matemáticas	*Mat, Math*	mathematics
mecánica	*Mec, Mech*	mech
medicina	*Med*	mec
metalurgia	*Metal*	met
meteorología	*Met, Meteo*	mete
México	*Méx, Mex*	Mexic
masculino y femenino	*mf*	mascu
militar	*Mil*	militar
minería	*Min*	mining
mitología	*Mit*	mytholc
masculino plural	*mpl*	masculir
masculino singular	*msing*	masculin
música	*Mús, Mus*	music
mitología	*Myth*	mythology
sustantivo	*n*	noun
Inglaterra del Norte	*N Engl*	North of England
náutica	*Náut, Naut*	nautical
negativo	*neg*	negative
Nicaragua	*Nic*	Nicaragua
sustantivo plural	*npl*	noun plural
sustantivo singular	*nsing*	noun singular
óptica	*Ópt, Opt*	optics
ornitología	*Orn*	ornithology
(a) sí mismo	*o.s.*	oneself
Panamá	*Pan*	Panama
Paraguay	*Par*	Paraguay
parlamento	*Parl*	parliament
por ejemplo	*p. ej.*	for example
personal	*pers*	personal
peyorativo	*pey, pej*	pejorative
farmacia	*Pharm*	pharmacy
filosofía	*Philos*	philosophy
fonética	*Phon*	phonetics
fotografía	*Phot*	photography
física	*Phys*	physics
fisiología	*Physiol*	physiology
plural	*pl*	plural
uso poético	*poét, poet*	poetic
política	*Pol*	politics
posesivo	*poses, poss*	possessive
participio de pasado	*pp*	past participle
prefijo	*pref*	prefix
preposición	*prep*	preposition
pronombre	*pron*	pronoun
psicología	*Psic, Psych*	psychology
tiempo pasado	*pt*	past tense
química	*Quím*	chemistry
marca registrada	®	registered trademark
radio	*Rad*	radio
ferrocarriles	*Rail*	railways
relativo	*rel*	relative
religión	*Rel*	religion
sustantivo	*s*	noun
alguien	*sb*	somebody
Cono Sur	*S. Cone*	Southern Cone
ciencia	*Sci*	science
escolar	*Scol*	school
Escocia	*Scot*	Scotland
costura	*Sew*	sewing
sustantivo femenino	*sf*	noun feminine
sustantivo femenino plural	*fpl*	noun feminine plural
singular	*sing*	singular
esquí	*Ski*	skiing
sustantivo masculino	*sm*	noun masculine
sustantivo masculino y femenino	*smf*	noun masculine and feminine
sustantivo masculino plural	*smpl*	noun masculine plural
sociología	*Sociol*	sociology
España	*Sp*	Spain
Bolsa	*St Ex*	Stock Exchange
algo	*sth*	something
subjuntivo	*subjun*	subjunctive
sufijo	*suf*	suffix
superlativo	*superl*	superlative
agrimensura	*Survey*	surveying
tauromaquia	*Taur*	bullfighting
también	*tb*	also
teatro	*Teat*	theatre
técnico	*Téc, Tech*	technical
telecomunicaciones	*Telec*	telecommunications
teatro	*Theat*	theatre
tipografía	*Tip*	typography
televisión	*TV*	television
tipografía	*Typ*	typography
universidad	*Univ*	university
Uruguay	*Uru*	Uruguay
Estados Unidos	*US*	United States
usualmente	*usu*	usually
véase	*V*	see
verbo	*vb*	verb
Venezuela	*Ven*	Venezuela
veterinaria	*Vet*	veterinary medicine
verbo intransitivo	*vi*	intransitive verb
verbo pronominal	*vpr*	pronominal verb
verbo transitivo	*vt*	transitive verb
verbo transitivo/intransitivo	*vti*	transitive/intransitive verb
zoología	*Zool*	zoology
lenguaje familiar, véase pág. xxiv	*	informal language, see page xxiv
lenguaje muy familiar, o argot, véase pág. xxiv	**	very informal language or slang, see page xxiv
lenguaje vulgar, véase pág. xxiv	***	offensive language, see page xxiv
lenguaje anticuado, véase pág. xxiv	†	old-fashioned term or expression, see page xxiv
lenguaje arcaico, véase pág. xxv	††	archaic term or expression, see page xxv
equivalencia cultural, véase pág. xxiii	≈	cultural equivalent, see page xxiii

DICCIONARIO
ESPAÑOL-INGLÉS
INGLÉS-ESPAÑOL

SPANISH-ENGLISH
ENGLISH-SPANISH
DICTIONARY

Collins
SPANISH DICTIONARY

Published by Collins
An imprint of HarperCollins Publishers
Westerhill Road
Bishopbriggs
Glasgow G64 2QT

Tenth Edition 2016

10 9 8 7 6 5 4 3 2

ISBN 978-0-00-815838-5

www.collinsdictionary.com

HarperCollins Publishers,
195 Broadway, New York, NY 10007

HARPERCOLLINS SPANISH UNABRIDGED DICTIONARY.
Tenth US Edition 2016

ISBN 978-0-06-257318-6

www.harpercollins.com

HarperCollins books may be purchased for educational, business, or sales promotional use. For information, please write to:
Special Markets Department,
HarperCollins Publishers,
195 Broadway, New York, NY 10007

Typeset by Macmillan Typesetting Solutions, Massachusetts, and Davidson Publishing Solutions, Glasgow

Printed and bound by Thomson Press India Ltd

A catalogue record for this book is available from the British Library.

If you would like to comment on any aspect of this book, please contact us at the given address or online.
E-mail: dictionaries@harpercollins.co.uk
facebook.com/collinsdictionary
@collinsdict

Acknowledgements
We would like to thank those authors and publishers who kindly gave permission for copyright material to be used in the Collins Corpus. We would also like to thank Times Newspapers Ltd for providing valuable data.

Find out more about HarperCollins and the environment at
www.harpercollins.co.uk/green

TENTH EDITION
DÉCIMA EDICIÓN

Series Editor • Director de publicaciones
Jethro Lennox

General Editors • Dirección general
Gerry Breslin Helen Newstead

Project Management • Dirección editorial
Teresa Álvarez Kerry Ferguson

Contributors • Colaboradores
Tony Gálvez Cordelia Lilly
Jose María Ruiz Vaca Roy Russell

With thanks to • Agradecimientos
Hugo Pooley

NINTH EDITION
NOVENA EDICIÓN

Series Editor • Director de publicaciones

Rob Scriven

General Editor • Dirección general

Catherine Love Gaëlle Amiot-Cadey

Project Management • Dirección editorial

Sabine Citron

Senior Editors • Responsables de redacción

Cordelia Lilly José A. Gálvez

Contributors • Equipo de redacción

José María Ruiz Vaca

José Martín Galera Lydia Batanaz Arteaga

Julie Muleba

Alison Sadler

Editorial Assistance • Ayudantes de redacción

Genevieve Gerrard Val McNulty

Cindy Paterson

Jill Williams

Joyce Littlejohn

Data Management • Informática

Thomas Callan

With thanks to/Agradecimientos

Beatriz Galimberti Jarman Carol Styles Carvajal Diarmuid Bradley

Helen Newstead Jeremy Butterfield Malihé Forghani Nowbari Marianne Noble

Sharon Hunter Susie Beattie Victoria Ordóñez Diví

SIXTH, SEVENTH AND EIGHTH EDITIONS
SEXTA, SÉPTIMA Y OCTAVA EDICIONES

Series Editor · Directora de publicaciones
Lorna Sinclair Knight

General Editor · Dirección general
Jeremy Butterfield

Project Management · Dirección editorial
Gerard Breslin

Senior Editors · Responsables de redacción
Teresa Álvarez García   Cordelia Lilly

Editorial Coordination · Coordinación editorial
Emma Aeppli   Sharon Hunter   Joyce Littlejohn   Val McNulty

Senior Contributors · Equipo de redacción
Fernando León Solís   Julie Muleba
Victoria Ordóñez Diví   José María Ruiz Vaca
Alison Sadler

Contributors · Colaboradores
Tom Bartlett   Joaquín Blasco   Diarmuid Bradley   Michael Britton
Claire Calder   Harry Campbell   Malihé Forghani-Nowbari   José Martín Galera
Nerea Gandarias Mendieta   Elena García Álvarez   Ben Goldstein   Bob Grossmith
Jane Horwood   Lesley Kingsley   Ana Cristina Llompart   Mª Ángeles Pérez Alonso
Ana Ramos   Mar Rodríguez Vázquez   Victoria Romero Cerro   Carol Styles Carvajal
Palmira Sullivan   Eduardo Vallejo   Stephen Waller

Editorial Assistance · Ayudantes de redacción
Elspeth Anderson   Susan Dunsmore   Alice Grandison   Angela Jack
Irene Lakhani   Cindy Mitchell   Maggie Seaton

Data Management · Informática
Jane Creevy   Paul Hassett   Sorcha Lenagh

FIFTH EDITION
QUINTA EDICIÓN

Editorial Staff • Redacción

Teresa Álvarez García   Gerard Breslin   Jeremy Butterfield
Sharon Hunter   Cordelia Lilly   José María Ruiz Vaca

Contributors • Colaboradores

Professor I. F. Ariza   Diarmuid Bradley   José Ramón Parrondo

Computing • Informática

Robert McMillan

THIRD AND FOURTH EDITIONS
EDICIONES TERCERA Y CUARTA

by • por

Colin Smith

in collaboration with • en colaboración con

Diarmuid Bradley   Teresa de Carlos   Louis Rodrigues
José Ramón Parrondo

Editorial Management • Dirección editorial

Jeremy Butterfield

Coordinating Editor • Coordinador de la obra

Gerard Breslin

Assistant Editors • Ayudantes de redacción

Sharon Hunter   Lesley Johnston

FIRST AND SECOND EDITIONS
PRIMERA Y SEGUNDA EDICIÓN

by • por

Colin Smith

in collaboration with • en colaboración con

Maria Boniface   Hugo Pooley   Arthur Montague   Mike Gonzalez
–
Manuel Bermejo   Marcos Eugenio Chang-Rodríguez

Colin Smith

In acknowledgement of his pioneering work in the field of English-Spanish lexicography, we would like to dedicate this book to Colin Smith. Not only was the first edition of the dictionary in 1971 the result of many years of devoted, scholarly labour on his part, he was also the main contributor to the second and third editions. In his memory and in his honour we have retained, with some slight changes, the section on word formation in Spanish which he wrote for the third edition. We in the editorial team are all indebted to him for the breadth of his vision and his constant encouragement, and hope that this latest edition is a fitting tribute to him, "il miglior fabbro".

Colin Smith

Queremos dedicar esta publicación a Colin Smith, por su gran trabajo pionero en el campo de la lexicografia en inglés y español. No sólo fue la primera edición del diccionario de 1971 el resultado de muchos años de trabajo riguroso y erudito por su parte, si no que además su contribución a la segunda y tercera ediciones fue primordial. En su memoria y en su honor hemos mantenido, con alguna pequeña variación, la sección dedicada a la formación de palabras en español que escribió para la tercera edición. Nuestro equipo editorial se halla en deuda con él por su amplitud de miras y continuo apoyo, por lo que esperamos que esta nueva edición sea un tributo apropiado para "il miglior fabbro".

Acknowledgements

Agradecimientos

Guillermo Arce, Pamela Bacarisse, David Balagué, Jennie Bachelor, Clive Bashleigh, Peter Beardsell, William Bidgood, Tom Bookless, Everett L. Boyd, T.R.M. Bristow, Prof R.F. Brown, John Butt, Max Cawdron, Nick Gardner, A. Bryson Gerrard, Robert Burakoff, Trevor Chubb, Sabine Citron, G.T. Colegate, Joe Cremona, Dr G.A. Davies, Eve Degnen, Maureen Dolan, Carmen and Pablo Domínguez, Fr Carlos Elizalde C.P., John England, María Jesús Fernández Prieto, José Miguel Galván Déniz, G.C. Gilham, Paul Gomez, Isobel Gordon, H.B. Hall, Stephen Harrison, Patrick Harvey, Tony Heathcote, David Henn, Leo Hickey, Ian Jacob, Leonor del Pino Jiménez, Concepción and Pilar Jiménez Bautista, A. Johnson, F. Killoran, Norman Lamb, Emilio Lorenzo, A. Madigan, A. McCallum, Rosa María Manchón, Rodney Mantle, Duncan Marshall, María Martín, Hazel Mills, Alan Morley, Brian Morris, Brian Mott, Bernard Murphy, Ana Newton, Patrick Nield, Richard Nott, Hugh O'Donnell, Chantal Pérez Hernández, Dan Quilter, Hugo Pooley, Chris Pratt, Brian Powell, Robert Pring-Mill, M. Dolores Ramis, Sr J. and Sra M. del Río, Brian Steel, C.H. Stevenson, Diana Streeten, Sra A. Espinosa de Walker, Sra M.J. Fernández de Wangermann, Ian Weetman, G. Weston, Richard Wharton, Roger Wright, Alan Yates

William Collins' dream of knowledge for all began with the publication of his first book in 1819. A self-educated mill worker, he not only enriched millions of lives, but also founded a flourishing publishing house. Today, staying true to this spirit, Collins books are packed with inspiration, innovation, and practical expertise. They place you at the centre of a world of possibility and give you exactly what you need to explore it.

Language is the key to this exploration, and at the heart of Collins Dictionaries is language as it is really used. New words, phrases, and meanings spring up every day, and all of them are captured and analysed by the Collins Corpus. Constantly updated, and with over 4.5 billion entries, this living language resource is unique to our dictionaries.

Words are tools for life. And a Collins Dictionary makes them work for you.

Find us at **www.collinsdictionary.com**.

Contents

Introduction xii

Using the dictionary xvi

Complex entries and language notes xxxiii

Cultural notes xxxiv

Spanish pronunciation and spelling xxxv

SPANISH-ENGLISH 1–949

Language in Use: a grammar of communication in Spanish and English 1–63

ENGLISH-SPANISH 955–2059

The Spanish verb 2063

The English verb 2073

Aspects of Word Formation in Spanish 2077

Numerals 2081

Weights and measures 2084

Time and dates 2087

Índice

Introducción xiv

Cómo utilizar el diccionario xvi

Entradas complejas y notas lingüísticas xxxiii

Notas culturales xxxiv

Pronunciación y ortografía del inglés xl

ESPAÑOL-INGLÉS 1–949

Lengua y Uso: gramática comunicativa del inglés y del español 1–63

INGLÉS-ESPAÑOL 955–2059

El verbo español 2063

El verbo inglés 2073

La formación de palabras en español 2077

Números 2081

Pesos y medidas 2084

La hora y las fechas 2087

Introduction

Since it was first published to great critical acclaim in 1971, the COLLINS SPANISH DICTIONARY has become one of the most highly respected reference works of its kind. The extent of its coverage together with the clarity and accuracy of the information it gives have made it a recognized authority in the field of Spanish-English English-Spanish lexicography.

As well as adding a wealth of new words and expressions that have recently come into the language, this edition continues to build on all the strengths that have made the COLLINS SPANISH DICTIONARY so popular, including features such as the Language in Use guide to self-expression and the innovative encyclopaedic and usage notes. As before, we have used the huge English and Spanish databases developed through the groundbreaking research into computational linguistics carried out by COLLINS in partnership with the University of Birmingham since the 1970s to refine existing entries, senses and phrases. These multi-million-word corpora are collections of texts held on computer, which provide numerous examples of how words are actually used in the widest possible variety of contexts, be it in newspapers, in literature, in official reports or in ordinary spoken language. In much the same way as scientists who analyse objective data to confirm their hypotheses, dictionary editors now have access to vast databases of hard facts and evidence to back up their own linguistic intuition. The result is a degree of accuracy and depth of coverage that would be impossible to achieve using traditional methods alone. Here is an example of how authentic usage, as documented in the Collins Corpus, is reflected in our dictionary entries:

disc. If the problem is	severe	and does not settle spontaneously
British system of justice took a	severe	blow. Let's hope that the
depressed and confidence has taken a	severe	blow from the turmoil in the
slow and tedious. I suffered from	severe	bouts of depression, migraine, fits
Pete suffered a fractured skull and	severe	brain damage. He went into a coma
Bosnia to Sarajevo because of the	severe	cold. Priorities will be blankets
the deeply damaged system. The	severe	conditions, which shocked EC
substantial loss of ozone could have	severe	consequences for life on Earth,
dictatorship here would be a very	severe	consequences in terms of trade,
and it will have especially	severe	consequences for the nations of the
his residence. This, at a time when	severe	constraints have been applied to
But at the same time he was a	severe	critic of American policy on the
said: "This bomb would have caused	severe	damage, injury and death within a
month, hurricane-force winds caused	severe	damage to property across much of
exploding under the bows, caused	severe	damage and slowed up the
Apart from anything else, the	severe	decline in Test-match crowds is
in the open and inflicting a	severe	defeat upon him, the pursuit of a
situation. The effect of the two	severe	defeats, and the continuous attack
interests adequately because of the	severe	defeats suffered in the preceding
Republic, has suffered several	severe	defeats and its very survival is
like cost, loss of child labour,	severe	discipline, outweigh the
Water companies claim that	severe	droughts are freak occurrences
to note that, despite its own	severe	economic problems, Turkey had
out at Warren after his son suffered	severe	facial injuries after beating
of sickness can therefore result in	severe	financial problems. With a PHI
City came to a virtual stop today.	Severe	flooding trapped people in their
to a new pipe-laying programme. The	severe	frost and rapid thaw caused small
and many families suffered	severe	hardship as a consequence. Little
the people continued to suffer	severe	hardship. Free-market policies
illness and yesterday awoke with a	severe	headache and stomach pains which
Hingham when he apparently died of a	severe	illness. The two were blindfolded
conditions such as TB or other	severe	illnesses; disorders of the
14, was airlifted to hospital with	severe	injuries. He was undergoing an
as he walked his dog. She had	severe	injuries to the head. The

severe [sɪˈvɪəʳ] (ADJ) (COMPAR: **severer**, SUPERL: **severest**) **1** (= *serious*) [*problem, consequence, damage*] grave, serio; [*injury, illness*] grave; [*defeat, setback, shortage*] serio; [*blow, reprimand*] fuerte, duro; [*pain, headache*] fuerte • **I suffered from ~ bouts of depression** padecía profundas *or* serias depresiones • **many families suffered ~ hardship as a consequence** muchas familias sufrieron enormes penurias a consecuencia de ello • **we have been under ~ pressure to cut costs** nos han presionado mucho para reducir gastos • **to suffer a ~ loss of blood** sufrir gran pérdida de sangre • **~ losses** (*Econ*) enormes *or* cuantiosas pérdidas *fpl*
2 (= *harsh*) [*weather, conditions, winter*] duro, riguroso; [*cold*] extremo; [*storm, flooding, frost*] fuerte
3 (= *strict*) [*person, penalty*] severo; [*discipline*] estricto • **I was his ~st critic** yo era su crítico más severo • **to be ~ with sb** ser severo con algn
4 (= *austere*) [*person, appearance, expression*] severo, adusto; [*clothes, style*] austero; [*hairstyle*] (de corte) serio; [*architecture*] sobrio

One of our greatest challenges, given the sheer wealth of information to be presented, was to make such a sophisticated reference work simple and quick to use. The result is a layout that is designed to make different senses, set structures and idioms easier to locate even in the longest entries, which have been given a special treatment all their own.

We are confident that the COLLINS SPANISH DICTIONARY will continue to be a valued companion for students, teachers, translators and language enthusiasts alike.

Introducción

Desde la primera edición, aparecida en 1971, el diccionario COLLINS de inglés-español ha sido una de las obras de consulta más respetadas e influyentes en su campo. La extensión del vocabulario incluido, junto a la claridad y la fiabilidad de su contenido han hecho de él un diccionario cuya calidad es ampliamente reconocida en el mundo de la lexicografía de español-inglés.

Además de añadir una profusión de neologismos y expresiones que han entrado en la lengua recientemente, esta nueva edición continúa con la línea trazada por anteriores ediciones, incluyendo elementos tan destacados como la guía de expresión "Lengua y uso" y las innovadoras notas enciclopédicas. Al mismo tiempo, continuamos refinando el tratamiento de las entradas, explorando en profundidad sus distintas acepciones y usos gracias a las bases de datos de inglés y español creadas a partir de la investigación en lingüística computacional llevada a cabo por COLLINS en colaboración con la universidad de Birmingham desde los años 70. Estas colecciones de textos son poderosas herramientas informáticas de análisis que muestran cómo funcionan las palabras en el mayor número de contextos posibles, tales como el periodístico, el de la administración, la literatura o la lengua hablada. Al igual que en las ciencias, en las que los investigadores analizan información objetiva para confirmar sus hipótesis, los lexicógrafos tienen ahora acceso a vastos bancos de datos con las pruebas que confirman sus propias intuiciones lingüísticas. El resultado es un nivel de exactitud y profundidad en el vocabulario incluido que sería imposible conseguir utilizando únicamente métodos tradicionales. Aquí abajo puede verse un ejemplo de cómo el uso real, documentado en *Collins Corpus*, se refleja en las entradas de nuestro diccionario:

y cuántos son productos de un apoyo	decidido	a otro candidato, como es usted en este
gobierno # El ministro mostró su apoyo	decidido	a que el Gobierno agote los plazos del
El portavoz de ciu manifestó un apoyo	decidido	a la resolución del Consejo General del
del teatro infantil y juvenil, el apoyo	decidido	a la autoría dramática autóctona y a la
municipal de Madrid ha dado apoyo	decidido	a la Escuela Normal de Ballet de Adolfo
Reclamamos de las instituciones un apoyo	decidido	al ballet clásico y denunciamos
Reserva Federal, dé una muestra de apoyo	decidido	al dólar, elevando los tipos de interés
sino también recompensas políticas: un	decidido	apoyo diplomático español y de la UE
Moscú, por su parte, critica a Bonn el	decidido	apoyo a la extensión de la Organización
cerealista y ganadera, encontramos un	decidido	apoyo a los demás sectores de la
momentos, Calvo Sotelo encontró un	decidido	apoyo a su propuesta entre la derecha.
a un alzamiento pacífico, vigoroso y	decidido	contra la injusticia, la corrupción, la
una pronta y pacífica conclusión con el	decidido	concurso de la OEA # dijo ayer el
de cinco millones de espectadores y el	decidido	elogio de la mayoría. De otro modo, el
Durante algunos minutos camino con paso	decidido,	contemplando de soslayo el desamparo
y de súbito le invade un sentimiento	decidido	de aversión por esta oscuridad helada,
sus comentaristas proviene de que este	decidido	adversario de las armas nucleares
como un hábil negociador y un	decidido	defensor del comercio multilateral y de
firmadas bajo tortura. Se mostró firme,	decidido,	defensor de otra justicia. El juez le
contemporáneo. Así lo vio ese otro	decidido	gnóstico, André Breton, por intermedio
nos podíamos esperar es que fuese un	decidido	impulsor de las matemáticas. En
que las cosas mismas". Santayana es un	decidido	materialista o, si se prefiere, un
de que aquél naciera), Jámblico, era	decidido	partidario de la teurgia, y su obra Los
de tensiones entre Felipe V, partidario	decidido	del reconocimiento, y el Consejo de
él. Simultáneamente, comenzaba a ser un	decidido	promotor del diálogo entre ETA y el
a San Sebastián, se ha dicho que era	decidido,	valiente, temperamental, vehemente.
verdadero y continuo, joven y vigoroso,	decidido	y leal, con un mundo soñado para la paz
clave dentro del equipo que parece estar	decidido	a abandonar el club cuando concluya su
durante una parte del día. No estaba nada	decidido	a abonarme. Me parecía mucho dinero,
al público, porque el Gobierno está	decidido	a asumir este compromiso, con y por la
que antes de partir y estaba totalmente	decidido	a casarme con tal de recuperarla,
evidentes dificultades, el padre está	decidido	a llevar adelante la división familiar,
defenderlo en la sesión próxima, y esta	decidido	a marcharse del Gobierno si se vota el
de tanta animadversión: el actor está	decidido	a montar un supercasino en la reserva

que jugarse la existencia. Que yo estoy	decidido	a sacar el asunto adelante y las
estadounidense, Bill Clinton, está	decidido	a seguir adelante con un proyecto de
que debe sufrir un artista cuando está	decidido	a seguir sin concesiones su verdadera
su segunda mujer. Les anunció que estaba	decidido	a suicidarse y todos los que le
de que me reconcilie, no lo haría. Estoy	decidido	a terminar con el matrimonio". El
crisis místicas, pero, sobre todo,	decidido	a convertirse en pintor, hizo progresos
que le reafirme en su posición de líder.	decidido	a luchar por el título, su trabajo ha
en esquí de fondo, un joven triatleta	decidido	a ser bombero o un empleado de artes
la categoría social de la dama.	decidido	a seguir el juego, el dueño del hotel
la oportuna aclimatación. Me levanté	decidido	a comenzar el suplicio de la escalada
asomó la cabeza por la ventanilla	decidido	a echar una mano y, cuando se quiso dar
en el caso, acudió ayer a la Audiencia	decidido	a declarar. Pero esta mañana (por
exploré el terreno diplomático,	decidido	a intentar por mi cuenta y riesgo lo
sesteando, pero el Zaragoza salió	decidido	a resolver el partido y supo aprovechar
de los encuestados afirma no estar	decidido	del todo. Conviene saber que la
pero él está ya practicamente	decidido.	Se presentará como candidato
hablando dos o tres minutos y se dirigió	decidido	hacia mí. Cuando pasó al lado de Celia
refleja sentimentalmente quien cabalga	decidido	hacia el poder. Chirac tiene la lista
de asalto. Salió de su casa, se encaminó	decidido	y enfiló la mirada hacia la oficina de
me dirigí a la terminal. La cruzé	decidido	y salí al exterior. Tomé un taxi. Pasé

decidido ADJ **1** (= *firme*) [*apoyo*] wholehearted; [*paso, gesto*] purposeful; [*esfuerzo, intento*] determined; [*defensor, partidario*] staunch, strong; [*actitud, persona*] resolute • **dio su apoyo ~ al proyecto** he gave his solid *o* wholehearted support to the project • **hubo un ~ apoyo a su propuesta entre la derecha** there was solid support for his proposal from the right • **andaba con paso ~** she walked purposefully *o* with a purposeful stride • **los más ~s saltaron al agua** the most resolute jumped into the water
2 • **estar ~: voy a dejar el trabajo, ya estoy ~** I'm going to leave my job, I've made up my mind *o* I've decided • **estar ~ a hacer algo** to be resolved *o* determined to do sth • **estaba decidida a irse con él** she'd made up her mind to go with him, she was resolved *o* determined to go with him

Frente a tan abundante información, uno de nuestros mayores desafíos era convertir esta herramienta de consulta tan sofisticada en una obra sencilla y fácil de usar. El resultado es una presentación diseñada para que las distintas acepciones, locuciones y modismos puedan localizarse fácilmente incluso en las entradas más largas, a las que se ha dado un tratamiento especial.

Estamos convencidos de que el diccionario COLLINS de inglés-español continuará siendo un valioso compañero para estudiantes, traductores, lingüistas y para todos los amantes de la lengua.

Using the dictionary

Word order

Alphabetical order is followed except in the cases mentioned below. For easier reference, abbreviations, acronyms and proper names are given alphabetically in the wordlist. Although traditionally **CH** and **LL** have been considered separate letters in Spanish and words containing them used to be given after other **C/L** combinations on the Spanish side, it is now the policy of the Association of Spanish Language Academies to order such words according to the universal Latin alphabet as in English. This is the policy followed in this dictionary. **Ñ** continues to be considered a separate letter and is therefore given between **N** and **O**.

If two or more variants follow one another alphabetically, they are usually treated in the same entry and the more common form given first.

If variant spellings are not alphabetically adjacent, each is treated as a separate headword and there is a cross-reference to the form treated in depth. Note, however, that English words whose endings can be spelt either **-ize** or **-ise**, **-ization** or **-isation** etc are always included at the **z** spelling.

For the alphabetical order of compounds see **Compounds** and for that of phrasal verbs see **Phrasal verbs**.

Cross-referring of headwords

Cross-references include alternative spellings, parts of irregular verbs, irregular plural forms, contracted forms and some prefixes and suffixes.

armor ['ɑ:mə^{r}] N (*US*) = **armour**
voy ▹ **ir**
gave [geɪv] PT *of* **give**

Homonyms

Superscript numbers are used to separate unrelated words which have the same spelling and pronunciation, e.g. **port**[1], **port**[2], **choclo**[1], **choclo**[2].

Pronunciation

As Spanish pronunciation is generally entirely predictable, pronunciation rules are given on pages xxxv-xxxviii and IPA phonetic transcriptions are only included on the Spanish side where the pronunciation of a given word or its inflections is at odds with these, as is the case for some words of foreign origin, e.g. **camping**.

camping ['kampin] SM (PL: **campings**['kampin])

Since English pronunciation is far less predictable, phonetic transcriptions are included for all headwords on the English side and for irregular plural inflections where appropriate.

amoeba [ə'mi:bə] N (PL: **amoebas**, **amoebae** [ə'mi:bi:]) ameba *f*, amiba *f*

For the pronunciation of multiword compounds, see the phonetic transcription given under each headword.

Special entries

Complex entries

Entries that are very long – often function words, delexical verbs or words which are used in a large number of set structures (**back**, **dar**) – are given special treatment in this dictionary. Complex entries with more than one part of speech begin with a special "menu" which shows how they are structured. Special notes inside the entry either explain important points of grammar and usage which cannot be properly demonstrated by examples alone, or refer you to another part of the dictionary. The beginning of each semantic category is clearly signposted with

Cómo utilizar el diccionario

Orden alfabético

Se sigue siempre el orden alfabético, excepto en los casos mencionados más abajo. Para facilitar la consulta del diccionario se incluyen en el texto las abreviaturas, siglas y nombres propios en el lugar que les corresponde alfabéticamente. Aunque **CH** y **LL** se consideraban tradicionalmente letras, la Asociación de Academias de la Lengua Española ya no las considera como tales, de acuerdo al alfabeto latino universal, por lo que se encontrarán alfabetizadas como **C+H** y **L+L**. La **Ñ** continúa siendo una letra independiente.

Si dos o más variantes van una a continuación de otra en el orden alfabético, aparecen normalmente en la misma entrada y la variante más frecuente suele ir primero.

Las variantes ortográficas que no van una a continuación de otra aparecen como entradas independientes y se da una remisión a la variante en la que se desarrolla la entrada. Las palabras inglesas que pueden escribirse con las terminaciones **-ize** o **-ise**, **-ization** o **-isation**, etc, aparecen siempre escritas con **z**.

Para el orden alfabético de los compuestos, véase **Compuestos** y para los verbos frasales, véase **Verbos frasales**.

Remisiones de una entrada a otra

Se envían a otras entradas las variantes ortográficas, las formas irregulares de los verbos, los plurales irregulares de las palabras inglesas, las formas contraídas y algunos prefijos y sufijos.

Homónimos

Se usan cifras voladitas para separar las palabras que tienen la misma grafía y pronunciación, p.ej. **port**[1], **port**[2], **choclo**[1], **choclo**[2].

Pronunciación

Al ser la pronunciación española por lo general previsible, se dan simplemente las normas de pronunciación en las páginas xxxv-xxxviii y sólo se incluyen las transcripciones en el alfabeto fonético internacional de aquellas palabras cuya pronunciación puede estar poco clara para los no hablantes de español, como es el caso de los extranjerismos, por ej. **camping**.

En la sección de inglés se incluye la transcripción fonética de todas las entradas, así como la del plural si es irregular, ya que la pronunciación inglesa es mucho menos previsible.

Para la pronunciación de los compuestos formados por dos palabras, véase la transcripción fonética de cada palabra.

Entradas especiales

Entradas complejas

A las entradas más largas, tales como algunos de los verbos más básicos y aquellas palabras que se usan en un gran número de expresiones fijas (**back**, **dar**), se les ha dado una presentación especial en este diccionario. Si tienen más de una categoría gramatical aparece un recuadro al comienzo de la entrada con todas ellas. En algunas de las entradas se verán o bien notas que explican puntos gramaticales importantes que no pueden aclararse sólo con ejemplos o bien remisiones a otra parte del diccionario. Al comienzo de cada acepción aparece un recuadro

indicators in boxes, and set structures have been given special prominence to make them easy to locate. Finally, in entries where there are long sequences of examples containing significant grammatical or lexical collocations, the examples are alphabetized on a key word.

con un indicador para dicha acepción. Las estructuras fijas aparecen resaltadas de forma especial para que sean fácilmente localizables. Por último, en las entradas en las que hay párrafos largos con importantes colocaciones gramaticales o léxicas, una palabra clave en la frase gobierna el orden alfabético de dichas frases.

Cultural notes
Extra information on culturally significant events, institutions, traditions and customs which cannot be given in an ordinary translation or gloss is given in the form of shaded boxed notes following the relevant entry. See index on page xxxiv.

Notas culturales
Se ha dado una información adicional sobre aquellos acontecimientos, instituciones, costumbres y tradiciones culturales importantes a los que no puede darse una traducción normal o una pequeña explicación. Dicha información aparece en un recuadro tras la entrada correspondiente. Véase el índice en la página xxxiv.

Language notes
These boxed notes are aimed at tackling certain areas of difficulty where even an advanced student may benefit from further explanation. They are designed to complement the dictionary entry in a clear and succinct fashion and to provide further helpful examples. The points covered in these notes were selected on the advice of practising teachers and academics. See index on page xxxiii.

Notas lingüísticas
Estas notas lingüísticas, cuyo objetivo es aclarar y explicar aquellas dificultades que pueda tener incluso un estudiante avanzado, están diseñadas para complementar la entrada del diccionario de una forma clara y esquemática, proporcionando para ello más ejemplos ilustrativos. Los puntos que se han tratado en dichas notas se han seleccionado con la ayuda de profesores de ambos idiomas. Véase el índice en la página xxxiii.

Finding your way through entries

Part-of-speech categories
Grammatical functions are distinguished by boxed abbreviations, for example:

Cómo orientarse dentro de una entrada

Categorías gramaticales
Las categorías gramaticales vienen marcadas por abreviaturas encuadradas, por ej.:

arder ▷ CONJUG 2a (VT) **1** (= *quemar*) to burn **2** (*esp LAm**) [*herida*] to sting, make smart

See list of abbreviations used inside the back cover.

Véase la lista de abreviaturas en el interior de las cubiertas del libro.

Sometimes two or more parts of speech are treated together on the Spanish side if the translations apply equally to each, for example:

En algunas ocasiones dos o más categorías gramaticales aparecen juntas en las entradas españolas si la traducción es válida para todas ellas, por ej.:

moldavo/a (ADJ), (SM/F) Moldavian, Moldovan

Meaning categories
The diverse meanings of the headword within each entry or part-of-speech category are separated by numbers, **1** ... **2** ..., occasionally subdivided into **1.1**, **1.2**, etc. A certain order is normally followed: basic and concrete senses first, figurative and familiar ones later.

Categorías semánticas
Las distintas acepciones de una entrada están separadas por números, **1** ... **2** ... y en ocasiones aparecen subdivididas en **1.1**, **1.2**, etc. Se sigue normalmente un cierto orden: primero los significados básicos y concretos, después los figurados y familiares.

sail [seɪl] (N) **1** (*Naut*) (= *cloth*) vela *f* • **the age of ~** la época de la navegación a vela • **in** *or* **under full ~** a toda vela, a vela llena • **to lower the ~s** arriar las velas • **to set ~** [*ship, person*] hacerse a la vela, zarpar • **we set ~ from Portsmouth** nos hicimos a la vela en Portsmouth • **to set ~ for Liverpool** zarpar hacia Liverpool, hacerse a la vela con rumbo a Liverpool • **to take in the ~s** amainar las velas • **under ~** a vela • IDIOM: • **to take the wind out of sb's ~s** bajarle los humos a algn **2** (*Naut*) (= *trip*) paseo *m* en barco • **it's three days' ~ from here** desde aquí se tarda tres días en barco • **to go for a ~** dar una vuelta en barco

Idioms, proverbs and set phrases
On the English side idioms are preceded by the label • IDIOM or • IDIOMS: and proverbs by • PROVERB: or • PROVERBS: while on the Spanish side idioms are labelled • MODISMO: or • MODISMOS: and proverbs • REFRÁN: or • REFRANES:. Both types of phrase are generally grouped at the end of the relevant sense category of the first invariable element in the phrase: e.g. **to ring the changes** and **to ring true/false** are all included under **ring**. Other types of set phrase are similarly given under the first lexical element, e.g. **red in the face** is given under **red**.

Modismos, refranes y estructuras
En la parte de inglés los modismos aparecen precedidos de las marcas • IDIOM: o • IDIOMS: y los refranes de las marcas • PROVERB: o • PROVERBS:. En la parte de español las marcas correspondientes son • MODISMO: o • MODISMOS: y • REFRÁN: o • REFRANES:. Ambos tipos de expresiones se hallarán agrupados normalmente al final de la categoría semántica correspondiente del primer elemento invariable de cada expresión. Por ej.: **to ring the changes** y **to ring true/false** aparecen en la entrada **ring**. Otros tipos de expresiones fijas aparecen también bajo el primer elemento léxico, por ej. se incluye **red in the face** en la entrada **red**.

The only exception to this is where certain very common English and Spanish verbs such as **make** or **tener** form the basis of a very large number of phrases, e.g. **to make an appointment**, **to make hay while the sun shines**, **to make sense**, **tener la impresión de que ...**, **tener sentido**, **tener interés**.

Since the entries for these verbs are very long, phrases are treated under the second element so that the user will find them more easily in the shorter entry; **to make an appointment** is thus under **appointment** and **tener interés** under **interés**.

There is, however, also intentional duplication of phrases where appropriate. Thus **año bisiesto** belongs under **año** under the first rule we have given; but it is also the sole phrase under the headword **bisiesto**. In many other cases phrases are duplicated because they illustrate something about both headwords.

En el caso de verbos muy frecuentes en ambas lenguas, tales como **make** o **tener**, que se usan con numerosas expresiones, dichas expresiones suelen aparecer en el segundo elemento, por ej.: **to make an appointment**, **to make hay while the sun shines**, **to make sense**, **tener la impresión de que ...**, **tener sentido**, **tener interés**.

Dado el tamaño de las entradas de estos verbos, la frase aparece bajo el segundo elemento para que sea más fácil de encontrar. Así, **to make an appointment** aparece bajo **appointment** y **tener interés** bajo **interés**.

Hay, sin embargo, muchos casos en los que dichas expresiones aparecen en ambas entradas. Es el caso de **año bisiesto**, que según la norma mencionada debe ir bajo la entrada **año**, pero que es también la única frase en **bisiesto**. En otras ocasiones se duplican las expresiones si ilustran algo sobre ambas entradas.

Repetition of the headword in the entry

To save space, where the headword occurs in its full form within the entry it is replaced by **~**. Where it might otherwise be confusing or the phrase is a common sign, the full form is used.

Repetición del lema en la entrada

Para ahorrar espacio, el lema se substituye por **~** cuando aparece completo dentro de la entrada. Se usa, sin embargo, la palabra completa en las frases cuando no hacerlo puede dar lugar a confusión o si dicha frase es un letrero.

smoking ['sməʊkɪŋ] (N) • **~ is bad for you** el fumar te perjudica • **~ or non-smoking?** ¿fumador o no fumador? • **to give up ~** dejar

pisar ▷ CONJUG 1a (VT) **1** (*= andar sobre*) to walk on • **¿se puede ~ el suelo de la cocina?** can I walk on the kitchen floor?
2 (*= poner el pie encima de*) to tread on, step on • **perdona, te he pisado** sorry, I trod *o* stepped on your foot • **vio una cucaracha y la pisó** she saw a cockroach and trod *o* stood on it • **~ el acelerador a fondo** to step on the accelerator, put one's foot down*
• **"prohibido pisar el césped"** "keep off the grass" • MODISMOS: • **ir pisando huevos** to tread carefully • **tiene un morro que se lo pisa*** he's a cheeky devil*

red [red] (ADJ) (COMPAR: **redder**, SUPERL: **reddest**) **1** (*gen*) [*apple, sweater, lips, pen*] rojo, colorado; [*flower, sky*] rojo; [*wine*] tinto • **the traffic lights are red** el semáforo está en rojo • **his eyes were red** (*from crying*) tenía los ojos rojos • **the red evening sun** el sol rojizo del atardecer • **bright red** rojo fuerte *or* chillón

Compounds in both languages are given in full, as are pronominal verbs in Spanish and phrasal verbs in English.

Los compuestos nominales aparecen completos en ambos idiomas, así como los verbos pronominales en español y los verbos frasales en inglés.

call ...
▸ **call off** (VT + ADV) **1** (*= cancel*) [*+ meeting, race*] cancelar, suspender; [*+ deal*] anular; [*+ search*] abandonar, dar por terminado • **the strike was called off** se desconvocó la huelga
2 [*+ dog*] llamar (*para que no ataque*)

levantar ...
(VPR) **levantarse 1** (*= alzarse*) **a** (*de la cama, del suelo*) to get up • **me levanto todos los días a las ocho** I get up at eight every day

Compounds

On the English-Spanish side of this dictionary, some entries include as their last category a section headed CPD or COMPOUND(S). In these will be found nouns made up of two or more separate words such as **sand dune** (under **sand**), **fast food** (under **fast**), **ear, nose and throat specialist** (under **ear**). Each compound is preceded by a triangle ▸, and the order is alphabetical.

Single-word nouns such as **blackbird**, and words usually written with a hyphen such as **by-your-leave**, appear as headwords in their own right.

Only compound words functioning as nouns are shown in compound categories. Adjective compounds which can be written with a hyphen or without, usually depending on whether they precede or

Compuestos

En la sección de inglés-español de este diccionario, algunas entradas incluyen una última categoría gramatical denominada CPD o COMPOUND(S). En ella se encontrarán los sustantivos formados por dos o más palabras como **sand dune** (bajo **sand**), **fast food** (bajo **fast**), **ear, nose and throat specialist** (bajo **ear**). Todos ellos aparecen precedidos de un triángulo ▸, y van por orden alfabético.

Los sustantivos compuestos (p. ej. **blackbird**) que gráficamente forman una sola palabra y aquellos escritos normalmente con guión (p. ej. **by-your-leave**) aparecen como entradas independientes.

Sólo aparecen bajo la categoría de compuestos aquellos que funcionan como sustantivo. Los compuestos que funcionan como adjetivo (que pueden escribirse con guión o sin él, según precedan

follow a noun, are shown as headwords in their hyphenated form.

o sigan a un sustantivo), aparecen como entradas independientes escritos con guión.

hard [hɑːd] (ADJ) ...
▸ **the hard core** (= *intransigents*) los incondicionales, el núcleo duro
hard-core ['hɑːdkɔː'] (ADJ) [*pornography*] duro; [*supporter, militant, activist*] acérrimo; [*conservative, communist*] acérrimo, empedernido ▹ **hard**

On the Spanish-English side compounds made up of a noun plus two or more separate words are shown within the relevant sense category of the first word, preceded by a triangle ▸.

En la sección de español-inglés los compuestos nominales formados por un sustantivo más una o más palabras aparecen por orden alfabético al final de la categoría semántica correspondiente y precedidos de un triángulo ▸.

copa (SF) **1** (= *recipiente*) (*para bebidas*) glass; (*para postres*) dessert glass • **huevo a la ~** (*And, Cono Sur*) boiled egg ▸ **copa balón** balloon glass, brandy glass ▸ **copa de champán** champagne glass ...
4 (*Dep*) (= *trofeo, competición*) cup ▸ **Copa de Europa** European Cup ▸ **Copa del Mundo** World Cup ▸ **Copa del Rey** (*Esp*) *Spanish FA Cup*

Phrasal verbs

Phrasal verbs like **light up**, **show off** are listed in their own alphabetical sequence at the end of the entry for the main verb and are highlighted by a triangle symbol ▸.

They are classified according to the following part of speech categories:-

VT + ADV	phrasal verbs with the patterns: **he took the lid off** **he took off the lid**
VI + ADV	phrasal verbs with the pattern: **the seat comes off**
VT + PREP	phrasal verbs with the pattern: **her new hairstyle takes ten years off her**
VI + PREP	phrasal verbs with the pattern: **she came off her bike**

Where the phrasal verb form is identical in one meaning to a category of the main verb, it may be included in the main verb entry.

Verbos frasales

Los verbos frasales como **light up**, **show off**, etc aparecen por orden alfabético al final de la entrada del verbo principal, marcados por un triángulo ▸.

Se les clasifica según las siguientes categorías gramaticales:

VT + ADV	verbos frasales con las estructuras: **he took the lid off** **he took off the lid**
VI + ADV	verbos frasales con la estructura: **the seat comes off**
VT + PREP	verbos frasales con la estructura: **her new hairstyle takes ten years off her**
VI + PREP	verbos frasales con la estructura: **she came off her bike**

Cuando el verbo frasal tiene el mismo significado que una de las categorías del verbo principal, puede ir incluido en la entrada de este último. Por ej., véase

hobble ['hɒbl] ...
(VI) (*also* **to hobble along**) cojear, andar cojeando • **to ~ to the door** ir cojeando a la puerta

Literal verb and preposition combinations are usually included in the entry for the main verb.

La combinación literal de verbo más preposición suele aparecer incluida en la entrada del verbo principal.

pound²
(VI)...
2 (= *strike*) • **the sea ~ed against** *or* **on the rocks** el mar azotaba las rocas *or* batía contra las rocas • **somebody began ~ing at** *or* **on the door** alguien empezó a aporrear la puerta

In the case of less common adverbs and prepositions the phrase may well appear under the adverb or preposition.

En el caso de los adverbios y preposiciones menos frecuentes la expresión puede estar en la entrada del adverbio o de la preposición.

astern [ə'stɜːn] (ADV) (*Naut*) a popa • **to fall ~** quedarse atrás • **to go ~** ciar, ir hacia atrás • **to make a boat fast ~** amarrar un barco por la popa • **~ of** detrás de

Plurals

Irregular plural forms of English nouns are given on the English-Spanish side while those of Spanish nouns are given on the Spanish-English side.

Plural inflections for Spanish nouns are shown where the following rules do not apply:

a) If a Spanish noun ends in a vowel it takes **-s** in the plural (e.g. **casa-s**, **tribu-s**).

Plurales

Los plurales irregulares de las entradas inglesas aparecen en la sección de inglés-español, mientras que los plurales irregulares de las entradas españolas aparecen en la sección de español-inglés.

Se han incluido los plurales de los sustantivos españoles que no siguen las siguientes normas:

a) Si el sustantivo termina en vocal se añade **-s** para formar el plural (p.ej. **casa-s**, **tribu-s**).

b) If it ends in a consonant (including for this purpose **y**) it takes **-es** in the plural (e.g. **pared-es**, **árbol-es**).

c) Nouns that end in stressed **í** take **-es** in the plural (e.g. **rubí-rubíes**). Exception: **esquí-esquís**.

d) Nouns that end in **-z** change this to **c** and add **-es** in the plural (e.g. **luz-luces**; **paz-paces**). The pronunciation is not affected.

e) The accent which is written on a number of endings of singular nouns is not needed in the plural (e.g. **nación-naciones**, **patán-patanes**, **inglés-ingleses**). Some words having no written accent in the singular need one in the plural (e.g. **crimen-crímenes**, **joven-jóvenes**).

There is little agreement about the plural of recent anglicisms and gallicisms, and some latinisms. Each case is treated separately in the dictionary.

Noun plurals in English are indicated after the headword only when they are truly irregular (e.g. **ox-oxen**), and in the few cases where a word in **-o** takes a plural in **-oes** (e.g. **potato-es**). In all other cases the basic rules apply:

a) Most English nouns take **-s** in the plural: **bed-s**, **site-s**, **photo-s**.

b) Nouns that end in **-s**, **-x**, **-z**, **-sh** and some in **-ch** [tʃ] take **-es** in the plural: **boss-es**, **box-es**, **dish-es**, **patch-es**.

c) Nouns that end in **-y** not preceded by a vowel change the **-y** to **-ies** in the plural: **lady-ladies**, **berry-berries** (but **tray-s**, **key-s**).

Plural forms of the headword which differ substantially from the singular form are listed in their alphabetical place in the word list with a cross-reference, and repeated under the singular form.

b) Si termina en consonante (la **y** se considera como consonante en esta posición) se añade **-es** para formar el plural (p.ej. **pared-es**, **árbol-es**).

c) Los sustantivos que terminan en **-í** acentuada forman el plural añadiendo **-es** (p.ej. **rubí-rubíes**). Excepción: **esquí-esquís**.

d) Los sustantivos que terminan en **-z** la cambian en **c** en plural (p.ej. **luz-luces; paz-paces**). Esto no afecta a la pronunciación.

e) La tilde de algunas terminaciones de los sustantivos en singular se suprime en el plural (p.ej. **nación-naciones**, **patán-patanes**, **inglés-ingleses**). Algunas palabras que no llevan tilde en singular la tienen en plural (p.ej. **crimen-crímenes**).

Debido a la confusión reinante en cuanto a la forma plural de los anglicismos y galicismos de reciente acuñación y de algún latinismo, se trata separadamente cada caso.

Los plurales de los sustantivos ingleses se incluyen tras el lema sólo cuando son irregulares (p.ej. **ox-oxen**), y en los pocos casos en los que una palabra terminada en **-o** forma el plural en **-oes** (p.ej. **potato-es**). En los demás casos se aplican las siguientes reglas:

a) La mayor parte de los sustantivos en inglés forman el plural añadiendo **-s**: **bed-s**, **site-s**, **photo-s**.

b) Los sustantivos terminados en **-s**, **-x**, **-z**, **-sh** y algunos en **-ch** [tʃ] forman el plural añadiendo **-es**: **boss-es**, **box-es**, **dish-es**, **patch-es**.

c) Los sustantivos terminados en **-y** no precedida por vocal forman el plural cambiando la **-y** en **-ies**: **lady-ladies**, **berry-berries** (pero **tray-s**, **key-s**).

Cuando es radicalmente distinto del singular, el plural aparece como entrada independiente con una remisión al singular, en donde aparecen ambas formas.

children ['tʃɪldrən] (NPL) *of* **child**

Spanish nouns which are invariable in the plural are marked INV or inv.

Los sustantivos españoles cuyo plural es idéntico al singular llevan la marca INV o inv.

campus (SM INV) (*Univ*) campus

bottle ... ▸ **bottle opener** abrebotellas *m inv*, destapador *m* (*LAm*)

Verbs

All Spanish verb headwords are referred by number and letter (e.g. ▹ CONJUG 2a) to the table of verb paradigms on pages 2064-2071. In a few cases in which verbs have slight irregularities or are defective, the fact is noted after the headword. English irregular or strong verbs have their principal parts noted in bold face after the headword; these are also listed on pages 2074-2075. Minor variations of spelling are listed on page 2076.

Verbos

Los verbos españoles llevan una remisión en número y letra (p.ej. ▹ CONJUG 2a) al cuadro de conjugaciones en las págs. 2064-2071. En los casos en los que el verbo es ligeramente irregular o defectivo, se nota tal hecho en la entrada. El pretérito y el participio de pasado de los verbos irregulares ingleses aparecen tras el lema en negrita y puede verse la lista de dichos verbos en las págs. 2074-2075. Las irregularidades ortográficas de los verbos ingleses constan en la pág. 2076.

Comparatives and superlatives

Where English adjectives have common inflected comparative and superlative forms, these are shown in the entry on the English-Spanish side.

Comparativos y superlativos

El comparativo y el superlativo de los adjetivos ingleses se incluyen en la entrada en la sección de inglés-español si son de uso frecuente.

easy ['i:zɪ] (ADJ) (COMPAR: **easier**, SUPERL: **easiest**)

Masculine and feminine nouns

On the Spanish-English side, parallel senses of nouns which change their endings predictably depending on whether they refer to a male or a female (e.g. **abuelo/abuela**, **profesor/profesora**) are treated under the entry for the masculine form even if there is also a separate entry for the feminine form in which other senses are treated.

Sustantivos masculinos y femeninos

Si el sustantivo tiene terminaciones de masculino y femenino, se incluyen bajo la forma del masculino las acepciones comunes (por ej.: **abuelo/abuela**, **profesor/profesora**). Las acepciones específicas del femenino aparecen como entradas independientes.

prima (SF) **1** [*de seguro*] premium
2 (= *gratificación*) bonus

primo/a (ADJ) **1** [*número*] prime
(SM/F) **1** (= *pariente*) cousin

Where a translation of a Spanish noun referring to a person varies depending on whether the referent is male or female, the masculine translation is separated from the feminine translation by a slash where this is not confusing.

Cuando las traducciones para el masculino y el femenino son distintas, aparecen separadas por una barra si la traducción así dada no lleva a confusión.

francés/esa ADJ ...
SM/F Frenchman/Frenchwoman

Gender information

On both sides of the dictionary gender information is given for Spanish nouns.

El género

Se da información sobre el género de los sustantivos españoles en ambas partes del diccionario.

English side		Sección de inglés-español
masculine noun (e.g. coche *m*)	*m*	sustantivo masculino (p.ej.: coche *m*)
feminine noun (e.g. aceituna *f*)	*f*	sustantivo femenino (p.ej.: aceituna *f*)
noun which is identical for masculine and feminine (e.g. hablante *mf*)	*mf*	sustantivo invariable en género (p.ej.: hablante *mf*)
masculine or feminine noun depending on the ending selected (e.g. profesor(a) *m/f*, niño/a *m/f*)	*m/f*	sustantivo masculino o femenino, según la terminación (p.ej.: profesor(a) *m/f*, niño/a *m/f*)
noun which can be either masculine or feminine (e.g. azúcar *m or f*)	*m or f*	sustantivo que puede ser masculino o femenino (p.ej.: azúcar *m or f*)
masculine noun used in the singular unlike the English (e.g. **capital assets** NPL activo *msing* fijo)	*msing*	sustantivo masculino usado en singular, a diferencia del inglés (p.ej.: **capital assets** NPL activo *msing* fijo)
feminine noun used in the singular unlike the English (e.g. **cash reserves** NPL reserva *fsing* en efectivo)	*fsing*	sustantivo femenino usado en singular, a diferencia del inglés (p.ej.: **cash reserves** NPL reserva *fsing* en efectivo)
masculine plural noun (e.g. consejos *mpl*)	*mpl*	sustantivo masculino plural (p.ej.: consejos *mpl*)
feminine plural noun (e.g. golosinas *fpl*)	*fpl*	sustantivo femenino plural (p.ej.: golosinas *fpl*)
masculine noun optionally used in the plural with the same meaning (e.g. remordimiento(s) *m(pl)*)	*m (pl)*	sustantivo masculino usado en ocasiones en plural con el mismo significado (p.ej.: remordimiento(s) *m(pl)*)
feminine noun optionally used in the plural with the same meaning (e.g. pasta(s) *f(pl)*)	*f (pl)*	sustantivo femenino usado en ocasiones en plural con el mismo significado (p.ej.: pasta(s) *f(pl)*)
Spanish side		**Sección de español-inglés**
masculine noun (e.g. **coche** SM)	SM	sustantivo masculino (p.ej.: **coche** SM)
feminine noun (e.g. **aceituna** SM)	SF	sustantivo femenino (p.ej.: **aceituna** SF)
noun which is identical for masculine and feminine (e.g. **hablante** SMF)	SMF	sustantivo invariable en género (p.ej.: **hablante** SMF)
masculine or feminine noun depending on the ending selected (e.g. **profesor(a)** SM/F, **tío/a** SM/F)	SM/F	sustantivo masculino o femenino, según la terminación (p.ej.: **profesor(a)** SM/F, **tío/a** SM/F)
masculine or feminine noun (e.g. **azúcar** SM o SF)	SM o SF	sustantivo masculino o femenino (p.ej.: **azúcar** SM o SF)
masculine plural noun (e.g. **alicates** SMPL)	SMPL	sustantivo masculino plural (p.ej.: **alicates** SMPL)
feminine plural noun (e.g. **afueras** SFPL)	SFPL	sustantivo femenino plural (p.ej.: **afueras** SFPL)

Gender in examples

Where a Spanish example is ambiguous as to the gender of the subject of a verb in the third person singular, either "he" or "she" may have been used in the translation to try to reflect the gender balance in the real world.

El género en los ejemplos

Cuando el género es ambiguo en los ejemplos españoles en los que se usa la forma de tercera persona del singular, la traducción al inglés puede ser tanto "he" como "she", en un intento de reflejar de esta forma el uso del género existente en la realidad.

Attributive use

Where a Spanish adjective is translated by a noun modifier in English which can only be used before the noun, this is labelled *antes de s*.

Uso aposicional

Cuando un adjetivo español se traduce por un sustantivo inglés que funciona como modificador de otro sustantivo y por lo tanto sólo puede ir antes del mismo, este hecho se indica tras la traducción.

papelero/a ADJ **1** (*Com*) paper (*antes de s*)

Regional labels

Words and expressions which are restricted to particular areas of the English- or Spanish-speaking worlds are marked as such:

ENGLISH REGIONAL LABELS

Australia
Brit (= Britain)
Canada
EEUU[1] (= United States of America)
Engl (= England)
Escocia[1] (= Scotland)
Irl (= Ireland)
N Engl (= North of England)
New Zealand (= New Zealand)
Scot[2] (= Scotland)
US[2] (= United States of America)
[1] Spanish-English side only
[2] English-Spanish side only

SPANISH REGIONAL LABELS

And (= Andes region: Bolivia, Chile, Colombia, Ecuador, Peru)
Arg (= Argentina)
Bol (= Bolivia)
CAm (= Central America: Costa Rica, El Salvador, Guatemala, Honduras, Nicaragua, Panama)
Caribe (Caribbean: Cuba, Puerto Rico, Santo Domingo)
Chile
Col (= Colombia)
Cono Sur[1] (= Southern Cone: Argentina, Chile, Paraguay, Uruguay)
Costa Rica
Cuba
Ecu (= Ecuador)
El Salvador
Esp[1] (= Spain)
Guat (= Guatemala)
Hond (= Honduras)
LAm (= Latin America: generally applicable to the whole region)
Mex[2]/Méx[1] (= Mexico)
Nic (= Nicaragua)
Pan (= Panama)
Par (= Paraguay)
Peru[2]
Puerto Rico
Santo Domingo
S. Cone[2] (= Southern Cone: Argentina, Chile, Paraguay, Uruguay)
Sp[2] (= Spain)
Uru (= Uruguay)
Ven (= Venezuela)
[1] Spanish-English side only
[2] English-Spanish side only

If the word is used particularly in a region, the regional label includes *esp* for especially: *esp L Am, esp Brit*

Indicating material

General indicating material takes the following forms:

In square brackets [ ]

1. Within verb entries, typical noun subjects of the headword.

> **stop** ...
> VI **1** (= *stop moving*) [*person, vehicle*] pararse, detenerse; [*clock, watch*] pararse

> **parir** ▸ CONJUG 3a VI [*mujer*] to give birth, have a baby; [*yegua*] to foal; [*vaca*] to calve; [*cerda*] to farrow; [*perra*] to pup

2. Within noun entries, typical noun complements of the headword.

Marcas de región

Aparecen marcadas como tales aquellas palabras y expresiones cuyo uso en el mundo anglófono o hispanohablante es restringido a una región determinada.

MARCAS DE REGIÓN PARA EL INGLÉS

Australia
Brit (= Reino Unido)
Canada
EEUU[1] (= Estados Unidos de América)
Engl (= Inglaterra)
Escocia[1]
Irl (= Irlanda)
N Engl (= norte de Inglaterra)
New Zealand (= Nueva Zelanda)
Scot[2] (Escocia)
US[2] (= Estados Unidos de América)
[1] en la sección de español-inglés
[2] en la sección de inglés-español

MARCAS DE REGIÓN PARA EL ESPAÑOL

And (= región andina: Bolivia, Chile, Colombia, Ecuador, Perú)
Arg (= Argentina)
Bol (= Bolivia)
CAm (= Centroamérica: Costa Rica, El Salvador, Guatemala, Honduras, Nicaragua, Panamá)
Caribe (Caribe: Cuba, Puerto Rico, Santo Domingo)
Chile
Col (= Colombia)
Cono Sur[1] (= Cono Sur: Argentina, Chile, Paraguay, Uruguay)
Costa Rica
Cuba
Ecu (= Ecuador)
El Salvador
Esp[1] (= España)
Guat (= Guatemala)
Hond (= Honduras)
LAm (= Latinoamérica)
Mex[2]/Méx[1] (= México)
Nic (= Nicaragua)
Pan (= Panamá)
Par (= Paraguay)
Perú[1]
Puerto Rico
Santo Domingo
S. Cone[2] (= Cono Sur : Argentina, Chile, Paraguay, Uruguay)
Sp[2] (= España)
Uru (= Uruguay)
Ven (= Venezuela)
[1] en la sección de español-inglés
[2] en la sección de inglés-español

Si una palabra o expresión se usa especialmente en una región, la marca de región puede incluir la abreviatura *esp*: *esp L Am, esp Brit*

Material indicador

Puede aparecer de las siguientes formas:

Entre corchetes [ ]

1. Dentro de los verbos, para los sustantivos que funcionan como sujeto de los mismos.

2. Dentro de los sustantivos, para los complementos nominales de dichos sustantivos.

bottom ['bɒtəm] N **1** *[of box, cup, sea, river, garden]* fondo *m*; *[of stairs, page, mountain, tree]* pie *m*; *[of list, class]* último/a *m/f*; *[of foot]* planta *f*; *[of shoe]* suela *f*; *[of chair]* asiento *m*;

tapa SF **1** *[de caja, olla, piano]* lid; *[de frasco]* top; *[de depósito de gasolina]* cap
2 *[de libro]* cover • **libro de ~s duras** hardback
3 *[de zapato]* heelplate

3. Typical noun complements of adjectives.

3. Dentro de los adjetivos, para los sustantivos a los que suelen modificar dichos adjetivos.

soft [sɒft] ADJ (COMPAR: **softer**, SUPERL: **softest**) **1** *(= not hard) [ground, water, cheese, pencil, contact lens]* blando; *[bed, mattress, pillow]* blando, mullido; *[metal]* maleable, dúctil;

duro/a ADJ **1** *(= resistente) [material, superficie, cama, agua]* hard; *[cable, alambre]* stiff; *[pan]* hard, stale; *[carne]* tough; *[legumbres]* hard; *[articulación, mecanismo]* stiff; *[músculo]* firm, hard

4. Typical verb or adjective complements of adverbs.

4. Dentro de los adverbios, para los verbos o adjetivos a los que suelen modificar dichos adverbios.

softly ['sɒftlɪ] ADV **1** *(= quietly) [walk, move]* silenciosamente, sin hacer ruido; *[say]* bajito, en voz baja; *[whistle]* bajito

dulcemente ADV *[sonreír, cantar]* sweetly; *[acariciar]* gently; *[amar]* tenderly, fondly; *[contestar]* gently, softly

In square brackets with +

Typical objects of verbs or of prepositions.

Entre corchetes con el signo +

Complemento nominal de verbos o preposiciones.

water ...
VT *[+ garden, plant]* regar; *[+ horses, cattle]* abrevar, dar de beber a; *[+ wine]* aguar,

crear ▷ CONJUG 1a VT **1** *(= hacer, producir) [+ obra, objeto, empleo]* to create ...
2 *(= establecer) [+ comisión, comité, fondo, negocio, sistema]* to set up; *[+ asociación, cooperativa]* to form, set up;

abide by VI + PREP *[+ rules]* atenerse a, obrar de acuerdo con; *[+ promise]* cumplir con; *[+ decision]* respetar, atenerse a; *[+ rules of competition]* ajustarse a, aceptar

In parentheses with =

Synonyms and mini-definitions.

Entre paréntesis con el signo =

Sinónimos y mini-definiciones.

wood [wʊd] N **1** *(= material)*
2 *(= firewood)* leña *f*
3 *(= forest)* bosque *m*;

oliva SF **1** *(= aceituna)* olive
2 *(= árbol)* olive tree

In parentheses ( )

Other information and hints which guide the user.

Entre paréntesis ( )

Otro tipo de información que oriente al usuario.

rise [raɪz] (VB: PT: **rose**, PP: **risen**) N ... *(in tone, pitch)* subida *f*, elevación *f*
2 *(= increase) (in number, rate, value)* aumento *m*; *(in price, temperature)* subida *f*, aumento *m*;

pintar ▷ CONJUG 1a VT **1** *(Arte) (con óleo, acuarela)* to paint; *(con lápices, rotuladores) (= dibujar)* to draw; *(= colorear)* to colour

Other indicators

Cultural equivalent sign ≈: is used when the source language headword or phrase has no precise equivalent in the target language and is therefore untranslatable. In such cases the nearest cultural equivalent is given.

Otros indicadores

Signo de equivalencia cultural ≈: usado cuando la entrada en la lengua origen no tiene un equivalente preciso en la traducción, por lo que es intraducible. En tal caso se da el equivalente cultural más próxima.

national ...
... ▸ **National Insurance** (*Brit*) ≈ Seguridad *f* Social ... ▸ **the National Lottery** (*Brit*) ≈ la lotería primitiva

ITV (SF ABR) (*Esp*) (= **Inspección Técnica de Vehículos**) ≈ MOT

An explanatory gloss (in italics) is given in cases where there is no cultural equivalent in the target language.

Si no hay un equivalente cultural en la lengua término se da una explicación en cursiva en dicha lengua.

RP (N ABBR) (*Brit*) (*Ling*) (= **Received Pronunciation**) *pronunciación estándar del inglés*

N[2] ... **20-N** *20 November, day of Franco's death*

Field labels

Labels indicating subject fields occur in the following cases:

Marcas de campo semántico

Se usan dichas marcas en los siguientes casos:

muñeca (SF) **1** (*Anat*) wrist

1. To differentiate various meanings of the headword.

1. Para diferenciar distintas acepciones de una palabra.

2. When the meaning in the source language is clear but may be ambiguous in the target language.

2. Cuando el significado en la lengua origen está claro pero puede ser ambiguo en la traducción.

retention [rɪ'tenʃən] (N) retención *f* (*also Med*)

cimera (SF) crest (*tb Heráldica*)

3. For technical terms.

3. Cuando se trata de una acepción técnica.

veer [vɪəʳ] (VI) (*also* **to veer round**) [*ship*] virar; [*car*] girar, torcer; [*wind*] cambiar de

A full list of the abbreviated field labels is given on the inside back cover of the dictionary.

Puede verse la lista completa de las abreviaturas de campo semántico en el interior de las cubiertas del diccionario.

Style labels

A dozen or so indicators of register are used to mark non-neutral words and expressions. These indicators are given for both source and target language and serve mainly as a warning to the reader using the foreign language. The following paragraphs explain the meaning of the most common style labels, of which a complete list is given with explanations on the inside back cover of the dictionary.

Marcas de estilo

Se usan una serie de indicadores de registro como marcas de palabras y expresiones sin un registro neutro para la lengua origen y para la traducción. Estas marcas sirven principalmente de advertencia para el lector que use el idioma extranjero. Los siguientes párrafos explican el significado de las marcas de estilo más frecuentes, cuya lista completa puede verse en el interior de las cubiertas del diccionario.

(i) The abbreviation *frm* (for formal) denotes formal language such as that used on an official form, in pronouncements and other formal communications.

(i) La abreviatura *frm* (de formal) denota un lenguaje usado en contextos formales como impresos oficiales, declaraciones y comunicados.

heretofore [ˌhɪətʊ'fɔːʳ] (ADV) (*frm*) (= *up to specified point*) hasta aquí; (= *up to now*) hasta ahora, hasta este momento; (= *previously*) con anterioridad

colegir ▸ CONJUG 3c, 3k (*frm*) (VT) **1** (= *juntar*) to collect, gather

(ii) * indicates that the expression, while not forming part of standard language, is used by all educated speakers in a relaxed situation, but would not be used in a formal essay or letter, or on an occasion when the speaker wishes to impress.

(ii) El asterisco * indica que la expresión no forma parte del lenguaje neutro, pero es usada en conversaciones y en la vida privada por todos los hablantes, aunque no se usaría en un ensayo, una carta oficial o en una ocasión en la que el hablante desee crear una impresión especial.

▸ **bomb along*** (VI + ADV) ir a toda marcha*, ir a toda hostia (*Sp**) • **we were bombing along at 150** íbamos a 150

chollo* (SM) **1** (= *buena oportunidad*) snip*, bargain

(iii) ⁑ indicates that the expression is used by some but not all educated speakers in a very relaxed situation. Such words should be handled with extreme care by the non-native speaker unless they are very fluent in the language and very sure of their company.

(iii) Dos asteriscos ⁑ indican que no todos los hablantes cultos usan en la vida privada la expresión a la que se refieren. Tales palabras o expresiones han de ser usadas con precaución por los hablantes no nativos a no ser que tengan un amplio dominio del idioma y conozcan bien a sus interlocutores.

clink[2]⁑ [klɪŋk] (N) (= *jail*) trena⁑ *f*

agua (SF) ...
mear ~ bendita⁑ to be a holy Joe*

(iv) ⁂ means "Danger!" Such words are liable to offend in any situation, and therefore are to be avoided by the non-native speaker.

(iv) Tres asteriscos ⁂ indican ¡peligro!. Tales palabras o expresiones pueden resultar ofensivas en una situación determinada y por lo tanto es preferible que los hablantes no nativos las eviten.

dick [dɪk] (N) **1** (*US**) sabueso *mf*
2** polla *f* (*Sp***), verga** *f*

polla (SF) ...
2** (= *pene*) prick**

(v) † denotes old-fashioned terms which are no longer in wide current use but which the foreign user will certainly find in reading, or may encounter in humorous use.

(v) † indica que un término es anticuado, apenas se usa en el lenguaje de hoy día, aunque pueden encontrarse en la literatura o en contextos humorísticos.

dashed†* [dæʃt] (ADJ) (*euph*) = **damned**

edad (SF) ...
to be of courting age†

(vi) †† denotes obsolete words which the user will normally only find in literature, or may encounter in humorous use.

(vi) †† denota palabras arcaicas que se pueden encontrar en la literatura o en contextos humorísticos.

amancebarse†† ▹ CONJUG 1a (VPR) to live together, cohabit

(vii) *liter* denotes an expression which belongs to literary language.

(vii) *liter* indica que una expresión pertenece al lenguage literario.

past [pɑːst] (ADV) ...
in times ~ antiguamente, antaño (*liter*)

(viii) The labels and symbols above are used to mark either an individual word or phrase, or a whole category, or even a complete entry. Where a headword is marked with asterisks, any phrases in the entry will only have asterisks if they are of a different register from the headword. All English compounds are marked even if their register is the same as that of the headword.

Where individual phrases rather than the whole entry or category are stylistically marked, the style label is included after the phrase in question.

(viii) Las marcas y símbolos que se acaban de explicar pueden ir acompañando a una palabra, una expresión, una categoría o toda una entrada. Si el lema lleva asteriscos, las frases incluidas en esa entrada sólo llevan asteriscos si tienen un registro diferente del lema. Todos los compuestos ingleses llevan la marca de registro aunque este sea el mismo que el del lema.

Si se trata de expresiones individuales, no de toda la entrada o categoría, la marca de estilo aparece al final de dichas expresiones.

eye ... to make (sheep's) eyes at sb*
lanzar miraditas insinuantes a algn, hacer ojitos a algn*

Note that the second asterisk refers only to *hacer ojitos a algn* and not to the translation given before the comma.

El segundo asterisco sólo se refiere a *hacer ojitos a algn* y no a la traducción dada antes de la coma.

Where a phrase contains alternatives and both/all are stylistically marked, the register is shown at the end of the phrase.

Si la frase incluye otras alternativas, se marca el registro al final de la frase si este se aplica a todas las variantes.

cabeza (SF) ... **andar** *o* **ir de ~***

Where a phrase contains alternatives and only one is stylistically marked, the register is shown as follows.

Si sólo una de las variantes necesita la marca de registro, ésta aparece como sigue:

apurada* (SF) (*LAm*) • **¿por qué no te echas** *o* **pegas una ~?** why don't you get a move on* *o* hurry up?

(only the first is informal)

(sólo la primera es informal)

acostumbrado (ADJ) ...
ya estoy ~ a que no me entiendan I'm used to *o* (*frm*) accustomed to not being understood

(only the second is formal)

(sólo la segunda es formal)

The user should not confuse the style label *liter* with the field label *Literat* which indicates that the term or expression so labelled belongs to the field of literature. Similarly, the user should note that the abbreviation *lit* indicates the literal as opposed to the figurative meaning of a word.

Conviene tener en cuenta que no significan lo mismo la marca de estilo *liter* y la marca de campo semántico *Literat*, que indica que se trata de un término o expresión perteneciente al campo de la literatura. Del mismo modo, hay que recordar que la abreviatura *lit* indica que se trata del sentido literal de una palabra, no del figurado.

Punctuation

A comma is used to separate translations which have the same or very similar meanings.

Puntuación

Se usa una coma para separar las traducciones que tienen el mismo significado, o con un significado muy similar.

perhaps [pəˈhæps] (ADV) quizá(s), tal vez
claro (ADJ) ... [*color*] light, pale

A semi-colon separates translations which are not interchangeable. Indicators are given to differentiate between non-interchangeable translations.

El punto y coma separa traducciones que no son intercambiables. Se dan indicadores para diferenciar estas traducciones.

chair [tʃɛəʳ] (N) **1** (*gen*) silla *f*; (= *armchair*) sillón *m*, butaca *f*; (= *wheelchair*) silla *f* (de ruedas); (= *seat*) lugar *m*, asiento *m*

asesinar ▹ CONJUG 1a (VT) **1** (= *matar*) to murder; (*Pol*) to assassinate

Alternative parts of phrases and translations are preceded by *or* (English-Spanish side) or *o* (Spanish-English side).

Las variantes de una frase o traducción aparecen precedidas de *or* en la sección de inglés-español y de *o* en la sección de español-inglés.

fall ...
(VI) **1 ... to ~ to** *or* **on one's knees** arrodillarse, caer de rodillas

cabeza (SF) **... andar** *o* **ir de ~***

An oblique / indicates alternatives in source language which are reflected exactly in the target language.

La barra indica alternativas en la lengua origen que se ven reflejadas igualmente en la lengua término.

fact-finding [ˈfækt,faɪndɪŋ] (ADJ) • **on a fact-finding tour/mission** en viaje/misión de reconocimiento

On the Spanish-English side an oblique is also used to indicate that the translation differs depending on whether the referent is male or female.

También se usa para separar las traducciones de masculino y femenino en la sección de español-inglés.

inglés/esa ...
(SM/F) Englishman/Englishwoman

Parentheses within illustrative phrases or their translations indicate that the material contained within them is optional.

El paréntesis dentro de las frases ilustrativas o de sus traducciones indica que el material contenido en ellos es opcional.

Fahrenheit ...
(CPD) ▸ **Fahrenheit thermometer** termómetro *m* de (grados) Fahrenheit

Equivalent phrases are separated by a dot •.

Las frases equivalentes aparecen separadas por un punto •.

charge ... • **to ~ sth (up) to sb** • **~ sth (up) to sb's account**

Cross-references

These are used to refer the user to the headword under which a certain compound, idiom or phrase has been treated (see **Idioms, proverbs and set phrases** above).

Remisiones

Se usan para enviar al usuario a las entradas en las que se encuentran otros compuestos, modismos y expresiones que incluyen la palabra en cuestión (véase más arriba **Modismos, refranes y expresiones**).

purse [pɜːs] (N) **1** (*Brit*) (*for money*) monedero *m* • **a well-lined ~** una bolsa llena • **it is beyond my ~** mis recursos no llegan a tanto, está fuera de mi alcance • IDIOM: • **to hold the ~ strings** administrar el dinero ▹ **public, silk**

They are also used to draw the user's attention to the full treatment of such words as numerals, days of the week and months of the year under certain key words.

También se usan para llamar la atención sobre las entradas en las que podrán encontrarse más frases y ejemplos relacionados con los numerales, los días de la semana y los meses del año.

January [ˈdʒænjʊərɪ] (N) enero *m* ▹ **July**

The key words which are treated in depth are:

English: **five, fifth, Tuesday, July**
Spanish: **seis, seiscientos, sexto, sábado, septiembre**

Dichas entradas son:

Inglés: **five, fifth, Tuesday, July**
Español: **seis, seiscientos, sexto, sábado, septiembre**

synonym / sinónimo

IPA phonetics / transcripción fonética

Spanish gender / género en español

homograph number / número de homógrafo

phrasal verb marked by ▶ / verbo frasal marcado con ▶

numbers for different senses / números para las distintas acepciones

~ replaces headword / ~ sustituye al lema

typical objects of verb / típicos objetos del verbo

compounds marked by ▶ / compuestos marcados con ▶

old-fashioned / anticuado

cross-reference to note / remisión a nota

American English / inglés americano

peninsular Spanish / español peninsular

very informal / muy familiar

British English / inglés británico

dally ['dælɪ] (VI) **1** (= *dawdle*) tardar • **to ~ over sth** perder el tiempo con algo ▹ **dilly-dally**
2 (= *amuse o.s.*) divertirse • **to ~ with** [+ *lover*] coquetear con, tener escarceos amorosos con; [+ *idea*] entretenerse con

Dalmatia [dæl'meɪʃə] (N) Dalmacia *f*

Dalmatian [dæl'meɪʃən] (N) (= *person*) dálmata *mf*
(ADJ) dálmata

dalmatian [dæl'meɪʃən] (N) (= *dog*) perro *m* dálmata

daltonism ['dɔːltənɪzəm] (N) daltonismo *m*

dam[1] [dæm] (N) (= *wall*) dique *m*, presa *f*; (= *reservoir*) presa *f*, embalse *m*
(VT) (*also* **dam up**) poner un dique a, represar; (*fig*) reprimir, contener
▸ **dampen down** (VT + ADV) (= *check*) [+ *demands*] contener; [+ *economy*] enfriar
▸ **dam up** (VT + ADV) = **dam**

dam[2]* [dæm] (ADJ) = **damn, damned**

dam[3] [dæm] (N) (*Zool*) madre *f*

damage ['dæmɪdʒ] (N) **1** (*gen*) daño *m*; (*visible, eg on car*) desperfectos *mpl*; (*to building, area*) daños (*pl*) • **to do** *or* **cause ~ to** [+ *building*] causar daños a; [+ *machine*] causar desperfectos en • **the bomb did a lot of ~** la bomba causó muchos daños • **not much ~ was caused to the car** el coche no sufrió grandes desperfectos
2 (*fig*) (*to chances, reputation etc*) perjuicio *m*, daño *m* • **to do** *or* **cause ~ to sth/sb** causar perjuicio a algo/algn, perjudicar algo/a algn • **the ~ is done** el daño ya está hecho
• IDIOM: • **what's the ~?*** (= *cost*) ¿cuánto va a ser?, ¿qué se debe?
3 damages (*Jur*) daños *mpl* y perjuicios
▹ **recover**
(VT) (= *harm*) dañar; [+ *machine*] averiar, causar desperfectos en; [+ *health, chances, reputation*] perjudicar • **to be ~d in a collision** sufrir daños en un choque
(CPD) ▸ **damage control operation** (US) campaña *f* para minimizar los daños
▸ **damage limitation, damage control** • **an exercise in ~ limitation** *or* **control** una campaña para minimizar los daños • **to be engaged in ~ limitation** *or* **control** esforzarse en minimizar los daños ▸ **damage limitation exercise** campaña *f* para minimizar los daños

damaged ['dæmɪdʒd] (ADJ) estropeado; (= *broken*) roto

damaging ['dæmɪdʒɪŋ] (ADJ) (*gen*) dañino; (*fig*) perjudicial (**to** para)

damascene ['dæməsiːn] (ADJ) damasquinado, damasquino
(VT) damasquinar

Damascus [də'mɑːskəs] (N) Damasco *m*

damask ['dæməsk] (ADJ) [*cloth*] adamascado; [*steel*] damasquinado
(N) (= *cloth*) damasco *m*; (= *steel*) acero *m* damasquinado
(VT) [+ *cloth*] adamascar; [+ *steel*] damasquinar
(CPD) ▸ **damask rose** rosa *f* de Damasco

dame [deɪm] (N) **1** • **Dame** (*Brit*) (= *title*) *título aristocrático para mujeres equivalente a "sir"*
2 (*esp Brit*†) dama *f*, señora *f*; (*Brit*) (*Theat*) *personaje de mujer anciana en las pantomimas británicas interpretado por un actor* ▹ PANTOMIME
3 (US†*) (= *woman*) tía* *f*, gachí *f* (*Sp**)

damfool‡ ['dæm'fuːl] (ADJ) = **damn-fool**

dammit‡ ['dæmɪt] (EXCL) ¡maldita sea!*
• IDIOM: • **as near as ~** (*Brit*) casi, por un pelo

damn [dæm] (VT) **1** (*Rel*) (= *condemn*) condenar • **the effort was ~ed from the start** desde el principio el intento estaba condenado a fracasar • **the critics ~ed the**

callana (SF) **1** (*LAm*) (*Culin*) flat earthenware pan
2 (*Cono Sur*) (*hum*) (= *reloj*) pocket watch
callandito* (ADV), **callandico*** (ADV) (= *sin ruido*) softly, very quietly; (= *furtivamente*) stealthily
callar ▹ CONJUG 1a (VI) **1** (= *dejar de hablar*) to be quiet • **¡calla, que no puedo oír la radio!** be *o* keep quiet, I can't hear the radio!, shut up *o* (*EEUU*) hush up, I can't hear the radio!* • **su madre le mandó ~** his mother ordered him to be quiet, his mother told him to shut up • **—Ernesto se casa —¡calla! ¡eso no puede ser!** "Ernesto is getting married" — "you're joking! that can't be true!"
2 (= *no hablar*) to say nothing, keep quiet • **al principio optó por ~** initially he decided to say nothing *o* keep quiet • **REFRÁN:** • **quien calla, otorga** silence is *o* gives *o* implies consent
(VT) **1** (= *hacer callar*) • **calló a los niños con un cuento** he got the children to be *o* keep quiet by reading them a story • **reparten dinero para ~ las protestas** they're giving out money to silence *o* quell complaints • **¡calla** *o* **cállate la boca!*** shut your mouth!‡, shut your face!‡
2 (= *ocultar*) to keep to o.s., keep quiet • **será mejor ~ este asunto** it's best to keep this matter to ourselves *o* keep this matter quiet
(VPR) **callarse 1** (= *dejar de hablar*) to stop talking, go quiet • **al entrar el profesor todos se ~on** when the teacher came in, everyone stopped talking *o* went quiet • **¡cállense, por favor!** please be quiet! • **si empieza a hablar, ya no se calla** once he starts talking, he doesn't stop
2 (= *no decir nada*) to say nothing, keep quiet • **en esas circunstancias es mejor ~se** in those circumstances, it would be best to say nothing *o* keep quiet
calle (SF) **1** (= *vía pública*) street; (*con más tráfico*) road • **una ~ muy céntrica** a street right in the centre of town • **~ abajo** down the street • **~ arriba** up the street
• **MODISMOS:** • **abrir ~** to make way, clear the way • **echar por la ~ de en medio** to push on, press on regardless • **se los lleva a todos de ~*** they just can't stay away from her, they find her irresistible • **llevar** *o* **traer a algn por la ~ de la amargura*** to make sb's life a misery* ▸ **calle cerrada** (*Ven, Col, Méx*), **calle ciega** (*Ven, Col*), **calle cortada** (*Cono Sur*) dead end, dead-end street, cul-de-sac ▸ **calle de doble sentido** two-way street ▸ **calle de sentido único**, **calle de una mano** (*Cono Sur*), **calle de una sola vía** (*Col*), **calle de un solo sentido** (*Chile*) one-way street ▸ **calle peatonal** pedestrianized street, pedestrian street ▸ **calle principal** main street ▸ **calle residencial** residential street (*with low speed limit and priority for pedestrians*) ▸ **calle sin salida** cul-de-sac, dead end, dead end street
▹ **aplanar, cabo**
2 (= *no casa*) **a • la ~**: • **he estado todo el día en la ~** I've been out all day • **se sentaba en la ~ a ver pasar a la gente** he used to sit out in the street *o* outside watching the people go by • **a los dos días de su detención ya estaba otra vez en la ~** two days after his arrest he was back on the streets again • **el grupo tiene ya tres discos en la ~** the group already have three records out • **irse a la ~** to go out, go outside • **¡iros a la ~ a jugar!** go and play outside! • **salir a la ~** (= *persona*) to go outside; (= *disco, publicación*) to come out • **llevo varios días sin salir a la ~** I haven't been out of the house *o* outside for several days • **el periódico salió ayer a la ~ por última vez** the

remisión a la tabla de conjugaciones / reference to verb tables
inglés americano / American English
refrán / proverb
* familiar / * informal
= sinónimo / = synonym
modismos / idioms
español de América / Latin American Spanish
compuestos marcados con ▶ / compounds marked by ▶
aclaración de la traducción / translation clarified
remisiones a otra entrada / cross-references
~ sustituye al lema / ~ replaces the headword

CPD ▸ **harvest festival** fiesta *f* de la cosecha ▸ **harvest home** (= *festival*) ≈ fiesta *f* de la cosecha; (= *season*) cosecha *f* ▸ **harvest moon** luna *f* llena ▸ **harvest time** cosecha *f*, siega *f*

harvester ['hɑːvɪstəʳ] N **1** (= *person*) [*of cereals*] segador(a) *m/f*; [*of fruit, vegetables*] recolector(a) *m/f*; [*of grapes*] vendimiador(a) *m/f*
2 (= *machine*) cosechadora *f*; (= *combine harvester*) segadora-trilladora *f*

harvesting ['hɑːvɪstɪŋ] N = **harvest**

has [hæz] VB *3rd pers sing present of* **have**

has-been* ['hæzbiːn] N vieja gloria *f*

hash¹ [hæʃ] N **1** (*Culin*) picadillo *m*
2* lío* *m*, embrollo *m* • **to make a ~ of sth** hacer algo muy mal • **he made a complete ~ of the interview** la entrevista le fue fatal
• IDIOM: • **to settle sb's ~** cargarse a algn*
CPD ▸ **hash browns** *croquetas de patata hervida y cebolla*

hash²* [hæʃ] N (= *hashish*) hachís *m*, chocolate‡ *m* (*Sp*), mota *f* (*CAm**)

hash³ [hæʃ] N (*Typ*) almohadilla *f*

hashish ['hæʃɪʃ] N hachís *m*

hasn't ['hæznt] = **has not**

hasp [hɑːsp] N (*for padlock*) hembrilla *f*; (*on window*) falleba *f*; (*on box, book*) cierre *m*

Hassidic [hə'sɪdɪk] ADJ hasídico

hassle ['hæsl] N* (= *problem, difficulty*) lío *m*, problema *m* • **no ~!** ¡no hay problema! • **it's not worth the ~** no vale la pena
VT molestar, fastidiar

hassle-free [ˌhæsəl'friː] ADJ [*experience, holiday, journey*] sin complicaciones • **the internet provides a hassle-free way of booking plane tickets** la Internet proporciona un medio sin complicaciones para la compra de billetes de avión

hassock ['hæsək] N (*Rel*) cojín *m*

hast†† [hæst] ▹ **have**

haste [heɪst] N prisa *f*, apuro *m* (*LAm*) • **to do sth in ~** hacer algo precipitadamente *or* de prisa • **to make ~** darse prisa, apurarse (*LAm*) • **to make ~ to do sth** apresurarse a hacer algo • PROVERBS: • **more ~ less speed** • **make ~ slowly** vísteme despacio que tengo prisa

hasten ['heɪsn] VT [+ *process*] acelerar; [+ *sb's end, downfall*] precipitar • **to ~ sb's departure** acelerar la partida *or* marcha de algn • **to ~ one's steps** apretar el paso • **to ~ death** precipitar *or* adelantar la muerte
VI apresurarse, darse prisa • **to ~ to do sth** apresurarse a hacer algo • **I ~ to add that ...** me apresuro a añadir que ... • **she ~ed to assure me that nothing was wrong** se apresuró a asegurarme que no pasaba nada
▸ **hasten away** VI + ADV marcharse precipitadamente (**from** de)
▸ **hasten back** VI + ADV volver con toda prisa
▸ **hasten on** VI + ADV seguir adelante con toda prisa

hastily ['heɪstɪlɪ] ADV **1** (= *hurriedly*) de prisa, apresuradamente • **I ~ suggested that ...** me apresuré a sugerir que ...
2 (= *rashly*) [*speak*] precipitadamente; [*judge*] a la ligera

hasty ['heɪstɪ] ADJ (COMPAR: **hastier**, SUPERL: **hastiest**) **1** (= *hurried*) apresurado, precipitado
2 (= *rash*) precipitado • **don't be so ~** no te precipites

hat [hæt] N sombrero *m* • **to raise one's hat** (*in greeting*) descubrirse • **to take off one's hat** quitarse el sombrero • IDIOMS: • **to eat one's hat**: • **I'll eat my hat if ...** que me maten si ... • **to hang one's hat up** jubilarse

---

equivalent in Spanish-speaking countries / equivalencia en países hispanohablantes

∗ informal / ∗ familiar

cross-reference / remisión a otra entrada

explanation (no Spanish equivalent) / explicación (sin equivalencia en español)

specialist field / campo semántico

Central American Spanish / español de Centroamérica

archaic / arcaico

Latin American Spanish / español de América

proverbs / refranes

examples / ejemplos

preposition often used / preposición usada normalmente

words which commonly co-occur / palabras que se usan a menudo juntas

common comparative and superlative forms / formas del comparativo y superlativo

idioms / modismos

creador(a) ADJ creative
SM/F **1** [*de movimiento, organización, personaje*] creator
2 (= *artista*) artist; (= *diseñador*) designer • **los grandes ~es del Renacimiento** the great artists of the Renaissance • **los ~es de moda juvenil** designers of youth fashion
SM • **el Creador** (*Rel*) the Creator

crear ▹ CONJUG 1a VT **1** (= *hacer, producir*) [+ *obra, objeto, empleo*] to create • **el hombre fue creado a imagen de Dios** man was created in the image of God • **~on una ciudad de la nada** they created a city out of nothing
2 (= *establecer*) [+ *comisión, comité, fondo, negocio, sistema*] to set up; [+ *asociación, cooperativa*] to form, set up; [+ *cargo, puesto*] to create; [+ *movimiento, organización*] to create, establish, found • **¿qué se necesita para ~ una empresa?** what do you need in order to set up *o* start a business? • **esta organización se creó para defender los derechos humanos** this organization was created *o* established *o* founded to defend human rights • **aspiraban a ~ un estado independiente** they aimed to create *o* establish *o* found an independent state
3 (= *dar lugar a*) [+ *condiciones, clima, ambiente*] to create; [+ *problemas*] to cause, create; [+ *expectativas*] to raise • **el bloqueo ha creado una situación insostenible** the blockade has created an untenable situation • **el vacío creado por su muerte** the gap left *o* created by her death • **la nicotina crea adicción** nicotine is addictive
4 (*liter*) (= *nombrar*) to make, appoint • **fue creado papa** he was made pope

creatividad SF creativity
creativo/a ADJ creative
SM/F (*tb* **creativo de publicidad**) copywriter
crece SM o SF (*Cono Sur*) = **crecida**
crecepelo SM hair-restorer
crecer ▹ CONJUG 2d VI **1** (= *desarrollarse*) [*animal, planta, objeto*] to grow • **el jazmín ha dejado de ~** the jasmine has stopped growing • **te ha crecido mucho el pelo** your hair's grown a lot • **me he dejado ~ la barba** I've grown a beard • **crecí en Sevilla** I grew up in Seville • **la princesa fue creciendo en belleza y sabiduría** the princess grew in beauty and wisdom
2 (= *aumentar*) [*cantidad, producción, sentimiento*] to grow; [*gastos*] to increase, rise; [*inflación*] to rise; [*desempleo*] to increase, grow, rise • **el número de heridos seguía creciendo** the number of wounded continued to grow • **la economía española ~á un 4%** the Spanish economy will grow by 4% • **crece el temor de un conflicto armado** there are growing fears of an armed conflict • **el viento fue creciendo en intensidad** the wind increased *o* grew in intensity • **~ en importancia** to grow in importance
3 (= *extenderse*) [*ciudad*] to grow; [*río, marea*] to rise; [*luna*] to wax
VPR **crecerse 1** (= *tomar fuerza*) • **pocos jugadores saben ~se ante la adversidad** there are few players who can stand up and be counted in the face of adversity
2* (= *engreírse*) to get full of o.s. • **con nada que le digas ya se crece** whatever you say to him he still gets all full of himself *o* his head still starts to swell
3 (*Cos*) • **en el cuello se le crece un punto** increase one stitch at the neck, add one stitch at the neck
creces SFPL **1** • **con ~** amply, fully • **superó**

campo semántico / specialist field

objetos típicos del verbo / typical objects of verb

números para las distintas acepciones / numbers for different senses

remisión a otra entrada / cross-reference

sujetos típicos del verbo / typical subjects of verb

ejemplos / examples

verbo pronominal / pronominal verb

in [ɪn]

PREPOSITION
ADVERB
ADJECTIVE
NOUN

menu
menú

PREPOSITION

*When **in** is the second element in a phrasal verb, eg **ask in**, **fill in**, **look in**, etc, look up the verb. When it is part of a set combination, eg **in the country**, **in ink**, **in danger**, **covered in**, look up the other word.*

where to look
envío a otra entrada

1 *(in expressions of place)* en; (= *inside*) dentro de • **it's in London/Scotland/Galicia** está en Londres/Escocia/Galicia • **in the garden** en el jardín • **in the house** en casa; (= *inside*) dentro de la casa • **our bags were stolen, and our passports were in them** nos robaron los bolsos, y nuestros pasaportes iban dentro

language tip
nota de uso

*When phrases like **in Madrid**, **in Germany** are used to identify a particular group, **de** is the usual translation:*

• **our colleagues in Madrid** nuestros colegas de Madrid • **the chairs in the room** las sillas de la habitación, las sillas que hay en la habitación *or* dentro de la habitación • **in here/there** aquí/allí dentro • **it's hot in here** aquí dentro hace calor

meaning indicator
indicador de acepción

2 *(in expressions of time)* **a** (= *during*) en • **in 1986** en 1986 • **in May/spring** en mayo/primavera • **in the eighties/the 20th century** en los años ochenta/el siglo 20 • **in the morning(s)/evening(s)** por la mañana/la tarde • **at four o'clock in the morning/afternoon** a las cuatro de la mañana/la tarde
b (= *for*) • **she hasn't been here in years** hace años que no viene
c (= *in the space of*) en • **I did it in 3 hours/days** lo hice en 3 horas/días • **it was built in a week** fue construido en una semana
d (= *within*) dentro de • **I'll see you in three weeks' time** *or* **in three weeks** te veré dentro de tres semanas • **he'll be back in a moment/a month** volverá dentro de un momento/un mes

3 *(indicating manner, medium)* en • **in a loud/soft voice** en voz alta/baja • **in Spanish/English** en español/inglés • **to pay in dollars** pagar en dólares • **it was underlined in red** estaba subrayado en rojo • **a magnificent sculpture in marble and copper** una magnífica escultura de *or* en mármol y cobre

4 *(= clothed in)* • **she opened the door in her dressing gown** abrió la puerta en bata • **they were all in shorts** todos iban en *or* llevaban pantalón corto • **he went out in his new raincoat** salió con el impermeable nuevo • **you look nice in that dress** ese vestido te sienta bien

*When phrases like **in the blue dress**, **in the glasses** are used to identify a particular person, **de** is the usual translation:*

• **the man in the hat** el hombre del sombrero • **the boy in the checked trousers** el chico de los pantalones de cuadros • **the girl in green** la chica vestida de verde ▹ **dressed**

5 *(giving ratio, number)* • **one person in ten** una

decir

VERBO TRANSITIVO
VERBO INTRANSITIVO
VERBO PRONOMINAL
SUSTANTIVO MASCULINO

menú
menu

▷ CONJUG 30

Para otras expresiones con el participio, ver ***dicho.***

remisión a otra entrada
where to look

VERBO TRANSITIVO **1** (*= afirmar*) to say • **ya sabe ~ varias palabras** she can already say several words, she already knows several words • **—tengo prisa —dijo** "I'm in a hurry," she said • **viene y dice: —estás despedido*** he goes "you're fired"* • **olvídalo, no he dicho nada** forget I said anything • **¿decía usted?** you were saying? • **como dicen los madrileños** as they say in Madrid • **como decía mi abuela** as my grandmother used to say • **como iba diciendo ...** as I was saying ... • **¿cómo ha dicho usted?** pardon?, what did you say? • **~ para** *o* **entre sí** to say to o.s.
decir que to say (that) • **mi amigo dice que eres muy guapa** my friend says (that) you're very pretty • **dicen que ...** they say (that) ..., people say (that) ... • **el cartel dice claramente que ...** the sign says clearly *o* clearly states that ... • **~ que sí/no** to say yes/no • **—¿viene? —dice que sí** "is she coming?" — "she says she is *o* she says so" • **la miré y me dijo que sí/no con la cabeza** I looked at her and she nodded/shook her head ▷ **adiós**

2 decir algo a algn to tell sb sth • **¿quién te lo dijo?** who told you? • **se lo dije bien claro, pero no me hizo caso** I told her quite clearly, but she didn't take any notice of me • **tengo algo que ~te** there's something I want to tell you, I've got something to tell you • **hoy nos dicen las notas** they're telling *o* giving us our results today
decir a algn que (*+ indic*) to tell sb (that) • **me dijo que no vendría** he told me (that) he wouldn't come • **ya te dije que no tiene ni idea** I told you he hasn't got a clue • **¿no te digo que no puedo ir?** I've already told you I can't go
decir a algn que (*+ subjun*) (*= ordenar*) to tell sb to do sth; (*= pedir*) to ask sb to do sth • **la profesora me dijo que esperara fuera** the teacher told me to wait outside • **le dije que fuera más tarde** I told her to go later • **dile que venga a cenar mañana con nosotros** ask him to come and have supper with us tomorrow • **te digo que te calles** I said shut up

estructuras fijas
set structures

3 (*= contar*) [*+ mentiras, verdad, secreto*] to tell • **~ tonterías** to talk nonsense ▷ **verdad**
4 (*= llamar*) to call • **¿cómo le dicen a esto en Perú?** what do they call this in Peru? • **se llama Francisco, pero le dicen Paco** his name is Francisco, but he's known as Paco • **le dicen "el torero"** he's known as "el torero" • **en México se le dice "recámara" al dormitorio** in Mexico they say "recámara" instead of "dormitorio" • **me dijo de todo** he called me all the names under the sun
5 (*= opinar*) to say • **podemos ir a Portugal, ¿tú qué dices?** we could go to Portugal, what do you say? • **¿tu familia qué dice de la boda?** what does your family say about the wedding?
6 (*rectificando*) • **había 8, digo 9** there were 8, I mean 9 • **dirá usted aquel otro** you must mean that other one • **¡qué digo!** what am

indicador de acepción
meaning indicator

Complex entries

all
any
as
ask
back
be
by
charge
do
for
get
give
go
good
hang
have
how
in
just
keep
know
make
mind
off
over
press
put
some
that
to
up
what
when
where
which
with

Language notes

ABLE, CAN
AFTER
AND
ASK
AVERAGE, HALF
BAD
BE
BECOME, GO, GET
BEFORE
BOTH
BUT
COME, GO
EASY, DIFFICULT, IMPOSSIBLE
ENOUGH
FORGET
GREAT, BIG, LARGE
GROUP
HOWEVER
HUNDRED
IF
LESS THAN, FEWER THAN
LET
LIKE
LOOK FOR
LOVE
MAJORITY, MOST
MINORITY
MORE THAN
MR, MRS, MISS
NEW
OFTEN
OLD
OR
POOR
PURE
REMEMBER
SAD
SINCE
SMALL
AS SOON AS
STILL
STRANGE, RARE
TAKE
THEN
THERE IS, THERE ARE
UNTIL
USED TO
WEAR
WHO, WHOM
WHOSE
WHY
YET
YOU

Entradas complejas

caer
coger
dar
de
decir
dejar
echar
estar
hacer
ir
llegar
llevar
mano
más
pasar
poder
poner
por
quedar
querer
sacar
salir
ser
tener
tirar
tomar
valer
venir
ver
vuelta

Notas lingüísticas

ABURRIDO
ACONSEJAR
ACOSTUMBRAR
ACUSAR
ALGUNO, ALGO
APENAS
ATENTAMENTE
AUNQUE
AYUDAR
BAJAR
CADA
CALIENTE
CANSADO
CANTIDAD
CÁRCEL
CASA
CASI
CIEN, CIENTO
CLÁSICO
COLEGIO
COLGAR
CÓMICO
CONOCER
CONSEJO
CUÁNTO
DECIR
DEJAR
DEMASIADO
DESDE
DIVERTIDO
DOS
DURANTE
ECONÓMICO
ELÉCTRICO
EN
ENFERMEDAD
ENTRAR
ESPERAR
EXPLICAR
HABLAR
HASTA
HOSPITAL
HÚMEDO
IGLESIA
KILOS, METROS, AÑOS
LLEGAR
MANERA, FORMA, MODO
MASCULINO
MUEBLE
NINGUNO
NOTICIA
OLVIDAR
PANTALONES, ZAPATOS, GAFAS
PAPEL
PAR
PAREJA
PASAR
PEDIR
PERSONA
PREFERIR
SABER
SALADO
SALIR
SER
SI
SUBIR
TODAVÍA
TODO
VACACIONES
VENIR
VIAJE

Cultural notes

A LEVELS
ACLU
ACT OF PARLIAMENT
AFFIRMATIVE ACTION
ALL-AMERICAN
FIFTH AMENDMENT
AMERICAN DREAM
ANGLO-SAXON
APRIL FOOLS' DAY
ARCHBISHOP
ASCOT
ATTORNEY
AULD LANG SYNE
BACKBENCHER
BANK HOLIDAY
BASEBALL
BED AND BREAKFAST
BEST MAN
BILL OF RIGHTS
BOOKER PRIZE
BOXING DAY
BRITAIN
BRITISH COUNCIL
BROADSHEETS AND TABLOIDS
BUDGET
BUREAU OF INDIAN AFFAIRS
BURNS NIGHT
BY-ELECTION
CABINET
CAJUN
CAPITOL
CAR BOOT SALE
CHECKS AND BALANCES
CHILDREN IN NEED
CHRISTMAS DINNER
CHURCHES OF ENGLAND/SCOTLAND
CITIZENS' ADVICE BUREAU
CITY NICKNAMES
COCKNEY
COLLEGE
COMIC RELIEF
COMMON LAW
COMMONWEALTH
COMPREHENSIVE SCHOOLS
CONGRESS
CONSTITUENCY
CONSTITUTION
CRICKET
DAR
DC – DISTRICT OF COLUMBIA
DEAN'S LIST
DEGREE
DIXIE
DOWNING STREET
DRIVE-IN
DRIVING LICENCE/DRIVER'S LICENSE
DUDE RANCH
EDINBURGH FESTIVAL
EISTEDDFOD
ELECTORAL COLLEGE
ENGLISH
ESTABLISHMENT
EXECUTIVE PRIVILEGE
STATE FAIR
FAIRNESS DOCTRINE
FCC
FDA
FOURTH OF JULY
FREEDOM OF INFORMATION ACT
FRONT BENCH
FULBRIGHT
GCSE
GLASTONBURY
GRADE
GRAMMAR SCHOOL
GRAND JURY
GRANT-MAINTAINED SCHOOL
GREEN-WELLIE BRIGADE
GREYHOUND RACING
GROUNDHOG DAY
GUY FAWKES NIGHT
HALLOWE'EN
HIGH SCHOOL
HIGHLAND GAMES
HOGMANAY
HOME COUNTIES
HONOURS LIST
IMPERIAL SYSTEM
IVY LEAGUE
LABOR DAY
LAND OF HOPE AND GLORY
LAWYERS
LEADER OF THE HOUSE
LEGION
LIBRARY OF CONGRESS
LIMERICK
LOLLIPOP LADY/MAN
LORD
MACY'S THANKSGIVING PARADE
MARGINAL SEAT
MASON-DIXON LINE
NAACP
NATIONAL GUARD
NATIONAL TRUST
NRA
NVQ
OFF-BROADWAY
OMBUDSMAN
OPEN UNIVERSITY
WE SHALL OVERCOME
OXBRIDGE
OXFAM
PAGE THREE
PANTOMIME
PEP RALLY
PHI BETA KAPPA
PILGRIM FATHERS
PLEDGE OF ALLEGIANCE
POET LAUREATE
POLITICALLY CORRECT
POPPY DAY
PREPARATORY SCHOOL
PRIMARIES
PRIVY COUNCIL
PROM
PUBLIC ACCESS TELEVISION
PULITZER
QC/KC
QUANGO
QUEEN'S/KING'S SPEECH
RA – ROYAL ACADEMY OF ARTS
RAG WEEK
REDBRICK UNIVERSITY
RHYMING SLANG
RSC – ROYAL SHAKESPEARE COMPANY
RUGBY
RULE BRITANNIA
SAVE THE CHILDREN
SLOANE RANGER
SMALL TOWN
SMITHSONIAN INSTITUTION
SORORITY/FRATERNITY
SPEAKER
SQUARE DANCE
STATE OF THE UNION ADDRESS
STATES' RIGHTS
SUNBELT
SUNDAY PAPERS
TEFL/EFL, TESL/ESL, ELT, TESOL/ESOL
TERRITORIAL ARMY
THANKSGIVING
THREE RS
V-E DAY
VICTORIAN
WASP
WESTMINSTER
WHIP
WHITEHALL
YANKEE
YEARBOOK
ZERO

Notas culturales

ACADEMIA
APELLIDO
ARAUCANO
ARPILLERA
BARAJA ESPAÑOLA
BOE
CABALGATA DE REYES
CAMINO DE SANTIAGO
CARLISMO
CARNAVAL
CARPA
CASA DE CONTRATACIÓN
CASTELLANO
CATALÁN
CAVA
CCOO
CHICHA
CHURROS
COCA
COMEDIA
COMUNIDAD AUTÓNOMA
CONGRESO DE LOS DIPUTADOS
LA CONSTITUCIÓN ESPAÑOLA
CORRIDO
CORTES GENERALES
COSTUMBRISMO
CRIANZA
CULTERANISMO, CONCEPTISMO
DENOMINACIÓN DE ORIGEN
LOS DESAPARECIDOS
DIADA NACIONAL DE CATALUNYA
DNI
DON/DOÑA
ENCOMIENDA
ENTREMÉS
EP – EDUCACIÓN PRIMARIA
ERTZAINTZA
ESCUELA OFICIAL DE IDIOMAS
ESO
ESPERPENTO
ESTANCO
EUSKERA
FALANGE ESPAÑOLA
FALLAS
FIESTAS
FOLLETÍN
FRANQUISMO
FUEROS
GALLEGO
GAUCHO
GENERACIÓN DEL 27/DEL 98
GENERALITAT
GESTORÍA
EL GORDO
GRINGO
GUARANÍ
GUARDIA CIVIL
GUERRA CIVIL ESPAÑOLA
DÍA DE LA HISPANIDAD
DÍA DE LOS (SANTOS) INOCENTES
JEREZ
LEÍSMO, LOÍSMO, LAÍSMO
LENGUAS COOFICIALES
LICENCIATURA
LOGSE
LOTERÍA
CONJUNTO MARIACHI
MARTES Y TRECE
MOVIDA MADRILEÑA
DÍA DE LOS MUERTOS
20-N
NÁHUATL
NOCHEBUENA
NOCHEVIEJA
ONCE
OPOSICIONES
OPUS DEI
PACTOS DE LA MONCLOA
PAGA EXTRAORDINARIA
PARADOR NACIONAL
PELADO
PERONISMO
PÍCARO
POLICÍA
PRENSA DEL CORAZÓN
PRESIDENTE DEL GOBIERNO
PROVINCIA
HACER PUENTE
PULQUE
QUECHUA
QUINIELA
RAE
REALISMO MÁGICO
RECONQUISTA
RESERVA
DÍA DE REYES
ROMERÍA
SACRA
SAINETE
SANFERMINES
SAN ISIDRO
SAN JUAN
SANTO
SEMANA SANTA
SENADO
SOBREMESA
SOLERA
TERTULIA
LA TRANSICIÓN
TRIBUNAL CONSTITUCIONAL
TUNA
TURRÓN
ZARZUELA

Spanish pronunciation and spelling

Pronouncing European Spanish

1 The pronunciation of European Spanish is generally quite clear from its spelling and the notes below should be sufficient for an English speaker to understand what written Spanish actually sounds like. Because Spanish pronunciation is so regular you will find that in Part I of the dictionary (Spanish into English) most of the headwords are not transcribed phonetically in IPA (International Phonetic Alphabet). Any words that do have a phonetic transcription are pronounced in a way that you would not expect, such as *reloj* [re'lo] for example, or they have been taken from another language and given a Spanish sound, often while keeping the original spelling.

The pronunciation described below could be called 'educated' Castilian. Pronunciation often heard in the Spanish regions, for example Andalusia, has not been covered. There are separate notes on the pronunciation of Latin American Spanish on p.xxxviii.

2 Placing the stress

There are simple rules for placing stress on Spanish words:

A If a word ends in a vowel, or in *n* or *s* (often an indication of the plural of verbs and nouns respectively), the penultimate syllable is stressed: *zapato, zapatos, divide, dividen, dividieron, antiviviseccionista, telefonea, historia, diluviaba.*

B If the word ends in a consonant other than *n* or *s*, the last syllable is stressed: *verdad, practicar, decibel, virrey, coñac, pesadez.*

C If the word needs to be stressed in some way contrary to rules **A** and **B**, an acute accent is written over the vowel to be stressed: *hablará, guaraní, rubí, esté, rococó, máquina, métodos, viéndolo, paralítico, húngaro.* The same syllable is stressed in the singular and plural forms of each word, but an accent may have to be added or suppressed in the plural: *crimen, crímenes, nación, naciones.* There are a few exceptions to this rule, e.g. *carácter, caracteres,* and *régimen, regímenes.* Only in a few verb forms does the stress fall further back than the antepenultimate syllable: *cántamelo, prohíbaselo.*

3 Dividing syllables

You will have seen in **2 A** above that in cases like *telefonea* and *historia* not all vowels count equally when dividing and stressing syllables. The convention is that *a, e* and *o* are 'strong' vowels while *i* and *u* are 'weak'. Bearing this in mind we can apply four rules:

A Where there is a combination of weak + strong vowels, forming a single syllable (called a diphthong), the stress falls on the strong vowel: *baila, cierra, puesto, peine, causa.*

B In a combination of weak + weak vowels, again forming a diphthong, the stress falls on the second element: *ruido, fuimos, viuda.*

C Where two strong vowels are combined they are pronounced as two distinct syllables, the stress falling according to rules **A** and **B** in section 2 above: *ma/es/tro* (three syllables), *con/tra/er* (three syllables), *cre/er* (two syllables).

D Any word that has a combination of vowels whose parts are not stressed according to the above rules is given an acute accent on the stressed part: *creído, período, baúl, ríe, tío.*
Note that in cases where IPA transcriptions are given for Spanish words, the stress mark ['] is inserted in the same way as explained for English. See **La pronunciación del inglés británico**, section 2.

4 Spanish letters and their sounds

All the examples given below are pronounced as in British English.

Vowels

Spanish vowels are pronounced clearly and quite sharply, and unlike English are not extended to form diphthongs (e.g. **side** [saɪd], **know** [nəʊ]). Unstressed vowels are relaxed only slightly (compare English **natural** ['nætʃrəl] with Spanish natural [natu'ral]). Stressed vowels are pronounced slightly more open and short before **rr** (compare **carro** with **caro**, **perro** with **pero**).

a	[a]	Not so short as **a** in English *pat, batter*, but not so long as in *rather, bar*	**pata** **amara**
e	[e]	In an open syllable (one which ends in a vowel) like **e** in English *they*, but without the sound of the **y**. In a closed syllable (one which ends in a consonant) the sound is shorter, like the **e** in *set, wet*	**me** **pelo** **sangre** **peldaño**
i	[i]	Not so short as **i** in the English *bit, tip*, but not so long as in *machine*	**iris** **filo**
o	[o]	In an open syllable (one which ends in a vowel) like **o** in the English *note*, but without the sound of [ʊ] which ends the vowel in this word. In a closed syllable (one which ends in a consonant) it is a shorter sound, but not quite so short as in the English *pot, cot*	**poco** **cosa** **bomba** **conté**
u	[u]	Like **u** in the English *rule* or **oo** in *food*. Silent after **q** and in the groups **gue**, **gui**, unless marked by a diaeresis (*argüir, fragüe, antigüedad*)	**luna** **pula** **aquel** **pague**
y	[i]	When used as a vowel – i.e. in the conjunction **y** meaning 'and', as well as at the end of words such as *voy, ley* – it is pronounced like **i**	

Diphthongs

(Single syllables consisting of two vowels. See also section 3 above)

ai, ay	[ai]	like **i** in the English *side*	**baile** **hay**
au	[au]	like **ou** in English *sound*	**áureo** **causa**
ei, ey	[ei]	like **ey** in the English *they*	**reina** **rey**
eu	[eu]	like the vowel sounds in the English **may-you**, without the sound of the **y**	**deuda** **feudo**
oi, oy	[oi]	like **oy** in the English *boy*	**oiga** **soy**

Semiconsonants

There are two semiconsonants in Spanish which appear in a variety of combinations as the first element. Not all the combinations are listed here.

i, y	[j]	like **y** in the English *yes*, *yacht* (See also the note under **y** in the list of consonants)	**bien** **hielo** **yunta** **apoyo**
u	[w]	like **w** in the English *well*	**huevo** **fuente** **agua** **guardar**

Consonants

b, v		These two letters have the same value in Spanish. There are two distinct pronunciations depending on position and context:	
	[b]	At the start of the breath group and after the written letters **m** and **n** (pronounced [m]) the sound is like the English **b**	**bomba** **boda** **enviar**
	[β]	In all other positions the sound is between an English **b** and **v** in which the lips do not quite meet (called a bilabial fricative, a sound unknown in English)	**haba** **severo** **yo voy** **de Vigo**
c		This letter has two different values:	
	[k]	**c** before **a**, **o**, **u** or a consonant is like the English **k** in keep, but without the slight aspiration which accompanies it	**calco** **acto** **cuco**
	[θ]	**c** before **e**, **i** is like the English **th** in *thin*. In parts of Andalusia and Latin America this is pronounced like **s** in English *same*, and is known as **seseo**. In words like *acción*, *sección* both types of c sound are heard [kθ]	**celda** **hacer** **cinco** **cecear**
ch	[tʃ]	like **ch** in the English *church*	**mucho** **chorro**
d		This letter has three different values depending on position and context:	
	[d]	At the start of the breath-group, and after **l**, **n** the sound is like the English **d**	**dama** **aldea** **andar**
	[ð]	Between vowels and after consonants other than **l**, **n** the sound is relaxed and similar to the English sound **th** [ð] in *this*. In parts of Spain and in casual speech it is further relaxed and even disappears, especially in the **-ado** ending	**pide** **cada** **pardo** **sidra**
		In the final position, the second type of [ð] is further relaxed or completely omitted. In eastern parts of Spain this final **d** may be heard as a **t**	**verdad** **usted** **Madrid** **callad**
f	[f]	like the English **f** in **f**or	**fama** **fofo**
g		This letter has three different values depending on position and context:	
	[x]	Before **e**, **i** it is the same as Spanish **j** (see below)	**Gijón** **general**

	[g]	At the start of the breath group and after **n** the sound is that of the English **g** in ***get***	**gloria** **rango** **pingüe**
	[ɣ]	In other positions the sound is as in the second type above, but it is fricative and not plosive Note that in the group **gue**, **gui** the **u** is silent (*guerra*, *guindar*) except when marked by a diaeresis (*antigüedad*, *argüir*). In the group **gua** all the letters are sounded (***gua**rdia*, ***gua**po*)	**haga** **agosto**
h		always silent	
j	[x]	a strong guttural sound not found in the English of England, but like the **ch** of Scots *loch*, Welsh *bach*, or German *Aachen*, *Achtung*. It is silent at the end of a word (*reloj*)	**jota** **jején** **baraja**
k	[k]	like the English letter **k** in *kick*, but without the slight aspiration which accompanies it	**kilo**
l	[l]	like English letter **l** in *love*	**lelo** **pañal**
ll	[ʎ]	similar to the English **lli** in *million*. In parts of Spain and most parts of Latin America it is pronounced as [j] and in other parts as [ʒ]. The pronunciation as [j] is rapidly becoming more widely accepted in Spain.	**calle** **ella** **lluvia** **millón**
m	[m]	like the letter **m** in English ***made***	**mano** **mamá**
n	[n]	like the letter **n** in English *none*, but before **v** is pronounced as **m**, the group making [mb] (e.g. ***en**viar*, ***sin** valor*)	**nadie** **pan** **pino**
ñ	[ɲ]	similar to the English sound **ni** [nj] in *onion*	**uña** **ñoño**
p	[p]	like English letter **p** in ***p**ut*, but without the slight aspiration which accompanies it. It is often silent in *septiembre*, *séptimo*	**padre** **patata**
q	[k]	like English **k** in *kick*, but without the slight aspiration which accompanies it. Always written in combination with **u**, which is silent.	**que** **quinqué** **bosque** **quiosco**
r	[r]	a single trill or vibration stronger than any **r** in the English of England, but like the Scots **r**. It is more relaxed in the final position and is silent in parts of Spain and Latin America. Pronounced like **rr** at the start of a word and also after **l**, **n**, **s**.	**coro** **quiere** **rápido** **real**
rr	[rr]	strongly trilled in a way that does not exist in English	**torre** **burro** **irreal**
s		Two pronunciations:	
	[s]	Except in the instances mentioned next, it is like the letter **s** in English *same*	**casa** **Isabel** **soso**
	[z]	Before a voiced consonant (**b**, **d**, **g**, **l**, **m**, **n**) it is usually pronounced like **s** in English *rose*, *phase*	**desde** **asgo** **mismo** **asno**
t	[t]	like English **t** in ***t**ame*, but without the slight aspiration which accompanies it	**título** **pata**
v		see **b**	
w		found in a few recent loanwords only; usually pronounced like Spanish **b**, **v** or like an English **v**, or kept as English **w**	**wáter** **week-end** **wolframio**
x		There are several possible pronunciations:	
	[ks]	Between vowels, **x** is pronounced like English **x** in *box* [ks], or	**máximo**
	[gs]	like **gs** in big stick [gs]	**examen**
	[s]	In a few words the **x** is pronounced between vowels like English **s** in *same*, but not by all Spanish speakers	**exacto** **auxilio**
	[s]	Before a consonant **x** is pronounced like English **s** in *same*, but not by all Spanish speakers	**extra** **sexto**
y	[j]	as a consonant or semiconsonant, **y** is pronounced as in English *yes*, *youth*. In emphatic speech in Spain and Latin America this is similar to **j** in the English word jam [dʒ]. In Argentina, Chile etc this **y** is pronounced like the **s** in English *leisure* [ʒ]	**mayo** **yo** **mayor** **ya**
z	[θ]	like the English **th** in ***th**in*. In parts of Andalusia and Latin America this is pronounced like the English **s** in *same*, and is known as **seseo**	**zapato** **zorro** **zumbar** **luz**

5 Additional notes on pronunciation

A The letter **b** is usually not pronounced in groups with **s** such as **obscuro**, **substituir**. In practice, such words are generally written **oscuro**, **sustituir** etc and this is the spelling under which they are treated in the dictionary.

B With one exception there are no real double consonants in Spanish speech. **cc** in words like **acción** is two separate sounds [kθ], while **ll** and **rr** have their own values (see table).

The exception is the **nn** group found in words with the prefix **in-**, e.g. **innato**, or occasionally **con-**, **sin-** as in **connatural**, **sinnúmero**. In these cases the **n** is pronounced double [nn].

C When taking loanwords from other languages the majority of Spanish speakers will adapt the pronunciation of these words, usually while keeping the original spelling. For some examples of this, see the main dictionary text under **chalet**, **jazz** and **shock**.

D No well-established Spanish word begins with what is called 'impure s', i.e. **s** plus a consonant as an initial group. When Spanish speakers have to pronounce a foreign word or name they will almost always add an initial e-sound, so that Smith becomes [ez'miθ] or [es'mis]. More recent anglicisms tend to be written in Spanish as **slip**, **slogan** etc, but are pronounced [ez'lip] and [ez'loɣan], while more established English loanwords are written **esnob**, **esplín** etc and are pronounced accordingly.

6 The letters of the Spanish alphabet

When letters of the alphabet are spoken one at a time, or when a word is spelled out letter by letter etc, the names of the letters are as follows:

a	[a]	**j**	['xota]	**r**	['ere]
b	[be] (*in LAm* [be'larɣa])	**k**	[ka]	**rr***	['erre]
c	[θe] *or* [se]	**l**	['ele]	**s**	['ese]
ch*	[tʃe]	**ll***	['eʎe]	**t**	[te]
d	[de]	**m**	['eme]	**u**	[u]
e	[e]	**n**	['ene]	**v**	['uβe] (*in LAm* [be'korta])
f	['efe]	**ñ**	['eɲe]	**w**	['uβe 'doβle] (*in LAm* ['doβle be])
g	[xe]	**o**	[o]	**x**	['ekis]
h	['atʃe]	**p**	[pe]	**y**	[i'ɣrjeɣa]
i	[i]	**q**	[ku]	**z**	['θeta] *or* ['seta]

The gender of the letters is feminine: '¿esto es una c o una t?' You also say 'una a' and 'la a', 'una h' and 'la h' (i.e. you do not apply the rule as in un ave, el agua).

*Though not strictly letters of the alphabet, these are considered separate sounds in Spanish.

Pronouncing Latin American Spanish

The pronunciation of Latin American Spanish varies widely from place to place, so the following notes are intended to give a general picture only. As a rule, the Spanish spoken in the upland areas of Latin America is similar to Castilian Spanish, while the lowland and coastal areas have many features of Andalusian pronunciation. Vowel sounds are all roughly the same, but there are differences in the way consonants are pronounced. These are listed below:

1 The Castilian [θ] sound (like the **th** in the English word ***th**in*) which is written **c** or **z** is pronounced as various kinds of **s** [s] throughout Latin America. This is known as **seseo**.

2 At the end of a syllable or a word, **s** is a slight aspiration, e.g. **las dos** [lah'doh], **mosca** ['mohka], but in parts of the Andes, upland Mexico and Peru the [s] sound is retained as in Castilian Spanish.

3 The Castilian written **ll** [ʎ] (like **lli** in the English word *mi**lli**on*) is pronounced in three different ways in Latin America. In parts of Colombia, all Peru, Bolivia, N. Chile and Paraguay it remains [ʎ]. In Argentina, Uruguay, upland Ecuador and part of Mexico it is pronounced [ʒ]. In the remaining areas it is pronounced [j]. When this last kind [j] is in contact with the vowels **e** and **i** it disappears altogether, and one finds incorrect written forms such as **gaína** (for **gallina**) and **biete** (for **billete**).

4 In all parts of Latin America you will often find confusion between the letters **l** and **r**: **clin** (for **crin**), **carma** (for **calma**) etc.

5 Written **h** is silent in Castilian, but in parts of Mexico and Peru this **h** is aspirated at the start of a word, so you may find incorrectly spelt forms such as **jarto** (for **harto**) and **jablar** (for **hablar**). Compare **halar/jalar** and other cases in the main dictionary text.

Spanish spelling

1 Use of capitals

As in English, capital letters are used to begin words in the following cases:

• for the first letter of the first word in a sentence

• for proper names (but see also below)

María, el Papa, el Rey, la Real Academia Española,

Viernes Santo, el Partido Laborista, Dios

Note that where the article is an integral part of the proper name, it also begins with a capital – **El Escorial, La Haya, La Habana** – but where the article is generally or optionally used with the name of a country, it does not begin with a capital – **la India, la Argentina**

• for abbreviations of titles:

Sr., D., Excm^{a}

In the following cases usage differs from English:

• names of days and months:

lunes, mayo

• the pronoun **yo**, unless it begins a sentence

• while capitals are used for names of countries, they are not used for the adjectives derived therefrom:

Francia, but **francés**

Similarly, adjectives derived from proper names do not begin with a capital:

... en los estudios lorquianos, las teorías einsteinianas

• in the titles of books, films, plays etc, only the first word begins with a capital letter:

Lo que el viento se llevó, Cien años de soledad

• points of the compass begin with lower case:

norte, sur etc

(though they are capitalized if part of a name: **Korea del Sur**)

• official and noble titles:

el duque de Alba, el ministro de Interior

Note that capital letters can be accentuated in the same way as lower case letters.

2 Punctuation

Other than the differences listed below, punctuation in English and Spanish is very similar.

A Exclamation marks and question marks

An inverted exclamation mark (¡) or question mark (¿) is required at the start of the exclamation or question in addition to the standard exclamation mark or question mark at the end. The position of these marks does not always coincide with the beginning of the sentence:

¡Qué calor hace!
Pues, ¿vamos o no vamos?
Son trece en total, ¿verdad?

B Full stops

These are used very much as in English, except that:

• they are generally used after abbreviations:
Sr. Solís

They are used in numbers where English uses a comma:

English	*Spanish*
10,587	10.587

C Commas

A comma is used instead of the decimal point:

English	*Spanish*
10.1	10,1 (*diez coma uno*)

D Colons

These are used instead of a comma after the name of the recipient of a letter, though nowadays the colon is often left out altogether in these contexts:

Querida Dolores:
Muy Señor mío:

E Semicolons

These are sometimes used where a comma or a full stop would be expected in English, to denote a longer pause between phrases:

Me habló de la familia, los amigos, el trabajo; sin embargo, no mencionó a su hijo.

F Hyphens

These are used very sparingly, since the tendency is for compound nouns and adjectives to be written as a single word:

antifranquista, proeuropeo, antihistamínico

When the two adjectives refer to different things, the hyphen is used:

el eje franco-alemán, el pensamiento anglo-americano

Hyphens are also used as in English to join nouns:

misiles tierra-aire, el eje Roma-Berlín

Confusion reigns in the use or absence of the hyphen in such combinations: **hombre rana, hombre-rana**. If the combination is brief there is a tendency to use the hyphen: **granja-escuela, grúa-puente, dos grúas-puente**. The Academy appears to rule against the hyphen but has hardly put its mind as yet to this relatively new and rapidly developing usage.

G The dash

1. The dash is often used to insert parenthetical material where English would use a comma:

la moción de censura fue aprobada por unanimidad — algo cada vez más raro en el parlamento — a últimas horas de la sesión.

2. The dash is used to represent continuous dialogue where English would use inverted commas. It is used both to show a change of speaker and the resumption of dialogue after a pause:

—¿Vas a venir? —dijo suavemente
—No puedo —contesté

Note that punctuation in direct speech is placed after the dash.

H Quotation marks

Traditionally "*comillas*" «...» were used to enclose quotations, unusual words, and so on. However, the tendency in some media these days is to use standard inverted commas, and the *El País* style guide, which is widely followed in Spain, recommends this.

3 Word division

The rules for splitting words in Spanish are not the same as for English. The main points are:

A A single consonant between vowels is grouped with the second of them: **pa-lo, Barcelo-na**.

B In a group of two consonants between vowels, the first is grouped with the preceding vowel and the second with the following vowel: **in-nato, des-mochar, paten-te**. But groups having **l** or **r** as the second element are considered as units and join the following vowel only: **re-probar, de-clarar**.

C A group consisting of consonant + **h** may be split: **ex-hibición, Al-hambra**.

D Remember that **ch**, **ll** and **rr** are considered as individual letters and must therefore never be split: **aprove-char, aga-lla, contra-revolucionario**.

E In a group of three consonants, the first two join the preceding vowel: **trans-porte, cons-tante**. The exception to this rule is if the third consonant in this group is **l** or **r** only the first consonant joins the preceding vowel while the second and third join the following vowel: **som-bra, des-preciar, con-clave**.

F Two vowels should never be separated, even where they form one syllable: **rui-do, maes-tro, pro-veer**.

G Where it is obvious that a word is made up of two more words which have an independent existence of their own, the composite word can be split in ways that contradict the above rules: **latino-americano, re-examinar, vos-otros.** The same applies to some prefixes: **des-animar, ex-ánime**.

Pronunciación y ortografía del inglés

La pronunciación del inglés británico

Como es sabido, la ortografía del inglés se ajusta a criterios históricos y etimológicos y en muchos puntos apenas ofrece indicaciones ciertas de cómo ha de pronunciarse cada palabra. Por ello nos ha parecido aconsejable y de utilidad para los hispanohablantes dar para cada palabra inglesa una pronunciación figurada o transcripción. Al tratar de explicar en estas notas los sonidos del inglés mediante comparaciones con los sonidos del español en un espacio reducido nos damos cuenta de que realizamos una labor que no pasa de ser aproximativa.

1 Sistema de signos

Se emplean los signos de la IPA (International Phonetic Association). Hemos seguido en general las transcripciones de Daniel Jones, *English Pronouncing Dictionary*, London, Dent, 14th ed., 1989. En el prólogo de esta obra el autor explica los principios que le han guiado en su trabajo.

2 Acentuación

En las transcripciones el signo ['] se coloca delante de la sílaba acentuada. El signo [ˌ] se pone delante de la sílaba que lleva el acento secundario o más ligero en las palabras largas, p.ej. **acceleration** [ækˌseləˈreɪʃən]. Dos signos de acento principal [' '] indican que las dos sílabas, o bien dos de las sílabas, se acentúan igualmente, p.ej. **A 1** [ˈeɪˈwʌn], **able-bodied** [ˈeɪblˈbɒdɪd].

3 Signos impresos en cursiva

En la palabra ***annexation*** [ˌænekˈseɪʃ*ə*n], la [*ə*] en cursiva indica que este sonido puede o no pronunciarse; bien porque muchos hablantes la pronuncian pero otros muchos no, o bien porque es un sonido que se oye en el habla lenta y cuidada pero que no se oye en el habla corriente y en el ritmo de la frase entera.

4 Transcripciones alternativas

En los casos donde se dan dos transcripciones, ello indica que ambas pronunciaciones son igualmente aceptables en el uso culto, p.ej. **medicine** [ˈmedsɪn, ˈmedɪsɪn], o bien que la pronunciación varía bastante según la posición de la palabra en la frase y el contexto fonético, p.ej. **an** [æn, ən, n].

5 Véase también la nota sobre la pronunciación del inglés norteamericano (pág. xliii).

6 El orden en que se explican los signos abajo es más o menos ortográfico y no estrictamente fonético.

Vocales

[æ]	sonido breve, bastante abierto, parecido al de **a** en *carro*	**bat** **apple**	[bæt] [ˈæpl]
[ɑː]	sonido largo parecido al de **a** en *caro*	**farm** **calm**	[fɑːm] [kɑːm]
[e]	sonido breve, bastante abierto, parecido al de **e** en *perro*	**set** **less**	[set] [les]
[ə]	'vocal neutra', siempre átona; parecida a la **e** del artículo francés *le* y a la **a** final del catalán (p.ej. *casa*, *porta*)	**above** **porter** **convey**	[əˈbʌv] [ˈpɔːtəʳ] [kənˈveɪ]
[ɜː]	forma larga del anterior, en sílaba acentuada; algo parecido al sonido de **eu** en la palabra francesa *leur*	**fern** **work** **murmur**	[fɜːn] [wɜːk] [ˈmɜːməʳ]
[ɪ]	sonido breve, abierto, parecido al de **i** en *esbirro*, *irreal*	**tip** **pity**	[tɪp] [ˈpɪtɪ]
[iː]	sonido largo parecido al de **i** en *vino*	**see** **bean** **ceiling**	[siː] [biːn] [ˈsiːlɪŋ]
[ɒ]	sonido breve, bastante abierto, parecido al de **o** en *corra*, *torre*	**rot** **wash**	[rɒt] [wɒʃ]
[ɔː]	sonido largo, bastante cerrado, algo parecido al de **o** en *por*	**ball** **board**	[bɔːl] [bɔːd]
[ʊ]	sonido muy breve, más cerrado que la **u** en *burro*	**soot** **full**	[sʊt] [fʊl]
[uː]	sonido largo, parecido al de **u** en *uno*, *supe*	**root** **fool**	[ruːt] [fuːl]
[ʌ]	sonido abierto, breve y algo oscuro, sin correspondencia en español; se pronuncia en la parte anterior de la boca sin redondear los labios	**come** **rum** **blood** **nourish**	[kʌm] [rʌm] [blʌd] [ˈnʌrɪʃ]

Diptongos

[aɪ]	sonido parecido al de **ai** en *fraile*, *vais*	**lie** **fry**	[laɪ] [fraɪ]
[aʊ]	sonido parecido al de **au** en *pausa*, *sauce*	**sow** **plough**	[saʊ] [plaʊ]
[eɪ]	sonido medio abierto, pero más cerrado que la **e** de *casé*; suena como si le siguiese una [i] débil, especialmente en sílaba acentuada	**fate** **say** **waiter** **straight**	[feɪt] [seɪ] [ˈweɪtəʳ] [streɪt]

[əʊ]	sonido que es una especie de **o** larga, sin redondear los labios ni levantar la lengua; suena como si le siguiese una [u] débil	**ago** **also** **atrocious** **note**	[ə'gəʊ] ['ɔ:lsəʊ] [ə'trəʊʃəs] [nəʊt]
[ɛə]	sonido que se encuentra únicamente delante de la **r**: el primer elemento se parece a la **e** de *perro*, pero es más abierto y breve; el segundo elemento es una forma débil de la 'vocal neutra' [ə]	**there** **rare** **fair** **ne'er**	[ðɛəʳ] [rɛəʳ] [fɛəʳ] [nɛəʳ]
[ɪə]	sonido cuyo primer elemento es una **i** medio abierta; el segundo elemento es una forma débil de la 'vocal neutra' [ə]	**here** **interior** **fear** **beer**	[hɪəʳ] [ɪn'tɪərɪəʳ] [fɪəʳ] [bɪəʳ]
[ɔɪ]	sonido cuyo primer elemento es una **o** abierta; seguido de una **i** abierta pero débil; parecido al sonido de **oy** en *voy* o de **oi** en *coime*	**toy** **destroy** **voice**	[tɔɪ] [dɪs'trɔɪ] [vɔɪs]
[ʊə]	sonido cuyo primer elemento es una **u** medio larga; el segundo elemento es una forma débil de la 'vocal neutra' [ə]	**allure** **sewer** **pure**	[ə'ljʊəʳ] [sjʊəʳ] [pjʊəʳ]

Consonantes

[b]	como la **b** de *tumbar, umbrío*	**bet** **able**	[bet] ['eɪbl]
[d]	como la **d** de *conde, andar*	**dime** **mended**	[daɪm] ['mendɪd]
[f]	como la **f** de *fofo, inflar*	**face** **snaffle**	[feɪs] ['snæfl]
[g]	como la **g** de *grande, rango*	**go** **agog**	[gəʊ] [ə'gɒg]
[h]	es una aspiración fuerte, algo así como la jota castellana [x] pero sin la aspereza gutural de aquélla	**hit** **reheat**	[hɪt] ['ri:'hi:t]
[j]	como la **y** de *cuyo, reyes*	**you** **pure** **million**	[ju:] [pjʊəʳ] ['mɪljən]
[k]	como la **c** de *cama* o la **k** de *kilómetro*, pero acompañada por una ligera aspiración inexistente en español	**catch** **kiss** **chord** **box**	[kætʃ] [kɪs] [kɔ:d] [bɒks]
[l]	como la **l** de *leer, pala*	**lick** **place**	[lɪk] [pleɪs]
[m]	como la **m** de *mes, comer*	**mummy** **roam**	['mʌmɪ] [rəʊm]
[n]	como la **n** de *nada, hablan*	**nut** **sunny**	[nʌt] ['sʌnɪ]
[ŋ]	como el sonido que tiene la **n** en *banco, rango*	**bank** **sinker** **singer**	[bæŋk] ['sɪŋkəʳ] ['sɪŋəʳ]
[p]	como la **p** de *palo, ropa*, pero acompañada por una ligera aspiración inexistente en español	**pope** **pepper**	[pəʊp] ['pepəʳ]
[r]	Es un sonido muy débil, casi semivocal, que no tiene la vibración fuerte que caracteriza la **r** española. Se articula elevando la punta de la lengua hacia el paladar duro. (NB: En el inglés de Inglaterra la **r** escrita se pronuncia únicamente delante de vocal; en las demás posiciones es muda. Véase abajo).	**rate** **pear** **fair** **blurred** **sorrow**	[reɪt] [pɛəʳ] [fɛəʳ] [blɜ:d] ['sɒrəʊ]
[ʳ]	Este signo en las transcripciones indica que la **r** escrita en posición final de palabra se pronuncia en el inglés británico en muchos casos cuando la palabra siguiente empieza con vocal. En algún dialecto inglés y sobre todo en los Estados Unidos esta **r** se pronuncia siempre, así cuando la palabra se pronuncia aislada como cuando la siguen otras (empezando con vocal o sin ella).	**bear** **humour** **after**	[bɛəʳ] ['hju:məʳ] ['ɑ:ftəʳ]
[s]	como la **s** (sorda) de *casa, sesión*	**sit** **scent** **cents** **pox**	[sɪt] [sent] [sents] [pɒks]
[t]	como la **t** de *tela, rata*, pero acompañada por una ligera aspiración inexistente en español	**tell** **strut** **matter**	[tel] [strʌt] ['mætəʳ]
[v]	Inexistente en español (aunque se encuentra en catalán y valenciano). En inglés es sonido labiodental, y se produce juntando el labio inferior con los dientes superiores.	**vine** **river** **cove**	[vaɪn] ['rɪvəʳ] [kəʊv]
[w]	como la **u** de *huevo, puede*	**wine** **bewail**	[waɪn] [bɪ'weɪl]

[z]	como la **s** (sonora) de *desde, mismo*	**zero**	[ˈzɪərəʊ]
		roses	[ˈrəʊzɪz]
		buzzer	[ˈbʌzəʳ]
[ʒ]	Inexistente en español, pero como la **j** de las palabras francesas *jour, jalousie*, o como la **g** de las palabras portuguesas *gente, geral*	**rouge**	[ruːʒ]
		leisure	[ˈleʒəʳ]
		azure	[ˈeɪʒəʳ]
	Este sonido aparece a menudo en el grupo [dʒ], parecido al grupo **dj** de la palabra francesa *adjacent*	**page**	[peɪdʒ]
		edge	[edʒ]
		jail	[dʒeɪl]
[ʃ]	Inexistente en español, pero como la **ch** de las palabras francesas *chambre, fiche*, o como la **x** de la palabra portuguesa *roxo*	**shame**	[ʃeɪm]
		ocean	[ˈəʊʃən]
		ration	[ˈræʃən]
		sugar	[ˈʃʊgəʳ]
	Este sonido aparece a menudo en el grupo [tʃ], parecido al grupo **ch** del español *mucho, chocho*	**much**	[mʌtʃ]
		chuck	[tʃʌk]
		natural	[ˈnætʃrəl]
[θ]	como la **z** de *zumbar*, o la **c** de *ciento*	**thin**	[θɪn]
		maths	[mæθs]
[ð]	forma sonorizada del anterior, algo parecido a la **d** de *todo, hablado*	**this**	[ðɪs]
		other	[ˈʌðəʳ]
		breathe	[briːð]
[x]	sonido que en rigor no pertenece al inglés de Inglaterra, pero que se encuentra en el inglés de Escocia y en palabras escocesas usadas en Inglaterra etc; es como la **j** de *joven, rojo*	**loch**	[lɔx]

7 Sonidos extranjeros

El grado de corrección con que un hablante de inglés pronuncia las palabras extranjeras que acaban de incorporarse al idioma depende – como en español – de su nivel cultural y de los conocimientos que pueda tener del idioma de donde se ha tomado la palabra. Las transcripciones que damos de tales palabras representan una pronunciación más bien culta. En las transcripciones la tilde [˜] indica que la vocal tiene timbre nasal (en muchas palabras de origen francés). En las pocas palabras tomadas del alemán aparece a veces la [x], para cuya explicación véase el cuadro de las consonantes.

8 Las letras del alfabeto inglés

Cuando se citan una a una, o cuando se deletrea una palabra para mayor claridad, o cuando se identifica un avión etc por una letra y su nombre, las letras suenan así:

a	[eɪ]	**j**	[dʒeɪ]	**s**	[s]
b	[biː]	**k**	[keɪ]	**t**	[tiː]
c	[siː]	**l**	[el]	**u**	[juː]
d	[diː]	**m**	[em]	**v**	[viː]
e	[iː]	**n**	[en]	**w**	[ˈdʌbljuː]
f	[ef]	**o**	[əʊ]	**x**	[eks]
g	[dʒiː]	**p**	[piː]	**y**	[waɪ]
h	[eɪtʃ]	**q**	[kjuː]	**z**	[zed] *(en EEUU* [ziː])
i	[aɪ]	**r**	[ɑːʳ]		

La pronunciación del inglés norteamericano

Empleamos las abreviaturas (*Brit*) (British) y (*US*) (United States).

1 Acentuación

Las palabras que tienen dos sílabas o más después del acento principal llevan en inglés americano un acento secundario que no tienen en inglés británico, p.ej.

	(*US*)	(*Brit*)
dictionary	ˈdɪkʃəˌnerɪ	ˈdɪkʃənrɪ
secretary	ˈsekrəˌterɪ	ˈsekrətrɪ

En algunos casos se acentúa en inglés americano una sílaba distinta de la que lleva el acento en inglés británico, p.ej:

primarily	praɪˈmærɪlɪ	ˈpraɪmərɪlɪ

Este cambio de acento se percibe ahora también, por influencia norteamericana, en el inglés de Inglaterra.

2 Entonación

El inglés americano se habla con un ritmo más lento y en un tono más monótono que en Inglaterra, debido en parte al alargamiento de las vocales que se apunta abajo.

3 Sonidos

Muchas de las vocales breves acentuadas en inglés británico se alargan mucho en inglés americano, y alguna vocal inacentuada en inglés británico se oye con más claridad en inglés americano, p.ej.

rapid	ˈræːpɪd	ˈræpɪd
capital	ˈkæːbɪdəl	ˈkæpɪtl

Una peculiaridad muy notable del inglés americano es la nasalización de las vocales antes y después de las consonantes nasales [m, n, ŋ].

En las vocales individuales también hay diferencias. El sonido [ɑː] en inglés británico en muchas palabras se pronuncia en inglés americano como [æ] o bien [æː], p.ej.

	(*US*)	(*Brit*)
grass	græs græːs	grɑːs
answer	ˈænsər ˈæːnsər	ˈɑːnsəʳ

El sonido [ɒ] en inglés británico se pronuncia en inglés americano casi como una [ɑ] oscura, p.ej.

dollar	ˈdɑlər	ˈdɒləʳ
hot	hɑt	hɒt
topic	ˈtɑpɪk	ˈtɒpɪk

El diptongo que se pronuncia en inglés británico [juː] en sílaba acentuada se pronuncia en la mayor parte de inglés americano sin [j], p.ej.

Tuesday	ˈtuːzdɪ	ˈtjuːzdɪ
student	ˈstuːdənt	ˈstjuːdənt

Pero muchas palabras de este tipo se pronuncian en inglés americano igual que en inglés británico, p.ej. **music**, **pure**, **fuel**.

En último lugar entre las vocales, se nota que la sílaba final **-ile** que se pronuncia en inglés británico [aɪl] es a menudo en inglés americano [əl] o bien [ɪl], p.ej.

missile	ˈmɪsəl ˈmɪsɪl	ˈmɪsaɪl

Existen otras diferencias en la pronunciación de las vocales de palabras individuales, p.ej. **tomato**, pero éstas se tratan individualmente en el texto del diccionario.

En cuanto a las consonantes, hay que destacar dos diferencias. La consonante sorda [t] entre vocales suele sonorizarse bastante en inglés americano, p.ej.

	(US)	*(Brit)*
united	jʊ'naɪdɪd	juː'naɪtɪd

o sufre lenición [t].

La *r* escrita en posición final después de vocal o entre vocal y consonante es por la mayor parte muda en inglés británico, pero se pronuncia a menudo en inglés americano, p.ej.

where	wɛər	wɛəʳ
sister	'sɪstər	'sɪstəʳ

Hemos tomado esto en cuenta en las transcripciones en el texto del diccionario. También en posición final de sílaba (no sólo de palabra) se nota esta pronunciación de la *r* escrita:

	(US)	*(Brit)*
burden	'bɜːrdn	'bɜːdn
jersey	'dʒɜːrzɪ	'dʒɜːzɪ

Conviene advertir que aun dentro del inglés de Estados Unidos hay notables diferencias regionales; la lengua de Nueva Inglaterra difiere bastante de la del Sur, la del Medio Oeste no es la de California, etc. Los datos que constan arriba no son más que indicaciones muy someras.

La ortografía del inglés

Vamos a hablar aquí de una serie de reglas ortográficas del inglés que pueden resultar de utilidad para los hablantes de español, así como de las diferencias ortográficas entre el inglés británico y el norteamericano. Nos referiremos, en primer lugar, al inglés británico.

1 Consonantes dobles

A En las palabras monosílabas que acaban en una sola consonante, esta consonante se dobla cuando se añade un sufijo que empieza por vocal.

Ej: **knot + -ed = knotted**; **cut + -er = cutter**; **hit + -ing = hitting**

EXCEPCIONES:
Cuando en la palabra hay dos vocales juntas.

Ej: **feel → feeling**

Cuando la consonante final es doble.

Ej: **hand → handed**

B En las palabras de dos o tres sílabas acabadas en consonante precedida de una sola vocal, esta consonante se dobla al añadírsele un sufijo, siempre que el énfasis de la raíz recaiga en la última sílaba.

Ej: **regret + -ing = regretting**; **transfer + -ed = transferred**; **begin + -er = beginner**

NOTA: cuando la última sílaba no va acentuada esto no ocurre.

Ej: **enter + -ed = entered**, **answer + -ing = answering**, **count + -er = counter**.

Sin embargo, existen algunas excepciones como:

kidnap → kidnapper, **kidnapped** etc; **worship → worshipping**, **worshipped** etc; **handicap → handicapped**, **handicapping**

C En algunas palabras acabadas en **-l**, esta **l** se suele hacer doble en los dos casos siguientes:

– en las palabras acabadas por **-l** precedida de una sola vocal.

Ej: **equal → equalling**; **instil → instilled**; **repel → repellent**

– en las palabras acabadas en dos vocales que formen un diptongo.

Ej: **real → really**; **fuel → fuelled**

2 Cuando desaparece la -e final

A En las palabras acabadas en una sola **-e** precedida de consonante, la **-e** desaparece cuando se añade un sufijo que empiece por vocal.

Ej: **care → cared**; **retrieve → retrieving**; **love → lovable**

NOTA: La excepción a esta regla la constituye la palabra **likeable** – aunque también existe la forma "likable" – así como algunas palabras que terminan por **-ce** o **-ge** (ver más abajo).

B Cuando se añade a la palabra un sufijo que empiece por consonante, la **-e** final se mantiene.

Ej: **hate → hateful**

EXCEPCIONES:

1. Cuando la palabra acaba en **-able** o **-ible** y se le añade el sufijo adverbial **-ly**.

Ej: **possible → possibly**; **arguable → arguably**

2. En determinadas palabras, entre las que cabe destacar:

whole → wholly; **argue → argument**; **judge → judgment**; **true → truly**; **due → duly**

3 Palabras terminadas en -ce y -ge

A Tanto en las palabras que terminan por **-ce** como en las que terminan por **-ge**, la **-e** final se mantiene al añadirles un sufijo que empiece por **a** o por **o**, a fin de que se mantenga el sonido suave de la **c** y la **g**.

Ej: **change → changeable**; **replace → replaceable**; **outrage → outrageous**

B En las palabras que terminan en **-ce**, la **-e** se convierte en **i** antes del sufijo **-ous**.

Ej: **space → spacious**; **malice → malicious**

4 Palabras terminadas en -y

A Cuando las palabras que terminan por **-y** van precedidas de una consonante, la **y** se convierte en **i** al añadírseles cualquier sufijo que empiece por vocal.

Ej: **try → tried**; **carry → carried**; **funny → funnier**; **easy → easily**

NOTA: Esto ocurre también en los sustantivos en singular acabados en **y** precedida de consonante, que forman el plural añadiendo el sufijo **-es**. Así: **baby → babies**; **lorry → lorries**. Y lo mismo en la formación de la tercera persona del presente: **hurry → she hurries**; **cry → she cries**.

EXCEPCIÓN: La única excepción a esta regla la constituye el sufijo **-ing**.

Ej: **try + ing = trying**; **carry + ing = carrying**.

B Cuando la **-y** va precedida de vocal, esta **y** se mantiene.

Ej: **convey → conveyed**; **lay → layer**

NOTA: Los sustantivos que acaban en **y** precedida de vocal tienen un plural regular. Así: **boy → boys**; **key → keys**. En los verbos acabados en **y** precedida de vocal la tercera persona del presente se forma añadiendo solamente una **s**: **say → she says**; **stay → he stays**.

5 Grupos vocálicos -ie- y -ei-

En la mayoría de los casos, el orden de las letras de estos grupos vocálicos en el interior de una palabra es **-ie-**, a menos que la **i** vaya precedida de **c**, en cuyo caso ocurre lo contrario.

Ej: **retrieve, believe** pero **receive, deceipt**

Sin embargo, existen unas cuantas excepciones a esta regla, que son, entre otras, las siguientes palabras:

beige	height	seize	weigh
eight	leisure	sleigh	weight
either	neighbour	their	weird
foreign	neither	veil	
freight	rein	vein	

6 Sustantivos terminados en -o

Estos sustantivos forman el plural añadiendo el sufijo **-es**.

Ej: **tomato, tomatoes**; **hero, heroes**; **potato, potatoes**.

EXCEPCIONES:
Cuando terminan en dos vocales.

Ej: **studio, studios**; **radio, radios**.

Cuando los sustantivos son, en origen, palabras abreviadas.

Ej: **kilo, kilos**; **photo, photos**.

7 Palabras terminadas en -ence y -ense

En inglés británico los verbos derivados de ciertos sustantivos que se escriben con **-c-** se escriben con **-s-**. Pero, como veremos más adelante, esto no ocurre en inglés americano.

Ej: **a licence** pero **to license**
the practice pero **to practise**

8 Mayúsculas

Las mayúsculas se emplean más en inglés que en español. Se emplean como en español al principio de palabra en los siguientes casos: en la primera palabra de la frase; en los nombres propios de toda clase; en los nombres, sobrenombres y pronombres posesivos de Dios, Jesucristo, la Virgen etc; en las graduaciones y títulos de las autoridades del estado, del ejército, de la iglesia y de las empresas.

Las mayúsculas se emplean en inglés en los siguientes casos donde se escribe minúscula en español:

A Los nombres de los días y meses: **Monday, Tuesday, May, June.**

B El pronombre personal de sujeto, primera persona: **I** (yo). Pero, a diferencia del español, en que se escribe Vd., Vds., el pronombre de segunda persona (igual que el resto de los pronombres) se escribe siempre con minúscula.

C Los gentilicios: **I like the French, two Frenchwomen, French cheese, to talk French, a text in old Castilian**. Sin embargo, el adjetivo de nacionalidad puede escribirse con minúscula en algún caso cuando se refiere a una cosa corriente y objeto conocido de todos, p. ej. **a french window, french beans, german measles, venetian blinds**.

D En los nombres y adjetivos derivados de otras clases de nombres propios: **a Darwinian explanation, a Thatcherite, the Elizabethans**.

E En los sustantivos y adjetivos principales en los títulos de libros, películas, artículos etc: **A Clockwork Orange, Gone with the Wind.**

9 Apóstrofes

El apóstrofe se usa fundamentalmente en inglés:

A En la formación del posesivo (el llamado posesivo sajón), para la que se añade una **s** precedida de apóstrofe al singular de cualquier sustantivo o al plural que no acabe en **-s**.

Ej: **my father's car**; **women's talk**

En los plurales de los sustantivos acabados en **-s** se añade solamente un apóstrofe.

Ej: **their friends' house; my daughters' social life**

B En determinadas contracciones de palabras, para señalar la omisión de una o más letras.

Ej: **I am → I'm**; **you are → you're**; **he is → he's**; **I had/ I would → I'd**; **you have → you've**; **does not → doesn't**; **I shall/will → I'll** etc

10 Diferencias ortográficas entre el inglés británico y el norteamericano

Palabras con el grupo vocálico -ou-

A En las palabras terminadas en **-our** en inglés británico derivadas del latín, la **u** se suprime en inglés americano. Así, por ejemplo: inglés británico **colour** = inglés americano **color**; inglés británico **labour** = inglés americano **labor**. (Esto no afecta a los monosílabos como **dour, flour, sour,** donde no hay diferencia).

B En inglés americano también se suprime la **u** cuando este grupo de letras se encuentra en el interior de la palabra. Así: inglés británico **mould** = inglés americano **mold**; inglés británico **smoulder** = inglés americano **smolder**.

Palabras terminadas en -re *(Brit)*

Cuando esta terminación va precedida de consonante y el énfasis no recae en esta sílaba en inglés británico, normalmente cambia a **-er** en inglés americano: inglés británico **centre** = inglés americano **center**; inglés británico **metre** = inglés americano **meter**; inglés británico **theatre** = inglés americano **theater**. (Pero no existe diferencia en **acre, genre, lucre, massacre, mediocre, ogre**).

Vocales finales

Ciertas vocales finales, que no tienen valor en la pronunciación, se escriben en inglés británico pero se suprimen en inglés americano: inglés americano **catalog** = inglés británico **catalogue**; inglés americano **prolog** = inglés británico **prologue**; inglés americano **program** = inglés británico **programme**; inglés americano **kilogram** = inglés británico **kilogramme**.

Diptongos de origen griego o latino

En inglés americano se suele simplificar los diptongos de origen griego o latino **ae, oe,** escribiéndose sencillamente **e**: inglés americano **anemia** = inglés británico **anaemia**; inglés americano **anesthesia** = inglés británico **anaesthesia**. En inglés americano se duda entre **subpoena** y **subpena**; en inglés británico se mantiene siempre el primero.

Palabras terminadas en -ence *(Brit)*

En algunos casos las palabras que en inglés británico terminan en **-ence** se escriben **-ense** en inglés americano: inglés británico **defence** = inglés americano **defense**; inglés británico **offence** = inglés americano **offense**.

Consonantes dobles

Algunas consonantes que en inglés británico se escriben dobles, en inglés americano se escriben sencillas: inglés británico **waggon** = inglés americano **wagon** (aunque **wagon** se admite también en el Reino Unido). Pero esto ocurre sobre todo en formas verbales, al añadirse sufijos a verbos que acaban en consonante (ver más arriba). Así, por ejemplo: inglés británico **kidnapped** = inglés americano **kidnaped**; inglés británico **worshipped** = inglés americano **worshiped**.

En el caso de la **l** o **ll** intervocálicas, mientras en inglés británico la **l** se hace doble antes de un sufijo en las palabras que terminan en **l** precedida de una sola vocal o de dos vocales que forman un diptongo (ver más arriba), en inglés americano estas palabras se escriben con una sola **l**. Así, por ejemplo: inglés británico **councillor** = inglés americano **councilor**; inglés británico **traveller** = inglés americano **traveler**. Sin embargo, en posición de final de sílaba o de palabra, la **l** en inglés británico es a menudo **ll** en inglés americano: así inglés americano **enroll, enrolls** = inglés británico **enrol, enrols**; inglés americano **skillful** = inglés británico **skilful**.

Uso familiar

En inglés americano se modifica algún otro grupo ortográfico del inglés, pero sólo en la escritura de tono familiar: inglés americano **tho** = inglés británico **though**; inglés americano **thru** = inglés británico **through**. También son más corrientes en inglés americano las formas como **Peterboro** (o bien **Peterboro'**), aunque éstas no son desconocidas en inglés británico.

Algunas palabras aisladas

Existe una serie de palabras aisladas que se escriben de modo diferente:

(US)	*(Brit)*	*(US)*	*(Brit)*
ax	axe	mustache	moustache
check	cheque	pajamas	pyjamas
cozy	cosy	plow	plough
disk	disc	skeptic	sceptic
gray	grey	tire	tyre
gypsy	gipsy		

Es importante observar, sin embargo, que existen algunas palabras que en inglés británico se escriben con ortografía americano, aunque en general su significado queda restringido a determinados contextos. Así, por ejemplo, encontramos **disk** y

program con ortografía norteamericana, pero referidos exclusivamente a la Informática, mientras que en todos los demás casos se escribe **disc** y **programme**.

11 La puntuación

Se usan los mismos signos que en español, con las siguientes excepciones:

A Los signos de admiración e interrogación

Los signos de apertura de admiración e interrogación (¡¿) no se emplean en inglés.

Ej.: **What is her name?**
Help!

B El paréntesis

En inglés el paréntesis se prefiere en muchos casos a la doble raya con función parentética (—...—).

Ej.: **Old people think that the pace of modern life (i.e. from 1940 onwards) is far too fast.**

C Las comillas

Se utilizan para abrir y cerrar el diálogo y la oración directa, en lugar de la raya.

Ej.: **"Would you like a cup of coffee?" she asked, smiling shyly.**

D La raya

En inglés informal se usa a menudo, en lugar de los dos puntos o del punto y coma, para indicar que lo que sigue es conclusión o resumen de lo anterior.

Ej.: **Everybody was trying to speak at the same time — the noise was deafening.**

Y también bien para separar un comentario o una idea del resto de la frase.

Ej.: **She told me everything she knew — at least that's what I thought at the time.**

E El guión

Se usa, como en español, para formar palabras compuestas de otras dos o más palabras, así como para dividir palabras al final de renglón (ver más abajo). También se usa en ocasiones en inglés británico para separar determinados prefijos, en los siguientes casos:

– cuando el prefijo acaba en la misma vocal con la que empieza la siguiente palabra.

Ej.: **co-opting, pre-eminent**

– cuando va delante de una palabra escrita con mayúscula.

Ej.: **anti-American, pre-Victorian**

– siempre que se trate de los prefijos **ex-** y **non-**.

Ej.: **ex-husband, non-proliferation**

12 La división de la palabra

Las reglas para dividir una palabra en final de renglón son menos estrictas en inglés que en español. En general se prefiere cortar la palabra tras vocal, **hori-zontal, vindi-cation**, pero se prefiere mantener como unidades ciertos sufijos comunes, **vindica-tion, glamor-ous**. De acuerdo con esto se divide la palabra dejando separada la desinencia **-ing**, p.ej. **sicken-ing**, pero si ésta está precedida por un grupo de consonantes, una de ellas se deja unida a **-ing**, p.ej. **tick-ling**. Los grupos de dos consonantes iguales se dividen: **pat-ter, yel-low, disap-pear**, así como los demás grupos consonánticos, que lo hacen de acuerdo con los elementos separables que forman la palabra: **dis-count, per-turb**.

DICCIONARIO ESPAÑOL-INGLÉS

SPANISH-ENGLISH DICTIONARY

Aa

A, a (SF) (= *letra*) A, a

a (PREP) **1** (*indicando dirección*) **a** (*hacia alguna parte*) to • **voy a la tienda/al parque** I'm going to the shop/to the park • **ir a trabajar** *o* **al trabajo** to go to work • **de aquí a Sevilla se tarda una hora** it's an hour from here to Seville • **mirar al norte** to look north(wards) • **de cara al norte** facing north • **torcer a la derecha** to turn (to the) right • **ir a casa** to go home
b (*hacia dentro*) into • **me caí al río/mar** I fell into the river/sea • **mirarse a los ojos** to look into each other's eyes • **subir a un avión** to get into a plane • **subirse a un tren** to get on a train
c • **llegar a** [+ *ciudad, país*] to arrive in; [+ *edificio*] to arrive at • **¿cuándo llegaste a Londres?** when did you arrive in London? • **no ha llegado todavía a la oficina** she still hasn't arrived at the office
d (= *encima de*) onto • **se subieron al tejado** they climbed onto the roof • **bajaron del tren al andén** they stepped out of the train onto the platform
2 (*indicando situación, distancia*) • **al final de la calle** at the end of the street • **a la orilla del río** on the riverbank • **al lado del cine** next to the cinema • **siéntate a mi lado** sit next to me, sit beside me • **nos pusimos a la sombra** we moved into the shade • **está a siete km de aquí** it is seven km (away) from here • **de este a aquel no hay mucha diferencia** there's not much difference between this one and that one • **a lo lejos** in the distance • **a la derecha** on the right • **a la izquierda** on the left • **estar a la mesa** to be at table • **estaba sentado a su mesa de trabajo** he was sitting at his desk
3 (*con expresiones de tiempo*) **a** (*en un momento concreto*) at • **a las ocho** at eight o'clock • **a los 55 años** at the age of 55 • **¿a qué hora llega el tren?** what time *o* when does the train arrive? • **estamos a tres de julio** it's the third of July • **a la mañana siguiente** the following morning • **a medianoche** at midnight • **a mediodía** at noon • **a la noche** at night • **a la tarde** in the afternoon; ▹ **tiempo**
b (*con tiempo transcurrido*) • **a la semana** a week later • **al año** a year later • **al año de vivir en Caracas** after living in Caracas for a year • **a los pocos días** after a few days, a few days later • **"Cervantes, a los 400 años de su muerte"** "Cervantes 400 years after his death", "Cervantes 400 years on" • **a los 18 minutos de juego** in the 18th minute, 18 minutes into the game • **a la que te descuidas ...** if you're not careful ..., before you know where you are ...
c (*indicando frecuencia*) • **dos veces al día** twice a day • **una vez a la semana** once a week • **día a día vamos mejorando** we're improving with every day, we're improving day by day
d • **al** (+ *infin*): • **al entrar yo** when I came in • **al verlo, lo reconocí inmediatamente** when I saw him, I recognized him immediately • **nos cruzamos al salir** we bumped into each other as we were going out • **estar al llegar** to be about to arrive • **al no llegar a tiempo, quedamos fuera de la prueba** since we didn't arrive on time, we were eliminated from the race
4 (*indicando modo*) • **a la americana** American-style • **una cocina a gas** a gas stove • **funciona a pilas y a la red** it runs on batteries and on mains electricity • **una camisa a cuadros** a check *o* checked shirt • **una camisa a rayas** a striped shirt • **a pie/caballo** on foot/horseback • **fui a pie** I walked • **fui a caballo** I rode • **a oscuras** in the dark • **a lápiz** in pencil • **lo derribó a puñetazos** she knocked him to the ground • **lo mataron a navajazos** they stabbed him to death • **sabe a queso** it tastes of cheese • **huele a vino** it smells of wine • **es muy agradable al tacto** it feels very nice • **beber algo a sorbos** to sip sth • **despertarse al menor ruido** to wake at the slightest sound • **a mano** by hand • **hay que lavarlo a mano** it should be washed by hand • **escrito a mano** hand-written • **hecho a mano** handmade • **una sábana bordada a mano** a hand-embroidered sheet
5 (*indicando cantidad, precio, velocidad*) • **a un precio elevado** at a high price • **a 3 euros el kilo** at *o* for 3 euros a kilo • **los huevos están a un euro la docena** eggs are a euro a dozen • **al 5 por ciento** at 5 per cent • **íbamos a más de 120km por hora** we were going at *o* doing over 120km an hour • **poco a poco** little by little
6 (*indicando finalidad*) **a** (*tras verbos*) to • **voy a verla** I'm going to see her • **ha ido a por agua a la fuente** she's gone to get some water from the fountain • **empezó a cantar** he began to sing, he started singing • **ha salido a tomar el aire** she's gone out for a breath of fresh air • **vengo a que me den un impreso** I've come to get a form
b (*tras sustantivos*) • **el criterio a adoptar** the criterion to be adopted • **asuntos a tratar** items to be discussed • **"precio a convenir"** "price negotiable" • **¿cuál es la cantidad a pagar?** what do we have to pay? • **este será el camino a seguir** this must be the path to take
7 (*con complemento de persona*) **a** (*como complemento indirecto*) to • **¿le has dado el libro a él?** did you give him the book?, did you give the book to him? • **le enseñé a Pablo el libro que me dejaste** I showed Pablo the book you lent me, I showed the book you lent me to Pablo • **el Barcelona marcó cinco goles al Madrid** Barcelona scored five against Madrid
b (*como complemento directo (no se traduce)*) • **vi al jefe** I saw the boss • **llamé al médico** I called the doctor
c (*indicando procedencia*) from • **se lo compré a él** I bought it from him
8 (*indicando condición*) • **a no ser esto así, me iría** if this were not the case, I'd leave
9 (*indicando desafío*) • **a que** I bet • **¿a que no sabes quién ha llamado?** (I) bet you can't guess who called • **¿a que no te atreves a tirarte de cabeza?** (I) bet you don't dare dive in headfirst
10 (*uso imperativo*) • **¡a callar!** be quiet! • **¡a trabajar!** down to work! • **¡a comer!** lunch is ready!
11 (= *en cuanto a*) • **a supersticioso no hay quien le gane** when it comes to being superstitious, there's nobody quite like him

A. (ABR) = **aprobado**

AA (ABR) (*Aer*) = **Aerolíneas Argentinas**

A.A. (ABR) (= **Alcohólicos Anónimos**) AA

AA.AA. (ABR) (= **Antiguos Alumnos**) FPs

AAE (SF ABR) (= **Asociación de Aerolíneas Europeas**) AEA

AA.EE. (ABR) = **Asuntos Exteriores**

Aarón (SM) Aaron

ab. (ABR) (= **abril**) Apr

abacá (SM) abaca, Manilla hemp

abacado (SM) (*Caribe*) avocado pear

abacería (SF) grocer's (shop), grocery store

abacero/a (SM/F) grocer

ábaco (SM) abacus

abacora (SF) (*LAm*) *type of tuna*

abacorar ▹ CONJUG 1a (VT) **1** (*And, Caribe*) (= *acosar*) to harass, bother; (= *sorprender*) to catch, surprise
2 (*Caribe*) (= *acometer*) to undertake boldly; (= *seducir*) to entice away
3 (*LAm*) (*Com*) to monopolize

abad (SM) abbot

abadejo (SM) **1** (= *pez*) [*de mar*] cod, codfish; [*de agua dulce*] ling; (*Caribe*) (= *pez espada*) swordfish
2 (= *insecto*) Spanish fly
3 (*Culin*) dried salted cod
4 (= *ave*) kinglet

abadengo (ADJ) abbatial, of an abbot
(SM) abbacy

abadesa (SF) **1** (*Rel*) abbess
2 (*LAm**) madam, brothel keeper

abadía (SF) **1** (= *convento*) abbey
2 (= *oficio*) abbacy

abajadero (SM) slope, incline

abajar ▹ CONJUG 1a (VT) (*LAm*) = **bajar**

abajeño/a (*LAm*) (ADJ) lowland, coastal
(SM/F) lowlander, coastal dweller

abajera (SF) (*Cono Sur*) saddlecloth

abajero (ADJ) (*LAm*) lower, under

abajino/a (*Cono Sur*) (ADJ) northern
(SM/F) northerner

abajo (ADV) **1** (*indicando posición*) **a** (*gen*) down • **~ en el río** down at the river • **ahí** *o* **allá** *o* **allí ~** down there • **aquí ~** down here • **de ~** lower, bottom • **yo duermo en la litera de ~** I sleep in the lower *o* bottom bunk • **la sábana**

de ~ the bottom sheet • **la parte de ~** the bottom • **el piso de ~** (= *planta inferior*) the next floor down; (= *planta baja*) the ground floor • **desde ~** from below • **más ~** (*en distancia*) further down; (*en altura*) lower down • **dos kilómetros más ~** two kilometres further down • **hay una farmacia un poco más ~** there's a chemist's further down the road • **unos escalones más ~** a few steps lower down • **vivo tres pisos más ~** I live three floors below • **de cintura para ~** from the waist down • **por ~** (= *en la parte inferior*) at the bottom; (= *por debajo*) underneath • **el abrigo está lleno de barro por ~** the bottom of the coat is all muddy • **tenía telarañas por ~** it had cobwebs underneath • **~ del todo** right at the bottom, at the very bottom; ▹ **boca**

b (*en edificio, casa*) downstairs • **~ están la cocina y el salón** the kitchen and lounge are downstairs • **te están esperando ~** they're waiting for you downstairs • **los vecinos de ~** the downstairs neighbours • **hay una fiesta en el apartamento de ~** there's a party in the flat downstairs

2 (*indicando dirección*) **a** (*con sustantivos*) • **aguas ~** downriver, downstream • **continuaron aguas ~ durante un rato** they continued downriver *o* downstream for a while • **sigamos aguas ~ del río** let's carry on down the river • **calle ~** down the street • **seguimos calle ~, hasta la plaza** we followed the street down to the square • **estuvimos calle arriba, calle ~, buscando al niño** we went up and down the street, looking for the child • **cuesta ~** down the hill • **escaleras ~** downstairs • **ladera ~** down the hillside • **río ~** downstream, downriver

b (*con preposición*) • **hacia ~** downward(s), down • **se iban deslizando hacia ~** they were sliding downward(s) *o* down • **caminaba con la cabeza hacia ~** he walked with his head bent down • **para ~**: • **me voy para ~** I'm going down • **no mires para ~** don't look down • **la economía va para ~** the economy is going downhill

c (*con verbo*) • **echar ~** [+ *puerta, barricada*] to break down; [+ *gobierno*] to bring down; [+ *paz*] to break up • **venirse ~** [*edificio, estructura, economía*] to collapse; [*planes, sueños*] to come to nothing; [*persona*] to go to pieces • **después del divorcio se vino ~** after the divorce he went to pieces • **este país se ha venido ~ por culpa de la guerra** this country has been ruined by war, war has brought this country to its knees

3 (*en un texto*) below • **en la foto de ~** in the photo below • **el ~ firmante** the undersigned

4 (*en una escala*) the bottom • **los cambios deben empezar por ~, a nivel local** change should begin at the bottom, at local level • **los de ~ siempre salimos perdiendo** those of us at the bottom (of the pile) are always the losers • **una revolución tiene que empezar desde ~** a revolution must start from the bottom up • **para ~**: • **los responsables, de ministro para ~, deben dimitir** those responsible, from the minister down, should resign • **de 30 años para ~** 30 years old and under

5 (*esp LAm*) (= *debajo*) underneath

6 • **~ de** (*LAm*) under • **~ de la camisa** under the shirt

EXCL down with! • **¡~ el gobierno!** down with the government!

abajofirmante SMF • **el ~ • la ~** the undersigned

abalanzadero SM (*Méx*) ford, cattle crossing

abalanzar ▹ CONJUG 1f VT **1** (= *lanzar*) to hurl, throw

2 (= *impeler*) to impel

3 (= *pesar*) to weigh

4 (= *equilibrar*) to balance

VPR **abalanzarse 1** (= *lanzarse*) to rush forward; [*multitud*] to surge forward • **todos se ~on hacia la salida** everyone rushed towards the exit • **~se sobre** to spring at, rush at; [*ave*] to pounce on

2 (*Cono Sur*) [*caballo*] to rear up

abaldonar ▹ CONJUG 1a VT † (= *degradar*) to degrade, debase; (= *insultar*) to affront

abalear* ▹ CONJUG 1a VT (*LAm*) to fire at, shoot up*; (*And*) (= *fusilar*) to shoot, execute

VI (*LAm*) to shoot off one's gun, fire in the air

abaleo* SM (*LAm*) shooting

abalorio SM glass bead • MODISMO: • **no vale un ~** it's worthless

abalumar* ▹ CONJUG 1a VT (*Méx*), **abalumbar*** ▹ CONJUG 1a VT (*Méx*) to pile up, stack

abanarse* ▹ CONJUG 1a VPR (*Cono Sur*) to show off

abanderado/a SM/F **1** (= *portaestandarte*) standard bearer

2 [*de un movimiento*] champion, leader

3 (*LAm*) (= *representante*) representative

4 (*Méx*) (= *linier*) linesman, assistant referee

abanderar ▹ CONJUG 1a VT **1** (*Náut*) to register

2 [+ *causa*] to champion; [+ *campaña*] to take a leading role in

abanderizar ▹ CONJUG 1f VT to organize into bands

VPR **abanderizarse** to band together; (*Cono Sur*) (*Pol*) to take sides, adopt a position

abandonado ADJ **1** (= *sin gente*) [*pueblo, vivienda vacía*] abandoned, deserted; [*fábrica, cantera*] disused; [*edificio en ruinas*] derelict

2 (= *desatendido*) [*jardín, terreno*] neglected • **la casa estaba muy abandonada, toda cubierta de polvo** the house was really neglected, completely covered in dust • **tienes ~s a los amigos** you've neglected your friends • **¡~ me tenías!** you'd forgotten all about me! • **tienen el negocio muy ~** they've allowed their business to decline • **dejar ~** [+ *cónyuge, hijo*] to abandon, desert; [+ *animal, casa, vehículo*] to abandon • **huyeron dejando abandonadas sus armas** they fled abandoning their weapons • **el autobús nos dejó ~s en la carretera** the bus left us stranded *o* abandoned us by the roadside

3 (= *despreocupado*) slack • **es muy ~ para las cosas de la casa** he's very slack about everything to do with the house

4 (= *desaliñado*) scruffy, shabby • **a ver si no eres tan ~ y te arreglas un poco** come on, tidy yourself up a bit and stop looking so scruffy *o* shabby

5 (= *solitario*) desolate, forlorn (*frm*)

abandonamiento SM = **abandono**

abandonar ▹ CONJUG 1a VT **1** (= *dejar abandonado*) [+ *cónyuge, hijo*] to abandon, desert; [+ *animal, casa, posesiones*] to abandon; [+ *obligaciones*] to neglect • **la abandonó por otra mujer** he abandoned *o* deserted her for another woman • **no me abandones nunca** never leave me • **tuvimos que ~ nuestras pertenencias en la huida** we had to abandon all our belongings when we fled • **no debes ~ las labores de la casa** you shouldn't neglect the housework • **~ el barco** to abandon ship • MODISMO: • **~ a algn a su suerte** *o* **a la buena de Dios** to abandon *o* leave sb to their fate

2 (= *marcharse de*) [+ *lugar, organización*] to leave • **pronto podrán ~ el hospital** they will soon be able to leave the hospital • **abandonó la reunión hecho una furia** he stormed out of the meeting • **miles de refugiados han abandonado la ciudad** thousands of refugees have abandoned the city

3 (= *renunciar a*) [+ *estudios, proyecto*] to give up, abandon; [+ *costumbre, cargo*] to give up; [+ *privilegio, título*] to renounce, relinquish • **hemos abandonado la idea de montar un negocio** we have given up *o* abandoned the idea of starting a business • **he decidido ~ la política** I've decided to give up *o* abandon politics • **si el tratamiento no da resultado lo ~emos** if the treatment doesn't work, we'll abandon it • **no es fácil ~ el tabaco** it's not easy to give up smoking • **la guerrilla ha prometido ~ las armas** the guerrillas have promised to lay down their arms • **se comprometieron a ~ sus reivindicaciones territoriales** they promised to renounce *o* relinquish their territorial claims

4 [*buen humor, suerte*] to desert • **el valor la abandonó** her courage deserted her • **nunca los abandona la alegría** they are always happy

VI **1** (*Atletismo*) (*antes de la prueba*) to pull out, withdraw; (*durante la prueba*) to pull out, retire

2 (*Boxeo*) to concede defeat, throw in the towel* *o* (*EEUU*) sponge

3 (*Ajedrez*) to resign, concede

4 (*Inform*) to quit

VPR **abandonarse 1** (= *no cuidarse*) to let o.s. go • **no deberías ~te aunque estés deprimida** you shouldn't let yourself go even though you're depressed • **aunque no se abandona nada parece cada vez más viejo** although he looks after himself very well he looks older every day

2 (= *entregarse*) to abandon o.s. • **nos abandonamos en manos de la suerte** we abandoned ourselves to the hand of fate • **~se a** [+ *alcohol, droga*] to give o.s. over *o* up to, abandon o.s. to; [+ *destino, suerte*] to abandon o.s. to; [+ *sueño*] to surrender to, give in to • **no te abandones a la desesperación** don't give in to despair

3 (= *desanimarse*) to lose heart, get discouraged

abandonismo SM defeatism

abandonista ADJ, SMF defeatist

abandono SM **1** (= *acción*) **a** [*de lugar*] • **ordenaron el ~ de la isla** they ordered people to abandon *o* leave the island • **el ~ de la zona por las tropas de ocupación** the withdrawal of the occupying forces from the region

b [*de actividad, proyecto*] abandonment • **votaron a favor del ~ del leninismo** they voted in favour of renouncing Leninism, they voted for the abandonment of Leninism • **ofrecen ayudas a los agricultores para el ~ de la producción** they are offering aid to farmers to cease production • **mi ~ del cargo se debió a problemas internos** I gave up the post because of internal problems

c (*Jur*) [*de cónyuge*] desertion; [*de hijos*] abandonment • **en caso de ~ de uno de los cónyuges** in the event of the desertion of either partner ▸ **abandono de deberes** dereliction of duty ▸ **abandono de la escuela** = **abandono escolar** ▸ **abandono del domicilio conyugal, abandono del hogar** desertion ▸ **abandono de tierras** land set aside, set-aside ▸ **abandono escolar** leaving school (*before school-leaving age*) • **problemas causados por el ~ escolar** problems caused by students leaving school early

2 (*Dep*) (*antes de la prueba*) withdrawal; (*durante la prueba*) retirement; (*Ajedrez*)

resignation • **ganar por ~** to win by default (*thanks to an opponent's withdrawal*)
3 (= *descuido*) neglect, abandon (*frm*) • **la iglesia se encontraba en un terrible estado de ~** the church was in a terrible state of neglect *o* abandon (*frm*) • **es lamentable el ~ que sufre la sanidad pública desde hace años** it's dreadful how public health has been so neglected for years • **darse al ~** to go downhill
4 (= *vicio*) indulgence • **llevaba una vida de excesos y ~** she led a life of excess and indulgence • **viven en el mayor ~** they live in utter degradation
5 (= *soledad*) desolation • **me invadió una sensación de ~** I was overcome by a feeling of desolation • **el pueblo presentaba un aspecto de ~** the town had a forlorn look about it
6 (*Méx*) (= *ligereza*) abandon, ease

abanicada SF fanning, fanning action

abanicar ▹ CONJUG 1g VT to fan
VPR **abanicarse** to fan o.s. • MODISMO: • **~se con algo** (*Cono Sur*‡) not to give a damn about sth*

abanico SM 1 (*para darse aire*) fan • **extender las cartas en ~** to fan out one's cards • **con hojas en ~** with leaves arranged like a fan ▸ **abanico de chimenea** fire screen ▸ **abanico eléctrico** (*Méx*) (= *ventilador*) electric fan
2 (= *gama*) range ▸ **abanico de posibilidades** range of possibilities ▸ **abanico de salarios, abanico salarial** wage scale
3 (*Náut*) derrick
4 (*Caribe*) (*Ferro*) points signal

abaniquear ▹ CONJUG 1a (*LAm*) VT to fan
VPR **abaniquearse** to fan o.s.

abaniqueo SM (*con abanico*) fanning, fanning movement; (= *manoteo*) gesticulation

abaniquero/a SM/F (= *fabricante*) fan maker; (= *comerciante*) dealer in fans

abarajar* ▹ CONJUG 1a VT (*Cono Sur*) [+ *golpe*] to parry, counter

abaratamiento SM price reduction

abaratar ▹ CONJUG 1a VT [+ *artículo*] to make cheaper, lower the price of; [+ *precio*] to lower
VPR **abaratarse** to get cheaper, come down (in price)

abarca SF sandal

abarcar ▹ CONJUG 1g VT 1 (*con los brazos*) to get one's arms round
2 (= *comprender*) to include, take in; (= *contener*) to contain, comprise • **el capítulo abarca tres siglos** the chapter covers three centuries • **sus conocimientos abarcan todo el campo de ...** his knowledge ranges over the whole field of ... • **abarca una hectárea** it takes up a hectare, it's a hectare in size
3 [+ *tarea*] to undertake, take on • REFRÁN: • **quien mucho abarca poco aprieta** don't bite off more than you can chew
4 (*LAm*) (= *acaparar*) to monopolize, corner the market in
5 (*con la vista*) to take in • **desde aquí se abarca todo el valle** you can take in the whole valley from here

abarque SM (*And*) (= *huevos*) clutch

abarquillar ▹ CONJUG 1a VT (= *arrollar*) to curl up, roll up; (= *arrugar*) to wrinkle
VPR **abarquillarse** (= *arrollarse*) to curl up, roll up; (= *arrugarse*) to crinkle

abarraganarse ▹ CONJUG 1a VPR to live together, set up home together

abarrajado* ADJ (*Cono Sur*) (= *libertino*) dissolute, free-living; (= *peleón*) quarrelsome, argumentative

abarrajar* ▹ CONJUG 1a VI (*Cono Sur*) to run away, flee
VPR **abarrajarse 1** (*And*) (= *caer de bruces*) to fall flat on one's face
2 (*And, Cono Sur*) (= *prostituirse*) to prostitute o.s., sell o.s.; (= *envilecerse*) to become corrupt, be perverted

abarrajo SM (*And*) fall, stumble

abarrancadero SM tight spot, jam

abarrancar ▹ CONJUG 1g VT to make cracks in, open up fissures in
VPR **abarrancarse 1** (= *caer*) to fall into a ditch *o* pit
2 (= *atascarse*) to get stopped up
3 (*Náut*) to run aground
4 (= *meterse en un lío*) to get into a jam

abarrotado ADJ [*sala, tren*] packed, jam-packed • **estar ~ de** [+ *personas*] to be packed *o* jam-packed with; [+ *objetos*] to be crammed *o* jam-packed with • **el cine estaba ~ (de gente)** the cinema was packed

abarrotar ▹ CONJUG 1a VT 1 (= *llenar*) to pack • **el público abarrotaba la sala** the hall was packed with people
2 (*Náut*) to stow, pack tightly
3 (*Com*) to overstock
VPR **abarrotarse 1** (= *llenarse*) to get packed
2 (*LAm*) (*Com*) to become saturated • **~se de** (*Méx*) to be stuffed with, be bursting with

abarrote SM 1 (*Náut*) packing
2 **abarrotes** (*LAm*) (= *ultramarinos*) groceries • **tienda de ~s** grocer's (shop), grocery store

abarrotería SF (*LAm*) grocer's (shop), grocery store

abarrotero/a SM/F (*LAm*) grocer

abastar ▹ CONJUG 1a VT to supply

abastardar ▹ CONJUG 1a VT to degrade, debase
VI to degenerate

abastecedor(a) ADJ supplying
SM/F 1 (= *proveedor*) supplier, purveyor (*frm*)
2 (*Méx*) (= *carnicero*) wholesale butcher, meat supplier

abastecer ▹ CONJUG 2d VT to supply, provide (**de** with)
VPR **abastecerse** • **~se de** [+ *víveres*] to stock up on • **las ciudades de la región se abastecen de agua de 14 embalses** the towns in the region get their water supply from 14 reservoirs

abastecimiento SM (= *acto*) supplying, provision; (= *servicio*) supply, provision; (= *víveres*) provisions (*pl*) ▸ **abastecimiento de agua** water supply

abastero SM (*Cono Sur, Méx*) wholesale butcher

abasto SM 1 (= *provisión*) supply • **dar ~ a** to supply • **dar ~ a un pedido** to fill an order, meet an order • **no da ~** there isn't enough (to go round) • **no puedo dar ~ (a)** (*fig*) I can't cope *o* keep up (with)
2 (*Cono Sur*) public meat market
3 (*Caribe*) grocer's (shop), grocery store

abatanado ADJ skilled, skilful, skillful (*EEUU*)

abatanar ▹ CONJUG 1a VT [+ *paño*] to beat, full; (= *maltratar*) to beat

abatatado ADJ (*Cono Sur*) shy, coy

abatatarse ▹ CONJUG 1a VPR (*Cono Sur*) to be shy, be bashful

abate SM (*Rel*) (*frec hum*) father, abbé

abatí SM (*And, Cono Sur*) maize, Indian corn (*EEUU*)

abatible ADJ • **asiento ~** tip-up seat; (*Aut*) reclining seat • **mesa de alas ~s** gate-leg(ged) table

abatido ADJ 1 (= *deprimido*) depressed, dejected • **estar muy ~** to be very depressed • **estar ~ por el dolor** to be writhing in pain • **tener la cara abatida** to be crestfallen, look dejected
2 (= *despreciable*) despicable, contemptible
3 (*Com, Econ*) depreciated

abatimiento SM 1 (= *derribamiento*) demolition, knocking down
2 (= *depresión*) depression, dejection
3 (= *moral*) contemptible nature

abatir ▹ CONJUG 3a VT 1 (= *derribar*) to demolish, knock down; [+ *tienda de campaña*] to take down; [+ *árbol*] to cut down, fell; [+ *ave*] to shoot down, bring down; [+ *bandera*] to lower, strike; [+ *persona*] to knock down
2 [*enfermedad, dolor*] to lay low, prostrate (*frm*)
3 (= *desanimar*) to depress, discourage; (= *humillar*) to humble, humiliate
VPR **abatirse 1** (= *caerse*) to drop, fall; [*pájaro, avión*] to swoop, dive • **~se sobre** to swoop on
2 (= *desanimarse*) to be depressed, get discouraged

abayuncar ▹ CONJUG 1g (*Méx*) VT [+ *vaca*] to throw, ground • **~ a algn*** to put sb on the spot
VPR **abayuncarse*** to become countrified

abbasí ADJ, SMF Abbasid

ABC SM ABR, **abc** SM ABR = abecé

Abderramán SM Abd-al-Rahman

abdicación SF abdication

abdicar ▹ CONJUG 1g VT to renounce, relinquish • **~ la corona** to give up the crown, abdicate
VI to abdicate • **~ de algo** to renounce *o* relinquish sth • **~ en algn** to abdicate in favour of sb

abdomen SM abdomen

abdominal ADJ abdominal
SM sit-up

abducción SF (*Med*) abduction

abductor SM (*Anat*) abductor

abecé SM 1 (= *abecedario*) ABC, alphabet
2 (= *lo básico*) rudiments (*pl*), basic elements (*pl*)

abecedario SM alphabet; (= *libro*) primer, spelling book

abedul SM birch ▸ **abedul plateado** silver birch

abeja SF 1 bee ▸ **abeja asesina** killer bee ▸ **abeja machiega** queen bee ▸ **abeja macho** male bee, drone ▸ **abeja maestra** queen bee ▸ **abeja neutra, abeja obrera** worker bee ▸ **abeja reina** queen bee
2 (*fig*) (= *hormiguita*) hard worker

abejar SM apiary

abejarrón SM bumblebee

abejaruco SM bee-eater

abejera SF beehive

abejón SM 1 (= *abejorro*) drone; (*Méx*) buzzing insect
2 • **hacer ~*** (*CAm*) (= *cuchichear*) to whisper; (*Caribe*) (= *silbar*) to boo, hiss

abejonear* ▹ CONJUG 1a VI (*Caribe*) to mumble, whisper

abejorro SM (= *insecto volador*) bumblebee; (= *coleóptero*) cockchafer

abejucarse ▹ CONJUG 1g VPR (*Méx*) to twist up, climb

abellacado ADJ villainous

abellacar ▹ CONJUG 1g VT to lower, degrade

aberenjenado ADJ violet-coloured, violet-colored (*EEUU*)

aberración SF aberration • **es una ~ bañarse cinco veces al día** it's crazy to have a bath five times a day

aberrante ADJ aberrant

aberrar ▹ CONJUG 1a VI to be mistaken, err

aberrear ▹ CONJUG 1a VT (*And*) to anger, annoy

Aberri Eguna SM *Basque national holiday,* ≈ Easter Sunday

abertura SF 1 (*gen*) opening, gap; (= *agujero*)

a

hole; (= *grieta*) crack; (= *corte*) slit; (= *brecha*) gap
2 (*Geog*) (= *cala*) cove; (= *valle*) wide valley, gap; (= *puerto*) pass
3 (*Cos*) vent
4 (= *franqueza*) openness, frankness

abertzale ADJ • **movimiento ~** (Basque) nationalist movement
SMF Basque nationalist

abetal SM fir plantation, fir wood

abeto SM fir, fir tree ▸ **abeto blanco** silver fir ▸ **abeto del norte, abeto falso, abeto rojo** spruce

abetunado ADJ dark-skinned

abetunar ▹ CONJUG 1a VT (*LAm*) to polish, clean

abey SM (*Caribe*) jacaranda tree

abiertamente ADV openly • **ha condenado ~ el terrorismo** she has openly condemned terrorism

abiertazo ADJ (*CAm*) generous, open-handed

abierto PP de abrir
ADJ 1 [*puerta, armario, boca, herida*] open • **tenía el libro ~ por la página 23** she had the book open at page 23 • **la puerta estaba un poco abierta** the door was ajar • **me miró con los ojos muy ~s** he looked at me with his eyes wide-open, he looked at me with wide-open eyes • **llevas la bragueta abierta** your flies are undone *o* open • **dejar ~** [+ *ventana, cortina, válvula*] to leave open; [+ *grifo*] to leave running, leave on • **dejó el tarro ~** he left the top off the jar; ▹ **boca, brazo, libro**
2 [*comercio, museo, oficina*] open • **"abierto"** "open" • **estar ~ las 24 horas** to be open 24 hours • **estar ~ al público** to be open to the public
3 (= *sin obstáculos*) [*competición, billete*] open • **un campeonato ~ a todos los menores de 25 años** a championship open to all those under 25 • **en campo ~** in the open
4 (= *extrovertido*) [*persona*] open, outgoing; [*carácter, mentalidad*] open • **tiene una mentalidad muy abierta** he's very open-minded, he's got a very open mind
5 • **estar ~ a** [+ *sugerencias, ideas*] to be open to • **tienen una actitud abierta al diálogo** they are open to dialogue
6 (= *directo*) [*contradicción, oposición*] open; [*desafío*] direct • **se encuentran en ~ desacuerdo con él** they openly disagree with him
7 (*TV*) • **en ~: emitir un programa en ~** to broadcast a programme unscrambled • **emisión en ~** unscrambled programme
8 (*Ling*) [*vocal, sonido*] open
SM (*Dep*) • **el Abierto** the Open

abigarrado ADJ 1 (= *de diversos colores*) multi-coloured, multi-colored (*EEUU*); [*animal*] piebald, brindled; [*escena*] vivid, colourful, colorful (*EEUU*)
2 (= *heterogéneo, variopinto*) motley
3 [*habla*] disjointed, uneven

abigarramiento SM 1 [*de colores*] variety
2 [*de ideas, objetos*] chaos

abigarrar ▹ CONJUG 1a VT *to paint etc in a variety of colours*

abigeato SM (*Méx*) cattle rustling

abigeo SM (*Méx*) cattle rustler

-abilidad ▹ **Aspects of Word Formation in Spanish 2**

abintestato ADJ intestate

abiótico ADJ abiotic

abisal ADJ [*pez, criatura, profundidades*] deep-sea (*antes de s*)

abiselar ▹ CONJUG 1a VT to bevel

Abisinia SF Abyssinia

abisinio/a ADJ, SM/F Abyssinian

abismado ADJ 1 (= *abstraído*) lost (*in thought*) • **estaba ~ en su lectura** he was engrossed in his reading • **estaba ~ en sus pensamientos** he was lost *o* deep in thought
2 (= *sorprendido*) astonished, amazed

abismal ADJ (= *enorme*) vast, enormous; [*diferencia*] irreconcilable

abismalmente ADV abysmally

abismante* ADJ (*LAm*) amazing, astonishing

abismar ▹ CONJUG 1a VT 1 (= *hundir*) • **~ a algn en la tristeza** to plunge sb into sadness
2 (= *humillar*) to cast down, humble
VPR **abismarse 1** • **~se en** to plunge into • **~se en el dolor** to abandon o.s. to grief
2 (*LAm*) (= *asombrarse*) to be amazed, be astonished

abismo SM 1 (= *sima*) abyss, chasm • **de sus ideas a las mías hay un ~** our views are worlds *o* poles apart
2 (= *profundidad*) depth(s); (*Rel*) hell • **desde los ~s de la Edad Media** from the dark depths of the Middle Ages • **estar al borde del ~** to be on the brink of ruin

abizcochado ADJ (*LAm*) spongy

Abjacia SF, **Abjasia** SF Abkhazia

abjacio/a ADJ, SM/F, **abjasio/a** ADJ, SM/F, **abjaso/a** ADJ, SM/F Abkhaz, Abkhazi, Abkhazian

abjuración SF (*Jur*) abjuration

abjurar ▹ CONJUG 1a VT to abjure, forswear
VI • **~ de** to abjure, forswear

ablación SF [*de órgano*] removal ▸ **ablación del clítoris, ablación femenina** female circumcision

ablactación SF (*Med*) weaning

ablactar ▹ CONJUG 1a VT (*Med*) to wean

ablandabrevas* SMF INV useless person, good-for-nothing

ablandador SM ▸ **ablandador de agua** water softener ▸ **ablandador de carnes** (*Méx*) meat tenderizer

ablandahigos* SMF INV = ablandabrevas

ablandamiento SM (*gen*) softening (up); (= *moderación*) moderation

ablandar ▹ CONJUG 1a VT 1 (= *poner blando*) to soften; (*Culin*) to tenderize; [+ *vientre*] to loosen
2 (= *conmover*) to touch; (= *mitigar*) to mitigate, temper; (= *calmar*) to soothe
3 (*LAm*) (*Aut*) to run in, break in (*EEUU*)
VI (*Meteo*) [*frío*] to become less severe; [*viento*] to moderate; [*elementos*] to decrease in force, die down
VPR **ablandarse** (= *ponerse blando*) to soften (up), get soft(er); [*persona*] to relent, soften; (*con la edad*) to mellow

ablande SM (*LAm*) (*Aut*) running-in

ablativo ADJ ablative
SM ablative ▸ **ablativo absoluto** ablative absolute

-able ▹ **Aspects of Word Formation in Spanish 2**

ablución SF ablution

ablusado ADJ (= *no tallado*) loose
SM (*Cono Sur*) loose garment

abnegación SF self-denial, abnegation (*frm*)

abnegado ADJ self-denying, self-sacrificing

abnegarse ▹ CONJUG 1h, 1j VPR to deny o.s., go without

abobado ADJ (= *que parece tonto*) stupid-looking; (= *asombrado*) bewildered

abobamiento SM (= *estupidez*) silliness, stupidity; (= *asombro*) bewilderment

abobar ▹ CONJUG 1a VT (= *entontecer*) to make stupid; (= *asombrar*) to daze, bewilder
VPR **abobarse** to become stupid

abocado ADJ [*vino*] smooth, pleasant; [*jerez*] medium-sweet

abocar ▹ CONJUG 1g VT to pour out, decant
VI 1 (*Náut*) to enter a river/channel
2 (= *ir a parar*) • **~ a** to lead to, result in, end up in • **estar abocado al desastre** to be heading for disaster • **verse abocado a un peligro** to see danger looming ahead
3 • **estar abocado a hacer algo** to be designed to do sth • **esta medida está abocada a mejorar la situación** this measure is designed to *o* is intended to improve the situation
VPR **abocarse 1** (= *aproximarse*) to approach • **~se con algn** to meet sb, have an interview with sb
2 • **~se a** (*Cono Sur*) to confront, face up to

abocardo SM (*Téc*) drill

abocastro SM (*And, Cono Sur*) ugly devil

abocetar ▹ CONJUG 1a VT to sketch

abochornado ADJ embarrassed

abochornante ADJ = bochornoso

abochornar ▹ CONJUG 1a VT (= *sofocar*) to suffocate; (= *avergonzar*) to shame, embarrass
VPR **abochornarse** to get flushed; [*planta*] to wilt • **~se de** to get embarrassed about

abocinado ADJ trumpet-shaped

abocinar ▹ CONJUG 1a VT (= *dar forma de bocina*) to shape like a trumpet; (*Cos*) to flare
VPR **abocinarse*** to fall flat on one's face

abodocarse ▹ CONJUG 1g VPR 1 (*CAm*) [*líquido*] to go lumpy
2 (*Méx**) to come out in boils

abofado ADJ (*Caribe, Méx*) swollen

abofarse ▹ CONJUG 1g VPR (*Méx*) to stuff o.s.

abofetear ▹ CONJUG 1a VT to slap, hit (in the face)

abogacía SF (= *abogados*) legal profession; (= *oficio*) the law

abogaderas SFPL (*LAm*), **abogaderías** SFPL (*LAm*) (*pey*) specious arguments, false arguments

abogado/a SM/F 1 lawyer, attorney(-at-law) (*EEUU*) • **ejercer de ~** to practise *o* (*EEUU*) practice law • **recibirse de ~** (*esp LAm*) to qualify as a lawyer ▸ **abogado/a auxiliar** (*Méx*) junior lawyer ▸ **abogado/a criminalista** criminal lawyer ▸ **abogado/a defensor(a)** defending counsel ▸ **abogado/a del Estado** public prosecutor, attorney general (*EEUU*) ▸ **abogado del diablo** devil's advocate ▸ **abogado/a de oficio** court-appointed counsel, duty solicitor, public defender (*EEUU*) ▸ **abogado/a de secano** barrack-room lawyer ▸ **abogado/a laboralista** labour lawyer, labor lawyer (*EEUU*) ▸ **abogado/a matrimonialista** divorce lawyer ▸ **abogado/a penalista** (*Méx*) criminal lawyer
2 (= *defensor, partidario*) champion, advocate

abogar ▹ CONJUG 1h VI to plead • **~ por** (= *defender en juicio*) to plead for, defend; (= *propugnar*) to advocate, champion

abolengo SM (= *linaje*) ancestry, lineage; (= *patrimonio*) inheritance • **de rancio ~** of ancient lineage

abolición SF abolition

abolicionismo SM abolitionism

abolicionista SMF abolitionist

abolir ▹ CONJUG 3a; defectivo VT to abolish

abollado ADJ dented

abolladura SF 1 (*en metal*) dent
2 (= *hinchazón*) bump; (= *cardenal*) bruise
3 (*Arte*) embossing

abollar ▹ CONJUG 1a VT 1 [+ *metal*] to dent
2 (*Med*) to raise a bump on
3 (*Arte*) to emboss, do repoussé work on
VPR **abollarse 1** [*metal*] to get dented
2 [*persona*] to get bruised

abollón SM dent

abollonar ▷ CONJUG 1a (VT) to emboss
abolsado (ADJ) baggy
abolsarse ▷ CONJUG 1a (VPR) to become baggy
abombachado (ADJ) baggy
abombado (ADJ) **1** (= *convexo*) convex; (= *abovedado*) domed; (= *saltón*) bulging
2 (*LAm*) (= *aturdido*) stunned
3 (*Méx**) (= *borracho*) tight*
4 (*LAm*) [*comida*] rotten • **estar ~** to smell bad, stink
abombar ▷ CONJUG 1a (VT) **1** (= *hacer convexo*) to make convex; (= *deformar*) to cause to bulge
2* (= *aturdir*) to stun; (= *desconcertar*) to disconcert, confuse
(VPR) **abombarse** (*LAm*) **1** (= *pudrirse*) to decompose, go off*
2* (= *emborracharse*) to get tight*
abominable (ADJ) abominable
abominablemente (ADV) abominably
abominación (SF) abomination • **es una ~** it's an abomination, it's detestable
abominar ▷ CONJUG 1a (VT) to abominate, detest
(VI) • **~ de** to curse
abonable (ADJ) payable, due
abonado/a (ADJ) **1** (*Com*) paid, paid-up
2 (*Agr*) fertilized
(SM/F) (*Telec*) (*a revista*) subscriber; (*Teat, Ferro*) season-ticket holder • **los ~s a la televisión por cable** cable TV subscribers
abonamiento (SM) = abono
abonanzar ▷ CONJUG 1f (VI) to grow calm, become settled
(VPR) **abonanzarse** to grow calm, become settled
abonar ▷ CONJUG 1a (VT) **1** (*Agr*) to fertilize • **abonan los campos cada primavera** they fertilize *o* put fertilizer on the fields every spring • **han abonado el jardín con estiércol** they've manured *o* put manure on the garden • **están abonando el terreno para cambiar la ley** they're preparing the ground for a change in the law
2 (= *pagar*) [+ *cuota, salario, renta*] to pay; [+ *cheque, giro*] to cash • **abonamos una cuota anual de ochenta euros** we pay an annual fee of eighty euros • **no nos han abonado las horas extras** we haven't been paid (for our) overtime • **"abonen al ser servidos"** "please pay as soon as you are served" • **la cajera no me quiso ~ el cheque** the cashier refused to cash the cheque • **tengo varios cheques para ~ en cuenta** I've got a few cheques to pay in • **me ~on los intereses en mi cuenta** the interest was credited to *o* paid into my account
3 (= *fomentar*) [+ *hipótesis, teoría*] to lend weight to, lend credence to; [+ *esperanza*] to add to, fuel • **eso abona nuestras sospechas** that adds to our suspicions
(VPR) **abonarse** • **~se a una revista** to subscribe to a magazine, take out a subscription to a magazine • **me he abonado a la ópera** I have bought a season ticket for the opera
abonaré (SM) promissory note, IOU
abonero/a (SM/F) **1** (*Méx*) (= *vendedor a plazos*) *street credit salesperson*
2 (*LAm*) (= *que recoge abonos*) collector
abono (SM) **1** (*Agr*) (= *fertilizante*) manure, fertilizer; (= *acto*) fertilizing, manuring
▸ **abono químico** chemical fertilizer, artificial manure
2 (*Com*) (= *pago*) payment; (= *plazo*) instalment, installment (EEUU); (= *crédito*) credit; (*LAm*) (= *entrega inicial*) down payment, deposit • **pagar por** *o* **en ~s** to pay by instalments *o* (EEUU) installments
3 (*a periódico, revista etc*) subscription; (*Teat, Ferro*) season ticket
4 (= *aval*) guarantee
5 (*Méx*) (= *recibo*) receipt
aboquillado (ADJ) tipped, filter-tipped
abordable (ADJ) **1** [*lugar*] accessible; [*tarea*] manageable; [*precio*] reasonable
2 [*persona*] approachable • **no es nada ~** he's a difficult man
abordaje (SM) **1** (*Náut*) (= *choque*) collision; (= *invasión*) boarding • **¡al ~!** all aboard!
2 [*de problema*] approach (**de** to); (*a persona*) accosting, approach
abordar ▷ CONJUG 1a (VT) **1** (= *acometer*) to tackle • **el libro aborda temas controvertidos** the book tackles some controversial subjects • **pidió más dinero para ~ el problema de la vivienda** he requested more money to tackle *o* deal with the housing problem
2 (= *tratar*) to deal with • **el ministro se negó a ~ la cuestión en la rueda de prensa** the minister refused to deal with the subject at the press conference
3 • **~ a algn** to approach sb • **abordó al profesor en el pasillo** he approached the teacher in the corridor • **una multitud de periodistas la abordó al salir** a crowd of journalists accosted her as she was leaving
4 (*Náut*) (= *atacar*) to board; (= *chocar con*) to ram
5 (*Méx*) [+ *bus*] to board, get on; (*Caribe*) (*Aer*) to board
(VI) (*Náut*) to dock
aborigen (ADJ) aboriginal
(SMF) aborigine, aboriginal
aborrascarse ▷ CONJUG 1g (VPR) to get stormy
aborrecer ▷ CONJUG 2d (VT) **1** (= *odiar*) to loathe, detest; (= *aburrirse con*) to become bored by
2 [+ *crías*] to desert, abandon
aborrecible (ADJ) loathsome, detestable
aborrecido (ADJ) hated, loathed
aborrecimiento (SM) (= *odio*) hatred, abhorrence; (= *aburrimiento*) boredom
aborregado (ADJ) • **cielo ~** mackerel sky
aborregarse ▷ CONJUG 1h (VPR) **1*** (= *seguir*) to follow like a sheep/like sheep, tag along
2 (*Meteo*) to cloud over
3 (*LAm**) to be silly, get silly
abortar ▷ CONJUG 1a (VI) (*accidentalmente*) to have a miscarriage; (*deliberadamente*) to have an abortion • **se puede ~ gratuitamente** you can have a free abortion
(VT) **1** (= *abandonar*) [+ *plan, aterrizaje*] to abort
2 (= *frustrar*) [+ *complot*] to foil, frustrate; [+ *motín, protesta*] to quell, put down • **el portero abortó el intento de gol** the goalkeeper frustrated the attempt at a goal
3 (*Inform*) to abort
abortero/a (SM/F) abortionist
abortista (ADJ) [*clínica*] abortion (*antes de s*); [*política*] pro-abortion
(SMF) **1** (= *partidario*) abortion campaigner
2 (= *criminal*) abortionist • **~ ilegal** backstreet abortionist
(SF) *woman who has had an abortion*
abortivo (ADJ) abortive
(SM) abortifacient
aborto (SM) **1** (*Med*) (*accidental*) miscarriage; (*provocado*) abortion; (*Jur*) (criminal) abortion ▸ **aborto clandestino** backstreet abortion ▸ **aborto espontáneo** miscarriage ▸ **aborto eugenésico** eugenic abortion ▸ **aborto habitual** repeated miscarriage ▸ **aborto ilegal** illegal abortion ▸ **aborto libre y gratuito** free abortion on demand
2 (*Bio*) monster, freak
3 (= *fracaso*) failure
4‡ ugly man/woman; (*aplicado a mujer*) old cow‡
abortón (SM) (*Vet*) premature calf
abotagado (ADJ) swollen, bloated
abotagamiento (SM) swelling
abotagarse ▷ CONJUG 1h (VPR) to swell up, become bloated
abotargado (ADJ) = abotagado
abotargamiento (SM) = abotagamiento
abotargarse ▷ CONJUG 1h (VPR) = abotagarse
abotonador (SM) buttonhook
abotonar ▷ CONJUG 1a (VT) **1** (= *abrochar*) to button up, do up
2 (*Méx*) (= *tapar*) to block, obstruct
(VI) [*planta*] to bud
(VPR) **abotonarse** (= *abrocharse*) to button up, do up
abovedado (ADJ) vaulted, arched
(SM) vaulting
abovedar ▷ CONJUG 1a (VT) to vault, arch
aboyar ▷ CONJUG 1a (VT) **1** (*Náut*) to mark with buoys
2 (*Méx*) to float
abozalar ▷ CONJUG 1a (VT) to muzzle
abr. (ABR) (= **abril**) Apr
abra¹ (SF) **1** (*Geog*) (= *cala*) inlet; (*entre montañas*) (mountain) pass
2 (*Geol*) (= *grieta*) fissure
3 (*LAm*) (= *claro*) clearing
abra² (SF) (*LAm*) panel, leaf (of a door)
abracadabra (SM) abracadabra
abracadabrante (ADJ) (= *aparatoso*) spectacular; (= *atractivo*) enchanting, captivating; (= *insólito*) unusual; (= *raro*) extravagant
abracar ▷ CONJUG 1g (VT) (*Méx*) = abrazar
Abraham (SM), **Abrahán** (SM) Abraham
abrasado (ADJ) **1** (= *quemado*) burnt, burned (EEUU), burnt up
2 • **estar ~** (= *avergonzado*) to burn with shame • **estar ~ en cólera** to be in a raging temper
abrasador (ADJ), **abrasante** (ADJ) burning, scorching
abrasar ▷ CONJUG 1a (VT) **1** (= *quemar*) to burn (up); (*con lejía*) to scorch • **murieron abrasados** they burned to death
2 [+ *plantas*] [*sol*] to dry up, parch; [*viento*] to sear; [*helada*] to cut, nip
3 (= *derrochar*) to squander, waste
4 (= *avergonzar*) to fill with shame
(VI) • **esta sopa abrasa** this soup's boiling
(VPR) **abrasarse 1** (= *quemarse*) to burn (up); [*tierra*] to be parched
2 • **~se de amores** to be passionately in love • **~se de calor** to be roasting *o* sweltering • **~se de sed** to be parched, have a raging thirst
abrasión (SF) (= *erosión*) abrasion; (*Med*) graze
abrasivo (ADJ), (SM) abrasive
abrazadera (SF) (= *soporte*) bracket, clamp; (*Tip*) (= *corchete*) bracket ▸ **abrazadera para papeles** paper clip
abrazar ▷ CONJUG 1f (VT) **1** [+ *persona*] to embrace, hug, hold
2 (= *adoptar*) [+ *fe*] to adopt, embrace; [+ *doctrina*] to espouse; [+ *oportunidad*] to seize; [+ *profesión*] to adopt, enter, take up
3 [+ *empresa*] to take charge of
4 (= *abarcar*) to include, take in
(VPR) **abrazarse** to embrace (each other), hug (each other) • **~se a** [*persona*] to embrace, hug; [*niño*] to cling to, clutch
abrazo (SM) **1** (= *acción*) hug, embrace
2 (*en cartas*) • **un ~ afectuoso** *o* **cordial** with best wishes *o* kind regards • **un fuerte ~ (de)** love from
abreboca (*LAm*) (ADJ) absent-minded
(SM) appetizer

abrebotellas (SM INV) bottle opener
abrecartas (SM INV) letter opener, paper knife
abrefácil (SM) • **un envase con ~** an easy-open carton
(ADJ) **1** [*envase*] easy-open • **"abrefácil"** "easy-open"
2 [*rueda*] quick-release
ábrego (SM) south-west wind
abrelatas (SM INV) tin opener, can opener (*EEUU*)
abrenuncio (EXCL) not for me!
abrevadero (SM) (*Zool*) (*natural*) watering place; (*Agr*) (= *pilón*) drinking trough
abrevar ▸ CONJUG 1a (VT) [+ *animal*] to water; [+ *tierra*] to water, irrigate; [+ *pieles*] to soak
(VI) (*Zool*) to drink
(VPR) **abrevarse** (= *regodearse*) • **~se en sangre** to wallow in blood
abreviación (SF) abridgement, shortening
abreviadamente (ADV) (= *sucintamente*) briefly, succinctly; (= *en forma resumida*) in an abridged form
abreviado (ADJ) (= *breve*) brief; (= *reducido*) shortened, abridged • **la palabra es forma abreviada de …** the word is short for …
abreviar ▸ CONJUG 1b (VT) **1** (= *acortar*) [+ *palabra*] to abbreviate; [+ *texto*] to abridge, reduce; [+ *discurso, estancia etc*] to shorten, cut short
2 (= *acercar*) [+ *fecha*] to bring forward; [+ *acontecimiento*] to hasten
(VI) (= *apresurarse*) to be quick • **bueno, para ~ …** well, to cut a long story short …
abreviatura (SF) abbreviation, contraction
abriboca (ADJ INV) (*Arg*) open-mouthed
abridor (SM) [*de botellas*] bottle opener; [*de latas*] tin opener, can opener (*EEUU*)
abrigada (SF), **abrigadero** (SM) shelter, windbreak ▸ **abrigadero de ladrones** (*Méx*) den of thieves
abrigado (ADJ) **1** (= *cubierto de ropa*) wrapped up (**con** in) • **iba ~ con una chaqueta** he was wrapped up in a jacket • **tengo los pies bien ~s** my feet are nice and warm
2 (= *que abriga*) [*ropa*] warm
3 (= *protegido*) [*lugar*] sheltered, protected (**de** from)
abrigador(a) (ADJ) (*And, Méx*) warm
(SM/F) *person who covers up for another*
abrigar ▸ CONJUG 1h (VT) **1** (*del frío*) [*persona*] to wrap up; [*ropa, manta*] to keep warm • **abriga bien a los niños** wrap the kids up well • **este gorro de lana te ~á las orejas** this woolly hat will keep your ears warm
2 (= *resguardar*) to shelter, protect (**de** from) • **los árboles nos abrigaban del viento** the trees sheltered *o* protected us from the wind
3 (= *ayudar*) to support • **tiene un buen equipo que le abriga** he's got a good team supporting him
4 (= *albergar*) [+ *ambición, sospecha, temor*] to harbour, harbor (*EEUU*); [+ *duda*] to entertain, harbour, harbor (*EEUU*); [+ *esperanza, ilusión*] to cherish, harbour, harbor (*EEUU*); [+ *opinión*] to hold
(VI) [*ropa, manta*] to be warm • **esta manta no abriga nada** this blanket isn't warm at all • **este jersey abriga mucho** this jumper is nice and warm
(VPR) **abrigarse 1** (*con ropa*) to wrap (o.s.) up • **salió a la nieve sin ~se** he went out in the snow without wrapping himself up • **¡abrígate bien!** wrap up well! • **usaban una manta para ~se** they used a blanket to keep themselves warm • **abrígate el cuello con la bufanda** cover your neck up with the scarf
2 (= *resguardarse*) to shelter, take shelter (**de** from) • **nos abrigamos de la tormenta bajo un árbol** we took shelter *o* sheltered from the storm under a tree • **se abrigaba en la presunción de inocencia** he sheltered behind the presumption of innocence
abrigo (SM) **1** (= *prenda*) coat • **un ~ de pieles** a fur coat • **un ~ de visón** a mink coat
2 (= *protección*) **a** (*contra el frío*) • **¿tienes suficiente ~?** are you warm enough? • **esta manta te servirá de ~** this blanket will keep you warm • **esta capa es un buen ~ para el invierno** this cloak is lovely and warm for the winter • **ropa de ~** warm clothes
b (*contra el viento, la lluvia*) shelter • **las rocas nos sirvieron de ~** the rocks sheltered us, the rocks gave us shelter • MODISMO: • **de ~** (*Esp*) [*gastos, presupuesto, pelea*] huge • **tiene una bronquitis de ~** she has really bad bronchitis • **ten cuidado porque es un tipo de ~** be careful - he's a dodgy character*
3 • **al ~ de a** (= *protegido por*) [+ *seto, roca*] in the shelter of; [+ *noche, oscuridad*] under cover of; [+ *ley, poder*] under, under the protection of • **la ciudad está situada al ~ de unas colinas** the town is sheltered by hills • **charlamos al ~ de la lumbre** we chatted by the fireside • **escaparon al ~ de la noche** they escaped under cover of darkness • **crearon empresas al ~ de la nueva ley** they set up companies under the protection of the new law • **se crearon pequeños bancos al ~ del proceso de industrialización** the process of industrialization led to the creation of small banks
b (= *protegido de*) [+ *tormenta, viento*] sheltered from; [+ *escándalo, desgracias*] protected from • **nos pusimos al ~ del viento** we took shelter *o* we sheltered from the wind • **por su posición estaba al ~ de semejantes infortunios** the nature of his position protected him from such misfortunes • **al ~ de las miradas indiscretas** away from prying eyes • **una sociedad al ~ de amenazas externas** a society immune to outside threats
4 (*Náut*) natural harbour, natural harbor (*EEUU*), haven
abril (SM) April • **en el ~ de la vida** in the springtime of one's life • **una chica de 15 ~es** a girl of 15 summers (*liter*) • MODISMO: • **estar hecho un ~** to look very handsome • REFRÁN: • **en ~ aguas mil** April showers bring May flowers; ▸ **septiembre**
abrileño (ADJ) April (*antes de s*)
abrillantado (ADJ) [*superficie*] polished; (*Culin*) glazed
(SM) [*de superficie*] polish(ing); (*Culin*) glaze, glazing
abrillantadora (SF) floor polisher
abrillantamuebles (SM INV) furniture polish
abrillantar ▸ CONJUG 1a (VT) (= *pulir*) to polish; [+ *piedra*] to cut; (*Culin*) to glaze; (= *mejorar*) to enhance, jazz up*
abrir ▸ CONJUG 3a (PP: **abierto**) (VT) **1** (*algo que estaba cerrado*) **a** [+ *puerta, armario, libro, ojos*] to open; [+ *cremallera, bragueta*] to undo • **abre la ventana** open the window • **~ una puerta/ventana de par en par** to open a door/window wide • **le abrían las cartas** they were opening his letters • **abre la boca** open your mouth; (*en el dentista*) open wide • **no encuentro la llave para ~ la puerta** I can't find the key to open *o* unlock the door • **abrid el libro por la página 50** turn to page 50 in the book, open the book at page 50 • MODISMO: • **en un ~ y cerrar de ojos** in the twinkling of an eye
b (*desplegando*) [+ *mapa, mantel*] to spread out; [+ *paraguas*] to open, put up; [+ *mano, abanico, paracaídas*] to open
c (*haciendo una abertura*) [+ *pozo*] to sink; [+ *foso, cimientos*] to dig; [+ *agujero, perforación*] to make, bore; [+ *camino*] to clear; (*LAm*) [+ *bosque*] to clear • **tuvimos que ~ camino cortando ramas** we had to cut a path through the branches • **he abierto un sendero en el jardín** I've made a path in the garden • **la explosión abrió una brecha en la pared** the explosion blew a hole in the wall • **las lluvias han abierto socavones en las calles** the rain has caused potholes to appear on the streets
d (*haciendo un corte*) [+ *sandía*] to cut open; [+ *herida*] to open • **abre el pan por la mitad** cut the loaf in half
e [+ *grifo, luz, agua*] to turn on; [+ *válvula*] to open • **abre el grifo del agua caliente** turn the hot water tap on • **abre un poco más el grifo** open the tap a bit more • **¿has abierto el gas?** have you turned the gas on?
2 (= *encabezar*) [+ *manifestación, desfile*] to lead, head; [+ *baile*] to open, lead off; [+ *lista*] to head
3 (= *inaugurar*) **a** [+ *acto, ceremonia*] to open • **se acaban de volver a ~ las negociaciones con los sindicatos** negotiations with the unions have been reopened • **el plazo para las solicitudes se abre en abril** applications may be made from April • **ya han abierto el plazo de matrícula** registration has already started
b (*Com*) [+ *negocio*] to set up, start; [+ *cuenta*] to open • **ha decidido ~ su propio negocio** she has decided to set up *o* start her own business • **han abierto un centro de atención al cliente** they've opened a customer service centre • **he abierto la cuenta con 400 euros** I opened the account with 400 euros • **~ un expediente a algn** (*investigación*) to open a file on sb; (*proceso*) to begin proceedings against sb • **~ una información** to open *o* start an inquiry
c (*Tip*) • **~ comillas** to open quotes • **~ paréntesis** to open brackets
d (*Mil*) • **¡abran fuego!** (open) fire!
4 (= *ampliar*) [+ *perspectivas*] to open up • **este acuerdo abre nuevas perspectivas de paz** this agreement offers new hope of peace • **vivir en el extranjero le abrió la mente** living abroad opened up his mind *o* made him more open-minded • **estos países han abierto sus economías** these countries have opened their economy up
5 [+ *apetito*] • **las vitaminas te ~án el apetito** taking vitamins will improve your appetite • **ese olor me está abriendo el apetito** that smell is making me hungry • **esta selección abre el apetito a los lectores** this selection is intended to whet the readers' appetite
(VI) **1** [*puerta, cajón*] to open • **esta puerta no abre** this door won't open
2 [*persona*] to open the door, open up • **¡abre, soy yo!** open the door *o* open up, it's me! • **llamé pero no abrió nadie** I knocked at the door, but nobody answered • **esta llave no abre bien** this key is a bit stiff
3 [*comercio, museo*] to open • **las tiendas abren a las diez** the shops open at ten o'clock • **los sábados no abrimos al público** we're not open to the public on Saturdays • **el banco abre de 9 a 1** the bank is open from 9 to 1 • **el almacén volverá a ~ en septiembre** the warehouse will reopen in September
4 [*flor*] to open
5 (*en operación quirúrgica*) • **vamos a tener que ~** we're going to have to open him up
6 (*Meteo*) to clear up • **parece que está empezando a ~** it looks like it's starting to clear up
7 (*Bridge*) to open • **~ de tres a un palo** to open

three in a suit • ~ **de corazones** to open (with a bid in) hearts
8 (*Caribe**) (= *huir*) to escape, run off
(VPR) **abrirse 1** [*paracaídas, paraguas, ventana, libro*] to open • **de repente se abrió la puerta** suddenly, the door opened • **se están abriendo las costuras** it's coming apart at the seams • **la madera se está abriendo** the wood is splitting
2 (= *extenderse*) • **ante nosotros se abría todo un mundo de posibilidades** a whole world of possibilities was opening up before us • **~se a algo** to open out onto sth • **la avenida se abre a una magnífica plaza** the avenue opens out onto a magnificent square
3 [*persona*] **a** • **no te abras tanto en las curvas** stay a bit closer to the side of the road when going round bends • **el delantero se abrió hacia la banda** the forward went wide
b • **intentaron ~se paso entre la muchedumbre** they tried to make their way through the crowd • MODISMO: • **~se camino en la vida** to make one's way in life
c‡ (= *largarse*) • **¡me abro!** I'm off! • **¡ábrete!** shove off!*
4 • **~se a: tenemos que ~nos más al progreso** we have to open up more to progress • **~se a** *o* **con algn** to confide in sb
5 (= *romperse, rajarse*) • **se le ha abierto la herida** his wound has opened • **~se la cabeza** to crack one's head open • **~se el tobillo** to twist one's ankle, sprain one's ankle • **~se las venas** to slash one's wrists
6 (*Meteo*) to clear, clear up
7 (*Méx*) (= *echar marcha atrás*) to backtrack, back-pedal

abrita (SF) (*CAm*) short dry spell

abrochador (SM) **1** (= *abotonador*) buttonhook
2 (*LAm*) (= *grapadora*) stapler, stapling machine

abrochar ▷ CONJUG 1a (VT) **1** [+ *botón, cremallera, vestido*] to do up; [+ *broche, hebilla*] to fasten • **¿me abrochas el vestido?** can you do up my dress? • **abróchale el abrigo al niño** do up the boy's coat • **¿me abrochas?** can you do me up? • **llevas los botones sin ~** your buttons are undone
2 (*LAm*) [+ *papeles*] to staple (together)
3 (*Méx*) (= *atar*) to tie up; (= *agarrar*) to grab hold of
4 (*And*) (= *reprender*) to reprimand
(VPR) **abrocharse** • **abróchate la camisa** do up your shirt • **el vestido se abrocha delante con cremallera** the dress does up at the front with a zip • **abróchate los zapatos** tie up your (shoe)laces • **abróchense el cinturón de seguridad** fasten your seat belts

abrogación (SF) abrogation, repeal

abrogar ▷ CONJUG 1h (VT) to abrogate, repeal

abrojo (SM) **1** (*Bot*) thistle; (*Mil*) caltrop
2 abrojos (*Náut*) submerged rocks, reefs; (*Méx*) (= *matorral*) thorn bushes

abroncar* ▷ CONJUG 1g (VT) (= *avergonzar*) to shame, make ashamed; (= *ridiculizar*) to ridicule; (= *aburrir*) to bore; (= *molestar*) to annoy; [+ *orador*] to boo, heckle, barrack; (= *reprender*) to give a lecture to, tick off
(VPR) **abroncarse** (= *enfadarse*) to get angry

abroquelarse ▷ CONJUG 1a (VPR) • ~ **con** *o* **de** to shield o.s. with, defend o.s. with

abrumado (ADJ) (= *agobiado*) overwhelmed; (= *oprimido*) weighed down; (= *cansado*) worn out, exhausted

abrumador (ADJ) **1** (= *agobiante*) crushing; (= *pesado*) burdensome • **es una responsabilidad ~a** it's a heavy responsibility
2 (= *importante*) [*mayoría*] overwhelming; [*superioridad*] crushing, overwhelming

abrumadoramente (ADV) **1** (= *de forma agobiante*) crushingly
2 (= *enormemente*) vastly, overwhelmingly

abrumar ▷ CONJUG 1a (VT) (= *agobiar*) to overwhelm; (= *oprimir*) to oppress, weigh down; (= *cansar*) to wear out, exhaust • ~ **a algn de trabajo** to overload *o* swamp sb with work • **le ~on con atenciones** they made too much of a fuss of him
(VPR) **abrumarse** (*Meteo*) to get foggy, get misty

abruptamente (ADV) abruptly

abrupto (ADJ) **1** [*cuesta*] steep; [*terreno*] rough, rugged
2 [*tono*] abrupt
3 [*cambio*] sudden

abrutado (ADJ) brutish, brutalized

ABS (SM ABR) (= **antilock braking system**) ABS

absceso (SM) abscess

abscisión (SF) incision

absenta (SF) absinth(e)

absentismo (SM) [*de obreros*] absenteeism; [*de terrateniente*] absentee landlordism
▸ **absentismo laboral** absenteeism from work

absentista (SMF) (= *obrero*) absentee; (= *terrateniente*) absentee landlord

ábside (SM) [*de iglesia*] apse; [*de tienda de campaña*] bell, bell end

absintio (SM) absinth(e)

absolución (SF) (*Rel*) absolution; (*Jur*) acquittal

absoluta (SF) **1** (= *declaración*) dogmatic statement, authoritative assertion
2 (*Mil*) discharge • **tomar la ~** to take one's discharge, leave the service

absolutamente (ADV) **1** (= *completamente*) absolutely • **es ~ imposible** it's absolutely impossible • **está ~ prohibido** it is absolutely forbidden • **el puente estaba ~ destruido** the bridge was completely destroyed
2 (*con negativos*) not at all, by no means • ~ **nada** nothing at all • **—¿así que no viene nadie? —absolutamente** "so nobody is coming?" — "nobody at all"

absolutismo (SM) absolutism
▸ **absolutismo ilustrado** enlightened dictatorship

absolutista (ADJ), (SMF) absolutist

absolutizar ▷ CONJUG 1f (VT) to pin down, be precise about

absoluto (ADJ) **1** (= *no relativo*) absolute • **los nacionalistas lograron mayoría absoluta** the nationalists got an absolute majority • **lo ~** the absolute
2 (= *máximo*) [*prioridad*] top; [*reposo, fe*] complete; [*verdad*] absolute • **tengo la absoluta certeza de que vino** I'm absolutely certain that he came • **son de absoluta necesidad** they are absolutely necessary *o* essential • **guardaron el más ~ silencio** they remained absolutely silent • **nunca lo supe con certeza absoluta** I never knew for sure • **viven en la miseria más absoluta** they live in the most abject poverty • **existe compenetración absoluta entre los dos** there is a perfect understanding between them, they understand each other perfectly
3 [*monarquía, poder*] absolute
4 • **en ~** not at all • **—¿es verdad? —no, en ~** "is it true?" — "no, absolutely not *o* no, not at all" • **—¿te importa? —en ~** "do you mind?" — "no, absolutely not *o* no, not at all" • **esa idea no me atrae en ~** that idea doesn't appeal to me at all *o* in the slightest • **no dijo nada en ~** he said absolutely nothing (at all) • **no es en ~ extraño** it is by no means odd

absolutorio (ADJ) • **fallo ~** verdict of not guilty

absolver ▷ CONJUG 2h (PP: **absuelto**) (VT) (*Rel*) to absolve; (*Jur*) to acquit, clear (**de** of)

absorbencia (SF) absorbency

absorbente (ADJ) **1** (*Quím*) absorbent
2 (= *interesante*) interesting, absorbing; [*tarea*] demanding; [*amor*] possessive, tyrannical
(SM) absorbent ▸ **absorbente higiénico** sanitary towel, sanitary napkin (*EEUU*)

absorber ▷ CONJUG 2a (VT) **1** [+ *líquido*] to absorb, soak up
2 [+ *información*] to absorb, take in; [+ *recursos*] to use up; [+ *energías*] to take up; [+ *atención*] to command
(VPR) **absorberse** • **~se en** to become absorbed *o* engrossed in

absorbible (ADJ) absorbable

absorbidad (SF) absorbency

absorción (SF) **1** [*de líquidos*] absorption
2 (= *atracción*) absorption
3 (*Com*) takeover

absorto (ADJ) absorbed, engrossed • **estar ~** (= *extasiado*) to be entranced; (= *pasmado*) to be amazed • **estar ~ (en sus pensamientos)** to be lost in thought • **estar ~ en un proyecto** to be engrossed in *o* taken up with a scheme

abstemio/a (ADJ) teetotal
(SM/F) teetotaller

abstención (SF) abstention

abstencionismo (SM) abstentionism

abstencionista (SMF) abstainer

abstenerse ▷ CONJUG 2k (VPR) (*gen*) to abstain • ~ **de hacer algo** to refrain from doing sth • **en la duda, abstente** when in doubt, don't • **"abstenerse intermediarios"** "no dealers" • **"abstenerse si no cumplen los requisitos"** "those without the necessary qualifications need not apply"

abstinencia (SF) (*gen*) abstinence; (*Rel*) fasting; [*de drogas*] withdrawal

abstinente (ADJ) (*Rel*) abstinent, observing abstinence

abstracción (SF) **1** (= *acto*) abstraction; (*pey*) (= *despiste*) absent-mindedness
2 • **hacer ~ de** to leave aside, except

abstractar ▷ CONJUG 1a (VT) [+ *publicaciones*] to abstract, make abstracts of

abstracto (ADJ) abstract • **en ~** in the abstract

abstraer ▷ CONJUG 2O (VT) to abstract
(VPR) **abstraerse** to be lost in thought, be preoccupied • **~se de** to detach o.s. from

abstraído (ADJ) (= *ensimismado*) withdrawn; (= *inquieto*) preoccupied

abstruso (ADJ) abstruse

absuelto (PP) *de* **absolver**

absurdamente (ADV) absurdly

absurdez (SF) absurdity

absurdidad (SF) absurdity

absurdo (ADJ) absurd • **es ~ que** it is absurd that • **lo ~ es que ...** the ridiculous thing is that ... • **teatro del ~** theatre *o* (*EEUU*) theater of the absurd
(SM) absurdity, (piece of) nonsense • **decir ~s** to talk nonsense

abubilla (SF) hoopoe

abucharar* ▷ CONJUG 1a (VT) (= *abuchear*) to boo, jeer; (= *excluir*) to ostracize, marginalize; (= *criticar*) to slate*, criticize; (= *avergonzar*) to put to shame • **quedarse abucharado** to be left out, be ostracized

abuchear ▷ CONJUG 1a (VT) to boo, jeer at • **ser abucheado** (*Teat*) to be booed, be hissed (at)

abucheo (SM) booing, jeering • **ganarse un ~** (*Teat*) to be booed, be hissed (at)

abuelado* (ADJ) (*Cono Sur*) spoiled by one's grandparents

a

abuelita SF **1** (*Cono Sur*) (= *gorra*) baby's bonnet
2 (*And*) (= *cuna*) cradle
abuelito/a* SM/F granddad/granny*, grandpa/grandma*; (*Méx*) grandfather/ grandmother
abuelo/a SM/F **1** (= *pariente*) grandfather/ grandmother • **mis ~s** my grandparents • **¡tu abuela!*** rubbish! • MODISMOS: • **¡cuéntaselo a tu abuela!*** pull the other one!*, go tell that to the marines! (*EEUU*) • **no necesitar abuela*** to blow one's own trumpet • **(éramos pocos) y parió la abuela*** and that was the last straw, and that was all we needed • **no tener abuela*** to be full of o.s.
2 (= *anciano*) old man/old woman • **está hecho un ~** he looks like an old man
3 (= *antepasado*) ancestor, forbear
abulense ADJ of/from Ávila
SMF native/inhabitant of Ávila • **los ~s** the people of Ávila
abulia SF total apathy
abúlico ADJ apathetic
abulón SM (*esp Méx*) abalone
abultado ADJ **1** (= *voluminoso*) bulky, unwieldy; [*labios, libro*] thick; (*Med*) swollen
2 (= *exagerado*) exaggerated
abultamiento SM **1** (= *voluminosidad*) bulkiness, (large) size; (*Med*) swelling
2 (= *exageración*) exaggeration
abultar ▷ CONJUG 1a VT **1** (= *aumentar*) to increase; (= *agrandar*) to enlarge; (= *hacer abultado*) to make bulky
2 (= *exagerar*) to exaggerate
VI **1** (= *tener bulto*) to be bulky, be big
2 (= *tener más importancia*) to increase in importance
abundamiento SM abundance, plenty • **a** *o* **por mayor ~** furthermore
abundancia SF **1** (= *multitud*) abundance • **hay gran ~ de olivos** there is a great abundance of olive trees • **en ~: hay copas en ~** there are plenty of glasses • **había bebida en ~** there was plenty to drink
2 (= *copiosidad*) abundance • **bendijo la ~ de la cosecha** he blessed the abundance of the harvest
3 (= *prosperidad*) • **su familia vive en la ~** his family are very well-off • **la sociedad de la ~** the affluent society • MODISMO: • **nadar en la ~** to be rolling in money; ▷ **cuerno**
abundante ADJ **1** (= *copioso*) abundant, plentiful • **el agua es ~ en toda la zona** water is abundant *o* plentiful throughout the area • **la fauna es ~ en el parque nacional** • **el parque nacional es ~ en fauna** there is abundant wildlife in the national park, there is a wealth of fauna in the national park • **un país ~ en minerales** a country which is rich in minerals, a country which abounds in minerals • **una ~ ración de calamares** a generous portion of squid • **teníamos ~ comida** we had plenty of food • **tienes que hervirlos en agua ~** you have to boil them in plenty of water • **la nubosidad será ~ en Galicia** there will be extensive cloud in Galicia
2 (*en plural*) a great many • **un texto con ~s citas** a text with a great many *o* numerous quotations • **los flamencos son muy ~s en toda la zona** there are a great many flamingos throughout the area • **existen ~s pruebas** there is plenty of proof
abundantemente ADV [*llover, sangrar*] heavily; [*crecer*] abundantly
abundar ▷ CONJUG 1a VI **1** (= *existir en abundancia*) to be plentiful • **el olivo abunda en el sur** olive trees are plentiful in the south • **este tipo de cáncer abunda entre personas sedentarias** this type of cancer is very common in *o* among sedentary people
2 (*frm*) (= *tener en abundancia*) • **~ en algo: la zona abunda en gas natural** the area is rich in natural gas, natural gas is plentiful in the area • **los periódicos abundan en anglicismos** the newspapers abound in *o* with anglicisms
3 (= *profundizar*) • **~ en algo** (*frm*) to elaborate on sth • **me gustaría ~ en ese comentario** I'd like to elaborate on this remark • **no quiso ~ más en el asunto** he declined to elaborate
4 (= *estar de acuerdo*) • **yo abundo en esa opinión** I absolutely *o* wholeheartedly agree
Abundio SM ▷ **tonto**
abundoso ADJ (*LAm*) abundant
abur* EXCL so long!
aburguesado ADJ • **un barrio ~** a gentrified area • **un hombre ~** a man who has become bourgeois, a man who has adopted middle-class ways
aburguesamiento SM embourgeoisement
aburguesar ▷ CONJUG 1a VT to gentrify
VPR **aburguesarse** [*persona*] to become bourgeois, adopt middle-class ways
aburrición SF (*LAm*) = **aburrimiento**
aburridamente ADV in a boring manner, boringly
aburrido ADJ (= *que aburre*) boring, tedious; (= *que siente aburrimiento*) bored • **un libro ~** a boring book • **una espera aburrida** a tedious wait • **¡estoy ~ de decírtelo!** I'm tired of telling you!

> **ABURRIDO**
>
> **¿"Bored" o "boring"?**
>
> ▷ *Usamos* **bored** *para referirnos al hecho de estar aburrido, es decir, de sentir aburrimiento:*
> **Si estás aburrida podrías ayudarme con este trabajo**
> If you're bored you could help me with this work
>
> ▷ *Usamos* **boring** *con personas, actividades y cosas para indicar que alguien o algo es aburrido, es decir, que produce aburrimiento:*
> **¡Qué novela más aburrida!**
> What a boring novel!
> **No me gusta salir con él; es muy aburrido**
> I don't like going out with him; he's very boring

aburridón ADJ (*And*) rather boring
aburridor ADJ (*LAm*) boring
aburrimiento SM boredom, tedium • **¡qué ~!** what a bore!
aburrir ▷ CONJUG 3a VT **1** (*gen*) to bore; (= *cansar*) to tire, weary
2‡ [+ *dinero*] to blow*; [+ *tiempo*] to waste
VPR **aburrirse** to be bored, get bored (**con, de, por** with) • **~se como una ostra** to be bored stiff
abusado/a (*Méx*) EXCL* (= *cuidado*) look out!, careful!
ADJ **1** (= *astuto*) sharp, cunning
2 (= *cauteloso*) watchful, wary
SM/F swot*, grind (*EEUU**)
abusador ADJ (*Cono Sur*) abusive
abusar ▷ CONJUG 1a VI **1** (= *extralimitarse*) to take advantage • **es muy generoso pero no debéis ~** he's very generous but you mustn't take advantage • **~ de** [+ *persona*] to take advantage of; [+ *amistad, hospitalidad, amabilidad, privilegio*] to abuse • **de los débiles todo el mundo abusa** everyone takes advantage of the weak • **el acusado abusó de su condición de policía** the defendant abused his position as a policeman • **no quiero ~ de su tiempo** I don't want to take up too much of your time • **si siguen abusando de mi paciencia, un día estallaré** if they continue to try my patience, one of these days I'm going to explode • **~ de la confianza de algn** (= *aprovecharse*) to take advantage of sb's good will; (= *traicionar*) to betray sb's trust
2 (= *usar en exceso*) • **está bien beber de vez en cuando pero sin ~** drinking every so often is fine as long as you don't overdo it • **~ de:** • **~ del tabaco** to smoke too much • **no conviene ~ de las grasas** it's not good to eat too much fat • **abusan de la jerga técnica** they use too much technical jargon
3 (= *usar mal*) • **~ de** [+ *dinero*] to misuse
4 (*sexualmente*) • **~ de algn** to (sexually) abuse sb
abusión SF (= *abuso*) abuse; (= *superstición*) superstition
abusivamente ADV unfairly
abusivo ADJ unfair; [*precio*] exorbitant, outrageous
abuso SM **1** (= *extralimitación*) [*de privilegios, cargo, fondos*] abuse • **se siguen cometiendo ~s en los derechos humanos** human rights abuses are still being committed • **cuando hay ~ de amistad** when unfair demands are made on friendship, when there are impositions made on friendship • **lo que te han cobrado es un ~** it's outrageous what they've charged you ▸ **abuso de autoridad** abuse of authority ▸ **abuso de confianza** (*Pol, Econ*) breach of trust, betrayal of trust • **su actitud me parece un ~ de confianza** I think he's taking liberties ▸ **abuso de poder** abuse of power
2 (= *uso excesivo*) [*de tabaco, drogas*] abuse; [*de disolventes, pesticidas*] overuse • **el ~ del alcohol puede traer consecuencias fatales** alcohol abuse can have fatal consequences • **especies en peligro por el ~ de la caza** endangered species through overhunting • **había un ~ de adjetivos en el texto** there was too much *o* excessive use of adjectives in the text • **recibió varias quejas por ~ de fuerza** he received several complaints of excessive use of force • **no es recomendable el ~ de la sal en la comida** it's not advisable to put too much salt in your food • **hicieron uso y ~ del teléfono** they used the phone to excess
3 (*tb* **abuso sexual**) sexual abuse ▸ **abuso de menores** child abuse ▸ **abusos deshonestos** indecent assault (*sing*)
abusón/ona* ADJ (= *egoísta*) selfish; (= *engreído*) big-headed*; (= *insolente*) abusive
SM/F selfish person, bighead* • **eres un ~** you're a selfish pig*
abute‡ ADV • **vivir de ~** to live well, live like a prince
abyección SF wretchedness, abjectness
abyecto ADJ wretched, abject
a.C. ABR (= **antes de Cristo**) BC
a/c. ABR **1** = **a cuenta**
2 (= **al cuidado de**) c/o
acá ADV **1** (*esp LAm*) (= *aquí*) here, over here • **acá y allá** *o* **acullá** here and there • **pasearse de acá para allá** to walk up and down *o* to and fro • **¡ven** *o* **vente para acá!** come over here! • **¡más acá!** more over this way! • **más acá de** on this side of • **tráelo más acá** move it this way, bring it closer • **está muy acá** it's right here • **no tan acá** not so close, not so far this way
2 (= *ahora*) at this time, now • **de** *o* **desde ayer acá** since yesterday • **de acá a poco** of late • **¿de cuándo acá?** since when?
3 (*LAm*) (= *como demostrativo*) this person *etc*

here • **acá le contará** he'll tell you about it • **acá es mi señora** this is my wife
acabada SF finish
acabadero* SM (*Méx*) • **el ~** the limit, the last straw
acabado ADJ **1** (= *completo*) finished
2 (= *viejo*) old, worn out • **estar ~** (*de salud*) to be a wreck • **está ~ como futbolista** he's finished as a footballer, his footballing days are over
3 (*LAm*) (= *flaco*) thin; (*Méx*) (= *rendido*) exhausted • **está muy ~** (*Méx*) he's looking very old
SM (*Téc*) finish • **buen ~** high finish ▸ **acabado brillo** gloss finish ▸ **acabado satinado** matt finish
acabador(a) SM/F (*Téc*) finisher
acabalar ▹ CONJUG 1a VT to complete
acaballadero SM stud farm
acaballado* ADJ (*Cono Sur*) clumsy, gauche
acaballar ▹ CONJUG 1a VT to cover
acabamiento SM (= *acto*) finishing, completion; (= *final*) end; (= *muerte*) death; (*LAm*) (= *agotamiento*) exhaustion
acabar ▹ CONJUG 1a VT **1** (= *terminar*) [+ *actividad, trabajo*] (*gen*) to finish; (= *dar el toque final a*) to finish off • **¿habéis acabado la instalación de la antena?** have you finished installing the aerial? • **me falta poco para ~ el jersey** I've nearly finished the jumper • **me quedan solo un par de horas para ~ este cuadro** it'll only take me another couple of hours to finish off this painting • **acabó sus días en prisión** he ended his days in prison
2 (= *consumir*) to finish • **ya hemos acabado el aceite** we've used up *o* finished the oil • **cuando acabe esta cerveza me voy** when I've finished this beer I'm going
3 (*LAm*) (= *hablar mal de*) • **~ a algn** to speak ill of sb
VI **1** (= *terminar*) to finish, end • **¿te falta mucho para ~?** are you nearly finished?, have you got long to go? • **la crisis lleva años y no acaba** the recession has been going on for years and there's no sign of it ending • **es cosa de nunca ~** there's no end to it • MODISMO: • **acabáramos:** • **acabáramos, ¿así que se trata de tu hijo?** oh, I see, so it's your son, then?; ▹ **cuento, rosario**
2 • **~ con a** [+ *comida*] to finish off; [+ *injusticia*] to put an end to, stop; [+ *relación*] to end; [+ *reservas*] to exhaust, use up; [+ *esperanzas*] to put paid to • **acabaron con la tarta en un minuto** they finished off the cake within a minute • **¿todavía no has acabado con la carta?** haven't you finished the letter yet? • **hay que ~ con tanto desorden** we must put an end to all this confusion • **hemos acabado con todas las provisiones** we've exhausted *o* used up all our supplies
b [+ *persona*] (= *atender*) to finish with; (= *matar*) to do away with • **cuando acabe con ella, te lavo la cabeza** when I'm done *o* finished with her, I'll wash your hair • **¡acabemos con él!** let's do away with him!* • **esto acabará conmigo** this will be the end of me
3 • **~ de hacer algo a** (*cuando se ha terminado*) • **acabo de llamarla por teléfono** I have just phoned her • **acababa de entrar cuando sonó el teléfono** I had just come in when the phone rang
b (*cuando se está haciendo*) • **cuando acabemos de pagarlo** when we finish paying for it • MODISMOS: • **para ~ de arreglarlo:** • **para ~ de arreglarlo, se fue sin despedirse** on top of everything, she left without even saying goodbye • **¡acaba de parir!*** spit it out!*
c • **no acabo de entender por qué lo hizo** I just can't understand why she did it • **no acabo de entender este concepto** I just can't seem to understand this concept • **ese candidato no me acaba de convencer** I'm not too sure about that candidate
4 (*con complemento de modo*) • **la película acaba bien** the film has a happy ending • **su relación acabó mal** their relationship came to an unhappy end • **si sigues así vas a ~ mal** if you carry on like that you'll come to a sticky end • **acabé harto de tantas fiestas** I ended up getting fed up of all those parties • **la palabra acaba con** *o* **por "z"** the word ends in a "z" • **~ en algo** to end in sth • **espero que no acabe en tragedia** I hope it won't end in tragedy • **el palo acaba en punta** the stick ends in a point • **unos zapatos que acaban en punta** a pair of pointed shoes • **la fiesta acabó en un baile** the party ended with everyone dancing • **después de tanto hablar, todo acabó en nada** after all that talk, it all came to nothing
5 • **~ haciendo algo** • **~ por hacer algo** to end up doing sth • **acabó aceptándolo** he ended up accepting it
6 (*en una relación*) to finish, split up • **hemos acabado** we've finished, we've split up • **¿cuánto hace que acabaste con ella?** how long is it since you split up with *o* finished with her?
7 (*LAm*‡) (= *eyacular*) to come‡
VPR **acabarse 1** (= *terminarse*) [*acto, reunión*] to finish, come to an end; [*reservas*] to run out • **la impresora te avisa cuando se acaba el papel** the printer tells you when the paper runs out • **todo se acabó para él*** he's had it* • **¡se acabó!** that's it! • **¡un minuto más y se acabó!** one more minute and that will be it! • **¡te quedas aquí y se acabó!** you're staying here and that's that! • **le das el dinero y se acabó** just give her the money and be done with it • MODISMO: • **... y (san) se acabó** ... and that's the end of the matter
2 (*con complemento indirecto*) • **se me ha acabado el tabaco** I'm out of cigarettes • **pronto se nos acabará la gasolina** we'll soon be out of petrol • **se me acabó la paciencia** my patience is exhausted *o* at an end, I've run out of patience
3 (*con valor enfático*) • **acábate el café y nos vamos** drink your coffee up and we'll go
4 [*persona*] (= *morir*) to die; (*esp LAm*) (= *cansarse*) to wear o.s. out
acabildar ▹ CONJUG 1a VT to get together, organize into a group
acabóse SM, **acabose** SM • **esto es el ~** this is the last straw • **la fiesta fue el ~** it was the party to end all parties, it was the best party ever
achetear ▹ CONJUG 1a VT to slap, punch
acachihuite SM (*Méx*) (= *paja*) straw, hay; (= *cesto*) straw basket
acacia SF acacia ▸ **acacia falsa** locust tree
acacito ADV (*LAm*) = **acá**
academia SF **1** (= *establecimiento*) academy; (*Escol*) (private) school • **la Real Academia** the Spanish Academy • **la Real Academia de la Historia** the Spanish Academy of History ▸ **academia de baile** dance school ▸ **academia de comercio** business school ▸ **academia de idiomas** language school ▸ **academia de música** school of music, conservatoire ▸ **academia militar** military academy
2 (= *sociedad*) learned society
académico/a ADJ academic
SM/F academician, member (of an academy) ▸ **académico/a de número** full member (*of an academy*)
acaecer ▹ CONJUG 2d VI to happen, occur • **acaeció que ...** it came about that ...
acaecimiento SM happening, occurrence
acahual SM (*Méx*) (= *girasol*) sunflower; (= *yerba*) tall grass
acáis‡ SMPL peepers‡, eyes
acalambrarse ▹ CONJUG 1a VPR to get cramp
acalaminado ADJ (*Cono Sur*) rough, uneven, bumpy
acalenturarse ▹ CONJUG 1a VPR to get feverish
acallamiento SM (= *silenciamiento*) silencing, quietening; (= *apaciguamiento*) pacification
acallar ▹ CONJUG 1a VT **1** (= *silenciar*) to silence, quieten, quiet (*EEUU*)
2 (= *calmar*) [+ *furia*] to assuage, pacify; [+ *crítica, duda*] to silence
acaloradamente ADV heatedly, excitedly
acalorado ADJ **1** (= *con calor*) heated, hot
2 (= *enardecido*) [*discusión*] heated; [*partidario*] passionate; (= *agitado*) agitated
acaloramiento SM **1** (= *calor*) heat
2 (= *enardecimiento*) vehemence, passion
acalorar ▹ CONJUG 1a VT **1** (= *calentar*) to make hot, warm up; (= *sobrecalentar*) to overheat
2 (= *enardecer*) to inflame, excite; [+ *pasiones*] to inflame; [+ *audiencia*] to work up; [+ *ambición*] to stir up, encourage
VPR **acalorarse 1** (= *sofocarse*) to get hot, become overheated
2 (= *enardecerse*) [*persona*] (*al actuar*) to get excited, get worked up (**por** about); (*al hablar*) to get worked up; [*discusión*] to become heated
acalórico ADJ low-calorie (*antes de s*), low in calories
acaloro SM anger
acalote SM (*Méx*) channel
acamar ▹ CONJUG 1a VT to beat down, lay
acamastronarse ▹ CONJUG 1a VPR (*LAm*) to get crafty, become artful
acampada SF camping • **ir de** *o* **hacer una ~** to go camping ▸ **acampada libre** camping rough, camping in the wild
acampado/a SM/F camper, motorhome (*EEUU*)
acampanado ADJ bell-shaped; [*pantalón*] flared, bell-bottomed
acampar ▹ CONJUG 1a VI to camp; (*Mil*) to encamp
VPR **acamparse** to camp
acampo SM pasture, common pasture
acanalado ADJ **1** (= *con canales*) grooved, furrowed
2 (*Arquit*) fluted
3 (*Téc*) [*hierro*] corrugated
acanaladura SF (= *canal*) groove, furrow; (*Arquit*) fluting

ACADEMIA

In Spain **academias** are private schools catering for students of all ages and levels outside normal school and working hours. Some specialize in particular skills such as computing, languages and music while others offer extra tuition in core school subjects and syllabuses. For people hoping to do well enough in the **oposiciones** to get a post in the public sector, there are **academias** offering special preparatory courses for these notoriously difficult competitive examinations.

▹ **OPOSICIONES**

acanalar ▷ CONJUG 1a VT **1** (= *hacer canales*) to groove, furrow
2 (*Arquit*) to flute
3 (*Téc*) [+ *hierro*] to corrugate

acanallado ADJ disreputable, low

acanelado ADJ cinnamon-flavoured *o* (*EEUU*) -flavored, cinnamon-coloured *o* (*EEUU*) -colored

acantilado ADJ [*risco*] steep, sheer; [*costa*] rocky; [*fondo del mar*] shelving
SM cliff

acanto SM acanthus

acantonamiento SM **1** (= *lugar*) cantonment
2 (= *acto*) billeting, quartering

acantonar ▷ CONJUG 1a VT (*Mil*) (= *colocar*) to station; (*en domicilio privado*) to billet

acaparación SF = **acaparamiento**

acaparador(a) ADJ **1** (= *acumulador*) • **las hormigas son animales ~es** ants are hoarders • **instintos ~es** acquisitive instincts
2 (= *egoísta*) (*con cosas*) selfish; (*con personas*) possessive
SM/F **1** [*de objetos, mercancías*] hoarder
2 (= *egoísta*) (*con cosas*) selfish person; (*con personas*) possessive person

acaparamiento SM **1** (= *acumulación*) hoarding, stockpiling • **hizo ~ de víveres** he hoarded *o* stockpiled provisions
2 (*Com*) (= *monopolio*) [*de ventas*] monopolizing; [*del mercado*] cornering
3 (= *apropiamiento*) • **se quejaron del ~ del teléfono por uno de ellos** they complained that one of them was hogging* *o* monopolizing the phone • **consiguió el ~ de todas las miradas** he managed to capture everyone's attention

acaparar ▷ CONJUG 1a VT **1** (= *acumular*) [+ *víveres, bienes*] to hoard • **~ provisiones para el invierno** to hoard food supplies for the winter
2 (= *tener la totalidad de*) **a** [+ *producción, poder, conversación*] to monopolize • **acaparan la distribución de gasolina en la zona** they have a monopoly on the distribution of petrol in the area • **~ el mercado de algo** to corner the market in sth • **han acaparado el mercado del vino** they have cornered the wine market
b (*pey*) to hog*, monopolize • **a ver si no acaparas el teléfono** don't hog* *o* monopolize the telephone, will you?
3 (= *quedarse con*) to take • **la película que acaparó todos los premios** the film which took all the prizes • **han acaparado un 25% del mercado de ventas a domicilio** they have captured *o* taken a 25% share of the home sales market • **la industria acapara la mayor parte de las ayudas del gobierno** industry gets most of the government aid
4 (= *poseer*) to hold • **la izquierda acapara todos los puestos en el ayuntamiento** the left holds all of the council posts • **la empresa acapara el 40% de la tierra** the company owns 40% of the land
5 (= *ocupar*) to take up • **el accidente acaparó las primeras páginas de todos los periódicos** the accident took up the front pages in all the newspapers • **el cantante acapara los titulares estos días** the singer is front page news these days
6 [+ *atención, interés*] to capture • **este asunto acaparó la atención de todos los políticos** this issue captured the attention of all the politicians • **le gustaba ~ las miradas de todo el mundo** he liked to hog the limelight*

acapetate SM (*Méx*) straw mat

acapillar‡ ▷ CONJUG 1a VT (*Méx*) to grab, take hold of

acápite SM (*LAm*) (= *párrafo*) paragraph; (= *título*) subheading • **punto ~** full stop, new paragraph

a cappella [aka'pela] ADV a cappella

acapullado ADJ in bud

acapulqueño/a ADJ of/from Acapulco
SM/F native/inhabitant of Acapulco • **los ~s** the people of Acapulco

acaracolado ADJ spiral (*antes de s*), winding, twisting

acaramelado ADJ **1** (*Culin*) • **con sabor ~** toffee-flavoured *o* (*EEUU*) -flavored • **de color ~** toffee-coloured *o* (*EEUU*) -colored
2 (*fig*) (= *dulce*) sugary, oversweet; (= *correcto*) over-polite • **estaban ~s** [*amantes*] they were all lovey-dovey*

acaramelar ▷ CONJUG 1a VT to coat with caramel
VPR **acaramelarse** to become besotted with each other

acarar ▷ CONJUG 1a VT (= *carear*) to bring face to face; (= *afrontar*) to face, face up to

acardenalar ▷ CONJUG 1a VT to bruise
VPR **acardenalarse** to get bruised, go black and blue

acarear ▷ CONJUG 1a VT = **acarar**

acariciador ADJ caressing

acariciar ▷ CONJUG 1b VT **1** (= *hacer caricias*) to caress, stroke; (= *sobar*) to fondle; [+ *animal*] to pat, stroke; (= *rozar*) to brush
2 [+ *esperanzas*] to cherish, cling to; [+ *proyecto*] to have in mind
VPR **acariciarse** (*uno al otro*) to caress each other • **se estaban acariciando en el asiento de atrás del coche** they were caressing *o* fondling each other on the back seat of the car • **se acariciaba la barba mientras pensaba en la respuesta** he stroked his beard while he thought about the answer

acaricida SM (*Cono Sur*) insecticide

ácaro SM mite ▸ **ácaro del polvo** dust mite

acarraladura* SF (*And, Cono Sur*) run, ladder

acarreadizo ADJ transportable, that can be transported

acarreado/a SM/F (*Méx*) *peasant bussed in by the government in order to vote*

acarrear ▷ CONJUG 1a VT **1** (= *transportar*) to transport, carry; (= *arrastrar*) to cart
2 (= *causar*) to cause, bring in its train *o* wake • **le acarreó muchos disgustos** it caused *o* brought him lots of problems • **acarreó la caída del gobierno** it led to the fall of the government

acarreo SM (= *flete*) haulage, carriage • **gastos de ~** transport charges

acarreto SM (*Caribe, Méx*) = **acarreo**

acartonado ADJ [*superficie*] like cardboard; (= *enjuto*) wizened

acartonar ▷ CONJUG 1a VT [+ *piel*] to weather
VPR **acartonarse** (= *ponerse rígido*) to grow stiff; (= *quedarse enjuto*) to become wizened

acartuchado* ADJ (*Cono Sur*) stuffy, stuck-up*

acarvamiento SM erosion

acaserarse* ▷ CONJUG 1a VPR (*And††*) to become attached; (*Com*) to become a regular customer (*of a shop*); (= *sentar la cabeza*) to settle down; (*And, Caribe*) (= *quedarse en casa*) to stay at home

acaso ADV **1** (*en preguntas retóricas*) • **¿~ no te lo he dicho cien veces?** haven't I told you a hundred times? • **¿~ tengo yo la culpa de lo que haga mi hermana?** (how) am I to blame for what my sister does? • **¿~ yo lo sé?** how would I know?
2 (*frm*) (= *quizá*) perhaps • **~ no es verdad lo que dicen** perhaps what they say is not true • **es ~ el más prestigioso galardón de poesía** it is perhaps the most prestigious poetry award • **~ venga** perhaps he will come
3 • **si ~: no quiero nada, si ~ algo de fruta** I don't want anything, except maybe perhaps some fruit • **está bueno, si ~ un poco dulce** it's quite good, if perhaps a bit too sweet • **no tienes que ir, si ~ lo llamas por teléfono** you don't have to go, just give him a phone call • **si ~ llama, dímelo** if by any chance he phones, let me know
4 • **por si ~** just in case • **yo por si ~ llevo impermeable** I'm wearing a raincoat just in case • **llévalo por si ~ hace falta** take it, just in case you need it • **por si ~ viniera** just in case he should come *o* were to come
SM (*frm*) chance • **al ~** at random • **por ~** • **por un ~** by (any) chance

acastañado ADJ hazel

acatamiento SM [*de ley*] observance (**de** of), compliance (**de** with); (= *respeto*) respect (**a** for)

acatar ▷ CONJUG 1a VT **1** (= *respetar*) to respect; [+ *ley*] to observe, comply with
2 (= *subordinarse a*) to defer to
3 (*LAm*) (= *notar*) to notice, observe
4 (*Cono Sur, Méx*) (= *molestar*) to annoy

acatarrado ADJ • **estar ~** to have a cold

acatarrar ▷ CONJUG 1a VT (*LAm*) (= *molestar*) to annoy, bother
VPR **acatarrarse 1** (= *resfriarse*) to catch a cold
2 (*Cono Sur**) (= *emborracharse*) to get boozed up*

acato SM = **acatamiento**

acatólico/a ADJ, SM/F non-Catholic

acaudalado ADJ well-off, affluent

acaudalar ▷ CONJUG 1a VT to acquire, accumulate

acaudillar ▷ CONJUG 1a VT to lead, command

ACB SF ABR (= **Asociación de Clubs de Baloncesto**) *the Spanish national basketball association*, ≈ NBA

acceder ▷ CONJUG 2a VI **1** (= *aceptar*) to agree • **se lo propuse y accedieron** I suggested it and they agreed • **~ a algo** to agree to sth • **el director ha accedido a nuestra petición** the director agreed *o* acceded (*frm*) to our request • **~ a hacer algo** to agree to do sth
2 • **~ a** (= *entrar*) **a** [+ *lugar*] to gain access to; [+ *grupo social, organización*] to be admitted to • **por esta puerta se accede al salón** you can gain access to the lounge through this door • **no pueden ~ al mercado laboral por no tener estudios** they have no access to the labour market because they have no qualifications • **este examen os permitirá ~ a la universidad** this exam will enable you to gain admittance to the university • **si ganan este partido, acceden a la final** if they win this match they go through to the final
b (*Inform*) [+ *fichero, Internet*] to access • **no está autorizado a ~ a la base de datos** he is not authorized to access the database
3 (= *conseguir*) • **~ a** [+ *información*] to gain access to, access • **fue la primera mujer en ~ a este puesto** she was the first woman to assume this post • **accedió a la secretaría general** he became secretary general • **las personas que no pueden ~ a una vivienda digna** people who have no access to decent housing • **los jóvenes tienen dificultades para ~ a un puesto de trabajo** young people have problems finding a job • **para ~ a estas becas es necesario ser europeo** only European citizens are eligible for these grants • **accedió a una graduación superior** he attained a higher rank, he was promoted to a higher rank • **~ al poder** to assume power • **~ a la propiedad de algo** to

become the owner of sth • **~ al trono** to succeed to the throne

accesibilidad SF accessibility (**a** to)

accesible ADJ **1** [*lugar, texto, lenguaje, estilo*] accessible
2 [*persona*] approachable
3 [*precio, producto*] affordable

accesión SF **1** (= *consentimiento*) assent (**a** to), acquiescence (**a** in)
2 (= *accesorio*) accessory
3 (*Med*) attack

accésit SM (PL: **accésits**) second prize

acceso SM **1** (= *posibilidad de entrar*) (*a edificio, institución, mercado, documentos*) access; (*a competición*) entry • **tenemos libre ~ a la biblioteca** we have free access to the library • **hay que garantizar el ~ público a la educación** we must guarantee public access to education • **tiene ~ a la información confidencial** she has access to confidential information • **"acceso prohibido"** • **"prohibido el acceso"** "no entry", "no admittance" • **(código de) ~ internacional** (*Telec*) international (dialling) code • **eso coincidió con su ~ al poder** this coincided with his assuming power • **dar ~ a** [+ *lugar*] to lead to; [+ *institución*] to give entry to; [+ *competición*] to provide a place in; [+ *información*] to give access to • **de fácil ~**: • **un puerto de fácil ~** a port with easy access • **los controles son de fácil ~** the controls are easily accessible • **~ gratuito** free admission ▸ **acceso al trono** accession
2 (= *llegada*) **a** (*en coche*) access • **no es posible el ~ por carretera** there is no access by road *o* no road access • **las inundaciones han cortado los ~s a la finca** floods have cut off access *o* the approaches to the estate • **carretera** *o* **vía de ~** (*a ciudad*) approach road; (*a autovía*) slip road
b [*de avión*] approach
3 (= *entrada*) entrance • **el ~ principal del museo** the main entrance to the museum • **puerta de ~** entrance gate *o* door
4 (*Univ*) (= *ingreso*) entrance • **le negaron el ~ a la carrera que quería** they didn't let him join the course he wished • **curso de ~** access course • **prueba de ~** entrance exam
5 (*Inform*) access ▸ **acceso aleatorio** random access ▸ **acceso directo** direct access ▸ **acceso en serie** serial access ▸ **acceso múltiple** multi-access ▸ **acceso remoto** remote access ▸ **acceso secuencial** sequential access
6 (= *ataque*) **a** (*Med*) [*de asma, fiebre*] attack; [*de tos*] fit
b [*de celos, cólera*] fit; [*de generosidad*] display • **en un ~ de ira** in a fit of rage

accesoria SF annex, outbuilding

accesorio ADJ accessory; [*gastos*] incidental
SM **1** (*gen*) accessory, attachment, extra; **accesorios** (*Téc*) accessories, spare parts; (*Aut*) spare parts; (*Teat*) props
2 (*de vestir*) accessory

accidentado/a ADJ **1** [*terreno*] rough, uneven
2 (= *turbado*) [*vida*] troubled, eventful; [*historial*] variable, up-and-down; [*viaje*] eventful
3 (*Med*) injured
4 (*Caribe*) (*Aut*) broken down; (*LAm*) (*euf*) (= *giboso*) hunchbacked
SM/F accident victim, casualty

accidental ADJ **1** (= *contingente*) accidental; (= *no deliberado*) unintentional; (= *fortuito*) [*encuentro*] casual, chance (*antes de s*)
2 (= *fugaz*) brief, transient • **un empleo ~** a temporary job

accidentalidad SF accident rate, number of accidents

accidentalmente ADV (= *por casualidad*) by chance; (= *sin querer*) accidentally, unintentionally

accidentarse ▹ CONJUG 1a VPR to have an accident; (*Méx*) (*Aut*) to (have a) crash

accidente SM **1** (= *suceso*) accident • **por ~** by accident, by chance • **una vida sin ~s** an uneventful life • **sufrir un ~** to have *o* meet with an accident • **hay ~s que no se pueden prever** accidents will happen ▸ **accidente aéreo** plane crash ▸ **accidente de carretera** road accident ▸ **accidente de circulación** traffic accident ▸ **accidente de coche** car accident ▸ **accidente laboral, accidente de trabajo** industrial accident ▸ **accidente de tráfico** road accident, traffic accident ▸ **accidente múltiple** multiple accident, pile-up
2 (*Med*) faint, swoon
3 (*Ling*) accidence
4 • **~s** [*de terreno*] unevenness (*sing*), roughness (*sing*)
5 • **~ de la cara** (*Méx*) (= *rasgo*) feature

acción SF **1** (= *actividad*) action • **es hora de pasar a la ~** it's time to take action • **¡luces, cámara, ~!** lights, camera, action! • **el programa de ~** the programme of action • **en ~** in action • **puso el plan en ~** he put the plan in action • **ponerse en ~** to go into action • **estar en ~** (*Cuba**) to be busy • **hombre de ~** man of action • **película de ~** action film, action movie (*esp EEUU*) ▸ **acción directa** (*Pol*) direct action
2 (= *acto*) act • **llevaron a cabo una ~ condenable** they committed a reprehensible act • **deben ser juzgados por sus acciones y no por sus palabras** they should be judged by their deeds, not by their words • **buena ~** good deed • **mala ~**: • **sufrirán justo castigo por sus malas acciones** they will receive fair punishment for their evil deeds • **es incapaz de una mala ~** he would never do anything bad • REFRÁN: • **unir la ~ a la palabra** to suit the deed to the word ▸ **acción de gracias** thanksgiving
3 (= *efecto*) [*de medicamento, viento*] action • **su ~ sobre el sistema nervioso** its action on the nervous system • **por ~ química** by chemical action • **una crema adelgazante de ~ rápida** a fast-acting slimming cream • **lo recomiendan por su ~ relajante** it is recommended for its relaxing effect • **de ~ retardada** [*bomba, mecanismo*] delayed-action (*antes de s*)
4 (*Mil*) (*gen*) action; (= *operación*) operation • **han condenado la ~ militar estadounidense** the American military action has been condemned • **una de las zonas de ~ de la guerrilla** one of the areas where the guerrillas are active • **una ~ que dejó varios heridos** an operation which left several wounded • **muerto en ~** killed in action • **fuerza** *o* **brigada de ~ rápida** rapid action force ▸ **acción de guerra** military operation
5 (*Teat, Literat, Cine*) (= *trama*) action • **la ~ se desarrolla en Italia** the action takes place in Italy ▸ **acción aparte** by-play
6 (= *movimiento*) [*de la cara, cuerpo*] movement • **sus acciones eran cada vez más lentas** her movements were slower and slower
7 (*Jur*) action ▸ **acción judicial, acción legal** (*gen*) legal action; (= *pleito*) lawsuit • **van a emprender acciones legales** they are going to take legal action • **han presentado una ~ judicial contra el periódico** they have taken out a lawsuit against the newspaper ▸ **acción penal** criminal action ▸ **acción popular** people's action
8 (*Com, Econ*) share • **capital en acciones** share capital • **emisión de acciones** share issue, stock issue ▸ **acción cotizada en bolsa** listed share, quoted share ▸ **acción de oro** golden share ▸ **acción liberada** fully-paid share ▸ **acción ordinaria** ordinary share, common stock (*EEUU*) ▸ **acción preferente** preference share, preferred stock (*EEUU*) ▸ **acción primitiva** ordinary share, common stock (*EEUU*) ▸ **acción prioritaria** priority share ▸ **acción sin voto** non-voting share

accionado SM shares (*pl*), shareholding • **~ mayoritario** majority shareholding

accionamiento SM (*Mec*) operation • **el mecanismo que controla el ~ del motor** the mechanism which controls the operation of the engine • **una capota de ~ eléctrico** an electrically-operated top • **un motor con ~ a distancia** a remote-controlled engine

accionar ▹ CONJUG 1a VT **1** (*Mec*) [+ *mecanismo, motor, alarma*] to activate, operate; [+ *bomba, misil*] to activate, trigger; [+ *interruptor*] to switch; [+ *palanca*] to pull
2 (*Inform*) to drive
VI to gesticulate

accionariado SM **1** (= *acciones*) shares (*pl*), total of shares, shareholding
2 (= *personas*) shareholders (*pl*)

accionarial ADJ share (*antes de s*) • **paquete ~** • **participación ~** shareholding

accionario ADJ share (*antes de s*), of stocks and shares, relating to stocks and shares

accionista SMF shareholder, stockholder • **~ mayoritario** majority shareholder

accisa SF excise duty

ACE SF ABR (= **Acción Católica Española**) *charitable and campaigning organization*

acebo SM holly, holly tree

acebuche SM **1** (= *árbol*) wild olive tree; (= *madera*) olive wood
2* (= *simplón*) yokel, hillbilly (*EEUU*)

acechadera SF (= *escondite*) hiding place; (*Caza*) hide, blind (*EEUU*)

acechador(a) SM/F spy, watcher

acechanza SF = acecho

acechar ▹ CONJUG 1a VT (= *observar*) to spy on, watch; (= *esperar*) to lie in wait for; [+ *caza*] to stalk; (= *amenazar*) to threaten, beset • **~ la ocasión** to wait one's chance

acecho SM (= *acto de espiar*) spying, watching; (*Mil*) ambush • **estar al** *o* **en ~** to lie in wait • **cazar al ~** to stalk

acechón* ADJ spying, prying • **hacer la acechona** to spy, pry

acecinar ▹ CONJUG 1a VT [+ *carne*] to salt, cure
VPR **acecinarse** (= *quedarse enjuto*) to get very thin

acedar ▹ CONJUG 1a VT (= *poner agrio*) **1** to turn sour, make bitter
2 (= *amargar*) to sour, embitter
VPR **acedarse** (= *ponerse agrio*) to turn sour; [*planta*] to wither, yellow

acedera SF sorrel

acedía SF **1** (*Culin*) acidity, sourness
2 (*Med*) heartburn
3 (*fig*) (= *desabrimiento*) unpleasantness
4 (= *pez*) plaice

acedo ADJ (= *agrio*) acid, sour; (= *desagradable*) sour, unpleasant, disagreeable

acéfalo ADJ (= *sin cabeza*) headless; (= *sin líder*) leaderless

aceitada‡ SF (*Cono Sur*) bribe, backhander*, sweetener (EEUU)

aceitar ▹ CONJUG 1a VT **1** (= *untar con aceite*) to oil
2 • **~ a algn** (*Caribe, Cono Sur**) (= *sobornar*) to bribe sb, grease sb's palm*

a

aceite SM **1** (*Culin, Med, Téc*) oil • MODISMO: • **echar ~ al fuego** to add fuel to the flames ▸ **aceite alcanforado** camphorated oil ▸ **aceite combustible** fuel oil ▸ **aceite de algodón** cottonseed oil ▸ **aceite de almendra** almond oil ▸ **aceite de ballena** whale oil ▸ **aceite de cacahuete** peanut oil ▸ **aceite de coco** coconut oil ▸ **aceite de colza** rapeseed oil ▸ **aceite de girasol** sunflower oil ▸ **aceite de hígado de bacalao** cod-liver oil ▸ **aceite de linaza** linseed oil ▸ **aceite de maíz** corn oil ▸ **aceite de oliva** olive oil ▸ **aceite de oliva refinado** refined olive oil ▸ **aceite de oliva virgen** virgin olive oil ▸ **aceite de ricino** castor oil ▸ **aceite de soja** soya oil ▸ **aceite esencial** essential oil ▸ **aceite lubricante** lubricating oil ▸ **aceite vegetal** vegetable oil
2‡ (= *droga*) hash*; (*Méx*) LSD

aceitera SF (*Culin*) oil bottle; (*Aut*) oilcan • **~s** oil and vinegar set

aceitero/a ADJ oil (*antes de s*)
SM/F oil merchant

aceitón SM thick oil, dirty oil

aceitoso ADJ oily

aceituna SF olive ▸ **aceituna de mesa** table olive ▸ **aceituna rellena** stuffed olive

aceitunado ADJ (= *verdoso*) olive (*antes de s*), olive-coloured *o* (*EEUU*) -colored; (= *de tez aceitunada*) olive-skinned

aceitunero/a SM/F (*Com*) dealer in olives; (*Agr*) olive picker

aceituno ADJ (*LAm*) [*color*] olive • **(de) color ~** olive-coloured *o* (*EEUU*) -colored
SM **1** (= *árbol*) olive tree
2‡ (= *guardia civil*) Civil Guard

aceleración SF (*Mec*) acceleration; (= *agilización*) speeding-up, hastening

acelerada SF acceleration, speed-up

aceleradamente ADV **1** (= *rápidamente*) rapidly
2 (= *precipitadamente*) hastily

acelerado ADJ **1** (= *rápido*) [*avance, crecimiento, ritmo*] rapid • **con el corazón ~** with her heart racing *o* beating fast • **andaban con paso ~** they walked at a brisk pace • **los ochenta fueron una década muy acelerada** the eighties was a decade of hectic activity
2 [*curso*] intensive, crash (*antes de s*)
3* [*persona*] hyper* • **se le ve muy ~ últimamente** he's been very hyper lately*

acelerador SM accelerator, gas pedal (*EEUU*) • **apretar *o* pisar el ~** (*lit*) to put one's foot down, step on the gas (*esp EEUU**); (*fig*) to step up the pace ▸ **acelerador de partículas** particle accelerator

acelerar ▹ CONJUG 1a VT **1** (*Aut*) [+ *coche*] to accelerate; [+ *motor*] to rev, rev up
2 (= *apresurar*) [+ *cambio, proceso*] to speed up; [+ *acontecimiento*] to hasten • **deben ~ los trámites de aduana** they must speed up customs procedures • **las conversaciones ~on el final de la guerra** the talks hastened the end of the war • **~ la marcha** to go faster • **~ el paso** to quicken one's pace, speed up • **~ el ritmo de algo** to speed sth up
3 (*Fís*) [+ *partícula, velocidad*] to accelerate
VI **1** (*Aut*) [*coche, conductor*] to accelerate • **no aceleres en las curvas** don't accelerate on the bends • **aceleró a fondo** he put his foot to the floor
2* (= *darse prisa*) to get a move on*, hurry up • **venga, acelera, que nos están esperando** come on, get a move on* *o* hurry up, they're waiting for us
VPR **acelerarse 1** (= *apresurarse*) [*cambio, proceso*] to speed up • **el proceso se acelera si se eleva la temperatura** the process speeds up if the temperature is raised • **eso no será posible si se acelera la inflación** this will not be possible if inflation goes up any faster • **el corazón se le aceleró** her heart beat faster, her heart started racing • **~se a hacer algo** to hurry to do sth, hasten to do sth
2* (= *ponerse nervioso*) to get over-excited
3 (*Fís*) (= *aumentar la velocidad*) to accelerate • **los objetos se aceleran en la caída** objects accelerate as they fall

acelerón SM **1** (*Aut*) sudden acceleration
2 (*fig*) (= *gran paso*) leap forward; (= *aumento*) rapid increase; (= *mejora*) rapid improvement

acelga SF Swiss chard

acémila SF **1** (= *mula*) beast of burden, mule
2 (= *persona torpe*) thick-headed person

acemilero SM muleteer

acendrado ADJ pure, unblemished • **de ~ carácter español** typically *o* thoroughly Spanish in nature

acendrar ▹ CONJUG 1a VT (= *purificar*) to purify; (*Téc*) (= *refinar*) to refine; (*Literat*) (= *pulir*) to refine

acensuar ▹ CONJUG 1d VT to tax

acento SM **1** (*Ling*) (*escrito*) accent; (*hablado*) stress, emphasis • **pon un ~ sobre la o** put an accent on the o • **el ~ cae en la segunda sílaba** the stress *o* emphasis is on the second syllable ▸ **acento agudo** acute accent ▸ **acento circunflejo** circumflex (accent) ▸ **acento ortográfico** written accent ▸ **acento tónico** tonic accent
2 (= *deje*) accent • **tiene ~ francés** he has French accent • **tiene un ~ muy cerrado** he has a very strong *o* broad accent • **con (un) fuerte ~ andaluz** with a strong Andalusian accent • **hablan inglés sin nada de ~** they speak English without a trace of an accent • **un hombre de ~ sudamericano** a man with a South American accent
3 (= *énfasis*) emphasis • **un programa de jazz con ~ latino** a jazz programme with the emphasis on Latin American jazz • **ha sido una campaña con ~ bipartidista** it has been a campaign with a two-party emphasis • **poner el ~ en algo** to put the emphasis on sth, emphasize *o* stress sth
4 (*frm*) (= *tono*) tone (of voice) • **lo anunció con ~ triunfal** he announced it with a note of triumph in his voice, he announced it in a triumphant tone of voice, he announced it triumphantly

acentor SM ▸ **acentor común** hedge sparrow, dunnock

acentuación SF accentuation

acentuado ADJ accented, stressed

acentuamiento SM increase

acentuar ▹ CONJUG 1e VT **1** (*Ling*) to accent, stress • **esta palabra se acentúa en la u** this word is stressed on the u
2 (= *subrayar*) to emphasize, accentuate
3 (*Inform*) to highlight
VPR **acentuarse** to become more noticeable, be accentuated • **se acentúa la tendencia a la baja en la Bolsa** the downward trend in the Stock Exchange is becoming more pronounced

aceña SF water mill

aceñero SM miller

acepción SF **1** (*Ling*) sense, meaning
2 (*en el trato*) preference • **sin ~ de persona** impartially

acepilladora SF planing machine

acepilladura SF wood shaving

acepillar ▹ CONJUG 1a VT **1** (= *cepillar*) to brush; (*Téc*) to plane, shave
2 (*LAm**) (= *adular*) to suck up to*

aceptabilidad SF acceptability

aceptable ADJ acceptable, passable

aceptación SF (= *acto*) acceptance; (= *aprobación*) approval; (= *popularidad*) popularity, standing • **mandar algo a la ~** (*Com*) to send sth on approval • **este producto tendrá una ~ enorme** this product will be widely welcomed • **no tener ~** to be unsuccessful

aceptado ADJ [*cheque, moneda, tarjeta*] accepted

aceptar ▹ CONJUG 1a VT **1** [+ *oferta, propuesta, dimisión*] to accept; [+ *cheque, moneda, tarjeta, trabajo*] to accept, take; [+ *condición*] to accept, agree to • **aceptó las tareas que se le asignaron** he accepted the tasks he was assigned • **la impresora solo acepta este tipo de papel** the printer only takes this type of paper • **se niega a ~ los hechos** he refuses to face the facts • **no han aceptado mi solicitud de trabajo** they have rejected my job application • **"no aceptamos devoluciones"** "no refunds given"
2 • **~ hacer algo** to agree to do sth • **aceptó rebajarnos el alquiler** he agreed to reduce our rent • **no ~ hacer algo** to refuse to do sth • **no acepta pagar su parte** he refuses to pay his share • **por fin ~on que se publicara** they finally agreed for it to be published, they finally allowed it to be published • **no acepta que las mujeres trabajen** he doesn't accept *o* agree that women should work
3 • **~ a algn** to accept sb • **no me ~on en la carrera de medicina** I wasn't accepted on the medical course • **me ~on muy bien en mi nuevo trabajo** I was made to feel very welcome in my new job • **¿aceptas a María por esposa?** do you take María to be your lawful wedded wife?

acepto ADJ acceptable, agreeable (**a, de** to), welcomed (**a, de** by)

acequia SF **1** (*Agr*) irrigation ditch, irrigation channel
2 (*LAm*) (= *riachuelo*) stream; (= *alcantarilla*) sewer

acera SF pavement, sidewalk (*EEUU*) • **los de la ~ de enfrente*** the gays

acerado ADJ **1** (*Téc*) steel (*antes de s*); (*con punta de acero*) steel-tipped
2 (= *mordaz*) sharp, cutting

acerar ▹ CONJUG 1a VT **1** (*Téc*) to make into steel
2 (= *vigorizar*) to harden; (= *hacer mordaz*) [+ *estilo*] to sharpen up, make more incisive
VPR **acerarse** to toughen o.s., harden o.s.

acerbamente ADV (*fig*) harshly, scathingly

acerbidad SF acerbity, harshness

acerbo ADJ [*sabor*] bitter, sour; (= *cruel*) harsh, scathing • **tener un odio ~ a algo** to despise *o* detest sth

acerca de PREP about

acercamiento SM **1** (*a un lugar*) approach • **maniobras de ~ a la pista** runway approach manoeuvres • **golpe de ~** (*Golf*) approach shot
2 (*a un tema*) introduction • **el documental es un excelente ~ a la mitología** the documentary is an excellent introduction to mythology
3 (= *reconciliación*) (*entre personas*) reconciliation; (*entre países, posiciones*) rapprochement • **su muerte fue motivo de ~ entre los hermanos** her death led to a reconciliation between the brothers • **la obra trata de conseguir el ~ con el público** the play seeks to forge a closer relationship with the audience • **fue el artífice del ~ entre China y EE.UU.** he was the architect of the rapprochement between China and the US

acercar ▹ CONJUG 1g VT **1** (= *aproximar*) (*gen*) to move closer; (*al hablante*) to bring closer • **acerca la silla a la mesa** move your chair closer to the table • **acercó la cámara a uno**

de los actores he moved the camera up to one of the actors • **acerca un poco la silla** bring your chair a bit closer • **acercó sus labios a los míos** he brought his lips close to mine • **un intento de ~ la cultura al pueblo** an attempt to bring culture to the people
2 (= *dar*) (*sin moverse*) to pass; (*desde más lejos*) to bring over • **acércame las tijeras** pass the scissors • **¿puedes ~me aquel paquete?** can you bring me over that parcel?
3 (= *llevar en coche*) to take • **¿me puedes ~ a casa?** can you take me home? • **¿quieres que te acerque al aeropuerto?** do you want me to take you to the airport?
4 (= *unir*) [+ *culturas, países, puntos de vistas*] to bring closer (together) • **hay intereses comunes que nos acercan** there are common interests that bring us closer (together) • **van a celebrar una nueva reunión para intentar ~ posturas** they are having another meeting to try and bring the two sides closer (together)
(VPR) **acercarse 1** (= *aproximarse*) **a** (*al hablante*) to come closer; (*a algo alejado del hablante*) to get closer • **acércate, que te vea** come closer so that I can see you • **no te acerques más, que te puedes quemar** don't get any closer, you could burn yourself • **al ver que se acercaban, el conductor se paró** when he saw them coming closer *o* approaching, the driver stopped • **unos pasos femeninos se acercaban por el pasillo** a woman's footsteps were coming up the corridor • **~se a: no te acerques tanto a la mesa** don't get so close to the table • **los periodistas no pudieron ~se al avión** the journalists couldn't get near the plane • **me acerqué a la ventana** I went up *o* over to the window • **señores pasajeros, nos estamos acercando a Heathrow** ladies and gentlemen, we're approaching Heathrow • **el paro se acerca al 10%** unemployment is approaching 10%
b (= *abordar*) • **~se a algn** (*al hablante*) to come up to sb; (*lejos del hablante*) to go up to sb • **se me acercó por la espalda** she came up behind me • **se le ~on para pedirle autógrafos** they went up to her to ask for autographs
c • **~se algo al oído** to put sth to one's ear
2 (*en el tiempo*) [*acontecimiento, momento*] to get closer, get nearer • **ya se acercan las vacaciones** the holidays are nearly here, the holidays are getting closer *o* nearer • **se acercaba la hora de despedirnos** it was nearly time to say goodbye • **~se a** [+ *fecha*] to approach; [+ *situación*] to get closer to • **se acercan a la edad de la jubilación** they are approaching retirement age • **nos acercábamos a la solución** we were getting closer to finding an answer
3 (= *ir*) • **acércate a la tienda y trae una botella de agua** go over to the shop and get a bottle of water • **tengo que ~me a comprar el periódico** I just have to go and buy the paper • **ya me ~é un día a visitaros** one of these days I'll pay you a visit *o* I'll come and see you • **acércate por la oficina cuando puedas** call by the office when you get the chance
4 (= *parecerse*) • **~se a algo** • **nuestros gustos se acercan más a la ópera** our tastes tend more towards opera • **los resultados se acercan bastante a lo que esperábamos** the results are fairly close to what we expected • **eso se acerca a la herejía** that is verging on heresy

ácere (SM) maple
acería (SF) steelworks, steel mill
acerico (SM) pincushion
acero (SM) steel • MODISMO: • **tener buenos ~s** (= *aguante*) to have guts*; (= *hambre*) to be ravenously hungry ▸ **acero al carbono** carbon steel ▸ **acero al manganeso** manganese steel ▸ **acero bruto** crude steel ▸ **acero colado** cast steel ▸ **acero fundido** cast steel ▸ **acero inoxidable** stainless steel ▸ **aceros especiales** special steels
acerote (SM) (= *holgazán*) idler, loafer
acérrimo (ADJ) [*partidario*] staunch; [*enemigo*] bitter
acerrojar ▹ CONJUG 1a (VT) to bolt
acertadamente (ADV) **1** (= *oportunamente*) aptly
2 (= *correctamente*) [*responder*] correctly; [*señalar, sugerir*] rightly
acertado (ADJ) **1** (= *correcto*) [*diagnóstico, respuesta*] right, correct; [*descripción, resumen*] accurate • **han sido tres respuestas acertadas** you had three right *o* correct answers • **estuvieron ~s en su elección** they made the right *o* correct choice • **el portero estuvo muy ~ en la segunda mitad** the goalkeeper didn't put a foot wrong in the second half
2 (= *apropiado*) [*comentario, título, regalo*] appropriate • **la música del funeral no fue muy acertada** the music was not very appropriate for a funeral • **tu contestación estuvo muy acertada** your reply was very appropriate • **fue la compra más acertada de mi vida** it was the best purchase of my life • **creo que tu elección ha sido muy acertada** I think you've made a very good choice
3 (= *sensato*) [*juicio, consejo, idea*] wise • **seguí el ~ consejo de mi padre** I followed my father's wise advice • **estuviste muy poco ~ al decir eso** that wasn't a very wise thing to say
acertante (ADJ) [*quiniela, boleto*] winning
(SMF) [*de quiniela, concurso*] winner • **esta semana han aparecido tres máximos ~s** this week three winners got the top prize
acertar ▹ CONJUG 1j (VT) [+ *respuesta*] to get right; [+ *adivinanza*] to guess • **gana el que acierte antes cinco preguntas** the winner is the first one to get five answers right *o* to answer five questions correctly • **¿cuántos números has acertado esta semana?** how many numbers did you get this week? • **a ver si aciertas lo que traigo** see if you can guess what I've brought you
(VI) **1** (*al disparar*) to hit the target • **rara vez aciertan** they rarely hit their targets • **la bala le acertó de lleno en el corazón** the bullet hit him right in the heart • **disparó a matar pero no acertó** he shot to kill but he missed
2 (= *adivinar*) to get it right • **¡has acertado!** you got it right! • REFRÁN: • **piensa mal y ~ás** think the worst and you won't be far wrong
3 (*al decir, hacer algo*) to be right • **aciertan cuando dicen que la corrupción no tiene solución** they're right when they say that there's no solution to corruption • **acertó al quedarse callado** he did the right thing keeping quiet, he was right to keep quiet • **~ con algo** (*al escoger*) to get sth right • **han acertado de pleno con el nuevo modelo de coche familiar** they've scored a real winner* *o* they've got it just right with their new family car • **habéis acertado con el regalo** you made just the right choice with that present • **~ en algo**: • **habéis acertado en la elección** you have made the right choice • **~on de pleno en sus pronósticos** their forecasts were totally accurate *o* correct
4 • **~ a hacer algo** (= *conseguir*) to manage to do sth; (*casualmente*) to happen to do sth • **acerté a encontrar la salida** I managed to find the exit • **no acerté a expresarme con claridad** I didn't manage to express myself clearly • **los médicos no aciertan a dar con lo que tiene** the doctors can't find out what's wrong with him • **no acierto a comprenderlo** I fail to understand it • **acertamos a pasar por delante de su casa** we happened to pass by his house
5 • **~ con** (= *encontrar*) to manage to find • **acerté con el interruptor** I managed to find the switch • **tras mucho pensarlo acertamos con la solución** after a lot of thought we managed to find the solution
6 [*planta*] to flourish, do well
acertijo (SM) riddle, puzzle
acervo (SM) **1** (*Jur*) undivided estate, common property • **aportar algo a nuestro ~ común** to contribute sth to our collective heritage ▸ **acervo arqueológico** arch(a)eological wealth, arch(a)eological riches (*pl*) ▸ **acervo cultural** cultural heritage
2 (= *montón*) heap, pile; (= *provisión*) stock, store
acetato (SM) acetate ▸ **acetato de vinilo** vinyl acetate
acético (ADJ) acetic
acetilénico (ADJ) acetylene (*antes de s*)
acetileno (SM) acetylene
acetona (SF) acetone
acetre (SM) (= *vasija*) small pail; (*Rel*) holy water vessel, portable stoup
acezar ▹ CONJUG 1f (VI) to puff, pant
achacable (ADJ) • **~ a** attributable to
achacar ▹ CONJUG 1g (VT) **1** • **~ algo a** to attribute sth to, put sth down to • **~ la culpa a algn** to lay the blame on sb
2 (*LAm**) (= *robar*) to pinch*, nick‡; (= *saquear*) to pillage, loot
achacoso (ADJ) sickly, ailing
achaflanar ▹ CONJUG 1a (VT) to chamfer, bevel
achafranar** ▹ CONJUG 1a (VI) (*Méx*) to fuck**, screw**
achahuistlarse ▹ CONJUG 1a (VPR) (*Méx*) to get depressed
achalay (EXCL), **achachay** (EXCL) (*And*) • **¡achalay!** brr!
achampañado (ADJ) champagne-flavoured *o* (EEUU) -flavored
achamparse ▹ CONJUG 1a (VPR) (*Cono Sur*) • **~ algo** to keep sth which does not belong to one
achancharse* ▹ CONJUG 1a (VPR) **1** (*And*) (= *ponerse perezoso*) to get lazy
2 (*Cono Sur*) (= *engordar*) to get fat
3 (*And*) (= *ponerse violento*) to become embarrassed
achantado* (ADJ) (*CAm*) bashful, shy
achantar ▹ CONJUG 1a (VT) (= *intimidar*) to intimidate; (= *humillar*) to take down a peg; (= *asustar**) to scare, frighten
(VPR) **achantarse 1** (= *intimidarse*) to back down, eat one's words • **~se por las buenas** to be easily intimidated
2 (= *esconderse*) to hide away
achaparrado (ADJ) [*árbol*] stunted; [*persona*] stocky, thickset
achapinarse ▹ CONJUG 1a (VPR) (*CAm*) to adopt the local customs
achaque (SM) **1** (*Med*) ailment, malady ▸ **achaques de la vejez** ailments *o* infirmities of old age ▸ **achaques mañaneros** morning sickness
2 (= *defecto*) defect, fault, weakness
3 (= *asunto*) matter, subject • **en ~ de** in the matter of, on the subject of
4 (= *pretexto*) pretext • **con ~ de** under the pretext of
achara (EXCL) (*CAm*) what a pity!
achares* (SMPL) jealousy • **dar ~ a algn** to make sb jealous

acharolado ADJ polished, varnished
achatado ADJ flattened
achatamiento SM **1** (= *allanamiento*) flattening
2 (*LAm*) (= *desmoralización*) loss of moral fibre • **sufrieron un ~** they lost heart, they felt down
achatar ▹ CONJUG 1a VT to flatten
VPR **achatarse 1** (= *allanarse*) to flatten, become flat
2 (*Cono Sur, Méx*) (= *declinar*) to grow weak, decline; (*LAm*) (= *desmoralizarse*) to lose heart, feel down
3 (*Cono Sur, Méx*) (= *avergonzarse*) to be overcome with shame, be embarrassed • **quedarse achatado** to be ashamed, be embarrassed
achicado ADJ childish, childlike
achicador SM scoop, baler
achicalado ADJ (*Méx*) sugared, honeyed
achicalar ▹ CONJUG 1a VT (*Méx*) to cover in honey, soak in honey
achicanado ADJ Chicano, characteristic of Mexican-Americans
achicar ▹ CONJUG 1g VT **1** (= *empequeñecer*) to make smaller; (= *hacer de menos*) to dwarf; [+ *espacios*] to reduce; (*Cos*) to shorten, take in; (= *descontar*) to minimize
2 (= *desaguar*) to bale *o* (*EEUU*) bail out; (*con bomba*) to pump out
3 (*fig*) (= *humillar*) to humiliate; (= *intimidar*) to intimidate, browbeat
4 (*And*) (= *matar*) to kill
5 (*And, Caribe*) (= *sujetar*) to fasten, hold down
VPR **achicarse 1** (= *empequeñecerse*) to get smaller; [*ropa*] to shrink
2 (*esp LAm*) (= *rebajarse*) to be intimidated, belittle o.s.
achicharradero SM inferno
achicharrado ADJ **1** (= *quemado*) burnt
2 (= *con mucho calor*) boiling (hot)
achicharrante ADJ • **calor ~** sweltering heat
achicharrar ▹ CONJUG 1a VT **1** (= *quemar*) to scorch; (*Culin*) to fry to a crisp; (*demasiado*) to burn • **el sol achicharraba la ciudad** the city was roasting in the heat
2* (= *fastidiar*) to bother, plague, pester
3 (*Chile**) (= *aplastar*) to flatten, crush
4‡ (= *matar*) to shoot, riddle with bullets
VI • **hace un sol que achicharra** it's absolutely roasting
VPR **achicharrarse** to get burnt • **¡me estoy achicharrando!** I'm getting burnt to a cinder!
achicharronar ▹ CONJUG 1a VT (*LAm*) to flatten, crush
achichiguar ▹ CONJUG 1i VT **1** (*Méx**) (= *mimar*) to cosset, spoil
2 (*Agr*) to shade
achichincle* SM (*Méx*) minion
achichuncle‡ SMF (*Méx*) creep‡, crawler‡, brown-nose (*EEUU*‡)
achicopalado* ADJ (*Méx*) depressed, gloomy
achicoria SF chicory, endive (*EEUU*)
achiguado* ADJ (*Méx*) spoiled
achiguarse ▹ CONJUG 1i VPR (*Cono Sur*) [*pared*] to bulge, sag; [*persona*] to get very fat
achilarse ▹ CONJUG 1a VPR (*And*) to turn cowardly
achimero SM (*CAm*) pedlar, peddler (*EEUU*), hawker
achimes SMPL (*CAm*) cheap goods, trinkets
achín SM (*CAm*) pedlar, peddler (*EEUU*), hawker
achinado ADJ **1** (*LAm*) (= *mestizo*) half-caste; (= *burdo*) coarse, common
2 [*aspecto*] Chinese-like, oriental; [*ojos*] slanting
achinar* ▹ CONJUG 1a VT to scare
VPR **achinarse** (*Cono Sur*) to become coarse
achiote SM (*LAm*) **1** (= *condimento*) annatto
2 (= *tinte*) annatto dye
achipolarse* ▹ CONJUG 1a VPR (*Méx*) to grow sad, get gloomy
achique SM **1** (= *empequeñecimiento*) making smaller; [*de espacios*] reduction
2 (= *desagüe*) baling; (*con bomba*) pumping
achiquillado ADJ (*esp Méx*) childish
achiquitar ▹ CONJUG 1a VT (*LAm*) to make smaller, reduce
achirarse ▹ CONJUG 1a VPR (*And*) (= *nublarse*) to cloud over; (= *oscurecerse*) to get dark
achís EXCL atishoo!
achispado ADJ tipsy
achispar* ▹ CONJUG 1a VT (*LAm*) to cheer up, liven up
VPR **achisparse** to get tipsy
-acho, -acha ▹ Aspects of Word Formation in Spanish 2
achocar ▹ CONJUG 1g VT **1** (= *tirar*) to throw against a wall, dash against a wall
2 (= *pegar*) to hit, bash*
3* (= *guardar*) to hoard, stash away*
achocharse ▹ CONJUG 1a VPR to get doddery, begin to dodder
achoclonarse ▹ CONJUG 1a VPR (*LAm*) to crowd together
achocolatado ADJ **1** [*color*] chocolate-brown
2 • **estar ~‡** (= *borracho*) to be canned‡
acholado ADJ (*LAm*) **1** half-caste, part-Indian
2 (= *acobardado*) cowed; (= *avergonzado*) abashed
acholar ▹ CONJUG 1a (*LAm*) VT (= *avergonzar*) to embarrass; (= *intimidar*) to intimidate, scare
VPR **acholarse 1** (= *acriollarse*) [*indígenas*] to have mestizo *o* half-breed ways, adopt mestizo *o* half-breed ways
2 (= *acobardarse*) to be cowed; (= *avergonzarse*) to be abashed, become shy; (= *sonrojarse*) to blush
acholo SM (*LAm*) embarrassment
-achón, -achona ▹ Aspects of Word Formation in Spanish 2
achoramiento‡ SM (*Cono Sur*) threat
achubascarse ▹ CONJUG 1g VPR to become threatening, cloud over
achuchado* ADJ **1** (= *difícil*) hard, difficult
2 • **estar ~** (*Cono Sur*) (= *palúdico*) to have malaria; (= *acatarrado*) to have a chill; (= *febril*) to be feverish; (= *asustado*) to be scared, be frightened
achuchar ▹ CONJUG 1a VT **1** (= *aplastar*) to crush, squeeze flat
2 (= *empujar*) to shove, jostle; (= *acosar*) to harass, pester
3 • **~ un perro contra algn** to set a dog on sb
VPR **achucharse 1** [*amantes*] to cuddle, fondle (one another), pet*
2 (*Cono Sur*) (*paludismo*) to catch malaria; (= *acatarrarse*) to catch a chill; (= *tener fiebre*) to get feverish; (= *asustarse*) to get scared
achuchón SM **1** (= *abrazo*) squeeze
2 (= *empujón*) shove, push
3 • **tener un ~** (*Med*) to be ill, be poorly
achucutado ADJ (*LAm*) (= *avergonzado*) abashed, ashamed; (= *deprimido*) gloomy, depressed; (= *agobiado*) overwhelmed
achucutarse ▹ CONJUG 1a VPR (*LAm*) (= *avergonzarse*) to be abashed, be ashamed; (= *estar afligido*) to be dismayed; (= *deprimirse*) to be depressed; (= *marchitarse*) to wilt
achucuyarse ▹ CONJUG 1a VPR (*CAm*) = **achucutarse**
achuicarse ▹ CONJUG 1g VPR (*Cono Sur*) (= *avergonzarse*) to be embarrassed; (= *apocarse*) to feel small
achulado ADJ, **achulapado** ADJ
1 (= *presumido*) cocky
2 (= *grosero*) coarse, uncouth
achumado* ADJ (*LAm*) drunk
achumarse* ▹ CONJUG 1a VPR (*LAm*) to get drunk
achunchar ▹ CONJUG 1a VT **1** (*And, Chile*) (= *avergonzar*) to shame
2 (*LAm*) (= *intimidar*) to scare
VPR **achuncharse 1** (*And, Chile*) (= *avergonzarse*) to be ashamed
2 (*LAm*) (= *intimidarse*) to get scared
achuntar ▹ CONJUG 1a (*Cono Sur*) VT (= *hacer bien*) to do properly, get right
VI (= *acertar*) to guess right; (= *dar en el clavo*) to hit the nail on the head
achuñuscar* ▹ CONJUG 1g VT (*Cono Sur*) to squeeze
achupalla SF (*LAm*) pineapple
achura SF (*Cono Sur*) offal
achurar ▹ CONJUG 1a VT (*Cono Sur*) [+ *animal*] to gut; [+ *persona*] to kill
VI (*LAm*) (= *salir ganando*) to benefit from, do well out of
achurrucarse ▹ CONJUG 1g VPR (*CAm*) (= *marchitarse*) to wilt
achurruscado* ADJ rumpled, crumpled up
achurruscar ▹ CONJUG 1g VT (*And, Cono Sur*) to rumple, crumple up
aciago ADJ ill-fated, fateful, black*
aciano SM cornflower
acíbar SM **1** (= *jugo*) aloes
2 (= *amargura*) sorrow, bitterness
acibarar ▹ CONJUG 1a VT **1** (= *poner acíbar*) to add bitter aloes to, make bitter
2 (= *amargar*) to embitter • **~ la vida a algn** to make sb's life a misery
acicalado ADJ **1** [*persona*] smart, spruce; (*pey*) tarted up*, overdressed
2 [*metal*] polished, bright and shiny
acicalar ▹ CONJUG 1a VT **1** [+ *persona*] to dress up, bedeck
2 [+ *metal*] to polish, burnish, shine
VPR **acicalarse** to smarten o.s. up, spruce o.s. up
acicate SM incentive
acicatear ▹ CONJUG 1a VT [+ *persona*] to spur on; [+ *imaginación*] to fire
acícula SF (*Bot*) needle
acidez SF (*Quím*) acidity; (*Culin*) sourness
acidia SF indolence, apathy, sloth
acidificar ▹ CONJUG 1g VT to acidify
VPR **acidificarse** to acidify
acidillo ADJ slightly sour
ácido ADJ **1** [*sabor, olor*] sour, acid
2 • **estar ~** (*LAm**) (= *fabuloso*) to be great*, be fabulous*
SM **1** (*Quím*) acid ▸ **ácido acético** acetic acid ▸ **ácido ascórbico** ascorbic acid ▸ **ácido carbólico** carbolic acid ▸ **ácido carbónico** carbonic acid ▸ **ácido cianhídrico** hydrocyanic acid ▸ **ácido clorhídrico** hydrochloric acid ▸ **ácido lisérgico** lysergic acid ▸ **ácido nicotínico** nicotinic acid ▸ **ácido nítrico** nitric acid ▸ **ácido nitroso** nitrous acid ▸ **ácido nucleico** nucleic acid ▸ **ácido oxálico** oxalic acid ▸ **ácido ribonucleico** ribonucleic acid ▸ **ácido sulfúrico** sulphuric acid ▸ **ácido úrico** uric acid
2* (= *droga*) LSD, acid*; (= *pastilla*) acid tab*, LSD tab*
acidófilo ADJ acidophilous
acidulante SM acidulant, acidifier
acídulo ADJ acidulous
acierto SM **1** (= *respuesta correcta*) (*en concurso, examen*) correct answer; (*en quiniela, diagnóstico*) correct forecast • **cuenta los ~s y los errores** count the correct and incorrect answers • **una quiniela con 15 ~s** a coupon with 15 correct forecasts

2 (= *buena decisión*) good move, good decision • **fue un ~ invitarla a la fiesta** it was a good move *o* decision to invite her to the party
3 (= *cualidad*) • **dudo del ~ de esa decisión** I doubt the wisdom of that decision • **con ~** (= *hábilmente*) skilfully, skillfully (*EEUU*); (= *correctamente*) rightly • **resolvió la situación con ~** she resolved the situation skilfully • **el periódico que con tanto ~ dirige** the paper which he edits so competently • **lo que con tanto ~ denominaron realismo** what they so rightly called realism • **tener el ~ de hacer algo** to have the good sense to do sth
4 (= *éxito*) success • **es una historia de ~s y fracasos** it's a story of successes and failures
5 (*Ftbl*) fine shot • **el gol llegó en un ~ de Cardeñosa** the goal came from a fine shot by Cardeñosa

aciguatado* (ADJ) (*Méx*) silly, stupid

aciguatarse ▷ CONJUG 1a (VPR) (*Caribe, Méx*) to grow stupid; (= *enloquecer**) to go crazy, lose one's head

acitrón (SM) 1 (*Culin*) candied citron
2 (*LAm*) (*Bot*) bishop's weed, goutweed

acitronar ▷ CONJUG 1a (VT) (*Méx*) to brown

acizañar* ▷ CONJUG 1a (VT) to stir things*, cause trouble

aclamación (SF) acclamation • **elegir a algn por ~** to elect sb by acclamation; **aclamaciones** applause (*sing*), acclaim (*sing*) • **entre las aclamaciones del público** amid applause from the audience

aclamar ▷ CONJUG 1a (VT) (= *proclamar*) to acclaim; (= *aplaudir*) to applaud • **~ a algn por jefe** to acclaim sb as leader, hail sb as leader

aclaración (SF) (*para hacer entender*) clarification; (*para dar razones*) explanation • **quisiera hacerles una ~** I'd like to clarify something • **exijo una ~ de tu comportamiento** I demand an explanation for your behaviour ▸ **aclaración marginal** marginal note

aclarado (SM) (*Esp*) rinse

aclarar ▷ CONJUG 1a (VT) 1 (= *explicar*) [+ *suceso, motivo*] to clarify; [+ *duda, malentendido*] to clear up; [+ *misterio*] to solve • **están tratando de ~ las circunstancias de su muerte** they are trying to clarify the circumstances surrounding her death • **todavía no se ha aclarado quién lo hizo** it is still not clear who did it • **con esto ya queda todo aclarado** with this now everything is clear • **dejaremos cinco minutos para ~ dudas** we'll leave five minutes to clear up any queries • **~ algo a algn** to explain sth to sb • **no pudo ~nos el motivo de su comportamiento** she couldn't explain the reasons for her behaviour • **me lo explicó dos veces pero no consiguió aclarármelo** she explained it to me twice but couldn't manage to make it clear • **le he escrito para ~ las cosas** I've written to him to make things clear • **~ que** to make it clear that • **quiero ~ que no soy racista** I want to make it clear that I am not a racist
2 (*Esp*) [+ *ropa, vajilla, pelo*] to rinse • **se debe ~ con agua fría** it should be rinsed in cold water
3 (= *diluir*) [+ *pintura, salsa*] to thin, thin down
4 (= *hacer más claro*) [+ *color, pelo*] to make lighter, lighten
5 [+ *bosque*] to clear
(VI) 1 (= *amanecer*) to get light • **ya estaba aclarando** it was already getting light
2 (= *despejarse las nubes*) to clear up • **en cuanto aclare, saldremos** as soon as it clears up, we'll go out
3 (*Esp*) (= *enjuagar*) to rinse
(VPR) **aclararse** 1 [*día, cielo*] to clear up
2 (= *hacerse más claro*) [*pelo, color*] to go lighter; [*mancha*] to fade
3 • **~se la voz** to clear one's throat
4 (*Esp**) [*persona*] • **con tantas instrucciones no me aclaro** I'm confused by all these instructions • **explícamelo otra vez, a ver si me aclaro** explain it to me again and let's see if I understand • **¡a ver si te aclaras!** (= *decídete*) make up your mind!; (= *explícate*) what are you on about?*

aclaratorio (ADJ) explanatory

aclayos‡ (SMPL) (*Méx*) eyes

aclimatación (SF) acclimatization, acclimation (*EEUU*); (= *aire acondicionado*) air conditioning

aclimatar ▷ CONJUG 1a (VT) to acclimatize, acclimate (*EEUU*)
(VPR) **aclimatarse** to acclimatize o.s., get acclimatized • **~se a algo** to get used to sth

acné (SF), **acne** (SF) acne

ACNUR (SM ABR) (= **Alto Comisariado de las Naciones Unidas para los Refugiados**) UNHCR

-aco, -aca ▷ Aspects of Word Formation in Spanish 2

acobardado (ADJ) intimidated

acobardamiento (SM) intimidation

acobardar ▷ CONJUG 1a (VT) (= *intimidar*) to intimidate, cow; (= *atemorizar*) to overawe, unnerve
(VPR) **acobardarse** (= *asustarse*) to be intimidated, get frightened; (= *echarse atrás*) to flinch, shrink back (**ante** from, at)

acobe* (SM) (*Caribe*) iron

acobrado (ADJ) copper-coloured *o* (*EEUU*) -colored, coppery

acocear ▷ CONJUG 1a (VT) (= *cocear*) to kick; (= *maltratar*) to ill-treat, trample on; (= *insultar*) to insult

acochambrar* ▷ CONJUG 1a (VT) (*Méx*) to make filthy

acocharse ▷ CONJUG 1a (VPR) to squat, crouch

acochinar‡ ▷ CONJUG 1a (VT) to bump off‡

acocil (SM) (*Méx*) freshwater shrimp • **estar como un ~** to be red in the face

acocote (SM) (*Méx*) *type of gourd used in the production of tequila and pulque*

acodado (ADJ) bent

acodalar ▷ CONJUG 1a (VT) to shore up, prop up

acodar ▷ CONJUG 1a (VT) [+ *brazo*] to lean, rest; [+ *tubo*] to bend; [+ *planta*] to layer
(VPR) **acodarse** to lean (**en** on) • **acodado en** leaning on • **~se hacia** to bend towards, curve towards

acodiciarse ▷ CONJUG 1b (VPR) • **~ a** to covet

acodo (SM) layer

acogedizo (ADJ) gathered at random

acogedor (ADJ) (= *hospitalario*) welcoming; [*ambiente*] friendly, cosy, cozy (*EEUU*), warm; [*cuarto*] snug, cosy, cozy (*EEUU*)

acoger ▷ CONJUG 2c (VT) 1 (= *albergar*) [+ *huésped, refugiado*] to take in; [+ *visitante*] to receive; [+ *fugitivo*] to harbour, harbor (*EEUU*), shelter • **nuestro país acogió a los exiliados** our country took in the exiles • **muchas familias acogen a estudiantes** many families provide accommodation for *o* take in students • **la ciudad acoge todos los años a miles de visitantes** the city receives thousands of visitors every year • **que Dios la acoja en su seno** may God receive her soul • **niños acogidos en centros públicos** children housed *o* accommodated in public centres • **el hotel que acoge a los periodistas extranjeros** the hotel where the foreign journalists are staying • **acogen en sus filas a antiguos terroristas** they number former terrorists among their ranks
2 (= *recibir*) [+ *noticia, idea, propuesta*] to receive • **acogieron la noticia con sorpresa** they were surprised at the news, they received the news with surprise • **nos acogieron con muestras de afecto** they received us with demonstrations of affection • **acogieron el plan como una oportunidad de reconvertir la industria** they welcomed the plan as an opportunity to restructure industry
3 (= *ser sede de*) [*ciudad*] to host; [*edificio, auditorio*] to be the venue for • **Atenas acogió por segunda vez los Juegos Olímpicos** Athens hosted the Olympics for the second time • **el palacio acoge un ciclo de conciertos** the palace is the venue for a concert season
4 (= *contener*) **a** [+ *espectadores*] to seat, hold • **el teatro podrá ~ a 1500 espectadores** the theatre will be able to seat *o* hold 1500 people
b [+ *obras*] • **este edificio acoge al Museo de la Ciencia** this building houses the Science Museum • **los pasillos del nuevo centro ~án una exposición fotográfica** the corridors of the new centre will accommodate a photographic exhibition • **la exposición acoge obras religiosas** the exhibition includes *o* contains religious works
(VPR) **acogerse** 1 (= *acudir*) • **~se a** [+ *ley, derecho*] to invoke • **se han acogido al derecho a no declarar** they have invoked the right not to testify • **se acogieron a la protección del santo** they turned to the saint for protection
2 (= *beneficiarse*) • **~se a:** • **los trabajadores que lo deseen podrán ~se a las bajas incentivadas** any workers who wish to may take voluntary redundancy • **~se a la amnistía** to accept the offer of amnesty

acogible (ADJ) (*Cono Sur*) acceptable

acogida (SF) 1 (= *recibimiento*) [*de noticia, producto, propuesta*] reception • **Madrid dispensó una fría ~ al espectáculo** Madrid afforded the show a very cold reception • **una calurosa ~** a warm welcome • **la ~ del disco fue muy favorable** the record was very favourably received • **tener buena/mala ~** to be well/poorly received • **¿qué ~ tuvo la idea?** how was the idea received? • **el centro de ~ de visitantes** the visitors' centre
2 (= *albergue*) **a** (*Pol*) [*de refugiado, emigrante*] • **tras la ~ de miles de refugiados** after accepting thousands of refugees • **un centro de ~** a reception centre • **país de ~** host country
b [*de personas necesitadas*] • **un centro de ~ de personas sin hogar** a homeless hostel, a shelter for the homeless • **un centro de ~ de menores** a children's refuge • **dar ~ a algn** to accept sb • **familia de ~** host family ▸ **acogida familiar** (*Jur*) fostering; ▷ **casa**
3 [*de ríos*] meeting place

acogimiento (SM) ▸ **acogimiento familiar, acogimiento judicial** fostering

acogollar ▷ CONJUG 1a (*Agr*) (VT) to cover up, protect
(VI) to sprout

acogotar ▷ CONJUG 1a (VT) (= *derribar*) to knock down, fell, poleaxe, poleax (*EEUU*); (= *dejar sin sentido*) to lay out; (*LAm*) (= *dominar*) to have at one's mercy; (= *agarrar*) to grab round the neck • **~ a algn** (*Cono Sur*) to harass sb for payment

acohombrar ▷ CONJUG 1a (VT) (*Agr*) to earth up

acojinar ▷ CONJUG 1a (VT) (*Téc*) to cushion

acojonador‡ (ADJ) (*esp Esp*) = **acojonante**

acojonamiento‡ (SM) (*esp Esp*) funk*, fear

acojonante‡ (ADJ) (*esp Esp*) (= *impresionante*) tremendous, brilliant*

a

acojonar‡ ▸ CONJUG 1a (*esp Esp*) VT
1 (= *atemorizar*) to put the wind up*, intimidate
2 (= *impresionar*) to impress; (= *asombrar*) to amaze, overwhelm
VPR **acojonarse 1** (= *acobardarse*) to back down; (= *inquietarse*) to get the wind up* • **¡no te acojones!** take it easy!*
2 (= *asombrarse*) to be amazed, be overwhelmed
3** (*de miedo*) to freak out*, shit o.s.**

acojone‡ SM, **acojono**‡ SM (*esp Esp*) funk*, fear

acolada SF accolade

acolchado ADJ [*tela*] quilted, padded; [*sobre*] padded
SM **1** [*de tela*] quilting; [*de sobre*] padding
2 (*Cono Sur*) eiderdown

acolchar ▸ CONJUG 1a VT **1** [+ *tela*] to quilt, pad
2 (= *amortiguar*) [+ *sonido*] to muffle; [+ *golpe*] to soften

acolchonado ADJ padded

acólito SM (*Rel*) acolyte; (= *monaguillo*) server, altar boy; (*fig*) (= *adlátere*) acolyte, minion

acollador SM (*Náut*) lanyard

acollar ▸ CONJUG 1l VT (*Agr*) to earth up; (*Náut*) to caulk

acollarar ▸ CONJUG 1a VT **1** [+ *bueyes*] to yoke, harness; [+ *perro*] to put a collar on; (= *atar*) to tie by the neck
2 (*Cono Sur*) to trap into marriage

acollerar ▸ CONJUG 1a VT, VI to gather, herd together
VPR **acollerarse** = **acollerar**

acomedido ADJ (*LAm*) (= *generoso*) helpful, obliging; (= *solícito*) concerned, solicitous

acomedirse ▸ CONJUG 3k VPR (*LAm*) to offer to help • **~ a hacer algo** to do sth willingly

acometedor ADJ (= *emprendedor*) energetic, enterprising; [*toro*] fierce

acometer ▸ CONJUG 2a VT **1** (= *atacar*) to attack, set upon; [*toro*] to charge
2 [+ *tarea*] to undertake, attempt; [+ *asunto*] to tackle, deal with; [+ *construcción*] to begin, start on
3 [*sueño*] to overcome; [*miedo*] to seize, take hold of; [*dudas*] to assail; [*enfermedad*] to attack • **le acometieron dudas** he was assailed by doubts, he began to have doubts • **me acometió la tristeza** I was overcome with sadness

acometida SF **1** (= *ataque*) attack, assault; [*de toro*] charge
2 (*Elec*) connection

acometimiento SM attack
▸ **acometimiento y agresión** (*Méx*) (*Jur*) assault and battery

acometividad SF **1** (= *energía*) energy, enterprise
2 (= *agresividad*) aggressiveness; [*de toro*] fierceness • **mostrar ~** to show some fight *o* pluck
3 (*Cono Sur*) (= *susceptibilidad*) touchiness

acomodable ADJ (= *adaptable*) adaptable; (= *que sirve*) suitable

acomodación SF (*gen*) accommodation; (= *adaptación*) adaptation; (= *arreglo*) arrangement

acomodadizo ADJ (= *complaciente*) accommodating, obliging; (= *manejable*) pliable

acomodado ADJ **1** (= *apropiado*) suitable, fit; [*precio*] moderate; [*artículo*] moderately priced
2 (= *rico*) well-to-do, well-off

acomodador(a) SM/F usher/usherette

acomodamiento SM **1** (= *cualidad*) suitability, convenience
2 (= *acto*) arrangement, agreement

acomodar ▸ CONJUG 1a VT **1** [+ *visitante, huésped*] to put up • **nos ~on en diferentes cuartos** they put us up in different rooms • **~on a los evacuados en la escuela** they put up *o* accommodated the evacuees in the school
2 (= *sentar*) • **nos ~on en nuestros asientos** they showed us to our seats
3 (= *poner cómodo*) to make comfortable
4 (= *albergar*) [*local*] to seat; [*vehículo*] to take • **una sala con capacidad para ~ a mil personas** a hall with a capacity of one thousand, a hall which can seat one thousand people
5 (*frm*) (= *adaptar*) • **~ algo a algo** to adapt sth to (suit) sth • **~on la historia a sus necesidades políticas** they adapted history to suit their political requirements • **tendrán que ~ la ley a la directiva europea** they will have to bring the law into line with the European directive • **tienes que ~ tus gastos a tus ingresos** you need to adjust your expenditure to your income
6 (*frm*) (= *conciliar*) [+ *colores*] to match; [+ *enemigos, rivales*] to reconcile
7 (*frm*) (= *suministrar*) • **~ a algn con algo** to supply *o* provide sb with sth
8 (*LAm*) (= *colocar*) to put • **acomoda aquí los libros** put the books here
9 (*Cono Sur, Méx*) (= *dar trabajo a*) to get a job for, fix up (with a job)* • **acomodó a su primo en la oficina** he got his cousin a job in the office, he fixed his cousin up (with a job) in the office*
10 (*Caribe*) (= *estafar*) to con*, trick
VPR **acomodarse 1** (= *ponerse cómodo*) • **¡acomódate!** make yourself comfortable • **se acomodó en el sillón** he settled down in the armchair • **se ~on en una mesa contigua a la nuestra** (*frm*) they sat at the next table to us
2 (= *adaptarse*) • **~se a algo** to adapt to sth • **yo me acomodo a todo** I'm easy*
3* (= *casarse*) to marry into money
4 (*frm*) • **~se de** to provide o.s. with
5 (*LAm*) (= *ajustarse*) [+ *ropa, gafas*] to adjust

acomodaticio ADJ = **acomodadizo**

acomodo SM **1** (= *arreglo*) arrangement; (= *acuerdo*) agreement, understanding
2 (= *puesto*) post, job; (*LAm*) (*pey*) (= *enchufe*) soft job, plum job
3 (*LAm*) (= *soborno*) bribe

acompañado/a ADJ **1** [*persona*] • **está ~** he's with someone • **los invitados no podrán ir ~s a la boda** guests can't take someone else along with them to the wedding • **~ de:** • **entró acompañada de su padre** she came in with her father, she came in accompanied by her father • **la enciclopedia viene acompañada de un diccionario** the encyclopaedia comes with a dictionary • **bien/mal ~** in good/bad company; ▸ **solo**
2 [*lugar*] busy, frequented
3 • **con falda acompañada** with skirt to match, with a skirt of the same colour *o* pattern
4 • **estar ~** (*Caribe**) to be drunk
SM/F (*LAm*) (= *amante*) lover; (= *cónyuge*) common-law husband/wife

acompañamiento SM **1** (= *cortejo*) (*como escolta*) escort; [*de rey*] retinue; [*de sepelio*] funeral procession; [*de boda*] wedding party
2 (*Mús*) accompaniment • **con ~ de piano** with piano accompaniment • **cantar sin ~** to sing unaccompanied
3 (= *acción*) accompaniment • **esta salsa sirve como ~ de pescados** this sauce makes a good accompaniment to fish • **filete y patatas como ~** steak served with potatoes
4 (= *consecuencias*) aftermath • **el terremoto y su ~** the earthquake and its aftermath
5 (*Teat*) (*en acotaciones escénicas*) retinue; (*en títulos de crédito*) supporting cast • **Macbeth y ~** Macbeth and his retinue

acompañanta SF (= *señora de compañía*) female companion, female chaperon; (*Mús*) accompanist

acompañante SMF (= *que acompaña*) companion, escort; (*Mús*) accompanist

acompañar ▸ CONJUG 1a VT **1** (*a alguna parte*) (*gen*) to go with, accompany (*frm*) • **no quiero que me acompañe nadie** I don't want anyone to go with me • **¿quieres que te acompañe al médico?** do you want me to go to the doctor's with you? • **¡te acompaño!** I'll come with you! • **iba acompañado de dos guardaespaldas** he had two bodyguards with him, he was accompanied by two bodyguards • **su abogado lo acompañó en la rueda de prensa** his lawyer was with him at the press conference • **~ a algn a casa** to see sb home • **~ a algn a la puerta** to see sb to the door, see sb out
2 (= *hacer compañía*) (*por un rato*) to keep company; (*como pareja*) to be companion to • **nos quedamos un rato para ~ a la abuela** we stayed a while to keep grandmother company • **su hermana la acompañó durante toda su enfermedad** her sister stood by her side throughout the illness • **la mujer que lo acompañó en sus últimos años** the woman who was his companion *o* who was companion to him in his last years • **~ a algn en algo** to join sb in sth • **se ofrecieron a ~me en la búsqueda** they offered to join me in the search • **le acompaño en el sentimiento** (*en un entierro*) please accept my condolences
3 (= *ocurrir al mismo tiempo*) to accompany • **el escándalo que acompañó al estreno de la ópera** the scandal that accompanied the opening of the opera
4 [*comida*] • **este vino acompaña bien al queso** this wine goes well with cheese • **~ algo con *o* de algo** to serve sth with sth • **se puede ~ de una salsa** it can be served with a sauce
5 [*documentos*] • **la solicitud debe ir acompañada de un certificado** the application should be accompanied by a certificate
6 (*Mús*) to accompany (**a, con** on) • **estuvo acompañado a la guitarra por Juan Maya** he was accompanied on the guitar by Juan Maya
7 (= *ser favorable*) • **a ver si la suerte nos acompaña** let's hope we're lucky, let's hope our luck's in • **parece que nos acompaña la mala suerte** we seem to be dogged by bad luck, we seem to be having a lot of bad luck • **el tiempo no nos acompañó** we were unlucky with the weather
VI **1** (= *hacer compañía*) to be company • **un perro acompaña mucho** a dog is good company
2 [*comida*] • **¿quieres un poco de pan para ~?** would you like some bread to go with it?
3 [*ser favorable*] to be favourable *o* (*EEUU*) favorable • **si la coyuntura económica acompaña** if the economic climate is favourable • **es una pena que el tiempo no ~a** it's a shame the weather wasn't more favourable • **si el tiempo acompaña** weather permitting
VPR **acompañarse** (*Mús*) to accompany o.s. (**con, de** on) • **se acompaña con la guitarra** she accompanies herself on the guitar

acompaño (SM) (*CAm, Méx*) meeting, group, crowd
acompasado (ADJ) **1** (*Mús*) (= *rítmico*) rhythmic, regular; (= *medido*) measured
2 (= *pausado*) slow, deliberate
acompasar ▹ CONJUG 1a (VT) **1** (*Mús*) to mark the rhythm of • **~ la dicción** to speak with a marked rhythm
2 (*Mat*) to measure with a compass
3 (= *ajustarse a*) to match, keep in step with
acomplejado (ADJ) neurotic, hung-up* • **está ~ por su nariz** he's got a complex about his nose, he's got a thing about his nose
acomplejante (ADJ) (*Cono Sur*) inhibiting, embarrassing
acomplejar ▹ CONJUG 1a (VT) • **~ a algn** to give sb a complex
(VPR) **acomplejarse** to get a complex (**con, por** about) • **¡no te acomplejes!** don't get so worked up!
acompletadores* (SMPL) (*Méx*) beans
acomunarse ▹ CONJUG 1a (VPR) to join forces
aconchabar* ▹ CONJUG 1a (VT) (*LAm*) to take on, hire
(VPR) **aconchabarse** to gang up*
aconchado/a* (SM/F) (*Méx*) sponger*, scrounger*
aconchar ▹ CONJUG 1a (VT) **1** (= *poner a salvo*) to push to safety
2 (*Náut*) (= *encallar*) to beach, run aground; [*viento*] to drive ashore
3 (*Méx**) (= *reprender*) to tell off*
(VPR) **aconcharse 1** (*Náut*) (= *volcarse*) to keel over; (= *encallarse*) run aground
2 (*Cono Sur*) [*líquido*] to settle, clarify
3* (= *vivir de otro*) to sponge*, live off somebody else
acondicionado (ADJ) • **bien ~** [*persona*] genial, affable, nice; [*objeto*] in good condition • **mal ~** [*persona*] bad-tempered, difficult; [*objeto*] in bad condition • **aire ~** air conditioning • **un laboratorio bien ~** a well-equipped laboratory
acondicionador (SM) conditioner
▸ **acondicionador de aire** air conditioner
acondicionamiento (SM) (*gen*) conditioning; (*Com*) shopfitting
▸ **acondicionamiento de aire** air conditioning
acondicionar ▹ CONJUG 1a (VT) **1** (= *arreglar*) to arrange, prepare; [+ *pelo*] to condition
2 (*Com*) to fit out
3 (= *aclimatar*) to air-condition
aconfesional (ADJ) [*estado*] non-denominational
acongojado (ADJ) distressed, anguished
acongojar ▹ CONJUG 1a (VT) to distress, grieve
(VPR) **acongojarse** to become distressed • **¡no te acongojes!** don't distress yourself!, don't get upset!
acónito (SM) (*Bot*) aconite, monkshood
aconsejable (ADJ) (= *conveniente*) advisable; (= *sensato*) sensible, politic • **nada** *o* **poco ~** inadvisable • **eso no es ~** that is not advisable • **no sería ~ que usted viniera** you would be ill-advised to come
aconsejado (ADJ) • **bien ~** sensible • **mal ~** ill-advised
aconsejar ▹ CONJUG 1a (VT) **1** (= *dar consejos a*) to advise • **~ a algn hacer algo** to advise sb to do sth
2 [+ *cuidado*] to advise, recommend; [+ *virtud*] to preach
(VPR) **aconsejarse** to seek advice, take advice • **~ con** *o* **de** to consult • **~ mejor** to think better of it

ACONSEJAR

Aconsejar a algn que haga algo *se traduce al inglés con* **advise** *+ objeto + infinitivo con* **to**, *es decir:* **advise sb to do sth**:

Le aconsejé que (no) cambiase de trabajo
I advised her (not) to change jobs
Le aconsejaré a mi hermana que se lo piense dos veces
I'll advise my sister to think it over carefully

Cuando se quiere aconsejar a una persona, en inglés se suele utilizar el condicional para que no parezca un mandato, como se ve en los siguientes ejemplos:

Le aconsejo que consulte a un abogado
I would advise you to see a lawyer
Te aconsejo que lo hagas
I'd advise you to do it

Para otros usos y ejemplos ver la entrada.

aconsonantar ▹ CONJUG 1a (VT), (VI) to rhyme (**con** with)
acontecedero† (ADJ) which could happen, possible
acontecer ▹ CONJUG 2d (VI) to happen, occur
acontecimiento (SM) event • **fue realmente un ~** it was an event of some importance • **fue todo un ~** it was quite an affair
acopiar ▹ CONJUG 1b (VT) (= *juntar*) to gather, gather together, collect; (*Com*) to buy up, get a monopoly of; [+ *miel*] to collect, hive
acopio (SM) **1** (= *acto*) gathering, collecting
2 (= *cantidad*) collection; (= *suministro*) store, stock; [*de madera*] stack; (*Cono Sur*) (= *abundancia*) abundance • **hacer ~** to stock up (**de** with), lay in stocks (**de** of)
acoplable (ADJ) attachable
acoplado (ADJ) • **un equipo bien ~** a well coordinated team
(SM) **1** (*Cono Sur*) (*Aut*) (= *remolque*) trailer, semitrailer (*EEUU*)
2 (*Cono Sur**) (= *parásito*) hanger-on*, sponger*; (= *intruso*) gatecrasher
acoplador (SM) ▸ **acoplador acústico** acoustic coupler
acoplamiento (SM) (*Mec*) coupling; (*Elec*) connection; (*Telec, TV*) link-up, hook-up; [*de astronaves*] docking, link-up; (*Zool*) mating ▸ **acoplamiento de manguito** sleeve coupling ▸ **acoplamiento en serie** series connection ▸ **acoplamiento universal** universal joint
acoplar ▹ CONJUG 1a (VT) **1** (= *unir*) (*Téc*) to couple; (*Elec*) to connect, join up; [+ *carros*] to join up, hook up; [+ *astronaves*] to dock, link up; (*LAm*) (*Ferro*) to couple (up)
2 (*Zool*) [+ *animales*] to mate, pair; [+ *bueyes*] to yoke, hitch
3 (*Dep*) to coordinate; [+ *personas*] to associate, bring together; [+ *opiniones*] to reconcile; [+ *proyectos, esfuerzos*] to coordinate
(VPR) **acoplarse 1** (*Zool*) to mate, pair
2 (*Aer*) to dock
3 (*Elec*) to cause feedback
4 (= *hacer las paces*) to make it up, be reconciled
acoplo (SM) (*Elec*) feedback
acoquinamiento (SM) intimidation
acoquinar ▹ CONJUG 1a (VT) to scare, intimidate, cow
(VPR) **acoquinarse** to get scared, take fright

acorar ▹ CONJUG 1a (VT) to distress, afflict, upset
acorazado (ADJ) [*cámara*] security (*antes de s*); [*vehículo*] reinforced, armoured, armored (*EEUU*), armour-plated, armor-plated (*EEUU*)
(SM) battleship
acorazar ▹ CONJUG 1f (VT) to armour-plate, armor-plate (*EEUU*)
(VPR) **acorazarse** (= *armarse de valor*) to steel o.s. (**contra** against); (= *hacerse insensible*) to become inured (**contra** to)
acorazonado (ADJ) heart-shaped
acorchado (ADJ) **1** (= *esponjoso*) spongy, cork-like
2 (*Med*) (= *insensible*) numb; [*boca*] furry
acorchar ▹ CONJUG 1a (VT) to cover with cork
(VPR) **acorcharse 1** [*patata*] to go spongy
2 (*Med*) [*pierna, dedos*] to go numb
acordada (SF) decree
acordadamente (ADV) unanimously, by common consent
acordar ▹ CONJUG 1l (VT) **1** (= *decidir*) [+ *precio, fecha*] to agree, agree on • **eso no es lo que acordamos** that is not what we agreed • **han acordado la suspensión provisional de las obras** it was agreed that the works should be suspended temporarily • **~ hacer algo** to agree to do sth • **~on retrasar la reunión** they agreed to put back the meeting • **~ que** to agree that • **acordamos que nadie saliera de la sala** we agreed that no one should leave the room
2 [+ *opiniones*] to reconcile; [+ *instrumentos*] to tune; [+ *colores*] to blend, harmonize
3 (= *recordar*) • **~ algo a algn**†† to remind sb of sth • **~ a algn de hacer algo** • **~ a algn que haga algo** (*And, Chile*) to remind sb to do sth
4 (*LAm*) (= *conceder*) to grant, accord (*frm*)
(VI) • **~ con algo** to go with sth, match sth
(VPR) **acordarse** to remember • **no me acuerdo** I don't *o* can't remember • **ya te lo traeré, si me acuerdo** I'll bring it for you, if I remember (to) • **no quiero ni ~me** I don't even want to think about it • **ahora que me acuerdo** now that I think of it, come to think of it • **~se de algo/algn** to remember sth/sb • **¿te acuerdas de mí?** do you remember me? • **nadie se acordaba del número** nobody could think of *o* remember the number • **ya no me acordaba de que tenía una reunión** I'd completely forgotten that I had a meeting • **no quiero ni ~me del frío que pasamos** I can hardly bear to think of how cold we were • **el otro día me acordé de ti cuando ...** I thought of you the other day when ... • **me acuerdo mucho de mi infancia** I often think about *o* recall my childhood • **desde que te has ido, me acuerdo mucho de ti** since you left, I've missed you a lot • **¡te ~ás de esta!** I'll teach you!, I'll give you something to remember me by! • **~se de hacer algo** to remember to do sth • **acuérdate de comprar pan** remember *o* don't forget to buy some bread • **~se de haber hecho algo** to remember doing sth • **me acuerdo de haber leído un artículo sobre eso** I remember reading an article about that • MODISMO: • **no se acuerda ni del santo de su nombre** he can hardly remember *o* he has trouble remembering his own name
acorde (ADJ) **1** • **~ a** *o* **con** [+ *situación, posición*] appropriate to; [+ *ley, directiva*] in conformity *o* compliance with • **su comportamiento fue ~ a** *o* **con las circunstancias** her behaviour was appropriate to the circumstances • **un motor ~ a** *o* **con las normas ecológicas** an engine that complies with environmental regulations

a

2 (*frm*) (= *coincidente*) • **estar ~s** to be agreed, be in agreement
3 (*Mús*) harmonious
SM (*Mús*) chord • **a los ~s de la marcha nupcial** to the strains of the wedding march
acordeón SM accordion ▸ **acordeón de botones** button accordion ▸ **acordeón de teclas, acordeón piano** piano accordion
acordeonista SMF accordionist
acordonado ADJ **1** (*Cos*) ribbed
2 [*calle*] cordoned-off; [*moneda, borde*] milled
3 (*LAm*) [*animal*] thin
acordonamiento SM **1** (*Cos*) ribbing
2 (= *acción*) [*de calle*] cordoning off; [*de moneda, borde*] milling
acordonar ▹ CONJUG 1a VT **1** [+ *zapatos*] to do up, lace up
2 [+ *lugar*] (*con guardias*) to cordon off; (*con cerca*) to surround
3 [+ *moneda, borde*] to mill
4 (*LAm*) [+ *terreno*] to prepare
acornar ▹ CONJUG 1l VT, **acornear** ▹ CONJUG 1a VT to gore
acorralamiento SM (= *cercamiento*) enclosing; (= *arrinconamiento*) cornering, trapping
acorralar ▹ CONJUG 1a VT (*Agr*) [+ *ganado*] to pen, corral; (= *arrinconar*) to corner; (= *intimidar*) to intimidate
acorrer ▹ CONJUG 2a VT to help, go to the aid of
VI to run up • **~ a algn** to hasten to sb
acortamiento SM shortening, reduction
acortar ▹ CONJUG 1a VT [+ *vestido, falda, traje*] to take up, shorten; [+ *artículo, texto*] to shorten, cut down; [+ *periodo, duración*] to shorten, reduce • **esta carretera ~á la distancia entre las dos ciudades** this road will shorten the distance between the two cities • **yendo por aquí acortamos camino** it's shorter if we go this way • **tuve que ~ las vacaciones** I had to cut short my holidays • **el Barcelona está acortando distancias con el Real Madrid** Barcelona is catching up with Real Madrid
VPR **acortarse** to get shorter • **empiezan a ~se los días** the days are getting shorter
acosador(a) SM/F **1** (*psicológico, laboral, escolar*) bully
2 (*sexual*) harasser
acosar ▹ CONJUG 1a VT **1** (= *atosigar*) to hound, harass; (*de forma premeditada*) [*una persona*] to bully; [*un grupo*] to mob • **~ a algn a preguntas** to pester sb with questions • **ser acosado sexualmente** to suffer (from) sexual harassment, be sexually harassed
2 (= *perseguir*) to pursue relentlessly
3 [+ *caballo*] to urge on
acosijar ▹ CONJUG 1a VT (*Méx*) = **acosar**
acoso SM **1** (= *atosigamiento*) harassment • **es víctima del ~ de la prensa** she's a victim of press harassment • **operación de ~ y derribo** (*Mil*) search and destroy operation • **una operación de ~ y derribo contra el presidente** a campaign to hound the president out of office ▸ **acoso escolar** (*por una persona*) bullying at school; (*por un grupo de personas*) mobbing (at school) ▸ **acoso laboral** workplace bullying, workplace harassment ▸ **acoso sexual** sexual harassment
2 (= *persecución*) relentless pursuit
acostado ADJ **1** (= *tumbado*) lying down
2 (= *en la cama*) in bed
acostar ▹ CONJUG 1l VT **1** (= *tender*) to lay down
2 (*en cama*) to put to bed
3 (*Náut*) to bring alongside
VPR **acostarse 1** (= *tumbarse*) to lie down; (= *ir a dormir*) to go to bed; (*LAm*) (= *dar a luz*) to give birth • **nos acostamos tarde** we went to bed late • **Pilar se acostó con Juan** Pilar went to bed *o* slept with Juan • **ella se acuesta con cualquiera** she sleeps around • **es hora de ~se** it's bedtime
2 (= *inclinarse*) to lean, bend
acostillado ADJ ribbed, with ribs
acostumbrado ADJ **1** (= *normal*) usual, customary (*frm*) • **se vieron en el lugar ~** they met at the usual *o* (*frm*) customary place • **se acostó antes de lo ~** she went to bed earlier than usual
2 • **~ a algo** used to sth • **no estoy acostumbrada al calor** I'm not used to the heat • **está ~ a trabajar de noche** he's used to working at night • **ya estoy ~ a que no me entiendan** I'm used to *o* (*frm*) accustomed to not being understood
3 • **bien ~: su marido está muy bien ~** her husband is very well trained • **mal ~: sus hijos están muy mal ~s** her children are very spoilt • **su mujer lo tiene muy mal ~** his wife spoils him (rotten)
acostumbramiento SM (*Cono Sur*) • **producir ~** to be addictive
acostumbrar ▹ CONJUG 1a VT • **~ a algn a algo** to get sb used to sth • **~ a algn a las dificultades** to get sb used to the problems • **~ a algn a hacer algo** to accustom sb to doing sth
VI • **~ (a) hacer algo** to be used *o* accustomed to doing sth, be in the habit of doing sth • **los sábados acostumbra (a) ir al cine** on Saturdays he usually goes to the cinema
VPR **acostumbrarse 1** • **~se a algo** to get accustomed *o* used to sth • **se acostumbró a tomar chocolate** he got into the habit of drinking chocolate • **está acostumbrado a verlas venir** he's not easily fooled
2 (*esp LAm*) • **aquí no se acostumbra decir eso** people don't say that *o* that isn't said here • **no se acostumbra** it isn't customary *o* usual
acotación SF **1** (= *linde*) boundary mark; (*Geog*) elevation mark
2 (*Tip*) (= *anotación*) marginal note
3 (*Teat*) stage direction
acotado ADJ enclosed, fenced
SM (*tb* **acotado de caza**) game preserve
acotamiento SM (*Méx*) hard shoulder, berm (*EEUU*), emergency lane
acotar ▹ CONJUG 1a VT **1** [+ *terreno*] (= *marcar*) to survey, mark out; (= *poner cotos en*) to limit, set bounds to; [+ *caza*] to fence in, protect
2 [+ *página*] to annotate; [+ *mapa*] to mark elevations on
3 [+ *árboles*] to lop
acotejar ▹ CONJUG 1a VT (*LAm*) [+ *cosas*] to put in order, arrange
VPR **acotejarse** (*LAm*) (= *acomodarse*) to come to an arrangement
acotillo SM sledgehammer
acoyundar ▹ CONJUG 1a VT to yoke
acr. ABR (= **acreedor**) Cr
acracia SF anarchy
ácrata ADJ anarchist(ic), libertarian
SMF anarchist, libertarian
acrático ADJ = **ácrata**
acre[1] ADJ **1** [*sabor*] sharp, bitter; [*olor*] acrid, pungent
2 [*temperamento*] sour; [*crítica*] sharp, biting, mordant
acre[2] SM acre
acrecencia SF **1** (*Jur*) accretion
2 = acrecentamiento
acrecentamiento SM increase, growth
acrecentar ▹ CONJUG 1j VT (= *aumentar*) to increase, augment; (= *ascender*) [+ *persona*] to advance, promote
VPR **acrecentarse** to increase, grow
acrecer ▹ CONJUG 2d VT to increase
acrecimiento SM increase, growth
acreditación SF (= *acto*) accreditation; (= *autorización*) authorization, sanctioning
acreditado ADJ (*Pol*) accredited; (= *estimado*) reputable • **nuestro representante ~** our official agent • **una casa acreditada** a reputable firm
acreditar ▹ CONJUG 1a VT **1** (= *dar reputación a*) to do credit to, give credit to • **y virtudes que le acreditan** and qualities which do him credit
2 (= *avalar*) to vouch for, guarantee; (= *probar*) to prove; (= *autorizar*) to sanction, authorize • **~ su personalidad** to establish one's identity
3 (*Pol*) [+ *embajador*] to accredit
4 (*Com*) to credit; (*And*) (= *fiar*) to sell on credit
VPR **acreditarse** to prove one's worth • **~se como** to get a reputation for • **~se en** to get a reputation in
acreditativo ADJ • **documentos ~s** supporting documents
acreedor(a) ADJ • **~ a** worthy of, deserving of
SM/F creditor ▸ **acreedor(a) común** unsecured creditor ▸ **acreedor(a) con garantía** secured creditor ▸ **acreedor(a) diferido/a** deferred creditor ▸ **acreedor(a) hipotecario/a** mortgagee
acreencia SF (*LAm*) (= *saldo acreedor*) credit balance; (= *deuda*) debt, amount owing *o* owed

ACOSTUMBRAR

▹ *La forma pronominal* **acostumbrarse a hacer algo** *se traduce al inglés por* **get used to** + *-ing:*
Te acostumbrarás a trabajar aquí
You'll get used to working here
Con el tiempo me acostumbré a estar sin él
In time I got used to being without him

▹ *La expresión* **estar acostumbrado a hacer algo** *se traduce por* **to be used to** + *-ing:*
Está acostumbrado a levantarse temprano
He's used to getting up early

Otra forma de traducir esta estructura al inglés es con la construcción **to be accustomed to** + *-ing, aunque tiene un registro formal:*
He's accustomed to getting up early

▹ *Cuando el verbo* **acostumbrar** *equivale a* **soler**, *se puede traducir de dos formas distintas en inglés, dependiendo de si la acción a la que se refiere ocurre en el pasado o en el presente.*

▹ *En el pasado, lo traducimos por* **used to** + *infinitivo:*
Cuando era niña acostumbraba a rezar todas las noches
When I was a child I used to pray every night
El año pasado acostumbrábamos a vernos todos los viernes
Last year we used to meet every Friday

▹ *En el presente se traduce por el adverbio* **usually** + *presente simple:*
Los domingos acostumbro a levantarme tarde
I usually get up late on Sundays

Para otros usos y ejemplos ver la entrada.

acremente ADV sharply, bitterly
acribadura SF sifting, sieving
acribar ▹ CONJUG 1a VT to sift, riddle
acribillado ADJ [*superficie*] pitted, pockmarked • **~ a** riddled with, peppered with • **~ de** filled with • **~ de picaduras** covered with stings
acribillar ▹ CONJUG 1a VT **1** to riddle, pepper • **~ a balazos** to riddle with bullets • **~ a puñaladas** to cover with stab wounds
2 (= *fastidiar*) to pester, badger • **~ a algn a preguntas** to bombard sb with questions
acridio SM (*LAm*) locust
acrílico ADJ acrylic
acrilonitrilo SM acrylonitrile
acriminación SF incrimination, accusation
acriminador(a) ADJ incriminating
SM/F accuser
acriminar ▹ CONJUG 1a VT (*Jur*) to incriminate, accuse; (*fig*) [+ *falta*] to exaggerate
acrimonia SF **1** (= *olor*) acridness, pungency; (= *sabor*) sharpness, sourness
2 (= *desabrimiento*) acrimony, bitterness
acrimonioso ADJ acrimonious
acriollado ADJ (*esp Cono Sur*) *adapted or adjusted to the customs of a Latin American country*
acriollarse ▹ CONJUG 1a VPR (*esp Cono Sur*) to go native
acrisolado ADJ (= *refinado*) pure • **una fe acrisolada** a faith tried and tested • **el patriotismo más ~** the noblest kind of patriotism • **de acrisolada honradez** of unquestionable honesty
acrisolar ▹ CONJUG 1a VT **1** (*Téc*) (= *purificar*) to purify, refine
2 (= *acendrar*) to bring out, prove
acristalado ADJ glazed
acristalamiento SM glazing • **los ~s** the windows, the glazing • **doble ~** double glazing
acristalar ▹ CONJUG 1a VT to glaze
acristianar ▹ CONJUG 1a VT (= *hacer cristiano*) to Christianize; [+ *niño*] to baptize
acritud SF = **acrimonia**
acrobacia SF acrobatics (*sing*) ▸ **acrobacia aérea** aerobatics (*sing*), aerial acrobatics (*sing*)
acróbata SMF acrobat
acrobático ADJ acrobatic
acrobatismo SM acrobatics (*sing*)
acromático ADJ colourless
acrónimo SM acronym
Acrópolis SF Acropolis
acróstico ADJ, SM acrostic
acta SF **1** [*de reunión*] minutes (*pl*) • **constar en ~:** • **las pruebas documentales constan en ~** the documentary proof is in the minutes • **pidieron que su oposición al plan constara en ~** they asked for their opposition to the plan to be noted • **que conste en ~** let it be noted in the record • **levantar ~ de** [+ *reunión, sesión parlamentaria*] to write up the minutes of; [+ *acontecimiento, delito*] to make a(n official) report on • **tomar ~ de algo** (*Cono Sur*) to take note of sth, bear sth in mind
2 [*de congreso*] proceedings (*pl*); [*de organismo*] records (*pl*)
3 (*Educ*) [*de notas*] student's achievement record
4 (= *certificado*) certificate ▸ **acta de bautismo** certificate of baptism ▸ **acta de defunción** death certificate ▸ **acta de diputado** (*Pol*) certificate of election ▸ **acta de matrimonio** marriage certificate ▸ **acta de nacimiento** birth certificate ▸ **acta matrimonial** marriage certificate
5 [*de acuerdo*] ▸ **acta constitutiva** charter ▸ **acta orgánica** (*LAm*) constitution ▸ **Acta Única Europea** Single European Act
6 (*Jur*) • **el juez levantó ~ del accidente** the judge drew up an official report on the accident ▸ **acta de acusación** bill of indictment ▸ **acta notarial** affidavit
7 (*Rel*) (= *relato*) ▸ **actas de los mártires** lives of the martyrs ▸ **actas de un santo** life of a saint
8 (*LAm*) (= *ley*) act, law
actinia SF actinia, sea anemone
actínico ADJ actinic
actinio SM actinium
actitud SF **1** (= *comportamiento, disposición*) attitude • **no vas a conseguir nada con esa ~** you won't get anywhere with that attitude • **tienes que cambiar tu ~ ante la vida** you must change your attitude to life • **han adoptado una ~ firme** they have taken a firm stand *o* a tough stance
2 (= *postura física*) posture • **tenía el mentón levantado, en ~ desafiante** he had his chin raised in a defiant posture • **adoptó una ~ pensativa** she adopted a thoughtful pose • **en ~ de: estaba en ~ de absoluta concentración** he was in state of total concentration • **las encontré en ~ de oración** I found them at prayer • **se incorporó en ~ de despedirse** he stood up as if he was going to leave
3 (= *estado de ánimo*) frame of mind, mood • **en ~ resignada** in a resigned mood *o* frame of mind
activación SF [*de mecanismo*] activation; [*de gestión, actividad*] expediting, speeding-up
activador SM (*Téc*) activator; (= *estímulo*) stimulus
activamente ADV actively
activar ▹ CONJUG 1a VT (= *poner en marcha*) to activate; [+ *trabajo*] to expedite, speed up, hurry along; [+ *fuego*] to brighten up, poke; [+ *mercado*] to stimulate
actividad SF **1** (= *acción*) activity • **ha habido una intensa ~ diplomática** there has been intense diplomatic activity • **estos son meses de escasa ~ en el sector hotelero** these months are not very busy in the hotel sector • **ha sido una jornada de escasa ~ bursátil** trading was slow *o* sluggish on the stock exchange today • **en ~: el volcán aún está en ~** the volcano is still active • **estuvo en ~ hasta su muerte** he worked right up until his death • **la recolección está en plena ~** the harvest is in full swing
2 (= *tarea profesional*) work • **los pescadores han reanudado su ~** the fishermen have gone back to work ▸ **actividad docente** teaching ▸ **actividad lucrativa** gainful employment
3 actividades (= *actos*) activities (*pl*) • **es sospechoso de ~es terroristas** he is suspected of terrorist activities • **~es culturales** cultural activities • **~es deportivas** sporting activities; ▹ **extraescolar**
activismo SM activism
activista SMF activist
activo ADJ **1** (= *que obra*) active; (= *vivo*) lively, energetic; (= *ocupado*) busy
2 (*Ling*) active
SM **1** (*Com*) assets (*pl*) ▸ **activo circulante** circulating assets (*pl*) ▸ **activo corriente** current assets (*pl*) ▸ **activo de la quiebra** bankrupt's estate ▸ **activo fijo** fixed assets (*pl*) ▸ **activo flotante** floating assets (*pl*) ▸ **activo inmaterial** intangible assets (*pl*) ▸ **activo intangible** intangible assets (*pl*) ▸ **activo invisible** invisible assets (*pl*) ▸ **activo líquido** liquid assets (*pl*) ▸ **activo neto** net worth ▸ **activo oculto** hidden assets (*pl*) ▸ **activo operante** operating assets (*pl*) ▸ **activo realizable** liquid assets (*pl*) ▸ **activos bloqueados** frozen assets ▸ **activos congelados** frozen assets ▸ **activos inmobiliarios** property assets, real-estate assets ▸ **activo tangible** tangible assets (*pl*) ▸ **activo y pasivo** assets and liabilities (*pl*)
2 (*Mil*) • **oficial en ~** serving officer • **estar en ~** to be on active service
acto SM **1** (= *acción*) act, action • **el ~ de escribir es un tipo de terapia** the act *o* action of writing is a kind of therapy • **no es responsable de sus ~s** he's not responsible for his actions • **la atraparon en el ~ de falsificar la firma** they caught her in the act of forging the signature • **hacer ~ de presencia** (= *asistir*) to attend, be present; (= *aparecer*) to appear; (= *dejarse ver brevemente*) put in an appearance • **morir en ~ de servicio** to die on active service • **el ~ sexual** the sexual *o* sex act ▸ **acto carnal** carnal act ▸ **acto de contrición** act of contrition ▸ **acto de desagravio** act of atonement ▸ **acto de fe** act of faith ▸ **acto de habla** speech act ▸ **acto reflejo** reflex action ▸ **Actos de los Apóstoles** Acts (of the Apostles)
2 (= *ceremonia*) • **celebrar un ~** to hold a function ▸ **acto inaugural** opening ceremony ▸ **acto oficial** official function ▸ **acto público** public engagement ▸ **acto religioso** (religious) service
3 (*Teat*) act
4 • **en el ~** (= *inmediatamente*) there and then • **la ingresaron y la operaron en el ~** she was admitted and operated on there and then *o* on the spot • **murió en el ~** he died instantly • **"reparaciones en el acto"** "repairs while you wait"
5 • **~ seguido** • **~ continuo** (*frm*) immediately after(wards)
actor ADJ (*Jur*) • **parte ~a** prosecution
SM **1** (*Teat, Cine*) actor • **primer ~** leading man ▸ **actor cinematográfico, actor de cine** film actor (*esp Brit*), movie actor (*EEUU*) ▸ **actor de doblaje** dubber ▸ **actor de reparto** supporting actor
2 (*Jur*) (= *demandante*) plaintiff
actriz SF actress • **primera ~** leading lady ▸ **actriz cinematográfica, actriz de cine** film actress (*esp Brit*), movie actress (*EEUU*) ▸ **actriz de doblaje** dubber ▸ **actriz de reparto** supporting actress
actuación SF **1** (= *intervención*) [*de cantante, deportista*] performance; [*de actor*] acting • **la primera ~ pública de la banda** the band's first public performance • **su ~ es lo peor de la película** the worst thing in the film is his acting ▸ **actuación en directo, actuación en vivo** live performance
2 (= *espectáculo*) • **todas sus actuaciones tuvieron un gran éxito de público** all his shows were a great success with the public • **habrá dos actuaciones de jazz** there will be two jazz sessions
3 (= *acción*) action • **sus líneas de ~** their plan of action • **las actuaciones policiales fueron vanas** police action was to no avail • **criticaron la ~ del presidente ante la crisis** they criticized the president's handling of the crisis
4 (= *conducta*) behaviour, behavior (*EEUU*), conduct • **la ~ de la policía en la manifestación** the behaviour *o* conduct of the police at the demonstration
5 actuaciones (*Jur*) (legal) proceedings
actual ADJ **1** (= *de ahora*) [*situación, sistema, gobernante*] current, present; [*sociedad*] contemporary, present-day; [*moda*] current, modern • **el ~ campeón de Europa** the reigning *o* current *o* present European champion • **en el momento ~** at the present

a

moment • **la ~ literatura francesa** French literature today, present-day French literature • **eso no le interesa a la juventud ~** that doesn't interest young people today • **el 6 del ~** the 6th of this month
2 (= *de actualidad*) [*cuestión, tema*] topical • **en la reunión trataron temas muy ~es** they dealt with highly topical issues in the meeting
3 (= *moderno*) up-to-date, fashionable • **ha cambiado su peinado por otro algo más ~** he's changed his hairstyle for a more up-to-date *o* fashionable one • **corbatas de diseño muy ~** very fashionable-looking ties • **emplean las técnicas más ~es** they use the most up-to-date *o* up-to-the-minute techniques, they use the latest techniques

actualidad SF **1** • **en la ~** (= *hoy día*) nowadays; (= *en este momento*) currently, at present, presently (*EEUU*) • **es un juego muy de moda en la ~** it's a very popular game nowadays • **hay en la ~ más de dos millones de parados** there are currently over two million unemployed, there are over two million unemployed at present
2 (= *cualidad*) • **las obras de Shakespeare no han perdido ~** the works of Shakespeare have not lost their topicality • **de ~** [*noticia, tema*] topical; [*modelo, diseño*] up-to-date, up-to-the-minute • **una cuestión de palpitante ~** a highly topical question • **poner algo de ~** to focus attention on sth • **eso ha puesto de ~ un problema olvidado** that has focused attention on a forgotten problem
3 (*Periodismo*) • **la ~** (= *asuntos*) current affairs (*pl*); (= *noticias*) news, current news • **una revista sobre la ~ francesa** a magazine on French current affairs • **y ahora vamos a pasar a la ~ internacional** and now (for) international news
4 actualidades (*en periódico*) current affairs; (*en cine*) newsreel (*sing*)

actualización SF (= *acto*) updating; (*Inform*) update, updating; (*Contabilidad*) discounting

actualizado ADJ **1** (= *informado*) up-to-date
2 [*aparato*] updated
3 [*software*] updated

actualizador ADJ modernizing

actualizar ▷ CONJUG 1f VT (= *poner al día*) to bring up to date, update; (*Inform*) to update; (*Contabilidad*) to discount
VPR **actualizarse 1** [*persona*] to keep up-to-date
2 [*datos, valores*] to be updated

actualmente ADV **1** (= *en este momento*) currently, at present, presently (*EEUU*) • **~ está rodando una nueva película** he's currently making a new film, he's making a new film at present
2 (= *hoy día*) nowadays • **~ se usan métodos más eficaces** nowadays more efficient methods are used

actuar ▷ CONJUG 1e VI **1** [*actor*] to act; [*cantante, banda, compañía, equipo*] to perform • **~ en una película** to act *o* be in a film
2 (= *obrar*) to act • **actúa como** *o* **de mediador en el conflicto** he's acting as a mediator in the conflict • **actúa de manera rara** he's acting *o* behaving strangely • **la indecisión no le dejaba ~** indecision prevented him from taking any action • **el árbitro actuó bien en el partido** the referee did a good job in the match
3 (*Jur*) (= *proceder*) to institute (legal) proceedings; [*abogado*] to act • **el abogado que actúa en nombre de mi familia** the lawyer acting for my family
4 (= *tener efecto*) to act • **la crema actúa directamente sobre la herida** the cream acts directly on the wound • **el freno actúa sobre la rueda trasera** the brake acts on the back wheel
VT (= *hacer funcionar*) to work, operate

actuarial ADJ actuarial

actuario/a SM/F **1** (*Jur*) clerk (of the court)
2 (*Econ*) actuary

acuache* SM, **acuachi*** SM (*Méx*) mate, buddy (*EEUU**), pal*

acuadrillar ▷ CONJUG 1a VT (= *juntar en cuadrilla*) to form into a band; (*Chile*) (= *acometer*) to set upon
VPR **acuadrillarse** to band together, gang up

acuanauta SMF deep-sea diver

acuaplano SM surfboarding

acuarela SF watercolour, watercolor (*EEUU*) • **pintor(a) a la ~** watercolourist, watercolorist (*EEUU*)

acuarelista SMF watercolourist, watercolorist (*EEUU*)

Acuario SM (*Astron, Astrol*) Aquarius • **es de ~** he's (an) Aquarius, he's an Aquarian

acuario SM aquarium
SMF INV (*Astrol*) Aquarius, Aquarian • **los ~ son así** that's what Aquariuses *o* Aquarians are like
ADJ INV (*Astrol*) Aquarius, Aquarian • **soy ~** I'm (an) Aquarius, I'm an Aquarian

acuárium SM aquarium

acuartelado ADJ (*Heráldica*) quartered

acuartelamiento SM (*Mil*) quartering, billeting; (= *disciplina*) confinement to barracks

acuartelar ▷ CONJUG 1a VT (*Mil*) to quarter, billet; (= *disciplinar*) to confine to barracks
VPR **acuartelarse** to withdraw to barracks

acuático ADJ aquatic, water (*antes de s*)

acuátil ADJ aquatic, water (*antes de s*)

acuatinta SF aquatint

acuatizaje SM touchdown (*on water*), landing (*on water*)

acuatizar ▷ CONJUG 1f VI to come down (*on water*), land (*on water*)

acuchamado ADJ (*Caribe*) (= *triste*) sad, depressed

acuchamarse ▷ CONJUG 1a VPR (*Caribe*) to get depressed

acuchillado ADJ **1** [*vestido*] slashed
2 (= *escarmentado*) wary, schooled by bitter experience

acuchillar ▷ CONJUG 1a VT **1** (= *cortar*) to knife, stab; [+ *vestido*] to slash
2 [+ *persona*] to stab (to death), knife
3 (*Téc*) to plane down, smooth
VPR **acuchillarse** • **se ~on** they fought with knives, they slashed at each other

acuchucar ▷ CONJUG 1g VT (*Cono Sur*) to crush, flatten

acucia SF (= *diligencia*) diligence, keenness; (= *prisa*) haste; (= *anhelo*) keen desire, longing

acuciadamente ADV (= *diligentemente*) diligently, keenly; (= *con prisa*) hastily; (= *con deseo*) longingly

acuciador ADJ = **acuciante**

acuciante ADJ pressing • **necesidad ~** dire necessity, urgent *o* pressing need

acuciar ▷ CONJUG 1b VT **1** (= *estimular*) to urge on; (= *dar prisa a*) to hasten; (= *acosar*) to harass; [*problema*] to press, worry • **acuciado por el hambre** driven on by hunger
2 (= *anhelar*) to yearn for, long for

acucioso ADJ (= *diligente*) keen, diligent

acuclillarse ▷ CONJUG 1a VPR to squat down

ACUDE SF ABR = **Asociación de Consumidores y Usuarios de España**

acudir ▷ CONJUG 3a VI **1** (*indicando movimiento*) (= *ir*) to go; (= *venir*) to come • **señor Martínez, acuda a información por favor** Mr Martínez, please go to the information desk • **dijo que ~ía a declarar voluntariamente** he said that he would testify voluntarily • **el perro acude cuando lo llamo** the dog comes when I call • **muchos profesores acuden cada año a nuestro congreso** every year many teachers come to *o* attend our conference • **miles de personas acudieron al aeropuerto** thousands of people turned up at *o* came to the airport • **solo diez trabajadores acudieron a sus puestos** only ten workers showed up for work • **acudieron en su ayuda** they went to his aid • **no acudió a la cita** he did not keep the appointment, he did not turn up (for the appointment) • **~ a una llamada** to answer a call • **~ al médico** to consult a doctor • **~ a la mente** to come to (one's) mind • **esta imagen acude a la mente de muchas personas** for many people this is the image that comes to mind • **~ a las urnas** to go to the polls
2 (= *participar*) to take part • **el pasado año acudieron 130 expositores** last year 130 exhibitors took part
3 (= *recurrir*) • **~ a** to turn to • **no tenemos a quién ~** we have nobody to turn to • **acudo a ustedes para quejarme sobre …** I am writing to complain about … • **~ a los tribunales** to go to court
4 (*Agr*) to produce, yield

acueducto SM aqueduct

ácueo ADJ aqueous

acuerdo SM **1** (= *decisión conjunta*) agreement; (*implícito, informal*) understanding; (*de negocios*) deal • **ambas partes quieren llegar a un ~** both parties wish to come to *o* reach an agreement • **tenemos una especie de ~ para no hacernos la competencia** we have a sort of understanding that we will not become competitors • **llegaron a un ~ sin necesidad de acudir a juicio** they settled out of court • **de común ~** by mutual agreement, by mutual consent • **de** *o* **por mutuo ~** by mutual agreement, by mutual consent • **tomar un ~:** • **no tomaron ni un solo ~ en la reunión** nothing was agreed on in the meeting • **se tomó el ~ de ofrecer ayuda a los países afectados** it was agreed to give aid to the affected countries ▸ **acuerdo de desarme** disarmament agreement, arms agreement ▸ **acuerdo de pago respectivo** (*Com*) knock-for-knock agreement, no-fault agreement (*EEUU*) ▸ **acuerdo de paz** peace agreement ▸ **acuerdo de pesca** fishing agreement ▸ **acuerdo de principio** agreement in principle ▸ **acuerdo entre caballeros** gentlemen's agreement ▸ **Acuerdo General sobre Aranceles Aduaneros y Comercio** General Agreement on Tariffs and Trade ▸ **acuerdo marco** framework agreement ▸ **acuerdo prematrimonial** prenuptial agreement ▸ **acuerdo tácito** unspoken agreement, tacit agreement ▸ **acuerdo verbal** verbal agreement
2 • **de ~ a** (*independiente*) OK, all right • **sí, de ~** yes, OK, yes, all right • **cada uno pondremos 40 euros ¿de ~?** we'll each put in 40 euros, OK *o* all right?
b • **estar de ~** to agree, be in agreement (*frm*) • **en eso estamos de ~** we agree on that, we're in agreement on that (*frm*) • **sigo sin estar de ~** I still don't agree • **estoy totalmente de ~ contigo** I totally agree with you • **estoy de ~ con que deberíamos mudarnos de casa** I agree that we should move house
c • **ponerse de ~** to come to an agreement,

reach (an) agreement • **aún no nos hemos puesto de ~** we still haven't come to an agreement, we still haven't reached (an) agreement • **no se ponían de ~ en nada** they couldn't agree on anything
d • de ~ con according to, in accordance with (*frm*) • **todo se hizo de ~ con las reglas** everything was done according to *o* (*frm*) in accordance with the regulations • **de ~ con el artículo 27** as laid down in article 27, in accordance with article 27 (*frm*) • **de ~ con estas fuentes, las dos mujeres fueron secuestradas** according to these sources, the two women were kidnapped • **una casa de ~ con sus necesidades** a house to suit their needs
acuícola ADJ aquatic
acuicultor(a) SM/F fish farmer
acuicultura SF aquaculture
acuidad SF sharpness
acuífero ADJ aquiferous, water-bearing
SM aquifer
acuilmarse ▷ CONJUG 1a VPR (*CAm*) (= *deprimirse*) to get depressed; (= *acobardarse*) to lose one's nerve
acuitadamente ADV sorrowfully, with regret
acuitar ▷ CONJUG 1a VT to afflict, distress, grieve
VPR **acuitarse** to grieve, be grieved (**por** at, by)
acular* ▷ CONJUG 1a VT **1** [+ *caballo*] to back (a against, into)
2 (= *acorralar*) to corner, force into a corner
VI (*And*) to back away
acullá ADV over there, yonder (*liter*)
acullicar ▷ CONJUG 1g VI (*And, Cono Sur*) to chew coca (leaves)
aculturación SF acculturation
aculturar ▷ CONJUG 1a VT to acculturate
acumuchar ▷ CONJUG 1a VT (*Cono Sur*) to pile up, accumulate
acumulación SF (= *acto*) accumulation; (= *reserva*) pile, stock • **una ~ de gas a** build-up of gas
acumulador ADJ accumulative
SM (= *batería*) storage battery; [*de calor*] storage heater
acumular ▷ CONJUG 1a VT [+ *posesiones*] to accumulate; [+ *datos*] to amass, gather
VPR **acumularse** to accumulate, gather, pile up • **se me acumula el trabajo** the work is piling up (on me)
acumulativo ADJ cumulative
acúmulo SM accumulation, build-up
acunar ▷ CONJUG 1a VT to rock, rock to sleep
acuñación SF [*de moneda*] minting; [*de frase*] coining
acuñar ▷ CONJUG 1a VT **1** [+ *moneda*] to mint; [+ *medalla*] to strike; [+ *frase*] to coin; [+ *rueda*] to wedge
2 (*Caribe*) (= *llevar a cabo*) to finish successfully
VPR **acuñarse** (*CAm*) to hit o.s., sustain a blow
acuosidad SF (= *calidad*) wateriness; [*de fruta*] juiciness
acuoso ADJ (= *con agua*) watery; [*fruta*] juicy
acupuntor(a) SM/F acupuncturist
acupuntura SF acupuncture
acupunturista SMF acupuncturist
acurrado ADJ **1** (*Caribe, Méx*) (= *guapo*) handsome
2 (*CAm*) (= *rechoncho*) squat, chubby
acurrucarse ▷ CONJUG 1g VPR to snuggle up, curl up
acusación SF (= *inculpación*) accusation; (*Jur*) (= *cargo*) charge, indictment; (= *acusador*) prosecution • **negar la ~** to deny the charge ▸ **acusación particular** • **la** particular (the counsel for) the prosecution
acusado/a ADJ **1** (*Jur*) accused
2 (= *marcado*) (*gen*) marked, pronounced; [*acento*] strong; [*contraste*] marked, striking; [*característica, rasgo, personalidad*] strong; [*color*] deep
SM/F accused, defendant
acusador(a) ADJ accusing, reproachful • **los letrados ~es** prosecuting counsel • **la parte ~a** the plaintiff
SM/F accuser ▸ **acusador(a) público/a** public prosecutor, procurator fiscal (*Escocia*), prosecuting *o* district attorney (*EEUU*)
acusar ▷ CONJUG 1a VT **1** (= *culpar*) to accuse • **~ a algn de algo** to accuse sb of sth • **nos acusan de racistas** they are accusing us of being racists • **~ a algn de hacer algo** to accuse sb of doing sth • **le acusan de promover la violencia** he is being accused of promoting violence
2 (*Jur*) (= *incriminar*) charge • **~ a algn de algo** to charge sb with sth • **le han acusado de asesinato** he has been charged with murder • **~ a algn de hacer algo** to charge sb with doing sth • **le acusan de malversar fondos** he is being charged with embezzling funds
3 (= *mostrar*) • **sus caras acusaban el cansancio** tiredness showed in their faces • **la empresa acusaba cierta desorganización** the company was showing signs of disorganization
4 (= *registrar*) to pick up, register • **este sismógrafo acusa la menor vibración** this seismometer picks up *o* registers the least vibration
5 (*Correos*) • **~ recibo de algo** to acknowledge receipt of sth
VPR **acusarse 1** (= *confesarse*) to confess • **~se de (haber hecho) algo** to confess to (having done) sth
2 (= *registrarse*) • **mañana se ~á un aumento de las temperaturas** temperatures will rise tomorrow, tomorrow there will be a rise in temperature • **esta deficiencia se acusa aquí claramente** this deficiency is clearly noticeable here, this deficiency shows clearly here

> **ACUSAR**
>
> ▷ *Traducimos* **acusar (de)** *por* **accuse (of)** *en la mayoría de los casos:*
>
> **Me acusó de haber mentido**
> He accused me of lying
> **¿De qué me estás acusando?**
> What are you accusing me of?
>
> ▷ *Traducimos* **acusar (de)** *por* **charge (with)** *cuando se trata de una acusación formal que llevará a la celebración de un juicio:*
>
> **No lo han acusado de ninguno de los cargos**
> He hasn't been charged with anything
> **Hasta ahora, la policía lo ha acusado solamente de uno de los asesinatos**
> So far, the police have only charged him with one of the murders
>
> *El verbo* **indict** *tiene un significado parecido a* **charge**, *pero solo se usa en contextos legales muy especializados.*
>
> *Para otros usos y ejemplos ver la entrada.*

acusativo ADJ, SM accusative
acusatorio ADJ accusatory, accusing
acuse SM ▸ **acuse de recibo** acknowledgement of receipt
acusetas* SMF INV (*And, Cono Sur*) telltale, sneak, tattler (*EEUU**)
acusete* SMF, **acusica*** SMF (*Esp*), **acusique*** SMF telltale, sneak, tattler (*EEUU**)
acusón/ona* ADJ telltale, sneaking
SM/F telltale, sneak, tattler (*EEUU**)
acústica SF acoustics
acústico ADJ acoustic
SM hearing aid
acutí SM (*LAm*) guinea pig
AD SF ABR (*Ven*) = **Acción Democrática**
ADA SF ABR (= **Ayuda del Automovilista**) ≈ AA, ≈ RAC, ≈ AAA (EEUU)
-ada ▷ **Aspects of Word Formation in Spanish 2**
ADAC SM ABR (= **avión de despegue y aterrizaje cortos**) VTOL
adagio SM (= *proverbio*) adage, proverb; (*Mús*) adagio
adalid SM leader, champion
adamado ADJ [*hombre*] effeminate, soft; [*mujer*] elegant, chic; (*pey*) flashy
adamascado ADJ damask
adamascar ▷ CONJUG 1g VT to damask
Adán SM Adam
adán SM (= *sucio*) scruffy fellow; (= *vago*) lazy fellow • MODISMO: • **estar hecho un ~** to be terribly shabby
adaptabilidad SF adaptability, versatility
adaptable ADJ (= *versátil*) adaptable, versatile; (*Tip*) compatible
adaptación SF adaptation
adaptador SM adapter, adaptor ▸ **adaptador universal** universal adapter *o* adaptor
adaptar ▷ CONJUG 1a VT **1** (= *acomodar*) to adapt; (= *encajar*) to fit, make suitable (**para** for); (= *ajustar*) to adjust
2 (*Inform*) to convert (**para** to)
VPR **adaptarse** to adapt (a to) • **saber ~se a las circunstancias** to be able to adapt to the circumstances
adaptativo ADJ adaptive
adaraja SF toothing
adarga SF *oval leather shield*
adarme SM • **ni un ~** not a whit • **no me importa un ~** I couldn't care less • **sin un ~ de educación** with no manners at all • **por ~s** in dribs and drabs
a. de C. ABR (= **antes de Cristo**) BC
adecentar ▷ CONJUG 1a VT to tidy up
VPR **adecentarse** to tidy o.s. up
adecuación SF adaptation
adecuadamente ADV suitably
adecuado ADJ **1** (= *apropiado*) [*actitud, respuesta, ropa, tratamiento*] appropriate; [*documento, requisito*] appropriate, relevant • **los medios ~s para resolver el problema** the appropriate means to solve the problem • **es el traje más ~ para la primavera** it is the most suitable *o* appropriate outfit for spring • **exigen un uso ~ de los recursos** they are demanding that resources be used appropriately *o* properly • **una actitud poco adecuada** an inappropriate attitude • **estar en el momento y el lugar ~s** to be in the right place at the right time • **esta no es la pieza adecuada** this is not the right part • **el hombre ~ para el puesto** the right man for the job • **lo más ~ sería ...** the best thing *o* the most appropriate thing would be to ...
2 (= *acorde*) • **~ a algo: un precio ~ a mis posibilidades** a price within my budget *o* reach
3 (= *suficiente*) [*dinero, tiempo*] sufficient
adecuamiento SM adjustment
adecuar ▷ CONJUG 1d VT to adapt • **han adecuado el planteamiento a la nueva situación** they've adapted their approach to the new situation *o* in line with the new

a

situation • **adecuó su charla a la edad de su audiencia** he adapted *o* tailored his speech to suit the age of the audience • **han adecuado los impuestos a la directiva europea** taxes have been adjusted in line with the European directive
VPR **adecuarse 1** (= *adaptarse*) to adapt • **no se adecuó a las nuevas circunstancias** he failed to adapt to the new circumstances • **tenemos que ~nos a los avances técnicos** we have to keep up with *o* keep abreast of technical progress
2 (*frm*) (= *ser apropiado*) to be suitable *o* right for sth • **este producto no se adecúa a lo que busco** this product is not suitable *o* right for what I want

adefesiero* ADJ (*And, Cono Sur*) (= *cómico*) comic, ridiculous; (= *torpe*) clumsy; (*en el vestido*) overdressed, camp*

adefesio SM **1** (= *persona rara*) queer bird, oddball*; (= *persona fea*) disaster*; (= *objeto feo*) monstrosity; (= *ropa fea*) outlandish attire, ridiculous attire • **estaba hecha un ~** she looked a sight
2 (= *disparate*) piece of nonsense, absurdity • **hablar ~s** to talk nonsense

adefesioso ADJ (*And, Cono Sur*) nonsensical, ridiculous

adehala SF (= *propina*) gratuity, tip; [*de sueldo*] bonus

a. de J.C. ABR (= **antes de Jesucristo**) BC

adela SF (*CAm*) bittersweet

adelaida SF (*Méx*) fuchsia

adelantado/a ADJ **1** (= *avanzado*) [*país, método, trabajo*] advanced • **las obras están ya muy adelantadas** the work is now very advanced • **lleva la tesis bastante adelantada** she's quite well ahead with her thesis • **estar** *o* **ir ~ en los estudios** to be well ahead in one's studies • **sus ideas eran bastante adelantadas entonces** his ideas were quite ahead of their time
2 [*reloj*] fast • **el despertador va unos minutos ~** the alarm clock is a few minutes fast
3 (= *precoz*) [*persona*] advanced, ahead of one's age • **está muy ~ para su edad** he's very advanced for his age, he's well ahead of his age
4 (= *prematuro*) [*cosecha, elecciones*] early • **es un regalo ~ de tu cumpleaños** it's an early birthday present
5 (= *de antemano*) [*pago*] advance • **por ~** in advance • **hay que sacar el billete por ~** you need to buy the ticket in advance
6 (= *atrevido*) forward, bold
7 (*Dep*) (*en una posición*) • **vio al portero ~ y disparó** he saw the goalkeeper out of goal and took a shot • **un pase ~** a forward pass
SM/F **1** (= *pionero*) pioneer • **ser un ~ en algo** to be a pioneer in sth
2 (*Hist*) governor (*of a frontier province*)

adelantamiento SM **1** (*Aut*) overtaking, passing (*esp EEUU*) • **realizó un ~ en una curva peligrosa** he overtook on a dangerous bend
2 (= *en el tiempo*) • **el ~ de las elecciones no ha sido posible** it has not been possible to bring forward the elections
3 (= *progreso*) progress

adelantar ▷ CONJUG 1a VT **1** (= *pasar por delante*) [+ *vehículo, rival*] to overtake, pass (*esp EEUU*) • **adelantó al resto del pelotón** he overtook the rest of the pack • **la oposición ha adelantado al gobierno en las encuestas** the opposition has overtaken the government in the polls
2 (= *mover de sitio*) [+ *ficha, meta*] to move forward • **~on la meta 300 metros** they moved the finishing line 300 metres forward
3 (*en el tiempo*) **a** [+ *fecha, acto*] to bring forward • **no van a ~ las elecciones** there is not going to be an early election, the election is not going to be brought forward • **no adelantemos acontecimientos** let's not get ahead of ourselves, let's not jump the gun*
b [+ *reloj*] to put forward • **hoy se adelantan los relojes una hora** today the clocks go forward (by) one hour
4 (= *conseguir*) • **no adelantamos nada con decírselo** we'll get nowhere by telling him • **¿qué adelantas con enfadarte?** getting upset won't get you anywhere
5 (= *anticipar*) **a** [+ *sueldo, dinero*] to pay in advance, advance • **me ~on parte de la paga de Navidad** they paid me some of my Christmas bonus in advance, they advanced me some of my Christmas bonus • **el dinero es para ~ pagas a las tropas** the money is for making advance payments to the troops
b [+ *información*] to disclose, reveal • **ha adelantado las líneas generales de su plan** he has disclosed *o* revealed the outline of his plan • **como adelantó este periódico, ha aumentado la tasa de paro** as this newspaper revealed, the unemployment rate has gone up • **lo único que puedo ~te es que se trata de una buena noticia** the only thing that I can tell you now is that it is good news
6 (= *apresurar*) [+ *trabajo*] to speed up • **yo voy poniendo la mesa para ~ trabajo** I'll start laying the table to speed things up • **~ el paso** to speed up, quicken one's pace
7 (*Dep*) [+ *balón*] to pass forward
VI **1** (*Aut*) to overtake, pass (*EEUU*) • **"prohibido ~"** "no overtaking", "no passing" (*EEUU*)
2 (= *avanzar*) to make progress • **por el atajo ~emos más** we'll make better progress if we take the shortcut • **llevamos un mes negociando sin ~ nada** we have spent a month negotiating without making any progress *o* headway
3 [*reloj*] to gain time • **ese reloj adelanta dos minutos diarios** that clock gains two minutes a day
VPR **adelantarse 1** (= *avanzar*) to go forward, move forward • **se adelantó para darle dos besos** she stepped *o* went *o* moved forward to kiss him • **nos adelantamos a su encuentro** we went forward to meet him • **se adelantó a codazos** she elbowed her way forward
2 (= *ir por delante*) to go ahead • **me ~é a inspeccionar el camino** I'll go ahead and check the way • **~se en el marcador** (*Dep*) to go ahead
3 (= *anticiparse*) [*cosecha, primavera*] to come early • **el calor se ha adelantado este año** the hot weather has come early this year
4 • **~se a a** [+ *deseos, preguntas*] to anticipate • **se adelantó a posibles preguntas** he anticipated possible questions
b [+ *persona*] (= *hacer antes*) to get in before; (= *dejar atrás*) to get ahead of • **yo iba a comprarlo pero alguien se me adelantó** I was going to buy it but someone beat me to it *o* got in before me • **un grupo de 19 corredores se adelantó al pelotón** a group of 19 runners got ahead of the pack • **es un diseñador que se adelanta a su tiempo** as a designer he is ahead of his time
5 [*reloj*] to gain time

adelante ADV **1** (*indicando dirección*) forward • **tráelo para ~** bring it forward • **echado para ~** (= *inclinado*) leaning forward; (= *seguro de sí mismo*) self-assured • **hacia ~** forward • **el espejo estaba inclinado hacia ~** the mirror was tilted forward • **un paso (hacia) ~** a step forward • **mirar hacia ~** to look ahead • **llevar ~ un proyecto** to carry out a project • **sacar ~ una empresa/un espectáculo** to get a company/a show off the ground • **sacar ~ a los hijos** to give one's children a good education in life • **salir ~** [*proyecto, propuesta*] to go ahead • **hay que trabajar mucho para salir ~** you have to work hard to get on (in life) • **si trabajamos juntos saldremos ~** if we all work together we'll get through this • **la orquesta no podrá salir ~ sin subvenciones** the orchestra won't be able to survive without subsidies • **seguir ~** to go on • **tuvimos una avería y no pudimos seguir ~** we broke down and couldn't go on any further • **mis hijos me dan fuerzas para seguir ~** my children give me the strength to keep going • **decidieron seguir ~ con sus proyectos** they decided to go ahead *o* carry on with their plans • **antes de seguir ~, ¿hay alguna pregunta?** before I go on, are there any questions?; ▷ **paso**
2 (*indicando posición*) • **la fila dos es demasiado ~** row two is too near the front *o* too far forward • **está más ~** it's further on • **la parte de ~** the front • **más ~** (*en una sala*) further forward; (*en texto*) below • **prefiero sentarme más ~** I'd rather sit further forward • **véase nota más ~** see note below
3 (*indicando tiempo*) • **en ~** from now on, in future • **en ~ las reuniones serán cada dos años** from now on *o* in future the meetings will be every two years • **desde el 13 de agosto en ~** from 13 August (onwards) • **de ahora en ~** • **de aquí en ~** from now on • **de hoy en ~** as from today • **más ~** later • **volveré a referirme al tema más ~** I will refer to the subject again later (on) • **decidimos dejar la reunión para más ~** we decided to leave the meeting till a later date *o* till later
4 (*indicando cantidad*) • **en ~** upwards • **de 50 euros en ~** from 50 euros (upwards) • **para niños de tres años en ~** for children of three and upwards
5 • **¡adelante!** (*autorizando a entrar*) come in!; (*animando a seguir*) go on!, carry on!; (*Mil*) forward!
6 • **~ de** (*LAm*) in front of • **se sentó ~ de mí** he sat in front of me

adelanto SM **1** (= *progreso*) **a** (= *acción*) advancement; (= *resultado*) step forward • **esa ley supone un gran ~** that law marks a great step forward • **eso representa un ~ sobre el método actual** that is an improvement on the current method
b adelantos (= *descubrimientos*) advances • **los ~s de la ciencia** the advances of science • **una cocina con los últimos ~s** a kitchen with the latest mod cons*
2 (*en tiempo*) • **piden el ~ de las elecciones** they are asking for the elections to be brought forward • **han conseguido el ~ de la edad de jubilación** they have managed to get the retirement age lowered • **el tren llegó con un ~ de 15 minutos** the train arrived 15 minutes early • **de ~:** • **con una hora de ~** an hour early • **su agenda está repleta con seis meses de ~** her diary is full six months ahead • **el reloj lleva diez minutos de ~** the clock is ten minutes fast • **llevaba tres minutos de ~ sobre el segundo corredor** he had a three-minute lead over the runner in second place
3 [*de información*] • **facilitaron un ~ de los resultados** they released some of the results in advance • **el artículo es solo un ~ de su próximo libro** the article is just a taster of

a

his latest book
4 [*de dinero*] (= *anticipo*) advance; (= *depósito*) deposit • **solicitó un ~ de quinientos euros** he asked for an advance of five hundred euros • **hay que hacer un ~ en metálico** it is necessary to make a cash deposit
5 (*Ajedrez*) (= *movimiento*) forward move
adelfa (SF) rosebay, oleander
adelgazador (ADJ) slimming, weight-reducing
adelgazamiento (SM) slimming
adelgazante (ADJ) slimming, weight-reducing
(SM) slimming product
adelgazar ▹ CONJUG 1f (VT) **1** (= *reducir el grosor*) to make thin, make slender; [+ *kilos*] to lose, take off; [+ *persona, figura*] to slim, reduce, slenderize (*EEUU*); [+ *palo*] to pare, whittle; [+ *punta*] to sharpen; [+ *voz*] to raise the pitch of
2 (*fig*) (= *purificar*) to purify, refine; [+ *entendimiento*] to sharpen
(VI) (= *perder peso*) to grow thin; (*con régimen*) to slim, lose weight
Adelpha [a'ðelfa] (SF ABR) (*Esp*) = **Asociación de Defensa Ecológica y del Patrimonio Histórico-artístico**
ademán (SM) **1** [*de mano*] gesture, movement; (= *postura*) posture, position • **en ~ de hacer algo** as if to do sth, getting ready to do sth • **hacer ~ de hacer** to make as if to do, make a move to do • **hacer ademanes** to gesture, make signs
2 ademanes (= *modales*) manners
además (ADV) **1** (= *también*) (*para añadir otro elemento*) also, in addition (*frm*); (*para reforzar un comentario*) what's more, besides, furthermore (*frm*), moreover (*frm*) • **hay, ~, pistas de tenis y campos de golf** there are also tennis courts and golf courses, in addition, there are tennis courts and golf courses (*frm*) • **y ~, me dijo que no me quería** and what's more *o* and besides, he told me he didn't love me • **estoy cansado y, ~, no me apetece** I'm tired, and what's more *o* besides, I don't feel like it • **quiero decirle, ~, que esa no era mi intención** furthermore *o* moreover I want to tell you that that was not my intention (*frm*)
2 • **~ de** as well as, besides, in addition to (*frm*) • **~ del alojamiento, necesitamos la comida** as well as *o* besides somewhere to stay we need food • **~ de una fotocopia, se requiere el documento original** as well as *o* (*frm*) in addition to a photocopy, we require the original document • **el examen fue largo, ~ de difícil** the exam was long as well as difficult • **~ de que** (+ *indic*) as well as (+ *ger*) • **~ de que estaba cansado, no había comido** as well as being tired he hadn't eaten
Adén (SM) Aden
ADENA (SF ABR) (*Esp*) = **Asociación para la Defensa de la Naturaleza**
adenoideo (ADJ) adenoidal
adentellar ▹ CONJUG 1a (VT) to sink one's teeth into
adentrarse ▹ CONJUG 1a (VPR) • **~ en** to go into, get inside; (= *penetrar*) to penetrate into • **~ en la selva** to go deep(er) into the forest • **~ en sí mismo** to become lost in thought
adentro (ADV) **1** (*esp LAm*) = **dentro**
2 • **mar ~** out at sea, out to sea • **tierra ~** inland • **¡adentro!** come in!
(PREP) • **~ de** (*LAm*) (= *dentro de*) inside • **~ mío** inside myself
(SM) **1** (*Cono Sur*) indoors, inside the house
2 adentros (*de persona*) innermost being (*sing*), innermost thoughts • **dijo para sus ~s** he said to himself • **reírse para sus ~s** to laugh inwardly
adepto/a (SM/F) (= *partidario*) follower, supporter; (*Rel*) adept, initiate; (*LAm**) (= *drogadicto*) drug addict
aderezado (ADJ) favourable, favorable (*EEUU*), suitable
aderezar ▹ CONJUG 1f (VT) **1** (= *preparar*) to prepare, get ready; (= *vestir*) to dress up; (= *adornar*) to embellish, adorn
2 (*Culin*) (= *sazonar*) to season, garnish; [+ *ensalada*] to dress; [+ *bebidas*] to prepare, mix; [+ *vinos*] to blend
3 [+ *máquina*] to repair; [+ *tela*] to gum, size
(VPR) **aderezarse** (= *prepararse*) to dress up, get ready
aderezo (SM) **1** (= *preparación*) preparation; (= *adorno*) decoration • **dar el ~ definitivo a algo** to put the finishing touch to sth
▸ **aderezo de casa** household equipment
▸ **aderezo de mesa** dinner service
2 (*Culin*) (= *aliño*) seasoning, dressing; (*Cos*) adornment; (= *reparación*) repair
3 (= *joyas*) set of jewels ▸ **aderezo de diamantes** set of diamonds
adeudado (ADJ) in debt
adeudar ▹ CONJUG 1a (VT) [+ *dinero*] to owe; [+ *impuestos*] to be liable for • **~ una suma en una cuenta** to debit an account for a sum
(VI) (= *emparentar*) to become related by marriage
(VPR) **adeudarse** to run into debt
adeudo (SM) (= *deuda*) debt; (*en aduana*) customs duty; (*en cuenta*) debit, charge
adeveras (*LAm*) • **de ~** (ADV) = **veras**
ADEVIDA (SF ABR) (*Esp*) = **Asociación en Defensa de la Vida Humana**
a.D.g. (ABR) (= **a Dios gracias**) D.G.
adherencia (SF) **1** (= *calidad*) adherence; (= *acción*) adhesion
2 (= *vínculo*) bond, connection
3 (*Aut*) road holding
4 • **tener ~s** to have connections
adherente (ADJ) adhesive, sticky • **~ a** (*fig*) adhering to
adherido/a (SM/F) adherent, follower
adherir ▹ CONJUG 3i (VT) (= *pegar*) to adhere, stick (**a** to)
(VI), (VPR) **adherirse** (= *pegarse*) to adhere, stick (**a** to) • **~se a** (= *seguir*) to follow; (= *afiliarse*) to join, become a member of
adhesión (SF) (*Téc*) adhesion; (= *apoyo*) adherence, support; (= *afiliación*) membership
adhesividad (SF) adhesiveness
adhesivo (ADJ) adhesive, sticky
(SM) adhesive
adicción (SF) addiction
adición (SF) **1** (*Mat*) addition; (= *sumar*) adding, adding up
2 (*Jur*) acceptance
3 (*Cono Sur*) (= *cuenta*) bill, check (*EEUU*)
adicional (ADJ) (= *complementario*) additional, extra; (*Inform*) add-on
adicionalidad (SF) additionality
adicionar ▹ CONJUG 1a (VT) (= *añadir*) to add (**a** to); (*Mat*) (= *sumar*) to add, add up
adictivo (ADJ) addictive
adicto/a (ADJ) **1** • **~ a algo** addicted to sth • **es ~ a la heroína** he's addicted to heroin, he's a heroin addict • **soy ~ a las ostras** I'm addicted to oysters • **es ~ al trabajo** he's a workaholic
2 (= *fiel*) [*admirador, amigo*] devoted • **un público ~ llenaba la sala** a devoted audience filled the hall
3 (= *partidario*) loyal • **la prensa adicta al Gobierno** sections of the press loyal to *o* supportive of the government • **las personas adictas al régimen franquista** supporters of the Franco regime
(SM/F) **1** (*a la droga, tele*) addict
2 (= *seguidor*) follower, supporter; (*LAm*) (*Dep*) supporter, fan
adiestrado (ADJ) trained
adiestrador(a) (SM/F) trainer
adiestramiento (SM) [*de animal*] training; (*Mil, Dep*) drilling, practice ▸ **adiestramiento con armas** weapons training
adiestrar ▹ CONJUG 1a (VT) [+ *animal*] to train; (*Mil*) (= *entrenar*) to drill; (= *guiar*) to guide, lead
(VPR) **adiestrarse** to practise, practice (*EEUU*), train o.s. • **~se a hacer** to teach o.s. to do
adifés (ADV) **1** (*CAm*) (= *con dificultad*) with difficulty
2 (*Caribe*) (= *a propósito*) on purpose, deliberately
adinerado (ADJ) wealthy, well-off
adinerarse ▹ CONJUG 1a (VPR) to get rich
ad infinitum (ADV) ad infinitum
adiós (EXCL) (*al irse*) goodbye!; (*al saludar*) hello! • MODISMO: • **¡~ Madrid, que te quedas sin gente!** good riddance!
(SM) goodbye, farewell • **decir(se) los adioses** to say one's farewells • **ir a decir ~ a algn** to go to say goodbye to sb • **decir ~ a algo** (= *renunciar*) to wave sth goodbye, give sth up
adiosito* (EXCL) (*esp LAm*) bye-bye!, cheerio!
adiposidad (SF), **adiposis** (SF INV) adiposity
adiposo (ADJ) adipose, fat
aditamento (SM) (= *complemento*) complement, addition; (= *accesorio*) accessory
aditivo (SM) additive ▸ **aditivo alimenticio** food additive
adivinación (SF) (= *predicción*) prophecy, divination; (= *conjeturas*) guessing; (= *solución*) solving • **por ~** by guesswork
▸ **adivinación de pensamientos** mind-reading
adivinador(a) (SM/F) fortune teller
adivinanza (SF) riddle, conundrum
adivinar ▹ CONJUG 1a (VT) **1** (= *acertar*) [+ *acertijo, adivinanza*] to solve • **¡adivina quién ha llamado!** guess who called! • **¡adivina por qué no vino!** guess why he didn't come! • **~ el pensamiento a algn** to read sb's mind *o* thoughts • **~ las intenciones a algn** to second-guess sb
2 (= *predecir*) to foresee • **~ el futuro** to foresee the future • **es fácil ~ lo que ocurrirá** it's easy to foresee *o* see what will happen
3 (= *entrever*) (*frm*) • **a lo lejos adivinó la figura de un hombre** in the distance he could just make out the figure of a man • **su primera novela deja ~ su genio** her first novel gives a glimpse of *o* hints at her genius
(VPR) **adivinarse** (*frm*) • **su silueta se adivinaba en la ventana** one could make out her silhouette in the window, her silhouette was just visible in the window • **en este texto se adivina su sensibilidad** in this text one gets a glimpse of his sensitivity • **en los parques ya se adivina la primavera** in the parks you can see the first signs of spring
adivino/a (SM/F) fortune-teller
adj. (ABR) (= **adjunto**) enc, encl
adjetivar ▹ CONJUG 1a (VT) (*Gram*) (= *dar valor de adjetivo*) to use adjectivally, use attributively; (= *modificar*) to modify
adjetivo (ADJ) adjectival
(SM) adjective
adjudicación (SF) **1** [*de premio*] award; (*en subasta*) knocking down, sale
2 (*Méx*) (*Jur*) adjudication, award
adjudicado (EXCL) sold!
adjudicador(a) (ADJ) adjudicating
(SM/F) adjudicator

adjudicar ▸ CONJUG 1g VT to award (a to) • **~ algo al mejor postor** to knock sth down to the highest bidder
VPR **adjudicarse** • **~se algo** to appropriate sth • **~se el premio** to win (the prize)

adjudicatorio/a SM/F (= *premiado*) award winner; (*en subasta*) successful bidder

adjuntar ▸ CONJUG 1a VT (= *incluir*) to append, attach; (*en carta*) to enclose • **adjuntamos factura** we enclose our account

adjunto/a ADJ **1** [*información*] attached • **rellene el formulario ~** please complete the attached form • **un órgano consultivo ~ a la Presidencia** a consultative body attached to the presidency • **en el documento ~ a esta carta** in the enclosed document
2 (= *ayudante*) assistant • **profesor(a) ~/a** assistant lecturer • **director(a) ~/a** assistant director
ADV (*en carta*) • **remitir** *o* **enviar algo ~** to enclose sth • **le envío ~ mi CV** I enclose my CV, please find enclosed my CV
SM/F **1** (= *ayudante*) • **el ~ al** *o* **del director** the assistant to the director, the director's assistant
2 (*en carta*) enclosure • **~s: un folleto informativo y un contrato** enc: one information leaflet and one contract
3 (*Ling*) adjunct

adlátere SM (= *compañero*) companion, associate; (*pey*) (= *subordinado*) minion, minder

adminículo SM accessory, gadget; **adminículos** emergency kit

administración SF **1** (= *organización*) administration; (= *dirección*) management, running • **en ~** in trust • **obras en ~** books handled by us, books for which we are agents ▸ **Administración de Correos** General Post Office ▸ **administración empresarial, administración de empresas** (= *curso*) business administration, business management ▸ **administración de lotería** lottery outlet ▸ **administración financiera** financial management ▸ **administración militar** commissariat ▸ **administración pública** civil service, public administration (*EEUU*)
2 (*Pol*) government, administration ▸ **administración central** central government ▸ **administración territorial** local government
3 (= *oficina*) headquarters (*pl*), central office; (*And*) [*de hotel*] reception
4 (*Caribe*) (*Rel*) extreme unction

administrador(a) SM/F [*de bienes, distrito*] administrator; [*de organización, empresa*] manager; [*de tierras*] agent, land agent • **es buena ~a de la casa** she uses the housekeeping money very efficiently ▸ **administrador(a) de aduanas** chief customs officer, collector of customs ▸ **administrador(a) de correos** postmaster/postmistress ▸ **administrador(a) de fincas** land agent ▸ **administrador(a) de redes** system administrator ▸ **administrador(a) judicial** (*Méx*) receiver

administrar ▸ CONJUG 1a VT **1** (= *organizar*) to administer; (*Com*) to manage, run
2 [+ *justicia, sacramento*] to administer
VPR **administrarse** to manage one's own affairs

administrativo/a ADJ administrative; (*Com*) managerial; (= *del gobierno*) of the government, of the administration
SM/F (= *funcionario*) clerk, office worker; (= *encargado*) administrator, administrative officer

admirable ADJ admirable

admirablemente ADV admirably

admiración SF **1** (= *aprecio*) admiration • **es conocida su ~ por el rey** his admiration for the king is well known • **un gesto digno de ~** an admirable gesture • **causar** *o* **despertar ~** to be (much) admired • **ganarse la ~ de algn** to win sb's admiration • **sentir** *o* **tener ~ a** *o* **por algn** to admire sb • **siento** *o* **tengo mucha ~ por él** I admire him greatly *o* very much • **le tengo mucha ~** I admire him greatly *o* very much
2 (= *asombro*) amazement • **ante la ~ de todos** to everyone's amazement
3 (*Tip*) exclamation mark

admirador(a) SM/F admirer

admirar ▸ CONJUG 1a VT **1** (= *estimar*) to admire • **~ algo/a algn** to admire sth/sb • **lo admiran por su coraje** he is admired for his courage • **sus progresos son de ~** his progress is admirable
2 (= *contemplar*) [+ *cuadro, panorama*] to admire • **admiramos el paisaje desde la cima** we admired the scenery from the top of the hill
3 (*frm*) (= *asombrar*) to amaze, astonish • **su descaro admiró a todos** everyone was amazed *o* astonished at *o* by his nerve • **me admira tu ingenuidad** your ingenuity amazes *o* astonishes me • **no es de ~ que haya triunfado** it's hardly surprising that she has won
VPR **admirarse** (*frm*) (= *asombrarse*) to be amazed, be astonished

admirativo ADJ admiring, full of admiration

admisibilidad SF admissibility

admisible ADJ [*conducta, crítica, propuesta*] acceptable, admissible (*frm*); [*excusa, nivel*] acceptable • **no es ~ que continúe esta situación** we cannot allow this situation to continue

admisión SF **1** (= *entrada*) (*en club, organización*) admission; (*en universidad*) acceptance • **"reservado el derecho de admisión"** "the management reserves the right to refuse admission" • **se ha ampliado el plazo de ~ de solicitudes** the closing date for applications has been extended • **las condiciones de ~ al concurso** the conditions of entry to the competition • **acto de ~** (*Jur*) validation (*of a suit*) • **prueba de ~** entrance examination
2 [*de error*] acceptance
3 (*Mec*) intake, inlet • **válvula de ~** inlet valve ▸ **admisión de aire** air intake

admitido ADJ **1** [*candidato, alumno*] admitted
2 [*opinión, teoría, vocablo*] accepted
3 [*producto*] permitted

admitir ▸ CONJUG 3a VT **1** (= *dejar entrar*) (*en organización*) to admit, accept; (*en hospital*) to admit • **el club no admite mujeres** the club does not admit *o* accept women members • **los extranjeros no son admitidos en la comunidad** foreigners are not accepted into the community • **fue admitido en la universidad** he was accepted for university
2 (= *aceptar*) [+ *opinión, regalo*] to accept • **se admiten apuestas** all bets accepted • **¿ha admitido la Academia esa palabra?** has the Academy accepted that word? • **"se admiten tarjetas de crédito"** "we take *o* accept credit cards" • **"no se admiten propinas"** "no tipping" • **el juez admitió la demanda a trámite** the judge granted leave to file a lawsuit
3 (= *permitir*) to allow, permit (*frm*) • **el contenido de plomo admitido en las gasolinas** the permitted lead content of petrol, the amount of lead allowed *o* permitted (*frm*) in petrol • **mi presupuesto no admite grandes despilfarros** my budget won't run to *o* does not allow extravagances • **este asunto no admite medias tintas** there's no room for half measures here • **la calidad de este vino no admite comparaciones** this is a wine of incomparable quality • **esto no admite demora** this cannot be put off, this will brook no delay (*frm*) • **no admite discusión** it is indisputable • **no admite duda(s)** it leaves no room for doubt • **no admite otra explicación** it allows of no other explanation
4 (= *reconocer*) [+ *culpabilidad, error*] to admit • **admito que la culpa ha sido mía** I admit that it was my fault • **admitió que había sido testigo** he admitted being a witness • **hay que ~ que no hay nada mejor** it has to be said that there's nothing better
5 (= *tener cabida para*) to hold • **la sala admite 500 personas** the hall holds 500 people

admón. ABR (= **administración**) admin

admonición SF warning ▸ **admonición escrita** written warning ▸ **admonición oral** verbal warning

admonitorio ADJ warning (*antes de s*)

ADN SM ABR (= **ácido desoxirribonucleico**) DNA • **prueba del ADN** DNA test
SF ABR (*Bol*) = **Acción Democrática Nacionalista**

adnominal ADJ, SM adnominal

-ado ▸ **Aspects of Word Formation in Spanish 2**

adobado SM pickled pork

adobar ▸ CONJUG 1a VT (= *preparar*) to prepare, dress; (= *cocinar*) to cook; [+ *carne*] to season, pickle; [+ *pieles*] to tan; [+ *narración*] to twist

adobe SM **1** (= *tabique*) adobe, sun-dried brick
2 (*Cono Sur*) (*hum*) (= *pie*) big foot
3 • **descansar haciendo ~s** (*Méx*) to moonlight, do work on the side

adobera SF **1** (*para ladrillos*) mould *o* (*EEUU*) mold for making adobes
2 (*Cono Sur, Méx**) (= *queso*) brick-shaped cheese; (= *molde*) cheese mould, cheese mold (*EEUU*)
3 (*Cono Sur*) (*hum*) (= *pie*) big foot

adobo SM **1** (= *preparación*) preparation, dressing; [*de pieles*] tanning
2 (= *salsa*) pickle, sauce; (*Méx*) (*picante*) red chilli sauce; (*para pieles*) tanning mixture

adocenado ADJ common-or-garden*

adocenarse ▸ CONJUG 1a VPR **1** (= *hacerse común*) to become commonplace
2 (= *decaer*) to become mediocre
3 (= *estancarse*) to remain stagnant, become fossilized

adoctrinación SF indoctrination

adoctrinador ADJ indoctrinating, indoctrinatory

adoctrinamiento SM indoctrination

adoctrinar ▸ CONJUG 1a VT to indoctrinate (en with)

adolecer ▸ CONJUG 2d VI • **~ de** (*Med*) to be ill with; (*fig*) to suffer from

adolescencia SF adolescence

adolescente ADJ adolescent
SMF (*Med*) adolescent; (= *joven*) teenager, teen (*EEUU**)

Adolfo SM Adolphus, Adolph, Adolf

adolorido ADJ (*LAm*) = **dolorido**

adonde CONJ (*esp LAm*) where

adónde (*esp LAm*) ADV INTERROG where?
CONJ where

adondequiera ADV wherever

Adonis SM Adonis • **es un ~** he's gorgeous*

adopción SF **1** [*de niño*] adoption

2 [*de medidas, decisiones*] • **es necesaria la ~ de medidas contra la crisis** we need to take *o* adopt measures against the crisis • **consiguió la ~ de un acuerdo** he managed to get an agreement adopted
3 [*de nacionalidad*] adoption, taking • **es español de ~** he's Spanish by adoption
adoptado/a (ADJ) adopted
(SM/F) adopted child
adoptante (ADJ) adoptive
(SMF) adoptive parent
adoptar ▹ CONJUG 1a (VT) **1** [+ *niño*] to adopt • **lo adoptó como hijo** she adopted him as her son
2 (= *tomar*) [+ *medida, decisión, postura, actitud*] to take; [+ *papel*] to take on • **~ una postura crítica frente al gobierno** to take a critical stance towards the government • **han adoptado el papel de víctimas** they have taken on the role of victims • **en la reunión no se adoptó ningún acuerdo concreto** nothing definite was agreed on in the meeting
3 [+ *postura física*] • **durante el sueño adopta una mala postura** he sleeps in a bad position • **deberías ~ una postura mejor al sentarte** you should sit better *o* with a better posture • **adoptó una postura provocativa con el cigarrillo** she struck a provocative pose with her cigarette
4 (= *empezar a usar*) [+ *nombre, nacionalidad*] to take, adopt; [+ *costumbres*] to adopt; [+ *sistema*] to adopt, introduce
adoptivo (ADJ) [*padres*] adoptive; [*hijo*] adopted • **patria adoptiva** country of adoption • **hijo ~ de la ciudad** honorary citizen
adoquín (SM) **1** (*para pavimentar*) paving stone, flagstone, cobble
2* (= *tonto*) idiot, clod
adoquinado (SM) paving, cobbles, flagstones
adoquinar ▹ CONJUG 1a (VT) to pave, cobble
adorable (ADJ) adorable
adoración (SF) adoration, worship • **una mirada llena de ~** an adoring look
▸ **Adoración de los Reyes** Epiphany
adorador (ADJ) adoring
adorar ▹ CONJUG 1a (VT) to adore, worship
adormecedor (ADJ) (= *soporífero*) that sends one to sleep, soporific; [*droga*] sedative; [*música, tono*] lulling, dreamy
adormecer ▹ CONJUG 2d (VT) (= *dar sueño*) to make sleepy, send to sleep; (= *sosegar*) to calm, lull
(VPR) **adormecerse 1** (= *amodorrarse*) to become sleepy, become drowsy; (= *dormirse*) to fall asleep, go to sleep; [*pierna, mano*] to go numb
2 • **~se en** (*fig*) to persist in
adormecido (ADJ) [*persona*] sleepy, drowsy; (= *aletargado*) inactive; [*miembro*] numb
adormecimiento (SM) (= *soñolencia*) sleepiness, drowsiness; [*de un miembro*] numbness
adormidera (SF) poppy
adormilado (ADJ) drowsy, half asleep
adormilarse ▹ CONJUG 1a (VPR), **adormitarse** ▹ CONJUG 1a (VPR) to doze
adornado (ADJ) • **~ con** [*habitación*] decorated with
adornar ▹ CONJUG 1a (VT) **1** (= *decorar*) to adorn, decorate (**de** with); (*Cos*) to trim (**de** with); (*Culin*) to garnish (**de** with)
2 [+ *persona*] (= *dotar*) to endow, bless (**de** with) • **le adornan mil virtudes** he is blessed with every virtue
adornista (SMF) decorator
adorno (SM) **1** (= *objeto*) ornament • **una casa llena de ~s** a house full of ornaments
▸ **adornos de navidad** Christmas decorations
2 (= *decoración*) ornamentation, adornment • **un estilo literario sin ~ superfluo** a literary style with no superfluous ornamentation *o* adornment • **de ~** decorative • **macetas de ~** decorative plant pots • **no se puede comer, está de ~** you can't eat it, it's just for decoration • **no funciona, está** *o* **es de ~** it doesn't work, it's just for show
3 (*Cos*) trim, trimming
4 (*Culin*) garnish
adosado (ADJ) • **casa adosada • chalet ~** semi-detached house, duplex (*EEUU*)
(SM) semi-detached house, duplex (*EEUU*)
adosar ▹ CONJUG 1a (VT) **1** • **~ algo a una pared** to lean sth against a wall, place sth with its back against a wall
2 (*LAm*) (= *juntar*) to join firmly; (= *adjuntar*) to attach, enclose (*with a letter*)
adquirido (ADJ) • **mal ~** ill-gotten
adquiriente (SMF) purchaser
adquirir ▹ CONJUG 3i (VT) **1** (= *comprar*) [+ *vivienda, billete*] to purchase; (*Econ*) [+ *derechos, acciones, empresa*] to acquire, purchase • **pueden ~se en cualquier tienda especializada** they are available in any specialist shop
2 (= *conseguir*) [+ *cultura, conocimientos, dinero*] to acquire; [+ *fama*] to gain, achieve • **viajando adquirió una gran experiencia** she gained great experience travelling • **ha adquirido renombre con una biografía de Stalin** he became renowned for his biography of Stalin
3 (= *adoptar*) [+ *costumbre*] to adopt; [+ *carácter, identidad*] to take on, acquire; [+ *nacionalidad*] to acquire, obtain; [+ *compromiso*] to undertake; [+ *color*] to take on • **adquirieron las costumbres locales** they adopted the local customs • **el problema adquirió proporciones de crisis** the problem took on *o* acquired crisis proportions • **la palabra "enchufe" adquirió el sentido que todos conocemos** the word "enchufe" took on *o* acquired the sense we are all familiar with • **deberían cumplir los compromisos adquiridos** they should fulfil the commitments they have undertaken • **el cielo adquirió un color rosado** the sky took on a pinkish colour • **el partido comenzó a ~ importancia** the party began to grow in importance • **hay que impedir que esas ideas adquieran fuerza** we have to prevent these ideas gaining a hold
adquisición (SF) **1** (= *compra*) acquisition, purchase • **he hecho unas nuevas adquisiciones** I've made some new acquisitions *o* purchases • **una casa de reciente ~** a newly-purchased house; ▹ **oferta**
2 (= *artículo comprado*) acquisition • **una de las mejores adquisiciones del museo** one of the museum's finest acquisitions • **este televisor ha sido una buena ~** the television has been a good buy
3 (= *persona*) acquisition • **la última ~ del Atlético** Atlético's latest signing *o* acquisition • **la cocinera ha sido una auténtica ~*** the cook is a real find*
4 [*de conocimientos, datos*] acquisition • **problemas en la ~ de un idioma extranjero** problems in foreign language acquisition
5 [*de costumbres*] adoption
adquisidor(a) (SM/F) buyer, purchaser
adquisitivo (ADJ) acquisitive • **poder ~ • valor ~** purchasing power
adquisividad (SF) acquisitiveness
adral (SM) rail, sideboard (*of a cart etc*)
adrede (ADV) on purpose, deliberately
adredemente (ADV) (*LAm*) = **adrede**
adrenalina (SF) adrenalin
Adriano (SM) Hadrian
Adriático (SM) Adriatic
adriático (ADJ) Adriatic • **el mar Adriático** the Adriatic Sea
adscribir ▹ CONJUG 3a (PP: **adscrito**) (VT) • **~ a** to appoint to, assign to • **estuvo adscrito al servicio de ...** he was attached to ...
ADSL (SM ABR) (= **asymmetric digital subscriber line**) ADSL, (ADSL) broadband
aduana (SF) **1** (= *institución*) customs; (= *oficina*) customs house; (= *impuesto*) customs duty • **derecho de ~** customs duty • **libre de ~** duty-free • **pasar por la ~** to go through customs
2‡ (= *escondite*) pad‡, hide-out; (= *refugio*) safe house; (*Méx*) (= *burdel*) brothel
aduanal (ADJ) customs (*antes de s*)
aduanero/a (ADJ) customs (*antes de s*)
(SM/F) customs officer
aducir ▹ CONJUG 3n (VT) (= *alegar*) to adduce, offer as proof; [+ *prueba*] to provide, furnish
adueñarse ▹ CONJUG 1a (VPR) • **~ de** (= *apropiarse*) to take possession of; (*fig*) to master
adujar ▹ CONJUG 1a (VT) to coil
adulación (SF) flattery, adulation
adulada* (SF) (*Méx*) flattery
adulador(a) (ADJ) flattering, fawning
(SM/F) flatterer
adular ▹ CONJUG 1a (VT) to flatter
adulate (ADJ), (SM) (*LAm*) = **adulón**
adulón/ona* (ADJ) fawning
(SM/F) toady, creep*, brown-nose (*EEUU*‡)
adulonería (SF) flattering, fawning
adulteración (SF) adulteration
adulterado (ADJ) adulterated
adulterar ▹ CONJUG 1a (VT) (= *viciar*) to adulterate
(VI) (= *cometer adulterio*) to commit adultery
adulterino (ADJ) (*gen*) adulterous; [*moneda*] spurious, counterfeit
adulterio (SM) adultery
adúltero/a (ADJ) adulterous
(SM/F) adulterer/adulteress
adultez (SF) adulthood
adulto/a (ADJ), (SM/F) adult, grown-up
adunar ▹ CONJUG 1a (VT) (*liter*) to join, unite
adunco (ADJ) bent, curved
adustez (SF) harshness, severity
adusto (ADJ) **1** (= *desabrido*) harsh, severe
2 (= *inexorable*) grim, stern
3 (= *hosco*) sullen
4 (= *caliente*) scorching hot
advenedizo/a (ADJ) (= *del extranjero*) foreign, from outside
(SM/F) (= *forastero*) foreigner, outsider; (*pey*) (= *arribista*) upstart; (*LAm*) (= *novato*) novice
advenimiento (SM) advent, arrival
▸ **advenimiento al trono** accession to the throne
adventicio (ADJ) adventitious
adverbial (ADJ) adverbial • **locución ~ • oración ~** adverbial phrase
adverbialización (SF) adverbialization
adverbialmente (ADV) adverbially
adverbio (SM) adverb
adversario/a (ADJ) opposing, rival
(SM/F) adversary, opponent
adversativo (ADJ) adversative
adversidad (SF) (= *problemas*) adversity; (= *revés*) setback, mishap
adverso (ADJ) [*lado*] opposite, facing; [*resultado etc*] adverse; [*suerte*] bad
advertencia (SF) **1** (= *aviso*) warning • **hizo caso omiso de mis ~s** he ignored my warnings • **un disparo de ~** a warning shot • **hacer una ~** to give a warning • **espero que esto os sirva de ~** let this be a warning to

you • REFRÁN: • **sobre ~ no hay engaño** forewarned is forearmed
2 (= *consejo*) • **hacer una ~** to give some advice, give a piece of advice • **una ~: conviene llevar ropa de abrigo** a word of advice: take warm clothes with you
3 (= *prefacio*) preface, foreword

advertido ADJ sharp

advertimiento SM = **advertencia**

advertir ▹ CONJUG 3i VT **1** (= *avisar*) to warn • **es la última vez que te lo advierto** that's the last time I'm going to warn you • **estás advertido** you have been warned • **~ a algn de algo** to warn sb about sth • **~ a algn que haga algo** to warn sb to do sth • **nos advirtió que no nos fiáramos de él** she warned us not to trust him • **te advierto que es la última vez que tolero que me insultes** I'm warning you that's the last time I'll allow you to insult me • **sí, iré, pero te advierto que tengo que estar de vuelta en casa pronto** yes, I'll go, but remember that I have to be back home early • **te advierto que no pienso ir** I have to let you know that I'm not going • **te advierto que tal vez habría sido mejor que no lo hubiera sabido** mind you, perhaps it would have been better if she hadn't found it
2 (= *aconsejar*) to advise, tell • **adviértele que se lleve el paraguas** advise *o* tell him to take his umbrella • **ya les advertí que si había algún problema me lo dijeran** I already told them to let me know if there were any problems
3 (= *notar*) [+ *olor, error*] to notice • **advertí en él un extraño comportamiento** I noticed some strange behaviour on his part • **el perro advirtió nuestra presencia** the dog noticed us • **en sus últimas obras se advierten una serie de cambios** one can see *o* observe some changes in her latest works • **~ que** to notice that • **¿ha advertido que su coche pierde aceite?** have you noticed that your car's leaking oil? • **advertimos que ya no corríamos peligro** we realised that we were no longer in danger
VI • **~ de** *o* **sobre algo** to warn of sth • **las señales advertían del peligro** the signs warned of danger

Adviento SM Advent

advocación SF (*Rel*) name, dedication • **una iglesia bajo la ~ de San Felipe** a church dedicated to St Philip

advocar ▹ CONJUG 1g VT (*LAm*) to advocate

ADVP ADJ ABR (= **adicto a drogas por vía parenteral**) *who uses drugs intravenously*
SM ABR IV drug user

adyacencia SF nearness, proximity • **en las ~s** in the vicinity

adyacente ADJ adjacent

AEDAVE SF ABR (= **Asociación Empresarial de Agencias de Viajes Españoles**) ≈ ABTA

AEE SF ABR (= **Agencia Europea del Espacio**) ESA

AELC SF ABR (= **Asociación Europea de Libre Comercio**) EFTA

aeración SF aeration

aéreo ADJ (*Fot*) aerial; [*tráfico*] air; (*Ferro*) overhead, elevated

aero... PREF aero...

aerobic SM aerobics

aeróbico ADJ aerobic

aerobismo SM (*Cono Sur*) aerobics

aerobús SM **1** (*Aer*) airbus
2 (*Caribe*) long-distance bus, coach, bus (*EEUU*)

aeroclub SM flying club

aerodeslizador SM, **aerodeslizante** SM hovercraft

aerodinámica SF aerodynamics (*sing*)

aerodinámico ADJ (*Fís*) aerodynamic; [*forma*] streamlined

aerodinamismo SM streamlining

aerodinamizar ▹ CONJUG 1f VT to streamline

aeródromo SM aerodrome, airdrome (*EEUU*)

aeroenviar ▹ CONJUG 1c VT to send by air

aeroescuela SF flying school

aeroespacial ADJ aerospace (*antes de s*)

aeroestación SF air terminal

aerofaro SM beacon

aerofobia SF fear of flying

aerofoto SF aerial photograph

aerofotográfico ADJ aerial photographic

aerofumigación SF crop dusting

aerogenerador SM wind turbine

aerografía SF spray painting, airbrushing

aerografiado ADJ spray-painted, airbrushed
SM spray painting, airbrushing

aerografista SMF spray paint artist

aerógrafo SM airbrush

aerograma SM aerogram, airmail letter

aeroligero SM microlight

aerolínea SF airline

aerolito SM meteorite

aeromodelismo SM aeromodelling, making model aeroplanes

aeromodelista SMF model aeroplane enthusiast

aeromodelístico ADJ model aeroplane (*antes de s*)

aeromodelo SM model aeroplane

aeromotor SM aero-engine

aeromozo/a SM/F (*LAm*) steward/stewardess, air steward/stewardess, flight attendant (*EEUU*)

aeronauta SMF aeronaut

aeronáutica SF aeronautics (*sing*)

aeronáutico ADJ aeronautical

aeronaval ADJ air-sea (*antes de s*) • **base ~** air-sea base

aeronave SF airship ▸ **aeronave espacial** spaceship

aeronavegabilidad SF airworthiness

aeronavegable ADJ airworthy

aeroparque SM (*Arg*) small airport

aeroplano SM aeroplane, airplane (*EEUU*)

aeroportuario ADJ airport (*antes de s*)

aeroposta SF (*LAm*) airmail

aeropuerto SM airport ▸ **aeropuerto de escala, aeropuerto de paso** stopover airport

aerosalsa SF salsaerobics (*sing*), salsacise

aerosol SM aerosol

aerostática SF ballooning

aerostato SM, **aeróstato** SM balloon, aerostat

aerotaxi SM air taxi

aeroterrestre ADJ air-ground (*antes de s*)

aerotransportado ADJ airborne

aerotransportar ▹ CONJUG 1a VT to airlift

aerotransporte SM air transport

aerotransportista SM carrier, air carrier

aeroturbina SF wind turbine

aerovía SF (= *ruta*) airway; (= *compañía*) airline

AES SM ABR (*Econ*) (= **Acuerdo Económico Social**) *wages pact*

a/f ABR = **a favor**

afabilidad SF affability, geniality

afable ADJ affable, genial

afablemente ADV affably, genially

afamado ADJ famous, noted (**por** for)

afamar ▹ CONJUG 1a VT to make famous
VPR **afamarse** to become famous, make a reputation

afán SM **1** (= *deseo*) eagerness • **en su ~ de marcar un gol** in his eagerness to score a goal • **con ~ de**: • **con ~ de agradar, repartió regalos para todos** in his eagerness to please he gave everyone presents • **por ~ de**: • **lo hizo por ~ de superarse** she did out of a desire to better herself • **lo hicieron por ~ de ganar tiempo** they did it in a bid to gain time • **tener ~ de algo** to be eager for sth ▸ **afán de conocimiento** thirst for knowledge ▸ **afán de lucro** • **el ~ de lucro** the profit motive • **actuaron sin ~ de lucro** they didn't do it to make money ▸ **afán de protagonismo** • **un juez con ~ de protagonismo** a judge who loves publicity *o* always wants to be in the limelight • **tu hermano tiene mucho ~ de protagonismo** your brother always wants to be the centre of attention ▸ **afán de superación** desire to better oneself ▸ **afán de venganza** thirst for revenge ▸ **afán de victoria** will to win, desire to win
2 (= *ahínco*) • **hacer algo con ~** to do sth eagerly • **rebuscó con ~ en los archivos** he searched eagerly through the files
3 (*frm*) (= *intención*) • **una obra con ~ didáctico** an educational work • **sin ~ efectista** with no desire for dramatic effect
4 (*LAm*) (= *prisa*) hurry • **tengo muchísimo ~** I'm in a tearing hurry • **ir con ~** to be in a hurry

afanador(a) SM/F (= *ladrón*) thief; (*Méx*) (= *obrero*) menial worker; [*de limpieza*] cleaner

afanaduría SF (*Méx*) casualty ward

afanar ▹ CONJUG 1a VT **1*** (= *birlar*) to pinch*, swipe*
2 (*CAm*) [+ *dinero*] to earn, make
3 (= *acosar*) to press, harass, bother; (*LAm*) (= *empujar*) to hustle
VPR **afanarse 1** (= *trabajar*) to toil, labour, labor (*EEUU*) (**en** at) • **~se por hacer algo** to strive to do sth
2 (*And*) (= *enfadarse*) to get angry

afanosamente ADV (= *con esmero*) diligently; (= *apasionadamente*) feverishly

afanoso ADJ **1** [*trabajo*] hard, heavy
2 (= *concienzudo*) [*temperamento*] industrious; [*actividad, búsqueda*] feverish, hectic

afantasmado ADJ conceited

afarolado ADJ (*LAm*) (= *emocionado*) excited, worked up

afarolarse ▹ CONJUG 1a VPR (*LAm*) (= *emocionarse*) to get excited, get worked up

afasia SF aphasia

afásico ADJ (*Psic*) aphasic; (= *mudo*) mute, dumb

AFE SF ABR (= **Asociación de Futbolistas Españoles**) ≈ FA, ≈ SFA

afeamiento SM **1** (*físicamente*) defacing, disfigurement
2 (= *censura*) condemnation, censure

afear ▹ CONJUG 1a VT **1** (= *hacer feo*) to make ugly, disfigure • **los errores que afean el texto** the mistakes which disfigure the text
2 (= *censurar*) to condemn, censure

afección SF **1** (= *cariño*) affection, fondness; (= *inclinación*) inclination • **afecciones del alma** emotions
2 (*Med*) trouble, disease ▸ **afección cardíaca** heart trouble ▸ **afección hepática** liver complaint ▸ **afección lumbar** back trouble

afeccionarse ▹ CONJUG 1a VPR (*Cono Sur*) • **~ a** to take a liking to, become fond of

afectación SF affectation

afectadamente ADV affectedly

afectado ADJ **1** (= *forzado*) [*acento, persona*] affected; [*estilo*] stilted, precious
2 (*Med*) (= *aquejado*) • **estar ~ del corazón** to have heart trouble • **estar ~** (*Méx*) to be consumptive; (*Cono Sur*) to be hurt

afectante ADJ (*Cono Sur*) disturbing, distressing

afectar ▹ CONJUG 1a VT **1** (*= repercutir sobre*) to affect • **el paro afecta especialmente a los jóvenes** unemployment affects young people in particular • **la falta de oxígeno afecta al cerebro** lack of oxygen affects the brain • **por lo que afecta al tema de la contaminación** as far as the question of pollution is concerned
2 (*= entristecer*) to sadden; (*= conmover*) to move • **su muerte nos afectó mucho** we were terribly saddened by his death • **me ~on mucho las imágenes del documental** I was very moved by the pictures in the documentary
3 (*frm*) (*= fingir*) to affect, feign • **~ ignorancia** to affect *o* feign ignorance
4 (*Jur*) to tie up, encumber
5 (*LAm*) [*+ forma*] to take, assume
6 (*LAm*) (*= destinar*) to allocate
VPR **afectarse** (*LAm*) (*= enfermar*) to fall ill
afectísimo ADJ affectionate • **suyo ~** yours truly
afectividad SF emotional nature, emotion • **falta de ~** (*en persona*) unemotional nature; (*en relación*) lack of emotion
afectivo ADJ affective
afecto ADJ **1** (*= apegado*) affectionate • **~ a** attached to
2 • **~ a** (*Jur*) (*= sujeto*) subject to, liable for
3 • **~ de** (*Med*) afflicted with
SM **1** (*= cariño*) affection, fondness (**a** for) • **tomar ~ a algn** to become attached to sb
2 (*= emoción*) feeling, emotion
afectuosamente ADV affectionately; (*en carta*) yours affectionately
afectuosidad SF affection
afectuoso ADJ affectionate
afeitada SF = **afeitado**
afeitado SM **1** [*de barba*] shave
2 (*Taur*) blunting of the horns, trimming of the horns
afeitadora SF electric razor, electric shaver
afeitar ▹ CONJUG 1a VT **1** (*= rasurar*) to shave; [*+ cola, planta*] to trim; (*Taur*) [*+ cuernos*] to blunt, trim; [*+ toro*] to blunt the horns of, trim the horns of • **¡que te afeiten!*** get your head seen to!*
2* (*= pasar*) to brush, brush past, shave
3 (*= maquillar*) to make up, paint, apply cosmetics to
VPR **afeitarse 1** (*= rasurarse*) to shave, have a shave
2 (*= maquillarse*) to make o.s. up, put one's make-up on
afeite SM make-up, cosmetic, cosmetics (*pl*)
afelpado ADJ plush, velvety
afeminación SF effeminacy
afeminado ADJ effeminate
SM effeminate man, poof‡, fag (*EEUU*‡)
afeminamiento SM effeminacy
afeminarse ▹ CONJUG 1a VPR to become effeminate
aferrado ADJ stubborn • **seguir ~ a** to stick to, stand by
aferrar ▹ CONJUG 1j VT **1** (*= asir*) to grasp, seize
2 (*Náut*) [*+ barco*] to moor; [*+ vela*] furl
VPR **aferrarse 1** (*= agarrarse*) to cling, hang on
2 • **~se a** *o* **en** (*= obstinarse en*) to stick to, stand by • **~se a un principio** to stick to a principle • **~se a una esperanza** to cling to a hope • **~se a su opinión** to remain firm in one's opinion
3 (*Náut*) [*barco*] to anchor, moor
afestonado ADJ festooned
affaire SM, (*Cono Sur*) SF affair, affaire
affidávit SM affidavit, sworn statement
affmo./a. ABR = **afectísimo/a**

Afganistán SM Afghanistan
afgano/a ADJ, SM/F Afghan
afianzado/a SM/F (*LAm*) (*= novio*) fiancé; (*= novia*) fiancée
afianzamiento SM **1** (*Téc*) strengthening, securing
2 (*Econ*) guarantee, security
3 (*Jur*) surety, bond
afianzar ▹ CONJUG 1f VT **1** (*= reforzar*) to strengthen, secure; (*= sostener*) to support, prop up; (*fig*) (*= apoyar*) to support, back
2 (*Com*) (*= avalar*) to guarantee, vouch for; (*= ser fiador*) to stand surety for
VPR **afianzarse** (*= sostenerse*) to steady o.s.; (*fig*) (*= establecerse*) to become strong, become established • **~se a** to catch hold of • **la reacción se afianzó después de la guerra** the reaction set in after the war
afiche SM (*esp LAm*) poster
afición SF **1** (*= apego*) fondness, liking (**a** for); (*= inclinación*) inclination (**a** towards) • **cobrar ~ a** • **tomar ~ a** to take a liking to • **tener ~ a** to like, be fond of
2 (*= pasatiempo*) hobby, pastime • **¿qué aficiones tiene?** what are his interests? • **pinta por ~** he paints as a hobby
3 • **la ~** (*Dep*) the fans • **aquí hay una gran ~** support is strong here
aficionado/a ADJ **1** (*= entusiasta*) keen, enthusiastic • **es muy ~** he's very keen • **es muy aficionada a la pintura** she's very keen on painting
2 (*= no profesional*) amateur • **un equipo de fútbol ~** an amateur football team
SM/F **1** (*= entusiasta*) (*de hobby*) enthusiast; (*como espectador*) lover • **un libro para los ~s al bricolaje** a book for DIY enthusiasts • **los ~s al teatro** theatre lovers • **todos los ~s a la música** all music lovers
2 (*= no profesional*) amateur • **tenis para ~s** amateur tennis • **partido de ~s** amateur game • **función de ~s** amateur performance • **somos simples ~s** we're just amateurs
3 [*de equipo, grupo*] fan, supporter • **gritaban los ~s** the fans were shouting
aficionar ▹ CONJUG 1a VT • **~ a algn a algo** to interest sb in sth
VPR **aficionarse** • **~se a algo** to get fond of sth, take a liking to sth
afidávit SM affidavit, sworn statement
áfido SM aphid
afiebrado ADJ feverish
afijo SM affix
afiladera SF grindstone, whetstone
afilado ADJ [*borde*] sharp; [*punta*] tapering, sharp
afilador SM (*= persona*) knife-grinder; (*Téc*) steel sharpener; (*= correa*) razor strop ▸ **afilador de lápices** pencil sharpener
afiladura SF sharpening
afilalápices SM INV pencil sharpener
afilar ▹ CONJUG 1a VT **1** [*+ herramienta*] (*= hacer más cortante*) to sharpen, put an edge on; (*= sacar punta*) to put a point on; [*+ cuchillo*] to whet, grind; [*+ navaja*] to strop
2 (*Cono Sur*) (*= flirtear*) to flatter, court; (*Chile***) (*= joder*) to fuck**, screw**
VPR **afilarse 1** [*cara*] to sharpen, grow thin; [*dedos*] to taper
2 (*LAm*) (*= prepararse*) to get ready
afiliación SF (*Pol*) affiliation; [*de sindicatos*] membership
afiliado/a ADJ affiliated (**a** to), member (*antes de s*); (*Com*) subsidiary • **los países ~s** the member countries
SM/F member
afiliarse ▹ CONJUG 1b VPR • **~ a** to affiliate to, join
afiligranado ADJ **1** (*Cos*) filigreed
2 (*= delicado*) delicate, fine; [*persona*] dainty

afilón SM (*= correa*) strop; (*= chaira*) steel
afilorar ▹ CONJUG 1a VT (*Caribe*) to adorn
afín ADJ **1** (*= lindante*) bordering, adjacent
2 (*= relacionado*) similar; [*persona*] related
SMF (*= pariente*) relation by marriage
afinación SF **1** (*Mús*) tuning
2 (*Aut*) tuning(-up)
3 (*= perfeccionamiento*) refining, polishing; (*= fin*) completion
afinado ADJ **1** (*Mús*) in tune
2 (*= acabado*) finished, polished
afinador(a) SM (*Mús*) tuning key
SM/F (*= persona*) tuner ▸ **afinador(a) de pianos** piano tuner
afinar ▹ CONJUG 1a VT **1** (*Mús*) to tune
2 (*Aut*) to tune up
3 (*= perfeccionar*) to put the finishing touch to, complete; (*= pulir*) to polish; (*Téc*) to purify, refine; [*+ puntería*] to sharpen, make more precise
VI to sing in tune, play in tune
VPR **afinarse** (*= pulirse*) to become polished
afincado/a ADJ settled
SM/F (*Cono Sur*) landowner
afincarse ▹ CONJUG 1g VPR [*persona*] to settle; [*creencia*] to take root
afinidad SF **1** (*= atracción*) affinity; (*= semejanza*) similarity; (*= parentesco*) relationship • **parentesco por ~** relationship by marriage
2 (*Quím*) affinity
afirmación SF affirmation
afirmado SM (*Aut*) road surface; (*Cono Sur*) (*= acera*) paving, paved surface
afirmar ▹ CONJUG 1a VT **1** (*= reforzar*) to make secure, strengthen
2 (*= declarar*) to assert, state; [*+ lealtad*] to declare, protest • **~ que** to affirm that • **~ bajo juramento** to swear under oath
3 (*LAm*) [*+ golpe*] to deal, give
VPR **afirmarse 1** (*= recobrar el equilibrio*) to steady o.s. • **~se en los estribos** (*= sujetarse*) to settle one's feet firmly in the stirrups; (*Cono Sur*) (*= aguantarse*) to grit one's teeth
2 • **~se en lo dicho** to stand by what one has said
afirmativa SF affirmative answer, yes*
afirmativamente ADV affirmatively • **contestar ~** to answer in the affirmative
afirmativo ADJ affirmative, positive • **en caso ~** if that is the case • **voto ~** vote in favour, vote for
aflatarse ▹ CONJUG 1a VPR (*LAm*) to be sad
aflautado ADJ high, fluty
aflicción SF affliction, sorrow
aflictivo ADJ distressing
afligente ADJ (*CAm, Méx*) distressing, upsetting
afligido ADJ **1** (*= apenado*) grieving, heartbroken • **los ~s padres** the bereaved parents
2 (*Med*) • **~ por** stricken with
SM • **los ~s** (*que padecen*) the afflicted; (*por deceso*) the bereaved
afligir ▹ CONJUG 3c VT **1** (*= afectar*) to afflict; (*= apenar*) to pain, distress
2 (*LAm*) (*= golpear*) to beat, hit
VPR **afligirse** to get upset • **no te aflijas** don't get upset, don't upset yourself (over it) • **no te aflijas tanto** you mustn't let it affect you like this, don't get so worked up*
aflojamiento SM (*= acto*) loosening, slackening; [*de esfuerzo, presión*] weakening
aflojar ▹ CONJUG 1a VT **1** (*= dejar suelto*) [*+ corbata, cinturón, nudo*] to loosen; [*+ tuerca, rosca*] to slacken, loosen; [*+ disciplina, restricción, política, presión*] to relax • **se sentó y se aflojó (el nudo de) la corbata** he sat down and loosened (the knot in) his tie

2 (= *relajar*) [+ *cuerda*] to slacken; [+ *músculo*] to relax
3 (= *ralentizar*) • **caminamos sin ~ el paso** *o* **la marcha** *o* **el ritmo** we walked without slackening our pace *o* without slowing down • **nuevas medidas para ~ la marcha de la economía** new measures to slow down the economy
4* [+ *vientre*] to loosen
5* [+ *dinero*] to fork out*, cough up*
VI 1 (*Meteo*) [*viento*] to drop; [*lluvia*] to ease off; [*calor*] to let up
2 [*fiebre*] to subside; [*tensión*] to ease, subside
3 [*ventas*] to tail off • **el negocio afloja en agosto** business slows down *o* eases up in August
4 (*al andar, correr, competir*) to ease up, let up • **no aflojó hasta conseguir la victoria** he did not ease up *o* let up until he won
VPR **aflojarse 1** [*algo apretado, cinturón, corbata*] to loosen; [*nudo, tuerca, rosca*] to come *o* work loose
2 [*algo tenso, cuerda*] to slacken
3 [*fiebre, interés*] to subside
4 (*Caribe***) (= *ensuciarse*) to shit o.s.**

afloración SF outcrop
aflorado ADJ fine, elegant
afloramiento SM = **afloración**
aflorar ▸ CONJUG 1a VI (*Geol*) to crop out, outcrop; (= *surgir*) to come to the surface, emerge
afluencia SF 1 (= *aflujo*) influx • **la ~ de turistas** the influx of tourists • **la ~ de capital extranjero** the influx of foreign capital • **hubo gran ~ de público** there was a good turnout • **la ~ a las urnas fue escasa** there was a low turnout at the polls
2 (*frm*) (= *elocuencia*) eloquence, fluency
afluente ADJ 1 [*agua, líquido*] inflowing
2 [*discurso*] eloquent, fluent
SM (*Geog*) tributary
afluir ▸ CONJUG 3g VI [*agua, líquido*] to flow (a into); [*gente*] to flock (**a** into, to)
aflujo SM (*Med*) afflux, congestion; (*Mec*) inflow, inlet
aflús* ADJ (*LAm*) broke*, flat (*EEUU**)
afluxionarse ▸ CONJUG 1a VPR (*LAm*) to catch a cold
afmo./a. ABR = **afectísimo/a**
afoetear†† ▸ CONJUG 1a VT (*And, Caribe*) to whip, beat
afonía SF loss of voice, aphonia
afónico ADJ 1 (= *sin voz*) voiceless; (= *ronco*) hoarse • **estar ~** to have lost one's voice
2 [*letra*] silent, mute
aforado/a ADJ [*provincia, territorio*] *with a regional charter* • **persona aforada** ▸ SM/F
SM/F *person with parliamentary immunity who can only be tried by the Supreme Court*
aforador SM gauger
aforar ▸ CONJUG 1a VT 1 (*Téc*) to gauge
2 (= *valorar*) to appraise, value
aforismo SM aphorism
aforístico ADJ aphoristic
aforjudo* ADJ (*Cono Sur*) silly, stupid
aforo SM 1 (*Téc*) gauging
2 (*Teat*) capacity • **el teatro tiene un ~ de 2.000** the theatre can seat 2,000
3 (= *valoración*) appraisal, valuation
4 (*Com*) import duty
aforrar ▸ CONJUG 1a VT 1 (= *forrar*) to line
2 (*Cono Sur**) (= *golpear*) to smack, punch
VPR **aforrarse 1** (= *abrigarse*) to wrap up warm, put on warm underclothes
2* (= *atiborrarse*) to stuff o.s.*, tuck it away*
afortunadamente ADV fortunately, luckily
afortunado ADJ (= *con suerte*) fortunate, lucky; (= *feliz*) happy • **poco ~** unsuccessful • **un comentario poco ~** a rather inappropriate comment

AFP SF ABR (= **alfa-fetoproteína**) AFP, afp
afrailado* ADJ (*LAm*) churchy*
afrancesado/a ADJ (*pey*) (= *que imita lo francés*) frenchified; (*Pol*) pro-French, supporting the French
SM/F (*pey*) (= *imitador de lo francés*) frenchified person; (*Pol*) pro-French person
afrancesamiento SM (= *sentimiento*) francophilism, pro-French feeling; (= *proceso*) gallicization, frenchification (*pey*)
afrancesarse ▸ CONJUG 1a VPR (= *asemejarse a lo francés*) to go French, become gallicized, acquire French habits; (*Pol*) to become a francophile
afrechillo SM (*Cono Sur*) bran
afrecho SM (= *salvado*) bran; (*LAm*) (= *serrín*) sawdust ▸ **afrecho remojado** mash
afrenta SF affront, insult
afrentar ▸ CONJUG 1a VT (= *insultar*) to affront, insult; (= *desacreditar*) to dishonour, dishonor (*EEUU*)
VPR **afrentarse** (= *avergonzarse*) to be ashamed (**de** of)
afrentoso ADJ (= *insultante*) insulting, outrageous; (= *vergonzoso*) shameful
África SF Africa ▸ **África Austral** Southern Africa ▸ **África del Norte** North Africa ▸ **África del Sur** South Africa ▸ **África negra** Black Africa
africaans SM Afrikaans
africado ADJ affricate
africanidad SF Africanness
africanista SMF (= *experto*) specialist in African affairs; (= *aficionado*) person interested in Africa
africano/a ADJ, SM/F African
afrijolar ▸ CONJUG 1a VT (*And*) to bother, annoy • **~ una tarea a algn** to give sb an unpleasant job to do
afrikaner ADJ, SMF (PL: **afrikaners**) Afrikaner
afro ADJ Afro • **peinado ~** Afro hairstyle
afro... PREF Afro...
afroamericano ADJ Afro-American
afroasiático ADJ Afro-Asian
afrobrasileño ADJ Afro-Brazilian
afrocaribeño ADJ Afro-Caribbean
afrocubano ADJ Afro-Cuban
afrodisíaco ADJ, SM, **afrodisiaco** ADJ, SM aphrodisiac
Afrodita SF Aphrodite
afronegrismo SM (*LAm*) *word borrowed from an African language*
afrontamiento SM confrontation
afrontar ▸ CONJUG 1a VT 1 [+ *dos personas*] to bring face to face
2 [+ *peligro*] to confront, face up to; [+ *problema*] to deal with, tackle
afrutado ADJ fruity
afta SF (*Med*) sore
after ['after] SM (PL: **afters** *o* **after**), **afterhours** ['afterauars] SM INV after-hours club
aftershave SM INV, **after-shave** SM INV ['afterʃeif] aftershave
aftersun SM INV, **after sun** SM INV ['after'san] aftersun
aftosa SF (*tb* **fiebre aftosa**) foot-and-mouth disease
afuera ADV (*esp LAm*) out, outside • **¡afuera!** out of the way!, get out! • **de ~** from outside • **por ~** on the outside • **las hojas de ~** the outer leaves, the outside leaves
PREP • **~ de** (*LAm*) outside
SFPL **afueras** outskirts
afuerano/a (*Chile*), **afuereño/a** (*Chile*), **afuerino/a** (*Chile*) ADJ strange, outside (*antes de s*)
SM/F [*de afuera*] outsider, stranger; (= *trabajador*) itinerant worker, casual worker

afuetear ▸ CONJUG 1a VT (*LAm*) to whip, beat
afufa‡ SF flight, escape • **tomar las ~s** to beat it*
afufar‡ ▸ CONJUG 1a VI, VPR **afufarse** to beat it*, get out quick
afufón‡ SM flight, escape
afusilar ▸ CONJUG 1a VT (*Méx*) to shoot
afutrarse ▸ CONJUG 1a VPR (*Cono Sur*) to dress up
ag. ABR (= **agosto**) Aug
agachada* SF trick, dodge*
agachadiza SF (= *ave*) snipe • **hacer la ~** to duck, try not to be seen
agachado/a* SM/F (*LAm*) down-and-out, bum (*EEUU**)
agachar ▸ CONJUG 1a VT [+ *cabeza*] to bend, bow • **~ las orejas*** to hang one's head
VPR **agacharse 1** (= *agazaparse*) to stoop, bend down, bend over; (= *acuclillarse*) to squat; (= *bajar la cabeza*) to duck; (= *encogerse*) to cower
2 (*fig*) (= *esconderse*) to go into hiding, lie low
3 (*LAm*) (= *ceder*) to give in, submit
4 (*Méx*) (= *callarse*) • **~se algo** to keep sth under one's hat
5 • **~se con algo** (*And, Méx*) (= *robar*) to make off with sth, pocket sth
6 (*LAm*) (= *prepararse*) to get ready
agache SM (*And*) (= *embuste*) fib, tale • **andar de ~** to be on the run
agachón‡ ADJ (*LAm*) weak-willed, submissive
agafar‡ ▸ CONJUG 1a VT to pinch*, nick*
agalbanado ADJ lazy, shiftless
agalla SF 1 (*Bot*) gall ▸ **agalla de roble** oak apple
2 [*de pez*] gill
3 **agallas*** (= *valor*) pluck, guts* • **tener (muchas) ~s** to be brave, have guts* • **es hombre de ~s** he's got guts*
4 (*LAm*) • **tener ~s** (= *ser glotón*) to be greedy; (= *ser tacaño*) to be mean; (= *ser descarado*) to have lots of cheek*
5 (*Cono Sur*) • **tener ~s** (= *ser astuto*) to be sharp, be smart
6 **agallas** (= *amígdalas*) tonsils; (= *anginas*) tonsillitis
agalludo (*Cono Sur*) ADJ 1 (= *valiente*) daring, bold
2 (= *tacaño*) mean, stingy
3 (= *glotón*) greedy
Agamenón SM Agamemnon
ágape SM banquet, feast
agareno/a ADJ Moslem
SM/F Moslem
agarrada SF 1 (= *pelea*) scrap, brawl; (= *riña*) row, run-in*
2 (*Dep*) tackle
agarradera SF (*LAm*), **agarradero** SM 1 (= *asidero*) handle, grip; [*de cortina*] cord
2 (= *amparo*) protection
3 **agarraderas** (= *influencias*) pull (*sing*), influence (*sing*) • **tener buenas ~s** to have friends in the right places
agarrado ADJ 1 mean, stingy
2 • **baile ~** slow dance
agarrador ADJ (*And, Cono Sur*) strong
agarrafar ▸ CONJUG 1a VT to grab hold of
agarrao* SM slow dance
agarrar ▸ CONJUG 1a VT 1 (= *asir*) **a** (*sujetando*) to hold (on to) • **agarra bien el bolso** hold on to your handbag firmly • **le señalaron falta por ~ a un jugador contrario** a free kick was given against him for holding on to one of the opposition • **lo tuvo bien agarrado hasta que llegó la policía** she held him until the police arrived • **entró agarrada del brazo de su padre** she came in holding her father's arm • **iban agarrados del brazo** they were walking arm in arm • **me agarró del brazo**

he took me by the arm
b (*con violencia*) to grab • **agarró al niño por el hombro** he grabbed the child by the shoulder • **la agarró de los pelos y no la soltaba** she grabbed her hair and refused to let her go
c (*con fuerza*) to grip • **la agarró fuertemente del brazo** he gripped her arm tightly
2 (= *capturar*) to catch • **ya han agarrado al ladrón** they've already caught the thief
3 [+ *resfriado*] to catch • **he agarrado un buen resfriado** I've caught a nasty cold • **lo tiene bien agarrado al pecho** she's got a nasty chesty cough • MODISMO: • **~la*** (= *emborracharse*) to get plastered*
4* (= *conseguir*) to get, wangle*
5 (*esp LAm*) (= *coger*) • **agarré otro pedazo de pastel** I took another piece of cake • **agarra el libro del estante** take the book off the shelf • **~ una flor** to pick a flower • **~ un tren** to catch a train • **la casa tiene tanto trabajo que no sé por dónde ~la** the house needs such a lot doing to it, I don't know where to start • **~ el vuelo** (= *despegar*) to take off
6 (*CAm, Caribe, Méx**) (= *captar*) to get*, understand
7 (*Cono Sur*) • **~ a palos a algn*** to beat sb up*
8 (*Caribe***) to fuck**
VI **1** (= *asir*) • **agarra por este extremo** hold it by this end, take hold of it by this end
2 (*Bot*) [*planta*] to take (root)
3 [*color*] to take
4 (*esp LAm*) (= *coger*) • **agarre por esta calle** take this street • **agarró y se fue*** he upped and went* • **~ para** (= *salir*) to set out for
VPR **agarrarse 1** (= *asirse*) to hold on • **¡agárrate bien!** hold (on) tight! • **~se a** *o* **de algo** to hold on to sth • **agárrate bien a la barandilla** hold on tight to the rail • **necesita algo adonde ~se** she needs something to hold on to • **me agarré al asiento con todas mis fuerzas** I held on to *o* gripped the seat with all my strength • **se ~on de los pelos** they tore at each other's hair • MODISMO: • **¡agárrate!*** wait for it!, listen to this! • **pues ahora agárrate, porque lo que te voy a contar es mucho peor** I hope you're sitting down, because what I'm going to tell you now is much worse • **—¿sabes que le ha tocado la quiniela? —¡agárrate!** "did you know she won the pools?" — "never!"
2 (*Aut*) [*coche, neumático*] to hold the road • **este coche se agarra muy bien en las curvas** this car holds the road very well on bends • **estos neumáticos se agarran con fuerza al asfalto** these tyres have excellent grip
3 (*como excusa*) • **~se a algo**: • **se agarra a cualquier excusa** any (old) excuse will do him • **se agarra a su mala salud para conseguir lo que quiere** she uses her poor health as an excuse to get whatever she wants • **se agarró a que era el mayor para hacerse cargo de la expedición** he used the fact that he was the oldest to take charge of the expedition
4* (= *cogerse*) • **se agarró una buena borrachera** he got well and truly plastered* • **me agarré un cabreo tremendo** I got really narked* • **se agarró un buen berrinche cuando se enteró** she threw a tantrum *o* fit when she found out
5 (*esp LAm*) (= *pelear*) to have a fight • **se ~on a tiros** they started shooting at each other • **se ~on a puñetazos** they started hitting each other • **la tenía agarrada conmigo** he had it in for me*
6 (*Culin*) (= *pegarse*) to stick

agarre SM **1** (*LAm*) (= *agarro*) hold; (*Aut*) road-holding, road-holding quality
2 (*And*) (= *asidero*) handle
3 (= *valor*) guts* (*pl*)
4 • **tener ~*** (= *tener influencia*) to have pull, be able to pull strings

agarrete ADJ (*And*) mean, stingy

agarro SM grasp, hold, clutch

agarrochar, agarrochear ▹ CONJUG 1a VT [+ *animal*] to jab with a goad; (*Taur*) to prick with a pike

agarrón SM **1** (= *tirón*) jerk, pull, tug
2 = agarrada

agarroso ADJ (*CAm*) sharp, acrid, bitter

agarrotado ADJ [*músculos*] stiff

agarrotamiento SM (= *apretón*) tightening; [*de músculos*] stiffening; (*Aut*) seizing up

agarrotar ▹ CONJUG 1a VT (= *atar*) to tie tight; [+ *persona*] to squeeze tight, press tightly; [+ *criminal*] to garrotte; [+ *músculos*] to stiffen • **esta corbata me agarrota** this tie is strangling me • **tengo los músculos agarrotados** I'm all stiff
VPR **agarrotarse** (*Med*) to stiffen, get numb; (*Aut*) to seize up

agasajado/a SM/F chief guest, guest of honour *o* (*EEUU*) honor

agasajador ADJ warm, welcoming

agasajamiento SM = agasajo

agasajar ▹ CONJUG 1a VT to entertain, fête

agasajo SM (= *acogida*) royal welcome; (= *regalo*) gift • **~s** hospitality

ágata SF agate

agatas ADV (*Cono Sur*) **1** (= *con dificultad*) with great difficulty, only with great difficulty
2 (= *apenas*) hardly, scarcely • **~ llegó, empezó a cantar** no sooner had he arrived than he started to sing

agauchado ADJ (*Cono Sur*) like a gaucho

agaucharse ▹ CONJUG 1a VPR (*Cono Sur*) to *imitate or dress like a gaucho*

agave SF agave, American aloe

agavilladora SF binder

agavillar ▹ CONJUG 1a VT [+ *trigo*] to bind, bind in sheaves; [+ *libro*] to bind
VPR **agavillarse** to gang up, band together

agazapar ▹ CONJUG 1a VT* to grab, grab hold of, nab*
VPR **agazaparse** (= *ocultarse*) to hide; (= *agacharse*) to crouch down, squat • **estaba agazapada tras las rocas** she was hidden behind the rocks • **tras esto se agazapa otra cosa** something else is concealed behind this

agencia SF **1** (= *empresa*) agency; (= *oficina*) office, bureau ▸ **agencia de cobro** debt-collecting agency ▸ **agencia de colocaciones** employment agency ▸ **agencia de contactos** dating agency ▸ **agencia de créditos** credit agency ▸ **agencia de damas de compañía** escort agency ▸ **agencia de información** news agency ▸ **agencia de noticias** news agency ▸ **agencia de patentes** patents office ▸ **agencia de prensa** news agency ▸ **agencia de promoción** development agency ▸ **Agencia de Protección de Datos** (*Esp*) *data protection agency* ▸ **agencia de publicidad** advertising agency ▸ **agencia de seguridad** security company ▸ **agencia de transportes** haulage company ▸ **agencia de turismo, agencia de viajes** travel agent's, travel agency ▸ **agencia exclusiva** exclusive agency ▸ **agencia inmobiliaria** estate agent's (office), real estate agency (*EEUU*) ▸ **agencia tributaria** Inland Revenue, Internal Revenue (*EEUU*) ▸ **agencia única** sole agency
2 (*Chile*) (= *montepío*) pawnshop

agenciar ▹ CONJUG 1b VT **1** (= *lograr*) to bring about, effect, engineer
2 (= *procurar*) to obtain, procure (**algo a algn** sth for sb); (*pey*) to wangle*, fiddle*
3 [+ *trato*] to negotiate
VPR **agenciarse 1** (= *apañarse*) to look after o.s. • **yo me las ~é para llegar allí** I'll manage to get there somehow, I'll work out how to get there • **bien sabe agenciárselas** he takes good care of number one
2 (= *proporcionarse*) • **~se algo** to get hold of sth, obtain sth

agenciero SM (*Cono Sur*) (= *agente*) agent, representative; [*de lotería*] lottery agent; (*Chile*) [*de montepío*] pawnbroker

agencioso ADJ active, diligent

agenda SF **1** (= *libro*) [*de citas, anotaciones*] diary, datebook (*EEUU*), notebook; [*de direcciones*] address book ▸ **agenda de bolsillo** pocket diary ▸ **agenda de despacho, agenda de mesa** desk diary ▸ **agenda de trabajo** engagement book ▸ **agenda electrónica** PDA
2 [*de reunión*] agenda
3 [*de actividades*] agenda, schedule • **una ~ apretada** a very busy agenda *o* schedule

agendar VT [+ *reunión, cita*] to schedule

agente SMF (= *representante*) agent; (= *policía*) policeman/policewoman; (*LAm*) (= *oficial*) officer, official ▸ **agente acreditado** accredited agent ▸ **agente comercial** business agent ▸ **agente de bolsa** stockbroker ▸ **agente de exportación** export agent ▸ **agente de negocios** business agent, broker ▸ **agente de prensa** press agent ▸ **agente de publicidad** (*Com*) advertising agent; (*Teat*) publicity agent ▸ **agente de seguridad** (*en vuelos comerciales*) sky marshal ▸ **agente de seguros** insurance agent ▸ **agente de tránsito** (*Arg, Méx*) traffic policeman/policewoman ▸ **agente de transportes** carrier ▸ **agente de turismo** travel agent, courier ▸ **agente de ventas** sales agent, sales rep, sales representative ▸ **agente de viajes** travel agent ▸ **agente especial** special agent ▸ **agente extranjero** foreign agent ▸ **agente inmobiliario** estate agent, real estate agent *o* broker (*EEUU*), realtor (*EEUU*) ▸ **agente literario** literary agent ▸ **agente marítimo** shipping agent ▸ **agente oficial** official agent, authorized agent ▸ **agente provocador** agent provocateur ▸ **agente secreto** secret agent ▸ **agentes sociales** social partners (*employers and unions*) ▸ **agente tributario** tax inspector ▸ **agente único** sole agent ▸ **agente viajero** commercial traveller, salesman
SM (*Quím*) agent ▸ **agente químico** chemical agent

agible ADJ feasible, workable

agigantado ADJ gigantic, huge • **a pasos ~s** by leaps and bounds

agigantar ▹ CONJUG 1a VT to enlarge, increase greatly • **~ algo** to exaggerate sth
VPR **agigantarse** (*gen*) to seem huge; [*crisis*] to get much bigger, get out of proportion

ágil ADJ (= *ligero*) agile, nimble; (= *flexible*) flexible, adaptable

agilidad SF **1** (= *ligereza*) agility, nimbleness; (= *flexibilidad*) flexibility, adaptability • **con ~** nimbly, quickly
2 (*Aut*) manoeuvrability, maneuverability (*EEUU*), handling

agilipollado* ADJ stupid, daft

agilipollarse* ▹ CONJUG 1a VPR to get all confused, act like an idiot

agilitar ▹ CONJUG 1a VT (= *hacer ágil*) to make agile; (= *facilitar*) to help, make it easy for; (*LAm*) (= *activar*) to activate, set in motion
VPR **agilitarse** (= *hacerse ágil*) to limber up

agilización SF (= *aceleración*) speeding-up; (= *mejora*) improvement
agilizar ▷ CONJUG 1f VT (= *acelerar*) to speed up; (= *mejorar*) to improve, make more flexible
VPR **agilizarse** to speed up
ágilmente ADV nimbly, quickly
agio SM (= *especulación*) speculation, agio; (*Méx*) (= *usura*) usury
agiotaje SM speculation
agiotista SMF (= *especulador*) speculator; (*Méx*) (= *usurero*) usurer
agitación SF **1** [*de mano*] waving, flapping; [*de bebida*] shaking, stirring; [*de mar*] roughness
2 (*Pol*) agitation; (= *bullicio*) bustle, stir; (= *intranquilidad*) nervousness; (= *emoción*) excitement
agitado ADJ **1** [*mar*] rough, choppy; [*aire*] turbulent; [*vuelo*] bumpy
2 (*fig*) (= *trastornado*) agitated, upset; (= *emocionado*) excited; [*vida*] hectic
SM stirring, mixing
agitador(a) SM (*Mec*) agitator, shaker; (*Culin*) stirrer
SM/F (*Pol*) agitator
agitanado ADJ gipsy-like, gypsy-like (EEUU)
agitar ▷ CONJUG 1a VT **1** [+ *mano, bandera, arma*] to wave • **agitaba un pañuelo** she was waving a handkerchief • **el viento agitaba las hojas** the wind stirred the leaves • **el pájaro agitaba las alas** the bird was flapping its wings
2 [+ *botella, líquido*] to shake • **agítese antes de usar** shake well before use • **agité al herido para que volviera en sí** I shook the injured man *o* I gave the injured man a shake to bring him round • **agitó el café con una cuchara** he stirred the coffee with a spoon
3 (= *inquietar*) to worry, upset • **los rumores del accidente la ~on** the rumours about the accident worried *o* upset her
4 (= *convulsionar*) [+ *multitud*] to stir up • **su asesinato agitó al país** his assassination stirred up the country
5 (= *esgrimir*) to use • **agitan el miedo a la guerra para ganar votos** they use the fear of war to win votes
VPR **agitarse 1** (= *moverse*) [*ramas*] to stir; [*bandera, toldo*] to flap; [*mar*] to get rough; [*barco*] to toss
2 (= *inquietarse*) to get worried *o* upset
3 (= *moverse inquieto*) • **el enfermo se agitaba en la cama** the patient was tossing and turning • **la acusada se agitaba nerviosa** the defendant shifted uneasily
aglomeración SF agglomeration
▸ **aglomeración de gente** mass of people
▸ **aglomeración de tráfico** traffic jam
▸ **aglomeración urbana** urban sprawl
aglomerado ADJ massed together, in a mass • **viven ~s** they live on top of each other
SM (= *madera*) chipboard, Masonite® (EEUU); (*Téc*) agglomeration ▸ **aglomerado asfáltico** asphalt, blacktop (*EEUU*)
aglomerar ▷ CONJUG 1a VT to agglomerate, crowd together
VPR **aglomerarse** (= *juntarse*) to agglomerate, form a mass; (= *apiñarse*) to crowd together
aglutinación SF agglutination
aglutinador ADJ agglutinative, cohesive • **fuerza ~a** unifying force, force that draws things together
aglutinadora SF unifying force
aglutinante ADJ agglutinative
aglutinar ▷ CONJUG 1a VT **1** (*Med*) to agglutinate
2 (= *unir*) to draw together, bring together
VPR **aglutinarse 1** (*Med*) to agglutinate
2 (= *unirse*) to come together, gel
agnosticismo SM agnosticism
agnóstico/a ADJ, SM/F agnostic
agobiado ADJ **1** [*persona*] • **estar ~: estamos ~s de trabajo** we're up to our eyes in work* • **estaba agobiada por tantas visitas** she found all these visitors overwhelming *o* a bit too much* • **no puedo hacerlo porque estoy ~ con otras cosas** I can't do it, I'm rushed off my feet with other things* *o* I've got too much else on*
2 [*lugar*] cluttered • **el dormitorio queda muy ~ con tantos muebles** the bedroom is very cluttered with all the furniture
3 • **ser ~ de hombros** (*Cono Sur*) to have a stoop
agobiador ADJ = **agobiante**
agobiante ADJ **1** [*calor, ambiente, lugar*] oppressive • **un día de verano ~** a stifling *o* sweltering summer's day
2 (= *insoportable*) [*trabajo, día*] stressful; [*pena, ritmo*] unbearable; [*responsabilidad*] overwhelming • **es ~ verla sufrir y no poder hacer nada** it's unbearable watching her suffer and being unable to do anything • **una ~ sensación de soledad** an overwhelming sense of loneliness
agobiar ▷ CONJUG 1b VT **1** (= *oprimir*) [*problemas, responsabilidad, pena*] to overwhelm; [*ropa*] to stifle • **estamos agobiados por las incesantes llamadas telefónicas** we're overwhelmed with constant phone calls • **agobiado por las deudas, tuvo que volver a trabajar** weighed down by debts, he was forced to go back to work • **este bochorno me agobia** I find this close weather oppressive *o* stifling
2 (= *angustiar*) • **le agobian mucho los espacios cerrados** he gets really anxious in enclosed spaces • **me agobian las grandes ciudades** big cities are too much for me*, I find big cities very stressful • **me agobia un montón oír el fútbol por la radio*** hearing football on the radio really gets to me*
3 (= *molestar*) to pester, harass • **estaban agobiándola con tantas preguntas** they were pestering *o* harassing her with so many questions
4* (= *meter prisa*) • **no me agobies, ya terminaré el trabajo cuando pueda** please, give me a break *o* get off my back, I'll finish the work when I can*
VPR **agobiarse*** • **no se agobia con nada** he doesn't let anything get on top of him *o* get to him* • **me agobié del calor que hacía** the heat was too much for me
agobio SM **1** (= *malestar*) • **el calor y el ~ provocaron algunos mareos entre el público** it was so hot and crowded that some of the audience fainted
2 (= *angustia*) • **soñaban con unas vacaciones lejos del ~ del trabajo doméstico** they dreamed of holidays away from the stress of housework • **¡cuántos deberes! ¡qué ~!*** so much homework! it's a nightmare!*
agolpamiento SM throng, crush
agolparse ▷ CONJUG 1a VPR (= *apiñarse*) to throng, crowd together; (= *acumularse*) [*problemas*] to come one on top of another; [*lágrimas*] to come in a flood • **~ en torno a algn** to crowd round sb
agonía SF **1** [*de muerte*] death agony, death throes (*pl*); (= *últimos momentos*) dying moments (*pl*) • **la época está en su ~** the period is in its death throes • **en su ~** on his death-bed • **acortar la ~ a un animal** to put an animal out of its misery
2 (= *angustia*) anguish; (= *deseo*) desire, yearning
agonías* SMF INV moaner, misery guts*
agónico ADJ (= *moribundo*) dying; (= *angustiante*) agonizing
agonioso ADJ (*LAm*) (= *egoísta*) selfish; (= *fastidioso*) bothersome • **es tan ~** he's such a pest
agonizante ADJ (= *moribundo*) dying; [*luz*] failing
SMF dying person
agonizar ▷ CONJUG 1f VI to be dying, be in one's death throes • **~ por hacer algo** to be dying to do sth
agonizos SMPL (*Méx*) worries, troubles
agora†† ADV (*LAm*) = **ahora**
ágora SF main square
agorafobia SF agoraphobia
agorafóbico/a SM/F agoraphobe
agorar ▷ CONJUG 1m VT to predict, prophesy
agorero/a ADJ (= *que presagia*) prophetic; (= *que presagia males*) ominous • **ave agorera** bird of ill omen
SM/F (= *adivino*) soothsayer, fortune teller
agostar ▷ CONJUG 1a VT **1** (= *quemar*) to parch, burn up
2 (= *marchitar*) to wither, kill before time
3 (*Méx*) (= *pastar*) to graze on rough ground
VPR **agostarse 1** (= *secarse*) to dry up, shrivel
2 (= *marchitarse*) to die, fade away
agosteño ADJ August (*antes de s*)
agosto SM August; (= *cosecha*) harvest; (= *época*) harvest time • **hacer su ~** to feather one's nest, make one's pile; ▸ **septiembre**
agotado ADJ **1** (= *cansado*) • **estar ~** to be exhausted, be worn out
2 (= *acabado*) [*mercancía, producto*] sold out; [*existencias, provisión*] finished, exhausted; [*libro*] out of stock
3 [*pila*] flat
agotador ADJ exhausting
agotamiento SM **1** (= *cansancio*) exhaustion ▸ **agotamiento nervioso** nervous strain ▸ **agotamiento por calor** heat exhaustion
2 [*de reservas*] depletion, draining
agotar ▷ CONJUG 1a VT **1** (= *cansar*) wear out, tire out • **las vacaciones me agotan** holidays wear *o* tire me out, holidays are exhausting • **este niño me agota las fuerzas** this child wears *o* tires me out
2 (= *terminar con*) [+ *recursos naturales, reservas*] to use up, exhaust; [+ *posibilidades*] to exhaust • **el público agotó las entradas en dos horas** all the tickets (were) sold out within two hours • **las jugueterías ~on sus existencias** the toyshops sold out • **han agotado todas las vías legales** they have exhausted all legal avenues • **antes de eso prefieren ~ la vía diplomática** they prefer to try all diplomatic options first • **agoté todos mis argumentos intentando convencerle** I ran out of arguments trying to persuade him • **agotamos todos los temas de conversación** we ran out of topics of conversation • **tanto papeleo me agota la paciencia** I lose patience with *o* get impatient with all this paperwork
3 • **he decidido ~ el plazo** I decided to take as much time as I was allowed • **he agotado todas las prórrogas** all my extensions have run out, I've used up all my extensions • **el gobierno pretende ~ la legislatura** the government aims to last out its term
VI (= *cansar*) • **correr cuando hace calor agota** running in the heat tires you out, running in the heat is exhausting
VPR **agotarse 1** (= *cansarse*) to get

exhausted, tire o.s. out, wear o.s. out • **me agoto pronto nadando** I soon get exhausted when I swim, I soon tire *o* wear myself out when I swim, swimming soon tires *o* wears me out
2 [*mercancía, artículo, género*] to sell out • **se han agotado las entradas para el concierto** tickets for the concert have sold out • **ese producto se nos ha agotado** we've sold out of that product, that product is *o* has sold out
3 [*recursos, reservas*] to run out • **se me agotó la gasolina** I ran out of petrol • **se me ~on los argumentos para defender mi tesis** I ran out of arguments to defend my thesis • **se me está agotando la paciencia** my patience is running out *o* wearing thin
4 [*prórroga, tiempo*] to run out • **el tiempo se iba agotando** time was running out • **el plazo se agota mañana** the deadline is tomorrow

agraceño ADJ tart, sour

agraciado/a ADJ **1** (= *atractivo*) graceful, attractive; (= *encantador*) charming • **poco ~** plain
2 (= *con suerte*) lucky • **ser ~ con** to be blessed with • **salir ~** to be lucky, be the winner
SM/F lucky winner

agraciar ▹ CONJUG 1b VT **1** (= *adornar*) to adorn; (= *ceder*) to grace; (= *hacer más atractivo*) to make more attractive
2 [+ *preso*] to pardon
3 • **~ a algn con algo** to bestow sth on sb

agradable ADJ (= *grato*) pleasant, agreeable • **es un sitio ~** it's a nice place • **el cadáver no era muy ~ para la vista** the body was not a pretty sight • **ser ~ al gusto** to taste good, be tasty

agradablemente ADV pleasantly, agreeably

agradar ▹ CONJUG 1a VT to please, be pleasing to • **esto no me agrada** I don't like this
VI to please • **su presencia siempre agrada** your presence is always welcome • **si le agrada le traeré más café** if you wish I'll bring you more coffee
VPR **agradarse** to like each other

agradecer ▹ CONJUG 2d VT (= *dar las gracias a*) to thank; (= *sentirse agradecido*) to be grateful for • **(te) agradezco tu ayuda** thanks for your help • **se lo agradezco** thank you, I am much obliged to you (*frm*) • **un favor que él no ~ía nunca lo bastante** a favour *o* (*EEUU*) favor he can never thank you enough for • **le ~ía me enviara** I would be grateful if you would send me • **eso no lo tiene que ~ a nadie** he has nobody to thank for that, he owes nobody thanks for that
VPR **agradecerse** • **¡se agradece!** much obliged!, thanks very much! • **una copita de jerez siempre se agradece** a glass of sherry is always welcome

agradecido ADJ **1** • **estar ~ (por algo)** to be grateful (for sth) • **estamos muy ~s** we are very grateful • **me miró agradecida** she looked at me gratefully • **¡muy ~!** many thanks!, I'm very grateful!, I appreciate it! • **le quedaría muy ~ si me enviara un ejemplar** I should be very grateful if you would send me a copy
2 • **ser ~** [*persona*] to be appreciative • **es muy agradecida, cualquier cosita la pone contenta** she's very appreciative, any little thing makes her happy
3 [*planta, tierra*] • **son terrenos muy ~s** this land is easy to grow things on, this land is very easy to cultivate • **los olivos son árboles muy ~s** olive trees are very easy to grow
4 (= *bien recibido*) • **tu visita es siempre agradecida** you're always welcome here

agradecimiento SM (= *gratitud*) gratitude; (= *aprecio*) appreciation

agrado SM **1** (= *cualidad*) affability • **con ~** willingly
2 (= *gusto*) • **ser del ~ de algn** to be to sb's liking • **tengo el ~ de informarle que ...** (*LAm*) I have pleasure in informing you that ..., I am glad to tell you that ...

ágrafo/a ADJ, SM/F illiterate

agramatical ADJ ungrammatical

agrandamiento SM enlargement

agrandar ▹ CONJUG 1a VT (= *hacer más grande*) to make bigger, enlarge; (= *exagerar*) to exaggerate, magnify
VPR **agrandarse** to get bigger

agranijado ADJ pimply

agrario ADJ agrarian • **política agraria** agricultural policy • **reforma agraria** land reform

agrarismo SM (*Méx*) agrarian reform movement

agrarista (*Méx*) ADJ • **movimiento ~** agrarian reform movement
SMF supporter of land reform

agravación SF, **agravamiento** SM (= *empeoramiento*) worsening; (*Med*) change for the worse

agravado SM • **robo con ~** robbery with aggravation

agravante ADJ aggravating
SM o SF additional problem; (*Jur*) aggravating circumstance • **con la ~ de que** with the further difficulty that • **robo con ~** robbery with aggravation • **con la ~ de la nocturnidad** (*Jur*) made more serious by the fact that it was done at night

agravar ▹ CONJUG 1a VT **1** (= *hacer más grave*) [+ *pena*] to increase; [+ *dolor*] to make worse; [+ *situación*] to aggravate; (*fig*) (= *oprimir*) to oppress, burden (**con** with)
2 (= *hacer más pesado*) to weigh down, make heavier
VI, VPR **agravarse** (= *empeorarse*) to worsen, get worse

agraviar ▹ CONJUG 1b VT (= *dañar*) to wrong; (= *insultar*) to offend, insult
VPR **agraviarse** to be offended, take offence, take offense (*EEUU*) (**de, por** at)

agravio SM (= *daño*) wrong, injury; (= *insulto*) offence, offense (*EEUU*), insult; (*Jur*) grievance, injustice ▸ **agravio comparativo** inequality, resentment arising from inequality ▸ **agravios de hecho** assault and battery

agravión ADJ (*Cono Sur*) touchy, quick to take offence

agravioso ADJ offensive, insulting

agraz SM **1** (= *uva*) sour grape; (= *jugo*) sour grape juice • **en ~** prematurely, before time
2 (*fig*) (= *amargura*) bitterness, ill-feeling

agrazar ▹ CONJUG 1f VT **1** (= *amargar*) to embitter
2 (= *fastidiar*) to vex, annoy
VI (= *saber amargo*) to taste sour, have a sharp taste

agrazón SM **1** (= *uva*) wild grape; (= *grosellero*) gooseberry bush
2 (*fig*) (= *enfado*) vexation, annoyance

agredir ▹ CONJUG 3a VT (*físicamente*) to assault, set upon; (*verbalmente*) to attack

agregado/a SM/F **1** (= *profesor*) assistant
2 (*Pol*) ▸ **agregado/a comercial** commercial attaché ▸ **agregado/a cultural** cultural attaché ▸ **agregado/a de prensa** press attaché ▸ **agregado/a militar** military attaché
3 (*LAm*) (= *aparcero*) sharecropper; (*Cono Sur*) (= *inquilino*) paying guest; (*Caribe*) (= *jornalero*) day labourer, day laborer (*EEUU*)
SM **1** (*Téc*) aggregate
2 (= *bloque*) concrete block

agregador SM (*tb* **agregador de noticias**) aggregator, news aggregator

agregaduría SF (*Pol*) office of attaché; (*Escol*) assistantship

agregar ▹ CONJUG 1h VT **1** (= *añadir*) to add • **~ algo a algo** to add sth to sth • **agregue el azúcar y remueva** add the sugar and stir • **—y no me satisface, agregó** "and I'm not satisfied," she added
2 [+ *trabajador, empleado*] to appoint • **fue agregado a la oficina de prensa** he was appointed to the press office
VPR **agregarse** • **~se a algo** to join sth • **se ~on a la fiesta** they joined the party

agremiar ▹ CONJUG 1b VT to form into a union, unionize
VPR **agremiarse** to form a union

agresión SF (= *acometida*) aggression; (*contra persona*) attack, assault • **pacto de no ~** non-aggression pact ▸ **agresión sexual** sexual assault

agresivamente ADV aggressively

agresividad SF (= *violencia*) aggressiveness; (= *vigor*) drive, punch, vigour, vigor (*EEUU*)

agresivo ADJ (= *violento*) aggressive; (= *vigoroso*) forceful, vigorous

agresor(a) ADJ • **país ~** aggressor country
SM/F (= *atacante*) aggressor, attacker; (*Jur*) assailant

agreste ADJ **1** (= *campestre*) rural, country
2 [*paisaje*] wild
3 (*fig*) (= *tosco*) rough, uncouth

agrete ADJ sourish

agriado ADJ **1** [*persona*] (= *resentido*) sour, resentful; (= *exasperado*) angry, irritated
2 (*Cono Sur*) (= *agrio*) sour, sharp

agriar ▹ CONJUG 1c VT **1** (= *avinagrar*) to turn sour
2 (*fig*) (= *amargar*) to sour; (= *fastidiar*) to vex, annoy
VPR **agriarse 1** (= *avinagrarse*) to turn sour
2 (= *amargarse*) to become embittered; (= *fastidiarse*) to get cross, get exasperated • **se le ha agriado el carácter** he's turned into a right creep*

agrícola ADJ agricultural, farming (*antes de s*)

agricultor(a) ADJ agricultural, farming (*antes de s*)
SM/F farmer ▸ **agricultor(a) de montaña** hill farmer

agricultura SF agriculture, farming ▸ **agricultura biodinámica, agricultura biológica** organic farming ▸ **agricultura de montaña** hill farming ▸ **agricultura de rozas y quema** slash-and-burn agriculture ▸ **agricultura de subsistencia** subsistence farming ▸ **agricultura ecológica** organic farming ▸ **agricultura intensiva** intensive farming ▸ **agricultura orgánica** organic farming

agricultural ADJ (*LAm*) agricultural, farming (*antes de s*)

agridulce ADJ bittersweet • **cerdo ~** sweet and sour pork

agriera SF (*LAm*) heartburn

agrietado ADJ (= *con grietas*) cracked; [*piel*] chapped

agrietar ▹ CONJUG 1a VT (= *resquebrajar*) to crack, crack open; [+ *piel*] to chap
VPR **agrietarse** (= *resquebrajarse*) to crack; [*piel*] to become chapped

agrifolio SM holly

agrimensor(a) SM/F surveyor

agrimensura SF surveying

agringado ADJ (*LAm*) like a gringo, like a foreigner

agringarse ▹ CONJUG 1h VPR (*LAm*) to act *o* behave like a gringo, act *o* behave like a foreigner

a

agrio ADJ **1** (*al gusto*) sour, tart; (*fig*) (= *desabrido*) bitter, disagreeable
2 [*camino*] rough, uneven; [*materia*] brittle; [*color*] garish
SM (= *zumo*) sour juice; **agrios** (= *frutas*) citrus fruits

agriparse ▹ CONJUG 1a VPR (*Cono Sur*) (= *coger gripe*) to get flu, get the flu (*esp EEUU*) • **estar agripado** to have flu *o* (*esp EEUU*) the flu

agriura SF (*LAm*) sourness, tartness

agro SM agriculture

agroalimentario ADJ food and agriculture (*antes de s*)

agrobiología SF agrobiology

agrobiológico ADJ agrobiological

agrobiólogo/a SM/F agrobiologist

agrocarburante SM, **agrocombustible** SM biofuel

agroenergética SF biofuel production

agroforestal ADJ agroforestry (*antes de s*)

agro-industria SF agro-industry

agronegocios SMPL agribusiness

agronomía SF agronomy, agriculture

agrónomo/a ADJ • **ingeniero ~** agricultural scientist
SM/F agronomist, agricultural expert

agropecuario ADJ farming (*antes de s*) • **sector ~** agriculture and fishing • **política agropecuaria** farming policy • **riqueza agropecuaria** agricultural wealth

agropesquero ADJ *relating to farming and fishing*

agroproducto SM farm produce

agroquímico ADJ, SM agrochemical

agrosistema SM agricultural ecosystem, farming ecosystem

agroturismo SM rural tourism

agroturístico ADJ rural tourism (*antes de s*)

agrupación SF **1** (= *grupo*) group, association; (= *reunión*) gathering; (= *unión*) union; (*Mús*) ensemble
2 (= *acción*) grouping; (= *reunión*) coming together

agrupamiento SM grouping

agrupar ▹ CONJUG 1a VT (= *reunir en grupo*) to group, group together; [+ *gente, datos etc*] to gather, assemble; (= *amontonar*) to crowd together
VPR **agruparse** (*Pol*) to form a group; (= *juntarse*) to gather together, come together (**en torno a** round)

agrura SF **1** (= *sabor agrio*) sourness, tartness
2 agruras (*Méx*) (*Med*) heartburn

agua SF **1** (*para beber, lavar*) water • **lavar en ~ fría** wash in cold water • **dame ~** give me a drink of water • **un motor refrigerado por ~** a water-cooled engine • **dos ~s con gas y una sin gas, por favor** two sparkling mineral waters and one still one, please • **ha sido un invierno de mucha ~** it's been a very wet winter, we've had a lot of rain this winter • **¡hombre al ~!** man overboard! • **lanzar un barco al ~** to launch a boat • **caer ~** to rain • **hace falta que caiga mucha ~** we need a lot of rain • **cayó ~ a mares** it poured down • **echarse al ~** (*lit*) to dive in; (*fig*) to take the plunge • **¡~ va!** look out!, careful! • **sin decir ~ va** without (any) warning • MODISMOS: • **bailar el ~ a algn** (*Esp*) (= *adular*) to dance attendance on sb; (*Méx**) (= *coquetear*) to flirt with sb • **bañarse en ~ de rosas** to see the world through rose-tinted spectacles • **hacérsele la boca ~ a algn** (*Esp*) • **hacérsele ~ la boca a algn** (*LAm*): • **se me hace la boca ~ solo de pensar en la sopa** just thinking about the soup makes my mouth water, my mouth is watering just thinking about the soup • **se le hace la boca ~ de pensar en los beneficios** he's drooling at the thought of the profit he'll make • **quedar en ~ de borrajas** [*promesas, proyectos*] to come to nothing • **cambiar el ~ al canario** *o* **a las aceitunas*** to take a leak* • **coger ~ en cesto** to labour in vain, be wasting one's time • **como ~ para chocolate** (*Méx**) furious • **estar con el ~ al cuello** to be in it up to one's neck* • **¿me da para mis ~s?** (*Méx*) how about a little something for me? • **echar a algn al ~** (*Chile**) to give sb away • **gastar el dinero como ~** to spend money like water • **como ~ de mayo** (*Esp*): • **esperan la privatización como ~ de mayo** they are eagerly awaiting privatization • **la noticia fue recibida como ~ de mayo en los mercados financieros** the news was welcomed with open arms on the financial markets • **este dinero nos viene como ~ de mayo** this money is a godsend, this money couldn't have come at a better time • **llevar el ~ a su molino** to turn things to one's own advantage • **mear ~ bendita‡** to be a holy Joe* • **es ~ pasada** that's all water under the bridge • **pescar en ~ turbia** to fish in troubled waters • **sacar ~ de las piedras** to work miracles • **de primera ~** (*Chile*) first hand • **ser como el ~ por San Juan** to be harmful, be unwelcome • REFRANES: • **~ que no has de beber déjala correr** don't be a dog in the manger • **nunca digas de esta ~ no beberé** never say never • **de las ~s mansas me libre Dios** still waters run deep • **~ pasada no mueve molino** it's no good crying over spilt milk • **lo que por ~ viene, por ~ se va** (*Col*) easy come, easy go* ▸ **agua bendita** holy water ▸ **agua blanda** soft water ▸ **agua corriente** running water ▸ **agua (de) cuba** (*Chile*) bleach ▸ **agua de cebada** barley water ▸ **agua de colonia** eau de cologne ▸ **agua de espliego** lavender water ▸ **agua de fregar** dishwater ▸ **agua de fuego** firewater ▸ **agua de fusión de la nieve** meltwater ▸ **agua de lavanda** lavender water ▸ **agua del grifo** tap water ▸ **agua de lluvia** rainwater ▸ **agua de mar** sea water ▸ **agua de rosas** rosewater ▸ **agua de seltz** seltzer, soda (water), seltzer water (EEUU) ▸ **agua destilada** distilled water ▸ **agua dulce** fresh water • **un pez de ~ dulce** a freshwater fish ▸ **agua dura** hard water ▸ **agua fuerte** *nitric acid solution* ▸ **agua Jane®** (*Uru*) bleach ▸ **agua mineral** mineral water • **~ mineral con gas** sparkling mineral water • **~ mineral sin gas** still mineral water ▸ **agua nieve** sleet • **cayó ~ nieve** it was sleeting ▸ **agua oxigenada** hydrogen peroxide ▸ **agua (de) panela** (*Col, Ven*) hot lemon ▸ **agua perra** (*Chile*) boiled water (*drunk for its cleansing properties*) ▸ **agua pesada** heavy water ▸ **agua potable** drinking water ▸ **agua salada** salt water • **un pez de ~ salada** a saltwater fish ▸ **agua tónica** tonic water; ▹ **claro, grabado, vía**
2 (*CAm, And*) (= *gaseosa*) fizzy drink, soda (EEUU); (= *infusión*) herbal tea • **~ de manzanilla** camomile tea
3 (*CAm*) (= *zumo*) juice • **~ de pera** pear juice
4 aguas [*de mar, río*] waters; [*de la marea*] tide (*sing*) • **las frías ~s del Atlántico** the cold waters of the Atlantic • **Dios creó las ~s** God created the seas and the oceans • **~s abajo** downstream, downriver • **~s arriba** upstream, upriver • **hacer ~s** [*barco*] to take in water; [*explicación, teoría*] to be full of holes, not to hold water; [*relación, organización, proyecto*] to founder • **nuestro mercado interno hacía ~** our domestic market was foundering *o* in trouble • **romper ~s**: • **rompió ~s camino del hospital** her waters broke on the way to the hospital • **tomar las ~s** to take the waters • MODISMOS: • **estar** *o* **nadar entre dos ~s** to sit on the fence • **volver las ~s a su cauce**: • **las ~s están volviendo a su cauce** things are returning to normal ▸ **aguas amnióticas** amniotic fluid (*sing*) ▸ **aguas de consumo** drinking water (*sing*) ▸ **aguas de escorrentía** run-off water (*sing*) ▸ **aguas de pantoque** bilge water (*sing*) ▸ **aguas fecales** sewage (*sing*) ▸ **aguas internacionales** international waters ▸ **aguas jurisdiccionales** territorial waters ▸ **aguas litorales** coastal waters ▸ **aguas llenas** high tide (*sing*) ▸ **aguas mayores** (*euf*) faeces (*sing*) (*frm*), feces (*sing*) (EEUU) (*frm*) • **hacer ~s mayores** to have a bowel movement ▸ **aguas menores** (*euf*) urine (*sing*) • **hacer ~s menores** to pass water ▸ **aguas muertas** neap tide (*sing*) ▸ **aguas negras, aguas residuales, aguas servidas** (*Cono Sur*) sewage (*sing*) ▸ **aguas subterráneas** groundwater (*sing*) ▸ **aguas superficiales** surface water (*sing*) ▸ **aguas termales** thermal springs ▸ **aguas territoriales** territorial waters
5 aguas (= *ondulación*) **a** [*de piedra preciosa*] veins • **la malaquita tenía unas ~s blancas** the malachite had white veins in it • **un papel azul haciendo ~s** a blue paper with a marbled design
b [*de tejado*] pitch, slope • **cubrir ~s** to put the roof on, top out • **tejado a dos ~s** gabled roof • **tejado a cuatro ~s** hipped roof
6 aguas (= *destello*) sparkle (*sing*) • **el diamante tenía unas ~s preciosas** the diamond sparkled beautifully, the diamond had a wonderful sparkle

aguacate SM **1** (= *fruto*) avocado pear; (= *árbol*) avocado pear tree
2 (*CAm**) (= *idiota*) idiot, fool
3 aguacates (*Méx***) balls**, bollocks**

aguacatero SM avocado tree

aguacero SM shower, heavy shower, downpour

aguacha SF foul water, stagnant water

aguachacha SF (*CAm*) weak drink, nasty drink

aguachado ADJ (*Cono Sur*) tame

aguachento ADJ (*And, Cono Sur*) (= *aguado*) watery

aguachinado ADJ (*Caribe*) (= *acuoso*) watery; (= *blando*) soft

aguachinarse ▹ CONJUG 1a VPR (*Méx*) to be flooded

aguachirle SF **1** (= *bebida*) slops (*pl*), dishwater
2 (= *bagatela*) trifle, mere nothing

aguacil SM (*Cono Sur*) dragonfly

aguacola SF (*Méx*) fish glue

aguada SF **1** (*Agr*) watering place
2 (*Náut*) water supply
3 (*Min*) flood
4 (*Arte*) watercolour, watercolor (EEUU), wash

aguadilla SF ducking • **hacer una ~ a algn** to duck sb, hold sb's head under water

aguado ADJ **1** (= *diluido*) [*sopa*] thin, watery; [*leche, vino*] watered down; [*café*] weak
2* (= *abstemio*) teetotal
3 (*LAm*) (= *débil*) weak
4 (*Méx*) (= *perezoso*) lazy, idle

aguador(a) SM/F water carrier, water seller

aguaducho SM **1** (= *arroyo*) freshet
2 (= *quiosco*) refreshment stall, small open-air café

aguafiestas SMF INV spoilsport, killjoy

aguafuerte SF **1** (*Quím*) nitric acid
2 (*Arte*) etching • **grabar algo al ~** to etch sth

aguafuertista SMF etcher

a

aguaitada SF (*LAm*) look, glance • **echar una ~ a** to take a look at
aguaitar ▷ CONJUG 1a VT 1 (*LAm*) (= *mirar*) to watch; (= *espiar*) to spy on, observe; (= *acechar*) to lie in wait for
2 (*And, Caribe*) (= *esperar*) to wait for
3 (*Cono Sur*) (= *ver*) to look, see
VI (*LAm*) • **~ por la ventana** to look out of the window
aguaje SM 1 (= *marea*) tide, spring tide; (= *corriente*) current; (= *estela*) wake
2 (= *provisión*) water supply; (*Agr*) watering trough
3 (*CAm*) (= *aguacero*) downpour
aguajirado ADJ (*Caribe*) withdrawn, timid
aguajirarse ▷ CONJUG 1a VPR (*Caribe*) (= *tomar costumbres campesinas*) to become countrified, acquire peasant's habits *etc*; (= *ser reservado*) to be withdrawn, be reserved
agualotal SM (*CAm*) swamp, marsh
aguamala SF (*And*) jellyfish
aguamanil SM (= *jarro*) water jug; (= *jofaina*) washbasin, bathroom sink
aguamar SM jellyfish
aguamarina SF aquamarine
aguamarse ▷ CONJUG 1a VPR (*And*) to get scared, be intimidated
aguamiel SF 1 (= *hidromiel*) sugared water
2 (*CAm, Méx*) (= *jugo del maguey*) fermented maguey juice, fermented agave juice
aguamuerta SF (*Cono Sur*) jellyfish
aguanieve SF sleet
aguano SM (*And*) mahogany
aguanoso ADJ 1 (= *lleno de agua*) wet, watery; [*tierra*] waterlogged
2 (*Méx*) (= *insípido*) [*persona*] wet*
aguantable ADJ bearable, tolerable
aguantaderas SFPL • **tener ~** to be patient, put up with a lot
aguantadero* SM (*Cono Sur*) hide-out
aguantador(a) ADJ (*LAm*) = **aguantón**
SM/F* fence*, receiver, receiver of stolen goods
aguantar ▷ CONJUG 1a VT 1 (= *soportar deliberadamente*) to put up with, endure • **aguanté el dolor como pude** I bore *o* put up with *o* endured the pain as best as I could • **tenemos que estar aguantando continuas ofensas** we have to put up with *o* endure continual insults • **no ~é tus impertinencias ni un minuto más** I won't stand for *o* take *o* put up with your cheek a minute longer • MODISMO: • **~ el chaparrón** to weather the storm
2 (= *tener capacidad de resistir*) to stand up to • **esta planta aguanta bien el calor** this plant withstands *o* can take heat well, this plant stands up well to heat • **aguanta bastante bien el trabajo en la mina** he stands up pretty well to the work in the mine • **no sé si podré ~ ese ritmo** I don't know if I'll be able to stand the pace • **sabe ~ bien las bromas** he can take a joke • **no ~**: • **no aguanto a los cotillas** I can't bear *o* stand gossips • **no aguanto ver sufrir a un animal** I can't bear *o* stand to see an animal suffering • **no aguantaba la rutina de los entrenamientos** he couldn't cope with *o* take the training programme • **no hay quien te aguante** you're impossible *o* insufferable • **este frío no hay quien lo aguante** this cold is just unbearable • **no hay quien aguante una ópera tan larga** who could sit through an opera that long?
3 (= *sostener*) [*persona*] to hold; [*muro, columna*] to support, hold up • **aguanta un momento el paquete** hold the parcel a minute • **la pierna que aguanta la guitarra** the leg that supports the guitar • **se rompió el cable que aguantaba la antena** the cable holding up *o* supporting the aerial broke • **estas vigas pueden ~ cualquier peso** these beams can take any weight • **esta estantería no podrá ~ tantos libros** these shelves won't take so many books
4 (= *contener*) [+ *respiración*] to hold; [+ *risa, llanto*] to hold back • **soy capaz de ~ la respiración durante dos minutos** I can hold my breath for two minutes • **el mundo aguantó la respiración temiendo un desastre** the world waited with bated breath, fearing a disaster • **apenas podía ~ la risa** she couldn't hold back her laughter • **~ las ganas de hacer algo** to resist the urge to do sth • **no pude ~ las ganas de decirle lo que pensaba** I couldn't resist telling her what I thought, I couldn't resist the urge to tell her what I thought • **se tuvo que ~ las ganas de llorar** she had to stifle her desire to cry
5 (= *durar*) to last • **este abrigo no ~á otro invierno** this coat won't last another winter
VI 1 [*persona*] • **ya no aguanto más** I can't bear it *o* stand it *o* take it any longer, I can't bear *o* stand *o* take any more • **cuando empezaba a correr no aguantaba más de diez minutos** when she started running she couldn't keep going *o* last for more than ten minutes • **~é en Madrid hasta que pueda** I'll hang on *o* hold on in Madrid as long as I can • **yo me emborracho enseguida, pero él aguanta mucho** I get drunk straight away but he can really hold his drink • **tienes que ~ hasta el año que viene con esos zapatos** you'll have to make do with those shoes until next year • **yo ya no aguanto mucho, a las diez estoy en la cama** I can't take the pace any more, I'm in bed by ten • **aguantan poco sin aburrirse** they have a low boredom threshold, they're easily bored • **bailaremos hasta que el cuerpo aguante** we'll dance till we drop • **es de guapo que no se puede ~*** he's drop dead gorgeous*, he's to die for*
2 [*clavo, columna*] to hold • **¿crees que este clavo ~á?** do you think this nail will hold? • **esa columna va a ~ poco** that pillar won't hold (out) much longer
3 (*LAm**) (= *esperar*) to hang on*, hold on • **¡aguanta!** hang on* *o* hold on a minute!
VPR **aguantarse** 1 (= *mantenerse*) • **estaba tan cansado que ya no me aguantaba de pie** I was so tired I could hardly stand • **~se de algo** to hang onto sth, hang on by sth • **me aguanté de una cuerda hasta que llegaron los bomberos** I hung onto a rope *o* I hung on by a rope until the firefighters came
2 (= *contenerse*) • **¿por qué tenemos que ~nos y no responder?** why do we have to keep quiet and not respond? • **¿no puedes ~te hasta que lleguemos a casa?** can't you hold on until we get home? • **~se de hacer algo** to hold back from doing sth
3 (= *conformarse*) • **no quería ir a la boda, pero me tuve que ~** I didn't want to go to the wedding but I had to grin and bear it • **¡si no te gusta el helado, ahora te aguantas!** if you don't like the ice cream, that's tough! *o* you can lump it!*
4 (= *soportarse*) • **cuando me duele la cabeza no me aguanto ni yo** when I have a headache I'm unbearable • **no sé cómo te aguantas** you're impossible *o* insufferable
5 (*Méx*) (= *callarse*) to keep quiet, keep one's mouth shut* • **¡aguántate!** calm down!
aguante SM 1 (= *paciencia*) patience • **no tengo ningún ~ con los niños** I have no patience with children • **no tiene ninguna capacidad de ~** she has no capacity for patience
2 (= *resistencia*) (*ante el dolor*) endurance; (*ante el cansancio*) stamina, staying power • **¿ya estás cansado? ¡qué poco ~ tienes!** are you tired already? you've no staying power *o* stamina! • **no pongas libros en esa mesa, que tiene muy poco ~** don't put books on that table, it can't take much weight
3 (*Caribe**) • **al ~ de algn** behind sb's back
aguantón ADJ (*Caribe, Méx*) long-suffering, extremely patient
SM (*Caribe**) • **te darás un ~** you'll have a long wait
aguapié SM weak wine, plonk*
aguar ▷ CONJUG 1i VT 1 [+ *vino*] to water, water down
2 (*fig*) (= *estropear*) to spoil, mar • **~ la fiesta a algn** to spoil sb's fun
3 (*CAm, Cono Sur*) [+ *ganado*] to water
aguarana SMF (*And*) primitive jungle Indian
aguardada SF wait, waiting
aguardadero SM, **aguardado** SM hide, blind (*EEUU*)
aguardar ▷ CONJUG 1a VT (= *esperar*) to wait for, await; (*con ansias*) to expect • **no sabemos el futuro que nos aguarda** we don't know what's in store for us
VI (= *esperar*) to wait • **aguarde usted** I'm coming to that • **¡aguarda te digo!** hold your horses!*
aguardentería SF liquor store
aguardentero/a SM/F liquor seller
aguardentoso ADJ [*licor, bebida*] alcoholic; [*voz*] husky, gruff
aguardiente SM brandy, liquor
▸ **aguardiente de caña** rum ▸ **aguardiente de cerezas** cherry brandy ▸ **aguardiente de manzana** applejack
aguardientoso ADJ (*LAm*) = **aguardentoso**
aguardo SM hide, blind (*EEUU*)
aguarrás SM turpentine
aguate SM (*Méx*) (= *espina*) prickle, spine
aguatero/a SM/F (*Méx*) (= *aguador*) water carrier, water seller
aguatocha SF pump
aguatoso ADJ (*Méx*) prickly
aguaturma SF Jerusalem artichoke
aguaviva SF (*Cono Sur*) jellyfish
aguayo SM (*And*) multicoloured woollen cloth *o* (*EEUU*) multicolored woolen cloth (*for adornment, or carried as shoulder bag*)
aguaza SF (*Med*) liquid (*from a tumour*); (*Bot*) sap
aguazal SM (= *charco*) puddle; (= *pantano*) swamp
aguazar ▷ CONJUG 1f VT to flood, waterlog
VPR **aguazarse** to flood, become waterlogged
agudeza SF 1 [*de los sentidos, de la mente*] acuteness, sharpness • **con una enorme ~ visual** with very keen *o* sharp vision
2 (= *ingenio*) wit, wittiness
3 (= *comentario, golpe*) witticism
agudización SF [*de los sentidos, de la mente*] sharpening; [*de crisis*] deterioration, worsening
agudizar ▷ CONJUG 1f VT [+ *los sentidos, la mente*] to sharpen, make more acute; [+ *crisis*] to aggravate
VPR **agudizarse** [*los sentidos, la mente*] to sharpen; (= *empeorarse*) worsen • **el problema se agudiza** the problem is becoming more acute • **la competencia se agudiza** competition is intensifying
agudo ADJ 1 (= *afilado*) [*filo*] sharp; [*instrumento*] sharp, pointed
2 (= *intenso*) [*enfermedad, dolor*] acute; [*acento*] acute
3 [*ángulo*] acute
4 (= *incisivo*) [*mente, sentido*] sharp, keen; [*ingenio*] ready, lively; [*crítica*] penetrating;

a

[*observación*] smart, clever; [*pregunta*] acute, searching
5 (= *gracioso*) witty
6 (*Mús*) [*nota*] high, high-pitched; [*voz, sonido*] piercing
agué (EXCL) (*CAm*) hello!
agüeitar ▹ CONJUG 1a (*LAm*) = **aguaitar**
agüera (SF) irrigation ditch
agüero (SM) omen, sign • **de buen ~** lucky • **ser de buen ~** to augur well • **de mal ~** of ill omen, unlucky • **pájaro de mal ~** bird of ill omen
aguerrido (ADJ) hardened, veteran
aguerrir ▹ CONJUG 3a; imperfecto (VT) to inure, harden
agüevar‡ ▹ CONJUG 1a (VT) (*CAm, Méx*) to put down, shame
(VPR) **agüevarse** to cower, shrink
aguijada (SF), **aguijadera** (SF) goad
aguijar ▹ CONJUG 1a (VT) [+ *buey, mula etc*] to goad; (*fig*) (= *incitar*) to urge, spur on
(VI) (= *acelerar el paso*) to hurry along, make haste
aguijón (SM) **1** (= *puya*) goad; [*de insecto*] sting; [*de planta*] prickle, spine • **dar coces contra el ~** to kick against the pricks, struggle in vain
2 (= *incitación*) stimulus, incitement • **el ~ de la carne** sexual desire
aguijonazo (SM) prick, prick with a goad, jab; (*Zool, Bot*) sting
aguijonear ▹ CONJUG 1a (VT) = **aguijar**
aguijoneo (SM) goading, provocation
águila (SF) **1** (= *ave*) eagle ▸ **águila calzada** booted eagle ▸ **águila culebrera** short-toed eagle ▸ **águila perdicera** Bonelli's eagle ▸ **águila pescadora** osprey ▸ **águila ratonera** buzzard ▸ **águila real** golden eagle • MODISMO: • **ser un ~** to be a genius, be terribly clever
2 (*Cono Sur*) (= *estafador*) cheat, swindler • **andar a palos con el ~*** to be broke
3 [*de moneda*] • **¿~ o sol?** (*Méx*) heads or tails?
aguileña (SF) columbine
aguileño (ADJ) [*nariz*] aquiline; [*rostro*] sharp-featured; [*persona*] hawk-nosed
aguilera (SF) eagle's nest, eyrie
aguilillo/a (SM/F) (*LAm*) fast horse
aguilón (SM) (= *ave*) large eagle; [*de grúa*] jib; (*Arquit*) gable, gable end; (*And*) (= *caballo*) large heavy horse
aguilucho (SM) (= *cría*) eaglet, young eagle; (*LAm*) (= *halcón*) hawk, falcon
aguinaldo (SM) **1** (= *propina*) Christmas box; (= *plus*) Christmas bonus
2 (*LAm*) (= *villancico*) Christmas carol
aguita‡ (SF) (*And*) cash, dough‡, bread‡
agüita (SF) (*Chile*) [*de menta*] herb tea, herbal tea
agüitado (ADJ) (*Méx*) depressed, gloomy
aguja (SF) **1** (*Cos, Med*) needle; [*de sombrero*] hatpin • **darle a la ~*** to shoot up‡ • MODISMO: • **buscar una ~ en un pajar** to look for a needle in a haystack ▸ **aguja capotera** darning needle ▸ **aguja de arria** (*LAm*) pack needle ▸ **aguja de gancho, aguja de ganchillo** crochet hook ▸ **aguja de hacer punto** knitting needle ▸ **aguja de marear** compass, compass needle • **conocer la ~ de marear** to know one's way around ▸ **aguja de media, aguja de tejer** (*LAm*) knitting needle ▸ **aguja de zurcir** darning needle ▸ **aguja hipodérmica** hypodermic needle ▸ **aguja imantada, aguja magnética** compass, compass needle
2 (= *indicador*) [*de reloj*] hand; (*Téc*) pointer, hand; (*Mil*) firing pin; [*de tocadiscos*] stylus, needle • **tumbar la ~*** (*Aut*) to step on the gas*, go full out
3 (*LAm*) (*Agr*) (= *estaca*) fence post
4 ▸ **aguja de pino** (*Bot*) pine needle
5 (= *chapitel*) spire, steeple
6 agujas (*Culin*) (= *costillas*) shoulder (*sing*), rib (*sing*)
7 agujas (*Ferro*) points, switch (*sing*) (*EEUU*)
8 (= *pez*) garfish
9 (*CAm, Méx*) (= *carne*) beef
agujazo (SM) prick, jab
agujereado (ADJ) full of holes
agujerear ▹ CONJUG 1a (VT) (= *hacer agujeros en*) to make holes in; (= *penetrar*) to pierce
agujero (SM) **1** (= *abertura*) hole • **hacer un ~ en** to make a hole in ▸ **agujero de hombre** manhole ▸ **agujero de ozono** ozone hole, hole in the ozone layer ▸ **agujero negro** black hole
2 (*Cos*) (*para agujas*) needle case; (*para alfileres*) pincushion
3 (*Econ*) (= *deuda*) hole, drain, deficit
agujeta (ADJ) (*Méx*) (= *listo*) sharp
(SF) **1** (*Méx*) (= *cordón*) shoelace
2 agujetas (*Esp*) (= *rigidez*) stiffness (*sing*) • **tengo ~s en las piernas** my legs are stiff
agujetero (SM) (*LAm*) (= *alfiletero*) pincushion
agujón (SM) hatpin
agur* (EXCL) cheerio!*, so long!
agusanado (ADJ) maggoty, wormy
agusanarse ▹ CONJUG 1a (VPR) to get maggoty
Agustín (SM) Augustine
agustino (ADJ), (SM), **agustiniano** (ADJ), (SM) Augustinian
agutí (SM) (*LAm*) guinea pig
aguzado (ADJ) (*LAm*) sharp, on the ball*
aguzamiento (SM) sharpening
aguzanieves (SF INV) wagtail
aguzar ▹ CONJUG 1f (VT) **1** (= *afilar*) to sharpen
2 (*fig*) (= *incitar*) to incite, stir up; [+ *ingenio*] to sharpen; [+ *apetito*] to whet • **~ el oído** to prick up one's ears • **~ la vista** to keep one's eyes peeled*
ah (EXCL) **1** (*para expresar sorpresa*) ah!, ha!, oh! • **¡ah del barco!** ship ahoy!
2 (*LAm*) (*para interrogar*) • **¿ah?** what?
a.h. (ABR) (= **año de la Hégira**) AH
ahechaduras (SFPL) chaff (*sing*)
ahechar ▹ CONJUG 1a (VT) to sift
aherrojamiento (SM) oppression
aherrojar ▹ CONJUG 1a (VT) (= *encadenar*) to put in irons, fetter; (*fig*) (= *someter*) to oppress
aherrumbrarse ▹ CONJUG 1a (VPR) [*metal*] to rust, get rusty; [*color*] to take on the colour of iron
ahí (ADV) **1** (*en un lugar*) there • **ponlo ahí** put it there • **ahí está Antonio** there's Antonio • **ahí llega el pelotón** here comes the pack • **esa de ahí es mi madre** that woman over there is my mother • **¿Nina, estás ahí?** Nina, are you there? • **de un salto puedo llegar hasta ahí enfrente** I can get over there in one jump • **ahí abajo** down there • **ahí arriba** up there • **ahí dentro** in there, inside • **ahí fuera** out there, outside • **ahí mero** (*Méx*) • **ahí mismo** right there • **vivo ahí mismo** I live right there • **ahí no más** (*LAm*) right (near) here • **por ahí** (*indicando dirección*) that way; (*indicando posición*) over there • **entra por ahí** go in that way • **busca por ahí** look over there • **las tijeras deben de estar por ahí** the scissors must be around somewhere • **hoy podemos ir a cenar por ahí** we can go out for dinner tonight, we can eat out tonight • **¿no dicen por ahí que vivimos en un país libre?** don't they say we live in a free country? • **lleva muchos años viviendo por ahí fuera** he has been living abroad for many years • **debe de tener unos cincuenta años o por ahí** she must be about fifty or so • **por ahí se le ocurre llamar** (*Cono Sur*) he might think to phone • **ahí tiene** there you are • **ahí tiene sus libros** there are your books • **¡ahí va!**: • **ahí va el balón, ¡cógelo!** there goes the ball, catch it! • **¡ahí va, qué bonito!** wow, it's lovely! • **¡ahí va, no me había dado cuenta de que eras tú!** well well! I didn't realise it was you • MODISMO: • **ahí donde lo ves** believe it or not • **ahí donde lo ves, come más que tú y yo juntos** believe it or not he eats more than you and me put together
2 (*en una situación*) • **la injusticia no acaba ahí** the injustice doesn't end there • **ahí está la clave de todo** that's the key to everything • **¡ahí está el problema!** that's the problem! • **ahí está, por ejemplo, el caso de Luis** there's the case of Luis, for example • **ahí estaba yo, con casi cincuenta años, y todavía soltero** there was I, about to turn fifty, and still a bachelor • **—¿está mejor tu mujer? —ahí anda** *o* (*LAm*) **ahí va** "is your wife better?" — "she's doing all right" • **¡hombre, haber empezado por ahí!** why didn't you say so before! • **de ahí** that's why • **de ahí las quejas de los inquilinos** that's why the tenants are complaining, hence the tenants' complaints (*frm*) • **de ahí que me sintiera un poco decepcionado** that's why I felt a bit let down • **de ahí se deduce que ...** from that it follows that ... • **hasta ahí**: • **hasta ahí llego yo** I can work that much out for myself • **bueno, hasta ahí de acuerdo** well, I agree with you up to there *o* that point • **¡hasta ahí podíamos llegar!** what a nerve!, that's the limit!, can you credit it! • **he ahí el dilema** that's the dilemma, there you have the dilemma • **ahí sí que** (*LAm*): • **si hubiéramos ido más rápido, ahí sí que nos matamos** if we'd gone any faster, we'd definitely have been killed • **ahí sí que me pillaste** you've really got me there • MODISMOS: • **¡ahí es nada!** imagine!, wow! • **ahí está el meollo** *o* **el quid de la cuestión** that's the crux of the matter, that's the whole problem • **hasta por ahí no más** (*Cono Sur*) up to a point
3 (*en el tiempo*) • **ahí mismo** (*LAm*) • **ahí no más** (*Chile*) there and then • **a partir de ahí** from then on
ahijado/a (SM/F) (= *hijo adoptivo*) godson/goddaughter; (*fig*) (= *protegido*) protégé/protégée
ahijar ▹ CONJUG 1a (VT) **1** [+ *niño*] to adopt; [+ *animal*] to adopt, mother
2 • **~ algo a algn** (= *imputar*) to impute sth to sb
ahijuna** (EXCL) (*LAm*) you bastard!**
ahilar ▹ CONJUG 1a (VT) (= *poner en fila*) to line up
(VI) (= *andar en fila*) to go in single file
(VPR) **ahilarse** (= *desmayarse*) to faint with hunger; [*planta*] to grow poorly; [*vino*] to turn sour, go off
ahincadamente (ADV) hard, earnestly
ahincado (ADJ) earnest
ahincar ▹ CONJUG 1g (VT) (= *instar*) to press, urge
(VPR) **ahincarse** (= *apresurarse*) to hurry up, make haste
ahinco (SM), **ahínco** (SM) (= *seriedad*) earnestness, intentness; (= *énfasis*) emphasis; (= *empeño*) effort; (= *resolución*) determination, perseverance • **con ~** eagerly, hard, earnestly
ahitar ▹ CONJUG 1a (VT) to cloy, surfeit
(VPR) **ahitarse** (= *empacharse*) to stuff o.s. (**de** with), give o.s. a surfeit (**de** of); (*Med*) (= *indigestarse*) give o.s. indigestion
ahíto (ADJ) **1** (= *empachado*) gorged, satiated

2 (*fig*) (= *harto*) • **estar ~ de** to be fed up with
3 (= *lleno*) full, packed tight
SM (= *empacho*) surfeit, satiety; (*Med*) (= *indigestión*) indigestion

AHN SM ABR (*Esp*) = **Archivo Histórico Nacional**

ahogadero SM **1** [*de animal*] throatband; [*de verdugo*] hangman's rope
2 (= *lugar caluroso*) • **esto es un ~** it's stifling in here

ahogado/a ADJ **1** [*persona*] (*en agua*) drowned; (*por falta de aire*) suffocated • **morir ~** (*en agua*) to drown; (*por falta de aire*) to suffocate
2 (= *apagado*) [*voz, llanto*] stifled; [*grito*] muffled
3 [*lugar*] cluttered • **la cocina está ahogada con tantos muebles** the kitchen looks cluttered with so much furniture
4 (= *sin dinero*) • **el club está ~ económicamente** the club is going under • **nos vimos ~s por las deudas** we were up to our eyes in debt
5 (*Méx**) (= *borracho*) drunk
SM/F drowned man/woman
SM (*And*) (= *salsa*) *sauce made with tomatoes, onions and peppers*; (= *guisado*) *stew made with tomatoes, onions and peppers*

ahogador SM (*Méx*) choke

ahogar ▷ CONJUG 1h VT **1** (= *matar*) (*en agua*) to drown; (*quitando el aire*) to suffocate • **lo ahogó en la bañera** she drowned him in the bath • **si riegas tanto el cactus lo vas a ~** if you keep watering the cactus so much you'll drown it • MODISMO: • **~ las penas** to drown one's sorrows
2 (= *asfixiar*) [*humo, espina, emoción*] to choke; [*angustia, pena*] to overcome • **el cuello de la camisa me está ahogando** the neck of this shirt is choking me • **su voz tiembla, ahogada por la emoción** her voice trembles, choked with emotion • **este calor me ahoga** this heat is suffocating me *o* is stifling • **la angustia me ahoga** I am overcome with anguish
3 (*económicamente*) [+ *empresa, país*] to cripple • **los impuestos ahogan a la pequeña empresa** taxation is crippling small businesses • **intentan ~ a Cuba con el bloqueo económico** they are trying to cripple Cuba with the economic blockade
4 (= *reprimir*) [+ *bostezo, tos*] to stifle; [+ *llanto*] to stifle, choke back
5 (= *detener*) [+ *fuego, llamas*] to smother; [+ *lucha, rebelión*] to crush, put down; [+ *voces, protestas*] to stifle; [+ *derechos, libertades*] to curtail; [+ *desarrollo, posibilidades, plan*] to hinder, block • **~on la rebelión en sangre** they crushed the rebellion with bloodshed • **las malas comunicaciones ahogan la expansión económica** bad communications are hindering *o* blocking economic expansion • **los aplausos ahogaban sus palabras** her words were drowned (out) by the applause • **el Barcelona ahogó las esperanzas del Deportivo** Barcelona put paid to *o* dashed Deportivo's hopes
6 (= *bloquear*) to block • **las hojas ahogan las alcantarillas** the drains were blocked (up) with leaves
7 (*Aut*) [+ *motor*] to flood
8 (*Ajedrez*) [+ *rey*] to stalemate
VPR **ahogarse 1** (*en agua*) (*accidentalmente*) to drown; (*suicidándose*) to drown o.s. • **se les ahogó el hijo en una piscina** their son drowned in a swimming pool • **no hay que regar tanto las plantas, porque se ahogan** you shouldn't water the plants so much, they'll get waterlogged • MODISMO: • **~se en un vaso de agua** to make a mountain out of a molehill
2 (= *asfixiarse*) **a** (*por falta de aire*) • **subió la cuesta ahogándose** she climbed the hill gasping for breath • **si subo las escaleras deprisa me ahogo** if I go up the stairs too quickly I get out of breath
b (*por el calor*) to suffocate • **me ahogo de calor** I'm suffocating with this heat, the heat is stifling
c (*con humo, espina*) to choke (**con** on)
3 (= *agobiarse*) • **me ahogo en los ascensores** I get claustrophobic in lifts • **se ahoga en un mar de indecisiones** she is drowning in a sea of indecision
4 (*Aut*) [*motor*] to flood

ahogo SM **1** (= *asfixia*) breathlessness • **una sensación de ~ le impedía hablar** a feeling of breathlessness prevented him from speaking • **el asma le produce ~** asthma makes him breathless
2 (= *angustia*) feeling of distress
3 (= *apuro económico*) financial difficulty • **hemos pasado unos ~s tremendos para comprar el piso** we went through tremendous difficulties to buy the flat

ahoguío SM (*Med*) = **ahogo**

ahondar ▷ CONJUG 1a VT to deepen, make deeper
VI • **~ en** to study thoroughly, explore
VPR **ahondarse** to go in more deeply, sink in more deeply

ahora ADV **1** (= *en este momento*) now • **hace ~ un mes** a month ago now • **~ o nunca** now or never • **ese color se lleva mucho ~** people wear that colour a lot these days *o* now • **el ~ primer ministro** the present prime minister • **de ~ en adelante** from now on • **de ~** of today • **la juventud de ~** the youth of today, today's youth • **no es una cosa de ~** it's not a recent thing • **desde ~** from now on • **hasta ~** up to now, so far • **~ mismo** right now • **~ mismo están reunidos** they're in a meeting at the moment *o* right now • **a partir de ~** from now on • **por ~** for the moment, for now • **es todo lo que podemos hacer por ~** it's all we can do for the moment *o* for now • **por ~ ha dirigido sólo dos películas** up to now he has only directed two films • **~ que** now that • **~ que lo dices** now that you mention it • **~ que lo pienso** come to think of it, now that I think of it • **~ resulta que ...** now it turns out that ... • **~ sí que me voy** I'm definitely going this time • **~ sí que os habéis equivocado** this time you're definitely wrong
2 (= *hace poco*) just now • **me lo acaban de decir ~** they've just told me • **acaban de llegar ~ mismito** they've just this minute arrived • **~ tiempo** (*Chile*) a while ago • **~ último** (*Chile*) recently
3 (= *enseguida*) in a minute • **~ lo apunto** I'll write it down in a minute • **~ mismo voy** I'll be right there, I'll be there in a minute • **¡hasta ~!** see you in a minute!
CONJ **1** (= *sin embargo*) • **~, yo entiendo que eso no fue lo acordado** I understand, though, that that is not what was agreed • **es muy barato; ~, si no te gusta no lo compro** it's very cheap; then again, if you don't like it I won't buy it • **~ bien** however • **~ que** although • **es listo, ~ que bastante vago** he's bright, although quite lazy
2 (*uso distributivo*) • **~ la quitan, ~ la ponen** one minute they take it away, the next they put it back • **la ducha escocesa, ~ caliente, ~ fría** the Scottish shower — one minute hot, the next cold

ahorcado/a ADJ (*Cono Sur**) flat broke*
SM/F hanged person

ahorcadura SF hanging

ahorcajarse ▷ CONJUG 1a VPR to sit astride • **~ en** to straddle

ahorcamiento SM hanging

ahorcar ▷ CONJUG 1g VT to hang • **a la fuerza ahorcan** there is no alternative • **¡que me ahorquen!** cross my heart!
VPR **ahorcarse** to hang o.s.

ahorita ADV (*esp LAm*), **ahoritica** ADV (*LAm*), **ahoritita** ADV (*Méx*) (= *en este momento*) right now, this very minute; (= *hace poco*) a minute ago, just now; (= *dentro de poco*) in a minute • **¡~ voy!** I'm just coming!, I'll be with you in a minute!

ahormar ▷ CONJUG 1a VT **1** (= *ajustar*) to fit, adjust (**a** to); (= *formar*) to shape, mould, to mold (*EEUU*); [+ *zapatos*] to break in, stretch; [+ *carácter*] to mould, mold (*EEUU*)
2 • **~ a algn** (= *poner en razón*) to make sb see sense

ahorquillado ADJ forked

ahorquillar ▷ CONJUG 1a VT **1** (= *apoyar*) to prop up
2 (= *formar*) to shape like a fork
VPR **ahorquillarse** to fork, become forked

ahorrador ADJ thrifty

ahorrar ▷ CONJUG 1a VT **1** [+ *dinero, energía, tiempo, trabajo*] to save • **así podrás ~ algo de electricidad** this way you will be able to save some electricity • **tienen bastante dinero ahorrado** they have quite a lot of money saved up *o* put by
2 (= *evitar*) [+ *disgustos, molestias, problemas*] to save; [+ *peligro*] to avoid • **me gustaría ~te las molestias** I'd like to save you the trouble • **te ~é los detalles** I'll spare you the details • **lo contó sin ~ detalles** she told it in great detail • **no ~ ataques/críticas contra algn** to show no mercy in one's attacks/criticism of sb • **no ~ elogios con algn** to be unstinting in one's praise of sb • **no ~ esfuerzos** to spare no effort, be unstinting in one's efforts
3†† [+ *esclavo*] to free
VI to save • **está ahorrando para comprarse un coche** he's saving (up) to buy a car • **no encienden la calefacción para ~** they don't put the heating on to save money *o* to economize
VPR **ahorrarse 1** [+ *dinero, tiempo*] to save • **al comprar esa casa se ahorró bastante dinero** buying that house saved him quite a lot of money • MODISMO: • **no ahorrárselas con nadie** to be afraid of nobody
2 (= *evitarse*) to save o.s. • **así te ahorras tener que ir al médico** this will save you *o* you'll save yourself having to go to the doctor's • **un regalo que te ahorras** it saves you having to buy a present, you save yourself having to buy a present • **podías haberte ahorrado los comentarios** I could have done without your comments • **por mí puedes ~te las molestias** as far as I'm concerned you can save yourself the trouble

ahorrativo ADJ (= *que no derrocha*) thrifty; (*pey*) (= *tacaño*) stingy, mean

ahorrillos SMPL small savings

ahorrista SMF saver

ahorro SM **1** (= *acto*) [*de dinero, energía, trabajo*] saving • **una política que fomenta el ~** a policy which promotes saving • **un plan de ~ energético** an energy saving scheme
2 ahorros (= *dinero*) savings • **he gastado todos mis ~s** I've spent all my savings • **con el tiempo he conseguido reunir unos ahorrillos** over time I've managed to get some savings together; ▷ **caja, libreta**
3 (= *cualidad*) thrift

ahoyar ▷ CONJUG 1a VT to dig holes in

ahuchar[1] ▷ CONJUG 1a VT to hoard, put by

ahuchar[2] ▷ CONJUG 1a VT (*And, Méx*) = **azuzar**

a

ahuecado (ADJ) • **voz ahuecada** deep voice
ahuecar ▸ CONJUG 1g (VT) **1** (= *excavar*) to hollow, hollow out • **~ la mano** to cup one's hand
2 (*Agr*) to loosen, soften; (*Cos*) to fluff out
3 [+ *voz*] to deepen
4 • **~ el ala** to make o.s. scarce
(VI) • **¡ahueca!*** beat it!*
(VPR) **ahuecarse** to show off
ahuesarse ▸ CONJUG 1a (VPR) (*And, Cono Sur*)
1* (= *pasar de moda*) to go out of fashion; [*alimentos*] to go off, go bad; [*mercancías*] to get spoiled
2 [*persona*] to get thin
ahuevado (ADJ) (*LAm*) silly, stupid
ahuizote (SM) **1** (*CAm, Méx*) (= *persona*) pain*, pain in the neck*, nuisance
2 (= *maleficio*) evil spell, curse
ahulado (SM) (*CAm, Méx*) oilskin • **~s** rubber shoes
ahumado (ADJ) **1** (*Culin*) smoked; (= *lleno de humo*) smoky; [*vidrio*] tinted
2* (= *borracho*) tight*, tipsy
(SM) **1** (= *acción*) smoking, curing
2* (= *borracho*) drunk
ahumar ▸ CONJUG 1a (VT) **1** (*Culin*) to smoke, cure
2 [+ *superficie*] to make smoky; [+ *sala*] to fill with smoke
3 [+ *colmena*] to smoke out
(VI) to smoke, give out smoke
(VPR) **ahumarse 1** [*comida*] to acquire a smoky flavour *o* (*EEUU*) flavor
2 [*cuarto*] to be smoky
3* (= *emborracharse*) to get tight*
ahusado (ADJ) tapering
ahusarse ▸ CONJUG 1a (VPR) to taper
ahuyentar ▸ CONJUG 1a (VT) **1** (= *espantar*) to frighten off, frighten away; (= *mantener a distancia*) to keep off
2 [+ *temores, dudas etc*] to banish, dispel • **~ las penas con vino** to drown one's sorrows in wine
(VPR) **ahuyentarse** to run away; (*Méx*) to stay away
AI (SF ABR) (= **Amnistía Internacional**) AI
AID (SF ABR) (= **Agencia Internacional para el Desarrollo**) AID
AIF (SF ABR) (= **Asociación Internacional de Fomento**) IDA
AIH [ai'atʃe] (SF ABR) = **Asociación Internacional de Hispanistas**
aimara, aimará (PL: **aimaraes**) (ADJ), (SMF) Aymara, Aymara Indian
(SM) (*Ling*) Aymara
aína (ADV) (*liter*) speedily
aindiado (ADJ) (*LAm*) Indian-like, Indianized
airadamente (ADV) angrily
airado (ADJ) **1** (= *enojado*) angry; (= *violento*) wild, violent • **joven ~** angry young man • **salió ~ del cuarto** he stormed out of the room
2 [*vida*] immoral, depraved
airar ▸ CONJUG 1a (VT) (= *enojar*) to anger; (= *irritar*) to annoy
(VPR) **airarse** to get angry (**de, por** at)
airbag ['erβag] (SM) (PL: **airbags**) airbag
aire (SM) **1** (= *elemento*) air • **una bocanada de ~ fresco** a breath of fresh air • **parece que me falta el ~** I feel as if I can't breathe • **ir a la montaña a respirar ~ puro** to go to the hills where the air is pure • **¡fuera de aquí, aire!*** get out of here! scram!* • **al ~**: • **lanzar algo al ~** to throw sth into the air • **la fruta se deja secar al ~** the fruit is left to dry uncovered • **un vestido con la espalda al ~** a backless dress • **estar en el ~** [*balón, paracaidista*] to be in the air; (*Radio*) to be on (the) air • **todo está en el ~ hasta que se conozcan los resultados** it's all up in the air until the results are known • **la polémica estaba en el ~** controversy hung in the air • **dejar una pregunta/problema en el ~** to leave a question/an issue up in the air • **al ~ libre** (*con verbo*) outdoors, in the open air; (*con sustantivo*) outdoor (*antes de s*), open-air (*antes de s*) • **el concierto se celebró al ~ libre** the concert was held outdoors *o* in the open air • **una piscina al ~ libre** an outdoor *o* open-air pool • **le gusta la vida al ~ libre** she loves the outdoor life • **actividades al ~ libre** outdoor activities • **salir al ~** (*Radio*) to go on (the) air • **saltar por los ~s** to blow up, explode • **tomar el ~** to get some fresh air • **salió a tomar un poco el ~** he went out to get *o* for some fresh air • **¡vete a tomar el ~!*** scram!*, clear off!* • **~ viciado** (*en habitación cerrada*) stale air; (*en fábrica, ciudad contaminada*) foul air • **volar por los ~s** to blow up, explode • **todas las esperanzas de paz han volado por los ~s** all hopes of peace have been dashed • MODISMOS: • **a mi/tu/su ~**: • **aprendieron a su ~** they learned in their own way • **le gusta hacer las cosas a su ~** he likes to do things his own way • **eso le permitió trabajar a su ~** that enabled her to work the way she wanted • **ir a su ~** to go one's own way, do one's own thing* • **beber los ~s por algn** to be madly in love with sb • **darle un ~ a algn**: • **le dio un ~ y perdió el habla** he had a stroke and lost the power of speech • **estar de buen/mal ~** to be in a good/bad mood • **mantenerse del ~** to live on thin air • **mudarse a cualquier ~** to change from one minute to the next • **ofenderse del ~** to be really touchy • **seguir el ~ a algn** to humour sb • **vivir del ~** to live on thin air ▸ **aire acondicionado** air conditioning • **un vehículo con ~ acondicionado** an air-conditioned vehicle ▸ **aire colado** cold draught, cold draft (*EEUU*) ▸ **aire comprimido** compressed air • **una escopeta de ~ comprimido** an air rifle ▸ **aire detonante** firedamp ▸ **aire líquido** liquid air
2 (*Meteo*) (= *viento*) wind; (= *corriente*) draught, draft (*EEUU*) • **no corre nada de ~** there isn't a breath of wind • **entra mucho ~ por la puerta** there's a strong draught coming in through the door • **hoy hace mucho ~** it's very windy today • **entraba un ~ muy agradable de la calle** there was a lovely breeze coming in from the street • **dar ~ a algn** to fan sb • **la prensa no da ~ al éxito del gobierno** the press is giving no coverage to the government's success • **darse ~** to fan o.s. • MODISMOS: • **¿qué ~s te traen por aquí?** what brings you here? • **cambiar** *o* **mudar de ~s** to have a change (of scene) ▸ **aires de cambio** (*Pol*) winds of change
3 (= *aspecto*) air • **los techos altos le daban un ~ señorial a la casa** high ceilings gave a stately air to the house • **le respondió con ~ cansado** he replied wearily • **su cara tiene un ~ familiar** there's something familiar about his face • **tienen ~ de no haber roto un plato en su vida** they look as if butter wouldn't melt in their mouths • MODISMO: • **darse ~s** to put on airs • **eso te pasa por darte ~s de superioridad** that's what happens when you think you're better than everyone else *o* when you put on airs • **no te des esos ~s de suficiencia conmigo** don't get on your high horse with me
4 (= *parecido*) • **¿no le notas un ~ con Carlos?** don't you think he looks a bit like Carlos? • **darse un ~ a algn** to look a bit like sb ▸ **aire de familia** family resemblance, family likeness
5 (= *aerofagia*) wind • **las lentejas me provocan mucho ~** lentils give me a lot of wind
6 (= *garbo*) style, panache • **lleva la ropa con mucho ~** she wears her clothes with great style *o* panache • **dio unos pases de muleta con buen ~** he did a few stylish passes with the cape
7 (*Mús*) air • **música con ~s populares** music with popular airs
aireación (SF) ventilation
aireado (SM) (= *ventilación*) ventilation; [*de vino*] aeration
aire-aire (ADJ) • **misil aire-aire** air-to-air missile
airear ▸ CONJUG 1a (VT) **1** (= *ventilar*) to air, ventilate; [+ *ropa*] to air • **~ la atmósfera** to clear the air
2 (= *difundir*) [+ *idea, cuestión*] to air; (*en prensa*) to discuss at length, give a lot of coverage to
3 (= *publicar*) to gossip about
(VPR) **airearse** (= *tomar el aire*) to take the air; (= *resfriarse*) to catch a chill
airecito (SM) breeze, gentle wind
aireo (SM) ventilation
aire-tierra (ADJ INV) • **misil aire-tierra** air-to-ground missile
airón (SM) **1** (= *ave*) heron
2 (= *penacho*) tuft, crest
airosamente (ADV) gracefully, elegantly • **salir ~ de algo** to come through sth unscathed
airosidad (SF) grace, elegance
airoso (ADJ) **1** (= *elegante*) graceful, elegant • **quedar ~** • **salir ~** to be successful, come out with flying colours • **salir ~ de algo** to come through sth unscathed
2 (= *ventilado*) airy; [*cuarto*] draughty; [*lugar expuesto*] windy; [*tiempo*] windy, blowy
aislación (SF) insulation ▸ **aislación de sonido** soundproofing ▸ **aislación térmica** insulation
aislacionismo (SM) isolationism
aislacionista (ADJ), (SMF) isolationist
aislado (ADJ) **1** (= *remoto*) isolated
2 (= *incomunicado*) cut off • **quedamos ~s por las inundaciones** we were cut off by the floods • **están ~s de la civilización** they are cut off *o* isolated from civilization
3 (= *suelto*) • **un caso ~** an isolated case
4 (*Elec*) insulated
aislador (ADJ) (*Elec*) insulating
(SM) (*Elec*) insulator
aislamiento (SM) **1** (= *acción*) isolation; (= *soledad*) loneliness, lonesomeness (*EEUU*) ▸ **aislamiento sensorial** sensory deprivation
2 (*Elec*) insulation ▸ **aislamiento acústico** soundproofing ▸ **aislamiento térmico** insulation
aislante (ADJ) insulating
(SM) (*Elec*) insulator; (= *suelo impermeable*) groundsheet
aislar ▸ CONJUG 1a (VT) **1** (= *dejar solo*) to isolate; (= *separar*) to separate, detach
2 [+ *ciudad, fortaleza*] to cut off
3 (*Elec*) to insulate
(VPR) **aislarse** to isolate o.s., cut o.s. off (**de** from)
AITA (SF ABR) (= **Asociación Internacional del Transporte Aéreo**) IATA
ajá (EXCL) (= *¡estupendo!*) splendid!; (*indicando sorpresa*) aha!
ajajay (EXCL) = **ajay**
ajamonarse* ▸ CONJUG 1a (VPR) to get plump, run to fat
ajar[1] (SM) garlic field, garlic patch
ajar[2] ▸ CONJUG 1a (VT) **1** (= *arrugar*) to crumple, crush
2 (= *despreciar*) to abuse, disparage
(VPR) **ajarse** (= *arrugarse*) [*piel*] to get

wrinkled; [*planta*] to wither, fade; [*chaqueta, vestido*] to get crumpled
ajarabezado ADJ • **vino ~** wine with syrup added
ajarafe SM (*Geog*) tableland; (*Arquit*) terrace, flat roof
ajardinado ADJ landscaped
ajardinar ▹ CONJUG 1a VT to landscape • **zona ajardinada** landscaped area
ajay EXCL (*LAm*) (*risa*) ha!
-aje ▹ **Aspects of Word Formation in Spanish 2**
ajedrea SF savory
ajedrecista SMF chess player
ajedrez SM chess • **un ~** a chess set
ajedrezado ADJ chequered, checkered (*EEUU*)
ajenjo SM (= *planta*) wormwood; (= *bebida*) absinth, absinthe
ajeno ADJ **1** (= *de otro*) • **con el dinero ~** with other people's money • **puso los huevos en un nido ~** it laid its eggs in another bird's nest • **esta semana juegan en campo ~** this week they are playing away from home • **a costa ajena** at somebody else's expense • **por cuenta ajena**: • **trabaja por cuenta ajena** he works for someone else • **trabajador por cuenta ajena** employed worker • **es matón por cuenta ajena** he's a hired thug • **meterse en lo ~** to interfere in other people's affairs; ▹ **vergüenza**
2 (= *no relacionado*) • **~ a** outside • **según fuentes ajenas a la empresa** according to sources outside the company • **"prohibido el paso a toda persona ajena a la obra"** "authorized staff only beyond this point" • **hablaron de cosas ajenas al trabajo** they talked about things unconnected with work • **el malhumor es ~ a su carácter** he's not at all bad-tempered in character, being bad-tempered is quite alien to his character (*frm*) • **reacciones ajenas a la racionalidad** irrational reactions • **el juez declaró que se mantendría ~ a la política** the judge declared that he would remain outside of politics • **por razones ajenas a nuestra voluntad** for reasons beyond our control
3 (= *indiferente*) • **no es ajena a los problemas de los ciudadanos** she is not indifferent to the population's problems • **nada de lo humano le es ~** (*liter*) everything human is his concern (*liter*) • **siguió leyendo, ~ a lo que sucedía** she carried on reading, oblivious to what was happening
4 (= *extraño*) strange • **todo le era ~ y desconocido** everything was strange and unknown
ajerezado ADJ sherry-flavoured *o* (*EEUU*) -flavored
ajete SM young garlic
ajetreado ADJ busy
ajetrearse ▹ CONJUG 1a VPR (= *atarearse*) to bustle about, be busy; (= *fatigarse*) to tire o.s. out
ajetreo SM (= *actividad*) hustle and bustle; (= *labor*) drudgery, hard work • **es un continuo ~** there's constant coming and going
ají SM (PL: **ajíes** *o* **ajises**) (*LAm*) (= *pimiento picante*) chilli; (= *pimiento dulce*) red pepper; (= *salsa*) chilli sauce • **MODISMOS**: • **estar hecho un ají** to be hopping mad • **ponerse como un ají** to go bright red, go bright red in the face • **refregarle a algn el ají** to criticize sb
ajiaceite SM *sauce of garlic and olive oil*
ajiaco SM (*LAm*) **1** (*Culin*) potato and chilli stew • **meterse el ~*** to eat
2 (= *lío*) mess, mix-up
ajibararse ▹ CONJUG 1a VPR (*Caribe*) = **aguajirarse**
ajigolones SMPL (*CAm, Méx*) troubles, difficulties
ajilar ▹ CONJUG 1a VI (*CAm, Méx*) to set out somewhere; (*Caribe*) to walk quickly
ajilimoje SM, **ajilimójili** SM *sauce of garlic and pepper* • **~s*** bits and pieces, things, odds and ends • **ahí está el ~*** that's the point, that's the trouble
ajillo SM chopped garlic • **al ~** with garlic, cooked in garlic
ajimez SM mullioned window
ajiseco SM (*And*) mild red pepper
ajises* (*LAm*) SMPL *de* **ají**
ajizarse* ▹ CONJUG 1f VPR (*Cono Sur*) to lose one's temper, get mad
ajo SM **1** (*Bot, Culin*) garlic • **un ajo** a clove of garlic; (= *salsa*) garlic sauce • **MODISMOS**: • **¡ajo y agua!*** you've just got to put up with it! • **harto de ajos** ill-bred, common • **(tieso) como un ajo** high and mighty, stuck-up* • **estar como el ajo** (*Cono Sur*) to feel miserable • **andar en el ajo** • **estar en el ajo** (= *involucrado*) to be mixed up in it; (= *enterado*) to be in on the secret • **revolver el ajo** to stir up trouble ▸ **ajo tierno** young garlic
2* (= *palabrota*) swearword, oath, curse • **MODISMOS**: • **echar ajos y cebollas** • **soltar ajos y cebollas** to swear like a trooper, let fly*
-ajo, -aja ▹ **Aspects of Word Formation in Spanish 2**
ajoaceite SM *sauce of garlic and oil*
ajoarriero SM *dish of cod with oil, garlic and peppers*
ajobar ▹ CONJUG 1a VT to carry on one's back, hump*
ajoblanco SM *cold garlic and almond soup*
ajobo SM (= *carga*) load; (= *pesadumbre*) burden
ajochar ▹ CONJUG 1a VT (*And*) = **azuzar**
ajonje SM, **ajonjo** SM birdlime
ajonjeo SM (*And*) compliment, nice remark
ajonjolí SM sesame
ajorca SF bracelet, bangle
ajornalar ▹ CONJUG 1a VT to employ by the day
ajotar ▹ CONJUG 1a VT (*CAm*) = **azuzar** (*Caribe*) (= *desdeñar*) to scorn; (= *rechazar*) to rebuff
ajoto SM (*Caribe*) rebuff
ajuar SM **1** [*de novia*] (= *objetos*) trousseau; (= *dote*) dowry
2 [*de niño*] layette
3 (= *muebles*) household furnishings (*pl*)
ajuarar ▹ CONJUG 1a VT to furnish, fit up
ajuiciado ADJ sensible
ajuiciar ▹ CONJUG 1b VT to bring to one's senses
ajumado/a* ADJ tight*, tipsy
SM/F drunk, drunkard
ajumarse* ▹ CONJUG 1a VPR to get tight*, get tipsy
ajuntar* ▹ CONJUG 1a VT (*entre niños*) to make friends with, be friends with • **¡ya no te ajunto!** I'm not your friend any more!
VPR **ajuntarse** (= *amancebarse*) to live together, live in sin; (*entre niños*) • **¡no me ajunto contigo!** I'm not your friend any more!
Ajuria Enea SF (= *residencia*) *residence of chief minister of Basque autonomous government*; (= *gobierno*) *Basque autonomous government*
ajurídico ADJ (*Cono Sur*) illegal
ajustable ADJ adjustable
ajustado ADJ **1** (= *ceñido*) tight, tight-fitting • **unos vaqueros ~s** a pair of tight *o* tight-fitting jeans • **la blusa le quedaba muy ajustada** the blouse was very tight on her
2 (= *con poco margen*) [*presupuesto*] tight; [*resultado*] tight, close • **tienen los precios más ~s del mercado** they have the most competitive prices in the market • **hemos tenido que venderlo todo a un precio muy ~** we had to sell everything at a very low profit • **los resultados de las elecciones han sido muy ~s** the election results were very tight *o* close • **la victoria fue muy ajustada** it was a very close victory
3 (= *acertado*) accurate • **un ~ retrato de la sociedad española** an accurate portrait of Spanish society • **~ a algo** in keeping with sth • **usó un lenguaje ~ a la ocasión** his language was in keeping with the occasion • **~ a la ley** in accordance with the law
ajustador SM **1** (*Téc*) fitter; (*Tip*) compositor
2 (*Col*) (= *sujetador*) (*tb* **ajustadores**) bra
3 (= *chaleco*) bodice
ajustamiento SM **1** [*de pieza, grifo*] (*al colocarla*) fitting; (*al apretarla*) tightening
2 (*Econ*) settlement
ajustar ▹ CONJUG 1a VT **1** (*Téc*) **a** [+ *pieza, grifo*] (*colocando*) to fit; (*apretando*) to tighten • **¿cómo se ajusta la baca al vehículo?** how does the roof rack fit onto the vehicle? • **necesito unos alicates para ~ la válvula** I need some pliers to tighten the valve
b (= *regular*) [+ *volumen, temperatura*] to adjust, regulate; [+ *asiento, retrovisor*] to adjust; [+ *cinturón*] to tighten
c (*Chile, Méx*) [+ *motor*] to fix • **hay que ~le el motor a la moto** we need to fix the motorbike's engine
2 (= *pactar*) [+ *acuerdo, trato*] to reach; [+ *boda*] to arrange; [+ *precio*] to agree on • **ya hemos ajustado el presupuesto con los albañiles** we have already agreed on the price with the builders • **el precio ha quedado ajustado en 500 euros** the price has been fixed *o* set at 500 euros • **~ cuentas con algn** (*lit*) to settle accounts with sb; (*fig*) to settle one's scores with sb
3 (= *adaptar*) to adjust (**a** to) • **deben ~ la producción a la demanda** they must adjust production to demand • **tuvieron una reunión para ~ diferencias** they had a meeting to settle their differences
4 (*euf*) (= *reducir*) • **han tenido que ~ el número de sucursales** the number of branches had to be rationalized (*euf*) • **este año hemos tenido que ~ drásticamente el presupuesto** this year we have had to sharply reduce our budget
5 (*Cos*) [+ *cintura, manga*] to take in • **hay que ~ la cintura** the waist needs taking in
6 (*Tip*) to compose
7† [+ *criado*] to hire, engage
8 (*CAm, Méx, Chile, Ven*) • **~ un golpe a algn** to deal sb a blow • **~ un garrotazo a algn** to beat sb with a club
VI **1** (= *encajar*) to fit • **este corcho no ajusta en la botella** this cork doesn't fit in the bottle • **rellena con masilla los empalmes que no ajusten** fill the joints that don't fit together with putty
2 (*Ven*) (= *agudizarse*) to get worse • **durante la noche me ajustó el dolor** the pain got worse during the night • **por el camino ajustó el aguacero** on the way, there was a sudden downpour
VPR **ajustarse 1** (= *ceñirse*) **a** [*persona*] • **¿me ayudas a ~me la corbata?** can you help me adjust my tie? • **salió del baño ajustándose los pantalones** he came out of the bathroom doing up his trousers
b [*zapato*] to fit; [*pantalón, vestido*] to cling

• **el zapato debe ~se al pie lo mejor posible** the shoe should fit the foot as well as possible • **se ajusta al cuerpo como una segunda piel** it clings to the body like a second skin; ▹ **cinturón**
2 (= *encajarse*) to fit • **el tapón no se ajustaba** the top didn't fit
3 (= *adaptarse*) • **~se a** [+ *situación, estilo*] to adapt to; [+ *necesidades*] to meet; [+ *presupuesto*] to be within; [+ *norma, regla*] to comply with • **los precios bajan para ~se a las demandas del mercado** prices go down to meet the demands of the market • **el motor se ajusta a la nueva normativa europea** the engine complies with the new European standards • **este contrato se ajusta al presupuesto de nuestro club** this contract is within our club's budget • **tendrán que ~se al guión** they will have to keep to *o* follow the script • **(no) se ajusta a derecho** it is (not) legally admissible
4 (= *coincidir*) • **la narración se ajusta a la verdad** the story agrees with the facts • **los rumores no siempre se ajustan a la realidad** rumours do not always reflect the real situation
5 (= *llegar a un acuerdo*) to come to an agreement (**con** with)

ajuste SM **1** (*Téc*) adjustment • **~ de zoom eléctrico** electric zoom adjustment • **estos tornillos necesitan algo de ~** these screws need a little tightening • **¿cómo se hace el ~ del brillo en este televisor?** how do you adjust the brightness on this television? • **~ fino** fine tuning; ▹ **carta**
2 (= *adaptación*) adjustment • **se producirán ~s de precios** price adjustments will occur • **mal ~** maladjustment ▸ **ajuste económico** economic adjustment ▸ **ajuste estructural** structural adjustment ▸ **ajuste financiero** financial settlement ▸ **ajuste de plantilla** (*Esp*) redeployment of labour *o* (*EEUU*) labor ▸ **ajuste laboral** redeployment of labour *o* (*EEUU*) labor ▸ **ajuste presupuestario** budget settlement ▸ **ajuste salarial** wage adjustment
3 (= *pacto*) • **ha habido un ~ de costes** there has been an adjustment in costs • **tras el ~ del precio** after fixing the price ▸ **ajuste de cuentas** settling of scores
4 (*Cos*) • **necesita unos pequeños ~s en la cintura** it needs to be taken in a little at the waist
5 (*Tip*) composition, make-up
6 (*Jur*) (= *honorarios*) retaining fee; (= *sobrepaga*) bonus ▸ **ajuste por aumento del costo de la vida** cost-of-living bonus
7 (*Méx*) [*de motor*] overhaul

ajusticiable SMF *person who may face capital punishment*

ajusticiamiento SM execution

ajusticiar ▹ CONJUG 1b VT to execute, put to death

ajustón SM (*And*) (= *castigo*) punishment; (= *mal trato*) ill-treatment

al ▹ **a**

ala SF **1** [*de insecto, pájaro*] wing • **de cuatro alas** four-winged • **de alas azules** blue-winged
2 [*de avión*] wing • **con alas en delta** delta-winged • **con alas en flecha** swept-wing ▸ **ala delta** hang glider
3 (*Pol*) wing • **el ala izquierda del partido** the left wing of the party
4 (*Mil*) wing, flank
5 [*de edificio*] wing
6 (= *parte sobresaliente*) [*de sombrero*] brim; [*de corazón*] auricle; [*del techo*] eaves (*pl*); [*de mesa*] leaf, flap
7 (*Dep*) (= *banda*) wing ▸ **ala derecha** outside-right ▸ **ala izquierda** outside-left
8 • MODISMOS: • **ahuecar el ala*** to beat it* • **arrastrar el ala** (= *cortejar*) to be courting; (= *estar deprimido*) to be depressed • **se le cayeron las alas del corazón** his heart sank • **cortar las alas a algn** to clip sb's wings • **dar alas a algn** to encourage sb • **del ala** (*Esp**): • **los 100 euros del ala** a cool 100 euros* • **ser como ala de mosca** to be paper thin, be transparent • **quedar tocado de ala** to be a lame duck • **tomar alas*** to get cheeky* • **volar con las propias alas** to stand on one's own two feet
SMF (*Dep*) winger • **medio ala** half-back, wing-half

Alá SM Allah

alabado SM **1** • **al ~** (*Cono Sur*) (= *amanecer*) at dawn
2 • **al ~** (*Méx*) (= *anochecer*) at nightfall

alabador ADJ eulogistic

alabamiento SM praise

alabancioso ADJ boastful

alabanza SF (*tb* **alabanzas**) praise • **en ~ de** in praise of • **cantar las ~s de algn** to sing sb's praises • **digno de toda ~** thoroughly praiseworthy, highly commendable

alabar ▹ CONJUG 1a VT to praise • **~ a algn de *o* por algo** to praise sb for sth
VPR **alabarse** to boast • **~se de** to boast of being • **se alaba de *o* por prudente** he prides himself on being sensible

alabarda SF halberd

alabardero SM (*Hist*) halberdier; (*Teat*) member of the claque, paid applauder

alabastrado ADJ, **alabastrino** ADJ alabastrine, alabaster (*antes de s*)

alabastro SM alabaster

álabe SM (*Mec*) wooden cog, tooth; [*de noria*] bucket; [*de árbol*] drooping branch

alabear ▹ CONJUG 1a VT to warp
VPR **alabearse** to warp

alabeo SM warp, warping • **tomar ~** to warp

alacalufe SMF (*Cono Sur*) *Indian inhabitant of Tierra del Fuego*

alacena SF cupboard, closet (*EEUU*)

alacrán SM **1** (= *escorpión*) scorpion
2 (*Cono Sur*) (= *chismoso*) gossip, scandalmonger

alacranear ▹ CONJUG 1a VI to gossip, spread scandal

alacraneo SM (*Cono Sur*) gossip, scandal

alacre ADJ (*Méx*) ready and willing

alacridad SF alacrity, readiness • **con ~** with alacrity, readily

alada SF flutter, fluttering

ALADI SF ABR = **Asociación Latinoamericana de Integración**

Aladino SM Aladdin

alado ADJ (= *con alas*) winged; (= *ligero*) swift

alafia SF (*CAm*) verbosity, wordiness

alafre (*Caribe*) ADJ wretched, miserable
SM wretch

alagartado ADJ motley, variegated, many-colored (*EEUU*)

alalá SM *traditional song in parts of northern Spain*

ALALC SF ABR (= **Asociación Latinoamericana de Libre Comercio**) LAFTA

alambicado ADJ **1** (= *destilado*) distilled
2 (= *intrincado*) [*proceso, estilo*] intricate; [*teoría, misterio*] complex
3 (= *afectado*) [*estilo*] precious; [*modales*] affected
4 (= *sutil*) subtle
5 (= *dado con escasez*) given sparingly, given grudgingly
6 (= *reducido*) • **precios ~s** rock-bottom prices

alambicamiento SM **1** (= *destilación*) distilling
2 (= *rebuscamiento*) preciosity, affectation

alambicar ▹ CONJUG 1g VT **1** (= *destilar*) to distil, distill (*EEUU*)
2 [+ *estilo*] to complicate unnecessarily
3 (= *escudriñar*) to scrutinize, investigate
4 (= *reducir*) (*gen*) to minimize, reduce to a minimum; [+ *precio*] to reduce to the minimum

alambique SM still • MODISMOS: • **dar algo por ~** to give sth sparingly *o* grudgingly • **pasar algo por ~** to go through sth with a fine-tooth comb

alambiquería SF (*Caribe*) distillery

alambiquero SM (*Caribe*) distiller

alambrada SF (= *red*) wire netting; (= *cerca*) wire fence; (*Mil*) barbed-wire entanglement ▸ **alambrada de espino, alambrada de púas** barbed-wire fence

alambrado SM (= *red*) wire netting; (= *cerca*) wire fence, wire fencing; (*Elec*) wiring, wiring system

alambrar ▹ CONJUG 1a VT (*Elec*) to wire; (*Agr*) to fence with wire

alambre SM wire • MODISMO: • **estar hecho un ~** to be as thin as a rake ▸ **alambre cargado** live wire ▸ **alambre de espino, alambre de púas** barbed wire ▸ **alambre de tierra** earth wire, ground wire (*EEUU*) ▸ **alambre espinoso** barbed wire ▸ **alambre forrado** covered wire

alambrera SF (= *red*) wire netting, chicken wire; (= *cobertera*) wire cover; (*para chimenea*) fireguard

alambrista SMF tightrope walker

alambrito SM (*LAm*) tall thin person

alambrón SM wire rod

alameda SF (*Bot*) poplar grove; (= *avenida*) avenue, boulevard

álamo SM poplar ▸ **álamo blanco** white poplar ▸ **álamo de Italia** Lombardy poplar ▸ **álamo negro** black poplar ▸ **álamo temblón** aspen

alamparse ▹ CONJUG 1a VPR • **~ por** to crave, have a craving for

alancear ▹ CONJUG 1a VT to spear, lance

alano[1] SM mastiff

alano[2] (*Hist*) ADJ of the Alani
SMPL **alanos** Alani

alar SM **1** [*de tejado*] eaves (*pl*)
2 (*LAm*) (= *acera*) pavement, sidewalk (*EEUU*)

alarde SM **1** display • **un ~ de patriotismo** a display of patriotism • **la decisión fue todo un ~ de serenidad** the decision was a feat of cool-headedness • **en un ~ de generosidad, me pagaron la cena** in a show *o* display of generosity they paid for my dinner • **en un ~ de falsa modestia** in a show of false modesty • **hacer ~ de**: • **siempre hace ~ de sus riquezas** he is always showing off his wealth • **siempre está haciendo ~ de sus triunfos sexuales** he's always boasting about *o* of his sexual prowess • **el grupo hizo ~ de su poder de convocatoria** the band demonstrated *o* displayed their pulling power, it was a demonstration of the pulling power of the band
2 (*Mil*†) review
3 **alardes** (*esp LAm*) (= *jactancias*) boasts

alardeado ADJ much-vaunted

alardear ▹ CONJUG 1a VI to boast, brag (**de** about)

alardeo SM boasting, bragging

alargadera SF (*Quím*) adapter; (*Téc*) extension

alargado ADJ long, extended

alargador SM (*Cono Sur*) extension lead

alargamiento SM (*gen*) lengthening; (= *prórroga*) extension; (*Arquit*) extension

alargar ▹ CONJUG 1h VT **1** (*en longitud*) [+ *cuerda, goma*] to stretch; [+ *pista de aterrizaje*]

to lengthen; [+ *cuello*] to crane; [+ *mano*] to stretch out; [+ *vestido*] to lengthen, let down
2 (*en tiempo*) [+ *visita*] to prolong, extend; [+ *discurso, espera*] to prolong; [+ *relato*] to spin out • **esto alargó nuestra espera** this prolonged our wait, this forced us to wait longer
3 [+ *cable de escalada*] to pay out
4 (= *dar*) to hand, pass (**a** to)
5 [+ *sueldo*] to increase, raise
6 [+ *paso*] to quicken
VPR **alargarse 1** (*en longitud*) to lengthen, get longer
2 (*en tiempo*) [*días*] to grow longer; [*relato*] to drag out; [*orador*] to go on for a long time • **~se en algo** to expatiate on sth, enlarge upon sth • **se alargó en la charla** he spun his talk out
3 (= *divagar*) to digress

alargo SM extension, lead

alarido SM shriek, yell • **dar ~s** to shriek, yell

alarife SMF **1** (*Constr*) (= *arquitecto*) master builder; (= *albañil*) bricklayer
2 (*Cono Sur*) (= *tipo listo*) sharp customer*; (= *mujer de vida alegre*) loose woman

alarma SF alarm • **falsa ~** false alarm • **dar la ~** to raise the alarm • **con creciente ~** with growing alarm, with growing concern • **timbre de ~** alarm bell • **voz de ~** warning note • **señal de ~** alarm signal ▸ **alarma aérea** air-raid warning ▸ **alarma antiincendios** fire alarm ▸ **alarma antirrobo** [*de coche*] car alarm, anti-theft alarm; [*de casa*] burglar alarm ▸ **alarma de incendios** fire alarm ▸ **alarma de ladrones** burglar alarm ▸ **alarma social** public alarm • **no había motivo para la ~ social** there was no cause for panic *o* public alarm

alarmante ADJ alarming

alarmantemente ADV alarmingly

alarmar ▹ CONJUG 1a VT (= *dar alarma*) to alarm; (= *asustar*) to frighten; (*Mil*) to alert, rouse
VPR **alarmarse** to get alarmed, be alarmed • **¡no te alarmes!** don't be alarmed!

alarmismo SM alarmism

alarmista ADJ alarmist
SMF alarmist

alauí ADJ, **alauita** ADJ Moroccan

Álava SF Álava

alavense = **alavés**

alavés/esa ADJ of/from Álava
SM/F native/inhabitant of Álava • **los alaveses** the people of Álava

alazán/ana ADJ sorrel
SM/F sorrel, sorrel horse

alazor SM safflower • **aceite de ~** safflower oil

alba SF **1** (= *amanecer*) dawn, daybreak • **al ~** at dawn • **al rayar** *o* **romper el ~** at daybreak
2 (*Rel*) alb

albacea SMF executor/executrix

Albacete SM Albacete

albacetense = **albaceteño**

albaceteño/a ADJ of/from Albacete
SM/F native/inhabitant of Albacete • **los ~s** the people of Albacete

albacora SF albacore, long fin tunny

albahaca SF basil

albanega SF hairnet

albanés/esa ADJ, SM/F Albanian
SM (*Ling*) Albanian

Albania SF Albania

albano = **albanés**

albanokosovar ADJ, SMF Kosovar Albanian

albañal SM (= *cloaca*) drain, sewer; (= *estercolero*) dung heap; (*fig*) (= *sitio sucio*) mess, muck heap*

albañil SMF builder, construction worker

albañilería SF (= *oficio*) bricklaying, building • **trabajo de ~** brickwork

albaquía SF balance due, remainder

albar ADJ white

albarán SM **1** (*Com*) delivery note, invoice
2 (= *señal*) "to let" sign

albarda SF (*para la carga*) packsaddle; (*CAm*) (= *silla de montar*) saddle • **~ sobre ~** piling it on, with a lot of unnecessary repetition • MODISMO: • **¡como ahora llueven ~s!** not on your life!

albardar ▹ CONJUG 1a VT to saddle, put a packsaddle on

albardear* ▹ CONJUG 1a VT (*CAm*) to bother, vex

albardilla SF **1** (= *silla de montar*) small saddle; (= *almohadilla*) cushion, pad
2 (*Arquit*) coping
3 (*Culin*) lard

albareque SM sardine net

albaricoque SM apricot

albaricoquero SM apricot tree

albariño SM (*type of*) *Galician wine*

albarrada SF **1** (= *muro*) wall
2 (*And*) (= *cisterna*) cistern

albatros SM INV albatross, double eagle (*EEUU*)

albayalde SM white lead

albazo SM **1** (*And, Méx*) dawn raid
2 (*Cono Sur*) dawn visit

albeador(a)* SM/F (*Cono Sur*) early riser

albear* ▹ CONJUG 1a VI (*Cono Sur*) to get up at dawn, get up early

albedrío SM (= *voluntad*) will; (= *capricho*) whim; (= *gusto*) pleasure • **libre ~** free will • **¡hágalo a su ~!** have it your way!

albéitar SM veterinary surgeon, veterinarian (*EEUU*)

albeitería SF veterinary medicine

alberca SF (= *depósito*) tank, reservoir; (*Méx*) (= *piscina*) swimming pool

albérchigo SM (= *fruto*) peach, clingstone peach; (= *árbol*) peach tree, clingstone peach tree

albergar ▹ CONJUG 1h VT **1** (= *acomodar*) [+ *visitante, refugiado, inmigrante*] to provide accommodation for; [+ *criminal, fugitivo*] to harbour • **fue condenado por ~ a un terrorista** he was found guilty of harbouring a terrorist
2 (= *dar cabida a*) [+ *espectadores, público*] to accommodate, hold; [+ *evento, celebración*] to host • **el estadio puede ~ a 30.000 personas** the stadium can accommodate *o* hold 30,000 people, the stadium has a capacity of 30,000 • **el edificio que alberga la sede del partido** the building which houses the party's headquarters • **este terreno ~á 300 chalets** this land will provide space for 300 houses
3 [+ *esperanza*] to cherish; [+ *dudas*] to have • **aún alberga los rencores de la infancia** he still harbours childhood resentments
VPR **albergarse 1** (= *refugiarse*) to shelter
2 (= *alojarse*) to stay

albergue SM (= *refugio*) shelter, refuge; (= *alojamiento*) lodging; [*de montaña*] refuge, mountain hut; (*Zool*) lair, den • **dar ~ a algn** to take sb in ▸ **albergue de animales** animal refuge ▸ **albergue de carretera** roadhouse ▸ **albergue juvenil** youth hostel ▸ **albergue nacional** state-owned tourist hotel

alberguista SMF youth hosteller

albero ADJ white
SM **1** (*Geol*) pipeclay
2 (= *paño*) dishcloth, tea towel

Alberto SM Albert

albillo ADJ white

albina SF salt lake, salt marsh

albinismo SM albinism

albino/a ADJ, SM/F albino

Albión SF Albion • **la pérfida ~** perfidious Albion

albis ADV • **quedarse en ~** not to know a thing, not have a clue • **me quedé en ~** my mind went blank

albo ADJ (*liter*) white

albogue SM (= *flauta*) rustic flute, shepherd's flute; (= *gaita*) bagpipes • **~s** (= *platillos*) cymbals

albóndiga SF meatball

albondigón SM large meatball

albor SM **1** (= *color*) whiteness
2 (= *luz*) dawn, dawn light ▸ **albor de la vida** childhood, youth
3 (*liter*) **albores** dawn • **a los ~es** at dawn • **en los ~es de la ciencia** at the dawn of science

alborada SF (= *alba*) daybreak, dawn; (*Mil*) reveille; (*Mús*) (*poét*) aubade, dawn song; (*Méx*) (*Rel*) night procession

alborear ▹ CONJUG 1a VI to dawn

albornoz SM **1** (= *de baño*) bathrobe
2 (= *prenda árabe*) burnous, burnouse

alborotadamente ADV (= *ruidosamente*) noisily; (= *con excitación*) excitedly

alborotadizo ADJ excitable

alborotado ADJ **1** [*persona*] (= *excitado*) agitated, excited; (= *ruidoso*) noisy; (= *precipitado*) hasty; (= *impetuoso*) reckless; (= *amotinado*) riotous
2 [*período*] troubled, eventful
3 [*mar*] rough

alborotador(a) ADJ (= *ruidoso*) boisterous, noisy; (*Pol*) (= *sedicioso*) seditious
SM/F (= *agitador*) agitator, troublemaker; (= *alumno*) troublemaker

alborotar ▹ CONJUG 1a VT (= *agitar*) to disturb, agitate; (= *amotinar*) to incite to rebel; (= *excitar*) to excite
VI to make a racket, make a row
VPR **alborotarse 1** [*individuo*] to get excited, get worked up; [*multitud*] to riot; [*mar*] to get rough
2 (*CAm*) (= *ponerse amoroso*) to become amorous
3 (*Cono Sur*) [*caballo*] to rear up

alboroto SM **1** (= *disturbio*) disturbance; (= *vocerío*) racket, row; (= *jaleo*) uproar; (= *motín*) riot; (= *pelea*) brawl • **armar un ~** to cause a commotion
2 (= *susto*) scare, alarm
3 alborotos (*CAm*) (= *rosetas de maíz*) popcorn (*sing*)

alborotoso/a (*And, Caribe*) ADJ troublesome, riotous
SM/F troublemaker

alborozado ADJ jubilant, overjoyed

alborozar ▹ CONJUG 1f VT to gladden, fill with joy
VPR **alborozarse** to be overjoyed, rejoice

alborozo SM joy, jubilation, rejoicing

albricias SFPL **1** (*como excl*) (= *¡felicidades!*) congratulations • **¡albricias! ¡lo conseguí!** whoopee! I got it!
2 (= *regalo*) gift (*sing*), reward (*sing*) (*to sb bringing good news*)

albufera SF lagoon

álbum SM (PL: **álbums, álbumes**) album; (*Mús*) (= *disco*) album; (= *elepé*) LP ▸ **álbum de recortes** scrapbook ▸ **álbum de sellos** stamp album ▸ **álbum doble** double album ▸ **álbum recopilatorio** compilation album

albumen SM (= *clara*) white of egg; (*Bot*) albumen

albúmina SF albumin

albuminoso ADJ albuminous

albur SM **1** (*Esp*) (= *pez*) bleak
2 (= *riesgo*) chance, risk
3 (*Méx*) (= *juego de palabras*) pun
4 (*Caribe*) (= *mentira*) lie

albura SF (= *blancura*) whiteness; [*de huevo*] white of egg

alburear ▸ CONJUG 1a VT (*CAm*) to disturb, upset
VI 1 (*And*) (= *enriquecerse*) to make money, get rich
2 (*Caribe*) (= *barrer para dentro*) to line one's pockets
3 (*Méx*) (= *decir albores*) to pun, play with words

ALCA SF ABR (= **Área de Libre Comercio de las Américas**) FTAA

alca SF razorbill

alcabala SF 1 (*Hist*) (= *tributo*) sales tax
2 (*LAm*) [*de policía*] roadblock

alcachofa SF 1 artichoke
2 ▸ **alcachofa de (la) ducha** shower head ▸ **alcachofa de regadera** rose
3 (*Radio**) microphone

alcahué* SM = **cacahuete**

alcahuete/a SM/F 1 (= *proxeneta*) (*hombre*) procurer, pimp; (*mujer*) procuress, go-between
2 (= *chismoso*) gossip
SM (*Teat*) drop curtain

alcahuetear ▸ CONJUG 1a VI to procure, pimp, to act as a go-between

alcahuetería SF procuring, pimping; **alcahueterías** pimping

alcaide SM (*Hist*) [*de castillo*] governor; [*de cárcel*] warder, guard (*EEUU*), jailer

alcaidía SF (= *cargo*) governorship; (= *edificio*) governor's residence

alcaldable SMF *candidate for mayor*

alcaldada SF abuse of authority

alcalde SM 1 [*de ayuntamiento*] mayor; (= *juez*) magistrate • **tener el padre ~** to have influence
2 (*LAm**) (= *alcahuete*) procurer, pimp

alcaldear* ▸ CONJUG 1a VI to lord it, be bossy

alcaldesa SF mayoress

alcaldía SF (= *oficio*) mayoralty, office of mayor; (= *oficina*) mayor's office; (= *edificio*) town hall, city hall (*EEUU*)

alcalducho* SM jumped-up mayor, power-mad mayor

álcali SM alkali

alcalino ADJ alkaline

alcaloide SM alkaloid

alcaloideo ADJ alkaloid

alcamonero ADJ (*Caribe*) meddlesome

alcamonías SFPL 1 (*Culin*) aromatic seeds (*for seasoning*)
2* (= *alcahuetería*) pimping

alcance SM 1 (= *posibilidad de acceso*) [*de brazo, persona*] reach; [*de pensamiento*] scope • **el escaso ~ de la mente humana** the limited scope of the human mind • **al ~ de algn** available to sb • **empleó todos los medios a su ~** she used all the means available to her • **no tenía el dinero a su ~** he didn't have access to the money, he didn't have the money available • **estar al ~ de algn** to be within sb's reach • **vi que estaba a mi ~ y lo cogí** I saw that it was within my reach and I grabbed it • **el récord estaba a nuestro ~** the record was within our grasp *o* reach • **estas joyas no están al ~ de cualquiera** not everyone can afford these jewels • **hizo lo que estaba a su ~ por ayudarme** he did what he could to help me • **estar fuera del ~ de algn** (= *alejado, imposible*) to be out of sb's reach, to be beyond sb's reach; (= *incomprensible*) to be over sb's head; (= *caro*) to be beyond sb's means • **"manténgase fuera del alcance de los niños"** "keep out of reach of children" • **quiero estar fuera del ~ de esas miradas** I don't want to be the object of those looks • **se encontraban fuera del ~ de los disparos** they were out of the gunfire • **al ~ de la mano** at hand, within arm's reach • **al ~ del oído** within earshot • **poner algo al ~ de algn** to make sth available to sb • **un intento de poner la cultura al ~ de todos** an attempt to make culture available to everyone • **al ~ de la vista** within sight • **cuando el faro estuvo al ~ de nuestra vista** when the lighthouse came into view *o* was within sight • **al ~ de la voz** within call
2 (= *distancia*) (*Mil*) range • **al ~** within range • **de corto ~** [*arma, misil*] short-range (*antes de s*); [*objetivo, proyecto*] short-term (*antes de s*) • **de gran** *o* **largo ~** [*faros*] full beam (*antes de s*), high beam (*antes de s*) (*EEUU*); [*arma, misil, micrófono*] long-range (*antes de s*); [*vuelo*] long haul (*antes de s*); [*efecto, repercusiones*] far-reaching • **de medio** *o* **mediano ~** [*arma, misil*] medium-range; ▸ **buzón**
3 (= *importancia*) [*de problema*] extent; [*de noticia, suceso*] importance, significance • **el ~ del problema** the extent of the problem • **esta huelga tiene mayor ~ para los trabajadores** this strike has greater importance *o* significance for the workers • **comprendió el verdadero ~ de lo ocurrido** she understood the true significance of what had happened • **una crisis de ~ planetario** a worldwide crisis
4 (= *persecución*) pursuit • **andar** *o* **ir a los ~s de algn** to press close on sb • **dar ~ a algn** (= *capturar*) to capture sb; (= *llegar a la altura*) to catch up with sb • **cuando la policía le dio ~** when the police captured him • **a punto estuvo de dar ~ al líder de la carrera** he was on the point of catching (up with) the leader of the race • **el Barcelona ha dado ~ al Madrid en el número de puntos** Barcelona have caught up with Madrid in number of points • **andar** *o* **ir en los ~s a algn** to spy on sb • **seguir el ~ a algn** (*Mil*) to pursue sb
5 (*Econ*) adverse balance, deficit
6 (*Tip*) stop-press, stop-press news
7 **alcances**: **a** (= *inteligencia*) grasp (*sing*) • **ideas superiores a sus ~s** ideas beyond his grasp • **de cortos** *o* **pocos ~s** not very bright • **es hombre de cortos ~s** he's not a very intelligent man, he's not too bright
b (*CAm*) (= *calumnias*) calumnies, malicious accusations
8 (*Chile*) • **hacer un ~** to clear sth up, clarify sth ▸ **alcance de nombres** • **no es su padre, es solo un ~ de nombres** he's not his father, it just happens that their names coincide

alcancía SF 1 (= *hucha*) money box; (*LAm*) (= *cepillo*) collection box, poor box
2 (*Méx‡*) (= *cárcel*) nick*, slammer‡, can (*EEUU‡*)

alcancil SM (*Cono Sur*) procurer, pimp

alcándara SF (*para ropa*) clothes rack; (*para aves*) perch

alcandora SF beacon

alcanfor SM camphor

alcanforado ADJ camphorated

alcanforar ▸ CONJUG 1a VT to camphorate
VPR **alcanforarse** (*And, CAm, Caribe*) to disappear, make o.s. scarce*

alcantarilla SF 1 (*para aguas de desecho*) (= *boca*) drain; (= *cloaca*) sewer; (= *conducto*) culvert, conduit
2 (*Caribe, Méx*) (= *fuente*) public fountain; (*And*) (*para goma*) *vessel for collecting latex*

alcantarillado SM sewer system, drains (*pl*)

alcantarillar ▸ CONJUG 1a VT to lay drains in

alcanzadizo ADJ easy to reach, easily reachable, accessible

alcanzado ADJ 1* (= *necesitado*) hard up*, broke* • **salir ~** to make a loss
2 (*And*) (= *fatigado*) tired; (= *atrasado*) slow, late

alcanzar ▸ CONJUG 1f VT 1 (*en carrera*) **a** [+ *persona*] (= *llegar a la altura de*) to catch up (with) • **la alcancé cuando salía por la puerta** I caught up with her *o* I caught her up just as she was going out of the door • **están a punto de ~ al grupo de cabeza** they are about to catch (up with) the leading group • **dentro de poco ~á a su padre en altura** he'll soon be as tall as his father
b [+ *ladrón, autobús, tren*] to catch • **no nos ~án nunca** they'll never catch us
2 (= *llegar a*) [+ *cima, límite, edad*] to reach • **por fin ~on la cima** they finally reached the summit • **alcanzó las cajas con un palo** she reached the boxes with a stick • **puede ~ una velocidad de 200km/h** it can reach speeds of up to 200km/h • **alcanzó el rango de general** he reached the rank of general • **la producción ha alcanzado las 20 toneladas** production has reached 20 tons • **el libro ha alcanzado ya las seis ediciones** the book is already in its sixth edition • **las montañas alcanzan los 5.000m** the mountains rise to 5,000m • **el termómetro llegó a ~ los cuarenta grados** temperatures rose as high as forty degrees • **~ la mayoría de edad** to come of age • **alcanzó la orilla a nado** he made it to the shore by swimming, he swam back to the shore • **no llegó a ~ la pubertad** he never made it as far as puberty
3 (= *conseguir*) [+ *acuerdo*] to reach; [+ *éxito, objetivo*] to achieve • **el acuerdo fue alcanzado tras muchos meses de conversaciones** the agreement was reached after many months of talks • **las expectativas no se corresponden con los resultados alcanzados** the expectations are out of proportion with the results that have been achieved • **~ la fama** to find fame, become famous • **~ la paz** to achieve peace
4 (= *afectar*) to affect • **el cambio nos ~á a todos** the change will affect us all • **una ley que alcanza sobre todo a los jubilados** a law which mainly affects *o* hits pensioners
5 [*bala*] to hit • **uno de los dos disparos alcanzó al presidente** the president was hit by one of the two shots • **la lancha fue alcanzada por un obús** the launch was hit by a shell
6 (*esp LAm*) (= *dar*) to pass • **alcánzame la sal, por favor** could you pass (me) the salt, please? • **¿me alcanzas las tijeras?** could you pass me the scissors?
7* (= *entender*) to grasp, understand • **no alcanza más allá de lo que le han enseñado** he's only capable of understanding what he's been taught
VI 1 (= *llegar*) to reach (**a, hasta** as far as) • **no alcanzo** I can't reach • **no alcanzaba al timbre** she couldn't reach (as far as) the doorbell • **hasta donde alcanza la vista** as far as the eye can see
2 • **~ a hacer algo** to manage to do sth • **no alcancé a verlo** I didn't manage to see him • **no alcanzo a ver cómo pudo suceder** I can't see how it can have happened • **no alcanzo a comprender sus razones** I just can't understand her reasons
3 (= *ser suficiente*) to be enough • **con dos botellas ~á para todos** two bottles will be enough for everyone • **el sueldo no me alcanza para nada** I can't make ends meet on my salary • **¿te alcanza para el tren?** (*esp LAm*) have you got enough money for the train?
4 (*LAm*) (= *ascender*) • **¿a cuánto alcanza todo?** how much does it all come to?

alcanzativo ADJ (*CAm*) suspicious

alcaparra SF caper

alcaraván SM stone curlew

alcaravea SF caraway
alcarreño/a ADJ of/from La Alcarria
SM/F native/inhabitant of La Alcarria • **los ~s** the people of La Alcarria
alcatraz SM gannet
alcaucil SM **1** (*Cono Sur*) artichoke
2 (*Cono Sur*‡) (= *informador*) informer, nark*; (= *alcahuete*) pimp
alcaudón SM shrike
alcayata SF meat hook, spike
alcayota SF squash, vegetable marrow
alcazaba SF citadel, castle
alcázar SM (*Mil*) fortress, citadel; (= *palacio*) royal palace; (*Náut*) quarter-deck
alcazuz SM liquorice
alce[1] SM (*Zool*) elk, moose • **~ de América** moose
alce[2] SM (*Naipes*) cut • **no dar ~ a algn** (*Cono Sur*) to give sb no respite, give sb no rest
alción SM (*Orn*) kingfisher; (*Mit*) halcyon
alcista (*Com, Econ*) ADJ • **mercado ~** bull market, rising market • **la tendencia ~** the upward trend
SMF bull, speculator
alcoba SF **1** (= *dormitorio*) bedroom; (*Méx*) (*Ferro*) couchette, sleeping compartment ▸ **alcoba de huéspedes** spare room, guest room
2 (= *mobiliario*) suite of bedroom furniture
alcohol SM alcohol • **lámpara de ~** spirit lamp ▸ **alcohol absoluto** absolute alcohol, pure alcohol ▸ **alcohol de quemar, alcohol desnaturalizado, alcohol metílico** methylated spirit ▸ **alcohol vínico** vinic alcohol
alcoholemia SF alcohol level of the blood • **control de ~** • **prueba de ~** • **test de ~** breath test, Breathalyser® test, Breathalyzer® (EEUU)
alcoholero ADJ alcohol (*antes de s*)
alcohólico/a ADJ alcoholic • **no ~** [*bebida*] non-alcoholic, soft
SM/F alcoholic
alcoholímetro SM Breathalyser®, Breathalyzer® (EEUU)
alcoholismo SM alcoholism
alcoholista* SMF (*Cono Sur*) drunk
alcoholizado ADJ • **está ~** he's an alcoholic • **morir ~** to die of alcoholism
alcoholizar ▹ CONJUG 1f VT to alcoholize
VPR **alcoholizarse** to become an alcoholic
alcor SM hill
Alcorán SM Koran
alcornoque SM **1** (= *árbol*) cork tree
2* (= *tonto*) idiot
alcorza SF **1** (*Culin*) icing, sugar paste
2 (*Cono Sur**) (= *tipo sensible*) crybaby, sensitive soul
alcorzar ▹ CONJUG 1f VT to ice
alcotán SM hobby
alcotana SF pickaxe, pickax (EEUU)
alcubilla SF cistern, reservoir
alcucero ADJ sweet-toothed
alcurnia SF ancestry, lineage • **de ~** of noble family, of noble birth
alcurniado ADJ aristocratic, noble
alcuza SF (*para aceite*) olive-oil bottle; (*LAm*) (= *vinagreras*) cruet, cruet stand
alcuzcuz SM couscous
aldaba SF **1** (*de puerta*) knocker, door knocker; (*para caballo*) hitching ring • **tener buenas ~s** to have friends in the right places
2 • **~s**‡ (= *tetas*) tits**‡
aldabada SF knock, knock on the door • **dar ~s en** to knock at
aldabilla SF latch
aldabón SM (= *aldaba*) large knocker, large door knocker; (= *asa*) handle
aldabonazo SM bang, loud knock, loud knock on the door • **dar ~s en** to bang at
aldea SF small village, hamlet
aldeanismo SM provincialism, parish-pump attitudes
aldeano/a ADJ **1** (= *de pueblo*) village (*antes de s*); (= *de campo*) rustic • **gente aldeana** country people
2 (*pey*) (= *pueblerino*) provincial, parish-pump (*antes de s*) • **actitud aldeana** parish-pump attitude
SM/F villager • **los ~s** the villagers
aldehuela SF hamlet
aldeorrio SM backward little place, rural backwater
alderredor ADV = **alrededor**
aldosterona SF aldosterone
aldrina SF aldrin
aleación SF (= *proceso*) alloying; (= *efecto*) alloy ▸ **aleación ligera** light alloy
aleado ADJ alloyed, alloy (*antes de s*)
alear[1] ▹ CONJUG 1a VT (*Téc*) to alloy
alear[2] ▹ CONJUG 1a VI **1** [*ave*] to flutter, flap, flap its wings; [*persona*] to move one's arms up and down
2 (= *cobrar fuerzas*) to improve • **ir aleando** to be improving
aleatoriamente ADV randomly, at random
aleatoriedad SF randomness
aleatorio ADJ (*Estadística*) random, contingent; (= *fortuito*) accidental, fortuitous
aleatorizar ▹ CONJUG 1f VT to randomize
alebrarse ▹ CONJUG 1j VPR **1** (= *pegarse al suelo*) to lie flat
2 (= *acobardarse*) to cower
alebrestar ▹ CONJUG 1a VT (*LAm*) (= *poner nervioso*) to excite, make nervous; (= *alterar*) to distress, disturb
VPR **alebrestarse 1** (= *ponerse nervioso*) to get excited; (= *alterarse*) to get distressed, become agitated; (= *rebelarse*) to rebel
2 (*And*) [*caballo*] to rear up
aleccionador ADJ (= *instructivo*) instructive, enlightening; [*castigo*] exemplary
aleccionamiento SM (= *instrucción*) instruction, enlightenment; (*Pol*) (*euf*) repression
aleccionar ▹ CONJUG 1a VT (= *instruir*) to instruct, enlighten; (= *castigar*) to teach a lesson to; (= *regañar*) to lecture
alechado ADJ (*LAm*) milky
alechugado ADJ (= *plisado*) pleated; (= *de volantes*) frilled, frilly
alechugar ▹ CONJUG 1h VT (= *doblar con pliegues*) to fold, pleat; (= *rizar*) to frill
aledaño ADJ adjoining, bordering
SM boundary, limit; **los aledaños** the outskirts
alefra* EXCL (*Caribe*) touch wood!, knock on wood! (EEUU)
alegación SF (*Jur*) declaration, declaration in court; (*Caribe, Cono Sur, Méx*) (= *discusión*) argument ▸ **alegación de culpabilidad** (*Méx*) (*Jur*) plea of guilty ▸ **alegación de inocencia** (*Méx*) (*Jur*) plea of not guilty
alegador(a) ADJ (*Cono Sur*) argumentative
SM/F argumentative person
alegal ADJ (*Cono Sur*) illegal
alegar ▹ CONJUG 1h VT **1** (*Jur*) to allege; (= *citar*) [+ *dificultad*] to plead; [+ *autoridad*] to quote; [+ *razones*] to put forward, adduce; [+ *méritos*] to cite, adduce • **~ que** to claim that, assert that • **alegando que ...** claiming that ..., on the grounds that ...
2 (*LAm*) (= *discutir*) to argue against, dispute
VI (*LAm*) to argue; (= *protestar*) to complain loudly, kick up a fuss
alegata SF (*LAm*) fight
alegato SM **1** (*Jur*) (*escrito*) indictment; (*oral*) allegation; (= *declaración*) statement, assertion
2 (*LAm*) (= *discusión*) argument, dispute
alegoría SF allegory
alegóricamente ADV allegorically
alegórico ADJ allegoric, allegorical
alegorizar ▹ CONJUG 1f VT to allegorize
alegrador ADJ cheering
alegrar ▹ CONJUG 1a VT **1** (= *poner contento*) to cheer up • **le mandamos flores para ~la un poco** we sent her some flowers to cheer her up a bit • **me alegra que me preguntes eso** I'm glad you asked me that • **nos alegra saber que ha aprobado** we're pleased to hear that you passed
2 (= *animar*) [+ *fiesta, reunión*] to liven up; [+ *casa, cuarto*] to brighten up, cheer up • **el rojo te alegra la cara** red gives your face a bit of colour • **¡alegra esa cara!** cheer up! • **los niños alegran el hogar con sus risas** the children liven up *o* cheer up the house with their laughter
3 [+ *fuego*] to poke
4 [+ *toro*] to excite, stir up
5 (*Náut*) [+ *cuerda*] to slacken
VPR **alegrarse 1** (= *complacerse*) to be happy, be pleased • **siempre se alegra cuando la visitamos** she's always happy *o* pleased when we go and visit her • **nos alegramos de *o* por tu decisión** we're very happy *o* pleased with your decision • **me alegro de verte** I'm pleased to see you, it's good to see you • **me alegro por ella** I'm happy *o* pleased for her • **—he aprobado —¡me alegro!** "I passed" — "I'm pleased to hear it!" • **me alegro muchísimo** I'm delighted • **—¿te importa que haya venido? —no, me alegro mucho** "do you mind me coming?" — "not at all, I'm pleased you've come" • **—ya puedo devolverte el dinero —me alegro de saberlo** "I can pay you back now" — "I'm glad to hear it" • **me alegro de que hayas venido, necesito tu ayuda** I'm glad you've come, I need your help • **me alegro de que saques el tema** I'm glad you mentioned that
2* (= *emborracharse*) to get merry *o* tipsy*
alegre ADJ **1** (= *feliz*) [*persona*] happy; [*cara, carácter*] happy, cheerful • **recibimos una ~ noticia** we received some happy news • **estar ~ (por algo)** to be happy (about sth) • **ser ~** to be cheerful *o* happy • **María es muy ~** María's a very cheerful *o* happy person
2 (= *luminoso*) [*día, habitación, color*] bright
3 [*música, fiesta*] lively
4* (= *borracho*) • **estar ~** to be merry *o* tipsy*
5 (= *irresponsable*) thoughtless
6 (= *inmoral*) [*vida*] fast; [*chiste†*] risqué, blue; ▹ **mujer**
alegremente ADV **1** (= *felizmente*) happily, cheerfully
2 (= *irresponsablemente*) gaily • **se lo gastó todo ~** he spent it all without a thought for tomorrow
alegría SF **1** (= *felicidad*) happiness, joy; (= *satisfacción*) gladness; (= *optimismo*) cheerfulness; (= *regocijo*) merriment • **¡qué ~!** how marvellous!, that's splendid! • **saltar de ~** to jump for joy ▸ **alegría vital** joie de vivre
2 (*pey*) (= *irresponsabilidad*) recklessness, irresponsibility
3 (*Bot*) ▸ **alegría de la casa** balsam
4 alegrías (*Mús*) *Andalusian song or dance*; (*Esp*‡) (= *genitales*) naughty bits‡
alegro SM allegro
alegrón SM **1** [*de felicidad*] thrill • **¡me dio un ~!** what a thrill I got!
2 [*de fuego*] sudden blaze, flare-up
alegrona SF (*LAm*) prostitute

alehop EXCL hup!

alejado ADJ **1** (= *distanciado*) remote • **en un pueblecito ~** in a remote little village • **vivimos algo ~s** we live quite far away, we live quite a distance away • **~ de** [*lugar*] distant from; [*persona*] away from • **un planeta muy ~ del sol** a planet very distant from the sun • **vive ~ de todo** he lives away from it all • **una lesión lo mantuvo ~ del fútbol** an injury kept him out of football • **ha pasado varios años alejada de los escenarios** she has spent several years off the stage • **viven completamente ~s de la realidad** they live completely cut off from the real world *o* from reality • **una sentencia muy alejada de la realidad actual** a sentence out of line with current thinking
2 (= *diferente*) removed (**de** from) • **muy ~ de nuestro concepto de libertad** very far removed from our concept of freedom

alejamiento SM **1** (= *distanciamiento*) (*gen*) distance; (*como actividad*) distancing • **se ha producido un pequeño ~ entre los dos planetas** the two planets have shifted slightly apart *o* away from each other • **la obra supone un ~ de la tradición teatral** the work represents a break with *o* a distancing from theatrical tradition
2 (*entre personas*) • **unos meses de ~ nos sentarán bien a los dos** a few months away from each other will do us both good, a few months apart will do us good • **se produjo un ~ entre el gobierno y los ciudadanos** there was a rift between the government and the people
3 [*de cargo*] removal
4 (= *actitud distante*) detachment

Alejandría SF Alexandria

alejandrino SM alexandrine

Alejandro SM Alexander ▸ **Alejandro Magno** Alexander the Great

alejar ▹ CONJUG 1a VT **1** (= *distanciar*) to move away (**de** from) • **aleja un poco más el jarrón** move the vase away a little
2 (= *hacer abandonar*) (*de lugar*) to keep away (**de** from); (*de puesto*) to remove (**de** from) • **ese olor aleja a los mosquitos** that smell keeps the mosquitoes away • **una enfermedad lo alejó de la vida pública** illness forced him to withdraw from public life • **lo hice para ~los de la tentación** I did it to keep them out of temptation's way • **~ a algn de algn** (= *distanciar*) to keep sb away from sb; (= *causar ruptura*) to cause a rift between sb and sb • **intentó ~la de mí** he tried to keep her away from me • **aquel asunto los alejó definitivamente** that matter caused a permanent rift between them
3 (= *desviar*) [+ *atención*] to distract; [+ *sospechas*] to remove; [+ *amenaza, peligro*] to remove • **tratan de ~ nuestra atención de los problemas** they are trying to distract our attention from the problems • **aleja de ti las tentaciones** stay out of temptation's way • **eso alejó el fantasma de la crisis** that removed the spectre of a crisis
VPR **alejarse 1** (= *irse lejos*) to go away, move away (**de** from) • **alejémonos un poco más** let's get *o* go *o* move a bit further away • **un coche rojo se alejaba del lugar** a red car was leaving the scene • **vieron ~se corriendo a dos jóvenes** they saw two youths running away • **se alejó lentamente** he walked off slowly • **no conviene ~se de la orilla** it's better not to go too far from the shore • **~se del buen camino** (*lit*) to lose one's way; (*fig*) to go *o* stray off the straight and narrow
2 (= *separarse*) • **~se de algo** • **la carretera se aleja de la costa** the road veers away from the coast • **en esta obra se aleja de los problemas sociales** in this work she moves away from social problems • **cada vez se alejan más del descenso** they are moving further away from relegation • **después de su divorcio se alejó de la vida social** after her divorce she withdrew from social life • **poco a poco se fueron alejando de sus amigos** they gradually drifted apart from their friends • **~se del tema** to get off the subject
3 (= *desaparecer*) [*peligro*] to recede; [*ruido*] to grow fainter • **la amenaza de una guerra se fue alejando poco a poco** the threat of war gradually receded • **se aleja la posibilidad de un nuevo recorte de los tipos de interés** the possibility of a new cut in interest rates is becoming increasingly unlikely
4 (= *diferir*) • **su comportamiento se aleja de lo normal** his behaviour is far from being normal • **lo que te he contado no se aleja de la verdad** what I have told you is not far from the truth • **la centralización del poder se aleja del espíritu de las sociedades cooperativas** the centralization of power is alien to the spirit of cooperative societies

alelado ADJ (= *aturdido*) stupefied, bewildered; (= *bobo*) foolish, stupid

alelamiento SM (= *aturdimiento*) bewilderment; (= *insensatez*) foolishness, stupidity

alelar ▹ CONJUG 1a VT to stupefy, bewilder
VPR **alelarse** to be stupefied, be bewildered

aleluya EXCL hallelujah!, hurray!
SM o SF (*Mús, Rel*) hallelujah, alleluia
SM **1** (= *Pascua*) Easter time
2 • **ir al ~** (*Caribe**) (= *pagar a escote*) to go Dutch*, share costs
SF **1** (= *alegría*) • **estar de ~** to rejoice
2 (*Arte*) (= *estampa*) Easter print, strip cartoon with rhyming couplets (*originally on religious themes*); (= *pintura mala**) daub, bad painting
3 (*LAm*) (= *excusa*) frivolous excuse
4 (*poét**) doggerel

alelúyico* ADJ evangelical

alemán/ana ADJ, SM/F German
SM (*Ling*) German

Alemania SF Germany

alentada SF big breath, deep breath • **de una ~** in one breath

alentado ADJ **1** (= *valiente*) brave; (= *orgulloso*) proud, haughty
2 (*Cono Sur*) (= *sano*) healthy
3 (*CAm, Méx*) (= *mejorado*) improved, better

alentador ADJ encouraging

alentar ▹ CONJUG 1j VT **1** (= *animar*) to encourage, hearten; [+ *oposición*] to stiffen; [+ *esperanzas*] to raise • **en su pecho alienta la esperanza de ...** he cherishes the hope of ... • **~ a algn a hacer algo** to encourage sb to do sth
2 (*LAm*) (= *aplaudir*) to clap, applaud
VI (= *brillar*) to burn, glow
VPR **alentarse 1** (= *animarse*) to take heart, cheer up
2 (*esp LAm*) (*Med*) to get better
3 (*And, CAm*) (= *dar a luz*) to give birth (**de** to)

aleonarse ▹ CONJUG 1a VPR (*Cono Sur*) to get excited, get worked up

aleoyota SF (*Cono Sur*) pumpkin

alepantado ADJ (*And*) absent-minded

alerce SM larch, larch tree

alergeno SM, **alérgeno** SM allergen

alergia SF allergy • **tener ~ a** to be allergic to (*tb fig*) ▸ **alergia a los frutos secos** nut allergy ▸ **alergia al polen, alergia polínica** pollen allergy, allergy to pollen ▸ **alergia primaveral** hay fever

alérgico/a ADJ allergic (**a** to)
SM/F allergic person

alergista SMF, **alergólogo/a** SM/F allergist, specialist in allergies

alergológico ADJ allergy (*antes de s*)

alero SM **1** (*Arquit*) eaves; (*Aut*) mudguard, fender (*EEUU*), wing • MODISMO: • **estar *o* seguir en el ~** (= *indeciso*) to be unsure, remain undecided
2 (*Dep*) winger

alerón SM aileron

alerta EXCL watch out!
ADJ, ADV alert, watchful • **estar ~** • **estar ojo ~** to be on the alert • **todos los servicios de auxilio están ~(s)** all the rescue services are on stand-by
SF alert • **dar la ~** • **dar la voz de ~** to raise the alarm • **en estado de ~** on the alert • **en ~ de 24 horas** on 24-hour stand-by ▸ **alerta previa** early warning ▸ **alerta roja** red alert

alertar ▹ CONJUG 1a VT to alert • **~ a algn de algo** to alert sb to sth
VI to be alert, keep one's eyes open

alesnado ADJ (*Caribe*) brave, intrepid

aleta SF **1** (*Zool*) [*de pez*] fin; [*de foca*] flipper; [*de pájaro*] wing, small wing; [*de natación*] flipper ▸ **aleta dorsal** dorsal fin
2 (*Mec*) [*de coche*] wing, fender (*EEUU*); [*de hélice*] blade

aletargado ADJ drowsy, lethargic

aletargamiento SM drowsiness, lethargy

aletargar ▹ CONJUG 1h VT (= *causar letargo*) to make drowsy, make lethargic
VPR **aletargarse** (= *padecer letargo*) to grow drowsy, become lethargic; (= *hibernar*) to become dormant, hibernate

aletazo SM **1** [*de ave*] wing beat, flap, flap of the wing; [*de pez*] movement of the fin
2 (*Cono Sur*) (= *bofetada*) punch, slap
3 (*CAm*) (= *hurto*) robbery; (= *estafa*) swindle

aletear ▹ CONJUG 1a VI [*ave*] to flutter, flap its wings; [*pez*] to move its fins; [*persona*] to wave one's arms

aleteo SM **1** [*de ave*] fluttering, flapping of the wings; [*de pez*] movement of the fins
2 (*Med*) (= *palpitación*) palpitation

aleudar ▹ CONJUG 1a VT to leaven, ferment with yeast
VPR **aleudarse** to rise

aleve ADJ treacherous, perfidious

alevín SM, **alevino** SM **1** (= *cría de pez*) fry, young fish
2 (= *joven principiante*) youngster, novice

alevosía SF **1** (= *traición*) treachery
2 (*Jur*) premeditation • **con ~** in a cold-blooded manner

alevoso/a ADJ treacherous
SM/F traitor

alfa[1] SF (= *letra*) alpha

alfa[2] SF (*LAm*) (= *alfalfa*) lucerne, alfalfa

alfabéticamente ADV alphabetically

alfabético ADJ alphabetic, alphabetical

alfabetismo SM literacy

alfabetización SF teaching people to read and write • **campaña de ~** literacy campaign

alfabetizado ADJ literate, that can read and write

alfabetizador(a) SM/F literacy tutor

alfabetizar ▹ CONJUG 1f VT **1** (= *clasificar*) to arrange alphabetically
2 (= *enseñar*) to teach to read and write

alfabeto SM alphabet ▸ **alfabeto Morse** Morse code ▸ **alfabeto romano** Roman alphabet

alfajor SM (*Cono Sur*) *sweet biscuit with filling*; (*Esp*) (= *polvorón*) *cake eaten at Christmas*

alfalfa SF lucerne, alfalfa

alfalfar SM lucerne field

alfandoque SM **1** (*LAm*) (*Culin*) cheesecake
2 (*And, Cono Sur*) (*Mús*) maraca

alfanje SM (= *sable*) cutlass; (= *pez*) swordfish

alfanumérico ADJ alphanumeric

alfaque SM (*Náut*) bar, sandbank

alfaquí SM Moslem doctor, ulema, expounder of the Law

alfar SM **1** (= *taller*) potter's workshop
2 (= *arcilla*) clay

alfarería SF (= *arte*) pottery; (= *tienda*) pottery shop

alfarero/a SM/F potter

alfarjía SF batten (*esp for door or window frames*)

alféizar SM (*Arquit*) (= *corte del muro*) splay, embrasure; [*de ventana*] window sill

alfeñicado* ADJ **1** (= *débil*) weakly, delicate
2 (= *afectado*) affected

alfeñicarse* ▸ CONJUG 1g VPR
1 (= *enflaquecerse*) to get terribly thin, look frail
2 (= *remilgarse*) to act affectedly, be overnice

alfeñique SM **1** (= *persona débil*) weakling
2 (= *afectación*) affectation
3 (*Culin*) toffee-like paste, almond-flavoured *o* (EEUU) -flavored sugar paste

alferecía SF epilepsy

alférez SMF (*Mil*) second lieutenant, subaltern; (*Rel*) official standard bearer (*in processions*) ▸ **alférez de fragata** midshipman, middie (EEUU*) ▸ **alférez de navío** sub-lieutenant, ensign (EEUU)

alfil SM bishop

alfiler SM **1** (*Cos*) pin; (= *broche*) brooch, clip • MODISMOS: • **aquí ya no cabe ni un ~** you can't squeeze anything else in • **prendido con ~es** shaky, hardly hanging together • **puesto con 25 ~es** dressed up to the nines ▸ **alfiler de corbata** tiepin ▸ **alfiler de gancho** (*Arg*) safety pin ▸ **alfiler de seguridad** (*LAm*) safety pin ▸ **alfiler de sombrero** hatpin ▸ **alfiler nodriza** (*Col*) safety pin
2 (= *propina*) • **~es** pin money, dress allowance • **pedir para ~es** to ask for a tip

alfilerar ▸ CONJUG 1a VT to pin together, pin up

alfilerazo SM (= *punzada*) pinprick • **tirar ~s a algn** (= *criticar*) to have a dig at sb

alfilerillo SM (*And, Cono Sur*) *type of spikenard used for animal feeding*

alfiletero SM (= *estuche*) needle case; (= *acerico*) pincushion

alfolí SM [*de granos*] granary; [*de sal*] salt warehouse

alfombra SF (*grande*) carpet; (*pequeña*) rug, mat ▸ **alfombra de baño** bath mat ▸ **alfombra de oración** prayer mat ▸ **alfombra mágica** magic carpet ▸ **alfombra voladora** flying carpet

alfombrado SM carpeting

alfombrar ▸ CONJUG 1a VT to carpet

alfombrero/a SM/F carpet maker

alfombrilla SF **1** rug, mat ▸ **alfombrilla roja** red carpet
2 (*Med*) (= *sarampión*) German measles; (*Caribe*) (= *sarpullido*) rash; (*Méx*) (= *viruela*) smallpox

alfonsí ADJ Alphonsine (*esp re Alfonso X, 1252-84*)

alfonsino ADJ Alphonsine (*esp re recent kings of Spain named Alfonso*)

Alfonso SM Alphonso • **~ X el Sabio** Alphonso the Wise (1252-84)

alforfón SM buckwheat

alforja SF [*de jinete*] saddlebag; (*en bicicleta*) pannier; (= *mochila*) knapsack • **~s** (= *provisión*) provisions (*for a journey*) • MODISMOS: • **sacar los pies de las ~s** to go off on a different tack • **para ese viaje no hacían falta ~s** there was no point in bringing all this stuff, you didn't have to go to such trouble • **pasarse a la otra ~** (*Cono Sur*) to overstep the mark, go too far

alforjudo ADJ (*Cono Sur*) silly, stupid

alforza SF (= *pliegue*) pleat, tuck; (= *cicatriz*) slash, scar

alforzar ▸ CONJUG 1f VT to pleat, tuck

Alfredo SM Alfred

alga SF seaweed, alga • **~ tóxica** toxic alga

algaida SF (*Bot*) bush, undergrowth; (*Geog*) dune

algalia SF **1** (= *perfume*) civet
2 (*Med*) catheter

algara SF (*Hist*) raid

algarabía SF **1** (= *griterío*) hullabaloo
2 (*Ling*) Arabic
3 (*Bot*) cornflower

algarada SF **1** (= *griterío*) outcry • **hacer** *o* **levantar una ~** to kick up a tremendous fuss
2 (*Hist*) cavalry raid, cavalry troop

Algarbe SM • **el ~** the Algarve

algarero ADJ noisy, rowdy

algarroba SF carob, carob bean

algarrobo SM carob tree, locust tree

algazara SF din, uproar

álgebra SF algebra ▸ **álgebra de Boole** Boolean algebra

algebraico ADJ algebraic

algecireño/a ADJ of/from Algeciras
SM/F native/inhabitant of Algeciras • **los ~s** the people of Algeciras

álgido ADJ (= *muy frío*) icy, chilly; [*momento*] crucial, decisive

algo PRON **1** (*en oraciones afirmativas*) something • **estaba buscando ~ más barato** I was looking for something cheaper • **—¿no habéis comido nada? —sí, ~ hemos picado** "haven't you eaten anything?" — "yes, we've had a little snack" • **~ así**: • **es músico o ~ así** he's a musician or something like that • **dura ~ así como tres horas** it's about three hours long • **~ de**: • **tuve ~ de miedo** I was a bit scared • **sé ~ de inglés** I know a little English • **nos dieron ~ de comer** they gave us something to eat • **hay ~ de verdad en lo que dicen** there is some truth in what they say • **tenía ~ de revolucionario** there was something of the revolutionary in him • **tengo ~ de prisa** I'm in a bit of a hurry • **tienen ~ de razón** they are right to a certain extent *o* in a way • **en ~**: • **queríamos ser útiles en ~** we wanted to be of some use • **se ha cambiado en ~ el plan** the plan has been changed slightly • **las dos hermanas se parecen en ~** there is a certain likeness between the two sisters • **estar en ~** (= *implicado*) to be involved in sth; (*Ven‡*) to be high on sth • **llegar a ser ~** to be something • **tomar ~** (*de beber*) to have a drink; (*de comer*) to have a bite (to eat) • **¿quieres tomarte ~?** would you like a drink? • **llegamos a las tres y ~** we arrived at three something • **al nacer pesó tres kilos y ~** she weighed just over three kilos at birth • MODISMOS: • **~ es ~** it's better than nothing • **creerse ~** to think one is somebody • **darle ~ a algn***: • **casi me da ~ cuando falló el penalti** I nearly died when he missed the penalty • **si no deja de comer dulces un día le va a dar ~** if he doesn't stop eating sweet things something will happen to him one day • **cuando le da por ~ …** when he gets something into his head … • **por ~ será** there must be a reason for it • **si lo dice el director, por ~ será** if the manager says so, he must have his reasons *o* there must be a reason for it • **ya es ~**: • **ha logrado un estilo propio, lo que ya es ~** she has achieved her own style, which is quite something
2 (*en oraciones interrogativas, condicionales*) (*gen*) anything; (*esperando respuesta afirmativa*) something • **¿hay ~ para mí?** is there anything *o* something for me? • **¿puedes darme ~?** can you give me something? • **¿le has dado ~ más de dinero?** have you given him any more money? • **¿no le habrá pasado ~?** nothing has happened to him, has it?
ADV **1** (*con adjetivo*) rather, a little • **estos zapatos son ~ incómodos** these shoes are rather *o* a little uncomfortable • **puede parecer ~ ingenuo** he may seem slightly *o* rather *o* a little *o* somewhat (*frm*) naive
2 (*con verbos*) a little • **me recuerda ~ a mi padre** he reminds me a little of my father • **la inflación ha subido ~ más de dos puntos** inflation has gone up by a little over two points
SM **1** • **un ~**: • **tiene un ~ que atrae** there's something attractive about him *o* there's something about him that's attractive • **había un ~ de tristeza en su expresión** there was something sad in his expression
2 (*Col*) *mid-afternoon snack*; ▸ ALGUNO, ALGO

algodón SM **1** (*Cos*) (= *material*) cotton; (= *planta*) cotton plant • MODISMO: • **se crió entre algodones** he was always pampered ▸ **algodón en rama** raw cotton ▸ **algodón labrado** patterned cotton ▸ **algodón pólvora** gun cotton
2 (*Med*) swab ▸ **algodón hidrófilo** cotton wool, absorbent cotton (EEUU)
3 [*de azúcar*] candy floss, cotton candy (EEUU)

algodonal SM cotton plantation

algodonar ▸ CONJUG 1a VT to stuff with cotton wool, wad

algodoncillo SM milkweed

algodoncito SM cotton wool bud, cotton bud, Q-tip® (EEUU)

algodonero/a ADJ cotton (*antes de s*)
SM/F (= *persona*) (= *cultivador*) cotton grower; (= *comerciante*) cotton dealer
SM (= *planta*) cotton plant

algodonosa SF cotton grass

algodonoso ADJ cottony

algorítmica SF algorithms (*pl*)

algorítmico ADJ algorithmic

algoritmo SM algorithm

algoterapia SF seaweed wrap treatment

alguacil SM (*Jur*) bailiff, constable (EEUU); (*Taur*) (*tb* **alguacilillo**) mounted official

alguicida SM algicide

alguien PRON (*gen*) somebody, someone; (*en frases interrogativas*) anybody, anyone • **si viene ~** if somebody comes, if anybody comes • **¿viste a ~?** did you see anybody? • **para ~ que conozca la materia** for anybody who is familiar with the subject • **~ se lo habrá dicho** somebody or other must have told him • **se cree ~** he thinks he's somebody

alguita‡ SF (*And*) money, dough‡

alguito (*LAm*) = algo

alguno/a ADJ (ANTES DE SM SING: **algún**)
1 (*antes de s*) (*en oraciones afirmativas*) some; (*en oraciones interrogativas, condicionales*) any • **algún día lo comprenderás** some day you'll understand • **tuvimos algunas dificultades** we had a few *o* some difficulties • **llámame si tienes algún problema** call me if you have any problems • **¿conoces algún hotel barato?** do you know a cheap hotel? • **hubo alguna que otra nube** there were one or two clouds, there was the odd cloud • **objetos de alguna importancia** objects of some importance • **en alguna parte** somewhere • **alguna vez** (*en oraciones afirmativas*) at some point; (*en oraciones interrogativas, condicionales*) ever • **todos lo hemos hecho alguna vez** we've all done it at one time or another *o* at some point • **alguna vez le he oído hablar de ella** I have heard him mention her sometimes • **¿has estado alguna vez en Nueva York?** have you ever been to New York?

a

2 (*después de s*) • **no tiene talento ~** he has no talent at all • **nos atacaron sin motivo ~** they attacked us for no reason at all • **sin interés ~** without the slightest interest • **sin valor ~** completely worthless; ▹ **duda**
3 **algunos** (= *varios*) several • **salvaron ~s cientos de vidas** they saved several hundred lives
PRON 1 (= *objeto*) one • **estará en ~ de esos cajones** it must be in one of those drawers • **de entre tantas camisas, seguro que alguna te gustará** out of all these shirts, there's bound to be one that you like • **~ que otro** one or two
2 (= *persona*) someone, somebody • **siempre hay ~ que protesta** there is always one *o* someone *o* somebody who complains • **~ de ellos** one of them
3 **algunos** (= *cosas*) some, some of them; (= *personas*) some, some of us/you *etc* • **vinieron ~s, pero no todos** some of them came, but not all • **~s no se han enterado todavía** some (people) haven't found out yet

ALGUNO, ALGO

"Some" y "any" en oraciones afirmativas e interrogativas

Frases afirmativas

▹ *En frases afirmativas debe usarse* **some** *o las formas compuestas de* **some**:
He leído algunos artículos interesantes sobre el tema
I have read some interesting articles on the subject
Algunos no están de acuerdo
Some people disagree
He comprado algo para ti
I've bought something for you

Frases interrogativas

▹ *En frases interrogativas que expresan algún tipo de ofrecimiento o petición y cuya respuesta se espera que sea positiva, también debe emplearse la forma* **some** *etc*:
Tienes muchos libros. ¿Me dejas alguno?
You've got lots of books. Can I borrow some?

▹ *En el resto de las frases interrogativas, empléese* **any** *o las formas compuestas de* **any**:
¿Se te ocurre alguna otra idea?
Do you have any other ideas?
¿Hay algún sitio donde podamos escondernos?
Is there anywhere we can hide?

Frases condicionales

▹ *La construcción* **si** + *verbo* + **algo** *o* **algún/alguna** *etc se traduce al inglés por* **if** + *sujeto* + *verbo* + **any** *o* **some**, *etc*:
Si necesitas algo, dímelo
If you need anything, let me know
Si quiere algunas cintas, no deje de pedirlas
If you would like some tapes, don't hesitate to ask

Hay que tener en cuenta que **some** *se utiliza cuando tenemos más certeza de que la condición se vaya a cumplir.*
▹ **NINGUNO**

Para otros usos y ejemplos ver **algo, alguno**

alhaja SF 1 (= *joya*) jewel, gem; (= *objeto precioso*) precious object, treasure; (= *mueble*) fine piece (of furniture)
2 (= *persona*) treasure, gem • **¡buena ~!** (*iró*) she's a fine one!
alhajado ADJ (*And*) wealthy
alhajar ▹ CONJUG 1a VT [+ *persona*] to adorn (*with jewels*); [+ *habitación*] to furnish, appoint, appoint in delicate taste
alhajero SM (*Cono Sur, Méx*), **alhajera** SF (*Cono Sur, Méx*) jewel box
alharaca SF fuss • **hacer ~s** to make a fuss, make a great song and dance
alharaquiento ADJ demonstrative, highly emotional
alhelí SM wallflower, stock
alheña SF 1 (*Bot*) (= *arbusto*) privet; (= *flor*) privet flower
2 (= *hongo*) blight, mildew
3 (*para teñir*) henna
alheñar ▹ CONJUG 1a VT to dye with henna
VPR **alheñarse** to become mildewed, get covered in mildew
alhóndiga SF corn exchange
alhucema SF lavender
aliacán SM jaundice
aliado/a ADJ allied
SM/F ally • **los Aliados** the Allies
SM (*Cono Sur*) (= *emparedado*) toasted sandwich; (= *bebida*) mixed drink
aliaga SF = **aulaga**
aliancista (*Esp*) (*Pol, Hist*) ADJ • **política ~** policy of Alianza Popular
SMF member of Alianza Popular
alianza SF 1 (= *pacto*) alliance • **la Alianza** (*Rel*) the Covenant • **Santa Alianza** Holy Alliance ▸ **la Alianza Atlántica** the Atlantic Alliance, NATO ▸ **Alianza para el Progreso** Alliance for Progress
2 (= *anillo*) wedding ring
aliar ▹ CONJUG 1c VT to ally, bring into an alliance
VPR **aliarse** to form an alliance • **~se con** to ally o.s. with, side with
alias ADV, SM INV alias
alicaído ADJ (= *débil*) drooping, weak; (= *triste*) downcast, depressed
Alicante SM Alicante
alicantina SF trick, ruse
alicantino/a ADJ of/from Alicante
SM/F native/inhabitant of Alicante • **los ~s** the people of Alicante
alicatado SM tiling
alicatar ▹ CONJUG 1a VT [+ *pared*] to tile; [+ *azulejo*] to shape, cut
alicate SM 1 = **alicates**
2 (*Arg*) (= *cortaúñas*) nail clippers (*pl*)
alicates SMPL pliers, pincers • **~ de corte** wire cutters
Alicia SF Alice • **"~ en el país de las maravillas"** "Alice in Wonderland" • **"~ a través del espejo"** "Alice through the Looking-glass"
aliciente SM (= *incentivo*) incentive, inducement; (= *atractivo*) attraction • **ofrece el ~ de** it has the attraction of • **ofrecer un ~** to hold out an inducement
alicorarse* ▹ CONJUG 1a VPR (*And*) to get boozed*
alicorear ▹ CONJUG 1a VT (*CAm*) to decorate, adorn
alicrejo SM (*CAm*) (= *animal feo*) *spider-like creature*; (*hum*) (= *rocín*) old horse, nag
alicurco ADJ (*Cono Sur*) sly, cunning
alienación SF (= *enajenación*) alienation; (*Psic*) alienation, mental derangement
alienado/a ADJ (= *marginado*) alienated; (*Psic*) insane, mentally ill
SM/F (= *marginado*) alienated person; (*Psic*) mentally ill person

alienador ADJ, **alienante** ADJ alienating, dehumanizing, inhuman
alienar ▹ CONJUG 1a VT = **enajenar**
alienígena ADJ (= *extranjero*) alien, foreign; (= *extraterrestre*) alien, extraterrestrial
SMF (= *extranjero*) alien, foreigner; (= *extraterrestre*) alien, extraterrestrial being
alienista SMF specialist in mental illness, psychiatrist, alienist (*EEUU*)
aliento SM 1 (= *hálito*) breath • **tiene mal ~** he has bad breath • **le huele el ~ a ajo** his breath smells of garlic
2 (= *respiración*) • **el ejercicio me dejó sin ~** the exercise left me breathless *o* out of breath • **contener el ~** to hold one's breath • **dar los últimos ~s** (*liter*) to breathe one's last (*liter*) • **faltar el ~**: • **me falta el ~** I'm out of breath • **recobrar** *o* **recuperar el ~** to get one's breath back • **tomar ~**: • **paró, tomó ~ y continuó hablando** he stopped to get his breath back, then went on talking
• MODISMOS: • **cortar a algn el ~** to take sb's breath away • **de un ~** (*frm*) (= *de una vez*) in one go
3 (*frm*) (= *ánimo*) courage, spirit • **cobrar ~** to take heart • **dar ~ a algn** to encourage sb
4 (= *tono*) • **una novela de hondo ~ patriótico** a novel with a deeply patriotic spirit, a profoundly patriotic novel
alifafe* SM ailment
aligación SF (= *aleación*) alloy; (= *vínculo*) bond, tie
aligeramiento SM (= *reducción de peso*) lightening; (= *aliviamiento*) easing, alleviation; (= *aceleración*) speeding-up
aligerar ▹ CONJUG 1a VT (= *hacer ligero*) to lighten; [+ *dolor*] to ease, relieve, alleviate; (= *abreviar*) to shorten; (= *acelerar*) to quicken • **voy a dar un paseo para ~ las piernas** I'm going for a walk to stretch my legs
VI (= *darse prisa*) to hurry, hurry up
VPR **aligerarse** [*carga*] to get lighter • **~se de ropa** to put on lighter clothing
aligustre SM privet
alijar[1] ▹ CONJUG 1a VT (*Téc*) to sandpaper
alijar[2] ▹ CONJUG 1a VT [+ *carga*] to lighten; [+ *barco*] to unload; [+ *contrabando*] to land, smuggle ashore
alijo SM 1 (= *aligeramiento*) lightening; (= *descarga*) unloading
2 (= *contrabando*) contraband, smuggled goods • **un ~ de armas** an arms cache, an arms haul • **un ~ de drogas** a drugs shipment, a consignment of drugs
alilaya SF (*And, Caribe*) (= *excusa*) lame excuse, flimsy excuse
SMF (*Méx*) (= *persona astuta*) cunning person, sharp character*
alimaña SF 1 (*Zool*) pest • **~s** vermin
2 (= *persona*) bloodsucker*
alimañero SM gamekeeper, vermin destroyer
alimentación SF 1 (= *acción*) feeding; (= *comida*) food • **el coste de la ~** the cost of food • **la ~ de los niños** the feeding of children ▸ **alimentación insuficiente** malnutrition ▸ **alimentación natural** natural food, health foods
2 (*Téc*) feed; (*Elec*) supply • **bomba de ~** feed pump ▸ **alimentación a la red** mains supply ▸ **alimentación automática de hojas** automatic sheet feeder ▸ **alimentación automática de papel** (automatic) paper feeder ▸ **alimentación por fricción** friction feed
alimentador SM (*Téc*) feeder ▸ **alimentador automático de hojas** automatic sheet feeder ▸ **alimentador automático de papel** (automatic) paper

feeder ▸ **alimentador de red** mains power supply
alimentar ▹ CONJUG 1a (VT) **1** (= *dar de comer a*) to feed • **alimentan el ganado con piensos** they feed the cattle with animal fodder • **tengo una familia que ~** I've got a family to feed
2 (= *nutrir*) to be nutritious *o* nourishing • **la comida rápida no te alimenta nada** fast food is not at all nutritious *o* nourishing
3 [+ *imaginación*] to fire, fuel; [+ *esperanzas, pasiones*] to feed, fuel; [+ *sentimiento, idea*] to foster • **ese tipo de comentario alimenta el rencor** that sort of remark fosters resentment • **sus historias ~on mi deseo de ir a Perú** her stories strengthened *o* fuelled my desire to go to Peru
4 [+ *hoguera, horno doméstico, fuego*] to feed, add fuel to; [+ *horno industrial*] to stoke • **el operario alimenta la máquina de *o* con combustible** the operator feeds fuel into the machine
5 (*Elec*) to supply
(VI) to be nutritious, be nourishing • **esta comida no alimenta nada** this food is not at all nutritious *o* nourishing • MODISMO: • **huele que alimenta*** it smells delicious
(VPR) **alimentarse 1** [*animal*] to feed • **se alimentan de carroña** they feed on carrion
2 [*persona*] • **en este país se alimentan fatal** people eat very poorly in this country • **se alimenta solo de productos naturales** she eats only natural foods • **durante el naufragio se ~on solo de fruta** while shipwrecked they lived *o* survived on fruit
3 (*Mec*) • **el motor se alimenta de gasoil** the engine runs on diesel
alimentario (ADJ) food (*antes de s*) • **la industria alimentaria** the food industry
alimenticio (ADJ) **1** (= *nutritivo*) nourishing, nutritive
2 (= *relativo a comida*) food (*antes de s*) • **productos ~s** foodstuffs • **valor ~** food value, nutritional value
alimento (SM) **1** (= *comida*) food • **de mucho ~** nourishing • **de poco ~** of little nutritional value ▸ **alimento de primera necesidad** staple food ▸ **alimentos integrales** whole foods ▸ **alimentos naturales** health foods
2 (= *apoyo*) encouragement, support; (= *incentivo*) incentive; [*de pasión*] fuel
3 alimentos (*Jur*) maintenance allowance (*sing*), alimony (*sing*) (EEUU)
alimentoso (ADJ) nourishing
alimoche (SM) Egyptian vulture
alimón • **al ~** (ADV) together, jointly, in collaboration
alindado (ADJ) foppish, dandified
alindar¹ ▹ CONJUG 1a (VT) (= *adornar*) to embellish, make pretty, make look nice; [+ *persona*] to doll up, prettify
alindar² ▹ CONJUG 1a (VT) [+ *tierra*] to mark off, mark out
(VI) (= *estar contiguo*) to adjoin, be adjacent
alinderar ▹ CONJUG 1a (VT) (*CAm, Cono Sur*) to mark out the boundaries of
alineación (SF) **1** (*Téc*) alignment • **estar fuera de ~** to be out of alignment, be out of true
2 (*Dep*) line-up
alineado (ADJ) • **países no ~s** non-aligned countries • **está ~ con el partido** he is in line with the party
alineamiento (SM) alignment • **no ~** non-alignment
alinear ▹ CONJUG 1a (VT) (*Téc*) to align; [+ *alumnos*] to line up, put into line; [+ *soldados*] to form up; (*Dep*) [+ *equipo*] to select, pick (**con** with)
(VPR) **alinearse** (= *ponerse en fila*) to line up; (*Mil*) to fall in; (*Inform*) to justify • **se ~on a lo largo de la calle** they lined up along the street
aliñador (SM) (*Cono Sur*) bonesetter
aliñar ▹ CONJUG 1a (VT) **1** (*Culin*) [+ *ensalada*] to dress; [+ *guiso*] to season
2 (= *adornar*) to adorn, embellish; (= *preparar*) to prepare
3 (*Cono Sur*) [+ *hueso*] to set
aliño (SM) **1** (*Culin*) [*de ensalada*] dressing; [*de guiso*] seasoning
2 (= *adorno*) adornment, embellishment
alioli (SM) (*Culin*) *sauce of garlic and oil*
alionar ▹ CONJUG 1a (VT) (*Cono Sur*) to stir up
alionín (SM) blue tit
alipego (SM) (*CAm*) **1** (= *plus*) extra, bonus (*added as part of a sale*)
2* (= *persona no invitada*) gatecrasher, intruder
aliquebrado (ADJ) crestfallen
alirón (EXCL) (= *¡bien!*) hurray!
(SM) • **cantar el ~** (*lit*) *to sing a chant celebrating one's team's victory*; (*fig*) to celebrate
alisado (ADJ) (= *liso*) smooth; (*Téc*) polished
(SM) (= *acción*) smoothing; (*Téc*) polishing, finishing
alisador (SM) (= *persona*) polisher; (= *herramienta*) smoothing blade, smoothing tool
alisadura (SF) (= *acción*) smoothing; (*Téc*) polishing • **~s** (= *raspaduras*) cuttings, shavings
alisamiento (SM) [*del pelo*] straightening
alisar¹ ▹ CONJUG 1a (VT) **1** [+ *vestido*] to smooth, smooth down; [+ *pelo*] to smooth, straighten, sleek
2 (*Téc*) to polish, finish
alisar² (SM), **aliseda** (SF) alder grove
alíscafo (SM), **aliscafo** (SM) hydrofoil
alisios (SMPL) • **vientos ~** trade winds
aliso (SM) alder, alder tree
alistamiento (SM) (= *matrícula*) enrolment, enrollment (EEUU); (*Mil*) enlistment
alistar ▹ CONJUG 1a (VT) **1** (= *registrar*) to list, put on a list; (= *matricular*) to enrol, enroll (EEUU); (*Mil*) to enlist
2 (= *disponer*) to prepare, get ready
3 (*CAm*) [+ *zapato*] to sew, sew up
(VPR) **alistarse 1** (= *matricularse*) to enrol *o* (EEUU) enroll; (*Mil*) to enlist, join up
2 (*LAm*) (= *vestirse*) to dress up; (= *prepararse*) to get ready
aliteración (SF) alliteration
aliterado (ADJ) alliterative
alitranca (SF) (*And, Cono Sur*) brake, braking device
aliviadero (SM) overflow channel
aliviado (ADJ) relieved
aliviador (ADJ) comforting, consoling
alivianarse* ▹ CONJUG 1a (VPR) (*Méx*) to play it cool, be cool, be laid-back*
aliviar ▹ CONJUG 1b (VT) **1** [+ *dolor, sufrimiento, problema*] to ease, relieve • **medidas para ~ los efectos de la catástrofe** measures to ease *o* relieve the effects of the disaster
2 [+ *carga, peso*] to lighten
3 (= *consolar*) to soothe • **el vino alivia las penas** wine soothes away your troubles • **me alivia saberlo** I'm pleased to hear it
4 (*frm*) • **~ el paso** to quicken one's step
5† (= *robar*) • **~ a algn de algo** to relieve sb of sth (*hum*)
(VI) (= *darse prisa*) to speed up
(VPR) **aliviarse 1** [*dolor*] to ease
2 [*enfermo*] to get better • **¡que te alivies!** get well soon!
alivio (SM) **1** (= *consuelo*) relief • **es un gran ~ haber aprobado por fin** it's a great relief to have passed at last, I'm relieved that I've passed at last • **¡qué ~!** what a relief! • **dio un suspiro de ~** he gave a sigh of relief
2 [*de un dolor*] • **los paños calientes le servirán de ~** the hot towels will ease *o* relieve his pain • **¡que siga el ~!** I hope you continue to improve!
3 (*Esp*) • **de ~*** awful, frightful • **me dio un susto de ~** he gave me an awful fright
4 ▸ **alivio de luto** half-mourning
aljaba (SF) **1** (*para flechas*) quiver
2 (*Cono Sur*) (*Bot*) fuchsia
aljama (SF) (*Hist*) **1** (= *barrio*) [*de moros*] Moorish quarter; [*de judíos*] Jewish quarter, ghetto
2 (= *mezquita*) mosque; (= *sinagoga*) synagogue
3 (= *reunión*) [*de moros*] gathering of Moors; [*de judíos*] gathering of Jews
aljamía (SF) *Spanish written in Arabic characters (14th-16th centuries)*
aljamiado (ADJ) • **texto ~** *text of Spanish written in Arabic characters*
aljibe (SM) **1** (= *tanque*) cistern, tank; (*Náut*) water tender; (*Aut*) oil tanker
2 (*And*) (= *pozo*) well; (= *calabozo*) dungeon, underground prison
aljofaina (SF) washbasin, washbowl
aljófar (SM) (= *perla*) pearl; [*de rocío*] dewdrop
aljofarar ▹ CONJUG 1a (VT) to bedew, cover with pearls of moisture
aljofifa (SF) floorcloth
aljofifar ▹ CONJUG 1a (VT) to wash, mop, mop up
allá (ADV) **1** (*indicando posición*) there, over there; (*dirección*) (over) there • **~ arriba** up there • **~ abajo** down there • **~ en Sevilla** down in Seville, over in Seville • **~ mismo** right there • **~ lejos** way off in the distance, away over there • **no tan ~** not so far • **más ~** further away, further over • **más ~ de** beyond • **más ~ de los límites** beyond the limits • **cualquier número más ~ de siete** any number higher than seven • **no sabe contar más ~ de diez** she can't count above ten, she can't count beyond ten • **por ~** thereabouts • **vamos ~** let's go there • **¡~ voy!** I'm coming! • MODISMOS: • **el más ~** the beyond, the great beyond • **no muy ~*** (= *valer poco*) not much cop* • **no está muy ~** (*de salud*) he isn't very well • **~ lo veremos** we'll see when we get there, we'll sort that one out later
2 • **~ tú** that's up to you, that's your problem • **¡~ él!** that's his lookout!*, that's his problem! • **~ cada uno** that's for the individual to decide
3 (*indicando tiempo*) • **~ en 1600** back in 1600, way back in 1600, as long ago as 1600 • **~ por el año 1960** round about 1960 • **~ en mi niñez** in my childhood days
allacito (ADV) (*LAm*) = allá
allanamiento (SM) **1** (= *nivelación*) levelling, leveling (EEUU); (= *alisadura*) smoothing; (*Mil*) razing
2 [*de obstáculos*] removal
3 (*Jur*) submission (**a** to)
4 (*esp LAm*) [*de policía*] raid • **el juez dispuso el ~ del domicilio** the judge granted the police a search warrant for the house ▸ **allanamiento de morada** breaking and entering
5 (= *pacificación*) pacification
allanar ▹ CONJUG 1a (VT) **1** (= *nivelar*) to level, level out, make even; (= *alisar*) to smooth, smooth down; (*Mil*) to raze (to the ground)
2 [+ *problema*] to iron out
3 (*Jur*) [+ *casa*] (= *robar*) to break into, burgle, burglarize (EEUU); (*esp LAm*) [*policía*] to raid
4 [+ *país*] to pacify, subdue
(VPR) **allanarse 1** (= *nivelarse*) to level out, level off

a

2 (= *derrumbarse*) to fall down, tumble down
3 (*fig*) (= *acceder*) to submit, give way • **~se a** to accept, agree to • **se allana a todo** he agrees to everything

allegadizo ADJ gathered at random, put together unselectively

allegado/a ADJ **1** (= *afín*) near, close • **según fuentes allegadas al ministro** according to sources close to the minister
2 [*pariente*] close • **los más ~s y queridos** one's nearest and dearest • **las personas allegadas a …** those closest to …
SM/F **1** (= *pariente*) relation, relative
2 (= *partidario*) follower

allegar ▸ CONJUG 1h VT **1** (= *reunir*) to gather (together), collect
2 (= *acercar*) • **~ una cosa a otra** to put something near something else
3 (= *añadir*) to add
VPR **allegarse 1** (*fig*) (= *adherirse*) • **~se a una opinión** to adopt a view • **~se a una secta** to become attached to a sect
2 (= *llegar*) to arrive, approach • **~se a algn** to go up to sb

allende (*liter*) ADV on the other side
PREP beyond • **~ los mares** beyond the seas • **~ los Pirineos** on the other side of the Pyrenees • **~ lo posible** impossible

allí ADV **1** (*indicando posición*) there • **~ arriba** up there • **~ dentro** in there • **~ cerca** near there • **de ~** from there • **de ~ para acá** back and forth • **por ~** over there, round there • **hasta ~** as far as that, up to that point • **~ donde va despierta admiración** wherever he goes he makes a favourable impression • **está tirado por ~*** he's hanging around somewhere
2 (*indicando tiempo*) • **de ~ a poco** shortly afterwards
3 (*expresiones*) • **de ~** (= *por lo tanto*) and so, and thus (*frm o liter*) • **de ~ que …** (= *por eso*) that is why …, hence … (*frm*) • **de ~ a decir que es un timo** but that's a long way from calling it a swindle • **hasta ~ no más** (*LAm*) that's the limit

allicito ADV (*LAm*) = **allí**

alma SF **1** (= *espíritu*) soul • **una oración por su ~** a prayer for his soul • **no había ni un ~ en la iglesia** there wasn't a soul in the church • **un pueblo de 2.000 ~s** a village of 2,000 souls • **tenía ~ de poeta** she had a poetic spirit • **es mi amigo del ~** he's my soulmate • **ni ~ viviente** not a single living soul ▸ **alma bendita** kind soul ▸ **alma cándida** poor innocent ▸ **¡alma de cántaro!** you idiot! ▸ **alma caritativa, alma de Dios** kind soul ▸ **alma en pena** lost soul ▸ **almas gemelas** soul mates, kindred spirits (*más frm*)
2 • MODISMOS: • **tener el ~ en su almario** to have what it takes • **le arrancó el ~** he was devastated • **estaba con el ~ en la boca** my heart was in my mouth • **se le cayó el ~ a los pies** his heart sank • **huir** *o* **ir como ~ que lleva el diablo** to flee *o* go like a bat out of hell • **se echó el ~ a las espaldas** he abandoned all scruples • **en el ~**: • **te lo agradezco en el ~** I'm eternally *o* deeply grateful • **me dolió en el ~** it broke my heart • **lo siento en el ~** I am truly sorry • **entregar el ~ (a Dios)** (*euf*) to depart this life • **hasta el ~**: • **me mojé hasta el ~** I got soaked to the skin • **vomitó hasta el ~** she was violently sick • **estar con el ~ en un hilo** *o* **en vilo** • **tener el ~ en un hilo** to have one's heart in one's mouth *o* (*EEUU*) throat • **en lo más hondo de mi ~** from the bottom of my heart, in my heart of hearts • **irse el ~ tras algo/algn** to fall in love with sth/sb, fall for sth/sb • **me llegó al ~** • **se me clavó en el ~** (= *me dolió*) I was deeply hurt; (= *me conmovió*) I found it deeply moving *o* touching • **de mi ~**: • **¡madre mía de mi ~!** • **¡Dios mío de mi ~!** good God!, good grief! • **¡hijo de mi ~!** (*con cariño*) my darling boy!, my precious child!; (*con ironía*) my dear child! • **¡mi ~!** *o* **¡~ mía!, ¿qué te ha pasado?** my love! what's wrong? • **partir** *o* **romper el ~ a algn** (= *hacer sufrir*) to break sb's heart; (= *golpear*‡) to beat sb up • **partirse el ~**: • **se parten el ~ trabajando** they work themselves into the ground • **se me parte el ~** it breaks my heart • **no puedo con mi ~** (*Esp**) I'm completely shattered*, I'm ready to drop* • **rendir el ~** to give up the ghost • **romperse el ~** (*LAm*) to break one's neck • **me salió del ~** I just said it without thinking, it just came out • **no tener ~** to have no soul • **con toda el ~**: • **lo deseo con toda el ~** I want it desperately • **la quiero con toda mi ~** I love her with all my heart • **lo odio con toda mi ~** I detest him, I hate his guts* • **tiró fuerte, con toda su ~** he pulled hard, with all his might • **vender el ~ al diablo** to sell one's soul to the devil • **le volvió el ~ al cuerpo** he recovered his composure
3 (= *parte vital*) [*de grupo, organización*] driving force; [*de asunto*] heart, crux • **hasta que no lleguemos al ~ del asunto** until we get to the heart *o* crux of the matter • **es el ~ de la fiesta** she's the life and soul of the party
4 (*Téc*) [*de cable*] core; [*de cuerda*] core, central strand; [*de cañón*] bore; [*de raíl*] web
5 (*Bot*) pith
6 (*And*) (= *cadáver*) corpse

almacén SM **1** [*de mercancías*] warehouse, store • **tener algo en ~** (= *de reserva*) to have sth in store; (*Com*) to stock sth ▸ **almacén de depósito** bonded warehouse ▸ **almacén depositario** (*Com*) depository
2 (*Mec, Mil*) magazine
3 (= *tienda*) shop, store • **almacenes** • **grandes almacenes** department store (*sing*) • **Almacenes Pérez** Pérez Department Store ▸ **almacén frigorífico** cold store
4 (*LAm*) (= *tienda de comestibles*) grocer's (shop)

almacenable ADJ that can be stored, storable

almacenado SM storage, warehousing

almacenaje SM **1** (= *servicio*) storage, storing ▸ **almacenaje de larga duración** long-term storage ▸ **almacenaje frigorífico** cold storage
2 (= *gastos*) storage charge

almacenamiento SM (*en almacén, depósito*) warehousing; (*Inform*) storage ▸ **almacenamiento de datos** data storage ▸ **almacenamiento primario** primary storage ▸ **almacenamiento secundario** secondary storage ▸ **almacenamiento temporal en disco** spooling, disk spooling

almacenar ▸ CONJUG 1a VT **1** (*como negocio*) to store, warehouse
2 [*cliente*] to put into storage; [+ *víveres*] to stock up (with)
3 (= *guardar*) to keep, collect; [+ *rencor, odio*] to store up
4 (*Inform*) to store

almacenero/a SM/F (*en almacén*) storekeeper; (*LAm*) (*en tienda*) shopkeeper, grocer, storekeeper (*EEUU*)

almacenista SMF (= *dueño*) warehouse owner; (= *vendedor*) wholesaler; (*LAm*) (*en tienda*) shopkeeper, grocer, storekeeper (*EEUU*)

almáciga SF, **almácigo** SM plantation, nursery

almádena SF sledgehammer

almadía SF raft

almadiarse ▸ CONJUG 1c VPR to be sick, vomit

almadraba SF (= *acto, arte*) tunny fishing; (= *lugar*) tunny fishery; (= *redes*) tunny net, tunny nets (*pl*)

almadreña SF wooden shoe, clog

almagre SM red ochre, red ocher (*EEUU*)

almajara SF hotbed, forcing frame

alma máter SF **1** (= *impulsor*) driving force
2 (*Univ*) alma mater

almanaque SM almanac • MODISMOS: • **hacer ~s** to muse • **echar a algn vendiendo ~s** (*And, Cono Sur*) to send sb away with a flea in his ear

almariarse ▸ CONJUG 1c VPR (*CAm, Cono Sur*) to be sick, vomit

almazara SF oil mill, oil press

almeja SF **1** (*Zool*) clam
2** [*de mujer*] cunt** • **mojar la ~** to have a screw**

almenado ADJ battlemented, crenellated

almenara SF (= *fuego*) beacon; (= *araña*) chandelier

almenas SFPL battlements

almendra SF **1** (*Bot*) almond • MODISMO: • **ser ~** (*Caribe*) (= *encanto*) to be a love, be a peach ▸ **almendra amarga** bitter almond ▸ **almendra garapiñada** sugared almond ▸ **almendra tostada** toasted almond
2 (= *semilla*) kernel, stone
3 [*de vidrio*] cut-glass drop (*of chandelier*)

almendrada SF almond milk shake, *drink made with milk and almonds*

almendrado ADJ **1** [*forma*] almond-shaped • **de ojos ~s** almond-eyed
2 [*sabor*] nutty
SM (= *dulce*) macaroon

almendral SM almond orchard

almendrera SF almond tree

almendrillo SM (*LAm*) almond tree

almendro SM almond tree

almendruco SM green almond

Almería SF Almería

almeriense ADJ of/from Almería
SMF native/inhabitant of Almería • **los ~s** the people of Almería

almete SM helmet

almez SM hackberry

almiar SM hayrick

almíbar SM syrup • **peras en ~** pears in syrup • MODISMO: • **estar hecho un ~** (= *amable*) to be all sweetness and light; (*pey*) (= *meloso*) to overdo the flattery ▸ **almíbar de pelo** (*LAm*) heavy syrup

almibarado ADJ **1** (= *con almíbar*) syrupy; (= *dulce*) honeyed, oversweet
2 (= *meloso*) sugary

almibarar ▸ CONJUG 1a VT (= *bañar en almíbar*) to preserve in syrup • **~ las palabras** to use honeyed words

almidón SM (= *fécula*) starch; (*Méx*) (= *engrudo*) paste

almidonado ADJ **1** [*ropa*] starched
2 [*persona*] (= *estirado*) stiff, starchy; (= *pulcro*) dapper, spruce

almidonar ▸ CONJUG 1a VT to starch • **los prefiero sin ~** I prefer them unstarched

almilla SF **1** (= *jubón*) bodice
2 (*Téc*) tenon
3 (*Culin*) breast of pork

alminar SM minaret

almirantazgo SM admiralty

almirante SMF admiral

almirez SM mortar

almizclado ADJ musky

almizcle SM musk

almizcleño ADJ musky

almizclera SF muskrat, musquash

almizclero SM musk deer

almo ADJ (*poét*) (= *vivificador*) nourishing; (= *digno de veneración*) sacred, venerable

almocafre SM weeding hoe

almodrote SM **1** (= *salsa*) cheese and garlic sauce
2 (*fig*) (= *baturrillo*) hotchpotch, hodgepodge (EEUU)

almofré SM (*LAm*), **almofrez** SM (*LAm*) sleeping bag, bedroll

almohada SF [*de cama*] pillow; (= *funda*) pillowcase; (= *cojín*) cushion • MODISMO: • **consultar algo con la ~** to sleep on sth ▸ **almohada mariposa** butterfly pillow ▸ **almohada neumática** air cushion

almohade ADJ, SMF Almohad

almohadilla SF **1** (= *almohada pequeña*) small pillow
2 (= *cojincillo*) (*para alfileres*) pincushion; (*para sellos*) inkpad ▸ **almohadilla de entintar** inkpad
3 (*Telec*) hash key
4 (*LAm*) (= *agarrador*) holder (*for iron*)
5 (*Arquit*) boss

almohadillado ADJ (= *acolchado*) padded, stuffed; (*Arquit*) dressed
SM dressed stone

almohadón SM (= *almohada grande*) large pillow, bolster; (*Rel*) hassock

almohaza SF currycomb

almohazar ▹ CONJUG 1f VT [+ *caballo*] to brush down, groom; [+ *piel*] to dress

almoneda SF (= *subasta*) auction; (= *liquidación*) clearance sale

almonedar, **almonedear** ▹ CONJUG 1a VT to auction

almorávide ADJ, SMF Almoravid

almorranas SFPL piles

almorta SF vetch

almorzar ▹ CONJUG 1f, 1l VT (*a mediodía*) to have for lunch, lunch on (*frm*); (*a media mañana*) to have for breakfast, have for brunch
VI (*a mediodía*) to have lunch, lunch (*frm*); (*a media mañana*) to have breakfast *o* brunch • **vengo almorzado** I've had lunch

almuecín SM, **almuédano** SM muezzin

almuerzo SM (*a mediodía*) lunch; (*a media mañana*) breakfast, brunch; [*de boda*] wedding breakfast ▸ **almuerzo de gala** official luncheon ▸ **almuerzo de negocios** business lunch ▸ **almuerzo de trabajo** working lunch

alnado/a SM/F stepchild

aló EXCL (*esp LAm*) (*Telec*) hello!

alobado‡ ADJ dim*, thick*

alocado/a ADJ (= *loco*) crazy, mad; (= *irresponsable*) wild; (= *distraído*) scatterbrained
SM/F madcap

alocar ▹ CONJUG 1g (*LAm*) VT to drive mad • **me alocan las pizzas** I love pizzas, I'm mad for pizzas*
VPR **alocarse** to fly off the handle*, go crazy

alocución SF speech, address, allocution (*frm*)

áloe SM (*Bot*) aloe; (*Farm*) aloes

alojado/a SM/F (*LAm*) guest, lodger, roomer (EEUU)

alojamiento SM (= *lugar de hospedaje*) lodging, lodgings (*pl*); (*Mil*) billet, quarters (*pl*); (*And*) (= *pensión*) small hotel, boarding house • **buscar ~** to look for accommodation • **dar ~** to put up, accommodate

alojar ▹ CONJUG 1a VT (= *hospedar*) to put up, accommodate; (*Mil*) to billet, quarter
VPR **alojarse** to stay; (*Mil*) to be billeted, be quartered • **~se en** to stay at, put up at • **la bala se alojó en el pulmón** the bullet lodged in the lung

alón ADJ (*LAm*) (= *de ala grande*) large-winged; [*sombrero*] broad-brimmed
SM wing (*of chicken*)

alondra SF lark, skylark

alongar ▹ CONJUG 1l VT = **alargar**
VPR **alongarse** to move away

alopecia SF alopecia

alpaca SF alpaca

alpargata SF rope-soled sandal, espadrille • **turismo de ~** travelling on the cheap*, tourism on a shoestring

alpargatería SF sandal shop

alpargatero/a ADJ* (= *de poca categoría*) low-class, down-market; (= *barato*) done on the cheap*
SM/F (= *fabricante*) *maker of canvas sandals*; (= *vendedor*) *seller of canvas sandals*

alpargatilla SMF crafty person

alpende SM shed, lean-to

Alpes SMPL Alps

alpestre ADJ (= *de los Alpes*) Alpine; (= *montañoso*) mountainous

alpinismo SM mountaineering, climbing

alpinista SMF mountaineer, climber

alpinístico ADJ mountaineering (*antes de s*), climbing (*antes de s*)

alpino ADJ Alpine

alpiste SM **1** (= *semillas*) birdseed, canary seed
2* (= *alcohol*) drink, booze*
3 (*LAm**) (= *dinero*) brass*

Al Qaeda SM o SF Al Qaeda

alquería SF farmhouse, farmstead

alquiladizo/a ADJ (= *que se alquila*) for rent, for hire; (= *que se puede alquilar*) that can be rented, that can be hired; (*pey*) (= *asalariado*) hireling
SM/F hireling

alquilado/a SM/F (*Caribe*) tenant

alquilador(a) SM/F (= *propietario*) renter, hirer; (= *usuario*) tenant, lessee

alquilar ▹ CONJUG 1a VT **1** [*propietario*] [+ *inmueble*] to let, rent, rent out; [+ *coche, autocar*] to hire, hire out; (*TV*) to rent, rent out • **"se alquila"** "to let", "for rent" (EEUU) • **aquí no se alquila casa alguna** there is no house to let here
2 [*usuario*] [+ *inmueble*] to rent; [+ *coche, autocar*] to hire; (*TV*) to rent • **turba alquilada** rent-a-mob* • **"por ~"** "to let", "for rent" (EEUU)
VPR **alquilarse 1** [*persona*] (*como asalariado*) to hire o.s. out; (*Caribe*) (*como sirviente*) to go into service
2 [*taxi*] to be for hire

alquiler SM **1** (= *acción*) [*de inmueble*] letting, renting; (*Téc*) plant hire; [*de coche, autocar*] hire, hiring • **coche de ~** hire car • **"alquiler sin conductor"** (*Esp*) "self-drive" ▸ **alquiler de úteros** surrogate motherhood, womb-leasing
2 (= *precio*) [*de inmueble*] rent, rental; [*de coche, autocar*] hire charge • **contrato de ~** tenancy agreement • **control de ~es** rent control • **exento de ~es** rent-free • **madre de ~** surrogate mother • **pagar el ~** to pay the rent • **subir el ~ a algn** to raise sb's rent • **vivir de ~** to live in rented accommodation

alquimia SF alchemy

alquimista SM alchemist

alquitara SF still

alquitarar ▹ CONJUG 1a VT to distil

alquitrán SM tar ▸ **alquitrán de hulla**, **alquitrán mineral** coal tar

alquitranado ADJ tarred, tarry
SM [*de carretera*] tarmac; (= *lienzo*) tarpaulin, tarp (EEUU)

alquitranar ▹ CONJUG 1a VT (= *untar con alquitrán*) to tar; [+ *carretera*] to tarmac

alrededor ADV **1** around • **todo ~** all around
2 • **~ mío** *etc* (*Cono Sur*) around me *etc*
3 • **~ de** (= *en torno a*) around • **todo ~ de la iglesia** all around the church • **mirar ~ de sí** • **mirar ~ suyo** to look around *o* about one
4 • **~ de** (= *aproximadamente*) about, in the region of • **~ de 200** about 200
SM (= *contorno*) • **mirar a su ~** to look around *o* about one • **~es** (*de un lugar*) surroundings, neighbourhood (*sing*), neighborhood (*sing*) (EEUU); [*de ciudad*] outskirts • **en los ~es de Londres** in the area round London, on the outskirts of London

Alsacia SF Alsace

Alsacia-Lorena SF Alsace-Lorraine

alsaciano/a ADJ, SM/F Alsatian

alt. ABR **1** (= **altura**) ht
2 (= **altitud**) alt.

alta SF **1** (*Med*) (*tb* **alta médica**) certificate of discharge • **dar a algn el ~ (médica)** • **dar de ~ a algn** to discharge sb
2 (*en club, organismo*) membership • **solicitó el ~ en el club de golf** he applied for membership of the golf club, he applied to be a member of the golf club • **solicité el ~ de la línea telefónica** I applied for a phone line • **causar ~** • **darse de ~** to join • **doce nuevos miembros han causado ~** twelve new members have joined • **darse de ~ en la empresa** to join the company • **nos dimos de ~ en la Seguridad Social** we registered with Social Security
3 (*Jur*) • **dar una propiedad de ~** to register a property at the Land Registry
4 (*Mil*) • **dar a algn de ~** to pass sb (as) fit

altamente ADV highly • **es ~ venenoso** it's highly poisonous • **documentos ~ secretos** top secret documents

altanería SF **1** (= *altivez*) haughtiness, arrogance
2 (*Caza*) hawking, falconry
3 (*Meteo*) upper air

altanero ADJ **1** (= *altivo*) haughty, arrogant
2 [*ave*] high-flying

altar SM altar • **llevar a algn al ~** to lead sb to the altar • MODISMOS: • **poner a algn en un ~** to put sb on a pedestal • **quedarse para adornar ~es** to be left on the shelf • **subir a los ~es** to be beatified, be canonized ▸ **altar mayor** high altar

altaricón* ADJ big-built, large

altavoz SM (*Radio*) loudspeaker; (*Elec*) amplifier

altea SF mallow

altear ▹ CONJUG 1a VT (*Cono Sur*) to order to stop, order to halt

alterabilidad SF changeability

alterable ADJ changeable

alteración SF **1** (= *cambio*) alteration, change
2 (= *aturdimiento*) upset, disturbance; (*Med*) irregularity of the pulse ▸ **alteración del orden público** breach of the peace
3 (= *riña*) quarrel, dispute
4 (= *agitación*) strong feeling, agitation

alterado ADJ (= *cambiado*) changed; [*orden*] disturbed; (= *enfadado*) angry; (*Med*) upset, disordered

alterar ▹ CONJUG 1a VT **1** (= *cambiar*) to modify, alter • **tuvimos que ~ los planes por la huelga** we had to modify *o* alter our plans because of the strike
2 (= *estropear*) [+ *alimentos*] to spoil; [+ *leche*] to sour • **la humedad alteró los alimentos** the humidity spoiled the food, the humidity made the food go bad
3 (= *conmocionar*) to shake, upset • **la noticia del accidente la alteró visiblemente** she was visibly shaken *o* upset by the news of the accident
4 • **~ el orden** to disturb the peace
5 (= *distorsionar*) [+ *verdad*] to distort, twist
VPR **alterarse 1** (= *estropearse*) [*alimentos*] to spoil, go bad; [*leche*] to go sour

a

2 [*voz*] to falter
3 (= *turbarse*) to be shaken, be upset • **se alteró con la noticia de su muerte** he was shaken *o* upset by the news of her death • **¡tranquila, no te alteres!** keep calm!, don't get upset! • **continuó hablando sin ~se** he continued speaking unperturbed
altercado (SM), **altercación** (SF) argument, altercation
altercar ▹ CONJUG 1g (VI) to argue, quarrel, wrangle
álter ego (SM) alter ego
alteridad (SF) otherness
alternación (SF) alternation
alternadamente (ADV) alternately
alternado (ADJ) alternate
alternador (SM) alternator
alternancia (SF) alternation ▸ **alternancia de cultivos** crop rotation ▸ **alternancia en el poder** power switching, taking turns in office
alternante (ADJ) alternating
alternar ▹ CONJUG 1a (VT) (*gen*) to alternate, vary; [+ *cultivos*] to rotate
(VI) **1** (= *turnar*) to alternate (**con** with); (*Téc*) to alternate, reciprocate
2 (= *relacionarse*) to mix, socialize; (= *ir a bares**) to go on a pub crawl*, go boozing* • **~ con un grupo** to mix with a group, go around with a group • **~ con la gente bien** to hobnob with top people • **tiene pocas ganas de ~** he doesn't want to mix, he is not inclined to be sociable • **~ de igual a igual** to be on an equal footing
(VPR) **alternarse** (= *hacer turnos*) to take turns, change about • **~se a los mandos** to take turns at the controls • **~se en el poder** to take turns in office
alternativa (SF) **1** (= *opción*) alternative, option, choice • **no tener ~** to have no alternative *o* option *o* choice • **tomar una ~** to make a choice
2 (= *sucesión*) alternation; (= *trabajo*) shift work, work done in relays ▸ **alternativa de cosechas** crop rotation
3 (*Taur*) *ceremony by which a novice becomes a fully qualified bullfighter* • **tomar la ~** *to become a fully qualified bullfighter*
4 alternativas (*en actitud*) ups and downs, vicissitudes, fluctuations • **las ~s de la política** the ups and downs *o* vicissitudes of politics
alternativamente (ADV) alternately
alternativo (ADJ) (*Elec*) alternating; [*cultura, prensa*] alternative • **fuentes alternativas de energía** alternative energy sources
alterne (SM) (*con gente*) mixing, socializing; (*euf*) (= *relaciones sexuales*) sexual contact, sexual contacts (*pl*) • **club de ~** singles club • **estas chicas no son de ~** these girls don't sleep around*, these girls are not easy lays‡; ▹ **chica**
alterno (ADJ) (*Bot, Mat*) alternate; (*Elec*) alternating • **tiempo con nubes alternas** there will be patches of clouds
altero (SM) (*Méx*), **alterón** (SM) (*And*) heap, pile
alteza (SF) **1** (= *altura*) height
2 (= *título*) • **Alteza** Highness • **Su Alteza Real** His/Her Royal Highness • **sí, Alteza** yes, your Highness
3 (= *elevación*) sublimity ▸ **alteza de miras** high-mindedness
altibajos (SMPL) ups and downs
altillo (SM) **1** (*Geog*) small hill, hillock
2 (*LAm*) (= *desván*) attic
3 (= *entreplanta*) mezzanine
altilocuencia (SF) grandiloquence
altilocuente (ADJ), **altílocuo** (ADJ) grandiloquent
altímetro (SM) altimeter
altimontano (ADJ) high mountain (*antes de s*), upland (*antes de s*)
altinal (SM) (*Méx*) pillar, column
altiplanicie (SF) high plateau
altiplánico (ADJ) high plateau (*antes de s*)
altiplano (SM) (= *meseta*) high plateau; (*LAm*) [*de los Andes*] high Andean plateau, altiplano
altiro* (ADV) (*Chile*) right away
altísimo (ADJ) very high • **el Altísimo** the Almighty
altisonancia (SF) high-flown style
altisonante (ADJ), **altísono** (ADJ) high-flown, high-sounding
altitud (SF) (*Aer*) height, altitude; (*Geog*) elevation • **a una ~ de** at a height *o* altitude of
altivamente (ADV) haughtily, arrogantly
altivarse ▹ CONJUG 1a (VPR) to give o.s. airs
altivez (SF), **altiveza** (SF) haughtiness, arrogance
altivo (ADJ) haughty, arrogant
alto[1] (ADJ) **1** (*en altura*) **a** [*edificio, persona*] tall; [*monte*] high • **está muy ~ para su edad** he is very tall for his age • **los pisos ~s tienen más luz natural** the top flats have more natural light • **jersey de cuello ~** polo neck jumper, turtleneck • **camino de alta montaña** high mountain path • **zapatos de tacón** *o* (*Cono Sur, Perú*) **taco ~** high-heeled shoes, high heels; ▹ **mar**[1]
b • **lo ~**: • **una casa en lo ~ de la cuesta** a house on top of the hill • **desde lo ~ del árbol** from the top of the tree • **lanzar algo de** *o* **desde lo ~** to throw sth down, throw sth down from above • MODISMO: • **por todo lo ~**: • **lo celebraron por todo lo ~** they celebrated it in style
2 (*en nivel*) [*grado, precio, riesgo*] high; [*clase, cámara*] upper • **se han alcanzado muy altas temperaturas** there have been very high temperatures • **tiene la tensión alta** he has high blood pressure • **los alumnos de los niveles más ~s** the highest level students • **la marea estaba alta** it was high tide, the tide was in • **ha pagado un precio muy ~ por su descaro** he paid a very high price for his cheekiness • **una familia de clase alta** an upper class family • **la cámara alta del Parlamento ruso** the upper house of the Russian parliament • **ocupa una alta posición en el gobierno** he occupies a high-ranking position in the government • **tiene un ~ sentido del deber** he has a strong sense of duty • **alta burguesía** upper-middle class • **~ cargo** (*puesto*) high-ranking position; (*persona*) senior official, high-ranking official • **alta cocina** haute cuisine • **~/a comisario/a** High Commissioner • **Alto Comisionado** High Commission • **alta costura** high fashion, haute couture • **de alta definición** high-definition (*antes de s*) • **~/a ejecutivo/a** top executive • **alta escuela** (*Hípica*) dressage • **un jugador de alta escuela** a top quality player • **altas esferas** upper echelons • **alta fidelidad** high fidelity, hi-fi • **altas finanzas** high finance • **alta frecuencia** high frequency • **~ funcionario** senior official, high-ranking official • **oficiales de alta graduación** senior officers, high-ranking officers • **~s hornos** blast furnace • **~s mandos** senior officers, high-ranking officers • **de altas miras**: • **es un chico de altas miras** he is a boy of great ambition • **alta presión** (*Téc, Meteo*) high pressure • **hoy continuarán las altas presiones** the high pressure system will continue today • **alta sociedad** high society • **alta tecnología** high technology • **temporada alta** high season • **alta tensión** high tension, high voltage • **alta traición** high treason • **alta velocidad** high speed • **Alta Velocidad Española** (*Esp*) *name given to high speed train system*
3 (*en intensidad*) • **el volumen está muy ~** the volume is very loud • **la calefacción está muy alta** the heating is very high • **en voz alta** [*leer*] out loud; [*hablar*] in a loud voice
4 (*en el tiempo*) • **hasta altas horas de la madrugada** until the early hours
5 [*estilo*] lofty, elevated
6 (= *revuelto*) • **estar ~** [*río*] to be high; [*mar*] to be rough
7 (*Geog*) upper • **el Alto Rin** the Upper Rhine
8 (*Mús*) [*nota*] sharp; [*instrumento, voz*] alto
9 (*Hist, Ling*) high • **~ antiguo alemán** Old High German • **la alta Edad Media** the high Middle Ages
(ADV) **1** (= *arriba*) high • **sube un poco más ~** go up a little higher • **ha llegado muy ~ en su carrera profesional** he's reached the top in his professional career • **lanzar algo ~** to throw sth high
2 (= *en voz alta*) • **gritar ~** to shout out loud • **hablar ~** (= *en voz alta*) to speak loudly; (= *con franqueza*) to speak out, speak out frankly • **¡más ~, por favor!** louder, please! • **pon la radio un poco más ~** turn the radio up a little • **pensar (en) ~** to think out loud, think aloud; ▹ **volar**
(SM) **1** (= *altura*) • **el muro tiene 5 metros de ~** the wall is 5 metres high • **mide 1,80 de ~** he is 1.80 metres tall • **en ~**: • **coloque los pies en ~** put your feet up • **con las manos en ~** (*en atraco, rendición*) with one's hands up; (*en manifestación*) with one's hands in the air • MODISMO: • **dejar algo en ~**: • **el resultado deja muy en ~ su reputación como el mejor del mundo** the result has boosted his reputation as the best in the world • **estas cosas dejan en ~ el buen nombre de un país** these things contribute to maintaining the country's good name
2 (*Geog*) hill • **el pueblo está en un ~** the town lies on a hill ▸ **Altos del Golán** Golan Heights
3 (*Arquit*) upper floor
4 (*Mús*) alto
5 ▸ **altos y bajos** ups and downs
6 • **pasar por ~** [+ *detalle, problema*] to overlook
7 (*Chile*) [*de ropa, cartas*] pile
8 (*Chile*) [*de tela*] length
9 • **los ~s** (*Cono Sur, Méx*) [*de casa*] upstairs; (*Geog*) the heights • **los ~s de Jalisco** the Jalisco heights
alto[2] (SM) **1** (= *parada*) stop • **dar el ~ a algn** to order sb to halt, stop sb • **hacer un ~** (*en viaje*) to stop off; (*en actividad*) to take a break • **a este bar vienen los camioneros que hacen un ~ en el camino** the lorry drivers stop off at this bar on the way • **hicieron un ~ en el trabajo para comer un bocadillo** they took a break from work to eat a sandwich • **poner el ~ a algo** (*Méx*) to put an end to sth ▸ **alto el fuego** (*Esp*) ceasefire
2 (*Aut*) (= *señal*) stop sign; (= *semáforo*) lights (*pl*)
(EXCL) • **¡alto!** halt!, stop! • **¡~ ahí!** stop there! • **¡~ el fuego!** cease fire!
altocúmulo (SM) altocumulus
altomedieval (ADJ) early medieval, of the High Middle Ages
altoparlante (SM) (*LAm*) loudspeaker
altorrelieve (SM) high relief
altostrato (SM) altostratus
altozanero (SM) (*Col*) porter
altozano (SM) **1** (= *otero*) small hill, hillock; [*de ciudad*] upper part
2 (*And, Caribe*) (= *atrio*) cathedral forecourt, church forecourt

altramuz SM lupin
altruismo SM altruism
altruista ADJ altruistic
SMF altruist
altura SF **1** *[de edificio, techo, persona]* height • **el agua llegó hasta una ~ de 30cms** the water reached a height of 30cms • **las dos estanterías tienen la misma ~** the two bookshelves are the same height • **se necesita tener una ~ superior a 1,80** you have to be over 1.80 metres tall • **hubo olas de hasta tres metros de ~** there were waves up to three metres high, there were waves of up to three metres in height • **a la ~ de algo**: • **la ventana quedaba a la ~ de mi cabeza** the window was level with my head • **sentí un dolor a la ~ de los riñones** I felt a pain around my kidneys • **se hizo un corte a la ~ del tobillo** he cut himself on the ankle ▸ **altura de caída** *[de cascada]* fall ▸ **altura de la vegetación** timber line
2 *(en el aire)* height, altitude • **el avión subió a una ~ de 10.000 pies** the plane rose to a height *o* an altitude of 10,000 feet • **nos encontramos a 3.000 metros de ~ sobre el nivel del mar** we are 3,000 metres above sea level • **volaba a muy poca ~ del suelo** it was flying just above the ground • **ganar** *o* **tomar ~** to climb, gain height • **el globo empezó a perder ~** the balloon began to lose height ▸ **altura de crucero** cruising height; ▹ **mal**
3 *(= nivel)* • **no llegó a la ~ que se exigía** he did not measure up to the standard required • **si lo insultas te estás rebajando a su ~** if you insult him you are just lowering yourself to his level • **no encuentra ningún rival a su ~** she can't find a rival to match her, she can't find a rival in her league • **un partido de gran ~** a really excellent game • **estar a la ~ de** *[+ persona]* to be in the same league as, be on a par with; *[+ tarea]* to be up to, be equal to • **no estamos a la ~ de los trabajadores japoneses** we are not in the same league as Japanese workers, we are not on a par with Japanese workers • **su último artículo no estaba a la ~ de los anteriores** his last article did not match up to the previous ones • **la novela no estaba a la ~ del concurso** the novel was not up to the standard set by the competition, the novel did not measure up to the competition standards • **supo estar a la ~ de las circunstancias** he managed to rise to the occasion • **no estábamos a la ~ de los acontecimientos** we didn't keep abreast of events • MODISMOS: • **dejar** *o* **poner a algn a la ~ del betún** *o (Arg, Uru)* **de un felpudo** *o (Chile)* **del unto*** *(estando presente)* to make sb feel small; *(estando ausente)* to lay into sb • **quedar a la ~ del betún** *(Esp)*: • **si no los invitamos quedaremos a la ~ del betún** if we don't invite them, it'll look really bad
4 *(Geog)* • **a la ~ de** on the same latitude as • **a la ~ de Cádiz** on the same latitude as Cádiz • **a la ~ del km 8** at the 8th km, at the 8th km point • **hay retenciones a la ~ de Burgos** there are tailbacks near Burgos • **¿a qué ~ de la calle quiere que pare?** how far along the street do you want me to stop?
5 *(Náut)* • **buque de ~** seagoing vessel • **pesca de ~** deep-sea fishing • **remolcador de ~** deep-sea tug, ocean-going tug
6 *(Dep)* *(= salto)* high jump; *(= distancia del suelo)* height • **acaban de superar la ~ de 1,90** they have managed to beat the height of 1.90
7 *(Mús)* pitch
8 *[de ideas, sentimientos]* sublimity, loftiness
9 alturas: **a** *(= lugar elevado)* *(Geog)* heights; *(Rel)* heaven *(sing)* • **en las ~s de Sierra Nevada** on the heights of Sierra Nevada • **¡Gloria a Dios en las ~s!** Glory to God in Heaven! • **estar en las ~s** *(Rel)* to be on high
b *[de organización]* upper echelons • **en las ~s abundan las intrigas palaciegas** court intrigues are plentiful in the upper echelons
c • **a estas ~s** *[de edad]* at my/your/his *etc* age; *[de tiempo]* at this stage • **a estas ~s no me preocupan las arrugas** at my age, wrinkles don't worry me • **a estas ~s del año las playas están casi vacías** at this stage of the year the beaches are almost empty • **a estas ~s nadie te va a preguntar nada** at this stage no one is going to ask you anything • **¿todavía no confías en mí a estas ~s?** you still don't trust me after all this time? • **a estas ~s no podemos volvernos atrás** having come this far we can't go back now, we can't go back at this stage
d† *(= pisos)* storey, story *(EEUU)* • **una casa de cinco ~s** a five-storey house
alubia SF kidney bean ▸ **alubia pinta** pinto bean ▸ **alubia roja** kidney bean
alucinación SF hallucination
alucinado ADJ **1** *(= trastornado)* suffering hallucinations
2* *(= fascinado)* gobsmacked* • **me quedé ~** I was gobsmacked
alucinador ADJ hallucinatory, deceptive
alucinante ADJ **1** *(Med)* hallucinatory
2 *(Esp*)* *(= fascinante)* attractive, beguiling; *(= misterioso)* mysterious; *(= genial)* great, fantastic*
3 *(Esp*)* *(= inconcebible)* absurd • **es ~** it's mind-blowing*
SM *(Méx)* hallucinogenic drug
alucinantemente ADV amazingly, incredibly
alucinar ▹ CONJUG 1a VT **1** *(= engañar)* to delude, deceive
2 *(Esp*)* *(= fascinar)* • **me alucinó lo que pasó** I was gobsmacked at what happened‡
VI **1** *(= padecer alucinaciones)* to hallucinate
2 *(Esp*)* *(= delirar)* • **¡tú alucinas!** you're seeing things! • **¡este tío alucina!** this guy must be joking!* • **yo alucino con esa canción** I love this song • **yo alucinaba al ver tanta cosa** I was gobsmacked at all the stuff I saw‡
VPR **alucinarse** to delude o.s. • **~se de algo*** to be gobsmacked at sth‡
alucine* SM delusion • **de ~** *(= genial)* fantastic*, great* • **¡qué ~!** *(= ¡es genial!)* this is brill!*
alucinógeno/a ADJ hallucinogenic
SM/F* acid head‡
SM *(Med)* hallucinogen
alucinosis SF INV hallucinosis
alud SM **1** *[de nieve]* avalanche
2 *(= afluencia)* wave
aludido ADJ aforesaid, above-mentioned • **darse por ~** to take the hint • **no darse por ~** to pretend not to hear • **no te des por ~** don't take it personally
aludir ▹ CONJUG 3a VI • **~ a** to allude to, mention
aluego ADV *(LAm)* = **luego**
alujado ADJ *(CAm, Méx)* bright, shining
alujar ▹ CONJUG 1a VT *(CAm, Méx)* to polish, shine
alumbrado/a ADJ* drunk
SM lighting ▸ **alumbrado de emergencia** emergency lighting ▸ **alumbrado de gas** gas lighting ▸ **alumbrado eléctrico** electric lighting ▸ **alumbrado fluorescente** fluorescent lighting ▸ **alumbrado público** street lighting
SM/F *(Rel)* illuminist • **los Alumbrados** the Illuminati
alumbramiento SM **1** *(Elec)* *(= acción)* lighting up; *(= sistema)* lighting, illumination
2 *(Med)* childbirth • **tener un feliz ~** to have a safe delivery
alumbrar ▹ CONJUG 1a VT **1** *(= iluminar)* *[+ cuarto, calle, ciudad]* to light; *[+ estadio, edificio, monumento]* to light up • **una sola bombilla alumbraba el cuarto** the room was lit by a single bulb • **la felicidad alumbró su rostro** his face lit up with happiness • **el sol alumbra la tierra** the sun illuminates the earth
2 *(= enfocar)* *(con linterna, foco)* • **ve delante y alumbra el camino** you go ahead and light the way • **alumbra aquí** shine the light here
3 *(frm)* *[+ asunto]* to shed light on
4 *(frm)* *(= instruir)* to enlighten
5 *[+ agua]* to find
6 *(Rel)* *[+ ciego]* to give sight to
VI **1** *(= dar luz)* to give light, shed light • **esta bombilla alumbra bien** this bulb gives a good light
2 *(frm)* *(= dar a luz)* to give birth
VPR **alumbrarse**† *(= emborracharse)* to get lit up*
alumbre SM alum
aluminio SM aluminium, aluminum *(EEUU)* • **papel de ~** cooking foil, kitchen foil, silver foil
aluminosis SF INV *(Constr)* *degeneration of cement used in construction*
alumnado SM **1** *(Univ)* student body; *(Escol)* roll, pupils
2 *(LAm)* *(= colegio)* college, school
alumno/a SM/F **1** *(Escol)* pupil; *(Univ)* student • **antiguo ~** *(Escol)* old boy, former pupil, alumnus *(EEUU)*; *(Univ)* old student, former student, alumnus *(EEUU)* ▸ **alumno/a externo/a** day pupil ▸ **alumno/a interno/a** boarder
2 *(Jur)* ward, foster child
alunarse ▹ CONJUG 1a VPR *(CAm)* to get saddle-sore *(horse)*
alunizaje SM **1** *(= aterrizaje en la luna)* landing on the moon, moon landing
2* *(= robo)* smash-and-grab raid
alunizar ▹ CONJUG 1f VI to land on the moon
alusión SF *(= mención)* allusion, reference; *(= indirecta)* hint • **hacer ~ a** to allude to, refer to
alusivo ADJ allusive
aluvial ADJ alluvial
aluvión SM **1** *(Geol)* alluvium ▸ **tierras de aluvión** alluvial soil *(sing)*, alluvial soils
2 *(fig)* *(= alud)* flood • **llegan en incontenible ~** they come in an unstoppable flood ▸ **aluvión de improperios** stream *o* torrent of abuse
aluvionado SM alluviation
álveo SM riverbed, streambed
alveolar ADJ alveolar
alvéolo SM, **alveolo** SM *(Anat)* alveolus; *[de panal]* cell; *(fig)* *(= laberinto)* network, honeycomb
alverja SF **1** *(= arveja)* vetch
2 *(LAm)* *(= guisante)* pea
alverjilla SF sweet pea
alza SF **1** *(= subida)* *[de precio, temperatura]* rise • **el ~ de los tipos de interés** the rise in interest rates • **la bolsa ha experimentado una fuerte ~** the stock market has risen sharply • **al ~** *[tendencia]* upward; *[inflación, precio]* rising • **revisar los precios al ~** to put prices up • **la Bolsa se mantuvo ayer al ~** the stock market continued its upward trend yesterday • **en ~** *[acciones, precio]* on the rise • **las acciones están en ~** the shares are rising *o* on the rise • **un artista en ~** a rising

a

star • **un joven escritor en ~** an up-and-coming writer • **jugar al ~** (*Econ*) to speculate on a rising market • **MODISMO:** • **hacer algo por la pura ~** to do sth just for the sake of it
2 (*Mil, Caza*) sights (*pl*) ▸ **alzas fijas** fixed sights ▸ **alzas graduables** adjustable sights
3 (*en zapato*) raised insole
alzacristales (SM INV) ▸ **alzacristales eléctrico** electric windows (*pl*)
alzacuello (SM), **alzacuellos** (SM INV) clerical collar, dog collar
alzada (SF) **1** [*de caballos*] height
2 (*Arquit*) elevation, side view
3 (*Jur*) appeal
alzado/a (ADJ) **1** (= *levantado*) raised • **con el puño ~** with a raised fist; ▹ **votación**
2 (*Econ*) [*cantidad, precio*] fixed; [*quiebra*] fraudulent; [*persona*] fraudulently bankrupt • **por un precio ~** for a lump sum; ▹ **tanto**
3 (*Méx, Ven*) (= *engreído*) big-headed
4 (*Chile, Col, Perú, Ven*) (= *sublevado*) arrogant, cocky*
5 (*LAm*) [*animal*] (= *arisco*) wild • **estar ~** (*Cono Sur*) to be on heat
6 (*And*) (= *borracho*) drunk
(SM/F) (= *persona sublevada*) rebel ▸ **alzado/a en armas** armed insurgent
(SM) **1** (*Arquit*) elevation
2 (*Tip*) gathering
alzamiento (SM) **1** (= *acción*) raising, lifting • **en el ~ del coche** in the raising *o* lifting of the car • **el juez ordenó el ~ del cadáver** the judge ordered the removal of the corpse
2 (= *sublevación*) revolt, uprising • **~ en armas** armed revolt, armed uprising
3 (*Com*) (*de precio*) rise, increase; (*en subasta*) higher bid ▸ **alzamiento de bienes** concealment of assets
alzaprima (SF) **1** (= *palanca*) lever, crowbar; (= *calce*) wedge
2 (*Mús*) bridge
3 (*Cono Sur*) (= *carro pesado*) heavy trolley, flat truck
alzaprimar ▹ CONJUG 1a (VT) (= *levantar*) to lever up, raise with a lever; (*fig*) (= *avivar*) to arouse, stir up
alzar ▹ CONJUG 1f (VT) **1** (= *levantar*) **a** [+ *objeto, persona*] to lift; [+ *objeto muy pesado*] to hoist; [+ *copa*] to raise • **no podía ~la del suelo** he could not lift her off the floor • **los manifestantes ~on sus banderas** the demonstrators raised *o* lifted up their flags • **alcemos nuestras copas por la victoria** let us raise our glasses to victory • **~on el telón unos minutos más tarde** the curtain went up a few minutes later
b [+ *brazo, cabeza, cejas*] to raise • **alzó los brazos al cielo** he raised up his arms to heaven • **alzó la mano para pedir la palabra** he put up *o* raised his hand to ask permission to speak • **~ la mirada** *o* **los ojos** *o* **la vista** to look up • **ni siquiera alzó la vista cuando entramos** she didn't even look up when we came in • **no alzó la mirada del libro ni un momento** he didn't look up *o* avert his gaze (*más frm*) from the book for one moment • **~ la voz** to raise one's voice • **a tu padre no le alces la voz** don't raise your voice at your father • **alza un poco más la voz, que no te oigo** speak up a little, I can't hear you • **alzan su voz contra la injusticia** they speak out against injustice • **siempre se ~án voces llamando a la unidad** there will always be calls for unity; ▹ **vuelo²**
2 (= *erigir*) [+ *monumento*] to raise; [+ *edificio*] to erect
3 [+ *mantel*] to put away
4 [+ *prohibición*] to lift
5 [+ *cosecha*] to gather in, bring in
6 (*Rel*) [+ *cáliz, hostia*] to elevate
7 (*Tip*) to gather
8 (= *recoger*) (*Méx*) (*del suelo*) to pick up; (*LAm*) (*a un bebé*) to pick up
9 (*Méx*) (= *ordenar*) [+ *casa, recámara*] to tidy up • **~ la mesa** to clear the table • **~ los trastes** to clear away the dishes
10 (*Méx*) [+ *dinero*] to save
(VPR) **alzarse 1** (= *ponerse en pie*) to rise • **cuando entró la novia todos se ~on** when the bride entered everyone stood up *o* rose to their feet
2 [*edificio, monte, monumento*] (= *tener una altura determinada*) to rise; (= *estar situado*) to stand • **la cordillera se alza 2.500m sobre el nivel del mar** the mountain range rises 2,500m above sea level • **en la plaza se alzaba la iglesia** the church stood in the square • **el rascacielos se alza por encima del parque** the skyscraper rises *o* towers over the park
3 (= *aumentar*) [*precio, temperatura*] to rise
4 (= *rebelarse*) to rise up, rise, revolt (**contra** against) • **~se en armas** to take up arms, rise up in arms
5 (= *llevarse*) • **~se con** [+ *premio, votos*] to win; [+ *dinero*] to run off with • **el Barcelona se alzó con el título de Liga** Barcelona won *o* took the League title • **se ~on con la mayoría absoluta** they won an absolute majority • **~se con el poder** to take power • **~se con la victoria** to win • **era el favorito indiscutible para ~se con la victoria** he was the undisputed favourite to win • **los primeros comicios en que los socialistas se han alzado con la victoria** the first elections in which the socialists have been victorious *o* have won • **MODISMO:** • **~se con el santo y la limosna** to make a clean sweep
6 (*Com*) to go fraudulently bankrupt
7 (*And*) (= *emborracharse*) to get drunk
8 (*Méx, Ven*) (= *volverse engreído*) to get big-headed
9 (*Chile, Col, Perú, Ven*) (= *rebelarse*) • **le llamé la atención a la muchacha y se me alzó** I told the maid off and she answered me back • **por nada se alza** he gets bolshy at the slightest thing*
10 • **~se de hombros** (*Méx*) to shrug one's shoulders
11 (*LAm*) [*animal*] (= *volverse arisco*) to run wild; (= *entrar en celo*) to be on heat
alzaválvulas (SM INV) tappet
alzo (SM) (*CAm*) theft
A.M. (SF ABR) (= **amplitud modulada**) AM
a.m. (ABR) (= **ante meridiem**) a.m., am
ama (SF) ▸ **ama de brazos** nurse, nursemaid ▸ **ama de cría** wet nurse ▸ **ama de cura** priest's housekeeper ▸ **ama de gobierno, ama de llaves** housekeeper ▸ **ama de leche** wet nurse ▸ **ama seca** nurse, nursemaid; ▹ **amo**
amabilidad (SF) (= *generosidad*) kindness; (= *cortesía*) courtesy • **tuvo la ~ de acompañarme** he was kind enough to come with me, he was good enough to come with me • **tenga la ~ de** (+ *infin*) please be so kind as to (+ *infin*)
amabilísimo (ADJ SUPERL) *de* **amable**
amable (ADJ) kind, nice • **es usted muy ~** you are very kind • **si es tan ~** if you would be so kind • **ser ~ con algn** to be kind to sb, be nice to sb • **¡qué ~ ha sido usted trayéndolo!** how kind of you to bring it! • **¡muy ~!** thanks very much, that's very kind, that's very kind of you • **sea tan ~ (como para)** • **si es tan ~ (como para)** (*LAm*) please be so kind as to
amablemente (ADV) kindly • **muy ~ me ayudó** he very kindly helped me
amachambrarse ▹ CONJUG 1a (VPR) (*Cono Sur*) = **amachinarse**
amacharse ▹ CONJUG 1a (VPR) (*LAm*) [*persona*] to dig one's heels in, refuse to be moved; [*caballo*] to refuse
amachinarse ▹ CONJUG 1a (VPR) (*LAm*) (= *amancebarse*) to set up house together • **~ con algn** to become sb's lover • **estar** *o* **vivir amachinado con** to live with
amacho (ADJ) (*CAm, Cono Sur*) (= *destacado*) outstanding; (= *fuerte*) strong, vigorous
amaderado (ADJ) woody
amado/a (ADJ) dear, beloved
(SM/F) lover, sweetheart
amador(a) (ADJ) loving, fond
(SM/F) lover
amadrigar ▹ CONJUG 1h (VT) to take in, give shelter to
(VPR) **amadrigarse** [*animal*] to go into its hole, burrow; [*persona*] (= *retraerse*) to go into retirement, hide o.s. away
amadrinar ▹ CONJUG 1a (VT) [+ *niño*] to be godmother to; [+ *soldado, regimiento*] to be patron to
amaestrado (ADJ) **1** [*animal*] trained; (*de circo*) performing
2 [*plan*] well-thought out, artful
amaestrador(a) (SM/F) trainer
amaestramiento (SM) training
amaestrar ▹ CONJUG 1a (VT) [+ *persona*] to train, teach; [+ *animal*] to train; [+ *caballo*] to break in
amagar ▹ CONJUG 1h (VT) (= *amenazar*) to threaten, portend (*liter*); (= *dar indicios de*) to show signs of
(VI) (= *estar próximo*) to threaten, be impending; (*Med*) (= *manifestarse*) to show the first signs; (*Esgrima*) to feint • **~ a hacer algo** to threaten to do sth, show signs of doing sth
(VPR) **amagarse 1*** (= *esconderse*) to hide
2 (*Cono Sur*) (= *tomar una postura amenazante*) to adopt a threatening posture
amago (SM) **1** (= *amenaza*) threat; (*fig*) (= *inicio*) beginning
2 (*Med*) (= *señal*) sign, symptom; (= *indicio*) hint • **un ~ de mapa** a rough map • **con un ~ de sonrisa** with the suggestion of a smile, with a faint smile ▸ **amago tormentoso** outbreak of bad weather
3 (*Esgrima*) feint
amainar ▹ CONJUG 1a (VT) [+ *vela*] to take in, shorten; [+ *furia*] to calm
(VI), (VPR) **amainarse** [*viento*] to abate, die down; [*ira*] to subside; [*esfuerzo*] to slacken
amaine (SM) **1** [*de velas*] shortening
2 [*de ira, viento*] abatement, moderation; [*de esfuerzo*] lessening, slackening
amaitinar ▹ CONJUG 1a (VT) to spy on
amaizado (ADJ) (*And*) rich
amalaya (EXCL) (*LAm*) = **ojalá**
amalayar ▹ CONJUG 1a (VT) (*And, CAm, Méx*) to covet, long for • **~ hacer algo** to long to do sth
amalgama (SF) amalgam
amalgamación (SF) amalgamation
amalgamar ▹ CONJUG 1a (VT) (*Quím*) to amalgamate; (*fig*) (= *combinar*) to combine, blend
(VPR) **amalgamarse** to amalgamate
Amalia (SF) Amelia
amamantar ▹ CONJUG 1a (VT) **1** (= *dar el pecho a*) to suckle, nurse
2 (*Caribe*) (= *mimar*) to spoil
amancebado†† (ADJ) • **estar** *o* **vivir ~s** to live together, cohabit
amancebamiento (SM) common-law union, cohabitation
amancebarse†† ▹ CONJUG 1a (VPR) to live together, cohabit
amancillar ▹ CONJUG 1a (VT) (= *manchar*) to stain; (= *deslustrar*) tarnish, dishonour, dishonor (*EEUU*)
amanecer ▹ CONJUG 2d (VI) **1** [*día*] to dawn

• **el día amaneció lloviendo** at daybreak it was raining • **amanece a las siete** it gets light at seven • **nos amaneció en Granada** the next morning found us in Granada, the next morning we woke up in Granada
2 [*persona, ciudad*] to wake up (in the morning) • **amanecimos en Vigo** the next morning found us in Vigo, the next morning we woke up in Vigo • **amaneció acatarrado** he woke up with a cold • **el pueblo amaneció cubierto de nieve** morning saw the village covered in snow, when the next day dawned the village was covered in snow • **amaneció rey** (*liter*) he woke up to find himself king • **amanecieron bailando** (*LAm*) they danced all night, they were still dancing at dawn • **¿cómo amaneció?** (*LAm*) how are you this morning?
(SM) dawn, daybreak • **al ~** at dawn, at daybreak
amanecida (SF) dawn, daybreak
amanerado (ADJ) (= *afectado*) mannered, affected; (*LAm*) (= *demasiado correcto*) excessively polite
amaneramiento (SM) affectation
amanerarse ▷ CONJUG 1a (VPR) to become affected
amanezca (SF) (*Caribe, Méx*) (= *alba*) dawn; (= *desayuno*) breakfast
amanezquera (SF) (*Caribe, Méx*) early morning, daybreak
amanita (SF) amanita
amanojar ▷ CONJUG 1a (VT) to gather by the handful, gather in bunches
amansa (SF) (*Cono Sur*) [*de fieras*] taming; [*de caballos*] breaking-in
amansado (ADJ) tame
amansador(a) (SM/F) (= *domador*) tamer; (*Méx*) [*de caballos*] horse breaker, horse trainer
amansadora (SF) (*Arg*) 1 (= *sala*) waiting room
2* (= *espera*) long wait (*at government office*)
amansamiento (SM) 1 (= *acto*) [*de fieras*] taming; [*de caballos*] breaking-in
2 (= *cualidad*) tameness
amansar ▷ CONJUG 1a (VT) [+ *caballo*] to break in; [+ *fiera*] to tame; [+ *persona*] to tame, subdue; [+ *pasión*] to soothe
(VPR) **amansarse** [*persona*] to calm down; [*pasión*] to moderate
amanse (SM) (*And, Méx*) [*de caballos*] breaking-in; [*de fieras*] taming
amante (ADJ) loving, fond • **nación ~ de la paz** peace-loving nation
(SMF) (= *hombre, mujer*) lover; (= *mujer*) mistress • **tuvo muchas ~s** he had many mistresses
amanuense (SMF) (= *escribiente*) scribe, amanuensis; (= *copista*) copyist; (*Pol*) secretary
amañado (ADJ) 1 (= *falso*) fake, faked
2 (= *diestro*) skilful, skillful (EEUU), clever
3 [*resultado, pelea*] fixed, rigged
amañador(a) (ADJ) (*And, Caribe*) having a pleasant climate
(SM/F)* fixer*
amañamiento (SM) (= *manipulación*) fiddling, trickery; (*Pol*) rigging, gerrymandering
amañanar ▷ CONJUG 1a (VI) [*persona*] to wake up; [*día*] to dawn
amañar ▷ CONJUG 1a (VT) 1 (*pey*) (= *manipular*) [+ *resultado*] to alter, tamper with; [+ *elección*] to rig; [+ *foto*] to fake; [+ *partido, jurado*] to fix; [+ *cuentas*] to cook*; [+ *excusa*] to cook up
2 (= *hacer bien*) to do skilfully, do skillfully (EEUU), do cleverly
(VPR) **amañarse** 1 [*ser diestro*] to be skilful *o* (EEUU) skillful, be expert; (= *adquirir destreza*) to become expert, get the hang of it
2 (= *acostumbrarse*) to become accustomed to • **ya se amaña en Quito** he's beginning to feel at home in Quito
3 (= *llevarse bien con*) • **~se con** to get along with
4 (*Caribe*) (= *mentir*) to tell lies, lie
amaño (SM) 1 (= *destreza*) skill, expertness, cleverness • **tener ~ para** to have an aptitude for
2 (= *ardid*) trick, guile
3 **amaños** (= *herramientas*) tools; (*Cono Sur*) (= *mañas*) underhand means
amapola (SF) poppy • **ponerse como una ~** to turn as red as a beetroot
amar ▷ CONJUG 1a (VT) to love
amaraje (SM) [*de hidroavión*] landing (*on the sea*); [*de nave espacial*] splashdown, touchdown ▸ **amaraje forzoso** ditching
amaranto (SM) amaranth
amarar ▷ CONJUG 1a (VI) [*hidroavión*] to land (*on the sea*); [*nave espacial*] to splash down, touch down; (*forzosamente*) to ditch
amarchantarse ▷ CONJUG 1a (VPR) (*Caribe, Méx*) • **~ en** to deal regularly with
amargado (ADJ) bitter, embittered • **estar ~** to be bitter
amargamente (ADV) bitterly
amargar ▷ CONJUG 1h (VT) [+ *comida*] to make bitter, sour; [+ *persona*] to embitter; [+ *ocasión*] to spoil • **~ la vida a algn** to make sb's life a misery • **a nadie le amarga un dulce** something's better than nothing
(VI) to be bitter, taste bitter
(VPR) **amargarse** 1 [*comida*] to get bitter
2 [*persona*] to become bitter *o* embittered
amargo/a (ADJ) 1 [*sabor*] bitter, tart • **más ~ que tueras** • **más ~ que la hiel** terribly bitter
2 (*fig*) (= *apenado*) bitter, embittered
3 (*Cono Sur*) (= *cobarde*) cowardly; (*Caribe*) (= *poco servicial*) unhelpful, offhand
(SM) 1 [*de sabor*] bitterness, tartness
2 **amargos** (= *licor*) bitters
3 (*Cono Sur*) (= *mate*) bitter tea, *bitter Paraguayan tea*
(SM/F) (*Cono Sur**) [*de mal genio*] grouch*; (= *vago*) shirker, skiver*
amargón (SM) dandelion
amargor (SM), **amargura** (SF) 1 (= *sabor*) bitterness, tartness
2 (*fig*) (= *aflicción*) bitterness; (= *pena*) grief, sorrow
amargoso (ADJ) (*LAm*) = **amargo**
amariconado‡, amaricado‡ (ADJ) effeminate
(SM) nancy boy‡, pansy*
Amarilis (SF) Amaryllis
amarilla (SF) (*Dep*) yellow card; ▷ **amarillo**
amarillear ▷ CONJUG 1a (VI) 1 (= *tirar a amarillo*) to be yellowish; (= *mostrarse amarillo*) to show yellow, look yellow
2 (= *volverse amarillo*) to go *o* turn yellow
3 (= *palidecer*) to pale
amarillecer ▷ CONJUG 2d (VI) to yellow, turn yellow
amarillejo (ADJ) yellowish
amarillento (ADJ) (= *que tira a amarillo*) yellowish; [*tez*] pale, sallow
amarillez (SF) (= *cualidad*) yellow, yellowness; [*de tez*] paleness, sallowness
amarillismo (SM) 1 (*Prensa*) sensationalist journalism
2 (*Pol**) *trade unionism which is in league with the bosses*
amarillista (ADJ) 1 [*prensa*] sensationalist
2 [*sindicato*] pro-management
amarillo (ADJ) [*color*] yellow; [*semáforo*] amber, yellow (EEUU); ▷ **prensa, sindicato**
(SM) 1 (= *color*) yellow ▸ **amarillo canario** canary yellow ▸ **amarillo limón** lemon yellow ▸ **amarillo mostaza** mustard yellow ▸ **amarillo paja** straw colour *o* (EEUU) color
2 (*Caribe*) ripe banana; ▷ **amarilla**
amarilloso (ADJ) (*LAm*) yellowish
amariposado* (ADJ) effeminate
amarra (SF) 1 (*Náut*) mooring line; (*LAm*) (= *cuerda*) rope, line, cord; (*Méx*) (= *rienda*) rein, lead
2 **amarras** (*Náut*) moorings • **cortar** *o* **romper las ~s** to break loose, cut adrift • **echar las ~s** to moor
3 **amarras** (= *protección*) protection (*sing*) • **tener buenas ~s** to have good connections
amarradera (SF) (*And*) (*para barcos*) mooring; (*Méx*) (= *cuerda*) rope, line, tether
amarradero (SM) (= *poste*) post, bollard; (*para barco*) berth, mooring
amarrado (ADJ) (*LAm*) mean, stingy
amarradura (SF) mooring
amarraje (SM) mooring charges (*pl*)
amarrar ▷ CONJUG 1a (VT) 1 (= *asegurar*) (*esp LAm*) to fasten, tie up; [+ *barco*] to moor, tie up; [+ *cuerda*] to lash, belay; (*Naipes*) to stack • **está de ~** he's raving mad • MODISMO: • **tener a algn bien amarrado** to have sb under one's thumb
2* (= *empollar*) to swot*, mug up*
(VI)* to get down to it in earnest
(VPR) **amarrarse*** • **amarrársela** (*And, CAm*) to get tight*
amarre (SM) (= *acto*) fastening, tying; (= *lugar*) berth, mooring
amarrete/a* (*Cono Sur*) (ADJ) mean, stingy*
(SM/F) miser, skinflint, tightwad (EEUU*)
amarro (SM) (*And*) (= *cuerda*) knotted string, knotted rope; (= *nudos*) mass of knots; (= *paquete*) bundle, packet, package (EEUU) ▸ **amarro de cigarrillos** packet of cigarettes
amarrocar ▷ CONJUG 1g (VI) (*Cono Sur*) to scrimp and save
amarronado (ADJ) chestnut, brownish
amarroso (ADJ) (*CAm*) acrid, sharp
amartelado (ADJ) lovesick • **andar** *o* **estar ~ con** to be in love with • **andan muy ~s** they're deeply in love
amartelamiento (SM) lovesickness, infatuation
amartelar ▷ CONJUG 1a (VT) 1 (= *dar celos a*) to make jealous
2 (= *enamorar*) to make fall in love; [+ *corazón*] to win, conquer
(VPR) **amartelarse** to fall in love (**de** with)
amartillar ▷ CONJUG 1a (VT) (= *martillar*) to hammer; [+ *rifle*] to cock
amartizaje (SM) Mars landing, landing on Mars
amasadera (SF) kneading trough
amasado (ADJ) (*Caribe*) 1 [*sustancia*] doughy
2 [*persona*] plump
amasador(a) (SM/F) kneader, baker
amasadora (SF) kneading machine
amasadura (SF) 1 (= *acto*) kneading
2 (= *hornada*) batch
amasamiento (SM) (*Culin*) kneading; (*Med*) massage
amasandería (SF) (*And, Cono Sur*) ≈ bakery
amasandero/a (SM/F) (*And, Cono Sur*) ≈ baker
amasar ▷ CONJUG 1a (VT) 1 (*Culin*) [+ *masa*] to knead; [+ *harina, yeso*] to mix, prepare
2 [+ *dinero*] to amass
3 (*Med*) to massage
4* (= *tramar*) to cook up*, concoct
amasiato (SM) (*Méx, Perú*) cohabitation, common-law marriage • **su ~ duró mucho tiempo** they lived together for a long time
amasigado (ADJ) (*And*) dark, swarthy
amasijar‡ ▷ CONJUG 1a (VT) (*Cono Sur*) to do in*

a

amasijo (SM) **1** (*Culin*) (= *acción*) kneading; (*Téc*) mixing
2 (= *material*) mixture; (= *mezcla*) hotchpotch, hodgepodge (*EEUU*), medley
3 (= *plan*) plot, scheme
4 (*Caribe*) (= *pan*) wheat bread
amasio/a (SM/F) (*CAm, Méx*) (= *amante*) lover; (= *mujer*) mistress
amate (SM) (*LAm*) fig tree
amateur (ADJ), (SMF) amateur
amateurismo (SM) amateurism
amatista (SF) amethyst
amatorio (ADJ) love (*antes de s*) • **poesía amatoria** love poetry
amauta (SM) (*And*) Inca elder
amayorado (ADJ) (*And*) precocious, forward
amazacotado (ADJ) (= *pesado*) heavy, awkward; (= *informe*) shapeless, formless; (*Literat*) ponderous, stodgy • **~ de detalles** crammed with details
amazona (SF) **1** (*Literat*) amazon; (*Dep*) horsewoman, rider; (= *mujer varonil*) (*pey*) mannish woman
2 (= *traje*) riding suit
Amazonas (SM) Amazon • **el río ~** the Amazon
Amazonia (SF) Amazonia
amazónico (ADJ) Amazon (*antes de s*), Amazonian
ambages (SMPL) • **hablar sin ~** to come straight to the point
ambagioso (ADJ) involved, circuitous, roundabout
ámbar (SM) amber ▸ **ámbar gris** ambergris
ambareado (ADJ) (*And**) chestnut, auburn
ambarino (ADJ) amber, yellow (*EEUU*)
Amberes (SM) Antwerp
ambición (SF) ambition
ambicionar ▹ CONJUG 1a (VT) (= *desear*) to aspire to, seek; (= *codiciar*) to lust after, covet • **~ ser algo** to have an ambition to be sth
ambiciosamente (ADV) ambitiously
ambicioso/a (ADJ) **1** (= *que tiene ambición*) ambitious
2 (*pey*) (= *egoísta*) proud, self-seeking
(SM/F) (*gen*) ambitious person; (= *oportunista*) careerist • **~ de figurar** social climber
ambidextro (ADJ), **ambidiestro** (ADJ) ambidextrous
ambientación (SF) **1** (= *estilo*) setting • **una novela de ~ oriental** a novel set in the Far East, a novel with an oriental setting • **la ~ estaba muy bien conseguida** they captured the atmosphere very well ▸ **ambientación musical** incidental music
2 (*Radio*) sound effects
3 (= *adaptación*) • **le cuesta bastante la ~ a los sitios nuevos** he finds it hard to adjust to new places
ambientado (ADJ) **1** [*película, obra*] • **un relato ~ en los años veinte** a story set in the twenties • **la película está muy bien ambientada** the film has a very good atmosphere
2 [*persona*] • **estar ~** to be settled in, be at home
3 (*Méx*) (= *climatizado*) air-conditioned
ambientador(a) (SM/F) (*Cine, TV*) dresser
(SM) air freshener
ambiental (ADJ) **1** (= *del aire*) • **hay un 70% de humedad ~** there is 70% humidity • **la luz ~ era insuficiente** the lighting was not strong enough; ▹ **música**
2 (= *medioambiental*) environmental • **contaminación ~** environmental pollution • **su entorno ~ fue muy negativo** he was in a very negative environment
ambientalismo (SM) environmentalism
ambientalista (ADJ), (SMF) environmentalist
ambientalmente (ADV) environmentally • **una zona ~ protegida** an environmentally protected area
ambientar ▹ CONJUG 1a (VT) **1** (= *dar ambiente a*) • **los fans ambientaban el partido** the fans gave the match some atmosphere • **~on la entrada del hotel con decorados exóticos** they livened up the hotel foyer with exotic decoration
2 [+ *película, obra*] to set
3 (= *orientar*) to orientate, direct
(VPR) **ambientarse 1** (= *adaptarse*) to settle in, adjust • **donde quiera que va, se ambienta rápidamente** wherever he goes, he manages to settle in *o* adjust quickly • **pondré un poco de música para que nos vayamos ambientando** I'll put some music on to get some atmosphere going
2 (= *orientarse*) to orientate o.s., get one's bearings
ambiente (ADJ INV) • **medio ~** environment • **ruido ~** environmental noise • **trabajamos con 120 decibelios de ruido ~** we work at a noise level of 120 decibels • **temperatura ~** room temperature • **"sírvase a temperatura ~"** "serve at room temperature"
(SM) **1** (= *aire*) • **el ~ de la sala estaba muy cargado de humo** there was a very smoky atmosphere in the room, the air was really smoky in the room • **habrá ~ soleado en la costa** it will be sunny on the coast, there will be sunny weather on the coast ▸ **ambiente artificial** air conditioning
2 (*creado por el entorno, la decoración*) atmosphere • **en medio de un ~ festivo** amid a festive atmosphere • **la madera da un ~ cálido al despacho** wood gives a warm feeling to *o* creates a warm atmosphere in the study • **no había un buen ~ en la oficina** there wasn't a good atmosphere in the office • **se respiraba un ~ de tensión** there was a feeling of tension • **cambiar de ~** to have a change of scene • **crónica de ~** background report • **micrófono de ~** field microphone; ▹ **música**
3 (= *animación*) • **¡qué ambientazo había en la plaza de toros!** what a great atmosphere there was in the bullring! • **el espléndido ~ cultural de París** the wonderful cultural life *o* ambience of Paris
4 (= *entorno*) environment • **con su familia se siente en su ~** with her family, she really feels in her element • **~ familiar** home environment • **~ laboral** work environment
5 ambientes (= *grupo social*) circles • **en ~s universitarios** in the university world, in university circles
6‡ (*tb* **ambiente homosexual**) • **el ~** the gay scene, the scene‡ • **de ~** [*bar, discoteca*] gay (*antes de s*)
7 (*Cono Sur*) (= *habitación*) room
ambigú (SM) buffet
ambiguamente (ADV) ambiguously
ambigüedad (SF) ambiguity
ambiguo (ADJ) **1** (= *impreciso*) ambiguous; (= *incierto*) doubtful, uncertain; (= *equívoco*) noncommittal, equivocal
2* (= *bisexual*) bisexual
3 (*Ling*) common
ambilado (ADJ) (*Caribe*) • **estar** *o* **quedar ~** (= *boquiabierto*) to be left open-mouthed; (= *embobado*) to be distracted
ámbito (SM) **1** (= *campo*) field; (= *límite*) boundary, limit • **dentro del ~ de** within the limits of, in the context of • **en el ~ nacional** on a nationwide basis, on a nationwide scale • **en todo el ~ nacional** over the whole nation, throughout the country • **en el ~ nacional y extranjero** at home and abroad
2 (*fig*) (= *esfera*) scope, range • **buscar mayor ~** to look for greater scope ▸ **ámbito de acción** sphere of activity
ambivalencia (SF) ambivalence
ambivalente (ADJ) ambivalent
ambladura (SF) • **a paso de ~** at an amble
amblar ▹ CONJUG 1a (VI) to amble, walk in a leisurely manner
ambo (SM) (*Arg*) two-piece suit
ambos (ADJ), (PRON) both • **vinieron ~** they both came • **~ tenéis los ojos azules** you've both got blue eyes • **~ a dos** both, both (of them) together
ambrosía (SF) ambrosia
Ambrosio (SM) Ambrose
ambucia (SF) (*Cono Sur*) (= *codicia*) greed, greediness; (= *hambre*) voracious hunger
ambuciento (ADJ) (*Cono Sur*) (= *codicioso*) greedy; (= *hambriento*) voracious
ambulancia (SF) (= *vehículo*) ambulance; (*Mil*) field hospital ▸ **ambulancia de correos** (*Esp*) post-office coach
ambulanciero/a (SM/F) ambulance man/woman
ambulante (ADJ) (= *que anda*) walking; [*circo, vendedor*] travelling, traveling (*EEUU*); [*biblioteca*] mobile; [*músico*] itinerant; [*actor*] strolling
(SMF) (= *vendedor callejero*) street seller, street vendor
ambulatoriamente (ADV) • **tratar un paciente ~** to treat sb as an out-patient
ambulatorio (SM) (= *clínica*) national health clinic; (= *sección*) out-patients department
(ADJ) • **tratar a algn en régimen ~** to treat sb as an out-patient
ameba (SF) amoeba, ameba (*EEUU*)
amedrentador (ADJ) frightening, menacing
amedrentar ▹ CONJUG 1a (VT) (= *asustar*) to scare, frighten; (= *intimidar*) to intimidate
(VPR) **amedrentarse** to be scared, be intimidated
amejoramiento (SM) (*LAm*) = **mejoramiento**
amejorar ▹ CONJUG 1a (VT) (*LAm*) = **mejorar**
amelcocharse ▹ CONJUG 1a (VPR) **1** (*Caribe*) to fall in love
2 (*Méx*) [*azúcar*] to harden, set
3 (= *ser coqueta*) to be coy, be prim
amelonado (ADJ) **1** (= *forma*) melon-shaped
2 • **estar ~*** (= *enamorado*) to be lovesick
amén (SM INV) **1** (*Rel*) amen • MODISMOS: • **decir ~ a todo** to agree to everything • **en un decir ~** in a trice
2 • **~ de** (= *salvo*) except for, aside from (*EEUU*); (= *además de*) in addition to, besides
3 • **~ de que** (= *a pesar de*) in spite of the fact that
(EXCL) amen!
-amen ▹ **Aspects of Word Formation in Spanish 2**
amenaza (SF) threat ▸ **amenaza amarilla** yellow peril ▸ **amenaza de bomba** bomb scare ▸ **amenaza de muerte** death threat
amenazador (ADJ), **amenazante** (ADJ) threatening, menacing
amenazar ▹ CONJUG 1f (VT) to threaten • **~ a algn de muerte** to threaten to kill sb • **me amenazó con despedirme** he threatened to fire me • **una especie amenazada de extinción** a species threatened with extinction • **la tarde amenazaba lluvia** it looked like rain in the evening • **~ violencia** to threaten violence
(VI) to threaten, impend • **~ con hacer algo** to threaten to do sth
amenguar ▹ CONJUG 1i (VT) **1** (= *disminuir*) to lessen, diminish
2 (= *despreciar*) to belittle
3 (= *deshonrar*) to dishonour, dishonor (*EEUU*)

amenidad SF pleasantness, agreeableness

amenización SF (= *mejoramiento*) improvement; [*de conversación*] enlivening; [*de estilo*] brightening up; [*de una reunión*] entertainment

amenizar ▹ CONJUG 1f VT (= *hacer agradable*) to make pleasant; [+ *conversación*] to enliven, liven up; [+ *estilo*] to brighten up; [+ *reunión*] to provide entertainment for, entertain

ameno ADJ (= *agradable*) pleasant, agreeable, nice; [*estilo*] engaging; [*libro*] enjoyable, readable; [*lectura*] light • **prefiero una lectura más amena** I prefer lighter reading • **es un sitio ~** it's a nice spot • **la vida aquí es más amena** life is more pleasant here

amento SM catkin

América SF (= *continente, Norteamérica*) America; (*LAm*) (= *Hispanoamérica*) South America, Spanish America, Latin America • **hacerse la ~** (*Cono Sur*) to make a fortune ▸ **América Central** Central America ▸ **América del Norte** North America ▸ **América del Sur** South America ▸ **América Latina** Latin America

americana SF coat, jacket ▸ **americana de sport** sports jacket; ▹ **americano**

americanada SF typically American thing, typically American thing to do

americanismo SM **1** (*Ling*) Americanism; (*LAm*) (= *imperialismo*) Yankee imperialism **2** (*Caribe, Méx*) (= *apego a lo americano*) *liking for North American ways etc*

americanista SMF **1** (= *estudioso*) Americanist, specialist in indigenous American culture; (= *literato*) specialist in American literature **2** (*CAm, Méx*) (= *aficionado*) *person with a liking for North American ways etc*

americanización SF Americanization

americanizado ADJ Americanized

americanizar ▹ CONJUG 1f VT to Americanize
VPR **americanizarse** to become Americanized

americano/a ADJ, SM/F (= *del continente, de Norteamérica*) American; (= *de Hispanoamérica*) Latin American, South American, Spanish American; ▹ **americana**

americio SM (*Quím*) americium

amerindio/a ADJ, SM/F American Indian, Amerindian

ameritado ADJ (*LAm*) worthy

ameritar ▹ CONJUG 1a VT (*LAm*) to deserve

amerizaje SM [*de hidroavión*] landing (*on the sea*); [*de nave espacial*] splashdown, touchdown

amerizar ▹ CONJUG 1f VI [*hidroavión*] to land (*on the sea*); [*nave espacial*] to splash down, touch down

amestizado ADJ *like a half breed*

ametrallador(a) SM/F machine gunner

ametralladora SF machine gun

ametrallamiento SM machine-gunning, machine-gun attack

ametrallar ▹ CONJUG 1a VT to machine-gun

amianto SM asbestos

amiba SF, **amibo** SM amoeba, ameba (EEUU)

amigable ADJ (= *amistoso*) friendly, sociable; (*Jur*) • **~ componedor** arbitrator

amigablemente ADV amicably

amigacho* SM (*pey*) mate, buddy (*EEUU*), bachelor friend • **ha salido con los ~s** he's out with the boys • **esos ~s tuyos** those cronies of yours

amigarse ▹ CONJUG 1h VPR (= *hacerse amigos*) to get friendly, become friends; [*amantes*] to set up house together

amigazo* SM (*Cono Sur*) pal*, buddy (EEUU), close friend

amígdala SF tonsil

amigdalitis SF INV tonsillitis

amigdalotomía SF tonsillectomy

amigo/a SM/F **1** friend • **Manuel es un ~ mío** Manuel is a friend of mine • **es una amiga de Sofía** she is a friend of Sofía's *o* of Sofía • **es un ~ de la infancia** he's a childhood friend • **es una amiga del colegio** she's a school friend • **el perro es el mejor ~ del hombre** a dog is a man's best friend • **hacer ~s** to make friends ▸ **amigo/a de confianza** very close friend, intimate friend ▸ **amigo/a del alma** soulmate ▸ **amigo/a de lo ajeno** (*hum*) thief ▸ **amigo/a en la prosperidad** fair-weather friend ▸ **amigo/a íntimo/a** very close friend, intimate friend ▸ **amigo/a por correspondencia** penfriend **2** (= *novio*) boyfriend/girlfriend **3** (*en oración directa*) • **pero, ~, ya no se puede hacer nada** there's nothing more we can do, my friend • **¡amigo! en ese tema ya no entro** hold on, I'm not getting mixed up in that!
ADJ **1** • **son muy ~s** they are good *o* close friends • **Gonzalo es muy ~ de Pepe** Gonzalo is a good *o* close friend of Pepe's *o* of Pepe • **hacerse ~s** to become friends • **al final me hice muy ~ de Antonio** in the end Antonio and I became good friends • **se perdonaron y quedaron tan ~s** they made it up and everything was fine • **lo pagamos a medias y todos tan ~s** we'll go halves on it and that'll be fine **2** • **ser ~ de algo** to be fond of sth • **soy ~ del buen vino** I'm fond of good wine • **no soy muy ~ de las multitudes** I'm not very fond of *o* keen on crowds • **soy ~ de hablar con franqueza** I like straight talking **3** [*país, fuego*] friendly

amigote SM mate*, sidekick*, buddy (*EEUU**); (*pey*) sidekick*, crony

amigovio/a* SM/F sex buddy*, friend with benefits*

amiguero ADJ (*LAm*) friendly

amiguete* SM (= *amigo*) mate*, buddy* (*EEUU*); (*con influencias*) influential friend, friend in the right place

amiguismo SM old-boy network, jobs for the boys

amiguito/a SM/F (= *novio*) boyfriend/ girlfriend; (= *amante*) lover

amiláceo ADJ starchy

amilanar ▹ CONJUG 1a VT to scare, intimidate
VPR **amilanarse** to get scared, be intimidated (**ante, por** at)

aminoácido SM amino acid

aminorar ▹ CONJUG 1a VT [+ *precio*] to cut, reduce; [+ *velocidad*] to reduce

amistad SF **1** (= *cariño*) friendship; (= *relación amistosa*) friendly relationship, friendly connection • **hacer** *o* **trabar ~ con** to strike up a friendship with, become friends with • **llevar ~ con** to be on friendly terms with • **hacer las ~es** to make it up • **romper las ~es** to fall out **2 amistades** (= *amigos*) friends; (= *relaciones*) acquaintances • **invitar a las ~es** to invite one's friends

amistar ▹ CONJUG 1a VT **1** (= *hacer amigos*) to bring together, make friends of; (= *reconciliar*) to bring about a reconciliation between **2** (*Méx*) (= *hacerse amigo de*) to befriend
VPR **amistarse** (= *hacerse amigos*) to become friends (**con** with), establish a friendship (**con** with); (= *reconciliarse*) to make it up

amistosamente ADV amicably, in a friendly way • **la carta termina ~** the letter ends in a friendly tone • **ayudémonos ~** let's help each other as friends

amistoso ADJ (= *amigable*) friendly, amicable; (*Dep*) friendly; (*Inform*) user-friendly
SM (*Dep*) friendly, friendly game

amnesia SF amnesia ▸ **amnesia temporal** blackout

amnésico/a ADJ, SM/F amnesiac, amnesic • **es ~** he suffers from memory loss *o* amnesia

amniocentesis SF INV amniocentesis

amniótico ADJ amniotic • **líquido ~** amniotic fluid

amnistía SF amnesty ▸ **Amnistía Internacional** Amnesty International

amnistiado/a ADJ amnestied
SM/F *person granted an amnesty*

amnistiar ▹ CONJUG 1c VT to amnesty, grant an amnesty to

amo/a SM/F **1** (= *de casa*) master/mistress • **¿está el amo?** is the master in? ▸ **amo/a de casa** house-husband/housewife **2** (= *propietario*) owner
SM (= *jefe*) boss • **ser el amo** to be the boss • **ese corredor es el amo de la pista** that runner rules the track; ▹ **ama**

amoblado (*LAm*) ADJ furnished
SM furniture

amoblamiento SM (*LAm*) furnishing

amoblar ▹ CONJUG 1l VT (*LAm*) to furnish

amodorrado ADJ sleepy

amodorramiento SM sleepiness, drowsiness

amodorrarse ▹ CONJUG 1a VPR **1** (= *adormecerse*) to get sleepy, get drowsy **2** (= *dormirse*) to go to sleep

amohinar ▹ CONJUG 1a VT to vex, annoy
VPR **amohinarse** to sulk

amohosado ADJ (*Cono Sur*) rusty

amojonar ▹ CONJUG 1a VT to mark out, mark the boundary of

amojosado ADJ (*Bol*) rusty

amoladera SF **1** (= *piedra*) whetstone, grindstone **2** (*LAm**) (= *tipo pesado*) nuisance, pain*

amolado ADJ **1** (*Cono Sur*) (= *fastidiado*) bothered, irritated **2** (*And, Méx*) (= *ofendido*) offended; (= *que molesta*) irritating, annoying **3** (*And*) (= *dañado*) damaged, ruined

amolador ADJ annoying
SM knife grinder

amoladura SF grinding, sharpening

amolar ▹ CONJUG 1l VT **1** (*Téc*) to grind, sharpen **2** (= *fastidiar*) to pester, annoy; (= *perseguir*) to harass, pester **3** (= *estropear*) to damage, ruin **4** (*Méx***) (= *arruinar*) to screw up**, fuck up** • **¡lo amolaste!** you screwed it up!**, you fucked it up!**
VPR **amolarse 1** (*esp LAm*) (= *enojarse*) to get cross, take offence *o* (*EEUU*) offense; (= *estropearse*) to be ruined **2**** = **joder 3** (= *enflaquecer*) to get thinner

amoldable ADJ adaptable

amoldar ▹ CONJUG 1a VT **1** (= *formar*) to mould, mold (EEUU) (**a, según** on) **2** (= *ajustar*) to adapt (**a** to), adjust (**a** to)
VPR **amoldarse** to adapt o.s., adjust o.s. (**a** to)

amonal SM ammonal

amonarse* ▹ CONJUG 1a VPR to get tight*

amondongado ADJ fat, flabby

amonedación SF coining, minting

amonedar ▹ CONJUG 1a VT to coin, mint

amonestación SF **1** (= *reprimenda*) reprimand; (= *advertencia*) warning; (= *consejo*) piece of advice; (*Ftbl*) caution, yellow card; (*Jur*) caution **2 amonestaciones** (*Rel*) marriage banns

• **correr las amonestaciones** to publish the banns

amonestador ADJ warning, cautionary

amonestar ▹ CONJUG 1a VT **1** (= *reprender*) to reprimand; (= *advertir*) to warn; (= *avisar*) to advise; (*Dep*) to caution, book; (*Jur*) to caution
2 (*Rel*) to publish the banns of

amoniacal ADJ [*nitrógeno, cloruro*] ammoniacal; [*compuesto, disolución*] ammonia (*antes de s*)

amoniaco, **amoníaco** ADJ [*nitrógeno, cloruro*] ammoniacal; [*compuesto, disolución*] ammonia (*antes de s*)
SM ammonia ▸ **amoniaco líquido** liquid ammonia

amononar ▹ CONJUG 1a VT (*Cono Sur*) to improve the appearance of, smarten up; (*pey*) to prettify

amontillado SM amontillado, amontillado wine

amontonadamente ADV in heaps

amontonado ADJ heaped, heaped up, piled up • **viven ~s** they live on top of each other

amontonamiento SM **1** (= *acción*) [*de mercancías, cajas*] piling up, heaping; [*de dinero*] hoarding; [*de datos*] accumulation; [*de gente*] crowding, overcrowding; [*de coches*] traffic jam
2 (= *montón*) [*de cajas*] heap, pile; [*de dinero*] stash; [*de gente*] crowd

amontonar ▹ CONJUG 1a VT **1** (= *apilar*) to pile (up), heap (up); [+ *datos*] to gather, collect; [+ *dinero*] to hoard; [+ *nieve, nubes*] to bank up • **viene amontonando fichas** he's been collecting data in large quantities • **~ alabanzas sobre algn** to heap praises on sb
2 (*And*) (= *insultar*) to insult
VPR **amontonarse 1** (= *apilarse*) to pile up; [*nubes*] to gather; [*hojas, nieve*] to drift; [*datos*] to accumulate; [*desastres*] to come one on top of another; [*gente*] to crowd, crowd together • **viven amontonados*** they're shacked up together* • **la gente se amontonó en la salida** people crowded into the exit, people jammed the exit • **se ~on los coches** the cars got into a jam
2* (= *enfadarse*) to fly off the handle*
3 (*And*) [*terreno*] to revert to scrub

amor SM **1** (= *pasión*) love (a for) • **por el ~ al arte** (*hum*) just for the fun of it • **hacer algo por ~ al arte** to do sth for nothing, do sth for free • **por el ~ de** for the love of • **por (el) ~ de Dios** for God's sake • **hacer algo con ~** to do sth lovingly, do sth with love • **lo hizo por ~** he did it for love • **casarse por ~** to marry for love • **matrimonio sin ~** loveless marriage • **una relación de ~-odio** a love-hate relationship • **hacer el ~** to make love • **hacer el ~ a** (= *cortejar*) to court; (= *hacer sexo*) to make love to ▸ **amor a primera vista** love at first sight ▸ **amor cortés** courtly love ▸ **amor de madre** mother love ▸ **amor fracasado** disappointment in love ▸ **amor interesado** cupboard love ▸ **amor libre** free love ▸ **amor maternal** mother love ▸ **amor platónico** platonic love ▸ **amor propio** amour propre, self-respect • **es cuestión de ~ propio** it's a matter of pride • **picarle a algn en el ~ propio** to wound sb's pride
2 (= *persona*) love, lover • **mi ~ • ~ mío** my love, my darling • **¡eres un ~!** you're a love!, you are sweet! • **primer ~** first love • **buscar un nuevo ~** to look for a new love • **tiene un ~ en la ciudad** he's carrying on an affair in town
3 • MODISMOS: • **ir al ~ del agua** to go with the current • **estar al ~ de la lumbre** to be close to the fire • **~ con el ~ se paga** one good turn deserves another; (*iró*) an eye for an eye
4 amores (= *amoríos*) love affair (*sing*), romance (*sing*) • **tener mal de ~es** to be lovesick • **¡de mil ~es! • ¡con mil ~es!** I'd love to!, gladly! • **los mil ~es de don Juan** Don Juan's countless affairs • **requebrar a algn de ~es** to court sb

amoral ADJ amoral

amoralidad SF amorality

amoratado ADJ (= *morado*) purple, purplish; (*de frío*) blue; (= *golpeado*) black and blue, bruised • **ojo ~** black eye, shiner*

amoratarse ▹ CONJUG 1a VPR (= *ponerse morado*) to turn purple, go purple; (*de frío*) to turn blue; (*por golpes*) to turn black and blue

amorcillo SM **1** (= *amorío*) flirtation, light-hearted affair
2 (= *Cupido*) Cupid

amordazar ▹ CONJUG 1f VT [+ *persona*] to gag; [+ *perro*] to muzzle; (*fig*) (= *hacer callar*) to gag, silence

amorfo ADJ amorphous, shapeless

amorío SM (*tb* **amoríos**) love affair, romance

amorochado ADJ (*LAm*) = **morocho**

amorosamente ADV lovingly, affectionately

amoroso ADJ **1** (= *cariñoso*) [*persona*] loving, affectionate; [*mirada*] amorous; [*carta*] love (*antes de s*) • **poesía amorosa** love poetry • **en tono ~** in an affectionate tone • **empezar a sentirse ~** to begin to feel amorous
2 (*fig*) [*tierra*] workable; [*metal*] malleable; [*tiempo*] mild
3 (*Cono Sur*) (= *dulce*) sweet, pretty, cute

amorrar ▹ CONJUG 1a VI (= *inclinar la cabeza*) to hang one's head; (*fig*) (= *enfurruñarse*) to be sullen, sulk; (*Náut*) to pitch, dip the bows under

amortajar ▹ CONJUG 1a VT to shroud

amortecer ▹ CONJUG 2d VT [+ *ruido*] to deaden, muffle; [+ *luz*] to dim; [+ *fuego*] to damp down; [+ *pasión*] to curb, control
VI (*Med*) to faint, swoon; [*ruido*] to become muffled, die away

amortecido ADJ • **caer ~** to fall in a swoon, faint away

amortecimiento SM **1** [*de ruido*] deadening, muffling; [*de luz*] dimming
2 [*de pasión*] controlling
3 (*Med*) fainting

amortiguación SF = **amortiguamiento**

amortiguador ADJ (*de ruido*) deadening, muffling; (*de luz*) softening
SM (*Mec, Aut*) shock absorber; (*Ferro*) buffer; (*Elec*) damper ▸ **amortiguador de luz** dimmer (switch) ▸ **amortiguador de ruido** silencer, muffler (*EEUU*)

amortiguamiento SM **1** [*de ruido*] deadening, muffling; [*de choque, golpe*] cushioning, absorption; [*de color*] toning down; [*de luz*] dimming, softening
2 (*Elec*) damping

amortiguar ▹ CONJUG 1i VT **1** [+ *ruido*] to deaden, muffle; [+ *choque*] to cushion, absorb; [+ *color*] to tone down; [+ *luz*] to dim, soften; [+ *fuego*] to damp down; (*Elec*) to damp
2 (*fig*) (= *mitigar*) to alleviate
VPR **amortiguarse 1** [*luz*] to grow dim; [*ruido*] to die down
2 (*Cono Sur*) [*planta*] to wither
3 (*Cono Sur*) (= *deprimirse*) to get depressed

amortizable ADJ redeemable

amortización SF **1** (*Econ*) [*de bono*] redemption; [*de préstamo*] repayment; [*de bienes*] depreciation; [*de puesto*] abolition
2 (*Jur*) amortization

amortizar ▹ CONJUG 1f VT **1** (*Econ*) [+ *capital*] to write off; [+ *bono*] to redeem; [+ *préstamo*] to pay off, repay; [+ *puesto*] to abolish • **~ algo por desvalorización** to write sth off for depreciation
2 (*Jur*) to amortize

amos‡ EXCL ▹ **ir**

amoscarse* ▹ CONJUG 1g VPR **1** (= *enojarse*) to get cross, be peeved*
2 (*Caribe, Méx*) (= *aturdirse*) to get confused; (= *avergonzarse*) to get embarrassed

amostazar* ▹ CONJUG 1f VT to make cross, peeve*
VPR **amostazarse 1** (= *enojarse*) to get cross, get peeved*
2 (*LAm*) (= *avergonzarse*) to be embarrassed, get embarrassed

amotinado/a ADJ (= *rebelde*) riotous; (*Mil, Náut*) mutinous
SM/F (*civil*) rioter; (*Pol*) rebel; (*Mil, Náut*) rebel, mutineer

amotinador(a) ADJ, SM/F = **amotinado**

amotinamiento SM (*civil*) riot; (*Pol*) rising, insurrection; (*Mil, Náut*) mutiny

amotinar ▹ CONJUG 1a VT to incite to riot/mutiny *etc*
VPR **amotinarse** (= *causar disturbios*) to riot; (*Pol*) to rise up; (*Mil, Náut*) to mutiny

amover ▹ CONJUG 2h VT to dismiss, remove, remove from office

amovible ADJ [*pieza*] removable, detachable; [*empleo*] temporary

amparador(a) ADJ protecting, protective
SM/F (= *protector*) protector/protectress; [*de criminal*] harbourer, harborer (*EEUU*)

amparar ▹ CONJUG 1a VT **1** (= *proteger*) to protect (**de** from), shelter; (= *ayudar*) to help • **~ a los pobres** to help the poor • **lo ampara el ministro** the minister protects him • **la ley nos ampara** the law is there to protect us
2 (*Jur*) [+ *criminal*] to harbour, harbor (*EEUU*)
3 (*Caribe*) (= *pedir prestado*) to borrow
VPR **ampararse 1** (= *buscar protección*) to seek protection, seek help • **~se con** *o* **de** *o* **en** to seek the protection of
2 (*de la lluvia*) to shelter

amparo SM **1** (= *protección*) • **buscó ~ en la familia** he sought refuge in his family • **mis nietos son mi único ~** my grandchildren are all I have • **al ~ de la ley** under the protection of the law • **actuaron al ~ de la oscuridad** they acted under cover of darkness • **viven al ~ de las donaciones de caridad** they live on *o* off charitable donations
2 (= *refugio*) shelter, refuge • **la cabaña da ~ contra la nieve** the hut provides shelter from the snow, the hut gives refuge from the snow • **dio ~ a los terroristas** she sheltered the terrorists
3 (*Jur*) • **recurso de ~** *appeal on the grounds of unconstitutionality*

ampáyar SM, **ampáyer** SM (*LAm*) referee, umpire

ampe EXCL (*And*) please!

amperímetro SM ammeter

amperio SM ampère, amp

ampliable ADJ (= *extensible*) extendable, which can be extended (a to); (*Inform*) expandable (a to)

ampliación SF (= *acción*) extension; (*Fot*) enlargement; (= *expansión*) expansion ▸ **ampliación de capital, ampliación de capitales** increase of capital

ampliado SM (*LAm*) (*Pol*) general meeting

ampliadora SF enlarger

ampliamente ADV (= *cumplidamente*) amply; (= *extensamente*) extensively • **satisfará ~ la demanda** it will more than meet the demand

ampliar ▹ CONJUG 1c VT **1** (*en tamaño*) to extend • **queremos ~ el salón** we want to extend the living room, we want to make the living room bigger • **lee mucho para ~ su**

vocabulario he reads a lot in order to extend *o* expand his vocabulary • **se fue a Inglaterra a ~ sus estudios** he went to England to broaden his studies
2 (*en número*) to increase • **van a ~ las plazas de profesor** they are going to increase the number of teaching posts • **no ~án la plantilla** they are not going to increase *o* expand the headcount *o* the payroll
3 [+ *prórroga, período*] to extend • **han ampliado el plazo de matrícula** they have put back the closing date for enrolment, they have extended the period for enrolment
4 (*Fot*) to enlarge
5 (*Com*) [+ *empresa, compañía*] to expand, grow; [+ *capital*] to increase • **deseamos ~ el campo de acción de la empresa** we want to extend *o* expand *o* broaden the company's area of business
6 [+ *sonido*] to amplify
7 [+ *idea, explicación*] to elaborate on
8 [+ *poderes*] to extend, widen
VPR **ampliarse** to expand • **~se a** to extend to

amplificación SF (*Téc*) amplification; (*LAm*) (*Fot*) enlargement

amplificador SM amplifier

amplificar ▸ CONJUG 1g VT (*Téc*) to amplify; (*LAm*) (*Fot*) to enlarge

amplio ADJ **1** (= *espacioso*) [*habitación, interior*] spacious; [*avenida, calle*] wide • **el terremoto afectó a una amplia zona del sur** the earthquake affected a wide area in the south • **compró una amplia extensión de terreno** he bought a vast tract *o* stretch of land
2 [*ropa*] loose(-fitting), roomy*; [*falda*] full
3 [*margen*] wide • **un ~ margen a ambos lados** a wide margin on each side • **los socialistas ganaron las elecciones por amplia mayoría** the socialists won the election with a large majority
4 [*conocimiento, vocabulario, poder, gama*] wide, extensive • **un ~ surtido de productos** a wide *o* extensive range of products
5 [*sentido*] broad • **en el sentido ~ de la expresión** in the broad sense of the term
6 [*repercusión*] far-reaching • **la noticia tuvo amplia difusión *o* ~ eco en la prensa** the news was widely *o* extensively reported • **su novela tuvo amplia resonancia entre los intelectuales** his novel had great influence among the intellectuals
7 [*informe*] full, detailed

amplitud SF **1** (= *espaciosidad*) [*de sala, habitación, interior*] spaciousness; [*de avenida, calle*] wideness; [*de terreno*] expanse, extent • **retiramos el sofá para dar ~ al cuarto** we moved the sofa to make the room bigger
2 [*de ropa*] looseness; [*de falda*] fullness
3 [*de conocimientos, vocabulario, poder, variedad*] extent ▸ **amplitud de criterio, amplitud de horizontes, amplitud de miras** broadmindedness
4 • **de gran ~** [*reforma, proyecto*] wide-ranging, far-reaching
5 (*Radio*) ▸ **amplitud de banda** bandwidth ▸ **amplitud de onda** amplitude

ampo SM (= *blancura*) dazzling whiteness; (= *copo de nieve*) snowflake • **como el ~ de la nieve** as white as the driven snow

ampolla SF (*en la piel*) blister; (*de inyección*) ampoule; (= *frasco*) flask • **la decisión levantó ~s entre los ministros** the decision got a few backs up in the Cabinet

ampollarse ▸ CONJUG 1a VPR to blister, form blisters

ampolleta SF **1** [*de arena*] hourglass; [*de termómetro*] bulb
2 (*LAm*) (= *bombilla*) bulb • MODISMO: • **encendérsele a algn la ~*** to have a brainwave

ampón ADJ (= *voluminoso*) bulky; [*persona*] stout, tubby

ampulosamente ADV bombastically, pompously

ampulosidad SF bombast, pomposity

ampuloso ADJ bombastic, pompous

amputación SF amputation

amputado/a SM/F amputee

amputar ▸ CONJUG 1a VT to amputate, cut off

amuchachado ADJ boyish

amuchar* ▸ CONJUG 1a VT (*And, Cono Sur*) to increase, multiply

amueblado ADJ furnished (**con, de** with)
SM (*Cono Sur*) hotel, hotel room (*used for sexual encounters and paid for by the hour*)

amueblamiento SM furnishing

amueblar ▸ CONJUG 1a VT to furnish (**de** with) • **sin ~** unfurnished

amuermado* ADJ bored

amuermante* ADJ (= *aburrido*) boring, dull; (= *ordinario*) banal, mundane

amuermar* ▸ CONJUG 1a VT to bore
VPR **amuermarse 1** (= *tener sueño*) to feel sleepy (*after a meal*); (*fig*) (= *aburrirse*) to get bored; (= *deprimirse*) to get depressed
2 (= *ponerse pesado*) to get very dull

amuinar* ▸ CONJUG 1a (*Méx*) VT to make cross, irritate
VPR **amuinarse** to get cross

amujerado ADJ effeminate

amularse ▸ CONJUG 1a VPR (*Méx*) [*persona*] to get stubborn, dig one's heels in; (*Com*) to become unsaleable, become a glut on the market

amulatado ADJ mulatto-like

amuleto SM amulet, charm

amunicionar ▸ CONJUG 1a VT to supply with ammunition

amuñecado ADJ doll-like

amura SF (*Náut*) (= *proa*) bow; (= *cabo*) tack

amurallado ADJ walled, fortified

amurallar ▸ CONJUG 1a VT to wall, fortify

amurar ▸ CONJUG 1a VI to tack

amurrarse ▸ CONJUG 1a VPR (*LAm*) to get depressed, become sad

amurriarse ▸ CONJUG 1b VPR (*Esp*) to get sad, get depressed

amurruñarse ▸ CONJUG 1a VPR (*Caribe*) (= *abrazarse*) to nestle together, cuddle up; (= *hacerse un ovillo*) to curl up

amusgar ▸ CONJUG 1h VT [+ *orejas*] to lay back, throw back; [+ *ojos*] to screw up, narrow
VPR **amusgarse** (*CAm*) to feel ashamed

Ana SF Ann, Anne

anabólico ADJ anabolic

anabolizante SM anabolic steroid

anacarado ADJ mother-of-pearl (*antes de s*)

anacardo SM (= *fruto*) cashew, cashew nut; (= *árbol*) cashew tree

anaco SM (*And*) poncho, Indian blanket

anacoluto SM anacoluthon

anaconda SF anaconda

anacoreta SMF anchorite

Anacreonte SM Anacreon

anacronía SF anachronism

anacrónico ADJ anachronistic

anacronismo SM anachronism

ánade SM duck ▸ **ánade friso** gadwall ▸ **ánade rabudo** pintail ▸ **ánade real** mallard ▸ **ánade silbón** wigeon

anadear ▸ CONJUG 1a VI to waddle

anadeo SM waddle, waddling

anadón SM duckling

anaeróbico ADJ, **anaerobio** ADJ anaerobic

anafe SM portable cooker

anáfora SF anaphora

anafórico ADJ anaphoric, anaphorical

anagrama SM anagram

anal ADJ anal

analcohólico ADJ non-alcoholic, soft

anales SMPL annals

analfa* ADJ, SMF = **analfabeto**

analfabetismo SM illiteracy ▸ **analfabetismo funcional** functional illiteracy

analfabeto/a ADJ illiterate
SM/F illiterate, illiterate person

analgesia SF analgesia

analgésico ADJ analgesic, painkilling
SM analgesic, painkiller

análisis SM INV **1** (= *examen*) analysis; (*detallado*) breakdown
2 (*Econ*) ▸ **análisis de costos** cost analysis ▸ **análisis de costos-beneficios** cost-benefit analysis ▸ **análisis de mercados** market research ▸ **análisis de viabilidad** feasibility study ▸ **análisis financiero** financial analysis
3 (*Med, Quím, Fís*) ▸ **análisis de sangre** blood test ▸ **análisis espectral** spectrum analysis ▸ **análisis orgánico** organic analysis
4 (*Ling*) analysis, parsing ▸ **análisis del discurso** discourse analysis ▸ **análisis funcional** functional analysis
5 (*Inform*) ▸ **análisis de la voz** speech analysis ▸ **análisis de sistemas** systems analysis

analista SMF (= *analizador*) analyst; (= *escritor de anales*) chronicler, annalist ▸ **analista de inversiones** investment consultant ▸ **analista de sistemas** systems analyst ▸ **analista financiero** financial analyst, market analyst

analista-programador(a) SM/F computer analyst and programmer

analítico ADJ analytic, analytical • **cuadro ~** analytic table

analizable ADJ analysable, analyzable (*EEUU*) • **fácilmente ~** easy to analyse *o* (*EEUU*) analyze

analizador(a) SM/F analyst

analizar ▸ CONJUG 1f VT to analyse, analyze (*EEUU*)

analogía SF (= *correspondencia*) analogy; (= *semejanza*) similarity • **por ~ con** on the analogy of

analógico ADJ (= *que se corresponde*) analogical; (*Inform*) analog

análogo ADJ analogous, similar (**a** to)
SM analogue • **limpiar con alcohol o ~** clean with alcohol or similar substance

ananá SM, **ananás** SM INV, **ananasa** SF (*And*) pineapple

anapesto SM anapaest

anaquel SM shelf

anaquelería SF shelves (*pl*), shelving

anaranjado ADJ orange, orange-coloured, orange-colored (*EEUU*)
SM orange, orange colour, orange color (*EEUU*)

anarco/a* SM/F anarchist

anarco... PREF anarcho...

anarcopunk SM anarchopunk

anarcosindicalismo SM anarcho-syndicalism

anarcosindicalista ADJ anarcho-syndical
SMF anarcho-syndicalist

anarquía SF anarchy

anárquico ADJ anarchic, anarchical

anarquismo SM anarchism

anarquista ADJ anarchist, anarchistic
SMF anarchist

anarquizante ADJ anarchic

anarquizar ▸ CONJUG 1f VT to cause

a

anarchy in, cause complete chaos in
anatema (SM) anathema
anatematizante (ADJ) • **palabras ~s** words of condemnation
anatematizar (VT), **anatemizar** ▹ CONJUG 1f (VT) **1** (*Rel*) to anathematize
2 (= *maldecir*) to curse
anatomía (SF) **1** (= *ciencia, cuerpo*) anatomy
2 (= *análisis*) anatomy
anatómicamente (ADV) anatomically
anatómico (ADJ) anatomical • **asiento ~** anatomically designed seat
anatomizar ▹ CONJUG 1f (VT) **1** (= *diseccionar*) to anatomize; (*Arte*) [+ *huesos, músculos*] to bring out, emphasize
2 (= *analizar*) to anatomize, dissect
anca (SF) **1** (= *cacha*) rump, haunch • **no sufre ~s*** he can't take a joke • MODISMO: • **llevar a algn a las ~s** *o* **en ~(s)** (*LAm*) to let sb ride pillion • **esto lleva el desastre en ~** (*LAm*) this spells disaster ▸ **ancas de rana** frog's legs
2 ancas* (= *posaderas*) behind (*sing*)
3 (*And*) (= *maíz*) toasted maize
ancestral (ADJ) (*de los antepasados*) ancestral; (= *antiguo*) ancient
ancestro (SM) (*esp LAm*) (= *persona*) ancestor; (= *linaje*) ancestry
anchamente (ADV) widely
ancheta (SF) **1** (= *lote*) small lot of goods; (= *negocio*) small business
2 (= *ganancia*) gain, profit; (*And, Méx*) (= *ganga*) bargain; (= *negocio*) profitable deal; (= *oportunidad*) chance to make easy money • **¡vaya ~!** • **¡buena ~!** some deal this turned out to be!
3 (*And, Cono Sur*) (= *palabrería*) prattle, babble
4 (*Caribe*) (= *broma*) joke; (= *estafa*) hoax
ancho (ADJ) **1** (= *amplio*) [*camino, puente, habitación*] wide; [*calle, sonrisa, manos*] broad; [*muro*] thick • **el salón es más ~ que largo** the living room is wider than it is long • **un tarro de boca ancha** a wide-necked bottle • **tenía las espaldas anchas** he had a broad back • **era muy ~ de hombros** he was very broad-shouldered • **plantas de hoja ancha** broad-leaved plants • **a lo ~ de algo** across sth • **colocaron una cuerda a lo ~ de la calle** they put a rope across the street • **había manifestantes a todo lo ~ de la avenida** there were demonstrators the length and breadth of the avenue • **por todo el ~ mundo** throughout the whole wide world, the world over; ▹ **Castilla, largo**
2 (= *holgado*) [*chaqueta, pantalón*] loose, loose-fitting; [*falda*] full; [*manga*] wide • **quedar** *o* (*Esp*) **estar** *o* (*Esp*) **venir ~ a algn** to be too wide for sb • **la chaqueta le quedaba muy ancha** the jacket was too wide for him • **esta camisa me viene ancha** this shirt is too big for me, this shirt is on the big side* • **le viene muy ~ el cargo** the job is too much for him • MODISMO: • **a sus anchas**: • **puedes hojear a tus anchas todos los libros** you can leaf through all the books at your leisure • **con ellos podrá discutir a sus anchas** you can discuss things freely with them • **aquí estoy a mis anchas** I feel at ease here • **ponerse a sus anchas** to make o.s. comfortable, spread o.s.; ▹ **manga**
3 (*Esp*) (= *cómodo, confortable*) • **aquí te puedes sentir bien ancha** you can make yourself comfortable *o* at home here • **en dos coches iremos más ~s** we'll be more comfortable in two cars, we'll have more room if we go in two cars • MODISMOS: • **quedarse tan ~** • **quedarse más ~ que largo**: • **le dijo cuatro verdades y se quedó tan ~** he gave him a piece of his mind and felt very pleased with himself • **no sabes lo ~ que me he quedado después de decírselo** it feels such a weight off my shoulders to have told him; ▹ **pancho**
4 (= *liberal*) liberal, broad-minded • **~ de conciencia** (*Esp*) not overscrupulous • **~ de miras** broad-minded
5 (= *orgulloso*) proud • **iba todo ~ con su traje nuevo** he was very proud in his new suit • **ponerse ~** to get conceited
(SM) **1** (= *anchura*) [*de camino, ventana*] width; [*de río*] width, breadth • **¿cuál es el ~ de la mesa?** what is the width of the table? • **todo el ~ de la habitación** the whole width of the room • **de ~**: • **tiene doce metros de ~** it is twelve metres wide • **las dos mesas tienen lo mismo de ~** both tables are the same width • **4 metros de largo por 2 de ~** 4 metres long by 2 metres wide ▸ **ancho de banda** band width; ▹ **doble**
2 (*Ferro*) (*tb* **ancho de vía**) gauge, gage (*EEUU*) • **~ europeo** European gauge • **~ internacional** international gauge • **~ normal** standard gauge
anchoa (SF) anchovy
anchor (SM) = **anchura**
anchote (ADJ) burly
anchoveta (SF) (*And*) anchovy (*for fishmeal*)
anchura (SF) **1** (= *amplitud*) [*de camino, ventana*] width; [*de río*] width, breadth • **de ~**: **un tronco de un metro de ~** a metre wide trunk • **tiene dos metros de ~** it is two metres wide ▸ **anchura alar** wingspan ▸ **anchura de banda** band width
2 (*Cos*) [*de falda*] fullness
3 (*Esp**) (= *descaro*) cheek* • **me habló con tanta ~** he talked to me with such a cheek *o* nerve* ▸ **anchura de conciencia** lack of scruple
anchuroso (ADJ) (= *ancho*) wide, broad; (= *espacioso*) spacious
ancianidad (SF) old age
anciano/a (ADJ) old, aged
(SM/F) [*de mucha edad*] old man/woman, elderly man/woman; (*Rel*) elder
ancilar (ADJ) ancillary
ancla (SF) anchor • **echar ~s** to drop anchor • **levar ~s** to weigh anchor ▸ **ancla de la esperanza** (*Náut*) sheet anchor; (*fig*) (= *única esperanza*) last hope
ancladero (SM) anchorage
anclaje (SM) **1** (*Náut*) (= *acción*) anchoring, anchorage; (= *fondeadero*) anchorage; (= *tributo*) mooring charge
2 (*Aut*) catch, clamp (*of a seat belt*)
anclar ▹ CONJUG 1a (VT) to anchor
(VI) to anchor, drop anchor • **estar anclado a/en algo** to be anchored to/in sth
ancón (SM) **1** (*Náut*) cove
2 (*Méx*) (= *rincón*) corner
3 (*And*) (= *camino*) mountain pass
áncora (SF) anchor ▸ **áncora de salvación** sheet anchor, last hope
andadas (SFPL) (*Caza*) tracks; (= *aventuras*) adventures; (*Chile, Méx*) walk (*sing*), stroll (*sing*) • **volver a las ~** to backslide, go back to one's old ways
andaderas (SFPL) baby walker (*sing*)
andadero (ADJ) passable, easy to traverse
andado (ADJ) (= *trillado*) worn, well-trodden; (= *corriente*) common, ordinary; [*ropa*] old, worn
andador(a) (ADJ) **1** (= *que anda rápido*) fast-walking • **es ~** he's a good walker
2 (= *viajero*) fond of travelling, fond of gadding about
3 (*Cono Sur*) [*caballo*] well-paced, long-striding
(SM/F) walker
(SM) **1** (*para niños*) baby walker; (*para enfermos*) Zimmer® frame
2 andadores [*de niño*] reins
(SF) (*Méx*) prostitute, streetwalker, hustler (*EEUU**)
andadura (SF) **1** (= *acción*) walking; (= *manera*) gait, walk; (= *de caballo*) pace
2 (*fig*) (= *camino*) path, course; (= *progreso*) progress; (= *avance*) advance • **comenzar nuevas ~s** to start again
ándale (EXCL) (*esp Méx*) come on!, hey!; ▹ **ándele, andar**
andalón (ADJ) (*Méx*) well-paced, long-striding
Andalucía (SF) Andalusia
andalucismo (SM) **1** (*Ling*) andalusianism, *word or phrase etc peculiar to Andalusia*
2 (= *sentimiento*) *sense of the differentness of Andalusia*; (*Pol*) *doctrine of or belief in Andalusian autonomy*
andaluz(a) (ADJ), (SM/F) Andalusian
(SM) (*Ling*) Andalusian
andaluzada* (SF) (= *cuento*) tall story, *piece of typical Andalusian exaggeration*; (= *acto*) *the sort of thing one expects from an Andalusian*
andamiaje (SM), **andamiada** (SF) (*Constr*) scaffolding; (*fig*) (= *estructura*) framework, structure
andamio (SM) (*Constr*) scaffold • **~s** scaffolding (*sing*) ▸ **andamio óseo** skeleton, bone structure
andana (SF) row, line • MODISMO: • **llamarse ~** to go back on one's word
andanada (SF) **1** (*Mil*) broadside; (*fig*) (= *reprensión*) reprimand, rocket* • **soltar la ~ a algn** to give sb a rocket* • **soltar una ~** to say sth unexpected, drop a bombshell* • **por ~s** (*Cono Sur*) in excess, to excess ▸ **andanada verbal** verbal broadside
2 (*Dep*) stand, grandstand; (*Taur*) *section of cheap seats*
3 (= *andana*) [*de ladrillos*] layer, row
andante (ADJ) (= *que anda*) walking • **caballero ~** knight errant
(SM) (*Mús*) andante
andanza (SF) (= *suerte*) fortune • **~s** (= *vicisitudes*) deeds, adventures
andar ▹ CONJUG 1p (VI) **1** (= *ir a pie*) to walk; (= *moverse*) to move; (= *viajar*) to travel around • **iremos andando a la estación** we'll walk to the station • **vinimos andando** we walked here, we came on foot • **el tren empezó a ~** the train started moving • **la máquina empezó a ~** the machine started up • **anduvieron por Jamaica y Cuba** they travelled around Jamaica and Cuba • **~ a caballo** to ride • **~ tras algo/algn** to be after sth/sb • **~ tras una chica** to be *o* chase after a girl
2 (= *funcionar*) to go, work • **el reloj no anda** the clock won't go, the clock isn't working • **el reloj anda bien** the clock keeps good time • **¿cómo anda esto?** how does this work?
3* (= *estar*) to be • **no sé por dónde anda** I don't know where he is • **anda por aquí** it's around here somewhere • **seguro que ese anda por Brasil** he's bound to be somewhere in Brazil • **~ alegre** to be *o* feel cheerful • **hay que ~ con cuidado** you have to be careful • **últimamente ando muy liado** I've been very busy lately • **~ bien de salud** to be well, be in good health • **andamos mal de dinero** we're badly off for money, we're short of money • **¿cómo andan las cosas?** how are things? • **¿cómo anda eso?** how are things going? • **¿qué tal andas?** how are you? • **¿cómo andas de tabaco?** how are you off for cigarettes? • **ando escaso de tiempo** I am pushed for time • **de ~ por casa**: • **ropa de ~ por casa** clothes for wearing around the house • **un montaje muy de ~ por casa** a rough-and-ready production • **justicia de ~ por casa** rough-and-ready justice • MODISMO: • **andan como Pedro por su casa** they act as if they owned the place

• REFRÁN: • **quien mal anda, mal acaba** you get what you deserve
4 (= *rebuscar*) • **¡no andes ahí!** keep away from there! • **~ en** to rummage around in • **han estado andando en el armario** they've been rummaging around in the cupboard • **no andes en mis cosas** keep out of my things
5 • **~ a:** • **siempre andan a gritos** they're always shouting • **andan a la greña** *o* **a la gresca** they're at each other's throats
6 • **~ con algn** to go around with sb • **anda con una chica francesa** he goes around with a French girl • REFRÁN: • **dime con quién andas y te diré quién eres** a man is known by the company he keeps
7 • **~ en** (= *estar implicado en*) to be involved in • **~ en pleitos** to be engaged *o* involved in lawsuits • **anda en la droga** he's involved with drugs • **sospecho que anda en ello Rosa** I suspect Rosa is involved • **¿en qué andas?** what are you up to?
8 • **~ haciendo algo** to be doing sth • **¿qué andas buscando?** what are you looking for? • **ando buscando un socio** I'm looking for a partner • **no andes criticándolo todo el tiempo** stop criticizing him all the time
9 • **~ por** (= *rondar*): • **anda por los 50** he's about 50 • **el pueblo anda por los 1.000 habitantes** the village has about 1,000 inhabitants • **anda por los 700 euros** it's around 700 euros
10 • MODISMO: • **andando el tiempo:** • **un niño que, andando el tiempo, sería rey** a child who, in time, would become king • **andando el tiempo la pena de muerte desaparecerá** the death penalty will eventually disappear
11 (*exclamaciones*) • **¡anda!** (= *¡no me digas!*) well I never!; (= *¡vamos!*) come on! • **¡anda!, no lo sabía** well I never, I didn't know that! • **anda, dímelo** go on, tell me • **anda, no me molestes** just stop annoying me, will you? • **anda, no te lo tomes tan a pecho** come on, there's no need to take it to heart like that • **¡anda, anda!** come on! • **¡ándale (pues)!** (*Méx**) (= *apúrese*) come on!, hurry up!; (= *adiós*) cheerio!; (= *gracias*) thanks!; (*encontrando algo*) that's it! • **¡andando!** right, let's get on with it! • **andando, que todavía hay mucho que hacer** let's get moving, there's still a lot to do • **¡anda ya!:** • **anda ya, no nos vengas con esnobismos** come on, don't be such a snob • **—dile que te gusta —¡anda ya, para que me suba el precio!** "tell her you like it" — "oh sure, so she can charge me more!"
(VT) **1** (= *recorrer a pie*) [+ *trecho*] to walk • **anduvimos varios kilómetros** we walked several kilometres • **me conocía muy bien el camino por haberlo andado varias veces** I knew the path very well, as I'd been down *o* walked it several times before
2 (*LAm*) (= *llevar*) [+ *ropa*] to wear; [+ *objeto*] to carry • **yo no ando reloj** I don't wear a watch
(VPR) **andarse 1** (= *irse*) to go off, go away • MODISMO: • **~se por las ramas** to beat about the bush
2 • **~se con:** • **ándate con cuidado** take care • **no puedes ~te con tonterías** you can't afford to mess about • **no ~se con contemplaciones** *o* **remilgos** not to stand on ceremony • **no podía ~se con demasiados remilgos a la hora de elegir marido** she couldn't be too fussy when choosing a husband • **no podemos ~nos con contemplaciones a la hora de buscar una solución a la crisis** we can't afford to worry about the niceties when looking for a solution to the crisis • **no se anda con chiquitas** he doesn't mess about • **no ~se con rodeos** not to beat about the bush
3 • **~se en** [+ *herida, nariz*] to pick; (= *permitirse*) to indulge in • **no te andes en la nariz** don't pick your nose • **se andaba en la herida** he was picking at his wound
4 • **todo se andará** all in good time
(SM) walk, gait • **es de ~es rápidos** he walks quickly • **a más** *o* **todo ~** at full speed, as quickly as possible • MODISMOS: • **a largo ~**† (= *al final*) in the end; (= *a largo plazo*) in the long run • **estar en un ~**† to be on the same level

andaras (SM) (*And*) Indian flute
andarica (SF) (*Asturias*) crab
andariego (ADJ) fond of travelling, restless
andarilla (SF) (*And*) *type of flute*
andarín (SM) walker • **es muy ~** he is a great walker
andarivel (SM) **1** (*Téc*) cable ferry
2 (*Náut*) (= *salvavidas*) lifeline
3 (*esp LAm*) (= *puente*) rope bridge; (= *cerco*) rope barrier; [*de piscina*] lane
4 (*And*) (= *adornos*) adornments (*pl*), trinkets (*pl*)
andas (SFPL) **1** (*Med*) (= *camilla*) stretcher (*sing*); (= *silla*) litter (*sing*), sedan chair (*sing*) • **llevar a algn en ~** (*lit*) to carry sb on a platform; (*fig*) to treat sb with great deference
2 (*Rel*) portable platform (*sing*); (= *féretro*) bier (*sing*)
ándele (EXCL) (*Méx*) (= *¡venga!*) come on!, hurry up!; (= *¡ya ves!*) see what I mean!; (= *¡ya lo creo!*) get away!*; (= *correcto*) exactly!
andén (SM) **1** (*Ferro*) platform ▸ **andén de salida** departure platform ▸ **andén de vacío** arrival platform
2 (*Náut*) quayside
3 (*CAm, Col*) (= *acera*) pavement, sidewalk (*EEUU*)
Andes (SMPL) Andes
andinismo (SM) (*LAm*) mountaineering, climbing • **hacer ~** to go mountaineering, go climbing
andinista (SMF) (*LAm*) mountaineer, climber
andino (ADJ) Andean, of/from the Andes
ándito (SM) (= *pasillo*) outer walk, corridor; (= *acera*) pavement, sidewalk (*EEUU*)
andoba* (SM) guy*, chap*
andolina (SF) swallow
andón (ADJ) (*LAm*) = **andador**
andonear ▹ CONJUG 1a (VI) (*Caribe*) [*persona*] to amble along, stroll along; [*caballo*] to trot
andorga* (SF) belly
andorina (SF) swallow
Andorra (SF) Andorra
andorrano/a (ADJ), (SM/F) Andorran
andorrear* ▹ CONJUG 1a (VI) (= *ajetrearse*) to bustle about, fuss around; (= *ir de acá para allá*) to gad about, move about a lot
andorrero/a (ADJ) bustling, busy
(SM/F) busy sort, gadabout
(SF) (*pey*) streetwalker, hustler (*EEUU**)
andrajo (SM) **1** rag, tatter • **~s** rags, tatters • **estar en ~s** • **estar hecho un ~** to be in rags • **ser un ~ humano** to be a wreck*
2 (= *pillo*) rascal, good-for-nothing
3 (= *bagatela*) trifle, mere nothing
andrajoso (ADJ) ragged, in tatters
Andrés (SM) Andrew
androcéntrico (ADJ) male-centred, androcentric
androcentrismo (SM) male-centredness, androcentricity
androfobia (SF) hatred of men
androgénico (ADJ) androgenic
andrógeno (SM) androgen
androginia (SF) androgyny
andrógino/a (ADJ) androgynous
(SM/F) androgyne
androide (SM) android
Andrómaca (SF) Andromache
andrómina* (SF) fib*, tale
andropausia (SF) male menopause
androsterona (SF) androsterone
andullo (SM) (*Cuba, Méx*) plug of tobacco
andurrial (SM) **1** (= *lodazal*) bog, quagmire; (= *zanja*) ditch; (= *descampado*) piece of waste ground
2 andurriales (= *lugar extraviado*) out-of-the-way place (*sing*) • **en esos ~es** in that godforsaken place
anduve, anduviera *etc* ▹ **andar**
anea (SF) bulrush
aneblar ▹ CONJUG 1j (VT) (= *cubrir de niebla*) to cover with mist; (= *anublar*) to obscure, darken, cast a cloud over
(VPR) **aneblarse** (= *cubrirse de niebla*) to get misty; (= *anublarse*) to get dark
anécdota (SF) anecdote, story • **este cuadro tiene una ~** there's a tale attached to this picture
anecdotario (SM) collection of stories
anecdótico (ADJ) (= *de anécdota*) anecdotal; (= *trivial*) trivial • **contenido ~** story content • **valor ~** story value, value as a story • **el estudio se queda en lo ~** the study does not rise above the merely superficial
anecdotismo (SM) anecdotal nature, anecdotal quality, merely anecdotal quality
anega (SF) (*Cono Sur*) = **fanega**
anegación (SF) flooding
anegadizo (ADJ) [*tierra*] subject to flooding, frequently flooded; [*madera*] heavier than water
anegado (ADJ) (= *inundado*) flooded
anegar ▹ CONJUG 1h (VT) **1** (= *ahogar*) to drown
2 (= *inundar*) to flood; (*fig*) (= *abrumar*) to overwhelm
(VPR) **anegarse 1** (= *ahogarse*) to drown
2 (= *inundarse*) to flood, be flooded • **~se en llanto** to dissolve into tears
3 (*Náut*) to sink, founder
anejo (ADJ) attached, joined on (**a** to)
(SM) (*Arquit*) annexe, outbuilding; [*de libro*] supplement, appendix
anemia (SF) anaemia, anemia (*EEUU*)
anémico (ADJ) anaemic, anemic (*EEUU*)
anemómetro (SM) anemometer, wind gauge ▸ **anemómetro registrador** wind-speed indicator
anémona (SF), **anémone** (SF) anemone ▸ **anémona de mar** sea anemone
aneroide (ADJ) aneroid
anestesia (SF) anaesthesia, anesthesia (*EEUU*) • **me operaron con ~** I was operated on under anaesthetic • **operar sin ~** to operate without (an) anaesthetic ▸ **anestesia general** general anaesthetic, general anesthetic (*EEUU*) ▸ **anestesia local** local anaesthetic, local anesthetic (*EEUU*)
anestesiante (ADJ), (SM) anaesthetic, anesthetic (*EEUU*)
anestesiar ▹ CONJUG 1b (VT) to anaesthetize, anesthetize (*EEUU*), give an anaesthetic to, give an anesthetic to (*EEUU*)
anestésico (ADJ), (SM) anaesthetic, anesthetic (*EEUU*)
anestesista (SMF) anaesthetist, anesthetist (*EEUU*)
anexar ▹ CONJUG 1a (VT) **1** (*Pol*) to annex
2 [+ *documento*] to attach, append
anexión (SF), **anexionamiento** (SM) annexation
anexionar ▹ CONJUG 1a (VT) to annex
(VPR) **anexionarse** to annex
anexo (ADJ) (= *anejo*) attached; (*en carta*) enclosed • **llevar** *o* **algo ~** • **tener algo ~** to have sth attached • **~ a la presente ...** (*Méx*) please find enclosed ...

a

SM (*Arquit*) annexe; (*Rel*) dependency; [*de carta*] enclosure
anfeta* SF = **anfetamina**
anfetamina SF amphetamine
anfetamínico/a SM/F **1** (= *adicto*) amphetamine addict, speed freak*
2* (= *pesado*) bore, pain*; (= *imbécil*) idiot
anfibio ADJ (*Zool*) amphibious; [*avión, vehículo*] amphibian
SM amphibian • **los ~s** the amphibia
anfibología SF ambiguity
anfibológico ADJ ambiguous
anfiteatro SM amphitheatre, amphitheater (*EEUU*); (*Univ*) lecture theatre *o* (*EEUU*) theater; (*Teat*) dress circle
▸ **anfiteatro anatómico** dissecting room
Anfitrión SM Amphitryon
anfitrión/ona SM/F host/hostess
ánfora SF **1** (= *cántaro*) amphora; (*Cono Sur**) [*de marihuana*] marijuana pouch
2 (*Méx*) (*Pol*) ballot box
anfractuosidad SF **1** (= *aspereza*) roughness, unevenness; [*de camino*] bend • **~es** rough places
2 (*Anat*) (*de cerebro*) sulcus anfractuosity
anfractuoso ADJ rough, uneven
angarillas SFPL [*de albañil*] handbarrow (*sing*); (*en bicicleta*) panniers; (*Culin*) cruet (stand) (*sing*)
angarrio ADJ (*And, Caribe*) terribly thin, thin as a rake*
angas SMPL • MODISMO: • **por ~ o por mangas** (*And*) like it or not
ángel SM **1** angel • **pasó un ~** (*silencio*) there was a sudden silence; (*en charla*) there was a lull in the conversation ▸ **ángel caído** fallen angel ▸ **ángel custodio, ángel de la guarda** guardian angel ▸ **ángel del infierno** hell's angel ▸ **ángel exterminador** angel of death
2 (= *gracia*) • **tener ~** to have charm, be very charming • **tener mal ~** to be a nasty piece of work*
angélica SF angelica
angelical ADJ, **angélico** ADJ angelic, angelical
angelino/a ADJ of/from Los Angeles
SM/F native/inhabitant of Los Angeles
• **los ~s** the people of Los Angeles
angelito SM (= *niño*) little angel; (*LAm*) (= *niño fallecido*) dead child • **¡angelito!** (*Cono Sur*) don't play the innocent!, pull the other one!* • **¡no seas ~!** (*Cono Sur*) don't be silly!
angelón* SM ▸ **angelón de retablo** fat old thing
angelopolitano/a (*Méx*) ADJ of/from Puebla
SM/F native/inhabitant of Puebla • **los ~s** the people of Puebla
angelote SM **1** (= *niño*) chubby child
2 (*LAm*) (= *persona*) decent person
3 (= *pez*) angel fish
ángelus SM INV angelus
angina SF **1** (*Med*) angina; (*Méx, Ven*) tonsil • **tener ~s** to have tonsillitis; (*gen*) to have a sore throat ▸ **angina de pecho** angina pectoris
2 • **~s** (*Esp*‡) (= *pecho*) tits*‡
angiosperma SF angiosperm
anglicanismo SM Anglicanism
anglicano/a ADJ, SM/F Anglican
anglicismo SM anglicism
anglicista ADJ • **tendencia ~** anglicizing tendency
SMF anglicist
angliparla SF (*hum*) Spanglish
anglo... PREF anglo...
angloamericano ADJ Anglo-American, British-American
angloespañol ADJ Anglo-Spanish, British-Spanish
anglófilo/a ADJ, SM/F anglophile
anglofobia SF anglophobia
anglófobo/a ADJ anglophobe, anglophobiç
SM/F anglophobe
anglófono/a ADJ English-speaking
SM/F English speaker
anglofrancés ADJ Anglo-French, British-French
anglonormando/a ADJ Anglo-Norman
• **islas Anglonormandas** Channel Isles
SM/F Anglo-Norman
SM (*Ling*) Anglo-Norman
angloparlante, anglohablante ADJ English-speaking
SMF English speaker
anglosajón/ona ADJ, SM/F Anglo-Saxon
SM (*Ling*) Anglo-Saxon
Angola SF Angola
angoleño/a ADJ, SM/F Angolan
angolés = **angoleño**
angora SF angora
angorina SF artificial angora
angostar ▷ CONJUG 1a VT (= *estrechar*) to narrow; (*Cono Sur*) (= *hacer pequeño*) to make smaller; [+ *ropa*] to take in
VPR **angostarse** to narrow, get narrow, get narrower
angosto ADJ narrow
angostura SF **1** (= *estrechez*) narrowness
2 (*Náut*) narrows (*pl*), strait; (*Geog*) narrow pass
3 (= *bebida*) angostura
angra SF cove, creek
ángstrom SM (PL: **ángstroms**) angstrom
anguila SF (= *pez*) eel • **~s** (*Náut*) slipway (*sing*)
angula SF elver, baby eel
angulación SF camera angle
angular ADJ angular; ▷ **piedra**
SM • **gran ~** wide-angle lens
Angulema SF Angoulême
ángulo SM (*Mat*) angle; (= *esquina*) corner; (= *curva*) bend, turning; (*Mec*) knee, bend • **de ~ ancho** (*Fot*) wide-angle • **en ~** at an angle • **está inclinado con un ~ de 45 grados** it is leaning at an angle of 45 degrees • **formar ~ con** to be at an angle to ▸ **ángulo agudo** acute angle ▸ **ángulo alterno** alternate angle ▸ **ángulo del ojo** corner of one's eye ▸ **ángulo de mira** angle of sight ▸ **ángulo de subida** (*Aer*) angle of climb ▸ **ángulo de toma** (*Fot*) angle of shooting ▸ **ángulo muerto** (*Aut*) blind spot ▸ **ángulo oblicuo** oblique angle ▸ **ángulo obtuso** obtuse angle ▸ **ángulo recto** right angle • **de *o* en ~ recto** right-angled
anguloso ADJ [*cara*] angular, sharp; [*camino*] winding, zigzagging
angurria SF (*esp LAm*) **1** (= *hambre*) desperate hunger • **comer con ~** to eat greedily
2 (= *angustia*) extreme anxiety
3 (= *tacañería*) stinginess*
angurriento ADJ (*esp LAm*), **angurrioso** (*Cono Sur*) ADJ **1** (= *glotón*) greedy
2 (= *ansioso*) anxious
3* (= *tacaño*) mean, stingy*
angustia SF **1** (= *miedo*) anguish, distress • **una mirada/sensación de ~** a look/feeling of anguish *o* distress • **un grito de ~** a cry of anguish, an anguished cry • **sentía un nudo de ~ en la garganta** I could feel a knot in my throat, from anguish • **¡estuve a punto de caerme por el acantilado! ¡qué ~!** I was just about to fall off the cliff! what an ordeal! • **da ~ ver esos niños tan delgados** it's distressing to see children as thin as that ▸ **angustia de muerte** death throes
2 (= *ansiedad*) (*por estrés, miedo*) anxiety; (*por inseguridad*) angst • **cada vez que voy en metro noto una terrible sensación de ~** every time I travel by underground I feel terribly anxious *o* I feel a terrible anxiety • **no podía contener la ~** he could not contain his anxiety • **su vejez estuvo llena de ~** he had an angst-ridden old age • **ataque de ~** anxiety attack, panic attack ▸ **angustia adolescente** adolescent angst ▸ **angustia existencial, angustia vital** (*Med*) state of anxiety; (*Psic*) angst
3* (= *náuseas*) • **me da ~ cuando como** I feel sick if I eat
SMF INV • **ser un ~s*** to be a worrier
angustiado ADJ **1** (= *asustado*) [*persona*] distressed; [*expresión, mirada*] anguished • **están muy ~s por la desaparición de su hija** they are very distressed about their daughter's disappearance • **recordaba el rostro ~ de su familia** I recalled the anguished look *o* look of anguish of their family • **nos hizo una súplica angustiada** he let out an anguished plea
2 (= *preocupado*) anxious • **está ~ por no tener trabajo** he is very worried *o* he is anxious about not having a job
3 (= *avaro*) grasping, mean
angustiante ADJ distressing
angustiar ▷ CONJUG 1b VT **1** (= *agobiar*) to distress • **la angustiaba verlo sufrir** she was distressed to see him suffer, seeing him suffer distressed her
2 (= *preocupar*) to make anxious • **los exámenes no me angustian** exams don't make me anxious
VPR **angustiarse 1** (= *agobiarse*) to be distressed (**por** at, on account of)
2 (= *preocuparse*) to get anxious • **no deberías ~te por un pequeño dolor** you shouldn't worry *o* get anxious about a slight pain
angustiosamente ADV **1** (= *con pena*) in an anguished voice • **—no iré —dijo ~** "I won't go," she said in an anguished voice • **estuvo llorando ~** he was crying inconsolably
2 (= *con preocupación*) anxiously
angustioso ADJ **1** (= *angustiado*) [*sensación*] distressed, anguished; [*voz, mirada*] anguished • **tres horas de angustiosa espera** three hours of anxious waiting
2 (= *agobiante*) [*habitación, espacio*] oppressive; [*problema, recuerdo, situación*] distressing • **tomar decisiones es siempre ~** taking decisions always makes one anxious • **pasamos unos momentos muy ~s** we went through moments of great anguish
3 (= *doloroso*) (*lit*) agonizing; (*fig*) heartbreaking • **sintió un ~ dolor** he felt an agonizing pain • **momentos de angustiosa soledad** moments of heartbreaking solitude
anhá EXCL (*Cono Sur*) = **anjá**
anhelación SF **1** (*Med*) panting
2 (= *ansia*) longing, yearning
anhelante ADJ **1** (= *jadeante*) panting
2 (= *ansioso*) eager • **esperar ~ algo** to long for sth
anhelar ▷ CONJUG 1a VT to long for, yearn for • **~ hacer algo** to be eager to do sth, long to do sth
VI (*Med*) to gasp, pant
anhelo SM longing, desire (**de, por** for) • **con ~** longingly • **tener ~s de** to be eager for, long for ▸ **anhelo de superación** urge to do better
anheloso ADJ **1** (*Med*) [*persona*] gasping, panting; [*respiración*] heavy, difficult, laboured, labored (*EEUU*)
2 (= *ansioso*) eager, anxious
anhídrido SM ▸ **anhídrido carbónico** carbon dioxide
Aníbal SM Hannibal

anidación SF, **anidada** SF nesting
anidamiento SM nesting
anidar ▹ CONJUG 1a VT to take in, shelter
VI **1** (*Orn*) to nest, make its nest; (*Inform*) to nest
2 (= *morar*) to live, make one's home • **la maldad anida en su alma** his heart is full of evil
anieblar ▹ CONJUG 1a = **aneblar**
aniego SM (*And, Cono Sur*), **aniegue** SM (*Méx*) flood
anilina SF aniline
anilla SF **1** [*de cortina*] curtain ring; [*de puro*] cigar band ▸ **anilla de desgarre** ring pull
2 (*Orn*) ring
3 anillas (*Gimnasia*) rings
anillado ADJ ringed, banded (*EEUU*), ring-shaped
SM ringing (*of birds*)
anillamiento SM ringing (*of birds*)
anillar ▹ CONJUG 1a VT (= *dar forma de anillo a*) to make into a ring, make rings in; (= *sujetar*) to fasten with a ring; (*Orn*) to ring
anillejo SM, **anillete** SM small ring, ringlet
anillo SM (*gen*) ring; [*de puro*] cigar band • **no creo que se me caigan los ~s por eso** I don't feel it's in any way beneath my dignity • **venir como ~ al dedo** to be just right, suit to a T ▸ **anillo de boda** wedding ring ▸ **anillo de compromiso** engagement ring ▸ **anillo de crecimiento** growth ring ▸ **anillo de pedida** engagement ring ▸ **anillo pastoral** bishop's ring
ánima SF **1** (*Rel*) soul • **las ~s** (= *oración*) the Angelus (*sing*) ▸ **ánima bendita, ánima del purgatorio, ánima en pena** soul in purgatory
2 (*Mil*) bore
3 (*Cono Sur*) (= *santuario*) wayside shrine
animación SF **1** (= *alegría*) life • **a la fiesta le faltaba un poco de ~** the party lacked a bit of life, the party was a bit dead* • **hemos logrado darle un poco de ~ al bar** we have managed to liven up the bar, we have managed to put some life into the bar • **su poesía goza de cierta ~** his poetry possesses a certain liveliness
2 (= *bullicio*) activity • **una intensa ~ en la Bolsa** an intense activity on the Stock Market • **una plaza con muchísima ~** a square with a lot of bustle *o* activity, a very lively square ▸ **animación suspendida** suspended animation
3 (= *impulso*) • **una campaña de ~ a la lectura** a reading promotion campaign • **coordinador de ~ social** social activities coordinator ▸ **animación (socio)cultural** • **en verano aumenta la ~ cultural** there are more cultural things going on in the summer • **departamento de ~ sociocultural** department of culture
4 (*Cine*) animation ▸ **animación por ordenador** computer animation
animadamente ADV [*charlar*] animatedly, in a lively way; [*bailar*] in a lively way
animado ADJ **1** (= *con ánimo*) • **no está muy ~ últimamente** he hasn't been in very high spirits recently • **estar ~ a hacer algo** to be keen to do sth
2 (= *alentado*) • **~ de** *o* **por algo/algn** encouraged by sth/sb, urged on by sth/sb • **~s por los hinchas** encouraged *o* urged on by the fans • **~s por el fanatismo** driven by fanaticism
3 [*lugar*] (= *alegre*) lively; (= *concurrido*) [*bar, mercado*] bustling, busy • **una fiesta muy animada** a very lively party • **una mañana muy animada en la Bolsa** a very lively morning on the Stock Market • **la boda estuvo animada por un grupo de música** the wedding was livened up by a band
4 (= *con vida*) animate • **un cortometraje ~** a short animation film; ▹ **dibujo**
5 (*Ling*) animate
animador(a) SM/F (*TV*) host/hostess, presenter ▸ **animador(a) cultural** (*en ayuntamiento*) events organiser; (*en hotel*) entertainment manager ▸ **animador(a) turístico(a)** tourist coordinator
animadora SF **1** (= *cantante*) night-club singer
2 (*Dep*) cheerleader
animadversión SF ill will, antagonism
animal ADJ **1** (= *de los animales*) animal • **instinto ~** animal instinct
2* (= *estúpido*) stupid • **el muy ~ no sabe la capital de España** he's so stupid he doesn't know what the capital of Spain is
3* (= *bruto*) • **¡deja ya de empujar, no seas tan ~!** stop pushing, you great oaf *o* brute • **no seas ~, trátala con cariño** don't be such a brute, be kind to her • **¡el muy ~ se comió tres platos!** he had three helpings, the oaf *o* pig!
SM animal • **los ~es salvajes** wild animals • **soy un ~ político** I am a political animal • **ser ~ de costumbres** to be a creature of habit • **MODISMOS:** • **ser un ~ de bellota*** to be as thick as two short planks* • **comer como un ~*** to eat like a pig • **trabajar como un ~*** to work like a slave, work all the hours God sends* ▸ **animal de carga** (= *burro, buey*) beast of burden • **¡me tratas como a un ~ de carga!** what did your last servant die of?* ▸ **animal de compañía** pet ▸ **animal de laboratorio** laboratory animal ▸ **animal de tiro** draught animal, draft animal (*EEUU*) ▸ **animal doméstico** [*de compañía*] pet; [*de granja*] domestic animal
SMF* **1** (= *estúpido*) fool, moron* • **¡animal!, tres y dos son cinco** you fool *o* moron*, three plus two makes five
2 (= *bruto*) brute • **el ~ de Juan seguía pegándole** that brute Juan kept on hitting him • **el ~ de Antonio se comió su plato y el mío** that pig Antonio ate all his own dinner and mine too • **eres un ~, lo has roto** you're so rough you've gone and broken it
animalada SF **1** (= *disparate*) silly thing (*to do o say*); (= *ultraje*) disgrace; (= *atrocidad*) outrage
2 (*LAm*) (= *rebaño*) group of animals, herd of animals
animalaje SM (*Cono Sur*) group of animals, herd of animals
animalejo SM (= *animal*) odd-looking creature, nasty animal; (= *bicho*) creepy-crawly*
animalidad SF animality
animalista ADJ **1** [*partido, manifestación*] animalist, pro-animal-rights
2 [*pintor, arte*] animalist
SMF **1** (= *activista político*) animal-rights campaigner, animalist
2 (= *artista*) animalist artist
animalizarse ▹ CONJUG 1f VPR to become brutalized
animalote SM big animal
animalucho SM (= *animal*) ugly brute; (= *bicho*) creepy-crawly*
animar ▹ CONJUG 1a VT **1** (= *alegrar*) [+ *persona triste*] to cheer up; [+ *habitación*] to brighten up • **unas flores la ~án** some flowers will cheer her up • **una sonrisa de ilusión animaba sus ojos** an excited smile brightened the look in her eyes
2 (= *entretener*) [+ *persona aburrida*] to liven up; [+ *charla, fiesta, reunión*] to liven up, enliven • **un humorista animó la velada** a comedian livened up *o* enlivened the evening
3 (= *alentar*) [+ *persona*] to encourage; [+ *proyecto*] to inspire; [+ *fuego*] to liven up • **había pancartas animando al equipo nacional** there were banners cheering on the national team • **te estaré animando desde las gradas** I'll be rooting for you *o* cheering you on from the crowd • **~ a algn a hacer** *o* **a que haga algo** to encourage sb to do sth • **esas noticias nos ~on a pensar que ...** that news encouraged us to think that ... • **ignoramos las razones que lo ~on a dimitir** we are unaware of the reasons for his resignation *o* the reasons that led him *o* prompted him to resign • **me animan a que siga** they're encouraging *o* urging me to carry on
4 (*Econ*) [+ *mercado, economía*] to stimulate, inject life into
5 (*Bio*) to animate, give life to
VPR **animarse 1** (= *alegrarse*) **a** [*persona*] to cheer up; [*cara, ojos*] to brighten up • **necesito una copa para ~me** I need a drink to cheer me *o* myself up • **¡venga, anímate!** come on, cheer up! • **se le animó la cara al verme** her face brightened up when she saw me
b [*charla, fiesta, reunión*] to liven up • **hace falta más alcohol si quieres que la fiesta se anime** we need more alcohol if you want the party to get going *o* liven up
2 (= *decidirse*) • **si te animas, hemos quedado en el cine** if you feel like it, we're meeting at the cinema • **cuando la economía va bien, la gente se anima y gasta** when the economy is doing well people feel more like spending • **si tú te animas, yo también** I'm game if you are • **nos vamos a París, ¿te animas?** we're going to Paris, do you fancy *o* feel like coming? • **~se a hacer algo: ¿alguien se anima a acompañarme?** does anyone feel like coming with me? • **hasta el abuelo se animó a bailar** even grandpa got up and had a dance • **nadie se anima a dar su opinión** nobody dares to give their opinion • **parece que no se anima a llover** it looks as if it's not going to rain after all
anime SM (*Caribe*) polyethylene
anímicamente ADV mentally
anímico ADJ mental • **estado ~** state of mind
animismo SM animism
animista ADJ animistic
SMF animist
animita SF (*Cono Sur*) roadside shrine
ánimo SM **1** (= *moral*) spirits (*pl*) • **tiene mejor ~** he is in better spirits • **hay que mantener el ~ arriba** you've got to keep your spirits up • **admiro su fortaleza de ~** I admire her strength of spirit • **apaciguar** *o* **aplacar los ~s** to calm things down • **estar bajo de ~** to be in low spirits • **caer(se) de ~** to lose heart, get disheartened • **calmar los ~s** to calm things down • **dar ~s a algn** to cheer sb up • **enardecer** *o* **encrespar los ~s** to rouse passions, inflame passions • **los ~s estaban muy encrespados** feelings were running high • **no consigo hacerme el ~ de levantarme temprano** I can't bring myself to get up early • **levantar el ~** to raise one's spirits • **recobrar el ~** to pick o.s. up • **estar sin ~** to be in low spirits • **no tengo el ~ para bromas** I'm not in the mood for jokes; ▹ **disposición, estado**
2 (= *aliento*) encouragement • **un mensaje de ~** a message of encouragement • **¡ánimo!** (*para alegrar*) come on!, cheer up!; (*ante un reto*) come on!, go for it! • **dar** *o* **infundir ~(s) a algn** to give encouragement to sb, encourage sb
3 (= *fuerza, coraje*) courage • **hay que afrontar el futuro con mucho ~** you have to face the future with great strength *o* courage • **no me encuentro con ~ de ir al cine** I don't feel up to going to the cinema
4 (= *intención*) intention • **no he venido con ~**

a

de pelea I haven't come here to fight *o* with the intention of fighting • **no había ~ de venganza en lo que dijo** there was nothing vengeful in what he said • **no estaba en mi ~ decir nada ofensivo** I didn't mean to say anything offensive • **lo dijo sin ~ de ofenderte** he meant no offence, he didn't mean to offend you • **una empresa sin ~ de lucro** a non-profit-making company; ▹ **presencia**
5 (= *pensamiento*) mind • **la idea estaba presente en el ~ de todos** the idea was uppermost in everyone's thoughts *o* minds • **el suceso dejó una huella profunda en mi ~** the incident marked me deeply
6 (= *alma*) soul, spirit

animosamente (ADV) (= *con valor*) bravely; (= *con brío*) with spirit, in lively fashion

animosidad (SF) animosity, ill will

animoso (ADJ) (= *valiente*) brave; (= *brioso*) spirited, lively

aniñado (ADJ) **1** [*aspecto*] childlike; [*conducta*] childish, puerile
2 (*Cono Sur*) (= *animoso*) spirited, lively
3 (*Cono Sur*) (= *guapo*) handsome

aniñarse ▹ CONJUG 1a (VPR) to act childishly

aniquilación (SF), **aniquilamiento** (SM) annihilation, destruction

aniquilador (ADJ) destructive

aniquilar ▹ CONJUG 1a (VT) **1** (= *destruir*) [+ *enemigo*] to annihilate, destroy; [+ *equipo rival*] to crush, annihilate
2 (= *matar*) to kill
(VPR) **aniquilarse 1** (*Mil etc*) to be annihilated, be wiped out
2 (= *deteriorarse*) to deteriorate, decline; (*Med*) to waste away; [*riqueza*] to be frittered away

anís (SM) **1** (*Bot*) anise, aniseed
2 (= *bebida*) anisette • MODISMOS: • **estar hecho un ~** (*And**) to be dressed up to the nines • **llegar a los anises** (*And**) to turn up late
3 (*And*) (= *energía*) strength, energy

anisado (ADJ) aniseed-flavoured, aniseed-flavored (*EEUU*)

anisakis (SM INV) anisakis

aniseros‡ (SMPL) (*And*) • MODISMOS: • **entregar los ~** to kick the bucket‡ • **vaciar los ~ a algn** to bump sb off‡

anisete (SM) anisette

anivelar ▹ CONJUG 1a (VT) = **nivelar**

aniversario (SM) [*de un suceso*] anniversary; (= *cumpleaños*) birthday

anjá (EXCL) **1** (*Caribe, Méx**) (= *¡claro!*) of course!; (= *¡eso es!*) that's it!
2 (*Caribe*) (= *¡bravo!*) bravo!; (*reprobación*) come off it!*

Anjeo (SM) Anjou

Ankara (SF) Ankara

ano (SM) anus

anoche (ADV) yesterday evening, last night • **antes de ~** the night before last

anochecedor(a) (SM/F) late bird, *person who keeps late hours*

anochecer ▹ CONJUG 2d (VI) **1** (= *venir la noche*) to get dark
2 • **anochecimos en Toledo** we got to Toledo as night was falling
(SM) nightfall, dusk • **al ~** at nightfall, at dusk • **antes del ~** before nightfall, before it gets dark

anochecida (SF) nightfall, dusk

anodino (ADJ) **1** (*Med*) anodyne (*frm*); (= *inocuo*) anodyne, harmless, inoffensive
2 [*persona*] dull
(SM) (*Med*) anodyne

ánodo (SM) anode

anomalía (SF) anomaly

anómalo (ADJ) anomalous

anona (SF) (*CAm, Méx*) scaly custard apple, sweetsop

anonadación (SF), **anonadamiento** (SM)
1 (= *asombro*) amazement, astonishment
2 (= *abatimiento*) discouragement; (= *humillación*) humiliation
3 (= *destrucción*) annihilation, destruction; (= *derrota*) crushing

anonadado (ADJ) stunned • **me quedé ~ ante un paisaje tan bello** I was stunned *o* left speechless by the beauty of the countryside • **vuestras opiniones me tienen ~** your opinions leave me utterly perplexed

anonadador (ADJ) crushing, overwhelming

anonadar ▹ CONJUG 1a (VT) to stun • **me anonadó su descaro** I was stunned *o* left speechless by her cheek
(VPR) **anonadarse 1** (= *ser derrotado*) to be crushed, be overwhelmed
2 (= *abatirse*) to get discouraged

anónimamente (ADV) anonymously

anonimato (SM), **anonimia** (SF) anonymity • **mantenerse en el ~** to remain anonymous

anónimo (ADJ) anonymous; ▹ **sociedad**
(SM) **1** (= *anonimato*) anonymity • **conservar *o* guardar el ~** to remain anonymous
2 (= *persona*) anonymous person
3 (= *carta*) anonymous letter; (= *carta maliciosa*) poison-pen letter; (= *documento*) anonymous document; (= *obra literaria*) unsigned literary work

anorak (SM) anorak

anorexia (SF) anorexia ▸ **anorexia nerviosa** anorexia nervosa

anoréxico/a (ADJ) anorexic
(SM/F) anorexic

anormal (ADJ) **1** (= *no normal*) abnormal
2* (= *imbécil*) silly, cretinous

anormalidad (SF) abnormality

anormalmente (ADV) abnormally, unusually

anotación (SF) **1** (= *nota*) (*por escrito*) note, annotation (*frm*); (*al hablar*) observation • **un manuscrito con anotaciones a mano de Cervantes** a manuscript with hand-written notes of Cervantes ▸ **anotación al margen** marginal note, note in the margin
▸ **anotación en cuenta** (*Com*) account entry
2 (= *acto*) • **era el encargado de la ~ de todos los resultados** he was in charge of noting down the results
3 (*Baloncesto*) point

anotador(a) (SM/F) **1** (*Literat*) annotator
2 (*Dep*) scorer
(SM) (*LAm*) scorecard

anotar ▹ CONJUG 1a (VT) **1** (= *apuntar*) **a** (*en cuaderno*) to make a note of, note down; (*en lista, tabla*) to enter, record • **anota la cifra total** make a note of *o* note down the total figure • **anotó la matrícula del coche** he took down the registration number of the car • **anota los resultados en las casillas** enter the results in the boxes • **se han olvidado de ~ los intereses** they have forgotten to record the interest rates
b (*Estadística*) [+ *velocidad, tiempo*] to log
2 (*esp Cono Sur*) (= *inscribir*) enrol, enroll (*EEUU*) • **¿me ~on en el registro?** have you written me down in the register?
• **anótame para la excursión** put me down for the outing
3 (*Literat*) [+ *texto, libro*] to annotate
4 (*Dep*) [+ *punto*] to score
(VPR) **anotarse 1** (*Dep*) [+ *punto, gol*] to score • **~se una victoria** to win a victory, gain a victory • MODISMO: • **¡anótate un tanto!*** give yourself a pat on the back!*
2 (*Econ*) [+ *precio*] to fetch; [+ *operación, puntos*] to register • **la serigrafía de Warhol se anotó 440.000 dólares** the Warhol screen print fetched 440,000 dollars • **el mercado bursátil se anotó 279,65 puntos** the stock market registered 279.65 points
3 (*esp Cono Sur*) (= *inscribirse*) to enrol, enroll (*EEUU*) • **—estamos organizando un viaje —¡yo me anoto!** "we're organizing a trip" — "count me in! *o* I'll come too!" • **—Ana va a ayudarnos —nosotros también nos anotamos** "Ana is going to help us" — "we'll help too"

anovulatorio (SM) (= *inhibidor*) anovulant; (= *píldora*) contraceptive pill

ANPE (SF ABR) = **Asociación Nacional del Profesorado Estatal**

anquilosado (ADJ) **1** [*músculo, miembro*] stiff; (*Med*) ankylosed (*frm*)
2 [*pensamiento, sociedad*] stagnant

anquilosamiento (SM), **anquilosis** (SF)
1 [*de músculo, pierna*] stiffness; (*Med*) ankylosis
2 [*de pensamiento, sociedad*] stagnation

anquilosar ▹ CONJUG 1a (VT) **1** [+ *músculo, pierna*] to get stiff; (*Med*) to ankylose (*frm*)
2 (= *detener*) to paralyze
(VI) (*Aut, Mec*) to seize up
(VPR) **anquilosarse** to stagnate

anquilostoma (SM) hookworm

ánsar (SM) goose

ansarino (SM) gosling

Anselmo (SM) Anselm

ansia (SF) **1** (= *anhelo*) yearning, longing • **~ de libertad/amor** yearning *o* longing for freedom/love • **~ de poder/riqueza/conocimiento/aventura** thirst for power/wealth/knowledge/adventure • **el ~ de superación** the will to outdo oneself • **el ~ de vivir la ayudó a recuperarse** the will to live helped her to recover • **el ~ de placeres** the desire for pleasure • **tenía ~s de verla** he was yearning *o* longing to see her • **comer con ~** to eat ravenously • **beber con ~** to drink thirstily • **besarse con ~** to kiss hungrily • **mirar con ~ a algn** to look longingly at sb
2 (= *ansiedad*) anxiety, worry; (= *angustia*) anguish
3 ansias (= *náuseas*) nausea (*sing*) • **tener ~s** to feel sick *o* nauseous

ansiado (ADJ) longed-for • **el momento tan ~** the long-awaited moment

ansiar ▹ CONJUG 1b (VT) to long for, yearn for • **~ hacer algo** to long to do sth, yearn to do sth
(VI) • **~ por algn** to be madly in love with sb

ansiedad (SF) **1** (= *preocupación*) anxiety, worry
2 (*Med*) anxiety, nervous tension

ansina (ADV) (*LAm*) = **así**

ansiolítico (ADJ) sedative
(SM) sedative, tranquillizer

ansiosamente (ADV) anxiously

ansioso (ADJ) **1** (= *preocupado*) anxious, worried; (= *deseoso*) eager, solicitous • **esperábamos ~s** we waited anxiously • **~ de *o* por algo** greedy for sth
2 (*Med*) (= *tenso*) anxious, suffering from nervous tension; (= *bascoso*) sick, queasy

anta (SF) **1** (= *ciervo*) elk, moose
2 (*LAm*) (= *danta*) tapir

antagónico (ADJ) antagonistic; (= *opuesto*) opposing

antagonismo (SM) antagonism

antagonista (SMF) antagonist

antagonístico (ADJ) = **antagónico**

antagonizar ▹ CONJUG 1f (VT) to antagonize

antañazo††* (ADV) a long time ago

antaño (*liter*) (ADV) long ago, in years past, in years gone by

antañón†* (ADJ) ancient, very old, of long ago

antañoso (ADJ) (*And*) ancient, very old

antara (SF) (*And*) Indian flute
antarca (ADV) (*And, Cono Sur*) on one's back • **caerse ~** to fall flat on one's back
antártico (ADJ) Antarctic
(SM) • **el Antártico** the Antarctic
Antártida (SF) Antarctica
ante[1] (SM) **1** (*Zool*) (= *ciervo*) elk, moose; (= *búfalo*) buffalo; (*Méx*) (= *tapir*) tapir
2 (= *piel*) suede
3 (*Méx*) (= *dulce*) macaroon
ante[2] (PREP) **1** (= *en presencia de*) [+ *persona*] before
2 (= *enfrentado a*) [+ *peligro*] in the face of, faced with; [+ *dificultad, duda*] faced with • **~ esta posibilidad** in view of this possibility • **~ tantas posibilidades** faced with so many possibilities • **estamos ~ un gran porvenir** we have a great future before us
3 • **~ todo** above all • **~ todo hay que recordar que ...** first of all let's remember that ...
-ante ▷ Aspects of Word Formation in Spanish 2
ante... (PREF) ante...
anteado (ADJ) buff-coloured, buff-colored (EEUU), fawn
anteanoche (ADV) the night before last
anteayer (ADV) the day before yesterday
antebrazo (SM) forearm
anteburro (SM) (*LAm*) tapir
antecámara (SF) (*Arquit*) anteroom, antechamber; (= *sala de espera*) waiting room; (*en parlamento*) lobby
antecedente (ADJ) previous, preceding • **visto lo ~** in view of the foregoing
(SM) **1** (*Mat, Fil, Gram*) antecedent
2 antecedentes (= *historial*) record (*sing*), history (*sing*); [*de enfermedad*] history (*sing*) • **tener buenos ~s** to have a good record • **no tener ~s** to have a clean record • **un hombre sin ~s** a man with a clean record • **en esta familia no hay ~s de esta dolencia** this family doesn't have a history of this complaint • **¿cuáles son sus ~s?** what's his background? • **estar en ~s** to be well informed • **poner a algn en ~s** to put sb in the picture ▸ **antecedentes delictivos, antecedentes penales, antecedentes policiales** criminal record
anteceder ▷ CONJUG 2a (VT) to precede, go before
antecesor(a) (ADJ) preceding, former
(SM/F) (*en cargo etc*) predecessor; (= *antepasado*) ancestor, forebear (*frm*)
antecocina (SF) scullery
antecomedor (SM) (*LAm*) *room adjoining the dining room*
antedatar ▷ CONJUG 1a (VT) to antedate
antedicho (ADJ) aforesaid, aforementioned
antediluviano (ADJ) antediluvian
anteiglesia (SF) (*Rel*) porch
antejuela (SF) (*CAm*) = **lentejuela**
antelación (SF) • **con ~** in advance, beforehand • **con mucha ~** long in advance, long beforehand
antelina (SF) suede
antellevar ▷ CONJUG 1a (VT) (*Méx*) to run over, knock down
antellevón (SM) (*Méx*) accident
antemano • **de ~** (ADV) in advance, beforehand
antena (SF) **1** (*Zool*) feeler, antenna • **tener ~ para** (= *intuición*) to have a feeling for, have a nose for
2 (*Náut*) lateen yard
3 (*Radio, TV, Telec*) aerial, antenna • **estar en ~** to be on the air • **permanecer en ~** to stay on the air • **salir en ~** to go out on the air, be broadcast • **el programa es el sexto en duración en ~** the programme is the sixth longest-running on TV ▸ **antena colectiva** communal aerial ▸ **antena de telefonía móvil** mobile-phone mast (*Brit*), cell site (*EEUU*), cell tower (*EEUU*) ▸ **antena de televisión** television aerial ▸ **antena direccional, antena dirigida** directional aerial ▸ **antena emisora** transmitting aerial ▸ **antena encerrada** built-in aerial ▸ **antena interior** indoor aerial ▸ **antena parabólica** satellite dish, dish antenna (*EEUU*) ▸ **antena receptora** receiving aerial
4 antenas* (= *oídos*) ears
antenatal (ADJ) antenatal, prenatal
antenombre (SM) title
anteojera (SF) **1**† spectacle case
2 anteojeras [*de caballo*] blinkers, blinders (*EEUU*)
anteojero/a† (SM/F) spectacle maker, optician
anteojo (SM) **1** (= *lente*) spyglass, telescope, small telescope ▸ **anteojo de larga vista** telescope
2 anteojos (*esp LAm*) (= *gafas*) glasses, spectacles, eyeglasses (*EEUU*); (*Aut, Téc etc*) goggles; (= *prismáticos*) binoculars; (*para la ópera*) opera glasses; [*de caballo*] blinkers, blinders (*EEUU*) ▸ **anteojos ahumados** smoked glasses ▸ **anteojos de concha** horn-rimmed spectacles ▸ **anteojos de sol, anteojos para el sol** sunglasses
antepagar ▷ CONJUG 1h (VT) to prepay
antepasado/a (ADJ) previous, before last
(SM/F) ancestor, forbear (*frm*) • **~s** ancestors
antepatio (SM) forecourt
antepecho (SM) [*de puente*] rail, parapet; [*de ventana*] ledge, sill; (*Mil*) parapet, breastwork
antepenúltimo (ADJ) last but two, antepenultimate (*frm*)
anteponer ▷ CONJUG 2q (VT) **1** (*lit*) to place in front (a of)
2 (*fig*) (= *preferir*) to prefer (a to)
(VPR) **anteponerse** to be in front (a of)
anteportal (SM) porch
anteproyecto (SM) preliminary plan ▸ **anteproyecto de ley** draft bill
antepuerto (SM) outer harbour *o* (*EEUU*) harbor
antepuesto (ADJ) preceding, coming before
antequerano/a (ADJ) of/from Antequera
(SM/F) native/inhabitant of Antequera • **los ~s** the people of Antequera
antera (SF) anther
anterior (ADJ) **1** (*en el espacio*) [*parte*] front • **el motor está en la parte ~ del coche** the engine is in the front (part) of the car • **las patas ~es** the forelegs
2 (*en una sucesión*) [*página, párrafo*] previous, preceding • **el capítulo ~** the previous *o* preceding chapter • **el capítulo ~ a este** the chapter before this one • **se subió en la parada ~** he got on at the stop before *o* at the previous stop • **retiro lo ~** I take back what I just said
3 (*en el tiempo*) previous • **en ~es ocasiones** on previous occasions • **el día ~** the day before • **un texto ~ a 1140** a text dating from before 1140 • **las horas ~es a la operación** the hours before the operation • **la discusión ~ al asesinato** the discussion prior to the killing • **los enfrentamientos ~es a la guerra** the clashes leading up to *o* preceding the war • **eso fue muy ~ a tu llegada** that was a long time before you arrived
4 (*Ling*) anterior
anterioridad (SF) priority • **con ~** previously, beforehand • **con ~ a esto** prior to this, before this
anteriormente (ADV) previously, before • **~, lo hacíamos así** we used to do it like this
antes (ADJ) before • **llame el día ~ para pedir cita** call the day before for an appointment • **ocurrió unos momentos ~** it happened a few moments earlier *o* before • **el tren ha llegado una hora ~** the train has arrived an hour early
(ADV) **1** (*en el tiempo*) **a** (*con relación a otro acontecimiento*) • **yo llegué ~** I arrived first • **el edificio que habían comenzado dos años ~** the building that had been started two years before *o* previously • **no te vayas sin ~ consultarle** don't go without *o* before consulting her first, don't go without consulting her beforehand, don't go until you've consulted her • **lo vio ~ que yo** he saw it first *o* before I did *o* before me • **~ de algo** before sth • **~ de 1900** before 1900 • **la cena estará lista para ~ de las nueve** dinner will be ready by *o* before nine • **una semana ~ de la firma del contrato** a week before *o* prior to (*más frm*) signing the contract • **~ de anoche** the night before last • **~ de ayer** the day before yesterday • **~ de terminado el discurso** before the speech was over • **~ de una semana no vamos a saber nada** we won't know anything for a week • **el año 27 ~ de Cristo** 27 BC, 27 before Christ • **~ de hacer algo** before doing sth • **~ de salir del coche, asegúrese de que están las ventanillas cerradas** before you get *o* before getting out of the car, make sure that the windows are closed • **mucho ~ de algo** long before sth • **mucho ~ de conocerte** a long time before I met you *o* meeting you, long before I met you *o* meeting you (*más frm*) • **~ de *o* que nada** (*en el tiempo*) first of all; (*indicando preferencia*) above all • **~ de nada dejad que me presente** first of all, allow me to introduce myself • **~ que nada, hay que mantener la calma** above all, we must keep calm • **somos, ~ que nada, demócratas** we are first and foremost democrats • **poco ~ de algo** just *o* shortly before sth • **~ de que** (+ *subjun*) before • **~ de que te vayas** before you go • **esperamos lograrlo ~ de que termine la década** we hope to achieve this before the end of the decade
b (*en el pasado*) • **~ fumaba un paquete de tabaco al día** before, I smoked a packet of cigarettes a day, I used to smoke a packet of cigarettes a day • **~ no pasaban estas cosas** these things didn't use to happen before *o* in the past • **de ~**: • **nuestra casa de ~** our old house, our previous house • **ya no tienen la alegría de ~** they don't have the joie de vivre they used to have • **ya no soy el mismo de ~** I'm not the same person I was *o* I used to be • **fue una boda de las de ~** it was an old-style wedding • **ya no se hacen películas como las de ~** they don't make films like they used to *o* like they did in the old days
c (= *hasta ahora*) before, before now • **nunca ~ he tenido problemas** I've never had any problems before
d (= *más temprano*) earlier • **no he podido venir ~** I couldn't come any earlier • **los viernes salimos un poco ~** on Fridays we leave a little earlier • **no te he podido llamar ~** I couldn't call you sooner *o* earlier • **cuanto ~** as soon as possible • **cuanto ~ mejor** the sooner the better • **lo ~ posible** as soon as possible
e (= *más joven*) at a younger age, at an earlier age • **cada vez se casan los hijos ~** kids get married at a younger *o* an earlier age these days
2 (*en el espacio*) before • **tres páginas ~** three pages before • **~ de algo** before sth • **la calle que hay ~ del semáforo** the street before the traffic lights

a

(CONJ) (*indicando preferencia*) sooner, rather • **preferimos ir en tren ~ que en avión** we prefer to go by train rather than by plane • **no cederemos: ~ gastamos todo nuestro dinero** we shall never give up: we would rather *o* sooner spend all our money • **~ bien** • **~ al contrario** but rather • **~ no** (*Chile, Méx*) just as well, luckily • **vi lo furiosa que estaba, ~ no te pegó** I saw how angry she was, just as well *o* luckily she didn't hit you • **~ que hacer algo** rather than doing sth • **~ que irme a la India, preferiría viajar por Europa** rather than going to India, I'd prefer to travel around Europe

antesala (SF) (= *habitación*) anteroom, antechamber • **en la ~ de** (= *al borde de*) on the verge of, on the threshold of • MODISMO: • **hacer ~** (= *esperar*) to wait to go in (*to see sb/do sth*); (= *pasar el tiempo*) to cool one's heels

antesalazo (SM) (*Méx*) long wait (*before admission*)

antetítulo (SM) introductory heading, prefatory heading

anteúltimo (ADJ) (*Cono Sur*) penultimate

anti... (PREF) anti...

antiabortista (ADJ) • **campaña ~** anti-abortion campaign
(SMF) anti-abortionist

antiaborto (ADJ INV) anti-abortion, pro-life

antiácaros (ADJ) anti-mite (*antes de s*)

antiácido (ADJ), (SM) antacid

antiadherencia (SF) non-stick properties (*pl*) • **prueba ~** non-stick test

antiadherente (ADJ) non-stick

antiaéreo (ADJ) anti-aircraft
(SM) (*LAm*) anti-aircraft gun

antialcohólico/a (ADJ) (*Med*) • **centro ~** detoxification unit • **grupo ~** alcoholics anonymous
(SM/F) teetotaller

antialérgico (ADJ) anti-allergic

antiamericano (ADJ) anti-American

antiapartheid (ADJ) anti-apartheid

antiarrugas (ADJ INV) anti-wrinkle, wrinkle (*antes de s*)

antiatómico (ADJ) • **refugio ~** fall-out shelter

antiatraco (ADJ INV), **antiatracos** (ADJ INV) • **dispositivo ~** anti-theft device, security device

antibacteriano (ADJ), (SM) antibacterial

antibalas (ADJ INV) bullet-proof

antibalístico (ADJ) antiballistic

antibelicista (ADJ) anti-war, pacifist
(SMF) pacifist

antibiótico (ADJ), (SM) antibiotic

antibloqueo (SM) • **sistema de ~ de frenos** ABS braking system, anti-lock braking system

antibombas (ADJ INV) • **refugio ~** bomb shelter

anticalcáreo (ADJ) • **dispositivo ~** anti-scaling device

anticanceroso (ADJ) anti-cancer, cancer (*antes de s*) • **tratamiento ~** cancer treatment

anticarro (ADJ INV) anti-tank

anticaspa (ADJ INV) dandruff (*antes de s*), anti-dandruff

anticelulítico (ADJ) anti-cellulite, cellulite (*antes de s*)

antichoque (ADJ INV), **antichoques** (ADJ INV) • **panel ~** shock-resistant panel

anticiclón (SM) anticyclone

anticiclonal (ADJ), **anticiclónico** (ADJ) anticyclonic

anticipación (SF) (= *adelanto*) • **hacer algo con ~** to do sth in good time • **llegar con ~** to arrive early, arrive in good time • **llegar con diez minutos de ~** to come ten minutes early • **reservar con ~** to book in advance, book early

anticipadamente (ADV) in advance, beforehand • **le doy las gracias ~** I thank you in advance

anticipado (ADJ) (= *con antelación*) early • **pago ~** advance payment • **gracias anticipadas** thanks in advance • **por ~** in advance, beforehand

anticipar ▷ CONJUG 1a (VT) **1** [+ *fecha, acontecimiento*] to bring forward • **~on las vacaciones** they took their holiday early • **no anticipemos los acontecimientos** let's not cross our bridges before we come to them, let's not get ahead of ourselves
2 [+ *factura etc*] to pay in advance; [+ *dinero*] to advance, lend, loan
3 • **~ algo con placer** (= *esperar*) to look forward to sth • **~ las gracias a algn** (= *adelantar*) to thank sb in advance
4 (= *prever*) to anticipate, foresee • **~ que ...** to anticipate that ...
(VPR) **anticiparse 1** [*acontecimiento*] to take place early
2 • **~se a un acontecimiento** to anticipate an event • **~se a algn** to beat sb to it • **usted se ha anticipado a mis deseos** you have anticipated my wishes • **~se a hacer algo** to do sth ahead of time, do sth before the proper time • **~se a una época** to be ahead of one's time

anticipo (SM) **1** [*de dinero*] advance • **pedir un ~** to ask for an advance
2 • **ser el ~ de algo** to be a foretaste of sth • **esto es solo un ~** this is just a foretaste, this is just a taste of what's to come
3 (*Jur*) retaining fee

anticlerical (ADJ), (SMF) anticlerical

anticlericalismo (SM) anticlericalism

anticlímax (SM INV) anticlimax

anticlinal (SM) **1** (*Geol*) anticline
2 (*LAm*) watershed

anticoagulante (ADJ), (SM) anticoagulant

anticoba (SF) brutal frankness, outspokenness

anticolesterol (ADJ) cholesterol-free, low in cholesterol

anticomunista (ADJ), (SMF) anti-communist

anticoncepción (SF) contraception, birth-control

anticoncepcional (ADJ) birth-control (*antes de s*), contraceptive

anticoncepcionismo (SM) contraception, birth control

anticonceptivo (ADJ) birth-control (*antes de s*), contraceptive • **métodos ~s** methods of birth control • **píldora anticonceptiva** contraceptive pill
(SM) contraceptive

anticongelante (ADJ), (SM) antifreeze

anticonstitucional (ADJ) unconstitutional

anticonstitucionalidad (SF) unconstitutionality

anticontaminante (ADJ) anti-pollution

anticorrosivo (ADJ) anticorrosive, antirust

anticristo (SM) Antichrist

anticuado (ADJ) [*maquinaria, infraestructura, tecnología*] antiquated; [*moda*] old-fashioned, out-of-date; [*técnica*] obsolete • **quedarse ~** to go out of date

anticuario/a (ADJ) antiquarian
(SM/F) (= *comerciante*) antique dealer; (= *coleccionista*) antiquarian, antiquary

anticuarse ▷ CONJUG 1d (VPR) (*Ling etc*) to become antiquated, go out of date; [*técnica*] to become obsolete

anticucho (SM) (*Perú, Chile*) kebab

anticuerpo (SM) antibody

antidemocráticamente (ADV) undemocratically

antidemocrático (ADJ) undemocratic

antideportivo (ADJ) unsporting, unsportsmanlike

antidepresivo (ADJ) antidepressant
(SM) antidepressant, antidepressant drug

antiderrapante (ADJ) non-skid

antideslizante (ADJ) (*Aut*) non-skid; [*piso*] non-slip
(SM) non-skid tyre, non-skid tire (*EEUU*)

antideslumbrante (ADJ) anti-glare

antidetonante (ADJ) anti-knock

antidisturbios (ADJ INV) • **policía ~** riot police, riot control police
(SMF) member of riot police

antidóping (ADJ INV), **antidopaje** (ADJ INV) • **control ~** drugs test, check for drugs

antídoto (SM) antidote (**contra** for, to)

antidroga (ADJ INV) • **brigada ~** drug squad • **campaña ~** anti-drug campaign • **tratamiento ~** treatment for drug addiction

antidúmping (ADJ INV) • **medidas ~** anti-dumping measures

antiecológico (ADJ) • **producto ~** product damaging to the environment, environmentally unsafe product

antieconómico (ADJ) uneconomic, uneconomical

antienvejecimiento (ADJ INV) anti-ageing

antier (ADV) (*LAm*) = **anteayer**

antiestático (ADJ) antistatic

antiestético (ADJ) unsightly, ugly

antiestrés (ADJ INV) anti-stress, stress (*antes de s*)

antifascismo (SM) anti-fascism

antifascista (ADJ), (SMF) anti-fascist

antifatiga (ADJ INV) • **píldora ~** anti-fatigue pill, pep pill*

antifaz (SM) **1** (= *máscara*) mask
2‡ (= *preservativo*) condom, johnny*, rubber (*EEUU**)

antifeminismo (SM) anti-feminism

antifeminista (ADJ), (SMF) anti-feminist

antífona (SF) antiphony

antifranquismo (SM) opposition to Franco

antifranquista (ADJ) anti-Franco
(SMF) opponent of Franco, person opposed to Franco

antifraude (ADJ INV) • **acción ~** action to combat fraud

antifriccional (ADJ) antifriction

antifrís (SM) (*LAm*) antifreeze

antifuego (ADJ INV) [*puerta, barrera*] fire (*antes de s*), fireproof • **lucha ~** firefighting

antigás (ADJ) • **careta ~** gas mask

antígeno (SM) antigen

antiglobalización (SF) anti-globalization • **grupo ~** anti-globalization group

antiglobalizador(a) (ADJ) anti-globalization (*antes de s*)

antigolpes (ADJ INV) shockproof

Antígona (SF) Antigone

antigripal (ADJ INV) • **vacuna ~** flu vaccine

antigualla (SF) (= *objeto*) old thing, relic; (= *cuento*) old story; (= *individuo*) has-been • **~s** old junk (*sing*)

antiguamente (ADV) in the past, in the old days • **~ las cosas eran de otra manera** things were different in the past *o* in the old days • **pongo en duda lo que ~ creía** now I'm questioning what I once thought

antigüedad (SF) **1** (= *época*) antiquity • **los artistas de la ~** the artists of antiquity, the artists of the ancient world • **alta ~** • **remota ~** high antiquity • **de toda ~** from time immemorial
2 (= *edad*) antiquity, age; (*en empleo*) seniority • **la fábrica tiene una ~ de 200 años** the factory has been going *o* in existence for

200 years
3 (= *objeto*) antique • **~es** antiques • **tienda de ~es** antique shop
antiguerra ADJ INV anti-war
antiguo/a ADJ **1** (= *viejo*) [*ciudad, costumbre*] old; [*coche*] vintage; [*mueble, objeto, libro*] antique • **las antiguas tradiciones** old traditions • **el Antiguo Testamento** the Old Testament • **rallies de coches ~s** vintage car rallies • **a la antigua (usanza)** in the old-fashioned way • **cocinan a la antigua usanza** they cook in the old style *o* in the old-fashioned way • **de** *o* **desde ~** from time immemorial • **una medicina usada desde muy ~** a medicine that has been used from time immemorial • **nuestra amistad viene de ~** our friendship dates back a long way • **en lo ~** in olden days (*liter*), in ancient times; ▹ **chapado, música**
2 (*Hist*) [*civilización, restos*] ancient • **la antigua Grecia** ancient Greece • **el palacio árabe más ~** the oldest Arab palace, the most ancient Arab palace • **Antiguo Régimen** ancien régime; ▹ **edad**
3 (= *anterior*) old, former • **la antigua capilla, ahora sala de exposiciones** the old *o* former chapel, now an exhibition hall • **un ~ novio** an old boyfriend, an ex-boyfriend • **mi ~ jefe** my former boss, my ex-boss • **la antigua Yugoslavia** the former Yugoslavia • **más ~** [*cliente, socio*] longest-standing; [*empleado, prisionero*] longest-serving • **el socio más ~** the most senior member, the longest-standing member, the oldest member • **es más ~ que yo en el club** he has been in the club longer than me; ▹ **alumno**
4 (= *anticuado*) [*traje, estilo, persona*] old-fashioned; [*mentalidad*] outdated • **lleva un peinado muy ~** she has a very old-fashioned hair style
SM/F **1** (= *anticuado*) • **tu madre es una antigua** your mother is really old-fashioned, your mother is a real fuddy-duddy*
2 (= *veterano*) • **el más ~** the oldest one • **los más ~s tienen derecho a votar primero** the oldest are entitled to vote first
3 (*Hist*) • **los ~s** the ancients
antihéroe SM antihero
antihigiénico ADJ unhygienic, insanitary
antihistamínico ADJ, SM antihistamine
antihumano ADJ inhuman
antiimperialismo SM anti-imperialism
antiimperialista ADJ, SMF anti-imperialist
antiincendios ADJ INV • **equipo ~** fire-fighting team • **servicio ~** fire-fighting services
antiinflacionista ADJ anti-inflationary
antiinflamatorio ADJ, SM anti-inflammatory
antillanismo SM *word or phrase peculiar to the Antilles*
antillano/a ADJ of/from the Antilles, West Indian
SM/F native/inhabitant of the Antilles, West Indian • **los ~s** the people of the Antilles, the West Indians
Antillas SFPL Antilles, West Indies • **el mar de las ~** the Caribbean, the Caribbean Sea
antilogaritmo SM antilogarithm
antilógico ADJ illogical
antílope SM antelope
antimacasar SM antimacassar
antimanchas ADJ INV • **superficie ~** stain-resistant surface
antimateria SF antimatter
antimilitarismo SM antimilitarism
antimilitarista ADJ, SMF antimilitarist
antimisil ADJ antimissile • **misil ~** antimissile missile
SM antimissile
antimonio SM antimony
antimonopolio ADJ INV, **antimonopolios** ADJ INV • **ley ~** anti-trust law
antimosquitos ADJ INV mosquito (*antes de s*) • **red ~** mosquito net
antinacional ADJ unpatriotic
antinatural ADJ unnatural
antiniebla ADJ INV • **faros ~** fog lamps
antinomia SF antinomy (*frm*), conflict of authority
antinuclear ADJ antinuclear
Antioquía SF Antioch
antioxidante ADJ antioxidant, anti-rust
SM antioxidant
antipalúdico ADJ antimalarial
antipara SF screen
antiparabólico* ADJ (*Caribe*) wild, over the top
antiparasitario ADJ antiparasitic
SM antiparasitic drug
antiparras* SFPL glasses, eyeglasses (*EEUU*), specs*
antipatía SF (= *sentimiento*) antipathy (**hacia** towards, **entre** between), dislike (**hacia** for); (= *actitud*) unfriendliness (**hacia** towards)
antipático ADJ unpleasant, disagreeable • **es un chico de lo más ~** he's a horrible *o* a thoroughly unpleasant boy • **me es muy ~** I don't like him at all • **en un ambiente ~** in an unfriendly environment, in an uncongenial atmosphere
antipatizar ▹ CONJUG 1f VI (*LAm*) to feel unfriendly • **~ con algn** to dislike sb
antipatriótico ADJ unpatriotic
antiperras SFPL (*And*) half-moon glasses, half-moon spectacles
antípodas SFPL antipodes
antipolilla ADJ INV mothproof
antiproteccionista ADJ anti-protectionist, free-trade (*antes de s*)
antiproyectil ADJ INV antimissile
antiquísimo ADJ ancient
antiquista (*Méx*) ADJ antiquarian
SMF antiquarian, antique dealer
antirrábico ADJ • **vacuna antirrábica** anti-rabies vaccine
antirracista ADJ, SMF anti-racist
antirreflectante ADJ anti-glare
antirreglamentariamente ADV unlawfully, illegally
antirreglamentario ADJ (= *ilegal*) unlawful, illegal; (*Dep*) foul
antirresbaladizo ADJ non-skid
antirretroviral ADJ anti-retroviral
SM anti-retroviral drug
antirrino SM antirrhinum
antirrobo ADJ INV • **sistema ~** anti-theft system
SM (*tb* **dispositivo antirrobo**) anti-theft device
antirruido ADJ INV • **sistema ~** noise-reduction system • **comisión ~** noise-abatement committee • **ley ~** noise-pollution law
antisemita ADJ anti-Semitic
SMF anti-Semite
antisemítico ADJ anti-Semitic
antisemitismo SM anti-Semitism
antiséptico ADJ, SM antiseptic
antisistema ADJ INV anti-capitalist
SMF INV anti-capitalist activist • **los ~** anti-capitalist activists
antisocial ADJ antisocial
antisubmarino ADJ anti-submarine
antisudoral (*LAm*) ADJ, SM deodorant
antitabaco ADJ INV • **campaña ~** anti-smoking campaign
antitabaquismo SM anti-smoking attitudes (*pl*)
antitabaquista ADJ anti-smoking
antitanque ADJ anti-tank
antitaurino ADJ anti-bullfighting
antiterrorismo SM counterterrorism
antiterrorista ADJ counterterrorist, antiterrorist (*antes de s*) • **Ley Antiterrorista** ≈ Prevention of Terrorism Act
antítesis SF INV antithesis
antitetánica SF anti-tetanus injection
antitético ADJ antithetic, antithetical
antitranspirante ADJ, SM anti-perspirant
antivaho ADJ INV • **dispositivo ~** demister, demisting device
antiviral ADJ, SM, **antivírico** ADJ, SM antiviral
antivirus SM INV antivirus
antiviviseccionista SMF antivivisectionist
antivuelco ADJ INV • **barra ~** anti-roll bar
antofagastino/a (*Cono Sur*) ADJ of/from Antofagasta
SM/F native/inhabitant of Antofagasta • **los ~s** the people of Antofagasta
antojadizo ADJ **1** (= *caprichoso*) • **es muy ~** he's always taking a fancy to something or other
2 (= *poco fiable*) unpredictable
antojado ADJ • **~ con** *o* **por** (= *con capricho de*) taken by, hankering after; [*mujer embarazada*] craving for
antojarse ▹ CONJUG 1a VPR **1** (= *apetecer*) • **antojársele a algn algo** to take a fancy to sth, want sth • **se me antoja una cervecita** I could go for a nice beer • **antojársele a algn hacer algo** to have a mind to do sth • **se le antojó ir al cine** he took it into his head to go to the cinema • **no se le antojó decir otra cosa** it didn't occur to him to say anything else • **no se me antoja ir** I don't feel like going
2 (= *parecer*) • **~ que** to imagine that • **se me antoja que no estará** I have the feeling that he won't be in • **¿cómo se le antoja esto?** how does this seem to you?
antojitos* SMPL (*Cono Sur*) (= *caramelos*) sweets, candy (*EEUU*); (*Méx*) (= *tapas*) snacks, nibbles
antojo SM **1** (= *capricho*) whim • **hacer a su ~** to do as one pleases • **cada uno a su ~** each to his own • MODISMO: • **no morirse de ~** (*Cono Sur*) to satisfy a whim
2 [*de embarazada*] craving • **tener ~s** to have cravings (*during pregnancy*)
3 (*Anat*) birthmark
antología SF (= *colección*) anthology; (*Arte*) retrospective • **un gol de ~** a goal for the history books, a goal that will go down in history
antológica SF (*Arte*) retrospective
antológico ADJ **1** (*Arte*) • **exposición antológica** retrospective
2 (= *destacado*) memorable • **un gol ~** a goal for the history books, a goal that will go down in history
antónimo SM antonym
Antonio SM Anthony
antonomasia SF antonomasia • **por ~** par excellence
antorcha SF **1** (= *tea*) torch ▸ **antorcha olímpica** • **la ~ olímpica** the Olympic torch
2 (= *guía*) mentor
antracita SF anthracite
ántrax SM anthrax
antro SM (= *cueva*) cavern; (= *local*) (*pey**) dive* ▸ **antro de corrupción** den of iniquity
antropocéntrico ADJ anthropocentric
antropofagia SF cannibalism
antropófago/a ADJ man-eating (*antes de s*), cannibalistic
SM/F cannibal • **~s** anthropophagi (*frm*), cannibals

a

antropoide ADJ, SMF anthropoid
antropoideo SM anthropoid
antropología SF anthropology
▸ **antropología social** social anthropology
antropológico ADJ anthropological
antropólogo/a SM/F anthropologist
antropomórfico ADJ anthropomorphic
antropomorfismo SM anthropomorphism
antruejo SM carnival (*three days before Lent*)
antucá SM (*Cono Sur*) sunshade, parasol
antuviada SF sudden blow, bump
antuvión* SM sudden blow, bump • **de ~** suddenly, unexpectedly
anual ADJ [*reunión, periodicidad*] yearly, annual; [*planta*] annual • **la cuota es de 100 euros ~es** the yearly *o* annual fee is 100 euros
anualidad SF **1** (*Econ*) annual payment ▸ **anualidad vitalicia** life annuity
2 (= *suceso*) annual occurrence
anualizado ADJ (*Econ*) annual
anualmente ADV annually, yearly
anuario SM (= *libro*) yearbook, annual; (= *guía*) directory ▸ **anuario militar** military list ▸ **anuario telefónico** telephone directory
anubarrado ADJ cloudy, overcast
anublar ▹ CONJUG 1a VT **1** [+ *cielo*] to cloud, cloud over; [+ *luz*] to obscure
2 [+ *planta*] to wither, dry up
VPR **anublarse 1** [*cielo*] to cloud over, become overcast
2 [*planta*] to wither, dry up
3 (= *desvanecerse*) to fade away
anudado ADJ knotted
anudar ▹ CONJUG 1a VT **1** (= *atar*) to knot, tie
2 [+ *cuento*] to resume, take up again
3 [+ *voz*] to choke, strangle
VPR **anudarse 1** [*cinta*] to get into knots
2 [*planta*] to remain stunted
3 • **se me anudó la voz (en la garganta)** I got a lump in my throat
anuencia SF consent
anuente ADJ consenting, consentient
anulación SF [*de contrato*] annulment, cancellation; [*de ley*] repeal
anular¹ ▹ CONJUG 1a VT **1** [+ *contrato*] to cancel, rescind; [+ *ley*] to repeal; [+ *decisión*] to override; [+ *matrimonio*] to annul
2 [+ *elecciones, resultado*] to declare null and void; [+ *gol, tanto*] to disallow • **han anulado la votación por irregularidad** they have declared the vote null and void because of irregularities
3 [+ *cita, viaje, evento*] to cancel • **~on el partido por causa de la lluvia** they cancelled the match because of the rain
4 [+ *cheque*] to cancel
5 [+ *efecto*] to cancel out, destroy
6 (*Mat*) to cancel out
7 [+ *persona*] to overshadow • **su potente carácter anula a sus amigos** her strong personality overshadows her friends
8 (*frm*) (= *incapacitar*) to deprive of authority, remove from office
VPR **anularse 1** (= *amilanarse*) to fade into the background • **se anula ante su padre** he fades into the background when his father is there
2 (= *neutralizarse*) • **los dos campos magnéticos se anulan** the two magnetic fields cancel each other out • **las dos sustancias se anulan mutuamente** the two substances neutralize each other
anular² ADJ ring-shaped, annular • **dedo ~** ring finger
SM ring finger
anunciación SF announcement
• **Anunciación** (*Rel*) Annunciation
anunciador(a) SM/F (*Méx*) (*Radio, TV*) announcer; (*Teat*) compere
anunciante SMF advertiser
anunciar ▹ CONJUG 1b VT **1** (= *hacer público*) to announce • **han anunciado la devaluación del euro** they have announced the devaluation of the euro • **el ministro anunció su dimisión** the minister announced that he was resigning • **la princesa anunció que se casaba** the princess announced that she was getting married • **anunciamos nuestra oposición a las privatizaciones** we declared our opposition to privatization
2 (= *convocar*) to call • **han anunciado una rueda de prensa para hoy** they have called a press conference for today • **el gobierno ~á hoy la convocatoria de elecciones** the government will call elections today
3 (*Com*) to advertise
4 (= *augurar*) • **no nos anuncia nada bueno** it is not a good sign, it bodes ill for us • **este viento anuncia tormenta** this wind means there is a storm coming • **el pronóstico del tiempo anuncia nevadas** they're forecasting snow, the weather forecast says there will be snow
5 (*frm*) (*a una visita*) to announce • **el mayordomo anunció a la Duquesa de Villahermosa** the butler announced the Duchess of Villahermosa • **¿a quién debo ~?** who shall I say it is?, what name should I say?
VPR **anunciarse 1** (*Com*) to advertise
2 (= *augurarse*) • **el festival se anuncia animado** it promises to be *o* looks like being a lively festival • **¿cómo se anuncia la cosecha este año?** how's the harvest looking this year?
anuncio SM **1** (*Com*) (*en un periódico*) advertisement, advert, ad*; (*en TV, radio*) advertisement, advert, commercial; (= *cartel*) poster • **poner un ~ en un periódico** to put an advertisement *o* advert *o* ad* in a newspaper • **"prohibido fijar** *o* **pegar anuncios"** "post *o* stick no bills" • **hombre ~** sandwich-board man ▸ **anuncio publicitario** advertisement, advert, commercial ▸ **anuncios clasificados** classified ads*, classified advertisements, classifieds ▸ **anuncios de relax** personal services ads ▸ **anuncios por palabras** classified ads, small ads*; ▹ **tablón**
2 (= *notificación*) announcement • **el ~ de su muerte causó mucha tristeza** the announcement of her death caused great sadness • **hoy se hará el ~ de su boda** their wedding will be announced today • **un ~ de bomba** a bomb warning
3 (= *presagio*) omen, sign • **fue un ~ de las desgracias futuras** it was an omen *o* a sign of the misfortunes to come • **es ~ de un futuro mejor** it heralds a better future • **esos nubarrones son ~ de tormenta** those black clouds mean there is a storm coming
anuo ADJ (*frm*) annual
anverso SM obverse
anzuelo SM (*para pescar*) fish hook; (= *aliciente*) bait, lure • **echar el ~** to offer a bait, offer an inducement • MODISMOS: • **picar en el ~** • **tragarse el ~** to swallow the bait
añada SF **1** (= *año*) year, season
2 (= *trozo de campo*) piece of field, strip
añadido ADJ (= *que se agrega*) added; (= *adicional*) additional, extra • **lo ~** what is added
SM **1** (*Tip*) addition
2 (= *pelo*) hairpiece
añadidura SF (= *lo que se agrega*) addition; (*Com*) extra • **dar algo de ~** to give something extra • **con algo de ~** with sth into the bargain • **por ~** in addition, on top of that
añadir ▹ CONJUG 3a VT **1** (= *agregar*) to add (a to)
2 [+ *encanto, interés*] to add, lend
añagaza SF (*Caza*) lure, decoy; (= *ardid*) ruse
añal ADJ **1** [*suceso*] yearly, annual
2 (*Agr*) year-old
SM yearling
añangá SM (*Cono Sur*) the devil
añango (*And*) ADJ [*niño*] sickly
SM small portion
añañay* EXCL (*Cono Sur*) great!*, super!*
añapar ▹ CONJUG 1a VT (*LAm*) to smash to bits
añar SM (*LAm*) • **hace ~es que ...** it's ages since ...
añascar ▹ CONJUG 1g VT to scrape together, get together bit by bit
añaz SM (*And*) skunk
añeja* SF (*Caribe*) old lady*, mum*
añejar ▹ CONJUG 1a VT to age
VPR **añejarse** [*vino*] to mature, age; (= *ranciarse*) to get stale, go musty
añejo ADJ **1** (*Culin*) [*vino, queso*] mature; [*jamón*] well-cured
2 (*pey*) (= *rancio*) stale, musty
3 [*noticia, historia*] old, stale
añicos SMPL pieces, fragments • **hacer un vaso ~** to smash a glass to bits *o* to smithereens • **hacer un papel ~** to tear a piece of paper into little *o* tiny bits • **hacerse ~** to shatter • **estar hecho ~** (= *cansado*) to be worn out, be shattered*
añil SM (*Bot*) indigo; (= *color*) indigo; (*para lavado*) blue, bluing
ADJ INV indigo
añilar ▹ CONJUG 1a VT (= *teñir*) to dye indigo; [+ *ropa*] to blue
añinos SMPL lamb's wool (*sing*)
año SM **1** (= *periodo de tiempo*) year • **el año pasado** last year • **el año próximo** • **el año que viene** next year • **el año entrante** the coming year • **el año antepasado** the year before last • **esperamos años y años** we waited years and years • **cinco toneladas al año** five tons a year • **al año de casado** a year after his marriage, after he had been married a year • **el año 66 después de Cristo** 66 A.D. • **en el año 1980** in 1980 • **en los años 60** in the sixties • **en estos últimos años** in recent years • **hace años** • **años ha** years ago • **los 40 años** • **los años difíciles** *o* **negros** (*Esp*) the Franco years (*1936-75*) • MODISMOS: • **estar de buen año** to look well-fed • **en el año de la nana** *o* **pera** *o* **polca** in the year dot, way back • **una lavadora del año de la nana** *o* **de la pera** a washing machine from the year dot • **el año verde** (*LAm*) never • REFRÁN: • **dentro de cien años, todos calvos** we all die in the end ▸ **año bisiesto** leap year ▸ **año civil, año común** calendar year ▸ **año de gracia** year of grace ▸ **año de nuestra salud** year of Our Lord ▸ **año económico** financial year ▸ **año escolar** school year ▸ **año fiscal** tax year ▸ **año lectivo** academic year ▸ **año luz** light-year • **100 años luz** 100 light-years • **los nórdicos están a años luz** the Scandinavians are light-years ahead (of the rest of us) • **el resto de corredores está a años luz de los dos campeones** the other runners are light-years behind the two champions ▸ **año natural** calendar year ▸ **Año Nuevo** New Year • **día de Año Nuevo** New Year's Day • **¡feliz año nuevo!** happy New Year! • **felicitar el año (nuevo) a algn** to wish sb (a) Happy New Year ▸ **año presupuestario** • **el año presupuestario va de noviembre a octubre** the budget covers

the period from *o* runs from November to October ▸ **año sabático** sabbatical (year) ▸ **año santo** Holy Year
2 [*de edad*] • **¿cuántos años tienes?** how old are you? • **tengo nueve años** I'm nine (years old) • **una niña de tres años** a three-year-old girl, a girl of three • **niños menores de un año** children under (the age of) one • **(nunca) en los años que tengo** never in all my life • **a mis años** at my age • **a sus años se mueve como una quinceañera** at *o* despite her age she still moves like a teenager • **cumplir años** to have one's birthday • **cumplir (los) 21 años** to have *o* celebrate one's 21st (birthday) • **entrado en años** elderly • **llevar diez años a algn** to be ten years older than sb • **¡por muchos años!** (*en cumpleaños*) many happy returns!; (*en brindis*) your *o* good health!; (*en presentación*†) how do you do? • **de pocos años** young • **quitarse años** (= *mentir*) to lie about one's age • **con ese lifting te has quitado diez años de encima** you look ten years younger after that face-lift • **sacar años a algn** to be older than sb • **le saca muchos años a su amiga** she is much older than her friend; ▸ KILOS, METROS, AÑOS
año-hombre SM (PL: **años-hombre**) man-year
añojal SM fallow land
añojo/a SM/F yearling
añorante ADJ yearning, longing
añoranza SF (= *recuerdos*) nostalgia, yearning, longing (**de** for); (*por pérdida*) sense of loss
añorar ▸ CONJUG 1a VT [+ *país*] to yearn for, miss, be homesick for; [+ *difunto, pérdida*] to mourn
VI to pine, grieve
añoso ADJ aged, full of years
añublar ▸ CONJUG 1a VI = **anublar**
añublo SM blight, mildew
añudar ▸ CONJUG 1a = **anudar**
añusgar ▸ CONJUG 1h VI (= *atragantarse*) to choke; (= *enfadarse*) to get angry
VPR **añusgarse** to get cross
aojada SF (*And*) skylight
aojar ▸ CONJUG 1a VT to put the evil eye on
aojo SM evil eye
aoristo SM aorist
aorta SF aorta
aovado ADJ oval, egg-shaped
aovar ▸ CONJUG 1a VI to lay eggs
aovillarse ▸ CONJUG 1a VPR to roll o.s. into a ball, curl up
AP SF ABR (*Esp*) (*Hist, Pol*) = **Alianza Popular**
Ap. ABR (= **apartado postal** *o* **de correos**) PO Box
APA SF ABR (= **Asociación de Padres de Alumnos**) ≈ PTA
apa[1] EXCL **1** (*Méx*) (= *¡Dios Santo!*) goodness me!, good gracious!
2 (= *ánimo*) cheer up!; (= *levántate*) get up!, up you get!; (= *recógelo*) pick it up!; (= *basta*) that's enough!
apa[2] • **al apa** ADV (*Cono Sur*) on one's back
apabullante ADJ shattering, crushing, overwhelming
apabullar ▸ CONJUG 1a VT [+ *rival*] to crush • **se le ve algo apabullado por las circunstancias** he was rather overwhelmed by the situation
VPR **apabullarse** to panic
apacentadero SM pasture
apacentar ▸ CONJUG 1j VT **1** (*Agr*) [+ *ganado*] to graze, feed
2 [+ *discípulos*] to teach; [+ *deseos, pasión*] to gratify
VPR **apacentarse 1** (*Agr*) [*ganado*] to graze, feed

2 (= *alimentarse*) to feed (**con, de** on)
apachar ▸ CONJUG 1a VT (*Perú*) to steal
apache SMF **1** (= *indio*) Apache, Apache Indian
2 (= *bandido*) crook, bandit
apacheta SF **1** (*And, Cono Sur*) (*Rel*) cairn, wayside shrine
2 (= *montón*) pile, heap
3 (*Pol*) clique; (= *confabulación*) ring, gang
4 (*Com*) ill-gotten gains (*pl*) • MODISMO: • **hacer la ~*** to make one's pile*
apachico SM (*LAm*) bundle
apachurrar ▸ CONJUG 1a VT (*esp LAm*) (= *aplastar*) to crush, squash; (= *romper*) to smash
apacibilidad SF (= *mansedumbre*) gentleness; [*de tiempo*] calmness
apacible ADJ (= *manso*) [*animal, persona*] gentle, mild; [*temperamento*] gentle, even; [*tiempo*] calm; [*viento*] gentle; [*tarde, noche*] pleasant • **es un tío muy ~** he's a very even-tempered *o* placid *o* mild-mannered guy
apaciblemente ADV gently, mildly
apaciguador ADJ pacifying, calming, soothing
apaciguamiento SM (= *tranquilidad*) calming down; (*Pol*) appeasement
apaciguar ▸ CONJUG 1i VT (= *tranquilizar*) to calm down; [+ *manifestantes*] to pacify, appease, mollify; (*Pol*) to appease
VPR **apaciguarse** to calm down, quieten down
apadrinamiento SM **1** [*de artista*] sponsorship, patronage
2 (= *apoyo*) backing, support
apadrinar ▸ CONJUG 1a VT **1** (*Rel*) [+ *niño*] to act as godfather to; [+ *novio*] to be best man for
2 [+ *artista*] to sponsor, be a patron to
3 (= *apoyar*) to back, support
4 [+ *duelista*] to act as second to
apadronarse ▸ CONJUG 1a VPR to register (as a resident)
apagadizo ADJ slow to burn, difficult to ignite
apagado ADJ **1** [*volcán*] extinct; [*cal*] slaked • **estar ~** [*fuego*] to be out; [*luz, radio*] to be off
2 [*sonido*] muted, muffled; [*voz*] quiet
3 [*color*] dull
4 [*persona, temperamento*] listless, spiritless; [*mirada*] lifeless, dull
SM switching-off • **botón de ~** off button, off switch
apagador SM **1** (= *extintor*) extinguisher
2 (*Mec*) silencer, muffler (*EEUU*); (*Mús*) damper
3 (*Cono Sur, Méx*) (= *interruptor*) switch
apagafuegos ADJ INV • **avión ~** fire-fighting plane
SM (= *avión*) fire-fighting plane
SMF (= *persona*) troubleshooter
apagar ▸ CONJUG 1h VT **1** [+ *fuego, vela, cerilla*] to put out; (*soplando*) to blow out • **apagó el cigarrillo en el cenicero** he put out *o* stubbed out his cigarette in the ashtray • **"por favor, apaguen sus cigarrillos"** "please extinguish all cigarettes" • MODISMO: • **(entonces) apaga y vámonos** let's forget it (then)
2 (*Elec*) to turn off, switch off • **apaga la luz/tele** turn *o* switch the light/TV off • **apagó el motor y salió del coche** she switched off the engine and got out of the car • **~ el sistema** (*Inform*) to close *o* shut down the system
3 [+ *sed*] to quench
4 [+ *ira*] to calm; [+ *rencor*] to pacify
5 [+ *dolor*] to take away, soothe
6 [+ *sonido*] to muffle, deaden; (*Mús*) to mute
7 [+ *color*] to tone down, soften

8 [+ *cal*] to slake
9 (*And, Caribe*) [+ *arma de fuego*] to empty, discharge
VPR **apagarse 1** [*fuego, vela*] to go out; (*con el viento*) to blow out; [*volcán*] to become extinct
2 [*luz*] to go out; [*aparato*] (*automáticamente*) to switch off, go off; (*por avería*) to stop working • **el motor se apaga en caso de incendio** the engine switches off if there is a fire • **la tele se me apagó durante el partido** the TV stopped working during the match
3 [*ira, rencor*] to subside, die away • **su entusiasmo se apagó con los años** his enthusiasm died away *o* subsided over the years
4 [*sonido*] to die away
5 [*persona*] to fade (away) • **su vida se apaga** his life is coming to an end *o* ebbing away • **su mirada se apagó con los años** the light went out of her eyes over the years
apagavelas SM INV candle snuffer
apagón SM power cut ▸ **apagón analógico** digital switchover ▸ **apagón informativo, apagón de noticias** news blackout
apagoso ADJ (*LAm*) = **apagadizo**
apaisado ADJ oblong
apajarado ADJ (*Cono Sur*) daft, scatterbrained
apalabrar ▸ CONJUG 1a VT **1** (= *convenir en*) to agree to • **estar apalabrado a una cosa** to be committed to sth
2 (= *encargar*) to bespeak; (= *contratar*) to engage
VPR **apalabrarse** to come to an agreement (con with)
apalabrear ▸ CONJUG 1a (*LAm*) = **apalabrar**
Apalaches SMPL • **montes ~** Appalachians
apalancado* ADJ **1** (= *apoltronado*) settled
2 (= *apoyado*) propped (up)
3 (= *estancado*) vegetating
apalancamiento SM leverage
apalancar ▸ CONJUG 1g VT **1** (= *para levantar*) to lever up
2 (= *para abrir*) to prise *o* (*EEUU*) prize off, lever off
3 (*Cono Sur**) • **~ a algn** to wangle a job for sb*
VPR **apalancarse 1** (= *apoltronarse*) to settle down • **se apalanca en el sofá y no se mueve en toda la tarde** he settles down on the sofa and doesn't budge all afternoon
2 (= *apoyarse*) to prop o.s. (up) • **se apalancó en la barra del bar y acabó borracho** he propped himself (up) on the bar and ended up drunk
3 (= *instalarse*) to settle in • **no quiero que se apalanque en mi piso** I don't want him taking up residence in my flat
4 (= *estancarse*) to vegetate, go to seed • **se mudó al pueblo y se apalancó** she moved to the village and just vegetated *o* went to seed
apalé EXCL (*Méx*) **1** (*sorpresa*) goodness me!
2 (*aviso*) look out!, watch it!
apaleada SF (*Cono Sur, Méx*) winnowing
apaleamiento SM beating, thrashing
apalear ▸ CONJUG 1a VT **1** (= *zurrar*) to beat, thrash; [+ *moqueta*] to beat • **~ oro** • **~ plata** to be rolling in money
2 (*Agr*) to winnow
apaleo SM (= *paliza*) beating; (*Agr*) winnowing
apalizar* ▸ CONJUG 1f VT to beat up*
apallar ▸ CONJUG 1a VT (*And*) to harvest
apamparse ▸ CONJUG 1a VPR (*Cono Sur*) to become bewildered
apanado ADJ (*LAm*) breaded, cooked in breadcrumbs
SM (*And*) beating
apanalado ADJ honeycombed

a

apanar ▸ CONJUG 1a (VT) (*LAm*) to coat in breadcrumbs
apancle (SM) (*Méx*) irrigation ditch
apandar‡ ▸ CONJUG 1a (VT) to rip off‡, knock off‡
apandillar ▸ CONJUG 1a (VT) to form into a gang
(VPR) **apandillarse** to gang up, band together
apando (SM) (*Méx*) punishment cell
apandorgarse ▸ CONJUG 1h (VPR) (*Perú*) to become lazy
apaniaguarse ▸ CONJUG 1i (VPR) (*And, Caribe*) to gang up
apanicar* ▸ CONJUG 1g (VT) (*Cono Sur*) to cause panic in, frighten
apaniguarse ▸ CONJUG 1i (VPR) = apaniaguarse
apantallado (ADJ) (*Méx*) (= *impresionado*) impressed, overwhelmed; (= *achatado*) overwhelmed, crushed • **quedar ~** (= *boquiabierto*) to be left open-mouthed
apantallar¹ ▸ CONJUG 1a (VT) to screen, shield
apantallar² ▸ CONJUG 1a (VT) (*Méx*) (= *impresionar*) to impress; (= *achatar*) to crush, overwhelm; (= *dejar boquiabierto*) to fill with wonder
apantanar ▸ CONJUG 1a (VT) to flood
apañado (ADJ) **1** (= *práctico*) [*persona*] clever; [*objeto*] handy
2 (= *ordenado*) neat, tidy
3* • **¡estás ~!** you've had it! • **estar ~ para hacer algo** to have difficulty in doing sth, have trouble doing sth • **estoy ~ si lo hago** I'll be in trouble if I do it • **~s estaríamos si confiáramos en eso** we'd be fools if we relied on that
4 (*económicamente*) • **los hijos quedarán bien ~s** the children will be well provided for
apañador(a) (SM/F) **1** (*Dep*) catcher
2* (= *amañador*) fixer*
apañar ▸ CONJUG 1a (VT) **1** (= *arreglar*) to fix • **¿me puedes ~ esta radio rota?** can you fix this broken radio for me?
2* (= *preparar*) to get ready • **apañó una cena con pocos ingredientes** he put together a dinner with just a few ingredients • **apañó la mesa antes de que llegaran los comensales** she got the table ready before the guests arrived • **apaña al niño que nos vamos pronto** get the child ready, we'll be going soon
3 (= *amañar*) [+ *elecciones*] to rig*, fix*
4 (*Méx*) (= *perdonar*) to forgive, let off
5 (*Cono Sur*) (= *encubrir*) [+ *crimen*] to cover up; [+ *criminal*] to harbour, harbor (*EEUU*), hide
(VPR) **apañarse 1** (*tb* **apañárselas**) to manage, get by • **yo me (las) apaño muy bien solo** I manage *o* get by very well on my own • **yo me (las) apaño con poco dinero** I get by *o* manage without much money • **ya me (las) ~é por mi cuenta** I'll manage *o* get by on my own • **apáñate(las) como puedas** you'll have to manage as best you can • **apáñate(las) con lo que tengas** make do with what you've got • **ya me (las) ~é para llegar a Sevilla** I'll find a way of getting to Seville somehow
2 (*esp Cono Sur*) • **~se algo** to get one's hands on sth, get hold of sth
apaño (SM) **1** (= *de algo roto*) • **me hizo un ~ en el lavabo** he fixed up the washbasin for me • **esta radio no tiene ~** this radio can't be fixed • **el problema del fraude no tiene ~** there's no answer to the problem of fraud
2 (= *chanchullo*) fix* • **el resultado del partido fue un ~** the match was a fix*, the match was fixed *o* rigged* • **hicieron un ~ para ganar las elecciones** the election was fixed *o* rigged*
3 (= *componenda*) deal • **un ~ entre los partidos evitó su dimisión** a deal between the parties avoided him having to resign
4** • **estar para un ~** to be a gorgeous piece of ass**
5† (= *amorío*) affair; (= *amante*) lover
apañuscar* ▸ CONJUG 1g (VT) **1** (= *ajar*) to rumple; (= *aplastar*) to crush
2 (= *robar*) to pinch*, steal
apapachar* ▸ CONJUG 1a (*Méx*) (VT) (= *mimar*) to spoil; (= *abrazar*) to cuddle, hug
apapachos* (SMPL) (*Méx*) (= *abrazos*) cuddles, hugs; (= *caricias*) caresses
aparador (SM) (= *mueble*) sideboard; (= *vitrina*) showcase; (*esp LAm*) (= *escaparate*) shop window • MODISMO: • **estar de ~** to be dressed up to receive visitors
aparadorista (SMF) (*Méx*) window dresser
aparar† ▸ CONJUG 1a (VT) **1** (= *disponer*) to arrange, prepare
2 [+ *manos*] to stretch out (*to catch sth*)
3 (*Agr*) to weed, clean
aparatarse ▸ CONJUG 1a (VPR) (*And, Cono Sur*) • **se aparata** it's brewing up for a storm, there's a storm coming
aparatejo* (SM) gadget
aparato (SM) **1** (*Téc*) machine • **uno de esos ~s para hacer café** one of those coffee machines *o* coffee-making things* • **un ~ para medir el nivel de contaminación** a device to measure pollution levels
▸ **aparato antirrobo** anti-theft device
▸ **aparato de escucha** listening device
▸ **aparato de medición** measuring instrument ▸ **aparato de relojería** clockwork mechanism ▸ **aparato fotográfico** photographic instrument, camera ▸ **aparato lector de microfilmes** microfilm reader ▸ **aparatos de mando** (*Aer*) controls ▸ **aparatos periféricos** (*Inform*) peripherals ▸ **aparatos sanitarios** bathroom fittings
2 (*Elec*) (= *electrodoméstico*) appliance; (= *televisor, radio*) set • **~ de uso doméstico** domestic appliance ▸ **aparato de radio** radio ▸ **aparato de televisión** television set ▸ **aparato eléctrico** electrical appliance
3 (*Telec*) phone, telephone • **al ~:** • —**¿puedo hablar con Pilar Ruiz?** —**al ~** "can I speak to Pilar Ruiz?" — "speaking" • **¡Gerardo, al ~!** Gerardo, telephone! • **colgar el ~** to put down the phone, hang up • **ponerse al ~** to come to the phone • **tener a algn al ~** to have sb on the line
4 (*Med*) • **ya respira sin ayuda del ~** she can now breathe without the apparatus *o* device ▸ **aparato auditivo** hearing aid
▸ **aparato circulatorio** circulatory system
▸ **aparato dental, aparato de ortodoncia** brace, braces (*pl*) (*EEUU*) ▸ **aparato digestivo** digestive system ▸ **aparato genital femenino** female genitalia
▸ **aparato genital masculino** male genitalia
▸ **aparato ortopédico** surgical appliance, orthopaedic aid, orthopedic aid (*US*)
▸ **aparato para sordos** hearing aid
▸ **aparato respiratorio** respiratory system
5 (*Gimnasia*) (= *máquina*) exercise machine, fitness machine; (= *anillas, barras*) piece of apparatus • **fallaron en casi todos los ~s** they failed on almost all the apparatus
6 (*Aer*) aircraft, airplane (*EEUU*)
7 (= *formalismo, artificio*) • **todo el ~ con el que viaja un rey** all the pomp and ceremony which accompanies a king when he travels • **el festival llevaba un gran ~ de protocolo** the festival was accompanied by a great show of protocol • **viaja sin ~ ceremonial** he travels without any ceremonial escort • **nos lo contó con gran ~ de misterio** she told us all about it with a great air of mystery
8 (*Pol*) (= *estructura*) [*de base*] machine; [*de control*] machinery • **el ~ del partido** the party machine, the party apparatus • **un fuerte ~ publicitario** a powerful publicity machine • **ven a la Iglesia como un ~ de poder** they see the Church as a power structure ▸ **aparato electoral** electoral machine ▸ **aparato estatal** state system, government machinery
9 (*Meteo*) • **una tormenta con gran ~ eléctrico** a storm with a great deal of thunder and lightning
10 (= *indicios*) signs (*pl*), symptoms (*pl*); (*Med*) symptoms (*pl*); (*Psic*) syndrome
11 (*Literat*) ▸ **aparato crítico** critical apparatus
12‡ (= *pene*) equipment*; (= *vagina*) pussy**
aparatosamente (ADV) spectacularly • **el torero fue volteado ~ en el aire** the bullfighter was tossed up in the air spectacularly • **se marcharon ~ de la reunión** they marched out of the meeting in a dramatic way
aparatosidad (SF) **1** (= *exageración*) showiness, ostentation
2 [*de accidente, caída*] spectacular nature
aparatoso (ADJ) **1** (= *exagerado*) [*persona, gestos*] showy, ostentatious; [*objeto, ropa*] flamboyant • **la boda fue muy aparatosa** the wedding was very extravagant *o* over the top* • **¡qué ~ eres al hablar!** you've got such a showy *o* flamboyant way of speaking
2 [*accidente, caída*] spectacular, dramatic
aparcacoches (SMF INV) car park attendant
aparcadero (SM) car park, parking lot (*EEUU*)
aparcamiento (SM), **aparcamento** (SM) (*CAm, Caribe*) **1** (= *acción*) parking
▸ **aparcamiento en doble fila** double parking
2 (= *lugar*) car park, parking lot (*EEUU*)
▸ **aparcamiento subterráneo** underground car park
3 (= *apartadero*) lay-by
aparcar ▸ CONJUG 1g (VT) **1** [+ *vehículo*] to park
2* (= *aplazar*) [+ *proyecto de ley*] to shelve; [+ *idea*] to put on the back burner
(VI) to park
aparcería (SF) **1** (*Com*) partnership; (*Agr*) share-cropping
2 (*Cono Sur*) (= *compañerismo*) comradeship, friendship
aparcero/a (SM/F) **1** (*Com*) co-owner, partner; (*Agr*) sharecropper
2 (*Cono Sur*) (= *compañero*) comrade, friend
apareamiento (SM) **1** [*de animales*] mating
2 [*de objetos*] matching, pairing
aparear ▸ CONJUG 1a (VT) **1** [+ *animales*] to mate
2 [+ *objetos*] to pair, match
(VPR) **aparearse** [*animales*] to mate
aparecer ▸ CONJUG 2d (VI) **1** (= *presentarse*) to appear, turn up* • **apareció en casa sin avisar** he appeared *o* turned up* at the house without warning • **apareció borracho** he turned up drunk
2 [*algo oculto*] to appear, turn up* • **aparecieron dos nuevos cadáveres en la fosa** two more bodies appeared *o* turned up* in the trench
3 [*algo perdido*] to reappear, turn up* • **ya ha aparecido mi paraguas** my umbrella has finally reappeared *o* turned up*
4 (= *surgir*) to appear • **han aparecido los primeros síntomas** the first symptoms have appeared • **han aparecido pintadas en la fachada del ayuntamiento** some graffiti has appeared on the front of the town hall
5 (= *editarse*) [*libro, disco*] to come out

6 (= *figurar*) [*dato, nombre*] to appear • **mi nombre no aparece en el censo electoral** my name does not appear on the electoral register, my name is not on the electoral register • **aparece brevemente en una película reciente** he appears briefly in a recent film

(VPR) **aparecerse** [*fantasma, espíritu*] to appear • **Nuestra Señora se apareció a Bernadette** Our Lady appeared to Bernadette

aparecido/a (SM/F) ghost

aparejado (ADJ) **1** (= *apto*) fit, suitable; (= *listo*) ready (**para** for)
2 (*fig*) • **ir ~ con** (= *ser inseparables*) to go hand in hand with • **llevar** *o* **traer algo ~** (= *traer consigo*) to entail sth

aparejador(a) (SM/F) **1** (*en una obra*) (= *capataz*) clerk of works; (*Arquit*) master builder; (= *encargado de la administración*) quantity surveyor
2 (*Náut*) rigger

aparejar ▹ CONJUG 1a (VT) (= *preparar*) to prepare, get ready; [+ *caballo*] to saddle, harness; (*Náut*) to fit out, rig out; [+ *lienzo*] to size, prime
(VPR) **aparejarse 1** (= *prepararse*) to get ready; (= *equiparse*) to equip o.s.
2 (*CAm, Caribe*) to mate, pair

aparejo (SM) **1** (= *acto*) preparation
2 (= *herramientas*) gear, equipment
3 [*de caballería*] (= *arreos*) harness; (*CAm, Méx*) (= *silla*) saddle; (*And*) (= *silla de mujer*) woman's saddle
4 (*Pesca*) ▸ **aparejo de anzuelos** set of hooks ▸ **aparejos de pesca** fishing tackle
5 (= *poleas*) lifting gear, block and tackle
6 (*Náut*) rigging
7 (*Arquit*) bond, bonding
8 (*Arte*) sizing, priming

aparellaje (SM) control gear

aparencial (ADJ) apparent

aparentar ▹ CONJUG 1a (VT) **1** (= *parecer*) to look • **no aparenta su edad** *o* **sus años** she doesn't look her age • **aparenta menos años de los que tiene** he looks younger than he is • **aparenta ser más joven de lo que es** he looks younger than he is
2 (= *fingir*) [+ *interés, sorpresa, indiferencia*] to feign • **aparentó ignorancia de su obra** (*frm*) she feigned ignorance of his work, she pretended not to know his work • **aparenta estar estudiando** he pretends to be studying • **tendrás que ~ que te encanta** you'll have to pretend you love it
(VI) to show off • **le gusta mucho ~** he really likes showing off

aparente (ADJ) **1** (= *no real*) apparent • **su interés es solo ~** he just pretends to be interested, he just feigns interest
2 (= *patente*) apparent • **no hubo lesión ~** there was no apparent injury • **sin motivo ~** for no apparent reason • **ganó la carrera sin esfuerzo ~** she won the race with no apparent effort
3* (= *atractivo*) attractive, smart • **tiene un novio muy ~** she has a very good-looking boyfriend • **esta figurilla está aquí muy ~** this figurine looks very good *o* goes very well here

aparentemente (ADV) **1** (= *según parece*) seemingly
2 (= *evidentemente*) visibly, outwardly

aparición (SF) **1** (= *acto*) appearance; (= *publicación*) publication • **un libro de próxima ~** a forthcoming book ▸ **aparición en público** public appearance
2 (= *aparecido*) apparition, spectre

apariencia (SF) (= *aspecto*) appearance • **tiene la misma ~ que el planeta Tierra** it has the same appearance as planet Earth • **la misma ~ del resto de los estudiantes** the same appearance as the rest of the students • **bajo su ~ despistada hay un genio** behind his absent-minded appearance he is a genius • **con ~ de**: • **una chica con ~ de alemana** a German-looking girl • **un jarabe con ~ de miel** a syrup that looks like honey • **de ~**: • **una herida de sospechosa ~** a suspicious-looking wound • **es rico solo de ~** he only appears to be rich • **en ~**: • **José, en ~ rudo, es muy cortés** although José may seem *o* appear rude on the surface, he is very polite • **en ~, el coche estaba perfecto** to all appearances, the car was in perfect condition • **guardar** *o* **salvar las ~s** to keep up appearances • **MODISMO**: • **las ~s engañan** appearances can be deceptive; ▹ **fiar**

aparragado/a (*Cono Sur*) (ADJ) stunted, dwarfish
(SM/F) dwarf

aparragarse ▹ CONJUG 1h (VPR) **1** (*CAm*) (= *hacerse un ovillo*) to roll up, curl up
2 (*Cono Sur*) (= *agacharse*) to squat, crouch down
3 (*CAm, Cono Sur, Méx*) (= *no crecer*) to remain stunted, stay small; (= *encogerse*) to shrink, grow small

apartadero (SM) (*Aut*) lay-by; (*Ferro*) siding

apartadijo (SM) **1** (= *porción*) small portion, bit
2 = **apartadizo**

apartadizo (ADJ) (= *huraño*) unsociable
(SM) recess, alcove, nook

apartado (ADJ) **1** (= *lejano*) remote, isolated • **un pueblo muy ~** a very remote *o* isolated village • **su casa está un poco apartada** her house is a bit out-of-the-way • **~ de** [*lugar*] far from; [*persona*] isolated from • **donde vivía, estaba ~ de todos nosotros** where he lived he was isolated from us all • **ha conseguido mantenerse ~ de los problemas** she's managed to keep out of the problems
2 (= *solitario*) [*vida, persona*] solitary
(SM) **1** (*Correos*) (*tb* **apartado de correos, apartado postal**) Post Office box, P.O. Box, box number • **~ de correos 325** P.O. Box 325
2 (= *sección*) (*Literat*) section; (*Jur*) section, sub-section • **vamos a empezar por el ~ dedicado a la economía** let's begin with the section on the economy • **en el ~ de sanidad han aumentado los gastos** in the area of health, costs have increased
3 (= *sala*) spare room, side room ▸ **apartado de localidades** ticket agency
4 (*Metal*) extraction

apartahotel (SM) aparthotel

apartamento (SM) apartment, flat ▸ **apartamentos turísticos** holiday apartments

apartamiento (SM) **1** (= *separación*) separation
2 (= *aislamiento*) seclusion, isolation
3 (= *lugar*) secluded spot, remote area

apartar ▹ CONJUG 1a (VT) **1** (= *alejar*) • **aparta las piezas blancas de las negras** separate the white pieces from the black ones • **aparta la sartén del fuego** take the pan off the heat • **lograron ~ la discusión de ese punto** they managed to turn the discussion away from that point • **no podía ~ mi pensamiento de ella** I couldn't get her out of my head • **~ la mirada/los ojos de algo** to look away from sth, avert one's gaze/one's eyes from sth (*liter*) • **apartó la mirada de la larga fila de casas** she looked away from *o* (*liter*) averted her gaze from the long row of houses • **no aparta los ojos de la comida** he can't keep his eyes off the food
2 (= *quitar de en medio*) • **tuvo que ~ los papeles de la mesa para colocar allí sus libros** he had to push aside the papers on the table to place his books there • **apartó el micrófono a un lado** she put the microphone aside *o* to one side • **apartó la cortina y miró a la calle** he drew *o* pulled back the curtain and looked out into the street • **le apartó los cabellos de la frente** she brushed her hair off her forehead • **avanzaban apartando la maleza** they made their way through the undergrowth, pushing *o* brushing it aside as they went
3 [+ *persona*] **a** (*de lugar*) • **lo apartó un poco para hacerle algunas preguntas** she took him to one side to ask him a few questions • **los guardaespaldas apartaban a las fans** the bodyguards pushed the fans aside *o* away • **aparta al niño de la ventana** move the child away from the window
b (*de otra persona*) (*lit*) to separate; (*fig*) to drift apart • **si no los apartamos se matarán** if we don't separate them they'll kill each other • **el tiempo los ha ido apartando** they have grown *o* drifted apart with time
c (*de actividad, puesto*) to remove • **el ministro lo apartó de su puesto** the minister removed him from his post • **su enfermedad la apartó de la política activa** her illness kept her away from playing an active role in politics • **si yo fuera el entrenador, lo ~ía del equipo** if I was the coach I would remove him from the team • **lo ~on de su intención de vender la casa** they dissuaded him from selling the house
4 (= *reservar*) to put aside, set aside • **si le interesa este vestido se lo puedo ~** if you like this dress I can put *o* set it aside for you • **"se apartan muebles"** "a deposit secures any piece of furniture" • **hemos apartado un poco de comida para él** we've put *o* set aside a little food for him • **picar las verduras y ~las a un lado** chop the vegetables and put them to one side
5 (*Correos*) to sort
6 (*Ferro*) to shunt, switch (*EEUU*)
7 (*Agr*) [+ *ganado*] to separate, cut out
8 (*Jur*) to set aside, waive
9 (*Min*) to extract
(VPR) **apartarse 1** (= *quitarse de en medio*) to move out of the way • **¿puedes ~te un poco?** can you move out of the way a bit? • **se apartó a tiempo para evitar el puñetazo** he moved aside *o* moved out of the way to avoid the punch • **se ~on para dejarla pasar** they moved aside to let her through • **¡apártense! ¡que está herido!** out of the way *o* stand clear! he's wounded! • **se apartó unos pasos** she moved *o* walked away a few paces • **~se de** [+ *persona, lugar, teoría*] to move away from; [+ *camino, ruta*] to stray from, wander off; [+ *actividad, creencia*] to abandon • **nos apartamos unos metros del vehículo** we moved a few metres away from the vehicle • **apártate del fuego** get *o* move away from the fire • **nunca se aparta de mi lado** she never leaves my side • **nunca se apartó de esta regla** he never strayed from this rule • **se apartó de la política** she left *o* abandoned politics • **no se aparta del teléfono por si suena** she's always sitting by the phone in case it rings • **consiguió ~se de la bebida** he managed to give up drinking • **¡apártate de mi vista!** get out of my sight! • **MODISMO**: • **~se del buen camino** to go off the straight and narrow
2 (= *distanciarse*) [*dos personas*] to part, separate; [*dos objetos*] to become separated • **con el tiempo se han ido apartando** they have drifted *o* grown apart with time

• **las cifras se apartan de las predicciones** the figures are far off the predictions • **esta novela se aparta del estilo del resto de su obra** this novel is a far cry from the style of the rest of his work • **el libro se aparta del realismo sentimentalista** the book diverges *o* strays from sentimentalist realism
3 (*Jur*) to withdraw from a suit
aparte (ADJ INV) separate • **guárdalo en un cajón ~** keep it in a different *o* separate drawer • **lo tuyo es un caso ~** you're a special case • **capítulo ~ merece la corrupción política** another question altogether is political corruption • **mantenerse ~** to keep away
(ADV) **1** (= *a un lado*) • **se la llevó ~ para contarle sus confidencias** he took her aside to confide in her • **bromas ~, ¿qué os parece que me vaya a vivir a El Cairo?** joking aside *o* seriously though, what do you think of me going to live in Cairo? • **diferencias ideológicas ~, perseguimos el mismo fin** ideological differences aside, we're after the same thing • **dejando ~ el norte, este país no es muy montañoso** leaving aside the north, this country is not very mountainous • **hacerle a algn ~** to exclude sb • **poner algo ~** to put sth aside • **la ropa sucia ponla ~** put the dirty clothes to one side, put aside the dirty clothes • **ser algo ~** to be something superior; ▹ **modestia**
2 (= *por separado*) separately • **tendremos que considerar eso ~** we'll have to consider that separately • **deberías lavar las toallas ~** you should wash the towels separately
3 (= *además*) besides • **~, yo ya soy mayorcita para que me manden** besides, I'm too old to be bossed about like that • **—¿y no paga el alquiler? —sí, eso ~** "and he doesn't pay the rent?" — "yes, that as well" • **300 euros, ~ impuestos** 300 euros, taxes aside • **~ hay un examen práctico** there is also a practical exam
(PREP) • **~ de** apart from • **~ del mal tiempo, las vacaciones fueron estupendas** apart from the bad weather, the holidays were great • **~ de que** apart from the fact that
(SM) **1** (*Teat*) aside • **hacer un ~ con algn** to take sb to one side
2 (*Tip*) paragraph, new paragraph • **punto y ~** new paragraph
apartheid (SM) apartheid
aparthotel (SM) aparthotel
apartidismo (SM) non-political nature, non-party character
apartidista (ADJ) apolitical, non-party (*antes de s*)
apasionadamente (ADV) **1** (= *con pasión*) passionately
2 (*pey*) (= *con parcialidad*) in a biased way, in a prejudiced way
apasionado/a (ADJ) **1** (= *con pasión*) [*persona*] passionate; [*discurso*] impassioned • **~ por algo** passionate about sth
2 (= *parcial*) biased, prejudiced
(SM/F) admirer, devotee • **los ~s de Góngora** devotees of Góngora, Góngora enthusiasts
apasionamiento (SM) (= *entusiasmo*) passion, enthusiasm; (= *fervor*) vehemence, intensity • **hacer algo con ~** to do sth with passion
apasionante (ADJ) exciting, thrilling
apasionar ▹ CONJUG 1a (VT) **1** (= *entusiasmar*) • **le apasiona el teatro de Shakespeare** he loves Shakespeare's plays • **le apasionan los ordenadores** he's mad about computers • **el grupo que apasiona a las quinceañeras** the group the teenagers are mad about • **a mí el fútbol no me apasiona** I'm not exactly passionate about football
2 (*frm*) (= *afligir*) to afflict, torment
(VPR) **apasionarse** to get excited • **cuando habla de literatura se apasiona** she gets very excited when she talks about literature • **~se con algo** to get excited about sth • **~se por algo: se apasionó por la idea de una Europa única** he became very excited by the idea of a United Europe • **~se por algn** to fall madly in love with sb
apaste (SM) (*CAm*), **apaxte** (SM) (*CAm*) clay pot, clay jug
apatía (SF) (= *abulia*) apathy; (*Med*) listlessness
apático (ADJ) (= *abúlico*) apathetic; (*Med*) listless
apátrida (ADJ) **1** (= *sin nacionalidad*) stateless
2 (*Cono Sur*) (= *sin patriotismo*) unpatriotic
(SMF) (*Cono Sur*) unpatriotic person
apatronarse ▹ CONJUG 1a (VPR) (*And, Cono Sur*) • **~ de algn** (= *amancebarse*) to find a protector in sb; (= *buscar empleo*) to seek a domestic post with sb; (*And*) (= *encargarse*) to take charge of sb
apatusco (SM) **1** (= *adornos*) frills (*pl*), adornments (*pl*)
2 (*Caribe*) (= *enredo*) trick; (= *fingimiento*) pretence, pretense (*EEUU*); (= *intrigas*) intrigue
APD (SF ABR) (*Esp*) = **Asociación para el Progreso de la Dirección**
Apdo. (ABR), **apdo.** (ABR) (= **apartado postal** *o* **de correos**) P.O. Box
apeadero (SM) **1** (*para montar*) mounting block, step
2 (*Ferro*) halt, stopping place
3 (= *alojamiento*) temporary lodging, pied-à-terre
apear ▹ CONJUG 1a (VT) **1** (= *ayudar a bajar*) to help down, help to alight (**de** from); [+ *objeto*] to take down, get down (**de** from); [+ *árbol*] to fell
2 [+ *caballo*] to hobble; [+ *rueda*] to chock
3 (*Arquit*) to prop up
4 [+ *problema*] to solve, work out; [+ *dificultad*] to overcome
5 (= *disuadir*) • **~ a algn de su opinión** to persuade sb that his opinion is wrong
6 • **~ el tratamiento a algn** (= *suprimir el tratamiento*) to drop sb's title
7* (= *despedir*) to give the boot*, sack* • **~ a algn de su cargo** to remove sb from his post
8 (*And*) (= *matar*) to kill
9 (*CAm*) (= *reprender*) to dress down*, tell off*
(VPR) **apearse 1** (= *bajarse*) (*de caballo, mula*) to dismount; (*de tren, autobús*) to get off, alight (*frm*) • **yo me apeo en la próxima parada** I'm getting off at the next stop • MODISMO: • **no ~se del burro** to refuse to climb *o* back down
2 • **~se en** (*LAm*) to stay at, put up at
3 • **~se de algo** (*And*) (= *librarse*) to get rid of sth
4 • **no apeársela** (*CAm*) (= *estar borracho*) to be drunk all the time
apechugar* ▹ CONJUG 1h (VI) **1** (= *empujar*) to push, shove • **¡apechuga!** (= *ánimo*) buck up!, come on!
2 • **~ con** (= *aguantar*) to put up with, swallow; [+ *cometido*] (= *cargar con*) to take on • **~ con las consecuencias** to take the consequences
(VT) **1** (*Cono Sur, Caribe*) (= *agarrar*) to grab, grab hold of, seize
2 (*And*) (= *sacudir*) to shake violently
(VPR) **apechugarse** • **~se con algo** to face up to sth, take the consequences of sth
apedazar ▹ CONJUG 1f (VT) **1** (= *remendar*) to mend, patch
2 (= *despedazar*) to tear to pieces, cut into pieces
apedrear ▹ CONJUG 1a (VT) (*como castigo*) to stone; (*en pelea*) to throw stones at
(VI) **1** (= *granizar*) to hail
2 (*Méx*‡) (= *apestar*) to stink, reek
(VPR) **apedrearse** (*Bot*) to be damaged by hail
apedreo (SM) **1** (= *acto*) stoning
2 (= *granizo*) hail
3 (*Bot*) damage by hail
apegadamente (ADV) devotedly
apegado (ADJ) attached, devoted (**a** to)
apegarse ▹ CONJUG 1h (VPR) • **~ a** to become attached to, become devoted to
apego (SM) attachment (**a** to), devotion (**a** to)
apelable (ADJ) (*Jur*) appealable, that can be appealed against, subject to appeal
apelación (SF) **1** (*Jur*) appeal • **sin ~** without appeal, final • **interponer ~** to appeal, lodge an appeal • **presentar su ~** to present one's appeal • **ver una ~** to consider an appeal
2 (= *remedio*) help, remedy • **no hay ~** • **esto no tiene ~** it's a hopeless case
apelante (SMF) appellant
apelar ▹ CONJUG 1a (VI) **1** (*Jur*) to appeal • **~ contra algo** to appeal (against) sth
2 • **~ a a** (= *invocar*) to appeal to • **apeló al sentido común para resolver el problema** he appealed to people's common sense to solve the problem • **apelamos al presidente a que cumpla sus compromisos** we appeal to the president to keep his promises
b (= *recurrir a*) to resort to • **tuvo que ~ a sus encantos personales** she had to resort to charm, she had to make use of her charm
(VT) (*Jur*) to appeal (against) • **han apelado la sentencia** they have appealed (against) the sentence
apelativo (SM) (*Ling*) appellative; (= *apellido*) surname
apeldar‡ ▹ CONJUG 1a (VT) • **~las** to beat it*
apellidar ▹ CONJUG 1a (VT) **1** (= *llamar*) to call
2†† (= *aclamar*) • **~ a algn por rey** to proclaim sb king
(VPR) **apellidarse** to be called • **¿cómo se apellida usted?** what's your surname?
apellido (SM) **1** (= *nombre de familia*) surname, family name ▸ **apellido de soltera** maiden name
2 (= *apodo*) nickname

APELLIDO
In the Spanish-speaking world most people use two **apellidos**, the first being their father's first surname, and the second their mother's first surname: e.g. the surname of the children of Juan **García López**, married to Carmen **Pérez Rodríguez**, would be **García Pérez**. Married women can either use the surnames they were born with or add their husband's first surname to theirs; so e.g. Carmen **Pérez Rodríguez** could also be known as Carmen **Pérez de García** or Carmen **Pérez Rodríguez de García**. In this particular case she could also be referred to as **la señora de García**. However most women continue to use their own surnames.

apelmazado (ADJ) **1** [*masa*] compact, solid; [*salsa, líquido*] thick, lumpy; [*pelo*] matted
2 [*estilo*] clumsy
apelmazar ▹ CONJUG 1f (VT) to compress
(VPR) **apelmazarse** to get lumpy
apelotonar ▹ CONJUG 1a (VT) to roll into a ball
(VPR) **apelotonarse** [*colchón*] to become lumpy; [*animal*] to curl up, curl up into a ball; [*gente*] to mass, crowd together
apenado (ADJ) **1** (= *triste*) sorry
2 (*LAm*) (= *avergonzado*) ashamed, embarrassed; (= *tímido*) shy, timid

apenar ▹ CONJUG 1a VT **1** (= *afligir*) to grieve, cause pain to
2 (*LAm*) (= *avergonzar*) to shame
VPR **apenarse 1** (= *afligirse*) to grieve, distress o.s. • **~se de** *o* **por algo** to grieve about sth, distress o.s. on account of sth
2 (*LAm*) (= *avergonzarse*) to be ashamed; (= *ser triste*) to be sorry, be sad; (= *ser tímido*) to be shy; (= *sonrojarse*) to blush • **no se apene, no tiene importancia** (*Méx*) don't worry, it doesn't matter

apenas ADV **1** (= *casi no*) hardly, scarcely • **~ consigo dormir** I can hardly *o* scarcely *o* barely sleep • **—¿has leído mucho últimamente? —apenas** "have you been reading much lately?" — "hardly anything" • **cocinan sin ~ aceite** they cook with hardly any oil • **siguió trabajando durante horas, sin ~ acusar el cansancio** he went on working for hours, with hardly any sign of tiredness • **~ nada** hardly anything • **no recuerdo ~ nada** I hardly remember anything • **no sé ~ nada de ese tema** I hardly know anything about that subject, I know almost nothing *o* next to nothing about that subject • **~ nadie** hardly anybody • **~ si**: • **~ si nos habló durante toda la cena** he hardly *o* barely *o* scarcely said a word to us throughout the whole dinner • **~ si nos queda dinero** we have hardly any money left
2 (= *casi nunca*) hardly ever • **ahora ~ voy** I hardly ever go now
3 (= *escasamente*) only • **faltan ~ cinco minutos** there's only five minutes to go • **hace ~ un año que nos conocimos** it's only a year ago that we met • **había muy pocos alumnos, ~ diez o doce** there were very few students, only *o* barely ten or twelve • **yo ~ tenía catorce años** I was barely fourteen, I was only just fourteen
4 (= *solamente*) only • **~ voy por la página cinco** I'm only on page five • **~ entonces me di cuenta de lo que pasaba** it was only then that I realized what was happening
CONJ (*esp LAm*) (= *en cuanto*) as soon as • **abandonaron la ciudad ~ amanecido** they left the city as soon as it got light • **~ llegue, te llamo** I'll phone you as soon as I arrive • **~ había cumplido quince años cuando …** he'd only just turned fifteen when …

apencar* ▹ CONJUG 1g VI to slog away*, slave away*

apendectomía SF appendectomy

apendejarse ▹ CONJUG 1a VPR (*Caribe*) (= *hacer el tonto*) to get silly, act the fool; (= *acobardarse*) to lose one's nerve

apéndice SM **1** (*Anat, Literat*) appendix; (*Jur*) schedule
2 (*fig*) (= *satélite*) appendage

apendicitis SF INV appendicitis

Apeninos SMPL Apennines

apenitas ADV (*And, Cono Sur*) = **apenas**

apensionado ADJ (*And, Cono Sur, Méx*) sad, depressed

apensionar ▹ CONJUG 1a VT (*And, Cono Sur, Méx*) to sadden, grieve
VPR **apensionarse** to become sad, get depressed

apeñuscarse ▹ CONJUG 1g VPR (*Cono Sur*) to crowd together

apeo SM **1** (*Jur*) surveying
2 (*Arquit*) (= *soporte*) prop, support; (= *andamio*) scaffolding
3 (*Agr*) felling

apeorar ▹ CONJUG 1a VI to get worse

aperado ADJ (*Cono Sur*) well-equipped

aperar ▹ CONJUG 1a VT **1** [+ *aparejo*] to repair
2 [+ *caballo*] to harness
3 (= *abastecer*) • **~ a algn de herramientas** to provide *o* equip sb with tools
VPR **aperarse** • **~se de algo** to equip o.s. with sth, provide o.s. with sth • **estar bien aperado para** to be well equipped for

apercancarse ▹ CONJUG 1g VPR (*Cono Sur*) to go mouldy, go moldy (EEUU)

aperchar ▹ CONJUG 1a VT (*CAm, Cono Sur*) to pile up, stack up

apercibimiento SM **1** (= *preparación*) preparation
2 (= *aviso*) warning
3 (*Jur*) caution

apercibir ▹ CONJUG 3a VT **1** (= *preparar*) to prepare; (= *proveer*) to furnish • **con los fusiles apercibidos** with rifles at the ready
2 (= *avisar*) to warn, advise
3 (*Jur*) to caution
4 (= *ver*) to notice, see
5 [+ *error etc*] = **percibir**
VPR **apercibirse** to prepare, prepare o.s., get ready (**para** for) • **~se de** (= *proveerse*) to provide *o* equip o.s. with; (= *percibir*) to notice

apercollar ▹ CONJUG 1l VT **1** (= *agarrar*) to seize by the neck
2 (= *matar*) to fell, kill (*with a blow on the neck*)
3‡ (= *detener*) to knock off‡, nick‡

apergaminado ADJ [*papel*] parchment-like; [*piel*] dried up, wrinkled; [*cara*] wizened

apergaminarse ▹ CONJUG 1a VPR [*papel*] to become like parchment; [*piel*] to dry up, get yellow and wrinkled

apergollar ▹ CONJUG 1a VT (*LAm*) (= *agarrar*) to grab by the throat; (= *engañar*) to trap, ensnare

aperital SM (*Cono Sur*) = **aperitivo**

aperitivo SM (= *comida*) appetizer; (= *bebida*) aperitif

apero SM **1** (*Agr*) (= *instrumento*) implement; (= *animales*) ploughing team, plowing team (EEUU)
2 (*LAm*) (= *arneses*) harness, trappings (*pl*); (*LAm*) (= *silla*) saddle
3 aperos (*Agr*) (= *equipo*) farm equipment (*sing*)

aperrarse* ▹ CONJUG 1a VPR (*Cono Sur*) to dig one's heels in

aperreado* ADJ wretched, lousy* • **llevar una vida aperreada** to lead a wretched *o* lousy* life

aperreador* ADJ bothersome, tiresome

aperrear ▹ CONJUG 1a VT **1** (= *azuzar perros contra*) to set the dogs on
2* (= *acosar*) to plague; (= *cansar*) to wear out, tire out
VPR **aperrearse* 1** (= *ser acosado*) to get harassed; (= *trabajar demasiado*) to slave away*, overwork
2 (*LAm*) (= *insistir*) to insist

aperreo* SM **1** (= *trabajo duro*) overwork; (= *problema*) harassment, worry
2 (*LAm*) (= *molestia*) nuisance; (= *ira*) rage • **¡qué ~ de vida!** it's a dog's life!, what a life!

apersogar ▹ CONJUG 1h VT [+ *animal*] to tether, tie up; (*Caribe*) (= *atar cosas juntas*) to string together

apersonado ADJ • **bien ~** presentable, nice-looking • **mal ~** unprepossessing

apersonarse ▹ CONJUG 1a VPR (*Jur*) to appear in person; (*Com*) to have a business interview

apertura SF **1** (= *acción*) opening • **la ~ de la caja torácica es una operación delicada** the opening of the rib cage is a delicate operation, opening the rib cage is a delicate operation • **la ~ del cajón activó la bomba** opening the box set off the bomb • **la ~ de la cuenta bancaria requiere tiempo** opening a bank account takes time • **la ~ de las puertas es automática** the doors open automatically
2 (= *comienzo*) start, beginning • **hoy se celebra la ~ del curso académico** today is the start *o* beginning of the new academic year • **la ~ del plazo de matrícula se ha aplazado** the starting date for enrolment has been postponed • **la ~ del juicio se realiza hoy** the trial opens today • **ceremonia de ~** opening ceremony • **sesión de ~** opening session
3 (*Fot*) aperture
4 (*Pol*) (= *liberalización*) opening-up • **la ~ política tras la muerte de Franco** the political opening-up after Franco's death
5 (*Jur*) [*de testamento*] reading • **~ de un juicio hipotecario** foreclosure
6 (*Ajedrez*) opening

aperturar ▹ CONJUG 1a VT to open

aperturismo SM (= *liberalización*) liberalization, relaxation; (*Pol*) (= *política*) policy of liberalization

aperturista ADJ [*tendencia etc*] liberalizing, liberal
SMF liberalizer, liberal

apesadumbrado ADJ sad, distressed

apesadumbrar ▹ CONJUG 1a VT to grieve, sadden
VPR **apesadumbrarse** to be grieved, distress o.s. (**con, de** about, at)

apesarar, apesararse ▹ CONJUG 1a = **apesadumbrar**

apescollar ▹ CONJUG 1l VT (*Cono Sur*) to seize by the neck

apesgar ▹ CONJUG 1h VT to weigh down

apestado ADJ **1** (= *maloliente*) stinking, reeking; (*Med*) plague-ridden
2 • **estar ~ de** (= *repleto*) to be infested with

apestar ▹ CONJUG 1a VT **1** (*Med*) to infect (*with the plague*)
2 (*con olor*) to stink out
3 (*fig*) (= *corromper*) to corrupt, spoil, vitiate (*frm*); (= *molestar*) to plague, harass;

APENAS

El adverbio **apenas** *tiene dos traducciones principales en inglés:* **hardly** *y* **scarcely**, *este último usado en lenguaje más formal.*

▹ *Estos adverbios se colocan normalmente detrás de los verbos auxiliares y modales y delante de los demás verbos:*

Apenas podía hablar después del accidente
He could hardly *o* scarcely speak after the accident
Apenas nos conocemos
We hardly *o* scarcely know each other

▹ *Sin embargo, en oraciones temporales, podemos colocar* **hardly** *y* **scarcely** *al principio de la oración si queremos reforzar la inmediatez de algo, o como recurso estilístico en cuentos y relatos. En este caso los adverbios van siempre seguidos de un verbo auxiliar, con lo que se invierte el orden normal del sujeto y del verbo en inglés, quedando la estructura* **hardly/scarcely** + **had** + *sujeto* + *participio* + **when** *…:*

Apenas me había acostado cuando oí un ruido extraño
Hardly *o* Scarcely had I gone to bed when I heard a strange noise

En este sentido se suele utilizar también **no sooner** + **had** + *sujeto* + *participio* + **than** *…:*

No sooner had I gone to bed than I heard a strange noise

Para otros usos y ejemplos ver la entrada.

(= *repugnar*) to sicken, nauseate
VI to stink, reek (**a** of)
VPR **apestarse 1** (*Med*) (*con la peste*) to catch the plague; (*And, Cono Sur*) (= *resfriarse*) to catch a cold
2 (*Bot*) to be blighted

apestillar ▷ CONJUG 1a VT (*Cono Sur*)
1 (= *agarrar*) to catch, grab hold of
2 (= *regañar*) to tell off, reprimand

apestoso ADJ **1** (= *hediondo*) stinking, reeking; [*olor*] awful, putrid
2 (= *asqueroso*) sickening, nauseating; (= *molesto*) annoying, pestilential

apetachar ▷ CONJUG 1a VT to patch, mend

apetecer ▷ CONJUG 2d VT **1** (= *desear*) to crave, long for
2 (= *atraer*) • **me apetece un helado** I feel like *o* I fancy an ice cream • **¿te apetece?** how about it?, would you like to?
VI • **la idea no apetece** the idea has no appeal *o* is not very attractive • **un vaso de jerez siempre apetece** a glass of sherry is always welcome

apetecible ADJ attractive, tempting

apetencia SF hunger (**de** for)

apetente ADJ hungry

APETI SF ABR = **Asociación Profesional Española de Traductores e Intérpretes**

apetite† SM **1** (= *condimento*) seasoning (*to whet one's appetite*)
2 (= *estímulo*) incentive

apetito SM **1** (= *gana de comer*) appetite (**de** for) • **abrir el ~** to whet one's appetite • **ese olor me está abriendo el ~** that smell is making me hungry • **comer con ~** to eat heartily *o* with appetite • **siempre tiene muy buen ~** he's always got a good *o* hearty appetite • **¿tienes ~?** are you hungry?
2 (= *deseo*) desire, relish (**de** for) • **me quitó el ~ de hacerlo** it destroyed my appetite for doing it ▸ **apetito sexual** sexual appetite

apetitoso ADJ **1** (= *gustoso*) appetizing; (= *sabroso*) tasty; (= *tentador*) tempting, attractive
2 (= *comilón*) fond of good food

apí SM **1** (*And*) *non-alcoholic maize drink*
2 (*And, Cono Sur*) (= *añicos*) • **el vaso se hizo apí** the glass was smashed to pieces

apiadar ▷ CONJUG 1a VT to move to pity
VPR **apiadarse** • **~se de** to pity, take pity on

apiado SM (*Cono Sur*) celery liqueur

apicarado ADJ roguish, mischievous

apicararse ▷ CONJUG 1a VPR to go off the rails*

ápice SM **1** (= *punta*) apex, top
2 [*de problema*] crux • **estar en los ~s de** to be well up in, know all about
3 (*fig*) (= *jota*) • **ni ~** not a whit • **no ceder un ~** not to yield an inch • **no importa un ~** it doesn't matter a bit

apichicarse ▷ CONJUG 1g VPR (*Cono Sur*) to squat, crouch

apicultor(a) SM/F beekeeper, apiarist (*frm*)

apicultura SF beekeeping, apiculture (*frm*)

apilado SM piling, heaping

apiladora SF stacker

apilar ▷ CONJUG 1a VT to pile up, heap up
VPR **apilarse** to pile up, mount

apilonar ▷ CONJUG 1a VT (*LAm*) = **apilar**

apimplado* ADJ sloshed*, pissed**, trashed (*EEUU*‡)

apiñado ADJ **1** (= *apretado*) crammed, packed (**de** with)
2 [*forma*] cone-shaped, pyramidal (*frm*)

apiñadura SF, **apiñamiento** SM crowding, congestion

apiñar ▷ CONJUG 1a VT (= *agrupar*) to crowd together, bunch together; (= *apretar*) to pack in; [+ *espacio*] to overcrowd, congest
VPR **apiñarse** to crowd together, press together • **la multitud se apiñaba alrededor de él** the crowd pressed round him

apio SM **1** (= *planta*) celery ▸ **apio nabo** celeriac
2 (*Esp*‡) (= *afeminado*) queer‡, poof‡, fag (*EEUU*‡)

apiolar‡ ▷ CONJUG 1a VT **1** (= *detener*) to nab*, nick‡
2 (= *matar*) to do in‡, bump off‡
VPR **apiolarse** (*Arg, Uru*) to wise up*

apiparse* ▷ CONJUG 1a VPR to stuff o.s.*

apir SM (*LAm*), **apiri** SM (*LAm*) mine worker

apirularse ▷ CONJUG 1a VPR (*Cono Sur*) to get dressed up to the nines

apisonadora SF (*con rodillo*) steamroller, road roller; (= *pisón*) tamp hammer

apisonar ▷ CONJUG 1a VT (*con rodillo*) to roll, roll flat; (*con pisón*) to tamp down, ram down

apitiquarse ▷ CONJUG 1a VPR (*And*) to get depressed

apitonar ▷ CONJUG 1a VT [+ *cáscara*] to pierce, break through
VI [*cuernos*] to sprout; [*animal*] to begin to grow horns
VPR **apitonarse*** (= *enfadarse*) to go into a huff*; [*dos personas*] (= *pelearse*) to have a slanging match*

apizarrado ADJ slate-coloured, slate-colored (*EEUU*)

aplacar ▷ CONJUG 1g VT (= *apaciguar*) [+ *persona*] to appease, placate; [+ *hambre*] to satisfy; [+ *sed*] to quench, satisfy • **intenté ~ los ánimos de todos** I tried to calm everyone down
VPR **aplacarse** [*tormenta*] to die down • **al final se ~on los ánimos** people finally calmed down

aplanacalles* SM INV (*LAm*) idler, layabout*

aplanado ADJ **1** [*superficie*] levelled, leveled (*EEUU*)
2* [*persona*] • **la noticia lo dejó ~** he was stunned by the news • **quedar ~** to be stunned

aplanador SM ▸ **aplanador de calles** idler, layabout

aplanamiento SM (= *nivelación*) levelling, leveling (*EEUU*), flattening; (= *derrumbe*) collapse

aplanar ▷ CONJUG 1a VT **1** (= *nivelar*) to level, make even • MODISMO: • **~ calles** (*LAm**) to loaf about
2 (*And*) [+ *ropa*] to iron, press
3* (= *asombrar*) to bowl over
VPR **aplanarse 1** (*Arquit*) to collapse, cave in
2 (= *desanimarse*) to get discouraged; (= *aletargarse*) to become lethargic, sink into lethargy

aplanchar ▷ CONJUG 1a VT (*LAm*) = **planchar**

aplastamiento SM crushing

aplastante ADJ overwhelming, crushing

aplastar ▷ CONJUG 1a VT **1** [+ *insecto etc*] to squash, crush
2 (*fig*) (= *vencer*) to crush, overwhelm; (*con argumentos*) to floor
VPR **aplastarse 1** (= *quedarse plano*) to be squashed; [*coche*] to crash, smash (**contra** on, against)
2 (= *espachurrarse*) to flatten o.s. • **se aplastó contra la pared** he flattened himself against the wall
3 (*Cono Sur*) (= *desanimarse*) to get discouraged, lose heart; (= *atemorizarse*) to get scared, take fright; (= *agotarse*) to wear o.s. out, tire o.s. out

aplatanado* ADJ **1** (= *soso*) lumpish, lacking all ambition; (= *aletargado*) weary, lethargic
2 • **está ~** (*Caribe*) (= *acriollado*) he has gone native

aplatanarse* ▷ CONJUG 1a VPR
1 (= *abandonarse*) to become lethargic, sink into lethargy
2 (*Caribe*) (= *acriollarse*) to go native

aplatarse ▷ CONJUG 1a VPR (*Caribe*) to get rich

aplaudir ▷ CONJUG 3a VT **1** [+ *actuación*] to applaud
2 (= *aprobar*) to welcome, approve
VI (= *dar palmadas*) to applaud, clap

aplauso SM **1** (= *palmadas*) applause • **un ~ cerrado** a warm round of applause • **~s** applause (*sing*), clapping (*sing*)
2 (= *aprobación*) approval, acclaim

aplausómetro SM clapometer

aplazamiento SM [*de acto*] postponement; (*Econ*) deferment

aplazar ▷ CONJUG 1f VT (= *posponer*) [+ *reunión, juicio*] (*antes de iniciarse*) to postpone, put back; (*ya iniciado*) to adjourn; [+ *pago*] to defer • **han aplazado el examen al martes** they have postponed the exam until Tuesday, they have put the exam back until Tuesday • **ha aplazado su decisión hasta su regreso** he has postponed *o* put off the decision until his return
VI (*CAm*) (= *suspender*) to fail

aplazo SM (*Arg, Uru*) fail

aplebeyado ADJ coarse, coarsened

aplebeyar ▷ CONJUG 1a VT to coarsen, degrade
VPR **aplebeyarse** to become coarse

aplicabilidad SF **1** [*de decisión, teoría*] applicability (**a** to) • **la ~ de los principios de Mendel al hombre** the applicability of Mendel's principles to man • **una norma de ~ inmediata** a norm that will be made applicable immediately
2 (*Téc*) applicability

aplicable ADJ **1** [*crema, pomada*] applicable • **"no es ~ a los niños"** "not to be used on children"
2 [*interés, método*] applicable • **un ejemplo ~ en la mayoría de los casos** an example applicable *o* that can be applied to the majority of cases • **~ a algn/algo** applicable to sb/sth • **el 3% de comisión ~ a los empresarios** the 3% charge applicable to businessmen • **una oferta ~ a mayores de 60 años** an offer applicable to over-60s

aplicación SF **1** (= *uso externo*) (*tb Med*) use, application (*frm*) • **recomiendan la ~ de compresas frías** they recommend the use *o* application (*frm*) of cold compresses • **una o dos aplicaciones diarias** to be applied once or twice daily • **"solo de aplicación externa"** "for external use only" • **tras la ~ de la primera capa de pintura** after applying the first coat of paint • **~ tópica** external use
2 (= *puesta en práctica*) [*de acuerdo, impuesto, medida*] implementation, application; [*de método*] implementation; [*de sanción, castigo*] imposition • **la ~ de las nuevas tecnologías en la industria** the implementation of new technologies in industry • **en ~ de la ley 9/1968** in accordance with law 9/1968 • **una brigada encargada de vigilar la ~ de las sanciones** a brigade in charge of overseeing the imposition of sanctions
3 (= *dedicación*) application • **le falta ~ en el estudio** he doesn't apply himself enough to his studies, he lacks application in his studies (*frm*)
4 (= *aplique*) (*Cos*) appliqué • **una puerta con hermosas aplicaciones de metal** (*Téc*) a door with beautiful metalwork overlay
5 aplicaciones (= *usos*) (*Téc*) uses, applications; (*Com, Inform*) applications • **un producto con múltiples aplicaciones en la**

industria a product with multiple uses in industry • **aplicaciones comerciales** business applications • **aplicaciones de gestión** management applications
6 (*Bol, Col, Ven*) (= *solicitud*) application • **enviar una ~** to send an application
aplicado ADJ 1 [*ciencia*] applied
2 (= *estudioso*) conscientious, diligent • **un niño muy ~** a very conscientious *o* diligent child • **es muy ~ en matemáticas** he works very hard at mathematics
aplicador ADJ applicator (*antes de s*)
SM applicator
aplicar ▷ CONJUG 1g VT 1 (= *poner*) **a** (*Med*) [+ *crema, pomada*] to apply; [+ *inyección, tratamiento*] to give, administer (*frm*) (**a** to) • **~ suavemente sobre la piel** apply lightly over the skin • **se debe ~ quimioterapia** it needs to be treated with chemotherapy
b (*frm*) [+ *pintura, pegamento*] to apply (*frm*)
2 (= *poner en práctica*) [+ *teoría*] to put into practice; [+ *técnica*] to use; [+ *principio*] to apply; [+ *descuento*] to give; [+ *sanción, castigo*] to impose, apply • **ahora tienes que ~ lo que has aprendido** now you have to put into practice what you have learnt • **su objetivo es ~ los acuerdos de paz** her aim is to put the peace agreements into practice *o* effect • **no se puede ~ la ley a su caso** the law cannot be applied to their case • **le ~on la legislación antiterrorista en el interrogatorio** he was questioned under anti-terrorist laws • **medidas que serán aplicadas progresivamente** measures that will be implemented step by step • **van a ~ una política de austeridad** they are going to impose a policy of austerity • **durante el verano aplicamos descuentos especiales** during the summer we offer *o* give special discounts
3 (= *dedicar*) • **~ a algo** [+ *esfuerzos, tiempo*] to devote to sth; [+ *recursos*] to apply to sth • **aplica tus esfuerzos a conseguir tus objetivos** devote your efforts to achieving your aims
VI (*Bol, Col, Ven*) to apply • **~ a algo** to apply for sth
VPR **aplicarse** 1 [+ *crema, pomada*] to apply (**a, en** to) • **aplíquese la pomada en la quemadura** apply the cream to the burn
2 (= *esforzarse*) • **si no te aplicas más, vas a suspender** if you don't work harder *o* if you don't apply yourself to your studies, you are going to fail • **~se en algo** to work hard at sth; ▷ **cuento¹**
aplique SM (= *lámpara*) wall lamp; (*Teat*) piece of stage décor; (*Cos*) appliqué
aplomado ADJ self-confident
aplomar ▷ CONJUG 1a VT 1 (*Arquit*) to plumb
2 (*Chile*) (= *dar vergüenza*) to embarrass
VPR **aplomarse** 1 (*Arquit*) to collapse, cave in
2 (*Chile*) (= *avergonzarse*) to get embarrassed
3 (= *ganar aplomo*) to become self-assured, gain confidence
aplomo SM (= *serenidad*) assurance, self-possession; (= *gravedad*) gravity, seriousness; (*pey*) (= *frescura*) nerve, cheek • **dijo con el mayor ~** he said with the utmost assurance • **perder el ~** to get worried, get rattled* • **¡qué ~!** what a nerve!, what a cheek!
apnea SF 1 (*durante el sueño*) apnoea, apnea (*EEUU*)
2 (*en buceo*) freediving
apocado ADJ (= *tímido*) timid; (= *humilde*) lowly; (= *falto de voluntad*) spiritless, spineless
apocalipsis SM INV apocalypse • **el Apocalipsis** (*Biblia*) Revelations
apocalíptico ADJ (= *del Apocalipsis, espantoso*) apocalyptic; [*estilo*] obscure, enigmatic
apocamiento SM 1 (= *timidez*) timidity; (= *humildad*) lowliness; (= *falta de voluntad*) spinelessness
2 (= *depresión*) depression, depressed state
apocar ▷ CONJUG 1g VT 1 (= *reducir*) to make smaller, reduce
2 (= *humillar*) to belittle, humiliate; (= *intimidar*) to intimidate • **nada me apoca** nothing scares me
VPR **apocarse** (= *intimidarse*) to shy away; (= *rebajarse*) to sell o.s. short, run o.s. down
apochongarse ▷ CONJUG 1h VPR (*Cono Sur*) to get scared, be frightened
apocopar ▷ CONJUG 1a VT to apocopate (*frm*), shorten
apócope SF apocope, apocopation • **"san" es ~ de "santo"** "san" is an apocopated form of "santo"
apócrifo ADJ apocryphal
apodar ▷ CONJUG 1a VT to nickname, dub
apoderado/a SM/F agent, representative; (*Jur*) proxy, attorney; (*Mús, Dep*) manager
apoderar ▷ CONJUG 1a VT 1 (= *autorizar*) to authorize, empower
2 (*Jur*) to grant power of attorney to
VPR **apoderarse** • **~se de** to seize, take possession of
apodíctico ADJ apodictic, necessarily true
apodo SM (= *mote*) nickname; (*Jur*) false name, alias
apódosis SF INV apodosis
apogeo SM (*Astron*) apogee; (= *punto culminante*) peak, height • **estar en el ~ de su fama** to be at the height of one's fame • **estar en todo su ~** to be on top form
apolillado ADJ moth-eaten
apolilladura SF moth hole
apolillar ▷ CONJUG 1a VT (*Cono Sur**) • **estarla apolillando** to be snoozing*
VPR **apolillarse** (*por la polilla*) to get moth-eaten; (= *hacerse viejo*) to get old
apolíneo ADJ (*Mit*) Apollonian; (*Literat*) classically handsome
apolismado ADJ (*And*) (= *enclenque*) sickly, weak; (*CAm*) (= *vago*) lazy; (*Méx, Caribe*) (= *deprimido*) gloomy, depressed; (*Caribe*) (= *estúpido*) stupid
apolismar ▷ CONJUG 1a VT (*LAm*) to ruin, destroy
VI (*CAm*) to laze about, idle
VPR **apolismarse** (*LAm*) (= *enfermar*) to grow weak, weaken; (= *deprimirse*) to get worried, get depressed; (= *desanimarse*) to lose heart
apoliticismo SM apolitical nature, non-political nature
apolítico ADJ (= *neutral*) apolitical; (*de interés general*) non-political
apoliyar ▷ CONJUG 1a VT = **apolillar**
Apolo SM Apollo
apologética SF apologetics (*sing*)
apologético ADJ apologetic
apología SF (= *defensa*) defence, defense (*EEUU*); (= *elogio*) eulogy • **una ~ del terrorismo** a statement in support *o* in defence of terrorism
apologista SMF apologist
apoltronado ADJ lazy, idle
apoltronarse ▷ CONJUG 1a VPR • **se apoltronó en el sofá** she settled down on the sofa • **desde que se jubiló se ha apoltronado** he has taken it very easy since he retired
apolvillarse ▷ CONJUG 1a VPR (*Cono Sur*) to be blighted
apoplejía SF apoplexy, stroke
apoplético ADJ apoplectic
apoquinar* ▷ CONJUG 1a VT to fork out*, cough up*
aporcar ▷ CONJUG 1g VT to earth up
aporrar* ▷ CONJUG 1a VI to dry up*, get stuck (*in a speech etc*)
VPR **aporrarse** to become a bore, become a nuisance
aporreado ADJ [*vida*] wretched, miserable; [*persona*] rascally
SM (*Caribe*) meat stew, chilli stew
aporreamiento SM beating
aporrear ▷ CONJUG 1a VT 1 (= *pegar*) to beat, club; (= *dar una paliza a*) to beat up
2 (*con el puño*) to thump, pound • **~ el piano** to hammer away at the piano
3 (*LAm*) (= *vencer*) to beat, defeat
4 (= *acosar*) to bother, pester
VPR **aporrearse** (= *pelearse*) to lay into each other; (= *trabajar*) to slave away*, slog*
aporreo SM 1 (= *paliza*) beating
2 (= *ruido*) thumping, pounding
3 (= *molestia*) bother, nuisance
aportación SF contribution • **aportaciones de la mujer** dowry (*sing*)
aportar ▷ CONJUG 1a VT 1 [+ *bienes, dinero*] to contribute • **aportó sus conocimientos de física nuclear** he contributed his knowledge of nuclear physics • **~ ideas** to contribute ideas • **su estudio no aporta nada nuevo** his study contributes nothing new • **aporta el 25% del calcio necesario** it provides 25% of the calcium requirement • **el viaje me aportó nuevas sensaciones** the journey brought me new experiences
2 [+ *pruebas*] to provide
VI (*Náut*) to reach port
VPR **aportarse** (*Chile*) (= *aparecer*) to show up
aporte SM (*LAm*) contribution ▸ **aporte calórico** calorie content ▸ **aporte jubilatorio** pension contribution
aportillar ▷ CONJUG 1a VT (= *romper*) to break down, break open; [+ *muro*] to breach
VPR **aportillarse** (= *desplomarse*) to collapse, tumble down
aposentar ▷ CONJUG 1a VT to lodge, put up
VPR **aposentarse** to lodge, put up (**en** at)
aposento SM (= *cuarto*) room; (= *hospedaje*) lodging
aposesionarse ▷ CONJUG 1a VPR • **~ de** to take possession of
aposición SF apposition • **en ~** in apposition
apositivo ADJ appositional
apósito SM dressing
aposta ADV on purpose, deliberately
apostadero SM (*Mil*) posting; (*Náut*) naval station
apostador(a) SM/F better, punter • **~(a) profesional** bookmaker
apostar¹ ▷ CONJUG 1a VT (*Mil*) to station, position • **había soldados apostados en todas las esquinas** there were soldiers stationed *o* positioned at every corner
VPR **apostarse** • **~se en un lugar** to position o.s. in *o* at a place
apostar² ▷ CONJUG 1l VT to bet (**a, en** on) • **he apostado diez euros en la quiniela** I've bet ten euros on the football pools • **~ algo a algo** to bet sth on sth • **aposté diez libras al ganador** I bet ten pounds on the winner • **ha apostado su futuro político a la victoria en las elecciones** he has staked his political future on the election victory • **~ algo a que** (+ *indic*) to bet sth that • **apuesto lo que sea a que es mentira** I'll bet you anything that it's a lie • **he apostado treinta euros con él a que no gana** I've bet him thirty euros that he won't win
VI to bet (**a, por** on) • **no me gusta ~ a los caballos** I don't like to bet *o* gamble on the horses • **~ por algo:** • **apostó por la calidad en vez de la cantidad** he opted *o* went for quality not quantity • **no todo el mundo apostaba por su éxito** not everyone believed in his success • **creía en el proyecto y apostó**

por nosotros he believed in the project and was behind us all the way *o* backed us all the way • **han apostado por una política de neutralidad** they have committed themselves to a policy of neutrality • **~ a que** to bet that • **apuesto a que no lo encontráis** I bet you don't find it • **—no creo que él sea culpable —pues yo apuesto a que sí** "I don't think he's guilty" — "I bet he is"
VPR **apostarse** to bet • **me apuesto cualquier cosa a que no vienen** I bet you anything they don't come • **¿qué te apuestas a que gano yo?** what do you bet that I'll win? • **apostárselas a** *o* **con algn** to compete with sb

apostasía SF apostasy

apóstata SMF apostate

apostatar ▹ CONJUG 1a VI **1** (*Rel*) to apostatize (**de** from)
2 (= *cambiar de bando*) to change sides

apostema SF abscess

a posteriori ADV **1** (= *después*) (*gen*) at a later stage; [*comprender*] with (the benefit of) hindsight
2 (*Lógica, Jur*) a posteriori

apostilla SF footnote

apostillar ▹ CONJUG 1a VT **1** (= *poner apostillas a*) to add notes to, annotate
2 (= *agregar*) to add, chime in with; [+ *observación*] to echo • **—sí, apostilló una voz** "yes," a voice added

apóstol SM (*Rel*) apostle
SMF [*de ideas, movimientos*] advocate

apostolado SM apostolate ▸ **apostolado seglar** lay ministry

apostólico ADJ apostolic

apostrofar ▹ CONJUG 1a VT **1** (= *dirigirse a*) to apostrophize (*frm*), address
2 (= *injuriar*) to insult

apóstrofe SM **1** (*en retórica*) apostrophe
2 (= *injuria*) insult; (= *reprensión*) rebuke, reprimand

apóstrofo SM apostrophe

apostura SF (= *esmero*) neatness; (= *elegancia*) elegance; (= *belleza*) good looks (*pl*)

apotegma SM apothegm, maxim

apoteósico ADJ huge, tremendous

apoteosis SF INV apotheosis

apoyabrazos SM INV armrest

apoyacabezas SM INV headrest

apoyador(a) SM (= *soporte*) support, bracket
SM/F (*Pol*) seconder

apoyalibros SM INV book end

apoyamuñecas SM INV wrist rest

apoyapié, apoyapiés SM INV footrest

apoyar ▹ CONJUG 1a VT **1** (= *reclinar*) to rest, lean • **apoya la cabeza en mi hombro** rest *o* lean your head on my shoulder • **no apoyes los codos en la mesa** don't put *o* lean your elbows on the table • **apoya la bicicleta contra la pared** lean the bicycle against the wall
2 (= *ayudar*) to support • **no me apoyan en nada de lo que hago** they don't support me in anything I do • **no ~emos más al gobierno** we will no longer support the government • **los nuevos datos apoyan mi teoría** the new information supports my theory
3 (= *basar*) to base • **apoya su argumento en los siguientes hechos** he bases his argument on the following facts
4 (= *secundar*) [+ *propuesta, idea*] to support
5 (*Arquit, Téc*) to support
VPR **apoyarse 1** (= *reclinarse*) to lean • **apóyate aquí** lean on this • **~se en algo/algn** to lean on sth/sb • **apóyate en mi hombro para pasar el arroyo** lean on my shoulder while we cross the stream • **~se contra algo** to lean against sth • **me apoyé contra la pared** I leaned against the wall • **la cúpula se apoya en tres pilares** the dome is supported by three pillars
2 (= *basarse*) • **~se en algo** to be based on sth • **¿en qué se apoya usted para decir eso?** on what do you base that statement?
3 (= *confiar*) • **~se en algn** to rely on sb • **se apoyó en sus amigos para pasar la crisis** she relied on her friends to get through the crisis

apoyatura SF **1** (= *apoyo*) support
2 (*Mús*) appoggiatura

apoyo SM **1** (= *ayuda*) support • **siempre cuento con el ~ de mis padres** I can always rely on my parents' support • **han retirado su ~ parlamentario** they've withdrawn their support in parliament • **~ económico** financial support • **~ psicológico** counselling, counseling (*EEUU*)
2 (*a una propuesta, idea*) support, backing
3 (= *apoyatura*) support • **el paraguas también me sirve de ~** my umbrella is also a support

apozarse ▹ CONJUG 1f VPR (*And, Cono Sur*) to form a pool

app SF (PL: **apps**) (*para móvil, Internet*) app • **descarga ~s gratis** download free apps

APRA SF ABR (*Perú*) (*Pol*) = **Alianza Popular Revolucionaria Americana**

apreciable ADJ **1** (= *perceptible*) appreciable, substantial; [*cantidad*] considerable • **~ al oído** audible
2 [*persona*] (= *digno de aprecio*) worthy, esteemed • **los ~s esposos** the esteemed couple

apreciación SF **1** (= *evaluación*) appreciation, appraisal; (*Com, Econ*) valuation, appraisal (*EEUU*) • **según nuestra ~** according to our estimation ▸ **apreciación del trabajo** job evaluation
2 (= *subida*) appreciation

apreciado ADJ worthy, esteemed • **"Apreciado Sr. ..."** "Dear Sir ..."

apreciar ▹ CONJUG 1b VT **1** (= *tener cariño a*) to be fond of, like • **aprecio mucho a tu padre** I'm very fond of your father
2 (= *valorar*) to value • **~ algo (en) mucho** to value sth highly • **~ algo (en) poco** to attach little value to sth, set little value on sth
3 (= *percibir*) [+ *comida, música*] to appreciate • **no sabe ~ un buen vino** he doesn't know how to appreciate a good wine
4 (*Econ*) [+ *moneda*] to revalue
5 (= *agradecer*) to appreciate • **aprecio mucho lo que han hecho por mí** I really appreciate what they've done for me
6 (= *detectar*) to notice, detect • **no apreció el sarcasmo en sus palabras** he didn't notice *o* detect the sarcasm in her words • **~on una fractura en el hueso** they detected *o* found a bone fracture • **este barómetro no aprecia cambios mínimos** this barometer doesn't detect *o* register very small changes
7 (*LAm*) (= *realzar*) to add value to, enhance, improve
VPR **apreciarse 1** (= *percibirse*) • **se aprecia la diferencia** you can tell *o* appreciate the difference • **como se aprecia en la radiografía ...** as you can see in the X-ray ... • **se ~á un aumento de las temperaturas** there will be a rise in temperature
2 [*moneda*] to appreciate, rise (in value); [*valor*] to appreciate, rise

apreciativo ADJ appreciative • **una mirada apreciativa** an appraising look, a look of appraisal

apreciatorio ADJ • **presión apreciatoria** upward pressure • **tendencia apreciatoria** upward tendency, tendency to rise

aprecio SM **1** (*Com, Econ*) valuation, appraisal (*EEUU*)
2 (= *estima*) appreciation • **no hacerle ~ algo** to pay no heed to sth • **tener a algn en gran ~** to hold sb in high regard • **en señal de mi ~** as a token of my esteem
3 (= *caso*) • **no hacer ~ de algo** (*Méx*) to pay no attention to sth, take no notice of sth

aprehender ▹ CONJUG 2a VT **1** [+ *individuo*] to apprehend, detain; [+ *bienes*] to seize
2 (*Fil*) to understand; (= *concebir*) to conceive, think; (= *concretar*) to pin down

aprehensible ADJ (= *comprensible*) understandable; (= *concebible*) conceivable • **una idea difícilmente ~** an idea which is difficult to pin down, an idea not readily understood

aprehensión SF **1** [*de individuo*] apprehension, capture; [*de bienes*] seizure
2 (*Fil*) (= *comprensión*) understanding; (= *percepción*) conception, perception

apremiador ADJ, **apremiante** ADJ urgent, pressing

apremiar ▹ CONJUG 1b VT **1** (= *apurar*) to urge, urge on, press; (= *obligar*) to force • **~ a algn a hacer algo** • **~ a algn para que haga algo** to press sb to do sth
2 (= *dar prisa a*) to hurry, hurry along
3 (= *oprimir*) to oppress; (= *acosar*) to harass
VI to be urgent • **apremiaba repararlo** it was in urgent need of repair work, it urgently needed repairing *o* to be repaired • **el tiempo apremia** time is pressing

apremio SM **1** (= *urgencia*) urgency, pressure; (= *obligación*) compulsion • **por ~ de trabajo/tiempo** because of pressure of work/time • **procedimiento de ~** compulsory procedure ▸ **apremio de pago** demand note
2 (*Jur*) writ, judgment
3 (= *opresión*) oppression; (= *acoso*) harassment

aprender ▹ CONJUG 2a VT to learn • **~ algo de memoria** to learn sth (off) by heart, memorize sth • **~ a hacer algo** to learn to do sth
VI to learn
VPR **aprenderse** ▹ VT

aprendiz(a) SM/F **1** [*de oficio*] apprentice; (*Com etc*) trainee, intern (*EEUU*) • **estar de ~ con algn** to be apprenticed to sb • MODISMO: • **~ de todo y oficial de nada** jack of all trades and master of none ▸ **aprendiz de brujo** sorcerer's apprentice ▸ **aprendiz(a) de comercio** business trainee
2 (= *novato*) beginner, novice; (*Dep*) novice, junior

aprendizaje SM **1** (*industrial etc*) apprenticeship; (*Com etc*) training period, internship (*EEUU*) • **hacer su ~** to serve one's apprenticeship • **pagar su ~*** to learn the hard way
2 (= *el aprender*) learning • **dificultades de ~** learning difficulties

aprensar ▹ CONJUG 1a VT **1** (*Téc*) to press, crush
2 (*fig*) (= *oprimir*) to oppress, crush; (= *afligir*) to distress

aprensión SF **1** (= *miedo*) apprehension, fear; (= *capricho*) odd idea; (= *hipocondría*) hypochondria, fear of being ill
2 (= *reparo*) misgiving; (= *escrúpulos*) squeamishness

aprensivo ADJ (= *preocupado*) apprehensive, worried; (= *escrupuloso*) squeamish

apresador(a) SM/F captor

apresamiento SM capture

apresar ▹ CONJUG 1a VT **1** (= *coger*) to catch; [+ *criminal*] to capture, catch; [+ *buque*] to take
2 [*animal*] to seize
3 (*Jur*) to seize

aprestado ADJ ready • **estar ~ para** (+ *infin*) to be ready to (+ *infin*)

aprestar ▹ CONJUG 1a VT (= *preparar*) to prepare, get ready; (*Arte*) to prime, size;

[+ tejido] to size
VPR **apretarse** to prepare, get ready • **~se a** *o* **para hacer algo** to prepare *o* get ready to do sth
apresto SM **1** (= *tratamiento*) stiffening, starching
2 (= *sustancia*) size
apresuradamente ADV hurriedly, hastily
apresurado ADJ (= *hecho con prisa*) hurried, hasty; [*paso*] quick
apresuramiento SM hurry, haste
apresurar ▹ CONJUG 1a VT (= *dar prisa a*) to hurry, hurry along; (= *acelerar*) to speed up; [+ *paso*] to quicken
VPR **apresurarse** to hurry, make haste • **~se a** *o* **por hacer algo** to hurry to do sth • **me apresuré a sugerir que ...** I hastily suggested that ..., I hastened to suggest that ...
apretadamente ADV tightly
apretadera SF **1** (= *correa, cuerda*) strap, rope
2 apretaderas* pressure (*sing*), insistence (*sing*)
apretado ADJ **1** [*tapa, tornillo, ropa*] tight • **no hagas el nudo tan ~** don't make the knot so tight • **el jersey te queda demasiado ~** the jumper is too tight on you • **le puso la venda bien apretadita en la pierna** she put the bandage tightly around his leg, she tightened the bandage around his leg
2 (= *difícil*) difficult • **hemos pasado por épocas muy apretadas** we have been through some quite difficult *o* hard times • **andamos muy ~s de dinero** we are very short of money • **una victoria muy apretada** a very close victory
3 (= *ocupado*) [*agenda, mañana*] busy • **un ~ programa de actividades** a very full *o* busy programme of activities
4 (= *apretujado*) (*en asiento, vehículo*) squashed, cramped • **si te sientas ahí, vamos a estar muy ~s** if you sit there we're going to be really squashed *o* cramped • **pusieron a los hinchas ~s contra las vallas** they shoved *o* pushed the fans against the barriers
5* (= *tacaño*) tight-fisted*, tight*
6* (= *tozudo*) pig-headed*
7 [*escritura*] cramped
8 (*Méx*) (= *presumido*) conceited
9 (*Caribe*) (*sin dinero*) broke*, flat (*EEUU**)
10 (*Ven*) (= *aprovechado*) • **usa el teléfono sin pedir permiso ¡qué ~ es!** he uses the phone without asking permission, he's got a real cheek*
apretar ▹ CONJUG 1j VT **1** [+ *tapa, tornillo, nudo*] to tighten
2 (= *pulsar*) [+ *interruptor, pedal, tecla*] to press; [+ *gatillo*] to squeeze, pull • **aprieta el botón derecho del ratón** press the right-hand button on the mouse • **~ el acelerador** to put one's foot down (on the accelerator), depress the accelerator (*frm*)
3 (= *apretujar*) **a** [+ *objeto*] to squeeze, grip; (*para que no caiga*) to clutch • **apretó bien los papeles en la cartera** he packed *o* squeezed the papers into the briefcase • **apretaba entre sus manos un ramo de flores** he was clutching a bunch of flowers in his hands • **con un puro apretado entre los dientes** with a cigar between his teeth • **hay que ~ el compost con los dedos** you have to press the compost down with your fingers • **~ los dientes** to grit one's teeth, clench one's teeth • **~ la mano a algn** to shake sb's hand • **~ el puño** to clench one's fist
b [+ *persona*] (*contra pared, suelo*) to pin, press; (*con los brazos*) to clasp, clutch • **me apretaba con todo su cuerpo contra la pared** he pinned *o* pressed me against the wall with his whole body • **la apretó con fuerza entre sus brazos** he clasped *o* clutched her tightly in his arms
4 (= *presionar*) • **~ a algn** to put pressure on sb • **nos aprieta mucho para que estudiemos** he puts a lot of pressure on us to study, he pushes us to study hard • MODISMO: • **~ las clavijas** *o* **las tuercas a algn** to put *o* tighten the screws on sb
5 • **~ el paso** to quicken one's pace
6 • **aprieta mucho la letra cuando escribe** he bunches up the words when he writes
7 (*Mil*) [+ *asedio*] to step up, intensify; [+ *bloqueo*] to tighten
VI **1** (= *oprimir*) [*zapatos*] to be too tight, pinch one's feet; [*ropa*] to be too tight • **estos zapatos aprietan** these shoes are too tight, these shoes pinch my feet • **este vestido me aprieta en la cintura** this dress is too tight for me around the waist; ▹ **zapato**
2 (= *aumentar*) [*dolor, frío*] to get worse; [*viento*] to intensify • **es media mañana y el hambre aprieta** it's half way through the morning and I'm beginning to feel hungry • **cuando el frío aprieta** when the cold gets worse, when it gets really cold • **donde más aprieta el calor** where the heat is at its worst
3 (= *presionar*) to put on the pressure, pile on the pressure* • **la oposición aprieta cada vez más** the opposition are putting on more and more pressure • **si le aprietan un poco más, confesará** if they put a bit more pressure on him, he'll confess • **~ con el enemigo** to close with the enemy; ▹ **Dios**
4 (= *esforzarse*) • **si apretáis un poco al final, aprobaréis** if you make an extra effort at the end, you'll pass
5 • **~ a hacer algo:** • **si aprieta a llover** if it starts to rain heavily • **apretamos a correr** we broke into a run
6 • **¡aprieta!** nonsense!, good grief!
7 (*Chile*) (= *irse con prisa*) • **apretemos que viene la profesora** let's run for it, the teacher's coming • **fueron los primeros en salir apretando después del golpe** they were the first ones to make a getaway after the coup
8‡ (*al defecar*) to push
VPR **apretarse 1** (= *arrimarse*) (*en asiento*) to squeeze up; (*para abrigarse*) to huddle together • **¿os podéis ~ un poco para hacerme sitio?** could you squeeze up a bit to make room for me? • **los diez sospechosos se apretaban en dos bancos** the ten suspects were squeezed together on two benches • **se aprietan unos contra otros en busca de calor** they huddle together for warmth
2 • **~se el cinturón** to tighten one's belt
apretón SM **1** (= *presión*) squeeze • **con un ~ en el brazo me indicó que me callase** he squeezed my arm *o* he gave my arm a squeeze to tell me to be quiet • **los apretones y empujones del metro** the pushing and shoving on the underground ▸ **apretón financiero** financial squeeze
2 (= *abrazo*) hug • **dar un ~ a algn** to give sb a hug ▸ **apretón de manos** handshake • **se dieron un ~ de manos** they shook hands
3 (= *apuro*) = **aprieto**
4 (= *esfuerzo*) push • **con un ~ más al final habría aprobado** with an extra effort at the end, he would have passed
5 (*en una carrera*) dash, sprint
6 (*euf*) [*de vientre*] urgent call of nature (*euf*)
apretujar ▹ CONJUG 1a VT (= *apretar*) to press hard, squeeze hard; (= *abrazar*) to hug, give a bear hug; (= *estrujar*) to crush, crumple • **estar apretujado entre dos personas** to be sandwiched *o* squashed between two people
VPR **apretujarse** (= *estrujarse*) to squeeze up, budge up* • **si os apretujáis un poco más cabemos todos** if you squeeze up *o* budge up* a bit more, we'll all fit in
apretujón SM **1** (= *apretón*) hard squeeze; (= *abrazo*) big hug, bear hug
2 (= *agolpamiento*) press, crush, jam
apretura SF **1** = **apretón, apretujón**
2 (= *pobreza*) poverty
aprieto SM **1** (= *apuro*) predicament • **estar** *o* **verse en un ~** to be in a predicament, be in a tight spot, be in an awkward situation • **poner a algn en un ~** to put sb in a predicament, put sb in an awkward situation • **la derrota puso en un ~ su continuidad como entrenador** the defeat put his continuation as trainer in jeopardy • **ayudar a algn a salir de un ~** to help sb out of trouble *o* out of a tight spot
2 (= *presión*) = **apretón**
a priori ADV **1** (= *antes*) (*gen*) beforehand; [*juzgar*] in advance
2 (*Lógica, Jur*) a priori
apriorismo SM *tendency to resolve matters quickly*
apriorístico ADJ **1** (= *deductivo*) a priori, deductive
2 (= *precipitado*) hasty, premature
aprisa ADV quickly, hurriedly
aprisco SM sheepfold
aprisionar ▹ CONJUG 1a VT (= *encarcelar*) to imprison, put in prison; (= *atar*) to bind, tie; (= *atrapar*) to trap; (= *aherrojar*) (*tb fig*) to shackle
aprismo SM (*And*) *doctrine of APRA*
aprista ADJ pertaining to APRA, supporting APRA
SMF supporter of APRA
aprobación SF **1** (*Pol*) [*de una ley*] passing • **la ~ parlamentaria de la ley** the passing of the law by Parliament • **esta ley requiere la ~ por referéndum** this law has to be ratified by a referendum • **el gobierno ha dado su ~ al tratado** the government has ratified the treaty
2 [*de informe, plan, acuerdo*] approval, endorsement • **necesito tu ~ para realizar la venta** I need your approval *o* endorsement to go ahead with the sale • **mis padres nunca me dieron su ~ para casarme** my parents never gave my marriage their approval
aprobado ADJ approved
SM pass, passing grade (*EEUU*)
aprobar ▹ CONJUG 1l VT **1** [+ *ley, proyecto de ley*] to pass; [+ *informe, plan, acuerdo*] to approve, endorse • **el parlamento aprobó el tratado** the treaty was approved *o* endorsed by Parliament
2 [+ *alumno, asignatura*] to pass • **¿aprobaste el examen?** did you pass the exam? • **no he aprobado las matemáticas** I haven't passed mathematics • **no me han aprobado la literatura** I didn't get a pass in literature
3 [+ *decisión, actitud*] to approve of • **no apruebo tu amistad con esa chica** I don't approve of your friendship with that girl • **mi familia aprobó mi decisión de casarme** my family approved of my decision to get married
VI to pass • **aprobé en francés** I passed (in) French
aprobatorio ADJ • **una mirada aprobatoria** an approving look
aproches SMPL **1** (*Mil*) approaches
2 (*LAm*) (= *vecindario*) neighbourhood (*sing*), neighborhood (*sing*) (*EEUU*), district (*sing*)
aprontamiento SM quick delivery, rapid service
aprontar ▹ CONJUG 1a VT (= *preparar*) to

a

prepare without delay; (= *entregar*) to deliver at once
VI (= *pagar*) to pay in advance
apronte SM (*Cono Sur*) **1** (*Dep*) heat, preliminary race
2 • **~s** preparations • **irse en los ~s** to waste one's energy on unnecessary preliminaries
apropiación SF appropriation
▸ **apropiación ilícita** illegal seizure, misappropriation ▸ **apropiación indebida de fondos** misappropriation of funds, embezzlement
apropiadamente ADV appropriately, fittingly
apropiado ADJ appropriate (**para** for), suitable (**para** for)
apropiamiento SM = **apropiación**
apropiar ▷ CONJUG 1b VT **1** (= *adecuar*) to adapt (**a** to), fit (**a** to)
2 • **~ algo a algn** (= *dar*) to give sth to sb; (*LAm*) (= *asignar*) to assign sth to sb; (= *otorgar*) to award sth to sb
VPR **apropiarse** • **~se (de) algo** to appropriate sth
apropincuarse ▷ CONJUG 1d VPR (*hum*) to approach
aprovechable ADJ • **unos cuantos consejos ~s** some useful pieces of advice • **estas tablas son ~s para hacer cajas** those boards can be used to make boxes • **esa camisa es ~ todavía** you can still wear that shirt, that shirt is still wearable
aprovechadamente ADV profitably
aprovechado/a ADJ **1** (= *usado*) • **terrenos muy poco ~s** lands that have not been made the best of • **bien ~** [*dinero, tiempo*] well-spent; [*espacio, recursos*] well-exploited; [*oportunidad*] well-taken, well-used • **el espacio está muy bien ~ en este apartamento** good use has been made of the space in this flat, the space in this flat has been really well exploited • **mal ~** [*dinero, tiempo, oportunidad*] wasted; [*espacio, recursos*] badly-exploited
2 (= *oportunista*) selfish, self-seeking • **no seas tan ~** don't be so selfish *o* self-seeking • **ese vendedor es muy ~** that salesman is a real opportunist
3 (= *ahorrador*) thrifty • **un contable muy ~** a very thrifty accountant
4 (= *aplicado*) [*trabajador*] industrious, hardworking; [*alumno*] resourceful
SM/F (= *oportunista*) • **es un ~** he's such a scrounger*, he's such an opportunist
aprovechamiento SM **1** (= *utilización*) use • **un mejor ~ del espacio** a better use of space • **carbón destinado a su ~ como combustible** coal intended to be used as fuel • **un sistema de ~ del suelo** a system of soil exploitation
2 (= *provecho*) • **sigue las asignaturas con ~** he is progressing in his studies • **conseguir** *o* **sacar el máximo ~ de algo** to get the maximum use *o* advantage out of sth, make the most of sth
aprovechar ▷ CONJUG 1a VT **1** (= *utilizar*) use • **algunas algas son aprovechadas en medicina** some algae are used in medicine • **un intento de ~ los recursos naturales de la zona** an attempt to take advantage of *o* use the area's natural resources • **ha sabido ~ la ocasión y hacer un buen negocio** he managed to take advantage *o* use the opportunity to make a profitable deal • **no quiso ~ su oferta** he chose not to take up their offer • **~ algo para hacer algo** to use sth to do sth, take advantage of sth to do sth • **aprovechó el descanso para tomarse un café** she used *o* took advantage of the break to have a coffee • **vamos a ~ este espacio para hacer un armario** we are going to use this space for a wardrobe • **aproveché que tenía la tarde libre para ir de compras** I took the opportunity of having an afternoon off to go shopping • **quiero ~ esta oportunidad para agradecerles a todos su apoyo** I want to take this opportunity to thank everyone for their support
2 (= *sacar el máximo provecho de*) [+ *tiempo, espacio, ocasión*] to make the most of; [+ *conocimientos, experiencia*] to make use of, make good use of • **hay que organizarse y saber ~ el tiempo** you have to be organized and know how to make the most of *o* get the most out of your time • **hemos movido los muebles para ~ mejor el espacio** we moved the furniture to make better use of the space • **sabe ~ muy bien su atractivo** he knows how to make the most of his good looks • **Sánchez aprovechó el cansancio de su rival** Sánchez capitalized on *o* took advantage of her opponent's tiredness
VI **1** (= *obtener provecho*) • **tú que eres soltera, aprovecha y disfruta** make the most of the fact that you're single and enjoy yourself • **su estrategia no le aprovechó para nada** his strategy did not prove to be of any use *o* advantage to him at all • **~ para hacer algo** to take the opportunity to do sth • **salió a pasear y aprovechó para hacer unas compras** he went out for a walk and took the opportunity to do some shopping • **aprovecha para pedirles el dinero que te deben** take the opportunity to ask them for the money they owe you • **¡que aproveche!** (*al comer*) enjoy your meal!, bon appétit!, enjoy! (*EEUU*)
2 (= *progresar*) to progress • **en ese curso no aprovechamos nada** we didn't get anywhere with that course
VPR **aprovecharse 1** (= *abusar*) to take advantage • **lo puedes usar, pero sin ~te** you can use it but don't take advantage • **todos se aprovechan de mí** everybody takes advantage of me
2 (*Esp*) (= *sacar provecho de*) to make the most of • **aprovechaos ahora que tenéis tiempo** make the most of it now that you have time • **la mayoría no se aprovecha de estos beneficios** most people don't take advantage of these benefits • **hay que ~se de que tenemos tiempo libre** we have to make the most of the fact that we have free time
3 (*en sentido sexual*) • **~se de** [+ *adulto*] to take advantage of; [+ *niño*] to abuse
aprovechón/ona* ADJ opportunistic
SM/F opportunist
aprovisionador(a) SM/F supplier
aprovisionamiento SM **1** (= *provisiones*) supply
2 (= *acto*) purchasing, buying
aprovisionar ▷ CONJUG 1a VT to supply
VPR **aprovisionarse** • **~se de algo** (*para usar*) to get one's supply of sth; (*para almacenar*) to stock up with sth
aprox. ABR (= **aproximadamente**) approx
aproximación SF **1** (*Mat*) approximation (**a** to)
2 (= *proximidad*) nearness, closeness • **no parece ni por ~ que vaya a ceder** he seems to be nowhere near giving up, he doesn't look remotely like giving up
3 (= *acercamiento*) approach (**a** to); (*Pol*) rapprochement
4 (*en lotería*) consolation prize
aproximadamente ADV approximately
aproximado ADJ (= *que se aproxima*) approximate; [*cálculo etc*] rough
aproximamiento SM = **aproximación**
aproximar ▷ CONJUG 1a VT to bring near, bring nearer (**a** to) • **~ una silla** to bring a chair over, draw up a chair
VPR **aproximarse 1** (= *arrimarse*) to come near, come closer • **~se a** (= *acercarse*) to near, approach • **el tren se aproximaba a su destino** the train was nearing *o* approaching its destination
2 • **~se a** [+ *cierta edad*] to be nearly, be getting on for
3 • **~se a** (= *intentar reconciliarse*) to approach, approximate to
aproximativo ADJ (= *que se aproxima*) approximate; [*cálculo etc*] rough
APS SM ABR (= **Advanced Photo System**) (*Inform*) APS
Aptdo. ABR, **aptdo.** ABR (= **apartado postal** *o* **de correos**) P.O. Box
aptitud SF **1** (= *conveniencia*) suitability, fitness (**para** for)
2 (= *capacidad*) aptitude, ability • **carece de ~** he hasn't got the talent • **demostrar tener ~es** to show promise ▸ **aptitud para los negocios** business sense
apto ADJ **1** (= *idóneo*) suitable (**para** for, to), fit (**para** for, to) • **~ para desarrollar** suitable for developing • **~ (para menores)** (*Cine*) suitable for children • **no ~ (para menores)** (*Cine*) unsuitable for children • **~ para el servicio** (*Mil*) fit for military service
2 (= *hábil*) competent, capable • **ser ~ para aprender** to be quick to learn
3 (*Escol*) pass (*antes de s*)
Apto. ABR (= **apartamento**) Apt
apuesta SF **1** (*en juego*) bet • **la ~ era de 100 euros** the bet was 100 euros, it was a 100-euro bet • **hagan sus ~s, señores** place your bets, ladies and gentlemen • **¿cuántas ~s has hecho esta semana en la quiniela?** how much did you bet on the pools this week?
2 (= *desafío*) • **te hago una ~ a que ...** I bet you that ...
3 (= *opción*) • **nuestra ~ por la modernización supondrá un aumento gradual de los gastos** our commitment to modernization will lead to a gradual increase in expenditure • **esa es una ~ de futuro** that is a future hope, that is a hope for the future
4 (*Bridge*) bid
apuesto ADJ **1** (= *guapo*) handsome, nice-looking
2 (= *pulcro*) neat, elegant; (*hum*) (= *peripuesto*) dapper, natty
Apuleyo SM Apuleius
apunamiento SM (*And, Cono Sur*) altitude sickness, mountain sickness
apunarse ▷ CONJUG 1a VPR (*And, Cono Sur*) to get altitude *o* mountain sickness
apuntación SF (= *nota*) note; (*Mús*) notation
apuntado ADJ **1** (= *con punta*) [*ventana, sombrero*] pointed; [*arco*] lancet
2 (= *escrito*) • **lo tengo ~ en alguna parte** I have it written down somewhere
3 (*Cono Sur**) (= *borracho*) merry*, tight*
apuntador(a) SM/F **1** (*Teat*) prompter
• MODISMO: • **no se salvó ni el ~*** no-one was spared
2 (*Méx*) (*Dep*) scorer
apuntalamiento SM propping-up, underpinning
apuntalar ▷ CONJUG 1a VT **1** (*Min, Arquit*) to prop up, shore up; (*Mec*) to strut
2 (= *respaldar*) to support, back
VPR **apuntalarse** (*C. Rica*) to have a snack
apuntamiento SM **1** [*de arma*] aiming
2 (= *anotación*) • **yo realicé el ~ de la mercancía** I noted down the merchandise
3 (*Jur*) judicial report
4 [*de arco, curva*] pointedness

a

5 [*de viga, muro*] support
apuntar ▹ CONJUG 1a (VT) **1** (= *dirigir*) [+ *cámara, pistola, misil*] to aim (**a** at), train (**a** on)
2 (= *sugerir*) to point out • **apuntó la necesidad de una huelga** he pointed out the need for a strike • **apuntó la posibilidad de que no hubiera sido un suicidio** she suggested the possibility that it mightn't have been suicide, she pointed out that it mightn't have been suicide
3 (= *anotar*) **a** (*en cuaderno*) make a note of, note down; (*en lista, tabla*) to enter, record • **apuntó la dirección en su agenda** she made a note of the address in her diary, she noted down the address in her diary • **apuntó la temperatura en un gráfico** she recorded *o* wrote down the temperature on a graph • **apúntalo en mi cuenta** put it on my account • **~ una cantidad a cuenta de algn** to charge a sum to sb's account
b (*Estadística*) [+ *velocidad, tiempo*] to log
4 (= *inscribir*) (*en lista*) to put down; (*en colegio, curso*) to enrol, enroll (EEUU); (*en concurso, competición*) to enter, put down • **¿me puedes ~ para la cena de Navidad?** could you put me down for the Christmas dinner? • **lo han apuntado en un colegio privado** they have enrolled him at a private school
5 (= *decir en voz baja*) (*a actor*) to prompt • **~ la respuesta a algn** to whisper the answer to sb
6 (= *afilar*) to sharpen, put a point on
7 (= *apostar*) [+ *dinero*] to bet
8 (*Cos*) to fasten
(VI) **1** (= *señalar*) (*con arma*) to aim; (*con dedo, objeto*) to point at • **no apuntes hacia ninguna persona** (*con arma*) don't aim at anybody *o* don't point your gun at anybody; (*con dedo*) don't point at anybody • **¡apunten! ¡disparen!** take aim! fire! • **~ con: todos le apuntaban con el dedo** everyone pointed their fingers at her • **no apuntes con la botella hacia la ventana** don't point the bottle at the window • **~ a algn con un arma** to aim a gun at sb, point a gun at sb • **me apuntó al pecho con un fusil** he aimed *o* pointed the gun at my chest • **apuntó con su pistola al cajero y se llevó todo el dinero** he held up the cashier with his gun and took all the money • **MODISMO**: • **~ y no dar** to fail to keep one's word
2 (= *dirigirse*) to point • **la proa apuntaba hacia el sur** the prow was pointing south • **sus declaraciones apuntaban en la dirección opuesta** his statements pointed in the opposite direction • **ese chico apunta demasiado alto** that kid sets his sights too high
3 (= *anotar*) to note down • **¿tienes dónde ~?** have you got something to note this down on? • **apunta, dos kilos de patatas y uno de uvas** note this down *o* make a note, two kilos of potatoes and a kilo of grapes
4 (= *surgir*) [*barba*] to sprout • **ya empezaba a ~ el día** the day was dawning • **una tendencia que ya comenzaba a ~ a finales del siglo** a tendency that had already begun to emerge at the end of the century • **el maíz apunta bien este año** (*LAm*) the corn is coming on nicely this year
5 • **~ a algo** to point to sth • **una hipótesis apunta al origen romano del yacimiento** one hypothesis suggests that the site is of Roman origin • **todo apunta a que van a ganar las elecciones** there is every indication *o* sign that they will win the elections, everything points to them winning the election • **todo parece ~ a que ...** everything seems to indicate that ...
6 (*LAm*) (= *apostar*) to bet, place bets
(VPR) **apuntarse 1** (= *inscribirse*) (*en lista*) to put one's name down; (*en colegio, curso*) to enrol, enroll (EEUU), register; (*en partido, asociación*) to join; (*en concurso, competición*) to enter, put one's name down • **como el viaje es tan barato nos hemos apuntado** as the trip is so cheap we've put our names down to go • **he ido a ~me al paro** I went to sign on the dole • **nos hemos apuntado a un plan de pensiones** we have taken out *o* joined a pension plan • **me he apuntado a un curso de inglés** I've signed up for an English course, I've enrolled on an English course • **~se a una moda** to follow a fashion
2* • **¿te apuntas a un café?** do you fancy a coffee? • **nos vamos de vacaciones a Cuba, ¿alguien se apunta?** we are going on holiday to Cuba, anyone interested? *o* does anyone fancy coming? • **si vais al cine el domingo, llamadme, que yo me apunto** if you're going to the cinema on Sunday, call me, I'll be up for it* • **MODISMO**: • **~se a un bombardeo** (*Esp*) to be game for anything, be up for anything*
3 (= *obtener*) • **~se un tanto** (*Dep*) to score a point; (*fig*) to chalk up a point, score a point, stay one up • **~se una victoria** to score a win, chalk up a win
4 (= *vislumbrarse*) • **a lo lejos se apuntaba la luz del faro** you could make out the lighthouse in the distance • **han seguido la dirección que ya se apuntaba al principio** they have continued in the direction that was evident from the start
5 [*vino*] to turn sour
6 (*Cono Sur**) (= *emborracharse*) to get tight*
apunte (SM) **1 apuntes** (= *notas*) notes • **¿me puedes pasar los ~s de la última clase?** could you give me the notes from the last class? • **ahora unos breves ~s sobre la actualidad** now for some short news items • **sacar ~s** (*Educ*) to take notes; (*Arte*) to make sketches • **tomar ~s** to take notes • **MODISMO**: • **llevar al ~ a algn** (*Cono Sur*) (= *hacer caso*) to take notice of sb; (= *vigilar*) to keep tabs on sb*
▸ **apuntes de campo** nature notes
2 (*Com*) (= *anotación*) entry; (*Cono Sur*) (= *listado*) list of debts, note of money owing
3 (*Arte*) sketch
4 (*Literat*) outline
5 (= *amago*) hint • **con un ~ de sonrisa en los labios** with the hint of a smile on his lips
6 (*Teat*) (= *persona*) prompter; (= *texto*) prompt book
7 (*Naipes*) (= *jugador*) punter; (= *apuesta*) bet
apuntillar ▹ CONJUG 1a (VT) **1** [+ *toro*] to finish off
2 (*fig*) (= *rematar*) to round off
apuñadura (SF) knob, handle
apuñalar ▹ CONJUG 1a (VT) to stab, knife • **~ a algn por la espalda** (*lit, fig*) to stab sb in the back • **~ a algn con la mirada** to look daggers at sb
apuñar ▹ CONJUG 1a (VT) **1** (= *asir*) to seize, seize in one's fist
2 (*Cono Sur*) (= *amasar, heñir*) to knead, knead with the fists
apuñear ▹ CONJUG 1a (VT), **apuñetear** ▹ CONJUG 1a (VT) to punch, strike
apurada* (SF) (*LAm*) • **¿por qué no te echas** *o* **pegas una ~?** why don't you get a move on* *o* hurry up? • **MODISMO**: • **a las ~s** (*Arg, Uru*) in a rush • **todo lo hace a las ~s** she rushes everything, she does everything in a rush • **andaba a las ~s** she was in a rush
apuradamente (ADV) **1** (= *con dificultad*) with great difficulty • **logramos salir ~ de aquel agujero** we managed to get out of that hole with great difficulty • **consiguieron la victoria ~** they gained a hard-fought victory, they gained victory with great difficulty
2 (= *con precisión*) precisely, exactly
3 (*LAm*) (= *de prisa*) hurriedly, in a rush
apurado (ADJ) **1** (= *falto*) (*de dinero*) hard up; (*de tiempo*) in a hurry, in a rush • **a final de mes siempre ando algo ~** I'm always a bit hard up at the end of the month • **siempre voy muy ~ de tiempo** I'm always in a hurry *o* rush • **tú vives ~** you're always stressed out • **MODISMO**: • **casarse ~** (*LAm*) to have a shotgun wedding
2 (= *difícil*) [*situación*] critical; [*triunfo, victoria*] hard-fought • **en tan ~ trance, decidieron entregarse** being in such a critical state, they decided to give in • **un ~ triunfo frente el Cáceres** a hard-fought victory against Cáceres
3 (= *avergonzado*) • **nunca te había visto tan apurada** I had never seen you so embarrassed • **estaba muy ~ porque iba a llegar tarde** I was really worried because I was going to be late
4 (*Esp*) (= *preciso*) [*limpieza, frenada*] precise, exact; [*afeitado*] close, smooth
(SM) (= *afeitado*) close shave • **la cuchilla que le proporciona el máximo nivel de ~** the razor that gives you the closest shave
apuramiento (SM) **1** (= *agotamiento*) exhaustion
2 (= *aclaración*) verification
3 (*Téc*) purification, refinement
apurar ▹ CONJUG 1a (VT) **1** (= *agotar*) [+ *bebida*] to drink up; [+ *comida*] to eat up; [+ *provisión, medios*] to use up, exhaust, finish off • **apuró hasta la última gota de agua** he drank up the last drop of water • **apura tu copa, que nos vamos** drink up, we're going • **apuró la copa hasta el final** he drained the glass • **tenemos que ~ todos los medios para conseguir nuestro objetivo** we have to exhaust all our means to achieve our aim • **apuró hasta el último momento de sus vacaciones** he stretched out his holiday until the last moment
2 (= *agobiar*) to put pressure on, pressurize • **deja que haga lo que pueda sin ~lo** let him do what he can without pressurizing him *o* putting him under pressure • **no dejes que el trabajo te apure** don't let your work get on top of you • **si se me apura, yo diría que es la mejor playa de España** if pushed, I would say that it is the best beach in Spain
3 (= *avergonzar*) to embarrass • **me apuraba oírla hablar de esa manera** it really embarrassed me to hear her speak like that
4 (= *comprobar*) [+ *detalles*] to check on; [+ *cuestión*] to study minutely; [+ *misterio*] to clear up, get to the bottom of
5 (*esp LAm*) (= *meter prisa*) to rush, hurry • **¡no me apures!** don't rush *o* hurry me!
6 (*Téc*) to purify, refine
(VI) (*Chile*) to be urgent • **este trabajo le apura mucho** this job is very urgent • **me apura ver al doctor** I have to see the doctor urgently
(VPR) **apurarse 1** (= *agobiarse*) to get upset, worry (**por** about, over) • **se apura por poca cosa** she gets upset *o* worries about the slightest thing • **¡no te apures, que todo se arreglará!** don't worry, everything will be all right!
2 (= *esforzarse*) to make an effort, go hard at it • **~se por hacer algo** to strive to do sth
3 (*esp LAm*) (= *apresurarse*) to hurry, hurry up • **¡apúrate!** get a move on! • **no te apures** there's no hurry
4 • **~se la barba** (*Esp*) to have a close shave
apuro (SM) **1** (= *aprieto*) predicament • **en caso de auténtico ~, siempre puedes vender**

las joyas if you're in real difficulty *o* in a real predicament you can always sell the jewels • **pueden servir para un caso de ~** they might be useful in an emergency • **vencieron con ~s, por 90-87** they won 90-87, not without a struggle • **vivimos sin ~s gracias a esa pensión** we have no financial worries thanks to that pension • **en ~s**: • **ayudan a empresas en ~s** they help companies in difficulty • **arriesgó su vida para socorrer a un anciano en ~s** he risked his life to help an old man in distress • **llámame si te ves en ~s** call me if you are in trouble • **se vieron en ~s para hacer el hojaldre** they found it difficult to make *o* had trouble making the puff pastry • **pasar ~s** [*de dinero*] to suffer hardship; (*al hacer algo*) to have difficulties • **antes de hacerse famoso pasó muchos ~s** before he became famous he suffered great hardship • **pasaron algunos ~s para llegar a la final** they had a bit of a struggle to reach the final • **poner a algn en ~s** to put sb in an awkward situation, make things awkward for sb • **sacar a algn de un ~** to get sb out of a mess • **me ha sacado de más de un ~** he has got me out of more than one mess • **gracias por sacarme del ~ delante de todos** thanks for getting me off the hook in front of everyone • **salir de un ~** to get out of a tight spot
2 (= *vergüenza*) embarrassment • **se desnudó sin ningún ~** he took off his clothes without any embarrassment • **en mi vida he pasado más ~** I've never been so embarrassed in all my life • **¡qué ~!** how embarrassing! • **me da ~** it embarrasses me, I'm embarrassed • **me da ~ hasta mirarla** I feel embarrassed just looking at her • **sigue dándome ~ entrar sola en los bares** I'm still too embarrassed to go into bars on my own
3 (*LAm*) (= *prisa*) rush • **tener ~** [*persona*] to be in a hurry, be in a rush; [*actividad*] to be urgent • **tenemos mucho ~ en llegar** we need to be there as soon as possible • **MODISMO**: • **casarse de ~** to have a shotgun wedding

apurón SM (*LAm*) (= *prisa*) great haste, great hurry; (*Cono Sur*) (= *impaciencia*) impatience • **andar a los apurones** (*Cono Sur*) to do things in a rush *o* hurry

apurruñar ▸ CONJUG 1a VT (*Caribe*) (= *maltratar*) to maltreat, handle roughly; (= *manosear*) to mess up, rumple

aquejado ADJ • **~ de** (*Med*) suffering from

aquejar ▸ CONJUG 1a VT **1** (= *afligir*) to bother, trouble; (= *importunar*) to worry, harass; (= *cansar*) to weary, tire out • **¿qué le aqueja?** what's up with him?
2 (*Med*) to afflict • **le aqueja una grave enfermedad** he suffers from a serious disease

aquel(la)[1] ADJ DEM that • **~los/as** those
SM (*Esp**) (= *gracia*) charm; (= *atractivo*) sex appeal • **tiene mucho ~** she's got it*, she certainly has sex appeal

aquel(la)[2] PRON DEM, **aquél(la)** PRON DEM that, that one • **~los/as** those, those ones • **estos son negros mientras ~los son blancos** these ones are black, whereas those ones are white • **~ que está en el escaparate** the one that's in the window • **todo ~ que ...** anyone who ... • **como ~ que dice** so to speak

*In the past the standard spelling for these demonstrative pronouns was with an accent (**aquél, aquélla, aquéllos** and **aquéllas**). Nowadays the **Real Academia Española** advises that the accented forms are only required where there might otherwise be confusion with the adjective.*

aquelarre SM **1** (= *reunión de brujas*) witches' coven
2 (= *barahúnda*) uproar, din

aquello PRON DEM INDEF that • **~ no tuvo importancia** that wasn't important • **~ no me gusta** I don't like that • **~ que te conté de mi hermano** that business about my brother I told you about • **~ de que no iba a venir fue mentira** when they said he wasn't coming it was a lie • **¡no se te olvide ~!** see you don't forget what I told you about *o* what I told you to do *etc!* • **~ fue de miedo*** that was awful, wasn't that awful?

aquerenciado ADJ (*Cono Sur, Méx*) in love, loving

aquerenciarse ▸ CONJUG 1b VPR **1** • **~ a un lugar** [*animal*] to become attached to a place
2 (*Cono Sur, Méx*) (= *enamorarse*) to fall in love

aqueridarse ▸ CONJUG 1a VPR (*Caribe*) to set up house together, move in together

aquí ADV **1** (*en el espacio*) here • **~ dentro** in here • **~ mismo** right here • **ven ~** come here • **soy de ~** I'm from (round) here • **la gente de ~** (the) people here • **a 2km de ~** 2km from here • **~ Pepe, ~ Manolo** this is Pepe and this is Manolo • **andar de ~ para allá** to walk up and down *o* to and fro • **hasta ~** so far, thus far (*frm*), as far as here • **por ~** round here • **por ~ cerca** round here somewhere • **venga por ~** come this way • **no pasó por ~** he didn't come this way • **he ~ la razón** (*frm*) herein lies the reason (*frm*) • **MODISMOS**: • **ni de ~ a Lima** *o* **la Luna** there's no comparison • **y ~ no ha pasado nada** and we'll say no more about it • **hubo un lío de ~ te espero*** there was a tremendous fuss
2 (*en el tiempo*) • **de ~ en adelante** from now on • **de ~ a un mes** a month from now • **de ~ a nada** in next to no time • **hasta ~** up till now
3 • **de ~ que** and so, that's why

aquiescencia SF acquiescence

aquiescente ADJ acquiescent

aquietar ▸ CONJUG 1a VT (= *sosegar*) to quieten down, calm down; [+ *temor*] to allay
VPR **aquietarse** to calm, calm down

aquijotado ADJ quixotic

aquilatar ▸ CONJUG 1a VT **1** [+ *metal*] to assay; [+ *joya*] to value, grade
2 (*fig*) (= *evaluar*) to size up, weigh up
VPR **aquilatarse** (*Cono Sur*) to improve

Aquiles SM Achilles

aquilón SM (*poét*) (= *viento*) north wind; (= *norte*) north

Aquisgrán SM Aachen, Aix-la-Chapelle

aquisito* ADV (*LAm*) = **aquí**

aquistar†† ▸ CONJUG 1a VT to win, gain

Aquitania SF Aquitaine

A.R. ABR = **Alteza Real**

ara[1] SF (= *altar*) altar; (= *piedra*) altar stone • **en aras de** in honour *o* (*EEUU*) honor of • **en aras de la exactitud** in the interests of precision

ara[2] SM (*LAm*) (= *pájaro*) parrot

árabe ADJ Arab • **lengua ~** Arabic • **palabra ~** Arabic word • **estilo ~** (*Arquit*) Mauresque
SMF **1** (= *de Arabia*) Arab
2 (*Méx*) (= *vendedor ambulante*) hawker, street vendor
SM (*Ling*) Arabic

arabesco ADJ, SM arabesque

Arabia SF Arabia ▸ **Arabia Saudí, Arabia Saudita** Saudi Arabia

arábigo ADJ [*número*] Arabic
SM (*Ling*) Arabic • **está en ~*** it's all Greek to me • **hablar en ~*** to talk double Dutch*

arábigoandaluz ADJ of Al-Andalus (*Muslim (southern) Spain*)

arabismo SM arabism

arabista SMF Arabist

arabizar ▸ CONJUG 1f VT to arabize

arable ADJ (*esp LAm*) arable

arácnido SM arachnid

arada SF **1** (*Agr*) (= *acción*) ploughing, plowing (*EEUU*)
2 (= *tierra*) ploughed land, plowed land (*EEUU*)
3 (= *jornada*) day's ploughing, day's plowing (*EEUU*)

arado SM **1** plough, plow (*EEUU*)
2 (= *reja*) ploughshare, plowshare (*EEUU*)
3 (*And*) (= *tierra*) ploughland, plowed land (*EEUU*), tilled land; (= *huerto*) orchard

arador SM ploughman, plowman (*EEUU*)

Aragón SM Aragon

aragonés/esa ADJ, SM/F Aragonese
SM (*Ling*) Aragonese

aragonesismo SM aragonesism, *word or phrase etc peculiar to Aragon*

araguato ADJ (*Caribe*) dark, tawny-coloured, tawny-colored (*EEUU*)
SM (*And, Caribe, Méx*) howler monkey

arahuaco ADJ, SM (*Ling*) Arawak

arambel SM **1** (*Cos*) patchwork hangings (*pl*), patchwork quilt
2 (= *triza*) rag, shred, tatter

arameo/a ADJ (*Ling*) Aramaic; [*pueblo*] Aramean
SM/F Aramean
SM (*Ling*) Aramaic

arana SF (= *trampa*) trick, swindle; (= *mentira*) lie

araná SM (*Caribe*) straw hat

arancel SM tariff, duty ▸ **arancel protector** protective tariff

arancelario ADJ tariff (*antes de s*), customs (*antes de s*) • **barrera arancelaria** tariff barrier • **protección arancelaria** tariff protection

arándano SM bilberry, blueberry ▸ **arándano agrio, arándano colorado, arándano encarnado** cranberry

arandela SF **1** (*Téc*) washer
2 [*de vela*] drip collar
3 (*And*) (= *chorrera*) frill, flounce
4 arandelas (*Col*) (= *pastelitos*) teacakes, buns

araña SF **1** (*Zool*) spider • **tela de ~** spider's web • **MODISMO**: • **matar la ~** (= *comer*) to take the edge off one's appetite; (= *perder el tiempo*) to waste time
2 (= *candelabro colgante*) chandelier ▸ **araña de mesa** candelabrum

arañar ▸ CONJUG 1a VT **1** (= *herir*) to scratch
2 (= *recoger*) to scrape together • **pasó los exámenes arañando** (*Arg*) he just scraped through the exams
3* [+ *beneficios*] to rake off, cream off

arañazo SM, **arañón** SM scratch

arañonero SM spider plant

arao SM guillemot

arar ▸ CONJUG 1a VT **1** (*Agr*) to plough, plow (*EEUU*), till
2 (*fig*) (= *hacer surcos en*) to mark, wrinkle

arara SM (*LAm*) parrot

arate‡ SM blood

araucano/a ADJ, SM/F Araucanian

ARAUCANO

The **Araucanos** or **Mapuches** from what is now Chile and western Argentina fiercely resisted both Inca and Spanish attempts to colonize them. Their indomitable spirit is celebrated in Alonso de Ercilla's epic poem **La Araucana**. Their language is today spoken by over 300,000 people and many words of Araucanian origin are used in Chilean and Argentinian Spanish. The name **Chile** is Araucanian for "Land's End".

araucaria SF araucaria, monkey-puzzle tree

arbitrador(a) SM/F arbiter, arbitrator
arbitraje SM **1** (= *juicio*) arbitration
▸ **arbitraje industrial** industrial arbitration
▸ **arbitraje laboral** industrial arbitration
2 (*Com*) arbitrage
3 (*Dep*) refereeing
arbitrajista SMF arbitrageur
arbitral ADJ of a referee, of an umpire
• **una decisión ~** a referee's ruling • **el equipo ~** the referee and his linesmen *o* assistant referees
arbitrar ▹ CONJUG 1a VT **1** [+ *disputa*] to arbitrate in; (*Tenis*) to umpire; (*Boxeo, Ftbl*) to referee
2 [+ *recursos*] to bring together; [+ *fondos*] to raise
VI **1** (= *actuar como árbitro*) to arbitrate; (*Dep*) to umpire, referee • **~ en una disputa** to arbitrate in a dispute • **~ entre A y B** to arbitrate between A and B
2 (*Fil*) to act freely, judge freely
VPR **arbitrarse** to get along, manage
arbitrariamente ADV arbitrarily
arbitrariedad SF **1** (= *cualidad*) arbitrariness
2 (= *acto*) arbitrary act; (= *ultraje*) outrage
arbitrario ADJ arbitrary
arbitrio SM **1** (= *libre albedrío*) free will
2 (= *medio*) means
3 (*Jur*) decision, judgment • **al ~ de** at the discretion of • **dejar al ~ de algn** to leave to sb's discretion
4 (= *impuesto*) excise tax ▸ **arbitrio municipal de plusvalía** municipal capital gains tax
arbitrismo SM arbitrariness, arbitrary nature
arbitrista SMF promoter of crackpot *o* utopian schemes
árbitro/a SM/F (*Jur*) arbiter, arbitrator; (*Tenis*) umpire; (*Boxeo, Ftbl*) referee
árbol SM **1** (*Bot*) tree • MODISMOS: • **los ~es no dejan ver el bosque** you can't see the wood for the trees • **estar en el ~** (*And*) to be in a powerful position ▸ **árbol de la ciencia** tree of knowledge, tree of knowledge of good and evil ▸ **árbol de Navidad** Christmas tree ▸ **árbol de Pascua** (*Cono Sur*) Christmas tree ▸ **árbol frutal** fruit tree ▸ **árbol genealógico** family tree
2 (*Mec*) shaft ▸ **árbol del cigüeñal** crankshaft ▸ **árbol de levas** camshaft
▸ **árbol de transmisión** transmission shaft
▸ **árbol motor** driving shaft
3 (*Náut*) mast ▸ **árbol mayor** mainmast
4 (*Inform*) tree
arbolado ADJ **1** [*tierra*] wooded, tree-covered; [*calle*] tree-lined, lined with trees
2 [*mar*] heavy
SM woodland
arboladura SF rigging
arbolar ▹ CONJUG 1a VT [+ *bandera*] to hoist, raise; [+ *buque*] to fit with masts; (= *esgrimir*) to brandish
VPR **arbolarse** [*caballo*] to rear up
arboleda SF grove, coppice
arboledo SM woodland
arbolejo SM small tree
arbóreo ADJ **1** (*Zool*) arboreal, tree (*antes de s*)
2 (*forma*) tree-like, tree-shaped
arborícola ADJ arboreal, tree-dwelling
arboricultor(a) SM/F forester
arboricultura SF forestry
arborización SF replanting, replanting of trees, reafforestation
arborizar ▹ CONJUG 1f VI to plant trees, replant trees
arbotante SM **1** (*Arquit*) flying buttress
2 (*Méx*) (= *lámpara*) wall lamp
arbustivo ADJ bushy
arbusto SM shrub, bush
arca SF **1** (= *cofre*) chest; (= *caja fuerte*) safe
• **ser un ~ cerrada** [*persona*] to be inscrutable
▸ **arca de hierro** strongbox ▸ **arcas públicas** public funds
2 (*Rel*) ▸ **Arca de la Alianza** Ark of the Covenant ▸ **Arca de Noé** Noah's Ark
3 (= *depósito*) tank, reservoir ▸ **arca de agua** water tower
4 (*Anat*) flank, side
arcabucero SM arquebusier, harquebusier
arcabuco SM thick forest, impenetrable vegetation
arcabuz SM arquebus, harquebus
arcada SF **1** (= *serie de arcos*) arcade
2 [*de puente*] arch, span • **de una sola ~** single-span
3 arcadas (*Med*) retching (*sing*) • **sentir ~s** to retch • **sentía ~s pensando aquello** the very thought of it made him feel sick
árcade ADJ, SMF Arcadian
Arcadia SF Arcady
arcádico ADJ, **arcadio** ADJ Arcadian
arcaduz SM **1** (= *caño*) pipe, conduit; [*de noria*] bucket
2 (*fig*) (= *medio*) channel, way, means
arcaico ADJ archaic
arcaísmo SM archaism
arcaizante ADJ [*estilo*] old-fashioned; [*tono*] nostalgic; [*persona*] fond of archaisms
arcángel SM archangel
arcano ADJ arcane, recondite
SM secret, mystery
arcar ▹ CONJUG 1g = **arquear**
arce SM maple, maple tree
arcediano SM archdeacon
arcén SM **1** [*de autopista*] hard shoulder; [*de carretera*] verge, berm (*EEUU*) ▸ **arcén de servicio** service area
2 (= *borde*) border, edge, brim; [*de muro*] curb, curbstone
archi... PREF arch...; (*en palabras compuestas, p.ej.*) • **archiconservador** ultra-conservative
• **archifresco** as fresh as one can get
• **archipopular** extremely popular • **un niño archimalo** a terribly naughty child • **un hombre archiestúpido** an utterly stupid man
archicomprobado ADJ all too well-known
archiconocido ADJ extremely well-known, famous
archidiácono SM archdeacon
archidiócesis SF INV archdiocese
archiduque SM archduke
archiduquesa SF archduchess
archienemigo/a SM/F arch enemy
archimillonario/a SM/F multimillionaire
archipámpano* SM big shot* • **el ~ de Sevilla** the Great Panjandrum
archipiélago SM **1** [*de islas*] archipelago
2 [*de problemas*] mass (of troubles), sea (of difficulties)
archirrepetido ADJ hackneyed, trite, over-used
archisabido ADJ extremely well-known
• **un hecho ~** common knowledge
architonto/a ADJ utterly silly
SM/F utter fool, complete idiot
archivado ADJ (*LAm*) out-of-date, old-fashioned
SM filing
archivador(a) SM/F (*en archivo*) archivist; (*en oficina*) filing clerk
SM (= *mueble*) filing cabinet; (= *carpeta*) file
archivar ▹ CONJUG 1a VT **1** (= *guardar en un archivo*) to file, store away; (*Inform*) to archive
2 (*fig*) [+ *plan*] to shelve, put on the back burner; (= *memorizar*) to put to the back of one's mind
3 (*LAm*) (= *retirar*) to take out of circulation
4 (*Cono Sur*) (= *encarcelar*) to jail
archivero/a SM/F [*de oficina*] filing clerk; (= *bibliotecario*) archivist • **~ público** registrar
archivista SMF (*LAm*) archivist
archivo SM **1** (= *sitio*) archive, archives (*pl*)
• **fotos de ~** library photos • **imágenes de ~** library pictures ▸ **Archivo Nacional** Public Record Office
2 (= *documentos*) • **~s** files • **buscaremos en los ~s** we'll look in the files ▸ **archivos policiales** police files, police records
▸ **archivo sonoro** sound archive
3 (*Inform*) file • **nombre de ~** file name
▸ **archivo adjunto** attachment ▸ **archivo comprimido** zip file ▸ **archivo de seguridad** backup file ▸ **archivo de transacciones** transactions file ▸ **archivo fuente** source file ▸ **archivo maestro** master file
4 • **de ~*** (= *viejo*) ancient, out of the ark
5 (*And*) (= *oficina*) office
6 (*Cono Sur, Méx*) (= *cárcel*) jail, prison
arcilla SF clay ▸ **arcilla cocida** baked clay
▸ **arcilla de alfarería, arcilla figulina** potter's clay ▸ **arcilla refractaria** fire clay
arcilloso ADJ clayey
arcipreste SM archpriest
arco SM **1** (*Anat, Arquit, Geom*) arch ▸ **arco de herradura** horseshoe arch, Moorish arch
▸ **arco detector de metales** metal detector
▸ **arco ojival** pointed arch ▸ **arco redondo** round arch ▸ **arco triunfal** triumphal arch
2 (= *arma*) bow ▸ **arcos y flechas** bows and arrows
3 (*Mús*) bow ▸ **arco de violín** violin bow
4 (*Pol*) (*tb fig*) ▸ **arco constitucional, arco parlamentario** *range of democratic parties represented in parliament* ▸ **arco político** political spectrum
5 (*Mat, Elec*) arc ▸ **arco iris** rainbow ▸ **arco voltaico** arc lamp
6 (*LAm*) (*Dep*) goal
arcón SM large chest
ARDE SF (*Nic*) (ABR) = **Alianza Revolucionaria Democrática**
ardedor ADJ (*Caribe, Méx*) quick-burning, easy to light
Ardenas SFPL Ardennes
ardentía SF (*Med*) heartburn; (*Náut*) phosphorescence
arder ▹ CONJUG 2a VT **1** (= *quemar*) to burn
2 (*esp LAm**) [*herida*] to sting, make smart
VI **1** (= *quemarse*) to burn • **~ sin llama** to smoulder, smolder (*EEUU*)
2 [*abono*] to ferment; [*trigo etc*] to heat up
3 (*poét*) (= *resplandecer*) to glow, shine, blaze; (= *relampaguear*) to flash
4 (*fig*) (= *consumirse*) to burn, seethe • **~ de** *o* **en amor** to burn with love • **~ de** *o* **en ira** to seethe with anger • **~ en guerra** to be ablaze with war • MODISMO: • **la cosa está que arde** things are coming to a head
VPR **arderse** to burn away, burn up; [*cosecha etc*] to parch, burn up
ardid SM ruse • **~es** tricks, wiles
ardido ADJ **1** (= *valiente*) brave, bold, daring
2 (*LAm*) (= *enojado*) cross, angry
ardiendo ADJ **1** (= *en llamas*) burning, blazing
2 (= *muy caliente*) scalding, steaming hot
ardiente ADJ **1** (= *que quema*) burning; (= *que brilla*) [*color*] blazing; [*flor*] bright red
2 [*deseo, interés*] burning; [*amor*] ardent, passionate; [*aficionado*] passionate; [*partidario*] fervent, ardent
ardientemente ADV ardently, fervently, passionately
ardilla SF **1** (*Zool*) squirrel • **andar como una ~** to be always on the go ▸ **ardilla de tierra** gopher ▸ **ardilla listada** chipmunk

2 (*LAm**) clever businessman/businesswoman, shrewd businessman/businesswoman; (*pey*) (= *trapichero*) wheeler-dealer*
ADJ INV * sharp, clever

ardiloso ADJ **1** (*And, Cono Sur*) (= *mañoso*) crafty, wily
2 (*Cono Sur*) (= *soplón*) loose-tongued

ardimiento¹ SM (= *acto*) burning

ardimiento² SM (= *bizarría*) courage, dash

ardita SF (*And, Caribe, Cono Sur*) = **ardilla**

ardite SM • **(no) me importa un ~** I don't give a damn • **no vale un ~** it's not worth a brass farthing

ardor SM **1** (= *calor*) heat
2 (*Med*) ▸ **ardor de estómago** heartburn
3 (= *fervor*) ardour, ardor (EEUU), eagerness; (= *bizarría*) courage, dash; [*de argumento*] heat, warmth • **en el ~ de la batalla** in the heat of battle

ardoroso ADJ **1** (= *caliente*) hot, burning • **en lo más ~ del estío** in the hottest part of the summer
2 (= *ferviente*) ardent, fervent

arduamente ADV arduously

arduidad SF arduousness

arduo ADJ arduous, hard

área SF **1** (= *zona, superficie*) area ▸ **área de castigo** (*Dep*) penalty area ▸ **área de descanso** (*Aut*) rest area ▸ **área de gol, área de meta** goal area ▸ **área de penalty** (*Dep*) penalty area ▸ **área de servicio** (*Aut*) service area
2 (*Inform*) ▸ **área de excedentes** overflow area
3 (= *campo*) • **en el ~ de los impuestos** in the field of taxation
4 (= *medida*) area (*100 square metres*)
5 ▸ **área metropolitana** metropolitan area, urban district ▸ **área verde** (*Caribe*) green area, park area

arena SF **1** (*Geol*) sand • MODISMO: • **sembrar en ~** to labour *o* (EEUU) labor in vain ▸ **arenas de oro** (*fig*) gold dust (*sing*) ▸ **arenas movedizas** quicksands
2 (*Med*) **arenas** stones
3 (*Dep*) arena

arenal SM **1** (= *terreno arenoso*) sandy spot
2 (*Golf*) bunker, sand trap (EEUU)
3 (*Náut*) sands (*pl*), quicksand

arenar ▹ CONJUG 1a VT **1** (= *restregar con arena*) to sand, sprinkle with sand
2 (*Téc*) to sand, polish with sand, rub with sand

arenga SF **1** (= *discurso*) harangue*, sermon*
2 (*Chile*) (= *discusión*) argument, quarrel

arengar ▹ CONJUG 1h VT to harangue

arenguear ▹ CONJUG 1a VI (*Cono Sur*) to argue, quarrel

arenillas SFPL (*Med*) stones

arenisca SF sandstone

arenisco ADJ sandy

arenoso ADJ sandy

arenque SM herring ▸ **arenque ahumado** kipper

areómetro SM hydrometer

arepa SF (*LAm*) corn pancake • **hacer ~s**** to make love (*lesbians*)

arepera SF (*LAm*) **1** (= *vendedora de arepas*) "arepa" seller
2** (= *tortillera*) lesbian

arepero SM (*Caribe*) poor wretch

arequipa SF (*And*) rice pudding

arequipeño/a ADJ of/from Arequipa
SM/F native/inhabitant of Arequipa • **los ~s** the people of Arequipa

arete SM earring • MODISMO: • **ir** *o* **estar de ~** (*Caribe*) to be a hanger-on

argamandijo* SM set of tools, tackle

argamasa SF mortar

argamasar ▹ CONJUG 1a VT to mortar
VI to mix mortar

árgana SF crane

árganas SFPL (*esp Cono Sur*) wicker baskets, panniers (*carried by horse*)

Argel SM Algiers

Argelia SF Algeria

argelino/a ADJ, SM/F Algerian

argén SM argent

argentado ADJ (*Téc*) silver-plated; [*voz*] silvery

argentar ▹ CONJUG 1a VT to silver-plate

argénteo ADJ = **argentino¹**

argentería SF [*de plata*] silver embroidery; [*de oro*] gold embroidery

Argentina SF (*tb* **la Argentina**) the Argentine, Argentina

argentinismo SM argentinism, *word or phrase etc peculiar to Argentina*

argentino¹ ADJ (*poét*) silver, silvery

argentino²/a ADJ, SM/F Argentinian, Argentine

argento SM (*poét*) silver ▸ **argento vivo** quicksilver

argo SM argon

argolla SF **1** (= *anilla*) ring; (*para caballo*) hitching ring; (= *aldaba*) door knocker; (= *gargantilla*) choker; [*de servilleta*] serviette ring; (*LAm*) (= *anillo*) [*de boda*] wedding ring; [*de novios*] engagement ring • **cambio de ~s** (*Cono Sur*) engagement
2 (*Dep*) *a game like croquet*

argollar ▹ CONJUG 1a VT **1** (*And*) [+ *cerdo*] to ring; (*Méx*) (= *enganchar*) to hitch to a ring
2 • **~ a algn** (*Méx*) to have a hold over sb (*because of a service rendered*)
VPR **argollarse** (*And*) to get engaged

argón SM argon

argonauta SM Argonaut

Argos SM Argus

argot [ar'got] SM (PL: **argots**) slang ▸ **argot pasota** dropout slang

argótico ADJ slang (*antes de s*)

argucia SF sophistry (*frm*), hair-splitting • **~s** nit-picking* (*sing*)

argüende SM (*LAm*) argument

argüir ▹ CONJUG 3g VT **1** (= *razonar*) to argue, contend; (= *indicar*) to indicate, point to; (= *inferir*) to deduce; (= *probar*) to prove, show • **esto arguye su poco cuidado** this shows his lack of care • **de ahí arguyo su buena calidad** that tells me it's good quality
2 (= *argumentar, justificarse*) to argue, claim • **arguyó que no era culpa suya** he claimed it wasn't his fault
3 (= *reprochar*) to reproach • **me argüían con vehemencia** they vehemently reproached me • **~ a algn (de) su crueldad** to reproach sb for their cruelty
VI to argue (**contra** against, **with**)

argumentable ADJ arguable

argumentación SF (= *acción*) arguing; (= *razonamiento*) argument, reasoning

argumentador ADJ argumentative

argumental ADJ (*Literat*) plot (*antes de s*) • **línea ~** line of the plot, storyline

argumentar ▹ CONJUG 1a VT, VI to argue • **~ que …** to argue that …, contend that …

argumentista SMF scriptwriter

argumento SM **1** [*de razonamiento*] argument (*tb Jur*) • **no me convencen tus ~s** I'm not convinced by your arguments *o* reasoning
2 (*Literat, Teat*) plot; (*TV etc*) storyline ▸ **argumento de la obra** plot summary, outline
3 (*LAm*) (= *discusión*) argument, discussion, quarrel

aria SF aria

aridecer ▹ CONJUG 2d VT to dry up, make arid
VI, VPR **aridecerse** to dry up, become arid

aridez SF aridity, dryness

árido ADJ arid, dry
SM **1 áridos** (*Com*) dry goods • **medida para ~s** dry measure
2 (= *hormigón*) sand and cement

Aries SM (*Astron, Astrol*) Aries • **es de ~** she's (an) Aries, she's an Arien

aries (*Astrol*) SMF INV Aries, Arien • **los ~ son así** that's what Aries *o* Ariens are like
ADJ INV Aries, Arien • **soy ~** I'm (an) Aries, I'm an Arien

ariete SM **1** (*Mil*) battering ram
2 (*Dep*) striker

arigua SF (*Caribe*) wild bee

arillo SM earring

ario/a ADJ, SM/F Aryan

ariqueño/a ADJ of/from Arica
SM/F native/inhabitant of Arica • **los ~s** the people of Arica

ariscar ▹ CONJUG 1g VT (*CAm, Caribe*) [+ *animal*] to pacify, control; [+ *persona*] to make suspicious
VPR **ariscarse** (*CAm, Caribe*) to run away

arisco ADJ [*animal*] unfriendly; [*persona*] unsociable, standoffish, surly

arista SF (*Bot*) beard; (*Geom*) edge; (*Alpinismo*) arête; (*Arquit*) arris

aristocracia SF aristocracy

aristócrata SMF aristocrat

aristocrático ADJ aristocratic

Aristófanes SM Aristophanes

aristón SM mechanical organ

Aristóteles SM Aristotle

aristotélico ADJ Aristotelian

aritmética SF arithmetic

aritmético/a ADJ arithmetical
SM/F arithmetician

Arlequín SM Harlequin

arlequín SM **1** (= *persona cómica*) buffoon
2 (= *helado*) Neapolitan ice cream

arlequinada SF (*Hist*) harlequinade; (= *bufonada*) buffoonery, piece of buffoonery

arlequinesco ADJ grotesque, ridiculous

Arlés SF Arles

arma SF **1** (*Mil*) weapon • **los guerrilleros entregaron las ~s** the guerrillas handed over their weapons • **un fabricante de ~s** an arms manufacturer • **nos apuntaba con un ~** he pointed a gun at us • **¡a las ~s!** to arms! • **¡~s al hombro!** shoulder arms! • **alzarse en ~s** to rise up in arms • **¡descansen ~s!** order arms! • **¡presenten ~s!** present arms! • **rendir las ~s** to lay down one's arms • **estar sobre las ~s** to be under arms • **tocar (al) ~** to sound the call to arms • **tomar las ~s** to take up arms • MODISMOS: • **de ~s tomar**: • **es una mujer de ~s tomar** she's not someone you mess around with • **limpiar el ~†**** to have a screw** • **pasar a algn por las ~s** (= *ejecutar*) to execute sb • **volver el ~ contra algn** to turn the tables on sb ▸ **arma arrojadiza** missile ▸ **arma atómica** atomic weapon ▸ **arma biológica** biological weapon ▸ **arma blanca** cold steel ▸ **arma convencional** conventional weapon ▸ **arma de combate** assault weapon ▸ **arma de doble filo** double-edged sword ▸ **arma de fuego** firearm ▸ **arma larga** shotgun ▸ **arma negra** fencing foil ▸ **arma química** chemical weapon ▸ **arma reglamentaria** service weapon, regulation weapon ▸ **armas cortas** small arms ▸ **armas de destrucción masiva** weapons of mass destruction
2 (= *medio*) weapon • **la movilización popular es su ~ más fuerte** popular mobilization is its most powerful weapon • **su sarcasmo es**

solo un ~ defensiva her sarcasm is just self-defence
3 (*Mil*) (= *cuerpo*) arm ▸ **arma de infantería** infantry arm
4 (*Mil*) • **las ~s** (= *profesión*) the military, the armed services
5 **armas** [*de escudo*] arms

armada SF **1** (*nacional*) navy; (*escuadra*) fleet • **la Armada Británica** the British Navy • **la Armada Invencible** the Spanish Armada • **un oficial de la ~** a naval officer
2 (*Cono Sur*) (= *lazo*) lasso

armadía SF = **almadía**

armadijo SM trap, snare

armadillo SM armadillo

armado ADJ **1** [*persona, lucha*] armed (**con, de** with) • **ir ~** to go armed, be armed • MODISMO: • **~ hasta los dientes** armed to the teeth
2 (= *montado*) mounted, assembled
3 [*hormigón*] reinforced
4 [*tela*] toughened
5 (*LAm*) (= *testarudo*) stubborn

armador(a) SM/F **1** (*Náut*) shipowner; (*Hist*) privateer
2 (*Mec*) fitter, assembler
SM **1** (= *vestido*) jerkin
2 (*LAm*) (= *chaleco*) waistcoat, vest (EEUU); (= *percha*) coat hanger

armadura SF **1** (*Mil, Hist*) armour, armor (EEUU) • **una ~** a suit of armour
2 (*Téc*) (= *armazón*) framework; (*en hormigón*) reinforcing bars; [*de gafas*] frame; (*Anat*) skeleton; (*Elec*) armature ▸ **armadura de la cama** bedstead
3 (*Mús*) key signature

armaduría SF (*LAm*) car assembly plant

Armagedón SM Armageddon

armamentismo SM arms build-up

armamentista ADJ arms (*antes de s*) • **carrera ~** arms race

armamento SM **1** (*Mil*) armament • **~s** armaments, arms; ▹ **carrera**
2 (*Náut*) fitting-out
3 (*Téc*) framework

armar ▹ CONJUG 1a VT **1** [+ *persona, ejército*] to arm (**con, de** with) • **un arsenal suficiente para ~ a un comando** enough weapons to arm a commando group • **vino armado de brocha y pintura** he came armed with a brush and paint • **se desconoce quién ha armado a los terroristas** it is not known who provided *o* supplied the terrorists with arms; ▹ **caballero**
2 (= *montar*) [+ *mueble, ventana, juguete*] to assemble, put together; [+ *tienda de campaña*] to pitch, put up; [+ *trampa*] to set; (*LAm*) [+ *rompecabezas*] to piece together, put together; [+ *cigarrillo*] to roll • **tuvimos que des~ la cama y volverla a ~** we had to take the bed apart and reassemble it *o* put it back together again
3* (= *organizar*) • **~ una bronca *o* un escándalo** to kick up a fuss • **~on un follón tremendo con lo del cambio de horario** they kicked up a real fuss about the timetable change • **amenacé con marcharme armando un escándalo y cedieron** I threatened to leave and create a scene, so they gave in • **el cuadro que ha armado tanta polémica** the painting which has caused such controversy • **por favor, id entrando despacio, sin ~ jaleo** go in slowly please, without making a racket • **armarla** to stir up trouble • **buena la armó con esa declaración** he really stirred up trouble with that statement • **pienso ~la hasta que consiga lo que quiero** I'm going to make a real fuss until I get what I want
4 [+ *hormigón*] to reinforce
5 (*Mil*) [+ *bayoneta*] to fix; [+ *rifle, cañón*] to load; [+ *arco*] to bend
6 (*Náut*) to fit out, commission
7 (*Cos*) [+ *chaqueta, solapa*] to stiffen • **una chaqueta sin ~** a loose jacket
8 • **~ un pleito** (*LAm**) to kick up a fuss*, get ready
VPR **armarse 1** [*soldado, atracador*] to arm o.s. (**con, de** with) • MODISMO: • **~se hasta los dientes** to be armed to the teeth
2 (= *proveerse*) • **~se de algo** to arm o.s. with sth • **los periodistas, armados de prismáticos y teleobjetivos** the journalists, armed with binoculars and telephoto lenses • **con este tráfico hay que ~se de paciencia** you need a lot of patience in traffic like this • **~se de valor** to pluck up courage
3* (= *organizarse*) • **¡que follón se armó!** there was a big fuss • **¡menudo escándalo se armó con lo de esa boda!** what a commotion there was with that wedding!* • **se está armando una crisis** a crisis is brewing; ▹ **Dios**
4 • **~se un lío***: **me armé un lío tremendo con todas las direcciones que me diste** I got into a real muddle* *o* mess with all the addresses you gave me
5 (*CAm*) to balk, shy
6 (*CAm, Caribe*) (= *obstinarse*) to become obstinate; (= *negarse*) to refuse point blank; (*Ven*) [*caballo*] to come to a halt
7 (*Méx**) (= *enriquecerse*) to make a packet*
8 • **~se con algo** (*Ven*) to run off with sth

armario SM [*de cocina*] cupboard, closet (EEUU); [*de ropa*] wardrobe, closet (EEUU) ▸ **armario botiquín** medicine chest *o* cabinet ▸ **armario empotrado** built-in cupboard ▸ **armario ropero** wardrobe, closet (EEUU)

armatoste SM **1** (= *objeto*) monstrosity; (*Mec*) contraption; (*Aut*) old crock*, jalopy*, old banger*
2 (= *persona*) bungling great fool*

armazón SM o SF **1** (= *armadura*) frame; (*fig*) (= *esqueleto*) framework; (*Aer, Aut*) body, chassis; [*de mueble*] frame
2 (*LAm*) (= *estantes*) shelving

armella SF eyebolt

Armenia SF Armenia

armenio/a ADJ, SM/F Armenian

armería SF **1** (= *museo*) military museum
2 (= *tienda*) gunsmith's, gunsmith's shop
3 (= *oficio*) gunmaking
4 (*Heráldica*) heraldry

armero SM **1** (= *artesano*) gunsmith; (= *fabricante*) arms manufacturer
2 (= *armario*) gun rack

armiño SM **1** (*Zool*) stoat
2 (= *piel*) ermine
3 (*Heráldica*) ermine

armisticio SM armistice

armón SM (*tb* **armón de artillería**) gun carriage, limber

armonía SF harmony • **en ~** in harmony (**con** with)

armónica SF harmonica, mouth organ; ▹ **armónico**

armónicamente ADV harmoniously

armonicista SMF harmonica player, mouth organist

armónico ADJ harmonic
SM (*Mús*) harmonic; ▹ **armónica**

armonio SM harmonium

armoniosamente ADV harmoniously

armonioso ADJ harmonious

armonizable ADJ • **ser ~** to be reconcilable (**con** with)

armonización SF (*Mús*) harmonization; (= *conciliación*) reconciliation • **ley de ~** coordinating law

armonizador ADJ • **ley ~a** coordinating law

armonizar ▹ CONJUG 1f VT (*Mús*) to harmonize; [+ *diferencias*] to reconcile
VI (*Mús*) to harmonize (**con** with) • **~ con** (= *avenirse*) to harmonize *o* be in keeping with; [*colores*] to tone in with

ARN SM ABR (= **ácido ribonucleico**) RNA

arnaco SM (*And*) useless object, piece of lumber

arnero SM (*LAm*) sieve

arnés SM **1** (*Mil, Hist*) armour, armor (EEUU)
2 (*en montañismo, paracaidismo*) harness ▸ **arnés de seguridad** safety harness
3 **arneses** (= *arreos*) harness (*sing*), trappings; (= *avíos*) gear (*sing*), tackle (*sing*)

árnica SF **1** (= *planta, tintura*) arnica
2 (*Dep*) • **pedir ~** to throw in the towel

aro¹ SM [*de tonel*] ring, hoop; [*de rueda*] rim; (= *servilletero*) napkin ring; (*And, Cono Sur*) (= *arete*) earring; **aros** (= *juego*) quoits • MODISMOS: • **hacer un aro** (*Cono Sur*) to have a break • **pasar por el aro** to fall into line ▸ **aro de émbolo** piston ring ▸ **aro de rueda** wheel rim

aro² SM (*Bot*) lords-and-ladies

aroma SM (= *perfume*) aroma, scent; [*de vino*] bouquet

aromaterapia SF aromatherapy

aromático ADJ aromatic, sweet-scented

aromatizador SM air-freshener

aromatizante SM flavouring, flavoring (EEUU), aromatic spice

aromatizar ▹ CONJUG 1f VT (= *perfumar*) to scent; [+ *aire*] to freshen; (*Culin*) to spice, flavour with herbs, flavor with herbs (EEUU)

arpa SF harp • MODISMO: • **tocar el ~*** to be a thief, live by thieving

arpado ADJ serrated

arpar¹ ▹ CONJUG 1a VT (= *arañar*) to scratch, claw, claw at; (= *hacer pedazos*) to tear, tear to pieces

arpar²‡ ▹ CONJUG 1a VT (*LAm*) (= *robar*) to pinch*, nick‡

arpegio SM arpeggio

arpeo SM grappling iron

arpero/a SM/F (*Méx*) (= *ladrón*) thief, burglar; (= *arpista*) harpist

arpía SF (*Mit*) harpy; (= *mujer*) old bag*

arpicordio SM harpsichord

arpillar ▹ CONJUG 1a VT (*CAm*) to pile up

arpillera SF sacking, sackcloth

> **ARPILLERA**
> **Arpillera** is the term used for the colourful pictures made in many parts of Latin America by appliquéing scraps of fabric onto a hessian backing. During the Pinochet dictatorship in Chile they became politically significant since working-class women used them to depict the reality of life under military rule. As these **arpilleras** escaped the scrutiny of the male-dominated regime, they provided women with a means of recording events as well as obtaining income from abroad.

arpir SM (*And, Cono Sur*) mine worker

arpista SMF (*Mús*) harpist; (*Cono Sur*) (= *ladrón*) thief, burglar

arpón SM harpoon

arponar ▹ CONJUG 1a VT, **arponear** ▹ CONJUG 1a VT to harpoon

arponero ADJ • **navío ~** whaler, whaling vessel

arquear ▹ CONJUG 1a VT **1** (= *doblar*) to arch, bend
2 [+ *lana*] to beat
3 (*Náut*) to gauge; (*LAm*) (*Com*) to tot up
VI (*Med*) to retch
VPR **arquearse** (= *doblarse*) to arch, bend; [*superficie*] to camber

a

arqueo (SM) **1** (*Arquit*) arching
2 (*Náut*) capacity; (*Com*) [*de caja*] filling up, cashing up ▸ **arqueo bruto** gross tonnage
arqueolítico (ADJ) Stone-Age (*antes de s*)
arqueología (SF) archaeology, archeology (*EEUU*) ▸ **arqueología industrial** industrial archaeology ▸ **arqueología submarina** underwater archaeology
arqueológico (ADJ) archaeological, archeological (*EEUU*) • **investigación arqueológica** dig, excavation
arqueólogo/a (SM/F) archaeologist, archeologist (*EEUU*)
arquería (SF) arcade, series of arches
arquero/a (SM/F) **1** (*Mil*) bowman, archer
2 (*Com*) cashier
3 (*LAm*) (*Dep*) goalkeeper
arqueta (SF) chest
arquetípico (ADJ) archetypal, archetypical
arquetipo (SM) archetype
Arquímedes (SM) Archimedes
arquimesa (SF) desk, escritoire
arquitecto/a (SM/F) architect
▸ **arquitecto/a de jardines, arquitecto/a paisajista** landscape gardener
▸ **arquitecto/a técnico/a** quantity surveyor
arquitectónicamente (ADV) architecturally
arquitectónico (ADJ) architectural
arquitectura (SF) architecture
▸ **arquitectura de jardines, arquitectura paisajista** landscape gardening
arquitrabe (SM) architrave
arrabal (SM) **1** (= *barrio de las afueras*) suburb • **~es** (= *afueras*) outskirts
2 (*LAm*) (= *barrio bajo*) slums (*pl*), slum quarter
arrabalero/a (ADJ) **1** (= *de las afueras*) suburban; (*pey*) (= *de barrio bajo*) of/from the poorer areas
2 (= *basto*) common, coarse
(SM/F) **1** (= *de las afueras*) suburbanite; (*pey*) (= *de barrio bajo*) person from the poorer areas
2 (= *persona basta*) common sort, coarse person
arrabio (SM) cast iron
arracacha (SF) (*And*) idiocy, silliness
arracacho (SM) (*And*) idiot
arracada (SF) pendant earring
arracimado (ADJ) clustered, in a cluster
arracimarse ▹ CONJUG 1a (VPR) to cluster together
arraigadamente (ADV) firmly, securely
arraigado (ADJ) [*costumbre*] deep-rooted; [*creencia*] deep-seated; [*persona*] property-owning
arraigar ▹ CONJUG 1h (VT) **1** (*fig*) (= *establecer*) to establish
2 (*LAm*) (*Jur*) to place under a restriction order
(VI) [*planta*] to take root
(VPR) **arraigarse 1** [*planta*] to take root
2 [*costumbre*] to take root, establish itself, take a hold; [*persona*] to settle, establish o.s.
arraigo (SM) **1** (*Bot*) rooting • **de fácil ~** easily rooted
2 (= *bienes*) land, real estate • **hombre de ~** man of property
3 [*de creencia etc*] deep-seatedness • **de mucho** *o* **viejo ~** deep-rooted
4 (= *influencia*) hold, influence • **tener ~** to have influence
5 • **orden de ~** (*Cono Sur, Méx*) restriction order
arralar ▹ CONJUG 1a (VT) (*Méx*) to thin out
arramblar ▹ CONJUG 1a (VI) • **~ con*** to make off with, pinch*
arrancaclavos (SM INV) claw hammer
arrancada (SF) (= *arranque*) sudden start; (= *aceleración*) sudden acceleration; (= *sacudida*) jerk, jolt; (*esp LAm*) (= *fuga*) sudden dash, escape attempt
arrancadero (SM) starting point
arrancado (ADJ)* (= *arruinado*) broke*, penniless
(SM) (*Aut*) starting, ignition
arrancador (SM) starter
arrancamiento (SM) [*de diente, pelo*] pulling out; [*de planta, árbol*] uprooting; [*de carteles*] tearing down; [*de bolso, arma*] snatching • **una campaña de ~ de carteles electorales** a campaign to tear down election posters
arrancar ▹ CONJUG 1g (VT) **1** (= *sacar de raíz*)
a [+ *planta, pelo*] to pull up; [+ *clavo, diente*] to pull out; [+ *pluma*] to pluck; [+ *ojos*] to gouge out; [+ *botón, esparadrapo, etiqueta*] to pull off, tear off; [+ *página*] to tear out, rip out; [+ *cartel*] to pull down, tear down • **he estado arrancando las malas hierbas del jardín** I've been pulling up the weeds in the garden • **le arrancó la oreja de un mordisco** he bit off his ear • **azulejos arrancados de las paredes de una iglesia** tiles that have been pulled off the walls of a church
b [*explosión, viento*] to blow off • **una explosión le arrancó las dos piernas** an explosion blew both his legs off • **el vendaval ha arrancado varios árboles** the gale has uprooted several trees • **el golpe le arrancó dos dientes** the blow knocked two of his teeth out; ▹ **cuajo, raíz**
c (*Med*) [+ *flema*] to bring up
2 (= *arrebatar*) to snatch (**a, de** from); (*con violencia*) to wrench (**a, de** from) • **le arrancó al niño de los brazos** she snatched the baby from his arms • **no podían ~le el cuchillo** they were unable to get the knife off him, they were unable to wrest *o* wrench the knife from him • **el viento me lo arrancó de las manos** the wind blew it out of my hands, the wind snatched it from my hands (*más frm*)
3 (= *provocar*) [+ *aplausos*] to draw; [+ *risas*] to provoke, cause • **el tenor arrancó una gran ovación** the tenor received a great ovation • **hemos conseguido ~le una sonrisa** we managed to get a smile out of him • **el beso arrancó algunos suspiros entre el público** when they kissed part of the audience let out a sigh • **~ las lágrimas a algn** to bring tears to sb's eyes
4 (= *separar*) • **~ a algn de** [+ *lugar*] to drag sb away from; [+ *éxtasis, trance*] to drag sb out of; [+ *vicio*] to wean sb off a bad habit • **no había forma de ~la del teléfono** there was no way I could drag her away from the phone
5 (= *obtener*) [+ *apoyo*] to gain, win; [+ *victoria*] to snatch; [+ *confesión, promesa*] to extract; [+ *sonido, nota*] to produce • **no hubo forma de ~le una palabra** we couldn't get a word out of him • **~ información a algn** to extract information from sb, get information out of sb
6 (*Aut*) [+ *vehículo, motor*] to start • **un motor de los que se arrancan con manivela** an engine that you crank up
7 (*Inform*) [+ *ordenador*] to boot, boot up, start up • **tengo problemas para ~ el ordenador** I have problems starting up *o* booting the computer
(VI) **1** [*vehículo, motor*] to start • **el coche no arranca** the car won't start *o* isn't starting • **esperé hasta que arrancó el tren** I waited until the train left
2 (= *moverse*) to get going, get moving • **¡venga, arranca!*** come on, get going *o* get moving!, come on, get a move on!*
3 (= *comenzar*) to start • **¿desde dónde arranca el camino?** where does the road start? • **el momento donde arrancó nuestra relación** the moment when our relationship started • **~ a hacer algo** to start doing sth, start to do sth • **arrancó a hablar a los dos años** she started talking *o* to talk when she was two • **arrancó a cantar/llorar** he broke *o* burst into song/tears • **~ de** to go back to, date back to • **esta celebración arranca del siglo XV** this celebration dates *o* goes back to the 15th century • **problemas que arrancan de muy antiguo** problems that go back a long way
4 (*Náut*) to set sail
5 (*Arquit*) [*arco*] to spring (**de** from)
6 (*Chile**) (= *escapar*) • **salieron arrancado** they ran away • **arranquemos de aquí** let's get away from here • **tuvieron que ~ del país** they had to get out of the country
• MODISMO: • **~ a perderse** to make a dash for it*
(VPR) **arrancarse 1** (= *quitarse*) [+ *pelo*] to pull out; [+ *botón*] to pull off • **he ido al dentista a ~me un diente** I went to the dentist to have a tooth pulled out *o* extracted
2 (= *empezar*) • **se ~on a cantar** they burst into song • **en mitad del paseo se arrancó a recitar un poema** in the middle of the walk she started to recite a poem • **~se por seguiriyas** to break into a seguidilla
3 (*Chile**) (= *escaparse*) • **se me arrancó el perro** my dog got away • **me arranqué de la oficina más temprano** I left the office earlier • **se ~on de la cárcel** they escaped from prison
4 (*Chile**) (= *aumentar*) to shoot up* • **hay que evitar que se arranque la inflación** we have to prevent inflation from shooting up*
5 (*Chile, Méx*) [*caballo*] to shy
arranchar ▹ CONJUG 1a (VT) **1** (*Náut*) [+ *velas*] to brace; [+ *costa*] to skirt, sail close to
2 (*And*) (= *arrebatar*) to snatch away (**a** from)
(VPR) **arrancharse 1** (= *reunirse*) to gather together; (= *comer*) to eat together
2 (*Caribe, Méx*) (= *acomodarse*) to settle in, make o.s. comfortable; (*Caribe*) (= *adaptarse*) to make the best of it
arrancón (SM) (*Méx*) = **arrancada**
arranque (SM) **1** (*Mec*) starting mechanism • **el motor tiene algunos problemas de ~** the engine has problems getting started
• MODISMO: • **ni para el ~** (*Méx**): • **¡10.000 pesos!, con eso ni para el ~** 10,000 pesos! that's nowhere near enough* • **no tengo ni para el ~** I haven't got nowhere near enough ▸ **arranque automático** starter motor ▸ **arranque en frío** cold start ▸ **arranque manual** crank start; ▹ **motor**
2 (= *comienzo*) beginning • **el ~ de esta tradición se remonta al siglo XVIII** the beginning of this tradition dates back to the 18th century • **el ~ de la historia es muy original** the beginning of the story is very original; ▹ **punto**
3 (= *impulso*) • **me falta ~ para embarcarme en esta empresa** I'm not bold enough to embark on this venture • **aprovechando este ~ de la economía** taking advantage of this burst in the economy • **necesita un poco más de ~ para ganar el partido** he needs a little more drive to win the match
4 (= *arrebato*) [*de generosidad, franqueza*] outburst; [*de ira, violencia*] fit; [*de energía*] burst • **en un ~ de generosidad** in an outburst of generosity • **en un ~ de celos** in a fit of jealousy
5 (= *ocurrencia*) witty remark • **tiene muy buenos ~s** he makes some very witty remarks
6 (= *base*) [*de columna, arco*] base; [*de escalera*] foot
arranquera* (SF) (*And, CAm, Caribe*),
arranquitis* (SF) (*And, CAm, Caribe*)

a

• MODISMO: • estar en la ~ to be completely broke*
arrapiezo SM 1 (= harapo) rag, tatter
2 (= mocoso) whippersnapper
arras SFPL 1 (Econ, Com) pledge (sing), security (sing)
2 (Hist) 13 coins given by bridegroom to bride
arrasador ADJ = arrollador
arrasamiento SM (= nivelación) levelling, leveling (EEUU); [de un edificio] demolishing; [de un territorio] devastation • **bombardeo de ~** carpet bombing
arrasar ▹ CONJUG 1a VT 1 (= nivelar) to level; [+ edificio] to demolish; (esp en guerra) to raze to the ground; [ciclón, terremoto] to devastate
2 (= colmar) to fill to the brim
VI 1 (Meteo) to clear
2 (= triunfar) to triumph, achieve a great success; (Pol etc) to sweep the board
VPR **arrasarse** (Meteo) to clear • **se le ~on los ojos de** o **en lágrimas** her eyes filled with tears
arrastracueros SM INV (Caribe) crook, shyster (EEUU)
arrastrada* SF whore, hooker (EEUU*); ▹ arrastrado
arrastradizo ADJ dangling, trailing
arrastrado/a ADJ 1 • **llevar algo ~** to drag sth along
2 (= pobre) poor, miserable • **andar ~** to have a wretched life
3 (= pícaro) wily, rascally
4 (LAm) (= servil) cringing, servile
SM/F (= pícaro) rogue, rascal; (Méx) (= necesitado) down-and-out; ▹ arrastrada
arrastrador SM (en impresora) tractor
arrastradora SF (Perú) prostitute
arrastrar ▹ CONJUG 1a VT 1 [+ objeto pesado] to drag; [+ carro] to pull; [+ caravana] to tow; [+ vestido, capa] to trail (along the ground) • **no arrastres la silla por el suelo** don't drag that chair (along the ground) • **~ los pies** to drag one's feet, shuffle along • **~ las palabras** to slur one's words
2 (= transportar) [río, viento] to sweep away o along • **la corriente arrastró las ramas** the current swept the branches away o along
3 (= atraer) to draw, attract • **su última película ha arrastrado mucho público** his latest film has drawn o attracted large audiences • **no te dejes ~ por esa idea** don't get carried away by that idea • **~ a algn a hacer algo** to sweep sb into doing sth
4 (= soportar) • **este país arrastra desde hace décadas el problema del paro** this country's been dogged by unemployment for decades • **arrastra un complejo de inferioridad desde la adolescencia** he's had an inferiority complex ever since he was a youth
5 (= provocar) [+ dificultad, problema] to bring with it • **su dimisión arrastró varias crisis financieras** his resignation brought with it several financial crises
6 (Bridge) [+ triunfos] to draw
VI 1 [vestido, capa] to trail (along the ground), drag • **te arrastra el vestido** your dress is trailing (along the ground) o dragging
2 (Bot) to trail
VPR **arrastrarse** 1 (= reptar) [bebé, serpiente] to crawl; [herido] to drag o.s. • **la oruga se arrastraba lentamente por el suelo** the caterpillar crawled along the ground • **la víctima se arrastró hasta la puerta** the victim dragged himself to the door
2 (= humillarse) to grovel • **se arrastró ante el profesor para conseguir el aprobado** he grovelled to the teacher so as to get a pass mark
arrastre SM 1 (= acción) dragging, pulling; (Aer) drag; (Pesca) trawling • **flota de ~** trawling fleet, fleet of trawlers ▸ **arrastre por correa** belt-drive
2 (Méx, CAm) (= influencia) influence • **tener mucho ~** to have friends in high places
3 (Taur) removal of dead animal • **estar para el ~*** to be knackered*
4 (Inform) ▸ **arrastre de dientes** tractor ▸ **arrastre de papel por fricción** friction feed ▸ **arrastre de papel por tracción** tractor feed
arrastrero ADJ trawler (antes de s) • **flota arrastrera** trawling fleet, fleet of trawlers
SM trawler
array SM (Inform) array ▸ **array empaquetado** packed array
arrayán SM myrtle
arre EXCL (= voz de arriero) gee up!; (LAm) (metiendo prisa) hurry up!, get a move on!
arreada SF (Cono Sur, Méx) (Agr) round-up; (Jur) cattle-rustling; (Mil) press-ganging
arreado ADJ (And, Cono Sur, Méx) sluggish, ponderous
arreador SM 1 (= arriero) muleteer; (And) (= capataz) foreman
2 (LAm) (= látigo) long whip
arrear ▹ CONJUG 1a VT 1 (= estimular) [+ ganado etc] to drive
2 (= poner arreos a) to harness
3 (CAm, Cono Sur, Méx) [+ ganado] to rustle
4* [+ golpe] to give
VI to hurry along • **¡arrea!** (= muévete) get moving!; (repulsa) get away!; (Esp) (asombro) Christ!, well I'm damned!; (admiración) look at that!
arrebañaduras SFPL leftovers
arrebañar ▹ CONJUG 1a VT (= juntar) to scrape together; [+ comida] to eat up, clear up
arrebatadamente ADV (= apresuradamente) suddenly, violently; (= impetuosamente) headlong, rashly • **hablar ~** to speak in a rush
arrebatadizo ADJ excitable, hot-tempered
arrebatado ADJ 1 (= apresurado) hasty, sudden, violent
2 (= impetuoso) rash, impetuous
3 (= absorto) rapt, bemused
4 (= extático) ecstatic
5 [cara] flushed
arrebatador ADJ [belleza] dazzling, breathtaking; [sonrisa] winning, captivating
arrebatamiento SM 1 (= acción) snatching away, seizure
2 (= abstracción) captivation; (= éxtasis) ecstasy, rapture; (= emoción) excitement; (= ira) anger
arrebatar ▹ CONJUG 1a VT 1 (= quitar violentamente) to snatch away, wrench (a from); [+ vida] to take; [viento etc] to carry off, carry away; [+ persona] to carry away, carry off, abduct (frm) • **le arrebató el revólver** he snatched the pistol from him • **le ~on la victoria** they snatched victory from under his very nose • **~ la vida a algn** to take sb's life
2 (= conmover) to stir; (= cautivar) to captivate; (= alegrar) to exhilarate • **se dejó ~ por su entusiasmo** he got carried away by his enthusiasm
3 (Agr) to parch
VPR **arrebatarse** 1 (= excitarse) to get carried away, get excited • **~se de cólera** to be overcome with anger
2 (Culin) to burn, overcook
arrebatiña SF scramble, scramble to pick sth up • **coger algo a la ~** to snatch sth up
arrebato SM (= ira) rage; (= éxtasis) ecstasy, rapture • **en un ~ de cólera** in an outburst of anger • **en un ~ de entusiasmo** in a sudden fit of enthusiasm
arrebiatarse ▹ CONJUG 1a VPR (CAm) (= unirse) to join up, join together; (Méx) (= decir amén a todo) to follow the crowd, agree automatically, agree automatically with everything
arrebol SM (= colorete) rouge; [de cielo] red glow; **arreboles** (= nubes) red clouds
arrebolar ▹ CONJUG 1a VT to redden
VPR **arrebolarse** 1 (= pintarse) to apply rouge
2 (= enrojecer) to blush
3 (Caribe) (= vestirse) to dress up
arrebozar ▹ CONJUG 1f VT 1 (= embozar) to cover, cover with a cloak; (= disimular) to conceal
2 (Culin) to cover, coat; [+ taza] to fill right up
VPR **arrebozarse** 1 (= embozarse) to cover one's face
2 (Entomología) to swarm
arrebujado ADJ wrapped-up
arrebujar ▹ CONJUG 1a VT 1 [+ objetos] to jumble together, jumble up
2 [+ niño] to wrap up, cover
VPR **arrebujarse** to wrap o.s. up (**con** in, with)
arrecha† SF (CAm, Méx) = arrechera
arrechar ▹ CONJUG 1a VT (LAm*) to arouse, excite
VI 1 (CAm) (= animarse) to show energy, begin to make an effort
2 (LAm*) (= estar cachondo) to feel randy*
VPR **arrecharse** (LAm*) 1 (= ponerse cachondo) to get aroused, get excited
2 (= enfadarse) to get angry
arrechera SF 1 (LAm) (= celo) [de animal] heat, mating urge; [de persona*] arousal
2 (Méx) (= capricho) whim, fancy
3 (Caribe) (= mal humor) bad mood
arrecho ADJ 1 (LAm*) (sexualmente) • **estar ~** [persona] to be in the mood, feel randy*; [animal] to be on heat
2 (LAm*) (= furioso) angry, furious
3 (CAm, Méx) (= vigoroso) vigorous; (= enérgico) energetic; (= valiente) brave
4 (Caribe) • **¡qué ~!** what fun!
SM 1 • **en ~** (CAm, Méx) [animal] on heat
2 • **es un ~** (CAm‡) (= fastidio) he's a bloody nuisance‡, he's a pain in the ass‡
arrechucho* SM 1 (= impulso) sudden impulse; [de cólera] fit, outburst; (= dificultad) unforeseen difficulty, new problem
2 (Med) turn
arreciar ▹ CONJUG 1b VI [tormenta] to get worse, intensify; [viento] to get stronger; [demanda] to intensify
VPR **arreciarse** 1 ▹ VI
2 (Med) to get stronger, pick up
arrecife SM reef ▸ **arrecife coralino, arrecife de coral** coral reef
arrecirse ▹ CONJUG 3b VPR (LAm) to be frozen stiff
arredo‡ EXCL • **¡~ vaya!** (CAm, Méx) get lost!*
arredomado ADJ (LAm) sly, artful
arredrar ▹ CONJUG 1a VT 1 (= asustar) to scare, frighten
2 (= hacer retirarse) to drive back; (= apartar) to remove, separate
VPR **arredrarse** 1 (= intimidarse) to be scared, be frightened • **~se ante algo** to shrink away from sth • **sin ~se** unmoved, undaunted
2 (= retirarse) to draw back, move away (**de** from)
arregazado ADJ [falda] tucked up; [nariz] snub
arregazar ▹ CONJUG 1f VT to tuck up
arregionado/a ADJ 1 (And, Méx) (= de mal genio) ill-tempered, sharp; (And) (= irreflexivo) impulsive; (And) (= mohino) sulky; (And) cross, angry
2 (Caribe) (= estimado) highly regarded
SM/F (Caribe) highly respected person

a

arreglada (SF) ▸ **arreglada de bigotes** (*Cono Sur**) dirty deal, shady business
arregladamente (ADV) in an orderly way
arreglado (ADJ) **1** (= *ordenado*) [*habitación, casa*] neat and tidy; [*conducta*] orderly
2 (= *acicalado*) smart, smartly dressed • **¿dónde irá tan arreglada?** where would she go looking so smart *o* so smartly dressed?
3 [*asunto, pelea*] (= *resuelto*) sorted out; (= *amañado*) arranged • **un matrimonio ~** an arranged marriage • **un precio ~** a reasonable price
4 • MODISMO: • **estar ~**: • **¡pues estamos ~s!** that's done it!*, we've really had it now!* • **estaría yo ~ si ahora tuviera que pagarlo todo** I would be in a fine mess now if I had to pay for it all myself* • **está arreglada si espera que yo la llame** if she expects me to call her, she's got another think coming* • **estamos ~s con tantos invitados** we are in a fine mess with so many guests coming* • **¡pues estamos ~s contigo!** you're nothing but trouble, you are!*
5 • **~ a algo** in accordance with sth • **un código ~ a la ley** a code in accordance with the law
6 (*LAm*) (= *esterilizado*) sterilized
arreglador(a) (SM/F) arranger
Arreglalotodo* (SM) • **el Señor ~** Mr Fixit*
arreglar ▸ CONJUG 1a (VT) **1** (= *reparar*) [+ *electrodoméstico, reloj*] to repair, fix, mend; [+ *coche*] to repair, fix; [+ *zapatos, vestido*] to mend, repair; [+ *casa*] to do up • **¿cuánto te ha costado ~ el coche?** how much did it cost you to have your car repaired *o* fixed? • **tengo que llevar estos zapatos a ~** I have to take these shoes to the mender's *o* to be mended • **quiero que le arreglen las mangas** I want to have the sleeves altered • **están arreglando la carretera de la costa** they are repairing the coast road • **vendrá un hombre a ~ el jardín** a man is coming to do the garden
2 (= *acicalar*) to get ready • **arregló a los niños para ir de paseo** she got the children ready for their stroll • **voy a que me arreglen el pelo** I'm going to have my hair done • **solo quiero que me arregle las patillas** I only want you to tidy up the sideburns • **¡a ti te voy a ~ yo!** (*iró*) I'll show you!*
3 (= *resolver*) [+ *asunto*] to sort out; [+ *conflicto, disputa*] to settle; [+ *problema*] to solve, sort out • **consiguió ~ lo del préstamo** he managed to sort out the loan • **no te preocupes por el dinero, yo lo ~é** don't worry about the money, I'll sort it out *o* I'll take care of that • **intentaron ~ el conflicto de forma diplomática** they tried to sort out *o* settle the conflict by diplomatic means • **tuvimos que ~ varios números en las cuentas** we had to correct some figures in the accounts • **pegándole no vas a ~ nada** you're not going to solve anything by hitting him • **este dinero les ~á la vida** this money will help sort their lives out • **si te crees que vas a ~ el mundo, vas listo** (*iró*) if you think you're going to put the world to rights, you've got another think coming* • **~ cuentas con algn** to settle accounts with sb
4 (= *ordenar*) [+ *casa, habitación*] to tidy, tidy up • **los sábados arreglo mi cuarto** I tidy my room on Saturdays • **estoy arreglando la mesa para la cena** I'm arranging the table for dinner
5 (= *organizar*) to arrange • **ya lo tenemos todo arreglado para la mudanza** we have got everything ready *o* arranged for the move • **lo arregló todo para que la entrevista fuera el lunes** he fixed up *o* arranged everything so the interview could be on Monday
6 (= *acordar*) [+ *detalles*] to settle; [+ *cita*] to arrange, fix up • **dime lo que habéis arreglado** tell me what you've arranged • **ya hemos arreglado el precio** we have already agreed (on) the price • **hemos arreglado que si yo no puedo hacerlo lo hará él** we have arranged that if I can't do it, he will
7 (*Mús*) to arrange
8 (*Culin*) [+ *ensalada*] to dress
9 (*LAm*) (= *amañar*) to arrange
10 (*LAm*) [+ *deuda*] to pay, repay • **le trabajé un mes y todavía no me arregla** (*Chile*) I worked for him for a month and still haven't been paid
11 (*LAm*) (= *esterilizar*) [+ *macho*] to castrate; [+ *hembra*] to spay
12 (*Chile*) [+ *registro, documento*] to update
(VPR) **arreglarse 1** (= *acicalarse*) to get o.s. ready; [+ *pelo, manos*] to do • **yo tardo poco en ~me** I won't take a moment to get myself ready • **se arregla mucho para ir a trabajar** she gets really dressed up to go to work • **~se la boca** to get one's teeth seen to • **~se la corbata** to adjust one's tie • **~se el pelo** [*uno mismo*] to fix one's hair; (*en peluquería*) to have one's hair done
2 (= *ponerse de acuerdo*) to come to an agreement • **no consiguieron ~se en el precio** they didn't manage to come to an agreement about the price • **~se a algo** to conform to sth • **las leyes deben ~se a los principios fundamentales** laws should conform to fundamental principles • **~se con algn**: • **me he arreglado con ella para cambiar los turnos** I've arranged to swap shifts with her
3 [*novios*] (= *reconciliarse*) to make up; (= *empezar a salir*†) to start courting† • **estuvieron un tiempo peleados, pero ya se han arreglado** they fell out for a while, but now they've made (it) up
4 (= *mejorarse*) to improve • **si las cosas no se arreglan la empresa tendrá que cerrar** if things don't improve the firm will have to close down • **si el tiempo se arregla, iremos a la playa** if the weather improves we'll go to the beach • **los problemas no se arreglan solos** problems don't sort themselves out
5 (= *apañarse*) to manage • **con este dinero me arreglo** I can get by *o* I can manage on this money • **~se con/sin algo** to manage with/without sth • **¿cómo os arregláis sin el coche?** how do you manage without the car? • **para comer me arreglo con un bocadillo** at lunch, I make do with a sandwich, I manage on a sandwich for lunch • MODISMO: • **arreglárselas*** to manage • **¿cómo te las arreglas para trabajar tanto y no cansarte?** how do you manage to work so hard and not get tired? • **sabe arreglárselas muy bien solito** he manages perfectly well on his own • **arreglárselas para hacer algo** to manage to do sth • **no sé cómo se las arregla para salir adelante con ese sueldo** I don't know how he manages to get by on that salary • **ya me las ~é para convencerlo** I'll find a way of convincing him
arreglista (SMF) arranger
arreglo (SM) **1** (= *reparación*) repair • **la cocina necesita unos pequeños ~s** the kitchen needs a few repairs • **"se hacen ~s"** [*de ropa*] "alterations"; [*de electrodomésticos*] "repairs done" • **el ~ del televisor son 75 euros** it's 75 euros to repair *o* mend *o* fix the TV • **el horno no tiene ~** the oven is beyond repair • **ese problema tiene fácil ~** that problem is easy to sort out *o* solve • **mi marido no tiene ~*** my husband is a hopeless case*
2 (= *aseo*) [*de persona*] appearance; [*de pelo, barba*] trim • **cuida mucho su ~ personal** he takes great care over his appearance • **un ~ de barba** a beard trim
3 (= *orden*) order • **vivir con ~** to live an orderly life
4 (= *acuerdo*) agreement • **tenemos un arreglillo con el jefe** we have made a little arrangement with the boss • **con ~ a** [+ *norma, ley*] in accordance with; [+ *circunstancias, criterio*] according to • **con ~ a lo dispuesto en el artículo 47** in accordance with the provisions of Article 47 • **los han ordenado con ~ a su tamaño** they have been arranged according to size • **llegar a un ~** to reach a compromise
▸ **arreglo de cuentas** settling of old scores
5 [*de amantes*] affair
6 (*Mús*) [*de obra original*] arrangement; (*a partir de texto literario*) setting
7 (*Inform*) array
8 ▸ **arreglo floral** flower arrangement • **clases de ~ floral** flower arranging classes
arregostarse ▸ CONJUG 1a (VPR) • **~ a** to take a fancy to
arregosto (SM) fancy, taste (**de** for)
arrejarse ▸ CONJUG 1a (VPR) (*Cono Sur*) (= *arriesgarse*) to take a risk
arrejuntado/a* (SM/F) live-in lover • **los ~s** the couple living together
arrejuntarse* ▸ CONJUG 1a (VPR) to set up house together, shack up together* • **vivir arrejuntados** to live together
arrejunte* (SM) cohabitation, living together
arrellanarse ▸ CONJUG 1a (VPR), **arrellenarse** ▸ CONJUG 1a (VPR) **1** (= *ponerse cómodo*) to lounge, sprawl • **~ en el asiento** to lie back in one's chair
2 (*en un trabajo*) to be happy in one's work
arremangado (ADJ) (= *vuelto hacia arriba*) turned up, tucked up; [*nariz*] turned up, snub
arremangar ▸ CONJUG 1h (VT) [+ *mangas, pantalones*] to roll up; [+ *falda*] to tuck up
(VPR) **arremangarse** (= *subirse las mangas*) to roll up one's sleeves; (= *subirse los pantalones*) to roll up one's trousers; (= *subirse la falda*) to tuck up one's skirt
arrematar* ▸ CONJUG 1a (VT) to finish, complete
arremeter ▸ CONJUG 2a (VT) [+ *caballo*] to spur on, spur forward
(VI) **1** (= *atacar*) to rush forward, attack • **~ a** *o* **contra algn** to attack sb, launch o.s. at sb • **el coche arremetió contra la pared** the car smashed into the wall
2 (*fig*) (= *chocar*) to offend good taste, shock the eye
arremetida (SF) **1** (= *ataque*) attack, assault; (= *empujón*) shove, push; (= *ímpetu*) onrush
2 [*de caballo*] sudden start
arremolinarse ▸ CONJUG 1a (VPR) [*gente*] to crowd around, mill around; [*corriente*] to swirl, eddy; [*bailadores, polvo*] to swirl, whirl
arrempujar* ▸ CONJUG 1a (VT) = **empujar**
arrendable (ADJ) • **casa ~** house to let, house available for letting
arrendador(a) (SM/F) **1** (= *propietario*) landlord/landlady; (*Jur*) lessor; (*Com*) franchisor
2 (= *inquilino*) tenant; (*Jur*) lessee; (*Com*) franchisee
arrendajo (SM) **1** (*Orn*) jay
2 (= *imitador*) mimic
arrendamiento (SM) **1** [*de casa, piso*] renting; [*de tierras*] leasing; [*de máquinas, servicios*] hiring • **tomar una casa en ~** to rent a house
▸ **arrendamiento financiero** leasing

2 (= *precio*) rent, rental
3 (= *contrato*) contract, agreement; (*Com*) (= *concesión*) franchise
arrendar¹ ▹ CONJUG 1j VT 1 [*propietario*] [+ *inmuebles*] to let, lease; [+ *máquinas*] to hire out
2 [*usuario*] [+ *inmuebles*] to rent, lease; [+ *máquinas*] to hire
arrendar² ▹ CONJUG 1j VT [+ *caballo*] to tie, tether (*by the reins*)
arrendatario/a SM/F 1 [*de vivienda*] (= *inquilino*) tenant; (*Jur*) lessee, leaseholder
2 [*de coche*] hirer
arrendero/a SM/F (*Cono Sur, Méx*) = **arrendatario**
arreo SM 1 (= *adorno*) adornment
2 **arreos** [*de caballo*] harness (*sing*), trappings; (= *avíos*) gear (*sing*)
3 (*LAm*) (= *animales*) drove, drove of cattle; (= *acto*) roundup
arrepentidamente ADV regretfully, repentantly
arrepentido/a ADJ (= *pesaroso*) sorry; (*Rel*) repentant • **terrorista ~** reformed terrorist • **estar ~ de algo** to regret sth, be sorry about sth • **se mostró muy ~** he was very sorry
SM/F (*Rel*) penitent; (= *terrorista*) reformed terrorist
arrepentimiento SM 1 (= *pesar*) regret; (*Rel*) repentance; [*de terrorista etc*] reformation
2 (*Arte*) (= *enmienda*) change (*made by the artist to a picture*)
arrepentirse ▹ CONJUG 3i VPR to repent, be repentant • **~ de algo** to regret sth • **~ de haber hecho algo** to regret doing sth, regret having done sth • **no ~ de nada** to have no regrets, not be sorry for anything
arrequín SM (*LAm*) 1 (= *ayudante*) helper, assistant
2 (*Agr*) leading animal, leading animal of a mule train
arrequives SMPL 1 (= *ropa*) finery (*sing*), best clothes; (= *adornos*) frills, trimmings
2 (= *circunstancias*) circumstances
arrestado ADJ bold, daring
arrestar ▹ CONJUG 1a VT (= *detener*) to arrest, detain; (= *encarcelar*) to imprison, put in prison • **~ en el cuartel** (*Mil*) to confine to barracks
VPR **arrestarse** • **~se a algo** to rush boldly into sth • **~se a todo** to be afraid of nothing
arresto SM 1 (*Jur*) (= *acción*) arrest; (= *detención*) remand; (*Mil*) detention, confinement • **estar bajo ~** to be under arrest ▸ **arresto domiciliario** house arrest ▸ **arresto mayor** (*Esp*) *imprisonment for from one month and a day to six months* ▸ **arresto menor** (*Esp*) *imprisonment for from one day to thirty days* ▸ **arresto preventivo** preventive detention
2 **arrestos** (= *arrojo*) daring (*sing*) • **tener ~s** to be bold, be daring
arrevesado ADJ (*LAm*) = **enrevesado**
arria SF (*LAm*) mule train, train of pack animals
arriada SF flood
arriado ADJ (*LAm*) = **arreado**
arrianismo SM Arianism
arriano/a ADJ, SM/F Arian
arriar ▹ CONJUG 1c VT 1 [+ *bandera*] to lower, strike; [+ *vela*] to haul down; [+ *cable*] to loosen
2 (= *inundar*) to flood
VPR **arriarse** to flood, become flooded
arriate SM 1 (*Bot*) (= *era*) bed, border
2 (= *camino*) road
arriba ADV 1 (*indicando situación*) above • **los platos y las tazas están ~** the cups and saucers are above • **allí ~** up there • **aquí ~** up here • **de ~**: • **el botón de ~** the top button • **los dientes de ~** my top *o* upper row of teeth • **la parte de ~** the top • **la parte de ~ del biquini** the bikini top • **los de ~** those above; (= *los que mandan*) the people *o* those at the top • **estos azulejos hacen juego con los de ~** these tiles match those above • **órdenes (que vienen) de ~** orders from above • **desde ~** from above • **visto desde ~ parece más pequeño** seen from above it looks smaller • **está más ~** it's higher *o* further up • **pon esos libros ~ del todo** put those books right at the top
2 (*indicando dirección*) • **escaparon (por la) calle ~** they escaped up the street • **de ~ abajo** from top to bottom, from head to foot • **rasgó el cuadro de ~ abajo** he slashed the painting from top to bottom • **me dio un masaje de ~ abajo** he massaged me from head to foot • **vestida de negro de ~ abajo** dressed completely in black, dressed in black from head to foot • **esa ley debe cambiar de ~ abajo** this act must be completely revised • **se puede mirar el catálogo de ~ abajo** you can read the catalogue through from beginning to end • **mirar a algn de ~ abajo** to look sb up and down • **andar para ~ y para abajo** • **ir de ~ para abajo** to run back and forth • **hacia ~** up(wards) • **mire hacia ~** look up • **hasta ~**: • **subí hasta ~** I climbed to the top • **llenar la copa hasta ~** to fill the glass to the brim • **el estadio está lleno hasta ~** the stadium is chock-a-block • **está hasta ~ de trabajo*** he's up to his eyes in work* • **llegar ~** to get to the top • **"este lado para ~"** "this side up" • **de la cintura para ~** from the waist up • **un juego para niños de ocho años para ~** a game for children of eight and over • **de diez dólares para ~** from ten dollars upwards; ▹ **agua, cuesta, patas**
3 (*en casa*) upstairs • **~ están los dormitorios** the bedrooms are upstairs • **los vecinos de ~** our upstairs neighbours • **grité de tal manera que los de ~ lo oyeron** I shouted so loud that the people upstairs heard me
4 (*en texto*) above • **lo escrito ~** what has been written above • **como hemos dicho más ~** as has been said above • **la persona ~ mencionada** the abovementioned *o* aforementioned person
5 • **~ de** (*esp LAm*) (= *encima de*) on top of; (= *por encima de*) above, over; (= *más alto que*) higher than, further up than; (= *más de*) more than • **lo dejé ~ del refrigerador** I left it on top of the fridge • **viven en el departamento ~ del mío** they live in the flat above mine • **el río ~ de la ciudad** the river above the town • **~ mío** (*esp Cono Sur*) over me, above me, on top of me
EXCL (= *a levantarse*) up you get! • **¡~ ese ánimo!** cheer *o* chin up! • **¡manos ~!** hands up! • **¡~ el telón!** raise the curtain! • **¡~ el Depor!** (*Dep*) up (with) Depor! • **¡~ el socialismo!** long live socialism!
arribada SF (*Náut*) arrival, entry into harbour *o* (*EEUU*) harbor • **entrar de ~** to put into port ▸ **arribada forzosa** unscheduled stop
arribaje SM (*Náut*) arrival, entry into harbour, entry into harbor (*EEUU*)
arribano ADJ (*Cono Sur*) upper, higher
arribar ▹ CONJUG 1a VI 1 (*esp LAm*) (= *llegar*) to arrive; (*Náut*) (= *llegar a puerto*) to put into port; (= *ir a la deriva*) to drift • **~ a** to reach
2 (*Med, Econ*) (= *convalecer*) to recover, improve
arribazón SF (= *abundancia de peces*) coastal abundance of fish, off-shore shoal; [*de dinero*] bonanza
arribeño/a SM/F 1 (*LAm*) (= *serrano*) highlander, inlander
2 (*Cono Sur*) (= *forastero*) stranger
arribismo SM social climbing
arribista SMF upstart, arriviste (*frm*)
arribo SM (*esp LAm*) arrival • **hacer su ~** to arrive
arriendo SM = **arrendamiento**
arriero SM muleteer
arriesgadamente ADV (= *peligrosamente*) riskily, dangerously; (= *intrépidamente*) daringly, boldly
arriesgado ADJ 1 [*acto*] risky, hazardous • **unas ideas arriesgadas** some dangerous ideas • **me parece ~ prometerlo** I would be rash to promise it
2 [*individuo*] (= *intrépido*) bold, daring; (*pey*) (= *impetuoso*) rash, foolhardy
arriesgar ▹ CONJUG 1h VT (= *poner en riesgo*) to risk, hazard; [+ *oportunidad*] to endanger, put at risk; [+ *conjetura*] to hazard, venture; [+ *dinero*] to stake
VPR **arriesgarse** to take a risk, expose o.s. to danger • **~se a hacer algo** to risk doing sth • **~se a una multa** to risk a fine • **~se en una empresa** to venture upon an enterprise
arrimadero SM (= *arrimo*) support; (= *apeadero*) mounting block, step
arrimadillo SM matting (*used as wainscot*)
arrimadizo/a ADJ (*fig*) parasitic
SM/F parasite, hanger-on
arrimado/a ADJ 1 [*imitación*] close
2 (*Col, Méx, Ven**) (= *aprovechado*) • **viven ~s con los suegros** they scrounge off their in-laws
3 (*Méx**) (= *juntos*) • **—¿son marido y mujer? —no, están ~s nomás** "are they married?" — "no, they're just living together"
SM/F 1 (*Col, Méx, Ven**) (= *aprovechado*) scrounger*
2 (*Caribe*) (= *intruso*) unwelcome guest
3 (*And*) (= *amante*) lover
4 (*Cono Sur**) (= *mantenido*) kept man/woman (*pey*)
arrimar ▹ CONJUG 1a VT 1 (= *acercar*) to move nearer, move closer (**a** to), to bring nearer, bring closer (**a** to) • **arrima tu silla a la mía** bring your chair nearer to mine • **~on el coche al bordillo a empujones** they pushed the car nearer to the kerb • **se saludan solo arrimando la cara** they just touch cheeks when they greet each other • **arrima el sofá contra la pared** move *o* push the sofa against the wall • **~ las espuelas a un caballo** to dig one's spurs into a horse • **~ un golpe a algn** (*Méx**) to hit sb, strike sb • **~ el oído a la puerta** to put one's ear to the door • **vivir arrimado a algn** (*gen*) to live with sb; (*con dependencia económica*) to live off sb; (*sexualmente*) to shack up with sb; ▹ **ascua, hombro**
2 (= *ignorar*) [+ *persona*] to ignore; [+ *proyecto*] to shelve • **el plan quedó arrimado** the plan was shelved • MODISMO: • **~ los libros** to give up studying, drop out*
3 (*Náut*) [+ *carga*] to stow
VPR **arrimarse** 1 (*a un lugar*) to come nearer, come closer (**a** to) • **arrímate un poco más a la pared** get a little nearer to the wall • **no te arrimes mucho al precipicio** don't get too close to the precipice • **se arrimó mucha gente a mirar** many people gathered round to look • **me arrimé a la pared para que no me vieran** I flattened myself against the wall so that they wouldn't see me • **se arrimó a la lumbre** she huddled closer to the fire
2 • **~se a algn** (*gen*) to come closer to sb; (*para pedir algo*) to come up to sb; (*buscando calor*) to snuggle up to sb; (*para sacar dinero*) to scrounge off sb* • **arrímate para que te vea mejor** come closer so I can see you better • **paraban la música si alguien se arrimaba demasiado a su pareja** they stopped the

a

music if anyone got too close to their partner • **bailaban muy arrimados** they were dancing cheek-to-cheek, they were dancing very close • **se me fue arrimando hasta que se sentó a mi lado** he edged closer until he was sitting right next to me • **se nos arrimó a preguntar la hora** he came up to us to ask the time • **se arriman a los que están en el poder** they ingratiate themselves with those in power • **se ~on a la casa de la madre del marido** they went to live with the husband's mother • **arrímate a mí** cuddle up to me, snuggle up to me; ▹ **sol**
3 (*Taur*) to fight close to the bull
4 (*Méx**) (= *vivir juntos*) to live together

arrimo SM **1** (= *ayuda*) protection • **al ~ de algn/algo** with the support of sb/with the help of sth • **prosperó al ~ de su tío** he prospered with his uncle's support • **nos resguardamos al ~ de un árbol** we sheltered under a tree
2 (= *apego*) attachment • **no siente ~ por nadie** he doesn't feel attached to anybody, he doesn't feel any attachment to anybody
3* (= *amorío*) affair
4 (*Constr*) partition
5 (*Chile*) (= *consola*) (*tb* **mesa de arrimo**) console table

arrimón SM (= *holgazán*) loafer, idler; (= *gorrón*) sponger* • **estar de ~** to hang about, loaf around

arrinconado ADJ (= *olvidado*) forgotten, neglected; (= *marginado*) out in the cold*; (= *remoto*) remote; (= *abandonado*) abandoned

arrinconar ▹ CONJUG 1a VT **1** [+ *objeto*] to put in a corner; [+ *enemigo*] to corner
2 (= *abandonar*) to lay aside, discard; (= *dar carpetazo a*) to shelve, put on the back burner; (= *apartar*) to push aside; (= *marginar*) to leave out in the cold*
VPR **arrinconarse** to become a recluse

arriñonado ADJ kidney-shaped

arriñonar* ▹ CONJUG 1a VT to wear out, exhaust • **estar arriñonado** to be knackered*

arriscadamente ADV boldly, resolutely

arriscado ADJ **1** (*Geog*) craggy
2 [*persona*] (= *resuelto*) bold, resolute; (= *animoso*) spirited; (= *ágil*) brisk, agile

arriscamiento SM boldness, resolution

arriscar¹ ▹ CONJUG 1g VT to risk
VPR **arriscarse** to take a risk

arriscar² ▹ CONJUG 1g VT (*And, Cono Sur, Méx*) (= *doblar*) to turn up, fold up, tuck up; (= *encrespar*) to stiffen; [+ *nariz*] to wrinkle
VI **1** (*And*) (= *enderezarse*) to draw o.s. up, straighten up
2 • **~ a** (*LAm*) to amount to
VPR **arriscarse 1** (= *engreírse*) to get conceited
2 (*And, CAm*) (= *vestir con elegancia*) to dress up to the nines

arriscocho ADJ (*And*) restless

arritmia SF (*Med*) arrhythmia

arrítmico ADJ **1** (*Med*) arrhythmic
2 (*Mús*) unrhythmical

arrivista = **arribista**

arrizar ▹ CONJUG 1f VT (*Náut*) [+ *vela*] to reef; (= *asegurar*) to fasten, lash down

arroba SF **1** (= *medida de peso*) 25 pounds; (= *medida de líquidos*) *a variable liquid measure* • MODISMO: • **por ~s*** tons*, loads* • **tiene talento por ~s** he has loads of talent, he oozes talent*
2 (*Internet*) (*en dirección electrónica*) at

arrobador ADJ entrancing, enchanting

arrobamiento SM (= *éxtasis*) ecstasy, rapture; (*Rel*) trance • **salir de su ~** to emerge from one's state of bliss, come back to earth*

arrobar ▹ CONJUG 1a VT to entrance, enchant
VPR **arrobarse** (= *embelesarse*) to go into ecstasies, be enraptured; [*místico etc*] to go into a trance

arrobo SM = **arrobamiento**

arrocero/a ADJ rice (*antes de s*) • **cultivo ~** rice cultivation • **industria arrocera** rice industry
SM/F (*Caribe*) gatecrasher

arrochelarse ▹ CONJUG 1a VPR (*And*) [*ganado*] to take a liking to a place; [*perro*] to refuse to go out; [*caballo*] to balk, shy

arrodajarse ▹ CONJUG 1a VPR (*CAm*) to sit cross-legged

arrodillado ADJ kneeling (down) • **estar ~** to be on one's knees, be kneeling down

arrodillarse ▹ CONJUG 1a VPR to kneel, kneel down, go down on one's knees

arrogancia SF (= *altanería*) arrogance, haughtiness; (= *orgullo*) pride

arrogante ADJ (= *altanero*) arrogant, haughty; (= *orgulloso*) proud

arrogantemente ADV (= *con altanería*) arrogantly, haughtily; (= *con orgullo*) proudly

arrogarse ▹ CONJUG 1h VPR • **~ algo** to assume sth, take sth on o.s.

arrojadamente ADV boldly

arrojadizo ADJ • **arma arrojadiza** missile, projectile

arrojado ADJ (= *valiente*) daring, dashing; (= *temerario*) reckless

arrojallamas SM INV flamethrower

arrojar ▹ CONJUG 1a VT **1** (= *lanzar*) to throw; (*con fuerza*) to hurl • **la niña arrojaba piedras al río** the girl was throwing stones into the river • **los hinchas ~on piedras contra la policía** the fans threw *o* hurled stones at the police • **arroja el papel al cubo de la basura** throw the paper into the wastepaper basket • **"no arrojar basura"** "no tipping"
2 [+ *humo, lava*] to send out
3 [+ *resultados, datos*] to produce • **la investigación ha arrojado datos muy negativos** the investigation has produced some very negative data • **la transacción arrojó un balance positivo** the transaction yielded a profit • **este estudio arroja (alguna) luz sobre el tema** this study sheds some light on the subject • **el accidente arrojó 80 muertos** (*LAm*) the accident left 80 dead
4 (= *expulsar*) to throw out • **lo arrojó de casa por su comportamiento** she threw him out of the house because of his behaviour
5 (*LAm*) (= *vomitar*) to bring up, vomit
VPR **arrojarse** (= *lanzarse*) to throw o.s.; (*con fuerza*) hurl o.s. • **se arrojó a mis brazos y lloró** he threw *o* flung himself into my arms and wept • **el ladrón se arrojó desde el quinto piso** the thief threw *o* hurled himself from the fifth floor • **el asesino se arrojó sobre su víctima** the killer threw *o* hurled himself on his victim

arrojo SM daring, fearlessness • **con ~** boldly, fearlessly

arrollado SM (*Cono Sur*) rolled pork

arrollador ADJ • **un ataque ~** a crushing attack • **por una mayoría ~a** by an overwhelming majority • **es una pasión ~a** it is a consuming passion • **tenía una personalidad ~a** she had an overwhelming *o* overpowering personality

arrollar¹ ▹ CONJUG 1a VT **1** (= *enrollar*) (*gen*) to roll up; [+ *cable, cuerda, hilo*] to coil, wind
2 (= *arrastrar*) [*río*] to sweep away, wash away; [+ *enemigo*] to rout; [+ *adversario*] to crush; [+ *peatón*] to run over, knock down • **~on a sus rivales** they crushed their rivals
3 [+ *persona*] (*en debate*) to crush; (= *asombrar*) to dumbfound, leave speechless

arrollar² ▹ CONJUG 1a VT = **arrullar**

arromar ▹ CONJUG 1a VT to blunt, dull

arropar ▹ CONJUG 1a VT **1** (= *vestir*) to wrap up, wrap up with clothes; (*en cama*) to tuck up, tuck up in bed
2 (*fig*) (= *proteger*) to protect
VPR **arroparse** to wrap o.s. up • **¡arrópate bien!** wrap up warm!

arrope SM (= *jarabe*) syrup; [*de mosto*] grape syrup; [*de miel*] honey syrup

arrorró SM (*LAm*) lullaby

arrostrado ADJ • **bien ~** nice-looking • **mal ~** ugly

arrostrar ▹ CONJUG 1a VT [+ *consecuencias*] to face, face up to; [+ *peligro*] to brave, face
VI **1** • **~ a algo** to show a liking for sth
2 • **~ con** [+ *consecuencias*] to face, face up to; [+ *peligro*] to brave, face
VPR **arrostrarse** • **~se con algn** to face up to sb

arroyada SF **1** (= *barranco*) gully, stream bed
2 (= *inundación*) flood, flooding

arroyo SM **1** (= *riachuelo*) stream, brook; (= *cauce*) watercourse; (*LAm*) (= *río*) river; (*Méx*) (= *barranco*) gully, ravine
2 (= *cuneta*) gutter • **poner a algn en el ~** to turn sb onto the streets • **sacar a algn del ~** to drag sb from the gutter • **ser del ~** to be an orphan

arroyuelo SM small stream, brook

arroz SM rice • MODISMO: • **hubo ~ y gallo muerto** (*Esp, Caribe**) it was a slap-up do*
▸ **arroz a la cubana** *rice with banana, tomato sauce and fried egg* ▸ **arroz blanco** white rice ▸ **arroz hervido** boiled rice ▸ **arroz hinchado** puffed rice ▸ **arroz con leche** rice pudding ▸ **arroz integral** brown rice

arrozal SM rice field, paddy field

arrufarse ▹ CONJUG 1a VPR (*Caribe*) to get annoyed, get angry

arruga SF **1** (*en piel*) wrinkle, line; (*en ropa*) crease
2 (*And**) (= *estafa*) swindle, con*; (= *deuda*) debt • **hacer una ~** (*And*) to cheat

arrugado ADJ [*cara etc*] wrinkled, lined; [*papel etc*] creased; [*vestido*] crumpled, creased up

arrugar ▹ CONJUG 1h VT [+ *cara*] to wrinkle, line; [+ *ceño*] to knit; [+ *papel*] to crumple, screw up; [+ *ropa*] to ruck up, crumple • **~ la cara** to screw up one's face • **~ el entrecejo** to knit one's brow, frown
VPR **arrugarse 1** [*cara*] to wrinkle, wrinkle up, get wrinkled; [*ropa*] to crease, get creased; [*planta*] to shrivel up
2 (*Méx**) (= *asustarse*) to get scared, get frightened

arrugue SM (*Caribe*) = **arruga**

arruinado ADJ **1** [*persona, reputación, vida*] ruined
2 (*Cono Sur, Méx*) (= *enclenque*) sickly, stunted; (*Cono Sur*) (= *miserable*) wretched, down and out

arruinamiento SM ruin, ruination

arruinar ▹ CONJUG 1a VT **1** (= *empobrecer*) to ruin
2 (= *destruir*) to wreck, destroy
3 (*LAm*) (= *desvirgar*) to deflower
VPR **arruinarse** [*compañía*] to be ruined; [*edificio*] to fall into ruins, fall down, collapse

arrullar ▹ CONJUG 1a VT [+ *niño*] to lull to sleep, sing to sleep; [+ *amante*] to say sweet nothings to
VI to coo
VPR **arrullarse** to bill and coo

arrullo SM (*Orn*) cooing; [*de amantes*] billing and cooing; [*de agua, olas*] murmur; (= *canción*) lullaby

arrumaco SM **1** (= *caricia*) caress
2 (= *halago*) piece of flattery • **andar con ~** to flatter
3 (= *vestido etc*) *eccentric item of dress or adornment*
4 arrumacos (= *cariñitos*) show of affection (*sing*), endearments

arrumaje SM stowage

arrumar ▹ CONJUG 1a VT **1** (*Náut*) to stow
2 (= *amontonar*) to pile up
VPR **arrumarse** to become overcast

arrumbar[1] ▹ CONJUG 1a VT **1** [+ *objeto*] (= *apartar*) to put aside, discard; (= *olvidar*) to neglect, forget
2 [+ *individuo*] (*en discusión*) to silence, floor; (= *apartar*) to remove

arrumbar[2] ▹ CONJUG 1a (*Náut*) VI to set course (**hacia** for)
VPR **arrumbarse** to take one's bearings

arrume SM (*And, Caribe*) pile, heap

arruncharse ▹ CONJUG 1a VPR (*And*) to curl up, roll up

arrurruz SM arrowroot

arrutanado ADJ (*And*) plump

arrutinarse ▹ CONJUG 1a VPR to get into a routine, get set in one's ways

arsenal SM **1** (*Náut*) naval dockyard; (*Mil*) arsenal • **el ~ nuclear** the nuclear arsenal
2 (= *conjunto numeroso*) storehouse, mine

arsenalera SF (*Cono Sur*) surgeon's assistant, theatre auxiliary

arsénico SM arsenic

arte SM o SF (*gen m en sing, f en pl*) **1** (= *pintura, música*) art • **~s** (*Univ*) arts • **~s y oficios** arts and crafts • **bellas ~s** fine arts • **~ de vivir** art of living • **el séptimo ~** the cinema, film • **~ de los trucos** conjuring • **por ~ de magia** by magic, as if by magic • MODISMO: • **no tener ~ ni parte en algo** to have nothing whatsoever to do with sth ▸ **arte abstracto** abstract art ▸ **artes decorativas** decorative arts ▸ **artes gráficas** graphic arts ▸ **artes marciales** martial arts ▸ **arte poética** poetics (*sing*) ▸ **arte pop** pop art ▸ **artes plásticas** plastic arts; ▹ **amor**
2 (= *habilidad*) skill; (= *astucia*) craftiness • **malas ~s** trickery (*sing*) • **por malas ~s** by trickery
3 (= *artificio*) workmanship, artistry • **sin ~** (*como adj*) clumsy; (*como adv*) clumsily
4 (*Literat*) ▸ **arte mayor** *Spanish verse of eight lines each of twelve syllables dating from the 15th century* ▸ **arte menor** *Spanish verse usually of four lines each of six or eight syllables*
5 (*Pesca*) • **~ de pesca** (= *red*) fishing net; (= *caña etc*) fishing tackle

artefacto SM **1** (*Téc*) device, appliance ▸ **artefacto explosivo** bomb, explosive device ▸ **artefacto incendiario** incendiary device ▸ **artefacto infernal** bomb, explosive device ▸ **artefacto nuclear** nuclear device ▸ **artefactos de alumbrado** light fittings, light fixtures ▸ **artefactos del baño** (*Arg, Uru*) bathroom fixtures
2 (*Arqueología*) artefact, artifact (*EEUU*)
3 (*Aut**) old crock, jalopy*, old banger*

artejo SM knuckle

arteramente ADV cunningly, artfully

arteria SF **1** (*Med*) artery
2 (= *calle*) artery • **la ~ principal de una ciudad** the main thoroughfare of a town

artería SF cunning, artfulness

arterial ADJ arterial

arterioesclerosis SF INV, **arteriosclerosis** SF INV arteriosclerosis

artero ADJ cunning, artful, crafty

artesa SF trough

artesanado SM artisans (*pl*)

artesanal ADJ craft (*antes de s*), handicraft (*antes de s*) • **industria ~** craft industry, handicraft industry • **productos ~es** crafts, handicrafts

artesanía SF (= *arte*) craftmanship; (= *productos*) crafts (*pl*), handicrafts (*pl*); (= *artes y oficios*) arts and crafts • **obra de ~** piece of craftsmanship • **zapatos de ~** craft shoes, hand-made shoes

artesano/a ADJ home-made, home-produced
SM/F craftsman/craftswoman, artisan

artesiano ADJ • **pozo ~** artesian well

artesón SM **1** [*de cocina*] kitchen tub
2 (*Arquit*) coffer, caisson; (= *adorno*) moulding, molding (*EEUU*)
3 (*And, Méx*) (= *bóveda*) vault; (= *arcos*) arcade, series of arches; (= *terraza*) flat roof, terrace

artesonado SM coffered ceiling

artesonar ▹ CONJUG 1a VT **1** (= *poner paneles a*) to coffer
2 (= *estucar*) to stucco, mould, mold (*EEUU*)

ártico ADJ Arctic
SM • **el Ártico** the Arctic

articulación SF **1** (*Anat*) articulation (*frm*), joint
2 (*Mec*) joint ▸ **articulación esférica** ball-and-socket joint ▸ **articulación universal** universal joint
3 (*Ling*) articulation

articuladamente ADV distinctly, articulately

articulado ADJ **1** [*persona*] articulate
2 (*Anat, Mec*) articulated, jointed; (*Aut*) [*volante*] collapsible
SM [*de ley, reglamento*] article

articular ▹ CONJUG 1a VT **1** (*Ling*) to articulate
2 (*Mec*) to articulate, join together
3 (*Jur*) to article
4 (*And, Cono Sur**) (= *regañar*) to tell off*, dress down*
VI (*Cono Sur*) (= *reñir*) to quarrel, squabble; (= *quejarse*) to grumble, moan*
VPR **articularse** • **~se en torno a** *o* **sobre** [*trama, programa*] to be made up of

articulista SMF columnist, contributor (*to a paper*)

artículo SM **1** (*Com*) article, item • **~s** commodities, goods ▸ **artículos alimenticios** foodstuffs ▸ **artículos de consumo** consumer goods ▸ **artículos de escritorio** stationery ▸ **artículos de marca** branded goods; (*Com*) proprietary goods ▸ **artículos de plata** silverware (*sing*) ▸ **artículos de primera necesidad** basic commodities, essentials ▸ **artículos de tocador** toiletries
2 (*escrito*) article; (*TV*) feature, report; (*en revista erudita*) article, paper; (*en libro de referencia*) entry, article ▸ **artículo de fondo** leader, editorial ▸ **artículo de portada** cover story, front-page article
3 (*Ling*) article ▸ **artículo definido** definite article ▸ **artículo indefinido** indefinite article
4 [*de ley, documento*] article, section, item

artífice SMF (*Arte*) artist, craftsman/craftswoman; (= *hacedor*) maker; (= *inventor*) inventor • **el ~ de la victoria** the architect of victory

artificial ADJ [*flor, luz, inseminación*] artificial; [*material*] artificial, man-made • **fuegos ~es** fireworks

artificialidad SF artificiality

artificializar ▹ CONJUG 1f VT to make artificial, give an air of artificiality to

artificialmente ADV artificially

artificiero/a SM/F explosives expert, bomb-disposal officer

artificio SM **1** (= *arte*) art, craft; (= *truco*) artifice; (= *astucia*) cunning, sly trick
2 (= *aparato*) device, appliance
3 (= *hechura*) workmanship, craftsmanship

artificiosamente ADV (= *ingeniosamente*) skilfully, skillfully (*EEUU*), ingeniously; (= *astutamente*) cunningly, artfully

artificioso ADJ (= *ingenioso*) skilful, skillful (*EEUU*), ingenious; (= *astuto*) cunning, artful, sly

artillería SF **1** (*Mil*) artillery ▸ **artillería antiaérea** anti-aircraft guns (*pl*) ▸ **artillería de campaña** field guns (*pl*) ▸ **artillería pesada** heavy artillery
2 (*Dep**) forward line

artillero SM **1** (*Mil*) artilleryman; (*Aer, Náut*) gunner; (*Min*) explosives expert
2 (*Dep**) forward

artilugio SM **1** (= *aparato*) gadget, contraption
2 (= *truco*) gimmick, stunt
3 (= *chisme*) thingummy*, gizmo (*EEUU**), whatsit*

artimaña SF **1** (*Caza*) trap, snare
2 (= *ingenio*) cunning

artista SMF **1** (*Arte*) artist
2 (*Teat, Cine*) artist, artiste ▸ **artista de cine** film actor/film actress ▸ **artista de teatro** actor/actress ▸ **artista de variedades** variety artist *o* artiste ▸ **artista invitado/a** guest artist *o* artiste
3* (= *persona hábil*) • **es un ~ haciendo paella** he's an expert at making paella

artísticamente ADV artistically

artístico ADJ artistic

artrítico ADJ arthritic

artritis SF INV arthritis ▸ **artritis reumatoide** rheumatoid arthritis

artrópodo SM arthropod; **artrópodos** SMPL (*como clase*) arthropoda

artroscopia SF arthroscopy

artrósico ADJ **1** • **estar ~** (*Med*) to have arthrosis
2 [*política, partido*] stagnant

artrosis SF INV osteoarthritis

Arturo SM Arthur

Artús SM • **el Rey ~** King Arthur

aruñón SM **1** (*And*) (= *ladrón*) thief, pickpocket
2 = **arañazo**

arveja SF **1** (*Bot*) vetch
2 (*LAm*) (= *guisante*) pea

arvejilla SF (*Arg, Uru*) sweet pea

Arz. ABR, **Arzbpo.** ABR (= **arzobispo**) Abp

arzobispado SM archbishopric

arzobispal ADJ archiepiscopal • **palacio ~** archbishop's palace

arzobispo SM archbishop

arzón SM saddle tree ▸ **arzón delantero** saddlebow

as SM **1** (*Naipes*) ace; (*dominó*) one ▸ **as de espadas** ace of spades • MODISMO: • **guardarse un as en la manga** to have an ace up one's sleeve
2* (= *campeón*) ace • **es un as** he's a star* ▸ **as del fútbol** star player ▸ **as del volante** champion driver, crack driver*
3 (*Tenis*) ace

asa[1] SF **1** (= *agarradero*) handle
2 (= *pretexto*) lever, pretext • MODISMO: • **ser muy del asa*** to be well in

asa[2] SF (*Bot*) (= *jugo*) juice

asadera SF (*Cono Sur*) baking tin

asadero ADJ roasting, for roasting
SM **1** (*Elec*) spit roaster; (= *lugar caluroso*) oven
2 (*Méx*) (= *queso blando*) cottage cheese

asado ADJ **1** (*Culin*) roast (*antes de s*), roasted • **carne asada** roast meat • **~ al horno** baked • **~ a la parrilla** grilled, broiled (*EEUU*) • **bien ~** well done • **poco ~** rare
2 (*LAm*) (= *enfadado*) cross, angry
3* • **estar ~** (*Caribe*) to be broke*
SM **1** (*Culin*) roast, joint

a

2 (*Cono Sur*) (= *comida*) barbecue; (= *carne asada*) barbecued meat
asador SM **1** (= *varilla*) spit; (= *aparato*) spit roaster ▸ **asador a rotación, asador rotatorio** rotary spit
2 (= *restaurante*) carvery
asadura SF **1** (*Anat*) **asaduras** entrails, offal (*sing*); (*Culin*) chitterlings • **MODISMO:** • **echar las ~s** to bust a gut*
2 (= *pachorra*) sluggishness, laziness • **tiene ~s** he's terribly lazy
SMF * stolid person, dull sort*
asaetear ▹ CONJUG 1a VT **1** to shoot, hit (*with an arrow*)
2 (*fig*) (= *acosar*) to bother, pester
asalariado/a ADJ wage-earning
SM/F **1** (= *empleado*) wage earner
2 (*pey*) (= *mercenario*) hireling • **es ~ de la Mafia** he's in the pay of the Mafia
asalariar ▹ CONJUG 1b VT to employ
asalmonado ADJ salmon coloured, salmon colored (*EEUU*)
asaltabancos SMF INV bank robber
asaltador(a) SM/F, **asaltante** SMF [*de persona*] attacker, assailant; [*de banco, tienda*] raider
asaltar ▹ CONJUG 1a VT **1** [+ *persona*] to attack, assault; (*Mil*) to storm; [+ *banco, tienda etc*] to break into, raid; (*en disturbios etc*) to loot, sack • **lo ~on cuatro bandidos** he was held up by four bandits • **anoche fue asaltada la joyería** the jeweller's was raided last night, last night there was a break-in at the jeweller's
2 [*dudas*] to assail; [*idea*] to cross one's mind • **le asaltó una idea** he was struck by an idea, an idea crossed his mind
3 [*desastre, muerte*] to fall upon, surprise, overtake
asalto SM **1** (= *atraco*) robbery • **~ a un banco** bank raid, bank robbery
2 (*Mil*) attack, assault • **el ~ al Parlamento** the attack *o* assault on parliament, the storming of parliament • **tomar por ~** to take by storm; ▹ **tropa**
3 (*Boxeo*) round
4 (*Esgrima*) ▸ **asalto de armas** fencing bout
5 (= *acoso*) hounding, harassment • **el continuo ~ de los paparazzi** the constant hounding *o* harassment by the paparazzi
6 (*Caribe, Méx*) (= *fiesta sorpresa*) surprise party
asamblea SF **1** (= *reunión*) meeting; [*de trabajadores*] mass meeting • **llamar a ~** (*Mil, Hist*) to assemble, muster
2 (= *congreso*) congress, assembly ▸ **asamblea general** general assembly ▸ **Asamblea Nacional** National Assembly
asambleario ADJ • **las decisiones asamblearias** the assembly's decisions • **los representantes ~s** the representatives to the assembly
asambleísta SMF member of the assembly
asapán SM (*Méx*) flying squirrel
asar ▹ CONJUG 1a VT **1** (*Culin*) to roast • **~ al horno** to bake • **~ a la parrilla** to grill, broil (*EEUU*)
2 (*fig*) (= *acosar*) to pester, plague (**con, a** with)
VPR **asarse** (*fig*) to be terribly hot, roast • **me aso de calor** I'm roasting, I'm boiling • **aquí se asa uno vivo** it's boiling hot here
asascuarse* ▹ CONJUG 1d VPR (*Méx*) to roll up into a ball
asaz ADV (*Literat*) very, exceedingly • **una tarea ~ difícil** an exceedingly difficult task
asbesto SM asbestos
ascendencia SF **1** (= *linaje*) ancestry; (= *origen*) origin • **de remota ~ normanda** of remote Norman ancestry
2 (= *dominio*) ascendancy; (= *influencia*) hold, influence
ascendente ADJ [*movimiento*] ascending; [*tendencia*] rising, increasing • **en una curva ~** in an upward curve • **la carrera ~ del pistón** the upstroke of the piston • **el tren ~** the up train
SM (*Astrol*) ascendant
ascender ▹ CONJUG 2g VI **1** (= *subir*) [*persona*] (*en montaña*) to climb up; (*en el aire*) to rise, ascend (*frm*) • **ascendieron hasta 3.500 metros** they climbed to 3,500 metres • **ascendieron por el otro lado del monte** they made their ascent on the other side of the mountain, they climbed up the other side of the mountain • **el globo ascendió por los aires** the balloon rose *o* ascended (*frm*) into the air • **ascendía por las escaleras** (*liter*) she ascended (*liter*) *o* climbed the steps
2 [*temperatura, presión*] to go up, rise
3 • **~ a** [*empleado, equipo, militar*] to be promoted to • **ascendió al cargo de presidente de la compañía** he was promoted to company president, he rose to the position of company president • **el Málaga ha ascendido a primera división** Málaga have gone up to the first division, Málaga have been promoted to the first division • **~ al trono** to ascend the throne
b [*cantidad*] to amount to, come to • **los beneficios ascendieron a miles de libras** the profits amounted *o* came to thousands of pounds • **el número de heridos asciende ya a 20** the number of wounded has now risen to *o* has now reached 20 • **¿a cuánto ascendió la factura?** how much did the bill come to?
VT [+ *empleado, militar*] to promote • **lo ascendieron a teniente** he rose *o* was promoted to the rank of lieutenant
ascendiente ADJ = **ascendente**
SMF (= *persona*) ancestor, forebear (*frm*)
SM (= *influencia*) ascendancy (*frm*), (powerful) influence (**sobre** over)
ascensión SF **1** (= *subida*) (*a montaña*) ascent; (*al poder*) rise • **la ~ al Mont Blanc** the ascent of Mont Blanc • **la ~ del comunismo** the rise of communism • **desde su ~ al trono** (*frm*) since his accession to the throne (*frm*)
2 [*de empleado, militar, equipo*] promotion (**a** to) • **su ~ a teniente** his promotion to lieutenant • **la ~ del Chelsea en la liga ha sido vertiginosa** Chelsea's rise in the league has been dramatic
3 (*Rel*) • **la Ascensión** the Ascension • **Día de la Ascensión** Ascension Day
ascensional ADJ [*curva, movimiento etc*] upward; (*Astron*) ascendant, rising
ascensionista SMF **1** (= *escalador*) mountain climber, mountaineer
2 (*en globo*) balloonist
ascenso SM **1** (= *subida*) (*a montaña*) ascent; (*al poder*) rise • **en el ~ al Everest** on the ascent of Everest • **se produjo el ~ de la burguesía al poder** the bourgeoisie rose to power
2 (= *aumento*) [*de temperatura, precio, popularidad*] rise; [*de beneficios, impuestos*] increase • **habrá un ~ general de las temperaturas** temperatures will go up *o* rise everywhere, there will be a rise in temperatures everywhere • **temperaturas en ~** rising temperatures, temperatures on the rise • **la Bolsa experimentó un ~ de 4,5 puntos** shares on the Stock Exchange rose by 4.5 points • **se quejan del ~ de los impuestos** they are complaining about the increase in taxes
3 (= *mejora*) rise • **preocupa el ~ electoral de los neofascistas** the increased popularity *o* the rise in popularity of the neo-fascists is giving cause for concern
4 [*de empleado, militar, equipo*] promotion (**a** to) • **soldados con posibilidades de ~** soldiers with promotion prospects • **su ~ a general** his promotion to the rank of general • **su ~ en la empresa ha sido impresionante** his rise within the company has been extraordinary • **acaban de conseguir el ~ a primera división** they have just managed to gain promotion to the first division
ascensor SM lift, elevator (*EEUU*); (*Téc*) elevator
ascensorista SMF lift attendant, elevator operator (*EEUU*)
ascesis SF asceticism
asceta SMF ascetic
ascético ADJ ascetic
ascetismo SM asceticism
asco SM **1** (= *sensación*) disgust, revulsion • **¡qué ~!** how disgusting!, how revolting! • **¡qué ~ de gente!** what awful *o* ghastly* people! • **coger ~ a algo** to get sick of sth • **dar ~ a algn** to sicken sb, disgust sb • **me das ~** you disgust me • **me dan ~ las aceitunas** I loathe olives • **hacer ~s a algo** to turn up one's nose at sth • **poner cara de ~** to look disgusted, pull a face • **morirse de ~** (*Esp**) to be bored to tears *o* to death
2 (= *objeto*) • **es un ~** it's disgusting • **estar hecho un ~** to be filthy • **poner a algn de ~** (*Méx**) to call sb all sorts of names
ascua SF live coal, ember • **¡~s!** ouch! • **MODISMOS:** • **arrimar el ~ a su sardina** to look after number one • **estar como ~ de oro** to be shining bright • **estar en ~s** to be on tenterhooks • **pasar por algo como sobre ~s** to rush through sth • **tener a algn sobre ~s** to keep sb on tenterhooks • **sacar el ~ con la mano del gato** • **sacar el ~ con mano ajena** to get somebody else to do the dirty work
aseadamente ADV (= *con limpieza*) cleanly; (= *con arreglo*) neatly, tidily
aseado ADJ (= *limpio*) clean; (= *arreglado*) neat, tidy
aseador(a) SM/F (*Chile*) cleaner
asear ▹ CONJUG 1a VT **1** (= *lavar*) to wash; (= *limpiar*) to clean up; (= *pulir*) to smarten up
2 (= *adornar*) to adorn, embellish (*frm*)
VPR **asearse** to tidy o.s. up, smarten o.s. up
asechanza SF trap, snare
asechar ▹ CONJUG 1a VT to set a trap for
asediador SM besieger
asediar ▹ CONJUG 1b VT **1** (*Mil*) to besiege; (*Náut*) to blockade
2 (= *molestar*) to bother, pester; [+ *amante*] to chase, lay siege to (*frm*)
asedio SM **1** (*Mil*) siege; (*Náut*) blockade
2 (*Econ*) run ▸ **asedio de un banco** run on a bank
asegún* ADV, PREP (*LAm*) = **según**
asegurable ADV insurable
aseguración SF insurance
asegurado/a ADJ **1** (= *con seguro*) insured (**de, contra** against, **en** for) • **la casa está asegurada contra incendios** the house is insured against fire • **solo estaba ~ contra daños a terceros** he was only insured for third party liability • **el coche no estaba ~** the car was uninsured *o* was not insured • **¿está ~ su coche a todo riesgo?** is your car fully insured?
2 (= *cierto*) • **el éxito de la huelga está ~** the success of the strike is assured • **tenemos el éxito ~** we are bound to be successful
SM/F • **el ~** (= *tomador*) the policyholder; (= *beneficiario*) the insured (*frm*)
asegurador(a) ADJ insurance (*antes de s*)
SM/F insurer • **~ indirecto** underwriter

aseguradora SF insurance company

asegurar ▹ CONJUG 1a VT **1** (= *sujetar*) to secure • **unos cables aseguran la carpa** the marquee is held in place *o* secured by cables • **hay que ~ mejor el cuadro a la pared** the painting needs to be more firmly fixed *o* secured to the wall • **~ algo con algo** to secure sth with sth • **aseguró con cola las patas del armario** he secured the legs of the wardrobe with glue • **~on los fardos con cuerdas** they fastened *o* secured the bundles with rope
2 (= *proteger*) [+ *zona, edificio*] to make secure (**contra** against)
3 (= *garantizar*) [+ *derecho*] to guarantee • **eso asegura el cumplimiento de los acuerdos** that ensures *o* guarantees that the agreements will be fulfilled • **si quieres ~te el aprobado, tienes que estudiar más** if you want to be certain of passing, you'll have to study more • **es posible, pero no lo aseguro** it's possible, but I can't tell you for sure • **es verdad, se lo aseguro** it's true, take my word for it *o* I assure you • **~ a algn que** to assure sb that • **nos ~on que no habría retrasos** they assured us that there would not be any delays
4 (= *declarar*) to maintain • **asegura que no salió de casa** he maintains that he didn't leave the house • **asegura no saber nada del asunto** he maintains *o* affirms that he knew nothing about the matter • **asegura estar dispuesto a ayudarnos** he says that he is willing to help us
5 (*Com, Econ*) [+ *vehículo, vivienda*] to insure (**de, contra** against, **en** for) • **han asegurado los cuadros en más de seis mil millones** the paintings have been insured for more than six thousand million • **deberías ~ el coche a todo riesgo** you should have your car fully insured, you should take out a comprehensive insurance policy on your car
VPR **asegurarse 1** (= *cerciorarse*) to make sure • **para ~nos del todo** in order to make quite sure • **ya me aseguro yo de que llegue a tiempo** I'll make sure that it arrives on time
2 (= *garantizarse*) to make sure of, assure o.s. of • **tuvo que luchar para ~se la victoria** he had a struggle to make sure of victory *o* to assure himself of victory • **han conseguido ~se su presencia en la final** they have made sure of their presence in the final
3 (*Com, Econ*) to insure o.s., take out an insurance policy

ASELE SF ABR = **Asociación para la Enseñanza del Español como Lengua Extranjera**

asemejar ▹ CONJUG 1a VT **1** (= *hacer parecido*) to make look alike, make similar; (= *copiar*) to copy
2 (= *comparar*) to liken, compare (**a** to)
VPR **asemejarse** (= *parecerse*) (*de carácter*) to be alike, be similar; (*de aspecto*) to look alike; (= *compararse*) to compare (**a** to) • **~se a** to be like, resemble

asendereado ADJ **1** [*camino*] beaten, well-trodden
2 [*vida*] wretched, miserable

asenderear ▹ CONJUG 1a VT • **~ a algn** to chase sb relentlessly, hound sb

asenso SM **1** (= *consentimiento*) assent • **dar su ~** to assent
2 (= *acto de creer*) credence • **dar ~ a** to give credence to

asentada SF sitting • **de una ~** at one sitting

asentaderas* SFPL behind* (*sing*), bottom (*sing*), seat (*sing*)

asentado ADJ **1** (= *instalado*) [*persona*] settled; [*tropas*] located, positioned; [*ciudad, campamento*] situated, located • **los israelíes ~s en Cisjordania** Israelis settled on the West Bank • **no está ~ del todo en su trabajo** he's still not totally settled in his job • **un escritor argentino ~ en Madrid** an Argentinian writer living in Madrid • **un campamento ~ a orillas del río** a camp situated *o* located on the riverbanks • **la iglesia estaba asentada sobre terreno arcilloso** the church was built on clay soil • **la mesa no está bien asentada** the table is wobbly
2 (= *establecido*) [*costumbre, tradición*] well-established; [*creencia*] deep-rooted, deeply-rooted, firmly held • **marcas firmemente asentadas en el mercado europeo** brands that are well-established in the European market • **una empresa asentada en España desde hace años** a company that has been established in Spain for many years • **la mafia está asentada aquí desde hace tiempo** the mafia has existed here for years • **sus argumentos están ~s en suposiciones** his arguments are based on suppositions
3 [*persona*] • **ser ~** to be well-balanced

asentador SM **1** [*de navajas*] razor strop
2 (*Com*) dealer, middleman

asentamiento SM **1** (= *acción*) [*de personas, partículas*] settlement
2 (= *lugar*) [*de personas*] settlement, establishment; [*de animales*] colony • **un ~ fenicio** a Phoenician settlement
3 (= *pueblo*) shanty town, township
4 (*Med*) settling

asentar ▹ CONJUG 1j VT **1** (= *colocar*) [+ *objeto*] to place, fix; [+ *tienda de campaña*] to pitch; [+ *campamento*] to set up, pitch
2 (= *establecer*) [+ *principio*] to lay down; [+ *opinión*] to state • **el documento en el que se asientan las bases de la paz** the document in which the foundations for peace are laid out *o* laid down • **como se asienta en las actas** as stated in the minutes
3 (= *sentar*) to seat, sit down • **lo ~on en el trono** they seated him on the throne
• MODISMOS: • **~ la cabeza** • **~ el juicio** to settle down
4 (= *aplanar*) [+ *tierra*] to firm down; [+ *costura*] to flatten
5 (= *afilar*) [+ *filo*] to sharpen; [+ *cuchillo*] to sharpen, hone
6 [+ *golpe*] to deal
7 (*Com*) [+ *pedido*] to enter, book; [+ *libro mayor*] to enter up • **~ algo al debe de algn** to debit sth to sb • **~ algo al haber de algn** to credit sth to sb
8 (*Constr*) [+ *cimientos*] to lay down
9 (*Téc*) [+ *válvula*] to seat
10 (*Méx*) (*frm*) to state • **asentó que la economía estaba en vías de recuperación** he stated that the economy was recovering
VI to be suitable, suit
VPR **asentarse 1** (= *estar situado*) [*ciudad*] to stand, be situated • **se asentaba sobre unos terrenos pantanosos** it stood *o* was situated on marshland
2 (= *posarse*) [*líquido, polvo*] to settle; [*ave*] to alight
3 (= *sentarse*) [*persona*] to sit down, seat o.s.
4 (= *consolidarse*) to settle • **parece que se asienta la moda de los vinos blancos jóvenes** young white wines seem to be becoming fashionable • **se ha asentado muy bien en ese papel** she has settled into that role very nicely
5 (= *basarse*) • **~se en** *o* **sobre algo** to be based on sth
6 (*Arquit*) to subside
7 (*LAm*) (= *adquirir madurez*) to settle down

asentimiento SM assent, consent

asentir ▹ CONJUG 3i VI **1** (= *mostrarse conforme*) to assent, agree • **~ con la cabeza** to nod, nod one's head in agreement
2 • **~ a** (= *consentir en*) to agree to, consent to; [+ *pedido*] to grant; [+ *convenio*] to accept • **~ a la verdad de algo** to recognize the truth of sth

asentista SMF contractor, supplier

aseñorado ADJ gentlemanly/ladylike

aseo SM **1** (= *acto*) washing, toilet (*frm*); (= *higiene*) cleanliness
2 aseos (= *retrete*) toilet (*sing*), rest room (*sing*) (EEUU)

Asepeyo SF ABR (= **Asistencia Sanitaria Económica para Empleados y Obreros**) *job-related health insurance scheme*

aséptico ADJ aseptic

asequible ADJ (= *alcanzable*) attainable; [*plan*] feasible; [*precio*] reasonable, within reach

aserción SF assertion

aserradero SM sawmill

aserrador(a) SM/F sawyer

aserradora SF power saw, chain saw

aserradura SF (= *corte de sierra*) saw cut; **aserraduras** (= *serrín*) sawdust (*sing*)

aserrar ▹ CONJUG 1j VT to saw, saw through

aserrín SM sawdust

aserruchar ▹ CONJUG 1a VT (*LAm*) = **aserrar**

asertar ▹ CONJUG 1a VT to assert, affirm

asertividad SF assertiveness

asertivo ADJ assertive

aserto SM assertion

asesinado/a SM/F murder victim, murdered person

asesinar ▹ CONJUG 1a VT **1** (= *matar*) to murder; (*Pol*) to assassinate
2 (= *molestar*) to pester, plague to death, pester the life out of*

asesinato SM (= *acto*) murder, homicide (EEUU); (*Pol*) assassination ▸ **asesinato en primer grado** murder in the first degree, first-degree murder (EEUU) ▸ **asesinato en segundo grado** murder in the second degree, second degree murder (EEUU)
▸ **asesinato frustrado** attempted murder
▸ **asesinato legal** judicial murder
▸ **asesinato moral** character assassination
▸ **asesinatos en serie** serial killings

asesino/a ADJ murderous
SM/F murder/murderess, killer; (*Pol*) assassin ▸ **asesino/a en serie, asesino/a múltiple** serial killer ▸ **asesino/a profesional** hired killer ▸ **asesino/a serial** (*LAm*) serial killer

asesor(a) ADJ advisory
SM/F adviser, consultant ▸ **asesor(a) administrativo/a** management consultant
▸ **asesor(a) de cuentas** tax accountant
▸ **asesor(a) de imagen** public relations adviser ▸ **asesora del hogar** (*Cono Sur*) maid
▸ **asesor(a) financiero/a** financial adviser
▸ **asesor(a) fiscal** tax accountant
▸ **asesor(a) jurídico/a** legal adviser
▸ **asesor(a) técnico/a** technical adviser *o* consultant

asesoramiento SM advice

asesorar ▹ CONJUG 1a VT **1** (*Jur*) to advise, give legal advice to, give professional advice to
2 (*Com*) to act as consultant to
VPR **asesorarse 1** • **~se con** to take advice from, consult
2 • **~se de una situación** to take stock of a situation

asesorato (SM) (*LAm*) **1** (= *acto*) advising
2 (= *oficina*) consultant's office
asesoría (SF) **1** (= *acto*) advising; (= *cargo*) consultancy ▸ **asesoría jurídica** legal advice ▸ **asesoría técnica** technical consultancy
2 (= *honorario*) adviser's fee
3 (= *oficina*) consultant's office
asestar ▹ CONJUG 1a (VT) **1** [+ *arma*] to aim (a at, in the direction of); [+ *tiro*] to fire
2 [+ *golpe*] to deal • **~ una puñalada a algn** to stab sb
aseveración (SF) assertion, contention
aseveradamente (ADV) positively
aseverar ▹ CONJUG 1a (VT) to assert
asexuado (ADJ) sexless
asexual (ADJ) asexual
asfaltado (ADJ) asphalt (*antes de s*), asphalted
(SM) **1** (= *proceso*) asphalting
2 (= *superficie*) asphalt surface; (*Aer*) tarmac
asfaltar ▹ CONJUG 1a (VT) to asphalt
asfáltico (ADJ) asphalt (*antes de s*), blacktop (EEUU)
asfalto (SM) asphalt, blacktop (EEUU); (*Aer*) tarmac • MODISMO: • **regar el ~**‡ to kick the bucket‡
asfixia (SF) (= *agobio*) suffocation, asphyxiation; (*Med*) asphyxia
asfixiador (ADJ), **asfixiante** (ADJ) suffocating; (*Med, Jur*) asphyxiating • **calor asfixiante** suffocating heat, stifling heat • **gas asfixiante** poison gas • **una política asfixiante para el comercio** a policy that stifles *o* strangles trade
asfixiar ▹ CONJUG 1b (VT) **1** (= *ahogar*) to suffocate; (*Med, Jur*) to asphyxiate • **asfixió a la víctima con un cojín** he suffocated the victim with a cushion • **se confirma que la víctima fue asfixiada** it has been confirmed that the victim was suffocated *o* asphyxiated • **este humo nos asfixia** this smoke is asphyxiating *o* suffocating us • **este calor seco me asfixia** this dry heat is suffocating • **los ~on con gas tóxico** they gassed them (to death) • **la asfixió bajo el agua** he drowned her
2 (= *agobiar*) • **el pequeño pueblo la asfixiaba** village life was suffocating *o* stifling her • **tanto trabajo lo asfixia** all this work is getting on top of him *o* getting to him *o* getting him down • **los impuestos han asfixiado el comercio** taxation has suffocated trade
(VPR) **asfixiarse 1** (= *ahogarse*) to suffocate, asphyxiate • **me asfixio con tanto humo** all this smoke is suffocating me • **murieron asfixiados en el incendio** they suffocated (to death) *o* asphyxiated in the fire
2 (= *agobiarse*) to suffocate, feel stifled • **estar asfixiado** (= *sin dinero*) to be broke*; (= *en aprieto*) to be up the creek‡ • **estoy asfixiado con tantos exámenes** all these exams are getting on top of me
3 [*negocio, economía, empresario*] to be strangled • **este país se asfixia a causa del embargo** this country is being strangled by the embargo
asgo ▹ asir
así (ADV) **1** (= *de este modo*) **a** (*con ser*) • **—te engañaron, ¿no es así? —sí, así es** "they deceived you, didn't they?" — "yes, they did", "they deceived you, isn't that so?" —"yes, it is" • **usted es periodista ¿no es así?** you're a journalist, aren't you? • **yo soy así** that's the way I am • **perdona, pero creo que eso no es así** excuse me, but I think that's not true • **así es como lo detuvieron** that's how *o* this is how they arrested him • MODISMO: • **¡(que) así sea!**: • **—solo les falta ganar la copa —que así sea** "all they have to do is win the cup" — "let's hope they do" • **—que el Señor esté con vosotros —así sea** "(may) God be with you" — "amen"
b (*con otros verbos*) like that, like this • **lo hizo así** he did it like that *o* like this • **esto no puede seguir así** things can't go on this way, this can't go on like this • **se iniciaba así una nueva etapa** thus *o* so a new phase began • **¡así se habla!** that's what I like to hear! • **así ocurrió el accidente** that's how *o* this is how the accident happened • **así me agradecen lo que hice por ellos** this is the thanks I get for what I did for them • **así están las cosas** that's the way things are • **puede leer el contrato si así lo desea** you can read the contract if you wish • **¿por qué te pones así? no es más que un niño** why do you get worked up like that? he's only a child • **—salúdelos de mi parte —así lo haré** "give them my best wishes"— "I will" • **dijo que llamaría y así lo hizo** he said he would call and he did
2 (*acompañando a un sustantivo*) like that • **un hombre así** a man like that, such a man (*más frm*) • **¿por una cosa así se han enfadado?** they got angry over a thing like that?
3 • **así de a** (+ *sustantivo*) • **tuvieron así de ocasiones de ganar y no las aprovecharon** they had so *o* this many chances to win but didn't take them
b (+ *adj, adv*) • **un baúl así de grande** a trunk as big as this, a trunk this big • **él todo lo hace así de rápido** he does everything that fast, that's how fast he does everything • **no para de comer y luego así está de gordita** she never stops eating, that's why she's so plump • **no creo que puedas hacerlo así de bien** I can't believe that you can do it that well • **así de feo era que ...** (*LAm*) he was so ugly that ...
4 • **así como a** (= *lo mismo que*) the same way as • **así como tú te portes conmigo, me portaré yo** I'll behave the same way as you do to me • **así en la Tierra como en el Cielo** on Earth as it is in Heaven
b (= *mientras que*) whereas, while • **así como uno de sus hijos es muy listo, el otro no estudia nada** whereas *o* while one of their children is very clever, the other doesn't study at all
c (= *además de*) as well as • **se necesita el original así como una copia** you need the original as well as a copy
5 (*otras locuciones*) • **así las cosas** with things as they are • **por así decirlo** so to speak • **no así** unlike • **los gastos fueron espectaculares, no así los resultados** the expenditure was astonishing, unlike the results • **¡así no más!** (*Méx**) (= *sin cuidado*) anyhow; (= *sin motivo*) just like that • **es un tema muy importante para tratarlo así no más** it's a very important issue, you can't just treat it any old how • **a mí me cuesta tanto y él lo hace así no más** I find it really hard, but he does it easily *o* just like that • **se fue así no más, sin decir nada** he left just like that, without saying anything • **lo echaron del trabajo así no más** they gave him the sack just like that* • **o así** about, or so • **20 dólares o así** about 20 dollars, 20 dollars or so • **llegarán el jueves o así** they'll arrive around Thursday, they'll arrive on Thursday or thereabouts • **así sin más** just like that • **y así sucesivamente** and so on and so forth • **así y todo** even so • MODISMOS: • **así así** so-so • **—¿cómo te encuentras hoy? —así así** "how do you feel today?" — "so-so" • **así o asá*** • **así o asao*** • **así que asá*** it makes no odds, one way or another • **así como así** • **así que así** just like that • **no gastan el dinero así como así** they don't spend money willy-nilly • **no se hace así como así** it's not as easy as all that • **así porque sí** just for the sake of it, just for the hell of it* • **y empezó a insultarme así porque sí** and he began to insult me just for the sake *o* hell of it* • **no hemos conseguido el éxito así porque sí** it's no accident that we've become successful • **así es la vida** such is life, that's life
(CONJ) **1** (= *aunque*) even if • **así tenga que recorrer el mundo entero, la encontraré** even if I have to travel the whole world, I'll find her
2 (= *consecuentemente*) so • **se gastó todo el dinero y así no pudo ir de vacaciones** he spent all the money, so he couldn't go on holiday • **esperan lograr un acuerdo, evitando así la huelga** they are hoping to reach an agreement and so avoid a strike, they are hoping to reach an agreement, thereby *o* thus avoiding a strike (*frm*) • **así pues** so • **ha conseguido una beca, así pues, podrá seguir estudiando** he got a grant, so he can carry on studying • **así (es) que** so • **estábamos cansados, así que no fuimos** we were tired so we didn't go
3 (= *ojalá*) • **¡así te mueras!** I hope you drop dead!*
4 (= *en cuanto*) • **así que** (+ *subjun*) as soon as • **así que te enteres, comunícamelo** as soon as you find out, let me know • **así que pasen unos años todo se olvidará** in a few years everything will be forgotten
Asia (SF) Asia ▸ **Asia Menor** Asia Minor
asiático/a (ADJ) Asian, Asiatic
(SM/F) Asian
asidero (SM) **1** (= *asa*) handle
2 (= *agarro*) hold, grasp
3 (= *pretexto*) pretext; (= *base*) basis • **eso no tiene ~** there is no basis for that, that is unfounded
asiduamente (ADV) (= *con persistencia*) assiduously; (= *con regularidad*) frequently, regularly
asiduidad (SF) **1** (= *persistencia*) assiduousness
2 (= *regularidad*) regularity
3 asiduidades attentions, kindnesses
asiduo/a (ADJ) (= *persistente*) assiduous; (= *frecuente*) frequent, regular; [*admirador*] devoted • **parroquiano ~** regular (customer) • **como ~ lector de su periódico** as a regular reader of your newspaper
(SM/F) regular, regular customer • **era un ~ del café** he was one of the café's regulars *o* regular customers • **es un ~ del museo** he is a frequent visitor to the museum
asiento (SM) **1** (= *mueble*) seat, chair; (= *lugar*) place; [*de bicicleta*] saddle • **no ha calentado el ~** he hasn't stayed long • **tomar ~** to take a seat ▸ **asiento de atrás** [*de coche*] rear seat; [*de moto*] pillion seat ▸ **asiento delantero** front seat ▸ **asiento expulsor, asiento lanzable, asiento proyectable** (*Aer*) ejector seat ▸ **asiento reservado** reserved seat ▸ **asiento trasero** = asiento de atrás
2 (= *sitio*) site, location
3 (= *fondo*) [*de jarrón, silla*] bottom; (= *nalgas**) bottom, seat
4 (*Mec*) seating ▸ **asiento de válvula** valve seating
5 (= *poso*) sediment
6 (*Arquit*) settling • **hacer ~** to settle, sink
7 (*Náut*) trim
8 (= *arraigo*) settling, establishment • **estar de ~** to be settled • **vivir de ~ con algn** to live in sin with sb

9 (*LAm*) (*tb* **asiento minero**) (= *población minera*) mining town
10 (*Com*) (= *contrato*) contract; (*en libro*) entry
▸ **asiento contable** book-keeping entry
▸ **asiento de cierre** closing entry
11 (*Pol*) treaty, peace treaty
12 (= *estabilidad*) stability; (= *juicio*) good sense, judgment • **hombre de ~** sensible man

asignable ADJ • **~ a** assignable to, which can be assigned to

asignación SF **1** (= *acto*) assignment, allocation; (= *cita*) appointment
2 (*Econ*) allowance ▸ **asignación de presupuesto** budget appropriation ▸ **asignación económica** allowance ▸ **asignación por kilometraje** ≈ mileage allowance ▸ **asignación presupuestaria** (*Caribe*) budget ▸ **asignación semanal** weekly allowance

asignado SM (*And*) wages paid in kind

asignar ▹ CONJUG 1a VT (= *adjudicar*) to assign; [+ *recursos etc*] to allocate, apportion; [+ *labor*] to set; (*Inform*) to allocate; [+ *persona*] to appoint; [+ *causas*] to determine

asignatario/a SM/F (*LAm*) heir/heiress, legatee

asignatura SF subject, course • **aprobar una ~** to pass a subject, pass in a subject ▸ **asignatura pendiente** (*Educ*) failed subject, resit subject; (= *asunto pendiente*) matter pending

asigunas* SFPL • **según ~** (*Caribe*) it all depends

asilado/a SM/F (*en institución*) inmate; (*Pol*) refugee, political refugee

asilar ▹ CONJUG 1a VT **1** (= *internar*) to put into a home, put into an institution
2 (= *albergar*) to take in, give shelter to; (*LAm*) (= *dar asilo político a*) to give political asylum to
VPR **asilarse 1** (= *refugiarse*) to take refuge (**en** in); (*Pol*) to seek political asylum
2 [*anciano etc*] to enter a home, enter an institution

asilo SM **1** (= *institución*) home, institution ▸ **asilo de ancianos** old people's home ▸ **asilo de huérfanos**† orphanage, children's home ▸ **asilo de locos** lunatic asylum ▸ **asilo de niños expósitos**† orphanage, children's home ▸ **asilo de pobres** poorhouse
2 (*Pol etc*) asylum; (*fig*) (= *abrigo*) shelter, refuge • **derecho de ~** right of sanctuary • **pedir (el) ~ político** to ask for political asylum

asilvestrarse ▹ CONJUG 1a VPR [*tierra*] to become wooded, revert to woodland; [*planta*] to establish itself in the wild

asimetría SF (= *falta de simetría*) asymmetry; (= *desequilibrio*) imbalance

asimétrico ADJ asymmetric, asymmetrical

asimiento SM **1** (= *acción*) seizing, grasping
2 (= *apego*) attachment

asimilable ADJ • **fácilmente ~** readily assimilated, easy to assimilate

asimilación SF assimilation

asimilado ADJ similar, related • **establecimientos hoteleros y ~s** hotels and the like
SM (*LAm*) professional, person attached to the army

asimilar ▹ CONJUG 1a VT to assimilate
VPR **asimilarse 1** (= *establecerse*) to become assimilated
2 • **~se a** (= *parecerse*) to resemble

asimismo ADV (= *igualmente*) likewise, in the same way; (= *también*) also

asín* ADV = **así**

asíncrono ADJ asynchronous

asintomático ADJ asymptomatic

asir ▹ CONJUG 3a; tiempo presente como salir
VT to grasp, take hold of (**con** with, **de** by)
• **ir asidos del brazo** to walk along arm-in-arm
VI (*Bot*) to take root
VPR **asirse** to take hold • **~se a** *o* **de** (= *agarrarse*) to seize • **~se de** (*fig*) (= *aprovecharse*) to avail o.s. of (*frm*), take advantage of • **~se con algn** to grapple with sb

Asiria SF Assyria

asirio/a ADJ, SM/F Assyrian

asisito ADV (*And*) = **así**

asísmico ADJ (*LAm*) • **construcción asísmica** earthquake-resistant building • **medidas asísmicas** anti-earthquake measures

asistencia SF **1** (*Escol etc*) attendance (**a** at); (*Teat*) audience • **¿había mucha ~?** were there many people there?
2 (= *ayuda*) help, assistance; (*Med*) care, nursing; (*en casa*) domestic help ▸ **asistencia en carretera** roadside assistance ▸ **asistencia intensiva** intensive care ▸ **asistencia letrada** legal aid ▸ **asistencia médica** medical care ▸ **asistencia pública** (*Cono Sur*) public health authority ▸ **asistencia sanitaria** health care ▸ **asistencia social** welfare work, social work ▸ **asistencia técnica** technical support
3 (*Méx*) (= *habitación*) spare room, guest room, den (*EEUU*)
4 **asistencias** (*Econ*) allowance (*sing*)

asistencial ADJ social security (*antes de s*), welfare (*antes de s*) (*EEUU*)

asistenta SF charwoman, daily help ▸ **asistenta social** social worker

asistente SMF **1** (= *ayudante*) assistant; (*Mil*) orderly; (*And*) (= *criado*) servant ▸ **asistente social** social worker
2 • **los ~s** (= *presentes*) those present

asistido/a ADJ • **~ por ordenador** computer-aided
SM/F (*And*, *Méx*) boarder, lodger, resident

asistir ▹ CONJUG 3a VI **1** (= *acudir*) to attend, go • **no se sabe cuántas personas ~án** it's not known how many people will attend *o* go • **¿va usted a ~?** will you be attending *o* going? • **~ a algo** to attend sth, go to sth • **no asistió a mi clase** he did not attend my lesson, he did not come to my lesson • **asiste a misa todos los domingos** he attends Mass every Sunday, he goes/comes to Mass every Sunday
2 (*Naipes*) to follow suit
VT **1** (= *ayudar*) • **~ a algn** to help sb, assist sb (*frm*) • **una institución que asiste a los inmigrantes** an organization that helps immigrants
2 (*Med*) • **~ a** [+ *paciente, enfermo*] to care for, look after; [+ *herido, accidentado*] to look after, help • **~ un parto** to deliver a baby
3 (= *presenciar*) • **~ a algo** to witness sth • **estamos asistiendo a una nueva revolución tecnológica** we are witnessing a new technological revolution
4 (*Jur*) • **su abogado le asistió en la declaración** his lawyer was present when he gave his statement
5 (*frm*) (= *respaldar*) • **le asiste el derecho a recurrir la sentencia** you have the right to appeal (against) the sentence • **le asiste la razón** he has right on his side
6 (*frm*) (= *atender*) to serve, wait on • **asistió a los invitados en el hotel** he served *o* waited on the hotel guests

askenazi ADJ, SMF Ashkenazi

asma SF asthma ▸ **asma bronquial** bronchial asthma

asmático/a ADJ, SM/F asthmatic

asnada* SF silly thing

asnal* ADJ asinine, silly

asnar ADJ • **ganado ~** donkeys

asnear* ▹ CONJUG 1a VI (*LAm*) (= *hacer tonterías*) to act the fool, do sth silly; (= *ser patoso*) to be clumsy

asnería* SF silly thing

asno/a SM/F **1** (*Zool*) donkey, ass
2 (= *tosco*) ass, fathead* • **¡soy un ~!** I'm an ass!*

asociación SF (= *acción*) association; (= *sociedad*) society, association; (*Com, Econ*) partnership • **por ~ de ideas** by association of ideas ▸ **asociación aduanera** customs union ▸ **asociación de padres de alumnos** parent-teacher association ▸ **asociación de vecinos** residents' association ▸ **asociación libre** free association ▸ **asociación obrera** trade union ▸ **asociación para el delito** criminal conspiracy

asociado/a ADJ associated; [*miembro etc*] associate
SM/F associate, member; (*Com, Econ*) partner

asocial ADJ asocial
SMF social misfit, socially maladjusted person

asociar ▹ CONJUG 1b VT **1** (= *relacionar*) to associate, connect • **se trata de ~ imágenes y números** it's all about associating *o* connecting images and numbers • **di con la solución asociando ideas** I came up with the solution by making (logical) connections • **~ algo con algo** to associate sth with sth, connect sth with sth • **asocio el azahar con Andalucía** I associate *o* connect orange blossom with Andalusia • **no quiero que me asocien con él** I don't want to be associated with him • **me suena, pero no puedo ~lo con nada** I know him, but I don't know where from *o* but I can't place him • **~ algo a algo** to link sth with *o* to sth • **asocian este gen al cáncer de mama** this gene is linked with *o* to breast cancer
2 (*Com, Econ*) to take into partnership
3 (= *unir*) [+ *recursos*] to pool, put together
VPR **asociarse 1** • **~se (con)** to join together (with), join forces (with) • **los sindicatos de izquierda se ~on** the left-wing trade unions joined together *o* joined forces
2 (*Com, Econ*) • **~se (con)** to go into partnership (with)
3 • **~se a algo** to join sth, become a member of sth • **Grecia buscaba ~se a la UE** Greece was seeking to join *o* become a member of the EU
4 [*circunstancias, hechos*] to combine

asocio SM (*LAm*) • **en ~** in association (**de** with)

asolación SF destruction, devastation

asolador ADJ devastating

asolanar ▹ CONJUG 1a VT to dry up, parch
VPR **asolanarse** to dry up, be ruined

asolar[1] ▹ CONJUG 1a = **asolanar**

asolar[2] ▹ CONJUG 1a VT to raze, raze to the ground, destroy
VPR **asolarse** [*líquidos*] to settle

asoleada SF (*LAm*) sunstroke

asoleado ADJ (*CAm*) **1** [*persona*] stupid
2 [*animal*] tired out

asoleadura SF (*Cono Sur*) sunstroke

asolear ▹ CONJUG 1a VT to put in the sun
VPR **asolearse 1** (= *tomar el sol*) to sunbathe
2 (*LAm*) (= *coger insolación*) to get sunstroke
3 (*CAm*) (= *atontarse*) to get stupid

asoleo SM (*Méx*) sunstroke

asomada SF **1** (= *aparición*) brief appearance
2 (= *vislumbre*) glimpse, sudden view

asomadero SM (*And*) viewing point, vantage point

asomar ▹ CONJUG 1a VT **1** [+ *cabeza, hocico*]

a

(*hacia arriba*) to lift; (*hacia fuera*) to poke out • **el animal asoma el hocico y husmea el aire** the animal lifts its snout and sniffs the air • **abrió la puerta y asomó la cabeza** she opened the door and poked her head round it • **asomó la cabeza por encima de la valla para mirar** he peeped over the fence • **asomó la cabeza por el hueco de la escalera** he leaned over the stairwell • **"prohibido asomar la cabeza por la ventanilla"** "do not lean out of the window" • **¿desde cuándo no asomas la cabeza por aquí?*** when was the last time you came round here?*
2 (*Taur*) • **~ el pañuelo** to raise the flag
VI **1** (= *verse*) [*sol, luna*] (*al salir*) to come up; (*entre las nubes*) to come out • **el sol empezó a ~ en el horizonte/por entre las nubes** the sun began to come up on the horizon/come out from behind the clouds • **en la ventana asoma el cañón de un fusil** the barrel of a gun appears at the window • **Jerusalén asoma entre los montes** Jerusalem comes into sight between the hills • **le asomaba la cartera por el bolsillo del pantalón** his wallet was sticking out of his trouser pocket • **el vestido le asomaba por debajo del abrigo** her dress was showing below her coat • **de pronto asomó un buque entre la niebla** a ship suddenly loomed up out of the fog
2* [*persona*] • **hace tiempo que no asoma por aquí** it's been a while since he came round here* • **se casó con el primero que asomó por la puerta** she married the first man *o* one who poked *o* stuck his head round the door*
3 (= *salir*) [*planta*] to come up; [*arruga, cana*] to appear; [*diente*] to cut • **ya empiezan a ~ los narcisos** the daffodils are beginning to come up now • **por la tarde le asomaba ya la barba** he already had five o'clock shadow*, by the afternoon his stubble was beginning to show • **ya le empiezan a ~ algunas canas** he has already got some grey hairs coming through *o* appearing • **ya le han asomado varios dientes** she has already cut several teeth
4 (= *comenzar*) • **nació apenas asomado el año** he was born at the very start of the new year, he was born when the new year had barely got underway
VPR **asomarse 1** [*persona*] • **algunos vecinos se ~on a mirar** some neighbours came out to look • **"prohibido asomarse"** "do not lean out of the window" • **~se a** *o* **por** [+ *precipicio, barandilla*] to lean over; [+ *ventana*] (*para mirar*) to look out of; (*sacando el cuerpo*) to lean out of • **me asomé a la ventana y vi que no estaba el coche** I looked out of the window and saw that the car wasn't there • **la vieron asomada a la ventana, regando las macetas** they saw her leaning out of the window, watering her plants • **asomaos a la terraza para ver la vista** come out on to the terrace to see the view • **¡ven, asómate a la puerta!** come on, come to the door! • **vamos a ~nos a las calles esta mañana** (*Radio, TV*) let's take a look at what's happening on the streets this morning • **si nos asomamos al panorama de la economía actual** if we take a brief look at the current economic situation
2 (= *mostrarse*) • **el ciprés se asomaba por encima de la tapia** the cypress showed above the wall, the cypress protruded over the top of the wall
3* (= *emborracharse*) to get tight*, get tipsy
4 (*And*) (= *acercarse*) to approach, come close, come close to

asombradizo ADJ easily alarmed
asombrador ADJ amazing, astonishing
asombrar ▷ CONJUG 1a VT **1** (= *extrañar*) to amaze, astonish • **nos asombra ese repentino cambio** we are amazed *o* astonished at this sudden change • **me asombra verte trabajar tanto** I'm amazed *o* astonished to see you working so hard • **este chico no deja de ~me** that boy never ceases to amaze me • **a mí ya nada me asombra** nothing surprises me any more
2 (*frm*) (= *hacer sombra*) to shade
3 (*frm*) (= *oscurecer*) [+ *color*] to darken
4 (*frm*) (*asustar*) to frighten
VPR **asombrarse 1** (= *extrañarse*) to be amazed, be astonished • **me asombré con** *o* **de su extraña reacción** I was amazed *o* astonished by his strange reaction • **se asombró (de) que lo supieras** she was amazed *o* astonished that you knew • **no me asombro por** *o* **de nada** nothing surprises me
2 (*frm*) (= *asustarse*) to take fright
3 (*CAm*) (= *desmayarse*) to faint
asombro SM **1** (= *sorpresa*) amazement, astonishment • **lo miró con ~** he looked at it with amazement *o* astonishment • **para ~ de todos** • **ante el ~ de todo el mundo** to everyone's amazement *o* astonishment • **tener cara** *o* **mirada de ~** to look amazed *o* astonished • **no salgo de mi ~** I can't get over it
2 (*frm*) (= *susto*) fear, fright
asombrosamente ADV amazingly, astonishingly
asombroso ADJ amazing, astonishing
asomo SM **1** (= *aparición*) appearance
2 (= *indicio*) sign, indication • **ante cualquier ~ de discrepancia** at the slightest hint of disagreement • **sin ~ de violencia** without a trace of violence • **ni por ~** (= *de ningún modo*) by no means • **¡ni por ~!** (= *¡ni en broma!*) no chance!, no way!
asonada SF **1** (= *personas*) mob, rabble
2 (= *motín*) riot, disturbance
asonancia SF **1** (*Literat*) assonance
2 (*fig*) (= *correspondencia*) correspondence, connection • **no tener ~ con** to bear no relation to
asonantar ▷ CONJUG 1a VT, VI to assonate (**con** with)
asonante ADJ assonant
SF assonant, assonant rhyme
asonar ▷ CONJUG 1l VI to assonate
asordar ▷ CONJUG 1a VT to deafen
asorocharse ▷ CONJUG 1a VPR (*LAm*) to get mountain sickness
asosegar ▷ CONJUG 1h, 1j = **sosegar**
aspa SF **1** (*Arquit*) crosspiece; [*de molino*] sail, arm; [*de ventilador*] blade • **en ~** X-shaped • **ventilador de ~** rotary fan
2 (*Mat*) multiplication sign
3 (*Téc*) reel, winding frame
4 (*Cono Sur*) (= *asta*) horn
aspadera SF reel, winder
aspado ADJ (*de forma*) X-shaped; [*persona*] with arms outstretched • **estar ~ en algo** to be all trussed up in sth
aspador SM reel, winder
aspamentero *etc* ADJ (*Cono Sur, Méx*) = **aspaventero** *etc*
aspamento SM (*Arg, Uru*) = **aspaviento**
aspar ▷ CONJUG 1a VT **1** (*Téc*) to reel, wind
2* (= *fastidiar*) to vex, annoy • **¡que te aspen!** get lost!* • **¡que me aspen si lo sé!** I'm buggered if I know!**, I'm blowed if I know!* • **lo hago aunque me aspen** wild horses wouldn't stop me doing it, I'll do it if it's the last thing I do
3 (*Rel*) to crucify

VPR **asparse 1** (= *retorcerse*) to writhe
2 (= *esforzarse*) to do one's utmost, go all out (**por algo** to get sth)
aspaventero/a ADJ excitable
SM/F excitable person
aspaviento SM exaggerated display of feeling • **hacer ~s** to make a great fuss
aspecto SM **1** (= *apariencia*) look • **no lo conozco, pero no me gusta su ~** I don't know him, but I don't like the look of him • **un señor con ~ de ejecutivo** a man who looks/looked like an executive • **un hombre de ~ saludable** a healthy-looking man • **tener ~ simpático** to look friendly • **¿qué ~ tenía?** what did he look like? • **el debate iba tomando un ~ desagradable** the discussion was starting to turn ugly • **tener buen ~** to look well • **tener mal ~**: • **Juan tiene muy mal ~** Juan isn't looking good *o* well at all • **esa herida tiene mal ~** that wound looks nasty ▸ **aspecto exterior** outward appearance
2 (= *punto*) aspect • **los ~s a tener en cuenta para el análisis** aspects to bear in mind when analysing the problem • **estudiar todos los ~s de una cuestión** to study all aspects of an issue • **en algunos ~s me parece una obra genial** in some respects I think it is a work of genius • **el ~ más destacado de la teoría** the strong(est) point of the theory • **bajo ese ~** from that point of view
3 (*Geog*) aspect
4 (*Arquit*) aspect
5 (*Ling*) aspect
6 • **al primer ~†** at first sight
aspectual ADJ aspectual
ásperamente ADV • **contestó ~** he answered gruffly • **criticar ~** to criticize bitterly
aspereza SF [*de terreno*] roughness, ruggedness; (= *acidez*) sourness, tartness; [*de carácter*] surliness • **contestar con ~** to answer harshly • **MODISMO**: • **limar ~s** to smooth things over
asperges SM INV **1** (= *aspersión*) sprinkling
2 (*Rel*) aspergillum
asperillo SM slight sour taste, slight bitter taste
asperjar ▷ CONJUG 1a VT (= *rociar*) to sprinkle; (*Rel*) to sprinkle with holy water
áspero ADJ **1** (*al tacto*) rough; [*terreno*] rough, rugged; [*filo*] uneven, jagged, rough
2 (*al gusto*) sour, tart
3 [*clima*] harsh; [*trato*] rough
4 [*voz*] rough, rasping; [*tono*] surly, gruff; [*temperamento*] sour; [*disputa etc*] bad-tempered
asperón SM sandstone
aspersión SF [*de agua etc*] sprinkling; (*Agr*) spraying • **riego por ~** watering by spray, watering by sprinklers
aspersor SM sprinkler
áspid SM, **áspide** SM asp
aspidistra SF aspidistra
aspillera SF loophole
aspiración SF **1** (*Zool, Med*) breathing in, inhalation; (*Ling*) aspiration; (*Mús*) short pause
2 (*Mec*) air intake
3 (= *anhelo*) aspiration; **aspiraciones** aspirations, ambition (*sing*) • **es un hombre sin aspiraciones** he's not an ambitious man, he's a man with no aspirations
aspirada SF aspirate
aspirado ADJ aspirate
aspirador ADJ • **bomba ~a** suction pump
SM (*tb* **aspirador de polvo**) vacuum cleaner, hoover® • **pasar el ~** to vacuum, hoover
aspiradora SF vacuum cleaner, hoover® • **pasar la ~** to vacuum, hoover

aspirante (ADJ) **1** [*persona*] aspiring
2 (= *aspirador*) • **bomba ~** suction pump
(SMF) candidate, applicant (**a** for) • **~ de marina** naval cadet
aspirar ▹ CONJUG 1a (VT) **1** [+ *aire*] to breathe in, inhale; [+ *líquido*] to suck in, take in; [+ *droga*] to sniff
2 (*Ling*) to aspirate
(VI) • **~ a algo** to aspire to sth • **no aspiro a tanto** I do not aim so high • **~ a hacer algo** to aspire to do sth, aim to do sth • **el que no sepa eso que no aspire a aprobar** whoever doesn't know that can have no hope of passing
aspirina (SF) aspirin
aspudo (ADJ) (*Cono Sur*) big-horned
asqueante (ADJ) nauseating, disgusting
asquear ▹ CONJUG 1a (VT) to disgust • **me asquean las ratas** I loathe rats, rats disgust me
(VPR) **asquearse** to be nauseated, feel disgusted
asquenazi (ADJ) Ashkenazi
(SMF) Ashkenazi
asquerosamente (ADV) disgustingly, revoltingly
asquerosidad (SF) **1** (= *suciedad*) filth • **estar hecho** *o* **ser una ~** to be filthy • **hacer ~es** to make a mess
2 (= *dicho*) obscenity; (= *truco*) dirty trick • **¡qué ~ acaba de decir!** what an obscene *o* a disgusting thing to say!
asqueroso (ADJ) **1** (= *repugnante*) disgusting, revolting; [*condición*] squalid; (= *sucio*) filthy
2 (= *de gusto delicado*) squeamish
asquiento (ADJ) (*And*) **1** (= *quisquilloso*) fussy
2 = **asqueroso**
asta (SF) **1** (= *arma*) lance, spear; (= *palo*) shaft; [*de banderas*] flagpole; [*de brocha*] handle • **a media ~** at half mast
2 (*Zool*) horn, antler • **dejar a algn en las ~s del toro** to leave sb in a jam *o* in a pickle*
astabandera (SF) (*LAm*) flagstaff, flagpole
ástaco (SM) crayfish
astado (ADJ) horned
(SM) bull
astear ▹ CONJUG 1a (VT) (*Cono Sur*) to gore
aster (SF) aster
asterisco (SM) asterisk • **señalar con un ~** • **poner ~ a** to asterisk, mark with an asterisk
asteroide (SM) asteroid
astigmático (ADJ) astigmatic
astigmatismo (SM) astigmatism
astil (SM) [*de herramienta*] handle, haft; [*de flecha*] shaft; [*de balanza*] beam
astilla (SF) **1** (= *fragmento*) splinter, chip; **astillas** (*para fuego*) kindling (*sing*) • **hacer algo ~s** to smash sth into little *o* tiny pieces • **hacerse ~s** to shatter into little *o* tiny pieces; ▹ **palo**
2 (*Esp**) (= *soborno*) small bribe, sweetener* • **dar ~ a algn** to give sb a cut* • **ese tío no da ~** he's a tight-fisted so-and-so*
astillar ▹ CONJUG 1a (VT) (= *hacer astillas*) to splinter, chip; (= *hacer pedazos*) to shatter, smash to pieces
(VPR) **astillarse** (= *levantarse astillas en*) to splinter; (= *hacerse pedazos*) to shatter, smash to pieces
astillero (SM) shipyard, dockyard
astracán (SM) astrakhan
astracanada* (SF) silly thing, silly thing to do
astrágalo (SM) (*Arquit, Mil*) astragal; (*Anat*) ankle bone, astragalus
astral (ADJ) astral
astreñir ▹ CONJUG 3h, 3k = **astringir**
astrilla (SF) (*Cono Sur*) = **astilla**
astringente (ADJ) astringent (*frm*), binding
(SM) astringent
astringir ▹ CONJUG 3e (VT) **1** (*Anat*) to constrict, contract; (*Med*) to bind
2 (= *constreñir*) to bind, compel
astro (SM) **1** (*Astron*) star, heavenly body • **el ~ Rey** the sun
2 (*Cine*) star
astrofísica (SF) astrophysics (*sing*)
astrofísico/a (SM/F) astrophysicist
astrolabio (SM) astrolabe
astrología (SF) astrology
astrológico (ADJ) astrological
astrólogo/a (SM/F) astrologer
astronauta (SMF) astronaut
astronáutica (SF) astronautics (*sing*)
astronave (SF) spaceship
astronometría (SF) astrometry
astronomía (SF) astronomy
astronómico (ADJ) astronomical
astrónomo/a (SM/F) astronomer
astroso (ADJ) **1** (= *sucio*) dirty; (= *desaliñado*) untidy, shabby
2 (= *malhadado*) ill-fated, ill-starred
3 (= *vil*) contemptible
astucia (SF) **1** (= *sagacidad*) astuteness, cleverness; (= *maña*) guile, cunning • **actuar con ~** to act cunningly, be crafty
2 • **una ~** a clever trick
astur (ADJ), (SMF) Asturian
asturiano/a (ADJ), (SM/F) Asturian
(SM) (*Ling*) Asturian
Asturias (SF) (*tb* **el Principado de Asturias**) Asturias ▸ **príncipe de Asturias** crown prince, ≈ Prince of Wales
asturleonés (ADJ) of/from Asturias and León
astutamente (ADV) (= *con sagacidad*) cleverly, smartly; (= *con maña*) craftily, cunningly
astuto (ADJ) (= *sagaz*) astute, clever; (= *mañoso*) crafty, sly
asueto (SM) time off, break • **día de ~** day off • **tomarse una tarde de ~** to take an afternoon off
asumible (ADJ) [*responsabilidad, riesgo*] acceptable, permissible; [*cambio, error*] acceptable
asumidamente (ADV) supposedly
asumir ▹ CONJUG 3a (VT) **1** (= *responsabilizarse de*) [+ *reto, tarea*] to take on; [+ *cargo*] to take up; [+ *mando*] to take over, assume (*más frm*) • **no han sido capaces de ~ la tarea de gobernar** they have been incapable of taking on the task of government • **el alcalde debería ~ sus responsabilidades por el accidente** the mayor should take *o* assume responsibility for the accident • **el gobierno asumió el compromiso de crear empleo** the government committed itself to creating employment *o* made a commitment to create employment • **ha asumido la cartera de Sanidad** he has been appointed Health Minister • **asumió la presidencia en 1999** he took up *o* assumed (*más frm*) the presidency in 1999 • **ha asumido la dirección de la empresa en un momento muy difícil** he has taken control of *o* has taken over the company at a very difficult time • **los socialistas asumieron el poder en 1982** the socialists came to power in 1982
2 (= *aceptar*) [+ *consecuencias*] to take, accept; [+ *crítica*] to accept; [+ *problema, enfermedad, derrota*] to come to terms with, accept • **un empresario debe invertir y ~ el riesgo** a businessman must invest and take the risk • **lo hice asumiendo el riesgo de ser castigado** I did it in the knowledge that I risked being punished • **estoy dispuesto a ~ todas las críticas** I am willing to accept all the criticism • **ya he asumido que no podré volver a esquiar** I've already come to terms with *o* accepted the fact that I won't be able to ski again • **la familia ha asumido su muerte con serenidad** the family has taken her death calmly
3 (= *adoptar*) to adopt, take • **asumieron una actitud crítica** they adopted *o* took a critical stance • **la población había asumido una actitud contraria a la presencia militar** people had come out against the military presence • **asumió el papel de víctima** he took on the role of victim
4 (= *adquirir*) to assume • **la cuestión del paro ha asumido una dimensión distinta** the question of unemployment has taken on *o* assumed a different dimension • **el fuego asumió enormes proporciones** the fire took on major proportions
5 (= *suponer*) • **~ que** to assume that • **asumieron que era cierto** they assumed that it was true
(VI) (*Pol*) to take office, take up office
asunceño/a (ADJ) of/from Asunción
(SM/F) native/inhabitant of Asunción • **los ~s** the people of Asunción
Asunción (SF) (*Geog*) Asunción
asunción (SF) assumption • **la Asunción** (*Rel*) the Assumption
asunto (SM) **1** (= *cuestión*) matter • **un ~ familiar grave** an urgent family matter • **vine a discutir unos ~s** I came to discuss several matters *o* issues • **no sé nada de ese ~** I don't know anything about it *o* the matter • **el ~ de los impuestos divide al gobierno** the government is divided on the matter *o* question *o* issue of taxes • **hemos tratado el ~ de nuestro divorcio** we've talked about the subject of our divorce • **~s a tratar agenda** • **no te metas en mis ~s** mind your own business • **¡esto es ~ mío!** that's my business *o* affair! • **¡~ concluido!** that's an end to the matter! • **—me ha llamado el jefe a su despacho —mal ~** "the boss has called me to his office" — "doesn't look good" • **ir al ~** to get down to business • **el ~ es que ...** the thing is (that) ... ▸ **asunto de honor** question of honour *o* (*EEUU*) honor
2 (*Jur*) case • **estuvo implicado en un ~ de desfalco** he was involved in a case of embezzlement
3 (*Pol*) • **el ~ Rumasa** the Rumasa affair • **Ministerio de Asuntos Exteriores** Foreign Ministry, Foreign Office, State Department (*EEUU*) ▸ **asuntos exteriores** foreign affairs
4 (= *aventura amorosa*) affair • **es ~ de faldas** there's a woman involved in this somewhere along the line ▸ **asunto de alcoba** bedroom intrigue
5 (*Cono Sur*) • **¿a ~ de qué lo hiciste?** why did you do it?
6 (*Caribe*) • **poner ~** to pay attention
7 (*Literat†*) (= *tema*) subject
asurar ▹ CONJUG 1a (VT) **1** (*Culin etc*) to burn; (*Agr*) to burn up, parch
2 (= *inquietar*) to worry
asurcar ▹ CONJUG 1g (VT) = **surcar**
asustadizo (ADJ) **1** [*persona*] (= *que se asusta mucho*) easily frightened; (= *nervioso*) nervy, jumpy
2 [*animal*] shy, skittish
asustado (ADJ) (= *con miedo*) frightened; (= *espantado*) startled
asustar ▹ CONJUG 1a (VT) (= *causar miedo a*) to frighten, scare; (= *espantar*) to alarm, startle
(VPR) **asustarse** to be frightened, get scared • **~se de algo** to be frightened by sth, get alarmed about sth • **¡no te asustes!** don't be alarmed! • **~se de hacer algo** to be afraid *o* scared *o* frightened to do sth

asusto SM (*And*) = susto

A.T. ABR (= **Antiguo Testamento**) OT

-ata ▸ Aspects of Word Formation in Spanish 2

atabacado ADJ **1** [*color*] tobacco-coloured, tobacco-colored (*EEUU*)
2 • **con aliento ~** (*Cono Sur*) with breath smelling of tobacco

atabal SM kettledrum

atabalear ▸ CONJUG 1a VI [*caballo*] to stamp; (*con dedos*) to drum

atacable ADJ attackable, assailable

atacado ADJ **1** (= *pusilánime*) fainthearted; (= *vacilante*) dithery, irresolute
2 (= *tacaño*) mean, stingy

atacador(a) SM (*Mil*) ramrod
SM/F attacker, assailant

atacadura SF fastener, fastening

atacante SMF attacker, assailant

atacar ▸ CONJUG 1g VT **1** [+ *enemigo, ciudad, fortaleza*] to attack
2 (*Med, Quím*) [*enfermedad, plaga, sustancia*] to attack • **ataca al hígado** it attacks the liver • **la gripe me ataca todos los inviernos** I get struck down by the flu every winter • **me estaba atacando el sueño** I was succumbing to sleep • **este niño me ataca los nervios*** that child gets on my nerves*
3 (= *criticar*) [+ *teoría, planteamiento, propuesta*] to attack • **~on despiadadamente su enfoque marxista** they mercilessly attacked her Marxist approach
4 (= *combatir*) [+ *problema*] to tackle, combat • **se pretende ~ el desempleo** the aim is to tackle *o* combat unemployment • **pretenden ~ la epidemia de meningitis** they aim to tackle *o* combat the meningitis epidemic
5 (= *abordar*) • **el gobierno debe ~ la reforma laboral** the government should get moving on labour reform* • **tengo que ~ a las matemáticas*** I'll have to get stuck into my maths* • **la orquesta atacó la novena de Beethoven** the band launched into Beethoven's Ninth • **¿puedo ~ al pastel?*** can I get stuck into the cake?*
VI to attack
VPR **atacarse** (*LAm**) to stuff o.s.*

atachable ADJ (*Méx*) compatible (**a** with)

atachar ▸ CONJUG 1a VT (*Méx*) to plug in

ataché SM (*CAm, Caribe*) paper clip

ataderas* SFPL garters

atadero SM (= *cuerda*) rope, fastening; (= *cierre*) fastening; (= *sitio*) place for tying; (*Méx*) (= *liga*) garter • **eso no tiene ~** you can't make head or tail of it, there's nothing to latch on to

atadijo SM loose bundle

atado ADJ **1** (= *amarrado*) tied
2 (= *tímido*) shy, inhibited; (= *indeciso*) irresolute
SM bundle • **~ de cigarrillos** (*Cono Sur*) packet of cigarettes

atadora SF binder

atadura SF **1** (= *acción*) tying, fastening
2 (= *cuerda*) string, rope; (*Agr*) tether
3 (= *enlace*) bond
4 (= *limitación*) limitation, restriction

atafagar ▸ CONJUG 1h VT **1** [+ *olor*] to stifle, suffocate
2 (= *molestar*) to pester the life out of

ataguía SF cofferdam, caisson

atajar ▸ CONJUG 1a VT **1** (= *interceptar*) to stop, intercept; [+ *ruta de fuga*] to cut off; (*Arquit*) to partition off; (*Dep*) to tackle; (*LAm*) (= *coger*) to catch, catch in flight • **~ un golpe** to parry a blow • **~ a algn** (*LAm*) to hold sb back (*to stop a fight*) • **me quiso ~ al almuerzo** (*LAm*) she wanted me to stay for lunch
2 [+ *debate*] to cut short; [+ *discurso etc*] to interrupt; [+ *proceso*] to end, stop, call a halt to; [+ *abuso*] to put a stop to • **este mal hay que ~lo** we must put an end to this evil
VI (= *tomar un atajo*) to take a short cut (**por** by way of, across); (*Aut*) to cut corners
VPR **atajarse 1** (= *detenerse*) to stop short
2 (= *avergonzarse*) to feel ashamed of o.s.; (= *aturdirse*) to be overcome by confusion, be all of a dither
3 (*Cono Sur*) (= *controlarse*) to keep one's temper, control o.s.

atajo SM **1** (*en camino*) short cut • **MODISMO**: • **echar por el ~** to seek a quick solution • **REFRÁN**: • **no hay ~ sin trabajo** short cuts don't help in the long run
2 (*Dep*) tackle

atalaje SM = **atelaje**

atalaya SF **1** (= *torre*) watchtower, observation post
2 (= *posición estratégica*) vantage point
SM lookout, observer

atalayador(a) SM/F lookout; (= *fisgón*) snooper, spy

atalayar ▸ CONJUG 1a VT (= *observar*) to observe; (= *vigilar*) to watch over, guard; (= *espiar*) to spy on

atañer ▸ CONJUG 2f; defectivo VI • **~ a** to concern, have to do with • **en lo que atañe a eso** with regard to that, concerning that • **eso no me atañe** it's no concern of mine, it has nothing to do with me

atapuzar ▸ CONJUG 1f (*Caribe*) VT to fill, stop up
VPR **atapuzarse** to stuff o.s.

ataque SM **1** (*Mil*) attack • **se dejó expuesto al ~** he left himself open to attack • **un ~ a** *o* **contra algo/algn** an attack on sth/sb • **lanzar un ~** to launch an attack • **volver al ~** to return to the attack • **pasar al ~** to go on the offensive • **¡al ~!** charge! ▸ **ataque aéreo** air raid, air strike ▸ **ataque a superficie** ground attack, ground strike ▸ **ataque fingido** sham attack ▸ **ataque frontal** frontal attack ▸ **ataque por sorpresa** surprise attack ▸ **ataque preventivo** pre-emptive strike ▸ **ataque suicida** suicide attack
2 (*Med*) attack • **le dio un ~ de tos** he had a coughing fit *o* a fit of coughing ▸ **ataque al corazón, ataque cardíaco** heart attack ▸ **ataque cerebral** brain haemorrhage *o* (*EEUU*) hemorrhage ▸ **ataque de nervios** nervous breakdown ▸ **ataque de pánico** panic attack ▸ **ataque epiléptico** epileptic fit ▸ **ataque fulminante** stroke
3 (= *arranque*) fit • **me entró** *o* **dio un ~ de risa** I got a fit of the giggles • **cuando se entere le da un ~*** she'll have a fit when she finds out* ▸ **ataque de celos** fit of jealousy ▸ **ataque de ira** fit of anger
4 (= *crítica*) attack • **~ a** *o* **contra algo/algn** attack on sth/sb • **un duro ~ a** *o* **contra la ley electoral** a fierce attack on the electoral law
5 (*Dep*) attack

atar ▸ CONJUG 1a VT **1** (= *amarrar*) to tie, tie up; [+ *cautivo*] to bind, tie up; (= *abrochar*) to fasten; [+ *animal*] to tether; [+ *gavilla*] to bind • **zapatos de ~** lace-up shoes • **está de ~** he's raving mad • **MODISMO**: • **dejar algo atado y bien atado** to leave no loose ends, leave everything properly tied up
2 (= *impedir el movimiento a*) to stop, paralyze • **MODISMOS**: • **~ corto a algn** to keep sb on a close rein • **~ la lengua a algn** to silence sb • **~ las manos a algn** to tie sb's hands • **verse atado de pies y manos** to be tied hand and foot
VI • **ni ata ni desata** this is getting us nowhere
VPR **atarse 1** (= *liarse*) to get into a muddle • **~se en una dificultad** to get tied up in a difficulty
2 (= *sentirse violento*) to be embarrassed, get embarrassed
3 (= *ceñirse*) • **~se a la letra** to stick to the literal meaning • **~se a una opinión** to stick to one's opinion, not budge from one's opinion

ataracea SF = **taracea**

atarantado ADJ (*Cono Sur*) impetuous

atarantar ▸ CONJUG 1a VT **1** (= *aturdir*) to stun, daze • **quedó atarantado** he was stunned, he was unconscious
2 (= *dejar atónito*) to stun, dumbfound
VPR **atarantarse 1** to be stunned, be dumbfounded
2 (*Chile*) (= *darse prisa*) to hurry
3 (*Méx*) (*comiendo*) to stuff o.s.
4 (*CAm*) (*bebiendo*) to get drunk

atarazana SF dockyard

atardecer ▸ CONJUG 2d VI to get dark • **atardecía** night was falling
SM dusk, evening • **al ~** at dusk

atardecida SF dusk, nightfall

atareado ADJ busy, rushed • **andar muy ~** to be very busy

atarear ▸ CONJUG 1a VT to assign a task to
VPR **atarearse** to work hard, keep busy • **~se con algo** to be busy doing sth

atarjea SF (= *conducto*) sewage pipe, drain; (*And*) (= *presa de agua*) reservoir

atarragarse ▸ CONJUG 1h VPR (*LAm*) to stuff o.s., overeat

atarugar ▸ CONJUG 1h VT **1** (= *llenar*) to stuff, cram
2 (= *asegurar*) to fasten
3 [+ *agujero*] to plug, stop, bung up
4* • **~ a algn** (= *hacer callar*) to shut sb up
VPR **atarugarse 1** (= *atragantarse*) to swallow the wrong way
2 (= *embrollarse*) to get confused, be in a daze
3* (= *atiborrarse*) to stuff o.s., overeat

atasajar ▸ CONJUG 1a VT to jerk

atascadero SM **1** (= *lodazal*) mire, bog
2 (= *obstáculo*) stumbling block

atascado ADJ [*cañería*] blocked; [*puerta, ventana*] jammed, stuck; [*papel*] jammed

atascar ▸ CONJUG 1g VT [+ *agujero etc*] to plug, bung up; [+ *cañería*] to clog up; [+ *fuga*] to stop; [+ *proceso*] to hinder
VPR **atascarse 1** (*en lodazal*) to get stuck; (*Aut*) to get into a jam; [*motor*] to stall • **se quedó atascado a mitad de la cuesta** he got stuck halfway up the climb
2 (*fig*) (= *no poder seguir*) to get bogged down; (*en discurso*) to dry up*
3 [*cañería*] to get clogged up
4 (*LAm*) (*Med*) to have an internal blockage

atasco SM (= *obstrucción*) obstruction, blockage; (*Aut*) traffic jam

ataúd SM coffin, casket (*EEUU*)

ataujía SF **1** (*Téc*) damascene, damascene work
2 (*CAm*) (= *desagüe*) conduit, drain

ataviar ▸ CONJUG 1c VT **1** (= *vestir*) to dress up, get up (**con, de** in)
2 (*LAm*) (= *adaptar*) to adapt, adjust, accommodate
VPR **ataviarse** to dress up, get o.s. up (**con, de** in)

atávico ADJ atavistic

atavío SM (= *atuendo*) getup • **~s** finery (*sing*)

atavismo SM atavism

ate SM (*Méx*) quince jelly

atecomate SM (*Méx*) tumbler

atediante ADJ boring, wearisome

atediar ▸ CONJUG 1b VT to bore, weary
VPR **atediarse** to get bored

ateísmo SM atheism

ateísta ADJ atheistic

atejonarse ▹ CONJUG 1a VPR (*Méx*) to hide

atelaje SM **1** (= *caballos*) team, team of horses
2 (= *arreos*) harness; (= *equipo*) equipment; (= *ajuar**) trousseau

atembado ADJ (*And*) silly, stupid

atemorizado ADJ (= *con miedo*) frightened

atemorizar ▹ CONJUG 1f VT to frighten, scare
VPR **atemorizarse** to get frightened, get scared (**de, por** at, by)

atempar* ▹ CONJUG 1a VI (*CAm*) to wait, hang around

atemperar ▹ CONJUG 1a VT **1** (= *moderar*) to temper, moderate
2 (= *ajustar*) to adjust, accommodate (**a** to) • **~ los gastos a los ingresos** (*Com*) to balance outgoings with income

atemporal ADJ timeless

atemporalado ADJ stormy

atemporalidad SF timelessness

Atenas SF Athens

atenazar ▹ CONJUG 1f VT (*fig*) to grip; [+ *duda etc*] to torment, beset • **~ los dientes** to grit one's teeth • **el miedo me atenazaba** I was gripped by fear

atención SF **1** (= *interés*) attention • **la novela mantiene la ~ del lector** the novel keeps the reader's attention • **esta emisora dedica especial ~ a la música** this station places particular emphasis on music *o* devotes particular attention to music • **¡~, por favor!** attention, please! • **siguen con ~ las explicaciones** they follow the explanations attentively • **garantizarán los derechos de todos, con especial ~ a las minorías** they will guarantee everybody's rights, particularly those of minorities • **en ~ a algo** (*frm*) in view of sth • **en ~ a los intereses de los clientes** in view of the clients' interests • **el premio le fue concedido en ~ a sus méritos** she was awarded the prize on merit • **llamar la ~ a algn** (= *atraer*) to attract sb's attention; (= *reprender*) to tell sb off • **siempre va llamando la ~ por como viste** the way he dresses always catches the eye *o* attracts attention • **me llamó la ~ no verte por allí** I was surprised not to see you there • **a mí el chocolate no me llama mucho la ~** I'm not too fond of *o* keen on chocolate • **nos llamó la ~ sobre el peligro que corrían los refugiados** he drew our attention to the danger that the refugees were in • **me llamaron la ~ por llegar tarde** they told me off for arriving late • **prestar ~** to pay attention (**a** to) • **léelo detenidamente, prestando especial ~ a la letra pequeña** read it carefully, paying particular attention to the small print • **prestad mucha ~ a lo que voy a decir** pay close attention to what I am going to say • **los niños necesitan que les presten mucha ~** children need to be given a lot of attention
2 (= *precaución*) care • **necesitas poner más ~ en lo que haces** you need to take greater care over what you do • **cuando vayas de vacaciones, ~ a los precios** when you go on holiday, watch out for the prices • **"¡atención! frenos potentes"** "beware! powerful brakes" • **¡atención!** look out!, careful!; (*Mil*) attention!; ▹ **toque**
3 (= *cortesía*) • **no tuvo ni la ~ de enviarle unas flores** he didn't even have the kindness *o* thought to send her flowers • **le agradezco la ~** that's very thoughtful of you • **ha tenido una bonita ~ regalándome el libro** it was a really nice thought of hers to buy me that book • **me colmó de atenciones** he showered me with attention
4 (= *asistencia*) • **vive rodeada de todas las atenciones necesarias** she has all the care and attention that she needs • **han descuidado la ~ al público** they have neglected the customers • **"horario de atención al público"** (*en oficina*) "hours of business"; (*en tienda*) "opening hours"
▸ **atención al cliente** customer service • **departamento de ~ al cliente** customer service department • **el personal de ~ al cliente** the staff who serve customers
▸ **atención médica** medical attention
▸ **atención personalizada** personalized service ▸ **atención primaria** primary health care ▸ **atención psicológica** counselling
▸ **atención psiquiátrica** psychiatric treatment • **centro de ~ psiquiátrica** psychiatric clinic ▸ **atención sanitaria** medical attention
5 atenciones (= *obligaciones*) duties, responsibilities
6 (*en correspondencia*) • **a la ~ de** for the attention of; (*en sobre*) attention

atencioso ADJ (*LAm*) = atento

atender ▹ CONJUG 2g VT **1** (= *ocuparse de*) **a** [+ *asunto*] to deal with • **atiende primero lo más urgente** deal with the most urgent things first • **para ~ los gastos de las vacaciones** to meet the holiday expenses
b [+ *paciente*] to look after • **en el hospital es donde mejor atendido está** you'll be better looked after in hospital • **están atendiendo a los animales heridos** they are looking after *o* seeing to *o* caring for the injured animals • **solo atienden los casos urgentes** they only deal with urgent cases • **necesitamos a alguien que atienda a la abuela** we need someone to look after *o* care for grandma
2 (= *recibir*) to see • **el propio presidente atendió al delegado** the president himself saw the delegate • **el doctor la ~á en un momento** the doctor will see you now
3 (*Com*) **a** [+ *cliente*] (*en tienda*) to serve; (*en oficina*) to see • **¿lo atienden, señor?** are you being served, sir? • **siéntese, enseguida la ~án** take a seat, they'll see you in a minute
b [+ *consulta, negocio, oficina*] (*como encargado*) to run; (*como trabajador*) to work in • **yo atiendo el negocio personalmente** I run the business myself • **atiendo la recepción cuando la secretaria no está** I work in reception *o* I man the reception desk when the secretary is not there • **el servicio de habitaciones está mal atendido** the room service is very sloppy
4 (= *prestar atención a*) [+ *ruego, petición*] to respond to, comply with (*frm*); [+ *necesidades, demanda*] to meet; [+ *compromiso, obligación*] to fulfil; [+ *reclamaciones, protesta, queja*] to deal with; [+ *aviso, consejo*] to heed • **deben ~ las demandas de la población** they should respond to the people's demands • **no atendieron la petición de extraditarlos a España** they did not comply with the request to extradite them to Spain (*frm*) • **los 25 autobuses son insuficientes para ~ la demanda** the 25 buses are not enough to meet the demand • **Señor, atiende nuestras súplicas** (*Rel*) Lord, heed our prayers
5 (*Telec*) [+ *teléfono, llamada*] to answer • **no había nadie para ~ el teléfono** there was nobody to answer the phone
6 (*Mec*) [+ *máquina*] to supervise
7 (*LAm*) (= *asistir a*) to attend, be present at
VI **1** (= *prestar atención*) to pay attention • **ahora, a ver si atendéis, que esto es importante** now, pay attention, this is important • **~ a algo/algn** to listen to sth/sb • **atended a lo que voy a decir** listen to what I'm going to say • **ahora atendedme un momento** pay attention to what I'm about to say • **¡tú atiende a lo tuyo!** mind your own business! • **atendiendo a** [+ *criterio, datos*] according to; [+ *situación, circunstancias*] bearing in mind, considering • **se han clasificado en distintos grupos atendiendo a su origen** they have been put into different groups according to their origin • **atendiendo a las circunstancias, lo recibiré personalmente** given the circumstances, I will see him in person, bearing in mind *o* considering the circumstances, I will see him in person; ▹ **razón**
2 (= *ocuparse de*) • **~ a** [+ *detalles*] to take care of; [+ *necesidades, demanda*] to meet • **lo primero que hace es ~ al desayuno de los niños** the first thing she does is to see to the kids' breakfast • **no quiso ~ a sus amenazas** he didn't heed their warnings • **~ a un giro** to honour *o* (*EEUU*) honor a draft • **~ a una orden** *o* **pedido** (*Com*) to attend to an order
3 (*Com*) (= *servir*) to serve • **¿quién atiende aquí?** who's serving here?
4 • **~ por** to answer to the name of • **extraviado caniche blanco; atiende por Linda** lost: white poodle; answers to the name of Linda
5 (*Telec*) [+ *teléfono, llamada*] to answer • **nadie atendió a nuestra llamada de socorro** nobody answered our distress call
6 (*Mec*) [+ *máquina*] to supervise

atendible ADJ [*petición, reivindicación*] worthy of consideration • **esa objeción no es ~** that is not a valid objection, that objection is not worthy of consideration

ateneo SM cultural association, cultural centre, cultural center (*EEUU*)

atenerse ▹ CONJUG 2k VPR • **~ a 1** (= *ceñirse a*) • **aténgase a lo que se le pregunta** confine yourself to answering the question
2 (= *cumplir*) • **~ a la ley** to abide by *o* obey the law • **aténgase a lo que se le ordena** follow the orders • **debes atenerte a lo acordado** you must stick to what has been agreed
3 (= *remitirse a*) • **me atengo a mis declaraciones previas** I stand by my previous statements • **simplemente nos atenemos a lo que has dicho** we are simply taking into account *o* bearing in mind what you said • **contigo nunca sé a qué atenerme** I never know what to expect with you • **si lo haces atente a las consecuencias** if you do it, you'll have to take the consequences
4 (= *adaptarse a*) to keep within • **atente a tus ingresos y no gastes tanto** keep within your income and don't spend so much • **viven ateniéndose a sus posibilidades** they live within their means

ateniense ADJ, SMF Athenian

atentado ADJ (= *prudente*) prudent, cautious; (= *moderado*) moderate
SM (= *ofensa*) offence, felony (*EEUU*); (= *crimen*) outrage, crime; (= *ataque*) assault, attack; (*Pol*) attempt • **~ a** *o* **contra la vida de algn** attempt on sb's life ▸ **atentado contra el pudor, atentado contra la honra** indecent assault ▸ **atentado golpista** attempted coup ▸ **atentado suicida** suicide bombing, suicide attack ▸ **atentado terrorista** terrorist attack

atentamente ADV **1** (= *con atención*) [*escuchar, observar*] attentively; [*leer*] carefully • **debes seguir ~ todos sus consejos** you should follow all his advice carefully
2 (= *cortésmente*) • **se dirigió a mí muy ~** she spoke to me very kindly • **lo saludó muy ~** she greeted him very warmly • **le saluda ~** (*en cartas formales*) yours faithfully, yours sincerely, sincerely yours (*EEUU*)

a

ATENTAMENTE

Para traducir **atentamente** *o* **le saluda atentamente** *al inglés británico hay que tener en cuenta la diferencia de uso entre* **Yours sincerely** *y* **Yours faithfully:**

▹ *Se traduce por* **Yours sincerely** *cuando hemos empezado la carta con* **Dear Mr/Mrs Brown**, *es decir, conocemos al destinatario y le queremos dar un tratamiento más cordial.*

▹ *Se traduce por* **Yours faithfully** *cuando no conocemos al destinatario de la carta y hemos empezado escribiendo* **Dear Sir, Dear Sirs** *o* **Dear Sir or Madam.**

▹ *En inglés americano se usa* **Sincerely yours** *en ambos casos.*

Para otros usos y ejemplos ver la entrada.

atentar ▹ CONJUG 1a VI • **~ a** *o* **contra** to commit an outrage against • **~ contra la honra de algn** to indecently assault sb • **~ contra la ley** to break the law • **~ contra la vida de algn** to make an attempt on sb's life
VT [+ *crimen etc*] to attempt, try to commit

atentatorio ADJ illegal, criminal • **un acto ~ a ...** an act which poses a threat to ..., an act which undermines ...

atento ADJ **1** (= *pendiente*) [*persona*] attentive; [*mirada*] watchful • **tenéis que estar ~s en clase** you have to be attentive in class, you have to pay attention in class • **estáte ~ y avísanos si lo ves** stay alert *o* keep a look out and let us know if you see him • **ante la mirada atenta del árbitro** under the referee's watchful eye • **estar ~ a** [+ *explicación*] to pay attention to; [+ *peligro*] to be on the alert for, be on the lookout for; [+ *movimiento, ruido*] to listen out for • **estuvo muy ~ a todo lo que le decíamos** he paid full attention to everything we told him • **hay que estar ~ a cualquier error** you have to watch *o* listen out for the slightest mistake • **está siempre ~ a las nuevas tendencias** he always keeps an eye out for the latest trends
2 (= *cortés*) attentive • **últimamente está muy ~ con ella** he has been very attentive to her recently • **fue muy ~ de tu parte** that was very thoughtful of you • **un dependiente muy ~** a very helpful *o* attentive sales assistant • **como indicaba en su atenta carta** (*frm*) as indicated in your kind letter (*frm*) • **su ~ y seguro servidor** (*frm*) yours truly
3 • **~ a algo** in view of sth, in consideration of sth (*frm*) • **~ a que** considering that, in view of the fact that

atenuación SF (= *aminoración*) attenuation; (*Ling*) understatement; [*de efectos etc*] lessening; (*Jur*) extenuation

atenuante ADJ extenuating • **circunstancias ~s** extenuating circumstances, mitigating circumstances
SM o SF extenuating circumstance, mitigating circumstance

atenuar ▹ CONJUG 1e VT (= *aminorar*) to attenuate; (*Jur*) [+ *crimen etc*] to extenuate; [+ *importancia*] to minimize; [+ *impresión etc*] to tone down; [+ *impacto*] to cushion, lessen
VPR **atenuarse** to weaken

ateo/a ADJ atheistic
SM/F atheist

ateperetarse ▹ CONJUG 1a VPR (*CAm, Méx*) to get confused, get bewildered

atepocate SM (*Méx*) tadpole

aterciopelado ADJ velvety

aterido ADJ stiff with cold

aterirse ▹ CONJUG 3a; imperfecto; úsase solo en infin y pp VPR to get stiff with cold

aterrada SF landfall

aterrador ADJ terrifying

aterraje SM (*Aer*) landing; (*Náut*) landfall

aterrar¹ ▹ CONJUG 1a VT to terrify
VPR **aterrarse** to be terrified (**de** by)

aterrar² ▹ CONJUG 1j VT **1** (= *derribar*) to pull down, demolish, destroy
2 (= *cubrir*) to cover with earth; (*Agr*) to earth up
3 (*CAm*) (= *obstruir*) to choke, obstruct
VI (*Aer*) to land; (*Náut*) to reach land
VPR **aterrarse** (*Náut*) to stand inshore • **navegar aterrado** to sail inshore

aterrazamiento SM terracing

aterrazar ▹ CONJUG 1f VT to terrace

aterrizaje SM (*Aer*) landing ▸ **aterrizaje a vientre** pancake landing ▸ **aterrizaje de emergencia** emergency landing, forced landing ▸ **aterrizaje de panza** pancake landing ▸ **aterrizaje de urgencia** emergency landing, forced landing ▸ **aterrizaje duro** hard landing ▸ **aterrizaje forzoso** emergency landing, forced landing ▸ **aterrizaje suave** soft landing ▸ **aterrizaje violento** crash landing

aterrizar ▹ CONJUG 1f VI to touch down, land

aterronar ▹ CONJUG 1a VT to cake, harden
VPR **aterronarse** to get lumpy

aterrorizado ADJ terrified

aterrorizador ADJ terrifying

aterrorizar ▹ CONJUG 1f VT (= *aterrar*) to terrify; (*Mil, Pol*) to terrorize

atersar ▹ CONJUG 1a VT to smooth

atesar ▹ CONJUG 1j VT (*LAm*) = **atiesar**

atesoramiento SM hoarding, accumulation

atesorar ▹ CONJUG 1a VT [+ *dinero, riquezas*] to hoard, accumulate; [+ *virtudes*] to possess

atestación SF (*Jur*) attestation; (*Pol*) deposition

atestado¹ SM (*Jur*) affidavit, statement ▸ **atestado policial** police statement

atestado² ADJ **1** (= *lleno*) packed • **~ de** packed with, crammed with, full of
2 (= *testarudo*) obstinate, stubborn

atestar¹ ▹ CONJUG 1a VT (*Jur*) to attest, testify to; (= *dar prueba de*) to vouch for • **una palabra no atestada** an unattested word, an unrecorded word

atestar² ▹ CONJUG 1j VT (= *llenar*) to pack, stuff (**de** with) • **~ a algn de frutas*** to stuff sb with fruit
VPR **atestarse** to stuff o.s. (**de** with)

atestiguación SF **1** (= *acción*) attestation
2 (*Jur*) deposition, testimony

atestiguar ▹ CONJUG 1i VT (*Jur*) to testify to, give evidence of; (= *dar prueba de*) to attest, vouch for

atezado ADJ **1** (= *bronceado*) tanned
2 (= *negro*) black

atezar ▹ CONJUG 1f VT **1** (*al sol*) to tan, burn
2 (= *ennegrecer*) to blacken, turn black
VPR **atezarse** to get tanned

atiborrado ADJ • **~ de** full of, stuffed with, crammed with

atiborrar ▹ CONJUG 1a VT to fill, stuff (**de** with) • **~ a un niño de dulces*** to stuff a child with sweets
VPR **atiborrarse** to stuff o.s. (**de** with)

ático SM (= *desván*) attic; (= *apartamento*) penthouse

atiesar ▹ CONJUG 1a VT to tighten, tighten up
VPR **atiesarse** (= *ponerse tieso*) to tighten; (*en la construcción*) to bind

atigrado ADJ (= *con manchas*) striped, marked like a tiger; [*gato*] tabby

atigronarse ▹ CONJUG 1a VPR (*Caribe*) to get strong

Atila SM Attila

atildado ADJ elegant, stylish

atildar ▹ CONJUG 1a VT **1** (*Tip*) to put a tilde over
2 (= *acicalar*) to tidy, clean, clean up
3 (= *criticar*) to criticize, find fault with
VPR **atildarse** to spruce o.s. up

atilincar ▹ CONJUG 1g VT (*CAm*) to tighten, stretch

atinadamente ADV (= *correctamente*) correctly; (= *sensatamente*) sensibly; (= *pertinentemente*) pertinently • **según dijo ~** as he rightly said

atinado ADJ (= *correcto*) accurate, correct; (= *sensato*) wise, sensible; (= *pertinente*) pertinent; (= *agudo*) penetrating • **unas observaciones atinadas** some pertinent remarks • **una decisión poco atinada** a rather unwise decision

atinar ▹ CONJUG 1a VI **1** (= *acertar*) to be right • **siempre atina** he always gets it right, he always hits the nail on the head • **el médico no le atina** the doctor doesn't know what's wrong with him, the doctor can't find out what's wrong with him • **~ a** *o* **con** *o* **en** to hit upon, find • **~ al blanco** to hit the mark
2 (= *conseguir*) • **~ a hacer algo** to succeed in doing sth
VT [+ *solución*] to hit upon, find; (= *acertar*) to guess right; (= *encontrar*) to succeed in finding

atingencia SF (*LAm*) **1** (= *relación*) connection, relationship
2 (= *obligación*) obligation
3 (= *reserva*) qualification; (= *aclaración*) clarification; (= *observación*) remark, comment

atingido ADJ **1** (*And, Cono Sur*) depressed, down-in-the-mouth; (= *débil*) feeble, weak; (= *tímido*) timid
2 (*And*) (= *sin dinero*) penniless
3 (*Méx*) (= *taimado*) sly, cunning

atingir ▹ CONJUG 3c VT **1** (*LAm*) to concern, relate to
2 (*And*) (= *oprimir*) to oppress

atiparse* ▹ CONJUG 1a VPR to stuff o.s.*

atípicamente ADV atypically, untypically

atipicidad SF atypical nature

atípico ADJ atypical, exceptional

atiplado ADJ high-pitched

atiplar ▹ CONJUG 1a VT [+ *voz*] to raise the pitch of
VPR **atiplarse** [*voz*] to go higher, become shrill; [*persona*] to talk in a high voice, talk in a squeaky voice

atipujarse ▹ CONJUG 1a VPR (*CAm, Méx*) to stuff o.s.

atirantar ▹ CONJUG 1a VT **1** (= *poner tirante*) to tighten, tauten • **estar atirantado entre dos decisiones** to be torn between two decisions
2 (*And, Cono Sur*) (= *estirar*) to stretch out on the ground
VPR **atirantarse** (*Méx**) (= *estirar la pata*) to kick the bucket*

atisba SM (*And*) (= *vigilante*) watchman, look-out; (= *espía*) spy

atisbadero SM peephole

atisbador(a) SM/F (= *guardia*) watcher; (= *espía*) spy

atisbar ▹ CONJUG 1a VT **1** (= *espiar*) to spy on, watch; (= *mirar*) to peep at • **~ a algn a través de una grieta** to peep at sb through a crack
2 (= *lograr ver*) to see, make out, discern (*frm*) • **atisbamos un rayo de esperanza** we can just see a glimmer of hope

atisbo SM **1** (= *acción*) spying, watching
2 (= *indicio*) inkling, indication

atizadero SM **1** (*para el fuego*) poker

2 (= *estímulo*) spark, stimulus

atizador SM 1 (*para el fuego*) poker
2 (*fig*) ▸ **atizador de la guerra** warmonger

atizar ▹ CONJUG 1f VT 1 [+ *fuego*] to poke, stir; [+ *horno*] to stoke; [+ *vela*] to snuff, trim
2 [+ *discordia*] to stir up; [+ *pasión*] to fan, rouse
3* [+ *golpe*] to give
VI • ¡atiza!* gosh!
VPR **atizarse*** 1 (= *fumar marihuana*) to smoke marijuana
2 (= *beberse*) • **se atizó el vaso** he knocked back the whole glass*

atizonar ▹ CONJUG 1a VT to blight, smut

Atlante SM Atlas

atlántico ADJ Atlantic
SM • **el (océano) Atlántico** the Atlantic, the Atlantic Ocean

Atlántida SF Atlantis

atlantista ADJ NATO (*antes de s*)
SMF NATO supporter

atlas SM INV atlas

atleta SMF athlete

atlético ADJ athletic

atletismo SM athletics (*sing*) • **copa del mundo de ~** athletics world cup ▸ **atletismo en pista cubierta, atletismo en sala** indoor athletics

atmósfera SF 1 (*Fís, Meteo*) atmosphere • **mala ~** (*Radio*) atmospherics (*pl*)
2 (*en sitio cerrado*) atmosphere
3 (*fig*) (= *ambiente*) atmosphere
4 (*fig*) (= *campo*) sphere, sphere of influence • **Juan tiene buena ~** (*LAm*) Juan enjoys considerable social standing, Juan stands well with everybody

atmosférico ADJ atmospheric

atoar ▹ CONJUG 1a VT to tow

atoc SM (*And*) fox

atocar ▹ CONJUG 1g VT (*LAm*) = **tocar**

atocha SF esparto

atochal SM esparto field

atochamiento SM (*Cono Sur*) traffic jam

atochar SM = **atochal**

atocinado* ADJ fat, tubby*

atocinar ▹ CONJUG 1a VT 1 (*Agr*) [+ *cerdo*] to cut up; [+ *carne*] to cure
2†* (= *asesinar*) to do in*, bump off*
VPR **atocinarse**†* 1 (= *sulfurarse*) to fly off the handle
2 (= *enamorarse*) to fall madly in love

atocle SM (*Méx*) *sandy soil rich in humus*

atol SM (*LAm*) cornflour drink

atolada SM (*CAm*) party

atole SM (*LAm*) cornflour drink

atoleada SF (*CAm*) party

atolería SF (*LAm*) *stall etc where "atol" is sold*

atolladero SM 1 (= *lodazal*) mire, morass
2 (= *aprieto*) jam*, fix* • **estar en un ~** to be in a jam *o* a fix* • **salir del ~** to get out of a jam *o* a fix* • **sacar a algn del ~** to get sb out of a jam *o* a fix*

atollar ▹ CONJUG 1a VI, VPR **atollarse**
1 (= *atascarse*) to get stuck in the mud, get bogged down
2 (= *meterse en un lío*) to get into a jam *o* a fix*

atolón SM atoll

atolondrado ADJ 1 (= *aturdido*) bewildered, stunned
2 (= *irreflexivo*) thoughtless, reckless; (= *casquivano*) scatterbrained; (= *tonto*) silly

atolondramiento SM 1 (= *aturdimiento*) bewilderment
2 (= *irreflexión*) thoughtlessness, recklessness

atolondrar ▹ CONJUG 1a VT (= *aturdir*) to bewilder; (= *pasmar*) to amaze
VPR **atolondrarse** (= *aturdirse*) to be bewildered; (= *quedarse pasmado*) to be amazed

atomía SF (*LAm*) 1 (= *acto*) evil deed, savage act
2 • **decir ~s** to shoot one's mouth off* (**a** to)

atómico ADJ atomic

atomista ADJ atomistic
SMF atomist

atomización SF (*con atomizador*) spraying; (*Pol*) atomization

atomizador SM atomizer, spray

atomizar ▹ CONJUG 1f VT 1 (*con atomizador*) to spray
2 (*Pol*) to atomize
VPR **atomizarse** to break up (**en** into), fragment

átomo SM atom • **ni un ~ de** not a trace of ▸ **átomo de vida** spark of life

atonal ADJ atonal

atonía SF lethargy, apathy

atónito ADJ amazed, astounded • **me miró ~** he looked at me in amazement *o* astonishment

átono ADJ atonic, unstressed

atontadamente ADV (= *aturdidamente*) in a bewildered way; (= *como tonto*) stupidly, foolishly

atontado ADJ 1 (= *aturdido*) bewildered, stunned
2 (= *tonto*) stupid, thick*

atontar ▹ CONJUG 1a VT 1 (*Med*) to stupefy
2 (= *aturdir*) to bewilder, stun
VPR **atontarse** to get bewildered, get confused

atontolinamiento SM bewilderment

atontolinar ▹ CONJUG 1a VT (= *pasmar*) to daze; (= *aturdir*) to stun • **quedar atontolinado** to be in a daze

atorafo ADJ (*Caribe*) anxious

atorar ▹ CONJUG 1a VT 1 (= *obstruir*) to stop up, obstruct; (= *inmovilizar*) to stop, immobilize
2 (*esp LAm*) to stop, hold up
VPR **atorarse** 1 (*esp LAm*) (= *atragantarse*) to choke, swallow the wrong way; (= *trabarse la lengua*) to get tongue-tied
2 (*Cono Sur*) (= *ponerse salvaje*) to get wild, get fierce

atormentado ADJ (= *afligido*) tormented

atormentador(a) ADJ tormenting
SM/F torturer

atormentar ▹ CONJUG 1a VT 1 (*Mil etc*) to torture
2 (= *causar aflicción*) to torment; (= *acosar*) to plague, harass; (= *tentar*) to tantalize
VPR **atormentarse** to torment o.s.

atornillador SM screwdriver

atornillar ▹ CONJUG 1a VT 1 (*Téc*) to screw down
2 (*Méx**) (= *molestar*) to bother, annoy, pester*

atoro SM (*LAm*) 1 (= *destrucción*) destruction
2 (= *aprieto*) difficulty, fix*, jam*

atorón SM (*LAm*) traffic jam

atorozarse ▹ CONJUG 1f VPR (*CAm*) to choke, swallow the wrong way

atorrante (*And, Cono Sur*) ADJ lazy
SMF tramp, bum (*EEUU**)

atorrantear ▹ CONJUG 1a VI (*Cono Sur*) to live like a tramp, be on the bum (*EEUU*)

atortolado ADJ • **están ~s** they're like two turtle-doves

atortolar ▹ CONJUG 1a VT (= *asustar*) to rattle, scare; (= *pasmar*) to shatter, flabbergast

atortujar ▹ CONJUG 1a VT to squeeze flat
VPR **atortujarse** (*CAm*) to be shattered, be flabbergasted

atorunado ADJ (*Cono Sur*) stocky, bull-necked

atosigador ADJ 1 (= *venenoso*) poisonous
2 (= *que importuna*) pestering, worrisome; (= *que presiona*) pressing

atosigante ADJ = **atosigador**

atosigar ▹ CONJUG 1h VT 1 (= *envenenar*) to poison
2 (= *importunar*) to harass, plague, pester*; (= *presionar*) to rush, put pressure on, pressurize
VPR **atosigarse** to slog away*, slave away*

atóxico ADJ non-poisonous

atrabancar ▹ CONJUG 1g VT to rush, hurry over
VPR **atrabancarse** to be in a fix*, get into a jam*

atrabiliario ADJ bad-tempered, irascible (*frm*)

atrabilis SF INV bad temper

atracadero SM pier

atracado ADJ (*CAm*) mean, stingy

atracador(a) SM/F (*en la calle*) mugger; (*en tienda, banco*) armed robber, raider ▸ **atracador(a) armado/a** armed robber ▸ **atracador(a) de bancos** bank robber
SM† [*de diligencias*] highwayman

atracar ▹ CONJUG 1g VT 1 (= *robar*) [+ *banco*] to hold up; [+ *individuo*] to mug; [+ *avión*] to hijack
2 (*Náut*) to bring alongside; [+ *astronave*] to dock (**a** with)
3 (= *atiborrar*) to stuff, cram
4 (*LAm*) (= *molestar*) to harass, pester; (= *zurrar*) to thrash, beat
5 (*Caribe*) (*Aut*) to park
VI (*Náut*) • **~ al** *o* **en el muelle** to berth at the quay
VPR **atracarse** 1 (= *atiborrarse*) to stuff o.s. (**de** with)
2 (*CAm, Méx*) (= *pelearse*) to brawl, fight
3 (*Caribe*) (= *acercarse*) to approach, come up • **~se a** to approach, come up to

atracción SF 1 (*Fís*) attraction ▸ **atracción gravitatoria** gravity, gravitational pull
2 (= *acción*) attraction; [*de persona*] attractiveness, appeal, charm ▸ **atracción sexual** sexual attraction
3 (*tb* **atracción de feria**) attraction, fairground attraction • **parque de atracciones** funfair; **atracciones** (*Teat*) (= *espectáculos*) attractions

atraco SM [*de banco etc*] holdup, robbery; [*de paseante*] mugging; [*de avión*] hijack, hijacking • **¡es un ~!** (*fig*) it's daylight robbery! ▸ **atraco a mano armada** armed robbery

atracón* SM blow-out*, chow-down (*EEUU**) • **darse un ~** to stuff o.s. (**de** with), to pig out* (**de** on)

atractivamente ADV attractively

atractividad SF attractiveness

atractivo ADJ attractive
SM attractiveness, appeal

atraer ▹ CONJUG 20 VT 1 (*Fís*) to attract
2 (= *hacer acudir a sí*) to draw, lure; [+ *apoyo etc*] to win, draw; [+ *atención*] to attract, engage; [+ *imaginación*] to appeal to • **dejarse ~ por** to allow o.s. to be drawn towards • **sabe ~(se) a la juventud** he knows how to win young people over
VPR **atraerse** • **se atrajo las simpatías de todos** he won everyone's affection, everyone liked him • **se atrajo el rencor del jefe** the boss began to resent him

atragantarse ▹ CONJUG 1a VPR 1 (*al comer*) to choke (**con** on), swallow the wrong way • **me atragranté con una espina** I choked on a fish bone, I got a fish bone stuck in my throat • **se me atragantó una miga de pan** a crumb went down the wrong way
2 (*al hablar*) to lose the thread of what one is saying
3* (= *caer mal*) • **el tío ese se me atraganta** that guy gets up my nose*, I can't stomach that guy*

atrague SM • **¡qué ~!** (*Caribe*) what an idiot!

atraillar ▹ CONJUG 1a VT to put on a leash

atramparse ▹ CONJUG 1a VPR **1** [*persona*] (= *caer en una trampa*) to fall into a trap; (= *meterse en un aprieto*) to get stuck, get o.s. into a jam*
2 [*tubo*] to clog, get blocked up; (= *atascarse*) to stick, catch, jam

atrancar ▹ CONJUG 1g VT **1** [+ *puerta*] to bar, bolt; [+ *cañería*] to clog, block up; (*fig*) [+ *escotillas*] to batten down
2 (*Cono Sur*) (= *estreñir*) to constipate
VI (*al andar*) to stride along, take big steps; (*al leer*) to skim
VPR **atrancarse 1** (= *atascarse*) to get bogged down (**en** in); (*Méx*) to jam; (*haciendo algo*) to get stuck
2 (*Méx**) (= *porfiarse*) to dig one's heels in, be stubborn
3 (*Cono Sur**) (= *estreñirse*) to get constipated

atranco SM = **atascadero**

atrapada SF save

atrapamaridos* ADJ INV • **mujer ~** *woman on the look-out for a husband*
SF INV *woman on the look-out for a husband*

atrapamoscas SM INV flypaper

atrapar ▹ CONJUG 1a VT **1** (*en trampa*) to trap; (= *apresar*) to capture; [+ *resfriado etc*] to catch • **quedaron atrapados en la montaña** they were trapped on the mountainside • **~ un empleo** to land a job
2 (= *engañar*) to take in, deceive

atraque SM **1** (*Náut*) mooring place, berth
2 [*de astronave*] link-up, docking

atrás ADV **1** (*posición*) **a** (= *a la espalda*) behind • **la pelota le vino de ~** the ball came from behind • **la tienda está ahí ~** the shop is back there • **~ mío** (*esp Cono Sur*) behind me • **quedarse ~** to fall behind, get left behind
b (= *al final*) at the back • **los alumnos de ~ estaban fumando** the pupils at the back were smoking • **más ~ se ve mejor la pantalla** you can see the screen better if you sit further back • **ese capítulo está más ~** that chapter is further back • **la parte de ~** the back, the rear • **está muy ~ en la fila** he is a long way down the queue • **las patas de ~** the back legs • **la rueda de ~** the back *o* rear wheel; ▹ **asiento**
2 (*dirección*) backwards • **dar un paso ~** to take a step back(wards) • **ir hacia** *o* **para ~** to go back(wards) • **échense ~, por favor** move back please • **lo has prometido y no puedes echarte ~** you can't back out now, you promised; ▹ **marcha**
3 (*en sentido temporal*) • **días ~** days ago • **cuatro meses ~** four months back • **este odio viene de ~** this hatred goes (a long) way back • **desde muy ~** for a very long time • **dejaron ~ sus rencores** they put aside their bitterness • **mirar ~** • **volver la vista ~** to look back
4 • **~ de** (*LAm*) = **detrás**
EXCL • **¡atrás!** back!, get back!

atrasado ADJ **1** (= *con retraso*) late, behind, behind time; [*pago*] overdue; [*número de revista etc*] back (*antes de s*) • **andar** *o* **estar ~** [*reloj*] to be slow • **estar un poco ~** [*persona*] to be a bit behind • **estar ~ en los pagos** to be in arrears • **estar ~ de medios** to be short of resources • **estar ~ de noticias** to lack up-to-date information
2 • **estar ~** (*CAm**) (= *sin dinero*) to be broke*
3 [*país*] backward; [*alumno etc*] slow, backward
SM • **es un ~** he's behind the times

atrasar ▹ CONJUG 1a VT [+ *progreso*] to slow down; [+ *salida etc*] to delay; [+ *reloj*] to put back
VI [*reloj*] to lose time, be slow • **mi reloj atrasa ocho minutos** my watch is eight minutes slow
VPR **atrasarse 1** (= *quedarse atrás*) to stay back, remain behind; [*tren etc*] to be late; [*reloj*] to be slow • **~se en los pagos** to be in arrears
2 (*LAm*) [*proyecto etc*] to suffer a setback; (*Cono Sur*) (= *lastimarse*) to hurt o.s. (**de** in); [*mujer*] to be pregnant

atraso SM **1** (= *retraso*) delay, time lag; [*de reloj*] slowness; [*de país etc*] backwardness • **el tren lleva ~** the train is late • **salir del ~** to catch up, make up lost time • **llegar con 20 minutos de ~** to arrive 20 minutes late • **¡esto es un ~!** this is just holding things up!
2 atrasos (*Com, Econ*) arrears; [*de pedidos etc*] backlog (*sing*), quantity pending (*sing*) • **cobrar ~s** to collect arrears
3 (*And*) (= *revés*) setback
4 • **tener un ~** (*LAm*) (*Med*) to have a period

atravesada SF (*LAm*) crossing, passage

atravesado ADJ **1** (= *de través*) • **la farola quedó atravesada en la calle** the lamppost fell across the street • MODISMO: • **tener ~***: • **lo tengo ~** I can't stand him • **tengo ~ este programa de tele** I can't stand this TV programme
2 (= *malintencionado*) treacherous
3 (= *bizco*) squinting, cross-eyed
4 (*Zool*) mongrel, cross-bred

atravesar ▹ CONJUG 1j VT **1** (= *colocar a través*) to put across • **atravesamos un tronco en el camino** we put a tree trunk across the road
2 (= *cruzar*) [+ *calle, puente, frontera*] to cross • **~on España en tren** they crossed *o* travelled across Spain by train • **esta avenida atraviesa la capital** this road passes through *o* crosses the capital • **el túnel atraviesa la montaña** the tunnel goes *o* passes under the mountain
3 (= *sufrir*) [+ *período, situación, crisis*] to go through • **mi familia atraviesa momentos difíciles** my family is going through a difficult time
4 (= *perforar*) [+ *cuerpo, órgano*] to go through • **la bala le atravesó el cráneo** the bullet went through his skull • **~ a algn con una espada** to run sb through with a sword
VPR **atravesarse 1** (= *colocarse a través*) • **un camión se nos atravesó en la carretera** a lorry came out into the road in front of us • **se me ha atravesado una raspa en la garganta** I've got a fishbone stuck in my throat • **~se en una conversación** to butt into a conversation
2* (= *hacerse insoportable*) • **se me ha atravesado Antonio** I've had all I can take of Antonio*

atrayente ADJ attractive

atrechar ▹ CONJUG 1a VI (*Caribe*) to take a short cut

atrecho SM (*Caribe*) short cut

atreguar ▹ CONJUG 1i VT to grant a truce to
VPR **atreguarse** to agree to a truce

atrenzo SM (*LAm*) (= *apuro*) trouble, difficulty • **estar en un ~** to be in trouble, have a problem

atreverse ▹ CONJUG 2a VPR **1** (= *osar*) to dare • **~ a hacer algo** to dare to do sth • **no me atrevo** • **no me atrevería** I wouldn't dare • **¿te atreves?** are you game?, will you? • **¡atrévete!** (= *amenaza*) just you dare! • **~ a una empresa** to undertake a task • **~ con un rival** to take on a rival • **se atreve con todo** he'll tackle anything • **me atrevo con una tarta** I could manage a cake
2 • **~ con algn** • **~ contra algn** (= *probar suerte*) to try one's luck with sb*; (= *insolentarse*) to be insolent to sb

atrevidamente ADV **1** (= *con audacia*) daringly, boldly
2 (= *con insolencia*) cheekily

atrevido/a ADJ **1** [*persona*] (= *audaz*) daring, bold; (= *insolente*) cheeky, sassy (*EEUU*) • **el periodista le hizo preguntas muy atrevidas** the reporter asked him some very daring *o* bold questions • **no seas tan ~ con el jefe** don't be so cheeky to the boss
2 [*chiste*] daring, risqué • **un escote muy ~** a very daring neckline
SM/F cheeky person

atrevimiento SM **1** (= *audacia*) daring, boldness
2 (= *insolencia*) insolence, cheek; (= *osadía*) forwardness

atrevismo SM ostentatiousness

atrezzo SM = **attrezzo**

atribución SF **1** (*Literat etc*) attribution
2 atribuciones (*Pol*) powers (*pl*), functions (*pl*)

atribuible ADJ attributable (a to) • **obras ~s a Góngora** works which are attributed to Góngora

atribuir ▹ CONJUG 3g VT **1** • **~ a algn/algo** to attribute to sb/sth; [+ *excusa*] to put down to sb/sth; (*Jur*) to impute to sb/sth
2 (*Pol*) • **las funciones atribuidas a mi cargo** the powers conferred on me by my post
VPR **atribuirse** • **~se algo** to claim sth for o.s. • **~se la responsabilidad de un atentado** to claim responsibility for an attack

atribulación SF affliction, tribulation

atribulado ADJ afflicted, suffering
SM • **los ~s** the afflicted, the suffering, the sufferers

atribular ▹ CONJUG 1a VT to grieve, afflict
VPR **atribularse** to grieve, be distressed

atributivo ADJ attributive

atributo SM **1** (= *cualidad*) attribute
2 (= *emblema*) emblem, sign of authority
3 (*Ling*) predicate

atril SM (*para libro*) bookrest, reading desk; (*Mús*) music stand; (*Rel*) lectern

atrincar ▹ CONJUG 1g VT (*LAm*) to tie up tightly
VPR **atrincarse** (*Méx*) to be stubborn, dig one's heels in

atrincherado ADJ entrenched

atrincheramiento SM entrenchment

atrincherar ▹ CONJUG 1a VT to fortify with trenches
VPR **atrincherarse 1** (*Mil*) to entrench o.s., dig in • **están muy fuertemente atrincherados** (*fig*) they are very strongly entrenched
2 • **~se en** (= *adoptar una postura*) to take one's stand on; (= *protegerse*) to take refuge in

atrio SM (*Hist*) atrium, inner courtyard; (*Rel*) vestibule, porch; [*de garaje*] forecourt

atrochar ▹ CONJUG 1a VI to take a short cut

atrocidad SF **1** (*Mil etc*) atrocity, outrage
2* (= *tontería*) foolish thing, silly thing • **decir ~es** to talk nonsense
3* (= *exageración*) • **¡qué ~!** how dreadful!, how awful! • **la comedia es una ~** the play is awful • **me gustan los helados una ~** I'm extremely fond of ice cream

atrofia SF atrophy ▸ **atrofia muscular** muscular atrophy

atrofiado ADJ [*músculo, miembro*] atrophied

atrofiar ▹ CONJUG 1b VT to atrophy
VPR **atrofiarse** to atrophy, be atrophied

atrojarse ▹ CONJUG 1a VPR (*Méx*) to be stumped (for an answer), be stuck (for an answer)

atrompetado ADJ bell-shaped • **nariz atrompetada** flared nostrils (*pl*)

atronadamente ADV recklessly, thoughtlessly

atronado ADJ reckless, thoughtless

atronador ADJ (= *ensordecedor*) deafening;

a

[aplausos] thunderous
atronamiento SM bewilderment, stunned state
atronar ▷ CONJUG 1l VT **1** (= *ensordecer*) to deafen
2 (= *aturdir*) to bewilder, stun
3 (*Taur*) (= *acogotar*) to fell with a blow on the neck
atropellada SF (*Cono Sur*) attack, onrush
atropelladamente ADV • **correr ~** to run helter-skelter • **hablar ~** to gabble • **decidir algo ~** to rush into a decision about sth
atropellado ADJ [*acto*] hasty, precipitate; [*estilo*] brusque, abrupt; [*ritmo*] violent
atropellador(a) SM/F hooligan
atropellaplatos* SMF INV clumsy servant
atropellar ▷ CONJUG 1a VT **1** (= *arrollar*) to knock down, run over • **la atropelló un taxi** she was knocked down *o* run over by a taxi • **una multitud de gente me atropelló mientras paseaba** a crowd of people barged into me as I was out walking
2 (= *humillar*) • **no te dejes ~ por nadie** don't let anyone walk (all) over you
3 (= *infringir*) [+ *derecho, constitución, estatuto*] to sweep aside, ride roughshod over
VI* (= *empujar*) to push • **oye, por favor, no atropelles** hey, stop pushing (and shoving), please
VPR **atropellarse 1** (= *empujarse*) • **entraron de uno en uno sin ~se** they went in one by one without pushing and shoving
2 (= *precipitarse*) to rush • **el actor se atropelló al recitar** the actor gabbled his recitation • **no te atropelles y hazlo con tranquilidad** don't rush, take your time
atropello SM **1** (*Aut*) accident; (= *empujón*) shove, push; (= *codeo*) jostling
2 (= *abuso*) abuse (**de** of), disregard (**de** for) • **los ~s del dictador** the crimes of the dictator
atroz ADJ **1** (= *terrible*) atrocious; (= *cruel*) cruel, inhuman; (= *escandaloso*) outrageous
2* (= *enorme*) huge, terrific; (= *malísimo*) dreadful, awful
atrozmente ADV **1** (= *terriblemente*) atrociously; (= *con crueldad*) cruelly; (= *escandalosamente*) outrageously
2* (= *muchísimo*) dreadfully, awfully
ATS SMF ABR (*Esp*) (= **ayudante técnico sanitario**) Registered Nurse
attaché SM attaché case
atto. ABR = **atento**
attrezzo SM (*Teat*) properties (*pl*); (= *equipo*) kit, gear
ATUDEM SF ABR (*Esp*) = **Asociación Turística de Estaciones de Esquí y Montaña**
atuendo SM **1** (= *vestido*) attire
2 (= *boato*) pomp, show
atufado* ADJ **1** (= *enojado*) cross, angry; (*And*) dazed
2 (*CAm, Caribe*) (= *vanidoso*) proud, stuck-up*
atufamiento* SM irritation, vexation
atufar* ▷ CONJUG 1a VT **1** [*olor*] to overcome, overpower
2 (= *molestar*) to irritate, vex
VPR **atufarse 1** [*vino*] to turn sour
2 [*persona*] to be overcome (*by smell or fumes*)
3 (= *enojarse*) to get cross, get angry (**con, de, por** at, with)
4 (*And*) (= *aturdirse*) to get bewildered, become confused; (*CAm, Caribe*) (= *engreírse*) to be proud, become vain
atufo* SM irritation, vexation
atulipanado ADJ tulip-shaped
atún SM **1** (= *pez*) tuna (fish) • MODISMO: • **querer ir por ~ y ver al duque** to want to have it both ways, want to have one's cake and eat it too
2* (= *imbécil*) nitwit*

atunero ADJ tuna (*antes de s*)
SM **1** (= *pescador*) tuna fisherman
2 (= *barco*) tuna fishing boat
aturar ▷ CONJUG 1a VT to close up tight
aturdidamente ADV **1** (= *atolondradamente*) in a bewildered way
2 (= *sin reflexionar*) thoughtlessly, recklessly
aturdido ADJ **1** (= *atolondrado*) bewildered, dazed
2 (= *irreflexivo*) thoughtless, reckless
aturdimiento SM, **aturdidura** SF (*Cono Sur*) **1** (= *atolondramiento*) bewilderment
2 (= *irreflexión*) thoughtlessness, recklessness
aturdir ▷ CONJUG 3a VT **1** (*físicamente*) (*con golpe*) to stun, daze; [*ruido*] to deafen; [*droga, movimiento, vino*] to make giddy, make one's head spin
2 (= *atolondrar*) to stun, dumbfound; (= *dejar perplejo*) to bewilder • **la noticia nos aturdió** the news stunned us, we were stunned by the news
VPR **aturdirse** (= *atolondrarse*) to be stunned; (= *quedarse perplejo*) to be bewildered
aturrullado* ADJ bewildered, perplexed
aturrullar* ▷ CONJUG 1a VT to bewilder, perplex
VPR **aturrullarse** to get flustered • **no te aturrulles cuando surja una dificultad** don't get flustered when a problem comes up
atusamiento SM smartness, elegance
atusar ▷ CONJUG 1a VT [+ *pelo*] (= *cortar*) to trim; (= *alisar*) to smooth, smooth down
VPR **atusarse** to dress up to the nines • **~se el bigote** to stroke one's moustache
audacia SF (= *atrevimiento*) boldness, audacity; (= *descaro*) cheek, nerve
audaz ADJ bold, audacious
audazmente ADV boldly, audaciously
audibilidad SF audibility
audible ADJ audible
audición SF **1** (*Med*) hearing
2 (*Teat*) audition • **dar ~ a algn** to audition sb, give sb an audition • **le hicieron una ~ para el papel** they gave him an audition for the part
3 (*Mús*) concert ▸ **audición radiofónica** radio concert
4 (*LAm*) (*Com, Econ*) audit
audiencia SF **1** (= *acto*) audience; (= *entrevista*) formal interview • **recibir a algn en ~** to grant sb an audience
2 (*Jur*) (= *tribunal*) court; (= *palacio*) assizes (*pl*); (= *sala*) audience chamber ▸ **audiencia pública** (*Pol*) public hearing
3 (= *personas*) audience; [*de periódico*] readership; (*Radio, TV*) audience • **índice de ~** ratings (*pl*), audience ratings (*pl*)
audífono SM **1** [*de sordo*] hearing aid
2 (*LAm*) (= *auricular*) receiver; **audífonos** (= *cascos*) headphones
audímetro SM audience meter
audio SM audio
audiofrecuencia SF audio frequency
audioguía SF audioguide
audiolibro SM audio book
audiómetro SM audiometer
audiovisual ADJ audiovisual
SM audiovisual presentation
auditar ▷ CONJUG 1a VT to audit
auditivo ADJ auditory (*frm*), hearing (*antes de s*)
SM receiver
audito SM audit, auditing
auditor(a) SM/F **1** (*Jur*) (*tb* **auditor(a) de guerra**) judge advocate
2 (*Econ*) auditor ▸ **auditor(a) de cuentas** auditor ▸ **auditor(a) externo/a** external auditor
3 (*Méx*) (*Ferro*) ticket inspector

auditora SF firm of auditors, auditors (*pl*)
auditoría SF (*Com, Econ*) audit, auditing ▸ **auditoría administrativa** management audit ▸ **auditoría de gestión** management audit ▸ **auditoría externa** external audit ▸ **auditoría financiera** financial audit ▸ **auditoría general** general audit ▸ **auditoría interna** internal audit ▸ **auditoría operativa** management audit
auditorio SM **1** (= *público*) audience
2 (= *local*) auditorium, hall
auge SM **1** (= *apogeo*) peak • **el agroturismo aún no ha alcanzado su ~** rural tourism has not yet reached its peak • **Internet conocerá su ~ en la próxima década** the internet will reach its peak in the next decade • **está en el ~ de su popularidad** he is at the peak *o* height of his popularity • **ya ha pasado el ~ del tecno** the heyday of techno is over
2 (= *ascendencia*) • **el rápido ~ del fundamentalismo** the rapid rise of fundamentalism • **un momento de ~ de la industria** a time of industrial growth • **una moda en ~** an increasingly popular fashion • **el feminismo está en ~** feminism is increasingly successful *o* influential, feminism is on the up and up* • **el sector turístico está en pleno ~** tourism is booming *o* experiencing a boom • **una empresa en pleno ~** a firm in full expansion
3 (*Astron*) apogee
Augías SM • **establos de ~** Augean Stables
augurar ▷ CONJUG 1a VT [*cosa*] to augur; [*individuo*] to predict, foresee • **~ que ...** to predict that ...
augurio SM **1** (= *presagio*) omen; (= *profecía*) prediction • **consultar los ~s** to take the auguries
2 augurios (= *deseos*) best wishes (**para** for) • **con nuestros ~s para ...** with our best wishes for ... • **mensaje de buenos ~s** goodwill message
augustal ADJ Augustan
Augusto SM Augustus
augusto ADJ august
aula SF (*Escol*) classroom; (*Univ*) lecture room ▸ **aula magna** assembly hall, main hall
aulaga SF furze, gorse
aulario SM lecture room building
áulico/a ADJ court (*antes de s*), palace (*antes de s*)
SM/F courtier
aullar ▷ CONJUG 1a VI to howl, yell
aullido SM howl, yell • **dar ~s** to howl, yell
aumentador SM booster
aumentar ▷ CONJUG 1a VT **1** [+ *tamaño*] to increase; (*Fot*) to enlarge; (*Ópt*) to magnify
2 [+ *cantidad*] to increase; [+ *precio*] to increase, put up; [+ *producción*] to increase, step up • **me van a ~ el sueldo** they are going to increase *o* raise my salary • **no aumentes la velocidad todavía** don't speed up yet • **esto aumentó el número de parados** this swelled the numbers of the unemployed
3 [+ *intensidad*] to increase • **su dimisión ha aumentado la tensión política** his resignation has increased political tension • **estas pastillas pueden ~ las molestias** these tablets can make the problem worse
4 (*Elec, Radio*) to amplify
VI **1** [*tamaño*] to increase
2 [*cantidad, precio, producción*] to increase, go up • **las temperaturas ~án mañana** temperatures will rise tomorrow • **el número de asesinatos ha aumentado en 200** the number of killings has increased *o* gone up by 200 • **este semestre aumentó la inflación en un 2%** inflation has increased *o* gone up by 2% over the last 6 months

3 [*intensidad*] to increase • **el calor aumenta por la tarde** the heat increases in the afternoon • **su popularidad ha aumentado** his popularity has increased *o* risen • **la crispación política aumenta por momentos** political tension is increasing *o* rising by the moment

4 • **~ de** to increase in • **~ de peso** [*objeto*] to increase in weight; [*persona*] to put on *o* gain weight • **~ de tamaño** to increase in size

aumentativo ADJ, SM augmentative

aumento SM **1** [*de tamaño*] increase; (*Fot*) enlargement; (*Ópt*) magnification

2 [*de cantidad, producción, velocidad, intensidad*] increase; [*de precio*] increase, rise • **un ~ del número de turistas** an increase in the number of tourists • **se registró un ~ de temperatura** an increase *o* rise in temperature was recorded • **un ~ del calor** a rise in temperature ▸ **aumento de peso** (*en objeto*) increase in weight; (*en persona*) weight gain ▸ **aumento de población** population increase ▸ **aumento de precio** rise in price ▸ **aumento de sueldo, aumento salarial** (pay) rise

3 (*Elec, Radio*) amplification

4 • **ir en ~** to be on the increase

5 (*Ópt*) magnification • **una lente de 30 ~s** a lens of 30x magnification • **unas gafas de mucho ~** glasses with very strong lenses

6 (*Méx*) (= *posdata*) postscript

aun ADV **1** (= *incluso*) even • **yo pagaría mil y aun dos mil** I'd pay a thousand, even two thousand • **aun siendo tan joven es muy responsable** even though he's so young he's very responsible • **aun los ricos sufrirán la crisis** (*frm*) even the rich will suffer the effects of the crisis

2 • **aun así: aun así, no creo que fuera** even so, I don't think I'd go • **es muy rica y aun así trabaja** she's very rich but she still works

3 • **aun cuando: aun cuando me lo rogara, no se lo daría** even if he begged me I wouldn't give it to him • **va en camisa aun cuando hace frío** he goes around in a shirt even when it's cold

4 • **ni aun** not even • **no lo aceptaría ni aun regalado** I wouldn't accept it even as a present • **ni aun pagándome haría yo eso** I wouldn't do that (even) if you paid me • **y ni aun así lo haría** and I wouldn't do it even then

aún ADV **1** (= *todavía*) (*temporal*) still, yet • **aún está aquí** he's still here • **aún no lo sabemos** we still don't know, we don't know yet • **¿no ha venido aún?** hasn't he come yet?; ▹ TODAVÍA

2 (= *incluso*) even • **y aún se permite el lujo de sermonearme** and he even goes so far as to lecture me • **más aún** even more • **la comida italiana me gusta más aún** I like Italian food even more *o* better • **si vienes lo pasaremos aún mejor** if you come we'll enjoy ourselves even more

3* (= *quizás*) perhaps, maybe • **—¿lo comprarás? —si lo rebajan, aún** "will you buy it?" — "if they reduce it, perhaps"

aunar ▹ CONJUG 1a VT to join, unite

VPR **aunarse** to unite

aunque CONJ although, though, even though • **~ estaba cansado vino con nosotros** although he was tired he came with us • **~ no me creas** even though you may not believe me • **~ llueva vendremos** we'll come even if it rains • **es guapa ~ algo bajita** she's pretty but rather short, she's pretty even if she is on the short side • **~ más ... ** however much ..., no matter how much ...

AUNQUE

Aunque *se puede traducir al inglés por* **although, though, even though** *o* **even if.**

▹ *Por regla general, cuando la cláusula introducida por* **aunque** *indica un hecho (***aunque** *+ indicativo), en inglés coloquial se traduce por* **though** *y en lenguaje más formal por* **although**:

Aunque había un montón de gente, al final pude encontrar a Carlos
Though there were a lot of people there, I managed to find Carlos

No esperaba eso de él, aunque entiendo por qué lo hizo
I did not expect that from him, although I can understand why he did it

▹ **Even though** *introduce la oración subordinada, enfatizando con más fuerza el contraste con la principal, cuando* **aunque** *va seguido de un hecho concreto, no una hipótesis, y equivale a* **a pesar de que**:

Llevaba un abrigo de piel, aunque era un día muy caluroso
She wore a fur coat, even though it was a very hot day

▹ *Si* **aunque** *tiene el sentido de* **incluso si** *(***aunque** *+ subjuntivo), se traduce por* **even if**:

Debes ir, aunque no quieras
You must go, even if you don't want to

Me dijo que no me lo diría, aunque lo supiera
He said he wouldn't tell me even if he knew

Para otros usos y ejemplos ver la entrada.

aúpa EXCL (*al levantar a un niño*) up!, upsadaisy!; (*para animar*) up!, come on! • **¡~ Toboso!** up Toboso!

ADJ* • **una función de ~** a slap-up do* • **una paliza de ~** a good thrashing* • **una tormenta de ~** a hell of a storm* • **es de ~** it's absolutely awful

au pair SMF au pair

aupar ▹ CONJUG 1a VT (= *levantar*) to help up; [+ *pantalón etc*] to hitch up; (= *ensalzar*) to praise • **sus discos la han aupado al primer puesto** her records have lifted her *o* shot her up to number one • **~ a algn al poder** to raise sb to power

aura SF **1** (= *brisa*) gentle breeze, sweet breeze

2 (= *popularidad*) popularity, popular favour, popular favor (*EEUU*)

3 (*LAm*) (= *pájaro*) vulture, buzzard (*EEUU*)

áureo ADJ **1** (*liter*) (= *de oro*) golden

2 (*Esp*) (*Hist*) • **nuestra literatura áurea** our literature of the Golden Age

aureola SF, **auréola** SF (*Rel*) halo, aureole (*frm*); (= *gloria*) fame

aureolar†† ▹ CONJUG 1a VT (*esp LAm*) [+ *persona*] to praise, extol the virtues of; [+ *reputación etc*] to enhance, add lustre to

aurícula SF auricle

auricular ADJ aural, of the ear • **el pabellón ~** the outer ear

SM **1** (= *dedo*) little finger

2 [*de teléfono*] receiver, handset; **auriculares** (= *cascos*) headphones, earphones

auriculoterapia SF auriculotherapy

aurífero ADJ gold-bearing

aurora SF (*lit, fig*) dawn ▸ **aurora boreal, aurora borealis** northern lights (*pl*)

auscultación SF sounding, auscultation (*frm*)

auscultar ▹ CONJUG 1a VT to sound, auscultate (*frm*)

ausencia SF absence • **condenar a algn en su ~** to sentence sb in his absence • **hacer buenas ~s de algn**† to speak kindly of sb in their absence, remember sb with affection • REFRÁN: • **en ~ del gato se divierten los ratones** when the cat's away the mice will play; ▹ **brillar**

ausentarse ▹ CONJUG 1a VPR (= *marcharse*) to absent o.s. (**de** from); (= *no acudir*) to stay away (**de** from)

ausente ADJ **1** (*físicamente*) absent (**de** from) • **estar ~ de** to be absent from, be missing from • **estar ~ de su casa** to be away from home

2 (*mentalmente*) daydreaming

SMF (*Escol etc*) absentee; (*Jur*) missing person

ausentismo SM (*LAm*) = **absentismo**

ausentista SMF (*LAm*) = **absentista**

auspiciado ADJ sponsored, backed

auspiciador(a) ADJ • **firma ~a** sponsoring firm

SM/F sponsor

auspiciar ▹ CONJUG 1b VT **1** (= *patrocinar*) to back, sponsor

2 (*LAm*) (= *desear éxito a*) to wish good luck to

auspicios SMPL **1** (= *patrocinio*) auspices, sponsorship (*sing*) • **bajo los ~ de** under the auspices of, sponsored by

2 (= *augurio*) omen • **buenos ~** good omen • **malos ~** bad omen

auspicioso ADJ auspicious

austeramente ADV (= *con frugalidad*) austerely; (= *con severidad*) sternly, severely

austericidio SM *suffering caused by austerity measures*

austeridad SF (= *frugalidad*) austerity; (= *severidad*) severity ▸ **austeridad económica** economic austerity

austero ADJ (= *frugal*) austere; (= *severo*) severe

austral ADJ **1** (= *del sur*) southern • **el Hemisferio Austral** the Southern Hemisphere

2 (*Cono Sur*) (= *del sur de Chile*) of/from southern Chile

SM (*Arg*) *monetary unit from 1985-1991*

Australia SF Australia

australiano/a ADJ, SM/F Australian

australopiteco/a SM/F, **australopitecus** SMF Australopithecus

Austria SF Austria

austríaco/a ADJ, SM/F, **austriaco/a** ADJ, SM/F Austrian

austro SM (*liter*) (= *sur*) south; (= *viento*) south wind

austro-húngaro ADJ Austro-Hungarian

autarquía SF **1** (*Pol*) autarchy (*frm*), self-government

2 (*Econ*) autarky (*frm*), national self-sufficiency

autazo SM (*LAm*) theft of a car

auténtica SF (*Jur*) (= *certificación*) certification; (= *copia*) authorized copy

auténticamente ADV authentically, genuinely

autenticar ▹ CONJUG 1g VT to authenticate

autenticidad SF authenticity

auténtico ADJ **1** (= *legítimo*) authentic; [*persona*] genuine • **un ~ espíritu de servicio** a true spirit of service • **es un ~ campeón** he's a real champion • **este es copia y no el ~** this one is a copy and not the real one • **días de ~ calor** days of real heat, really hot days

2* (= *estupendo*) great*, brilliant*

autentificar ▹ CONJUG 1g VT to authenticate

autería SF (*Cono Sur*) (= *presagio*) evil omen, bad sign; (= *brujería*) witchcraft
autero/a¹ SM/F (*LAm*) (= *ladrón*) car thief
autero/a² SM/F (*Cono Sur*) **1** (= *pesimista*) pessimist, defeatist
2 (= *gafe*) jinx*
autillo SM tawny owl
autismo SM autism
autista ADJ autistic
SMF autistic, autistic person • **es un ~** he's autistic
autístico ADJ autistic
autito SM (*Cono Sur*) ▸ **autitos chocadores** bumper cars, dodgems (*Brit*)
auto¹ SM (*esp Cono Sur*) car, automobile (*EEUU*) ▸ **auto de choque** bumper car, dodgem (*Brit*)
auto² SM **1** (*Jur*) edict, judicial decree ▸ **auto de comparecencia** summons, subpoena (*EEUU*) ▸ **auto de ejecución** writ of execution ▸ **auto de prisión** warrant for arrest ▸ **auto de procesamiento** charge, indictment
2 autos (= *documentos*) proceedings, court record (*sing*) • **estar en ~s** to be in the know • **poner a algn en ~s** to put sb in the picture
3 (*Rel, Teat*) mystery play, religious play ▸ **auto del nacimiento** nativity play ▸ **auto sacramental** eucharistic play
4 (*Hist*) ▸ **auto de fe** auto-da-fé • **hacer un ~ de fe de algo**† (*fig*) to burn sth
auto... PREF auto..., self-...
autoabastecerse ▸ CONJUG 2d VPR (= *autoproveerse*) to supply o.s. (**de** with); (= *ser autosuficiente*) to be self-sufficient
autoabastecimiento SM self-sufficiency
autoacusación SF self-accusation
autoacusarse ▸ CONJUG 1a VPR to accuse o.s.
autoadherente ADJ self-adhesive
autoadhesivo ADJ self-adhesive
autoadministrarse ▸ CONJUG 1a VPR
1 • **~ una droga** to take a drug
2 (*Pol*) to govern o.s., be self-governing
autoadulación SF self-praise
autoafirmación SF assertiveness
autoaislarse ▸ CONJUG 1a VPR to isolate o.s.
autoalarma SF car alarm
autoalimentación SF (*Inform*) ▸ **autoalimentación de hojas** automatic paper feed
autoanálisis SM INV self-analysis
autoanalizador SM analyser, auto-analyser
autoanalizarse ▸ CONJUG 1f VPR to analyze o.s., do self-analysis
autoaprendizaje SM self-study • **curso de ~** self-study course • **programa de ~** self-study programme, self-study program (*EEUU*)
autoaprovisionamiento SM self-sufficiency
autoayuda SF self-help
autobiografía SF autobiography
autobiográfico ADJ autobiographic, autobiographical
autobomba SF fire engine
autobombearse ▸ CONJUG 1a VPR to blow one's own trumpet
autobombo SM self-praise, self-glorification • **hacerse el ~** to blow one's own trumpet
autobronceador SM self-tanning lotion
autobús SM bus; (*LAm*) [*de distancia*] coach, bus (*EEUU*) ▸ **autobús de dos pisos** double-decker, double-decker bus ▸ **autobús de línea** long-distance coach ▸ **autobús escolar** school bus
autobusero/a ADJ bus (*antes de s*)
SM/F bus driver

autocalificarse ▸ CONJUG 1g VPR • **~ de** to describe o.s. as
autocar SM coach, bus (*EEUU*) ▸ **autocar de línea** long-distance coach, inter-city coach ▸ **autocar de línea regular** scheduled coach
autocaravana SF camper, motor home (*EEUU*), camping vehicle
autocargador ADJ • **camión ~** self-loading truck
autocarril SM (*LAm*) railway car
autocartera SF holding of its own shares (*by a company*)
autocensura SF self-censorship
auto-choque SM bumper car, dodgem (*Brit*)
autocine SM drive-in cinema
autoclave SM (*Med*) autoclave
autocompasión SF self-pity
autocomplaciente ADJ self-satisfied
autocomprobación SF self-test
autoconcederse ▸ CONJUG 2a VPR • **~ un título** to grant o.s. a title
autoconfesado ADJ self-confessed
autoconfesarse ▸ CONJUG 1a VPR to confess o.s.
autoconfesión SF self-confession
autoconfianza SF self-confidence
autoconservación SF self-preservation
autoconsumo SM [*de alimentos*] personal consumption; [*de bienes*] personal use
autocontrol SM **1** (= *autodominio*) self-control, self-restraint
2 (*Téc*) self-monitoring
autoconvencerse ▸ CONJUG 2d VPR to convince o.s.
autocracia SF autocracy
autócrata SMF autocrat
autocrático ADJ autocratic
autocremarse ▸ CONJUG 1a VPR to set fire to o.s., burn o.s. (to death)
autocrítica SF self-criticism
autocrítico ADJ self-critical
autocross SM INV autocross
autóctono ADJ indigenous, native
autocue SM autocue
autodefensa SF self-defence, self-defense (*EEUU*)
autodefinirse ▸ CONJUG 3a VPR to define o.s., state one's position
autodegradación SF self-abasement
autodenominarse ▸ CONJUG 1a VPR to call o.s.
autodestrucción SF self-destruction
autodestructible ADJ, **autodestructivo** ADJ self-destructive, self-destructing
autodestruirse ▸ CONJUG 3g VPR to self-destruct
autodeterminación SF self-determination
autodidacta ADJ [*persona*] self-taught; [*formación, método*] autodidactic (*frm*)
SMF autodidact, self-taught person
autodidacto/a ADJ, SM/F = **autodidacta**
autodisciplina SF self-discipline
autodisciplinado ADJ self-disciplined
autodisparador SM self-timer
autodominio SM self-control
autódromo SM racetrack, racing circuit
autoedición SF desktop publishing
autoelevador SM, **autoelevadora** SF (*Cono Sur*) forklift truck
autoempleo SM self-employment
autoengaño SM self-deception, self-delusion
autoerótico ADJ autoerotic
autoescuela SF driving school
autoestima SF self-esteem
autoestop SM = **autostop**
autoestopista SMF = **autostopista**

autoevaluación SF self-assessment
autoexcluirse ▸ CONJUG 3g VPR to exclude o.s.
autoexploración SF self-examination
autoexpresión SF self-expression
autofacturación SF auto check-in
autofecundación SF self-fertilization
autofelicitación SF self-congratulation
autofinanciable ADJ, **autofinanciado** ADJ self-financing
autofinanciarse ▸ CONJUG 1b VPR to finance o.s.
autógena SF welding
autógeno ADJ autogenous
autogestión SF self-management
autogiro SM autogiro
autogobernarse ▸ CONJUG 1j VPR to govern o.s., be self-governing
autogobierno SM self-government
autogol SM own goal
autogolpe SM *coup organized by the government itself to allow it to take extra powers*
autógrafo SM autograph
autohipnosis SF INV autohypnosis, self-hypnosis
autoimpuesto ADJ self-imposed
autoincluirse ▸ CONJUG 3g VPR to include o.s.
autoinculpación SF **1** (= *autoacusación*) self-incrimination
2 (*Jur*) plea of guilty
autoinculparse ▸ CONJUG 1a VPR to incriminate o.s.
autoinducido ADJ self-induced
autoinfligido ADJ self-inflicted
autoinmune ADJ autoimmune
autoinmunidad SF autoimmunity
autoinmunitario ADJ, **autoinmunológico** ADJ autoimmune
autolavado SM car-wash
autolesionarse ▸ CONJUG 1a VPR to inflict injury on o.s., injure o.s.
autolimpiable ADJ self-cleaning
autollamarse ▸ CONJUG 1a VPR to call o.s.
automación SF automation
automarginación SF dropping-out
automarginado/a ADJ • **persona automarginada** drop-out
SM/F drop-out
automarginarse ▸ CONJUG 1a VPR to drop out • **~ de** to drop out of
autómata SM automaton, robot ▸ **autómata industrial** industrial robot
automática SF **1** (= *ciencia*) automation
2 (= *lavadora*) washing machine
3 (*Mil*) automatic
automáticamente ADV automatically
automaticidad SF automaticity
automático ADJ automatic • **lavadora automática** (automatic) washing machine
SM **1** (*Cono Sur*) (= *restaurante*) self-service restaurant, automat (*EEUU*)
2 (= *cierre*) press stud, popper, snap (fastener) (*EEUU*)
automatismo SM automatism
automatización SF automation ▸ **automatización de fábricas** factory automation ▸ **automatización de oficinas** office automation
automatizado ADJ automated
automatizar ▸ CONJUG 1f VT to automate
automedicarse ▸ CONJUG 1g VPR to treat o.s.
automedonte SM (*LAm*) (*hum*) coachman
automercado SM (*Caribe*) supermarket
automoción SF **1** (= *transporte*) transport, road transport
2 (= *automóvil*) • **la industria de la ~** the car industry, the automobile industry (*EEUU*) • **gasóleo de ~** diesel for automobiles
automodelismo SM model car racing

a

automodelista SMF model car enthusiast
automontable ADJ self-assembly
automotor ADJ **1** (= *autopropulsado*) self-propelled
2 (*LAm*) car (*antes de s*), automobile (*antes de s*) (*EEUU*)
SM **1** (*Ferro*) diesel train
2 (*LAm*) (= *vehículo*) motor vehicle
automóvil ADJ **1** (= *autopropulsado*) self-propelled
2 car (*antes de s*), automobile (*antes de s*) (*EEUU*)
SM car, automobile (*EEUU*) • **ir en ~** to drive, go by car, travel by car ▸ **automóvil de alquiler** hire car ▸ **automóvil de carreras** racing car ▸ **automóvil de choque** bumper car, dodgem (*Brit*) ▸ **automóvil de importación** imported car, foreign car
automovilismo SM motoring ▸ **automovilismo deportivo** motor racing
automovilista SMF motorist, driver
automovilístico ADJ car (*antes de s*), auto (*antes de s*) (*EEUU*) • **accidente ~** car accident • **industria automovilística** car industry
automutilación SF self-harm
automutilarse ▹ CONJUG 1a VPR to self-harm
autonomía SF **1** (= *independencia*) autonomy; (= *autogobierno*) self-government • **Estatuto de Autonomía** (*Esp*) Devolution Statute
2 (= *territorio*) autonomous region, autonomy
3 (*Aer, Náut*) range • **el avión tiene una ~ de 5.000km** the aircraft has a range of 5,000km • **de gran ~** long range ▸ **autonomía de vuelo** range
4 [*de pila, batería*] battery range
autonómico ADJ (*Pol*) autonomous, self-governing • **elecciones autonómicas** elections for the autonomous regions • **política autonómica** policy concerning the autonomies • **el proceso ~** the process leading to autonomy • **región autonómica** autonomous region
autonomismo SM separatism, movement towards autonomy
autónomo/a ADJ **1** (*Pol*) autonomous, self-governing
2 (*Inform*) stand-alone, off-line
3 [*persona*] self-employed • **trabajo ~** self-employment
SM/F self-employed person
autopatrulla SM (*Méx*) patrol car
autopegado ADJ self-sealing
autopiano SM (*Caribe*) pianola
autopista SF motorway, freeway (*EEUU*) ▸ **autopista de la información** information superhighway ▸ **autopista de peaje** toll road, turnpike (*EEUU*) ▸ **autopista perimetral** ring road, bypass
autopolinización SF self-pollination
autopreservación SF self-preservation
autoproclamado ADJ self-proclaimed
autoproclamarse ▹ CONJUG 1a VPR to proclaim o.s.
autoprofesor SM teaching machine
autoprogramable ADJ • **ordenador ~** intelligent computer
autopropulsado ADJ self-propelled
autopropulsión SF self-propulsion
autopropulsor ADJ self-propelling
autoprotección SF self-protection
autoprotegerse ▹ CONJUG 2c VPR to protect o.s.
autopsia SF post mortem, autopsy • **hacer** *o* **practicar la ~ a algn** to carry out an autopsy on sb
autopublicidad SF self-advertisement • **hacer ~** to indulge in self-advertisement

autor(a) SM/F **1** [*de obra*] author, writer; [*de idea*] creator, originator, inventor • **el ~ de la novela** the author of the novel • **el ~ del cuadro** the painter • **el ~ de mis días** my father
2 [*de delito*] perpetrator • **los presuntos ~es del crimen** the suspected killers • **el ~ intelectual** the mastermind • **el ~ material** *the person directly responsible (for the crime)*
autoreferencial ADJ self-referential
autoría SF authorship • **la ~ del atentado** the responsibility for the attack
autoridad SF **1** (= *potestad*) authority • **las ~es** the authorities • **~es aduaneras** customs authorities • **¡abran a la ~!** open up in the name of the law! • **entregarse a la ~** to give o.s. up (*to the police*) ▸ **autoridad de sanidad** health authorities (*pl*) ▸ **autoridad local** local authority
2 (= *persona*) authority
3 (= *boato*) pomp, show
autoritariamente ADV in an authoritarian manner
autoritario/a ADJ, SM/F authoritarian
autoritarismo SM authoritarianism
autoritativo ADJ authoritative
autorización SF authorization, permission • **~ para hacer algo** authorization *o* permission to do sth
autorizadamente ADV officially, authoritatively
autorizado ADJ **1** (= *oficial*) authorized, official
2 (= *fiable*) authoritative
3 (*Com*) approved • **la persona autorizada** the officially designated person, the approved person
autorizar ▹ CONJUG 1f VT **1** (= *dar facultad a*) to authorize, empower; (= *permitir*) to approve, license • **~ a algn para** (+ *infin*) to authorize sb to (+ *infin*), empower sb to (+ *infin*) • **el futuro no autoriza optimismo alguno** the future does not warrant *o* justify the slightest optimism
2 (*Jur*) to legalize
autorradio SF car radio
autorrealización SF self-fulfilment
autorrealizado ADJ self-fulfilled
autorrealizarse ▹ CONJUG 1f VPR to feel fulfilled
autorregulable ADJ self-adjusting
autorregulación SF self-regulation
autorretrato SM self-portrait
autoservicio SM **1** (= *tienda*) self-service store, self-service shop
2 (= *restaurante*) self-service restaurant
autosostenerse ▹ CONJUG 2k VPR to pay one's own way, be self-supporting
autostop SM hitch-hiking • **hacer ~** to hitch-hike, thumb lifts • **viajar en ~** to hitch-hike • **fuimos haciendo ~ de Irún a Burgos** we hitch-hiked from Irún to Burgos, we hitched a lift from Irún to Burgos
autostopismo SM hitch-hiking
autostopista SMF hitch-hiker
autosuficiencia SF **1** (*Econ*) self-sufficiency
2 (*pey*) (= *petulancia*) smugness
autosuficiente ADJ **1** (*Econ*) self-sufficient
2 (*pey*) (= *petulante*) smug
autosugestión SF autosuggestion
autotanque SM tanker, tank truck (*EEUU*)
autotitularse ▹ CONJUG 1a VPR to title o.s., call o.s.
autoventa ADJ INV • **vendedor ~** travelling salesman, representative who travels by car
autovía SF main road, trunk road, state highway (*EEUU*) ▸ **autovía de circunvalación** bypass, ring road

autovivienda SF caravan, trailer
Auvernia SF Auvergne
auxiliar[1] ADJ **1** (*Univ*) assistant (*antes de s*)
2 (*Ling*) auxiliary
3 [*plantilla*] ancillary
SMF **1** (= *subordinado*) assistant ▸ **auxiliar administrativo** administrative assistant ▸ **auxiliar de cabina** steward/stewardess ▸ **auxiliar de clínica, auxiliar de enfermería** auxiliary nurse, nursing auxiliary, nurse's aide (*EEUU*) ▸ **auxiliar de laboratorio** lab assistant, laboratory assistant ▸ **auxiliar de vuelo** steward/stewardess ▸ **auxiliar domiciliario** domestic, home help, home helper (*EEUU*) ▸ **auxiliar sanitario** health worker ▸ **auxiliar técnico sanitario** nurse
2 (*Univ*) ▸ **auxiliar de conversación** conversation assistant ▸ **auxiliar de lengua inglesa** English language assistant
3 (*Dep*) linesman, assistant referee ▸ **auxiliar técnico** (*LAm*) (*Dep*) coach, trainer
auxiliar[2] ▹ CONJUG 1b VT **1** (= *ayudar*) to help, assist; [+ *agonizante*] to attend
2 (*Pol etc*) to aid, give aid to
auxilio SM help, assistance (*más frm*) • **primeros ~s** (*Med*) first aid • **acudir en ~ de algn** to come to sb's aid • **pedir ~** to ask for help *o* assistance • **prestar ~** to give help *o* assistance ▸ **auxilio espiritual** (*Rel*) consolations of religion (*pl*); (= *sacramentos*) last rites (*pl*) ▸ **auxilio social** welfare service
Av. ABR (= **Avenida**) Av., Ave
a/v ABR (*Com*) = **a vista**
avada‡ SM (*Caribe*) queer‡, fag (*EEUU‡*)
avahar ▹ CONJUG 1a VT to blow on, warm with one's breath
VI, VPR **avaharse** to steam, give off steam *o* vapour
aval SM **1** (*Com*) endorsement; [*de firma*] guarantee • **dar su ~ a** [+ *fiador*] to be a guarantor for; (*Econ*) to underwrite ▸ **aval bancario** banker's reference
2 (*Pol*) backing, support
avalancha SF **1** [*de nieve*] avalanche
2 (*fig*) • **una ~ de gente** a flood *o* torrent of people • **una ~ de cartas** an avalanche of letters
avalar ▹ CONJUG 1a VT **1** (*Econ*) to underwrite; [+ *individuo*] to act as guarantor for
2 (*Com*) to endorse, guarantee; [+ *persona*] (= *responder de*) to answer for
avalentado ADJ, **avalentonado** ADJ boastful, arrogant
avalista SMF (*Econ*) guarantor; (*Com*) endorser
avalorar ▹ CONJUG 1a VT **1** (*Com*) to appraise
2 (= *animar*) to encourage
avaluación SF (*LAm*), **avaluada** (*LAm*) SF valuation, appraisal
avaluar ▹ CONJUG 1e VT to value, appraise (en at)
avalúo SM valuation, appraisal
avancarga SF ▸ **cañón de avancarga** muzzle loader
avance SM **1** (= *movimiento*) advance • **el ~ de las tropas** the advance of the troops • **el ~ del feminismo** the advance of feminism
2 (= *progreso*) advance • **grandes ~s en el terreno de la genética** major advances in the field of genetics • **Pedro ha hecho grandes ~s en matemáticas** Pedro has made great progress in mathematics • **la reunión concluyó sin ~s** no progress had been made by the end of the meeting
3 (*Econ*) advance (payment)
4 (*Cine*) (= *tráiler*) trailer • **un ~ de la programación matinal** (*TV*) a look ahead at the morning's programmes ▸ **avance informativo** news headlines, advance news summary

a

5 (*Com*) (= *balance*) balance; (= *cálculo*) estimate
6 (*Elec*) lead
7 (*Mec*) feed
8 (*Cono Sur*) (= *ataque*) attack, raid
9 (*Cono Sur*) (= *regalo*) tempting offer, inducement (*made to secure sb's goodwill*)
10 (*CAm*) (= *robo*) theft
avante ADV (*esp LAm*) (= *adelante*) forward; (*Náut*) forward, ahead • **todo ~** (*Náut*) full steam ahead • **¡avante!** forward! • **salir ~** to get ahead, get on in the world
avanzada SF (*Mil*) (= *soldados*) advance party, advance guard; (= *puesto*) outpost
avanzadilla SF (= *patrulla*) scout, patrol; (= *avanzada*) advance party
avanzado ADJ (= *adelantado*) advanced; [*pómulo*] prominent; [*diseño*] advanced; [*ideas, tendencia*] advanced, avant-garde, progressive • **de edad avanzada** • **~ de edad** advanced in years • **a una hora avanzada** at a late hour
avanzar ▷ CONJUG 1f VT 1 (= *mover*) to move forward, advance • **avanzó la ficha cuatro casillas** he moved the counter forward four spaces, he advanced the counter four spaces • **avanza un poco tu silla** move your chair forward a bit
2 [+ *dinero*] to advance
3 [+ *opinión, propuesta*] to put forward
4 [+ *resultado*] to predict; [+ *predicción*] to make
5 (*Caribe*) (= *vomitar*) to vomit
VI 1 (= *ir hacia adelante*) to advance, move forward • **el ejército avanzó de madrugada** the army advanced *o* moved forward at dawn • **no me esperéis, seguid avanzando** don't wait for me, carry on
2 (= *progresar*) to make progress • **estudio mucho pero no avanzo** I work hard but I don't make any progress *o* headway • **ha avanzado mucho en química** she has made great progress in chemistry • **las conversaciones de paz no parecen ~** the peace talks do not seem to be progressing *o* making (any) progress • **la genética avanza a ritmo vertiginoso** genetics is progressing *o* advancing at a dizzy speed
3 [*noche, invierno*] to draw on, approach
VPR **avanzarse** • **~se algo** (*CAm, Méx*) to steal sth
avanzo SM (*Com*) (= *balance*) balance sheet; (= *cálculo*) estimate
avaricia SF avarice, greed, greediness
avariciosamente ADV avariciously, greedily
avaricioso ADJ, **avariento** ADJ avaricious, greedy
avariosis SF INV (*LAm*) syphilis
avaro/a ADJ miserly, mean • **ser ~ de** *o* **en alabanzas** to be sparing in one's praise • **ser ~ de palabras** to be a person of few words
SM/F miser
avasallador ADJ overwhelming
avasallamiento SM subjugation
avasallar ▷ CONJUG 1a VT 1 (= *subyugar*) to subjugate
2 • **~ a algn** (= *obligar*) to steamroller sb (*into agreement or compliance*)
VPR **avasallarse** to submit, yield
avatar SM 1 (= *encarnación*) incarnation; (= *transformación*) change, transformation • **~es** (= *vicisitudes*) ups and downs
2 (= *etapa*) phase; (= *ola*) wave ▸ **avatar destructivo** wave of destruction
3 (*en videojuegos*) avatar
Avda. ABR (= **Avenida**) Av., Ave
AVE SM ABR (= **Alta Velocidad Española**) *high speed train*
ave SF (= *pájaro*) bird; (*esp LAm*) (= *pollo*) chicken ▸ **ave acuática, ave acuátil** water bird ▸ **ave canora, ave cantora** songbird ▸ **ave de corral** chicken, fowl ▸ **ave del paraíso** bird of paradise ▸ **ave de paso** bird of passage ▸ **ave de presa, ave de rapiña** bird of prey ▸ **ave marina** sea bird ▸ **ave negra** (*Cono Sur*) crooked lawyer ▸ **ave nocturna** night bird (*tb fig*) ▸ **aves de corral** poultry (*sing*) ▸ **ave zancuda** wader, wading bird
avechucho* SM ragamuffin, ne'er-do-well
avecinarse ▷ CONJUG 1a VPR to approach, come near
avecindarse ▷ CONJUG 1a VPR to take up one's residence, settle
avefría SF lapwing
avejentado ADJ [*piel, rostro*] old • **le encontré ~ para su edad** I thought he looked old for his age
avejentar ▷ CONJUG 1a VT • **el pelo blanco te avejentaba mucho** your grey hair made you look much older *o* put years on you
VI, VPR **avejentarse** to age
avejigar ▷ CONJUG 1h VT to blister
VPR **avejigarse** to blister
avellana SF 1 (*Bot*) hazelnut
2 (*Perú*) firecracker
avellanado ADJ 1 [*color*] nutbrown
2 [*piel*] wrinkled, wizened
3 [*sabor*] nutty
avellanal SM hazel wood
avellanar[1] SM hazel wood
avellanar[2] ▷ CONJUG 1a VT (*Téc*) to countersink
VPR **avellanarse** to become wrinkled
avellanedo SM hazel wood
avellano SM hazel nut tree
avemaría SF 1 (*Rel*) (= *cuenta*) rosary bead; (= *oración*) Ave Maria, Hail Mary
2 • **al ~** at dusk • **en un ~** in a twinkling, in a jiffy* • **saber algo como el ~*** to know sth inside out
avena SF oats (*pl*) ▸ **avena loca, avena morisca, avena silvestre** wild oats (*pl*)
avenado ADJ half-crazy, touched*, nuts*
avenal SM oatfield
avenamiento SM drainage
avenar ▷ CONJUG 1a VT to drain
avenencia SF (= *acuerdo*) agreement; (*Com*) deal
avenida SF 1 (= *calle*) avenue
2 [*de río*] flood, spate
avenido ADJ • **están muy bien ~s** [*personas*] they get on well; [*pareja*] they're well matched • **están muy mal ~s** [*personas*] they get on badly; [*pareja*] they're badly matched
avenimiento SM agreement, compromise
avenir ▷ CONJUG 3a VT to reconcile, bring together
VI to come to pass
VPR **avenirse** 1 (*Com etc*) to come to an agreement; [*hermanos etc*] to get on well together • **no se avienen** they don't get on
2 • **~se con algo** (= *estar de acuerdo*) to be in agreement with sth; (= *resignarse*) to resign o.s. to sth • **~se con algn** to reach an agreement with sb • **¡allá te las avengas!*** that's your look-out!*, that's up to you!
3 • **~se a hacer algo** to agree to do sth
aventado ADJ (*LAm*) daring
aventador SM (*para fuego*) fan, blower; (*Agr*) winnowing fork
aventadora SF winnowing machine
aventajadamente ADV outstandingly, extremely well
aventajado ADJ outstanding • **~ de estatura** exceptionally tall
aventajar ▷ CONJUG 1a VT 1 (= *superar*) to surpass, excel (**en** in); (*en carrera*) to outstrip; (*CAm*) (*Aut*) to overtake • **~ con mucho a algn** to beat sb easily, be far better than sb, leave sb standing* • **Juan aventaja a Pablo por cuatro puntos** Juan leads Pablo by four points
2 (= *mejorar*) to improve, better
3 (= *preferir*) to prefer
VPR **aventajarse** (= *adelantarse*) to get ahead • **~se a** to surpass, excel
aventar ▷ CONJUG 1j VT 1 [+ *fuego*] to fan, blow; (*Agr*) to winnow
2 (= *expulsar*) to chuck out*, throw out; (*LAm*) (= *arrojar*) to throw
3 (= *lanzar al aire*) to cast to the winds; [*viento*] to blow away; (*Caribe*) (*Agr*) to dry in the wind
VPR **aventarse** 1 [*vela etc*] to fill with air, swell up
2‡ (= *largarse*) to beat it*
3 (= *atacar*) to attack
4 (*LAm*) (= *tirarse*) to throw o.s.; (= *arriesgarse*) to take risks
aventón* SM (*Méx*) (= *empujón*) push, shove • **pedir ~** to hitch a lift, hitch a ride (*EEUU*)
aventura SF 1 (= *suceso*) adventure • **nos contó las ~s de su viaje** he told us of the adventures he had had on his journey • **una película de ~s** an adventure film
2 (= *riesgo*) • **invertir ahora es una ~** investing at this time is a gamble • **se fue a América a buscar trabajo a la ~** he went to America and took a chance on *o* gambled on finding work, he went to America on the off-chance of finding work • **se lanzaron a la ~ de montar un negocio** they embarked on the venture of setting up a business
3* (= *amorío*) fling*, brief affair • **tuvo una ~ con un estudiante** she had a fling* *o* a brief affair with a student
4 (*frm*) (= *contingencia*) chance, contingency
aventurado ADJ risky, hazardous • **es ~ suponer ...** it's a bit too much to suppose that ...
aventurar ▷ CONJUG 1a VT (= *arriesgar*) to venture, risk; [+ *opinión etc*] to hazard; [+ *capital*] to risk, stake
VPR **aventurarse** to dare, take a chance • **~se a hacer algo** to venture to do sth, risk doing sth • REFRÁN: • **el que no se aventura no pasa la mar** nothing ventured, nothing gained
aventurero/a ADJ adventurous, enterprising
SM/F adventurer/adventuress
SM (*Mil*) mercenary, soldier of fortune; (*pey*) (= *arribista*) social climber
avergonzado ADJ • **estar ~** to be ashamed (**de, por** about, at)
avergonzar ▷ CONJUG 1f, 1l VT (= *hacer pasar vergüenza*) to shame, put to shame; (= *poner en un aprieto*) to embarrass
VPR **avergonzarse** 1 (= *sentir vergüenza*) to be ashamed (**de, por** about, at, of) • **~se de hacer algo** to be ashamed to do sth • **se avergonzó de haberlo dicho** he was ashamed at having said it
2 (= *sentirse violento*) to be embarrassed
avería[1] SF 1 (*Com etc*) damage; (*Mec*) breakdown • **en caso de ~ llame al 3474** in the event of a breakdown call 3474 • **el coche tiene una ~** there's something wrong with the car
2 (*Cono Sur*) (= *matón*) tough guy*, thug; (= *criminal*) dangerous criminal • **ser de ~** to be dangerous
avería[2] SF (*Orn*) (= *pajarera*) aviary; (= *aves*) flock of birds
avería[3] SF (*Com, Náut*) average ▸ **avería gruesa** general average
averiado ADJ 1 (*Mec*) broken down, faulty • **los faros están ~s** the lights have failed,

a

there's something wrong with the lights • **"Averiado"** "Out of order"
2 [*fruto etc*] damaged, spoiled
averiar ▷ CONJUG 1c (VT) (*Mec*) to cause a breakdown in, cause a failure in; (= *estropear*) to damage
(VPR) **averiarse 1** (*Mec*) to have a breakdown; (= *estropearse*) to get damaged • **debe de haberse averiado** [*coche*] it must have broken down; [*ascensor*] it must be out of order • **se averió el arranque** the starter failed, the starter went wrong
2 (*Méx*) (= *perder la virginidad*) to lose one's virginity
averiguable (ADJ) verifiable
averiguación (SF) **1** (= *comprobación*) verification; (= *investigación*) inquiry, investigation
2 (*CAm, Méx*) (= *riña*) quarrel, argument
averiguadamente (ADV) certainly
averiguado (ADJ) certain, established • **es un hecho ~** it is an established fact
averiguador(a) (SM/F) investigator
averiguar ▷ CONJUG 1i (VT) to find out, establish (*frm*) • **debemos ~ cuándo llega el tren** we must find out when the train arrives • **averigua cuál es su hermano** find out who the brother is • **nunca ~on quién era el asesino** they never found out *o* (*frm*) established *o* discovered who the killer was • **~ la solución** to find out the answer • **ya han averiguado la identidad del padre** they have found out *o* (*frm*) established *o* discovered the identity of the father • **~ las causas de un problema** to find out *o* (*frm*) establish the causes of a problem • **un estudio para ~ el alcance de la tragedia** a study to find out *o* (*frm*) establish the extent of the tragedy • **han averiguado que el presidente malversaba fondos** it has been established *o* discovered that the president was embezzling funds • **—¿quién ha roto el vaso? —¡averigua!** "who broke the glass?" — "who knows!"
(VI) (*CAm, Méx**) (= *pelear*) to quarrel
(VPR) **averiguarse** (*tb* **averiguárselas**) (*esp Méx*) to manage, get by • **yo me (las) averiguo muy bien solo** I manage *o* get by very well on my own • **yo me (las) averiguo con poco dinero** I get by *o* manage without much money • **ya me (las) ~é por mi cuenta** I'll manage *o* get by on my own • **averíguate(las) como puedas** you'll have to manage as best you can • **averíguate(las) con lo que tengas** make do with what you've got • **ya me las ~é para llegar a Barcelona** I'll find a way of getting to Barcelona somehow • **~se** *o* **averiguárselas con algn: tú olvídate, ya me (las) ~é yo con él** don't worry about it, I'll sort it out with him • **~se** *o* **averiguárselas bien con algn** to get on (well) with sb • **ellos dos se las averiguan bien** the two of them get on well (together)
averiguata (SF) (*Méx*) argument, fight
averigüetas* (SMF INV) (*And*) snooper, busybody
averrugado (ADJ) warty
aversión (SF) (= *repulsión*) aversion; (= *aborrecimiento*) disgust, loathing • **~ hacia** *o* **por algo** aversion to sth • **~ a algn** aversion for sb • **cobrar ~ a algn/algo** to take a strong dislike to sb/sth
avestruz (SM) **1** (= *ave*) ostrich ▸ **avestruz de la pampa** rhea
2 (*LAm**) (= *imbécil*) dimwit*, idiot
avetado (ADJ) veined, streaked
avetoro (SM) bittern
avezado (ADJ) accustomed, inured • **los ya ~s en estos menesteres** those already experienced in such activities
avezar ▷ CONJUG 1f (VT) to accustom, inure (a to)
(VPR) **avezarse** to become accustomed • **~se a algo** to get used to sth, get hardened to sth, get inured to sth (*frm*)
aviación (SF) **1** (= *locomoción*) aviation ▸ **aviación comercial** commercial aviation
2 (*Mil*) air force • **la ~ francesa** the French air force
AVIACO (SF ABR) (*Esp*) (= **Aviación y Comercio S.A.**) *airline*
aviado (ADJ) **1** • **estar ~** (*Arg*) to be well off, have all one needs
2 • **estar ~** (*en un lío*) to be in a mess • **¡~s estamos!** what a mess we're in!, we're in a right mess!
aviador(a)[1] (SM/F) **1** (*Aer*) (= *piloto*) pilot, airman; (= *tripulante*) crew member; (*Mil*) member of the air force
2 (*Méx**) phantom employee
aviador(a)[2] (SM/F) (*And, Caribe*) (= *financiador*) mining speculator, mining financier; (= *prestamista*) moneylender, loan shark*
aviar ▷ CONJUG 1c (VT) **1** (= *preparar*) to get ready, prepare; (= *ordenar*) to tidy up; (= *proveer*) to supply (**de** with)
2 (*LAm*) (= *prestar dinero a*) to advance money to
3 • **~ a algn** (= *dar prisa a*) to hurry sb up, gee sb up* • **¡vamos aviando!** let's get a move on!
(VPR) **aviarse** to get ready • **~se para hacer algo** to get ready to do sth
aviario (SM) aviary
aviatorio (ADJ) (*LAm*) • **accidente ~** air crash, plane crash
avícola (ADJ) poultry (*antes de s*) • **granja ~** poultry farm
avicultor(a) (SM/F) poultry farmer
avicultura (SF) poultry farming
ávidamente (ADV) (= *con entusiasmo*) avidly, eagerly; (= *con codicia*) greedily
avidez (SF) (= *entusiasmo*) avidity, eagerness (**de** for); (= *codicia*) greed, greediness (**de** for) • **con ~** (= *con entusiasmo*) avidly, eagerly; (= *con codicia*) greedily
ávido (ADJ) (= *entusiasta*) avid, eager (**de** for); (= *codicioso*) greedy (**de** for) • **~ de sangre** bloodthirsty
aviejarse ▷ CONJUG 1a (VPR) to age before one's time
avieso (ADJ) **1** (= *torcido*) distorted, crooked
2 (= *perverso*) perverse, wicked; (= *siniestro*) sinister; (= *rencoroso*) spiteful
(SM) (*And*) abortion
avifauna (SF) birds (*pl*), bird life
avilantarse ▷ CONJUG 1a (VPR) to be insolent
avilantez (SF) insolence
avilés/esa (ADJ) of/from Ávila
(SM/F) native/inhabitant of Ávila • **los avileses** the people of Ávila
avilesino/a (ADJ) of/from Avilés
(SM/F) native/inhabitant of Avilés • **los ~s** the people of Avilés
avillanado (ADJ) boorish, uncouth
avinagrado (ADJ) [*sabor*] sour, acid; [*individuo*] sour, jaundiced
avinagrar ▷ CONJUG 1a (VT) to sour
(VPR) **avinagrarse** [*individuo*] to be crotchety; [*vino etc*] to turn sour
Aviñón (SM) Avignon
avío (SM) **1** (= *prevención*) preparation, provision; [*de pastor*] provisions for a journey
2 (*LAm*) (*Agr*) loan
3 • **hacer su ~*** (= *enriquecerse*) to make one's pile*; (*iró*) (= *armarla*) to make a mess of things
4 • **¡al ~!** (= *¡en marcha!*) get cracking!, get on with it!
5 avíos (= *equipo*) gear (*sing*)
avión (SM) **1** (*Aer*) aeroplane, plane, aircraft, airplane (*EEUU*) • **por ~** (*Correos*) by airmail • **enviar artículos por ~** to send goods by plane • **ir en ~** to go by plane, go by air ▸ **avión a chorro** jet plane ▸ **avión ambulancia** air ambulance ▸ **avión a reacción** jet plane ▸ **avión cisterna** fire-fighting plane ▸ **avión de carga** freight plane, cargo plane ▸ **avión de caza** fighter, pursuit plane ▸ **avión de chorro** jet plane ▸ **avión de combate** fighter, pursuit plane ▸ **avión de despegue vertical** vertical take-off plane ▸ **avión de papel** paper dart ▸ **avión de pasajeros** passenger aircraft ▸ **avión de reacción** jet plane ▸ **avión de transporte** transport plane ▸ **avión espía** spy plane ▸ **avión sanitario** air ambulance
2 (*Orn*) martin
3 • **hacer el ~ a algn*** (= *hacer daño*) to do sb down, cause sb harm; (*esp And*) (= *estafar*) to cheat sb
4 (*CAm*) (= *juego*) hopscotch
avionazo (*esp Méx*) (SM) plane crash, accident to an aircraft
avioncito (SM) ▸ **avioncito de papel** paper dart
avionero (SM) (*And, Cono Sur*) airman
avioneta (SF) light aircraft
aviónica (SF) aviation, avionics (*sing*)
avionístico (ADJ) aeroplane (*antes de s*), flying (*antes de s*) • **miedo ~** fear of flying
avisadamente (ADV) sensibly, wisely
avisado (ADJ) sensible, wise • **mal ~** rash, ill-advised
avisador(a) (SM) (= *timbre*) electric bell; (*Culin*) timer ▸ **avisador de incendios** fire alarm
(SM/F) **1** (= *informante*) informant; (= *mensajero*) messenger; (= *denunciador*) informer
2 (*Cine, Teat*) programme seller
avisar ▷ CONJUG 1a (VT) **1** (= *informar*) to tell, notify (*frm*) • **¿por qué no me avisaste?** why didn't you tell me? • **avísale cuando acabes** tell him *o* let him know when you finish • **la policía ya ha avisado a los familiares** the police have now told *o* (*frm*) notified *o* (*frm*) informed the family • **me avisó (de) que no comería en casa** she told me she wouldn't be eating at home • **nos avisó (de) que se casaba** he told us he was getting married • **lo hizo sin ~** he did it without telling anyone • **se presentó en casa sin ~** he turned up at home without telling anyone *o* without warning • **me ~on con una semana de antelación** they gave me a week's notice
2 (= *llamar*) to call • **~ un taxi** to call a taxi • **~ al médico** to call the doctor, send for the doctor • **"avisamos grúa"** (*Esp*) "cars parked here will be towed away"
3 (= *advertir*) to warn • **te aviso (de) que te denunciaré si no pagas** I warn you I shall report you if you don't pay • **un dispositivo que avisa (de) que la línea está interceptada** a device that warns you that the line is bugged
aviso (SM) **1** (= *notificación*) notice • **recibimos un ~ por escrito** we received written notice *o* notice in writing • **"Aviso: cerrado el lunes"** "Notice: closed Mondays" • **hasta nuevo ~** until further notice • **sin previo ~** without warning *o* notice • **salvo ~ contrario** unless otherwise informed • **dar ~ a algn de algo** to notify *o* inform sb of sth • **mandar ~** to send word ▸ **aviso de bomba** bomb alert
2 (= *advertencia*) warning • **el bombardeo fue un ~ a los rebeldes** the bombing was a

warning to the rebels • **poner a algn sobre ~** to warn sb • **ya está usted sobre ~** you have been warned
3 (*Com, Econ*) demand note • **según (su) ~** as per order, as ordered ▸ **aviso de envío** dispatch note ▸ **aviso de mercancías** advice note
4 (*Inform*) prompt
5 (*esp LAm*) (*Com*) advertisement ▸ **aviso económico** classified advertisement ▸ **aviso mural** poster, wall poster ▸ **avisos clasificados** (*Cono Sur*), **avisos limitados** (*Col*) classified advertisements
avispa (SF) 1 (= *insecto*) wasp
2 (= *persona*) sharp person, clever person
avispado (ADJ) 1 (= *astuto*) sharp, clever; (*pey*) (= *taimado*) sly, wily
2 (*LAm*) (= *nervioso*) jumpy*, nervous
avispar ▸ CONJUG 1a (VT) [+ *caballo*] to spur on; (= *despabilar*) to prod
(VPR) **avisparse** (= *despabilarse*) to liven up; (= *preocuparse*) to fret, worry; (*LAm*) (= *alarmarse*) to become alarmed
avispero (SM) 1 (= *nido*) wasps' nest
2 (*Med*) carbuncle
3* (= *enredo*) hornet's nest, mess • **meterse en un ~** to get o.s. into a jam*
avispón (SM) hornet
avistamiento (SM) sighting
avistar ▸ CONJUG 1a (VT) to sight, catch sight of
(VPR) **avistarse** to have an interview (**con** with)
avitaminosis (SF INV) vitamin deficiency
avituallamiento (SM) provisioning, supplying
avituallar ▸ CONJUG 1a (VT) to provision, supply with food
(VPR) **avituallarse** to provision o.s.
avivado/a* (*Cono Sur*) (ADJ) forewarned, alerted
(SM/F) smart alec*, wise guy (*EEUU**)
avivar ▸ CONJUG 1a (VT) [+ *fuego*] to stoke, stoke up; [+ *color*] to brighten; [+ *dolor*] to intensify; [+ *pasión*] to excite, arouse; [+ *disputa*] to add fuel to; [+ *interés*] to stimulate; [+ *esfuerzo*] to revive; [+ *efecto*] to enhance, heighten; [+ *combatientes*] to urge on
(VPR) **avivarse** (= *cobrar vida*) to revive, take on new life; (= *animarse*) to cheer up, become brighter • **¡avívate!** look alive!, snap out of it!
avizor (ADJ) • **estar ojo ~** to be on the alert, be vigilant
(SM) watcher
avizorar ▸ CONJUG 1a (VT) to watch, spy on
avocastro (SM) (*Cono Sur*) = **abocastro**
avorazado (ADJ) (*Méx*) greedy, grasping
AVT (SF ABR) (= **Asociación de víctimas del terrorismo**) *organization which supports the victims of terrorism*
avutarda (SF) great bustard
axial (ADJ) axial
axila (SF) armpit
axiológico (ADJ) axiological
axioma (SM) axiom
axiomático (ADJ) axiomatic
axis (SM INV) axis
ay (EXCL) 1 (*dolor*) ow!, ouch!
2 (*pena*) oh!, oh dear! • **¡ay de mí!** whatever shall I do? • **¡ay del que lo haga!** woe betide the man who does it!
3 (*sorpresa*) oh!, goodness!
(SM) (= *gemido*) moan, groan; (= *suspiro*) sigh; (= *grito*) cry • **un ay desgarrador** a heartrending cry
aya (SF) governess
ayatolá (SM), **ayatollah** (SM) ayatollah
Ayax (SM) Ajax
ayer (ADV) yesterday • **repitieron el capítulo de ~** yesterday's episode was repeated • **~ por la mañana** yesterday morning • **antes de ~** the day before yesterday • **~ eran terroristas, hoy en día comparten el gobierno** yesterday they were terrorists, today they are part of the government • **~ mismo** (*Esp*) • **~ mismamente** *o* (*LAm*) **no más** only yesterday • **parece que fue ~** it seems like (only) yesterday • **no es (cosa) de ~** it's nothing new • MODISMO: • **no nací ~** I wasn't born yesterday
(SM) • **el ~** (*liter*) yesteryear (*liter*) • **las canciones del ~** the songs of yesteryear (*liter*) • **el Madrid del ~** the Madrid of yesteryear (*liter*), old Madrid
ayllu (SM) (*And*) Indian commune
aymara (ADJ), (SMF), **aymará** (ADJ), (SMF) Aymara
ayo (SM) tutor
ayote (SM) (*Méx, CAm*) (= *calabaza*) pumpkin; (*hum*) (= *cabeza*) nut‡, noggin (*EEUU*‡), bonce‡ • **dar ~s a algn** to jilt sb, give sb the elbow • **la fiesta fue un ~** (*Méx*) the party was a disaster
ayotoste (SM) armadillo
ayte. (ABR) (= **ayudante**) asst
Ayto (ABR) = **Ayuntamiento**
ayuda (SF) 1 (= *asistencia*) help, assistance (*más frm*) ▸ **ayuda a domicilio** home help, home helper (*EEUU*) ▸ **ayudas a la navegación** aids to navigation, navigational aids ▸ **ayuda compensatoria** ≈ income support, welfare (*EEUU*) ▸ **ayuda económica** economic aid ▸ **ayuda humanitaria** humanitarian aid ▸ **ayuda visual** visual aid ▸ **ayudas audiovisuales** audiovisual aids ▸ **ayudas familiares** family allowances
2 (*Med*) (= *enema*) enema; (*LAm*) (= *laxante*) laxative
(SM) (= *paje*) page ▸ **ayuda de cámara** valet
ayudado (SM) (*Taur*) *two-handed pass with the cape*
ayudador(a) (SM/F) helper
ayudanta (SF) helper, assistant
ayudante (SMF) (= *que ayuda*) helper, assistant; (*Mil*) adjutant; (*Téc*) technician; (*Golf*) caddie; (*Escol, Univ*) assistant ▸ **ayudante de dirección** (*Teat etc*) production assistant ▸ **ayudante de laboratorio** lab(oratory) assistant, lab(oratory) technician ▸ **ayudante del electricista** electrician's assistant, electrician's helper (*EEUU*) ▸ **ayudante de realización** (*TV*) production assistant ▸ **ayudante ejecutivo** executive assistant ▸ **ayudante técnico sanitario** Registered Nurse
ayudantía (SF) (= *cargo*) assistantship; (*Mil*) adjutancy; (*Téc*) post of technician
ayudar ▸ CONJUG 1a (VT) (= *asistir*) to help, assist, aid • **~ a algn a hacer algo** to help sb to do sth • **¿me puedes ~ con la limpieza esta tarde?** can you help me out with the cleaning this afternoon? • **me ayudó a bajar del autobús** he helped me off the bus • **me ayuda muchísimo** he's a great help to me, he helps me a lot
(VPR) **ayudarse** (*mutuamente*) to help each other; (= *valerse de*) to make use of, use • REFRÁN: • **ayúdate y Dios te ~á** God helps those who help themselves
ayudista (SMF) (*Cono Sur*) supporter
ayudita* (SF) small contribution
ayunar ▸ CONJUG 1a (VI) (= *no comer*) to fast • **~ de algo** (*fig*) (= *privarse*) to go without sth
ayunas (SFPL) • **salir en ~** to go out without any breakfast • **estar** *o* **quedarse en ~** (= *ser ignorante*) to be completely in the dark; (= *no caer*) to miss the point
ayuno (SM) fast, fasting • **guardar ~** to fast • **día de ~** fast day
(ADJ) 1 (*Rel etc*) fasting
2 (= *privado*) deprived • **estar ~ de algo** to know nothing about sth
ayuntamiento (SM) 1 (= *corporación*) district council, town council, city council
2 (= *Casa Consistorial*) town hall, city hall
3 (= *cópula*) sexual intercourse • **tener ~ con algn** to have intercourse with sb
ayuntar ▸ CONJUG 1a (VT) 1 (*Náut*) to splice
2 (*And*) (*Agr*) to yoke, yoke together
ayuya (SF) (*Cono Sur*) flat roll, scone
azabachado (ADJ) jet-black
azabache (SM) (*Min*) jet • **~s** jet trinkets
azacán/ana (SM/F) drudge, slave • **estar hecho un ~** to be worked to death
azacanarse ▸ CONJUG 1a (VPR) to drudge, slave away
azada (SF) hoe
azadón (SM) large hoe, mattock, pickax (*EEUU*)
azadonar ▸ CONJUG 1a (VT) to hoe
azafata (SF) 1 (*Aer*) air hostess, stewardess, flight attendant; (*TV*) hostess; (*Náut*) stewardess; (= *compañera*) escort (*supplied by escort agency*) ▸ **azafata de congresos** conference hostess ▸ **azafata de vuelo** air hostess, flight attendant
2 (*Cono Sur*) = **azafate**
3 (*Hist*) lady-in-waiting
azafate (SM) flat basket, tray
azafrán (SM) saffron
azafranado (ADJ) [*color*] saffron-coloured, saffron-colored (*EEUU*); [*sabor*] saffron-flavoured, saffron-flavored (*EEUU*)
azafranar ▸ CONJUG 1a (VT) (*Culin*) (= *dar color a*) to colour with saffron, color with saffron (*EEUU*); (= *sazonar*) to flavour with saffron, flavor with saffron (*EEUU*)
azagaya (SF) assegai, javelin
azahar (SM) orange blossom
azalea (SF) azalea
azar (SM) 1 (= *suerte*) chance, fate • **al ~** at

AYUDAR

Ayudar *se puede traducir por* **help, assist** *y* **aid.**

▸ *La manera más frecuente de traducir* **ayudar** *es por* **help.** *Si* **help** *va seguido de un verbo, este puede ir en infinitivo con o sin* **to:**
¿Puedes ayudarnos?
Can you help (us)?
Siempre le ayuda con la tarea
He always helps her with her homework
¿Me puedes ayudar a preparar la cena?
Can you help me (to) get dinner ready?

▸ **Ayudar** *se traduce por* **assist** *en un registro bastante más formal y se construye frecuentemente en la estructura* **to assist somebody with something:**
La comadrona ayudó al médico con el parto
The midwife assisted the doctor with the delivery

▸ **Ayudar** *se traduce por* **aid** *en inglés formal en el contexto de asesorar o prestar ayuda a un grupo de personas necesitadas:*
... los intentos de Estados Unidos de ayudar a los refugiados kurdos ...
... attempts by the United States to aid Kurdish refugees ...

Para otros usos y ejemplos ver la entrada.

random • **por ~** accidentally, by chance • **juego de ~** game of chance • **los ~es de la vida** life's ups and downs • **no es un ~ que ...** it is no mere accident that ..., it is not a matter of chance that ... • **decir al ~** to say to nobody in particular
2 (= *desgracia*) accident, piece of bad luck
azararse¹ ▸ CONJUG 1a (VPR) **1** (= *malograrse*) to go wrong, go awry
2 = **azorar**
azararse² ▸ CONJUG 1a (VPR) (= *ruborizarse*) to blush, redden
azarear ▸ CONJUG 1a (VT), (VPR) **azarearse** = azorar
azarosamente (ADV) (= *con riesgo*) hazardously; (= *con percances*) eventfully
azaroso (ADJ) **1** (= *arriesgado*) risky, hazardous; [*vida*] eventful
2 (= *malhadado*) unlucky
Azerbaiyán (SM) Azerbaijan
azerbaiyaní (ADJ), (SMF) Azerbaijani
azerbaiyano/a (ADJ), (SM/F) Azerbaijani
azerí (ADJ) Azeri
(SMF) (= *persona*) Azeri
(SM) (*Ling*) Azeri
ázimo (ADJ) unleavened
aznarismo (SM) *policies and following of José María Aznar - Spanish Prime Minister from 1996 to 2004*
aznarista (ADJ) *related to José María Aznar or his policies*, Aznar (*antes de s*); [*intelectual, círculos*] pro-Aznar
(SMF) Aznar supporter
-azo, -aza ▸ **Aspects of Word Formation in Spanish 2**
azocar ▸ CONJUG 1g (VT) (*Caribe*) to pack tightly
azófar (SM) brass
azogado (ADJ) restless, fidgety • **temblar como un ~** to shake like a leaf, tremble all over
(SM) silvering
azogar ▸ CONJUG 1h (VT) (= *cubrir con azogue*) to coat with quicksilver; [+ *espejo*] to silver
(VPR) **azogarse** to be restless, be fidgety
azogue (SM) mercury, quicksilver • **ser un ~** to be always on the go • **tener ~** to be restless, be fidgety
azolve (SM) (*Méx*) sediment, deposit
azonzado (ADJ) (*Cono Sur*) silly, stupid
azor (SM) goshawk
azora (SF) (*LAm*) = **azoramiento**
azorado (ADJ) **1** (= *alarmado*) alarmed, upset
2 (= *turbado*) embarrassed, flustered
3 (= *emocionado*) excited
azoramiento (SM) **1** (= *alarma*) alarm
2 (= *turbación*) embarrassment, fluster
3 (= *emoción*) excitement
azorar ▸ CONJUG 1a (VT) **1** (= *alarmar*) to alarm
2 (= *turbar*) to embarrass, fluster
3 (= *emocionar*) to excite; (= *animar*) to urge on, egg on
(VPR) **azorarse 1** (= *alarmarse*) to get alarmed, get rattled*
2 (= *sentirse violento*) to be embarrassed, get flustered
Azores (SFPL) Azores
azoro (SM) **1** (*esp LAm*) = **azoramiento**
2 (*CAm*) (= *fantasma*) ghost
azorrillarse ▸ CONJUG 1a (VPR) (*Méx*) to hide away, keep out of sight
azotacalles (SMF INV) idler, loafer
azotaina (SF) beating, spanking • **¡te voy a dar una ~!** I'm going to give you a good hiding!*
azotamiento (SM) whipping, flogging
azotar ▸ CONJUG 1a (VT) **1** (= *latigar*) to whip, flog; (= *zurrar*) to thrash, spank; (*Agr*) to beat; [*lluvia, olas*] to lash • **un viento huracanado azota la costa** a hurricane is lashing the coast
2 • MODISMO: • **~ las calles** to loaf around the streets
(VPR) **azotarse** (*Méx*) (= *darse aires*) to put on airs, fancy o.s.
azotazo (SM) [*de látigo*] stroke, lash; [*de mano*] spank
azote (SM) **1** (= *látigo*) whip, scourge
2 (= *golpe*) [*de látigo*] stroke, lash; [*de mano*] spanking • **ser condenado a 100 ~s** to be sentenced to 100 lashes ▸ **azotes y galeras** the same old stuff
3 (= *calamidad*) scourge • **Atila, el ~ de Dios** Attila, the Scourge of God
azotea (SF) **1** (*Arquit*) (= *terraza*) flat roof, terrace roof; (*And, Cono Sur*) (= *casa*) flat-roofed adobe house
2‡ (= *cabeza*) bonce‡, head • **estar mal de la ~** to be round the bend *o* twist‡, be off one's head
azotera (SF) (*LAm*) (= *acto*) beating, thrashing; (= *látigo*) cat-o'-nine-tails
AZT (SM ABR) (= **azidotimidina**) AZT
azteca (ADJ), (SMF) Aztec
azúcar (SM o SF) (*en LAm gen SF*) sugar
▸ **azúcar blanca/o** white sugar ▸ **azúcar blanquilla/o** white sugar ▸ **azúcar cande, azúcar candi** sugar candy, rock candy
▸ **azúcar de caña** cane sugar ▸ **azúcar de cortadillo** lump sugar ▸ **azúcar Demerara** demerara sugar, brown sugar ▸ **azúcar en polvo** (*Col*) icing sugar, confectioners' sugar (*EEUU*) ▸ **azúcar en terrón** lump sugar
▸ **azúcar extrafina/o, azúcar fina/o** caster sugar ▸ **azúcar flor** (*Chile*), **azúcar glas** (*Arg, Uru*), **azúcar impalpable** (*Arg*) icing sugar (*Brit*), confectioners' sugar (*EEUU*) ▸ **azúcar lustre** caster sugar ▸ **azúcar mascabada/o** cane sugar ▸ **azúcar morena/o, azúcar negra/o** brown sugar
azucarado (ADJ) sugary, sweet
azucarar ▸ CONJUG 1a (VT) **1** (= *agregar azúcar a*) to sugar, add sugar to; (= *bañar con azúcar*) to ice with sugar, coat with sugar
2 (*fig*) (= *suavizar*) to soften, mitigate; (= *endulzar*) to sweeten
azucarera (SF) sugar refinery
azucarería (SF) (*Caribe, Méx*) sugar shop
azucarero (ADJ) sugar (*antes de s*); [*zona*] sugar-producing, sugar-growing
(SM) sugar bowl
azucena (SF) white lily, Madonna lily
▸ **azucena rosa** belladonna lily ▸ **azucena tigrina** tiger lily
azud (SM), **azuda** (SF) (= *noria*) waterwheel; (= *presa*) dam, irrigation dam, mill dam
azuela (SF) adze
azufre (SM) (*Quím*) sulphur, sulfur (*EEUU*); (*Rel etc*) brimstone
azufroso (ADJ) sulphurous, sulfurous (*EEUU*)
azul (ADJ) blue • **sangre ~** noble blood, blue blood
(SM) (= *color*) blue; (= *grado*) blueness ▸ **azul celeste** sky blue ▸ **azul claro** light blue
▸ **azul de cobalto** cobalt blue ▸ **azul de mar** navy blue ▸ **azul de ultramar** ultramarine
▸ **azul eléctrico** electric blue ▸ **azul marino** navy blue ▸ **azul de Prusia** Prussian blue
▸ **azul pavo** peacock blue ▸ **azul turquesa** turquoise
azulado (ADJ) blue, bluish
azular ▸ CONJUG 1a (VT) to colour blue, color blue (*EEUU*), dye blue
(VPR) **azularse** to turn blue
azulear ▸ CONJUG 1a (VI) **1** (= *volverse azul*) to go blue, turn blue
2 (= *tirar a azul*) to be bluish; (= *mostrarse azul*) to show blue, look blue
azulejar ▸ CONJUG 1a (VT) to tile
azulejería (SF) **1** (= *azulejos*) tiling
2 (= *industria*) tile industry
azulejista (SMF) tiler
azulejo (SM) **1** (= *ladrillo vidriado*) glazed tile; (*en el suelo*) floor tile
2 (*Caribe*‡) (= *policía*) cop*
3 (*Méx*) (= *color*) bluish colour, bluish color (*EEUU*)
4 (*Méx*) (= *pez*) *sardine-like fish*
azulenco (ADJ) bluish
azulete (SM) blue (*for washing*)
azulgrana (ADJ INV) **1** [*color*] blue and scarlet
2 (*Dep*) of Barcelona Football Club
(SMPL INV) • **los Azulgrana** the Barcelona club, the Barcelona team
azulina (SF) cornflower
azulino (ADJ) bluish
azulón (ADJ), (SM) deep blue
azuloso (ADJ) (*LAm*) bluish
azumagarse ▸ CONJUG 1h (VPR) (*Cono Sur*) to rust, get rusty
azumbrado* (ADJ) tight*
azumbre (SM) *liquid measure (= 2.016 litres)*
azur (SM) azure
azurumbado (ADJ) (*CAm, Méx*) (= *tonto*) silly, stupid; (= *borracho*) drunk
azuzar ▸ CONJUG 1f (VT) **1** • **~ a los perros a algn** to set the dogs on sb, urge the dogs to attack sb
2 (*fig*) [+ *persona*] to egg on, urge on, incite; [+ *emoción*] to stir up, fan**agregador** (SM) (*tb* **agregador de noticias**) aggregator, news aggregator

Bb

B, b SF [be] (= *letra*) B, b • **se escribe con B de Barcelona** it's written with a B

B. ABR (*Rel*) = **Beato/a**

baba SF **1** (= *saliva*) [*de adulto*] spittle, saliva; [*de niño*] dribble; [*de perro*] slobber • **echar ~** to drool, slobber; [*niño*] to dribble • **mala ~*** (= *malhumor*) bad temper; (= *mal genio*) nasty character • MODISMO: • **se le caía la ~** he was thrilled to bits *o* pieces
2 (= *mucosidad*) (*en nariz*) mucus; [*de caracol*] slime, secretion
3 (*Col, Ven*) small crocodile

babador SM bib

babalao* SM (*Cuba*) quack

babasfrías SM INV (*And, Méx*) fool

babaza SF **1** (= *mucosidad*) [*de caracol*] slime; [*de nariz*] mucus
2 (*Zool*) slug

babear ▹ CONJUG 1a VI **1** (= *echar saliva*) [*adulto*] to slobber, drool; [*niño*] to dribble
2 (= *quedarse admirado*) to drool (**por** over)
VPR **babearse 1** (*Méx**) • **~se por algo** to yearn for sth, drool at the thought of sth
2 (*Cono Sur*) to feel flattered, glow with satisfaction

Babel SM Babel • **Torre de ~** Tower of Babel

babel SM o SF bedlam

babeo SM [*de adulto*] slobbering, drooling; [*de niño*] dribbling; [*de perro*] slobbering

babero SM **1** [*de bebé*] (*para el pecho*) bib; (*más grande*) apron
2 (*para el colegio*) smock

babi* SM **1** [*de bebé*] bib
2 (*para el colegio*) smock

Babia SF • MODISMO: • **estar en ~** to be daydreaming, be in the clouds

babieca ADJ simple-minded, stupid
SMF dolt

babilla SF (*Vet*) stifle

Babilonia SF (= *ciudad*) Babylon; (= *reino*) Babylonia

babilonia SF bedlam; ▹ **babilonio**

babilónico ADJ Babylonian

babilonio/a ADJ, SM/F Babylonian; ▹ **babilonia**

bable SM *Asturian dialect*

babor SM port, port side • **a ~** to port, on the port side • **poner el timón a ~** • **virar a ~** to turn to port, port the helm • **¡tierra a ~!** land to port! • **de ~** port (*antes de s*)

babosa SF slug; ▹ **baboso**

babosada* SF **1** (*CAm, Méx*) (= *disparate*) piece of stupidity • **¡~s!** rubbish! • **decir ~s** to talk nonsense *o* rubbish
2 (*LAm*) (= *persona inútil*) dead loss*, useless thing*

babosear ▹ CONJUG 1a VT **1** [*perro*] to slobber over
2 (= *halagar*) to drool over
3 (*Méx**) (= *manosear*) to manhandle
4 (*CAm, Méx‡*) (= *tratar de bobo*) to take for a fool, treat like a fool
5 (= *tratar superficialmente*) • **muchos han baboseado este problema** lots of people have taken a superficial look at this problem
6 (*CAm*) to insult
VI **1** (= *echar saliva*) [*adulto*] to slobber, drool; [*niño*] to dribble; [*perro*] to slobber
2 (*Méx*) (= *holgazanear*) to mess about

baboseo SM **1** (= *saliva*) [*de adulto*] drooling, slobbering; [*de niño*] dribbling; [*de perro*] slobbering
2 (= *halago excesivo*) infatuation, drooling

baboso/a ADJ **1** (= *con baba*) [*adulto*] drooling, slobbering; [*niño*] dribbling; [*perro*] slobbering; [*caracol*] slimy
2 [*persona*] (= *sentimental*) slushy; (= *sensiblero*) mushy, foolishly sentimental; (= *adulador*) fawning, snivelling; (= *sucio*) dirty
3 (*LAm*) (= *tonto*) silly
4 (*CAm**) rotten*, caddish*
SM/F (*Méx, CAm*) fool, idiot; (*pey*) drip*; ▹ **babosa**

babucha SF **1** (= *zapatilla*) slipper • MODISMO: • **llevar algo a ~** (*Cono Sur*) to carry sth on one's back
2 (= *prenda*) (*Caribe*) child's bodice; (*LAm*) loose blouse, smock
3 babuchas (*Caribe*) rompers; (*Méx*) high-heeled boots

babuino SM baboon

babujal SM (*Caribe*) witch, sorcerer

baby SM **1** (*LAm*) (= *bebé*) baby; (*Aut*) small car, mini • **~ fútbol** table football
2 = **babi**

baca SF **1** (= *portaequipajes*) luggage rack, roof rack
2 (= *techo*) [*de autocar*] top; (*contra la lluvia*) rainproof cover

bacal SM (*Méx*) corncob

bacalada‡ SF sweetener*, backhander*, payola (*EEUU*)

bacaladero ADJ cod (*antes de s*) • **flota bacaladera** cod fleet

bacaladilla SF blue whiting

bacalao SM **1** (= *pez*) cod, codfish • MODISMOS: • **cortar el ~*** to be the boss, have the final say, run the show • **¡te conozco, ~!*** I've rumbled you!* • **ser un ~*** to be as thin as a rake
2 (*Cono Sur*) miser, scrooge*
3 (*Esp***) cunt**

bacán* ADJ posh*, classy*
SM (= *rico*) wealthy man; (= *protector*) sugar daddy*; (= *señorito*) playboy; (= *elegante*) toff*, dude (*EEUU*)

bacanal ADJ bacchanalian
SFPL **bacanales** orgy (*sing*)

bacanalear ▹ CONJUG 1a VI (*CAm*) to have a wild time

bacane SM (*Caribe*) driving licence, driver's license (*EEUU*)

bacanería* SF (*Cono Sur*) (= *elegancia*) sharp dressing, nattiness; (= *ostentación*) vulgar display, ostentation

bacano* ADJ (*Col*) great*

bacante SF **1** (*Mit*) bacchante
2 (= *mujer ebria*) drunken and noisy woman

bacará SM, **bacarrá** SM baccarat

bacelador* SM (*Caribe*) con man

bacelar ▹ CONJUG 1a VT (*Caribe*) to con, trick

bacenica SF (*LAm*) = **bacinica**

baceta SF (*Naipes*) pack, stock

bacha SF (*Caribe*) spree, merry outing

bachata SF (*Caribe*) spree

bachatear ▹ CONJUG 1a VI (*Caribe*) to go on a spree, go out for a good time

bachatero SM (*Caribe*) reveller, carouser

bache SM **1** (*Aut*) hole, pothole ▸ **bache de aire** (*Aer*) air pocket
2 (= *mal momento*) bad patch, rough patch • **atravesar un ~** to go through a bad *o* rough patch • **remontar el** *o* **salir del ~** to get through the bad *o* rough patch, pull through • **salvar el ~** to get the worst over, be over the worst ▸ **bache económico** slump, depression

bacheado ADJ [*carretera*] pot-holed

bachicha SF **1** (*Cono Sur*) (*pey*) (= *italiano*) dago**, wop**, guinea (*EEUU***)
2 (*Méx*) (= *restos*) leftovers (*pl*); (= *colilla*) cigarette end, cigar stub; [*de bebida*] dregs (*pl*)
3 (*Méx*) (*Econ*) nest egg, secret hoard

bachiche SM (*And*) (*pey*) = **bachicha**

bachiller ADJ †† garrulous, talkative
SMF (*Escol*) secondary school graduate, high school graduate (*EEUU*)
SM **1** (*Escol*†) ▹ **bachillerato**
2†† (*hum*) (= *charlatán*) windbag*

bachillera†† SF (= *erudita*) bluestocking; (= *gárrula*) chatterbox*; (= *astuta*) cunning woman, scheming woman

bachillerato SM **1** (*Escol*) *higher secondary-education course* ▸ **bachillerato comercial** certificate in business studies ▸ **bachillerato del magisterio** certificate for students going on to do teacher training ▸ **bachillerato elemental** lower examination, ≈ GCSE ▸ **bachillerato laboral** certificate in agricultural *o* technical studies ▸ **bachillerato superior** higher certificate, ≈ A level; ▹ **ESO**
2 (*Univ, Hist*) bachelor's degree

bachillerear†† ▹ CONJUG 1a VI to talk a lot, prattle away

bachillería†† SF **1** (= *cotorreo*) talk, prattle
2 (= *disparate*) piece of nonsense

bacía SF (= *recipiente*) (*gen*) basin; [*de afeitar*] barber's bowl, shaving bowl

bacilar ADJ bacillary

bacilarse ▹ CONJUG 1a VPR (*And*) to have a good time

bacilo SM bacillus, germ

bacilón* ADJ brilliant, great
SM (*And*) fun, good time; ▸ **vacilón**

bacín SM **1** (= *recipiente*) (*para orinar*) chamber pot; [*de mendigo*] beggar's bowl
2 (= *cepo*) poor box
3 (= *persona miserable*) wretch, cur

bacinete SM (*LAm*) lavatory pan

bacinica (SF) small chamber pot
backstage [bakes'teis] (SM) (= *lugar*) backstage area; (= *gente*) (backstage) crew
Baco (SM) Bacchus
bacón (SM) bacon
bacteria (SF) bacterium, germ; **bacterias** bacteria, germs ▸ **bacteria asesina** killer bacteria (*pl*)
bacterial (ADJ), **bacteriano** (ADJ) bacterial
bactericida (ADJ) antibacterial, bactericidal, germicidal
(SM) bactericide, germicide
bactérico (ADJ) bacterial
bacteriología (SF) bacteriology
bacteriológico (ADJ) bacteriological
bacteriólogo/a (SM/F) bacteriologist
bacteriosis (SF INV) bacteriosis
báculo (SM) **1** (= *bastón*) stick, staff ▸ **báculo pastoral** crozier, bishop's staff
2 (= *apoyo*) prop, support • **ser el ~ de la vejez de algn** to be sb's comfort in old age
badajada (SF), **badajazo** (SM) **1** [*de campana*] stroke, chime
2 (= *cotilleo*) piece of gossip
3 (= *tontería*) rubbish, garbage
badajear ▸ CONJUG 1a (VI) to swing to and fro
badajo (SM) **1** [*de campana*] clapper
2* (= *charlatán*) chatterbox
badajocense, **badajoceño/a** (ADJ) of/from Badajoz
(SM/F) native/inhabitant of Badajoz • **los ~s** the people of Badajoz
badana (SF) sheepskin • MODISMO: • **sobarle** *o* **zurrarle la ~ a algn*** to give sb a good hiding*
badaza (SF) (*Caribe*) strap (*for standing passenger*)
badén (SM) (*Aut*) (= *bache*) dip; (*para agua*) gutter
badil (SM), **badila** (SF) fire shovel
badilejo (SM) (*And*) trowel, builder's trowel
bádminton (SM) badminton
badulaque (SM) **1** (= *idiota*) idiot, nincompoop
2 (*Cono Sur**) rogue
badulaquear ▸ CONJUG 1a (VI) **1** (= *ser idiota*) to be an idiot, act like an idiot
2 (*Cono Sur**) to be a rogue, be dishonest
bafle (SM), **baffle** (SM) speaker, loudspeaker
bagaje (SM) **1** (= *conocimientos*) experience, background ▸ **bagaje cultural** cultural background
2 (*Mil*) (= *equipaje*) baggage, equipment
3 (= *mula*) pack mule
bagatela (SF) **1** (= *objeto*) trinket, knick-knack
2 (= *nimiedad*) trifle • **una ~** a mere trifle • **son ~s** they're not worth worrying about
3 (*Mús*) bagatelle
bagayero/a* (SM/F) (*Cono Sur*) smuggler
bagayo/a‡ (*Cono Sur*) (SM/F) (= *persona inútil*) useless lump, berk‡
(SM) (= *lío*) bundle, tramp's bundle; (= *carga*) heavy *o* awkward burden; (= *cosas robadas*) loot; (= *contrabando*) contraband goods (*pl*)
(SF) (= *mujer fea*) old hag*
bagazo (SM) **1** (= *residuo*) chaff, husks (*pl*); [*del azúcar*] sugar cane pulp, sugar cane mash
2 (*LAm*) (= *persona inútil*) dead loss*
Bagdad (SM) Baghdad
bagre (ADJ) **1** (*LAm*) vulgar, coarse
2 (*CAm*) clever, sharp
(SMF) (*LAm‡*) (= *persona astuta*) sly person; (= *fea*) ugly mug‡
(SM) (*LAm*) (= *pez*) catfish • MODISMO: • **pica el ~** (*Cono Sur**) I'm starving
bagrero (ADJ) (*And*) fond of ugly women
bagual (*Cono Sur*) (ADJ) **1** [*caballo*] wild, untamed
2 (= *huraño*) unsociable
(SM) **1** (= *caballo salvaje*) wild horse, untamed horse • MODISMO: • **ganar los ~es** (*Hist*) to escape, get to safety
2 (= *huraño*) unsociable person
baguala (SF) *type of folk music originating from north-east Argentina*
bagualada (SF) (*Cono Sur*) **1** [*de caballos*] herd of wild horses
2 (= *torpeza*) stupid thing, stupid thing to do
bagualón (ADJ) (*Cono Sur*) half-tamed
baguío (SM) hurricane, typhoon
bah (EXCL) (*indicando desdén*) bah!, pooh!, phooey (*EEUU**); (*indicando incredulidad*) never!
Bahamas (SFPL) • **las islas ~** the Bahamas
bahareque (SM) = **bajareque**
baharí (SM) sparrowhawk
bahía (SF) bay
baho (SM) (*CAm*) (*Culin*) *dish of meat and yucca*
bahorrina (SF) **1** (= *suciedad*) dirt, filth
2 (= *gentuza*) riffraff, scum
bahreiní (ADJ), (SMF) Bahreini
bailable (ADJ) • **música ~** music that you can dance to
(SM)† dance number
bailada (SF) (*LAm*) dance
bailadero (SM) (= *sala*) dance hall; (= *pista*) dance floor
bailador(a) (ADJ) dancing
(SM/F) dancer
bailaor(a) (SM/F) flamenco dancer
bailar ▸ CONJUG 1a (VI) **1** (= *danzar*) to dance • **sacar a algn a ~** to ask sb to dance, ask sb for a dance • **le bailaban los ojos de alegría** her eyes sparkled with happiness • MODISMOS: • **este es otro que bien baila** here's another one (of the same kind) • **¡que me quiten lo bailado** *o* **bailao!*** nobody can take away the good times I've had! • **~ con la más fea**: • **siempre me toca ~ con la más fea** I always draw the short straw • **~ al son que tocan**: • **los políticos bailan al son que le tocan los militares** the politicians toe the line given them by the military
2 [*peonza*] to spin (round)
3 [*mueble*] to be wobbly, be unsteady
4* [*ropa, calzado*] to be miles too big* • **he adelgazado y me bailan los pantalones** I've lost weight and my trousers are miles too big for me*
(VT) **1** (= *danzar*) to dance • **~ flamenco** to dance flamenco • **~ el vals** to waltz, dance the waltz • **~ un vals** to dance a waltz
2 [+ *peonza*] to spin
3 (*LAm**) (= *timar*) • **le ~on la herencia** they cheated her out of her inheritance
(VPR) **bailarse** • **~se a algn** (*Méx**) to thrash sb
bailarín/ina (ADJ) dancing
(SM/F) dancer; (*tb* **bailarín/ina de ballet**) (= *hombre*) ballet dancer; (= *mujer*) ballet dancer, ballerina • **primera bailarina** prima ballerina ▸ **bailarina del vientre** belly dancer ▸ **bailarín/ina de claqué** tap dancer
bailata‡ (SF) = **baile**
baile (SM) **1** (= *acción*) dancing • **lo mío no es el ~** dancing is not my thing*; ▸ **academia, pareja, pista**
2 (= *pieza*) dance • **¿me concede este ~?** (*frm*) may I have this dance? (*frm*) ▸ **baile agarrado** slow dance
3 (= *arte*) dance • **la sardana, el ~ típico de Cataluña** the sardana, the traditional dance of Catalonia ▸ **baile clásico** ballet ▸ **baile de salón** ballroom dancing ▸ **baile flamenco** flamenco dancing ▸ **baile folklórico**, **baile popular** folk dancing
4 (= *fiesta*) dance; (*formal*) ball • **me han invitado a un ~** I have been invited to a dance ▸ **baile de candil** (*LAm*) village dance ▸ **baile de contribución** (*CAm, Caribe*) public dance ▸ **baile de disfraces** fancy-dress ball ▸ **baile de etiqueta** (formal) ball ▸ **baile de fantasía**, **baile de máscaras** (*LAm*) masked ball ▸ **baile de medio pelo** (*LAm*) village dance
5 (*Med*) ▸ **baile de San Vito** St Vitus' dance
6 (*Ftbl*) • **hacer el ~*** *to dribble the ball aimlessly, playing for time*
7 (= *confusión*) • **hubo un ~ de cifras antes del anuncio de la victoria** the figures went first one way and then the other before the final victory was announced
bailecito (SM) (*LAm*) folk dance
bailón (ADJ) • **es muy ~** he loves dancing
bailongo (ADJ) dance (*antes de s*) • **música bailonga** music for dancing, music you can dance to
bailotear ▸ CONJUG 1a (VI) to dance about, jump about
bailoteo* (SM) dancing • **estuvieron toda la noche de ~** they were out all night dancing
baivel (SM) bevel
baja (SF) **1** (= *descenso*) fall, drop • **se produjo una ~ continuada de las temperaturas** there was a continued fall *o* drop in temperatures • **una ~ repentina de los beneficios** a sudden fall *o* drop in profits • **sigue la ~ en la cotización del euro** the euro continues to fall • **el gobierno anunció una ~ de los tipos de interés** the government announced a cut in interest rates • **a la ~** [*evolución, tendencia*] downward • **se ha producido una orientación del mercado a la ~** the market has started on a downward trend • **el precio del algodón sigue a la ~** the price of cotton continues to fall • **la patronal está presionando los salarios a la ~** employers are forcing wages down • **abrir a la ~** (*Bolsa*) to open down • **cerrar a la ~** (*Bolsa*) to close down • **la Bolsa cerró a la ~ en el día de ayer** the Stock Exchange closed down *o* was down at the close of trading yesterday • **corregir algo a la ~** to adjust sth downwards • **cotizarse a la ~** (*Bolsa*) to trade low • **estar en ~** to be in decline • **su reputación estuvo en ~ en los últimos meses** his reputation was on the *o* in decline over the last few months • **la Bolsa está en ~** there is a downward trend in the Stock Exchange, the Stock Exchange is in decline
2 (= *cese*) (*en organización, suscripción, trabajo*) • **hubo tantas ~s que el club tuvo que cerrar** so many people left that the club had to close down • **la ~ de dos de los países miembros** the departure of two member countries • **el nuevo estilo de la revista ha causado numerosas ~s** the new style of the magazine has led many people to cancel their subscription • **dar de ~** [+ *socio*] to expel; [+ *abogado, médico*] to strike off; [+ *militar*] to discharge; [+ *empleado*] to dismiss, fire; [+ *empresa, sociedad*] to dissolve; [+ *coche*] to take out of circulation; [+ *avión, tren*] to decommission; [+ *teléfono, luz*] to have disconnected • **la dieron de ~ del club por no pagar la suscripción** her membership of the club was cancelled because she had failed to pay her subscription • **la dirección decidió dar de ~ al nuevo profesor** the board decided to dismiss the new teacher • **hemos dado de ~ la luz** we had the electricity disconnected • **darse de ~** [*de club, institución, partido*] to leave; [*de revista, periódico*] to cancel one's subscription • **numerosos suscriptores han decidido darse de ~ de la revista** many readers have decided to cancel their

subscription to the magazine • **nos dimos de ~ del teléfono** we had the telephone disconnected • **pedir la ~** to hand in one's resignation ▸ **baja incentivada** voluntary redundancy ▸ **baja por incentivo** voluntary redundancy ▸ **baja por jubilación** retirement ▸ **baja por jubilación anticipada** early retirement ▸ **baja voluntaria** (*por dimisión*) voluntary redundancy; (*por jubilación*) early retirement
3 (= *ausencia laboral*) • **dar de ~**: • **se le dará de ~ a partir del día de la operación** she will be on sick leave from the day of the operation • **estar de ~** to be on sick leave, be off sick • **pedir la ~** to ask for *o* apply for sick leave ▸ **baja laboral** leave ▸ **baja maternal** maternity leave ▸ **baja médica** sick leave ▸ **baja permanente** indefinite sick leave ▸ **baja por enfermedad** sick leave • **el número de ~s por enfermedad** the number of people taking sick leave ▸ **baja por maternidad** maternity leave ▸ **baja por paternidad** paternity leave ▸ **baja retribuida** paid leave
4 (*Dep*) (*por descalificación*) suspension; (*por lesión*) injury • **el equipo sufrió dos ~s por sendas tarjetas rojas** the team lost two players for red card offences • **el partido registró varias ~s en ambos equipos** there were several injuries for both teams during the match
5 (*Esp*) (*Med*) (= *certificado*) medical certificate, sick note*
6 (*Mil*) (= *víctima*) casualty • **hasta la fecha no ha habido ninguna ~** there have been no casualties to date

bajá SM pasha

bajacaliforniano/a ADJ of/from Baja California
SM/F native/inhabitant of Baja California • **los ~s** the people of Baja California

bajada SF **1** (= *camino*) • **la ~ hasta el río** (= *sendero*) the path down to the river; (= *carretera*) the road down to the river • **una ~ muy difícil para un esquiador sin experiencia** a very difficult slope for an inexperienced skier
2 (= *acción*) descent • **en la ~ alcanzamos los 150km/h** on the way down *o* descent we got up to 150km/h • **salimos antes de la ~ del telón** we left the theatre before the curtain went down • MODISMO: • **ser una ~ de pantalones** (*LAm**) to be a shameful action ▸ **bajada de aguas** gutter ▸ **bajada de bandera** minimum (taxi) fare
3 (= *disminución*) fall, drop • **una drástica ~ de las temperaturas** a dramatic fall *o* drop in temperature • **sufrió una ~ de azúcar** his sugar level fell *o* dropped ▸ **bajada de tensión** fall *o* drop in blood pressure
4 (*Esp‡*) [*de drogas*] • **cuando le da la ~ del éxtasis** when he's coming down from ecstasy

bajamar SF low tide, low water

bajante SF o SM drainpipe, downspout (*EEUU*)

bajar ▸ CONJUG 1a VT **1** (= *llevar abajo*) to take down; (= *traer abajo*) to bring down • **¿has bajado la basura?** have you taken the rubbish down? • **¿me bajas el abrigo?, hace frío aquí fuera** could you bring my coat down? it's cold out here • **te he bajado la maleta del armario** I got your suitcase down from the wardrobe • **la bajó del caballo** he helped her down off the horse • **¿me baja a la Plaza Mayor?** (*en taxi*) could you take me to the Plaza Mayor?
2 (= *mover hacia abajo*) [+ *bandera, ventanilla*] to lower; [+ *persiana*] to put down, lower • **~ el telón** to lower the curtain • **dimos un paseo para ~ la comida** we had a walk to help us digest our meal
3 (*con partes del cuerpo*) [+ *brazos*] to drop, lower • **bajó la vista** *o* **los ojos** he looked down • **bajó la cabeza** she bowed *o* lowered her head
4 (= *reducir*) [+ *precio*] to lower, put down; [+ *fiebre, tensión, voz*] to lower • **los comercios han bajado los precios** businesses have put their prices down *o* lowered their prices
5 [+ *radio, televisión, gas*] to turn down • **baja la radio que no oigo nada** turn the radio down, I can't hear a thing • **¡baja la voz, que no estoy sordo!** keep your voice down, I'm not deaf!
6 • **~ la escalera** (*visto desde arriba*) to go down the stairs; (*visto desde abajo*) to come down the stairs
7 (= *perder*) to lose • **bajé seis kilos** I lost six kilos
8 (*Inform*) to download
9 (= *humillar*) to humble, humiliate
10 (*Caribe‡*) (= *pagar*) to cough up*, fork out*
11 (*And‡*) (= *matar*) to do in‡
VI **1** (= *descender*) (*visto desde arriba*) to go down; (*visto desde abajo*) to come down • **baja y ayúdame** come down and help me • **¡ahora bajo!** I'll be right down!
2 (= *apearse*) (*de autobús, avión, tren, moto, bici, caballo*) to get off; (*de coche*) to get out • **~ de** [+ *autobús, avión, tren, moto, bici, caballo*] to get off; [+ *coche*] to get out of
3 (= *reducirse*) [*temperatura, fiebre, tensión arterial*] to go down, fall, drop; [*hinchazón, calidad*] to go down • **han bajado los precios** prices have fallen *o* come *o* gone down • **el dólar bajó frente al euro** the dollar fell against the euro • **los coches han bajado de precio** cars have come down in price • **el partido bajó de cinco diputados a dos** the party went down from five deputies to two
4 • **~ de** (= *perder*): • **el avión empezó a ~ de altura** the plane started to lose height • **el ejercicio te hará ~ de peso** exercise will help you to lose weight
5 • **no ~ de** (= *no ser menos de*): • **el regalo no ~á de 15 euros** you won't pay less than 15 euros for the present • **la venta no ha bajado nunca de mil** sales have never fallen below a thousand • **los termómetros no han bajado de 30 grados** temperatures haven't dropped below 30 degrees
6 [*regla*] to start • **me acaba de ~ la regla** my period has just started
VPR **bajarse 1** (*de árbol, escalera, silla*) to get down (**de** from) • **¡bájate de ahí!** get down from there!
2 (*de autobús, tren, avión, moto, bici*) to get off; (*de coche*) to get out • **~se de** [+ *autobús, tren, avión, moto, bici*] to get off; [+ *coche*] to get out of • **se bajó del autobús antes que yo** he got off the bus before me
3 • **~se algo de Internet** to download sth from the internet
4 • **~se del vicio*** to kick the habit*
5 (= *inclinarse*) to bend down • **~se a recoger algo** to bend down to pick sth up
6 (= *rebajarse*) to lower o.s. • **~se a hacer algo vil** to lower o.s. to do sth mean
7 (*Cono Sur*) (= *alojarse*) to stay, put up • **~se en** to stay at; ▹ **pantalón**

bajareque SM **1** (*LAm*) (= *tapia*) mud wall
2 (*Caribe*) (= *cabaña*) hovel, shack
3 (*CAm*) (= *llovizna*) fine drizzle
4 (*CAm*) (= *caña*) bamboo

bajativo SM (*Cono Sur*) digestif

bajel SM (*liter*) (= *barco*) vessel, ship

bajera SF **1** (*Arquit*) lower ground floor, basement
2 (*And, CAm, Caribe*) (= *hojas*) *lower leaves of the tobacco plant*; (= *tabaco*) rough tobacco, inferior tobacco
3 (*And, CAm, Caribe*) (= *persona sin importancia*) insignificant person, nobody
4 (*Cono Sur*) horse blanket

bajero ADJ **1** (= *de abajo*) lower, under- • **falda bajera** underskirt • **sábana bajera** bottom sheet
2 (*CAm*) (*en cuesta, bajada*) downhill, descending

bajetón ADJ (*LAm*) short, small

bajeza SF **1** (= *maldad*) vileness, baseness
2 (= *acto malvado*) mean deed, vile deed

bajial SM (*LAm*) (= *terreno bajo*) lowland; (= *terreno inundado*) flood plain

bajini*, **bajinis*** • **por lo ~(s)** ADV [*decir*] very quietly, in an undertone

bajío SM **1** (*Náut*) shoal, sandbank
2 (*LAm*) lowland • **el Bajío** (*Méx*) *the fertile plateau of northern Mexico*
3 bajíos (*Méx*) *flat arable land on a high plateau*

bajista ADJ downward • **tendencia ~** downward *o* bearish trend
SMF (*Mús*) bassist
SM (*Econ*) bear

bajo ADJ **1** (= *de poca altura*) [*objeto*] low; [*persona*] short; [*parte*] lower, bottom; [*tierra*] low-lying; [*agua*] shallow • **una silla muy baja** a very low chair • **mi hermano es muy ~** my brother is very short • **en la parte baja de la ciudad** in the lower part of the town • **planta baja** ground floor, first floor (*EEUU*) • **los ~s fondos** the underworld (*sing*)
2 (= *inclinado*) • **contestó con la cabeza baja** she answered with her head bowed • **con los ojos ~s** with downcast eyes
3 (= *reducido, inferior*) [*precios, temperaturas, frecuencia*] low; [*calidad*] low, poor • **de baja calidad** low-quality, poor-quality • **de ~ contenido en grasas** low-fat • **~ en calorías** low-calorie • **la temporada baja** the low season • **estar ~ de algo**: • **estar ~ de ánimo** *o*

BAJAR

De vehículos

▹ **Bajar(se) de** *un vehículo privado o de un taxi se traduce por* **get out of**, *mientras que* **bajar(se) de** *un vehículo público (tren, autobús, avión etc) se traduce por* **get off**:
Bajó del coche y nos saludó
She got out of the car and said hello
No baje del tren en marcha
Don't get off the train while it is still moving

▹ *Debe emplearse* **get off** *cuando nos referimos a bicicletas, motos y animales de montura:*
Se bajó de la bicicleta
He got off his bicycle

Otros verbos de movimiento

▹ **Bajar la escalera/la cuesta** *etc, por regla general, se suele traducir por* **come down** *o por* **go down**, *según la dirección del movimiento (hacia o en sentido contrario del hablante), pero* **come** *y* **go** *se pueden substituir por otros verbos de movimiento si la oración española especifica la forma en que se baja mediante el uso de adverbios o construcciones adverbiales:*
Bajó las escaleras deprisa y corriendo
She rushed down the stairs
Bajó la cuesta tranquilamente
He ambled down the hill

Para otros usos y ejemplos ver la entrada.

de moral to be in low spirits • **estar ~ de forma (física)** to be unfit, be out of shape
4 [*sonido*] faint, soft; [*voz, tono*] low • **hablar en voz baja** to speak quietly *o* in a low voice • **decir algo por lo ~** to say sth under one's breath • **hacer algo por lo ~** to do sth secretly
5 [*etapa*] • **en la baja Edad Media** in the late Middle Ages • **~ latín** Low Latin
6 [*oro, plata*] *with a high level of impurities*
7 [*color*] (= *apagado*) dull; (= *pálido*) pale
8 (= *humilde*) low, humble; [*clase*] lower; [*condición*] lowly; [*barrio*] poor; [*tarea*] menial
9 (*pey*) (= *vulgar*) common, ordinary; (= *mezquino*) base, mean
10 • **por lo ~** (= *a lo menos*) at (the) least
SM **1** (*Cos*) [*de vestido*] hem; [*de pantalones*] turn-up, cuff (*EEUU*)
2 [*de edificio*] (= *piso*) ground floor, first floor (*EEUU*) • **vivo en un ~** I live on the ground floor ▸ **bajo comercial** ground-floor *o* (*EEUU*) first-floor business premises
3 (*Mús*) (= *instrumento*) bass; (= *voz*) bass; (= *guitarrista*) bass (guitar) player, bassist • **Elena toca el ~ en un grupo** Elena plays bass (guitar) in a group ▸ **bajo profundo** basso profundo
4 bajos [*de edificio*] ground floor (*sing*), first floor (*sing*) (*EEUU*); [*de coche*] underside; (*euf*) [*del cuerpo*] private parts
5 (= *hondonada*) hollow
6 (*Náut*) = **bajío**
ADV [*volar*] low; [*tocar, cantar*] quietly, softly • **el avión volaba muy ~** the plane was flying very low • **hablar ~** (= *en voz baja*) to speak quietly, speak softly; (= *tener una voz suave*) to be softly spoken, be soft spoken • **¡más ~, por favor!** quieter, please!
PREP **1** (= *debajo de*) under • **Juan llevaba un libro ~ el brazo** Juan was carrying a book under his arm • **~ cero** below zero • **estamos a dos grados ~ cero** it's two degrees below zero • **~ la lluvia** in the rain • **~ tierra** underground • **toda la familia está ya ~ tierra** the whole family are dead and buried
2 (= *dependiente de, sometido a*) under • **~ Napoleón** under Napoleon • **~ los efectos de la droga** under the influence of drugs • **~ el título de ...** under the title of ... • **~ mi punto de vista** from my point of view • **~ el reinado de** in the reign of • **está ~ la tutela de su tío** her uncle is her legal guardian; ▹ **fianza, juramento, llave**

bajo-barítono SM bass-baritone

bajón SM **1** (= *descenso*) [*de presión, temperatura*] fall, drop; [*de salud*] decline, worsening; (*Com, Econ*) sharp fall • **dar** *o* **pegar un ~** [*persona, salud*] to go downhill; [*precios*] to fall away sharply; [*mercado*] to slump ▸ **bajón de moral** slump in morale
2 (*Mús*) bassoon
3‡ withdrawal symptoms (*pl*) (*after drug use*)

bajoneado* ADJ (*Arg, Uru*) down

bajorrelieve SM bas-relief

bajuno ADJ [*truco*] base, underhand

bajura SF **1** • **pesca de ~** shallow-water fishing, coastal fishing
2 (*de poca altura*) lowness
3 (*de tamaño pequeño*) smallness, small size
4 (*Caribe*) (*Geog*) lowland

bakaladero/a* ADJ rave (*antes de s*)
SM/F raver

bakalao* ADJ INV rave (*antes de s*)
SM rave, rave music • **la ruta del ~** *weekend-long tour of a series of rave parties*

bala SF **1** (= *proyectil*) bullet • **una ~ perdida lo alcanzó en el hombro** he was hit in the shoulder by a stray bullet • **sonaron dos disparos de ~** two gunshots rang out • **disparar una ~** to fire a bullet • **a prueba de ~s** bullet-proof • **un chaleco a prueba de ~s** a bullet-proof vest • MODISMOS: • **como una ~** like a shot • **entró como una ~** he came shooting in, he came in like a shot • **el tren pasó como una ~** the train shot *o* flew past • **comió como una ~ y se fue** he bolted his food down and left • **no le entran ~s** (*Chile*) he's as hard as nails* • **ni a ~** (*Méx, Col**) no way* • **estar** *o* **quedar con la ~ pasada** (*Chile*) to be seething • **ser una ~** (*Caribe**) to be a pain in the neck* • **tirar con ~** not to pull one's punches ▸ **bala de cañón** cannonball ▸ **bala de fogueo** blank (cartridge) ▸ **bala de goma** plastic bullet, rubber bullet ▸ **bala de salva** blank round ▸ **bala fría** spent bullet ▸ **bala trazadora** tracer bullet
2 (= *fardo*) bale • **una ~ de heno** a bale of hay
3 (*Tip*) ▸ **bala de entintar** ink(ing) ball
4 (*LAm*) (*Dep*) shot • **lanzamiento de ~** shot put
SMF* (= *juerguista*) • MODISMO: • **ser un ~ perdida** to be a good-for-nothing

balaca SF **1** (*LAm*) (= *baladronada*) boast, brag
2 (*And*) (= *boato*) show, pomp

balacada SF (*Cono Sur*) = **balaca**

balacear ▹ CONJUG 1a VT (*CAm, Méx*) to shoot, shoot at

balacera SF (*CAm, Méx*) (= *tiroteo*) shooting, exchange of shots; (= *balas*) hail of bullets; (= *enfrentamiento armado*) shoot-out

balada SF (*Mús*) ballad, ballade; (*Literat*) ballad

baladí ADJ trivial, paltry

baladista SMF (= *compositor*) writer of ballads; (= *cantante*) ballad singer

baladrar ▹ CONJUG 1a VI to scream, howl

baladre SM oleander, rosebay

baladrero ADJ loud, noisy

baladro SM scream, howl

baladrón/ona ADJ boastful
SM/F braggart, bully

baladronada SF (= *dicho*) boast, brag; (= *hecho*) piece of bravado

baladronear ▹ CONJUG 1a VI (= *decir*) to boast, brag; (= *hacer*) to indulge in bravado

bálago SM **1** (= *paja*) straw, long straw
2 (= *jabón*) soapsuds (*pl*), lather

balance SM **1** (*Econ*) [*de una cuenta*] balance; (= *documento*) balance (sheet); (*Com*) [*de existencias*] stocktaking, inventory (*EEUU*) • **hacer ~** [*de una cuenta*] to draw up a balance; [*de existencias*] to take stock, do the stocktaking ▸ **balance consolidado** consolidated balance sheet ▸ **balance de comprobación** trial balance ▸ **balance de pagos** balance of payments ▸ **balance de situación** balance sheet
2 (= *resultado*) • **el ~ de víctimas mortales en el accidente** the death toll in the accident, the number of dead in the accident • **el equipo tiene un ~ de dos victorias y tres derrotas** so far the team have had two wins and three defeats • **un abogado con un buen ~ de casos ganados** a lawyer who has won a good proportion of his cases
3 (= *evaluación*) [*de hecho, situación*] assessment, evaluation • **los puntos negros en el ~ del año académico** the black spots in the assessment *o* evaluation of the academic year • **hizo ~ de los cinco años de su gobierno** he assessed *o* evaluated *o* took stock of the five years of his government
4 (= *balanceo*) to-and-fro motion; [*de un barco*] roll, rolling
5 (= *indecisión*) vacillation
6 (*Caribe*) (= *mecedora*) rocking chair

balanceado SM (*Boxeo*) swing

balancear ▹ CONJUG 1a VT to balance
VPR **balancearse 1** (= *oscilar*) [*persona*] (*al andar*) to move to and fro; (*en mecedora, columpio*) to rock; [*péndulo*] to swing; [*barco, avión*] to roll
2 (= *vacilar*) to hesitate, waver, vacillate (*frm*)

balanceo SM **1** (= *vaivén*) (*al andar*) to-and-fro motion; (*al mecerse*) rocking; [*de barco, avión*] roll, rolling
2 (*LAm*) (*Aut*) (*tb* **balanceo de ruedas**) wheel balancing

balancín SM **1** (= *barra*) [*de balanza*] balance beam; [*de equilibrista*] balancing pole; (*para llevar cargas*) yoke
2 (*para mecerse*) (= *columpio*) seesaw, teeter-totter (*EEUU*); (= *mecedora*) rocking chair; (= *juguete*) child's rocking toy
3 (*Mec*) (*en motor*) rocker, rocker arm; [*de carro*] swingletree; [*de máquina*] beam
4 (*Náut*) outrigger

balandra SF yacht, sloop

balandrán SM cassock

balandrismo SM yachting

balandrista SMF yachtsman/yachtswoman

balandro SM yacht, sloop

balanza SF **1** (= *instrumento*) scales (*pl*); (*Quím*) balance • MODISMO: • **estar en la ~** to be in the balance ▸ **balanza de cocina** kitchen scales (*pl*) ▸ **balanza de cruz** grocer's scales (*pl*) ▸ **balanza de laboratorio** precision scales (*pl*) ▸ **balanza de muelle** spring balance ▸ **balanza de precisión** precision scales (*pl*) ▸ **balanza romana** steelyard
2 (*Com, Pol*) balance ▸ **balanza comercial, balanza de pagos** balance of payments ▸ **balanza de poder, balanza política** balance of power ▸ **balanza por cuenta corriente** balance on current account
3 (*frm*) (= *sensatez*) judgment

balaquear ▹ CONJUG 1a VI to boast

balar ▹ CONJUG 1a VI to bleat, baa

balasto[1] SM (*Ferro*) sleeper, tie (*EEUU*)

balasto[2] SM (*Cono Sur, Méx*) (*gen*) ballast; (*Téc*) aggregate

balastro SM = **balasto[2]**

balata SF (*LAm*) (*Aut*) brake lining

balaustrada SF balustrade

balaustre SM baluster

balay SM (*LAm*) wicker basket

balazo SM (= *tiro*) shot; (= *herida*) bullet wound • **matar a algn de un ~** to shoot sb dead

balboa SF *Panamanian currency unit*

balbucear ▹ CONJUG 1a VT, VI [*adulto*] to stammer, stutter; [*niño*] to babble

balbuceo SM [*de adulto*] stammering, stuttering; [*de niño*] babbling

balbuciente ADJ [*persona, voz*] stammering, stuttering; [*niño*] babbling

balbucir ▹ CONJUG 3f VT, VI (*se usan únicamente las formas que tienen i en la desinencia*) = **balbucear**

Balcanes SMPL • **los ~** the Balkans • **los montes ~** the Balkan Mountains • **la península de los ~** the Balkan Peninsula

balcánico ADJ Balkan

balcanización SF Balkanization

balcarrias SFPL, **balcarrotas** SFPL (*And*) sideburns

balcón SM **1** (= *terraza pequeña*) balcony
2 (= *mirador*) vantage point

balconada SF row of balconies

balconeador(a) SM/F (*Cono Sur*) onlooker, observer

balconear ▹ CONJUG 1a VT (*Cono Sur*) to watch closely (*from a balcony*); (*en juego*) to sneak a look at
VI (*CAm*) [*amantes*] to talk at the window

balconero SM cat burglar

balconing [bal'konin] SM balconing, *jumping from a balcony into the pool* • **hacer ~** to do balconing

balda SF shelf

baldada SF (*Cono Sur*) bucketful

baldado/a PP *de* baldar
ADJ **1** (= *lisiado*) crippled

2* (= *agotado*) • **estar ~** to be knackered*
SM/F cripple, disabled person
baldaquín SM, **baldaquino** SM canopy
baldar ▸ CONJUG 1a VT **1** (= *lisiar*) to cripple
2* (= *agotar*) to shatter
3 (*Naipes*) to trump
balde¹ SM (= *cubo*) bucket, pail ▸ **balde de la basura** (*LAm*) trash can
balde² SM **1** • **de ~** (= *gratis*) (for) free, for nothing • **obtener algo de ~** to get sth (for) free, get sth for nothing • **vender algo medio de ~** to sell sth for a song
2 • **estar de ~** (= *ser superfluo*) to be unwanted; (= *estorbar*) to be in the way
3 • **en ~** in vain • **los años no pasan en ~** the years don't go by in vain • **por lo menos el viaje no ha sido en ~** at least the journey wasn't in vain • **¡ni en ~!** (*LAm*) no way!*, not on your life!
4 • **¡no de ~!** (*CAm*) goodness!, I never noticed!
baldear ▸ CONJUG 1a VT **1** (= *limpiar*) (*con cubos de agua*) to wash (down), swill with water; (*con manguera*) to hose down
2 (*Náut*) to bale out, bail out (EEUU)
baldeo SM **1** (= *limpieza*) (*con cubos de agua*) washing-down; (*con manguera*) hosing down
2‡ (= *navaja*) chiv‡, knife
baldío ADJ **1** (= *sin cultivos*) [*campo*] fallow, uncultivated; [*terreno*] waste
2 (= *inútil*) vain, useless
3 (= *ocioso*) lazy, idle
SM (*Agr*) (= *campo sin cultivos*) uncultivated land, fallow land; (= *solar*) wasteland
baldón SM (= *afrenta*) affront, insult; (= *deshonra*) blot, stain
baldonar ▸ CONJUG 1a VT (= *insultar*) to insult; (= *deshonrar*) to blot, disgrace
baldosa SF **1** (*para el suelo*) floor tile
2 (*LAm*) (= *lápida*) tombstone
baldosado SM (= *suelo*) (*en casa*) tiled floor, tiling; (*en el exterior*) paving
baldosar ▸ CONJUG 1a VT [+ *suelo*] to tile; [+ *camino*] to pave (*with flagstones*)
baldoseta SF small tile
baldosín SM tile
balduque SM red tape
baleado/a SM/F (*CAm, Méx*) shooting victim, person who has been shot
balear¹ ▸ CONJUG 1a (*CAm, Méx*) VT (= *disparar contra*) to shoot, shoot at; (= *matar*) to shoot down, shoot dead • **morir baleado** to be shot dead
VPR **balearse** (*esp LAm*) to exchange shots, shoot at each other
balear² ADJ Balearic
SMF native/inhabitant of the Balearic Isles • **los ~es** the people of the Balearic Islands
Baleares SFPL (*tb* **islas Baleares**) Balearics, Balearic Islands
baleárico ADJ Balearic
baleo SM **1** (*CAm, Méx*) (= *tiroteo*) shooting
2 (*Méx*) (= *abanico*) fan
balero SM **1** (*LAm*) (= *juguete*) cup-and-ball toy
2 (*Méx*) (*Mec*) ball bearing
3 (*Cono Sur‡*) head, nut‡, noggin (EEUU‡)
balido SM bleat, baa
balín SM pellet; **balines** buckshot (*sing*)
balinera SF (*And*) ball bearing, ball bearings (*pl*)
balística SF ballistics (*sing*)
balístico ADJ ballistic
balita SF **1** (= *balín*) pellet
2 (*Cono Sur*) (= *canica*) marble
baliza SF **1** (= *boya*) (*Náut*) buoy, marker; (*Aer*) beacon, marker
2 balizas (*LAm*) (*Aut*) sidelights, parking lights
balizaje SM, **balizamiento** SM ▸ **balizaje de pista** (*Aer*) runway lighting, runway beacons (*pl*)
balizar ▸ CONJUG 1f VT (*Náut*) to mark with buoys; (*Aer*) to light o mark with beacons
ballena SF **1** (*Zool*) (= *animal*) whale; (= *hueso*) whalebone • **parece una ~*** she's like a beached whale* ▸ **ballena azul** blue whale
2 (*Cos*) [*de corsé*] bone, stay
ballenato SM whale calf
ballenear ▸ CONJUG 1a VI to whale, hunt whales
ballenera SF whaler, whaling ship
ballenero ADJ whaling • **industria ballenera** whaling industry
SM **1** (= *pescador*) whaler
2 (= *barco*) whaler, whaling ship
ballesta SF **1** (*Hist*) crossbow
2 (*Mec*) spring • **las ~s** the springs, the suspension (*sing*)
ballestero SM (*Hist*) crossbowman
ballestrinque SM clove hitch
ballet [ba'le] SM (PL: **ballets** [ba'les]) (= *disciplina, espectáculo*) ballet; (= *grupo de bailarines*) troupe of dancers, dance troupe ▸ **ballet acuático** synchronized swimming
balletístico ADJ ballet (*antes de s*)
balneario ADJ • **estación balnearia** spa
SM **1** (*Med*) spa, health resort
2 (*LAm*) seaside resort
balneoterapia SF balneotherapy
balompédico ADJ soccer (*antes de s*), football (*antes de s*)
balompié SM soccer, football
balón SM **1** (*Dep*) ball • MODISMOS: • **achicar balones*** • **echar balones fuera*** to dodge the issue ▸ **balón de boxeo** boxing ball, punchball ▸ **balón de playa** beach ball ▸ **balón de reglamento** regulation ball ▸ **balón suelto** loose ball
2 (= *recipiente*) (*Quím*) bag (*for gas*); (*Meteo*) balloon; (*Arg*) (= *vaso*) balloon glass; (*And, Cono Sur*) (= *bombona*) drum, canister ▸ **balón de oxígeno** oxygen cylinder • **la noticia fue un ~ de oxígeno para la economía** the news gave the economy a real boost
3 (*Com*) bale
balonazo SM • **me dio un ~** he thumped me with the ball
baloncestista SMF basketball player
baloncestístico ADJ basketball (*antes de s*)
baloncesto SM basketball
balonmanear ▸ CONJUG 1a VI (*Dep*) to handle, handle the ball
balonmanista SMF handball player
balonmano SM handball
balonvolea SM volleyball
balota SF (*Perú*) ballot
balotaje SM (*Méx*) (= *votación*) balloting, voting; (= *recuento*) counting of votes
balotar ▸ CONJUG 1a VI (*Perú*) to ballot, vote
balsa¹ SF **1** (*Náut*) (= *embarcación*) raft ▸ **balsa de salvamento, balsa salvavidas** life raft ▸ **balsa neumática** rubber dinghy
2 (*Bot*) balsa, balsa wood
balsa² SF **1** (= *charca*) pool, pond • **el pueblo es una ~ de aceite** the village is as quiet as the grave
2 (*Méx*) (= *pantano*) swamp, marshy place
balsadera SF, **balsadero** SM ferry, ferry station
balsámico ADJ **1** (*de bálsamo*) balmy
2 (= *relajante*) soothing
bálsamo SM **1** (= *sustancia*) balsam, balm
2 (= *consuelo*) balm, comfort
3 (*Cono Sur*) [*de pelo*] hair conditioner
balsar SM (*And, Caribe*) overgrown marshy place
balsear ▸ CONJUG 1a VT **1** [+ *río*] to cross by ferry, cross on a raft
2 [+ *personas, mercancías*] to ferry across
balsero/a SM/F **1** (= *conductor de balsa*) ferryman/ferrywoman
2 balseros boat people (*especially Cuban, seeking refuge in the USA*)
balsón¹ SM (*Méx*) (= *pantano*) swamp, bog; (= *agua estancada*) stagnant pool
balsón² ADJ (*And*) fat, flabby
balsoso ADJ (*And*) soft, spongy
Baltasar SM Balthazar; (*Biblia*) Belshazzar
báltico ADJ Baltic • **los estados ~s** the Baltic states • **el mar Báltico** the Baltic, the Baltic Sea
baluarte SM bastion
balumba SF **1** (= *masa*) (great) bulk, mass
2 (= *montón*) pile, heap
3 (*LAm*) (= *alboroto*) noise, uproar
balumbo SM bulky thing, cumbersome object
balumoso ADJ (*LAm*) bulky, cumbersome
baluquero SM (*Econ*) forger
balurdo ADJ (*LAm*) flashy
SM (*Cono Sur**) crooked deal*
bamba¹ SMF (*Caribe*) black man/black woman
bamba² SF **1** (*Esp*) (= *zapatilla*) plimsoll, sneaker (EEUU)
2 (*CAm, Ven*) (= *moneda*) silver coin
3 (*And*) (*Bot*) bole, swelling (*on tree trunk*)
4 (*And*) (= *gordura*) fat, flabbiness
bamba³† SF (*Esp*) fuzz‡, police
bambalear ▸ CONJUG 1a VI = **bambolear**
bambalina SF (*Teat*) drop, drop scene • **entre ~s** behind the scenes
bambalúa SM (*LAm*) clumsy fellow, lout
bambarria* SMF idiot, fool
bamboleante ADJ **1** (= *inestable*) [*persona, mesa*] wobbly; [*paso*] unsteady
2 [*pantalones*] baggy
bambolear ▸ CONJUG 1a VI, VPR **bambolearse** (*al andar*) to sway; [*péndulo, lámpara*] to swing, sway; [*silla, mesa*] to wobble; [*tren*] to sway
bamboleo SM [*de péndulo, lámpara*] swinging, swaying; [*de silla, mesa*] wobbling, unsteadiness; [*de tren*] rolling
bambolla* SF (= *ostentación*) show, ostentation; (= *farsa*) sham
bambollero* ADJ showy, flashy
bambú SM bamboo
bambudal SM (*And*) bamboo grove
banal ADJ (= *poco importante*) [*comentario, tema*] banal; [*persona*] ordinary, commonplace
banalidad SF **1** (= *cualidad*) [*de comentario, tema*] banality; [*de persona*] ordinariness
2 banalidades small talk (*sing*), trivialities • **intercambiar ~es con algn** to swap small talk with sb, exchange trivialities with sb
banalizar ▸ CONJUG 1f VT to trivialize
banana SF (*esp LAm*) (= *fruta*) banana; (= *árbol*) banana tree
bananal SM (*LAm*), **bananera** SF (*LAm*) banana plantation
bananero ADJ **1** (*LAm*) (= *de bananas*) banana (*antes de s*) • **compañía bananera** banana company • **plantación bananera** banana plantation
2 (*Pol*) third-world (*antes de s*), backward • **república bananera** banana republic
3* vulgar, coarse
SM banana tree
banano SM **1** (= *árbol*) banana tree
2 (*LAm*) (= *fruta*) banana
banas SFPL (*Méx*) (*Rel*) banns
banasta SF large basket, hamper
banasto SM large round basket
banca SF **1** (*Com, Econ*) banking • **horas de ~** banking hours • **la Banca** the banking community, the banks (*pl*) ▸ **banca**

comercial commercial banking ▸ banca electrónica e-banking ▸ banca industrial merchant banking, investment banking ▸ banca online, banca por Internet online banking ▸ banca telefónica telephone banking
2 (en juegos) bank • hacer saltar la ~ to break the bank • tener la ~ to be banker, hold the bank
3 (= puesto) stand, stall
4 (LAm) (= asiento) bench
5 (Cono Sur) (= influencia) pull, influence • tener (gran) ~ to have (lots of) pull o influence

bancada SF 1 (= banco) stone bench
2 (Mec) bed, bedplate
3 (Náut) thwart, (oarsman's) seat ▸ bancada corrediza [de remo] sliding seat

bancal SM 1 (Agr) (= terraza) terrace; (= terreno cultivado) patch, plot
2 (Mec) runner, bench cover

bancar ▹ CONJUG 1g (Cono Sur) VT 1 (= pagar) to pay for
2 (= aguantar) to put up with
VPR bancarse • ~se algo/a algn to put up with sth/sb

bancario/a ADJ bank (antes de s), banking • giro ~ bank draft
SM/F bank clerk, bank employee

bancarrota SF 1 (Econ) bankruptcy • declararse en o hacer ~ to go bankrupt
2 (= fracaso) failure

bancazo SM (Méx) bank robbery

banco SM 1 (= asiento) (al aire libre) bench, seat; (en iglesia) pew; [de carpintero] bench ▸ banco azul (Pol) ministerial benches (pl) ▸ banco de abdominales sit-up bench ▸ banco de pruebas (lit) test bed; (fig) testing ground
2 (Com, Econ) bank ▸ banco central central bank ▸ banco comercial commercial bank ▸ banco de ahorros savings bank ▸ banco de crédito credit bank ▸ banco de inversiones investment bank ▸ banco de liquidación clearing house ▸ banco ejidal (Méx) cooperative bank ▸ banco emisor issuing bank ▸ banco en casa home banking ▸ banco fiduciario trust company ▸ banco mercantil merchant bank ▸ Banco Mundial World Bank ▸ banco por acciones joint-stock bank
3 (= reserva) [de información, órganos] bank ▸ banco de alimentos food bank ▸ banco de datos data bank ▸ banco de esperma sperm bank ▸ banco de memoria memory bank ▸ banco de sangre blood bank
4 (Geog) (en el mar) bank, shoal; (= estrato) stratum, layer; (And) (= suelo aluvial) deposit (of alluvial soil); (Caribe) (= tierra elevada) raised ground ▸ banco de arena sandbank ▸ banco de hielo ice field, ice floe ▸ banco de niebla fog bank ▸ banco de nieve snowdrift
5 [de peces] shoal, school

banda SF 1 (= grupo) [de música] band; [de delincuentes, amigos] gang; [de guerrilleros] band; [de partidarios] party, group; [de aves] flock • negociaciones a tres ~s three-party talks, trilateral negotiations • MODISMO: • cerrarse en ~ to stand firm, be adamant ▸ banda armada armed gang ▸ banda juvenil youth gang, street gang ▸ banda terrorista terrorist group
2 (= cinta) (en la ropa) band, strip; [de gala] sash ▸ banda gástrica (Med) gastric band ▸ banda magnética magnetic strip ▸ banda transportadora conveyor belt
3 (= franja) [de tierra] strip, ribbon; [de carretera, pista de atletismo] lane ▸ banda ancha broadband ▸ banda de frecuencia band, waveband ▸ la banda de Gaza the Gaza Strip ▸ banda de rodaje, banda de rodamiento (Aut) tread ▸ banda de sonido sound track ▸ la Banda Oriental (esp Cono Sur) Uruguay ▸ banda salarial wage scale ▸ banda sonora [de película] soundtrack; (en carretera) rumble strip
4 (= lado) [de río] side, bank; [de monte] side, edge; [de barco] side • de la ~ de acá on this side • dar un barco a la ~ to careen a ship • irse a la ~ to list • MODISMO: • coger a algn por ~: • ¡como te coja por ~! I'll get even with you!
5 (Dep) sideline, touchline • fuera de ~ out of play, in touch • sacar de ~ to take a throw-in, throw the ball in ▸ línea de banda sideline, touchline
6 (Billar) cushion

bandada SF 1 (Zool) [de aves] flock; [de peces] shoal
2 (LAm) = banda

bandazo SM 1 (= sacudida) (al andar) lurch, jolt; (Náut) heavy roll; (LAm) (Aer) air pocket, sudden drop • dar ~s: • el coche iba dando ~s the car swerved from side to side • caminaba dando ~s he stumbled along, he reeled from side to side
2 (= cambio repentino) marked shift

bandear ▹ CONJUG 1a VT 1 (CAm) (= perseguir) to pursue, chase; (= pretender) to court
2 (CAm) (= herir) to wound severely; (Cono Sur) (con comentario) to hurt
3 (Cono Sur) (= cruzar) to cross, go right across
VPR bandearse 1 (= ir de un lado a otro) to move to and fro; (Méx) (Náut) to move to the other side of a boat
2 (Cono Sur) (Pol) to change parties
3 (Méx) (= vacilar) to vacillate; (= cambiar de dirección) to go one way and then another
4 (Esp*) (= arreglárselas) to shift for o.s., get by on one's own

bandeja SF 1 (para llevar a la mesa, en nevera) tray • MODISMO: • poner o servir algo en ~ (de plata) a algn to hand sth to sb on a plate • te lo han puesto en ~ they've made it very easy for you ▸ bandeja de alimentación de papel (Inform) paper-feed tray ▸ bandeja de entrada in-tray ▸ bandeja de quesos cheeseboard ▸ bandeja de salida out-tray ▸ bandeja para horno oven tray
2 (Cono Sur) (en carretera) central reservation, median strip (EEUU)

bandera SF 1 [de país, ciudad] flag; [de regimiento] colours, colors (pl) (EEUU) • la ~ está a media asta the flag is (flying) at half mast • arriar la ~ to lower o strike the colours • izar la ~ to raise o hoist the flag • jurar ~ to swear allegiance to the flag • MODISMO: • estar hasta la ~* to be packed out ▸ bandera a cuadros, bandera ajedrezada chequered flag, checkered flag (EEUU) ▸ Bandera Azul Blue Flag ▸ bandera blanca white flag ▸ bandera de conveniencia flag of convenience ▸ bandera de esquina corner flag ▸ bandera de la paz white flag ▸ bandera de parlamento (Hist) flag of truce, white flag ▸ bandera de popa ensign ▸ bandera de proa jack ▸ bandera negra, bandera pirata Jolly Roger, skull and crossbones ▸ bandera roja red flag ▸ la bandera roja y gualda the Spanish flag
2 (= idea) banner • bajo la ~ de la renovación under the banner of change and renewal
3 [de taxi] • bajar la ~ to pick up a fare
4 • MODISMO: • de ~ (Esp†) fantastic • se ha comprado un coche de ~ she's bought a fantastic car • es una mujer de ~ she's one hell of a woman*
5 (Inform) marker, flag

banderazo SM • el ~ de llegada the chequered flag, the checkered flag (EEUU) • el ~ de salida the starting signal • dar el ~ de salida to signal the start, give the starting signal

bandería SF (= bando) faction; (= parcialidad) bias, partiality

banderilla SF 1 (Taur) banderilla • MODISMOS: • clavar ~s a algn to goad sb • poner un par de ~s a algn to taunt sb, provoke sb ▸ banderilla de fuego banderilla with attached firecracker
2 (Culin) savoury appetizer, savory appetizer (EEUU)
3 (LAm) scrounging

banderillear ▹ CONJUG 1a VT (Taur) to stick the banderillas into the neck of the bull

banderillero SM (Taur) banderillero, bullfighter who uses the banderillas

banderín SM (para adornar) small flag, pennant; (Ferro) signal flag ▸ banderín de enganche recruiting centre, recruiting post ▸ banderín de esquina corner flag

banderita SF (= bandera pequeña) little flag; [de caridad] flag (sold for charity) • día de la ~ flag day

banderizo ADJ 1 (= faccioso) factional, factionalist
2 (= alterado) fiery, excitable

banderola SF 1 (= bandera pequeña) banderole; (Mil) pennant ▸ banderola de esquina corner flag
2 (Cono Sur) (= travesaño) transom

bandidaje SM, bandidismo SM banditry

bandido SM 1 (= delincuente) bandit, outlaw
2* • ¡bandido! you rogue!, you beast!

bando SM 1 (= edicto) edict, proclamation
2 bandos (Rel) banns
3 (= facción) (Pol) faction, party; (Dep) side • uno del otro ~* one of them* • pasarse al otro ~ to change sides

bandola SF 1 (Mús) mandolin
2 (And) (= capa) bullfighter's cape
3 (Caribe) (= fuete) knotted whip

bandolera SF bandoleer • llevar algo en ~ to wear sth across one's chest; ▹ bandolero

bandolerismo SM brigandage, banditry

bandolero/a SM/F bandit
SM (Hist) highwayman; ▹ bandolera

bandolina SF mandolin

bandoneón SM (Cono Sur) large accordion

bandullo‡ SM belly, guts* (pl) • llenarse el ~ to stuff o.s.*

bandurria SF bandurria (lute-type instrument)

Banesto SM ABR = Banco Español de Crédito

bangaña SF (LAm), bangaño SM (LAm)
1 (Bot) calabash, gourd, squash (EEUU)
2 (= vasija) vessel made from a gourd

Bangladesh SM Bangladesh

bangladesí ADJ, SMF Bangladeshi

banjo SM banjo

banner ['baner] SM (PL: banners) (Internet) banner ad

banquear ▹ CONJUG 1a VT 1 (Aer) to bank
2 (LAm) to level, flatten out

banqueo SM 1 terraces (pl), terracing
2 (Aer) bank, banking

banquero/a SM/F banker

banqueta SF 1 (= taburete) stool; (= banquillo) low bench; (Aut) bench seat ▸ banqueta de piano piano stool
2 (CAm, Méx) (= acera) pavement, sidewalk (EEUU)

banquetazo* SM spread*, blow-out*

banquete SM banquet, feast ▸ banquete anual annual dinner ▸ banquete de boda(s) wedding reception ▸ banquete de gala state banquet

banquetear ▹ CONJUG 1a VI to banquet, feast

banquillo SM (= *asiento*) bench; (*Dep*) bench, team bench; (*Jur*) dock • **el portero tuvo que quedarse en el ~** the goalkeeper had to stay *o* remain on the bench ▸ **banquillo de los acusados** dock
banquina SF (*Arg, Uru*) hard shoulder, berm (*EEUU*)
banquisa SF ice field, ice floe
banquito SM (*Arg*) stool
bantam SF **1** (*tb* **gallina de bantam**) bantam
2 (*LAm*) (= *persona*) small restless person
bántam SM (*esp LAm*) (*Dep*) bantamweight
bantú ADJ, SMF Bantu
banyo SM (*LAm*) banjo
bañada SF (*LAm*) **1** (= *baño*) (*en bañera*) bath; (*en mar, río*) swim, dip
2 [*de pintura*] coat
bañadera SF **1** (*LAm*) bathtub, bath
2 (*Arg*) open-top bus
bañado SM **1** (*LAm*) (= *pantano*) swamp, marshland
2 (*And*) (= *charco*) rain pool
3 (*Téc*) bath
bañador(a) SM/F bather, swimmer
SM **1** (= *prenda*) [*de mujer*] bathing costume, swimsuit, bathing suit; [*de hombre*] (swimming) trunks (*pl*)
2 (*Téc*) tub, trough
bañar ▸ CONJUG 1a VT **1** • **~ a algn** to bath sb, bathe sb (*EEUU*), give sb a bath • **bañé al bebé esta mañana** I bathed the baby this morning, I gave the baby a bath this morning
2 (*Culin*) • **una galleta bañada en coñac** a biscuit dipped *o* soaked in brandy • **he bañado el pastel de** *o* **con chocolate** I've covered the cake with chocolate icing, I've iced the cake with chocolate
3 (= *dar una capa de*) to plate • **esta pulsera está bañada en oro** this bracelet is gold-plated
4 (= *cubrir*) • **bañado en sangre/sudor** [*persona*] bathed *o* drenched in blood/sweat; [*ropa*] drenched in blood/sweat • **tenía la cara bañada en lágrimas** her face was bathed in *o* wet with tears
5 [*mar, lago*] to wash (*liter*) • **el Mediterráneo baña las costas catalanas** the Catalan coast is washed by the Mediterranean • **la capital está bañada por el Guadalquivir** the Guadalquivir runs through the capital
6 [*luz, sol*] to flood, bathe • **el sol bañaba de luz su cuarto** the sun flooded his room with light, the sun bathed his room in light
VPR **bañarse 1** (*en bañera*) to have a bath, take a bath; (*en mar, piscina*) to swim • **siempre me baño por la mañana** I always have *o* take a bath in the morning • **en verano vamos a ~nos al río** in the summer we go swimming in the river • **"prohibido bañarse"** "no bathing"
2 • **¡anda a ~te!** (*Cono Sur**) get lost!*, go to hell!‡
bañata* SM (*Esp*) swimsuit, bathing costume
bañera SF bath, bathtub ▸ **bañera de hidromasaje** whirlpool bath
bañero/a SM/F (*Cono Sur*) lifeguard
bañista SMF **1** (*en mar, río*) bather
2 (*Med*) (*en balneario*) patient
baño SM **1** (= *bañera*) bath, bathtub • **cuarto de ~** bathroom; (= *aseo*) toilet, bathroom (*esp EEUU*)
2 (= *acción*) (*en bañera*) bath; (*en el mar, piscina*) swim • **darse** *o* **tomar un ~** (*en bañera*) to have *o* take a bath; (*en mar, piscina*) to have a swim, go for a swim • **playas aptas para el ~** beaches suitable for bathing ▸ **baño de asiento** hip bath ▸ **baño de burbujas** foam bath, bubble bath ▸ **baño de ducha** showerbath ▸ **baño de espuma** foam bath, bubble bath ▸ **baño de fuego** baptism of fire ▸ **baño de masas, baño de multitudes** walkabout • **darse un ~ de masas** *o* **multitudes** to go on a walkabout, mingle with the crowd ▸ **baño de pies** foot bath ▸ **baño de sangre** bloodbath ▸ **baño de sol** • **darse** *o* **tomar un ~ de sol** to sunbathe ▸ **baño de vapor** steam bath ▸ **baño ocular** eyebath ▸ **baño ruso** (*Cono Sur*) steam bath ▸ **baño turco** Turkish bath
3 (*Culin*) • **le dio un ~ de licor a las galletas** she soaked the biscuits in liqueur • **le he dado un ~ de chocolate al pastel** I've covered the cake with chocolate icing, I've iced the cake with chocolate ▸ **baño María** bain-marie
4 [*de oro, plata*] plating; [*de pintura*] coat • **el pendiente tiene un ~ de plata** the earring is silver-plated ▸ **baño de revelado** developing bath
5 (*Arte*) wash
6 baños (*Med*) spa (*sing*) • **ir a ~s†** to take the waters†, bathe at a spa (*EEUU*) ▸ **baños termales** thermal baths
7 (= *paliza*) • **darle un ~ a algn*** to thrash sb*, wipe the floor with sb*
8 (*Caribe*) (= *lugar*) cool place
bao SM (*Náut*) beam
baobab SM baobab
baptismo SM • **el ~** the Baptist faith
baptista ADJ, SMF Baptist
baptisterio SM baptistery
baque SM bang, thump
baqueano/a ADJ, SM/F = **baquiano**
baquelita SF bakelite
baqueta SF **1** (*Mil*) ramrod • **MODISMOS**: • **correr ~s** • **pasar por ~s** to run the gauntlet • **mandar a ~** to rule tyrannically • **tratar a algn a (la) ~** to treat sb harshly
2 (*Mús*) [*de tambor*] drumstick; (*CAm, Méx*) [*de marimba*] hammer
baquetazo SM • **tratar a algn a ~ limpio*** to give sb a hard time
baqueteado ADJ [*persona*] experienced; [*mueble*] worse for wear, battered
baquetear ▸ CONJUG 1a VT **1** (= *fastidiar*) to annoy, bother
2 (= *maltratar*) to treat harshly • **ha sido baqueteado por la vida** life's been hard on him
baqueteo SM annoyance, bother • **es un ~** it's an imposition, it's an awful bind*
baquetudo ADJ (*Caribe*) sluggish, slow
baquía SF (*LAm*) **1** (= *conocimientos locales*) local expertise
2† (= *habilidad*) expertise, skill
baquiano/a ADJ **1** (*LAm*) (= *que conoce una región*) familiar with a region
2 (*esp LAm*) (= *experto*) expert, skilful, skillful (*EEUU*) • **REFRÁN**: • **para hacerse ~ hay que perderse alguna vez** one learns the hard way
SM/F **1** (*LAm*) (= *guía*) guide, scout; (*Náut*) pilot
2 (*esp LAm*) (= *experto*) expert; (= *experto local*) local expert, *person with an intimate knowledge of a region*
báquico ADJ (*liter*) Bacchic (*liter*)
báquiro SM (*Col, Ven*) peccary
bar SM bar ▸ **bar de alterne, bar de citas** singles bar ▸ **bar de copas** nightclub
baraca SF *charismatic gift of bringing good luck blessing*
barahúnda SF (= *alboroto*) uproar
baraja SF **1** (= *juego de cartas*) pack of cards; (*Méx*) cards • **jugar ~** (*LAm*) to play cards • **MODISMOS**: • **jugar a** *o* **con dos ~s** to play a double game, double deal • **romper la ~** to break off the engagement, end the conflict
2 barajas (= *pelea*) fight (*sing*), set-to* (*sing*)

> **BARAJA ESPAÑOLA**
> The Spanish deck of cards differs from its British and American counterpart, known in Spain as the **baraja francesa**. The four Spanish suits, **oros**, **copas**, **espadas** and **bastos** ("golden coins", "goblets", "swords" and "clubs") each contain nine numbered cards, although for certain games only seven are used, and three picture cards: **sota**, **caballo** and **rey** (jack, queen, king).

barajadura SF shuffle, shuffling
barajar ▸ CONJUG 1a VT **1** [+ *cartas*] to shuffle
2 (= *considerar*) [+ *nombres, candidatos*] to consider, weigh up • **se baraja la posibilidad de que ...** the possibility that ... is being weighed up *o* considered, there is discussion about the possibility that ... • **las cifras que se barajan ahora** the figures now being put *o* bandied about
3 (= *mezclar*) to jumble up, mix up
4 (*Cono Sur, Méx*) [+ *asunto*] (= *confundir*) to confuse; (= *demorar*) to delay
5 (*Cono Sur*) (= *ofrecer*) to pass round, hand round
6 (*Cono Sur*) (= *agarrar*) to catch (*in the air*) • **MODISMO**: • **~ algo en el aire** to see the point of sth
VI to quarrel, squabble
VPR **barajarse 1** (*esp LAm*) (= *pelear*) to fight, brawl
2 (= *mezclarse*) to get jumbled up, get mixed up
barajo EXCL (*LAm*) (*euf*) = **carajo**
SM (*And*) (= *pretexto*) pretext, excuse; (= *salida*) loophole
barajuste SM (*Caribe*) stampede, rush
baranda[1] SF **1** [*de balcón*] rail, railing; [*de escalera*] handrail
2 (*Billar*) cushion
baranda[2]‡ SM chief, boss
barandal SM (= *pasamanos*) handrail; (= *soporte de pasamanos*) base, support; (= *balaustrada*) balustrade
barandilla SF [*de balcón*] rail, railing; [*de escalera*] banisters (*pl*), bannisters (*pl*); (*And*) altar rail
barata SF **1** (*Méx*) (= *venta*) sale, bargain sale; (= *mercado*) street market
2 (*And*) (= *sección de gangas*) bargain counter; (= *tienda*) cut-price store • **MODISMO**: • **a la ~*** (= *sin orden*) any old how* • **tratar a algn a la ~** to treat sb with scorn
3 (*Chile*) (= *cucaracha*) cockroach, roach (*EEUU*)
baratear ▸ CONJUG 1a VT (= *vender barato*) to sell cheaply; (= *vender perdiendo dinero*) to sell at a loss
baratejo* ADJ cheap and nasty, trashy
baratero/a ADJ **1** (*esp LAm*) (= *barato*) cheap; [*tendero*] cut-price (*antes de s*), discount (*antes de s*) • **tienda baratera** shop offering bargains, cut-price store, discount store
2 (*Cono Sur*) [*regateo*] haggling
SM/F **1** (*en el juego*) *person who extracts money from winning gamblers*
2 (*LAm*) (= *tendero*) cut-price shopkeeper, discount storekeeper
3 (*Cono Sur*) (= *persona que regatea*) haggler
baratez SF (*Caribe*), **baratía** SF (*And*) cheapness
baratija SF **1** (= *objeto*) trinket; (= *cosa insignificante*) trifle
2 baratijas (*Com*) cheap goods; (*pey*) trash (*sing*), junk (*sing*)
baratillero SM seller of cheap goods
baratillo SM **1** (= *artículos usados*)

b

secondhand goods (*pl*); (= *artículos baratos*) cheap goods (*pl*)
2 (= *tienda*) secondhand shop, junk shop; (= *sección de gangas*) bargain counter
3 (= *saldo*) bargain sale • **cosa de ~** trash, junk
4 (= *mercadillo*) street market

barato ADJ **1** (= *económico*) cheap • **este vestido es muy ~** this dress is very cheap • **el café sale más ~ a granel** coffee is cheaper if you buy it in bulk • REFRÁN: • **lo ~ sale caro** buying cheap things is false economy, cheap things turn out expensive in the end
2 (= *de mala calidad*) [*música, imitación*] cheap; [*novela*] trashy
3 (= *indigno*) [*demagogia, electoralismo*] cheap • **esa actitud es patriotismo ~** that attitude is just cheap patriotism
ADV cheap, cheaply • **el coche nos costó ~** the car was cheap • **en este restaurante se come muy ~** you can eat very cheaply in this restaurant • **vivo muy ~** I live very cheaply
SM (= *mercadillo*) street market

baratón ADJ (*And, CAm, Méx*) [*argumento*] weak, feeble; [*comentario*] well-worn, trite
SM (*CAm*) (= *ganga*) bargain; (= *saldo*) sale

baratura SF low price, cheapness

baraúnda SF = **barahúnda**

barba SF **1** (= *pelo*) beard • **llevar** *o* **tener ~** to have a beard • **lleva** *o* **tiene ~ de tres días** he's got three days' stubble, he's got three days' growth of beard • **tiene la ~ cerrada** *o* **muy poblada** he's got a very thick beard, his beard grows thickly • **arreglarse** *o* **hacerse** *o* **recortarse la ~** to trim one's beard • **dejarse ~: me estoy dejando ~** I'm growing a beard • **por ~: dos naranjas por ~** two oranges apiece *o* per head • MODISMOS: • **colgar ~s al santo** to give sb his due • **hacer algo en las ~s de algn** to do sth right under sb's nose • **hacerle la ~ a algn** (*Méx*) (= *adular*) to fawn on sb, flatter sb • **llevar a algn de la ~** to lead sb by the nose • **mentir por la ~** to lie through one's teeth • **tener pocas ~s** to be inexperienced • **a ~ regalada** abundantly • **subirse a las ~s de algn** to be cheeky to sb • **tirarse de las ~s** to be tearing one's hair (out) • **un hombre con toda la ~** a real man, a regular guy (*EEUU**) • REFRÁN: • **cuando las ~s de tu vecino veas pelar pon las tuyas a remojar** you should learn from other people's mistakes ▸ **barba de chivo** goatee (beard) ▸ **barba honrada** distinguished personage
2 (= *mentón*) chin
3 [*de ave*] wattle; [*de mejillón, cabra*] beard ▸ **barba de ballena** whalebone
4 (*Bot*) [*de raíz*] beard
SM (*Teat†*) (= *papel*) old man's part; (= *actor*) *performer of old men's roles*; (= *villano*) villain

Barba Azul SM Bluebeard

barbacana SF [*de defensa*] barbican; (= *tronera*) loophole, embrasure

barbacoa SF **1** (= *asadero*) barbecue
2 (*CAm, Méx, Ven*) (= *carne*) barbecued meat
3 (*LAm*) (= *cama*) bed (*made with a hurdle supported on sticks*)
4 (*And*) (= *estante*) rack (*for kitchen utensils*)
5 (*And*) (= *desván*) loft, attic
6 (*And*) tap dance

Barbada SF • **la ~** Barbados

barbado ADJ bearded, with a beard
SM **1** (= *hombre con barba*) man with a beard; (= *hombre adulto*) full-grown man
2 (*Bot*) cutting (*with roots*) • **plantar de ~** to transplant, plant out

Barbados SM Barbados

barbar ▸ CONJUG 1a VI **1** (= *dejarse barba*) to grow a beard
2 (*Bot*) to strike root

Bárbara SF Barbara

bárbaramente ADV **1** (= *cruelmente*) cruelly, savagely
2* (= *estupendamente*) tremendously* • **pasarlo ~** to have a tremendous time*

barbáricamente ADV barbarically

barbárico ADJ barbaric

barbaridad SF **1** (= *desatino*) • **es una ~ conducir con esta niebla** it's madness to drive in this fog • **es capaz de hacer cualquier ~** he's capable of anything, he will stop at nothing • **decir ~es** (= *tonterías*) to talk nonsense • **¡qué ~!**: • **¡qué ~! ¿cómo puedes comer tanto?** that's incredible *o* amazing! how can you eat so much? • **¡qué ~! ¡consentirle que hable así a sus padres!** that's awful! letting him talk to his parents like that! • **¡qué ~! ¡qué bien hablas el inglés!** that's incredible *o* amazing! your English is really good!
2 (= *brutalidad*) atrocity • **las ~es que se cometieron en la guerra** the atrocities committed during the war • **las pruebas con animales son una ~** it is horrible to experiment on animals
3 (= *palabrota*) • **cuando se enfada dice** *o* **suelta muchas ~es** he says some terrible things when he gets angry
4 • **una ~*** (= *mucho*) (*como adv*): • **comimos una ~** we ate loads *o* tons *o* masses*, we stuffed ourselves* • **cuesta una ~** it costs a fortune • **nos divertimos una ~** we had a great *o* fantastic time* • **nos gustó una ~** we thought it was great *o* fantastic* • **habló una ~** he talked his head off* • **se nota una ~** it sticks out a mile* • **me quiere una ~** he loves me to death* • **había una ~ de gente** there were loads *o* tons *o* masses of people*

barbarie SF **1** (= *atraso*) barbarism
2 (= *crueldad*) barbarity, cruelty

barbarismo SM **1** (*Ling*) barbarism
2 = **barbarie**

bárbaro/a ADJ **1** (*Hist*) barbarian
2 (= *cruel*) barbarous, cruel; (= *espantoso*) awful, frightful
3 (= *grosero*) rough, uncouth; (= *inculto*) ignorant
4* (= *increíble*) tremendous*, smashing* • **un éxito ~** a tremendous *o* smashing success* • **es un tío ~** he's a great *o* fantastic guy* • **hace un frío ~** it's freezing • **¡qué ~!** (= *estupendo*) great!, terrific!; (= *horrible*) how awful!
ADV* (= *estupendamente*) brilliantly • **lo pasamos ~** we had a tremendous time* • **canta ~** she signs brilliantly, she's a terrific singer
EXCL (*Cono Sur**) fine!, OK!*
SM/F **1** (*Hist*) barbarian
2 (= *bruto*) uncouth person • **conduce como un ~** he drives like a madman • **gritó como un ~** he gave a tremendous shout, he shouted like mad

barbarote* SM brute, savage

barbas* SM INV beardie*, bearded guy*

barbear ▸ CONJUG 1a VT **1** (*LAm*) to shave
2 (*CAm, Méx*) (= *lisonjear*) to fawn on, flatter
3 (*Méx*) [+ *ganado*] to throw, fell
4 (*esp LAm*) (= *alcanzar*) to come up to, be as tall as
5 (*CAm*) (= *fastidiar*) to annoy, bore
6* (= *ver*) to see, spot
7 (*CAm**) (= *regañar*) to tell off
VI **1** • **~ con** (*esp LAm*) (= *alcanzar*) to come up to, be as tall as
2 (*CAm**) (= *entrometerse*) to stick one's nose in, poke one's nose in

barbechar ▸ CONJUG 1a VT **1** (= *dejar en barbecho*) to leave fallow
2 (= *arar*) to plough for sowing, plow for sowing (*EEUU*)

barbechera SF fallow, fallow land

barbecho SM **1** (= *terreno*) fallow, fallow land • **estar en ~** (*Agr*) to be left fallow; (*fig*) to be in preparation • MODISMO: • **firmar como en un ~** to sign without reading
2 (= *tierra arada*) ploughed land ready for sowing
3 (= *preparación*) preparation for sowing

barbería SF **1** (= *peluquería*) barber's, barber's shop
2 (= *arte*) hairdressing

barbero ADJ (*CAm, Méx**) (= *adulador*) grovelling; [*niño*] affectionate, cuddly
SM **1** (= *peluquero*) barber • **"El ~ de Sevilla"** "The Barber of Seville"
2 (*Guat, Méx**) flatterer

barbeta* SMF (*Cono Sur*) fool

barbetear ▸ CONJUG 1a VT (*Méx*) [+ *ganado*] to throw (to the ground) *o* fell (*by twisting the head of*)

barbicano ADJ grey-bearded, white-bearded

barbihecho ADJ freshly shaven

barbijo SM (*And, Cono Sur*) **1** (= *correa*) chinstrap
2 (= *chirlo*) slash, scar
3 (= *pañuelo*) headscarf (*knotted under the chin*)

barbilampiño ADJ **1** (= *sin barba*) beardless, clean-shaven
2 (= *de cara de niño*) baby-faced
3 (= *inexperto*) inexperienced
SM (= *novato*) novice, greenhorn

barbilindo ADJ (= *pulcro*) dapper, spruce; (*pey*) dandified, foppish

barbilla SF chin, tip of the chin

barbiponiente ADJ **1** (= *con barba incipiente*) beginning to grow a beard, with a youthful beard
2 (= *inexperto*) inexperienced, green

barbiquejo SM **1** = **barbijo**
2 (*Caribe*) (= *bocal*) bit

barbiturato SM barbiturate

barbitúrico ADJ, SM barbiturate

barbo SM barbel ▸ **barbo de mar** red mullet, goatfish (*EEUU*)

barbón SM **1** (= *hombre con barba*) bearded man, man with a (big) beard; (= *anciano*) greybeard, old hand
2 (*Zool*) billy goat

barbotear ▸ CONJUG 1a VT, **barbotar** ▸ CONJUG 1a VT to mutter, mumble

barboteo SM muttering, mumbling

barbudo ADJ bearded
SM (*a veces pey*) bearded man

barbulla SF hullabaloo

barbullar ▸ CONJUG 1a VI to jabber away, talk noisily

Barça SM • **el ~** (*Esp**) Barcelona Football Club

barca SF boat, small boat ▸ **barca de pasaje** ferry ▸ **barca de pesca, barca pesquera** fishing boat

barcada SF **1** (= *carga*) boat load
2 (= *viaje*) boat trip; (= *travesía*) ferry crossing

barcaje SM toll

barcarola SF barcarole

barcaza SF barge ▸ **barcaza de desembarco** (*Mil*) landing craft

Barcelona SF Barcelona

barcelonés/esa ADJ of/from Barcelona
SM/F native/inhabitant of Barcelona • **los barceloneses** the people of Barcelona

barchilón/ona SM/F **1** (*And*) (= *enfermero*) nurse
2 (*And, Cono Sur*) (= *curandero*) quack doctor

barcia SF chaff

barcino ADJ reddish-grey

barco SM (= *embarcación*) boat; [*de gran tamaño*] ship, vessel (*frm*) • **en ~** by boat, by ship • MODISMO: • **como ~ sin timón** irresolutely, lacking a firm purpose ▸ **barco almirante** flagship ▸ **barco cablero** cable ship ▸ **barco carbonero** collier ▸ **barco cisterna** tanker ▸ **barco contenedor** container ship ▸ **barco de apoyo** support ship ▸ **barco de carga** cargo boat ▸ **barco de guerra** warship ▸ **barco de pesca** fishing boat ▸ **barco de vapor** steamer ▸ **barco de vela** sailing boat, sailboat (EEUU) ▸ **barco meteorológico** weather ship ▸ **barco minero** collier ▸ **barco náufrago** wreck ▸ **barco nodriza** supply ship ▸ **barco patrullero** patrol boat ▸ **barco pesquero** fishing boat ▸ **barco vivienda** houseboat; ▹ abandonar

barco-madre (SM) (PL: **barcos-madre**) mother ship

barda (SF) **1** protective covering on a wall; (*Méx*) high hedge, fence, wall
2 bardas top (*sing*) of a wall, walls
3‡ jacket

bardal (SM) wall topped with brushwood

bardana (SF) burdock

bardar ▹ CONJUG 1a (VT) to thatch

bardo (SM) bard

baremar ▹ CONJUG 1a (VT) to assess

baremo (SM) **1** (= *escala de valores*) scale
2 (= *criterio*) yardstick, gauge, gage (EEUU)
3 (*Mat*) ready reckoner

bareo* (SM) • **ir de ~** to go drinking, go on a pub crawl*

barillero (SM) (*Méx*) hawker, street vendor

bario (SM) barium

barítono (SM) baritone

barjuleta (SF) knapsack

barloventear ▹ CONJUG 1a (VI) **1** (*Náut*) to beat to windward
2 (= *vagar*) to wander about

Barlovento • **islas de ~** (SFPL) Windward Isles

barlovento (SM) windward • **a ~** to windward • **de ~** windward (*antes de s*) • **ganar el ~ a** to get to windward of

barman (SM) (PL: **barmans**) barman, bartender

Barna. (ABR) = **Barcelona**

barniz (SM) **1** (= *sustancia*) (*para dar brillo*) varnish; (*para cerámica*) glaze; (*en metal*) gloss, polish • **dar (de) ~ a algo** to varnish sth ▸ **barniz de uñas** nail varnish
2 (= *cualidad superficial*) veneer
3 (*Aer*) dope

barnizado (SM) varnishing

barnizar ▹ CONJUG 1f (VT) **1** (= *cubrir con barniz*) [+ *madera, mueble*] to varnish; [+ *cerámica*] to glaze
2 (= *encubrir*) to put a gloss on

barométrico (ADJ) barometric

barómetro (SM) barometer ▸ **barómetro aneroide** aneroid barometer

barón (SM) **1** (= *título*) baron; (*Pol*) chief, big wig*
2 (*Caribe**) pal*, buddy (EEUU)

baronesa (SF) baroness

baronía (SF) barony

baronial (ADJ) baronial

barquero/a (SM/F) [*de barcaza, barca*] boatman/boatwoman; [*de embarcadero*] ferryman/ferrywoman

barquía (SF) skiff, rowing boat, rowboat (EEUU)

barquilla (SF) **1** (*Aer*) [*de globo*] basket; [*de dirigible*] gondola, car
2 (*Náut*) log
3 (*LAm*) = **barquillo**

barquillo (SM) (*Culin*) rolled wafer; (= *helado*) cornet, cone

barquinazo (SM) **1** (= *caída*) tumble, hard fall
2 (= *movimiento brusco*) (*Aut*) bump, jolt; (*And*) sudden start

barra (SF) **1** (= *pieza alargada*) bar; [*de metal*] bar, ingot; (*en armario*) rail; (*en un bar*) bar, counter; (*en autoservicio*) counter; (*Mec*) rod; [*de bicicleta*] crossbar • **beber en la ~** to drink at the bar • **la bandera de las ~s y estrellas** the Stars and Stripes • MODISMOS: • **a ~s derechas** honestly • **no pararse en ~s** to stick at nothing ▸ **barra americana** singles bar ▸ **barra antivuelco** anti-roll bar ▸ **barra de carmín** lipstick ▸ **barra de cereales** cereal bar ▸ **barra de chocolate** (*Cono Sur*) bar of chocolate, chocolate bar, candy bar (EEUU) ▸ **barra de cortina** curtain rod ▸ **barra de desplazamiento vertical** (*Inform*) scrollbar ▸ **barra de equilibrio(s)** beam ▸ **barra de espaciado** space bar ▸ **barra de herramientas** (*Inform*) toolbar ▸ **barra de labios** lipstick ▸ **barra de pan** French stick, French loaf ▸ **barra espaciadora** space bar ▸ **barra estabilizadora** anti-roll bar ▸ **barra fija** horizontal bar, fixed bar ▸ **barra libre** free bar ▸ **barras asimétricas** asymmetric bars ▸ **barras paralelas** parallel bars
2 (*Tip*) (*tb* **barra oblicua**) oblique stroke, slash ▸ **barra inversa** backslash
3 (*Heráldica*) stripe, bar
4 (*Náut*) bar, sandbank
5 (*Jur*) (= *banquillo*) dock • **llevar a algn a la ~** to bring sb to justice • **la Barra** (*Méx*) the Bar, the legal profession, the Bar Association (EEUU)
6 (*Mús*) bar
7 (*Cono Sur*) (= *público*) (*en concierto, espectáculo*) audience, spectators (*pl*); (*Dep*) fans (*pl*), supporters (*pl*) • **había mucha ~** there was a big audience ▸ **barra brava** *gang of hard-line supporters*
8 (*Cono Sur*) (= *pandilla*) gang; (= *camarilla*) clique, coterie
9 (*Caribe*) river mouth, estuary

Barrabás (SM) Barrabas • MODISMO: • **ser un ~** [*adulto*] to be wicked; [*niño*] to be mischievous, be naughty

barrabasada (SF) mischief, piece of mischief

barraca[1] (SF) **1** (= *cabaña*) hut, cabin; [*de obreros*] workmen's hut; (*en Valencia*) small farmhouse
2 (= *chabola*) shanty, hovel • **una zona de ~s** an area of shantytown
3 (*en feria*) stall, booth ▸ **una barraca de feria** a fairground stall *o* booth ▸ **barraca de tiro al blanco** shooting gallery ▸ **barraca persa** (*Cono Sur*) cut-price store
4 (*And*) (= *depósito*) large storage shed; (*en mercado*) market stall
5 • MODISMO: • **creerse algo a la ~** to believe sth implicitly

barraca[2] (SF) (*LAm*) (*Mil*) barracks

barracón (SM) **1** (= *cabaña*) big hut; (*Caribe*) (*Agr*) farmworkers' living quarters
2 (*en feria*) (= *caseta*) large booth, stall; (= *espectáculo*) sideshow ▸ **barracón de espejos, barracón de la risa** hall of mirrors

barracuda (SF) barracuda

barragana (SF) (= *concubina*) concubine; (= *esposa*††) morganatic wife

barrajes (SMPL) (*And*) shanty town (*sing*)

barranca (SF) gully, ravine

barrancal (SM) place full of ravines

barranco (SM) **1** (= *hondonada*) gully, ravine
2 (= *precipicio*) cliff; [*de río*] steep riverbank
3 (= *obstáculo*) difficulty, obstacle

barraquismo (SM) problem of the slums, shanty town problem

barrar ▹ CONJUG 1a (VT) to daub, smear (de with)

barreal (SM) (*Cono Sur*) (= *tierra*) heavy clay land; (*CAm*) (= *pantano*) bog

barrear ▹ CONJUG 1a (VT) (= *poner barricadas*) to barricade, fortify; (= *bloquear con una barra*) to bar, fasten with a bar

barredera (SF) **1** (= *vehículo*) street sweeper, road sweeper ▸ **barredera de alfombras, barredera mecánica** carpet sweeper
2 (= *persona*) street sweeper, road sweeper

barredor (SM) (*tb* **barredor de frecuencia**) frequency sweeper

barredura (SF) **1** (= *acción*) sweep, sweeping
2 barreduras (= *restos*) sweepings; (= *basura*) rubbish (*sing*), refuse (*sing*), garbage (EEUU)

barreminas (SM INV) minesweeper

barrena (SF) **1** (= *taladro*) (*para pared*) drill; (*para asfalto*) pneumatic drill; (*Min*) rock drill, mining drill ▸ **barrena de guía** centre *o* (EEUU) center bit ▸ **barrena de mano, barrena pequeña** gimlet
2 (*Aer*) • **entrar en ~** to go into a spin

barrenado* (ADJ) • **estar ~** to be dotty*

barrenar ▹ CONJUG 1a (VT) **1** (= *taladrar*) [+ *madera, metal*] to drill, bore; [+ *roca*] to blast; [+ *barco*] to scuttle
2 (= *volar*) to blast
3 (= *frustrar*) to foil, frustrate
4 (*Jur*) to violate, infringe

barrendero/a (SM/F) street sweeper, road sweeper

barrenillo (SM) **1** (*Zool*) borer
2 (*Caribe*) (= *empeño*) foolish persistence; (*Cono Sur, Méx*) (= *preocupación*) constant worry; (= *manía*) pet idea

barreno (SM) (= *perforación*) borehole; (*Min*) blasthole • **dar ~ a un barco** to scuttle a ship

barreño (SM) washing bowl, washbowl

barrer ▹ CONJUG 2a (VT) **1** (*con escoba*) to sweep; [+ *suelo*] to sweep, sweep clean; [+ *habitación*] to sweep (out); [+ *objeto*] to sweep aside, sweep away
2 (*Mil, Náut*) to sweep *o* rake (*with gunfire*)
3 (= *eliminar*) [+ *obstáculo*] to sweep aside, sweep away; [+ *rival*] to sweep aside, overwhelm; [+ *dudas*] to sweep aside, dispel • **los candidatos del partido barrieron a sus adversarios** the party's candidates swept their rivals aside • MODISMO: • **~ con todo** to make a clean sweep
(VI) **1** (= *con escoba*) to sweep up
2 (= *llevarse*) • MODISMOS: • **~ para *o* hacia dentro** to look after number one • **comprar algo al ~** (*Cono Sur*) to buy sth in a job lot
(VPR) **barrerse 1** (*Méx*) [*caballo*] to shy, start
2 (*Méx**) (= *humillarse*) to grovel

barrera (SF) **1** (= *obstáculo*) barrier • **levantó la ~ para dejarnos pasar** he lifted the barrier to let us through • **crema ~** barrier cream • **contraconcepción *o* anticonceptivo de ~** barrier contraception • **método anticonceptivo de ~** barrier method • **ya ha traspasado la ~ de los treinta** he has passed the 30-year-old mark ▸ **barrera aduanera, barrera arancelaria** tariff barrier ▸ **barrera comercial** trade barrier ▸ **barrera coralina** coral reef ▸ **barrera de color** colour *o* (EEUU) color bar ▸ **barrera de contención** containing wall ▸ **barrera del sonido** sound barrier • **este avión supera *o* traspasa *o* rompe la ~ del sonido** this plane can break the sound barrier ▸ **barrera de seguridad** safety barrier ▸ **barrera generacional** generation gap ▸ **barrera protectora** safety barrier ▸ **barrera racial** colour *o* (EEUU) color bar
2 (*en carretera*) roadblock ▸ **barrera de peaje, barrera de portazgo** toll gate, turnpike
3 (*Ferro*) crossing gate
4 (*Taur*) (= *valla*) barrier; (= *primera fila*) first row; ▹ **toro**
5 (*Dep*) [*de jugadores*] wall

b

6 (*Mil*) (= *barricada*) barricade; (= *parapeto*) parapet ▸ **barrera de fuego** barrage ▸ **barrera de fuego móvil** creeping barrage
7 (= *impedimento*) barrier, obstacle • **poner ~s a algo** to hinder sth, obstruct sth

barrero ADJ (*Cono Sur*) [*caballo*] that likes heavy going
SM (= *tierra fangosa*) muddy ground; (*And, Cono Sur*) (= *saladar*) salt soil

bar-restaurante SM bar-cum-restaurant

barretina SF *Catalan cap*

barriada SF (= *barrio*) quarter, district; (*LAm*) (= *chabolas*) slum, shanty town

barrial SM 1 (*Méx*) (= *tierra*) heavy clay land
2 (*LAm*) (= *pantano*) bog

barrica SF large barrel, cask

barricada SF barricade

barrida SF (*con escoba*) sweep, sweeping; [*de policía*] sweep, raid; (*en elecciones*) landslide

barrido SM (*con escoba*) sweep, sweeping; (*Elec*) scan, sweep • MODISMO: • **vale tanto para un ~ como para un fregado** he can turn his hand to anything

barriga SF 1 (*Anat*) belly; (= *panza*) paunch • **echar ~** to get middle-age spread • **estás echando ~** you're getting a bit of a belly* • **con la cerveza echas ~** beer makes you fat • **me duele la ~** I have a sore stomach • **hacer una ~ a una chica*** to get a girl in the family way • **llenarse la ~** to stuff o.s. • **tener ~*** (= *estar encinta*) to be in the family way*; (= *ser gordo*) to be fat • MODISMO: • **rascarse** *o* **tocarse la ~*** to do damn-all*
2 (= *parte abultada*) [*de jarra*] belly, rounded part; [*de muro*] bulge

barrigón/ona, barrigudo/a ADJ potbellied
SM/F (*And, Caribe**) child, kid*

barriguera SF girth, horse's girth

barril SM 1 (= *tonel*) (*gen*) barrel; [*de madera*] cask; [*de metal*] keg • **cerveza de ~** draught *o* (*EEUU*) draft beer, beer on draught • MODISMOS: • **comer del ~** (*And*) to eat poor-quality food • **ser un ~ de pólvora** to be a powder keg ▸ **barril de petróleo** barrel of oil
2 (*LAm*) (= *cometa hexagonal*) hexagonal kite

barrila* SF row • **dar la ~** to kick up a fuss

barrilería SF 1 (= *almacén*) barrel store
2 (= *tienda, taller*) cooper's shop
3 (= *arte*) cooperage

barrilero/a SM/F cooper

barrilete SM 1 (= *barril*) [*de metal*] keg; [*de madera*] cask
2 [*de revólver*] chamber
3 (*Téc*) clamp
4 (*Méx*) (*Jur*) junior barrister
5 (*Cono Sur*) (= *cometa de juguete*) kite
SF (*Cono Sur*) restless woman

barrilla SF (*Bot, Quím*) barilla, saltwort

barrillo SM (= *grano*) pimple; (*con la cabeza negra*) blackhead

barrio SM 1 (= *distrito*) area, district, neighborhood (*EEUU*) • **una casa en un ~ residencial** a house in a residential area *o* district *o* (*EEUU*) neighborhood • **el ~ de Gracia** Gracia district • **mi ~** my part of town, my neighborhood (*EEUU*) • **un piso en un ~ céntrico** a flat in the centre of town • **vive en el ~ judío de Córdoba** he lives in the Jewish quarter of Cordova • **los ~s de la periferia** the outlying suburbs *o* areas, the outskirts • **tiendas de ~** local shops, corner shops, neighborhood stores (*EEUU*) • **cine de ~** local cinema • MODISMOS: • **el otro ~*** the next world • **irse al otro ~*** to snuff it* • **mandar a algn al otro ~*** to do sb in* ▸ **barrio bruja** (*And*) shanty town ▸ **barrio chino** [*de mayoría china*] Chinatown, Chinese quarter; [*de prostitución*] (*Esp*) red-light district ▸ **barrio comercial** [*de negocios*] business quarter, commercial district; [*de tiendas*] shopping area, shopping district ▸ **barrio de chabolas** shanty town ▸ **barrio de tolerancia** (*And*) red-light district ▸ **barrio dormitorio** commuter suburb, dormitory suburb ▸ **barrio exterior** outer suburb ▸ **Barrio Gótico** *historic district with principally Gothic architecture* ▸ **barrio latino** Latin quarter ▸ **barrio miseria**† shanty town ▸ **barrio obrero** working-class area, working-class district, working-class neighborhood (*EEUU*) ▸ **barrios bajos** poorer areas (of town) ▸ **barrios marginales** poorer areas (of town)
2 (*LAm*) shanty town

barriobajero ADJ 1 [*zona, vida*] slum (*antes de s*)
2 (= *vulgar*) vulgar, common

barrisco • **a ~** ADV jumbled together, in confusion, indiscriminately

barritar ▸ CONJUG 1a VI [*elefante*] to trumpet

barrito SM trumpeting

barrizal SM mire

barro SM 1 (= *lodo*) mud • **me llené de ~** I got covered in mud
2 (*Arte*) (= *arcilla*) potter's clay • **~ cocido** baked clay • **una vasija de ~** a clay pot
3 (= *loza*) earthenware • **un cacharro de ~** an earthenware dish; **barros** earthenware (*sing*), crockery (*sing*)
4‡ (= *dinero*) dough‡, brass* • **tener ~ a mano** to be in the money
5 (*Cono Sur**) (= *desacierto*) • **hacer un ~** to drop a clanger*
6 (*Anat*) pimple
7 ▸ **barros jarpa** (*Chile*), **barros luca** (*Chile*) *toasted ham and cheese sandwich*

barroco ADJ 1 [*estilo, período*] baroque
2 (= *recargado*) elaborate
SM (= *estilo*) baroque, baroque style; (= *período*) baroque period

barroquismo SM 1 (= *estilo barroco*) baroque, baroque style
2 (= *adorno excesivo*) excess

barroso ADJ 1 (= *con barro*) muddy
2 [*color*] mud-coloured, mud-colored (*EEUU*); [*ganado*] reddish; (*CAm*) (= *blancuzco*) off-white
3 (*Anat*) pimply

barrote SM 1 [*de celda*] bar • **los ~s de la ventana** the bars on the window
2 [*de silla*] rung

barruntar ▸ CONJUG 1a VT (= *adivinar*) to guess, conjecture; (= *sospechar*) to suspect

barrunte SM sign, indication

barrunto SM 1 (= *adivinanza*) guess, conjecture; (= *indicio*) sign, indication; (= *sospecha*) suspicion; (= *presentimiento*) foreboding
2 (*Caribe, Méx*) (*Meteo*) *north wind which brings rain*

Barsa SM = Barça

bartola SF • MODISMO: • **echarse** *o* **tenderse a la ~*** to be lazy, take it easy*

bartolear ▸ CONJUG 1a VI (*Cono Sur*) to be lazy, take it easy*

bartolina SF (*CAm, Méx*) dark cell, dungeon

Bartolo SM *forma familiar de* **Bartolomé**

bartolo* ADJ (*Méx*) thick*, stupid

Bartolomé SM Bartholomew

bartulear ▸ CONJUG 1a VI (*Cono Sur*) to think hard, rack one's brains

bártulos* SMPL things, belongings; (*Téc*) tools • **liar los ~** to pack up one's things *o* belongings

barucho* SM (*pey*) seedy bar

barullento ADJ (*Cono Sur*) noisy, rowdy

barullo SM 1 (= *alboroto*) racket; (= *confusión*) confusion • **armar ~** to make a racket • **esta habitación está hecha un ~** this room is a mess
2 • **a ~** in abundance, in great quantities

barzón SM saunter, stroll • **dar barzones** to saunter around, stroll around

barzonear ▸ CONJUG 1a VI to saunter around, stroll around

basa SF 1 (*Arquit*) base (*of a column*)
2 (= *fundamento*) basis, foundation

basal ADJ (*Med*) basal

basalto SM basalt

basamentar ▸ CONJUG 1a VT = **basar**

basamento SM (*Arquit*) base

basar ▸ CONJUG 1a VT [+ *teoría, argumento*] to base • **basó su teoría en los más modernos descubrimientos** he based his theory on the very latest discoveries
VPR **basarse** 1 (= *tener como base*) • **~se en algo** to be based on sth • **la película está basada en hechos reales** the film is based on actual events
2 (= *usar como base*) • **para la novela me basé en la vida de mi abuela** the novel was inspired by the life of my grandmother, I based the novel on the life of my grandmother • **¿en qué te basas para decir eso?** what basis *o* grounds have you got for saying that?

basca SF 1* (= *grupo*) crowd; (= *pandilla*) gang, pals (*pl*)
2 (= *impulso*) • **le dio la ~** he had a sudden urge
3 (= *rabieta*) fit of rage, tantrum
4 **bascas** (*esp LAm*) (*Med*) nausea (*sing*), sick feeling (*sing*) • **le entraron ~s** he felt nauseated, he felt sick • **dar ~s a algn** to turn sb's stomach

bascosidad SF 1 (= *porquería*) filth, dirt
2 (*And*) (= *obscenidad*) obscenity

bascoso ADJ 1 (= *delicado*) squeamish, easily upset; (*Med*) queasy
2 (*LAm*) (= *nauseabundo*) nauseating, sick-making*
3 (*And*) (= *obsceno*) obscene

báscula SF (= *con plato*) scales (*pl*), weighing machine; (*romana*) steelyard; (*para camiones*) weighbridge ▸ **báscula biestable** flip-flop, toggle ▸ **báscula de(l) baño** bathroom scales (*pl*) ▸ **báscula de cocina** kitchen scales (*pl*) ▸ **báscula de puente** weighbridge

basculable ADJ (*Aut*) [*luz*] directional, with swinging beam

basculante SM tipper, dumper, dump truck (*EEUU*)

báscula-puente SF weighbridge

bascular ▸ CONJUG 1a VI 1 (= *inclinarse*) to tilt, tip up; (= *columpiarse*) to seesaw; (= *mecerse*) to rock to and fro
2 (*Pol*) to swing
3 (*Inform*) to toggle

base SF 1 (= *parte inferior*) base • **la ~ de la columna** the base of the pillar • **este jarrón tiene muy poca ~** this vase has a very narrow base • **la fecha de caducidad viene en la ~ del paquete** the use-by date is on the base *o* the bottom of the pack • **la ~ del cráneo** the base of the skull
2 (= *fondo*) [*de pintura*] background; [*de maquillaje*] foundation • **sobre una ~ de amarillo** on a yellow background • **primero se coloca una ~ de tomate** start by laying a tomato base
3 (= *fundamento*) basis • **ese artículo no tiene ~ científica alguna** that article has no scientific basis at all • **la ~ del éxito está en el trabajo** the key to success is hard work • **carecer de ~** [*acusación*] to lack foundation, be unfounded; [*argumento*] to lack justification, be unjustified • **de ~** [*error, dato*] basic, fundamental; [*activista, apoyo*] grass-roots (*antes de s*) • **en ~ a** (*uso periodístico*):

b

• **un programa elaborado en ~ a criterios subjetivos** a programme based on subjective criteria • **en ~ a lo que acabamos de ver** based on what we have just seen • **en ~ a que: no publicaron la carta en ~ a que era demasiado larga** they didn't publish the letter because it was too long • **partir de una ~**: • **un juez tiene que partir de una ~ de neutralidad absoluta** a judge must start out from a position of absolute neutrality • **partiendo de esta ~, nos planteamos la necesidad ...** on this assumption, we think it necessary ... • **partir de la ~ de que ...** to take as one's starting point that ... • **sentar las ~s de algo** to lay the foundations of sth • **Chomsky sentó las ~s de la gramática generativa** Chomsky laid the foundations of generative grammar • **su visita sentó las ~s para una futura cooperación** her visit paved the way for *o* laid the foundations of future cooperation • **sobre la ~ de algo** on the basis of sth • **hay que negociar sobre la ~ de resoluciones previas** we must negotiate on the basis of previous resolutions • **MODISMO**: • **coger a algn fuera de ~** (*CAm, Caribe*) to catch sb out ▸ **base de poder** power base
4 (= *componente principal*) • **la leche es la ~ de su alimentación** his diet is milk-based • **la ~ de este jabón es la soda** this soap is soda-based • **a ~ de algo**: • **una dieta a ~ de arroz** a rice-based diet, a diet based on rice • **un plato a ~ de verduras** a vegetable-based dish, a dish based on vegetables • **este aparato funciona a ~ de ultrasonidos** this machine works with ultrasound • **sólo conseguirás salir adelante a ~ de mucho esfuerzo** you will only get ahead by working hard • **a ~ de hacer algo** by doing sth • **así, a ~ de no hacer nada, poco vas a conseguir** you won't achieve much by doing nothing • **a ~ de insistir, la convenció para comprar la casa** by *o* through his insistence, he persuaded her to buy the house • **MODISMO**: • **a ~ de bien** (*Esp**): • **hoy hemos trabajado a ~ de bien** we've done loads of work today* • **nos divertimos a ~ de bien** we had a whale of a time* • **cenamos a ~ de bien** we had a really good meal ▸ **base imponible** (*Econ*) taxable income
5 (= *conocimientos básicos*) grounding • **le falta un poco de ~** he doesn't have the proper grounding • **este manual le aportará una buena ~ de química** this handbook will give you a good grounding in chemistry
6 (*Mil*) base ▸ **base aérea** air base ▸ **base aeronaval** naval air base ▸ **base avanzada** forward base ▸ **base de lanzamiento** launch site ▸ **base de operaciones** operations base ▸ **base espacial** space station ▸ **base militar** military base ▸ **base naval** naval base
7 bases: **a** (= *condiciones*) [*de concurso*] conditions, rules; [*de convocatoria*] requirements
b (*Pol*) • **las ~s** the rank and file
8 (*Inform*) ▸ **base de datos** database ▸ **base de datos documental** documentary database ▸ **base de datos relacional** relational database
9 (*Mat*) (*en una potencia*) base
10 (*Quím*) base
11 (*Téc*) base, mounting
12 (*Agrimensura*) base, base line
13 (*Ling*) (*tb* **base derivativa**) base form
14 (*Béisbol*) base
15‡ (= *droga*) base
(SMF) (*Baloncesto*) guard
(ADJ INV) **1** (= *de partida*) [*campamento, campo*] base (*antes de s*); [*puerto*] home (*antes de s*) • **dejamos el campamento ~ por la mañana** we left base camp in the morning
2 (= *básico*) [*idea*] basic; [*documento, texto*] provisional, draft • **han aprobado el texto ~ para el nuevo convenio** they have approved the provisional *o* draft text of the new agreement • **alimento ~** staple (food) • **color ~** base colour *o* (*EEUU*) color; ▸ **salario, sueldo**

baseballista (SMF) (*LAm*) baseball player

basebolero/a (ADJ) (*Caribe*) baseball (*antes de s*)
(SM/F) (*Caribe*) baseball player

básica (SF) = **EGB**

básicamente (ADV) basically

básico (ADJ) basic

Basilea (SF) Basle, Basel

basílica (SF) basilica

basilisco (SM) (*Mit*) basilisk; (*Méx*) iguana • **MODISMOS**: • **estar hecho un ~** to be furious • **ponerse como un ~** to get terribly angry

básket (SM) basketball

basoto (ADJ) of/from Lesotho

basquear ▹ CONJUG 1a (*LAm*) (VI) (= *sentir náuseas*) to be nauseated, feel sick • **hacer ~ a algn** to make sb feel sick, turn sb's stomach

básquet (SM) (*tb* **pelota básquet**) basketball

basquetbolero/a (ADJ) (*LAm*) basketball (*antes de s*)
(SM/F) (*LAm*) basketball player

basquetbolista (SMF) (*LAm*) basketball player

basquetbolístico (ADJ) (*LAm*) basketball (*antes de s*)

basquiña (SF) skirt

basta (SF) tacking stitch, basting stitch

bastante (ADJ) **1** (= *suficiente*) enough (para for) • **hay ~ sitio para todos** there is enough room for everyone • **¿no tienes ya ~s?** haven't you got enough? • **no había ~ público** there wasn't a big enough audience
2 (= *mucho*) quite a lot of, a fair amount of • **han dejado ~ comida** they've left quite a lot of *o* a fair amount of food • **hace ~ frío** it's quite cold • **se marchó hace ~ rato** he left quite some time ago • **la calidad deja ~ que desear** the quality leaves much to be desired
3 (= *muchos*) quite a lot of, quite a few • **había ~s invitados en la recepción** there were quite a lot of *o* quite a few guests at the reception • —**¿tienes muchos cuadros?** —**bastantes** "do you have many paintings?"— "quite a few"
4 (*Méx*) (= *demasiado*) too much
(ADV) **1** (= *suficiente*) enough • **ya has comido ~** you've eaten enough • **no tenemos ~ para ir de vacaciones** we haven't enough to go on holiday • **ya tienen ~ como para que vayamos también nosotros con nuestros problemas** they've got enough on their plate already without us taking our problems along • **es lo ~ alto como para alcanzarlo** he's tall enough to reach it
2 (= *de forma considerable*) (*con verbos*) quite a lot; (*con adjetivos, adverbios*) quite • **los niños han cambiado ~** the children have changed a fair amount *o* quite a lot • **lo he visto ~ últimamente** I've seen a fair amount of him *o* quite a lot of him recently • **me gusta ~** I quite like it, I like it quite a lot • **el libro está ~ bien** it's a fairly good book, it's quite a good book • **estoy ~ cansado** I'm rather *o* quite tired • **habla inglés ~ bien** she speaks quite good English, her English is quite good • **vivo ~ lejos** I live quite a long way away

bastantemente (ADV) sufficiently

bastar ▹ CONJUG 1a (VI) **1** (= *ser suficiente*) to be enough • **eso me basta** that's enough for me • **esta información debería ~ al juez** this information should be enough for the judge • **baste decir que ...** suffice it to say that ... • **como ejemplo, baste decir que los beneficios han aumentado en un 20%** by way of example, suffice it to say that profits have risen by 20% • **~ para hacer algo** to be enough to do sth • **suele ~ una esponja para absorber el agua** a sponge is usually enough *o* all it takes to soak up the water • **me bastó una foto para reconocerlo** one look at a photo was enough to recognize him, one look at a photo was all it took for me to recognize him • **una mirada bastó para hacerme callar** one look was enough to make me shut up, one look was all it took to make me shut up • **me bastó leer el primer párrafo para saber que era un genio** I only had to read the first paragraph to know that he was a genius • **basta que ... para que ...**: • **basta que queramos llegar pronto a casa, para que haya un atasco** just when we want to get home quickly, there's a traffic jam • **basta saber que ...** it is enough to know that ...
2 (*terciopersonal*) • **con eso basta** that's enough • **me basta con tu palabra** your word's good enough for me • **con la intención basta** it's the thought that counts • **basta con dar una vuelta por la ciudad para ...** you only need to take a walk round the city to ... • **no basta con ...** it's not enough to ... • **no basta con decir que uno no es culpable, hay que demostrarlo** it's not enough to say you're not guilty, you have to prove it
3 (*exclamación*) • **¡basta!** • **¡basta ya!** that will do!, that's enough! • **¡basta de charla!** that's enough chatter! • **¡basta de tonterías!** that's enough nonsense! • **¡basta ya de llorar!** that's enough crying!
4 • **MODISMOS**: • **hasta decir basta**: • **nevó hasta decir basta** it snowed like there was no tomorrow • **bailamos hasta decir basta** we danced till we dropped • **es honrado hasta decir basta** he's as honest as the day is long • **~ y sobrar** to be more than enough • **con esa comida basta y sobra para un mes** that food is more than enough for a month • **no hablamos alemán, nos basta y sobra con el inglés** we don't speak German, English is all we need
(VPR) **bastarse** • **yo sola me basto para cuidarlo** I'm well capable of looking after him on my own • **se bastan y se sobran para llevar ellos el negocio** they're more than capable of running the business themselves • **~se a sí mismo** to be self-sufficient

bastardear ▹ CONJUG 1a (VT) to bastardize
(VI) **1** (*Bot*) to degenerate
2 (= *degenerar*) to degenerate, fall away

bastardía (SF) **1** (= *cualidad*) bastardy
2 (= *bajeza*) meanness, baseness
3 (= *acción vil*) wicked thing

bastardilla (SF) (*Tip*) (*tb* **letra bastardilla**) italic type, italics (*pl*) • **en ~** in italics • **poner en ~** to italicize

bastardo/a (ADJ) **1** (= *ilegítimo*) bastard
2 (= *mezquino*) mean, base
3 (*Bot*) (= *híbrido*) hybrid, mixed
(SM/F) bastard

bastear ▹ CONJUG 1a (VT) to tack, stitch loosely

bastedad (SF), **basteza** (SF) coarseness, vulgarity

bastero/a (SM/F) (*Méx*) pickpocket

bastes‡ (SMPL) (*Esp*) fingers

bastez (SF) coarseness, vulgarity

b

bastidor SM **1** (= *armazón*) (*Téc, Cos*) frame, framework; [*de ventana*] frame; [*de lienzo*] stretcher; [*de vehículo*] chassis
2 (*Teat*) wing • **entre ~es** behind the scenes • **estar entre ~es** to be offstage • **dirigir entre ~es** to pull the strings
3 (*And, Cono Sur*) (= *celosía*) lattice window
4 (*Caribe*) (= *catre*) metal bedstead
5 (*Caribe, Méx*) (= *colchón*) interior sprung mattress
bastilla SF hem
bastillar ▹ CONJUG 1a VT to hem
bastimentar ▹ CONJUG 1a VT to supply, provision
bastimento SM **1** (= *provisiones*) supply
2 (*Náut*) vessel
bastión SM bastion
basto ADJ **1** [*superficie, piel*] coarse
2 [*persona, comportamiento*] rude, vulgar
SM **1** (*Naipes*) ace of clubs; **bastos** clubs (*one of the suits in the Spanish card deck*) • **MODISMO**: • **pintan ~s** things are getting tough, the going's getting tough; ▸ **BARAJA ESPAÑOLA**
2 (= *albarda*) packsaddle
3 (*LAm*) **bastos** soft leather pad (*used under the saddle*)
bastón SM **1** (*para andar*) (walking) stick • **necesita llevar ~ para andar** he needs a stick for walking ▸ **bastón alpino, bastón de alpinista** alpenstock ▸ **bastón de esquí** ski stick ▸ **bastón de estoque** swordstick ▸ **bastón de montaña** alpenstock
2 [*de policía*] truncheon, billy (club) (*EEUU*); [*de militar*] baton • **MODISMOS**: • **empuñar el ~** to take command • **meter el ~** to intervene ▸ **bastón de mando** baton, sign of authority
3 (*Heráldica*) vertical bar, pallet
bastonazo SM (= *golpe*) blow (*with a stick*)
bastoncillo SM **1** (*para los oídos*) cotton bud, Q-tip® (*EEUU*)
2 (*Anat*) rod, retinal rod
bastoncito SM **1** [*de pan*] bread stick
2 (*para los oídos*) cotton bud, Q-tip® (*EEUU*)
bastonear ▹ CONJUG 1a VT to beat (*with a stick*), hit (*with a stick*)
bastonera SF umbrella stand
bastonero/a SM/F **1** [*de bailes*] master of ceremonies (*at a dance*), compere, emcee (*EEUU*)
2 (*Caribe*) scoundrel, tough nut*
bastón-taburete SM shooting stick
basuco* SM cocaine base, unpurified cocaine
basura SF **1** (= *desechos*) (*en casa*) rubbish, garbage (*EEUU*); (*por el suelo*) litter • **hay mucha ~ en la calle** there's a lot of litter in the street • **"prohibido arrojar basuras (y escombros)"** "no dumping", "no tipping" ▸ **basura espacial** space junk ▸ **basura radiactiva** radioactive waste
2 (= *contenedor*) (*en casa*) dustbin, trash can (*EEUU*); (*en la calle*) litter bin, trash can (*EEUU*) • **tirar algo a la ~** to put *o* throw sth in the bin
3 (= *persona o cosa despreciable*) trash, rubbish • **es una ~*** he's a shocker*, he's a rotter* • **la novela es una ~** the novel is rubbish
basural SM (*LAm*) rubbish dump
basurear ▹ CONJUG 1a VT • **~ a algn** (*Cono Sur*) (= *empujar*) to push sb along; (= *humillar*) to humiliate sb; (= *insultar*) to be rude to sb, rubbish sb*
basurero/a SM/F (= *persona*) dustman/ dustwoman, garbage collector (*EEUU*)
SM **1** (= *vertedero*) rubbish dump; (*Agr*) dung heap
2 (*LAm*) (= *cubo*) litter bin, trash can (*EEUU*)
basuriento ADJ (*And, Cono Sur*) full of rubbish

Basutolandia SF (*Hist*) Basutoland
bata[1] SF **1** (*para levantarse de la cama*) dressing gown; (*encima de la ropa*) housecoat; [*de playa*] wrap
2 [*de médico*] white coat; [*de científico*] laboratory coat, lab coat ▸ **bata blanca** white coat
3 (= *guardapolvo*) overall, smock
bata[2]‡ SF mother
batacazo SM **1** (= *porrazo*) thump
2 (*LAm*) (= *golpe de suerte*) stroke of luck, fluke
bataclán SM (*LAm*) striptease show, burlesque show (*EEUU*)
bataclana SF (*LAm*) striptease girl, stripper
batahola* SF (= *ruido*) din, hullabaloo*; (= *jaleo*) rumpus*
bataholear ▹ CONJUG 1a VI, **batajolear** ▹ CONJUG 1a VI (*And*) (= *pelear*) to brawl; (= *ser travieso*) to be mischievous, play pranks
batalla SF **1** (= *lucha*) battle • **librar** *o* **trabar ~** to do battle ▸ **batalla campal** pitched battle
2 (= *sufrimiento*) fight, struggle • **ropa de ~** everyday clothes (*pl*)
3 (*Aut*) wheelbase
batallador(a) ADJ battling, fighting
SM/F (= *luchador*) battler, fighter; (*Dep*) fencer
batallar ▹ CONJUG 1a VI (= *luchar*) to battle, fight
batallita SF • **contar ~s*** to go over old times
batallón ADJ • **cuestión batallona** vexed question
SM battalion ▸ **batallón de castigo, batallón disciplinario** punishment squad
batán SM **1** (= *lugar*) fulling mill; (= *herramienta*) fulling hammer
2 (*Cono Sur*) (= *tintorería*) dry cleaner's
3 (*And*) (= *espesura de tela*) thickness (*of cloth*)
batanar ▹ CONJUG 1a VT **1** (*Téc*) to full
2* to beat, thrash
batanear ▹ CONJUG 1a VT = **batanar**
batanero/a SM/F fuller
bataola SF = **batahola**
batasuno/a ADJ of Herri Batasuna
SM/F member/supporter of Herri Batasuna
batata ADJ **1** (*Cono Sur*) (= *tímido*) bashful, shy
2 (*Caribe, Cono Sur*) (= *simple*) simple, gullible
3 (*Caribe*) (= *llenito*) chubby, plump; (= *rechoncho*) squat
SF **1** (*Bot*) sweet potato, yam
2 (*Cono Sur*) (= *timidez*) bashfulness, embarrassment
3 (*And, Caribe*) (= *pantorrilla*) calf (*of the leg*)
4 (*Cono Sur**) (= *coche*) car, auto(mobile) (*EEUU*)
batatar SM (*LAm*) sweet potato field
batatazo* SM (*esp LAm*) (= *golpe de suerte*) stroke of luck, fluke
batayola SF (*Náut*) rail
bate SM (*esp LAm*) bat, baseball bat • **MODISMO**: • **estar al ~ de algo** (*CAm, Caribe*) to be in charge of sth ▸ **bate de béisbol** baseball bat ▸ **bate de polo** polo stick
batea SF **1** (= *bandeja*) tray
2 (*LAm*) (= *artesa para lavar*) washing trough
3 (*Min*) washing pan
4 (*Ferro*) flat car, low waggon
5 (*Náut*) flat-bottomed boat, punt
bateador(a) SM/F batter
batear ▹ CONJUG 1a VT to hit
VI **1** (*esp LAm*) (*Dep*) to bat
2 (*Caribe**) (= *tragar*) to overeat
batel SM small boat, skiff
batelero/a SM/F boatman/boatwoman
batelón SM (*LAm*) canoe
batería SF **1** (*Elec*) battery • **se ha agotado la ~** the battery is flat • **MODISMO**: • **(re)cargar las ~s** to recharge one's batteries ▸ **batería de arranque** starter battery ▸ **batería seca** dry battery
2 (= *fila*) [*de luces*] bank, battery; (*en teatro*) footlights (*pl*); (*para gallinas*) battery; [*de soldados*] battery • **aparcar en ~** to park at an angle to the kerb
3 (*Mús*) (= *instrumento*) drums (*pl*); [*de orquesta*] percussion instruments (*pl*) • **¿tocas la ~?** do you play the drums?
4 (*Culin*) ▸ **una batería de cocina** a set of kitchen equipment
5 (*LAm*) (*Béisbol*) hit, stroke
6 (*And*) (= *ronda de bebidas*) round
7 (*Méx*) • **dar ~** to raise a rumpus • **dar ~ a algn*** to make trouble for sb, make a lot of work for sb
SMF (= *persona*) (*en grupo*) drummer
baterista SMF (*LAm*) drummer
batey SM (*Caribe*) outbuildings (*pl*) (*of sugar refinery*)
batiburrillo SM hotchpotch, hodgepodge (*EEUU*)
baticola SF **1** [*de montura*] crupper
2 (*And*) (= *taparrabos*) loincloth
3 (*Cono Sur*) (= *pañal*) nappy, diaper (*EEUU*)
batida SF **1** (= *búsqueda*) **a** (*Caza*) beating **b** [*de policía, ejército*] (*buscando algo*) search; (*haciendo detenciones*) raid • **por las noches salíamos a hacer una ~** we used to comb *o* search the area at night • **dieron una ~ por el centro de la ciudad** they carried out a raid in the city centre
2 (= *acuñación*) minting
3 (*And*) (= *persecución*) chase
4 (*And, Caribe*) (= *paliza*) beating, thrashing
batido PP *de* **batir**
ADJ **1** [*camino*] well-trodden, beaten
2 [*seda*] shot
SM **1** (= *bebida*) milk shake, shake (*esp EEUU*) • **un ~ de frutas** a fruit shake
2 (= *golpe*) beat, beating • **se oía un ~ de tambores** you could hear drums beating *o* the beat of drums
3 (*Culin*) (= *rebozo*) batter
batidor(a) SM/F **1** (*Caza*) beater; (*Mil*) scout
2 (*Orfebrería*) ▸ **batidor(a) de oro** gold beater
3 (*Arg*) (= *delator*) informer
SM **1** (*Culin*) whisk ▸ **batidor mecánico** egg beater, egg whisk
2 (= *peine*) wide-toothed comb
3 (*CAm*) (= *vasija*) wooden bowl, mixing bowl
batidora SF **1** (*eléctrica*) (food) mixer, blender ▸ **batidora de brazo** hand blender
2 (*manual*) whisk
batiente ADJ ▹ **mandíbula**
SM **1** (= *marco de puerta*) jamb; (= *marco de ventana*) frame, case; (= *hoja de puerta*) leaf, panel
2 (*Náut*) open coastline
3 (*Mús*) damper
batifondo SM (*Cono Sur*) uproar, tumult
batín SM **1** (= *bata de hombre*) [*de casa*] dressing gown; [*de playa*] beach-wrap
2 (= *chaqueta*) smoking jacket
batintín SM gong
batir ▹ CONJUG 3a VT **1** (= *vencer, superar*) [+ *adversario, enemigo*] to beat; [+ *récord*] to break, beat • **batieron al Osasuna por 4 a 1** they beat Osasuna 4-1 • **el cáncer ha sido batido en muchos frentes** cancer has been beaten on many fronts • **batió el récord mundial de 400 metros vallas** she broke *o* beat the world 400 metres hurdles record • **las ventas han batido todos los récords este año** sales have broken *o* beaten all records this year
2 (*Culin*) [+ *huevos*] to beat, whisk; [+ *nata, crema*] to whip;

b

[+ *mantequilla, margarina*] to cream; [+ *leche*] (*para hacer mantequilla*) to churn • **se bate el queso con el huevo** beat the cheese with the egg
3 (= *recorrer*) (*Mil*) to comb, search; (*Caza*) to beat • **la policía batió la zona pero no encontró nada** the police combed *o* searched the area but found nothing
4 (= *agitar*) [+ *alas*] to flap; [+ *pestañas*] to flutter; [+ *brazos*] to flap, wave • **~ palmas** to clap one's hands • **~ el vuelo** to fly off, take flight
5 (= *golpear*) **a** [+ *tambor, metal*] to beat • **el ~ de los martillos contra el metal** the sound of hammers beating the metal, the clang of hammers on metal
b [*lluvia, olas, viento*] to beat on *o* against; [*sol*] to beat down on • **las olas batían la orilla de la playa** the waves were beating on *o* against the shore • **el viento batía con fuerza las ventanas** the wind was pounding on *o* against the windows
c [+ *moneda*] to mint; ▹ **cobre**
6 (= *derribar*) [+ *edificio*] to knock down, demolish; [+ *privilegio*] to do away with
7 (*Mil*) [+ *muro*] to batter, pound • **los cañones batieron las murallas de la ciudad** the cannons battered *o* pounded the city walls
8 (= *cardar*) [+ *lana*] to comb out, card; [+ *pelo*] to backcomb
9 (*And*) (= *enjuagar*) [+ *ropa*] to rinse (out)
10 (*Arg*) (= *denunciar*) to inform on
(VI) 1 [*lluvia, olas, viento*] to beat • **el viento batía con fuerza contra los cristales** the wind pounded on *o* against the windows
2 [*puerta, persiana*] • **se oía el ~ de una puerta** you could hear a door banging • **baten las persianas con el viento** the blinds rattle in the wind
3 [*tambor*] to ring out, sound
(VPR) **batirse** 1 (= *luchar*) to fight • **se batió contra la enfermedad con todas sus fuerzas** she fought the illness with all her strength • **~se con algn** to fight sb, have a fight with sb • **~se en duelo** to fight a duel
2 • **~se en retirada** to beat a retreat
batiscafo (SM) bathyscaph, bathyscaphe
batista (SF) cambric, batiste
bato¹ (SM) simpleton
bato²‡ (SM) father
batonista (SF) drum majorette
batracio (SM) batrachian
Batuecas (SFPL) • **las ~** • MODISMO: • **estar en las batuecas** to be daydreaming, be in a world of one's own
batueco* (ADJ) stupid, silly
batuque* (SM) (*Cono Sur*) uproar
batuquear* ▹ CONJUG 1a (VT) (*And, Méx*) (= *batir*) to shake, shake up
baturrillo (SM) hotchpotch, hodgepodge (*EEUU*)
baturro/a (ADJ) (= *rudo*) uncouth, rough
(SM/F) Aragonese peasant
batusino/a (SM/F) idiot, fool
batuta (SF) (*Mús*) baton • MODISMO: • **llevar la ~** to be the boss, be firmly in command
batzoki (SM) political party bar/ headquarters
baudio (SM) (*Inform*) baud
baúl (SM) 1 (= *arca*) trunk • MODISMO: • **el ~ de los recuerdos** the back of the mind ▸ **baúl armario** wardrobe trunk ▸ **baúl camarote** cabin trunk ▸ **baúl de viaje** portmanteau ▸ **baúl mundo** large trunk, Saratoga trunk ▸ **baúl ropero** wardrobe trunk
2 (*LAm*) (*Aut*) boot, trunk (*EEUU*)
3* (= *vientre*) belly
bauprés (SM) bowsprit
bausa (SF) (*And, Méx*) (= *pereza*) laziness, idleness
bausán (SM), **bausana** (SF) 1 (= *figura*) dummy; (*fig*) simpleton
2 (*And*) (= *holgazán*) good-for-nothing
bausano (SM) (*CAm*) idler, lazy person
bauseador (SM) (*And*) idler, lazy person
bautismal (ADJ) baptismal
bautismo (SM) baptism, christening • MODISMO: • **romper el ~ a algn**‡ to knock sb's block off‡ ▸ **bautismo de fuego** baptism of fire ▸ **bautismo del aire** maiden flight
Bautista (ADJ) Baptist • **Iglesia ~** Baptist Church • **San Juan ~** St John the Baptist
(SMF) Baptist • **el ~** the Baptist
bautizar ▹ CONJUG 1f (VT) 1 (*Rel*) to baptize, christen • **la ~on con el nombre de Teresa** she was christened Teresa
2 (= *nombrar*) [+ *objeto, barco*] to christen, name
3 (= *poner apodo*) to nickname, dub
4 (= *diluir*) [+ *vino*] to water, dilute; [+ *persona*] to drench, soak
bautizo (SM) 1 (= *acto*) baptism, christening
2 (= *celebración*) christening party
bauxita (SF) bauxite
bávaro/a (ADJ), (SM/F) Bavarian
Baviera (SF) Bavaria
baya (SF) berry
bayajá (SM) (*Caribe*) headscarf
báyer‡ (SF) (*Cono Sur*) dope‡, pot‡
bayeta (SF) 1 (= *trapo de cocina*) (cleaning) cloth • **¿has pasado la ~ por la mesa?** have you wiped the table?
2 (= *tejido*) flannel
3 (*Billar*) baize
4 (*And*) (= *pañal*) nappy, diaper (*EEUU*)
bayetón (SM) 1 (= *trapo*) bearskin, thick woollen cloth
2 (*And*) (= *poncho largo*) long poncho
bayo (ADJ) bay
(SM) 1 (= *caballo*) bay, bay horse
2 (*Méx*) bean
Bayona (SF) Bayonne
bayoneta (SF) bayonet ▸ **bayonetas caladas** fixed bayonets • **luchar a ~s caladas** to fight with fixed bayonets
bayonetazo (SM) (= *arremetida*) bayonet thrust; (= *herida*) bayonet wound
bayonetear ▹ CONJUG 1a (VT) (*LAm*) to bayonet
bayoya (SM) (*Caribe*) row, uproar • **es un ~ aquí** it's pandemonium here
bayunca (SF) (*CAm*) bar, saloon
bayunco/a (ADJ) (*CAm*) (= *tonto*) silly, stupid; (= *tímido*) shy; (= *grosero*) crude, vulgar
(SM/F) (*CAm*) uncouth peasant (*name applied by Guatemalans to other Central Americans*)
baza (SF) 1 (*Naipes*) trick • **hacer una ~** to make *o* win a trick ▸ **baza de honor** honours trick
2 (*en asunto, negocio*) (= *recurso*) weapon; (= *oportunidad*) chance • **han usado el miedo como ~ electoral** they have used fear as an electoral weapon • **Carlos es una de las principales ~s del equipo** Carlos is one of the team's main weapons • **el equipo supo aprovechar sus ~s** the team made the most of its chances • **jugar una ~**: • **si juega bien su ~, conseguirá el trabajo** if he plays his cards right, he'll get the job • **no es el momento de jugar su principal ~** this is not the time to play their trump card • **están jugando su última ~** they are playing their last hand • **Alemania juega una ~ muy firme para el Mundial** Germany has a good chance of winning the World Cup • MODISMOS: • **meter ~*** to butt in • **le encanta meter ~ aunque no tenga ni idea del tema** she loves butting in even though she has no idea about the subject • **cuando habla no deja meter ~ a nadie** when he's speaking he doesn't let anybody get a word in edgeways • **sacar ~ de algo** (*Esp*) to turn sth to one's (own) advantage • **es de los que siempre sacan ~ de todo** he's one of those people who always turns everything to their own advantage
bazar (SM) 1 (= *mercado*) bazaar
2 (= *tienda*) (= *grandes almacenes*) large retail store; (= *juguetería*) toy shop; (*LAm*) bazaar, charity fair; (*Méx*) second-hand shop; (*Cono Sur*) (= *ferretería*) ironmonger's, ironmonger's shop
bazo (ADJ) yellowish brown
(SM) (*Anat*) spleen
bazofia (SF) 1 (= *sobras*) leftovers (*pl*), scraps (*pl*) of food; (*para cerdos*) pigswill
2 (= *producto de mala calidad*) pigswill, hogwash (*EEUU*)
bazooka (SF), **bazuca** (SF) bazooka
bazucar ▹ CONJUG 1g (VT), **bazuquear** ▹ CONJUG 1a (VT) (= *agitar*) to stir; (= *sacudir*) to shake, jolt
bazuqueo (SM) (= *agitación*) stirring; (= *sacudida*) shaking, jolting ▸ **bazuqueo gástrico** rumblings (*pl*) in the stomach
BCE (SM ABR) (= **Banco Central Europeo**) ECB
BCG (SM ABR) (= **Bacilo Calmette-Guérin**) BCG
Bco. (ABR) (= **Banco**) bk
be¹ (SF) *name of the letter B* • MODISMOS: • **be por be** in detail • **esto tiene las tres bes** (= *bueno, bonito y barato*) this is really very nice, this is just perfect ▸ **be chica** (*Méx*) V ▸ **be larga** (*LAm*), **be grande** (*Méx*) B
be² (SM) baa
beata‡ (SF) (*Econ*) one peseta; ▹ **beato**
beatería (SF) (= *santidad*) affected piety; (= *hipocresía*) cant, sanctimoniousness
beaterío* (SM) goody-goodies* (*pl*), sanctimonious people (*pl*)
beatificación (SF) beatification
beatificar ▹ CONJUG 1g (VT) to beatify
beatífico (ADJ) beatific
beatitud (SF) (= *santidad*) beatitude; (= *bendición*) blessedness • **su Beatitud** His Holiness
beatnik ['bitnik] (SMF) (PL: **beatniks** ['bitnik]) beatnik
beato/a (ADJ) 1 (*Rel*) (= *beatificado*) blessed
2 (= *piadoso*) devout, pious; (= *santurrón*) sanctimonious
3 (*frm, hum*) (= *feliz*) happy
(SM/F) 1 (*Rel*) lay brother/sister
2 (= *devoto*) devout man/woman
3 (*pey*) (= *hombre*) holy Joe*; (= *mujer*) excessively pious woman, sanctimonious woman; ▹ **beata**
Beatriz (SF) Beatrice
bebe/a (SM/F) (*Cono Sur*) baby
bebé (SM) baby • **~ foca** baby seal • **dos ~s panda** two baby pandas ▸ **bebé de diseño** designer baby; ▹ **bebé-probeta**
bebecina (SF) (*And*) (= *embriaguez*) drunkenness; (= *juerga*) drinking spree
bebedera (SF) 1 (*And*) (= *embriaguez*) habitual drunkenness
2 (*CAm, Méx*) (= *juerga*) drinking bout, drunken spree
bebedero (ADJ) drinkable, good to drink
(SM) 1 (*para aves*) water bowl; (*en jaula*) water dispenser
2 (*para ganado*) drinking trough
3 [*de botijo, jarro*] spout
4 (*Chile, Méx*) drinking fountain
5 (*And*) (*Com*) *establishment selling alcoholic drinks*
bebedizo (ADJ) drinkable
(SM) (*medicinal*) potion; (*mágico*) love potion, philtre, philter (*EEUU*)
bebedor(a) (ADJ) hard-drinking
(SM/F) drinker; (*pey*) heavy drinker

▸ **bebedor(a) empedernido/a** hardened drinker

bebendurria SF 1 (= *juerga*) drinking spree 2 (*And, Méx*) (= *borrachera*) drunkenness 3 (*Cono Sur*) (= *fiesta*) drinking party

bebé-probeta SMF (PL: **bebés-probeta**) test-tube baby

beber ▹ CONJUG 2a VT 1 [+ *agua, leche, cerveza*] to drink • **¿qué quieres (de) ~?** what would you like to drink? • **no bebe alcohol** he doesn't drink • **~ algo con la lengua** to lap sth up • **~ algo a sorbos** to sip sth • **~ algo a tragos** to gulp sth, gulp sth down 2 (*frm*) (= *absorber*) to drink in • **bebían las palabras del orador** they were drinking in the speaker's words • **toda su filosofía la bebió de Platón** all his philosophy comes from Plato
VI 1 (*gen*) to drink • **no debes ~ y comer a la vez** you shouldn't eat and drink at the same time • **bebió de la botella** he drank straight from the bottle
2 (= *beber alcohol*) to drink • **—¿quieres vino? —no, gracias, no bebo** "would you like some wine?" — "no thanks, I don't drink" • **su padre bebe muchísimo** his father drinks a lot, his father is a heavy drinker • **si bebes, no conduzcas** don't drink and drive
• MODISMO: • **~ como un cosaco** to drink like a fish
3 (= *brindar*) • **~ por algo/algn** to drink to sth/sb • **bebimos por mi nuevo hijo** we drank to my new son; ▹ **salud**
VPR **beberse** to drink • **bébetelo que nos vamos** drink up, we're going • **se lo bebió todo** he drank it all (up)
SM drinking • **disfruto con el buen ~** I like a (good) drink

beberaje SM (*Cono Sur*) drink (*esp alcoholic*)

bebercio* SM booze*

bebereca* SF (*And*) booze*

beberecua* SF (*And*) 1 (= *juerga*) boozing* 2 = bebereca

beberrón/ona ADJ, SM/F = bebedor

bebestible ADJ (*LAm*) drinkable
SMPL **bebestibles** drinks

bebezón SF (*Caribe*) 1 (= *bebida*) drink, booze* 2 (= *embriaguez*) drunkenness; (= *juerga*) drinking spree

bebezona* SF booze-up*

bebible ADJ drinkable • **no ~** undrinkable

bebida SF 1 (= *líquido*) drink, beverage ▸ **bebida no alcohólica** soft drink, non-alcoholic drink ▸ **bebida refrescante** soft drink
2 (*tb* **bebida alcohólica**) drink, alcoholic drink • **dado a la ~** hard-drinking • **darse** *o* **entregarse a la ~** to take to drink • **tener mala ~** to get violent with drink

bebido PP *de* **beber**
ADJ • **estar ~** to be drunk

bebistrajo* SM nasty drink, filthy drink

bebito/a SM/F (*Cono Sur*) little baby

BEBS ABR (*Inform*) (= **basura entra, basura sale**) GIGO

beca SF 1 (= *ayuda*) (*por méritos o en concurso*) scholarship; (*ayuda económica general*) grant ▸ **beca de investigación** research grant 2 (= *vestido*) sash, hood

becacina SF snipe

becada SF (*Orn*) woodcock

becado/a ADJ [*estudiante*] who holds a scholarship; [*investigador*] who holds an award • **está aquí ~** he's here on a grant
SM/F (*por méritos o en concurso*) scholarship holder; (*por ayuda económica general*) grant holder

becar ▹ CONJUG 1g VT to award a scholarship/grant to

becario/a SM/F 1 (= *con beca*) = **becado** 2 (= *estudioso*) scholar, fellow

becerrada SF (*Taur*) fight with young bulls

becerrillo SM calfskin

becerro SM 1 (= *animal*) yearling calf, bullock ▸ **becerro de oro** golden calf 2 (= *piel*) calfskin 3 (*Rel, Hist*) cartulary, register

bechamel SF béchamel sauce

becuadro SM (*Mús*) natural sign

Beda SM Bede

bedel(a) SM/F [*de facultad*] ≈ head porter; [*de colegio*] ≈ janitor; [*de edificio oficial, museo*] caretaker

bedoya SM (*And*) idiot

beduino/a ADJ, SM/F Bedouin; (*pey*) savage

befa SF jeer, taunt

befar ▹ CONJUG 1a VT, VPR **befarse** • **~(se) de** to scoff *o* jeer at, taunt

befo ADJ 1 (= *de labios gruesos*) thick-lipped 2 (= *zambo*) knock-kneed
SM (= *labio*) lip

begonia SF begonia

behaviorismo SM behaviourism, behaviorism (*EEUU*)

behaviorista ADJ, SMF behaviourist, behaviorist (*EEUU*)

BEI SM ABR (= **Banco Europeo de Inversiones**) EIB

beibi‡ SF girlfriend, bird‡, chick (*EEUU‡*)

beicon SM bacon

beige [beis] ADJ, SM beige

Beirut SM Beirut

beis ADJ (*Esp*) beige
SM 1 (*Esp*) beige 2 (*Méx*) baseball

béisbol SM baseball

beisbolero/a ADJ (*LAm*) baseball (*antes de s*)
SM/F (*esp LAm*) (= *jugador*) baseball player; (= *aficionado*) baseball fan

beisbolista SM (*esp LAm*) baseball player

beisbolístico ADJ baseball (*antes de s*)

bejuco SM (*LAm*) (= *caña*) reed, liana
• MODISMO: • **no sacar ~** (*Caribe**) to miss the boat

bejuquear ▹ CONJUG 1a VT (*LAm*) (= *zurrar*) to beat, thrash

bejuquero SM (*And*) confused situation, mess

bejuquillo SM 1 (*Caribe, Méx*) (*Bot*) *variety of liana* 2 (*And*) (= *vainilla*) vanilla

bejuquiza SF (*And*) beating, thrashing

Belcebú SM Beelzebub

beldad SF (*liter*) 1 (= *cualidad*) beauty 2 (= *persona*) beauty, belle

beldar ▹ CONJUG 1j VT to winnow (*with a fork*)

belduque SM (*CAm, Méx*) pointed sword

Belén SM Bethlehem

belén SM 1 [*de Navidad*] nativity scene, crib, crèche (*EEUU*) ▸ **belén viviente** *representation of the Nativity by real people* 2 (= *confusión*) bedlam; (= *lugar*) madhouse
• MODISMO: • **meterse en belenes** to get into a mess, get into trouble

belenista SMF maker of nativity scenes

beleño SM henbane

belfo ADJ, SM = **befo**

belga ADJ, SMF Belgian

Bélgica SF Belgium

bélgico ADJ Belgian

Belgrado SM Belgrade

Belice SM Belize

beliceño/a ADJ, SM/F Belizean

belicismo SM warmongering, militarism

belicista ADJ warmongering, militaristic
SMF warmonger

bélico ADJ 1 [*actitud*] warlike 2 [*material, juguete*] war (*antes de s*)

belicosidad SF (= *actitud*) warlike spirit; (= *agresividad*) belligerence, aggressiveness

belicoso ADJ (= *guerrero*) warlike; (= *agresivo*) bellicose, aggressive

beligerancia SF belligerency

beligerante ADJ belligerent • **no ~** non-belligerent

belinún/una SM/F (*Cono Sur*) simpleton, blockhead*

belitre SMF 1 (= *granuja*) rogue, scoundrel 2 (*And, CAm*) (= *niño*) (*astuto*) shrewd child; (*inquieto*) restless child

bellaco/a ADJ 1 [*persona*] (= *malvado*) wicked; (= *astuto*) cunning, sly; (= *pícaro*) rascally
2 (*Cono Sur, Méx*) [*caballo*] vicious, hard-to-control; (*And, CAm*) brave
SM/F (= *bribón*) scoundrel, rogue
SM (*Cono Sur, Méx*) (= *caballo*) difficult horse

belladona SF deadly nightshade

bellamente ADV (= *hermosamente*) beautifully; (= *con gran elegancia*) finely

bellaqueada SF (*Cono Sur*) bucking, rearing

bellaquear ▹ CONJUG 1a VI 1 (= *engañar*) to cheat, be crooked* 2 (*And, Cono Sur*) (= *encabritarse*) to shy; (= *ser terco*) to dig one's heels in

bellaquería SF 1 (= *acto*) dirty trick 2 (= *cualidad*) (= *maldad*) wickedness; (= *astucia*) cunning, slyness

belleza SF 1 (= *cualidad*) beauty, loveliness 2 (= *persona bella*) beauty • **es una ~ (de mujer)** she's a beautiful woman • **Juan es una ~ (de hombre)** Juan is a very handsome man
3 (= *cosa bella*) beauty • **las ~s de Mallorca** the beauties of Majorca
4 • **de ~** beauty (*antes de s*)

bello ADJ 1 (= *hermoso*) beautiful, lovely • **es una bella persona** he's a lovely person • **Bellas Artes** Fine Art 2 (= *elegante*) fine

bellota SF 1 [*de encina*] acorn 2 [*de clavel*] bud 3 (*Anat**) Adam's apple 4 (*para perfumes*) perfume box, pomander 5 ▸ **bellota de mar, bellota marina** sea urchin

bemba‡ SF (*LAm*) lip

bembo (*LAm*), **bembudo** (*LAm*) ADJ thick-lipped
SM thick lip

bemol SM 1 (*Mús*) flat
2 **bemoles*** (*euf*) • MODISMOS: • **esto tiene muchos** *o* **tres ~es** this is a tough one • **¡tiene ~es la cosa!** (*iró*) that's just bloody great!*

bencedrina® SF Benzedrine®

benceno SM benzene

bencina SF 1 (*Quím*) benzine 2 (*Chile*) petrol, gas(oline) (*EEUU*)

bencinera SF (*Chile*) (= *estación de servicio*) petrol *o* (*EEUU*) gas station; (= *bomba*) petrol *o* (*EEUU*) gas pump

bencinero/a SM/F (*Cono Sur*) petrol station attendant, gas station attendant (*EEUU*)

bendecir ▹ CONJUG 3o VT 1 [+ *persona, agua, casa, vino, pan*] to bless • **~ la comida** *o* **la mesa** to say grace 2 (= *loar*) to praise

bendición SF 1 [*de persona, agua*] blessing, benediction • **echar la ~** to give one's blessing (a to) • MODISMO: • **echar la ~ a algo:** • **será mejor echarle la ~*** it will be best to have nothing more to do with it ▸ **bendición de la mesa** grace (*before meals*) ▸ **bendiciones nupciales** wedding ceremony (*sing*)
2 • MODISMO: • **... que es una ~:** • **lo hace que**

es una ~ he does it splendidly • **llovió que era una ~ de Dios** there was such a lovely lot of rain
bendiga *etc*, **bendije** *etc* ▹ bendecir
bendito/a ADJ **1** [*persona, casa*] blessed; [*santo*] saintly; [*agua*] holy • **¡~s los ojos que te ven!** you're a sight for sore eyes! • **¡bendita la madre que te parió!** what a daughter for a mother to have! • **¡~ sea Dios!** thank goodness! • MODISMO: • **venderse como pan ~** to sell like hot cakes
2 (*iró*) (= *maldito*) blessed
3 (= *dichoso*) happy; (= *afortunado*) lucky
4 (= *de pocas luces*) simple, simple-minded
SM/F **1** (= *santo*) saint
2 (= *bobo*) simpleton, simple soul • **es un ~** he's so sweet • MODISMO: • **dormir como un ~** to sleep like a log
SM **1** (*Cono Sur*) (= *oración*) prayer
2 (= *hornacina*) wayside shrine
3 (= *cabaña*) native hut
benedícite SM grace
benedictino ADJ Benedictine
SM Benedictine • MODISMO: • **es obra de ~s** it's a monumental task
Benedicto SM Benedict
benefactor(a) ADJ beneficent; ▹ estado
SM/F benefactor
beneficencia SF **1** (= *virtud*) doing good
2 (*tb* **asociación de beneficencia**) charity, charitable organization • **vivir de la ~** to live on charity ▸ **beneficencia social** social welfare
beneficiado/a SM/F • **el único ~ ha sido el intermediario** the only one to benefit was the middleman
SM (*Rel*) incumbent, beneficiary
beneficial ADJ *relating to ecclesiastical benefices* • **terreno ~** glebe, glebe land
beneficiar ▹ CONJUG 1b VT **1** (= *favorecer*) to benefit • **el acuerdo solo beneficia a las economías más desarrolladas** the agreement only benefits the more developed economies • **la empresa más beneficiada por esta ayuda** the company which benefitted most from this aid • **esta huelga no beneficia a nadie** this strike is of no benefit to anyone • **esa conducta no te va a ~** such behaviour will do you no favours *o* won't do you any good • **el ex director beneficiaba a sus amigos mediante las adjudicaciones de obras** the ex-director favoured his friends by awarding them work contracts • **la lluvia beneficia al campo** rain is good for the countryside
2 (*Com*) to sell at a discount
3 (*Min*) (= *extraer*) to extract; (= *tratar*) to process
4 (*LAm*) [+ *animal*] (= *descuartizar*) to butcher; (= *matar*) to slaughter
5 (*CAm*) [+ *persona*] to shoot, kill
VI to be of benefit • **de momento ninguna de estas técnicas ~á** for the moment none of these techniques will be of any benefit
VPR **beneficiarse 1** (= *obtener provecho*) to benefit • **los bancos son los que más se benefician** it's the banks that profit *o* benefit most • **el campo es el que más se beneficia con la lluvia** it's the countryside that gets most benefit from the rain, it's the countryside that benefits most from the rain • **~se de algo** to benefit from sth • **los suscriptores se ~án de esta oferta** subscribers will benefit from this offer
2 • **~se a algn** (*Esp‡*) (*sexualmente*) to lay sb‡; (*CAm*) (= *matar*) to shoot sb
beneficiario/a SM/F [*de herencia, póliza*] beneficiary; [*de beca, subsidio*] recipient; [*de cheque*] beneficiary, payee • **sus hijos son los principales ~s de su éxito** his children are the main beneficiaries of his success
beneficiencia SF (*Méx*) welfare
beneficio SM **1** (= *ventaja*) benefit • **los manipulan para su ~** they manipulate them to their own advantage *o* for their own benefit • **concederle a algn el ~ de la duda** to give sb the benefit of the doubt • **a ~ de algn** in aid of sb • **un recital a ~ de los niños de Somalia** a recital in aid of the children of Somalia • **en ~ de algn**: • **aprovechó las cualidades literarias de su mujer en ~ propio** he exploited his wife's literary talent to his own advantage *o* for his own benefit • **estaría dispuesto a retirarse en ~ de otro aspirante** he would be prepared to withdraw in favour of another candidate • **en *o* por tu propio ~, es mejor que no vengas** for your own good *o* benefit *o* in your own interests, it's best if you don't come ▸ **beneficio de justicia gratuita** legal aid; ▹ oficio
2 (*Com, Econ*) profit • **estos bonos han producido enormes ~s** these bonds have yielded enormous profits • **obtener *o* tener ~s** to make a profit • **obtuvieron 1.500 millones de ~ el año pasado** they made a profit of 1,500 million last year ▸ **beneficio bruto** gross profit ▸ **beneficio de explotación** operating profit, trading profit ▸ **beneficio distribuible** distributable profit ▸ **beneficio económico** financial gain ▸ **beneficios excesivos** excess profits ▸ **beneficio líquido** (*en un balance*) net profit; (*en una transacción*) net profit, clear profit ▸ **beneficio neto** = **beneficio líquido** ▸ **beneficio no realizado** unrealized profit ▸ **beneficio operativo** operating profit, trading profit ▸ **beneficio por acción** earnings per share (*pl*) ▸ **beneficios antes de impuestos** pre-tax profits, profits before tax ▸ **beneficios imprevistos** windfall profits ▸ **beneficios marginales** fringe benefits ▸ **beneficios postimpositivos** after-tax profits, profits after tax ▸ **beneficios preimpositivos** pre-tax profits ▸ **beneficios previstos** anticipated profits ▸ **beneficios retenidos** retained profits; ▹ margen
3 (= *función benéfica*) benefit (performance)
4 (= *donación*) donation
5 (*Rel*) living, benefice
6 (*Min*) [*de mina*] exploitation, working; [*de mineral*] (= *extracción*) extraction; (= *tratamiento*) processing, treatment
7 (*LAm*) (= *descuartizamiento*) butchering; (= *matanza*) slaughter
8 (*CAm*) [*de café*] coffee processing plant
beneficiosamente ADV • **influir ~ en algo** to have a beneficial effect on sth, be beneficial to sth
beneficioso ADJ **1** (= *provechoso*) beneficial • **una solución beneficiosa para todos** a beneficial solution for everyone • **el ejercicio es ~ para la salud** exercise is beneficial to health
2 (*Com*) profitable
benéfico ADJ **1** (= *acción, influencia*) beneficial
2 (= *caritativo*) charitable • **concierto ~** charity concert • **función benéfica** charity performance • **obra benéfica** charity • **organización *o* sociedad benéfica** charity, charitable organization
Benemérita SF • **la ~** (= *la Guardia Civil*) the Civil Guard; ▹ GUARDIA CIVIL
benemérito/a ADJ **1** (= *merecedor*) worthy, meritorious
2 (= *destacado*) distinguished • **el ~ hispanista** the distinguished hispanist
SM/F • **un ~ de la patria** a national hero
beneplácito SM approval, consent • **dar su ~** to give one's blessing *o* consent
benevolencia SF (= *bondad*) benevolence, kindness; (= *jovialidad*) geniality
benevolente ADJ, **benévolo** ADJ
1 (= *bondadoso*) benevolent, kind • **estar ~ con algn** to be well-disposed towards sb, be kind to sb
2 (= *jovial*) genial
Bengala SF Bengal • **el golfo de ~** the Bay of Bengal
bengala SF **1** (= *luz de aviso*) flare; (= *fuego*) Bengal light
2 (*Bot*) rattan
bengalí ADJ Bengali
SMF (= *persona*) Bengali
SM (*Ling*) Bengali
Bengasi SM Bengazi
benignamente ADV **1** (= *amablemente*) kindly, benignly; (= *con gentileza*) graciously, gently
2 (= *ligeramente*) mildly
benignidad SF **1** [*de persona*] kindness
2 (*Meteo, Med*) mildness
benigno ADJ **1** [*persona*] kind, benevolent
2 [*clima*] mild
3 (*Med*) [*tumor*] benign, non-malignant; [*ataque, caso*] mild
Benito SM Benedict
benito ADJ, SM = **benedictino**
Benjamín SM Benjamin
benjamín/ina SM/F **1** (*más joven*) baby of the family, youngest child
2 (*Dep*) young player
SM (= *botella*) half bottle
benjasmín (*Cono Sur*) = **benjamín**
benzina SF (*Cono Sur*) = **bencina**
beo** SM cunt**
beocio‡ ADJ stupid
beodez SF drunkenness
beodo/a ADJ drunk
SM/F drunk, drunkard
beorí SM American tapir
beque (*CAm*) ADJ stammering
SMF stammerer
bequista SMF (*CAm, Caribe*) = **becario**
berbecí SMF (*Méx*) quick-tempered person
berbén SM (*Méx*) scurvy
berberecho SM cockle
berberí ADJ, SMF = **bereber**
Berbería SF Barbary
berberisco ADJ Berber
berbiquí SM carpenter's brace ▸ **berbiquí y barrena** brace and bit
BERD SM ABR (= **Banco Europeo para la Reconstrucción y el Desarrollo**) EBRD
berdel SM mackerel
bereber ADJ, SMF, **beréber** ADJ, SMF, **berebere** ADJ, SMF Berber
berengo/a (*Méx*) ADJ foolish, stupid
SM/F idiot
berenjena SF **1** aubergine, eggplant (EEUU)
2 (*Caribe**) nuisance, bother
berenjenal SM **1** aubergine field, eggplant field (EEUU)
2 (= *lío*) mess, trouble • **en buen ~ nos hemos metido** we've got ourselves into a fine mess
bereque ADJ (*CAm*) cross-eyed
bergante SM scoundrel, rascal
bergantín SM brig
Beri SM • MODISMO: • **andar *o* ir con las de ~** (= *tener genio*) to have a violent temper; (= *tener malas intenciones*) to have evil intentions
beriberi SM (*Med*) beriberi (fever)
berilio SM beryllium
berilo SM (*Min*) beryl
berkelio SM berkelium
Berlín SM Berlin ▸ **Berlín Oeste** (*Hist*) West Berlin

berlina SF **1** (*Aut*) saloon car, sedan (*EEUU*)
2 (*Cono Sur*) doughnut, donut (*EEUU*)

berlinés/esa ADJ Berlin (*antes de s*)
SM/F Berliner

berma SF (*Chile*) (*Aut*) hard shoulder, berm (*EEUU*), emergency lane

bermejo ADJ **1** (= *rojizo*) [*color*] reddish, ginger; [*gato*] ginger; (*Cuba, Méx*) [*toro, vaca*] light brown
2 (*Caribe*) (= *único*) matchless, unsurpassed

bermellón SM vermilion

bermuda SF (*LAm*) meadow grass

Bermudas SFPL (*tb* **islas Bermudas**) Bermuda

bermudas SMPL Bermuda shorts • **unas ~** a pair of Bermuda shorts

Berna SF Berne

bernardina* SF yarn, tall story

Bernardo SM Bernard

bernés/esa ADJ of/from Berne
SM/F native/inhabitant of Berne • **los berneses** the people of Berne

berraco* SM noisy brat

berrear ▸ CONJUG 1a VI **1** (= *gritar*) [*animal*] to bellow; [*niño*] to howl, bawl
2 (*Mús*) (*hum*) to bawl
VPR **berrearse** to squeal‡, grass‡

berrenchín SM = **berrinche**

berreo* SM howling, bawling

berreta* ADJ (*Cono Sur*) cheap, flashy

berretín* SM (*Cono Sur*) (= *obsesión*) obsession, mania; (= *terquedad*) pigheadedness

berrido SM **1** (= *grito*) [*de animal*] lowing; [*de niño*] howl
2 berridos bawling (*sing*)

berrinche* SM **1** (= *rabieta*) rage, tantrum • **coger** *o* **llevarse un ~** to fly into a rage
2 (*LAm‡*) (= *hedor*) pong‡, stink

berrinchudo* ADJ **1** [*persona*] cross, bad-tempered
2 (*Méx*) [*animal*] on heat

berro SM **1** (*Bot*) watercress
2 (*Caribe*) (= *enojo*) rage, anger

berza SF cabbage • MODISMO: • **mezclar ~s con capachos** to get things in a shocking mess ▸ **berza lombarda** red cabbage
SMF INV **berzas*** = **berzotas**

berzal SM cabbage patch

berzotas* SMF INV twit*, chump*

besamanos SM INV (*Hist*) (= *recepción*) royal audience; (= *saludo*) forelock touching

besamel SF white sauce, bechamel sauce

besana SF *land to be ploughed*

besar ▸ CONJUG 1a VT **1** (*con los labios*) to kiss • MODISMO: • **~ a algn la mano** to pay one's humble respects (a to)
2 (= *tocar con suavidad*) to graze, touch
VPR **besarse 1** (*con los labios*) to kiss, kiss one another
2* (= *chocar con la cabeza*) to bump heads

besazo SM big kiss, smacker*

beso SM **1** (= *con los labios*) kiss • **dar un ~ a algn** to kiss sb, give sb a kiss • **echar** *o* **tirar un ~ a algn** • **dar un ~ volado a algn** to blow sb a kiss ▸ **beso de la muerte** kiss of death ▸ **beso de tornillo, beso lingual** French kiss
2 (= *choque*) bump, collision

besograma SM kissagram

besotear ▸ CONJUG 1a VT (*Méx*) = **besuquear**

bestia ADJ* **1** (= *bruto*) • **ese tío ~ le ha vuelto a pegar a su mujer** that brute *o* animal* has been beating his wife again • **no lo vayas a asustar ¡no seas ~!** you're not going to frighten him, are you? don't be such a brute *o* such an animal!* • **los hinchas llegaron en plan ~** (*Esp*) the supporters came looking for trouble • MODISMO: • **poner a algn ~** (*Esp***): • **esa tía me pone ~** I've really got the hots for her‡
2 • **a lo ~: un deporte parecido a la lucha libre pero más a lo ~** a sport that's similar to wrestling but more rough • **lo tuyo son mentiras a lo ~** your lies are real whoppers* • **todo lo haces a lo ~** you make a mess of everything you do • **hoy hemos entrenado a lo ~** we trained really hard today • **comimos a lo ~** we really stuffed ourselves*, we pigged out* • **conducen a lo ~** they drive like idiots • **bebe a lo ~** he drinks like a fish
3 (= *ignorante*) thick* • **es tan ~ que no sabe ni sumar** he's so thick he can't even add up* • **¡anda, no seas ~! ¡eso no puede ser verdad!** don't be an idiot! that can't be true!
4 (*con admiración, asombro*) • **¡qué ~! ¡ha ganado todos los partidos!** she's amazing *o* incredible! she's won all the matches! • **¡qué ~! ¡se come cuatro huevos diarios!** it's amazing! she eats four eggs a day! • **¡qué ~ eres, le has ganado al campeón!** what a star! you beat the champion!
SMF* (= *bruto*) • **¡eres un ~!** you're a brute!, you're an animal!* • **el muy ~ se ha bebido media botella de whisky él solo** that animal drank half a bottle of whisky on his own* • **es un ~ con el trabajo** he works like a dog*
SF (*Zool*) beast • MODISMO: • **ser una mala ~** to be a nasty piece of work* ▸ **bestia de arrastre** draught animal, draft animal (*EEUU*) ▸ **bestia de carga** beast of burden, pack animal ▸ **bestia de tiro** draught animal, draft animal (*EEUU*) ▸ **bestia feroz, bestia salvaje** wild animal, wild beast ▸ **bestia negra, bestia parda** bête noire

bestiada* SF • **una ~ de algo** masses of sth, tons of sth* • MODISMO: • **disfrutar ~s** to enjoy o.s. hugely

bestial ADJ **1** (= *violento*) beastly, bestial • **instintos ~es** beastly *o* bestial instincts • **fue un crimen ~** it was a beastly *o* brutal crime
2* (= *enorme*) terrific*, tremendous* • **la máquina hacía un ruido ~** the machine made a terrific *o* tremendous noise* • **tengo un sueño ~** I'm incredibly tired • **tengo unas ganas ~es de irme de vacaciones** I'm just dying to go on holiday*
3 (*Esp**) (= *estupendo*) smashing*, super* • **¡es un tío ~!** he's a smashing *o* super guy!* • **pasamos un rato ~** we had a smashing *o* super time*, we had a whale of a time*

bestialidad SF **1** (= *cualidad*) beastliness, bestiality
2 (= *acción brutal*) act of brutality • **en las guerras se cometen muchas ~es** in wars many acts of brutality are committed
3* (= *disparate*) • **comer tanto es una ~** eating so much is just gross* • **no dice más que ~es** he's so coarse
4* (= *cantidad excesiva*) • **la cena nos costó una ~** the meal cost us a fortune *o* packet* • **los precios han subido una ~** prices have rocketed* • **he dormido una ~** I slept for absolutely ages* • **una ~ de** a mass of*, tons of* • **había una ~ de gente** there were masses of people*, there were tons of people*
5 (*en sentido sexual*) bestiality

bestialismo SM bestiality

bestialmente ADV **1** (= *violentamente*) savagely • **fue ~ asesinado** he was savagely murdered
2* (= *enormemente*) • **era ~ rico** he was filthy rich*
3 (*Esp**) (= *estupendamente*) • **lo pasamos ~** we had a great *o* super time*, we had a whale of a time*

bestiario SM bestiary

best-seller SM (PL: **best-sellers**) bestseller

besucar* ▸ CONJUG 1g VT = **besuquear**

besucón/ona* ADJ • **es muy ~** he's always dishing out kisses*
SM/F • **es un ~** he's always dishing out kisses*

besugo SM sea bream • **ojos de ~** bulging eyes
SMF* idiot

besuguera SF **1** (*Culin*) fish pan
2 (*Náut*) fishing boat
3 (*Galicia*) (= *pez*) bream

besuquear* ▸ CONJUG 1a VT to cover with kisses
VPR **besuquearse** (= *besarse*) to kiss (each other) a lot; (= *magrearse*) to neck*, smooch*

besuqueo* SM (*con besos*) kissing; (*con arrumacos*) necking*, smooching*

beta SF beta

betabel (*Méx*) ADJ* old, ancient
SM beetroot, beet (*EEUU*)

betabloqueador SM betablocker

betarraga SF (*LAm*), **betarrata** SF beetroot, beet (*EEUU*)

betel SM betel

Bética SF (*Literat*) Andalusia; (*Hist*) Baetica

bético ADJ **1** (*Literat*) Andalusian
2 (= *del Betis*) of Real Betis F.C.

betonera SF (*Cono Sur*) concrete mixer

betún SM **1** (*para zapatos*) shoe polish • **dar (de) ~ a algo** to polish sth • MODISMO: • **darse ~*** to show off
2 (*Quím*) (*tb* **betún asfáltico**) bitumen ▸ **betún de Judea, betún judaico** asphalt; ▹ **altura**

betunero/a SM/F shoeblack, bootblack

bezo SM (= *labio*) thick lip; (*Med*) proud flesh

bezudo ADJ thick-lipped

bi... PREF bi...

biaba* SF (*Cono Sur*) punch • **dar la ~ a algn** (= *golpear*) to beat sb up; (= *derrotar*) to defeat sb, crush sb

bianual ADJ, SM (*Bot*) biannual

bianualmente ADV biannually

biatlón SM biathlon

Bib. ABR (= **Biblioteca**) Lib

biberón SM feeding bottle, baby's bottle • **voy a dar el ~ al niño** I'm going to give the baby his bottle

Biblia SF Bible • **la Santa ~** the Holy Bible • MODISMOS: • **es la ~ (en verso)*** it's the tops* • **saber la ~ en verso** to know everything

bíblico ADJ biblical

biblio... PREF biblio...

bibliobús SM mobile library, bookmobile (*EEUU*)

bibliofilia SF bibliophily, love of books

bibliófilo/a SM/F bibliophile, book lover

bibliografía SF bibliography

bibliográfico ADJ bibliographic(al)

bibliógrafo/a SM/F bibliographer

bibliomanía SF bibliomania

bibliometría SF bibliometry

bibliométrico ADJ bibliometric

bibliorato SM (*Cono Sur*) box file

biblioteca SF **1** (= *edificio*) library ▸ **biblioteca ambulante** mobile library, bookmobile (*EEUU*) ▸ **biblioteca circulante** [*de préstamo*] lending library; (*ambulante*) circulating library ▸ **biblioteca de consulta** reference library ▸ **biblioteca de préstamo** lending library ▸ **biblioteca pública** public library ▸ **biblioteca universitaria** university library
2 (= *mueble*) bookcase, bookshelves (*pl*)

bibliotecario/a ADJ library (*antes de s*) • **servicios ~s** library services
SM/F librarian

bibliotecnia SF, **bibliotecología** SF, **biblioteconomía** SF library science,

librarianship
biblioteconomista SMF librarian
bicameral ADJ (*Pol*) two-chamber, bicameral
bicameralismo SM *system of two-chamber government*
bicampeón/ona SM/F two-times champion, twice champion
bicarbonatado ADJ bicarbonated, fizzy
bicarbonato SM bicarbonate
▸ **bicarbonato sódico, bicarbonato de soda** (*Quím*) bicarbonate of soda; (*Culin*) baking soda
bicentenario ADJ, SM bicentenary
bíceps SM (PL: **bíceps**) biceps
bicha SF **1*** (= *serpiente*) snake • MODISMO: • **mentar la ~** to bring up an unpleasant subject ▸ **bicha negra** bête noire, pet aversion
2 (*CAm*) (= *niña*) child, little girl
3 (*And*) (= *olla*) large cooking pot
bichadero SM (*Cono Sur*) watchtower, observation tower
bichará SM (*Cono Sur*) poncho (*with black and white stripes*)
bicharraco/a* SM/F **1** (*Zool*) (= *animal*) creature; (= *insecto*) creepy-crawly*
2 (*iró*) (= *niño*) little monster
biche ADJ **1** (*LAm*) (= *no maduro*) unripe, immature
2 (*Cono Sur*) (= *débil*) weak; (= *de mal color*) pale, off-colour
3 (*Méx**) (= *fofo*) soppy*, empty-headed
SM (*And*) large cooking pot
bicheadero SM (*Cono Sur*) = **bichadero**
bichear ▸ CONJUG 1a VT (*esp Cono Sur*) (= *mirar*) to observe; (= *espiar*) to spy on
bicherío SM (*LAm*) (= *insectos*) insects (*pl*), bugs (*pl*), creepy-crawlies* (*pl*)
bichero SM **1** (*en barca*) boat hook
2 (*Pesca*) gaff
bichi‡ ADJ (*Méx*) naked, starkers‡
bichicori* ADJ (*Méx*) skinny
bichito SM **1** small creature, little insect
2‡ (= *ácido*) LSD tablet
bicho SM **1** (*Zool*) (*gen*) small animal; (= *insecto*) bug, creepy-crawly*; (*Taur*) bull; (*Cuba, Cono Sur*) (= *gusano*) maggot, grub; (*And*) (= *serpiente*) snake; (*LAm*) (= *animal extraño*) odd-looking creature • MODISMOS: • **de puro ~** (*LAm*) out of sheer pig-headedness • **matar el ~** to quench one's thirst • **tener ~** to be dying of thirst • REFRÁN: • **~ malo nunca muere** the devil looks after his own
2 bichos vermin (*sing*), pests
3* (= *persona*) oddball* • **mal ~** rogue, villain • **es un mal ~** he's a nasty piece of work, he's a rotter* • **todo ~ viviente** every living soul, every man-jack of them ▸ **bicho raro** weirdo*
4* (*pey*) (= *niño*) brat* • **sí, bichito** yes, my love
5 (*CAm*) (= *niño*) child, little boy
6 (*And*) (= *peste aviar*) fowl pest
7 (*Mil*) squaddie*, recruit
8 (*Caribe*) (= *chisme*) what's-it*, thingummy*
9 (*CAm, Méx***) (= *pene*) prick**
bichoco ADJ (*Cono Sur*) (= *inútil*) useless; (*para el trabajo*) unfit to work
bici* SF bike*
bicicleta SF bicycle, cycle • **andar** *o* **ir en ~** to cycle • **montar en ~** to ride a bike
▸ **bicicleta de carreras** racing bicycle
▸ **bicicleta de ejercicio, bicicleta de gimnasio** exercise bike ▸ **bicicleta de montaña** mountain bike ▸ **bicicleta estática, bicicleta fija, bicicleta gimnástica** exercise bike
bicicletero/a* ADJ bicycle (*antes de s*)
SM/F cyclist
biciclo†† SM velocipede††
bicicross SM INV cyclo-cross
bicilíndrico ADJ two-cylinder (*antes de s*), twin-cylinder (*antes de s*)
bicimoto SM (*CAm*) moped
bicoca SF **1** (*Esp**) (= *trabajo fácil*) cushy job*; (= *ganga*) bargain
2 (*LAm*) (*Rel*) (= *solideo*) skullcap, calotte
3 (*And, Cono Sur*) (= *golpe*) slap, smack; (*con los dedos*) snap of the fingers
bicolor ADJ two-colour, two-color (*EEUU*); (*Aut*) two-tone
bicultural ADJ bicultural
bicúspide ADJ bicuspid
SM bicuspid
BID SM ABR (= **Banco Interamericano de Desarrollo**) IDB
bidé SM, **bidet** [bi'de] SM (PL: **bidés** *o* **bidets**) bidet
bidel SM (*LAm*) bidet
bidimensional ADJ two-dimensional
bidireccional ADJ bidirectional
• **~ simultáneo** full duplex
bidón SM (= *barril*) (*grande*) drum; (*pequeño*) can ▸ **bidón de aceite** oil drum ▸ **bidón de basura** rubbish bin, trash can (*EEUU*)
biela SF (*Téc*) connecting rod
bielástico ADJ with two-way stretch
bielda SF winnowing fork
bieldar ▸ CONJUG 1a VT to winnow (*with a fork*)
bieldo SM winnowing rake
Bielorrusia SF Belorussia
bielorruso/a ADJ, SM/F Belorussian
bien ADV **1** (= *satisfactoriamente*) well • **hablas ~ el español** you speak good Spanish, you speak Spanish well • **el libro se ha vendido ~** the book has sold well • **no veo muy ~** I can't see very well • **lo sé muy ~** I know that perfectly well • **viven ~** they live well • **me gusta la carne ~ hecha** I like my meat well-done • **~ gracias, ¿y usted?** fine thanks, and you? • **¡muy ~!** very good!; (*aprobando un discurso*) hear, hear! • **¡qué ~!** great!, excellent! • **oler ~** to smell good • **saber ~** to taste good
2 (= *correctamente*) • **¿has puesto ~ la rueda?** have you put the wheel on properly? • **si no cierras la tapa ~, se saldrá el líquido** if you don't screw the top on properly, the liquid will leak out • **se limpia ~ el pescado** clean the fish thoroughly *o* well • **¡~ hecho!** well done! • **has contestado ~** you gave the right answer, you answered correctly • **no consigo hacerlo ~** I can't seem to do it right • **haces ~** you're (quite) right • **hacer ~ en**: • **hiciste ~ en decírselo** you were right to tell him, you did the right thing in telling him
3 • **estar ~**: • **¿estás ~?** are you all right?, are you OK? • **aquí se está ~** it's nice here • **¡está ~!, lo haré** O.K. *o* all right, I'll do it! • **¡pues sí que estamos ~!** this is a fine mess we're in! • **ese libro está muy ~** that book's very good, that's a very good book • **estás muy ~ con ese sombrero** you look really nice in that hat • **la casa está muy ~** the house is really nice • **está muy ~ que ahorres dinero** it's very good that you're saving • **que esté(s) ~** (*Col**) bye* • **¡eso no está ~!** (*a un niño*) that's not very nice! • **te está ~ la falda** the skirt fits you fine • **¡ya está ~!** that's enough! • **ya está ~ de quejas** that's (quite) enough complaining • **estar ~ de algo**: • **estar ~ de salud** to be well, be in good health • **estar ~ de dinero** to be well off • **no está ~ de la cabeza** he isn't right in the head
4 (= *de acuerdo*) • **¡bien!** all right!, O.K.! • **—¿quieres que vayamos al cine? —bien** "shall we go to the cinema?" — "O.K. *o* all right" • **si a ustedes les parece ~** if it's all right with *o* by you
5 (= *muy*) • **un café ~ caliente** a nice hot coffee • **un coche ~ caro** a pretty expensive car • **~ temprano** pretty early • **estoy ~ seguro** I am pretty certain • **eso es ~ tonto** that's pretty silly • **esperamos hasta ~ entrada la noche** we waited until very late at night, we waited until well into the night
6 • **~ de** (= *muchos*): • **~ de veces** lots of times • **¡te han dado ~ de regalos!** you got a lot of presents! • **bebe ~ de café** he drinks a lot of coffee
7 (= *de buena gana*) • **yo ~ iría, pero …** I'd gladly go, but …, I'd be happy to go, but … • **~ me tomaría ahora un café** I'd love a coffee now
8 (= *fácilmente*) easily • **~ se ve que …** it is easy to see that … • **¡~ podía habérmelo dicho!** he could have told me!
9 (*locuciones*) • **estar a ~ con algn** to be on good terms with sb • **de ~ en ~** *o* **mejor** better and better • **~ que mal** one way or another, by hook or by crook • **más ~** rather • **más ~ bajo** on the short side, rather short • **más ~ creo que …** I actually think … • **pues ~** well • **tener a ~ hacer algo** to see fit to do sth • **sus padres tienen a ~ que se vaya a vivir con su tía** her parents have seen fit to send her to live with her aunt • **le ruego tenga a ~ inscribirme en la lista** please be so kind as to include me on the list, I would be grateful if you would include me on the list • **le ruego tenga a ~ comunicarlo a sus lectores** please be kind enough to inform your readers • **~ es verdad que …** it is of course true that … • **¿y ~?** well?
CONJ **1** • **si ~** although • **si ~ es cierto que …** although it's true that …
2 • **no ~ … ni ~** (*Cono Sur*): • **no ~ llegó, empezó a llover** no sooner had he arrived than it started to rain, as soon as he arrived it started to rain
3 (*en alternancia*) • **~ por avión, ~ en tren** either by air or by train • **~ se levantó, ~ se sentó** whether he stood up or sat down
ADJ [*persona*] well-to-do; [*restaurante, barrio*] posh* • **son gente ~** they're well-to-do • **son de casa ~** they come from a good home
SM **1** (= *bondad*) good • **el ~ y el mal** good and evil • **hacer el ~** to do good • **hombre de ~** good man
2 (= *provecho*) good • **el ~ común** *o* **público** the common good • **en ~ de** for the good of • **hacer algo para el ~ de** to do sth for the good of • **es por tu ~** it's for your own good
3 (*apelativo*) • **mi ~** my dear, my darling
4 bienes (= *géneros*) goods; (= *propiedad*) property (*sing*), possessions; (= *riqueza*) riches, wealth (*sing*) ▸ **bienes activos** active assets ▸ **bienes de capital** capital goods
▸ **bienes de consumo** consumer goods
▸ **bienes de consumo duraderos** consumer durables ▸ **bienes de equipo** capital goods
▸ **bienes de inversión** capital goods ▸ **bienes de la tierra** agricultural produce (*sing*)
▸ **bienes de producción** industrial goods
▸ **bienes de servicio** services ▸ **bienes dotales** dowry (*sing*) ▸ **bienes duraderos** durables ▸ **bienes fungibles** perishables
▸ **bienes gananciales** shared possessions
▸ **bienes inmuebles** real estate (*sing*)
▸ **bienes mostrencos** unclaimed property (*sing*) ▸ **bienes muebles** personal property (*sing*), goods and chattels ▸ **bienes públicos** government property (*sing*) ▸ **bienes raíces** real estate (*sing*), realty (*sing*) (*EEUU*) ▸ **bienes relictos** estate (*sing*), inheritance (*sing*)
▸ **bienes semovientes** livestock (*sing*)
▸ **bienes terrestres** worldly goods

bienal ADJ biennial
SF biennial exhibition, biennial show
bienamado ADJ beloved
bienandante ADJ (= *feliz*) happy; (= *próspero*) prosperous
bienandanza SF (= *felicidad*) happiness; (= *prosperidad*) prosperity
bienaventuradamente ADV happily
bienaventurado ADJ **1** (*Rel*) blessed
2 (= *feliz*) happy, fortunate
3 (= *ingenuo*) naïve
bienaventuranza SF **1** (*Rel*) (= *vida eterna*) bliss, eternal bliss
2 las Bienaventuranzas the Beatitudes
3 (= *felicidad*) happiness; (= *bienestar*) well-being, prosperity
bienestar SM (= *satisfacción*) well-being, welfare; (= *comodidad*) comfort ▸ **bienestar social** social welfare • **estado de ~ social** welfare state
bienhablado ADJ well-spoken
bienhadado ADJ lucky
bienhechor(a) ADJ beneficent, generous
SM/F benefactor/benefactress
bienhechuría SF (*Caribe*) improvement (*to property*)
bienintencionado ADJ well-meaning
bienio SM two-year period
bienoliente ADJ sweet-smelling, fragrant
bienpensante ADJ sanctimonious, goody-goody*
SMF do-gooder*, goody-goody*
bienquerencia SF (= *afecto*) affection; (= *buena voluntad*) goodwill
bienquerer ▸ CONJUG 2t VT to like, be fond of
SM (= *afecto*) affection; (= *buena voluntad*) goodwill
bienquistar ▸ CONJUG 1a VT to bring together, reconcile
VPR **bienquistarse** to become reconciled • **~se con algn** to gain sb's esteem
bienquisto ADJ well-liked, well-thought-of (*con, de, por* by)
bienudo* ADJ (*Cono Sur*) well-off
bienvenida SF **1** (*a un lugar*) welcome • **dar la ~ a algn** to welcome sb • **calurosa ~** warm welcome • **fiesta de ~** welcome party
2 (= *saludo*) greeting
bienvenido ADJ, EXCL • **¡bienvenido!** welcome! • **¡bienvenidos a bordo!** welcome on board! • **siempre serás ~ aquí** you will always be welcome here
bienvivir ▸ CONJUG 3a VI (= *vivir con comodidad*) to live in comfort; (*de acuerdo con las reglas*) to live decently, lead a decent life
bies SM • **al ~** (*Cos*) on the cross
bifásico ADJ (*Elec*) two-phase
bife SM (*Cono Sur*) **1** (= *filete*) steak, beefsteak
2 (= *bofetada*) slap
bífido ADJ [*lengua*] forked; ▸ **espina**
bifidus SM INV, **bífidus** SM INV • **yogur con ~ activo** yoghurt with live *o* active bifidus
bifocal ADJ bifocal • **gafas ~es** bifocals
SMPL o SFPL **bifocales** bifocals
bifronte ADJ two-faced
biftec SM steak, beefsteak
bifurcación SF (= *división*) [*de calle*] fork; (*Elec*) junction; (*Inform, Ferro*) branch
bifurcado ADJ forked
bifurcarse ▸ CONJUG 1g VPR [*camino*] to fork, branch off; [*vía*] to diverge
bigamia SF bigamy
bígamo/a ADJ bigamous
SM/F bigamist
bigardear* ▸ CONJUG 1a VI to loaf around, laze around
bigardo/a ADJ (= *vago*) lazy, idle; (= *libertino*) licentious
SM/F (= *vago*) idler; (= *libertino*) libertine
bígaro SM, **bigarro** SM winkle
bignonia SF ▸ **bignonia del Cabo** Cape honeysuckle
bigornia SF (double-headed) anvil
bigotazo SM huge moustache, huge mustache (*EEUU*)
bigote SM **1** (*tb* **bigotes**) moustache, mustache (*EEUU*) • **~ de cepillo** toothbrush moustache • MODISMOS: • **chuparse los ~s** (*Cono Sur*) to lick one's lips • **de ~*** terrific*, marvellous; (*pey*) awful • **menear el ~*** to eat, scoff*
2 (*Zool*) whiskers (*pl*) ▸ **bigotes de morsa** walrus moustache
bigotudo ADJ with a big moustache *o* (*EEUU*) mustache
bigudí SM curler, hair curler
bijirita SF (*Caribe*) **1** (= *cometa*) kite
2 • MODISMO: • **empinar la ~*** (= *beber*) to booze*, drink a lot; (= *enriquecerse*) to make money by dubious methods
bikini SM, (*Arg*) SF bikini
bilabial ADJ (*Ling*) bilabial
bilateral ADJ bilateral
bilateralmente ADV bilaterally
bilbaíno/a ADJ of/from Bilbao
SM/F native/inhabitant of Bilbao • **los ~s** the people of Bilbao
Bilbao SM Bilbao
bilbilitano/a ADJ of/from Calatayud
SM/F native/inhabitant of Calatayud • **los ~s** the people of Calatayud
Bilbo SM = **Bilbao**
bilet SM (*Méx*) lipstick
biliar ADJ bile (*antes de s*), gall (*antes de s*) • **cálculo ~** gallstone
bilingüe ADJ bilingual
bilingüismo SM bilingualism
bilioso ADJ **1** (*Med*) bilious
2 (= *irritable*) bilious, peevish
bilis SF INV (*Med*) bile • MODISMOS: • **descargar la ~ en** *o* **contra algn** to vent one's spleen on sb • **se le exalta la ~** he gets very cross • **eso me revuelve la ~** it makes my blood boil • **tragar ~** to put up with it
billar SM **1** (= *juego*) billiards; (*con 22 bolas*) snooker • **mesa de ~** billiard table/snooker table ▸ **billar americano** pool ▸ **billar automático, billar romano** pin table
2 (= *mesa*) billiard table/snooker table
3 billares [*de billar*] billiard hall/snooker hall/pool hall; [*de otros juegos*] amusement arcade
billete SM **1** (*Econ*) note, bill (*EEUU*) • **un ~ de cinco libras** a five-pound note • **un ~ de 100 dólares** a 100-dollar bill • MODISMO: • **tener ~ largo** (*Cono Sur**) to be rolling in it* ▸ **billete de banco** banknote
2 [*de transporte*] ticket • **¿puedes comprarme** *o* **sacarme el ~?** can you buy me a ticket? • **medio ~** half fare • **un ~ de libre circulación** a travel-card ▸ **billete azul** *ticket for off-peak travel* ▸ **billete de avión** plane ticket ▸ **billete de ida** single *o* (*EEUU*) one-way ticket ▸ **billete de ida y vuelta** return *o* (*EEUU*) round-trip ticket ▸ **billete electrónico** e-ticket ▸ **billete kilométrico** *concessionary ticket allowing free travel for a certain number of kilometres* ▸ **billete sencillo** single *o* (*EEUU*) one-way ticket
3 (*esp LAm*) [*de cine, espectáculo*] ticket • **ya están los ~s a la venta** tickets are now on sale ▸ **billete de abono** season ticket ▸ **billete de favor** complimentary ticket
4 [*de lotería*] ticket
5† (= *carta*) note, short letter ▸ **billete amoroso** love letter, billet-doux
billetera SF, **billetero** SM wallet, billfold (*EEUU*)
billón SM billion, trillion (*EEUU*)
billonario/a SM/F billionaire
bilobulado ADJ bilobate
bilongo SM (*Cuba*) (= *mal de ojo*) evil eye • **echar ~ en** to put the evil eye on, cast a spell on • **tener ~** to bristle with difficulties
bilonguear ▸ CONJUG 1a VT (*Caribe*) to cast a spell on, put the evil eye on
bimba¹* SF top hat, topper*
bimba²* SF (*Méx*) (= *embriaguez*) drunkenness; (= *borrachera*) drunken spree, binge
bimba³‡ SF wallet, billfold (*EEUU*)
bimbalete SM (*Méx*) (= *columpio*) swing; (*basculante*) seesaw, teeter-totter (*EEUU*)
bimbollo SM (*Méx*) bun
bimensual ADJ **1** (= *cada dos meses*) bimonthly, two-monthly
2 (= *dos veces al mes*) fortnightly, semimonthly (*EEUU*)
bimensualmente ADV every two months
bimensuario ADJ bimonthly, two-monthly
SM bimonthly publication
bimestral ADJ bimonthly, two-monthly
bimestralmente ADV bimonthly, every two months
bimestre ADJ bimonthly, two-monthly
SM **1** (= *período*) two-month period
2 (= *pago*) bimonthly payment, two-monthly payment
bimilenario ADJ bimillenary
SM bimillenary, two-thousandth anniversary
bimotor ADJ twin-engined
SM twin-engined plane
binadera SF, **binador** SM weeding hoe
binar ▸ CONJUG 1a VT to hoe, dig over
binario ADJ **1** (*Mat, Inform*) binary
2 (*Mús*) two-four
bincha SF (*And, Cono Sur*) hairband
bingo SM **1** (= *juego*) bingo • **hacer ~** (*lit*) to get a (full) house; (*fig*) to hit the target, turn up trumps
2 (= *sala*) bingo hall
binguero/a SM/F bingo hall attendant
binoculares SMPL **1** (= *prismáticos*) binoculars; (*Teat*) opera glasses
2 (= *quevedos*) pince-nez (*sing*)
binóculo SM pince-nez
binomio SM **1** (*Mat*) binomial
2 (= *pareja*) • **el ~ ejército-gobierno** the government-army pairing
bio... PREF bio...
bío ADJ INV organic • **productos ~** organic products
bioactivo ADJ bioactive
bioagricultura SF organic farming
biocarburante SM biofuel
biociencia SF bioscience
biocombustible SM biofuel
biodegradable ADJ biodegradable
biodegradación SF biodegradation
biodegradar ▸ CONJUG 1a VT to biodegrade
VPR **biodegradarse** to biodegrade
biodetergente SM biodegradable detergent
biodiésel ADJ, SM biodiesel
biodiversidad SF biodiversity
bioestadística SF biostatistics (*pl*), vital statistics (*pl*)
bioética SF bioethics (*sing*)
bioético/a ADJ bioethical
SM/F bioethicist, expert in bioethics
biofísica SF biophysics (*sing*); ▸ **biofísico**
biofísico/a SM/F biophysicist; ▸ **biofísica**
biogás SM biogas
biogénesis SF biogenesis
biogenética SF genetic engineering
biografía SF biography
biografiado/a SM/F subject of a biography, biographee
biografiar ▸ CONJUG 1c VT to write the

biography of
biográfico (ADJ) biographical
biógrafo/a (SM/F) biographer
(SM) (LAm†) (= cine) cinema, movie theater (EEUU)
bioingeniería (SF) bioengineering
biología (SF) biology ▸ **biología aplicada** applied biology ▸ **biología celular** cell biology ▸ **biología marina** marine biology ▸ **biología molecular** molecular biology ▸ **biología vegetal** plant biology
biológico (ADJ) [ciclo, origen, padre] biological; [alimento] organic • **cultivo ~** organically-grown produce • **guerra biológica** biological warfare
biólogo/a (SM/F) biologist
biomagnetismo (SM) biomagnetism
biomasa (SF) biomass
biombo (SM) folding screen
biomédico (ADJ) biomedical
biometría (SF) biometry, biometrics (sing)
biométrico (ADJ) [datos, tecnología, mecanismo] biometric
biónico (ADJ) bionic
bioorgánico (ADJ) bio-organic
biopiratería (SF) biopiracy
bioprospección (SF) bioprospecting
bioprospector(a) (ADJ) [empresa] bioprospecting (antes de s)
biopsia (SF) biopsy
bioquímica (SF) biochemistry
bioquímico/a (ADJ) biochemical
(SM/F) biochemist
biorritmo (SM) biorhythm
bioscopia (SF) bioscopy
bioseguridad (SF) biosafety
biosensor (SM) biosensor
biosfera (SF) biosphere
biosíntesis (SF INV) biosynthesis
biosintético (ADJ) biosynthetic
biotecnología (SF) biotechnology
biotecnológico (ADJ) biotechnological
biotecnólogo/a (SM/F) biotechnologist
bioterrorismo (SM) bioterrorism
bioterrorista (SMF) bioterrorist
(ADJ) bioterrorist (antes de s)
biótico (ADJ) biotic
biotipo (SM) biotype
biotopo (SM) biotope
biotransformación (SF) biotransformation
bióxido (SM) dioxide ▸ **bióxido de carbono** carbon dioxide
BIP (SM ABR) (= **Banco Internacional de Pagos**) BIS
bip (SM) pip, beep
bipartidismo (SM) two-party system
bipartidista (ADJ) two-party (antes de s)
bipartido (ADJ) bipartite, two-party (antes de s)
bipartito (ADJ) = **bipartido**
bípedo (SM) biped
biplano (SM) biplane
biplaza (ADJ INV) two-seater (antes de s)
(SM) (Aer) two-seater
bipolar (ADJ) (Med) bipolar
bipolaridad (SF) bipolarity
bipolarizar ▸ CONJUG 1f (VT) to bipolarize
biquini (SM), (Arg) (SF) bikini
BIRD (SM ABR) (= **Banco Internacional para la Reconstrucción y el Desarrollo**) IBRD
birdie (SM) (Golf) birdie
BIRF (SM ABR) = **Banco Internacional de Reconstrucción y Fomento**
birimbao (SM) Jew's harp
birlar* ▸ CONJUG 1a (VT) (= quitar) to pinch*, nick* • **me han birlado la bici** my bike's been nicked o pinched* • **le birló la novia** he pinched his girl* • **le ~on el empleo** he was done out of the job*
birlibirloque (SM) • MODISMO: • **por arte de ~** as if by magic
birlocha (SF) 1 (= cometa) kite
2 (Méx‡) (= auto) old banger‡, jalopy
birlonga (SF) • MODISMO: • **hacer algo a la ~** to do sth carelessly, do sth sloppily
Birmania (SF) Burma
birmano/a (ADJ), (SM/F) Burmese
birome (SF) (Cono Sur) (= bolígrafo) ballpoint pen, Biro®; (= lápiz) propelling pencil
birra* (SF) beer
birreactor (ADJ) twin-jet (antes de s)
(SM) twin jet, twin-jet plane
birreta (SF) (Rel) biretta, cardinal's hat
birrete (SM) 1 (= gorro) (Univ) mortarboard; (Jur) judge's cap
2 (Rel) = **birreta**
birrí (SM) (And) snake
birria (SF) 1 (esp Esp) (= cosa fea) monstrosity; (= cosa inútil) useless object • **la novela es una ~*** the novel is rubbish o trash • **entre tanta ~** among so much trash
2 (And*) (= obsesión) set idea
3 (Cono Sur, Méx) (= bebida) tasteless drink; (Méx) (= guiso) stew
4 • MODISMO: • **jugar de ~** (LAm) to play half-heartedly
5 (CAm*) (= cerveza) beer
birriondo (ADJ) (LAm) 1* (= asustadizo) jumpy, highly strung
2‡ (= cachondo) randy*, horny*
birrioso* (ADJ) awful
biruji (SM) (esp Cono Sur) chilly wind
birutilla (SF) (Cono Sur) pot scourer
birutillar ▸ CONJUG 1a (VT) (Cono Sur) to polish
bis (ADV) (= dos veces) twice; (en una calle) • **vive en el 24 bis** he lives at 24B
(SM) (Teat) encore • **la banda hizo dos bises** the band played two encores • **¡bis!** encore!
bisabuelo/a (SM/F) great-grandfather/ great-grandmother • **~s** great-grandparents
bisagra (ADJ) • **acontecimiento ~** decisive event, event that marks a watershed • **partido ~** party that holds the balance of power
(SF) 1 (Téc) hinge
2* [de caderas] waggle, wiggle
bisar ▸ CONJUG 1a (VT) 1 to give as an encore, repeat
2 (Cono Sur) to encore, demand as an encore
(VI) to give an encore
bisbisar ▸ CONJUG 1a (VT) to mutter, mumble
bisbisear ▸ CONJUG 1a (VT) (= murmurar) to mutter, mumble; (Cono Sur) to whisper
bisbiseo (SM) muttering, mumbling
bisbita (SF) pipit
biscote (SM) rusk, melba toast (EEUU)
biscúter (SM) (Aut) three-wheeler
bisecar ▸ CONJUG 1g (VT) to bisect
bisel (SM) 1 (Téc) bevel, bevel edge
2 (Mús) finger hole, keyhole
biselado (ADJ) bevel (antes de s), bevelled
biselar ▸ CONJUG 1a (VT) to bevel
bisemanal (ADJ) twice-weekly
bisemanalmente (ADV) twice-weekly
bisexuado (ADJ) hermaphrodite, twin-sex
bisexual (ADJ), (SMF) bisexual
bisexualidad (SF) bisexuality
bisgra‡ (SF) (Caribe) armpit
bisiesto (ADJ) • **año ~** leap year
bisilábico (ADJ), **bisílabo** (ADJ) two-syllabled
bismuto (SM) bismuth
bisnieto/a (SM/F) great-grandson/ great-granddaughter • **~s** great-grandchildren
bisnis‡ (SM INV) (= clientela) (prostitute's) clients, clientèle
bisojo (ADJ) = **bizco**
bisonte (SM) bison
bisoñada (SF) (= comentario) naïve remark; (= acto) naïve thing to do
bisoñé (SM) toupée
bisoñez (SF) inexperience
bisoño (ADJ) (= principiante) green, inexperienced; (Mil) raw
(SM) (= principiante) greenhorn; (Mil) raw recruit, rookie*
bisté (SM), **bistec** (SM) (PL: **bistés** o **bistecs**)
1 (= filete) steak, beefsteak
2‡ tongue • MODISMO: • **achantar el ~** to shut one's trap‡
bistongo (ADJ) (CAm, Caribe, Méx) spoiled, indulged
bisturí (SM) scalpel
bisunto (ADJ) greasy, grubby
bisutería (SF) costume jewellery o (EEUU) jewelry, imitation jewellery o (EEUU) jewelry
bit (SM) (Inform) bit ▸ **bit de parada** stop bit ▸ **bit de paridad** parity bit
bitácora (SF) (Náut) binnacle
bitensional (ADJ) (Elec) equipped to work on two different voltages
bíter (SM) bitters
bitio (SM) bit
bitoque (SM) 1 [de barril] bung, spigot
2 (CAm) (= desagüe) drain
3 (LAm) (= cánula) short tube, injection tube (of a syringe)
4 (Cono Sur) (= canilla) tap, faucet (EEUU)
5 (Cono Sur) (= bulto) bump, swelling
bituminoso (ADJ) bituminous
bivalvo (ADJ), (SM) bivalve
bivio (SM) (LAm) road junction
Bizancio (SM) Byzantium
bizantino/a (ADJ) 1 (Hist) Byzantine
2 (= baldío) idle, pointless; (= irreal) over-subtle, unreal • **discusión bizantina** pointless argument
3 (fig) (= decadente) decadent
(SM/F) Byzantine
bizarramente (ADV) 1 (= valientemente) gallantly, bravely
2 (= generosamente) generously, splendidly
bizarría (SF) 1 (= valor) gallantry, bravery
2 (= generosidad) generosity
bizarro (ADJ) 1 (= valiente) gallant, brave
2 (= generoso) generous
bizbirindo (ADJ) (Méx) lively, bright
bizcar ▸ CONJUG 1g (VT) [+ ojo] to wink
(VI) to squint, be cross-eyed
bizco/a (ADJ) cross-eyed, squinting • **mirada bizca** squint, look cross-eyed look • **ponerse ~** to squint, look cross-eyed • MODISMOS: • **dejar a algn ~** to leave sb open-mouthed • **quedarse ~** to be flabbergasted
(SM/F) cross-eyed person, someone with a squint
(ADV) • **mirar ~** to squint, look cross-eyed
bizcochera (SF) biscuit barrel, biscuit tin
bizcochería (SF) (Méx) pastry shop
bizcocho (SM) 1 (Culin) (= pastel) sponge cake; (más pequeño) sponge finger, lady finger (EEUU) • MODISMO: • **embarcarse con poco ~** to set out unprepared ▸ **bizcocho borracho** sponge soaked in wine and syrup
2 (Náut) hardtack
3 (= cerámica) biscuit ware
4 (Méx) (= galleta) biscuit
5 (Méx**) (= órgano sexual) cunt**
bizcochuelo (SM) (Arg, Uru) sponge cake; (Col) cake made with cornmeal
bizcorneado (ADJ) (Caribe) cross-eyed, squinting
bizcornear ▸ CONJUG 1a (VI) (Caribe) to squint
bizcorneto (ADJ) (And, Méx) = **bizco**
Bizkaia (SF) Biscay (Basque province)
bizma (SF) poultice
bizmar ▸ CONJUG 1a (VT) to poultice
biznieto/a (SM) = **bisnieto**
bizquear ▸ CONJUG 1a (VI) to squint
bizquera* (SF) (esp LAm) squint

bla-bla-bla SM claptrap, hot air

blanca SF **1** (*Hist*) *old Spanish copper coin* • **MODISMOS**: • **estar sin ~*** • **no tener ~*** to be broke*, be skint*
2 (*Mús*) minim, half note (EEUU)
3 (*Ajedrez*) white piece • **yo llevo las ~s** I'll be white
4 (*Dominó*) blank ▶ **blanca doble** double blank
5‡ (= *cocaína*) coke‡; (= *heroína*) smack‡; ▸ **blanco**

Blancanieves SF Snow White

blanco/a ADJ **1** (= *de color blanco*) white • **el pantalón ha quedado blanquísimo** the trousers have come out really white • **se te está poniendo el pelo ~** your hair is going white • **un vino ~** a white wine • **es de color ~** it's white • **MODISMO**: • **~ como la nieve** as white as snow
2 [*raza*] white • **una mujer blanca** a white woman
3 (= *pálido*) [*cara, cutis*] fair • **soy muy ~ de piel** I'm very fair-skinned • **estar ~** [*cara*] to be pale; [*cuerpo*] to be white • **tenía la cara muy blanca** his face was very pale • **el más ~ de toda la playa** the whitest person on the beach • **MODISMO**: • **~ como la cera** *o* **como el papel** *o* **como la pared** as white as a sheet
4 (*Literat*) [*verso*] blank
SM/F (= *persona*) white man/woman • **el ladrón era un ~, fuerte, de 1,80** the thief was white, heavily built, 6ft tall • **llegó acompañado de dos ~s** he arrived with two white people • **los ~s** white people; ▸ **trata**
SM **1** (= *color*) white • **me gusta el ~ para vestir** I like wearing white • **calentar algo al ~** to heat sth till it is white-hot • **de ~**: • **casarse de ~** to get married in white, have a white wedding • **pintar algo de ~** to paint sth white • **vestirse de ~** to wear white • **en ~ y negro** black and white • **imágenes en ~ y negro** black and white pictures • **MODISMOS**: • **decir que lo ~ es negro** to swear that black is white • **no distinguir lo ~ de lo negro** to be unable to tell right from wrong • **poner los ojos en ~** to roll one's eyes • **verlo todo ~ o negro** to see everything in black and white ▶ **blanco de España** whiting ▶ **blanco de plomo** white lead ▶ **blanco y negro** (*Culin*) *iced coffee with cream*; ▸ **carpintero, punta**
2 (= *parte blanca*) ▶ **blanco de la uña** half-moon ▶ **blanco del huevo** white of the egg, egg white ▶ **blanco del ojo** white of the eye • **MODISMO**: • **no parecerse a algn ni en el ~ de los ojos** to look nothing like sb
3 (= *blancura*) whiteness
4 (= *objetivo*) target • **el puente era un ~ fácil** the bridge was an easy target • **apunta al ~** aim for the target • **dar en el ~** (*lit*) to hit the target • **tus críticas han dado en el ~** your criticisms were right on target *o* were spot on • **has dado en el ~ escogiendo esta carrera** you did exactly the right thing in choosing that degree course • **ese comentario tuyo dio en el ~, por eso dolió tanto** that remark of yours hit home, that's why it hurt so much • **hacer ~** to hit the target • **hacer ~ en algo** to hit sth • **la patrullera hizo ~ en dos lanchas** the patrol boat hit two launches • **la prensa la hizo ~ de sus críticas** the press singled her out for criticism, she was the target of attacks by the press • **lo hicieron ~ de sus sátiras** they held him up to ridicule • **ser (el) ~ de** [*+ crítica*] to be the target of; [*+ burla*] to be the butt of • **se convirtió en el ~ de sus críticas** he became the target of their criticism • **la modelo fue el ~ de todas las miradas** the model was the centre of attention, all eyes were on the model ▶ **blanco móvil** moving target; ▸ **tiro**
5 (= *espacio sin escribir*) blank, blank (space) • **un ~ entre las dos palabras** a blank (space) between the two words
6 • **en ~** blank • **una página en ~** a blank page • **un cheque en ~** a blank cheque • **rellene los espacios en ~** fill in the blanks • **dejar algo en ~** to leave sth blank • **he dejado el examen en ~** I left the exam paper blank, I didn't write anything on the exam paper • **dejé varias preguntas en ~ en el examen** there were several questions I didn't answer in the exam • **votar en ~** to return a blank ballot paper • **MODISMOS**: • **pasar la noche en ~** not to sleep a wink*, have a sleepless night • **quedarse en ~**: • **el concursante se quedó en ~** the contestant's mind went blank • **no pude contestar porque se me quedó la mente en ~** I couldn't answer because my mind went blank
7 (= *pausa*) gap, break • **hay varios ~s entre las clases** there are several gaps *o* breaks between classes
8 (= *mancha blanca*) (*pequeña*) white spot; (*más grande*) white patch
9 (*Puerto Rico*) (= *formulario*) blank, blank form
10 • **los Blancos** (*Uru*) (*Pol*) *political party*; ▸ **blanca**

blancón ADJ (*And*) white-skinned

blancor SM whiteness

blancote ADJ **1** sickly white, unhealthily white
2* (= *cobarde*) yellow*, cowardly
SM* yellow belly*, coward

blancura SF whiteness

blancuzco ADJ (= *parecido al blanco*) whitish; (= *blanco sucio*) dirty-white, off-white

blandamente ADV **1** (*al tacto*) (= *sin aspereza*) mildly, gently; (= *mullido*) tenderly
2 (*en el trato*) indulgently

blandear¹ ▸ CONJUG 1a VT = **blandir**

blandear² ▸ CONJUG 1a VT (= *convencer*) to convince, persuade
VI, VPR **blandearse** (= *ceder*) to soften, yield, give way • **~ con algn** to humour sb, humor sb (EEUU)

blandengue* ADJ soft, weak
SMF softie*

blandenguería* SF softness, weakness

blandiporno* ADJ INV • **película ~** soft-porn film

blandir ▸ CONJUG 3a; defectivo; no utilizado en presente VT to brandish, flourish
VPR **blandirse** to wave to and fro, swing

blando/a ADJ **1** (= *tierno*) [*madera, droga, agua*] soft; [*pasta*] smooth; [*carne*] tender; (*pey*) flabby • **~ de boca** [*caballo*] tender-mouthed • **~ de carnes** flabby • **~ al tacto** soft to the touch
2 (= *indulgente*) [*persona*] soft, indulgent; [*carácter*] soft, delicate; [*política*] soft, wet • **~ de corazón** soft-hearted, sentimental • **ser ~ con el crimen** to be soft on crime • **llevar una vida blanda** to live an easy life
3 (= *cobarde*) cowardly
SM/F (*Pol*) soft-liner, moderate; (*Mil*) dove

blandón SM (*Rel*) (= *vela delgada*) wax taper; (= *candelabro*) large candlestick

blandorro/a* ADJ [*sabor*] tasteless, insipid; [*sonrisa*] weak, sheepish
SM/F **1** (= *pusilánime*) weakling, wimp*
2 (= *cobarde*) coward

blanducho ADJ (*pey*) [*madera, superficie*] soft; [*carne*] flabby (*pey*)

blandujo ADJ softish

blandura SF **1** (= *suavidad*) [*de madera, cama*] softness; [*de carne*] tenderness; [*de agua, pasta*] softness
2 (= *templanza*) [*de clima*] mildness
3 (= *dulzura*) gentleness, tenderness
4 blanduras endearments, sweet nothings

blanduzco ADJ softish

blanqueada SF **1** (*LAm*) (= *blanqueo*) [*de ropa*] bleaching; [*de pared, casa*] whitewashing
2 (*Méx*) (*Dep**) whitewash

blanqueado ADJ [*pared, casa*] whitewashed
SM = **blanqueo**

blanqueador(a) SM/F bleacher

blanquear ▸ CONJUG 1a VT **1** (= *poner blanco*) [*+ dientes*] to whiten; [*+ ropa*] to bleach; [*+ pared, fachada*] to whitewash; [*+ oro, plata*] to blanch • **la nieve blanqueaba el paisaje** the snow turned the landscape white, the snow whitened the landscape
2 (*Esp**) [*+ dinero*] to launder*; [*+ falta, persona culpable*] to whitewash
VI to turn white, go white • **el pelo le blanqueó con los años** his hair went *o* turned white over the years • **ya blanquea la nieve en las montañas** the mountains are now covered in white (snow)

blanquecer ▸ CONJUG 2d VT = **blanquear**

blanquecino ADJ off-white, whitish

blanqueo SM [*de dientes*] whitening; [*de pared, casa*] whitewashing; [*de ropa*] bleaching ▶ **blanqueo de dinero** money laundering

blanquiazul ADJ **1** blue and white
2 (*Dep*) of Espanyol football club
SMF Espanyol player/supporter *etc* • **los ~es** Espanyol football club/team *etc*

blanquillo ADJ whitish • **azúcar ~** white sugar • **trigo ~** white wheat
SM **1** (*CAm, Méx*) (= *huevo*) egg
2 (*Chile, Perú*) (= *durazno*) white peach
3 (*Caribe, Cono Sur*) (= *pez*) whitefish

blanquimiento SM bleach, bleaching solution

blanquín SM ▶ **blanquín de gallina** (*Caribe*) (*euf*) hen's egg

blanquinegro ADJ black-and-white

blanquita‡ SF (*Caribe*) cocaine

blasfemador(a) ADJ blasphemous
SM/F blasphemer

blasfemamente ADV blasphemously

blasfemar ▸ CONJUG 1a VI **1** (*Rel*) to blaspheme (**contra** against)
2 (= *decir tacos*) to curse, swear

blasfemia SF **1** (*Rel*) blasphemy
2 (= *taco*) swearword, curse

blasfemo/a ADJ, SM/F = **blasfemador**

blasón SM **1** (*Heráldica*) (= *escudo*) coat of arms; (= *ciencia*) heraldry
2 (= *honor*) honour, honor (EEUU), glory

blasonar ▸ CONJUG 1a VT **1** [*+ escudo*] to emblazon
2 (= *encomiar*) [*+ persona*] to praise, extol
VI to boast, boast about

blaugrana ADJ of Barcelona Football Club
SMF • **los ~(s)** (= *jugadores*) the Barcelona team; (= *hinchas*) the Barcelona fans

blazer SM blazer

bleck SM (*Cono Sur*) pitch, tar • **MODISMO**: • **dar una mano de ~ a algn** to discredit sb, blacken sb's name

bledo SM ▸ **importar²**

bleque SM (*Cono Sur*) = **bleck**

blindado ADJ [*vehículo*] armour-plated, armor-plated (EEUU); [*chaleco*] bullet-proof; [*cable*] shielded • **carro ~** armoured *o* (EEUU) armored car • **puerta blindada** reinforced door
SM armoured *o* (EEUU) armored vehicle

blindaje SM [*de vehículo*] armour-plating, armor-plating (EEUU); [*de cable*] shield

blindar ▸ CONJUG 1a VT [*+ vehículo*] to armour-plate, armor-plate (EEUU); [*+ cable*] to shield

b.l.m. ABR (= **besa la mano**) *courtesy formula*

bloc SM (PL: **blocs**) (*para notas*) pad, writing pad ▶ **bloc de dibujos** sketch pad ▶ **bloc de ejercicios** jotter, exercise book ▶ **bloc de**

b

notas [*de estudiante*] notepad; [*de periodista*] reporter's notebook ▸ **bloc de taquigrafía** shorthand book
blocaje (SM) (= *bloqueo*) (*Dep*) tackle, stop; (*Mil*) blockade; (*Mec*) gripping, locking
blocao (SM) (*Mil*) blockhouse
blocar ▹ CONJUG 1g (VT) (*Dep*) [+ *jugador*] to tackle; [+ *balón*] to stop, trap
blof (SM) (*LAm*) bluff • **hacer un ~ a algn** to bluff sb
blofear ▹ CONJUG 1a (*LAm*) (VI) to boast, brag
blofero (ADJ) (*LAm*) boastful, bragging
blofista (SMF) (*LAm*) boaster, braggart
blog [blox] (SM) (PL: **blogs**) (*Internet*) blog
blogger ['bloger] (SMF) (PL: **bloggers**) blogger
blogosfera (SF) blogosphere
bloguear ▹ CONJUG 1a (VI) to blog
blogueo (SM) blogging, weblogging (*frm*)
bloguero/a (SM/F) blogger
blonda (SF) **1** (= *encaje*) blond lace
2 (*Cono Sur*) (= *rizo*) curl
blondo (ADJ) **1** (*liter*) (= *rubio*) blond, fair, flaxen (*liter*)
2 (*LAm*) (= *liso*) soft, smooth, silken
3 (*CAm*) (= *lacio*) lank
4 (*Cono Sur, Méx*) (= *rizado*) curly
bloque (SM) **1** (= *trozo*) [*de piedra, mármol*] block; [*de helado*] brick ▸ **bloque de casas** block, block of houses ▸ **bloque de cilindros** cylinder block ▸ **bloque de hormigón** block of concrete ▸ **bloque de papel** = **bloc** ▸ **bloque de pisos** block of flats (*Brit*), apartment building (*EEUU*) ▸ **bloque de sellos** block of stamps ▸ **bloque de viviendas** block of flats ▸ **bloque publicitario** commercial break
2 (= *bloqueo*) (*en tubo, salida*) block, blockage, obstruction
3 (*Pol*) bloc • **el ~ comunista** the communist bloc • **en ~** en bloc
4 (*Inform*) block
bloqueado (ADJ) (*Inform*) locked
bloqueante (ADJ) paralysing, inhibiting (SM) (= *droga*) inhibitor, anticatalyst
bloquear ▹ CONJUG 1a (VT) **1** (= *obstaculizar*) [+ *entrada, salida*] to block (off); [+ *camino, proyecto, proceso*] to block • **un tractor bloqueaba la carretera** the road was blocked by a tractor, a tractor was blocking the road • **~on la puerta con un sillón** they blocked *o* barricaded the door with an armchair • **los manifestantes ~on la calle en protesta** the demonstrators blocked the street as a protest • **la oposición bloqueó la ley en la cámara** the opposition blocked the bill in parliament • **la policía nos bloqueó el paso** the police barred our way
2 (= *atascar*) [+ *mecanismo*] to jam (up), block; [+ *cerradura, línea telefónica*] to jam; [+ *volante*] to lock • **los oyentes ~on la centralita de la emisora** listeners jammed the radio station's switchboard
3 (= *aislar*) to cut off • **quedaron bloqueados por la nieve** they were cut off by the snow
4 (*Mil*) to blockade
5 (*Com, Econ*) to freeze • **fondos bloqueados** frozen assets
6 (*Dep*) [+ *jugador*] to tackle; [+ *balón*] to stop, trap
(VPR) **bloquearse 1** (= *paralizarse*) [*persona*] • **me bloqueé en el examen** my mind went blank in the exam, I had a (mental) blank in the exam • **cuando me habla me bloqueo** when he speaks to me I get completely tongue-tied • **me quedé bloqueado ante tanta información** I was overwhelmed by the amount of information • **siempre me bloqueo ante el peligro** I always freeze in the face of danger
2 (= *atascarse*) [*mecanismo*] to jam (up); [*cerradura, línea telefónica, centralita*] to jam; [*frenos, volante*] to lock
bloqueo (SM) **1** (*Mil*) blockade • **burlar** *o* **forzar el ~** to run the blockade
2 (*Com, Econ*) ▸ **bloqueo de fondos** freezing of assets ▸ **bloqueo informativo** news blackout
3 ▸ **bloqueo mental** mental block
b.l.p. (ABR) (= **besa los pies**) *courtesy formula*
bluejean (SM INV) (*LAm*) jeans (*pl*), denims (*pl*)
Bluetooth® (SF) Bluetooth® • **tecnología ~** Bluetooth® technology
blufar *etc* ▹ CONJUG 1a (VI) = **blofear** *etc*
bluff (SM) bluff
blumes (SMPL) • MODISMO: • **tener ~** (*Caribe**) to be fussy, be finicky
blusa (SF) **1** (= *camisa*) blouse
2 (= *mono*) overall
3 (= *bata*) smock
blusero/a (ADJ) blues (*antes de s*), rhythm and blues (*antes de s*)
(SM/F) blues fan, rhythm and blues fan
blusón (SM) (= *camisa grande*) long shirt, loose shirt; [*de pintor*] smock
Blvr. (ABR) (= **Bulevar**) Blvd
BM (SM ABR) (= **Banco Mundial**) WB
BN (ABR) (*Esp*) (= **Biblioteca Nacional**) (SM ABR) (*Perú*) = **Banco de la Nación**
b/n (ABR) (= **blanco y negro**) b/w
B.° (ABR) **1** (*Econ*) (= **Banco**) bk
2 (*Com*) = **beneficiario**
boa (SF) boa
boardilla (SF) = **buhardilla**
boatiné (SF) • **bata de ~** padded dressing-gown
boato (SM) show, ostentation
bob (SM) bobsleigh
bobada (SF) silly thing, stupid thing • **esto es una ~** this is nonsense • **este programa es una ~** this programme is stupid • **decir ~s** to say silly things, talk nonsense • **¡no digas ~s!** come off it!, don't talk nonsense! • **hacer ~s** to do stupid things • **cuando está borracho no para de hacer ~s** when he's drunk he's always doing stupid things
bobales* (SMF INV) nitwit*, dolt
bobalicón/ona (ADJ) utterly stupid (SM/F) nitwit, clot*, dumbbell (*EEUU**)
bobamente (ADV) (= *tontamente*) stupidly; (= *inocentemente*) naïvely
bobático* (ADJ) silly, half-witted
bobear ▹ CONJUG 1a (VI) (= *hacer tonterías*) to fool about, do silly things; (= *decir tonterías*) to talk nonsense, say silly things
bobelas* (SMF INV) idiot, chump*
bobera (SF) = **bobería**
boberá (SMF) (*Caribe*) fool
bobería (SF) **1** (= *cualidad*) silliness, idiocy
2 = **bobada**
bobeta (ADJ) (*Cono Sur*) silly, stupid (SMF) (*Cono Sur*) fool, idiot
bobetas (SMF INV) (*And*) fool, idiot
bobicomio (SM) (*And*) lunatic asylum
bóbilis (ADV) • MODISMO: • **de ~** (= *gratis*) free, for nothing; (= *sin esfuerzo*) without lifting a finger
bobina (SF) (= *carrete*) (*Cos*) reel; (*Téc, Pesca*) spool; (*Fot*) spool, reel; (*Aut, Elec*) coil ▸ **bobina de encendido** ignition coil
bobinado (SM) (*Elec*) winding
bobinadora (SF) winder, winding machine
bobinar ▹ CONJUG 1a (VT) to wind
bobo/a (ADJ) (= *tonto*) silly, stupid; (= *ingenuo*) simple, naïve • MODISMO: • **estar** *o* **andar ~ con algo** to be crazy about sth
(SM/F) (= *tonto*) idiot, fool; (*Teat*) clown, funny man • MODISMOS: • **entre ~s anda el juego** (*iró*) they're well matched, one's as bad as the other • **a los ~s se les aparece la madre de Dios** fortune favours fools
(SM/F) **1** (*Caribe**) (= *reloj*) watch
2 (*Cono Sur*) (= *corazón*) heart, ticker*
boboliche (SMF) (*And*) fool
bobsleigh ['bobslei] (SM) bobsleigh
boca (SF) **1** (*Anat*) mouth • **no debes hablar con la ~ llena** you shouldn't talk with your mouth full • **tengo que arreglarme la ~** I must get my teeth seen to • **aceituna de ~** eating olive • **(respiración) ~ a ~** mouth-to-mouth resuscitation • **¡cállate la ~!*** shut up!*, shut your mouth!‡ • **~ abajo** face down • **estar tumbado ~ abajo** to be lying face down • **se cuelgan los manojos ~ abajo** hang the bunches upside down • **~ arriba** face up • **poner a algn ~ arriba** to turn sb on his back ▸ **boca de escorpión** wicked tongue ▸ **boca de mar** (*Culin*) crab stick
2 • **en ~ de**: • **suena extraño en ~ de un socialista** it sounds odd coming from a socialist • **está en ~ de todos** it's on everybody's lips • **puso esa frase en ~ de un personaje suyo** he gave that phrase to one of his characters • **por ~ de** through • **hablan por ~ del negociador** they speak through the negotiator • **lo sabemos por ~ de los propios autores del delito** we know so from the people responsible for the crime
3 • MODISMOS: • **no abrió la ~ en toda la tarde** he didn't open his mouth *o* he didn't say a word all afternoon • **buscar la ~ a algn** (= *hacer hablar*) to try to draw sb out; (= *provocar*) to provoke sb • **coserse la ~*** to keep quiet, keep mum* • **dar ~*** to gab*, chat • **de ~ en ~**: • **la cosa anda de ~ en ~** the story is doing the rounds • **ella anda de ~ en ~** everyone is talking about her • **de ~ para afuera**: • **apoyó la idea de ~ para afuera** he paid lip-service to the idea • **eso lo dice de ~ para afuera** he's just saying that, that's what he says (but he doesn't mean it) • **decir algo con la ~ chica** *o* **pequeña** to say sth without really meaning it • **sin decir esta ~ es mía** without a word to anybody • **hablar por ~ de ganso** to parrot other people's opinions • **hacer ~** to whet sb's appetite • **se me hace la ~ agua** my mouth is watering • **irse la ~ a algn**: • **se me fue la ~** it just slipped out • **llenársele la ~ a algn**: • **esa Europa con la que se les llena la ~** this Europe that they're always talking about • **se le llena la ~ del coche** all he can talk about is the car • **meter a algn en la ~ del lobo** to put sb on the spot • **meterse en la ~ del lobo** to put one's head in the lion's mouth • **(oscuro) como ~ de lobo** pitch black • **partir la ~ a algn*** to smash sb's face in* • **a pedir de ~**: • **todo salió a pedir de ~** it all turned out perfectly • **quedarse con la ~ abierta** to be dumbfounded • **me lo has quitado de la ~** you took the words right out of my mouth • **¡que tu ~ sea santa!** (*Caribe*) I hope you're right! • **tapar la ~ a algn** to keep sb quiet, shut sb up* • **torcer la ~** (= *hacer un gesto*) to make a wry face; (= *burlarse*) to sneer • REFRANES: • **en ~ cerrada no entran moscas** silence is golden • **el que tiene ~ se equivoca** we all make mistakes, to err is human • **por la ~ muere el pez** silence is golden, it's best to keep one's own counsel; ▹ **sabor**
4 (= *abertura, entrada*) [*de túnel, cueva, vasija*] mouth; [*de tonel*] bunghole; [*de puerto*] entrance; [*de arma*] muzzle • MODISMO: • **a ~ de jarro**: • **beber a ~ de jarro** to drink to excess • **disparar a ~ de jarro** to shoot point-blank, shoot at close range ▸ **boca de incendios** hydrant ▸ **boca del estómago** pit of the stomach ▸ **boca de metro**

underground *o* *(EEUU)* subway entrance
▸ **boca de mina** pithead, mine entrance
▸ **boca de riego** hydrant ▸ **boca de río** river mouth, estuary
5 *[de vino]* flavour, flavor *(EEUU)* • **tener buena ~** to have a good flavour
6 *[de crustáceo]* pincer
7 *[de herramienta]* cutting edge
8 ▸ **boca de dragón** *(Bot)* snapdragon
9 *(Inform)* slot
10 bocas *(= personas)* mouths • **son seis ~s las que tengo que alimentar** I have six mouths to feed
(SM) **1** ▸ **boca a boca** • **aplicar** *o* **hacer** *o* **practicar el ~ a ~ a algn** to give sb mouth-to-mouth resuscitation, give sb the kiss of life
2‡ *[de cárcel]* screw‡, warder

bocabajear ▸ CONJUG 1a (VT) *(LAm)* to put down, crush

bocabajo (SM) *(Caribe)* beating

bocacalle (SF) side street • **la primera ~ a la derecha** the first turning *o* road on the right

bocacha (SF) **1‡** bigmouth‡
2 *(Mil, Hist)* blunderbuss

bocacho (ADJ) *(Cono Sur*)* big-mouthed

Bocacio (SM) Boccaccio

bocadear ▸ CONJUG 1a (VT) to cut up *(for eating)*

bocadillería (SF) *(Esp)* snack bar, sandwich bar

bocadillo (SM) **1** *(Esp)* sandwich *(made with French bread)* • **un ~ de queso** a cheese baguette
2 *(en historietas)* balloon, bubble

bocadito (SM) **1** *(= mordisco)* morsel, bit
2 bocaditos *(And)* snack *(sing)*, appetizer *(sing)* • MODISMO: • **a ~s** piecemeal
3 *(Caribe)* *(= cigarrillo) cigarette wrapped in tobacco leaf*

bocado (SM) **1** *(= de comida)* mouthful; *(= aperitivo)* snack • **~ exquisito** titbit • **no he probado ~ en todo el día** I've not had a bite to eat all day • **intentaba hablar entre ~ y ~** I was trying to talk between mouthfuls • **tomar un ~** to have a bite to eat • MODISMOS: • **no hay para un ~** that's not nearly enough • **el ~ del león** the lion's share • **~ sin hueso** sinecure, soft job
2 *(= mordisco)* bite • **le arrancó la oreja de un ~** he bit his ear off • **pegar un ~ a algo/algn** to bite sth/sb • **le he dado solo un ~ a tu tortilla** I've only had a bite out of your omelette
3 *(para caballo)* bit
4 ▸ **bocado de Adán** Adam's apple
5* *(= astilla)* sweetener*, backhander*, payola *(EEUU)*
6 *(And)* *(= veneno)* poison, animal poison

bocajarro (ADV) • **a ~** *[disparar]* at point-blank range • **decir algo a ~** to say sth bluntly, say sth without mincing one's words

bocal (SM) **1** *(= jarro)* pitcher, jar
2 *(Mús†)* mouthpiece

bocallave (SF) keyhole

bocamanga (SF) **1** *(Cos)* cuff, wristband
2 *(Méx)* *(= agujero)* hole for the head *(in a cape)*

bocamina (SF) *(Min)* pithead, mine entrance

bocana (SF) estuary

bocanada (SF) **1** *(= ráfaga)* *[de humo]* puff; *[de viento, aliento]* gust, blast • MODISMO: • **echar ~s** to boast, brag
2 *[de vino]* mouthful, swallow
3 ▸ **bocanada de gente** crush of people

bocaracá (SM) *(CAm)* snake

bocarada (SF) *(LAm)* = **bocanada**

bocarte (SM) anchovy

bocasucia* *(Arg, Uru)* (ADJ) foul-mouthed
(SMF) • **ser un ~** to swear like a trooper

bocata* (SM) sandwich

bocatería* (SF) ≈ sandwich bar

bocatero/a (SM/F) *(Caribe)* loudmouth*, braggart

bocatoma (SF) *(LAm)* water intake, inlet pipe

bocazas* (SMF INV) bigmouth*

bocera (SF) smear on the lips

boceras* (SMF INV) loudmouth*

bocetista (SMF) sketcher

boceto (SM) *(= esquema)* sketch, outline; *(= diseño)* design; *(= maqueta)* model, mock-up

bocha (SF) **1** *(= bola)* bowl • **juego de las ~s** bowls
2 *(Cono Sur‡)* *(= cabeza)* nut*, noggin *(EEUU‡)*

bochar ▸ CONJUG 1a (VT) **1** *(LAm)* *(= rechazar)* to rebuff, reject • **~ a algn** to give sb a dressing down
2 *(Arg*)* *(= suspender)* to fail, flunk*

boche (SM) **1** *(Chile)* husks *(pl)*, chaff
2 *(LAm)* *(= rechazo)* snub • **dar ~ a algn** to snub sb
3 *(And, Cono Sur)* row, fuss

bochinche (SM) **1** *(= jaleo)* uproar, commotion
2 *(And, Caribe)* *(= chisme)* piece of gossip
3 *(Méx)* *(= baile)* rave-up*; *(= fiesta)* wild party
4 *(Méx)* *(= bar)* seedy bar, dive*
5 *(Méx)* *(= tienda)* local store
6 *(Caribe)* muddle, mess

bochinchear ▸ CONJUG 1a (VI) *(LAm)* to make a commotion

bochinchero/a *(esp LAm)* (ADJ) rowdy, brawling
(SM/F) *(LAm)* brawler

bochinchoso (ADJ) **1** *(LAm)* *(= chismoso)* gossiping, gossipy
2 *(And)* *(= agresivo)* rowdy, noisy
3 *(= quisquilloso)* fussy, finicky

bocho (SM) • **ser un ~** *(Cono Sur)* to be brainy, be clever

bochorno (SM) **1** *(= calor)* sultry weather, stuffy weather*
2 *(Med)* hot flush
3 *(= vergüenza)* embarrassment, shame • **¡qué ~!** how embarrassing!

bochornoso (ADJ) **1** *[tiempo, día]* close*, stuffy*
2 *(= vergonzoso)* degrading, shameful • **es un espectáculo ~** it is a degrading spectacle, it is a shameful sight

bocina (SF) **1** *(Mús, Aut)* horn • **tocar la ~** *(Aut)* to sound one's horn, blow one's horn
▸ **bocina de niebla** foghorn
2 *(= megáfono)* megaphone
3 *(LAm)* *(= trompetilla)* ear trumpet
4 *(Méx)* *(Telec)* mouthpiece
5 *(Cono Sur)* *(= soplón)* grass‡, informer, fink *(EEUU‡)*

bocinar ▸ CONJUG 1a (VI) *(Aut)* to sound one's horn, blow the horn, hoot

bocinazo (SM) *(Aut)* toot, blast *(of the horn)* • MODISMO: • **dar el ~‡** to grass‡

bocinero/a (SM/F) horn player

bocio (SM) goitre, goiter *(EEUU)*

bock [bok] (SM) (PL: **bocks** [bok]) beer glass, tankard

bocón/ona (ADJ) **1** *(= jactancioso)* boastful, big-mouthed‡
2 *(Caribe, Cono Sur)* *(= gritón)* loud-mouthed; *(= chismoso)* backbiting, gossipy
3 *(Méx)* *(= poco discreto)* indiscreet
(SM/F) bigmouth‡

bocoy (SM) hogshead, large cask

boda (SF) **1** *(= ceremonia)* wedding, marriage; *(= convite)* reception, wedding reception
2 *(= aniversario)* ▸ **bodas de diamante** *[de pareja]* diamond wedding *(sing)*, diamond wedding anniversary *(sing)*; *[de asociación]* diamond jubilee *(sing)* ▸ **bodas de oro** *[de pareja]* golden wedding *(sing)*, golden wedding anniversary *(sing)*; *[de asociación]* golden jubilee *(sing)* ▸ **bodas de plata** *[de pareja]* silver wedding *(sing)*, silver wedding anniversary *(sing)*; *[de asociación]* silver jubilee *(sing)*

bodega (SF) **1** *(= depósito)* *[de alimentos]* storeroom; *[de vinos]* wine cellar; *[de una casa]* cellar
2 *(tb* **bodega de carga***)* *(Aer, Náut)* hold
3 *(= tienda)* *[de vinos, licores]* wine shop; *(LAm)* *[de comestibles]* grocer's shop, grocery store *(EEUU)*
4 *(esp LAm)* *(= bar)* bar

bodegaje (SM) *(Chile)* storage

bodegón (SM) **1** *(= restaurante)* cheap restaurant
2 *(Arte)* still life

bodegonista (SMF) still-life painter

bodeguero/a (ADJ) *(Caribe)* coarse, common
(SM/F) **1** *[de vino]* *(= productor)* wine producer; *(= encargado)* cellarman/cellarwoman; *(= dueño)* owner of a bodega
2 *(And, Caribe)* *(= tendero)* grocer

bodijo* (SM) *(= boda)* quiet wedding; *(pey)* misalliance

bodolle (SM) *(Cono Sur)* billhook

bodoque (SM) **1** *[de ballesta]* small ball, pellet
2 *(CAm, Méx)* *(Med)* *(= bulto)* lump, swelling; *(= bolita)* lump, ball
3 *(Méx)* *(= tonto)* dimwit*
4 *(CAm)* *(= manojo)* bunch
5 *(Méx)* *(= cosa mal hecha)* badly-made thing

bodorrio (SM) **1** *(= boda)* *(pey)* poor wedding
2 *(Méx)* *(= fiesta)* rowdy party

bodrio (SM) **1*** *(= porquería)* rubbish, garbage *(EEUU)*, trash • **la película era un ~** the film was rubbish *o* a load of tosh* • **un ~ de sitio** an awful place
2 *(esp LAm)* *(= confusión)* mess

body [boði] (SM) (PL: **bodies**) body stocking
▸ **body milk** body lotion

BOE (SM ABR) *(Esp)* (= **Boletín Oficial del Estado**) ≈ Hansard, ≈ The Congressional Record *(EEUU)*

> **BOE**
> The **Boletín Oficial del Estado** is a daily Spanish government publication in which new laws, directives and executive decisions are published together with advertisements for public-sector posts and contracts. It is provided free of charge to all government agencies and state organizations including schools, embassies and public libraries.

bóer (ADJ) Boer
(SMF) (PL: **bóers**) Boer

bofe (SM) *(Zool)* lung • MODISMO: • **echar los ~s*** to slog one's guts out • **echar los ~s por algo*** to go all out for sth

bofetada (SF) *(= tortazo)* slap in the face; *(= puñetazo)* punch, punch in the face • **dar de ~s a algn** to hit *o* punch *o* slap sb • **darse de ~s** *[personas]* to come to blows; *[colores]* to clash

bofetón (SM) punch, punch in the face

bofia‡ (SF) • **la ~** the pigs‡ *(pl)*
(SMF) pig‡, cop*

boga¹ (SF) *(= moda)* fashion, vogue • **la ~ de la minifalda** the fashion for the miniskirt • **estar en ~** to be in fashion, be in vogue • **poner algo en ~** to establish a fashion for sth

boga² (SF) *(Ferro)* bogey

boga³ (SMF) *(= remador)* rower, oarsman/oarswoman
(SF) rowing

bogada (SF) stroke *(of an oar)*

bogador(a) SM/F, **bogante** SMF rower, oarsman/oarswoman
bogar ▷ CONJUG 1h VI to row
bogavante SM **1** (*Náut*) stroke, first rower
2 (*Zool*) lobster
Bogotá SF Bogotá
bogotano/a ADJ of/from Bogotá
SM/F native/inhabitant of Bogotá • **los ~s** the people of Bogotá
bogotazo SM **1** (*LAm*) *Bogotá rising of 1948*
2 (*And*) ruin, destruction, pillage
bohardilla SF = **buhardilla**
Bohemia SF Bohemia
bohémico ADJ (*Geog*) Bohemian
bohemio/a ADJ, SM/F **1** (*Geog*) Bohemian
2 (= *poco convencional*) bohemian
bohío SM (*LAm*) (= *choza*) hut, shack
boicot SM (PL: **boicots**) boycott • **hacer el ~ a algo** to boycott sth
boicotear ▷ CONJUG 1a VT to boycott
boicoteo SM boycott, boycotting
boicotero SM (*LAm*) boycott
boina SF beret
SMF ▸ **boina verde** commando
boite [bwat] SF, **boîte** [bwat] SF nightclub
boj SM (= *planta*) box; (= *madera*) boxwood
boje ADJ (*Méx*) silly, stupid
bojote SM **1** (*LAm*) (= *paquete*) bundle, package
2 • **un ~ de** a lot of, a load of*
3 (*CAm*) (= *trozo*) lump, chunk
4 (*Caribe*) (= *alboroto*) fuss, row
bol SM **1** (= *cuenco*) bowl; (*para ponche*) punchbowl
2 (*LAm*) (= *lavafrutas*) finger bowl
3 (*Dep*) ninepin
4 (*Pesca*) dragnet
bola SF **1** (= *cuerpo esférico*) ball; [*de helado*] scoop; (= *canica*) marble • **van a sacar la ~ premiada** they're going to pick the winning ball • **del susto se me ha hecho una ~ en el estómago** my stomach knotted up with fright • MODISMO: • **estar hecho una ~** (= *gordo*) to be round as a barrel, be chubby*; (= *acurrucado*) to be curled up (in a ball) ▸ **bola de alcanfor** mothball ▸ **bola de contar** abacus bead ▸ **bola de cristal** crystal ball ▸ **bola de fuego** (*Mil*) fireball; (*Meteo*) ball lightning ▸ **bola del mundo** globe ▸ **bola de naftalina** mothball ▸ **bola de nieve** snowball ▸ **bola de tempestad, bola de tormenta** storm signal ▸ **bola negra** black ball; ▷ **pie, queso**
2 (*Dep*) ball; [*de petanca*] boule • MODISMOS: • **andar como ~ huacha** (*Chile*) • **andar como ~ sin manija** (*Arg, Uru*) to be at a loose end • **dar ~** (*Cono Sur**) to take notice • **se lo he dicho mil veces pero no me da ~** I've told him a thousand times but he doesn't take any notice *o* a blind bit of notice • **¡dale ~!** what, again! • **dar la ~** (*Esp*†‡) to be released (from jail) • **dejar que ruede la ~** to let things take their course • **escurrir la ~** to take French leave • **ir a su ~** (*Esp**) to do one's own thing* • **aquí cada uno va a su ~** everyone does their own thing here* • **tú (ve) a tu ~** just do your own thing* • **parar ~(s)** (*Col, Ven*) to pay attention • **no me paró ~s** he didn't take any notice, he didn't pay attention • **pasar la ~*** to pass the buck* • **pasarse de la ~** (*Caribe**) to go too far • **no rascar ~** (*Esp*‡) not to lift a finger* ▸ **bola de billar** billiard ball, snooker ball • MODISMO: • **tener la cabeza como una ~ de billar** to be as bald as a coot ▸ **bola de partido** (*Esp*) (*Tenis*) match ball ▸ **bola de set** (*Esp*) (*Tenis*) set point
3 (*en lana, algodón*) bobble • **para que no le salgan ~s es mejor lavarlo a mano** it's best to wash it by hand to stop bobbles • **hacerse ~s** [*jersey, abrigo*] to get bobbly; (*Méx**) [*persona*] to get o.s. tied up in knots
4 (*Esp*) (= *músculo*) [*del brazo*] biceps; [*de la pantorrilla*] calf muscle • **sacar ~** to flex one's muscles
5‡ (= *cabeza*) nut*, noggin (*EEUU*‡) • **tú estás mal de la ~** you're nuts* • MODISMO: • **cambiar la ~** (*Caribe**) to change one's mind
6 bolas** (= *testículos*) balls** • MODISMOS: • **en ~s**‡ (= *desnudo*) naked • **tíos en ~s** naked men • **aquí todo el mundo va** *o* **está en ~s** everyone goes round naked *o* in the nude here • **en esta cala está permitido ponerse en ~s** they allow nude bathing on this beach • **tras el incendio nos quedamos en ~s** the fire completely cleaned us out* • **hasta las ~s**** pissed off** • **estoy hasta las ~s de él** I'm pissed off with him** • **me tiene hasta las ~s con sus tonterías** I'm pissed off with his fooling around**, I've had it up to here with his fooling around* • **pillar a algn en ~s**‡ to catch sb on the hop* • **¡qué ~s!** (*Caribe, Cono Sur**) what a nerve!*
7* (= *mentira*) fib • **¡vaya ~ que nos metiste!** what a fib you told us! • **este niño nos quiere meter una ~** that boy's trying to put one past us* • **¡qué ~ más grande!** what a whopper!* • **¿no te habrás tragado esa ~?** you didn't swallow that one, did you?*, you didn't fall for it, did you?*
8 (= *rumor*) • **correr la ~** to spread the word • **¿quién ha corrido la ~ de que se van a vivir al extranjero?** who's been spreading the word that they're going to move abroad?
9 (*Méx*) • **dar ~** to polish shoes
10 (*Naipes*) (grand) slam • **media ~** small slam
11 (*Náut*) signal (with discs)
12 (*Tip*) golf ball
13 (*Mec*) ball bearing
14 (*Méx*) (= *jaleo*) row, hubbub; (= *pelea*) brawl • MODISMO: • **se armó la ~** all hell broke loose*
bolacear ▷ CONJUG 1a VI (*Cono Sur*) to talk rubbish
bolaco SM (*Cono Sur*) ruse, device
bolada SF **1** (= *lanzamiento*) (*Ftbl*) throw; (*Atletismo*) putt; (*Billar*) stroke
2 (*LAm*) (= *suerte*) stroke of luck, lucky break; (= *ganga*) bargain, good deal
3 (*Cono Sur*) ▸ **bolada de aficionado** intervention (*by a third party*)
4 (*LAm*) (= *mentira*) fib, lie
5 (*Méx*) (= *chiste*) joke, witty comment; (= *engaño*) trick, con*
6 (*Cono Sur*) (= *golosina*) titbit, treat
bolado SM **1** (*LAm**) (= *asunto*) deal, affair • **esta noche tengo un ~** I've got something on tonight
2 (*Méx*) (= *amorío*) love affair, flirtation
3 (*CAm*) clever stroke
4 (*CAm*) (= *cuento*) fib, tale; (= *chisme*) rumour, piece of gossip
5 (*LAm**) (= *favor*) • **¡hazme un ~!** do me a favour!*
bolamen** SM balls** (*pl*)
bolardo SM bollard
bolata SM ex-con‡, old lag‡
bolate SM (*And*) = **volate**
bolazo SM **1** (*Cono Sur*) (= *tontería*) silly remark, piece of nonsense; (= *noticia falsa*) false news; (= *mentira*) fib, lie; (= *error*) mistake, error • MODISMO: • **mandarse un ~** to put one's foot in it
2 (*Méx*) • MODISMO: • **al** *o* **de ~** at random
bolchevique ADJ, SMF Bolshevik
bolchevismo SM Bolshevism
bolea SF (*Dep*) volley
boleada[1] SF (*Méx*) shoeshine
boleada[2] SF (*Cono Sur**) hunt, hunting expedition (*with bolas*)
boleado[1] (*Cono Sur*) ADJ • **estar ~** to have lost one's touch
boleado[2] SM (*Méx*) shoeshine
boleador(a) SM/F (*Méx*) (= *limpiabotas*) shoeshine boy/girl
boleadoras SFPL (*Cono Sur*) bolas; ▷ **GAUCHO**
bolear ▷ CONJUG 1a VT **1** (= *lanzar*) [+ *pelota*] to throw • **has boleado esa pelota demasiado baja** you threw that ball too low
2 (*LAm*) (= *cazar*) *to catch with bolas*
3 (*LAm*) (= *vencer*) to floor, flummox*
4 (*LAm*) [+ *candidato*] to reject, blackball; [+ *obrero**] to sack*, fire*
5 (*Méx*) [+ *zapatos*] to polish, shine
VI (*Billar*) to play for fun, knock the balls about
VPR **bolearse 1** (*Cono Sur*) (= *darse la vuelta*) [*caballo*] to rear and fall; [*coche*] to overturn
2 (*Cono Sur*) (= *avergonzarse*) to be shamefaced
boleco ADJ (*CAm*) drunk
bolera SF bowling alley, skittle alley
bolería SF (*Méx*) shoeshine shop
bolero[1] ADJ truant
bolero[2] SM (*Mús*) bolero
bolero[3] SM (*Méx*) bootblack, shoeshine boy
boleta SF **1** (*LAm*) (= *billete*) ticket; (= *recibo*) receipt ▸ **boleta de calificaciones** (*Méx*) report
2 (*LAm*) [*de voto*] ballot paper, voting paper; (*Cono Sur*) (*Jur*) draft
3 (*Cono Sur**) • MODISMOS: • **hacer la ~ a algn** to bump sb off* • **ser ~** to be condemned to death
boletería SF (*LAm*) **1** (= *agencia*) ticket agency; (*en estación*) ticket office, booking office; (*Teat*) box office
2 (*Dep*) (= *recaudación*) gate, takings (*pl*)
boletero/a SM/F (*LAm*) ticket clerk, ticket seller
boletín SM **1** (= *publicación informativa*) bulletin; (*Univ*) journal, review; (*Escol*) report ▸ **boletín de inscripción** registration form ▸ **boletín de noticias** news bulletin ▸ **boletín de pedido** order form ▸ **boletín de precios** price list ▸ **boletín de prensa** press release ▸ **boletín de suscripción** subscription form ▸ **boletín electrónico** e-newsletter ▸ **boletín facultativo** medical report ▸ **boletín informativo** news bulletin, news sheet ▸ **boletín meteorológico** weather report *o* forecast ▸ **boletín naviero** shipping register ▸ **Boletín Oficial del Estado** (*Esp*) ≈ Hansard, ≈ The Congressional Record (*EEUU*); ▷ **BOE**
2 (= *billete*) ticket
3 (*Mil*) pay warrant
boleto SM **1** [*de quiniela*] coupon ▸ **boleto de apuestas** betting slip ▸ **boleto de lotería** lottery ticket ▸ **boleto de quinielas** pools coupon
2 (*LAm*) (= *billete*) ticket ▸ **boleto de ida y vuelta** return *o* (*EEUU*) round-trip ticket ▸ **boleto electrónico** e-ticket
3 • MODISMO: • **de ~** (*LAm*) at once
boli* SM pen, Biro®, ballpoint pen
bolichada SF lucky break, stroke of luck • MODISMO: • **de una ~** at one go
boliche[1] SM **1** (= *juego*) bowls (*sing*), bowling
2 (= *bola*) jack
3 (= *bolos*) skittles (*sing*)
4 (= *bolera*) bowling alley
5 (= *juguete*) cup-and-ball toy
6 (= *red*) small dragnet
7 (= *horno*) small furnace, smelting furnace
boliche[2] SM **1** (*LAm*) (= *tenducha*) small grocery store; (*Cono Sur*) (= *café*) cheap snack bar
2 (*And*) (= *tahona*) cheap bakery

3 (*Cono Sur*) (= *garita*) gambling den

boliche³* SM (*LAm*) Bolivian

bolichera SF (*Perú*) fishing boat

bolichero/a SM/F (*LAm*) grocer, shopkeeper

bólido SM **1** (*Aut*) racing car • **iba como un ~*** he was really shifting*
2 (*Náut*) powerboat, speedboat
3 (*Astron*) meteorite

bolígrafo SM pen, ballpoint pen, Biro®

bolilla SF **1** (*Cono Sur*) (= *canica*) marble
2 (*Cono Sur*) (*Univ*) (piece of paper bearing) examination question • **dar ~ a algo** to take notice of sth

bolillo SM **1** (*Cos*) bobbin (*for lacemaking*)
2 (*LAm*) (*Mús*) drumstick
3 (*Méx*) (= *panecillo*) bread roll

bolina SF **1** (= *cabo*) bowline; (= *sonda*) lead, sounding line • **de ~** close-hauled • **navegar de ~** to sail close to the wind
2* (= *jaleo*) racket, row

bolinga‡ ADJ • **estar ~** to be canned*
SF • **estar de ~** to be on the booze* • **ir de ~** to go on the booze*

bolita SF **1** (= *bola pequeña*) (*hueca*) small ball; (*maciza*) pellet; (*Cono Sur*) (= *canica*) marble
2 (*Cono Sur*) (*Pol*) ballot paper

bolívar SM *Venezuelan currency unit*
• MODISMO: • **no verle la cara a Bolívar*** to be broke*

Bolivia SF Bolivia

bolivianismo SM bolivianism, *word/phrase etc peculiar to Bolivia*

boliviano/a ADJ, SM/F Bolivian

bollera‡ SF dyke**; ▹ bollero

bollería SF (= *dulces*) pastries (*pl*); (= *establecimiento*) baker's (shop), pastry shop

bollero/a SM/F baker, pastry cook *o* chef; ▹ **bollera**

bollo SM **1** (*Culin*) [*de pan*] bread roll; (*dulce*) scone, bun • MODISMOS: • **perdonar el ~ por el coscorrón** to realize that it's more trouble than it's worth • **no pela ~** (*Caribe*) he never gets it wrong
2 (*en el coche*) dent • **tengo el coche lleno de ~s** my car is full of dents
3 (*Med*) bump, lump
4 (*Cos*) puff
5 (= *confusión*) confusion, mix-up
• MODISMOS: • **armar un ~** to make a fuss
• **meter a algn en un ~** to get sb into trouble
6 **bollos** (*And*) (= *problemas*) troubles
7 (*CAm, Caribe***) cunt**

bollón SM **1** (= *tachón*) stud, ornamental stud
2 (= *pendiente*) button earring

bolo¹ SM **1** (= *cilindro*) skittle, ninepin (*EEUU*) • MODISMOS: • **andar en ~** (*And*) to be naked • **ir en ~** (*Caribe*) to run off, run away • **tumbar ~** (*And*) to do well, bring it off
2 **bolos** (= *juego*) skittles (*sing*), ninepins (*EEUU*) (*sing*) • MODISMO: • **echar a rodar los ~s** to stir up trouble, make mischief
3 (*Med*) large pill
4 (*Naipes*) slam
5 (= *moneda*) (*Caribe*) one-peso coin; (*Ven*) one-bolívar coin
6 (*Méx*) (= *regalo*) christening present (*from godparents*)
7** (= *pene*) prick**

bolo² (*CAm, Cuba, Méx*) ADJ drunk
SM drunk

bolo³‡ SM (*Mús*) gig, concert

bolón SM **1** (*Cono Sur*) (= *piedra*) quarry stone
2 (*Cuba, Méx*) (= *muchedumbre*) mob

Bolonia SF Bologna

bolonio/a* SM/F dunce, ignoramus

boloñesa SF bolognese sauce, meat sauce

bols SM INV (= *cuenco*) bowl

bolsa SF **1** (*para llevar algo*) bag • **una ~ de caramelos** a bag of sweets • **una ~ de patatas** *o* (*LAm*) **papas fritas** a packet *o* bag of crisps • **una ~ de papel** a paper bag • **una ~ de plástico** a plastic bag • MODISMO: • **hacer algo ~** (*Cono Sur**) to ruin sth • **le pegaron hasta dejarlo hecho ~** they beat him to a pulp ▸ **bolsa de agua caliente** hot-water bottle ▸ **bolsa de asar** roasting bag ▸ **bolsa de asas** carrier bag ▸ **bolsa de aseo** toilet bag ▸ **bolsa de basura** (*para cubo grande*) rubbish bag, bin bag, garbage bag (*EEUU*); (*para cubo pequeño*) bin liner ▸ **bolsa de cultivo** growbag ▸ **bolsa de deportes** sports bag ▸ **bolsa de hielo** ice-pack ▸ **bolsa de la compra** shopping bag ▸ **bolsa de mano** overnight bag, travelling bag ▸ **bolsa de palos** (*Golf*) golf bag ▸ **bolsa de playa** beach bag ▸ **bolsa de tabaco** tobacco pouch ▸ **bolsa para el mareo** sickbag
2 (*Méx*) [*de mujer*] handbag
3 (= *bolsillo*) pocket
4 (*Zool*) [*de canguro*] pouch; [*de calamar*] sac
5 (*Anat*) [*de sangre, pus*] build-up • **una pequeña ~ de pus** a small build-up of pus • **tenía unas ~s enormes en los ojos** she had huge bags under her eyes ▸ **bolsa de aguas** amniotic sac • **ya ha roto la ~ de aguas** her waters have broken ▸ **bolsa escrotal** scrotum ▸ **bolsa lacrimal** tear duct
6 (= *acumulación*) [*de gas, personas*] pocket • **muchos votos procedían de la ~ de indecisos** many of their votes came from those who were undecided • **una enorme ~ de desempleo** a huge number of unemployed, very high levels of unemployment ▸ **bolsa de agua** pocket of water ▸ **bolsa de aire** air pocket ▸ **bolsa de gas** pocket of gas ▸ **bolsa de petróleo** pocket of oil ▸ **bolsa de pobreza** pocket of poverty
7 (= *arruga*) (*en papel pintado*) bubble • **esa blusa te hace ~s** that blouse goes all baggy *o* doesn't hang right on you
8 (*Econ*) (= *mercado*) • **la Bolsa** the Stock Exchange, the Stock Market • **perdieron casi todo jugando a la ~** they lost almost everything playing the market • **las empresas que cotizan en ~** quoted *o* listed companies • **sacar una emisión a ~** to float an issue on the stock market *o* exchange ▸ **bolsa de cereales** corn exchange ▸ **bolsa de divisas** currency market, foreign exchange market ▸ **bolsa de empleo** employment office ▸ **bolsa de granos** corn exchange ▸ **bolsa de la propiedad** property section, property page(s) ▸ **bolsa de trabajo** employment exchange ▸ **bolsa negra** (*Chile*) black market
9 [*de dinero*] • **solo busca engordar la ~** all he's trying to do is line his pockets* • **¡la ~ o la vida!** your money or your life!
• MODISMOS: • **no abrir la ~** to be tight with one's money • **hacer algo a la ~** (*Chile*) to do sth at somebody else's expense ▸ **bolsa de estudios** (study) grant ▸ **bolsa de viaje** travel grant
10 (*Boxeo*) purse

bolsear ▹ CONJUG 1a VT • **la ~on** she had her handbag stolen • **~ a algn** (*CAm, Méx*) to pick sb's pocket
VI **1** (*CAm, Méx*) (= *robar*) to pick pockets
2 (*CAm, Cono Sur, Méx*) (= *estafar*) to cheat, swindle

bolsicón SM (*And*) thick flannel skirt

bolsicona SF (*And*) peasant woman

bolsillo SM **1** [*de chaqueta, pantalón*] pocket • **lo pagué de mi ~** I paid it out of my own pocket • **guardar algo en el ~** to put sth in one's pocket • MODISMOS: • **doler a algn en el ~** to hurt sb's pocket • **meterse a algn en el ~** to have sb eating out of one's hand; (*Pol**) to buy sb off • **rascarse el ~*** to pay up, fork out* • **tener a algn en el ~** to have sb eating out of one's hand, have sb in one's pocket • **tentarse el ~** to consider one's financial circumstances
2 • **de ~** pocket (*antes de s*), pocket-size • **acorazado de ~** pocket battleship • **edición de ~** pocket edition

bolsín SM kerb market (*in stocks and shares*)

bolsiquear ▹ CONJUG 1a VT (*Cono Sur*) • **~ a algn** (= *registrar*) to search sb's pockets, go through sb's pockets; (= *robar*) to pick sb's pockets

bolsista SMF **1** (*Econ*) stockbroker
2 (*CAm, Méx*) (= *ratero*) pickpocket

bolsita SF (*tb* **bolsita de té**) tea bag

bolso SM **1** [*de mano*] bag, handbag, purse (*EEUU*) ▸ **bolso de aseo** toilet bag ▸ **bolso de bandolera** shoulder bag ▸ **bolso de viaje** travelling bag, traveling bag (*EEUU*)
2 (= *monedero*) purse, moneybag, pocketbook
3 (*Náut*) • **hacer ~** [*vela*] to fill, belly out

bolsón ADJ **1** (*And*) (= *tonto*) silly, foolish
2 (*Caribe*) (= *perezoso*) lazy
SM **1** (*Perú*) (= *bolso*) bag, handbag, purse (*EEUU*)
2 (*Bol*) (*Min*) lump of ore
3 (*LAm*) [*de escuela*] satchel, schoolbag
4 (*Méx*) (= *lago*) lagoon
5 (*And*) (= *tonto*) fool

bolsonada SF (*And, Cono Sur*) silly thing to do

boludear‡ ▹ CONJUG 1a VI (*Cono Sur*) to piss about**

boludez‡ SF (*Cono Sur*) **1** (= *cosa fácil*) piece of cake*
2 (= *acto*) stupid thing to do
3 **boludeces** shit** (*sing*), crap** (*sing*)

boludo/a‡ (*Cono Sur*) ADJ thick*, stupid
SM/F arsehole**, asshole (*EEUU***), jerk (*EEUU**)

bomba SF **1** (*Mil*) bomb • **arrojar** *o* **lanzar una ~** (*desde un avión*) to drop a bomb; (*desde el suelo*) to throw a bomb • **poner una ~** to plant a bomb • **a prueba de ~(s)** bomb-proof • **un muro de hormigón a prueba de ~s** a bomb-proof concrete wall • **tiene un estómago a prueba de ~** he's got a cast-iron stomach • **es de una honestidad a prueba de ~** he is as honest as the day is long • MODISMO: • **caer** *o* **sentar como una ~** [*noticia*] to come as a bombshell, be a bombshell • **la cena me cayó como una ~** dinner did not agree with me at all • **las especias me sientan como una ~ en el estómago** spices really upset my stomach ▸ **bomba atómica** atomic bomb ▸ **bomba cazabobos** booby-trap bomb ▸ **bomba de acción retardada** time bomb ▸ **bomba de dispersión** cluster bomb ▸ **bomba de efecto retardado** time bomb ▸ **bomba de fósforo** incendiary bomb ▸ **bomba de fragmentación** fragmentation bomb ▸ **bomba de hidrógeno** hydrogen bomb ▸ **bomba de humo** (*lit*) smoke bomb; (*fig*) smokescreen • **es una ~ de humo para encubrir otras cosas** it is a smokescreen to cover up other things ▸ **bomba de implosión** suction bomb ▸ **bomba de mano** (hand) grenade ▸ **bomba de mortero** mortar bomb, mortar shell ▸ **bomba de neutrones** neutron bomb ▸ **bomba de profundidad** depth charge ▸ **bomba de racimo** (*Cono Sur*) cluster bomb ▸ **bomba de relojería** time bomb ▸ **bomba fétida** stink bomb ▸ **bomba fosfórica** incendiary bomb ▸ **bomba H** H-bomb ▸ **bomba incendiaria** incendiary bomb ▸ **bomba lacrimógena**

tear-gas canister, tear-gas bomb ▸ **bomba lapa** limpet mine ▸ **bomba nuclear** nuclear bomb ▸ **bomba sucia** dirty bomb ▸ **bomba volante** flying bomb
2 (*Téc*) [*de agua, de aire*] pump • **la ~ de la bicicleta** the bicycle pump • **dar a la ~** to pump, work the pump ▸ **bomba aspirante** suction pump ▸ **bomba bencinera** (*Chile*) petrol station, gas station (*EEUU*) ▸ **bomba de aire** (air) pump ▸ **bomba de alimentación** feed pump ▸ **bomba de cobalto** (*Med*) cobalt bomb ▸ **bomba corazón-pulmón** (*Med*) heart-lung machine ▸ **bomba de engrase** grease gun ▸ **bomba de gasolina** (*en motor*) fuel pump; (*en gasolinera*) petrol *o* (*EEUU*) gas(oline) pump ▸ **bomba de inyección (de combustible)** (fuel) injection pump ▸ **bomba de pie** foot pump ▸ **bomba de succión** suction pump ▸ **bomba impelente** force pump ▸ **bomba impulsora** force pump
3 (*Periodismo*) **a** (= *notición*) bombshell • **la dimisión del presidente fue una auténtica ~** the president's resignation was a real bombshell • **esta boda ha sido la ~ del año** this wedding has been the big news of the year • **noticia ~** bombshell
b* (= *éxito*) smash hit* • **este disco será una ~** this record will be a smash hit*
4 (*Mús*) slide
5 [*de lámpara*] glass, globe
6 (*And, Caribe*) (= *burbuja*) bubble; (= *pompa de jabón*) soap bubble
7 (*Col, Ven*) (*tb* **bomba gasolinera**) petrol station, gas station (*EEUU*)
8 (*Chile*) [*de bomberos*] (= *vehículo*) fire engine; (= *estación*) fire station; (= *cuerpo*) fire brigade
9 (*And, Ven*) (= *globo*) balloon; (*Caribe*) (= *cometa*) round kite
10 (*Caribe*) (= *tambor*) big drum; (= *baile*) *dance accompanied by a drum*
11 (*CAm, Perú*) (= *borrachera*) drunkenness • **estar en ~** to be drunk
12 (*LAm*) (= *rumor*) false rumour; (= *mentira*) lie; (*Caribe*) (= *noticia falsa*) hoax
(ADJ INV) (*Esp*†*) (= *estupendo*) • **estar ~** [*persona*] to be gorgeous* • **esa tía está ~** that girl is gorgeous* • **éxito ~*** phenomenal success • **el grupo está teniendo un éxito ~ en su gira** the group is having a phenomenally successful tour
(ADV) (*Esp**) • **pasarlo ~** to have a whale of a time*, have a super time*

bombachas (SFPL) **1** (*And, Cono Sur*) (= *pantalón*) baggy trousers
2 (*Cono Sur*) (= *bragas*) panties

bombacho (ADJ) baggy, loose-fitting
(SMPL) **bombachos** (= *pantalones*) baggy trousers; [*de golf*] plus-fours

bomba-lapa (SF) (PL: **bombas-lapa**) limpet mine

bombardear ▹ CONJUG 1a (VT) **1** (= *lanzar bombas*) (*desde el aire*) to bomb; (*desde tierra*) to bombard, shell
2 (= *lanzar preguntas*) to bombard (**a, con** with) • **~ a algn a preguntas** to bombard sb with questions

bombardeo (SM) **1** (*Mil*) (*desde el aire*) bombing; (*con artillería*) bombardment, shelling ▸ **bombardeo aéreo** (*contable*) air raid, air attack; (*incontable*) air bombardment (**contra, sobre** on) ▸ **bombardeo de saturación** saturation bombing ▸ **bombardeo en picado** dive bombing; ▹ **apuntar**
2 [*de preguntas*] bombardment

bombardero (ADJ) bombing
(SM) (*Aer*) bomber

bombardino (SM) (*Mús*) tuba, bass saxhorn

bombasí (SM) fustian

bombástico (ADJ) (= *grandilocuente*) bombastic; (*Caribe*) (= *elogioso*) complimentary, eulogistic

bomba-trampa (SF) (PL: **bombas-trampa**) booby-trap bomb

Bombay (SM) Mumbai, Bombay

bombazo (SM) **1** (= *explosión*) explosion
2* (= *notición*) bombshell
3* (= *éxito*) smash hit* • **esa película puede ser un ~** that film could be a smash hit*

bombeador (SM) **1** (*Cono Sur*) (*Aer*) bomber
2 (*Cono Sur*) (= *explorador*) scout; (= *espía*) spy

bombear ▹ CONJUG 1a (VT) **1** (*Téc*) [+ *agua, sangre*] to pump
2 (*Ftbl*) to lob • **un balón bombeado** a high ball
3 (*Mil*) to shell
4 (*Cos*) to pad
5 (= *alabar*) to praise up, inflate the reputation of
6 (*Cono Sur*‡) (= *espiar*) to spy on, observe closely
7 (*And, Ven*) (= *despedir*) to sack*, fire*
8 (*CAm*) (= *robar*) to steal
(VI) (*Caribe*) (= *emborracharse*) to get drunk
(VPR) **bombearse** [*techo, pared*] to bulge; [*madera*] to warp

bombeo (SM) **1** (= *acción*) pumping • **estación de ~** pumping station
2 (= *convexidad*) [*de superficie*] bulge; [*de madera*] warp

bombero/a (SM/F) **1** (*de incendios*) firefighter, fireman • **cuerpo de ~s** fire brigade • **llamar a los ~s** to call the fire brigade
2 (= *persona problemática*) troublemaker; ▹ **idea**
3 (*Arg*) (*Mil*) (= *explorador*) spy, scout
4 (*LAm*) (*Aut*) petrol-pump attendant, gas station attendant (*EEUU*)

bombilla (SF) **1** (*Elec*) bulb, light bulb
• MODISMO: • **se le encendió la ~** (= *se dio cuenta*) the penny dropped; (= *tuvo una idea genial*) he had a brilliant idea ▸ **bombilla de flash**, **bombilla fusible** flash bulb
2 (*Náut*) ship's lantern
3 (*Cono Sur*) (= *tubito*) *tube for drinking maté*; (= *pajita*) drinking straw
4 (*Méx*) (= *cuchara*) ladle

bombillo (SM) **1** (*LAm*) (*Elec*) light bulb
2 (*Téc*) U-bend, trap

bombín (SM) **1** (= *sombrero*) bowler hat, derby (*EEUU*)
2 (*Cono Sur*) [*de aire*] pump

bombita (SF) (*Cono Sur*) light bulb

bombo (ADJ) **1** (= *aturdido*) dumbfounded, stunned
2 (*LAm*) (= *tibio*) lukewarm
3 (*Cuba*) (= *comida*) tasteless, insipid; [*persona*] stupid, thick*
4 (*Méx*) [*carne*] bad, off
(SM) **1** (*Mús*) bass drum • **tengo la cabeza como un ~** my head's throbbing *o* buzzing
• MODISMOS: • **estar con ~*** to be in the family way* • **hacer un ~ a una chica*** to put a girl in the family way* • **anunciar algo a ~ y platillo** to announce sth amid a lot of hype, go in for a lot of publicity about sth • **poner a algn ~** (*Méx**) (= *insultar*) to hurl insults at sb; (= *golpear*) to hit sb
2 (*en sorteos*) drum
3* (= *elogio exagerado*) exaggerated praise; (*Teat, Cine*) hype* • **dar ~ a algn** to praise sb to the skies • **darse ~** to blow one's own trumpet*
4 (*Cono Sur*) • MODISMO: • **mandar a algn al ~**‡ to knock sb off‡ • **irse al ~** to come to grief, fail
5 (*Náut*) barge, lighter
6 (*Caribe*) (= *sombrero*) bowler hat, derby (*EEUU*)

bombón (SM) **1** [*de chocolate*] chocolate
2* (= *objeto*) beauty, gem; (= *chica*) peach*, smasher*
3* (= *chollo*) gift*, cinch‡

bombona (SF) **1** ▸ **bombona de butano** gas cylinder
2 (= *garrafón*) carboy

bombonera (SF) **1** (= *caja*) sweet box; (= *lata*) sweet tin, sweet box
2* (= *lugar*) cosy little place

bombonería (SF) sweetshop, confectioner's, confectioner's shop, candy store (*EEUU*)

bómper (SM) (*CAm, Caribe*) bumper, fender (*EEUU*)

Bón. (ABR) (= **Batallón**) Battn

bonachón (ADJ) (= *de buenas intenciones*) good-natured, easy-going; (*pey*) simple, naïve

bonachonamente (ADV) (= *con buenas intenciones*) good-naturedly, in an easy-going way; (*pey*) naïvely

bonaerense (ADJ) of/from Buenos Aires
(SMF) native/inhabitant of Buenos Aires • **los ~s** the people of Buenos Aires

bonancible (ADJ) [*viento*] light

bonanza (SF) **1** (*Náut*) fair weather, calm conditions • **ir en ~** (*Náut*) to have fair weather; (= *prosperar*) to go well, prosper
2 (*Min*) bonanza
3 (= *prosperidad*) prosperity, boom • **estar en ~** (*Com*) to be booming • **ir en ~** go well, prosper

bonazo (ADJ) = **buenazo**

bonchar* ▹ CONJUG 1a (VI) (*Caribe*) (= *hacer una fiesta*) to have a party; (= *pasarlo bien*) to have a good time

bonche[1] (SM) (*LAm*) (= *montón*) load, bunch

bonche[2]* (SM) (*Caribe*) **1** (= *fiesta*) party
2 (= *cosa divertida*) amusing thing; (= *persona divertida*) amusing person

bonche[3]* (SM) petting*, necking*

bonchón/ona (SM/F) fun-loving person

bondad (SF) (= *cualidad*) goodness; (= *amabilidad*) kindness • **tener la ~ de hacer algo** to be so kind as to do sth, be good enough to do sth • **tenga la ~ de pasar** please go in • **tenga la ~ de no fumar** please refrain from smoking

bondadosamente (ADV) **1** (= *amablemente*) kindly
2 (= *con buenas intenciones*) good-naturedly

bondadoso (ADJ) (= *amable*) kind-hearted; (= *de buenas intenciones*) good-natured

bondi (SM) (*Cono Sur*) tram

bonete (SM) (*Rel*) biretta; (*Univ*) mortarboard • **¡bonete!** (*CAm**) not on your life!, no way!* • MODISMO: • **a tente ~** doggedly, insistently

bonetería (SF) (*esp Méx*) haberdasher's (shop), notions store (*EEUU*)

bóngalo (SM), **bongaló** (SM) bungalow

bongo (SM) (*Náut*) (*LAm*) large canoe; (*And*) small punt

bongó (SM) (*Caribe*) bongo, bongo drum

boni‡ (SM) = **boniato**

boniata (ADJ) (*LAm*) edible, non-poisonous
(SF) (*Caribe*) edible yucca, cassava

boniato (SM) sweet potato, yam

bonificación (SF) **1** (= *pago*) bonus; (*esp Agr*) betterment, improvement (*in value*)
2 (*Com*) (= *descuento*) allowance, discount
3 (*Dep*) allowance of points

bonificar ▹ CONJUG 1g (VT) **1** (*Agr*) to improve
2 (*Com*) to allow, discount
(VPR) **bonificarse** to improve

bonísimo (*frm*) (ADJ) *superl de* **bueno**

bonitamente (ADV) (= *con delicadeza*) nicely, neatly; (= *con maña*) craftily

bonitero (ADJ) bonito (*antes de s*)
(SM) **1** (= *pescador*) bonito fisherman

2 (= *barco*) bonito fishing boat
bonito¹ ADJ **1** (= *bello*) pretty • **María es un ~ nombre** María is a pretty name • **Amelia tiene una cara bonita** Amelia has a pretty face • **el pueblo más ~ de Andalucía** the prettiest village in Andalusia • **es un bebé muy ~** he's a very pretty baby, he's a lovely baby • **un hombre ~** (*Cono Sur*) a handsome man • **¡qué ~! ¡contestarle así a tu padre!** (*iró*) that's nice, answering your father back like that! • **¡~ follón se armó!*** (*iró*) there was certainly a bit of a row! • **lo ~**: • **lo ~ sería que no hubiera guerras** it would be nice if there were no wars • **quedar ~**: • **ese cuadro queda ahí muy ~** that picture looks very nice there • **el vendedor me lo pintó todo muy ~** the salesman painted me a very pretty picture of it • MODISMO: • **~ como un sol** as pretty as a picture
2 (= *considerable*) • **una bonita cantidad** *o* **suma** a tidy little sum*, a pretty penny*
ADV (*LAm**) nicely • **ella canta ~** she sings nicely • **se te ve ~** it looks good on you
bonito² SM (= *pez*) tuna, bonito
bonitura SF (*LAm*) beauty, attractiveness
bono SM **1** (= *vale*) voucher, certificate ▸ **bono de metro** underground pass
2 (*Econ*) bond ▸ **bono de caja** debenture bond ▸ **bono del estado** government bond ▸ **bono del Tesoro** Treasury bond ▸ **bono de tesorería** debenture bond
bono-bus SM (PL: **bono-buses**) (*Esp*), **bonobús** SM (PL: **bonobuses**) (*Esp*) bus pass
bono-loto SF, **bonoloto** SF *state-run weekly lottery;* ▸ LOTERÍA
bono-metro SM underground pass
bonsai SM bonsai
bonzo SM bonze • **quemarse a lo ~** to set o.s. alight
boñiga SF, **boñigo** SM [*de vaca*] cow pat; [*de caballo*] horse dung
booleano ADJ (*Mat*) Boolean
boom [bum] SM boom • **dar ~ a un problema** to exaggerate a problem, make a meal of a problem ▸ **boom inmobiliario** property boom
boomerang [bume'ran] SM (PL: **boomerangs**) boomerang
boqueada SF gasp • **dar la última ~** to breathe one's last
boquear ▸ CONJUG 1a VT to say, utter, pronounce
VI **1** (= *quedar boquiabierto*) to gape, gasp
2 (= *estar expirando*) to be at one's last gasp
3 (= *terminar*) to be in its final stages
boquera SF **1** (*Agr*) sluice
2 (*Med*) lip sore
boqueras‡ SMF INV screw‡, warder
boqueriento ADJ **1** (*Med*) suffering from lip sores
2 (*Cono Sur*) (= *miserable*) wretched, miserable
boquerón SM **1** (= *pez*) fresh anchovy
2 (= *abertura*) wide opening, big hole
3* (= *persona*) = **malagueño**
boquete SM **1** (= *agujero*) hole • **abrieron un ~ en el muro** they made a hole in the wall
2 (= *abertura*) gap, opening
boqui‡ SMF screw‡, warder
boquiabierto ADJ open-mouthed • **quedarse ~** to be dumbstruck
boquiancho ADJ wide-mouthed
boquiblando ADJ [*caballo*] tender-mouthed
boquifresco* ADJ (= *descarado*) outspoken, cheeky*, sassy (*EEUU**)
boquilla SF **1** (*Mús*) mouthpiece
2 (= *extremo*) [*de manga*] nozzle; [*de cocina*] burner; [*de biberón*] teat, nipple (*EEUU*); [*de pipa*] stem; (*para fumar*) cigarette holder • **cigarros con ~** tipped cigarettes
3 • MODISMO: • **de ~**: • **apoyó la idea de ~** he paid lip-service to the idea • **eso lo dice de ~** he's just saying that, that's what he says (but he doesn't mean it) • **promesa de ~** insincere promise, promise not meant to be kept
4 (*And*) (= *chisme*) rumour, piece of gossip
boquillazo SM (*And*) rumour, talk
boquillero ADJ (*Caribe*) smooth-talking, sweet-talking
boquirroto ADJ talkative, garrulous
boquirrubio ADJ **1** (= *gárrulo*) talkative; (= *de mucha labia*) glib; (= *indiscreto*) indiscreet, loose-tongued
2 (= *simple*) simple, naïve
SM fop, dandy
boquita SF • **~ de piñón** pursed lips (*pl*)
boquitinguero ADJ (*Cono Sur*) gossipy
boquituerto ADJ wry-mouthed
boquiverde* ADJ foul-mouthed
boraciar ▸ CONJUG 1b VI (*Cono Sur*) to boast, brag
bórax SM borax
borbollar ▸ CONJUG 1a VI, **borbollear** ▸ CONJUG 1a VI **1** (= *burbujear*) to bubble, boil up
2 (= *chisporrotear*) to splutter
borbollón SM = **borbotón**
borbollonear ▸ CONJUG 1a VI = **borbollar**
Borbón SM Bourbon
borbónico ADJ Bourbon (*antes de s*)
borbotar ▸ CONJUG 1a VI **1** (= *hacer burbujas*) to bubble; (*al hervir*) to boil, boil up, boil over
2 (= *nacer*) to gush forth, well up
borbotón SM (= *de agua, líquido*) bubbling, boiling • **salir a borbotones** [*agua, sangre*] to gush out • **hablar a borbotones** to talk nineteen to the dozen
borceguí SM (= *botín*) high shoe, laced boot; [*de bebé*] bootee
borda SF (*Náut*) **1** gunwale, rail • **motor de fuera ~** outboard motor • MODISMO: • **echar** *o* **tirar algo por la ~** to throw sth overboard
2 (= *vela*) mainsail
3 (= *choza*) hut
bordada SF (*Náut*) tack • **dar ~s** (*lit*) to tack; (*fig*) to pace to and fro
bordado SM embroidery, needlework
bordadora SF needlewoman
bordadura SF embroidery, needlework
bordalesa* SF (*Cono Sur*) *wine barrel holding 225 litres*
bordante SMF (*Caribe, Méx*) lodger, roomer (*EEUU*)
bordar ▸ CONJUG 1a VT **1** (*Cos*) to embroider • **bordado a mano** hand-embroidered
2 (= *hacer perfectamente*) to do supremely well • **ha bordado su papel** she was excellent in her part
borde¹ SM **1** [*de asiento, andén, pañuelo*] edge; [*de plato*] rim, lip; [*de vaso, sombrero*] brim; [*de carretera, camino*] side; [*de ventana*] ledge; [*de río*] edge, bank • **se sentó en el ~ del sofá** she sat down on the edge of the sofa • **fotos con los ~s en blanco** photos with white borders *o* edges • **sembró semillas en los ~s del césped** he sowed some seeds at the sides *o* edges of the lawn • **iba andando por el ~ de la carretera** she was walking by the roadside *o* by the side of the road • **en el ~ del Sena** on the banks of the Seine ▸ **borde de ataque** (*Aer*) leading edge ▸ **borde de la acera** kerb, curb (*EEUU*) ▸ **borde de salida** (*Aer*) trailing edge
2 • **al ~ de** [+ *precipicio, lago, cráter*] at *o* on the edge of; [+ *quiebra, histeria, crisis*] on the verge of • **el régimen está al ~ del colapso** the regime is on the verge of collapse *o* on the point of collapsing • **estamos al mismo ~ del desastre** we are on the very brink of disaster • **su carrera política está al ~ del abismo** her political career is teetering on the edge of the abyss • **están al ~ de los cuarenta años** they're close to forty, they're hitting *o* pushing forty* • **al ~ del mar** beside the sea • **al ~ de la muerte** at death's door • **estuvo al ~ de la muerte por congelación** she nearly froze to death
borde² (*Esp*) ADJ **1‡** (= *antipático*) nasty • **estuviste muy ~ con él** you were very nasty to him • **estuvo toda la mañana en plan ~** he was in a strop‡ *o* in a foul mood* all morning • **ponerse ~ (con algn)** to get stroppy (with sb)*, get nasty (with sb)
2 [*planta, árbol*] wild
3†† [*niño*] illegitimate
SMF‡ • **¡eres un ~!** you're a nasty piece of work!*
bordear ▸ CONJUG 1a VT **1** (= *rodear*) to skirt (round) • **tuvimos que ~ la montaña** we had to skirt round the mountain • **navegamos bordeando la costa** we sailed along the edge of the coast
2 [*calle, árboles*] (= *estar alrededor de*) to border, border on; (= *flanquear*) to line • **la calle que bordeaba el parque** the street bordering (on) the park • **un paseo que bordea el mar** a promenade running along the sea • **un camino bordeado de cipreses** a road lined with cypress trees
3 (= *acercarse a*) [+ *edad*] to be approaching, be close to; [+ *genialidad, obsesión*] to border on • **bordea los sesenta años** he's approaching sixty, he's close to sixty • **su comportamiento bordea la estupidez** his behaviour borders on stupidity
4 (*Cono Sur*) (= *evitar*) • **~ un asunto** to skirt round *o* avoid a (tricky) subject
VI (*Náut*) to tack
bordejada SF (*Caribe*) (*Náut*) tack
bordejar ▸ CONJUG 1a VI (*Caribe*), **bordejear** ▸ CONJUG 1a VI (*Caribe*) (*Náut*) to tack
bordelés/esa ADJ of/from Bordeaux
SM/F native/inhabitant of Bordeaux • **los bordeleses** the people of Bordeaux
bordería* SF stroppiness* • **decir ~s** to be rude
bordillo SM kerb, curb (*EEUU*)
bordin SM (*And, Caribe, Méx*) boarding house
bordinguero/a SM/F (*And, Caribe, Méx*) landlord/landlady
bordo SM **1** (*Náut*) • **a ~** aboard, on board • **"bienvenidos a ~"** "welcome aboard" • **estar a ~ del barco** to be on board the ship • **con ordenador de a ~** with on-board computer • **ir a ~** (*Náut*) to go on board; (*Aer*) to board • **de alto ~**: • **buque de alto ~** big ship, seagoing vessel • **personaje de alto ~** distinguished person, influential person
2 (= *bordada*) tack • **dar ~s** to tack
3 (*Méx*) (*Agr*) roughly-built dam
4 (*Cono Sur*) (= *dique*) raised furrow
5 (*CAm*) [*de montaña*] peak, summit
bordó (*Arg*) ADJ INV, SM maroon
bordón SM **1** (= *bastón*) [*de peregrino*] staff; [*de ciego*] stick
2 (= *ayuda*) helping hand
3 (*Mús*) (= *cuerda*) bass string; (= *registro*) bass stop, bourdon
4 (*Literat*) refrain
5 (*And, CAm*) (= *hijo menor*) youngest son
bordona SF (*Cono Sur*) *sixth string of the guitar;* **bordonas** bass strings of the guitar
bordoncillo SM pet word, pet phrase
bordonear ▸ CONJUG 1a VT (*Mús*) to strum
VI (*And*) (= *zumbar*) to hum
bordoneo SM (*Mús*) strumming
boreal ADJ northern • **el hemisferio ~** the

northern hemisphere
borgesiano ADJ, **borgiano** ADJ Borgesian, characteristic of J L Borges
Borgoña SF Burgundy
borgoña SM (*tb* **vino de borgoña**) Burgundy
bórico ADJ boric
boricua ADJ, SMF, **borinqueño/a** ADJ, SM/F Puerto Rican
Borja SM (= *familia italiana*) Borgia
borla SF [*de cortina*] tassel; [*de gorro*] pompom; (*Univ*) tassel • **tomar la ~** (*Univ*) to take one's master's degree *o* doctorate ▸ **borla de empolvarse** powder puff
borlete SM (*Méx*), **borlote** SM (*Méx*) row, uproar
borne SM (*Elec*) terminal
borneadizo ADJ easily warped, flexible
bornear ▹ CONJUG 1a VT **1** (= *torcer*) to twist, bend
2 (*Arquit*) to put in place, align
3 (*Méx*) [+ *pelota*] spin
VPR **bornearse** to warp, bulge
borneco ADJ (*Cono Sur*) small, short
borneo SM **1** (= *torcimiento*) twisting, bending
2 (*Arquit*) alignment
3 (*Náut*) swinging at anchor
boro SM (*Quím*) boron
borona SF **1** (= *maíz*) maize, corn (EEUU)
2 (= *mijo*) millet
3 (*CAm*) (= *migaja*) crumb
borra SF **1** (= *relleno*) (*para colchones*) flock; (*para cojines*) stuffing
2 (= *pelusa*) [*de polvo*] fluff; (*Bot*) down ▸ **borra de algodón** cotton waste ▸ **borra de seda** floss silk
3 (*Zool*) yearling ewe
4 (= *sedimento*) sediment, lees ▸ **borra de vino** (*Arg, Uru*) (= *color*) maroon
5* (= *charla insustancial*) empty talk; (= *tonterías*) trash, rubbish
borrachear* ▹ CONJUG 1a VI to booze*, get drunk habitually
borrachera SF **1** (= *estado*) drunkenness • **coger** *o* **pillar** *o* **agarrar** *o* (*Méx*) **ponerse una ~** to get drunk • **quitarse la ~** to sober up
2 (= *juerga*) spree, binge
borrachez SF drunkenness, drunken state
borrachín SM boozer*
borracho/a ADJ **1** [*persona*] • **está ~** he's drunk • **es muy ~** he's a drunkard, he's a heavy drinker • MODISMO: • **estar ~ como una cuba** to be plastered*, be blind drunk*
2 (= *poseído*) drunk, blind (**de** with)
3 (*Culin*) [*bizcocho*] tipsy (*soaked in liqueur o spirit*); [*fruta*] marinated
4 (*de color*) violet
SM/F drunkard, drunk
borrado SM erasure
borrador SM **1** (= *versión*) [*de texto*] first draft, rough copy; [*de pintura, dibujo*] rough sketch • **hacer un nuevo ~** to do a redraft
2 (= *cuaderno*) scribbling pad, scratch pad (EEUU); (*Com*) daybook
3 (*para pizarra*) rubber, duster, eraser (EEUU)
borradura SF erasure, crossing out
borraja SF borage; ▹ **agua**
borrajear ▹ CONJUG 1a VT, VI to scribble, scrawl
borrar ▹ CONJUG 1a VT **1** (= *hacer desaparecer*)
a [+ *palabra, dibujo*] (*con goma*) to rub out, erase; (*con borrador*) to rub off, clean off • **la fecha había sido cuidadosamente borrada** the date had been carefully rubbed out *o* erased • **borra lo que has puesto en la pizarra** rub off *o* clean off what you've put on the blackboard • **bórralo con Tippex** white it out with Tipp-Ex®, tippex it out • MODISMO: • **~ a algn/algo del mapa** to wipe sb/sth off the map
b [+ *señal, mancha*] to remove; [+ *pintada*] to clean off; [+ *huellas*] to wipe off, rub off
c [+ *mensaje, fichero*] to delete, erase; [+ *canción, película*] to tape over, erase • **he borrado todos los mensajes del contestador** I've erased *o* deleted all the messages on the answering machine • **¿no habrás borrado el partido de fútbol?** you haven't taped over *o* erased the football match, have you?
d [+ *impresión*] to wipe away, erase • **he borrado de mi mente aquellas imágenes** I have wiped away *o* erased those images from my mind • **consiguió ~ aquellos malos recuerdos** he managed to wipe away *o* erase all those painful memories • **era como si se hubieran borrado 40 años de la historia** it was as if 40 years of history had been wiped clean *o* erased • **no podía ~ de su cara las huellas del cansancio** he was unable to wipe away the signs of fatigue from his face
2 (= *limpiar*) [+ *disquete, cinta*] to erase; [+ *pantalla*] to clear • **~ la pizarra** to clean the blackboard
3 (= *dar de baja a*) • **~ a algn de** [+ *clase, actividad*] to take sb out of, remove sb from; [+ *lista, curso*] to take sb off, remove sb from • **borró a los niños de la clase de natación** she took the children out of the swimming class, she removed the children from the swimming class • **bórranos de la excursión del sábado** take us off the list for Saturday's outing, count us out of Saturday's outing*
4 (*Fot*) (= *poner borroso*) to blur
5 (*Pol*) • **~ a algn** (*euf*) to deal with sb, dispose of sb
VPR **borrarse 1** (= *darse de baja*) • **~se de** [+ *club, asociación*] to cancel one's membership of, resign from; [+ *curso*] to drop out of • **se borró de la biblioteca** she cancelled her library membership • **siempre hay alguien que se borra del curso al principio** there's always somebody who drops out of the course at the beginning
2 (= *desaparecer*) [*señal, marca*] to fade away; [*imagen, recuerdo*] to fade; [*duda, sospecha, temor*] to disappear, be dispelled; [*sonrisa*] to vanish • **se había borrado el código** the code number had faded away • **eso se borra con agua** that comes off *o* washes off with water • **lo que pasó aquel día se me ha borrado con el tiempo** the memory of what happened that day has faded with time • **no se han borrado las sospechas entre la pareja** the suspicion between the two of them has not disappeared *o* been dispelled
3 (*Fot*) to fade
borrasca SF **1** area of low pressure, depression • **viene una ~ por el Atlántico** there's low pressure *o* a low approaching from the Atlantic
2 (= *tormenta*) (*en tierra*) storm; (*en el mar*) squall
3 (= *peligro*) peril, hazard; (= *mala racha*) setback
4* (= *juerga*) orgy, spree
borrascoso ADJ **1** [*tiempo*] stormy; [*viento*] squally, gusty
2 (= *problemático*) stormy, tempestuous
borrasquero ADJ riotous, wild
borregada* SF student rag*, prank
borregaje SM (*Cono Sur*) flock of lambs
borrego/a SM/F **1** (*Zool*) (= *oveja joven*) lamb, yearling lamb; (= *oveja adulta*) sheep
2 (= *persona*) • **le siguieron como ~s** they followed him like sheep
SM **1** (*Cuba, Méx**) hoax
2 borregos (= *nubes*) fleecy clouds; (*Náut*) foamy crests of waves, white horses, white caps (EEUU)
borreguil ADJ meek, like a lamb
borreguillo SM fleece ▸ **forro de borreguillo** fleece lining
borricada SF silly thing, piece of nonsense
borrico/a SM/F **1** (*Zool*) donkey/she-donkey
2 (= *persona*) fool
SM (*Téc*) sawhorse, sawbuck (EEUU)
borricón* SM, **borricote*** SM (= *hombre paciente*) long-suffering person
borriquete SM (*Arte*) easel; (*Téc*) sawhorse, sawbuck (EEUU)
borrón SM **1** (= *mancha*) blot, stain
• MODISMO: • **hacer ~ y cuenta nueva** (= *olvidar el pasado*) to let bygones be bygones; (= *empezar de nuevo*) to wipe the slate clean
2 (= *vergüenza*) blemish
3 (*Literat*) rough draft; (*Arte*) preliminary sketch • **estos borrones** (*iró*) these humble jottings
borronear ▹ CONJUG 1a VT **1** (= *garabatear*) to scribble, scrawl
2 (= *hacer borrador de*) to make a rough draft of
borrosamente ADJ hazily • **veía todo ~** everything was blurred
borroso ADJ **1** (= *indistinguible*) [*foto, imagen*] blurred, indistinct; [*escrito*] smudgy • **lo veo todo ~** everything is blurred
2 [*idea, recuerdo*] vague, hazy
boruca* SF row, din
borujo SM lump, pressed mass, packed mass
borujón SM **1** (*Med*) bump, lump
2 (= *lío*) bundle
boruquear ▹ CONJUG 1a VT (*Méx*) (= *revolver*) to mix up, mess up; (= *inmiscuirse*) to stir up
boscaje SM **1** (= *bosque*) thicket, grove
2 (*Arte*) woodland scene
Bosco SM • **el ~** Hieronymus Bosch
boscoso ADJ wooded
Bósforo SM • **el (estrecho del) ~** the Bosp(h)orus
Bosnia SF Bosnia ▸ **Bosnia Herzegovina** Bosnia Herzegovina
bosnio/a ADJ, SM/F Bosnian
bosorola SF (*CAm, Méx*) sediment, dregs (*pl*)
bosque SM **1** (= *terreno con árboles*) wood; (*más denso*) forest
2 (*LAm**) (= *selva*) jungle, rainforest ▸ **bosque pluvial** rainforest
bosquecillo SM copse, small wood
bosquejar ▹ CONJUG 1a VT **1** (*Arte*) to sketch
2 (= *dar forma a*) [+ *idea*] to sketch, outline; [+ *plan*] to draft
bosquejo SM **1** (*Arte*) sketch
2 (= *forma provisional*) [*de idea*] sketch, outline; [*de plan*] draft
bosquete SM copse, small wood
bosquimán/ana SM/F, **bosquimano/a** SM/F African bushman/bushwoman
bosta SF (= *excremento*) dung, droppings (*pl*); (*para estiércol*) manure
bostezar ▹ CONJUG 1f VI to yawn
bostezo SM yawn
bota SF **1** (= *calzado*) boot • MODISMOS: • **morir con las ~s puestas** to die with one's boots on • **ponerse las ~s*** (= *enriquecerse*) to strike it rich; (= *comer mucho*) to have a blow-out* ▸ **botas camperas** cowboy boots ▸ **botas de agua** gumboots, wellingtons (*esp Brit*), rubber boots (*esp EEUU*) ▸ **botas de campaña** cowboy boots ▸ **botas de esquí** ski boots ▸ **botas de fútbol** football boots ▸ **botas de goma, botas de hule** (*Méx*) gumboots, wellingtons (*esp Brit*), rubber boots (*esp EEUU*) ▸ **botas de media caña** ankle boots ▸ **botas de montaña** mountain boots ▸ **botas de montar** riding boots

2 ▸ **bota de vino** _wineskin bottle_
3 (= _tonel_) large barrel
4 (= _medida_) 516 litres

botada SF (_LAm_) (= _tirada_) [_de objeto, pelota_] throw, throwing; [_de basura_] throwing away; [_de trabajador*_] sacking*

botadero SM **1** (_LAm_) (= _vertedero_) rubbish dump
2 (_And_) (= _vado_) ford

botado/a ADJ **1** (= _descarado_) cheeky, sassy (EEUU*)
2 (_Méx*_) (= _barato_) dirt cheap
3 (_CAm_) (= _despilfarrador_) spendthrift
4 (_And_) (= _resignado_) resigned; (= _dispuesto para todo_) ready for anything, resolute
5 (_CAm, Méx_) (= _borracho_) blind drunk
SM/F **1** (_LAm_) (_tb_ **niño/a botado/a**) foundling
2 (_And_) (= _vago_) good-for-nothing, bum (EEUU*)

botador(a) SM/F (_LAm_) (= _despilfarrador_) spendthrift
SM **1** (_Náut_) pole, punt pole
2 (= _sacaclavos_) nail-puller, claw-hammer

botadura SF **1** (_Náut_) launching
2 (_LAm_) = **botada**

botafuego SM **1** (_Mil††_) linstock
2* (= _persona_) quick-tempered person

botalodo SM (_And, Caribe_) mudguard, fender (EEUU)

botalón SM **1** (_Náut_) outrigger ▸ **botalón de foque** jib-boom
2 (_And, Cono Sur_) (= _viga_) beam, prop
3 (_And_) (= _poste_) post, stake; [_de atar_] hitching post

botamanga SF (_Arg, Uru_) [_de pantalón_] turn-up, cuff (EEUU); [_de manga_] cuff

botana SF (_Méx_) snack, appetizer

botanearse* ▹ CONJUG 1a VPR • **~ a algn** (_LAm_) to speak ill of sb, drag sb's name through the dirt

botaneo* SM (_LAm_) gossip, malicious gossip, slander

botánica SF botany

botánico/a ADJ botanical
SM/F botanist

botanista SMF botanist

botar ▹ CONJUG 1a VT **1** (_Dep_) [+ _pelota_] to bounce
2 (_Náut_) [+ _barco_] to launch; [+ _timón_] to put over
3 (_LAm_) (= _tirar_) to throw away, throw out, chuck out*; (= _despedir_) to fire*, sack* • **~ un saque de esquina** to take a corner kick • **lo ~on de su trabajo** he was fired _o_ sacked*
4 (_LAm_) (= _derrochar_) to fritter away, squander
5 (_Chile, Col, Ven_) (= _derramar_) to spill
6 (_Chile, Col, Ven_) (= _derribar_) [+ _florero, persona_] to knock over; [+ _árbol_] to knock down
VI **1** (_Esp_) [_pelota_] to bounce; [_coche_] to bump, jolt; [_caballo_] to rear up
2 (_Esp_) [_persona_] to jump • **estaba botando de alegría** she was jumping for joy • MODISMO: • **está que bota*** he's hopping mad*

botarata* SMF (_LAm_) (= _despilfarrador_) spendthrift

botaratada SF wild scheme, nonsensical idea

botarate* SMF **1** (= _loco_) madcap
2 (= _imbécil_) idiot
3 (_LAm_) (= _despilfarrador_) spendthrift

botarel SM buttress

botarga SF motley, clown's outfit

botavara SF **1** (_Náut_) boom
2 (_Caribe_) [_de carro_] pole, shaft

bote[1] SM **1** [_de pelota_] bounce • **dar un ~** to bounce
2 (_Esp_) (= _salto_) [_de persona, caballo_] jump • **se levantó de un ~** he jumped up, he leapt to his feet • **dar** _o_ **pegar un ~** [_persona_] to jump; [_coche_] to bump, jolt • MODISMOS: • **a ~ pronto*** (just) off the top of one's head* • **dar el ~ a algn*** to chuck sb out*, give sb the boot*, give sb the push* • **darse el ~** (_Esp*_) to beat it* • **de ~ y voleo** instantly
3 (= _arremetida_) (_con un arma_) thrust; (_con el cuerpo_) lunge

bote[2] SM **1** (= _recipiente_) [_de vidrio_] jar; [_de plástico_] container; [_de metal_] (_para conservas, pintura_) can, tin; (_para bebidas_) can • **un ~ de colonia** a bottle of cologne • **de ~** canned, tinned • **esta sopa es de ~** this is canned _o_ tinned soup • **es rubia de ~*** she's a fake blonde • MODISMOS: • **chupar del ~** (_Esp*_) to line one's own pocket*, feather one's own nest* • **estar de ~ en ~*** to be packed, be jam-packed* • **estar en el ~** (_Esp*_) [_título, premio_] to be in the bag*, be all sewn up* • **meterse a algn en el ~** (_Esp*_) to talk sb round, sweet-talk sb* • **pegarse el ~ con algn** to get on with sb like a house on fire* • **tener algo en el ~** (_Esp*_) to have sth in the bag*, have sth all sewn up* • **tener a algn (metido) en el ~** (_Esp*_) to have sb in one's pocket* ▸ **bote de basura** (_Méx_) dustbin, trash can (EEUU) ▸ **bote de cerveza** (_Esp_) (_lleno_) can of beer; (_vacío_) beer can ▸ **bote de cuestación** collecting tin ▸ **bote de humo** smoke canister
2 (_como propina_) • **hoy hemos sacado un ~ de 40 euros** we got 40 euros in tips today • **un euro para el ~** a euro for the tips box • "**bote**" "tips"
3 (= _fondo común_) kitty • **poner un ~** to have a kitty • **pusimos un ~ de diez libras cada uno** we each put ten pounds into the kitty
4 (_en lotería, quiniela_) jackpot • **hay un ~ de 300 millones** the jackpot is 300 million
5 (_CAm, Méx, Ven‡_) (= _cárcel_) jail, nick*, can (EEUU*)

bote[3] SM (= _barca_) [_de pesca_] boat; (_deportivo_) skiff ▸ **bote de a ocho** racing eight ▸ **bote de carrera** skiff ▸ **bote de paseo** rowing boat, rowboat (EEUU) ▸ **bote de paso** ferryboat ▸ **bote de remos** rowing boat, rowboat (EEUU) ▸ **bote de salvamento** lifeboat ▸ **bote hinchable** inflatable dinghy ▸ **bote neumático** rubber dinghy ▸ **bote patrullero** patrol boat ▸ **bote salvavidas** lifeboat

botella SF **1** (= _envase_) bottle • **de** _o_ **en ~** bottled • **cerveza de ~** bottled beer • **media ~** half bottle • **~ de vino** (= _contenido_) bottle of wine; (= _envase_) wine bottle ▸ **botella de Leiden** Leyden jar
2 (_Caribe_) (= _prebenda_) sinecure, soft job (_in government_)

botellazo SM blow with a bottle

botellería SF (_Cono Sur_) wine shop

botellero SM wine rack

botellín SM small bottle, half bottle

botellón* SM (_Esp_) open-air drinking session (_involving groups of young people_)

botepronto SM (_Dep_) half-volley; ▹ **bote[1]**

botería SF (_Cono Sur_) shoe shop

bote-vivienda SM (PL: **botes-vivienda**) houseboat

botica SF **1** (= _establecimiento_) chemist's, chemist's shop, pharmacy (EEUU), drugstore • MODISMO: • **de todo como en ~** everything under the sun
2‡ (= _cremallera_) trouser fly, flies (_pl_)

boticario/a SM/F chemist, druggist (EEUU)

botija SF **1** (= _vasija_) earthenware jug • MODISMOS: • **estar como una ~** to be as round as a barrel • **poner a algn como ~ verde** (_CAm_) to insult sb
2 (_CAm_) (= _tesoro_) buried treasure
SMF (_Uru*_) (= _chaval_) kid*

botijo SM **1** (= _recipiente_) _earthenware drinking jug with spout and handle_
2* [_de policía_] water cannon

botijón* ADJ (_Méx_) pot-bellied

botijuela SF (_LAm_) **1** (= _jarro_) earthenware jug
2 (= _tesoro_) buried treasure

botillería SF (_Chile_) off-licence, liquor store (EEUU)

botillero SM (_Méx_) shoemaker, cobbler

botín[1] SM [_de guerra_] booty, plunder; [_de ladrón_] loot

botín[2] SM **1** (= _calzado_) ankle boot
2 (= _polaina_) legging, spat
3 (_Chile_) (= _borceguí_) bootee
4 (_Cono Sur_) (= _calcetín_) sock

botina SF (= _calzado_) high shoe; [_de bebé_] bootee

botiquín SM **1** (= _armario_) medicine cabinet; (= _conjunto de medicinas_) first-aid kit ▸ **botiquín de emergencia, botiquín de primeros auxilios** first-aid kit
2 (= _enfermería_) first-aid post, first-aid station (EEUU), sick bay
3 (_Caribe_) (_hum_) (_para bebidas_) drinks cupboard

boto ADJ **1** [_punta_] blunt
2 (= _torpe_) dull, dim
SM _wineskin bottle_

botón SM **1** (_Cos, Téc_) button • **apretar** _o_ **pulsar el ~** to press the button • MODISMO: • **¡ni un ~!*** not a sausage!* ▸ **botón de alarma** alarm, alarm button ▸ **botón de arranque** starter, starter switch ▸ **botón de contacto** push-button ▸ **botón de destrucción** destruct button ▸ **botón de muestra** sample, illustration ▸ **botón de presión** push-button
2 (_Bot_) bud ▸ **botón de oro** buttercup

botonadura SF buttons (_pl_), set of buttons

botonar ▹ CONJUG 1a (_LAm_) VT to button, button up
VI to bud, sprout

botones SM INV bellboy, bellhop (EEUU)

Botox® ['botoks] SM Botox®

Botsuana SF Botswana

botulismo SM botulism

boutique [bu'tik] SF boutique ▸ **boutique del pan** _fashionable bakery specializing in foreign and wholefood bread_

bóveda SF **1** (_Arquit_) vault ▸ **bóveda celeste** vault of heaven ▸ **bóveda craneal** cranial cavity ▸ **bóveda de cañón** barrel vault
2 (= _cueva_) cave, cavern

bovedillas* SFPL • MODISMO: • **subirse a las ~** to go up the wall*

bovino ADJ bovine • **carne bovina** beef • **ganado ~** cattle
SM bovine • **ovinos y ~s** sheep and cattle • **carne de ~** beef

box SM **1** (_Aut_) pit • **entrar en boxes** to go into the pits, make a pit stop
2 (_Equitación_) stall
3 (_LAm_) (= _boxeo_) boxing

boxeador(a) SM/F boxer

boxear ▹ CONJUG 1a VI to box

boxeo SM boxing

bóxer SMF boxer, boxer dog

boxístico ADJ, **boxeril** ADJ (_Cono Sur_) boxing (_antes de s_)

boya SF (_Náut_) buoy; (_Pesca_) float ▸ **boya de campana** bell buoy

boyada SF drove of oxen

boyante ADJ **1** (_Náut_) buoyant
2 (= _próspero_) [_persona_] buoyant; [_negocio_] prosperous

boyar ▹ CONJUG 1a VI to float

boyazo SM (_CAm, Cono Sur_) punch

boyé SM (_Cono Sur_) snake

boyera SF, **boyeriza** SF cattle shed

boyero/a SM/F (= _persona_) oxherd, drover
SM **1** (= _perro_) cattle dog

2 (*And*) (= *aguijada*) goad, spike
bozada SF (*And*) halter
bozal SM 1 [*de perro*] muzzle
2 (*LAm*) [*de caballo*] halter
ADJ 1 (= *nuevo*) [*recluta*] new, raw; [*animal*] wild, untamed
2 (= *tonto*) stupid
3 (*LAm*) [*negro*] pure
4 (*LAm*) *speaking broken Spanish*
bozo SM 1 [*de adolescente*] fuzz
2 (= *boca*) mouth, lips (*pl*)
3 (= *cabestro*) halter, headstall
bracamonte SM (*And*) ghost
bracear ▹ CONJUG 1a VT 1 (*Náut*) to measure in fathoms
2 [+ *horno*] to tap
VI 1 (= *mover los brazos*) to swing one's arms; (*al nadar*) to swim
2 (= *luchar*) to wrestle, struggle
bracero SM 1 (*Agr*) (= *jornalero*) farmhand, farm labourer *o* (*EEUU*) laborer
2 (= *peón*) labourer, laborer (*EEUU*), navvy
3 • **ir de ~** to walk arm-in-arm
bracete SM • **ir del ~** to walk arm-in-arm
bracmán SM Brahman, Brahmin
braco ADJ pug-nosed
SM (*tb* **perro braco**) setter
braga SF 1 **bragas** [*de mujer*] knickers, panties • MODISMOS: • **dejar a algn en ~s*** to leave sb empty-handed • **estar en ~s*** to be broke*, be skint* • **estar hecho una ~*** to be knackered* • **pillar a algn en ~s*** to catch sb with his pants down*
2 [*de niño*] nappy, diaper (*EEUU*)
3 (*Náut, Téc*) sling, rope (*for hoisting*)
bragado ADJ gritty
bragadura SF (*Cos*) crotch
braga-faja SF panty girdle
bragapañal SM disposable nappy, disposable diaper (*EEUU*)
bragazas* SM INV henpecked husband
braguero SM (*Med*) truss
bragueta SF (*Cos*) fly, flies (*pl*), zipper (*EEUU*) • MODISMOS: • **estar como ~ de fraile** (*Cono Sur*) to be very solemn • **oír por la ~*** (= *estar sordo*) to be stone-deaf; (= *entender mal*) to misunderstand; (= *ser torpe*) to be pretty thick* • **ser hombre de ~** to be a real man
braguetazo* SM marriage for money • **dar el ~** to marry for money
braguetero ADJ 1 (= *lascivo*) lecherous, randy
2 (*LAm*) (*al casarse*) *who marries for money*; (*And, Caribe*) (= *vividor*) *who lives on a woman's earnings* • **todos saben que es ~** everyone knows he married for money
SM lecher, womanizer
braguillas SM INV brat
braguitas SFPL panties
brahmán SM Brahman, Brahmin
braille ['braile] SM Braille
brainstorming ['breinstormin] SM (PL: **brainstormings**) (= *actividad*) brainstorming • **una sesión de ~** a brainstorming session • **hacer un ~** to have a brainstorming session
brama SF (*Zool*) rut, rutting season
bramadero SM (*LAm*) tethering post
bramante SM twine, string
bramar ▹ CONJUG 1a VI 1 (*Zool*) [*toro, elefante*] to bellow; [*león*] to roar
2 [*persona*] • **están que braman con el alcalde*** they're hopping mad with the mayor
3 (*Meteo*) [*viento*] to howl, roar; [*mar*] to thunder
bramido SM [*de toro, elefante*] bellow, bellowing; [*de león*] roar, roaring
brandy SM brandy
branquia SF gill • **~s** gills
brasa SF live coal, hot coal • **carne a la ~** grilled meat, barbecued meat • MODISMOS: • **atizar la ~** to stir things up, add fuel to the flames • **estar en ~s** to be on tenterhooks • **estar hecho una ~** to be very flushed
brasear ▹ CONJUG 1a VT to braise
brasería SF grill
brasero SM 1 (= *como calefacción*) [*de carbón*] brazier; (*eléctrico*) heater
2 (*Méx*) fireplace
3 (*And*) (= *hoguera*) large bonfire
4 (*Méx*) (= *hornillo*) small stove
brasier SM (*Méx*) bra
Brasil SM Brazil
brasileño/a ADJ, SM/F, **brasilero/a** ADJ, SM/F Brazilian
Brasilia SF Brasilia
brassier SM (*Méx*) bra
brava SF 1 (*Méx*) (= *disputa*) row, fight • MODISMO: • **a la ~** like it or not • **a la ~ tendrás que ir** you'll have to go whether you like it or not
2 (*Caribe*) • MODISMO: • **dar una ~ a algn** to lean on sb*, intimidate sb
bravata SF 1 (= *amenaza*) threat
2 (= *fanfarronada*) boast, brag • **echar ~s** to boast, talk big*
braveador(a) ADJ blustering, bullying
SM/F bully
bravear ▹ CONJUG 1a VI 1 (= *jactarse*) to boast, talk big
2 (= *bravuconear*) to bluster
bravera SF vent, window (*in an oven*)
bravero/a (*Caribe*) ADJ bullying
SM/F bully
braveza SF 1 (= *ferocidad*) [*de animal*] ferocity, savageness; [*del viento*] fury
2 (= *valor*) bravery
bravío ADJ 1 (*Zool*) (= *feroz*) ferocious, savage; (= *indómito*) wild, untamed
2 (*Bot*) wild
3 (= *rudo*) uncouth, coarse
SM ferocity
bravo ADJ 1 [*animal*] fierce, ferocious; ▹ **toro**
2 [*persona*] (= *malhumorado*) bad-tempered; (= *jactancioso*) boastful, swaggering; (= *valentón*) boastful, swaggering • **ponerse ~ con algn** to get angry with sb
3 [*mar*] rough, stormy; [*paisaje*] rugged; ▹ **costa²**
4 (= *excelente*) fine, excellent
5 (*LAm*) (*Culin*) hot, spicy
EXCL bravo!, well done!
SM thug
bravucón/ona ADJ swaggering
SM/F braggart
bravuconada SF boast
bravura SF 1 (= *ferocidad*) ferocity
2 (= *valor*) bravery
3 = **bravata**
braza SF 1 (*Natación*) breaststroke • **nadar a ~** to swim breaststroke ▸ **braza de espalda** back stroke ▸ **braza de mariposa** butterfly stroke
2 (*Náut*) ≈ fathom
brazada SF 1 (= *movimiento*) movement of the arms
2 (*Remo*) stroke
3 (*Natación*) stroke, style
4 (= *cantidad*) armful
5 (*LAm*) (*Náut*) (= *braza*) ≈ fathom
brazado SM armful
brazal SM 1 (= *banda de tela*) armband
2 (*Agr*) irrigation channel
brazalete SM 1 (= *joya*) bracelet
2 (= *banda de tela*) armband
brazo SM 1 [*de persona*] arm; [*de animal*] foreleg • **se echó a los ~s de su madre** he threw himself into his mother's arms • **dar el ~ a algn** to give sb one's arm • **le dio el ~ al bajar del autobús** he gave her his arm as they got off the bus • **coger a algn del ~** to take sb by the arm • **cogió a su hermano del ~** she took her brother by the arm • **iban (cogidos) del ~** they were walking arm in arm • **llevar a algn en ~s** to carry sb in one's arms • MODISMOS: • **con los ~s abiertos** with open arms • **dar el ~ a torcer** to give way, give in • **luchar a ~ partido** to fight tooth and nail • **ser el ~ derecho de algn** to be sb's right-hand man/woman ▸ **brazo de gitano, brazo de reina** (*Cono Sur*) (*Culin*) swiss roll; ▹ **huelga, cruzado**
2 [*de sillón, tocadiscos, grúa, cruz*] arm ▸ **brazo de lámpara** lamp bracket ▸ **brazo de lámpara de gas** gas bracket ▸ **brazo de lectura, brazo lector** pick-up arm
3 (= *sección*) ▸ **brazo armado** military wing ▸ **brazo político** political wing ▸ **brazo secular** secular arm
4 (*Geog*) ▸ **brazo de mar** inlet, arm of the sea, sound • MODISMO: • **estar** *o* **ir hecho un ~ de mar** to be dressed up to the nines* ▸ **brazo de río** channel, branch of river
5 [*de árbol*] branch, limb
6 (*liter*) (= *fuerza*) arm • **el ~ de la ley** the long arm of the law
7 **brazos** (= *trabajadores*) hands, men
brazuelo SM (*Zool*) shoulder
brea SF 1 (= *alquitrán*) tar, pitch
2 (= *cubierta*) tarpaulin, tarp (*EEUU*)
break [brek] SM (*Mús*) break dancing
brear ▹ CONJUG 1a VT 1 (= *maltratar*) to abuse, ill-treat • **~ a algn a golpes** *o* **palos** to beat sb up
2 (= *embromar*) to make fun of, tease
brebaje SM potion; (*hum*) brew, concoction
brecha SF 1 (= *abertura*) breach, opening • **abrir ~ en una muralla** to breach a wall • **batir en ~** (*Mil*) to breach; (*fig*) to get the better of • MODISMOS: • **estar en la ~** to be in the thick of things • **hacer ~ en algn** to make an impression on sb • **seguir en la ~** to go on with one's work, keep at it
2 (*entre personas*) rift; (*entre opiniones*) gap ▸ **brecha generacional** generation gap
3 (*Med*) gash, wound
brecina SF (*Bot*) heath
breck [brek] SM (*Cono Sur*) = **breque**
brécol SM broccoli
brega SF 1 (= *lucha*) struggle • **andar a la ~** to slog away
2 (= *riña*) quarrel, row
3 (= *broma*) trick, practical joke • **dar ~ a algn** to play a trick on sb
bregar ▹ CONJUG 1h VI 1 (= *luchar*) to struggle, fight (**con** against, with)
2 (= *reñir*) to quarrel
3 (= *trabajar mucho*) to slog away • **tendremos que hacerlo bregando** we shall have to do it by sheer hard work
breguetear ▹ CONJUG 1a VI (*And*) to argue
breje‡ SM (*Esp*) • **¿cuántos ~s tienes?** how old are you?
brejetero ADJ (*Caribe*) trouble-making, mischief-making
breke SM (*CAm*) (*Aut*) brake
bren SM bran
breña SF, **breñal** SM scrub, rough ground
breñoso ADJ (= *con maleza*) rough, scrubby; (= *con zarzas*) brambly
breque SM (*LAm*) 1 (= *carroza*) brake
2 (*Ferro*) guard's van, baggage car (*EEUU*)
3 (*Mec*) brake
brequear ▹ CONJUG 1a VT, VI (*LAm*) to brake
brequero SM (*And, CAm, Méx*) brakeman
Bretaña SF Brittany

brete SM **1** (= *cepo*) shackles (*pl*)
2 (= *apuro*) predicament • **estar en un ~** to be in a jam* • **poner a algn en un ~** to put sb on the spot
3 (*Caribe***) screw**, lay**

bretel SM (*LAm*) [*de vestido*] strap

bretón/ona ADJ, SM/F Breton
SM **1** (*Ling*) Breton
2 bretones (= *coles*) Brussels sprouts

breva SF **1** (*Bot*) early fig • MODISMOS: • **¡no caerá esa ~!** no such luck! • **pelar la ~** (*Cono Sur*) to steal • **poner a algn como una ~** to beat sb black and blue
2 (= *puro*) flat cigar; (*Caribe*) [*de calidad*] good-quality cigar
3 (*LAm*) (= *tabaco*) chewing tobacco
4* (= *puesto*) plum, plum job; (= *gaje*) perk*
5 (= *cosa fácil*) • **es una ~** it's a cinch‡, it's a pushover* • **para él es una ~** it's chickenfeed to him*

breve ADJ **1** (= *corto*) short, brief • **una ~ rueda de prensa** a short *o* brief press conference • **continuaremos tras un ~ descanso** we shall continue after a short break *o* a brief pause • **un brevísimo periodo de tiempo** a very short period of time • **enviaron una nota muy ~, solo dos líneas** they sent a very short note, just two lines long • **seré muy ~** I shall be very brief • **dimos un ~ repaso a la lección** we briefly went over the lesson • **expuso el problema en ~s palabras** he briefly explained the problem • **en ~s palabras, se negó a dimitir** in short, he refused to resign • **en ~** (= *pronto*) shortly, before long
2 [*vocal*] short
SM **1** (*Prensa*) short news item • **"~s"** "news in brief"
2 (*Rel*) papal brief
SF (*Mús*) breve

brevedad SF [*de mensaje*] shortness; [*de texto*] brevity; [*de estilo*] conciseness • **con** *o* **a la mayor ~ (posible)** as soon as possible • **bueno, para mayor ~ ...** well, to be brief ... • **llamado por ~ ...** called for short ...

brevemente ADV briefly, concisely

brevería SF (*Tip*) note, short news item; (*en conversación*) snippet • **"Breverías"** (= *sección de periódico*) "News in Brief"

brevete SM **1** (= *nota*) note, memorandum
2 (*LAm*) (*Aut*) driving licence *o* (*EEUU*) license

breviario SM (*Rel*) breviary; (= *compendio*) compendium

brezal SM moor, heath

brezar ▹ CONJUG 1f VT to rock, lull (*in a cradle*)

brezo SM **1** (*Bot*) heather
2 [*de pipa*] briar

briaga SF (*Méx*) drunkenness

briago ADJ (*Méx*) drunk

briba SF vagabond's life, idle life • **andar** *o* **vivir a la ~** to loaf around, be on the bum (*EEUU*)

bribón/ona ADJ **1** (= *vago*) lazy
2 (= *criminal*) dishonest, rascally
SM/F **1** (= *vagabundo*) vagabond, vagrant
2 (= *holgazán*) loafer
3 (= *granuja*) rascal, rogue

bribonada SF dirty trick, piece of mischief

bribonear ▹ CONJUG 1a VI **1** (= *gandulear*) to idle, loaf around
2 [*ser granuja*] to be a rogue, play dirty tricks

bribonería SF **1** (= *briba*) vagabond's life, idle life
2 (= *picardía*) roguery

bribonesco ADJ rascally, knavish

bricbarca SF *large sailing ship*

bricolador(a) SM/F do-it-yourself enthusiast, DIY enthusiast

bricolage SM do-it-yourself, DIY

bricolagista SMF do-it-yourself enthusiast, DIY enthusiast

bricolaje SM do-it-yourself, DIY

bricolajista SMF, **bricolero/a** SM/F do-it-yourself enthusiast, DIY enthusiast

brida SF **1** [*de caballo*] bridle • **ir a toda ~** to go at top speed • MODISMO: • **tener a algn a ~ corta** to keep sb on a tight rein, keep sb under strict control
2 (*Téc*) (= *abrazadera*) clamp; [*de tubería*] flange
3 (*Ferro*) fishplate
4 (*Med*) adhesion

bridge [briʒ, britʃ] SM (*Naipes*) bridge

bridgista [bri'ʒista] SMF bridge player

bridgístico [bri'ʒistiko] ADJ bridge (*antes de s*) • **el mundo ~** the bridge world

bridón SM [*de caballo*] snaffle; (*Mil*) bridoon

briega SF **1** (= *pelea*) fight, brawl
2 (= *trabajo duro*) slog

brigada SF **1** (*Mil*) brigade
2 (= *grupo*) [*de obreros*] gang; [*de policía*] squad ▸ **brigada antidisturbios** riot squad ▸ **brigada antidrogas** drug squad ▸ **brigada de bombas** bomb-disposal unit ▸ **brigada de delitos monetarios** fraud squad ▸ **brigada de estupefacientes** drug squad ▸ **brigada fluvial** river police ▸ **brigada móvil** flying squad ▸ **brigada sanitaria** sanitation department ▸ **Brigadas Internacionales** International Brigades
SMF (*Mil*) sergeant major

brigadier SM brigadier, brigadier-general (*EEUU*)

brigadilla SF squad, detachment

brigadista SMF • **~ internacional** member of the International Brigade

brigán SM (*CAm, Caribe*) (*Hist*) brigand, bandit

brigandaje SM (*CAm, Caribe*) (*Hist*) brigandage, banditry

brigantino/a ADJ of/from Corunna
SM/F native/inhabitant of Corunna • **los ~s** the people of Corunna

Brígida SF Bridget

Briján SM • MODISMO: • **saber más que ~** to be very smart, know the lot

brik SM (PL: **briks**) carton

brillante ADJ **1** (= *reluciente*) [*luz, sol, color*] (*gen*) bright; (*muy fuerte*) brilliant; [*superficie pulida*] shiny; [*pelo*] glossy, shiny; [*joyas, lentejuelas*] sparkling, glittering • **un estampado amarillo ~** a bright *o* brilliant yellow pattern • **los focos eran demasiado ~s** the floodlights were too bright • **un vestido de satén ~** a shiny satin dress • **¡qué ~ ha quedado el suelo!** the floor is really shiny now! • **frota los zapatos hasta que estén bien ~s** polish the shoes until they are nice and shiny • **tenía los ojos ~s por la emoción** her eyes sparkled with excitement
2 (= *excelente*) brilliant • **al final de su ~ carrera deportiva** at the end of her brilliant sporting career • **su actuación fue absolutamente ~** her performance was absolutely outstanding *o* brilliant • **su ~ conversación** her sparkling conversation
SM diamond, brilliant • **un anillo de ~s** a diamond ring

brillantemente ADV
1 (= *extraordinariamente*) brilliantly • **respondió ~ a sus preguntas** he answered her questions brilliantly • **la orquesta ha despedido ~ la temporada** the orchestra bid a brilliant farewell to the season
2 (= *con brillo*) brightly

brillantez SF **1** (= *brillo*) (*gen*) brightness; (*más fuerte*) brilliance
2 (= *excelencia*) brilliance • **ahí está la ~ de la novela** that is the brilliance of the novel • **con ~** brilliantly • **hemos cumplido nuestro objetivo con ~** we have achieved our aim brilliantly • **ganaron el partido con ~** they won the match in brilliant style • **dar ~ a algo** to add a bit of sparkle to sth
3 (= *boato*) splendour, splendor (*EEUU*)

brillantina SF brilliantine, hair cream

brillar ▹ CONJUG 1a VI **1** (= *relucir*) [*luz, sol*] to shine; [*estrella, ojos*] to shine, sparkle; [*metal, superficie, pelo*] (*gen*) to shine; (*por estar mojado, grasiento*) to glisten; [*joyas, lentejuelas*] to sparkle, glitter • **la luz de la vela brillaba en la oscuridad** the light of the candle shone in the dark • **le brillaban los ojos de alegría** her eyes shone *o* sparkled with happiness • **¡cómo te brillan los zapatos!** what shiny shoes! • **el mar brillaba a la luz de la luna** the sea glistened in the moonlight • **le brillaba la cara por el sudor** his face glistened with sweat
2 (= *sobresalir*) to shine • **Argentina brilló en la segunda mitad** Argentina shone in the second half • MODISMOS: • **~ con luz propia** to stand out on one's own • **~ por su ausencia**: • **el ingenio ha brillado por su ausencia** there has a been a distinct lack of ingenuity • **en la cena las bebidas ~on por su ausencia** there was a distinct lack of drinks at dinner

brillazón SF (*Cono Sur*) mirage

brillo SM **1** (= *resplandor*) [*de luz, sol, estrella*] (*gen*) brightness; (*más fuerte*) brilliance; [*de pantalla*] brightness; [*de tela, pelo, zapatos, superficie*] shine, sheen; [*de papel, foto*] glossiness; [*de joyas, lentejuelas*] sparkle, glitter • **estas luces emiten demasiado ~** these lights are too bright • **el ~ de la luna sobre el agua** the moonlight shining on the water • **lo noté en el ~ de sus ojos** I noticed it in her sparkling eyes • **el ~ de la navaja lo asustó** he was frightened by the gleam of the knife • **estos zapatos no tienen ~** these shoes have no shine • **¿le revelamos las fotos con ~?** would you like gloss photos?, would you like a gloss finish to the photos? • **se puede ajustar el ~** the brightness can be adjusted • **dar** *o* **sacar ~ a** [+ *suelo, plata, zapatos*] to polish, shine; [+ *muebles*] to polish • **este producto da mucho ~ a la madera** this product gives wood an excellent shine ▸ **brillo de labios** lip gloss ▸ **brillo de uñas** clear nail polish, clear nail varnish
2 (= *esplendor*) brilliance, splendour, splendor (*EEUU*) • **fueron cautivados por el ~ de la profesión** they were captivated by the splendour of the profession • **la ausencia de varios jugadores importantes ha restado ~ al torneo** the absence of several important players has taken the shine off the tournament

brilloso ADJ (*LAm*) shiny

brin SM fine canvas, duck

brincar ▹ CONJUG 1g VT [+ *pasaje*] (*en lectura*) to skip, miss out
VI **1** (*esp LAm*) (= *saltar*) [*niño*] to jump (up and down); (*con un solo pie*) to hop; [*cordero*] to skip about, gambol • MODISMOS: • **está que brinca** he's hopping mad • **~ de cólera** to fly into a rage
2 (= *rebotar*) to bounce
VPR **brincarse** • **~se a algn** (*And*‡) to bump sb off‡

brinco SM (= *salto*) (*gen*) jump, leap; (*al correr*) skip • **de** *o* **en un ~** at one bound • **dar ~s** to hop (about), jump (about) • **pegar un ~** to jump, give a start • MODISMOS: • **a ~s** by fits and starts • **¿para qué son tantos ~s estando el suelo parejo?** (*CAm, Méx*) what's all the fuss about? • **quitar los ~s a algn** to take sb down a peg

brindar ▹ CONJUG 1a VT **1** (= *ofrecer*) to offer,

afford • **los árboles brindaban sombra** the trees afforded shade • **~ a algn (con) algo** to offer sth to sb • **le brinda la ocasión** it gives *o* affords him the opportunity • **bríndame un cigarro** (*hum*) give me a cigarette • **me brindó una copa** he bought me a drink
2 (= *dedicar*) to dedicate (**a** to)
VI • **~ por algn/algo** to drink to sb/sth, toast sb/sth • **~on por los novios** they drank a toast to the newly-weds • **¡brindemos por la unidad!** here's to unity!
VPR **brindarse** • **~se a hacer algo** to offer to do sth • **se brindó a ayudarme** he offered to help me

brindis SM INV **1** (*para celebrar algo*) toast • **hacer un ~ por algn/algo** to toast sb/sth, drink a toast to sb/sth
2 (= *dedicatoria*) dedication, ceremony of dedication
3 (*And, Caribe*) (= *recepción*) official reception; (= *fiesta*) cocktail party

brío SM **1** (= *ánimo*) spirit, verve • **es hombre de ~s** he's a man of spirit, he's a man of mettle
2 (= *decisión*) determination • **cortar los ~s a algn** to clip sb's wings
3 (= *elegancia*) elegance

briosamente ADV **1** (= *con ánimo*) with spirit, dashingly, with verve
2 (= *con decisión*) resolutely
3 (= *elegantemente*) elegantly

brioso ADJ **1** (= *animoso*) spirited, full of verve
2 (= *decidido*) determined
3 (= *elegante*) elegant

briqueta SF briquette

brisa SF breeze

brisca SF *Spanish card game similar to whist but in which it is not necessary to follow suit*

brisera SF (*LAm*), **brisero** SM (*LAm*) windshield (*for a lamp*)

brisita SF • **tener** *o* **pasar una ~** to be hungry, have an empty stomach

británico/a ADJ British
SM/F British person, Briton, Britisher (*EEUU*) • **los ~s** the British

britano/a (*Hist, Literat*) ADJ British
SM/F Briton

brizna SF **1** (= *hebra*) [*de hierba*] blade; [*de judía*] string
2 (= *trozo*) piece, fragment; (*muy pequeño*) scrap • **no me queda ni una ~** I haven't a scrap left
3 (*LAm*) drizzle

briznar ▷ CONJUG 1a VI (*LAm*) to drizzle

broca SF **1** (*Cos*) reel, bobbin
2 (*Mec*) (drill) bit
3 [*de zapato*] tack

brocado SM brocade

brocal SM **1** (= *borde*) rim, mouth
2 [*de pozo*] curb, parapet
3 (*Méx*) kerb, curb (*EEUU*)

brocha SF **1** (= *para pintar*) paintbrush, large paintbrush • **pintor de ~ gorda** (*lit*) painter and decorator; (*fig*) bad painter
2 ▸ **brocha de afeitar** shaving brush
3 (*Cono Sur*) skewer, spit
4 (*CAm**) (= *zalamero*) creep‡
ADJ (*CAm*) meddling, creeping*, servile • **MODISMO:** • **hacerse ~** (*CAm*) to play the fool

brochada SF, **brochazo** SM brushstroke

broche SM **1** (*Cos*) clasp, fastener ▸ **broche de gancho** hook and eye ▸ **broche de presión** press stud (*Brit*), snap fastener (*EEUU*)
2 (= *joya*) brooch • **MODISMOS:** • **el ~ final** • **el ~ de oro** the finishing touch
3 (*LAm*) (*para papel*) paperclip; (*Cono Sur*) (*para ropa*) clothes peg, clothespin (*EEUU*)

brocheta SF skewer

brochón ADJ (*Caribe*) flattering
SM whitewash brush

brócoli SM, **bróculi** SM broccoli

bróder* SM (PL: **bróders**) (*CAm*) lad, fellow*

broker SM (PL: **brokers**) (*Cono Sur*) (*Econ*) broker

brollero ADJ (*Caribe*) troublemaking, mischief-making

broma SF **1** (= *cachondeo*) • **ni en ~** never, not on any account • **lo decía en ~** I was only joking, I was only kidding* • **estar de ~** to be in a joking mood • **tomar algo a ~** to take sth as a joke
2 (= *chiste*) joke • **no es ninguna ~** it's no joke, this is serious • **la ~ me costó caro** the affair cost me dear • **no hay ~s con la autoridad** you can't play games with the authorities • **~s aparte ...** joking aside ... • **¡déjate de ~s!** quit fooling!, joke over! • **gastar ~s** to tell jokes • **gastar una ~ a algn** to play a joke on sb • **estar para ~s:** • **¡para ~s estoy!** (*iró*) a fine time for joking! • **no está para ~s** he's in no mood for jokes • **entre ~s y veras** half-joking(ly) ▸ **broma pesada** practical joke, hoax
3 (*Caribe, Cono Sur*) (= *decepción*) disappointment; (= *molestia*) vexation, annoyance
4 (*Zool*) shipworm

bromato SM bromate

bromazo SM unpleasant joke, stupid practical joke

bromear ▷ CONJUG 1a VI to joke, crack jokes* • **creía que bromeaba** I thought he was joking

bromista ADJ • **es muy ~** he's full of jokes, he's a great one for jokes
SMF (= *chistoso*) joker; (= *gracioso*) practical joker, leg-puller* • **lo ha hecho algún ~** some joker did this

bromuro SM bromide

bronca* SF **1** (= *follón*) row • **armar una ~** to kick up a fuss • **se armó una ~ tremenda** there was an almighty row* • **buscar ~** to be looking for a fight, be spoiling for a fight • **dar una ~ a algn** (*Teat, Taur*) to give sb the bird*
2 (= *regañina*) ticking off* • **nos echó una ~ fenomenal** he came down on us like a ton of bricks*
3 (= *ruido*) racket*
4 (*Cono Sur*) (= *rabia*) anger, fury • **me da ~** it makes me mad*

broncamente ADV (= *con dureza*) roughly, harshly; (= *con malos modos*) rudely

bronce SM **1** (= *aleación*) bronze • **una medalla de ~** a bronze medal • **MODISMOS:** • **ligar ~** (*Esp**) to get a suntan • **ser de ~** to be inflexible, be deaf to all appeals ▸ **bronce de campana** bell metal ▸ **bronce de cañon** gunmetal ▸ **bronce dorado** ormolu
2 (= *latón*) brass
3 (*Mús*) brass instruments
4 (*Arte*) bronze, bronze statue
5 (= *moneda*) copper coin
6 (*LAm*) (= *campana*) bell

bronceado ADJ **1** [*persona, piel*] tanned, brown
2 (*color*) bronze, bronze coloured *o* (*EEUU*) colored
SM **1** [*de piel*] tan, suntan
2 (*Téc*) bronze finish

bronceador SM suntan lotion

broncear ▷ CONJUG 1a VT **1** [+ *piel*] to tan, bronze
2 (*Téc*) to bronze
VPR **broncearse** to get a tan, get a suntan

broncería SF (*Cono Sur*) ironmonger's (shop), ironmongery, hardware store (*EEUU*)

bronco ADJ **1** [*superficie*] rough, coarse
2 [*metal*] brittle
3 [*voz*] gruff, hoarse; (*Mús*) rasping, harsh
4 [*actitud, porte*] gruff, rude
5 [*caballo*] unbroken

broncodilatador SM bronchodilator

bronconeumonía SF bronchopneumonia

broncopulmonar ADJ broncho-pulmonary

bronquedad SF **1** [*de superficie*] roughness
2 [*de metal*] brittleness
3 [*de voz*] gruffness, harshness

bronquial ADJ bronchial

bronquina* SF = **bronca**

bronquinoso* ADJ (*Caribe*) quarrelsome, brawling

bronquios SMPL bronchial tubes • **estaba malo de los ~** he had a bad chest

bronquítico/a ADJ bronchitic
SM/F bronchitis sufferer

bronquitis SF INV bronchitis ▸ **bronquitis crónica** chronic bronchitis

broquel SM shield

broquelarse ▷ CONJUG 1a VPR to shield o.s.

broquero SM (*Méx*) brace

broqueta SF skewer

brota SF bud, shoot

brotar ▷ CONJUG 1a VI **1** (*Bot*) [*planta, semilla*] to sprout, bud; [*hoja*] to sprout, come out; [*flor*] to come out
2 [*agua*] to spring up; [*río*] to rise; [*lágrimas, sangre*] to well (up)
3 (= *aparecer*) to spring up • **han brotado sectas por todos sitios** sects have sprung up all over the place • **las protestas populares ~on de la crisis económica** popular protest sprang from the recession • **como princesa brotada de un cuento de hadas** (*liter*) like a princess out of a fairy tale
4 (*Med*) (= *epidemia*) to break out; (= *erupción, grano, espinilla*) to appear • **le ~on granos por toda la cara** spots appeared all over his face, he came out in spots all over his face

brote SM **1** (*Bot*) shoot ▸ **brotes de soja** bean sprouts, bean shoots
2 (= *aparición*) [*de rebelión*] outbreak; [*de enfermedad*] outbreak • **un ~ de violencia** an outbreak of violence • **un ~ de sarampión** an outbreak of measles
3 (= *erupción cutánea*) rash

broza SF **1** (*Bot*) dead leaves, brushwood
2 (*en discurso*) rubbish, trash, garbage (*EEUU*)
3 (= *brocha*) hard brush
4 (*Tip*) printer's brush

brucelosis SF INV brucellosis

bruces • **de ~** ADV face down • **caer de ~** to fall flat on one's face • **estar de ~** to lie face downwards, lie flat on one's stomach

bruja ADJ • **estar ~** (*Caribe, Méx*‡) to be broke*, be flat (*EEUU**) • **ando bien ~**‡ I'm skint‡
SF **1** (= *hechicera*) witch
2* (= *arpía*) old hag*; (*Méx*) woman
3 (*Caribe, Cono Sur*) (= *fantasma*) spook*, ghost; (= *puta*) whore
4 (*Orn*) barn owl

Brujas SF Bruges

brujear ▷ CONJUG 1a VT (*Caribe*) (*tb fig*) to stalk, pursue
VI **1** (= *hacer brujería*) to practise witchcraft
2 (*Caribe, Méx*) (= *ir de juerga*) to go on a spree

brujería SF **1** (= *hechizos*) witchcraft, sorcery, (black) magic
2 (*Caribe*) (= *pobreza*) poverty

brujeril ADJ witch-like

brujo ADJ enchanting
SM **1** (= *hechicero*) wizard, sorcerer
2 (*LAm*) shaman, medicine man*

brújula SF **1** (*Náut*) compass • **MODISMO:** • **perder la ~** to lose one's bearings ▸ **brújula de bolsillo** pocket compass
2 (= *mira*) guide, norm

brujulear ▹ CONJUG 1a VT **1** [+ *cartas*] to uncover (*gradually*)
2* (= *adivinar*) to guess
3 (= *tratar de conseguir*) to intrigue for, try to wangle
VI **1** to manage, get along, keep going
2 (*And, Caribe*) to go on the booze*, go on a bender‡
brulote SM **1** (*Chile*) rude word, dirty word
2 (*Cono Sur*) (= *escrito*) obscene letter
bruma SF (= *niebla*) mist, fog; (*en el mar*) sea mist ▸ **bruma del alba** morning mist
brumoso ADJ misty, foggy
bruno ADJ dark brown
bruñido ADJ polished, burnished
SM **1** (= *acto*) polish, polishing ▸ **bruñido de zapato** shoeshine
2 (= *brillo*) shine, gloss
bruñidor(a) SM/F polisher, burnisher
bruñir ▹ CONJUG 3h VT **1** (= *sacar brillo a*) [+ *metal, mármol*] to polish, burnish
2 (= *maquillar*) to make up (*with cosmetics*)
3 (*CAm*) (= *molestar*) to pester
VPR **bruñirse** to make up, make o.s. up
bruscamente ADV **1** (= *repentinamente*) suddenly, brusquely, sharply
2 (= *rudamente*) sharply, abruptly
brusco ADJ **1** (= *repentino*) [*descenso, curva, declive*] sharp; [*movimiento*] sudden; [*cambio*] abrupt, sudden
2 (= *grosero*) [*actitud, porte*] curt, brusque; [*comentario*] rude
SM (*Bot*) butcher's broom
Bruselas SF Brussels
bruselas SFPL tweezers • **unas ~** a pair of tweezers
bruselense ADJ of/from Brussels
SMF native/inhabitant of Brussels • **los ~s** the people of Brussels
brusquedad SF **1** (= *cambio repentino*) suddenness
2 (= *rudeza*) brusqueness, abruptness • **hablar con ~** to speak sharply
brut SM *kind of very dry wine or champagne*
brutal ADJ **1** (= *salvaje*) brutal
2* (= *genial*) terrific*
3 (*CAm*) (= *asombroso*) incredible, amazing
brutalidad SF **1** (= *cualidad*) brutality
2 (= *acción*) • **una ~** an act of brutality
3 (= *estupidez*) stupidity
4* • **me gusta una ~** I think it's great, I love it
brutalizar ▹ CONJUG 1f VT (= *tratar mal*) [+ *persona, animal*] to brutalize, treat brutally; [+ *mujer*] to rape
VPR **brutalizarse** to become brutalized
brutalmente ADV brutally
bruteza SF **1** (= *brutalidad*) brutality
2 (= *tosquedad*) coarseness, roughness
Bruto SM Brutus
bruto/a ADJ **1** (= *salvaje*) brutish • **¡no seas ~!** don't be so rough!
2 (= *estúpido*) stupid, ignorant • **¡no seas ~!** don't be an idiot! • **es muy ~** he's pretty thick*
3 (= *inculto*) uncouth
4 (= *sin alterar*) [*materias*] raw; [*medidas*] gross • **en ~** [*superficie, terreno*] rough; [*diamantes*] uncut • **hierro en ~** crude iron, pig iron • **peso ~** gross weight • **petróleo ~** crude oil • **producto ~** gross product • **salario ~** gross salary • **a lo ~** roughly, crudely • MODISMO: • **más ~ que un adoquín** as dumb as an ox
5 • **pegar a algn en ~** (*Caribe*) to beat sb mercilessly
6 (*Cono Sur*) (= *de mala calidad*) poor-quality, inferior
SM (*animal*) brute, beast
SM/F **1** (= *salvaje*) brute, boor • **¡bruto!** you beast!
2 (= *idiota*) idiot
bruza SF **1** (= *cepillo*) coarse brush; (*para caballos*) horse brush
2 (*Tip*) printer's brush
Bs.As. ABR (= **Buenos Aires**) BA
Bto./a. ABR (*Rel*) = **Beato/a**
bto. ABR (= **bruto**) gr
bu* SM bogeyman • **hacer el bu a algn** to scare sb
búa SF pimple
buba SF, **bubón** SM (= *inflamación*) bubo
bubónico ADJ • **peste bubónica** bubonic plague
bubute SM (*Caribe*) beetle
bucal ADJ [*higiene*] oral • **por vía ~** orally, by mouth
bucanero SM buccaneer
bucarán SM buckram
Bucarest SM Bucharest
búcaro SM **1** (= *jarrón*) vase
2 (= *arcilla*) clay, fragrant clay
buccino SM whelk
buceador(a) SM/F diver
bucear ▹ CONJUG 1a VI **1** (= *nadar bajo el agua*) to swim under water; (= *sumergirse*) to dive
2 (= *investigar*) to explore, look below the surface
buceo SM diving ▸ **buceo de saturación** saturation diving
buchaca SF (*CAm, Caribe*) (= *bolso*) saddlebag; (*Billar*) pocket
buchada SF mouthful (*of liquid*)
buchante‡ SM shot
buche SM **1** (= *estómago*) (*Orn*) crop; (*Zool*) maw; (*liter*) belly • MODISMOS: • **guardar algo en el ~** to keep sth very quiet • **llenar el ~*** to fill one's belly • **sacar el ~*** to show off • **sacar el ~ a algn*** to make sb talk
2 (= *trago*) mouthful; (*And*) shot, slug (*EEUU*) (*of drink*) • **hacer ~s con algo** to rinse one's mouth out with sth
3 (*Cos*) (= *bolsa*) bag; (= *arruga*) wrinkle, pucker • **hacer ~** to be baggy, wrinkle up
4 (*LAm*) (*Med*) (= *bocio*) goitre, goiter (*EEUU*); (= *paperas*) mumps
5 (*And*) (= *chistera*) top hat
6 (*Caribe*) (= *tonto*) fool, idiot
buchí SM (*CAm*) rustic, peasant
buchinche SM (*Caribe*) (= *casa*) hovel; (= *tienda*) pokey little shop
bucle SM **1** [*de pelo*] curl, ringlet
2 (= *curva*) curve, bend; (*Aer, Inform*) loop ▸ **bucles anidados** nested loops
bucodental ADJ [*salud, higiene*] oral; [*tratamiento, clínica*] dental
bucólica SF **1** (*Literat*) bucolic poem, pastoral poem
2* meal
bucólico ADJ bucolic, pastoral
Buda SM Buddha
budín SM **1** (= *dulce*) pudding; (*LAm*) (= *pastel*) cake • **~ de pescado** fish pie
2* (= *persona*) • **esa chica es un ~** that girl's a peach *o* a smasher*
budismo SM Buddhism
budista ADJ, SMF Buddhist
budleia SF buddleia
buen ADJ ▹ **bueno**
buenamente ADV **1** (= *fácilmente*) easily, without difficulty
2 (= *de buena gana*) willingly
buenamoza SF (*And*) (*euf*) jaundice
buenaventura SF **1** (= *suerte*) good luck, good fortune
2 (= *adivinación*) fortune • **decir** *o* **echar la ~ a algn** to tell sb's fortune
buenazo/a ADJ (= *buena persona*) kindly, good-natured; (= *sufrido*) long-suffering
SM/F good-natured person • **el ~ de Marcos** good old Marcos • **ser un ~** to be kind-hearted, be soft (*pey*)
buenmozo ADJ (*Cono Sur*) good-looking, handsome
bueno/a ADJ (ANTES DE SM SING: **buen**)
1 (*gen*) good; [*tiempo*] fine, good, fair • **es un buen libro** it's a good book • **está muy ~ este bizcocho** this sponge cake is lovely *o* really good • **tiene buena voz** she has a good voice • **les gusta la buena vida** they like the good life • **es buen traductor** he's a good translator • **hace buen tiempo** the weather's fine *o* good *o* fair • **los ~s tiempos** the good old days • **la mano buena** (*hum*) the right hand • **¡~ está!** (*LAm*) that's enough! • **¡qué ~!** (*esp LAm*) excellent!, great! • **lo ~ es que ...** the best thing is that ..., the best part is that ... • **lo ~ fue que ni siquiera quiso venir** the best thing *o* part was that he didn't even want to come • REFRÁN: • **lo ~, si breve, dos veces ~** brevity is the soul of wit
2 (= *bondadoso*) [*persona*] kind, good • **fue muy ~ conmigo** he was very kind *o* good to me • **es usted muy ~** you are very kind • **sé ~** be good • **es buena persona** he's a nice person, he's a good sort • MODISMO: • **es más ~ que el pan** he's a good soul
3 (= *apropiado*) good • **este es un buen momento para comprar** this is a good time to buy • **no es ~ que esté solo** it's not good for him to be alone • **ser ~ para** to be good for • **esta bebida es buena para la salud** this drink is good for your health
4 (*de salud*) • **estar ~** to be well • **ponerse ~** to get better
5* (= *atractivo*) • **está muy ~** he's a bit of all right*, he's gorgeous*
6 (= *considerable*) good, large • **un buen número de ...** a good *o* large number of ... • **una buena cantidad de dinero** a large amount of money • **un buen trozo de ...** a nice big piece of ... • **le eché un buen rapapolvo** I gave him a good telling-off • **le di un buen susto** I gave him a real fright • **ganó ~s duros** she earned a good deal of money
7 (*iró*) • **¡buen conductor!** a fine driver you are!, some driver you are! • **¡esa sí que es buena!** that's a good one! • **¡buena la has liado** *o* **hecho!** you've really gone and done it now! • **¡en buen lío me he metido!** I've got myself into a fine mess! • **¡estaría ~!*** I should hope not! • **estaría ~ que ...** it would be just great if ... • **luego verás lo que es ~*** then you'll see • **le pusieron ~*** (= *lo pegaron*) they beat the living daylights out of him*; (= *lo criticaron*) they slagged him off* • **le dio un tortazo de los ~s** he gave him a hell of a thump*
8 (*en saludos*) • **¡buenas!** hello! • **~s días** good morning • **buenas tardes** (*a primera hora*) good afternoon; (*más tarde*) good evening • **¿qué hay de ~?** what's new?
9 • MODISMOS: • **estar de buenas** to be in a good mood • **estar en la buena** (*And*) (*de buen humor*) to be in a good mood; (= *tener suerte*) to be in luck • **hacer algo a la buena de Dios** to do sth any-old-how • **por las buenas**: • **resolver algo por las buenas** to settle sth amicably • **irás por las buenas o por las malas** you'll go whether you like it or not • **si no me obedeces por las buenas, tendrás que hacerlo por las malas** you can either do as I say willingly, or I'll have to force you to do it • **de buenas a primeras** suddenly, without warning • **decir una noticia a algn de buenas a primeras** to spring a piece of news on sb
ADV • **¡bueno!** all right!, O.K.!; (*Méx*) (*Telec*) hello! • **~, pues ...** well ... • **~, resulta que ...** well, it so happens that ... • **~, ¿y qué?** well, so what?, well? • **¡pero ~, cómo puedes ser tan bruto!** honestly, how can you be so

b

stupid! • **pero ~, no nos vamos a meter en historias** but anyway, let's not go into this
SM/F **1** • **el ~** [*de la película*] the goody*, the good guy*
2 • **el ~ de Manolo** good old Manolo
buenón* ADJ nice-looking, good-looking
Buenos Aires SM Buenos Aires
buenrollismo* SM **1** (= *buena onda*) good vibes* *pl* • **un disco lleno de ~** a record with lots of good vibes*
2 (= *optimismo excesivo*) relentless positivity • **no puedo con ese ~ que tiene** I can't stand his relentless positivity
buey SM **1** (*Zool*) ox ▸ **buey almizclado** musk ox ▸ **buey corneta** (*And, Cono Sur*) one-horned ox; (*fig*) (= *entrometido*) busybody, nosey-parker* • MODISMO: • **nunca falta un ~ corneta** (*And, Cono Sur*) there's always someone who can't keep his mouth shut ▸ **buey de Francia** crab ▸ **buey de mar** *variety of crab or crawfish* ▸ **buey marino** manatee ▸ **buey muerto** (*Caribe*) bargain
2 • MODISMOS: • **como ~es** enormous • **chinches como ~es** bedbugs the size of elephants, enormous bedbugs • **cuando vuelen los ~es** when pigs fly • **hablar de ~es perdidos** (*Cono Sur*) to waste one's breath • **pegar ~es** (*CAm*) to go to sleep • **poner los ~es antes que el carro** to put the cart before the horse • **saber con los ~es que ara** (*Caribe*) to know who your friends are • **sacar el ~ de la barranca** (*Méx*) to bring it off • **ser un ~ para algo**: • **es un ~ para el trabajo** he's a tremendous worker • **~ suelto** free agent; (= *soltero*) bachelor
3 (*LAm*) (= *cornudo*) cuckold
4 (*Caribe*) (= *dineral*) big sum of money
bueyada SF (*LAm*) drove of oxen
bufa* ADJ (*Caribe, Méx*) tight*, drunk
SF **1** (= *broma*) joke, piece of clowning
2 (*Caribe*) (= *embriaguez*) drunkenness
búfalo ADJ (*Caribe**) great*, fantastic*
SM buffalo
bufanda SF **1** (= *prenda*) scarf
2‡ (= *soborno*) sweetener*, back-hander*
3 (= *gaje*) perk*
bufar ▸ CONJUG 1a VI [*toro*] to snort; [*gato*] to spit • **está que bufa** he's furious • **~ de ira** to snort with rage
VPR **bufarse** (*Méx*) [*pared*] to bulge
bufarrón* SM (*Cono Sur*) pederast, child molester
bufé SM (PL: **bufés**) = **bufet**
bufeo SM (*CAm, Caribe, Méx*) (= *atún*) tunny; (= *delfín*) dolphin
bufet SM (PL: **bufets**) **1** (= *cena*) buffet supper, cold supper; (= *almuerzo*) buffet lunch ▸ **bufet libre** fixed buffet, set-price buffet • **"bufet libre: 10 euros"** "eat as much as you like for 10 euros"
2 (= *comedor*) [*de hotel*] dining room
3 (= *restorán*) restaurant
4 (= *mueble*) sideboard
bufete SM **1** (= *mesa*) desk
2 [*de abogado*] (= *oficina*) lawyer's office; (= *negocio*) legal practice • **establecer su ~** to set up in legal practice
3 (*Culin*) = **bufet**
buffer SM (*Inform*) buffer
buffet SM (PL: **buffets**) = **bufet**
bufido SM snort
bufo ADJ **1** (= *cómico*) comic, farcical • **ópera bufa** comic opera
2 (*Caribe*) spongy
SM **1** (= *payaso*) clown, funny man; (*Mús*) buffo
2 (*Cono Sur‡*) (= *homosexual*) queer‡, fag (*EEUU‡*)
bufón ADJ funny, comical
SM **1** (= *payaso*) clown
2 (*Hist*) jester

bufonada SF **1** (= *comentario*) jest; (= *acto*) piece of buffoonery
2 (*Teat*) farce
bufonear ▸ CONJUG 1a VI, VPR **bufonearse**
1 (= *bromear*) to joke, jest
2 (= *payasear*) to clown, play the fool
bufonesco ADJ **1** (= *gracioso*) funny, comical
2 (= *de payaso*) clownish
bufoso* SM (*Arg*) gun, shooter*
buga* SM **1** (*Aut*) car, wheels* (*pl*)
2 (= *persona*) straight person*, heterosexual
buganvilla SF bougainvillea
bugle SM bugle
bugui-bugui SM boogie-woogie
buhardilla SF, **buharda** SF **1** (= *desván*) loft
2 (= *ventana*) dormer window, dormer (*EEUU*)
búho SM **1** (*Orn*) owl, long-eared owl ▸ **búho real** eagle owl
2 (= *persona*) unsociable person, recluse
buhonero SM pedlar, ped(d)ler (*EEUU*), hawker
buido ADJ **1** (= *puntiagudo*) sharp, pointed
2 (= *estriado*) fluted, grooved
buitre SM (*Orn*) vulture ▸ **buitre alimoche** Egyptian vulture ▸ **buitre leonado** griffon vulture
SMF* (= *persona gorrona*) scrounger*
buitrear ▸ CONJUG 1a VT **1*** (= *gorronear*) to scrounge*
2 (*LAm*) (= *matar*) to kill
3 (*And, Cono Sur**) (= *vomitar*) to throw up, vomit
VI (*And, Cono Sur*) to be sick, vomit
buitrón SM fish trap
buja SF (*Méx*) (*Aut*) axle box
bujarra‡ SM, **bujarrón‡** SM queer‡, fag (*EEUU‡*)
buje SM axle box, bushing
bujería SF trinket, knick-knack
bujero‡ SM hole
bujía SF **1** (*Aut*) spark plug
2 (*Elec*) candle power
3† (= *vela*) candle; (= *candelero*) candlestick
4 (*CAm*) (= *bombilla*) light bulb
bula SF (*Rel*) bull • MODISMOS: • **no poder con la ~*** to have no strength left for anything • **no me vale la ~ de Meco** I'm done for
bulbiforme ADJ bulbiform
bulbo SM **1** (*Anat, Bot, Med*) bulb
2 (*Méx*) valve, tube (*EEUU*)
3 (*Cono Sur*) (*Elec*) bulb
bulboso ADJ bulbous
buldog [bul'dog] SM (PL: **buldogs**) bulldog
bule SM (*Méx*) (*Bot*) gourd, squash (*EEUU*); (= *cántaro*) water pitcher • MODISMO: • **llenarse hasta los ~s** to stuff o.s.* • REFRÁN: • **el que nace para ~ hasta jícara no para** you can't escape your destiny
bulerías SFPL *Andalusian song accompanied with clapping and dancing*
bulevar SM boulevard, avenue
Bulgaria SF Bulgaria
búlgaro/a ADJ, SM/F Bulgarian
SM (*Ling*) Bulgarian
bulimia SF bulimia, binge-eating syndrome (*EEUU*)
bulín SM (*Cono Sur*) **1** [*de soltero*] bachelor flat
2 (= *burdel*) room (*used for sexual encounters*)
bulla SF **1** (= *bullicio*) row, racket • **armar** *o* **meter ~** to make a row, make a racket*
2 (= *bronca*) quarrel, brawl • **meter algo a ~** to throw sth into confusion
3 (= *prisa*) hurry • **tengo mucha ~** I'm in a real hurry • **métele ~** hurry him up *o* along
4 (= *muchedumbre*) crowd, mob
5 • **ser el hombre de la ~** (*Caribe*) to be the man of the moment
bullabesa SF fish soup, bouillabaisse
bullaje SM noisy crowd, mob
bullanga SF disturbance, riot
bullanguero/a ADJ riotous, rowdy

SM/F **1** (= *persona ruidosa*) noisy person
2 (= *alborotador*) troublemaker
bullaranga SF (*LAm*) **1** (= *bullicio*) noise, row
2 (= *disturbio*) riot
bullarengue‡ SM bottom, woman's bottom
bulldog SM (*Zool*) bulldog
bulldozer [bul'doθer] SM (PL: **bulldozers** [bul'doθer]) bulldozer
bullebulle* SMF (= *entrometido*) busybody; (= *intranquilo*) fusspot, fussbudget (*EEUU**)
bullero ADJ (*LAm*) = **bullicioso**
bullicio SM **1** (= *ruido*) din, hubbub
2 (= *actividad*) activity, bustle
3 (= *confusión*) confusion
4 (= *disturbio*) disturbance
bulliciosamente ADV **1** (= *ruidosamente*) [*protestar*] noisily; [*jugar*] boisterously
2 (= *con gran actividad*) busily
bullicioso ADJ **1** (= *ruidoso*) [*lugar*] noisy; [*niño*] boisterous
2 (= *con actividad*) busy, bustling
bullir ▸ CONJUG 3h VI **1** [*agua*] (= *hervir*) to boil; (= *agitarse*) to bubble (up) • **el agua bullía ligeramente** the water bubbled gently; ▸ **sangre**
2 (= *moverse*) to move, stir • **no bullía** he didn't move, he never stirred • **Londres está que bulle de juventud** London is bursting with young people • **la ciudad bullía de actividad** the town was humming with activity • **bullía de indignación** he was seething with indignation
3 [*insectos*] to swarm
VT to move, stir • **no bulló pie ni mano** he did not lift a finger
VPR **bullirse** to move, stir
bulo SM hoax
bulón SM bolt
bulto SM **1** (= *abultamiento*) bulge • **se le notaba un ~ debajo de la chaqueta** you could see a shape *o* bulge under his jacket • MODISMOS: • **buscar el ~ a algn*** to provoke *o* push sb • **menear el ~ a algn*** to thrash sb
2 (= *silueta*) shape • **vimos un ~ moviéndose entre los árboles** we saw a shape moving in the trees • **sin gafas solo distingo los ~s** without glasses I can only make out shapes • **ir al ~** (*Taur*) to go for the body; (*Ftbl*) to go for the man
3 (= *volumen*) space, room • **no ocupa** *o* **hace ~** it doesn't take up any space *o* room • **he comprado regalos que ocupen poco ~** I've bought presents that won't take up much space *o* that are not too bulky • **error de ~** glaring error • **de mucho ~** (*lit*) bulky; (*fig*) important • **de poco ~** (*lit*) small; (*fig*) unimportant • **llevaba dos bolsas de poco ~** she carried two small bags • **no discutamos por cosas de poco ~** let's not argue about unimportant things • MODISMOS: • **a ~** at a rough guess • **así, a ~, debe de haber unas mil botellas** at a rough guess there must be about a thousand bottles • **calcular algo a ~** to work sth out roughly, make a rough estimate of sth • **decir algo a ~**: • **di algo a ~** just have a guess • **escurrir el ~*** (= *desaparecer*) to duck out*; (= *cambiar de tema*) to dodge the issue* • **ir de ~** • **hacer ~** to swell the number(s), make up the number(s) • **allí solo estábamos para hacer ~** we were only there to make up *o* swell the numbers • **no hay que hacer nada, solo ir de ~** we don't have to do anything, we just have to be there *o* to go along
4 (= *paquete*) [*de compra*] bag; [*de ropa, papel*] bundle; [*de equipaje*] piece of luggage *o* (*EEUU*) baggage • **vino cargado de ~s del supermercado** he arrived laden with bags from the supermarket • **el camión trajo todos los ~s pesados** the truck brought all

the heavy loads • **pon los ~s en el maletero** put the luggage in the boot, put the baggage in the trunk (*EEUU*) ▸ **bulto de mano** item of hand luggage
5 (*Med*) (= *quiste*) lump; (= *chichón*) bump • **le salió un ~ en el cuello** he got a lump on his neck • **del golpe me salió un ~ en la frente** I got a bump on my forehead when I hit myself
6 (= *estatua*) statue
7 (*Mil*‡) squaddie*, recruit
8 (*Ven*) [*de escolar*] satchel, bag
bululú* (SM) (*Ven*) excitement, fuss
bumerán (SM) boomerang
bumerang [bume'ran] (SM) (PL: **bumerangs** [bume'ran]) boomerang
bunga (SF) (*Caribe*) lie
bungalow ['boŋgalo, buŋga'lo] (SM) (PL: **bungalows** ['boŋgalo, buŋga'lo]) bungalow
bungee ['banji] (SM) bungee jumping
bungo (SM) (*CAm*) = **bongo**
buniato (SM) = **boniato**
bunjo (SM) • **hacer ~** (*Caribe*) to hit the jackpot
búnker ['buŋker] (SM) (PL: **búnkers** ['buŋker]) **1** (*Mil*) bunker
2 (*Golf*) bunker, sand trap (*EEUU*)
3 (*Pol*) reactionary clique, reactionary core
búnquer (SM) = **búnker**
buñolería (SF) **1** (= *panadería*) *bakery where "buñuelos" are made*
2 (= *tienda*) *shop where "buñuelos" are sold*
buñuelo (SM) **1** (*Culin*) fritter, ≈ doughnut, ≈ donut (*EEUU*)
2* (= *chapuza*) botched job, mess
BUP (SM ABR) (*Esp*) (*Escol*) (= **Bachillerato Unificado y Polivalente**) *former secondary-school certificate and course for 14-17 age group*
buque (SM) **1** (= *barco*) ship, boat • **ir en ~** to go by ship, go by sea ▸ **buque almirante** flagship ▸ **buque anfibio** amphibious craft ▸ **buque carguero** freighter ▸ **buque cisterna** tanker ▸ **buque correo** mailboat ▸ **buque costero** coaster ▸ **buque de abastecimiento** supply ship ▸ **buque de carga** freighter ▸ **buque de desembarco** landing craft ▸ **buque de guerra** warship; (*Hist*) man-of-war ▸ **buque de línea** liner; (*Hist*) ship of the line ▸ **buque de pasajeros** passenger ship ▸ **buque de ruedas** paddle-steamer ▸ **buque de vapor** steamer, steamship ▸ **buque de vela** sailing ship ▸ **buque escolta** escort vessel ▸ **buque escuela** training ship ▸ **buque espía** spy ship ▸ **buque factoría** factory ship ▸ **buque fanal, buque faro** lightship ▸ **buque granelero** bulk-carrier ▸ **buque hospital** hospital ship ▸ **buque insignia** flagship ▸ **buque mercante** merchantman, merchant ship ▸ **buque minador** minelayer ▸ **buque nodriza** mother ship ▸ **buque portacontenedores** container ship ▸ **buque portatrén** train ferry ▸ **buque velero** sailing ship
2 (= *cabida*) capacity
3 (= *casco*) hull
buqué (SM) bouquet (*of wine*)
buraco (SM) (*Cono Sur*) hole
burata‡ (SF) (*Caribe*) cash, dough‡
burbuja (SF) bubble • **un refresco sin ~s** a still drink • **un refresco con ~s** a fizzy drink • **hacer ~s** [*persona*] to blow bubbles; [*gaseosa*] to fizz
burbujeante (ADJ) bubbly, fizzy
burbujear ▸ CONJUG 1a (VI) [*agua hirviendo*] to bubble; [*champán, gaseosa*] to fizz
burbujeo (SM) bubbling
burda‡ (SF) door
burdégano (SM) hinny
burdel (SM) brothel
Burdeos (SM) Bordeaux
burdeos (ADJ INV) maroon, dark red
(SM INV) (*tb* **vino de burdeos**) claret, Bordeaux, Bordeaux wine
burdo (ADJ) **1** [*persona*] coarse, rough
2 [*excusa, mentira*] clumsy
burear* ▸ CONJUG 1a (*And*) (VT) to con*, trick
(VI) to go out on the town*
bureo* (SM) **1** (= *diversión*) entertainment, amusement • **ir de ~** to go out on the town*
2 (= *paseo*) stroll • **darse un ~** to go for a stroll
bureta (SF) burette
burgalés/esa (ADJ) of/from Burgos
(SM/F) native/inhabitant of Burgos • **los burgaleses** the people of Burgos
burgo (SM) hamlet
burgomaestre (SM) burgomaster
burgués/esa (ADJ) **1** (= *de clase media*) middle-class • **pequeño ~** lower middle-class
2 (*Pol*) (*pey*) bourgeois
3 (= *de la ciudad*) town (*antes de s*)
(SM/F) **1** (*de clase media*) middle-class person; (*Pol*) (*pey*) bourgeois • **pequeño ~** lower middle-class person; (*Pol*) (*pey*) petit bourgeois
2 (= *ciudadano*) townsman/townswoman
burguesía (SF) middle-class, bourgeoisie • **alta ~** upper middle class • **pequeña ~** lower middle class; (*Pol*) (*pey*) petit bourgeoisie
buril (SM) burin, engraver's chisel
burilar ▸ CONJUG 1a (VT) to engrave
burka (SM), (*a veces*) (SF) burqa
burla (SF) **1** (= *mofa*) gibe, taunt • **hacer ~ de algn** to make fun of sb, mock sb • **hace ~ de todo** he makes fun of *o* mocks everything
2 (= *broma*) joke • **fue una ~ cruel** it was a cruel trick
3 burlas joking (*sing*), fun (*sing*) • **de ~s** in fun, tongue in cheek • **gastar ~s con algn** to make fun of sb • **entre ~s y veras** half-joking(ly)
burladero (SM) **1** (*Taur*) covert (*barrier behind which the bullfighter protects himself from the bull*)
2 (*Aut*) traffic island; (*en túnel*) recess
burlador(a) (ADJ) mocking
(SM/F) **1** (= *cínico*) mocker
2 (= *bromista*) practical joker
(SM) † Don Juan
burlar ▸ CONJUG 1a (VT) **1** (= *engañar*) [+ *persona*] to deceive, trick; [+ *enemigo*] to outwit; [+ *vigilancia*] to defeat; [+ *bloqueo*] to run
2 (= *frustrar*) [+ *ambición, plan*] to thwart, frustrate; [+ *esperanzas*] to ruin, frustrate
3 (= *seducir*) to seduce
4* (= *saber usar*) to know how to use, be able to handle • **ya burla la moto** she can handle the bike now*
(VPR) **burlarse 1** (= *bromear*) to joke, banter • **yo no me burlo** I'm serious, I'm not joking
2 • **~se de algn** to mock sb, make fun of sb
burlería (SF) **1** (= *mofa*) mockery
2 (= *engaño*) trick, deceit
3 (= *cuento*) tall story, fairy tale
4 (= *bromas*) fun
burlesco (ADJ) **1** (= *cómico*) funny, comic
2 (*Literat*) burlesque
burlete (SM) draught excluder, weather strip (*EEUU*)
burlisto (ADJ) (*Cono Sur, CAm, Méx*) = **burlón**
burlón/ona (ADJ) (= *bromista*) [*persona*] mocking, teasing; [*risa, voz*] sardonic • **dijo ~** he said teasingly
(SM/F) **1** (= *bromista*) joker
2 (= *mofador*) mocker, scoffer
(SM) (*Méx**) mockingbird
burlonamente (ADV) (= *en broma*) mockingly, teasingly; (= *sarcásticamente*) sardonically, derisively
buró (SM) **1** (= *escritorio*) bureau, (roll-top) desk
2 ▸ **buró político** (*Pol*) executive committee
3 (*Méx*) (= *mesita de noche*) bedside table, night stand *o* table (*EEUU*)
burocracia (SF) bureaucracy
burócrata (SMF) **1** (*pey*) bureaucrat
2 (= *funcionario*) civil servant, administrative official, public official
burocrático (ADJ) **1** (*pey*) bureaucratic
2 (= *de los funcionarios*) official, civil service (*antes de s*)
burocratizar ▸ CONJUG 1f (VT) to bureaucratize
burofax (SM) registered fax (*sent via the Spanish Post Office*)
buromática (SF), **burótica** (SF) office automation, office computerization
burqa (SM), (*a veces*) (SF) burqa
burra (SF) **1** (*Zool*) donkey, she-donkey; ▸ **burro**
2 (*Esp**) (= *bicicleta*) bike
burrada (SF) **1** (= *tontería*) stupid thing • **decir ~s** to talk nonsense • **hacer ~s** to do stupid things • **no hagas ~s con el coche** don't do anything stupid with the car
2* (= *mucho*) • **me gusta una ~** I like it a lot • **sabe una ~** he knows a hell of a lot* • **una ~ de cosas** a whole heap of things, loads of things*
burrajo (ADJ) (*Méx*) vulgar, rude
burrear‡ ▸ CONJUG 1a (VT) **1** (= *robar*) to rip off‡
2 (= *engañar*) to con*
burrero/a (ADJ) (*Cono Sur*) (*hum*) horse-loving, race-going
(SM/F) **1** (*Méx*) mule driver, donkey driver
2 (*Caribe*) (= *malhablado*) coarse person, foul-mouthed person
3 (*Cono Sur*) (*hum*) horse-lover
(SM) (*CAm*) (= *burros*) *large herd of donkeys*
burricie* (SF) stupidity
burro (ADJ) **1*** (= *estúpido*) stupid • **¡qué ~! ¡no sabe la capital de Italia!** what a fool *o* moron*, he doesn't know the capital of Italy!
2 (= *bruto*) • **¡deja de empujar, no seas ~!** stop pushing, you great oaf *o* you big brute!* • **¡el muy ~ se comió el pastel entero!** he ate the whole cake, the pig!*
3 (= *obstinado*) pig-headed* • **ponerse ~** to dig one's heels in, be pigheaded*
(SM) **1** (*Zool*) donkey; (*Cono Sur*) (*hum*) racehorse; (= *perdedor en carrera*) also-ran • **salto de ~** (*Méx*) leapfrog • MODISMOS: • **apearse** *o* **bajar(se) del ~*** to back down • **a pesar de las críticas, el gobierno no se apea** *o* **baja del ~** in spite of the criticism, the government refuses to back down • **¡el niño no se apea** *o* **baja del ~!** this kid doesn't know when he's beaten! • **bajar del ~ a algn** to take sb down a peg (or two)*, put sb in his/her place* • **caer ~s aparejados** (*Caribe**) to rain cats and dogs • **caerse del ~*** to admit defeat • **es un ~ cargado de letras** he's a pompous ass* • **comer ~**: • **esto comió ~** (*Cono Sur**) it got lost, it vanished • **el ~ grande, ande o no ande*** never mind the quality, feel the width* • **no ver tres en un ~***: • **sin gafas no veo tres en un ~** without my glasses I'm as blind as a bat* • **en el bosque no se veía tres en un ~** in the wood you couldn't see your hand in front of your face* • **poner a algn a caer de un ~*** to savage sb, tear sb to shreds • **ver ~s negros** (*Cono Sur**) to see stars • **si los ~s volaran** pigs might fly • **si los ~s volaran, todos nos haríamos ricos con ese negocio** this business could make us rich, and pigs might fly ▸ **burro de agua** (*Caribe, Méx*) big wave ▸ **burro de carga** • **trata a su empleados como ~s de carga** he treats his workers like slaves
2* (= *estúpido*) fool, moron* • **¡burro!, tres y dos son cinco** you fool *o* moron*, three plus two makes five!
3* (= *bruto*) • **eres un ~, lo has roto** you're so rough you've gone and broken it • **el ~ de Juan seguía pegándole** that brute Juan kept on hitting him • **el ~ de Antonio se comió su**

plato y el mío that pig Antonio ate all his own dinner and mine too* • **MODISMO**: • **trabaja como un ~** he works like a slave, he works all the hours God sends*
4 (= *obstinado*) stubborn fool • **es un ~ y no lo vas a convencer** he's so pig-headed* *o* stubborn you'll never persuade him
5 (*Naipes*) ≈ old maid
6 (*Téc*) sawhorse, sawbuck (*EEUU*) ▸ **burro de planchar** (*Méx*) ironing board
7 (*Méx*) (= *escalera*) stepladder
8 (*And, Caribe*) (= *columpio*) swing
burrumazo* SM (*Caribe*) blow, thump
bursátil ADJ stock-exchange (*antes de s*), stock-market (*antes de s*) • **crisis ~** stock-market crisis • **desplome ~** stock-market crash
bursitis SF INV bursitis
burucuyá SF (*Arg, Para*) passionflower
burujaca SF (*LAm*) saddlebag
burujo SM = **borujo**
burundanga SF (*Cuba*) **1** (= *objeto sin valor*) piece of junk • **es ~** it's just a piece of junk • **de ~** worthless
2 (= *lío*) mess, mix-up
burusca SF (*CAm*) kindling
bus SM **1** (= *autobús*) bus, coach
2 (*Inform*) bus ▸ **bus de expansión** expansion bus ▸ **bus de memoria** memory bus
busa‡ SF • **tener ~** (*Esp*) to feel hungry
busaca SF **1** (*And, Caribe*) saddlebag
2 (*Caribe*) satchel
busca SF search • **la niebla dificultaba la ~** the search was hampered by fog • **están analizando la muestra a la ~ de impurezas** they are analysing the sample in search of impurities *o* to search for impurities • **en ~ de** in search of • **salieron en ~ del niño desaparecido** they set off in search of the missing child • **empezó a llamar por teléfono a todas partes en mi ~** he began phoning around everywhere to try and find me • **se marcharon en ~ de fortuna** they went off to seek their fortune ▸ **busca y captura** • **el juez dictó orden de ~ y captura del fugitivo** the judge ordered the fugitive's (immediate) capture • **estar en ~ y captura** to be wanted, be on the run*
SM (*Esp*) (= *mensáfono*) bleeper*, pager
buscabullas* SMF (*Caribe, Méx*) troublemaker
buscada SF = **busca**
buscador(a) SM/F (= *persona*) ▸ **buscador(a) de agua** water-diviner ▸ **buscador(a) de diamantes** diamond prospector ▸ **buscador(a) de fortuna** fortune-seeker ▸ **buscador(a) de oro** gold prospector ▸ **buscador(a) de setas** mushroom-gatherer ▸ **buscador(a) de talentos** talent spotter, talent scout ▸ **buscador(a) de tesoros** treasure hunter
SM **1** (*Internet*) search engine
2 (= *mecanismo*) scanner
buscaniguas SM INV (*And, CAm*) squib, cracker
buscapersonas SM INV = **busca**
buscapié SM hint
buscapiés SM INV jumping jack, firecracker (*EEUU*)
buscapleitos SMF INV (*LAm*) troublemaker
buscar ▸ CONJUG 1g VT **1** (= *tratar de encontrar*)
a [+ *persona, objeto perdido, trabajo*] to look for • **estuvieron buscando a los montañeros** they were searching for *o* looking for the mountaineers • **llevo meses buscando trabajo** I've been job-hunting for months, I've been looking for a job for months • **el ejército busca a un comando enemigo** the army is searching for *o* looking for an enemy commando unit • **el terrorista más buscado del país** the most wanted terrorist in the country • **"se busca piso"** "flat wanted" • **"chico busca chica"** "boy seeks girl" • **el acomodador me buscó un asiento al fondo** the usher found me a seat at the back • **las plantas buscan la luz** plants grow towards the light • **MODISMO**: • **~le tres pies al gato** (= *buscar complicaciones*) to complicate matters, make things difficult; (= *buscar defectos*) to split hairs, nitpick* • **REFRÁN**: • **busca y encontrarás** seek and you shall find
b (*en diccionario, enciclopedia*) to look up • **busca el número en la guía** look up the number in the directory
c (*con la vista*) to try to spot, look for • **lo busqué entre el público pero no lo vi** I tried to spot him *o* looked for him in the crowd but I didn't see him
2 (= *tratar de conseguir*) [+ *solución*] to try to find • **no sé lo que buscas con esa actitud** I don't know what you're aiming to *o* trying to achieve with that attitude • **con esta novela se busca la creación de un estilo diferente** this novel attempts to *o* aims to create a different style • **yo no busco la fama** I'm not looking for fame • **solo buscaba su dinero** he was only out for *o* after her money • **como tienen una niña ahora van buscando la parejita** as they've got a girl they're trying for a boy now • **~ excusas** to make excuses • **~ hacer algo** to seek to do sth, try to do sth • **siempre buscaba hacerlo lo mejor posible** she always sought *o* tried to do the best possible thing • **ir a ~ algo/a algn**: • **ha ido a ~ una servilleta** she's gone to fetch *o* get a napkin • **ve a ~ a tu madre** go and fetch *o* get your mother • **voy a ~ tabaco** I'll go and get some cigarettes • **MODISMOS**: • **~la** • **~ pelea** to be looking for a fight, be looking for trouble • **vino buscando pelea** he was looking for trouble *o* a fight, he was spoiling for a fight* • **~ la ruina a algn** to be the ruin of sb • **este hijo mío me va a ~ la ruina** this son of mine will be the ruin of me
3 (= *recoger*) to pick up, fetch • **¿vais a ir a ~me a la estación?** are you going to pick me up *o* fetch me from the station? • **vino a ~ sus plantas** she came to pick up *o* fetch her plants
4 (*Inform*) to search
5 (= *preguntar por*) to ask for • **¿quién me busca?** who is asking for me?
VI to look • **ya puedes dejar de ~, aquí tienes las llaves** you can stop looking, here are the keys • **¿has buscado bien?** have you looked properly? • **busca en la página 45** look on page 45 • **¡busca!** (*al perro*) fetch!
VPR **buscarse 1** [+ *marido, trabajo*] to find (o.s.); [+ *ayuda, patrocinador*] to get, find • **deberías ~te un ayudante** you should find yourself an assistant • **ya tendrías que ~te trabajo** you should find yourself a job *o* start looking for a job • **MODISMO**: • **~se la vida*** (= *ganar dinero*) to try to earn *o* make a living; (= *arreglárselas solo*) to manage on one's own, get by on one's own • **yo me busco la vida como puedo** I (try to) earn *o* make a living as best as I can • **no me vengas con historias, búscate la vida** stop bothering me, sort it out for yourself
2 [+ *problemas*] • **no te busques más problemas** don't bring more problems on yourself, don't make more trouble for yourself • **él se lo buscó** he brought it on himself, he asked for it* • **MODISMO**: • **buscársela*** to ask for trouble, ask for it* • **te la estás buscando** you're asking for it, you're asking for trouble • **él se la buscó** he asked for it*
buscarruidos SM INV rowdy, troublemaker
buscas* SFPL (*LAm*) perks*, profits on the side
buscatesoros SMF INV treasure hunter, treasure seeker
buscavidas SMF INV **1** (= *persona ambiciosa*) go-getter
2 (= *fisgón*) snooper, nosey-parker*
buscón/ona ADJ (= *deshonesto*) thieving, crooked
SM/F †† (= *ladronzuelo*) petty thief, rogue
buscona SF (*pey*) whore
buseca SF **1** (*And, Caribe*) small bus, minibus
2 (*Cono Sur*) thick stew
busilis* SM INV difficulty, snag • **ahí está el ~** that's the problem • **dar en el ~ del asunto** to reach the crux of the matter
búsqueda SF search (**de** for) • **continúa la ~ de los desaparecidos** the search for the missing people continues • **hacer una ~** to do a search • **a *o* en ~ de algo** in search of sth • **estamos trabajando en la ~ de una vacuna** we're working on finding a vaccine ▸ **búsqueda del tesoro** treasure hunt ▸ **búsqueda de votos** canvassing ▸ **búsqueda y sustitución** (*Inform*) find and replace
busto SM **1** (= *escultura*) bust ▸ **busto parlante** talking head
2 (*Anat*) chest
butaca SF **1** (= *sillón*) armchair, easy chair ▸ **butaca orejera** wing-chair
2 (*Teat*) seat ▸ **butaca de platea, butaca de patio** seat in the stalls *o* (*EEUU*) orchestra
butacón SM large armchair
butanero SM gas-bottle delivery man
butano SM (*tb* **gas butano**) butane, butane gas • **bombona de ~** (large butane) gas cylinder • **color ~** orange
butaque SM (*LAm*) small armchair
buten ADV • **de ~*** terrific*, tremendous*
butifarra SF **1** (= *embutido*) *Catalan sausage* • **MODISMO**: • **hacer (la) ~ a algn*** ≈ to give sb the two-fingers sign, make an obscene gesture to sb
2* (= *media*) *badly-fitting stocking*
3 (*Perú*) *meat and salad roll*
4 • **MODISMO**: • **tomar a algn para la ~** (*Cono Sur**) to make a laughing stock of sb
butiondo ADJ lewd, lustful
butrón* SM **1** (= *agujero*) *hole made to effect a break-in*
2 (= *robo*) burglary, break-in
butronero* SM burglar
butuco ADJ (*CAm*) short, squat
buz SM respectful kiss, formal kiss • **hacer el buz** to bow and scrape
buzamiento SM (*Geol*) dip
buzar ▸ CONJUG 1f VI (*Geol*) to dip
buzo¹ SM diver
buzo² SM (*And, Cono Sur*) (= *chándal*) tracksuit; (= *mono*) jumpsuit
buzón SM **1** (*Correos*) (*en casa*) letterbox, mailbox (*EEUU*); (*en calle*) postbox, letterbox, mailbox (*EEUU*) • **echar una carta al ~** to post a letter • **MODISMOS**: • **cerrar el ~‡** to keep one's trap shut* • **vender un ~ a algn** (*Cono Sur**) to sell sb a dummy, pull the wool over sb's eyes ▸ **buzón de alcance** late-collection postbox ▸ **buzón de sugerencias** suggestions box ▸ **buzón de voz** voice mail
2 (*Inform*) mailbox ▸ **buzón de entrada** inbox
3 (= *tapón*) plug
4 (= *compuerta*) sluice
5 (*Pol*) *courier in secret organization*
buzonear ▸ CONJUG 1a VT to deliver door-to-door
buzoneo SM direct mail
buzonero/a SMF (*LAm*) postal employee (*who collects from letterboxes*)
byte SM (*Inform*) byte

C

Cc

C[1], **c** [θe], (*esp LAm*) [se] SF (= *letra*) C, c
C[2] ABR (= **centígrado**) C
C. ABR (= **Compañía**) Co
c. ABR **1** (= **capítulo**) ch, c., chap
2 (= **cuenta**) a/c, acc., acct.
c^3 ABR (= **centímetros cúbicos**) cc
C-14 ABR (= **carbono 14**) C.14 • **datación por C-14** C.14 dating
C/ ABR (= **Calle**) St
c/ ABR **1** (= **cuenta**) a/c, acc., acct.
2 (= **capítulo**) ch, c., chap
3 (= **carretera**) Rd
Cª ABR (= **compañía**) Co.
ca EXCL not a bit of it!, never!
C.A. ABR **1** (*Elec*) (= **corriente alterna**) AC
2 (*Esp*) (*Pol*) = **Comunidad Autónoma**
3 (*Dep*) (= **Club Atlético**) AC
cabal ADJ **1** (= *exacto*) • **llegó a las doce ~es** he arrived at exactly twelve o'clock, he arrived at twelve o'clock precisely • **5 euros ~es** exactly 5 euros
2 (*frm*) (= *completo*) • **una ~ formación humanística** a thorough classical education • **esto nos proporciona una idea ~ del asunto** this provides us with a clearer and fuller picture of the matter
3 (= *sensato*) upright
SMPL **cabales** • **no está en sus ~es** she isn't in her right mind • **perdió sus ~es por ella** he lost his mind over her
EXCL † • **¡cabal!** perfectly correct!, right!
cábala SF **1** (*Rel*) kabbalah
2 (= *intriga*) cabal, intrigue
3 cábalas (= *conjeturas*) • **hacer ~s** to speculate, conjecture
cabalgada SF (*Hist*) (= *tropa*) troop of riders; (= *incursión*) cavalry raid
cabalgador SM rider, horseman
cabalgadura SF [*de montar*] mount, horse; [*de carga*] beast of burden
cabalgar ▸ CONJUG 1h VT **1** [*jinete*] to ride
2 [*semental*] to cover, serve
VI to ride, go riding • **~ en mula** to ride (on) a mule • **~ sin montura** • **~ a pelo** to ride bareback
cabalgata SF **1** (= *desfile*) mounted procession, cavalcade ▸ **cabalgata de Reyes** Twelfth Night procession
2 [*de jinete*] ride

CABALGATA DE REYES
The **cabalgata de Reyes** is a float parade held on 5 January, the eve of Epiphany, in most Spanish towns and cities. It celebrates the coming of the Three Kings with their gifts for the infant Jesus. In the course of the **cabalgatas**, the Three Kings throw sweets into the crowd.
▸ DÍA DE REYES

cabalidad SF • **a ~** perfectly, adequately
cabalista SMF schemer, intriguer
cabalístico ADJ (= *de la cábala*) cabalistic; (= *misterioso*) occult, mysterious
caballa SF (Atlantic) mackerel
caballada SF **1** (*Zool*) drove of horses
2 (*LAm*) (= *animalada*) stupid thing to do • **has hecho una ~** that was a stupid thing to do
caballaje SM horsepower
caballar ADJ horse (*antes de s*), equine • **ganado ~** horses (*pl*) • **cara ~** horse-face
caballazo SM (*LAm*) collision between two horsemen, accident involving a horse
caballejo SM **1** (= *poney*) pony
2 (= *rocín*) old horse, nag*
caballerango SM (*Méx*) groom
caballerear ▸ CONJUG 1a VI to play the gentleman
caballeresco ADJ **1** (*Hist*) knightly, chivalric • **literatura caballeresca** chivalresque literature, books of chivalry • **orden caballeresca** order of chivalry
2 [*sentimiento*] fine, noble; [*carácter*] gentlemanly, noble; [*conducta*] chivalrous
caballerete SM **1** (= *jovenzuelo*) young man
2 (= *presumido*) cocky youngster, Jack-the-lad*
caballería SF **1** (= *montura*) mount, steed (*liter*); (= *caballo*) horse; (= *mula*) mule ▸ **caballería de carga** beast of burden
2 (*Mil*) cavalry ▸ **caballería ligera** light cavalry, light horse
3 (*Hist*) chivalry; (= *orden*) order of chivalry • **libros de ~s** books of chivalry ▸ **caballería andante** knight errantry
4 • **andarse en ~s** to overdo the compliments
5 (*CAm, Caribe, Cono Sur, Méx*) (*Agr*) *a land measurement of varying size (usually 42 hectares)*
caballericero SM (*CAm, Caribe*) groom
caballeriza SF **1** (= *cuadra*) stable; [*de cría*] stud, horse-breeding establishment ▸ **caballeriza de alquiler** livery stable
2 (= *empleados*) stable hands (*pl*), grooms (*pl*)
caballerizo SM groom, stableman ▸ **caballerizo del rey** equerry ▸ **caballerizo mayor del rey** master of the king's horse
caballero SM **1** (= *hombre educado*) gentleman • **es todo un ~** he is a real gentleman; ▸ **pacto**
2 (*fórmula de cortesía*) • **¿qué desea tomar, ~?** what would you like to drink, sir? • **señoras y ~s** ladies and gentlemen
3 (= *hombre*) • **camisa de ~** man's shirt • **peluquería de ~s** gents' hairdresser's • **servicio de ~s** gents, men's toilets, men's • **ropa de ~** menswear • **"caballeros"** (= *servicios*) "gents", "gentlemen"
4 (*Hist*) knight • **los ~s de la Tabla Redonda** the Knights of the Round Table • **armar ~ a algn** to knight sb • **el Caballero de la Triste Figura** the Knight of the Doleful Countenance, Don Quixote • **~ de Santiago** Knight of (the Order of) Santiago ▸ **caballero andante** knight errant
caballerosamente ADV (= *con cortesía*) like a gentleman, in a gentlemanly fashion; (= *con nobleza*) chivalrously
caballerosidad SF (= *cortesía*) gentlemanliness; (= *nobleza*) chivalry
caballeroso ADJ (= *cortés*) gentlemanly; (= *noble*) chivalrous • **poco ~** ungentlemanly
caballerote SM (*pey*) so-called gentleman, gentleman unworthy of the name
caballete SM (*Arte*) easel; (*Téc*) trestle; [*de tejado, de tierra labrada*] ridge; [*de chimenea*] cowl; (*Anat*) bridge (of the nose) ▸ **caballete de pintor** painter's easel ▸ **caballete de serrar** sawhorse, sawbuck (*EEUU*) ▸ **caballete para bicicleta** bicycle clamp, bicycle rest
caballista SMF (= *jinete*) horseman/woman; (= *experto*) expert on horses
caballito SM **1** (= *caballo*) little horse, pony • MODISMO: • **llevar a algn a ~** to give sb a piggy-back ▸ **caballito del diablo** dragonfly ▸ **caballito de mar** sea horse ▸ **caballito de niño** (*para mecerse*) rocking horse; (*con palo (y rueda)*) hobby-horse ▸ **caballito marino** sea horse
2 (*Méx*) (= *compresa*) sanitary towel, sanitary napkin (*EEUU*)
3 caballitos [*de feria*] merry-go-round (*sing*), carousel (*sing*) (*esp EEUU*)
caballo SM **1** (= *animal*) horse • **a ~**: **una mujer a ~** a woman on horseback *o* riding a horse • **vino a ~** he came on horseback, he rode here • **me gusta montar a ~** I like (to go) horse riding • **paseo a ~** (horse) ride • **tropas de a ~** mounted troops • MODISMOS: • **de ~**‡ huge, massive • **una dosis de ~** a huge dose, a massive dose • **una depresión de ~** a terrible depression, a really deep depression • **a ~ entre**: • **Andalucía, a ~ entre oriente y occidente** Andalusia, halfway between the east and the west • **vivo a ~ entre Madrid y Barcelona** I spend my time between Madrid and Barcelona, I spend half my time in Madrid, half in Barcelona • **como ~ desbocado** rashly, hastily • **ir a mata ~*** to go at breakneck speed, go like the clappers* • REFRÁN: • **a ~ regalado no le mires el diente** don't look a gift horse in the mouth ▸ **caballo blanco**† white knight ▸ **caballo de batalla** • **han convertido el asunto en su ~ de batalla personal** the issue has become their hobbyhorse • **esto se convirtió en el ~ de batalla de la reunión** this became the bone of contention in the meeting ▸ **caballo de carga** packhorse ▸ **caballo de carreras** racehorse ▸ **caballo de caza** hunter ▸ **caballo de guerra** warhorse, charger ▸ **caballo de manta, caballo de silla** saddle horse ▸ **caballo de tiro** carthorse, plough horse, plow horse (*EEUU*) ▸ **Caballo de Troya** Trojan horse
2 (*Ajedrez*) knight; (*Naipes*) *equivalent of queen in the Spanish pack of cards*
3 (*Mec*) (*tb* **caballo de fuerza, caballo de vapor**) horsepower • **un motor de 100 ~s** a 100 horsepower engine • **¿cuántos ~s tiene este coche?** what horsepower is this car?, what's this car's horsepower? • **un dos ~s** a

2CV ▸ **caballo de vapor decimal** metric horsepower
4 (*Dep*) ▸ **caballo con arcos** pommel horse, side horse ▸ **caballo de saltos** vaulting horse, long horse
5 [*de carpintero*] sawhorse, sawbuck (*EEUU*)
6‡ (= *heroína*) smack‡, sugar‡
caballón (SM) (*Agr*) ridge
caballuno (ADJ) horse-like, horsy
cabalmente (ADV) (= *exactamente*) exactly; (= *bien*) properly; (= *completamente*) completely, fully; (= *a conciencia*) thoroughly
cabanga (SF) (*CAm*) nostalgia, blues*, homesickness • **estar de ~** to be homesick
cabaña (SF) **1** (= *choza*) hut, cabin; (*pobre*) hovel, shack ▸ **cabaña de madera** log cabin
2 (*Billar*) baulk
3 (*Agr*) (= *rebaño*) (large) flock; (= *ganado*) livestock
4 (*Cono Sur*) (= *estancia*) cattle-breeding ranch
cabañero (SM) herdsman
cabañuelas (SFPL) (*LAm*) folk weather predictions, *weather predictions made by country people, based on weather variations in the first few days of January and August*; (*And*) (= *lluvias*) first summer rains; (*Méx*) (= *periodo*) first twelve days of January (*used to predict the weather*)
cabaré (SM), **cabaret** [kaβa're] (SM) (PL: **cabarés** *o* **cabarets**) (= *espectáculo*) cabaret, floor show; (= *boîte*) cabaret, nightclub
cabaretera (SF) (= *bailarina*) cabaret entertainer, cabaret dancer, showgirl; (= *chica de alterne*) night-club hostess
cabaretero (ADJ) of a nightclub • **con ambiente ~** with a nightclub atmosphere
cabás (SM) schoolbag, satchel
cabe¹ (PREP) (*liter*) close to, near to
cabe² (SM) (*Dep*) header
cabe³ (SM) (= *golpe*) • **dar un ~ a algo** to harm sth, do harm to sth • **dar un ~ al bolsillo** to make a hole in one's pocket ▸ **cabe de pala** windfall, lucky break
cabeceada (SF) (*LAm*) nod (of the head), shake of the head • **dar ~s** to nod off • **echarse una ~** to have a nap
cabecear ▹ CONJUG 1a (VT) **1** [+ *balón*] to head
2 [+ *vino*] to strengthen; [+ *vinos*] to blend
3 (*Cos*) to bind (the edge of)
(VI) **1** (*al dormir*) to nod off; (= *negar*) to shake one's head; [*caballo*] to toss its head
2 [*barco*] to pitch; [*carruaje*] to lurch, sway; [*carga*] to shift, slip
cabeceo (SM) **1** (*al dormir*) nod; (= *negativa*) shake of the head; [*de caballo*] toss of the head
2 [*de un barco*] pitching; [*de un carruaje*] lurching, lurch; [*de una carga*] shifting, slipping
cabecera (SF) **1** [*de página*] top; [*de artículo*] heading; [*de carta*] opening; (*Inform*) title-page • **la noticia apareció en la ~ de todos los periódicos** the news made the headlines in all the newspapers • **ha ocupado la ~ de todos los telediarios** it has been headline news on every news programme ▸ **cabecera de cartel** main attraction
2 [*de río*] headwaters (*pl*)
3 [*de manifestación*] head, front
4 [*de cama*] headboard • **tenía una bandera a la ~ de la cama** he had a flag at the head of the bed; ▹ **libro, médico**
5 [*de mesa*] head • **se sentaron en la ~ de la mesa** they sat at the head of the table
6 [*de organización, ministerio*] top (level) • **desde la ~ del ministerio** from top ministerial level
cabecero (SM) headboard, bedhead
cabeciduro (ADJ) (*And, Caribe*) stubborn, pigheaded
cabecilla (SMF) ringleader
cabellera (SF) **1** (= *pelo*) hair, head of hair; (= *postizo*) switch, hairpiece • MODISMO: • **soltarse la ~*** to let one's hair down
2 (*Astron*) tail
cabello (SM) hair • **analizaremos solo un ~** we shall analyse just a single hair • **llevaba el ~ recogido atrás** she had *o* wore her hair tied back • **te deja los ~s brillantes** it leaves your hair shiny ▸ **cabello de ángel** *confectionery and pastry filling made of pumpkin and syrup*
cabelludo (ADJ) (= *peludo*) hairy, shaggy; (*Bot*) fibrous
caber ▹ CONJUG 2l (VI) **1** (= *haber espacio para*) to fit (**en** into) • **tu guitarra no cabe en mi armario** your guitar won't fit in my cupboard • **en este baúl no cabe** it won't fit in *o* go into this trunk, there's no room for it in this trunk • **en mi coche caben dos maletas más** there's room for two more suitcases in my car • **¿cabe alguien más?** is there room for anyone else? • **¿cabemos todos?** is there room for us all? • **no cabe nadie más** there's no room for anyone else • **en este baúl ya no cabe más** there's no more room (for anything) in this trunk • MODISMOS: • **¡no me cabe en la cabeza!** I can't understand it! • **no ~ en sí** (= *estar feliz*) to be beside o.s.; (= *ser engreído*) to be big-headed*, to be full of o.s. • **no cabe en sí de contento** *o* **gozo** he's beside himself with joy, he's over the moon
2 (= *tener cabida*) • **en la bandeja de papel caben 100 hojas** the paper tray will hold 100 sheets • **en este depósito caben 20 litros** this tank holds 20 litres • **un sofá donde caben dos** a two-seater sofa
3 • **~ por** to go through • **eso no cabe por esta puerta** that won't go through this door
4 (*Mat*) • **veinte entre cinco cabe a cuatro** five into twenty goes four (times)
5 [*ser posible*] **a** [+ *explicación*] to be possible • **solo caben dos explicaciones** there are only two possible explanations • **la única explicación que cabe es que ...** the only possible explanation is that ... • **todo cabe en ese chico** that boy is capable of anything, nothing would surprise me from that boy • **no cabe en él hacerlo** he doesn't have it in him to do it • **ya no caben más lamentaciones** it's no use complaining • **no cabe perdón** it's inexcusable
b (+ *infin*) • **cabe imaginar distintas posibilidades** different possibilities can be imagined • **la persona más generosa que cabe imaginar** the most generous person you could imagine, the most generous person imaginable • **cabe intentar otro sistema** it would be worth trying another system • **cabe preguntar si ...** one might *o* could ask whether ...
c • **dentro de lo que cabe** under the circumstances • **se trata al animal lo mejor posible dentro de lo que cabe** the animal is treated as well as possible under the circumstances • **nos llevamos bastante bien, dentro de lo que cabe** we get on quite well, under the circumstances *o* considering • **no cabe duda de que ...** there is *o* can be no doubt that ... • **no cabe más que**: • **no cabe más que esperar a ver lo que pasa** we can only wait *o* all we can do is wait *o* the only thing for it is to wait and see what happens • **no cabe más que obedecer** there's no option but to obey • **cabe la posibilidad de que ...**: • **¿no cabe la posibilidad de que usted haya sido utilizada?** is it not possible that you might have been used? • **cabe la posibilidad que en unos días nos comuniquen algo** (there is a chance that) we may hear from them in a few days • **el flash no resulta aconsejable, puesto que cabe la posibilidad de asustar a los animales** it's best not to use a flash as it is liable to frighten the animals • **si cabe**: • **a mí me parece que es aún mejor, si cabe** I think it's even better, if that's possible • **ahora está más amable, si cabe** she's even friendlier now • **mejoraremos, si cabe, el servicio posventa** we will improve our after-sales service, wherever possible
6 (= *corresponder*) • **me cabe el honor/la satisfacción de presentarles (a) ...** I have the honour/it gives me great pleasure to introduce ... • **me cupo el privilegio de ...** I had the privilege of ... • **me cupo la responsabilidad de dirigir el país** the responsibility of running the country fell to me • **le cupieron 120 dólares** his share was 120 dollars, he got 120 dollars (as his share); ▹ **suerte**
cabestrar ▹ CONJUG 1a (VT) to halter, put a halter on
cabestrillo (SM) sling • **con el brazo en ~** with one's arm in a sling
cabestro (SM) **1** (= *brida*) halter • MODISMO: • **llevar a algn del ~** to lead sb by the nose
2 (= *buey*) leading ox, bell-ox
3* (= *cornudo*) cuckold; (= *lerdo*) thickie*
cabeza (SF) **1** [*de persona*] head • **se rascó la ~** he scratched his head • **me duele la ~** I've got a headache, my head aches • **los aviones pasan por encima de nuestras ~s** the planes are flying overhead • **afirmar con la ~** to nod (one's head) • **agarrarse la ~** to hold one's head in one's hands • **asentir con la ~** to nod (one's head) • **caer de ~** to fall headfirst *o* headlong • **se tiró al agua de ~** he dived headfirst into the water • **marcar de ~** (*Dep*) to score with a header • **lavarse la ~** to wash one's hair • **levantar la ~** (= *mirar*) to look up • **negar con la ~** to shake one's head • **por ~**: • **cinco dólares por ~** five dollars a head, five dollars per person • **se me va la ~** I feel giddy • **volver la ~** to look round, turn one's head • **al oírlos volví la ~** when I heard them I looked round *o* turned my head • **me da vueltas la ~** my head's spinning
2 • MODISMOS: • **andar** *o* **ir de ~*** to be snowed under • **andar en ~** (*LAm*) to go bareheaded • **cortar ~s**: • **será necesario cortar ~s** heads will have to roll • **esconder la ~** to keep one's head down • **írsele a algn de la ~**: • **se me fue de la ~** it went right out of my mind • **jugarse la ~** to risk one's neck • **lanzarse de ~ a** (= *atacar*) to rush headlong at; (= *precipitarse*) rush headlong into • **levantar ~** to get back on one's feet again • **el Sporting sigue sin levantar ~** Sporting still haven't managed to end their poor run of form, Sporting haven't managed to turn the corner • **el país no termina de levantar ~** the country still hasn't managed to turn the corner • **hay sectores como la construcción que empiezan a levantar ~** some sectors, such as construction, are starting to pick up • **estar mal de la ~*** • **no estar bien de la ~***: • **hace falta estar mal de la ~ para hacer eso** you'd have to be out of your mind to do that • **no quiero acabar mal de la ~** I don't want to go off my head • **mantener la ~ fuera del agua** to keep one's head above water • **meter la ~ en la arena** to bury one's head in the sand • **meter algo en la ~ a algn**: • **por fin le metimos en la ~ que ...** we finally got it into his head that ... • **metérsele a algn en la ~**: • **se le ha metido en la ~ hacerlo solo** he's taken *o* got it into his head to do it alone • **esa melodía la tengo metida en la ~** I can't get that tune

out of my head • **pasársele a algn por la ~**: • **jamás se me pasó por la ~** it never entered my head • **perder la ~ por** to lose one's head over • **es ~ de pescado** (*Cono Sur**) it's sheer nonsense • **hablar ~s de pescado** (*Cono Sur**) to talk drivel, talk through the back of one's head* • **tener ~ de pollo** (*Cono Sur**) to have a memory like a sieve • **quitar algo de la ~ a algn** to get sth out of sb's head • **romper la ~ a algn** to smash sb's face in • **romperse la ~** to rack one's brains • **sacarse una idea de la ~** to get an idea out of one's head • **sentar ~** to settle down • **subirse a la ~**: • **el vino se me subió a la ~** the wine went to my head • **tener ~** to be bright • **tengo la ~ como un bombo** my head is ringing • **tener la ~ dura** to be stubborn • **tener la ~ sobre los hombros** to have one's head screwed on (the right way) • **tener mala ~** (= *tener mala memoria*) to have a bad memory; (= *ser despistado*) to be absent-minded • **estar tocado de la ~** to be soft in the head • **traer de ~ a algn** to drive sb mad • **vestirse por la ~**† (= *ser mujer*) to be female; (= *ser sacerdote*) to be a cleric; ▹ **calentar**

3 (= *frente*) • **a la ~ de**: • **a la ~ de la manifestación** at the head *o* front of the demonstration • **con Pérez a la ~ del gobierno** with Pérez at the head of the government • **ir en ~** to be in the lead • **ir en ~ de la lista** to be at the top of the list, head the list

4 (= *distancia*) head • **ganar por una ~ (escasa)** to win by a (short) head • **le saca una ~ a su hermano** he is a head taller than his brother

5 (*de montaña*) top, summit

6 (= *objeto*) ▸ **cabeza atómica** atomic warhead ▸ **cabeza buscadora** homing head, homing device ▸ **cabeza de ajo** bulb of garlic ▸ **cabeza de biela** (*Mec*) big end ▸ **cabeza de dragón** (*Bot*) snapdragon ▸ **cabeza de escritura** (*Tip*) golf ball ▸ **cabeza de guerra** warhead ▸ **cabeza de impresión** (*Inform*) head, printhead ▸ **cabeza de partido** administrative centre ▸ **cabeza de plátanos** (*LAm*) bunch of bananas ▸ **cabeza de playa** beachhead ▸ **cabeza de puente** bridgehead ▸ **cabeza explosiva** warhead ▸ **cabeza grabadora** recording head ▸ **cabeza impresora** (*Inform*) head, printhead ▸ **cabeza nuclear** nuclear warhead ▸ **cabeza sonora** recording head

(SMF) **1** (= *líder*) head, leader • **es ~ de las fuerzas armadas** he's head *o* the leader of the armed forces • **es ~ del grupo rebelde** he's the leader of the rebel group

2 ▸ **cabeza caliente** extremist ▸ **cabeza cuadrada*** bigot ▸ **cabeza de chorlito*** scatterbrain ▸ **cabeza de familia** head of the household ▸ **cabeza de serie** (*Dep*) seed ▸ **cabeza de serrín*** airhead* ▸ **cabeza de turco** scapegoat ▸ **cabeza dura** stubborn person • **es un ~ dura** he's as stubborn as a mule ▸ **cabeza hueca** idiot ▸ **cabeza pelada** (*Hist*) Roundhead ▸ **cabeza rapada** skinhead ▸ **cabeza sin seso** idiot ▸ **cabeza visible** head, leader

cabezada (SF) **1** (= *cabezazo*) head butt, butt; (= *porrazo*) blow on the head • MODISMO: • **darse de ~s** to rack one's brains

2 (= *cabeceo*) shake of the head, nod • **dar ~s** to nod (sleepily), doze • **dar** *o* **echar una ~** have a nap

3 (*Náut*) pitch, pitching • **dar ~s** to pitch

4 (= *parte de arreos*) head stall; [*de bota*] instep; [*de zapato*] vamp

5 (*And, Cono Sur*) saddle tree

6 (*Caribe, Cono Sur*) [*de río*] headwaters

cabezadita (SF) • **echar una ~*** to have a snooze*, doze

cabezahueca (SMF) idiot

cabezal (SM) **1** (= *almohada*) pillow, bolster; [*de dentista etc*] headrest; (*Med*) pad, compress

2 (*Inform*) head; [*de vídeo, cassette*] head

3 • **~ de enganche** (*Aut*) towbar

cabezazo (SM) (*gen*) head butt, butt; (= *porrazo*) bump on the head; (*Dep*) header

cabezo (SM) (*Geog*) hillock, small hill; (*Náut*) reef

cabezón (ADJ) **1*** (= *cabezudo*) bigheaded, with a big head; (= *terco*) pigheaded

2 [*vino*] heady

(SM) **1*** (= *cabeza*) big head

2 (*Cos*) hole for the head

3 (= *cuello*) collar band • **llevar a algn de los cabezones** to drag sb along against his will

4 cabezones (*en un río*) white water (*sing*)

cabezonada* (SF) pig-headed thing to do

cabezonería* (SF) pig-headedness

cabezota* (ADJ) pig-headed

(SMF) pig-headed person

cabezudo (ADJ)* = **cabezón**

(SM) *carnival figure with an enormous head*

cabezuela (SF) (*Bot*) head (of a flower); (= *capullo*) rosebud

cabida (SF) **1** (= *capacidad*) (*en depósito, caja*) capacity; (*en vehículo*) space, room • **necesitamos un depósito de mayor ~** we need a tank with a greater capacity • **en este autobús no hay ~ para 20 personas** this bus can't hold *o* take 20 people, there isn't space *o* room in this bus for 20 people • **dar ~ a**: • **el auditorio puede dar ~ a más de mil espectadores** the concert hall can accommodate more than a thousand people, the concert hall has a capacity of more than a thousand • **los hoteles no podrán dar ~ a tantos turistas** the hotels will not be able to accommodate so many tourists • **con el nuevo tratado se da ~ a los países del Este** the new treaty opens the way for *o* embraces the Eastern bloc countries • **tener ~**: • **el teatro tiene ~ para 600 personas** the theatre holds 600 people, the theatre has a capacity of 600 • **la impresora tiene ~ para 200 hojas** the printer can hold *o* take up to 200 sheets

2 (= *aceptación*) • **no hay ~ para la superstición** there is no place *o* room for superstition • **dar ~ a**: • **en este periódico no se da ~ a las ideas de vanguardia** there's no place *o* room for avant-garde ideas in this newspaper • **ya no le vamos a dar más ~ en esta casa** he will no longer be welcome in this house • **tener ~**: • **personajes de ese tipo no tienen ~ en nuestro programa** there is no place *o* room in our programme for characters like that

3 (*Náut*) capacity

4 (= *terreno*) area

cabildear ▹ CONJUG 1a (VI) (= *presionar*) to lobby; (= *conspirar*) to intrigue

cabildeo (SM) (= *presión*) lobbying; (= *intrigas*) intriguing, intrigues (*pl*)

cabildero/a (SM/F) lobbyist, member of a pressure group; (*pey*) intriguer

cabildo (SM) **1** (*Rel*) (= *personas*) chapter; (= *junta*) chapter meeting

2 (*Pol*) (= *ayuntamiento*) town council; (*Parl*) lobby ▸ **cabildo insular** (*en Canarias*) inter-island council

3 (*Caribe*) [*de negros*] gathering of black people; (= *reunión desordenada*) riotous assembly

cabilla** (SF) • **dar ~ a algn** to fuck sb**, screw sb**

cabillo (SM) end; (*Bot*) stalk, stem

cabina (SF) **1** [*de discjockey, intérprete*] booth; (*tb* **cabina telefónica, cabina de teléfono(s)**) telephone booth, telephone box • **no te pude llamar porque no había ninguna ~** I couldn't call you because there was no phone box ▸ **cabina de grabación** recording booth ▸ **cabina de prensa** press box ▸ **cabina de proyección** projection room ▸ **cabina electoral** voting booth

2 [*de tren, camión*] cab

3 (*Aer*) [*de pasajeros*] cabin; [*de pilotos*] cockpit ▸ **cabina a presión** pressurized cabin ▸ **cabina de mando** (*Aer*) flight deck, cockpit

4 (*Náut*) bridge

cabinada (SF) cabin cruiser

cabinero/a (SM/F) (*Col*) (= *hombre*) steward, flight attendant (*EEUU*); (= *mujer*) air hostess, stewardess, flight attendant (*EEUU*)

cabinista (SMF) projectionist

cabio (SM) (= *viga*) beam, joist; [*del techo*] rafter; (*en puerta, ventana*) lintel, transom

cabizbajo (ADJ) dejected, downcast, crestfallen

cabla (SF) (*LAm*) trick

cable (SM) **1** (*Elec*) (= *hilo*) wire; (*con cubierta aislante*) cable • **tiene varios ~s sueltos** there are several loose wires • **el ~ del micrófono/amplificador** the microphone/amplifier cable *o* lead • MODISMOS: • **se le cruzaron los ~s*** he totally flipped* • **se le pelaron los ~s** (*CAm**) he got all mixed up ▸ **cable de alta tensión** high-voltage cable ▸ **cable de cobre** copper wire

2 (*Mec*) [*de acero*] cable • MODISMO: • **echar un ~ a algn*** to give sb a helping hand ▸ **cable de remolque** towline, towrope

3 (*Telec*) cable, wire • **televisión por ~** cable television, cable TV ▸ **cable coaxial** coaxial cable ▸ **cable de fibra óptica** fibreoptic cable, optical fibre, optical fiber (*EEUU*) ▸ **cable óptico** optical cable

4 (= *cablegrama*) cable • **enviar un ~ a algn** to cable sb

cableado (SM) wiring

cablear ▹ CONJUG 1a (VT) to wire up

cablegrafiar ▹ CONJUG 1c (VI) to cable, wire

cablegráfico (ADJ) cable (*antes de s*) • **transferencia cablegráfica** cable transfer

cablegrama (SM) cable, cablegram

cablero (SM) cable ship

cablevisión (SF) cable television, cable TV

cablista (ADJ) (*LAm*) sly, cunning

cabo (SM) **1** (= *trozo pequeño*) [*de cuerda, hilo*] thread; [*de vela, lápiz*] stub • **falta cortar los cabitos de hilo** the loose threads just need cutting off • **iluminamos la habitación con un ~ de vela** we used the stub *o* end of a candle to light the room with • **escribía con un cabito** he was writing with a pencil stub ▸ **cabo de vela** (*Náut*) rope, cable

2 (*locuciones*) • **al ~** (*frm*) (= *al final*) in the end; (= *después de todo*) at the end of the day • **al ~, su dedicación a la música ha rendido sus frutos** in the end, his dedication to music has borne fruit, his dedication to music has finally borne fruit • **al ~, su gran satisfacción era oír los aplausos** at the end of the day, his greatest satisfaction was to hear the applause • **al ~ de** after • **al ~ de tres meses** after three months, three months later • **llevar a ~** [+ *acción, investigación, tarea*] to carry out; [+ *viaje*] to make • **estamos llevando a ~ un proyecto en colaboración con la universidad** we are carrying out a joint project with the university • **ya hemos llevado a ~ la recogida de firmas** we have already collected the signatures • **en esta piscina se llevarán a ~ las pruebas de natación** the swimming events will take place in this pool • MODISMOS: • **atar ~s**: • **atando ~s, me di cuenta de que …** I put two

and two together and realized that ... • de ~ a ~ • de ~ a rabo from beginning to end, from start to finish • me leí el libro de ~ a rabo en un día I read the book from beginning to end *o* from start to finish in a day • me recorrí el pueblo de ~ a rabo y no encontré ningún restaurante I went all through the village and didn't find a single restaurant • estar al ~ de la calle de algo (*Esp*) to be fully aware of sth • no dejar ningún ~ suelto (*preparando algo*) to leave nothing to chance; (*investigando algo*) to tie up all the loose ends; ▹ fin
3 (= *graduación*) [*de militar*] corporal; [*de policía*] sergeant ▸ cabo de escuadra corporal ▸ cabo de mar petty officer ▸ cabo primero first officer
4 (*Geog*) cape ▸ Cabo Cañaveral Cape Canaveral ▸ cabo de Buena Esperanza Cape of Good Hope ▸ cabo de Hornos Cape Horn ▸ Cabo Verde Cape Verde
5 (*Remo*) stroke

cabotaje SM cabotage, coasting trade, coastal traffic

caboverdiano/a ADJ, SM/F Cape Verdean

cabra SF 1 (*Zool*) goat; (= *hembra*) nanny goat, she-goat; (= *almizclero*) musk deer • MODISMO: • estar como una ~ to be crazy • REFRÁN: • la ~ siempre tira al monte a leopard does not change its spots, what's bred in the bone will out in the flesh ▸ cabra montés Spanish ibex
2 (*LAm*) (= *truco*) trick, swindle; (= *dado*) loaded dice
3 (*Cono Sur*) (= *carro*) light carriage; [*de carpintero*] sawhorse, sawbuck (*EEUU*)
4 (*Cono Sur**) (= *niña*) little girl
5 (= *moto*) motorbike; ▹ cabro

cabracho SM large-scaled scorpion fish

cabrahígo SM wild fig

cabrales SM INV *strong cheese from Asturias*

cabré *etc* ▹ caber

cabreado‡ ADJ pissed off✱✱

cabreante‡ ADJ infuriating, maddening

cabrear‡ ▹ CONJUG 1a VT to piss off✱✱
VPR cabrearse 1 (= *enfadarse*) to get pissed off✱✱
2 (= *sospechar*) to get suspicious
3 (*Cono Sur*) (= *aburrirse*) to get bored

cabreo‡ SM • ¡menudo ~ lleva! she's really pissed off!✱✱ • coger un ~ to fly off the handle*, fly into a rage

cabreriza SF goat shed, goat house

cabrerizo/a SM/F goatherd
ADJ (= *de las cabras*) goat (*antes de s*)

cabrero/a ADJ (*Cono Sur**) bad-tempered • ponerse ~ to fly off the handle*
SM/F goatherd

cabrestante SM capstan, winch

cabria SF hoist, derrick ▸ cabria de perforación drilling rig

cabrio SM rafter

cabrío ADJ goatish • macho ~ billy goat, he-goat
SM (= *rebaño*) herd of goats

cabriola SF 1 (= *movimiento*) gambol, skip • hacer ~s [*persona*] to caper about; [*caballo*] to buck, prance around; [*cordero*] to gambol
2 (*Caribe*) (= *travesura*) prank, piece of mischief

cabriolar ▹ CONJUG 1a VI [*persona*] to caper (about), prance (around); [*caballo*] to buck; [*cordero*] to gambol

cabriolé SM cabriolet

cabriolear ▹ CONJUG 1a VI = cabriolar

cabritada* SF dirty trick

cabritas SFPL (*Chile*) popcorn (*sing*)

cabritilla SF kid, kidskin

cabrito SM 1 (*Zool*) kid • a ~ astride
2* (= *cabrón*) swine*; (= *cornudo*) cuckold; [*de prostituta*] client • ¡cabrito! you swine!*
3 cabritos (*Chile*) (= *palomitas*) popcorn (*sing*)

cabro/a SM (*LAm*) (*Zool*) (= *macho*) he-goat, billy goat
SM/F (*Cono Sur**) 1 (= *niño*) small child, kid; (= *amante*) lover, sweetheart
2‡ (= *homosexual*) queer‡, fag (*EEUU*‡); ▹ cabra

cabrón/ona✱✱ SM (= *cornudo*) cuckold
SM/F 1 • ¡cabrón! you bastard!✱✱ • es un ~ he's a bastard✱✱ • el muy ~ le robó el coche the bastard stole his car✱✱ • el tío ~ ese that bastard✱✱
2 (*LAm*) [*de burdel*] brothel keeper; (*And, Cono Sur*) (= *chulo*) pimp; (*CAm, Cono Sur*) (= *traidor*) traitor; (*And*) (= *maricón*) queer‡, fag (*EEUU*‡) • ¡cabrón! (= *idiota*) you stupid berk!‡

cabronada✱✱ SF 1 (= *mala pasada*) dirty trick • hacer una ~ a algn to play a dirty trick on sb
2 (= *lata*) fag*, bugger✱✱

cabronazo✱✱ SM bastard✱✱, bugger✱✱ • ¡jo, ~! (*hum*) hey, you old bastard!✱✱

cabroncete* SM little twerp*

cabruno ADJ goat (*antes de s*)

cábula SF (*LAm*) 1 (= *complot*) intrigue, cabal
2 (= *trampa*) trick, stratagem
3 (= *amuleto*) amulet

cabulear ▹ CONJUG 1a VI (*And, CAm, Caribe*) to scheme

cabulero (*And, CAm, Caribe*) ADJ tricky, cunning, scheming
SM trickster, schemer

cabuya SF (*LAm*) (*Bot*) pita, agave; (= *fibra*) pita fibre; (*Náut*) (= *cuerda*) rope, cord, *especially one made from pita fibre* • MODISMOS: • dar ~ (*Caribe*) to put things off • ponerse en la ~* to cotton on* • vérsele a algn las ~s to see what sb is up to, see what sb's (little) game is

caca* SF 1 (*lenguaje infantil*) poo*, poop (*EEUU**), number two* • ¿quieres hacer ~? do you want to do a poo?* • el niño tiene *o* se ha hecho ~ the child has pooed himself* • ¡caca! (= *no toques*) dirty!
2 (= *birria*) rubbish, crap✱✱ • tenemos un ejército que es una ~ our army is rubbish, our army is crap✱✱ • estoy hecha una ~ I feel like shit✱✱

caca-can* SM pooper-scooper*

cacaguatal SM (*CAm*) cocoa field

cacahual SM (*LAm*) cacao plantation

cacahuete SM, **cacahuate** (*Méx*) SM peanut, monkey nut; (= *planta*) groundnut • aceite de ~ peanut oil

cacao SM 1 (*Bot*) cacao; (= *bebida*) cocoa • ~ en polvo cocoa powder • MODISMOS: • pedir ~ (*LAm*) to give in, beg for mercy • ser gran ~ to have influence • no valer un ~ (*LAm*) to be worthless
2* (= *jaleo*) fuss, to-do • MODISMOS: • armar *o* montar un ~ to cause havoc • se armó un buen ~ all hell broke loose* • tener un ~ en la cabeza* to be all mixed up ▸ cacao mental* mental confusion

cacaotal SM cocoa plantation

cacaraña SF 1 (= *señal*) pockmark
2 (*CAm*) (= *garabato*) scribble

cacarañado ADJ pitted, pockmarked

cacarañar ▹ CONJUG 1a VT 1 [*viruelas*] to pit, scar, pockmark
2 (*Méx*) (= *arañar*) to scratch; (= *pellizcar*) pinch

cacarear ▹ CONJUG 1a VT to boast about, make much of • ese triunfo tan cacareado that much-trumpeted victory
VI [*gallina*] to cluck; [*gallo*] to crow

cacareo SM [*de gallo*] crowing; [*de gallina*] clucking; (*fig*) boasting, crowing

cacarico ADJ (*CAm*) numb

cacarizo ADJ (*Méx*) pitted, pockmarked

cacastle SM (*CAm, Méx*) (= *esqueleto*) skeleton; (= *canasta*) large wicker basket; (= *armazón*) wicker carrying frame

cacatúa SF 1 (*Orn*) cockatoo
2* (= *vieja*) old bat*, old bag*, old cow*

cacaxtle SM (*CAm, Méx*) = cacastle

cacera SF ditch, irrigation channel

cacereño/a ADJ of/from Cáceres
SM/F native/inhabitant of Cáceres • los ~s the people of Cáceres

cacería SF 1 (= *actividad*) hunting, shooting • ir de ~ to go hunting, go shooting
2 (= *partida*) hunt, shoot, shooting party • organizar una ~ to organize a hunt ▸ cacería de brujas witch-hunt ▸ cacería de zorros fox hunt
3 (= *animales cazados*) bag, total of animals etc bagged
4 (*Arte*) hunting scene

cacerola SF pan, saucepan

cacerolazo SM (*Cono Sur*) banging on pots and pans (*as political protest*)

cacha SF 1 [*de arma*] butt
2‡ (*Anat*) (= *muslo*) thigh; cachas (= *muslos*) thighs; (= *culo*) bottom (*sing*) • MODISMOS: • estar ~s (= *ser musculoso*) to have plenty of muscles, be well set-up; (= *ser atractivo*) to be dishy*; [*mujer*] to be hot stuff* • hasta las ~s up to the hilt, completely
3 (*And*) (= *cuerno*) horn
4 (*And*) [*de gallo*] *metal spur attached to the leg of a fighting cock*
5 (*And*) (= *arca*) large chest
6 (*Chile**) (= *burla*) • sacar ~(s) a *o* de algn to make fun of sb
7 (*LAm*) (= *cachete*) cheek
8 (*CAm**) (= *apaño*) crooked deal*
9 (*CAm*) (= *oportunidad*) opportunity
10 • MODISMOS: • estar a medias ~s (*Méx**) to be tipsy • estar fuera de ~ to be out of danger • hacer la ~ (*CAm**) to put one's back into it • hacer ~s (*CAm**) to try hard • ¡qué ~! (*CAm**) what a nuisance!

cachaciento ADJ (*CAm, Cono Sur*) = cachazudo

cachaco* SM 1 (*Perú*) (= *policía*) copper*, cop*
2 (*And, Caribe*) (= *petimetre*) fop, dandy; (= *desaliñado*) scruff*
3 (*Caribe**) (= *entrometido*) busybody, nosey-parker*
4 (*Col*) (= *bogotano*) person from Bogotá

cachada SF 1 (*LAm*) (= *embestida*) butt, thrust; (*Taur*) goring
2 (*Cono Sur*) (= *broma*) joke, leg-pull*

cachador* (*Cono Sur*) ADJ fond of practical jokes
SM practical joker

cachafaz* ADJ (*LAm*) (= *pillo*) rascally; (= *taimado*) crafty; (= *fresco*) cheeky*, sassy (*EEUU**)

cachalote SM sperm whale

cachancha SF (*Caribe*) patience • estar de ~ con algn* to suck up to sb*

cachaña SF (*Chile*) 1 (*Orn*) small parrot
2 (= *broma*) hoax, leg-pull*; (= *mofas*) mockery, derision
3 (= *arrogancia*) arrogance
4 (= *estupidez*) stupidity
5 (= *arrebatiña*) rush, scramble (for sth)

cachañar ▹ CONJUG 1a VT (*Chile*) • ~ a algn to pull sb's leg; (*Cono Sur*) = cachar¹

cachar¹ ▹ CONJUG 1a VT 1 (*And, CAm*) (= *cornear*) to butt, gore
2 (*Cono Sur*) (= *ridiculizar*) to make fun of, ridicule; (= *fastidiar*) to annoy, irritate
3 (*And, Cono Sur*✱✱) (= *follar*) to screw✱✱
4 (*Méx**) (= *registrar*) to search
5 (= *romper*) to smash, break, break in pieces; [+ *madera*] to split; (*Agr*) to plough up

cachar² ▸ CONJUG 1a (VT) **1** (*Cono Sur*) [+ *bus etc*] to catch
2 (*CAm*) (= *obtener*) to get, obtain; (*CAm, Cono Sur*) (= *robar*) to steal
3 (*Cono Sur, Méx*) [+ *delincuente*] to surprise, catch in the act
4 (*Cono Sur*) [+ *sentido etc*] to penetrate; [+ *persona, razón*] to understand • **sí, te cacho** sure, I get it*
5 (*And, CAm, Caribe*) (*Dep*) [+ *pelota*] to catch

cacharpari (SM) (*Perú*) farewell banquet

cacharpas (SFPL) (*LAm*) (= *trastos*) useless objects, lumber (*sing*), junk (*sing*); (= *cosas sueltas*) odds and ends

cacharpaya (SF) (*And, Cono Sur*) (= *fiesta*) send-off, farewell party; (*Cono Sur*) (= *despedida*) farewell; (= *festividad*) minor festivity

cacharpearse ▸ CONJUG 1a (VPR) (*LAm*) to dress up

cacharra‡ (SF) gun, pistol, rod (*EEUU**)

cacharrazo* (SM) bash*, bang • **darse** *o* **pegarse un ~** (*Aut*) to prang the car*

cacharrear ▸ CONJUG 1a (VT) (*CAm, Caribe*) to throw into jail, jail

cacharrería (SF) **1** (= *tienda*) crockery shop • **como un elefante en una ~** like a bull in a china shop
2 (= *cacharros*) crockery, pots (*pl*)
3 (*And*) (= *ferretería*) ironmongery

cacharro (SM) **1** [*de cocina*] pot, dish • **fregar los ~s** to do *o* wash the dishes ▸ **cacharros de cocina** pots and pans
2* (= *trasto*) useless object, piece of junk; (*Aut*) old crock, jalop(p)y; (*And*) trinket
3* (= *aparato*) gadget
4‡ (= *pistola*) rod‡, pistol
5 (*CAm, Caribe*) (= *cárcel*) jail

cachativa (SF) • **tener ~** (*Cono Sur*) to be quick on the uptake

cachaza (SF) **1** (= *lentitud*) • **lo hace todo con mucha ~** he does everything very slowly • **¡menuda ~, llegaremos tarde por su culpa!** he's so slow, we're going to be late because of him!
2 (= *licor*) ≈ rum

cachazo (SM) (*LAm*) (= *golpe*) butt (*with the horns*); (= *herida*) goring

cachazudo/a (ADJ) (= *lento*) slow; (= *flemático*) calm, easy-going
(SM/F) (= *lento*) slowcoach*, slowpoke (*EEUU**); (= *tranquilo*) phlegmatic person

cache¹* (ADJ) (*Arg*) tacky, kitsch

cache² (SM O SF) (*Inform*) cache, cache memory

caché (SM) = cachet
(ADJ) (*Inform*) cached

cachear ▸ CONJUG 1a (VT) **1** (= *registrar*) to search, frisk (for weapons)
2 (*LAm*) (*Taur*) to butt, gore
3 (*LAm*) (= *pegar*) to punch, slap
4 (= *abrir*) to split, cut open

cachejo* (SM) (*Esp*) • **un ~ (de) pan** a little bit of bread • **aquel ~ de partido** that awful game

cachemir (SM), **cachemira** (SF) cashmere

Cachemira (SF) Kashmir

cacheo (SM) searching, frisking (for weapons)

cachería (SF) **1** (*And, CAm*) (*Com*) small business, sideline
2 (*Cono Sur**) (= *falta de gusto*) bad taste; (= *desaseo*) slovenliness

cachero (ADJ) **1** (*CAm, Caribe*) (= *embustero*) deceitful
2 (*CAm*) (= *trabajador*) hard-working, diligent
(SM) (*LAm*) sodomite

cachet [ka'tʃe] (SM) (PL: **cachets** [ka'tʃes]) **1** (= *sello distintivo*) cachet; (= *carácter*) character, temperament
2 [*de artista*] fee

cachetada (SF) (*LAm*) (= *golpe*) slap, clip on the ear; (= *paliza*) beating

cachetazo (SM) **1** (*LAm*) (= *bofetada*) slap, punch; (*fig*) snub
2 (*LAm*) (= *trago*) swig*, slug (*EEUU**)
3 (*CAm, Caribe**) (= *favor*) favour, favor (*EEUU*) • **¡hazme un ~!** do me a favour!

cachete (SM) **1** (= *golpe*) slap, punch in the face • **darse de ~s con algn** to fight with sb
2 (= *arma*) dagger
3 (= *mejilla*) (fat) cheek; (*Med*) swollen cheek
4 (*CAm*) (= *favor*) favour, favor (*EEUU*)
5 cachetes (*Cono Sur**) (= *culo*) bottom (*sing*)

cacheteada (SF) (*Cono Sur*) slap, box on the ear

cachetear ▸ CONJUG 1a (VT) (*LAm*) (= *pegar*) to slap *o* smack in the face
(VI) (*Cono Sur*) (= *comer*) to eat well

cachetero (SM) **1** (= *puñal*) dagger
2 (*Taur*) *bullfighter who finishes the bull off with a dagger*

cachetina* (SF) fist fight, punch-up*

cachetón (ADJ)* **1** (*LAm*) (= *de cara rechoncha*) plump-cheeked, fat-faced
2 (*Méx*) (= *descarado*) impudent, barefaced; (*Cono Sur*) (= *orgulloso*) proud, haughty
3 (*CAm*) (= *atractivo*) attractive, congenial

cachi* (ADJ) (*Arg*) tacky, kitsch

cachicamo (SM) (*And, Caribe*) armadillo

cachicán† (ADJ) sly, crafty
(SM) **1** (*Agr*) foreman
2* (= *hombre astuto*) sly character

cachicuerno (ADJ) [*arma*] with a horn handle

cachifo/a* (SM/F) **1** (*Col*) (= *jovenzuelo*) kid*
2 (*Ven*) (= *criado*) servant

cachila* (SF) (*Cono Sur*) old heap*, old banger*

cachimba (SF) **1** (= *pipa*) pipe
2 (*CAm*) (= *cartucho*) empty cartridge
3 (*Cono Sur*) (= *pozo*) *shallow well or water hole*
4 (*Cuba*‡) (= *prostituta*) tart‡, slut‡
5 • MODISMO: • fregar la ~ a algn* to get on sb's nerves
(ADJ)* fantastic*, great*; ▸ **cachimbo**

cachimbazo* (SM) (*CAm*) **1** (= *golpe*) thump, blow
2 (= *trago*) shot, slug (*EEUU**)

cachimbo/a (SM/F) **1** (*Caribe*) (= *pobre*) poor man/woman
2 (*Perú*) (*Univ*) fresher, freshman; ▸ **cachimba**
(SM) **1** (*LAm*) (= *pipa*) pipe • **chupar ~** (*Ven*) to smoke a pipe; (*hum*) [*niño*] to suck one's thumb
2 (*Caribe*) (= *ingenio*) small sugar mill
3 (*CAm**) (= *montón*) pile, heap
4 (*And*) (*Mil*) soldier, squaddie*

cachimbón* (ADJ) (*CAm*) smart, sharp

cachipolla (SF) mayfly

cachiporra (SF) **1** (= *porra*) truncheon, cosh, (billy) club (*EEUU*)
2 (*Cono Sur**) (= *jactancioso*) braggart

cachiporrazo* (SM) blow with a truncheon *etc*

cachiporrear* ▸ CONJUG 1a (VT) (*Mús etc*) to bash*, pound
(VPR) **cachiporrearse** (*Cono Sur*) to brag, boast

cachito (SM) **1** (= *trocito*) a bit, a little • **a ~s** bit by bit
2 (*LAm**) (= *poquito*) • **espera un ~** just a minute, hang on a sec* • **un ~ de café** a drop of coffee
3 (*And*) (= *juego de dados*) dice game; (= *cubilete*) dice cup

cachivache (SM) **1** (= *vasija*) pot
2 cachivaches (= *trastos*) trash (*sing*), junk (*sing*)

cacho¹ (SM) **1*** (= *miga*) crumb; (= *trozo*) bit, small piece • **¡~ de gloria!** my precious! • **¡~ de ladrón!** you thief! • **es un ~ de pan*** he's really kind, he's got a heart of gold • **a ~s** bit by bit • **caerse a ~s** to fall apart, be falling to pieces
2 (*LAm*) (= *cuerno*) horn; (*Cono Sur*) (*para beber*) cup (made of horn)
3 (*And, Cono Sur*) (= *dados*) dice, set of dice; (= *cubilete*) dice cup • **jugar al ~** to play dice
4 (*Cono Sur*) [*de plátanos*] bunch
5 (*Cono Sur*) (= *géneros*) unsaleable *o* unsold goods (*pl*); (= *objeto*) useless thing
6 (*LAm*) (= *chiste*) funny story, joke; (= *broma*) prank, practical joke; (*Caribe*) (= *mofa*) mockery, derision
7 (*Caribe*‡) (= *marijuana*) joint‡, spliff‡
8 (*Caribe***) (= *pene*) prick**
9 (*Cono Sur*) (= *problema*) problem; (= *apuro*) jam*, tricky situation
10 • MODISMOS: • ¡~s para arriba! (*Cono Sur**) that's marvellous!, splendid! • **echar ~ a algn** (*And**) to outshine sb, go one better than sb • **empinar el ~** (*LAm**) (= *beber*) to drink • **estar fuera de ~** to be in safe keeping, be out of danger • **pegar los ~s a algn** (*CAm**) to cheat on sb, be unfaithful to sb • **raspar el ~ a algn** (*Cono Sur**) to tell sb off*

cacho² (SM) (= *pez*) [*de río*] chub; [*de mar*] (red) surmullet

cachón (SM) (= *ola*) wave, breaker; (= *cascada*) small waterfall

cachondear* ▸ CONJUG 1a (*CAm, Méx*) (VI) (= *acariciar*) to pet*, make out (*EEUU*‡); (= *besarse*) to snog‡, smooch*
(VPR) **cachondearse 1** to take things as a joke • **~se de algn** to take the mickey out of sb‡, make fun of sb
2 (*LAm**) to get turned on*

cachondeo* (SM) **1** (= *bromas*) joking; (= *guasa*) laugh*, messing about; (= *burla*) teasing, nagging • **estar de ~** to be in the mood for a laugh • **hacer algo en plan de ~** to do sth for a lark *o* a laugh • **tomar a ~** to treat as a joke • **para ella la vida es un ~ continuo** life for her is just one big joke
2 (= *juerga*) • **estar de ~** to live it up, have a great time
3 (= *jaleo*) trouble • **armar un ~** to make a fuss
4 (= *desastre*) farce, mess • **¡esto es un ~!** what a farce this is!, what a mess!

cachondez* (SF) **1** [*de animal*] heat
2 [*de persona*] randiness*

cachondo* (ADJ) **1** [*animal*] on heat
2 (= *persona*) randy*, horny* • **ser ~** to be sexy • **estar ~** to feel randy *o* horny*
3 (= *juerguista*) fun-loving, riotous
4 (= *gracioso*) funny, amusing, jokey
• **~ mental** crazy but likable

cachorro/a (SM/F) **1** (*Zool*) (*gen*) cub; (= *perro*) puppy, pup
2 (*LAm*) (= *persona*) uncouth person
• **¡cachorro!** (*Caribe**) you brute!, you rat!*

cachuca‡ (SF) (*And*) nick‡, can (*EEUU**), prison

cachucha‡ (SF) (*Col, Méx*) cap

cachucho (SM) **1** (= *pez*) sea bream
2 (= *alfiletero*) pin box
3 (*And*) (= *sustento*) daily bread • **ganarse el ~** to make a living

cachudo (ADJ) **1** (*Méx*) (= *con cuernos*) horned
2 (*Col*) (= *rico*) wealthy
3 (*Cono Sur*) suspicious, distrustful; (= *taimado*) cunning
4 (*Méx*) (= *triste*) long-faced, miserable
(SM) • **el ~** the devil, the horned one

cachuela (SF) **1** (*Culin*) *stew made from pig or rabbit offal*
2 (*LAm*) (*en un río*) rapids (*pl*)

cachupín/ina (SM/F) (*CAm, Méx*) (*Hist*) (*pey*)

Spanish settler
cachureo SM (*Cono Sur*) bric-a-brac, junk, bits and pieces (*pl*)
cachuzo* ADJ (*Arg*) worn-out, old
cacica SF (*LAm*) (*= jefe*) woman chief; (*= esposa*) chief's wife; (*Pol*) wife of a local boss *etc*
cacicada SF (*= arbitrariedad*) despotic act, high-handed act; (*= abuso*) abuse of authority
cacillo SM ladle
cacimba SF **1** (*And, Caribe, Cono Sur*) beach well; (*Caribe*) [*de árbol*] *hollow of tree where rain water is collected*; (*And*) (*= wáter*) outdoor privy
2 (*Caribe, Méx*) (*= casucha*) hovel, slum
cacique SM **1** (*LAm*) (*Hist*) chief, headman; (*Pol*) local party boss; (*fig*) petty tyrant, despot
2 (*Cono Sur*) (*= vago*) *person who lives idly in luxury*
3 (*And, CAm, Méx*) (*= ave*) oriole
caciquil ADJ despotic, tyrannical
caciquismo SM (*Pol*) (system of) dominance by the local party boss; (*fig*) petty tyranny, despotism
cacle SM (*Méx*) rough leather sandal
caco* SM **1** (*= ladrón*) thief; (*= carterista*) pickpocket; (*= criminal*) crook*
2 (*= cobarde*) coward
cacofonía SF cacophony
cacofónico ADJ cacophonous
cactus SM INV, **cacto** SM cactus
cacumen* SM (*= inteligencia*) brains (*pl*); (*= agudeza*) nous* (*sing*)
cada ADJ INV **1** (*uso distributivo*) (*con elementos individuales*) each; (*con números, tiempo*) every • **~ uno de los jugadores dispone de cuatro fichas** each player has four counters • **habrá una mesa por ~ ocho invitados** there will one table for every eight guests • **han aumentado los beneficios en todos y ~ uno de los sectores** profits have risen in each and every sector • **~ cual busca la felicidad como quiere** we all seek *o* each one of us seeks happiness in our own way
2 (*indicando frecuencia*) every • **juega al fútbol ~ domingo** he plays football every Sunday • **~ cierto tiempo** every so often, every now and then • **~ dos días** every couple of days, every other day • **los problemas de ~ día** everyday problems • **cinco de ~ diez** five out of every ten • **¿~ cuánto tiempo?** how often? • **~ que** (*Méx*) whenever, every time (that) • **~ vez que** whenever, every time (that) • **~ vez que voy al extranjero** whenever *o* every time (that) I go abroad • MODISMO: • **~ dos por tres** every other minute, all the time • **~ dos por tres sonaba el teléfono** the phone rang every other minute *o* all the time
3 (*indicando progresión*) • **~ vez más** more and more • **te necesito ~ vez más** I need you more and more • **encontrar trabajo es ~ vez más difícil** finding a job is increasingly difficult *o* is (getting) more and more difficult • **me siento ~ vez más viejo** I feel (I'm getting) older and older • **~ vez mejor** better and better • **~ vez menos** less and less • **~ vez peor** worse and worse
4 (*uso enfático*) • **¡tienes ~ cosa!** the things you come out with! • **¡oye una ~ historia!** the things you hear nowadays! • **¡se compra ~ coche!** you should see the cars he buys!
cadalso SM (*Jur*) (*= patíbulo*) scaffold; (*Téc*) stand, platform
cadarzo SM floss, floss silk
cadáver SM [*de persona*] (dead) body, corpse; [*de animal*] body, carcass • **¡sobre mi ~!** • **¡por encima de mi ~!** over my dead body! • **ingresó ~** he was dead on arrival (at hospital) ▸ **cadáver en el armario** (*fig*) skeleton in the cupboard
cadavérico ADJ cadaverous, ghastly; (*= pálido*) deathly pale
caddie SMF, **caddy** ['kadi] SMF (*Golf*) caddie
cadena SF **1** [*de eslabones, joyería*] chain • **se me salió la ~ de la bici** the chain came off my bike, my bike chain came off • **la ~ del perro** the dog chain • **la ~ del reloj** the watch chain • **tirar de la ~ (del wáter)** to flush the toilet, pull the chain • **no echó la ~ de la puerta** he didn't put the door-chain on ▸ **cadena (antirrobo)** chain ▸ **cadena de distribución** distribution chain ▸ **cadena de oruga** caterpillar track
2 (*Radio, TV*) (*= canal*) channel ▸ **cadena de televisión** TV channel
3 (*Audio*) ▸ **cadena de sonido** sound system ▸ **cadena musical** music centre, sound system
4 (*Com*) [*de hoteles, tiendas, restaurantes*] chain ▸ **cadena comercial** retail chain
5 ▸ **cadena montañosa** mountain range
6 (*= sucesión*) [*de acontecimientos, átomos*] chain; [*de atentados*] string, series • **en ~: colisión en ~** multiple collision, (multiple) pile-up • **efecto en ~** knock-on effect • **reacción en ~** chain reaction • **trabajo en ~** assembly-line work ▸ **cadena alimenticia** food chain ▸ **cadena de caracteres** (*Inform*) character string ▸ **cadena de ensamblaje** assembly line ▸ **cadena de fabricación** production line ▸ **cadena de montaje** assembly line ▸ **cadena de producción** production line
7 ▸ **cadena perpetua** (*Jur*) life imprisonment, life • **el juez lo condenó a ~ perpetua** the judge sentenced him to life (imprisonment)
8 cadenas (*Aut*) tyre *o* (*EEUU*) tire chains • **es obligatorio el uso de ~s** the use of tyre chains is compulsory
cadencia SF **1** (*= ritmo*) cadence, rhythm
2 (*Mús*) (*en frase musical*) cadence; [*de solista*] cadenza
3 (*= frecuencia*) • **a una ~ de 1.000 unidades diarias** at the rate of 1,000 units per day
cadencioso ADJ [*voz*] melodious; [*música*] rhythmic(al); [*andares*] swinging
cadeneta SF (*Cos*) chain stitch ▸ **cadeneta de papel** paper chain
cadenilla SF, **cadenita** SF small chain; (*= collar*) necklace
cadera SF hip • **ponerse una prótesis de ~** to have a hip replacement
caderamen* SM big hips (*pl*), massive hips (*pl*)
cadetada SF thoughtless action, irresponsible act
cadete SM (*Mil etc*) cadet; (*Dep*) junior; (*LAm*) (*= aprendiz*) apprentice; (*en oficina*) office boy
cadí SM (*Hist*) cadi
Cádiz SM Cadiz
cadmio SM cadmium
caducar ▸ CONJUG 1g VI **1** (*Com, Jur*) to expire, lapse; [*permiso, plazo*] to run out; [*costumbre*] to fall into disuse • **esta oferta caduca el 31 de mayo** valid until 31 May, this offer runs until 31 May • **el abono ha caducado** the season ticket has expired
2 [*comida*] to be *o* go past its sell-by date
caducidad SF expiry, expiration (*EEUU*) • **fecha de ~** (*gen*) expiry date; [*de alimentos*] sell-by date, best-before date
caduco ADJ **1** (*Bot*) deciduous • **árbol de hoja caduca** deciduous tree
2 [*persona*] senile, decrepit
3 [*ideas etc*] outdated, outmoded
4 [*belleza*] faded
5 [*placer etc*] fleeting
6 (*Com, Jur*) lapsed, expired, invalid • **quedar ~** to lapse, be out of date, have expired
caduquez SF senility, decrepitude
C.A.E. ABR (*Com*) (*= cóbrese al entregar*) COD
caedizo ADJ (*= inestable*) unsteady; (*= débil*) weak; (*Bot*) deciduous
SM (*And*) (*= edificio*) shed; (*= techo*) sloping roof

CADA

▸ **Cada** *se traduce por* **each** *cuando queremos individualizar, cuando se conocen o se le quiere dar importancia a los elementos dentro del grupo:*

A cada miembro del personal se le asignó una tarea específica
Each member of staff was allocated a specific task
Quiero tener una charla con cada uno de vosotros
I want to have a chat with each of you

▸ *Se traduce por* **every** *cuando el número de elementos del grupo no se conoce o no importa, cuando se está generalizando:*

Cada empresa funciona de una manera distinta
Every company works differently
Cada día me dice una cosa diferente
Every day he tells me something different
Cada vez que viene nos trae un regalo
Every time he comes he brings us a present

En expresiones como **cada dos meses/cada tres años** *etc*, **cada** *se traduce por* **every**:

Se hace una revisión cada tres meses
He has a check-up every three months

▸ *Cuando hablamos solo de dos cosas o personas,* **cada** *solamente se puede traducir por* **each**:

Es importante que cada gemelo desarrolle su propia personalidad
It is important that each twin develops his own personality

Cuando **each** *o* **every** *forman parte del sujeto, el verbo va en singular.*

Para otros usos y ejemplos ver la entrada.

caer

VERBO INTRANSITIVO
VERBO PRONOMINAL

▸ CONJUG 2n

Para las expresiones **caer en la cuenta, caer en desuso, caer en el olvido, caer enfermo, caer redondo, caerse de risa**, *ver la otra entrada.*

VERBO INTRANSITIVO

1 *persona, objeto* **a** (*desde la posición vertical*) to fall • **me hice daño al ~** I fell and hurt myself • **cayó al suelo y se dio un golpe en la cabeza** he fell to the ground and hit his head • **tropezó y cayó de espaldas** she stumbled and fell on her back • **cayó muerto de un tiro** he was shot dead • **hacer ~ algo** to knock sth over • **al pasar hizo ~ la lámpara**

he knocked the lamp over as he brushed past
b (*desde una altura*) to fall • **cayó de un tercer piso** he fell from the third floor • **el niño cayó al río** the child fell into the river • **cayó una bomba en el mercado** a bomb fell on the market • **el avión cayó al mar** the plane came down in the sea • **el coche cayó por un barranco** the car went over a cliff • **dejar ~** [+ *objeto*] to drop; [+ *comentario*] to slip in • **se sobresaltó y dejó ~ la bandeja** she gave a start and dropped the tray • **dejó ~ que estaba buscando otro trabajo** he mentioned that he was looking for another job • **dejarse ~** (*sobre sofá, cama*) to fall; (= *visitar*) to drop in, drop by • **se dejó ~ sobre la cama** he fell onto the bed • **suele dejarse ~ por aquí** he usually drops in *o* by • **~ sobre algo/algn** to fall on sth/sb • **una gran piedra cayó sobre el tejado** a large stone fell on the roof • **cayeron sobre nosotros rocas enormes** huge boulders fell on us • **los presos cayeron sobre el guarda** the prisoners fell on the warder • **los fotógrafos cayeron sobre ella** the photographers pounced on her • **queremos que caiga sobre él todo el peso de la Ley** we want the full weight of the law to be brought to bear on him • **MODISMO**: • **estar al ~** to be imminent • **su excarcelación está al ~** his release is imminent *o* is expected any day • **el jefe está al ~** the boss will be here any moment
2 (*lluvia, helada*) • **la lluvia caía incesantemente sobre Madrid** the rain was falling continuously on Madrid • **cayó un chaparrón** there was a heavy shower • **¡qué nevada ha caído!** what a heavy snowfall!, what a heavy fall of snow! • **cayó un rayo en la torre** the tower was struck by lightning
3 (= *colgar*) to hang, fall • **es una tela que cae mucho** it's a fabric which hangs *o* falls nicely • **le caía un mechón sobre la frente** a lock of hair fell across his forehead
4 (= *bajar*) [*precio, temperatura*] to fall, drop • **~á la temperatura por debajo de los veinte grados** the temperature will fall *o* drop below twenty degrees • **el dólar cayó más de cinco centavos** the dollar fell over five cents • **la bolsa de Nueva York ha vuelto a ~** the New York stock exchange has fallen again; ▹ **picado**
5 (= *ser derrotado*) [*soldados, ejército*] to be defeated; [*deportista, equipo*] to be beaten; [*ciudad, plaza*] to fall, be captured; [*criminal*] to be arrested • **cayó en la final ante su rival polaco** he was beaten in the final by his Polish rival • **ha caído el gobierno** the government has fallen
6 (= *morir*) to fall, die • **muchos cayeron en el campo de batalla** many fell *o* died on the field of battle • **cayó como un valiente** he died a hero • **cayeron abatidos por las balas** they were killed by the gunfire • **MODISMOS**: • **~ como chinches** • **~ como moscas** to drop like flies
7 • **~ en** (= *incurrir*): • **~ en un engaño** to be tricked • **no debemos ~ en el triunfalismo** we mustn't give way to triumphalism *o* to crowing over our triumphs • **~ en el error de hacer algo** to make the mistake of doing sth • **~ en la tentación** to give in *o* yield to temptation • **y no nos dejes ~ en la tentación** (*Biblia*) and lead us not into temptation • **MODISMO**: • **~ bajo**: • **¡qué bajo has caído!** (*moralmente*) how low can you get!, how can you sink so low?; (*socialmente*) you've certainly come down in the world!; ▹ **trampa**
8 (= *darse cuenta*) • **no caigo** I don't get it*, I don't understand • **ya caigo** I see, now I understand, now I get it* • **~ en que** to realize that
9 (*fecha*) to fall, be • **su cumpleaños cae en viernes** her birthday falls *o* is on a Friday • **¿en qué cae el día de Navidad?** what day is Christmas Day?, what day does Christmas fall on?
10 (= *tocar*) • **el premio gordo ha caído en Madrid** the first prize (in the lottery) *o* the jackpot went to Madrid • **~le a algn**: • **le pueden ~ muchos años de condena** he could get a very long sentence • **le puede ~ una multa de 50 dólares** he could get a 50 dollar fine • **MODISMO**: • **¡la que nos ha caído encima!** that's just what we needed!; ▹ **suerte**
11 (= *estar situado*) to be • **¿por dónde cae eso?** whereabouts is that? • **eso cae más hacia el este** that lies *o* is further to the east
12 • **~ dentro de** (= *estar comprendido en*): • **no cae dentro de mis atribuciones** it is not within my powers • **esta cuestión no cae dentro del ámbito de este trabajo** that falls outside the scope of this study • **eso cae dentro de la responsabilidad de los ayuntamientos** that falls within the remit of town councils
13 (= *causar impresión*) • **no les caí** (*CAm*) I didn't hit it off with them, I didn't get on well with them, they didn't take to me • **~ bien a algn**: • **me cae (muy) bien** I (really) like him, I like him (very much) • **no me cae nada bien** I don't like him at all • **Pedro no le cayó bien a mi padre** Pedro didn't make a very good impression on my father, my father didn't really take to Pedro • **~ gordo** *o* **fatal a algn***: • **me cae gordo** *o* **fatal el tío ese** I can't stand that guy • **~ mal a algn**: • **me cae mal** I don't like him
14 (= *sentar*) **a** [*información, comentario*] • **me cayó fatal lo que me dijiste** I was very upset by what you said, what you said really upset me • **la noticia cayó como un mazazo** the news was a blow
b [*ropa*] • **~le bien a algn** to suit sb • **~le mal a algn** not to suit sb
15 (= *terminar*) • **al ~ la noche** at nightfall • **al ~ la tarde** at dusk
VERBO PRONOMINAL **caerse**
1 (*persona, objeto*) **a** (*desde la posición vertical*) [*persona, objeto*] to fall over; [*edificio*] to collapse, fall (down) • **¿te has caído?** did you fall over? • **¡cuidado, no te caigas!** watch out or you'll fall over! • **tropecé y estuve a punto de ~me** I tripped and nearly fell (over) • **se cayó y se torció el tobillo** she fell (over) and twisted her ankle • **se ha caído el perchero** the coat stand has fallen over • **el edificio se está cayendo** the building is falling down • **~se al suelo** to fall to the ground
b (*desde una altura*) to fall • **se cayó al agua** she fell into the water • **se cayó por la ventana** he fell out of the window • **~se de algo** to fall off sth • **se cayó del caballo** he fell off his horse • **los libros se cayeron del estante** the books fell off the shelf • **el niño se cayó de la cama** the child fell out of bed
c • **caérsele algo a algn: se me cayeron las monedas** I dropped the coins • **se me ha caído el guante** I've dropped my glove • **sin el botón se te van a ~ los pantalones** without the button your trousers will fall down
2 (= *desprenderse*) [*hoja*] to fall off; [*diente*] to fall out • **se me está cayendo el pelo** my hair is falling out • **se me ha caído un botón de la chaqueta** a button has come off my jacket
3 • **~se de: se cae de cansancio** he's so tired he could drop • **me caigo de sueño** I'm so sleepy I could drop, I'm asleep on my feet • **el edificio se cae de viejo** the building is so old it's falling to bits *o* it's on the point of collapsing

café SM **1** (*Bot*) (= *bebida*) coffee • **~ ~** real coffee, coffee that really is coffee ▸ **café americano** large black coffee ▸ **café cerrero** (*And*) strong black coffee ▸ **café completo** (*Cono Sur*) continental breakfast ▸ **café con leche** white coffee, coffee with milk, coffee with cream (*EEUU*); (= *homosexual‡*) queer‡, fag (*EEUU‡*) ▸ **café cortado** coffee with a dash of milk ▸ **café descafeinado** decaffeinated coffee ▸ **café en grano** coffee beans (*pl*) ▸ **café exprés** expresso coffee ▸ **café helado** iced coffee ▸ **café instantáneo** instant coffee ▸ **café irlandés** Irish coffee ▸ **café molido** ground coffee ▸ **café negro** (small) black coffee ▸ **café pintado** (*And*), **café quemado** (*Caribe*) coffee with a drop of milk ▸ **café solo** black coffee ▸ **café soluble** instant coffee ▸ **café tinto** (*LAm*) black coffee ▸ **café torrefacto** roasted coffee ▸ **café tostado** roasted coffee
2 (= *cafetería*) café, coffee shop ▸ **café cantante** café with entertainment
3 (*Cono Sur**) (= *reprimenda*) ticking-off*
4 • **MODISMO**: • **mal ~***: • **estar de mal ~** to be in a bad mood; (*CAm*) to be out of sorts • **tener mal ~** (= *genio*) to have a nasty temper; (= *intenciones*) to have evil intentions
5 • **color ~** brown • **~ avellana** (*como adj*) nut-brown
cafecito SM (*LAm*) black coffee
café-concierto SM café which provides musical entertainment
cafeína SF caffein(e)
cafeinómano/a ADJ addicted to coffee *o* caffeine
SM/F coffee *o* caffeine addict
cafetal SM **1** (= *plantío*) coffee plantation
2 (*CAm*) (= *árbol*) coffee tree
cafetalero/a (*LAm*) ADJ coffee (*antes de s*), coffee-growing • **industria cafetalera** coffee industry
SM/F coffee grower
cafetalista SMF (*LAm*) coffee grower
cafetear* ▹ CONJUG 1a VT (*Cono Sur*) to tick off*, tell off*
café-teatro SM (= *lugar*) *café with live theatre*; (= *espectáculo*) live entertainment; (= *comedia*) stand-up comedy
cafetera SF **1** (= *aparato*) coffee maker, coffee machine; (= *jarra*) coffee pot • **MODISMO**: • **estar como una ~*** to be off one's head *o* rocker* ▸ **cafetera automática** coffee machine ▸ **cafetera de filtro** filter coffee maker ▸ **cafetera exprés** espresso coffee maker
2 (*Aut**) old banger*, jalop(p)y*; [*de policía*] police car; ▹ **cafetero**
cafetería SF **1** (*gen*) café, coffee shop; (= *autoservicio*) cafeteria; (*Ferro*) buffet, refreshment car (*EEUU*)
2 (*LAm*) (= *tienda*) retail coffee shop
cafetero/a ADJ **1** [*finca, sector*] coffee (*antes de s*); [*país*] coffee producing • **industria cafetera** coffee industry
2 (= *aficionado al café*) • **soy muy ~** I really like (my) coffee
3 (= *aficionado a los cafés*) fond of going to cafés • **es muy ~** he spends a lot of time in cafés
SM/F* (= *dueño*) café proprietor, café owner; (= *cultivador*) coffee grower; (= *comerciante*) coffee merchant; ▹ **cafetera**
cafetín SM small café
cafeto SM coffee tree

cafetucho SM seedy little café
cafiche‡ SM (*Cono Sur*) pimp, ponce‡
cafichear‡ ▸ CONJUG 1a VI (*Cono Sur*) to live off sb else, ponce‡
caficho‡ SM (*Cono Sur*) pimp, ponce‡
caficultor(a) SM/F (*CAm*) coffee grower
caficultura SF (*CAm*) coffee growing
cáfila SF group, flock (*esp on the march*) • **una ~ de disparates** a string of nonsense
cafiolo‡ SM (*Cono Sur*) pimp, ponce‡
cafre SMF **1** [*de África*] Kaffir
2 (= *bruto*) savage • **como ~s** like savages, like beasts
ADJ **1** (*de África*) Kaffir
2 (= *brutal*) uncouth, boorish
caftán SM caftan, kaftan
cagaaceite SM missel thrush, mistle thrush
cagada** SF **1** (= *excremento*) shit**, crap** • **~s de perro** dog shit** (*sing*)
2 (= *error*) cock-up**, fuck-up**, screw-up (*EEUU***)
3 (= *tonterías*) crap**, balls** (*pl*) • **decir una ~** to talk a load of crap**
4 (= *porquería*) crap** • **el discurso fue una ~** the speech was total crap**
cagadera** SF (*LAm*) • **tener ~** to have the shits** *o* trots* *o* runs*
cagadero** SM bog‡, john (*EEUU‡*)
cagado** ADJ shit-scared** • **no se atreve a salir, está ~ de miedo** he daren't go out, he's shit-scared** • **no seas tan ~** don't be such a gutless coward
cagajón* SM horse-dung, mule-dung
cagalera** SF • **tener ~** to have the shits** *o* trots* *o* runs* • **¡menuda ~!** what a mess!
cagar** ▸ CONJUG 1h VI (= *defecar*) to shit**, have a shit**, take a shit (*EEUU***)
• MODISMO: • **¡está que no caga!** he's on cloud nine!
VT **1** [+ *ropa*] to dirty, soil
2 • MODISMOS: • **~la** to blow it*, balls up** • **¡la hemos cagado!** we've ballsed up!**, we've blown it!‡ • **ir cagando leches** to bomb along* • **irse cagando leches** to leg it*, scarper*
3 (*Arg*) (= *dañar*) to harm
4 (*Arg*) (= *defraudar*) to rip off*
VPR **cagarse 1** to shit o.s.** • **se cagó en los pantalones** he shat himself**, he messed his pants
2 • MODISMOS: • **~se de miedo** to shit o.s.** • **~se de risa** to piss o.s. (laughing)** • **me cago de risa con los chistes de tu hermano** your brother's jokes really crack me up* • **~se en algn/algo** not to give a toss‡ *o* a shit** *o* a fuck** about sb/sth • **¡me cago en diez** *o* **en la mar** *o* **en la leche!** bloody hell!**, shit!** • **¡cada vez que bebía se cagaba en la madre de todo el mundo!** whenever he drank he'd start effing and blinding at everything and everyone *o* telling everyone to go to hell* • **¡me cago en la puta** *o* **en la hostia!** fucking hell!** • **¡me cago en la leche que mamaron!** screw them!** • **¡me cago en el gobierno!** to hell with *o* sod the government!* • **... y se caga la perra ...** (*Esp*) and you never saw anything like it • **~se patas abajo**: • **tenía tanto miedo que se cagó patas abajo** he was so frightened, he shat himself**
3 • MODISMO: • **que te cagas** (*como adj*) damn‡, bloody‡ • **¡en la sierra hace un frío que te cagas!** it's bloody freezing in the mountains!‡ • **el jefe tiene una cara que te cagas** the boss has got a bloody nerve‡ • **la película estaba que te cagabas** the film was bloody brilliant‡ • **la tía estaba que te cagas** she was drop dead gorgeous*
cagarruta SF **1** [*de animal*] pellet, dropping
2 • **es una ~ de su padre** (*Esp‡*) he's the spitting image of his father
cagatintas* SMF INV **1** (= *oficinista*) penpusher, pencil pusher (*EEUU*)
2 (*And*) (= *avaro*) miser
cagón/ona** ADJ **1** = **cagado**
2 [*bebé*] • **ser ~** to keep dirtying one's nappies
SM/F **1** (= *cobarde*) wimp*
2 (= *bebé*) • **ser un ~** to keep dirtying one's nappies
caguama SF (*Méx*) large turtle
cague** SM • **le entró un ~ de mucho cuidado** he was scared shitless**
cagüen** = **cago en** ▸ **cagar**
cagueruelas‡ SFPL the runs‡, the trots‡
cagueta‡ SMF, **caguetas‡** SMF INV, **caguica‡** SMF INV chicken
caguitis‡ SF INV • **entrarle ~ a algn** to get the wind up*
Cahispa SF ABR = **Caja Hispana de Previsión**
cahuín SM (*Chile*) **1** (= *borrachera*) drunkenness
2‡ (= *lío*) cock-up‡, screw-up (*EEUU***)
3 (= *reunión*) rowdy gathering
caída SF **1** (= *accidente*) fall; [*de caballo*] fall, tumble • **tuvo una aparatosa ~ de la moto** he had a spectacular fall from his motorbike • **sufrir una ~** to have a fall, take a tumble • **durante un campeonato regional, sufrió una grave ~ del caballo** during a regional championship, he had a bad fall *o* tumble off his horse ▸ **caída de agua** waterfall ▸ **caída de cabeza** • **sufrir una ~ de cabeza** to fall headfirst, take a header* ▸ **caída en barrena** spiral fall
2 [*de gobierno, imperio*] fall, collapse; [*de un gobernante*] downfall • **la ~ del Muro de Berlín** the collapse *o* fall of the Berlin Wall • **la crisis ocasionó la ~ del gobierno** the crisis brought down the government • **la ~ del Imperio Romano** the fall of the Roman Empire • **la ~ de Napoleón se produjo en Waterloo** Waterloo was Napoleon's downfall
3 (= *pérdida*) [*de cabello, dientes*] loss • **un champú contra la ~ del cabello** a shampoo that helps prevent hair loss
4 (*Dep*) ▸ **caída al vacío, caída libre** free fall
5 (= *descenso*) [*de precios, ventas*] fall, drop; [*de divisa*] fall • **la espectacular ~ de precios afectó con gran dureza a numerosas economías** many economies were hard hit by the dramatic fall *o* drop in prices • **el gobierno está decidido a frenar la ~ de la libra** the government is determined to curb the fall of the pound • **~ de la temperatura** drop in temperature • **~ de tensión** (*Med*) drop in blood pressure; (*Elec*) drop in voltage • **~ de la actividad económica** downturn in the economy • **~ en picado** sharp fall • **el banco intervino para evitar la ~ en picado del dólar** the bank intervened to stop the dollar taking a nose-dive *o* plummeting
6 • **a la ~ del sol** *o* **de la tarde** at sunset
7 (= *desprendimiento*) fall • **había una continua ~ de piedras desde la cima de la montaña** rocks fell continuously from the top of the mountain
8 (= *inclinación*) [*de terreno*] slope; (*brusco*) drop
9 [*de tela, ropa*] hang • **esta chaqueta tiene buena ~** this jacket hangs well ▸ **caída de hombros** slope of the shoulders ▸ **caída de ojos** • **tenía una ~ de ojos entre coqueta y malvada** the way she lowered her eyes was somewhere between coquettish and wicked
10 (*Rel*) • **la Caída** the Fall
11 ▸ **caída radiactiva** radioactive fallout
12 caídas: **a*** (= *golpes*) witty remarks • **¡qué ~s tiene!** isn't he witty?
b (= *lana*) low-grade wool (*sing*)
caído ADJ (*gen*) fallen; [*cabeza*] hanging; [*hombros*] drooping; [*cuello*] turndown; [*flor etc*] limp, drooping • **estar ~ de sueño** to be dead tired
SM **1** (= *muerto*) • **los ~s** the fallen • **los ~s por España** (*en el bando franquista*) those who died for Spain • **monumento a los ~s** war memorial, monument to the fallen
2 (*Méx*) (= *soborno*) backhander*, sweetener*
caifán* SM (*Méx*) pimp*, ponce*
caigo *etc* ▸ **caer**
caimacán SM (*And*) (= *persona importante*) important person, big shot*; (= *estrella*) ace, star, expert
caimán SM **1** (= *cocodrilo*) caiman, alligator
2 (*And*) (= *iguana*) iguana
3 (*LAm*) (= *estafador*) con man, swindler
4 (*Méx*) (*Téc*) chain wrench
5 (*And*) (= *gandul*) lazybones*
caimanear ▸ CONJUG 1a (*LAm*) VT (= *estafar*) to swindle, cheat
VI (= *cazar*) to hunt caiman *o* alligators
caimiento SM **1** (= *acto*) fall, falling; (*Med*) decline
2 (= *desfallecimiento*) dejection
Caín SM Cain • MODISMOS: • **pasar las de ~*** to go through hell* • **venir con las de ~*** to have evil intentions
cainismo SM fratricidal violence, fratricidal treachery
cainita ADJ (*frm*) • **odio ~** brotherly hatred • **un país ~** a country where brother hates brother
caipiriña SF caipirinha
cairel SM (= *peluca*) wig; (*Cos*) fringe
cairelear ▸ CONJUG 1a VT to trim, fringe
Cairo SM • **el ~** Cairo
caita (*Cono Sur*) ADJ INV (= *montaraz*) wild, untamed; (= *huraño*) unsociable, withdrawn
SM (= *trabajador*) migratory agricultural worker
caite SM (*CAm*) rough sandal
caitearse ▸ CONJUG 1a VPR • **caiteárselas** (*CAm*) to run away, beat it*
caja SF **1** (= *recipiente*) box; [*de cervezas, refrescos*] crate • **una ~ de cartón** a cardboard box • **la ~ tonta*** (= *tele*) the box*, the goggle-box*, the idiot box (*EEUU**) ▸ **caja china** Chinese box ▸ **caja de cerillas** (*llena*) box of matches; (*vacía*) matchbox ▸ **caja de colores** box of crayons ▸ **caja de herramientas** toolbox ▸ **caja de Pandora** Pandora's box ▸ **caja de sorpresas** (= *juego*) jack-in-the-box • **ser una ~ de sorpresas** to be full of surprises ▸ **caja de zapatos** shoebox ▸ **caja negra** [*de avión*] black box
2 (*Com*) (*en supermercado*) checkout; (*en tienda*) till, cash desk; (*en banco*) window, cash desk • **robaron todo el dinero que había en la ~** they stole all the money in the till • **para pagar, pase por ~** please pay at the cash desk *o* till *o* checkout • **entrar en ~**: • **ha entrado muy poco dinero en ~** takings have been low • **hacer ~** to cash up • **después de cerrar hacen ~** after closing they cash up • **hicieron una ~ de 5.000 euros** they took (in) 5,000 euros • **ingresar en ~**: • **hemos ingresado 5.000 euros en ~** we have taken (in) 5,000 euros ▸ **caja B** B account, secret account *o* fund, slush fund ▸ **caja de ahorros** savings bank ▸ **caja de caudales** safe, strongbox ▸ **caja de pensiones** pension fund ▸ **caja de resistencia** emergency fund, contingency fund ▸ **caja fuerte** safe, strongbox ▸ **Caja Postal de Ahorros** ≈ Post Office Savings Bank ▸ **caja registradora** cash register, cash till
3 [*de reloj*] case, casing; [*de radio, TV*] casing, housing; [*de fusil*] stock ▸ **caja de cambios**

(*Mec*) gearbox ▸ **caja de empalmes** junction box ▸ **caja de fusibles** fuse box ▸ **caja del cigüeñal** crankcase ▸ **caja de registro** manhole, inspection hole
4 [*de parking*] pay station
5 (*Mús*) (= *tambor*) drum; [*de piano*] case; [*de violín*] soundbox • MODISMO: • **despedir** *o* **echar a algn con ~s destempladas** to send sb packing*, throw *o* kick sb out ▸ **caja de música** music box ▸ **caja de resonancia** [*de un instrumento*] soundbox • **sirve de ~ de resonancia a los terroristas** it's a sounding board for terrorists ▸ **caja de ritmos** drum machine, beatbox*
6 (*Anat*) ▸ **caja craneana** skull, cranial cap ▸ **caja de dientes*** set of choppers* ▸ **caja torácica** thoracic cavity
7* (= *ataúd*) box*, coffin ▸ **caja de muerto** coffin, casket (EEUU)
8 (*Bot*) seed case, capsule
9 (*Tip*) case ▸ **caja alta** upper case ▸ **caja baja** lower case
10 (*Mil*) • **entrar en ~** to join up, enlist ▸ **caja de reclutamiento, caja de reclutas** recruiting office
11 (*Cono Sur*) (= *lecho de río*) (dried up) riverbed
cajear* ▸ CONJUG 1a VT (*And, CAm*) to beat up*
cajero/a SM/F (*gen*) cashier; (*en banco*) cashier, (bank) teller; (*en supermercado etc*) checkout operator
SM ▸ **cajero automático** cash dispenser, automated *o* automatic teller machine (*frm*)
cajeta SF **1** (*LAm*) (= *dulce de leche*) fudge, soft toffee; (*Méx*) (= *dulce de jalea*) jelly; (*CAm, Méx*) (= *caramelo*) sweet, candy (EEUU)
2 (*CAm, Méx*) (*para dulces*) round sweet box
3 (*And, CAm*) [*de animal*] lip
4 • MODISMO: • **de ~** (*CAm, Méx*) (*iró*) first-class, super
5 (*Méx**) (= *cobarde*) coward; (= *enclenque*) wimp*
6 (*Cono Sur***) (= *vagina*) cunt**
cajete SM (*Méx*) **1** (= *cazuela*) earthenware pot *o* bowl
2* (= *wáter*) toilet, loo*, john (EEUU‡)
3‡ (= *culo*) bum‡, ass (EEUU‡)
cajetilla SF **1** (= *paquete*) packet, pack (EEUU) ▸ **cajetilla de cigarrillos, cajetilla de tabaco** packet *o* (EEUU) pack of cigarettes
2 (*Caribe*) (= *dientes*) teeth (*pl*)
SM (*Cono Sur**) (= *petimetre*) dude*, toff*; (= *urbanita*) city slicker (EEUU); (= *afeminado*) poof‡, queen‡, fag (EEUU‡)
cajista SMF compositor, typesetter
cajón SM **1** [*de mueble*] drawer ▸ **cajón de sastre** • **esta palabra es un ~ de sastre** this is a catch-all term • **esta sección es un ~ de sastre** this section is a bit of a ragbag *o* mixed bag
2 (= *caja*) big box, crate ▸ **cajón de embalaje** crate, packing case ▸ **cajón de suspensión, cajón hidráulico** caisson
3 (*Méx*) (= *puesto*) stall ▸ **cajón de ropa** draper's (shop), dry-goods store (EEUU)
4 (*Dep*) ▸ **cajón de salida** starting gate
5 • MODISMO: • **de ~***: • **eso es de ~** that goes without saying
6 (*And, Cono Sur*) (= *ataúd*) coffin, casket (EEUU)
7 (*LAm*) (*Geog*) ravine
caju SM cashew (nut)
cajuela SF (*Méx*) (*Aut*) boot, trunk (EEUU)
cajún ADJ Cajun
SM (= *lenguaje*) Cajun
cal SF lime • MODISMOS: • **cerrar algo a cal y canto** to shut sth firmly *o* securely • **de cal y canto** firm, strong • **dar una de cal y otra de arena** to apply a policy of carrot and stick ▸ **cal apagada, cal muerta** slaked lime ▸ **cal viva** quicklime
cala[1] SF **1** (*Geog*) (= *ensenada*) cove
2 (*Náut*) hold
3 (*Pesca*) fishing ground
cala[2] SF **1** (*Culin*) [*de fruta*] sample slice • **hacer ~ y cata** to test for quality
2 (*Med*) (= *supositorio*) suppository; (= *sonda*) probe
3 (*Aut*) dipstick
cala[3]* SF (*Esp*) peseta
cala[4]‡ SM (*Mil*) glasshouse‡, prison
calabacear* ▸ CONJUG 1a VT (*Univ*) [+ *candidato*] to fail; [+ *amante*] to jilt
calabacera SF pumpkin (plant)
calabacín SM **1** (*Bot*) courgette, zucchini (EEUU)
2 (= *idiota*) dolt
calabacita SF (*Esp*) courgette, zucchini (EEUU)
calabaza SF **1** (*Bot*) pumpkin; (= *recipiente*) gourd, calabash
2 (= *idiota*) dolt
3* (= *cabeza*) bonce‡, nut*, noggin (EEUU‡)
4 • **dar ~s a** [+ *candidato, estudiante*] to fail; [+ *amante*] to jilt; (= *ofender*) to snub, offend • **llevarse** *o* **recibir ~s** [*estudiante*] to fail; [*amante*] to be jilted • **salir ~** to be a flop*, prove a miserable failure
calabazada SF (= *cabezada*) head butt; (= *golpe en la cabeza*) blow on the head
calabazazo SM bump on the head
calabazo SM **1** (*Bot*) pumpkin, gourd, squash (EEUU)
2 (*Caribe*) (*Mús*) drum
calabobos* SM INV drizzle
calabozo SM (= *prisión*) prison; (= *celda*) prison cell; (*Mil*) military prison; (*esp Hist*) dungeon
calabrote SM (*Náut*) cable-laid rope, cable rope
calache* SM (*CAm*) thing, thingummyjig*, thingamajig (EEUU*) • **reúne tus ~s** get your things, get your bits and pieces
calada SF **1** (= *mojada*) soaking
2 [*de red*] lowering
3 [*de ave*] swoop, dive
4 [*de tabaco*] puff, drag*
5* (= *regañada*) ticking-off* • **dar una ~ a algn** to tick sb off*, haul sb over the coals
caladero SM fishing ground
calado ADJ **1** (= *mojado*) soaked • **estar ~ (hasta los huesos)** to be soaked (to the skin)
2 (*Cos*) openwork (*antes de s*)
3 [*gorro etc*] • **con la boina calada hasta las orejas** with his beret pulled down over his ears
4 [*bayoneta*] fixed
SM **1** (*Téc*) fretwork; (*Cos*) openwork
2 (*Náut*) depth of water; [*de barco*] draught, draft (EEUU) • **en iguales ~s** on an even keel
3 (*fig*) depth; (= *alcance*) scope; (= *importancia*) importance • **una razón de mayor ~** a more convincing reason • **un descubrimiento de gran ~** a very important discovery
4 (*Mec*) stall, stalling
calafate SM caulker, shipwright
calafatear ▸ CONJUG 1a VT to caulk, plug up
calaguasca SF (*LAm*) rum
calagurritano/a ADJ of Calahorra
SM/F native/inhabitant of Calahorra • **los ~s** the people of Calahorra
calamaco SM (*Méx*) (*Culin*) kidney bean
calamar SM squid ▸ **calamares a la romana** squid rings fried in batter
calambrazo* SM attack of cramp
calambre SM **1** (*muscular*) • **me dan ~s** I get cramp ▸ **calambre de escribiente** writer's cramp
2 (*Elec*) shock • **un cable que da ~** a live wire
calambur SM (*LAm*) pun
calamidad SF (= *desastre*) calamity, disaster; (= *persona*) • **es una ~** he's a dead loss* • **estar hecho una ~** to be in a very bad way • **¡vaya ~!** what terrible luck!
calamina SF **1** (*Med, Min*) calamine
2 (*Chile, Bol, Perú*) (= *chapa*) corrugated iron
calaminado ADJ (*LAm*) bumpy, uneven
calamita SF lodestone; (= *aguja*) magnetic needle
calamitosamente ADV calamitously, disastrously
calamitoso ADJ calamitous, disastrous
cálamo SM (*Bot*) stem, stalk; (*Mús*) reed; (*Mús Hist*) flute; (= *pluma*) pen • **empuñar el ~** to take up one's pen • **menear ~** to wield a pen
calamocano* ADJ **1** (= *borracho*) merry*, tipsy
2 (= *cariñoso*) doting
calamoco SM icicle
calamorra* SF head, nut‡
calamorrada* SF (= *cabezada*) head butt; (= *golpe en la cabeza*) bump on the head
calandraco ADJ (*And, Cono Sur*) (= *fastidioso*) annoying, tedious; (= *casquivano*) scatterbrained
calandria[1] SF (*Orn*) calandra lark
calandria[2] SF **1** (*Téc*) calender
2 (*Econ‡*) one peseta
3 (= *argot*) underworld slang, argot
SMF* (= *persona*) malingerer
calaña SF sort • **gente de esa ~** people of that ilk *o* sort
calañés SM (*Andalucía*) *hat with a turned-up brim*
calar[1] ADJ calcareous (*frm*), lime (*antes de s*)
SM limestone quarry
calar[2] ▸ CONJUG 1a VT **1** [*líquido, lluvia, humedad*] to soak (through) • **la lluvia me caló la ropa** the rain soaked *o* drenched my clothes • **~ a algn (hasta) los huesos** to cut sb (through) to the bone • **un frío y una humedad que calan los huesos** cold and damp that cut through to the bone
2* (= *percatar*) to suss (out)* • **lo calé nada más conocerlo** I had him sussed as soon as I'd met him* • **¡nos ha calado!** he's sussed *o* rumbled us!*, we've been sussed *o* rumbled!*
3 (*Téc*) [+ *metal, madera*] to fret • **sierra de ~** fret saw
4 [+ *bayoneta*] to fix
5 [+ *mástil*] to fix, fit; [+ *vela*] to lower; [+ *red*] to cast • **el buque cala 12 metros** the ship draws 12 metres, the ship has a draught of 12 metres
6 (*And*) (= *aplastar*) to crush, flatten; (= *humillar*) to humiliate
VI (= *penetrar*) • **esa moda no caló en España** that fashion did not take on *o* catch on in Spain • **su defensa caló en el jurado** the arguments in his defence got through to the jury • **una ideología que está calando en la sociedad** an ideology that is catching on in society • **esta opinión ha calado entre la población** this opinion has taken deep root among the public • **su mensaje caló hondo en nuestra generación** her message had a deep effect *o* made a deep impression on our generation
VPR **calarse 1** (= *mojarse*) to get soaked, get drenched • **me calé hasta los huesos** I got soaked to the skin
2 [*material, ropa*] to let water in, get wet; [*zapatos*] to let water in • **esos zapatos se calan** those shoes will let water in as soon as it rains
3 [*motor, vehículo*] to stall • **se le caló el coche** his car stalled

4 [+ *sombrero, gorra*] to pull down; [+ *gafas, careta*] to put on • **se caló el sombrero hasta la frente** he pulled his hat down over his forehead
calarredes SM INV trawler
calatear ▷ CONJUG 1a VT (*Perú*) to undress
calato ADJ (*Perú*) (= *desnudo*) naked; (*fig*) penniless, broke*
calavera SF **1** (*Anat*) skull
2 (*Méx*) (*Aut*) tail-light, rear light
3 (*Entomología*) death's-head moth
SM (= *juerguista*) reveller; (= *locuelo*) madcap; (= *libertino*) rake, roué; (= *canalla*) rotter†, cad†, heel†
calaverada SF madcap escapade
calaverear ▷ CONJUG 1a VI to live it up*; (*pey*) to lead a wild life, live recklessly
calca SF **1** (*Perú*) (= *granero*) barn, granary
2 (*LAm*) (= *copia*) copy
calcado ADJ (= *idéntico*) • **ser ~ a algo** to be just like sth • **ese bolso es ~ al mío** that bag is just like mine • **ser ~ a algn** to be the spitting image of sb • **es ~ a su padre** he's the spitting image of his father
SM (*Téc*) tracing
calcañal SM, **calcañar** SM, **calcaño** SM heel
calcar ▷ CONJUG 1g VT **1** (*Téc*) to trace, make a tracing of
2 (= *plagiar*) to copy, imitate • **~ A en B** (= *copiar*) to model A on B, base A on B
calcáreo ADJ calcareous, lime (*antes de s*)
calce SM **1** (*Mec*) (= *llanta*) (steel) tyre; (= *cuña*) wedge, shim; (= *punta*) iron tip
2 (*And*) (= *empaste*) filling (*of a tooth*)
3 (*Méx*) (*Tip*) [*de documento*] foot (of a document), lower margin; (= *firma*) signature • **firmar al ~** to sign at the foot *o* bottom of the page
4 (*Cono Sur*) (= *oportunidad*) chance, opportunity
cal. cen. ABR (= **calefacción central**) c.h.
calcés SM masthead
calceta SF **1** • **hacer ~** to knit
2 (= *media*) (knee-length) stocking
3 (= *hierro*) fetter, shackle
calcetería SF **1** (= *oficio*) hosiery
2 (= *tienda*) hosier's (shop)
calcetero/a SM/F hosier
calcetín SM sock • **MODISMO:** • **darle la vuelta al ~** to turn things upside-down ▸ **calcetín de viaje**‡ French letter, rubber (*esp EEUU*‡)
calcha SF (*Cono Sur*) **1** (= *ropa*) clothing; [*de cama*] bedding; (= *arreos*) harness
2 (= *cerneja*) fetlock
3 (= *flequillo*) fringe (of hair)
4 (= *harapos*) tatters (*pl*), strands (*pl*)
calchona SF (*Cono Sur*) ghost, bogey; (*fig*) hag
calchudo ADJ (*Cono Sur*) shrewd, cunning
calcícola ADJ calcicolous
SF calcicole
calcificación SF calcification
calcificado ADJ calcified
calcificante ADJ calcifying
calcificar ▷ CONJUG 1g VT, VPR **calcificarse** to calcify
calcífugo ADJ calcifugous
calcina SF concrete
calcinación SF calcination
calcinar ▷ CONJUG 1a VT **1** (= *quemar*) to burn, reduce to ashes, blacken • **las ruinas calcinadas del edificio** the charred remains of the building • **cuerpos calcinados** charred bodies • **murió calcinado** he burned to death
2* (*fastidiar*) to bother, annoy
VPR **calcinarse** to calcine
calcio SM calcium

calco SM **1** (*Téc*) tracing
2 (*Ling*) calque (**de** on), loan translation (**de** from)
3 (= *imitación*) copy, imitation • **ser un ~ de algn** to be the spitting image of sb
4 calcos‡ (= *pies*) plates‡, feet; (= *zapatos*) shoes
calcomanía SF transfer, decal (*EEUU*)
calculable ADJ calculable
calculado ADJ [*riesgo, decisión, intento*] calculated; [*moderación, elegancia, ambigüedad*] studied
calculador ADJ **1** (*gen*) calculating
2 (*LAm*) (= *egoísta*) selfish, mercenary
calculadora SF calculator; (*Hist*) calculating machine ▸ **calculadora de bolsillo** pocket calculator
calcular ▷ CONJUG 1a VT **1** (*Mat*) (*exactamente*) to calculate, work out • **debes ~ la cantidad exacta** you must calculate *o* work out the exact number • **~ la distancia entre dos puntos** to calculate *o* work out the distance between two points • **calculé mal la distancia y me caí** I misjudged the distance and fell
2 (*estimativamente*) • **~ que** to reckon (that) • **calculo que debe de tener unos cuarenta años** I reckon *o* (*esp EEUU*) figure he must be about 40 (years old) • **¿cuánto calculas que puede costar?** how much do you reckon it might cost? • **se calcula que habrá unos diez heridos** about ten people are estimated to have been wounded • **calculo que llegará mañana** I reckon *o* (*esp EEUU*) figure he'll come tomorrow
3 (= *planear*) to work out, figure out • **lo calculó todo hasta el más mínimo detalle** he worked *o* figured it all out down to the last detail
4* (= *imaginar*) • **—¿tienes ganas de ir? —¡calcula!** "are you looking forward to going?" — "what do you think? *o* you bet (I am)!"*
5 (*Arquit*) [+ *puente, bóveda*] to design, plan
cálculo SM **1** (*gen*) calculation, reckoning; (= *conjetura*) estimate, conjecture; (*Mat*) calculus • **según mis ~s** by my reckoning, by my calculations • **obrar con mucho ~** to act cautiously • **hoja de ~** spreadsheet • **libro de ~s hechos** ready reckoner ▸ **cálculo de costo** costing, pricing (*EEUU*) ▸ **cálculo de probabilidades** theory of probability ▸ **cálculo diferencial** differential calculus ▸ **cálculo mental** mental arithmetic
2 (*Med*) stone ▸ **cálculo biliar** gallstone
Calcuta SF Calcutta
calda SF **1** (= *calentamiento*) (*gen*) heating; (*en hornos de fundición*) stoking
2 caldas (= *baños*) hot springs, hot mineral baths
caldeado ADJ lively • **ambiente ~** (= *animado*) lively atmosphere; (= *tenso*) heated atmosphere • **los ánimos estaban ~s** feelings were running high
caldeamiento SM warming, heating
caldear ▷ CONJUG 1a VT (= *calentar*) to warm (up), heat (up); (*Téc*) to weld • **~ los ánimos de la gente** to work people up
VPR **caldearse** [*local*] to get hot; [*ambiente*] to get tense *o* heated
caldeo SM warming, heating; (*Téc*) welding
caldera SF (*Téc*) boiler; (= *caldero*) cauldron; (*Cono Sur*) (= *cacerola*) pot; (= *tetera*) teapot; (= *pava*) kettle; (*And*) crater • **MODISMO:** • **las ~s de Pe(d)ro Botero** hell
calderero SM boilermaker ▸ **calderero remendón** tinker
caldereta SF **1** (*Culin*) [*de pescado*] fish stew; [*de cordero*] lamb stew

2 (= *caldera pequeña*) small boiler; (= *cacerola*) stewpan
3 (*Rel*) holy water vessel
4 (*Caribe*) (= *viento*) warm wind from the sea
calderilla SF **1** (*Econ*) small change • **en ~** in small change
2 (*Rel*) holy water vessel
caldero SM cauldron, copper
calderón SM **1** (*Mús*) pause (sign)
2 (= *caldera grande*) large boiler, cauldron
3 (*Tip*) paragraph sign, section mark
calderoniano ADJ relating to Calderón • **héroe ~** Calderonian hero • **estudios ~s** Calderón studies
caldo SM **1** (= *sopa*) soup, broth; (= *consomé*) (clear) soup • **con un caldito te sentirás mejor** you'll feel better with some nice hot soup *o* broth inside you
2 [*de guiso*] juice • **tómate el ~ del estofado** have some of the juice from the stew • **la salsa se hace con el ~ de la carne** the sauce is made from the stock *o* juice of the meat • **hierva las verduras/los huesos para hacer el ~** boil the vegetables/the bones to make a stock • **cubitos de ~** stock cubes
3 ▸ **caldo de cultivo** (*Bio*) culture medium; (*fig*) breeding ground • **el ~ de cultivo del fascismo** the breeding ground of fascism
4 • **MODISMOS:** • **cambiar el ~ a las aceitunas**‡ to have a leak‡ • **hacer el ~ gordo a algn*** to make things easy for sb, make it easy for sb • **se le hacía ~ la cabeza** (*Cono Sur*) he worried a lot about it • **poner a algn a ~*** (= *regañar*) to tell sb off, give sb a ticking off* • **REFRÁN:** • **si no quieres ~, taza y media** *o* **dos tazas** it never rains but it pours
5 (= *vino*) wine • **los ~s jerezanos** the wines of Jerez
6 (= *aceite*) oil
7 (*Méx*) sugar cane juice
caldoso ADJ [*sopa*] watery, thin; [*arroz*] soggy
calducho SM (*Cono Sur*) day off
cale SM slap, smack
calé ADJ gipsy (*antes de s*), gypsy (*antes de s*)
SMF gipsy, gypsy
calefacción SF heating • **sistema de ~** heating (system) ▸ **calefacción central** central heating
calefaccionable ADJ • **espejo exterior ~** heated wing mirror
calefaccionar ▷ CONJUG 1a VT (*Cono Sur*) to heat (up)
calefactor ADJ heating (*antes de s*) • **sistema ~** heating system
SM heater
calefón SM (*Cono Sur*) water heater, boiler ▸ **calefón a gas** gas-fired water heater *o* boiler
caleidoscópico ADJ kaleidoscopic
caleidoscopio SM kaleidoscope
calendar ▷ CONJUG 1a VT to schedule, programme, program (*EEUU*)
calendario SM calendar; [*de reforma etc*] timetable; [*de trabajo etc*] schedule • **MODISMO:** • **hacer ~s** to muse, dream ▸ **calendario de pared** wall calendar ▸ **calendario de taco** tear-off calendar
caléndula SF marigold
calentador SM heater ▸ **calentador de agua** water heater ▸ **calentador de cama** (*Hist*) bedwarmer, warming pan ▸ **calentador de gas** gas-fired boiler *o* water heater ▸ **calentador de inmersión** immersion heater ▸ **calentador eléctrico** electric fire ▸ **calentadores de piernas** legwarmers
calentamiento SM **1** (= *acción*) (*a temperatura alta*) heating; (*a temperatura media*) warming • **a consecuencia de un ~**

excesivo as a result of overheating ▸ **calentamiento de la atmósfera, calentamiento del planeta, calentamiento global** global warming
2 (*Dep*) warm-up

calentar ▹ CONJUG 1j VT **1** [+ *líquido, metal, mineral, comida*] (*a temperatura alta*) to heat (up); (*a temperatura media*) to warm (up) • **¿caliento un poco más la sopa?** shall I heat (up) the soup a bit more? • **tómate este café, que te caliente un poco el estómago** have this coffee, it will warm you up inside • **¿dónde puedo ~ la voz?** where can I warm up? • **estaban calentando piernas antes del partido** they were doing leg warm-up exercises before the match • **~ motores** (*lit*) to warm up the engines; (*fig*) to gather momentum • **los coches ya están calentando motores** the cars are already warming up their engines • **ya calentaba motores la huelga general** the general strike was already gathering momentum • MODISMO: • **~ la cabeza** *o* **los cascos a algn*** (= *marear*) to pester sb; (= *empujar*) to egg sb on • **tras ~le mucho la cabeza han conseguido convencerlo** after endlessly pestering him they finally convinced him • **le ~on los cascos hasta que se metió en la pelea** they egged him on until he finally joined in the fight; ▹ **rojo**
2 [+ *ambiente, ánimos*] • **no fueron capaces de ~ los ánimos de los asistentes** they couldn't get the audience fired up • **el torero inició la faena de rodillas para ~ al público** the bullfighter began with kneeling passes to get the spectators warmed up
3* (*sexualmente*) to turn on*
4 (*esp LAm**) (= *enojar*) to make cross, make mad (*esp EEUU**)
5* (= *zurrar*) • **~ bien a algn** to give sb a good hiding
6 (*Chile**) [+ *examen, materia*] to cram for*
VI **1** (= *dar calor*) [*sol*] to get hot; [*estufa, radiador, fuego*] to give off heat, give out heat • **cuando caliente más el sol** when the sun gets hotter • **el radiador apenas calienta** the radiator hardly gives off *o* gives out any heat
2 (*Dep*) to warm up, limber up
VPR **calentarse 1** (= *caldearse*) [*persona*] to warm o.s. up; [*plancha, sartén*] to heat up, get hot; [*habitación*] to warm up; [*motor, coche*] (*al encenderse*) to warm up; (*en exceso*) to overheat • **nos calentamos a la lumbre** we warmed ourselves up by the fire • MODISMO: • **~se la cabeza** *o* **los cascos (por algo)*** to agonize (about sth), fret (over sth)
2* (= *animarse*) • **se calentaban con los aplausos del público** they got a buzz from the audience's applause* • **los ánimos se ~on y acabaron a golpes** feelings began to run high *o* things got heated and it ended in a punch-up
3* (*sexualmente*) to get turned on*
4 (*LAm**) (= *enojarse*) to get cross, get mad (*esp EEUU**)
5 (*Cono Sur**) (= *disgustarse*) to get upset

calentito ADJ [*lugar*] nice and warm; [*comida*] nice and hot • **aquí estaremos ~s** we'll be nice and warm here • **una sopa calentita** a nice plate of hot soup

calentón‡ ADJ randy*, horny*
SM **1** (*And, Cono Sur**) randy devil*, horny devil*
2 • **darse el ~** • **tener un ~** to feel randy *o* horny*

calentorro/a‡ SM/F randy *o* horny devil*

calentura SF **1** (*Med*) fever, (high) temperature • **estar con** *o* **tener ~** to be feverish, have a temperature • MODISMO: • **tener ~ de pollo** (*hum*) to pretend to be ill
2 (*en labios*) cold sore
3 (*Chile*) tuberculosis
4 (*And, Cono Sur*) (= *cachondez**) randiness*, horniness*
5 (*LAm*) (= *furia*) anger

calenturiento ADJ **1** (*Med*) feverish
2 (= *impúdico*) dirty, prurient; (= *exaltado*) rash, impulsive • **las mentes calenturientas** (*Pol etc*) the hotheads
3 (*Cono Sur*) (= *tísico*) consumptive, tubercular

calenturón* SM high fever

calenturoso ADJ feverish

calera SF (= *cantera*) limestone quarry; (= *horno*) limekiln

calero ADJ lime (*antes de s*)
SM limekiln

calés‡ SMPL bread‡ (*sing*), money (*sing*)

calesa SF chaise, calash, buggy

calesera SF *Andalusian jacket*

calesín SM gig, fly

calesita SF (*And, Cono Sur*) merry-go-round, carousel (EEUU)

caleta SF **1** (*Geog*) cove, small bay, inlet
2 (*And*) (= *barco*) coasting vessel, coaster
3 (*And*) (= *escondite*) cache

caletero/a SM/F **1** (*Caribe*) (= *estibador*) docker, port worker
2 (*Caribe*) (*en tienda*) shop assistant, salesclerk (EEUU)
SM (*LAm*) (*Ferro*) milk train

caletre* SM gumption*, brains (*pl*) • **no le cabe en el ~** he can't get it into his thick head*

calibración SF calibration

calibrado ADJ calibrated

calibrador SM (*gen*) gauge, gage (EEUU); [*de mordazas*] calliper(s) ▸ **calibrador de alambre** wire gauge

calibraje SM calibration

calibrar ▹ CONJUG 1a VT (*Téc*) to calibrate; (*fig*) (= *evaluar*) to gauge, gage (EEUU), measure

calibre SM **1** (= *diámetro*) [*de bala, proyectil, casquillo*] calibre, caliber (EEUU); [*de pistola, rifle, cañón*] calibre, bore; [*de tubo, conducto, tornillo*] calibre • **de alto** *o* **gran** *o* **grueso ~** large-bore • **de bajo** *o* **pequeño ~** small-bore • **casquillos del ~ 9 parabellum** .9 Parabellum cases • **nunca he visto un coche de tal ~** I've never seen such a massive car
2 (= *importancia*) calibre • **no tenemos un poeta del ~ de Lorca** we do not have a poet of the calibre of Lorca • **tienen problemas de gran ~** they have problems of a serious nature
3 (*Cono Sur*) • **palabras de grueso ~** rude words, crude language (*sing*) • **un chiste de grueso ~** a crude joke

calicanto SM (*Caribe, Cono Sur*) (= *muro*) stone wall; (= *muelle*) jetty

calicatas‡ SFPL (= *culo*) backside* (*pl*)

caliche SM **1** (*LAm*) saltpetre bed, caliche; (= *terreno*) nitrate-bearing ground
2 (*Cono Sur*) (= *jalbegue*) *crust of whitewash which flakes from a wall*
3 • **echar un ~**‡ to have a screw‡

calicó SM calico

calidad SF **1** [*de objeto, material, producto*] quality; [*de servicio*] quality, standard • **la ~ del agua ha empeorado** the quality of the water has worsened • **han mejorado la ~ de la enseñanza** they have improved the quality *o* standard of education, they have raised standards in education • **de (buena) ~** good-quality, quality (*antes de s*) • **fruta de (buena) ~** good-quality fruit, quality fruit • **turismo de ~** quality tourism • **vinos de ~** quality wines • **de mala ~** low-quality, poor-quality ▸ **calidad de vida** quality of life
2 (= *condición*) position, status • **su ~ de presidente se lo prohíbe** his position *o* status as president prohibits him from doing so • **en ~ de: te lo digo en ~ de amigo** I'm telling you as a friend
3 (*Inform*) ▸ **calidad de borrador** draft quality, draft ▸ **calidad de carta, calidad de correspondencia** letter quality ▸ **calidad de texto** text quality

cálido ADJ (*gen*) hot; [*color, sonrisa*] warm; [*aplausos*] enthusiastic

calidoscópico ADJ kaleidoscopic

calidoscopio SM kaleidoscope

calienta *etc* ▹ **calentar**

calientabiberones SM INV bottle warmer

calientabraguetas‡ SF INV prick-teaser‡, prick-tease‡, cock-teaser‡

calientacamas SM INV electric blanket

calientafuentes SM INV hotplate, plate warmer

calientapiernas SMPL legwarmers

calientapiés SM INV (*gen*) foot warmer; [*de agua caliente*] hot-water bottle

calientaplatos SM INV hotplate, plate warmer

calientapollas‡ SF INV (*Esp*) prick-teaser‡, prick-tease‡, cock-teaser‡

caliente ADJ **1** (= *que quema*) hot • **no toques la plancha, que está ~** don't touch the iron, it's hot • **un café bien ~** a piping hot coffee • **dieron la noticia cuando todavía estaba ~** the news was released hot off the press • **comer ~** to have a hot meal, have some hot food • **servir algo ~** to serve sth hot • MODISMOS: • **en ~**: • **tuvo que responderle en ~** he had to answer him there and then *o* on the spur of the moment • **así, en ~, no sé qué decirle** offhand, I don't know what to say • **agarrar a algn en ~** (*Méx**) to catch sb red-handed
2 (= *no frío*) warm • **esta cerveza está ~** this beer is warm • **si te abrigas con la manta estarás más calentito** if you wrap the blanket around you, you'll feel warmer • **el cuerpo estaba todavía ~ cuando lo tocaron** the body was still warm to the touch • **me gusta el pan calentito** I like my bread nice and warm • REFRÁN: • **ande yo ~ y ríase la gente** (*en el vestir*) I dress for comfort, not for show; (*en el comportamiento*) I do my own thing and don't care what people say
3 (= *violento*) [*época, lugar*] turbulent;

CALIENTE

A la hora de traducir el adjetivo **caliente**, *hay que tener en cuenta la diferencia en inglés entre los adjetivos* **warm** *y* **hot**.

▹ *Se utiliza* **warm** *cuando nos referimos a algo que está templado, que no quema o que no está suficientemente frío:*

El biberón del niño ya está caliente
The baby's bottle is warm now

¡Esta cerveza está caliente!
This beer is warm!

▹ *Se emplea* **hot** *cuando estamos hablando de una temperatura alta, que puede quemar:*

No toques la sartén, está muy caliente
Don't touch the frying pan, it's very hot

Me apetece un café calentito
I fancy a nice hot cup of coffee

Para otros usos y ejemplos ver la entrada.

[*discusión*] heated; [*batalla*] raging; (*LAm*) [*persona*] angry, mad* • **los sindicatos anunciaron un otoño ~** trade unions warned of a turbulent autumn ahead • **~ de cascos** hot-headed
4 (*en juegos*) warm • **¡caliente, caliente!** warm!, getting warmer!
5* (*en sentido sexual*) • **estar ~** to feel horny‡ • **poner ~ a algn** to turn sb on*, make sb horny‡ • **ponerse ~** to get turned on*, get horny‡
califa SM caliph
califal ADJ caliphal • **la Córdoba ~** Cordova under the Caliphs, the Cordova of the Caliphs
califato SM caliphate
calificación SF **1** (*Escol etc*) grade, mark
2 [*de una película*] rating, certificate • **la película recibió la ~ X** the film was awarded an X certificate, the film was X-rated
3 (= *descripción*) description
4 (= *posición*) rating, standing
calificado ADJ **1** (= *competente*) qualified, competent; [*obrero*] skilled
2 (= *conocido*) well-known, eminent
3 (*Jur*) [*prueba*] undisputed; [*robo*] proven
4 (*Méx*) (*Jur*) qualified, conditional
calificar ▸ CONJUG 1g VT **1** • **~ algo/a algn como** *o* **de algo** to describe sth/sb as sth, call sb/sth sth • **calificó su política como** *o* **de racismo encubierto** he called their policy covert racism, he described their policy as covert racism • **el párroco lo calificó de impertinente** the parish priest described him as *o* called him impertinent • **documentos calificados como alto secreto** documents classified as top secret
2 (*Escol*) [+ *examen*] to mark, grade (*EEUU*); [+ *alumno*] to give a mark to, give a grade to (*EEUU*)
3 (*frm*) (= *ennoblecer*) to distinguish
VPR **calificarse** (*LAm*) (*Pol*) to register as a voter
calificativo ADJ qualifying
SM • **solo merece el ~ de ...** it can only be described as ... • **lo que han hecho estos gamberros no tiene ~s** what these hooligans have done beggars belief
California SF California
california SF (*Cono Sur*) **1** (= *carrera*) horse-race
2 (*Téc*) wire stretcher
californiano/a ADJ, SM/F Californian
calígine (*poét*) SF (= *neblina*) mist; (= *oscuridad*) gloom
caliginoso ADJ (*poét*) (*con neblina*) misty; (= *oscuro*) gloomy
caligrafía SF (= *arte*) calligraphy; (= *letra*) handwriting
caligrafiar ▸ CONJUG 1c VT to write in a stylish hand
caligráfico ADJ calligraphic
calilla SF (*LAm*) **1** (= *persona*) bore
2 (= *molestia*) nuisance
3 (= *engaño*) hoax; (= *broma*) tired *o* old joke
calima SF = calina
calimocho SM wine and cola
calina SF haze, mist
calinoso ADJ hazy, misty
calipso SM calypso
caliqueño SM **1** (= *cigarro*) type of cheap cigar
2** prick** • **echar un ~** to have a screw**
calistenia SF callisthenics (*sing*), calisthenics (*sing*) (*EEUU*)
cáliz SM **1** (*Rel*) chalice, communion cup; (= *copa*) goblet, cup ▸ **cáliz de amargura** bitter cup, cup of sorrow
2 (*Bot*) calyx
caliza SF limestone
calizo ADJ • **piedra caliza** limestone • **tierra caliza** limy soil
callada SF • **a la** *o* **de ~** on the quiet, secretly • **dar la ~ por respuesta** to say nothing in reply
calladamente ADV (= *silenciosamente*) quietly, silently; (= *en secreto*) secretly
callado ADJ **1** [*carácter*] quiet, reserved
2 (= *silencioso*) quiet • **todo estaba muy ~** everything was very quiet • **tener algo ~** to keep quiet about sth, keep sth secret • **¡qué ~ te lo tenías!** you kept pretty quiet about it! • **más ~ que un muerto** as quiet as a mouse* • **pagar para tener ~ a algn** to pay to keep sb quiet, pay for sb's silence • **nunca te quedas ~** you always have an answer for everything
callampa SF (*Chile*) **1** (= *hongo*) mushroom; (= *paraguas*) umbrella, brolly*
2 callampas (= *suburbios*) shanty town (*sing*)
callana SF **1** (*LAm*) (*Culin*) flat earthenware pan
2 (*Cono Sur*) (*hum*) (= *reloj*) pocket watch
callandito* ADV, **callandico*** ADV (= *sin ruido*) softly, very quietly; (= *furtivamente*) stealthily
callar ▸ CONJUG 1a VI **1** (= *dejar de hablar*) to be quiet • **¡calla, que no puedo oír la radio!** be *o* keep quiet, I can't hear the radio!, shut up *o* (*EEUU*) hush up, I can't hear the radio!* • **su madre le mandó ~** his mother ordered him to be quiet, his mother told him to shut up • **—Ernesto se casa —¡calla! ¡eso no puede ser!** "Ernesto is getting married" — "you're joking! that can't be true!"
2 (= *no hablar*) to say nothing, keep quiet • **al principio optó por ~** initially he decided to say nothing *o* keep quiet • REFRÁN: • **quien calla, otorga** silence is *o* gives *o* implies consent
VT **1** (= *hacer callar*) • **calló a los niños con un cuento** he got the children to be *o* keep quiet by reading them a story • **reparten dinero para ~ las protestas** they're giving out money to silence *o* quell complaints • **¡calla** *o* **cállate la boca!*** shut your mouth!‡, shut your face!‡
2 (= *ocultar*) to keep to o.s., keep quiet • **será mejor ~ este asunto** it's best to keep this matter to ourselves *o* keep this matter quiet
VPR **callarse 1** (= *dejar de hablar*) to stop talking, go quiet • **al entrar el profesor todos se ~on** when the teacher came in, everyone stopped talking *o* went quiet • **¡cállense, por favor!** please be quiet! • **si empieza a hablar, ya no se calla** once he starts talking, he doesn't stop
2 (= *no decir nada*) to say nothing, keep quiet • **en esas circunstancias es mejor ~se** in those circumstances, it would be best to say nothing *o* keep quiet
calle SF **1** (= *vía pública*) street; (*con más tráfico*) road • **una ~ muy céntrica** a street right in the centre of town • **~ abajo** down the street • **~ arriba** up the street • MODISMOS: • **abrir ~** to make way, clear the way • **echar por la ~ de en medio** to push on, press on regardless • **se los lleva a todos de ~*** they just can't stay away from her, they find her irresistible • **llevar** *o* **traer a algn por la ~ de la amargura*** to make sb's life a misery* ▸ **calle cerrada** (*Ven, Col, Méx*), **calle ciega** (*Ven, Col*), **calle cortada** (*Cono Sur*) dead end, dead-end street, cul-de-sac ▸ **calle de doble sentido** two-way street ▸ **calle de sentido único, calle de una mano** (*Cono Sur*), **calle de una sola vía** (*Col*), **calle de un solo sentido** (*Chile*) one-way street ▸ **calle peatonal** pedestrianized street, pedestrian street ▸ **calle principal** main street ▸ **calle residencial** residential street (*with low speed limit and priority for pedestrians*) ▸ **calle sin salida** cul-de-sac, dead end, dead end street; ▹ **aplanar, cabo**
2 (= *no casa*) **a · la ~**: • **he estado todo el día en la ~** I've been out all day • **se sentaba en la ~ a ver pasar a la gente** he used to sit out in the street *o* outside watching the people go by • **a los dos días de su detención ya estaba otra vez en la ~** two days after his arrest he was back on the streets again • **el grupo tiene ya tres discos en la ~** the group already have three records out • **irse a la ~** to go out, go outside • **¡iros a la ~ a jugar!** go and play outside! • **salir a la ~** (= *persona*) to go outside; (= *disco, publicación*) to come out • **llevo varios días sin salir a la ~** I haven't been out of the house *o* outside for several days • **el periódico salió ayer a la ~ por última vez** the paper came out yesterday for the last time • MODISMOS: • **coger la ~*** to up and leave* • **dejar a algn en la ~** to put sb out of a job • **echar a algn a la ~** to throw sb out on the street • **echarse a la ~** to take to the streets • **hacer la ~** (*euf*) to walk the streets • **poner a algn (de patitas) en la ~*** to kick sb out • **quedarse en la ~** (= *sin trabajo*) to be out of a job; (= *sin vivienda*) to be homeless • **tomar la ~** to take to the streets; ▹ **hombre**
b • **de ~**: • **ropa de ~** (= *no de estar en casa*) *clothes for wearing outside the house*; (= *no de gala*) everyday clothes (*pl*) • **iba vestido de ~** (*Mil*) he was wearing civilian clothes, he was wearing civvies*
3 • **la ~** (= *gente*) the public • **vamos a oír ahora la opinión de la ~** we're now going to hear what members of the public think • **la presión de la ~** the pressure of public opinion
4 (*Natación, Atletismo*) lane; (*Golf*) fairway
5 (*Aer*) ▸ **calle de rodadura, calle de rodaje** taxiway
calleja SF = callejuela
callejear ▸ CONJUG 1a VI to wander (about) the streets, stroll around; (*pey*) to loaf around, hang about
callejera SF street-walker
callejero ADJ **1** (*gen*) street (*antes de s*) • **accidente ~** street accident • **disturbios ~s** street riots • **mercado ~** street market
2 [*persona*] • **son muy ~s** they are always out and about; ▹ **perro**
SM **1** (*guía*) street directory, street plan
2 (*Aut*) runabout
callejón SM (= *calleja*) alley, passage; (*And*) (= *calle*) main street; (*Taur*) space between inner and outer barriers; (*Geog*) narrow pass ▸ **callejón sin salida** cul-de-sac, dead end; (*fig*) blind alley • **las negociaciones están en un ~ sin salida** the negotiations are at an impasse, the negotiations are stalemated • **gente de ~** (*And*) low-class people
callejuela SF **1** (= *calle*) side street, small street; (= *pasaje*) alley, passage
2 (= *subterfugio*) subterfuge; (*fig*) way out (of the difficulty)
callicida SM corn cure
callista SMF chiropodist, podiatrist (*EEUU*)
callo SM **1** (*Med*) [*de pie*] corn; [*de mano*] callus, callosity (*frm*) • MODISMOS: • **criar ~s** to become inured, become hardened • **dar el ~** (*Esp**) to slog, work hard, slave away*
2* (= *persona fea*) • **María/Juan es un ~** María/Juan is as ugly as sin
3 callos (*Culin*) tripe (*sing*)
callosidad SF callosity (*frm*), hard patch (*on hand etc*)
calloso ADJ calloused, rough
calma SF **1** (= *tranquilidad*) calm • **la ~ ha vuelto al equipo** calm has been restored to

the team • **en la ~ de la noche** in the calm of the night • **¡calma!** (*en una discusión*) calm down!; (*ante un peligro*) keep calm! • **cuando llegaron los niños se acabó la ~** when the children arrived, the peace and quiet ended • **pasó la noche en ~** he had a peaceful night • **hubo un periodo de ~ entre las elecciones municipales y las legislativas** there was a lull between the local and the general elections • **con ~** calmly • **conservar** *o* **mantener la ~** to keep calm, stay calm • **perder la ~** to lose one's cool* • **tomárselo con ~** to take it easy*
2 (= *relajo excesivo*) • **me atendieron con una ~ increíble** they served me in a very relaxed fashion
3 (*Náut, Meteo*) calm • **navegamos con la mar en ~** we sailed in a calm sea ▸ **calma chicha** dead calm
calmadamente ADV calmly
calmado ADJ calm • **estar ~** to be calm • **sería mejor esperar a que las cosas estén más calmadas** it would be better to wait until things have calmed down *o* are calmer
calmante ADJ soothing, sedative
SM sedative, tranquillizer
calmar ▹ CONJUG 1a VT **1** (= *relajar*) [+ *persona*] to calm (down); [+ *ánimos*] to calm; [+ *nervios*] to calm, steady • **intenté ~la pero seguía llorando** I tried to calm her down but she kept crying • **estas pastillas le ayudarán a ~ la ansiedad** these pills will help reduce *o* relieve your anxiety • **esta medida ~á la tensión en el país** this measure will reduce tension in the country
2 (= *aliviar*) [+ *dolor, picor*] to relieve; [+ *tos*] to soothe; [+ *sed*] to quench
VPR **calmarse 1** [*persona*] to calm down • **¡cálmese!** calm down!
2 (*Meteo*) [*viento*] to drop; [*olas*] to calm down • MODISMO: • **~se las aguas:** • **las aguas se ~án tras las elecciones** things will quieten down after the elections
3 (*Econ*) [*mercado*] to settle down
calmazo SM dead calm
calmécac SM (*Méx*) (*Hist*) *Aztec school for priests*
calmo[1] ADJ [*aguas, mar, persona*] calm; [*ambiente*] peaceful
calmo[2] ADJ (*esp LAm*) [*tierra*] barren
calmosamente ADV **1** (= *con tranquilidad*) calmly
2 (= *lentamente*) slowly, sluggishly
calmosidad SF **1** (= *tranquilidad*) calm, calmness
2 (= *lentitud*) slowness, sluggishness
calmoso ADJ **1** (= *tranquilo*) calm
2 (= *lento*) slow, sluggish
caló SM gipsy dialect, gypsy dialect
calofriarse ▹ CONJUG 1c VPR = **escalofriarse**
calofrío SM = **escalofrío**
calor SM, (*a veces*) SF **1** (= *alta temperatura*) heat • **no puedo dormir con este ~** I can't sleep in this heat • **no soporto los ~es del verano** I can't cope with the heat in summer • **un material resistente al ~** a heat-resistant material • **¡qué ~!** it's really hot! • **nos sentamos al ~ de la chimenea** we sat by the heat of the fire, we sat by the warm fireside • **dar ~:** • **el fuego da un ~cito muy agradable** the fire gives off a very pleasant heat • **esta camiseta me da demasiado ~** this shirt is too hot *o* warm • **entrar en ~** to get warm • **un café para entrar en ~** a coffee to warm you/us up • **hacer ~** to be hot • **hace muchísimo ~** it's very hot • **mañana hará mucho ~** it will be very hot tomorrow • **pasar ~** to be hot • **nunca he pasado tanto ~ como hoy** I've never been *o* felt as hot as today • **tener ~** to be hot • **tengo mucho ~** I'm very hot; ▹ **asar**
2 (= *afecto*) warmth and affection • **un niño falto de ~** a child deprived of warmth and affection ▸ **calor humano** human warmth
3 calores [*de la menopausia*] hot flushes, hot flashes (EEUU)
caloría SF calorie
calórico ADJ caloric
calorífero ADJ heat-producing, heat-giving
SM (= *sistema*) heating system; (= *estufa*) furnace, stove; (= *radiador*) heater, radiator ▸ **calorífero mural** wall radiator
calorífico ADJ calorific • **potencia calorífica** calorific value
calorifugar ▹ CONJUG 1h VT [+ *caldera, tubo*] to lag
calorífugo ADJ (= *resistente*) heat-resistant, non-conducting; (= *incombustible*) fireproof
calorro/a* SM/F gipsy, gypsy
calostro SM colostrum
calote* SM (*Cono Sur*) swindle, trick, con* • **dar ~** to skip payments, leave without paying
calotear* ▹ CONJUG 1a VT (*Cono Sur*) to swindle, con*
calta SF (*tb* **calta palustre**) marsh marigold
caluga SF (*Cono Sur*) toffee
caluma SF (*Perú*) gap, pass (*in the Andes*)
calumnia SF (= *difamación*) slander, calumny (*frm*); (*Jur*) (*oral*) slander (**de** of); (*escrita*) libel (**de** on)
calumniador(a) SM/F (= *difamador*) slanderer; (*en prensa etc*) libeller
calumniar ▹ CONJUG 1b VT (= *difamar*) to slander; (*en prensa etc*) to libel • REFRÁN: • **calumnia, que algo queda** if you throw enough mud, some sticks
calumnioso ADJ (= *difamatorio*) slanderous; (*en prensa etc*) libellous, libelous (EEUU)
calurosamente ADV warmly, enthusiastically
caluroso ADJ [*día, tiempo*] warm, hot; [*recibimiento*] warm, enthusiastic; [*aplausos*] enthusiastic
calva SF (= *cabeza*) bald head; (= *parte sin pelo*) bald patch; (*en alfombra, piel, tela*) bare patch, worn place; [*de bosque etc*] clearing
Calvados SM Calvados
calvario SM **1** (= *vía crucis*) Stations of the Cross (*pl*) ▸ **el Calvario** (*Biblia*) Calvary
2 (= *martirio*) torment • **su matrimonio fue un ~** her marriage was a torment (to her) • **pasar un ~** to suffer agonies
calvatrueno†* SM **1** (= *calvo*) bald pate
2 (= *tarambana*) madcap
calvero SM **1** [*de bosque*] glade, clearing
2 (= *cantera*) clay pit
calvicie SF baldness ▸ **calvicie precoz** premature baldness
calvinismo SM Calvinism
calvinista ADJ Calvinist, Calvinistic
SMF Calvinist
Calvino SM Calvin
calvo ADJ **1** [*persona*] bald; [*piel*] bald, hairless • **un señor ~ con gafas** a bald man with glasses • **quedarse ~** to go bald • MODISMO: • **más ~ que una bola de billar** as bald as a coot; ▹ **tanto**
2 [*terreno*] bare, barren
SM bald man
calza SF **1** (*Mec*) wedge, chock • **poner ~ a** to wedge, chock, scotch
2* (= *media*) stocking
3 (*Col*) (*Med*) (= *empaste de dientes*) filling
4 calzas† (= *medias*) hose (*pl*); (= *pantalón*) breeches • MODISMO: • **estar en ~s prietas** to be in a fix
calzada SF (= *carretera*) road; [*de casa*] drive; (*LAm*) (= *avenida*) avenue; (*Caribe*) (= *acera*) pavement, sidewalk (EEUU) • **el coche se salió de la ~** the car went off *o* left the road ▸ **calzada romana** Roman road
calzado ADJ • **conviene ir ~** it's better to wear shoes, one has to wear something on one's feet • **~ con** wearing • **iba calzada con unos zapatos rojos** she was wearing red shoes
SM footwear • **vendemos todo tipo de ~** we sell all types of footwear *o* shoes • **fábrica de ~** shoe factory
calzador SM shoehorn; (*And, Cono Sur*) pen-holder
calzar ▹ CONJUG 1f VT **1** [+ *zapatos etc*] (= *llevar*) to wear; (= *ponerse*) to put on • **calzaba zapatos verdes** she was wearing green shoes • **¿qué número calza usted?** what size shoes do you wear *o* take?, what size do you take? • MODISMO: • **el que primero llega se la calza** first come first served
2 [+ *niño etc*] to put shoes on; (= *proveer de calzado*) to provide with footwear, supply with shoes • **me ayudó a ~me las botas** he helped me to put my boots on
3 (*Mil etc*) [+ *armas*] to bear
4 (*Téc*) [+ *rueda etc*] to scotch, chock; (*con cuña*) to put a wedge (under); (= *bloquear*) to block; (= *asegurar*) to secure
5 (*Col*) [+ *diente*] to fill
6 (= *poner punta a*) to tip, put an iron tip on
VI **1** • **calza bien** he wears good shoes
2* • MODISMOS: • **calza poco** • **no calza mucho** he's pretty dim*
VPR **calzarse 1** • **~se los zapatos** to put one's shoes on
2* • **~se un empleo** to get a job • **~se a algn** to keep sb under one's thumb
3 • **~se a algn**** to screw sb**
calzo SM **1** (*gen*) wedge; (*Mec*) shoe, brake-shoe; (*Náut*) skid, chock
2 (*Ftbl*) professional foul (*euf*)
calzón SM **1** (*Esp*) (= *pantalón corto*) shorts (*pl*) • MODISMOS: • **amarrarse los calzones** to act resolutely • **hablar a ~ quitado** (= *hablar claro*) to call a spade a spade, speak openly *o* frankly; (*sin parar*) to talk without stopping • **ponerse los calzones** to wear the trousers • **tener (muchos) calzones** (*Méx*) to be tough ▸ **calzón de baño**† bathing trunks (*pl*)
2 (*LAm*) (= *ropa interior*) [*de mujer*] pants (*pl*), knickers (*pl*), panties (*pl*) (*esp EEUU*); [*de hombre*] underpants, pants, shorts (EEUU)
3 (*LAm*) [*de bebé*] ▸ **calzón desechable** disposable nappy ▸ **calzón de vinilo** plastic pants
4 • **calzones rotos** (*Cono Sur*) (*Culin*) doughnuts, donuts (EEUU)
calzonarias SFPL (*And, Col*), **calzonarios** SMPL (*Pan*) pants, knickers, panties (*esp EEUU*)
calzonazos* SM INV (= *marido*) henpecked husband; (= *tonto*) stupid twit*; (= *débil*) wimp*
calzoncillos SMPL underpants, pants, shorts (EEUU) ▸ **calzoncillos del nueve largo***, **calzoncillos marianos*** long johns*
calzoneras SFPL (*Méx*) trousers buttoned down the sides
calzoneta SF (*CAm, Méx*) swimming trunks (*pl*)
calzonudo ADJ (*And, CAm, Cono Sur*) (= *estúpido*) stupid; (= *débil*) weak-willed, timid; (*Méx*) (= *enérgico*) energetic; (= *audaz*) bold, brave
CAM SF ABR = **Comunidad Autónoma de Madrid**
cama SF **1** bed • **una ~ para los invitados a**

spare bed • **una habitación con dos ~s** a twin-bedded room • **está en la ~ durmiendo** he's asleep in bed, he's in bed sleeping • **caer en ~** to fall ill • **estar en ~** to be in bed • **guardar ~** to stay in bed • **hacer la ~** to make the bed • **irse a la ~** to go to bed • **llevarse a algn a la ~** to get sb into bed • **meterse en la ~** to go to bed • **mojar la ~** to wet the bed, wet one's bed ▸ **cama camera** three-quarter bed ▸ **cama de agua** water bed ▸ **cama de campaña** camp bed ▸ **cama de matrimonio** double bed ▸ **cama de tijera** folding bed ▸ **cama doble** double bed ▸ **cama elástica** trampoline ▸ **cama individual** single bed ▸ **cama litera** bunk bed ▸ **cama nido** truckle bed, trundle bed (*EEUU*) ▸ **cama plegable** folding bed ▸ **cama redonda** group sex ▸ **cama solar** sunbed ▸ **cama turca** divan bed • REFRÁN: • **quien mala ~ hace en ella yace** you've made your bed and now you must lie in it
2 [*de carro*] floor
3 (*Geol*) layer
camachuelo SM bullfinch
camada SF **1** (*Zool*) litter, brood; (= *pandilla*) gang, band • **son lobos de una ~** they're birds of a feather
2 (*Geol*) layer; (*Arquit*) course (of bricks); [*de huevos, frutas*] layer
camafeo SM cameo
camagua SF (*CAm*) ripening maize, ripening corn (*EEUU*); (*Méx*) unripened maize
camal SM **1** (= *cabestro*) halter
2 (= *palo*) pole (*from which dead pigs are hung*); (*And*) (= *matadero*) slaughterhouse, abattoir
camaleón SM chameleon
camaleónico ADJ chameleon-like
camalote SM camalote (*aquatic plant*)
camama* SF (= *mentira*) lie; (= *engaño*) trick
camamila SF camomile
camanance SM (*CAm*) dimple
camanchaca* SF (*Cono Sur*) thick fog, pea-souper*
camándula SF **1** (= *rosario*) rosary
2 (= *astucia*) • **tener muchas ~s*** to be full of tricks, be a sly sort
camandulear ▹ CONJUG 1a VI to be sanctimonious, be falsely devout; (*LAm*) (= *intrigar*) to intrigue, scheme; (= *vacilar*) to bumble, avoid taking decisions
camandulería SF sanctimoniousness, false devotion
camandulero/a ADJ (= *beato*) sanctimonious, falsely devout; (= *taimado*) sly, tricky; (*LAm*) (= *enredador*) intriguing, scheming; (= *zalamero*) fawning, bootlicking*
SM/F (= *gazmoño*) prude, prig; (= *hipócrita*) hypocrite; (= *vividor*) sly sort, tricky person; (*LAm*) (= *intrigante*) intriguer, schemer
cámara SF **1** [*de fotos, televisión*] camera • **a ~ lenta** in slow motion • **a ~ rápida** in fast-forward ▸ **cámara de cine** film camera ▸ **cámara de fotos** camera ▸ **cámara de seguridad** security camera ▸ **cámara de vídeo** video camera ▸ **cámara digital** digital camera ▸ **cámara fotográfica** camera ▸ **cámara oculta** hidden camera ▸ **cámara oscura** camera obscura; ▹ **chupar**
2† (= *habitación*) chamber ▸ **cámara acorazada** [*de archivo*] strongroom, vaults (*pl*); [*de banco*] vaults (*pl*) ▸ **cámara ardiente** funeral chamber ▸ **cámara de aislamiento** isolation room ▸ **cámara de descompresión** decompression chamber ▸ **cámara de gas** [*de ejecución*] gas chamber ▸ **cámara de tortura** torture chamber ▸ **cámara frigorífica** cold-storage room, refrigerated container ▸ **cámara mortuoria** funeral chamber ▸ **cámara nupcial** bridal chamber
3 (*Pol*) house, chamber ▸ **Cámara Alta** Upper House, Upper Chamber ▸ **Cámara Baja** Lower House, Lower Chamber ▸ **Cámara de Comercio** Chamber of Commerce ▸ **Cámara de los Comunes** House of Commons ▸ **Cámara de (los) Diputados** Chamber of Deputies ▸ **Cámara de los Lores** House of Lords ▸ **Cámara de Representantes** House of Representatives ▸ **Cámara de Senadores** Senate ▸ **cámara legislativa** legislative chamber ▸ **Cámara Regional** regional parliament
4 (*Hist*) [*de palacio*] royal chamber • **médico de ~** royal doctor • **gentilhombre de ~** gentleman-in-waiting; ▹ **ayuda**
5 (*Náut*) (= *camarote*) cabin; [*de oficiales*] wardroom ▸ **cámara de cartas** chart house ▸ **cámara de motores** engine room
6 [*de neumático*] (inner) tube • **cubierta sin ~** tubeless tyre, tubeless tire (*EEUU*)
7 (*Mec*) ▸ **cámara de combustión** combustion chamber ▸ **cámara de compresión** compression chamber ▸ **cámara de oxígeno** oxygen tent
8 (*Anat*) cavity
9 cámaras (*Med*†) diarrhoea (*sing*), diarrhea (*sing*) (*EEUU*) • MODISMO: • **tener ~s en la lengua** to tell tales (out of school)
SMF camera operator, cameraman/camerawoman
camarada SMF **1** (*en partido político*) comrade
2 (*en el trabajo*) colleague; (*en el colegio*) school friend
3 (= *amigo*) pal*, mate*, buddy (*EEUU**)
camaradería SF (*en partido político*) comradeship; (*entre amigos*) camaraderie, matiness*; (*en deportes*) camaraderie, team spirit
camarata‡ SM waiter
camarera SF (*en hotel*) maid, chambermaid; (*en casa*) parlourmaid
camarero/a SM/F **1** (*en restaurante*) waiter/waitress ▸ **camarero/a principal** head waiter/waitress, maître d'(hôtel)
2 (*Náut*) steward/stewardess; (*Aer*) steward/stewardess, flight attendant (*EEUU*)
SM (*Hist*) chamberlain ▸ **camarero mayor** (*Hist*) royal chamberlain
camareta SF (*Náut*) cabin ▸ **camareta alta** deckhouse
camarico SM (*Cono Sur*) **1** (= *lugar*) favourite place
2 (= *amor*) love affair
camarilla SF **1** [*de presidente etc*] entourage; (*pey*) clique, coterie
2 (*en organización*) faction; (*en partido*) (party) caucus; (*en cuerpo legislativo*) lobby, pressure group
3 (= *cuarto*) small room
camarín SM **1** (*Teat*) dressing room; (= *tocador*) boudoir; (= *cuarto pequeño*) side room
2 (*Rel*) (*para imagen*) chapel; (*para joyas*) *room where jewels etc belonging to an image are kept*
3 (*LAm*) [*de tren*] sleeping compartment; [*de barco*] cabin; [*de ascensor*] lift car, elevator car (*EEUU*)
camarista SMF (*Arg*) member of Court of Appeal
camarógrafo/a SM/F cameraman/camerawoman
camarón SM **1** (*Zool*) shrimp
2 (*CAm*) (= *propina*) tip, gratuity
3 (*And**) (= *traidor*) turncoat • **hacer ~** to change sides, go over to the other side *o* camp
4 (*CAm**) (= *trabajo*) casual *o* occasional work
5 (*Cono Sur*) (= *litera*) bunk (bed)
camaronear ▹ CONJUG 1a VI **1** (*Méx*) (= *pescar camarones*) to go shrimping
2 (*And*) (*Pol*) to change sides
camaronero SM (*And*) kingfisher
camarote SM (*Náut*) cabin ▸ **camarote de lujo** first-class cabin, stateroom
camarotero SM (*LAm*) steward, cabin servant
camaruta* SF bar girl
camastro SM rickety old bed
camastrón ADJ* sly, untrustworthy
SM (*CAm*) (= *cama*) large bed, double bed
camayo SM (*Perú*) (*Agr*) foreman, overseer (*of a country estate*)
cambado ADJ (*And, Caribe, Cono Sur*) bow-legged
cambalache SM **1** (= *trueque*) swap, exchange
2 (*LAm*) (= *tienda*) second-hand shop, junk shop
cambalachear ▹ CONJUG 1a VT to swap, exchange
cambar ▹ CONJUG 1a VT (*Caribe, Cono Sur*) = combar
cámbaro SM crayfish
cambiable ADJ **1** (= *modificable*) changeable
2 (= *intercambiable*) exchangeable (**por** for)
cambiadiscos SM INV record-changer
cambiadizo ADJ changeable
cambiado ADJ **1** (= *diferente*) • **estás muy cambiada desde la última vez que te vi** you've really changed since the last time I saw you
2 (= *intercambiado*) reversed • **sus padres tenían los papeles ~s** the parents' roles were reversed
cambiador SM [*de dinero*] moneychanger; [*de productos*] barterer; (*LAm*) (*Ferro*) pointsman, switchman (*EEUU*)
cambiante ADJ (= *variable*) [*situación*] changing; [*tiempo, viento*] changeable; [*persona, carácter*] moody • **vivimos en un mundo ~** we live in an ever-changing world
SMF (= *cambista*) moneychanger
SM **1** (= *tela*) iridescent fabric
2 cambiantes (*en nácar, tela*) changing colours, iridescence (*sing*)
cambiar ▹ CONJUG 1b VT **1** (= *modificar*) to change • **tendremos que ~ el color de nuestro logotipo** we'll need to change the colour of our logo • **eso no cambia mucho las cosas** that doesn't change things much
2 (= *intercambiar*) to exchange, swap* • **te cambio el rotulador verde por el rojo** I'll exchange my green pen for that red one, I'll swap you the green pen for the red one* • **¿me cambias el sitio?** can we change places?, can we swap places?*
3 (= *reemplazar*) to change • **¿les has cambiado el agua a los peces?** have you changed the water in the fish tank? • **ha ido a ~le los pañales al niño** she's gone to change the baby's nappy • **¿me lo puede ~ por otra talla?** could I change *o* exchange this for another size?
4 (= *trasladar*) to move • **van a ~ la oficina al piso de arriba** they are going to move the office up a floor • **nos van a ~ de aula** they are moving us to another classroom
5 (*Econ, Com*) to change • **tengo que ~ 800 euros en** *o* (*LAm*) **a libras** I have to change 800 euros into pounds • **¿tienes para ~me 50 euros?** have you got change for a 50-euro note?
VI **1** (= *volverse diferente*) [*persona, situación*] to change; [*voz*] to break • **desde que te fuiste nada ha cambiado** nothing has changed since you left • **nada lo hará ~** nothing will make him change • **si es así, la cosa cambia**

C

if it's true, that changes things, well that's a different story then • **con doce años ya le había cambiado la voz** his voice had already broken at the age of twelve
2 • ~ **de** [+ *actitud, canal, dirección*] to change; [+ *casa*] to move • **cuando no le interesa algo, cambia de tema** whenever he isn't interested in something, he changes the subject • **su vida cambió de rumbo 180 grados** the course of her life changed completely • **tú lo que necesitas es ~ de aires** what you need is a change of scene • ~ **de dueño** to change hands • ~ **de idea** *u* **opinión** to change one's mind • ~ **para mejor/peor** to change for the better/worse; ▹ **camisa, tercio**
3 (*Transportes*) to change • **tienes que ~ en King's Cross** you have to change at King's Cross
4 (*Radio*) • **¡cambio!** over! • **¡cambio y corto!** • **¡cambio y fuera!** over and out!
(VPR) **cambiarse 1** [*persona*] to change, get changed • **me cambio y estoy lista** I'll just change *o* I'll just get changed and then I'll be ready
2 [+ *peinado, ropa, camisa*] to change • **¿te has cambiado el peinado?** have you changed your hairstyle?
3 • **~se de algo** to change sth • **llovió tanto que tuve que ~me de chaqueta** it rained so much that I had to change jackets • **para ~se de médico hay que rellenar este formulario** to change doctors you need to fill in this form • **~se de casa** to move house
4 (= *intercambiarse*) to exchange, swap* • **¿nos cambiamos las camisetas?** shall we exchange *o* swap* T-shirts? • **siempre están cambiándose la ropa** they are always borrowing each other's clothes • **~se por algn** to change places with sb, swap places with sb* • **no me ~ía por ella** I wouldn't want to swap* *o* change places with her
cambiario (ADJ) (*Econ*) exchange (*antes de s*) • **estabilidad cambiaria** stability of *o* in the exchange rate • **liberalización cambiaria** freeing of exchange controls *o* rates *etc*
cambiavía (SM) (*Caribe, Méx*) (*Ferro*)
1 (= *persona*) pointsman, switchman (*EEUU*)
2 (= *agujas*) points (*pl*), switch (*EEUU*)
cambiazo* (SM) (*Com*) switch • **dar el ~** to switch the goods • **dar el ~ a algn** to switch the goods on sb
cambio (SM) **1** (= *variación*) change • **ha habido un ~ de planes** there has been a change of plan • **el matrimonio supuso un ~ radical en mi vida** marriage meant a complete change in my life • **el entrenador ha hecho ya tres ~s en lo que va de partido** the coach has already made three substitutions *o* changes so far in the match • **estamos en la época de ~ entre el otoño y el invierno** we are in the changeover period between autumn and winter • **necesito un ~ de aires** I need a change of scene • **siempre nos veíamos durante el ~ de clase** we always used to meet in the break between classes • **un ~ para mejor/peor** a change for the better/worse ▸ **cambio climático** climatic change ▸ **cambio de agujas** (*Ferro*) points junction, switch junction (*EEUU*) ▸ **cambio de domicilio** change of address ▸ **cambio de gobierno** (*completo*) change of government; (*parcial*) reshuffle ▸ **cambio de guardia** changing of the guard ▸ **cambio de impresiones** exchange of views ▸ **cambio de la marea** turn of the tide ▸ **cambio de línea** (*Inform*) line feed ▸ **cambio de marchas** (= *acción*) gear change; (= *mecanismo*) gear stick, gearshift (*EEUU*) • **hacer el ~ de marchas** to change gear • **un coche con ~ automático de marchas** a car with an automatic gearbox ▸ **cambio de opinión** change of opinion, turn in opinion ▸ **cambio de página** (*Inform*) form feed ▸ **cambio de pareja** change of partners (*in dancing*) ▸ **cambio de rasante** • **prohibido adelantar en un ~ de rasante** no overtaking on the brow of a hill ▸ **cambio de sentido** change of direction ▸ **cambio de sexo** sex change ▸ **cambio de tercio** (*Taur*) change of stage (*in a bullfight*) • **se produjo un ~ de tercio en la conversación** the conversation changed direction *o* subject ▸ **cambio de velocidades** = **cambio de marchas** ▸ **cambio de vía** (*Ferro*) points (*pl*), switches (*pl*) (*EEUU*) • **hacer el ~ de vía** to go through the points *o* switches ▸ **cambio genético** genetic change
2 (= *intercambio*) exchange, swap* • **hicimos un ~ de coche** we exchanged cars, we swapped cars* • **salimos ganando con el ~** the exchange worked out in our favour
3 (*Econ*) **a** (= *dinero suelto*) change • **no tengo ~ para el teléfono** I don't have any change for the phone • **¿tienes ~ de 50 euros?** do you have change for 50 euros?, can you change 50 euros? • **quédese con el ~** keep the change • **te han dado mal el ~** they've given you the wrong change
b [*de moneda extranjera*] (= *tipo*) exchange rate • **son 40 dólares al ~** that is 40 dollars at the current exchange rate • **al ~ del mes de febrero** at the February exchange rate • **"Cambio"** "Bureau de Change", "Change" ▸ **cambio a término** forward exchange ▸ **cambio de divisas** foreign exchange
4 • **a ~** in return, in exchange • **lo ganó todo sin ceder nada a ~** he won it all without giving anything in return • **"admitimos su coche usado a ~"** "cars taken in part exchange", "trade-ins accepted" • **a ~ de** in return for, in exchange for • **reclamaba dinero a ~ de su silencio** he demanded money in return *o* exchange for keeping quiet (about it)
5 • **en ~** whereas • **yo nunca llego a tiempo, en ~ ella es muy puntual** I never arrive on time, whereas she is very punctual • **¿pero qué ha sucedido en ~?** but instead, what has happened?
cambista (SMF) money changer
Camboya (SF) Cambodia, Kampuchea
camboyano/a (ADJ), (SM/F) Cambodian, Kampuchean
cambray (SM) cambric
cambrón (SM) (= *espino*) buckthorn; (= *zarza*) bramble
cambrona* (SF) (*Cono Sur*) tough cotton cloth
cambucho (SM) (*Cono Sur*) (= *cono*) paper cone; (= *cesta*) straw basket for waste paper *o* dirty clothes; (= *tapa*) straw cover (*for a bottle*); (= *cuartucho*) miserable little room
cambujo/a (*CAm, Méx*) (ADJ) [*animal*] black; [*persona*] dark, swarthy
(SM/F) mestizo
cambullón* (SM) (*LAm*) (= *estafa*) swindle; (= *compló*) plot, intrigue; (= *cambio*) swap, exchange
cambur (SM) (*Ven*) **1** (= *plátano*) banana; (= *árbol*) banana tree
2* (= *prebenda*) government post, soft job, cushy number*; (= *dinero*) windfall
3 (= *funcionario*) public servant, state employee
cambuto (ADJ) (*Perú*) (= *pequeño*) small, squat; (= *gordito*) chubby
camelar ▹ CONJUG 1a (VT) **1** (= *persuadir*) to cajole, win over • **tener camelado a algn** to have sb wrapped round one's little finger
2 [+ *mujer*] (= *flirtear*) to flirt with, make up to*; (= *conquistar*) to attract
3 (*Méx*) (= *mirar*) to look into, look towards *etc*; (= *espiar*) to spy on; (= *perseguir*) to pursue, hound
camelia (SF) camellia
camelista (SMF) **1** (= *cuentista*) joker
2 (= *halagador*) flatterer, bootlicker*
camellar* ▹ CONJUG 1a (VI) (*Caribe*) to work (hard)
camellear‡ ▹ CONJUG 1a (VI) to push drugs, be a pusher
camelleo‡ (SM) drug-pushing
camellero (SM) camel driver
camello (SM) **1** (*Zool*) camel ▸ **camello bactriano** Bactrian camel
2‡ (= *traficante*) dealer*, pusher*
3 (*Náut*) camel
camellón (SM) **1** (*Méx*) (*Aut*) central reserve *o* reservation, median strip (*EEUU*)
2 (= *bebedero*) drinking trough
3 (*Agr*) ridge (*between furrows*)
camelo* (SM) **1** (= *timo*) swindle • **¡esto es un ~!** it's all a swindle! • **me huele a ~** it smells fishy*, there's something funny going on here
2 (= *mentira*) humbug • **dar ~ a algn** (= *reírse*) to make fun of sb; (= *engañar*) to put one over on sb • **a mí me da que es un ~** I don't believe a word of it*
3 (= *flirteo*) flirtation; (= *coba*) blarney
cameo (SM) cameo appearance
camerino (SM) (*Teat*) dressing room; (*Méx*) (*Ferro*) roomette
camero (ADJ) **1** [*colcha, sábana*] for a three-quarter bed • **cama camera** three-quarter bed
2 (*Caribe*) (= *grande*) big
Camerún (SM) Cameroon
camerunés/esa (ADJ) Cameroonian
(SM/F) Cameroonian
camilla (SF) (*Med*) stretcher; (= *sofá*) couch, sofa; (= *cuna*) cot; (= *mesa*) table with a heater underneath
camillero/a (SM/F) stretcher-bearer
camilucho (SM) (*Cono Sur, Méx*) Indian day labourer
caminante (SMF) (= *viajero*) traveller, traveler (*EEUU*), wayfarer (*liter*); (*a pie*) walker
caminar ▹ CONJUG 1a (VI) **1** (= *andar*) to walk • **iban caminando por el parque** they were walking in the park • **fuimos caminando a casa de María** we walked to María's house • **hemos venido caminando** we walked (here), we came on foot • **salen a ~ después de comer** they go (out) for a walk after lunch • **~ sin rumbo** to walk *o* wander about aimlessly
2 (= *progresar*) to move • **el cortejo caminaba en silencio** the funeral procession was moving silently • **caminamos hacia una sociedad sin clases** we are moving towards a classless society
3 (*LAm*) (= *funcionar*) to work • **esto no camina** this doesn't work
(VT) to walk • **caminamos cuatro kilómetros** we walked four kilometres
caminata (SF) (= *paseo largo*) long walk; (*campestre*) hike, ramble
caminero (ADJ) • **peón ~** navvy, road labourer, road laborer (*EEUU*)
(SM) (*LAm*) road builder
caminito (SM) ▸ **caminito de rosas** (*fig*) primrose path
camino (SM) **1** (*sin asfaltar*) track; (= *sendero*) path; (= *carretera*) road • **un ~ de montaña** a mountain path • **~ de tierra** dirt track • **~ sin firme** unsurfaced road • MODISMO: • **todos los ~s conducen a Roma** all roads lead to Rome ▸ **Caminos, Canales y Puertos** (*Univ*)

Civil Engineering ▸ **camino de acceso** access road ▸ **camino de Damasco** road to Damascus ▸ **camino de entrada** access road ▸ **camino de herradura** bridle path ▸ **camino de ingresos, camino de peaje** toll road ▸ **camino de rosas** • **la vida no es ningún ~ de rosas** life's no bed of roses ▸ **Camino de Santiago** *pilgrims' route to Santiago de Compostela*, Way of St James ▸ **camino de sirga** towpath ▸ **camino forestal** forest track; (*para paseos*) forest trail ▸ **camino francés** (*Hist*) = **Camino de Santiago** ▸ **camino real** highroad (*tb fig*) ▸ **camino trillado** • **~s turísticos no trillados** tourist routes that are off the beaten track • **experimentan con nuevas técnicas, huyen de los ~s trillados** they are experimenting with new techniques and avoiding conventional approaches *o* the well-trodden paths • **este escritor ha recorrido los ~s trillados de sus antecesores** this writer has been down the well-trodden paths followed by his predecessors ▸ **camino vecinal** minor road

2 (= *ruta*) **a** (*lit*) way, route; (= *viaje*) journey • **volvimos por el ~ más corto** we took the shortest way *o* route back • **¿sabes el ~ a su casa?** do you know the way to his house? • **es mucho ~** it's a long way • **está a varios días de ~** it's several days' journey away • **después de tres horas de ~** after travelling for three hours • **nos quedan 20 kms de ~** we still have 20 kms to go • **¿cuánto ~ hay de aquí a San José?** how far is it from here to San José? • **~ de Lima** on the way to Lima • **iba ~ de Nueva York** I was on my way to New York • **abrirse ~ entre la multitud** to make one's way through the crowd • **de ~ a**: • **lo puedo recoger de ~ al trabajo** I can collect it on my way to work • **la farmacia me queda de ~** the chemist's is on my way • **echar ~ adelante** to strike out • **en el ~** on the way, en route • **nos encontramos en el ~ a Zaragoza** we met on the way to Zaragoza • **tienen dos niños, y otro en ~** they have two children, and another on the way • **ponerse en ~** to set out *o* off • **a medio ~** halfway (there) • **a medio ~ paramos para comer** halfway there, we stopped to eat • **se quedaron a mitad de ~** they only got halfway (there) • **a mitad de ~ entre Dublín y la frontera** halfway between Dublin and the border • **la verdad está a mitad de ~ entre las dos posturas** the truth is somewhere between the two views

b (*fig*) (= *medio*) path, course • **es el ~ a la fama** it's the path to fame • **es el ~ al desastre** it's the road to ruin • **el ~ a seguir**: • **yo te explico el ~ a seguir** I'll tell you the way *o* route • **me indicaron el ~ a seguir para resolver el problema** they showed me what needed to be done to solve the problem • **censurar estos programas no es el ~ a seguir** censoring these programmes isn't the solution *o* the right thing to do • MODISMOS: • **abrirse ~ en la vida** to get ahead (in life) • **allanar el ~**: • **eso sería allanar el ~ a sus adversarios** that would make things easy for their rivals • **los nervios de su rival le allanaron el ~** her opponent's nerves made it easy for her • **errar el ~** to lose one's way • **estar en ~** to be on the way • **estamos en ~ de solucionar el problema** we're on the way to solving the problem • **está en ~ de desaparecer** it's on its way out • **ir ~ de**: • **va ~ de convertirse en un gran centro financiero** it is on its way to becoming a major financial centre • **vamos ~ del desastre** we are heading for disaster • **ir por buen ~** to be on the right track • **traer a algn por buen ~** (= *orientar*) to put sb on the right track *o* road; (= *desengañar*) to set sb straight • **ir por mal ~** to be on the wrong track • **las cosas van por buen ~** things are going well • **llevar a algn por mal ~** to lead sb astray • **quedarse en el ~**: • **varios corredores se quedaron en el ~** several runners didn't make it to the end • **un 70% sacó el diploma y el resto se quedó en el ~** 70 per cent of them got the diploma, the rest didn't make it • **ir por su ~** to go one's own sweet way • **en vez de seguir las normas él fue por su ~** instead of following the rules he just went his own sweet way *o* did his own thing • **no me fijo en mis rivales, yo sigo por mi ~** I don't take any notice of what my rivals are doing, I just do my own thing • **tirar por el ~ de en medio** to take the middle way

3 (*Inform*) path

4 (*And, Cono Sur*) (= *alfombra, tapete*) runner, strip of carpet *o* matting ▸ **camino de mesa** table runner

> **CAMINO DE SANTIAGO**
>
> The **Camino de Santiago** is a medieval pilgrim route stretching from the Pyrenees to Santiago de Compostela in northwest Spain, where tradition has it that the body of Saint James the Apostle (Spain's patron saint) is buried. Those who had made the long, dangerous journey returned proudly wearing on their hat or cloak the **venera** or **concha** (scallop shell) traditionally associated with this pilgrimage - Saint James' body had reportedly been found covered in scallops. Today this symbolic shell can still be seen all along the **Camino de Santiago**, carved on ancient buildings and painted on modern-day road signs marking the historic route for the benefit of tourists and pilgrims.
>
> In astronomy the **Camino de Santiago** is another name for the **Vía Láctea** (Milky Way), hence the title of Buñuel's famous satirical film about the route to Compostela.

camión (SM) (*Aut*) lorry, truck (*esp EEUU*); [*de reparto*] van; [*de caballos*] heavy wagon, dray; (*Méx*) bus; (= *carga*) lorryload, truckload (*esp EEUU*) • **dos camiones de alimentos** two lorryloads of food • **estar como un ~*** to be a smasher*, be gorgeous ▸ **camión articulado** articulated lorry, trailer truck (EEUU) ▸ **camión blindado** armoured truck, armored truck (EEUU) ▸ **camión bomba** lorry bomb, truck bomb ▸ **camión cisterna** tanker, tank wagon ▸ **camión de agua** water cart, water wagon ▸ **camión de bomberos** fire engine ▸ **camión de caja a bajo nivel** low loader ▸ **camión de carga** haulage truck ▸ **camión de la basura** dustcart, refuse lorry, garbage truck (EEUU) ▸ **camión de mudanzas** removal van, moving van (EEUU) ▸ **camión de reparto** delivery van ▸ **camión de riego** water cart, water wagon ▸ **camión de volteo** (*Méx*) dump truck ▸ **camión frigorífico** refrigerator lorry, refrigerated truck ▸ **camión ganadero** cattle truck ▸ **camión vivienda** camper van ▸ **camión volquete** dump truck, tipper truck

camionaje (SM) haulage, trucking (EEUU)

camionero/a (SM/F) **1** lorry driver, truck driver (EEUU)
2 (*Méx*) (*en autobús*) bus driver

camioneta (SF) (= *camión*) van, light truck; (= *coche*) estate car, station wagon (EEUU); (*CAm*) (= *autobús*) bus; (*Caribe*) minibus ▸ **camioneta de reparto** delivery van ▸ **camioneta detectora** detector van ▸ **camioneta de tina** (*CAm*) pick-up (truck)

camión-grúa (SM) (PL: **camiones-grúa**) tow truck, towing vehicle

camionista (SM) = camionero

camión-tanque (SM) (PL: **camiones-tanque**) tanker

camisa (SF) **1** (= *prenda*) shirt • MODISMOS: • **cambiar de ~** to change sides • **jugarse hasta la ~** to put one's shirt on it*, bet one's last penny • **no llegarle a algn la ~ al cuerpo**: • **no le llegaba la ~ al cuerpo** he was simply terrified • **meterse en ~ de once varas** to get into it way over one's head • **perder hasta la ~** to lose everything, lose the shirt off one's back ▸ **camisa de dormir** nightdress ▸ **camisa de fuerza** straitjacket; ▹ **manga**
2 (*LAm*) garment, article of clothing
3 (= *piel*) [*de serpiente*] slough; [*de guisante, trigo*] skin
4 (*Mec*) case, casing ▸ **camisa de agua** water jacket ▸ **camisa de gas** gas mantle
5 [*de libro*] dust jacket

camisería (SF) (= *tienda*) outfitter's; (= *taller*) shirtmaker's

camisero (ADJ) [*blusa, vestido*] shirt (*antes de s*)
(SM) (*que confecciona*) shirt maker; (= *vendedor*) outfitter

camiseta (SF) **1** (*interior*) vest, singlet, undershirt (EEUU); (*exterior*) T-shirt • **una ~ de algodón** a cotton vest • **una ~ sin mangas** a sleeveless vest • **una ~ de tirantes** a vest • MODISMO: • **ponerse la ~** (*Cono Sur**) to roll up one's sleeves, put one's back into it
2 (*Dep*) shirt, jersey, strip • **la ~ de la selección nacional** the national team shirt *o* jersey • MODISMO: • **sudar la ~*** to sweat blood ▸ **camiseta de deporte** sports shirt, sports jersey
3 (*LAm*) nightdress

camisilla (SF) (*Caribe, Cono Sur*) = **camiseta**

camisola (SF) (*Méx*) sports shirt

camisolín (SM) stiff shirt front, dickey

camisón (SM) [*de mujer*] nightdress, nightgown; [*de hombre*] nightshirt

camita[1] (ADJ), **camítico** (ADJ) (*de Cam*) Hamitic

camita[2] (SF) (= *cama*) small bed, cot

camomila (SF) camomile

camón (SM) (= *cama grande*) big bed; (*Arquit*) oriel window ▸ **camón de vidrios** glass partition

camorra (SF) fight, row, set-to* • **armar ~** to kick up a row • **buscar ~** to go looking for trouble

camorrear* ▹ CONJUG 1a (VI) (*CAm, Cono Sur*) to have a row

camorrero/a (ADJ), (SM/F) = **camorrista**

camorrista (ADJ) rowdy, troublemaking
(SMF) rowdy, hooligan

camotal (SM) (*LAm*) sweet potato field *o* plot

camote (SM) **1** (*LAm*) (= *batata*) sweet potato; (*Méx*) (= *bulbo*) tuber, bulb
2 (*CAm, Cono Sur*) (*Med*) bump, swelling
3 (*Cono Sur*) (= *piedra*) large stone
4 (*Cono Sur*) (= *persona*) bore
5 (*CAm*) [*de pierna*] calf
6 (*CAm**) (= *molestia*) nuisance, bother
7 (*LAm*) (= *amor*) love; (= *enamoramiento*) crush* • **tener un ~ con algn** to have a crush on sb*
8 (*And, Cono Sur**) (= *amante*) lover, sweetheart
9 (*Cono Sur*) (= *mentirilla*) fib
10 (*And, Cono Sur*) (= *tonto*) fool
11 (*LAm**) • **poner a algn como ~** to give sb a telling off* • MODISMO: • **tragar ~** (= *tener miedo*) to have one's heart in one's mouth; (= *balbucir*) to stammer

camotear ▹ CONJUG 1a (VI) **1** (*Méx*) (= *vagar*) to wander about aimlessly
2 (*CAm*) (= *molestar*) to be a nuisance, cause trouble
(VT) **1** (*Cono Sur*) (= *estafar*) to rob, fleece*;

(= *engañar*) to take for a ride*
2 (*CAm*) (= *molestar*) to annoy
campa SF open field, open space
ADJ INV • **tierra ~** treeless land
campal ADJ • **batalla ~** pitched battle
campamentista SMF camper
campamento SM camp, encampment
• **~ para prisioneros** prison camp • **~ de refugiados** refugee camp ▸ **campamento de base** base camp ▸ **campamento de trabajo** labour *o* (*EEUU*) labor camp ▸ **campamento de verano** holiday camp
campana SF **1** [*de iglesia, puerta*] bell; [*de orquesta*] bell, chime • **a ~ tañida** • **a toque de ~** to the sound of bells • MODISMOS: • **echar** *o* **lanzar las ~s a vuelo** to celebrate • **aún es pronto para echar las ~s al vuelo** it's still too early to celebrate *o* to start spreading the good news • **estar ~** (*Caribe**) to be fine • **hacer ~(s)*** to play truant • **oír ~s (y no saber de dónde vienen)** not to have a clue
2 (*Téc*) [*de la chimenea*] hood ▸ **campana de humos, campana extractora** extractor hood
3 (*Buceo*) ▸ **campana de buzo, campana de inmersión** diving bell
4 (*Cono Sur*) (= *campo*) country(side)
SMF (*LAm**) (= *vigilante*) look-out • **hacer de ~** to keep watch
campanada SF **1** [*de campana*] stroke, peal
2 (= *escándalo*) scandal, sensation • **detener al Ministro sería una ~ tremenda** arresting the Minister would cause a tremendous scandal *o* stir • **dar la ~** to cause (quite) a stir
campanario SM **1** [*de iglesia etc*] belfry, bell tower, church tower
2 (*pey*) • **de ~** mean, narrow-minded
• **espíritu de ~** parochial *o* parish-pump attitude
campanazo SM **1** = campanada
2 (*And*) (= *advertencia*) warning
campaneado ADJ much talked-of
campanear ▹ CONJUG 1a VI **1** (*Mús*) to ring the bells
2 (*LAm**) [*ladrón*] to keep watch
campaneo SM pealing, chiming
campanero SM (*Téc*) bell founder; (*Mús*) bell ringer
campaniforme ADJ bell-shaped
campanilla SF **1** (= *campana*) small bell, handbell; (*eléctrica*) bell • **de (muchas) ~s** high-class, grand
2 (= *burbuja*) bubble
3 (*Anat*) uvula
4 (*Cos*) tassel
5 (*Bot*) bellflower, campanula ▸ **campanilla blanca, campanilla de febrero** snowdrop
campanillazo SM loud ring, sudden ring
campanillear ▹ CONJUG 1a VI to ring, tinkle
campanilleo SM ringing, tinkling
campanología SF campanology, bell-ringing
campanólogo/a SM/F campanologist, bell-ringer
campante ADJ **1** (= *despreocupado*) • **siguió tan ~** he went on as if nothing had happened *o* without batting an eyelid • **allí estaba tan ~** there he sat as cool as a cucumber
2 (= *destacado*) outstanding
campanudo ADJ **1** [*objeto*] bell-shaped; [*falda*] wide, flared
2 [*estilo*] high-flown, bombastic, windy*; [*orador*] pompous • **dijo ~** he said pompously
campánula SF bellflower, campanula
▸ **campánula azul** bluebell
campaña SF **1** (*Pol, Com*) campaign • **una ~ antidroga** an anti-drugs campaign, a campaign against drugs • **una ~ de recogida de firmas** a petition • **hacer ~** to campaign
▸ **campaña de descrédito, campaña de desprestigio** smear campaign ▸ **campaña de imagen** image campaign ▸ **campaña de protesta** protest campaign ▸ **campaña de publicidad** advertising campaign
▸ **campaña de ventas** sales campaign
▸ **campaña electoral** election campaign
▸ **campaña publicitaria** advertising campaign
2 (*Mil*) campaign • **la ~ de Rusia** the Russian campaign; ▹ **hospital, tienda, traje²**
3 (= *campo*) countryside; (= *llano*) plain
campañol SM vole
campar ▹ CONJUG 1a VI **1** (*Mil etc*) to camp
2 (= *sobresalir*) to stand out, excel • **~ por sus respetos** to please o.s.
campear ▹ CONJUG 1a VI **1** (*Agr*) [*ganado*] to go to graze, go out to pasture; [*persona*] to work in the fields
2 (*Bot*) to show green
3 (*Mil*) to reconnoitre; (*LAm*) to scour the countryside
4 • **ir campeando*** to carry on, keep going
5 (*LAm*) (= *ir de camping*) to camp, go camping
6 (*And*) (= *atravesar*) to make one's way through
7 (*And*) (= *fardar*) to bluster
campechana SF **1** (*Caribe, Méx*) (= *bebida*) cocktail
2 (*Méx*) [*de mariscos*] seafood cocktail
campechanería SF, **campechanía** SF (= *cordialidad*) good nature, cheerfulness; (= *franqueza*) frankness, openness; (= *generosidad*) generosity
campechano ADJ **1** (= *cordial*) good-natured, cheerful, genial; (= *franco*) frank, open; (= *generoso*) generous; (= *amigable*) comradely
2 (*Caribe**) (= *campesino*) peasant (*antes de s*)
campeón/ona SM/F champion
▸ **campeón/ona de venta** best seller
campeonar ▹ CONJUG 1a VI to win the championship, emerge as champion
campeonato SM **1** (*Dep*) championship
• **el ~ de Liga** the League championship • **los ~s de pista cubierta** the indoor championships
2 (*Esp**) • **de ~: se armó una bronca de ~** there was one hell of an argument* • **se agarra unas borracheras de ~** he gets incredibly *o* unbelievably drunk, he gets blind drunk*
campeonísimo/a SM/F undisputed champion
campera SF (*Arg*) windcheater, bomber jacket* ▸ **campera de duvet** (*Cono Sur*) quilted jacket
campero ADJ **1** (= *al descubierto*) unsheltered, (out) in the open • **fiesta campera** open-air party • **ganado ~** stock that sleeps out in the open
2 (*LAm*) [*persona*] knowledgeable about the countryside; (= *experto en agricultura*) expert in farming matters
3 [*animal*] trained to travel in difficult country, sure-footed
SM (*Col*) (= *vehículo*) four-wheel drive (vehicle)
camperuso/a* (*Caribe*) ADJ **1** (= *rural*) rural, rustic
2 (= *huraño*) reserved, stand-offish
SM/F (= *campesino*) peasant
campesinado SM peasantry, peasants (*pl*)
campesino/a ADJ [*población*] rural; [*familia, revuelta*] peasant (*antes de s*) • **una organización campesina** an organization representing peasant farmers • **siempre ocultó su origen ~** she always concealed her rustic *o* peasant origins • **la vida campesina** country life, rural life
SM/F **1** (= *persona del campo*) country person
2 (= *labrador*) farmer; (= *labrador pobre*) peasant
3 (*And*) (= *indio*) Indian
campestre ADJ **1** country (*antes de s*), rural
2 (*Bot*) wild
camping ['kampin] SM (PL: **campings** ['kampin]) **1** (= *actividad*) camping • **estar** *o* **ir de ~** to go camping • **hacer ~** to go camping
2 (= *lugar*) campsite, campground (*EEUU*)
campiña SF (= *campo*) countryside, open country; (*cultivado*) flat stretch of farmland, large area of cultivated land
campirano/a SM/F (*LAm*) **1** (= *campesino*) peasant; (*pey*) rustic, country bumpkin, hick (*EEUU**)
2 (*Agr*) (= *perito*) expert in farming matters; (= *guía*) guide, pathfinder; (= *jinete*) skilled horseman; (= *ganadero*) stockbreeding expert
campiruso/a ADJ, SM/F (*Caribe*) = camperuso
campista¹ SMF camper
campista² ADJ **1** (*CAm, Caribe*) rural, country (*antes de s*)
2 (*LAm*) = **campero**
SM (*CAm*) herdsman, cattleman, herder (*EEUU*)
campisto ADJ (*CAm*) rural, country (*antes de s*)
SM **1** (*CAm*) (= *campesino*) peasant
2 (*CAm*) (*Agr*) (= *veterinario*) amateur vet
campo SM **1** (= *terreno no urbano*) country
• **viven en el ~** they live in the country *o* countryside • **los domingos salimos al ~** on Sundays we go out to the country • **el ~ está precioso** the countryside looks beautiful
• **la gente del ~** country people *o* folk • **a ~ raso** out in the open ▸ **campo a través** cross-country • **campeonato de ~ a través** cross-country championship • **los tres prisioneros huyeron ~ a través** the three prisoners fled cross-country
2 (*Agr*) (*para cultivar*) • **un ~ de trigo** a wheat field • **~s de amapolas** poppy fields • **los obreros del ~** farm workers, agricultural workers • **los productos del ~** farm produce, country produce • **trabajar en el ~** to work the land ▸ **campo de cultivo** (*lit*) farm land; (*fig*) breeding ground
3 (*Dep*) (= *estadio*) ground; (= *cancha*) pitch, field (*EEUU*) • **jugaron en el ~ del Barcelona** they played at Barcelona's ground • **el portero tuvo que abandonar el ~** the goalkeeper had to leave the pitch *o* field • **el equipo perdió en su ~** the team lost at home
▸ **campo de deportes** sports ground
▸ **campo de fútbol** football pitch ▸ **campo de golf** golf course ▸ **campo de juego** playing field
4 (= *espacio delimitado*) ▸ **campo de aterrizaje** landing field ▸ **Campo de Gibraltar** *Spanish territory around the border with Gibraltar* ▸ **campo de minas** minefield ▸ **campo de tiro** firing range • **estar dentro del ~ de tiro de algn** to be in sb's firing range ▸ **campo petrolífero** oilfield ▸ **campo santo** cemetery, churchyard ▸ **Campos Elíseos** (*en París*) Champs Elysées; (*Mit*) Elysian Fields
5 (*Mil*) (= *campamento*) camp • **levantar el ~** (*Mil*) to break camp, strike camp; (= *irse*) to make tracks* • MODISMO: • **dejar el ~ libre** to leave the field open ▸ **campo de aviación** airfield, airdrome (*EEUU*) ▸ **campo de batalla** battlefield • **quedar en el ~ de batalla** to fall in battle ▸ **campo de concentración** concentration camp
▸ **campo de ejercicios** exercise ground
▸ **campo de entrenamiento** training camp
▸ **campo de exterminio** extermination

camp ▸ **campo de maniobras** training camp ▸ **campo de pruebas** testing ground ▸ **campo de refugiados** refugee camp ▸ **campo de trabajo** [*de castigo*] labour *o* (*EEUU*) labor camp; [*de vacaciones*] work camp
6 (= *grupo*) field ▸ **campo alfanumérico** alphanumeric field ▸ **campo léxico** lexical field ▸ **campo numérico** numeric field ▸ **campo semántico** semantic field
7 (= *ámbito*) field • **el ~ de las ciencias** the field of science • **investigación de ~** field investigation ▸ **campo de acción, campo de actuación** scope, room for manoeuvre *o* (*EEUU*) maneuver ▸ **campo de investigación** field of investigation ▸ **campo gravitatorio** gravity field, field of gravity ▸ **campo magnético** magnetic field ▸ **campo visual** field of vision, visual field; ▹ **trabajo**
8 (*Arte*) background
9 (*Heráldica*) field
10 (*And*) (= *estancia*) farm, ranch; (*Cono Sur*) (= *tierra pobre*) barren land; (*And, Cono Sur*) (*Min*) mining concession
11 (*LAm*) (= *espacio*) space, room • **no hay ~** there's no room *o* space

camposantero SM cemetery official

camposanto SM churchyard, graveyard, cemetery

Campsa SF ABR (*Esp*) = **Compañía Arrendataria de Monopolio de Petróleos, S.A.**

campus SM INV (*Univ*) campus

campusano, campusio, campuso SM (*CAm*) peasant

camuesa SF pippin, dessert apple

camueso SM **1** (*Bot*) apple tree
2* (= *tonto*) dolt, blockhead*, clod (*EEUU**)

camuflado ADJ camouflaged; [*coche policial*] unmarked

camuflaje SM camouflage

camuflar ▹ CONJUG 1a VT to camouflage

can SM **1** (*hum*) (= *perro*) dog, mutt*, pooch*
2 (*Mil*) trigger
3 (*Arquit*) corbel

cana¹ SF (*tb* **canas**) white *o* grey *o* (*EEUU*) gray hair • MODISMOS: • **echar una ~ al aire*** to let one's hair down • **faltar a las ~s** to show a lack of respect for one's elders • **peinar ~s** to be getting on

cana² (*LAm**) SF **1** (= *cárcel*) jail; (= *celda*) prison cell • **caer en ~** to land in jail
2 (= *policía*) police
SM (= *policía*) policeman

canabis SM cannabis

canaca SMF **1** (*And, Cono Sur***) (= *chino*) Chink**, Chinese
2 (*Cono Sur*) (= *dueño*) brothel-keeper; (= *burdel*) brothel

Canadá SM • **el ~** Canada

canadiense ADJ, SMF Canadian
SM (*tb* **chaqueta canadiense**) lumber jacket

canal SM **1** (*Náut, Geog*) (*natural*) channel; (*artificial*) canal • **Canal de la Mancha** English Channel • **Canal de Panamá** Panama Canal ▸ **Canal de Suez** Suez Canal
2 (*Agr, Téc*) (= *conducto*) channel ▸ **canal de desagüe** drain ▸ **canal de drenaje** drainage channel ▸ **canal de riego** irrigation channel
3 (*Anat*) canal, tract ▸ **canal del parto** birth canal ▸ **canal digestivo** digestive tract
4 (*TV*) channel • **no cambies de ~** don't change *o* switch channels ▸ **canal autonómico** *television channel of an autonomous region* ▸ **canal de pago** pay channel, subscription channel ▸ **canal de televentas** shopping channel ▸ **canal de televisión** television channel ▸ **canal por cable** cable channel ▸ **canal temático** thematic channel, theme channel ▸ **canal vía satélite** satellite channel
5 (= *medio*) channel • **el problema se resolvió por los ~es habituales** the problem was resolved through the usual channels ▸ **canal de chat** (*Internet*) chat room ▸ **canal de distribución** distribution channel ▸ **canales de comunicación** channels of communication, communication channels
6 (*Caribe*) (*Aut*) lane
SF **1** (*Téc*) pipe, conduit ▸ **canal maestra** main pipe
2 (*Arquit*) [*de columna*] groove • **~es** fluting (*sing*)
3 (*Agr*) dressed carcass • **peso en ~** dressed weight

canaladura SF = **acanaladura**

canalé SM • **jersey de ~** ribbed sweater

canaleta SF (*Cono Sur*) (= *canalón*) gutter (*on roof*); (= *tubería*) pipe, conduit

canalete SM paddle

canalización SF **1** [*de un río*] canalization
2 [*de inversiones etc*] channelling, channeling (*EEUU*)
3 (*Téc*) piping; (*Elec*) wiring; [*de gas etc*] mains (*pl*); (*LAm*) [*de cloacas*] sewerage system, drains

canalizar ▹ CONJUG 1f VT **1** [+ *río*] to canalize; [+ *agua*] to harness; (*por tubería*) to pipe; [+ *aguas de riego*] to channel
2 [+ *inversiones etc*] to channel, direct
3 (*Elec*) [+ *impulso, mensaje*] to carry

canalizo SM navigable channel

canalla* SMF swine* • **¡canalla!** you swine!
SF rabble, riffraff • **la ~ periodística** *o* **de la prensa** the press mob*

canallada SF (= *hecho*) dirty trick; (= *dicho*) nasty remark, vile thing to say

canallesco ADJ mean, despicable • **diversión canallesca** low form of amusement

canalón SM **1** (= *cañería*) (*en el tejado*) gutter, guttering; (= *bajante*) drainpipe
2 canalones (*Culin*) cannelloni

canana SF **1** (*Mil*) cartridge belt
2 (*LAm*) (*Med*) goitre
3 (*Caribe*) (= *mala pasada*) mean trick, dirty trick
4 cananas (*LAm*) (= *esposas*) handcuffs

canapé SM **1** (= *sofá*) sofa, couch
2 (*Culin*) canapé

Canarias SFPL (*tb* **las islas Canarias**) the Canaries, the Canary Islands

canario¹/a ADJ from/of the Canary Islands
SM/F Canary Islander, native/inhabitant of the Canary Islands • **los ~s** the people of the Canary Islands

canario² SM **1** (*Orn*) canary
2** prick**
3 (*LAm*) (= *amarillo*) canary yellow
EXCL* well I'm blowed!*

canarión/ona SM/F native/inhabitant of Gran Canaria

canasta SF **1** (= *cesta*) (round) basket; (*para comida*) hamper; (*Com*) crate ▸ **canasta familiar** (*LAm*) weekly shopping basket ▸ **canasta para papeles** wastepaper basket
2 (*Baloncesto*) basket ▸ **canasta triple** three-point shot
3 (*Naipes*) canasta
4 (*Méx, Col*) (*Aut*) luggage rack

canastero/a SM/F basket maker, basketweaver

canastilla SF **1** [*de bebé*] (baby's) layette
2 (*And, Caribe, Cono Sur*) [*de novia*] trousseau; (*hum*) bottom drawer, hope chest (*EEUU*)
3 (= *cestita*) small basket; (*Méx*) (= *papelera*) wastepaper basket ▸ **canastilla de la costura** sewing basket

canastillo SM **1** (= *bandeja*) wicker tray, small basket
2 [*de bebé*] (baby's) layette

canasto SM **1** (= *cesto*) large basket; [*de comida*] hamper; (*Com*) crate
2 (*Col*) (= *criado*) servant
3 • **¡canastos!** good heavens!

cáncamo SM (*Náut*) eyebolt ▸ **cáncamo de argolla** ringbolt

cancamurria* SF = **murria**

cancamusa* SF trick • **armar una ~ a algn** to throw sand in sb's eyes

cancán SM **1** (= *baile*) cancan
2 (= *enagua*) stiff, flounced petticoat
3 cancanes (*Cono Sur*) (= *pantimedias*) tights, pantyhose (*sing*) (*EEUU*)

cáncana SF (*Cono Sur*) [*de asar*] spit; [*de vela*] candlestick; (*And*) (= *persona*) thin person

cancanco* SM (*Caribe*) (*Aut*) breakdown

cancanear ▹ CONJUG 1a VI **1** (= *gandulear*) to loiter, loaf about
2 (*Cono Sur*) (= *bailar*) to dance the cancan
3 (*And, CAm, Méx*) (= *tartamudear*) to stammer; (= *expresarse mal*) to express o.s. with difficulty; (= *leer mal*) to read haltingly

cancaneo SM (*And, CAm, Méx*) (*al leer*) faltering; (= *tartamudeo*) stammering

cáncano SM louse • MODISMO: • **andar como ~ loco** to go round in circles

cancel SM **1** (= *contrapuerta*) storm door, windproof door
2 (= *tabique*) partition, thin wall; (*Méx*) (= *mampara*) folding screen

cancela SF wrought-iron gate

cancelación SF cancellation; (*Inform*) deletion

cancelar ▹ CONJUG 1a VT **1** [+ *pedido, suscripción, tarjeta*] to cancel; [+ *cuenta bancaria*] to close
2 [+ *reunión, concierto, viaje, proyecto*] to cancel • **~on el vuelo a causa de la nieve** they cancelled the flight because of the snow
3 [+ *deuda*] to pay off • **tendré que ahorrar para ~ el crédito** I'll have to save up to pay off my debt
4 (*LAm*) (= *pagar*) to pay, settle

cancelaría SF papal chancery

Cáncer SM (*Astron, Astrol*) Cancer • **es de ~** (*LAm*) she's (a) Cancer, she's a Cancerian

cáncer SM (*Med*) cancer ▸ **cáncer cervical, cáncer de cuello uterino** cervical cancer, cancer of the cervix ▸ **cáncer de los huesos** bone cancer ▸ **cáncer de mama** breast cancer ▸ **cáncer de ovario** ovarian cancer ▸ **cáncer de pecho** breast cancer ▸ **cáncer de pulmón** lung cancer
SMF INV (*Astrol*) Cancer, Cancerian • **los ~ son así** that's what Cancers *o* Cancerians are like
ADJ INV (*Astrol*) Cancer, Cancerian • **soy ~** I'm (a) Cancer, I'm a Cancerian

cancerado ADJ (*Med*) cancerous; (*fig*) corrupt

cancerarse ▹ CONJUG 1a VPR **1** (*Med*) [*tumor*] to become cancerous; [*persona*] to get cancer
2 (*fig*) to become corrupt

cancerbero SM **1** (= *guardameta*) goalkeeper
2 (*Mit*) • **el Cancerbero** Cerberus

cancerígeno ADJ carcinogenic

cancerología SF (= *estudio*) study of cancer, cancer research; (= *tratamiento*) cancer treatment

cancerólogo/a SM/F cancer specialist

canceroso/a ADJ cancerous
SM/F cancer patient, cancer sufferer

cancha SF **1** (*Dep*) (= *de tenis, baloncesto*) court; [*de fútbol*] ground ▸ **cancha de bolos** (*LAm*) bowling alley ▸ **cancha de golf** (*LAm*) golf course
2 (*Cono Sur*) (= *espacio*) room • **abrir ~** to make way, make room • MODISMOS: • **estar en su ~**

to be in one's element • **dar ~ a algn**: • **hay que dar ~ a los jóvenes escritores** we have to give a chance to young writers • **medios de difusión que dan mucha ~ a los terroristas** media that give a lot of coverage *o* exposure to terrorists
3 (*en aeropuerto*) ▸ **cancha de aterrizaje** (*Cono Sur*) landing strip, runway
4 (*LAm*) (= *experiencia*) experience • **tener ~** to be experienced
5 (*LAm*) (= *hipódromo*) racecourse, racetrack (*EEUU*) • MODISMO: • **en la ~ se ven los pingos** *o* **gallos** actions speak louder than words
6 (*LAm*) (= *maíz*) toasted corn
7 (*And**) (= *tajada*) cut

canchar ▹ CONJUG 1a (VT) (*And, Cono Sur*) to toast

canche (ADJ) **1** (*CAm*) (= *rubio*) blond(e)
2 (*And*) [*comida*] poorly seasoned, tasteless

canchero/a (ADJ) (*Cono Sur*) (*Dep*) experienced
(SM/F) **1** (*LAm*) (*Dep*) (= *cuidador*) groundsman/groundswoman; (= *jugador*) experienced player
2 (= *experto*) experienced person
3 (*Cono Sur*) (= *vago*) layabout, loafer

canchón (SM) (*And*) enclosed field

cancilla (SF) gate

canciller (SMF) **1** (= *presidente*) chancellor • **la ~ Merkel** Chancellor Merkel
2 (*LAm*) (*Pol*) (= *ministro*) ≈ Foreign Secretary, ≈ Secretary of State (*EEUU*), Minister for Foreign Affairs

cancilleresco (ADJ) chancellery (*antes de s*), chancery (*antes de s*); (= *diplomático*) diplomatic

cancillería (SF) (*en embajada*) chancery, chancellery; (*LAm*) (= *ministerio*) ministry of foreign affairs, foreign ministry

canción (SF) **1** (*Mús*) song ▸ **canción de amor** love song ▸ **canción de cuna** lullaby ▸ **canción infantil** nursery rhyme ▸ **canción protesta** protest song
2 (*Literat*) ballad ▸ **canción de gesta** chanson de geste, epic poem

cancionero (SM) (*Mús*) song book; (*Literat*) anthology, collection of verse

cancionista† (SMF) **1** (= *compositor*) songwriter
2 (= *cantante*) singer, vocalist; [*de baladas*] ballad singer

canco (SM) **1** (*Cono Sur*) (= *jarro*) earthenware jug; (= *tiesto*) flowerpot; (= *orinal*) chamberpot
2 cancos (*And, Cono Sur*) (= *nalgas*) buttocks; (= *caderas*) hips

cancro (SM) (*Bot*) canker; (*Med*) cancer

candado (SM) **1** (*gen*) padlock; [*de libro*] clasp, hasp • **cerrar algo con ~** to padlock sth • **poner algo bajo siete ~s** to lock sth safely away ▸ **candado digital** combination lock
2 (*And*) (= *barba*) goatee beard

candanga (SM) (*Méx*) • **el ~** the devil

candar ▹ CONJUG 1a (VT) to lock

cande (ADJ) • **azúcar ~** sugar candy, rock candy

candeal (ADJ) • **pan ~** white bread • **trigo ~** bread wheat
(SM) (*Cono Sur*) (*Culin*) egg flip

candela (SF) **1** (= *vela*) candle; (= *candelero*) candlestick; (*Fís*) candle power • **en ~** (*Náut*) vertical • MODISMOS: • **acabársele la ~ a algn‡**: • **se le acabó la ~** he snuffed it‡ • **arrimar ~ a algn*** to give sb a tanning* • **estar con la ~ en la mano** to be at death's door
2 (*esp LAm*) (= *fuego*) fire; (*para cigarro*) light • **pegar** *o* **prender ~ a** to set fire to, set alight • MODISMOS: • **dar ~*** to be a nuisance • **dar ~ a algn*** to rough sb up*
3 (*Bot*) blossom

candelabro (SM) candelabra

Candelaria (SF) Candlemas

candelaria (SF) (*Bot*) mullein

candelejón* (ADJ) (*And*) simple, slow

candelero (SM) **1** (= *candelabro*) candlestick; (= *lámpara*) oil lamp • MODISMO: • **en (el) ~**: • **estar en el ~** [*persona*] to be in the spotlight *o* limelight; [*tema*] to be in the news • **poner algo en ~** to bring sth into the limelight • **tema en ~** hot topic, subject of great current interest
2 (*Náut*) stanchion

candelilla (SF) **1** (= *vela*) small candle
2 (*Bot*) catkin
3 (*LAm*) (= *luciérnaga*) glow worm; (*Cono Sur*) (= *libélula*) dragonfly; (*And*) (= *niño*) lively child
4 (*Caribe, Cono Sur*) (*Cos*) hem, border

candelizo (SM) icicle

candelo (ADJ) (*And*) reddish-blond(e)

candencia (SF) white heat

candente (ADJ) **1** [*metal*] (= *rojo*) red-hot; (= *blanco*) white-hot
2 [*cuestión*] burning • **un tema de ~ actualidad** a red-hot issue, a subject that everyone is talking about

candi (ADJ) • **azúcar ~** sugar candy, rock candy

candidatizar ▹ CONJUG 1f (VT) to propose, nominate

candidato/a (SM/F) **1** (= *aspirante*) candidate (**a** for); (*para puesto*) applicant (**a** for)
2 (*Cono Sur‡*) sucker‡

candidatura (SF) **1** (*a un cargo*) candidature, candidacy • **presentar su ~** to put o.s. forward for a post, stand for a post
2 (= *lista*) list of candidates; (= *papeleta*) ballot paper

candidez (SF) **1** (= *simpleza*) simplicity, ingenuousness; (= *inocencia*) naïveté; (= *estupidez*) stupidity
2 (= *comentario*) silly remark

candidiasis (SF) (*Med*) thrush, candidiasis (*frm*)

cándido (ADJ) **1** (= *simple*) simple, ingenuous; (= *inocente*) naïve; (= *estúpido*) stupid
2 (*poét*) snow-white

candil (SM) **1** (= *lámpara*) oil lamp; (*Méx*) (*tb* **candil de prisma**) chandelier • MODISMO: • **(poder) arder en un ~** [*vino*] to pack a powerful punch, be very strong; [*tema etc*] to be pretty strong stuff
2 (*Zool*) tine, small horn

candileja (SF) **1** (= *depósito*) oil reservoir of a lamp; (= *lámpara*) small oil lamp
2 candilejas (*Teat*) footlights

candinga¹ (SF) (*Cono Sur*) impertinence, insistence

candinga² (SM) (*Méx*) • **el ~** the devil

candiota (SF) wine cask

candiotero (SM) cooper

candombe (SM) (*LAm*) African dance

candomblé (SM) candomblé

candonga (SF) **1*** (= *lisonjas*) blarney, flattery; (= *truco*) trick; (= *broma*) playful trick, hoax, practical joke; (= *guasa*) teasing • **dar ~ a algn** to tease sb, kid sb*
2 candongas (*And*) (= *pendientes*) earrings
3‡ (= *moneda*) one peseta
4‡ (*Anat*) scrotum
5‡ (= *mujer*) whore, tart‡, slut‡

candongo* (ADJ) (= *zalamero*) smooth, oily; (= *taimado*) sly, crafty; (= *vago*) lazy
(SM) (= *cobista*) creep‡, toady*, flatterer; (= *taimado*) sly sort; (= *vago*) shirker, idler, lazy blighter‡

candonguear* ▹ CONJUG 1a (VT) (= *bromear*) to tease, kid*
(VI) (= *vaguear*) to shirk, dodge work

candonguero* (ADJ) = **candongo**

candor (SM) **1** (= *inocencia*) innocence, lack of guile; (= *candidez*) frankness, candidness
2 (*poét*) pure whiteness

candorosamente (ADV) (= *con inocencia*) innocently, guilelessly, simply; (= *con franqueza*) frankly, candidly

candoroso (ADJ) (= *inocente*) innocent, guileless; (= *franco*) frank, candid

candungo (SM) (*Perú*) idiot

canear* ▹ CONJUG 1a (VT) to bash*, hit

caneca (SF) **1** (*Méx*) (= *vasija*) glazed earthenware pot; (*Cono Sur*) (= *balde*) wooden bucket; (*Col*) (*para basura*) rubbish bin, garbage can (*EEUU*); (*Caribe*) (= *bolsa de agua*) hot water bottle; (*And*) (= *lata*) can, tin; [*de petróleo etc*] drum; (= *porrón*) wine bottle (with a spout)
2 (*Cuba*) (= *medida*) liquid measure of 19 l

caneco (ADJ) (*And*) tipsy

canela (SF) **1** (*Bot, Culin*) cinnamon • MODISMO: • **ser ~ fina** *o* **en rama**: • **Ana es ~ fina** *o* **en rama** Ana is wonderful • **este torero es ~ fina** he's a brilliant bullfighter • **prueba estas gambas, son ~ fina** try these prawns, they're exquisite ▸ **canela en polvo** ground cinnamon ▸ **canela en rama** stick cinnamon; ▹ **flor**
2 (*Caribe*) (= *mulata*) mulatto girl
(EXCL) (*euf*) good gracious!

canelero (SM) cinnamon tree

canelo (ADJ) cinnamon(-coloured *o* (*EEUU*) -colored)
(SM) cinnamon tree • MODISMO: • **hacer el ~*** to act *o* play the fool

canelón (SM) **1** = **canalón**
2 (= *carámbano*) icicle
3 (*CAm*) (= *rizo*) corkscrew curl
4 canelones (*Culin*) cannelloni

canesú (SM) **1** (= *parte superior*) yoke
2 (= *prenda*) underbodice, camisole

caney (SM) **1** (*Ven*) (= *cabaña*) log cabin, hut; (*Caribe*) [*de jefe*] chief's house; (*And, Caribe*) (= *cobertizo*) large shed
2 (*LAm*) [*de río*] river bend

canfín (SM) (*CAm, Caribe*) petrol, gasoline (*EEUU*)

cangalla* (SMF) (*LAm*) coward

cangallar* ▹ CONJUG 1a (VT) (*And, Cono Sur*) to pinch*, swipe‡

cangilón (SM) **1** (= *jarro*) pitcher; [*de metal*] metal tankard; [*de noria*] bucket, scoop
2 (*LAm*) (= *carril*) cart track, rut

cangrejo (SM) **1** [*de mar*] crab; [*de río*] crayfish • **está más rojo que un ~** (*por el sol*) he is as pink *o* red as a lobster • MODISMO: • **avanzar como los ~s** to make little headway
2 (*Náut*) gaff
3 (*And*) (= *idiota*) idiot; (= *granuja*) rogue, crafty person
4 (*LAm*) (= *misterio*) mystery, enigma
5‡ (= *moneda*) 25-peseta coin

cangri‡ (SM) **1** (= *cárcel*) nick‡, can (*EEUU‡*), prison
2 (*Rel*) church
3 (= *moneda*) 25-peseta coin

cangro (SM) (*And, CAm, Méx*) cancer

canguelo* (SM), **canguis*** (SM) • **le entró el ~ justo antes de entrar** he got the jitters just before he went in* • **tener ~** to have the jitters*

canguro (SM) **1** (*Zool*) kangaroo
2 (= *impermeable*) cagoule
3 (= *mochila*) baby-sling, baby-carrier (*worn on the chest*)
4 (*Náut*) ferry
(SMF)* [*de niños*] baby-sitter • **esta noche hago de ~** I'm baby-sitting tonight • —**¿a qué te dedicas?** —**trabajo de ~** "what do you

do for a living?" — "I do some baby-sitting"

caníbal ADJ **1** (= *antropófago*) cannibal(istic), man-eating
2 (= *feroz*) fierce, savage
SMF cannibal

canibalesco ADJ cannibalistic

canibalismo SM **1** (= *antropofagia*) cannibalism
2 (= *ferocidad*) fierceness, savageness

canibalizar ▹ CONJUG 1f VT to cannibalize

canica SF **1** (= *bola*) marble
2 canicas (= *juego*) marbles; (= *testículos***) balls**

caniche SMF poodle

canicie SF greyness, grayness (*EEUU*), whiteness (*of hair*)

canícula SF **1** (= *verano*) dog days (*pl*); (= *calor*) midsummer heat
2 (= *mediodía*) midday sun
3 • **Canícula** Dog Star, Sirius

canicular ADJ • **calores ~es** midsummer heat
SMPL **caniculares** dog days

canicultura SF dog breeding

canijo* ADJ **1** (= *pequeño*) puny; (= *endeble*) weak, sickly
2 (*Méx*) (= *astuto*) sly

canilla SF **1** (= *espinilla*) (*tb* **canilla de la pierna**) shinbone, shin; (*esp LAm*) (= *pierna*) shank, thin leg
2 (= *cúbito*) (*tb* **canilla del brazo**) armbone, ulna
3 (*Orn*) wing bone
4 (*Téc*) bobbin, reel
5 (*esp LAm*) (= *grifo*) tap, faucet (*EEUU*); [*de tonel*] spigot, tap • **irse como una ~*** • **irse de ~*** to have the trots‡
6 [*de tela*] rib
7 (*Méx*) • **a ~** by hook or by crook • **tener ~** to be very strong
8 (*Caribe*) (= *cobardía*) cowardice

canillento ADJ (*And*) long-legged

canillera SF **1** (*Dep*) shin guard
2 (*LAm*) (= *miedo*) fear; (= *cobardía*) cowardice

canillita SM (*And, Cono Sur*) newsboy

canillón ADJ, **canilludo** ADJ (*LAm*) long-legged

canina SF dog dirt

caninez SF ravenous hunger

canino ADJ canine, dog (*antes de s*) • **exposición canina** dog show • **hambre canina** ravenous hunger • **tener un hambre canina** to be ravenous
SM canine (tooth)

canje SM exchange

canjeable ADJ (*gen*) exchangeable; (*Econ*) exchangeable for cash, cashable

canjear ▹ CONJUG 1a VT [+ *prisioneros*] to exchange; [+ *cupón*] to cash in

cannabis SM cannabis

cano ADJ **1** [*pelo, barba*] (= *gris*) grey, gray (*EEUU*); (= *blanco*) white • **una mujer de pelo ~** a grey-haired *o* (*EEUU*) gray-haired *o* white-haired woman
2 [*persona*] (= *con pelo gris*) grey-haired, gray-haired (*EEUU*); (= *con pelo blanco*) white-haired

canoa SF **1** (*gen*) canoe ▸ **canoa automóvil** motor boat, launch ▸ **canoa fuera borda** outboard motorboat
2* (= *porro*) joint*
3 (*LAm*) (= *conducto*) conduit, pipe; (= *comedero*) feeding trough; [*de gallinas*] chicken coop; [*de palomas*] dovecot

canódromo SM dog track

canoero/a SM/F (*LAm*), **canoísta** SMF canoeist

canólogo/a SM/F expert on dogs

canon SM (PL: **cánones**) **1** (= *modelo*) canon (*frm*) • **una novela que sigue los cánones tradicionales** a novel which follows the traditional norms *o* canons • **el ~ de belleza** the model of beauty
2 (*Rel*) canon • MODISMO: • **como mandan los cánones**: • **se niega a dimitir, como mandan los cánones de la dignidad política** he is refusing to resign, as the norms of political dignity require • **primero tomamos un vinito, como mandan los cánones** (*hum*) first let's have our requisite glass of wine
3 (= *impuesto*) tax, levy ▸ **canon de arrendamiento** rate of rental ▸ **canon del agua** water charge, water rate ▸ **canon de traspaso** (*Dep*) transfer fee
4 (*Mús*) canon

canonical ADJ of a canon *o* prebendary, canonical

canonicato SM **1** (*Rel*) (= *prebenda*) canonry
2* (= *empleo*) sinecure, cushy job*

canónico ADJ canonical • **derecho ~** canon law

canóniga SF nap before lunch • MODISMO: • **coger una ~*** to have one too many

canónigo SM canon

canonista SM canon lawyer, expert in canon law

canonización SF canonization

canonizar ▹ CONJUG 1f VT (*Rel*) to canonize; (*fig*) to applaud, show approval of

canonjía SF **1** (*Rel*) (= *prebenda*) canonry
2* (= *empleo*) sinecure, cushy job*

canoro ADJ melodious, sweet, tuneful • **ave canora** songbird

canoso ADJ **1** [*persona*] (= *con pelo gris*) grey-haired, gray-haired (*EEUU*); (= *con pelo blanco*) white-haired
2 [*pelo, barba*] (= *gris*) grey, gray (*EEUU*); (= *blanco*) white

canotaje SM boating

canotier SM, **canotié** SM straw hat, boater

cansadamente ADV **1** (= *fatigadamente*) wearily, in a tired way
2 (= *de forma aburrida*) tediously, boringly

cansado ADJ **1** (= *fatigado*) [*persona*] tired (**de** from); [*aspecto, apariencia*] weary, tired; [*ojos*] tired, strained • **lo noto ~ últimamente** he's been looking tired lately • **es que nació cansada** (*iró*) she was born lazy • **con voz cansada** with a weary voice; ▹ **vista**
2 (= *harto*) • **estar ~ de algo** to be tired of sth • **estoy ~ de que me hagan siempre la misma pregunta** I'm tired of always being asked the same question • **estamos más que ~s de tanta corrupción** we are sick and tired of all this corruption • **¡ya estoy ~ de vuestras tonterías!** I've had enough of this nonsense of yours! • **estar ~ de hacer algo** to be tired of doing sth • **estoy ~ de tanto viajar** I'm tired of so much travelling • **sus amigos, ~s de esperarlo, se habían ido** tired of waiting, his friends had left
3 (= *pesado*) tiring • **debe de ser ~ corregir tantos exámenes** it must be tiring marking *o* to mark so many exams, marking so many exams must be tiring
4 • MODISMO: • **a las cansadas** (*Cono Sur*) at long last

cansador ADJ (*Cono Sur*) tiring

cansancio SM **1** (= *fatiga*) tiredness • **ante los primeros síntomas de ~** at the first signs of tiredness *o* weariness • **ya empezaban a acusar el ~** they were already beginning to feel tired *o* weary • **estar muerto de ~** to be dead tired
2 (= *hastío*) boredom • **ha dejado el trabajo por ~** he left his job out of boredom • MODISMO: • **hasta el ~** endlessly • **lo hemos discutido hasta el ~** we've discussed it endlessly

cansar ▹ CONJUG 1a VT **1** (= *fatigar*) to tire, tire out • **no canse más a la paciente con sus preguntas** don't tire the patient (out) with your questions • **me cansa mucho trabajar en el jardín** I get really tired working in the garden, working in the garden really tires me out, I find working in the garden really tiring • **~ la vista** to strain one's eyes, make one's eyes tired
2 (= *aburrir*) • **no quiero ~os con tanta gramática** I don't want to bore you with too much grammar • **me cansa ir siempre a los mismos bares** I get tired of *o* bored with always going to the same old bars, it's boring always going to the same old bars
3 (*Agr*) [+ *tierra*] to exhaust
VI **1** (= *fatigar*) to be tiring • **conducir cansa mucho** driving is very tiring
2 (= *hartar*) • **los niños cansan a veces** children can sometimes be tiresome *o* trying
VPR **cansarse 1** (= *fatigarse*) to get tired • **me canso mucho subiendo las escaleras** I get very tired going up stairs • **se cansa con nada** the slightest effort makes him tired, he gets tired at the slightest effort • **cuando ando mucho se me cansan las piernas** when I walk a lot my legs get very tired • **se me cansan los ojos con la televisión** television strains my eyes, my eyes get tired watching television
2 (= *hartarse*) to get bored • **~se de algo** to get tired of sth, get bored with sth • **se cansó de él y lo dejó** she got tired of him *o* got bored with him and left him • **~se de hacer algo** to get tired of doing sth • **me cansé de esperar y me fui** I got tired of waiting and left • **no me canso de repetirle que deje de fumar** I'm always telling him to stop smoking

cansera* SF bother; (*LAm*) wasted effort

cansinamente ADV (= *con cansancio*) wearily; (= *sin vida*) lifelessly

cansino ADJ **1** (= *lento*) weary • **andaba con paso ~** he walked wearily, he walked with a weary step
2 (= *pesado*) tiring

cantable ADJ suitable for singing, to be sung; (*Mús*) cantabile, melodious
SM *sung part of a "zarzuela"*

Cantabria SF (*gen*) Cantabria; (*frec*) Santander

CANSADO

¿"Tired" o "tiring"?

Hay que tener en cuenta la diferencia entre **tired** *y* **tiring** *a la hora de traducir* **cansado**.

▹ *Lo traducimos por* **tired** *cuando queremos indicar que estamos o que nos sentimos cansados:*

Se sintió cansado y se marchó
He felt tired and left
Estoy cansado de trabajar
I'm tired of working
Estábamos cansados del viaje
We were tired after the journey

▹ *Lo traducimos por* **tiring** *cuando queremos indicar que algo es* **cansado**, *es decir, que nos produce cansancio:*

Conducir 140 kms. todos los días es muy cansado
Driving 140 kms every day is very tiring

Para otros usos y ejemplos ver la entrada.

C

cantábrico (ADJ) Cantabrian • **mar Cantábrico** Bay of Biscay • **los (montes) ~s** the Cantabrian Mountains

cántabro/a (ADJ), (SM/F) Cantabrian

cantada* (SF) (*Méx*) squealing*, grassing*, ratting (EEUU*)

cantadera (SF) (*LAm*) loud singing, prolonged singing

cantado (ADJ) • **MODISMO**: • **estar ~** to be totally predictable

cantador(a) (SM/F) folksinger, singer of popular songs

cantal (SM) **1** (= *piedra*) boulder; (= *bloque*) stone block
2 (= *pedregal*) stony ground

cantaleta (SF) (*LAm*) (= *repetición*) boring repetition *o* chorus, tedious refrain; (= *quejas*) constant nagging

cantaletear ▹ CONJUG 1a (VT) (*LAm*)
1 (= *repetir*) to repeat ad nauseam, say over and over
2 (= *embromar*) to laugh at, make fun of

cantalupo (SM), **cantalupa** (*CAm*) (SF) cantaloupe

cantamañanas* (SMF INV) bullshitter⁑

cantante (SMF) singer • **es ~ de un grupo de rock** he's a singer in a rock band ▸ **cantante de ópera** opera singer
(ADJ) singing; ▹ **voz**

cantaor(a) (SM/F) Flamenco singer

cantar ▹ CONJUG 1a (VI) **1** (*Mús*) to sing • **cantas muy bien** you sing very well • **en esa región hablan cantando** (*fig*) they talk in a singsong way in that region • **los monjes cantaban en la abadía** the monks chanted *o* sang in the abbey; ▹ **voz**
2 [*pájaro*] to sing; [*gallo*] to crow; [*cigarra, grillo*] to chirp
3 (*liter*) (= *alabar*) to sing of, sing the praises of • **los poetas que le cantan a la mar** the poets who sing of *o* sing the praises of the sea
4‡ (= *revelar*) to spill the beans*; (*a la policía*) to squeal* • **MODISMOS**: • **~ de plano** to tell all, make a full confession • **los hechos cantan por sí solos** the facts speak for themselves
5‡ (= *oler mal*) to stink*, reek • **te cantan los pies** your feet really stink* *o* reek
(VT) **1** [+ *canción*] to sing; [+ *mantra, canto gregoriano*] to chant; [+ *misa*] to sing, say; [+ *número de lotería*] to call out • **MODISMOS**: • **~las claras*** to call a spade a spade • **~ a algn las cuarenta*** to give sb a piece of one's mind* • **su madre le cantó las cuarenta cuando llegó a casa** his mother gave him a piece of her mind when he got home* • **~ victoria**: • **es muy pronto para ~ victoria, la crisis política continúa** it is too early to claim victory, the political crisis continues • **—creo que ya está solucionado —no cantes victoria** "I think it's sorted out" — "don't speak too soon" *o* "don't count your chickens (before they're hatched)"
2 (*liter*) [+ *mérito, belleza*] to praise, eulogize
3 (= *revelar*) to confess • **cantó todo lo que sabía** he confessed all that he knew
(SM) **1** (= *canción*) song; (*Rel*) chant
2 (*Literat*) • **el Cantar de los Cantares** the Song of Songs • **MODISMO**: • **eso es otro ~** that's another story ▸ **cantar de gesta** chanson de geste, epic poem; ▹ **gallo¹**

cántara (SF) **1** (= *recipiente*) large pitcher
2 (= *medida*) *liquid measure = 16.13 litres*

cantarería (SF) **1** (= *tienda*) pottery shop, earthenware shop
2 (= *cerámica*) pottery

cantarero (SM) potter, dealer in earthenware

cantárida (SF) (= *insecto*) Spanish fly; (*Med*) cantharides

cantarín/ina (ADJ) [*persona*] fond of singing; [*arroyo*] tinkling, babbling; [*voz*] singsong, lilting
(SM/F) singer

cántaro (SM) **1** (= *vasija*) pitcher, jug; (= *cantidad*) jugful • **a ~s** in plenty • **MODISMO**: • **llover a ~s** to rain cats and dogs, rain buckets

2 cántaros‡ (= *pechos*) tits⁑

cantata¹ (SF) (*Mús*) cantata

cantata²‡ (SF) (= *soplo*) tip-off

cantautor(a) (SM/F) singer-songwriter

cante (SM) **1** (*Mús*) ▸ **cante flamenco, cante jondo** Andalusian gipsy singing, Flamenco singing
2 (= *extravagancia*) • **dar el ~*** to make a fool of o.s. • **con ese peinado vas a dar el ~** you'll look really silly with that haircut • **ser un ~*** to be ridiculous • **no puedes salir con ese sombrero, es un ~** you can't go out wearing that hat, it looks ridiculous
3‡ (= *soplo*) tip-off (to the police)

cantegril (SM) (*Uru*) shanty town, slum

cantera (SF) **1** (*Min*) quarry, pit ▸ **cantera de arena** sandpit ▸ **cantera de piedra** stone quarry
2 [*de artistas etc*] source; (*Dep*) reserve of young players • **Escocia es una ~ de grandes futbolistas** Scotland produces many talented footballers

canterano/a (ADJ) reserve (*antes de s*)
(SM/F) reserve player

cantería (SF) **1** (*Min*) quarrying, stone cutting
2 (*Arquit*) masonry, stonework
3 (= *piedra*) piece of masonry, stone, ashlar

cantero (SM) **1** (*Min*) quarryman; (*Arquit*) stonemason
2 (= *cabo*) end, extremity ▸ **cantero de pan** crust of bread
3 (*Cono Sur*) [*de plantas*] bed, plot; [*de flores*] flowerbed; (*And, Méx*) [*de caña*] plot of sugar cane

cántico (SM) (*Rel*) canticle; (*fig*) song

cantidad (SF) **1** (= *medida*) amount, quantity • **hay que poner la misma ~ de azúcar que de harina** you have to add the same amount *o* quantity of sugar as of flour • **según la ~ de trabajo que tengas** depending on the amount of work you have • **hay que sumar ambas ~es** you have to add the two amounts together • **en ~: hemos recibido mercancía en ~** we have received huge amounts *o* quantities of stock • **MODISMO**: • **en ~es industriales** (*hum*): • **bebo café en ~es industriales** I drink coffee by the bucketful *o* by the gallon ▸ **cantidad de movimiento** (*Fís*) momentum
2 [*de personas, animales, cosas*] number • **había gran ~ de gente** there was a large number of people • **¿has visto la ~ de discos que tienes?** do you realize just how many records you've got?
3* (= *gran cantidad*) **a** • **~ de** loads of* • **tengo ~ de trabajo** I've got loads of work* • **vino a verme ~ de gente** loads of people came to see me* • **tengo ~ de cosas que hacer** I've loads to do*
b (*LAm*) • **cualquier ~*** loads* • **—¿había mucha gente? —¡cualquier ~!** "were there many people?" — "loads!"* • **cualquier ~ de errores** loads of mistakes*
4 [*de dinero*] sum, amount • **por una pequeña ~ se lo enviamos a su domicilio** for a small sum *o* amount we'll deliver it to your house • **hay que abonar una ~ a cuenta** a payment must be made on account • **pagaron ~es millonarias por los derechos de la película** they paid millions for the film rights ▸ **cantidad alzada** flat rate ▸ **cantidad a pagar** amount to pay ▸ **cantidad bruta** gross amount ▸ **cantidad neta** net amount ▸ **cantidad simbólica** nominal fee
5 [*de sílaba*] quantity
(ADV) (*esp Esp‡*) • **sabe ~ de eso** he knows loads about that* • **le va el alcohol ~** he's into drinking in a big way‡ • **me gustas ~** I like you a lot, I think you're really cool‡ • **ese asunto es ~ de chungo** the whole thing's really dodgy* • **ese tío está ~ de bueno** that guy's really hunky*

CANTIDAD

Cantidad, *como sustantivo, se puede traducir al inglés por* **amount**, **number**, **sum**, **quantity** *y* **figure**.

▹ *Cuando* **cantidad** *expresa cuánto tenemos, necesitamos u obtenemos de algo se traduce por* **amount**, *palabra que se usa en el contexto de nombres incontables:*

Le preocupaba la cantidad de trabajo que tenía que hacer
He was worried about the amount of work he had to do

NOTA: Se puede decir **a large amount** *y* **a small amount**, *pero es incorrecto decir* **a big amount** *o* **a little amount**.

▹ *Cuando hablamos de una* **cantidad** *de personas, animales o cosas, (nombres en plural),* **cantidad** *se traduce por* **number**. *Con la expresión* **the number of** *el verbo va en singular y con* **a number of** *en plural:*

En los últimos 30 años la cantidad de consumidores de electricidad ha aumentado en un 50 por ciento
In the last 30 years, the number of electricity consumers has risen by 50 per cent

Me esperaban una gran cantidad de recibos sin pagar
A large number of bills were waiting for me

NOTA: Hay que tener en cuenta que con **number** *también podemos utilizar* **large** *y* **small**, *pero no* **big** *ni* **little**.

▹ *Hablando de dinero,* **cantidad** *se traduce por* **sum**. *Puede aparecer con* **large**, **small** *o* **huge**:

Los fabricantes gastan enormes cantidades de dinero en anunciar sus productos
Manufacturers spend huge sums of money on advertising their products

▹ *Una* **cantidad** *que se puede medir o contar se puede traducir por* **quantity**. *Puede ir acompañado de* **large** *o* **small**:

Quiero un kilo de patatas y la misma cantidad de manzanas
I'd like a kilo of potatoes and the same quantity of apples

Sólo necesitas una cantidad muy pequeña
You only need a very small quantity

Amount *también es posible en el contexto de sustancias incontables:*

You only need a very small amount

▹ *Una* **cantidad** *específica, expresada numéricamente, se traduce por* **figure**, *que puede aparecer con los adjetivos* **high** *y* **low**:

Al final se decidieron por una cantidad de veinte mil libras
Finally, they decided on a figure of twenty thousand pounds

Para otros usos y ejemplos ver la entrada.

cantiga SF, **cántiga** SF song, poem
cantil SM (*en roca*) shelf, ledge; [*de costa*] coastal shelf; (= *risco*) cliff
cantilena SF **1** (= *canción*) ballad, song
2 = cantinela
cantillos SMPL (= *juego*) jacks
cantimplora SF (*para agua*) water bottle, canteen; (*para licores*) hip flask; (*Téc*) syphon; (*And*) powder flask • **¡cantimplora!** (*And**) not on your life!
cantina SF **1** (*Ferro*) buffet, refreshment car; (*Mil etc*) canteen, cafeteria (EEUU); (= *café-bar*) snack bar; (*LAm*) bar, saloon; (*Cono Sur*) (= *restaurante*) cheap restaurant
2 (= *bodega*) wine cellar
3 (= *para llevar comida*) hamper; (*And*) [*de leche*] milk churn
4 cantinas (*Méx*) (= *alforjas*) saddlebags
cantinela SF • **la misma ~** the same old story • **y toda esa ~*** and all that jazz*
cantinero/a SM/F (= *bárman*) barman/ barmaid, bartender; (= *dueño*) publican
cantinflismo SM (*Méx*) babble, empty chatter
cantío SM (*Caribe*) folksong, popular song
cantiral SM stony ground, stony place
canto¹ SM **1** (*Mús*) (= *arte*) singing; (= *canción*) song; (*Rel*) chant • **estudió ~ en Barcelona** she studied singing in Barcelona • **clases de ~** singing lessons • **se oían los ~s alegres de los niños** you could hear the joyful songs of the children ▸ **canto de sirena** siren call, siren song ▸ **canto gregoriano** Gregorian chant, (Gregorian) plainsong ▸ **canto llano** plainsong
2 [*de pájaro*] song; [*de gallo*] crow; [*de grillo, chicharra*] chirp ▸ **canto del cisne** swan song
3 (*liter*) song, hymn • **un ~ a la libertad** a hymn *o* song to freedom
canto² SM **1** (= *borde*) [*de mesa, libro*] edge • **de ~: el libro cayó de ~** the book fell on its side • **pon el libro de ~** stand the book on end *o* on its side • MODISMOS: • **al ~***: • **cada vez que se veían, pelea al ~** every time they saw each other there was inevitably an argument, every time they saw each other an argument was the order of the day • **faltar el ~ de un duro**: • **ha faltado el ~ de un duro para que se caiga** he was *o* came this close to falling ▸ **canto de pan** heel of bread, crust (of bread)
2 (= *piedra*) pebble • MODISMO: • **darse con un ~ en los dientes*** to think o.s. lucky, count o.s. lucky • **si no llega a los 10 euros nos podemos dar con un ~ en los dientes** we can think *o* count ourselves lucky if it comes to less than 10 euros ▸ **canto rodado** pebble
cantón¹ SM **1** (*Pol*) canton
2 (*Mil*) cantonment
3 (= *esquina*) corner
cantón² SM (*Cos*) cotton material
cantonada SF • **dar ~ a algn** to dodge sb, shake sb off
cantonal ADJ cantonal
cantonear ▹ CONJUG 1a VI to loaf around
cantonera SF **1** (= *anaquel*) corner shelf; (= *escuadra*) corner bracket, angle iron; (= *mesita*) corner table; (= *armario*) corner cupboard; [*de libro, mueble etc*] corner piece
2* (= *prostituta*) streetwalker, hustler (EEUU*)
cantonero SM loafer, idler, good-for-nothing
cantonés/esa ADJ, SM/F Cantonese
SM (*Ling*) Cantonese
cantor(a) ADJ singing, that sings • **ave ~a** songbird
SM/F (= *persona*) singer; (*Orn*) songbird
Cantórbery SM Canterbury
cantorral SM stony ground, stony place
cantoso* ADJ showy*
cantuariense ADJ of/from Canterbury
cantuja SF (*Perú*) underworld slang
cantúo‡ ADJ • **una mujer cantúa** a woman with a smashing figure*
canturía SF (= *canto*) singing, vocal music; (= *ejercicio*) singing exercise; (*pey*) monotonous singing, droning
canturrear ▹ CONJUG 1a VT, VI to sing softly, croon; (*con la boca cerrada*) to hum
canturreo SM soft singing, crooning; (*con la boca cerrada*) humming
canutazo‡ SM telephone call
canutero SM (*LAm*) barrel (*of pen*)
canuto SM **1** (= *tubo*) small tube, small container
2* (= *porro*) joint*
3 (*Bot*) internode
4* (= *persona*) telltale, tattletale (EEUU)
5* (= *teléfono*) phone, blower*
6 (*Cos*) needle case
ADJ * **1** super*, smashing*
2 • MODISMO: • **pasarlas canutas** to have a rough time of it
canzonetista SF vocalist, crooner
caña SF **1** (= *junco*) reed; (= *tallo*) stem, stalk • **un techo de ~** a roof of reed thatch • **azúcar de ~** cane sugar • **ron de ~** cane rum • MODISMOS: • **dar** *o* **meter ~‡**: • **la policía le dio ~ a los manifestantes** the police laid into the demonstrators* • **la prensa le ha dado ~ al gobierno** the press has really laid into the government, the press has really given the government some stick* • **le han metido ~ al jefe para que nos aumente el sueldo** they've been going on at my boss to give us a pay rise • **tendrás que darle** *o* **meterle ~ si quieres acabarlo pronto** you'll have to get stuck into it if you want to finish it soon • **le mete mucha ~ al coche** he really steps on the gas • **las ~s se vuelven lanzas** a joke can easily turn into something unpleasant ▸ **caña de azúcar** sugar cane ▸ **caña de bambú** cane ▸ **caña dulce, caña melar** sugar cane; ▹ **miel**
2 (*tb* **caña de pescar**) fishing rod
3 (= *vaso*) • **una ~ (de cerveza)** a small glass of beer • **¡dos ~s!** two beers please • **una ~ de vino** a tall wineglass, a long glass
4 (*Anat*) [*de la pierna*] shinbone; [*de caballo*] shank
5 [*de bota*] leg • **botas de media ~** calf-length boots
6 [*de columna*] shaft
7 (*esp LAm*) (= *aguardiente*) cane liquor • **estar con la ~ mala** (*Cono Sur**) to have a hangover*
8 (*Min*) gallery
9 (*Náut*) [*de ancla*] shank; [*de timón*] tiller, helm
10 (*Caribe**) (= *trago*) swig*, drink
11 (*And, Caribe*) (= *bulo*) false rumour; (= *bravata*) bluff, bluster
12 (*LAm*) (= *pajita*) (drinking) straw
13†** (= *pene*) prick**
cañabrava SF (*LAm*) reed
cañada SF **1** (= *barranco*) gully, ravine; (= *valle*) glen
2 (*Agr*) (= *camino*) cattle track, drover's road
3 (*LAm*) (= *arroyo*) stream; (= *terreno*) low-lying wet place
cañadón SM (*Cono Sur*) *low-lying part of a field flooded in wet weather*
cañamar SM hemp field
cañamazo SM embroidery canvas
cañamelar SM sugar-cane plantation
cañameno ADJ hempen
cañamero ADJ hemp (*antes de s*)
cañamiel SF sugar cane
cáñamo SM (*Bot*) hemp; (= *tela*) hemp cloth; (*CAm, Caribe, Cono Sur*) (= *cuerda*) hemp rope ▸ **cáñamo agramado** dressed hemp ▸ **cáñamo índico** (*CAm*), **cáñamo indio** Indian hemp, marijuana plant
cañamón SM hemp seed; (*para pájaros*) birdseed
cañata‡ SF (glass of) beer
cañavera SF reed grass
cañaveral SM **1** (*Bot*) reedbed
2 (*Col*) (*Agr*) sugar-cane plantation
cañazo SM (*And*) cane liquor • MODISMO: • **dar ~ a algn** to play a trick on sb
cañear* ▹ CONJUG 1a VI to drink, carouse
cañengo ADJ (*And, Caribe*), **cañengue** ADJ (*And, Caribe*) (= *débil*) weak, sickly; (= *flaco*) skinny
cañeo* SM drinking, carousal
cañería SF **1** (= *tubo*) pipe; (= *sistema*) pipes (*pl*), piping; (= *desaguadero*) drain
2 (*Mús*) organ pipes
3‡ (= *vena*) main line‡
cañero ADJ **1** (*LAm*) sugar-cane (*antes de s*) • **machete ~** sugar-cane knife
2 (*And, Caribe*) (= *mentiroso*) lying; (= *fanfarrón*) boastful
SM **1** (*Téc*) pipe fitter
2 (*LAm*) (*Agr*) owner *o* manager of a sugar-cane plantation
3 (*And, Caribe*) (= *mentiroso*) bluffer; (= *fanfarrón*) boaster
cañete SM small pipe
cañí ADJ, SMF = **calé**
cañita SF (*And*) (drinking) straw
cañiza SF coarse linen
cañizal SM, **cañizar** SM (*natural*) reedbed; (*Agr*) sugar-cane plantation
cañizo SM wattle
caño SM **1** (= *tubo*) tube, pipe; (*Mús*) pipe; [*de fuente*] jet, spout; (*Arquit*) gutter; (= *alcantarilla*) drain, (open) sewer; (*And*) (= *grifo*) tap, faucet (EEUU)
2 (*Min*) gallery
3 (= *bodega*) wine cellar
4 (*Náut*) navigation channel, deep channel; (*And, Caribe*) (= *río*) narrow navigable river
cañón SM **1** [*de artillería*] cannon • **el castillo estaba defendido por 30 cañones** the castle was defended by 30 cannons ▸ **cañón antiaéreo** anti-aircraft gun ▸ **cañón antitanque** anti-tank gun ▸ **cañón de agua** water cannon ▸ **cañón de avancarga** muzzle loader ▸ **cañón de campaña** field gun ▸ **cañón de nieve (artificial)** snow cannon
2 [*de escopeta*] barrel • MODISMO: • **ni a ~** *o* **cañones** (*Chile, Perú*) not at all ▸ **cañón arponero** harpoon ▸ **cañón de ánima rayada, cañón rayado** rifled barrel, rifled bore; ▹ **escopeta**
3 [*de pipa*] stem; [*de pluma*] quill, calamus
4 (= *valle*) canyon, gorge • **el Gran Cañón del Colorado** the Grand Canyon
5 (*And*) (= *puerto de montaña*) pass; (= *vereda*) mountain path
6 (*Mús*) (organ) pipe
7 (*Arquit*) [*de ascensor*] shaft
8 (*Téc*) [*de televisor*] (electron) gun ▸ **cañón de luz** spot(light) ▸ **cañón láser** laser gun
9 (*And*) (*Bot*) trunk
ADJ INV† (= *estupendo*) fabulous*, marvellous, marvelous (EEUU*) • **una mujer ~** one hell of a woman‡
ADV† • MODISMO: • **pasarlo ~** to have a whale of a time*
cañonazo SM **1** (*Mil*) cannon shot; **cañonazos** (= *fuego*) cannon fire (*sing*) • **salva de 21 ~s** 21-gun salute ▸ **cañonazo de advertencia** (*Náut*) warning shot, shot across the bows
2 (*Ftbl*) shot, volley, fierce shot
cañonear ▹ CONJUG 1a VT to shell, bombard

c

VPR **cañonearse** (*Cono Sur**) to get tight*
cañoneo SM shelling, bombardment
cañonera SF **1** (*Náut*) (*tb* **lancha cañonera**) gunboat
2 (*LAm*) (= *pistolera*) holster
3 (*Mil, Hist*) embrasure
cañonero/a SM/F (*LAm*) (*Dep*) striker
SM (*Mil*) gunboat
cañusero/a SM/F (*And*) owner of a sugar-cane plantation
cañutero SM pincushion
cañuto SM = **canuto**
caoba SF mahogany
caolín SM kaolin
caos SM INV chaos • **su mesa de trabajo era un ~ total** his desk was complete chaos, his desk was a complete mess • **esta ciudad es un auténtico ~** this city is a complete shambles* ▸ **caos circulatorio** traffic chaos
caótico ADJ chaotic
caotizar ▹ CONJUG 1f VT to throw into disarray, cause chaos in
C.A.P. SM ABR (= **Certificado de Aptitud Pedagógica**) ≈ PGCE
cap. ABR, **cap.º** ABR (= **capítulo**) ch, c., chap
capa SF **1** (= *prenda*) cloak, cape • **una comedia de ~ y espada** a cloak-and-dagger play • MODISMOS: • **andar** *o* **estar de ~ caída** (= *estar triste*) to look *o* be crestfallen, be down in the mouth; (= *estar en decadencia*) to be in *o* on the decline • **defender algo a ~ y espada** to fight tooth and nail for sth • **hace de su ~ un sayo** he does as he pleases ▸ **capa de agua** (= *chubasquero*) raincape ▸ **capa torera** bullfighter's cape
2 (= *estrato*) layer • **la ~ atmosférica** the atmosphere • **las ~s de la atmósfera** the layers *o* strata of the atmosphere • **la ~ de ozono** the ozone layer • **amplias ~s sociales** *o* **de la población** broad strata of society • **un corte de pelo a ~s** a layered cut • **madera de tres ~s** three-ply wood ▸ **capa freática** aquifer, phreatic stratum
3 (= *recubrimiento*) • **una ~ de hielo** a sheet of ice • **una ~ de nieve** a blanket of snow • **los muebles tenían una densa ~ de polvo** the furniture had a thick layer of dust • **una fina ~ de grasa** a film of grease • **le di dos ~s de pintura** I gave it two coats of paint • **el pastel tiene dos ~s de chocolate** the cake has two layers of chocolate
4 (*Náut*) • **estar** *o* **ponerse a la ~** to lie to
5 (*frm*) • **so** *o* **bajo ~ de** (= *bajo la apariencia de*) in *o* under the guise of; (= *con el pretexto de*) on *o* under the pretext of, as a pretext for • **so** *o* **bajo ~ ética, predican un puritanismo extremo** in *o* under the guise of ethics, they are preaching extreme puritanism • **so** *o* **bajo ~ de modernizar la empresa han reducido la plantilla** on *o* under the pretext of modernizing the company they have cut back the staff
capaburro SM (*LAm*) piranha
capacha* SF **1** (*Cono Sur*) (= *cárcel*) nick*, slammer*, can (*EEUU**) • **caer en la ~** to fall into the trap
2 (= *espuerta*) basket
capacheca SF (*And, Cono Sur*) street vendor's barrow *o* stall
capacho SM **1** (= *cesto*) wicker basket, big basket; (*Téc*) hod; (*LAm*) (= *alforja*) saddlebag
2 (*And, Cono Sur*) (= *sombrero*) old hat
capacidad SF **1** [*de vehículo, teatro, depósito*] capacity • **una sala con ~ para 900 personas** a hall with a capacity of 900 people • **un disquete con ~ de 1.44 MB** a diskette with a capacity of 1.44 MB • **"capacidad: 40 viajeros sentados"** "seating capacity: 40" • **un avión con ~ para 155 pasajeros** a 155-seater aircraft, an aircraft that can carry 155 passengers ▸ **capacidad de almacenamiento** storage capacity ▸ **capacidad de carga** carrying capacity, freight capacity ▸ **capacidad útil** effective capacity; ▹ **medida**
2 (= *habilidad*) ability • **necesitamos una persona con ~ para afrontar desafíos** we require a person with the ability to face challenges • **esas bacterias tienen una mayor ~ de reproducción** those bacteria have a greater capacity for reproduction • **su ~ para manejar el balón era asombrosa** his ball skills were amazing • **no tiene ~ para los negocios** he has no business sense *o* business acumen ▸ **capacidad adquisitiva** (*Com*) purchasing power, buying power ▸ **capacidad de aprendizaje** learning ability ▸ **capacidad de convocatoria** [*de orador*] pulling power; [*de huelga, manifestación*] appeal, popular appeal ▸ **capacidad de decisión** decision-making ability ▸ **capacidad de ganancia** (*Com*) earning power, earning capacity ▸ **capacidad de trabajo** • **tiene una enorme ~ de trabajo** she can get through a tremendous amount of work, she has an enormous capacity for hard work ▸ **capacidad financiera** financial standing ▸ **capacidad física** physical capacity ▸ **capacidad intelectual** intellectual ability ▸ **capacidad mental** mental ability
3 (= *autoridad*) authority • **no tenemos ~ para modificar las decisiones del gobierno** we do not have the authority to alter government decisions
4 (*Jur*) capacity ▸ **capacidad civil** civil capacity ▸ **capacidad legal** legal capacity
capacitación SF **1** (*Educ*) • **conseguir la ~ de piloto** to qualify as a pilot
2 (*Jur*) capacitation
capacitado ADJ • **el candidato más ~** the best-qualified candidate • **estar ~ para hacer algo** to be qualified to do sth • **los únicos ~s para alcanzar los cuartos de final** the only ones capable of reaching the quarter-finals
capacitar ▹ CONJUG 1a VT **1** (= *preparar*) to prepare • **una formación que no capacita a los jóvenes para incorporarse en el mercado laboral** training which fails to give young people the skills they need to enter the job market, training which fails to prepare young people for the job market
2 (= *habilitar*) to qualify • **este título me capacita para ejercer como abogado** this qualification qualifies *o* entitles me to work as a lawyer
VPR **capacitarse** • **~se para algo** to qualify for sth
capacitor SM capacitor
capadura SF castration
capar ▹ CONJUG 1a VT **1** [+ *animal*] to castrate, geld
2 (*fig*) to reduce, cut down, curtail
3 (*Caribe, Méx*) (*Agr*) to cut back, prune
4 (*And, Caribe*) [+ *comida*] to start on
caparazón SM **1** (= *concha*) shell • **encerrarse en su ~** to withdraw into one's shell • **salir de su ~** to come out of one's shell
2 (*para caballo*) (*con comida*) nosebag; (= *manta*) caparison
caparrón SM bud
caparrosa SF copperas, vitriol ▸ **caparrosa azul** copper sulphate
capataz SMF foreman/forewoman, overseer
capaz ADJ **1** (= *competente*) capable, able • **es una persona muy ~** he is a very capable *o* able person • **~ de hacer algo** capable of doing sth • **antibióticos capaces de curar la infección** antibiotics capable of curing the infection • **no han sido capaces de localizar las joyas** they were unable to find the jewels • **una película ~ de hacerme llorar** a film that can make me cry • **no es ~ ni de freír un huevo** he can't even fry an egg • **¡es ~ de no venir!** he's quite capable of not coming! • **es ~ de cualquier tontería** he can do some really stupid things, he's capable of the stupidest things • **ser ~ para algo** to be capable of sth • **~ para testar** (*Jur*) competent to make a will
2 (= *que se atreve*) • **¿no me crees ~?** do you think I won't? • **ser ~** to dare • **¿a que no eres ~?** you wouldn't dare!, I bet you wouldn't! • **si eres ~, dime eso otra vez** just say that again, if you dare! • **ser ~ de hacer algo**: • **si soy ~ de hacerlo** if I can bring myself to do it • **no fue ~ de tirarse a la piscina** he just couldn't bring himself to dive into the pool • **fui ~ de decirle lo que pensaba** I managed to tell him what I thought
3 (= *con capacidad*) • **un auditorio ~ para 1.200 personas** an auditorium with a capacity of 1,200 people, an auditorium that holds 1,200 people
4 (*LAm**) • **~ que**: • **~ que llueva** it might rain • **~ que se perdió** he might have got lost • **es ~ que venga mañana** he might come tomorrow
capazo SM (= *cesto*) large basket; (*para niño*) Moses basket, (wicker) carrycot
capcioso ADJ cunning, deceitful • **pregunta capciosa** trick question
capea SF *bullfight with young bulls*
capeador SM *bullfighter who uses the cape*
capear ▹ CONJUG 1a VT **1** (*Taur*) wave the cape at; (*fig*) to take in, deceive
2 (*Náut*) • **~ el temporal** (*lit, fig*) to ride out *o* weather the storm
3 (= *esquivar*) to dodge
4 (*Culin*) to top, cover (**con** with)
VI (*Náut*) to ride out the storm
capellada SF (= *puntera*) toecap; (= *remiendo*) patch
capellán SM chaplain ▸ **capellán castrense, capellán de ejército** military chaplain, padre*
capellanía SF chaplaincy
capelo SM **1** (*Rel*) (= *sombrero*) cardinal's hat; (= *dignidad*) cardinalate
2 (*Cono Sur, Méx*) (= *tapa*) bell glass, glass cover
3 (*LAm*) (*Univ*) ▸ **capelo de doctor** doctor's gown
capero SM hallstand, hatstand
Caperucita Roja SF (Little) Red Riding Hood
caperuza SF [*de tela*] (pointed) hood; (*Mec*) hood, cowling; [*de bolígrafo*] cap, top ▸ **caperuza de chimenea** chimney cowl
Cap. Fed. ABR (*Arg*) = **Capital Federal**
capi[1]* SM = **capitán**
capi[2] SF (*And, Cono Sur*) (= *harina*) white maize flour; (= *maíz*) maize, corn (*EEUU*); (= *vaina*) unripe pod
capi[3]* SF (*esp LAm*) capital (city)
capia SF (*And, Cono Sur*) white maize flour
capiango SM (*Cono Sur*) clever thief
capicúa ADJ palindromic (*frm*)
SM palindrome (*frm*), symmetrical number (*e.g. 12321*)
capigorra SM, **capigorrón** SM idler, loafer
capilar ADJ hair (*antes de s*), capillary • **loción ~** hair lotion • **tubo ~** capillary
SM capillary
capilaridad SF capillarity
capilla SF **1** (*Rel*) chapel ▸ **capilla ardiente** funeral chapel ▸ **capilla de la Virgen** Lady

Chapel ▸ **capilla mayor** choir, chancel
2 • **estar en (la) ~** [*condenado a muerte*] to be awaiting execution; (= *estar en peligro*) to be in great danger; (= *estar sobre ascuas*) to be on tenterhooks
3 (*Mús*) choir
4 (*Tip*) proof sheet • **estar en ~s** to be at the proof stage, be in proof
5 (= *camarilla*) group of supporters, following
6 (= *caperuza*) cowl; (*Téc*) hood, cowl
capiller, capillero (SM) churchwarden, sexton
capillo (SM) 1 [*de bebé*] baby's bonnet; [*de halcón*] hood
2 (*Bot, Zool*) = **capullo**
capirotazo (SM) flip, flick
capirote (SM) 1 (*Univ, Orn*) hood
2 (= *golpe*) flip, flick
3 • **tonto de ~** dunce, complete idiot
4 (*Culin*) cloth strainer (*for coffee etc*)
capirucho (SM) hood
capiruchu (SM) (*CAm*) *child's toy consisting of wooden cup and ball*
capisayo (SM) (*And*) vest, undershirt (EEUU)
capitación (SF) poll tax, capitation
capital (ADJ) 1 (= *clave*) [*nombre, personaje*] key; [*rasgo*] main • **una figura ~ de la democracia española** a key figure in Spanish democracy • **su obra ~ es el Quijote** his supreme work is Don Quixote • **esta pregunta es de importancia ~** this question is of paramount *o* cardinal *o* capital importance • **esto tuvo una importancia ~ en su vida** this was of paramount *o* cardinal importance in his life • **los puntos ~es de su discurso** the cardinal *o* main points of her speech • **la ciudad ~** the capital city
2 (= *mortal*) • **pecado ~** mortal sin • **la pena ~** capital punishment
3 (*LAm*) • **letra ~** capital letter
(SM) (*Econ*) [*de empresa*] capital; [*de persona*] capital, money • **la empresa ha ampliado el ~** the company has increased its capital ▸ **capital activo** working capital ▸ **capital en acciones** share capital, equity capital ▸ **capital extranjero** • **la entrada de ~ extranjero** the inflow of foreign capital • **han vendido la empresa al ~ extranjero** they have sold the company to foreign capital *o* investors ▸ **capital fijo** fixed capital ▸ **capital flotante** floating capital ▸ **capital humano** human resources (*pl*) ▸ **capital privado** private capital ▸ **capital riesgo** risk capital, venture capital
(SF) 1 [*de país*] capital (city); [*de provincia*] main city, provincial capital • **soy de Málaga ~** I am from the city of Málaga (*as opposed to the province*) • **Praga, la ~ europea de la cerveza** Prague, the beer capital of Europe
2 (*Tip*) decorated initial capital
capitalidad (SF) capital status, status as capital
capitalino/a (*LAm*) (ADJ) of/from the capital
(SM/F) 1 native/inhabitant of the capital • **los ~s** those that live in the capital
2* city slicker*
capitalismo (SM) capitalism ▸ **capitalismo de Estado** state capitalism ▸ **capitalismo monopolista** monopoly capitalism ▸ **capitalismo salvaje** ruthless capitalism
capitalista (ADJ), (SMF) capitalist
capitalización (SF) capitalization; [*de interés*] compounding
capitalizar ▸ CONJUG 1f (VT) 1 to capitalize; [+ *interés*] to compound
2 (*fig*) to capitalize on, turn to one's advantage
capitán (SM) (*gen*) captain; (*fig*) leader, chief; (*Méx*) (*en hotel*) maître d'(hôtel) ▸ **capitán de corbeta** lieutenant commander ▸ **capitán de fragata** commander ▸ **capitán del puerto** harbour *o* (EEUU) harbor master ▸ **capitán de navío** captain ▸ **capitán general** [*de ejército*] ≈ field marshal; [*de armada*] chief of naval operations
capitana (SF) 1 (*Dep, Mil*) (woman) captain; (*Hist*) captain's wife
2 (*Náut*) flagship
capitanear ▸ CONJUG 1a (VT) [+ *equipo*] to captain; [+ *rebeldes*] to lead, command
capitanía (SF) 1 (*Mil*) (= *rango*) captaincy; (= *edificio*) headquarters (*pl*) ▸ **capitanía del puerto** harbour master's office ▸ **capitanía general** (= *puesto*) *command of a military district*; (= *edificio*) *headquarters of a military district*
2 (*Náut*) (= *derechos*) harbour dues (*pl*), harbor dues (*pl*) (EEUU)
capitel (SM) (*Arquit*) capital
capitolio (SM) (= *edificio grande*) large edifice, imposing building; (= *acrópolis*) acropolis • **el Capitolio** the Capitol
capitoné (SM) 1 [*de mudanzas*] removal van, moving van (EEUU), furniture van
2 (*Cono Sur*) quilt, quilted blanket
capitonear ▸ CONJUG 1a (VT) (*Cono Sur*) to quilt
capitoste* (SM) (= *jefe*) bigwig*, boss; (= *tirano*) petty tyrant
capitulación (SF) 1 (*Mil*) capitulation, surrender ▸ **capitulación sin condiciones** unconditional surrender
2 (= *convenio*) agreement, pact • **capitulaciones (de boda *o* matrimoniales)** marriage contract (*sing*), marriage settlement (*sing*)
capitular¹ ▸ CONJUG 1a (VT) 1 [+ *condiciones*] to agree to, agree on
2 (*Jur*) to charge (**de** with), impeach
(VI) 1 (*Mil*) (= *rendirse*) to capitulate, surrender
2 (= *pactar*) to come to terms, make an agreement (**con** with)
capitular² (ADJ) (*Rel*) chapter (*antes de s*) • **sala ~** chapter house, meeting room
capitulear ▸ CONJUG 1a (VI) (*And, Cono Sur*) (*Parl*) to lobby
capituleo (SM) (*And, Cono Sur*) (*Parl*) lobbying
capítulo (SM) 1 [*de libro*] chapter; [*de ley*] section • **eso es ~ aparte** that's another question altogether • **esto merece ~ aparte** this deserves separate treatment
2 (= *reprensión*) reproof, reprimand ▸ **capítulo de culpas** charge, impeachment
3 (= *tema*) subject, matter • **en el ~ de las pensiones …** on the subject of pensions … • **ganar ~** to make one's point
4 (= *contrato*) ▸ **capítulos matrimoniales** marriage contract (*sing*), marriage settlement (*sing*)
5 (= *junta*) meeting (*of a council*); (*Rel*) chapter • MODISMO: • **llamar a algn a ~** to call sb to account, take sb to task
6 (*Rel*) chapter house
capo (SM) (= *jefe*) boss; (= *persona influyente*) bigwig*; (= *perito*) expert; [*de la mafia*] capo; (*esp Col*) drug baron • **es un ~** (*en arte, profesión*) he's a real pro*, he's brilliant
(ADJ INV) great*, fabulous*
capó (SM) (*Aut*) bonnet, hood (EEUU); (*Aer*) cowling
capoc (SM) kapok
capón¹* (SM) rap on the head
capón² (ADJ) castrated
(SM) 1 (= *pollo*) capon; (= *hombre**) eunuch
2 (*Cono Sur*) (= *cordero*) castrated sheep, wether; (= *carne*) mutton
3 (*Cono Sur**) (= *novato*) novice, greenhorn
caponera (SF) 1 (*Agr*) chicken coop, fattening pen; (*fig*) place of easy living, open house
2‡ (= *cárcel*) clink‡
caporal (SM) (*Mil*) corporal; (= *jefe*) chief, leader; (*esp LAm*) (= *capataz*) foreman (*on cattle ranch*)
capot [ka'po] (SM) (*Aut*) bonnet, hood (EEUU)
capota (SF) 1 (= *prenda*) bonnet
2 [*de carruaje, cochecito*] hood; (*Aut*) hood, top (EEUU); (*Aer*) cowling ▸ **capota plegable** folding hood, folding top (EEUU)
capotar ▸ CONJUG 1a (VI) (*Aut*) to turn over, overturn; (*Aer*) to nose-dive; (*fig*) to fall down, collapse
capote (SM) 1 (= *capa*) cloak; (*Mil*) cape, capote • MODISMOS: • **de ~** (*Méx*) on the sly, in an underhand way • **darse ~** (*Méx*) to give up one's job • **dijo algo para su ~** he said sth to himself • **echar un ~ a algn** to give *o* lend sb a helping hand • **hacer ~** (*Arg**) to be very successful
2 (*Taur*) (bullfighter's) cape ▸ **capote de brega** *cape used in the first part of the bullfight* ▸ **capote de paseo** *bullfighter's ceremonial capelet*
capotear ▸ CONJUG 1a (VT) 1 (*Taur*) to play with the cape
2 (= *engañar*) to deceive, bamboozle
3 (= *esquivar*) to dodge, duck
4 (*Cono Sur*) (*Naipes*) to win all the tricks against, whitewash*
capotera (SF) 1 (*LAm*) (= *colgador*) clothes hanger
2 (*Cono Sur*) (= *azotaina*) beating
3 (*CAm*) (= *lona*) tarpaulin, tarp (EEUU)
capotudo (ADJ) frowning, scowling
capricho (SM) 1 (= *antojo*) whim, (passing) fancy, caprice (*liter*) • **tiene sus ~s** he has his little whims • **es un ~ nada más** it's just a passing fancy • **por puro ~** just to please o.s. • **entra y sale a su ~** he comes and goes as he pleases • **hacer algo a ~** to do sth any old how
2 (= *cualidad*) whimsicality, fancifulness
3* (*amante*) plaything*
4 (*Mús*) caprice, capriccio; (*Arte*) caprice
caprichosamente (ADV) capriciously
caprichoso (ADJ) 1 [*persona*] capricious
2 [*idea, novela etc*] whimsical, fanciful
caprichudo (ADJ) stubborn, obstinate, unyielding (*about one's odd ideas*)
Capricornio (SM) (*Astron, Astrol*) Capricorn • **es de ~** (*LAm*) he's (a) Capricorn, he's a Capricornean
capricornio (*Astrol*) (SMF INV) Capricorn, Capricornean • **los ~ son así** that's what Capricorns *o* Capricorneans are like
(ADJ INV) Capricorn, Capricornean • **soy ~** I'm (a) Capricorn, I'm a Capricornean
cápsula (SF) (*Med, Aer*) capsule; [*de botella*] cap; [*de tocadiscos*] pick-up; [*de cartucho*] case; (*Caribe*) cartridge ▸ **cápsula de mando** command module ▸ **cápsula espacial** space capsule ▸ **cápsula fulminante** percussion cap
capsular (ADJ) capsular • **en forma ~** in capsule form
captación (SF) ▸ **captación de capital** (*Econ*) capital raising ▸ **captación de clientes** • **es la encargada de la ~ de clientes** she's in charge of attracting new customers ▸ **captación de datos** data capture ▸ **captación de fondos** fundraising ▸ **captación de votos** vote-winning
captador (SM) (*Téc*) sensor
captafaros (SM INV) (*tb* **placa de captafaros**) reflector
captar ▸ CONJUG 1a (VT) 1 (= *atraer*) [+ *dinero, capital*] to raise; [+ *votos*] to win; [+ *clientes,*

audiencia] to attract • **con la campaña ~on miles de nuevos votantes** through the publicity campaign they won thousands of new voters • **intentaron ~ nuevos clientes** they tried to attract new clients • **esto no logró ~ el interés del público** this failed to capture public interest • **llora para ~ la atención de sus padres** he cries to get his parents' attention
2 [+ *emisora, señal*] to pick up • **no capto BBC1** I don't *o* can't pick up BBC1 • **un aparato que capta las señales acústicas** a device that picks up *o* captures sound signals • **esta antena no capta bien las imágenes** you don't get a good picture with this aerial, this aerial doesn't give a good picture • **un videoaficionado captó esta escena** this scene was caught on amateur video
3 (= *comprender*) [+ *sentido, esencia*] to get, grasp • **supo ~ la importancia política del asunto** she managed to grasp the political significance of the matter • **no ha sabido ~ el mensaje del electorado** she has failed to pick up on *o* get *o* understand the message from the electorate • **no captó la indirecta** he didn't get *o* take the hint
4 [+ *aguas*] to collect • **el pantano capta las aguas de lluvia** the reservoir collects rainwater

captor(a) (SM/F) captor

captura (SF) [*de prisionero, animal*] capture; [*de droga*] seizure; [*de pesca*] catch ▸ **captura de carbono** carbon capture ▸ **captura de datos** data capture ▸ **captura y almacenamiento de carbono** carbon capture and storage

capturar ▹ CONJUG 1a (VT) [+ *prisionero, animal*] to capture; [+ *droga*] to seize

capturista (SMF) (*Méx*) typist; (*en computadora*) computer operator, keyboarder

capucha (SF) **1** [*de prenda*] hood; (*Rel*) hood, cowl ▸ **capucha antihumo** smoke hood
2 (= *acento*) circumflex accent

capuchina (SF) **1** (*Bot*) nasturtium
2 (*Rel*) Capuchin sister

capuchino (SM) **1** (*Rel*) Capuchin
2 (*LAm*) (*Zool*) Capuchin monkey
3 (= *café*) cappuccino (coffee)

capucho (SM) cowl, hood

capuchón (SM) **1** [*de pluma*] top, cap
2 [*de prenda*] hood
3 (*Fot*) hood
4 ▸ **capuchón de válvula** (*Aut*) valve cap
5 (= *prenda*) capuchin, lady's hooded cloak

capujar ▹ CONJUG 1a (VT) (*Cono Sur*)
1 (= *atrapar*) to catch in the air, snatch out of the air; (= *arrebatar*) to snatch
2 (= *anticiparse*) to say what sb was about to say

capullada** (SF) daft thing to do/say

capullo¹ (SM) **1** (= *flor*) bud ▸ **capullo de rosa** rosebud
2 (*Zool*) cocoon
3** (*del pene*) head • MODISMO: • **porque no me sale del ~** because I don't want to
4 [*de bellota*] cup
5 (*tela*) coarse silk cloth

capullo²/a** (SM/F) (= *imbécil*) twit* • **¡eres un ~!** you're a daft sod!**

caqui (SM) khaki, olive drab (EEUU)
• MODISMO: • **marcar el ~** to do one's military service

caquino (SM) (*Méx*) • **reírse a ~s** • **reírse a ~ suelto** to laugh uproariously, cackle

cara (SF) **1** (= *rostro*) face • **tiene la ~ alargada** he has a long face • **en la fiesta me encontré con varias ~s conocidas** I saw several familiar faces at the party • **se los tiré a la ~** I threw them in his face • **los banqueros sin ~** the faceless bankers • **conocido como "~ cortada"** known as "Scarface" • **~ a ~**: **se encontraron ~ a ~** they met face to face • **un encuentro ~ a ~** a face-to-face encounter • **asomar la ~** to show one's face • **de ~**: • **corrimos con el viento de ~** we ran into the wind • **el sol les daba de ~** the sun was shining in their eyes • **el viento me pegaba de ~** the wind was blowing into my face • **de ~ a**: • **nos sentamos de ~ al sol** we sat facing the sun • **de ~ al norte** facing north • **reformas de ~ a las próximas elecciones** reforms with an eye on the next elections *o* for the next elections • **no soy nada optimista de ~ al futuro** I'm not at all optimistic about the future • **hay que estar prevenidos de ~ a afrontar los cambios** we have to be prepared for the changes • **volver la ~ hacia algn** to turn one's face towards sb • **no vuelvas la ~ atrás** don't look back • **no se puede volver la ~ ante la corrupción** you cannot turn a blind eye to corruption
• MODISMOS: • **caérsele a algn la ~ de vergüenza**: • **se le tendría que caer la ~ de vergüenza** she ought to be ashamed of herself • **se le caía la ~ de vergüenza** he blushed with embarrassment • **cruzar la ~ a algn** to slap sb in the face • **dar la ~** to face the consequences • **dar la ~ por algn** to come to sb's defence • **a ~ descubierta** openly • **decir algo en la ~ de algn** to say sth to sb's face • **a dos ~s**: • **actuar a dos ~s** to engage in double-dealing • **echar algo a la ~***: • **lo mejor que te puedes echar a la ~** the very best you could wish for • **echar algo en ~ a algn** to reproach sb for sth • **echaron en ~ a los estudiantes su escasa participación** they reproached the students for not joining in enough • **le echan en ~ haber abandonado su país** they accuse him of having abandoned his country • **hacer ~ a** [+ *dificultades*] to face up to; [+ *enemigo*] to stand up to • **huir la ~ a algn** to avoid sb • **lavar la ~ a algo** to make sth look presentable • **le lavó la ~ al piso** she made the flat look presentable • **querían lavar la ~ al partido** they wanted to make the party look better • **mirar a algn a la ~** to look sb in the face • **partir la ~ a algn** to smash sb's face in • **cuidado con lo que dices o te parto la ~** just watch it or I'll smash your face in • **partirse la ~ con algn** to have a fight with sb • **partirse la ~ por algo** to fight for sth • **plantar ~ a** [+ *persona, críticas*] to stand up to; [+ *problema*] to face up to, confront • **por la ~***: • **entrar por la ~ en una fiesta** to gatecrash a party • **es alcalde por la ~** he's only mayor because of his connections • **está viviendo con sus padres y cobrando el paro por la ~** he's living with his parents and getting away with claiming dole money at the same time • **no me lo van a dar por mi ~ bonita** they're not going to hand it to me on a plate • **romper la ~ a algn** to smash sb's face in • **sacar la ~ por algn** to stick up for sb • **nos veremos las ~s** you haven't seen the last of me
2 (= *expresión*) • **poner mala ~** to grimace, make a (wry) face • **no pongas esa ~** don't look like that • **puso ~ de alegría** his face lit up • **tener ~ de**: • **tenía ~ de querer pegarme** he looked as if he wanted to hit me • **tener ~ de estar aburrido** to look bored • **tener buena ~** [*enfermo*] to be looking well; [*comida*] to look appetizing • **tener mala ~** [*enfermo*] to look ill; [*comida*] to look bad • MODISMOS: • **poner ~ de circunstancias** to look serious • **tener ~ de acelga** (*por enfado*) to have a face a mile long; (*por enfermedad*) to look pale, look washed out • **tener ~ de aleluya** to look overjoyed, be beaming with joy • **tener ~ de chiste** to be wearing a ridiculous expression • **tener ~ de corcho** to be a cheeky devil* • **tener ~ de estatua** to have a wooden expression • **tener ~ de hereje** to be as ugly as sin • **tener ~ de (justo) juez** to look stern • **tener ~ de monja boba** to look all innocent • **tener ~ de palo** to have a wooden expression • **tener ~ de pascua(s)** to be grinning from ear to ear • **tener ~ de pocos amigos** to look very unfriendly • **tener ~ de vinagre** to have a sour face
3* (= *descaro*) cheek*, nerve*; (= *valor*) nerve* • **¡qué ~ más dura!*** what a cheek *o* nerve!* • **¡qué ~ tienes!** what a cheek you've got!*, you've got a nerve!* • **¿con qué ~ le voy a pedir eso?** how do you expect me to have the nerve to ask her for that?* • **tener ~ para hacer algo** to have the nerve to do sth*
• MODISMOS: • **tener más ~ que espalda** • **tener más ~ que un elefante con paperas** to be a cheeky devil*
4 (= *lado*) [*de moneda, montaña, figura geométrica*] face; [*de disco, planeta, papel*] side; [*de tela*] face, right side; (*Arquit*) face, front • **escribir por ambas ~s** to write on both sides • **intentaron ascender por la ~ norte** they tried to climb the north face • **~ A** (*en disco*) A side • **~ adelante** facing forwards • **~ atrás** facing backwards • **~ o cruz** • **~ o ceca** (*Arg*) heads or tails • **echar** *o* **jugar** *o* **sortear algo a ~ o cruz** to toss for sth • **lo echamos a ~ o cruz** we tossed for it • MODISMO: • **~ y cruz**: • **~ y cruz de una cuestión** both sides of a question

caraba‡ (SF) • **es la ~** it's the absolute tops‡; (*pey*) it's the last straw

carabao (SM) Philippine buffalo

cárabe (SM) amber

carabela (SF) caravel

carabina (SF) **1** (*Mil*) carbine, rifle
• MODISMO: • **ser la ~ de Ambrosio*** to be a dead loss* ▸ **carabina de aire comprimido** airgun
2 (= *persona*) chaperone • **hacer** *o* **ir de ~** to go as chaperone, play gooseberry*

carabinero (SM) **1** (*Mil*) rifleman, carabineer; [*de frontera*] border guard; (*LAm*) policeman
2 (*Zool*) prawn

cárabo (SM) tawny owl

Caracas (SF) Caracas

caracha* (SF) (*LAm*) mange, itch

carachento* (ADJ) (*LAm*), **carachoso*** (ADJ) (*LAm*) mangy, scabby

caracho (ADJ) violet-coloured
(EXCL) • **¡caracho!** (*And**) sugar!*, shoot!*, I'll be darned! (EEUU*)

caracol (SM) **1** (*Zool*) snail; (*esp LAm*) (= *concha*) (sea) shell, snail shell ▸ **caracol comestible** edible snail ▸ **caracol de mar** winkle
2 (= *rizo*) curl
3 (*Arquit*) spiral; (*Cono Sur*) *circular shopping centre* • **escalera de ~** spiral staircase, winding staircase • **subir en ~** [*humo*] to spiral up, corkscrew up • **hacer ~es** [*persona*] to weave about, zigzag; (*pey*) to reel, stagger; [*caballo*] to prance about
4 • **¡~es!** (*euf**) (*sorpresa*) good heavens!; (*ira*) damn it!

caracola (SF) (*Zool*) large shell

caracoleante (ADJ) winding, spiral

caracolear ▹ CONJUG 1a (VI) [*caballo*] to prance about, caracole

caracolillo (SM) kiss-curl

carácter (SM) (PL: **caracteres**) **1** [*de persona*] character • **tiene un ~ muy fuerte** he has a strong personality • **no tiene ~** he lacks character, he's a weak character • **tener el ~ abierto** to be open, have an open nature • **tener buen ~** to be good-natured • **persona**

de ~ person of *o* with character • **una persona de mucho ~** person with a strong character *o* a lot of personality • **de ~ duro** hard-natured • **imprimir ~** to be character-building, build up character • **pasé un año en el ejército y eso imprime ~** I spent a year in the army, and that builds up character • **tener mal ~** to be ill-tempered • **tener el ~ reservado** to be of a quiet *o* reserved disposition

2 [*de edificio, estilo*] character • **una casa con mucho ~** a house with a lot of character

3 (= *índole*) nature • **algunos datos de ~ biográfico** some biographical data • **problemas de ~ general** problems of a general nature • **una visita con ~ oficial/privado** an official/private visit • **información de ~ reservado** information of a confidential nature • **la despenalización tiene ~ retroactivo** the decriminalization will be applied retrospectively • **un aumento de sueldo con ~ retroactivo** a backdated pay rise • **la estación se utilizará para trenes de ~ urbano** the station will be used by trains serving the city • **con ~ de urgencia** as a matter of urgency

4 (*Bio*) trait, characteristic ▸ **carácter adquirido** acquired characteristic ▸ **carácter dominante** dominant trait, dominant characteristic ▸ **carácter hereditario** hereditary trait ▸ **carácter recesivo** recessive trait

5 (*Tip*) character • **una pintada con caracteres árabes** (a piece of) graffiti written in Arabic • **está escrito con caracteres góticos** it is written in Gothic (script) ▸ **caracteres de imprenta** block letters ▸ **carácter de letra** handwriting

6 (*Inform*) character ▸ **carácter alfanumérico** alphanumeric character ▸ **carácter comodín** wild character ▸ **carácter de cambio de página** form feed character ▸ **carácter de petición** prompt ▸ **carácter libre** wildcard character

7 (*LAm*) (*Literat, Teat*) character

caracteriológico ADJ character (*antes de s*) • **cambio ~** character change, change of character

característica SF characteristic, feature

característicamente ADV characteristically

característico/a ADJ characteristic (**de** of)
SM/F (*Teat*) character actor/actress

caracterizable ADJ (that can be) characterized

caracterización SF characterization

caracterizado ADJ (= *distinguido*) distinguished, of note; (= *especial*) special, peculiar, having special characteristics; (= *típico*) typical

caracterizar ▹ CONJUG 1f VT **1** (*gen*) to characterize; (= *distinguir*) to distinguish, set apart; (= *tipificar*) to typify
2 (*Teat*) [+ *papel*] to play with great effect
3 (= *honrar*) to confer (a) distinction on, confer an honour on
VPR **caracterizarse 1** • **~se por algo** to be characterized by sth
2 (*Teat*) to make up, dress for the part

caracú SM (*LAm*) bone marrow

caradura SMF cheeky person, sassy person (*EEUU*) • **¡caradura!** you've got a cheek *o* a nerve!*
SF cheek*, nerve*

carajear ▹ CONJUG 1a VT (*Cono Sur*) to insult, swear at

carajiento ADJ (*And*) foul-mouthed

carajillo SM *coffee with a dash of brandy, anis etc*

carajito* SM (*LAm*) kid*, small child

carajo‡ SM **1** (*con valor enfático*) • **—me debes dinero —¡qué dinero ni qué ~!** "you owe me some money" — "I don't owe you a damn *o* bloody thing!" *o* "like hell I do!"‡ • **¡qué ~, si no quiere venir que se quede!** if he doesn't want to come he can damn well *o* bloody well stay!‡
2 • **un ~**: • **no entendí un ~** I didn't understand a damn *o* bloody thing‡ • **me importa un ~** I couldn't give a damn* *o* toss‡ • **no vale un ~** it isn't worth a thing *o* penny • **—llévame a mi casa —¡y un ~!** "take me home" — "like hell I will!"*
3 • **al ~**: • **¡al ~ con los libros!** to hell with the books!* • **irse al ~**: **¡vete al ~!, estoy harto de ti** go to hell! I'm sick of you‡ • **¿que te ha tocado la lotería? ¡vete al ~!** you've won the lottery? like hell (you have)!* • **todo el trabajo se fue al ~** all the work went down the tubes* • **mandar al ~**: **si te molesta, mándalo al ~** if he bothers you, tell him to piss off‡
4 • **del ~**: • **hace un frío del ~** it's bloody freezing* • **una bronca del ~** a hell of a row • **¡esta paella está del ~!** this is a damn good paella!, this paella is bloody brilliant‡
5 (= *pene*) prick‡, dick‡ • MODISMO: • **en el quinto ~** in the back of beyond*
EXCL • **¡carajo!** damn (it)!* • **¡cállate ya, ~!** shut up, damn it!* • **¡~, qué viento!** this damn *o* bloody wind!‡ • **¡~ con el coche!** this damn *o* bloody car!‡, damn this car!‡

caramanchel SM **1** (*LAm*) (= *cabaña*) hut, shack
2 (*And*) (= *puesto*) street vendor's stall

caramba EXCL (*indicando sorpresa*) good gracious!; (*indicando extrañeza*) how strange!; (*indicando protesta*) for crying out loud!

carámbano SM icicle

carambola SF (*Billar*) (= *juego*) billiards (*sing*); (= *golpe*) cannon, carom (*EEUU*) • **¡carambolas!** (*LAm*) (*euf**) hell!*, wow!* • MODISMO: • **por ~** by fluke

caramel SM sardine

caramelear* ▹ CONJUG 1a VT (*And*) (= *engañar*) to con*, deceive; (= *engatusar*) to suck up to*, flatter

caramelizado ADJ coated with caramel

caramelizar ▹ CONJUG 1f VT to coat with caramel

caramelo SM **1** (= *golosina*) sweet, piece of candy (*EEUU*)
2 (*Culin*) caramel • **un jersey color ~** a caramel-coloured *o* (*EEUU*) caramel-colored jersey • **a punto de ~** [*azúcar*] caramelized • MODISMO: • **estar a punto de ~** [*proyecto*] to be ripe for implementation • **el acuerdo está ya a punto de ~** the agreement is on the verge of success • **—¿se ha convencido? —no, pero está a punto de ~** "is he persuaded?" — "no, but he's not far off it" • **un par de horas en la cárcel te ponen a punto de ~** a couple of hours in jail soon softens you up
3 (= *incentivo*) sweetener • **es solo un ~ para evitar protestas** it's just a sweetener to stop us protesting • **agitan el ~ de los subsidios para ganar votos** they're waving the carrot of subsidies to attract votes • **su apoyo es un ~ envenenado** his support is a sugar-coated pill

caramillo SM **1** (*Mús*) flageolet
2 (= *montón*) untidy heap
3 (= *chisme*) piece of gossip • **armar un ~** to make mischief, start a gossip campaign
4 (= *jaleo*) fuss, trouble

caramilloso† ADJ fussy

caranchear ▹ CONJUG 1a VT (*Cono Sur*) to irritate, annoy

carancho SM **1** (*Perú*) (= *búho*) owl
2 (*Cono Sur*) (= *buitre*) vulture, turkey buzzard (*EEUU*)

caranga SF (*And, CAm*), **carángano** SM (*LAm*) louse

carantamaula† SF **1** (= *careta*) grotesque mask
2‡ (= *cara*) ugly mug‡; (= *persona*) ugly person

carantoña SF **1** (= *caricia*) caress; (= *zalamería*) sweet talk • **no me vengas con ~s** don't give me any of your sweet talk • **hacer ~s a algn** (= *acariciar*) to caress sb; (= *halagar*) to sweet-talk sb, butter sb up
2 (= *careta*) grotesque mask • MODISMO: • **es una ~*** she's mutton dressed up as lamb*
3‡ (= *cara*) ugly mug‡

caraota SF (*Ven*) bean

carapacho SM shell, carapace • **meterse en su ~** to go into one's shell

carapintada ADJ ultra right-wing
SMF rebel, right-wing ultranationalist

caraqueño/a ADJ of/from Caracas
SM/F native/inhabitant of Caracas • **los ~s** the people of Caracas

caráspita EXCL (*Cono Sur*) damn!

carátula SF **1** (= *portada*) [*de vídeo*] case; [*de disco*] sleeve
2 (= *careta*) mask • **la ~** (*Teat*) the stage, the theatre
3 (*Méx*) (= *muestra de reloj*) face, dial

caratular ▹ CONJUG 1a VT (*Cono Sur*) to entitle, call

caravana SF **1** (*Aut*) [*de camiones, coches*] convoy; (= *atasco*) tailback, line of traffic (*EEUU*) • **ir en ~** to go in convoy • **las ~s que se forman en el camino de la playa** the tailbacks of traffic heading for the beach
2 (= *remolque*) caravan, trailer (*EEUU*)
3 (*Hist*) caravan
4 (*Caribe*) (= *trampa*) bird trap
5 (*Méx*) (= *cortesía*) flattering remark, compliment • **bailar** *o* **correr** *o* **hacer la ~ a algn** to overdo the compliments with sb
6 caravanas (*Cono Sur*) (= *pendientes*) large earrings

caravanera SF, **caravansera** SF, **caravasar** SM caravanserai

caravaning [kara'βanin] SM caravanning, RV *o* camper vacationing (*EEUU*)

caravanismo SM caravanning, RV *o* camper vacationing (*EEUU*)

caravanista SMF caravaner

caray EXCL = **caramba**

carbohidrato SM carbohydrate

carbólico ADJ carbolic

carbón SM **1** (*Min*) coal ▸ **carbón bituminoso** soft coal, bituminous coal ▸ **carbón de leña** charcoal ▸ **carbón de piedra** coal ▸ **carbón menudo** small coal, slack ▸ **carbón pardo** brown coal ▸ **carbón térmico** steam coal ▸ **carbón vegetal** charcoal • MODISMO: • **¡se acabó el ~!** that's that, then!
2 (*Tip*) (*tb* **papel carbón**) carbon paper • **copia al ~** carbon copy
3 (*Arte*) charcoal • **dibujo al ~** charcoal drawing
4 (*Elec*) carbon
5 (*Agr*) smut

carbonada SF **1** (= *cantidad de carbón*) large load of coal
2 (*And, Cono Sur*) (= *guiso*) meat stew; (= *carne*) chop, steak
3 (*Cono Sur*) (= *sopa*) thick soup, broth; (= *picadillo*) mince, ground meat (*EEUU*)

carbonatado ADJ carbonated

carbonato SM carbonate ▸ **carbonato de calcio** calcium carbonate ▸ **carbonato**

sódico sodium carbonate
carboncillo SM charcoal • **un retrato al ~** a portrait in charcoal
carbonear ▹ CONJUG 1a VT **1** (= *convertir en carbón*) to make charcoal of
2 (*Cono Sur*) (= *incitar*) to push, egg on
carbonera SF **1** (= *mina*) coalmine
2 (*en casa*) coal bunker
3 (*Téc*) charcoal kiln; ▹ **carbonero**
carbonería SF coalyard
carbonero/a ADJ coal (*antes de s*) • **barco ~** collier • **estación carbonera** coaling station
SM/F (= *vendedor*) coal merchant, coalman; ▹ **fe**
SM **1** (*Náut*) collier
2 (*Orn*) coal tit; ▹ **carbonera**
carbónico ADJ carbonic
SM (*Cono Sur*) (*tb* **papel carbónico**) carbon, carbon paper
carbonífero ADJ carboniferous • **la industria carbonífera** the coal industry
carbonilla SF **1** (*Min*) coal dust
2 (*Aut*) carbon, carbon deposit
3 (*LAm*) (*Arte*) charcoal
carbonización SF (*Quím*) carbonization
carbonizado ADJ [*cuerpo, madera*] charred; [*ropa, papeles, coche*] burnt • **quedar ~** (= *quemado*) to be charred, be burnt to a cinder; (= *electrocutado*) to be electrocuted
carbonizar ▹ CONJUG 1f VT **1** (*Quím*) to carbonize
2 (= *quemar*) to burn
3 [+ *madera*] to make charcoal of
VPR **carbonizarse** (*Quím*) to carbonize
carbono SM carbon ▸ **carbono 14** carbon 14
carbonoso ADJ carbonaceous
carborundo SM carborundum
carbunclo SM **1** (*Min*) carbuncle
2 (*Med*) anthrax
carbunco SM (*Med*) anthrax
carburador SM carburettor, carburetor (EEUU)
carburante SM fuel
carburar ▹ CONJUG 1a VI **1** (*Aut*) to carburet
2* (= *dar buen rendimiento*) • **esta lavadora no carbura** this washing machine is not working very well • **no he dormido bien y hoy no carburo** I haven't slept well and I can't think straight today *o* I'm not very with it today*
carburo SM carbide ▸ **carburo de silicio** silicon carbide
carca* ADJ, SMF INV **1** (= *reaccionario*) reactionary
2 (= *anticuado*) square* • **¡qué tío más ~!** what a square!
carcacha* SF (*Méx*) (*Aut*) old crock
carcaj SM **1** (= *para flechas*) quiver
2 (*Méx*) rifle case
carcajada SF loud laugh, guffaw • **reírse a ~s** to roar with laughter • **soltar una ~** to burst out laughing
carcajeante ADJ [*conducta*] riotous; [*abrazo*] hearty; [*decisión*] ridiculous, laughable
carcajear ▹ CONJUG 1a VI, VPR **carcajearse** to roar with laughter
carcamal* SM old crock*
carcamán¹ SM **1** (*Náut*) tub, hulk
2 (*And, Caribe**) old crock*, wreck
carcamán²/ana SM/F **1** (*Caribe**) (= *persona*) low-class person
2 (*And, Caribe**) (= *inmigrante*) poor immigrant
3 (*Cono Sur*) (*Pol*) diehard, reactionary
carcancha SF (*Méx*) bus
carcasa SF **1** (= *armazón*) casing
2 (*Aut*) [*de motor*] chassis; [*de neumático*] carcass
3 [*de móvil*] fascia
carcayú SM wolverine
cárcel SF **1** (= *prisión*) prison, jail • **poner** *o* **meter a algn en la ~** to jail sb, send sb to jail ▸ **cárcel de régimen abierto** open prison ▸ **cárcel del pueblo** people's prison ▸ **cárcel modelo** model prison
2 (*Téc*) clamp

CÁRCEL

Uso del artículo

A la hora de traducir expresiones como **a la cárcel, en la cárcel, desde la cárcel** *etc, hemos de tener en cuenta el motivo por el que alguien acude al recinto o está allí.*

▹ *Se traduce* **a la cárcel** *por* **to jail** *o* **to prison, en la cárcel** *por* **in jail** *o* **in prison, desde la cárcel** *por* **from jail** *o* **from prison** *etc, cuando alguien va o está allí en calidad de preso:*
¿Cuánto tiempo estuvo en la cárcel?
How long was he in jail *o* prison?
No sabemos por qué los metieron en la cárcel
We don't know why they were sent to jail *o* prison

▹ *Se traduce* **a la cárcel** *por* **to the jail** *o* **to the prison, en la cárcel** *por* **in the jail** *o* **in the prison, desde la cárcel** *por* **from the jail** *o* **from the prison** *etc, cuando alguien va o está allí por otros motivos:*
Fueron a la cárcel a inspeccionar el edificio
They went to the jail *o* prison to inspect the building
Las visitas no pueden estar en la cárcel más de media hora
Visitors may only stay at the jail *o* prison for half an hour

Para otros usos y ejemplos ver la entrada.

carcelario ADJ prison (*antes de s*)
carcelería SF imprisonment, detention
carcelero ADJ prison (*antes de s*)
SM warder, jailer, guard (EEUU)
carcinogén SM carcinogen
carcinogénesis SF INV carcinogenesis
carcinogénico ADJ carcinogenic
carcinógeno SM carcinogen
carcinoma SM carcinoma
carcocha SF (*And*) = **carcacha**
carcoma SF **1** (= *insecto*) woodworm
2 (= *preocupación*) anxiety, perpetual worry
carcomer ▹ CONJUG 2a VT **1** [+ *madera*] to eat into, eat away
2 [+ *salud*] to undermine
VPR **carcomerse 1** (*Arquit*) to be worm-eaten
2 (*Med*) to waste away
carcomido ADJ **1** [*madera*] infested with woodworm
2 (= *podrido*) rotten, decayed
carcoso ADJ (*And*) dirty, mucky
carda SF **1** (*Bot*) teasel
2 (*Téc*) teasel, card
3 (= *acto*) carding
4* (= *reprimenda*) reprimand • **dar una ~ a algn** to rap sb's knuckles
cardamomo SM cardamom
cardán SM universal joint
cardar ▹ CONJUG 1a VT **1** (*Textiles*) to card, comb • MODISMO: • **~ la lana a algn*** to tell sb off, rap sb's knuckles
2 [+ *pelo*] to backcomb
3** (= *copular*) to screw**, fuck**
cardenal SM **1** (*Rel*) cardinal
2 (*Med*) bruise
3 (*Orn*) cardinal, cardinal bird
4 (*Chile*) (*Bot*) geranium
cardenalato SM cardinalate
cardenalicio ADJ • **capelo ~** cardinal's hat
cardencha SF (*Bot, Téc*) teasel
cardenillo SM verdigris
cárdeno ADJ [*color*] purple, violet; [*agua*] opalescent
cardiaco/a, cardíaco/a ADJ **1** cardiac, heart (*antes de s*) • **ataque ~** heart attack
2* • **estar ~ con algo** to be delighted with sth
SM/F sufferer from a heart complaint
cárdigan SM (*esp LAm*) cardigan
cardinal ADJ cardinal
cardio... PREF cardio...
cardiocirujano/a SM/F heart surgeon
cardiograma SM cardiogram
cardiología SF cardiology
cardiológico ADJ cardiological
cardiólogo/a SM/F cardiologist
cardiopatía SF heart disease
cardiopulmonar ADJ (*Med*) cardiopulmonary
cardiorrespiratorio ADJ cardiorespiratory
cardiosaludable ADJ good for the heart
cardiovascular ADJ cardiovascular
cardo SM thistle • MODISMO: • **es un ~*** (= *insociable*) he's a prickly customer*; (= *feo*) he's as ugly as sin*
cardón SM (*Cono Sur*) *species of giant cactus*
cardumen SM, **cardume** SM **1** (*Pesca*) shoal
2 (*And, Cono Sur**) (= *muchos*) mass • **un ~ de gente** a mass of people, a load of people*
carea SM sheepdog
carear ▹ CONJUG 1a VT [+ *personas*] to bring face to face; [+ *textos*] to compare
VPR **carearse** to come face to face
carecer ▹ CONJUG 2d VI **1** • **~ de** to lack • **carece de talento** he lacks talent, he has no talent • **no carecemos de dinero** we don't lack for money, we're not short of money • **eso carece de sentido** that doesn't make sense
2 (*Cono Sur*) (= *hacer falta*) • **carece hacerlo** we/you have to do it, it is necessary to do it • **carece no dejarla** we must not let her
carecimiento SM lack, need
carel SM side, edge
carena SF **1** (*Náut*) careening • **dar ~ a algo** to careen sth
2†* ragging*, teasing, hazing (EEUU*) • **dar ~ a algn** to rag sb*, tease sb, haze sb (EEUU*)
carenar ▹ CONJUG 1a VT to careen
carencia SF **1** (= *ausencia*) lack; (= *escasez*) lack, shortage, scarcity (*frm*) • **una ~ absoluta de recursos económicos** a total lack of economic resources • **la ~ de agua y alimentos empieza a ser preocupante** the lack *o* shortage *o* scarcity of water is starting to become worrying • **para compensar las ~s vitamínicas** to make up for vitamin deficiencies • **sufrió graves ~s emocionales y materiales** he suffered extreme emotional and material deprivation
2 (*Econ*) (= *periodo*) *period free of interest payments and debt repayments*
carenciado ADJ (*Cono Sur*) deprived
carencial ADJ • **estado ~** state of want • **enfermedad ~** deficiency disease
carente ADJ • **~ de** lacking in, devoid of (*frm*)
carentón ADJ (*Cono Sur*) large-faced
careo SM (*Jur*) confrontation, face-to-face meeting • **someter a los sospechosos a un ~** to bring the suspects face to face
carero* ADJ [*tienda*] expensive, dear, pricey*
carestía SF **1** (= *escasez*) scarcity, shortage

• **época de ~** period of shortage
2 (*Com*) high price, high cost ▸ **carestía de la vida** high cost of living

careta SF mask • **quitar la ~ a algn** to unmask sb ▸ **careta antigás** gas mask ▸ **careta de esgrima** fencing mask ▸ **careta de oxígeno** oxygen mask

careto‡ SM ugly mug‡ • **¡vaya ~ que tiene!** what an ugly mug!‡

carey SM **1** (= *material*) tortoiseshell
2 (*Zool*) turtle

carga SF **1** (= *cargamento*) **a** [*de camión, lavadora*] load; [*de barco*] cargo; [*de tren*] freight • **el camión volcó con toda la ~** the lorry overturned with a full load • **la lavadora admite cinco kilos de ~** the washing machine has a maximum load of five kilos
b (= *acto*) loading • **"zona reservada para carga y descarga"** "loading and unloading only" • **andén de ~** loading platform • **de ~ frontal** front-loading (*antes de s*) • **de ~ superior** top-loading (*antes de s*)
c (= *peso*) load • **no puedo con tanta ~** I can't take *o* manage such a heavy load • **la ~ que aguantaba la columna** the weight supported by the column ▸ **carga aérea** air cargo ▸ **carga de fractura** breaking load ▸ **carga de pago** payload ▸ **carga de rotura** breaking load ▸ **carga fija, carga muerta** dead load ▸ **carga útil** payload; ▷ **bestia, buque**
2 (= *responsabilidad*) burden • **no quiero ser una ~ para mis hijos** I don't want to be a burden to my children • **la ~ de la prueba** (*Jur*) the burden of proof • **yo soy quien lleva la ~ de esta casa** I'm the one who takes responsibility for everything in this house • **no sabes la ~ que me quitas de encima** you can't imagine what a weight off my mind that is ▸ **carga de trabajo** workload ▸ **carga financiera** (*por gastos*) financial burden; (*por intereses*) financial expense, financing cost ▸ **carga fiscal, carga impositiva** tax burden ▸ **carga lectiva** *hours of attendance at lectures or seminars* ▸ **cargas familiares** dependants, dependents (EEUU) ▸ **cargas sociales** social security contributions ▸ **carga tributaria** tax burden
3 (= *contenido*) • **el discurso tenía una fuerte ~ emocional** the speech was charged with great emotion • **se caracteriza por un exceso de ~ ideológica** it is characterized by its excessive ideological content ▸ **carga viral** viral load
4 (*en armas*) charge • **una ~ de tres kilos de explosivo** three kilos of explosives ▸ **carga de pólvora** (*Min*) gunpowder charge ▸ **carga de profundidad** depth charge ▸ **carga explosiva** explosive charge
5 (= *recambio*) [*de pluma*] cartridge; [*de bolígrafo*] refill • **se le ha acabado la ~ al mechero** the lighter has run out of fuel
6 (= *ataque*) (*Mil, Dep*) charge • **¡a la ~!** charge! • MODISMO: • **volver a la ~**: • **a los pocos minutos el equipo volvió a la ~** a few minutes later the team returned to the attack • **el grupo vuelve a la ~ con un nuevo disco** the group are back with a new record ▸ **carga de caballería** cavalry charge ▸ **carga policial** police charge
7 (*Elec*) [*de un cuerpo*] charge; [*de generador, circuito*] load ▸ **carga eléctrica** electrical charge, electric charge ▸ **carga estática** static

cargada SF **1** (*Méx*) • MODISMO: • **ir a la ~** to jump on the bandwagon
2 (*Cono Sur**) nasty practical joke

cargaderas SFPL (*And*) braces, suspenders (EEUU)

cargadero SM **1** (*Min*) (*en estación*) loading platform, goods platform; (*en puerto*) loading bay
2 (*Arquit*) lintel

cargado PP *de* **cargar**
ADJ **1** (= *con cargamento*) loaded • **el ascensor iba demasiado ~** the lift was overloaded • **la furgoneta iba cargada hasta los topes** the van was packed full • **déjame que te ayude, que vas muy cargada** let me help you, you've got such a lot to carry • **~ de algo**: • **los árboles estaban ya ~s de fruta** the trees were already weighed down *o* loaded down with fruit • **se presentó ~ de regalos** he arrived weighed down *o* loaded down with presents • **viajaba cargada de maletas** she was travelling with a ton of luggage, she was travelling loaded down with *o* weighed down with luggage • **iba cargada de joyas** she was dripping with jewels • **estamos muy ~s de trabajo** we're snowed under (with work), we're overloaded with work • **un país ~ de deudas** a country burdened *o* weighed down with debt • **la dejó cargada de hijos** he left her a brood of children to look after • **estar ~ de años** to be weighed down with age • **fue un partido ~ de tensión** it was a match fraught with tension • **ser ~ de espaldas** *o* **hombros** to be round-shouldered • **estar ~ de razón** to be totally in the right
2 (= *fuerte*) [*café, bebida alcohólica*] strong • **este gin tonic está muy ~** this gin and tonic is too strong
3 [*ambiente*] (= *no respirable*) stuffy; (= *lleno de humo*) smoky; (= *tenso*) fraught, tense • **abre la ventana que esto está muy ~** open the window, it's very stuffy in here • **el ambiente de la reunión estaba cada vez más ~** the atmosphere in the meeting became increasingly fraught *o* tense
4 (*Meteo*) (= *bochornoso*) close, overcast
5 (*Mil*) [*arma*] loaded; [*bomba, mina*] live
6 (*Elec*) [*batería, pila*] charged; [*cable*] live
7 [*dados*] loaded
8 [*ojos*] heavy • **tener los ojos ~s de sueño** to have one's eyes heavy with sleep
9* (= *borracho*) tanked up‡ • **salimos bien ~s del bar** when we left the bar we were really tanked up‡

cargador(a) SM/F (= *persona*) [*de camión*] loader; [*de barco*] docker; [*de horno*] stoker; (*Méx*) porter ▸ **cargador(a) de muelles** docker
SM **1** (*Téc*) [*de pistola, metralleta*] magazine; [*de cañón*] chamber; [*de bolígrafo*] filler; [*de pluma*] cartridge; [*de móvil*] charger ▸ **cargador de acumuladores, cargador de baterías** battery charger ▸ **cargador de discos** (*Inform*) disk pack ▸ **cargador de pilas** battery charger
2 (*Mil, Hist*) ramrod
3 cargadores (*Col*) (= *tirantes*) braces, suspenders (EEUU)

cargadora SF (*And, Caribe*) nursemaid

cargamento SM **1** [*de barco, avión*] (= *mercancías*) cargo; (= *remesa*) shipment • **el ~ del buque** the ship's cargo • **el último ~ de cigarrillos** the last shipment of cigarettes • **se han incautado de un ~ de armas** they have seized an arms shipment ▸ **cargamento de retorno** return cargo
2 [*de camión, tren*] load

cargante* ADJ [*discurso, personaje*] annoying; [*tarea*] irksome; [*persona*] trying • **¡qué tío más ~!** what a pain that bloke is!*

cargar ▷ CONJUG 1h VT **1** [+ *peso*] (= *echar*) to load; (= *llevar*) to carry • **~on los sacos en dos camiones** they loaded the sacks onto two lorries • **iba cargando la pesada cruz** he was carrying the heavy cross • **iba cargando al niño sobre los hombros** he was carrying the child on his shoulders • **cargó a sus espaldas una enorme mochila** he swung a huge rucksack up onto his back • **cuando cargaba el peso sobre la pierna mala** when he shifted the weight onto his bad leg
2 (= *llenar*) **a** [+ *vehículo, pistola, lavadora, cámara*] to load • **han terminado de ~ el avión** they've finished loading the plane • **~on el coche hasta arriba de maletas** they loaded the car up with suitcases
b (= *llenar de combustible*) [+ *mechero, pluma*] to fill; [+ *batería, pilas*] to charge; [+ *horno*] to stoke
c (*en exceso*) • **has cargado la sopa de sal** you've overdone the salt *o* put too much salt in the soup • **tratamos de no ~ a los alumnos con demasiadas horas de clase** we try not to overburden the students with too many teaching hours • MODISMOS: • **~ la mano** • **~ las tintas** to exaggerate
d [+ *imaginación, mente*] to fill • **le cargó la cabeza de ideas disparatadas** she filled his head with wild ideas
e (*Inform*) to load
3 (= *cobrar*) **a** (*en cuenta*) to charge • **~ una cantidad en cuenta a algn** to charge an amount to sb's account • **me lo pueden ~ en mi cuenta** you can charge it to my account • **~ una factura con un porcentaje por servicio** to add a service charge to a bill
b [+ *contribución*] to charge for; [+ *impuesto*] to levy
4 (= *hacer recaer*) • **~ las culpas (de algo) a algn** to blame sb (for sth), put the blame (for sth) on sb • **buscan a alguien a quien ~ la culpa** they are looking for somebody to blame *o* to put the blame on • **~ la culpabilidad en** *o* **sobre algn** to hold sb responsible, put the blame on sb
5 (= *agobiar*) • **~ a algn de algo**: **el ser campeones nos carga de responsabilidad** being champions places a lot of responsibility on our shoulders • **~ a algn de nuevas obligaciones** to burden sb with new duties • **~ a algn de deudas** to encumber sb with debts
6 (= *acusar*) to charge, accuse • **~ algo a algn** • **~ a algn con algo** to charge sb with sth, accuse sb of sth • **~ a algn de poco escrupuloso** to accuse sb of being unscrupulous, charge sb with being unscrupulous
7 (= *soportar*) [+ *culpa*] to take; [+ *responsabilidad*] to accept; [+ *carga*] to shoulder • **cargó toda la responsabilidad del fracaso** he accepted full responsibility for the disaster
8* (= *fastidiar*) • **esto me carga** this gets on my nerves*, this bugs me* • **deja de ~me** stop being such a pain*
9* (= *suspender*) to fail
10 (*Mil*) (= *atacar*) to charge, attack
11 (*Náut*) [+ *vela*] to take in
12 [+ *dados*] to load
13 (*LAm*) (= *llevar*) • **¿cargas dinero?** have you got any money on you? • **~ anteojos** to wear glasses • **~ revólver** to carry a gun
14 (*And, Cono Sur*) [*perro*] to attack, go for
VI **1** (= *echar carga*) (*Aut*) to load up; (*Náut*) to take on cargo
2 • **~ con a** [+ *objeto*] (= *levantar*) to pick up; (= *llevar*) to carry
b [+ *culpa, responsabilidad*] to take; [+ *consecuencias*] to suffer • **la empresa ~á con los gastos del viaje** the company will bear the travel expenses
3 (= *atacar*) • **la policía cargó contra los manifestantes** the police charged the

C

demonstrators • **el presidente cargó contra la prensa** the president attacked the press • **~ sobre algn** (= *presionar*) to urge sb, press sb; (= *molestar*) to pester sb
4 (= *apoyarse*) • **~ en** *o* **sobre algo** [*persona*] to lean on *o* against sth; [*muro, bóveda*] to rest on sth, be supported by sth
5 (*Ling*) [*acento*] to fall (**en, sobre** on)
6 (*Meteo*) to turn, veer (**a** to, **hacia** towards)
VPR **cargarse 1** (= *llenarse*) • **~se de** [+ *fruta, dinero*] to be full of, loaded with; [+ *culpa, responsabilidad*] to take • **mis pulmones se ~on de humo** my lungs filled with smoke • **el árbol se había cargado de manzanas** the tree was heavy laden with apples • **~se de hijos** to have lots of children • **~se de paciencia** to summon up one's patience
2* (= *destruir*) [+ *jarrón, juguete*] to smash, break; [+ *esperanzas, vida*] to ruin • **¡te lo has cargado!*** you've gone and knackered it*
3 [*aire, ambiente*] • **la atmósfera se cargó antes de la tormenta** the atmosphere became oppressive before the storm • **el ambiente se cargó de humo** the air became filled with smoke
4 [*cielo*] to become overcast
5 (*Elec*) to become charged
6* (= *hartarse*) • **me he cargado ya de tantas lamentaciones tuyas** I've had enough of your moaning
7* (= *enfadarse*) to get annoyed
8 (*Esp**) • **~se a algn** (= *suspender*) to fail sb; (= *matar*) to bump sb off*, do sb in‡; (= *eliminar*) to get rid of sb, remove sb
9 • **cargársela*** to get into hot water*, get it in the neck* • **te la vas a ~** you're in for it*, you've had it*

cargazón SF **1** (= *carga*) load; (*Náut*) cargo, shipment
2 (*Med*) heaviness ▸ **cargazón de espaldas** stoop
3 (*Meteo*) bank of heavy cloud
4 (*Cono Sur*) heavy crop of fruit (*on tree*)

cargo SM **1** (= *puesto*) post • **ocupa el ~ de comisario europeo desde hace tres años** he has held the office *o* post of European Commissioner for three years • **dejó el ~ de embajador en 1992** he left his post as ambassador in 1992 • **alto ~** (= *persona*) top official, senior official; (= *puesto*) high-ranking position, top post • **ha dimitido un alto ~ directivo** a top *o* senior official has resigned • **han quedado vacantes tres altos ~s** three high-ranking positions *o* top posts have become vacant • **desempeñar un ~** to hold a position • **jurar el ~** to be sworn in • **poner el ~ a disposición de algn** (*euf*) to offer up one's post to sb ▸ **cargo público** (= *puesto*) public office; (= *persona*) person in public office
2 • **a ~ de a** (= *responsable de*) in charge of, responsible for • **las tropas a ~ de los refugiados** the troops in charge of *o* responsible for the refugees • **los detectives a ~ de la investigación** the detectives in charge of *o* heading the investigation
b (= *bajo la responsabilidad de*) • **la presentación del programa estuvo a ~ de una actriz desconocida** the programme was presented by an unknown actress • **"formación a ~ de la empresa"** "training will be provided" • **la clausura del festival estará a ~ de Plácido Domingo** Plácido Domingo will be the main attraction of the festival's closing ceremony • **un concierto a ~ de la orquesta de cámara de la ciudad** a concert performed by the city's chamber orchestra • **la llamada irá a mi ~** I'll pay for the phone call • **las reparaciones correrán a ~ del dueño** the cost of repairs will be met by the owner, repairs will be paid for by the owner • **tener algo a su ~** to be in charge of sth, be responsible for sth • **20 policías tenían a su ~ la seguridad del monarca** 20 policemen were in charge of *o* responsible for the king's security • **los niños que tengo a mi ~** the children in my care *o* charge (*frm*)
3 • **hacerse ~ de** (= *encargarse*) to take charge of; (= *pagar*) to pay for; (= *entender*) to realize • **cuando él murió, su hijo se hizo ~ del negocio** when he died, his son took charge of *o* took over the business • **el ejército se hizo ~ del poder** the army took over power *o* took control • **el abuelo se hizo ~ del niño** the boy's grandfather took care of him • **deben hacerse ~ de los daños causados a los muebles** they should pay for breakages to the furniture • **la empresa no quiso hacerse ~ de la reparación** the company refused to meet the costs of repair • **me hago ~ de la importancia de estas conversaciones** I am aware of *o* realize how important these talks are • **—estamos pasando unos momentos difíciles —sí, ya me hago ~** "we're going through difficult times" — "yes, I understand *o* realize"
4 (*Com*) charge • **podrá recibir información sin ~ alguno** you can receive information free of charge • **paga siempre con ~ a su cuenta corriente** he always charges payments directly to his current account ▸ **cargo por gestión** [*de un billete electrónico*] administration fee
5 (*Jur*) charge • **el fiscal retiró los ~s contra el acusado** the prosecution dropped all the charges against the defendant • **fue puesto en libertad sin ~s** he was released without charges ▸ **cargo de conciencia** • **tengo ~ de conciencia por el tiempo perdido** I feel guilty about all that wasted time; ▹ **pliego, testigo**
6 (*Chile, Perú*) (= *certificación*) date stamp (*providing proof of when a document was submitted*)

cargosear* ▹ CONJUG 1a VT (*LAm*) to pester, annoy
cargoso* ADJ (*LAm*) annoying
carguera SF (*And, Caribe*) nursemaid
carguero SM **1** (= *vehículo*) (*Náut*) cargo boat; (*Aer*) freight plane ▸ **carguero militar** military transport craft
2 (*And, Cono Sur*) (= *bestia de carga*) beast of burden
carguío SM load
cari ADJ (*Cono Sur*) grey, gray (*EEUU*)
cariacontecido ADJ crestfallen, down in the mouth
cariado ADJ [*muela*] decayed
cariadura SF caries, decay
cariancho ADJ broad-faced
cariar ▹ CONJUG 1b VT to cause to decay, cause decay in
VPR **cariarse** to decay, become decayed
cariátide SF caryatid
caribe ADJ **1** (*Geog*) Caribbean • **mar Caribe** Caribbean, Caribbean Sea
2 (*LAm*) (= *caníbal*) cannibalistic
SM/F Carib
caribeño/a ADJ Caribbean
SM/F Carib
caribú SM caribou
caricato SM (*Cono Sur, Méx*) = **caricatura**
caricatura SF **1** [*de persona*] caricature
2 (*en periódico, dibujos animados*) cartoon
caricaturesco ADJ absurd, ridiculous
caricaturista SMF **1** (= *dibujante*) caricaturist
2 [*de periódico, dibujos animados*] cartoonist
caricaturización SF caricaturization, caricaturing
caricaturizar ▹ CONJUG 1f VT to caricature
caricia SF (*a persona*) caress; (*a animal*) pat, stroke • **hacer ~s a** to caress, stroke
caricioso ADJ caressing, affectionate
CARICOM SM ABR (= **Caribbean Community and Common Market**) CARICOM
caridad SF charity • **vive de la ~ de las gentes del barrio** she lives on *o* off the charity of the local people • **obra de ~** act of charity • **condonarle la deuda es una obra de ~** writing off his debt is an act of charity • **hizo muchas obras de ~** she did many charitable deeds • **dinero destinado a obras de ~** money given to charity, charity money • **¡una limosna, por ~!** could you spare some change *o* a little money (out of charity), please? • REFRÁN: • **la ~ empieza por uno mismo** charity begins at home
caries SF INV **1** (*Med*) tooth decay, caries • **está recomendado contra la ~** it's recommended for the prevention of tooth decay • **tengo una ~ en la muela del juicio** I've got some decay in my wisdom tooth
2 (*Agr*) blight
carigordo* ADJ fat-faced
carilampiño ADJ **1** (= *afeitado*) clean-shaven
2 (= *joven*) smooth-faced, beardless
carilargo* ADJ **1** (= *de cara larga*) long-faced
2 (= *enfadado*) annoyed
carilla SF **1** [*de folio, página*] side
2 (= *careta*) bee veil
carilleno* ADJ round-faced, full-faced
carillo* ADJ a bit expensive, on the dear side
carillón SM carillon
carimbo SM (*LAm*) branding iron
cariño SM **1** (= *afecto*) love, affection • **demostró mucho ~ por sus hijas** he showed great love *o* affection for his daughters • **falta de ~** lack of affection • **palabras de ~** affectionate words • **coger ~ a algn/algo** to grow *o* become fond of sb/sth, become attached to sb/sth • **con ~**: • **trata a sus plantas con mucho ~** she takes loving care of her plants • **lo recuerdo con ~** I have fond memories of it, I remember it with great affection • **con ~, Luis** (*en carta*) love (from) Luis • **dar ~ a algn** to be affectionate to sb • **sentir ~ por algn** to be fond of sb, like sb • **tener ~ a algn/algo** to be fond of sb/sth, like sb/sth • **tomar ~ a algn/algo** to grow *o* become fond of sb/sth, become attached to sb/sth
2 (*apelativo*) darling, honey* • **ven aquí, ~** come here darling
3 (= *caricia*) • **dar** *o* **hacer (un) ~ a algn** to caress sb, stroke sb
4 (*LAm*) (= *regalo*) gift, token (of affection)
5 cariños (= *saludos*) love • **Rosa te manda muchos ~s** Rosa sends her love
cariñosamente ADV affectionately, lovingly, fondly
cariñoso ADJ affectionate, loving
carioca ADJ of/from Rio de Janeiro
SMF native/inhabitant of Rio de Janeiro • **los ~s** the people of Rio de Janeiro
cariparejo* ADJ poker-faced, inscrutable
carirraído* ADJ brazen, shameless
carirredondo* ADJ round-faced
carisellazo SM (*And*) toss of a coin • **echar un ~** to toss a coin, spin a coin
carisma SM charisma
carismático ADJ charismatic
carita SF (= *cara pequeña*) little face • MODISMOS: • **de ~** (*And*) first-class • **dar** *o* **hacer ~** (*Méx*) [*mujer*] to return a smile, flirt, flirt back • **hacer ~s** (*And*) to make faces
caritativamente ADV charitably

caritativo (ADJ) charitable (**con, para** to)

cariz (SM) **1** (= *aspecto*) look • **este asunto está tomando mal ~** this is beginning to look bad, I don't like the look of this • **en vista del ~ que toman las cosas** in view of the way things are going
2 (*Meteo*) outlook

carlanca (SF) **1** (= *collar*) spiked dog-collar
2 (*And, CAm*) (= *grillo*) shackle, fetter
3 (*CAm, Cono Sur*) (= *persona*) bore, pest, drag; (= *aburrimiento*) boredom, tedium; (= *enojo*) annoyance, irritation
4 carlancas (= *picardía*) tricks, cunning (*sing*) • **tener muchas ~s** to be full of tricks

carlinga (SF) cockpit, cabin

carlismo (SM) Carlism

> **CARLISMO**
> The controversial change which Ferdinand VII of Spain made to the law in order to allow his daughter Isabella to succeed him instead of his brother, Carlos María Isidro de Borbón, gave rise to Carlism, a movement supporting Carlos's claim to the throne. It also sparked off a series of armed conflicts. The First Carlist War (1833-1839) was declared by Carlos when Isabella came to the throne, the Second (1860) was started by his son of the same name, and the Third (1872-76) by a grandson, another Don Carlos. The last Carlist pretender, Alfonso, died in 1936 without descendants, although that did not prevent the **Falange Española** from later backing the Carlist cause in an attempt to prevent the current king, Juan Carlos, being designated Franco's successor. To this day there is still a Carlist party in Spain.
> ▸ **FALANGE ESPAÑOLA**

carlista (ADJ), (SMF) Carlist

carlistada (SF) Carlist attack, Carlist uprising

Carlitos (SM) (*forma familiar de* **Carlos**) Charlie

Carlomagno (SM) Charlemagne

Carlos (SM) Charles

Carlota (SF) Charlotte

carlota (SF) (*Culin*) charlotte

carmelita (ADJ) **1** (*Rel*) Carmelite
2 (*LAm*) light brown, tan
(SMF) Carmelite • **~ descalzo** discalced Carmelite

carmelitano (ADJ) Carmelite

carmelito (ADJ) (*LAm*) light brown, tan

Carmelo (SM) Carmelite convent

Carmen (SM) (*Rel*) Carmelite Order

carmen[1] (SM) (*en Granada*) villa with a garden

carmen[2] (SM) (*liter*) song, poem

carmenar* ▸ CONJUG 1a (VT) **1** (= *cardar*) [+ *lana*] to card, teasel; [+ *seda*] to unravel; [+ *pelo*] to disentangle • **~ a algn*** to pull sb's hair
2* (= *estafar*) to fleece, swindle

carmesí (ADJ), (SM) crimson

carmín (SM) **1** (= *color*) carmine
2 (= *pintalabios*) lipstick
3 (*Bot*) dog rose

carminativo (ADJ) carminative

carmíneo (ADJ) carmine, crimson

carnada (SF) bait

carnal (ADJ) **1** (*Rel*) carnal, of the flesh
2 [*pariente*] full, blood (*antes de s*) • **hermano ~** full brother • **primo ~** first cousin • **tío ~** real uncle
(SM) (*Méx**) pal*, buddy (*EEUU**)

carnalidad (SF) lust, carnality

carnaval (SM) **1** (= *fiesta*) carnival
2 (*Rel*) Shrovetide • **martes de ~** Shrove Tuesday

> **CARNAVAL**
> **Carnaval** is the traditional period of fun, feasting and partying that precedes the start of Lent (**Cuaresma**). The most important day is probably Shrove Tuesday (**Martes de Carnaval**), but throughout **Carnaval** there are fancy-dress parties, parades and firework displays. In some places in Spain, the changeover from **Carnaval** to Lent on Ash Wednesday is marked by the **Entierro de la Sardina**. This is a grotesque funeral parade in which the symbolic cardboard figure of a sardine is marched through the streets and finally ceremonially burnt or buried.

carnavalero (ADJ), **carnavalesco** (ADJ) carnival (*antes de s*)

carnavalito (SM) (*And, Chile*) folk song and dance

carnaza (SF) **1** (= *cebo*) (*para peces*) groundbait; (*para leones*) scraps (*pl*) of meat
2 [*de escándalo, suceso*] • **dar ~ a la gente** to feed people (with) juicy titbits

carne (SF) **1** (*Culin*) meat • **MODISMOS:** • **poner toda la ~ en el asador** to pull out all the stops, give it one's all • **no ser ~ ni pescado** to be neither fish nor fowl, be neither one thing nor the other • **ser ~ de algo***: • **son ~ de cañón** they are cannon-fodder • **son ~ de prestamista** they are prime targets for moneylenders • **eran ~ de prisión** they were prime candidates to end up in prison ▸ **carne adobada** marinated meat ▸ **carne asada** roast meat ▸ **carne blanca** white meat ▸ **carne bovina, carne de bovino** beef ▸ **carne congelada** frozen meat ▸ **carne cruda** raw meat ▸ **carne de carnero** mutton ▸ **carne de cerdo, carne de chancho** (*LAm*) pork ▸ **carne de cordero** lamb ▸ **carne de res** (*LAm*) beef ▸ **carne deshilachada** (*CAm, Méx*) stewed meat ▸ **carne de ternera** veal ▸ **carne de vaca** beef ▸ **carne de venado** venison ▸ **carne magra, carne mollar** lean meat ▸ **carne marinada** (*LAm*) salt meat ▸ **carne molida** (*LAm*), **carne picada** mince, ground meat (*esp EEUU*) ▸ **carne porcina** pork ▸ **carne roja** red meat ▸ **carne salvajina** game ▸ **carnes blandas** (*Cono Sur*) white meat (*sing*) ▸ **carne tapada** stewed meat, stew
2 (*Anat*) flesh • **MODISMOS:** • **de ~ y hueso:** • **las marionetas parecían actores de ~ y hueso** the puppets were just like real-life actors • **ser de ~ y hueso** to be only human • **me enamoro como cualquier chica de mi edad, soy de ~ y hueso** I fall in love like any girl of my age, I'm only human • **en ~ y hueso** in the flesh • **en ~ viva:** • **tenía las rodillas en ~ viva** his knees were raw • **un programa que muestra el horror en ~ viva** a programme that shows the full horror ▸ **carne de gallina** gooseflesh, goose pimples (*pl*), goose bumps (*pl*) (*EEUU*) • **me pone la ~ de gallina** [*de frío, emoción*] it gives me goose pimples *o* (*EEUU*) goose bumps; [*de miedo*] it gives me the creeps, it makes my flesh crawl
3 carnes [*de persona*] • **de abundantes ~s** amply proportioned • **criar** *o* **echar ~s** to put on weight • **entrado** *o* **metido en ~s** plump, overweight • **algo metidita en ~s** somewhat plump • **de pocas ~s** thin, skinny
4 (*Rel*) flesh • **la ~ es débil** the flesh is weak • **el Verbo se hizo ~** the Word was made flesh • **los pecados de la ~** sins of the flesh
5 (*Bot*) flesh, pulp; (*LAm*) [*de árbol*] heart(wood) ▸ **carne de membrillo** quince jelly
(ADJ) • **color ~** flesh-coloured, flesh-colored (*EEUU*) • **medias de color ~** flesh-coloured tights

carné (SM) = carnet

carneada (SF) (*Cono Sur*) slaughter, slaughtering

carnear ▸ CONJUG 1a (VT) **1** (*Cono Sur*) [+ *ganado*] to slaughter; [+ *persona*] to murder, butcher
2 (*Chile*) to deceive, take in*

carnecería (SF) = carnicería

carnerada (SF) flock of sheep

carnerear ▸ CONJUG 1a (VI) (*Cono Sur*) to blackleg, be a strikebreaker

carnerero (SM) shepherd

carnero (SM) **1** (*Zool*) sheep, ram • **MODISMOS:** • **no hay tales ~s** there's no such thing • **cantar para el ~‡** to kick the bucket‡, peg out‡ ▸ **carnero de la sierra** (*LAm*), **carnero de la tierra** (*LAm*) llama, alpaca, vicuña ▸ **carnero de simiente** breeding ram ▸ **carnero marino** seal
2 (*Culin*) mutton
3 (= *piel*) sheepskin
4 (*Cono Sur*) (= *esquirol*) blackleg, scab*
5 • **MODISMO:** • **botarse** *o* **echarse al ~** (*Cono Sur*) to chuck it all up*, throw in the towel

carnestolendas (SFPL) Shrovetide (*sing*)

carnet [kar'ne] (SM) (PL: **carnets** [kar'nes]) • **tiene ~ del partido socialista** he has a membership card for the Socialist party • **un miembro con ~** a card-carrying member • **una fotografía tamaño ~** a passport-sized photo ▸ **carnet de conducir** driving licence, driver's license (*EEUU*) • **sacarse el ~ de conducir** to get one's driving licence ▸ **carnet de estudiante** student card ▸ **carnet de identidad** identity card; ▸ DNI ▸ **carnet de prensa** press pass ▸ **carnet de socio** membership card ▸ **carnet por puntos** penalty-points driving licence, *type of driving licence in which drivers start with a certain number of points that can be reduced or lost if they commit driving offences, potentially culminating in the loss of the licence*

carnicería (SF) **1** (*Com*) butcher's, butcher's shop
2 (= *matanza*) slaughter, carnage • **ha sido una ~ de inocentes** it was a slaughter of the innocent(s)
3 (*And*) slaughterhouse

carnicero/a (ADJ) **1** (= *carnívoro*) carnivorous, meat-eating
2 (= *cruel*) cruel, bloodthirsty
(SM/F) **1** (= *persona*) butcher
2 (= *carnívoro*) carnivore, meat-eater

cárnico (ADJ) meat (*antes de s*) • **industria cárnica** meat industry

carnitas (SFPL) (*Méx*) barbecued pork (*sing*)

carnívoro (ADJ) carnivorous, meat-eating
(SM) carnivore, meat-eater

carnosidad (SF) **1** (= *masa carnosa*) fleshy part
2 (= *gordura*) corpulence, fleshiness
3 (*Med*) proud flesh

carnoso (ADJ) meaty

carnudo (ADJ) fleshy

caro (ADJ) **1** (= *costoso*) expensive, dear • **un coche carísimo** a very expensive car • **costar ~** to be expensive, cost a lot • **el abrigo me costó muy ~** my coat was very expensive, my coat cost a lot • **le costó ~ tal atrevimiento** his daring cost him dear • **pagar ~ algo** to pay dearly for sth • **pagó cara su insolencia** he paid dearly for his insolence • **salir ~:** • **un piso amueblado sale más ~** a furnished flat is more expensive • **en total el viaje nos salió muy ~** altogether the trip was *o* proved very expensive
2 (= *querido*) (*liter*) dear, beloved • **las cosas que nos son tan caras** the things which are so dear to us • **¡mi ~ amigo!** my dear *o*

beloved friend!
(ADV) • **vender ~: esa tienda vende ~** that shop is expensive
carocas†* (SFPL) **1** (= *lisonjas*) flattery (*sing*)
2 (= *caricias*) caresses
carocha* (SF) (*Méx*) old banger*, jalopy*
caroleno (SM) (*Méx*) backslang
Carolina[1] (SF) Caroline
Carolina[2] (SF) (*Geog*) ▸ **Carolina del Norte** North Carolina ▸ **Carolina del Sur** South Carolina
carolingio (ADJ) Carolingian
carón (*LAm*) (ADJ) broad-faced
(SM)‡ mug‡, face
carona (SF) **1** (*Equitación*) (= *paño*) saddlecloth; (= *parte del caballo*) saddle
• MODISMO: • **andar con las ~s ladeadas** (*Cono Sur*) to have problems
2 (*Cono Sur*) bed
carota* (SMF) cool customer*
carótida (SF) carotid, carotid artery
carozo (SM) **1** cob of maize, corncob (*EEUU*)
2 (*LAm*) [*de fruta*] stone, pit (*EEUU*)
carpa[1] (SF) (= *pez*) carp ▸ **carpa dorada** goldfish
carpa[2] (SF) **1** [*de circo*] big top
2 (= *toldo*) awning
3 (*esp LAm*) (= *tienda de campaña*) tent
4 (*Méx*) travelling show

> **CARPA**
> In Mexico a **carpa** is a travelling show held under a big top. Originating in the nationalistic aftermath of the Mexican revolution, **carpas** toured agricultural communities and mining towns offering a menu of satire, slapstick humour, dramatic sketches and humorous monologues, as well as acrobatics, tightrope walking and other circus entertainments. It was in the **carpa** that the Mexican comic character, **Cantinflas**, started life.
> ▸ PELADO

carpanta (SF) **1*** (= *hambre*) ravenous hunger
2 (*Méx*) gang
Cárpatos (ADJ) • **montes ~** Carpathians
carpeta (SF) **1** (*para papeles, documentos*) folder, file • MODISMO: • **cerrar la ~** to close the file (*in an investigation*) ▸ **carpeta de anillas** ring binder ▸ **carpeta de información** information folder, briefing kit
2 (= *cartera*) briefcase
3 [*de mesa*] table cover
4 (*LAm*) (= *pupitre*) table, desk
carpetazo (SM) • MODISMO: • **dar ~ a algo** to shelve sth, do nothing about sth
carpetovetónico (ADJ) terribly Spanish, Spanish to the core
carpiano (ADJ) (*Med*) carpal • **síndrome del túnel ~** carpal tunnel syndrome
carpidor (SM) (*LAm*), **carpidora** (SF) (*LAm*) weeding hoe
carpincho (SM) (*Cono Sur*) capybara
carpintear ▸ CONJUG 1a (VI) **1** (*como profesional*) to carpenter
2 (*como aficionado*) to do woodwork (*as a hobby*)
carpintería (SF) **1** (= *arte, oficio*) carpentry, joinery
2 (= *afición*) woodwork
3 (= *taller*) carpenter's shop
carpintero (SM) **1** (*Téc*) carpenter
▸ **carpintero de blanco** joiner ▸ **carpintero de buque** ship's carpenter, shipwright
▸ **carpintero de carretas, carpintero de prieto** cartwright, wheelwright
▸ **carpintero de ribera** = **carpintero de buque**
2 (*Orn*) woodpecker
carpir ▸ CONJUG 3a (VT) (*LAm*) to weed, hoe
carraca (SF) **1** (*Mús, Dep*) rattle
2 (= *vehículo viejo*) (= *coche*) banger*, jalopy*; (= *barco*) tub
3 (*Téc*) ratchet brace
4 • MODISMO: • **echar ~** (*And*) to lie
carraco (ADJ) feeble, decrepit
(SM)* (= *coche*) old banger*, jalopy*
carrada (SF) (*Cono Sur*) = **carretada**
carral (SM) barrel, vat
carralero (SM) cooper
carrasca (SF) kermes oak • MODISMO: • **ser de ~*** to be absolutely awful
carrascoloso‡ (ADJ) (*LAm*) grumpy*, touchy, irritable
carraspear ▸ CONJUG 1a (VI) (*al hablar*) to be hoarse, have a frog in one's throat; (*al aclararse*) to clear one's throat
carraspeo (SM) • **es incómodo oír en el cine los continuos ~s** it's unpleasant hearing people continuously clearing their throats in the cinema
carraspera (SF) hoarseness
carrasposo (ADJ) **1** (*Med*) hoarse, with a sore throat
2 (*LAm*) rough, harsh
carrera (SF) **1** (= *acción*) (*tb Béisbol*) run • **tuvimos que pegarnos una ~ para no perder el tren** we had to run for it so as not to miss the train • **emprendí una loca ~ en dirección a la salida** I made a mad dash *o* rush for the exit • **¿nos echamos una ~ hasta el muro?** race you to the wall! • **nos fuimos de una ~ y llegamos en cinco minutos** we ran for it *o* rushed over and got there in five minutes • MODISMOS: • **a la ~** at (full) speed, hurriedly • **consiguieron escapar a la ~** they managed to make a quick getaway • **siento tener que dar explicaciones tan a la ~** I'm sorry to have to explain in such a rush • **tuvo que hacer el trabajo a la ~** he had to rush through the job *o* do the job in a rush • **a ~ tendida** at full speed, flat out* ▸ **carrera de aterrizaje** landing run ▸ **carrera de despegue** take-off run ▸ **carrera del oro** gold rush
2 (= *competición*) race • **las ~s de Fórmula 1** Formula 1 races ▸ **carrera armamentista, carrera armamentística** arms race
▸ **carrera campo a través** cross country race
▸ **carrera ciclista** (bi)cycle race ▸ **carrera contrarreloj** (*lit*) time trial; (*fig*) race against time ▸ **carrera corta** dash, sprint ▸ **carrera de armamentos** arms race ▸ **carrera de caballos** horse race ▸ **carrera de coches** motor race ▸ **carrera de ensacados** (*Cono Sur*) sack race ▸ **carrera de fondo** long-distance race ▸ **carrera de galgos** greyhound race ▸ **la Carrera de Indias** (*Hist*) the Indies run ▸ **carrera de medio fondo** middle-distance race ▸ **carrera de obstáculos** (*Atletismo, Equitación*) steeplechase; (*para niños*) obstacle race
▸ **carrera de relevos** relay, relay race
▸ **carrera de resistencia** long-distance race
▸ **carrera de sacos** sack race ▸ **carrera de vallas** (*Atletismo*) hurdles; (*Equitación*) steeplechase ▸ **carrera espacial** space race
▸ **carrera pedestre** walking race ▸ **carrera popular** fun run
3 (*tb* **carrera universitaria**) (university) course • **no sabe qué hará cuando termine la ~** he doesn't know what he'll do after university *o* when he finishes his course • **está en primero de ~** she's in her first year (at university) • **quiere que sus hijos estudien una ~** she wants her children to go to university • **había comenzado a estudiar la ~ de Medicina** she had started studying medicine • **dar ~ a algn** to pay sb through college • **hacer una ~**: • **estoy haciendo la ~ de Económicas** I'm doing a degree in economics • **tener ~** to have a (university) degree ▸ **carrera de ciencias** science degree
▸ **carrera de letras** arts degree
4 (*tb* **carrera profesional**) career • **tuvo una brillante ~ como actriz** she had an outstanding career as an actress • **se encuentra en uno de los momentos más difíciles de su ~ política** this is one of the most difficult moments of her political career • **diplomático de ~** career diplomat • **militar de ~** career officer • **hacer ~** to advance one's career, pursue a career • **quiso hacer ~ en el partido** he tried to pursue a career *o* advance his career in the party • **muchos prefieren hacer ~ en el extranjero** many prefer to pursue careers abroad • MODISMOS: • **hacer ~ de *o* con algn** to make headway with sb • **no hago ~ con este niño** I can't make any headway *o* I'm getting nowhere with this child • **hacer la ~*** to be on the game* ▸ **carrera artística** [*de actor*] career as an actor; [*de pintor, escultor*] artistic career ▸ **carrera cinematográfica** film career ▸ **carrera literaria** literary career, career as a writer ▸ **carrera militar** career as a soldier, military career ▸ **carrera política** political career, career as a politician
5 (*en medias*) run, ladder
6 (= *recorrido*) [*de desfile*] route; [*de taxi*] ride, journey; [*de barco*] run, route; [*de estrella, planeta*] course • **la ~ del sol** the course of the sun
7 (= *avenida*) avenue
8 (*Mec*) [*de émbolo*] stroke; [*de válvula*] lift
▸ **carrera ascendente** upstroke ▸ **carrera descendente** downstroke
9 (= *hilera*) row, line; [*de ladrillos*] course
10 (= *viga*) beam, rafter
11 (*Mús*) run
carrerilla (SF) • **a ~** non-stop, continuously • **de ~** on the trot, in succession • **lo dijo de ~** he reeled it off in one go • **tomar ~** to take a run up
carrerista (ADJ) fond of racing
(SMF) **1** (= *aficionado a carreras de caballos*) racing man/woman, racegoer, professional punter
2 (= *ciclista*) racing cyclist
3 (*Pol*) careerist, career politician
(SF)* streetwalker, hustler (*EEUU**)
carrero (SM) carter, cart driver
carreta (SF) **1** (= *carro*) (*cubierta*) waggon, wagon; (*sin cubrir*) cart • MODISMO: • **tener la ~ llena** (*Caribe*) to be weighed down by problems ▸ **carreta de bueyes** oxcart
▸ **carreta de mano** = **carretilla**
2 (*Col, Ven*) wheelbarrow
carretada (SF) waggonload, wagonload, cart load • MODISMO: • **a ~s**: • **había pan a ~s** there was loads of bread • **llegaron a ~s** they came by the waggonload
carretaje (SM) cartage, haulage
carrete (SM) **1** (*Fot*) film
2 (*Cos*) reel, bobbin • MODISMOS: • **dar ~ a algn*** to keep sb amused *o* entertained
• **tiene ~ para rato*** she could gab all day*
3 (*Elec*) coil ▸ **carrete de encendido** (*Aut*) ignition coil ▸ **carrete de inducción** induction coil
4 (*Pesca*) reel
carretear ▸ CONJUG 1a (VT) **1** [+ *carga*] to cart, haul
2 [+ *carro*] to drive
3 (*Aer*) to taxi
carretel (SM) **1** (*Pesca*) reel, fishing reel
2 (*Náut*) log reel
carretela (SF) **1** (*Hist*) coach, carriage

2 (*CAm*) (= *carro*) cart
carretera (SF) road, highway (*esp EEUU*) • **la ~ entre Barcelona y Sitges** the Barcelona-Sitges road, the road between Barcelona and Sitges • **de ~**: • **bar de ~** roadside bar • **accidente de ~** road accident, traffic accident • **control de ~** roadblock • **por ~**: • **un viaje por ~** a road journey, a journey by road • **transporte por ~** road transport • **circulación por ~** (road) traffic • **hemos venido por ~** we drove here ▸ **carretera comarcal** local road, ≈ B road ▸ **carretera de acceso** approach road ▸ **carretera de circunvalación** bypass, ring road, beltway (*EEUU*) ▸ **carretera de cuota** (*Méx*) toll road ▸ **carretera general** main road ▸ **carretera nacional** ≈ A road, ≈ state highway (*EEUU*) ▸ **carretera radial** arterial road
carretero (ADJ) • **camino ~** vehicular road
(SM) **1** (= *transportista*) cartwright, wheelwright • **MODISMOS**: • **fumar como un ~** to smoke like a chimney • **jurar como un ~** to swear like a trooper
2 (*LAm*) road
carretilla (SF) **1** (*tb* **carretilla de mano**) handcart, barrow ▸ **carretilla de horquilla, carretilla elevadora** fork-lift truck
2 (*Hort*) wheelbarrow
3 (*en tienda*) trolley, cart (*EEUU*)
4 (= *buscapiés*) squib, cracker
5 (*Cono Sur*) (= *quijada*) jaw, jawbone
6 (*Col*) (= *serie*) lot, series
7 • **MODISMO**: • **de ~**: • **saber algo de ~** to know sth by heart • **aprender algo de ~** to learn sth parrot fashion *o* by rote
carretón (SM) small cart ▸ **carretón de remolque** trailer
carricero (SM) ▸ **carricero común** reed warbler
carricoche (SM) covered wagon, caravan, gipsy caravan
carricuba (SF) water cart
carriel (SM) (*And, CAm*) leather case
carril (SM) **1** (*en carretera*) lane • **el camión invadió el ~ izquierdo** the truck wandered into the left lane ▸ **carril bici** cycle lane, bikeway (*EEUU*) ▸ **carril bus** bus lane ▸ **carril de acceso** slip road ▸ **carril de aceleración** acceleration lane ▸ **carril de adelantamiento** overtaking lane, fast lane
2 (*Ferro*) (= *vía*) rail; (*Caribe, Cono Sur*) (= *tren*) train
3 (= *camino*) track, lane
4 (*Agr*) [*del arado*] furrow
5 (*LAm*) (*Dep*) (= *calle*) lane
carrilano (*Chile*) (ADJ) railway (*antes de s*), railroad (*antes de s*) (*EEUU*)
(SM) railway labourer, railroad laborer (*EEUU*)
carril-bici (SM) (PL: **carriles-bici**) cycle lane, bikeway (*EEUU*)
carril-bus (SM) (PL: **carriles-bus**) bus lane
carrilera (SF) **1** (= *rodera*) rut, track
2 (*Caribe*) (*Ferro*) siding
carrilero (SM) **1** (*And*) (*Ferro*) railwayman, railroad man (*EEUU*)
2 (*Cono Sur*‡) (= *embaucador*) con man*
carrillera (SF) **1** (*Zool*) jaw
2 [*de casco*] chinstrap
carrillo (SM) **1** (*Anat*) cheek, jowl • **MODISMO**: • **comer a dos ~s** to stuff o.s.*, stuff one's face*
2 (*Téc*) pulley
carrindanga* (SF) (*Cono Sur*) old banger*, jalopy*
carriola (SF) truckle bed
carrito (SM) **1** (*para llevar cosas*) (*en supermercado*) trolley, cart (*EEUU*); (*en hotel*) tea trolley, serving trolley ▸ **carrito de bebidas** drinks trolley ▸ **carrito de golf** golf trolley ▸ **carrito de postres** dessert trolley
2 (*Caribe*) (= *taxi*) taxi
carrizal (SM) reedbed
carrizo (SM) **1** (*Bot*) reed
2 carrizos (*And, Méx*) (= *piernas*) thin *o* spindly legs, pins‡, gams (*EEUU**)
3 • **MODISMO**: • **no nos ayudan un ~** (*Ven*) they do nothing at all to help us
carro (SM) **1** (= *carreta*) cart, waggon, wagon • **MODISMOS**: • **aguantar ~s y carretas** to put up with anything • **apearse** *o* **bajarse del ~*** to leave off, give it a rest* • **¡para el ~!*** hold your horses! • **pararle el ~ a algn*** to tell sb to stop • **poner el ~ delante de las mulas** *o* **los bueyes** to put the cart before the horse • **subirse al ~** to climb *o* jump on the bandwagon • **tirar del ~** to do all the donkey work • **untar el ~ a algn** to grease sb's palm ▸ **carro alegórico** float ▸ **carro aljibe** water cart ▸ **carro de golf** golf buggy ▸ **carro de guerra** (*Hist*) chariot ▸ **carro de la compra** shopping trolley, shopping cart (*EEUU*)
2 (*Mil*) tank ▸ **carro blindado** armoured car, armored car (*EEUU*), armour-plated car, armor-plated car (*EEUU*) ▸ **carro de asalto, carro de combate** tank
3 (*LAm*) (= *coche*) car; (= *taxi*) cab, taxi; (= *vagón*) carriage, car (*esp EEUU*); (= *autobús*) bus, coach ▸ **carro comedor** (*Méx*) dining car, restaurant car ▸ **carro correo** mail van ▸ **carro cuba** tank truck ▸ **carro de mudanzas** removal van, moving van (*EEUU*) ▸ **carro dormitorio** (*Méx*) sleeping car ▸ **carro fúnebre** hearse ▸ **carros chocones** (*Méx*), **carros locos** (*Col*) bumper cars, dodgems (*Brit*) ▸ **carro tranvía, carro urbano** tramcar, streetcar (*EEUU*)
4 [*de máquina de escribir*] carriage
5 (= *carga*) cartload • **un ~ de problemas** a whole load of problems
carrocería (SF) **1** (*Aut*) bodywork
2 (= *taller*) coachbuilder's, body shop
carrocero/a (SM/F) coachbuilder, car-body maker
carrocha (SF) eggs (*pl*) (*of insect*)
carromato (SM) covered wagon, caravan, gypsy caravan
carroña (SF) carrion
carroñero (ADJ) **1** [*persona*] vile, foul
2 • **animal ~** animal which feeds on carrion
carroño (ADJ) **1** (= *putrefacto*) rotten, putrid, foul
2 (*And*) (= *cobarde*) cowardly
carroza (SF) **1** (= *vehículo*) [*de caballos*] coach, carriage; [*de carnaval*] float ▸ **carroza fúnebre** hearse
2 (*Náut*) awning
(SMF) **1** (= *viejo*) old boy*, old geezer‡; (= *vieja*) old girl*
2 (= *carca*) old fogey*
(ADJ INV)* **1** (= *viejo*) old
2 (= *carca*) • **es muy ~** he's an old fogey*
carruaje (SM) carriage
carrujo‡ (SM) (*LAm*) joint‡, reefer‡
carrusel (SM) **1** [*de verbena*] merry-go-round, roundabout, carousel (*EEUU*)
2 (*Fot*) carousel, circular slide tray
3 [*de regalos*] revolving display
carry-all (SM) (*Cono Sur*) estate car, station wagon (*EEUU*)
carta (SF) **1** (*Correos*) letter • **echar una ~ (al correo)** to post a letter • **MODISMOS**: • **a ~ cabal** thoroughly, in every respect • **era honrado a ~ cabal** he was totally honest • **es un caballero a ~ cabal** a true *o* real gentleman • **tomar ~s en el asunto** to step in ▸ **carta abierta** open letter ▸ **carta adjunta** covering letter ▸ **carta certificada** registered letter ▸ **carta de acuse de recibo** letter of acknowledgement ▸ **carta de amor** love letter ▸ **carta de asignación** letter of allotment ▸ **carta de aviso** letter of advice ▸ **carta de despido** letter of dismissal, pink slip (*EEUU**) ▸ **carta de dimisión** letter of resignation ▸ **carta de pésame** letter of condolence ▸ **carta de presentación** letter of introduction • **esta exposición es la mejor ~ de presentación del pintor** this exhibition is the best introduction to the painter ▸ **carta de recomendación** (*para un trabajo*) letter of recommendation; (*como presentación*) letter of introduction ▸ **carta de solicitud** (letter of) application ▸ **carta pastoral** pastoral letter ▸ **carta postal** (*LAm*) postcard ▸ **carta tipo** standard letter ▸ **carta urgente** special-delivery letter
2 (*Jur, Com*) (= *documento*) ▸ **carta blanca** carte blanche • **dar ~ blanca a algn** to give sb carte blanche • **tener ~ blanca** to have a free hand, have carte blanche ▸ **carta de ciudadanía** naturalization papers (*pl*) ▸ **carta de crédito** letter of credit • **~ de crédito documentaria** documentary letter of credit • **~ de crédito irrevocable** irrevocable letter of credit ▸ **carta de emplazamiento** summons ▸ **carta de hidalguía** letters patent of nobility (*pl*) ▸ **carta de intenciones** letter of intent ▸ **carta de naturaleza** naturalization papers (*pl*) • **MODISMO**: • **adquirir** *o* **tomar ~ de naturaleza** to come to be like one of the natives, be thoroughly accepted ▸ **carta de pago** receipt, discharge in full ▸ **carta de pedido** (*Com*) order ▸ **carta de portes** bill of lading ▸ **carta de venta** bill of sale ▸ **carta ejecutoria** letters patent of nobility (*pl*) ▸ **carta verde** (*Aut*) green card, certificate of insurance (*EEUU*) ▸ **cartas credenciales** credentials
3 (= *estatuto*) charter • **la Carta de las Naciones Unidas** the United Nations Charter ▸ **Carta de Derechos** Bill of Rights ▸ **Carta Magna** (= *constitución*) constitution; (*Brit*) (*Hist*) Magna Carta ▸ **Carta Social (Europea)** (European) Social Charter
4 (*Naipes*) card • **una baraja de ~s españolas** a pack of Spanish (playing) cards • **echar las ~s a algn** to tell sb's fortune (*with cards*) • **fui a una pitonisa a que me echara las ~s** I went to a fortune-teller to have my fortune told with cards • **jugar a las ~s** to play cards • **MODISMOS**: • **¡~ canta!** there it is in black and white! • **enseñar las ~s** to show one's hand • **poner las ~s boca arriba** *o* **sobre la mesa** to put *o* lay one's cards on the table • **no saber a qué ~ quedarse** not to know what to think, be undecided • **a ~s vistas** openly, honestly ▸ **carta de figura** picture card
5 (*Culin*) menu • **a la ~** à la carte; [*televisión*] on demand ▸ **carta de vinos** wine list
6 (= *mapa*) (*Geog*) map; (*Náut*) chart ▸ **carta acotada** contour map ▸ **carta astral** star chart ▸ **carta bomba** letter-bomb ▸ **carta de flujo** flowchart ▸ **carta de marear** chart ▸ **carta de navegación, carta de viaje, carta de vuelo** flight plan ▸ **carta geográfica, carta marítima** chart ▸ **carta meteorológica** weather chart, weather map ▸ **carta náutica, carta naval** chart
7 (*TV*) ▸ **carta de ajuste** test card
carta-bomba (SF) (PL: **cartas-bomba**) letter-bomb
cartabón (SM) **1** (= *instrumento*) [*de dibujante*] set square, triangle (*EEUU*); [*de carpintero*] square, set square
2 (*Mil*) quadrant
cartagenero/a (ADJ) of/from Cartagena
(SM/F) native/inhabitant of Cartagena • **los ~s** the people of Cartagena

cartaginés/esa (ADJ), (SM/F) Carthaginian
Cartago (SF) Carthage
cartapacio (SM) **1** (= *cuaderno*) notebook
2 (= *carpeta*) folder
carta-tarjeta (SF) (PL: **cartas-tarjeta**) letter card
cartear ▷ CONJUG 1a (VI) (*Naipes*) to play low (VPR) **cartearse** to correspond (**con** with) • **se ~on durante dos años** they wrote to each other for two years
cartel (SM) **1** (= *póster*) poster • **el ~ del Festival** the poster for the Festival • **"se prohíbe fijar carteles"** "stick no bills", "post no bills" • **ser cabeza de ~** to be top of the bill • **en ~: esa película ya no está en ~** that film is not showing yet, that film is not on yet • **"Cats" lleva años en ~** "Cats" has been running for years
2 (= *letrero*) sign • **no vi el ~ de "prohibido fumar"** I didn't see the no smoking sign
3 (= *fama*) • **tener ~** to be well known • **un torero de ~** a star bullfighter
cártel (SM) cartel, trust
cartela (SF) **1** (= *papel*) slip of paper, bit of card
2 (*Arquit*) console
cartelera (SF) [*de cine*] hoarding, billboard; (*en periódico*) entertainments (*pl*), what's on section* • **se mantuvo en la ~ durante tres años** it ran for three years
cartelero (SM) billsticker, billposter
cartelista (SMF) poster artist, poster designer
cartelón (SM) large notice
carteo (SM) correspondence, exchange of letters
cárter (SM) (*Mec*) housing, case ▸ **cárter de cigüeñal** crankcase
cartera (SF) **1** (= *monedero*) [*de hombre*] wallet, billfold (*EEUU*); [*de mujer*] purse, billfold (*EEUU*)
2 (*LAm*) (= *bolso*) handbag, purse (*EEUU*)
3 [*de colegial*] satchel, schoolbag
4 (*para documentos*) briefcase • MODISMO: • **en ~** in the pipeline • **tenemos en ~ varios proyectos** we have several projects in the pipeline ▸ **cartera de mano** briefcase
5 (*Pol*) • **renunció a la ~ de Cultura** he turned down the post of Minister of Culture • **el actual titular de la ~ de Interior** the present Minister of the Interior • **ministro sin ~** minister without portfolio
6 (*Com, Econ*) ▸ **cartera de acciones** stock portfolio, share portfolio ▸ **cartera de pedidos** order book ▸ **cartera de valores** securities portfolio
7 (*Cos*) (*en bolsillo*) pocket flap; ▷ **cartero**
carterero/a (SM/F) (*Cono Sur*) pickpocket
carterista (SMF) pickpocket
carterita (SF) ▸ **carterita de fósforos** (*esp LAm*) book of matches
cartero/a (SM/F) postman/postwoman, mailman/mailwoman (*EEUU*); ▷ **cartera**
cartesiano/a (ADJ), (SM/F) Cartesian
cartilaginoso (ADJ) cartilaginous
cartílago (SM) cartilage
cartilla (SF) **1** (*Escol*) primer, first reader • MODISMOS: • **cantar** *o* **leer la ~ a algn** to take sb to task, give sb a severe ticking off • **no saber (ni) la ~** not to know a single thing
2 (= *documento*) ▸ **cartilla de ahorros** bank book ▸ **cartilla de identidad** identity card ▸ **cartilla del paro** unemployment card ▸ **cartilla de racionamiento** ration book ▸ **cartilla de seguridad, cartilla de seguro** social security card
3 (*Rel*) certificate of ordination
4 (*Mil*) record
cartografía (SF) cartography, mapmaking
cartografiado (SM) mapping
cartográfico (ADJ) cartographic, cartographical
cartógrafo/a (SM/F) cartographer, mapmaker
cartomancia (SF) fortune-telling (*with cards*)
cartomante (SMF) fortune-teller (*who uses cards*)
cartón (SM) **1** (= *material*) cardboard ▸ **cartón acanalado** corrugated cardboard ▸ **cartón alquitranado** tar paper ▸ **cartón de embalaje** wrapping paper ▸ **cartón de encuadernar** millboard ▸ **cartón piedra** papier mâché
2 (= *caja*) ▸ **cartón de huevos** (*lleno*) box of eggs; (*vacío*) egg box ▸ **cartón de leche** (*lleno*) carton of milk; (*vacío*) milk carton ▸ **cartón de tabaco** pack of cigarettes
3 (*Arte*) cartoon
4 [*de bingo*] card
cartoné (SM) • **en ~** [*libro*] in boards, bound in boards
cartón-madera (SM) hardboard
cartuchera (SF) **1** (*para pistola*) cartridge belt
2* (*en muslos*) saddlebags
cartuchería (SF) cartridges (*pl*), ammunition
cartucho (SM) **1** (*Mil*) cartridge ▸ **cartucho en blanco** blank cartridge
2 (= *bolsita*) paper cone; [*de monedas*] roll
3 ▸ **cartucho de datos** (*Inform*) data cartridge
Cartuja (SF) (*Rel*) Carthusian order
cartuja (SF) Carthusian monastery
cartujano (ADJ), (SM) Carthusian
cartujo (SM) Carthusian
cartulaje‡ (SM) pack of cards
cartulario (SM) cartulary
cartulina (SF) card • **una ~** a piece of card ▸ **cartulina amarilla** (*Ftbl*) yellow card ▸ **cartulina roja** (*Ftbl*) red card
carura (SF) **1** (*And, CAm, Cono Sur*) (= *lo costoso*) high price, dearness
2 (*And, CAm, Cono Sur*) (= *objeto*) expensive thing • **en esta tienda solo hay ~s** everything in this shop is dear
3 (*Cono Sur*) (= *carestía*) lack, shortage
CASA (SF ABR) (*Esp*) = **Construcciones Aeronáuticas, S.A.**
casa (SF) **1** (= *vivienda*) house • **una ~ en el campo** a house in the country, a country house • **ir de ~ en ~ vendiendo** to sell things from door to door ▸ **casa adosada** *terraced villa* ▸ **Casa Blanca** • **la Casa Blanca** the White House ▸ **casa consistorial** town hall ▸ **casa cuartel** *Civil Guard police station including living quarters for families of policemen* ▸ **casa cuna** (*Hist*) foundling home; (*moderna*) day-nursery, crèche ▸ **casa de acogida** (*para enfermos, menores*) hostel; (*para mujeres maltratadas*) refuge ▸ **casa de alquiler** • **vivo en una ~ de alquiler** I live in rented accommodation ▸ **casa de asistencia** boarding house ▸ **casa de azotea** penthouse ▸ **casa de baños** public bathhouse ▸ **casa de bebidas†** drinking house ▸ **casa de beneficencia†** poor-house ▸ **casa de bombas** pumphouse ▸ **casa de campaña** (*LAm*) tent ▸ **casa de campo** country house ▸ **casa de citas** brothel ▸ **casa de comidas** *cheap restaurant* ▸ **casa de corrección†** young offenders institution, reformatory (*EEUU*) ▸ **casa de correos** post office ▸ **casa de cultura** *municipal arts centre* ▸ **casa de Dios** house of God ▸ **casa de ejercicios** retreat house ▸ **casa de fieras** zoo ▸ **casa de guarda** lodge ▸ **casa de huéspedes** boarding house ▸ **casa de juego** gambling house ▸ **casa de labor, casa de labranza** farmhouse ▸ **la Casa de la Moneda** *Chilean presidential palace* ▸ **casa de locos** (= *manicomio*) madhouse, asylum; (= *lugar caótico*) madhouse ▸ **casa de maternidad** maternity hospital ▸ **casa de muñecas** doll's house ▸ **casa de pisos** block of flats, apartment block ▸ **casa de putas*** brothel ▸ **casa de seguridad** (*Cono Sur*) (*Pol*) safe house ▸ **casa de socorro** first-aid post ▸ **casa de tolerancia†** house of ill repute ▸ **casa de vecindad** tenement block ▸ **casa de vicio†** brothel ▸ **casa encantada** haunted house ▸ **casa mortuoria** house of the deceased ▸ **casa pareada** semi-detached house ▸ **casa parroquial** parish house ▸ **casa religiosa** [*de monjes*] monastery; [*de monjas*] convent ▸ **casa rodante** caravan, trailer ▸ **la Casa Rosada** *Argentinian presidential palace* ▸ **casa rural** (*de alquiler*) holiday cottage; (= *pensión*) rural B & B ▸ **casa solariega** (*habitada*) family seat, ancestral home; (*usada como museo*) stately home
2 (= *hogar*) home • **estábamos en ~** we were at home • **se fue a ~** she went home • **estábamos en ~ de Juan** we were at Juan's (place) • **¿dónde tiene usted su ~?** where is your home? • **está usted en su ~** make yourself at home • **es una ~ con alegría** it's a happy home, it's a happy household • **la ~ de Lorca en Fuentevaqueros** Lorca's former home in Fuentevaqueros • **abandonar la ~** to leave home • **de ~**: • **un animal de ~** a pet, a family pet • **ropa de ~** clothes for wearing around the house • **estoy vestido de ~** I'm in the clothes I wear around the house • **en ~** at home • **debes dejar claro quién manda en ~** you should make it quite clear who's in charge at home • **¿está la señora en (la) ~?** is the lady of the house in?, is the lady of the house at home? • **me he dejado los libros en (mi) ~** I've left my books at home • **está fuera de ~** she's out, she's not at home • **ir a ~** to go home • **ir hacia ~** to head for home • **ir a ~ de Juan** to go to Juan's (place) • **llevar la ~** to run the household • **poner ~** to set up house • **poner ~ a una mujer** to set a woman up in a little place • **estar por la ~** to be about the house • **salir de ~** to leave home • **sentirse como en su ~** to feel at home • **siéntase como en su ~** make yourself at home • **ser de la ~** to be like one of the family ▸ **casa natal** • **la ~ natal de Lorca** the house where Lorca was born ▸ **casa paterna** parents' home ▸ **casa y comida** board and lodging
3 • MODISMOS: • **de andar por ~**: • **zapatos de andar por ~** shoes for wearing around the house • **una explicación de andar por ~** a rough-and-ready explanation • **psicoanálisis de andar por ~** homespun psychoanalysis • **como una ~***: • **una rata como una ~** a massive great rat • **una mentira como una ~** a whopper* • **un penalti como una ~** a clear-cut penalty • **está en ~ Dios*** it's miles away* • **echar la ~ por la ventana** to spare no expense • **echaron la ~ por la ventana comprándonos regalos para la boda** they really went to town on buying us presents for our wedding* • **empezar la ~ por el tejado** to put the cart before the horse • **franquear la ~ a algn** to open one's house to sb • **hacer ~** to get rich • **poner a algn en ~** to do sb a great favour • **poner su ~ en orden** to put one's own house in order • **no tener ~ ni hogar** to be homeless • **esto es la ~ de Tócame Roque** everyone just does as they like in this house, it's utter chaos in this house
4 (= *asociación*) ▸ **casa de España** *club for expatriate Spaniards* ▸ **casa de Galicia** *Club for expatriate Galicians* ▸ **Casa del Pueblo** (*Pol*)

social club run by Spanish socialist party
5 (*Dep*) home ground • **la ~ del Real Madrid** Real Madrid's (home) ground • **equipo de ~** home team • **jugar en ~** to play at home • **jugar fuera de ~** to play away (from home) • **perdieron en ~ ante el Betis** they lost at home to Betis
6 (*en juegos*) home • **si sacas tres seguidos, te vuelves a tu ~** if you get three in a row you go back to the beginning *o* go back to home
7 (*en bar, restaurante*) • **un postre de la ~** one of our own special desserts • **una botella de vino de la ~** a bottle of house wine • **hoy invita la ~** it's on the house today
8 (= *empresa*) firm, company ▸ **casa armadora** shipping company ▸ **casa bancaria** banking house ▸ **casa central** head office ▸ **casa de banca** banking house ▸ **casa de discos** record company ▸ **casa de empeños** pawnshop ▸ **casa de (la) moneda** mint ▸ **casa de modas** fashion house ▸ **casa de préstamos** pawnshop ▸ **casa discográfica** record company ▸ **casa editorial** publishing house ▸ **casa matriz** (= *oficina*) head office; (= *empresa*) parent company
9 (= *linaje*) house • **la Casa de Saboya** the House of Savoy • **la Casa de Austria** the Hapsburgs ▸ **casa real** royal household

CASA

Uso de la preposición "to" con "home"

A la hora de traducir expresiones como **ir a casa, volver a casa, venir a casa,** *hay que tener en cuenta que* **home** *sigue directamente al verbo (sin* **to**):

Quiero irme a casa
I want to go home
No puede volver a casa
He can't go back home

Sin embargo, **to** *sí se pone cuando* **home** *viene calificado:*

Quiere volver a su antigua casa
She wants to return to her former home

Para otros usos y ejemplos ver la entrada.

CASA DE CONTRATACIÓN

The **Casa de Contratación** was responsible for the regulation of Spain's trade with her Latin American colonies. Founded in 1503 by the Crown, the **Casa de Contratación** supervised all transatlantic ships operating between certain ports in Spain and Latin America, notably between Cádiz in Spain and Veracruz in Mexico. The **Casa** also collected the levy (known as the **quinto**) of a fifth of all colonial gold and silver, and regulated the African slave trade with Cartagena de Indias, Colombia. As the volume of trade increased, the **Casa** operated armed fleets to protect shipments from piracy.

casabe (SM) cassava
casa-bote (SF) (PL: **casas-bote**) houseboat
casaca (SF) **1** (= *prenda*) dress coat; (*And, Cono Sur*) blouson, zip jacket • MODISMO: • **cambiar de ~** to be a turncoat ▸ **casaca de montar** riding coat
2* (= *boda*) wedding, marriage
casación (SF) cassation, annulment
casacón (SM) greatcoat
casa-cuartel (SF) (PL: **casas-cuarteles**) residential barracks (*for Civil Guard*)
casadero (ADJ) marriageable, old enough to get married • **una muchacha en edad casadera** a girl of marriageable age, a girl old enough to get married
casado/a (ADJ) married • **¿está** *o* (*LAm*) **es usted casada?** are you married? • **está ~ con mi prima** he's married to my cousin • **todas sus hijas están muy bien casadas** all her daughters have married well
(SM/F) married man/woman • **estuvo saliendo con un ~** she was going out with a married man • **Pierce es su apellido de casada** Pierce is her married name • **no está contenta con su vida de casada** she is dissatisfied with married life • **los ~s** (= *hombres*) married men; (= *hombres y mujeres*) married people • **los recién ~s** the newlyweds
(SM) **1** (*Tip*) imposition
2 (*LAm*) (*Culin*) *two separate varieties of food eaten together*
casal (SM) **1** (*en el campo*) (= *casa*) country house; (= *granja*) farmhouse; (= *solar*) ancestral home
2 (*Cono Sur*) (= *pareja*) [*de esposos*] married couple; [*de animales*] pair
casamata (SF) casemate
casamentero/a (SM/F) matchmaker
casamiento (SM) (= *unión*) marriage; (= *ceremonia*) wedding, wedding ceremony ▸ **casamiento a la fuerza** shotgun wedding ▸ **casamiento de conveniencia** marriage of convenience ▸ **casamiento por amor** love match
casampolga (SF) (*CAm*) (*Zool*) black widow spider
Casandra (SF) Cassandra
casapuerta (SF) entrance hall, vestibule
casar ▹ CONJUG 1a (VT) **1** (= *unir en matrimonio*) to marry • **los casó el cura del pueblo** they were married by the village priest
2 (= *dar en matrimonio*) to marry off • **ya ha casado a todas sus hijas** she's married off all her daughters
3 (= *hacer coincidir*) to match up • **casa los estampados antes de coser las telas** match up the patterns before sewing the pieces together
4 (*Tip*) to impose
(VI) **1** (= *armonizar*) • **estas dos piezas casan perfectamente** these two pieces go together *o* fit together perfectly • **hay una serie de datos que no casan** there are a number of details that don't tally *o* match up • **sus dos declaraciones no casan** her two statements do not match up *o* tally • **~ con algo: el color de la alfombra no casa con el del sofá** the colour of the carpet doesn't go with that of the sofa • **mis noticias no casan con las tuyas** the news I have doesn't tally with *o* match yours • **tanta modestia no casa con sus ansias de poder** such modesty doesn't go with *o* tally with his craving for power
2 (*frm*) (= *contraer matrimonio*) • **casó con una chica del pueblo** he married *o* he got married to a girl from the town
(VPR) **casarse** to marry, get married • **¿cuándo te casas?** when are you getting married? • **se casó con una italiana** he married an Italian woman, he got married to an Italian woman • MODISMO: • **no ~se con nadie:** • **respeta a todo el mundo, pero no se casa con nadie** he respects everyone but doesn't side with any of them; ▹ **civil, iglesia, nupcias, penalti**
casa-refugio (SF) (PL: **casas-refugio**) refuge for battered wives
casatienda (SF) shop with dwelling accommodation, shop with flat over it
casba (SF), **casbah** (SF) kasbah
casca (SF) **1** (= *corteza*) bark (*for tanning*)
2 (= *uvas*) marc (*of grapes*)
3 ▸ **cascas almibaradas** candied peel
cascabel (SM) little bell • MODISMOS: • **de ~ gordo** pretentious • **ser un ~** to be a scatterbrain • **echar** *o* **soltar el ~** to drop a hint • **poner el ~ al gato** to bell the cat; ▹ **serpiente**
(SF) (*LAm*) rattlesnake, rattler (*EEUU**)
cascabela (SF) (*LAm*) rattlesnake, rattler (*EEUU**)
cascabelear ▹ CONJUG 1a (VT) to take in*, beguile
(VI) **1** (*LAm*) (= *tintinear*) to jingle, tinkle
2 (= *ser atolondrado*) to be a scatterbrain
3 (*Cono Sur*) (= *refunfuñar*) to moan, grumble
cascabeleo (SM) jingling, tinkling
cascabelero/a* (ADJ) scatterbrained
(SM/F) scatterbrain
cascabillo (SM) **1** (= *campanilla*) little bell
2 (*Bot*) husk, shuck (*EEUU*)
cascada (SF) waterfall, cascade
cascado (ADJ) **1** [*objeto*] broken, broken down
2 [*persona*] worn out
3 (*Mús*) [*voz*] cracked; [*piano*] tinny
cascajo (SM) **1** (= *grava*) gravel, piece of gravel
2 [*de vasija*] fragments (*pl*), shards (*pl*)
3 (= *trasto*) junk, rubbish, garbage (*EEUU*)
• MODISMO: • **estar hecho un ~*** to be a wreck*
cascajoso (ADJ) gritty, gravelly
cascanueces (SM INV) nutcracker • **un ~** a pair of nutcrackers
cascar ▹ CONJUG 1g (VT) **1** (= *romper*) [+ *nuez*] to crack; [+ *huevo*] to break, crack; [+ *taza, plato*] to chip
2* (= *pegar*) • **cuando se entere tu padre, te casca** when your father finds out, he'll thump you *o* give you a bashing* • **cuando se pelea con sus amigos, siempre le cascan** when he fights with his friends they always give him a bashing*
3* (= *poner*) • **me ~on una multa por aparcar mal** I was landed with *o* slapped with a fine for parking in the wrong place*
4 (= *chivar*) to squeal*, tell*
5 • MODISMO: • **~la‡** (= *morirse*) to kick the bucket* • **la cascó la semana pasada** he kicked the bucket last week*
(VI)* (= *charlar*) to chatter, natter*
(VPR) **cascarse 1** (= *romperse*) [*nuez*] to crack; [*huevo*] to break, crack; [*taza, plato*] to chip • **se le ha cascado la voz** his voice has gone
2 • MODISMO: • **cascársela**** to wank**, jerk off**
cáscara (SF) **1** (= *cubierta*) [*de huevo, nuez*] shell; [*de grano*] husk, shuck (*EEUU*); [*de fruta*] peel, rind, skin • **patatas cocidas con ~** potatoes in their jackets • MODISMOS: • **ser de la ~ amarga*** to be wild, be a troublemaker; (*Pol*) have radical ideas; (*sexualmente*) to be the other sort • **dar ~s de novillo a algn** (*LAm*) to thrash sb ▸ **cáscara de huevo** eggshell ▸ **cáscara de limón** lemon peel ▸ **cáscara de plátano** banana skin ▸ **cáscara sagrada** (*Farm*) cascara
2* (*euf*) • **¡cáscaras!** well I'm blowed!*
• MODISMO: • **no hay más ~s** there's no other way out*
3 cáscaras (*And‡*) (= *ropa*) clothes, togs*, threads (*EEUU**)
4 • MODISMO: • **tener ~** (*CAm**) to have a cheek*
cascarazo* (SM) **1** (*And, Caribe*) (= *puñetazo*) punch
2 (*And*) (= *azote*) lash
3 (*Caribe*) (= *trago*) swig*, slug (*EEUU**)
cascarear* ▹ CONJUG 1a (VT) (*And, CAm*) to belt*, smack

C

VI (*Méx**) to scrape a living

cascarilla ADJ (*Caribe, Cono Sur*) (= *enojadizo*) touchy, quick-tempered

SF **1** (*Caribe, Cono Sur*) quick-tempered person

2 (*And, Cono Sur*) (*Med*) medicinal herb

cascarón SM eggshell, broken eggshell • MODISMOS: • **meterse en su ~** to go into one's shell • **está recién salido del ~** he's a bit wet behind the ears

cascarrabias SMF INV grouch*

cascarria SF (*Cono Sur*) **1*** (= *mugre*) filth, muck

2 (*Agr*) sheep droppings (*pl*)

cascarriento* ADJ (*Cono Sur*) filthy, greasy, mucky*

cascarrón* ADJ gruff, abrupt, rough

cascarudo ADJ thick-shelled, having a thick skin

SM (*Cono Sur*) beetles (*collectively*)

casco SM **1** [*de soldado*] helmet; [*de obrero*] protective helmet, safety helmet, hard hat; [*de motorista, ciclista*] (crash) helmet • **los ~s azules (de la ONU)** the (UN) blue helmets ▸ **casco de acero** steel helmet ▸ **casco de bicicleta** cycle helmet

2 [*de ciudad*] ▸ **casco antiguo** • **el ~ antiguo de la ciudad** the old quarter *o* part of the city ▸ **casco histórico** • **el ~ histórico de la ciudad** the historic city centre *o* (*EEUU*) center ▸ **casco urbano** built-up area ▸ **casco viejo** • **el ~ viejo de la ciudad** the old quarter *o* part of the city

3 (= *envase*) empty bottle • **te dan 50 céntimos al devolver el ~** they give you 50 cents back on the empty (bottle) • **había ~s (de botellas) por todo el parque** there were empty bottles *o* empties all over the park

4 cascos [*de walkman*] headphones

5 cascos* (= *cabeza*) nut* (*sing*) • MODISMOS: • **alegre** *o* **ligero de ~s** (= *irreflexivo*) reckless, foolhardy; (= *frívolo*) flighty • **sentar los ~s** to settle down; ▹ **calentar**

6 (= *pezuña*) hoof

7 (= *trozo*) [*de fruta*] segment, piece; [*de cebolla*] slice; [*de vasija*] fragment, shard

8 (*Náut*) [*de barco*] hull

9 (*Mec*) [*de cableado*] casing

10 (*LAm*) (= *edificio vacío*) empty building

11 (*LAm*) (*Agr*) ranch house, ranch and outbuildings; (*Cono Sur*) [*de hacienda*] part, section

12 [*de sombrero*] crown

cascorros* SMPL (*Méx*) shoes

cascorvo* ADJ (*CAm*) bow-legged

cascote SM piece of rubble • **~s** rubble (*sing*)

cascundear ▹ CONJUG 1a VT (*CAm*) to beat, thrash

cáseo SM curd

caseoso ADJ cheesy, like cheese

casería SF **1** (= *casa*) country house

2 (*LAm*†) (= *clientela*) customers (*pl*), clientèle

caserío SM country house

caserna SF (*LAm*) barracks (*pl*)

casero/a ADJ **1** (= *hecho en casa*) [*comida, sopa, artefacto*] homemade; [*remedio*] household, home (*antes de s*) • **cocina casera** home cooking • **un vídeo ~** a home video • **eso es filosofía casera** that is homespun philosophy • **tareas caseras** housework (*sing*), domestic chores • **de fabricación casera** homemade • **sufrió un pequeño accidente ~** she had a minor domestic accident, she had a small accident at home

2 (= *hogareño*) • **soy muy ~** I'm the home-loving sort, I'm the stay-at-home type • **llevan una vida muy casera** they're always at home

3 (*Dep*) • **una victoria casera** a home win, a win for the home side • **un árbitro ~** *a referee biased in favour of the home team*

SM/F **1** (= *propietario*) landlord/landlady

2 (*en casa de campo*) caretaker

3 (= *inquilino*) tenant, occupier

4 (= *persona hogareña*) home bird*, homebody (*EEUU*)

5 (*LAm*) (= *cliente*) customer, client

6 (*Caribe*) (= *repartidor*) delivery man/woman

caserón SM large house, ramshackle house

caseta SF **1** (= *lugar cerrado*) [*de bañista*] changing room; (*en exposición*) stand; (*en mercado*) stall ▸ **caseta del timón** (*Náut*) wheelhouse ▸ **caseta de perro** kennel, doghouse (*EEUU*)

2 [*de feria*] stall

3 (*Ftbl*) dugout • **mandar a algn a la ~** to send sb for an early bath, send sb off

casete [ka'set] SF (= *cinta*) cassette

SM (= *aparato*) cassette player

casetera SF (*LAm*) cassette deck

cash [katʃ] SM (PL: **cash**) (*tb* **cash and carry**) cash-and-carry store

casi ADV **1** (= *indicando aproximación*) almost, nearly • **está ~ terminado** it's almost *o* nearly finished • **son ya ~ las tres** it's almost *o* nearly three o'clock • **¡huy!, ~ me caigo** oops! I almost *o* nearly fell over • **hace ~ un año que empezó la guerra** it's almost a year since war broke out • **nada ha cambiado en los ~ dos años transcurridos** nothing has changed in what is almost two years • **despidieron a la ~ totalidad de la plantilla** they sacked virtually *o* practically the entire staff • **estaba congelado, o ~** it was frozen, or very near it • **ocurre lo mismo en ~ todos los países** the same thing happens in virtually *o* practically all countries • **—¿habéis terminado? —casi, casi** "have you finished?" — "just about *o* very nearly" • **~ nada** almost *o* virtually nothing, hardly anything • **no sabemos ~ nada de lo que está ocurriendo** we know almost *o* virtually nothing about what's going on, we know hardly anything about what's going on • **100 dólares ..., ¡~ nada!** (*iró*) 100 dollars, a mere trifle! • **~ nunca** hardly ever, almost never • **~ nunca hay sitio en la biblioteca** there is hardly ever any room in the library • **~ siempre** almost always

2 (*indicando indecisión*) almost • **no sé, ~ prefiero no ir** I don't know, I think I'd rather not go • **~ sería mejor empezar otra vez** it might be better to start again

casilla SF **1** (= *caseta*) [*de jardín*] hut, shed; (*en parque, jardín zoológico*) keeper's lodge; (*en mercado*) stall; [*de guardagujas*] pointsman's *o* (*EEUU*) switchman's hut ▸ **casilla electoral** (*Méx*) polling-station

2 (= *compartimento*) (*para cartas*) pigeonhole, mail box (*EEUU*); [*de caja*] compartment; [*de formulario*] box; [*de papel*] ruled column, section ▸ **casilla de correos, casilla postal** post office box (number), P.O. Box ▸ **casilla electrónica** (*LAm*) email address

3 (*en ajedrez, damas*) square • MODISMOS: • **sacar a algn de sus ~s** to infuriate sb, drive sb up the wall* • **salirse de sus ~s** to fly off the handle*

4 (= *cabina*) (*en tren, camión*) cab

5 (*Teat*) box office

6 (*And*) (= *retrete*) lavatory, bathroom (*EEUU*)

7 (*Caribe*) (= *trampa*) bird trap

casillero SM **1** (*para cartas*) (*en oficina*) pigeonholes (*pl*), set of pigeonholes; (*en oficina de correos*) sorting rack

2 (*para equipaje*) luggage locker

3 (*Ftbl**) scorer

casimba SF (*LAm*) = **cacimba**

casimir SM cashmere

casimiro ADJ (*LAm*) (*hum*) cross-eyed

casinista SM clubman, member of a casino

casino SM **1** [*de juego*] casino

2 (*club social*) club

3 (*Cono Sur*) (= *comedor*) canteen

Casio SM Cassius

casis SF INV (*tb* **casis de negro**) blackcurrant (bush) ▸ **casis de rojo** redcurrant (bush)

casita SF small house, cottage • **los niños están jugando a las ~s** the children are playing houses

caso SM **1** (= *circunstancia*) **a** (*gen*) case • **ahí**

CASI

Las dos traducciones principales de **casi** *en inglés son* **almost** *y* **nearly**:

Estoy casi lista
I'm almost *o* nearly ready

Eran casi las cuatro cuando sonó el teléfono
It was almost *o* nearly four o'clock when the telephone rang

Nos vemos casi todos los días
We meet almost *o* nearly every day

▹ *Cuando* **almost** *y* **nearly** *acompañan a un verbo, se colocan detrás de este si se trata de un verbo auxiliar o modal y delante en el caso de los demás verbos:*

Casi me rompo la muñeca
I almost *o* nearly broke my wrist

Mi hijo ya casi habla
My son can almost *o* nearly talk

Sin embargo, hay algunos casos en los que no podemos utilizar **nearly**:

▹ *delante de adverbios que terminan en* **-ly**

"¿Qué estáis haciendo aquí?" nos preguntó casi con enfado
"What are you doing here?" he asked almost angrily

▹ *delante de* **like**:

Se comporta casi como un niño
He behaves almost like a child

▹ *acompañando a adjetivos o sustantivos que, normalmente, no pueden ser modificados:*

El mono tenía una expresión casi humana
The monkey had an almost human expression

Me pareció casi un alivio
I found it almost a relief

▹ *delante de palabras de sentido negativo, como* **never, no, none, no-one, nothing** *y* **nowhere**; *en estos casos, muchas veces se traduce también por* **practically**:

No dijo casi nada
She said almost *o* practically nothing

No había casi nadie en la fiesta
There was almost *o* practically no-one at the party

En estos casos también se puede usar la construcción **hardly** + **ever/any/anything** *etc:*

She said hardly anything
There was hardly anyone at the party

Para otros usos y ejemplos ver la entrada.

tienes el ~ de Pedro take Pedro's case • **en esos ~s la policía corta la circulación** in such cases the police block the road off • **en el ~ de Francia** in France's case, in the case of France • **me creía en el ~ de informarles** I felt obliged to inform you
b • **en ~ afirmativo** if so • **en (el) ~ contrario** if not, otherwise • **en cualquier ~** in any case • **en ~ de** in the event of • **esto protege al conductor en ~ de accidente** this protects the driver in the event of an accident • **en ~ de necesidad** if necessary • **en ~ de no ser posible** should it not be possible • **en (el) ~ de que venga** if he comes, should he come • **en ~ de que llueva, iremos en autobús** if it rains, we'll go by bus • **en ese ~** in that case • **en el mejor de los ~s** at best • **en ~ necesario** if necessary • **en ~ negativo** if not, otherwise • **en el peor de los ~s** at worst • **en su ~** where appropriate • **su finalidad es el cuidado y, en su ~, educación de los niños** their aim is to care for and, where appropriate, educate the children • **en tal ~** in such a case • **en todo ~** in any case • **en último ~** as a last resort, in the last resort • **en uno u otro ~** one way or the other; ▹ **extremo**[1]
c • **darse el ~**: • **todavía no se ha dado el ~** such a situation hasn't yet arisen • **dado el ~ que tuvieras que irte, ¿a dónde irías?** in the event that you did have to go, where would you go? • **el ~ es que ...**: • **el ~ es que se me olvidó su nombre** the thing is I forgot her name • **el ~ es que tiene razón** the fact is (that) she's right • **el ~ es que no me gustó** basically I didn't like it • **el ~ es que me entiendan** the main thing is to make myself understood • **hablar al ~** to keep to the point • **hacer al ~** to be relevant • **pongamos por ~ que ...** let us suppose that ... • **pongamos por ~ a Luis** let's take Luis as an example • **ponte en mi ~** put yourself in my position • **según el ~** as the case may be • **necesitan una o dos sesiones de rayos, según el ~** they need either one or two X-ray treatment sessions, as the case may be *o* depending on the circumstances • **sustitúyase, según el ~, por una frase u otra** replace with one or other of the phrases, as appropriate • **según lo requiera el ~** as the case may require, depending on the requirements of the case in question • **este ejemplo debería servir para el ~** this example should serve our purpose *o* should do • **no tiene ~** (*Méx*) there's no point (in it) • **¡vamos al ~!** let's get down to business! • **vaya por ~ ...** to give an example ... • **venir al ~** to be relevant • **no venir al ~** to be beside the point • **verse en el ~ de hacer algo** to be obliged to do sth
2 (*Med*) case • **ha habido tres ~s de meningitis** there have been three cases of meningitis ▸ **caso clínico** clinical case
3 (= *asunto*) affair; (*Jur*) case • **el ~ Hess** the Hess affair • **la juez encargada del ~** the judge hearing the case • **es un ~ perdido** [*situación*] it's a hopeless case; [*persona*] he's a dead loss, he's hopeless ▸ **caso de autos** case in hand ▸ **caso de conciencia** question of conscience ▸ **caso fortuito** (*Jur*) act of God; (= *suceso imprevisto*) unforeseen circumstance ▸ **caso límite** extreme case
4 • **hacer ~ a** *o* **de algo** to take notice of sth, pay attention to sth • **no me hacen ~** they take no notice of me, they pay no attention to me • **no le hagas ~** don't take any notice of him • **¡no haga usted ~!** take no notice! • **hazle ~, que ella tiene más experiencia** listen to her, she has more experience • **maldito el ~ que me hace*** a fat lot of notice he takes of me* • **ni ~**: • **tú a todo lo que te diga ¡ni ~!*** take no notice of what he says! • **se lo dije, pero ni ~** I told him, but he took absolutely no notice • **hacer ~ omiso de algo** to ignore sth
5 (*Ling*) case

casona (SF) large house
casorio* (SM) **1** (= *matrimonio precipitado*) hasty marriage, unwise marriage
2 (*Méx*) (= *boda*) wedding, marriage
caspa (SF) dandruff
Caspio (ADJ) • **mar ~** Caspian Sea
caspiroleta (SF) (*And, Caribe, Cono Sur*) eggnog, egg flip
cáspita (EXCL) my goodness!
casposo (ADJ) covered in dandruff
casquería (SF) tripe and offal shop
casquero/a (SM/F) seller of tripe and offal
casquete (SM) **1** (= *casco*) (*Mil*) helmet; (*Mec*) cap ▸ **casquete de hielo** icecap ▸ **casquete de nieve** snowcap ▸ **casquete polar** polar icecap
2 (= *gorra*) skullcap
3 • **echar un ~**** to have a screw**
casquijo (SM) gravel
casquillo (SM) **1** (= *cápsula*) (*Téc*) ferrule, tip; (*Mil*) cartridge case ▸ **casquillo de bala** bullet shell
2 (*LAm*) horseshoe
casquinona (SF) (*And*) (= *botella*) beer bottle; (= *cerveza*) beer
casquivano/a (ADJ) scatterbrained
(SM/F) scatterbrain
cassette (SF) = **casete**
casta (SF) **1** (= *clan*) caste • **el sistema de ~s de la India** the Indian caste system
2 (= *estirpe*) stock • **es de ~ de aristócratas** she is of aristocratic stock • **eso me viene de ~** it's in my blood • REFRÁN: • **de ~ le viene al galgo** it's in the blood *o* genes
3 (= *grupo social*) class • **la ~ militar** the military class
4 (= *calidad*) class • **el equipo jugó con ~** the team played with class • **un toro de ~** a thoroughbred bull • **un torero de ~** a top class bullfighter
5 (*Méx*) (*Tip*) font
castamente (ADV) chastely, purely
castaña (SF) **1** (= *fruto*) chestnut • MODISMOS: • **conducir a toda ~*** to drive flat out • **sacar a algn las ~s del fuego** to get sb off the hook • **ser una ~*** to be a drag* • **¡toma ~!*** (*indicando disfrute*) take that!; (*indicando sorpresa*) just imagine! ▸ **castaña de agua** water chestnut ▸ **castaña de cajú** (*Arg, Uru*) cashew nut ▸ **castaña de Indias** horse chestnut ▸ **castaña del Brasil, castaña de Pará** Brazil nut
2* (= *golpe*) punch • **darse una ~** to give o.s. a knock
3* (= *borrachera*) • **cogerse una ~** to get pissed**
4 [*de pelo*] bun, chignon
5 (= *vasija*) demijohn
6* (= *año*) • **tiene 71 ~s** he's 71 (years old)
castañar (SM) chestnut grove
castañazo* (SM) (= *puñetazo*) punch, thump; (= *choque*) bump
castañero/a (SM/F) chestnut seller
castañeta (SF) **1** (*con dedos*) snap (*of the fingers*)
2 castañetas (*Mús*) castanets
castañetazo (SM) snap, crack, click
castañetear ▹ CONJUG 1a (VT) **1** [+ *dedos*] to snap
2 (*Mús*) to play on the castanets
(VI) **1** (= *sonar*) [*dedos*] to snap, click; [*dientes*] to chatter; [*huesos*] to crack • **~ con los dedos** to snap one's fingers
2 (*Mús*) to play the castanets
castañeteo (SM) **1** (= *sonido*) [*de dedos*] snapping; [*de dientes*] chattering; [*de huesos*] cracking
2 (*Mús*) sound of the castanets
castaño (ADJ) [*pelo*] chestnut, chestnut-coloured, chestnut-colored (*EEUU*); [*ojos*] brown • MODISMO: • **esto pasa de ~ oscuro** this is beyond a joke
(SM) (*Bot*) chestnut tree • MODISMO: • **pelar el ~** (*Caribe**) to hoof it* ▸ **castaño de Indias** horse chestnut tree
castañuela (SF) castanet • MODISMO: • **estar como** *o* **hecho unas ~s** to be very merry, be in high spirits
castañuelo (ADJ) [*caballo*] chestnut-coloured, chestnut-colored (EEUU), brown
castellanizar ▹ CONJUG 1f (VT) to hispanicize, give a Spanish form to
castellano/a (ADJ) (*Pol*) Castilian; (*Ling*) Spanish
(SM/F) Castilian
(SM) (*Ling*) Castilian, Spanish

CASTELLANO
In the Spanish-speaking world **castellano** rather than **español** is a very common term for the Spanish language. Under the Spanish Constitution **castellano** is Spain's official language, but in some of the **Comunidades Autónomas** it shares official status with another language. Use of one or other term in Spain will depend on where the speaker is from, and where they place themselves in the linguistic debate.
▹ **LENGUAS COOFICIALES, COMUNIDAD AUTÓNOMA**

castellanohablante, castellanoparlante (ADJ) Castilian-speaking, Spanish-speaking
(SMF) Castilian speaker, Spanish speaker
castellonense (ADJ), (SMF) = **castellonés**
castellonés/esa (ADJ) of/from Castellón
(SM/F) native/inhabitant of Castellón • **los castelloneses** the people of Castellón
casticidad (SF), **casticismo** (SM) **1** (*Ling*) purity, correctness
2 [*de costumbres*] traditional character, authenticity
casticista (ADJ), (SMF) purist
castidad (SF) chastity, purity
castigador(a) (SM/F) ladykiller/seductress
castigar ▹ CONJUG 1h (VT) **1** (*por delito, falta*) **a** [+ *delincuente, pecador, culpable*] to punish (**por** for); [+ *niño*] (*gen*) to punish; (*sin salir*) to ground, keep in • **es un delito que puede ser castigado con 15 años de prisión** it is a crime punishable by 15 years' imprisonment • **la profesora me dejó castigado al terminar las clases** the teacher kept me in *o* made me stay behind after school • **la ~on por decir mentiras** she was punished for telling lies • **lo ~on sin postre** he was not allowed any dessert as punishment • **~ la carne** (*Rel*) to mortify the flesh
b (*Dep*) to penalize (**por** for) • **lo ~on con tarjeta amarilla** he was given a yellow card • **el árbitro los castigó con un penalti** the referee awarded a penalty against them
c (*Com, Pol*) to punish • **Cuba fue castigada con sanciones comerciales** Cuba was punished with economic sanctions • **el socialismo salió muy castigado de las urnas** socialism suffered heavy losses in the elections
2 (= *perjudicar*) [*guerra, crisis*] to afflict, affect; [*calor*] to beat down on; [*frío*] to bite into • **el sol castigó con dureza a los tenistas** the sun beat down mercilessly on the tennis players • **la ciudad más castigada por los**

bombardeos the city worst hit by the bombing
3 (*físicamente*) (= *maltratar*) to damage, harm • **castigamos a nuestro cuerpo con los excesos en la bebida** we harm our bodies with excessive drinking • **~ el hígado** (*iró*) to damage one's liver
4 [+ *caballo*] to ride hard • **~ mucho a un caballo** to ride a horse very hard
5 (= *corregir*) [+ *estilo*] to refine; [+ *texto*] to correct, revise
6 (= *enamorar*) to seduce
7 (*Com*) [+ *gastos*] to reduce
8 (*Méx*) (= *apretar*) [+ *tornillo, cuerda*] to tighten (up)
castigo SM 1 (*por delito, falta*) punishment • **celda de ~** punishment cell • **una cosa así no puede quedarse sin ~** such an act cannot go unpunished • **el gobierno ha sufrido un duro ~ en las urnas** the government has suffered heavy losses in the elections ▸ **castigo corporal** corporal punishment ▸ **castigo divino** divine retribution
2 (*Dep*) penalty • **área de ~** penalty area, penalty box • **golpe de ~** (*Rugby*) penalty, penalty kick
3 (= *tormento*) • **ese cantante es un ~ que no nos merecemos** we don't deserve to have a singer like that inflicted upon us • **el partido fue un ~ para los aficionados** the match was purgatory for the fans • **la artillería sometió durante horas a la ciudad a un duro ~** the artillery pounded the city for hours on end
4 (*Literat*) correction
Castilla SF Castile ▸ **Castilla la Nueva** New Castile ▸ **Castilla la Vieja** Old Castile
• **MODISMO:** • **¡ancha es ~!** it takes all sorts!
castilla SF (*Cono Sur, Méx*) 1 (*Ling*) Castilian, Spanish • **MODISMO:** • **hablar la ~** to speak Spanish
2 • **MODISMO:** • **de ~** (*Hist*) Spanish, from the old country
Castilla-León SM Castile and León
castillejo SM 1 (*Arquit*) scaffolding
2 [*de niño*] babywalker
castillo SM castle • **MODISMO:** • **~s en el aire** castles in the air ▸ **castillo de arena** sandcastle ▸ **castillo de fuego** firework set piece ▸ **castillo de naipes** house of cards ▸ **castillo de popa** aftercastle ▸ **castillo de proa** forecastle
casting ['kastin] SM (*Cine*) casting
castizo ADJ 1 (= *tradicional*) traditional
2 (= *auténtico*) pure, authentic • **es un tipo ~** he's one of the best • **un aragonés ~** a true-blue Aragonese, an Aragonese through and through
3 (*Ling*) pure, correct
casto ADJ chaste, pure
castor SM beaver
castoreño SM 1 (= *sombrero*) beaver
2 (*Taur*) picador's hat
castóreo SM (*Farm*) castor
castra SF 1 (*Bot*) (= *acto*) pruning
2 (= *época*) pruning season
castración SF 1 (*Zool*) castration, gelding
2 (*Bot*) pruning
3 (*Agr*) extraction of honeycombs
castrado ADJ castrated
SM eunuch
castrar ▸ CONJUG 1a VT 1 (*Zool*) [+ *toro*] to castrate; [+ *caballo*] to geld; [+ *gato*] to doctor
2 (*Bot*) to prune, cut back
3 (= *debilitar*) to impair, weaken
castrense ADJ army (*antes de s*), military
castrista ADJ Castroist, Castroite • **el régimen ~** the Castro regime
SMF Castroist, Castroite
castro SM 1 (= *fortaleza*) hill-fort
2 (*Hist*) Iron-Age settlement
casual ADJ 1 (= *fortuito*) chance (*antes de s*) • **un encuentro ~** a chance encounter • **es un hecho ~ y aislado** it's an isolated, chance happening • **su éxito no es ~, sino fruto del trabajo** his success cannot be put down to chance but is the product of hard work • **el descubrimiento de la obra fue ~** the work was discovered by chance • **nada es ~** nothing happens by chance • **de forma** *o* **manera ~** by chance • **no es ~ que ...** it's no coincidence that ...
2 (*Ling*) case (*antes de s*) • **desinencia ~** case ending
SM • **por un ~*** by any chance
casualidad SF 1 (= *azar*) chance; (= *coincidencia*) coincidence • **¿cree en el destino o en la ~?** do you believe in destiny or in chance? • **sería mucha ~** *o* **ya sería ~ que os pusieseis enfermos los dos al mismo tiempo** it would be too much of a coincidence if you both fell ill at the same time • **nuestra victoria no ha sido fruto de la ~** our victory was no fluke • **da la ~ de que ...** it (just) so happens that ... • **dio la ~ de que ...** it just so happened that ... • **ese día dio la ~ de que decidí salir a dar una vuelta** that day I happened to decide to go out for a walk, as luck would have it I decided to go out for a walk that day • **de** *o* **por ~** by chance • **tuve muchísima suerte en el accidente: estoy vivo de ~** I was really lucky in the accident: it's purely by chance *o* pure chance that I'm still alive • **un día entró de ~** he dropped in *o* by one day • **nos enteramos casi por ~** we found out almost by accident • **¿no tendrás un pañuelo, por ~?** you wouldn't happen to have a handkerchief, would you? • **no meten un gol ni por ~** they've got no chance *o* hope of scoring a goal • **no toca un libro ni por ~** he would never think of picking up a book • **¡qué ~!** what a coincidence! • **¡qué ~ verle aquí!** what a coincidence meeting you here!, fancy meeting you here!
2 (= *suceso casual*) coincidence • **fue una pura ~** it was sheer coincidence • **mi carrera profesional es una suma de ~es** my career has been a series of coincidences • **por una de esas ~es de la vida** by one of life's little coincidences
3 **casualidades** (*CAm*) (= *víctimas*) casualties
casualmente ADV by chance, fortuitously (*frm*) • **~ lo vi ayer** I happened to see him yesterday
casuario SM cassowary
casuca SF, **casucha** SF hovel
casuista SMF casuist
casuística SF casuistry
casulla SF chasuble
cata[1] SM o SF 1 (= *acto*) tasting, sampling ▸ **cata de vino** wine tasting
2 (= *porción*) sample
3 (*LAm*) (*Min*) trial excavation, test bore
4 • **MODISMO:** • **ir en ~ de algo*** to go looking for sth
cata[2] SF (*LAm*) (= *loro*) parrot
catabre SM (*And, Caribe*) gourd
catacaldos† SM INV 1 (= *persona inconstante*) rolling stone
2 (= *entrometido*) busybody, meddler
3 (*Arte*) dilettante
cataclismismo SM doomwatching
cataclismista SMF doomwatcher
cataclismo SM cataclysm
catacumbas SFPL catacombs
catadióptrico SM catseye, Catseye®
catador SM 1 [*de comida*] taster, sampler
2 [*de vinos*] taster
catadura SF 1 (= *acto*) tasting, sampling
2 (= *aspecto*) looks (*pl*), appearance • **de mala ~** nasty-looking
catafalco SM catafalque
catafotos SMPL (*Aut*) cat's-eyes
catajarria SF (*Caribe*) string, series
catalán/ana ADJ, SM/F Catalan, Catalonian
SM (*Ling*) Catalan

> **CATALÁN**
> Catalan is a romance language whose earliest literature dates back to the 12th century. In the Middle Ages Catalan military expansion spread the use of the language beyond modern Catalonia, but following the unification of Castile and Aragon the language lost ground to Castilian. During the Franco régime the use of Catalan and other minority national languages was prohibited in the media and in public institutions. This, together with the influx of Castilian-speaking immigrants, posed a threat to the survival of the language. Since 1979, when Catalonia's autonomous government, the **Generalitat**, was re-established and Catalan gained **lengua cooficial** status, the language has returned to public life in Catalonia and is flourishing. Indeed, many Catalan authors publish first in Catalan and only later in Castilian. Outside Catalonia, Catalan is also spoken by large numbers of people in the Balearic Islands and Andorra. **Valenciano**, a language spoken in the Valencia region, is closely related.
> ▷ **LENGUAS COOFICIALES**

catalanismo SM 1 (*Ling*) catalanism, *word or phrase etc peculiar to Catalonia*
2 (= *tendencia*) *sense of the differentness of Catalonia*; (*Pol*) doctrine of Catalan autonomy, belief in Catalan autonomy
catalanista ADJ that supports *etc* Catalan autonomy • **el movimiento ~** the movement for Catalan autonomy • **la familia es muy ~** the family strongly supports Catalan autonomy
SMF supporter *etc* of Catalan autonomy
catalanizar ▸ CONJUG 1f VT to make Catalan, make a Catalan version of
catalejo SM spyglass, telescope
catalepsia SF catalepsy
cataléptico/a ADJ, SM/F cataleptic
Catalina SF Catherine
catálisis SF INV catalysis
catalítico ADJ catalytic
catalizador SM 1 (*Quím*) catalyst
2 (*Aut*) catalytic converter
catalizar ▸ CONJUG 1f VT to catalyse
catalogable ADJ classifiable
catalogación SF cataloguing, cataloging (*EEUU*)
catalogar ▸ CONJUG 1h VT 1 (*en catálogo*) to catalogue, catalog (*EEUU*)
2 (= *clasificar*) to classify (**de as**) • **una zona catalogada de interés artístico** an area classified *o* designated as "of artistic interest"
catálogo SM catalogue, catalog (*EEUU*) • **el libro está fuera de ~** the book is out of print ▸ **catálogo colectivo** union catalogue ▸ **catálogo de materias** subject index ▸ **catálogo de viajes** travel brochure
Cataluña SF Catalonia
catamarán SM catamaran
cataplasma SF 1 (*Med*) poultice
2* (= *persona*) bore
cataplines* SMPL goolies**
cataplum EXCL bang!, crash!
catapulta SF catapult, slingshot (*EEUU*)
catapultar ▸ CONJUG 1a VT to catapult

catapum (EXCL) bang!, crash!
catapún* (ADJ) • **una cosa del año ~** an ancient old thing* • **películas del año ~** films from the year dot
catar ▷ CONJUG 1a (VT) **1** (*Culin*) to taste, sample
2 (= *examinar*) to examine, inspect
3 (= *mirar*) to look at • **¡cata! • ¡cátale!** just look at him!
4 [+ *colmenas*] to extract honeycombs from
catarata (SF) **1** (*Geog*) waterfall, cataract ▸ **cataratas del Niágara** Niagara Falls
2 (*Med*) cataract
catarral (ADJ) catarrhal
catarriento (ADJ) (*LAm*) = **catarroso**
catarro (SM) (*Med*) (= *resfriado*) cold; (= *mucosidad*) catarrh • **pescarse** *o* **pillarse un ~** to catch a cold ▸ **catarro crónico del pecho** chest trouble
catarroso (ADJ) with a cold; (*Med*) catarrhal
catarsis (SF INV) catharsis
catártico (ADJ) cathartic
catasalsas† (SM INV) = **catacaldos**
catastral (ADJ) relating to the property register • **valores ~es** property values, land values
catastro (SM) property register, land registry
catástrofe (SF) catastrophe, disaster • **esta guerra ha supuesto una ~ para el país** this war has been a catastrophe *o* a disaster for the country • **~ aérea/ferroviaria** air/rail disaster • **la fiesta fue una ~** the party was a disaster ▸ **catástrofe natural** natural disaster
catastróficamente (ADV) catastrophically, disastrously
catastrófico (ADJ) catastrophic, disastrous
catastrofismo (SM) alarmism
catastrofista (ADJ) alarmist
(SMF) alarmist
catatán (SM) (*Cono Sur*) punishment
catatar ▷ CONJUG 1a (VT) (*And*) to ill-treat
catatónico (ADJ) (*Med*) catatonic
catauro (SM) (*Caribe*) basket
catavinos (SM INV) **1** (= *enólogo*) wine taster
2 (= *copa*) wine taster's glass
3* (= *bebedor*) boozer*
cate (SM) **1** (= *golpe*) punch, bash*
2* (= *suspenso*) • **dar un ~ a algn** to fail sb, flunk sb (*EEUU**)
catear ▷ CONJUG 1a (VT) **1** (= *buscar*) to search
2 (= *probar*) to test, try
3* [+ *candidato, estudiante, examen*] to fail, flunk (*EEUU**)
4 (*LAm*) (*Min*) to prospect
5 (*Méx*) [*policía*] to raid
catecismo (SM) catechism
catecúmeno/a (SM/F) catechumen
cátedra (SF) **1** (*en universidad*) chair, professorship • **ostentar una ~** to hold a chair (**de** in) • **hablar ex ~** (*Rel*) to speak ex cathedra; (*fig*) to speak with authority • **hacer oposiciones** *u* **opositar para una ~** to compete for a chair *etc* by public competitive examination • **sentar ~ sobre algo** to pontificate about sth
2 (*en enseñanza secundaria*) post of head of department
3 (= *aula*) seminar room
4 (*Caribe**) wonder, marvel • **es ~ • está la ~** it's marvellous
(ADJ) (*Caribe*) wonderful, marvellous, excellent
catedral (SF) cathedral • **MODISMO**: • **como una ~*** enormous, gigantic
catedralicio (ADJ) cathedral (*antes de s*)
catedrático/a (SM/F) **1** [*de universidad*] professor ▸ **catedrático/a de inglés** professor of English
2 (*en enseñanza secundaria*) head of department ▸ **catedrático/a de inglés** head of English, head of the English department
cátedro* (SM) = **catedrático**
categoría (SF) **1** (*en clasificación*) category • **existen tres ~s diferentes** there are three different categories • **obtuvo la ~ de cinturón amarillo** he got his yellow belt • **hoteles de máxima ~** top-class *o* top-flight hotels • **de primera ~** [*hotel, servicio*] first-class (*antes de s*) ▸ **categoría gramatical** part of speech ▸ **categoría laboral** work category ▸ **categoría profesional** professional status ▸ **categoría social** social group
2 (= *calidad*) quality • **fue un espectáculo de ~** it was a top-quality show • **telenovelas de ínfima ~** soap operas of the very worst kind • **han confirmado su reconocida ~ artística** they have confirmed their recognized status *o* standing as artists • **no hay hoy ningún maestro de su ~** nowadays there are no maestros of his calibre *o* in his class • **es hombre de cierta ~** he is a man of some standing • **productos de baja ~** poor quality products • **de ~** [*deportista, artista*] top-class (*antes de s*) • **es una orquesta de ~** it is a top-class orchestra
3 (= *apartado*) (*en premio*) category; (*en deporte*) event • **en la ~ de ensayo** in the essay section *o* category • **en la ~ femenina** in the women's event
4 (= *rango profesional*) grade; (*Mil*) rank • **fue ascendido a la ~ de director general** he was promoted (to the position of) director general • **oficial de baja ~** low-ranking officer
categóricamente (ADV) categorically
categórico (ADJ) [*respuesta*] categorical; [*mentira*] outright, downright; [*orden*] express
categorización (SF) categorization
categorizar ▷ CONJUG 1f (VT) to categorize
catenaria (SF) (*Elec, Ferro*) overhead power cable
cateo (SM) (*Méx*) search, raid
catequesis (SF INV) (*Rel*) catechesis
catequista (SMF) (*Rel*) catechist
catequizar ▷ CONJUG 1f (VT) **1** (*Rel*) to catechize, instruct in Christian doctrine
2* (= *convencer*) to win over, talk round
catering ['katerin] (SM INV) catering ▸ **empresa de catering** caterer's, catering firm
caterva (SF) throng, crowd • **venir en ~** to come in a throng, come thronging
catetada* (SF) piece of nonsense
catéter (SM) catheter
catetismo* (SM) slow-wittedness, boorishness, stupidity
cateto/a* (SM/F) yokel*, hick (*EEUU**)
catimbao (SM) (*And, Cono Sur*) clown, carnival clown
catinga (SF) **1** (*And, Cono Sur*) (= *olor corporal*) [*de persona*] body odour; [*de animales*] strong smell
2 (*Cono Sur*) (= *soldado*) soldier
catingoso (ADJ) (*And, Cono Sur*), **catingudo** (ADJ) (*And, Cono Sur*) stinking, foul-smelling
catire/a (*Caribe, Col*) (ADJ) (= *de pelo rubio*) fair, fair-haired; (= *de piel blanca*) fair-skinned
(SM/F) [*de pelo rubio*] fair-haired person; [*de piel blanca*] fair-skinned person
catisumba (SF) (*CAm*), **catisumbada** (SF) (*CAm*) • **una ~ de algo** lots of sth, loads of sth
catita (SF) (*LAm*) parrot
catitear ▷ CONJUG 1a (VI) (*Cono Sur*) to dodder, shake (*with old age*)
catiusca (ADJ) (*Esp*) • **botas ~s** wellington boots
(SF) wellington boot, welly*
catoche (SM) (*Méx*) bad mood, bad temper
catódico (ADJ) cathodic, cathode (*antes de s*)
cátodo (SM) cathode
catolicidad (SF) catholicity
catolicismo (SM) Catholicism, Roman Catholicism
católico/a (ADJ) (*Rel*) Catholic, Roman Catholic • **no ~** non-Catholic • **MODISMO**: • **no estar muy ~*** to be under the weather
(SM/F) Catholic
Catón (SM) Cato
catón (SM) **1** (= *crítico*) severe critic
2 (= *libro*) primer, first reading book • **eso está en el ~** that is absolutely elementary
catorce (ADJ INV), (PRON) (*gen*) fourteen; (*ordinal, en la fecha*) fourteenth • **le escribí el día ~** I wrote to him on the fourteenth
(SM) (= *número*) fourteen; (= *fecha*) fourteenth; ▹ **seis**
catorceavo (SM) fourteenth part
(ADJ) fourteenth; ▹ **sexto**
catorrazo (SM) (*Méx*), **catorro** (SM) (*Méx*) punch, blow
catracho/a* (*CAm*) (*pey*) (ADJ) of/from El Salvador, Salvadorean
(SM/F) native/inhabitant of El Salvador, Salvadorean • **los ~s** the people of El Salvador
catre (SM) **1** (= *litera*) cot • **MODISMO**: • **cambiar el ~** to change the subject ▸ **catre de tijera, catre de viento** campbed, folding bed
2* (= *cama*) bed
3 ▸ **catre de balsa** (*Cono Sur*) (= *barquito*) raft
catrecillo (SM) folding seat
catrera* (SF) (*Cono Sur*) bunk, bed
catrín† (SM) (*CAm, Méx*) toff*, dude (*EEUU**)
catsup (SM) ketchup, catsup (*EEUU*)
Catulo (SM) Catullus
caucarse ▷ CONJUG 1g (*Cono Sur*) (VPR)
1 [*persona*] to get old
2 [*comida*] to go stale
caucasiano/a (ADJ), (SM/F) Caucasian
caucásico/a (ADJ), (SM/F) Caucasian
Cáucaso (SM) Caucasus
cauce (SM) **1** (= *lecho*) [*de río, arroyo*] riverbed; [*de canal*] bed; (= *curso*) course • **el ~ del río se seca en verano** the riverbed dries up in the summer • **desviaron el ~ del río** they changed *o* diverted the course of the river • **tras las riadas, las aguas han vuelto a su ~** the river has returned to its normal level after the floods
2 (= *medio*) channel, means • **por ~s legales** through legal channels *o* means • **han actuado fuera de los ~s oficiales** they have acted outside the official channels • **tras el encuentro, las negociaciones volvieron a su ~** following that encounter, negotiations returned to their normal course • **MODISMO**: • **dar ~ a algo**: • **este juego da ~ a la imaginación de los niños** this game provides a channel *o* outlet for children's imagination
3 (*Agr*) irrigation channel
cauch (SM) (*CAm, Caribe*) couch
cauchal (SM) rubber plantation
cauchar (SM) (*And*) rubber plantation
(VI) ▷ CONJUG 1a (*And*) to tap, tap trees for rubber
cauchera (SF) **1** (*Bot*) rubber plant, rubber tree
2 (*And*) (= *cauchal*) rubber plantation
cauchero/a (ADJ) rubber (*antes de s*) • **industria cauchera** rubber industry
(SM/F) (*LAm*) worker in a rubber plantation
caucho¹ (SM) **1** (= *material*) rubber ▸ **caucho en bruto** natural rubber ▸ **caucho esponjoso** foam rubber ▸ **caucho natural** natural rubber ▸ **caucho sintético** synthetic rubber
2 (*LAm*) (*Aut*) tyre, tire (*EEUU*)
3 (*LAm*) (= *impermeable*) raincoat, mac
4 (*And*) (= *manta*) waterproof blanket; (= *zapato*) rubber shoe
caucho² (SM) (*Caribe*) couch
cauchutado (ADJ) rubberized

C

cauchutar ▷ CONJUG 1a VT to rubberize

caución SF **1** (= *cautela*) caution, wariness
2 (*Jur*) security, bond • **admitir a algn a ~** to grant sb bail

caucionar ▷ CONJUG 1a VT **1** (= *prevenir*) to prevent, guard against
2 (*Jur*) to bail, go bail for

C

caudal SM **1** [*de río*] volume (of water) • **el ~ del río es el normal para esta época del año** the volume of water in the river is normal for this time of year • **el ~ del río desciende en verano** the level of the river goes down in the summer • **la ciudad se abastece del ~ del Guadalquivir** the city draws its water supply from the Guadalquivir
2 (= *fortuna*) fortune, wealth • **malgastó todo su ~** he squandered his entire fortune *o* all his wealth ▸ **caudal público, caudales públicos** public funds; ▷ **caja**
3 [*de información, datos, ideas*] wealth, volume

caudaloso ADJ **1** [*río*] wide, fast-flowing; (*liter*) mighty
2 (= *abundante*) copious, abundant

caudillaje SM **1** (= *jefatura*) leadership • **bajo el ~ de algn** under the leadership of sb
2 (*LAm*) (*Pol*) (*pey*) tyranny, rule by political bosses

caudillismo SM autocratic government

caudillo SM **1** (*Mil*) leader, chief • **el Caudillo** (*Esp*) the Caudillo, Franco
2 (*Pol*) boss*
3 (*LAm*) (= *tirano*) tyrant; (= *líder*) political boss, leader

caula SF (*CAm, Cono Sur*) plot, intrigue

cauri SM cowrie

causa[1] SF **1** (= *motivo*) cause • **la niebla pudo haber sido la ~ del accidente** the accident could have been caused by fog, the fog could have been the cause of *o* reason for the accident • **algunos protestaron sin ~ justificada** some protested for no good reason *o* without true cause • **por ~s ajenas a nuestra voluntad** for reasons beyond our control • **el fuego se inició por ~s desconocidas** it is not known how the fire was started • **veamos cuál es la ~ de todo esto** let us see what the reason for this is • **relación ~-efecto** cause and effect relationship ▸ **causa final** final cause ▸ **causa primera** first cause; ▷ **conocimiento, doctor**
2 • **a** *o* **por ~ de** because of • **el concierto fue aplazado a ~ de la lluvia** the concert was postponed because of rain • **dos personas han muerto a ~ de una explosión** two people have died in an explosion • **no quiero que sufras por mí ~** I don't want you to suffer for my sake *o* on my account
3 (= *ideal*) cause • **la ~ palestina** the Palestinian cause • **es por una buena ~** it's for a good cause • **hacer ~ común con algn** to make common cause with sb ▸ **causa perdida** lost cause
4 (*Jur*) (*tb* **causa judicial**) lawsuit, case ▸ **causa criminal** criminal prosecution

causa[2] SF **1** (*Cono Sur*) (= *tentempié*) snack, light meal
2 (*Perú*) (= *plato*) *fish and potato pie, served cold*

causal ADJ **1** [*factor, relación*] causal
2 (*Ling*) • **oración ~** clause of reason
SF reason, grounds (*pl*)

causalidad SF causality

causante ADJ • **la explosión ~ del incendio** the explosion that caused the fire
SMF **1** (= *origen*) cause • **el mal tiempo fue el ~ del retraso** the delay was caused by bad weather • **eres el ~ de todas mis desgracias** you are the cause of all my misfortunes
2 (*Méx*) taxpayer
3 (*Jur*) [*de sucesión*] • **el ~** the deceased

causar ▷ CONJUG 1a VT [+ *problema, consecuencia, víctima*] to cause; [+ *impresión*] to make • **su mal carácter le causa muchos problemas** his temper causes him a lot of problems • **el tobillo aún le causa algún problema** his ankle is still giving him trouble • **la explosión causó heridas a dos personas** the explosion injured two people, the explosion left two people injured • **la noticia ha causado gran preocupación** the news has caused enormous concern • **sus declaraciones han causado el efecto esperado** her statements have produced *o* had the desired effect • **el poema le causó una honda impresión** the poem made a great impression on him • **su frialdad me causa un profundo dolor** I find his coolness very hurtful • **~ asombro a algn** to amaze sb • **~ emoción a algn** to move sb • **~ extrañeza a algn** to puzzle sb • **~ risa a algn** to make sb laugh

causativo ADJ causative

causear ▷ CONJUG 1a VI (*Chile*) to have a snack

causeo SM (*Cono Sur*) = **causa[2]**

cáustica SF caustic

cáustico ADJ caustic

cautamente ADV cautiously, warily, carefully

cautela SF **1** (= *cuidado*) caution, wariness • **con mucha ~** very cautiously • **tener la ~ de hacer algo** to take the precaution of doing sth
2 (*pey*) (= *astucia*) cunning

cautelar[1] ADJ precautionary • **prisión ~** preventive detention

cautelar[2] ▷ CONJUG 1a VT **1** (= *prevenir*) to prevent, guard against
2 (*LAm*) (= *defender*) to protect, defend
VPR **cautelarse** to be on one's guard (**de** against)

cautelosamente ADV **1** (= *con cautela*) cautiously, warily, carefully
2 (*pey*) (= *astutamente*) cunningly, craftily

cauteloso ADJ **1** (= *cuidadoso*) cautious, wary, careful
2 (*pey*) (= *astuto*) cunning, crafty

cauterio SM **1** (*Med*) cautery, cauterization
2 (= *remedio*) drastic remedy

cauterizador ADJ cauterizing
SM cautery, cauterant

cauterizar ▷ CONJUG 1f VT **1** (*Med*) to cauterize
2 (= *atajar*) to eradicate

cautivador ADJ, **cautivante** ADJ captivating

cautivar ▷ CONJUG 1a VT **1** (= *hacer prisionero a*) (*Mil*) to capture, take prisoner
2 (= *hechizar*) to captivate • **su belleza me cautivó** her beauty captivated me

cautiverio SM, **cautividad** SF **1** [*de prisionero*] captivity
2 [*de siervo*] bondage, serfdom

cautivo/a ADJ, SM/F captive

cauto ADJ cautious, wary, careful

cava[1] SM cava

> **CAVA**
> A sparkling white or occasionally rosé Spanish wine, **cava** is produced mainly in the **Penedès** region using the traditional techniques developed in Champagne, France. To maintain the constant temperature important to the process, the wine is stored and fermented in cellars or **cavas**, hence the name. Varieties of **cava** include: medium (**semiseco**), dry (**seco**), very dry (**brut**) and the extra dry variety especially recommended by connoisseurs called **brut nature**.

cava[2] SF **1** (= *lugar*) (= *para el vino*) wine cellar; [*de garaje*] pit
2 (*Caribe*) (= *nevera*) icebox

cava[3] SF (= *acción*) digging

cavador(a) SM/F digger ▸ **cavador(a) de oro** gold digger

cavadura SF digging, excavation

cavar ▷ CONJUG 1a VT (*en el suelo*) [+ *fosa, hoyo*] to dig; [+ *pozo*] to sink; (*Agr*) [+ *tierra*] to dig over; [+ *cepas*] to dig round
VI **1** (*en el suelo*) to dig
2 (= *investigar*) to delve (**en** into), go deeply (**en** into)
3 (= *meditar*) to meditate profoundly (**en** on)

cavazón SF digging, excavation

caverna SF cave, cavern

cavernícola ADJ **1** (= *de caverna*) cave-dwelling, cave (*antes de s*) • **hombre ~** caveman
2 (*Pol**) reactionary
SMF **1** (= *habitante de caverna*) cave dweller
2 (*Pol**) reactionary, backwoodsman

cavernoso ADJ **1** (= *hueco*) [*lugar*] cavernous; [*montaña*] full of caves, honeycombed with caves
2 [*voz*] resounding, deep

caviar SM caviar, caviare

cavidad SF cavity ▸ **cavidad bucal** oral cavity ▸ **cavidad nasal** nasal cavity ▸ **cavidad oral** oral cavity

cavilación SF **1** (= *meditación*) deep thought, rumination
2 (= *sospecha*) suspicion

cavilar ▷ CONJUG 1a VI to think deeply, ponder

cavilosear ▷ CONJUG 1a VI **1** (*Caribe*) (= *ilusionarse*) to harbour illusions; (= *vacilar*) to vacillate, hesitate
2 (*CAm*) (= *chismear*) to gossip

cavilosidad SF suspicion

caviloso ADJ **1** (= *obsesionado*) brooding, suspicious
2 (*CAm*) (= *chismoso*) gossipy, backbiting
3 (*And*) (= *agresivo*) quarrelsome, touchy; (= *quisquilloso*) fussy, finicky

cayado SM **1** (*Agr*) crook
2 (*Rel*) crozier

cayena SF cayenne pepper

cayendo *etc* ▷ **caer**

cayo SM (*Caribe*) islet, key ▸ **Cayo Hueso** Key West

cayubro ADJ (*And*) reddish-blond, red-haired

cayuca‡ SF (*Caribe*) head, bean*

cayuco SM (*LAm*) *small Indian canoe*

caz SM **1** [*de riego*] irrigation channel
2 [*de molino*] millrace

caza SF **1** (= *acción*) hunting; (*con fusil*) shooting • **la ~ del jabalí** boar hunting • **la ~ del zorro** foxhunting • **la ~ de la perdiz** partridge shooting • **~ con hurón** ferreting • **a la ~ de algo**: • **los periodistas andan siempre a la ~ de noticias** journalists are always on the hunt for *o* out in pursuit of news • **van a la ~ de nuevos talentos** they are on the hunt for new talent • **dar ~ a** (= *perseguir*) to give chase to, pursue; (= *alcanzar*) to hunt down • **dieron ~ al ciervo** they gave chase to *o* pursued the deer • **dieron orden de dar ~ al fugitivo** they ordered the fugitive to be hunted down • **los corredores consiguieron dar ~ al escapado** the runners managed to catch (up with) the breakaway leader • **ir de ~** to go hunting; (*con fusil*) to go (out) shooting • MODISMO: • **levantar la ~** to put up the game ▸ **caza de brujas** witchhunt ▸ **caza de control** culling ▸ **caza del hombre** manhunt ▸ **caza furtiva** poaching ▸ **caza mayor** game hunting ▸ **caza menor** small

game hunting; (*con fusil*) small game shooting ▸ **caza submarina** underwater fishing ▸ **caza y captura** • **estar a la ~ y captura de la noticia** to be on the hunt for news • **operación de ~ y captura de criminales** operation to track down and catch criminals; ▹ **coto**¹
2 (= *animal cazado*) game; (*Culin*) game ▸ **caza mayor** big game ▸ **caza menor** small game
SM (*Aer*) fighter (plane) ▸ **caza de escolta** escort fighter

cazaautógrafos SMF INV autograph hunter

cazabe SM (*LAm*) (*Culin*) cassava bread, cassava flour

caza-bombardero SM fighter-bomber

cazaclavos SM INV nail puller

cazadero SM hunting ground

cazador(a) SM/F (*gen*) hunter; (*a caballo*) huntsman/huntswoman ▸ **cazador(a) de alforja, cazador(a) de pieles** trapper ▸ **cazador(a) furtivo/a** poacher

cazadora SF jacket ▸ **cazadora de cuero, cazadora de piel** leather jacket ▸ **cazadora tejana** denim jacket

cazador-recolector SM (PL: **cazadores-recolectores**) hunter-gatherer

cazadotes SM INV fortune-hunter

cazaejecutivos SMF INV (*Com*) headhunter

cazafortunas SMF INV fortune hunter, gold digger

cazagenios SMF INV **1** (*Univ*) talent scout, talent spotter
2 (*Com*) headhunter

cazamariposas SM INV butterfly net

cazaminas SM INV minesweeper

cazamoscas SM INV flycatcher

cazanazis SMF INV Nazi-hunter

cazar ▹ CONJUG 1f VT **1** [+ *animales*] to hunt; (*con fusil*) to shoot
2 [+ *ladrón, fugitivo*] to hunt down
3 [+ *corredor, ciclista*] to catch (up with)
4 [+ *votos*] to capture; [+ *electores, votantes*] to win (over)
5* (= *atrapar*) to land* • **al final cazó un magnífico empleo** in the end he landed an excellent job* • **su aspiración es ~ un hombre para casarse** her ambition is to land herself a husband*
6* (= *sorprender*) to catch • **los cazó robando** he caught them stealing
7* (= *comprender*) to understand • **es el mejor alumno, lo caza todo enseguida** he's the best pupil, he understands *o* gets* everything at once; ▹ **vuelo**²
VI to hunt • **salir a ~** to go (out) hunting; (*con fusil*) to go (out) shooting

cazarrecompensas SMF INV bounty hunter

cazasubmarinos SM INV **1** (*Náut*) (= *en superficie*) destroyer; (*sumergible*) hunter-killer
2 (*Aer*) anti-submarine craft

cazatalentos SMF INV talent scout, talent spotter

cazatanques SM INV • **avión ~** anti-tank aircraft

cazatesoros SMF INV treasure hunter

cazaturistas ADJ INV • **lugar ~** tourist trap, touristy place

cazcalear†* ▹ CONJUG 1a VI to fuss around, buzz about

cazcarrias SFPL splashes of mud (*on one's clothes*)

cazcarriento ADJ splashed with mud, mud-stained

cazo SM **1** (= *cacerola*) saucepan ▸ **cazo de cola** gluepot
2 (= *cucharón*) ladle
3‡ (= *chulo*) pimp

cazolero SM milksop

cazoleta SF **1** [*de cocina*] pan, small pan
2 [*de pipa*] bowl
3 [*de sostén*] cup
4 [*de espada*] guard
5 [*de escudo*] boss
6 (*Mec*) housing

cazón SM dogfish

cazonete SM (*Náut*) toggle

cazuela SF **1** (= *recipiente*) [*de metal*] pan; [*de barro*] casserole (dish)
2 (= *guiso*) stew, casserole
3 (*Teat*) gods (*pl*)

cazurrismo SM dim-wittedness

cazurro ADJ **1** (= *torpe, lento en comprender*) dim, dim-witted • **¡cómo puedes ser tan ~!** how can you be so dim *o* dim-witted!
2 (= *huraño*) surly, sullen
3 (= *testarudo*) stubborn

cazuz SM ivy

CC SF ABR (*Esp*) (*Pol*) = **Coalición Canaria**
ABR **1** (*Aut*) = **Código de la Circulación**
2 (*Pol*) = **Comité Central**
3 = **Cuerpo Consular**

cc ABR (= **con copia**) (*Inform*) cc

C.C. ABR (*Elec*) (= **corriente continua**) DC

c.c. ABR (= **centímetros cúbicos**) cc

c/c ABR (= **cuenta corriente**) C/A, a/c (EEUU)

CCAA SFPL ABR (*Esp*) (*Pol*) = **Comunidades Autónomas**

CCI SF ABR (= **Cámara de Comercio Internacional**) ICC

CCOO SFPL ABR (*Esp*) (= **Comisiones Obreras**) *Communist trade union*

CCOO
Comisiones Obreras is the Spanish communist trade union federation. Banned under the dictatorship of General Franco, it was relegalized following Franco's death and is nowadays one of Spain's two largest trade unions, together with the **UGT**.

CD SM ABR (= **compact disc**) CD

C.D. ABR **1** (= **Cuerpo Diplomático**) CD
2 = **Club Deportivo**

c/d ABR **1** (= **en casa de**) c/o
2 (*Com*) = **con descuento**

C. de J. ABR (= **Compañía de Jesús**) S.J.

CD-I [θeðe'i] SM ABR (= **Compact Disc Interactive**) CD-I

C.D.N. SM ABR (*Esp*) (= **Centro Dramático Nacional**) ≈ RADA

CD-R SM ABR (= **compact disc recordable**) CD-R

CD-ROM [θeðe'rom] SM ABR (= **Compact Disc Read-Only Memory**) CD-ROM

CD-RW SM ABR (= **compact disc rewritable**) CD-RW

CDS SM ABR (*Esp*) (*Pol*) = **Centro Democrático y Social**

Cdte., cdte. ABR (= **comandante**) (*en ejército*) ≈ Maj; (*en marina*) Cdr, Cmdr; [*de avión*] ≈ Capt

CDU SF ABR = **Clasificación Decimal Universal**

CE SF ABR (= **Comunidad Europea**) EC
SM ABR = **Consejo de Europa**

ce SF C (*name of the letter c*) • MODISMOS: • **ce por be** down to the tiniest detail • **por ce o por be** somehow or other

ceba SF **1** (*Agr*) fattening
2 [*de arma*] priming
3 [*de horno*] stoking

cebada SF barley ▸ **cebada perlada** pearl barley

cebadal SM barley field

cebadera SF **1** (*Agr*) nosebag
2 (*Téc*) hopper

cebadero SM **1** (= *comerciante*) barley dealer
2 (= *mula*) leading mule (*of a team*)
3 (= *sitio*) feeding place
4 (*Téc*) *mouth for charging a furnace*

cebado ADJ (*LAm*) [*animal*] man-eating
SM **1** (*Agr*) fattening
2 [*de arma de fuego*] priming

cebador SM (*Cono Sur*) (*Aut*) choke

cebadura SF = **ceba**

cebar ▹ CONJUG 1a VT **1** [+ *animal*] to fatten (up) • **ceban a los pavos con piensos artificiales** they fatten up the turkeys on artificial feeds • **cuando voy a casa mi madre me ceba*** when I go home my mother feeds me up
2 [+ *anzuelo, cepo, trampa*] to bait
3 [+ *fuego, horno*] to feed, stoke (up); [+ *arma*] to prime
4 (*frm*) [+ *pasión, odio*] to feed, nourish; [+ *cólera*] to feed
5 (*Cono Sur*) [+ *mate*] to brew
VI [*tuerca, tornillo*] to catch, grip; [*clavo*] to go in
VPR **cebarse** • **~se con** *o* **en algn: la oposición se cebó con** *o* **en el presidente** the opposition launched a savage *o* furious attack on the president • **el paro se ceba especialmente en los jóvenes** unemployment hits young people particularly hard • **estaba enfadada y se cebó conmigo** she was angry and took it out on me *o* vented her anger on me

cebeísmo SM enthusiasm for CB radio

cebeísta SMF CB radio enthusiast

cebellina SF (*Zool*) sable

cebiche SM (*Cono Sur*) (*Culin*) *raw fish or shellfish dish*

cebo SM **1** (*Pesca*) bait
2 (*Agr*) feed, fodder
3 (*Téc*) fuel
4 [*de arma*] charge, primer

cebolla SF **1** (*Bot*) (= *hortaliza*) onion; [*de tulipán*] bulb ▸ **cebolla de Cambray** spring onion ▸ **cebolla escalonia** shallot
2* (= *cabeza*) nut*

cebollado ADJ (*LAm*) cooked with onions

cebollana SF chive

cebolleta SF **1** (*Bot*) (= *cebolla*) spring onion, green onion (EEUU); (= *cebollana*) chive
2‡ (= *pene*) prick**

cebollina SF, **cebollino** SM **1** (= *cebolleta*) spring onion, green onion (EEUU)
2 (= *semilla*) onion seed
3 (= *cebollana*) chive

cebollita SF (*LAm*) (*Bot*) (*tb* **cebollita china**) spring onion

cebollón SM **1** (*Cono Sur*) (*pey*) old bachelor
2‡ (= *borrachera*) • **llevaba un ~ enorme cuando salió del bar** he was plastered when he left the bar*

cebollona SF (*Cono Sur*) (*pey*) old maid*, spinster

cebolludo ADJ **1** (*Bot*) bulbous
2* [*persona*] vulgar

cebón ADJ fat, fattened
SM fattened animal

ceboruco SM **1** (*Caribe*) (= *arrecife*) reef
2 (*Méx*) (= *terreno quebrado*) rough rocky place
3 (*Caribe*) (= *maleza*) brush, scrub, scrubland

cebra SF zebra

cebú SM zebu

CECA SF ABR **1** (= **Comunidad Europea del Carbón y del Acero**) ECSC
2 = **Confederación Española de Cajas de Ahorro**

Ceca SF • **andar** *o* **ir de la ~ a la Meca** to go hither and thither, chase about all over the place

ceca SF (*Econ*) mint

CECE SF ABR = **Confederación Española de**

Centros de la Enseñanza
cecear ▹ CONJUG 1a VI (*por defecto*) to lisp; (*Ling*) to pronounce "s" as "th"
ceceo SM (*por defecto*) lisp; (*Ling*) pronunciation of "s" as "th"
ceceoso ADJ lisping, with a lisp
Cecilia SF Cecily
Cecilio SM Cecil
cecina SF **1** (= *carne seca*) cured meat, smoked meat
2 (*Cono Sur*) jerked meat, jerked beef
CEDA SF ABR (*Esp*) (*Hist*) = **Confederación Española de Derechas Autónomas**
ceda SM ▸ **ceda el paso** (*Aut*) priority, right of way
cedazo SM sieve
cedente SMF (*Jur*) assignor
ceder ▹ CONJUG 2a VT **1** [+ *propiedad*] to transfer; [+ *territorio*] to cede (*frm*), hand over • **me cedió el asiento** she let me have her seat, she gave up her seat (for me) • **cedió los derechos de autor a su familia** she gave up *o* over the authorial rights to her family • **el director ha cedido el puesto a su colaborador** the director has decided to hand over the post to his colleague • **~ la palabra a algn** to give the floor to sb (*frm*), call upon sb to speak • **"ceda el paso"** "give way", "yield" (*EEUU*) • **~ terreno a algn/algo** to give ground to sb/sth
2 (*Dep*) [+ *balón*] to pass
VI **1** (= *transigir*) to give in, yield (*frm*) • **los negociadores tendrán que ~** the negotiators will have to give way *o* yield • **~ a algo** to give in to sth, yield to sth • **~ al chantaje** to give in *o* yield to blackmail • **~ ante algn/algo** to give in to sb/sth, yield to sb/sth • **no ~emos a *o* ante sus amenazas** we will not give in to *o* yield to his threats • **~ en algo**: • **no ceden en su empeño de ganar la liga** they're not giving in *o* up in their endeavour to win the league
2 (= *disminuir*) [*viento*] to drop, die down; [*lluvia*] to ease up; [*frío*] to abate, ease up; [*fiebre*] to go down; [*dolor*] to lessen
3 [*suelo, viga*] to give way, give • **el techo cedió y se derrumbó** the roof gave (way) and collapsed
4 (= *dar de sí*) [*zapatos, prenda, elástico*] to stretch, give • **el tejido ha cedido y me queda ancho** the material has stretched *o* given and now it's too big for me
cederrón SM CD-ROM
cedible ADJ transferable
cedilla SF cedilla
cedizo ADJ [*carne*] high, tainted
cedro SM cedar
cedrón SM (*Cono Sur*) (*Culin*) lemon verbena
cédula SF **1** (= *documento*) document • **dar ~ a algn** to license sb ▸ **cédula ciudadanía** (*Col*) identity card, ID ▸ **cédula de aduana** customs permit ▸ **cédula de cambio** bill of exchange ▸ **cédula de identidad** (*LAm*) identity card, ID ▸ **cédula en blanco** blank cheque, blank check (*EEUU*) ▸ **cédula hipotecaria** mortgage bond ▸ **cédula personal** identity card, ID ▸ **cédula real** royal letters patent
2 (= *ficha*) index card
3 (*Com*) warrant
cedulista SMF (*Econ*) holder (*of a certificate etc*)
CEE SF ABR (= **Comunidad Económica Europea**) EEC
cefalea SF migraine
cefálico ADJ cephalic
céfiro SM zephyr
cegador ADJ blinding • **brillo ~** blinding glare
cegajoso ADJ weepy, bleary-eyed
cegamiento SM [*de tubería*] blockage
cegar ▹ CONJUG 1h, 1j VT **1** (= *deslumbrar*) to blind • **el camión me cegó con las luces** the lights of the lorry blinded me
2 (= *ofuscar*) [+ *persona*] to blind • **le ciega la pasión** he is blinded by passion
3 (= *obstruir*) [+ *tubería, agujero*] to block up, stop up; [+ *pozo*] to block up; [+ *puerta, ventana*] to wall up
VI to go blind, become blind
VPR **cegarse 1** (= *ofuscarse*) to be blinded (de by) • **se cegó de furia** he was blinded by anger
2 (= *obstruirse*) to block
cegato* ADJ, **cegatón*** ADJ half blind*
cegatoso ADJ = cegajoso
cegué ▹ **cegar**
ceguera SF, **ceguedad** SF **1** (= *pérdida de visión*) blindness ▸ **ceguera nocturna** night blindness
2 (= *obcecación*) blindness (to reason)
CEI SF ABR (= **Comunidad de Estados Independientes**) CIS
ceiba SF (*LAm*) (*Bot*) ceiba tree, kapok tree
ceibo SM (*LAm*) (*Bot*) (cockspur) coral tree
Ceilán SM (*Hist*) Ceylon
ceilanés/esa ADJ, SM/F (*Hist*) Ceylonese
ceja SF **1** (*Anat*) eyebrow • **~s pobladas** bushy eyebrows, thick eyebrows • **arquear las ~s** to raise one's eyebrows • **fruncir las ~s** to knit one's brows, frown • MODISMOS: • **estar endeudado hasta las ~s*** to be up to one's eyes in debt • **meterse algo entre ~ y ~*** to get sth firmly into one's head • **tener a algn entre ~ y ~*** to have no time for sb • **quemarse las ~s*** to burn the midnight oil
2 (*Téc*) rim, flange
3 (*Cos*) edging
4 (*Arquit*) projection
5 (*Geog*) brow, crown
6 (*Mús*) bridge
cejar ▹ CONJUG 1a VI **1** (= *retroceder*) to move back, go back; (*en discusión*) to back down • **no ~** to keep it up, keep going • **no ~ en sus esfuerzos** to keep at it • **no ~ en su trabajo** to keep up the work • **sin ~** unflinchingly
2 (= *ceder*) to give way, back down
cejijunto ADJ with eyebrows very close together
cejilla SF (*Mús*) bridge
cejudo ADJ with bushy eyebrows
celacanto SM coelacanth
celada SF **1** (= *emboscada*) ambush, trap • **caer en la ~** to fall into the trap
2 (*Hist*) helmet
celador(a) SM/F (= *vigilante*) [*de edificio*] guard; [*de cárcel*] warder, guard (*EEUU*); [*de centro escolar*] porter; [*de museo*] attendant, warder; [*de hospital*] hospital porter; [*de aparcamiento*] parking attendant
celaje SM **1** (= *nubes*) (*Meteo*) sky with coloured *o* (*EEUU*) colored clouds; (*Náut*) clouds (*pl*) • **~s** sunset clouds
2 (*Arte*) cloud effect
3 (*Arquit*) skylight
4 (= *presagio*) sign, promising sign, token
5 (*And, Caribe*) (= *fantasma*) ghost • MODISMO: • **como un ~** in a flash
celar[1] ▹ CONJUG 1a VT (= *vigilar*) [+ *paciente, seguridad*] to watch over; (*en un examen*) to invigilate • **~ la justicia** to see that justice is done
VI • **~ por *o* sobre algo** to watch over sth
celar[2] ▹ CONJUG 1a VT (= *ocultar*) to conceal, hide
celda SF cell ▸ **celda de castigo** solitary confinement cell
celdilla SF **1** [*de colmena*] cell
2 (*Arquit*) niche
cele ADJ (*CAm*) **1** [*color*] light green
2 [*fruta*] unripe
celebérrimo ADJ *superl de* **célebre**
celebración SF **1** (= *realización*) • **tras la ~ de las elecciones** after the elections were held • **durante la ~ del pleno municipal** during the council meeting
2 (= *fiesta*) celebration • **una ~ familiar** a family celebration • **un año de grandes celebraciones** a year of great celebrations
3 (*Rel*) [*de misa, festividad*] celebration • **coincidiendo con la ~ del Ramadán** coinciding with the celebration of Ramadan
4 (= *alabanza*) celebration
celebrante SM (*Rel*) celebrant, officiating priest
celebrar ▹ CONJUG 1a VT **1** (= *festejar*) [+ *aniversario, acontecimiento*] to celebrate • **siempre celebramos la Navidad en familia** we always celebrate Christmas as a family • **estamos celebrando que hemos aprobado los exámenes** we're celebrating passing our exams • **en mayo se celebra el día de los trabajadores** Labour Day is in May • **el día 22 se celebra la fiesta de santa Cecilia** the 22nd is the feast day of Saint Cecilia • **tu santo se celebra el día 19 de marzo** your saint's day is on 19 March
2 (= *llevar a cabo*) [+ *congreso, juicio, elecciones, fiesta*] to hold; [+ *acuerdo, contrato*] to sign • **la reunión se ~á el viernes por la tarde** the meeting will take place *o* will be held on Friday afternoon • **el partido no pudo ~se a causa de la lluvia** the match could not be played because of rain
3 (*frm*) (= *alegrarse de*) • **lo celebro** I'm delighted • **lo celebro por él** I'm very pleased for him • **celebro comprobar que conserva su sentido del humor** I'm delighted *o* very pleased to see that he's still got his sense of humour • **celebro que hayas aceptado ese trabajo** I'm delighted *o* very pleased that you've accepted that job • **celebro que no sea nada grave** I'm glad it's nothing serious
4 (= *alabar*) [+ *valor, belleza*] to celebrate, praise; [+ *ventajas*] to preach, dwell on; [+ *bromas, gracias*] to laugh at
5 (*Rel*) [+ *boda, ceremonia*] to perform • **~ una misa** to celebrate mass, say mass
VI [*sacerdote*] to celebrate mass, say mass
célebre ADJ famous, celebrated, noted (**por** for)
celebridad SF **1** (= *fama*) celebrity, fame
2 (= *persona famosa*) celebrity
celeque ADJ (*CAm*) green, unripe
célere ADJ (*liter*) rapid, swift
celeridad SF speed, swiftness • **con ~** quickly, promptly
celeste ADJ **1** (= *del cielo*) heavenly
2 [*color*] sky blue
celestial ADJ **1** (*Rel*) celestial
2 (= *delicioso*) heavenly
celestina SF procuress
celestinazgo SM procuring
celíaco/a ADJ, SM/F coeliac, celiac (*EEUU*)
celibato SM celibacy
célibe ADJ, SMF celibate
célico ADJ (*liter*) heavenly, celestial
celidonia SF celandine
celinda SF (*Bot*) mock orange
cellisca SF sleet
cellisquear ▹ CONJUG 1a VI to sleet
cello[1] SM (*Mús*) cello
cello[2] SM = celo[2]
celo[1] SM **1** (= *diligencia*) zeal • **hacer algo con ~** to do sth zealously *o* with zeal ▸ **celo profesional** professional commitment, commitment to one's job; ▹ **huelga**
2 (*Rel*) zeal
3 (*Zool*) [*de hembra*] oestrus, estrus (*EEUU*); [*de*

macho] rut • una hembra en ~ a female on heat o in season • estar en ~ to be on heat, be in season
4 celos jealousy (sing) • los ~s la consumen she's eaten up with jealousy • dar ~s a algn to make sb jealous • tener ~s de algn to be jealous of sb
celo²® SM (= cinta adhesiva) Sellotape®, Scotchtape® (EEUU), sticky tape
celo³ SM (Mús) cello
celofán SM cellophane
celosamente ADV 1 (= con fervor) zealously
2 (pey) (= sin confianza) suspiciously, distrustfully
3 (= con celos) jealously
celosía SF 1 (= enrejado) lattice, lattice window
2 (= contraventana) slatted shutter
3 (= celos) jealousy
celoso ADJ 1 [marido, hermano] jealous (de of)
2 (= ferviente) zealous; (en el trabajo) conscientious
3 (= desconfiado) suspicious, distrustful
4 (LAm) (Mec) highly sensitive
5 (And) [barca] unsteady, easily upset
6 (LAm) [arma] delicate, liable to go off • este es un fusil ~ this gun is quite liable to go off
Celsius ADJ INV (escala) Celsius • grado ~ degree Celsius
celta ADJ Celtic
SMF Celt
SM (Ling) Celtic
Celtiberia SF Celtiberia
celtibérico/a ADJ, SM/F Celtiberian
celtíbero/a ADJ, SM/F Celtiberian
céltico ADJ Celtic
célula SF 1 (Bio, Elec) cell ▸ célula de combustible fuel cell ▸ célula de silicio silicon chip ▸ célula fotoeléctrica photoelectric cell ▸ célula fotovoltaica photovoltaic cell ▸ célula germen germ cell ▸ célula grasa fat cell ▸ célula madre stem cell • investigación con ~s madre stem cell research ▸ célula nerviosa nerve cell ▸ célula sanguínea blood cell
2 (Pol) cell ▸ célula terrorista terrorist cell
3 (Aer) airframe
celular ADJ cellular, cell (antes de s) • tejido ~ cell tissue; ▹ coche¹
SM (LAm) (= teléfono) mobile (phone) (Brit), cellphone (EEUU) ▸ celular con cámara camera phone
celulítico ADJ [célula, proceso] cellulite (antes de s); [persona] with cellulite
celulitis SF INV cellulitis
celuloide SM celluloid • llevar algo al ~ to make a film of sth
celulosa SF cellulose
CEM SM ABR = Centro de Estudios de la Mujer
CEMA SM ABR (= curso en línea masivo y abierto) MOOC
cementación SF (Téc) case-hardening, cementation
cementar ▹ CONJUG 1a VT (Téc) to case-harden, cement
cementera SF cement works
cementerio SM (municipal) cemetery; (en iglesia) graveyard ▸ cementerio de coches used-car dump, junkyard (EEUU) ▸ cementerio nuclear nuclear waste dump
cementero ADJ cement (antes de s)
cementista SM cement worker
cemento SM 1 [de construcción] cement ▸ cemento armado reinforced concrete ▸ cemento Portland Portland cement ▸ cemento reforzado reinforced concrete
2 (LAm) (= pegamento) glue
3 [de diente] cement
cemita SF (LAm) white bread roll
CEN SM ABR (Esp) = Consejo de Economía Nacional
cena SF (a última hora) supper; (como comida principal) dinner • nos invitó a una ~ en el restaurante he invited us to dinner at a restaurant • la Última Cena the Last Supper ▸ Cena de Baltasar Belshazzar's Feast ▸ cena de gala dinner function, formal dinner; (Pol) state banquet ▸ cena de negocios business dinner ▸ cena de trabajo working dinner
cena-bufete SF (PL: cenas-bufete) buffet supper
cenáculo SM group, coterie
cenador SM arbour, arbor (EEUU)
cenaduría SF (Méx) eating house, restaurant
cena-espectáculo SF (PL: cenas-espectáculo) dinner show, dinner with a floor show
cenagal SM 1 (= pantano) bog, quagmire
2 (= desorden) mess, nasty business
cenagoso ADJ muddy
cena-homenaje SF (PL: cenas-homenaje) formal dinner, celebratory dinner • ofrecer una cena-homenaje a algn to hold a dinner for sb
cenar ▹ CONJUG 1a VI (a última hora) to have supper; (como comida principal) to have dinner; (en ocasión formal) to dine (frm) • cenamos a las diez de la noche we have supper at ten o'clock • los británicos cenan a las seis the British have dinner at six o'clock • el rey cenó en la embajada de Alemania the king had dinner at o (frm) dined at the German Embassy • vengo cenado I've had dinner o supper already, I've had (my) dinner, I've already eaten • me han invitado a ~ they've asked me to dinner • salir a ~ to go out to dinner, dine out (frm)
VT (a última hora) to have for supper; (como comida principal) to have for dinner • siempre ceno algo muy ligero I always have a very light supper
cenceño ADJ thin, skinny; ▹ pan
cencerrada SF noise made with cowbells, pots and pans etc, on festive occasions or in mockery
cencerrear ▹ CONJUG 1a VI 1 [campanillas] to jingle
2 [motor] to rattle
3 (Mús) to make a dreadful noise
cencerreo SM 1 [de campanillas] jangle
2 [de motor] rattle, clatter
3 (Mús) dreadful noise
cencerro SM cowbell • MODISMOS: • a ~s tapados stealthily, on the sly • estar como un ~* to be round the bend*
cendal SM 1 (= gasa) gauze
2 (= tela fina) fine silk stuff, sendal
cenefa SF 1 (Cos) edging, border
2 (Arquit) border
cenetista ADJ • política ~ policy of the CNT
SMF member of the CNT
cenicero SM ashtray
cenicienta SF • soy la ~ de la casa I'm the dogsbody round here • la Cenicienta Cinderella
ceniciento ADJ ashen (liter), ash-coloured, ash-colored (EEUU)
cénit SM, **cenit** SM zenith
ceniza SF 1 (= polvo) ash • reducir algo a ~s to reduce sth to ashes • MODISMO: • huir de las ~s y dar en las brasas to jump out of the frying pan into the fire
2 cenizas [de persona] ashes, mortal remains
cenizo ADJ 1 [color] ashen (liter), ash-coloured, ash-colored (EEUU)
2* (= de mala suerte) • es un avión ~ it's a plane with a jinx on it*
SM 1* (= mala suerte) jinx* • tener el ~ to have a jinx on one* • MODISMO: • entrar el ~ en casa to have a spell of bad luck
2 (= persona) jinx*
3 (Bot) goosefoot
cenobio SM monastery
cenobita SMF c(o)enobite
cenojil SM garter
cenorrio* (hum) SM posh dinner*, slap-up do*
cenotafio SM cenotaph
cenote SM (CAm, Méx) natural well
censado SM census-taking
censal ADJ = censual
censar ▹ CONJUG 1a VT to take a census of
censista SMF census official, census taker
censo SM 1 (= lista) census • elaborar o hacer un ~ to take a census ▸ censo de población population census ▸ censo electoral electoral roll, list of registered voters (EEUU)
2 (Hist, Econ) (= tributo) tax; (= alquiler) (annual) ground rent
censor(a) SM/F 1 (Pol) censor
2 (Com, Econ) ▸ censor(a) de cuentas auditor ▸ censor(a) jurado/a de cuentas chartered accountant, certified public accountant (EEUU)
3 (= crítico) critic
censual ADJ 1 [demografía] census (antes de s), relating to a census
2 (Econ) mortgage (antes de s)
3 (= de elecciones) electoral, relating to the electoral roll
censura SF 1 (= supresión) censorship • la ~ de prensa press censorship • sometieron todos sus libros a la ~ they censored all his books
2 (= institución) censors (pl) • el autor tuvo problemas con la ~ the author had problems with the censors
3 (= condena) censure (frm), criticism • lanzó palabras de ~ contra los políticos he spoke words of censure (frm) o criticism against the politicians • digno de ~ reprehensible; ▹ moción, voto
4 (Com, Econ) ▸ censura de cuentas auditing
censurable ADJ reprehensible
censurar ▹ CONJUG 1a VT 1 (Pol) to censor
2 [+ obra, película] to censor
3 (= criticar) to censure (frm), criticize
censurista ADJ censorious
SMF critic, faultfinder
cént ABR (= céntimo) c
centaura SF centaury
centauro SM centaur
centavo SM 1 (partitivo) hundredth, hundredth part
2 (Econ) cent
centella SF 1 (= chispa) spark
2 (= rayo) flash of lightning • salió como una ~ del cuarto he was out of the room as quick as a flash o in a flash
centelleante ADJ [luz, diamante] sparkling; [estrella] twinkling; [metal] gleaming, glinting; [fuego] flickering
centellear ▹ CONJUG 1a VI [luz, diamante] to sparkle; [estrella] to twinkle; [metal] to gleam, glint; [fuego] to flicker
centelleo SM [de luz, diamante] sparkle; [de estrella] twinkle; [de metal] glint
centena SF, **centenada** SF hundred
centenal SM 1 (Agr) rye field
2 (= centena) hundred
centenar¹ SM hundred • a ~es by the hundred, in hundreds, in their hundreds
centenar² SM (Agr) rye field
centenario/a ADJ centenary
SM/F centenarian, hundred-year-old person
SM centenary, centennial

centeno SM rye
centésima SF hundredth, hundredth part
centesimal ADJ centesimal
centésimo ADJ hundredth • **centésima parte** hundredth
SM **1** *(partitivo)* hundredth, hundredth part; ▹ **sexto**
2 *(LAm)* *(= moneda)* centésimo, *one-hundredth part of a balboa etc*
centígrado ADJ centigrade
centigramo SM centigram
centilitro SM centilitre, centiliter (EEUU)
centímetro SM centimetre, centimeter (EEUU); ▹ **KILOS, METROS, AÑOS**
céntimo SM **1** hundredth part
2 *[de euro]* cent • **no vale un ~** it's worthless
centinela SMF *(Mil)* sentry, guard • **estar de ~** to be on guard • **hacer ~** to keep watch, be on the look-out
centiplicado ADJ hundredfold
centolla SF, **centollo** SM spider crab
centón SM **1** *(Cos)* patchwork quilt
2 *(Literat)* cento
centrado ADJ **1** *(= en el centro)* in the middle
2 *(= equilibrado)* balanced
central ADJ **1** *(= principal)* **a** *[personaje, idea]* central, main • **el personaje ~ de la novela** the central *o* main character in the novel • **el tema ~ de la reunión** the main subject of the meeting
b *[oficina]* head *(antes de s)*; *[banco]* central; *[ordenador]* mainframe *(antes de s)* • **la oficina ~ del banco** the head office of the bank • **la empresa tiene su sede ~ en Nueva York** the company's headquarters is in New York; ▹ **calefacción**
2 *(= del medio)* *[región, zona]* central • **en la zona ~ de la imagen** in the centre of the image • **la parte ~ de la plaza** the centre of the square
3 *(= no regional)* *[gobierno, administración]* central
SF **1** *(tb* **oficina central***)* *[de empresa]* head office; *(a nivel internacional)* headquarters • **la ~ de la OMS en Ginebra** the headquarters of the WHO in Geneva ▸ **central de abasto** *(Méx)* market ▸ **central de correos** main post office, general post office ▸ **central de teléfonos** telephone exchange ▸ **central obrera, central sindical** trade union confederation ▸ **central telefónica** telephone exchange
2 *(= factoría)* plant, station; *(tb* **central nuclear***)* nuclear power station • **la ~ de Chernobyl** Chernobyl nuclear power station ▸ **central azucarera** *(Cuba, Perú)* sugar mill ▸ **central de bombeo** pumping-station ▸ **central de energía** power station ▸ **central depuradora** sewage works *(pl)* ▸ **central eléctrica** power station ▸ **central hidroeléctrica** hydroelectric power station ▸ **central lechera** dairy ▸ **central térmica** power station • **~ térmica de fuel-oil/de gas** oil-fired/gas-fired power station
SMF *(Ftbl)* central defender
centralidad SF centrality, central importance
centralismo SM centralism
centralista[1] ADJ, SMF centralist
centralista[2] SM *(Caribe)* sugar-mill owner
centralita SF *(Telec)* switchboard
centralización SF centralization
centralizado ADJ centralized • **cierre ~** central locking
SM centralization
centralizar ▹ CONJUG 1f VT to centralize
centrar ▹ CONJUG 1a VT **1** *(= colocar)* *[+ imagen, texto]* to centre, center (EEUU) • **la foto no está bien centrada** the photo is not centred correctly • **el cuadro no está centrado** the picture isn't straight • **~ el balón** to knock the ball into the centre
2 *(= concentrar)* *[+ investigación]* to focus, centre, center (EEUU); *[+ esfuerzos]* to concentrate; *[+ atención]* to focus • **la policía centró las investigaciones en torno a dos jóvenes delincuentes** the police investigation focused *o* centred on two young criminals, the police focused *o* centred their investigation on two young criminals • **he centrado mi nueva obra en solo dos personajes** my new play focuses on *o* centres on only two characters • **los cuadros de Goya ~on el interés del público** Goya's paintings captured the interest of the public
VI *(Dep)* to centre, center (EEUU)
VPR **centrarse 1** • **~se en** *[estudio, investigación, debate, programa]* to be focused on, centre on, center on (EEUU); *[obra, película, exposición]* to be focused on • **la atención internacional se centraba en El Salvador** international attention focused on *o* centred on El Salvador • **sus investigaciones se centran en la Europa medieval** her research focuses on *o* centres on medieval Europe • **un mercado centrado exclusivamente en los jóvenes** a market aimed exclusively at *o* geared exclusively toward young people
2 *(= equilibrarse)* to settle down • **tuvo una época muy loca pero después se centró** he went through a very wild period but then he settled down
3 *(= acomodarse)* to settle in, find one's feet
céntrico ADJ central • **está muy ~** it's very central • **un restaurante ~** a restaurant in the centre of town, a downtown restaurant (EEUU)
centrífuga SF centrifuge
centrifugadora SF **1** *(para ropa)* spin-dryer
2 *(Téc)* centrifuge
centrifugar ▹ CONJUG 1h VT **1** *[+ ropa]* to spin-dry
2 *(Téc)* to centrifuge
centrífugo ADJ centrifugal
centrípeto ADJ centripetal
centrismo SM centrism, *political doctrine of the centre*
centrista ADJ centrist
SMF centrist, *member of a centrist party*
centro SM **1** *(= medio)* centre, center (EEUU) • **las regiones del ~ del país** the central areas of the country, the areas in the centre of the country • **pon el jarrón en el ~ de la mesa** put the vase in the middle *o* centre of the table • **el balón se hallaba en el ~ del campo** the ball was in midfield • **MODISMO:** • **estar en su ~** to be in one's element ▸ **centro de gravedad** centre of gravity ▸ **centro de mesa** centrepiece ▸ **centro neurálgico** nerve centre
2 *[de ciudad]* centre, center (EEUU) • **no se puede aparcar en el ~** you can't park in the centre (of town), you can't park downtown (EEUU) • **un edificio del ~ de Madrid** a building in the centre of Madrid *o* in Madrid town centre *o* (EEUU) in downtown Madrid • **"centro ciudad"** "city centre", "town centre" • **ir al ~** to go into town, go downtown (EEUU)
3 *(Pol)* centre, center (EEUU) • **ser de ~** *[persona]* to be a moderate; *[partido]* to be in the centre • **los partidos de ~ izquierda** the parties of the centre left, the centre-left parties
4 *(= foco)* *[de huracán]* centre, center (EEUU); *[de incendio]* seat • **ha sido el ~ de varias polémicas últimamente** he has been at the centre *o* heart of various controversies lately • **el gobierno se ha convertido en el ~ de las críticas** the government has become the target of criticism • **ser el ~ de atención** *o* **atracción** *o* **interés** to be the focus *o* centre of attention • **Zaire fue el ~ del interés internacional** Zaire was the focus of *o* was at the centre of international attention • **ser un ~ de intrigas** to be a hotbed of intrigue • **ser el ~ de las miradas:** • **Roma es estos días el ~ de todas las miradas** all eyes are on Rome at the moment
5 *(= establecimiento)* centre, center (EEUU) • **dos alumnos han sido expulsados del ~** two students have been expelled from the school *o* centre • **~s con más de 500 trabajadores** companies with over 500 workers ▸ **centro cívico** community centre ▸ **centro comercial** shopping centre, shopping mall ▸ **centro cultural** *(en un barrio, institución)* (local) arts centre; *[de otro país]* cultural centre ▸ **centro de abasto** *(Méx)* market ▸ **centro de acogida** • **~ de acogida de menores** children's home • **~ de acogida para mujeres maltratadas** refuge for battered women • **~ de acogida de refugiados** refugee reception centre ▸ **centro de atención de día** day-care centre ▸ **centro de atención primaria** primary care centre ▸ **centro de beneficios** profit centre ▸ **centro de bronceado** tanning salon ▸ **centro de cálculo** computer centre ▸ **centro de coordinación** *[de la policía]* operations room ▸ **centro de datos** data processing centre ▸ **centro de decisión** decision-making centre ▸ **centro de detención** detention centre ▸ **centro (de determinación) de costos** *(Com)* cost centre ▸ **centro de día** day centre ▸ **centro de distribución** distribution centre ▸ **centro de enseñanza** *(gen)* educational institution; *(= colegio)* school ▸ **centro de enseñanza media, centro de enseñanza secundaria** secondary school ▸ **centro de enseñanza superior** higher education institution ▸ **centro de jardinería** garden centre, garden center (EEUU) ▸ **centro de llamadas** call centre ▸ **centro de planificación familiar** family planning clinic ▸ **centro de proceso de datos** data processing centre ▸ **centro de protección de menores** child protection centre ▸ **centro de rastreo** *(Astron)* tracking centre ▸ **centro de salud** health centre ▸ **centro de trabajo** workplace • **en los ~s de trabajo** in the workplace ▸ **centro docente** educational institution ▸ **centro escolar** school ▸ **centro espacial** space centre ▸ **centro médico** *(gen)* medical establishment; *(= hospital)* hospital ▸ **centro penitenciario** prison, penitentiary (EEUU) ▸ **centro recreacional** *(Cuba, Ven)* sports centre, leisure centre ▸ **centro sanitario** = **centro médico** ▸ **centro universitario** *(= facultad)* faculty; *(= universidad)* university
6 *(= población)* ▸ **centro de población** population centre ▸ **centro turístico** *(= lugar muy visitado)* tourist centre; *(diseñado para turistas)* tourist resort ▸ **centro urbano** urban area, city
7 *(= ropa)* *(CAm)* *(= juego)* trousers and waistcoat, pants and vest (EEUU); *(And, Caribe)* *(= enaguas)* underskirt; *(And)* *(= falda)* thick flannel skirt
SMF *(Ftbl)* centre • **delantero ~** centre-forward • **medio ~** centre-half
centroafricano/a ADJ Central African
SM/F native *o* inhabitant of the Central African Republic
Centroamérica SF Central America
centroamericano/a ADJ, SM/F Central American

centroasiático ADJ Central Asian

centrocampismo SM midfield play

centrocampista SMF (*Dep*) midfielder • **los ~s** the midfield

centrocampo SM midfield

centroderecha SM centre-right

Centroeuropa SF Central Europe

centroeuropeo/a ADJ, SM/F Central European

centroizquierda SM centre-left

cénts ABR (= **céntimos**) c

centuplicar ▸ CONJUG 1g VT to increase a hundredfold, centuplicate (*frm*)

céntuplo ADJ hundredfold, centuple
SM centuple

centuria SF century

centurión SM centurion

cenutrio* SM twit*, twerp*

cénzalo SM mosquito

cenzontle SM (*CAm, Méx*) mockingbird

ceñido ADJ **1** [*vestido*] figure-hugging; [*traje*] tight-fitting; [*vaqueros*] skintight
2 (= *reducido*) • **una novela ceñida a las normas clásicas** a novel that sticks close to classical principles • **~ y corto** brief and to the point
3 [*curva*] tight

ceñidor SM sash, girdle

ceñir ▸ CONJUG 3h, 3k VT **1** (= *ajustar*) • **el vestido le ceñía el cuerpo** the dress clung to *o* hugged her body, the dress was really tight-fitting • **la faja le ceñía el talle** the sash fitted tightly around her waist
2 (*Cos*) to take in • **habrá que ~ más el talle** the waist will need to be taken in more
3 (*liter*) (= *rodear*) to surround, encircle • **la muralla que ciñe la ciudad** the wall that surrounds *o* encircles the city • **un lazo de terciopelo le ceñía la cintura** she had a velvet ribbon around her waist, a velvet ribbon encircled *o* (*liter*) girdled her waist • **ceñí su cuerpo con mis brazos** I wrapped my arms around his body
4 (*liter*) (= *llevar puesto*) • **la corona que ciñó nuestro rey** the crown that our king wore, the crown that rested on the head of our king
VPR **ceñirse 1** (= *reducirse*) • **~se a algo: esta biografía se ciñe a la vida personal del autor** this biography limits itself *o* restricts itself to the author's personal life • **me voy a ~ a algunos detalles significativos** I am going to limit *o* restrict myself to certain relevant details
2 (= *atenerse*) • **~se a algo: no se ciñeron a lo acordado** they did not keep to *o* stick to the agreement • **será difícil ~se al presupuesto** it will be difficult to keep to *o* keep within *o* stay within the budget • **por favor, cíñase a las preguntas del fiscal** please keep to the questions of the public prosecutor, please limit yourself to answering the questions of the public prosecutor
3 (*frm*) (= *ponerse*) to put on • **quiso ~se de nuevo el traje de novia** she wanted to put on her wedding dress again • **se ciñó la correa alrededor de la cintura** she put the belt around her waist • **se ciñó la gorra y se marchó** he put *o* pulled his hat on and left • **~se la corona** to be crowned, take the crown (*liter*) • **~se la espada**†† to put on one's sword, gird one's sword (*liter*)

ceño SM **1** (= *expresión*) frown, scowl • **arrugar** *o* **fruncir el ~** to frown, knit one's brows • **mirar con ~ a algn** to frown at sb, scowl at sb, give black looks to sb
2 [*de las nubes, del mar*] threatening appearance

ceñudo ADJ frowning, scowling

CEOE SF ABR (= **Confederación Española de Organizaciones Empresariales**) ≈ CBI

CEP SM ABR (*Esp*) (= **Centro de Educación de Profesores**) *teacher training centre*

cepa SF **1** (= *tronco*) [*de árbol*] stump; [*de vid*] stock
2 [*de persona*] stock • **es de buena ~ castellana** he's of good Castilian stock • **es un inglés de pura ~** he's English through and through, he's every inch an Englishman
3 (*Arquit*) pier
4 (*Bio*) strain
5 (*Méx*) (= *hoyo*) pit, trench

CEPAL SF ABR (= **Comisión Económica para América Latina y el Caribe**) ECLAC

cepero SM trapper

cepillado SM **1** [*de ropa, dientes, pelo*] brushing • **se elimina con un suave ~** you can get rid of it with a gentle brushing
2 [*de madera*] planing

cepilladura SF = **cepillado**

cepillar ▸ CONJUG 1a VT **1** [+ *ropa, dientes, pelo*] to brush
2 [+ *madera*] to plane, plane down
3* (= *suspender*) to fail, flunk (*esp EEUU**)
4* (= *adular*) to flatter, butter up
5* (= *robar*) to rip off*
6* (= *ganar*) to win, take (**a** from)
VPR **cepillarse 1** [+ *dientes, pelo*] to brush
2 • **~se a algn*** (= *matar*) to bump sb off*; (= *copular con**) to screw sb**
3* (= *robar*) • **~se algo** to rip sth off*

cepillo SM **1** (*para ropa, dientes, pelo*) brush • **lleva el pelo cortado al ~** he has a crew cut ▸ **cepillo de baño** toilet brush ▸ **cepillo de dientes** toothbrush ▸ **cepillo de púas (metálicas)** wire brush ▸ **cepillo para el pelo** hairbrush ▸ **cepillo para la ropa** clothes brush ▸ **cepillo para las uñas** nailbrush
2 (*para barrer*) brush ▸ **cepillo para el suelo** scrubbing brush
3 (*para madera*) plane
4 (*Rel*) poorbox, alms box
5 (*LAm*) (= *adulador*) flatterer, bootlicker*

cepillón/ona‡ ADJ soapy*
SM/F creep‡

cepo SM **1** (*Caza*) trap, snare ▸ **cepo conejero** snare ▸ **cepo lobero** wolf-trap
2 (*Aut*) (wheel) clamp
3 [*de yunque, ancla*] stock
4 (*Bot*) branch, bough
5 (*Rel*) poorbox, alms box

ceporrez* SF idiocy

ceporro* SM **1** (= *idiota*) twit*, idiot
2 (= *gordo*) • **estar como un ~** to be very fat

Cepsa SF ABR (*Com*) = **Compañía Española de Petróleos, Sociedad Anónima**

CEPYME SF ABR = **Confederación Española de la Pequeña y Mediana Empresa**

cequión SM (*Cono Sur*) *large irrigation channel*

cera SF **1** wax • **depilarse a la ~** • **hacerse la ~** to wax one's legs *o* arms *etc* • MODISMO: • **ser como una ~** to be as gentle as a lamb ▸ **cera de abejas** beeswax ▸ **cera de los oídos** earwax ▸ **cera de lustrar** wax polish ▸ **cera de para suelos** floor polish
2 ceras [*de colmena*] honeycomb (*sing*)
3 (*And, Méx*) (= *vela*) candle

cerafolio SM chervil

cerámica SF **1** (*Arte*) ceramics (*sing*), pottery
2 (= *conjunto de objetos*) ceramics (*pl*), pottery

cerámico ADJ ceramic

ceramista SMF potter

cerbatana SF **1** (*Mil*) blowpipe
2 (= *juguete*) peashooter
3 (*Med*) ear trumpet

cerca[1] SF (= *valla*) [*de madera, alambre*] fence; [*de piedra, ladrillo*] wall ▸ **cerca eléctrica** electrified fence, electric fence ▸ **cerca viva** hedge

cerca[2] ADV **1** (*indicando proximidad*) (*de aquí o allí*) near, nearby; (*entre objetos, personas*) close • **no había un hospital ~** there wasn't a hospital near there *o* nearby • **está aquí ~** it's very *o* just near here • **¿está ~ la estación?** is the station near here *o* nearby? • **está tan ~ que puedo ir andando** it's so near here *o* so close I can just walk • **las casas están tan ~ que se pueden oír las conversaciones de los vecinos** the houses are so close (to each other) that you can hear what the neighbours are saying • **quería tener más ~ a los amigos** he wanted to be nearer (to) *o* closer to his friends • **las vacaciones están ya ~** the holidays are nearly here, the holidays are not far off now • **~ de** near (to), close to • **viven ~ de la playa** they live near (to) *o* close to the beach • **estaba sentada ~ de mí** she was sitting near me • **se sentía muy ~ de su familia** she felt very close to her family
2 • **de ~ a** (= *a poca distancia*) [*ver*] close up; [*seguir, observar, vigilar*] closely • **no veo bien de ~** I can't see things close up, I'm long-sighted • **visto de ~, parece mayor** when you see him close up *o* at close quarters, he seems older • **pudo ver de ~ la pobreza** she got to see poverty close at hand *o* at close quarters • **el coche iba a gran velocidad, seguido de ~ por su escolta** the car was travelling at a high speed, followed closely by its escort • **seguí de ~ la guerra a través de los periódicos** I followed the war closely in the newspapers
b (= *en persona*) in person • **para todos aquellos que no puedan ver la exposición de ~** for all those unable to see the exhibition in person • **he tenido la oportunidad de conocer de ~ a muchos famosos** I have had the opportunity of meeting many famous people personally *o* in person • **los que lo conocen de ~ hablan muy bien de él** those who know him well speak very highly of him • **la crisis me ha afectado muy de ~** the crisis has affected me personally • **no conoce de ~ los problemas de la población** he does not have first-hand *o* personal knowledge of the people's problems
3 • **~ de** (= *casi*) nearly • **hay ~ de ocho toneladas** there are nearly eight tons of it • **~ de 2.500 personas** nearly 2,500 people • **son ~ de las seis** it's nearly six o'clock • **estar ~ de hacer algo** to come close to doing sth • **he estado ~ de tirar el libro por la ventana** I've come close to throwing that book out of the window • **estuvimos tan ~ de conseguir la victoria ...** we were so close to obtaining victory ...
4 (*esp Cono Sur*) • **~ nuestro/mío** near us/me
SM† **1** (= *aspecto*) • **tiene buen ~** it looks all right close up
2 cercas (*Arte*) foreground (*sing*)

cercado SM **1** (= *recinto*) enclosure; (= *huerto*) enclosed garden, orchard
2 (= *valla*) fence, wall ▸ **cercado eléctrico** electrified fence
3 (*And*) (= *ejido*) communal lands
4 (*And*) (*Hist*) *state capital and surrounding towns*

cercanía SF **1** (= *proximidad*) nearness, proximity
2 cercanías (= *alrededores*) neighbourhood (*sing*), neighborhood (*EEUU*) (*sing*), vicinity (*sing*); (= *suburbios*) outskirts, suburbs • **tren de ~s** suburban train, commuter train

cercano ADJ **1** [*lugar*] nearby • **entraron en un bar ~** they went to a nearby bar • **acudió a la comisaría más cercana** he went to the nearest police station • **sentía la presencia cercana de su madre** he felt the presence of his mother nearby • **~ a** close to, near, near

to • **un hotel ~ al aeropuerto** a hotel close to *o* near (to) the airport • **una cifra cercana a los tres millones de dólares** a figure close to three million dollars
2 [*amigo, pariente*] close • **su colaborador más ~** his closest collaborator • **~ a** close to • **según fuentes cercanas al ministerio** according to sources close to the ministry • **personas cercanas a la organización terrorista** people closely linked to the terrorist organization
3 (*en el tiempo*) • **en el futuro ~** in the near future • **cree cercana la firma del acuerdo** he believes that they are close to signing the agreement • **ahora, cuando está ~ el primer aniversario de su muerte** now, as the first anniversary of her death approaches
Cercano Oriente SM Near East
cercar ▹ CONJUG 1g VT **1** [+ *campo, terreno*] to enclose; (*con vallas*) to fence in, wall in
2 [+ *persona*] to surround, ring
3 (*Mil*) [+ *pueblo, ciudad*] to surround, besiege; [+ *tropas*] to cut off, surround
cercén ADV • **cortar a ~** to sever • **cortar un brazo a ~** to sever an arm
cercenar ▹ CONJUG 1a VT **1** (= *recortar*) to cut *o* trim the edges of
2 [+ *brazo, pierna*] to sever
3 (= *reducir*) [+ *gastos*] to cut down, reduce; [+ *texto*] to shorten, cut down
cerceta SF teal, garganey
cerciorar ▹ CONJUG 1a VT • **~ a algn de algo** to convince sb of sth
VPR **cerciorarse** • **~se de algo** make sure *o* certain of sth • **cerciórense de que las luces están apagadas** make sure *o* certain that the lights are switched off
cerco SM **1** (*Agr*) (= *recinto*) enclosure
2 (*LAm*) (= *valla*) fence, hedge • **MODISMO**: • **saltar el ~** (*Cono Sur*) to jump on the bandwagon
3 (*Téc*) [*de rueda*] rim; [*de tonel*] hoop
4 (= *borde externo*) [*de estrella*] halo; [*de mancha*] ring
5 (= *corrillo*) social group, circle
6 (*Mil*) siege • **alzar** *o* **levantar el ~** to raise the siege • **poner ~ a algo** to lay siege to sth, besiege sth
7 (*Arquit*) casing, frame
cercón ADV (*LAm*) rather close
cerda SF **1** (*Zool*) sow; ▹ **cerdo**
2 (= *pelo*) [*de cepillo, jabalí, tejón*] bristle; [*de caballo*] horsehair
3‡ (= *puta*) slut‡
cerdada SF dirty trick
cerdear ▹ CONJUG 1a VI **1** (*Mús*) to rasp, screech
2* (= *aplazar*) to put things off
Cerdeña SF Sardinia
cerdito/a SM/F piglet
cerdo[1] SM **1** (*Zool*) pig, hog (EEUU) • **todos los políticos son unos ~s** all politicians are bastards *o* swine* • **MODISMO**: • **comer como un ~** (= *mucho*) to stuff o.s; (= *sin modales*) to eat like a pig • **REFRÁN**: • **a todos los ~s les llega su San Martín** everyone gets their just deserts sooner or later, everyone gets their comeuppance in the end ▸ **cerdo ibérico** Iberian pig ▸ **cerdo marino** porpoise; ▹ **cerda**
2 (*Culin*) pork • **carne de ~** pork
cerdo²/a* ADJ **1** (= *sucio*) filthy, dirty
2 (= *malhablado*) • **no digas palabrotas, no seas tan ~** don't swear *o* curse, don't be so foul-mouthed *o* crude
3 (= *maleducado*) • **no eructes en público, no seas ~** don't belch in public, don't be such a pig *o* don't be so gross!
4 (= *canalla*) rotten*
SM/F **1** (= *sucio*) slob* • **¡mira cómo tienes la habitación! ¡eres un ~!** look at the state of your room! you're a real slob! *o* you're filthy!*
2 (= *malhablado*) foul-mouthed pig
3 (= *maleducado*) • **es un ~, siempre habla con la boca llena** he's such a pig *o* so gross eating with his mouth full all the time*
4 (= *canalla*) swine*; ▹ **cerda**
cerdoso ADJ bristly
cereal ADJ cereal, grain (*antes de s*)
SM **1** (= *grano*) cereal, grain ▸ **cereal forrajero** fodder grain
2 **cereales** [*de desayuno*] cereal (*sing*), cereals • **he tomado ~es para desayunar** I've had cereal for breakfast
cerealista ADJ grain-producing (*antes de s*)
SMF cereal farmer; (*Com*) grain dealer
cerealístico ADJ grain (*antes de s*), cereal (*antes de s*)
cereal-pienso SM (PL: **cereales-pienso**) fodder grain
cerebelo SM cerebellum
cerebral ADJ **1** (= *del cerebro*) cerebral, brain (*antes de s*)
2 (*pey*) (= *calculador*) scheming, calculating
cerebralismo SM intellectualism, cerebralism
cerebro SM **1** (*Anat*) brain • **MODISMOS**: • **estrujarse el ~*** to rack one's brains • **ser un ~*** to be brilliant, be really brainy ▸ **cerebro electrónico** electronic brain ▸ **cerebro gris** éminence grise
2 (= *dirigente*) brains (*pl*) • **es el ~ del equipo** he's the brains of the team
ceremonia SF **1** (= *acto*) ceremony ▸ **ceremonia de apertura** opening ceremony ▸ **ceremonia de clausura** closing ceremony ▸ **ceremonia inaugural** inaugural ceremony ▸ **ceremonia religiosa** religious ceremony, (religious) service
2 (= *afectación*) formality, ceremoniousness • **es muy llano y le molesta tanta ~** he's very straightforward and all this formality annoys him • **¡déjate de ~s!** don't stand on ceremony! • **sin ~: el rey nos habló sin ~s** the king spoke to us plainly *o* without any ceremony • **se despidió sin ~s** he said goodbye without a fuss
ceremonial ADJ, SM ceremonial
ceremoniosamente ADV ceremoniously
ceremonioso ADJ [*reunión, saludo, visita*] formal; [*ambiente*] ceremonious
céreo ADJ (*liter*) waxen (*liter*)
cerería SF wax-chandler's shop, chandlery
cerero SM wax chandler
cereza SF **1** (= *fruta*) cherry • **un jersey rojo ~** a cherry-red jumper ▸ **cereza silvestre** wild cherry
2 (*LAm*) (= *cáscara*) husk of coffee bean
cerezal SM cherry orchard
cerezo SM cherry tree
cerilla SF **1** (= *fósforo*) match
2 (*Anat*) earwax
3 (*Rel*) wax taper
cerillazo* SM • **pegar un ~ a algo** to set a match to sth
cerillero/a SM/F match seller
cerillo SM (*LAm*) match
cernedor SM sieve
cerneja SF fetlock
cerner ▹ CONJUG 2g VT **1** (*filtrar*) [+ *harina*] to sift, sieve; [+ *tierra*] to sieve
2 (= *observar*) to scan, watch
VI **1** (*Bot*) to bud, blossom
2 (*Meteo*) to drizzle
VPR **cernerse 1** [*ave*] to hover; [*avión*] to circle
2 [*amenaza*] • **~se sobre algo/algn** to hang over sth/sb
3 (*al andar*) to waddle
cernícalo SM **1** (*Orn*) kestrel
2* (= *persona torpe*) lout, dolt
3 • **coger un ~*** to get tight*
4 (*And*) (*Orn*) hawk, falcon
cernidillo† SM **1** (= *modo de andar*) swagger, rolling gait
2 (*Meteo*) drizzle
cernido SM **1** (= *acto*) sifting
2 (= *harina*) sifted flour
3 (*And*) (*Meteo*) drizzle
cernidor SM sieve
cernidura SF sifting
cero SM **1** (*Fís, Mat*) zero • **ocho grados bajo ~** eight degrees below zero • **desde las ~ horas** from twelve o'clock midnight • **MODISMOS**: • **estoy a ~ de dinero** I'm broke* • **empezar** *o* **partir de ~** to start from scratch • **tendremos que partir nuevamente de ~** we'll have to start from scratch again • **ser un ~ a la izquierda** to be useless ▸ **cero absoluto** absolute zero
2 (*Ftbl, Rugby*) nil, zero (*EEUU*) • **ganaron por tres goles a ~** they won by three goals to nil, they won three nil • **empataron a ~** they drew nil-nil, it was a no-score draw • **estamos 40 a ~** (*Tenis*) it's 40-love
3 (*Educ*) nought • **me han puesto un ~** I got nought out of ten
4* (= *coche-patrulla*) police car
ceroso ADJ waxen (*liter*), waxy
cerote SM **1** (*Téc*) wax, shoemaker's wax
2* (= *miedo*) panic
3 (*CAm, Méx*) (= *excremento*) piece of human excrement, stool • **MODISMOS**: • **estar hecho un ~** (*And*) • **tener ~** (*Cono Sur, Méx*) to be covered in muck
cerotear ▹ CONJUG 1a VT [+ *hilo*] to wax
cerquillo SM **1** (*LAm*) (= *flequillo*) fringe, bangs (*pl*) (EEUU)
2 [*de monje*] *fringe of hair round the tonsure*
3 (*Téc*) seam, welt
cerquita* ADV quite near, close by
cerradero ADJ (= *dispositivo*) locking, fastening • **caja cerradera** box that can be locked, box with a lock
SM (= *mecanismo de cierre*) locking device; (*en cerradura*) strike, keeper; [*de monedero*] purse strings
cerrado ADJ **1** (= *no abierto*) [*puerta, ventana, boca*] closed; [*puño*] clenched; [*curva*] sharp, tight • **escuchaban música con los ojos ~s** they were listening to music with their eyes closed • **respira con la boca cerrada** breathe with your mouth closed • **"cerrado"** "closed" • **"cerrado por vacaciones"** "closed for holidays", "closed for vacation" (*EEUU*) • **"cerrado por reformas"** "closed for refurbishment" • **la puerta no estaba cerrada con llave** the door was not locked • **se lo dio en un sobre ~** he gave it to her in a sealed envelope • **¿está el grifo bien ~?** is the tap turned off properly? • **esa fábrica lleva varios años cerrada** that factory has been closed for years • **el caso está ~** the case is closed • **el mitin se celebró en un recinto ~** the rally was held indoors • **huele a ~** it smells stuffy in here • **~ a** closed to • **los jardines están ~s al público** the gardens are closed to the public • **el aeropuerto permanece ~ al tráfico aéreo** the airport remains closed to all air traffic; ▹ **puerta**
2 (= *apretado*) [*barba*] thick, full; [*bosque*] dense, thick; [*ambiente, atmósfera*] stuffy • **el candidato fue recibido con una cerrada ovación** the presidential candidate was given a rapturous welcome; ▹ **descarga**
3 [*cielo*] cloudy, overcast; [*noche*] dark, black • **era ya noche cerrada cuando llegamos a casa** it was completely dark by the time we got home
4 (*Ling*) [*acento*] broad, strong; [*vocal*] closed

• tiene un acento muy ~ she has a very broad *o* strong accent • hablaba con ~ acento gallego he spoke with a broad *o* strong *o* thick Galician accent
5 [*persona*] a (= *intransigente*) • la gente de este pueblo es muy cerrada the people in this village don't much like strangers • no está a ningún tipo de sugerencias he is open to all suggestions
b (= *torpe*) (*tb* cerrado de mollera) dense, thick*
c (= *reservado*) reserved
6 (*Com*) [*precio*] fixed • a precio ~ at a fixed price
cerradura (SF) (*Mec*) lock ▸ cerradura de combinación combination lock ▸ cerradura de golpe, cerradura de muelle spring lock ▸ cerradura de seguridad safety lock
cerraja (SF) 1 (*Mec*) lock
2 (*Bot*) sow thistle
cerrajería (SF) 1 (= *oficio*) locksmith's craft, locksmith's trade
2 (*Com*) locksmith's, locksmith's shop
cerrajero/a (SM/F) locksmith
cerrar ▹ CONJUG 1j (VT) 1 (*hablando de un objeto abierto*) [+ *puerta, ventana, boca*] to close, shut; [+ *cremallera*] to do up; [+ *camisa*] to button, do up; [+ *cortina*] to draw; [+ *paraguas, válvula*] to close; [+ *carta*] to seal; [+ *costura, herida*] to sew up • no puedo ~ esta maleta I can't close *o* shut this suitcase • cierra los ojos close *o* shut your eyes • ~ algo de golpe to slam sth shut • cerró el libro de golpe she banged *o* slammed the book shut • los colegios ~on sus puertas a causa de la huelga the schools closed because of the strike • cerré la puerta con llave I locked the door • cierra el pico* shut your trap‡ • ~ el puño to clench one's fist; ▹ fila
2 (= *desconectar*) [+ *gas, grifo, radiador*] to turn off
3 (= *bloquear*) [+ *agujero, brecha, tubo*] to block (up); [+ *frontera, puerto*] to close • una roca cerraba la entrada a la cueva a rock was obstructing the entrance to the cave • han cerrado la frontera they have closed the border • ~ el paso a algn to block sb's way • trató de entrar, pero le ~on el paso he tried to get in, but they blocked *o* barred his way
4 [+ *tienda, negocio*] (*al final de la jornada*) to close, shut; (*para siempre*) to close, close down
5 [+ *jardín, terreno*] (*con cerca*) to fence in; (*con muro*) to wall in
6 (= *poner fin a*) a [+ *debate, narración, programa*] to close, end • ~ el sistema (*Inform*) to shut down the system
b [+ *desfile*] to bring up the rear of • los manifestantes que cerraban la marcha the demonstrators bringing up the rear *o* at the rear • cierra la cabalgata la carroza de Santa Claus the last float in the procession is the one with Santa Claus
7 • ~ un trato to seal a deal
(VI) 1 (*hablando de un objeto abierto*) [*puerta, ventana*] to close, shut; [*bragueta*] to do up; [*paraguas, válvula*] to close; [*herida*] to close up • la puerta cierra mal the door won't close *o* shut properly • un estuche que cierra con llave a jewellery box with a lock
2 [*persona*] • cierra, que se va a escapar el gato close *o* shut the door or the cat will get out • te dejo las llaves para que cierres I am leaving you the keys so you can lock up
3 [*tienda, negocio*] to close, shut • ¿a qué hora cierran las tiendas el sábado? what time do the shops close *o* shut on Saturday? • cerramos a las nueve we close at nine • las discotecas no cierran en toda la noche the discos stay open all night
4 (*Econ*) (*en la Bolsa*) to close
5 (*en dominó*) to block; (*en Scrabble*) to use one's tiles up • ¡cierro! I'm out!
6 (= *atacar*) • ~ con *o* contra algn to grapple with sb • ~ con el enemigo to engage the enemy at close quarters
(VPR) **cerrarse** 1 [*puerta, ventana*] to close, shut; [*bragueta*] to do up; [*paraguas, válvula*] to close; [*herida*] to close up • la puerta se cerró detrás de mí the door closed *o* shut behind me • la ventana se cerró de golpe the window slammed shut • este sofá-cama se cierra con gran facilidad this sofa-bed is very easy to fold away • se me cierran los ojos I can't keep my eyes open
2 [*persona*] • ciérrate bien el abrigo do your coat up properly • ~se la cremallera to do one's zip up
3 (*Com*) to close, shut • la tienda se cierra a las nueve the shop closes *o* shuts at nine • el museo se cerró por obras the museum closed for refurbishment
4 (= *obcecarse*) • ~se a algo: • no hay que ~se a nada sin probarlo primero you should never dismiss anything without trying it first • no puedes ~te a la evidencia you can't ignore the evidence • ~se en algo: • se ~on en una actitud beligerante they persisted with a belligerent attitude • ~se en hacer algo to persist in doing sth • MODISMO: • ~se en banda (= *mostrarse inflexible*) to refuse to budge; (= *unirse*) to close ranks
5 (= *terminar*) to close, end • el trimestre se cerró con un aumento del desempleo the quarter closed *o* ended with a rise in unemployment • se ha cerrado el plazo para las votaciones the period for voting has closed *o* is over
6 [*cielo*] to cloud over, become overcast; [*invierno, noche*] to close in
7 (*Mil*) to close ranks
cerrazón (SF) 1 (= *obstinación*) bloody-mindedness
2 (= *torpeza*) dimwittedness
3 [*del cielo*] threatening sky, storm clouds (*pl*)
cerrero (ADJ) 1 [*animal*] wild
2 [*persona*] rough, uncouth
3 (*LAm*) (= *sin azúcar*) unsweetened, bitter
cerril (ADJ) 1 [*terreno*] rough, mountainous
2 [*animal*] untamed, unbroken
3 [*persona*] (= *brusca*) rough, uncouth; (= *de miras estrechas*) small-minded
cerrilismo (SM) 1 (= *brusquedad*) roughness, uncouthness
2 (= *estrechez de miras*) small-mindedness
cerrillar ▹ CONJUG 1a (VT) [+ *moneda*] to mill
cerro (SM) 1 (*Geog*) hill • MODISMO: • andar *o* echarse *o* ir por los ~s de Úbeda to wander off the point, go off at a tangent
2 (*Zool*) back • MODISMO: • ir en ~ to ride bareback
3 (*Téc*) *bunch of cleaned hemp or flax*
4 (*And*) (= *montón*) heap, load • un ~ de algo a heap of sth, a load of sth
cerrojazo (SM) slamming • dar un ~ (*lit*) to slam the bolt; (*fig*) to end unexpectedly
cerrojo (SM) 1 (= *mecanismo*) bolt, latch • echar el ~ to bolt the door
2 (*Dep*) (*tb* táctica de cerrojo) defensive play, negative play
certamen (SM) competition, contest ▸ certamen de belleza beauty contest
certeramente (ADV) accurately
certero (ADJ) 1 (= *correcto*) [*respuesta*] accurate; [*decisión*] correct, right; [*acto*] sure
2 [*tiro*] well-aimed • es un cazador ~ he's a crack shot
certeza (SF) 1 (= *seguridad*) certainty • tener la ~ de que ... to know for certain that ..., be sure that ... • ¿lo sabes con ~? do you know (that) for certain?
2 (= *precisión*) accuracy
certidumbre (SF) 1 (= *seguridad*) certainty
2 (= *confianza*) conviction
certificable (ADJ) certifiable
certificación (SF) 1 (= *acción*) certification
2 (*Correos*) registration
3 (*Jur*) affidavit
certificado (ADJ) 1 (*Correos*) [*carta, paquete*] registered • envié la carta por correo ~ I sent the letter by registered mail *o* post
2 (= *aprobado*) certified • el avión estaba ~ para volar the plane was certified to fly
(SM) 1 (= *documento*) certificate ▸ certificado de acciones (*Com*) share *o* stock certificate ▸ certificado de aptitud certificate of attainment ▸ certificado de autenticidad certificate of authenticity ▸ certificado de ciudadanía naturalization papers (*pl*) ▸ certificado de defunción death certificate ▸ certificado de depósito certificate of deposit ▸ certificado de escolaridad *completion certificate for compulsory education* ▸ certificado de estudios school-leaving certificate ▸ certificado de garantía certificate of guarantee ▸ certificado de nacimiento birth certificate ▸ certificado de origen certificate of origin ▸ certificado de penales good-conduct certificate ▸ certificado de vacuna vaccination certificate ▸ certificado escolar = certificado de escolaridad ▸ certificado médico medical certificate
2 (*Correos*) registered item
certificar ▹ CONJUG 1g (VT) 1 (*Jur*) to certify • ~ que ... to certify that ...
2 (*Correos*) to register
certitud (SF) certainty
cerúleo (ADJ) (*liter*) cerulean (*liter*), sky blue
cerumen (SM) earwax
cerval (ADJ) deer (*antes de s*), deer-like
cervantino (ADJ) Cervantine • estilo ~ Cervantine style, style of Cervantes • estudios ~s Cervantes studies, studies of Cervantes
cervantista (SMF) Cervantes scholar, specialist in Cervantes
cervatillo (SM) fawn
cervato (SM) fawn
cervecera (SF) brewery
cervecería (SF) (= *bar*) bar, public house, beer hall (*EEUU*)
cervecero/a (ADJ) beer (*antes de s*) • la industria cervecera the brewing industry
(SM/F) brewer
cerveza (SF) beer • una caña de ~ a glass of beer *o* lager ▸ cerveza de barril draught beer, draft beer (*EEUU*) ▸ cerveza de malta malt beer ▸ cerveza de sifón (*CAm*) = cerveza de barril ▸ cerveza embotellada bottled beer ▸ cerveza negra stout ▸ cerveza rubia lager
cervical (ADJ) 1 (= *del cuello*) neck (*antes de s*), cervical
2 (= *del útero*) cervical
Cervino (SM) • el monte ~ Mont Cervin, the Matterhorn
cerviz (SF) 1 (= *nuca*) nape (of the neck) • MODISMOS: • bajar *o* doblar la ~ to submit, bow down • de dura ~ stubborn, headstrong
2 (= *útero*) cervix
cervuno (ADJ) deer-like
cesación (SF) cessation, suspension ▸ cesación del fuego ceasefire ▸ cesación de pagos suspension of payments
cesante (ADJ) 1 [*empleado*] redundant, laid-off; (*esp LAm*) unemployed
2 [*funcionario*] suspended • el ministro ~ the outgoing minister
3 [*embajador*] recalled

C

SMF redundant worker, laid-off worker (*EEUU*)
cesantear ▸ CONJUG 1a VT (*Cono Sur*) to dismiss, sack*
cesantía SF (*esp LAm*) (= *desempleo*) unemployment; (= *paga*) redundancy money, redundancy payment; [*de funcionario*] suspension
cesar ▸ CONJUG 1a VI **1** (= *parar*) to stop • **un ruido que no cesa** an incessant noise • **no ~ de hacer algo**: • **el paro no cesa de aumentar** unemployment is constantly increasing • **no cesaba de repetirlo** he kept repeating it • **no cesa de hablar** he never stops talking • **sin ~** incessantly, nonstop • **repetía sin ~ que siempre estaríamos juntos** she kept saying that we would always be together
2 (= *dimitir*) to leave, quit (*EEUU*) • **acaba de ~ como presidente de la empresa** he has just left his job as company director • **~ en su cargo** [*empleado*] to resign, leave one's job; [*alto cargo*] to leave office
VT **1** (= *despedir*) to dismiss • **ha sido cesado de su cargo en el ministerio** he has been dismissed from his post at the ministry
2 (= *parar*) [+ *ataque*] to stop
César SM Caesar • REFRÁN: • **dar al ~ lo que es del ~ y a Dios lo que es de Dios** to render unto Caesar that which is Caesar's and unto God that which is God's
cesaraugustano/a ADJ, SM/F = **zaragozano**
cesárea SF (*Med*) Caesarean, Caesarean section • **le han tenido que hacer una ~** she had to have a Caesarean (section)
cesáreo ADJ **1** Caesarean
2 (*Med*) • **operación cesárea** Caesarean section
cese SM **1** (= *parada*) cessation • **un acuerdo sobre el ~ de la violencia** an agreement on the cessation of violence • **un ~ temporal de los bombardeos** a temporary halt *o* cessation to the bombing • **el ~ de (las) hostilidades** the cessation of hostilities ▸ **cese de alarma** (*Mil*) all-clear signal ▸ **cese de pagos** suspension of payments ▸ **cese el fuego** ceasefire
2 (= *despido*) dismissal • **dar el ~ a algn** to dismiss sb
3 (= *dimisión*) resignation • **entregué mi ~ al jefe** I handed in my resignation *o* gave in my notice to the boss
CESEDEN SM ABR (*Esp*) = **Centro Superior de Estudios de la Defensa Nacional**
CESID SM ABR, **Cesid** SM ABR (*Esp*) (= **Centro Superior de Información de la Defensa**) *military intelligence service*
cesio SM caesium, cesium (*EEUU*)
cesión SF **1** [*de territorio*] cession (*frm*), giving up
2 (*Jur*) granting, transfer ▸ **cesión de bienes** surrender of property
cesionario/a SM/F grantee, assignee
cesionista SMF grantor, assignor
césped SM **1** (= *planta*) grass ▸ **césped artificial** artificial turf, Astroturf®
2 (= *terreno plantado*) lawn
3 (*Dep*) pitch
cesta SF **1** (= *canasta*) basket • MODISMO: • **llevar la ~*** to play gooseberry, be a third wheel (*EEUU*) ▸ **cesta de costura** sewing basket ▸ **cesta de la compra** shopping basket; (*Econ*) *cost of a week's shopping* ▸ **cesta de Navidad** Christmas box, Christmas hamper ▸ **cesta de picnic** picnic hamper
2 (*en baloncesto, pelota vasca*) basket
cestada SF basketful
cestería SF **1** (= *arte*) basketmaking
2 (= *conjunto de cestas*) wickerwork, basketwork • **silla de ~** wicker chair, wicker-work chair
3 (= *tienda*) basketwork shop
cestero/a SM/F basketmaker
cestillo SM **1** (= *cesto pequeño*) small basket
2 [*de globo*] basket
cesto SM **1** (= *canasta*) basket, hamper ▸ **cesto de la colada** linen basket, clothes basket
2 • MODISMO: • **estar hecho un ~*** to be very drowsy
3* (= *gamberro*) lout
cesura SF caesura
cetáceo ADJ, SM cetacean
cetárea SF, **cetaria** SF shellfish farm
cetme SM rifle
cetorrino SM basking shark
cetrería SF falconry, hawking
cetrero SM **1** (*Caza*) falconer
2 (*Rel*) verger
cetrino ADJ [*tez*] sallow; [*persona, temperamento*] melancholy
cetro SM **1** (= *bastón de mando*) sceptre, scepter (*EEUU*) • MODISMO: • **empuñar el ~** to ascend the throne
2 (= *poder*) sway, dominion
3 (*LAm*) (*Dep*) crown, championship
CEU SM ABR (*Esp*) (= **Centro de Estudios Universitarios**) *private university*
Ceuta SF Ceuta
ceutí ADJ from *o* of Ceuta
SMF native *o* inhabitant of Ceuta • **los ~es** the people of Ceuta
C.F. ABR (= **Club de Fútbol**) FC
cf. ABR (= **compárese**) cf
CFC SM ABR (= **clorofluorocarbono**) CFC
cfr. ABR (= **confróntese**) cf
CG SF ABR (*Esp*) (*Pol*) = **Coalición Galega**
cg ABR (= **centígramo(s)**) cg
CGC-L SM ABR (*Esp*) = **Consejo General de Castilla y León**
CGPJ SM ABR (*Esp*) (= **Consejo General del Poder Judicial**) *government body which oversees legal profession*
CGS SF ABR (*Guat, El Salvador*) = **Confederación General de Sindicatos**
CGT SF ABR **1** (*Méx, Perú, Esp*) = **Confederación General de Trabajadores**
2 (*Arg*) = **Confederación General del Trabajo**
Ch, ch [tʃe] SF *combination of consonants forming one letter in the Spanish alphabet but treated as separate letters for alphabetization purposes*
ch. ABR (= **cheque**) ch
cha SM Shah
chabacanear ▸ CONJUG 1a VI (*LAm*) to say *o* do coarse things
chabacanería SF **1** (= *mal gusto*) vulgarity, bad taste
2 (= *comentario grosero*) • **una ~** a coarse *o* vulgar remark
chabacanizar ▸ CONJUG 1f VT to trivialize
chabacano¹ ADJ [*chiste*] vulgar, coarse, in bad taste; [*objeto*] cheap; [*trabajo*] shoddy
chabacano² SM (*Méx*) apricot, apricot tree
chabola SF shack • **~s** shanty town
chabolismo SM *problem of shanty towns*
chabolista ADJ slum (*antes de s*), shanty-town (*antes de s*)
SMF slum dweller, shanty-town dweller
chabón/ona* ADJ daft, stupid
SM/F twit*
chaca* SF • MODISMO: • **estar en la ~** (*Caribe*) to be flat broke*
chacal SM jackal
chacalín/ina (*CAm*) SM/F **1** (= *niño*) kid*, child
2 (= *camarón*) shrimp
chacanear ▸ CONJUG 1a VT **1** (*Cono Sur*) [+ *caballo*] to spur violently
2 (*Cono Sur*) (= *fastidiar*) to pester, annoy
3 (*And*) (= *usar*) to use daily
chacaneo SM • MODISMO: • **para el ~** (*And*) for daily use, ordinary
chácara¹ SF **1** (*LAm*) sore, ulcer
2 (*CAm*) large bag (*made of leather*)
chácara² SF (*LAm*) = **chacra**
chacarera SF *Argentinian folk dance*; ▸ **chacarero**
chacarería SF **1** (*LAm*) (*Agr*) market gardens (*pl*), truck farms (*pl*) (*EEUU*)
2 (*And, Cono Sur*) (= *industria*) horticulture, market gardening, truck farming (*EEUU*)
chacarero/a SM/F (*LAm*) (= *granjero*) small farmer, market gardener, truck farmer (*EEUU*); ▸ **chacarera**
SM (*Chile*) (*tb* **sandwich chacarero**) sandwich
ADJ (*LAm*) small farm (*antes de s*)
chacha* SF **1** (= *criada*) maid, housemaid
2† (= *niñera*) nanny, nursemaid
chachacaste SM (*CAm*) liquor, brandy
chachachá SM, **cha-cha-cha** SM
1 (= *baile*) cha-cha-cha, cha-cha
2 (= *juego*) solitaire
chachal SM (*CAm*) charm necklace
chachalaca* (*CAm, Méx*) ADJ chatty
SF chatterbox
chachar ▸ CONJUG 1a VT (*LAm*) [+ *coca*] to chew
cháchara SF **1** chatter, chit-chat* • **estar de ~*** to chatter, gab*
2 chácharas (*Méx*) (= *trastos*) junk (*sing*)
3 (*And*) (= *chiste*) joke
chacharachas SFPL (*Cono Sur*) useless ornaments
chacharear ▸ CONJUG 1a VT (*Méx*) to deal in
VI to chatter, gab*
chacharería SF (*Cono Sur, Méx*) trinkets (*pl*)
chacharero/a ADJ chattering
SM/F **1*** (= *parlanchín*) chatterbox
2 (*Méx*) (= *vendedor*) rag-and-bone man
chachi* ADJ great*, brill* • **¡qué ~!** that's great!, that's brill!* • **¡estás ~!** you look great!*
ADV great*, brill* • **nos lo pasamos ~** we had a great* time
chachipén ADJ, ADV = **chachi**
chacho* SM **1** (= *chico*) boy, lad
2 (*CAm*) (= *gemelo*) twin
3 (*Méx*) (= *criado*) servant
chachos SMPL (*CAm*) Siamese twins
chacina SF **1** (= *carne para embutidos*) pork
2 (= *embutidos*) cold meats (*pl*), cold cuts (*pl*) (*EEUU*)
3 (= *cecina*) dried meat
chacinería SF pork butcher's, pork butcher's shop
chacinero ADJ pork (*antes de s*) • **industria chacinera** pigmeat industry
chacó SM shako
chacolí SM *sharp-tasting Basque wine*
chacolotear ▸ CONJUG 1a VI to clatter
chacoloteo SM clatter, clattering
chacón SM Philippine lizard
chacota* SF • **estar de ~** to be in a joking mood • **echar** *o* **tomar algo a ~** to make fun of sth
chacotear ▸ CONJUG 1a VI to have fun
VPR **chacotearse** • **~se de algo** to make fun of sth
chacoteo SM (*Cono Sur*) = **chacota**
chacotería SF (*Cono Sur*) = **chacota**
chacotero ADJ, **chacotón** ADJ (*Cono Sur*) fond of a joke
chacra SF (*And, Cono Sur*) small farm
chacuaco ADJ (*LAm*) coarse, rough
SM **1** (*CAm*) (= *cigarro*) roughly-made cigar
2 (*CAm, Méx*) (= *colilla*) cigar stub
Chad SM Chad
chadiano/a ADJ, SM/F Chadian

chador (SM) chador
chafa* (ADJ) (*Méx*) useless
chafallar ▹ CONJUG 1a (VT) to botch, botch up
chafallo (SM) botched job
chafalonía (SF) (*And*) *worn-out gold jewellery*
chafalote (ADJ) (*Cono Sur*) (= *ordinario*) common, vulgar
(SM) **1** = **chafarote**
2 (*LAm***) (= *pene*) prick**
chafar ▹ CONJUG 1a (VT) **1** (= *aplastar*) [+ *pelo*] to flatten; [+ *ropa*] to crumple, crease; [+ *patatas*] to mash
2 [+ *persona*] • ~ *o* **dejar chafado a algn** to crush sb, take the wind out of sb's sails* • **quedó chafado** he was speechless
3 (= *estropear*) to ruin, spoil • ~ **las vacaciones a algn** to ruin sb's holidays • **le ~on el negocio** they messed up the deal for him
4 (*Cono Sur*) (= *engañar*) to hoax, deceive
chafardear ▹ CONJUG 1a (VI) to gossip
chafardeo (SM) gossip
chafardero/a (ADJ) • **es muy ~** he's a terrible gossip
(SM/F) gossip
chafarote (SM) **1** (= *alfanje*) cutlass
2* (= *espada*) sword
3 (*LAm*) machete
4 (*CAm*‡) (= *policía*) cop*
chafarrinada (SF) spot, stain
chafarrinar ▹ CONJUG 1a (VT) to blot, stain
chafarrinón (SM) spot, stain • **MODISMO**: • **echar un ~ a algn**† to smear *o* slander sb
chafiro (SM) (*CAm, Méx*), **chafirro** (SM) (*CAm, Méx*) knife
chaflán (SM) **1** (= *inclinación*) bevel • **la casa que hace ~** the house on the corner
2 (= *casa*) corner house
chaflanar ▹ CONJUG 1a (VT) to bevel, chamfer
chaflar* ▹ CONJUG 1a (VT) (*Chile*) to expel, fire*
chagra (SF) (*Ecu*) = **chacra**
(SM) (*And*) peasant farmer
chagrín (SM) shagreen
chagua (SF) (*And*) gang
chaguar ▹ CONJUG 1i (VT) (*Cono Sur*) [+ *ropa*] to wring, wring out; [+ *vaca*] to milk
cháguar (SM) (*LAm*) (= *fibra*) agave fibre, hemp
cháguara (SF) (*Cono Sur*) = **cháguar**
chagüe (SM) (*CAm*) swamp, bog
chagüite (SM) (*CAm, Méx*) (= *pantano*) swamp; (= *campo*) flooded field; (= *bananal*) banana plantation
chagüitear* ▹ CONJUG 1a (VI) (*CAm, Méx*) to chat, natter*
chah (SM) Shah
chai‡ (SF) bird*, chick (*EEUU*‡)
chaine (SM) (*And, CAm*) shoeshine
chainear ▹ CONJUG 1a (VT) (*CAm*) to shine, polish
chaira (SF) **1** [*de afilar*] sharpening steel
2 [*de zapatero*] shoemaker's knife
chairar ▹ CONJUG 1a (VT) (*Cono Sur*) to sharpen
chal (SM) shawl ▸ **chal de noche** evening wrap
chala (SF) **1** (*And, Cono Sur*) [*de maíz*] maize leaf, maize husk
2 (*Cono Sur**) money, dough* • **MODISMO**: • **pelar la ~ a algn** to fleece sb*
3 (*Cono Sur*) (= *zapato*) sandal
chalado* (ADJ) crazy* • **¡estás ~!** you're crazy!* • **¡ven acá, ~!** come here, you idiot! • **estar ~ por algo/algn** to be crazy about sth/sb*
chaladura* (SF) crankiness*
chalán (SM) **1** [*de caballos*] dealer, horse dealer
2 (= *estafador*) shady businessman, shark
3 (*LAm*) horse breaker
chalana (SF) barge, lighter
chalanear ▹ CONJUG 1a (VT) **1** (= *tratar con maña*) [+ *persona*] to beat down; [+ *negocio*] to bring off
2 (*LAm*) (= *adiestrar*) to break in, tame
3 (*Cono Sur**) (= *acosar*) to pester
4 (*CAm*) (= *burlarse de*) to make fun of
(VI) to bargain shrewdly
chalaneo (SM), **chalanería** (SF) **1** (= *trato*) hard bargaining, horse trading
2 (= *trampas*) trickery, deception
chalaquear* ▹ CONJUG 1a (*CAm*) (VT) to trick, con*
(VI) to chatter away, rabbit on*
chalar* ▹ CONJUG 1a (VT) to drive crazy *o* round the bend*
(VPR) **chalarse** to go crazy*, go off one's rocker* • **se ha chalado por ella** he's crazy *o* nuts about her • **se chaló por su vecina** he fell madly in love with his neighbour • **se ha chalado por las motos** he's crazy about motorbikes
chalchihuite (SM) (*Méx*) jade
chale‡ (SMF) (*Méx*) (*pey*) Chink*
chalé (SM) = **chalet**
chaleco (SM) [*de traje*] waistcoat, vest (*EEUU*); [*de lana*] sleeveless pullover • **MODISMOS**: • **a ~** (*CAm, Méx*) by hook or by crook • **quedar como ~ de mono** (*Cono Sur*) to lose one's credibility ▸ **chaleco antibalas** bulletproof vest ▸ **chaleco de fuerza** (*LAm*) straitjacket ▸ **chaleco de seguridad** (*Aut*) reflective safety vest ▸ **chaleco salvavidas** life jacket, life preserver (*EEUU*)
chalecón (ADJ) (*Méx*) tricky, deceitful
(SM) con man*
chalequear ▹ CONJUG 1a (VT) (*Cono Sur, Méx*) (= *estafar*) to trick; (= *robar*) to steal
chalet [tʃa'le] (SM) (PL: **chalets** [tʃa'les])
1 (= *casa con jardín*) (*independiente*) detached house; (*en hilera*) terraced house; [*de campo*] villa, cottage; [*de una sola planta*] bungalow; [*de montaña*] chalet ▸ **chalet adosado** terraced house ▸ **chalet pareado** semi-detached house, duplex (*EEUU*)
2 (*Dep*) clubhouse
chalina (SF) **1** (= *corbata ancha*) cravat
2 (*LAm*) scarf
chalón (SM) (*LAm*) shawl, wrap
chalona (SF) (*LAm*) dried meat, dried mutton
chalote (SM) shallot
chalupa¹ (SF) **1** (= *embarcación*) launch, boat ▸ **chalupa salvavidas** lifeboat
2 (*Méx*) small canoe
chalupa² (SF) (*Méx*) (*Culin*) stuffed tortilla
chalupa³* (ADJ) crazy • **volver ~ a algn** to drive sb crazy
chamaco/a (SM/F) (*esp Méx*) **1** (= *niño*) kid
2 (= *novio*) boyfriend/girlfriend
chamada (SF) **1** (= *leña*) brushwood
2 (= *incendio*) brushwood fire
3* (= *humo*) smoke
chamagoso* (ADJ) (*Méx*) (= *mugriento*) filthy; (= *chabacano*) crude, rough
chamal (SM) (*And, Cono Sur*) blanket (*worn by Indian women as tunic, men as trousers*)
chamanto (SM) (*Chile*) ruana dress, poncho
chamar* ▹ CONJUG 1a (VT), (VI) to smoke
chámara (SF), **chamarasca** (SF) **1** (= *leña*) kindling, brushwood
2 (= *incendio*) brush fire, blaze
chamarilero/a (SM/F), **chamarillero/a** (SM/F) second-hand dealer
chamarra (SF) **1** (= *chaqueta*) sheepskin jacket, leather jacket
2 (*CAm, Méx*) (= *manta*) rough blanket, poncho
3 (*CAm**) (= *engaño*) con*, swindle
chamarrear* ▹ CONJUG 1a (VT) (*CAm*) to con*, swindle
chamarrero (SM) (*Caribe*) quack doctor
chamarro (SM) (*LAm*) **1** (= *manta*) coarse woollen *o* (*EEUU*) woolen blanket
2 (= *serape*) poncho, woollen *o* (*EEUU*) woolen cape
chamba¹ (SF) **1** (*And*) (= *tierra*) turf, sod; (= *charca*) pond, pool; (= *zanja*) ditch
2 (*Méx**) (= *trabajo*) work, business; (= *sueldo*) wages (*pl*), pay; (= *sueldo bajo*) low pay; (= *chollo*) soft job*
3 (*Caribe, Méx**) dough‡, bread (*EEUU*‡)
chamba²* (SF) luck • **por ~** by a fluke • **¡vaya ~ que has tenido!** you lucky thing!
chambeador(a)* (*Méx*) (ADJ) hard-working
(SM/F) hard worker, slogger*
chambear* ▹ CONJUG 1a (*Méx*) (VI) to earn one's living
chambelán (SM) chamberlain
chamberga* (SF) coat
chambergo (SM) **1** (= *sombrero*) [*de ala ancha*] broad-brimmed soft hat; (*Hist*) cocked hat
2* (= *chaquetón*) coat
chambero (SM) (*Méx*) draughtsman, draftsman (*EEUU*)
chambón/ona* (ADJ) **1** (= *patoso*) clumsy
2 (= *afortunado*) lucky
3 (= *desaseado*) slovenly
(SM/F) fluky player • **MODISMO**: • **hacer algo a la chambona** (*And*) to do sth in a rush
chambonada* (SF) **1** (= *torpeza*) awkwardness, clumsiness
2 (= *suerte*) luck
3 (= *error*) blunder
chambonear* ▹ CONJUG 1a (VI) **1** [*ser torpe*] to botch up
2 (= *tener suerte*) to have a stroke of luck, win by a fluke
chamborote (ADJ) (*And, CAm*) long-nosed
chambra¹ (SF) **1** (= *bata*) housecoat
2 (= *blusa*) blouse
3 (= *chaqueta*) loose jacket
chambra² (SF) (*Caribe*) (= *alboroto*) din, hubbub
chambra³ (SF) (*Caribe*) (= *machete*) machete, broad knife
chambrana (SF) (*And, Caribe*) row, uproar
chambre‡ (SM) (*CAm*) tittle-tattle, gossip
chambroso‡ (ADJ) (*CAm*) gossipy
chamburgo (SM) (*And*) pool, stagnant water
chamelicos* (SMPL) (*And, Cono Sur*) (= *trastos*) lumber (*sing*), junk (*sing*); (= *ropa*) old clothes
chamiza (SF) **1** [*de techo*] thatch, thatch palm
2 (= *leña*) brushwood
chamizo (SM) **1** (= *cabaña*) thatched hut
2 (= *chabola*) shack
3 (= *mina*) illegal coalmine
4 (= *leño*) half-burned log; (= *árbol*) half-burned tree
chamo/a* (SM/F) (*LAm*) kid*, child
chamorro (ADJ) [*cabeza*] shorn, close-cropped
(SM) ▸ **chamorro de cerdo** (*Méx*) leg of pork
champa (SF) **1** (*And, Chile*) (= *tierra*) sod, turf
2 (*And, Chile*) [*de pelo*] (= *greña*) mop of hair; (= *maraña*) tangled mass
3 (*CAm*) (= *cobertizo*) shed; (= *tienda de campaña*) tent
champán (SM) champagne
champanero (ADJ) champagne (*antes de s*)
champanizar ▹ CONJUG 1f (VT) [+ *vino*] to add a sparkle to
Champaña (SF) Champagne
champaña (SM) champagne
champañazo (SM) (*Cono Sur*) champagne party
champañero (ADJ) champagne (*antes de s*)
champi* (SM) = **champiñón**

champiñón SM mushroom

championes SMPL (*Uru*) trainers (*Brit*), sneakers (*EEUU*)

champú SM shampoo ▸ **champú acondicionador** conditioning shampoo ▸ **champú anticaspa** anti-dandruff shampoo

champudo ADJ (*LAm*) [*pelo*] dishevelled, messy; [*persona*] long-haired

champurrado SM (*LAm*) **1** [*de bebidas*] mixture of alcoholic drinks, cocktail
2* (= *lío*) mess
3 (*Méx*) [*de chocolate*] *thick chocolate drink*

champurrar ▹ CONJUG 1a VT (*esp LAm*) [+ *bebidas*] to mix, make a cocktail of

champurreado SM (*Cono Sur*) **1** (*Culin*) hastily-prepared dish
2 (= *prisa*) hash, botch
3 = champurrado

champurrear ▹ CONJUG 1a VT (*Caribe*)
1 [+ *bebidas*] to mix, make a cocktail of
2 = chapurrear

chamuchina* SF (*LAm*) **1** (= *turba*) rabble, mob
2 (= *niños*) crowd of small children, mob of kids*
3 (*And, Caribe*) (= *jaleo*) row, shindy*; (= *riña*) row, quarrel

chamullar‡ ▹ CONJUG 1a VT to speak, talk • **yo también chamullo el caló** I can talk slang too • **¿qué chamullas tú?** what are you burbling about?
VI **1** (= *hablar*) to speak, talk • **chamullaban en árabe** they were jabbering away in Arabic
2 (*Cono Sur*) to cook up a story

chamuscado ADJ [*pelo*] singed; [*ropa, madera, muebles*] scorched; [*comida*] burnt

chamuscar ▹ CONJUG 1g VT **1** (= *quemar*) to scorch, singe
2 (*Méx*) (= *vender barato*) to sell cheap
VPR **chamuscarse 1** (= *quemarse*) to get scorched, singe
2 (*And**) to fly off the handle*

chamusquina SF **1** (= *quemadura*) singeing, scorching
2 (= *riña*) row, quarrel • MODISMO: • **esto huele a ~** there's trouble brewing
3 (*And, CAm*) (= *niños*) bunch of kids*

chamuyar ▹ CONJUG 1a VI (*Arg, Uru*) = chamullar

chan SM (*CAm*) local guide

chanada* SF trick, swindle

chanar‡ ▹ CONJUG 1a VT (*tb* **chanar de algo**) to understand sth

chanca SF (*And, Cono Sur*) **1** (= *molienda*) grinding, crushing
2 (= *paliza*) beating

chancaca SF **1** (*CAm*) [*de maíz*] maize cake, wheat cake
2 (*LAm*) (= *azúcar*) dark brown sugar
3 (*And*) (*Med*) sore, ulcer

chancadora SF (*Chile*) grinder, crusher

chancar ▹ CONJUG 1g VT (*LAm*) **1** (= *moler*) to grind, crush
2 (= *pegar*) to beat, ill-treat
3 (*And, Cono Sur*) (= *estropear*) to botch, bungle

chance SM, (*a veces*) SF (*LAm*)
1 (= *oportunidad*) chance • **dale ~** let him have a go
2 (= *suerte*) good luck
CONJ (*Méx*) maybe, perhaps

chancear ▹ CONJUG 1a VI, VPR **chancearse 1** (= *bromear*) to joke, make jokes (**de** about) • **~se de algn** to make fun of sb
2 (= *jugar*) to fool about, play around (**con** with)

chancero ADJ fond of a joke

chancha SF **1** (*LAm*) (*Zool*) sow
2 (*Cono Sur*) (= *carro*) small wooden cart; (= *bicicleta**) bike*
3 (*And*) • MODISMO: • **hacer la ~*** to play truant, play hooky (*EEUU*)

chanchada* SF (*LAm*) dirty trick

chánchamo SM (*Méx*) (*Culin*) tamale

cháncharas SFPL • MODISMO: • **andar en ~ máncharas** to beat about the bush

chanchería SF (*LAm*) pork butcher's, pork butcher's shop

chanchero SM (*LAm*) pork butcher

chanchi* ADJ, ADV = chachi

chanchito* SM (*LAm*) • **mi ~** my darling

chancho (*LAm*) ADJ dirty, filthy
SM **1** (= *cerdo*) pig, hog (*EEUU*); (= *carne*) pork • MODISMOS: • **son como ~s** they're as thick as thieves • **hacerse el ~ rengo** to pretend not to notice • **quedar como ~** to come off badly ▸ **chancho salvaje** wild boar
2 (*Ajedrez*) blocked piece
3 (*Cono Sur*) = **chancadora**
4 (*Cono Sur*) [*de suelos*] floor polisher

chanchono* SM lie

chanchullero/a* ADJ crooked, bent*
SM/F crook

chanchullo* SM fiddle*, wangle* • **andar en ~s** to be on the fiddle*, be mixed up in something shady

chanciller SM = **canciller**

chancillería SF chancery

chancla SF **1** (= *zapatilla*) flip-flop, thong (*EEUU*)
2 (= *zapato viejo*) old shoe

chancleta SF **1** flip-flop, thong (*EEUU*) • **ir en ~s** to wear flip-flops • MODISMOS: • **estar hecho una ~*** to be a wreck* • **tirar la ~** (*Cono Sur*) to have a good time
2 (*LAm*) baby girl
3 (*Caribe*) accelerator
SMF* good-for-nothing

chancletero ADJ (*LAm*), **chancletudo** ADJ (*LAm*) **1** (= *ordinario*) common, low-class
2 (= *desaseado*) scruffy

chanclo SM **1** (= *zueco*) clog
2 [*de goma*] overshoe, galosh

chancón/ona* SM/F (*And*) swot*, grind (*EEUU**)

chancro SM chancre

chandal SM (PL: **chandals**), **chándal** SM (PL: **chándals**) tracksuit

chanelar* ▹ CONJUG 1a VT to catch on to, twig*

chanfaina SF **1** (*Culin*) cheap stew
2 (*And, CAm*) (= *enredo*) mess; (= *suerte*) lucky break

chanfle SM **1** (*Cono Sur**) cop*
2 (*LAm*) = **chaflán**

chanflón ADJ **1** (= *deforme*) misshapen
2 (= *basto*) crude, coarse

changa SF **1** (*And, Cono Sur*) (= *chapuza*) odd job
2 (*And*) (= *propina*) tip (*to a porter*)
3 (*Caribe*) (= *broma*) joke; ▹ **chango**

changador SM (*And, Cono Sur*) (= *mozo de cordel*) porter; (= *trabajo*) odd job

changango SM (*Cono Sur*) (= *guitarra*) small guitar

changarín* SM (*Arg*) casual labourer, casual laborer (*EEUU*)

changarro SM (*Méx*) small shop

changarse‡ ▹ CONJUG 1h VPR to break, break down, go wrong

chango/a ADJ **1** (*Méx*) (= *listo*) quick, sharp • **¡ponte ~!** wake up!
2 (*Chile*) (= *tonto*) silly
3 (*Caribe, Méx*) (= *juguetón*) mischievous, playful
4 (*Cono Sur*) (= *molesto*) annoying
5 • **la gente está changa** (*Méx*) there are lots of people
SM/F **1** (*Méx*) small monkey
2 (*Cono Sur, Méx*) (= *niño*) kid; (= *criado*) young servant; ▹ **changa**

changuear ▹ CONJUG 1a VI (*And, Caribe, Méx*) = chancear

changüí†* SM **1** (= *chiste*) joke
2 (= *engaño*) trick • **dar ~ a algn** (= *engañar*) to trick sb; (= *tomar el pelo*) to tease sb

changuito SM **1** (*Arg, Uru*) shopping trolley (*Brit*), shopping cart (*EEUU*)
2 changuitos (*Méx*) • **hacer ~s** to keep one's fingers crossed

changurro SM crab

chanquetes SMPL whitebait (*pl*)

chanta‡ SMF (*Cono Sur*) (= *fanfarrón*) loudmouth*; (= *informal*) fraud

chantaje SM blackmail • **hacer ~ a algn** to blackmail sb ▸ **chantaje emocional** emotional blackmail

chantajear ▹ CONJUG 1a VT to blackmail

chantajista SMF blackmailer

chantar ▹ CONJUG 1a VT **1** • **~ algo a algn** to tell sb sth to his face
2 (*Perú, Chile**) (= *arrojar*) to throw, chuck • **~ a algn en la cárcel** to throw sb in jail, put sb in jail • **~ a algn en la calle** to throw sb out
3 (*Cono Sur*) (= *abandonar*) to leave in the lurch; (= *engañar*) to deceive, trick
4 (*And, Cono Sur*) [+ *golpe*] to give

chantre SM (*Rel*) precentor

chanza SF **1** (= *chiste*) joke • **de o en ~** in fun, as a joke • **estar de ~** to be joking
2 chanzas (= *diversión*) fun (*sing*)

chañaca SF (*Cono Sur*) **1** (*Med*) itch, rash
2 (= *mala reputación*) bad reputation

chao* EXCL bye*, cheerio*, so long (*esp EEUU**), see ya (*esp EEUU**)

chapa SF **1** (= *material*) sheet metal • **la escultura incorpora ~ y madera** the sculpture includes sheet metal and wood
2 (= *lámina*) • **una ~ de metal** a metal sheet, a sheet of metal • **una ~ de madera** a wooden panel • **una ~ de acero** a steel plate • **la ~ del coche** the panel of the car • **una mesa revestida con ~ de nogal** a table covered with a walnut veneer ▸ **chapa acanalada, chapa ondulada** corrugated iron (sheet)
3 [*de policía*] badge; [*de adorno*] badge • **lleva la cazadora llena de ~s** he has badges all over his jacket
4 [*de botella*] cap, top
5 (*Cono Sur*) [*de matrícula*] ▸ **chapa de patente** licence *o* (*EEUU*) license plate
6 chapas (= *juego*) *game of throwing bottle tops*
7 (*Esp‡*) *one-hundred-peseta coin* • MODISMO: • **estar sin ~†** not to have a farthing *o* cent
8 • MODISMO: • **hacer ~s‡** (= *prostituirse*) to turn tricks‡
9 (*LAm*) (= *cerradura*) lock; (= *tirador*) (door) handle
10 • **hombre de ~†** sensible man

chapado ADJ [*metal*] plated; [*muebles*] veneered, finished • **~ de roble** with an oak veneer, with an oak finish • **~ de oro** gold-plated • MODISMO: • **~ a la antigua** old-fashioned, of the old school

chapalear ▹ CONJUG 1a VI = **chapotear**

chapaleo SM = **chapoteo**

chapapote SM (*Méx*) (= *pez*) tar, pitch; (= *asfalto*) asphalt

chapar ▹ CONJUG 1a VT **1** (= *cubrir*) [+ *metal*] to plate; [+ *muebles*] to veneer, finish; [+ *pared*] to tile
2 [+ *frase, observación*] to come out with • **le chapó un "no" como una casa** he gave him a flat "no"
3‡ (= *cerrar*) [+ *local, negocio*] to shut, close
4 (*Perú*) (= *asir*) to seize; (= *atrapar*) to catch; (= *espiar*) to spy on
VI **1‡** (= *estudiar*) to swot*, cram*
2‡ (= *dormir*) to kip*, sleep

chaparra SF **1** (= *árbol*) kermes oak
2 (= *maleza*) brush, scrub
chaparrada SF = **chaparrón**
chaparral SM thicket (*of kermes oaks*), chaparral
chaparrear ▸ CONJUG 1a VI (= *llover*) to pour down
chaparreras SFPL (*Méx*) leather chaps
chaparro/a ADJ **1** (= *rechoncho*) squat
2 (*esp LAm*) (= *bajito*) short
SM dwarf oak, kermes oak
SM/F **1** (= *persona*) short chubby person
2 (*Méx*) child, kid*
chaparrón SM **1** (*Meteo*) downpour, cloudburst • **MODISMO**: • **aguantar el ~** to face the music*
2 [*de insultos*] barrage; [*de cartas*] flood
chapata SF ciabatta
chapatal SM muddy place
chape SM (*And, Cono Sur*) tress, pigtail
chapear ▸ CONJUG 1a VT **1** = **chapar**
2 (*LAm*) (*Agr*) to weed
3 (= *sonar*) to rattle
4 • **~ a algn** (*Caribe*) to cut sb's throat
VI (*LAm*) to clear the ground
chapeau [tʃa'po] EXCL bravo!, well done!
SM **1** • **MODISMO**: • **hacer ~** to take off one's hat (**ante** to)
2 (= *felicitación*) congratulations
chapeo‡ SM hat
chapero‡ SM **1** (= *prostituto*) rent boy*
2 (= *homosexual*) queer**, poof**, fag (EEUU‡)
chapeta SF flush (*on the cheeks*)
chapetón ADJ (*LAm**) (= *novato*) inexperienced, green*; (= *torpe*) clumsy, awkward
SM **1** (*LAm**) *European greenhorn in Latin America*
2 (*Méx*) horse brass
3 (= *lluvia*) downpour
chapetonada SF **1** (*And**) *illness suffered by Europeans on arrival in Latin America*
2 (*Ecu*) (= *novatada*) blunder
3 (*And, Cono Sur*) (= *torpeza*) awkwardness, clumsiness
4 (*Caribe*) (= *aguacero*) sudden downpour
chapín ADJ (*LAm*) bowlegged, with crooked feet
SM **1** (= *zueco*) clog
2 (*CAm*) Guatemalan
chapinada SF (*CAm*) (*hum*) *action typical of a Guatemalan*, dirty trick
chapiri‡ SM hat
chápiro* SM • **¡por vida del ~!** • **¡voto al ~!** damn it!
chapisca SF (*CAm*) maize harvest
chapista SM **1** (*Téc*) tinsmith
2 (*Aut*) panel beater
chapistería SF body shop
chapita* SF (*And*) cop*
chapitel SM (*Arquit*) [*de columna*] capital; [*de torre*] spire
chapo¹ ADJ (*Méx*) stunted, dwarf (*antes de s*)
chapo² SM (*Méx*) (*Culin*) maize porridge
chapó EXCL bravo!, well done!
SM • **MODISMO**: • **hacer ~** to take one's hat off (**ante** to)
chapodar ▸ CONJUG 1a VT **1** [+ *árbol*] to prune
2 (= *reducir*) to cut down, reduce
chapola SF (*And*) butterfly
chapolín SM (= *juego*) pool
chapopote SM (*Méx*) = **chapapote**
chapote SM (*CAm, Caribe, Méx*) (= *pez*) pitch, tar; (= *asfalto*) asphalt
chapotear ▸ CONJUG 1a VI (*en el agua*) to splash about • **~ en el barro** to splash around in the mud
chapoteo SM splashing
chaptalizar ▸ CONJUG 1f VT to chaptalize, add sugar to
chapucear ▸ CONJUG 1a VT **1** [+ *trabajo*] to botch, make a mess of
2 (*Méx*) (= *estafar*) to swindle
chapuceramente ADV shoddily
chapucería SF **1** (= *cualidad*) shoddiness
2 (= *chapuza*) botched job, shoddy piece of work
chapucero/a ADJ **1** [*trabajo*] shoddy, slapdash
2 [*persona*] sloppy, slapdash
SM/F bungler
chapulín SM **1** (*Méx*) large grasshopper
2 (*CAm**) child, kid*
chapupa* SF • **MODISMO**: • **me salió de pura ~** (*CAm*) it was pure luck, it was sheer fluke
chapuro SM (*CAm*) asphalt
chapurrear* ▸ CONJUG 1a VT, **chapurrar*** ▸ CONJUG 1a VT • **chapurrea el italiano** he speaks broken *o* bad Italian
chapuz SM **1** = **chapuza**
2 (= *chapuzón*) ducking
chapuza SF **1** (= *trabajo mal hecho*) botched job, shoddy piece of work
2 (= *trabajo ocasional*) odd job • **siempre está haciendo ~s en la casa** he's always doing odd jobs around the house
3 (*Méx*) trick, swindle
chapuzar ▸ CONJUG 1f VT to duck
VI, VPR **chapuzarse** to dive, dive in
chapuzas* SMF INV botcher*
chapuzón SM **1** (= *zambullida*) dip, swim • **darse un ~** to go for a dip, go for a swim
2 [*de cápsula*] splashdown
3 (*LAm**) cloudburst, downpour
chaqué SM morning coat
chaquet [tʃa'ke] SM (PL: **chaquets** [tʃa'kes]) = **chaqué**
chaqueta SF jacket • **MODISMOS**: • **cambiar de ~** to change sides • **volarse la ~** (*CAm***) to toss off** ▸ **chaqueta de cuero** leather jacket ▸ **chaqueta de punto** cardigan
chaquetar ▸ CONJUG 1a VT, VI (*Méx*) = **chaquetear**
chaquete SM backgammon
chaquetear* ▸ CONJUG 1a VT to slag off‡, criticize
VI **1** (= *cambiar de política*) to change sides, be a turncoat, turn traitor
2 (= *acobardarse*) to go back on one's word, chicken out*, rat*
chaquetero/a* SM/F turncoat
chaquetón SM three-quarter coat
charada SF charade
charadrio SM plover
charal SM (*Méx*) small fish • **MODISMO**: • **estar como ~*** to be as thin as a rake
charaludo* ADJ (*Méx*) thin
charamusca SF **1** (*LAm*) (*tb* **charamuscas**) firewood, kindling
2 (*Cono Sur, Méx*) (= *dulce*) candy twist
3 (*Caribe*) (= *alboroto*) noise, row
charanga SF **1** (*Mús, Mil*) brass band; ▸ **España**
2* (= *jaleo*) hullabaloo*, racket*
3 (*LAm*) (= *baile*) informal dance, hop*
charango SM (*LAm*) *small 10-stringed guitarlike instrument originally made from the shell of an armadillo*
charanguero ADJ = **chapucero**
charape SM (*Méx*) *type of "pulque"*
charca SF pond, pool
charchina* SF (*LAm*) old crock, old banger‡, jalopy
charco SM pool, puddle • **MODISMO**: • **cruzar** *o* **pasar el ~** to cross the water; (*esp*) to cross the Pond (*the Atlantic*)
charcón¹ ADJ (*And, Cono Sur*) thin, skinny
charcón² SM pool (*in a river*)
charcutería SF **1** (= *productos*) cooked pork products (*pl*)
2 (= *tienda*) pork butcher's, pork butcher's shop
charcutero/a SM/F pork butcher
charla SF **1** (= *conversación*) chat • **MODISMO**: • **es de ~ común** it's common knowledge
2 (= *chismes*) gossip
3 (= *conferencia*) talk ▸ **charla literaria** literary talk, informal literary lecture ▸ **charla radiofónica** radio talk
charla-coloquio SF (PL: **charlas-coloquio**) talk (*followed by debate*)
charlado* SM • **echar un ~** to have a chat
charlador ADJ talkative
charladuría SF (*tb* **charladurías**) prattle
charlar ▸ CONJUG 1a VI **1** (= *conversar*) to chat (**de** about)
2 (= *chismear*) to gossip
charlatán/ana ADJ **1** (= *hablador*) talkative
2 (= *chismoso*) gossipy
SM/F **1** (= *hablador*) chatterbox
2 (= *chismoso*) gossip
3 (= *estafador*) trickster, confidence trickster, con man*
4 (= *vendedor aprovechado*) smooth-tongued salesman
charlatanear ▸ CONJUG 1a VI to chatter away
charlatanería SF **1** (= *locuacidad*) talkativeness; (*pey*) hot air
2 (= *chismorreo*) gossip
3 (= *engaños*) quackery, charlatanism
4 [*de vendedor*] sales talk, patter
charlatanismo SM = **charlatanería**
charlestón SM charleston
charleta SMF (*Cono Sur*) **1** (= *hablador*) chatterbox
2 (= *chismoso*) gossip
charli‡ SM 1,000-peseta note
charlista SMF speaker, lecturer
Charlot SM Charlie Chaplin
charlota SF *type of frozen cream cake*
charlotada SF **1** (*Teat*) gag
2 (*Taur*) mock bullfight
charlotear ▸ CONJUG 1a VI to chatter, talk a lot
charloteo SM chatter
charnego/a SM/F (*pey*) *Southern Spanish immigrant who has settled in Catalonia*
charnela SF, **charneta** SF hinge
charol SM **1** (= *barniz*) varnish • **MODISMO**: • **darse ~** to brag
2 (= *cuero*) patent leather
3 (*LAm*) (= *bandeja*) tray
charola SF **1** (*LAm*) (= *bandeja*) tray
2 charolas (*CAm*) (= *ojos*) eyes
charolado ADJ polished, shiny
charolar ▸ CONJUG 1a VT to varnish
charolés ADJ, SM Charolais
charpa SF (*CAm*) **1** (*Mil*) pistol belt, sword belt
2 (*Med*) sling
charquear ▸ CONJUG 1a VT (*LAm*) **1** [+ *carne*] to dry, jerk
2 [+ *persona*] to slash, cut to pieces
charquecillo SM (*And*) (*Culin*) dried salted fish
charqui SM **1** (*LAm*) (= *carne*) jerked beef, jerky (EEUU)
2 (*Cono Sur*) (= *frutas*) dried fruit; (= *legumbres*) dried vegetables (*pl*) • **MODISMO**: • **hacer ~ a algn** = **charquear**
charquicán SM (*Cono Sur*) (*Culin*) *dish of dried meat and vegetables*
charra SF **1** (*Salamanca*) (= *campesina*) peasant woman; (= *mujer de clase baja*) low-class woman, coarse woman
2 (*CAm*) (= *sombrero*) broad-brimmed hat
3 (*And*) (= *grano*) itch, pimple
4 (*CAm***) (= *pene*) prick**, tool**; ▸ **charro**

charrada SF **1** (= *adorno*) flashy ornament
2 (= *torpeza*) coarseness
3 (*Mús*) country dance
charral SM (*CAm*) scrub, scrubland
charramasca SF (*CAm*) firewood, kindling
charrán¹ SM (*Orn*) tern
charrán² SM rascal, villain
charranada* SF dirty trick
charrar‡ ▹ CONJUG 1a VI **1** (= *hablar*) to talk, burble
2 (= *soplar*) to blab
charrasca SF **1** (*LAm*) knife
2†† trailing sword
charrasquear* ▹ CONJUG 1a VT **1** (*Méx*) (= *apuñalar*) to knife, stab
2 (*And, CAm, Caribe*) (= *rasguear*) to strum
charré SM trap, dog-cart
charreada SF (*Méx*) public fiesta
charrería SF (*Méx*) horsemanship
charretera SF **1** (*Mil*) epaulette
2 (*Cos*) shoulder pad
charro ADJ **1** [*gente*] rustic
2 (= *de mal gusto*) [*ropa*] loud, gaudy; [*objeto*] flashy, showy
3 (= *salmantino*) Salamancan
4 (*Méx*) [*costumbres*] traditional, picturesque; ▹ **CONJUNTO MARIACHI**
SM **1** (= *pueblerino*) rustic
2 (*Méx*) (= *vaquero*) typical Mexican
3 (*Méx*) (= *sombrero*) wide-brimmed hat
4 (*Méx**) corrupt union boss
5 (*Salamanca*) peasant; ▹ **charra**
charrúa ADJ, SMF (*Cono Sur*) Uruguayan
chart (PL: **charts**) (*Bolsa*) SM (= *gráfico*) market forecast, stock market forecast
SMF (= *analista*) market analyst
chárter ADJ INV • **vuelo ~** charter, charter flight
SM (PL: **chárters** ['tʃarter]) charter, charter flight
chartista ADJ market (*antes de s*), stock market (*antes de s*)
SMF market analyst
chasca SF **1** (= *leña*) brushwood (*from pruning trees*)
2 (*And, Cono Sur*) (= *greña*) mop of hair, tangled hair
chascar ▹ CONJUG 1g VT **1** (= *hacer sonar*) [+ *lengua*] to click; [+ *dedos*] to snap; [+ *látigo*] to crack; [+ *grava*] to crunch
2 [+ *comida*] to swallow
VI [*leña*] to crackle
chascarrillo SM funny story
chasco SM **1** (= *desilusión*) disappointment • **dar un ~ a algn** to disappoint sb • **llevarse un ~** to be disappointed, be let down • **¡vaya ~ que me llevé!** I was just sick about that!, I felt really let down
2 (= *broma*) trick, joke • **dar un ~ a algn** to play a trick on sb
chascón ADJ (*Chile*) (= *greñudo*) with a tangled mop of hair
chasis SM INV, **chasís** SM INV (*LAm*) **1** (*Aut*) chassis • **MODISMO**: • **quedarse en el ~*** to get terribly thin
2 (*Fot*) plateholder
chasque SM (*LAm*) = **chasqui**
chasquear¹ ▹ CONJUG 1a VT **1** (= *decepcionar*) to disappoint, let down
2 (= *engañar*) to play a trick on, fool
3 [+ *promesa*] to break
chasquear² ▹ CONJUG 1a VT, VI = **chascar**
VPR **chasquearse** (*And**) to make a mess of things, mess things up*
chasqui SM (*LAm*) (*Hist*) messenger, courier
chasquido SM (= *ruido seco*) [*de lengua*] click; [*de dedos*] snap; [*de madera*] crack
chasquilla SF (*And, Cono Sur*), **chasquillas** SFPL (*And, Cono Sur*) (= *flequillo*) fringe, bangs (*pl*) (EEUU)

chat SM (*Internet*) chat room
chata SF **1** (*Med*) bedpan
2 (*Náut*) barge
3 (*Cono Sur*) (*Ferro*) flatcar
4* (= *escopeta*) sawn-off shotgun
chatarra SF scrap, scrap iron • **vender para ~** to sell for scrap ▸ **chatarra espacial** space junk
chatarrería SF scrapyard, scrap merchant's, junkyard (EEUU)
chatarrero/a SMF scrap dealer, scrap merchant
chatear* ▹ CONJUG 1a VI **1** (*Internet*) to chat
2 (*en bar*) to have a few glasses of wine
chateo* SM **1** (*Internet*) chatting
2 drinking • **ir de ~** to go out for a few glasses of wine
chatero/a ADJ chat
SM/F chat-room user
chati* SMF love, darling
chato ADJ **1** [*nariz*] snub
2 (= *plano*) [*objeto*] flattened, blunt; [*barco*] flat
3 (*Arquit*) low, squat
4 (*And, Chile*) [*persona*] short
5 (*Méx*) (= *pobre*) poor, wretched • **MODISMO**: • **quedarse ~*** to be disappointed (**con** at)
SM tumbler, wine tumbler
chatón SM large mounted stone
chatre ADJ (*And, Cono Sur*) smartly-dressed • **MODISMO**: • **está hecho un ~** he's looking very smart
chatungo* ADJ = **chato**
chau EXCL = **chao**
chaucha ADJ INV (*LAm*) **1** (*Agr*) early
2 (*Med*) [*nacimiento*] premature; [*mujer*] who gives birth prematurely
3 (*Cono Sur*) (= *malo*) poor-quality; (= *soso*) insipid, tasteless, characterless; (= *de mal gusto*) in poor taste
SF **1** (*LAm*) (= *patata*) early potato
2 (*Cono Sur*) (= *judía verde*) string bean
3 (*Perú*) (= *comida*) food • **MODISMO**: • **pelar la ~** (*And, Cono Sur*) to brandish *o* use one's knife
4 (*Chile, Perú**) (= *dinero*) dough* • **le cayó la ~** the penny dropped
5 chauchas (*Cono Sur**) peanuts*, trifles
chauchau SM (*Chile, Perú*) stew, chow*
chauchera SF (*And, Cono Sur*) purse, coin purse (EEUU)
chauchero SM (*Cono Sur*) **1** (= *recadero*) errand boy
2 (= *trabajador*) poorly-paid worker
chaufa SF (*LAm*) Chinese fried rice
chauvinismo SM chauvinism
chauvinista ADJ, SMF chauvinist
chava‡ SMF (*CAm, Méx*) = **chaval**
chaval(a)* SM/F lad/lass, boy/girl, kid* • **es todavía un ~** he's only a kid still
chavalada* SF = **chavalería**
chavalería* SF young people, kids* (*pl*)
chavalo* SM (*Nic*) lad, kid*
chavalongo SM (*Cono Sur*) **1** (= *fiebre*) fever
2 (= *insolación*) sunstroke
3 (= *modorra*) drowsiness, drowsy feeling
chavea* SMF lad, kid*
chaveta SF **1** (*Téc*) cotter, cotter pin • **MODISMOS**: • **perder la ~*** to go off one's rocker* • **perder la ~ por algn** to lose one's head over sb
2 (*LAm*) (= *navaja*) broad-bladed knife
ADJ INV • **estar ~‡** to be nuts*
chavetear ▹ CONJUG 1a VT (*And, Caribe*) to knife
chavo/a SM • **no tener** *o* **estar sin un ~** to be skint*, be stony broke*
SM/F (*Méx, CAm**) guy*/girl
chavó* SM lad, kid*
chayote SM chayote, vegetable pear (EEUU)

chayotera SF chayote, chayote plant
che¹ SF Ch (*name of the letter ch*)
che² EXCL (*Cono Sur*) hey!; (*en conversación*) man, boy, friend
che³* SM (*Chile*) Argentinian
checa SF **1** (= *policía*) secret police
2 (= *comisaría*) secret police headquarters; (= *cárcel‡*) nick‡, jail
checar ▹ CONJUG 1g VT (*esp Méx*) = **chequear**
cheche SM (*Caribe*) bully, braggart
chechear ▹ CONJUG 1a VT (*Cono Sur*) = **vosear**
checheno/a ADJ Chechen
SM/F Chechen
chécheres SMPL (*And, CAm*) (= *cosas*) things, gear (*sing*); (= *cachivaches*) junk (*sing*), lumber (*sing*)
chechón ADJ (*Méx*) spoilt, pampered
checo/a ADJ, SM/F Czech
SM (*Ling*) Czech
checoslovaco/a ADJ, SM/F Czechoslovakian
Checoslovaquia SF Czechoslovakia
chef SM (PL: **chefs**) chef
cheira SF = **chaira**
Chejov SM Chekhov
chele ADJ (*CAm*) fair, blond/blonde
chelear ▹ CONJUG 1a VT (*CAm*) to whiten, whitewash
cheli* SM **1** bloke*, guy* • **ven acá, ~** come here, man
2 (*Ling*) Madrid slang
chelín SM shilling
chelista SMF cellist
chelo¹ ADJ (*Méx*) fair, blond/blonde
chelo² SM (*Mús*) (= *instrumento*) cello; (= *músico*) cellist
chepa SF hump
SMF hunchback
cheposo/a ADJ hunchbacked
SM/F hunchback
cheque SM cheque, check (EEUU) • **un ~ por 400 euros** a cheque for 400 euros • **cobrar un ~** to cash a cheque • **extender un ~** to make out *o* write a cheque • **pagar con ~** to pay by cheque ▸ **cheque abierto** open cheque ▸ **cheque abierto cruzado** crossed cheque ▸ **cheque al portador** cheque payable to bearer ▸ **cheque bancario** banker's cheque ▸ **cheque caducado** out-of-date cheque ▸ **cheque conformado** certified cheque ▸ **cheque cruzado** crossed cheque ▸ **cheque de compensación** clearing cheque ▸ **cheque de viaje, cheque de viajero** traveller's cheque ▸ **cheque en blanco** blank cheque ▸ **cheque nominativo** order cheque • **un ~ nominativo a favor de Luis González** a cheque made out to *o* made payable to Luis González ▸ **cheque regalo** gift voucher ▸ **cheque sin fondos** bounced cheque
chequear ▹ CONJUG 1a VT **1** (*esp LAm*) (= *comprobar*) [+ *cuenta, documento, salud*] to check; [+ *persona*] to check on, check up on
2 (*LAm*) [+ *equipaje*] to check in
3 (*LAm*) [+ *cheque*] to make out, write
4 (*Méx*) (*Aut*) to service
chequeo SM **1** (*Med*) check-up
2 (*Aut*) service
chequera SF (*LAm*) cheque book, checkbook (EEUU)
cherife SM (*LAm*) sheriff
cherna SF wreckfish
chero* SM (*CAm*) pal*, mate*, buddy (EEUU*)
cheruto SM cheroot
cherva SF castor oil plant
cheto/a* (*Arg, Uru*) ADJ posh*
SM/F posh person*
cheurón SM chevron
chévere* ADJ (*Col, Ven*) great*, fabulous*
SM (*Caribe*) bully, braggart

chevió (SM), **cheviot** (SM) cheviot
chibola (SF) (*CAm*) **1** (= *refresco*) fizzy drink, pop*, soda (*EEUU*)
2 = chibolo
3 (= *canica*) marble
chibolo (SM) (*And, CAm*) bump, swelling
chic (ADJ INV) chic, smart
(SM) elegance
chica (SF) **1** (= *criada*) maid, servant
2 ▸ **chica de alterne** bar-girl, bar-room hostess ▸ **chica de conjunto** chorus girl; ▹ chico
chicana (SF) (*Méx*) chicanery
chicanear ▹ CONJUG 1a (VI) (*Méx*) to use trickery, be cunning
chicanería (SF) (*LAm*) chicanery
chicanero (ADJ) **1** (*Méx*) tricky, crafty
2 (*And*) (= *tacaño*) mean
chicano/a (ADJ) Chicano, Mexican-American
(SM/F) Chicano, Mexican immigrant in the USA
chicar* ▹ CONJUG 1g (VI) (*And*) to booze*, drink
chicarrón/ona (ADJ) strapping, sturdy
(SM/F) strapping lad/sturdy lass
chicato* (ADJ) (*Cono Sur*) short-sighted, near-sighted (*EEUU*)
chicha[1] (SF) **1** (*LAm*) (= *bebida*) maize liquor, corn liquor (*EEUU*) • MODISMOS: • **ni ~ ni limonada** *o* **limoná*** neither fish nor fowl, neither one thing nor the other • **estas cosas están como ~** (*And**) there are hundreds *o* any number of these things • **sacar la ~ a algo/algn** (*Cono Sur**) to milk sth/sb dry ▸ **chicha de uva** unfermented grape juice
2 (*And, CAm**) (= *berrinche*) rage, bad temper • **estar de ~** to be in a bad mood

CHICHA
Chicha is a strong alcoholic drink made from fermented maize and produced in Peru, where it is associated with ceremonial and ritual occasions. It is now an element of what is known as **chicha** culture, a dynamic blend of traditional Indian and modern imported styles and fashions created out of the migration of the rural poor to major cities. **Chicha** music has become the most popular music in Peru. It combines the traditional Andean **huayno** with tropical, Afro-Hispanic music and electronic instruments.

chicha[2]* (SF) meat • MODISMOS: • **tiene poca(s) ~(s)** she's as thin as a rake* • **de ~ y nabo** insignificant
chicha[3] (ADJ) • **calma ~** (*Náut*) dead calm
chícharo (*LAm*) (SM) **1** (= *guisante*) pea
2 (= *garbanzo*) chickpea
chicharra (SF) **1** (*Entomología*) harvest bug, cicada • MODISMOS: • **es como ~ en verano** it's nasty, it's unpleasant • **canta la ~** it's terribly hot, it's roasting*
2 (= *persona habladora*) chatterbox
3 (*Elec*) (= *timbre*) bell, buzzer; (*Telec*) bug*, bugging device
4 (*CAm, Caribe*) (= *chicharrón*) crackling (*of pork*)
5‡ (= *droga*) reefer*
6‡ (= *monedero*) purse, coin purse (*EEUU*)
chicharrero[1] (SM) **1** (= *horno*) oven, hothouse
2* (= *lugar muy caliente*) oven, furnace
chicharrero[2]**/a** (ADJ) of/from Tenerife
(SM/F) native/inhabitant of Tenerife • **los ~s** the people of Tenerife
chicharro (SM) horse-mackerel
chicharrón (SM) **1** (*Culin*) • **chicharrones (de cerdo)** pork scratchings, pork cracklings (*EEUU*) • MODISMO: • **estar hecho un ~*** [*carne*] to be burnt to a cinder; [*persona*] to be as red as a lobster*
2 (*por el sol*) lobster*
3 (*Caribe*) (= *adulador*) flatterer
chiche (ADJ) (*CAm*) easy, simple • **está ~** it's a cinch*
(ADV) (*CAm*) easily
(SM) **1** (*CAm, Méx**) (= *pecho*) breast, tit‡
2 (*Cono Sur*) (= *joya*) trinket; (= *juguete*) small toy
(SF) (*Méx*) nursemaid
chichear ▹ CONJUG 1a (VT), (VI) to hiss
chicheo (SM) hiss, hissing
chichera‡ (SF) (*CAm*) jail, clink‡, can (*EEUU**)
chichería (SF) (*And*) **1** (= *bar*) chicha bar
2 (= *fábrica*) chicha brewery
chichero (SM) **1** (= *vendedor*) chicha seller
2 (= *fabricante*) chicha maker
chichi* (SF) **1** (= *vulva*) fanny**, beaver (*EEUU**)
2 (*Méx*) (= *teta*) tit**
3 (*Méx*) (= *niñera*) nursemaid
chichicaste (SM) (*CAm*) **1** (*Bot*) nettle
2 (*Med*) nettle rash
chichigua (SF) **1** (*CAm, Méx*) (= *niñera*) nursemaid
2 (*Caribe*) (= *cometa*) kite
3 (*Méx*) (= *animal manso*) tame animal; (= *hembra*) nursing animal
4 (*Méx**) pimp
chicho (SM) **1** (= *bucle*) curl, ringlet
2 (= *bigudí*) curler, roller
chichón[1]* (ADJ) **1** (*Cono Sur*) (= *jovial*) merry, jovial
2 (*CAm*) (= *fácil*) easy, straightforward • **está ~** it's a piece of cake*
chichón[2] (SM) (= *bulto*) lump, swelling
chichonear ▹ CONJUG 1a (VI) (*Cono Sur*) to joke
chichonera (SF) helmet
chichus (SM) (*CAm*) flea
chicle (SM) chewing gum ▸ **chicle de globo** bubble gum ▸ **chicle sin azúcar** sugar-free chewing gum
chiclear ▹ CONJUG 1a (VI) (*CAm, Méx*)
1 (= *cosechar*) to extract gum
2 (= *masticar chicle*) to chew gum
chiclero (SM) (*Méx, CAm*) gum collector
chico/a (ADJ) **1** (= *pequeño*) small, little • MODISMOS: • **dejar ~ a algn** to put sb in the shade • **quedarse ~** to be humiliated; ▹ **patria, perra**
2 (= *joven*) young • **yo era muy ~, pero me acuerdo de ella** I was very young but I remember her • **de ~ no me gustaban las verduras** I didn't like vegetables when I was little, as a child, I didn't like vegetables
(SM/F) **1** (= *joven*) boy/girl • **me gusta un ~ de Barcelona** there's a guy* *o* boy from Barcelona I like • **es un buen ~** he's a good lad • **el entrenador tiene bien preparados a sus ~s** the trainer has his lads well prepared • **las chicas de la oficina** the girls at the office
2 (= *niño*) boy/girl • **los ~s de la clase** the boys in the class ▸ **chico de la calle** street kid* ▸ **chico de los recados** office boy, messenger boy
3 (= *hijo*) boy/girl • **no nos hemos divorciado aún por los ~s** we haven't got divorced yet because of the kids* *o* children
4 (= *novio*) boyfriend/girlfriend • **¿sales con algún ~?** are you going out with anyone?, have you got a boyfriend?
5 (*apelativo*) **a** (*a un adulto*) • **mira, ~, déjalo** OK, just leave it, will you? • **chica, ¡qué cambiada estás!** hey! *o* you know, you look so different! • **¡hola, ~s! ¿qué tal?** hi, guys! how're you doing?* • **hola chicas ¡ya estoy aquí!** hi, girls, here I am!
b (*a un niño*) • **¡oye, ~! ¿quieres ganarte un poco de dinero?** hey! do you want to earn yourself a bit of money? • **chica, ¡no corras!** don't run, dear!; ▹ **chica**
(SM) (*LAm*) (*Naipes*) game, round; (*Billar*) game; (*Snooker*) frame
chicolear* ▹ CONJUG 1a (VI) **1** (*Méx*) (= *flirtear*) to flirt, say nice things
2 (*And*) (= *divertirse*) to amuse o.s., have a good time
(VPR) **chicolearse** (*And*) to amuse o.s.
chicoleo (SM) (*Méx*) **1** (= *piropo*) compliment
2* (= *flirteo*) flirting
3 (*And*) (= *cosa infantil*) childish thing • **no andemos con ~s** let's be serious
chicolero (ADJ) flirtatious
chicoria (SF) chicory
chicota (SF) (*pey*) big girl
chicotazo (SM) (*LAm*) lash
chicote (SM) **1*** (= *chico*) big chap*, fine lad
2 (*Náut*) piece of rope, rope end
3 (*LAm*) whip, lash
4* (= *puro*) cigar; (= *colilla*) cigar stub
chicotear ▹ CONJUG 1a (*LAm*) (VT) **1** (= *azotar*) to whip, lash
2 (= *pegar*) to beat up
3 (*And*) (= *matar*) to kill
(VI) [*cola*] to lash about
chifa (SM) (*Chile, Perú*) Chinese restaurant
chifla (SF) (*Dep*) **1** (= *sonido*) hissing, whistling
2 (= *silbato*) whistle
chifladera* (SF) (*CAm, Méx*) crazy idea
chiflado/a* (ADJ) crazy*, barmy* • **esa chica le tiene ~** he's crazy about that girl • **estar ~ con** *o* **por algo/algn** to be crazy about sth/sb
(SM/F) nutter*, nutcase*
chifladura (SF) **1** = chifla
2* (= *locura*) craziness • **una ~** a crazy idea, a wild scheme • **su ~ es el ajedrez** he is crazy *o* mad about chess • **ese amor no es más que una ~** what he calls love is just a foolish infatuation
chiflar[1] ▹ CONJUG 1a (VT) **1** [+ *silbato*] to blow
2 (*Teat*) to hiss, boo, whistle at
3* (= *beber*) to drink, knock back*
4* (= *encantar*) to entrance, captivate; (= *volver loco*) to drive crazy • **esa chica le chifla** he's crazy about that girl • **me chiflan los helados** I just adore ice cream • **me chifla ese grupo** I think that group is fantastic*
(VI) **1** (*esp LAm*) to whistle, hiss
2 (*CAm, Méx*) [*ave, pájaro*] to sing
(VPR) **chiflarse*** **1** • **~se con** *o* **por algo/algn** to go crazy about sth/sb
2 • MODISMO: • **chiflárselas** (*CAm*) to snuff it*
chiflar[2] ▹ CONJUG 1a (VT) (*Téc*) [+ *cuero*] to pare, pare down
chiflato (SM) whistle
chifle (SM) **1** (= *silbido*) whistle
2 [*de ave*] call, bird call
3 (*CAm, Caribe*) (*Hist*) powder horn, powder flask
chiflete (SM) whistle
chiflido (SM) (*esp LAm*) **1** (= *silbido*) whistle
2 (= *siseo*) hiss
chiflón (SM) **1** (*LAm*) (= *viento*) (sudden) draught *o* (*EEUU*) draft (*of air*)
2 (*CAm, Caribe, Cono Sur*) [*de río*] rapids (*pl*), very strong current; (*CAm*) waterfall
3 (*Méx*) (= *caz*) flume, race
4 (*Méx*) (= *tobera*) nozzle
chigüín/ina* (SM/F) (*CAm*) kid*
chihuahua (SM) Chihuahua
chií (ADJ), (SMF) Shiite, Shiah
chiíta (ADJ), (SMF), **chiita** (ADJ), (SMF) Shiite, Shiah
chilaba (SF) jellaba(h)
chilacayote (SM) (*LAm*) gourd
chilango/a (*Méx*) (ADJ) of/from Mexico City
(SM/F) native/inhabitant of Mexico City

• **los ~s** the people of/from Mexico City
chilaquiles SMPL (*Méx*) *tortilla fried in thick chilli or green tomato sauce*
chilco SM (*Chile*) wild fuchsia
Chile SM Chile
chile SM **1** (*Bot, Culin*) chilli, chilli pepper ▸ **chile con carne** chilli con carne ▸ **chile morrón** (*Méx*) pepper
2 (*CAm**) (*tb* **chiles**) (= *broma*) joke
chilear* ▹ CONJUG 1a VI (*CAm*) to tell jokes
chilena SF overhead kick, scissors kick
chilenismo SM Chilenism (*word or phrase peculiar to Chile*)
chileno/a ADJ, SM/F Chilean
chilicote SM (*And, Cono Sur*) (*Entomología*) cricket
chilindrón SM • **al ~** cooked with tomatoes and peppers
chilla¹ SF (= *tabla*) thin board, weatherboard, clapboard (*EEUU*)
chilla² SF (*Chile*) (= *zorro*) small fox
chilla³ SF (*Méx*) **1** (= *pobreza*) poverty • **estar en la ~** to be very poor
2 (*Teat*) gods, gallery
chillador ADJ howling, screeching, screaming
chillante ADJ **1** (= *que chilla*) howling, screeching
2 = **chillón**
chillar ▹ CONJUG 1a VI **1** (= *gritar*) [*persona*] to shriek, scream; [*gato, animal salvaje*] to screech, yowl; [*ratón*] to squeak; [*cerdo*] to squeal; [*ave*] to screech, squawk; [*radio*] to blare • MODISMOS: • **el cochino chilló** (*Caribe, Méx*) he let the cat out of the bag*, he squealed* • **no ~** (*LAm*) to keep one's mouth shut, not say a word
2 (*Mec*) [*frenos*] to screech, squeal
3 [*colores*] to scream, jar, be loud
4 (*LAm*) (= *llorar*) to bawl
VPR **chillarse 1** (*LAm*) (= *quejarse*) to complain (**con** to), protest (**con** to)
2 (*And, Caribe, Méx**) (= *enojarse*) to get cross; (= *ofenderse*) to take offence, get into a huff
3 (*CAm*) (= *sofocarse*) to get embarrassed
chillería SF row, hubbub
chillido SM [*de persona*] shriek, scream; [*de gato, animal salvaje*] screech, yowling; [*de ratón*] squeak; [*de cerdo*] squeal; [*de ave*] screech, squawk
chillo SM **1** (*CAm*) (= *deuda*) debt
2 (*Caribe*) (= *muchedumbre*) rabble, mob
3 (*And*) (= *ira*) anger; (= *protesta*) loud protest
chillón¹/ona* ADJ **1** [*persona*] loud, shrill, noisy
2 [*sonido, tono*] shrill
3 [*color*] loud, garish, lurid • **un naranja ~** a loud *o* garish *o* lurid orange colour
4 (*LAm*) (= *quejumbroso*) moaning, whingeing*
SM/F (*LAm*) **1** (= *quejón*) moaner, whinger
2 (= *gritón*) loudmouth*
chillón² SM (*Téc*) small nail, panel pin, finishing nail (*EEUU*)
chillonamente ADV [*hablar, quejarse*] loudly, shrilly; [*vestir*] loudly
chilpayate* SM (*Méx*) kid*
chilposo ADJ (*Cono Sur*) ragged, tattered
chimal SM (*Méx*) dishevelled hair, mop of hair
chimar ▹ CONJUG 1a VT **1** (*CAm, Méx*) (= *molestar*) to annoy, bother
2 (*CAm*) (= *arañar*) to scratch
3 (*CAm**‡) (= *copular*) to fuck*‡, screw*‡
chimba¹ SF **1** (*And, Cono Sur*) (= *orilla*) opposite bank (of a river); (= *barrio*) suburb
2 (*And*) (= *vado*) ford
chimba² SF (*And*) (= *trenza*) pigtail
chimbar ▹ CONJUG 1a VT (*And, Cono Sur*) to ford
chimbe SM = **chimba¹**

chimbero ADJ (*Cono Sur*) **1** (*de chimba*) slum (*antes de s*)
2 (= *grosero*) coarse, rough
chimbo ADJ * **1** (*Col, Ven*) (= *gastado*) worn-out, wasted, old
2 (*Col*) (= *falso*) fake; [*cheque*] dud*
SM (*And*) piece of meat
chimenea SF **1** (*en el tejado*) chimney; [*de fábrica*] smokestack, chimney ▸ **chimenea de aire** air shaft ▸ **chimenea refrigeradora** cooling tower
2 (*dentro de casa*) fireplace, hearth • **encender la ~** to light the fire ▸ **chimenea francesa** fireplace
3 [*de barco*] funnel
4 (*Min*) shaft
5* (= *cabeza*) nut‡, noggin (*EEUU**), head • MODISMO: • **estar mal de la ~** to be wrong in the head*
chimentos* SMPL (*Arg, Uru*) gossip (*sing*)
chimichurri SM (*Cono Sur*) strong barbecue sauce
chimiscolear ▹ CONJUG 1a VI (*Méx*)
1 (= *chismear*) to go around looking for gossip
2 (= *curiosear*) to poke one's nose in*
chimiscolero/a SM/F (*Méx*) gossip, busybody
chimpancé SMF chimpanzee
chimpín SM (*And*) brandy, liquor
chimuelo ADJ (*LAm*) toothless
china¹ SF **1** (= *porcelana*) china, chinaware
2 (= *piedra*) pebble • MODISMOS: • **poner ~s** to put obstacles in the way • **tocarle a algn la ~**: • **nos tocó la ~ de ser niños en los cincuenta** we had the misfortune *o* bad luck to be children in the fifties • **te ha tocado la ~ de cuidar de los niños** you drew the short straw, you've got to look after the children
3‡ [*de droga*] lump, piece
4 (= *seda*) China silk
5 chinas (= *juego*) *game played with pebbles*
6 (*And*) (= *trompo*) spinning-top
7 (= *abanico*) fan, blower
8 (*Caribe, Méx*) (= *naranja*) orange; ▹ **chino**
china² SF (*And, Cono Sur*) (= *niñera*) nursemaid; ▹ **chino**
China SF China
chinaca‡ SF • **la ~** (*Méx*) the plebs*, the proles
chinado‡ ADJ crazy
chinaloa‡ SF (*Méx*) heroin, smack‡
chinampa SF (*Méx*) man-made island (*for cultivation on lakes*)
chinar‡ ▹ CONJUG 1a VT to carve up*, slash
chinarro SM large pebble, stone
chinazo SM blow from a stone • MODISMO: • **le tocó el ~*** he had bad luck
chinchada SF (*Cono Sur*) tug-of-war
chinchal SM (*Caribe*) [*de tabaco*] tobacco stall; (= *tienda*) small shop
chinchar* ▹ CONJUG 1a VT to pester, annoy • **me chincha tener que hacerlo** it annoys *o* bugs* me having to do it
VPR **chincharse** to get annoyed, get cross • **¡para que te chinches!** so there! • **¡y que se chinchen los demás!** and the others can go jump in the lake!* *o* can get stuffed!‡
chincharrero SM (*And*) small fishing boat
chinche SM o SF **1** bedbug • MODISMO: • **caer** *o* **morir como ~s** to die like flies
2 (= *chincheta*) drawing pin, thumbtack (*EEUU*)
3 (= *molestia*) nuisance
4 (*Cono Sur**) (= *rabieta*) pique, irritation
SMF (= *persona molesta*) nuisance; (*And, CAm*) naughty child
chincheta SF drawing pin, thumbtack (*EEUU*)
chinchetear ▹ CONJUG 1a VT to pin up

chinchibí SM (*And, CAm, Cono Sur*), **chinchibirra** SF (*Cono Sur*) ginger beer
chinchilla SF chinchilla
chinchín¹ SM **1** (= *música*) street music
2 (*Cono Sur*) (= *sonajero*) baby's rattle
chinchín² SM (*Caribe*) drizzle
chin-chin EXCL chin-chin, cheers
chinchón SM *aniseed spirit from the town of Chinchón*
chinchona SF quinine
chinchorrería SF **1** (= *pesadez*) fussiness
2 (= *chisme*) piece of gossip
chinchorrero ADJ **1** (= *quisquilloso*) fussy (*about details*)
2 (= *chismoso*) gossipy
chinchorro SM **1** (= *red*) dragnet
2 (= *chalupa*) rowing boat, rowboat (*EEUU*)
3 (*LAm*) (= *hamaca*) hammock; (= *vivienda*) poor tenement
4 (*Caribe*) (= *tienda*) little shop
chinchoso ADJ **1** full of bugs
2 = chinchorrero
3 (= *pesado*) tiresome
chinchudo* ADJ (*Cono Sur*) • **estar ~** to be in a grumpy mood
chinchulines SMPL (*Cono Sur*) (*Culin*) chitterlings, chitlins
chindar‡ ▹ CONJUG 1a VT to chuck out*
chinear ▹ CONJUG 1a VT (*CAm*) **1** (= *llevar en brazos*) to carry in one's arms
2 (= *mimar*) to spoil
VI (*Cono Sur*) *to have an affair with someone of mixed race*
chinel‡ SM guard
chinela SF **1** (= *zapatilla*) slipper
2 (= *chanclo*) clog
chinero¹ SM china cupboard
chinero² ADJ (*And, Cono Sur*) *fond of mixed-race girls*
chinesco ADJ Chinese; ▹ **sombra**
chinetero ADJ (*Cono Sur*) = **chinero²**
chinga* SF (*CAm*) **1** (= *colilla*) fag end, cigar stub
2 (= *posos*) dregs (*pl*)
3 (*CAm, Caribe*) (= *pequeña cantidad*) drop, small amount • **una ~ de agua** a drop of water
4 (*Caribe*) (= *borrachera*) drunkenness
5 (*Méx**) (= *paliza*) beating-up
chingada*‡ SF (*CAm, Méx*) **1** (= *acto sexual*) fuck*‡, screw*‡ • **hijo de la ~** bastard*‡, son of a bitch (*EEUU**‡)
2 (= *molestia*) bloody nuisance*‡
chingadazo* SM (*CAm, Méx*) bash*, punch
chingado*‡ ADJ (*CAm, Méx*) lousy*‡, bloody*‡ • **estar ~** to be cross, be upset
chingadura SF (*Cono Sur*) failure
chingana SF **1** (*And, Cono Sur*) dive*, tavern; [*de baile*] cheap dance hall
2 (*Cono Sur*) (= *fiesta*) wild party
chinganear ▹ CONJUG 1a VI (*And, Cono Sur*) to go out on the town, live it up*
chinganero/a (*And, Cono Sur*) ADJ fond of living it up*, wildly social
SM/F owner of a "chingana"
chingar ▹ CONJUG 1h VT **1** (= *beber con exceso*) to knock back*
2*‡ (= *copular*) to fuck*‡, screw*‡ • MODISMOS: • **no chingues** (*Méx*) don't mess me around* • **¡chinga tu madre!** (*Méx*) fuck off!*‡
3 (*CAm*) [+ *cola*] to dock, cut off
VI **1** to get pissed*‡
2 (*CAm, Méx**) to lark about*
VPR **chingarse*** **1** (= *emborracharse*) to get pissed*
2 (*CAm, Méx*) to fail • **la fiesta se chingó** the party was a disaster*
chingo ADJ **1** (*CAm*) [*vestido*] short; [*cuchillo*] blunt; [*animal*] tailless
2 (*CAm*) (= *desnudo*) naked, half-naked
3 (*Ven*) (= *pequeño*) small

4 (*Ven**) [*persona*] snub-nosed; [*nariz*] snub
5 (*Ven**) (= *loco*) • **estar ~ por algo** to be crazy about sth
SM **1** (*And*) (= *caballo*) colt
2 (*And, CAm*) (= *barca*) small boat
3 chingos (*CAm*) underclothes
4 (*Méx**) • **un ~ de algo** loads of sth*
chingón* SM (*Méx*) big shot*, boss
chingue SM (*Chile*) skunk
chinguear *etc* ▷ CONJUG 1a VT (*CAm*) = **chingar**
chinguirito SM **1** (*Caribe, Méx*) (= *licor*) rough liquor, firewater
2 (*And, Caribe*) (= *trago*) swig*
chinita SF (*And, Cono Sur*) (*Zool*) (= *mariquita*) ladybird, ladybug (*EEUU*)
chinito/a SM/F **1** (*Cono Sur*) (= *criado*) servant/maid
2 (*LAm*) (*apelativo*) dear, dearest
3 (*And, Caribe, Cono Sur*) (= *indio*) Indian boy/Indian girl
chino[1]/a ADJ Chinese • **barrio ~** red-light district
SM/F **1** (= *persona*) Chinese man/woman
• MODISMOS: • **quedar como un ~** (*Cono Sur**) to come off badly • **trabajar como un ~** (*esp Cono Sur**) to work like a dog • **es trabajo de ~s*** it's slave labour *o* (*EEUU*) labor
2 (*LAm*) (= *mestizo*) mestizo, person of mixed race (*of Amerindian and European parentage*); (= *indio*) Indian, Amerindian
3 (*LAm*) (= *criado*) servant/maid
SM **1** (*Ling*) Chinese • MODISMOS: • **hablar en ~*** to talk gobbledygook • **ni que hablara en ~** it was all Greek to me • **me suena a ~*** (*idioma*) it sounds like double Dutch to me; (*tema*) it's all Greek to me
2 (*Culin*) conical strainer
3 (*And, CAm*) (= *cerdo*) pig, hog (*EEUU*)
4 chinos (*Méx*) (= *rizos*) curls
5 (*Arg, CAm*) (= *rabia*) anger • **le salió el ~** he lost his temper • **tener un ~** to be angry; ▷ **china**
chino[2] SM (*Geol*) pebble, stone
chino... PREF Sino...
chinólogo/a SM/F expert in Chinese affairs, Sinologist; (*hum*) China watcher
chinorri‡ SF bird*, chick (*EEUU*‡)
chip SM **1** (*Inform*) chip • MODISMO: • **cambiarse el ~*** to get up to date, get with it ▸ **chip de memoria** memory chip ▸ **chip de silicio** silicon chip
2 (*Culin*) crisp, chip (*EEUU*)
3 (*Golf*) chip, chip shot
chipe* ADJ (*CAm*) **1** (= *enfermizo*) weak, sickly
2 (= *llorón*) whining, snivelling
SMF (*And, CAm, Méx*) baby of the family
chipear ▷ CONJUG 1a VT (*CAm*) to bother, pester
VI (*And, CAm*) to moan, whine
chipén†‡ ADJ • MODISMO: • **de ~** super*, smashing*
ADV marvellously, really well • **comer de ~** to have a super meal*
SF • **la ~** the truth
chipi ADJ, SMF = **chipe**
chipiar* ▷ CONJUG 1a VT (*CAm*) to bother, pester
chipichipi* SM (*CAm, Méx*) continuous drizzle
chipichusca* SF whore, hooker (*EEUU*‡)
chipil* ADJ (*Méx*) sad, gloomy
chipión* SM (*CAm*) telling-off*
chipirón SM baby squid
chipote SM (*Méx*) bump
chipotear ▷ CONJUG 1a VT (*CAm*) to slap
Chipre SF Cyprus
chipriota ADJ, SMF Cypriot
chiquear ▷ CONJUG 1a VT (*Méx*) **1** (= *mimar*) to spoil, indulge
2 (= *dar coba a*) to flatter, suck up to*
VPR **chiquearse 1** (*Méx*) (= *mimarse*) to be pampered
2 (*CAm*) (= *contonearse*) to swagger along, sway one's hips
chiqueo SM **1** (*Caribe, Méx*) (= *caricia*) caress
2 (*CAm*) (= *contoneo*) swagger
chiquero SM **1** (= *pocilga*) pigsty, pigpen (*EEUU*)
2 (*Taur*) bull pen
3 (*Cono Sur*) hen run
ADJ [*persona*] fond of kids
chiquilicuatro* SM, **chiquilicuatre*** SM nobody, insignificant person • **es un ~** he's a nobody
chiquilín* SM (*CAm, Cono Sur, Méx*) tiny tot, small boy
chiquillada SF **1** childish prank • **esos son ~s** that's kid's stuff*
2 (*esp LAm**) (= *niños*) kids* (*pl*), group of children
chiquillería SF kids* (*pl*)
chiquillo/a SM/F kid*, child
chiquirín SM (*CAm*) (*Entomología*) cricket
chiquirritín* ADJ, **chiquirrito*** ADJ small, tiny
chiquitear ▷ CONJUG 1a VI **1** (= *jugar*) to play like a child
2* (= *beber*) to tipple
chiquitín/ina* ADJ tiny
SM/F tiny tot
chiquito/a ADJ (*esp LAm**) small
• MODISMO: • **es ~ pero matón** he may be small but he's tough
SM/F* kid* • MODISMO: • **no andarse con chiquitas** not to beat about the bush
SM **1** (= *vaso*) small glass of wine
2 (*Cono Sur**) (= *pedacito*) • **un ~** a bit, a little
chiquitura SF **1** (*CAm*) (= *nimiedad*) small thing
2 (*CAm*) = **chiquillada**
chira SF **1** (*And*) (= *andrajo*) rag, tatter
2 (*CAm*) (= *llaga*) wound, sore
chirajos SMPL **1** (*CAm*) (= *trastos*) lumber, junk
2 (*And*) (= *andrajos*) rags, tatters
chirajoso ADJ (*CAm*) ragged, tattered
chircal SM (*And*) brickworks (*pl*), tileworks (*pl*)
chiri‡ SM joint‡
chiribita SF **1** (= *chispa*) spark • MODISMO: • **estar que echa ~s*** to be hopping mad
2 chiribitas* (= *destellos*) spots before the eyes • MODISMO: • **los ojos le hacían ~s** her eyes sparkled, her eyes lit up
3 (*Bot*) daisy
chiribitil SM **1** (= *desván*) attic, garret
2 (= *cuchitril*) cubbyhole
chiribito SM poker
chirigota SF **1*** (= *broma*) joke • **fue motivo de ~** it got a laugh, it caused some amusement • **estar de ~** to be joking • **tomarse algo a ~** to take sth as a joke *o* in good heart; (*pey*) to treat sth too lightly
2 (*en carnaval*) *group that sings humorous and satirical songs during Carnival*
chirigotero ADJ full of jokes, facetious
chirimbolo* SM **1** (= *trasto*) thingummyjig*, thingamajig (*EEUU**)
2 chirimbolos (= *bártulos*) things, gear* (*sing*)
chirimía SF shawm
chirimiri SM drizzle
chirimoya SF **1** (= *fruta*) custard apple, cherimoya (*EEUU*)
2‡ (= *cabeza*) nut*, noggin (*EEUU**), head
chirimoyo SM **1** (= *planta*) custard apple tree, cherimoya tree (*EEUU*)
2 (*Cono Sur**) dud cheque*
chirinada SF **1** (*Cono Sur*) (= *fracaso*) failure, disaster
2 = **chirinola**
chiringuito SM refreshment stall, refreshment stand
chirinola SF **1** (= *discusión*) heated discussion
2 (= *nimiedad*) trifle, bagatelle
3 (= *juego*) skittles (*pl*)
chiripa SF **1*** (= *casualidad*) fluke, stroke of luck • **de** *o* **por ~** by a fluke, by chance
2 (*Billar*) lucky break
chiripá SM (*Cono Sur*) Amerindian breeches (*pl*), *kind of blanket worn as trousers* • **gente de ~** country people, peasants
chiripero ADJ lucky, fluky
SM lucky sort
chirís* SMF (*CAm*) kid*, child
chirivía SF **1** (*Bot*) parsnip
2 (*Orn*) wagtail
chirivisco SM (*CAm*) firewood, kindling
chirla[1] SF mussel, clam
chirla[2]‡ SF armed hold-up
chirlata* SF whore, hooker (*EEUU*‡)
chirle ADJ **1** [*sopa*] insipid
2 (= *aburrido*) flat, dull, wishy-washy* • **poeta ~** mere versifier, third-rate poet
chirlo SM **1** (= *corte*) gash, slash (*in the face*)
2 (= *cicatriz*) scar, long scar
3 (*Arg**) (= *cachete*) slap
chirola* SF **1** (*CAm, Caribe*) (= *cárcel*) nick*, jail, can (*EEUU**)
2 (*Arg*) **chirolas** (= *monedas*) • **unas pocas ~s** a few pennies
chirona‡ SF nick*, jail, can (*EEUU**) • **estar en ~** to be in the nick* • **lo metieron en ~** he was banged up‡
chiros SMPL (*And*) rags, tatters
chiroso ADJ (*And, CAm*) ragged, tattered
chirota SF (*CAm*) tough woman
chirote* ADJ (*And*) daft*
chirri‡ SM joint‡
chirriado ADJ (*And*) (= *gracioso*) witty; (= *alegre*) merry, jovial
chirriante ADJ squeaky
chirriar ▷ CONJUG 1b VI **1** (*Zool*) [*grillo*] to chirp, sing; [*ave*] to screech, squawk
2 [*bisagra, puerta*] to creak, squeak
3 [*frenos*] to screech, squeal
4 (*And*) (= *tiritar*) (*de frío*) to shiver
chirrido SM **1** (*Zool*) [*de grillo*] chirp, chirping; [*de ave*] screech, screeching, squeak, squeaking
2 [*de bisagra, puerta*] creak, creaking, squeak, squeaking
3 [*de frenos*] screeching, squealing
chirrión SM **1** (= *carro*) tumbrel
2 (*And, CAm, Méx*) (= *látigo*) whip
3 (*CAm*) (= *sarta*) string, line
4 (*CAm*) (= *charla*) chat, conversation (*esp between lovers*)
chirrionar ▷ CONJUG 1a VT (*Méx*) to whip, lash
chirrisco ADJ **1** (*CAm, Caribe*) (= *diminuto*) very small, tiny • **viejo ~** dirty old man
2 (*Méx**) [*mujer*] flirtatious
chirucas SFPL *canvas mountain boots*
chirumen* SM nous*, savvy*
chirusa* SF (*Cono Sur*) (= *niña*) girl, kid*; (= *mujer*) poor woman
chis EXCL (*pidiendo silencio*) sh!; (*llamando a alguien*) hey!, psst!
chischís SM (*And, CAm, Caribe*) drizzle
chiscón SM hovel
chisgarabís* SM meddler, nosey-parker*
chisguete* SM swig*, drink
chisme SM **1*** (= *cosa*) thing • **¿y este ~ para qué sirve?** and what's this thing for? • **tiene la cartera llena de ~s** her bag is full of all sorts of things *o* bits and pieces • **un ~ para cortar metal** a thing *o* whatnot* *o* thingummyjig* for cutting metal with

2 (= *cotilleo*) • **se sabe todos los ~s** he knows all the gossip • **me contó un ~ sobre Juan** she told me the gossip about Juan

chismear ▹ CONJUG 1a VI to gossip, spread scandal

chismería SF, **chismerío** SM (*Cono Sur*) gossip, scandal

chismero/a ADJ, SM/F = **chismoso**

chismografía SF gossip

chismorrear ▹ CONJUG 1a VI = **chismear**

chismorreo SM = **chismería**

chismoso/a ADJ gossiping, scandalmongering
SM/F gossip

chispa SF **1** [*de luz, fuego*] spark • MODISMOS: • **echar ~s: está que echa ~s*** he's hopping mad* • **perder ~** to lose one's/its sparkle
2 (= *gota de lluvia*) drop • **caen ~s** it's just spitting
3 (= *pizca*) bit, tiny amount • **una ~ de café** a tiny drop of coffee • **una ~ de sal** a pinch of salt • **ni ~** not the least bit • **eso no tiene ni ~ de gracia** that's not in the least bit funny • **si tuviera una ~ de inteligencia** if he had an ounce of intelligence
4 (= *ingenio*) wit • **la historia tiene ~** the story's quite amusing • **Juan tiene ~** John's quite witty • MODISMO: • **es de ~ retardada*** he's slow on the uptake
5* (= *borrachera*) drunkenness • **coger** *o* **pillar una ~** to get sloshed* • **estar con** *o* **tener la ~** to be tight*
6 (*CAm, Méx*) • **dar ~** to work, be successful, yield results
7 (*And*) (= *rumor*) rumour, rumor (EEUU)
8 (*And*) (= *arma*) gun, weapon
ADJ INV **1** (= *borracho*) • **estar ~*** to be sloshed*
2 (*Méx*) (= *divertido*) funny, amusing
SM* (*tb* **chispas**) electrician

chisparse* ▹ CONJUG 1a VPR **1** (*And*) (= *emborracharse*) to get tight*
2 (*CAm, Méx*) (= *huir*) to run away, slip off

chispazo SM **1** spark • MODISMO: • **primeros ~s** first signs
2 = **chisme**

chispeante ADJ sparkling, scintillating

chispear ▹ CONJUG 1a VI **1** [*leña, fuego*] to throw out sparks
2 (= *destellar*) to sparkle, scintillate
3 (*Meteo*) to drizzle

chispero[1] ADJ (*And, Caribe*) gossiping, scandalmongering
SM (*CAm*) **1**†† (= *encendedor*) lighter
2 (*Aut*) spark plug, sparking plug

chispero[2]/a* ADJ of low-class Madrid
SM/F low-class inhabitant of Madrid

chispita* SF • **una ~ de vino** a drop of wine

chisporrotear ▹ CONJUG 1a VI [*aceite*] to spit; [*carne*] to sizzle; [*leña*] to crackle; [*fuego*] to throw out sparks

chisporroteo SM [*de aceite*] spitting, spluttering; [*de carne*] sizzling; [*de leña*] sparking, crackling

chisquero SM pocket lighter

chist EXCL = **chis**

chistada SF bad joke

chistar* ▹ CONJUG 1a VI • **nadie chistó** nobody said a word • **a ese no le chista nadie** you don't dare answer him back • **no ~** not to say a word • **sin ~** without a word

chiste SM joke • **caer en el ~** to get the joke, get it • **dar en el ~** to guess right • **hacer ~ de algo** • MODISMO: • **tomar algo a ~** to take sth as a joke • **tiene ~** it's funny • **no veo el ~** I don't get it ▸ **chiste verde** blue joke, dirty joke

chistera SF **1** (= *sombrero*) top hat ▸ **chistera de mago** magician's hat
2 (*Pesca*) fish basket
3 (*Dep*) *variety of pelota racket*

chistosamente ADV funnily, amusingly

chistoso/a ADJ funny, amusing
SM/F wit, funny person

chistu SM = **txistu**

chistulari SM = **txistulari**

chita[1] SF • MODISMO: • **a la ~ callando** (= *sin molestar*) unobtrusively; (= *con disimulo*) on the quiet, on the sly

chita[2] SF **1** (*Anat*) anklebone • MODISMOS: • **dar en la ~*** to hit the nail on the head • **no se me da una ~*** • **(no) me importa una ~*** I don't care two hoots (**de** about)
2 (= *juego*) *boys' game played with an anklebone*
3 (*Méx*) (= *saco*) net bag; (= *dinero*) money; (= *ahorros*) small amount of money saved, nest egg

chita[3]* EXCL (*Chile*) (= *caramba*) damn!*, Jesus!* • **¡por la ~!** damn it!*

chiticalla* SMF quiet sort

chiticallando ADV = **chita[1]**

chitón EXCL sh!

chiva SF **1** (*Zool*) kid; (= *cabra*) nanny goat • MODISMO: • **estar como una ~*** to be crazy
2 (*LAm*) (= *barba*) goatee, goatee beard
3 (*CAm*) (= *manta*) blanket, bedcover
• **~s** bedclothes
4 (*And, CAm*) (= *autobús*) bus; (= *coche*) car
5 (*Caribe, Cono Sur*) (= *niña*) naughty little girl; (*CAm, Cono Sur*) (= *marimacho*) mannish woman; (*And, Caribe, Cono Sur*) (= *vividora*) immoral woman
6 (*CAm, Cono Sur*) (= *rabieta*) rage, tantrum
7 (*Caribe*) (= *mochila*) knapsack
8 chivas (*Méx**) (= *trastos*) junk (*sing*)
9 (*Cono Sur**) fib, tall story • MODISMO: • **meter una ~** to cook up a story
10 (*Caribe**) (= *delator*) grass‡, informer
ADJ (*CAm**) (= *despabilado*) alert, sharp
EXCL (*CAm**) look out!, careful!

chivar* ▹ CONJUG 1a VT (*LAm*) (= *fastidiar*) to annoy, upset
VPR **chivarse 1** (= *dar un chivatazo*) to squeal* (**a, con** on), grass* (**a, de** on) • **se chivó a la policía** he squealed *o* grassed to the police* • **~se a la maestra** to tell the teacher
2 (*LAm*) to get annoyed

chivata‡ SF **1** (= *linterna*) torch
2 (= *pluma*) fountain-pen

chivatazo* SM tip-off • **dar el ~** to inform, give a tip-off

chivatear ▹ CONJUG 1a VI **1** = **chivar**
2 (*Cono Sur*) to shout
3 (*And, Cono Sur*) (= *saltar*) to jump about; (= *retozar*) to indulge in horse-play, have a noisy free-for-all
4 (*Caribe*) (= *impresionar*) to create a big impression
VPR **chivatearse** (*Caribe*) to get scared

chivato SM **1*** (= *soplón*) informer
2 (*Zool*) kid
3 (*Ven**) prominent person
4 (*LAm*) (= *niño*) child, kid*
5 (*And*) (= *pillo*) rascal, villain
6 (*And*) (= *aprendiz*) apprentice, mate
7 (*Cono Sur*) (= *aguardiente*) cheap liquor, firewater
8 (*Aut*) indicator, indicator light
9 (= *busca*) pager, beeper

chivearse* ▹ CONJUG 1a VPR (*CAm*) to get embarrassed

chivera SF (*And, CAm*) goatee, goatee beard

chivero SM **1** (*And*) (= *conductor*) bus driver
2 (*And*) (= *matón*) brawler
3 (*Caribe*) (= *intrigante*) intriguer

chiviroso* ADJ (*CAm*) outgoing, extrovert

chivitería SF (*Uru*) steakburger stall

chivito SM (*Uru*) steakburger ▸ **chivito canadiense** *meat, egg and salad sandwich*

chivo SM **1** (*Zool*) billy goat • MODISMO: • **esto huele a ~** (*Caribe, Cono Sur**) this smells fishy, there's something fishy about this* ▸ **chivo expiatorio** scapegoat
2 (*Cono Sur*) (= *rabia*) fit of anger • MODISMOS: • **comer ~** (*And, Caribe**) • **ponerse como ~** (*CAm, Caribe**) to be furious
3 (*CAm*) (= *dados*) dice; (= *juego*) game of dice
4 (*Caribe*) (= *estafa*) fraud; (= *intriga*) plot, intrigue; (= *acto de contrabando*) smuggling; (= *géneros*) contraband, smuggled goods (*pl*)
5 (*Méx*) (= *jornal*) day's wages; (= *anticipo*) advance; (= *soborno*) backhander*, sweetener*
6 (*Caribe*) (= *golpe*) punch, blow
7 (*And, CAm*) (= *niño*) naughty boy, scamp
8 (*CAm**) (= *guatemalteco*) Guatemalan
9 (*CAm*‡) (= *chulo*) pimp
10‡ (= *maricón*) poofter‡
ADJ (*CAm**) **1** (= *guatemalteco*) Guatemalan
2 • **andas bien ~** you're looking very smart

chivón/ona (*Caribe*) ADJ annoying, irritating
SM/F bore

chocante ADJ **1** (= *sorprendente*) startling, striking
2 (= *raro*) odd, strange • **lo ~ es que** the odd thing about it is that
3 (= *escandaloso*) shocking, scandalous
4 (*esp LAm*) (= *pesado*) tiresome; (= *desagradable*) offensive, unpleasant

chocantería SF (*LAm*) **1** (= *descaro*) impertinence
2 (= *chiste*) coarse joke

chocar ▹ CONJUG 1g VI **1** (= *colisionar*) [*coches, trenes*] to collide, crash; [*barcos*] to collide • **los dos coches ~on de frente** the two cars crashed head on *o* were in a head-on collision • **~ con** *o* **contra** [+ *vehículo*] to collide with, crash into; [+ *objeto*] to bang into; [+ *persona*] to bump into • **para no ~ contra el avión** to avoid crashing into *o* colliding with the plane • **el buque chocó con una mina** the ship struck a mine • **el balón chocó contra el poste** the ball hit the post • **chocaban unos contra otros por los pasillos** people bumped into each other in the corridors
2 (= *enfrentarse*) [*opiniones, personalidades*] to clash • **~ con** [+ *ideas, intereses*] to run counter to, be at odds with; [+ *obstáculos, dificultades*] to come up against, run into; [+ *personas*] to clash with • **esa propuesta choca con los intereses de EEUU** that proposal runs counter to *o* is at odds with American interests • **no choca con ninguna idea religiosa** it does not clash with any religion • **esa sería una de las mayores dificultades con las que ~ían en este proyecto** that would be one of the biggest problems they would come up against in this project • **por su carácter chocaba a menudo con sus compañeros de trabajo** he often clashed with his colleagues because of his confrontational nature
VT **1** (= *sorprender*) to shock • **¿no te choca la situación actual?** don't you find the current situation shocking? • **me chocó muchísimo lo que dijo** I was really shocked by what he said, what he said really shocked me • **me choca que no lo hayan hecho** I am surprised that they haven't done it • **no me choca que haya dimitido** I'm not surprised that he's resigned
2 (= *hacer chocar*) [+ *vasos*] to clink; [+ *manos*] to shake • **¡chócala!*** • **¡choca esos cinco!*** put it there!* • **~ la mano de algn** to shake hands with sb
3 (*Méx*) (= *asquear*) to disgust • **me choca su actitud** I find his attitude offensive
VPR **chocarse** (*Méx*) (*Aut*) to have a crash

chocarrear ▷ CONJUG 1a (VI) **1** (= *tontear*) to clown, act the fool
2 (= *contar chistes*) to tell rude jokes
chocarrería (SF) **1** (= *cualidad*) coarseness, vulgarity
2 • **una ~** a dirty joke
chocarrero (ADJ) coarse, vulgar
chocha (SF) (*tb* **chochaperdiz**) woodcock; ▷ **chocho³**
chochada* (SF) (*CAm*) (= *nimiedad*) triviality • **~s** bits and pieces
chochaperdiz (SF) woodcock
chochear ▷ CONJUG 1a (VI) **1** (*por la edad*) to dodder, be senile
2 (*por el cariño*) to be soft
chochecientos* (ADJ) umpteen*
chochera (SF) **1** (= *cualidad*) senility
2 (= *acción*) sentimental act
3 (= *adoración*) • **tener ~ por algn** to dote on sb, be crazy about sb
4 (*And, Cono Sur*) (= *preferido*) favourite, favorite (EEUU), pet
chochez (SF) = **chochera**
chochín (SM) **1** (*Orn*) wren
2‡ (= *novia*) bird‡, chick (EEUU‡)
chochita (SF) wren
chocho¹ (ADJ) **1** (= *senil*) doddering, senile
2 (= *embelesado*) soft, doting, sentimental • **estar ~ por algn** to dote on sb, be soft on sb
3 (*Cono Sur*) (= *contento*) delighted, pleased
(EXCL) (*CAm**) no kidding!*, really?
chocho² (SM) **1** (= *caramelo*) candy stick; **chochos** (= *golosinas*) sweets, candy (*sing*) (EEUU) ▸ **chochos de vieja** *lupin seeds sold at street stalls, fairs etc for eating*
2** (= *vulva*) pussy**
3* (= *lío*) rumpus*, shindy*
chocho³/a* (ADJ) (*CAm*) (= *nicaragüense*) Nicaraguan
(SM/F) **1** (= *drogadicto*) drug addict
2 (*CAm*) (= *nicaragüense*) Nicaraguan; ▷ **chocha**
chochoca‡ (SF) (*CAm*) nut‡, noggin (EEUU‡), head
chocholear ▷ CONJUG 1a (VT) (*And*) to spoil, pamper
chock (SM) (*And, Caribe*) (*Aut*) choke
choclo¹ (SM) **1** (= *zueco*) clog • MODISMO: • **meter el ~** (*Méx**) to put one's foot in it
2 (*Méx*) low-heeled shoe
choclo² (SM) **1** (*LAm*) (*Agr*) (= *planta*) maize, corn (EEUU); (= *mazorca*) corncob; (= *granos*) sweetcorn
2 choclos (*Cono Sur*) [*de niño*] (= *brazos*) children's arms; (= *piernas*) children's legs
3 (*And*) • **un ~ de algo** a group of sth, a lot of sth
4 (*Cono Sur*) (= *dificultad*) difficulty, trouble; (= *molestia*) annoyance; (= *carga*) burden, task
choclón (SM) (*Chile*) crowd
choco¹ (*Chile*) (SM) poodle
choco² (ADJ) (*And, Cono Sur*) (= *rojo*) dark red; (= *chocolate*) chocolate-coloured, chocolate-colored (EEUU); (= *moreno*) swarthy, dark
choco³ (ADJ) (*Chile*) **1** (= *manco*) one-armed
2 (= *cojo*) one-legged
3 (= *tuerto*) one-eyed
(SM) **1** (*Cono Sur*) (= *tocón*) stump (*of tree*)
2 (*And*) (= *sombrero*) top hat
3 (*Méx***) (= *vulva*) cunt**
choco⁴ (SM) (*Zool*) cuttlefish
choco⁵‡ (SM) (= *droga*) = **chocolate**
chocolatada (SF) *party or gathering at which one drinks hot chocolate*
chocolate (ADJ) (*LAm*) chocolate-coloured, chocolate-colored (EEUU)
(SM) **1** (*para comer*) chocolate; (*para beber*) drinking chocolate, cocoa ▸ **chocolate blanco** white chocolate ▸ **chocolate con leche** milk chocolate ▸ **chocolate negro** plain chocolate
2‡ (= *hachís*) hash*, pot* • **darle al ~** to be hooked on drugs
3 (*LAm*) (*hum*) blood • MODISMOS: • **dar a algn agua de su propio ~** (*Méx**) to give sb a taste of his own medicine • **sacar el ~ a algn** to make sb's nose bleed, give sb a bloody nose
chocolatera (SF) **1** chocolate pot
2* piece of junk
chocolatería (SF) **1** (= *fábrica*) chocolate factory
2 (= *tienda*) chocolate shop
chocolatero (ADJ) (= *de chocolate*) chocolate (*antes de s*) • **no soy muy ~** I'm not very fond of *o* keen on chocolate, I'm not a great one for chocolate *o* a great chocolate eater*
(SM) **1** (*And*) (*para chocolate*) chocolate pot
2 (*Caribe, Méx*) (= *viento*) strong northerly wind
chocolatina (SF) chocolate bar
chocolear ▷ CONJUG 1a (*And*) (VT) to dock, cut off the tail of
(VI) to get depressed
chófer (SMF), **chofer** (SMF) (*LAm*) **1** [*de coche*] driver
2 [*de autobús*] bus driver
cholada (SF) (*And*) (*pey*) *action typical of a "cholo"*
cholar‡ ▷ CONJUG 1a (VT) to nick‡, pinch*
cholería (SF) (*And*), **cholerío** (SM) (*And*) *group of "cholos"*
cholga (SF) (*Cono Sur*) mussel
cholla* (SF) **1** (= *cabeza*) nut*, noggin (EEUU*), head
2 (= *cerebro*) brains (*pl*)
3 (*CAm*) (= *herida*) wound, sore
4 (*And, CAm*) laziness, slowness
chollo* (SM) **1** (= *buena oportunidad*) snip*, bargain • **el piso es un ~ por ese precio** the apartment is a snip* *o* a bargain at that price • **¡qué ~ de trabajo!** what a cushy job!*
2 (= *amorío*) love affair
cholludo (ADJ) (*And, CAm*) lazy, slow
cholo/a (ADJ) **1** (*LAm*) half-breed*, mestizo
2 (*Chile*) (= *miedoso*) cowardly
(SM/F) **1** (*And, Cono Sur*) (= *mestizo*) dark-skinned person
2 (*CAm*) (= *indio*) half-civilized Indian
3 (*Cono Sur*) (= *indio*) Indian
4 (*LAm*) (= *peruano*) Peruvian
5 (*Cono Sur*) (= *cobarde*) coward
6 (*And*) (*apelativo*) darling, honey (EEUU)
chomba (SF) (*Chile*), **chompa** (SF) (*And, Cono Sur*) sweater, jumper
chompipe (SM) (*CAm*) turkey
chomskiano (ADJ) Chomskyan
chonchón (SM) (*Chile*) lamp
chonco (*CAm*) (ADJ) = **choco³**
(SM) stump
chongo (SM) **1** (*Méx*) (= *moño*) bun
2 (*Cono Sur*) (= *cuchillo*) blunt knife, worn-out knife
3 (*Caribe*) (= *caballo*) old horse
4 (*CAm, Méx*) **chongos** (= *trenzas*) pigtails
chonta (SF) (*And*) palm shoots (*pl*)
chontal (ADJ) **1** (*CAm*) (= *salvaje*) wild, uncivilized; (= *rebelde*) rebellious; (= *revoltoso*) unruly
2 (*And, CAm, Caribe*) (= *inculto*) uncivilized; (= *grosero*) rough, coarse
3 (*Caribe*) (= *de habla inculta*) rough-spoken
(SM) (*And*) peach palm
chop (SM) (*Chile*) **1** (= *vaso*) large beer glass
2 (= *cerveza*) draught beer, draft beer (EEUU)
chopa* (SF) jacket
chopazo* (SM) (*Cono Sur*), **chope** (SM) (*Cono Sur*) punch, bash*
chopera (SF) poplar grove
chopería (SF) (*Chile*) bar, beer bar
chopito (SM) baby squid
chopo (SM) **1** (*Bot*) black poplar ▸ **chopo de Italia, chopo lombardo** Lombardy poplar
2 (*Mil**) gun • MODISMO: • **cargar con el ~** to join up
chopp (SM) (*Chile*) = **chop**
choque (SM) **1** [*de vehículos*] crash, collision ▸ **choque frontal** head-on collision ▸ **choque múltiple** multiple crash, pile-up; ▷ **coche¹**
2 (= *desavenencia*) clash • **hubo un ~ entre ambos ministros** there was a clash between the two ministers • **un ~ de personalidades** a personality clash • **un ~ de culturas** a clash of cultures
3 (= *lucha*) clash • **hubo varios ~s entre la población civil** there were several clashes between civilians; ▷ **fuerza, tropa**
4 (*Dep*) (= *partido*) encounter, clash
5 (= *conmoción*) • **su muerte fue un ~ para ella** his death was a shock for her • **sufrí un ~ cultural al llegar a este país** I had a culture shock when I came to this country
6 (*Med*) shock
choquezuela (SF) kneecap
chorar‡ ▷ CONJUG 1a (VT) **1** [+ *casa*] to burgle, burglarize (EEUU)
2 [+ *objeto*] to rip off‡
chorbo/a‡ (SM/F) **1** (= *novio*) boyfriend; (= *novia*) girlfriend, bird*, chick (EEUU‡)
2 (= *tío*) bloke‡, guy*; (= *tía*) bird*, chick (*esp* EEUU‡)
chorcha (SF) **1** (*Méx*) (= *fiesta*) noisy party • **una ~ de amigos** a group of friends (*out for a good time*)
2 (*CAm*) (*Orn*) crest, comb
3 (*CAm*) (*Med*) goitre
4 (*CAm***) (= *clítoris*) clit‡, clitoris
chorchero (ADJ) (*Méx*) party-loving
chorchi‡ (SM) soldier
chorear* ▷ CONJUG 1a (VI) (*Chile*) (= *refunfuñar*) to grumble, complain • **estar choreado** to be miffed*, be upset
(VT) **1** (*Chile*) (= *hartar*) • **me chorea** it gets up my nose*
2 (*Cono Sur, Perú*) (= *robar*) to pinch*, nick*
choreo (SM) (*Chile*) complaint
chori* (SM) **1** (= *cuchillo*) chiv‡, knife
2 = **chorizo**
choricear* ▷ CONJUG 1a (VT) to rip off‡, lift*
choricería* (SF) crookedness*, corruption
choricero* (SM) = **chorizo**
choripán (SM) (*Arg, Uru*) sausage sandwich
chorizada‡ (SF) **1** (= *engaño*) swindle, con*
2 (= *robo*) theft
chorizar* ▷ CONJUG 1f (VT) (= *robar*) to nick* • **me han chorizado la bici** they've nicked my bike*
chorizo (SM) **1** (*Culin*) *hard pork sausage*
2 (*en circo*) balancing pole
3* (= *ratero*) small-time crook*; (= *maleante*) criminal; (= *carterista*) pickpocket
4 (*And, Cono Sur*) (*Culin*) • **bife de ~** rump steak
5 (*And, Cono Sur*) (*Arquit*) *mixture of clay and straw used in plastering*
6 (*And**) (= *idiota*) idiot
7 (*Caribe*) (= *mulato*) mulatto**
chorlito (SM), **chorlitejo** (SM) (*Orn*) plover; ▷ **cabeza**
chorlo/a (SMF) (*And, CAm, Caribe*) great-great-grandchild
choro¹‡ (SM) **1** (= *persona*) thief, burglar
2 (*Ling*) thieves' slang
choro² (SM) (*And, Cono Sur*) (*Zool*) mussel
chorote (SM) **1** (= *bebida*) (*Méx, Ven*) drinking chocolate (*with brown sugar*); (*And*) thick drinking chocolate
2 (*Caribe*) (= *bebida espesa*) *any thick drink*; (= *bebida aguada*) watery drink; (= *café*) coffee
3 (*And*) (= *chocolatera*) unglazed chocolate pot
chorra (SF) **1‡** (= *suerte*) luck • **¡qué ~ tiene!**

how jammy can you get!* • de ~ by chance
2 (Cono Sur) underworld slang
3✱✱ (= pene) prick✱✱
SMF ‡ (= idiota) fool, idiot

chorrada SF 1 [de líquido] extra drop
• MODISMO: • dar algo con ~ to give sth and a bit extra
2* (= objeto insignificante) knick-knack • le regalaremos cualquier ~ we'll give her some little thing
3* (= tontería) • la película es una ~ the film is nonsense* • no digas ~s stop talking drivel
4‡ [de orina] • echar la ~ to have a piss✱✱

chorrar‡ ▷ CONJUG 1a VT = chorar

chorrear ▷ CONJUG 1a VI 1 (= salir a chorros) to gush (out), spout • la sangre le chorreaba por la frente blood was gushing (out) o spouting from his forehead • estar chorreando de sudor to be dripping with sweat
2 (= gotear) to drip • la ropa chorrea todavía the clothes are still dripping water o wringing wet
3 [dinero] to trickle in, come in in dribs and drabs • chorrean todavía las solicitudes applications are still trickling in o coming in in dribs and drabs
VT 1 (Mil*) (= regañar) to tick off*, dress down*
2 (= verter) to pour
3 (Cono Sur) (= robar) to pinch*
4 (And) (= mojar) to soak
VPR chorrearse • ~se algo* to pinch sth

chorreo SM 1 (= flujo) gushing, spouting
2 (= goteo) dripping
3 [de dinero] trickle (de on)
4* (= reprimenda) ticking-off*, dressing-down*
5 ▸ chorreo mental‡ nonsense, rubbish, garbage (EEUU)

chorreón SM 1 (= cascada) cascade
2 (= de aceite, vinagre) ▷ chorretón

chorrera SF 1 (= pitorro) spout
2 chorreras (Cos) frill (sing); ▷ jamón
3 (Méx) (= montón) stream, string • una ~ de algo a stream o string of sth
4 (Caribe*) (= regañina) ticking-off*, dressing-down*

chorrero‡ ADJ jammy‡, lucky

chorretada SF 1 (= chorro) squirt, jet
2 = chorrada

chorretón SM 1 (= chorro) • echa un buen ~ de aceite put plenty of oil on it • un ~ de agua de colonia a splash of cologne
2 (= mancha) dribble

chorrillo SM steady trickle

chorro SM 1 [de líquido] jet, stream • salía un buen ~ de agua del grifo there was a strong flow of water from the tap • se añade un chorrito de leche add a drop of milk • beber a ~ to drink without touching the bottle
2 (Téc) jet, blast • un avión con propulsión a ~ jet-propelled plane • motor a ~ jet engine ▸ chorro de arena sandblast ▸ chorro de vapor steam jet
3 (= montón) stream, string • un ~ de insultos a stream o string of insults • un ~ de palabras a torrent of words • un ~ de voz a verbal blast, a really loud voice • MODISMO: • a ~s in plenty, in abundance • llover a ~s to pour (down) • salir a ~s to gush forth, come spurting out • hablar a ~s to talk nineteen to the dozen
4‡ (= suerte) jam‡, luck • ¡qué ~ tiene! he's so jammy!‡
5 (Cono Sur*) (= ladrón) thief, pickpocket
6 (And) [de látigo] lash
7 (CAm) (= grifo) tap, faucet (EEUU)
8 (Caribe*) (= reprimenda) ticking-off*, dressing-down*

chorvo/a‡ SM/F = chorbo

chota SF • MODISMO: • estar como una ~* to be crazy o mad*

chotacabras SM INV nightjar, goatsucker (EEUU)

chotear* ▷ CONJUG 1a VT 1 (LAm) (= burlarse de) to make fun of
2 (And) (= mimar) to spoil, pamper
3 (CAm) [+ sospechoso] to shadow, tail
VPR chotearse 1 (= bromear) to joke (de about)
2 (= confesar) to cough‡, inform

choteo* SM kidding*, joking • estar de ~ to be kidding*

chotis SM INV traditional dance of Madrid
• MODISMO: • ser más agarrado que un ~* to be tight-fisted

choto ADJ 1 (CAm) (= abundante) abundant, plentiful
2 (= de poco valor) crummy‡
3 (= viejo) clapped-out*
SM 1 (Zool) (= cabrito) kid; (= ternero) calf
• MODISMO: • ser un viejo ~ to be a stupid old twit*
2 (Cono Sur‡) (= pene) prick✱✱

chotuno ADJ [cabrito, ternero] sucking, very young; [cordero] weakly • MODISMO: • oler a ~ to smell bad

chova SF crow, rook ▸ chova piquirroja chough

chovinismo etc SM = chauvinismo etc

chow-chow ['tʃautʃau] SM (PL: chow-chow) chow

choza SF hut, shack

chozno/a SM/F great-great-great-grandchild

christmas ['krismas] SF, **chrisma** ['krisma] SM (PL: christmas ['krismas]) Christmas card

chubasco SM 1 (Meteo) heavy shower ▸ chubasco de nieve brief snowstorm
2 (= contratiempo) setback • aguantar el ~ to weather the storm

chubascoso ADJ squally, stormy

chubasquero SM 1 (= impermeable) cagoule, foul-weather gear (EEUU)
2‡ (hum) French letter

chucán ADJ (CAm) 1 (= gracioso) buffoonish
2 (= grosero) coarse, rude

chúcaro ADJ (LAm) 1 (= salvaje) wild, untamed
2 (= tímido) shy

chucear ▷ CONJUG 1a VT (LAm) to prick, goad

chucha SF 1 (Zool) bitch
2* (apelativo) sweetheart
3 (And) (Zool) opossum
4 (And) (= olor) B.O.
5 (And) (= juego) hide-and-seek
6 (And, Cono Sur✱✱) (= vulva) cunt✱✱
7† (= peseta) peseta

chuchada SF (CAm) trick, swindle

chuche* SF sweet, candy (EEUU)

chuchear[1] ▷ CONJUG 1a VI to hunt, trap, fowl

chuchear[2] ▷ CONJUG 1a VI = cuchichear

chuchería SF 1 (= golosina) sweet, candy (EEUU)
2 (= bocada) titbit
3 (= adorno) trinket

chuchito SM = chucho

chucho ADJ 1 (CAm*) (= tacaño) mean, stingy*
2 (And) [fruta] soft, watery; [persona] wrinkled
3 (Méx) (chismoso) gossipy
SM 1 (= perro callejero) mongrel • ¡chucho! down boy!
2 (= pastel) custard-filled doughnut
3* (= novio) sweetheart
4 (Caribe) (Ferro) switch
5 (Caribe) (= látigo) rawhide whip
6 (Cono Sur) (= cárcel) jail
7 (LAm) (= escalofrío) shakes (pl), shivers (pl); (= fiebre) fever • entrarle a algn el ~* to get the jitters*
8 (CAm*) (= persona ostentosa) spiv*
9 (LAm‡) (= canuto) joint*, reefer*
10 (And, CAm, Méx) (Culin) tamale

chuchoca* SF (Cono Sur) • MODISMO: • estar en la ~ to be in the thick of it, be where the action is

chuchumeca* SF (And, Cono Sur) whore, tart*, hooker (EEUU*)

chuchumeco* SM 1 (Méx) (= enano) dwarf, runt
2 (= tacaño) mean person, skinflint
3 (Cono Sur) (= enfermizo) sickly person; (= derrochador) wastrel
4 (And) (= viejo) old dodderer
5 (And, Caribe*) (= encopetado) toff*, dude (EEUU*)
6 (Caribe*) (= idiota) idiot

chuchurrío* ADJ 1 [flor, planta] wilted
2 [persona] down

chuco ADJ 1 (And, CAm, Méx) [pescado] high, off
2 (CAm) (= asqueroso) disgusting, filthy

chucrú SM, **chucrut** SM, **chucruta** SF sauerkraut

chueca SF 1 (Bot) stump
2 (Anat) round head of a bone
3 (= broma) practical joke, prank • gastar una ~ a algn to play a joke on sb

chueco ADJ (LAm) 1 (= torcido) crooked, bent
• un negocio ~ a crooked deal*
2 (= patizambo) bandy-legged
3 (And, Cono Sur) (= patituerto) pigeon-toed
4 (Méx) (= manco) one-armed; (= con una sola pierna) one-legged
5 (Méx) (= de mala vida) loose-living; (= sospechoso) suspicious

chufa SF 1 (= tubérculo) tiger nut • horchata de ~ drink made from tiger nuts
2* (= puñetazo) bash*, punch
3†* (= peseta) peseta

chufeta SF = chufleta

chufla SF joke, merry quip • a ~ jokingly
• tomar algo a ~ to take sth as a joke

chuflarse ▷ CONJUG 1a VPR to joke, make jokes

chuflay SM (Cono Sur) (= bebida) punch

chufleta SF 1 (= broma) joke
2 (= mofa) taunt

chufletear ▷ CONJUG 1a VI 1 (= bromear) to joke
2 (= mofarse) to jeer

chuico SM (Chile) demijohn

chula SF 1 (= madrileña) woman from the back streets (of Madrid), low-class woman, coarse woman
2 (= charra) loud wench, flashy female, brassy girl
3 (LAm) (= novia) girlfriend

chulada SF 1 (= grosería) coarse thing
2 (= truco) mean trick
3* • ¡qué ~ de moto! wow! what a fantastic bike!*
4* = chulería

chulángano†‡ SM roughneck‡, tough*

chulapa SF Madrid girl in traditional dress

chulear* ▷ CONJUG 1a VT 1 (= reírse de) to make fun of
2 (= afanar) to pinch*, swipe*
3 [+ prostitutas] to live off

chulería SF 1 (= encanto) natural charm, winning ways
2 (= vulgaridad) commonness, vulgarity
3 (= bravuconada) • déjate de ~s conmigo don't get all cocky with me*
4* (= cosa bonita) • esa moto es una ~ that bike is really nice • me he comprado una ~

de camiseta I've bought a really nice *o* gorgeous T-shirt

chulesco ADJ = chulo

chuleta SF **1** [*de carne*] chop, cutlet ▸ **chuleta de cerdo** pork chop ▸ **chuleta de cordero** lamb chop ▸ **chuleta de ternera** veal chop, veal cutlet
2 (*Cos*) insert
3 (*Téc*) filling
4* (= *golpe*) punch, bash*
5 (*Escol**) crib*, trot (*EEUU*)
6 chuletas* (= *patillas*) sideburns, sideboards
7 (*Golf**) divot
SM* (= *fanfarrón*) show-off*; (= *persona agresiva*) pushy person*; (= *fresco*) cheeky individual*
ADJ INV cheeky*, smart (*EEUU**), sassy (*EEUU**)

chuletada SF barbecue, cookout (*EEUU*) (*mainly consisting of chops*)

chuletón SM large steak, T-bone steak

chulillo SM (*And*) tradesman's assistant

chulleco ADJ (*Cono Sur*) twisted, crooked

chullo SM (*Perú*) woollen cap

chulo ADJ* **1** (= *arrogante*) cocky* • **vino uno muy ~ y me insultó** this guy comes up to me all cocky *o* bold as brass and insulted me* • **una mujer se abanicaba, muy chula ella, en la ventana** a woman was fanning herself in the window, bold as brass *o* as brazen as you like • **ponerse ~: se puso en plan ~** he got all cocky* • **no te pongas ~ conmigo** don't get cocky with me*
2 (= *bonito*) • **¡qué vestido más ~!** what a lovely dress! • **¡qué ~ me ha quedado el dibujo!** my drawing looks great! • **chica, estás chulísima** (*LAm*) you look gorgeous
ADV (*CAm, Méx**) well • **jugar ~** to play well
SMF (*Hist*) *typical working-class person from Madrid*
SM **1*** (*tb* **chulo putas**) pimp
2 (*Col**) (= *buitre*) vulture, buzzard (*EEUU*)
3 (*Taur*) *bullfighter's assistant*

chulón ADJ (*CAm*) naked

chuma SF (*And, Cono Sur*) drunkenness

chumacera SF **1** (*Mec*) ball bearing
2 (*Náut*) rowlock, oarlock (*EEUU*)

chumado* ADJ (*Arg*) drunk, tight*

chumarse* ▸ CONJUG 1a VPR (*Arg*) to get drunk

chumbar ▸ CONJUG 1a VT **1** (*Cono Sur*) [*perro*] to attack, go for • **¡chúmbale!** at him, boy!
2 (*And*) (= *fusilar*) to shoot
3 (*And*) [+ *bebé*] to swaddle

chumbe SM (*LAm*) sash

chumbera SF prickly pear

chumbo SM **1** (*Bot*) prickly pear
2 (*And***) (= *pene*) prick**

chumeco SM (*CAm*) apprentice

chuminada* SF **1** (= *tontería*) silly thing, piece of nonsense
2 (= *detalle*) petty detail

chumino** SM cunt**

chumpa SF (*CAm*) jacket

chumpi SM (*And*) = **chumbe**

chumpipe SM (*CAm*) turkey

chumpipear ▸ CONJUG 1a VI (*CAm*) to wander about

chunche* SM (*CAm*) whatsit*, thingumabob*

chuncho/a (*Perú*) (*pey*) ADJ **1** (= *salvaje*) savage, rustic
2 (= *inculto*) uncivilized
3 (= *tímido*) bashful, shy
SM/F savage Indian

chunco ADJ (*And, CAm*) = **choco**[3]

chuneco/a* (*CAm*) ADJ, SM/F Jamaican

chunga* SF fun • **contar ~s** to crack jokes* • **decir algo de ~** to say sth jokingly *o* in fun • **estar de ~** to be in a joking mood • **en plan de ~** for a laugh

chungarse* ▸ CONJUG 1h VPR = **chunguearse**

chungo‡ ADJ **1** [*lavadora, televisor*] bust*; [*fruta*] rotten
2 (= *desagradable*) nasty
3 (= *feo*) ugly, hideous
4 (= *con mala pinta*) dodgy*, dicey*
5 (= *enfermo*) • **he estado un poco ~** I've been feeling a bit rop(e)y *o* dodgy*

chungón/ona* SM/F joker, tease

chunguearse* ▸ CONJUG 1a VPR to crack jokes* • **~ de algn** to make fun of sb

chuño SM (*LAm*) potato starch

chupa[1] SF • MODISMO: • **poner a algn como ~ de dómine** to give sb a real ticking off* • **en la prensa le pusieron como ~ de dómine** they gave him a tremendous pasting in the press*

chupa[2]* SF (= *chaqueta*) leather jacket

chupa[3] SF (*LAm*) (= *borrachera*) drunkenness; (= *reunión*) drinking session

chupachupa‡ SMF sucker‡

chupacirios* SMF INV holy Willie*

chupada SF **1** [*de biberón, caramelo*] suck
2 (*en pipa*) pull, puff • **dar ~s a la pipa** to puff away at one's pipe • MODISMO: • **se cree la última ~ del mate** (*Cono Sur**) he thinks he's the cat's pyjamas *o* the bee's knees*

chupadero* SM (*Arg*) (*1975-81*) *secret military prison*

chupado/a ADJ **1** (= *flaco*) gaunt, skinny* • **está ~ de cara** his face looks *o* he looks very gaunt, he looks very hollow-cheeked
2 [*falda*] tight
3 • **estar ~ de frío** to be pinched with cold
4 • **estar ~*** (= *borracho*) to be drunk
5 • **está ~*** (= *fácil*) it's dead easy*
SM/F (*Cono Sur**) (= *desaparecido*) missing person

chupador SM **1** teething ring
2 (*LAm**) (= *borracho*) drunkard

chupaflor SM (*LAm*) hummingbird

chupagasolina* ADJ INV gas-guzzling*, heavy on petrol
SM INV gas-guzzler*

chupalla SF (*Cono Sur, Méx*) straw hat

chupamangas‡ SM INV (*And, Cono Sur*), **chupamedias‡** SM INV (*And, Cono Sur*) creep‡, bootlicker*, brown-nose (*EEUU‡*)

chupamirto SM (*Caribe, Méx*) hummingbird

chupandina* SF (*Cono Sur*) boozy party*

chupar ▸ CONJUG 1a VT **1** (= *succionar*) [+ *biberón, caramelo, bolígrafo*] to suck; [+ *pipa*] to puff at, puff on • **el trabajo le está chupando la salud** his work is undermining his health • **chupó lo que pudo mientras estuvo en la organización** he milked the organization for all he could while he was there • **le chupan el dinero** they're milking him dry • MODISMOS: • **~ cámara*** to get as much (media) exposure as possible • **~ el balón*** (*Ftbl*) to hog the ball • **~ la sangre a algn** to bleed sb dry, take sb for everything they've got
2* (= *aguantar*) to put up with, take • MODISMO: • **~ banquillo** (*Ftbl*) to sit on the substitutes' bench
3 [*planta*] [+ *agua*] to absorb, take in, take up
4* (= *beber*) to drink, knock back*
5 • **chupársela a algn**** to suck sb off**
VI to suck • MODISMO: • **~ del bote*** to line one's pocket
VPR **chuparse 1** (= *succionar*) • **~se el dedo** (*lit*) to suck one's finger • **¿tú te crees que me chupo el dedo?** (*fig*) do you think I was born yesterday?, do you take me for a mug?* • MODISMO: • **~se los dedos***: • **la paella estaba para ~se los dedos** the paella was absolutely delicious • **hacen unas hamburguesas para ~se los dedos** their hamburgers are to die for *o* are finger-licking good (*hum*)
2* (= *aguantar*) • **nos chupamos toda la conferencia de pie** we had to go through the whole of the lecture standing • **tuve que ~me cuatro horas de tren** I had to sit in a train for four hours • **~se un insulto** (*LAm*) to swallow an insult • MODISMO: • **¡chúpate esa!** put that in your pipe and smoke it!*
3 (*Med*) to waste away

chupasangres* SM INV (*Cono Sur*) (*pey*) bloodsucker

chupatintas* SM INV (*pey*) penpusher, pencil pusher (*EEUU*)

chupe SM **1** (*And, Cono Sur*) (*Culin*) (= *guiso*) stew
2 (*Cono Sur*) (= *tapa*) snack

chupeta SF (*Náut*) roundhouse

chupete SM **1** [*de niño*] dummy, pacifier (*EEUU*)
2 (*LAm*) (= *pirulí*) lollipop
3 (*LAm*) (= *chupada*) suck
4 • MODISMO: • **de ~** delicious

chupetear ▸ CONJUG 1a VT [+ *polo*] to suck; [+ *helado*] to lick
VI to suck, suck slowly

chupeteo SM sucking

chupetín SM (*Arg, Uru*) lollipop

chupetón* SM lovebite, hickey (*EEUU**)

chupi* ADJ super*, brilliant*
ADV • **pasarlo ~** to have a great time*

chupín SM (*Arg*) fish and potato stew

chupinazo SM **1** (= *disparo*) loud bang
2 (*Dep*) hard kick, fierce shot

chupinudo* ADJ = **chupi**

chupito* SM [*de bebida alcohólica*] shot*

chupo SM **1** (*LAm*) (*Med*) boil
2 (*And*) (= *biberón*) baby's bottle

chupón/ona SM/F* (= *parásito*) sponger*
SM **1** (*Bot*) sucker
2 (= *piruleta*) lollipop ▸ **chupón de caramelo** toffee apple
3 (*LAm*) (= *chupete*) dummy, pacifier (*EEUU*); (= *biberón*) baby's bottle
4 (*Méx*) teat
5 (*And, Caribe*) [*de pipa*] puff, pull
6 (*And*) boil

chupóptero* SM bloodsucker

churdón SM (= *fruta*) raspberry; (= *planta*) raspberry cane; (= *jarabe*) raspberry syrup, raspberry purée

churi‡ SM chiv‡, knife

churo[1] ADJ (*And, Cono Sur*) handsome, attractive

churo[2] SM **1** (*And*) (*Mús*) *coiled wind instrument*
2 (*And*) (= *escalera*) spiral staircase
3 (*And*) (= *rizo*) curl
4 (*And*) (= *cárcel*) nick‡, jail, can (*EEUU**)

churra[1] SF (*And, Cono Sur*) girl

churra[2]* SF (= *suerte*) luck, jam‡

churrasco SM **1** (= *filete a la parrilla*) barbecued meat
2 (*Cono Sur*) (= *filete*) steak

churrasquear ▸ CONJUG 1a VI (*Cono Sur*) to eat steak

churrasquería SF barbecue stall

churre[1] SF thick grease, grime

churre[2] SM (*And*) bloke‡, guy*

churrería SF shop or stall selling churros

churrero/a ADJ‡ lucky, jammy‡
SM/F *person who makes and sells "churros"*

churrete SM dirty mark (*esp on a child's face*)

churretear ▸ CONJUG 1a VT (*LAm*) to stain, dirty

churretón SM dirty mark (*esp on a child's face*)

churria SF **1** (*Méx, Col*) stain
2 churrias (*And, CAm, Caribe**) (= *diarrea*)

runs*, trots*
churriento ADJ 1 (= *sucio*) filthy
2 (*LAm*) (= *suelto*) loose
churrigueresco ADJ 1 (*Arquit*) churrigueresque
2 (= *excesivamente adornado*) excessively ornate
churro ADJ [*lana*] coarse
SM 1 (*Culin*) *flour fritter eaten with coffee or hot chocolate* • MODISMO: • **venderse como ~s** to sell like hot cakes
2* (= *chapuza*) botch, mess • **el dibujo ha salido hecho un ~** the sketch came out all wrong
3* (= *suerte*) fluke
4 (*And, Cono Sur**) attractive person, dish*
5** (= *pene*) prick**
6 (*Méx**) bad film

CHURROS
Churros, long fritters made with flour and water, are popular in much of Spain and are often eaten with thick hot chocolate either for breakfast or as a snack. In Madrid, they eat a thicker variety of **churro** called a **porra**.

churrullero ADJ talkative, gossipy
churruscar ▷ CONJUG 1g VT to fry till crisp
VI to sizzle
VPR **churruscarse** to burn
churrusco[1] SM burnt toast
churrusco[2] ADJ (*And, CAm*) [*pelo*] kinky, curly
churumbel* SM 1 (= *niño*) kid*
2 (= *tipo*) bloke*, guy*
churumbela SF 1 (*Mús*) flageolet
2 (*CAm*) maté cup
3 (*And*) (= *pipa*) short-stemmed pipe
4 (*And*) (= *preocupación*) worry, care
churumen* SM nous*, savvy*
chus EXCL • MODISMO: • **no decir ~ ni mus*** not to say a word
chuscada SF witty remark, joke
chusco[1] ADJ 1 (= *gracioso*) funny, droll
2 (*And*) [*perro*] mongrel; [*caballo*] ordinary; [*persona*] coarse, ill-mannered
chusco[2] SM • **un ~ de pan** a hunk of bread
chuse SM (*And*) blanket
chusma SF rabble, riffraff
chusmaje SM (*LAm*) = **chusma**
chuspa SF (*LAm*) bag, pouch
chusquero* SM (*Mil*) ranker
chut SM 1 (*Dep*) shot (*at goal*)
2‡ (= *de droga*) shot*, fix‡
chuta[1]‡ SF 1 (= *jeringuilla*) needle
2 = **chut**
chuta[2]‡ EXCL • **¡chuta!** (*Cono Sur*) good God!, good heavens!
chutador(a) SM/F (*Dep*) shooter
chutar ▷ CONJUG 1a VI 1 (*Dep*) to shoot (*at goal*)
2 • **está que chuta*** [*persona*] he's hopping mad*; [*comida*] it's scalding hot
3* (= *ir bien*) to go well • **dale diez euros y va que chuta** give him ten euros and he'll be more than happy
VPR **chutarse*** [+ *heroína*] to shoot up*
chutazo* SM fierce drive, fierce shot (*at goal*)
chute SM 1 (*Dep*) shot (*at goal*)
2* [*de droga*] shot*, fix*
chuzar ▷ CONJUG 1f VT (*And*) to prick
chuzo SM 1 (= *bastón*) spiked stick
2 (= *aguijón*) prick, goad; (*CAm*) [*de alacrán*] sting • MODISMOS: • **caer ~s de punta*** to rain cats and dogs, pelt down* • **echar ~s*** to brag
3 (*Mil, Hist*) pike
4 (*And*) shoe
5 (*Cono Sur*) (= *zapapico*) pickaxe, pickax (*EEUU*)
6 (*Caribe, Cono Sur*) (= *látigo*) whip
7 (*CAm*) (= *pico*) beak
8** (= *pene*) prick**
ADJ (*CAm**) [*pelo*] lank
chuzón ADJ 1 (= *astuto*) wily
2 (= *ingenioso*) witty, amusing
chuzonada SF piece of tomfoolery, piece of buffoonery
CI SM ABR (= **coeficiente de inteligencia** *o* **intelectual**) IQ
SF ABR (*LAm*) (= **cédula de identidad**) ID
CIA SF ABR (*Estados Unidos*) (= **Central Intelligence Agency**) CIA
cía SF hip bone
Cía. ABR (= **Compañía**) Co
cianhídrico ADJ hydrocyanic
cianotipia SF, **cianotipo** SM blueprint
cianuro SM cyanide ▸ **cianuro potásico** potassium cyanide
ciar ▷ CONJUG 1c VI 1 (= *ir hacia atrás*) to go backwards, back up; (*Náut*) to go astern
2 (= *cambiar de opinión*) to back down
ciática SF sciatica
ciático ADJ sciatic
cíber SM (= **cibercafé**) internet café
ciber... PREF cyber...
ciberacoso SM cyberbullying
ciberamenaza SF cyberthreat
ciberataque SM cyberattack
cibercafé SM internet café
cibercultura SF cyberculture
ciberdelito SM cybercrime
ciberespacial ADJ cyberspace (*antes de s*)
ciberespacio SM cyberspace
ciberespiar VT to cyberspy on
VI to cyberspy
ciberespionaje SM cyberspying, cyberespionage
cibernauta SMF cybernaut, internet user, web surfer
cibernética SF cybernetics (*sing*)
cibernético ADJ cybernetic
ciberokupa SM cybersquatter
ciberpunk SM cyberpunk
ciberseguridad SF information security, online security, cybersecurity
cibersexo SM cybersex
ciberterrorismo SM cyberterrorism
ciberterrorista SMF cyberterrorist
cibertienda SF online shop (*esp Brit*), online store (*esp EEUU*)
cicatear ▷ CONJUG 1a VI to be stingy, be mean
cicatería SF stinginess, meanness
cicatero/a ADJ stingy, mean
SM/F miser, skinflint
cicatriz SF 1 [*de herida*] scar
2 (= *mal recuerdo*) scar
cicatrización SF healing, cicatrization (*frm*)
cicatrizar ▷ CONJUG 1f VT to heal
VPR **cicatrizarse** to heal, heal up, form a scar
Cicerón SM Cicero
cicerone SMF guide, cicerone
ciceroniano ADJ Ciceronian
ciclamato SM cyclamate
ciclamen SM, **ciclamino** SM cyclamen
cíclico ADJ cyclic, cyclical
ciclismo SM cycling ▸ **ciclismo de montaña** mountain biking ▸ **ciclismo en ruta** road racing
ciclista ADJ cycle (*antes de s*) • **vuelta ~** cycle race
SMF cyclist
ciclo SM 1 (*en hechos repetidos*) cycle • **un ~ reproductor de corta duración** a short reproductive cycle • **empieza un nuevo ~ económico** a new economic cycle is beginning ▸ **ciclo circadiano** circadian cycle ▸ **ciclo de carbón** carbon cycle ▸ **ciclo de instrucción** instruction cycle ▸ **ciclo del nitrógeno** nitrogen cycle ▸ **ciclo de vida** life cycle ▸ **ciclo menstrual** menstrual cycle ▸ **ciclo vital** life cycle
2 [*de conferencias*] series; [*de cine, conciertos*] season
3 (*Escol*) • **el segundo ~ de primaria** the second stage of primary school
4 (*Literat*) cycle • **las historias del ~ artúrico** the stories of the Arthurian cycle
ciclo-cross SM INV cyclo-cross
ciclomotor SM moped
ciclón SM cyclone • MODISMO: • **como un ~**: • **entró como un ~ en la cocina** he burst into the kitchen • **salió como un ~ del despacho** she dashed out of the office ▸ **ciclón tropical** tropical cyclone
cíclope SM Cyclops
ciclópeo ADJ gigantic, colossal
ciclorama SM cyclorama
ciclostil SM cyclostyle
ciclostilado ADJ cyclostyled
ciclostilar ▷ CONJUG 1a VT to cyclostyle
ciclostilo SM = **ciclostil**
ciclotrón SM cyclotron
cicloturismo SM touring by bicycle
cicloturista SMF touring cyclist
-cico, -cica ▷ Aspects of Word Formation in Spanish 2
CICR SM ABR (= **Comité Internacional de la Cruz Roja**) ICRC
cicuta SF hemlock
cidiano ADJ relating to the Cid • **estudios ~s** Cid studies
cidra SF citron
cidracayote SM (*LAm*) gourd, calabash
cidro SM citron, citron tree
ciegamente ADV blindly
ciego/a ADJ 1 (= *invidente*) blind • **es ~ de nacimiento** he has been blind from *o* since birth, he was born blind • **la justicia es ciega** justice is blind • **dejar ~ a algn** to blind sb • **las luces me dejaron ~ por un momento** the lights blinded me for a moment • **el accidente la dejó ciega** she was blinded in the accident • **estar ~** to be blind • **pero ¿estás ~? ¿no ves que el semáforo está en rojo?** are you blind or what? can't you see the lights are red? • **quedarse ~** to go blind • **se quedó ~ después del accidente** he was blinded in the accident, he went blind as a result of the accident • MODISMO: • **más ~ que un topo** as blind as a bat
2 (*por ofuscación*) **a** [*persona*] blind • **~ a** blind to • **~ a las necesidades del resto del mundo** blind to the needs of the rest of the world • **~ de celos** blind with jealousy • **~ de dolor** in absolute agony • **~ de ira** *o* **rabia** blind with rage
b [*violencia*] mindless, senseless; [*fanatismo*] mindless
3 (= *total*) [*confianza, fe*] unquestioning, blind (*pey*) • **tenían una confianza ciega en su líder** they had unquestioning *o* (*pey*) blind faith in their leader • **exijo una obediencia ciega** I demand unquestioning obedience
4 (= *bloqueado*) [*arco, entrada*] blind; [*conducto, tubo*] blocked
5‡ (= *borracho*) blind drunk*, pissed‡; (*con drogas duras*) high*; (*con drogas blandas*) stoned‡ • **ponerse ~ a** *o* **de algo** (= *borracho*) to get pissed on sth‡, get trashed on sth (*EEUU*‡); (*con drogas duras*) to get high on sth*; (*con drogas blandas*) to get stoned on sth‡; (*comiendo*) to stuff o.s. with sth*
6 • **a ciegas a** (= *sin ver*) • **andar** *o* **caminar a ciegas** to grope one's way • **avanzamos a ciegas hasta encontrar el interruptor** we groped our way to the light switch • **buscó a ciegas la puerta** he searched blindly for the door, he groped about searching for the door • **volar a ciegas** to fly blind
b (= *sin pensar*) [*actuar, decidir*] in the dark; [*obedecer*] unquestioningly, blindly (*pey*)

• **creíamos a ciegas todo lo que decía el partido** we unquestioningly *o* (*pey*) blindly believed everything the party said, we believed everything the party said without question; ▹ **cita**
(SM/F) (= *invidente*) blind man/blind woman • **una organización de ~s** an organization for the blind, a blind people's organization
(SM) **1** (*Esp*‡) • **¡qué ~ llevaba!** [*de alcohol*] he was blind drunk* *o* pissed!‡; [*de drogas duras*] he was high as a kite*; [*de drogas blandas*] he was stoned out of his mind‡
2 (*Anat*) caecum, cecum (*EEUU*)
3 (*Caribe*) (= *claro*) forest clearing

cielito (SM) **1** (*Mús*) *Argentinian folk dance*
2 (= *apelativo cariñoso*) my love, sweetheart

cielo (SM) **1** (*Astron, Meteo*) sky • **el ~ está cubierto** the sky is overcast *o* cloudy • **el ~ estaba despejado** it was a cloudless *o* clear day • **a ~ abierto** [*mina, explotación*] opencast, open cut (*EEUU*) • **a ~ descubierto** in the open • **MODISMOS:** • **cambiar del ~ a la tierra** (*Chile*) to change out of all recognition • **llegar** *o* **venir (como) caído** *o* **llovido del ~** (*inesperado*) to come (totally) out of the blue; (*muy oportuno*) to be a godsend • **irse al ~ con todo y zapatos** (*Méx*): • **tú te vas al ~ con todo y zapatos** you'll be blessed in heaven • **juntársele a algn el ~ con la tierra** (*LAm*): • **se le juntó el ~ con la tierra** he lost his nerve • **poner a algn por los ~s** to praise sb to the skies • **remover ~ y tierra** to move heaven and earth • **tocar el ~ con las manos** (*Cono Sur, Perú, Col*): • **conseguir que me ayude es tocar el ~ con las manos** getting him to help me would be virtually impossible • **si me lo ganara sería como tocar el ~ con las manos** if I won it, it would be like a dream come true • **venírsele a algn el ~ abajo**: • **se le vino el ~ abajo** the heavens opened
2 (*Rel*) heaven • **Padre Nuestro que estás en los ~s** Our Father who art in heaven • **¡cielos!** good heavens! • **ganar el ~** to win salvation • **ir al ~** to go to heaven • **MODISMOS:** • **clamar al ~**: • **es una injusticia que clama al ~** it is a gross injustice • **¡esto clama al ~!** it's an outrage!, it's outrageous! • **estar en el séptimo ~** to be in seventh heaven • **ganar el ~ con rosario ajeno** to cash in on other people's hard work • **ver el ~ abierto**: • **cuando me ofrecieron el trabajo vi el ~ abierto** when I was offered the job I saw my chance • **vimos el ~ abierto cuando dijo que podíamos quedarnos en su casa** it was a great relief when he said we could stay in his house
3* (*uso afectivo*) • **¡mi ~!** • **¡~ mío!** my love, sweetheart • **el jefe es un ~** the boss is a real sweetie* • **¡has fregado los platos! eres un ~** you've washed the dishes! you're a real angel
4 (= *parte superior*) [*de la boca*] roof; [*de una cama*] canopy; (*CAm*) [*de un coche*] roof ▸ **cielo máximo** (*Aer*) ceiling
5 (*Arquit*) (*tb* **cielo raso**) ceiling

ciempiés (SM INV) centipede

cien¹ (ADJ), (PRON) (*antes de s, apócope de ciento*) a hundred, one hundred • **~ mil** a hundred thousand • **las últimas ~ páginas** the last hundred pages • **diez por ~** ten per cent • **es de lana ~ por ~** it's pure wool, it's a hundred per cent wool • **es español ~ por ~** he's Spanish through and through • **lo apoyo al ~ por ~** I support it wholeheartedly • **MODISMOS:** • **estar hasta el ~** (*And*) to be on one's last legs • **me pone a ~*** (= *enfadar*) it drives me up the wall*; (= *calentar sexualmente*) it makes me feel horny *o* randy*; ▹ **seis**

> **CIEN, CIENTO**
>
> ▹ *La traducción de* **cien(to)** *puede ser* **a hundred** *o* **one hundred**:
>
> **Tengo que escribir cien páginas**
> I've got to write a *o* one hundred pages
> **Murió a la edad de ciento veinte años**
> He died at the age of a *o* one hundred and twenty
>
> *Sin embargo, hay que utilizar siempre* **one hundred**:
>
> ▹ *cuando* **cien(to)** *va detrás de otra cifra:*
> **El curso cuesta dos mil ciento noventa libras**
> The course costs two thousand one hundred and ninety pounds
>
> ▹ *cuando se quiere precisar que se trata de* **cien(to)** *y no de doscientos etc:*
> I said "one hundred" not "two hundred"
>
> *Para otros usos y ejemplos ver* **cien¹**, **ciento**

cien²‡ (SM) bog‡, lavatory, john (*EEUU**)

ciénaga (SF) marsh, swamp

ciencia (SF) **1** (= *conocimiento*) science • **los avances de la ~** the advances of science • **MODISMOS:** • **saber algo a ~ cierta** to know sth for certain *o* for a fact • **no tener mucha ~**: • **esto no tiene mucha ~** there's nothing difficult about it ▸ **ciencia ficción** science fiction ▸ **ciencia infusa** • **lo sabe por ~ infusa** (*iró*) he has God-given intelligence
2 (= *doctrina*) science, sciences (*pl*) • **un hombre de ~** a man of science ▸ **ciencias naturales** natural science (*sing*) ▸ **ciencias ocultas** occultism (*sing*) ▸ **ciencias sociales** social science, social sciences (*pl*)
3 ciencias (*Educ*) science (*sing*), sciences • **estudia una carrera de ~s** she's doing a science degree ▸ **Ciencias de la Educación** Education (*sing*) ▸ **Ciencias de la Información** Media Studies ▸ **Ciencias Económicas** Economics (*sing*) ▸ **Ciencias Empresariales** Business Studies ▸ **Ciencias Exactas** Exact Sciences ▸ **Ciencias Físicas** Physical Science (*sing*) ▸ **Ciencias Políticas** Political Science (*sing*)

ciencia-ficción (SF) science fiction

Cienciología (SF) Scientology

cieno (SM) **1** (= *lodo*) mud
2 (= *depósito fluvial*) silt

cienoso (ADJ) muddy, miry

científicamente (ADV) scientifically

cientificidad (SF) scientific nature

científico/a (ADJ) scientific
(SM/F) scientist ▸ **científico/a social** social scientist

cientifismo (SM) scientific spirit

cientista (SMF) (*LAm*) scientist • **~ social** social scientist

ciento (ADJ), (PRON) a hundred, one hundred • **~ veinte** one hundred and twenty, a hundred and twenty
(SM) **1** a hundred, one hundred • **~s de personas** hundreds of people • **te lo he dicho ~s de veces** I've told you hundreds of times • **varios ~s de profesores** several hundred teachers • **a** *o* **por ~s: casos como este se producen a** *o* **por ~s** there are cases like this by the hundred, there are hundreds of cases like this • **las víctimas se cuentan a** *o* **por ~s** the death toll runs into hundreds • **MODISMOS:** • **dar ~ y raya a algn** to be more than a match for sb • **~ y la madre***: • **¡allí había ~ y la madre!** the world and his wife were there*, there were loads of people there*; ▹ **CIEN, CIENTO**
2 • **por ~** per cent • **el cuarenta y dos por ~ de los estudiantes** forty-two per cent of the students • **hay un cinco por ~ de descuento** there is a five per cent discount • **el ~ por ~** a *o* one hundred per cent • **el ~ por ~ de las participantes son mujeres** a *o* one hundred per cent of the participants are women • **los hoteles están al ~ por ~ de su capacidad** the hotels are full to capacity, the hotels have a hundred per cent occupancy

cierne (SM) blossoming, budding • **en ~(s)** (*Bot*) in blossom; (*fig*) in its infancy • **es un ajedrecista en ~s** he's a budding chess champion

cierra *etc* ▹ **cerrar**

cierre (SM) **1** (= *acto*) [*de verja, puerta*] (*gen*) closing, shutting; (*con llave*) locking; (*automático*) central locking; [*de edificio, establecimiento, frontera*] closing • **un dispositivo especial controla el ~ de la puerta** the door is closed *o* shut by a special device • **se está incumpliendo el horario de ~ de los bares** bars are not observing closing time • **cuatro horas después del ~ de los colegios electorales** four hours after the polling stations closed • **el mal tiempo obligó al ~ del aeropuerto** the airport was forced to close due to the bad weather ▸ **cierre empresarial, cierre patronal** lockout
2 (= *fin*) [*de una emisión*] closedown; [*de campaña electoral*] end, close; [*de la Bolsa*] close; [*de año fiscal*] end • **el mitin de ~ de la campaña electoral** the final rally of the electoral campaign • **al ~**: • **al ~ de esta edición de noticias** at the end of this news bulletin • **al ~ de impresión** at the time of going to press • **al ~ de la sesión de ayer** at the close of trading yesterday • **precio de ~** closing price
3 [*de negocio, carretera, instalaciones*] closure • **los vecinos piden el ~ de la factoría** local residents are demanding the closure of the factory • **muchos comerciantes se verán obligados al ~ de sus comercios** many traders will find themselves having to close down their businesses
4 (= *mecanismo*) [*de maleta, puerta*] catch; [*de collar, pulsera, libro*] clasp; [*de vestido*] fastener, snap fastener ▸ **cierre antirrobo** anti-theft lock ▸ **cierre centralizado** (*Aut*) central locking ▸ **cierre de dirección** (*Aut*) steering lock ▸ **cierre eclair** (*Chile*) zip, zip fastener, zipper (*esp EEUU*) ▸ **cierre hermético** airtight seal ▸ **cierre metálico** (= *persiana*) metal shutter; (= *cremallera*) metal zip ▸ **cierre relámpago** (*Cono Sur, Perú*) zip, zip fastener, zipper (*esp EEUU*)
5 • **echar el ~ a** (*a un local, comercio*) (*temporalmente*) to close; (*definitivamente*) to close down • **estaba echando el ~ a la tienda** he was locking the shop up *o* locking up the shop
b (*Esp**) (= *callar*) • **¡echa el ~!** give it a rest! • **echar el ~ a algn** to shut sb up

cierrecler (SM) (*Chile*) zip, zip fastener, zipper (*esp EEUU*)

cierro (SM) (*Chile*) fence

ciertamente (ADV) certainly • **no era ~ uno de los más inteligentes** he was certainly not one of the brightest

cierto (ADJ) **1** (= *verdadero*) true • **los rumores resultaron ser ~s** the rumours turned out to be true • **¿es ~ eso?** is that really so?, is that true? • **ha mejorado mucho, ¿no es ~?** it has improved a lot, don't you think? • **es ~, es mejor que nos vayamos** yes *o* you're right, I think we'd better go • **~, es un problema grave** it's certainly a serious problem

C

• **estar en lo ~** to be right • **lo ~ es que** the fact is that, the truth of the matter is that • **nadie habló sobre ello pero lo ~ es que todos estaban preocupados** nobody talked about it but the fact is *o* the truth of the matter is that everyone was worried • **es ~ que** it's true that • **no es ~ que mi mujer me haya abandonado** it is not true that my wife has walked out on me
2 (= *seguro*) certain, sure • **les espera una muerte cierta** they are heading for certain death • **hay indicios ~s de mejoría** there are clear signs of improvement • **lo único ~ es que …** the only sure thing is that … • **saber algo de ~** to know sth for certain
3 (*uso indefinido*) **a** (*en sing*) a certain • **cierta persona que yo conozco** a certain person I know • **no me gusta ~ tipo de literatura** there's a certain type of literature which I don't like • **ocurre con cierta frecuencia** it happens fairly frequently • **en todos sus movimientos había un ~ aire de misterio** everything he did had a certain air of mystery about it • **me alejé de allí con una cierta sensación de preocupación** I left there feeling a little anxious, I left there with a certain feeling of anxiety • **~ día de mayo** one day in May • **en cierta ocasión** on one occasion, once • **durante ~ tiempo** for a while • **estuvieron buscándolo durante ~ tiempo** they looked for it for a while • **las monedas nacionales se mantendrían en uso durante un ~ tiempo** national currencies would continue to be used for a (certain) time; ▹ **edad, manera, modo, punto, sentido**
b (*en pl*) some, certain • **es mejor no hablar de ciertas cosas** some *o* certain things are better not discussed
4 • **por ~** by the way, incidentally • **por ~, ¿qué es de tu hermano?** by the way, *o* incidentally, what's your brother doing now? • **un libro que, por ~, recomiendo totalmente** a book which, by the way, *o* incidentally, I would thoroughly recommend

cierva (SF) hind

ciervo (SM) (*Zool*) (*gen*) deer; (*macho*) stag, buck; (*Culin*) venison ▸ **ciervo común** red deer ▸ **ciervo volante** stag beetle

cierzo (SM) north wind

CIF (SM ABR) (= **Cédula de Identificación Fiscal**) company or personal tax code

cifosis (SF INV) (*Med*) kyphosis

cifra (SF) **1** (= *dígito*) figure • **las ~s dadas por el Ministerio** the figures provided by the Ministry • **un número de seis ~s** a six-figure number ▸ **cifras de ventas** sales figures
2 (= *cantidad*) number • **piensa una ~** think of a number • **la ~ de parados es preocupante** the number of unemployed people is worrying • **la ~ oficial de muertos** the official death toll • **ganan ~s astronómicas** they earn astronomical sums
3 • **en ~** (= *codificado*) coded, in code

cifradamente (ADV) **1** (= *en clave*) in code
2 (= *resumiendo*) in brief, in a shortened form

cifrado (ADJ) [*mensaje*] coded, in code
(SM) (en)coding, ciphering

cifrar ▹ CONJUG 1a (VT) **1** [+ *mensaje*] to code, write in code; (*Ling*) to encode
2 [+ *esperanzas, ilusiones*] to pin, place (**en** on)
3 [+ *ganancias, pérdidas*] to calculate • **cifran las pérdidas por el terremoto en miles de millones** losses caused by the earthquake have been calculated at billions
4 [+ *discurso, explicación*] (= *compendiar*) to summarize; (= *abreviar*) to abbreviate
(VPR) **cifrarse** • **todas las esperanzas se cifran en él** all hopes are centred on him

cigala (SF) Dublin Bay prawn

cigarra (SF) cicada

cigarral (SM) (*de Toledo*) *country house on the banks of the Tagus*

cigarrera (SF) **1** (= *estuche*) cigar case
2 (= *obrera*) cigar maker; (= *vendedora*) cigar seller

cigarrería (SF) (*LAm*) (= *tienda*) tobacconist's (shop), tobacco *o* smoke shop (EEUU); (= *fábrica*) tobacco factory

cigarrero (SM) (= *obrero*) cigar maker; (= *vendedor*) cigar seller

cigarrillo (SM) cigarette • **cajetilla** *o* **paquete de ~s** pack(et) of cigarettes • **cartón de ~s** box of cigarettes • **liar un ~** to roll a cigarette ▸ **cigarrillo electrónico** electronic cigarette

cigarrito (SM) cheroot

cigarro (SM) **1** (= *cigarrillo*) cigarette
2 (*tb* **cigarro puro**) cigar ▸ **cigarro habano** Havana cigar

cigoto (SM) zygote

ciguato (ADJ) **1** (*Caribe, Méx*) (= *simple*) simple, stupid
2 (*Caribe, Méx*) (= *pálido*) pale, anaemic, anemic (EEUU)

cigüeña (SF) **1** (*Orn*) stork
2 (*Mec*) crank, handle; (*Náut*) winch, capstan
3 (*CAm*) (*Mús*) barrel organ
4 (*Caribe*) (*Ferro*) bogie, bogy

cigüeñal (SM) crankshaft

CIJ (SF ABR) (= **Corte Internacional de Justicia**) ICJ

cija (SF) (= *cuadra*) sheep shed; (= *pajar*) hayloft

cilampa (SF) (*CAm*) drizzle

cilampear ▹ CONJUG 1a (VI) (*CAm*) to drizzle

cilantro (SM) (*Bot, Culin*) coriander

cilicio (SM) (= *vestidura áspera*) hair shirt; (*con pinchos*) *spiked belt or chain etc worn by penitents*

cilindrada (SF) cylinder capacity

cilindradora (SF) steamroller, road roller

cilindraje (SM) cylinder capacity

cilindrar ▹ CONJUG 1a (VT) to roll, roll flat

cilíndrico (ADJ) cylindrical

cilindrín‡ (SM) cigarette, fag* • **incinerar el ~** to light up

cilindro (SM) **1** (*Mat, Téc*) cylinder; (*en máquina de escribir*) roller ▸ **cilindro compresor, cilindro de caminos** steamroller, road roller
2 (*Méx*) (= *organillo*) barrel organ
3* (= *sombrero de copa*) top hat

cilla (SF) **1** (= *granero*) tithe barn, granary
2 (= *diezmo*) tithe

cima (SF) **1** [*de montaña*] top, summit • **la ~ del Aconcagua** the top *o* summit of Aconcagua • **dieron ~ a la montaña** they reached *o* got to the summit *o* top of the mountain • **las ~s más altas de los Alpes** the highest peaks in the Alps
2 (= *cúspide*) • **está en la ~ de su carrera** she is at the peak *o* height of her career • **llegó a la ~ del éxito profesional** she achieved the pinnacle of success in her profession • **conoció las más altas ~s del poder** he knew *o* experienced the very heights of power • **han dado ~ a las negociaciones** they brought the negotiations to a successful conclusion
3 [*de árbol*] top

cimarra (SF) • **hacer ~** (*Cono Sur*) to play truant

cimarrón/ona (ADJ) **1** (*LAm*) (*Bot, Zool*) wild, untamed
2 (*LAm*) [*persona*] (= *inculto*) rough, uncouth; (= *vago*) lazy • **negro ~** (*Hist*) runaway slave, fugitive slave
3 (*Cono Sur*) [*mate*] bitter, unsweetened
(SM/F) (*Hist*) runaway slave, maroon
(SM) (*Cono Sur*) unsweetened mate

cimarronear ▹ CONJUG 1a (VI) (*LAm*) to run away

cimba (SF) **1** (*And*) (= *cuerda*) plaited rope of hard leather
2 (*And*) (= *trenza*) pigtail
3 (*And*) (= *escala*) rope ladder

címbalo (SM) cymbal

cimbel (SM) **1** (= *señuelo*) decoy (*tb fig*)
2‡ [*de hombre*] prick**

cimborio (SM), **cimborrio** (SM) **1** (*Arquit*) (= *cúpula*) dome; (= *base*) base of a dome
2 (*Min*) roof

cimbrar ▹ CONJUG 1a (VT) **1** (= *agitar*) to shake, swish, swing; (= *curvar*) to bend
2 • **~ a algn*** to clout sb (with a stick) • **le cimbró de un porrazo** he clouted him with his stick

cimbreante (ADJ) swaying

cimbrear ▹ CONJUG 1a (VT) (= *hacer oscilar*) to swish, swing; (= *curvar*) to bend; (= *agitar*) to shake
(VI) to swing round
(VPR) **cimbrearse 1** (= *balancearse*) to sway; (= *curvarse*) to bend; (= *agitarse*) to shake • **~se al viento** to sway in the wind
2 (= *andar con garbo*) to walk gracefully

cimbreño (ADJ) [*vara*] pliant, flexible; [*talle*] willowy, lithe

cimbreo (SM) (= *balanceo*) swaying; (= *agitación*) shaking; (= *curvado*) bending

cimbrón (SM) **1** (*And, CAm, Cono Sur*) (= *sacudida*) shudder
2 (*LAm*) [*de lazo*] crack
3 (= *tirón*) jerk, yank*, tug
4 (*Cono Sur, Méx*) (= *espadazo*) *blow with the flat of a sword*
5 (*And*) (= *dolor*) sharp pain

cimbronada (SF), **cimbronazo** (SM) **1** (*And, Cono Sur, Méx*) = **cimbrón**
2 (*Caribe*) earthquake

cimentación (SF) **1** (= *cimientos*) foundation
2 (= *acción*) laying of foundations

cimentar ▹ CONJUG 1j (VT) **1** (*Arquit*) to lay the foundations of *o* for
2 (= *fundar*) to found, establish
3 (= *reforzar*) [+ *relaciones, cooperación*] to strengthen, cement
4 [+ *oro*] to refine

cimera (SF) crest (*tb Heráldica*)

cimero (ADJ) (= *superior*) [*pico*] highest, topmost; [*puesto*] highest; [*proyecto, figura*] crowning, finest

cimiento (SM) (*Arquit*) foundation; [*de amistad, sociedad*] foundation • **abrir los ~s** to dig the foundations • **echar los ~s de algo** to lay the foundations for sth

cimitarra (SF) scimitar

cimpa (SF) (*And*) = **cimba**

cinabrio (SM) cinnabar

cinc (SM) zinc

cincel (SM) chisel

cincelado (SM) (= *labrado*) chiselling; (= *grabado*) engraving

cincelador (SM) **1** (= *persona*) (*en metal*) engraver; (*en piedra*) stone cutter
2 (= *herramienta*) (chipping) chisel, chipping hammer

cincelar ▹ CONJUG 1a (VT) **1** [+ *piedra, mármol*] to chisel, carve, cut; [+ *metal*] engrave
2 [+ *proyecto*] to fine-tune; [+ *memorias*] to be specific about

cincha (SF) **1** [*de caballo*] girth, saddle strap
• MODISMO: • **a revienta ~s** (= *apresuradamente*) at breakneck speed, hurriedly; (*LAm*) (= *con renuencia*) reluctantly
2 (*para sillas*) webbing
3 (*And*) • **tener ~** to have some black/Indian blood in one

cinchada (SF) (*Cono Sur, Méx*) tug-of-war

cinchar ▹ CONJUG 1a (VT) [+ *caballo*] to girth, secure the girth of; (*Téc*) to band, hoop, secure with hoops

VI (*Cono Sur**) (= *trabajar*) to work hard
• **~ por** (= *apoyar*) to root for
cincho SM (*gen*) belt, girdle; (= *aro*) iron hoop, metal band; (*CAm, Caribe, Méx*) = **cincha**
cinchona SF (*LAm*) quinine bark
cinco ADJ INV, PRON (*gen*) five; (*ordinal, en la fecha*) fifth • **las ~** five o'clock • **le escribí el día ~** I wrote to him on the fifth
• **MODISMOS**: • **estar sin ~*** • **no tener ni ~*** to be broke* • **le dije cuántas son ~** I told him a thing or two • **no estar en sus ~*** to be off one's rocker* • **saber cuántas son ~** to know what's what • **tener los ~ muy listos*** to be light-fingered • **¡vengan esos ~!*** shake on it!*
SM **1** (= *número*) five; (= *fecha*) fifth; (*Educ*) five (*the pass mark*) • **sacar un ~ pelado** to scrape through*
2 (*Ven*) (= *guitarra*) five-stringed guitar
3 (*Méx**) (= *trasero*) bottom, backside*
4 (*CAm, Méx*) (= *moneda*) five-peso piece; ▹ **seis**
cincuenta ADJ INV, PRON, SM (*gen*) fifty; (*ordinal*) fiftieth • **los (años) ~** the fifties
• **MODISMO**: • **cantar las ~ a algn** to haul sb over the coals; ▹ **seis**
cincuentañero/a ADJ fiftyish, about fifty
SM/F *person of about fifty, person in his/her fifties*
cincuentavo SM fiftieth part; ▹ **sexto**
cincuentena SF fifty, about fifty • **una ~ de** fifty-odd, fifty or so
cincuentenario SM 50th anniversary
cincuenteno ADJ fiftieth; ▹ **sexto**
cincuentón/ona ADJ fifty-year old, fiftyish
SM/F *person in his/her fifties*
cine SM **1** (= *arte*) cinema • **el ~ español** Spanish cinema • **hacer ~** to make films *o* movies (*esp EEUU*) • **de ~**: **actor de ~** film actor, movie actor (*EEUU*) • **festival de ~** film festival • **era una casa de ~*** it was a fairytale house, the house was like something out of a film • **me lo pasé de ~*** I had a fantastic *o* brilliant time, I had a whale of a time* ▸ **cine de acción** action films (*pl*), action movies (*pl*) (*esp EEUU*) ▸ **cine de animación** animated films (*pl*) ▸ **cine de arte y ensayo** art cinema ▸ **cine de autor** auteur cinema ▸ **cine de aventuras** adventure films (*pl*), adventure movies (*pl*) (*esp EEUU*) ▸ **cine de terror** horror films (*pl*), horror movies (*pl*) (*esp EEUU*) ▸ **cine mudo** silent films (*pl*), silent movies (*pl*) (*esp EEUU*) ▸ **cine negro** film noir ▸ **cine sonoro** talking films (*pl*), talkies* (*pl*)
2 (= *local*) cinema, movie theater (*EEUU*) • **¿quieres ir al ~?** do you want to go to the cinema *o* (*esp EEUU*) the movies? ▸ **cine de barrio** local cinema, local (movie) theater (*EEUU*) ▸ **cine de verano** open-air cinema, open-air movie theater (*EEUU*)
cine... PREF cine...
cineasta SMF film maker, moviemaker (*EEUU*)
cine-club SM (PL: **cine-clubs, cine-clubes**) film club
cinefilia SF love of the cinema
cinéfilo/a SM/F (= *aficionado*) film fan, movie fan (*EEUU*); (= *especialista*) film buff*, movie buff (*EEUU*)
cinegética SF hunting, the chase
cinegético ADJ hunting (*antes de s*), of the chase
cinema SM cinema, movie theater (*EEUU*)
cinemateca SF film library, film archive
cinemático ADJ cinematic
cinematografía SF cinematography, films, film making, movie making (*EEUU*)
cinematografiar ▹ CONJUG 1a VT to film
cinematográfico ADJ film (*antes de s*), cinematographic (*frm*)
cinematógrafo SM **1** (= *cine*) cinema, movie theater (*EEUU*)
2 (= *aparato*) (film) projector
cineración SF incineration
cinerama SM cinerama
cinerario ADJ **1** [*urna*] cinerary
2 = **ceniciento**
cinéreo ADJ ash-grey, ash-gray (*EEUU*), ashen (*liter*)
cineteca SF (*LAm*) film archive
cinética SF kinetics (*sing*)
cinético ADJ kinetic
cingalés/esa ADJ Sinhalese
SM/F Sinhalese • **los cingaleses** the Sinhalese
SM (*Ling*) Sinhalese
cíngaro/a ADJ gipsy
SM/F gipsy (*esp Hungarian*)
cinguería SF (*Cono Sur*) (= *obra*) sheet-metal work; (= *taller*) sheet-metal shop
cinguero SM (*Cono Sur*) sheet-metal worker
cínicamente ADV cynically
cínico/a ADJ cynical
SM/F cynic
cinismo SM cynicism • **¡qué ~!** how cynical!, what a nerve!*
cinofilia SF **1** (*gen*) dog-fancying, dog-breeding
2 (= *personas*) dog-fanciers, dog-breeders
cinólogo/a SM/F canine expert
cinta SF **1** (= *tira*) ribbon • **se recogió el pelo con una ~** she tied her hair back with a ribbon ▸ **cinta adhesiva** adhesive tape ▸ **cinta aislante, cinta de aislar** (*CAm, Méx*) insulating tape ▸ **cinta elástica** elastic ▸ **cinta métrica** tape measure
2 [*de vídeo, sonido*] tape ▸ **cinta de audio** audio tape ▸ **cinta de casete** cassette tape ▸ **cinta de vídeo** video tape ▸ **cinta limpiadora** head cleaner, head-cleaning tape ▸ **cinta magnética** magnetic tape ▸ **cinta magnetofónica** audio tape ▸ **cinta virgen** blank tape
3 (*Cine*) film
4 (*Téc*) ▸ **cinta de equipajes** baggage *o* luggage carousel ▸ **cinta transportadora** conveyor belt
5 (*Culin*) ▸ **cinta de cerdo, cinta de lomo** loin of pork
6 (*Bot*) spider plant
cinteado ADJ beribboned
cintero SM **1** [*de mujer*] girdle
2 (= *cuerda*) rope
cintillo SM **1** [*de sombrero*] hatband; (*LAm*) (*para pelo*) hairband
2 (= *anillo*) small ring with jewels
3 (*Tip*) heading, collective heading
4 (*Caribe*) (= *bordillo*) kerb, curb (*EEUU*)
cinto SM (= *cinturón*) belt; [*de traje típico, militar*] girdle, sash • **armas de ~** side arms ▸ **cinto negro** black belt
cintura SF **1** (*Anat*) waist • **me rodeó la ~ con los brazos** she put her arms around my waist • **tiene poca ~** she has a slim waist • **tengo 76cm de ~** my waist (measurement) is 76cm • **de ~ para abajo** from the waist down • **con la dieta redujo unos centímetros de ~** with his diet he reduced his waistline by a few centimetres, with his diet he took a few centimetres off his waistline ▸ **cintura de avispa** wasp waist
2 [*de falda, pantalón*] waist • **un pantalón ancho de ~** a pair of trousers that are loose-fitting around the waist • **un vestido alto de ~** a high-waisted dress • **MODISMO**: • **meter a algn en ~** to bring sb into line, make sb toe the line
cinturilla SF waistband
cinturón SM **1** (*gen*) belt; [*de traje típico, militar*] girdle, sash; [*de espada*†] sword belt
• **MODISMO**: • **apretarse** *o* **ajustarse el ~** to tighten one's belt ▸ **cinturón bomba** bomb belt ▸ **cinturón de castidad** chastity belt ▸ **cinturón de explosivos** explosives belt, explosive belt ▸ **cinturón de salvamento** lifebelt, life preserver (*EEUU*) ▸ **cinturón de seguridad** safety belt ▸ **cinturón salvavidas** lifebelt, life preserver (*EEUU*)
2 (= *zona*) belt, zone • **el ~ industrial de Madrid** the Madrid industrial belt ▸ **cinturón de miseria** slum area; (*Méx*) [*de chabolas*] shanty town ▸ **cinturón verde** green belt
3 (*Dep*) belt
4 (= *carretera*) ▸ **cinturón de circunvalación, cinturón de ronda** ring road, bypass, beltway (*EEUU*)
ciña, ciñendo *etc* ▹ **ceñir**
CIP SM ABR **1** (*Esp*) = **Club Internacional de Prensa**
2 (*Esp*) = **Centro de Investigación para la Paz**
3 (*Perú*) = **Centro Internacional de la Papa**
cipayo SM **1** (*Brit*) (*Mil, Hist*) sepoy
2 (*Cono Sur*) (*Pol*) *politician in the service of foreign commerce*
cipe SM (*LAm*) sickly baby
cipo SM (= *monumento*) memorial stone; (= *mojón*) milestone, signpost
cipote ADJ **1** (*And, Caribe*) (= *estúpido*) stupid, thick*
2 (*CAm*) (= *rechoncho*) plump, chubby
SM **1** (*CAm, Caribe*) (= *chico*) lad, youngster
2 (*Esp***) (= *pene*) prick**
3 (*CAm*) (= *maza*) Indian club
4* (= *idiota*) chump*, blockhead*, clod (*EEUU**)
5 (*And**) • **~ de chica** smashing girl* • **~ de película** great film*
6‡ (= *barriga*) belly, guts*
cipotear** ▹ CONJUG 1a VT (*Esp*) to screw**
ciprés SM cypress (tree)
cipresal SM cypress grove
CIR SM ABR (*Esp*) (*Mil*) = **Centro de Instrucción de Reclutas**
circadiano ADJ circadian
circense ADJ circus (*antes de s*), of the circus
circo SM **1** (= *espectáculo*) circus ▸ **circo ambulante** travelling circus, traveling circus (*EEUU*) ▸ **circo romano** Roman circus
2 (*Geol*) cirque ▸ **circo glaciar** glacier cirque, glacial cirque
circonio SM zirconium
circuir ▹ CONJUG 3g VT to encircle, surround
circuitería SF circuitry
circuito SM **1** (= *pista*) circuit, track • **un ~ de fórmula-1** a formula-1 circuit ▸ **circuito de carreras** racetrack, racecourse (*esp EEUU*), (motor) racing circuit ▸ **circuito urbano** city circuit, town circuit
2 (= *círculo*) circuit • **el mejor tenista del ~ profesional** the best tennis player on the professional circuit • **sus películas forman parte del ~ comercial** his films are mainstream commercial films
3 (*Elec*) circuit • **corto ~** short circuit
4 (*Telec*) ▸ **circuito cerrado (de televisión)** closed-circuit (television)
5 (= *gira*) tour • **un ~ en autobús por Andalucía** a bus tour around Andalusia
circulación SF **1** (*Aut*) traffic • **calle de gran ~** busy street • **en el continente la ~ es por la derecha** on the Continent they drive on the right ▸ **circulación prohibida** no traffic ▸ **circulación rodada** vehicular traffic • **"cerrado a la circulación rodada"** "closed to vehicular traffic *o* vehicles" ▸ **circulación única** (*Méx*) one way (traffic)
2 (*Med*) circulation ▸ **circulación de la**

C

sangre, circulación sanguínea circulation of the blood
3 (*Econ*) circulation • **estar fuera de ~** to be out of circulation, be no longer current • **poner algo en ~** to issue sth, put sth into circulation ▸ **circulación fiduciaria** paper money, paper currency
circulante ADJ 1 (*gen*) circulating; [*biblioteca*] mobile
2 (*Econ*) [*capital*] working
circular ▷ CONJUG 1a VI 1 [*vehículo*] to run • **el metro no circula los domingos** the underground does not run on Sundays, there is no underground service on Sundays • **este tren circula a muy alta velocidad** this train goes *o* travels *o* runs at very high speeds • **mañana ~án muchos vehículos por las carreteras** there will be many vehicles on the roads tomorrow • **circule por la izquierda** drive on the left
2 [*peatón*] to walk • **por favor, circulen por la acera** please walk on the pavement • **¡circulen!** move along!
3 [*ciudadano, mercancía*] to move around • **los españoles pueden ~ libremente por la UE** Spaniards can move around freely *o* have free movement within the EU
4 [*moneda*] to be in circulation
5 [*sangre*] to circulate; [*agua*] to flow
6 [*rumor*] to go round, circulate
VT to circulate
ADJ (= *redondo*) circular • **un edificio ~** a circular building • **un salón con** *o* **de forma ~** a circular *o* round hall • **el autobús tiene un recorrido ~** the bus follows *o* has a circular route • **una carta ~** a circular
SF (= *carta*) circular
circularidad SF circularity
circulatorio ADJ 1 (*gen*) circulatory
2 (*Aut*) traffic (*antes de s*) • **colapso ~** traffic jam, traffic stoppage
círculo SM 1 (= *circunferencia*) circle • **las sillas estaban puestas en ~** the chairs were set out in a circle ▸ **círculo de giro, círculo de viraje** turning circle ▸ **círculo máximo** great circle ▸ **círculo polar antártico** Antarctic Circle ▸ **círculo polar ártico** Arctic Circle ▸ **círculo vicioso** vicious circle
2 (= *grupo*) circle • **los ~s íntimos del ministro confirmaron su dimisión** sources close to the minister confirmed his resignation
3 (= *club*) club
4 (= *campo*) scope, compass, extent
circun... PREF circum...
circuncidar ▷ CONJUG 1a VT 1 (*Med*) to circumcise
2 (= *restringir*) to curtail; (= *moderar*) to moderate
circuncisión SF circumcision
circunciso/a ADJ (*Med*) circumcised
SM/F (*gen*) circumcised man/woman; (*Hist*) *term used in the past to refer to either a Jew or a Moor*
circundante ADJ surrounding
circundar ▷ CONJUG 1a VT to surround
circunferencia SF circumference
circunferir ▷ CONJUG 3i VT to circumscribe, limit
circunflejo SM circumflex
circunlocución SF, **circunloquio** SM circumlocution, roundabout expression
circunnavegación SF circumnavigation
circunnavegar ▷ CONJUG 1a VT to sail round, circumnavigate
circunscribible ADJ circumscribable
circunscribir ▷ CONJUG 3a (PP: **circunscrito**) VT to circumscribe (a to)
VPR **circunscribirse** (= *limitarse*) to be limited, be confined (a to)
circunscripción SF (*gen*) circumscription; (*Mil*) district; (*Pol*) constituency, electoral district
circunspección SF circumspection, prudence
circunspecto ADJ [*persona*] circumspect; [*palabras*] carefully chosen, guarded
circunstancia SF circumstance • **dadas las ~s** in *o* under the circumstances • **estar a la altura de las ~s** to rise to the occasion • **en las ~s actuales** under present circumstances, the way things are at the moment ▸ **circunstancias agravantes** aggravating circumstances ▸ **circunstancias atenuantes** extenuating *o* mitigating circumstances
circunstanciado ADJ detailed
circunstancial ADJ 1 (*gen*) circumstantial; [*caso*] incidental • **mi estancia en Lima era ~** I just happened to be in Lima
2 (= *temporal*) [*arreglo, acuerdo*] makeshift, temporary
circunstante ADJ 1 (= *que rodea*) surrounding
2 (= *presente*) present
SMF • **los ~s** those present
circunvalación SF • **carretera de ~** ring road, bypass, beltway (*EEUU*)
circunvecino ADJ adjacent, neighbouring, neighboring (*EEUU*), surrounding
cirial SM processional candlestick
cirílico ADJ, SM Cyrillic
cirio SM 1 (*Rel*) (wax) candle
2* (= *jaleo*) squabble • **montar un ~** to kick up a row
cirquero SM (= *empresario*) circus impresario; (*Méx*) (= *trabajador*) acrobat
cirro SM cirrus
cirrocúmulo SM cirrocumulus
cirrosis SF INV cirrhosis ▸ **cirrosis hepática** cirrhosis of the liver
cirrostrato SM cirrostratus
ciruela SF plum ▸ **ciruela claudia** greengage ▸ **ciruela damascena** damson ▸ **ciruela pasa, ciruela seca** prune ▸ **ciruela verdal** greengage
ciruelo SM 1 (*Bot*) plum tree
2** (= *pene*) prick**
3* (= *necio*) dolt, idiot
cirugía SF surgery ▸ **cirugía estética** cosmetic surgery ▸ **cirugía plástica** plastic surgery
ciruja SMF (*Cono Sur*) scavenger (*on rubbish dumps*)
cirujano/a SM/F surgeon ▸ **cirujano/a plástico/a** plastic surgeon
ciscar ▷ CONJUG 1g VT 1 (= *ensuciar*) to dirty *o* soil *o* mess up (*frm*)
2 (*Cuba, Méx**) (= *avergonzar*) to put to shame
3 (*Caribe, Méx*) (= *meterse con*) to provoke, needle*
VPR **ciscarse** 1 (*euf*) (= *hacerse de vientre*) to do one's business*; (*encima*) to mess oneself • **los que se ciscan en las teorías** those who thumb their noses at theories • **¡me cisco en todo!*** blast it!*
2 (*Cuba, Méx**) (= *avergonzarse*) to feel ashamed
3 (*Caribe, Méx*) (= *ofenderse*) to get upset, take offence
cisco SM 1 (*Min*) coaldust, dross
• MODISMOS: • **estar hecho (un) ~*** to be a wreck, be all in • **hacer algo ~** to tear sth to bits, smash sth to smithereens
2* (= *riña*) row, shindy* • **armar un ~** • **meter ~** to kick up a row, make trouble
3 (*Méx*) (= *miedo*) fear, fright
ciscón ADJ (*Caribe, Méx*) touchy
Cisjordania SF the West Bank
cisjordano/a ADJ of/from the West Bank
SM/F native/inhabitant of the West Bank • **los ~s** the people of the West Bank
cisma SM 1 (*Rel*) schism; (*Pol*) split; (= *desacuerdo*) discord, disagreement
2 (*And*) (= *remilgo*) prudery
3 (*And*) (= *chismes*) gossip
cismático ADJ 1 (*Rel*) schismatic(al); (*fig*) troublemaking, dissident
2 (*And*) (= *remilgado*) prudish
3 (*And*) (= *chismoso*) gossipy
cisne SM 1 (*Orn*) swan
2 (*Cono Sur*) (= *borla de empolvarse*) powder puff
Cister SM, **Císter** SM Cistercian Order
cisterciense ADJ, SM Cistercian
cisterna SF cistern, tank • **buque ~** tanker
cistitis SF INV cystitis
cita SF 1 (= *encuentro*) **a** (*con médico, profesional*) appointment • **tengo ~ con el dentista** I have a dental appointment, I have an appointment at the dentist's • **concertar una ~** to make an appointment, arrange an appointment • **pedir ~** to make an appointment
b [*de novios*] date • **tener una ~** to have a date ▸ **cita a ciegas** blind date
2 (= *reunión*) meeting • **tengo una ~ con la junta directiva** I have a meeting with the board of directors • **los ciudadanos tienen una ~ con las urnas el domingo** the country goes to the polls on Sunday • **acudir a una ~** to attend a meeting • **darse ~** (= *quedar citado*) to arrange to meet; (= *encontrarse*) to gather • **los mejores atletas del mundo se han dado ~ aquí hoy** the world's top athletes have gathered here today • **lugar de ~** meeting place • **este café es lugar de ~ de escritores famosos** this café is a meeting place for famous writers; ▸ **casa**
3 (= *punto de encuentro*) event • **los Juegos Olímpicos son la ~ más importante del deporte mundial** the Olympic Games are the most important sporting event in the world • **ser ~ obligada**: • **este festival es ~ obligada para los amantes de la danza** this festival is a must for lovers of dance • **estos días París se convierte en ~ obligada para los diseñadores de moda** for these few days, Paris becomes the only place to be for fashion designers
4 (= *mención literal*) [*de escrito, libro*] quotation; [*de parte de discurso, declaraciones*] quote • **una ~ de Quevedo** a quotation from Quevedo • **varias ~s del presidente** several quotes from the president • **la ~ más famosa de Groucho Marx** Groucho Marx's most famous quote • **un diccionario de ~s** a dictionary of quotations ▸ **cita textual** direct quote • **se escribe así cuando se trata de una ~ textual** it's written like this when it's a direct quote • **"es intolerable" (~ textual de un compañero de la oficina)** "it's intolerable", as a colleague from work said, in the words of a colleague from work, "it's intolerable"
citable ADJ quotable
citación SF 1 [*de un libro*] quotation
2 (*Jur*) summons, citation ▸ **citación a licitadores** invitation to tender ▸ **citación judicial** summons, subpoena
citadino/a (*LAm*) ADJ urban
SM/F urban *o* city dweller
citado ADJ aforementioned • **en el ~ país** in the aforementioned country
citar ▷ CONJUG 1a VT 1 (= *mencionar*) **a** [+ *ejemplo, caso*] to quote, cite • **el informe cita a Francia, Italia e Irlanda** the report quotes *o* cites France, Italy and Ireland • **todo tipo de plásticos, entre los que podemos ~ el nilón** all kinds of plastics, such as nylon for example
b [+ *frase, autor, fuentes*] to quote • **cita a Platón en su libro** he quotes Plato in his

book • **las fuentes citadas por el periódico** the sources quoted by the newspaper • **~ textualmente** to quote word for word, quote verbatim • **~on textualmente varios párrafos** they quoted several paragraphs word for word *o* verbatim • **no quería que ningún "imbécil" —cito textualmente— le quitara el puesto** he wasn't having any "idiot" — and I quote — taking the job away from him
2 (= *convocar*) • **la ~on a las nueve de la mañana** she was given an appointment for nine in the morning • **¿está usted citado?** do you have an appointment? • **la cité para ultimar unos detalles** I arranged to see her to go over some details
3 (*Jur*) [*juez*] to summon; [*abogado, defensa, fiscal*] to call • **~ a algn a declarar** to summon sb to give evidence • **tiene facultades para ~ testigos** he has the power to call witnesses
4 (*Taur*) to incite, provoke
VPR **citarse 1** [*varias personas*] to arrange to meet • **nos citamos a las cuatro** we arranged to meet at four • **quedamos citados para el día siguiente** we made a date for the following day • **~se con algn** to arrange to meet sb
2 [*novios*] to make a date

cítara SF zither
-cito, -cita (*tb* **-ecito, -ecita**) ▹ **Aspects of Word Formation in Spanish 2**
citófono SM (*And*) buzzer
citología SF **1** (= *análisis*) cervical smear, smear test, Pap smear
2 (*Bio*) cytology
citológico ADJ (*Med*) cytological
citotóxico ADJ cytotoxic
citrato SM citrate
cítrico ADJ citric
SMPL **cítricos** citrus fruits
citrícola ADJ citrus (*antes de s*)
citrón SM lemon
citronela SF lemon balm
CiU ABR (*Esp*) (*Pol*) (= **Convergència i Unió**) *Catalan political coalition*
ciudad SF **1** (*de gran tamaño*) city; (*más pequeña*) town • **se levanta temprano para ir a la ~** he gets up early to go into the city *o* into town • **la ~ de Granada** (the city of) Granada • **la Ciudad Condal** *name for the city of Barcelona* • **la Ciudad del Turia** *name for the city of Valencia* ▸ **Ciudad del Cabo** Cape Town ▸ **Ciudad del Vaticano** Vatican City ▸ **Ciudad de México** Mexico City ▸ **ciudad dormitorio** dormitory town, bedroom community (EEUU) ▸ **ciudad natal** home town, native city, native town ▸ **ciudad perdida** (*Méx*) shanty town
2 (= *instalaciones*) ▸ **ciudad deportiva** sports complex ▸ **ciudad sanitaria** hospital complex ▸ **ciudad universitaria** university campus
ciudadanía SF **1** (= *habitantes*) citizens (*pl*), citizenry (*frm*)
2 (= *status*) citizenship • **derechos de ~** rights of citizenship ▸ **ciudadanía de honor** freedom of the city
ciudadano/a ADJ civic, city (*antes de s*) • **el orgullo ~** civic pride
SM/F citizen • **el ~ de a pie** the man in the street • **~ de honor** freeman of the city • **~ del mundo** citizen of the world • **~s de segunda clase** second-class citizens
ciudadela SF **1** (*Mil*) citadel, fortress
2 (*LAm*) (= *casa pobre*) tenement block
ciudad-estado SF (PL: **ciudades-estado**) city-state
ciudadrealeño/a ADJ of/from Ciudad Real
SM/F native/inhabitant of Ciudad Real • **los ~s** the people of Ciudad Real
civeta SF civet cat
civeto SM civet
cívico ADJ [*deber*] civic; [*persona*] public-spirited, civic-minded
SM **1** (*Arg*) (= *vaso de cerveza*) large glass of beer
2 (*LAm*) (= *policía*) policeman
civil ADJ **1** (= *no militar*) [*autoridad, aviación*] civil; [*vida, víctima, población*] civilian • **guerra ~** civil war • **va vestido de ~** he's wearing civilian clothes, he's in civilian clothes • **la sociedad ~** civil society
2 (= *no religioso*) civil • **matrimonio ~** civil wedding, registry office wedding • **contrajo matrimonio ~** he got married in a registry office (wedding) • **casarse por lo ~** to have a civil wedding, have a registry office wedding, be married in a civil ceremony
3 (*Jur*) [*responsabilidad, desobediencia*] civil; ▹ **código, derecho, gobernador, guardia, protección, registro**
SMF **1** (= *persona no militar*) civilian
2 (= *guardia*) civil guard
civilidad SF civility, courtesy, politeness
civilismo SM (*Cono Sur*) pro-civilian-government stance
civilización SF civilization
civilizado ADJ civilized
civilizador ADJ civilizing
civilizar ▹ CONJUG 1f VT to civilize
VPR **civilizarse** to become civilized
civilizatorio ADJ civilizing
civismo SM sense of civic responsibility, public-spiritedness
cizalla SF, **cizallas** SFPL **1** (= *tijeras*) wire cutters, metal shears; (= *guillotina*) guillotine
2 (= *fragmento*) shavings, metal clippings
cizaña SF **1** (*Bot*) darnel; (*Biblia*) tares
2 (= *discordia*) discord • **meter** *o* **sembrar ~** to sow discord (**entre** among), create a rift (**entre** between)
3 (= *vicio*) vice, corruption, harmful influence
cizañar ▹ CONJUG 1a VT, **cizañear** VT to sow discord among
cizañero/a SM/F troublemaker, mischief-maker
cl ABR (= **centilitro(s)**) cl
clac SM (PL: **claques**) opera hat, cocked hat
SF claque
clamar ▹ CONJUG 1a VT [+ *justicia, venganza*] to clamour for, clamor for (EEUU), cry out for; [+ *inocencia*] to proclaim
VI (= *protestar*) to protest • **~ contra** to protest against, cry out against • **~ por** to clamour for, clamor for (EEUU), to cry out for • MODISMO: • **~ al cielo** *o* **a Dios** to be an absolute outrage • **una injusticia que clama al cielo** an absolutely outrageous injustice
clamidia SF chlamydia
clamor SM **1** (= *griterío*) clamour, clamor (EEUU), roar • **el ~ de los espectadores** the clamour *o* roar of the spectators
2 (= *protesta*) outcry • **un gran ~ contra la corrupción** a great outcry against corruption • **este poema es un ~ contra la violencia** this poem is a protest against death
3 [*de campana*] toll
clamorear ▹ CONJUG 1a VT = **clamar**
VI [*campana*] to toll
clamoreo SM **1** (= *griterío*) clamour(ing), clamor(ing) (EEUU), prolonged shouting
2 (= *ruegos*) beseeching, pleading
3 (= *protestas*) sustained outcry, vociferous protests ▸ **clamoreos de protesta** vociferous protests
clamorosamente ADV clamorously
clamoroso ADJ **1** [*éxito*] resounding, enormous; [*acogida, recibimiento*] rapturous
2 (= *vociferante*) clamorous
clan SM (*Hist*) clan; [*de gángsters*] family, mob*
clandestinamente ADV clandestinely
clandestinidad SF secrecy, clandestinity, secret nature • **en la ~** in secrecy • **movimiento en la ~** (*Pol*) underground movement • **pasar a la ~** to go into hiding, go underground
clandestinista SM (*LAm*) bootlegger
clandestino/a ADJ **1** [*reunión, cita*] secret, clandestine; [*boda*] secret; [*pasos*] stealthy
2 (*Pol*) [*actividad, movimiento*] clandestine, underground; [*agente*] secret, undercover; [*inmigrante*] illegal • **andar ~** (*LAm*) (*Pol*) to be underground
SM/F illegal immigrant
SMPL **clandestinos** (*And*) shacks
clánico ADJ clannish, clan (*antes de s*)
claque SF claque
claqué SM tap dancing
claqueta SF clapperboard
clara SF **1** [*de huevo*] egg white • **bata las ~s a punto de nieve** whisk the egg whites until they form peaks • **una ~ de huevo** the white of an egg, an egg white
2 (*Esp*) (= *cerveza con gaseosa*) shandy, lager shandy
3 (= *calva*) bald patch
claraboya SF skylight
claramente ADV clearly • **es una medida ~ inadecuada** this measure is clearly inadequate
clarea SF *white wine with cinnamon, sugar and spices added*
clarear ▹ CONJUG 1a VI **1** (*Meteo*) (= *despejarse*) to clear up
2 (*al amanecer*) [*día*] to dawn, break; [*cielo*] to grow light • **ya empieza a ~** it's starting to get light now
3 (= *escasear*) • **con la altura el monte ya clarea** as you go up the vegetation becomes more sparse • **ya le empieza a ~ el pelo** he's beginning to lose his hair
4 (= *transparentarse*) [*tela*] to be transparent • **ya empiezan a ~le las sienes** he's beginning to go grey at the temples
VT (= *iluminar*) to light up; (= *aclarar*) to make lighter
VPR **clarearse 1** [*tela*] to be transparent
2* (= *delatarse*) to give the game away
clareo‡ SM • **darse un ~** (= *pasear*) to take a stroll; (= *irse*) to hoof it*
clarete SM (= *tinto claro*) light red wine; [*de Burdeos*] claret
claridad SF **1** (= *luminosidad*) light • **me despierta la ~** the light wakes me • **en la ~ de la mañana** in the light of the morning, in the brightness of the morning light (*liter*) • **este cuarto tiene mucha ~** this room is very light
2 [*de explicación*] clarity • **explicar/expresar algo con ~** to explain sth clearly
3 (= *nitidez*) [*de sonido, voz*] clarity; [*de imagen*] sharpness, clarity • **oír/ver algo con ~** to hear/see sth clearly
4 (= *sinceridad*) frankness • **hablar con ~** to speak frankly
claridoso ADJ (*CAm, Méx*) blunt, plain-spoken
clarificación SF **1** (= *aclaración*) clarification
2 [*de vino, licor*] clarification
3 (= *iluminación*) illumination, lighting (up)
clarificador ADJ = **clarificante**
clarificante ADJ [*experiencia, charla*] illuminating, enlightening; [*notas, teoría*] explanatory
SM clarifier, clarifying agent

clarificar ▸ CONJUG 1g (VT) **1** [+ *asunto, problema*] to clarify
2 [+ *líquidos*] to clarify
3 (= *iluminar*) to illuminate, light (up)

clarín (SM) **1** (*Mús*) (= *instrumento*) bugle, trumpet; [*de órgano*] clarion
2 (*Chile*) (*Bot*) sweet pea
(SMF) (= *instrumentista*) bugler

clarinada* (SF) uncalled-for remark

clarinazo (SM) warning signal

clarinero (SM) bugler

clarinete (SM) (= *instrumento*) clarinet
(SMF) (= *persona*) clarinettist

clarinetista (SMF) clarinettist

clarión (SM) chalk, white crayon

clarisa (ADJ) • **monja ~** Poor Clare nun
(SF) Poor Clare

clarividencia (SF) **1** (= *adivinación*) clairvoyance
2 (= *previsión*) farsightedness; (= *discernimiento*) discernment; (= *intuición*) intuition

clarividente (ADJ) **1** (= *que adivina el futuro*) clairvoyant
2 (= *previsor*) far-sighted; (= *discerniente*) discerning; (= *intuitivo*) intuitive
(SMF) clairvoyant

claro (ADJ) **1** (= *no oscuro*) [*piel*] fair; [*color*] light, pale • **un vestido verde ~** a light *o* pale green dress • **pelo castaño ~** light brown hair • **una alemana de ojos ~s** a blue-eyed German girl
2 (= *evidente*) **a** (*con sustantivos*) [*ejemplo, prueba, ventaja*] clear; [*inconveniente*] obvious; [*desastre*] total, absolute • **esto es un ~ reflejo de que el sistema no funciona** this is a clear indication that the system does not work • **España ganó por un ~ 15-6** Spain won a decisive 15-6 victory, Spain were clear winners by 15-6 • **... aseguró, en clara referencia a sus superiores** ... he asserted, clearly referring *o* in an obvious reference to his superiors
b (*con verbos*) • **dejar algo ~** to make sth clear • **ha dejado bien ~ que no quiere vernos más** he has made it quite clear he does not want to see us again • **dejar las cosas claras** *o* **en ~** to get things clear, get things straight* • **estar ~** to be clear • **el futuro del equipo no está muy ~** the future of the team is not very clear • **¿está ~?** is that clear? • **estar ~ que** to be clear that, be obvious that • **está ~ que así no vamos a ninguna parte** it's clear *o* obvious that we'll get nowhere like this • **no está nada ~ que nuestro partido vaya a ganar las elecciones** it's not at all clear that our party will win the election • **quedar ~** to be clear • **si te lees la bibliografía, te quedará todo más ~** if you read the books on the reading list, it'll all be clearer to you *o* you'll have a better idea of things • **así quedarán claras nuestras intenciones** this way our intentions will be (quite) clear • **tener algo ~** to be sure of sth, be clear about sth • **ni siquiera tengo ~ lo que me espera mañana** I'm not even sure *o* clear what's in store for me tomorrow • **es importante tener nuestro objetivo bien ~** it is important to be sure of our objective • **no lo tengo nada ~** I'm not at all sure, I don't really know
c • MODISMOS: • **a las claras**: • **prefiero decírselo a las claras** I prefer to tell him straight (out) • **su triunfo deja bien a las claras el buen momento que atraviesa** his victory is a clear indication *o* sign that he is on excellent form • **ser más ~ que el agua** • **ser ~ como la luz del día** to be crystal-clear • **las cuentas claras**: • **me gustan las cuentas claras** I like to have *o* keep things clear • **el ministro ha presentado las cuentas claras al Parlamento** the minister has been quite straightforward with Parliament • **llevarlo** (*Esp*) *o* **tenerlo ~** (*iró*): • **lo tienes ~** things won't be easy for you • **sacar algo en ~ (de algo)**: • **solo hemos sacado en ~ que no pretende dimitir** all that we can safely *o* definitely say is that he has no intention of resigning • **lo único que la policía consiguió sacar en ~ durante el interrogatorio** the only definite thing the police got from the interview • **no he sacado nada en ~ de esa conferencia** I'm still none the wiser after that lecture • **ver algo ~**: • **no ven ~ cómo van a poder terminar a tiempo** they can't really see how they are going to finish on time • **el ministro ve ~ que se puede lograr un acuerdo** the minister is optimistic about reaching an agreement • **lo vi ~ en cuanto oí la noticia** it became clear to me when I heard the news • **sus padres no veían muy ~ el tema** his parents weren't too sure about the matter
3 (= *poco espeso*) [*té, café*] weak; [*caldo*] thin
4 (= *luminoso*) [*día, mañana*] bright; [*habitación, casa*] light, bright
5 (= *transparente*) [*agua*] clear; [*tejido*] transparent
6 (= *nítido*) [*sonido, voz*] clear; [*imagen*] sharp, clear
7 (= *escaso*) [*pelo*] thin; [*bosque*] light, sparse
8 (= *preciso*) [*idea*] clear • **tiene las ideas muy claras** he really knows what he wants from life • **una mente clara** (*lit*) a clear mind; (*fig*) a clear thinker
9 (= *sincero*) frank • **ser ~** to be frank
(ADV) **1** (= *con precisión*) [*oír, ver, hablar*] clearly
2 (= *sinceramente*) frankly • **hablar ~** to speak frankly, be frank • MODISMO: • **~ y raspado** (*Ven*) frankly and to the point
3 (*tras invitaciones, peticiones*) sure • **—¿puedo usar tu coche mañana? —¡claro!** "can I use your car tomorrow?" — "sure!" • **—¿queréis venir a cenar? —¡claro!** "would you like to come to dinner?" — "sure!"
4 (*uso enfático*) • **¡claro! por eso estaba ayer tan rara** of course! that's why she was acting so funny yesterday • **a menos que, ~ está, él también la conozca** unless of course he knows her too • **—¿por qué no te disfrazas tú? —¡~, para que os riáis de mí todos!** "why don't you dress up?" — "oh sure, so you can all laugh at me!" • **~ que**: • **~ que nadie se imaginaba lo que vendría después** of course nobody could imagine what would happen afterwards • **¡~ que no!** of course not! • **~ que no es verdad** of course it isn't true • **¡~ que sí!** yes, of course!
(SM) **1** (*Meteo*) bright spell, sunny interval • **habrá nubes y ~s** it will be cloudy with bright spells *o* sunny intervals • **un pequeño ~ entre las nubes** a slight break in the clouds ▸ **claro de luna** moonlight
2 [*de tiempo*] lull • **aprovechamos un clarillo para salir a comprar** we took advantage of a little lull to go and do some shopping • MODISMO: • **velar de ~ en ~** to lie awake all night
3 (= *espacio despejado*) (*entre personas*) space; (*entre árboles*) clearing; [*de pelo*] bald patch • **se pueden ver algunos ~s en la sala** there are a few (empty) spaces in the hall
4 (*en un texto*) gap, space; (*en discurso*) pause
5 (*Arquit*) (= *claraboya*) skylight; (= *abertura*) window (opening)
6 (*Caribe*) (*Culin*) guava jelly
7 (*Caribe*) (= *bebida*) sugar-cane brandy

claroscuro (SM) chiaroscuro

clase (SF) **1** (*Escol*) **a** (= *lección*) lesson, class • **una ~ de historia** a history lesson *o* class • **~ de música** music lesson • **~ de conducir** driving lesson • **dar** *o* (*Chile*) **hacer ~(s)** [*profesor*] to teach; (*Esp*) [*alumno*] to have lessons • MODISMO: • **fumarse** *o* **saltarse** *o* **soplarse la ~*** to skip class*, skive off*
b (= *instrucción*) school • **hoy no tengo ~** I don't have school today • **los viernes salgo de ~ a las cuatro** on Fridays I finish school at four • **faltar a ~** to miss school, be absent
c (= *aula*) classroom
d (= *grupo de alumnos*) class • **es el primero de la ~** he is top of the class • **la gente de mi ~** my classmates, my class • **compañero de ~** classmate ▸ **clase nocturna** evening class ▸ **clase particular** private lesson • **doy ~s particulares de francés** I teach private lessons in French • **"se dan clases particulares"** "private tuition offered"
2 (*Univ*) **a** (*práctica*) (= *lección, instrucción*) class; (= *aula*) classroom • **hoy no tengo ~** I don't have any classes today • **dar** *o* (*LAm*) (*frm*) **dictar ~** [*profesor*] to teach; [*alumno*] (*Esp*) to have classes
b (= *lección*) lecture • **hoy no voy a ~** I'm not going to any lectures today, I'm not going to University today • **dar ~** [*profesor*] to teach, lecture; [*alumno*] to have lectures • **doy ~ de Derecho Civil** I teach civil law
c (= *aula*) lecture room ▸ **clase magistral** master class
3 (= *tipo*) kind, sort • **gente de todas ~s** all kinds *o* sorts of people, people of all kinds • **les deseo toda ~ de felicidad** I wish you every happiness • **con toda ~ de detalles** in great detail, down to the last detail
4 (= *calidad*) quality • **productos de primera ~** top-quality products
5 (*en viajes*) class • **primera ~** first class • **viajar en primera ~** to travel first class • **segunda ~** second class, standard class • **un billete de segunda ~** a second class ticket ▸ **clase económica** economy class ▸ **clase preferente** club class ▸ **clase turista** tourist class
6 (= *elegancia*) class • **una persona con ~** someone with class • **tener ~** to have class • **tu hermana tiene mucha ~** your sister has a lot of class, your sister's very classy
7 (*Sociol*) class • **la lucha de ~s** the class struggle • **las ~s acomodadas** the well-to-do, the moneyed classes • **la ~ dirigente** *o* **dominante** the ruling class • **la ~ médica** the medical profession • **la ~ política** politicians (*pl*), the political establishment (*Sociol*) • **las ~s privilegiadas** the privileged classes ▸ **clase alta** upper class • **una joven de ~ alta** an upper-class girl ▸ **clase baja** lower class • **un chico de ~ baja** a lower-class boy ▸ **clase media** middle class • **una familia de ~ media** a middle-class family ▸ **clase media-alta** upper-middle class ▸ **clase media-baja** lower-middle class ▸ **clase obrera** working class • **la mentalidad de la ~ obrera** the working-class mentality ▸ **clase social** social class
8 (*Bio, Bot*) class
9 (*Mil*) ▸ **clases de tropa** non-commissioned officers
(ADJ) (*And**) first-rate, classy*

clásicas (SFPL) (*Univ*) classics

clasicismo (SM) classicism

clásico (ADJ) **1** (*Arte, Mús*) classical
2 (= *característico*) classic • **el ~ error de los estudiantes ingleses** the classic mistake of students of English • **es la clásica plazuela española** it is a typical Spanish square
3 (= *de época*) [*coche*] vintage
4 [*costumbre*] time-honoured • **le dio el ~ saludo** he gave him the time-honoured greeting
5 (= *destacado*) outstanding, remarkable

SM 1 (= *obra, película*) classic
2 (= *artista, escritor*) outstanding figure, big name*

CLÁSICO

¿"Classic" o "classical"?

Hay que tener en cuenta que el adjetivo **clásico** *se puede traducir por* **classic** *o por* **classical**:

▷ *Se traduce por* **classic** *cuando el sustantivo al que acompaña reúne todas las características propias de su especie o cuando nos referimos a películas, libros etc de una calidad extraordinaria:*

Es el clásico ejemplo de niño mimado
He's a classic example of a spoilt child
... una de las historias de detectives clásicas de esa época ...
... one of the classic detective stories of that time ...

▷ *Se traduce por* **classical** *cuando* **clásico** *hace referencia a la música clásica o a asuntos relacionados con las civilizaciones griega y romana:*

Cuanta más música clásica escucho más me gusta
The more classical music I listen to the more I enjoy it
El Partenón es uno de los ejemplos más significativos de la arquitectura clásica
The Parthenon is one of the most significant examples of classical architecture

Para otros usos y ejemplos ver la entrada.

clasificable ADJ classifiable
clasificación SF 1 (= *categorización*) classification
2 (= *ordenación*) [*de documentos*] classification; (*Inform, Correos*) sorting
3 (*Náut*) rating
4 (*en torneo*) qualification
5 (= *lista*) table, league
clasificado ADJ [*anuncios*] classified; [*película*] rated
SMPL **clasificados** (*LAm*) classifieds
clasificador SM 1 (= *mueble*) filing cabinet ▸ **clasificador de cartas** letter file
2 (= *aparato*) collator
3 (= *persona*) classifier
clasificar ▷ CONJUG 1g VT 1 (= *categorizar*) to classify • **lo ~on bajo la letra B** they classified it under the letter B
2 (= *ordenar*) [+ *documentos*] to classify; (*Correos, Inform*) to sort
VPR **clasificarse** (*Dep*) • **mi equipo se clasificó en segundo lugar** my team came *o* was placed second • **no se clasificó el equipo para la final** the team did not qualify for the final
clasificatoria SF (= *ronda*) qualifying round; (*Atletismo*) heat
clasificatorio ADJ [*fase, prueba*] qualifying • **tabla clasificatoria** league table
clasismo SM 1 (= *actitud discriminatoria*) classism
2 (= *estructura social*) class structure
clasista ADJ 1 [*actitud*] class-conscious, classist; (*pey*) snobbish • **Gran Bretaña es aún una sociedad muy ~** Britain is still a very class-conscious society • **un análisis ~** a classist analysis
2 (= *de clases*) class (*antes de s*)
SMF class-conscious person; (*pey*) snob
claudia SF greengage
claudicación SF giving way, abandonment of one's principles, backing down ▸ **claudicación moral** failure in one's moral duty
claudicar ▷ CONJUG 1g VI 1 (= *rendirse*) to give in • **no claudicó ante el chantaje** he did not give in to the blackmail
2 (= *renunciar*) • **~ de algo** to renounce sth • **no podemos ~ de nuestras convicciones** we cannot renounce our convictions
3† (= *cojear*) to limp
4† (= *engañar*) to act deceitfully
5† (= *vacilar*) to waver, stall
Claudio SM Claudius
claustral SMF (*Univ*) member of the Senate
claustro SM 1 (*Rel*) cloister
2 (*Univ*) staff, faculty (*EEUU*); (= *junta*) senate; (= *asamblea*) staff meeting
3 (*Anat*) ▸ **claustro materno** womb
claustrofobia SF claustrophobia
claustrofóbico ADJ claustrophobic
cláusula SF clause ▸ **cláusula de exclusión** (*Com*) exclusion clause ▸ **cláusula de reajuste de los precios** escalation clause ▸ **cláusula de rescisión** cancellation clause ▸ **cláusula de revisión** trigger clause
clausura SF 1 [*de local, edificio*] closure
2 [*de olimpiada, congreso*] closing ceremony; [*de tribunal*] closing session • **discurso de ~** closing speech
3 (*Rel*) (= *recinto*) cloister; (= *reclusión religiosa*) cloister, religious seclusion • **convento de ~** enclosed convent, enclosed monastery
4 (*Méx*) (*Jur*) [*de negocio*] closing down
clausurar ▷ CONJUG 1a VT 1 [+ *debate, curso*] to close, bring to a close
2 [+ *negocio, edificio*] to close, close down
3 (*LAm*) [+ *casa*] to close (up)
clava SF club, cudgel
clavada SF 1 (= *salto*) dive
2‡ • **pegar una ~ a algn** to rip sb off‡, overcharge sb
clavadista SMF (*CAm, Méx*) (*Dep*) diver
clavado ADJ 1 (= *fijo*) (*con clavos, puntas*) nailed
2 (= *decorado*) [*mueble*] studded with nails
3 [*ropa*] just right
4 • **dejar a algn ~** to leave sb speechless • **quedó ~** he was speechless *o* dumbfounded
5 • **a las cinco clavadas** at five sharp *o* on the dot
6 (= *idéntico*) • **es Pedro ~** he's the spitting image of Pedro • **es** *o* (*LAm*) **está ~ a su padre** he's the spitting image of his father
7 • **¡clavado!** exactly!, precisely!
SM (= *salto*) dive • **dar un ~** to dive, take a dive
clavar ▷ CONJUG 1a VT 1 (= *hincar*) [+ *clavo*] to hammer in • **le clavó un cuchillo en el cuello** he stuck a knife in his throat • **me clavé un alfiler mientras cosía** I stuck a needle in(to) my finger while I was sewing • **le clavó las uñas en la cara** she dug her nails into his face • **~ banderillas** (*Taur*) *to thrust banderillas into the bull's neck*
2 (= *fijar*) (*con clavos*) to nail • **ha clavado unas tablas en la puerta** he has nailed some panels onto the door • **clavó con chinchetas un póster de su equipo** he pinned up a poster of his team • MODISMO: • **~ la mirada** *o* **los ojos en algn/algo** to fix one's gaze *o* one's eyes on sb/sth
3 [+ *joya*] to set, mount
4 (*Ftbl*) [+ *pelota*] to hammer, drive • **el delantero clavó el balón en la red** the forward hammered *o* drove the ball into the net
5‡ (= *cobrar de más*) to rip off* • **me ~on 350 euros por una cena** I got ripped off to the tune of 350 euros for a meal • **—pagué cuarenta euros —pues, te han clavado** "I paid forty euros" — "you were ripped off"
6* (= *hacer perfecto*) • **—¿cómo has hecho el examen? —lo he clavado** "how did the exam go?" — "it was spot on"*
7 (*Méx‡*) (= *robar*) to swipe*, nick*, pinch*
VPR **clavarse 1** [*espina, astilla*] • **se me ha clavado una astilla en la mano** I've got a splinter in my hand • **se me clavó una raspa en la garganta** a fishbone got stuck in my throat
2 (*reflexivo*) • **se clavó la espada** he stabbed himself with his sword
3 (*CAm, Méx*) (*Dep*) to dive
clave SF 1 (= *código*) code • **la ~ de la caja fuerte** the code of *o* to the safe • **la ~ secreta** the secret code • **en ~** in code • **hablan en ~** they speak in code • **mensaje en ~** coded message, message in code ▸ **clave de acceso** (*Inform*) password ▸ **clave de búsqueda** (*Inform*) search key ▸ **clave de clasificación** (*Inform*) sort key
2 (= *quid*) key • **la ~ del problema** the key to the problem • **una de las ~s para entender el tema** one of the keys to understanding the subject
3 (*Mús*) clef ▸ **clave de fa** bass clef ▸ **clave de sol** treble clef
4 (= *sentido*) • **una interpretación en ~ económica** an economic interpretation, an interpretation from an economic viewpoint *o* perspective • **una novela escrita en ~ de humor** a novel written in a humorous style *o* tone
5 (*Arquit*) keystone
SM (*Mús*) harpsichord
ADJ (= *esencial*) [*tema, punto, factor, personaje*] key (*antes de s*) • **una figura ~ en la política catalana** a key figure in Catalan politics • **cuestión ~** key question • **palabra ~** keyword
clavecín SM spinet
clavel SM carnation • MODISMO: • **no tener un ~*** to be broke*
clavellina SF pink
clavelón SM marigold, African marigold
clavero¹ SM (*Bot*) clove tree
clavero² SM (= *llavero*) key-holder
claveteado SM studding, studs
clavetear ▷ CONJUG 1a VT 1 (= *adornar*) [+ *puerta, mueble*] to stud, decorate with nails
2 [+ *cordón*] to put a metal tip on, tag
3 [+ *trato*] to clinch, close
clavicémbalo SM harpsichord, clavicembalo
clavicordio SM clavichord
clavícula SF collarbone, clavicle
clavidista SMF (*Méx*) (*Dep*) diver
clavija SF (*Carpintería*) peg, dowel, pin; (*Mús*) peg; (*Elec*) plug • MODISMO: • **apretar las ~s a algn** to put the screws on sb* ▸ **clavija de dos patas, clavija hendida** cotter pin, split pin
clavijero SM 1 (*Mús*) pegbox
2 (= *percha*) clothes rack
clavillo SM, **clavito** SM 1 (*Téc*) pivot, pin ▸ **clavillo de tijeras** pin, rivet
2 (*Bot*) clove
clavo SM 1 [*de carpintero*] nail; [*de adorno*] stud • MODISMOS: • **agarrarse a un ~ ardiendo**: • **estoy tan desesperado que me agarraría a un ~ ardiendo** I'm so desperate I'd do anything *o* I'm capable of anything • **los estudiantes se agarran a esta ley como a un ~ ardiendo** the students are pinning their hopes on this law as their last hope • **como un ~**: • **llegó a las dos en punto, como un ~** she arrived at two o'clock on the dot • **a las doce, como un ~, llamaba a la puerta** at twelve o'clock, as regular as clockwork, he would call at the door • **dar en el ~** to hit the

nail on the head • **dar una en el ~ y ciento en la herradura** to be more often wrong than right • **entrar de ~** to squeeze in • **¡por los ~s de Cristo!** for heaven's sake! • **remachar el ~** (= *empeorar*) to make matters worse • **meter algo de ~** to slip sth in • **ser una verdad de ~ pasado** to be patently obvious • REFRÁN: • **un ~ saca a otro ~** a new worry helps to take the pain away *o* take your mind off the old one ▸ **clavo romano** brass-headed nail ▸ **clavo sin cabeza** panel pin
2 [*de botas de fútbol*] stud; [*de zapatillas de correr*] spike
3 [*de montañismo*] piton
4 (*Bot*) (*tb* **clavo de olor**) clove
5 (= *callo*) corn
6 (*Med*) (= *pieza metálica*) (metal) pin, (metal) rod
7 (*CAm, Méx*) (*Min*) *rich vein of ore*
8 (*And, Cono Sur*) (= *cosa desagradable*) • **es un ~ tener que levantarse temprano** it's a real pain *o* bind having to get up so early • **¡vaya ~ que te han vendido!** they've sold you a dud!*
9 (*CAm, Méx*) (= *problema*) problem, snag
claxon (SM) (PL: **claxons** *o* **cláxones**) horn • **tocar el ~** to sound *o* blow one's horn, hoot, honk
claxonar ▹ CONJUG 1a (VI) to sound *o* blow one's horn, hoot, honk
claxonazo (SM) hoot, toot (on the horn), honk
clemátide (SF) clematis
clemencia (SF) (= *misericordia*) mercy, clemency; (*Jur*) leniency
clemente (ADJ) (= *misericordioso*) merciful, clement; (*Jur*) lenient
clementina (SF) clementine, tangerine
Cleopatra (SF) Cleopatra
cleptomanía (SF) kleptomania
cleptómano/a (ADJ), (SM/F) kleptomaniac
clerecía (SF) 1 (= *oficio*) priesthood
2 (= *grupo*) clergy
clergyman [klerxi'man] (ADJ INV) • **traje ~** *modernized form of priest's attire (adopted in Spain 1962)*
clerical (ADJ) clerical
(SM) (*CAm, Caribe*) clergyman, minister
clericalismo (SM) clericalism
clericato (SM), **clericatura** (SF) priesthood
clericó (SM) (*Cono Sur*) mulled wine
clérigo (SM) (*católico*) priest; (*anglicano*) clergyman, priest
clero (SM) clergy
clic (SM) click • **hacer ~ en algo** (*Inform*) to click on sth • **hacer doble ~ en algo** to double-click on sth
clicar ▹ CONJUG 1a (VI) (*Inform*) to click • **clica en el icono** click on the icon • **~ dos veces** to double-click
cliché (SM) 1 (*Tip*) stencil
2 (= *tópico*) cliché
3 (*Fot*) negative
click (SM) = clic
cliente (SMF) [*de tienda, bar, restaurante, banco*] customer; [*de empresa*] customer, client; [*de hotel*] guest, customer • **el ~ siempre tiene la razón** the customer is always right ▸ **cliente fijo, cliente habitual** regular customer
clientela (SF) (*Com*) clientele, customers (*pl*); (*Med*) practice, patients (*pl*)
clientelar (ADJ) 1 (*de patrocinio*) of *o* relating to political patronage
2 (*de corrupción*) of *o* relating to corruption • **redes ~es dedicadas a extraer sobornos** networks of corruption dedicated to extracting bribes
clientelismo (SM) patronage system
clima (SM) (*Meteo*) climate; [*de reunión*] atmosphere; [*de situación*] climate ▸ **clima artificial** (*LAm*) air conditioning ▸ **clima de opinión** climate of public opinion
climatérico (ADJ) climacteric
climático (ADJ) climatic
climatización (SF) air conditioning
climatizado (ADJ) air-conditioned
climatizador (SM) air conditioning, climate control (system)
climatizar ▹ CONJUG 1f (VT) to air-condition
climatología (SF) (= *ciencia*) climatology; (= *tiempo*) weather
climatológico (ADJ) climatological • **estudios ~s** studies in climate *o* climatic change
climatólogo/a (SM/F) climatologist
clímax ['klimas] (SM INV) climax
clinch [klinʃ] (SM) (*LAm*), **clincha** (SF) (*LAm*) clinch
clínica (SF) 1 (= *hospital*) clinic; [*de formación*] teaching hospital ▸ **clínica ambulatoria** outpatients' department ▸ **clínica de reposo** convalescent home, rest home
2 (*Univ*) clinical training; ▹ **clínico**
clínicamente (ADV) clinically • **~ muerto** clinically dead
clínico/a (ADJ) [*asistencia, análisis*] clinical • **hospital ~** teaching hospital
(SMF) (= *médico*) consultant; ▹ **clínica**
clip (SM) (PL: **clips** [klis]) 1 [*de sujeción*] (*para papeles*) paper clip; [*de collar, pulsera*] fastener; [*de pantalón*] trouser-clip
2 (*LAm*) (= *pendiente*) clip-on earring
3 [*de vídeo*] videoclip
clíper (SM) clipper
cliqueable (ADJ) clickable
cliquear ▹ CONJUG 1a (VI) to click • **cliquea en el icono** click on the icon
clisar ▹ CONJUG 1a (VT) to stereotype, stencil
clisé (SM) 1 (*Tip*) cliché, stereotype plate; (*Fot*) negative
2 (= *tópico*) cliché
clisos‡ (SMPL) peepers‡, eyes
clitoridectomía (SF) clitoridectomy
clítoris (SM INV) clitoris
clo (SM) cluck • **hacer clo** to cluck
cloaca (SF) sewer, drain
cloacal (ADJ) 1 [*sistema*] sewage (*antes de s*)
2 (*hum*) [*chiste*] lavatorial
cloch, cloche (SM) (*CAm, Méx*) clutch
clon (SM) clone
clonación (SF), **clonaje** (SM) cloning
clonar ▹ CONJUG 1a (VT) to clone
clónico (ADJ) clonal, cloned
(SM) (*Inform*) clone
cloquear ▹ CONJUG 1a (VI) to cluck
cloqueo (SM) clucking
cloración (SF) chlorination
clorador (SM) chlorinator
cloral (SM) chloral
clorar ▹ CONJUG 1a (VT) to chlorinate
cloratita (SF) chloratite
clorhídrico (ADJ) hydrochloric
clorinar ▹ CONJUG 1a (VT) to chlorinate
clorinda (SF) (*Cono Sur*) bleach
cloro (SM) chlorine
clorofila (SF) chlorophyl(l)
clorofluorocarbono (SM) chlorofluorocarbon
cloroformar ▹ CONJUG 1a (VT) (*LAm*), **cloroformizar** ▹ CONJUG 1f (VT) to chloroform
cloroformo (SM) chloroform
cloruro (SM) chloride ▸ **cloruro de cal** chloride of lime ▸ **cloruro cálcico** calcium chloride ▸ **cloruro de hidrógeno** hydrogen chloride ▸ **cloruro de polivinilo** polyvinyl chloride ▸ **cloruro sódico** sodium chloride
closet (SM), **clóset** (SM) (*LAm*) (*gen*) (built-in) cupboard; (*para ropa*) (built-in) wardrobe, closet (*EEUU*)
clown [klawn] (SM) (PL: **clowns**) clown
clownesco (ADJ) clownish
club (SM) (PL: **clubs** *o* **clubes**) 1 (= *sociedad*) club ▸ **club de fans** fan club ▸ **club de fútbol** football club ▸ **club de golf** golf club ▸ **club deportivo** sports club ▸ **club de tiro** shooting club, rifle club ▸ **club náutico** yacht club
2 (= *bar*) club ▸ **club de alterne** hostess club ▸ **club de carretera** roadside brothel ▸ **club nocturno** night club
clubista (SMF) club member
clueca (SF) broody hen
clueco (ADJ) 1 [*gallina*] broody
2 (*Cono Sur*) (= *enfermizo*) sickly, weak
3 (*Caribe**) (= *engreído*) stuck-up*
cluniacense (ADJ), (SM) Cluniac
clutch (SM) (*Méx*) clutch
cm (ABR) (= **centímetro(s)**) cm
cm² (ABR) (= **centímetros cuadrados**) sq. cm
cm³ (ABR) (= **centímetros cúbicos**) cc
CNA (SM ABR) (= **Congreso Nacional Africano**) ANC
CNC (SM ABR) (*Col*) = **Consejo Nacional del Café**
CNEA (SF ABR) (*Arg*) = **Comisión Nacional de Energía Atómica**
Cnel. (ABR) (= **Coronel**) Col
CNI (SF ABR) (*Chile*) (= **Central Nacional de Informaciones**) *Chilean secret police*
CNMV (SF ABR) = **Comisión Nacional del Mercado de Valores**
CNT (SF ABR) 1 (*Esp*) (= **Confederación Nacional del Trabajo**) *anarchist trade union*
2 (*Cono Sur, Méx*) (= **Confederación Nacional de Trabajadores**) *trade union*
co... (PREF) co...
coa (SF) 1 (*CAm, Caribe, Méx*) (*Agr*) (*para cavar*) long-handled narrow spade; (*para sembrar*) pointed stick for sowing seed
2 (*Cono Sur*) (= *argot*) underworld slang
coacción (SF) coercion, compulsion • **con ~** under duress
coaccionador (ADJ) constraining, compelling
coaccionar ▹ CONJUG 1a (VT) to coerce, pressure
coach (SMF) life coach
coactivo (ADJ) coercive
coacusado/a (SM/F) co-defendant
coadjutor(a) (SM/F) assistant, coadjutor (*frm*)
coadyuvar ▹ CONJUG 1a (VI) • **coadjuvar a** to contribute to
coagulación (SF) [*de sangre*] coagulation, clotting; [*de leche*] curdling
coagulante (SM) coagulant
coagular ▹ CONJUG 1a (VT) [+ *sangre*] to coagulate, clot, congeal; [+ *leche*] to curdle
(VPR) **coagularse** to coagulate; [*sangre*] to coagulate, clot, congeal; [*leche*] to curdle
coágulo (SM) clot, coagulum (*frm*) ▸ **coágulo de sangre, coágulo sanguíneo** blood clot
coalescente (ADJ) coalescent
coalición (SF) coalition • **gobierno de ~** coalition government
coalicionarse ▹ CONJUG 1a (VPR) to form a coalition
coaligado/a (ADJ) • **estar ~s** to be allied
(SM/F) ally
coaligarse ▹ CONJUG 1h (VPR) to make common cause (**con** with)
coartada (SF) alibi • **alegar una ~** to produce an alibi
coartar ▹ CONJUG 1a (VT) to limit, restrict
coaseguro (SM) coinsurance
coatí (SM) (*LAm*) coati
coautor(a) (SM/F) joint author, co-author
coaxial (ADJ) coaxial
coba (SF) 1 (= *adulación*) soft soap*, cajolery • **dar ~ a algn** to suck up to sb, play up to sb
2 (= *mentirilla*) fib; (= *truco*) neat trick
cobalto (SM) cobalt

cobarde ADJ (*en lucha, aventura*) cowardly; (*ante sangre, alturas*) faint-hearted; (= *tímido*) timid
SMF coward
cobardear ▸ CONJUG 1a VI to be a coward, show cowardice, act in a cowardly way
cobardemente ADV in a cowardly way
cobardía SF (= *miedo*) cowardice, cowardliness; (= *timidez*) faint-heartedness, timidity
cobardón SM shameful coward, great coward
cobaya SF guinea pig ▸ **cobaya humana** human guinea pig
cobayismo SM *use of animals or humans in medical experiments*
cobayo SM guinea pig
cobear* ▸ CONJUG 1a VI (*Ven*) to lie
cobertera SF **1** (= *tapadera*) lid, cover; [*de reloj*] watchcase
2 (*Bot*) white water lily
3† (= *alcahueta*) procuress
cobertizo SM **1** (*para animales, útiles*) shed
2 (= *refugio*) shelter ▸ **cobertizo de aviación** hangar ▸ **cobertizo de coche** carport
3 (= *tejadillo*) lean-to
cobertor SM bedspread, coverlet
cobertura SF **1** (*Radio, TV*) [*de noticia, acontecimiento*] coverage • **la ceremonia recibió amplia ~ informativa** the ceremony was widely covered, the ceremony received wide news coverage
2 (*Radio, TV, Telec*) (= *ámbito*) range • **este teléfono solo tiene ~ nacional** this phone only has a range within this country • **no hay ~** (*al interlocutor*) you're breaking up; (*al acompañante*) I can't get a signal; (*dicho por la empresa de telefonía*) there's no network coverage • **una emisora de ~ regional** a regional radio station
3 [*de un crédito*] cover ▸ **cobertura de desempleo** unemployment benefit, unemployment insurance (*EEUU*)
▸ **cobertura de dividendo** dividend cover
▸ **cobertura del seguro** insurance cover
▸ **cobertura sanitaria** health care
▸ **cobertura social** welfare (services) (*pl*)
4 (= *cubierta*) • **el fuego ha dañado la ~ vegetal** the fire has damaged the vegetation
cobija SF **1** (*Arquit*) ridge tile
2 (*LAm*) (= *manta*) blanket; [*de vestir*] poncho • **las ~s** the bedclothes • MODISMO: • **pegársele a algn las ~s** to oversleep
3 (*Caribe*) (= *techo*) roof (of palm leaves)
cobijar ▸ CONJUG 1a VT **1** (= *proteger*) to protect, shelter; (= *hospedar*) to take in, give shelter to; (*Pol, Jur*) to harbour, harbor (*EEUU*)
2 (*And, Caribe*) (= *techar*) to thatch, roof with palms
VPR **cobijarse** to (take) shelter
cobijo SM (= *protección, hospedaje*) shelter
cobista* ADJ greasy*, smarmy*
SMF bootlicker*, toady*
cobo SM (*Caribe*) **1** (*Zool*) sea snail
2 (= *persona*) unsociable person, shy person • **ser un ~** to be shy, be withdrawn
cobra¹ SF (*Zool*) cobra
cobra² SF (*Caza*) retrieval
cobrable ADJ, **cobradero** ADJ [*cheque*] cashable; [*precio*] chargeable; [*suma*] recoverable
cobrador(a) SM/F **1** (*Com*) collector ▸ **cobrador del frac**® debt collector (*working for company* ***Cobrador del Frac***®*, whose livery includes a tailcoat*)
2 (*en bus, tren*) conductor/conductress
cobranza SF **1** = cobro
2 (*Caza*) retrieval

cobrar ▸ CONJUG 1a VT **1** (= *pedir como pago*) to charge • **cobran 200 dólares por arreglarlo** they charge 200 dollars to repair it • **¿qué me va usted a ~?** what are you going to charge me? • **¿cuánto os cobra de alquiler?** how much rent does she charge you? • **me han cobrado demasiado** they've charged me too much, they've overcharged me • **¿me cobra, por favor?** how much do I owe you?, can I have the bill, please? • **¿me cobra los cafés?** how much do I owe you for the coffees?
2 (= *recibir*) • **no han cobrado el dinero prometido** they haven't been paid *o* received the money they were promised • **no hemos cobrado los dividendos** we haven't received any dividends • **cobran un sueldo anual de nueve millones** they get *o* earn *o* receive an annual salary of nine million • **¿cuánto cobras al año?** how much do you get *o* earn a year? • **nuestro vecino está cobrando el paro** our neighbour is on unemployment benefit • **cantidades a** *o* **por ~** amounts payable, amounts due • **cuentas a** *o* **por ~** accounts receivable • MODISMO: • **~ palos** (= *paliza*) to get a beating; (= *crítica*) to get *o* receive a lot of criticism
3 (= *recoger dinero de*) [+ *deuda, alquiler, impuesto*] to collect; [+ *cheque*] to cash; [+ *subsidio, pensión*] to draw • **voy a ir a ~ el desempleo** I'm going to draw my unemployment benefit • **tienen problemas para ~ las multas** they have problems collecting the fines
4 (= *adquirir*) • **los ordenadores han cobrado una gran importancia** computers have become very important • **~ actualidad** to become topical • **~ cariño a algn** to grow fond of sb • **~ fama** to become famous • **~ fama de inteligente/ladrón** to acquire a reputation for being intelligent/a thief • **~ fuerzas** to gather one's strength • **~ vida** [*personaje, juego*] to come alive • **el campo reverdece y cobra vida** the field turns green again and is infused with new life • **en la película todo cobra vida propia** the film takes on a life of its own
5 (= *recuperar*) [+ *pieza de caza*] to retrieve, fetch; [+ *cuerda*] to pull in, take in
6 (*LAm*) • **~ a algn** to press sb for payment
VI **1** (= *recibir dinero*) **a** (*como sueldo*) to be paid • **cobra los viernes** he gets paid on Fridays • **te pagaré en cuanto cobre** I'll pay you as soon as I get my wages • **el lechero vino a ~** the milkman came for his money, the milkman came to be paid • **los atletas cobran por participar en la carrera** the athletes get paid *o* receive a fee for taking part in the race
b (*por servicio*) to charge • **ahora cobran por renovar la tarjeta** they have introduced a charge for renewing your card • **no cobramos por llevarlo a domicilio** we don't charge for delivery • **~ por los servicios prestados** to charge for services rendered
2* (= *recibir golpes*) • **¡vas a ~!** you're (in) for it!
VPR **cobrarse 1** (= *recibir dinero*) • **¡cóbrese, por favor!** can I pay, please? • **¡se cobra aquí, por favor!** pay over here, please!
2 • **~se un favor** to call in a favour • **~se (la) venganza** to take one's revenge
3 [+ *muertos, víctimas*] to claim • **el accidente se cobró la vida de tres personas** the accident claimed the lives of three people
4 • **~se de una pérdida** to make up for a loss
5 (*Med*) (= *volver en sí*) to come to
cobre SM **1** (*Min*) copper; (*LAm**) (= *céntimo*) cent • **no tengo un ~** I haven't a cent/penny • MODISMOS: • **batir(se) el ~** (= *trabajar mucho*) to work with a will, work hard, hustle (*EEUU*); (*en discusión*) to get worked up • **batirse el ~ por** (+ *infin*) to go all out to (+ *infin*)
2 (*Culin*) copper pans (*pl*)
3 (*Mús*) brass
4 (*LAm*) • MODISMO: • **enseñar el ~** to show one's true colours
cobreado ADJ copperplated
cobreño ADJ (= *de cobre*) copper (*antes de s*); (= *parecido al cobre*) coppery
cobrero SM coppersmith
cobrizo ADJ coppery, copper-coloured, copper-colored (*EEUU*)
cobro SM **1** (= *recaudación*) [*de cheque*] cashing, encashment (*frm*); [*de salario, subsidio*] receipt, collection; [*de pensión*] collection, drawing; [*de factura, deuda*] collection • **endurecerán los requisitos para el ~ de pensiones** they will tighten up the requirements for drawing *o* collecting pensions • **protestó por el ~ de 50 euros por el servicio** he complained about the 50-euro charge for the service • **cargo** *o* **comisión por ~** collection charge ▸ **cobro revertido** • **llamada a ~ revertido** reverse charge call, collect call (*EEUU*) • **llamar a ~ revertido** to reverse the charges, call collect (*EEUU*), call toll-free (*EEUU*)
2 (= *pago*) • **nos comprometemos a garantizar el ~ de las pensiones** we make a guarantee that the pensions will be paid
3† • **poner algo en ~** to put sth in a safe place, put sth out of harm's way • **ponerse en ~** to take refuge
coca¹ SF **1** (*Bot*) coca; (= *droga*) coke*
2 (*Méx**) • MODISMO: • **de ~** free

COCA

In Peru, Colombia and Bolivia, the leaves of the Erythroxylon coca plant have traditionally been chewed as a mild stimulant and for a variety of medicinal purposes. As such, they are sold quite legally in street markets. Since **coca** is also the raw material for cocaine, peasant farmers in remote areas grow it to sell to the illegal drugs trade. Cartels in Cali and Medellín control most of the processing, shipment and distribution of cocaine and retain most of the profits. The cocaine industry brings few benefits to the vast majority of Latin Americans and the power struggle between the drug barons and government is responsible for widespread violence.

coca² SF **1*** (= *cabeza*) head, nut*, noggin (*EEUU**)
2‡ (= *golpe*) rap on the nut‡
3 [*de pelo*] bun, coil
4 (*en cuerda*) kink
coca³* SF Coke®, Coca-Cola®
cocacho SM (*And, Cono Sur*) tap on the head
cocacolo/a SM/F (*And*) frivolous teenager
cocacolonización SF (*hum*) Americanization
cocada SF **1** (*CAm*) (*Culin*) coconut sweet
2 (= *viaje*) length of a journey
3 (*And*) (*Aut*) tyre *o* (*EEUU*) tire grip
4 (*Bol, Perú*) coca plug
cocaína SF cocaine
cocaínico ADJ cocaine (*antes de s*)
cocainomanía SF cocaine addiction
cocainómano/a SM/F cocaine addict
cocal SM coca plantation
cocalero/a ADJ coca (*antes de s*)
SM/F coca grower
cocción SF **1** (*Culin*) (*gen*) cooking; (= *hervor*) boiling; (= *duración*) cooking time • **el agua de ~** cooking liquid ▸ **cocción al horno** baking ▸ **cocción al vapor** steaming
2 (*Téc*) firing, baking

cóccix SM INV coccyx

cocear ▹ CONJUG 1a VT, VI to kick (**contra** against)

cocer ▹ CONJUG 2b, 2h VT **1** (*Culin*) (= *hervir*) to boil • **cocemos la leche antes de tomarla** we boil the milk before drinking it; ▹ **haba**
2 (*Culin*) (= *guisar*) to cook • **cueza el pescado a fuego suave** cook the fish over a gentle heat • **~ al vapor** to steam • **~ al horno** to bake
3 (*Téc*) [+ *ladrillos, cerámica*] to fire
VI [*vino*] to ferment
VPR **cocerse 1** (= *hervir*) to boil
2 (= *guisarse*) to cook; (*al vapor*) to steam; (*al horno*) to bake • **la carne tarda más en ~se que el pescado** meat takes longer to cook than fish
3* (= *tramarse*) • **algo raro se está cociendo en el comité** something strange is brewing in the committee • **voy a ver qué se cuece por aquí** I'm going to see what's going on here
4* (= *pasar calor*) to bake*, roast*, boil* • **en este piso se cuece uno en verano** this apartment is baking *o* roasting *o* boiling in summer*
5‡ (= *emborracharse*) to get plastered‡, get smashed‡

cocha SF (*And, Cono Sur*) (= *charca*) pool; (= *pantano*) swamp; (= *laguna*) lagoon; ▹ **cocho**

cochambre SF (= *mugre*) filth, muck • **esa silla es una ~** that chair is filthy *o* disgusting • MODISMO: • **caer en la ~** to sink very low

cochambroso ADJ filthy

cochayuyo SM (*LAm*) edible seaweed

cochazo* SM whacking great car*

coche[1] SM **1** (= *automóvil*) car, automobile (EEUU); (*frm*) • **fuimos a Almería en ~** we drove to Almeria, we went to Almeria by car • **una exposición de ~s antiguos** a vintage car show ▸ **coche blindado** armoured car, armored car (EEUU) ▸ **coche bomba** car bomb ▸ **coche celular** police van, patrol wagon (EEUU) ▸ **coche de alquiler** hire car ▸ **coche de bomberos** fire engine ▸ **coche de caballos** coach, carriage ▸ **coche de carreras** racing car ▸ **coche de choque** bumper car, dodgem (*Brit*) ▸ **coche de cortesía** courtesy car ▸ **coche de época** vintage car ▸ **coche de línea** coach, long distance bus (*esp EEUU*) ▸ **coche de muertos** hearse ▸ **coche de ocasión** used car, second-hand car ▸ **coche deportivo** sports car ▸ **coche de punto**† taxi ▸ **coche de turismo** private car ▸ **coche escoba** (*Ciclismo*) sag wagon ▸ **coche fúnebre** hearse ▸ **coche K** unmarked police-car ▸ **coche mortuorio** hearse ▸ **coche patrulla** patrol car ▸ **coche radio-patrulla** radio patrol car ▸ **coche usado** used car, second-hand car ▸ **coche Z, coche zeta** police car, patrol car • MODISMO: • **en el ~ de San Fernando** on Shanks's pony, on Shanks's mare (EEUU)
2 (*Ferro*) coach, car (*esp* EEUU), carriage ▸ **coche cama** sleeping car, sleeper, Pullman (EEUU) ▸ **coche comedor** dining car, restaurant car ▸ **coche de correos** mail van ▸ **coche de equipajes** luggage van, baggage car (EEUU) ▸ **coche de literas** couchette car ▸ **coche de viajeros** passenger coach ▸ **coche directo** through carriage
3 [*de bebé*] pram, baby carriage (EEUU)
4 (*Méx*) (= *taxi*) taxi, cab

coche[2] SM (*CAm, Méx*) (= *animal*) pig, hog (*esp* EEUU); (= *carne*) pork ▸ **coche de monte** wild pig *o* boar

coche-bomba SM (PL: **coches-bomba**) car bomb

coche-cabina SM (PL: **coches-cabina**) bubble-car

coche-cama SM (PL: **coches-cama**) sleeping car, sleeper, Pullman (EEUU)

cochecillo SM small carriage *etc* ▸ **cochecillo de inválido** invalid carriage

cochecito SM **1** (= *juguete*) toy car ▸ **cochecito de niño** toy car
2 (*para bebé*) pram, baby carriage (EEUU); (*para niño*) pushchair, (baby) buggy, stroller (EEUU)
3 (*Med*) wheelchair

coche-comedor SM (PL: **coches-comedor**) dining-car, restaurant car

coche-correo SM (PL: **coches-correo**) (*Ferro*) mail-van, mobile sorting-office

coche-cuba SM (PL: **coches-cuba**) tank lorry, water wagon

coche-habitación SM (PL: **coches-habitación**) caravan, trailer (EEUU)

cochemonte SM (*CAm*) wild pig, wild boar

coche-patrulla SM (PL: **coches-patrulla**) patrol car

cochera SF [*de coches*] carport; [*de autobuses*] depot; [*de trenes*] engine shed; [*de tranvías*] tram shed, tram depot; [*de carruajes*] coach house ▸ **cochera de alquiler** livery stable

cocherada SF (*Méx*) coarse *o* vulgar expression

coche-restaurante SM (PL: **coches-restaurante**) dining car, restaurant car

cochería SF (*Arg*) undertaker's

cochero ADJ • **puerta cochera** carriage entrance
SM coachman • MODISMO: • **hablar (en) ~** (*Méx*) to use coarse language ▸ **cochero de punto**† cabman, cabby*

cocherón SM (*Ferro*) engine-shed, locomotive depot

coche-salón SM (PL: **coches-salón**) (*Ferro*) saloon coach

cochina SF sow; ▹ **cochino**

cochinada SF **1** (= *suciedad*) filth, filthiness
2 (= *comentario*) filthy remark
3 (= *cosa*) filthy object, dirty thing
4 (= *canallada*) dirty trick • **hacer una ~ a algn** to play a dirty trick on sb

Cochinchina SF Cochin China; ▹ **Conchinchina**

cochinear* ▹ CONJUG 1a VI to talk dirty

cochinería SF = **cochinada**

cochinilla SF **1** (*Zool*) woodlouse
2 (*Culin*) cochineal
3 • **de ~** (*Cuba, Méx*) trivial, unimportant

cochinillo SM (= *animal*) piglet; (= *carne*) suck(l)ing pig

cochino/a ADJ **1** (= *sucio*) filthy, dirty
2 [*trabajo, sueldo, vacaciones*] rotten*, lousy*; [*mentira*] filthy*, rotten*; [*tiempo*] rotten*, lousy*, filthy* • **esta vida cochina** this rotten *o* miserable life*
SM/F **1** (= *animal*) pig, hog (*esp EEUU*) ▸ **cochino de leche** sucking pig, suckling pig
2 (= *mala persona*) swine*
3 (= *guarro*) filthy pig*; ▹ **cochina**

cochiquera SF, **cochitril** SM pigsty (*tb fig*)

cocho/a* (*LAm*) ADJ old
SM/F old man/old woman; ▹ **cocha**

cochón SM (*Hond*) poof‡, queer‡, fag (EEUU‡)

cochoso ADJ (*And*) filthy

cochura† SF **1** (= *acto*) = **cocción**
2 (= *hornada*) batch of (loaves, cakes, bricks *etc*)

cocido ADJ **1** (*Culin*) boiled, cooked • **bien ~** well done
2 (= *borracho*) • **estar ~*** to be sloshed*
3 (= *acalorado*) • **estar ~*** to be roasting*
4 • **estar ~ en algo*** to be well versed in sth, be expert at sth
SM (*Esp*) stew (*of meat, bacon, chickpeas etc*) • MODISMO: • **ganarse el ~** to earn one's living

cociente SM (*Mat*) quotient; (*Dep*) [*de goles*] goal average ▸ **cociente intelectual** intelligence quotient, IQ

cocina SF **1** (= *habitación*) kitchen • **muebles de ~** kitchen units • MODISMO: • **llegar hasta la ~** (*Dep*) to slice *o* burst through the defence ▸ **cocina amueblada** fitted kitchen; ▹ **batería, cuchillo**
2 (= *aparato*) stove, cooker ▸ **cocina de gas** gas cooker, gas stove ▸ **cocina de petróleo** (*LAm*) oil stove ▸ **cocina económica** range ▸ **cocina eléctrica** electric cooker, electric stove (*esp EEUU*)
3 (= *actividad*) cooking, cookery; (= *arte*) cuisine, cookery • **no me gusta nada la ~** I don't like cookery *o* cooking at all • **libro de ~** cookery book, cookbook (EEUU) • **la ~ valenciana** Valencian cuisine, Valencian cookery • **alta ~** haute cuisine ▸ **cocina casera** home cooking

cocinada SF (*LAm*) (period of) cooking, cooking time

cocinado SM cooking

cocinar ▹ CONJUG 1a VT to cook
VI **1** (= *guisar*) to cook
2 (= *tramar*) to plot, cook up* • **deben estar cocinando algo** they must be plotting something, they must be up to something
VPR **cocinarse 1** (*comida*) to cook
2 (= *tramarse*) • **¿qué se está cocinando aquí?** what's going on here?

cocinero/a SM/F cook

cocineta SF (*LAm*) **1** (= *cuarto*) kitchenette, small kitchen
2 (= *aparato*) small cooker, small stove

cocinilla SF **1** (= *cuarto*) kitchenette, small kitchen
2 (= *aparato*) (*cocina pequeña*) small cooker, small stove; [*de alcohol*] spirit stove, alcohol stove (EEUU); (= *escalfador*) chafing dish

cocker ['koker] SM cocker spaniel, cocker

coco[1] SM **1** (*Bot*) (= *fruto*) coconut; (= *árbol*) coconut palm
2‡ (= *cabeza*) nut*, noggin (EEUU*), head • **se ha dado un golpe en el ~** he banged his head, he banged himself on the nut* • **no anda muy bien del ~** she's not right in the head* • **tuve que romperme el ~ para resolver el problema** I had to rack my brains to come up with an answer to the problem • MODISMOS: • **comer el ~ a algn**: • **la tele les ha comido el ~** the TV has got them brainwashed • **mira, tío, no me comas el ~** hey, stop going on about it • **comerse el ~** to worry (one's head); ▹ **comedura**
3 (= *prodigio*) whizz* • **mi hermano es un ~ para las matemáticas** my brother is a whizz at maths*

coco[2] SM **1** (= *fantasma*) bogeyman, boogeyman (EEUU*) • **¡que viene el ~!** the bogeyman's coming!
2 (= *persona fea*) • **es un ~** he's an ugly devil, he's ugly as sin*
3 • **hacer ~s a algn** (= *carantoñas*) to make eyes at sb; (= *halagos*) to coax sb, wheedle sb

coco[3] SM **1** (= *bacteria*) coccus
2 (= *insecto*) weevil

cocoa SF (*LAm*) cocoa ▸ **cocoa en polvo** cocoa powder

cococha SF *in cod and hake, fleshy part of the jaw, considered a delicacy*

cocodrilo SM crocodile

cocol SM (*Méx*) sesame seed bun

cocoliche SM (*Cono Sur*) (*Ling*) *hybrid Spanish of Italian immigrants*

cócona SF (*Caribe*) tip

coconote SM (*Méx*) **1** (= *niño*) chubby child
2 (= *adulto*) squat person

cocoroco ADJ (*Cono Sur**) (= *engreído*) stuck-up*; (= *descarado*) insolent, cheeky*, sassy (EEUU*)

cocorota SF nut*, noggin (EEUU*), head

cocoso ADJ worm-eaten

cocotal SM coconut plantation, coconut grove

cocotero SM coconut palm

cóctel ['koktel, 'kotel] SM (PL: **cóctels** *o* **cócteles**) **1** (= *bebida*) cocktail
2 (= *snack, entrante*) cocktail ▸ **cóctel de frutas** fruit cocktail ▸ **cóctel de gambas** prawn cocktail ▸ **cóctel de mariscos** seafood cocktail
3 (= *reunión*) cocktail party • **ofrecer un ~ en honor de algn** to hold a cocktail party in sb's honour
4 ▸ **cóctel (Molotov)** petrol bomb, Molotov cocktail

coctelera SF cocktail shaker

cocuyo SM (*LAm*) **1** (= *insecto*) firefly, glowfly (EEUU)
2 (*Aut*) rear light

cod. ABR = **código**

coda SF **1** (*Mús*) coda
2 (*Téc*) wedge

codal SM **1** (*Bot*) layered vine shoot
2 (*Arquit*) strut, prop

codaste SM stern post

codazo SM **1** (= *golpe*) • **darle un ~ a algn** (*disimuladamente*) to give sb a nudge, nudge sb; (*con fuerza*) to elbow sb • **abrirse paso a ~s** to elbow one's way through
2 (*Méx*) • **MODISMO:** • **dar ~ a algn** to tip sb off, warn sb

codear ▹ CONJUG 1a VT **1** (= *empujar con el codo*) to elbow, jostle, nudge
2 (*And, Cono Sur*) (= *insistir*) • **~ a algn** to keep on at sb, pester sb
VI **1** (= *empujar con el codo*) (*disimuladamente*) to nudge; (*con fuerza*) to elbow, jostle • **abrirse paso codeando** to elbow one's way through
2 (*And, Cono Sur**) to sponge*, live by sponging*
VPR **codearse** (= *alternar*) • **~se con** to hobnob with, rub shoulders with

codeína SF codeine

CODELCO SF ABR (*Chile*) = **Corporación del Cobre**

codeo* (*LAm*) SM **1** (= *sablazo*) sponging*
2 (= *insistencia*) pestering

codera SF (= *parche*) elbow patch; [*de protección*] elbow guard

codeso SM laburnum

códice SM codex

codicia SF (= *avaricia*) greed; (*por lo ajeno*) covetousness

codiciable ADJ desirable, covetable

codiciado ADJ [*medalla, trofeo*] coveted; [*zona, casa*] sought-after • **obtuvo el ~ título** he won the coveted title

codiciar ▹ CONJUG 1b VT [+ *dinero, bienes*] to desire; [+ *lo ajeno*] to covet

codicilo SM codicil

codiciosamente ADV greedily, covetously

codicioso ADJ covetous, greedy

codificación SF **1** (*Jur*) codification
2 [*de mensajes, textos*] encoding ▸ **codificación de barras** bar coding

codificado SM • **el programa se emitirá en ~** the programme will be encrypted
ADJ coded

codificador SM encoder

codificar ▹ CONJUG 1g VT **1** (*Jur*) to codify
2 [+ *mensaje, información*] to encode, code; (*TV*) to encrypt, scramble

código SM **1** (= *reglamento*) code ▸ **código civil** civil code ▸ **código de conducta** code of conduct ▸ **Código de Derecho Canónico** Canon Law Code ▸ **código de la circulación** highway code ▸ **código de leyes** statute book ▸ **código deontológico** code of practice, ethics (*esp EEUU*) ▸ **código ético** code of ethics ▸ **código militar** military law ▸ **código penal** penal code
2 [*de signos, números*] code • **teclee su ~ secreto** key in your password ▸ **código binario** binary code ▸ **código de acceso** access code ▸ **código de barras** bar code ▸ **código de colores** colour code, color code (EEUU) ▸ **código de máquina** (*Inform*) machine code ▸ **código de operación** (*Inform*) operational code ▸ **código de señales** signal code ▸ **código genético** genetic code ▸ **código hexadecimal** hexadecimal code ▸ **código legible por máquina** machine-readable code ▸ **código máquina** (*Inform*) machine code ▸ **código postal** postcode, zip code (EEUU)

codillo SM **1** (*Zool*) (= *articulación*) elbow; (= *pata*) upper foreleg; [*de cerdo*] knuckle ▸ **codillo de cerdo** (*Méx*) (*Culin*) pig's trotter
2 (*Téc*) elbow (joint), bend
3 (*Bot*) stump (of a branch)

codirigir ▹ CONJUG 3c VT to co-direct

codo¹ SM **1** (*Anat*) elbow; [*de caballo*] knee • **MODISMOS:** • **a base de ~s:** • **sacó la oposición a base de ~s** he won the post by sheer hard work *o* through sheer hard graft • **comerse los ~s de hambre** to be utterly destitute • **dar con el ~** *o* **de ~ a algn** (*CAm*) to nudge sb • **empinar el ~*** to have a few*, bend the elbow* • **hablar por los ~s** to talk nineteen to the dozen, talk a blue streak (EEUU) • **hacer ~s** • **hincar los ~s** to swot* • **morderse un ~** (*Méx, Cono Sur*) to restrain o. s. • **partirse** *o* **romperse los ~s** to slog* • **ser del ~** • **ser duro de ~** (*CAm*) to be mean ▸ **codo de tenista** tennis elbow
2 • **MODISMO:** • **codo a codo:** • **hubo un ~ a ~ por el segundo puesto** there was a close battle for second place, it was neck and neck for second place • **las elecciones serán un ~ a ~ entre socialistas y nacionalistas** the elections are going to be a close-run thing *o* a neck-and-neck affair between the Socialists and Nationalists • **fue un combate ~ a ~** it was a neck-and-neck fight
3 • **MODISMO:** • **codo con codo** (*como adverbio*): • **enemigos políticos se sentaron ~ con ~ en el funeral** political foes sat down together *o* sat side by side with each other at the funeral, political foes rubbed shoulders with each other at the funeral • **en las elecciones quedaron ~ con ~ con los socialistas** in the elections they were neck and neck with the Socialists • **luchar ~ con ~** to fight shoulder to shoulder, fight side by side • **trabajar ~ con ~** to work side by side *o* closely together
4 [*de camisa, chaqueta*] elbow
5 [*de tubería*] elbow, bend
6 (= *medida*) cubit

codo²‡ ADJ (*Méx*) (= *tacaño*) mean, stingy

codorniz SF quail

COE SM ABR = **Comité Olímpico Español**

coedición SF [*de libro*] joint publication; (= *acto*) joint publishing

coeditar ▹ CONJUG 1a VT to publish jointly

coeducación SF coeducation

coeducacional ADJ coeducational

coeficiente SM (*Mat*) coefficient; (*Econ*) rate; (*Med*) degree ▸ **coeficiente aerodinámico** drag factor ▸ **coeficiente de caja** cash deposit requirement ▸ **coeficiente de incremento** rate of increase ▸ **coeficiente de inteligencia** intelligence quotient, IQ ▸ **coeficiente de penetración aerodinámica** drag factor ▸ **coeficiente intelectual, coeficiente mental** intelligence quotient, IQ

coercer ▹ CONJUG 2b VT to constrain (*frm*)

coerción SF coercion (*frm*)

coercitivamente ADV coercively

coercitivo ADJ coercive

coestrella SMF co-star

coetáneo/a ADJ, SM/F contemporary (con with) • **es famoso entre sus ~s** he is famous among his peers *o* contemporaries

coevo ADJ coeval

coexistencia SF coexistence ▸ **coexistencia pacífica** peaceful coexistence

coexistente ADJ coexistent

coexistir ▹ CONJUG 3a VI to coexist (**con** with)

cofa SF top ▸ **cofa mayor** maintop

cofabricar ▹ CONJUG 1g VT to manufacture jointly

cofia SF [*de enfermera, criada, monja*] cap; (= *redecilla*†) hairnet

cofinanciación SF joint financing

cofinanciar ▹ CONJUG 1b VT to finance jointly

cofrade SMF member (of a brotherhood), brother

cofradía SF (*Rel*) brotherhood, fraternity; (= *gremio*) guild, association; [*de ladrones etc*] gang; ▹ **SEMANA SANTA**

cofre SM (= *caja*) chest; (*para joyas*) casket, jewellery *o* (EEUU) jewelry box, jewel case; (*Méx*) (*Aut*) bonnet, hood (EEUU)

cofrecito SM casket

cofundador(a) SM/F co-founder

cogedero ADJ [*fruto*] ripe for picking
SM handle

cogedor SM [*de polvo, basura*] dustpan; [*de ceniza*] (small) shovel

coger

VERBO TRANSITIVO
VERBO INTRANSITIVO
VERBO PRONOMINAL

▹ CONJUG 2c

*Para las expresiones **coger desprevenido, coger in fraganti**, ver la otra entrada.*

VERBO TRANSITIVO

1 (= *con la mano*) **a** (= *tomar*) to take • **¿puedo ~ este?** can I take this one? • **~ un libro de un estante** to take a book from a shelf • **coge un poco más de queso** have a bit more cheese • **~ a algn de la mano** to take sb by the hand • **ir cogidos de la mano** to walk along holding hands *o* hand in hand
b (= *levantar*) to pick up • **cogió la guitarra y se puso a tocar** he picked up the guitar and started to play • **coge al niño, que está llorando** pick up the baby, he's crying • **cogió el bolso y salió de casa** she picked up her handbag and went out
c (*con fuerza*) to grasp • **la cogió por la muñeca y no la soltó** he grabbed her by the wrist and wouldn't let go
d (= *sostener*) to hold • **coge bien el bolígrafo** hold the biro properly • **no ha cogido un fusil en la vida** he's never held a gun in his life
2 (= *escoger*) to pick • **cogió el azul** she picked the blue one • **coge el que más te guste** take *o* pick the one you like best • **has cogido un mal momento** you've picked a bad time
3 (+ *flor, fruta*) to pick
4 (= *quitar*) (*gen*) to take; (= *pedir prestado*) to borrow • **me coge siempre las cerillas** he's always taking my matches • **¿quién ha cogido el periódico?** who's taken the newspaper? • **¿te puedo ~ el bolígrafo?** can I

borrow your pen? • **te he cogido la regla** I've borrowed *o* pinched your ruler*

5 (*= apuntar*) to take (down) • **cogió la dirección del cliente** she took (down) the customer's address • **~ apuntes** to take notes

6 (*esp Esp*) (*= conseguir*) to get • **¿nos coges dos entradas?** would you get us two tickets? • **cógeme un buen sitio** get me a good place • **he cogido un billete de avión** I've bought an air ticket • **~ hora para el dentista/en la peluquería** to make an appointment to see *o* with the dentist/at the hairdresser's

7 (*= adquirir*) **a** [*+ enfermedad*] to catch • **~ un resfriado** to catch a cold • **el niño cogió sarampión** the child got *o* caught measles • **~ frío** to get cold • **ha cogido una insolación** she's got sunstroke

b [*+ costumbre, hábito*] to get into; [*+ acento*] to pick up • **ha cogido la costumbre de morderse las uñas** she has got into the habit of biting her nails • **ha cogido la manía de las quinielas** he's caught the pools craze • **cogieron acento irlandés** they picked up an Irish accent

c [*+ fuerzas*] to gather; [*+ velocidad*] to gather, pick up

8 (*= atrapar*) **a** (*esp Esp*) [*+ persona, pez, balón*] to catch • **¡coge la pelota!** catch the ball! • **¡por fin te he cogido!** caught you at last! • **les cogieron con varios kilos de heroína** they were caught with several kilos of heroin

b (*esp Esp*) [*toro*] (*= cornear*) to gore; (*= voltear*) to toss

c (*esp Esp*) [*coche*] (*= atropellar*) to knock down, run over

d (*Mil*) to take prisoner, capture • **han cogido a quince soldados** fifteen soldiers have been taken prisoner *o* have been captured

9 (*esp Esp*) (*= sorprender*) to catch • **la cogieron robando** they caught her stealing • **~ a algn en una mentira** to catch sb lying, catch sb in a lie • **la guerra nos cogió en Francia** the war found *o* caught us in France • **la noche nos cogió todavía en el mar** the night caught us still at sea • **antes que nos coja la noche** before night overtakes us *o* comes down on us • **MODISMOS:** • **~ a algn detrás de la puerta** • **~ a algn en la hora tonta** to catch sb at a disadvantage • **~ de nuevas a algn** to take sb by surprise

10 (*= empezar a sentir*) • **~ aversión a algo** to take a strong dislike to sth • **~ cariño a algn** to grow *o* become fond of sb, become attached to sb • **~ celos de algn** to become jealous of sb

11 (*= tomarse*) to take • **no sé si podré ~ vacaciones** I don't know if I'll be able to take any holidays • **¿vas a ~ fiesta mañana?** are you going to take tomorrow off?, are you going to take the day off tomorrow?

12 (*= entender*) [*+ sentido, giro*] to get • **¿no has cogido el chiste?** don't you get the joke?

13 (*esp Esp*) (*= aceptar*) [*+ empleados, trabajo*] to take on; [*+ alumnos*] to take in; [*+ pacientes*] (*en hospital*) to take in; (*en consultorio*) to take on • **acabo de ~ una secretaria nueva** I've just taken on a new secretary

14 (*= alquilar*) to take, rent • **cogimos un apartamento** we took *o* rented an apartment

15 (*= viajar en*) [*+ tren, avión, autobús*] to take • **vamos a ~ el tren** let's take *o* get the train • **quiero ~ el tren de las tres** I want to catch the three o'clock train

16 (*= ir por*) to take • **coja la primera calle a la derecha** take the first street on the right • **no cojas las curvas tan rápido** don't take the bends so fast

17 (*= recibir*) [*+ emisora, canal*] to pick up, get • **con esta radio cogemos Radio Praga** we can pick up *o* get Radio Prague on this set

18 (*= retener*) [*+ polvo*] to gather, collect • **esta moqueta coge mucho polvo** this carpet gathers *o* collects a lot of dust • **los perros cogen pulgas** dogs get *o* catch fleas

19 (*= aprender*) to pick up • **los niños lo cogen todo enseguida** children pick things up very quickly

20 (*= incorporarse a*) • **cogí la conferencia a la mitad** I joined the discussion halfway through • **cogí la obra casi al final** the play was almost over when I got there

21 (*Méx, Arg, Ven*)** (*sexualmente*) to fuck**, screw**

VERBO INTRANSITIVO

1 (*= estar*) to be • **¿coge muy lejos de aquí?** is it very far from here? • **el cine coge bastante cerca** the cinema is quite near here • **el banco me coge de camino** the bank's on my way

2 (*= ir*) • **~ por:** • **cogió por esta calle** he went down this street

3 (*Esp*)* (*= caber*) to fit • **aquí no coge** there's no room for it here, it doesn't fit (in) here

4 (*planta*) to take

5 (*Méx, Arg, Ven*)** (*sexualmente*) to fuck**, screw**

6 • **MODISMO:** • **cogió y se fue*** he just upped and left *o* offed*

VERBO PRONOMINAL **cogerse**

1 (*= sujetarse*) • **~se a** *o* **de algo** to hold on to sth • **se cogió a** *o* **de las rejas** he held on to the bars • **cógete a** *o* **de la cuerda** hold on to the rope • **~se a algn** to hold on to sb • **cógete a mí, que aquí resbala** hold on to me, it's slippery here

2 (*enfático*) **a** (*= pillarse*) [*+ catarro, gripe*] to catch • **~se los dedos en la puerta** to catch one's fingers in the door • **~se una borrachera** to get drunk

b (*= tomarse*) [*+ vacaciones*] to take • **hace tiempo que no me cojo unas vacaciones** it's a long time since I took a holiday

c (*= agarrar*) [*+ objeto*] to grab • **cógete una silla** grab a chair

cogestión (SF) joint management

cogida (SF) **1** (*Taur*) (*= cornada*) goring • **sufrir una ~** to be gored
2 (*Agr*) (*= cosecha*) harvest; (*Pesca*) catch; (*= acto*) [*de moras, fresas*] picking, gathering; [*de cereales*] harvesting
3 (*LAm***) screw**, fuck**

cogido (SM) (*Cos*) fold, gather, tuck

cogienda (SF) **1** (*And, Caribe*) = **cogida**
2 (*Méx***) fucking**, screwing**

cognado (ADJ), (SM) cognate

cognición (SF), **cognitividad** (SF) cognition

cognitivo (ADJ), **cognoscitivo** (ADJ) cognitive

cogollo (SM) **1** (*Bot*) [*de lechuga, col*] heart; [*de árbol*] top; (*LAm*) [*de caña de azúcar*] sugar-cane top; (*= brote*) shoot, sprout
2 (*= lo mejor*) best part, cream • **el ~ de la sociedad** the cream of society
3 [*de asunto, problema*] heart, crux; [*de ciudad*] centre, center (*EEUU*)
4 (*Caribe*) (*= sombrero*) straw hat

cogorza* (SF) • **pescar una ~** to get plastered*

cogotazo (SM) (*= golpe*) blow on the back of the neck; (*Boxeo*) rabbit punch

cogote (SM) **1** (*Anat*) back of the neck, nape • **coger a algn por el ~** to take sb *o* grab sb *o* pick sb up by the scruff of the neck • **MODISMOS:** • **estar hasta el ~** to have had it up to here • **ponérselas en el ~** (*CAm‡*) to beat it*
2 • **de ~** (*Cono Sur*) [*animal*] fat • **carne de ~** (*Cono Sur*) rubbish, trash, garbage (*EEUU*)

cogotudo‡ (ADJ) (*And, Cono Sur*) well-heeled*, filthy rich*; (*Caribe*) powerful
(SM) (*LAm*) (*= nuevo rico*) self-made man, parvenu • **es un ~** he's got friends in high places

coguionista (SMF) co-scriptwriter

cogujada (SF) woodlark

cogulla (SF) cowl

cohabitación (SF) (*= vida en común*) cohabitation (*frm*); (*Pol*) coexistence

cohabitar ▷ CONJUG 1a (VI) (*= vivir juntos*) to live together, cohabit (*frm*); (*Pol*) to coexist

cohechar ▷ CONJUG 1a (VT) to bribe, offer a bribe to

cohecho (SM) bribery

coheredero/a (SM/F) coheir/coheiress, joint heir/joint heiress

coherencia (SF) **1** [*de ideas, razonamiento, exposición*] coherence
2 [*de acciones, proyecto, política*] consistency
3 (*Fís*) cohesion

coherente (ADJ) **1** [*texto, idea, exposición, argumentación*] coherent • **no sería ~ cumplir con sus órdenes** it wouldn't make sense to follow his orders
2 [*proyecto, política*] consistent • **~ con** in line with, in tune with

coherentemente (ADV) **1** (*= razonar, exponer, pensar*) coherently
2 (*= actuar*) consistently

cohesión (SF) cohesion

cohesionado (ADJ) united, unified

cohesionador (ADJ) • **elemento ~** unifying force

cohesionar ▷ CONJUG 1a (VT) to unite, draw together

cohesivo (ADJ) cohesive

cohete (SM) **1** (*gen*) rocket ▸ **cohete de señales** flare, distress rocket ▸ **cohete espacial** (space) rocket ▸ **cohete luminoso** flare, distress rocket
2 (*Méx**) (*= pistola*) piece*, pistol
3 (*Cono Sur*) • **al ~** to no effect
4 (*Méx*) (*= mecha*) blasting fuse
(ADJ) (*CAm, Méx**) (*= borracho*) drunk, tight*

cohetería (SF) **1** (*= fábrica*) fireworks factory; (*= tienda*) fireworks shop
2 (*= ciencia*) rocketry

cohibición (SF) **1** (*Jur*) restraint
2 (*Med*) inhibition

cohibido (ADJ) **1** (*= tímido*) shy, timid, self-conscious; (*= incómodo*) awkward, ill-at-ease • **sentirse ~** to feel awkward *o* ill-at-ease
2 (*Jur*) restrained, restricted
3 (*Med*) inhibited

cohibir ▷ CONJUG 3a (VT) **1** (*= incomodar*) to make awkward *o* ill-at-ease; (*= avergonzar*) to make shy, embarrass
2 (*Jur*) to restrain, restrict
3 (*Med*) to inhibit
(VPR) **cohibirse 1** (*= incomodarse*) to feel awkward *o* ill-at-ease; (*= avergonzarse*) to feel embarrassed, become shy
2 (*Med*) to feel inhibited

cohombro (SM) cucumber

cohonestar ▷ CONJUG 1a (*frm*) (VT) **1** [*+ acto*] to cover up
2 [*+ diferencias*] to reconcile

cohorte (SF) cohort

COI (SM ABR) (= **Comité Olímpico Internacional**) IOC

coima (SF) **1** (*LAm**) (*= soborno*) backhander*, sweetener*, bribe; (*= acto*) bribing, bribery
2‡ (*en el juego*) rake-off*
3†† (*= concubina*) concubine; (*= puta*) whore

coimacracia* (SF) (*Perú*) rule of graft

Coimbra (SF) Coimbra

coime (SM) **1** (*And*) (*= camarero*) waiter
2† (*= chulo*) pimp, ponce

3† (*en el juego*) gambling operator
coimear ▹ CONJUG 1a (VT) (*And, Cono Sur*) (= *sobornar*) to bribe; (= *aceptar sobornos*) to take bribes from
coimero/a (*And, Cono Sur*) (ADJ) easily bribed, bent‡
(SM/F) bribe-taker • **son unos ~s** they are all bent‡
coincidencia (SF) 1 (= *casualidad*) coincidence • **es pura ~** it's just a coincidence, it's pure coincidence • **dio la ~ de que yo también estaba allí** it was a coincidence that I was also there
2 (= *acuerdo*) agreement • **en ~ con** in agreement with
coincidente (ADJ) coincident • **ser ~ con algn/algo** to be coincident with sb/sth
coincidentemente (ADV) coincidentally
coincidir ▹ CONJUG 3a (VI) 1 (*en el tiempo*) to happen at the same time, occur simultaneously (*frm*), to coincide • **para que se produzca una explosión han de ~ varias circunstancias** for an explosion to occur several circumstances must happen at the same time • **~ con algo** to coincide with sth • **la exposición coincide con el 50 aniversario de su muerte** the exhibition coincides with the 50th anniversary of his death • **mis vacaciones nunca coinciden con las de los niños** my holidays are never at the same time as my children's • **no puedo ir al concierto porque coincide con el examen** I can't go to the concert because it clashes with the exam
2 (*en un lugar*) to happen to meet • **coincidimos en el teatro** we happened to meet at the theatre • **he coincidido con él en varias fiestas pero nunca nos han presentado** I've happened to be at some of the same parties as him but we've never been introduced • **el punto en que las dos líneas coinciden** the point at which both lines meet
3 (= *estar de acuerdo*) **a** • **~ con algn** to agree with sb • **coincido plenamente contigo en este punto** I fully agree with you on this point • **~ en algo**: • **todos coinciden en que esta es su mejor película** everyone agrees that this is his best film • **los observadores internacionales coinciden en afirmar que ...** international observers all agree that ...
b [*informes, versiones, resultados*] to coincide • **las conclusiones de ambos estudios coinciden** the conclusions of the two studies coincide • **ambos ensayos coinciden en sus conclusiones** both essays reach the same conclusion • **~ con algo** to agree with sth, coincide with sth • **los hechos no coinciden exactamente con las declaraciones del testigo** the facts don't exactly agree with the witness's statement
4 (= *ajustarse*) [*huellas, formas*] to match, match up • **~ con algo** to match (up with) sth • **sus huellas dactilares no coinciden exactamente con las del asesino** his fingerprints don't match the murderer's exactly *o* don't match up exactly with the murderer's
cointérprete (SMF) fellow actor
coinversión (SF) joint investment
coipo (SM), **coipu** (SM) (*LAm*) coypu
coirón (SM) (*And*) thatch
coito (SM) intercourse, coitus (*frm*) ▸ **coito anal** anal intercourse, anal sex
cojan *etc* ▹ **coger**
cojear ▹ CONJUG 1a (VI) 1 [*persona*] (= *estar cojo*) to limp, hobble (along); (= *ser cojo*) to be lame • **cojea de la pierna izquierda** (*temporalmente*) she's limping on her left leg; (*permanentemente*) she's lame in her left leg, she has a limp in her left leg • MODISMOS: • **cojean del mismo pie** they're two of a kind • **sabemos de qué pie cojea** we know his weak points *o* weaknesses
2 [*mueble*] to wobble, be wobbly
cojera (SF) (= *estado*) lameness; (*al andar*) limp
cojijo† (SM) 1 (*Entomología*) bug, small insect
2 (= *queja*) peeve*, grudge, grumble
cojijoso† (ADJ) peevish, grumpy
cojín (SM) 1 (= *almohadilla*) cushion ▸ **cojín elevador** booster seat, booster cushion
2‡ (*euf*) = **cojón**
cojinete (SM) 1 (= *almohadilla*) small cushion
2 (*Mec*) bearing ▸ **cojinete a bolas, cojinete de bolas** ball bearing ▸ **cojinete de rodillos** roller bearing
3 (*Ferro*) chair
4 **cojinetes** (*And, Caribe, Méx*) saddlebags
cojinillos (SMPL) (*CAm, Méx*) saddlebags
cojo[1]/a (ADJ) 1 (= *de andar defectuoso*) lame • **está un poco ~ por la caída** he's a bit lame from the fall • **~ de un pie** lame in one foot • **salió ~ del campo de juego** he left the ground limping; ▹ **pata**
2 (= *con una sola pierna, pata*) one-legged • **el típico pirata ~** the typical one-legged pirate • **se quedó ~ en la guerra** he lost a leg in the war
3 [*mueble, objeto*] wobbly
4 (= *incompleto*) [*equipo, organización*] weak, lame • **su expulsión dejó ~ al equipo** his sending-off left the team weak
(SM/F) 1 [*de andar defectuoso*] lame person
2 (*con una sola pierna*) one-legged person
• REFRÁN: • **el ~ echa la culpa al empedrado** a bad workman blames his tools
cojo[2] ▹ **coger**
cojón** (SM) 1 (= *testículo*) ball‡ • MODISMOS: • **con cojones**: • **es un tío con cojones** he's got balls** *o* guts* • **echar cojones a algo** to brave sth out • **estar hasta los cojones**: • **estoy hasta los cojones de este trabajo** I'm really pissed off with this job‡, I'm fed up to the back teeth with this job* • **ya estoy hasta los cojones de que me insulte** I'm totally pissed off with being insulted‡ • **hago lo que me sale de los cojones** I do what I damn well like *o* bloody well like‡ • **¡olé sus cojones!** good for him! • **pasarse algo por (el forro de) los cojones**: • **me lo paso por los cojones** I don't give a fuck** *o* toss‡ about it • **tener cojones**: • **no tienes cojones de decírmelo a la cara** you haven't got the balls to tell me to my face** • **tocar los cojones a algn**: • **este tío me está tocando los cojones** this guy is pissing me off‡ • **tocarse los cojones**: • **se pasa el día tocándose los cojones** he spends all day doing fuck all** *o* sod all‡
2 (*como exclamación*) • **callaos ya, ¡cojones!** shut up, for fuck's sake!** • **¡los cojones!** • **¡y un ~!**: —**dame el dinero** —**¡(y) un ~** *o* **los cojones!** "give me the money" — "go fuck yourself!"**
3 (*como intensificador*) • **¿qué cojones haces aquí?** what the fuck are you doing here?** • **pero, ¿quién cojones se han creído que son?** who the fuck do they think they are?** • **de cojones**: • **¡hace un frío de cojones!** it's fucking freezing!** • **con dos sueldos viven de cojones** with two salaries they have a fucking great life** • **de los cojones**: • **no aguanto al periodista ese de los cojones** I can't stand that fucking journalist** • **por cojones**: • **tienes que hacerlo por cojones** you fucking well have to do it**
4 • **un ~** (*como adverbio*): • **cuesta un ~** it's worth a fucking fortune** • **no me importa un ~ lo que tú digas** I don't give a fuck what you think** • **ese tío sabe un ~** he knows fucking loads**
cojonudamente‡ (ADV) brilliantly, awesomely (*EEUU**)
cojonudo‡ (ADJ) 1 (*Esp*) (= *estupendo*) brilliant*, awesome (*EEUU**) • **un tío ~** a great bloke‡ *o* guy* • **¡qué ~!** great stuff!*
2 (= *grande*) huge, colossal; (= *muy importante*) very important; (= *destacado*) outstanding
3 (= *gracioso*) really funny
4 (*LAm*) (= *holgazán*) lazy, slow; (= *tonto*) stupid
cojudear‡ ▹ CONJUG 1a (*LAm*) (VT) to con*, swindle
(VI) to mess about
cojudez** (SF) (*And, Cono Sur*) nonsense, stupidity • **¡déjate de cojudeces!** stop pissing around!**
cojudo/a (ADJ) 1 [*animal*] (= *sin castrar*) entire, not castrated; (= *semental*) used for stud purposes
2 (*Cono Sur***) (= *estúpido*) stupid
(SM/F) cretin*, stupid prick**
cok [kok] (SM), **coke** ['koke] (SM) (*LAm*) (*Min*) coke
col (SF) cabbage ▸ **col china** Chinese leaves (*pl*), bok choy (*EEUU*) ▸ **col de bruselas** (Brussels) sprout ▸ **col de Saboya** savoy (cabbage) ▸ **col lombarda** red cabbage ▸ **col rizada** curly kale ▸ **col roja** red cabbage
• REFRÁN: • **entre col y col, lechuga** variety is the spice of life
col. (ABR) 1 (= **columna**) col
2 = **colaboradores** • **y ~** et al.
col.ª (ABR) (= **columna**) col
cola[1] (SF) 1 [*de animal, avión, cometa*] tail
• MODISMOS: • **tener ~ de paja** (*Uru**) to feel guilty • **traer ~**: • **la decisión del árbitro va a traer ~** this is not the last we will hear of the referee's decision ▸ **cola de caballo** (= *en el pelo*) pony tail; (= *planta*) horsetail ▸ **cola de milano, cola de pato** (*Téc*) dovetail ▸ **cola de rata** (*Pesca*) fly line
2 [*de frac*] tail; [*de vestido*] train
3 (= *hilera*) queue, line (*EEUU*) • **hay una ~ enorme en la taquilla del cine** there's a huge queue at the box office • **se formó una ~ de dos kilómetros debido al accidente** a two-kilometre tailback formed because of the accident • **¡a la ~!** get in the queue!, get in line! (*EEUU*) • **hacer ~** to queue (up), line up (*EEUU*) • **ponerse a la ~** to join *o* get into the queue, join *o* get into the line (*EEUU*)
4 (= *parte final*) [*de manifestación*] tail end, back; [*de carrera*] back • **el ciclista estaba en** *o* **a la ~ del pelotón** the cyclist was at the back of *o* at the tail end of the pack • **los equipos en la ~ de la tabla** the teams at the foot *o* bottom of the table • **estamos a la ~ de las sociedades civilizadas** we are at the bottom of the league of civilized societies • **el equipo está en el tercer puesto por la ~** the team is sitting third place from (the) bottom
5* (= *pene*) willy*, weenie (*EEUU**)
6 (*Ven*) (*Aut*) • **pedir ~** to ask for a lift *o* ride (*EEUU*)
7 (*Cono Sur**) (= *trasero*) bum‡, bottom, butt‡ (*EEUU*); (= *cóccix*) coccyx
cola[2] (SF) (= *pegamento*) glue, gum; (*para decorar*) size • **pintura a la ~** distemper; (*Arte*) tempera • MODISMOS: • **comer ~** (*Cono Sur*) to be let down, be disappointed • **no pegar ni con ~**: • **esas cortinas no pegan ni con ~** those curtains just don't go with the rest • **el final de la película no pega ni con ~** the ending of the film is totally unconvincing • **el verde y el azul no pegan ni con ~** green and blue just don't go together ▸ **cola de carpintero** wood glue ▸ **cola de contacto**

contact adhesive ▸ **cola de impacto** impact adhesive ▸ **cola de pescado** fish glue ▸ **cola de retal** size

cola³ (SF) **1** (= *planta*) cola, kola
2 (= *bebida*) cola, Coke®
3 (*And*) (= *refresco*) fizzy drink ▸ **cola de naranja** orangeade

cola⁴* (SM) (*Chile*) poof‡, queer‡

colaboración (SF) **1** (= *cooperación*) collaboration • **escrito en ~ con mi tutor** written in collaboration with my tutor ▸ **colaboración ciudadana** help from the public
2 (*en periódico*) (*gen*) contribution; (= *artículo*) article
3 [*de congreso*] paper
4 (= *donativo*) contribution

colaboracionismo (SM) collaboration

colaboracionista (SMF) collaborator, collaborationist

colaborador(a) (SM/F) **1** (*en trabajo, misión*) collaborator, co-worker
2 (*en periódico, revista*) contributor
3 (*en congreso*) contributor
4 (*con dinero*) contributor

colaborar ▹ CONJUG 1a (VI) to collaborate • **ambas organizaciones ~on estrechamente** the two organizations collaborated closely *o* worked closely together • **te necesitamos ¡colabora!** we need you, come and join us! • **~ a algo** to contribute to sth • **colaboró a la resolución del problema** he contributed to solving the problem • **~ con algn** to collaborate with sb • **~ con algo**: • **colaboramos con los movimientos pacifistas** we are collaborating with the peace groups • **colaboró con cien euros** he contributed a hundred euros • **~ en algo**: • **nuestra empresa ~á en el proyecto** our company is to collaborate on the project • **el viento colaboró en la propagación del incendio** the wind contributed to the spread of the fire • **~ en un periódico** to contribute to a newspaper, write for a newspaper

colaborativo (ADJ) collaborative

colación (SF) **1** (= *mención*) • **sacar** *o* **traer a ~** to mention, bring up
2 (= *refrigerio*) light meal, collation (*frm*)
3 (= *comparación*) collation, comparison
4 (*LAm*) (= *dulce*) box of sweets
5 (*Univ*) conferral

colacionar ▹ CONJUG 1a (VT) to collate, compare

colada (SF) **1** (= *lavado*) washing • **hacer la ~** to do the washing • **día de ~** washday • **tender la ~** to hang out the washing • **todo saldrá en la ~** it will all come out in the wash
2 (= *lejía*) bleach, lye
3 (*Geol*) outflow
4 (*Agr*) sheep run, cattle run; ▹ **colado**

coladera (SF) **1** (*Culin*) strainer
2 (*Méx*) (= *alcantarilla*) sewer

coladero (SM) (*para té, infusión*) strainer; (*con agujeros*) colander; [*de malla*] sieve • MODISMO: • **dejar como un ~** to riddle with bullets

coladicto/a (SM/F) glue-sniffer‡

colado/a (ADJ) **1** [*metal*] cast
2 • MODISMO: • **estar ~ por algn*** to be madly in love with sb
3 • **aire ~** draught, draft (*EEUU*)
(SM/F) (= *intruso*) intruder; (*en fiesta, recepción*) gatecrasher; ▹ **colada**

colador (SM) (*para té, infusión*) strainer; (*con agujeros*) colander; [*de malla*] sieve • MODISMO: • **dejar como un ~** to riddle with bullets

coladura (SF) **1** (= *filtración*) straining
2* (= *metedura de pata*) clanger*, blunder
3 coladuras grounds, dregs

colágeno (SM) collagen

colapsado (ADJ) [*tráfico, circulación*] at a standstill; [*centralita*] jammed • **el tráfico en el centro está ~ por culpa de un accidente** traffic in the city centre *o* (*EEUU*) center is at a standstill due to an accident • **la centralita de la empresa recibió tantas llamadas que quedó colapsada** there were so many calls that the company switchboard was jammed

colapsar ▹ CONJUG 1a (VT) **1** (= *derribar*) to cause to collapse
2 [+ *tráfico, circulación*] to bring to a halt *o* standstill; [+ *puerta*] to jam, block; [+ *entrada*] to block
(VI), (VPR) **colapsarse** (= *derrumbarse*) to collapse, go to pieces

colapso (SM) **1** (*Med*) • **el boxeador sufrió un ~** the boxer collapsed ▸ **colapso cardíaco** heart failure ▸ **colapso cardiovascular** circulatory collapse ▸ **colapso respiratorio** respiratory failure
2 [*de régimen, imperio, empresa*] collapse • **el país está al borde del ~ económico** the country is on the verge of economic collapse
3 (= *paralización*) • **el accidente provocó el ~ del tráfico** the accident caused traffic to come to a standstill *o* to grind to a halt

colar ▹ CONJUG 1l (VT) **1** [+ *leche, infusión, verduras, caldo*] to strain
2* (*furtivamente*) **a** [+ *objetos*] to sneak • **consiguió ~lo por la aduana** he managed to sneak it through customs • **le coló un gol al portero** he sneaked a goal past the keeper
b • **~ algo a algn** (= *dar algo malo*) to palm sth off on sb, palm sb off with sth; (= *hacer creer algo*) to spin sb a yarn about sth* • **quiso ~nos varias monedas falsas** he tried to palm off some forged coins on us *o* palm us off with some forged coins • **me coló una peras podridas** he palmed off some rotten pears on me, he slipped me some rotten pears • **el ladrón intentó ~les que era el revisor de la luz** the burglar tried to pass himself off as the electricity man, the burglar tried to spin them a yarn about being the electricity man • **¡a mí no me la cuelas!** don't give me any of that!*
c • **~ a algn** (*en espectáculo, cine*) to sneak sb in
3 [+ *metal*] to cast
4 (= *blanquear*) [+ *ropa*] to bleach
(VI) **1*** (= *ser creído*) • **diles que estás enfermo, igual cuela** say you're ill, they might swallow it* • **me parece que tu historia no va a ~** I don't think your story will wash*, I don't think they'll swallow your story* • **tienes que copiar muy bien la firma para que cuele el cheque** you'll need to copy the signature very well if you want the cheque to go through
2* (= *beber*) to booze*, tipple
(VPR) **colarse 1** (= *filtrarse*) • **el agua se cuela por las rendijas** the water seeps (in) through *o* gets in through the cracks • **se le coló el balón** the ball slipped past him • **la moto se iba colando entre la fila de coches** the motorbike slipped through the line of cars
2 [*personas*] (*sin pagar*) to get in without paying; (*en lugar prohibido*) to sneak in; (*en fiesta*) to gatecrash • **intentaron ~se en el concierto** they tried to get into the concert without paying • **se coló silenciosamente en la habitación** he sneaked quietly into the room • **un equipo de segunda división se había colado en las semifinales** a second division team had slipped through to the semifinals
3 [*error*] • **se le ~on varias faltas al revisar el texto** he overlooked several mistakes when revising the text
4 (*en una cola*) to jump the queue, cut in line (*EEUU*) • **se me intentó ~** he tried to jump the queue in front of me • **¡oiga, no se cuele!** excuse me, there's a queue!
5 (*Esp**) (= *equivocarse*) to get it wrong* • **¡huy! ¡me colé!** oops! I got it wrong!* • **ahí te has colado porque yo no dije nada de eso** you got it wrong there, because I didn't say anything about that
6 (*Esp*) (= *enamorarse*) • **~se por algn** to fall for sb

colateral (ADJ) collateral

colca (SF) (*And*) (= *troje*) barn, granary; (= *almacén*) storeroom; (= *ático*) attic store, loft

colcha (SF) bedspread, counterpane

colchón (SM) **1** (*gen*) mattress • MODISMO: • **servir de ~ a** to act as a buffer for ▸ **colchón de aire** airbed; (*Téc*) air cushion ▸ **colchón de muelles** spring mattress, interior sprung mattress ▸ **colchón de plumas** feather bed ▸ **colchón neumático** airbed
2 (= *precio*) floor price, reserve price; (= *fondos*) reserve fund

colchoneta (SF) mat

colcrén (SM) cold cream

cole* (SM) = **colegio**

colear ▹ CONJUG 1a (VT) **1** [+ *toro*] to hold on to the tail of
2 (*LAm**) (= *regañar*) to nag, give a hard time*
3 (*CAm*) (= *seguir*) to tail, follow
(VI) **1** [*perro*] to wag its tail; [*caballo*] to swish its tail; [*pez*] to wriggle
2 (*fig*) • **el asunto todavía colea** the affair is still not settled • MODISMO: • **estar vivito y coleando** to be alive and kicking
3 (*CAm, Caribe*) (*en edad*) • **colea en los 50** he's close on 50, he's knocking on 50*
(VPR) **colearse** (*Caribe*) **1** (*Aut*) to skid (out of control)
2 [*huésped*] to arrive unexpectedly *o* uninvited

colección (SF) collection • **es de ~** (*Méx*) it's a collector's item

coleccionable (ADJ) collectable
(SM) (= *objeto*) collectable; (*Prensa*) pull-out section

coleccionador(a) (SM/F) collector

coleccionar ▹ CONJUG 1a (VT), (VI) to collect

coleccionismo (SM) collecting

coleccionista (SMF) collector

colecho (SM) co-sleeping, bed-sharing

colecta (SF) **1** (= *recaudación*) collection (for charity)
2 (*Rel*) collect

colectar ▹ CONJUG 1a (VT) to collect

colecticio (ADJ) **1** (*Mil*) raw, untrained
2 • **tomo ~** omnibus edition, collected works

colectivamente (ADV) collectively

colectivero (SM) (*LAm*) (mini-)bus driver, *driver of a "colectivo"*

colectividad (SF) (*gen*) collectivity; (= *grupo*) group, community • **en ~** collectively

colectivismo (SM) (*Pol*) collectivism

colectivista (ADJ) (*Pol*) collectivist

colectivización (SF) collectivization

colectivizar ▹ CONJUG 1f (VT) to collectivize

colectivo (ADJ) **1** [*responsabilidad, esfuerzo*] collective; [*obra, proyecto*] collective, group (*antes de s*) • **el transporte ~** collective transport • **acción colectiva** joint action; ▹ **convenio, inconsciente, negociación**
2 (*Ling*) collective
(SM) **1** (= *grupo*) group • **el ~ más desfavorecido de la sociedad** the least favoured group in society
2 (*LAm*) (= *autobús*) bus; (= *taxi*) taxi

colector (SM) **1** (*Elec*) collector; (*Mec*) sump, trap • **~ de aguas residuales** main sewer

C

▸ **colector solar** solar panel
2† (= *recaudador*) collector

colega SMF **1** [*de trabajo*] colleague
2 (= *amigo**) mate*, pal*, buddy (*EEUU**); (*en oración directa*) man*

colegiado/a ADJ **1** [*médico, profesor, ingeniero*] member of a professional body • **has de estar ~ para ejercer de profesor** you have to be a member of the professional association of teachers to work as a teacher • **decisión colegiada** decision voted on by members • **tribunal ~** bench of judges
2 (*LAm*) (= *cualificado*) qualified
SM/F (*Dep*) referee; (*Med*) doctor

colegial(a) ADJ **1** (*Escol*) school (*antes de s*)
2 (*Rel*) collegiate
3 (*Méx*) (= *inexperto*) raw, green*, inexperienced
SM/F schoolboy/schoolgirl

colegialidad SF **1** (= *cuerpo*) college; (= *asociación, institución*) collegiate, membership
2 (= *cualidad*) collegiality, corporate feeling

colegiarse ▷ CONJUG 1a VPR to become a member of a professional body

colegiata SF collegiate church

colegiatura SF, **colegiaturas** SFPL (*Méx*) school fees, university fees

colegio SM **1** (*Escol*) school • **mañana no hay ~** there's no school tomorrow • **ir al ~** to go to school • **los niños están en el ~** the children are at school • **estudió en este ~** he went to this school ▸ **colegio confesional** faith school ▸ **colegio de curas** Catholic boys school (*run by priests*) ▸ **colegio de monjas** convent school ▸ **colegio de pago** fee-paying school ▸ **colegio mayor** (*Univ*) hall of residence; (*Hist*) college ▸ **colegio privado** private school ▸ **colegio público** state school, public school (*EEUU*) ▸ **Colegio Universitario** university college
2 (= *corporación*) ▸ **colegio cardenalicio** College of Cardinals ▸ **colegio de abogados** bar (association) ▸ **colegio de arquitectos** architects' association ▸ **Colegio de cardenales** College of Cardinals ▸ **colegio de médicos** medical association
3 (*Pol*) ▸ **colegio electoral** (= *lugar*) polling station; (= *electores*) electoral college

colegir ▷ CONJUG 3c, 3k (*frm*) VT **1** (= *juntar*) to collect, gather
2 (= *inferir*) to infer (**de** from) • **de lo cual colijo que …** from which I deduce *o* gather that …

coleóptero SM coleopteran, coleopteron

cólera SF **1** (= *ira*) anger, rage • **descargar la ~ en** to vent one's anger on • **montar en ~** to fly into a rage
2 (*Anat*) bile
SM (*Med*) cholera

colérico ADJ (= *furioso*) angry, furious; (= *malhumorado*) irritable, bad-tempered

colero SM (*Chile*) top hat

colesterol SM cholesterol

coleta SF **1** [*de pelo*] ponytail; (*Taur*) pigtail • **gente de ~** bullfighters • MODISMO: • **cortarse la ~** to quit, retire, hang up one's spurs* • **me cortaré la ~ si …*** I'll eat my hat if …
2 (= *adición*) postscript, afterthought

coletazo SM **1** [*de animal*] *blow or thrash or swipe with the tail*
2 (*Aut*) swaying movement • **dar ~s** to sway about • MODISMO: • **está dando los últimos ~s** [*régimen, sistema*] it's in its death throes; [*moda*] it's had its day; [*huracán*] it's petering out

coletero SM scrunchy

coletilla SF (*en carta, discurso*) postscript, afterthought; (*en frase*) tag

coleto SM **1*** • MODISMOS: • **decir para su ~** to say to o.s. • **echarse algo al ~** (= *comer*) to put sth away; (= *beber*) to drink sth down • **echarse un libro al ~** to get through *o* polish off a book*
2 (*Caribe*) (= *fregasuelos*) mop
3 (*Hist*) doublet, jerkin

colgadero SM (= *gancho*) peg; (= *percha*) hanger

colgadizo ADJ hanging, loose
SM (= *tejadillo*) piece of roofing; (*Caribe*) (= *techo*) flat roof

colgado PP *de* colgar
ADJ **1** (= *pendiente*) • **la bombilla colgada del techo** the light bulb hanging from the ceiling • **este cuadro estuvo ~ muchos años en el museo de la ciudad** this picture hung for many years in the city museum • **me dejaron ~ del teléfono** I was left hanging on the phone • **está ~ del teléfono todo el día** he's on the phone all day long; ▷ **colgar**
2 (= *ahorcado*) hanged, hung
3* [*asignatura*] • **tengo la física colgada** I have to resit *o* retake physics • **me han dejado el inglés ~** I've failed English
4 • **dejar ~ a algn*** (*en una situación difícil*) to leave sb in the lurch*; (*en una cita*) to stand sb up* • **se fue del país y me dejó ~ con todas las facturas del negocio** he's left the country and left me in the lurch with all the company invoices to sort out* • **vendrás ¿no?, espero que no me dejes ~** you'll be there, won't you? I hope you're not going to stand me up*
5‡ (= *drogado*) spaced out‡; (= *chiflado*) nuts*; (= *sin dinero*) broke*, short of money • **estoy ~ de deudas** I'm up to my neck in debts*
6‡ (= *enviciado*) • **~ de algo** hooked on sth* • **estar ~ del bingo** to be hooked on bingo* • **estar ~ de las emociones fuertes** to be hooked on big thrills* • **estar ~ de la tele** to be glued to the TV*
7‡ (= *enamorado*) • **estoy muy ~ de ella** I'm crazy about her*
8 (*Chile**) (= *ignorante*) clueless* • **salí muy ~ de la clase** I left the class completely clueless* • **estoy muy ~ en geografía** I haven't got a clue about geography*, I'm clueless in geography*
SMF‡ **1** (= *drogadicto*) druggie*
2 (= *chiflado*) nutter*

colgadura SF (*tb* **colgaduras**) hangings (*pl*), drapes (*pl*); (= *tapiz*) tapestry ▸ **colgaduras de cama** bed hangings *o* curtains

colgajo SM **1** (= *trapo*) strip, shred
2 (*Bot*) bunch (*of grapes hung to dry*)
3 (*Med*) flap of skin

colgante ADJ hanging • **jardín ~** hanging garden; ▷ **puente**
SM **1** (= *joya*) pendant
2 (*Arquit*) festoon
3 (*Caribe*) [*de reloj*] watch chain

colgar ▷ CONJUG 1h, 1l VT **1** (= *colocar pendiendo*) [+ *cuadro, diploma*] to hang, put up; [+ *colada, banderines*] to hang out; [+ *cartel, letrero, lámpara, cortina*] to put up; [+ *ropa*] (*en armario*) to hang up; (*para secar*) to hang out • **cuelga el abrigo en la percha** hang your coat on the hook • **cada día cuelgan el cartel de "no hay billetes"** every day the "tickets sold out" sign goes up • **le colgó un collar al** *o* **del cuello** he put *o* hung a necklace around her neck • MODISMOS: • **~ las botas** to hang up one's boots • **~ los estudios** to give up one's studies • **~ los hábitos** to leave the priesthood • **~ los libros** to give up one's studies • **~ la raqueta** to hang up one's racket • **~ el uniforme** to hang up one's uniform
2 (= *ahorcar*) to hang • **¡que lo cuelguen!** hang him!, string him up!*
3 [+ *teléfono*] to put down • **~ a algn** to hang up on sb, put the phone down on sb • **colgó el teléfono** he hung up • **dejar el teléfono mal colgado** to leave the phone off the hook
4 (= *atribuir*) [+ *apodo, mote*] to give • **le ~on el mote de "el lobo"** they nicknamed him "el lobo" • **enseguida te cuelgan la etiqueta de envidioso** they label you as jealous straight away • **~ la culpa a algn** to pin the blame on sb; ▷ **sambenito**
VI **1** [*cuadro, lámpara*] to hang • **~ de** [+ *techo*] to hang from; [+ *pared*] to hang on • **hay telarañas colgando del techo** there are cobwebs hanging from the ceiling • **lo encontraron con la jeringuilla aún colgando del brazo** he was found with the syringe still hanging from his arm • **de la pared colgaba un espejo** there was a mirror hanging on the wall • **llevar algo colgado a** *o* **del cuello** to wear sth round one's neck
2 (= *caer suelto*) [*rizos, tirabuzones*] to hang down • **le colgaban dos ricitos sobre la frente** she had two little curls hanging down over her forehead • **la ropa le colgaba por todas partes** his clothes were hanging off him
3 (*al teléfono*) to hang up • **han colgado** they've hung up, they've put the phone down • **no cuelgue, por favor** please, hold the line
VPR **colgarse 1** (= *estar suspendido*) • **~se de** to hang from • **se colgó de una grúa durante**

COLEGIO

Uso del artículo

A la hora de traducir expresiones como **al colegio/a la escuela** *o* **en el colegio/en la escuela, desde el colegio/desde la escuela** *etc, hemos de tener en cuenta el motivo por el que alguien acude al recinto o está allí:*

▷ *Se traduce* **al colegio/a la escuela** *por* **to school, en el colegio** *o* **en la escuela** *por* **at school** *y* **desde el colegio** *o* **desde la escuela** *por* **from school** *cuando alguien va o está allí en calidad de alumno:*

El primer día que fui al colegio me pasé toda la mañana llorando
The first day I went to school I spent the whole morning crying

Juan todavía está en el colegio. Lo han castigado
Juan's still at school. He's been given a detention

▷ *Se traduce* **al colegio/a la escuela** *por* **to the school, en el colegio/en la escuela** *por* **at the school** *y* **desde el colegio/desde la escuela** *por* **from the school** *cuando alguien va o está en el centro por otros motivos:*

Ayer fueron mis padres al colegio para hablar con el director
Yesterday my parents went to the school to talk to the headmaster

Podemos quedar en el colegio y luego ir a tomar algo
We can meet at the school and then go for a drink

Para otros usos y ejemplos ver la entrada.

varias horas he hung from a crane for several hours • **~se del brazo de algn** to take hold of sb's arm, take sb by the arm • **~se del cuello de algn** to throw one's arms around sb's neck • **~se del teléfono**: • **se colgó del teléfono durante más de una hora** she was on the phone for over an hour

2 (= *ahorcarse*) to hang o.s.

3 (= *ponerse*) to put on • **se colgó el bolso del** *o* **al hombro** she put her bag on her shoulder

4 (*Esp‡*) (= *con drogas*) to flip*, blow one's head‡

5 (*Chile, Méx*) *to plug illegally into the mains*

COLGAR

¿"Hanged" o "hung"?

▷ *Cuando* **colgar** *significa* **ahorcar, hang** *es un verbo regular y* **hanged** *es tanto el pasado como el participio:*

> **Le colgaron al amanecer**
> He was hanged at dawn

▷ *En el resto de los casos* **hang** *es irregular, y* **hung** *es la forma tanto de pasado como de participio:*

> **He colgado el cuadro en mi habitación**
> I've hung the picture in my room

Para otros usos y ejemplos ver la entrada.

colibrí SM hummingbird

cólico SM colic

colicuar ▷ CONJUG 1d VT (= *derretir*) to melt; (= *disolver*) to dissolve
VPR **colicuarse** (= *derretir*) to melt; (= *disolver*) to dissolve; [*gas*] to liquefy

colifato* (*Cono Sur*) ADJ nuts‡, crazy
SM madman, nutcase‡

coliflor SF cauliflower

coligado ADJ allied, coalition (*antes de s*) • **estar ~s** to be allied, be in league
SM ally

coligarse ▷ CONJUG 1h VPR to unite, join together, make common cause (**con** with)

coliguacho SM (*Cono Sur*) horsefly

coligüe SM (*Arg, Chile*) bamboo

colilla SF cigarette butt, cigarette end, fag end‡ • MODISMO: • **ser una ~*** to be past it, be all washed up*

colimba* (*Arg*) SM recruit, conscript, draftee (EEUU)
SF military service • **hacer la ~** to do one's military service

colimbo¹ SM (*Orn*) diver, loon (EEUU)

colimbo² SM (*Arg*) recruit, conscript, draftee (EEUU)

colín SM (*Caribe*) cane knife

colina SF hill

colinabo SM kohlrabi

colindante ADJ adjacent, adjoining, neighbouring, neighboring (EEUU)

colindar ▷ CONJUG 1a VI to adjoin, be adjacent • **~ con** [*país*] to have a border with; [*casa, finca*] to adjoin

colirio SM eye drops (*pl*)

colirrojo SM redstart

colís SM (*And*) cane knife

Coliseo SM Coliseum

colisión SF 1 [*de vehículos*] collision, crash ▸ **colisión de frente** head-on collision ▸ **colisión en cadena** multiple collision, multiple pile-up ▸ **colisión frontal** head-on collision ▸ **colisión múltiple** multiple collision, multiple pile-up
2 (*entre personas, intereses, ideas*) clash

colisionar ▷ CONJUG 1a VI to collide • **~ con** *o* **contra** [*tren, autobús, coche*] to collide with; [*persona, ideas*] to clash with, conflict with

colista SM (*Dep*) bottom team (in the league)
SMF person standing in a queue, person standing in a line (EEUU)

colita¹ SF (*Ven*) (*Aut*) lift • **hacer ~** to hitchhike, thumb a lift

colita²‡ SF [*de niño*] willy*, weenie (EEUU*)

colitis SF INV colitis

colla SMF (*Bol, Perú*) Indian from the altiplano

collado SM 1 (= *colina*) hill; (*más pequeña*) hillock
2 (= *puerto*) mountain pass

collage [koˈlaːʒ] SM collage

collalba SF (*Orn*) wheatear

collar SM 1 (= *adorno*) necklace; (= *insignia*) chain (of office) ▸ **collar de perlas** pearl necklace
2 [*de perro*] (dog) collar; (*Zool*) collar, ruff
3 (*Mec*) collar, ring
4 ▸ **collar de fuerza** stranglehold

collarín SM surgical collar ▸ **collarín ortopédico** orthopaedic collar

colleja SF 1 (*planta*) campion
2* (*golpe*) slap on the back of the neck

collera SF 1 (*Agr*) horse collar
2 **colleras** (*Cono Sur*) (= *gemelos*) cufflinks

collie [ˈkoli] SM collie

collín SM (*CAm*), **collines** SM (*And*) cane knife, machete

colmado ADJ [*vaso*] full to the brim (**de** with), full (**de** of); [*río*] overflowing (**de** with); [*plato, cuchara*] heaped (**de** with) • **una cucharada colmada** a heaped tablespoonful • **una carrera colmada de incidentes** an eventful race
SM (= *tienda*) grocer's shop, grocery store (EEUU); (*Andalucía*) (= *bodega*) retail wine shop; (= *restaurante*) cheap seafood restaurant

colmar ▷ CONJUG 1a VT 1 (= *llenar*) [+ *vaso, recipiente*] to fill to the brim, fill to overflowing, fill right up (**de** with); [+ *cuchara, plato*] to heap (**de** with)
2 [+ *ambición, esperanzas*] to fulfil, fulfill (EEUU), realize
3 • **~ a algn de algo**: **~ a algn de honores** to shower sb with honours *o* (EEUU) honors • **~ a algn de improperios** to heap insults *o* abuse on sb, shower sb with insults *o* abuse • **~ a algn de alabanzas** to heap praise on sb

colmatación SF silting

colmena SF 1 [*de abejas*] beehive, hive • **este edificio/barrio es una ~** this building is a warren
2 (*Méx*) (= *abeja*) bee; (= *conjunto*) bees

colmenar SM apiary

colmenero/a SM/F beekeeper

colmillo SM (*Anat*) eye tooth, canine (tooth); (*Zool*) fang; [*de elefante, morsa, jabalí*] tusk • **enseñar los ~s** to show one's teeth, bare one's teeth • MODISMOS: • **escupir por el ~** to talk big*, brag • **tener ~s** (*Méx*) to be long in the tooth* • **tener el ~ torcido** to be an old fox • **¡ya tengo ~s!** (*Méx*) you can't fool me!

colmillón SM (*LAm*) greed

colmilludo ADJ 1 (= *dentudo*) with big teeth *o* fangs *o* tusks
2* (= *sagaz*) sharp, alert

colmo SM • **¡eres el ~! ¡deja ya de quejarte!** you really take the biscuit! just stop complaining! • **¡esto es el ~! ¡ya no lo aguanto más!** this is the last straw! I can't stand it any longer! • **tu hermano es el ~, no paro de reírme con él** your brother is hilarious *o* is something else*, he makes me laugh so much • **el ~ de la elegancia** the height of elegance • **para ~** to top it all, to cap it all • **y, para ~, se le rompió el ordenador** and to top *o* cap it all his computer broke • **para ~ de desgracias** *o* **de males** to make matters worse • MODISMO: • **ser el ~ de los ~s**: • **que la mismísima policía le robe es ya el ~ de los ~s** to be robbed by the police themselves really is the limit

colocación SF 1 (= *acto*) (*gen*) placing; [*de bomba*] planting; [*de baldosa, moqueta, primera piedra*] laying; [*de cuadro*] hanging • **la simple ~ de un espejo frente a otro da sensación de espacio** simply placing one mirror opposite another creates an impression of space • **una fuga de gas producida por la incorrecta ~ del regulador** a gas leak caused by the incorrect installation of the regulator *o* by installing the regulator incorrectly • **la campaña consistirá en la ~ de carteles en lugares públicos** the campaign will consist of putting up posters in public places
2 (= *empleo*) job • **no encuentro ~** I can't find a job • **agencia de colocaciones** employment agency
3 (= *situación*) positioning • **el balón no entró gracias a la buena ~ del portero** thanks to the good positioning of the goalkeeper, the ball did not go in • **he cambiado la ~ de los muebles** I've rearranged the furniture
4 (*Com*) [*de acciones*] placing, placement

colocado ADJ 1 (*en trabajo*) • **estar ~** to be in work, have a job • **mi hija está muy bien colocada** my daughter has a very good job
2 (*Esp‡*) (= *drogado*) high*; (= *borracho*) smashed*, plastered*, trashed (EEUU‡)
3 • **apostar para ~** to back (a horse) for a place
4 (*Chile**) • **estar ~** to be well in* • **estar ~ con algn** to be well in with sb*

colocar ▷ CONJUG 1g VT 1 (= *situar*) (*gen*) to place; [+ *cartel*] to put up; [+ *bomba*] to plant, place; [+ *tropas*] to position, place; [+ *baldosa, moqueta, primera piedra*] to lay; [+ *cuadro*] to hang; (*Náut*) [+ *quilla*] to lay down • **coloca en cada plato una bola de helado** place a scoop of ice cream on each plate • **colocamos la estatua en el centro** we placed the statue in the centre • **de un solo pase colocó la pelota en la portería** he put *o* placed the ball in the net with just one touch • **coloca las tazas en su sitio** put the cups away • **~on carteles en el colegio** they put posters up around the school • **~ un producto en el mercado** to place a product on the market
2 (= *ordenar*) [+ *muebles, objetos, libros*] to arrange • **tenemos que ~ los muebles de otro modo** we need to arrange the furniture differently • **he colocado las revistas por orden alfabético** I've arranged the magazines in alphabetical order • **colocó a los niños en fila** he lined the children up
3 (= *dar trabajo*) • **~ a algn** [*agencia*] to get sb a job; [*empresario, jefe*] to give sb a job • **ha colocado a su hermano como camarero en su bar** he got his brother a job as a waiter in his bar
4 (*Econ*) [+ *acciones, dinero*] to place
5† (= *casar*) to marry off • **tiene a todas sus hijas bien colocadas** she has all her daughters nicely married off
6* (= *endilgar*) • **~ algo a algn** to palm sth off on sb, palm sb off with sth • **nos han colocado un vídeo que no funciona** they've palmed us off with a video that doesn't work • **no sé a quién ~ estas enciclopedias** I don't know who to palm these encyclopaedias off on • **otra vez quería ~nos el mismo rollo** he tried to fob us off with the same old story again*
VI (*Esp‡*) [*drogas, alcohol*] • **este vino coloca** this wine is pretty strong stuff

VPR **colocarse 1** (*en un lugar*) (*de pie*) to stand; (*sentado*) to sit • **colócate aquí** stand here • **siempre se coloca en el mismo asiento** she always sits in the same seat • **me coloqué en primera fila** I took my place in the front row
2 (*en una clasificación*) • **se acaban de ~ en quinto lugar** they have just moved into fifth place • **el programa se ha colocado en el primer lugar de la lista de audiencia** the programme is now top of the ratings *o* has reached the top of the ratings
3 (*en un trabajo*) to get a job • **se ha colocado como** *o* **de enfermera** she's got a job as a nurse
4 (*Esp*‡) (= *emborracharse*) to get pissed‡, get trashed (*EEUU*‡) (**con** on); (= *drogarse*) to get high* (**con** on)

colocata‡ SMF (= *borracho*) drunk*; (= *drogado*) junkie*

colocho (*CAm*) ADJ (= *rizo*) curly(-haired)
SMPL **colochos 1** (= *rizos*) curls
2 (= *virutas*) wood shavings

colocolo SM (*Chile*) **1** (= *gato montés*) cod-cod, *type of wildcat*
2 (= *monstruo*) mythical monster

colocón‡ SM • **cogerse un ~** to get high‡

colodrillo SM back of the neck

colofón SM **1** (*Tip*) colophon
2* (= *culminación*) culmination

colofonia SF rosin, colophony

Colombia SF Colombia

colombianismo SM *word/phrase etc peculiar to Colombia*

colombiano/a ADJ of/from Colombia
SM/F native/inhabitant of Colombia • **los ~s** the Colombians, the people of Colombia

colombicultor(a) SM/F pigeon-breeder

colombicultura SF pigeon-breeding

colombino ADJ of Columbus, relating to Columbus

colombofilia SF pigeon breeding, pigeon-fancying

colombófilo/a SM/F pigeon-fancier

colon SM (*Anat*) colon

Colón SM Columbus

colón SM monetary unit of Costa Rica and El Salvador

Colonia SF Cologne

colonia[1] SF **1** (= *territorio*) colony • **las antiguas ~s españolas** the former Spanish colonies
2 (= *comunidad*) [*de personas*] community; [*de animales, células*] colony • **la ~ norteamericana en Madrid** the American community in Madrid ▸ **colonia bacteriana** bacterial colony
3 (= *grupo de edificios*) ▸ **colonia obrera** working-class housing scheme ▸ **colonia penal** penal colony
4 (= *campamento*) summer camp • **irse de ~s** to go (off) to summer camp ▸ **colonia de vacaciones** holiday camp ▸ **colonia de verano** summer camp
5 (*Méx*) residential suburb, residential area • **Colonia Quintanilla del D.F.** the Quintanilla area of the capital ▸ **colonia proletaria** shanty town
6 (= *cinta*) silk ribbon

colonia[2] SF (*tb* **agua de colonia**) cologne, eau de Cologne

coloniaje SM (*LAm*) (= *época*) colonial period; (= *sistema*) colonial government; (*pey*) (= *esclavitud*) slavery

colonial ADJ [*época*] colonial; [*alimentos, productos*] overseas (*antes de s*), imported (*originally referring to imports from Spanish colonies*)

colonialismo SM colonialism

colonialista ADJ, SMF colonialist

colonización SF [*de país, territorio*] colonization

colonizador(a) ADJ [*proceso, país, lengua*] colonizing
SM/F [*de país, territorio*] colonist, colonizer

colonizar ▸ CONJUG 1f VT **1** [+ *país, territorio*] to colonize
2 (*Bio*) to colonize

colono/a SM/F **1** [*de país, territorio*] colonist; (= *nativo de una colonia*) colonial
2 (*Agr*) tenant farmer
3 (*Caribe*) [*de azúcar*] sugar planter
4 (*And*) (*Hist*) (= *indio*) Indian bound to an estate

coloqueta‡ SF **1** (= *detención*) arrest • **dar una ~ a** to nick‡, arrest
2 (= *redada*) police sweep
3 = **colocata**

coloquial ADJ colloquial

coloquialmente ADV colloquially

coloquiante SMF (= *hablante*) speaker; (*en charla, debate*) person taking part in a discussion • **mi ~** the person I was (*etc*) talking to

coloquiar ▸ CONJUG 1b VI to talk, discuss

coloquio SM **1** (= *debate*) discussion • **un ~ sobre el aborto** a discussion about abortion • **charla-coloquio** • **conferencia-coloquio** talk followed by a discussion
2 (= *congreso*) conference, symposium • **un ~ internacional sobre el comercio** an international trade conference *o* symposium
3 (*frm*) (= *diálogo*) dialogue, dialog (*EEUU*), colloquy (*frm*)

color SM, (*a veces*) SF **1** (= *coloración*) colour, color (*EEUU*) • **los ~es del arco iris** the colours of the rainbow • **el ~ azul** blue • **¿de qué ~ es?** what colour is it? • **¿de qué ~ tiene los ojos?** what colour are her eyes?, what colour eyes does she have? • **es de ~ verde** it's green • **una falda (de) ~ rojo** a red skirt • **un traje (de) ~ canela** a cinnamon-coloured suit • **lo quisiera en ~ verde** I'd like it in green • **a ~** colour (*antes de s*), color (*antes de s*) (*EEUU*) • **fotocopias a ~** colour photocopying • **a todo ~** full-colour • **dar ~ a algo** to colour sth in • **le dio ~ al dibujo** he coloured in the drawing • **de ~:** • **ropa de ~** coloured *o* (*EEUU*) colored clothes • **viste de ~** she wears coloured clothes • **en ~** colour (*antes de s*) • **película en ~** colour film • **televisión en ~** colour television • **tomar** *o* **coger ~:** • **esa tela no ha tomado** *o* **cogido bien el ~** that material has not dyed at all well • **cuando la cebolla haya tomado ~** when the onion has gone *o* turned golden brown • **el proyecto empieza a tomar** *o* **coger ~** the project is starting to take shape ▸ **color apagado** subdued colour ▸ **color pastel** pastel colour ▸ **color primario** primary colour
2 [*de la cara*] colour, color (*EEUU*) • **tener buen ~** to have good colour • **tener mal ~** to look off colour • MODISMOS: • **ponerse de mil ~es** to go bright red • **sacar los ~es a algn** to make sb blush • **le salieron los ~es** she blushed, she flushed red
3 (= *raza*) colour, color (*EEUU*) • **sin distinción de sexo o ~** regardless of sex or colour • **persona de ~** coloured person
4 (= *tipismo*) • **la feria ha perdido el ~ de antaño** the festival has lost the flavour *o* (*EEUU*) flavor *o* feel it used to have ▸ **color local** local colour
5 • MODISMOS: • **de ~ de rosa:** • **lo describió todo de ~ de rosa** she described it all in very rosy terms • **verlo todo de ~ de rosa** to see everything through rose-tinted *o* rose-coloured spectacles • **la vida no es de ~ de rosa** life isn't all roses • **no hay ~*** there's no comparison • **subido de ~** [*chiste*] risqué; [*discusión*] heated
6 colores (*tb* **lápices de colores**) coloured pencils, crayons • **una caja de ~es** a box of coloured pencils *o* crayons
7 colores (*Dep*) colours • **una bufanda con los ~es del Barcelona** a scarf with the Barcelona colours • **los ~es nacionales** the national colours
8 (= *cosmético*) blusher, rouge • **ponerse ~** to put on blusher *o* rouge
9 (= *interés*) colour • **el partido no tuvo ~** the game lacked colour
10†† • **so ~ de** under pretext of

coloración SF (*gen*) coloration, colouring, coloring (*EEUU*); (*Zool*) coloration

colorado ADJ **1** (= *rojo*) red • MODISMOS: • **~ como un tomate** as red as a beetroot *o* (*EEUU*) beet • **poner ~ a algn** to make sb blush • **ponerse ~** to blush
2 (*LAm*) [*chiste*] blue
SM **1** (= *color*) red
2 (*Caribe*) (= *escarlatina*) scarlet fever
3 • **los Colorados** *Uruguayan political party*

colorante ADJ colouring, coloring (*EEUU*)
SM colouring (matter)

colorar ▸ CONJUG 1a VT (= *pintar*) to colour, color (*EEUU*); (= *teñir*) to dye, tint • **~ algo de amarillo** to colour/dye sth yellow

coloratura SF coloratura

coloreado ADJ (= *pintado*) coloured, colored (*EEUU*); (= *teñido*) tinted
SM (= *pintado*) colouring, coloring (*EEUU*); (= *teñido*) tinting

colorear ▸ CONJUG 1a VT **1** = **colorar**
2 (= *justificar*) to justify, put in a favourable light; (= *quitar importancia a*) to whitewash, gloss over
VI **1** [*frutos*] to ripen
2 (= *tirar a rojo*) to be reddish
3 (= *ponerse colorado*) to redden

colorete SM rouge, blusher

colorido SM colour(ing), color(ing) (*EEUU*) ▸ **colorido local** local colour

colorín ADJ (*Cono Sur*) strawberry *o* reddish blond(e)
SM **1** (= *color*) bright colour, bright color (*EEUU*) • **con muchos colorines** all bright and colourful • **¡qué colorines tiene el niño!** what rosy cheeks the little fellow has! • **y ~, colorado, este cuento se ha acabado** and they all lived happily ever after, and that is the end of the story
2 (*Orn*) goldfinch
3 (*Med*) measles

colorinche* (*Arg, Perú*) ADJ loud*
SM loud colour*, loud color (*EEUU**)

colorir ▸ CONJUG 3a; defectivo VT **1** (= *pintar*) to colour, color (*EEUU*)
2 (*fig*) = **colorear**
VI to take on a colour, take on a color (*EEUU*), colour up, color up (*EEUU*)

colorista ADJ colouristic, coloristic (*EEUU*)
SMF colourist, colorist (*EEUU*)

colosal ADJ [*edificio, montaña*] colossal; [*comida, fiesta*] amazing*, fantastic*

colosalmente ADV immensely

coloso SM **1** (= *titán*) colossus • **el ~ del norte** (*esp LAm*) *the United States*
2 (*Cono Sur*) (*Aut*) trailer

coludo ADJ (*Cono Sur*) long-tailed

columbario SM columbarium

Columbina SF Columbine

columbrar ▸ CONJUG 1a (*liter*) VT **1** (= *divisar*) to make out, glimpse
2 (= *conjeturar*) to guess
3 [+ *solución*] to begin to see

columna SF **1** (*Arquit*) column

C

2 (*Tip*) [*de periódico*] column • **~ periodística** newspaper column • **un documento escrito a dos ~s** a document in two columns, a two-column document
3 [*de soldados, tanques*] column • **~ blindada** armoured *o* (*EEUU*) armored column; ▹ **quinto**
4 (*Anat*) (*tb* **columna vertebral**) spine, spinal column, backbone • **son la ~ vertebral del equipo** they form the backbone of the team • **la más firme ~ de la democracia** the steadiest pillar of democracy
5 (*Aut*) ▸ **columna de dirección** steering column
6 (*Téc*) [*de mercurio*] column

columnata SF colonnade

columnista SMF columnist

columpiar ▹ CONJUG 1b VT • **~ a algn** (*en columpio*) to push sb; (*en mecedora*) to rock sb
VPR **columpiarse** 1 (*en columpio*) to swing; (*en mecedora*) to rock
2* (= *meter la pata*) to drop a clanger*
3† (*fig*) to swing to and fro, seesaw

columpio SM 1 [*de niños*] swing ▸ **columpio basculante, columpio de tabla** seesaw, teeter-totter (*EEUU*)
2 (*LAm*) (= *mecedora*) rocking chair

colusión SF collusion

colza SF (*Bot*) rape, colza • **aceite de ~** rape-seed oil

coma¹ SM (*Med*) coma • **en ~** in a coma • **entrar en (estado de) ~** to go into a coma • **salir del (estado de) ~** to come out of the coma ▸ **coma diabético** diabetic coma ▸ **coma profundo** deep coma

coma² SF 1 (*Tip*) comma • MODISMO: • **sin faltar** *o* **sin saltarse una ~**: • **recitó todo el poema sin saltarse una ~** he recited the whole poem word perfect *o* without leaving out a single word; ▹ **punto**
2 (*Mat*) ≈ point (*Spanish uses a comma in place of a point*) • **doce ~ cinco** twelve point five ▸ **coma decimal** decimal point ▸ **coma flotante** floating point
3 (*Mús*) comma

comadre SF 1 (= *chismosa*) gossip
2 (= *vecina*) neighbour, neighbor (*EEUU*); (= *amiga*) friend
3 (= *madrina*) godmother
4 (*Med*) (= *partera*) midwife
5 (= *alcahueta*) go-between, procuress
6‡ (= *maricón*) pansy‡

comadrear ▹ CONJUG 1a VI to gossip

comadreja SF weasel

comadreo SM, **comadrería** SF chatting, nattering*

comadrona SF midwife

comal SM (*CAm, Méx*) (clay) griddle

comanche ADJ, SMF Comanche

comandancia SF 1 (= *función*) command
2 (= *grado*) rank of major
3 (= *central*) headquarters (*pl*)
4 (= *zona*) area under a commander's jurisdiction
5 (*Méx*) police station

comandanta SF 1 (*gen*) commander; (*Mil*) major; (*Hist*) major's wife
2 (*Náut*) flagship

comandante SMF 1 (= *jefe*) commander, commandant; (*Aer*) (*tb* **comandante de vuelo**) captain • **segundo ~** copilot, second pilot; (*tb* **comandante de policía**) (*Méx*) chief of police, chief superintendent ▸ **comandante en jefe** commander-in-chief
2 (= *grado*) major

comandar ▹ CONJUG 1a VT to command

comandita SF limited partnership, silent partnership (*EEUU*) • **en ~*** all together, as a team • **fuimos todos en ~ a hablar con el jefe** we all went together to talk to the boss

comanditario ADJ • **socio ~** sleeping partner, silent partner (*EEUU*)

comando SM 1 (*Mil*) (= *grupo*) commando unit, commando group ▸ **comando de acción** active service unit ▸ **comando de información** intelligence unit ▸ **comando suicida** suicide squad ▸ **comando terrorista** terrorist cell, terrorist squad
2 (*Mil*) (= *soldado*) commando
3 (*Mil*) (= *mando*) command
4 (*Téc*) control; (*Inform*) command ▸ **comando a distancia** remote control ▸ **comando vocal** voice command
5 (= *prenda*) duffle coat

comarca SF *administrative division comprising a number of municipalities*

comarcal ADJ [*carretera*] local; [*emisora*] regional

comarcano ADJ neighbouring, neighboring (*EEUU*), bordering

comarcar ▹ CONJUG 1g VI to border (**con** on), be adjacent (**con** to)

comatoso ADJ comatose

comba SF 1 (= *curvatura*) bend; (*en viga*) warp, sag
2 (= *cuerda*) skipping rope, jump rope (*EEUU*) • **saltar a la ~** to skip, jump rope (*EEUU*) • **dar a la ~** to turn the skipping rope
3 (= *juego*) skipping, jumping rope (*EEUU*)
4 • MODISMO: • **no pierde ~** he doesn't miss a trick

combado ADJ warped

combadura SF 1 = **comba**
2 (*Aut*) camber

combar ▹ CONJUG 1a VT (= *curvar*) to bend, curve
VPR **combarse** (= *hacer curva*) to bend, curve; (= *alabearse*) to bulge, warp; [*techo*] to sag

combate SM (*Mil*) combat; (*Boxeo*) contest, fight; [*de ideas, sentimientos*] conflict • **estar fuera de ~** (*lit, fig*) to be out of action; (*Boxeo*) to be knocked out • **dejar** *o* **poner a algn fuera de ~** (*lit, fig*) to put sb out of action; (*Boxeo*) to knock sb out • **ganar por fuera de ~** to win by a knockout ▸ **combate a muerte** fight to the death ▸ **combate naval** naval battle, sea battle ▸ **combate singular** single combat

combatiente SMF combatant • **no ~** non-combatant

combatir ▹ CONJUG 3a VI [*ejército, soldado*] to fight • **su padre combatió en la Guerra** his father fought in the War • **ha combatido por conseguir un acuerdo** she has fought to achieve an agreement
VT [+ *fraude, desempleo, injusticia, enfermedad*] to combat, fight; [+ *frío*] to fight (off) • **dedicó todo su esfuerzo a ~ al enemigo** he put all his strength into fighting *o* combating the enemy • **combatió las tesis capitalistas** he fought against capitalist ideologies • **un buen libro para ~ el aburrimiento** a good book to fight off *o* combat boredom • **medidas para ~ el fuego** fire-fighting measures

combatividad SF fighting spirit

combativo ADJ combative, spirited

combazo SM (*Cono Sur*) punch

combés SM waist

combi¹* SF 1 (= *prenda*) slip
2 (= *ardid*) fiddle*, wangle*

combi²* SF, **combinable** SF
1 (= *furgoneta*) combi (van)
2 (*Méx*) (= *bus*) minibus

combinación SF 1 [*de elementos, factores*] combination • **una elegante ~ de colores** an elegant combination of colours
2 [*de números*] combination • **sabía la ~ de la caja fuerte** he knew the combination of the safe • **la ~ ganadora del sorteo** the winning combination (of the draw)
3 (*Quím*) compound
4 [*de transportes*] connection • **hay muy buena ~ de autobuses** there is a very good bus connection
5 (= *prenda*) slip
6 (*Literat*) ▸ **combinación métrica** stanza form, rhyme scheme

combinacional ADJ combinatory, combinational

combinadamente ADV jointly, in combination with (**con** with)

combinado SM 1 [*de bebidas*] cocktail
2 (*Cono Sur*) radiogram
3 (= *equipo*) selection, team

combinar ▹ CONJUG 1a VT 1 [+ *esfuerzos, movimientos*] to combine; [+ *colores*] to match, mix
2 [+ *plan, proyecto*] to devise, work out
VPR **combinarse** 1 [*personas*] to get together, join together • **~se para hacer algo** to get *o* join together to do sth
2 (*Méx*) (= *alternarse*) to take it in turns

combinatoria SF (*Mat*) combinatorial analysis

combinatorio ADJ combinatorial, combinative • **análisis ~** (*Mat*) combinatorial analysis

combo ADJ (= *combado*) bent; (= *arqueado*) bulging; (= *torcido*) warped
SM 1 (*LAm*) (= *martillo*) sledgehammer
2 (*And, Cono Sur*) (= *golpe*) slap; (= *puñetazo*) punch
3 (*Col**) (= *pandilla*) gang

combustible ADJ combustible
SM (= *carburante*) fuel ▸ **combustible fósil** fossil fuel ▸ **combustible líquido** liquid fuel

combustión SF combustion ▸ **combustión espontánea** spontaneous combustion

comebolas* SM INV (*Caribe*) sucker*, mug*

comecocos* SM INV 1 (= *obsesión*) obsession, hang-up*; (= *pasatiempo*) brainteaser, idle pastime, absorbing but pointless activity; (= *lavacerebros*) brainwashing exercise
2 (= *preocupación*) nagging worry
3 (= *videojuego*) Pacman®
SMF INV 1 (= *preocupación*) worry
2 (= *persona*) • **es todo un ~ y los tiene a todos haciendo lo que él quiere** he brainwashes everyone into doing what he wants

COMECON SM ABR (= **Council for Mutual Economic Assistance**) Comecon

comedero SM 1 (*Agr*) feeding trough, trough; (*Orn*) feeding box, feeder
2 (= *comedor*) dining room; [*de animal*] feeding place
3 (*Caribe*) (= *prostíbulo*) brothel
4 (*And*) (= *sitio favorito*) haunt, hang-out*
ADJ † (= *comestible*) eatable, edible

comedia SF 1 (*Teat*) (= *obra cómica*) comedy • **alta ~** high comedy • **La divina ~** The Divine Comedy ▸ **comedia de costumbres** comedy of manners ▸ **comedia de enredo** comedy of intrigue ▸ **Comedia del Arte** commedia dell'arte ▸ **comedia musical** musical ▸ **comedia negra** black comedy
2 (*Teat*) (= *obra dramática*) play • **una ~ en un acto** a one-act play ▸ **comedia de capa y espada** cloak-and-dagger play
3 (*TV*) ▸ **comedia de situación** situation comedy, sitcom*
4 (= *fingimiento*) play-acting • **¡déjate ya de tanta ~!** stop your play-acting! • **hacer ~** to play-act • **¡deja de hacer ~ y di la verdad!** stop play-acting *o* pretending and tell the truth!

COMEDIA

The Spanish **comedias** written by dramatists of the Golden Age, or **Edad de Oro**, were five-act plays performed in open-air theatres. They involved stock characters similar to those of the Italian Commedia dell'Arte: a beautiful lady, her suitor, servants and go-betweens. In these **comedias**, which were not always comical in nature, action and a moral theme took precedence over character. Cloak and dagger episodes were built around plots involving disguises and mistaken identity. They dealt primarily with affairs of the nobility, while peasants were there to provide comic relief or to enhance particular pastoral themes. One of the most prolific **comedia** writers was Lope de Vega, who wrote on religious, historical and social themes. Other major **comedia** writers were Pedro Calderón de la Barca and Tirso de Molina, from whose pen came the figure of the archetypal seducer, Don Juan, in **El Burlador de Sevilla y Convidado de Piedra** (1630).

comediante/a SM/F **1** (*Teat*) (= *actor*) actor/actress
2 (= *humorista*) (= *hombre, mujer*) comedian; (*solo mujer*) comedienne
3 (= *farsante*) play-actor

comedidamente ADV (= *moderadamente*) moderately; (= *cortésmente*) courteously

comedido ADJ **1** (= *moderado*) moderate, restrained
2 (*esp LAm*) (= *solícito*) obliging

comedieta SF light comedy

comedimiento SM **1** (= *moderación*) moderation, restraint
2 (*esp LAm*) (= *solicitud*) helpfulness

comedio† SM **1** [*de territorio, lugar*] middle
2 (= *intervalo*) interval

comediógrafo/a SM/F playwright

comedirse ▹ CONJUG 3k VPR **1** (*en conducta*) (= *mostrar moderación*) to show restraint • **~ en las palabras** to choose one's words carefully
2 • **~ a** (*LAm*) (+ *infin*) to offer to (+ *infin*), volunteer to (+ *infin*)

comedón SM blackhead

comedor SM **1** (*en casa*) dining room; (*en barco, tren*) restaurant; (*en colegio, facultad*) dining hall, lunch room (EEUU); (*en trabajo*) canteen; ▹ **salón**
2 (= *mobiliario*) dining-room suite
ADJ • **Juan es muy buen ~** Juan's a big eater, Juan likes his food

comedura SF • **~ de coco** *o* **de tarro*** = comecocos

comefuegos SMF INV fire-eater

comegente‡ SM (*And, Caribe*) glutton

comehostias* SMF INV goody-goody*

comején SM **1** (= *insecto*) termite, white ant
2 (*And*) (= *glotón*) glutton
3 (*And*) (= *preocupación*) nagging worry, gnawing anxiety

comelitona SF (*Méx*) = **comilona**

comelón/ona ADJ, SM/F (*LAm*) = **comilón**

comelona SF (*LAm*) = **comilona**

comemierdas** SMF INV shit**

comendador SM knight commander (*of a military order*)

comendatorio ADJ • **carta comendatoria** letter of recommendation

comensal SMF **1** (= *compañero de mesa*) fellow diner (*frm*) • **habrá 13 ~es** there will be 13 for dinner, there will be 13 people dining (*frm*) • **mis ~es** my fellow diners (*frm*)
2 (*And*) (*en hotel*) guest

comensurabilidad SF commensurability

comentador(a) SM/F commentator

comentar ▹ CONJUG 1a VT **1** (= *explicar*) [+ *poema, texto*] to comment on
2 (= *hablar de*) [+ *noticia, hecho*] to discuss • **no pude ~ la situación con nadie** I couldn't discuss the situation with anyone • **antes prefiero ~lo con mi mujer** I'd like to discuss it with my wife first • **es un secreto, no lo comentes** it's a secret, don't tell anyone (about it) *o* don't mention it to anyone
3 (= *decir*) • **le estaba comentando que estás muy cambiada** I was saying to *o* telling him that you've changed a lot • **me han comentado que se casa** I've heard *o* I gather he's getting married • **me han comentado que es un buen libro** I've heard that it's a good book
4 (*TV, Radio*) [+ *partido*] to commentate on
VI **1** (= *opinar*) • **no quiso ~ al respecto** she didn't want to comment on it • **~ sobre algo** to comment on sth
2* (= *charlar*) to chat • **comentando con los amigos, se le escapó el secreto** he let slip the secret while chatting to *o* talking to friends

comentario SM **1** (= *observación*) comment • **hizo varios ~s irónicos sobre mi familia** he made some sarcastic comments *o* remarks about my family • **esto merece ~ aparte** this deserves separate comment • **"sin ~s"** "no comment" • **el tema no merece ~** the matter does not deserve mention • **sin más ~, pasemos a ver la película** without further ado, let's watch the film • **hacer un ~: le hizo un ~ al oído** she said something in his ear • **no hizo ~ alguno al respecto** he made no comment on the matter
2 (= *redacción*) essay • **un ~ sobre "El Quijote"** an essay on "Don Quixote" ▸ **comentario de texto** (*literario*) (literary) commentary; (*lingüístico*) textual analysis
3 comentarios (= *cotilleo*) gossip (*sing*) • **dar lugar a ~s** to lead to gossip

comentarista SMF commentator • **~ deportivo** sports commentator

comento (*frm*) SM **1** (= *observación*) comment
2 (*de un texto*) commentary
3 (= *embuste*) lie

comenzar ▹ CONJUG 1f, 1j VT to begin, start, commence (*frm*) • **comenzamos el rodaje ayer** we began *o* started *o* commenced (*frm*) filming yesterday • **comenzó la charla con un agradecimiento** she began *o* started the talk with a word of thanks • **comenzó su carrera literaria hace dos décadas** she began her literary career two decades ago • **la empresa comienza la construcción hoy** the company starts the construction work today • **hemos comenzado mal el año** we started the year badly • **comenzamos el recorrido en la iglesia** we start our trip at the church
VI [*proyecto, campaña, historia, proceso*] to begin, start • **¿puedo ~?** may I start *o* begin?, can I start *o* begin? • **el partido comienza a las ocho** the match starts *o* begins at eight • **comenzó diciendo que estaba de acuerdo conmigo** she began by saying that she agreed with me • **comenzó a los diez años haciendo recados** he began *o* started at the age of ten as a messenger boy • **al ~ el año** at the start *o* beginning of the year • **~ a hacer algo** to start *o* begin doing sth, start *o* begin to do sth • **la nieve comenzó a caer de nuevo** the snow started falling again, the snow began to fall again • **comencé a trabajar a los dieciocho años** I started *o* began working at eighteen • **podéis ~ a comer** you can start eating • **los invitados ya han comenzado a llegar** the guests have started arriving *o* to arrive • **aquel día comenzó a tener problemas con el oído** that day she began having trouble with her hearing • **~ con algo**: • **la película comienza con una pelea** the film starts *o* begins with a fight • **para ~** to start with • **para ~, una sopa de verduras** to start with, vegetable soup • **~ por**: • **no sé por dónde ~** I don't know where to start *o* begin • **la reforma ha comenzado por la educación** reform has started *o* begun with education • **comenzó por agradecernos nuestra presencia** she started *o* began by thanking us for coming • **para sentirte mejor, comienza por comer bien** in order to feel better, start by eating well • **su nombre comienza por m** his name begins with m • **todos sois culpables, comenzando por ti** you're all guilty, starting with you

comer ▹ CONJUG 2a VT **1** [+ *comida*] to eat • **¿quieres ~ algo?** would you like something to eat? • **no tienen qué ~** they have nothing to eat • MODISMO: • **sin ~lo ni beberlo**: • **sin ~lo ni beberlo, me vi envuelto en un caso de contrabando de drogas** without really knowing how, I found myself involved in a drug smuggling case • **ha recibido una herencia sin ~lo ni beberlo** he's come into an inheritance without having done anything to deserve it; ▹ **coco¹, tarro**
2 (= *almorzar*) to have for lunch, eat for lunch • **los domingos suelo ~ paella** on Sundays I usually have paella for lunch
3 (= *hacer desaparecer*) • **el pelo te come la cara** your hair's covering half your face • **esto come las existencias** this devours the stocks • **poco a poco el polvo fue comiendo la casa** dust gradually took over the house • **~ terreno**: • **la derecha les está comiendo terreno** the right is gaining ground on them • **el equipo se dejó ~ el terreno** the team conceded a lot of ground
4 (= *destruir, consumir*) • **un ácido que come la plata** an acid that corrodes silver • **el agua comió la piedra** the water wore down the stone • **eso les come la moral** that's eating away at their morale • **le come la envidia por dentro** she is eaten up *o* consumed with envy
5 (= *escocer*) • **el picor me come la pierna** my leg's stinging
6 (*Ajedrez*) to take
VI **1** (= *ingerir alimento*) to eat • **¿qué hay para ~?** what have we got to eat?, what is there to eat? • **los leones tienen que cazar para ~** lions have to hunt to eat • **¡come y calla!** shut up and eat your food!* • **~ de algo** (= *tomar comida*) to eat sth; (= *vivir*) to live off sth • **come de los platos de los demás** she eats other people's food • **no todos podemos ~ de lo que cultivamos** not all of us can live off what we grow ourselves • **~ fuera** to eat out • MODISMOS: • **~ con los ojos**: • **siempre comes con** *o* **por los ojos** your eyes are bigger than your stomach • **~ como una vaca** *o* **fiera** to eat like a horse • **no ~ ni dejar ~** to be a dog in the manger • **el mismo que come y viste** the very same
2 (= *tomar la comida principal*) (*esp Esp*) (*a mediodía*) to have lunch; (*LAm*) (*por la noche*) to have dinner • **comemos a la una** we have lunch at one • **me gusta ~ fuerte y cenar poco** I like to have a big lunch and a light evening meal
3 • **dar de ~** to feed • **estaba dando de ~ al niño** she was feeding her child • **dar de ~ a las gallinas** to feed the hens • **ni siquiera nos dio de ~** she didn't even give us anything to eat
4 (*And***) • **~ a algn** to screw sb**

C

(VPR) **comerse 1** [+ *comida*] to eat • **solo me he comido un bocadillo** all I've had to eat is a sandwich • **¿quién se ha comido mi queso?** who's eaten my cheese? • **se lo comió todo** he ate it all (up) • **~se las uñas** to bite one's nails • **MODISMOS**: • **~se a algn a besos** to smother sb in kisses • **~se a algn con los ojos** *o* **la vista** to devour sb with one's eyes • **¿cómo se come eso?** what on earth is that? • **está para comérsela*** she's really gorgeous *o* tasty* • **~se el mundo** to conquer the world • **~se a algn por pies** to take sb in completely; ▹ **coco¹, rosca, tarro, vista**
2 (= *destruir*) • **el sol se ha ido comiendo los colores de la alfombra** the sun has bleached the carpet, the sun has caused the colours of the carpet to fade • **el ácido se ha comido el metal** the acid has eaten the metal away • **MODISMO**: • **se comen unos a otros** they're at daggers drawn
3 [+ *capital, recursos*] to eat up • **en un mes se comió toda la herencia** he blew his entire inheritance within a month
4 (= *saltarse*) [+ *párrafo*] to miss out; [+ *consonante*] to swallow • **se come las palabras** he swallows his words
(SM) • **tan necesario como el ~** as necessary as eating • **era muy parco en el ~** he didn't eat much, he wasn't a big eater • **el buen ~** good food • **Fernando es de buen ~** Fernando enjoys his food

comerciabilidad (SF) marketability, saleability

comerciable (ADJ) **1** (*Com*) marketable, saleable • **valores ~s** marketable securities
2† (= *sociable*) sociable

comercial (ADJ) **1** (= *de tiendas*) [*área, recinto*] shopping (*antes de s*) • **un centro ~** a shopping centre
2 (= *financiero*) [*carta, operación*] business (*antes de s*); [*balanza, déficit, guerra, embargo*] trade (*antes de s*); [*intercambio, estrategia*] commercial • **el interés ~ de la empresa** the commercial *o* trading interests of the company • **su novela alcanzó un gran éxito ~** his novel was very successful commercially, his novel achieved great commercial success • **han reanudado las relaciones ~es** they have resumed trading relations; ▹ **agente, local**
3 [*aviación, avión, piloto*] civil
4 [*cine, teatro, literatura*] commercial • **una película muy ~** a very commercial film
(SMF) (= *vendedor*) salesperson

comercializable (ADJ) marketable, saleable

comercialización (SF) (= *explotación comercial*) commercialization; (= *puesta en mercado*) marketing

comercializar ▹ CONJUG 1f (VT) (= *explotar comercialmente*) to commercialize; (= *lanzar al mercado*) to market

comercialmente (ADV) commercially

comerciante (SMF) **1** (*gen*) trader, dealer; (*a gran escala*) merchant; (= *tendero*) shopkeeper, storekeeper (*EEUU*)
▸ **comerciante al por mayor** wholesaler
▸ **comerciante al por menor** retailer
▸ **comerciante exclusivo** sole trader
2 (= *interesado*) • **es un ~** he's very money-minded

comerciar ▹ CONJUG 1b (VI) [*dos empresas*] to do business (together); [*naciones*] to trade • **~ con** [+ *empresa*] to do business with, have dealings with; [+ *país*] to trade with; [+ *mercancías*] to deal in, trade in, handle

comercio (SM) **1** (= *actividad*) trade, commerce • **medidas para favorecer el ~ con Francia** measures to promote trade *o* commerce with France • **defensores del libre ~** champions of free trade • **el ~ de textiles** the textile trade ▸ **comercio de exportación** export trade ▸ **comercio de importación** import trade ▸ **comercio E, comercio electrónico** e-commerce
▸ **comercio exterior** foreign trade
▸ **comercio interior** domestic trade
▸ **comercio internacional** international trade ▸ **comercio justo** (*Com*) fair trade
▸ **comercio minorista** retail trade; ▹ **cámara**
2 (= *tienda*) shop, store (*EEUU*) • **¿a qué hora cierran hoy los ~s?** what time do the shops *o* stores close today? • **ha comenzado la huelga del ~** the shopkeepers' *o* (*EEUU*) storekeepers' strike has started
3 (= *intercambio*) ▸ **comercio carnal** sexual intercourse ▸ **comercio social** social intercourse

comestible (ADJ) (= *digerible*) edible
(SMPL) **comestibles 1** (= *alimentos*) food (*sing*); (*Com*) foodstuffs; (*en tienda, supermercado*) groceries • **tienda de ~s** grocer's (shop), grocery (*EEUU*)
2 (= *provisiones*) provisions

cometa¹ (SM) (*Astron*) comet

cometa² (SF) kite ▸ **cometa delta** (*And*), **cometa voladora** (*And*) hang glider

cometer ▹ CONJUG 2a (VT) [+ *crimen, delito, pecado*] to commit; [+ *atentado*] to carry out; [+ *error*] to make • **ha cometido una falta de ortografía** she made a spelling mistake • **el tenista cometió dos dobles faltas** the tennis player made two double faults • **no ~ás actos impuros** thou shalt not commit impure acts

cometido (SM) task, mission • **tiene un ~ difícil en este viaje** she has a difficult task *o* mission on this trip • **el detective cumplió con su ~** the detective fulfilled his task *o* mission • **el ~ del Metro es el transporte de viajeros** the task of the Metro is to transport passengers

comezón (SF) **1** (= *picor*) itch, itching; [*de calor*] tingle, tingling sensation • **siento ~ en el brazo** my arm itches, my arm is tingling
2 (= *inquietud*) itch (**por** for) • **sentir ~ de hacer algo** to feel an itch to do sth

comi* (SF) = **comisaría**

comible (ADJ) eatable

Comibol (SF ABR) (*Bol*) = **Corporación Minera de Bolivia**

cómic ['komik] (SM) (PL: **cómics** ['komik]) comic

comicastro/a (SM/F) ham (actor/actress)*

comicidad (SF) funniness, comicalness

comicios (SMPL) elections, voting (*sing*)

cómico/a (ADJ) **1** (= *gracioso*) comic(al), funny
2 (*Teat*) comedy (*antes de s*) • **autor ~** playwright
(SM/F) **1** (*Teat*) (comic) actor/actress
2 (= *humorista*) comedian/comedienne

comida (SF) **1** (= *alimento*) food • **le echas mucha sal a la ~** you put too much salt on your food • **sirvió la ~ en cuencos** she served the food in bowls • **nos hemos quedado sin ~** we've got no food left • **no me gusta la ~ india** I don't like Indian food • **mamá está haciendo** *o* **preparando la ~** mum is making lunch • **no sirven ~ después de las tres** they don't serve food *o* meals after three o'clock • **acábate la ~** finish your meal ▸ **comida a domicilio** meals on wheels (*pl*) ▸ **comida basura** junk food ▸ **comida casera** home cooking ▸ **comida infantil** baby food
▸ **comida para gatos** cat food ▸ **comida para perros** dog food ▸ **comida precocinada, comida preparada** ready meals (*pl*), precooked meals (*pl*) ▸ **comida rápida** fast food ▸ **comida reconfortante** comfort food
2 (= *acto de comer*) meal • **ganamos una ~ para dos personas** we won a meal for two • **tómese una pastilla después de cada ~** take one tablet after meals • **hacemos la ~ fuerte al mediodía** we have our main meal at midday ▸ **comida de negocios** business lunch ▸ **comida de trabajo** working lunch
3 (*esp Esp*) (= *almuerzo*) lunch • **la hora de la ~** lunch time
4 (*LAm*) (= *cena*) dinner, evening meal
5‡ ▸ **comida de coco, comida de tarro** • **en la mili le han hecho una ~ de coco** *o* **tarro** they brainwashed him when he was in the army • **este libro es una ~ de coco** *o* **tarro** this book is pretty heavy stuff*

comidilla (SF) **1** • **ser la ~ del barrio** to be the talk of the town
2 (= *pasatiempo*) hobby, special interest

comido (ADJ) **1** • **estar ~** to have had lunch *etc* • **vengo ~** I've had lunch (before coming)
2 • **MODISMO**: • **es lo ~ por lo servido** it doesn't pay, it's not worth while

comience (SM) (*And*) = **comienzo**

comienzo (SM) **1** (= *principio*) [*de película, historia, partido*] beginning, start; [*de proyecto, plan*] beginning; [*de enfermedad*] onset • **desde el ~ supe que el asesino era el mayordomo** I knew the butler was the murderer from the beginning *o* the start • **ese fue el ~ de una serie de desastres** that was the first in a series of disasters • **al ~: al ~ no entendía nada** at first I didn't understand anything • **al ~ de la primavera** in early Spring, at the start of Spring • **los ~s: en los ~s de este siglo** at the beginning of this century • **en los ~s del proceso democrático** in the early *o* initial stages of the democratic process

---

CÓMICO

¿"Comic" o "comical"?

El adjetivo **cómico** *se puede traducir por* **comic** *y* **comical**, *pero estos no son intercambiables.*

Comic

▹ *Algo que es* **cómico** *porque se hace o se dice con la intención de hacer reír a la gente se traduce al inglés por* **comic**:
El efecto cómico se consigue poniéndose ropa que te queda grande
Comic effect is achieved by wearing clothes that are too big

▹ **Cómico** *también se traduce por* **comic** *para describir algo perteneciente o relativo a la comedia*:
... un actor cómico ...
... a comic actor ...

Hay que tener en cuenta que en este caso **comic** *nunca funciona como atributo.*

Comical

▹ **Cómico** *se traduce por* **comical** *para describir algo o a alguien que resulta gracioso o absurdo (a menudo porque es raro o inesperado)*:
Su gesto rozaba lo cómico
Her expression was almost comical
Hay algo en él ligeramente cómico
There is something slightly comical about him

Para otros usos y ejemplos ver la entrada.

• **una etapa muy difícil en sus ~s** a very difficult stage, initially
2 • **dar ~** [*acto, curso*] to start, begin, commence (*frm*) • **la ceremonia dio ~ a las cinco de la tarde** the ceremony started *o* began *o* (*frm*) commenced at five o'clock
3 • **dar ~ a** [+ *acto, ceremonia*] to begin, start; [+ *carrera*] to start; [+ *etapa*] to mark the beginning of • **su último libro daba ~ a una nueva etapa** his last book marked the beginning of a new phase • **el director dio ~ al curso académico** the headmaster inaugurated the academic year

comillas (SFPL) quotation marks, quotes (*EEUU*) • **entre ~** in inverted commas, in quotes (*EEUU*)

comilón/ona (ADJ) greedy
(SM/F) (= *buen comedor*) big eater; (= *glotón*) glutton, pig*

comilona* (SF) feast, blowout*

cominero/a (ADJ) fussy
(SM/F) fusspot*, fussbudget (*EEUU*), fussy person

comino (SM) cumin, cumin seed
• MODISMOS: • **no vale un ~** it's not worth tuppence • **(no) me importa un ~** • **no se me da un ~** I couldn't give a toss‡, I couldn't care less (**de** about)

Comintern (SF ABR) (= **Communist International**) Comintern

comiquero (ADJ) comic

comiquita (SF) (*Ven*) (= *tira cómica*) comic strip; (= *dibujos animados*) cartoon

comisaría (SF) 1 [*de policía*] police station, precinct (*EEUU*)
2 (*Mil*) administrative office; (*Náut*) purser's office

comisariado (SM) 1 (= *delegación*) commission
2 (*Pol*) commissary

comisariato (SM) administrative office

comisario/a (SM/F) 1 (= *delegado*) commissioner • **alto ~** high commissioner ▸ **comisario/a europeo/a** European commissioner
2 [*de policía*] superintendent, captain (*EEUU*)
3 (*Pol*) commissar
4 (*Mil*) administrative officer, service corps officer
5 [*de exposición*] organizer
6 (*Náut*) purser
7 [*de hipódromo*] steward ▸ **comisario/a de carreras** course steward

comiscar ▹ CONJUG 1g (VT) to nibble (at)

comisión (SF) 1 (= *encargo*) assignment, task, commission (*frm*); (= *misión*) mission, assignment
2 (*Pol*) commission; (= *junta*) committee ▸ **comisión de seguimiento** watchdog committee ▸ **Comisión Europea** European Commission ▸ **comisión investigadora** investigating committee, board of enquiry, board of inquiry (*EEUU*) ▸ **Comisiones Obreras** Communist trade union ▸ **comisión mixta** joint committee ▸ **comisión parlamentaria** parliamentary committee ▸ **comisión permanente** standing committee ▸ **comisión planificadora** planning board
3 (*Econ*) board
4 (*Com*) (= *pago*) commission • **a ~** on a commission basis ▸ **comisión porcentual** percentage commission (**sobre** on) ▸ **comisión sobre las ventas** sales commission
5 (= *ejecución*) commission; [*de ultraje*] perpetration • **pecado de ~** sin of commission
6 ▸ **comisión de servicio(s)** (= *destino provisional*) secondment, temporary transfer; (= *permiso de ausencia*) leave of absence

comisionado/a (SM/F) 1 (= *delegado*) commissioner
2 (= *miembro*) (*Pol*) committee member; (*Com, Econ*) board member

comisionar ▹ CONJUG 1a (VT) to commission

comisionista (SMF) commission agent, person working on a commission basis

comiso (SM) (*Jur*) 1 (= *acto*) seizure, confiscation
2 (= *géneros*) confiscated goods

comisquear ▹ CONJUG 1a (VT) = **comiscar**

comistrajo (SM) bad meal, awful food

comisura (SF) corner, angle, commissure (*frm*) ▸ **comisura de los labios** corner of the mouth

comité (SM) committee ▸ **comité de apelación** committee *o* board of appeal ▸ **comité de dirección** steering committee ▸ **comité de empresa** works committee, shop stewards' committee ▸ **Comité de No Intervención** Non-Intervention Committee ▸ **comité de redacción** (*gen*) drafting committee; (*Prensa*) editorial committee ▸ **Comité Directivo** (*Dep*) board (of management) ▸ **comité ejecutivo** executive board

comitiva (SF) (= *cortejo*) retinue • **la ~ del rey** the King's retinue • **la ~ de fotógrafos que sigue todos sus pasos** (*fig*) (*hum*) the retinue of photographers who follow his every move ▸ **comitiva fúnebre** cortège, funeral procession

como (ADV) 1 (*indicando semejanza*) like • **tienen un perro ~ el nuestro** they've got a dog like ours • **se portó ~ un imbécil** he behaved like an idiot • **es ~ un pez** it's like a fish • **juega ~ yo** he plays like me *o* like I do • **~ este hay pocos** there are few like this *o* him • **sabe ~ a queso** it tastes a bit like cheese • **blanco ~ la nieve** as white as snow • **tuvo resultados ~ no se habían conocido antes** it had results such as had never been known before
2 (*introduciendo ejemplo*) such as • **hay peces, ~ truchas y salmones** there are fish, such as trout and salmon • **tiene ventajas, ~ son la resistencia y durabilidad** it has advantages, such as *o* like strength and durability
3 (*indicando modo*) **a** (+ *indic*) • **lo hice ~ me habían enseñado** I did it as I had been taught • **hazlo ~ te dijo ella** do it like* *o* the way she told you • **toca ~ canta** she plays like* *o* the same way as she sings • **no es ~ me lo imaginaba** it isn't as *o* like* I imagined it • **prefiero ~ lo haces tú** I prefer it the way you do it • **la manera ~ sucedió** the way (in which) it happened • **fue así ~ comenzó** that was how it began • **lo levanté ~ pude** I lifted it as best I could • **tal ~:** • **tal ~ lo había planeado** just as *o* the way I had planned it
b (+ *subjun*) • **hazlo ~ quieras** do it however you want *o* like • **hazlo ~ puedas** do your best, do the best you can • **~ sea** at all costs • **tratan de mantenerse en el poder ~ sea** they will do whatever it takes to stay in power • **está decidido a salvar ~ sea la vida del niño** he's determined to do whatever it takes to save the child's life • **sea ~ sea** in any case • **hay que evitar que nos eliminen sea ~ sea** we must avoid getting knocked out at all costs
4 (= *en calidad de*) as • **lo usé ~ cuchara** I used it as a spoon • **asistió ~ espectador** he attended as a spectator • **lo dice ~ juez** he says it speaking as a judge • **vale más ~ poeta** he is better as a poet
5 (= *más o menos*) about, around • **había ~ cincuenta** there were about *o* around fifty • **vino ~ a las dos** he came at about *o* around two • **sentía ~ tristeza** she felt a sort *o* kind of sadness
6 (*con valor causal*) • **libre ~ estaba** free as he was
(CONJ) 1 (+ *indic*) (= *ya que*) as, since • **~ no tenía dinero** as *o* since I had no money
2 (+ *indic*) (= *según*) as • **~ dice mi profesor** as my teacher says • **~ se ve en el gráfico** as you can see from the diagram • **tal (y) ~ están las cosas** the way things are, as things stand • **tal ~ están los precios de las motos** ... with motorbike prices as they are at the moment ...
3 (+ *indic*) (= *cuando*) as soon as • **así ~ nos vio lanzó un grito** as soon as he saw us he shouted
4 (+ *indic*) (= *que*) • **verás ~ les ganamos** we'll beat them, you'll see • **ya verás ~ no vienen** I bet they won't come • **de tanto ~:** • **tienen las manos doloridas de tanto ~ aplaudieron** they clapped so much their hands hurt • **de tanto ~ odio a los dos, no sé a quien odio más** I hate them both so much, I don't know which I hate the most
5 (+ *subjun*) (= *si*) if • **~ vengas tarde, no comes** if you're late you'll get nothing to eat • **~ sea cierto, ¡estamos perdidos!** if it's true, we're done for! • **¡~ lo pierdas!** you'd better not lose it!, don't you lose it! • **~ no:** • **~ no lo haga en seguida** ... if he doesn't do it at once ..., unless he does it at once ... • **no salimos, ~ no sea para ir al cine** we only go out if it's to go to the cinema, we don't go out unless it's to go to the cinema
6 • **~ que** as if • **¡~ que yo soy tonto y me creo esas mentiras!** as if I was stupid enough to believe lies like that! • **¡~ que te van a pagar!** don't tell me they're going to pay you! • **hizo ~ que no nos veía** he pretended not to see us • **al tragar nota ~ que le molesta** he shows discomfort when swallowing
7 • **~ si** as if, as though • **siguió leyendo, ~ si no hubiera oído nada** he kept on reading, as if *o* as though he hadn't heard • **sentí ~ si fuera a caerme** I felt as if *o* as though I was about to fall • **~ si no hubiera pasado nada** as if *o* as though nothing had happened • **se comporta ~ si me odiara** he behaves as if *o* as though he hated me • **~ si fuera a llover** as if *o* as though it was going to rain
8 • **~ para:** • **¡es ~ para denunciarlos!** it's enough to make you want to report them to the police! • **tampoco es ~ para enfadarse tanto** there's no need to get so angry about it
9 (*CAm, Méx*) • **a ~ dé** *o* **diera lugar** at any cost;
▹ **así, pronto, querer**

cómo (ADV) 1 (*interrogativo*) **a** (= *de qué modo*) how? • **¿~ se hace?** how do you do it? • **¿~ se escribe?** how do you spell it? • **¿~ están tus nietos?** how are your grandchildren? • **¿~ está usted?** how are you? • **¿~ te llamas?** what's your name? • **¿~ te va?** how are you doing? • **¿~ lo has pasado en la fiesta?** how was the party? • **¿y eso tú ~ lo sabes?** but, how do you know? • **no sé ~ hacerlo** I don't know how to do it • —**¿~ va el Barcelona?** —**el primero** "how's Barcelona doing" — "they're first" • **¿~ soportas a ese idiota?** how do you put up with that idiot? • **¿~ se te ocurrió llamarlo tan tarde?** what(ever) were you thinking of, ringing him so late? • **no me digas ~ tengo que comportarme** don't you tell me how to behave • **fue así ~ comenzó todo** that was how it all began • **no había ~ seguir su ritmo** there was no way of keeping up with him
b (*en descripciones*) • **¿~ es tu casa?** what's

your house like? • **¿~ es tu hermano?** what's your brother like? • **¿~ es de alto el armario?** how tall is the cupboard?, what height is the cupboard? • **¿~ está de alto tu niño?** how tall is your child?
c (= *¿por qué?*) why? • **¿~ es que no viniste?** why didn't you come? • **—no fui a la fiesta —¿~ no?** "I didn't go to the party" — "why not *o* how come?" • **—¿me dejas este libro? —¡~ no!** "can I borrow this book?" — "of course!"
d (*indicando extrañeza*) what? • **¿cómo? ¿que tú no lo sabías?** what? you mean you didn't know? • **¿y ~ es eso?** how come?, how can that be? • **¿~ que Mónica no vino a la boda?** what do you mean, Monica didn't come to the wedding? • **¿~ te atreves?** how dare you! • **—pues no lo haré —¿~ que no?** "I won't do it"— "what do you mean, you won't do it?" • **¿~ que no sabes nada? no me lo creo** "what do you mean, you don't know anything about it? I don't believe you"
e (= *¿perdón?*) sorry?, what's that? • **¿~ dice?** I beg your pardon?
f • **¿a ~?: ¿a ~ están** *o* **son las peras?** how much are the pears? • **¿a ~ estamos hoy?** what's the date today?
2 (*exclamativo*) • **¡~ llueve!** look at the rain! • **¡~ corre!** he can certainly run! • **¡hay que ver ~ está el tiempo!** what terrible weather! • **¡~ me gusta ir a la playa!** I love going to the beach! • **—toma, un regalito —¡~ eres!** "here's a small present" — "you shouldn't have!" • **—no quiero prestarte dinero —¡~ eres!** "I won't lend you any money" — "you mean thing!" • **¡~ te has puesto de harina!** you're covered in flour! • **está lloviendo ¡y ~!** just look at the rain!
EXCL • **¡cómo! ¿solo cuatro libros?** what do you mean, only four books! • **¡pero ~! ¿todavía no has acabado?** what are you doing! haven't you finished yet?
SM • **el ~ y el por qué de las cosas** the whys and wherefores • **aclaró el ~ y el dónde podremos pescar** he explained the conditions for us to be allowed to fish

cómoda SF chest of drawers

cómodamente ADV (= *confortablemente*) comfortably; (= *convenientemente*) conveniently

comodidad SF **1** (= *confort*) comfort • **vivir con ~** to live in comfort
2 (= *conveniencia*) convenience • **pensar en su propia ~** to consider one's own interest • **venga a su ~** come at your convenience
3 comodidades (= *servicios*) comforts, amenities; (*LAm*) (*Com*) commodities, goods ▸ **comodidades de la vida** good things of life, life's comforts

comodín SM **1** (*Naipes*) joker
2 (= *excusa*) pretext, stock excuse
3 (*Ling*) catch-all, all-purpose word
4 (*Inform*) wildcard
5 (*Mec*) useful gadget
ADJ (*And, Caribe, Méx*) = **comodón**

cómodo ADJ **1** (= *confortable*) [*cama, silla, habitación*] comfortable; [*trabajo, tarea*] agreeable
2 (= *conveniente*) [*instrumento, objeto*] handy; [*arreglo, horario*] convenient
3 (= *descansado*) comfortable • **así estarás más ~** you'll be more comfortable this way • **ponerse ~** to make o.s. comfortable
4 [*persona*] (= *perezoso*) lazy; (= *tranquilo*) laid-back*

comodón/a ADJ (= *regalón*) comfort-loving; (= *pasivo*) easy-going, liking a quiet life; (= *perezoso*) lazy
SM/F (= *perezoso*) lazybones* • **es un ~** he likes his home comforts

comodonería SF love of comfort

comodoro SM commodore

comoquiera CONJ **1** • **~ que** (+ *indic*) since, in view of the fact that
2 • **~ que** (+ *subjun*) in whatever way • **~ que sea eso** however that may be

comp. ABR (= **compárese**) cp

compa* SMF **1** (*CAm, Méx*) (= *compañero*) pal*, buddy (*EEUU**)
2 (*Nic*) (*Hist*) Nicaraguan freedom fighter

compacidad SF compactness

compact SM (PL: **compacts**) (*tb* **compact disc**) compact disc

compactación SF compacting, compression

compactado ADJ compacted

compactadora SF compacter

compactar ▹ CONJUG 1a VT to compact, compress

compacto ADJ compact • **disco ~** compact disc
SM (*Mús*) compact hi-fi system

compadecer ▹ CONJUG 2d VT (= *apiadarse de*) to pity, be sorry for; (= *comprender*) to sympathize with
VPR **compadecerse 1** • **~se de** ▹ VT
2† • **~se con** to fit with

compadrada SF (*Cono Sur*) cheek, insolence

compadrazgo SM **1** (= *parentesco*) status of godfather
2 (*LAm*) (= *amistad*) close friendship

compadre SM **1** (= *padrino*) godfather
2 (*esp LAm**) (= *amigo*) friend, pal*, buddy (*esp EEUU**); (*en oración directa*) friend
3 (*Cono Sur*) (= *jactancioso*) braggart, loudmouth; (= *engreído*) show-off*; (= *matón*) bully

compadrear ▹ CONJUG 1a VI **1** (*esp LAm**) [*amigos*] to be mates*, be buddies (*EEUU**)
2 (*Cono Sur*) (= *jactarse*) to brag, show off; (= *presumir*) to put on airs; (= *amenazar*) to give threatening looks

compadreo SM (*esp LAm*) companionship, close contact

compadrito SM (*Cono Sur*) = **compadre**

compaginable ADJ compatible • **motivos difícilmente ~s** motives that are hard to reconcile

compaginación SF (= *armonización*) arrangement, combination; [*de papeles impresos*] putting in order, collation; (*Tip*) makeup

compaginar ▹ CONJUG 1a VT **1** (= *armonizar*) to combine • **~ el trabajo con la familia** to combine work and having a family
2 (= *ordenar*) to put together, put in order
3 (*Tip*) to make up
VPR **compaginarse** (= *concordar*) to agree, tally • **~se con** (*gen*) to tally with; [+ *colores*] to blend with • **esa conducta no se compagina con su carácter** this behaviour is out of character for him

compañerismo SM (= *camaradería*) comradeship, friendship; (*Dep etc*) team spirit

compañero/a SM/F **1** (*gen*) companion; (*Dep, Naipes*) partner; (*Dep*) [*de equipo*] team-mate ▸ **compañero/a de armas** comrade-in-arms ▸ **compañero/a de baile** dancing partner ▸ **compañero/a de cama** bedfellow ▸ **compañero/a de candidatura** running mate ▸ **compañero/a de clase** schoolmate, classmate ▸ **compañero/a de cuarto** roommate ▸ **compañero/a de infortunio** companion in misfortune ▸ **compañero/a de juego** playmate ▸ **compañero/a de piso** flatmate, roommate (*EEUU*) ▸ **compañero/a de rancho** messmate ▸ **compañero/a de trabajo** (*en fábrica*) workmate, fellow worker; (*en oficina*) colleague ▸ **compañero/a de viaje** fellow traveller, fellow traveler (*EEUU*) ▸ **compañero/a sentimental** partner
2 • **dos calcetines que no son ~s** two odd socks, two socks which do not match • **¿dónde está el ~ de este?** where is the one that goes with this?, where is the other one (of the pair)?
3 (*Pol*) brother/sister • **¡compañeros!** comrades!

compañía SF **1** (*gen*) company • **en ~ de** with, accompanied by, in the company of • **pasé la tarde en ~ de unos amigos** I spent the afternoon with *o* (*frm*) in the company of some friends • **hacer ~ a algn** to keep sb company • **andar en malas ~s** • **frecuentar malas ~s** to keep bad company
2 (*Com, Teat, Rel*) company • **Pérez y Compañía** Pérez and Company ▸ **compañía afiliada** associated company ▸ **compañía concesionadora** franchiser ▸ **compañía de bandera** national company ▸ **Compañía de Jesús** Society of Jesus ▸ **compañía de seguros** insurance company ▸ **compañía inversionista** investment trust ▸ **compañía naviera** shipping company ▸ **compañía (no) cotizable** (un)listed company ▸ **compañía pública** public company ▸ **compañía tenedora** holding company
3 (*Mil*) company

comparabilidad SF comparability

comparable ADJ comparable (**a** to, **con** with)

comparación SF **1** (= *cotejo*) comparison • **en ~ con** in comparison with, beside • **es sin ~** it is beyond compare
2 (*Literat*) simile

comparado ADJ **1** [*estudio, proyecto*] comparative
2 • **~ con** compared with *o* to

comparar ▹ CONJUG 1a VT to compare (**a** to, **con** with, to) • **~ dos archivos** (*Inform*) to compare two files • **he estado comparando los precios** I've been comparing prices • **por favor, no compares, esta casa es mucho mejor que la que tenías antes** there's no comparison, this house is much better than the one you had before
VPR **compararse** • **~se a** *o* **con** to compare with *o* to • **él no puede ~se a ti** *o* **contigo** he doesn't stand *o* bear comparison with you, he comes nowhere near you*

comparativo ADJ, SM comparative

comparecencia SF (*Jur*) appearance (in court) • **su no ~** his non-appearance • **orden de ~** summons, subpoena (*EEUU*)

comparecer ▹ CONJUG 2d VI (*Jur*) to appear (in court) • **~ ante un juez** to appear before a judge

comparecimiento SM = **comparecencia**

comparencia SF (*Cono Sur*) = **comparecencia**

comparendo SM (*Jur*) (= *orden*) summons; (= *documento*) subpoena

comparsa SF **1** [*de carnaval*] group
2 (*Teat*) • **la ~** the extras (*pl*)
3 (= *persona subordinada*) puppet
SMF **1** (*Teat*) extra
2 (*Caribe*) (= *bailadores*) dance troupe

comparsería SF extras, supernumeraries

compartible ADJ **1** (= *que se puede compartir*) which can be shared
2 (= *aceptable*) [*opinión*] acceptable, readily shared

compartido ADJ [*habitación*] shared

compartimentación SF compartmentalization

compartimentado ADJ compartmentalized

compartimentar ▸ CONJUG 1a (VT) to compartmentalize
compartimento (SM), **compartimiento** (SM) **1** (= *acción*) division, sharing; (= *distribución*) distribution
2 (*Transportes*) compartment
▸ **compartimento de equipajes** luggage compartment, baggage compartment (*esp EEUU*) ▸ **compartimento estanco** watertight compartment
3 (*Aer*) ▸ **compartimento de bombas** bomb bay ▸ **compartimento de carga** hold
compartir ▸ CONJUG 3a (VT) **1** [+ *casa, cuarto, comida, ropa*] to share • ~ **algo con algn** to share sth with sb • **comparto habitación con otro estudiante** I share a room with another student
2 [+ *ganancias*] to share (out), divide (up); [+ *gastos*] to share • **compartimos las ganancias a medias** we shared (out) *o* divided (up) the profits between us • **comparten los gastos del viaje** they are sharing the costs of the trip
3 [+ *opinión*] to share; [+ *objetivos*] to agree with; [+ *sentimientos*] to share • **no comparto ese criterio** I do not share that view
compás (SM) **1** (*Mús*) time; (= *ritmo*) beat, rhythm; (= *división*) bar, measure (*EEUU*) • **a** ~ in time • **al** ~ **de la música** in time to the music • **fuera de** ~ off beat, not in time • **martillar a** ~ to hammer rhythmically • **llevar el** ~ to keep time • **perder el** ~ to lose the beat • **entraron a los compases de un vals** they came in to the strains of a waltz • **mantenemos el** ~ **de espera** we are still waiting ▸ **compás de 2 por 4** 2/4 time ▸ **compás de vals** waltz time
2 (*Mat*) (*tb* **compás de puntas**) compass, pair of compasses
3 (*Náut*) compass
compasado (ADJ) measured, moderate
compasar ▸ CONJUG 1a (VT) **1** (*Mat*) to measure (with a compass)
2 [+ *gastos, tiempo*] to adjust
3 (*Mús*) to divide into bars
compasión (SF) (= *pena*) compassion, sympathy; (= *piedad*) pity • **no siento** ~ **por ella** I have no sympathy for her • **¡por** ~**!** for pity's sake! • **tener** ~ **de** to take pity on, feel sorry for • **mover a algn a** ~ to move sb to pity • **tener pronta** ~ be easily moved to pity
compasivamente (ADV) (*gen*) compassionately, pityingly; (= *comprensivamente*) sympathetically
compasividad (SF) = **compasión**
compasivo (ADJ) compassionate
compatibilidad (SF) compatibility
compatibilización (SF) harmonization
compatibilizar ▸ CONJUG 1f (VT) to harmonize, reconcile, bring into line, make compatible (**con** with)
compatible (ADJ) (*Inform*) compatible (**con** with)
compatriota (SMF) compatriot, fellow countryman/countrywoman
compeler ▸ CONJUG 2a (VT) to compel • ~ **a algn a** (+ *infin*) to compel sb to (+ *infin*)
compendiar ▸ CONJUG 1b (VT) to abridge, condense, summarize
compendio (SM) (= *tratado breve*) compendium; (*Univ, Téc*) summary • **en** ~ briefly, in short
compendiosamente (ADV) briefly, succinctly
compendioso (ADJ) [*libro, discurso*] (= *abreviado*) condensed, abridged; (= *sucinto*) brief, succinct
compenetración (SF) mutual understanding, fellow feeling, natural sympathy
compenetrarse ▸ CONJUG 1a (VPR) **1** (= *entenderse*) to understand one another • ~ **con algo/algn** to identify with sth/sb • **estamos muy compenetrados** we understand each other very well
2 (*Quím*) to interpenetrate, fuse
compensación (SF) **1** (= *pago*) compensation • **como** *o* **en** ~ as compensation • **le ofreció 100.000 dólares como** ~ he offered him 100,000 dollars compensation
▸ **compensación económica** financial compensation ▸ **compensación por daños y perjuicios** damages (*pl*) ▸ **compensación por despido** severance pay, redundancy payment
2 (= *recompensa*) • **no espero ninguna** ~ **por mis desvelos** I don't expect any reward for my efforts • **este trabajo me ofrece muy pocas compensaciones** this job is very unrewarding • **en** ~**: tendrán que devolver sus tierras, pero en** ~**, …** they will have to give up their land, but in return *o* in exchange, … • **en** ~ **por lo mal que se portó ayer** to make up for his (bad) behaviour yesterday
3 (= *equilibrio*) • **medidas de** ~ compensatory measures • **un mecanismo de** ~ **de precios** a compensatory price mechanism
4 (*Jur*) [*de deudas*] compensation, redress
5 (*Econ*) clearing • **cámara de** ~ clearing house
compensador (ADJ) compensating, compensatory
compensar ▸ CONJUG 1a (VT) **1** (= *indemnizar*) to compensate (**por** for) • ~ **económicamente a algn** to compensate sb financially • **lo** ~**on con 100 dólares por los cristales rotos** he received 100 dollars compensation for the broken windows • **¿cómo puedo** ~**te por lo que has hecho por mí?** how can I repay you for what you have done for me?
2 (= *equilibrar*) [+ *pérdida, falta*] to compensate for, make up for; [+ *efecto, bajada*] to compensate for, offset; [+ *gastos*] to repay, reimburse; [+ *error*] to make amends for • **le ponen luz artificial para** ~ **la falta de sol** they put in artificial lighting to compensate for *o* make up for the lack of sunlight • **espero que el resultado le compense la molestia** I hope the result makes it worth your trouble
3 (*Mec*) [+ *ruedas*] to balance
4 (*Econ*) [+ *cheque*] to clear
(VI) • **no compensa** it's not worth it, it's not worthwhile • **te compensa hacerlo** it's worth you doing it, it's worth your while doing it *o* to do it • **compensa gastarse más dinero ahora y ahorrarlo después** it pays to spend more now and save money later, it's worth spending more now to save money later on • **el esfuerzo no compensa** it's not worth the effort • **no me compensa el tiempo que he invertido** it isn't worth the time I've spent on it
compensatoriamente (ADV) by way of compensation
compensatorio (ADJ) [*indemnización*] compensatory; [*educación*] remedial
competencia (SF) **1** (= *rivalidad*) competition • **nos enfrentamos a la** ~ **de los productos norteamericanos** we are faced by competition from American products • **existe una fuerte** ~ **entre las dos empresas por el control del mercado externo** the two companies are vying for control of the foreign market, there is fierce competition between the two companies for control of the foreign market • ~ **desleal** unfair competition • ~ **despiadada** ruthless competition • **en** ~ **con algn/algo** in competition with sb/sth • **en** ~ **directa con el sector privado** in direct competition with the private sector • **actúan en** ~ **con el estado** they are in competition with the state • **hacer la** ~ **a algn/algo** to compete with sb/sth • **dos compañías nos hacen la** ~ we have two companies to compete with • **¿me quieres hacer la** ~**?** are you trying to compete with me? • **libre** ~ free competition
2 (= *rival*) competition • **han conseguido hundir a la** ~ they have managed to beat the competition • **ahora trabaja para la** ~ she's working for the competition now • **la** ~ **tiene mejores ofertas** our competitors have better offers, the competition has better offers
3 (= *capacidad*) competence, ability • **no dudo de tu** ~ **como abogado** I am not questioning your competence *o* ability as a lawyer
▸ **competencia lingüística** linguistic competence, linguistic ability
4 (= *responsabilidad*) • **ese tema no es de mi** ~ that matter is outside my jurisdiction *o* my competence • **esta decisión es** ~ **exclusiva del gobierno** this decision is the exclusive jurisdiction of the government, only the government is competent to deal with this decision • **las** ~**s legales del Consejo de Administración** the jurisdiction *o* areas of competence of the Administrative Council
5 competencias (*Pol*) powers • ~**s transferidas a las comunidades autónomas** powers devolved *o* transferred to the autonomous regions
6 (*LAm*) (*Dep*) competition
competente (ADJ) **1** (= *responsable*) competent (*frm*) • **la autoridad** ~ the proper *o* (*frm*) competent authority • **esto se elevará al ministerio** ~ this will be sent to the appropriate ministry *o* to the ministry concerned • **de fuente** ~ from a reliable source • **ser** ~ **para hacer algo** to be competent to do sth (*frm*)
2 (= *capaz*) competent • **necesitamos gente** ~ we need competent people • **es muy** ~ **en su especialidad** he is very competent in his field
competentemente (ADV) competently
competer ▸ CONJUG 2a (VI) • ~ **a algn** to be the responsibility of sb • **un tema que compete al Ministerio del Exterior** a matter that comes under the jurisdiction of *o* that is the responsibility of the Foreign Office • **es al gobierno a quien compete mantener la seguridad** it falls to the government to maintain law and order, it is the government that is responsible for maintaining law and order • **este tema compete exclusivamente al director** this subject is the exclusive concern *o* responsibility of the director
competición (SF) **1** (= *enfrentamiento*) competition • **deporte de** ~ competitive sport
2 (= *concurso*) competition, contest • **mañana comenzará la** ~ **de tiro con arco** the archery competition starts tomorrow • **acaba de comenzar la** ~ **electoral** the electoral race has begun
competido (ADJ) [*carrera*] hard-fought, close-run
competidor(a) (ADJ) (*gen*) competing, rival
(SM/F) **1** (*gen*) competitor; (*Com*) rival (**a** for)
2 (*en concurso*) contestant
competir ▸ CONJUG 3k (VI) **1** (= *enfrentarse*) to compete • ~ **con** *o* **contra algo/algn** to compete with *o* against sth/sb • **son incapaces de** ~ **con** *o* **contra gente más joven** they are incapable of competing with *o* against younger people • ~ **en algo** to compete in sth • **los equipos que** ~**án en este**

campeonato the teams competing in this championship • **~ en el mercado** (*Com*) to compete in the market • **~ por algo** to compete for sth • **cuatro películas compiten por el Oscar** four films are competing for the Oscar
2 (= *compararse*) • **~ con algo**: • **no hay nada que pueda ~ con un buen vino** you can't beat a good wine, nothing can compare with a good wine • **es el único modelo que compite en precio con sus rivales** it's the only model which can compete *o* compare with its rivals in terms of price • **en cuanto a resistencia Miguel no puede ~ con Andrés** when it comes to stamina Miguel is no match for Andrés

competitivamente ADV competitively

competitividad SF competitiveness

competitivo ADJ competitive

compilación SF compilation • **tiempo de ~** (*Inform*) compile time

compilador(a) SM/F (= *persona*) compiler
SM (*Inform*) compiler ▸ **compilador incremental** incremental compiler

compilar ▹ CONJUG 1a VT to compile

compincharse ▹ CONJUG 1a VPR to band together, team up • **estar compinchados*** to be in cahoots* (**con** with)

compinche* SMF **1** (= *amigo*) pal*, mate*, buddy (*EEUU**)
2 (= *cómplice*) partner in crime, accomplice

compita* SMF (*Nic*) (*Hist*) comrade*, Nicaraguan freedom fighter

complacencia SF **1** (= *placer*) pleasure, satisfaction
2 (= *agrado*) willingness • **lo hizo con ~** he did it gladly
3 (= *indulgencia*) indulgence • **tiene excesivas ~s con los empleados** he is too indulgent towards his employees
4 (*LAm*) (= *autosatisfacción*) complacency

complacer ▹ CONJUG 2w VT **1** (*gen*) to please; [+ *cliente*] to help, oblige; [+ *jefe*] to humour • **nos complace anunciarles …** we are pleased to announce … • **¿en qué puedo ~le?** (*Com*) (*frm*) can I help you?, what can I do for you?
2 [+ *deseo*] to indulge, gratify
VPR **complacerse** • **~se en hacer algo** to take pleasure in doing sth • **el Banco se complace en comunicar a su clientela que …** the bank is pleased to inform its customers that …

complacido ADJ pleased, satisfied • **me miró ~** he gave me a pleased look • **quedamos ~s de la visita** we were pleased with our visit

complaciente ADJ **1** (= *indulgente*) indulgent; [*marido*] complaisant
2 (= *solícito*) obliging, helpful

complejidad SF complexity

complejo ADJ (*gen*) complex
SM **1** (*Psic*) complex ▸ **complejo de culpa**, **complejo de culpabilidad** guilt complex ▸ **complejo de Edipo** Oedipus complex ▸ **complejo de Electra** Electra complex ▸ **complejo de inferioridad** inferiority complex ▸ **complejo de superioridad** superiority complex ▸ **complejo persecutorio** persecution complex
2 (= *instalaciones*) complex ▸ **complejo deportivo** sports complex, sports centre *o* (*EEUU*) center ▸ **complejo industrial** industrial complex ▸ **complejo petroquímico** petrochemical complex ▸ **complejo recreativo** leisure complex, leisure centre *o* (*EEUU*) center ▸ **complejo residencial** housing development ▸ **complejo turístico** tourist development
3 (*Quím*) complex ▸ **complejo vitamínico** vitamin complex

complementación SF complementation • **un ejemplo ideal de la ~ entre la iniciativa privada y la estatal** a perfect example of how public and private initiatives complement one another

complementar ▹ CONJUG 1a VT to complement
VPR **complementarse** to complement each other

complementariamente ADV in addition (a to), additionally

complementariedad SF complementarity

complementario ADJ (*gen*) complementary • **visita complementaria** follow-up visit
SM (*en lotería*) bonus number

complemento SM **1** (*Mat*) complement
2 (*Ling*) complement, object ▸ **complemento directo** direct object ▸ **complemento circunstancial** adverbial ▸ **complemento indirecto** indirect object ▸ **complemento preposicional** prepositional complement
3 (= *parte*) • **el vino es un ~ de la buena comida** wine is the ideal complement to good food • **sería el ~ de su felicidad** it would complete her happiness
4 • **oficial de ~** (*Mil*) reserve officer
5 (= *pago*) ▸ **complemento de destino** extra allowance (attached to a post) ▸ **complemento de productividad** performance-related bonus ▸ **complemento de sueldo** bonus, extra pay ▸ **complemento por peligrosidad** danger money ▸ **complemento salarial** bonus, extra pay
6 (*Cine*) short, supporting feature
SMPL **complementos** (*Aut*) [*de moda*] accessories

completa SF (*Caribe*) full (cheap) meal

completamente ADV completely

completar ▹ CONJUG 1a VT **1** (= *terminar*) to complete, finish; (= *perfeccionar*) to finish off, round off; (*Méx*) to match • **me falta un sello para ~ la serie** I need one stamp to complete the series • **completó su formación en varias universidades norteamericanas** she finished off her education at a number of American universities
2 [+ *pérdida*] to make good

completas SFPL compline

completez SF completeness

completo ADJ **1** (= *entero*) [*dieta*] balanced; [*colección*] complete; [*texto, informe*] full, complete; [*felicidad*] complete, total; [*panorama*] full • **tomamos una comida ligera pero completa** we had a light but full meal • **un coche con equipamiento ~** a car with a full range of fittings • **un laboratorio de idiomas con equipamiento ~** a fully-equipped language lab • **las poesías completas de San Juan de la Cruz** the complete poems of San Juan de la Cruz • **trabajar a tiempo ~** to work full time; ▹ **jornada, obra, pensión**
2 (= *lleno*) full; [*hotel*] full, fully booked • **"completo"** (*en pensión, hostal*) "no vacancies"; (*en taquilla*) "sold out" • **al ~: el tren está al ~** the train is full • **el hotel estaba al ~** the hotel was fully booked *o* full • **asistió el ayuntamiento al ~** the entire council was present
3 (= *total*) [*éxito, fracaso*] complete, total • **la película fue un ~ fracaso** the film was a complete *o* total flop • **por ~** [*desaparecer, desconocer*] completely • **ha quedado destruido por ~** it was completely destroyed • **se me olvidó por ~** I completely forgot • **la niebla cubrió por ~ el paisaje** the fog completely covered the countryside • **está dedicado por ~ a su trabajo** he is totally dedicated to his work • **su partido apoyaba por ~ la iniciativa** his party fully supported the initiative, his party gave its full support to the initiative • **el problema quedará resuelto por ~** the problem will be solved once and for all
4 (= *terminado*) • **la novela está ya casi completa** the novel is almost finished
5 (= *bien hecho*) • **ha entregado un trabajo muy ~** he's handed in a very thorough piece of work • **este libro es pequeño, pero bastante ~** this book is small, but quite comprehensive
6 (= *polifacético*) [*actor, deportista*] all-round • **un atleta muy ~** an all-round athlete
SM (*Chile*) hot dog (*with salad*)

complexión SF **1** (*Anat*) build, constitution • **un hombre de ~ fuerte** a well-built man, a man with a strong constitution
2 (*LAm*) (= *tez*) complexion

complexionado ADJ • **bien ~** strong, tough, robust • **mal ~** weak, frail

complexional ADJ constitutional

complicación SF **1** (= *problema*) complication • **han surgido complicaciones** complications have arisen • **una persona sin complicaciones** an uncomplicated person
2 (= *cualidad*) complexity • **no captó la ~ del asunto** he did not grasp the complexity of the matter

complicado ADJ (= *complejo*) complicated, complex; (*Med*) [*fractura*] compound; [*estilo*] elaborate; [*persona*] complex; [*método*] complicated, involved; (*Jur*) involved, implicated

complicar ▹ CONJUG 1g VT **1** (*gen*) to complicate
2 (*Jur*) to involve, implicate (**en** in)
VPR **complicarse 1** (*gen*) to get complicated • **~se la vida** to make life difficult for o.s.
2 • **~se en algo** to get involved *o* mixed up in sth

cómplice SMF accomplice

complicidad SF complicity, involvement (**en** in)

compló SM, **complot** SM (PL: **complots**) plot, conspiracy, intrigue

complotado/a SM/F plotter, conspirator

complotar ▹ CONJUG 1a VI to plot, conspire

complutense ADJ of Alcalá de Henares

componedor(a) SM/F • **~ de huesos** bonesetter

componenda SF **1** (= *arreglo temporal*) temporary arrangement
2 (= *acuerdo sucio*) shady deal

componente ADJ (*gen*) component, constituent
SM **1** (= *miembro*) member
2 (= *parte*) (*Quím*) component; (*Mec*) part, component; (*Culin*) ingredient ▸ **componentes lógicos** (*Inform*) software
3 (*Meteo*) • **un viento de ~ norte** a northerly wind

componer ▹ CONJUG 2q (PP: **compuesto**) VT
1 (= *constituir*) [+ *comité, jurado, organización*] to make up • **los doce miembros que componen la junta** the twelve members who make up the board • **componen el jurado once personas** the jury is made up of eleven people • **los cuadros que componen esta exposición** the pictures that make up this exhibition, the pictures in this exhibition
2 (= *escribir*) [+ *poesía, sinfonía, canción*] to compose, write; [+ *poema, tratado, redacción*] to write • **compuso la música de varios ballets** he composed *o* wrote the music for several ballets

3 (= *arreglar*) [+ *objeto roto*] to mend, repair, fix; (*Med*) [+ *hueso*] to set • **a este no hay quien le componga*** he's a hopeless case
4 (= *curar*) [+ *estómago*] to settle; [+ *espíritu*] to soothe; [+ *abuso*] to set to rights, correct
5 (*Tip*) [+ *texto*] to typeset, set, compose
6 (*Culin*) to prepare
VPR **componerse 1** • **~se de** to consist of • **se compone de seis partes** it consists of six parts • **la cena se compone de dos platos y postre** dinner consists of two courses and dessert
2 (= *arreglarse*) to dress up • **le gusta ~se para salir** she likes to dress up to go out
3 [*tiempo atmosférico*] to improve, clear up
4 (*Méx*) [*persona*] to recover, get better
5 • **componérselas*** to manage • **me las compuse cómo pude y salí adelante** I managed as best I could and carried on • **siempre se las compone para salirse con la suya** he always manages to get his own way • MODISMO: • **¡allá** *o* **que se las componga (como pueda)!*** that's his problem, that's his funeral*
componible ADJ **1** [*objeto roto*] repairable, worth mending
2 (= *que se puede conciliar*) reconcilable, capable of settlement
comportable ADJ bearable
comportamental ADJ behavioural, behavioral (EEUU)
comportamiento SM **1** behaviour, behavior (EEUU) • **un premio al buen ~** a prize for good behaviour ▸ **comportamiento antisocial** antisocial behaviour ▸ **comportamiento sexual** sexual behaviour, sexual behavior (EEUU) ▸ **comportamiento social** social behaviour, social behavior (EEUU)
2 [*de mercado, automóvil*] performance • **el ~ de la Bolsa** the performance of the stock market ▸ **comportamiento en carretera** road performance
comportar ▹ CONJUG 1a VT **1** (= *significar*) to involve • **no comporta obligación alguna** it carries no obligation, you are under no obligation
2 (= *aguantar*) to bear, endure, put up with
3 (*And, Cono Sur*) (= *causar*) to entail, bring with it
VPR **comportarse** to behave • **~se como es debido** to behave properly, conduct o.s. in a proper fashion (*frm*) • **~se mal** to misbehave, behave badly
comporte SM **1** = comportamiento
2 (= *porte*) bearing, carriage
composición SF **1** (*Mús, Quím, Arte*) composition
2 (*Educ*) essay
3 ▸ **composición de lugar** stocktaking, inventory • **hacerse una ~ de lugar** to take stock (of one's situation)
4 (*Tip*) typesetting ▸ **composición por ordenador** computer typesetting
5 [*de desacuerdo*] settlement; [*de personas*] reconciliation ▸ **composición procesal** (*Jur*) out-of-court settlement
6 (= *arreglo*) arrangement
compositor(a) SM/F **1** (*Mús*) composer
2 (*Tip*) compositor
3 (*Cono Sur*) (= *curandero*) quack doctor, bonesetter
compost ['kompos] SM compost
compostación SF, **compostaje** SM composting
compostelano/a ADJ of/from Santiago de Compostela
SM/F native/inhabitant of Santiago de Compostela • **los ~s** the people of Santiago de Compostela
compostura SF **1** (= *dignidad*) composure • **perder la ~** to lose one's composure
2 (= *arreglo*) mending, repair • **estar en ~** to be under repair
3 (= *constitución*) composition, make-up; (= *estructura*) structure
4† (= *condimento*) condiment, seasoning
5† (= *aseo*) neatness; (= *adorno*) adornment
6† (= *acuerdo*) arrangement, agreement, settlement
compota SF compote, preserve ▸ **compota de manzanas** stewed apples
compotera SF dessert dish
compra SF **1** (= *proceso*) purchase, purchasing, buying • **hacer la ~** to do the shopping • **tengo que ir a la ~** I've got to do the shopping, I've got to go shopping • **ir de ~s** to go shopping • **prueba de ~** proof of purchase • **ticket de ~** receipt ▸ **compra a crédito** buying on credit ▸ **compra a granel** (*Com*) bulk buying ▸ **compra al contado** cash purchase ▸ **compra a plazos** hire purchase, installment plan (EEUU) ▸ **compra por catálogo** mail order ▸ **compra proteccionista** (*Com*) support buying ▸ **compra y venta** buying and selling
2 (= *artículo*) purchase • **es una buena ~** it's a good buy
comprador(a) SM/F (*Com*) buyer, purchaser; (*en tienda*) shopper, customer ▸ **comprador(a) principal** head buyer
comprar ▹ CONJUG 1a VT **1** (= *adquirir*) [+ *casa, comida, regalo*] to buy, purchase (*frm*) • **¿te has comprado por fin la bici?** did you buy the bike in the end? • **~ algo a algn** (*para algn*) to buy sth for sb, buy sb sth; (*de algn*) to buy sth from sb • **le compré un vestido a mi hija** I bought a dress for my daughter, I bought my daughter a dress • **siempre le compro la carne a este carnicero** I always buy my meat from this butcher • **si decides vender el coche, yo te lo compro** if you decide to sell the car, I'll buy it from *o* off you • **~ algo al contado** to pay cash (for sth), pay sth in cash • **~ algo al detalle** to buy sth retail • **~ algo a plazos** to buy sth on hire purchase • **~ algo al por mayor** to buy sth wholesale • **~ algo al por menor** to buy sth retail • **~ deudas** to factor
2 (= *sobornar*) to bribe, buy off* • **intentaron ~ al juez** they tried to bribe *o* buy off* the judge • **el árbitro está comprado** they've bribed the referee
VI (= *hacer la compra*) to buy, shop • **nunca compro en grandes almacenes** I never buy *o* shop in department stores
compraventa SF **1** (*gen*) buying and selling, dealing • **negocio de ~** second-hand shop
2 (*Jur*) contract of sale
comprender ▹ CONJUG 2a VT **1** (= *entender*) to understand • **espero que comprendan nuestras razones** I hope that they understand our reasons • **compréndeme, no me quedaba más remedio** you have to understand, I had no choice • **te comprendo perfectamente** I understand perfectly • **no acabo de ~ qué es lo que pasa** I still don't understand what's going on • **no comprendo cómo ha podido pasar esto** I don't see *o* understand how this could have happened • **hacer ~ algo a algn**: • **esto bastó para hacernos ~ su posición** this was all we needed to understand his position • **hacerse ~** to make o.s. understood
2 (= *darse cuenta*) to realize • **al final comprendió que yo no iba a ayudarle** he finally realized I wasn't going to help him • **comprendemos perfectamente que haya gente a quien le molesta el tabaco** we fully understand *o* appreciate that some people are bothered by smoking
3 (= *incluir*) to comprise (*frm*) • **la colección comprende cien discos y cuarenta libros** the collection consists of *o* (*frm*) comprises a hundred records and forty books • **el primer tomo comprende las letras de la A a la G** the first volume covers *o* (*frm*) comprises letters A to G • **está todo comprendido en el precio** the price is all-inclusive • **el período comprendido entre 1936 y 1939** the period from 1936 to 1939 *o* between 1936 and 1939; ▹ **edad**
VI **1** (= *entender*) to understand • **¿comprendes?** do you understand? • **no hay forma de hacerle ~** there is no way to make him understand
2 (= *darse cuenta*) • **¡ya comprendo!** now I see!, I get it (now)!* • **como tú ~ás, no soy yo quién para juzgarlo** as you will appreciate *o* understand, I'm not the best person to judge him
comprensible ADJ **1** (= *justificable*) understandable • **es ~ que haya actuado así** it's understandable that he behaved in that way • **no es ~ que no haya dicho nada** it's hard to understand why he hasn't said anything
2 (= *inteligible*) • **eso no le resulta ~ a nadie** nobody can understand that • **un arte ~** an accessible art
comprensiblemente ADV understandably
comprensión SF **1** (= *entendimiento*) understanding • **los dibujos nos ayudan a la ~ del texto** the drawings help us to understand the text *o* help our understanding of the text • **un ejercicio de ~ auditiva** a listening comprehension test
2 (= *actitud comprensiva*) understanding • **ha mostrado una gran ~ con nuestros problemas** he has shown great understanding of our problems
comprensivo ADJ understanding
compresa SF **1** (*para mujer*) sanitary towel, sanitary napkin (EEUU)
2 (*Med*) compress
compresibilidad SF compressibility
compresible ADJ compressible
compresión SF compression
compresor SM compressor
comprimible ADJ compressible
comprimido ADJ (*gen*) compressed
SM (*Med*) pill, tablet ▸ **comprimido para dormir** sleeping pill
comprimir ▹ CONJUG 3a VT **1** (*Téc*) to compress (**en** into); (= *prensar*) to press (down), squeeze down; (*Inform*) to zip; (= *condensar*) to condense
2 (= *controlar*) to control; [+ *lágrimas*] to hold back
VPR **comprimirse** (*gen*) to get compressed; [*personas*] to squeeze *o* squash together
comprobable ADJ verifiable, capable of being checked • **un alegato fácilmente ~** an allegation which is easy to prove
comprobación SF (= *proceso*) checking, verification; (= *datos*) proof • **de difícil ~** hard to prove • **en ~ de ello** as proof of what I say ▸ **comprobación general de cuentas** (*Com*) general audit
comprobador SM tester ▸ **comprobador de lámparas** valve tester
comprobante ADJ • **documento ~** supporting document
SM (= *documento*) proof, supporting document; (*Com*) receipt, voucher
comprobar ▹ CONJUG 1l VT **1** (= *examinar*) [+ *billete, documento, frenos*] to check • **compruebe el aceite antes de salir de viaje**

check your oil before setting out • **compruebe el cambio antes de salir de la tienda** check your change before leaving the shop • **comprobó la hora y decidió marcharse** he checked the time and decided to leave • **tendré que ~ si se han cumplido los objetivos** I shall have to see *o* check whether the objectives have been met • **necesito algún documento para ~ su identidad** I need some document that proves your identity, I need some proof of identity • **compruebe nuestros productos usted mismo** try our products for yourself

2 (= *confirmar*) [+ *teoría, existencia*] to prove; [+ *eficacia, veracidad*] to verify, confirm • **pudimos ~ que era verdad** we were able to verify *o* confirm *o* establish that it was true • **comprobó sus ideas experimentalmente** he proved his arguments through experiments

3 (*frm*) (= *darse cuenta*) to realize • **~on que el candidato era demasiado joven** they realized that the candidate was too young

comprometedor ADJ compromising

comprometer ▹ CONJUG 2a VT **1** (= *poner en evidencia*) to compromise • **aquellas cartas lo comprometían** those letters compromised him

2 (= *implicar*) • **~ a algn en algo** (*futuro*) to involve sb in sth; (*pasado*) to implicate sb in sth

3 (= *obligar*) • **~ a algn a algo** to commit sb to sth • **esta firma no le compromete a nada** this signature does not commit you to anything

4 (= *arriesgar*) [+ *conversaciones, éxito, reputación, paz*] to jeopardize • **han comprometido la neutralidad del país** they have jeopardized the neutrality of the country • **su rebelión comprometió la vida de los rehenes** his rebellion endangered *o* jeopardized the hostages' lives

5 (= *apalabrar*) [+ *habitación, entrada*] to reserve, book • **ya he comprometido la casa** I've already promised the house to someone

6 (= *invertir*) to invest, tie up • **ha comprometido todo su capital en esta empresa** he has invested all his capital in this company, all his capital is tied up in this company

7 (*frm*) (= *afectar*) • **la bala le comprometió el pulmón** the bullet damaged his lung • **la gangrena le ha comprometido la rodilla** the gangrene has spread to *o* affected his knee

VPR **comprometerse 1** (= *contraer un compromiso*) to commit o.s. • **no te comprometas demasiado pronto** don't commit yourself too soon • **~se a algo** to commit o.s. to sth • **la compañía se compromete a una subida de 250 euros mensuales** the company is committed to a pay rise of 250 euros a month • **se compromete con él a cosas que luego no cumple** he makes him promises he then doesn't keep • **~se en algo** to commit o.s. to sth • **~se a hacer algo** to commit o.s. to doing sth, undertake to do sth • **se han comprometido a reducir el paro** they have committed themselves to reducing unemployment, they have undertaken to reduce unemployment • **me comprometí a ayudarte y lo haré** I promised to help you and I will, I said I'd help you and I will • **me comprometo a terminar el trabajo para el viernes** I promise to finish the work by Friday

2 (= *implicarse socialmente*) to commit o.s., make a commitment • **~se políticamente (con algo)** commit o.s. politically (to sth), to make a political commitment (to sth)

3 (= *citarse*) • **ya me he comprometido para el sábado** I've arranged to do something else on Saturday • **~se con algn** to arrange to see sb

4 [*novios*] to get engaged • **se han comprometido y se casarán pronto** they have got engaged and will be getting married soon • **~se con algn** to get engaged to sb

comprometido ADJ **1** (= *difícil*) awkward, embarrassing • **nos vimos en una situación muy comprometida** we found ourselves in a very awkward *o* embarrassing situation

2 (*socialmente*) [*escritor, artista*] politically committed, engagé; [*arte*] politically committed • **un artista no ~** art which is not politically committed, art without any political commitment • **estar ~ con algo** to be committed to sth • **está ~ con la causa** he's committed to the cause

3 (*por cita, trabajo*) • **ya están ~s para jugar el sábado** they've already arranged to play on Saturday, they've booked to play on Saturday • **ya estaba ~ con otro proyecto** he was already committed to another project • **estar ~ a hacer algo** to be committed to doing sth

4 (*antes del matrimonio*) engaged • **estar ~ con algn** to be engaged to sb

compromisario/a SM/F convention delegate

compromiso SM **1** (= *obligación*) **a** (*por acuerdo, ideología*) commitment • **el gobierno reiteró su ~ con el plan de paz** the government reiterated its commitment to the peace plan • **nuestro ~ con la cultura** our commitment to cultural projects • **esperamos que cumplan con su ~ de bajar los impuestos** we hope they will honour their commitment to lowering taxes • **sin ~** without obligation • **pida presupuesto sin ~** ask for an estimate without obligation

b (*por convenciones sociales*) • **aunque no tenemos ~ con ellos, los vamos a invitar** we're going to invite them even though we're under no obligation to • **si le regalas ahora algo, la pondrás en el ~ de invitarte a cenar** if you give her a present now, you'll make her feel obliged to take you out to dinner • **por ~** out of a sense of duty • **fui a la boda por ~** I felt obliged to go to the wedding, I went to the wedding out of a sense of duty • **por ~ no lo hagas** don't feel obliged to do it • **verse en el ~** to feel obliged • **me vi en el ~ de tener que invitarlos a cenar** I felt obliged to invite them to dinner ▸ **compromiso político** political commitment ▸ **compromiso público** public commitment ▸ **compromiso social** social commitment

2 (= *aprieto*) • **poner a algn en un ~** to put sb in an awkward position

3 (= *acuerdo*) agreement; (*con concesiones mutuas*) compromise • **aceptar un ~** to accept a compromise • **una fórmula de ~** a compromise, a compromise formula • **una solución de ~** a compromise solution ▸ **compromiso histórico** historic agreement ▸ **compromiso verbal** unwritten agreement

4 (= *cita*) **a** (*con otras personas*) engagement • **ahora, si me disculpan, tengo que atender otros ~s** now, if you will excuse me, I have other engagements • **mañana no puede ser, tengo un ~** tomorrow is impossible, I'm otherwise engaged • **¿tienes algún ~ para esta noche?** do you have anything arranged for tonight?

b (*Dep*) match • **en su próximo ~ frente al Zaragoza** in their next match against Zaragoza

5 [*de matrimonio*] engagement • **han roto su ~** they have broken off their engagement • **soltero y sin ~** single and unattached ▸ **compromiso matrimonial** engagement, engagement to marry

6 (*Med*) • **una afección cardíaca con ~ hepático** a heart condition affecting the liver

compuerta SF **1** (*en canal*) sluice, floodgate; (*en puerta*) hatch

2 (*Inform*) gate

compuesto VB (*pp de* **componer**) • **estar ~ de** to be composed of, consist of • **un caldo ~ de apio y cebolla** a soup (made) of celery and onion • **un grupo ~ por 15 personas** a group of 15 people

ADJ **1** (*Mat, Econ, Ling, Quím*) compound; (*Bot*) composite

2 (= *elegante*) dressed up, smart • MODISMO: • **compuesta y sin novio** all dressed up and nowhere to go

3 (= *tranquilo*) composed

SM **1** (*Quím*) compound ▸ **compuesto químico** chemical compound

2 (*Ling*) compound, compound word

3 (*Med, Odontología*) compound

compulsa SF **1** (= *cotejo*) checking, comparison

2 (*Jur, Admin*) certified true copy, attested copy

compulsar ▹ CONJUG 1a VT **1** (= *comparar*) to collate, compare

2 (*Jur, Admin*) to make an attested copy of

compulsión SF compulsion

compulsivamente ADV compulsively

compulsivo ADJ **1** [*deseo, hambre*] compulsive

2 (= *obligatorio*) compulsory

compulsorio ADJ (*LAm*) compulsory

compunción SF (*liter*) (= *arrepentimiento*) compunction, remorse; (= *tristeza*) sorrow

compungido ADJ (= *arrepentido*) remorseful, contrite; (= *triste*) sad, sorrowful

compungir ▹ CONJUG 3c VT (= *arrepentir*) to make remorseful, arouse feelings of remorse in

VPR **compungirse** (= *arrepentirse*) to feel remorseful (**por** about, because of), feel sorry (**por** for); (= *entristecerse*) to feel sad, be sorrowful

compurgar ▹ CONJUG 1h VT (*And, Cono Sur, Méx*) [+ *ofensa*] to purge; (*Méx*) (*Jur*) [+ *pena*] to serve out

computación SF (*esp LAm*) **1** (= *cálculo*) calculation

2 (*esp LAm*) (*Inform*) computing • **cursos de ~** computer courses

computacional ADJ (*esp LAm*) computational, computer (*antes de s*)

computador SM (*esp LAm*), **computadora** SF (*esp LAm*) computer ▸ **computador personal, computadora personal** personal computer ▸ **computador portátil, computadora portátil** (*gen*) portable computer; (*pequeño*) laptop computer ▸ **computador central, computadora central** mainframe computer ▸ **computador de mesa, computadora de mesa, computador de sobremesa, computadora de sobremesa** desktop computer ▸ **computador digital, computadora digital** digital computer

computadorización SF computerization

computadorizado ADJ computerized

computadorizar ▹ CONJUG 1f VT to computerize

computar ▹ CONJUG 1a VT to calculate, compute (**en** at)

computarización SF computerization

computarizado ADJ computerized

computarizar ▹ CONJUG 1f (VT) to computerize
computerización (SF) computerization
computerizado (ADJ) computerized
computerizar ▹ CONJUG 1f (VT) to computerize
computista (SMF) computer user
cómputo (SM) (= *cálculo*) calculation, computation; (*Méx*) (= *suma*) total • **según nuestros ~s** according to our calculations
COMSAT (SM ABR) (= **satélite de comunicaciones**) Comsat, COMSAT
comulgante (SMF) communicant
comulgar ▹ CONJUG 1h (VT) (*Rel*) to administer communion to
(VI) **1** (*Rel*) to take communion, receive communion
2 • **~ con** (*gen*) to like, accept, agree with; [+ *ideas*] to share; [+ *personas*] to sympathize with • **hay varias cosas con las que ella no comulga** there are several things that she doesn't agree with; ▹ **rueda**
comulgatorio (SM) communion rail, altar rail
común (ADJ) **1** (= *compartido*) [*afición, intereses*] common; [*amigo*] mutual • **tienen una serie de características comunes** they share a series of features, they have a series of common features *o* features in common • **a través de un amigo ~** through a mutual friend • **~ a algn/algo** common to sb/sth • **una situación ~ a todos los países europeos** a situation common to all European countries • **lo ~ a todas las democracias** what all democracies share in common, a feature common to all democracies
2 (= *colectivo*) [*causa, frente, espacio*] common; [*gastos*] communal • **tener algo en ~** to have sth in common • **su pasión por el fútbol es lo único que tienen en ~** their passion for football is all they have in common • **no tenemos nada en ~** we have nothing in common • **la pareja tuvo dos hijos en ~** the couple had two children together • **hacer algo en ~** to do sth together • **poner en ~** [+ *iniciativas, problemas*] to share; ▹ **acuerdo, bien, denominador, fosa, lugar, mercado, sentido**
3 (= *frecuente*) [*enfermedad, opinión*] common, widespread; [*costumbre*] widespread; [*cualidad*] common, ordinary • **el consumo de alcohol es una práctica ~** alcohol consumption is very common *o* widespread • **el concierto fue más largo de lo ~** the concert was longer than usual • **~ y corriente** perfectly ordinary • **fuera de lo ~** exceptional, extraordinary • **tiene una voz única, algo fuera de lo ~** she has a unique voice, quite exceptional *o* extraordinary • **por lo ~** as a rule • **~ y silvestre** (*LAm*) perfectly ordinary; ▹ **delincuente, nombre**
4 (*Esp*) (*Educ*) [*asignatura*] core
(SM) **1** • **el ~ de los mortales** ordinary mortals, any ordinary person • **el ~ de las gentes** the common man • **bienes del ~** public property
2* (= *retrete*) toilet, bathroom
3 (*Pol*) (*en el Reino Unido*) • **los Comunes** the Commons • **la Cámara de los Comunes** the House of Commons
comuna (SF) **1** (= *comunidad*) commune
2 (*LAm*) (= *municipio*) municipality, county (*EEUU*)
comunacho/a (SM/F) (*Cono Sur*) (*pey*) commie*
comunal (ADJ) communal, community (*antes de s*)
comunalmente (ADV) communally, as a community
comunicable (ADJ) **1** [*opinión, conocimiento*] • **una emoción difícilmente ~** an emotion difficult to communicate *o* convey
2 [*persona*] sociable
comunicación (SF) **1** (= *conexión*) communication • **¿tenemos otra vez ~ con el estadio?** has communication with the stadium been restored? • **no existe ~ entre los dos pueblos** there is no way of getting from one town to the other, there is no means of communication between the two towns • **entre nosotros falla la ~** we just don't communicate well, we have poor communication ▸ **comunicación de masas** mass communication ▸ **comunicación no verbal** non-verbal communication; ▹ **medio**
2 (= *contacto*) contact • **no hemos tenido más ~ con él** we have had no further contact with him • **establecer ~ con algn** to establish contact with sb • **estar en ~ con algn** to be in contact *o* touch with sb • **ponerse en ~ con algn** to get in contact *o* touch with sb, contact sb
3 (*por teléfono*) • **cortar la ~** to hang up • **dijo su nombre y se cortó la ~** he said his name and the line went dead *o* we were cut off
4 comunicaciones (= *conjunto de medios*) communications • **se han interrumpido las comunicaciones a causa del temporal** communications have been interrupted due to bad weather • **el satélite facilitará las comunicaciones** the satellite will facilitate communications
5 (= *escrito*) (= *mensaje*) message; (= *informe*) report; (*Pol*) communiqué
6 (*Univ*) (*en congreso*) paper • **presentar una ~ (sobre algo)** to give *o* present a paper (on sth)
7 (*Literat*) rhetorical question
comunicacional (ADJ) communication (*antes de s*)
comunicado (ADJ) **1** [*habitaciones*] connected • **las dos habitaciones están comunicadas** the two rooms are connected
2 [*pueblo, zona*] • **la urbanización está muy mal comunicada** the housing estate has poor transport connections *o* is not easily accessible • **el pueblo está bien ~ por tren** the town has good train connections, the town is easily accessible by train
(SM) (= *notificación*) statement, press release, communiqué (*frm*) • **han hecho público un ~ con la lista de los candidatos** they have issued a statement *o* press release *o* (*frm*) communiqué with the list of candidates ▸ **comunicado conjunto** joint statement, joint communiqué (*frm*) ▸ **comunicado de prensa** press release ▸ **comunicado oficial** official statement
comunicador(a) (SM/F) communicator • **un buen ~** a good communicator
comunicante (SMF) **1** (= *informador*) informant • **según ~ anónimo** according to an anonymous *o* unnamed source
2 (*en congreso*) speaker; ▹ **vaso**
comunicar ▹ CONJUG 1g (VT) **1** (= *decir*) **a** [+ *decisión, resultado*] to announce • **ha comunicado su decisión de abandonar la orquesta** he has announced his decision to leave the orchestra • **ha sido el encargado de ~ la noticia** he was given the task of announcing the news • **no pudo ~ la situación exacta del velero** he was unable to give *o* state the yacht's exact position • **según ~on fuentes del gobierno** according to government sources
b • **~ algo a algn** to inform sb of sth • **una vez comunicado el hallazgo a la policía** once the police had been informed of the discovery • **le ~on su despido por carta** they informed her of her dismissal by letter • **cuando le ~on la noticia** when they told her the news • **~ a algn que** to inform sb that • **comunicamos a los señores pasajeros que ...** we would like to inform passengers that ... • **nos comunican desde Lisboa que ...** we have heard from Lisbon that ...
2 (*al teléfono*) • **¿me comunica con la dirección, por favor?** could I speak to the manager, please?, could you put me through to the manager, please?
3 (= *transmitir*) [+ *sensación, entusiasmo*] to convey, communicate, transmit; (*Fís*) [+ *movimiento, fuerza*] to transmit • **nos comunicó su miedo** his fear spread to us *o* communicated itself to us
4 (= *unir*) to connect • **el pasillo comunica ambas oficinas** the offices are connected by a corridor • **han comunicado el comedor con la cocina** the dining-room and the kitchen have been knocked together
(VI) **1** (*Esp*) [*teléfono*] to be engaged • **su teléfono comunicaba todo el tiempo** her telephone was engaged all the time • **está comunicando** • **comunica** it's engaged; ▹ **señal**
2 [*cuarto, habitación*] to connect • **la cocina comunica con el comedor** the kitchen connects with the dining-room
3 (*Esp*) [*persona*] • **sabe ~ con la gente** she's a good communicator
(VPR) **comunicarse 1** (= *establecer comunicación*) **a** (*uso recíproco*) to communicate • **se comunican en inglés/por fax** they communicate in English/by fax, they use English/fax (to communicate) • **aunque no nos vemos, nos comunicamos a menudo** although we don't see each other, we're often in touch *o* in contact
b (*uso transitivo*) • **nos comunicamos nuestras impresiones** we exchanged impressions
c • **~se con algn** to communicate with sb • **necesitan una emisora con la que ~se con nosotros** they need a radio to communicate with us • **se comunicó telefónicamente con su esposa** he spoke to his wife on the phone • **en mi trabajo tengo que ~me con gente de muchos países** my work brings me into contact with people from many different countries
2 (= *entenderse*) • **~se bien con algn** to connect well with sb • **hay gente con la que me comunico muy bien** there are some people I connect with really well • **se comunica mal con sus empleados** he can't communicate with his employees
3 (= *transmitirse*) • **el entusiasmo del capitán se comunicó a toda la tripulación** the captain's enthusiasm spread to *o* communicated itself to the whole crew
4 (= *unirse*) to be connected (**con** to) • **sus habitaciones se comunicaban** they had adjoining rooms, their rooms were connected • **el salón se comunica con la cocina a través de un pasillo** the living room is connected to the kitchen by a corridor
comunicatividad (SF) communicativeness, powers of communication
comunicativo (ADJ) [*método, función, persona*] communicative • **tiene una gran capacidad comunicativa** he is a great communicator, he has great communicative skills • **es muy poco ~** he's very uncommunicative
comunicología (SF) communication theory
comunicólogo/a (SM/F) communication theorist
comunidad (SF) **1** (*gen*) community; (= *sociedad*) society, association; (*Rel*) community; (*And*) commune (*of free Indians*)

• **de** *o* **en ~** (*Jur*) jointly ▸ **comunidad autónoma** (*Esp*) autonomous region ▸ **Comunidad Británica de Naciones** British Commonwealth ▸ **Comunidad de Estados Independientes** Commonwealth of Independent States ▸ **comunidad de vecinos** residents' association ▸ **Comunidad (Económica) Europea** European (Economic) Community ▸ **Comunidad Europea del Carbón y del Acero** European Coal and Steel Community ▸ **comunidad lingüística** speech community
2 (= *pago*) [*de piso*] service charge, charge for communal services

COMUNIDAD AUTÓNOMA
In Spain the **comunidades autónomas** are any of the 19 administrative regions consisting of one or more provinces and having political powers devolved from Madrid, as stipulated by the 1978 Constitution. They have their own democratically elected parliaments, form their own cabinets and legislate and execute policies in certain areas such as housing, infrastructure, health and education, though Madrid still retains jurisdiction for all matters affecting the country as a whole, such as defence, foreign affairs and justice. The **Comunidades Autónomas** are: Andalucía, Aragón, Asturias, Islas Baleares, Canarias, Cantabria, Castilla y León, Castilla-La Mancha, Cataluña, Extremadura, Galicia, Madrid, Murcia, Navarra, País Vasco, La Rioja, Comunidad Valenciana, Ceuta and Melilla.
The term **Comunidades Históricas** refers to Galicia, Catalonia and the Basque Country, which for reasons of history and language consider themselves to some extent separate from the rest of Spain. They were given a measure of independence by the Second Republic (1931-1936), only to have it revoked by Franco in 1939. With the transition to democracy, these groups were the most vociferous and successful in their demand for home rule, partly because they already had experience of federalism and had established a precedent with autonomous institutions like the Catalan **Generalitat**.

comunión (SF) communion • **Primera Comunión** First Communion • **hacer la Primera Comunión** to take one's First Communion
comunismo (SM) communism
comunista (ADJ) communist
(SMF) communist • **~ libertario** libertarian communist
comunitariamente (ADV) communally
comunitario (ADJ) **1** [*centro, servicios, cooperación*] community (*antes de s*); [*jardín, pasillos*] communal
2 (= *de la comunidad europea*) Community (*antes de s*)
(SM) (= *país*) EC member state
comunizar ▹ CONJUG 1f (VT) to communize
comúnmente (ADV) commonly • **como ~ se cree** as is commonly believed • **lo que ~ se llama mal de amores** what is commonly called love sickness
con (PREP) **1** (*indicando compañía, instrumento, medio*) with • **vivo con mis padres** I live with my parents • **¿con quién vas a ir?** who are you going with? • **atado con cuerda** tied with string • **lo tomo con limón** I take it with lemon • **con su ayuda** with his help • **ducharse con agua fría** to have a cold shower • **lo he escrito con bolígrafo** I wrote it in pen • **andar con muletas** to walk on *o* with crutches • **con este sol no hay quien salga** no one can go out in this sun • **con el tiempo** in the course of time, with time
2 (*indicando características, estado*) • **un hombre con principios** a man of principle • **llegó con aspecto relajado** she arrived looking relaxed • **un amigo con aspecto de jugador de rugby** a friend who is built like a rugby player • **gente joven con ganas de divertirse** young people out for a good time • **murió con 60 años** she died at the age of 60
3 (*indicando combinación*) and • **pan con mantequilla** bread and butter • **vodka con naranja** vodka and orange • **café con leche** white coffee • **arroz con leche** rice pudding
4 (*indicando contenido*) • **una cazuela con agua caliente** a pan of hot water • **un maletín con dinero** a briefcase full of money • **encontraron una maleta con 800.000 dólares** they found a suitcase containing 800,000 dollars *o* with 800,000 dollars in it
5 (*indicando modo*) • **se levantó con rapidez** he got up quickly • **ábrelo con cuidado** open it carefully • **anda con dificultad** she walks with difficulty • **desayunamos con apetito** we ate our breakfast with relish • **estar con algo** • **estar con dolor de muelas/la pierna escayolada** to have toothache/one's leg in plaster • **está con la gripe** he's got flu • **con mucho gusto** certainly, by all means
6 (*como complemento personal de algunos verbos*) to • **¿con quién hablas?** who are you speaking to? • **voy a hablar con Luis** I'll talk to Luis • **se ha casado con Jesús** she's married Jesús, she's got married to Jesús • **estoy emparentado con la duquesa** I am related to the duchess • **no sabemos lo que va a pasar con nosotros** we don't know what's going to happen to us • **me escribo con ella** she and I write to each other
7 (*tras adjetivos*) to, towards • **amable con todos** kind to *o* towards everybody • **ser insolente con el jefe** to be disrespectful to *o* towards the boss
8 (*con decimales*) • **once con siete** (11,7) eleven point seven (11.7) • **un dólar con cincuenta centavos** one dollar fifty cents
9 (= *pese a*) in spite of • **con tantas dificultades, no se descorazonó** in spite of all *o* for all the difficulties he didn't lose heart • **con ser su madre, le odia** even though she is his mother she hates him • **con todo (y con eso), la gente se lo pasó bien** in spite of everything, people had a good time
10 (*en exclamaciones*) • **¡vaya con el niño!*** the cheeky monkey!* • **¡con lo bien que se está aquí!** and it's so nice here too! • **no me dejó ni un trocito, con lo que me gustan esos caramelos** he didn't even let me have a tiny piece, and he knows how much I like those sweets
11 (*indicando una condición*) **a** (+ *infin*) • **con estudiar un poco apruebas** with a bit of studying you should pass • **cree que con confesarlo se librará del castigo** he thinks that by owning up he'll escape punishment • **con decirle que no voy, se arreglará todo** when I tell him I'm not going, everything will be fine • **con llegar a las seis estará bien** if you come by six it will be fine • **con llegar tan tarde nos perderemos la comida** by arriving so late we're going to miss the meal
b • **con que** (+ *subjun*) • **con que me digas tu teléfono basta** if you just give me your phone number that'll be enough • **con que me invite, me conformo** as long as *o* provided that she invites me, I don't mind • **basta con que nos remita la tarjeta cumplimentada** all you have to do is send us the completed card; ▹ **tal**
Conacyt (SM ABR) (*Méx*) = **Consejo Nacional de Ciencia y Tecnología**
CONADEP (SF ABR) (*Arg*) (*Pol*) = **Comisión Nacional sobre la Desaparición de Personas**
Conasupo (SF ABR) (*Méx*) (= **Compañía Nacional de Subsistencias Populares**) *government buying and selling organization for subsidized food, clothes and furniture*
conato (SM) **1** (= *intento*) attempt • **hizo un ~ de entrar** he made an attempt to get in ▸ **conato de robo** attempted robbery
2 (*frm*) (= *esfuerzo*) • **poner ~ en algo** to put an effort into sth
concatenación (SF) linking, concatenation (*frm*) ▸ **concatenación de circunstancias** chain *o* series of circumstances
concatenar ▹ CONJUG 1a (VT) to link together
concavidad (SF) concavity, hollow, cavity
cóncavo (ADJ) concave
(SM) hollow, cavity
concebible (ADJ) conceivable, thinkable • **no es ~ que ...** it is unthinkable that ...
concebir ▹ CONJUG 3k (VT) **1** (= *crear*) [+ *plan, proyecto*] to conceive, devise; [+ *personaje*] to create; [+ *historia*] to think up, invent
2 (= *imaginar*) to conceive of, imagine • **no concibo una tarde de verano sin una siesta** I can't conceive of *o* imagine a summer afternoon without a siesta
3 (= *entender*) • **una forma diferente de ~ las cosas** a different way of seeing things • **eso es amor concebido solo como pasión** this is love viewed only as passion • **concebía el Estado como su propiedad personal** he thought *o* considered the State his personal property • **no concibe que haya gente con ideas mejores que las suyas** he can't comprehend that there are people with better ideas than his
4 (= *engendrar*) [+ *hijo*] to conceive • **el gol nos hizo ~ esperanzas de victoria** the goal brought *o* gave us hopes of victory • **esto le hizo ~ la sospecha de que pasaba algo** this planted the suspicion in his mind *o* made him suspect that something was wrong
(VI) (= *quedar encinta*) to conceive, become pregnant • **concibió a una avanzada edad** she conceived *o* became pregnant at a late age
conceder ▹ CONJUG 2a (VT) **1** (= *dar*) [+ *beca, premio*] to award, grant; [+ *crédito, permiso, deseo, entrevista*] to grant • **su mujer no quería ~le el divorcio** his wife didn't want to grant *o* give him a divorce • **el juez les concedió el divorcio** the judge granted them a divorce • **solo concedió unos minutos para unas preguntas** he only allowed a few minutes for some questions • **el árbitro les concedió el gol** the referee awarded them the goal • **le concedieron el honor de presidir el congreso** they conferred on him the honour of presiding over the conference • **¿me concede el honor de este baile?** may I have the pleasure of this dance?
2 (*frm*) (= *admitir*) to concede, admit • **concedo que el error fue mío** I concede *o* admit it was my mistake
concejal(a) (SM/F) town *o* city councillor, town *o* city councilman/councilwoman (*EEUU*)
concejalía (SF) post of town *o* city councillor, post of town councilman (*EEUU*), seat on the town *o* city council
concejil (ADJ) (= *del concejo*) council (*antes de s*); (= *municipal*) municipal, public

concejo SM council • **~ municipal** town council, city council
concelebrar ▷ CONJUG 1a VT to concelebrate
concentración SF **1** (= *centralización*) concentration, centralization • **contra la ~ de poder en Madrid** against the concentration *o* centralization of power in Madrid
2 (*mental*) concentration
3 (= *mitin*) gathering, meeting, rally; (*Dep*) [*de equipo*] base • **una ~ en pro de los derechos humanos** a gathering in support of human rights • **una ~ de motos** a motorcycling rally
4 (*Educ*) ▸ **concentración escolar** *rural school at centre of a catchment area*
5 (*LAm*) (*Com*) merger
concentrado ADJ concentrated
SM **1** (*Culin*) extract, concentrate
▸ **concentrado de carne** meat extract
2 (*Pol*) demonstrator
concentrar ▷ CONJUG 1a VT to concentrate
VPR **concentrarse 1** (= *reunirse*) to gather (together), assemble • **se ~on cientos de personas** hundreds of people gathered (together)
2 (*mentalmente*) to concentrate (**en** on)
• **concéntrate en lo que estás haciendo** concentrate on what you're doing
3 (= *estar concentrado*) to concentrate, be concentrated • **el interés se concentra en esta lucha** interest is centred on this fight
concéntrico ADJ concentric
concepción SF **1** (*Bio*) conception • **la Inmaculada Concepción** the Immaculate Conception
2 (= *idea*) conception, idea
3 (= *facultad*) understanding
conceptismo SM conceptism, *witty, allusive and involved style of esp 17th century*;
▷ CULTERANISMO, CONCEPTISMO
conceptista ADJ [*estilo, novela*] witty, allusive and involved
SMF (= *escritor*) writer in the style of conceptism
concepto SM **1** (= *idea*) concept, notion
• **formarse un ~ de algo** to get an idea of sth
• **un ~ grandioso** a bold conception, a bold plan
2 (= *opinión*) view, judgment • **en mi ~** in my view • **formarse un ~ de algn** to form an opinion of sb • **¿qué ~ has formado de él?** what do you think of him? • **tener buen ~ de algn, tener en buen ~ a algn** to think highly of sb
3 (= *condición*) heading, section • **bajo ningún ~** in no way, under no circumstances • **bajo todos los ~s** from every point of view, in every way, in every respect • **en *o* por ~ de** as, by way of • **se le pagó esa cantidad en *o* por ~ de derechos** he was paid that amount as royalties • **deducciones en *o* por ~ de seguro** deductions for social security • **por dicho ~** for this reason • **por ningún ~** in no way
4 (*Literat*) conceit
conceptual ADJ conceptual
conceptualización SF conceptualization
conceptualizar ▷ CONJUG 1f VT to conceptualize
conceptualmente ADV conceptually
conceptuar ▷ CONJUG 1e VT to judge, deem (*frm*) • **le conceptúo poco apto para eso** I think *o* consider him unsuited for that • **~ a algn de *o* como ...** to regard sb as ..., deem sb to be ... (*frm*)
conceptuosamente ADV (= *con ingenio*) wittily; (*pey*) over-elaborately, in a mannered way
conceptuoso ADJ (= *ingenioso*) witty, full of conceits; (*pey*) overelaborate, mannered
concerniente ADJ • **~ a** concerning, relating to • **en lo ~ a** with regard to, concerning
concernir ▷ CONJUG 3i; defectivo VI • **~ a** to concern • **eso a mi no me concierne** that does not concern me, that is of no concern to me, that is not of my concern • **por lo que a mi concierne** as far as I am concerned • **en lo que concierne a...** with regard to ..., concerning ...
concertación SF **1** (= *acto*) harmonizing; (= *coordinación*) coordination; (= *reconciliación*) reconciliation • **política de ~** consensus politics (*pl*) ▸ **concertación social** social harmony
2 (= *pacto*) agreement, pact
concertadamente ADV (= *metódicamente*) methodically, systematically; (= *ordenadamente*) in an orderly fashion; (= *armoniosamente*) harmoniously
concertado ADJ **1** (= *metódico*) systematic, concerted; (= *ordenado*) ordered; (= *armonioso*) harmonious
2 [*centro, colegio, hospital*] officially approved, state assisted
concertar ▷ CONJUG 1j VT **1** (*frm*) [+ *entrevista*] to arrange, set up • **~ una cita** to arrange *o* make an appointment
2 [+ *salario, precio*] to agree (on); [+ *póliza, seguro*] to take out • **~ un acuerdo** to reach an agreement • **han concertado una estrategia** they have agreed (on) a strategy • **hemos concertado suprimir dos puntos del acuerdo** we have agreed to delete two points from the agreement • **le ~on matrimonio cuando tenía diez años** they arranged her marriage when she was ten years old
3 (*Mús*) (= *armonizar*) [+ *voces*] to harmonize; [+ *instrumentos*] to tune (up)
VI **1** (*frm*) [*cifras, datos*] to agree, match (up)
2 (*Ling*) to agree
3 (*Mús*) [*voces*] to harmonize; [*instrumentos*] to be in tune
VPR **concertarse** • **~se para hacer algo** (*frm*) to agree to do sth
concertina SF (= *instrumento*) concertina
concertino/a SM/F leader of the orchestra, concertmaster (EEUU)
concertista SMF soloist, solo performer
• **~ de guitarra** concert guitarist • **~ de piano** concert pianist
concesión SF **1** (*en acuerdo, negociación*) concession, granting
2 (*Jur, Pol*) [*de nacionalidad, libertad*] granting
3 [*de un premio*] award
4 (*Com*) [*de fabricación*] licence, license (EEUU); [*de venta*] franchise; [*de transporte*] concession, contract
concesionario/a SM/F (*Com*) (*gen*) licence holder, license holder (EEUU), licensee; [*de venta*] franchisee, authorized dealer; [*de transportes*] contractor ▸ **concesionario/a exclusivo/a** sole agency, exclusive dealership
concesivo ADJ concessive
Concha SF *forma familiar de* **María de la Concepción**
concha SF **1** (*Zool*) shell • **MODISMOS**:
• **meterse en su ~** to retire into one's shell
• **tener muchas ~s** to be very sharp, be a sly one • **tiene más ~s que un galápago** he's as slippery as an eel ▸ **concha de perla** (*And*) mother-of-pearl; ▷ CAMINO DE SANTIAGO
2 (= *carey*) tortoiseshell
3 [*de porcelana*] flake, chip
4 (*Teat*) prompt box
5 (*And, Caribe*) (= *descaro*) nerve, cheek* • **¡qué ~ la tuya!** you've got a nerve!, you've got a cheek!*
6 (*And*) (= *pereza*) sloth, sluggishness
7 (*LAm*) (*euf*) = **coño** • **MODISMO**: • **¡~(s) de tu madre!** bastard!*‡, son of a bitch! (EEUU*‡)
8 (*Caribe*) (= *cartucho*) cartridge case
9 (*Caribe*) (= *piel*) peel; (= *corteza*) bark
conchabado/a SM/F (*LAm*) servant
conchabar ▷ CONJUG 1a VT **1** (*LAm*) [+ *persona*] to hire for work, engage, employ
2 (= *mezclar*) to mix, blend
3 (*And, Cono Sur*) (= *trocar*) to barter
VPR **conchabarse 1** (= *confabularse*) to gang up (**contra** on), conspire, plot (**contra** against) • **los dos estaban conchabados** the two were in cahoots*
2 (*LAm*) (= *colocarse, esp como criado*) to hire o.s. out, get a job (as a servant)
conchabo SM **1** (*LAm*) (= *contratación*) hiring, engagement • **oficina de ~** (*Cono Sur*) employment agency for domestics
2 (*Cono Sur*) (= *permuta*) barter(ing)
cónchale EXCL (*Caribe*) • **¡cónchale!** well!, goodness!, jeez (EEUU*)
Conchinchina* SF • **MODISMO**: • **estar en la ~** to be miles away, be on the other side of the world
Conchita SF = **Concha**
conchito SM (*And, Cono Sur*) youngest child, baby of the family
concho[1] SM **1** (*LAm*) (= *poso*) dregs (*pl*), sediment; (= *residuo*) residue • **MODISMOS**:
• **hasta el ~** to the very end • **irse al ~** (*Cono Sur*) to go down, go under, sink
2 conchos (= *sobras*) left-overs
concho[2]* EXCL (*euf*) sugar!*
concho[3] SM (*Caribe*) (= *taxi*) taxi
concho[4] (*CAm*) ADJ crude, vulgar
SM (= *campesino*) peasant; (*pey*) (= *paleto*) rustic, country bumpkin, hick (EEUU)
concho[5] SM (*And, Cono Sur*) = **conchito**
conchudo/a* ADJ (*And, Cono Sur*) sluggish, slow
SM/F **1** (*And, Cono Sur*) (= *idiota*) bloody idiot‡, jerk (EEUU*)
2 (*Puerto Rico*) (= *persona terca*) stubborn person, pigheaded person
conciencia SF **1** (= *moralidad*) conscience
• **pesará sobre su ~** it will weigh on his conscience • **no tienes ~, tratar así a tu pobre madre** you have no conscience, treating your poor mother like that • **en ~** in all conscience • **en ~ no podemos permitir que se produzca esa situación** in all conscience, we cannot allow that situation to arise • **actuar *u* obrar en ~** to act in good conscience • **votar en ~** to vote according to one's conscience • **libertad de ~** freedom of conscience • **tener la ~ limpia** to have a clear conscience • **tener mala ~** to have a guilty *o* bad conscience • **remorder a algn la ~**: • **me remuerde la ~ por haberle mentido** I've got a guilty *o* bad conscience about lying to him
• **tener la ~ tranquila** to have a clear conscience ▸ **conciencia de culpa** guilty conscience; ▷ **ancho, anchura, cargo, gusanillo, objetor, preso**
2 • **a ~** (= *con dedicación*) conscientiously; (= *con mala intención*) on purpose • **trabaja a ~** she works conscientiously • **me tuve que preparar a ~ para el examen** I had to prepare very thoroughly for the exam • **una casa construida a ~** a solidly *o* well built house
• **lo has hecho a ~ para fastidiarme** you deliberately did it to annoy me, you did it on purpose to annoy me
3 (= *capacidad de juicio*) awareness • **debería haber una mayor ~ sobre los riesgos del alcohol** people should be more aware of the risks of alcohol, there should be greater awareness of the risks of alcohol • **lo ha hecho con plena ~ del daño que podía causar** he did it in full knowledge of the

damage he might cause, he was fully aware of the damage he might cause when he did it • **a ~ de que ...** fully aware that ..., in the certain knowledge that ... • **despertar la ~ de algn** to raise sb's consciousness *o* awareness • **tener ~ de algo**: • **no tienen ~ de nación** they have no sense of national identity • **tenían plena ~ de lo que hacían** they were fully aware of what they were doing • **tomar ~ de algo** to become aware of sth • **tomar ~ de que ...** to become aware that ... ▸ **conciencia crítica** critical awareness ▸ **conciencia de clase** class consciousness ▸ **conciencia social** social conscience
4 (*Med*) consciousness • **perder la ~** to lose consciousness

concienciación SF (*Esp*) • **una campaña de ~ ciudadana** a campaign to raise public awareness

concienciado ADJ (*Esp*) socially aware

concienciar ▹ CONJUG 1b (*Esp*) VT (= *sensibilizar*) • **~ a algn de un problema** to raise sb's awareness of an issue • **un anuncio para ~ a los conductores de que no beban** an advert to raise drivers' awareness about drink-driving
VPR **concienciarse** • **~se de algo** to become aware of sth

concientización SF (*LAm*) = **concienciación**

concientizado ADJ (*LAm*) = **concienciado**

concientizar ▹ CONJUG 1f VT (*LAm*) = **concienciar**

concienzar ▹ CONJUG 1f VT = **concienciar**

concienzudamente ADV conscientiously • **trabaja ~** she works conscientiously • **un informe realizado ~** a painstaking report

concienzudo ADJ **1** [*estudiante, trabajador*] conscientious
2 [*estudio, esfuerzo*] painstaking, thorough

concierto SM **1** (*Mús*) (= *función*) concert; (= *obra*) concerto ▸ **concierto de arias** song recital ▸ **concierto de cámara** chamber concert ▸ **concierto sinfónico** symphony concert
2 (*frm*) (= *acuerdo*) agreement • **de ~ con** in agreement with • **quedar de ~ acerca de** to be in agreement with regard to • **los fabricantes, en ~ con los vendedores, se han negado a la exportación de los vehículos** the manufacturers, together with the retailers, have refused to export the vehicles
3 (*Pol*) (= *orden*) order • **la incorporación de España al ~ europeo** Spain's admission into Europe; ▹ **orden**

conciliable ADJ reconcilable • **dos opiniones no fácilmente ~s** two opinions which it is not easy to reconcile

conciliábulo SM secret meeting, secret discussion

conciliación SF **1** (*entre personas*) conciliation, reconciliation • **la ~ de la vida laboral y familiar** finding a balance between work and family life
2 (= *afinidad*) affinity, similarity

conciliador(a) ADJ conciliatory
SM/F conciliator

conciliar[1] ▹ CONJUG 1b VT **1** [+ *enemigos*] to reconcile; [+ *ideas*] to harmonize, bring into line• **~ el trabajo y familia** to find a balance between work and family life
2 • **~ el sueño** to get to sleep
3 [+ *respeto, antipatía*] to win, gain
VPR **conciliarse** [+ *respeto, antipatía*] to win, gain

conciliar[2] ADJ (*Rel*) of a council, council (*antes de s*)
SM council member

conciliatorio ADJ conciliatory

concilio SM council • **el Segundo Concilio Vaticano** the Second Vatican Council

concisamente ADV concisely, briefly

concisión SF conciseness, brevity

conciso ADJ concise, brief

concitar ▹ CONJUG 1a VT **1** (= *provocar*) to stir up, incite (**contra** against)
2 (= *reunir*) to gather, assemble, bring together

conciudadano/a SM/F fellow citizen

conclave SM, **cónclave** SM conclave

concluir ▹ CONJUG 3g VT **1** (= *finalizar*) [+ *estudios, trabajo*] to finish, complete, conclude (*frm*) • **~emos las obras en 2014** work will finish in 2014, the work will be completed in 2014 • **regresó a España tras ~ su visita oficial a China** he returned to Spain after concluding *o* ending his official visit to China
2 (= *alcanzar*) [+ *acuerdo, pacto*] to reach
3 (= *deducir*) to conclude • **el informe concluye que ese no es el factor más importante** the report concludes that this is not the most important factor • **~ algo de algo** to deduce sth from sth
VI (*frm*) (= *finalizar*) [*acto, proceso, evento*] to conclude, finish, end; [*era, etapa*] to end, come to an end; [*plazo*] to expire • **el acto concluyó con un brindis** the ceremony concluded *o* finished *o* ended with a toast • **las negociaciones concluyeron en un tratado de paz** the talks ended in a peace treaty • **cuando la investigación concluya** when investigations are complete *o* have been completed • **y para ~ ...** and finally ...
VPR **concluirse** to end • **así se concluye un nuevo capítulo de esta serie** so ends *o* so we conclude another chapter in this series

conclusión SF conclusion • **en ~** in conclusion, finally • **llegar a la ~ de que ...** to come to the conclusion that ... • **extraiga usted las conclusiones oportunas** draw your own conclusions

concluyente ADJ conclusive, decisive

concluyentemente ADV conclusively, decisively

concolón SM (*LAm*) scrapings

concomerse ▹ CONJUG 2a VPR • MODISMO: • **~ de impaciencia*** to be itching with impatience

concomitante ADJ concomitant

conconete SM (*Méx*) child, little one

concordancia SF **1** (= *acuerdo*) agreement; (= *armonía*) harmony
2 (*Ling*) concord, agreement
3 (*Mús*) harmony
4 concordancias (*Literat*) concordance (*sing*)

concordante ADJ concordant

concordar ▹ CONJUG 1l VT **1** (= *armonizar*) to reconcile, bring into line
2 (*Ling*) to make agree
VI **1** (= *armonizar*) to agree (**con** with), tally (**con** with), correspond (**con** to) • **esto no concuerda con los hechos** this does not square with *o* fit in with the facts • **los dos concuerdan en sus gustos** the two have the same tastes
2 (*Ling*) to agree

concordato SM concordat

concorde ADJ • **estar ~s** to be agreed, be in agreement • **estar ~ en hacer algo** to agree to do sth • **poner a dos personas ~s** to bring about agreement between two people

concordia SF **1** (= *armonía*) concord, harmony; (= *conformidad*) conformity
2 (= *anillo*) double finger-ring
3 • **Línea de la Concordia** (*Cono Sur*) frontier between Chile and Peru

concreción SF **1** (= *precisión*) precision • **le falta ~ al expresarse** she lacks precision in expressing herself • **intenta responder a las preguntas con mayor ~** try to be more precise when you reply to the questions
2 (= *materialización*) realization • **llegó el momento de la ~ de sus deseos** the time for realizing her dreams arrived • **su falta de ~ a la hora de marcar goles** their failure to make an impression when it came to scoring
3 (*Fís*) concretion
4 (*Med*) stone

concretamente ADV **1** (= *específicamente*) specifically • **se refirió ~ a dos** he specifically mentioned two • **estoy buscando esta película ~** I'm looking for this film in particular, I'm specifically looking for this film • **estuvimos en Inglaterra, ~ en Manchester** we were in England, in Manchester to be exact *o* precise
2 (= *exactamente*) exactly • **¿qué dijo ~?** what exactly did he say?

concretar ▹ CONJUG 1a VT **1** (= *precisar*) to specify; (= *concertar*) to settle • **los expertos prepararán un documento que ~á los términos del acuerdo** experts are to draw up a document which will specify the terms of the agreement • **el portavoz no quiso ~ más datos** the spokesman declined to go into details *o* to be more specific • **en la reunión no concretamos nada** we didn't settle (on) anything specific at the meeting, nothing specific came out of the meeting • **pusieron una fecha tope para ~ los acuerdos** they gave a deadline for the details of the agreement to be settled • **llámame para ~ los detalles** call me to fix *o* settle the details
2 (= *resumir*) to sum up • **has concretado mi pensamiento en unas pocas palabras** you've summed up my thoughts in a few words
3 (= *materializar*) **a** (*LAm*) [+ *sueños, esperanzas*] • **la publicación de sus poemas vino a ~ uno de sus grandes deseos** the publication of his poems was the realization of one of his dearest wishes
b (*Chile*) [+ *oferta, donación*] to materialize
4 (*Chile*) (*Constr*) to concrete
VI **1** (= *puntualizar*) • **concretemos** let's be more specific
2 (*Ftbl*) (= *marcar*) • **no lograron ~ ante puerta** they were unable to make any impression in front of goal
VPR **concretarse 1** (= *materializarse*) **a** [*ley, prohibición*] to come into force; [*esperanzas*] to be fulfilled; [*sueños*] to come true • **queda por ver cómo se concretan en la práctica los puntos del acuerdo** it remains to be seen how the points contained in the agreement work out in practice • **nunca llegó a ~se su proyecto** his project never came to anything, nothing came of his project • **su ayuda nunca llegó a ~se** their help never materialized *o* was never forthcoming
b • **~se en algo**: **un avance de la derecha que se concretó en su triunfo electoral** an advance by the right which resulted in its electoral win • **el proyecto se concretaba en tres objetivos principales** in essence the project had three main objectives
2 (= *limitarse*) • **~se a algo** to limit o.s. to sth, confine o.s. to sth • **el profesor se concretó al siglo XVIII** the teacher limited *o* confined himself to the 18th century • **~se a hacer algo** to limit *o* confine o.s. to doing sth

concretizar ▹ CONJUG 1f VT = **concretar**

concreto ADJ **1** (= *específico*) [*medida, propuesta*] specific, concrete; [*hecho, resultado*] specific; [*fecha, hora*] definite, particular • **una forma concreta de llevarlo a la práctica** a specific way of putting it into practice • **voy a poner algunos ejemplos ~s** I'm going to give a few specific examples • **en un plazo breve tendremos datos más ~s** we will have more specific *o* precise

information shortly • **no me dijo ninguna hora concreta** he didn't tell me any definite *o* particular time • **en este caso ~** in this particular case • **lo importante son los hechos ~s** the most important thing is the actual facts
2 (= *no abstracto*) concrete • **un nombre ~** a concrete noun
3 • **en ~ a** (*con verbos*) • **nos referimos, en ~, al abuso del alcohol** we are referring specifically to alcohol abuse • **he viajado mucho por África, en ~, por Kenia y Tanzania** I've travelled a lot in Africa, specifically in Kenya and Tanzania *o* in Kenya and Tanzania to be precise • **¿qué dijo en ~?** what exactly did he say?
b (*con sustantivos*) • **¿busca algún libro en ~?** are you looking for a particular *o* specific book?, are you looking for any book in particular? • **no se ha decidido nada en ~** nothing definite *o* specific has been decided
(SM) (*LAm*) (= *hormigón*) concrete ▸ **concreto armado** reinforced concrete
concubina (SF) concubine
concubinato (SM) concubinage
concúbito (SM) copulation
conculcación (SF) (*gen*) infringement; [*de ley*] violation
conculcar ▸ CONJUG 1g (VT) (*gen*) to infringe (on); [+ *ley*] to break, violate
concupiscencia (SF) **1** (= *lujuria*) lustfulness, concupiscence (*frm*)
2 (= *codicia*) greed, avarice
concupiscente (ADJ) **1** (= *lujurioso*) lustful, lewd, concupiscent (*frm*)
2 (= *avaro*) greedy, avaricious
concurrencia (SF) **1** (= *coincidencia*) concurrence; (= *simultaneidad*) simultaneity, coincidence
2 (= *público*) (*Dep*) spectators (*pl*); (*Cine, Teat*) audience
3 (= *asistencia*) attendance, turnout • **había una numerosa ~** there was a big attendance *o* turnout
4 (*Com*) competition
concurrente (ADJ) **1** [*suceso*] concurrent
2 (*Com*) competing
(SMF) **1** (= *asistente*) person present, person attending • **los ~s** those present, the audience
2 (*en carrera, competición*) entrant • **este año ha aumentado el número de ~s en la maratón** the number of people entering the marathon has gone up this year
concurrido (ADJ) [*local*] crowded, much frequented; [*calle*] busy, crowded; (*Teat etc*) popular, well-attended, full (of people)
concurrir ▸ CONJUG 3a (VI) **1** (= *acudir*) • **~ a algo** to attend sth • **cien personas concurrieron a la subasta** a hundred people attended the auction • **diez millones de votantes ~án a las urnas** ten million voters will go to the polls
2 (= *participar*) to take part • **al certamen podrá ~ el que lo desee** anyone who wishes may take part in the competition • **tres bailarinas concurren al premio** three dancers are competing for the prize • **todos los partidos que concurren a las elecciones** all parties taking part in the election • **concurre como candidato a la presidencia** he's running as a candidate for the presidency
3 (*frm*) (= *combinarse*) • **concurrieron los factores necesarios para la desertificación** the necessary factors for desertification were present • **si concurren las circunstancias siguientes** given *o* in the following circumstances • **en ella concurren las mejores cualidades** she combines the best qualities • **~ en algo: numerosos factores concurren en el éxito de esta empresa** many factors combine to make this company a success • **~ a algo: las circunstancias que concurrieron a la ruina del campo** the circumstances that combined to bring about the demise of the countryside, the circumstances that contributed to the demise of the countryside
4 (= *confluir*) [*ríos, calles*] to meet, converge
concursado/a (SM/F) insolvent debtor, bankrupt
concursante (SMF) **1** (*para un empleo*) candidate
2 (*en juego, concurso*) contestant; (*Dep*) competitor
concursar ▸ CONJUG 1a (VI) **1** (*por un empleo*) to compete • **va a ~ por la vacante** he is going to apply *o* compete for the vacancy
2 (*en un concurso*) to take part
(VT) (*Jur*) to declare insolvent, declare bankrupt
concurso (SM) **1** (*Com*) tender • **presentar algo a ~** to open sth up to tender, put sth out to tender
2 (= *competición*) competition, contest; (*TV, Radio*) quiz, game show • **un ~ de poesía** a poetry competition • **queda ya fuera de ~** he's out of the running now ▸ **concurso de belleza** beauty contest ▸ **concurso de ideas** (*Arquit*) design competition ▸ **concurso de pastoreo** sheepdog trials (*pl*) ▸ **concurso de redacción** essay competition ▸ **concurso de saltos** show-jumping contest *o* competition ▸ **concurso hípico** horse show, show-jumping contest *o* competition ▸ **concurso radiofónico** radio quiz show
3 (= *examen*) examination, open competition • **ganar un puesto por ~** to win a post in open competition ▸ **concurso de méritos** competition for posts ▸ **concurso oposición** public competition
4 ▸ **concurso de acreedores** (*Jur*) meeting of creditors
5 (= *coincidencia*) coincidence, concurrence
6 (= *ayuda*) cooperation, help • **con el ~ de** with the help of • **prestar su ~** to help, collaborate
(ADJ) • **corrida ~** bullfighting competition • **programa ~** TV game show • **cata ~** wine-tasting competition
concurso-subasta (SM) (PL: **concursos-subasta**) competitive tendering
concusión (SF) **1** (*Med*) concussion
2 (*Econ*) extortion
concusionario/a (SM/F) extortioner
condado (SM) (= *demarcación territorial*) county; (*Hist*) earldom
condal (ADJ) • **Ciudad Condal** Barcelona
conde (SM) earl, count • **el Conde Fernán González** Count Fernán González
condecoración (SF) (= *acción*) decoration; (= *insignia*) decoration, medal; (= *divisa*) badge
condecorar ▸ CONJUG 1a (VT) to decorate (con with)
condena (SF) **1** (= *pronunciamiento*) sentence, conviction; (= *período*) term (of imprisonment) • **cumplir una ~** to serve a sentence • **el año pasado hubo diez ~s por embriaguez** last year there were ten convictions for drunkenness • MODISMO: • **ser algn la ~ de otra** (*Méx*) to be the bane of sb's life ▸ **condena a perpetuidad, condena de reclusión perpetua** life sentence, sentence of life imprisonment
2 (= *desaprobación*) condemnation
condenable (ADJ) reprehensible
condenación (SF) **1** (*gen*) condemnation; (*Rel*) damnation; (= *censura*) disapproval, censure; (*Jur*) = **condena**
2 • **¡condenación!** damn!, damnation!
condenadamente* (ADV) • **es un trabajo ~ duro** it's bloody hard work‡ • **una mujer ~ lista** a damn *o* darned clever woman*
condenado/a (ADJ) **1** (*Jur*) condemned, convicted; (*Rel*) damned
2 (= *destinado*) [*cambio, reforma, ley*] doomed • **la reforma estaba condenada al fracaso** the reform was doomed to failure • **~ al olvido** destined for oblivion • **el buque ~** the doomed *o* fated vessel • **una especie condenada a la extinción** a species doomed to extinction • **instituciones condenadas a desaparecer** institutions doomed to disappear
3* (= *maldito*) damn*, flaming* (*euf*) • **¡aquel ~ teléfono!** that damn *o* flaming *o* wretched phone!*, that bloody phone!‡
4* [*niño*] mischievous, naughty
5 (*Cono Sur*) (= *listo*) clever; (= *astuto*) sharp
(SM/F) **1** (*Jur*) prisoner • **el ~ a muerte** the condemned man • MODISMO: • **trabaja como un ~** he works like a Trojan
2 (*Rel*) damned soul
3 • **el ~ de mi tío*** that wretched *o* damned uncle of mine*
condenar ▸ CONJUG 1a (VT) **1** (= *desaprobar, criticar*) to condemn
2 (*Jur*) to convict, find guilty, sentence; (*a pena capital*) to condemn • **~ a algn a tres meses de cárcel** to sentence sb to three months in jail, give sb a three-month prison sentence • **le ~on por ladrón** they found him guilty of robbery • **~ a algn a una multa** to sentence sb to pay a fine
3 (*Rel*) to damn
4 (*Arquit*) to wall up, block up
5†* (= *fastidiar*) to vex, annoy
(VPR) **condenarse 1** (*Jur*) to confess, own up; (= *reprocharse*) to blame o.s.
2 (*Rel*) to be damned
3†* (= *enfadarse*) to get cross, get irate
condenatorio (ADJ) condemnatory • **declaración condenatoria** statement of condemnation
condensación (SF) condensation
condensado (ADJ) condensed
condensador (SM) condenser
condensar ▸ CONJUG 1a (VT) to condense
(VPR) **condensarse** to condense, become condensed
condesa (SF) countess
condescendencia (SF) **1** (= *deferencia*) obligingness; (= *indulgencia*) affability • **aceptar algo por ~** to accept sth so as not to hurt feelings
2 (*pey*) • **tratar a algn con ~** to patronize sb
condescender ▸ CONJUG 2g (VI) to acquiesce, comply, agree • **~ a** to consent to, say yes to • **~ a los ruegos de algn** to agree to sb's requests • **~ en hacer algo** to agree to do sth
condescendiente (ADJ) **1** (= *deferente*) obliging; (= *afable*) affable; (= *conforme*) acquiescent
2 (*pey*) • **ser ~ con algn** to patronize sb
condición (SF) **1** (= *requisito*) condition • **lo haré con una ~** I'll do it on one condition • **ha puesto como ~ el que se respeten los derechos humanos** he has made it a condition that human rights be respected • **están negociando las condiciones de la entrega de los rehenes** they are negotiating the conditions for the release of the hostages • **las condiciones del contrato** the terms *o* conditions of the contract • **a ~ de que ...** • **con la ~ de que ...** on condition that ... • **te dejaré salir con la ~ de que no vuelvas**

tarde I'll let you go out provided (that) *o* on condition (that) you don't come back late • **acepté a ~ de que no dijera nada a nadie** I agreed on condition that he didn't say anything to anyone • **~ indispensable** essential condition • **~ previa** precondition • **entregarse** *o* **rendirse sin condiciones** to surrender unconditionally • **rendición sin condiciones** unconditional surrender • **~ sine qua non** essential condition, sine qua non ▸ **condiciones de favor** concessionary terms ▸ **condiciones de pago** terms of payment, payment terms ▸ **condiciones de uso** instructions for use ▸ **condiciones de venta** terms of sale, conditions of sale ▸ **condiciones económicas** [*de contrato*] financial terms; [*de profesional*] fees; ▹ **pliego**
2 condiciones: **a** (= *situación*) conditions • **las condiciones de luz eran muy buenas** the light conditions were very good • **si se dan las condiciones adecuadas, ganaremos las elecciones** if the conditions are right, we will win the election • **viven en condiciones infrahumanas** they live in subhuman conditions • **en condiciones normales** under normal conditions *o* circumstances • **estar en (buenas) condiciones** [*lugar, máquina*] to be in good condition; [*alimentos*] to be fresh; [*deportista*] to be fit • **el terreno de juego está en perfectas condiciones** the pitch is in perfect condition • **el coche se encuentra en excelentes condiciones** the car is in excellent condition • **esa leche no está en buenas condiciones** that milk is not fresh • **estar en condiciones de** *o* **para hacer algo** [*enfermo*] to be well *o* fit enough to do sth; [*deportista*] to be fit (enough) to do sth • **la industria automovilística no está en condiciones de enfrentarse a la competencia** the car industry is not in a condition to face up to competition • **estar en malas condiciones** [*coche, libro, campo de juego*] to be in bad condition • **me devolvieron el libro en pésimas condiciones** they returned the book to me in a terrible state *o* condition • **el queso estaba en malas condiciones** the cheese had gone bad, the cheese was off
b • **en condiciones** (= *decente*) proper • **no tengo tiempo de echarme una siesta en condiciones** I don't have time for a proper siesta • **antes de irnos lo dejaremos todo en condiciones** we'll leave everything in order before we go
c (= *cualidades*) • **no tiene condiciones para la pintura** she is not cut out to be a painter • **no reúne las condiciones necesarias para este trabajo** he doesn't fulfil the requirements for this job • **el edificio no reúne condiciones para museo** the building is not suitable for use as a museum ▸ **condiciones de trabajo** working conditions ▸ **condiciones de vida** living conditions ▸ **condiciones físicas** physical condition (*sing*) • **el equipo se encuentra en excelentes condiciones físicas** the team is in excellent physical condition • **no está en condiciones físicas de boxear** he is not physically fit (enough) to box ▸ **condiciones laborales** working conditions ▸ **condiciones sanitarias** [*de bar, restaurante*] health requirements; [*de hospital*] sanitary conditions; ▹ **igualdad, inferioridad**
3 (= *naturaleza*) condition • **la ~ humana** the human condition • **el derecho a no ser discriminada por su ~ de mujer** the right not to be discriminated against on the grounds of being *o* because one is a woman • **tiene muy buena ~** he's very good-natured
4 (= *clase social*) social background • **personas de distinta ~** people of different social backgrounds • **personas de humilde ~** people from a humble background
5 (= *posición*) position • **su ~ de artista no lo autoriza a hacer eso** his position as an artist does not allow him to do this • **les pidieron algún documento acreditativo de su ~ de pasajeros** they were asked for some documentary evidence proving that they were passengers • **en su ~ de presidente** in his capacity as president

condicionado (ADJ) conditional • **la oferta está condicionada a la demanda** the offer is conditional on demand • **prestó su apoyo ~ a una serie de ayudas económicas** he gave his support, conditional on a financial aid package

condicional (ADJ) (*tb Ling*) conditional • **hizo una oferta ~** she made a conditional offer • **nos prestó su ayuda de forma ~** he gave us his help on a conditional basis *o* subject to certain conditions; ▹ **libertad**

condicionalmente (ADV) conditionally

condicionamiento (SM) conditioning

condicionante (ADJ) determining
(SM o SF) determining factor, determinant

condicionar ▹ CONJUG 1a (VT) **1** (= *influir*) to condition, determine • **¿en qué medida condiciona el clima su forma de vida?** to what extent does the climate condition *o* determine your way of life?
2 (= *supeditar*) • **~ algo a algo** to make sth conditional on sth • **condicionó su apoyo a la retirada del otro candidato** he made his support conditional on the withdrawal of the other candidate

condigno (ADJ) proper, corresponding

condimentación (SF) seasoning

condimentado (ADJ) seasoned

condimentar ▹ CONJUG 1a (VT) (*gen*) to flavour, flavor (*EEUU*), season; (*con especias*) to spice

condimento (SM) (*gen*) seasoning, flavouring, flavoring (*EEUU*); (= *aliño*) dressing

condiscípulo/a (SM/F) fellow student, fellow pupil

condolencia (SF) condolence, sympathy

condolerse ▹ CONJUG 2h (VPR) • **~ de** *o* **por** to sympathize with, feel sorry for

condominio (SM) **1** (*Jur*) joint ownership; (*Pol*) condominium
2 (*LAm*) (= *piso*) condominium, condo*, apartment (*owned by the occupant*)

condón (SM) condom ▸ **condón femenino** female condom

condonación (SF) **1** [*de pena*] remission, reprieve
2 [*de deuda*] cancellation

condonar ▹ CONJUG 1a (VT) **1** (*Jur*) • **~ una pena** to lift a sentence
2 (*Econ*) [+ *deuda*] to cancel, forgive

cóndor (SM) condor

conducción (SF) **1** (*Com*) management; [*de líquidos*] piping; (*por cable*) wiring; (*Fís*) conduction
2 (*Aut*) driving • **coche de ~ interior** saloon car ▸ **conducción descuidada, conducción imprudente, conducción negligente** careless driving ▸ **conducción por la derecha** right-hand drive ▸ **conducción temeraria** reckless driving
3 (*Téc*) (= *tubo*) pipe; (= *cable*) cabling ▸ **conducción de agua** water pipe ▸ **conducción principal de agua** water main ▸ **conducción principal de gas** gas main
4 (*TV, Radio*) presentation

conducente (ADJ) • **~ a** conducive to, leading to

conducir ▹ CONJUG 3n (VT) **1** (*Aut*) to drive
2 (= *llevar*) to take, lead • **este pasillo conduce a los pasajeros al avión** this corridor leads *o* takes passengers to the plane • **el general condujo al ejército a la victoria** the general led the army to victory • **la secretaria nos condujo hasta la salida** the secretary showed us out
3 [+ *electricidad, calor*] to conduct; [+ *agua, gas*] to convey
4 (*frm*) (= *estar a cargo de*) [+ *negocio, empresa*] to manage; [+ *equipo*] to lead; [+ *debate*] to chair, lead
5 (*TV, Radio*) to present
(VI) **1** (*Aut*) to drive • **¿sabes ~?** can you drive?, do you know how to drive? • **si bebes, no conduzcas** don't drink and drive
2 (= *llevar*) • **~ a algo** to lead to sth • **esta carretera conduce al aeropuerto** this road leads to the airport, this road takes you to the airport • **un infarto que le condujo a la muerte** a heart attack which led to his death • **¿esa actitud a qué conduce?** where will that attitude get you? • **esto no nos conduce a ninguna parte** *o* **a nada** this is getting us nowhere
(VPR) **conducirse** (*frm*) (= *comportarse*) to behave, conduct o.s. (*frm*), bear o.s. (*liter*)

conducta (SF) **1** (= *comportamiento*) conduct, behaviour, behavior (*EEUU*) • **le dieron un permiso de tres días por buena ~** he was allowed home for three days because of his good conduct *o* behaviour • **una persona de ~ irreprochable** a person whose conduct has been beyond reproach • **la ~ sexual de los españoles** the sexual habits *o* behaviour of Spaniards • **mala ~** misconduct, misbehaviour • **cambiar de ~** to mend one's ways ▸ **conducta compulsiva** compulsive behaviour
2 (*Com*) direction, management

conductibilidad (SF) conductivity

conductismo (SM) behaviourism, behaviorism (*EEUU*)

conductista (ADJ), (SMF) behaviourist, behaviorist (*EEUU*)

conductividad (SF) = **conductibilidad**

conductivo (ADJ) conductive

conducto (SM) **1** [*de agua, gas*] pipe, conduit; (*Anat*) duct, canal; (*Elec*) lead, cable • **~s** (*Aut*) leads ▸ **conducto alimenticio** alimentary canal ▸ **conducto biliar** bile duct ▸ **conducto de desagüe** drain ▸ **conducto de humo** flue ▸ **conducto lacrimal** tear duct
2 (= *medio*) channel; (= *persona*) agent, intermediary • **por ~ de** through, by means of • **por los ~s normales** through the usual channels

conductor(a) (ADJ) (*Fís*) • **un material ~** a conductive material • **el agua salada es mejor ~ que el agua dulce** salt water is much more conductive than fresh water • **un material ~ de la electricidad** a material that conducts electricity
(SM/F) **1** [*de coche, camión, autobús*] driver; [*de moto*] rider • **este impuesto afectará a todos los ~es de vehículos** this tax will affect all motorists
2 (*TV, Radio*) presenter
3 (*LAm*) (*Mús*) conductor
4 (*frm*) (= *dirigente*) leader
(SM) (*Fís*) conductor • **no ~** non-conductor

conductual (ADJ) behavioural, behavioral (*EEUU*)

condueño/a (SM/F) joint owner, part owner, co-owner

conduje *etc* ▸ **conducir**

condumio* (SM) grub‡, chow (*EEUU*‡), food

conectable (ADJ) connectable (a to)

conectado (ADJ) connected • **estar ~** [*aparato*] to be on; [*cable*] to be live

conectar ▹ CONJUG 1a VT **1** [+ *cables, tubos*] to connect (up) • **he conectado el ordenador a Internet** I've connected the computer to the internet • **todavía no hemos conectado la luz en el piso nuevo** we still haven't had the electricity connected in the new flat • **conecta el televisor para ver las noticias** switch on the television to watch the news • **~ un aparato eléctrico a tierra** to earth *o* (*EEUU*) ground an electrical appliance; ▹ **masa²**
2 (= *enlazar*) • **~ algo con algo** to link sth to sth • **esta autovía ~á Granada con Almería** this dual carriageway will link Granada and *o* to Almería • **la secretaria no me quiso ~ con el jefe** the secretary wouldn't put me through to the boss • **una oración que me conecta con Dios** a prayer which puts me in touch with God
3 (= *relacionar*) • **no logro ~ una cosa con la otra** I can't see how one thing connects with another, I can't see how everything ties in together • **conectó todos los datos y resolvió el problema** he put all the facts together and solved the problem
VI **1*** (= *congeniar*) • **Ana y Eugenia conectan bien** Ana and Eugenia have a lot in common • **un autor que ha sabido ~ con el público** an author who knows how to get through to *o* reach the public • **no hemos logrado ~ con el electorado** we didn't manage to get through to the electorate
2 (= *enlazar*) • **esta carretera ~á con la autopista** this road will link up to *o* provide a link to the motorway • **este tren conecta con el de Málaga** this train connects (up) with the Málaga train • **la obra conecta con la tradición poética española** the work ties in with Spanish poetic tradition
3 (*TV, Radio*) • **conectamos con nuestro corresponsal en Londres** and now it's over to our correspondent in London, and now we're going over to our correspondent in London
VPR **conectarse** (*Inform*) • **~se a Internet** to get connected to the internet

conectividad SF connectivity

conectivo ADJ connective

conector SM connector

coneja SF doe (rabbit)

conejar SM (rabbit) hutch

conejera SF **1** (= *madriguera*) warren, burrow; (= *jaula*) rabbit hutch
2‡ (= *tasca*) den, dive‡

conejillo SM ▸ **conejillo de Indias** guinea pig

conejita* SF bunny girl

conejo SM **1** (*Zool*) rabbit ▸ **conejo casero** (*gen*) tame rabbit; (= *mascota*) pet rabbit ▸ **conejo de monte, conejo silvestre** wild rabbit
2 (*Anat***) (= *órgano sexual*) pussy**
3 (*CAm*) (= *detective*) detective, sleuth* • **andar de ~** (*LAm*) to be (operating) under cover
4 (*Mil*) recruit*, squaddie*
ADJ (*CAm*) (= *soso*) flat, unsweetened; (= *amargo*) bitter, sour

conejuna SF rabbit fur, coney

conexión SF **1** (= *relación*) connection • **no encuentro la ~ entre los dos hechos** I don't see the connection between the two facts • **no existe ~ entre lo que declaró y lo que sucedió** what he said bears no relation to what happened • **pretenden establecer ~ con nuestro partido** their aim is to establish links with our party • **gritaba cosas sin ~ ninguna** he was shouting incoherently
2 (*Elec*) connection • **en caso de mala ~, apague el aparato** if there is a bad connection, switch off the machine • **hemos solicitado la ~ a la red eléctrica** we have applied to have the electricity connected • **~ a tierra** earth, ground (*EEUU*)
3 (*TV, Radio, Telec*) • **tenemos ~ con nuestro corresponsal en Londres** we are going over to our London correspondent • **seguimos en ~ telefónica con el presidente** we still have a telephone link with the president ▸ **conexión en directo** live link-up
4 (*Inform*) interface ▸ **conexión en paralelo** parallel interface
5 conexiones (= *contactos*) contacts • **tenía conexiones en el Ministerio** he had contacts at the Ministry • **conexiones familiares** family connections

conexionarse ▹ CONJUG 1a VPR (= *ponerse en contacto*) to get in touch; (= *hacer contactos*) to make connections, establish contacts

conexo ADJ connected, related

confabulación SF **1** (= *complot*) plot, conspiracy; (= *intriga*) intrigue
2 (*Com*) ring

confabularse ▹ CONJUG 1a VPR
1 (= *conchabarse*) to plot, conspire, scheme
2 (*Com*) to form a ring

confección SF **1** (= *preparación*) making-up, preparation
2 (*Cos*) dressmaking • **industria de la ~** clothing industry • **traje de ~** ready-to-wear suit • **es una ~ Pérez** it's a Pérez creation ▸ **confección de caballero** menswear
3 (*Farm*) concoction, preparation

confeccionado ADJ • **~ a la medida** made to measure

confeccionador SM (*Prensa*) layout man

confeccionar ▹ CONJUG 1a VT **1** [+ *lista*] to make out, write; [+ *informe*] to prepare, write up
2 (*Cos*) to make (up)
3 (*Culin*) to make, bake
4 (*Farm*) to concoct, make up

confeccionista SMF clothing manufacturer

confederación SF confederation

confederado/a ADJ, SM/F confederate

confederal ADJ federal

confederarse ▹ CONJUG 1a VPR to confederate, form a confederation

conferencia SF **1** (*Pol*) (= *congreso*) conference, meeting ▸ **conferencia cumbre** summit, summit conference ▸ **conferencia de desarme** disarmament conference ▸ **conferencia de prensa** press conference ▸ **conferencia de ventas** sales conference ▸ **conferencia episcopal** synod
2 (= *charla*) lecture • **dar una ~** to give a lecture
3 (*Telec*) call • **facilidad de ~ múltiple** follow-on call facility ▸ **conferencia a cobro revertido** reverse charge *o* call, collect call (*EEUU*) ▸ **conferencia de persona a persona** personal call, person-to-person call (*EEUU*) ▸ **conferencia interurbana** long-distance call
4 (*Inform*) conference, conferencing

conferenciante SMF lecturer

conferenciar ▹ CONJUG 1b VI to confer (**con** with), be in conference (**con** with)

conferencista SMF (*LAm*) lecturer

conferir ▹ CONJUG 3i (*frm*) VT **1** [+ *premio*] to award (**a** to); [+ *honor*] to confer (**a** on), bestow (**a** on)
2 (= *proporcionar*) to lend, give • **los cuadros confieren un aire de dignidad a la sala** the paintings lend an air of dignity to the room
3 (= *cotejar*) [+ *documentos*] to compare (**con** with)

confesante SM penitent

confesar ▹ CONJUG 1j VT **1** (= *admitir*) [+ *error*] to admit, acknowledge; [+ *crimen*] to confess to, own up to
2 (*Rel*) [+ *pecados*] to confess; [*sacerdote*] to confess, hear the confession of
VI (= *admitir*) to confess, own up
• MODISMO: • **~ de plano** to own up
VPR **confesarse** (*Rel*) to confess, make one's confession • **me confesé de mis pecados** I confessed my sins • **ayer me confesé** I made my confession yesterday
• MODISMO: • **¡que Dios nos coja confesados!** God help us!, Lord have mercy!

confesión SF confession

confesional ADJ **1** (= *religioso*) confessional, denominational
2 (*de la confesión*) confessional • **secreto ~** secrecy of confession

confesionario SM, **confesonario** SM confessional (box)

confeso/a ADJ **1** (*Jur*) self-confessed
2 (*Hist*) (= *judío*) converted
SMF (*Hist*) converted Jew
SM (*Rel*) lay brother

confesor SM confessor

confeti SM confetti

confiabilidad SF reliability, trustworthiness

confiable ADJ reliable, trustworthy

confiadamente ADV **1** (= *con seguridad*) confidently
2 (= *ingenuamente*) trustingly

confiado ADJ **1** (= *seguro*) confident • **está muy ~** he's very confident • **se presentó muy ~ ante el juez** he seemed very confident when he appeared before the judge • **~ en algo** confident of sth • **se mostró ~ en que obtendría el puesto** he seemed confident that he would obtain the post • **~ en sí mismo** self-confident
2 (= *ingenuo*) trusting
3 (= *vanidoso*) vain, conceited

confianza SF **1** (= *credibilidad*) confidence • **ese abogado tuyo no me inspira ~** that lawyer of yours doesn't exactly fill me with confidence • **en un clima de ~** in an atmosphere of trust • **de ~** [*producto*] reliable • **una persona de ~** (= *competente*) a reliable person; (= *honrada*) a trustworthy person • **hable con alguien de su ~** speak to someone you trust • **un producto de mi entera ~** a product I have complete faith *o* confidence in • **defraudar la ~ de algn** to let sb down • **ganarse la ~ de algn** to win sb's confidence • **dar *o* conceder un margen de ~ a algn** to place one's trust in sb • **perder la ~ en algo/algn** to lose faith in sth/sb • **perder la ~ de algn** to lose sb's confidence • **poner su ~ en algn** to put *o* place one's trust in sb • **preso de ~** trusty • **puesto de ~** position of responsibility • **recuperar la ~ de *o* en algo** to regain one's faith *o* confidence in sth • **tener ~ en algn** to have faith *o* confidence in sb ▸ **confianza ciudadana** public confidence ▸ **confianza mutua** mutual trust; ▹ **hombre, moción**
2 (= *seguridad*) confidence • **dar ~ a algn** to give sb confidence, make sb confident • **ya no le duele el pie y eso le da más ~ al andar** her foot no longer hurts so she's more confident walking • **infundir ~ a algn** to inspire confidence in sb • **tener ~ en algo** to be confident of sth • **tienen plena ~ en su victoria** they are fully confident of victory • **tener ~ en que ...** to be confident that ... ▸ **confianza en sí mismo** self-confidence • **necesitas tener más ~ en ti mismo** you need to have more confidence in yourself, you need more self-confidence
3 (= *amistad*) • **no te preocupes porque estemos nosotros delante, que hay ~** don't

mind us, we're all friends here • **entre amigos debe haber ~** friends should trust each other • **con ~**: • **te lo digo con toda ~** I'm being completely open with you • **podéis tratarme con toda ~** you can treat me as one of yourselves • **de ~**: • **puedes hablar delante de él, es de ~** you can speak freely in front of him, he's a friend • **un amigo de ~** a close friend, an intimate friend • **en ~**: • **(dicho sea) en ~** *o* **hablando en ~, no me fío nada de él** between you and me, I don't trust him at all • **aquí estamos en ~** we're all friends here • **tener ~ con algn** to be on close terms with sb • **díselo tú, que tienes más ~ con ella** you tell her, you're closer to her
4 confianzas (= *libertades*) • **se toma demasiadas ~s contigo** he takes too many liberties with you, he's a bit too familiar with you • **detesto las ~s con los criados** I hate it when people are too familiar with their servants • **¿qué ~s son esas?** don't be so familiar!

confianzudo (ADJ) **1** (= *demasiado familiar*) overfamiliar, fresh
2 (*LAm*) (= *entrometido*) meddlesome

confiar ▹ CONJUG 1c (VT) • **~ algo a algn** [+ *misión, tarea, cuidado, educación*] to entrust sb with; [+ *secreto, preocupaciones*] to confide to sb; [+ *voto*] to give sb • **le ~on una misión imposible** they entrusted him with an impossible mission • **la aplicación del acuerdo se ~á a la ONU** the UN will be entrusted with *o* will be responsible for implementing the agreement • **les ~on la gestión de la publicidad** they were put in charge of publicity • **confíenos sus ahorros** trust your savings to us • **confió a sus hijos al cuidado de sus abuelos** he left his children in the care of their grandparents • **le confié por qué no había ido aquella noche** I confided to him why I hadn't gone that night • **~ algo al azar** to leave sth to fate
(VI) • **~ en algn/algo** to trust sb/sth • **confío en ti** I trust you • **confiemos en Dios** let us trust in God • **no deberías ~ en su palabra** you shouldn't trust his word *o* what he says • **confío plenamente en la justicia** I have complete faith *o* confidence in justice • **confían en él para que resuelva el problema** they trust him to solve the problem • **~ en hacer algo**: • **confiamos en poder ganar la partida** we are confident that we can win the game, we are confident of winning the game • **~ en que** to hope that • **confiemos en que todo salga bien** let's hope that everything goes well • **confío en que podáis echarme una mano** I trust that you can give me a hand • **confían en que este libro sea un gran éxito** they are confident this book will be a success
(VPR) **confiarse 1** (*con excesiva seguridad*) • **no te confíes, te queda mucho por estudiar** you shouldn't be so over-confident *o* sure of yourself, you still have a lot more to study
2 (= *sincerarse*) • **~se a algn** to confide in sb
3 (= *entregarse*) • **~se a algo** to entrust o.s. to sth

confidencia (SF) (= *secreto*) confidence, secret; (*a policía*) tip-off • **hacer ~s a algn** to confide in sb, tell sb secrets

confidencial (ADJ) confidential

confidencialidad (SF) confidentiality • **en la más estricta ~** in the strictest confidence

confidencialmente (ADV) confidentially

confidente/a (SM/F) **1** (= *amigo*) confidant/confidante, intimate friend
2 (*Jur*) informer; (= *agente secreto*) secret agent ▸ **confidente policial** police informer

configurabilidad (SF) configurability

configuración (SF) **1** (*gen*) shape, configuration • **la ~ del terreno** the lie of the land • **la ~ del futuro** the shape of things to come
2 (*Inform*) configuration ▸ **configuración de bits** bit configuration

configurar ▹ CONJUG 1a (VT) to shape, form

confín (SM) **1** (= *límite*) boundary
2 (= *horizonte*) horizon
3 confines [*de la tierra, atmósfera*] confines, limits; (= *parte exterior*) remote parts, outermost parts, edges

confinación (SF), **confinamiento** (SM) confinement

confinar ▹ CONJUG 1a (VT) (*Jur*) to confine (**a, en** in); (*Pol*) to banish, exile (**a** to)
(VI) (= *limitar*) • **~ con** to border on (*tb fig*)
(VPR) **confinarse** (= *encerrarse*) to shut o.s. away

confirmación (SF) confirmation (*tb Rel*)

confirmado (ADJ) [*reserva*] confirmed

confirmar ▹ CONJUG 1a (VT) **1** [+ *noticia, rumor, temor*] to confirm • **esto confirma mis peores sospechas** this confirms my worst suspicions • **según ~on fuentes policiales** as police sources confirmed, according to police sources • REFRÁN: • **la excepción confirma la regla** the exception proves the rule
2 [+ *vuelo, cita*] to confirm • **el presidente confirmó su asistencia a la reunión** the president confirmed that he would be attending the meeting
3 (= *reafirmar*) [+ *sentencia*] to confirm • **esta victoria le confirma como el mejor atleta mundial** this win confirms him as the best athlete in the world • **esto me confirma más en mi postura** this makes me more convinced that I'm right
4 (*Rel*) to confirm
(VPR) **confirmarse 1** (*Rel*) to be confirmed
2 (= *reafirmarse*) • **me confirmo en la creencia de que es culpable** I stand by my belief that he is guilty

confirmatorio (ADJ) confirmatory

confiscación (SF) confiscation

confiscado (ADJ) confiscated

confiscar ▹ CONJUG 1g (VT) to confiscate

confisgado (ADJ) (*CAm*) mischievous, naughty

confitado (ADJ) • **fruta confitada** crystallized fruit

confitar ▹ CONJUG 1a (VT) **1** (= *conservar*) (*en almíbar*) to preserve (in syrup); (*con azúcar*) to candy
2 (= *endulzar*) (*tb fig*) to sweeten

confite (SM) sweet, candy (EEUU)

confitería (SF) **1** (= *arte*) confectionery
2 (= *tienda*) confectioner's (*frm*), sweet shop, candy store (EEUU); (*And, Cono Sur*) (= *cafetería*) café and cake shop

confitero/a (SM/F) confectioner

confitura (SF) (= *mermelada*) preserve, jam; (= *fruta escarchada*) crystallized fruit

conflagración (SF) **1** (= *perturbación*) flare-up, outbreak ▸ **conflagración bélica** outbreak of war
2 (= *incendio*) conflagration

conflictividad (SF) **1** (= *tensiones*) tensions and disputes (*pl*) • **la ~ laboral** industrial disputes, labour *o* (EEUU) labor troubles ▸ **conflictividad social** social unrest
2 (= *cualidad*) controversial nature

conflictivo (ADJ) [*sociedad*] troubled; [*asunto*] controversial; [*sistema*] unstable; [*situación*] tense, troubled • **la edad conflictiva** the age of conflict • **punto ~** point at issue • **zona conflictiva** troubled region, trouble spot

conflicto (SM) **1** (= *enfrentamiento*) conflict • **esto provocó un ~ entre China y Taiwán** this caused a conflict between China and Taiwan • **el ~ vasco** the Basque conflict • **estar en ~** to be in conflict • **los intereses de las dos empresas están en ~** the interests of the two companies are in conflict • **sus ideas y las mías están en ~** we have conflicting ideas • **los agricultores españoles están en ~ con los franceses** Spanish farmers are in dispute with the French • **las partes en ~** (*Pol*) the warring parties *o* factions; (*Jur*) the parties in dispute • **entrar en ~ con algo/algn** to come into conflict with sth/sb ▸ **conflicto armado** armed conflict ▸ **conflicto bélico** military conflict ▸ **conflicto de intereses** conflict of interests, clash of interests ▸ **conflicto generacional** generation gap ▸ **conflicto laboral** labour dispute, labor dispute (EEUU)
2 (= *dilema*) dilemma
3 (*Psic*) conflict

conflictual (ADJ) = conflictivo

confluencia (SF) confluence

confluente (ADJ) confluent
(SM) confluence

confluir ▹ CONJUG 3g (VI) **1** [*ríos*] to meet, come together
2 [*gente*] to gather

conformación (SF) **1** (= *forma*) structure, configuration
2 (= *constitución*) • **la ~ de la plantilla** the line-up of the team

conformado (ADJ) **1** (= *formado*) • **los asientos son firmes y bien ~s** the seats are firm and well-shaped
2 (= *resignado*) resigned
(SM) (*Téc*) moulding, molding (EEUU), shaping

conformar ▹ CONJUG 1a (VT) **1** (= *dar forma a*) [+ *proyecto, educación, escultura*] to shape • **¿tiene conformado ya su equipo?** has he chosen his team yet?
2 (= *constituir*) to make up • **seis de los ocho cuentos que conforman este libro** six of the eight stories that make up this book • **un universo conformado por millones de estrellas** a universe composed of *o* made up of millions of stars • **una exposición conformada por 25 esculturas** an exhibition composed of *o* made up of 25 sculptures
3 (= *adaptar*) • **trataba de ~ su vida a ese ideal** he tried to make his life conform to that ideal, he tried to shape his life around that ideal • **el pueblo no debe ~ su voluntad a la de sus gobernantes** the people's will should not be subject to that of their governors
4 (= *contentar*) [+ *persona*] to keep happy • **lo conforma con regalos** she keeps him happy with presents • **no me vas a ~ dándome dinero** you won't keep me quiet by giving me money
5 [+ *cheque, talón*] to authorize, endorse
6 [+ *enemigos*] to reconcile
(VI) • **~ con algn** to agree with sb
(VPR) **conformarse 1** (= *estar satisfecho*) • **~se con algo** to be happy with sth • **yo me conformo con cualquier cosa para cenar** I'm happy to have anything for dinner • **yo me conformo con lo que tengo** I'm happy *o* satisfied with what I have • **no se conforma con nada** he's never happy *o* satisfied • **tuvo que ~se con la medalla de plata** she had to settle for the silver medal, she had to be satisfied with the silver medal • **de momento me conformo con no perder dinero** at the moment I'm just happy not to be making a loss • **el hombre ya no se conforma con transformar la naturaleza** Man is no longer content *o* satisfied with transforming nature • **no hay que ~se con**

pensar, hay que actuar thinking is not enough, we have to act
2 (= *corresponderse*) • **~se con** [+ *reglas, política*] to comply with • **eso no se conforma con nuestra política de pagos** that does not comply with our pay policy • **no parece ~se con el original** it doesn't seem to correspond to the original
3 (= *tomar la forma*) • **~se como** to take the form of • **la representación se conforma como un viaje existencial** the performance takes the form of an existential journey

conforme (ADJ) **1** (= *satisfecho*) • **¿conforme?** (are we) agreed? • **¡conforme!** agreed!, all right! • **he revisado el contrato, está todo ~** I've gone over the contract, everything is in order • **estar ~ con algo/algn** to be happy *o* satisfied with sth/sb • **no está ~ con el precio** he's not happy *o* satisfied with the price • **estar ~ en que** to agree that • **todos se mostraron ~s en que había que buscar otra solución** everyone agreed *o* was agreed that another solution had to be found • **todos están ~s en apoyar esta propuesta** everyone agrees *o* is agreed that we should support this proposal • **quedarse ~**: • **no se quedó ~ con la propina** he wasn't happy *o* satisfied with the tip • **parece que ha quedado algo más ~ después de la explicación** he seems a little happier after that explanation
2 • **~ con** (= *correspondiente a*) consistent with • **el resultado ha estado ~ con nuestras esperanzas** the result is consistent with our expectations
3 • **~ a** (= *según*) according to • **serán juzgados ~ a las leyes libanesas** they will be tried under Lebanese law, they will be tried according to Lebanese law • **todo marcha ~ a lo previsto** everything is going according to plan • **actuaron ~ a las instrucciones que les dieron** they acted in accordance with the instructions they received, they acted according to instructions; ▸ **derecho**
(CONJ) **1** (= *como*) as • **lo hice ~ me dijiste** I did it as you told me to • **todo quedó ~ estaba** everything remained as it was
2 (= *a medida que*) as • **~ entraban, se iban sentando** as they came in, they sat down • **~ avanza el verano aumenta el calor** as summer progresses, the heat increases • **~ subes la calle, a mano derecha** on the right as you go up the street
(SM) (= *aprobación*) approval, authorization • **dar** *o* **poner el ~** to authorize • **el juez dio su ~ a la liberación del prisionero** the judge authorized the prisoner's release • **necesito que me des tu ~ a esta factura** I need you to approve *o* authorize payment of this invoice

conformidad (SF) **1** (= *acuerdo*) agreement • **no hubo ~ con respecto a ese tema** there was no agreement on this subject
2 (= *consentimiento*) consent • **dar su ~ a algo** to give one's consent to sth • **hasta que no dé su ~** until he gives his consent
3 (*frm*) (= *resignación*) resignation, forbearance • **soportar algo con ~** to put up with sth with resignation • REFRÁN: • **el tiempo da la ~** time heals all wounds, time is a great healer
4 • **de** *o* **en ~ con algo** (*frm*) in accordance with sth (*frm*)

conformismo (SM) conformism, conventionality

conformista (ADJ), (SMF) conformist

confort [kon'for(t)] (SM) (PL: **conforts** [kon'for(t)]) **1** (= *comodidad*) comfort • **"todo confort"** "all mod cons"
2 (*Cono Sur*) (*euf*) (= *papel higiénico*) toilet paper

confortabilidad (SF) comfort

confortable (ADJ) comfortable
(SM) (*And*) sofa

confortablemente (ADV) comfortably

confortante (ADJ) **1** (= *consolador*) comforting
2 (*Med*) soothing

confortar ▸ CONJUG 1a (VT) **1** (= *consolar*) to comfort
2 (*Med*) to soothe

confortativo (ADJ) **1** (= *consolador*) comforting, consoling
2 (*Med*) soothing
(SM) **1** (= *consuelo*) comfort, consolation
2 (*Med*) tonic, restorative

confraternidad (SF) fraternity, brotherhood

confraternización (SF) fraternization

confraternizar ▸ CONJUG 1f (VI) to fraternize (**con** with)

confrontación (SF) **1** (= *enfrentamiento*) confrontation ▸ **confrontación nuclear** nuclear confrontation
2 (*Literat*) comparison

confrontar ▸ CONJUG 1a (VT) **1** [+ *peligro*] to confront, face, face up to
2 (= *carear*) to bring face to face • **~ a algn con otro** to confront sb with sb else
3 [+ *textos*] to compare, collate
(VI) to border (**con** on)
(VPR) **confrontarse** • **~se con** to confront, face up to

Confucio (SM) Confucius

confundible (ADJ) • **fácilmente ~ con** easily mistaken for, easily confused with

confundido (ADJ) **1** (= *equivocado*) • **puede que esté ~, pero creo que te he visto antes** I could be mistaken *o* wrong, but I think I've seen you before
2 (= *confuso*) confused • **se quedó confundida después de tantas preguntas** she was confused after so many questions • **—algo falla aquí, dijeron ~s** "there's something wrong here," they said in some confusion

confundir ▸ CONJUG 3a (VT) **1** (= *equivocar*) to confuse • **en este planteamiento se están confundiendo causa y efecto** this approach confuses cause and effect • **no confundamos las cosas, por favor** let's not confuse things, please • **siempre os confundo por teléfono** I always get you mixed up on the phone • **confundimos el camino** we went the wrong way • **~ algo/a algn con algo/algn** to get sth/sb mixed up with sth/sb, mistake sth/sb for sth/sb • **la confundí con su hermana gemela** I got her mixed up with her twin sister, I mistook her for her twin sister • **no se debe ~ a Richard Strauss con Johann Strauss** Richard Strauss should not be confused with Johann Strauss • **su sabor no se puede ~ con nada** its taste is unmistakable; ▸ **culo, velocidad**
2 (= *mezclar*) [+ *papeles*] to mix up • **me confundieron todas las facturas** they mixed up all the bills
3 (= *desconcertar*) to confuse • **sus palabras nos confundieron a todos** we were all confused by what he said • **técnicas para ~ al adversario** techniques for confusing your opponent • **me confunde con tanta palabrería** he confuses me *o* gets me confused with all that talk of his, I find all that talk of his confusing
4 (= *turbar*) to overwhelm • **me confundía con tantas atenciones** her kindness was overwhelming, I was overwhelmed by all her kindness
(VPR) **confundirse 1** (= *equivocarse*) to make a mistake • **me he confundido al mandar el mensaje** I made a mistake when I sent the message • **~se de**: • **lo siento, se ha confundido de número** I'm sorry, you have the wrong number • **~se en**: • **se confundió en un cero al hacer la multiplicación** he got a zero wrong *o* he made a mistake over a zero when doing the multiplication • **para no ~me en la espesa niebla** so as not to lose my way *o* get lost in the thick fog • **es bastante normal ~se en los aparcamientos** it's quite easy to get mixed up in car parks
2 (= *mezclarse*) • **realidad y fantasía se confunden en la mente del protagonista** reality and fantasy become confused in the mind of the main character • **~se con algo**: • **el mar se confundía con el cielo** the sea blended with the sky • **los policías se confundían con los manifestantes** the police mingled with the demonstrators • **se confundió con la multitud** he disappeared into the crowd

confusamente (ADV) • **hablaba ~** his speech was muddled *o* confused • **lo recuerdo ~** I have a vague *o* hazy memory of it

confusión (SF) **1** (= *equivocación*) confusion • **lo que provocó la ~** what caused the confusion • **para evitar confusiones** to avoid confusion • **ha habido una ~ en los nombres** there was a mix-up with the names, there was some confusion with the names • **esta carta no es para mí, debe de tratarse de una ~** this letter is not for me, there must be some mistake • **por ~** by mistake
2 (= *desconcierto*) confusion • **el terremoto produjo una gran ~ en las calles** the earthquake caused great confusion in the streets • **tiene una gran ~ de ideas** his ideas are very confused • **la recuerdo con bastante ~** I have a hazy *o* vague memory of her
3 (= *turbación*) • **sentí tal ~ que no pude ni dar las gracias** I was so overwhelmed that I couldn't even say thank you • **tantas alabanzas me produjeron una gran ~** I found all that praise overwhelming

confusional (ADJ) • **estado ~** confused state, state of confusion

confusionismo (SM) confusion, uncertainty • **sembrar el ~ y desconcierto** to spread alarm and despondency

confusionista (ADJ) muddle-headed
(SMF) muddle-headed person

confuso (ADJ) **1** (= *poco claro*) [*ideas, noticias*] confused; [*recuerdo*] hazy; [*ruido*] indistinct; [*imagen*] blurred • **tiene las ideas muy confusas** he has very confused ideas, his ideas are very mixed up • **llegaban noticias confusas** confused reports were coming in • **una situación muy confusa** a very confused situation
2 (= *desconcertado*) confused • **nunca lo había visto tan ~** I had never seen him so confused • **no sé qué decir, estoy ~** I don't know what to say, I'm overwhelmed

confutar ▸ CONJUG 1a (VT) to confute

conga (SF) conga

congal (SM) (*Méx*) brothel

congelación (SF) **1** [*de alimentos, líquidos*] freezing
2 (*Med*) frostbite
3 (*Econ*) freeze, freezing ▸ **congelación de créditos** credit freeze ▸ **congelación de salarios** wage freeze
4 ▸ **congelación de imagen** [*de vídeo*] freeze-frame

congelado (ADJ) **1** [*carne*] frozen, chilled; [*grasa*] congealed • **¡estoy ~!** I'm frozen *o* freezing!
2 (*Med*) frostbitten
3 (*Econ*) frozen, blocked

congelador (SM) **1** (= *electrodoméstico*) freezer, deep freeze ▸ **congelador horizontal** chest freezer ▸ **congelador vertical** cabinet freezer
2 (*Náut*) frozen-food vessel

C

congeladora SF deep freeze, freezer
congelar ▷ CONJUG 1a VT **1** [+ *carne, agua*] to freeze; [+ *sangre, grasa*] to congeal
2 (*Med*) to affect with frostbite
3 (*Econ*) to freeze, block; [+ *proceso*] to suspend, freeze
4 [+ *imagen de vídeo*] to freeze
VPR **congelarse 1** [*carne, agua*] to freeze; [*sangre, grasa*] to congeal
2 (*Med*) to get frostbitten
congénere SM fellow, person *etc* of the same sort • **el criminal y sus ~s** the criminal and others like him
congeniar ▷ CONJUG 1b VI to get on (**con** with) • **congeniamos con los dos hermanos** we hit it off with the two brothers
congenital ADJ (*LAm*) = **congénito**
congénitamente ADV congenitally
congénito ADJ congenital
congestión SF congestion
congestionado ADJ **1** [*circulación*] congested
2 (*Med*) [*pecho, pulmones, nariz*] congested • **tener el pecho ~** to be chesty
3 [*rostro*] flushed, red
congestionamiento SM (*Caribe*) traffic jam
congestionar ▷ CONJUG 1a VT to congest, produce congestion in
VPR **congestionarse** to become congested • **se le congestionó la cara** his face became flushed *o* turned read
congestivo ADJ (*Med*) congestive
conglomeración SF conglomeration
conglomerado SM **1** (*Geol, Téc*) conglomerate
2 (= *aglomeración*) conglomeration
conglomerar ▷ CONJUG 1a VT, VPR **conglomerarse** to conglomerate
Congo SM • **el ~** the Congo • MODISMO: • **¡vete al ~!**‡ get lost!‡
congo/a SM/F (*LAm*) black man/woman, black person
congoja SF anguish, distress
congola SF (*And*) pipe
congoleño/a ADJ, SM/F Congolese
congolés/esa ADJ, SM/F = **congoleño**
congosto SM narrow pass, canyon
congraciador ADJ ingratiating
congraciamiento SM ingratiation
congraciante ADJ ingratiating
congraciar ▷ CONJUG 1b VT to win over
VPR **congraciarse** to ingratiate o.s. (**con** with)
congratulación SF congratulation • **congratulaciones** congratulations
congratular ▷ CONJUG 1a VT to congratulate (**por** on)
VPR **congratularse** to congratulate o.s., be pleased • **de eso nos congratulamos** we are glad about that
congregación SF **1** (= *asamblea*) gathering, assembly; (= *sociedad*) brotherhood, guild
2 (*Rel*) congregation • **la ~ de los fieles** the (Catholic) Church
congregacionalista ADJ congregational
SMF congregationalist
congregar ▷ CONJUG 1h VT to bring together
VPR **congregarse** to gather, congregate
congresal SMF (*LAm*) = **congresista**
congresional ADJ congressional
congresista SMF delegate, member (*of a congress*); (*en EEUU*) member of Congress
congreso SM **1** [*de científicos, profesionales, políticos*] conference • **un ~ médico** a medical conference; ▸ **congreso anual** annual conference; ▷ **palacio**
2 (*Pol*) • **Congreso** (*en Reino Unido*) ≈ Parliament; (*en EEUU*) ≈ Congress
▸ **Congreso de los Diputados** (*Esp*) (*Pol*) ≈ House of Commons, ≈ House of Representatives (*EEUU*)

CONGRESO DE LOS DIPUTADOS
The **Congreso de los Diputados**, the lower house in the Spanish Parliament, has 350 seats. Members (**diputados**) are elected by proportional representation for a maximum term of four years. The house itself chooses the prime minister (**Presidente del Gobierno**) by majority vote and he/she is invited in turn by the King to form the government.
▷ CORTES GENERALES, SENADO

congresual ADJ parliamentary, congressional
congrio SM conger, conger eel
congruencia SF **1** (*Mat*) congruence
2 (= *coherencia*) suitability
congruente ADJ, **congruo** ADJ **1** (*Mat*) congruent, congruous (**con** with)
2 (= *coherente*) suitable
cónico ADJ [*forma*] conical; [*sección*] conic
conífera SF conifer
conífero ADJ coniferous
conimbricense ADJ of/from Coimbra
SMF native/inhabitant of Coimbra
conjetura SF conjecture, surmise • **por ~** by guesswork • **son meras ~s** it's just guesswork
conjeturable ADJ that can be guessed at • **es ~ que ...** one may conjecture that ...
conjetural ADJ conjectural
conjeturar ▷ CONJUG 1a VT to guess, guess at, surmise (**de, por** from, **que** that)
conjugación SF conjugation
conjugado ADJ (*Ling*) finite
conjugar ▷ CONJUG 1h VT **1** (*Ling*) to conjugate
2 (= *reunir*) to combine • **es difícil ~ los deseos de los dos** it is difficult to please them both • **la obra conjuga cualidades y defectos** the work has both good qualities and defects
VPR **conjugarse 1** (*Ling*) to be conjugated
2 (= *unirse*) to fit together, blend
conjunción SF conjunction
conjuntado ADJ **1** (= *coordinado*) coordinated
2 (= *unido*) united, combined
conjuntamente ADV jointly, together • **~ con** together with
conjuntar ▷ CONJUG 1a VT **1** (= *coordinar*) to coordinate
2 (= *unir*) to unite, combine
VI • **~ con** to go with, match
conjuntero/a* SM/F band member
conjuntivitis SF INV conjunctivitis
conjuntivo ADJ conjunctive
conjunto ADJ joint, combined • **operaciones conjuntas** (*Mil*) combined operations
SM **1** (= *totalidad*) whole • **formar un ~** to form a whole • **impresión de ~** overall impression • **vista de ~** all-embracing view • **en ~** as a whole, altogether • **hay que estudiar esos países en ~** you have to study these countries as a whole • **en su ~** in its entirety ▸ **conjunto monumental** *collection of historic buildings*
2 (= *ropa*) ensemble • **un ~ de falda y blusa** a matching skirt and blouse
3 (*Mús*) [*de cámara*] ensemble; (*pop*) group • **un ~ de música pop** a pop group
4 (*Teat*) chorus • **chica de ~** chorus girl
5 (*Dep*) (= *equipo*) team
6 [*de muebles*] suite ▸ **conjunto de baño** bathroom suite
7 (*Mat, Inform*) set ▸ **conjunto integrado de programas** integrated software suite
8 (*Mec*) unit, assembly
conjura SF, **conjuración** SF plot, conspiracy
conjurado/a SM/F plotter, conspirator
conjurar ▷ CONJUG 1a VT **1** (*Rel*) to exorcise, cast out
2 [+ *peligro*] to ward off; [+ *pensamiento*] to rid o.s. of
3 (= *rogar*) to entreat (*frm*), plead with
VI • **~ contra algn** to plot *o* conspire against sb
VPR **conjurarse** to get together in a plot, plot together, conspire together
conjuro SM **1** (*Rel*) exorcism; (= *hechizo*) spell • **al ~ de sus palabras** under the spell of his words
2 (= *ruego*) entreaty (*frm*), plea
conllevar ▷ CONJUG 1a VT **1** [+ *sentido*] to convey, carry
2 (= *implicar*) to imply, involve
3 (= *aguantar*) to bear, put up with • **~ las penas de otro** to take sb else's troubles on one's shoulders
conmemoración SF commemoration
conmemorar ▷ CONJUG 1a VT to commemorate
conmemorativo ADJ commemorative
conmigo PRON with me • **¿por qué no vienes ~?** why don't you come with me? • **se portó muy bien ~** he was very good to me • **atento ~** kind to *o* towards me • **no estoy satisfecho ~ mismo** I'm not proud of myself
conmilitón SM fellow soldier
conminación SF **1** (= *amenaza*) threat
2 (*Méx*) (*Jur*) judgement
conminar ▷ CONJUG 1a VT **1** (= *amenazar*) to threaten (**con** with)
2 (= *avisar*) to warn officially
3 (*Méx*) (= *desafiar*) to challenge
conminatorio ADJ threatening, warning
conmiseración SF sympathy, commiseration
conmoción SF **1** (*Geol*) shock, tremor
2 (*Med*) ▸ **conmoción cerebral** concussion
3 (= *perturbación*) shock • **producir una ~ desagradable a algn** to give sb a nasty shock
4 (*Pol*) disturbance • **una ~ social** a social upheaval
conmocionado ADJ (*Med*) shocked, concussed
conmocionar ▷ CONJUG 1a VT **1** (= *conmover*) to move, affect deeply
2 (= *turbar*) to shake profoundly, cause an upheaval in
3 (*Med*) to put into shock, concuss
conmovedor ADJ moving, touching, poignant
conmovedoramente ADV touchingly, movingly
conmover ▷ CONJUG 2h VT **1** (*Geol*) to shake
2 (= *enternecer*) to move, touch
3 (= *turbar*) to upset
VPR **conmoverse 1** (*Geol*) to shake, be shaken
2 (= *enternecerse*) to be moved *o* be touched
conmuta SF (*And, Cono Sur*) change, alteration
conmutable ADJ commutable
conmutación SF **1** [*de pago, pena*] commutation
2 (*Inform*) switching ▸ **conmutación de mensajes** message switching ▸ **conmutación de paquetes** packet switching
conmutador SM **1** (*Elec*) switch
2 (*LAm*) (*Telec*) (= *centralita*) switchboard
conmutar ▷ CONJUG 1a VT **1** (= *trocar*) to exchange (**con, por** for); (= *transformar*) to convert (**en** into)

2 (*Jur*) to commute (**en, por** to)

connatural ADJ innate, inherent (**a** in)

connaturalizarse ▷ CONJUG 1f VPR to become accustomed (**con** to), to become acclimatized, become acclimated (*EEUU*) (**con** to)

connivencia SF connivance • **estar en ~ con** to be in collusion with

connivente ADJ • **ser ~ con algo** to collude *o* be collusive with sth

connotación SF **1** (= *sentido*) connotation
2 (= *parentesco*) distant relationship

connotado ADJ (*LAm*) (= *famoso*) famous, renowned; (= *destacado*) outstanding

connotar ▷ CONJUG 1a VT to connote

cono SM cone

conocedor(a) ADJ expert (**de** in), knowledgeable (**de** about) • **muy ~ de** very knowledgeable about
SM/F expert (**de** in), connoisseur (**de** of) • **es buen ~ de ganado** he's a good judge of cattle

conocencia SF (*esp LAm*) girlfriend, sweetheart

conocer ▷ CONJUG 2d VT **1** [+ *persona*] **a** (= *saber quién es*) to know • **conozco a todos sus hermanos** I know all his brothers and sisters • **¿de qué lo conoces?** where do you know him from? • **la conozco de haber trabajado juntos** I know her from having worked with her • **¿conoces a Pedro?** have you met Pedro?, do you know Pedro? • **no me conoce de nada** he doesn't know me from Adam • **la conozco de oídas** I've heard of her, I know of her • **lo conozco de vista** I know him by sight
b (= *ver por primera vez*) to meet • **la conocí en Sevilla** I met her in Seville
c (= *saber cómo es*) to get to know • **cuando la conozcas mejor** when you get to know her better • **la única forma de ~lo es vivir con él** the only way to get to know him is to live with him • MODISMOS: • **la conozco como la palma de la mano** I know her like the back of my hand • **la conozco como si la hubiera parido** I know her inside out, I can read her like a book
d (= *reconocer*) to recognize, know • **te he conocido por el modo de andar** I recognized *o* knew you from the way you walk
2 (= *tener conocimiento de*) [+ *método, resultado*] to know; [+ *noticia*] to hear • **conozco un camino más corto** I know a shorter way • **ella conoce una forma más fácil de hacerlo** she knows an easier way to do it • **el enfermo debe ~ la verdad** the patient must be told *o* must know the truth • **conozco las dificultades** I know (about) the difficulties • **no conocía tus dotes de pintor** I didn't know what a good painter you were • **conocía la existencia de los documentos** she knew of the documents' existence • **queremos ~ de cerca la situación** we want to get to know the situation at first hand • **investigaciones destinadas a ~ la verdad** investigations aimed at establishing the truth • REFRÁN: • **más vale lo malo conocido que lo bueno por ~** better the devil you know than the devil you don't
3 [+ *país, ciudad*] • **me encantaría ~ China** I would love to go to China • **no conozco Buenos Aires** I've never been to Buenos Aires, I don't know Buenos Aires • **quiero ~ mundo** I want to see the world
4 (= *dominar*) to know • **conoce su oficio** he knows his job • **no conozco mucho el tema** I don't know much about the subject • **conoce cuatro idiomas** she speaks *o* knows four languages
5 (= *experimentar*) • **ha conocido dos guerras mundiales** she has lived through two world wars • **los muchos terremotos que ha conocido Italia** the many earthquakes there have been in Italy • **todavía no ha conocido el amor** he's never known love
6 (= *distinguir*) to know, tell • **conoce cuáles son buenos y cuáles malos** he knows *o* can tell which are good and which are bad • **por tu cara se te conoce que estás sano** you can tell from your face that you are healthy
7 • **dar a ~** [+ *información*] to announce; [+ *declaración, informe, cifras*] to release • **dio a ~ sus intenciones** she announced her intentions, she made her intentions known • **dieron a ~ el ganador del premio a través de la radio** the prize was announced on the radio • **no dieron a ~ su paradero por motivos de seguridad** they didn't reveal where they were staying for security reasons • **los hechos se dieron a ~ en enero** the facts came to light in January • **darse a ~** [*persona*] to become known, make a name for o.s. • **se dio a ~ en una película de Almodóvar** he made his name in an Almodóvar film • **darse a ~ a algn** to make o. s. known to sb
8 (*Jur*) [+ *causa*] to try
VI **1** (= *saber*) • **~ de algo**: • **¿alguien conoce de algún libro sobre el tema?** does anybody know (of) a book on the subject?
2 (*Jur*) • **~ de** *o* **en una causa** to try a case
VPR **conocerse 1** (*uso reflexivo*) • **~se a sí mismo** to know o.s.
2 (*uso recíproco*) **a** (= *tener relación con*) to know each other, know one another • **¿os conocéis?** have you met?, do you know each other? • **ya nos conocemos, no hace falta que nos presentes** we've already met, there's no need to introduce us
b (*por primera vez*) to meet • **¿dónde os conocisteis?** where did you (first) meet? • **se conocieron en un baile** they met at a dance
c (= *familiarizarse*) to get to know each other, get to know one another • **Juan y yo nunca llegamos a ~nos bien** Juan and I never really got to know each other
3 (= *reconocerse*) [*uno mismo*] to recognize o.s.; [*dos personas*] to recognize each other • **no me conocía en la foto** I didn't recognize myself in the photo • **se miraron pero no se conocieron** they looked at each other but didn't recognize each other
4 (= *saber*) to know • **me lo conozco de memoria** I know it off by heart
5 (*uso impersonal*) • **se conocen varios casos** several cases are known • **se conocen con el nombre de composites** they are known as composites • **a esta enfermedad no se le conoce cura** this illness has no known cure • **no se le conoce ninguna novia** he doesn't have a girlfriend as far as anyone knows • **se conoce que ...** apparently ..., it seems that ... • **se conoce que se lo han contado** apparently he's been told about it, it seems that he's been told about it • **se conoce que no le ha sentado bien** he's obviously not best pleased

conocible ADJ knowable

conocido/a ADJ **1** (= *público*) [*dato*] known; [*persona*] well-known • **un médico ~** a well-known doctor • **un hecho conocidísimo** a very well-known fact • **más ~ por Michel** better known as Michel
2 (= *familiar*) familiar • **su cara me es conocida** I recognize his face, his face is familiar
SM/F acquaintance

conocimiento SM **1** (= *saber*) knowledge • **un ~ profundo del tema** a thorough knowledge of the subject • **conocimientos** (= *nociones*) knowledge (*sing*) • **tengo algunos ~s musicales** I have some knowledge of music • **mis pocos ~s de filosofía/cocina** my limited knowledge of philosophy/cookery • **tener ~s generales de algo** to have a general knowledge of sth
2 (= *información*) knowledge • **el encuentro tuvo lugar sin ~ público** the meeting took place without the public's knowledge • **dar ~ de algo**: • **dimos ~ del robo a la policía** we informed the police about the robbery • **llegar a ~ de algn** to come to sb's attention *o* notice • **tener ~ de algo**: • **aún no tenemos ~ de su detención** we still do not know that he has been arrested • **no tenemos ~ del accidente** we are unaware of the accident • **se les informó al tenerse ~ del suceso** they were informed as soon as it was known what had happened • **poner algo en ~ de algn** to bring sth to sb's attention • **desea ponerlo en ~ público** he wants it brought to the public's attention, he wishes it to be made public • **el Ministro ha puesto en ~ del rey su decisión** the minister has informed the king of his decision ▸ **conocimiento de causa** • **hacer algo con ~ de causa** to be fully aware of what one is doing • **hablar con ~ de causa** to know what one is talking about
3 (= *consciencia*) consciousness • **estuvo sin ~ durante unos minutos** he was unconscious for a few minutes • **perder el ~** to lose consciousness • **quedarse sin ~** to lose consciousness • **recobrar** *o* **recuperar el ~** to regain consciousness
4 (= *sentido común*) common sense • **los niños no tienen ~** children have no common sense
5 (*Jur*) cognizance (*frm*)
6 (*Com*) ▸ **conocimiento de embarque** bill of lading ▸ **conocimiento de embarque aéreo** air waybill

conorte SM (*LAm*) comfort

Cono Sur SM (*Pol*) Argentina, Chile and Uruguay, Southern Cone

conozca *etc* ▷ **conocer**

conque* CONJ so, so then • **¿~ te pillaron?** so they caught you then?
SM **1** (= *condición*) condition, reservation • **~s** ifs and buts
2* (= *dinero*) wherewithal, means

CONOCER

▷ **Conocer**, *aplicado a personas o cosas, se traduce generalmente por* **know**:

> **No conozco muy bien a su familia**
> I don't know his family very well
> **Nos conocemos desde que éramos pequeños**
> We have known each other since we were little
> **Conoce Manchester como la palma de la mano**
> He knows Manchester like the back of his hand

▷ *Sin embargo, cuando queremos indicar que se trata del primer encuentro, se debe utilizar* **meet**:

> **La conocí en una fiesta**
> I (first) met her at a party
> **¿Conoces a Carmen? Ven que te la presento**
> Have you met Carmen? Come and I'll introduce you

Para otros usos y ejemplos ver la entrada.

C

conqué* (SM) (*LAm*) = conque
conquense (ADJ) of/from Cuenca
(SMF) native/inhabitant of Cuenca • **los ~s** the people of Cuenca
conquista (SF) conquest • **ir de ~** (*fig*) to be dressed to kill
conquistador(a) (ADJ) conquering
(SM/F) conqueror
(SM) **1** (*Hist*) conquistador
2* (= *seductor*) ladykiller
conquistar ▹ CONJUG 1a (VT) **1** (*Mil*) to conquer • **los países conquistados por los romanos** the countries conquered by the Romans
2 [+ *puesto, simpatía*] to win; [+ *adversario*] to win round, win over; (= *enamorar*) to win the heart of • **la conquistó con su sonrisa** he won her over with his smile • **~ el título de campeón** to win the championship title • **los escaladores no lograron ~ la montaña** the climbers failed to conquer the mountain
consabido (ADJ) **1** (= *conocido*) well-known; [*frase*] old, oft-repeated
2 (= *susodicho*) above-mentioned
consagración (SF) **1** (*Rel*) consecration, dedication
2 [*de costumbre*] establishment
consagrado (ADJ) **1** (*Rel*) consecrated (**a** to), dedicated (**a** to)
2 (= *tradicional*) hallowed, traditional • **según la expresión consagrada** in the time-honoured *o* (*EEUU*) -honored phrase • **principios ~s en la constitución** principles enshrined in the constitution • **un actor ~** an established actor
consagrar ▹ CONJUG 1a (VT) **1** (*Rel*) to consecrate, dedicate (**a** to); [+ *emperador*] to deify
2 [+ *esfuerzo, tiempo, vida*] to devote, dedicate (**a** to); [+ *monumento, placa*] to put up (**a** to)
3 [+ *fama*] to confirm • **este triunfo lo consagra como un cirujano excepcional** this success confirms him as a really exceptional surgeon
(VPR) **consagrarse 1** (*por fama*) to establish o.s.
2 • **~se a** to devote o.s. to
consanguíneo (ADJ) related by blood, consanguineous (*frm*)
consanguinidad (SF) blood relationship, consanguinity (*frm*)
consciencia (SF) = conciencia
consciente (ADJ) **1** • **ser ~ de algo** to be conscious *o* aware of sth
2 (*Med*) • **estar ~** to be conscious
3 (*Jur*) fully responsible
4 (= *sensato*) responsible
(SM) conscious, conscious mind
conscientemente (ADV) consciously
conscripción (SF) (*esp LAm*) conscription, draft (*EEUU*)
conscripto (SM) (*esp LAm*) conscript, draftee (*EEUU*)
consecución (SF) [*de resultado, visado, beca, permiso*] obtaining; [*de meta*] attainment, achievement; [*de premio, campeonato*] winning • **les ayudó en la ~ de trabajo** he helped them find work • **para la ~ de estos objetivos** in order to attain these goals (*frm*), to achieve these goals
consecuencia (SF) **1** (= *resultado*) consequence • **esto es ~ de una mala gestión** this is the consequence *o* result of bad management • **una decisión de ~s imprevisibles** a decision with unforeseeable consequences • **a ~ de algo** as a result of sth • **falleció a ~ de las heridas** he died as a result of his injuries • **atenerse a las ~s** to take *o* accept the consequences • **hazlo, pero atente a las ~s** do it, but you'll have to take *o* accept the consequences • **como ~** as a result, in consequence (*frm*) • **como ~, está al borde de la bancarrota** as a result *o* in consequence he is on the verge of bankruptcy • **ha muerto como ~ del frío** it died from *o* as a result of the cold • **esto tuvo** *o* **trajo como ~ el aumento del paro** this led to *o* resulted in an increase in unemployment • **en ~** (*frm*) consequently • **no se trata, en ~, de ningún principiante** so *o* therefore *o* consequently, this can't be a beginner we are talking about • **está enamorado y, en ~, feliz** he is in love, and therefore he is happy • **padecer las ~s** to suffer the consequences • **tener ~s**: • **tuvo graves ~s para la economía** it had serious consequences for the economy • **el accidente no tuvo ~s graves** the accident was not serious • **últimas ~s**: • **llevar algo hasta sus últimas ~s** to take sth to its logical conclusion ▸ **consecuencia directa** direct consequence, direct result
2 (= *conclusión*) conclusion • **sacar ~s de algo** to draw conclusions from sth
▸ **consecuencia lógica** logical conclusion
3 (= *coherencia*) • **actuar** *u* **obrar en ~** to act accordingly • **se comportó en ~ con sus ideas** he acted in accordance with his beliefs
4 (= *importancia*) importance
5 (*esp LAm*) (= *honradez*) integrity
consecuente (ADJ) **1** (= *coherente*) consistent (**con** with) • **una actuación ~ con su ideología** behaviour consistent with their ideology
2 (*Fil*) consequent
3 (= *importante*) important • **no demasiado ~** not very important
4 (*LAm*) (= *honrado*) • **una persona ~** an honourable person, a person of integrity
consecuentemente (ADV) consistently
consecutivamente (ADV) one after the other, one after another, consecutively
consecutivo (ADJ) consecutive
conseguible (ADJ) obtainable, attainable
conseguido (ADJ) successful
conseguir ▹ CONJUG 3d, 3k (VT) [+ *meta, objetivo*] to achieve; [+ *resultado*] to obtain, achieve; [+ *premio, campeonato*] to win; [+ *entradas, empleo, dinero*] to get; [+ *documento, visado, beca, permiso*] to get, obtain; [+ *acuerdo*] to reach • **siempre consigue lo que se propone** he always achieves what he sets out to do • **consiguieron la victoria por tres millones de votos** they won by three million votes • **consiguieron la mayoría absoluta** they won *o* gained an absolute majority • **si insistimos lo ~emos** if we keep trying we'll manage it • **ha conseguido un estilo muy personal** she has achieved a very individual style • **~ hacer algo** to manage to do sth • **he conseguido aprobar el examen** I managed to pass the exam • **no conseguí dar con la solución** I didn't manage to find the answer • **no consigo entender tu argumento** I just don't quite understand your argument • **~ que algn haga algo** to get sb to do sth • **al final conseguí que me devolvieran el dinero** I got them to give me my money back in the end, I got my money back from them in the end • **vas a ~ que papá se enfade** you'll make daddy cross
conseja (SF) old wives' tale
consejería (SF) **1** (*Esp*) (*Pol*) ministry in a regional government
2 (= *concejo*) council, commission
consejero/a (SM/F) **1** (= *asesor*) adviser
2 (*Téc*) consultant; (*Com*) director; (*en comisión*) member of a board *etc* ▸ **consejero/a de publicidad** advertising consultant
▸ **consejero/a delegado/a** managing director, chief executive officer (*EEUU*)
▸ **consejero/a militar** military adviser
3 [*de autonomía*] minister in a regional government
consejillo (SM) inner cabinet, kitchen cabinet
consejo (SM) **1** (= *sugerencia*) advice • **un ~** a piece of advice • **~s** advice (*sing*) • **su ~** his advice • **¿quieres que te dé un ~?** would you like me to give you some advice? • **¿qué ~ me das?** what would you suggest?, how would you advise me? • **pedir ~ a algn** to ask sb for advice, ask sb's advice ▸ **consejo pericial** expert advice
2 (= *organismo*) (*Pol*) council; (*Com*) board; (*Jur*) tribunal ▸ **consejo asesor** advisory board ▸ **consejo de administración** board of directors ▸ **consejo de disciplina** disciplinary board ▸ **Consejo de Europa** Council of Europe ▸ **consejo de guerra** court-martial ▸ **consejo de guerra sumarísimo** drumhead court-martial
▸ **consejo de ministros** (= *entidad*) cabinet; (= *reunión*) cabinet meeting ▸ **consejo de redacción** editorial board ▸ **Consejo de Seguridad** Security Council ▸ **Consejo General del Poder Judicial** (*Esp*) *governing body of the Spanish judiciary*

CONSEJO

▹ *Para traducir la palabra* **consejo** *al inglés, hemos de tener en cuenta que el sustantivo* **advice** *es incontable y lleva el verbo en singular:*

Te voy a dar un consejo
Let me give you some advice
Los consejos que me diste han sido muy útiles
The advice you gave me has been very useful
Actuó siguiendo los consejos de su abogado
He acted on his lawyer's advice

▹ *Cuando queremos referirnos a un* **consejo** *en particular o a un número determinado de consejos, lo traducimos con la expresión* **piece/pieces of advice** *o a veces* **bit/bits of advice**:

Te voy a dar un consejo
Let me give you a piece *o* a bit of advice
Tengo dos buenos consejos para quien quiere vender su casa
I have two useful pieces of advice for anyone selling their house

Para otros usos y ejemplos ver la entrada.

consenso (SM) **1** (*esp Pol*) consensus
2 (= *consentimiento*) consent
consensuado (ADJ) [*texto*] agreed • **llegaron a un acuerdo ~** they achieved a consensus • **es una solución consensuada** it's a solution that has been reached by consensus
consensual (ADJ) agreed • **unión ~** common-law marriage
consensuar ▹ CONJUG 1e (VT) to agree on, reach an agreement on, reach a consensus on
consentido/a (ADJ) **1** (= *mimado*) spoiled, spoilt
2 [*marido*] complaisant
(SM/F) • **es una consentida** she's totally spoiled
consentidor (ADJ) [*madre*] indulgent; [*marido*] complaisant

consentimiento (SM) consent
consentir ▸ CONJUG 3i (VT) **1** (= *permitir*) to allow; (= *tolerar*) to tolerate • **¡eso no se puede ~!** we can't have *o* allow that! • **aquí no te consienten hablar** they don't let you speak here • **no te consiento que vayas** I can't allow you to go
2 (= *soportar*) to stand, bear • **la plataforma no consiente más peso** the platform will not bear *o* take any more weight • **el abrigo consiente un arreglo más** the overcoat will bear repairing once more
3 (= *mimar*) to spoil
(VI) to agree, consent, say yes • **~ en hacer algo** to agree to do sth
(VPR) **consentirse** to break, give, give way
conserje (SMF) [*de facultad*] ≈ head porter; [*de colegio*] ≈ janitor; [*de hotel*] hall porter; [*de edificio oficial, museo*] caretaker ▸ **conserje de noche** night porter
conserjería (SF) porter's office, porter's lodge
conserva (SF) **1** (= *proceso*) preserving
2 (*Culin*) (= *alimentos*) preserve, preserves (*pl*); (= *mermelada*) jam; (= *encurtido*) pickle • **no comemos muchas ~s** we don't eat much tinned *o* (*EEUU*) canned food • **en ~** tinned, canned (*EEUU*) • **atún en ~** tinned *o* (*EEUU*) canned tuna • **~s de carne** tinned *o* (*EEUU*) canned meat ▸ **conservas alimenticias** tinned *o* (*EEUU*) canned food
3 (*Náut*) convoy • **navegar en (la) ~** to sail in convoy
conservación (SF) **1** [*del medio ambiente*] conservation • **instinto de ~** instinct of self-preservation ▸ **conservación de la energía** energy conservation ▸ **conservación de la naturaleza** nature conservation ▸ **conservación de suelos** soil conservation
2 (*Culin*) preservation ▸ **conservación refrigerada** cold storage
3 (*Arquit*) maintenance, upkeep ▸ **gastos de conservación** maintenance costs
conservacionismo (SM) conservationism
conservacionista (ADJ) conservationist, conservation (*antes de s*)
(SMF) conservationist
conservado (ADJ) • **estar muy bien ~** [*persona*] to look very well for one's age, be very well-preserved (*hum*); [*mueble*] to be in very good condition (*frm*)
conservador(a) (ADJ) **1** (*Pol*) conservative, Tory
2 (*Culin*) preservative
(SM/F) **1** (*Pol*) conservative, Tory
2 [*de museo*] curator, keeper • **~ adjunto** assistant keeper
conservadurismo (SM) conservatism
conservante (SM) preservative
conservar ▸ CONJUG 1a (VT) **1** (= *mantener*) [+ *calor*] to retain, conserve; [+ *tradición, costumbre*] to preserve • **el frío conserva los alimentos** the cold preserves food • **con este sistema de cierre se conserva más la energía** this lock system saves *o* conserves more energy • **todavía conservamos el piso de Madrid** we are still keeping on the flat in Madrid • **todavía conservo las amistades del colegio** I still keep up the friendships I had at school • **conserva intactas sus facultades mentales** she is still in full possession of her mental faculties • **conservo un recuerdo magnífico de esas vacaciones** I have wonderful memories of that holiday • **un producto para ~ la piel tersa** a product to keep the skin smooth • **conservaba un aspecto juvenil** she still looked youthful • **ante todo hay que ~ la calma** above all we must keep calm; ▸ **línea**
2 (= *guardar*) [+ *secreto*] to keep • **conservo todas mis fotografías en un baúl** I keep all my photographs in a chest • **aún conservo varias cartas suyas** I still have several of his letters • **el museo conserva los mejores cuadros del pintor** the museum has *o* houses the artist's best paintings • **consérvese en lugar seco y fresco** store in a cool dry place
3 (*Culin*) (= *poner en conserva*) to preserve
(VPR) **conservarse 1** [*tradición, costumbre, ruinas*] to survive • **los alimentos se conservan mejor en la nevera** food keeps better in a fridge • **se han conservado intactos en el ámbar** they have been preserved intact in the amber • **aquel hecho todavía se conserva en la memoria británica** that fact is still fresh in the British memory *o* is still remembered in Britain
2 [*persona*] • **¡qué bien se conserva!** he looks very well for his age!, he's very well preserved (*hum*) • **se conserva muy joven para su edad** she keeps herself looking young • **se conserva en forma** he keeps himself fit *o* in shape
conservatismo (SM) conservatism
conservativo (ADJ) preservative
conservatorio (SM) **1** (*Mús*) conservatoire, conservatory
2 (*LAm*) (= *invernáculo*) greenhouse
3 (*Cono Sur*) (= *escuela*) private school
conservero (ADJ) canning (*antes de s*) • **la industria conservera** the canning industry
considerable (ADJ) considerable • **hubo un retraso ~** there was a considerable delay • **hemos tenido pérdidas ~s** we have suffered substantial *o* considerable losses
considerablemente (ADV) considerably
consideración (SF) **1** (= *deliberación*) consideration • **ese asunto merece la mayor ~** that matter deserves serious consideration • **en ~** under consideration • **dos elementos entran en ~ a la hora de decidir** two factors should be taken into consideration when making a decision • **someter algo a la ~ de algn** to put sth to sb for consideration • **tener** *o* **tomar algo en ~** to take sth into consideration
2 (= *punto a considerar*) • **hizo hincapié en la ~ de que ...** he stressed the fact that ... • **aquí pueden hacerse algunas consideraciones** a few points can be made here • **tales consideraciones no se ajustan a la realidad** such statements *o* views do not reflect reality • **sin querer entrar en consideraciones acerca de su propia actuación** without entering into a discussion of his actual performance
3 (= *concepción*) conception • **la ~ del idioma como poder político** the conception of language as political power
4 (= *importancia*) status • **tiene la ~ de lengua nacional** it has the status of a national language • **de ~** [*herida, daños*] serious • **daños de poca ~** minor damage • **sufrió quemaduras de diversa ~** he suffered burns of varying degrees of seriousness
5 (= *atención*) consideration • **eso sería una falta de ~ hacia nuestros invitados** that would be showing a lack of consideration towards our guests • **nos trataron con gran ~** they were very considerate to us • **¡qué falta de ~!** how inconsiderate! • **en ~ a algo/algn** out of consideration for sth/sb • **lo dejaron libre en ~ a sus circunstancias** he was released out of consideration for his circumstances • **le dieron un premio en ~ a su trabajo** they awarded her a prize in recognition of her work • **sin ~**: • **tratar a algn sin ~** to show no consideration for sb • **sin ~ a la libertad de la persona** with no regard for personal freedom • **tener ~ a** *o* **con algn** to show consideration to sb • **no tuvieron ninguna ~ con las víctimas** they showed no consideration for the victims
6 (= *estima*) regard • **tengo una gran ~ por él** I have (a) great regard for him, I hold him in high regard
7 (*en cartas*) • **le saludo con mi más distinguida ~** (*frm*) I remain yours faithfully (*frm*) • **De mi (mayor) ~** (*LAm*) Dear Sir/Madam
consideradamente (ADV) considerately
considerado (ADJ) **1** (= *atento*) considerate • **ojalá todos fueran tan ~s como tú** if only everybody was as thoughtful *o* considerate as you • **ser ~ con algn** to be considerate to sb
2 (= *estimado*) • **está ~ (como) el mejor corredor del mundo** he is considered (to be) the best runner in the world • **el robo está ~ un delito** robbery is regarded as *o* considered a crime • **estar bien ~** to be highly regarded • **su profesión no está muy bien considerada** his profession is not very highly regarded • **estar mal ~** (= *no aceptado*) to be frowned upon; (= *menospreciado*) to be undervalued
considerando (SM) (*Jur*) point, item, statement
considerar ▸ CONJUG 1a (VT) **1** (= *reflexionar sobre*) to consider • **considera las ventajas y los inconvenientes de tu decisión** think about *o* consider the advantages and disadvantages of your decision • **tengo que ~ el tema con detenimiento** I must give this matter some thought
2 (= *tener en cuenta*) • **considerando lo que cuesta, la calidad podría ser mejor** considering what it costs, the quality could be better • **considera que esta puede ser tu última oportunidad** bear in mind that this could be your last chance
3 (= *creer*) • **~ algo/a algn (como) (+ adj)** to consider sth/sb to be (+ *adj*) • **lo considero imposible** I consider it (to be) impossible • **se le considera culpable del robo** he is believed to be *o* considered to be guilty of the robbery • **se le considera como uno de los grandes pintores de este siglo** he is considered (to be) *o* regarded as one of the great painters of this century • **lo considero hijo mío** I look on him *o* regard him as my own son • **~ que** to believe that, consider that • **considero que deberíamos hacer algo** I believe *o* consider that we should do something
4 (*Jur*) • **considerando...** whereas ... (*word with which each item in a judgement begins*)
(VPR) **considerarse** to consider o.s. • **yo me considero bastante guapo** I consider myself quite good-looking • **me considero una persona normal** I consider myself (to be) a normal person
consigna (SF) **1** (= *orden*) order • **seguir** *o* **cumplir las ~s del Gobierno** to follow government orders ▸ **consignas de vuelo** operating instructions for a flight, operational orders for a flight
2 (= *eslogan*) slogan
3 [*de equipaje*] left-luggage office, checkroom (*EEUU*) ▸ **consigna automática** left-luggage locker
consignación (SF) **1** (*Com*) consignment, shipment
2 (*Econ*) allocation
3 (*Méx*) (*Jur*) remand
consignador (SM) consignor
consignar ▸ CONJUG 1a (VT) **1** (*Com*) to send, dispatch (**a** to)
2 (*Econ*) (= *asignar*) to assign (**para** to, for);

C

[+ *créditos*] to allocate
3 (= *registrar*) to record, register; (= *escribir*) to set down, state • **olvidé ~ mi nombre** I forgot to write my name in, I forgot to state my name • **el hecho no quedó consignado en ningún libro** the fact was not recorded *o* set down in any book
4 (*CAm, Méx*) (*Jur*) to remand, hold for trial

consignatario/a SM/F 1 (*Com*) consignee; (*Náut*) broker, agent
2 (*Jur*) trustee
3 [*de carta*] recipient, addressee

consigo¹ ▹ **conseguir**

consigo² PRON 1 (= *con él*) with him; (= *con ella*) with her; (= *con uno mismo*) with you, with one; (= *con usted*) with you; (= *con ellas, ellos*) with them • **siempre lleva ~ un paraguas** he always carries an umbrella with him • **siempre hay que llevar un pañuelo ~** you *o* (*más frm*) one should always carry a handkerchief • **¿tienen su pasaporte ~?** do you have your passports with you? • **mis hermanas no llevaban dinero ~** my sisters didn't have any money with *o* on them • **llevar *o* traer algo ~**: • **la separación llevó *o* trajo ~ terribles consecuencias** the separation had terrible consequences • **el acuerdo llevará *o* traerá ~ un incremento de las ventas** the agreement will result in increased sales • MODISMO: • **no tenerlas todas ~**: • **lo preparó todo bien y aun así no las tenía todas ~** he prepared it all well enough but he still wasn't quite sure about it
2 • **~ mismo** with himself • **estaba contento ~ mismo** he was pleased with himself • **vive en paz ~ misma** she is at peace with herself • **hablaba ~ misma** she was talking to herself • **no puede ser amable quien no está contento ~ mismo** you can't be nice to others when you are not happy with yourself • **no son sinceros ~ mismos** they are not being honest with themselves • **son muy exigentes ~ mismos** they ask a lot of themselves

consiguiente ADJ 1 (= *resultante*) consequent, resulting
2 • **por ~** consequently, therefore

consiguientemente ADV consequently, therefore

consistencia SF consistence, consistency

consistente ADJ 1 [*materia*] (= *sólido*) solid, firm, tough; (= *espeso*) thick
2 [*argumento*] sound, valid
3 • **~ en** consisting of
4 [*persona, conducta*] consistent

consistir ▹ CONJUG 3a VI 1 • **~ en** (= *componerse de*) to consist of • **la decoración consiste en un cuadro y un jarrón** the decoration consisted of a picture and a vase • **este periódico consiste en varias secciones fijas** this newspaper is made up of various regular sections
2 • **~ en** (= *ser*): • **el juego consiste en adivinar palabras** the object of the game is to guess words • **su misión consiste en aclarar el problema** her task is to solve the problem • **su atractivo consiste en su timidez** her shyness is what makes her attractive • **el secreto *o* truco consiste en añadir un poco de vino** the secret lies in adding a little wine • **todo consiste en saber qué es lo importante** it's all a question of knowing what's important • **¿en qué consiste el trabajo?** what does the job involve *o* entail? • **¿en qué consiste para ti la democracia?** what does democracy mean for you? • **su política consiste en decir cosas impresionantes** his policy consists of saying things to impress

consistorial ADJ 1 (*Rel*) consistorial
2 • **casa ~** town hall

consistorio SM 1 (*Rel*) consistory
2 (*Pol*) town council; (= *edificio*) town hall

consocio SMF fellow member; (*Com*) co-partner, associate

consola SF 1 (= *mesa*) console table
2 (*Inform, Mús*) console ▸ **consola de mandos** control console ▸ **consola de videojuegos** games console

consolación SF consolation

consolador ADJ consoling, comforting
SM (*sexual*) dildo

consolar ▹ CONJUG 1l VT to console, comfort • **me consuela de no haber ido** it's one consolation for not having gone
VPR **consolarse** to console o.s. (**por** about)

consolatorio ADJ consolatory

consolidación SF consolidation

consolidado ADJ (*Econ*) [*pasivo*] consolidated

consolidar ▹ CONJUG 1a VT 1 (= *afianzar*) to consolidate, strengthen • **hemos consolidado nuestra amistad** we've strengthened our friendship • **una democracia consolidada** a consolidated democracy
2 (*Arquit*) to shore up • **~ la estructura del edificio** to shore up the structure of the building
3 (*Econ*) to fund
VPR **consolidarse** to strengthen

consomé SM consommé, clear soup

consonancia SF 1 (= *conformidad*) • **en ~ con** in accordance *o* harmony with
2 (*Mús*) harmony, consonance (*frm*)
3 (*Literat*) consonance, rhyme

consonante ADJ 1 (*Mús*) harmonious, consonant (*frm*)
2 (*Ling*) consonantal
3 (*Literat*) rhyming
SF (*Ling*) consonant

consonántico ADJ consonantal

consonar ▹ CONJUG 1l VI 1 (*Mús*) (*tb fig*) to be in harmony, harmonize
2 (*Literat*) to rhyme (**con** with)

consorciarse ▹ CONJUG 1b VPR to form a consortium *o* syndicate, go into partnership

consorcio SM 1 (*Com*) consortium, syndicate
2 (= *unión*) relationship
3 [*de circunstancias*] conjunction

consorte SMF 1 (= *esposo/a*) consort, spouse • **príncipe ~** prince consort
2 (= *compañero*) partner, companion
3 **consortes** (*Jur*) accomplices

conspicuo ADJ eminent, famous

conspiración SF conspiracy

conspirador(a) SM/F conspirator

conspirar ▹ CONJUG 1a VI to conspire, plot (**con** with, **contra** against) • **~ para hacer algo** to conspire to do sth

conspirativo ADJ conspiratorial

constancia SF 1 (= *perseverancia*) perseverance • **la ~ en los estudios le llevó al éxito** he achieved success through perseverance in *o* by persevering at his studies
2 (= *evidencia*) • **no existe ~ de ello** there is no record of it • **escribo para dar *o* dejar ~ de estos hechos** I am writing to put these facts on record • **quiso dejar ~ de su visita** she wanted to leave some token of her visit • **quiero que quede ~ de mi intervención** I want my contribution to be put *o* go on record • **tengo ~ de que todo es cierto** I have proof that it is all true
3 (*LAm*) (= *comprobante*) documentary proof, written evidence

constante ADJ 1 (= *continuado*) constant • **la búsqueda ~ de la verdad** the constant search for truth • **un día de lluvia ~** a day of constant *o* persistent rain
2 (= *frecuente*) constant • **recibía ~s advertencias de su jefe** she was getting constant warnings from her boss
3 (= *perseverante*) [*persona*] persevering
4 (*Fís*) [*velocidad, temperatura, presión*] constant
SF 1 (= *factor predominante*) • **el mar es una ~ en su obra** the sea is a constant theme *o* an ever-present theme in his work • **el paro es una ~ en la economía española** unemployment is a permanent feature of the Spanish economy ▸ **constante histórica** historical constant
2 (*Mat*) constant
3 (*Med*) ▸ **constantes vitales** vital signs

constantemente ADV constantly

Constantino SM Constantine

Constantinopla SF Constantinople

Constanza SF Constance

constar ▹ CONJUG 1a VI 1 (= *ser evidente*) • **consta que ...** it is a fact that ... • **me consta que ...** I have evidence that ...
2 (= *aparecer, figurar*) • **~ (en)** to appear (in), be given (in *o* on) • **no consta en el catálogo** it isn't listed in the catalogue • **en el carnet no consta su edad** his age is not stated on the licence *o* (*EEUU*) license • **y para que así conste ...** and for the record ... • **hacer ~** to put on record • **que consten los hechos** let's put the record straight
3 • **que conste: que conste que no estoy de acuerdo** for the record, I disagree • **conste que yo no lo aprobé** let it be clearly understood that I did not approve • **que conste que lo hice por ti** believe me, I did it for your own good
4 (= *componerse*) • **~ de** to consist of, be composed of
5 (*Literat*) to scan

constatable ADJ observable, evident • **es ~ que ...** it can be observed that ...

constatación SF confirmation, verification

constatar ▹ CONJUG 1a VT 1 (= *confirmar*) • **estos datos constatan la existencia de vida en el planeta** this data proves the existence of life on the planet • **la autopsia constata que fue un ataque al corazón** the post mortem confirms that it was a heart attack • **pude ~ que era verdad** I was able to establish that it was true • **yo mismo pude ~ su calidad** I was able to see the quality of it for myself
2 (= *afirmar*) to state • **—el presidente ha vuelto a ganar —constató el portavoz** "the president has won again," stated the spokesman

constelación SF constellation

constelado ADJ (*Meteo*) starry, full of stars; (*fig*) bespangled (**de** with)

consternación SF consternation, dismay

consternado ADJ • **estar ~** to be dismayed • **dejar ~** = **consternar**

consternar ▹ CONJUG 1a VT to dismay
VPR **consternarse** to be dismayed (**con** by)

constipación SF = **constipado**

constipado ADJ • **estar ~** to have a cold
SM (*Med*) cold • **coger un ~** to catch a cold

constiparse ▹ CONJUG 1a VPR to catch a cold

constitución SF 1 (= *creación*) setting up • **vamos a proceder a la ~ de un comité de representantes** we are going to set up a committee of representatives
2 (= *composición*) • **a causa de la nueva ~ del gobierno** because of the make-up of the new cabinet • **la ~ del equipo hace pensar que el entrenador quiere un juego de**

ataque the line-up suggests that the coach favours an attacking game
3 (= *complexión*) constitution • **es de ~ débil** he has a weak constitution
4 (*Pol*) constitution • **la Constitución** the Constitution • **jurar la Constitución** to swear allegiance to the Constitution

LA CONSTITUCIÓN ESPAÑOLA
Since its first one of 1812, Spain has had no fewer than nine constitutions, including the current one, which brought stability to Spanish political life. Drawn up by the democratically elected **UCD** government, the **Constitución de 1978** symbolizes the spirit of reconciliation that prevailed during Spain's transition to democracy (1975-82), and has helped the country through a period of radical but peaceful change. The Constitution was ratified by Parliament on 31 October 1978 and approved by a referendum on 6 December, finally receiving the royal assent on 27 December 1978. Apart from setting forth general principles on the nature of the Spanish state, it deals with such issues as the powers of the **comunidades autónomas** (regional governments), the role of the Crown in a parliamentary monarchy, and the status of Spain's different languages.
▹ **COMUNIDAD AUTÓNOMA, LENGUAS COOFICIALES**

constitucional (ADJ) constitutional
constitucionalidad (SF) constitutionality
constitucionalmente (ADV) constitutionally
constituir ▹ CONJUG 3g (VT) (*frm*) **1** (= *crear, fundar*) [+ *comité, asamblea*] to set up, constitute (*frm*); [+ *empresa*] to set up • **constituyeron una comisión de investigación** a committee of inquiry was set up *o* (*frm*) constituted • **constituyeron la empresa entre tres socios** the company was set up by three partners
2 (= *estar formado por*) to make up, constitute • **el comité lo constituyen 12 miembros** the committee is made up *o* composed of 12 members, the committee comprises 12 members • **estar constituido por** to be made up of, be composed of, comprise
3 (= *representar*) to constitute (*frm*) • **la pesca constituye la principal riqueza de la región** fishing represents *o* (*frm*) constitutes the region's main source of wealth • **una llamada anónima no constituye delito** making an anonymous call does not constitute a crime (*frm*) • **para mí constituye un gran honor** this represents a great honour for me • **eso no constituye ninguna molestia** that is no inconvenience at all • **los Beatles pronto llegaron a ~ una leyenda** the Beatles soon became a legend
4 (= *nombrar*) • **constituyeron la nación en república** the country was made a republic • **lo constituyó en heredero de su imperio** she designated him heir to her empire • **~ a algn en árbitro** to appoint sb as arbitrator
(VPR) **constituirse 1** (= *formarse*) [*sociedad, empresa*] to be set up; [*estado*] to be constituted • **¿en qué fecha se constituyó la sociedad?** when was the company set up?
2 (= *convertirse*) to become • **el pueblo se constituyó en un importante centro turístico** the town became a major tourist centre • **se han constituido en una amenaza para el proceso de paz** they have become a threat to the peace process • **~se como** *o* **en** (*Com, Pol*): **la factoría se ~á en empresa autónoma** the factory will be set up as *o* will become an independent company • **el país tiene derecho a ~se en estado independiente** the country has the right to constitute itself as *o* to become an independent state
3 (*frm*) (= *personarse*) • **~se en un lugar** to present o.s. at a place
constitutivo (ADJ) [*elemento*] constituent • **va contra los valores ~s del orden social** it goes against the fundamental values of social order • **ser ~ de delito** to constitute a crime
(SM) constituent element
constituyente (ADJ) **1** [*asamblea, congreso*] constituent
2 [*elemento, sintagma*] constituent
(SM) **1** (= *elemento*) constituent • **uno de los ~s del sintagma nominal** one of the constituents *o* constituent parts of the noun phrase
2 (*Pol*) constituent member
constreñir ▹ CONJUG 3h, 3k (VT) **1** (= *limitar*) to restrict
2 (= *obligar*) • **~ a algn a hacer algo** to compel *o* force *o* (*frm*) constrain sb to do sth
3 (*Med*) to constrict
constricción (SF) constriction
construcción (SF) **1** (= *acción*) construction, building • **en (vía de) ~** under construction
▸ **construcción de buques** shipbuilding
▸ **construcción de carreteras** road building
▸ **construcción naval** shipbuilding
2 (= *sector laboral*) construction industry
3 (= *estructura*) structure
4 (*Ling*) construction
constructivamente (ADV) constructively
constructivismo (SM) constructivism
constructivista (ADJ), (SMF) constructivist
constructivo (ADJ) constructive
constructo (SM) construct
constructor(a) (ADJ) building, construction (*antes de s*)
(SM/F) builder ▸ **constructor(a) cinematográfico(a)** set designer, set builder ▸ **constructor(a) de buques** shipbuilder ▸ **constructor(a) naval** shipbuilder
constructora (SF) (*tb* **empresa constructora**) construction company
construible (ADJ) suitable for building
construir ▹ CONJUG 3g (VT) **1** [+ *barco, carretera, hospital*] to build
2 (*Ling, Geom*) to construct
(VPR) **construirse** (*Ling*) • **este verbo se construye con "en"** this verb takes "en"
consuegro/a (SMF) father-in-law/mother-in-law of one's son/daughter
consuelda (SF) comfrey
consuelo (SM) solace, comfort • **llorar sin ~** to weep inconsolably • **premio de ~** consolation prize
consuetudinario (ADJ) **1** (= *usual*) habitual, customary; (*hum*) [*borracho*] hardened
2 • **derecho ~** common law
cónsul (SMF) consul ▸ **cónsul general** consul general
consulado (SM) (= *cargo*) consulship; (= *sede*) consulate
consular (ADJ) consular • **Sección Consular** Consular Section
consulta (SF) **1** (= *pregunta*) enquiry • **para cualquier ~, llamen a partir de las cinco** if you have any enquiries, please call after five o'clock • **hice una ~ telefónica al banco** I telephoned the bank to make an enquiry • **¿le puedo hacer una ~?** can I ask you something? • **servicio de ~** enquiry service
▸ **consulta de saldo** statement request;
▹ **biblioteca, libro, obra**
2 (*Med*) (= *visita*) consultation; (= *local*) surgery, consulting room, office (EEUU) • **horas de ~** *u* **horario de ~** surgery hours • **el pediatra pasa ~ a las tres** the paediatrician has a surgery *o* sees patients at three • **el doctor no pasa ~ a domicilio** the doctor does not make home visits
3 (*Pol*) (= *referéndum*) referendum ▸ **consulta electoral** elections (*pl*) ▸ **consulta popular** referendum, plebiscite
4 **consultas** (= *negociaciones*) • **se llegó a un acuerdo tras intensas ~s** an agreement was reached after intense negotiations • **ronda** *o* **rueda de ~s** round of talks
5 (*Jur*) review
6 (*Inform*) enquiry
consultable (ADJ) • **~ por todos** which can be consulted by anybody
consultación (SF) consultation
consultar ▹ CONJUG 1a (VT) **1** (= *pedir opinión*) to consult • **decidieron irse sin ~me** they decided to go without consulting me • **es mejor que consultes a un médico** you'd better go to *o* see a doctor • **~ algo con algn** to discuss sth with sb • **lo ~é con mi abogado** I'll discuss it with my lawyer • **MODISMO:** • **~ algo con la almohada** to sleep on sth
2 [+ *diccionario, libro, base de datos, archivo*] to consult • **consulté las páginas web en gallego** I consulted the web pages in Galician • **consulta la palabra en el diccionario** look the word up in the dictionary • **consulté el saldo de mi cuenta** I checked my account balance
(VI) • **~ con algn: no lo haré sin ~ antes contigo** I won't do it without discussing it with you first
consúlting [kon'sultin] (SM) (PL: **consúltings** [kon'sultin]) business consultancy
consultivo (ADJ) consultative
consultor(a) (SM/F) consultant
▸ **consultor(a) en dirección de empresas** (*Com*) management consultant
(SM) (*Inform*) ▸ **consultor de ortografía** spellchecker
consultora (SF) consultancy, consultancy firm
consultoría (SF) consultancy, consultancy firm ▸ **consultoría de dirección, consultoría gerencial** management consultancy (firm)
consultorio (SM) **1** (*Med*) surgery, doctor's office (EEUU)
2 [*de abogado*] office
3 [*de revista*] (*tb* **consultorio sentimental**) problem page, agony column
4 (*Radio*) phone-in (*for listeners' queries*)
consumación (SF) **1** (*Jur*) commission, perpetration
2 [*de matrimonio*] consummation
consumado (ADJ) (= *perfecto*) consummate, perfect; (= *imbécil*) thorough, out-and-out
(SM)* **1** (= *cosas robadas*) loot, swag*
2 (= *droga*) hash*
consumar ▹ CONJUG 1a (VT) **1** (= *acabar*) to complete; [+ *trato*] to close, complete
2 [+ *crimen*] to commit; [+ *asalto, robo*] to carry out
3 [+ *matrimonio*] to consummate
4 (*Jur*) [+ *sentencia*] to carry out
5 (*And, CAm*) (= *hundir*) to submerge
consumerismo (SM) = **consumismo**
consumible (ADJ) • **bienes ~s** consumer goods
consumición (SF) **1** (= *acción*) consumption
2 (= *bebida*) drink; (= *comida*) food • **no pagó su ~** he did not pay for what he had (to eat/drink) ▸ **consumición mínima** cover charge
consumido (ADJ) **1** [*fruta*] shrivelled, shrunken

2 [*persona*] (= *flaco*) skinny
3 (= *tímido*) timid; (= *inquieto*) fretful, easily upset

consumidor(a) SM/F consumer
• **productos al ~** consumer products
▸ **consumidor(a) de drogas** drug user, drug taker

C

consumir ▹ CONJUG 3a VT **1** [+ *comida, bebida, droga*] to consume (*frm*) • **en este bar se consume más vino que cerveza** more wine than beer is drunk *o* (*frm*) consumed in this bar • **consúmase inmediatamente después de abierto** consume immediately after opening • **solo consumo alimentos frescos** I only eat fresh food • **en casa no consumimos leche de cabra** we don't drink goat's milk at home • **no pueden sentarse aquí si no van a ~ nada** you can't sit here if you're not going to have anything to eat or drink • **consuma productos andaluces** buy Andalusian products • **consumir preferentemente antes de ...** best before ...
2 [+ *energía, gasolina*] to use, consume (*frm*) • **mi coche consume muy poco** my car uses very little fuel • **consume gran cantidad de gasolina en el despegue** it consumes vast quantities of fuel on take-off • **la moto consume cinco litros a los 100kms** the motorbike does 100kms to (every) five litres
3 [+ *tiempo*] to take up
4 (= *extinguir*) [+ *salud*] to destroy • **el cáncer lo está consumiendo** cancer is destroying him, he's being wasted away by cancer • **estos niños me están consumiendo la paciencia** these children are trying *o* taxing my patience, my patience is wearing thin with these children • **el tejado fue consumido por las llamas** the roof was consumed by the flames
5 (= *desesperar*) • **los celos lo consumen** he is consumed *o* eaten up with jealousy • **su terquedad me consume** his stubbornness gets on my nerves
6 (*And, CAm*) (= *sumergir*) to submerge
VI **1** (= *comer*) to eat; (= *beber*) to drink • **por favor, váyase si no va a ~** please leave if you're not going to eat or drink
2 (= *gastar*) to consume • **el mercado nos impulsa a ~ sin parar** the market encourages us to consume constantly
VPR **consumirse 1** [*líquido*] to boil away; [*salsa*] to reduce
2 [*vela, cigarro*] to burn down • **se le consumió el cigarro entre los dedos** the cigarette burned out between his fingers • **se le estaba consumiendo el cigarro mientras hablaba** his cigarette was burning down as he spoke
3 [*enfermo, anciano*] to waste away
4 [*tiempo*] to run out
5 (= *desesperarse*) • **se consume de envidia al ver mis triunfos** he's green with envy at my success • **se consumía de pena tras la muerte de su hija** she was consumed with grief after the death of her daughter • **me consumía en deseos de abrazarlo** I had a burning desire to embrace him, I was consumed with a desire to embrace him (*liter*)

consumismo SM consumerism

consumista ADJ consumer (*antes de s*), consumerist
SMF consumer

consumo SM **1** [*de productos*] consumption • **el ~ de bebidas alcohólicas** alcohol consumption • **una charla sobre el ~ de drogas** a talk on drug use • **ha aumentado nuestro ~ de gas** our gas consumption has gone up, we are using more gas • **ordenadores de bajo ~** low-energy computers • **bienes de ~** consumer goods • **fecha de ~ preferente** best-before date • **precios al ~** retail prices • **sociedad de ~** consumer society
2 **consumos** (*Econ*) municipal tax on food

consunción SF consumption

consuno • **de ~** ADV with one accord

consustancial ADJ consubstantial • **ser ~ con** to be inseparable from, be all of a piece with

contabilidad SF (= *práctica*) accounting, book-keeping; (= *profesión*) accountancy • **yo llevo la ~** I keep the books • **libros de ~** account books • **"Contabilidad"** "Accounts", "Accounts Department" ▸ **contabilidad analítica** variable costing *o* (*EEUU*) pricing ▸ **contabilidad creativa** creative accountancy ▸ **contabilidad de costos** cost accounting ▸ **contabilidad de doble partida** double-entry book-keeping ▸ **contabilidad de gestión** management accounting ▸ **contabilidad de inflación** inflation accounting ▸ **contabilidad financiera** financial accounting ▸ **contabilidad por partida simple** single-entry book-keeping

contabilizable ADJ eligible for inclusion

contabilización SF accounting, accountancy

contabilizadora SF accounting machine, adding machine

contabilizar ▹ CONJUG 1f VT **1** (*Econ*) to enter in the accounts
2 (= *tener en cuenta*) to reckon with, take into account

contable ADJ countable
SMF (= *tenedor de libros*) book-keeper; (= *licenciado*) accountant

contactar ▹ CONJUG 1a VI • **~ con** to contact, get in touch with

contacto SM **1** (= *acto de tocar*) contact • **el ~ físico** physical contact • **entrar en ~ con algo** to come into contact with sth
2 (= *trato*) touch • **hace años que perdí ~ con ella** I lost touch with her years ago • **estar en ~ con algn** to be in touch with sb • **nos mantenemos en ~ por teléfono** we keep in touch by phone • **ponerse en ~ con algn** to get in touch with sb, contact sb
3 (*Aut*) ignition
4 (*Elec*) contact
5 (*Méx*) (= *enchufe*) plug
6 (= *encuentro*) meeting
7 (*Fot*) contact print
8 **contactos** (= *conocidos*) contacts • **sección de ~s** [*de un periódico*] contact section, contacts • **agencia de ~s** dating agency

contado ADJ (= *reducido*) • **un ~ número de países** a small number of countries • **en contadas ocasiones** on rare occasions • **contadas veces** seldom, rarely • **son ~s los que ...** there are few who ... • **pero son contadísimos los que pueden** but those who can are very few and far between
• MODISMO: • **tiene los días ~s** his days are numbered
SM **1** (*Com*) • **al ~** for cash, cash down • **lo pagué al ~** I paid cash for it • **pago al ~** cash payment • **precio al ~** cash price
2 • **por de ~** (= *por supuesto*) naturally, of course • **tomar algo por de ~** to take sth for granted
3 (*And*) (= *plazo*) instalment, installment (*EEUU*)

contador(a) ADJ counting
SM/F **1** (*esp LAm*) (*Com*) book-keeper, accountant; (*Jur*) receiver
2 (*And*) (= *prestamista*) pawnbroker, moneylender
SM **1** (*Náut*) • **~ (de navío)** purser
2 (*Téc*) meter ▸ **contador de agua** water meter ▸ **contador de aparcamiento** parking meter ▸ **contador de electricidad** electricity meter ▸ **contador de gas** gas meter ▸ **contador de revoluciones** tachometer ▸ **contador de taxi** taximeter ▸ **contador Geiger** Geiger counter

contaduría SF **1** (= *profesión*) accountancy
2 (= *oficina*) accountant's office; (*And*) [*del prestamista*] pawnbroker's, pawnshop
3 (*Teat*) box office

contagiado ADJ infected

contagiar ▹ CONJUG 1b VT **1** (*Med*) [+ *enfermedad*] to pass on, transmit (*frm*), give (**a** to); [+ *víctima*] to infect (**con** with) • **no quiero ~te** I don't want to give it to you
2 (*fig*) (= *transmitir*) to infect (**con** with) • **me ha contagiado su optimismo** his optimism has rubbed off on me
VPR **contagiarse 1** (*Med*) [*enfermedad*] to be contagious, be catching; [*persona*] to become infected • **~se de algo** to become infected with sth, catch sth • **tiene la gripe y no quiere que los niños se contagien** he has (the) flu and doesn't want the children to catch it
2 (*fig*) (= *transmitirse*) to be contagious • **el mal ejemplo se contagia** a bad example is contagious *o* catching • **me contagié de alegría al verla tan contenta** I was overjoyed when I saw how happy she was

contagio SM **1** (*Med*) infection, contagion
2 (*fig*) contamination

contagioso ADJ **1** (*Med*) [*enfermedad*] contagious; [*enfermo*] infected, infectious
2 (*fig*) catching; [*risa*] infectious

contáiner SM container

contaje SM count, counting

contaminación SF **1** (*Meteo*) [*de aire, mar*] pollution; [*de alimentos, agua potable*] contamination ▸ **contaminación acústica** noise pollution ▸ **contaminación ambiental** environmental pollution ▸ **contaminación atmosférica** air pollution ▸ **contaminación del aire** air pollution ▸ **contaminación genética** genetic pollution
2 (*textual*) corruption; (*Literat*) influence

contaminado ADJ [*aire, mar*] polluted; [*alimentos*] contaminated; [*agua potable*] contaminated, polluted

contaminador(a) SM/F polluter

contaminante SM pollutant

contaminar ▹ CONJUG 1a VT **1** [+ *aire, mar*] to pollute; [+ *alimentos, agua potable*] to contaminate; [+ *ropa*] to soil
2 [+ *texto*] to corrupt; (*Literat*) to influence, affect
3 (*Rel*) to profane
VPR **contaminarse** [*alimentos, agua potable*] to be contaminated, become contaminated (**con** with, **de** by); [*agua, aire*] to become polluted

contante ADJ • **dinero ~ (y sonante)** cash

contar ▹ CONJUG 1l VT **1** (= *calcular*) [+ *objetos, números, puntos*] to count; [+ *dinero*] to count, count up • **estaba contando los minutos que quedaban para el final** I was counting the minutes till the end • **cuenta cuántos alumnos hay en la clase** count how many pupils there are in the class
2 (= *relatar*) to tell • **nos contó un cuento muy bonito** she told us a very nice story • **cuéntanos lo que ocurrió** tell us what happened • **¿qué les voy a ~ que ustedes no sepan?** what can I tell you that you don't already know? • **el paro está peor y la corrupción, ¿qué le voy a ~?** unemployment has got worse and as for corruption, what can I say? • **si pierdo el trabajo, ya me ~ás de qué vamos a vivir** you tell me what we'll live on if I lose my job • **¿y a mí qué me**

cuentas? so what? • **¡a mí me lo vas a ~!** you're telling me!*, tell me about it!* • **se cuenta que ...** it is said that ... • MODISMO: • **¡una obra que ni te cuento!*** one hell of a fine work*; ▹ **abuelo**

3 (= *tener la edad de*) • **la Constitución española cuenta 20 años** the Spanish constitution is 20 years old • **María cuenta 32 años** María is 32 years of age

4 (= *incluir*) to count • **lo cuento entre mis amigos** I count him among my friends • **a mí ya me cuentan como adulto** I'm counted as an adult now • **seis en total, sin ~me a mí** six altogether, not counting me • **1.500 sin ~ las propinas** 1,500, excluding tips, 1,500, not counting tips • **se le cuenta entre los más ricos** he is reckoned among the richest

5 (= *tener en cuenta*) to remember, bear in mind • **cuenta que es más fuerte que tú** remember *o* don't forget he's stronger than you are

VI **1** (*Mat*) to count • **sabe ~ hasta 20** he can count (up) to 20 • **~ con los dedos** to count on one's fingers • MODISMO: • **parar de ~***: • **hay dos sillas, una mesa y para ya de ~** there are two chairs, a table, and that's it

2 (= *relatar*) to tell • **luego te ~é** I'll tell you later • **ojalá tengas suerte con la entrevista de trabajo, ya me ~ás** I hope the job interview goes well, I look forward to hearing all about it • **es muy largo de ~** it's a long story • MODISMO: • **cuenta y no acaba (de hablar)** he never stops talking

3 (= *importar, valer*) to count • **aquí lo que cuenta es la ganancia final** what counts here is the final profit • **el último gol no cuenta** the last goal doesn't count • **este examen no cuenta para la nota final** this exam doesn't count towards the final mark • **~ por dos**: • **los domingos una hora cuenta por dos** on Sundays one hour counts as two • **come tanto que cuenta por dos** he eats enough for two • MODISMO: • **la intención es lo que cuenta** it's the thought that counts

4 • **~ con a** (= *confiar en*) to count on • **cuenta conmigo** you can rely *o* count on me • **no cuentes con mi ayuda** don't count on my help • **cuento con que no llueva** I'm counting on it not raining

b (= *tener presente*) • **tienes que ~ con el mal estado de la carretera** you have to take into account *o* remember the bad state of the road • **lo calcularon sin ~ con nosotros** they worked it out without taking us into account • **cuenta con que es más fuerte que tú** bear in mind *o* remember he's stronger than you are • **no contábamos con eso** we hadn't bargained for that • **sin ~ con que ...** leaving aside the fact that ...

c (= *incluir*) to count in • **cuenta conmigo para la cena** count me in for dinner • **lo siento, pero para eso no cuentes conmigo** I'm sorry but you can count me out of that • **no contéis con nosotros para el viernes, estaremos ocupados** don't expect us on Friday, we'll be busy

d (= *tener*) to have • **el polideportivo cuenta con una piscina olímpica** the sports centre has *o* boasts an Olympic-size swimming pool • **cuenta con varias ventajas** it has a number of advantages • **una democracia que tan solo cuenta con dieciséis años de existencia** a democracy that has only existed for sixteen years

VPR **contarse 1** (*al saludar*) • **¿qué te cuentas?*** how's things?*

2 • **~se entre** (= *incluirse*): • **me cuento entre sus admiradores** I count myself among his admirers, I consider myself one of his admirers • **su película se cuenta entre las nominadas al óscar** his film is amongst those nominated for an Oscar

3 • **~se por** (= *calcularse*): • **sus seguidores se cuentan por miles** he has thousands of supporters, his supporters number several thousand • **los muertos se cuentan por centenares** the dead number several hundred

contemplación SF **1** (= *observación*) (*gen*) contemplation

2 (= *meditación*) meditation

3 contemplaciones: **a** (= *indulgencia*) indulgence (*sing*) • **tener demasiadas contemplaciones con algn** to be too indulgent towards sb, be too soft on sb • **tratar a algn con contemplaciones** to treat sb leniently

b (= *ceremonias*) • **no andarse con contemplaciones** not to stand on ceremony • **sin contemplaciones** without ceremony • **no me vengas con contemplaciones** don't come to me with excuses

contemplar ▹ CONJUG 1a VT **1** (= *observar*) [+ *paisaje, edificio, cuadro*] to gaze at, contemplate • **se pasa horas contemplando el mar** she spends hours gazing at *o* contemplating the sea • **contemplaba su imagen en el espejo** she gazed at *o* contemplated her reflection in the mirror • **contemplaba a Juan en silencio** she gazed at Juan in silence • **desde aquí se contempla el valle entero** from here you can see the whole valley • **desde aquí se contempla una vista espectacular** there is a spectacular view from here • **la exposición podrá ~se aquí en octubre** the exhibition can be seen here in October • **pude ~ la belleza de Elena** (*frm*) I was able to look on Elena's beauty

2 (= *analizar*) • **debemos ~ su obra desde otra perspectiva** we must look at *o* consider his work from another perspective

3 (= *mimar*) to indulge • **no contemples tanto a tus hijos** don't indulge your children so much

4 (*frm*) (= *considerar*) [+ *idea, posibilidad*] to consider

5 [*ley, tratado*] to provide for • **el acuerdo contempla una subida del 3%** the agreement provides for an increase of 3% • **la ley contempla los casos siguientes** the law provides for the following cases

VI (*Rel*) to meditate

contemplativo ADJ **1** [*vida, persona*] contemplative

2 (= *indulgente*) indulgent (**con** towards)

contemporáneo/a ADJ, SM/F contemporary

contemporización SF (= *acomodación*) temporizing; (*Pol*) appeasement

contemporizador(a) ADJ excessively compliant

SM/F temporizer

contemporizar ▹ CONJUG 1f VI (= *acomodarse*) to be compliant, show o.s. ready to compromise; (*pey*) to temporize (**con** with) • **~ con algn** to hedge with sb; (*Pol*) to appease sb

contención SF **1** (*Mil*) containing, containment • **muro de ~** retaining wall • **operación de ~** holding operation

2 (= *restricción*) restraint • **sin ~** freely, without restraint ▸ **contención salarial** pay restraint

3 (= *rivalidad*) contention

4 (*Jur*) suit

contencioso ADJ **1** (*Jur*) contentious

2 [*carácter*] captious; [*asunto*] contentious

SM (= *disputa*) dispute; (= *problema*) problem; (= *punto conflictivo*) point of disagreement

contender ▹ CONJUG 2g VI **1** (= *lidiar*) to contend (**con** with, **sobre** over); (= *competir*) to compete • **~ en unas oposiciones** to take part in a competitive examination

2 (*Mil*) to fight

contendiente ADJ contending

SMF contestant, contender

contenedor SM **1** (*gen*) container ▸ **contenedor de basura(s)** rubbish skip ▸ **contenedor de escombros** skip, builder's skip ▸ **contenedor de vidrio** bottlebank

2 (*Náut*) container ship

contenedorización SF (*Com*) containerization

contener ▹ CONJUG 2k VT **1** (= *incluir*) to contain • **el maletín contenía explosivos** the suitcase contained explosives • **el libro contenía un capítulo dedicado a su vida** the book contained a chapter on her life • **"no contiene alcohol"** "alcohol-free", "does not contain alcohol"

2 (= *frenar*) [+ *gente, muchedumbre*] to contain, hold back; [+ *revuelta, epidemia, infección*] to contain; [+ *invasión, lágrimas, emoción*] to contain, hold back; [+ *aliento, respiración*] to hold; [+ *hemorragia*] to stop; [+ *bostezo*] to stifle; [+ *inflación*] to check, curb; [+ *precios, déficit, consumo*] to keep down • **para ~ la tendencia al alza de los precios** to check the tendency for prices to rise • **no pude ~ la risa** I couldn't help laughing

3 (*Cono Sur*) (= *significar*) to mean

VPR **contenerse** (= *controlarse*) to control o.s., restrain o.s. • **me contuve para no llorar** I controlled *o* restrained myself so as not to cry

contenerización SF containerization

contenerizar ▹ CONJUG 1f VT to containerize

contenido ADJ **1** [*persona*] restrained, controlled

2 [*risa, emoción*] suppressed

SM **1** [*de recipiente, paquete*] contents (*pl*) • **el ~ de la maleta** the contents of the suitcase • **alimentos con un alto ~ de proteínas** foods with a high protein content

2 [*de programa, proyecto*] content • **el ~ político de la campaña** the political content of the campaign

contenta SF **1** (*Com*) endorsement; (*Mil*) good-conduct certificate

2 (*LAm*) (*Jur*) release, acknowledgement

contentadizo ADJ (*tb* **bien contentadizo**) easy to please • **mal ~** hard to please

contentamente ADV contentedly

contentamiento SM contentment

contentar ▹ CONJUG 1a VT **1** (= *complacer*) [+ *persona*] to please; (*frm*) [+ *deseo*] to satisfy • **decidió casarse para ~ a su familia** he decided to get married to please his family • **~ los deseos de todos** to satisfy everyone's wishes • **para ~ al cliente** to keep the customer happy

2 (*LAm*) (= *reconciliar*) • **~ a dos personas** to reconcile two people

3 (*Com*) to endorse

VPR **contentarse 1** • **~se con algo**: **se contenta con cualquier cosa** he's happy with anything • **Israel no se contentó con esa enmienda** Israel was not satisfied with that amendment • **no quedaba vino, y me tuve que ~ con agua** there was no wine left so I had to make do with water • **el atleta se tuvo que ~ con un segundo puesto** the athlete had to be content with *o* had to settle for second place • **no se contenta con orientarme, sino que trata de controlarme** he's not content with just giving me guidance, he tries to control me • **me contento con saber que estás bien** I'm

happy just knowing that you are all right • **me contento con que lo termines a tiempo** I'll be happy if you just finish it on time
2 (*LAm*) (= *reconciliarse*) • **~se con algn** to become reconciled with sb

contento ADJ 1 (= *alegre, feliz*) happy • **¿estás ~?** are you happy? • **estoy contenta de vivir aquí** I'm happy living here • **viven muy ~s en su casita del campo** they live very happily in their country cottage • **se pone muy ~ cuando viene la abuela** he's always pleased when his grandmother comes • **estar loco de ~** • **no caber en sí de ~** (*frm*) to be overjoyed • MODISMO: • **estar más ~ que unas castañuelas** *o* **que unas pascuas** to be as happy as a sandboy
2 (= *satisfecho*) pleased • **no ~s con sus excusas, lo denunciaron** not satisfied with his excuses, they reported him • **estar ~ con algn/algo** to be pleased with sb/sth • **estoy contenta con mis hijos** I'm pleased with my children • **están muy ~s con el coche** they're very pleased with the car • **estar ~ de hacer algo** to be happy *o* pleased to do sth • **dejar a algn ~** to satisfy sb • **quedar ~ con algo** to be satisfied with sth • **no quedaron ~s con el trabajo** they were not satisfied with the work • **le das una golosina y se queda tan ~** he's perfectly happy if you give him a sweet • **lo escribió con b y se quedó tan ~** he wrote it with a b but didn't seem to let that bother him • **tener ~ a algn** to keep sb happy *o* satisfied • **contenta me tienes, hijo** (*iró*) oh, wonderful!, oh, great!*
3 (= *bebido*) merry • **no me emborraché, pero estaba ~** *o* **contentillo** I didn't get drunk but I was quite merry
SM (*frm*) (= *alegría*) happiness, joy • **el anuncio fue motivo de ~** the announcement gave cause for happiness *o* joy

contentura SF (*CAm, Caribe*) = **contento**

conteo SM count, counting; (*Méx*) (*Dep*) count ▸ **conteo regresivo** (*LAm*) countdown

contera SF 1 (*Téc*) tip, metal tip, ferrule
2 (= *remate*) little extra, small addition • **por ~** to crown *o* cap it all, as a final blow

contertuliano/a SM/F, **contertulio/a** SM/F fellow member (*of a social set*) ▸ **contertulianos/as de café** café companions

contesta SF (*LAm*) answer

contestable ADJ questionable, debatable

contestación SF 1 (= *respuesta*) answer, reply • **mala ~** sharp retort, piece of backchat • **dejar una carta sin ~** to leave a letter unanswered
2 ▸ **contestación a la demanda** (*Jur*) defence *o* (*EEUU*) defense plea
3 (*Pol*) protest • **movimiento de ~** protest movement

contestado ADJ contentious, controversial

contestador ADJ (*LAm*) cheeky, saucy, sassy (*EEUU**)
SM ▸ **contestador automático** answering machine, answerphone, Ansaphone®

contestar ▹ CONJUG 1a VT 1 (= *responder*) to answer, reply; [+ *saludo*] to return • **contesté todas las preguntas** I answered all the questions • **~ al teléfono** to answer the telephone • **~ una carta** to reply to a letter • **le pregunté que si vendría y contestó que sí** I asked him if he would come and he replied that he would
2 (= *replicar*) to answer back • **no le contestes así a tu madre** don't answer your mother back like that, don't talk back to your mother like that
3 (*Jur*) to corroborate, confirm
VI 1 (= *responder*) to answer, reply • **abstenerse de ~** to make no reply • **no contestan** there's no reply *o* answer
2 (*Pol*) to protest

contestatario/a ADJ rebellious • **movimiento ~** protest movement
SM/F non-conformist

contesto SM (*And, Cono Sur, Méx*††) answer, reply

contestón* ADJ given to answering back, argumentative

contexto SM 1 (= *marco*) context • **sacar algo (fuera) de ~** to take sth out of context • **~ histórico** historical context
2 (*Téc*) web, tangle

contextual ADJ contextual

contextualizar ▹ CONJUG 1f VT to provide a context for, set in a context

contextura SF 1 (*Téc*) contexture
2 (*Anat*) build, physique

contienda SF contest, struggle

contigo PRON with you; (*Rel*) with thee • **quiero ir ~** I want to go with you • **necesito hablar ~** I need to talk to you • **estamos ~** we're behind you, we're on your side

contigüidad SF contiguity

contiguo ADJ adjacent, contiguous (*frm*) (a to) • **en un cuarto ~** in an adjoining room

continencia SF continence

continental ADJ continental

continentalidad SF continental nature

continente ADJ continent
SM 1 (*Geog*) continent • **el viejo ~** Europe, the Old World
2 (= *recipiente*) container
3 (= *aspecto*) bearing • **de ~ distinguido** with an air of distinction, with a distinguished air • **de ~ duro** harsh-looking

contingencia SF (*gen*) contingency; (= *posibilidad*) eventuality, possibility

contingentación SF quota system

contingentado ADJ subject to a quota system

contingentar ▹ CONJUG 1a VT to make subject to quotas

contingente ADJ contingent
SM 1 (*Mil*) contingent
2 (*Com*) quota ▸ **contingente de importación** import quota
3 = **contingencia**

continuación SF 1 [*de acto, proceso, calle*] continuation • **el instinto de supervivencia asegura la ~ de la especie** the survival instinct ensures the continuation of the species • **el mal tiempo impidió la ~ del desfile** the bad weather prevented the parade from continuing • **mañana veremos la ~ de la serie** the series will be continued tomorrow • **esta película es la ~ de Rocky** this film is the sequel to Rocky
2 • **a ~** (*en conversación*) next; (*en texto*) below • **a ~ viene una canción dedicada a todos nuestros oyentes** coming up next, a song dedicated to all our listeners • **el fin, como veremos a ~, justifica los medios** the end, as we shall now see, justifies the means • **a ~ vamos a presentarles a Margarita Pracatán** and now I would like to welcome Margarita Pracatán • **el poeta habló a ~ de su nuevo libro** the poet went on to speak about his new book, next the poet spoke about his new book • **según se expone a ~** as stated below
3 • **a ~ de** following, after • **a ~ del sorteo ofrecerán una rueda de prensa** following *o* after the draw, they will give a press conference • **se sentaron uno a ~ del otro** they sat down one after another

continuadamente ADV continually

continuado ADJ continual
SM (*Cono Sur*) *a cinema showing films in continuous performance*

continuamente ADV 1 (= *repetidamente*) constantly, continually • **el teléfono sonaba ~** the telephone was ringing constantly *o* continually
2 (= *sin interrupción*) constantly, continuously • **el prisionero ha de ser vigilado ~** the prisoner has to be watched constantly *o* continuously

continuar ▹ CONJUG 1e VT to continue • **el tren continuó su marcha** the train continued its journey • **continuó sus estudios en Barcelona** she continued her studies in Barcelona • **~emos la clase mañana** we will go on with *o* continue the lesson tomorrow • **continuó su vida como antes** he went on with *o* continued with his life as before
VI 1 [*historia, espectáculo, guerra*] to continue, go on • **la búsqueda continuó durante toda la noche** the search continued *o* went on all night • **continúe, por favor** please continue, please go on • **la serie continúa la semana que viene** the series continues next week • **"~á"** "to be continued" • **pase lo que pase, la vida continúa** come what may, life goes on
2 (*en una situación*) • **la puerta continúa cerrada** the door is still shut, the door remains shut (*frm*) • **continúa muy grave** she is still in a critical condition, she remains in a critical condition (*frm*) • **continúa en el mismo puesto de trabajo** she is still in the same post, she remains in the same post (*frm*) • **continuaba en Noruega** he was still in Norway • **~ con algo** to continue with sth, go on with sth • **continuó con su trabajo** he continued with *o* went on with his work • **Pablo continúa con Irene** Pablo is still (together) with Irene • **~ con salud** to be still in good health, remain in good health (*frm*) • **~ haciendo algo**: • **continuó leyendo** she continued to read *o* reading, she went on reading • **la policía ~á investigando el caso** the police are to continue *o* go on investigating the case • **a pesar de todo, continúa diciendo lo que piensa** in spite of everything, she continues to speak her mind *o* she still speaks her mind • **continúa lloviendo** it's still raining • **continuaba trabajando para ellos** he still worked for them • **en cualquier caso continúo siendo optimista** in any case, I remain optimistic *o* I am still optimistic
3 [*camino, carretera*] to continue, go on, carry on • **el camino continúa hasta la costa** the road continues *o* goes on *o* carries on (all the way) to the coast

continuidad SF 1 (= *permanencia*) continuity • **el nuevo presidente supondrá una cierta ~ política** the new president will represent a certain political continuity
2 (= *continuación*) continuation • **estas elecciones serán cruciales para la ~ del proceso de paz** these elections will be crucial for the continuation of the peace process • **su ~ en el equipo está fuera de dudas** his continuation in the team is beyond doubt, there is no doubt whatsoever that he will remain *o* stay in the team
3 (*Cine, TV*) continuity

continuismo SM (*Pol*) preservation of the status quo

continuista SMF *person who maintains the status quo*

continuo ADJ 1 (= *ininterrumpido*) [*línea, fila*] continuous; [*dolor, movimiento, crecimiento*] constant, continuous; [*pesadilla, molestia*] constant • **marque el número cuando oiga**

una señal continua dial the number when you hear a continuous tone • **la presencia continua de los militares lo hacía todo más difícil** the constant *o* continuous presence of the soldiers made everything more difficult; ▸ **evaluación, sesión**
2 (= *frecuente, repetido*) [*llamadas, amenazas, críticas, cambios*] constant, continual • **no aguanto sus continuas quejas** I can't bear his constant *o* continual complaining
3 (*Fís*) [*movimiento*] perpetual
4 (*Elec*) [*corriente*] direct
5 (*Ling*) continuous
6 • **de ~** = **continuamente**
SM (*Fís*) continuum

contonearse ▸ CONJUG 1a VPR [*hombre*] to swagger; [*mujer*] to swing one's hips, wiggle one's hips

contoneo SM [*de hombre*] swagger; [*de mujer*] hipswinging, wiggle

contorcerse ▸ CONJUG 2b, 2h VPR to writhe, twist

contorno SM **1** (= *perfil*) outline; (*Geog*) contour; [*de moneda*] edge
2 (= *medida*) girth • **el ~ de cintura es de 26 pulgadas** her waist measurement is 26 inches • **el ~ de un árbol** the girth of a tree
3 contornos neighbourhood (*sing*), neighborhood (*sing*) (*EEUU*), surrounding area (*sing*) • **Caracas y sus ~s** Caracas and its environs • **en estos ~s** in these parts, hereabouts

contorsión SF contortion • **hacer contorsiones** to writhe

contorsionarse ▸ CONJUG 1a VPR to contort o.s.

contorsionista SMF contortionist

Contra SF • **la ~** (*Nic*) (*Hist*) the Contras (*pl*)

contra PREP **1** (*indicando oposición*) against • **no tengo nada ~ ti** I have nothing against you • **son cinco ~ uno** it's five against one • **una campaña ~ la discriminación** a campaign against discrimination • **el Sevilla juega ~ el Betis** Seville are playing (against) Betis • **un ataque ~ objetivos militares** an attack on military targets • **unas pastillas ~ el mareo** some (anti-)travel sickness pills • **~ la opinión de la mayoría, yo me opongo** contrary to the opinion of the majority, I oppose it • **en ~**: • **¿quién está en ~?** who is against? • **tres votos a favor y dos en ~** three votes in favour and two against • **lo tenemos todo en ~** the odds are stacked against us • **tengo a toda la familia en ~** the whole family is against me • **el Barcelona tenía el marcador en ~** the score was not in Barcelona's favour • **en ~ de algo** against sth • **estoy en ~ de la subida de los impuestos** I'm against an increase in taxes • **en ~ de lo que habíamos pensado** contrary to what we had thought • **por ~** on the other hand
2 (*indicando posición*) against • **apoyó la bici ~ la pared** she leaned the bike against the wall • **me abrazó fuerte ~ su pecho** she hugged me tightly to her breast
3 (*indicando dirección*) against • **fue muy cansado remar ~ la corriente** it was very tiring rowing against the current • **se chocó ~ la valla** he crashed into the fence
4 (*Com, Econ*) • **cobrará el dinero ~ entrega del boleto ganador** you will receive the money when you produce the winning ticket; ▸ **reembolso**
SF **1*** (= *contraria*) • **hacer la ~ a algn: no me hagas más la ~** stop being so obstructive, stop taking the opposite line all the time • **llevar la ~ a algn** to contradict sb • **no le gusta que le lleven la ~** he doesn't like to be contradicted • **¿por qué siempre tienes que llevar la ~?** why do you always have to be so contrary?
2 (*LAm*) (*Med*) antidote
3 (*Bridge*) double
SM (= *inconveniente*) disadvantage, drawback • **la fama también tiene sus ~s** fame also has its disadvantages *o* drawbacks; ▸ **pro**
EXCL* damn it* • **¡ya me has confundido otra vez, ~!** now you've got me all mixed up again, damn it!*

contra... PREF counter-..., contra...
• **contramanifestación** counter-demonstration
• **contrapropaganda** counter-propaganda

contraanálisis SM follow-up test, counter-test

contrabajista SMF [*de orquesta*] double-bass player; [*de rock*] bass guitarist

contrabajo SM **1** (= *instrumento*) double bass
2 (= *cantante, voz*) low bass, contrabasso
SMF (= *músico*) double bass player, double bassist

contrabalancear ▸ CONJUG 1a VT to counterbalance

contrabalanza SF counterbalance

contrabandear ▸ CONJUG 1a VI to smuggle, live by smuggling

contrabandista SMF smuggler ▸ **contrabandista de armas** gunrunner

contrabando SM **1** (= *actividad*) smuggling • **introducir** *o* **pasar algo de ~** to smuggle sth in • **lo trajeron al país de ~** they smuggled it into the country • **géneros de ~** smuggled goods • **amores de ~** (*fig*) clandestine love affairs ▸ **contrabando de armas** gun-running ▸ **contrabando de drogas** drug smuggling
2 (= *mercancías*) contraband, smuggled goods (*pl*)

contracampaña SF counter-campaign

contracargo SM counter-charge

contracarro ADJ INV • **defensas ~** anti-tank defences, anti-tank defenses (*EEUU*)

contracción SF **1** [*de una enfermedad*] contraction
2 [*de compromiso, deuda*] contracting; [*de matrimonio*] contraction (*frm*)
3 [*de músculo, metal*] contraction
4 (*Ling*) contraction

contracepción SF contraception ▸ **contracepción de barrera** barrier contraception ▸ **contracepción oral** oral contraception

contraceptivo ADJ, SM contraceptive

contrachapado ADJ • **madera contrachapada** plywood
SM plywood

contracifra SF key, key to a code

contracorriente SF cross-current • **ir a ~** (*lit*) to go against the current, go upstream; (*fig*) to go against the tide

contráctil ADJ contractile

contractual ADJ contractual

contractualmente ADV contractually

contractura SF muscular contraction

contracubierta SF back cover (*of book*)

contracultura SF counter-culture

contracultural ADJ alternative, of the counter-culture

contracurva SF second bend, bend the other way

contradecir ▸ CONJUG 3o VT to contradict
VPR **contradecirse** to contradict o.s.

contradicción SF contradiction • **espíritu de ~: había en él cierto espíritu de ~** there were certain contradictions in his nature • **eres el espíritu de la ~, ahora piensas una cosa y luego cambias de idea** you're so contrary, one minute you think one thing, the next minute you've changed your mind • **~ de** *o* **en los términos** contradiction in terms • **están en ~** they stand in contradiction to each other

contradictoriamente ADV contradictorily

contradictorio ADJ contradictory

contradique SM outer harbour *o* (*EEUU*) harbor wall

contradón SM reciprocal gift

contraefecto SM counter-effect

contraejemplo SM counter-example

contraempuje SM counter-thrust

contraer ▸ CONJUG 2o VT **1** [+ *enfermedad*] to contract (*frm*), catch
2 [+ *compromiso*] to make, take on; [+ *obligación*] to take on, contract (*frm*); [+ *deuda, crédito*] to incur, contract (*frm*) • **~ matrimonio (con algn)** to marry (sb) • **contrajo parentesco con la familia real** (*frm*) she married into the royal family
3 [+ *costumbre*] to get into, acquire (*frm*)
4 [+ *músculo, nervio*] to contract • **tenía el rostro contraído por el dolor** his face was contorted *o* twisted with pain • **tanta pobreza le contrajo el corazón** such poverty made his heart bleed
5 [+ *metal, objeto*] to cause to contract • **la humedad contrae las cuerdas** dampness causes the ropes to contract
VPR **contraerse 1** [*músculo, nervio*] to contract • **se le quedó el músculo contraído** his muscle contracted *o* tightened
2 [*objeto, material*] to contract
3 (*Ling*) to contract

contraespionaje SM counter-espionage

contraetiqueta SF second label, label on the back

contrafallar ▸ CONJUG 1a VT to overtrump

contrafuerte SM **1** (*Arquit*) buttress; (*Geog*) spur; (*Mil*) outwork
2 [*de calzado*] stiffener

contragambito SM counter-gambit

contragolpe SM **1** (= *reacción*) counter-blow
2 (*Dep*) counter-attack

contragolpear ▸ CONJUG 1a VI to strike back

contrahacer ▸ CONJUG 2r VT **1** (= *copiar*) to copy, imitate
2 [+ *moneda*] to counterfeit; [+ *documento, prueba*] to forge, fake; [+ *libro*] to pirate

contrahaz SM wrong side

contrahecho ADJ **1** (*Anat*) hunchbacked
2 (= *falso*) [*moneda*] counterfeit; [*documento, prueba*] fake, faked, forged; [*libro*] spurious

contrahechura SF [*de moneda*] counterfeit; [*de documento, prueba*] forgery, fake; [*de libro*] pirated edition, spurious edition

contraído ADJ **1** (= *encogido*) contracted
2 (*And*) (= *diligente*) diligent, industrious

contraimagen SF mirror image; (*pey*) negative image

contraincendios ADJ INV • **aparato ~** fire-prevention apparatus, fire-alarm system

contraindicación SF counter-indication

contrainformación SF disinformation

contrainforme SM counter-report

contrainsurgencia SF counter-insurgency

contrainteligencia SF counter-intelligence

contrairritante SM counterirritant

contralmirante SM, **contraalmirante** SM rear admiral

contralor SM (*LAm*) comptroller

contraloría SF (*LAm*) treasury inspector's office

contralto ADJ contralto

SMF (= *mujer*) contralto; (= *hombre*) counter tenor

contraluz SM view against the light • **a ~** against the light

contramaestre SMF (*Náut*) boatswain; (*Téc*) foreman/forewoman

contramandar ▷ CONJUG 1a VT to countermand

contramandato SM counter-order

contramanifestación SF counter-demonstration

contramano SM • **ir a ~** to go the wrong way • **eso queda a ~** that's in the other direction

contramarcha SF **1** (*Mil*) countermarch
2 (*Aut*) reverse • **dar ~ (a)** to reverse; (*fig*) to go into reverse

contramarchar ▷ CONJUG 1a VI to countermarch

contramatar ▷ CONJUG 1a VT • **~ a algn** (*LAm*) to bang sb against the wall
VPR **contramatarse 1** (*LAm*) (= *chocarse*) to crash into sth, collide with sth
2 • **~se de hacer algo** (*Méx*) to repent of having done sth, regret doing *o* having done sth

contramedida SF counter-measure

contramenaza SF, **contraamenaza** SF counter-threat

contranatural ADJ unnatural

contraofensiva SF counter-offensive

contraoferta SF counter-offer

contraorden SF countermand

contraparte SF (*And*) other party

contrapartida SF **1** (*Com, Econ*) balancing entry
2 (= *compensación*) compensation • **pero como ~ añade que ...** but in contrast she adds that ... • **como ~ de** as *o* in compensation for, in return for • **dar algo de ~ de algo** to give sth in return for sth

contrapelo SM • **a ~** the wrong way • **acariciar un gato a ~** to stroke a cat the wrong way • **todo lo hace a ~** he does everything the wrong way round • **intervino muy a ~** he spoke up in a most unfortunate way

contrapesar ▷ CONJUG 1a VT **1** (= *hacer contrapeso*) to counterbalance
2 (= *compensar*) to offset, compensate for

contrapeso SM **1** (*Téc*) counterpoise, counterweight; (*Com*) makeweight
2 [*de equilibrista*] balancing pole
3 (*fig*) counterweight

contrapié • **a ~** ADV • **mi oponente me cogió a ~** my opponent caught me off balance, my opponent wrongfooted me • **me pillaron a ~ al llegar antes de lo esperado** I was caught off balance when they arrived earlier than expected

contrapoder SM anti-establishment movement

contraponer ▷ CONJUG 2q VT **1** (= *cotejar*) to compare, set against each other
2 (= *oponer*) to oppose • **~ A a B** to set up A against B • **a esta idea ellos contraponen su teoría de que ...** against this idea they set up their theory that ...

contraportada SF back cover

contraposición SF **1** (= *cotejo*) comparison
2 (= *oposición*) contrast, clash • **en ~ a** in contrast to • **pero en ~, ...** but on the other hand, ...

contraprestación SF compensation

contraproducente ADJ counterproductive • **tener un resultado ~** to have a boomerang effect, boomerang

contraproductivo ADJ counterproductive

contraprogramación SF competitive programming

contraprogramar ▷ CONJUG 1a VI to set competitive schedules

contrapropuesta SF counter-proposal

contrapuerta SF storm door

contrapuesto ADJ conflicting, opposing

contrapuntear ▷ CONJUG 1a VI (*And*) to compete in a verse duel; (*fig*) to compete

contrapunteo SM **1** (*And, Caribe, Cono Sur*) (= *riña*) argument, quarrel
2 (*And, Cono Sur*) (*Literat*) improvised verse duel
3 (*And, Caribe, Cono Sur*) (= *debate*) debate • **en ~** (*And*) in competition

contrapuntístico ADJ (*Mús*) contrapuntal; (*fig*) contrasting

contrapunto SM **1** (*Mús*) (*tb fig*) counterpoint
2 (*LAm*) (= *concurso de poesía*) poetic competition with improvised verses • **de ~** in competition

contrargumento SM, **contraargumento** SM counter-argument

contrariado ADJ upset, annoyed, put out

contrariamente ADV • **~ a lo que habíamos pensado** contrary to what we had thought

contrariar ▷ CONJUG 1c VT **1** (= *contradecir*) to contradict
2 (= *oponer*) to oppose, go against; (= *dificultar*) to impede, thwart • **solo lo hace por ~nos** he only does it to be contrary *o* awkward *o* difficult
3 (= *fastidiar*) to vex, annoy

contrariedad SF **1** (= *obstáculo*) obstacle; (= *contratiempo*) setback, trouble; (= *pega*) snag, trouble
2 (= *disgusto*) vexation, annoyance • **producir ~ a algn** to annoy sb
3 (= *oposición*) contrary nature

contrario/a ADJ **1** (= *rival*) [*partido, equipo*] opposing • **el abogado de la parte contraria** the opposing party's lawyer • **no llegaron nunca a la portería contraria** they never got near the other *o* opposing side's goal • **se pasó al bando ~** he went over to the other *o* opposing side
2 (= *opuesto*) [*extremo, efecto, significado, sexo*] opposite • **tuvo el resultado ~ al deseado** it had the opposite of the desired effect • **mi opinión es contraria a la vuestra** I have the opposite opinion to you • **soy ~ al aborto** I am opposed to *o* against abortion • **se mostraron ~s al acuerdo** they came out against the agreement, they were opposed to the agreement • **su actitud es contraria a los intereses del país** his attitude is against *o* contrary to the nation's interests
• **dirección contraria**: • **tomamos la dirección contraria** we went in the opposite direction • **lo multaron por ir en dirección contraria** he was fined for travelling in the wrong direction • **intereses ~s** conflicting *o* opposing interests • **pie ~**: • **se puso el zapato en el pie ~** she put her shoe on the wrong foot • **sentido ~**: • **un coche que venía en sentido ~** a car coming in the opposite direction • **el portavoz se expresó en sentido ~** the spokesperson expressed the opposite view • **en sentido ~ a las agujas del reloj** anti-clockwise • **viento ~** headwind; ▷ **caso**
3 (*en locuciones*) • **al ~** on the contrary, quite the opposite • **no me disgusta la idea, al ~, me encanta** I don't dislike the idea, on the contrary *o* quite the opposite, I think it would be wonderful • **—¿te aburres? —¡que va, al ~!** "are you bored?" — "no way, quite the opposite!" • **se puso el jersey al ~** he put his jumper on inside out • **antes al ~** • **muy al ~** (*frm*) on the contrary • **al ~ de**: • **todo salió al ~ de lo previsto** everything turned out the opposite of what we expected • **al ~ de lo que creíamos, hizo muy buen tiempo** contrary to what we thought, the weather turned out very nice • **siempre va al ~ de todo el mundo** she always has to be different to everyone else, she always does the opposite to everyone else • **al ~ que** *o* **de ella, yo no estoy dispuesto a aguantar** unlike her, I'm not willing to put up with it • **lo ~**: • **¿qué es lo ~ de alto?** what is the opposite of tall? • **nunca he dicho lo ~** I never said anything else *o* different • **soy inocente, hasta que no se demuestre lo ~** I am innocent until proven otherwise • **a mí me pasa lo ~ que a ti** for me it's different than for you • **de lo ~** otherwise, or else • **salga o, de lo ~, llamaré a la policía** please leave, otherwise *o* or else I'll call the police • **por el ~**: • **los inviernos, por el ~, son muy fríos** the winters, on the other hand *o* on the contrary, are very cold • **parece ir todo bien, y por el ~, la situación es muy complicada** it all appears to be going well, when in fact the situation is rather difficult • **todo lo ~** quite the opposite, quite the reverse • **—¿es feo? —no, todo lo ~** "is he ugly?" — "no, quite the opposite *o* reverse" • **no hay descenso de precios, sino todo lo ~** prices are not going down, quite the opposite *o* reverse, in fact • **es todo lo ~ de su marido** she is the exact opposite of her husband • **ha sucedido todo lo ~ de lo que esperábamos** exactly the opposite of what we expected has happened
SM/F opponent
SM (= *opuesto*) opposite • **¿cuál es el ~ del negro?** what is the opposite of black?
SF • MODISMO: • **llevar la contraria**: • **¿por qué siempre tienes que llevar la contraria?** why do you always have to be so contrary? • **siempre me lleva la contraria en todo** he always contradicts me about everything • **no le gusta que le lleven la contraria** he doesn't like to be contradicted

contrarreembolso SM cash on delivery

Contrarreforma SF Counter-Reformation

contrarreloj ADV against the clock
ADJ • **prueba ~** time trial
SF time trial

contrarréplica SF rejoinder

contrarreplicar ▷ CONJUG 1g VI to answer back

contrarrestar ▷ CONJUG 1a VT **1** (= *resistir*) to resist; (= *oponerse*) to oppose
2 (= *compensar*) to counteract • **~ el efecto de una vacuna** to counteract the effect of a vaccine
3 [+ *pelota*] to return

Contrarrevolución SF (*Nic*) (*Hist*) *armed opposition to the Sandinista government of the 1980s*

contrarrevolución SF counter-revolution

contrarrevolucionario/a ADJ, SM/F counterrevolutionary

contrasentido SM **1** (= *contradicción*) contradiction • **aquí hay un ~** there is a contradiction here
2 (= *disparate*) piece of nonsense; (= *inconsecuencia*) inconsistency • **es un ~ que él actúe así** it doesn't make sense for him to act like that

contraseña SF **1** (= *seña*) countersign, secret mark
2 (*Mil, Inform*) password
3 (*Teat*) (*tb* **contraseña de salida**) pass-out ticket

contrastar ▷ CONJUG 1a VT **1** [+ *metal*] to assay; [+ *medidas*] to check; [+ *radio*] to monitor; [+ *hechos*] to check, confirm
2 (= *resistir*) to resist

VI 1 (= *hacer contraste*) to contrast (**con** with)
2 • **~ a** *o* **con** *o* **contra** (= *resistir*) to resist; (= *hacer frente a*) to face up to
contraste SM 1 (= *oposición*) contrast • **en ~ con** in contrast to • **por ~** in contrast • **hacer ~ con** to contrast with ▸ **contraste de pareceres** difference of opinion
2 (*TV*) contrast
3 [*de pesos y medidas*] (*tb* **marca del contraste**) (= *sello*) hallmark; (= *acción*) assay; (= *persona*) inspector of weights and measures; (= *oficina*) weights and measures office
contrastivo ADJ (*Ling*) contrastive
contrata SF contract
contratacar ▸ CONJUG 1g VT, VI, **contraatacar** ▸ CONJUG 1g VT, VI to counter-attack
contratación SF 1 [*de albañil, fontanero*] hiring; [*de abogado*] hiring, contracting (*frm*); [*de empleado*] recruitment • **se ha prohibido la ~ de jugadores extranjeros** the signing of foreign players has been banned • **este año ha habido diez mil nuevas contrataciones** this year there have been ten thousand new contracts
2 [*de vehículo, servicio*] hiring, hire
contratante SMF (*Com*) contractor; (*Jur*) contracting party
contrataque SM, **contraataque** SM counter-attack
contratar ▸ CONJUG 1a VT 1 [+ *empleado*] to take on; [+ *albañil, abogado*] to hire; [+ *jugador, artista*] to sign (up) • **le ~on por un año** they took her on for a year, they gave her a one-year contract • **contrató a dos fontaneros para arreglar las tuberías** he hired two plumbers to fix the pipes • **han contratado nuevo personal** they have taken on *o* recruited new staff • **me han contratado por horas** they have hired me by the hour
2 (= *alquilar*) [+ *vehículo, servicio*] to hire
3 [+ *obra*] to put out to contract
contratenor SM counter-tenor
contraterrorismo SM counter-terrorism
contraterrorista ADJ • **medidas ~s** measures against terrorism, anti-terrorist measures
contratiempo SM 1 (= *revés*) setback, reverse; (= *accidente*) mishap, accident
2 (*Mús*) • **a ~** offbeat
contratista SMF contractor ▸ **contratista de obras** building contractor, builder
contrato SM contract (**de** for)
• **incumplimiento de ~** breach of contract
• **renovación del ~** renewal of contract
▸ **contrato a precio fijo** fixed-price contract
▸ **contrato a término** forward contract
▸ **contrato basura** mickey-mouse contract
▸ **contrato bilateral** bilateral agreement
▸ **contrato de alquiler** [*de casa*] lease, leasing agreement; [*de coche*] rental contract, hire contract ▸ **contrato de arrendamiento** rental agreement ▸ **contrato de compraventa** contract of sale ▸ **contrato de mantenimiento** maintenance contract, service agreement ▸ **contrato de sociedad** deed of partnership ▸ **contrato de trabajo** contract of employment, contract of service
▸ **contrato indefinido** permanent contract
▸ **contrato verbal** verbal agreement
contratuerca SF locknut
contravalor SM exchange value
contravención SF contravention, violation
contraveneno SM antidote (**de** to)
contravenir ▸ CONJUG 3r VT to contravene, infringe
VI • **~ a** to contravene, infringe
contraventana SF shutter
contrayendo ▸ contraer
contrayente SMF • **los ~s** the bride and groom
contribución SF 1 (= *colaboración*) contribution • **su ~ a la victoria** his contribution to the victory, his part in the victory • **poner a ~** to make use of, put to use
2 (*Econ*) tax; **contribuciones** taxes, taxation (*sing*) • **exento de contribuciones** tax-free, tax-exempt (*EEUU*) • **pagar las contribuciones** to pay one's taxes
▸ **contribución directa** direct tax
▸ **contribución municipal** rates (*pl*)
▸ **contribución territorial urbana** rates (*pl*)
contribuidor(a) SM/F contributor
contribuir ▸ CONJUG 3g VI 1 (= *colaborar*) to contribute • **cada uno contribuyó con diez euros** each person contributed ten euros
• **~ a hacer algo** to help to do sth • **~ al éxito de algo** to contribute to *o* help towards the success of sth
2 (*Econ*) to pay, pay in taxes
contribuyente SMF taxpayer
contrición SF contrition
contrincante SMF opponent, rival
contristar ▸ CONJUG 1a (*frm*) VT to sadden
VPR **contristarse** to grow sad, grieve
contrito ADJ (*frm*) contrite
control SM 1 (= *dominio, vigilancia*) control
• **nunca pierde el ~** he never loses control
• **bajo ~** under control • **fuera de ~** out of control • **perder el ~** to lose control (of o.s.)
• **hacerse con el ~ de algo** to take control *o* charge of sth • **~ de** *o* **sobre sí mismo** self-control ▸ **control armamentista** arms control ▸ **control de alquileres** rent control
▸ **control de calidad** quality control
▸ **control de cambio** exchange control
▸ **control de costos** cost control ▸ **control de créditos** credit control ▸ **control de existencias** stock control ▸ **control de la circulación** traffic control ▸ **control de la demanda** demand management ▸ **control de la natalidad** birth control ▸ **control del tráfico** traffic control ▸ **control de natalidad** birth control ▸ **control de precios** price control ▸ **control nuclear** nuclear inspection ▸ **control presupuestario** budget control
2 (= *inspección*) (*Jur*) inspection, check; (*Com, Econ*) audit, auditing
3 (= *puesto*) (*tb* **control de carretera**) roadblock; (*tb* **control de frontera**) frontier checkpoint • **montar un ~** to set up a roadblock ▸ **control de pasaportes** passport inspection ▸ **control policial en carretera** police roadblock
4 [*de un aparato*] control ▸ **control del volumen** volume control ▸ **control de tonalidad** tone control ▸ **control remoto** remote control
5 (= *examen*) (*Educ*) test
6 (*Med*) test ▸ **control antidopaje** drugs test, dope test ▸ **control antidoping** drug test, dope test ▸ **control de alcoholemia** Breathalyser® test
controlable ADJ controllable
controladamente ADV in a controlled way
controlado ADJ [*experimento*] controlled
• **no se preocupen, está todo ~** don't worry, everything's under control
controlador(a) SM/F 1 (*Aer*) (*tb* **controlador aéreo**) air-traffic controller
2 • **~ de estacionamiento** traffic warden
3 (*LAm*) (*Ferro*) inspector, ticket-collector
controlar ▸ CONJUG 1a VT 1 (= *dominar*) [+ *situación, emoción, balón, vehículo, inflación*] to control • **los rebeldes controlan ya todo el país** the rebels now control the whole country, the rebels are now in control of the whole country • **mis padres quieren ~me la vida** my parents want to control my life • **no pudo ~ el impulso de pegarle** he couldn't control the urge to hit him • **medidas para ~ la calidad** quality-control measures • **los bomberos consiguieron ~ el fuego** the firefighters managed to bring the fire under control • **no controlo muy bien ese tema*** I'm not very hot on that subject*
2 (= *vigilar*) • **inspectores para ~ el proceso electoral** observers to monitor the electoral process • **deberías ~ tu peso** you should watch your weight • **contrólame al niño mientras yo estoy fuera*** can you keep an eye on the child while I'm out • **estoy encargado de ~ que todo salga bien** I'm responsible for checking *o* seeing that everything goes well • **controla que no hierva el café*** make sure the coffee doesn't boil, see that the coffee doesn't boil
3 (= *regular*) to control • **este termostato controla la temperatura** this thermostat controls the temperature
VI* • **he bebido tanto que ya no controlo** I've drunk so much I can't see straight*
VPR **controlarse** (= *dominarse*) to control o. s. • **¡no te exaltes, contrólate!** don't get worked up, control yourself! • **no pude ~me y le dije todo lo que pensaba** I couldn't control *o* stop *o* help myself and told him exactly what I thought • **deberías ~te con el tabaco** you should watch how much you smoke, you should try and keep your smoking down
controversia SF controversy
controversial ADJ controversial
controvertible ADJ controversial
controvertido ADJ controversial
controvertir ▸ CONJUG 3i VT to dispute, question
VI to argue
contubernio SM 1 (= *confabulación*) conspiracy
2 (= *cohabitación*) cohabitation
contumacia SF 1 (= *terquedad*) obstinacy, stubborn disobedience
2 (*Jur*) contempt, contempt of court
contumaz ADJ 1 (= *terco*) obstinate, stubbornly disobedient
2 [*bebedor*] inveterate, hardened, incorrigible
3 (*Jur*) guilty of contempt, guilty of contempt of court
4 (*Med*) disease-carrying, germ-laden
contumazmente ADV obstinately
contumelia SF contumely
contumerioso ADJ (*CAm*) finicky, fussy
contundencia SF 1 [*de instrumento*] bluntness
2 [*de argumentación, razonamiento*] forcefulness, convincing nature; [*de prueba*] conclusiveness
contundente ADJ 1 [*arma*] offensive; [*instrumento*] blunt
2 (= *aplastante*) [*argumento*] forceful, convincing; [*prueba*] conclusive; [*derrota, victoria*] crushing, overwhelming; [*tono*] forceful; [*efecto, método*] severe; [*arbitraje*] strict, severe; [*juego*] tough, hard, aggressive
contundir ▸ CONJUG 3a VT to bruise, contuse
conturbar ▸ CONJUG 1a VT to dismay, perturb
VPR **conturbarse** to be troubled, become uneasy
contusión SF bruise, contusion (*frm*)
contusionar ▸ CONJUG 1a VT (= *magullar*) to bruise; (= *dañar*) to hurt, damage
contuso ADJ bruised

C

conuco (SM) (*Ven*) smallholding
conuquero (SM) (*Ven*) smallholder, farmer
conurbación (SF) conurbation
convalecencia (SF) convalescence
convalecer ▷ CONJUG 2d (VI) to convalesce, recover (**de** from)
convaleciente (ADJ), (SMF) convalescent
convalidable (ADJ) which can be validated
convalidación (SF) validation • **tengo que solicitar la ~ de mis títulos** I need to have my qualifications validated
convalidar ▷ CONJUG 1a (VT) to validate
convección (SF) convection
convecino/a (SM/F) neighbour, neighbor (*EEUU*)
convectivo (ADJ) convective
convector (SM) convector
convencer ▷ CONJUG 2b (VT) **1** • **~ a algn (de algo)** to convince sb (of sth), persuade sb (of sth) • **me convencieron de su inocencia** they convinced *o* persuaded me he was innocent *o* of his innocence • **al final la convencí de que era verdad** I eventually convinced *o* persuaded her it was true • **no me ~éis de lo contrario** you won't convince *o* persuade me otherwise
2 • **~ a algn (de *o* para hacer algo)** to persuade sb (to do sth) • **me han convencido de *o* para que los vote** they persuaded me to vote for them • **no iba a salir, pero al final me convencieron** I wasn't going to go out, but in the end they persuaded me (to)
3 (= *satisfacer*) • **no nos convence del todo la propuesta** we are not entirely convinced about the proposal, the proposal is not entirely convincing • **ninguno de los dos candidatos me convence** neither of the two candidates seems very convincing *o* good to me • **su último disco no me convence nada** I'm not very impressed with her latest record, her latest record doesn't do much for me • **el torero convenció a su afición** the bullfighter did not disappoint his fans • **parece buena gente, pero no me acaba de ~** he seems nice enough but I'm not too sure about him • **su intervención no convenció a los votantes** his speech failed to win over the voters
(VPR) **convencerse** • **al final se convenció y dejó de intentarlo** he eventually thought better of it and stopped trying • **¡convéncete ya, esa enfermedad no tiene cura!** I wish you'd understand, there's no cure for this illness! • MODISMO: • **~se de algo**: • **se convencieron de mi inocencia** they were persuaded of my innocence • **¿te convences ahora de que decía la verdad?** do you believe now that I was telling the truth? • **me convencí de que lo mejor era callarse** I came to the conclusion that it would be better to keep quiet • **tuvo que volver a casa para ~se de que había apagado todas las luces** he had to go back home to reassure *o* convince himself that he had switched off all the lights
convencido (ADJ) [*pacifista, cristiano*] committed, convinced • **estar ~ de algo** to be convinced of sth, be certain of sth, be sure of sth
convencimiento (SM) **1** (= *creencia*) conviction, certainty • **llegar al ~ de algo** to become convinced of sth • **llevar algo al ~ de algn** to convince sb of sth • **tener el ~ de que** to be convinced that
2 (= *acción*) convincing, persuasion
convención (SF) convention ▸ **Convención de Ginebra** Geneva Convention
convencional (ADJ) conventional
convencionalismo (SM) conventionalism
convencionero (ADJ) (*And, Méx*) comfort-loving, self-indulgent
convencionista (SMF) (*Méx*) *follower of Convención movement led by Zapata and Villa (1914-15)*
convenible (ADJ) **1** (= *apropiado*) suitable, fitting
2 [*precio*] fair, reasonable
3 [*persona*] accommodating
conveniencia (SF) **1** (= *utilidad*) [*de una acción*] advisability • **insistió en la ~ de adelantar las elecciones** she insisted on the advisability of bringing forward the election • **ser de la ~ de algn** to be convenient to sb, suit sb
2 (= *provecho propio*) • **a su ~** at your (own) convenience • **por ~: lo hace por ~** he does it because it suits him *o* because it's in his own interest(s) • **se ha casado por ~** she made a marriage of convenience • **te lo digo por tu ~** I'm telling you for your own sake *o* in your own interests • **cambios dictados por ~s partidistas** changes dictated by party interests ▸ **conveniencias sociales** social conventions; ▷ **bandera, matrimonio, pabellón**
3 conveniencias† (= *propiedad*) property (*sing*); (= *renta*) income (*sing*); [*de criado*] perquisites
4† (= *acuerdo*) agreement
5† (= *puesto*) domestic post, job as a servant
conveniente (ADJ) **1** (= *aconsejable*) advisable • **el comité hará lo que considere *o* estime ~** the committee will do as it sees fit, the committee will do what it considers advisable • **ser ~ hacer algo** to be advisable to do sth • **es ~ no tomar grasas en exceso** it is advisable not to eat too much fat • **es ~ que**: • **es ~ que consulte con su abogado** it is advisable to consult your lawyer • **sería ~ que habláramos sobre el tema** it would be advisable *o* desirable for us to talk about the matter • **sería ~ que nos levantásemos temprano** it might be a good idea for us to get up early *o* if we got up early
2 (= *indicado*) suitable • **la clase de cultivo ~ a cada tierra** the kind of crop suitable for each type of soil
3 (= *provechoso*) convenient • **a usted le resultaría más ~ un fondo de pensiones** you would find a pension fund more convenient • **para nosotros es ~ la existencia de la competencia** the existence of competition is good for us *o* is in our interest
4 (= *correcto*) proper • **se sentó frente a ella, guardando la ~ distancia** he sat down opposite her, keeping a proper distance
convenientemente (ADV) **1** (= *como debe ser*) [*arreglar, reparar, comportarse*] properly • **está permitido fumar solo en las zonas de espera si están ~ separadas** smoking is only permitted in waiting areas if they are properly separated
2 (*para conveniencia de algn*) conveniently • **la información fue ~ censurada** the information was conveniently censored
convenio (SM) agreement ▸ **convenio colectivo** collective bargain, general wages agreement ▸ **convenio comercial** trade agreement ▸ **convenio de nivel crítico** threshold agreement ▸ **convenio laboral** trade agreement ▸ **convenio salarial** wages agreement
convenir ▷ CONJUG 3r (VI) **1** (= *ser adecuado*) • **~ hacer algo**: • **conviene recordar que este es un tema serio** it should be remembered that this is a serious matter • **conviene reservar asiento** reservation is advisable • **convendría hacer algo al respecto** it might be desirable *o* advisable *o* appropriate to do something about it • **necesitaban reunirse para reflexionar sobre lo que convenía hacer** they needed to get together to reflect on the most appropriate course of action • **~ que**: • **no conviene que nos vean juntos** we shouldn't be seen together, it is not advisable that we are seen together • **convendría que perdiese unos kilos** it might be a good idea *o* advisable to lose a few kilos
2 (= *ser de interés*) to suit • **elija las fechas que mejor le convengan** choose the dates that suit you best • **esa hora no me conviene** that time is not convenient for me, that time doesn't suit me • **esa amistad no te convenía nada** that friendship was not good *o* right for you • **lo que más le conviene es reposo absoluto** the best thing for him *o* what he needs is complete rest • **~ a algn hacer algo**: • **me conviene quedarme aquí** the best thing for me is to stay here, it is best for me to stay here • **no te conviene fumar** it's not good for you to smoke, smoking isn't good for you • **te convendría olvidar ese asunto** you would be well advised to forget all about this business
3 • **~ en algo** to agree on sth • **conveníamos en la necesidad de un cambio** we agreed on the need for change • **~ en hacer algo** to agree to do sth • **convinimos en dejar de vernos** we agreed to stop seeing each other • **~ en que** to agree that • **todos convienen en que está loco** everyone agrees that he is mad • **convinieron en que el plazo fuese de dos años** they agreed that it would be for a period of two years
(VT) [+ *precio, hora*] to agree on, agree • **convinimos la hora y el lugar** we agreed (on) a time and a place • **nos vimos a la hora convenida** we saw each other at the agreed time • **eso es más de lo convenido** that is more than what was agreed (on) • **"precio/sueldo a ~"** "price/salary to be agreed", "price/salary negotiable" • **~ hacer algo** to agree to do sth • **hemos convenido no trabajar los sábados** we have agreed not to work on Saturdays
conventilleo (SM) (*And, Cono Sur*) gossip
conventillero/a (*And, Cono Sur*) (ADJ) gossipy
(SM/F) scandalmonger, gossip
conventillo (SM) (*esp LAm*) tenement house
convento (SM) [*de monjes*] monastery; [*de monjas*] convent, nunnery
conventual (ADJ) conventual
convergencia (SF) **1** (*Mat, Fís, Econ*) convergence
2 (= *tendencia común*) common tendency, common direction • **~ de izquierdas** (*Pol*) grouping *o* coming together of left-wing forces
convergente (ADJ) **1** (*Mat, Fís*) convergent, converging
2 (= *concurrente*) having a common tendency, tending in the same direction
3 (*Esp*) (*Pol*) *of the Catalan coalition Convergència i Unió*
convergentemente (ADV) • **~ con** together with, jointly with
converger ▷ CONJUG 2c (VI), **convergir** ▷ CONJUG 3c (VI) **1** (*Mat, Fís*) to converge (**en** on)
2 (*fig*) to tend in the same direction (**con** as) • **sus esfuerzos convergen en un fin común** their efforts are directed towards the same objective
3 (*Pol*) to come together
conversa (SF) (*esp LAm*) (= *charla*) talk, chat; (= *lisonjas*) smooth talk; ▷ **converso**
conversación (SF) conversation, talk • **cambiar de ~** to change the subject • **trabar**

~ con algn to strike up a conversation with sb

conversacional ADJ [tono] conversational; [estilo] colloquial

conversada* SF (LAm) chat

conversador(a) ADJ talkative, chatty SM/F 1 (= persona locuaz) conversationalist 2 (LAm) (= zalamero) smooth talker

conversar ▷ CONJUG 1a VT 1 (And, Cono Sur) (= contar) to tell, relate; (= informar) to report 2 (Caribe) (= ligar) to chat up* VI 1 (= charlar) to talk, chat 2 (Mil) to wheel

conversata SF (Cono Sur) talk, chat

conversión SF 1 (= cambio) conversion 2 (Mil) wheel

converso/a ADJ converted SM/F convert; (Hist) converted Jew/Jewess; ▷ conversa, RECONQUISTA

conversón/ona (And) ADJ talkative, gossiping SM/F talkative person, gossip

conversor SM converter

convertibilidad SF convertibility

convertible ADJ convertible SM (LAm) (Aut) convertible

convertidor SM converter ▸ convertidor catalítico catalytic converter

convertir ▷ CONJUG 3i VT 1 • ~ algo en algo to turn sth into sth • ~ a algn en algo to turn sb into sth • convirtió el pañuelo en una paloma he turned the handkerchief into a dove • la victoria le convirtió en un héroe the victory turned him into a hero, the victory made him a hero • han convertido el corral en un invernadero they've converted the yard into a greenhouse • ~ metros en centímetros to convert metres to centimetres • ~ dólares en libras to convert dollars to pounds 2 (a una religión, ideología) to convert • convirtió a su hijo al catolicismo she converted her son to catholicism 3 (Dep) [+ penalti] to convert, score; [+ gol, tanto] to score VPR convertirse 1 • ~se en algo to turn into sth • el riachuelo se convirtió en un torrente the stream turned into o became a torrent • la rana se convirtió en un príncipe the frog turned into a prince • con la empresa se convirtió en millonario the company made him a millionaire • todos sus deseos se convirtieron en realidad all her wishes came true 2 (Rel) to be converted, convert • se convirtió al Islam he converted to Islam

convexidad SF convexity

convexo ADJ convex

convicción SF conviction

convicto/a ADJ convicted SM/F (LAm) convict

convidada SF round (esp of drinks) • dar o pagar una ~ to stand a round

convidado/a SM/F guest

convidar ▷ CONJUG 1a VT 1 (= invitar) to invite • ~ a algn a hacer algo to invite sb to do sth • ~ a algn a una cerveza to buy sb a beer 2 (= incitar) • ~ a to stir to, move to • el ambiente convida a la meditación the atmosphere is conducive to meditation VPR convidarse 1 (= invitarse) to invite o.s. along 2 (= ofrecerse) to volunteer, offer one's services

convincente ADJ convincing

convincentemente ADV convincingly

convite SM 1 (= invitación) invitation 2 (= función) banquet, feast ▸ convite a escote Dutch treat

convivencia SF 1 [de personas] cohabitation, living together • ~ en familia living with a family 2 (fig) (Pol) coexistence 3 (Rel) • irse de ~s to go on a retreat

convivencial ADJ social

conviviente SMF (Chile) partner

convivir ▷ CONJUG 3a VI 1 (= vivir juntos) to live together • ~ con algn to live with sb 2 (= coexistir) [personas] to live together, live together in harmony; [ideologías, razas] to coexist

convocación SF calling, convening

convocante SMF organizer

convocar ▷ CONJUG 1g VT 1 [+ elecciones, referéndum, huelga] to call; [+ asamblea, reunión] to call, convene; [+ manifestación] to call for; [+ concurso, oposiciones] to announce • convocó una conferencia de prensa he called a press conference • han convocado un congreso extraordinario para el lunes they have called o convened a special conference for Monday • ~ Cortes (Hist) to convoke parliament 2 • ~ a algn: ~on a los periodistas a una rueda de prensa they called journalists to a press conference • ~on a todos los presos en el patio they summoned all the prisoners to the yard • los españoles serán convocados a las urnas en abril Spaniards will go to the polls in April • los jugadores convocados por el entrenador the players selected by the trainer

convocatoria SF 1 (= anuncio) [de concurso, oposiciones] official announcement • se ha anunciado la ~ del congreso socialista the socialist congress has been called o convened • han anunciado la ~ de elecciones generales they have announced the date for the general election • ~ (pública) de plazas docentes public notice o announcement of selection for teaching places • en la última ~ el premio fue declarado desierto in the last competition the prize was not awarded • ~ de huelga strike call 2 (= ronda) • ha aprobado todo en la ~ de septiembre she passed everything in September's exams • en primera ~, el candidato precisa el 51% de los votos in the first round the candidate needs 51% of the votes

convólvulo SM convolvulus

convoy SM 1 (Mil, Náut) convoy; (Ferro) train 2 (frm) (= séquito) retinue 3 (= vinagrera) cruet, cruet stand 4 (Caribe) (= ensalada) salad

convoyar ▷ CONJUG 1a VT 1 (= escoltar) to escort 2 (Cono Sur) (= financiar) to back, sponsor VPR convoyarse (Caribe) to connive together, plot

convulsión SF 1 (Med) convulsion 2 (Geol) tremor 3 (Pol) upheaval

convulsionar ▷ CONJUG 1a VT to convulse

convulsivamente ADV convulsively

convulsivo ADJ convulsive

convulso ADJ convulsed (de with)

conyugal ADJ conjugal (frm), married • vida ~ married life

conyugalidad SF married life

cónyuge SMF spouse, partner; cónyuges married couple (sing), husband and wife

coña** SF piss-taking** • estar de ~ to be taking the piss** • ¡esto es la ~! this is a fucking joke!** • tomar algo a ~ to take sth as a joke

coñá SM = coñac

coñac [koˈɲa] SM (PL: coñacs [koˈɲas]) brandy, cognac

coñazo‡ SM pain* • dar el ~ to be a real pain

coñe‡ EXCL = coño

coñearse** ▷ CONJUG 1a VPR to take the piss**

coñete ADJ (Chile, Perú) mean

coño¹** SM (= sexo femenino) cunt** • MODISMOS: • ser el ~ de la Bernarda to be a disgrace • estar hasta el ~ de algn/algo to have had it up to here with sb/sth • el quinto ~ the arse end of nowhere**, the back of beyond* • viven en el quinto ~ they live out in the arse end of nowhere** • lo hice porque me salió del ~ I did it because I bloody well felt like it‡ EXCL 1 (como expresión de enfado) hell!*, damn!*, shit!** • ¡vámonos ya, ~! come on, let's get a bloody move on!‡ • ¡ni hablar, ~, ni hablar! not on your bloody life!‡ • ¿cómo ~? how the fuck?** • ¿dónde ~? where the fuck?** • ¿por qué ~? why the fuck?** • ¿qué ~? what the fuck?** • ¿a ti qué ~ te importa? what the fuck does it matter to you?** • ¿qué ~ quieres? what the fuck do you want?** • que lo haga él, ¡qué ~! let him do it, for Christ's sake!* • ¡qué libro ni qué ~! what bloody book!‡ • —no puedo salir esta noche, tengo un compromiso —¡qué compromiso ni qué ~! tú sales hoy porque lo digo yo "I can't go out tonight, I'm busy" — "busy my arse! you're going out today because I'm telling you"** ▸ coño de madre (Ven**) bastard**, motherfucker (esp EEUU**) 2 (como expresión de alegría) bugger me!** • ¡esto hay que celebrarlo, ~! well bugger me! this calls for a celebration!**

coño²/a SMF (LAm) (pey) (= español) nickname for Spaniard

cooficial ADJ • dos lenguas ~es two languages equally recognized as official

cooficialidad SF • la ~ de dos lenguas the equal official status of two languages

cool* [kul] ADJ INV cool*

cooperación SF cooperation

cooperador(a) ADJ cooperative, collaborating, participating SM/F collaborator, co-worker

cooperante SMF voluntary worker, overseas voluntary worker

cooperar ▷ CONJUG 1a VI to cooperate (en in, con with) • ~ a hacer algo to cooperate in doing sth • ~ a un mismo fin to work for a common aim • ~ en to collaborate in, work together on • los factores que ~on al fracaso the factors which together led to failure, the factors which contributed to the failure

cooperativa SF cooperative, co-op* ▸ cooperativa agrícola agricultural cooperative ▸ cooperativa de crédito credit union ▸ cooperativa industrial industrial cooperative

cooperativismo SM cooperativism; (como movimiento) cooperative movement

cooperativista SMF member of a cooperative

cooperativización SF cooperativization

cooperativizar ▷ CONJUG 1f VT to cooperativize

cooperativo ADJ cooperative

cooptación SF cooption

cooptar ▷ CONJUG 1a VT to coopt (a on, to)

coordenada SF coordinate

coordinación SF coordination

coordinado ADJ (= armonizado) coordinated; (Mil) [operación] combined SMPL coordinados (= ropa) separates

coordinador(a) ADJ coordinating SM/F coordinator

coordinadora SF coordinating committee

coordinar ▷ CONJUG 1a VT (= armonizar)

[+ *movimientos, actividades, equipo, esfuerzo, trabajo*] to coordinate • **se reunieron para ~ una respuesta al conflicto** they met to coordinate a response to the conflict • **tiene dificultades para ~ sus ideas** he has difficulties in organizing his thoughts
VI * • **ha bebido tanto que ya no coordina** he's had so much to drink that his coordination has gone • **hasta que no me tomo un café por las mañanas no coordino** I can't think straight in the mornings until I've had a coffee

copa SF **1** (= *recipiente*) (*para bebidas*) glass; (*para postres*) dessert glass • **huevo a la ~** (*And, Cono Sur*) boiled egg ▸ **copa balón** balloon glass, brandy glass ▸ **copa de champán** champagne glass ▸ **copa de coñac** brandy glass ▸ **copa flauta** champagne flute
2 (= *contenido*) drink • **os invito a una ~** let me buy you a drink • **una ~ de coñac te quitará el frío** a glass of brandy will warm you up • **ir(se)** *o* **salir de ~s** to go out for a drink • **tomarse una ~** to have a drink • **se tomó una ~ de más** he had one too many
3 [*de árbol*] top, crown • MODISMO: • **como la ~ de un pino***: • **es un artista como la ~ de un pino** he's a real star • **es una idiotez como la ~ de un pino** that's the stupidest thing I've ever heard
4 (*Dep*) (= *trofeo, competición*) cup ▸ **Copa de Europa** European Cup ▸ **Copa del Mundo** World Cup ▸ **Copa del Rey** (*Esp*) *Spanish FA Cup* ▸ **Copa Libertadores** (*LAm*) Latin American inter-national cup
5 copas (*Naipes*) *one of the suits in Spanish card deck, represented by a goblet*; ▹ BARAJA ESPAÑOLA
6 [*de sombrero*] crown; ▹ **sombrero**
7 [*de sujetador*] cup
8 (*And*) (*Aut*) hubcap

copado ADJ thick, with dense foliage
copago SM copayment, copay
copal SM **1** (*CAm, Méx*) (= *resina*) resin
2 (*Hist*) incense
copantes SMPL (*CAm, Méx*) stepping stones
copar ▹ CONJUG 1a VT **1** (*Mil*) to surround, cut off
2 (*Econ*) to corner • **~ el mercado** to corner the market
3 (*Pol*) • **han copado todos los escaños** they've made a clean sweep of all the seats
4 (*Naipes*) (*tb* **copar la banca**) to win, win all the tricks
5 (*Méx*) (= *monopolizar*) to monopolize
coparticipación SF joint participation (**en** in)
copartícipe SMF **1** (= *socio*) partner; (= *colaborador*) collaborator (**en** in)
2 (*Dep*) fellow participant, fellow competitor
copazo* SM *mixed drink of e.g. rum and Coke*
COPE SF ABR (= **Cadena de Ondas Populares Españolas**) *radio network*
copear ▹ CONJUG 1a VI **1*** (= *beber*) to booze*, tipple*
2 (*Com*) to sell wine (*etc*) by the glass
Copei SM ABR (*Ven*) (= **Comité Organizador para Elecciones Independientes**) *Christian Democrat party*
Copenhague SM Copenhagen
copeo SM • **ir de ~*** to go drinking
copera SF (*Cono Sur*) hostess
Copérnico SM Copernicus
copero ADJ cup (*antes de s*)
SM (*Cono Sur*) waiter
copete SM **1** [*de persona*] tuft (of hair), quiff; [*de caballo*] forelock; [*de pájaro*] tuft, crest • MODISMOS: • **estar hasta el ~*** to be really fed up • **de alto ~** aristocratic, upper-crust*
2 (= *altanería*) arrogance • **tener mucho ~** to be haughty, be stuck-up*

copetín SM (*Cuba, Cono Sur*) drink, aperitif
copetón ADJ **1** (*LAm*) = **copetudo**
2 (*And**) • **estar ~** to be tight*
copetudo ADJ **1** (*Zool*) tufted, crested
2 (= *engreído*) haughty, stuck-up*
copia SF **1** (= *reproducción*) [*de fotografía, documento*] copy; (*Econ*) duplicate ▸ **copia al carbón** carbon copy ▸ **copia carbónica** (*Cono Sur*) carbon copy ▸ **copia certificada** certified copy ▸ **copia de calco** (*Cono Sur*) carbon copy ▸ **copia de respaldo**, **copia de seguridad** (*Inform*) back-up copy • **hacer una ~ de seguridad** to back up, make a back-up copy ▸ **copia en color** colour *o* (*EEUU*) color copy ▸ **copia en limpio** fair copy ▸ **copia fotostática** photostat, photocopy ▸ **copia impresa** (*Inform*) hard copy
2 (= *imitación*) [*de obra de arte, edificio*] copy
3 (*liter*) (= *abundancia*) abundance, plenty
copiado SM copying
copiador(a) SM/F (= *persona*) copier, copyist
SM (*tb* **libro copiador**) letter-book
copiadora SF photocopier, Xerox® machine
copiante SMF copyist
copiar ▹ CONJUG 1b VT **1** (= *reproducir*) to copy (**de** from); [+ *estilo*] to imitate
2 [+ *dictado*] to take down • **~ al pie de la letra** to copy word for word • **~ por las dos caras** (*Téc*) to make a double-sided copy
VI (*en un examen*) to cheat
copichuela* SF social drink
copihue SM (*Chile*) Chilean bell flower (*national symbol of Chile*)
copilotar ▹ CONJUG 1a VT (*Aut*) to be the co-driver of; (*Aer*) to copilot
copiloto SMF **1** (*Aut*) co-driver
2 (*Aer*) co-pilot
copión/ona* SM/F **1** (= *alumno*) cheat
2 (= *imitador*) copycat*
copiosamente ADV copiously, abundantly, plentifully
copioso ADJ (= *abundante*) copious, abundant; [*lluvia*] heavy
copipega SM copy and paste
copipegar VT to copy and paste
copista SMF copyist
copistería SF copy shop
copita SF glass, small glass • **una ~ de jerez** a little glass of sherry • **tomarse unas ~s** to have a drink or two, have a couple of drinks
copla SF **1** (*Literat*) verse (*esp of 4 lines*)
2 (*Mús*) popular song, ballad; **coplas** verses • **hacer ~s** to write verse • MODISMOS: • **andar en ~s** to be the talk of the town • **la misma ~*** the same old song* • **quedarse con la ~**: • **¿os vais quedando con la ~?** do you follow?, do you get my drift? • **no valen ~s** it's no use your arguing *o* apologizing ▸ **coplas de ciego** doggerel
3 (*LAm*) (*Téc*) pipe joint
copo SM **1** [*de lino*] small bundle ▸ **copo de algodón** cotton ball ▸ **copo de nieve** snowflake ▸ **copos de avena** oatmeal (*sing*), rolled oats ▸ **copos de maíz** cornflakes
2 (*LAm*) [*de árbol*] tree top
3 (*Cono Sur*) (= *nubes*) piled-up clouds (*pl*)
copón SM (= *copa*) large cup; (*Rel*) pyx • **un susto del ~*** a tremendous fright, a hell of a fright‡ • **y todo el ~*** and all that stuff*, and all that*
coprocesador SM co-processor
coproducción SF joint production
coproducir ▹ CONJUG 3n VT to co-produce, produce jointly
coprofilia SF coprophilia
copropiedad SF co-ownership
copropietario/a SM/F co-owner, joint owner

copto/a ADJ Coptic
SM/F Copt
SM (*Ling*) Coptic
copucha SF (*Cono Sur*) gossip
copuchar ▹ CONJUG 1a VI (*Cono Sur*) to gossip
copuchento ADJ (*Cono Sur*) lying
copudo ADJ bushy, thick
cópula SF **1** (*Bio*) copulation ▸ **cópula carnal** copulation, sexual intercourse
2 (*Ling*) conjunction
copulador ADJ copulatory
copular ▹ CONJUG 1a VI to copulate (**con** with)
copulativo ADJ copulative
coque SM coke
coquear ▹ CONJUG 1a VI (*And, Cono Sur*) to chew coca
coqueluche SF whooping cough
coquero/a SM/F cocaine addict
coqueta SF (= *mueble*) dressing table; ▹ **coqueto**
coquetamente ADV coquettishly
coquetear ▹ CONJUG 1a VI to flirt (**con** with)
coqueteo SM, **coquetería** SF (= *cualidad*) flirtatiousness, coquetry; (= *acto*) flirtation
coqueto/a ADJ **1** [*vestido*] smart, natty*, attractive
2 (= *juguetón*) flirtatious, flirty
3 (= *presumido*) • **es muy ~** he's very fussy about his appearance, he's very clothes-conscious
SMF **1** (= *juguetón*) flirt
2 (= *presumido*) • **es una coqueta** she's very fussy about her appearance, she's very clothes-conscious; ▹ **coqueta**
coquetón ADJ **1** [*objeto*] neat*
2 [*persona*] = **coqueto**
coquilla SF (*Cono Sur*) shell
coquitos SMPL • **hacer ~** to make faces (**a** at)
Cor. ABR (= **Coronel**) Col
coracha SF leather bag
coraje SM **1** (= *valor*) courage • **debes tener ~ y enfrentarte a la realidad** you have to be brave *o* have courage and face up to reality • **no tuvo el ~ de admitir su fallo** she wasn't brave enough to admit her mistake
2* (= *rabia*) • **hemos perdido el autobús, ¡qué ~!** we've missed the bus, what a pain!* • **me da ~ que me mientas** it makes me mad* *o* it really annoys me when you lie to me • **me da ~ verlo pasear con mi novia** it makes me mad to see him walking around with my girlfriend*
corajina SF fit of rage
corajudo ADJ **1** (= *irascible*) quick-tempered
2 (= *valiente*) brave, gutsy*
coral[1] (*Mús*) ADJ choral
SM chorale
SF choir
coral[2] SM (*Zool*) coral
SF (= *serpiente*) coral snake
coralina SF coralline
coralino ADJ coral (*antes de s*), coralline
corambre SF hides, skins
Corán SM Koran
corana SF (*And, Cono Sur*) sickle
coránico ADJ Koranic
coraza SF **1** (*Mil, Hist*) cuirass; (= *protección*) protection
2 (*Náut*) armour-plating, armor-plating (*EEUU*)
3 (*Zool*) shell
4 (*Aut*) radiator cover
corazón SM **1** (*Anat*) heart • **le falló el ~** his heart failed, he had heart failure • **estar enfermo** *o* **mal del ~** to have heart trouble *o* problems • **padecer** *o* **sufrir del ~** to have a weak heart, have heart trouble *o* problems • **ser operado a ~ abierto** to have open heart surgery; ▹ **ataque**
2 • MODISMOS: • **abrir el ~ a algn** to open

one's heart to sb, pour one's heart out to sb • **no caberle a algn el ~ en el pecho**: • **cuando me lo dijeron no me cabía el ~ en el pecho** when they told me I was over the moon* • **de ~** sincerely • **te lo digo de ~** I mean it sincerely • **de buen ~** kind-hearted • **de gran ~** big-hearted • **de todo ~**: • **se lo agradezco de todo ~** I thank you with all my heart *o* from the bottom of my heart • **la quería con todo mi ~** I loved her with all my heart • **ser duro de ~** to be hard-hearted • **encoger a algn el ~**: • **aquellas imágenes me encogieron el ~** those scenes made my heart bleed • **un grito en la noche me encogió el ~** a scream during the night made my heart miss a beat • **llegar al ~ de algn**: • **sus palabras me llegaron al ~** I was deeply touched by her words, her words touched my heart • **con el ~ en la mano** with one's hand on one's heart • **partir** *o* **romper el ~ a algn** to break sb's heart • **tener el ~ en la boca** *o* **en un puño** to have one's heart in one's mouth, be on tenterhooks • **tener un ~ de oro** to have a heart of gold • **tener el ~ de piedra** to have a heart of stone • **no tener ~** to have no heart, be heartless • **una mujer sin ~** a heartless woman • **no tener ~ para hacer algo** not to have the heart to do sth; ▷ **vuelco**

3 (*Prensa*) • **la prensa del ~** gossip magazines (*pl*) • **una revista del ~** a gossip magazine

4 (*apelativo*) • **sí, ~** yes, sweetheart • **¡hijo de mi ~!** (my) darling!

5 (= *centro*) [*de ciudad, zona, alcachofa*] heart; [*de manzana*] core • **limpie las manzanas y quíteles el ~** wash and core the apples

6 corazones (*Naipes*) hearts

corazonada SF **1** (= *presentimiento*) hunch
2 (= *impulso*) impulsive act

corazoncito* SM • **tener su ~** to have a heart

corbata SF tie, necktie (*EEUU*) ▸ **corbata de humita** (*Chile*) bow tie ▸ **corbata de lazo, corbata de moño** (*LAm*) bow tie ▸ **corbata de smoking** black tie ▸ **corbata michi** (*And*) bow tie

corbatín SM bow tie

corbeta SF corvette

corca SF woodworm

Córcega SF Corsica

corcel SM steed, charger

corcha SF cork bark, piece of cork bark

corchea SF quaver, eighth (note) (*EEUU*)

corchero ADJ cork (*antes de s*) • **industria corchera** cork industry

corcheta SF eye (*of hook and eye*)

corchete SM **1** (*Cos*) (= *broche*) hook and eye; (= *macho*) hook
2 corchetes (*Tip*) square brackets ▸ **corchetes agudos** angled brackets
3 (*Chile*) (= *grapa*) staple

corchetear ▷ CONJUG 1a VT (*Cono Sur*) to staple, staple together

corchetera SF (*Chile*) stapler

corcho SM **1** [*de botella*] cork • **sacar el ~ de la botella** to uncork the bottle
2 (= *corteza*) cork bark • **de ~** cork (*antes de s*) ▸ **corcho bornizo, corcho virgen** virgin cork
3 (= *estera*) cork mat
4 (= *zueco*) cork-soled clog
5 (*Pesca*) float

corcholata SF (*Méx*) metal bottle top

córcholis* EXCL good Lord!, dear me!

corchoso ADJ corklike, corky

corcor SM (*CAm, Caribe*) gurgle • **beber ~*** to swig*, knock it back*

corcova SF **1** (*Med*) hump, hunch
2 (*And, Cono Sur*) (= *fiesta*) all-night party

corcovado/a ADJ hunchbacked
SM/F hunchback

corcovar ▷ CONJUG 1a VT to bend, bend over

corcovear ▷ CONJUG 1a VI **1** (= *brincar*) [*persona*] to prance about, cut capers; [*caballo*] to buck
2 (*And, Caribe, Cono Sur*) (= *quejarse*) to grumble, grouse*
3 (*Méx*) (= *tener miedo*) to be frightened, be afraid

corcovo SM **1** (= *brinco*) prance, caper; [*de caballo*] buck
2* (= *torcimiento*) crookedness*

cordada SF roped team

cordaje SM (= *cuerdas*) cordage, ropes; [*de raqueta*] strings; (*Náut*) rigging

cordal SM hill range

cordel SM cord, line • **a ~** in a straight line

cordelería SF **1** (= *cuerdas*) cordage, ropes; (*Náut*) rigging
2 (= *oficio*) ropemaking
3 (= *fábrica*) ropeyard, ropeworks

cordelero/a SM/F cordmaker, ropemaker

cordería SF cordage, cords, ropes

corderillo SM lambskin

cordero/a SM/F (*Zool*) lamb • MODISMOS: • **¡no hay tales ~s!** it's nothing of the sort! • **es (como) un ~** he wouldn't say "boo" to a goose, he's as quiet as a mouse ▸ **cordero asado** roast lamb ▸ **Cordero de Dios** Lamb of God ▸ **cordero lechal** young lamb
SM (= *piel*) lambskin

corderuna SF lambskin

cordial ADJ **1** (= *afectuoso*) warm, cordial
2 (*Med*) invigorating
SM cordial, tonic

cordialidad SF warmth, cordiality

cordialmente ADV warmly, cordially; (*en carta*) sincerely

cordillera SF mountain range, mountain chain

cordillerano ADJ (*Cono Sur*) Andean

cordita SF cordite

Córdoba SF (*Esp*) Cordova; (*Arg*) Cordoba

córdoba SM (*Nic*) *monetary unit of Nicaragua*

cordobán SM cordovan, cordovan leather

cordobana SF • MODISMO: • **andar a la ~** to go around stark naked

cordobés/esa ADJ, SM/F Cordovan

cordón SM **1** (= *cuerda*) cord, string; [*de zapato*] lace, shoelace • **lana de tres cordones** three-ply wool • **aparcar en ~** to park in a (straight) line
2 (*Náut*) strand; (*Mil*) braid; **cordones** (*Mil*) aiguillettes
3 (*Elec*) flex, wire (*EEUU*), cord (*EEUU*) ▸ **cordón detonante** (*Cono Sur*) fuse
4 (*Anat*) cord ▸ **cordón umbilical** umbilical cord
5 [*de policía*] cordon ▸ **cordón sanitario** cordon sanitaire
6 (*Arquit*) cordon
7 (*Cono Sur*) (= *bordillo*) kerb, curb (*EEUU*)
8 (*Geog*) ▸ **cordón de cerros** (*And, Caribe, Cono Sur*) chain of hills
9 (*And, Caribe*) (= *licor*) liquor, brandy

cordoncillo SM **1** [*de tela*] rib; (= *bordado*) braid, piping
2 [*de moneda*] milled edge

cordura SF **1** (*Med*) sanity
2 (= *sensatez*) good sense • **con ~** sensibly, wisely

Corea SF Korea ▸ **Corea del Norte** North Korea ▸ **Corea del Sur** South Korea

coreano/a ADJ, SM/F Korean

corear ▷ CONJUG 1a VT to chorus; [+ *eslogan*] shout in unison, chant; (*Mús*) to sing in chorus, sing together • **su opinión es coreada por ...** his opinion is echoed by ...

coreografía SF choreography

coreografiar ▷ CONJUG 1c VT to choreograph

coreográfico ADJ choreographic

coreógrafo/a SM/F choreographer

Corfú SM Corfu

coriana SF (*And*) blanket

corifeo SM **1** (*Hist*) coryphaeus
2 (= *portavoz*) leader, spokesman

corindón SM corundum

corintio ADJ Corinthian

Corinto SM Corinth

corinto ADJ INV maroon, purplish
SM maroon, purplish colour

corista SMF (*Rel, Mús*) chorister
SF (*Teat*) chorus girl

coritatis* ADV • **estar en ~** to be in the buff*

cormorán SM cormorant

cornada SF butt, goring • **dar una ~ a** to gore

cornadura SF [*de toro*] horns (*pl*); [*de ciervo*] antlers (*pl*)

cornalina SF cornelian, carnelian

cornamenta SF **1** [*de toro*] horns (*pl*); [*de ciervo*] antlers (*pl*)
2 (*hum*) [*de marido*] cuckold's horns • MODISMO: • **poner la ~ a algn** to cuckold sb

cornamusa SF (= *gaita*) bagpipe; (= *cuerna*) hunting horn

córnea SF cornea

corneal ADJ corneal

cornear ▷ CONJUG 1a VT to butt, gore

corneja SF crow ▸ **corneja calva** rook ▸ **corneja negra** carrion crow

córneo ADJ horny, corneous (*frm*)

córner ['korner] SM (PL: **córners**) **1** (*Dep*) corner, corner kick • **¡córner!** (*excl*) corner! • **enviar a ~** to send (out) for a corner • **sacar un ~** to take a corner
2 (*LAm*) (*Boxeo*) corner

cornerina SF cornelian, carnelian

corneta SF (= *instrumento*) bugle; (*Caribe*) (*Aut*) horn ▸ **corneta acústica** ear trumpet ▸ **corneta de llaves** cornet ▸ **corneta de monte** hunting horn
SMF bugler, cornet player

cornetear ▷ CONJUG 1a VI (*Caribe*) (*Aut*) to sound one's horn

cornetín/ina SM (= *instrumento*) cornet
SM/F (= *instrumentista*) cornet player

cornetista SMF bugler

corneto ADJ (*CAm*) bow-legged

cornezuelo SM ergot

cornflaques SMPL (*LAm*), **cornflés** SMPL (*LAm*) cornflakes

cornial ADJ horn-shaped

córnico ADJ Cornish
SM (*Ling*) Cornish

corniforme ADJ horn-shaped

cornisa SF cornice • **la Cornisa Cantábrica** the Cantabrian coast

cornisamento SM entablature

corno SM (*Mús*) horn ▸ **corno de caza** hunting horn ▸ **corno inglés** cor anglais, English horn (*EEUU*)

Cornualles SM Cornwall

cornucopia SF **1** (*Mit*) cornucopia, horn of plenty
2 (= *espejo*) *small ornamental mirror*

cornudo ADJ **1** (*Zool*) horned
2 [*marido*] cuckolded
SM cuckold

cornúpeta SM (*Taur*) bull; (*hum*) cuckold

coro SM **1** (= *agrupación*) choir • **canto en un ~** I sing in a choir • **niño de ~** choirboy
2 (= *composición*) (*en obra musical, tragedia*) chorus • **una chica del ~** a girl from the chorus, a chorus girl • **un ~ de críticas** a chorus of criticism • **decir algo a ~** to say sth in a chorus *o* in unison • **hacer ~ de** *o* **a las palabras de algn** to echo sb's words

• MODISMO: • **hacer ~ a algn** to back sb up
3 (*Arquit*) choir
4 [*de ángeles*] choir ▸ **coro celestial** celestial choir, heavenly choir
corola SF corolla
corolario SM corollary
corona SF 1 [*de rey, reina*] crown; [*de santo*] halo; (*tb* **corona de flores**) (*para la cabeza*) garland ▸ **corona de espinas** crown of thorns ▸ **corona de laurel** (*lit*) laurel wreath
2 [*de difuntos*] wreath ▸ **corona funeraria**, **corona mortuoria** funeral wreath; ▹ **ceñir**
3 • **la Corona** (= *monarquía*) the Crown; (*Hist*) (= *reino*) the kingdom • **el heredero de la ~** the crown prince • **en la mayor parte de la Corona de Castilla** throughout most of the Kingdom of Castile
4 [*de muela*] (*natural*) crown; (*artificial*) crown, artificial crown
5 (*Mec*) [*de coche*] crown wheel; [*de bicicleta*] chain wheel; [*de reloj*] winder, crown
6 (*Econ*) [*de Suecia, Islandia, Rep. Checa*] crown
7 (*Astron*) corona; (*Meteo*) halo • **la ~ solar** the sun's corona
8 [*de monje*] tonsure
coronación SF 1 [*de rey*] coronation
2 (= *fin*) end, culmination
3 (*Arquit*) = **coronamiento**
4 (*Ajedrez*) queening
coronamiento SM 1 (= *fin*) end, culmination
2 (*Arquit*) crown
coronar ▹ CONJUG 1a VT 1 [+ *persona*] to crown • **~ a algn rey** to crown sb king
2 • **~ la cima** to reach the summit
3 (= *completar*) to crown, culminate, end • **coronó su trayectoria deportiva con una gran victoria en Wimbledon** he crowned *o* culminated *o* ended his sporting career with a great win at Wimbledon • **~ algo con éxito** to crown sth with success • **para ~lo** to crown it all
4 (*Ajedrez, Damas*) to queen
5 (*And, Caribe, Cono Sur*) (= *poner los cuernos a*) to cuckold, make a cuckold of
coronario ADJ coronary
coronel SM/F colonel ▸ **coronel de aviación** group captain, colonel (EEUU)
coronela SF (*Hist*) colonel's wife
coronilla SF crown, top of the head • **andar** *o* **bailar** *o* **ir de ~** to bend over backwards to please sb • **dar de ~** to bump one's head • **estar hasta la ~** to be utterly fed up (**de** with)
coronta SF (*And, Cono Sur*) deseeded corncob
corotear ▹ CONJUG 1a VI (*And*) to move house
coroto SM 1 (*Ven*) (= *poder*) power • **tomar el ~** to take power
2 **corotos** (*Col, Ven**) (= *trastos*) odds and ends
corpacho* SM, **corpanchón*** SM, **corpazo*** SM carcass*
corpiño SM (= *almilla*) bodice; (*LAm*) (= *sostén*) bra
corporación SF corporation
corporal ADJ corporal, bodily • **castigo ~** corporal punishment • **ejercicio ~** physical exercise • **higiene ~** personal hygiene
corporativismo SM corporate spirit
corporativista ADJ corporatist
corporativo ADJ corporate
corporeidad SF corporeal nature
corporeizar ▹ CONJUG 1f VT (= *encarnar*) to embody
VI (= *aparecer*) to materialize, turn up
VPR **corporeizarse** (= *tomar cuerpo*) to come about
corpóreo ADJ corporeal, bodily
corpulencia SF burliness, stoutness • **cayó con toda su ~** he fell with his full weight
corpulento ADJ [*persona*] burly, heavily-built; [*árbol*] stout, solid, massive
Corpus SM Corpus Christi
corpus SM INV corpus, body ▸ **corpus lingüístico** language corpus
corpúsculo SM corpuscle
corral SM 1 (*Agr*) (= *patio*) farmyard; [*de aves*] poultry yard; (= *redil*) pen, corral (EEUU); [*de pesca*] weir • MODISMO: • **hacer ~es** to play truant ▸ **corral de abasto** (*Cono Sur*) slaughterhouse ▸ **corral de carbonera** coal dump, coalyard ▸ **corral de madera** timberyard ▸ **corral de vacas*** slum ▸ **corral de vecindad** tenement
2 [*de niño*] playpen
corralillo SM, **corralito** SM playpen
corralón SM 1 (= *patio*) large yard; (= *madería*) timberyard
2 (*Perú*) (= *terreno*) vacant site *o* (EEUU) lot
correa SF 1 (= *cinturón*) belt; (= *tira*) strap; (= *ronzal*) tether; (*para afilar una navaja*) strop • **la ~ de mi reloj** my watchstrap, my watchband (EEUU) • MODISMO: • **besar la ~††** to eat humble pie
2 [*de perro*] leash, lead
3 (*Mec*) ▸ **correa de seguridad** safety belt ▸ **correa de transmisión** driving belt, drive ▸ **correa de transporte** conveyor belt ▸ **correa de ventilador, correa del ventilador** (*Aut*) fan belt ▸ **correa sin fin** endless belt ▸ **correa transportadora** conveyor belt
4 (= *aguante*) give, elasticity • MODISMO: • **tener ~**: • **por cualquier cosa se enfada, tiene muy poca ~** she gets angry at the slightest thing, she has a very short fuse
correaje SM (= *correas*) straps (*pl*); (*Agr*) harness; (*Mil*) leathers (*pl*); (*Téc*) belting
correalizador(a) SM/F co-director
correcalles SF INV streetwalker, hooker (EEUU*)
correcaminata SF fun run
corrección SF 1 (= *arreglo*) correction ▸ **corrección de pruebas** (*Tip*) proofreading ▸ **corrección por líneas** (*Inform*) line editing
2 (= *censura*) rebuke, reprimand; (= *castigo*) punishment
3 (= *perfección*) correctness
4 (= *cortesía*) courtesy, good manners
correccional SM reformatory
correcorre SM (*Caribe*) headlong rush, stampede
correctamente ADV 1 (= *exactamente*) correctly, accurately
2 (= *decentemente*) correctly, politely
correctivo ADJ, SM corrective
correcto ADJ 1 [*respuesta*] correct, right • **¡correcto!** right!
2 (= *educado*) [*persona*] correct; [*conducta, comportamiento*] courteous; [*vestido*] proper, fitting • **estuvo muy ~ conmigo** he was very polite to me
3 [*rasgos*] regular, well-formed
corrector(a) SM/F ▸ **corrector(a) de estilo** (*Prensa*) copy editor ▸ **corrector(a) de pruebas** (*Tip*) proofreader
SM 1 (= *líquido*) correcting fluid
2 ▸ **corrector ortográfico** (*Inform*) spell checker, spelling checker
3 (*tb* **corrector dental**) brace, tooth brace
corredera SF 1 (*Téc*) slide; (= *ranura*) track, rail, runner • **puerta de ~** sliding door
2 (*Náut*) log
3 [*de molino*] upper millstone
4 (= *cucaracha*) cockroach
5 (*Dep*) racetrack
6 (*Cono Sur*) (= *rápidos*) rapids (*pl*)
corredero SM 1 (*Méx*) (*Dep*) racetrack
2 (*And*) (= *lecho de río*) old riverbed
corredizo ADJ [*puerta*] sliding; [*nudo*] running, slip (*antes de s*); [*grúa*] travelling, traveling (EEUU)
corredor(a) SM/F 1 (*Dep*) (= *atleta*) runner; [*de coches*] driver ▸ **corredor(a) automovilista** racing driver ▸ **corredor(a) ciclista** racing cyclist ▸ **corredor(a) de fondo, corredor(a) de larga distancia** long-distance runner ▸ **corredor(a) de pista** track athlete
2 (= *agente*) agent, broker ▸ **corredor(a) de apuestas** bookmaker ▸ **corredor(a) de bienes raíces** estate agent, real estate agent *o* broker (EEUU) ▸ **corredor(a) de bodas††** matchmaker ▸ **corredor(a) de bolsa** stockbroker ▸ **corredor(a) de casas** house agent ▸ **corredor(a) de comercio** business agent ▸ **corredor(a) de fincas** estate agent, real estate agent *o* broker (EEUU) ▸ **corredor(a) de fincas rurales** land agent ▸ **corredor(a) de oreja††** gossip ▸ **corredor(a) de propiedades** (*Cono Sur*) estate agent, real estate agent *o* broker (EEUU) ▸ **corredor(a) de seguros** insurance broker
SM 1 (= *pasillo*) corridor, passage ▸ **corredor de la muerte** death row ▸ **corredor de popa** (*Náut*) stern gallery
2 (*Geog, Mil*) corridor ▸ **corredor aéreo** corridor, air corridor
3 (*Méx*) (*Caza*) beater
4 (*Mil††*) raider
correduría SF brokerage
corregible ADJ rectifiable
corregido ADJ [*examen*] marked
corregidor SM (*Hist*) chief magistrate
corregidora SF (*Hist*) wife of the chief magistrate
corregimiento SM (*Col*) small town
corregir ▹ CONJUG 3c, 3k VT 1 (= *rectificar*) [+ *error, defecto, rumbo, pruebas de imprenta*] to correct; [+ *vicio*] to get rid of; [+ *comportamiento*] to improve; [+ *tendencia*] to correct, counteract; (*Econ*) [+ *déficit*] to counteract • **¡deja ya de ~me!** stop correcting me! • **me gusta que me corrijan cuando hablo en inglés** I like people to correct me when I speak English • **corrígeme si me equivoco, pero creo que aquí hemos estado ya** correct me if I'm wrong, but I think we've been here before
2 (*Educ*) [+ *examen, dictado, tareas*] to mark, grade (EEUU)
VPR **corregirse** 1 [*persona*] to reform, mend one's ways
2 [*defecto*] • **nadando se te ~á la desviación de columna** swimming will help to correct the curvature of your spine • **la miopía no puede ~se sola** shortsightedness does not cure itself
correlación SF correlation
correlacionar ▹ CONJUG 1a VT to correlate
correlativo ADJ, SM correlative
correligionario/a SM/F 1 (*Rel*) co-religionist
2 (*Pol*) • **el presidente y sus ~s** the president and his fellow party members
correlón ADJ 1 (*LAm*) [*persona*] fast, good at running
2 (*Méx, Ven*) (= *cobarde*) cowardly
correntada SF (*Cono Sur*) rapids (*pl*), strong current
correntón ADJ 1 (= *activo*) busy, active
2 (= *bromista*) jokey, jolly, fond of a lark
SM (*And, Caribe*) strong current
correntoso ADJ (*LAm*) [*río*] strong-flowing, rapid; [*agua*] torrential
correo SM 1 (= *correspondencia*) post, mail • **¿ha llegado el ~?** has the post *o* mail come?
2 (= *servicio*) post, mail • **echar algo al ~**

• **poner algo en el ~** to post sth, mail sth (*esp EEUU*) • **llevar algo al ~** to take sth to the post • **por ~** by post, through the post • **a vuelta de ~** by return (of post) ▸ **correo aéreo** airmail ▸ **correo basura** (*por carta*) junk mail; (*por Internet*) spam, junk email ▸ **correo certificado** registered post ▸ **correo electrónico** email, electronic mail ▸ **correo urgente** special delivery ▸ **correo web** webmail
3 (= *oficina*) • **Correos** post office (*sing*) • **ir a ~s** to go to the post office • **Dirección General de Correos** General Post Office
4 • **el ~** (*Ferro*) the mail train, the slow train
5 (= *mensajero*) courier; (*Mil*) dispatch rider ▸ **correo de gabinete** Queen's Messenger, diplomatic courier (EEUU)

correosidad (SF) **1** (*Culin*) toughness, leatheriness
2 (= *flexibilidad*) flexibility

correoso (ADJ) **1** (*Culin*) tough, leathery
2 (= *flexible*) flexible
3 [*asunto, situación*] difficult, tricky*

correr ▸ CONJUG 2a (VI) **1** (= *ir deprisa*) [*persona, animal*] to run; [*vehículo*] to go fast • **tuve que ~ para alcanzar el autobús** I had to run to catch the bus • **se me acercó corriendo** he ran up to me • **subió las escaleras corriendo** he ran up the stairs • **corrió a decírselo** he ran to tell him • **¡cómo corre este coche!** this car's really fast!, this car can really go some! • **no corras tanto, que hay hielo en la carretera** don't go so fast, the road's icy • **echar a ~** to start running, break into a run • **el ladrón echó a ~** the thief ran off • MODISMO: • **~ como un galgo** *o* **gamo** to run like a hare
2 (= *darse prisa*) to hurry, rush • **¡corre!** hurry (up)! • **corre que llegamos tarde** hurry (up) or we'll be late • **no corras que te equivocarás** don't rush it or you'll make a mistake • **me voy corriendo, que sale el tren dentro de diez minutos** I must dash, the train leaves in ten minutes • **llega el jefe, más vale que te vayas corriendo** the boss is coming so you'd better get out of here • **hacer algo a todo ~** to do sth as fast as one can • **salieron a todo ~** they rushed out as fast as they could
3 (= *fluir*) [*agua*] to run, flow; [*aire*] to flow; [*grifo, fuente*] to run • **el río corre muy crecido** the river is running very high • **corre mucho viento** there's a strong wind blowing, it's very windy • **voy a cerrar la ventana porque corre un poco de aire** I'm going to shut the window because there's a bit of a draught *o* draft (EEUU) • **el camino corre por un paisaje pintoresco** the road runs *o* goes through picturesque countryside • **han corrido ríos de tinta sobre el asunto** reams and reams have been written on the subject • **por sus venas corre sangre china** he has Chinese blood
• **~ paralelo a**: • **una cadena montañosa que corre paralela a la costa** a chain of mountains that runs parallel to the coast • **la historia de los ordenadores corre paralela a los adelantos en materia de semiconductores** the history of computers runs parallel to advances in semiconductor technology • MODISMO: • **dejar las cosas ~** to let matters take their course; ▹ **sangre**
4 [*tiempo*] • **el tiempo corre** time is getting on *o* pressing • **¡cómo corre el tiempo!** time flies! • **el mes que corre** the current month, the present month • **corría el año 1965** it was 1965 • **al** *o* **con el ~ del tiempo** over the years • **en estos** *o* **los tiempos que corren** nowadays, these days • **en los tiempos que corren es difícil encontrar personas tan honradas** it's hard to find people as honest as him these days *o* nowadays • **es un tipo demasiado sensible para los tiempos que corren** he's too sensitive for this day and age
5 (= *moverse*) [*rumor*] to go round; [*creencia*] to be widespread • **el dinero corre con fluidez** money is constantly changing hands • **las noticias corren muy deprisa** news travels fast • **corre por ahí un documento muy interesante** there's a very interesting document going around • **la noticia corría de boca en boca** the news was on everyone's lips • **la noticia corrió como la pólvora** the news spread like wildfire
6 (= *hacerse cargo*) • **eso corre de mi cuenta** I'll take care of that • **~ a cargo de algn**: • **eso corre a cargo de la empresa** the company will take care of that • **la entrega del premio corrió a cargo del ministro de Cultura** the prize was presented by the Minister for Culture • **la música corrió a cargo de la RPO** the music was provided by the RPO • **la traducción ha corrido a cargo de Cortázar** the translation is by Cortázar • **~ con algo**: • **~ con los gastos** to meet *o* bear the expenses • **el inversor corre con los riesgos** the investor bears the risk • **~ con la casa** to run the house, manage the house
7 (*Econ*) [*sueldo*] to be payable; [*moneda*] to be valid • **su sueldo ~á desde el primer día del mes** his salary will be payable from the first of the month
8 • **~ a** *o* **por** (= *venderse*) to sell at
(VT) **1** (*Dep*) [+ *distancia*] to run; [+ *prueba*] to compete in • **corre cinco kilómetros diarios** she runs five kilometres a day • **corrí 50 metros hasta alcanzar la carretera** I ran for 50 metres until I reached the road • **Carl Lewis has decidido no ~ los 100 metros** Carl Lewis has decided not to run (in) *o* compete in the 100 metres • **corrió la Vuelta a España** he competed in the Tour of Spain • **ha corrido medio mundo** he's been round half the world
2 (= *desplazar*) [+ *objeto*] to move along; [+ *silla*] to move; [+ *balanza*] to tip; [+ *nudo*] to adjust; [+ *vela*] to unfurl • **corre un poco la silla para allá** move the chair (along) that way a little • **corrió el pestillo** she bolted the door • **corre la cortina** draw the curtain; ▹ **velo**
3 (= *hacer correr*) [+ *caballo*] to run, race; [+ *caza*] to chase, pursue • **~ un toro** *to run in front of and avoid being gored by a charging bull for sport*
4 (= *tener*) [+ *riesgo*] to run; [+ *suerte*] to suffer, undergo • **corren el riesgo de ser encarcelados** they run the risk of being sent to prison • **no quería ~ la misma suerte de su amigo** he didn't want to suffer *o* undergo the same fate as his friend • **no corréis peligro** you're not in (any) danger • **el acuerdo no parece ~ peligro** the agreement doesn't seem to be in danger; ▹ **prisa**
5 (= *extender*) • **el agua corrió la pintura** the water made the paint run • **las lágrimas le corrieron el maquillaje** her tears made her make-up run • **has corrido la tinta por toda la página** you've smeared the ink across the page
6 (*Mil*) (= *invadir*) to raid; (= *destruir*) to lay waste
7 (*Com*) to auction
8 (= *abochornar*) to embarrass
9 (*esp LAm**) (= *expulsar*) to chuck out* • **lo corrieron de la casa con gritos y patadas** they chucked him kicking and screaming out of the house*
10 • **~la*** (= *ir de juerga*) to live it up*
(VPR) **correrse 1** (= *desplazarse*) [*objeto, persona*] to move; [*peso*] to shift • **el tablero se ha corrido unos centímetros** the board has moved a few centimetres • **córrete un poco** move over *o* up a bit • **córrete un poco hacia este lado** move this way a bit • **el dolor se me ha corrido hacia la pierna** the pain has moved to my leg • **~se de asiento** to move up a seat
2 (= *extenderse*) [*colores, maquillaje, tinta*] to run • **se me han corrido las medias** I've got a ladder *o* (EEUU) run in my tights
3 • **~se la clase*** to skive off*, play hooky (*EEUU**)
4* (= *avergonzarse*) to be embarrassed; (= *aturdirse*) to be disconcerted
5 (*CAm, Caribe, Méx*) (= *huir*) to take flight, run away; (= *acobardarse*) to get scared, take fright
6** (= *tener un orgasmo*) to come**
7 (*Perú***) to screw**; ▹ **juerga**

correría (SF) **1** (*Mil*) raid, foray
2 (= *viaje*) trip, excursion; **correrías** travels

correspondencia (SF) **1** (= *cartas*) mail, post • **abrir la ~** to open the mail • **despachar la ~** to deal with *o* attend to the mail ▸ **correspondencia entrante** incoming mail ▸ **correspondencia privada** private correspondence
2 (= *relación por correo*) correspondence • **estar en ~ con algn** to be in correspondence with sb • **mantener ~ con algn** to correspond with sb • **un curso de dibujo por ~** a correspondence course in drawing • **jugar al ajedrez por ~** to play chess by correspondence
3 (*en el metro*) connection • **"~ con las líneas 3 y 5"** "change here for lines 3 and 5"
4 (= *relación recíproca*) correspondence
5 (*Mat*) correspondence

corresponder ▸ CONJUG 2a (VI) **1** (= *tocar*) **a** (*en reparto*) • **nos correspondieron diez euros a cada uno** each of us got ten euros as our share
b (*como derecho*) • **le corresponde un tercio de los beneficios** a third share of the profits goes to him • **me corresponde un día de vacaciones cada dos semanas** I am due one day's holiday every two weeks • **este hecho no ocupa el lugar que le corresponde en la historia de España** this event does not occupy the place it should in Spanish history, this event is not accorded the importance it deserves in Spanish history
c (*en sorteo, competición*) [*honor, victoria*] to go to • **el honor de representar a su país correspondió a Juan Blanco** the honour of representing his country fell to *o* went to Juan Blanco • **la victoria final correspondió a Escartín** the final victory was Escartín's, the final victory went to Escartín • **al primer premio le correspondieron 30.000 euros** the winner of the first prize received 30,000 euros
2 (= *incumbir*) • **~ a algn** [*responsabilidad*] to fall to sb • **esta decisión le corresponde al director** this decision is for the director (to take), this decision falls to the director • **le corresponde a ella decidir** it's up to her to decide • **nos corresponde a todos garantizar la calidad** it's everyone's job to ensure quality • **a mí no me corresponde criticarlo** it is not for me to criticize him, it is not my place to criticize him • **"a quien corresponda"** "to whom it may concern"
3 (= *deberse*) • **~ a algo: de los 50 millones de ganancias, 40 corresponden a ventas en el extranjero** out of profits of 50 million, 40 million comes from overseas sales *o* overseas sales account for 40 million • **la**

mayor parte de nuestra deuda corresponde a préstamos norteamericanos most of our debt is a result of American loans, American loans account for most of our debt
4 (*frm*) (= *ser adecuado*) • **~ a: se vistió como correspondía a la ocasión** she dressed suitably for the occasion • **fue recibido como corresponde a una persona de su cargo** he was received in a manner befitting a person of his rank, he was received as befitted a person of his rank
5 (= *concordar*) • **~ a** *o* **con** to match with, match up with • **su versión de los hechos no corresponde a la realidad** her version of the events does not match up with *o* correspond to *o* tally with the truth • **el presunto delincuente, cuyas iniciales corresponden a las siglas R.C.A.** the alleged perpetrator of the crime, whose initials are R.C.A. • **los dos cadáveres hallados corresponden a los dos secuestrados** the two bodies found are those of the two kidnap victims • **esa forma de actuar no corresponde con sus principios** such behaviour is not in keeping with his principles
6 (= *retribuir*) • **~ a** [+ *cariño, amor*] to return; [+ *favor, generosidad*] to repay, return • **ella lo amaba, pero él no le correspondía** she loved him but he did not return her love *o* love her back *o* love her in return • **un amor no correspondido** unrequited love • **nunca podré ~ a tanta generosidad** I can never adequately repay *o* return such generosity • **pero ella le correspondió con desprecio** but she responded with contempt, but all she gave in return was contempt
7 (*Mat*) to correspond
8 (*Ferro*) • **~ con algo** to connect with sth
VPR **corresponderse 1** (= *ajustarse*) • **~se con algo** to match sth • **esas muestras no se correspondían con las del laboratorio** these samples did not match (up with) the laboratory ones • **el éxito deportivo no siempre se ha correspondido con una buena organización** sporting success has not always been matched by good organization • **eso no se corresponde con su modo de actuar** that is not in keeping with his usual behaviour
2 (= *coordinarse*) [*colores, piezas*] to match, go together
3 (*por carta*) • **~se con algn** to correspond with sb

correspondiente ADJ **1** (= *apropiado*) appropriate • **adjunto le envío fotocopia de toda la documentación ~** I enclose a photocopy of all the appropriate documentation
2 • **~ a: los datos ~s al año anterior** the figures for the previous year • **facturas ~s a gastos de viajes** invoices for travel expenses • **en el número ~ al 15 de agosto pasado, la revista ...** in its issue of 15 August, the magazine ... • **el partido ~ a la décima jornada de la liga** the match of the tenth day of the league championship
3 (= *respectivo*) respective • **dos épocas distintas, con sus ~s conflictos ideológicos** two different eras, with their respective ideological conflicts • **cada regalo con su tarjeta ~** each present with its own card • **entregó el premio y su ~ banda a la ganadora** he awarded the prize and accompanying sash to the winner
SMF [*de academia*] corresponding member

corresponsabilidad SF joint responsibility

corresponsable ADJ jointly responsible (**de** for)

corresponsal SMF correspondent, newspaper correspondent ▸ **corresponsal de guerra** war correspondent

corretaje SM brokerage

corretear ▹ CONJUG 1a VT **1** (*LAm*) (= *acosar*) to harass
2 (*CAm*) (= *ahuyentar*) to scare off
3 (*Cono Sur*) [+ *trabajo*] to hurry along, push*
VI **1** (= *ir de prisa*) to run about
2 (= *vagar*) to loiter, hang about the streets

correteo SM • **andar en ~s** (*CAm*) to rush about

corretero/a SM/F busy person, gadabout

correvedile SMF, **correveidile** SMF (= *acusica*) tell-tale; (= *chismoso*) gossip

corrida SF **1** (= *carrera*) run • **dar una ~** to make a dash • **decir algo de ~** to rattle off sth • **en una ~** in an instant
2 • **~ (de toros)** (*Taur*) bullfight • MODISMO: • **tener ~ de toros (en casa)** to have a big family row
3** (= *orgasmo*) orgasm
4 (*Geol*) outcrop
5 (*Chile*) (= *fila*) row, line
6 (*Caribe, Cono Sur*) (= *fiesta*) party, rave-up*, hot party (EEUU)
7 (*Méx*) (= *recorrido*) run, journey

corrido ADJ **1** [*habitación, galería*] continuous
2 [*cortinas*] drawn
3 (= *avergonzado*) abashed, embarrassed • **~ de vergüenza** covered with shame
4 (= *experimentado*) worldly-wise, sharp • **es una mujer corrida** she's a woman who has been around
5 (*con expresiones temporales*) • **tres noches corridas** three nights running • **hasta muy corrida la noche** far into the night
6 [*peso, medida*] extra, extra large • **un kilo ~** a good kilo, a kilo and a bit
7 [*estilo*] fluent, confident • **de ~** fluently • **decir algo de ~** to rattle sth off • **se sabía la lección de ~** he knew it all right through, he could say it all from memory
8 (*Méx*) • **comida corrida** fixed price menu
SM **1** (*Méx*) (= *balada*) ballad
2 (*Perú*) (= *fugitivo*) fugitive from justice

> **CORRIDO**
> **Corridos** are Mexican ballads, usually sung by a solo voice and accompanied on the guitar. Traditionally they were used to narrate important events to semi-literate communities, and favourite themes include the Mexican Revolution and Mexican migration to the USA. The **corrido** is similar in form to the Spanish **romance** from which it derives, but deals with the common people's struggle for justice, rather than the chivalrous deeds of the aristocracy.

corriente ADJ **1** (= *frecuente*) [*error, apellido*] common • **las intoxicaciones son bastante ~s en verano** cases of food poisoning are fairly common in summer • **la cocaína era ~ en sus fiestas** cocaine was commonly used *o* commonplace was at their parties • **aquí es ~ que la policía te pida la documentación** here it's quite common for the police to ask you for identification • **una combinación de cualidades que no es ~ encontrar en una misma persona** a combination of qualities not commonly *o* often found in the same person • **un término de uso ~** a common term, a term in common use • **poco ~** unusual
2 (= *habitual*) usual, customary • **lo ~ es llamar antes de venir** the usual thing is to phone before coming, it's customary to phone before coming • **es ~ que la familia de la novia pague la boda** it's customary for the bride's family to pay for the wedding, the bride's family usually pays for the wedding
3 (= *no especial*) ordinary • **no es nada especial, es solo un anillo ~** it's nothing special, it's just an ordinary ring • **fuera de lo ~** out of the ordinary • **normal y ~** perfectly ordinary • **salirse de lo ~** to be out of the ordinary • MODISMO: • **~ y moliente** (*Esp*) very ordinary • **tiene un trabajo ~ y moliente** he has a very ordinary job, he has a run-of-the-mill job
4 (*en curso*) [*déficit, mes, año*] current • **el día 2 del ~ mes de marzo** (on) the second of this month; ▹ **cuenta, gasto, moneda**
5 [*agua*] running
6† (= *en regla*) in order • **tiene ~ la documentación** his papers are in order • **todo está ~ para nuestra partida** everything is ready *o* fixed up for our departure • **estar** *o* **ir ~ en algo** to be up to date with sth • **está ~ en los pagos** he is up to date with his payments
SM **1** • **al ~ a** (= *al día*) up to date • **estoy al ~ de mis pagos a Hacienda** I'm up to date with *o* on my tax payments • **poner algo al ~** to bring sth up to date
b (= *informado*) • **estar al ~ (de algo)** to know (about sth) • **puedes hablar sin miedo, ya estoy al ~** you can talk freely, I know (all) about it • **¿estaba usted al ~?** did you know (about it)? • **mantener a algn al ~ (de algo)** to keep sb up to date (on sth), keep sb informed (about sth) • **poner a algn al ~ (de algo)** to bring sb up to date (on sth), inform sb (about sth) • **ponerse al ~ (de algo)** to get up to date (with sth), catch up (on sth) • **tener a algn al ~ (de algo)** to keep sb up to date (on sth), keep sb informed (about sth)
2 (*en cartas*) • **el día 9 del ~** *o* **de los ~s** the 9th of this month
SF **1** [*de fluido*] current • **la ~ lo arrastraba hacia el mar** the current was carrying him out to sea • MODISMOS: • **dejarse llevar por la ~** to follow the crowd *o* stream, go with the flow (*esp EEUU*) • **ir** *o* **navegar** *o* **nadar contra (la) ~** to swim *o* go against the tide • **seguir la ~ a algn** to humour *o* (*EEUU*) humor sb • **cuando se pone a hablar así es mejor seguirle la ~** when he starts talking like that it's best to humour him ▸ **corriente de agua** stream of water ▸ **corriente de Humboldt** Humboldt Current ▸ **corriente de lava** lava flow, stream of lava ▸ **corriente del Golfo** Gulf Stream ▸ **corriente sanguínea** bloodstream ▸ **corriente submarina** undercurrent, underwater current
2 [*de aire*] draught, draft (*EEUU*) • **hay mucha ~** it's very draughty ▸ **corriente de aire** (*gen*) draught, draft (*EEUU*); (*Téc*) air current, air stream ▸ **corriente en chorro** jet stream ▸ **corriente térmica** thermal
3 (*Elec*) current • **anoche se cortó la ~** there was a power cut last night • **el cable tiene ~** the wire is live • **dar ~:** • **no toques ese cable que da ~** don't touch that wire, it's live • **me dio (la) ~** I got a shock, I got an electric shock ▸ **corriente alterna** alternating current ▸ **corriente continua** direct current ▸ **corriente difásica** two-phase current ▸ **corriente directa** direct current ▸ **corriente eléctrica** electric current ▸ **corriente trifásica** three-phase current
4 (= *tendencia*) (*ideológica*) tendency; (*artística*) trend • **una ~ más radical dentro del partido** a more radical tendency within the party • **la ~ renovadora de la derecha** the trend towards renewal on the Right • **las ~s modernas del arte** modern trends in art

▸ **corriente de opinión** current of opinion
▸ **corriente de pensamiento** school of thought
corrientemente (ADV) usually, normally
corrillero/a (SM/F) idler, person with time to gossip
corrillo (SM) (= *grupo*) huddle, small group; (*pey*) clique, coterie
corrimiento (SM) **1** (*Geol*) slip ▸ **corrimiento de tierras** landslide
2 (*Med*) (= *secreción*) discharge; (*Caribe, Cono Sur*) (= *reúma*) rheumatism; (*And*) (= *flemón*) tooth abscess
3 (= *vergüenza*) embarrassment
4 (*Inform*) scrolling
corrincho (SM) **1** (= *muchedumbre*) mob
2 (*And*) (= *jaleo*) uproar, row
3 (*And*) (= *emoción*) excitement; (= *prisa*) haste
corro (SM) **1** [*de gente*] ring, circle • **la gente hizo ~** the people formed a ring *o* circle
2 (= *baile*) ring-a-ring-a-roses • **los niños cantan esto en ~** the children sing this in a ring
3 (*Econ*) pit, ring (*in the stock exchange*)
4 (*Agr*) plot, small field, patch
corroboración (SF) corroboration
corroborar ▹ CONJUG 1a (VT) to corroborate
corroborativo (ADJ) corroborative
corroer ▹ CONJUG 2a (VT) **1** (*Téc*) to corrode
2 (*Geol*) to erode
3 (= *reconcomer*) to corrode, eat away • **le corroen los celos** he is eaten up with jealousy
(VPR) **corroerse** to corrode, become corroded
corroído (ADJ) [*pieza, hierro*] corroded
corromper ▹ CONJUG 2a (VT) **1** (= *pudrir*) [+ *madera*] to rot; [+ *alimentos*] to turn bad
2 (= *estropear*) [+ *costumbres, lengua, joven*] to corrupt; [+ *placeres*] to spoil
3 (= *sobornar*) to bribe
4* (= *enojar*) to vex, annoy
(VI)* to smell bad, stink*
(VPR) **corromperse 1** (= *pudrirse*) [*madera*] to rot; [*alimentos*] to go bad
2 [*personas*] to become corrupted
corrompido (ADJ) **1** [*cosas*] rotten, putrid
2 [*personas*] corrupt
corroncha (SF) (*And, CAm*) crust, scale
corroncho (ADJ) **1** (*Caribe*) (= *torpe*) slow, sluggish
2 (*And*) [*persona*] difficult, prickly
corronchoso (ADJ) (*And, CAm, Caribe*) (= *burdo*) rough, coarse; (= *escamoso*) crusty, scaly
corrongo (ADJ) (*CAm, Caribe*) (= *excelente*) first-rate, splendid; (= *encantador*) charming, attractive
corrosión (SF) (*Quím*) corrosion; (*Geol*) erosion
corrosivo (ADJ) [*sustancia*] corrosive; [*lenguaje, estilo*] caustic
(SM) corrosive
corrte. (ABR) (= **corriente, de los corrientes**) inst
corrugación (SF) contraction, shrinkage
corrupción (SF) **1** (= *pudrición*) rot, decay
2 (*moral*) corruption
3 (*Jur*) corruption, graft; (= *soborno*) graft, bribery • **en el gobierno existe mucha ~** there is a lot of corruption in the government ▸ **corrupción de menores** corruption of minors ▸ **corrupción urbanística** bribery and corruption (*relating to the granting of planning permission*)
4 [*de lengua, texto*] corruption
corruptela (SF) **1** (= *corrupción*) corruption
2 (= *abuso*) corrupt practice, corrupt practise (*EEUU*), abuse
corruptible (ADJ) **1** [*persona*] corruptible, bribable
2 [*alimentos*] perishable
corrupto (ADJ) corrupt
corruptor(a) (ADJ) corrupting
(SM/F) corrupter, perverter
corsario (SM) privateer, corsair
corsé (SM) corset; (*fig*) straitjacket
corso¹/a (ADJ), (SM/F) Corsican
corso² (SM) (*Náut, Hist*) privateering, piratical enterprise
corta (SF) felling, cutting
cortaalambres (SM INV) wire cutters
cortabolsas (SM INV) pickpocket
cortacésped (SM) lawnmower
cortacircuitos (SM INV) circuit breaker, trip switch
cortacorrientes (SM INV) circuit breaker, trip switch
cortacutícula (SF) cuticle scissors
cortada (SF) **1** (*LAm*) (= *corte*) cut; (= *atajo*) short cut
2 [*de pan*] slice
3 (*Tenis*) stroke giving backspin
cortadillo (SM) **1** (= *vaso*) small glass, small tumbler
2 (= *azúcar*) lump of sugar
3* (= *ligue*) affair
cortado (ADJ) **1** (= *recortado, partido*) cut • **la carne cortada en trozos grandes** meat cut into large chunks • **~ a pico** [*montaña, acantilado*] steep, sheer, precipitous
2 (= *pasado*) [*leche, mayonesa*] off • **tener** *o* **sentir el cuerpo ~** to feel off colour
3 [*piel, labios*] chapped
4 [*calle, carretera*] closed • **"carretera cortada por obras"** "closed for roadworks"
5 [*café*] coffee with a little milk
6 [*estilo*] (*gen*) disjointed; (*al hablar*) clipped
7 [*película*] cut
8* [*persona*] shy • **es un tío muy ~** he's a really shy bloke* • **está ~ porque no os conoce** he's shy because he doesn't know you • **dejar ~** to cut short • **me dejó ~ en mitad de lo que estaba diciendo** he cut me short in the middle of what I was saying • **quedarse ~**: • **no te quedes ~, hombre, di algo** come on, don't be shy, say something • **me quedé ~ cuando entré en la habitación y los vi besándose** I was left speechless when I came into the room and found them kissing
9 • **estar ~** (*esp LAm**) (= *arruinado*) to be broke*
(SM) **1** (= *café*) coffee with a little milk
2 (*Ballet*) leap
cortador(a) (ADJ) cutting
(SM/F) cutter
(SM) ▸ **cortador de cristal** glass cutter
cortadora (SF) cutter, cutting-machine
▸ **cortadora de césped** lawnmower
cortadura (SF) **1** (= *incisión*) cut; (*grande*) slash, slit
2 (*Geog*) narrow pass, defile
3 cortaduras (= *recortes*) cuttings, clippings
cortafrío (SM) cold chisel
cortafuego (SM), **cortafuegos** (SM INV) fire-break, fire lane (*EEUU*); (*Inform*) firewall
cortahuevos (SM INV) egg-slicer
cortahumedades (SM INV) damp course
cortalápices (SM INV) pencil sharpener
cortante (ADJ) **1** [*instrumento*] cutting, sharp
2 [*viento*] cutting, biting • **hace un frío ~** it's bitterly cold
3 [*respuesta*] sharp, cutting
(SM) (= *trinchador*) cleaver, chopper
cortapapel (SM) (*LAm*), **cortapapeles** (SM INV) (*para cartas*) paper knife; (*Téc*) paper cutter, guillotine
cortapega (SM) cut and paste
cortapegar (VT) to cut and paste
cortapicos (SM INV) earwig
cortapisa (SF) **1** (= *restricción*) restriction, condition • **sin ~s** with no strings attached
2 (= *traba*) snag, obstacle • **poner ~s a algo/algn** to restrict *o* hold back sth/sb • **se pone ~s para sí mismo** he makes obstacles for himself • **hablar sin ~s** to talk freely
3 (= *gracia*) charm, wit
cortaplumas (SM INV) penknife
cortapuros (SM INV) cigar cutter
cortar ▹ CONJUG 1a (VT) **1** (*con algo afilado*) (*gen*) to cut; (*en trozos*) to chop; (*en rebanadas*) to slice • **corta la manzana por la mitad** cut the apple in half • **¿quién te ha cortado el pelo?** who cut your hair? • **corta el apio en trozos** cut *o* chop the celery into pieces
2 (= *partir*) [+ *árbol*] to cut down; [+ *madera*] to saw • **~ la cabeza a algn** to cut sb's head off
3 (= *dividir*) to cut • **la línea corta el círculo en dos** the line cuts *o* divides the circle in two
4 (= *interrumpir*) **a** [+ *comunicaciones, agua, corriente*] to cut off; [+ *carretera, puente*] (= *cerrar*) to close; (= *bloquear*) to block • **han cortado el gas** the gas has been cut off • **las tropas están intentando ~ la carretera que conduce al aeropuerto** the troops are trying to cut off the road to the airport • **han cortado el tráfico durante unos minutos** they've closed the road to traffic for a few minutes • **"carretera cortada al tráfico"** "road closed" • **sus seguidores han cortado la calle** her followers have blocked off the road • **nos ~on la retirada** they cut off our retreat • **~ la hemorragia** to stop the bleeding
b [+ *relaciones*] to break off; [+ *discurso, conversación*] to cut short • **~ la comunicación** to hang up
5 (= *suprimir*) to cut • **la censura cortó una de las escenas** the censors cut one of the scenes
6 [*frío*] to chap, crack • **el frío me corta los labios** the cold is chapping *o* cracking my lips
7 (*Dep*) [+ *balón*] to slice
8 [+ *baraja*] to cut
9* [+ *droga*] to cut*
(VI) **1** (= *estar afilado*) to cut • **estas tijeras no cortan** these scissors are blunt *o* don't cut; ▹ **sano**
2 (*Inform*) • **"~ y pegar"** "cut and paste"
3 (*Meteo*) • **hace un viento que corta** there's a bitter *o* biting wind
4 (= *acortar*) • **podemos ~ por el parque** we can take a shortcut through the park • **es mejor que cortéis por el atajo** it would be better if you took the shortcut
5 • **~ con** (= *terminar*): • **~ con el pasado** to make a break with the past • **hay que ~ con este comportamiento** we must put a stop to this behaviour • **es absurdo ~ con tu tía por culpa de su marido** it's ridiculous to break off contact with your aunt because of her husband • **ha cortado con su novia** he's broken up with *o* finished with his girlfriend
6 • **¡corta!*** give us a break!*; ▹ **rollo**
7 (*Naipes*) to cut
8 (*Radio*) • **¡corto!** over! • **¡corto y cierro!** over and out!
9 (*LAm*) (*Telec*) to hang up • **cortó** he hung up
(VPR) **cortarse 1** (*con algo afilado*) **a** [*persona*] to cut o.s. • **te vas a ~** you're going to cut yourself
b • **me corté el dedo con un cristal** I cut my finger on a piece of glass • **~se las uñas** to cut one's nails • **ha ido a ~se el pelo** she's gone to get her hair cut, she's gone to the hairdresser's, she's gone for a haircut • **se cortó las venas** she slashed her wrists
• MODISMO: • **cortársela**‡: • **si no acepta, me la corto** I'll be bloody amazed if he doesn't accept it‡

2 (= *rajarse*) [*manos, labios*] to get chapped; [*material*] to split, come apart
3 (*Culin*) [*mayonesa, natillas*] to curdle; [*leche*] to go off, curdle
4* (= *cohibirse*) to get embarrassed • **no te cortes** don't be shy • **no se corta a la hora de decir lo que piensa** she doesn't hold back at all when it comes to saying what she thinks • MODISMO: • **no ~se un pelo**: • **el entrenador, que no se corta un pelo, ha culpado al árbitro de la derrota** the coach, never one to hold back, has blamed the referee for the defeat
5 (= *interrumpirse*) [*luz*] to go off, go out • **se ha cortado la comunicación** the line's gone dead • **se cortó la llamada** I was cut off
6 (*Cono Sur**) (= *separarse*) to become separated (from the others), get left behind; (= *irse*) to clear off*; (*en trato*) to get left out • **~se solo** to go off on one's own
7 (*Cono Sur**) (= *morirse*) to die

cortauñas SM INV nail clippers
cortavidrios SM INV glass cutter
cortavientos SM INV windbreak
corte[1] SM **1** (= *incisión, herida*) cut • **le hizo un ~ a la madera** he made a cut in the wood • **tienes un pequeño ~ en la pierna** you have a small cut on your leg • **hacerse un ~** to cut o.s. • **me he hecho un ~ en el dedo** I've cut my finger ▸ **corte longitudinal** lengthwise section, longitudinal section ▸ **corte transversal** cross section
2 (*tb* **corte de pelo**) cut, haircut ▸ **corte a navaja** razor cut ▸ **corte a tijera** scissor cut
3 (*Cos*) (= *diseño*) cut • **un traje de ~ muy moderno** a suit with a very modern cut ▸ **corte y confección** dressmaking
4 (= *interrupción*) cut • **persisten los ~s de agua** the water keeps being cut off • **la censura dejó la película sin ~s** the censor did not cut the film ▸ **corte de carretera** (*para obras, accidente*) road closure; (*como protesta*) roadblock ▸ **corte de corriente** power cut ▸ **corte de digestión** stomach cramp ▸ **corte de luz** power cut ▸ **corte publicitario** commercial break
5 (= *estilo*) • **literatura de ~ tradicional** traditional (type) literature • **un discurso de ~ fascista** a speech with fascist undertones • **un sistema fiscal de ~ occidental** a western-style taxation system
6 (= *trozo*) ▸ **corte de carne** cut of meat ▸ **corte (de helado)** wafer, ice cream sandwich (*EEUU*)
7* (= *respuesta contundente*) • **dar un ~ a algn: ¡vaya ~ que te dieron!** that was one in the eye for you, wasn't it! • **dale un buen ~ y no te molestará más** tell him where to go and he won't bother you any more* ▸ **corte de mangas** *rude gesture made with the arm and hand which is the equivalent of giving the V-sign or, in the US, the finger* • **le hizo un ~ de mangas a los fotógrafos** he made a *o* the V-sign at the photographers, he gave two fingers to the photographers, he gave the photographers the finger (*EEUU*) • **sus declaraciones son un ~ de mangas a la Constitución** his statements are a two-fingered salute to the Constitution
8* (= *vergüenza*) • **es un ~ que te vean tus padres fumando** it's embarrassing when your parents see you smoking • **¡qué ~, me besó delante de todos!** how embarrassing! he kissed me in front of everyone! • **me da ~ que me vean contigo** I'm embarrassed to be seen with you • **me da mucho ~ hablar en público** I get really embarrassed if I have to speak in public • **llevarse un ~: me llevé un buen ~ cuando supe que tenía novio** I felt really silly when I found out she had a boyfriend
9 (= *borde*) edge • **con ~s dorados** with gilt edges • **dar ~ a algo** to sharpen sth, put an edge on sth
10 [*de disco*] track
11 (*Min*) stint
12 (*Cono Sur*) (= *importancia*) • **darse ~s** to put on airs

corte[2] SF **1** [*de un rey*] (= *residencia*) court; (= *séquito*) court, entourage, retinue • **los ciudadanos de la ~** the court dwellers ▸ **corte celestial** heavenly court; ▹ **villa**
2 • **hacer la ~ a algn** (= *cortejar*) to pay court to sb; (= *halagar*) to win favour with sb, lick sb's boots*, suck up to sb* • **no deja de hacerme la ~ a ver si le presto dinero** he keeps licking my boots *o* sucking up to me so that I'll lend him some money
3 (*Jur*) law court ▸ **Corte de Justicia** Court of Justice ▸ **Corte Internacional de Justicia** International Court of Justice ▸ **Corte Suprema** Supreme Court
4 (= *ciudad*) capital, capital city • **La Corte** Madrid
5 • **las Cortes** (*Pol*) Spanish parliament • **el Presidente disolvió las Cortes** the President dissolved Parliament • **una manifestación frente a las Cortes** a demonstration outside the Parliament building ▸ **Cortes Constituyentes** constituent assembly ▸ **Cortes de Castilla-La Mancha** Regional Assembly of Castile and La Mancha ▸ **Cortes de Castilla y León** Regional Assembly of Castile and León ▸ **Cortes Generales** Parliament

CORTES GENERALES
The Spanish parliament consists of a lower house, the **Congreso de los Diputados**, and an upper house, the **Senado**. Members of the lower house are called **diputados** and members of the **Senado** are **senadores**.
▹ CONGRESO DE LOS DIPUTADOS, SENADO

cortedad SF **1** [*de tiempo*] shortness, brevity; [*de espacio*] smallness; (*tb* **cortedad de alcances**) stupidity ▸ **cortedad de vista** shortsightedness
2 (= *escasez*) dearth, lack
3 (= *timidez*) shyness, bashfulness ▸ **cortedad de ánimo** diffidence
cortejar ▹ CONJUG 1a VT to court, woo
cortejo SM **1** (= *séquito*) entourage, retinue
2 (*Rel*) procession ▸ **cortejo fúnebre** funeral cortège, funeral procession ▸ **cortejo nupcial** wedding party
3 (= *acción*) wooing, courting
cortés ADJ **1** (= *atento*) courteous, polite
2 • **amor ~** courtly love
cortesana SF courtesan
cortesanía SF politeness
cortesano ADJ of the court, courtly • **ceremonias cortesanas** court ceremony
SM courtier
cortesía SF **1** (= *conducta*) courtesy, politeness • **visita de ~** courtesy call • **entrada de ~** complimentary ticket • **días de ~** (*Com*) days of grace • **por ~** as a courtesy
2 (= *etiqueta*) social etiquette • **la ~ pide que ...** etiquette demands that ...
3 [*de carta*] formal ending
4 (= *reverencia*) [*de hombre*] bow; [*de mujer*] curtsy • **hacer una ~ a algn** [*hombre*] to bow to sb; [*mujer*] to curtsy to sb
5 (= *regalo*) present, gift
cortésmente ADV courteously, politely
córtex SM cortex
corteza SF **1** [*de árbol*] bark; [*de pan*] crust; [*de fruta*] peel, skin; [*de queso, tocino*] rind • **se añade una ~ de limón** add a bit of lemon peel ▸ **corteza cerebral** cerebral cortex ▸ **corteza de cerdo** pork rind ▸ **corteza terrestre** earth's crust
2 (= *exterior*) outside, outward appearance
3 (= *grosería*) roughness, coarseness
corticoide SM corticoid
cortijo SM farmhouse
cortina SF (*para ventana*) curtain, drape (*EEUU*); (*Téc*) retaining wall; (*fig*) screen • MODISMOS: • **correr la ~** to draw a veil over sth • **descorrer la ~** to draw back the veil ▸ **cortina de ducha** shower curtain ▸ **cortina de fuego** (*Mil*) barrage ▸ **cortina de hierro** (*Pol*) iron curtain ▸ **cortina de humo** smoke screen ▸ **cortina de tienda** tent flap ▸ **cortina musical** (*Cono Sur*) (*TV*) musical interlude
cortinado SM (*Cono Sur*) curtains (*pl*)
cortinilla SF lace curtain
cortisona SF cortisone
corto ADJ **1** [*longitud, distancia*] short • **llevaba el pelo muy ~** she had very short hair • **una camisa de manga corta** a short-sleeved shirt • **vinimos por el camino más ~** we came by the shortest route • **un relato ~** a short story • **el vestido se le ha quedado ~** the dress has got too short for her • **el tiro se quedó ~** the shot fell short; ▹ **pantalón**
2 [*periodo, visita, reunión*] short, brief • **en un ~ espacio de tiempo** in a short space of time • **los días se van haciendo más ~s** the days are getting shorter • **la película se me hizo muy corta** the film was over *o* went very quickly; ▹ **plazo**
3 (= *escaso*) [*ración*] small • **dos niñas de corta edad** two very young girls • **~ de algo**: • **un café con leche, pero ~ de café** a coffee with plenty of milk, a milky coffee • **~ de oído** hard of hearing • **ando** *o* **voy ~ de dinero** I'm short of money • **ando** *o* **voy muy ~ de tiempo** I'm short of time, I'm pressed *o* pushed for time • **~ de vista** shortsighted, nearsighted (*EEUU*) • **quedarse ~**: • **costará unos tres millones, y seguro que me quedo ~** it will cost three million, and I'm probably underestimating • **le dijo lo que pensaba de él, pero se quedó ~** she told him what she thought of him, but it still wasn't enough • **nos quedamos ~s con la bebida en la fiesta** we didn't have enough drink for the party • **esta ley se queda corta en sus pretensiones** this law does not go far enough
4 (= *tímido*) shy • MODISMO: • **ni ~ ni perezoso** as bold as brass
5 (= *torpe*) dim*, thick* • MODISMO: • **es más ~ que las mangas de un chaleco*** he's as thick as two short planks*; ▹ **alcance, entendederas**
SM **1** (*Cine*) short, short film, short movie (*EEUU*)
2 [*de cerveza, vino*] small glass; [*de café*] black coffee
SF • **a la corta o a la larga** sooner or later
cortocircuitar ▹ CONJUG 1a VT to short-circuit
cortocircuito SM short-circuit • **poner(se) en ~** to short-circuit
cortometraje SM short
cortón[1] SM (*Entomología*) mole cricket
cortón[2]* ADJ **1** (= *tímido*) bashful, timid
2 • **es muy ~** (*CAm*) (= *que interrumpe*) he's always interrupting
cortopunzante ADJ (*Cono Sur*) sharp
Coruña SF • **La ~** Corunna
coruñés/esa ADJ of/from Corunna
SM/F native/inhabitant of Corunna • **los coruñeses** the people of Corunna
corva SF back of the knee
corvadura SF (= *curvatura*) curvature; (*Arquit*) arch
corvejón SM [*de caballo*] hock; [*de gallo*] spur

corveta ADJ (*CAm*) bow-legged
SF curvet, prance

corvetear ▹ CONJUG 1a VI to curvet, prance

corvina SF sea bass, croaker

corvo ADJ (= *curvo*) curved, bent; [*nariz*] hooked

corza SF doe

corzo/a SM/F roe deer

cosa SF **1** (= *objeto*) thing • **¿qué es esa ~ redonda?** what's that round thing? • **cogí mis ~s y me fui** I picked up my things and left • **no es otra ~ que una bolsa de plástico** it's nothing more than a plastic bag, it's just a plastic bag • **para el dolor de cabeza no tengo otra ~ que aspirina** all I have for headaches is aspirin • **~s de comer** things to eat • **las ~s del jardín** the gardening things • MODISMOS: • **es ~ fina*** it's excellent stuff* • **es ~ de ver** it's well worth seeing, you have to see it
2 (*uso indefinido*) • **¿alguna ~ más?** anything else? • **o ~ así**: • **20 kilos o ~ así** 20 kilos or thereabouts • **y ~s así** and suchlike • **cualquier ~** anything • **haría cualquier ~ por ella** I'd do anything for her • **este vino no es cualquier ~** this isn't just any old wine • **gran ~**: • **el coche no vale gran ~** the car isn't worth much • **no ha servido de gran ~** it hasn't been much use • **la película no fue gran ~** the film wasn't up to much • **como futbolista no es gran ~** he's not a great footballer, he's not much of a footballer • **poca ~**: • **lo qué recibieron a cambio fue poca ~** they didn't get much in return, they got very little in return • **vive bien con poca ~** she lives well on very little • **no te preocupes por tan poca ~** don't worry about a little thing like that • **jugamos a las cartas, leemos y poca ~ más** we play cards, read and do little else *o* and that's about it • **la vida es tan corta y somos tan poca ~** life is so short and we're so insignificant • **la chica es muy poquita ~** there's not much of her • **una ~** something • **hay una ~ que no me gusta** there is one thing I don't like • **¿me puedes decir una ~?** can you tell me something? • **una ~, se me olvidaba preguntarte por el precio** by the way, I forgot to ask you about the price • **en general está muy bien, solo una ~ …** on the whole, it's very good, there's just one thing …
3 (= *asunto*) • **eso es ~ tuya** that's your affair • **es ~ fácil** it's easy • **¿has visto ~ igual?** did you ever see the like? • **¡qué ~ más extraña!** how strange! • **es ~ de nunca acabar** there's no end to it • **esa es ~ vieja** so what's new?, that's ancient history • **¡vaya una ~!** well!, there's a thing! • **la ~ es que …** the thing is (that) … • **la ~ puede acabar mal** things could end badly • **la ~ no está tan clara** it's not that clear • **la ~ está en considerar el problema desde otro ángulo** the thing to do *o* the trick is to consider the problem from another angle • **no es ~ de broma** *o* **risa** it's no laughing matter • **no es ~ de que lo dejes todo** there's no need for you to give it all up • **no sea ~ que** in case • **trae el paraguas, no sea ~ que llueva** bring your umbrella in case it rains • **otra ~**: • **no se hablaba de otra ~** people talked about nothing else • **¿hay otra ~ que pueda hacer?** is there anything else I can do? • **eso es otra ~** that's another matter *o* thing (entirely) • **otra ~ es que la ley imponga 40 horas semanales para todos** it's another matter entirely for the law to oblige everyone to work 40 hours a week • **otra ~ sería si …** it would be quite another matter if … • **~ rara**: • **y, ~ rara, nadie lo vio** and, oddly *o* funnily enough, nobody saw it • MODISMOS: • **a otra ~, mariposa** it's time to move on • **como quien no quiere la ~**: • **lo miraba como quien no quiere la ~** she cast a casual glance at the boy • **se levantó y se fue como quien no quiere la ~** she got up and left as inconspicuously as possible • **como si tal ~**: • **me devolvió el libro roto como si tal ~** he gave me back the damaged book as if nothing had happened • **le dije que había sido seleccionado para el trabajo y se quedó como si tal ~** I told him he had got the job and he barely reacted • **decir una ~ por otra** to lie
4 (= *nada*) • **no hay ~ peor** there's nothing worse • **jamás he visto ~ semejante** I've never seen anything like it, I've never seen the like of it • **¡no hay tal ~!** nothing of the sort! • **nunca he dicho nada sobre ese tema ni ~ que se le parezca** I never said anything about that subject or anything like it • MODISMO: • **no es ninguna ~ del otro jueves** *o* **mundo** it's nothing to write home about
5 cosas: **a** (= *acciones, asuntos*) • **¡son ~s de Juan!** that's Juan all over!, that's just like Juan! • **son ~s de la edad** it's just old age • **¡~s de niños!** boys will be boys! • **¡qué ~s dices!** you do say some silly things! • **¡tienes unas ~s!** the things you say! • **meterse en ~s de otros** to stick one's nose in other people's business • MODISMO: • **decir cuatro ~s a algn** to give sb a piece of one's mind
b • **las ~s** (= *situación*) things • **las ~s van mejor** things are going better • **tal como están las ~s** as things stand • **así las ~s, se marchó de la reunión** at this point, she left the meeting • **¡lo que son las ~s!** just imagine!, fancy that! • MODISMO: • **las ~s de palacio van despacio** it all takes time, the mills of God grind slowly
6 • **~ de** (*indicando tiempo*) about • **es ~ de un par de semanas** it takes about a couple of weeks • **en ~ de diez minutos** in about ten minutes
7‡ (*droga*) hash*
8 (*LAm*) (*como conj*) • **~ que**: • **camina lento, ~ que no te canses** walk slowly so (that) you don't get tired • **no le digas nada, ~ que no se ofenda** don't say anything to him, that way he won't get offended, don't say anything to him in case he gets offended

cosaco/a ADJ, SM/F **1** (= *soldado*) Cossack • MODISMO: • **beber como un ~** to drink like a fish
2 (*Cono Sur*) (= *policía*) mounted policeman

coscacho SM (*And, Cono Sur*) rap on the head

coscarana SF cracknel

coscarse* ▹ CONJUG 1g VPR to catch on, get it*

coscoja SF kermes oak

coscolino ADJ **1** (*Méx*) (= *malhumorado*) peevish, touchy; [*niño*] naughty
2 (*moralmente*) of loose morals

coscorrón SM **1** (= *golpe*) bump on the head
2 (= *contratiempo*) setback, knock

coscurro SM hard crust, hard crust of bread

cosecha SF **1** (= *recogida*) harvest; (= *temporada*) harvest, harvest time • **la ~ de 1972** (= *vino*) the 1972 vintage • **una buena ~ de éxitos políticos** a whole crop of political successes • **la película recibió una ~ de premios** the film received a whole crop of prizes
2 (= *producto*) crop • **de ~ propia** home-grown, home-produced • MODISMO: • **cosas de su propia ~** things of one's own invention • **no añadas nada de tu ~** don't add anything that you've made up
3 (= *producción*) yield

cosechado SM harvesting

cosechadora SF combine harvester, combine (*EEUU*)

cosechar ▹ CONJUG 1a VT **1** (= *recoger*) [+ *cereales*] to harvest, reap; [+ *frutas*] to harvest, pick
2 (= *cultivar*) to grow, cultivate • **aquí solo cosechan patatas** the only thing they grow here is potatoes
3 (= *ganar*) [+ *admiración, premios*] to win; [+ *respeto*] to win, earn; [+ *fracasos, éxitos*] to achieve; [+ *enemigos*] to earn, make • **no cosechó sino disgustos** all he got was troubles

cosechero/a SM/F harvester

cosechón SM bumper crop

coseno SM cosine

coser ▹ CONJUG 2a VT **1** [+ *vestido*] to sew, sew up; [+ *botón*] to sew on, stitch on • **es cosa de ~ y cantar** it's easy as pie*, it's as simple as ABC*
2 (*Med*) to stitch, stitch up; (*Náut*) to lash • **~ con grapas** to staple
3 (= *unir*) to unite, join closely (**con** to)
4 • MODISMOS: • **~ a algn a balazos** to riddle sb with bullets • **~ a algn a puñaladas** to stab sb repeatedly, carve sb up* • **lo encontraron cosido a puñaladas** his body was found full of stab wounds
VI to sew
VPR **coserse** • **~se con algn** to become closely attached to sb

cosher ADJ INV kosher

cosiaca SF (*LAm*) small thing

cosido SM sewing, needlework

cosificación SF treating as an object • **el capitalismo conduce a la ~ de los obreros** capitalism leads to the workers being treated as objects

cosificar ▹ CONJUG 1g VT to treat as an object

cosignatario/a SM/F cosignatory

cosijoso ADJ (*CAm, Méx*) **1** (= *molesto*) bothersome, annoying
2 (= *displicente*) peevish, irritable

cosmética SF cosmetics (*pl*)

cosmético ADJ, SM cosmetic

cosmetizar ▹ CONJUG 1f VT to make cosmetic improvements to

cosmetólogo/a SM/F cosmetician

cósmico ADJ cosmic

cosmódromo SM cosmodrome

cosmogonía SF cosmogony

cosmografía SF cosmography

cosmógrafo/a SM/F cosmographer

cosmología SF cosmology

cosmológico ADJ cosmological

cosmólogo/a SM/F cosmologist

cosmonauta SMF cosmonaut

cosmopolita ADJ, SMF cosmopolitan

cosmos SM INV cosmos

cosmovisión SF world view

coso[1] SM (= *recinto*) enclosure; (*esp Taur*) bullring

coso[2] SM (= *insecto*) woodworm

coso[3]* SM (*esp Cono Sur*) (= *cosa*) thingummy*, thingamajig (*EEUU**), what-d'you-call-it

cospel SM (*Arg*) telephone token

cosquillar ▹ CONJUG 1a VT to tickle

cosquillas SFPL tickling, tickling sensation • **buscar las ~ a algn** to tease sb • **me hace ~** it tickles • **hacer ~ a algn** to tickle sb • **siento ~ en el pie** my foot tickles • **tener ~** to be ticklish • MODISMOS: • **no sufre ~** • **tiene malas ~** he's touchy, he can't take a joke

cosquillear ▹ CONJUG 1a VT to tickle • **me cosquillea la idea de …** I've a notion to …, I've half a mind to …

cosquilleo (SM) tickling, tickling sensation
cosquilloso (ADJ) **1** (= *que tiene cosquillas*) ticklish
2 (= *quisquilloso*) touchy, prickly*
costa¹ (SF) **1** • **a ~ de algo/algn: nos estuvimos riendo a ~ suya** we had a laugh at his expense • **lo ha conseguido a ~ de muchos sacrificios** he has achieved it by making many sacrifices • **quiere quedarse en el poder a ~ de lo que sea** he wants to remain in power at all costs *o* no matter what *o* whatever happens • **a toda ~** at all costs • **hay que impedir a toda ~ que esto se repita** we must prevent this from happening again at all costs
2 costas (*Jur*) costs • **condenar a algn en ~s** to order sb to pay costs
costa² (SF) **1** (*Geog*) [*del mar*] coast • **pasamos las vacaciones en la ~** we spend our holidays on the coast • **la ~ mediterránea** the Mediterranean coast • **la ~ del Pacífico** the Pacific coast • **la ~ del Atlántico es muy accidentada** the Atlantic coastline is very rugged ▸ **la Costa Azul** the Côte d'Azur ▸ **la Costa Blanca** the Costa Blanca ▸ **la Costa Brava** the Costa Brava ▸ **la Costa del Sol** the Costa del Sol ▸ **la Costa de Oro** the Gold Coast
2 (*Náut*) shore • **fuimos bordeando la ~ hasta el puerto** we hugged the shore all the way to the port ▸ **costa afuera** offshore
3 (*Cono Sur*) [*de un río*] bank, riverbank; [*de un lago*] shore
costabravense (ADJ) of the Costa Brava
Costa de Marfil (SF) Ivory Coast
costado (SM) **1** [*de objeto*] side • **neumáticos de ~ blanco** white-walled tyres
2 (*Anat*) side • **de ~** [*tumbarse*] on one's side; [*moverse*] sideways • **español por los cuatro ~s** Spanish through and through
3 (*Náut*) side; (*Mil*) flank
4 (*Méx*) (*Ferro*) platform
costal (SM) sack, bag • **MODISMO**: • **estar hecho un ~ de huesos** to be all skin and bone, be a bag of bones
costalada (SF), **costalazo** (SM) (= *caída*) bad fall • **darse una ~** to fall on one's back
costalar ▷ CONJUG 1a (VI) (*Cono Sur*) to roll over
costanera (SF) **1** (= *costado*) side, flank
2 (= *cuesta*) slope
3 (*Cono Sur*) (= *paseo marítimo*) seaside promenade, seaside drive
4 (*Caribe*) (*alrededor de un pantano*) firm ground (*surrounding a swamp*)
5 costaneras (*Arquit*) rafters
costanero (ADJ) **1** (= *que está en cuesta*) sloping
2 (= *costero*) coastal
costar ▷ CONJUG 1l (VT) **1** (*en dinero*) to cost • **la lámpara cuesta 45 euros** the lamp is *o* costs 45 euros • **¿cuánto te ha costado el libro?** how much did you pay for the book?, how much did the book cost (you)? • **¿cuánto cuesta este libro?** how much is this book?, how much does this book cost? • **el porte no me ha costado nada** it didn't cost me anything to have it delivered, the delivery didn't cost me anything • **reparar el tejado me ha costado un dineral** it cost me a fortune to have the roof mended
• **MODISMO**: • **~ un ojo de la cara*** to cost an arm and a leg*
2 (*en esfuerzo, tiempo*) • **me ha costado lo mío llegar adonde he llegado** it's taken a lot to get where I am • **cada traducción nos cuesta muchas horas de trabajo** each translation takes us many hours of work • **~ trabajo**: • **cuesta poco trabajo ser amable** it doesn't take much to be pleasant, it's not so hard to be pleasant • **¿te ha costado trabajo encontrar la casa?** did you have trouble finding the house? • **MODISMOS**: • **cueste lo que cueste** whatever it takes • **~ Dios y ayuda**: • **me costó Dios y ayuda convencerla** I had a hard job *o* time persuading her; ▸ **sangre**
3 (*en consecuencias*) to cost • **ese error te ~á el puesto** that mistake will cost you your job *o* will lose you your job • **el accidente por poco le cuesta la vida** the accident nearly cost him his life • **la violación le costó doce años de cárcel** the rape earned him twelve years in prison, he got twelve years in prison for the rape
(VI) **1** (*en dinero*) • **este abrigo me ha costado muy barato** this coat was very cheap
2 (*en dificultad*) to be hard, be difficult • **al principio cuesta, pero luego se hace más fácil** it's hard *o* difficult at first but then it gets easier • **cuesta reconocerlo, pero es verdad** it's hard *o* difficult to admit it, but it's true • **~ a algn**: • **lo que más me cuesta es el inglés** the thing I find hardest *o* most difficult is English • **me cuesta creer que seas hermano suyo** I find it hard *o* difficult to believe that you are his brother • **¿por qué no me llamas? ¡si no te cuesta nada!** why don't you give me a call? it's not so hard *o* difficult! • **no me cuesta nada llevarte** it's no trouble to give you a lift
3 (*en consecuencias*) • **~ caro a algn** to cost sb dear • **un error que le costó caro** a mistake that cost him dear • **eso que acabas de decir te va a ~ caro** you'll pay dearly for what you've just said
Costa Rica (SF) Costa Rica
costarricense (ADJ), (SMF) Costa Rican
costarriqueñismo (SM) *word or phrase peculiar to Costa Rica*
costarriqueño/a (ADJ), (SM/F) Costa Rican
costasoleño (ADJ) of the Costa del Sol
coste (SM) (*Esp*) cost • **el ~ global de la operación** the overall cost of the operation • **el ~ social de la guerra** the social cost of the war • **a precio de ~** at cost, at cost price ▸ **coste de compra** initial cost ▸ **coste de fabricación** manufacturing cost ▸ **coste de la vida** cost of living ▸ **coste de mantenimiento** upkeep, maintenance cost ▸ **coste de reemplazo** replacement cost ▸ **coste efectivo** actual cost ▸ **coste neto** net cost ▸ **coste real** real cost ▸ **costes salariales** wage costs ▸ **costes de explotación** operating costs ▸ **costes de producción** production costs ▸ **costes financieros** financial costs ▸ **coste, seguros y flete** cost, insurance and freight, C.I.F. ▸ **costes laborales unitarios** unitary labour *o* (EEUU) labor costs
costear¹ ▷ CONJUG 1a (VT) (= *financiar*) to pay for, finance (*más frm*); (*Com, Econ*) to finance; (*Radio, TV*) to back, sponsor • **costea los estudios a su sobrino** he is paying for his nephew's education, he is financing his nephew's studies • **no lo podemos ~** we can't afford it
(VPR) **costearse** • **~se los estudios** to pay for one's studies • **~se los caprichos** to pay for one's little indulgences
costear² ▷ CONJUG 1a (VT) (*Náut*) to sail along the coast of; [+ *río*] to sail close to the banks of
costear³ ▷ CONJUG 1a (VT) (*Cono Sur*) [+ *ganado*] to pasture
coste-eficacia (SM) cost-efficiency
costeño/a (ADJ) coastal
(SM/F) (*LAm*) coastal dweller
costera (SF) **1** [*de paquete*] side
2 (*Geog*) slope
3 (= *costa*) coast
4 (*Pesca*) fishing season
costero (ADJ) coastal; [*barco, comercio*] coasting
costilla (SF) **1** (*Anat*) rib
2 (*Culin*) sparerib ▸ **costilla de cerdo** pork chop, pork cutlet
3* • **MODISMOS**: • **todo carga sobre mis ~s** everything falls on my shoulders • **medir las ~s a algn** to beat sb
4* (= *mujer*) wife, better half*
costillar (SM) **1** (*Anat*) ribcage
2 (*Culin*) ribs (*pl*)
costilludo (ADJ) broad-shouldered, strapping
costipado (ADJ), (SM) = **constipado**
costo (SM) **1** (*esp LAm*) (*Econ*) cost ▸ **costo de expedición** shipping charges (*pl*); ▷ **coste**
2 (*LAm*) (= *esfuerzo*) trouble, effort
3 (*Esp‡*) (= *hachís*) dope‡
costosamente (ADV) expensively
costoso (ADJ) costly, expensive
costra (SF) **1** (= *corteza*) crust
2 (*Med*) scab
3 [*de vela*] snuff
costroso (ADJ) **1** (= *con corteza*) crusty
2 (*Med*) scabby
costumbre (SF) **1** (*tradicional*) custom; **costumbres** customs, ways • **las ~s de esta provincia** the customs of this province • **novela de ~s** novel of (local) customs and manners
2 [*de una persona*] habit • **persona de buenas ~s** respectable person, decent person • **he perdido la ~** I've got out of the habit • **tener la ~ de hacer algo** • **tener por ~ hacer algo** to be in the habit of doing sth
3 • **de ~** (*adj*) usual; (*adv*) usually • **como de ~** as usual • **más que de ~** more than usual
costumbrismo (SM) (*Literat*) *literature of local customs and manners*

COSTUMBRISMO
Costumbrismo is a literary genre which emerged in Spain in the 1830s. It concentrated on a detailed depiction of social and regional traditions and customs and often contrasted them with the changes brought by industrial development. Among the most noted writers of this movement were Fernán Caballero, Pedro Antonio de Alarcón, Juan Valera and José María de Pereda.

costumbrista (ADJ) (*Literat*) of local customs and manners
(SMF) *writer about local customs and manners*
costura (SF) **1** (= *puntadas*) seam • **sin ~** seamless • **sentar las ~s** to press the seams • **MODISMO**: • **sentar las ~ a algn*** to give sb a hiding*
2 (= *labor*) sewing, needlework; (= *confección*) dressmaking • **alta ~** haute couture, high fashion • **la ~ italiana** Italian fashion
3 (*Náut*) seam
costurar ▷ CONJUG 1a (VT), (VI), **costurear** (VT), (VI) (*LAm*) = **coser**
costurera (SF) dressmaker, seamstress
costurero (SM) (= *caja*) sewing box; (= *cuarto*) sewing room
cota¹ (SF) **1** (*Hist*) ▸ **cota de malla** coat of mail
2 (*Caribe*) (= *blusa*) blouse
cota² (SF) **1** (*Geog*) height above sea level; (= *altura*) height, level • **misil de baja ~** low-flying missile • **volar a baja ~** to fly low
2 (= *cifra*) number, figure ▸ **cota de popularidad** level of popularity
cotarro (SM) **1*** (= *grupo*) • **MODISMOS**: • **alborotar el ~** to stir up trouble • **dirigir el ~** to be the boss, rule the roost

2† (= *albergue*) night shelter for tramps • MODISMO: • **andar** *o* **ir de ~ en ~** to wander about, gad about
3 (*Cono Sur**) (= *colega*) mate*, pal*, buddy (EEUU*)

coteja SF (*LAm*) equal, match

cotejar ▹ CONJUG 1a VT **1** (= *comparar*) to compare, collate
2 (*And, Caribe*) (= *arreglar*) to arrange

cotejo ADJ (*LAm*) similar, same
SM **1** (= *comparación*) comparison, collation
2 (*Dep*) match, game

cotelé SM (*Chile*) corduroy

cotense SM (*And, Cono Sur, Méx*), **cotensia** SF (*And, Cono Sur*), **cotensio** SM (*Cono Sur*) coarse hemp fabric

coterna SF (*And*) broad hat

coterráneo/a ADJ from the same country, from the same region
SM/F compatriot, fellow-countryman/-woman • **un ~ le dio trabajo a Reilly en México** a fellow-countryman gave Reilly work in Mexico

cotí SM ticking

cotidianeidad SF daily nature, routine character

cotidiano ADJ daily, everyday • **la vida cotidiana** daily life, everyday life

cotiledón SM cotyledon

cotilla* SMF gossip

cotillear* ▹ CONJUG 1a VI to gossip

cotilleo* SM gossip, gossiping

cotillero/a SM/F = cotilla

cotillón SM ≈ New Year's Eve party

cotín SM (*Dep*) backhand return

cotitular SMF joint owner

cotiza SF (*LAm*) rough sandal

cotizable ADJ [*valor*] quotable

cotización SF **1** (*Econ*) price ▸ **cotización de apertura** opening price ▸ **cotización de cierre, cotización de clausura** closing price
2 [*de club*] dues (*pl*), subscription; (*a la Seguridad Social*) National Insurance contributions (*pl*) ▸ **cotización empresarial** employer contribution
3 (= *cambio*) exchange rate

cotizado ADJ (= *solicitado*) in demand, sought-after; (= *estimado*) valued, esteemed • **uno de los corredores más ~s del ciclismo español** one of the most highly regarded Spanish cyclists • **un fotógrafo italiano, ~ internacionalmente** an internationally esteemed *o* acclaimed Italian photographer

cotizante SMF contributor

cotizar ▹ CONJUG 1f VI **1** (= *contribuir*) to make contributions, pay contributions • **no tiene pensión porque nunca ha cotizado** he doesn't have a pension because he hasn't made *o* paid any contributions • **~ a la Seguridad Social** to pay National Insurance contributions
2 (*Econ*) • **nuestra empresa cotiza ahora en Bolsa** our company is now quoted on the Stock Exchange • **al cierre cotizó a 3,21 euros** it closed at 3.21 euros, at the close it stood at 3.21 euros
VT **1** (= *pagar*) [+ *cuota, recibo, impuesto*] to pay
2 (*Caribe, Cono Sur*) (= *valorar*) to value (**en** at)
3 (*Cono Sur*) (= *prorratear*) to share out proportionally
4 (*And, Caribe*) (= *vender*) to sell
VPR **cotizarse 1** (*Com, Econ*) [*acciones*] to stand at, be quoted at; [*divisa*] to stand at • **estas acciones se están cotizando a once dólares** these shares are standing *o* (being) quoted at eleven dollars • **este es el valor que más se cotiza** this is the most commonly quoted price • **el dólar se cotizó hoy a 102,32 yenes** the dollar stood at 102.32 yen today
2 (= *valorarse*) to be valued • **esos vídeos se cotizan en el mercado negro a 100 dólares cada uno** those videos are worth 100 dollars each on the black market, those videos are valued on the black market at 100 dollars each • **los conocimientos de inglés se cotizan muy alto** knowledge of English is highly valued

coto[1] SM **1** (= *reserva*) reserve ▸ **coto cerrado** closed shop • **los académicos son un ~ cerrado** the academic world is a closed shop ▸ **coto de caza** game preserve ▸ **coto de pesca** fishing preserve ▸ **coto forestal** forest reserve, forest estate ▸ **coto privado** private reserve ▸ **coto redondo** large estate
2 • **poner ~ a algo** to put a stop to sth • **medidas para poner ~ a la violencia** measures to put a stop to the violence
3 (= *mojón*) boundary stone
4 (*Com*) (= *acuerdo*) price-fixing agreement
5 (*Bridge*) rubber

coto[2] SM (*LAm*) (*Med*) goitre, goiter (EEUU)

cotón SM **1** (= *tela*) printed cotton, cotton fabric
2 (*Méx*) (= *camisa*) shirt; (= *blusa*) blouse

cotona SF **1** (*LAm*) (= *camisa*) *tightly woven cotton shirt*
2 (*Méx*) (= *cazadora*) leather jacket, suede jacket
3 (*Caribe*) (= *camisón*) child's nightdress

cotonete SM (*Méx*) cotton bud, Q-tip® (EEUU)

cotorina SF (*Méx*) jerkin

cotorra SF **1** (*Orn*) (= *loro*) parrot; (= *urraca*) magpie
2* (= *persona*) chatterbox*, windbag* (*pey*)

cotorrear* ▹ CONJUG 1a VI to chatter

cotorreo* SM **1** (= *plática*) chatter
2 (*Méx**) (= *diversión*) fun, good time

cotorrera SF female parrot; = cotorra

cotorro* ADJ (*Méx*) (= *platicón*) chatty, talkative; (= *alborotado*) loud, noisy

cototo SM (*Cono Sur*) bump, bruise, bruise on the head

cotudo ADJ **1** (*LAm*) suffering from goitre *o* goiter (EEUU)
2 (*And*) (= *tonto*) stupid

cotufa SF **1** (*Bot*) Jerusalem artichoke
2 cotufas (*LAm*) popcorn (*sing*)

coturno SM buskin; (*Hist*) cothurnus • MODISMO: • **de alto ~** lofty, elevated

COU SM ABR (*Esp*) (= **Curso de Orientación Universitaria**) *formerly, preparatory one-year course for the university entrance examinations*

covacha SF **1** (= *cueva*) small cave
2 (= *vivienda*) hovel
3 (*LAm*) (= *trastera*) lumber room, storage space
4 (*And*) (= *puesto*) vegetable stall
5 (*Caribe*) (= *perrera*) kennel

covachuela SF hovel

covadera SF (*LAm*) guano deposit

cover* SM (*Prensa*) cover story; (*Mús*) cover version

covin SM, **covín** SM (*Cono Sur*) popcorn

cowboy [kao'βoi] SM (PL: **cowboys**) cowboy

coxcojilla SF, **coxcojita** SF hopscotch

coxis SM INV coccyx

coy SM **1** (*Náut*) hammock
2 (*And, Caribe*) (= *cuna*) cradle

coyón* ADJ (*Méx*) cowardly

coyotaje* SM (*Méx*) fixing*

coyote SM **1** (*Zool*) coyote, prairie wolf
2 (*Méx, CAm**) (= *intermediario*) fixer*; (= *sablista*) con man*; (= *guía*) *guide for would-be immigrants to US*
3 (*Méx*) (*Com, Econ*) speculator, dealer in shares *etc*

coyotear ▹ CONJUG 1a (*Méx*) VI **1** (*Com, Econ*) to deal in shares, speculate in shares
2 (= *ser intermediario*) to act as go-between; (= *ser sablista*) to be a con man*

coyunda SF **1** (*CAm*) (= *correa*) strap; (= *dogal*) halter; (= *tralla*) lash, *part of whip*
2 (*hum*) (*conyugal*) yoke, yoke of marriage

coyuntura SF **1** (*Anat*) joint
2 (= *momento*) juncture • **en esta ~** at this juncture, at this moment in time • **esperar una ~ favorable** to wait for a suitable moment ▸ **coyuntura crítica** critical moment, critical juncture, conjuncture (*frm*)
3 (= *situación*) situation • **la ~ política** the political situation

coyuntural ADJ relating to the moment *o* situation *etc*, relating to the present moment *o* situation *etc* • **datos ~es** relevant data • **medidas ~es** immediately relevant measures • **solución ~** interim solution

coyunturalismo SM opportunism

coyunturalmente ADV responding to the demands of the moment

coz SF **1** (= *patada*) kick • **dar (de) coces a** to kick • **tirar coces** to lash out (*tb fig*) • MODISMO: • **dar coces contra el aguijón** to kick against the pricks
2 [*de fusil*] (= *retroceso*) recoil, kick; (= *culata*) butt
3 [*de agua*] backward flow
4 (= *insulto*) insult, rude remark • **tratar a algn a coces** to treat sb like dirt

CP ABR **1** (*Esp*) = **Caja Postal**
2 (*Esp*) (*Com*) (= **contestación pagada**) RP
3 (*LAm*) (= **casilla postal**) PO Box

CP/M SM ABR (= **Central Program for Microprocessors**) CP/M

CPN ABR (*Esp*) = **Cuerpo de la Policía Nacional**

cps, cps. ABR (= **caracteres por segundo**) (*Inform*) cps

crac[1] SM (*Com, Econ*) crash • **el viernes del Crac** Black Friday • **el ~ del 29** the 1929 Stock Exchange crash ▸ **crac financiero** financial crash

crac[2] EXCL crack!, snap! • **hizo crac y se abrió** it went snap! *o* crack! and came open

crack SM **1** (*LAm*) (*Dep*) (= *persona*) top player, star player; (= *caballo*) champion horse
2* (= *droga*) crack‡

cracker SMF (*Inform*) cracker

crampón SM crampon

craneal ADJ (*Med*) cranial • **traumatismo ~** cranial traumatism

craneano ADJ (*Med*) cranial

cranear* ▹ CONJUG 1a VT (*Cono Sur*) to dream up
VPR **cranearse** (*Chile, Perú*) to dream up

cráneo SM skull, cranium (*frm*) • MODISMOS: • **ir de ~***: • **voy de ~** it's all going wrong for me • **va a ir de ~ si hace eso*** he'll be in trouble if he does that • **ir de ~ con algn*** to be on bad terms with sb • **esto me lleva** *o* **trae de ~*** this is driving me crazy *o* nuts*

crápula SF (= *embriaguez*) drunkenness; (= *disipación*) dissipation
SM wastrel

crapuloso ADJ (= *borracho*) drunken; (= *disoluto*) dissolute, dissipated

craquear ▹ CONJUG 1a VT to crack

craqueo SM cracking

crasitud SF fatness

craso ADJ **1** (= *gordo*) [*persona*] fat; [*líquido*] greasy, thick
2 [*error*] gross, crass
3 (*And, Cono Sur*) (= *grosero*) coarse

cráter (SM) crater
crawl [krol] (SM) crawl, front crawl
crayón (SM) crayon, chalk
crayota (SF) (*And*) wax crayon
creación (SF) **1** (= *acción*) **a** [*de obra, objeto, empleo, ambiente*] creation • **para la ~ artística es necesaria la libertad de expresión** freedom of expression is necessary for artistic creation • **alterna la ~ literaria con la profesión periodística** she divides her time between literary work and journalism • **un empleo de nueva ~** a newly created position **b** [*de empresa, asociación*] • **incentivos para la ~ de empresas** incentives aimed at creating new businesses • **piden la ~ de una comisión de investigación** they are asking for a committee of inquiry to be set up • **empresas de nueva ~** newly-created businesses • **Canadá es miembro de la OTAN desde su ~** Canada has been a member of NATO since its creation *o* foundation
2 (= *cosa creada*) creation • **presentará sus últimas creaciones en Milán** he will show his latest creations *o* designs in Milan • **su última ~ teatral** his latest work for the stage
3 • **la Creación** (*Rel*) the Creation
creacionismo (SM) creationism
creacionista (SMF) creationist
creador(a) (ADJ) creative
(SM/F) **1** [*de movimiento, organización, personaje*] creator
2 (= *artista*) artist; (= *diseñador*) designer • **los grandes ~es del Renacimiento** the great artists of the Renaissance • **los ~es de moda juvenil** designers of youth fashion
(SM) • **el Creador** (*Rel*) the Creator
crear ▷ CONJUG 1a (VT) **1** (= *hacer, producir*) [+ *obra, objeto, empleo*] to create • **el hombre fue creado a imagen de Dios** man was created in the image of God • **~on una ciudad de la nada** they created a city out of nothing
2 (= *establecer*) [+ *comisión, comité, fondo, negocio, sistema*] to set up; [+ *asociación, cooperativa*] to form, set up; [+ *cargo, puesto*] to create; [+ *movimiento, organización*] to create, establish, found • **¿qué se necesita para ~ una empresa?** what do you need in order to set up *o* start a business? • **esta organización se creó para defender los derechos humanos** this organization was created *o* established *o* founded to defend human rights • **aspiraban a ~ un estado independiente** they aimed to create *o* establish *o* found an independent state
3 (= *dar lugar a*) [+ *condiciones, clima, ambiente*] to create; [+ *problemas*] to cause, create; [+ *expectativas*] to raise • **el bloqueo ha creado una situación insostenible** the blockade has created an untenable situation • **el vacío creado por su muerte** the gap left *o* created by her death • **la nicotina crea adicción** nicotine is addictive
4 (*liter*) (= *nombrar*) to make, appoint • **fue creado papa** he was made pope
creatividad (SF) creativity
creativo/a (ADJ) creative
(SM/F) (*tb* **creativo/a de publicidad**) copywriter
crece (SM o SF) (*Cono Sur*) = **crecida**
crecepelo (SM) hair-restorer
crecer ▷ CONJUG 2d (VI) **1** (= *desarrollarse*) [*animal, planta, objeto*] to grow • **el jazmín ha dejado de ~** the jasmine has stopped growing • **te ha crecido mucho el pelo** your hair's grown a lot • **me he dejado ~ la barba** I've grown a beard • **crecí en Sevilla** I grew up in Seville • **la princesa fue creciendo en belleza y sabiduría** the princess grew in beauty and wisdom
2 (= *aumentar*) [*cantidad, producción, sentimiento*] to grow; [*gastos*] to increase, rise; [*inflación*] to rise; [*desempleo*] to increase, grow, rise • **el número de heridos seguía creciendo** the number of wounded continued to grow • **la economía española ~á un 4%** the Spanish economy will grow by 4% • **crece el temor de un conflicto armado** there are growing fears of an armed conflict • **el viento fue creciendo en intensidad** the wind increased *o* grew in intensity • **~ en importancia** to grow in importance
3 (= *extenderse*) [*ciudad*] to grow; [*río, marea*] to rise; [*luna*] to wax
(VPR) **crecerse 1** (= *tomar fuerza*) • **pocos jugadores saben ~se ante la adversidad** there are few players who can stand up and be counted in the face of adversity
2* (= *engreírse*) to get full of o.s. • **con nada que le digas ya se crece** whatever you say to him he still gets all full of himself *o* his head still starts to swell
3 (*Cos*) • **en el cuello se le crece un punto** increase one stitch at the neck, add one stitch at the neck
creces (SFPL) **1** • **con ~** amply, fully • **superó las expectativas con ~** she far exceeded *o* surpassed all expectations • **superó con ~ el récord** he beat the record by a long way *o* a long chalk, he smashed the record • **pagar con ~ un error** to pay dearly for a mistake • **pagó con ~ lo que debía** he paid back the full amount and more, he gave back everything he owed and more • **había cumplido su obligación con ~** he had amply carried out his obligation • **devolver un favor/el cariño con ~** to return a favour/sb's affection hundredfold
2 (*Cos*) room to let out • **para los niños se hace la ropa con ~** children's clothes are made to be let out
crecida (SF) [*de río*] (= *aumento del cauce*) rise in level; (= *inundación*) flooding
crecido (ADJ) **1** [*persona*] • **está muy ~ para su edad** he's very tall *o* big for his age • **está ya crecidita para saber lo que se hace** (*iró*) she's old enough to know what she's doing
2 [*río*] high • **el río siempre viene ~ a la altura del puente** the level of the river is always higher where it goes under the bridge • **los ríos van ~s por los deshielos de la primavera** the rivers are swollen from the spring thaws, river levels are high from the spring thaws
3 [*cantidad, número*] large
4 [*pelo, barba*] • **tienes el pelo mucho más ~ que cuando te vi la última vez** your hair is much longer than last time I saw you • **llevaba la barba crecida de un día** he had a day's growth (on his chin)
5 (= *engreído*) vain, conceited
creciente (ADJ) **1** [*tendencia, demanda, volumen*] growing, increasing • **existe un ~ interés por las nuevas tecnologías** there is growing *o* increasing interest in new technology
2 [*luna*] waxing; ▷ **cuarto**
(SM) (*Astron*) [*de la luna*] crescent ▸ **el Creciente Rojo** the Red Crescent
(SF) [*de río*] flood ▸ **creciente del mar** flood tide
crecientemente (ADV) increasingly
crecimiento (SM) **1** (*en seres vivos*) growth • **el deporte favorece el ~** sport is good for growth • **tiene problemas de ~** he has growth problems
2 (= *aumento*) growth • **bajo ~** low growth rate • **modelos de ~ económico** models of economic growth • **el ~ del gasto público** the growth *o* increase in public spending • **una población en ~** a growing population
▸ **crecimiento cero** (*Econ*) zero growth
▸ **crecimiento demográfico** population growth ▸ **crecimiento negativo** (*Econ*) negative growth ▸ **crecimiento sostenido** sustained growth ▸ **crecimiento vegetativo** (*Sociol*) natural increase
credencial (ADJ) accrediting; ▷ **carta**
(SF) **1** (= *documento*) document confirming appointment
2 credenciales credentials
credibilidad (SF) credibility
crediticio (ADJ) credit (*antes de s*)
crédito (SM) **1** (= *fe*) credit • **dar ~ a algo** to believe sth, credit sth • **no podía dar ~ a sus oídos/ojos** he could hardly believe his ears/eyes
2 (= *fama*) standing, reputation • **persona (digna) de ~** reliable person • **tiene ~ de muy escrupuloso** he has the reputation of being thoroughly honest
3 (*Com, Econ*) credit • **a ~** on credit • **abrir ~ a** to give credit to ▸ **crédito a corto plazo** short-term credit ▸ **crédito a la exportación** export credit ▸ **crédito a largo plazo** long-term credit ▸ **crédito al consumidor** consumer credit ▸ **crédito bancario** bank credit ▸ **crédito de aceptación** acceptance credit ▸ **crédito de vivienda** mortgage ▸ **crédito diferido** deferred credit ▸ **crédito hipotecario** mortgage loan ▸ **crédito personal** personal credit ▸ **crédito puente** bridging loan, bridge loan (*EEUU*) ▸ **crédito renovable, crédito rotativo** revolving credit
4 (*Univ*) credit
5 (*Cine, TV*) • **~s** credits
credo (SM) (*Rel*) creed • **el Credo** the Creed
credulidad (SF) credulity
crédulo/a (ADJ) gullible, credulous
(SM/F) • **es tan ~** he's so gullible
creederas (SFPL) • **tiene buenas ~** he's very gullible
creencia (SF) belief (**en** in) • **en la ~ de que ...** in the belief that ...
creencial (ADJ) relating to belief
creer ▷ CONJUG 2e (VI) **1** (= *pensar*) • **es de Madrid, según creo** I believe she's from Madrid • **no creo** I don't think so • **es difícil, no creas** it's hard enough, I can tell you
2 • **~ en** to believe in • **creen en Dios** they believe in God • **creo en la igualdad** I believe in equality • **¿crees en los fantasmas?** do you believe in ghosts?
(VT) **1** (= *considerar cierto*) to believe • **nadie me cree** nobody believes me • **créame** believe me, take my word for it • **no creo lo que dijo** I don't believe what she said • **¡ya lo creo!**: • **—¿quieres un café? —¡ya lo creo!** "do you want some coffee?" — "you bet!"* • **¡ya lo creo que está roto!** you bet it's broken!, it certainly is broken! • **¿que yo voy a ir andando hasta el faro? ¡ya lo creo!** (*iró*) you think I'm going to walk all the way to the lighthouse? you must be joking!* • **¿que tú no sabías lo del examen? ¡sí, sí, ya lo creo!** (*iró*) you didn't know about the exam? oh, sure you didn't!*
2 (= *pensar*) to think • **creen haber descubierto el motivo** they think (that) they've discovered the reason • **~ que** to think (that) • **no creo que pueda ir** I don't think I'll be able to go • **creo que es sincera** I think she's sincere, I believe her to be sincere • **creo que sí** I think so • **creo que no** I don't think so • **no puedo ~ que esto esté pasando** I can't believe this is happening • **no se vaya usted a ~ que ...** don't go thinking that ..., I wouldn't want you to think that ...

3 (= *considerar*) to think • **no lo creía capaz de hacerlo** I didn't think him capable of doing it • **lo creo mi deber** I think *o* consider it (to be) my duty

VPR **creerse 1** (= *considerar cierto*) to believe • **no me lo creo** I don't believe it • **eso no se lo ~á nadie** no one will believe that • **se cree todo lo que le dicen** he believes everything he's told • **hace falta que yo me lo crea** I remain to be convinced • **¡que te crees tú eso!*** you must be joking!* • **¡no te lo crees ni tú!*** come off it!*

2 (= *pensar*) to think • **¿de dónde te crees que sacan el dinero?** where do you think they get the money? • **¿pero tú qué te crees, que soy millonario?** what do you think I am, a millionaire or something?

3 (= *considerarse*) to think • **se cree muy listo** he thinks he's pretty clever • **¿quién te crees que eres?** who do you think you are? • **se cree alguien** he thinks he's somebody • **¿qué se ha creído?** who does he think he is?

creíble ADJ believable, credible • **¿es ~ que ...?** is it conceivable that ...?

creíblemente ADV credibly

creído/a ADJ **1** (= *engreído*) conceited

2 (= *crédulo*) credulous, trusting

SM/F • **es un ~** he's very full of himself

crema SF **1** (*en cosmética, de zapatos*) cream ▸ **crema antiarrugas** anti-wrinkle cream ▸ **crema base** foundation cream ▸ **crema bronceadora** suntan lotion, suntan cream ▸ **crema de afeitar** shaving cream ▸ **crema de belleza** beauty cream ▸ **crema de día** day cream ▸ **crema de manos** hand cream ▸ **crema de noche** night cream ▸ **crema depilatoria** hair removing cream, depilatory cream ▸ **crema de protección solar** sun protection cream ▸ **crema de zapatos** shoe cream ▸ **crema hidratante** moisturizer, moisturizing cream ▸ **crema nutritiva** nourishing cream

2 (= *licor*) cream liqueur, crème

3 (*Culin*) (*tb* **crema de leche**) cream • **~ líquida** single cream, pouring cream • **una ~ de champiñones** cream of mushroom (soup) ▸ **crema agria** sour cream, soured cream ▸ **crema batida** whipped cream ▸ **crema catalana** *dessert similar to crème brûlée* ▸ **crema de cacahuete** peanut butter ▸ **crema de cacao, crema de chocolate** chocolate filling ▸ **crema inglesa** custard ▸ **crema pastelera** confectioner's cream, custard, crème pâtissière

4 • **la ~** (= *lo mejor*) the cream • **la ~ de la sociedad** the cream of society

5 (*Tip*) (= *diéresis*) diaeresis, dieresis (*EEUU*)

6 (*Cono Sur*) • MODISMO: • **dejar la ~*** to make a hash of things*, put one's foot in it

ADJ INV [*color*] cream, cream-coloured, cream-colored (*EEUU*) • **una chaqueta ~ claro** a light cream *o* cream-coloured jacket • **un coche color ~** a cream(-coloured) car

cremación SF cremation

cremallera SF **1** (*en material*) zip, zipper (*EEUU*) • **cerrar la ~** do the zip *o* zipper up • **cierre de ~** zip, zip fastener, zipper (*EEUU*) • MODISMO: • **echar la ~*** to shut up*, button up*

2 (*Téc*) rack ▸ **cremallera y piñón** rack and pinion

cremar ▸ CONJUG 1a VT (*Méx*) to cremate

crematístico ADJ financial, economic

crematorio ADJ • **horno ~** crematorium

SM crematorium

crémor SM (*tb* **crémor tártaro**) cream of tartar

cremosidad SF creaminess

cremoso ADJ creamy

crencha SF parting, part (*EEUU*)

creosota SF creosote

crep[1] SM (= *tela*) crêpe, crepe, crape; (= *caucho*) crêpe (rubber), crepe (rubber)

crep[2] SM, **crepa** SF (*LAm*) (*Culin*) pancake, crêpe

crepar‡ ▸ CONJUG 1a VI (*Cono Sur*) to peg out‡, kick the bucket‡

crepe SM o SF = **crep**[2]

crepé SM **1** = **crep**[1]

2 (*Méx*) (= *peluca*) wig

crepería SF pancake restaurant, crêperie

crepitación SF [*de leño*] crackling; [*de bacon*] sizzling

crepitar ▸ CONJUG 1a VI [*leño*] to crackle; [*bacon*] to sizzle

crepuscular ADJ twilight (*antes de s*), crepuscular (*liter, frm*) • **luz ~** twilight

crepúsculo SM twilight, dusk

cresa SF **1** (= *larva*) larva

2 [*de abeja*] eggs of the queen bee

crescendo SM crescendo • **ir en ~** to increase, get louder *o* greater *etc*

Creso SM Croesus

crespo ADJ **1** (= *rizado*) [*pelo*] curly; [*hoja*] curled

2 [*estilo*] involved, tortuous

3 [*persona*] cross, angry

SM (*esp Caribe*) (= *rizo*) curl, ringlet

crespón SM crêpe, crepe, crape

cresta SF **1** (*Orn*) (*gen*) crest; [*de gallo*] comb

2 (*Geog*) crest

3 [*de ola*] crest • MODISMO: • **en la ~ de la ola** on the crest of a wave

4 (= *peluca*) wig, toupée

crestería SF (*Arquit*) (= *coronamiento*) cresting; (= *almenas*) crenellations (*pl*)

crestomatía SF anthology, collection of texts

crestón SM **1** [*de celada*] crest

2 (*Min*) outcrop

Creta SF Crete

creta SF chalk

cretáceo ADJ cretaceous

cretense ADJ, SMF Cretan

cretinada SF silly thing to do *o* say *etc*, stupid thing to do *o* say *etc*

cretinez SF stupidity

cretinismo SM cretinism

cretino/a ADJ cretinous

SM/F cretin

cretona SF cretonne

cretoso ADJ chalky

creyendo *etc* ▸ **creer**

creyente SMF believer • **no ~** non-believer, unbeliever

cría SF **1** (*Agr*) (= *actividad*) rearing; (*para la reproducción*) breeding • **hembra de ~** breeding female ▸ **cría caballar** horse breeding ▸ **cría de ganado** cattle breeding, stockbreeding ▸ **cría de peces** fish farming

2 (*Zool*) (= *camada*) litter; (= *individuo*) baby animal • **una ~ de ballena** a baby whale • **una ~ de león** a lion cub

criadero SM **1** (*Bot*) nursery

2 (*Zool*) breeding place, breeding ground ▸ **criadero de ostras** oyster bed ▸ **criadero de peces** fish hatchery, fish farm

3 (*Geol*) vein, seam

criadilla SF **1** (*Culin*) testicle ▸ **criadillas de tierra** truffles

2 (= *pan*) small loaf, roll

3 (= *patata*) potato, tuber

criado/a ADJ reared, brought up • **bien ~** well-bred • **mal ~** ▸ **malcriado**

SM/F **1** (= *sirviente*) (= *hombre*) servant; (= *mujer*) servant, maid ▸ **criado/a para todo** servant with general duties ▸ **criado/a por horas** (= *hombre*) *servant paid by the hour*; (= *mujer*) daily, *maid paid by the hour*

2 (*Naipes*) jack, knave

criador(a) SM/F breeder

SM • **el Criador** (*Rel*) the Creator

criajo/a* SM/F wretched child, urchin

criandera SF (*LAm*) nursemaid, wet nurse

crianza SF **1** (*Agr*) (= *actividad*) rearing; (*para la reproducción*) breeding

2 (*Med*) lactation

3 [*de vinos*] vintage ▸ **vinos de crianza** vintage wines

4 (= *educación*) breeding • **mala ~** lack of breeding • **sin ~** ill-bred

> **CRIANZA**
> Quality Spanish wine is often graded **Crianza**, **Reserva** or **Gran Reserva** according to the length of bottle-ageing and barrel-ageing it has undergone. **Crianza** wines are in their third year, reds having spent at least twelve months in cask and whites six.
> ▸ **RESERVA**

criar ▸ CONJUG 1c VT **1** (= *educar*) [+ *niño*] to bring up, raise (*esp EEUU*) • **los crió su abuela hasta los diez años** they were brought up *o* raised by their grandmother till they were ten • REFRÁN: • **Dios los cría y ellos se juntan** birds of a feather flock together

2 (= *amamantar*) to nurse, suckle, feed • **al niño lo crió su tía** the baby was nursed *o* suckled *o* fed by his aunt • **~ con biberón** to bottle-feed • **~ con el pecho** to breast-feed

3 [+ *ganado*] to rear, raise; [+ *aves de corral*] to breed; (*para competición*) to breed • REFRÁN: • **cría cuervos (que te sacarán los ojos)**: • **qué mala suerte tuvo con sus hijos; ya sabes, cría cuervos ...** she's been so unlucky with her children, after all she's done for them they've repaid her with nothing but ingratitude

4 [+ *hortalizas*] to grow • MODISMO: • **~ malvas**: • **ya está criando malvas** he's pushing up the daisies*

5 (= *producir*) • **los perros crían pulgas** dogs get fleas • **~ barriga** to get a belly* • **~ carnes** to put on weight • **esta tierra no cría malas hierbas** this soil doesn't produce any weeds • **~ polvo** to gather dust

VI **1** (= *tener crías*) to breed • **la gaviota suele ~ en las rocas** seagulls usually breed on rocks

2 (= *madurar*) [*vino*] to age, mature

VPR **criarse** to grow up • **se ~on juntos** they grew up together • **se ha criado con sus abuelos** he was brought up *o* raised by his grandparents • MODISMO: • **~se en buena cuna** *o* **en buenos pañales** to be born with a silver spoon in one's mouth

criatura SF **1** (= *ser creado*) creature • **las ~s de Dios** God's creatures

2 (= *niño pequeño*) child • **todavía es una ~** he's only *o* still a child

3 (*dicho cariñosamente*) • **la criaturita estaba asustada** the poor little thing *o* the poor creature was frightened • **¡pobre ~!** poor little thing! • **pero ~, ¿cómo no te has dado cuenta antes?** you silly thing, how come you didn't realize before?

criba SF **1** (= *instrumento*) sieve

2 (= *acto*) sifting, selection • MODISMOS: • **hacer una ~** to sort out the sheep from the goats • **superar la ~** to slip through the net

cribar ▸ CONJUG 1a VT to sieve, sift

cric SM jack

Crimea SF Crimea

crimen SM **1** (= *asesinato*) murder; (= *delito grave*) crime ▸ **crimen contra la humanidad** crime against humanity ▸ **crimen de guerra** war crime ▸ **crimen de sangre** violent crime ▸ **crimen organizado** organized crime ▸ **crimen pasional** crime of

passion, crime passionnel (*frm*)
2* (= *barbaridad*) • **es un ~ dejar aquí al niño** it's criminal to leave the child here
criminal ADJ [*comportamiento, acto*] criminal • **es ~ desperdiciar tanta comida** it's criminal *o* a crime to waste so much food
SMF (= *asesino*) murderer, killer • **un ~ sin escrúpulos** a ruthless murderer *o* killer
▸ **criminal de guerra** war criminal
criminalidad SF 1 (= *cualidad*) criminality
2 (= *índice*) crime rate
criminalista SMF 1 (*Univ*) criminologist
2 (*Jur*) criminal lawyer
criminalística SF criminology
criminalizar ▹ CONJUG 1f VT to criminalize • **~ un acto** to make an act a criminal offence
criminógeno ADJ conducive to crime, encouraging criminal tendencies
criminología SF criminology
criminólogo/a SM/F criminologist
crin SF (*Zool*) mane; (*Téc*) horsehair
crinolina SF crinoline
crinudo ADJ (*LAm*) long-maned
crío/a SM/F kid*, child; (*pey*) little brat* • **¡no seas ~!** grow up!, don't be such a baby!
criogénico ADJ cryogenic
criogenizar ▹ CONJUG 1f VT to freeze cryogenically
criollaje SM (*LAm*) Creoles (*pl*)
criollismo SM (*Chile*) local saying
criollo/a ADJ 1 (*Hist*) Creole; (= *de origen español*) of Spanish extraction
2 (*LAm*) (= *no extranjero*) native, native to America
SM/F 1 (*Hist*) Creole
2 (*LAm*) Peruvian/Colombian/Ecuadorean, etc, *native of a particular Latin American country, as opposed to a foreigner* • **un español y dos ~s** a Spaniard and two natives
3 (*And*) (= *cobarde*) coward
SM (*Ling*) Creole • **como dicen en ~** as they say in Latin America/Peru *etc*
criosfera SF cryosphere
cripta SF crypt
críptico ADJ cryptic
cripto... PREF crypto...
criptocomunista SMF crypto-communist
criptografía SF cryptography
criptográfico ADJ cryptographic, cryptographical
criptógrafo/a SM/F cryptographer
criptograma SM cryptogram
criptología SF cryptology
críquet SM cricket
crisálida SF chrysalis
crisalidar ▹ CONJUG 1a VI to pupate
crisantemo SM chrysanthemum
crisis SF INV 1 (*Econ, Pol, Sociol*) crisis • **la situación económica está pasando por una nueva ~** the economy is undergoing *o* going through a new crisis • **lo que está en ~ es el propio sistema** the system itself is in crisis • **nuestro matrimonio está en ~** our marriage is in crisis *o* going through a crisis • **hacer ~** to reach crisis point, come to a head ▸ **crisis de fe** crisis of faith ▸ **crisis de gobierno** government crisis ▸ **crisis de identidad** identity crisis ▸ **crisis de la vivienda** housing crisis ▸ **crisis de los cuarenta** midlife crisis ▸ **crisis económica** economic crisis ▸ **crisis energética** energy crisis ▸ **crisis ministerial** cabinet reshuffle
2 (*Med*) • **alguien a quien recurrir en momentos de ~** someone to turn to in moments of crisis ▸ **crisis cardíaca** cardiac arrest, heart failure ▸ **crisis de ansiedad** anxiety attack ▸ **crisis epiléptica** epileptic fit, epileptic attack ▸ **crisis nerviosa** nervous breakdown ▸ **crisis respiratoria** respiratory failure
crisma[1] SF 1 (*Rel*) chrism
2‡ (= *cabeza*) nut‡, noggin (EEUU‡), head • **romper la ~ a algn** to knock sb's block off‡ • **romperse la ~** to split one's head open
crisma[2] SM, (*a veces*) SF (*tb* **crismas**) (*Esp*) Christmas card
SF (*Méx*) Christmas present
crismón SM *monogram of Christ*
crisol SM (*Téc*) crucible; (*fig*) melting pot
crispación SF tension, nervousness
crispado ADJ tense, on edge
crispante ADJ infuriating
crispar ▹ CONJUG 1a VT 1 [+ *músculo*] to cause to twitch, cause to contract • **con el rostro crispado por la ira** with his face contorted with anger • **eso me crispa (los nervios)** that gets on my nerves* • **tengo los nervios crispados** my nerves are all on edge
2 (= *enfadar*) • **~ a algn*** to annoy sb intensely, really get on sb's nerves*
VPR **crisparse** [*músculo*] to twitch, contract; [*cara*] to contort; [*nervios*] to get all on edge; [*situación*] to become tense, get tenser
crispetas SFPL (*And*) popcorn (*sing*)
cristal SM 1 (= *vidrio normal*) glass; (= *vidrio fino*) crystal • **una puerta de ~** a glass door • **un vaso de ~** a glass • **una estatuilla de ~** a crystal statuette ▸ **cristal ahumado** smoked glass ▸ **cristal antibalas** bullet-proof glass ▸ **cristal blindado** reinforced glass ▸ **cristal cilindrado** plate glass ▸ **cristal de Bohemia** Bohemian glass ▸ **cristal de Murano** Venetian glass ▸ **cristal de patente** (*Náut*) bull's-eye ▸ **cristal de seguridad** safety glass ▸ **cristal esmerilado** frosted glass ▸ **cristal inastillable** shatterproof glass ▸ **cristal soplado** blown glass ▸ **cristal tallado** cut glass
2 (= *trozo de cristal*) piece of glass • **me he cortado con un ~** I've cut myself on a piece of glass • **hay ~es en el suelo** there's broken glass *o* there are pieces of broken glass on the floor • **se ha roto el ~ de la mesa** the glass table top has got cracked ▸ **cristales emplomados** leaded lights
3 [*de ventana*] window pane; [*de coche*] window; [*de gafas*] lens • **¿puedes subir un poco el ~?** can you wind the window up a bit? ▸ **cristal bifocal** bifocal lens ▸ **cristal de aumento** lens, magnifying glass
4 (*Min*) crystal ▸ **cristal de cuarzo** quartz crystal ▸ **cristal de roca** rock crystal ▸ **cristal de sílice** silica crystal ▸ **cristal líquido** liquid crystal
5 (= *espejo*) glass, mirror
cristalera SF 1 (= *ventana*) (*fija*) window; (*corredera*) French windows (*pl*)
2 (= *aparador*) display cabinet
cristalería SF 1 (= *arte*) glassmaking
2 (= *fábrica*) glassworks; (= *tienda*) glassware shop
3 (= *vasos*) glassware; (= *juego*) set of glasses
cristalero SM (*Cono Sur*) glass cabinet
cristalinamente ADV transparently
cristalino ADJ (*Fís*) crystalline; [*agua, explicación*] crystal-clear
SM crystalline lens
cristalización SF 1 (*Fís*) crystallization
2 [*de proyecto, idea*] realization
cristalizar ▹ CONJUG 1f VT to crystallize
VI 1 (*Fís*) to crystallize
2 [*proyecto, idea*] to crystallize, take shape
VPR **cristalizarse** 1 (*Fís*) to crystallize
2 [*proyecto, idea*] to crystallize, take shape
cristalografía SF crystallography
cristalógrafo/a SM/F crystallographer
cristero/a SM/F (*Méx*) *Catholic militant*
cristianamente ADV in a Christian way • **morir ~** to die in a state of grace
cristianar ▹ CONJUG 1a VT 1 (= *bautizar*) to christen, baptize
2 [+ *vino*] to water
cristiandad SF Christendom
cristianismo SM Christianity
cristianizar ▹ CONJUG 1f VT to Christianize
cristiano/a ADJ 1 (*Rel*) Christian
2 • **vino ~** unwatered wine
SM/F (*Rel*) Christian ▸ **cristiano nuevo** (*Hist*) *converted Jew or Moor* ▸ **cristiano viejo** (*Hist*) *Christian with no Jewish or Moorish blood*
SM 1 (= *persona*) person • **eso lo sabe cualquier ~** anyone knows that • **eso no hay ~ que lo entienda** that is beyond anyone's comprehension • **no hay ~ que lo sepa** no one knows that • **este ~*** yours truly*
2 • **hablar en ~** (= *claramente*) to talk sense; (= *en español*) to speak Spanish
Cristo SM (*Rel*) 1 (= *Jesucristo*) Christ • **en el año 41 antes de ~** in 41 B.C. • **en el año 80 después de ~** in 80 A.D. • MODISMOS: • **donde ~ dio las tres voces*** • **donde ~ perdió la sandalia*** in the back of beyond*
2 (= *imagen*) figure of Christ • **un ~ barroco** a Baroque figure of Christ
cristo SM 1 (= *crucifijo*) crucifix • MODISMOS: • **poner a algn como un ~*** (= *criticar*) to tear sb to shreds, call sb every name under the sun; (= *pegar*) to give sb a real thumping* • **hecho un ~*** in a terrible mess • **volvió hecho un ~ de la pelea** he returned from the fight in a terrible mess *o* looking a terrible sight • **ni ~***: • **eso no lo entiende ni ~** no one on earth can understand that, absolutely no one can understand that • **no había ni (un) ~ en la manifestación** there wasn't a soul at the demonstration • **todo ~***: • **eso lo sabe ya todo ~** everyone knows that, every Tom, Dick and Harry knows that*
2* (= *pelea*) • **¡vaya ~!** what a to-do!* • **armar *o* montar un ~** to raise hell, make an almighty fuss*
Cristóbal SM Christopher ▸ **Cristóbal Colón** Christopher Columbus
criterio SM 1 (= *método*) criterion • **este es el ~ de selección que hemos seguido** this is the selection criterion that we have followed • **tenemos que unificar ~s** we have to agree on our criteria • **con ese mismo ~ también podríamos afirmar lo contrario** by the same token *o* criterion one could also state the opposite
2 (= *juicio*) judgement • **me impresiona su falta de ~** I'm struck by his lack of judgement *o* (*frm*) discernment • **tiene buen ~** he has good *o* sound judgement • **lo dejo a su ~** I leave it to your discretion *o* judgement
3 (= *punto de vista*) opinion, view • **no comparto ese ~** I do not share that opinion *o* view • **en mi ~** in my opinion *o* view • **diferencia de ~s** difference of opinion • **formarse un ~ sobre algo** to form an opinion of sth • **depende del ~ de cada uno** it depends on each person's *o* individual's viewpoint
criterioso* ADJ (*Cono Sur*) level-headed, sensible
crítica SF 1 (= *censura*) criticism • **recibir duras ~s** to be severely criticized, come in for severe criticism • **lanzó duras ~s contra el Gobierno** he levelled fierce criticism at the Government, he launched a fierce attack on the Government
2 (*en periódico, revista*) review; (= *ensayo, libro*) critique
3 • **la ~** (= *los críticos*) the critics (*pl*) • **ser bien recibido por la ~** to be well received by the critics

4 (= *actividad*) criticism; (= *chismes*) gossip ▸ **crítica literaria** literary criticism ▸ **crítica teatral** dramatic criticism; ▹ **crítico**
criticable ADJ [*conducta, actitud*] reprehensible • **no es ~ que se te oponga** you can't blame him for standing against you
criticador(a) ADJ critical
SM/F critic
críticamente ADV critically
criticar ▹ CONJUG 1g VT **1** (= *censurar*) to criticize • **la actuación de la policía fue criticada por la oposición** the police behaviour was criticized by the opposition
2 (= *hablar mal*) • **siempre está criticando a la gente** he's always criticizing people, he's always finding fault with people
3 (*Arte, Literat, Teat*) [+ *libro, obra*] to review
VI to gossip
criticastro/a SM/F hack critic, ignorant critic
criticidad SF critical nature • **fase de ~** critical phase
crítico/a ADJ critical • **encontrarse en un estado ~** (*Med*) to be in a critical condition
SM/F critic ▸ **crítico/a cinematográfico/a** film critic ▸ **crítico/a de arte** art critic ▸ **crítico/a de cine** film critic ▸ **crítico/a literario/a** literary critic ▸ **crítico/a musical** music critic; ▹ **crítica**
criticón/ona* ADJ hypercritical, critical, faultfinding • **es muy ~** he's always finding fault with people, he's hypercritical, he's so critical
SM/F faultfinder
critiquizar ▹ CONJUG 1f VT to be overcritical of, indulge in petty criticism of
CRM SM ABR = **certificado de regulación monetaria**
Croacia SF Croatia
croar ▹ CONJUG 1a VI to croak
croata ADJ, SMF Croat, Croatian • **los ~s** the Croats, the Croatians
croché SM crochet • **hacer ~** to crochet
crochet [kro'tʃe] SM **1** (*Cos*) crochet
2 (*Boxeo*) hook
crocitar ▹ CONJUG 1a VI to crow, caw
croissan SM, **croissant** [krwa'zan] SM croissant
croissantería [krwazante'ria] SF croissant shop
crol SM (*Natación*) crawl
cromado ADJ chromium-plated, chrome
SM chromium plating, chrome
cromático ADJ chromatic
cromatografía SF chromatography
cromatograma SM chromatogram
crómlech SM stone circle
cromo SM **1** (*Quím*) chromium, chrome
2 (= *estampa*) picture card; (*Rel*) religious card • MODISMO: • **iba hecho un ~*** he was a sight*
3 (*Tip*) coloured print, colored print (*EEUU*)
cromosoma SM chromosome
cromosomático ADJ, **cromosómico** ADJ chromosomal
cromoterapia SF chromotherapy, colour therapy
crónica SF **1** [*de periódico*] feature, article; (*Radio, TV*) report • **"Crónica de sucesos"** "News in Brief" ▸ **crónica deportiva** sports page ▸ **crónica de sociedad** society column, gossip column ▸ **crónica literaria** literary page
2 (*Hist*) chronicle; (*fig*) account, chronicle
3 Crónicas (*Biblia*) Chronicles
crónico ADJ [*enfermedad, déficit, problema*] chronic; [*vicio*] ingrained
cronificación SF • **en fase de ~** becoming chronic
cronificar ▹ CONJUG 1g VT (*Prensa*) to chronicle
VI (*Med*) to become chronic
VPR **cronificarse** (*Med*) to become chronic
cronista SMF **1** [*de periódico*] reporter, columnist ▸ **cronista de radio** radio commentator ▸ **cronista deportivo** sports writer ▸ **cronista de sucesos** accident and crime reporter ▸ **cronista social** society columnist
2 (*Hist*) chronicler
crono SM **1** (= *reloj*) stopwatch
2 (*tiempo*) time, recorded time • **ganó con un ~ de 6,59** she won with a time of 6.59 • **hacer** o **marcar un ~ de** to do a time of, get a time of
SF time-trial
cronografista SMF (*Cono Sur*) timekeeper
cronograma SM (*Cono Sur*) timetable, schedule
cronología SF chronology
cronológicamente ADV chronologically, in chronological order
cronológico ADJ chronological • **en orden ~** in chronological order
cronometrada SF (*Dep*) time-trial
cronometrador(a) SM/F timekeeper
cronometraje SM timekeeping, timing • **~ electrónico** electronic timekeeping • **~ manual** manual timekeeping
cronometrar ▹ CONJUG 1a VT to time
cronómetro SM (*Téc*) chronometer; (*Dep*) stopwatch
croquet [kro'ke] SM croquet
croqueta SF croquette • **~ de pescado** fish croquette • **~ de pollo** chicken croquette
croquis SM INV sketch • **hacer un ~** to do o draw a sketch
cross [kros] SM INV **1** (*Atletismo*) (= *deporte*) cross-country running; (= *carrera*) cross-country race
2 (*Motociclismo*) (= *deporte*) moto(r)cross; (= *carrera*) moto(r)cross race
crostón SM crouton
crótalo SM **1** (*Zool*) rattlesnake, rattler (*EEUU**)
2 crótalos (*Mús*) castanets
croto* SM (*Cono Sur*) bum, layabout*
cruasán SM croissant
cruce SM **1** (*Aut*) [*de carreteras, autopistas*] junction, intersection; [*de cuatro esquinas*] crossroads; (*para peatones*) crossing, crosswalk (*EEUU*) • **"cruce peligroso"** "dangerous junction" ▸ **cruce a nivel** level crossing, grade crossing (*EEUU*) ▸ **cruce de peatones, cruce peatonal** pedestrian crossing, crosswalk (*EEUU*)
2 • **luces de ~** dipped headlights • **poner la luz** o **las luces de ~** to dip one's lights
3 (= *acto*) • **hubo un ~ de acusaciones entre ellos** there was an exchange of accusations between them • **se produjo un ~ de miradas entre ellos** their eyes met • MODISMO: • **tener un ~ de cables*** to lose one's head* ▸ **cruce de aros** (*Ven*) engagement ceremony (*involving the exchange of rings*)
4 (*Telec*) crossed line • **hay un ~ en las líneas** the wires are crossed
5 (*Bio*) (= *proceso*) crossbreeding; (= *resultado*) cross • **ser un ~ de** o **entre un animal y otro** to be a cross o crossbreed between one animal and another
6 (*Mat*) intersection, point of intersection
7 (*Ling*) cross, mutual interference
crucerista SMF cruise passenger
crucero SM **1** (= *barco*) cruise ship, (cruise) liner; (*Mil*) cruiser ▸ **crucero de batalla** battle cruiser ▸ **crucero de lujo** luxury cruise ship, luxury (cruise) liner ▸ **crucero pesado** heavy cruiser
2 (= *viaje*) cruise • **hacer un ~** to go on a cruise • **velocidad de ~** cruising speed ▸ **crucero de placer, crucero de recreo** pleasure cruise
3 (*Arquit*) [*de templo*] transept
4 (= *viga*) crosspiece
5 (*Aut*) [*de carreteras*] crossroads; (*Ferro*) crossing
6 (= *persona*) crossbearer
7 (*Astron*) ▸ **Crucero (Austral)** Southern Cross
8 (= *misil*) cruise missile
cruceta SF **1** (= *viga*) crosspiece; (*Náut, Mec*) crosstree
2 (*Mec*) crosshead
3 (*Cono Sur*) (= *torniquete*) turnstile
crucial ADJ crucial
crucificar ▹ CONJUG 1g VT (*Rel*) to crucify • **si llega a perecer alguien, te crucifico** if anyone gets killed, I'll crucify you
crucifijo SM crucifix
crucifixión SF crucifixion
cruciforme ADJ cruciform
crucigrama SM crossword (puzzle)
crucigramista SMF crossword enthusiast
cruda* SF (*LAm*) (= *resaca*) hangover
crudamente ADV starkly
crudelísimo ADV (*superl de* **cruel**) (*liter*) most cruel, terribly cruel
crudeza SF **1** [*de imágenes, descripción*] coarseness, crudeness, crudity • **expresar algo con ~** to put sth crudely
2 [*del invierno*] harshness, bleakness
3 (*Culin*) [*de carne*] rawness; [*de frutas*] unripeness
4 [*de comida*] indigestibility
5 [*de agua*] hardness
6 (= *comida*) undigested food (in the stomach)
crudo ADJ **1** (*Culin*) **a** (= *sin cocinar*) [*carne*] raw; [*verduras*] raw, uncooked
b (= *poco hecho*) underdone • **las patatas están crudas** the potatoes are underdone o are not properly cooked
2 • **de color ~ natural** • **un jersey de color ~** a natural-coloured o (*EEUU*) natural-colored jersey
3 (*Téc*) [*producto*] untreated; [*seda*] raw; [*lino*] unbleached
4 [*clima, invierno*] harsh, severe
5 [*descripción*] crude, coarse; [*imágenes*] harrowing • **la cruda realidad** the harsh reality
6* (= *difícil*) • **lo tienen ~ para encontrar un trabajo** they're having a hard o tough time finding a job • **lo tendrán ~ si piensan que ...** they'll have a tough time of it if they think that ... • **lo veo muy ~** it doesn't look (too) good
7 [*agua*] hard
SM **1** (= *petróleo*) crude (oil)
2 (*LAm**) (= *resaca*) hangover
3 (*Perú*) (= *arpillera*) sackcloth
cruel ADJ cruel • **fue una ~ ironía** it was a cruel irony • **el destino ~** cruel fate • **ser ~ con algn** to be cruel to sb
crueldad SF **1** (= *cualidad*) cruelty • **tratar a algn con ~** to treat sb cruelly
2 (= *acción*) cruelty • **¡es una ~!** that's so cruel!, it's such a cruel thing to do o say!
cruelmente ADV cruelly
cruento ADJ (*liter*) bloody, gory
crujía SF (*Arquit*) corridor, gallery; (*Med*) ward; (*Náut*) midship gangway; [*de cárcel*] wing • MODISMO: • **pasar ~** to have a tough time of it
crujido SM **1** [*de papel, hojas, seda*] rustle, rustling; [*de madera, mueble, rama*] creak, creaking; [*de nieve, grava*] crunch, crunching; [*de leña ardiendo*] crackle, crackling
2 [*de articulaciones, huesos*] crack, cracking; [*de dientes*] grinding
crujiente ADJ [*galleta*] crunchy; [*pan*]

crunchy, crusty; [*seda*] rustling; [*madera*] creaking
crujir ▹ CONJUG 3a VI **1** [*papel, seda, hojas*] to rustle; [*madera, mueble, rama*] to creak; [*leña ardiendo*] to crackle; [*galletas, nieve, grava*] to crunch
2 [*articulación, hueso*] to crack; [*dientes*] to grind • **le crujen los dientes** his teeth are grinding • **hacer ~ los nudillos** to crack one's knuckles
crupier SMF croupier
crustáceo SM crustacean
cruz SF **1** (= *figura*) cross • **en ~** cross-shaped • **coloque los dos palos en ~** put the two sticks in a cross-shape *o* in the shape of a cross • **con los brazos en ~** with one's arms outstretched • **firmar con una ~** to make one's mark • **hacerse cruces** to cross o.s. • **se hacía cruces cada vez que oía una palabrota** he crossed himself every time he heard a swearword • MODISMOS: • **cargar la ~** (*Méx**) to have a hangover • **¡~ y raya!** that's quite enough!, no more! • **a partir de ahora, a los Pérez, ¡~ y raya!** that's it, I'm through with the Pérez family! *o* I've had it with the Pérez family! • **por estas que son cruces** by all that is holy • **quedar en ~** to be in an agonizing situation ▸ **cruz de hierro** iron cross ▸ **Cruz del Sur** Southern Cross ▸ **cruz de Malta** Maltese Cross ▸ **cruz de mayo** (*LAm*), **cruz gamada** swastika ▸ **cruz griega** Greek cross ▸ **cruz latina** Latin cross ▸ **Cruz Roja** Red Cross
2 (= *suplicio*) • **¡qué ~ tengo con estos hijos!** these kids of mine are a nightmare!* • **cada uno lleva su ~** each of us has his cross to bear
3 [*de espada*] hilt; [*de ancla*] crown; (*Tip*) dagger
4 [*de moneda*] tails • **¿cara o ~?** heads or tails?
5 (*Zool*) withers (*pl*)
cruza SF (*LAm*) **1** (*Bio*) cross, hybrid
2 (*Agr*) second ploughing *o* (*EEUU*) plowing
cruzada SF **1** (*Hist*) (*tb fig*) crusade • **una ~ contra el terrorismo** a crusade against terrorism
2 • **La Cruzada** *the Civil War of 1936-39 (in official Spanish usage up to 1975)*
cruzadilla SF (*CAm*) level crossing, grade crossing (EEUU)
cruzado ADJ **1** (= *atravesado*) • **se sentó con las piernas cruzadas** he sat down with his legs crossed • **con los brazos ~s** with one's arms folded *o* crossed • **no podemos quedarnos con los brazos ~s** we can't sit back and do nothing, we can't just sit idly by and do nothing
2 [*chaqueta, americana*] double-breasted
3 [*cheque*] crossed
4 (*Zool*) crossbred
5 (*And**) hopping mad*, furious
SM **1** (*Hist*) crusader
2 (= *moneda*) cruzado (*Brazilian currency unit*)
cruzador(a)* SM/F (*Méx*) shoplifter
cruzamiento SM **1** (*Bio*) crossing
2 (*Ferro*) crossover
cruzar ▹ CONJUG 1f VT **1** [+ *calle, río, frontera, puente*] to cross • **han cruzado el Atlántico** they've crossed the Atlantic • **~ la (línea de) meta** to cross the finishing line • **al ~ la puerta** *o* **el umbral del palacio** when you set foot inside the palace • **~on el lago a nado** they swam across the lake
2 [*arrugas, líneas*] • **profundas arrugas le cruzaban la cara** her face was covered in wrinkles • **una profunda cicatriz le cruzaba la mano** a deep scar ran across his hand • **el corte le cruzó la espalda de un lado a otro** the cut ran right across his back
3 (= *poner cruzado*) • **~ un palo sobre otro** to place one stick across another • **~ la espada con algn** to cross swords with sb • **~ los dedos** (*lit, fig*) to cross one's fingers • **el equipo se juega la Copa —cruzo los dedos— mañana** the team is playing for the Cup tomorrow — (I'm keeping my) fingers crossed • **~ las piernas** to cross one's legs
4 [+ *palabras*] to exchange • **no ~on ni una palabra** they didn't exchange a (single) word
5 [+ *apuestas*] to place, make
6 (*Bio*) [+ *plantas, razas*] to cross
7 (*Náut*) to cruise
8 (*esp LAm*) (*Agr*) *to plough a second time in a criss-cross pattern*
9 (*And, Cono Sur*) (= *atacar*) to fight, attack
10 (*Ven*) • **~ (los) aros** to celebrate the engagement ceremony (*involving the exchange of rings*)
VI [*peatón*] to cross • **cruza ahora, que no vienen coches** cross now, there are no cars coming • **~ por el puente** to cross over the bridge • **~ por el paso de peatones** to cross at the zebra crossing
VPR **cruzarse 1** [*dos cosas*] [*líneas*] to intersect, cross; [*caminos*] to cross • **nuestras cartas se ~on** our letters crossed in the post • **se ~on las miradas de los dos** their eyes met • MODISMO: • **se le ~on los cables*** (*por enfado*) he just lost it*, he flipped*; (*por confusión*) he just lost track*
2 [*personas, vehículos*] **a** (= *encontrarse*) to pass each other • **iban tan deprisa que se ~on sin darse cuenta** they were in such a hurry that they passed each other without even noticing • **se cruzó con ella en la escalera** he passed her on the stairs • **hace tiempo que no me cruzo con él** I haven't seen him for a long time
b (= *pasar por delante*) • **se le cruzó otro coche y para evitarlo, se salió de la carretera** another car pulled out in front of him and he swerved off the road to avoid it • **dos hechos que se ~on en su camino cambiaron su vida** two things that happened to him changed his life
3 • **~se con algn** (*And*) to fight sb, attack sb
4 (*Chile**) (= *ponerse bravucón*) • **se le cruzó por un asunto de dinero** he took him on over money matters • **se cruza con cualquiera que lo contradiga** he'll stand up to anybody who contradicts him • **no te me cruces** don't get cocky with me*
5 (*Ven*) • **~se (los) aros con algn** to exchange rings with sb
CSD SM ABR (*Esp*) (= **Consejo Superior de Deportes**) ≈ Sports Council
c.s.f. ABR (= **coste, seguro, y flete**) c.i.f.
CSIC [θe'sik] SM ABR (*Esp*) = **Consejo Superior de Investigaciones Científicas**
CSN SM ABR (*Esp*) = **Consejo de Seguridad Nuclear**
CSP SM ABR (*Esp*) = **Cuerpo Superior de Policía**
cta. ABR, **c.ta** ABR (= **cuenta**) a/c, acc., acct
cta. cte. ABR (= **cuenta corriente**) C/A, a/c (EEUU)
cta. cto. ABR (= **carta de crédito**) L/C
ctdad. ABR (= **cantidad**) qty
cte. ABR (= **corriente, de los corrientes**) inst
CTI SM ABR (= **Centro de Tratamiento Intensivo**) ICU
CTM SF ABR (*Méx*) = **Confederación de Trabajadores de México**
ctra. ABR (= **carretera**) Rd
CTV SF ABR (*Ven*) = **Confederación de Trabajadores de Venezuela**
cu SF Q (*name of the letter q*)
c/u ABR (= **cada uno**) ea
cuacar ▹ CONJUG 1g (*And, Caribe, Cono Sur*) VT • **no me cuaca** (= *no quiero*) I don't want to; (= *no me cuadra*) it doesn't suit me
cuácara SF (*And*) (= *levita*) frock coat; (*Cono Sur*) (= *blusa*) workman's blouse
cuache (*CAm*) ADJ, SMF = **cuate**
cuaco SM **1** (*LAm*) (= *rocín*) nag
2 (= *bolsista*) bag snatcher
cuaderna SF (*Náut*) (= *madera*) timber, lumber (EEUU); (= *costilla*) rib, frame
cuadernillo SM **1** (*gen*) booklet • **~ de sellos** book of stamps
2 (*Tip*) quinternion
3 (*Rel*) liturgical calendar
cuadernito SM notebook
cuaderno SM **1** (*para notas*) notebook; (*Escol*) jotter, exercise book, workbook (EEUU) • **~ de espiral** spiral notebook, spiral-bound notebook ▸ **cuaderno de bitácora** (*Náut*) logbook ▸ **cuaderno de campo** field diary ▸ **Cuaderno de Cortes** (*Hist*) official parliamentary record ▸ **cuaderno de navegación** logbook ▸ **cuaderno de trabajo** logbook
2* (= *baraja*) pack of cards
cuadra SF **1** (*para caballos*) stable • **los mejores son los caballos de la ~ Martín** the best horses are from the Martín stable • **tienes la habitación que parece una ~*** your room looks like a pigsty*, your room is an absolute tip* ▸ **cuadra de carreras** racing stable
2 (*LAm*) (= *manzana*) block • **vivo a dos ~s de aquí** I live two blocks from here
3 [*de hospital*] ward
4 (*Mil*) (= *barracón*) barracks (*pl*)
5 (= *sala*) hall, large room; (*And*) reception room
6 (*And*) (= *casa*) small rural property (*near a town*)
7 (= *medida*) (*Cono Sur*) ≈ 125.50 metres; (*And, CAm, Caribe, Uru*) ≈ 83.5 metres
cuadrada SF (*Mús*) breve
cuadrado/a ADJ **1** (*Mat*) square • **dos metros ~s** two square metres • MODISMO: • **tenerlos ~s**** to have balls**
2 [*objeto, superficie*] square
3 (= *corpulento*) • **estar ~** to be well-built, be hefty*
4 (*Caribe, Cono Sur*) (= *grosero*) coarse, rude
5 (*And*) (= *elegante*) graceful, elegant
6 (*LAm**) (= *poco flexible*) • **ser ~** to be narrow-minded
7 (*Arg, Uru**) (= *poco inteligente*) dense, stupid
8 (*Chile, Ven**) • **estar ~ con algn** to side with sb • **el pueblo está ~ con el presidente** the people are siding with the president
SM/F (= *persona poco inteligente*) idiot
SM **1** (*Mat, Geom*) square • **cinco (elevado) al ~** five square(d), the square of five ▸ **cuadrado mágico** magic square
2 (= *regla*) ruler, parallel ruler
3 (*Téc*) die
4 (*Cos*) gusset
5 (*Tip*) quad, quadrat
6 (*Caribe, Cono Sur**) (= *persona*) boor, oaf
Cuadragésima SF Quadragesima
cuadragésimo ADJ **1** (= *ordinal*) fortieth
2 (= *partitivo*) • **una cuadragésima parte** one fortieth; ▹ **sexto**
cuadrangular ADJ quadrangular
cuadrángulo ADJ quadrangular
SM quadrangle
cuadrante SM **1** (*Mat, Náut*) quadrant • **el ~ noroccidental de la Península** the northwestern part *o* corner of the Peninsula
2 [*de radio*] dial; [*de reloj*] face ▸ **cuadrante (solar)** sundial

cuadrar ▷ CONJUG 1a (VI) **1** [*cuentas, cifras*] to tally • **los números no cuadran** the numbers don't tally • **~ con algo** to square with sth, tally with sth
2 [*misterio, historia*] to fit together • **todo parecía ~ perfectamente** everything seemed to fit together perfectly • **~ con algo** to fit in with sth • **su reacción no cuadraba con lo que me habían dicho de él** his reaction was at odds with *o* didn't fit in with what they had told me about him
3 [*estilo, muebles*] to go, look right • **una silla Luis XIV no cuadra en esta habitación** a Louis XIV chair doesn't go in this room *o* doesn't look right in this room • **~ con algo** to go with sth
4 • **~ a algn** to suit sb • **los papeles dramáticos le cuadran muy bien a un actor como él** dramatic roles suit an actor like him very well • **ven mañana si te cuadra** come tomorrow if it suits you *o* if that's convenient
5 • **~ hacer algo** to be ready to do sth
6 (*Ven**) (= *quedar*) to arrange to meet • **cuadramos para encontrarnos después del cine** we arranged to meet after the cinema • **¿a qué hora cuadraste con él?** what time did you arrange to meet him?
7 (*Col**) (= *ennoviar*) • **Juan y Ana se han cuadrado** Juan and Ana are going out • **~se con algn** to go out with sb
8 (*Chile, Ven**) • **~se con algn** to side with sb • **el pueblo se cuadró con el ministro** the people sided with the minister
9 (*Chile**) • **~se con algo** to donate sth
10 (*Col, Ven, Perú*) (= *aparcar*) to park
11 (*Perú, Ven**) • **~se a algn** to take sb on • **se me cuadró y por poco me pega** he took me on and nearly hit me
(VT) **1** (*Mat*) to square
2 (*Téc*) to square, square off
3 (*Perú*) (= *aparcar*) [+ *carro*] to park
(VPR) **cuadrarse 1** [*soldado*] to stand to attention
2 (*en una actitud*) to dig one's heels in
3 (*Caribe*) (= *enriquecerse*) to make one's pile*; (= *tener éxito*) to come out on top

cuadratín (SM) (*Tip*) quadrat, quad, space
cuadratura (SF) (*Mat*) quadrature • **la ~ del círculo** squaring the circle
cuádriceps (SM) quadriceps
cuadrícula (SF) (*Tip*) grid, ruled squares; [*de mapa*] grid
cuadriculado (ADJ) • **papel ~** squared paper, graph paper • **mapa ~** grid map
cuadricular ▷ CONJUG 1a (VT) to draw squares on, draw a grid on
(ADJ) [*papel*] ruled in squares, squared; [*tela*] chequered, checkered (*EEUU*)
cuadrilátero (ADJ) quadrilateral, four-sided
(SM) (*Mat*) quadrilateral; (*Boxeo*) ring
cuadrilla (SF) **1** [*de amigos*] party, group; [*de obreros*] gang, team • **una ~ de chiquillos** a bunch of kids* • **¡menuda ~!** a fine bunch they are! ▸ **cuadrilla de demolición** demolition squad
2 (*Taur*) *bullfighting team*
3 (*Mil*) squad ▸ **cuadrilla de noche** night shift, night squad
cuadrillazo (SM) (*And, Cono Sur*) gang attack
cuadrillero (SM) **1** (= *jefe*) [*de grupo*] group leader; [*de banda*] gang leader
2 (*esp And, Cono Sur*) (*pey*) hooligan
3 (= *trabajador*) worker (*in a team*)
cuadrilongo (ADJ) oblong
(SM) oblong
cuadringentésimo (ADJ) four hundredth
cuadripartido (ADJ) quadripartite
cuadrito (SM) (*Culin*) cube • **cortar en ~s** to dice
cuadrivio (SM) quadrivium

cuadro (SM) **1** (= *cuadrado*) square • **una camisa/un vestido a *o* de ~s** a checked *o* check shirt/dress • **~s escoceses** tartan (pattern) • MODISMOS: • **quedarse a ~s*** to be flabbergasted* • **en ~**: • **el equipo llegó en ~ al partido** they brought a drastically reduced side *o* team to the match • **hacerse la vida de ~s *o* cuadritos** (*Méx*) to make things complicated • **ser del otro ~** (*Uru**) to be gay
2 (*Arte*) (= *pintura*) painting; (= *reproducción*) picture • **dos ~s de Velázquez** two paintings by Velázquez, two Velázquez paintings • **pintar un ~** to do a painting, paint a picture • MODISMO: • **ir hecho un ~** to be a (real) sight* ▸ **cuadro de honor** roll of honour, honor roll (*EEUU*)
3 (= *escena*) (*Teat*) scene; (*fig*) scene, sight • **fue un ~ desgarrador** it was a heart-breaking scene *o* sight • **desde el avión los escaladores ofrecían un ~ impresionante** seen from the plane the climbers were an impressive sight • **llegaron calados hasta los huesos y llenos de barro ¡vaya ~!** they arrived soaked to the skin and covered in mud, what a sight (they were)! ▸ **cuadro viviente, cuadro vivo** tableau vivant
4 (= *gráfico*) table, chart ▸ **cuadro de diálogo** dialog box ▸ **cuadro sinóptico** synoptic chart
5 (= *tablero*) panel ▸ **cuadro de conmutadores, cuadro de distribución** (*Elec*) switchboard ▸ **cuadro de instrumentos** (*Aer*) instrument panel; (*Aut*) dashboard ▸ **cuadro de mandos** control panel
6 (= *armazón*) [*de bicicleta, ventana*] frame
7 cuadros (*tb* **cuadros de mando**) (*en empresa*) managerial staff; (*Admin, Pol*) officials; (*Mil*) commanding officers ▸ **cuadros dirigentes** (*en empresa*) senior management; (*Admin, Pol*) senior officials; (*Mil*) senior officers ▸ **cuadros medios** (*en empresa*) middle management; (*Admin, Pol*) middle-ranking officials; (*Mil*) middle-ranking officers ▸ **cuadros superiores** = cuadros dirigentes
8 (*Med*) symptoms (*pl*), set of symptoms • **el paciente presentaba un ~ vírico** the patient presented with viral symptoms (*frm*), the patient showed symptoms of a virus ▸ **cuadro clínico** symptoms (*pl*), clinical symptoms (*pl*)
9 (= *descripción*) picture • **un verdadero ~ de la sociedad** a true picture of society ▸ **cuadro de costumbres** (*Literat*) *description of local customs*
10 (*en jardín, huerto*) bed, plot
11 (*Mil*) (= *formación*) square • MODISMO: • **formar el ~** to close ranks
12 (*Dep*) team • **el ~ argentino** the Argentinian team
13 (*Cono Sur*) (= *matadero*) slaughterhouse, abattoir
14 (*Cono Sur*) (= *bragas*) knickers (*pl*), panties (*pl*)
15 (*And*) (= *pizarra*) blackboard
cuadrúpedo (SM) quadruped, four-footed animal
cuádruple (ADJ) quadruple, fourfold
(SM) • **yo he pagado el ~** I paid four times that • **el ~ del salario mínimo** four times the minimum salary
cuadruplicado (ADJ) quadruplicate • **por ~** in quadruplicate
cuadruplicar ▷ CONJUG 1g (VT) to quadruple • **hemos cuadruplicado nuestras ventas este año** we have quadrupled our sales this year • **las pérdidas cuadruplican las del año pasado** losses are four times last year's
(VPR) **cuadruplicarse** to quadruple, increase fourfold
cuádruplo (ADJ) fourfold, quadruple
(SM) = **cuádruple**
cuajada (SF) [*de leche*] curd; (= *requesón*) curd cheese, cottage cheese; (*como postre*) junket
cuajado (ADJ) **1** [*leche*] curdled; [*sangre*] coagulated, congealed
2 (= *lleno*) • **~ de** full of, filled with • **un cielo ~ de estrellas** a star-spangled sky, a star-studded sky, a sky studded with stars • **una corona cuajada de diamantes** a diamond-studded crown, a crown studded with diamonds • **una tapia cuajada de pintadas** a wall covered in graffiti • **una situación cuajada de peligros** a situation fraught with dangers • **un texto ~ de problemas** a text bristling with problems
3 (= *asombrado*) • **estar ~** to be dumbfounded
4 (= *dormido*) • **quedarse ~** to fall asleep
(SM) ▸ **cuajado de limón** lemon curd
cuajaleche (SM) **1** (*Culin*) cheese rennet
2 (*Bot*) bedstraw
cuajar ▷ CONJUG 1a (VT) **1** [+ *leche*] to curdle; [+ *gelatina*] to set; [+ *sangre*] to coagulate, clot; [+ *grasa*] to congeal
2 • **~ algo de** (= *cubrir*) to cover sth with, adorn sth with; (= *llenar*) to fill sth with • **cuajó el tablero de cifras** he covered the board with figures
(VI) **1** [*nieve*] to lie; [*leche*] to curdle
2 [*moda, producto*] to catch on, take off; [*plan*] to take shape; [*idea, propuesta*] to be well received, be acceptable; [*truco*] to come off, work • **el acuerdo no cuajó** the agreement didn't come off *o* work out
3 (*Méx*) (= *charlar*) to chat
(VPR) **cuajarse 1** [*leche*] to curdle; [*sangre*] to congeal, coagulate; [*gelatina*] to set
2 • **~se de** to fill (up) with
3 (= *dormirse*) to fall fast asleep
cuajarón (SM) clot
cuajo (SM) **1** (*Zool, Culin*) rennet • **~ en polvo** powdered rennet
2 • **arrancar algo de ~** to tear sth out by its roots • **arrancar una puerta de ~** to wrench a door out of its frame • **extirpar un vicio de ~** to eradicate a vice completely
3 (= *cachaza*) phlegm, calmness • **tiene mucho ~** he's very phlegmatic
4 • **coger un ~*** to cry one's eyes out; ▷ **llorar**
5 (*Méx**) (= *charla*) chatter
6 (*Méx**) (= *mentirijilla*) fib
7 (*Méx**) (= *proyecto*) pipe dream
8 (*Méx*) (*Escol*) (= *recreo*) playtime, recess (*EEUU*)
9 (*Méx*) (= *látigo*) short whip
cual (PRON) **1** • **el ~/la ~/los ~es/las ~es a** (*aplicado a cosas*) which • **un balcón desde el ~ se puede ver toda la bahía** a balcony from which you can see the whole bay • **obtuvo una beca, gracias a la ~ pudo subsistir varios años** he got a grant, which gave him enough to live on for several years • **el estado al ~ se ha solicitado la extradición** the country from which extradition has been requested
b (*aplicado a personas*) (*como sujeto*) who; (*como objeto*) who, whom; (*tras preposición*) whom • **se reunieron con el presidente, el ~ les informó del asunto** they had a meeting with the president, who briefed them on the affair • **tengo gran amistad con el director, al ~ conozco desde hace muchos años** the director, who *o* whom I have known for many years, is a great friend of mine • **había ocho chicos, tres de los ~es hablaban en inglés** there were eight boys, three of whom were speaking in English

2 • **lo ~** which • **se rieron mucho, lo ~ me disgustó** they laughed a lot, which upset me • **con lo ~** with the result that • **se han construido dos escuelas más, con lo ~ contaremos con más de 2.000 plazas escolares** two more schools have been built, with the result that *o* which means that we will have more than 2,000 school places • **llegué tarde, con lo ~ no pude entrar** I arrived late, which meant I couldn't get in • **por lo ~** and therefore, consequently
3 • **cada ~**: • **miembros de distintas religiones, cada ~ con su libro sagrado** members of different religions, each (one) with their holy book • **cada ~ puede hacer lo que crea conveniente** everyone may do what they think fit • **depende del gusto de cada ~** it depends on individual taste, it depends on each individual's taste • **allá cada ~** everyone must look out for themselves • **allá cada ~ con su conciencia** that is a matter for each individual's conscience
4 • **sea ~ sea** *o* **fuese** *o* **fuere** whatever • **nuestra postura no variará sea ~ sea el resultado de las elecciones** our position will not change whatever the outcome of the election (is *o* may be) • **quiere entrar en un club de golf, sea ~ sea** he wants to join a golf club, and any one will do
(ADV), (CONJ) (*liter*) like • **en la novela su amada se suicida ~ nueva Ofelia** in the novel his loved one commits suicide like a modern-day Ophelia • **frágil ~ mariposa** as delicate as a butterfly • **~ si** as if • **todos aplaudieron su sugerencia, ~ si de una idea genial se tratara** everyone applauded his suggestion, as if it were the most brilliant idea; ▹ **tal**
(ADJ) (*Jur*) said, aforementioned • **los ~es bienes** the said *o* aforementioned property

cuál (PRON) **1** (*interrogativo*) what, which (one) • **¿~ quieres?** which (one) do you want? • **¿~ es su opinión sobre el tema?** what's your opinion on the subject? • **¿~ es el que dices?** which one are you talking about? • **ignora ~ será el resultado** he does not know what the outcome will be
2 • **a ~ más**: • **son a ~ más gandul** each *o* one is as lazy as the other • **una serie de coches a ~ más rápido** a series of cars each faster than the last • **gritaban a ~ más** one was shouting louder than the other • **~ más ~ menos** some more, some less
3 (*exclamativo*) • **¡~ no sería mi asombro!** imagine the surprise I got!, imagine my surprise! • **¡~ gritan esos malditos!** (*frm*) how those wretched people shout!
(ADJ) (*esp Méx, Perú, Ven*) which? • **¿~ libro dices?** which book do you mean? • **¿~es carros?** which cars? • **tú ¿a ~ colegio vas?** which school do you go to?

cualidad (SF) **1** (= *virtud*) quality; (= *talento*) talent • **tiene buenas ~es** he has good qualities • **su principal ~ era la lealtad** loyalty was their main virtue, their foremost quality was loyalty • **defectos y ~es** faults and virtues • **hizo una demostración de sus ~es como actriz** she demonstrated her talent as an actress • **jóvenes que apuntan ~es** promising young people
2 (= *atributo*) attribute, characteristic
3 (*Fís, Fil*) property

cualificado (ADJ) **1** [*obrero*] skilled, qualified • **obrero no ~** unskilled worker
2 • **estar ~ para hacer algo** to be qualified to do sth
3 = **calificado**

cualitativamente (ADV) qualitatively

cualitativo (ADJ) qualitative

cualquier(a) (PL: **cualesquier(a)**) (ADJ INDEF) **1** (*antes de s*) any • **como en ~ otro país europeo** as in any other European country • **~ día se presenta aquí** he could turn up here any day • **~ persona de por aquí te diría lo mismo** anyone from round here would tell you the same • **en ~ caso** in any case • **~ cosa** anything • **en un lugar como este puede ocurrir ~ cosa** in a place like this anything could happen • **en ~ lugar del mundo** anywhere in the world • **en ~ momento** at any time, (at) any moment • **MODISMO**: • **~ tiempo pasado fue mejor** the grass is always greener (on the other side of the fence)
2 (*después de s*) any • **—¿cuál prefieres? —me da igual, uno ~a** "which one do you prefer?" — "it doesn't matter, any one (will do)" • **sucedió un día ~a** it happened on a day like any other day • **el presidente tendrá que ir a juicio, como un ciudadano ~a** the president will have to go to court, like any ordinary citizen • **este no es un coche ~a** this is not just any old car
3 (*LAm*) (= *bastante*) • **tienen ~ cantidad de juguetes** they have loads of toys* • **puede comer ~ cantidad y no se llena** he can eat loads and not get full*

cualquiera (PL: **cualesquiera**) (PRON INDEF) **1** (= *cualquier persona*) anyone, anybody; (= *cualquier cosa*) any one • **en un club como ese no admiten a ~** they don't accept just anyone *o* anybody into that club • **~ puede ser candidato a la presidencia** anyone *o* anybody can stand for president • **esos precios están al alcance de ~** those prices are within everyone's *o* everybody's means • **tal como gritaban los niños, ~ diría que los estaba torturando** the way the children were screaming anyone would think I was torturing them • **puedes coger ~** you can choose any one (you like) • **es una costumbre como otra ~** it is a custom like any other
2 • **~ de** any, any of • **puede acudir a ~ de las sucursales del banco** you can go to any branch *o* any of the branches of the bank • **~ de mis alumnos podría realizar este proyecto** any *o* any one of my pupils could do this project • **~ de los dos** either (one) of them, either of the two • **llama a Pedro o a Carlos, ~ de los dos** call Pedro or Carlos, either (one) of them *o* either of the two • **~ de los dos equipos** either team *o* either (one) of the two teams
3 • **~ que** (+ *subjun*) **a** (*en general*) whatever; (*ante una elección*) whichever • **~ que sea el color de su piel** whatever the colour of their skin • **~ que sea tu problema** whatever your problem is, no matter what your problem is • **respetaremos el resultado de la votación, ~ que sea** we will respect the result of the vote, whatever that may be • **es caro, pero ~ que compres te va a costar una fortuna** it's expensive, but whichever (one) you buy it'll cost you a fortune
b (= *persona*) anyone who, anybody who • **~ que lo conozca te diría lo mismo** anyone *o* anybody who knows him *o* whoever knows him would tell you the same
4 (*en exclamaciones*) • **¡~ sabe!** who knows? • **¡~ le interrumpe ahora!** I wouldn't interrupt him at the minute! • **¡así ~!** it's all right for some!*
(SM) • **un ~** a nobody • **yo no me caso con un ~** I'm not marrying just anybody
(SF) (*pey*) • **una ~** a hussy*

cuan (ADV) (*liter*) • **tan estúpidos ~ criminales** as stupid as they are criminal

cuán (ADV) how • **¡~ agradable fue todo eso!** how delightful it all was!

cuando (CONJ) **1** (*con valor temporal*) (*en un momento concreto*) when; (*en cualquier momento*) whenever • **~ llegué a su casa él ya se había ido** when I got to his house he had already left • **te lo diré ~ nos veamos** I'll tell you when I see you • **ven ~ quieras** come when(ever) you like • **~ iba allí lo veía** whenever I went there I saw him, I used to see him when(ever) I went there • **me acuerdo de ~ jugábamos en el patio** I remember when we used to play in the yard • **lo dejaremos para ~ estés mejor** we'll leave it until you're better
2 (*con valor condicional, causal*) if • **~ él lo dice, será verdad** if he says so, it must be true • **~ no te ha dicho nada todavía, es que no piensa invitarte** if he hasn't said anything yet, that means he isn't thinking of inviting you
3 (*con valor adversativo*) when • **yo lo hago todo, ~ es él quien debería hacerlo** I'm the one that does it all, when it should be him; ▹ **aun**
(ADV) **1** • **fue entonces ~ comprendí la importancia del problema** it was then that *o* that was when I understood the seriousness of the problem • **en abril es ~ más casos hay** April is when there are most cases, it's in April that there are most cases • **de ~ en ~** • **de vez en ~** from time to time, now and again, every so often
2 • **~ más** at (the) most • **tardaremos, ~ más, una semana** it will take us a week at (the) most *o* at the outside • **~ menos** at least • **esperamos llegar, ~ menos, a las semifinales** we are hoping to reach the semifinals, at least • **~ mucho** at (the) most • **~ no** if not • **docenas, ~ no cientos, de películas** dozens, if not hundreds, of films
(PREP) • **eso fue ~ la guerra** that was during the war • **ocurrió ~ la boda** it happened at the time of the wedding • **~ niño yo era muy travieso** as a child *o* when I was a child I was very naughty

cuándo (ADV) **1** (*en oraciones interrogativas*) when • **¿~ te lo dijo?** when did he tell you? • **no sé ~ será** I don't know when it will be • **no me ha dicho aún desde ~ sabe la noticia** he hasn't told me yet how long he has known the news (for) • **¿de ~ acá?** since when? • **¿desde ~?** since when? • **¿desde ~ os conocéis?** how long have you known each other? • **¿desde ~ trata uno así a su padre?** since when do you treat your father like that? • **¿hasta ~?** how long? • **¿hasta ~ vamos a aguantar esta injusticia?** how long are we going to put up with this injustice? • **¿hasta ~ ya no te veo?** when will I see you again *o* next?, how long will it be till I see you again? • **¿para ~ ...?** when ... by? • **¿para ~ estará listo el proyecto?** when will the project be ready (by)? • **¿para ~ una edición de sus obras completas?** when are we (ever) going to see an edition of his complete works? • **MODISMO**: • **no tener para ~** (*Chile**): • **a este paso no tenemos para ~ terminar** we're never going to finish at this rate • **—¿esta lista ya? —¡no tiene para ~!** "is she ready yet?" — "she'll be a long time yet!"
2 • **¡~ no!** (*LAm*) just to make a change! • **se le perdieron las llaves ¡~ no!** he lost his keys, just to make a change!

cuandoquiera (CONJ) • **~ que ...** whenever ...

cuantía (SF) **1** (= *cantidad*) **a** (= *importe*) quantity, amount • **¿cómo se calcula la ~ de la pensión?** how is the amount *o* level of pension calculated? • **el fraude asciende a la ~ de cinco millones** the fraud amounts to

more than five million
b (= *alcance*) extent • **se ignora la ~ de las pérdidas** the extent of the losses is not known
2 (= *importancia*) importance • **de mayor ~** more important, more significant • **de menor ~** • **de poca ~** unimportant, of little account
cuántico (ADJ) • **teoría cuántica** quantum theory
cuantificable (ADJ) quantifiable
cuantificación (SF) quantifying • **hacer una ~ de** to quantify
cuantificador (SM) quantifier
cuantificar ▷ CONJUG 1g (VT) **1** [+ *daños, pérdidas*] to quantify (*frm*), assess
2 (*Fís*) to quantize
3 (*Lógica*) to quantify
cuantimás* (ADV) • **~ que** all the more so because
cuantioso (ADJ) [*suma, beneficios, daños*] substantial, considerable; [*pérdidas*] substantial, heavy • **el terremoto causó ~s daños materiales** the earthquake caused substantial *o* considerable material damage
cuantitativamente (ADV) quantitatively
cuantitativo (ADJ) quantitative
cuanto (ADJ) **1** (*indicando cantidad*) • **daremos ~s créditos se precisen** we will give as many loans as (are) needed *o* whatever loans are needed • **~s hombres la ven se enamoran de ella** all the men that see her fall for her
2 (*en correlación*) • **~ más** the more • **~s más invitados vengan más comida habrá que preparar** the more guests come, the more food we'll have to prepare • **~ menos** the less • **~ menos dinero tiene la gente, menos gasta en salir a comer** the less money people have, the less they spend on eating out • **~s menos errores hagas mejor** the fewer mistakes you make, the better
3 • **unos ~s** (= *no muchos*) a few; (= *bastantes*) quite a few • **solo unos ~s funcionarios permanecerán en el país** only a few officials will stay in the country • **he leído unos ~s libros suyos** I've read quite a few of his books
(PRON) **1** (*indicando cantidad*) all • **tiene todo ~ desea** he has everything *o* all (that) he wants • **tome ~ quiera** take as much as you want, take all you want
2 (*en correlación*) • **~s más** the more • **~s más mejor** the more the better • **~s menos** the fewer
3 • **unos ~s** (= *no muchos*) a few; (= *bastantes*) quite a few • **lo sabíamos unos ~s, pero la mayoría no** a few of us knew, but most people didn't • **hay unos ~s en clase que no hacen más que molestar** there are a few people in the class who do nothing but cause trouble • **—¿cuántos vinieron? —unos ~s** "how many people came?" — "quite a few"
(ADV), (CONJ) **1** (*expresando correlación*) • **~ antes mejor** the sooner the better • **~ más** the more • **~ más intentes convencerlo, menos caso te hará** the more you try to persuade him, the more he will ignore you • **~ más corto mejor** the shorter, the better • **~ menos** the less • **~ menos se hable sobre este asunto mejor** the less (that is) said about this issue, the better
2 (*locuciones*) **a** • **~ antes** as soon as possible • **tiene que estar terminado ~ antes** it has to be finished as soon as possible • **ven ~ antes** come as soon as you can *o* as soon as possible
b • **en ~** (= *tan pronto como*) as soon as; (= *en calidad de*) as • **en ~ lo supe me fui** as soon as I heard I left • **iré en ~ pueda** I'll go as soon as I can • **el cuento infantil, en ~ género literario** children's stories, as a literary genre
c • **en ~ a** as regards, as for • **en ~ a tu aumento de sueldo, lo discutiremos en diciembre** as regards *o* as for your pay rise, we'll discuss it in December • **el sistema tiene ventajas en ~ a seguridad y comodidad** as regards *o* with regard to safety and comfort, the system has advantages • **en ~ a mí** as for me
d • **en ~ que** insofar as
e • **~ más** especially • **siempre está nervioso, ~ más en época de exámenes** he's always nervous, all the more so *o* especially at exam time • **no escribe a nadie, ~ más a nosotros** he doesn't write to anyone, let alone us
f • **~ menos** to say the least • **esta interpretación es, ~ menos, discutible** this interpretation is debatable to say the least
g • **por ~** in that, inasmuch as (*frm*) • **es un delito por ~ vulnera los derechos constitucionales** it is a crime in that *o* inasmuch as (*frm*) it violates constitutional rights • **llama la atención por ~ supone de innovación** it attracts attention because of its novelty value
cuánto (ADJ) **1** (*en oraciones interrogativas*) **a** (*en singular*) how much • **¿cuánta sal echo?** how much salt shall I add? • **¿~ tiempo ...?** how long ...? • **¿~ tiempo llevas viviendo en Perú?** how long have you been living in Peru (for)?
b (*en plural*) how many • **¿~s días libres tienes al año?** how many days off do you have a year? • **¿cuántas personas había?** how many people were there? • **no sabe ~s cuadros hay en su casa** he doesn't know how many paintings there are in his house
2 (*en exclamaciones*) • **¡cuánta gente!** what a lot of people! • **¡~ tiempo perdido!** think of all the time that's been wasted! • **¡cuántas viviendas han construido desde que me fui!** they've built so many houses since I left! • **¡~ borracho hay por las calles!*** the streets are full of drunks!
(PRON) **1** (*en preguntas, uso indirecto*) **a** (*tb* **cuánto dinero**) how much • **¿~ has gastado?** how much have you spent? • **no sé ~ es** I don't know how much it is • **no me ha dicho ~ es** he hasn't told me how much it is • **¿a ~ están las peras?** how much are (the) pears?
b (*tb* **cuánto tiempo**) how long • **¿~ durará esto?** how long will this last? • **¿cada ~?** how often?
c (*en plural*) how many • **¿~s de vosotros apoyaríais la huelga?** how many of you would support the strike? • **¿a ~s estamos?** what's the date today?, what date is it today?
2 (*en exclamaciones*) • **¡~ has gastado!** you've spent a fortune! • **¡~ has tardado!** you've been ages!, you took ages! • **¡~s has comprado!** you've bought so many!, you've bought loads!
3 • **no sé ~s**: • **el señor no sé ~s** Mr So-and-So, Mr something-or-other • **el señor Anastasio no sé ~s** Mr Anastasio something-or-other
(ADV) **1** (*en preguntas, uso indirecto*) **a** (*de cantidad*) how much • **¿~ pesas?** how much do you weigh? • **no sé ~ quieres** I don't know how much you want
b (*de distancia*) how far • **¿~ hay de aquí a Bilbao?** how far is it from here to Bilbao? • **¿~ falta para llegar al pueblo?** how much further is the town?, how far is it to the town from here?
2 (*en exclamaciones*) • **¡~ has crecido!** how you've grown! • **¡~ trabajas!** how hard you work! • **¡~ me alegro!** I'm so glad!

> **CUÁNTO**
>
> **¿Cuánto tiempo?**
>
> ▷ *Cuando se habla de la duración de algo,* **cuánto** *se traduce al inglés por* **how long** *y se utiliza el pretérito perfecto cuando la acción comenzó en el pasado y continúa todavía:*
>
> **¿Cuánto tiempo llevas esperando?**
> How long have you been waiting?
> **¿Cuánto hace que nos conocemos?**
> How long have we known each other?
>
> ▷ *En otros contextos, no debe utilizarse el pretérito perfecto:*
>
> **¿Cuánto tardasteis en llegar a Barcelona?**
> How long did it take you to get to Barcelona?
> **¿Cuánto dura la película?**
> How long is the film?
>
> *Para otros usos y ejemplos ver la entrada.*

cuaquerismo (SM) Quakerism
cuáquero/a (ADJ), (SM/F) Quaker
cuarcita (SF) quartzite
cuarenta (ADJ INV), (PRON), (SM) (*gen*) forty; (= *cuadragésimo*) fortieth • **los (años) ~** the forties • **los ~ rugientes** the Roaring Forties • **"Los ~ principales"** (*Radio, TV*) "the Top Forty" (*Spanish hit parade*) • **MODISMOS**: • **cantar las ~** (*Naipes*) *to have the king and queen of trumps* • **cantar las ~ a algn** to tell sb a few home truths, tell sb a thing or two • **esas son otras ~** (*Arg, Perú*) that's a different story • **REFRÁN**: • **hasta el ~ de mayo no te quites el sayo** ne'er cast a clout till May be out; ▷ **seis**
cuarentañero/a (ADJ) fortyish, about forty (SM/F) person of about forty, person in his *o* her forties
cuarentavo (ADJ) **1** (= *ordinal*) fortieth
2 (= *partitivo*) • **la cuarentava parte** a fortieth
(SM) fortieth
cuarentena (SF) **1** (= *número*) about forty, forty-odd • **ambos rondan la ~** they're both around forty (years old) • **una ~ de** some forty, forty or so
2 (= *aislamiento*) quarantine • **poner a algn en ~** (*Med*) to put sb in quarantine, quarantine sb; (*fig*) to send sb to Coventry • **poner un asunto en ~** to suspend judgement on a matter
3 (*Rel*) (= *cuaresma*) Lent
cuarentón/ona (ADJ) forty-something • **es ya ~** he's in his forties, he's forty-something
(SM/F) person in their forties
cuaresma (SF) Lent; ▷ **CARNAVAL**
cuaresmal (ADJ) Lenten
cuark (SM) (PL: **cuarks**) quark
cuarta (SF) **1** (*Mat*) quarter
2 (= *palmo*) span
3 (*Aut*) fourth gear, fourth • **meter la ~** to go into fourth (gear), put it *o* the car into fourth (gear)
4 (*Náut*) point (*of the compass*)
5 (*Méx*) (= *látigo*) *a short whip used for horse-riding*
6 (*Cono Sur*) (*Agr*) extra pair of oxen
7 • **MODISMOS**: • **a la ~** short of money • **la situación económica nos trae a todos a la ~** the economic situation has left us all broke *o* short of money • **a fin de mes siempre andamos a la ~** at the end of the month we're always short of money • **es muy tacaño, nos tiene a todos a la ~** he's very mean, we're crying out for money • **andar de la ~ al pértigo** (*Cono Sur*) • **vivir a la ~** (*Cono

Sur, Méx) to be on the bread line
cuartago SM pony
cuartazos* SM INV fat person, lump*
cuarteado ADJ cracked
cuartear ▹ CONJUG 1a VT **1** [+ *res*] to cut up
2 (*Mat*) to divide into four
3 [+ *carretera*] to zigzag up
4 (*Náut*) • **~ la aguja** to box the compass
5 (*Caribe, Méx*) (= *azotar*) to whip, beat
VI **1** (*Taur*) to dodge, step aside
2 (*Naipes*) to make a fourth (player), make up a four
VPR **cuartearse 1** (= *agrietarse*) to crack, split
2 (*Taur*) to dodge, step aside
3 (*Méx*) (= *desdecirse*) to go back on one's word
cuartel SM **1** (*Mil*) barracks • **vida de ~** army life, service life • **estar de ~†** to be on half-pay ▸ **cuartel de bomberos** (*Arg, Uru*) fire station ▸ **cuarteles de invierno** (*Mil*) winter quarters; (*fig*) winter retreat (*sing*) ▸ **cuartel general** headquarters (*pl*)
2 (= *tregua*) • **no hubo ~ para los revoltosos** no mercy was shown to the rebels • **no dar ~** to give no quarter, show no mercy • **guerra sin ~** all-out war • **lucha sin ~** fight to the death
3 (= *cuarta*) quarter
4 (= *distrito*) quarter, district
5 (*Heráldica*) quarter
6 (*Hort*) bed
cuartelazo SM, **cuartelada** SF military uprising
cuartelero ADJ barracks (*antes de s*) • **utiliza un lenguaje ~** he swears like a trooper • **rancho ~** *food eaten by soldiers in barracks*
SM (*And*) waiter
cuartelillo SM **1** [*de policía*] police station; [*de bomberos*] fire station, fire *o* station house (*EEUU*)
2‡ [*de droga*] dealer's share (*of drug deal*) • **dar ~ a algn‡** to give sb their share
cuartería SF (*Caribe, Cono Sur*) bunkhouse (*on a ranch*)
cuarterón/ona SM **1** (= *peso*) quarter pound, quarter
2 (*Arquit*) [*de ventana*] shutter; [*de puerta*] panel
SM/F (*LAm*) quadroon
cuarteta SF quatrain
cuarteto SM **1** (*Mús*) (= *conjunto, composición*) quartet, quartette ▸ **cuarteto de viento** wind quartet
2 (*Literat*) quatrain
cuartil SM quartile
cuartilla SF **1** (= *hoja*) (*en general*) sheet (of paper); (= *medio folio*) A5 sheet of paper • **un sobre tamaño ~** an A5 envelope
2 [*de caballo*] pastern
3 (= *cuarta parte*) fourth part (*of a measure*)
4 cuartillas (*Tip*) copy; (= *apuntes*) notes, jottings
cuarto ADJ (*ordinal*) fourth • **en ~ lugar** in fourth place • **la cuarta parte** a quarter; ▹ **sexto**
SM **1** (= *habitación*) room; (= *dormitorio*) bedroom, room • **el ~ de los niños** the children's room • MODISMOS: • **echar su ~ a espaldas** to stick one's oar in • **hacer ~ a algn** (*Col*) to shelter sb ▸ **cuarto de aseo** toilet, cloakroom, bathroom (*EEUU*) ▸ **cuarto de baño** bathroom ▸ **cuarto de desahogo** lumber room ▸ **cuarto de estar** living room, sitting room ▸ **cuarto de juego** playroom ▸ **cuarto frío** (*Culin*) cold store ▸ **cuarto intermedio** (*Arg, Uru*) • **estar en ~ intermedio** to be in recess • **pasar a ~ intermedio** to adjourn the session ▸ **cuarto oscuro** (*Fot*) darkroom; (= *trastero*) broom cupboard; (*Arg, Uru*) voting booth ▸ **cuarto trastero** lumber room
2 (= *cuarta parte*) quarter • **un ~ de millón de dólares** a quarter of a million dollars • **un ~ (de) kilo** a quarter (of a) kilo • **(abrigo) tres ~s** three-quarter length coat • MODISMOS: • **de tres al ~** worthless, third-rate • **tres ~s de lo mismo**: • **su amigo es un inútil, y él ... tres ~s de lo mismo** his friend is useless, and he's not much better • **en otros países ocurre tres ~s de lo mismo** it's the same story *o* it's more of the same in other countries ▸ **cuarto creciente** first quarter ▸ **cuarto de luna** quarter of the moon ▸ **cuarto menguante** last quarter ▸ **cuartos de final** quarter finals
3 (*en la hora*) quarter • **son las seis menos ~** • **es un ~ para las seis** (*LAm*) it's a quarter to six • **a las seis y ~** at (a) quarter past six • MODISMO: • **tener algn/algo su ~ de hora** (*LAm*) to be all the rage • **tuvo su ~ de hora, ahora nadie lo lleva** it had its day *o* it was all the rage, now nobody wears it anymore ▸ **cuarto de hora** quarter of an hour • **tardó tres ~s de hora** it took him *o* he took three quarters of an hour
4 [*de animal*] [*de cerdo, vaca*] joint • **un ~ de pollo** a chicken quarter, a quarter chicken; **cuartos** legs ▸ **cuartos delanteros** forequarters ▸ **cuartos traseros** hindquarters
5 (= *moneda*) *coin used in Spain in former times*; **cuartos*** (= *dinero*) dough* (*sing*) • **es hombre de muchos ~s** he's got pots of money* • MODISMOS: • **aflojar los ~s** to cough up* • **estar sin un ~** to be broke* • **dar ~s al pregonero** (*Esp*) to tell everyone one's private business • **por cinco ~s** (*Esp*) for a song • **¡qué coche ni qué ocho ~s!** car, my foot! • **no tener un ~** to be broke*
6 (*Tip*) quarto • **libro en ~** quarto volume
7 • **estar de ~** (*Mil*) to be on watch
8†† (= *piso*) small flat • **poner ~** to set up house • **poner ~ a la querida** to set one's mistress up in a little place
9†† (= *servidumbre*) household, servants (*pl*)
cuartofinalista SMF quarter-finalist
cuartón SM dressed timber, beam, plank; **cuartones** dressed timber (*sing*), beams, planks
cuartucho SM (= *habitación*) poky little room; (= *casucha*) hovel
cuarzo SM quartz ▸ **cuarzo hialino** rock crystal ▸ **cuarzo rosa, cuarzo rosado** rose quartz
cuás* SM (*Méx*) bosom pal*
cuásar SM quasar
cuasi ADV (*liter*) = **casi**
cuasi... PREF quasi-...
cuate (*CAm, Méx*) ADJ twin
SMF **1** (= *gemelo*) twin
2 (= *compadre*) mate*, pal*, buddy (*EEUU**)
3 (= *tipo*) guy*/girl
SM (= *escopeta*) double-barrelled gun
cuaternario ADJ quaternary; (*Geol*) Quaternary
SM • **el ~** the Quaternary
cuatrear ▹ CONJUG 1a, **cuatrerear** ▹ CONJUG 1a (*Cono Sur*) VT [+ *ganado*] to rustle, steal
VI to act treacherously
cuatrero/a SM/F [*de ganado*] rustler, stock thief; [*de caballos*] horse thief
ADJ (*CAm*) treacherous, disloyal
cuatrienal ADJ four-year (*antes de s*), quadrennial (*frm*) • **un plan ~** a four-year plan
cuatrifónico ADJ quadraphonic
cuatrillizo/a SM/F quadruplet
cuatrimestral ADJ **1** (= *de cuatro meses*) four-monthly, every four months • **son exámenes ~es** they are four-monthly exams, the exams are every four months
2 (= *de cuatro meses*) four-month(-long) • **una asignatura ~** a four-month(-long) course, a course which lasts for four months
cuatrimestralmente ADV every four months
cuatrimestre SM four-month period
cuatrimotor ADJ four-engined
SM four-engined plane
cuatriplicado ADJ quadruplicate • **por ~** in quadruplicate
cuatro ADJ INV, PRON **1** (*gen*) four; (*ordinal, en la fecha*) fourth • **cada ~ días** every four days • **las ~** four o'clock • **le escribí el día ~** I wrote to him on the fourth
2 (= *pocos*) • **solo había ~ muebles** there were only a few sticks of furniture • **te escribo solo ~ líneas para decirte que ...** I'm just dropping you a line to tell you that ... • **cayeron ~ gotas** a few drops fell • **más de ~ lo creen** quite a few people believe it • MODISMO: • **solo había ~ gatos** the place was dead*, there was hardly a soul
SM **1** (*gen*) four; (= *fecha*) fourth • **el ~ de octubre** (on) the fourth of October, (on) October the fourth; ▹ **seis**
2 (*Méx*) (= *trampa*) trick, fraud; (= *error*) blunder
3 (*Ven*) (*Mús*) four-stringed guitar
4 (*Aut*) ▸ **cuatro latas*** Renault 4L ▸ **cuatro por cuatro** four-wheel drive vehicle ▸ **cuatro ojos*** (*smf inv*) four-eyes*
cuatrocientos/as ADJ, PRON, SMPL/SFPL four hundred; ▹ **seiscientos**
cuatrojos* SMF INV four-eyes*
cuba¹ SF **1** (= *tonel*) cask, barrel; (= *tina*) tub, vat; (*Ferro*) tank car; (*para el agua de lluvia*) rainwater butt • MODISMO: • **estar como una ~** to be as drunk as a lord ▸ **cuba de riego** water wagon, street sprinkler
2* (= *panzudo*) pot-bellied person
cuba² SM (*And*) (= *hijo*) youngest child
Cuba SF Cuba • MODISMO: • **más se perdió en ~** it's not the end of the world
cubaje SM (*LAm*) volume, contents
cubalibre SM, **cuba-libre** SM (PL: **cubas-libres** *o* **cuba-libres**) [*de ron*] (white) rum and Coke®; [*de ginebra*] gin and Coke®
cubanismo SM cubanism, *word or phrase etc peculiar to Cuba*
cubano/a ADJ, SM/F Cuban
cubata* SM = **cubalibre**
cubero SM cooper
cubertería SF cutlery, flatware (*EEUU*) • **una ~ de plata** a set *o* canteen of silver cutlery, a silver flatware service (*EEUU*)
cubeta SF **1** (*Fot, Quím*) tray
2 [*de barómetro, termómetro*] bulb
3 (*para hielo*) ice tray
4 (= *tonel*) keg, small cask ▸ **cubeta de siembra** seed box
cubetera SF (*Cono Sur*) ice tray
cubicaje SM cubic capacity; (*Aut*) cylinder capacity
cubicar ▹ CONJUG 1g VT **1** (*Mat*) to cube
2 (*Fís*) to determine the volume of
cúbico ADJ cubic • **un objeto ~** a cubic *o* cube-shaped object • **metro ~** cubic metre • **raíz cúbica** cube root, cubic root
cubículo SM cubicle
cubierta SF **1** (= *cobertura*) cover(ing); [*de libro*] cover, jacket; [*de edificio*] roof • **~ de lona** tarpaulin
2 [*de rueda*] tyre, tire (*EEUU*) • **~ sin cámara** tubeless tyre
3 (*Náut*) deck • **salir a ~** to go up *o* out on deck ▸ **cubierta de aterrizaje** flight deck ▸ **cubierta de botes** boat deck ▸ **cubierta de paseo** promenade deck ▸ **cubierta de popa** poop deck ▸ **cubierta de proa** foredeck ▸ **cubierta de vuelo** flight deck ▸ **cubierta**

principal main deck
4 (*Méx*) (= *funda*) sheath
5 (= *pretexto*) cover, pretext
6 (= *sobre*) envelope • **bajo esta ~** under the same cover, enclosed herewith • **bajo ~ separada** under separate cover

cubierto PP *de* **cubrir**
ADJ **1** (*gen*) covered (**de** with, in) • **un cheque no ~** a bad *o* unbacked cheque
2 [*cielo*] overcast
3 [*vacante*] filled • **la plaza está ya cubierta** the place has already been filled
4 (*Aut*) • **poco ~** [*neumático*] threadbare, worn
5 (= *tocado*) [*persona*] with a hat
SM **1** (= *techumbre*) cover • **a** *o* **bajo ~** under cover • **estar a ~ de algo** to be safe from sth • **ponerse a ~** to take shelter, take cover • **ponerse a ~ de algo** to shelter from sth
2 (*para comer*) a piece of cutlery • **coge el ~ con la mano derecha** take the spoon/fork/ knife with your right hand • **los ~s** the cutlery
3 (= *servicio de mesa*) place setting • **falta un ~, porque somos ocho** we're a place short, there are eight of us
4 (= *comida*) • **pagaron 200 dólares por ~** they paid 200 dollars each *o* per head • **precio del ~** price per person *o* per head

cubil SM den, lair

cubilete SM **1** [*de dados*] cup
2 (= *cuenco*) basin, bowl; (= *copa*) goblet
3 (*Culin*) (= *molde*) mould, mold (*EEUU*); (= *bandeja*) pastry tray
4 (*LAm*) (= *intriga*) intrigue
5 (*LAm*) (= *chistera*) top hat; (= *hongo*) bowler hat

cubiletear ▸ CONJUG 1a VT **1** (*en el juego*) to shake the dice cup
2 (= *intrigar*) to intrigue, scheme

cubiletero/a SM/F conjurer

cubismo SM cubism

cubista ADJ, SMF cubist

cubitera SF ice-tray

cubito SM **1** (*tb* **cubito de hielo**) ice cube
2 ▸ **cubito de caldo** stock cube
3 [*de niño*] bucket

cúbito SM ulna

cubo SM **1** (= *balde*) bucket, pail • **~ para el carbón** coal scuttle ▸ **cubo de (la) basura** (*en casa*) dustbin, trash can (*EEUU*); (*en la calle*) litter bin, trash can (*EEUU*)
2 (= *contenido*) bucketful, bucket, pailful, pail
3 (*Mat*) cube • **cinco elevado al ~** five cubed
4 (*Geom*) cube ▸ **cubo de Rubik®** Rubik('s) cube ®
5 (*Mec*) barrel, drum
6 [*de rueda*] hub
7 [*de molino*] millpond
8 (*Arquit*) round turret

cuboflash SM (*Fot*) flashcube

cubrebocas SM INV (*Med*) mask

cubrebotones SM INV button-cover

cubrecama SM coverlet, bedspread

cubrecorsé SM camisole

cubremesa SF table cover

cubreobjetos SM INV (*Bio*) slide cover

cubrerradiadores SM INV *cover for radiator*

cubrerrueda SF mudguard, fender (*EEUU*)

cubretetera SM tea cosy, tea cozy (*EEUU*)

cubrimiento SM [*de objeto*] covering; [*de noticia*] coverage

cubrir ▸ CONJUG 3a (PP: **cubierto**) VT
1 (= *ocultar*) **a** [+ *superficie, objeto*] to cover • **un velo le cubría el rostro** a veil covered her face • **las nubes cubrían la cima de la montaña** the mountain top was covered by clouds • **habían cubierto el suelo de papeles** they had covered the floor with papers
b [*agua*] • **lo cubrieron las aguas** the waters closed over it • **no te metas donde te cubra el agua** don't go out of your depth
c (= *poner techo a*) to roof, roof over • **queremos ~ parte del patio** we want to roof (over) part of the patio
d [+ *fuego*] to make up, bank up
2 (= *llenar*) [+ *agujero*] to fill in; [+ *hueco*] to fill • **cubrieron el hoyo con la tierra del jardín** they filled in the hole with soil from the garden • **~ el hueco existente en el mercado** to fill the existing gap in the market • **~ a algn de alabanzas** to heap praises on sb • **~ a algn de atenciones** to lavish attention on sb • **~ a algn de besos** to smother sb with kisses • **~ a algn de improperios** to shower sb with insults • **~ a algn de oprobio** to bring shame on sb
3 (= *proteger*) (*Dep, Mil*) to cover • **intenta llegar a las líneas enemigas: nosotros te ~emos** try to get to the enemy lines: we'll cover you • **~ su retirada** to cover one's retreat
4 (= *recorrer*) [+ *ruta, distancia*] to cover • **cubrió 80 kms en una hora** he covered 80 km in an hour • **el autocar cubría el trayecto entre León y Madrid** the coach was travelling between León and Madrid
5 (= *ocupar*) [+ *vacante, plaza*] to fill
6 (= *pagar*) [+ *gastos, déficit, préstamo*] to cover • **esto apenas cubre los gastos** this scarcely covers the expenses
7 (= *satisfacer*) [+ *necesidades, demanda*] to meet • **esto cubre todas nuestras necesidades** this meets all our needs
8 (*Prensa*) [+ *suceso*] to cover • **todos los periódicos cubrieron la noticia** all the newspapers covered the event
9 (*Zool*) (= *montar*) to cover
10 (= *disimular*) [+ *emoción*] to cover up, conceal • **cubre su tristeza con una falsa alegría** she covers up *o* conceals her sadness with a false cheerfulness • MODISMO: • **~ las apariencias** *o* **las formas** to keep up appearances
VPR **cubrirse 1** [*persona*] **a** (= *ocultarse*) to cover o.s. • **~se la cabeza** to cover one's head • **~se el rostro** to cover one's face
b (= *ponerse el sombrero*) to put on one's hat
2 (= *llenarse*) • **~se de algo** to be covered with *o* in sth • **el campo se cubre de flores en primavera** the countryside is covered with flowers in spring • **~se de gloria** (*lit*) to cover o.s. with *o* in glory; (*iró*) to show o.s. up
3 (= *protegerse*) to cover o.s. • **~se contra un riesgo** to cover *o* protect o.s. against a risk • MODISMO: • **~se las espaldas** to cover o.s., cover one's back
4 (*Meteo*) [*cielo*] to become overcast

cuca SF **1*** (= *peseta*) peseta
2** [*de hombre*] prick**; (*CAm*) [*de mujer*] pussy**
3 (= *cucaracha*) cockroach, roach*
4 (= *jugador*) compulsive gambler
5 **cucas** (= *dulces*) sweets, candy (*EEUU*)

cucambé SM (*And*) hide-and-seek

cucamente ADV (= *con astucia*) shrewdly; (= *taimadamente*) slyly, craftily

cucamonas* SFPL (= *palabras*) sweet nothings; (= *caricias*) caresses; (= *magreo*) fondling (*sing*), petting* (*sing*) • **ella me hizo ~** she gave me a come-hither look

cucaña SF **1** (= *juego*) greasy pole
2* (= *chollo*) cinch*, piece of cake*; (= *prebenda*) plum job*, soft job*; (= *ganga*) bargain

cucañero/a* SM/F (= *astuto*) smart cookie*, shrewd person; (= *parásito*) hanger-on

cucar ▸ CONJUG 1g VT **1** (= *guiñar*) to wink
2 (= *burlarse de*) to deride, poke fun at
3 (*LAm*) (= *instar*) to urge on, incite, provoke

cucaracha SF **1** (*Zool*) cockroach
2 (*Méx**) (= *coche*) old crock, old banger
3‡ (= *droga*) roach‡
4 (*Inform*) chip
SM* priest

cucarachero SM **1** (*And, Caribe*) (= *parásito*) parasite, hanger-on
2 (*And*) (= *adulador*) flatterer, creep‡

cucha SF (*Arg*) (= *cama*) bed; (= *caseta de perro*) kennel

cuchara SF **1** (*para comer*) spoon
• MODISMOS: • **con la ~ grande** (*esp LAm*): • **despacharse** *o* **servirse con la ~ grande** to look after number one* • **meter algo a algn con ~** to spoon-feed sb sth • **meter (la) ~** (*en conversación*) to butt in; (*en asunto*) to shove one's oar in • **soplar ~*** to eat • **soplar ~ caliente*** to eat well ▸ **cuchara de café** coffee spoon, ≈ teaspoon ▸ **cuchara de palo** wooden spoon ▸ **cuchara de postre** dessert spoon ▸ **cuchara de servir** serving spoon, tablespoon ▸ **cuchara de sopa** soup spoon
2 (*Téc*) scoop, bucket
3 (= *cucharón*) ladle
4 (*LAm*) (= *llana*) flat trowel • **albañil de ~** skilled bricklayer
5 (*CAm, Chile**) • **hacer ~(s)** to pout
6 • **militar de ~*** officer who has risen from the ranks, ranker
SMF (*Méx**) (= *carterista*) pickpocket

cucharada SF spoonful • **una ~ colmada** a heaped spoonful • **una ~ rasa** a level spoonful • **comer algo a ~s** to eat sth by the spoonful ▸ **cucharada de café** teaspoonful ▸ **cucharada de sopa, cucharada sopera** tablespoonful

cucharadita SF teaspoonful

cucharear ▸ CONJUG 1a VT **1** (*Culin*) to spoon out, ladle out
2 (*Agr*) to pitch, pitchfork

cucharetear ▸ CONJUG 1a VI **1** (*con cuchara*) to stir (with a spoon)
2 (= *entrometerse*) to meddle

cucharilla SF, **cucharita** SF **1** [*de café, té*] teaspoon
2 (*Pesca*) spoon
3 (*Golf*) wedge

cucharón SM **1** (*Culin*) ladle • MODISMO: • **tener el ~ por el mango** to be the boss, be in control
2 (*Téc*) scoop, bucket

cuche SM (*CAm*) pig, hog (*esp EEUU*)

cuché SM art paper

cucheta SF (*Arg, Uru*) bunk beds (*pl*)

cuchi (*Perú*) EXCL *call to a pig or hog*
SM pig, hog (*esp EEUU*)

cuchichear ▸ CONJUG 1a VI to whisper (a to)

cuchicheo SM whispering

cuchilear* ▸ CONJUG 1a VT (*LAm*) to egg on

cuchilla SF **1** blade ▸ **cuchilla de afeitar** razor blade
2 (= *cuchillo*) large kitchen knife; [*de carnicero*] chopper, cleaver
3 [*de arado*] coulter, colter (*EEUU*)
4 (*LAm*) (= *cortaplumas*) penknife
5 (*Geog*) ridge, crest; (*Chile*) (= *colinas*) sharp ridge; (*Caribe*) (= *cumbre*) mountain top

cuchillada SF **1** (= *corte*) stab; (= *herida*) stab wound • **me di una ~ en el dedo** I cut my finger with a knife • **murió de una ~ en la garganta** she died from a knife wound *o* stab wound to the throat • **dar una ~ a algn** to stab sb • **matar a algn a ~s** to stab sb to death • **fue asesinado a ~s** he was stabbed to death • **hubo ~s** there was a serious fight; (*fig*) the knives really came out • **una ~ de cien reales††** a long gash, a severe wound • MODISMO: • **dar ~** (*Teat**) to make a hit
2 (*Cos*) slash, slit

cuchillazo SM = **cuchillada**

cuchillería SF **1** (= *cubiertos*) cutlery, flatware (EEUU)
2 (= *tienda*) cutler's (shop), flatware store (EEUU)

cuchillero ADJ (*LAm*) quarrelsome, fond of brawling
SM cutler

cuchillo SM **1** (*gen*) knife • MODISMOS: • **pasar a ~** to put to the sword • **remover el ~ en la llaga** to turn the knife in the wound ▸ **cuchillo de carne** steak knife ▸ **cuchillo de caza** hunting knife ▸ **cuchillo de cocina** kitchen knife ▸ **cuchillo del pan** breadknife ▸ **cuchillo de trinchar** carving knife
2 (*Arquit*) upright, support
3 ▸ **cuchillo de aire** sharp draught, sharp draft (EEUU)
4 (= *colmillo*) fang, tusk
5 (*Cos*) gore

cuchipanda* SF blow-out*, chow-down (EEUU‡) • **ir de ~** to go out on the town

cuchitril SM **1** (= *cuartucho*) hole*, hovel
2 (*Agr*) (= *pocilga*) pigsty, pigpen (EEUU)

cucho[1] SM (*And*) = **cuchitril**

cucho[2]**/a** SM/F **1** (*CAm*) (= *jorobado*) hunchback
2 (*Méx*) (= *manco*) limbless person
3 (*Cono Sur*) (= *gato*) puss

cucho[3]* ADJ (*Méx*) (= *deprimido*) gloomy, depressed

cuchuche SM • **ir a ~** (*CAm*) to ride piggyback

cuchuflé SM (*Caribe*) = **cuchuflí**

cuchufleta* SF **1** (= *broma*) joke, crack*
2 (*Méx*) (= *baratija*) trinket, trifle

cuchuflí* SM (*Caribe*) uncomfortable place; (= *celda*) cell

cuchugos SMPL (*And, Caribe*) saddlebags

cuchumbo SM (*CAm*) (= *embudo*) funnel; (= *balde*) bucket, pail; [*de dados*] dice box; (= *juego*) game of dice

cuclillas SFPL • **en ~** squatting, crouching • **ponerse en ~** to squat • **sentarse en ~** to sit on one's heels

cuclillo SM **1** (*Orn*) cuckoo
2* (= *cornudo*) cuckold

cuco/a ADJ **1** [*persona*] (= *taimado*) sly, crafty; (= *astuto*) shrewd
2 (= *bonito*) pretty, cute
SM/F* (= *persona*) wily bird*, sly one
SM **1** (*Orn*) cuckoo
2 (= *oruga*) grub, caterpillar
3* (= *jugador*) gambler
4 • MODISMO: • **hacer ~ a algn** (*Méx*) to poke fun at sb
5 (*Cono Sur*) (= *sabelotodo*) smart guy*, wise guy*, know-all*
6 (*Caribe***) (= *sexo femenino*) cunt**
7 (*And, Cono Sur*) (= *fantasma*) bogeyman

cucú SM (= *canto*) cuckoo

cucuche (*CAm*) SM • **ir a ~** to ride astride

cucufato/a* (*And, Cono Sur*) ADJ (= *hipócrita*) hypocritical, two-faced*; (= *mojigato*) prudish
SM/F (= *hipócrita*) hypocrite; (= *mojigato*) prude; (= *loco*) nut‡

cuculí SM (*And, Cono Sur*) wood pigeon

cucurucho SM **1** [*de papel*] (paper) cone, (paper) twist, cornet; (*para helado*) cone, cornet
2 (= *helado*) (ice-cream) cone
3 (*Rel*) penitent's hood, pointed hat
4 (*Aut*) cone
5 (*And, CAm, Caribe*) (= *cumbre*) top, summit, apex
6 (*Caribe*) (= *cuchitril*) hovel, shack

cucurucú SM, **cucurrucú** SM (*LAm*) cockadoodledoo

cueca SF (*And, Cono Sur*) *popular handkerchief dance*; (*Chile*) *Chilean national dance*

cuelga SF **1** (= *acto*) hanging (*of fruit etc to dry*); (= *racimo*) bunch (*of drying fruit etc*)
2 (= *regalo*) birthday present
3 (*And, Cono Sur*) (*Geog*) fall (*in the level of a stream etc*)

cuelgacapas SM INV (*en pared*) coat rack; (*de pie*) coat stand

cuelgue‡ SM **1** [*de drogas*] high‡ • **lleva un ~** he's completely high *o* spaced out‡, he's really out of it *o* off his head‡
2 [*de vergüenza*] • **¡qué ~!** how awful!, how embarrassing!

cuellicorto ADJ short-necked

cuellilargo ADJ long-necked

cuello SM **1** (*Anat*) neck • **cortar el ~ a algn** to cut sb's throat • MODISMOS: • **apostar el ~***: • **me apuesto el ~ a que no te atreves** I bet you anything you don't dare • **erguir el ~** to be stuck-up* • **jugarse el ~*** to stick one's neck out, put one's neck on the line • **levantar el ~** to get on one's feet again ▸ **cuello del útero, cuello uterino** cervix, neck of the womb
2 [*de prenda*] collar; (= *talla*) (collar) size • MODISMO: • **de ~ blanco** white-collar (*antes de s*) ▸ **cuello (a la) caja** crew neck ▸ **cuello alto** polo neck, turtle neck ▸ **cuello blando** soft collar ▸ **cuello (de) cisne** polo neck, turtleneck (*esp EEUU*) ▸ **cuello de pajarita** wing collar ▸ **cuello de pico** V-neck ▸ **cuello de quita y pon** detachable collar ▸ **cuello de recambio** spare collar ▸ **cuello postizo** detachable collar
3 [*de botella*] neck ▸ **cuello de botella** (*Aut*) bottleneck

Cuenca SF Cuenca

cuenca SF **1** (*Geog*) bowl; (*fluvial*) basin • **la ~ del Ebro** the Ebro basin ▸ **cuenca hullera, cuenca minera** coalfield
2 [*del ojo*] socket
3 (*Hist*) (= *escudilla*) wooden bowl, begging bowl

cuenco SM **1** (= *recipiente*) earthenware bowl
2 (= *concavidad*) hollow; [*de cuchara*] bowl ▸ **cuenco de la mano** hollow of the hand

cuenta SF **1** (*Mat*) (= *operación*) calculation, sum • **hacer una ~** to do a calculation • **echar** *o* **hacer ~s**: • **vamos a hacer ~s de lo que ha costado la fiesta** let's work out how much the party cost • **no paraba de echar ~s con los dedos** she kept doing sums *o* adding things up on her fingers • MODISMOS: • **hacer las ~s de la lechera** to indulge in wishful thinking, count one's chickens before they are hatched • **la ~ de la vieja**: • **su hijo tiene 35, así que por la ~ de la vieja ella debe de tener 60** her son's 35, so I guess she must be 60; ▹ **claro**
2 (= *cálculo*) count • **llevar la ~ (de algo)** to keep count (of sth) • **perder la ~ (de algo)** to lose count (of sth) • **salir a ~**: • **sale más a ~** it works out cheaper • **no sale a ~** it isn't worth it • MODISMOS: • **hacer algo con su ~ y razón** to be fully aware of what one is doing • **más de la ~**: • **habla más de la ~** she talks too much • **ha bebido más de la ~** he's had one too many • **me cobraron más de la ~** they charged me over the odds • **pesa más de la ~** it weighs more than it should • **salirle las ~s a algn**: • **al Estado no le salen las ~s** the State isn't able to balance its books • **le salieron mal las ~s** his plans went wrong ▸ **cuenta atrás** countdown • **ha empezado la ~ atrás para las próximas Olimpiadas** the countdown to the next Olympics has already begun
3 (= *factura*) bill; [*de restaurante*] bill, check (EEUU) • **¿nos puede traer la ~?** could we have *o* could you bring us the bill, please? • **pasar la ~ a algn** to send sb the bill • **pedir la ~** to ask for the bill • **vivir a ~ de algn** to live at sb's expense • MODISMO: • **presentar las ~s del Gran Capitán** to make excessive demands
4 (*Econ*) (*en banco*) account • **habían cargado los gastos en mi ~** they had charged the expenses to my account • **"únicamente en ~ del beneficiario"** "payee only" • **a ~** on account • **un dividendo a ~** an interim dividend • **retenciones a ~ del impuesto sobre la renta** income tax deducted at source • **le dieron una cantidad a ~ de lo que le debían** they paid him part of the money they owed him • **abonar una cantidad en ~ a algn** to credit a sum to sb's account • **abrir una ~** to open an account • **liquidar una ~** to settle an account ▸ **cuenta a plazo (fijo)** fixed-term deposit account ▸ **cuenta bancaria** bank account ▸ **cuenta corriente** current account, checking account (*EEUU*) ▸ **cuenta de ahorro(s)** deposit account, savings account ▸ **cuenta de amortización** depreciation account ▸ **cuenta de asignación** appropriation account ▸ **cuenta de caja** cash account ▸ **cuenta de capital** capital account ▸ **cuenta de crédito** credit account, loan account ▸ **cuenta de depósitos** deposit account ▸ **cuenta de diversos** sundries account ▸ **cuenta de gastos** expense account ▸ **cuenta de gastos e ingresos** income and expenditure account ▸ **cuenta de pérdidas y ganancias** profit and loss account ▸ **cuenta en participación** joint account ▸ **cuenta pendiente** unpaid bill, outstanding account ▸ **cuenta personal** personal account ▸ **cuenta por cobrar** account receivable ▸ **cuenta por pagar** account payable ▸ **cuenta presupuestaria** budget account ▸ **cuenta vivienda** mortgage account
5 (*Internet*) account ▸ **cuenta de correo** email account
6 (*en disputa*) • **ajustar ~s con algn** to settle one's scores with sb • **lo está buscando para ajustar ~s** he is searching for him because he has a few scores to settle with him • **voy a ajustarle las ~s** I'm going to have it out with him • **ajustar viejas ~s con algn** to settle an old score with sb • **arreglar las ~s a algn** (*Méx**) to punish sb • **tener ~s pendientes con algn** to have unfinished business with sb • **no querer ~s con algn** to want nothing to do with sb
7 (= *explicación*) • **dar ~ de algo** (= *informar*) to recount sth, report sth; (= *acabar*) to finish sth off • **tiene que darle ~ a ella de sus actos** he has to account to her for his actions • **no tiene que dar ~s a nadie** he's not answerable to anyone • **dar buena ~ de una botella** to finish off a bottle • **exigir** *o* **pedir ~s a algn** to call sb to account, bring sb to book • **rendir ~s a algn** to report to sb • **en resumidas ~s** in short, in a nutshell
8 (= *consideración*) • **caer en la ~ (de algo)** to catch on (to sth), see the point (of sth) • **por fin cayó en la ~** he finally caught on, the penny finally dropped • **cuando cayó en la ~ de que lo engañaban** when he realized that they were deceiving him • **darse ~** (= *enterarse*) to realize; (= *ver*) to notice • **perdona, no me había dado ~ de que eras vegetariano** sorry, I didn't realize (that) you were a vegetarian • **¿te has dado ~ de que han cortado el árbol?** did you notice (that) they've cut down the tree? • **hay que darse ~ de que ...** one must not forget that ... • **¡date ~! ¿tú crees que es posible tener tanta cara?**

just look at that, can you believe that anyone could have such a cheek! • **¿te das ~?** (*Arg*) can you believe it! • **habida ~ de eso** bearing that in mind • **haz ~ de que no voy** (*esp LAm*) just imagine I'm not going • **tener en ~** to take into account, bear in mind • **también hay que tener en ~ su edad** you must also take her age into account, you must also bear in mind her age • **imponen sus ideas sin tener en ~ la opinión de la gente de la calle** they impose their ideas without taking ordinary people's opinions into consideration • **es otra cosa a tener en ~** that's another thing to remember *o* be borne in mind • **tomar algo en ~ a algn** to hold sth against sb • **está borracho y no sabe lo que dice, no se lo tomes en ~** he's drunk and doesn't know what he's saying, don't take any notice of him *o* don't hold it against him • **traer ~**: • **no me trae ~ ir** it's not worth my while going • **trae ~ emplear a más gente** it's worth employing more people • **lo harán por la ~ que les trae** *o* **tiene** they'll do it if they know what's good for them

9 (= *responsabilidad*) • **esta ronda corre de mi ~** this round's on me • **por mi ~** (= *solo*) on my own • **yo he de resolver esto por mi ~** I have to resolve this on my own • **trabajar por ~ ajena** to be an employee • **trabajar por ~ propia** to work for o.s., be self-employed • **por ~ y riesgo de algn** at one's own risk • **lo hizo por su ~ y riesgo, sin consultar a nadie** she did it off her own bat, without consulting anyone; ▹ **apañar**

10 (*en embarazo*) • **está fuera de ~s** • **ha salido de ~s** she's due

11 [*de rosario, collar*] bead • **~s de cristal** glass beads

cuentacorrentista (SMF) account holder, holder of a current account

cuentacuentos (SMF INV) storyteller

cuentagotas (SM INV) dropper • **MODISMO**: • **a** *o* **con ~** drop by drop, bit by bit

cuentakilómetros (SM INV) **1** [*de distancias*] mileometer, milometer, odometer (*esp EEUU*)

2 (= *velocímetro*) speedometer

cuentarrevoluciones (SM INV) rev counter, tachometer (*frm*)

cuente *etc* ▹ **contar**

cuentear ▹ CONJUG 1a (VT) **1** (*And*) (= *pretender*) to court; (= *felicitar*) to compliment

2 (*Méx**) (= *tomar el pelo*) to kid*, have on*

(VI) (*CAm*) to gossip

cuenterete (SM) (*CAm*) (= *chisme*) piece of gossip; (= *cuento*) tall story, tale

cuentero/a* (SM/F) (*Cono Sur*) **1** (= *mentiroso*) liar, fibber*

2 (= *estafador*) confidence trickster, con man*

cuentista (SMF) **1** (*Literat*) (= *escritor*) short-story writer; (= *narrador*) storyteller

2 (= *chismoso*) gossip; (= *soplón*) telltale

3 (= *mentiroso*) liar, fibber*

4 (*esp LAm**) (= *estafador*) confidence trickster, con man*

cuentística (SF) genre of the short story

cuento¹ (SM) **1** (= *historia corta*) short story; (*para niños*) story, tale • **el ~ de Blancanieves** the tale *o* story of Snow White • **contar un ~** to tell a story • **de ~**: • **un héroe de ~** a storybook *o* fairytale hero • **una casita de ~** a fairytale house • **ir con el ~**: • **en seguida le fue con el ~ a la maestra** he went straight off and told the teacher • **MODISMOS**: • **aplicarse el ~** to take note • **el ~ de la lechera**: • **eso es como el ~ de la lechera** it's a case of wishful thinking • **es el ~ de nunca acabar** it's a never-ending story ▸ **cuento corto** short story ▸ **cuento de hadas** a fairytale • **vive en un ~ de hadas** she lives in a fairytale world ▸ **cuento infantil** children's story

2* (= *mentira*) • **no le duele nada, no es nada más que ~** it doesn't hurt at all, he's just putting it on • **todo eso es puro ~ para no ir al colegio** he just made it all up because he doesn't want to go to school • **¡no me cuentes ~s!** • **¡no me vengas con ~s!** • **¡déjate de ~s!** don't give me that!* • **eso se me hace ~** (*Cono Sur**) I don't believe that for a minute, come off it!* • **tener ~**: • **tu hermanito tiene mucho ~** your little brother is a big fibber* • **MODISMOS**: • **tener más ~ que siete viejas** to have the gift of the gab* • **vivir del ~** to live by one's wits ▸ **cuento chino** tall story, cock-and-bull story* • **¡no me vengas con ~s chinos!** don't give me that (rubbish)!* ▸ **el cuento del tío** (*And, Cono Sur*) confidence trick, confidence game (*EEUU*) ▸ **cuento de viejas** old wives' tale

3 (*otras locuciones*) • **¿a ~ de qué?**: • **¿a ~ de qué sacas ese tema ahora?** what are you bringing that up for now? • **traer algo a ~** to bring sth up • **venir a ~**: • **eso no viene a ~** that's irrelevant, that doesn't come into it, that has nothing to do with it • **todo esto viene a ~ de lo que acaba de pasar** this all has some bearing on what has just happened • **lo dijo sin venir a ~** she said it for no reason at all

4 (*frm*) (= *cómputo*) • **sin ~** countless

cuento² (SM) [*de bastón*] point, tip

cuera (SF) **1** (*LAm*) (= *piel*) hide; (= *correa*) leather strap

2 (*Méx*) (= *chaqueta*) leather jacket

3 cueras (*CAm*) leggings (*for riding*)

4 (*And, CAm, Caribe*) (= *paliza*) flogging

cuerazo (SM) (*LAm*) lash

cuerda (SF) **1** (*gruesa*) rope; (*fina*) string, cord; (*para saltar*) skipping rope, jump rope (*EEUU*) • **un metro de ~** a metre (length) of rope • **ató la caja con un trozo de ~** she tied up the box with a piece of string • **se ha roto la ~ de la persiana** the cord on the blind has broken • **MODISMOS**: • **bajo ~**: • **ha conseguido un visado bajo ~** she's got hold of a visa under the counter • **han llegado a un acuerdo bajo ~** they have reached an agreement in secret, they have made a secret agreement • **estirar la ~**: • **estiraron la ~ para derrocar al gobierno** they put pressure on to bring the government down ▸ **cuerda de plomada** plumbline ▸ **cuerda de salvamento** lifeline ▸ **cuerda floja** tightrope • **MODISMO**: • **caminar en la ~ floja** to walk a tightrope ▸ **cuerda salvavidas** lifeline

2 (*Mec*) [*de reloj*] winder; [*de juguete*] clockwork mechanism • **se me ha roto la ~ del reloj** the winder on my watch has broken • **un reloj de ~** a wind-up watch • **dale ~ al reloj** wind up the clock • **el juguete funciona con ~** it's a clockwork toy • **MODISMOS**: • **dar ~ a algn***: • **no para de hablar, parece que le han dado ~** he never stops talking, you'd think he'd been wound up • **quedarle ~ a algn***: • **a ese viejo aún le queda mucha ~** the old boy's still got plenty of life *o* steam left in him* • **tener ~***: • **después de dos años sin verse, estos tienen ~ para rato*** after two years apart, those two have got enough to keep them going for a while yet

3 (*Mús*) [*de instrumento*] string • **un cuarteto de ~** a string quartet • **sección de ~** string section, strings (*pl*) • **MODISMO**: • **son de la misma ~** they're as bad as each other

4 (*Anat*) ▸ **cuerdas vocales** vocal cords

5 cuerdas (*Boxeo*) ropes; (*Hípica*) rails • **MODISMO**: • **contra las ~s** on the ropes • **el escándalo puso al gobierno contra las ~s** the scandal put the government on the ropes

6 (*Mat, Arquit*) chord

7 (*Pesca*) *style of fishing with three or more flies mounted on struts tied to the main line*

cuerdamente (ADV) **1** (= *sensatamente*) sanely

2 (= *prudentemente*) wisely, sensibly

cuerdo (ADJ) **1** [*persona*] sane

2 [*acto*] sensible, wise

cuereada (SF) (*LAm*) beating, hiding*

cuerear ▹ CONJUG 1a (VT) **1** (*LAm*) [+ *animal*] to skin; [+ *persona*] to beat, whip, flay

2 • **~ a algn** (*Caribe, Cono Sur*) to tear a strip off sb

cuerito (SM) • **de ~ a ~** (*LAm*) from end to end

cueriza (SF) (*LAm*) beating, hiding*

cuerna (SF) **1** (*Zool*) horns (*pl*); [*de ciervo*] antlers (*pl*)

2 (= *vaso*) drinking horn

3 (*Caza*) horn, hunting horn

cuerno (SM) **1** (*Zool*) horn; [*de ciervo*] antler • **el Cuerno de África** the Horn of Africa • **¡cuerno(s)!** gosh!*, blimey!‡ • **MODISMOS**: • **¡(y) un ~!** my foot!, you must be joking! • **coger al toro por los ~s** to take the bull by the horns • **estar en los ~s (del toro)** to be in a jam* • **irse al ~** [*negocio*] to fail, go to the wall*; [*proyecto*] to fall through • **¡que se vaya al ~!** he can go to hell! • **mandar a algn al ~** to tell sb to go to hell* • **mandar algo al ~** to consign sth to hell • **poner los ~s a algn** to cheat on sb, cuckold sb† • **romperse los ~s** to break one's back working, work one's butt off (*EEUU**) • **¡así te rompas los ~s!** I hope you break your neck! • **saber a ~ quemado**: • **esto me sabe a ~ quemado** it makes my blood boil ▸ **cuerno de la abundancia** horn of plenty

2 (*Culin*) roll, croissant

3 (*Mil*) wing

4 (*Mús*) horn ▸ **cuerno alpino** alpenhorn

cuero (SM) **1** (= *piel*) (*curtida*) leather; (*sin curtir*) skin, hide; [*de conejo*] pelt • **una chaqueta de ~** a leather jacket • **MODISMOS**: • **andar en ~s** to go about stark naked • **dejar a algn en ~s** to clean sb out* ▸ **cuero adobado** tanned skin ▸ **cuero cabelludo** scalp ▸ **cuero charolado** patent leather ▸ **cuero de cocodrilo** (*Cono Sur*) crocodile skin

2 (= *odre*) wineskin

3‡ (= *borracho*) old soak‡ • **MODISMO**: • **estar hecho un ~** to be (as) drunk as a lord, be (as) drunk as a skunk (*esp EEUU**)

4 [*de grifo*] washer

5 (*LAm*) (= *látigo*) whip • **MODISMO**: • **arrimar** *o* **dar el ~ a algn** to give sb a beating *o* thrashing

6 (*Dep*) (= *balón*) ball

7 (*And, Caribe*) (*pey*) (= *prostituta*) whore, hooker (*EEUU**); (*And*) (= *solterona*) old maid; (*Caribe‡*) (= *vieja*) old bag‡; (*And, Méx**) (= *amante*) mistress

8 (*CAm, Caribe**) (= *descaro*) cheek*, nerve*

9‡ (= *cartera*) wallet

cuerpada* (SF) (*Chile*) • **tiene buena ~** she's got a good body

cuerpazo* (SM) **1** (= *cuerpo grande*) huge frame, mighty bulk

2 (= *cuerpo sexy*) bod*

cuerpear ▹ CONJUG 1a (VI) (*Cono Sur*) to dodge

cuerpo (SM) **1** (*Anat*) body • **me dolía todo el ~** my body was aching all over, I was aching all over • **se le metió el frío en el ~** he caught a chill • **nos sacó dos ~s de ventaja** she was two lengths ahead of us • **MODISMO**: • **~ a ~**: • **fue una lucha ~ a ~** it was hand-to-hand combat • **un ~ a ~ entre los dos políticos** a head-on *o* head-to-head confrontation

between the two politicians • **de ~ entero** [*retrato, espejo*] full-length • **de medio ~** [*retrato, espejo*] half-length • **~ serrano** (*hum*) body to die for • **¡~ a tierra!** hit the ground! • **dar con el ~ en tierra** to fall down, fall to the ground • MODISMOS: • **en ~ y alma** body and soul, wholeheartedly • **a ~ gentil**: • **salió a ~ gentil** he went out without wrapping up properly • **un combate a ~ gentil** a hand-to-hand fight • **a ~ limpio** (= *sin ayuda*) unaided • **a ~ de rey**: • **vive a ~ de rey** he lives like a king • **nos trataron a ~ de rey** they treated us like royalty • **hacer del ~** (*euf*) to defecate, have a bowel movement • **hurtar el ~** to sneak away, sneak off • **hurtó el ~ y eludió a sus vecinos** he sneaked off *o* away and avoided his neighbours • **pedirle a algn algo el ~**: • **hice lo que en ese momento me pedía el ~** I did what my body was telling me to do at that moment
2 (= *cadáver*) body, corpse • **encontraron el ~ entre los matorrales** they found the body *o* corpse in the bushes • **de ~ presente: su marido aún estaba de ~ presente** her husband had not yet been buried • **funeral de ~ presente** funeral service, funeral
3 (= *grupo*) • **el ~ social** society ▸ **cuerpo de baile** corps de ballet ▸ **cuerpo de bomberos** fire brigade, fire department (EEUU) ▸ **cuerpo de doctrina** body of teaching ▸ **cuerpo de leyes** body of laws ▸ **cuerpo de policía** police force ▸ **cuerpo de sanidad** medical corps ▸ **cuerpo diplomático** diplomatic corps ▸ **cuerpo electoral** electorate ▸ **cuerpo legislativo** legislative body
4 (= *parte*) [*de mueble*] section, part; [*de un vestido*] bodice; (= *parte principal*) main body • **un armario de dos ~s** a cupboard in two sections *o* parts
5 (= *objeto*) body, object ▸ **cuerpo celeste** heavenly body ▸ **cuerpo compuesto** compound ▸ **cuerpo del delito** corpus delicti ▸ **cuerpo extraño** foreign body ▸ **cuerpo geométrico** geometric shape ▸ **cuerpo simple** element
6 (= *consistencia*) [*de vino*] body • **un vino de mucho ~** a full-bodied wine • **dar ~ a algo**: • **el suavizante que da ~ a su cabello** the conditioner that gives your hair body • **hay que darle un poco más ~ a la salsa** the sauce needs thickening a bit more • **sugirieron varios puntos para dar ~ al proyecto** they suggested several points to round out *o* give more substance to the project • **tomar ~** [*plan, proyecto, personaje, historia*] to take shape • **batió las claras hasta que tomaron ~** she beat the egg whites until they were fluffy *o* stiff • **el vino va tomando ~ con los años** aging gives the wine more body
7 (*Tip*) [*de letra*] point, point size • **negritas del ~ seis** six-point bold

cuerudo (ADJ) **1** (*LAm*) [*caballo*] slow, sluggish
2 (*LAm*) (= *incordiante*) annoying
3 (*Cono Sur*) (= *valiente*) brave, tough
4 (*CAm, Caribe*) (= *descarado*) impudent, cheeky*, sassy (EEUU*)

cuervo (SM) **1** (= *ave*) raven; (*Cono Sur*) (= *buitre*) vulture, buzzard (EEUU) ▸ **cuervo marino** cormorant
2* (= *cura*) priest

cuesco (SM) **1** (*Bot*) stone
2* (= *pedo*) fart‡
3 (*Mec*) millstone (*of oil mill*)

cuesta (SF) **1** (= *pendiente*) hill, slope • **mi casa está al final de la ~** my house is at the top of the hill • **una ~ empinada** a steep slope • **bajamos la ~ corriendo** we ran down the hill • **~ abajo** downhill • **ir ~ abajo** to go downhill • **~ arriba** uphill • **me canso más cuando voy ~ arriba** I get more tired when I go uphill • **se me hace muy ~ arriba estudiar tan tarde** I find it a struggle to study so late at night • **la ~ de enero** *period of financial stringency following Christmas spending*
2 • **a ~s** on one's back • **siempre va con su guitarra a ~s** he always goes around with his guitar on his back *o* slung over his shoulder • **llevé al niño a ~s a la cama** I carried the child up to bed on my back *o* shoulders • **se recorrieron Europa con la mochila a ~s** they went backpacking all around Europe • **se echa todas las responsabilidades a ~s** she takes all the responsibilities on her own shoulders

cuestación (SF) charity collection

cueste *etc* ▹ **costar**

cuestión (SF) **1** (= *asunto*) matter, question • **quedan algunas cuestiones por resolver** there are still a few matters *o* questions to be resolved • **eso es otra ~** that's another matter • **¡sigue gritando, la ~ es no dejarme tranquilo!*** (*iró*) carry on shouting, don't mind me! • **no sé por qué, pero la ~ es que ahora soy más pobre*** I don't know why, but the fact is that I'm poorer now than I was • **~ de**: • **una ~ de honor** a matter of honour • **resolver el problema no es solo ~ de dinero** the answer to the problem is not just a question of money • **su entrega a la policía es ~ de tiempo** it's only a matter of time before he gives himself up to the police • **todo es ~ de proponérselo** it's all a matter *o* question of telling yourself you can do it • **será ~ de irse ya a casa** it's time we were thinking of going home • **puedes beber, pero no es ~ de que te emborraches** you can have a drink or two, but there's no need to get drunk • **para solucionarlo tan solo es ~ de que lo habléis** all you have to do to solve the problem is talk it over • **en ~** in question • **la persona en ~ resultó ser mi padre** the person in question turned out to be my father • **falleció en ~ de segundos** she died in a matter of seconds • **en ~ de política social hemos avanzado poco** we have made little progress in terms of social policy; ▹ **quid, vida**
2 (= *pregunta*) question • **el examen se compone de tres cuestiones** the exam is made up of three questions • **la ~ está en saber si ella estaba al corriente** the question is whether she knew ▸ **cuestión de confianza** vote of confidence
3 (= *duda*) • **poner algo en ~** to call sth into question, raise doubts about sth

cuestionable (ADJ) questionable

cuestionador (ADJ) questioning

cuestionamiento (SM) questioning

cuestionar ▹ CONJUG 1a (VT) to question
(VI) to argue
(VPR) **cuestionarse** to ask o.s., question

cuestionario (SM) [*de sondeo*] questionnaire; (*Escol, Univ*) question paper

cuestor¹ (SM) (*Hist*) quaestor, questor (EEUU)

cuestor²(a) (SM/F) charity collector

cuete (ADJ) (*Méx**) drunk
(SM) **1** (*And, CAm, Méx*) (= *pistola*) pistol
2 (*CAm, Méx*) = **cohete**
3 (*Méx**) (= *embriaguez*) drunkenness
4 (*Méx*) (*Culin*) steak

cuetearse ▹ CONJUG 1a (VPR) (*And*)
1 (= *explotar*) to go off, explode
2‡ (= *morirse*) to kick the bucket‡

cueva (SF) **1** (*Geog*) cave ▸ **cueva de ladrones** den of thieves
2 (*para vino*) cellar, vault
3 (*Cono Sur***) (= *vagina*) pussy**
4 • **tener ~** (*Cono Sur*‡) (= *suerte*) to be lucky

cuévano (SM) pannier, deep basket

cuezo (SM) • MODISMO: • **meter el ~*** to poke *o* stick one's nose in*

cui (PL: **cuis, cuises**) (SM) (*LAm*) guinea pig

cuica (SF) (*And*) earthworm

cuico/a (SM/F) **1** (*Cono Sur*) (= *forastero*) foreigner, outsider
2 (*And, Cono Sur*) (*pey*) (= *boliviano*) Bolivian; (*Caribe*) (= *mejicano*) Mexican
3 (*Méx**) (= *policía*) pig‡, cop*

cuidadero/a (SM/F) keeper

cuidado (SM) **1** (= *precaución*) **a** (*como advertencia directa*) • **¡cuidado!** look out!, watch out! • **¡~ con el techo!** mind the ceiling! • **¡~ con los rateros!** watch out for pickpockets! • **"cuidado con el perro"** "beware of the dog" • **¡mucho ~ con lo que haces!** be very careful what you do! • **~ con hacer algo**: • **cuidadito con abrir la boca** keep your mouth shut, remember! • **¡~ con perderlo!** mind you don't lose it!
b • **tener ~ (con algo)** to be careful (of sth) • **¡ten ~!** careful! • **ten ~ con el paquete** careful with the parcel • **hay que tener ~ con los coches al cruzar la carretera** you must be aware of cars when you cross the road • **tener ~ con algn** to watch out for sb, watch sb*, be careful of sb • **tener ~ de no hacer algo** to be careful *o* take care not to do sth • **debe tener ~ de no tomar mucho el sol** you should be careful *o* take care not to sunbathe too much
c • **andarse con ~** to tread carefully, tread warily • **¡ándate con ~!** watch how you go!, watch your step!
2 (= *atención*) care • **las prendas delicadas deben lavarse con ~** delicate garments should be washed with care • **analicemos con ~ el último de los ejemplos** let's analyse the last of the examples carefully • **poner/tener ~ en algo** to take care over sth • **pondremos especial ~ en la programación dedicada a los niños** we will take special care in planning children's programming • **han tenido sumo ~ en subrayar que no es su responsabilidad** they have taken the greatest care to stress that it is not their responsibility
3 [*de niño, enfermo, planta, edificio*] care • **recibió los ~s de varias enfermeras** she received medical care from a number of nurses • **los ~s regulares de manos y pies** regular hand and foot care • **¿es ese el pago que merecen nuestros ~s amorosos?** is that all the reward we get for our tender loving care? • **estar al ~ de** (= *encargado de*) [+ *niños, familia, plantas*] to look after; [+ *proyecto*] to be in charge of; (= *cuidado por*) [*niños, jardín*] to be in the care of; [*departamento, sección*] to be run by • **antes la mujer tenía que quedarse al ~ de la casa** formerly women had to stay at home and look after the house • **una organización dedicada al ~ de minusválidos** an organization dedicated to caring for the disabled • **el monasterio está al ~ de la edición de miles de documentos** the monastery is in charge of editing thousands of documents • **dejó a su hija al ~ de una amiga** she left her daughter in the care of a friend • **la sección de publicidad está al ~ de Sr. Moyano** Mr Moyano is in charge of the advertising department ▸ **cuidado paliativo** palliative care ▸ **cuidado personal** personal care ▸ **cuidados intensivos** intensive care (*sing*) • **unidad de ~s intensivos** intensive care unit ▸ **cuidados médicos** medical care (*sing*) ▸ **cuidados paliativos** palliative care (*sing*)
4 (= *preocupación*) worry, concern • **pierda usted ~, ya me hago yo cargo de todo** don't

worry about it, I'll take care of everything • dar ~ to give cause for concern • estar con ~ • sentir ~ to be anxious, be worried
• MODISMOS: • tener o traer sin ~: • me tiene sin ~ lo que pase a partir de ahora I don't care at all o I couldn't care less what happens from now on • ¡allá ~s! let others worry about that!, that's their funeral!*
5 • de ~* [chapuza, bromista] real • les echó una bronca de ~ he gave them a real telling-off* • son unos racistas de ~ they're real racists • es un tacaño de ~ he's really stingy • está enfermo de ~ he is really o seriously ill • traía una intoxicación de ~ she had bad food poisoning • un enemigo de ~ a fearsome enemy
(ADJ) [aspecto] impeccable; [trabajo, selección] meticulous, careful • una película con una ambientación muy cuidada a film in which careful attention has been paid to the setting • una cuidada edición de la obra a beautifully-produced edition of the work • el interior del coche está muy ~ the interior of the car is impeccable

cuidador(a) (SM/F) 1 [de niños] childminder; [de enfermos] carer
2 [de caballos] trainer; [de zoo] keeper, zookeeper; [de terreno] caretaker
3 (Boxeo) second

cuidadosamente (ADV) carefully

cuidadoso (ADJ) 1 (= atento) [persona, observación, estrategia] careful • es muy ~ con sus cosas he's very careful with his things • es muy ~ de su aseo personal he takes a lot of care over his personal hygiene
2 (= prudente) careful • hay que ser ~ con gente así you have to be careful with people like that
3 (= solícito) attentive

cuidar ▸ CONJUG 1a (VT) 1 (= atender) [+ familia, jardín, edificio] to look after, take care of; [+ rebaño] to tend • las personas que deciden quedarse en casa y ~ a sus hijos people who decide to stay at home and look after their children • se dedica a ~ niños por las noches she does baby-sitting in the evenings • una organización que cuida a los huérfanos de guerra an organization caring for orphans of war
2 (= preocuparse por) [+ muebles, propiedades, entorno, salud] to look after, take care of • no cuidan nada la casa they don't look after the house at all, they don't take any care of the house • se preocupa mucho de ~ la línea she watches her figure very carefully
3 (= poner atención en) [+ detalles, ortografía] to pay attention to, take care over • en ese restaurante cuidan mucho los detalles they pay great attention to detail o take great care over the details in that restaurant • el director cuidó al máximo la puesta en escena de la obra the director took the greatest care over the production of the play • cuida mucho su imagen liberal she carefully cultivates her liberal image
(VI) 1 • ~ de to look after, take care of • ¿quién ~á de ti? who will look after you?, who will take care of you? • ~ de hacer algo to take care to do sth • siempre cuidaba de mantener el termo lleno de agua caliente he always took care to keep the thermos full of hot water • cuide de no caer careful you don't fall • ~ de que to make sure that • cuide de que no pase nadie make sure nobody gets in • cuidó de que todo saliera bien he made sure that everything went smoothly
2 • ~ con† to be careful of • cuida con esa gente be careful of those people
(VPR) cuidarse 1 [persona] to look after o.s., take care of o.s. • desde que se quedó viudo ha dejado de ~se since he lost his wife he hasn't been looking after himself properly o taking proper care of himself • se cuida mucho she takes good care of herself • ¡cómo te cuidas! you do know how to look after yourself well! • ¡cuídate! (al despedirse) take care!
2 • ~se de algo (= encargarse) to take care of sth; (= preocuparse) to worry about sth • los organizadores se cuidan del alojamiento y las comidas the organizers take care of accommodation and meals • no se cuida del qué dirán she doesn't worry about what people think • ~se de hacer algo to be careful to do sth, take care to do sth • todos se cuidan de no ser los primeros en hacerlo everyone is careful not to o takes care not to be the first to do it • ~se muy mucho de hacer algo to take good o great care to do sth

cuido†† (SM) care • en o para su ~ for your own good

cuita[1] (SF) (liter) (= preocupación) worry, trouble; (= pena) grief, affliction; (civil, doméstico) strife • contar sus ~s a algn to tell sb one's troubles

cuita[2] (SF) (CAm, Méx) (= estiércol) poultry manure; (= excremento) dung

cuitado (ADJ) (liter) 1 (= preocupado) worried, troubled
2 (= tímido) timid

cuitlacoche (SM) (Méx) black mushroom (that grows on corn)

cuja (SF) 1 (= cama) bedstead
2 (CAm, Méx) (= sobre) envelope

cujinillos (SMPL) (Guat, Méx) saddlebags

culada (SF) • darse una ~* to drop a clanger*

culamen* (SM) bottom, bum*, butt (esp EEUU*)

culandrón‡ (SM) queer‡, fag (EEUU‡)

culantrillo (SM) maidenhair

culantro (SM) coriander

culata (SF) 1 (Mec) [de fusil] butt; [de cañón] breech; [de cilindro] head
2 (Zool) haunch, hindquarters
3 (= parte trasera) rear, back
4 (Cono Sur) (= cobertizo) hut, shelter

culatazo (SM) kick, recoil

culé* (SMF) supporter of Barcelona Football Club

culear ▸ CONJUG 1a (VT) (And, Cono Sur, Méx**) to fuck**, screw**
(VI) 1* (= mover el culo) to waggle one's bottom, waggle one's backside
2 (And, Cono Sur, Méx**) (= fornicar) to fuck**, screw**

culebra (SF) 1 (Zool) snake • hacer ~ to zigzag ▸ culebra de anteojos cobra ▸ culebra de cascabel rattlesnake, rattler (EEUU*)
2 (Mec) worm (of a still)
3* (= alboroto) disturbance, disorder
4 (And) (= cuenta) debt, bill
5 (Méx) (= manguera) hosepipe

culebrear ▸ CONJUG 1a (VI) [culebra] to wriggle, wriggle along; [carretera] to zigzag, wind; [río] to wind, meander

culebreo (SM) [de culebra] wriggling; [de carretera] zigzag, winding; [de río] winding, meandering

culebrina (SF) 1 (Meteo) forked lightning
2 (Hist) culverin

culebrón* (SM) soap opera, soap*

culeco (ADJ) 1 (LAm) [gallina] broody
2 (LAm) [persona] home-loving
3 (And, Caribe, Cono Sur) (= enamorado) • estar ~ to be head over heels in love
4 • estar ~ con algo (And, CAm, Caribe, Méx*) (= satisfecho) to be very pleased about sth, be over the moon about sth; (= orgulloso) to be very proud of sth

culera (SF) seat (of trousers)

culeras* (SMF INV) coward, chicken*

culero/a (ADJ) lazy
(SM) 1 (= pañal) nappy, diaper (EEUU)
2 (CAm‡) (= maricón) poof‡, queer‡, fag (EEUU‡)
(SM/F)* 1 [de drogas] drug courier, drug smuggler
2 (Méx) (= cobarde) coward

culí (SM) coolie

culibajo* (ADJ) short, dumpy

culigordo* (ADJ) big-bottomed, broad in the beam*

culillo* (SM) 1 (And, CAm, Caribe) (= miedo) fear
2 • tener ~ (Caribe) to be in a rush

culín (SM) (= gota) drop • solo queda un ~ de vino there's only a tiny drop of wine left

culinario (ADJ) culinary, cooking (antes de s)

culipandear ▸ CONJUG 1a (VI) (Caribe) to stall, hedge

culmen (SM) 1 (= colmo) • el ~ de la ignorancia the height of ignorance; (= persona) the epitome of ignorance
2 (= punto culminante) • el ~ de su carrera the crowning moment of his career • llegar a su ~ to reach its height
(ADJ) • el momento ~ de su carrera the crowning moment of her career • el momento ~ de la campaña electoral the culminating moment of the electoral campaign, the climax of the electoral campaign

culminación (SF) culmination

culminante (ADJ) 1 (Geog) highest, topmost
2 [momento] culminating • el momento ~ de la revolución the culminating moment of the revolution, the climax of the revolution • este fue el momento ~ de su carrera this was the crowning moment of his career • en el momento ~ de la fiesta, se apagaron las luces at the high point of the party, the lights went out • el punto ~ de la novela the climax of the novel

culminar ▸ CONJUG 1a (VT) [+ objetivo] to reach, attain; [+ acuerdo] to conclude; [+ tarea, carrera] to finish
(VI) to culminate (en in)

cúlmine (ADJ) (And) = culminante

culo (SM) 1* (= nalgas) backside*, bum‡, arse**, ass (EEUU**), butt (EEUU‡); (= ano) arsehole**, asshole (EEUU**) • le dio un puntapié en el ~ he kicked him in the backside* • le limpió el culito al niño he wiped the baby's bottom • caer de ~ to fall on one's backside* • dar a algn por el ~** (= sexualmente) to bugger sb; (= fastidiar) to piss sb off** • me da por ~ tener que trabajar tan temprano it really pisses me off having to go to work so early** • ¡que te den por (el) ~!** fuck you!**, screw you!** • MODISMOS: • confunde el ~ con las témporas‡ he can't tell his arse from his elbow** • el ~ del mundo‡: • está en el ~ del mundo it's in the back of beyond • es el ~ del mundo it's the arsehole of the world** • dejar a algn con el ~ al aire* to leave sb stranded • ir con el ~ a rastras* to be in a fix o jam* • ir de ~‡: • con tanta llamada, esta mañana voy de ~ with all these calls this morning I'm way behind* • si no apruebas esta asignatura vas de ~ if you don't pass this subject you've had it* • en cuanto al paro, el país va de ~ the country's unemployment record is disastrous • lamer el ~ a algn‡ to lick sb's arse o (EEUU) ass**, kiss sb's arse o (EEUU) ass** • meterse algo por el ~**: • ¡métetelo por el ~! stick it up your ass!** • mojarse el ~‡: • para conseguirlo tendrás que mojarte el ~ you won't achieve that without getting your feet wet* • partirse el ~‡: • me partí el ~ de risa con él I laughed myself silly with

him • **se parten el ~ por encontrar entradas** they're pulling their hair out trying to get tickets • **pasarse algo por el ~**‡ not to give a shit about sth‡ • **perder el ~ por algn/algo**‡: • **pierde el ~ por ella** he's nuts about her* • **pierde el ~ por conocerlos** she's dying to be introduced to them • **ser un ~ de mal asiento**: • **se mudó cinco veces en un año, es un ~ de mal asiento** she moved house five times in one year, she just can't stay in one place • **tomar por ~**‡: • **¡vete a tomar por ~!**‡ screw you!‡, fuck off!‡, piss off!‡ • **¡que se vayan a tomar por ~!**‡ they can go screw themselves‡, they can fuck *o* piss off‡ • **si nos pillan nos vamos todos a tomar por ~** if they catch us we'll all be fucked *o* screwed‡ • **el proyecto se fue a tomar por ~** the project went down the toilet‡ • **les mandó a tomar por ~** he told them to fuck off *o* piss off‡ • **un día se hartó y mandó el trabajo a tomar por ~** one day he got fed up with it and jacked his job in* • **su casa está a tomar por ~** her house is in the back of beyond • **~ que veo, ~ que deseo** if I see something I like then I have to have it
2* [*de vaso, botella*] bottom • **el vaso se rompió por el ~** the bottom of the glass broke • **—¿queda cerveza? —sí, un culillo** "is there any beer left in there?" — "yes, a drop" • **se bebió los ~s de todos los vasos** he drank the dregs of all the glasses • **gafas de ~ de vaso** pebble glasses

culón ADJ = **culigordo**

culote SM, **culottes** SMPL **1** (*Dep*) cycling shorts (*pl*)
2 (= *prenda íntima*) French knickers (*pl*)

culpa SF **1** (= *responsabilidad*) fault, blame • **es ~ suya** it's his fault, he's to blame • **la ~ fue de los frenos** the brakes were to blame • **no le alcanza ~** (*frm*) no blame attaches to him, he is blameless • **cargar con la ~ a algn** to pin *o* put the blame on sb • **echar la ~ a algn de algo** to blame sb for sth • **siempre me echan la ~ a mí** they're always blaming me *o* saying it's my fault • **por ~ del mal tiempo** because of the bad weather • **tener la ~ de algo** to be to blame for sth • **nadie tiene la ~** nobody is to blame, it's nobody's fault • **tú tienes la ~** you're to blame, it's your fault
2 (*Jur*) guilt
3 (= *pecado*) sin • **pagar las ~s ajenas** to pay for somebody else's sins

culpabilidad SF **1** (= *culpa*) guilt, culpability (*frm*) • **admitió su ~ públicamente** he made a public admission of his guilt, he admitted his guilt publicly • **sentimiento de ~** guilt feelings (*pl*), feelings of guilt (*pl*) • **complejo de ~** guilt complex
2 (*Jur*) guilt • **veredicto de ~** verdict of guilty
3 (= *responsabilidad*) responsibility

culpabilizar ▹ CONJUG 1f VT = **culpar**

culpable ADJ **1** [*persona*] guilty • **confesarse ~** to plead guilty • **declarar ~ a algn** to find sb guilty • **la persona ~** the person to blame *o* at fault, the culpable person (*frm*); (*Jur*) the guilty person, the culprit
2 [*acto*] blameworthy • **con descuido ~** with culpable negligence (*frm*)
SMF **1** (= *responsable*) person to blame, person at fault
2 (*Jur*) (= *responsable de un delito*) culprit; (= *condenado por un delito*) offender, guilty party

culpado/a ADJ guilty
SM/F culprit; (*Jur*) the accused

culpar ▹ CONJUG 1a VT (= *acusar*) to blame • **~ a algn de algo** to blame sb for sth

culposo ADJ (*esp LAm*) guilty, culpable

cultamente ADV (= *de manera culta*) in a cultured way; (*pey*) (= *con afectación*) affectedly, in an affected way

culteranismo SM (*Literat*) *latinized, precious and highly metaphorical style (esp 17th century)*

> **CULTERANISMO, CONCEPTISMO**
> **Culteranismo** and **conceptismo** were opposing literary fashions which developed in the early 17th century in Spain. Luis de Góngora was the main exponent of **culteranismo**, also known as **gongorismo**. His poetry was very learned in style, full of metaphor, classical allusions, neologisms and deliberate syntactic playfulness. By contrast, **conceptismo**, as championed by Francisco de Quevedo, meant very precise, economic and rational language with complex ideas presented in a simple and succinct style. Góngora, who was much vilified in his time, and not only by Quevedo, found posthumous favour with generations of modern Spanish poets, most notably the **Generación del 27**.
> ▹ GENERACIÓN DEL 27/DEL 98

culterano/a (*Literat*) ADJ *latinized, precious and highly metaphorical*
SM/F writer in the style of "culteranismo"

cultismo SM learned word

cultista ADJ learned

cultivable ADJ cultivable, arable

cultivado ADJ [*campo, superficie*] cultivated; [*persona*] cultured, cultivated; [*perla*] cultured

cultivador¹ SM (*Agr*) cultivator

cultivador²(a) SM/F farmer, grower • **~ de vino** winegrower • **~ de café** coffee grower, coffee planter

cultivar ▹ CONJUG 1a VT **1** (*Agr*) [+ *tierra*] to farm, cultivate, till; [+ *cosecha*] to grow, raise
2 (*Bio*) to culture
3 [+ *amistad, arte, estudio*] to cultivate; [+ *talento*] to develop; [+ *memoria*] to develop, improve

cultivo SM **1** (= *acto*) cultivation, growing
2 (= *cosecha*) crop • **el ~ principal de la región** the chief crop of the area • **rotación de ~s** crop rotation
3 (*Bio*) culture; ▹ **caldo**

culto ADJ **1** [*persona*] cultured, educated; (*pey*) (= *afectado*) affected
2 [*palabra, frase*] learned
SM **1** (*Rel*) (= *veneración*) worship; (= *ritual*) cult (a of) • **libertad de ~** freedom of worship • **el ~ a Zeus** the cult of Zeus • **rendir ~ a** (*lit*) to worship; (*fig*) to pay homage *o* tribute to
2 (= *admiración*) cult • **de ~** cult (*antes de s*) • **una película de ~** a cult movie ▸ **culto a la personalidad** personality cult

cultrún SM (*Cono Sur*) drum

cultura SF **1** (= *civilización*) culture • **la ~ griega** Greek culture • **la ~ clásica** Classical culture
2 (= *saber*) • **Juan tiene mucha ~** Juan is very knowledgeable *o* widely-read • **un hombre de gran ~** a very knowledgeable *o* cultured man ▸ **cultura de masas** popular culture ▸ **cultura general** general knowledge ▸ **cultura popular** popular culture
3 (= *artes*) culture • **este gobierno no invierte en ~** this government is not investing in culture • **Ministerio de Cultura** Minister of Culture

cultural ADJ cultural • **tiene un bajo nivel ~** he's not very (well-)educated

culturalmente ADV culturally

culturismo SM body building

culturista SMF body builder

culturización SF education, enlightenment

culturizar ▹ CONJUG 1f VT to educate, enlighten
VPR **culturizarse** to educate o.s., improve one's mind

cuma SF **1** (*CAm*) (= *cuchillo*) curved machete, curved knife
2 (*And*) (= *mujer*) woman (*of the village*); (= *comadre*) gossip

cumbancha SF (*Caribe*) spree, drinking bout

cumbia SF (= *música*) *Colombian dance music*; (= *baile*) *popular Colombian dance*

cúmbila SM (*Caribe*) pal*, buddy (*esp EEUU*)

cumbo SM **1** (*CAm*) (= *chistera*) top hat; (= *hongo*) bowler hat, derby (*EEUU*)
2 (*CAm*) (= *taza*) narrow-mouthed cup

cumbre SF (*Geog*) summit, top; (*fig*) top, height • **conferencia en la ~** (*Pol*) summit, summit conference • **está en la ~ de su poderío** he is at the height of his power • **hacer ~** to make it to the top
ADJ INV • **conferencia ~** summit conference • **momento ~** culminating point • **es su libro ~** it's his most important book

cume SM (*CAm*), **cumiche** SM (*CAm*) baby of the family

cumpa* SM (*LAm*) pal*, buddy (*esp EEUU*)

cumpleañero/a SM/F (*LAm*) birthday boy/birthday girl

cumpleaños SM INV birthday • **¡feliz ~!** happy birthday!, many happy returns!

cumplido ADJ **1** (= *perfecto*) complete, full • **un ~ caballero** a perfect gentlemen
2 (= *amplio*) [*ropa*] full; [*ración*] large, plentiful
3 (= *cortés*) courteous, correct; (= *formal*) formal
4 • **tiene sesenta años ~s** he's sixty years old
SM **1** (= *alabanza*) compliment
2 (= *cortesía*) • **visita de ~** courtesy call • **por ~** (= *por cortesía*) out of politeness, as a matter of courtesy; (= *por obligación*) out of a sense of duty • **¡sin ~s!** no ceremony, please! • **andarse con ~s** • **usar ~s** to stand on ceremony, be formal • **cambiar los ~s de etiqueta** to exchange formal courtesies

cumplidor ADJ reliable, trustworthy

cumplimentar ▹ CONJUG 1a VT
1 [+ *formulario*] to complete, fill in
2 [+ *órdenes*] to carry out; [+ *deber*] to perform
3 (*frm*) [+ *superior, jefe*] to pay one's respects to (**por** on)

cumplimentero ADJ formal, ceremonious

cumplimiento SM **1** (= *satisfacción*) • **el ~ de su promesa le reportará buena fama** fulfilling *o* keeping his promise will earn him a good reputation • **el ~ de sus obligaciones** keeping *o* fulfilling his obligations • **le felicitó por el ~ de todos los objetivos propuestos** he congratulated him on achieving all the proposed aims
2 [*de ley*] observance, compliance • **una ley de obligado ~ para los ciudadanos** a law that is binding on all citizens • **en ~ de lo estipulado por el acuerdo** in adherence to the terms stipulated in the agreement • **dar ~ a** to fulfil • **falta de ~** non-fulfilment
3 [*de condena*] • **pasará tres años en prisión en ~ de la condena** he will spend three years in prison in order to complete his sentence
4 (*Com*) expiry, expiration (*EEUU*)

cumplir ▹ CONJUG 3a VT **1** (= *llevar a cabo*) [+ *amenaza*] to carry out; [+ *promesa*] to keep; [+ *objetivo, sueño*] to achieve; [+ *ambición*] to fulfil, fulfill (*EEUU*), achieve; [+ *papel*] to play • **los contratan para ~ las misiones más difíciles** they are hired to carry out *o* do the most difficult tasks • **la cárcel no cumple su función preventiva** prison is failing to fulfil its role as *o* failing to act as a deterrent • **los parques naturales cumplen la función de**

proteger nuestro patrimonio natural nature reserves serve to protect our natural heritage • **cumplió su palabra de aumentarnos el sueldo** he kept his promise to give us a pay rise • **les ha acusado de no ~ su palabra** he has accused them of failing to keep *o* breaking their word
2 (= *obedecer*) [+ *ley, norma, sentencia*] to observe, obey; [+ *orden*] to carry out, obey • **solo estoy cumpliendo órdenes** I'm only carrying out *o* obeying orders • **~ la voluntad del difunto** to carry out the wishes of the deceased • **hacer ~ la ley/un acuerdo** to enforce the law/an agreement
3 (= *alcanzar*) [+ *condición, requisito*] to comply with, fulfil, fulfill (*EEUU*), meet • **estos productos no cumplen las condiciones sanitarias exigidas** these products do not comply with *o* fulfil *o* meet the necessary health requirements • **cumplió su deseo de viajar a la India** he fulfilled his wish of travelling to India
4 (= *realizar*) [+ *condena, pena*] to serve; [+ *servicio militar*] to do, complete • **está cumpliendo 30 días de arresto** he is serving 30 days detention • **tiene el servicio militar cumplido** he has done *o* completed his military service
5 (*con periodos de tiempo*) **a** [+ *años*] • **hoy cumple ocho años** she's eight today, it's her eighth birthday today • **el rey cumple hoy años** today is the King's birthday • **cumple 40 años en diciembre** she'll be 40 in December • **cuando cumplas los 21 años** when you're 21, when you reach the age of 21 • **¿cuántos años va a ~?** how old is he going to be? • **¡que cumplas muchos más!** many happy returns!
b [+ *aniversario, días*] • **la democracia cumple su vigésimo aniversario** democracy is celebrating its twentieth anniversary • **el premio cumple su cincuentenario** the prize is currently in its fiftieth year • **el paro en el transporte cumple hoy su cuarto día** this is the fourth day of the transport strike
6 (*Naipes*) [+ *contrato*] to make
(VI) **1** (= *terminar*) [*plazo*] to end, expire; [*pago*] to fall due
2 (= *hacer lo correcto*) to do one's duty • **tengo la tranquilidad de haber cumplido** at least I can say that I did my duty *o* what was expected of me • **es muy profesional y siempre cumple** she is very professional - she never lets you down • **yo siempre cumplo en mi trabajo** I always do my job properly • **mi marido no cumple en la cama** (*hum*) my husband isn't performing (in bed) • **prepárales una sopita y con eso cumples** just make them a bit of soup, that's as much as can be expected of you
3 • **~ con** [+ *compromiso, acuerdo*] to honour, honor (*EEUU*); [+ *ley*] to observe, obey; [+ *condición, requisito, criterio*] to fulfil, fulfill (*EEUU*), comply with, meet • **estaba cumpliendo con su deber** he was doing his duty • **~ con los trámites de la aduana** to go through customs • **tendrá que ~ con lo estipulado en el acuerdo** he will have to comply with what was stipulated in the agreement • **tendrán que ~ con el calendario acordado** they will have to comply with the schedule we agreed on • **para ~ con los criterios de Maastricht** in order to comply with *o* meet the Maastricht criteria • **~ con la iglesia** to fulfil one's religious obligations
4 • **~ por algn** to act on sb's behalf
5 (*frm*) (= *corresponder*) • **lo he recibido dos veces, con la amabilidad que me cumple** I've received him twice, with the friendliness that is expected of me
6 (*Mil*) to finish one's military service
(VPR) **cumplirse 1** (= *realizarse*) [*deseo, sueño, vaticinio*] to come true; [*plan, proyecto*] to be implemented
2 (= *acabarse*) [*plazo*] to expire • **se cumplió el plazo de dos años del visado** the two years of the visa expired • **el viernes se cumple el plazo para entregar las solicitudes** Friday is the deadline *o* last day for handing in applications • **la jornada se cumplió sin incidentes** the day passed off without incident • **hoy se cumple el 40 aniversario de su muerte** today is the 40th anniversary of her death • **ayer se cumplió un año desde que fui puesto en libertad** it was a year yesterday since I was released • **ayer se cumplió el quinto día de la campaña electoral** yesterday was the fifth day of the election campaign

cumquibus (SM INV) (*hum*) • **el ~** the wherewithal (*hum*)

cumucho (SM) (*Cono Sur*) **1** (= *multitud*) gathering, mob, crowd
2 (= *cabaña*) hut, hovel

cumulativo (ADJ) cumulative

cúmulo (SM) **1** (= *montón*) heap, accumulation (*frm*) • **un ~ de datos** a heap of facts • **un ~ de obstáculos** a whole series of obstacles • **es un ~ de virtudes** he's full of virtues, he's a paragon of virtue
2 (*Meteo*) cumulus

cumulonimbo (SM) cumulonimbus

cuna (SF) **1** [*de bebé*] cot, crib (*EEUU*); (*con balancines*) cradle • **canción de ~** lullaby • **casa ~** children's home ▸ **cuna portátil** carrycot
2 (= *lugar de nacimiento*) [*de persona*] birthplace; [*de tendencia, movimiento*] cradle • **Málaga, la ~ de Picasso** Málaga, the birthplace of Picasso • **Atenas, la ~ de las olimpiadas** Athens, the birthplace of the Olympics • **Escocia, la ~ del golf** Scotland, the home of golf
3 (= *linaje*) • **de ~ humilde** of humble birth *o* stock *o* origin • **de noble ~** of noble birth • MODISMO: • **criarse en buena ~** to be born with a silver spoon in one's mouth
4 cunas (= *juego*) cat's cradle (*sing*)

cundir ▹ CONJUG 3a (VI) **1** (= *rendir*) to produce a good quantity • **hoy no me ha cundido el trabajo** I didn't get very far with my work today, I didn't get much work done today • **no me cunde el tiempo** I'm not getting very far, I'm not getting a lot done, I'm not making very much headway
2 (= *extenderse*) to spread • **la noticia cundió** the news spread • **cunde el rumor que ...** there's a rumour going round that ... • **¡que no cunda el pánico!** there's no need for panic!, don't panic!
3 (= *multiplicarse*) to increase • **van cundiendo los efectos del paro** the effects of unemployment are multiplying
4 (= *hincharse*) [*arroz*] to swell

cunear ▹ CONJUG 1a (VT) to rock, cradle
(VPR) **cunearse** to rock, sway; (*al andar*) to swing along

cuneco/a (SM/F) (*Ven*) baby of the family

cuneiforme (ADJ) cuneiform

cuneta (SF) **1** [*de calle*] gutter; [*de carretera*] ditch • MODISMOS: • **dejar a algn en la ~**: • **Juan deja a Pedro en la ~** Juan leaves Pedro standing, Juan leaves Pedro way behind • **quedarse en la ~** to get left behind, miss the bus*
2 (*CAm, Méx*) [*de acera*] kerb, curb (*EEUU*)

cunicultura (SF) rabbit breeding

cuña (SF) **1** (*Téc*) wedge; [*de rueda*] chock
2 (*Tip*) quoin
3 • **meter ~** to sow discord
4* (= *pez gordo*) big shot*, fat cat* • **tener ~s** to have a lot of influence *o* pull
5 (*CAm, Caribe*) (*Aut*) two-seater car
6 (*Radio, TV*) spot, slot; (*Prensa*) space filler, brief item ▸ **cuña publicitaria** commercial

cuñadismo* (SM) nepotism, old boy network

cuñado/a (SM/F) brother-/sister-in-law

cuñete (SM) keg

cuño (SM) **1** (*Téc*) die-stamp • **de nuevo ~** [*palabra*] newly-coined; [*persona*] new-fledged
2 (= *sello*) stamp, mark

cuota (SF) **1** (= *parte proporcional*) share • **han aumentado sus ~s de poder en el gobierno** they've increased their share of power within the government ▸ **cuota de mercado** market share ▸ **cuota de pantalla** (*TV*) share of the viewing figures ▸ **cuota electoral** share of the vote
2 (= *parte asignada*) quota • **una reducción en la ~ española de producción de aceite** a reduction in Spain's oil production quota
3 (= *cantidad fija*) [*de club*] membership fee, membership fees (*pl*); [*de sindicato*] dues (*pl*) ▸ **cuota de conexión** connection charge, connection fee ▸ **cuota de enganche** down payment ▸ **cuota de inscripción** (*a un curso*) enrolment fee, enrollment fee (*EEUU*); (*a una conferencia*) registration fee ▸ **cuota de instalación** installation charge, installation fee ▸ **cuota de socio** membership fee ▸ **cuota inicial** (*LAm*) down payment ▸ **cuota patronal** employer's contribution (*to national insurance*)
4 (*LAm*) (= *plazo*) • **por ~s** by instalments *o* (*EEUU*) installments

cuotidiano (*frm*) (ADJ) = **cotidiano**

cupaje (SM) blending, blending of wines

cupe *etc* ▹ **caber**

cupé (SM) coupé

Cupido (SM) Cupid

cupiera *etc* ▹ **caber**

cuplé (SM) *type of light, sometimes risqué song originally sung in variety shows*

cupletista (SF) cabaret singer, singer of "cuplés"

cupo (SM) **1** (*Econ, Com*) quota ▸ **cupo de azúcar** sugar quota ▸ **cupo de importación** import quota
2 (*LAm*) capacity • **no hay ~** there's no room • **"no hay cupo"** (*Teat*) "house full", "sold out"
3 (*Mil*) draft • **excedente de ~** exempt from military service

cupolino (SM) hubcap

cupón (SM) (= *vale*) coupon; [*de lotería*] ticket • **~ de (los) ciegos** (*Esp*) *ticket for the lottery for the blind* ▸ **cupón de dividendos** dividend voucher ▸ **cupón de franqueo internacional** international reply coupon ▸ **cupón de interés** interest warrant ▸ **cupón de racionamiento** ration coupon ▸ **cupón de regalo** gift voucher, gift token, gift certificate (*EEUU*) ▸ **cupón de respuesta internacional** international reply coupon ▸ **cupón obsequio** gift voucher, gift token, gift certificate (*EEUU*)

cuponazo* (SM) special lottery prize

cuprero (ADJ) (*Chile*) copper (*antes de s*)

cúpula (SF) **1** (*Arquit*) dome, cupola
2 (*Náut*) turret
3 (*Bot*) husk, shell
4 (*Pol*) party leadership, leading members; (*Com, Econ*) top management

cuquería (SF) craftiness

cura[1] (SM) **1** (*Rel*) priest • **sí, señor ~** yes, father ▸ **cura obrero** worker priest ▸ **cura párroco** parish priest
2† (= *yo mismo*) I, myself • **este ~** yours truly* • **no se ofrece este ~** this poor devil isn't

volunteering

cura² SF **1** (*Med*) (= *curación*) cure; (= *tratamiento*) treatment • **no tiene ~** (*lit*) there is no cure for it; (*fig*) there's no remedy, it's quite hopeless • **tiene ~** it can be cured, it is curable • **primera ~** first aid ▸ **cura de choque** shock treatment ▸ **cura de reposo** rest therapy ▸ **cura de sueño** sleep therapy ▸ **cura de urgencia** emergency treatment, first aid
2 ▸ **cura de almas** (*Rel*) cure of souls

curable ADJ curable

curaca¹ SM (*And*) (= *cacique*) Indian chief, Indian native authority

curaca² SF (*And*) (= *ama*) priest's housekeeper

curación SF (*Med*) (= *proceso*) cure, healing; (= *tratamiento*) treatment • **primera ~** first aid

curadillo SM **1** (*Culin*) dried cod
2 (*Téc*) bleached linen

curado ADJ **1** (*Culin*) cured; [*pieles*] tanned, prepared
2 (*And, Cono Sur*) (= *borracho*) drunk
3 (= *endurecido*) hardened, inured • **estar ~ de espanto(s)** to have seen it all before
SM (*Culin*) curing

curador(a) SM/F **1** (*Jur*) (= *tutor*) guardian; (= *administrador*) executor
2 [*de museo*] curator
3 [*de enfermos*] healer ▸ **curador(a) por fe** faith-healer

curalotodo ADJ INV cure-all
SM cure-all

curanderismo SM folk medicine; (*pey*) quack medicine, quackery

curandero/a SM/F quack, quack doctor

curar ▹ CONJUG 1a VT **1** (*Med*) (= *tratar*) to treat; (= *sanar*) to cure • **le están curando el resfriado con antibióticos** they're treating her cold with antibiotics • **este tratamiento me curó la bronquitis** this treatment cured my bronchitis • **le curó la herida con alcohol** she treated *o* dressed his wound with alcohol • **no le consiguió ~ la herida** he couldn't get his wound to heal • **para ~ los males de la sociedad** (*fig*) to cure all of society's ills • REFRÁN: • **el tiempo lo cura todo** time is a great healer
2 [+ *carne, pescado*] to cure; [+ *queso*] to mature; [+ *piel*] to tan; [+ *tela*] to bleach; [+ *madera*] to season
VI (*Med*) [*fármaco, medicamento*] to work; (*frm*) [*paciente*] to get better, recover
VPR **curarse 1** (*Med*) [*paciente*] to get better, recover; [*herida*] to heal (up) • **no se me ha curado la herida todavía** my wound still hasn't healed (up) • **~se de algo: ya me he curado de la gripe** I've got over the flu now • **nunca se curó del mal de amores** he never got over his unrequited love; ▹ **salud**
2 (*frm*) (= *preocuparse*) • **~se de algo: nunca se curó de agradar a sus súbditos** he never made any effort to please his subjects
3 (*And, Cono Sur**) (= *emborracharse*) to get drunk; (*Méx**) (*de resaca*) to have the hair of the dog*

curare SM curare, curari

curasao SM curaçao

curativo ADJ curative

curato SM curacy, parish

curazao SM curaçao

curca SF (*And, Cono Sur*) (= *joroba*) hump

curco/a (*And, Cono Sur*) ADJ hunchbacked
SM/F hunchback

curcuncho/a (*And, Chile*) SM (= *joroba*) hump
SM/F (= *jorobado*) hunchback

curda* ADJ sloshed*, pissed**, trashed (EEUU‡) • **estar ~** to be sloshed*, be pissed**, be trashed (EEUU‡)
SF drunkenness • **agarrar una ~** to get sloshed*, get pissed**, get trashed (EEUU‡) • **estar (con la) ~** • **estar en ~** (*Cono Sur*) to be sloshed*, be pissed**, be trashed (EEUU‡) • **tener una ~** to be sloshed*, be pissed**, be trashed (EEUU‡)

curdo/a ADJ Kurdish
SM/F Kurd

cureña SF gun carriage • **a ~ rasa** out in the open, exposed to the elements

curia SF **1** (*Rel*) (*tb* **curia romana**) papal Curia
2 (*Jur*) legal profession, the Bar, the Bar Association (EEUU)

curiana SF cockroach

curiara SF (*Ven*) dugout canoe

curiche* SM (*Cono Sur*) black man

curiosamente ADV **1** (= *extrañamente*) curiously, oddly
2 (= *pulcramente*) neatly, cleanly

curiosear ▹ CONJUG 1a VT **1** (= *husmear*) to nose out
2 (= *mirar*) (*en una tienda*) to look over, look round
VI **1** (= *husmear*) to snoop, pry
2 (= *mirar*) (*en una tienda*) to look round, wander round; (= *explorar*) to poke about • **~ por las tiendas** to wander round the shops • **~ por los escaparates** to go window-shopping

curiosidad SF **1** (= *interés*) curiosity; (= *indiscreción*) inquisitiveness • **despertar la ~ de algn** to arouse sb's curiosity • **estar muerto de ~** to be dying of curiosity • **tenemos ~ por saber si ...** we are curious to know if ... • **la ~ de noticias me llevó allí** the quest for news took me there
2 (= *objeto*) curiosity, curio
3 (= *aseo*) neatness, cleanliness
4 (= *esmero*) care, carefulness, conscientiousness

curioso/a ADJ **1** [*persona*] curious; (= *indiscreto*) inquisitive • **estar ~ por saber** to be curious to know • **~ de noticias** eager for news
2 (= *raro*) [*acto, objeto*] curious, odd • **¡qué ~!** how odd!, how curious!
3 (= *aseado*) neat, clean, tidy
4 (= *cuidadoso*) careful, conscientious
SM/F **1** (= *presente*) bystander, onlooker
2 (= *interesado*) • **los ~s de la literatura** those interested in literature
3 (= *cotilla*) busybody

curiosón/ona SM/F busybody

curita SF (*LAm*) plaster, sticking plaster, Band-Aid® (EEUU)

currante* SMF worker

currar* ▹ CONJUG 1a VI, **currelar*** ▹ CONJUG 1a VI to work

curre* SM, **currelo*** SM work

curricular ADJ curriculum (*antes de s*)

currículo SM curriculum

curriculum SM, **currículum** SM (*tb* **curriculum vitae**) curriculum vitae, résumé (EEUU)

currinche SM **1** (*Tip*) apprentice journalist, cub reporter
2* (= *persona insignificante*) little man, nonentity

currito* SM working man, working bloke*

Curro SM *forma familiar de* **Francisco**

curro ADJ **1** (= *elegante*) smart; (= *ostentoso*) showy, flashy
2 (= *presumido*) cocky, brashly confident
SM **1*** = **curre**
2 (= *golpe*) bash*, punch • **dar un ~** to beat up
3 (*Arg**) (= *estafa*) rip-off‡

curroadicto/a* SM/F workaholic

currusco* SM hard crust (*at the end of French bread*)

currutaco/a ADJ **1** (= *ostentoso*) showy, loud
2 (*LAm*) (= *bajito*) short, squat
SM/F **1** (*LAm*) (= *persona bajita*) shortie*
2† (= *petimetre*) toff*, dandy
3 currutacos (*CAm*) (= *diarrea*) diarrhoea (*sing*), diarrhea (*sing*) (EEUU)

curry SM **1** (= *especia*) curry powder • **pollo al ~** curried chicken
2 (= *plato*) curry

cursante SMF (*LAm*) student

cursar ▹ CONJUG 1a VT **1** [+ *orden, mensaje*] to send, dispatch; [+ *solicitud*] to deal with
2 [+ *asignatura*] to study; [+ *curso*] to take, attend • **~ Matemáticas** to read Maths
3 (*frm*) [+ *sitio*] to frequent
VI • **el mes que cursa** the present month

cursi ADJ **1** [*persona*] (= *amanerado*) affected; (= *remilgado*) prissy; (*en sus gustos*) twee
2 [*objeto*] twee
SMF • **es una ~** (= *amanerada*) she's so affected; (= *niña remilgada*) she's so prissy; (*en sus gustos*) she's so twee

cursilada SF = **cursilería**

cursilería SF **1** (= *cualidad*) (= *amaneramiento*) (*gen*) affectation; [*de niña remilgada*] prissiness; (= *mal gusto*) tweeness
2 (= *acto*) • **no soporto las ~s que dice** I can't stand her affected way of speaking • **hizo la ~ de cortarle el pelo al caniche** he was twee enough to get the poodle's hair cut

cursillista SMF member, member of a course

cursillo SM (= *curso*) short course; (= *conferencias*) short series of lectures

cursilón/ona SM/F = **cursi**

cursiva SF (*Tip*) italics (*pl*); (= *escritura*) cursive writing

cursivo ADJ (*Tip*) italic; [*escritura*] cursive

curso SM **1** (*Escol, Univ*) (= *año escolar*) year; (= *clase*) year, class (*esp* EEUU) • **este ~ empieza el dos de septiembre** this school year begins on the second of September • **los alumnos del segundo ~** second year pupils, the second years • **es el único chico de mi ~** he's the only boy in my year ▸ **curso escolar** school year, academic year
2 (= *estudios*) course • **un ~ de informática** a course in computing • **apertura/clausura de ~** beginning/end of term ▸ **curso acelerado** crash course, intensive course ▸ **curso de actualización** refresher course ▸ **curso de formación** training course ▸ **Curso de Orientación Universitaria** = **COU** ▸ **curso de reciclaje** refresher course ▸ **curso intensivo** crash course, intensive course ▸ **curso lectivo** academic year ▸ **curso por correspondencia** correspondence course
3 [*de río*] course ▸ **curso de agua, curso fluvial** watercourse
4 (= *desarrollo*) course • **un nuevo tratamiento que retrasa el ~ de la enfermedad** a new treatment which delays the course of the illness • **deja que las cosas sigan su ~** let matters take their course • **seguimos por la tele el ~ de la carrera** we watched the progress *o* course of the race on TV • **la recuperación del enfermo sigue su ~ normal** the patient is recovering normally • **en ~**: • **el proceso judicial está en ~** the case is under way *o* in progress • **el año en ~** the present year, the current year • **en el ~ de**: • **en el ~ de la entrevista** during the interview, in *o* during the course of the interview • **en el ~ de la vida** in the course of a lifetime • **en el ~ de los años** over the years
5 (*frm*) • **dar ~ a algo**: • **dar ~ a una solicitud** to deal with an application • **estaba dando ~ a las instrucciones recibidas** she was carrying out the instructions she had received • **dio ~ a su indignación** she gave

vent to her anger • **dar libre ~ a algo: dio libre ~ a sus pensamientos** he gave free rein to his thoughts • **dimos libre ~ a la imaginación** we let our imagination run wild
6 (*Com*) • **moneda de ~ legal** legal tender
cursor SM **1** (*Téc*) slide
2 (*Inform*) cursor
curtido ADJ **1** [*cuero*] tanned
2 [*piel*] hardened, leathery; [*cara*] (*por sol*) tanned; (*por intemperie*) weather-beaten
3 (= *experimentado*) • **estar ~ en** to be expert at, be skilled in
SM **1** (= *acto*) tanning
2 (= *cuero*) tanned leather, tanned hides (*pl*)
curtidor SM tanner
curtiduría SF, **curtiembre** SF (*LAm*) tannery
curtir ▸ CONJUG 3a VT **1** [+ *cuero*] to tan
2 [+ *piel*] to tan, bronze
3 (= *acostumbrar*) to harden, inure
VPR **curtirse 1** (*por sol*) to become tanned; (*por intemperie*) to get weather-beaten
2 (= *acostumbrarse*) to become inured (**contra** to)
3 (*LAm*) (= *ensuciarse*) to get o.s. dirty
curul SF (*Col*) (*Pol*) seat (in parliament)
curva SF **1** [*de carretera, camino*] bend ▸ **curva en herradura** hairpin bend
2 (*Mat*) curve ▸ **curva de demanda** (*Com*) demand curve ▸ **curva de indiferencia** indifference curve ▸ **curva de la felicidad** (*hum*) paunch, beer-belly ▸ **curva de nivel** contour line ▸ **curva de rentabilidad** (*Com*) break-even chart
3 curvas* [*de mujer*] vital statistics • **¡tiene unas ~s!** what a body she's got!
curvar ▸ CONJUG 1a VT [+ *material*] to bend; [+ *labios*] to curl
VPR **curvarse** [*material*] to bow; [*estante*] to sag, bend; [*madera*] to warp
curvatura SF curvature ▸ **curvatura terrestre** Earth's curvature
curvilíneo ADJ curved, curvilinear
curvo ADJ **1** (= *curvado*) curved, bent
2 (*And*) (= *estevado*) bow-legged
3 (*Caribe*) (= *zurdo*) left-handed
cusca SF **1** • **hacer la ~ a algn*** to play a dirty trick on sb
2 (*CAm*) (= *coqueta*) flirt
3 (*Méx‡*) (= *puta*) tart*, hooker (*EEUU‡*), whore
cuscha SF (*CAm*) liquor, rum
cuscurrante ADJ crunchy, crisp
cuscurro SM crouton
cuscús SM INV couscous
cusma SF (*Perú*) sleeveless shirt, tunic
cuspa SF (*And*) weeding
cuspar ▸ CONJUG 1a VT (*And*) to weed
cúspide SF **1** (*Anat*) cusp
2 (*Geog*) summit, peak; (*fig*) pinnacle, apex
3 (*Mat*) apex
cusqui SF • **hacer la ~*** to bug*, annoy
custodia SF **1** (= *cuidado*) care, safekeeping, custody • **bajo la ~ de** in the care *o* custody of ▸ **custodia policial** police protection ▸ **custodia preventiva** protective custody
2 (= *escolta*) guard, escort
3 (*Rel*) monstrance
custodiar ▸ CONJUG 1b VT **1** (= *vigilar*) to guard, watch over
2 (= *cuidar de*) to take care of, look after
3 (= *proteger*) [+ *derechos, libertades*] to defend
custodio/a ADJ • **ángel ~** guardian angel
SM/F (= *guardián*) custodian; (*Méx, Perú*) police officer
customizar VT to customize
cususa SF (*CAm*) home-made liquor, home-made rum
CUT SF ABR (*Chile*) = **Central Unitaria de Trabajadores**
cutacha SF (*LAm*) = **cuma**
cutama SF **1** (*Chile*) (= *saco*) bag; (= *alforja*) saddlebag
2 (= *torpe*) clumsy person
cutáneo ADJ cutaneous, skin (*antes de s*)
cutaras SFPL (*CAm, Caribe, Méx*), **cutarras** SFPL (*CAm*) sandals, rough shoes
cúter SM cutter
cutí SM ticking
cutícula SF cuticle
cutis SM INV skin, complexion
cuto ADJ **1** (*And, CAm*) [*persona*] (= *tullido*) maimed, crippled; (= *desdentado*) toothless
2 (*And, CAm*) [*objeto*] damaged, spoiled
3 (*And*) (= *corto*) short
cutre* ADJ **1** [*persona*] (= *tacaño*) mean, stingy; (= *vulgar*) vulgar, coarse
2 [*lugar*] squalid, shabby • **un sitio ~** a dive*, a hole*
3 [*objeto*] tacky*
cutrería* SF **1** [*de persona*] (= *tacañería*) meanness, stinginess; (= *vulgaridad*) vulgarity, coarseness
2 [*de lugar*] (= *miseria*) squalidness, shabbiness • **su bar es una auténtica ~** his bar is a real dive *o* hole*
3 [*de objeto*] • **ese vestido me parece una ~** I think that dress is tacky*
cutter ['kuter] SM (PL: **cutters**) [*de carpintero*] Stanley knife®, razor knife (*EEUU*); (*para papel*) artist's scalpel
cuy, cuye (PL: **cuis** *o* **cuyes**) SM (*LAm*) guinea pig
cuya SF (*Caribe, Cono Sur*) gourd, drinking vessel
cuyano/a* ADJ, SM/F (*Chile*) Argentinian
cuye SM = **cuy**
cuyo ADJ REL **1** [*de persona*] of whom (*frm*), whose; [*de cosa*] of which, whose • **la señora en cuya casa nos hospedábamos** the lady in whose house we were staying • **el asunto ~s detalles conoces** the matter of which you know the details
2 • **en ~ caso** in which case • **por cuya razón** and for this reason
SM †* (= *amante*) lover
cuz EXCL • **¡cuz cuz!** (*dicho a un perro*) here boy!
cuzqueño/a ADJ of/from Cuzco
SM/F native/inhabitant of Cuzco • **los ~s** the people of Cuzco
C.V. SM ABR (= **curriculum vitae**) CV
SMPL ABR (= **caballos de vapor**) HP, h.p.
C y F ABR (= **costo y flete**) CAF, c.a.f., C and F
czar SM = **zar**

Dd

d

D, d [de] SF (= *letra*) D, d

D. ABR **1** (= **Don**) ▹ DON/DOÑA
2 (*Econ*) = **debe**
3 (= **diciembre**) Dec

Da. ABR, **D.ª** ABR (= **Doña**) ▹ DON/DOÑA

dable ADJ possible, feasible • **en lo que sea ~** as far as possible • **no es ~ hacerlo** it is not possible *o* feasible to do it

dabuti‡ ADJ (= *estupendo*) super*, smashing*
ADV • **pasarlo ~** to have a great time

DAC SM ABR (*LAm*) (= **diseño asistido por computador**) CAD

daca†† EXCL hand it over!; ▹ **toma**

dación SF • **~ en pago** (*Jur*) surrender in lieu of foreclosure

dacrón® SM Dacron®

dactilar ADJ • **huellas ~es** fingerprints

dactílico ADJ dactylic

dáctilo SM dactyl

dactilografía SF typing, typewriting

dactilografiar ▹ CONJUG 1c VT to type

dactilógrafo/a SM/F typist

dactilograma SM (*Méx*) fingerprint

dadá SM, **dadaísmo** SM dadaism

dadaísta ADJ Dadaist
SMF Dadaist

dadista SMF (*Méx*) dice player

dadito SM (*Culin*) small cube • **cortar en ~s** to dice

dádiva SF **1** (= *regalo*) gift
2 (= *compensación*) sop

dadivosidad SF generosity, open-handedness

dadivoso ADJ generous, open-handed

dado[1] SM **1** (*en juegos*) die; **dados** dice • **echó** *o* **tiró los ~s** he threw the dice • **jugar a los ~s** to play dice
2 (*Arquit*) dado
3 (*Mec*) block

dado[2] ADJ **1** (= *determinado*) • **en un caso ~** in a given case • **dada su corta edad** in view of his youth • **dadas estas circunstancias** in view of *o* given these circumstances
2 • **ser ~ a algo** to be given to sth • **es muy ~ a discutir** he is much given to arguing
3 • MODISMO: • **ir ~***: • **si crees que te voy a pagar las vacaciones, vas ~** if you think I'm going to pay for your holidays, you've another think coming!
4 • **~ que** (+ *subjun*) provided that, so long as; (+ *indic*) given that

dador(a) SM/F **1** (*Com*) drawer
2 [*de carta*] bearer
3 (*Naipes*) dealer

Dafne SF Daphne

daga SF **1** (= *espada corta*) dagger
2 (*Caribe*) (= *machete*) machete

dagazo SM (*Caribe, Méx*) stab wound

daguerrotipo SM daguerreotype

daifa SF **1** (= *querida*) mistress, concubine
2 (= *prostituta*) prostitute

daiquiri SM, **daiquirí** SM daiquiri

dalia SF dahlia

Dalila SF Delilah

daliniano ADJ Daliesque

dallar ▹ CONJUG 1a VT to scythe, mow with a scythe

dalle SM scythe

Dalmacia SF Dalmatia

dálmata SMF **1** (= *persona*) Dalmatian
2 (= *perro*) dalmatian, dalmatian dog
ADJ Dalmatian

daltónico ADJ, **daltoniano** ADJ colour-blind, color-blind (*EEUU*)

daltonismo SM colour blindness, color blindness (*EEUU*)

dama SF **1** (= *señora*) lady • **~s y caballeros** ladies and gentlemen • **primera ~** (*Teat*) leading lady; (*Pol*) First Lady (*EEUU*) ▸ **dama de compañía** (*LAm*) lady companion ▸ **la Dama de Hierro** the Iron Lady ▸ **dama de honor** [*de reina*] lady-in-waiting; [*de novia*] bridesmaid ▸ **dama de noche** night jasmine ▸ **dama joven** (*Teat*) ingénue ▸ **dama regidora** carnival queen
2 (= *mujer noble*) lady
3 (= *amante*) lady, mistress • **el poeta y su ~** the poet and his lady *o* mistress
4 (= *pieza*) (*Ajedrez, Naipes*) queen; (*Damas*) king
5 damas (*juego*) draughts, checkers (*EEUU*)

damajuana SF, **damasana** (*LAm*) SF demijohn

Damasco SM Damascus

damasco SM **1** (= *tela*) damask
2 (= *ciruela*) damson
3 (*LAm*) (= *árbol*) apricot tree; (= *albaricoque*) apricot

damasquinado ADJ [*espada, metal*] damascene
SM damascene, damascene work

damasquinar ▹ CONJUG 1a VT to damascene, damask

damasquino ADJ **1** [*espada, metal*] damascene, damask
2 (*de Damasco*) Damascene

damero SM **1** (= *pasatiempo*) *type of crossword*
2 (= *tablero*) draughtboard, checkerboard (*EEUU*)

damesana SF (*LAm*) demijohn

damisela SF (*Hist*) damsel; (*pey*) courtesan, prostitute

damita SF (*CAm*) young lady

damnificado/a SM/F victim

damnificar ▹ CONJUG 1g VT [+ *persona*] to injure, harm; [+ *cosa*] to damage

Damocles SM Damocles

dandi, dandy SM dandy, fop
ADJ INV • **estilo ~** dandy style

dandismo SM foppishness, foppish ways

danés/esa ADJ Danish
SM/F **1** (= *persona*) Dane
2 (= *perro*) (*tb* **gran danés**) Great Dane
SM (= *idioma*) Danish

Daniel SM Daniel

danta SF (*LAm*) **1** (= *tapir*) tapir
2 (= *anta*) elk, moose

Dante SM Dante

dantesco ADJ **1** (*Literat*) of Dante, relating to Dante • **la obra dantesca** Dante's works
2 (= *horrible*) nightmarish • **un espectáculo ~** a nightmarish sight

dantzari [dan'sari] SMF *Basque folk-dancer*

Danubio SM Danube

danza SF **1** (= *arte*) dance ▸ **danza contemporánea** contemporary dance
2 (= *baile*) dance • MODISMO: • **siempre está en ~** he's always on the go* ▸ **danza de apareamiento** courtship dance, mating display ▸ **danza de espadas** sword dance ▸ **danza de figuras** square dance ▸ **danza de la muerte** dance of death, danse macabre ▸ **danza de los siete velos** dance of the seven veils ▸ **danza del vientre** belly dance ▸ **danza de salón** ballroom dancing ▸ **danza guerrera** war dance ▸ **danza macabra** = **danza de la muerte**
3* (= *negocio sucio*) shady affair; (= *lío*) mess • **meterse en la ~** to get caught up in a shady affair
4* (*jaleo*) row, rumpus* • **armar una ~** to kick up a row *o* rumpus* • MODISMO: • **no metas los perros en ~** let sleeping dogs lie

danzante/a SM/F **1** (= *bailarín*) dancer
2* (= *persona activa*) live wire; (= *entrometido*) busybody; (= *zascandil*) scatterbrain, featherbrain (*EEUU*)

danzar ▹ CONJUG 1f VI **1** (= *bailar*) to dance • MODISMO: • **llevo toda la mañana danzando*** I've been on the go all morning*
2* (= *entrometerse*) to meddle
VT to dance

danzarín/ina ADJ (= *nervioso*) jumpy
SM/F **1** (= *bailarín*) dancer • **danzarina del vientre** belly dancer
2 = **danzante**

dañado ADJ **1** [*edificio, pelo, fruta*] damaged
2 [*persona*] twisted, perverted

dañar ▹ CONJUG 1a VT **1** [+ *objeto, pelo, piel, salud*] to damage, harm • **el alcohol le ha dañado el hígado** alcohol has damaged his liver • **la recesión ha dañado el tejido social** the recession has damaged the social fabric • MODISMO: • **~ la vista**: • **es tan feo que daña la vista** it's an eyesore
2 [+ *cosecha*] to damage, spoil
3 [+ *reputación, carrera, proyecto*] to damage, harm • **es un intento de ~ su imagen pública** it's an attempt to damage *o* harm his public image
VPR **dañarse 1** (= *hacerse daño*) to be hurt, be injured • **el ciclista se dañó al caer** the cyclist was hurt *o* injured when he fell off • **se dañó el brazo escalando** she hurt *o* injured her arm while climbing
2 [*objeto*] to be damaged • **los cimientos no llegaron a ~se en el incendio** the foundations were not damaged in the fire
3 [*cosecha*] to be damaged, be spoiled

dañinear ▹ CONJUG 1a (*Cono Sur*) VT
1 = **dañar**
2 (= *robar*) to steal

dañino/a ADJ **1** (*para la salud*) harmful

• **animales ~s** vermin (*sing*), pests
2 (*para el desarrollo de algo*) damaging (**para** to)
(SM/F) (*Cono Sur*) thief
daño (SM) **1** (*a algo*) damage, harm • **el granizo ha producido grandes ~s a los cultivos** the hail has caused extensive damage to crops • **estas medidas han ocasionado un gran ~ a la industria** these measures have caused a great deal of harm to the industry • **~s y perjuicios** damages ▸ **daños colaterales** collateral damage
2 (*a alguien*) (*físico, emocional*) pain; (*económico*) harm • **¡ay, qué ~!** ow, that hurts! • **en ~ de** (*frm*) to the detriment of • **por mi ~** (*frm*) to my cost • **causar** *o* **hacer ~ a algn** to hurt sb • **¡suelta, que me haces ~!** let go, you're hurting me! • **el ajo me hace ~** garlic doesn't agree with me, garlic disagrees with me • **tanta comida picante hace ~ al estómago** all that spicy food is bad for the stomach • **hacerse ~** to hurt o.s. • **¿te has hecho ~?** have you hurt yourself? • **se hizo ~ en el pie** he hurt his foot ▸ **daños corporales** physical injury (*sing*)
3 (*Med*) (= *mal*) problem, trouble • **los médicos no saben dónde está el ~** the doctors can't tell where the problem *o* trouble is
4 (*LAm*) (= *maleficio*) spell, curse
dañoso (ADJ) harmful
DAO (SM ABR) (= **diseño asistido por ordenador**) CAD

dar

VERBO TRANSITIVO
VERBO INTRANSITIVO
VERBO PRONOMINAL

▷ CONJUG 1q

*Para las expresiones **dar importancia, dar ejemplo, dar las gracias, dar clases, dar a conocer, dar a entender, darse prisa**, ver la otra entrada.*

(VERBO TRANSITIVO)
1 (= *entregar, conceder*) [+ *objeto, mensaje, permiso*] to give; [+ *naipes*] to deal (out); [+ *noticias*] to give, tell • **le dio un bocadillo a su hijo** he gave his son a sandwich • **se lo di a Blanca** I gave it to Blanca • **me dieron un diploma por mi buen comportamiento** I was given a diploma for good conduct • **le dieron el primer premio** he was awarded *o* given first prize • **déme dos kilos** I'll have two kilos, two kilos, please • **ir dando cuerda** to pay out rope • **dar los buenos días a algn** to say good morning to sb, say hello to sb
2 (= *realizar*) [+ *paliza*] to give; [+ *paso*] to take • **dar un alarido** to shriek • **dar una bofetada a algn** to slap sb • **dar un golpe a algn** to hit sb • **dio un golpe en la mesa** he banged on the table • **dar un grito** to let out a cry, give a cry • **dar un paseo** to go for a walk, take a walk • **dar un suspiro** to heave *o* give a sigh, sigh
3 (= *celebrar*) [+ *fiesta*] to have, throw • **la embajada dará una recepción** the embassy will hold a reception
4 (= *encender*) [+ *luz*] to turn on • **¿has dado el gas?** have you turned on the gas?
5 (= *presentar*) [+ *obra de teatro*] to perform, put on; [+ *película*] to show, screen • **dan una película de Almodóvar** there's an Almodóvar film on, they're showing *o* screening an Almodóvar film • **¿qué dan hoy en la tele?** what's on TV tonight?
6 (= *hacer sonar*) [*reloj*] to strike • **el reloj dio las tres** the clock struck three • **ya han dado las ocho** it's past *o* gone eight o'clock
7 (= *producir*) [+ *fruto*] to bear; [+ *ganancias, intereses*] to yield • **dar flores** to flower • **este negocio da mucho dinero** there's a lot of money in this business • **una inversión que da un 7% de interés** an investment that pays *o* yields 7% interest
8 (= *tener como resultado*) • **el cálculo dio 99** the sum worked out at 99 • **el atleta dio positivo en el control antidoping** the athlete tested positive for drugs
9 (= *hacer sentir*) [+ *placer*] to give • **me dio mucha alegría verla** I was very pleased to see her • **las babosas me dan asco** I find slugs disgusting *o* revolting • **este jersey me da demasiado calor** this jumper is too hot, I'm too hot in this jumper • **da gusto hablar con él** he's really nice to talk to • **tu padre me da miedo** I'm scared *o* frightened of your father • **me da pena tener que tirarlo** it's a pity to have to throw it away • **el vino me da sueño** wine makes me sleepy
10* (= *fastidiar*) to ruin • **vinieron a visitarme y me dieron la tarde** they came to visit and ruined my afternoon • **¡me estás dando las vacaciones!** you're ruining the holiday for me!
11 dar por (= *considerar*) to consider • **doy el asunto por concluido** I consider the matter settled, I regard the matter as settled • **le dieron por desaparecido** they gave him up for lost • **doy el dinero por bien empleado** I consider it money well spent • **lo daba por seguro** he was sure *o* certain of it • **lo podemos dar por terminado** we can consider it finished
12 • MODISMOS: • **¡y dale!** (= *¡otra vez!*) not again! • **estar/seguir dale que dale** *o* **dale que te pego** *o* (*LAm*) **dale y dale** to go/keep on and on • **la vecina está dale que dale al piano** our neighbour is pounding away at the piano • **estoy dale que dale a este problema** I've been bashing away at this problem* • **a mí no me la das*** you can't fool me • **¡ahí te las den todas!*** you just couldn't care less! • **por si vienen mal dadas** in case of emergency; (*ahorrar*) for a rainy day • **para dar y tomar**: • **tenemos botellas para dar y tomar** we've got loads *o* stacks of bottles • **aquí hay basura para dar y tomar** there's tons of rubbish here • **me da que ...** I have a feeling (that)... • **me da que no va a venir** I have a feeling (that) he's not going to come
(VERBO INTRANSITIVO)
1 (= *entregar*) to give • **dame, yo te lo arreglo** give it here, I'll fix it for you • REFRÁN: • **a quien dan no escoge** beggars can't be choosers
2 (= *entrar*) • **me dieron ganas de vomitar** I felt like being sick • **si te da un mareo siéntate** if you feel giddy, sit down • **le dio un fuerte dolor en el costado** he felt a sudden sharp pain in his side • **le dio un infarto** he had a heart attack
3 (= *importar*) • **¡qué más da!** • **¡da igual!** it doesn't matter!, never mind! • **¿qué más te da?** what does it matter to you? • **¿qué más da un sitio que otro?** surely one place is as good as another!, it doesn't make any difference which place we choose • **lo mismo da** it makes no difference *o* odds • **me da igual** • **lo mismo me da** • **tanto me da** it's all the same to me, I don't mind
4 (*seguido de preposición*) **dar a** (= *estar orientado*) [*cuarto, ventana*] to look out onto, overlook; [*fachada*] to face • **mi habitación da al jardín** my room looks out onto *o* overlooks the garden
darle a (= *hacer funcionar*) [+ *botón*] to press; (= *golpear*) to hit; [+ *balón*] to kick • **dale a la tecla roja** hit *o* press the red key • **darle a la bomba** to pump, work the pump • **dale más fuerte a la bomba** pump harder • **¡dale!** hit him! • **no es capaz de darle al balón de cabeza** he can't head the ball
dar con (= *encontrar*) [+ *persona*] to find; [+ *idea, solución*] to hit on, come up with • **dimos con él dos horas más tarde** we found him two hours later • **al final di con la solución** I finally hit on the solution, I finally came up with the solution • **no doy con el nombre** I can't think of the name • **dar consigo en** to end up in • **dio consigo en la cárcel** he ended up in jail
dar contra (= *golpear*) to hit • **el barco dio contra el puente** the ship hit the bridge
dar de • **dar de palos a algn** to give sb a beating • **dar de puñetazos a algn** to punch sb • **dar de barniz a algo** to varnish sth • **dar de beber a algn** to give sb something to drink • **dar de comer a algn** to feed sb • **dar de sí** [*comida, bebida*] to go a long way • **lo que cada uno puede dar de sí** what each person can contribute
dar en [+ *blanco, suelo*] to hit; [+ *solución*] to hit on, come up with • **el sol me da en la cara** the sun is in my eyes • **dar en hacer algo** to take to doing sth • **han dado en llamarle Boko** they've taken to calling him Boko
darle a algn por hacer algo • **le ha dado por no venir a clase** he has taken to cutting classes • **les dio por venir a vernos** they took it into their heads to come and see us • **últimamente le ha dado por el golf** he's taken up golf lately • **al chico le daba por dormirse en la clase** the boy was always falling asleep in class • **la casa que a alguien le dio por llamar Miramar** the house that someone had the bright idea of calling Miramar
dar para (= *ser suficiente*) to be enough for • **con eso da para cuatro personas** this is enough for four people • **mi pobre cabeza no da para más hoy** I don't think my poor head can take any more today
5 dar que hablar to set people talking • **una película que da en qué pensar** a thought-provoking film, a film which gives you a lot to think about
(VERBO PRONOMINAL) **darse**
1 (= *entregarse*) to give in
2 (= *golpearse*) to hit o.s. • **¿dónde te has dado?** where did you hit yourself? • **darse con** *o* **contra** to bump into • **me he dado contra la esquina del armario** I bumped into the edge of the cupboard; ▷ **nariz**
3 (= *ocurrir*) [*suceso*] to happen • **si se da el caso** if that happens • **se han dado muchos casos** there have been a lot of cases • **se dio una situación extraña** a strange situation arose
4 (= *crecer*) to grow • **esa planta no se da en el sur** that plant doesn't grow in the south • **los pepinos se dan bien en esta tierra** cucumbers grow well on this land • **el cultivo se da bien este año** the crop is doing well this year
5 (*seguido de preposición*) **darse a** to take to • **darse a la bebida** to take to drink, start drinking
darse de sí [*cuero, tela*] to give, stretch
dárselas de to make o.s. out to be • **se las da de experto** he makes himself out to be an expert • **¡no te las des de listo!** stop acting clever!
darse por • **no se dio por aludido** he didn't take the hint • **darse por ofendido** to take offence • **darse por perdido** to give o.s. up for lost • **con llegar me doy por satisfecho** I'll be quite happy if we just get there • **me doy**

d

por vencido I give up, I give in
6 **dársele bien a algn** • **se me dan bien las ciencias** I'm good at science • **se le dan muy bien las matemáticas** she's very good at maths
dársele mal a algn • **se me dan muy mal los idiomas** I'm very bad at languages • **no se me da mal** I'm not doing too badly at it
7 • MODISMOS: • **no se me da un higo** *o* **bledo** *o* **rábano*** I don't care two hoots* • **dársela (con queso) a algn*** to fool sb, put one over on sb*

d

Dardanelos (SMPL) Dardanelles
dardo (SM) dart • **jugar a los ~s** to play darts
dares* (SMPL) • **~ y tomares** arguments, bickering (*sing*) • **andar en ~ y tomares con algn** to bicker with sb, squabble with sb
Darío (SM) Darius
dársena (SF) 1 (*Náut*) dock ▸ **dársena de marea** tidal basin
2 (*Aut*) bus shelter
darviniano (ADJ), **darwiniano** (ADJ) Darwinian
darvinismo (SM), **darwinismo** (SM) Darwinism
darvinista (ADJ), (SMF), **darwinista** (ADJ), (SMF) Darwinian
data (SF) 1 (= *fecha*) date and place (*on document*) • **es de larga ~** it is long-established, it goes back a long way
2 (*Com*) item
datable (ADJ) datable, that can be dated
datación (SF) date, dating • **de difícil ~** hard to date ▸ **datación con carbono** carbon dating
datáfono (SM) dataphone
datar ▸ CONJUG 1a (VT) to date
(VI) • **~ de** to date from, date back to • **esto data de muy atrás** this goes a long way back
datero* (SM) (*Cono Sur*) tipster
dátil (SM) 1 (*Bot*) date
2 (*Zool*) date mussel
3 **dátiles‡** (= *dedos*) fingers
datilera (SF) date palm
dativo (SM) (*Ling*) dative
dato (SM) 1 (= *información*) piece of information • **un ~ interesante** an interesting fact *o* piece of information • **no tenemos todos los ~s** we don't have all the facts • **otro ~ que tener en cuenta es ...** another thing to bear in mind is ... ▸ **datos de entrada** input data ▸ **datos de salida** output data ▸ **datos estadísticos** statistics ▸ **datos móviles** mobile data ▸ **datos personales** personal details, particulars
2 (*Mat*) datum
David (SM) David
dB (ABR) (= **decibelio**) dB
d.C. (ABR) (= **después de Cristo**) AD
dcha. (ABR) (= **derecha**) R
d. de C. (ABR) (= **después de Cristo**) AD
DDT (SM ABR) (= **diclorodifeniltricloroetano**) DDT

de

PREPOSITION

1 (*relación*) of • **las calles de Madrid** the streets of Madrid • **el alcalde de Valencia** the mayor of Valencia • **cabo de Buena Esperanza** Cape of Good Hope • **la ciudad de Madrid** the city of Madrid • **en el mes de agosto** in the month of August • **un libro de consulta** a reference book • **un millón de euros** a million euros • **la carretera de Valencia** the Valencia road, the road to Valencia • **el interés del préstamo** the interest on the loan • **la llave de mi cuarto** the key to my room • **en el día de hoy** today • **tuvieron la desgracia de perder el partido** they were unlucky enough to lose the match • **ya era hora de que vinieses** it's about time you got here • **el hecho de que yo no supiera nada** the fact that I didn't know anything about it
2 (*pertenencia*) • **la casa de Isabel** Isabel's house • **el coche de mi amigo** my friend's car • **un familiar de mi vecina** a relative of my neighbour's • **los coches de mis amigos** my friends' cars • **el vestuario de las actrices** the actresses' dressing room • **la señora de Pérez** Pérez's wife, Mrs Pérez • **es de ellos** it's theirs • **esa contestación es muy de ella** that answer is typical of her
3 (*característica, material*) • **una cadena de oro** a gold chain • **no es de oro** it's not gold • **una puerta de cristal** a glass door • **una cocina de gas** a gas cooker • **este modelo es de electricidad** this model uses electricity, this is an electric model • **ropa de buena calidad** good-quality clothes • **un billete de primera clase** a first-class ticket • **la niña de pelo largo** the girl with the long hair • **ese tío del sombrero** that chap with *o* in the hat • **pintado de rojo** painted red • **lo tengo de varios colores distintos** I have it in several different colours
4 (*contenido*) • **una caja de bombones** a box of chocolates • **una copa de vino** (*llena*) a glass of wine; (*vacía*) a wine glass • **una bolsita de té** a tea bag • **estaba hecha un saco de nervios** she was a bundle of nerves
5 (*origen, distancia, espacio temporal*) from • **soy de Galicia** I'm from Galicia • **Julia no es de aquí** Julia is not from round here • **los de Madrid son los mejores** the ones from Madrid are the best, the Madrid ones are the best • **es de buena familia** he's from a good family • **vuelo 507 (procedente) de Londres** flight 507 from London • **vive a 20km de Madrid** she lives 20km from Madrid • **aléjate del fuego** move away from the fire • **marcó un gol a dos minutos del final del partido** he scored two minutes from the end of the match • **el tren de Santiago** the Santiago train • **el avión pasó a muy poca altura del suelo** the plane flew by at very low altitude • **salir del cine** to come out of the cinema
de ... a ... • **vivió de 1898 a 1937** he lived from 1898 to 1937 • **de mi casa a la suya hay 5km** it is 5km from my house to his • **de mayo a julio** from May to July • **del 15 al 30** from the 15th to the 30th
6 (*causa*) • **murió de viejo** he died from old age • **me dolían los pies de tanto andar** my feet were sore from all that walking • **de puro cansado** out of sheer tiredness • **no podía moverse de miedo** he was rigid with fear • **estar loco de alegría** to be wild with joy • **saltar de alegría** to jump for joy
7 (*manera*) • **lo derribó de un solo puñetazo** he felled him with a single blow • **se puso a mi lado de un salto** he jumped to my side • **se lo bebió de un trago** he drank it all down in one go
de ... en ... • **iban entrando de dos en dos** they came in two by two • **bajó la escalera de tres en tres** he came down the stairs three at a time • **de puerta en puerta** from door to door
8 (*= respecto de*) • **estar mejor de salud** to be in better health, be better • **es fuerte de brazos** he has strong arms • **paralizado de las dos piernas** paralysed in both legs • **es muy estrecho de hombros** he doesn't have very broad shoulders
9 (*tema*) about • **un libro de biología** a biology book, a book on *o* about biology • **hablaba de política** he was talking about politics • **no sé nada de él** I don't know anything about him • **una clase de francés** a French class
10 (*uso*) • **máquina de coser** sewing machine • **goma de mascar** chewing gum
11 (*cantidad, medida, valor*) • **un chico de quince años** a fifteen-year-old boy • **un viaje de dos días** a two-day journey • **un embarazo de siete meses** a seven-month pregnancy • **una moneda de 5 pesos** a 5-peso coin • **tiene un metro de alto** it's a metre high
12 (*con horas y fechas*) • **a las siete de la mañana** at seven o'clock in the morning, at seven a.m. • **son las dos de la tarde** it's two o'clock in the afternoon, it's two p.m. • **muy de mañana** very early in the morning • **el 3 de mayo** 3 May (*leído May the third o the third of May*)
13 (*tiempo*) • **de día** during the day(time) • **de noche** at night • **de niño** as a child • **de mayor voy a ser médico** when I grow up I'm going to be a doctor
14 (*proporción*) • **tres de cada cuatro** three out of every four
15 (*uso partitivo*) of • **uno de nosotros** one of us • **comió un poco de pastel** she ate a bit of cake • **¡había una de gente!*** there were loads of people there!*
16 (*autoría*) by • **un libro de Cela** a book by Cela, a book of Cela's • **las películas de Almodóvar** Almodóvar's films
17 (*como complemento agente*) by • **fue amado de todos** he was loved by all • **el rey entró seguido de su séquito** the king entered, followed by his entourage • **tiene dos hijos de su primera mujer** he has two children by his first wife
18 (*en aposición a sustantivos o adjetivos*) • **el bueno/pobre de Pedro** good/poor old Pedro • **el imbécil de Fernández** that idiot Fernández • **es un encanto de persona** he's a lovely person
19 (*en comparaciones*) than • **es más difícil de lo que creía** it's more difficult than I thought • **más/menos de siete** more/less than seven • **más de 500 personas** more than *o* over 500 people
20 (*con superlativos*) in • **el peor alumno de la clase** the worst pupil in the class • **el más caro de la tienda/mundo** the most expensive in the shop/world • **es el coche más caro del mercado** it's the dearest car on the market
21 (*+ infin*) • **un problema fácil de resolver** an easily solved problem • **un libro agradable de leer** a nice book to read
ser de (+ *infin*) • **es de admirar su lealtad** his loyalty is admirable • **es de esperar que recibamos una pronta respuesta** it is to be hoped that we receive a prompt reply • **sería de desear que actualizaran su información** it would be desirable for them to update their information
22 (*dependiente de formas verbales*) • **la acusaban de hipócrita** they accused her of being a hypocrite • **colmar de elogios a algn** to shower praise on sb • **se dio cuenta de que lo sabía** she realized (that) she knew it • **de esto se deduce que ...** from this it can be deduced that ... • **disfrutar de la vida** to enjoy life • **¿qué esperabas de él?** what did you expect from him? • **limpiar algo de polvo** to dust sth • **llenar algo de algo** to fill sth with sth • **se sirvió de sus amigos para salir de un mal trago** he turned to his friends to help him through a difficult patch • **trabaja de camarero** he works as a waiter • **lo uso de despensa** I use it as a pantry • **vestido de azul** dressed in blue

23 (*uso condicional*) if • **de ser posible** if possible • **de haberlo sabido no habría venido** if I had known, I wouldn't have come • **de resultar esto así** if this turns out to be true • **de no ser así** if it were not so, were it not so • **de no** (*LAm*) (= *si no*) otherwise

dé ▹ **dar**

deambulador SM walking frame, Zimmer®

deambular ▹ CONJUG 1a VI to wander (about)

deambulatorio SM (*Rel*) ambulatory

deán SM (*Rel*) dean

debacle SF debacle, disaster

debajo ADV **1** (= *en la parte de abajo*) underneath • **antes de pintar la silla, pon un periódico ~** before you paint the chair, put some newspaper underneath • **el libro que está ~** the book underneath • **solo lleva una camiseta (por) ~** he's only got a T-shirt on underneath • **ahí ~** down there • **ahí ~ hay un árbol** there's a tree down there • **de ~:** • **la capa de ~ no se ve** you can't see the layer underneath *o* beneath • **el piso de ~** the flat below
2 • **~ de** under • **~ de este árbol** under *o* beneath this tree • **vive en el piso ~ del nuestro** he lives in the flat below ours • **pasamos (por) ~ del puente** we went under *o* underneath the bridge • **me gusta nadar (por) ~ del agua** I like swimming underwater *o* under the water • **el Barcelona sigue por ~ del Atlético** Barcelona is still (trailing) behind Atlético • **el rango por ~ del de capitán** the rank below that of captain • **por ~ de la media** below average • **trabajan por ~ de sus posibilidades** they are working below their capabilities

debate SM debate • **un ~ parlamentario** a parliamentary debate • **no entro en el ~ de si es bueno o malo** I won't enter into the debate about whether it is good or bad • **tuvimos un pequeño ~ sobre la película** we had a little discussion *o* debate about the film • **conceptos como el marxismo están a ~** concepts like Marxism are being re-evaluated • **poner** *o* **sacar un tema a ~** to raise an issue for discussion

debatir ▹ CONJUG 3a VT **1** [+ *ley, presupuesto*] to debate
2 [+ *punto de vista, problema*] to discuss, debate
VPR **debatirse 1** (= *luchar*) to struggle • **~se entre la vida y la muerte** to be fighting for one's life
2 (= *forcejear*) to writhe

debe SM (*en cuenta*) debit side • **asentar algo al ~ de algn** to debit sth to sb • **~ y haber** debit and credit

debelador(a) SM/F conqueror

debelar ▹ CONJUG 1a VT to conquer

deber ▹ CONJUG 2a VT [+ *dinero, explicación, respeto*] to owe • **me debes cinco dólares** you owe me five dollars • **¿qué le debo?** (*en bares, tiendas*) how much (is it)?, how much do I owe you? • **me deben muchos favores** they owe me a lot of favours • **te debo una disculpa** I owe you an apology • **el teatro español debe mucho a Buero Vallejo** Spanish theatre owes a lot to Buero Vallejo • **todo lo que he conseguido se lo debo a mi padre** I have my father to thank for everything I have achieved, I owe everything I have achieved to my father
VI **1** (+ *infin*) (*obligación*) • **debo intentar verla** I must try to see her • **no debes preocuparte** you mustn't worry • **no debes comer tanto** you shouldn't eat so much • **como debe ser** as it ought to *o* should be • **~ía cambiarse cada mes** it ought to *o* should be changed every month • **habrías debido traerlo** you ought to have *o* should have brought it • **no ~ías haberla dejado sola** you shouldn't have left her alone • **debíamos haber salido ayer** we were to have *o* should have left yesterday
2 (+ *infin*) (*suposición*) • **debe (de) ser brasileño** he must be a Brazilian • **debe (de) hacer mucho frío allí** it must be very cold there • **debe (de) ser así** it must be like that, that's how it must be • **he debido (de) perderlo** I must have lost it • **no debe (de) ser muy caro** it can't be very dear • **no debe (de) tener mucho dinero** he can't have much money • **no debía (de) tener más de dieciocho años** she couldn't have been more than eighteen • **no debía (de) andar lejos de los 200.000 libros** it can't have been far off 200,000 books • **no debía (de) quedar ninguno vivo** it is unlikely that any survived
VPR **deberse 1** • **~se a algo** (= *tener por causa*) to be due to sth • **el retraso se debió a una huelga** the delay was due to a strike • **el accidente se debió al mal tiempo** the accident was caused by the bad weather • **se debe a que no hay carbón** it is because (of the fact that) there's no coal • **puede ~se a que ...** it may be because ... • **¿a qué se debe esto?** what is the reason for this?, why is this? • **¿a qué se debe el aumento?** what is the reason for the increase? • **no se sabe realmente a qué se debe la inestabilidad** we don't really know the reason for the instability
2 • **~se a algn** (= *tener obligación hacia*) to have a duty to sb • **yo me debo a mis lectores** I have a duty to my readers • **se debe a su pueblo** he has a duty to his people
SM **1** (= *obligación*) duty • **mi ~ es advertir al Gobierno** it's my duty to warn the Government • **era mi ~ de hijo** it was my duty as a son • **es un ~ para con la comunidad** it's a duty to the community • **nunca hubiera faltado a su ~** he would never have failed in *o* to do his duty • **cumplir con un ~** to perform a duty, carry out a duty • **últimos ~es** last rites ▸ **deber ciudadano** civic duty
2 (= *deuda*) debt
3 deberes (*Escol*) homework (*sing*) • **~es de francés** French homework • **hacer los ~es del colegio** to do one's homework • **el profe me ha puesto unos ~es** the teacher has set me some homework

debidamente ADV [*ajustar, comer*] properly; [*cumplimentar*] duly • **si te comportas ~** if you behave properly • **un documento ~ redactado** a properly drawn up document

debido ADJ **1** (= *adecuado*) due, proper • **a su ~ tiempo** in due course • **con el ~ respeto** with all due respect • **con las debidas precauciones** with all due *o* the necessary precautions • **en debida forma** duly • **como es ~** as is (only) right and proper • **no lo hizo como es ~** he didn't do it properly • **una fiesta como es ~** a proper *o* real party • **un padre como es ~ no haría eso** a true father would not do that • **más de lo ~** more than necessary
2 • **~ a** owing to, because of • **~ a ello** owing to *o* because of this • **~ a la falta de agua** owing to *o* because of the water shortage • **~ a que** owing to *o* because of the fact that

débil ADJ **1** [*persona*] (*gen*) weak; (*extremadamente*) feeble; (*por mala salud o avanzada edad*) frail • **se encuentra un poco ~ de salud** his health is rather frail, he is in rather poor health
2 [*carácter*] weak; [*esfuerzo*] feeble, half-hearted
3 (= *poco intenso*) [*voz, ruido*] faint; [*luz*] dim
SMF • **es un ~ mental** he's a bit mentally deficient; ▹ **económicamente**

debilidad SF **1** (= *falta de fuerzas*) (*gen*) weakness; (*extrema*) feebleness; (*por mala salud o avanzada edad*) frailty ▸ **debilidad senil** senility
2 [*de carácter*] weakness; [*de esfuerzo*] feebleness, half-heartedness • **la ~ de su fuerza de voluntad** his lack of willpower
3 (= *poca intensidad*) [*de voz, ruido*] faintness; [*de luz*] dimness
4 (= *inclinación*) • **los niños son mi ~** I love *o* adore children • **tengo ~ por el chocolate** I have a weakness for chocolate • **tener ~ por algn** to have a soft spot for sb

debilitación SF weakening, debilitation

debilitado ADJ (*Med*) [*persona*] run-down; [*sistema inmunológico*] weakened, damaged • **mi madre tiene la salud muy debilitada** my mother is in very poor health

debilitador ADJ, **debilitante** ADJ debilitating

debilitamiento SM = **debilitación**

debilitar ▹ CONJUG 1a VT **1** (*Med*) [+ *persona, sistema inmunológico*] to weaken, debilitate; [+ *salud*] to weaken
2 [+ *resistencia*] to weaken, impair
VPR **debilitarse 1** [*persona*] to grow weaker, weaken
2 [*voz, luz*] to grow *o* become fainter

débilmente ADV [*sonreír, golpear, moverse*] weakly; [*protestar, quejarse*] half-heartedly; [*lucir, brillar*] dimly

debitar ▹ CONJUG 1a VT (*Com*) to debit

débito SM **1** (*Com*) (= *debe*) debit; (= *deuda*) debt ▸ **débito directo** (*LAm*) (*Com*) direct debit ▸ **débitos varios** (*LAm*) [*de hotel*] sundries
2 ▸ **débito conyugal** conjugal duty, marital duty

debocar* ▹ CONJUG 1g VT, VI (*LAm*) to vomit, throw up

Débora SF Deborah

debú SM (PL: **debús**), **debut** [de'βu] SM (PL: **debuts**) début

debutante ADJ novice (*antes de s*) • **jugador ~** new player, new cap
SMF **1** (= *principiante*) beginner; (*en sociedad*) debutante
2 (*Dep*) new player • **el ~ marcó en el minuto 29** the new player scored in the 29th minute (of his first match)

debutar ▹ CONJUG 1a VI to make one's debut

década SF **1** (= *decenio*) decade • **la ~ de los noventa** the nineties
2 (= *serie*) set of ten, series of ten

decadencia SF (= *proceso*) decline, decay; (= *estado*) decadence • **estar en franca ~** to be in full decline • **caer en ~** to fall into decline

decadente ADJ [*moral, sociedad*] decadent; [*imperio, salud*] declining

decaer ▹ CONJUG 2n VI **1** [*imperio, país*] to decline • **desde que cerraron la fábrica el pueblo ha decaído** since they closed the factory the town has gone downhill
2 (= *disminuir*) [*entusiasmo, interés*] to wane, fade (away); [*esperanzas*] to fade • **su ánimo decayó tras la muerte de su padre** he lost heart after his father's death • **¡ánimo, que no decaiga!** bear up, don't lose heart! • **¡que no decaiga la fiesta!** come on, let's keep the party going!
3 (= *empeorar*) [*salud*] to fail, decline; [*enfermo*] to deteriorate, fail
4 (*Com*) [*demanda*] to fall off; [*calidad*] to decline, fall off

5 • **~ en algo: ha decaído en belleza** her beauty has faded • **su fuerza dramática decae en intensidad al final** its dramatic force declines in intensity at the end
6 (*Náut*) to drift, drift off course

decagramo SM decagram

decaído ADJ down, low • **estar ~** to be down *o* low

decaimiento SM **1** (= *decadencia*) decline, decay
2 (= *empeoramiento*) [*de salud*] weakening; [*de ánimo*] discouragement
3 (*Com*) falling-off

decalaje SM shift of time, time lag

decalitro SM decalitre, decaliter (EEUU)

decálogo SM decalogue

decámetro SM decametre, decameter (EEUU)

decanato SM **1** (= *cargo*) deanship
2 (= *despacho*) dean's office

decano/a SM/F **1** (*Univ*) dean
2 [*de junta, grupo*] (= *de mayor edad*) senior member; (= *de más antigüedad*) doyen/doyenne

decantación SF **1** (*Téc*) decanting, decantation (*frm*)
2 (= *preferencia*) leaning (**hacia** towards)

decantamiento SM leaning

decantar[1] ▹ CONJUG 1a VT [+ *vino*] to decant; [+ *líquido*] to pour off
VPR **decantarse** • **~se hacia algo** to move towards sth, evolve in the direction of sth • **~se por algo/algn** to opt for sth/sb, choose sth/sb • **~se por hacer algo** to opt to do sth, choose to do sth

decantar[2] ▹ CONJUG 1a VT to praise • **el tan decantado edificio** (*iró*) this much-vaunted building

decapado SM [*de pintura*] stripping

decapante SM [*de pintura*] paint stripper

decapar ▹ CONJUG 1a VT [+ *pintura, barniz*] to strip

decapitar ▹ CONJUG 1a VT to behead, decapitate

decasílabo ADJ decasyllabic, ten-syllable
SM decasyllable

decatlón SM decathlon

deceleración SF deceleration

decena SF **1** (= *diez*) • **una ~ de barcos** (= *diez*) ten ships; (= *aproximadamente diez*) some *o* about ten ships • **~s de miles de manifestantes** tens of thousands of demonstrators
2 decenas (*Mat*) tens • **contar por ~s** to count in tens • **vender por ~s** to sell in tens

decenal ADJ decennial • **plan ~** ten-year plan

decencia SF **1** (= *pudor*) decency; (= *decoro*) decorum; (= *honestidad*) respectability • **faltar a la ~** to offend against decency *o* propriety
2 (= *aseo*) cleanliness, tidiness

decenio SM decade

decente ADJ **1** (= *pudoroso*) decent; (= *honesto*) respectable
2 (= *aceptable*) [*sueldo, empleo*] decent
3 (= *aseado*) clean, tidy

decentemente ADV **1** (= *con pudor*) [*comportarse*] respectably, decently; [*vestir*] respectably
2 (= *aseadamente*) tidily

decepción SF disappointment • **llevarse** *o* **sufrir una ~** to be disappointed

decepcionado ADJ disappointed • **estar ~ con algo** to be disappointed with sth

decepcionante ADJ disappointing

decepcionar ▹ CONJUG 1a VT to disappoint

decesado/a SM/F (*LAm*) deceased person

deceso SM (*LAm*) decease, passing

dechado SM **1** (= *modelo*) model • **no es ningún ~ de perfección** it isn't a model of perfection • **es un ~ de virtudes** she's a paragon of virtue
2 (*Cos*) sampler

decibel SM, **decibelio** SM decibel

decibélico ADJ loud, noisy

decible ADJ expressible • **eso no es ~** that cannot be expressed, there are no words to say it

decididamente ADV **1** (= *con decisión*) decisively • **tenemos que afrontar ~ el futuro** we have to face the future decisively • **entró ~ en la sala** he entered the room purposefully
2 (= *obviamente*) decidedly • **un poema ~ romántico** a decidedly romantic poem
3 (= *sin duda*) definitely • **~, vuelven a estar de moda los tacones** high heels are definitely back in fashion

decidido ADJ **1** (= *firme*) [*apoyo*] wholehearted; [*paso, gesto*] purposeful; [*esfuerzo, intento*] determined; [*defensor, partidario*] staunch, strong; [*actitud, persona*] resolute • **dio su apoyo ~ al proyecto** he gave his solid *o* wholehearted support to the project • **hubo un ~ apoyo a su propuesta entre la derecha** there was solid support for his proposal from the right • **andaba con paso ~** she walked purposefully *o* with a purposeful stride • **los más ~s saltaron al agua** the most resolute jumped into the water
2 • **estar ~: voy a dejar el trabajo, ya estoy ~** I'm going to leave my job, I've made up my mind *o* I've decided • **estar ~ a hacer algo** to be resolved *o* determined to do sth • **estaba decidida a irse con él** she'd made up her mind to go with him, she was resolved *o* determined to go with him

decidir ▹ CONJUG 3a VT **1** (= *tomar una decisión*) to decide • **¿habéis decidido lo que vais a hacer?** have you decided what you are going to do? • **después de pensarlo mucho he decidido que sí** after giving it a lot of thought, I've decided to go ahead • **~ hacer algo** to decide to do sth • **decidieron no ir** they decided not to go
2 (= *determinar*) [+ *futuro, resultado*] to decide; [+ *asunto, disputa*] to settle, resolve • **el penalti decidió el partido** the penalty decided the match • **el resultado de los exámenes ~á su futuro** the exam results will decide her future
3 (= *convencer*) • **¿qué fue lo que al final te decidió?** what finally made up your mind?, what finally decided you?, what finally made you decide? • **la huelga de trenes me decidió a ir en coche** the rail strike made me decide to take the car
VI to decide • **nadie va a ~ por ellos** no one will make the decision *o* decide for them • **tuvo que ~ entre varias opciones** she had to choose *o* decide from a number of options • **el juez decidió en nuestro favor** the judge ruled in our favour • **~ sobre algo** to decide on sth, make a decision on sth
VPR **decidirse** to decide, make up one's mind • **no me he decidido todavía** I haven't decided *o* made up my mind yet • **¡decídete ya, que se hace tarde!** make up your mind! it's getting late • **~se a hacer algo** to decide to do sth, make up one's mind to do sth • **si me decido a marcharme de París ...** if I decide to *o* make up my mind to leave Paris ... • **ojalá se decida a visitarnos** I hope she decides to visit us • **parece que no se decide a llover** it looks as if it's not going to rain just yet • **~se por algo** to decide on sth • **se decidió por el más barato** she decided on the cheapest

decidor(a) ADJ **1** (= *gracioso*) witty, amusing
2 (= *elocuente*) fluent, eloquent
SM/F **1** (= *chistoso*) wit, witty talker
2 (= *narrador*) fluent speaker, eloquent speaker

decil SM decile

decilitro SM decilitre, deciliter (EEUU)

décima SF **1** [*de segundo, grado*] tenth • **tiene 37 y tres ~s** his temperature is 37.3 (degrees) • **tiene solo unas ~s (de fiebre)** he's only got a slight temperature
2 (*Rel*) tithe
3 (*Literat, Hist*) *a ten-line stanza*

decimación SF decimation

decimal ADJ decimal
SM decimal
SF ▸ **decimal periódica** recurring decimal

decimalización SF decimalization

decimalizar ▹ CONJUG 1f VT to decimalize

decímetro SM decimetre, decimeter (EEUU)

décimo ADJ tenth; ▹ **sexto**
SM **1** (*Mat*) tenth
2 (*tb* **décimo de lotería**) ≈ lottery ticket; ▹ **LOTERÍA, EL GORDO**

decimoctavo ADJ eighteenth; ▹ **sexto**

decimocuarto ADJ fourteenth; ▹ **sexto**

decimonónicamente ADV in the style of the 19th century

decimonónico ADJ nineteenth-century (*antes de s*)

decimonono ADJ, **decimonoveno** ADJ nineteenth; ▹ **sexto**

decimoprimero ADJ eleventh; ▹ **sexto**

decimoquinto ADJ fifteenth; ▹ **sexto**

decimosegundo ADJ twelfth; ▹ **sexto**

decimoséptimo ADJ seventeenth; ▹ **sexto**

decimosexto ADJ sixteenth; ▹ **sexto**

decimotercero ADJ, **decimotercio** ADJ thirteenth; ▹ **sexto**

decir

VERBO TRANSITIVO
VERBO INTRANSITIVO
VERBO PRONOMINAL
SUSTANTIVO MASCULINO

▹ CONJUG 30

Para otras expresiones con el participio, ver ***dicho***.

VERBO TRANSITIVO

1 (= *afirmar*) to say • **ya sabe ~ varias palabras** she can already say several words, she already knows several words • **—tengo prisa —dijo** "I'm in a hurry," she said • **viene y dice: —estás despedido*** he goes, "you're fired"* • **olvídalo, no he dicho nada** forget I said anything • **¿decía usted?** you were saying? • **como dicen los madrileños** as they say in Madrid • **como decía mi abuela** as my grandmother used to say • **como iba diciendo ...** as I was saying ... • **¿cómo ha dicho usted?** pardon?, what did you say? • **~ para** *o* **entre sí** to say to o.s.
decir que to say (that) • **mi amigo dice que eres muy guapa** my friend says (that) you're very pretty • **dicen que ...** they say (that) ..., people say (that) ... • **el cartel dice claramente que ...** the sign says clearly *o* clearly states that ... • **~ que sí/no** to say yes/no • **—¿viene? —dice que sí** "is she coming?" — "she says she is *o* she says so" • **la miré y me dijo que sí/no con la cabeza** I looked at her and she nodded/shook her head; ▹ **adiós**
2 decir algo a algn to tell sb sth • **¿quién te lo dijo?** who told you? • **se lo dije bien claro,**

pero no me hizo caso I told her quite clearly, but she didn't take any notice of me • **tengo algo que ~te** there's something I want to tell you, I've got something to tell you • **hoy nos dicen las notas** they're telling *o* giving us our results today

decir a algn que (+ *indic*) to tell sb (that) • **me dijo que no vendría** he told me (that) he wouldn't come • **ya te dije que no tiene ni idea** I told you he hasn't got a clue • **¿no te digo que no puedo ir?** I've already told you I can't go

decir a algn que (+ *subjun*) (= *ordenar*) to tell sb to (+ *infin*); (= *pedir*) to ask sb to (+ *infin*) • **la profesora me dijo que esperara fuera** the teacher told me to wait outside • **le dije que fuera más tarde** I told her to go later • **dile que venga a cenar mañana con nosotros** ask him to come and have supper with us tomorrow • **te digo que te calles** I said shut up

3 (*= contar*) [+ *mentiras, verdad, secreto*] to tell • **~ tonterías** to talk nonsense; ▷ **verdad**

4 (*= llamar*) to call • **¿cómo le dicen a esto en Perú?** what do they call this in Peru? • **se llama Francisco, pero le dicen Paco** his name is Francisco, but he's known as Paco • **le dicen "el torero"** he's known as "el torero" • **en México se le dice "recámara" al dormitorio** in Mexico they say "recámara" instead of "dormitorio" • **me dijo de todo** he called me all the names under the sun

5 (*= opinar*) to say • **podemos ir a Portugal, ¿tú qué dices?** we could go to Portugal, what do you say? • **¿tu familia qué dice de la boda?** what does your family say about the wedding?

6 (*rectificando*) • **había 8, digo 9** there were 8, I mean 9 • **dirá usted aquel otro** you must mean that other one • **¡qué digo!** what am I saying?

7 (*texto*) to say • **no puedo leer lo que dice** I can't read what it says • **no me dice nada este libro** this book leaves me cold • **como dice el refrán ...** as the saying goes...

8 (*+ misa*) to say

9 (*locuciones en indicativo*) • **digo ...** (*Méx*) well, er ... • **mis súbditos se presentarán ante mí ¡he dicho!** my subjects shall appear before me: I have spoken! • **y dice bien** and he is quite right • **como quien dice** (= *de alguna manera*) so to speak; (= *aproximadamente*) in a way, more or less • **aunque no es el director es, como quien dice, el que manda en la empresa** although he isn't the manager, he's the person in charge, so to speak, of the company • **está, como quien dice, aquí al lado** it's just round the corner, as they say • **como quien no dice nada** quite casually, as though it wasn't important • **lo mismo digo** likewise • **—gracias por todo —lo mismo digo** "thank you for everything" — "likewise!" *o* "thanks to you too!" • **pero dice mal** but he is wrong • **pues si esto te parece mucha gente, no te digo nada en verano** if you think this is a lot of people, you should see it in summer • **no lo digo por ti** I'm not referring to you, I'm not getting at you • **sí, porque tú lo digas** yes, sir, aye, aye, captain! (*iró*) • **¿qué me dices?** (*sorpresa*) you don't say!, well I never!; (*incredulidad*) come off it! • **si tú lo dices** if you say so • **eso digo yo** that's (just) what I say • **deberías buscar trabajo, vamos, digo yo** you ought to look for a job, that's what I say, if you ask me, you ought to look for a job • **¡si te lo digo yo!** of course it's true! • **¡lo digo yo y basta!** you will do it because I say so! • **¡y que lo digas!** you can say that again! • **MODISMOS**: • **~ digo donde dijo Diego** to take back what one said earlier • **no dijo ni pío** • **no dijo esta boca es mía** she never once opened her mouth • **REFRÁN**: • **dime con quien andas y te diré quien eres** a man is known by the company he keeps

10 (*locuciones en infinitivo*) • **dar que ~ (a la gente)** to make people talk, set tongues wagging • **es ~** that is (to say) • **mi prima, es ~, la hija de Ana** my cousin, that is (to say) Ana's daughter • **ir a ~**: • **¡a mí me lo vas a ~!** you're telling me! • **es mucho ~** that's saying something • **ni que ~ tiene que ...** it goes without saying that ... • **no hay más que ~** there's nothing more to say • **para ~lo con otras palabras** to put it another way, in other words • **~ por ~** to talk for talking's sake • **por así ~lo** so to speak • **querer ~** to mean • **¿qué quiere ~ "spatha"?** what does "spatha" mean? • **¿qué quiere usted ~ con eso?** what do you mean by that? • **¿querrás ~ un millón, no un billón?** do you mean a million rather than a billion? • **ya es ~** that's saying something • **les ha costado más cara que mi casa, y eso ya es ~** it cost them more than my house did, and that's saying something

11 (*locuciones en subjuntivo, imperativo*) • **no es que yo lo diga, pero ...** it's not because I say so, but ... • **es, digamos, un comerciante** he's a dealer, for want of a better word, he's a sort of dealer • **¡haberlo dicho!** • **¡me lo hubieras dicho!** you could have told me *o* said! • **digámoslo así** so to speak, for want of a better word • **digan lo que digan** whatever they say • **y no digamos ...** not to mention ... • **y su madre, no digamos** not to mention his mother • **no es muy guapa que digamos** she's not what you'd call pretty, she's not exactly pretty • **no estuvo muy cortés, que digamos** he wasn't what you'd call polite, he wasn't exactly polite • **¡no me digas!** (*sorpresa*) you don't say!, well I never!; (*incredulidad*) come off it! • **¿qué quieres que te diga?** what can I say?

12 (*locuciones en condicional*) • **¿cómo (lo) diría yo?** how shall I put it? • **¿cómo diríamos?** how shall I put it? • **¡quién lo diría!** would you believe it!, who would have thought it!

13 el qué dirán • **pero no quiso por el qué dirán** but she didn't want to because of what people might say • **se preocupa mucho por el qué dirán** she's always worried about what people will say *o* think

VERBO INTRANSITIVO

1 (*invitando a hablar*) • **—¿te puedo pedir un favor? —dime** "can I ask you a favour?" —"go ahead" • **¿diga?** • **¿dígame?** (*al teléfono*) hello? • **usted dirá** (*invitando a hablar*) go ahead; (*sirviendo bebida*) say when; (*en tienda*) can I help you? • **—¿te gustaría cambiar de coche? —¡hombre, ya me dirás!** "would you like a new car?" — "you bet I would!"

2 (*= indicar*) • **su nombre no me dice nada** her name doesn't mean anything to me • **su mirada lo dice todo** her expression says it all *o* speaks volumes • **eso dice mucho de su personalidad** that says a lot about her personality • **una situación que tan mal dice de nuestro gobierno** a situation which shows our government in such a bad light

VERBO PRONOMINAL **decirse**

1 (*uso reflexivo*) • **yo sé lo que me digo** I know what I'm talking about *o* saying • **me dije que no volvería a hacerlo** I promised myself *o* told myself I wouldn't do it again • **él se lo dice todo** he seems to have all the answers • **al verlo me dije: —han pasado muchos años** when I saw him, I said *o* thought to myself, "it's been a long time"

2 (*uso impersonal*) • **se dice** it is said, they *o* people say • **no se diría eso ahora** you'd never say such a thing nowadays • **¿cómo se dice "cursi" en inglés?** what's the English for "cursi"?, how do you say "cursi" in English? • **se les ha dicho que ...** they have been told that ... • **y no se diga ...** not to mention ... • **no se diga que ...** never let it be said that ... • **se diría que no está** she doesn't seem to be here • **alto, lo que se dice alto, no es** he's not what you'd call tall, he's not exactly tall • **hablar portugués, lo que se dice hablar, no sé** I can't really speak Portuguese properly • **esto es lo que se dice un queso** now this is what I call a cheese • **MODISMO**: • **eso se dice muy pronto** that's easier said than done

DECIR

¿"Say" o "tell"?

▷ **Decir** *se puede traducir por* **say** *o por* **tell**. *Por regla general,* **say** *simplemente dice y* **tell** *informa u ordena hacer algo.*

▷ **Decir** *generalmente se traduce por* **say** *en estilo directo. Normalmente no lleva un complemento de persona pero si se menciona a quién se está dirigiendo el hablante, el complemento de persona tiene que ir precedido por la preposición* **to:**

"Ya son las tres", dije
"It's already three o'clock," I said
"¡Qué tiempo más malo!" Eso fue lo único que me dijo
"What awful weather!" That's all he said to me

▷ *En estilo indirecto,* **decir** *se puede traducir por* **say** *cuando simplemente se cuenta lo que alguien ha dicho. Si* **say** *lleva complemento de persona, este se coloca después del complemento directo:*

Dijo que se tenía que marchar
He said he had to leave
Me dijo algo que no entendí
He said something to me that I didn't understand

▷ **Decir** *se traduce por* **tell** *cuando se informa o se ordena hacer algo. Suele llevar un objeto de persona sin la preposición* **to:**

Me dijo que tenía una entrevista de trabajo
He told me he had a job interview
¡Te he dicho que no lo toques!
I told you not to touch it!

▷ *Hay algunos usos idiomáticos en los que* **decir** *se traduce por* **tell** *aunque no lleva complemento de persona. Por ejemplo:* **to tell the truth** *(decir la verdad) y* **to tell a lie** *(decir una mentira).*

Otros verbos

▷ *Si* **decir** *va acompañado de un calificativo en español, a menudo se puede traducir al inglés por otros verbos que no sean* **say** *o* **tell:**

"Lo he perdido todo", dijo entre sollozos
"I've lost everything," she sobbed
Dijo con voz ronca algo sobre necesitar un médico
He croaked something about needing a doctor

Para otros usos y ejemplos ver la entrada.

3 (= *llamarse*) to be called • **esta plaza se dice de la Revolución** this is called Revolution Square

SUSTANTIVO MASCULINO

1 (= *dicho*) saying • MODISMO: • **es un ~** it's a manner of speaking • **pongamos, es un ~, que Picasso naciera en Madrid** let's suppose, just for the sake of argument, that Picasso had been born in Madrid

2 • **a ~ de** according to • **a ~ de la gente mayor** according to the older generation • **a ~ de todos** by all accounts

d

decisión (SF) **1** (= *determinación*) decision; (*Jur*) judgment • **forzar una ~** to force the issue • **tomar una ~** to make *o* take a decision ▸ **decisión por mayoría** majority decision
2 (= *firmeza*) decisiveness
3 (= *voluntad*) determination

decisivo (ADJ) [*resultado, factor, influencia, papel*] decisive; [*argumento*] winning; [*voto*] deciding • **una etapa decisiva de mi vida** a crucial *o* decisive stage in my life

decisorio (ADJ) decision-making • **poderes ~s** decision-making powers • **proceso ~** decision-making process
(SM) (*Méx*) (*Jur*) judgment, verdict

declamación (SF) (*gen*) declamation; [*de poema*] recital, recitation

declamador(a) (SM/F) orator

declamar ▸ CONJUG 1a (VT)
(VT) (*gen*) to declaim; [+ *versos, poema*] to recite
(VI) to declaim

declamatorio (ADJ) declamatory

declaración (SF) **1** (= *proclamación*) declaration ▸ **declaración de amor** declaration of love ▸ **declaración de derechos** (*Pol*) bill of rights ▸ **declaración de guerra** declaration of war ▸ **declaración de intenciones** declaration of intent ▸ **declaración de principios** declaration of principles ▸ **declaración de quiebra** declaration of bankruptcy
2 declaraciones (*a la prensa*) statement (*sing*) • **no quiso hacer declaraciones a los periodistas** he refused to talk to journalists, he refused to make a statement to journalists ▸ **declaraciones conjuntas** joint statement (*sing*)
3 (*a Hacienda*) tax return • **hacer la ~** to do one's tax return ▸ **declaración conjunta** joint tax return ▸ **declaración de aduana(s)** customs declaration ▸ **declaración de impuestos, declaración de ingresos, declaración de la renta** income tax return
4 (*Jur*) (*ante la policía, en juicio*) statement • **firmó una ~ falsa** he signed a false statement • **las declaraciones de los testigos son contradictorias** the evidence given by the witnesses is contradictory, the witnesses' statements are contradictory • **prestar ~** (*ante la policía*) to make a statement; (*en un juicio*) to give evidence, testify • **tomar la ~ a algn** to take a statement from sb ▸ **declaración de culpabilidad** plea of guilty, guilty plea ▸ **declaración de inocencia** plea of not guilty, not guilty plea ▸ **declaración inmediata** (*Méx*) verbal statement ▸ **declaración judicial** statement in court ▸ **declaración jurada** sworn statement, affidavit
5 [*de incendio, epidemia*] outbreak
6 (*Naipes*) bid

declaradamente (ADV) openly

declarado (ADJ) [*actitud, intención*] professed • **un ateo ~** a professed atheist

declarante (SMF) **1** (*Jur*) deponent
2 (*Naipes*) bidder

declarar ▸ CONJUG 1a (VT) **1** (= *proclamar*) [+ *guerra, independencia*] to declare • **Japón declaró la guerra a China** Japan declared war on China • **fue declarado el estado de sitio** a state of siege was declared • **el tribunal declaró la inconstitucionalidad de la ley** the court declared the law unconstitutional • **yo os declaro marido y mujer** I pronounce you man and wife • MODISMOS: • **tener declarada la guerra a algo** to have declared war on sth • **tener declarada la guerra a algn** to have it in for sb*
2 (= *considerar*) to declare • **el tribunal médico lo declaró no apto para el servicio militar** the medical board declared him unfit for military service • **el bosque fue declarado zona protegida** the forest was declared a conservation area • **fue declarada abierta la competición** the competition was declared open • **el premio fue declarado desierto** the prize was not awarded • **este matrimonio podría ~se nulo** this marriage could be annulled • **~ culpable a algn** to find sb guilty • **~ inocente a algn** to find sb innocent
3 (= *manifestar*) (*en público, ante el juez*) to state; (*como anuncio, noticia*) to announce • **declaró su apoyo a la democracia** he stated his support for democracy • **el ministro declaró no saber nada del asunto** the minister stated that he knew nothing of the matter • **según declaró un portavoz del gobierno** as a government spokesperson announced
4 (*Com*) (*en la aduana, a Hacienda*) to declare • **¿(tiene) algo que ~?** (do you have) anything to declare? • **"nada que declarar"** "nothing to declare"
5 (*Naipes*) to bid • **declaró dos picos** she bid two spades • **declaró menos de lo que tenía** he underbid
(VI) **1** (*Jur*) (= *testificar*) to give evidence, testify • **fue llamada a ~ por el juez** the judge called her to give evidence *o* to testify • **~ en falso** to commit perjury
2 (= *declarar impuestos*) to submit one's tax return
3 (*Naipes*) to bid
(VPR) **declararse 1** (= *reconocerse*) to declare o.s. • **se han declarado objetores de conciencia** they have declared themselves conscientious objectors • **~se a favor de algo** to declare o.s. in favour of sth • **~se en bancarrota** *o* **quiebra** to declare o.s. bankrupt • **poco después de ~se abiertamente homosexual** shortly after coming out as a homosexual, shortly after announcing in public that he was a homosexual • **~se culpable** to plead guilty • **~se en huelga** to go on strike • **~se inocente** to plead not guilty • **~se en suspensión de pagos** to call in the receivers
2 • **~se a algn** to declare one's love to sb • **se le declaró en el jardín** he declared his love to her in the garden • **¿se te ha declarado ya?** has he told you he loves you yet?
3 [*epidemia, guerra*] to break out • **se declaró un incendio en el almacén** a fire broke out in the warehouse • **el incendio se declaró en la cocina y se extendió por toda la casa** the fire started in the kitchen and spread throughout the house

declaratoria (*Jur*) (ADJ) declaratory
(SF) declaration

declinable (ADJ) declinable

declinación (SF) **1** (*Ling*) declension
2 (*Astron, Náut*) declination
3 (= *decaimiento*) decline, falling-off

declinar ▸ CONJUG 1a (VT) **1** (= *rechazar*) [+ *honor, invitación*] to decline; (*Jur*) to reject • **declinamos cualquier responsabilidad** we cannot accept responsibility • **~ hacer algo** to decline to do sth
2 (*Ling*) to decline
(VI) **1** (= *decaer*) to decline, decay
2 (*liter*) [*día*] to draw to a close
3 [*terreno*] to slope (away *o* down)
4 (*Ling*) to decline

declive (SM) **1** [*de terreno, superficie*] incline, gradient • **un terreno en ~** sloping ground
2 (= *decadencia*) decline • **en ~: es una ciudad en ~** it's a city in decline • **una ideología en ~** an ideology in decline *o* on the wane • **el consumo de alcohol está** *o* **va en ~** alcohol consumption is declining *o* is on the decline

decocción (SF) decoction

decodificador (SM) = **descodificador**

decodificar ▸ CONJUG 1g (VT) = **descodificar**

decolaje (SM) (*And, Chile*) take-off

decolar ▸ CONJUG 1a (VI) (*And, Chile*) to take off

decolorado (ADJ) [*pelo*] bleached; [*piel, ropa*] discoloured, discolored (*EEUU*)

decolorante (SM) bleaching agent

decolorar ▸ CONJUG 1a (VT) [+ *pelo*] to bleach; [+ *piel, ropa*] to discolour, discolor (*EEUU*)
(VPR) **decolorarse** [*pelo*] to get bleached; [*piel, ropa*] to get discoloured, become discolored (*EEUU*), fade • **el pelo se me ha decolorado con el sol** the sun has bleached my hair

decomisar ▸ CONJUG 1a (VT) to seize, confiscate

decomiso (SM) seizure, confiscation

descongestionante (SM) decongestant

deconstrucción (SF) deconstruction

deconstruir ▸ CONJUG 3g (VT) (*Literat*) to deconstruct

decoración (SF) **1** (= *adorno*) decoration ▸ **decoración de escaparates** window dressing ▸ **decoración de interiores, decoración del hogar** interior decorating
2 (*Cine, Teat*) set, scenery

decorado (SM) (*Cine, Teat*) scenery, set

decorador(a) (SM/F) **1** [*de interiores*] decorator, interior decorator ▸ **decorador(a) de escaparates** window dresser
2 (*Teat*) set designer

decorar[1] ▸ CONJUG 1a (VT) [+ *casa, habitación*] to decorate (**de** with)

decorar[2] ▸ CONJUG 1a (VT) **1** (= *aprender*) to learn, memorize
2 (= *recitar*) to chorus

decorativo (ADJ) decorative

decoro (SM) **1** (= *decencia, dignidad*) decorum, decency ▸ **decoro virginal** maidenly modesty
2 (= *honor*) honour, honor (*EEUU*), respect

decorosamente (ADV) decorously

decoroso (ADJ) [*conducta, lenguaje*] decorous; [*empleo, sueldo*] decent

decrecer ▸ CONJUG 2d (VI) **1** (= *disminuir*) [*importancia, interés*] to decrease; [*nivel de agua*] to subside, go down
2 [*días*] to draw in

decreciente (ADJ) decreasing, diminishing

decrecimiento (SM), **decremento** (SM) decrease

decrépito (ADJ) decrepit

decrepitud (SF) decrepitude

decretar ▸ CONJUG 1a (VT) **1** (= *ordenar*) to order; (*por decreto*) to decree • **~ que** to decree that
2 [+ *premio*] to award (**a** to) • **el árbitro ha decretado penalti** the referee has awarded a penalty
3 (*Méx*) [+ *dividendo*] to declare

VI (*Jur*) to deliver a judgment

decretazo* SM *decree that comes into force without being agreed on by a majority*

decreto SM decree, order; (*Parl*) act • **real ~** royal decree • **por real ~** (*lit*) by royal decree; (*fig*) compulsorily, willy-nilly

decreto-ley SM (PL: **decretos-leyes**) order in council, government decree

decúbito SM (*Med*) ▸ **decúbito prono** prone position ▸ **decúbito supino** supine position

decuplar ▷ CONJUG 1a VT, **decuplicar** ▷ CONJUG 1g VT to multiply tenfold, increase tenfold

décuplo ADJ tenfold
SM • **es el ~ de lo que era** it is ten times what it was, it has increased tenfold

decurso SM (*liter*) • **en el ~ de los años** over the years • **en el ~ del tiempo** in the course of time

dedada SF (= *cantidad*) (*lit*) thimbleful; (*fig*) very small quantity • **una ~ de mermelada** a spot *o* dab of jam • **una ~ de pimienta** a pinch of pepper • MODISMO: • **dar una ~ de miel a algn** to give sb a crumb of comfort

dedal SM **1** (*Cos*) thimble
2 (= *cantidad*) thimbleful

dedalera SF foxglove

dédalo SM **1** (= *laberinto*) labyrinth
2 (= *lío*) tangle, mess

dedazo SM fingermark

dedicación SF **1** (= *entrega*) dedication (**a** to) • **las profesiones de ~ humanitaria** the caring professions • **con ~ exclusiva** *o* **plena** full-time (*antes de s*) • **trabajar con ~ plena** to work full-time • **"dedicación plena"** "full-time"
2 [*de discurso, libro*] dedication
3 (*Rel*) consecration

dedicado ADJ (*Inform*) dedicated

dedicar ▷ CONJUG 1g VT **1** [+ *obra, canción*] to dedicate • **dedico este poema a mis padres** this poem is dedicated to my parents • **me dedicó una copia firmada de su última novela** she presented me with a signed copy of her latest novel • **quisiera ~ unas palabras de agradecimiento a ...** I should like to address a few words of thanks to ... • **el festival dedicó un homenaje al actor** the festival paid tribute to the actor
2 [+ *tiempo, espacio, atención*] to devote, give; [+ *esfuerzo*] to devote • **dedico un día a la semana a ordenar mis papeles** I devote *o* give one day a week to organizing my paperwork • **ha dedicado toda su vida a los derechos humanos** she has dedicated *o* devoted her whole life to human rights • **dedica este terreno al cultivo del tulipán** he uses this land for growing tulips • **un programa dedicado a los deportes de invierno** a programme about *o* on winter sports
3 (*Rel*) to dedicate, consecrate
VPR **dedicarse 1** (*como profesión*) • **~se a: se dedica a la enseñanza** he is a teacher, he's in teaching • **¿a qué se dedica usted?** what do you do (for a living)? • **se dedican a arreglar electrodomésticos** they repair domestic appliances
2 (*como afición*) • **~se a: se dedica a ver la tele todo el día** he spends the whole day watching TV • **en el verano se dedicó a la cerámica** he spent the summer doing *o* making pottery • **¡dedícate a lo tuyo!** mind your own business!
3 (= *entregarse*) • **~se a** to devote o.s. to • **se dedicó completamente a cuidar de sus padres** she devoted herself entirely to looking after her parents

dedicatoria SF dedication, inscription

dedicatorio ADJ dedicatory

dedil SM fingerstall

dedillo SM • **conocer algo al ~** to know sth like the back of one's hand • **cumplir una orden al ~** to follow an order to the letter • **saber algo al ~** to have sth at one's fingertips

dedismo* SM arbitrary selection, arbitrary nomination

dedo SM **1** [*de mano, guante*] finger; [*de pie*] toe • **con la punta** *o* **la yema de los ~s** with one's fingertips • **apuntar** *o* **señalar algo/a algn con el ~** (*señalando*) to point at sth/sb; (*acusando*) to point the finger at sth/sb • **meterse el ~ en la nariz** to pick one's nose • MODISMOS: • **a ~***: • **vine a ~** I hitched here* • **he viajado por toda Alemania a ~** I hitched all round Germany* • **ha entrado a ~** he got the job because he knew somebody, he got the job through contacts • **han adjudicado a ~ todas las obras** they handed out all the building contracts to people they knew • **contarse con los ~s** to count on one's fingers • **mis amigos se pueden contar con los ~s de una mano** I can count my friends on the fingers of one hand • **dale un ~ y se toma hasta el codo** give him an inch and he'll take a mile • **escaparse de entre los ~s** to slip through one's fingers • **hacer ~** (*Esp**) to hitch* • **hacer ~s** (*Mús*) to practise one's scales • **no levantar** *o* **mover un ~** not to lift a finger • **pillarse** *o* **cogerse los ~s** (*Esp*) to get one's fingers burned • **poner el ~ en la llaga** (*de error*) to put one's finger on it; (*de tema delicado*) to touch a raw nerve • **poner el ~ en el renglón** (*Méx*) to put one's finger on it ▸ **dedo anular** ring finger ▸ **dedo auricular** little finger ▸ **dedo cordial, dedo (del) corazón, dedo (de en) medio** middle finger ▸ **dedo (en) martillo** hammer toe ▸ **dedo gordo** [*de la mano*] thumb; [*del pie*] big toe ▸ **dedo índice** index finger, forefinger ▸ **dedo meñique** [*de la mano*] little finger, pinkie (*EEUU, Escocia**); [*del pie*] little toe ▸ **dedo pulgar** thumb; ▷ **anillo, chupar, cruzar, ligero**
2 (= *medida*) [*de altura, grosor*] *about an inch*; [*de cantidad*] drop • **cayeron cuatro ~s de nieve** about four inches of snow fell • **hay que meterle el bajo unos dos ~s** you'll have to turn up the trousers a couple of inches • **ponme un ~ de coñac** give me a drop of brandy • **dos deditos nada más** just a little drop • MODISMOS: • **estar a dos ~s de algo** to be *o* come within an inch *o* an ace of sth • **no tener dos ~s de frente*** to be as thick as two short planks* • **si tuvieras dos ~s de frente no te habrías metido en este lío** if you had any sense at all you wouldn't have got into this mess

dedocracia* SF *arbitrary exercise of power*

deducción SF **1** (*Fil*) (= *método*) deduction; (= *razonamiento*) inference
2 (*Com*) deduction

deducible ADJ **1** (= *inferible, lógico*) deducible (**de** from) • **según es fácilmente ~** as may readily be deduced
2 (*en la declaración de la renta*) tax-deductible, deductible (EEUU)

deducir ▷ CONJUG 3n VT **1** (= *inferir*) [+ *razonamiento, conclusión*] to deduce, infer (**de** from); [+ *fórmula*] to derive (**de** from)
2 (= *descontar*) to deduct • **deducidos los gastos** less charges
VPR **deducirse** • **de su discurso se deduce que va a haber grandes cambios** judging by what he said in his speech, there are going to be some big changes

deductivo ADJ deductive

defalcar ▷ CONJUG 1g VT = **desfalcar**

defecación SF defecation

defecar ▷ CONJUG 1g VI to defecate

defección SF defection

defectible ADJ **1** (= *que puede fallar*) fallible, imperfect
2 (= *defectuoso*) faulty

defectivo ADJ (*Ling*) defective

defecto SM **1** [*de persona*] (*físico*) defect; (*de personalidad*) fault, shortcoming • **un ~ congénito** a congenital defect • **el ~ que tiene es su mal genio** his one fault *o* shortcoming is his bad temper, the one flaw in his character is his bad temper • **su único ~ es que no sabe escribir a máquina** his only shortcoming is that he can't type ▸ **defecto de fonación, defecto del habla, defecto de pronunciación** speech defect, speech impediment ▸ **defecto de visión** • **tiene un ~ de visión** he has defective eyesight ▸ **defecto físico** physical defect
2 [*de máquina, sistema*] fault; [*de tela, vestido, ornamento*] flaw, defect • **el ~ de tu teoría es su superficialidad** the flaw in your theory is its superficiality • **tiene un ~ de fábrica** *o* **fabricación** it has a manufacturing defect *o* fault, it's faulty *o* defective
3 (*Jur*) ▸ **defecto de forma** technicality ▸ **defecto legal** legal defect
4 • **en su ~: Manolo, o en su ~, Gonzalo** Manolo, or failing him *o* failing that, Gonzalo • **por ~** (*Inform*) by default • MODISMO: • **pecar por ~**: • **antes no paraba de hablar y ahora peca por ~** before, she never stopped talking, and now she's gone to the other extreme *o* she's gone too far the other way • REFRÁN: • **más vale pecar por exceso que por ~** too much is better than too little

defectuosamente ADV defectively, faultily

defectuoso ADJ defective, faulty

defender ▷ CONJUG 2g VT (*Mil*) [+ *país, territorio, intereses*] to defend; [+ *causa, ideas*] to defend, champion; (*Jur*) to defend • **defiende sus opiniones con buenos argumentos** he defends his opinions with good arguments • **el Real Madrid defiende el título de campeón** Real Madrid are defending the championship title, Real Madrid are the defending champions • **nos defendió de los atracadores** he defended us against the muggers • **defiendo la tesis doctoral el mes que viene** I'm having a viva on *o* (EEUU) I'm defending my doctoral thesis next month
VPR **defenderse 1** (= *protegerse*) • **~se de** *o* **contra** [+ *calor, lluvia, sol*] to protect o.s. from; [+ *agresor, ataque*] to defend o.s. from *o* against • **se defendió del lobo con un palo** he defended himself against the wolf with a stick
2 (= *desenvolverse*) to get by • **me defiendo en inglés** I can get by *o* along in English • **gana poco pero se defiende** she doesn't earn much but she gets by • **ya eres mayor, ya puedes ~te solo** you're old enough, you can get by *o* manage on your own now • **—¿sabes algo de ordenadores? —me defiendo** "do you know anything about computers?" — "I get by *o* I know a bit" • **se defendió muy bien en la entrevista** she performed very well in the interview • MODISMO: • **~se como un gato panza arriba** to fight tooth and nail (to defend o.s.)

defendible ADJ defensible

defendido/a SM/F (*Jur*) • **mi ~** my client

defenestración SF (*hum*) abrupt dismissal, sudden removal

defenestrar ▷ CONJUG 1a VT (*hum*) to boot out (*hum*), oust, remove

defensa SF **1** (= *protección*) defence, defense

(EEUU) • **la ~ del territorio nacional** the defence of national territory • **la cueva nos sirvió de ~ contra la lluvia** the cave offered us protection from the rain • **en ~ de los derechos civiles** in defence of civil rights • **salió en ~ de su hermano** he came to his brother's defence • **en ~ propia** in self-defence • **(Ministerio de) Defensa** Ministry of Defence, Defense Department (EEUU) ▸ **defensa pasiva** civil defence ▸ **defensa personal** self-defence ▸ **defensas costeras** coastal defences
2 (*Jur*) (= *abogado, argumentación*) defence, defense (EEUU)
3 (*Dep*) • **la ~** (= *jugadores*) the defence, the defense (EEUU)
4 **defensas** (*Med*) defences, defenses (EEUU) • **está bajo de ~s** his (body's) defences are low, his resistance is low
5 **defensas** [*de toro*] horns; [*de elefante, jabalí*] tusks
6 (*Náut*) fender
7 (*Méx*) bumper, fender (EEUU)
SMF (*Dep*) defender ▸ **defensa escoba, defensa libre** sweeper

defensiva SF defensive • **estar a la ~** to be on the defensive

defensivo ADJ defensive • **política defensiva** defence policy, defense policy (EEUU)
SM defence, defense (EEUU), safeguard

defensor(a) SM/F 1 (= *protector*) [*de territorio, intereses*] defender; [*de causa, idea, derechos*] defender, champion • **mi pastor alemán es un ~ feroz** my Alsatian is a fierce guard dog ▸ **defensor(a) del menor** children's commissioner, children's ombudsman ▸ **defensor(a) del pueblo** ombudsman
2 (*Jur*) defence lawyer, defense attorney *o* lawyer (EEUU) • **el ~ interrogó al testigo** counsel for the defence *o* defending counsel cross-examined the witness
3 (*Dep*) [*de título*] defender
ADJ 1 (= *protector*) • **una asociación ~a de los derechos de los marginados** an organization which defends *o* protects the rights of the underprivileged • **una organización ~a de los derechos civiles** a civil rights organization
2 (*Jur*) • **abogado ~** defence lawyer, defense attorney *o* lawyer (EEUU)

defeño/a ADJ of/from Mexico City
SM/F native/inhabitant of Mexico City

deferencia SF deference • **fue la única que nos trató con ~** she was the only one to treat us with deference *o* respect • **no tuvo la ~ de informarnos** he didn't have the courtesy to let us know • **en** *o* **por ~ a** *o* **hacia algn** out of *o* in deference to sb

deferente ADJ deferential

deferir ▷ CONJUG 3k VT (*Jur*) to refer, delegate
VI • **~ a algo** to defer to sth

deficiencia SF 1 (= *defecto*) defect (**de** in, of)
2 (= *falta*) deficiency ▸ **deficiencia auditiva** hearing impairment ▸ **deficiencia mental, deficiencia psíquica** mental deficiency, mental handicap ▸ **deficiencia visual** visual impairment

deficiente ADJ 1 (= *imperfecto*) [*mercancía, motor*] defective; [*sistema, estructura*] inadequate • **los ~s sistemas de seguridad** the inadequacy of the security systems
2 (= *falto*) deficient (**en** in)
SMF ▸ **deficiente mental, deficiente psíquico** mentally handicapped person ▸ **deficiente visual** visually handicapped person

déficit SM (PL: **déficits**) 1 (*Com, Econ*) deficit ▸ **déficit comercial, déficit exterior** trade deficit ▸ **déficit por cuenta corriente** current account deficit ▸ **déficit presupuestario** budget deficit
2 (= *falta*) lack, shortage

deficitario ADJ 1 (*Econ*) [*empresa, operación*] loss-making • **financiación/reducción deficitaria** financing/reduction of the deficit • **tiene una cuenta deficitaria** his account is overdrawn
2 • **ser ~ en algo** to be short of sth, be lacking in sth

definible ADJ definable

definición SF 1 [*de palabra*] definition • **por ~** by definition
2 (*Téc*) definition

definido ADJ 1 [*línea*] clearly defined; [*preferencia*] definite, clear • **bien ~** well defined, clearly defined • **~ por el usuario** (*Inform*) user-defined
2 [*carácter*] tough, manly
3 (*Ling*) definite

definir ▷ CONJUG 3a VT 1 [+ *concepto, palabra*] to define
2 (= *calificar*) to describe • **definió el partido como aburrido** she described the match as boring
3 (= *aclarar*) [+ *actitud, posición*] to define; [+ *contorno, silueta*] to define, make sharp
4 (= *establecer*) [+ *poder, jurisdicción*] to define, establish • **esta ley define las competencias de cada administración** this law defines *o* establishes the powers of each authority
5 (*Inform*) to define
VPR **definirse** 1 (= *calificarse*) to define o.s. • **se definió como liberal** he defined himself as a liberal
2 (= *decidirse*) • **la comisión aún no se ha definido con respecto al tema** the commission has not yet defined its position on the subject, the commission has not yet said where it stands on the subject • **el gobierno se definió a favor del pacto** the government came out in favour of the agreement

definitivamente ADV 1 (= *con seguridad*) definitely • **~ nos casamos el 14 de marzo** we are definitely getting married on 14 March
2 (= *para siempre*) permanently • **se ha instalado ~ en la capital** he has settled permanently in the capital, he has settled in the capital for good • **eliminaron ~ el virus** they permanently eliminated the virus, they eliminated the virus for ever *o* for good *o* once and for all • **son teorías ~ superadas** these theories have now been permanently superseded
3 (= *claramente*) definitely • **~, es la peor película del año** it's definitely the worst film of the year • **un autor ~ encasillable en el modernismo** an author who can definitely be classed as modernist

definitivo ADJ 1 (= *final*) definitive, final • **la clausura definitiva de la línea ferroviaria** the permanent closure of the railway line
2 (= *inamovible*) [*proyecto, fecha, respuesta*] definite • **este es el plan, pero no es ~** this is the plan, but it's not definite • **ya es ~ que las elecciones son en mayo** the election will now definitely be in May
3 [*prueba*] definitive, conclusive
4 • **en definitiva: es, en definitiva, una pésima película** in short, it's a terrible film • **en definitiva, que no quieres venir** so you don't want to come then? • **este es, en definitiva, el mejor pacto alcanzable** all in all *o* all things considered, this is the best deal we can expect to achieve

definitorio ADJ defining, distinctive

deflación SF deflation

deflacionar ▷ CONJUG 1a VT to deflate

deflacionario ADJ, **deflacionista** ADJ deflationary

deflactación SF (*Cono Sur*) deflation

deflactar ▷ CONJUG 1a VT (*Cono Sur*) to deflate

deflector SM (*Téc*) baffle, baffle plate

defoliación SF defoliation

defoliante SM defoliant

defoliar ▷ CONJUG 1b VT to defoliate

deforestación SF deforestation

deforestar ▷ CONJUG 1a VT to deforest

deformación SF 1 (= *alteración*) [*de manos, superficie*] deformation; [*de madera*] warping
2 (*Radio*) distortion
3 (*Mec*) strain
4 ▸ **deformación profesional** • **—¡deja ya de hacer preguntas! —soy detective, es ~ profesional** "stop asking questions!" — "I'm a detective, it's a habit you pick up in this job"

deformado ADJ [*cuerpo, rostro*] deformed; [*imagen, vista*] distorted

deformante ADJ • **espejo ~** distorting mirror

deformar ▷ CONJUG 1a VT 1 [+ *cuerpo*] to deform • **la artritis puede ~ los miembros** arthritis can deform limbs
2 [+ *objeto*] to distort, deform • **el impacto deformó el chasis** the impact distorted *o* deformed the chassis • **si sigues tirando del jersey, lo ~ás** if you keep pulling at your sweater you'll pull it out of shape • **no te pongas mis zapatos que me los deformas** don't wear my shoes, you'll put them out of shape • **el calor deformó la madera** the heat warped the wood
3 [+ *imagen, realidad*] to distort
VPR **deformarse** 1 [*cuerpo, miembro*] to become deformed
2 [*madera, puerta*] to become warped, become twisted • **se le deformó el sombrero con la lluvia** her hat lost its shape in the rain, the rain made her hat lose its shape • **se le ~on los zapatos de tanto caminar** his shoes got out of shape from so much walking
3 [*imagen*] to distort, become distorted

deforme ADJ 1 (= *de forma anormal*) [*espécimen, cuerpo*] deformed; [*cabeza, sombra*] misshapen
2 (= *feo*) ugly

deformidad SF 1 (= *forma anormal*) deformity, malformation
2 (= *defecto moral*) shortcoming

defragmentar ▷ CONJUG 1a VT [+ *disco, ordenador*] to defragment, defrag*

defraudación SF 1 (= *desfalco*) defrauding ▸ **defraudación de impuestos, defraudación fiscal** tax evasion
2 (= *engaño*) deceit
3 (= *decepción*) disappointment

defraudador(a) SM/F fraudster*

defraudar ▷ CONJUG 1a VT 1 (= *decepcionar*) [+ *persona*] to disappoint; [+ *esperanzas*] to dash, disappoint; [+ *amigos*] to let down • **este libro no te ~á** you won't be disappointed by this book
2 (*Com*) [+ *acreedores*] to cheat, defraud • **~ impuestos** to evade one's taxes
3 (*Fís*) to intercept, cut off

defraudatorio ADJ fraudulent

defuera ADV • **por ~** outwardly, on the outside

defunción SF decease • **"cerrado por defunción"** "closed owing to bereavement"

defuncionar‡ ▷ CONJUG 1a VT to do in‡

DEG SMPL ABR (= **derechos especiales de giro**) SDR

degeneración SF 1 (= *proceso*) degeneration (**en** into)
2 (= *estado*) degeneracy

degenerado/a ADJ degenerate

SM/F (*moralmente*) degenerate; (*sexualmente*) pervert

degenerar ▷ CONJUG 1a VI **1** (= *empeorar*) [*enfermedad*] to get worse; [*discusión, situación*] to degenerate (**en** into) • **la manifestación degeneró en una sangrienta revuelta** the demonstration degenerated into a bloody riot
2 (= *decaer*) to decline

degenerativo ADJ degenerative

deglución SF swallowing

deglutir ▷ CONJUG 3a VT, VI to swallow

degollación SF **1** [*de persona*] throat cutting; (*Jur*) beheading
2 (= *masacre*) massacre ▸ **Degollación de los Inocentes** Slaughter of the Innocents

degolladero SM **1** (*Anat*) throat, neck
2 (*Hist*) scaffold, block (*for executions*)
• MODISMO: • **ir al ~** to expose o.s. to mortal danger; (*hum*) to put one's head in the lion's mouth
3 (= *matadero*) slaughterhouse

degollador SM (*Hist*) executioner

degollar ▷ CONJUG 1m VT **1** (= *cortar la garganta de*) [+ *persona*] to cut the throat of, slit the throat of; [+ *animal*] to slaughter • **lo ~on** they cut *o* slit his throat
2 (= *decapitar*) [+ *persona*] to behead; [+ *toro*] to kill badly, butcher
3 (= *masacrar*) to massacre
4 (= *arruinar*) [+ *comedia, papel*] to murder
5 (*Cos*) to cut low in the neck

degradable ADJ degradable • **un plástico no ~** a non-degradable plastic

degradación SF **1** (= *deterioro*) [*de la salud*] deterioration; [*del litoral*] deterioration, degradation (*frm*); [*de calidad*] worsening, decline
2 (= *bajeza*) degradation
3 (*Mil*) demotion
4 (*Geol*) impoverishment

degradado SM (*Inform*) gradient fill

degradante ADJ degrading

degradar ▷ CONJUG 1a VT **1** (= *deteriorar*) [+ *salud*] to cause to deteriorate; [+ *litoral*] to spoil; [+ *calidad*] to lower, make worse
2 (*Mil*) to demote, downgrade
3 (*Inform*) [+ *datos*] to corrupt
4 (*Geol*) [+ *suelo*] to impoverish
VPR **degradarse** to demean o.s., degrade o.s.

degüello SM **1** [*de arma*] shaft
2 • **a ~**: **entrar a ~ en una ciudad** to put the people of a city to the sword • **tirarse a ~ contra algn** to lash out against sb

degustación SF tasting, sampling

degustar ▷ CONJUG 1a VT to taste, sample

dehesa SF **1** (= *pastos*) pasture, meadow
2 (= *finca*) estate

deíctico ADJ, SM deictic

deidad SF **1** (= *dios*) deity ▸ **deidad pagana** pagan god, pagan deity
2 (= *divinidad*) divinity

deificación SF deification

deificar ▷ CONJUG 1g VT **1** (*Rel*) to deify
2 [+ *cantante, ídolo*] to deify, idolize
3 [+ *persona, hijo*] to put on a pedestal

deísmo SM deism

deísta ADJ deistic, deistical
SMF deist

deixis SF INV deixis

dejación SF **1** (*Jur*) abandonment, relinquishment
2 (*And, CAm*) (= *descuido*) carelessness

dejada SF (*Tenis*) let

dejadez SF **1** (*en el trabajo*) (= *falta de esfuerzo*) laziness; (= *falta de cuidado, atención*) carelessness
2 (= *falta de aseo*) slovenliness

dejado ADJ **1** (= *desaliñado*) (*en las costumbres*) slovenly; (*en la apariencia*) scruffy • **es tan ~ que ni siquiera lava los platos** he's so slovenly he doesn't even bother to do the washing up • **va siempre muy ~** he's always very scruffy • **está muy dejada desde que vive en el campo** she's got very scruffy since she started living in the country • **con ese aspecto tan ~ nunca conseguirás trabajo** you'll never get a job looking so scruffy
2 (= *negligente*) careless, sloppy • **comete esos errores porque es un ~** he makes those mistakes because he's so careless *o* sloppy • **eres muy ~ con tu familia** you don't bother much about *o* with your family • **no te escribe porque es una dejada** she doesn't write to you because she can't really be bothered; ▷ **Dios**

dejamiento SM = **dejadez**

dejar

VERBO TRANSITIVO
VERBO INTRANSITIVO
VERBO PRONOMINAL

▷ CONJUG 1a

Para las expresiones ***dejar caer, dejarse caer, dejar que desear, dejar dicho, dejarse llevar, dejar paso***, *ver la otra entrada.*

VERBO TRANSITIVO

1 (= *poner, soltar*) to leave • **he dejado las llaves en la mesa** I've left the keys on the table • **se lo dejo en la conserjería** I'll leave it for you at the porter's office • **dejé 1.500 euros de entrada** I put down 1,500 euros as a deposit • **podemos ~le los niños a mi madre si salimos** we can leave the children with my mother if we go out • **~ algo aparte** to leave sth aside • **~ atrás** [+ *corredor, vehículo adelantado, competidor*] to leave behind • **dejó atrás a los demás corredores** he left the other runners behind • **se vino de Holanda, dejando atrás a su familia** he came over from Holland, leaving his family behind • **~ a algn muy atrás** to leave sb a long way behind • **~ algo a un lado** to set sth aside

2 (*al desaparecer, morir*) to leave • **el agua ha dejado una mancha en la pared** the water has left a stain on the wall • **te deja un sabor demasiado dulce después de comerlo** it leaves a sickly aftertaste in your mouth • **dejó todo su dinero a sus hijos** he left all his money to his children • **dejó dos niñas pequeñas** she left two small girls • **deja escritas tres novelas** he leaves three completed novels behind

3 (= *guardar*) • **¿me habéis dejado algo de tarta?** have you left *o* saved me some cake? • **deja algo de dinero para cuando lo necesites** put some money aside for when you need it

4 (= *abandonar*) **a** [+ *actividad, empleo*] to give up • **dejó el esquí después del accidente** he gave up skiing after the accident • **ha dejado los estudios por el fútbol** he has given up his studies to pursue a career in football • **lo dejamos porque era muy difícil** we gave up because it was too hard • **lo dejamos por imposible** we gave it up as being impossible • **~ la bebida** to give up drink, stop drinking
b [+ *persona, lugar*] to leave • **~on al niño en la puerta de una iglesia** they left the child outside a church • **su novio la ha dejado** her boyfriend has left her • **dejé su casa al amanecer** I left his house at dawn
c (*en coche*) to drop off • **¿te dejo en tu casa?** shall I drop you off at your place?

5 (= *no molestar*) • **deja ya el ordenador, que lo vas a romper** leave the computer alone, you're going to break it • **déjame, quiero estar solo** leave me be, I want to be alone • **¡déjalo!** (= *¡no hagas eso!*) stop it!; (= *no te preocupes*) forget it!, don't worry about it! • **~ así las cosas** to leave things as they are • **dejémoslo así** let's leave it at that • **¡déjame en paz!** • **¡déjame tranquilo!** leave me alone!

6 (= *posponer*) • **~ algo para** to leave sth till • **~ algo para mañana** to leave sth till tomorrow • **~ algo para después** to leave sth till later • **he dejado el italiano para cuando tenga más tiempo** I've put off learning Italian till I have more time

7 (= *prestar*) to lend • **le dejé mi libro de física** I lent him my physics book • **¿me dejas diez euros?** can you lend me ten euros? • **¿me dejas el coche?** can I borrow the car?, will you lend me the car?

8 (= *permitir*) (+ *infin*) to let • **mis padres no me dejan salir de noche** my parents won't let me go out at night • **quiero pero no me dejan** I want to but they won't let me • **~ entrar a algn** to let sb in • **~ pasar a algn** to let sb through *o* past • **~ salir a algn** to let sb out
dejar que (+ *subjun*) • **~ que las cosas vayan de mal en peor** to let things go *o* allow things to go from bad to worse

9 (*indicando resultado*) (+ *adj*) • **dejó la ventana abierta** she left the window open • **lo ha dejado muy triste** it has left him very sad • **me dejó confundido** she left me confused, she confused me • **nos dejó a todos asombrados** he stunned us all • **hay algo que quiero ~ bien claro** there is one thing I want to make perfectly clear • **~on el jardín tal como estaba** they left the garden as it was • **~ algo como nuevo**: • **me han dejado el abrigo como nuevo** my coat was as good as new when it came back from them • **esa ducha me ha dejado como nueva** I feel like a different person after that shower

10 (= *producir*) [+ *dinero*] • **el negocio le deja lo justo para vivir** the business brings in just enough for him to live on • **ese fondo de inversión apenas me deja intereses** that investment fund barely pays any interest

11 **dejar que** (= *esperar*) • **deja que acabe de llover** wait for it to stop raining • **~on que pasara el temporal antes de zarpar** they waited for the storm to pass before setting sail • **deja que me toque la lotería y verás** just wait till I win the lottery, then you'll see

12 (= *omitir*) to leave out, forget

VERBO INTRANSITIVO

(*con una actividad*) • **deja, ya lo hago yo** leave it, I'll do it • **deja, yo lo pago** no *o* it's all right, I'll pay for it
dejar de hacer algo (*por un momento*) to stop doing sth; (*por una temporada*) to give up doing sth, stop doing sth • **cuando deje de llover** when it stops raining, when the rain stops • **¡deja de hacer eso!** stop that! • **yo dejé de ir hace muchos años** I gave up *o* stopped going years ago • **no puedo ~ de fumar** I can't give up *o* stop smoking • **cuando murió su padre dejó de comer** when her father died she stopped eating *o* she went off her food
no dejar de (+ *infin*) • **no deja de preguntarme por ti** he's always asking me about you • **eso no deja de tener gracia** it has its funny side • **no deja de ser raro que no haya venido** it's rather odd that she hasn't come • **no por eso deja de ser una tontería lo que has dicho** that doesn't change the fact that what you said was stupid • **no puedo ~ de**

asombrarme I can't help being astonished • **no dejes de visitarlos** don't fail to visit them, make sure you visit them • **no dejes de comprar el billete** make sure you buy the ticket

VERBO PRONOMINAL **dejarse**

1 (*= abandonarse*) to let o.s. go • **empezó a ~se después de tener su primer hijo** she started to let herself go after she had her first child

2 (*= olvidar*) to leave • **se dejó el bolso en un taxi** she left her bag in a taxi • **me he dejado el dinero en casa** I've left my money at home • **me he dejado la luz encendida** I've left the light on

3 (*= dejar crecer*) to grow • **~se las uñas largas/el pelo largo** to grow long nails/hair • **~se barba** to grow a beard

4 (*= permitir*) (+ *infin*) • **~se convencer** to allow o.s. to be persuaded • **no se dejó engañar** he was not to be deceived • **el gato no se dejaba acariciar** the cat wouldn't let anyone stroke it • **—¿está bien la película? —se deja ver** "is the film any good?" — "it's watchable"; ▹ **vencer**

5 (*= poderse*) (+ *infin*) • **se dejó oír una débil voz** a weak voice could be heard • **ya se deja sentir el frío** it's starting to get colder

6 **dejarse de** (= *terminar de*) • **déjate de rollos y vamos al grano** stop messing around and let's get to the point • **déjate de bromas** stop kidding around • **¡déjate de tonterías!** stop messing about *o* being silly! • **déjate de tanto hablar y estudia** stop talking all the time and do some studying • **¡déjate de andar y vamos a coger el coche!** forget about walking, let's take the car!

DEJAR

Dejar en el sentido de prestar se puede traducir al inglés empleando **borrow** *o* **lend. Borrow** *se usa cuando el sujeto es quien pide (significa tomar prestado) y* **lend** *cuando el sujeto es quien da (significa dejar prestado):*

¿Me dejas tus botas de esquiar?
Can I borrow your ski boots? *o* Can you lend me your ski boots?
¿Me podrías dejar tu reloj?
Could I borrow your watch? *o* Could you lend me your watch?

NOTA: **Borrow** *y* **lend** *no se utilizan normalmente con cosas que no pueden trasladarse de un sitio a otro:*

¿Me dejas tu casa de campo este fin de semana?
Can I use your house in the country this weekend?

Para otros usos y ejemplos ver la entrada.

deje (SM) accent

dejo (SM) 1 (= *sabor*) aftertaste • **tiene un ~ raro** it has an odd aftertaste
2 [*de arrogancia, laxitud*] touch
3 (*Ling*) accent, trace of accent

del = **de + el** ▹ **de**

Del. (ABR) = **Delegación**

delación (SF) denunciation

delantal (SM) 1 (*Culin*) apron • **~ de cuero** leather apron
2 (*Escol*) pinafore

delante (ADV) 1 in front • **no hay ningún edificio ~** there are no buildings in front • **en el coche me gusta sentarme ~** I like to sit in the front of the car, when I'm in a car I like to sit in the front • **los más bajos que se pongan ~** can the shorter ones come to the front? • **no hables de Antonio con mis amigos ~** don't talk about Antonio in front of my friends • **no tengo el documento ~** I don't have the document in front of me • **entró al puerto (con) la popa ~** it entered the harbour stern first • **de ~**: • **la parte de ~** the front part • **siempre se sentaba en el banco de ~** she always sat on the front bench • **el coche de ~** the car in front • **hacia ~**: • **hizo un movimiento hacia ~** he moved forward(s) • **por ~**: • **yo iba por ~ con la linterna** I went in front with the torch • **un vestido que se abre por ~** a dress that opens at the front • **tenemos todavía cuatro horas por ~** we still have four hours in front of us • **todavía tiene mucha vida por ~** she still has her whole life ahead of her • **destruye al que se le pone por ~** he destroys anyone who gets in his way • **resuelve todos los problemas que se le pongan por ~** he solves any problem you put in front of him; ▹ **llevar**
2 • **~ de** in front of • **se colocó ~ de mí** he stood in front of me • **había un camión ~ del cine** there was a lorry in front of the cinema • **te espero ~ del cine** I'll meet you outside the cinema
3 (*esp Cono Sur*) • **~ mío/tuyo** in front of me/you • **en tu ~** in front of you

delantera (SF) 1 [*de casa, vestido*] front
2 (*Dep*) (= *línea de ataque*) forward line • **coger** *o* **tomar la ~ a algn** (*en carrera*) to take over the lead from sb; (*al contestar*) to beat sb to it • **llevar la ~** to be in the lead • **llevar la ~ a algn** to be ahead of sb • **sacar la ~ a algn** to steal a march on sb
3 (*Teat*) front row
4 (*Anat‡*) knockers‡ (*pl*), tits‡ (*pl*)
5 **delanteras** (= *calzones*) chaps; (= *mono*) overalls

delantero/a (ADJ) 1 (= *de delante*) [*parte, fila, rueda*] front (*antes de s*); [*patas de animal*] fore (*antes de s*), front
2 [*línea, posición*] (*Dep*) forward; (*en progreso*) first, foremost
(SM/F) (*Dep*) forward ▸ **delantero centro** centre-forward, center-forward (*EEUU*) ▸ **delantero extremo** outside forward, wing forward ▸ **delantero interior** inside forward

delatar ▹ CONJUG 1a (VT) 1 [*persona*] to denounce, inform against • **los delató a la policía** he reported them to the police
2 [*actitud, mirada*] to betray, give away
(VPR) **delatarse** to give o.s. away • **con su nerviosismo acabó delatándose** in the end his nerves gave him away

delator(a) (ADJ) [*sonrisa, comentario*] revealing; [*mancha*] incriminating
(SM/F) informer

delco (SM) (*Aut*) distributor

delectación (SF) delectation

delegación (SF) 1 (= *acto*) delegation ▸ **delegación de poderes** (*Admin*) devolution
2 (= *sucursal*) (*Com*) local office; [*del Estado*] *local office of a government department* ▸ **delegación del gobierno** *office of the government delegate to an autonomous community*
3 (= *representantes*) delegation • **la ~ fue a cumplimentar al Ministro** the delegation went to pay its respects to the minister ▸ **delegación comercial** trade mission
4 (*Méx*) (= *comisaría*) main police station; (= *municipio*) municipal district

delegado/a (SM/F) (= *representante*) delegate; (*Com*) representative, agent; (*Educ*) representative ▸ **delegado/a de alumnos, delegado/a de curso** student representative ▸ **delegado/a del Gobierno** (*Esp*) *government delegate to an autonomous community* ▸ **delegado/a sindical** shop steward

delegar ▹ CONJUG 1h (VT) to delegate • **~ algo en algn** to delegate sth to sb

deleitable (ADJ) delightful, delectable

deleitación (SF), **deleitamiento** (SM) delectation

deleitar ▹ CONJUG 1a (VT) to delight, charm
(VPR) **deleitarse** to delight (**con, en** in) • **~se en hacer algo** to delight in doing sth

deleite (SM) delight, pleasure • **los ~s de la carne** the pleasures of the flesh

deleitosamente (ADV) delightfully

deleitoso (ADJ) delightful, pleasing

deletéreo (ADJ) deleterious

deletrear ▹ CONJUG 1a (VT) 1 [+ *apellido, palabra*] to spell
2 (= *descifrar*) to decipher, interpret
3 (*Cono Sur*) (= *escudriñar*) to observe in great detail, look minutely at

deletreo (SM) 1 [*de apellido, palabra*] spelling, spelling-out
2 (= *desciframiento*) decipherment, interpretation

deleznable (ADJ) 1 (= *despreciable*) atrocious
2 [*arcilla, superficie*] crumbly
3 [*argumento, construcción*] weak

délfico (ADJ) Delphic

delfín (SM) 1 (*Zool*) dolphin
2 (*Pol*) designated successor, heir apparent
3 (*Hist*) dauphin

delfinario (SM) dolphinarium

Delfos (SM) Delphi

delgadez (SF) 1 [*de persona*] (= *flaqueza*) thinness; (= *esbeltez*) slimness
2 [*de tabla, muro*] thinness; [*de hilo*] fineness
3† (= *delicadeza*) delicateness
4† (= *agudeza*) sharpness

delgado (ADJ) 1 [*persona*] (= *esbelto*) slim; (= *flaco*) thin • **una jovencita muy delgada** a very slim young girl • **tienes los brazos demasiado ~s** your arms are too thin • **se ha quedado muy ~ con la enfermedad** he's got very thin from being ill • MODISMO: • **~ como un fideo** as thin as a rake
2 [*tabla, placa, muro, hebra*] thin; [*hilo*] fine
3 (*Méx*) (= *aguado*) weak, thin
4† [*tierra*] poor
5† (= *delicado*) delicate
6† (= *agudo*) sharp, clever
(ADV) ▹ **hilar**

delgaducho (ADJ) skinny*

deliberación (SF) deliberation

deliberadamente (ADV) deliberately

deliberado (ADJ) deliberate

deliberar ▹ CONJUG 1a (VT) 1 (= *debatir*) to debate
2 (= *decidir*) • **~ hacer algo** to decide to do sth
(VI) to deliberate (**sobre** on), discuss (**si** whether) • **el juez se retiró a ~** the judge retired to deliberate

deliberativo (ADJ) deliberative

delicadamente (ADV) delicately

delicadez (SF) 1 = **delicadeza**
2 (= *debilidad física*) weakness
3 (*frm*) (= *sensibilidad excesiva*) hypersensitivity

delicadeza (SF) 1 (= *suavidad*) [*de tejido, piel*] softness; [*de tela*] fineness; [*de color*] softness
2 (= *cuidado*) gentleness • **la ~ con que transportó al enfermo** the gentleness with which she moved the patient • **con mucha ~** very gently
3 (= *amabilidad*) • **tuvo la ~ de ayudarme a bajar** he was kind enough to help me down, he did me the kindness of helping me down • **no tuvo la ~ de comunicárnoslo** he didn't have the decency to let us know
4 (= *tacto*) tact, delicacy • **tuvo mucha ~ al presentar su queja** she made the complaint very tactfully *o* with great tact *o* with great

delicacy • **tendrás que presentar la queja con mucha ~** you will have to make the complaint very tactfully *o* delicately • **falta de ~** tactlessness, indelicacy
5 (= *dificultad*) delicacy, delicate nature • **no comprendió la ~ de la situación** he did not understand the delicacy *o* delicate nature of the situation
6 (= *finura*) [*de rasgos*] delicacy • **la ~ con que ejecutó la pieza** the delicacy with which she performed the piece • **describió la ~ del ambiente de palacio** she described the refined atmosphere at the palace • **me enamoró la ~ de sus modales** I fell in love with his exquisite manners
7 (= *sensibilidad excesiva*) hypersensitiveness
delicado (ADJ) **1** (= *suave*) [*tejido, piel*] delicate; [*tela*] fine; [*color*] soft
2 (= *frágil*) [*máquina*] sensitive; [*salud*] delicate • **está ~ del estómago** he has a delicate stomach
3 (= *fino*) [*rasgos*] delicate, fine; [*gusto*] delicate, subtle
4 (= *difícil*) [*situación*] delicate, tricky; [*punto*] sore; [*tema*] delicate
5 [*persona*] (= *difícil de contentar*) hard to please, fussy; (= *sensible*) hypersensitive; (= *discreto*) tactful; (= *atento*) considerate • **es muy ~ con la comida** he's very choosy about his food*
delicia (SF) delight • **tiene un jardín que es una ~** he has a delightful garden • **un libro que ha hecho las ~s de muchos niños** a book which has delighted many children
deliciosamente (ADV) delightfully
delicioso (ADJ) **1** [*momento, sonido*] delightful
2 [*comida, bebida*] delicious
delictivo (ADJ) criminal (*antes de s*)
Delilá (SF) Delilah
delimitación (SF) delimitation
delimitar ▹ CONJUG 1a (VT) to delimit
delincuencia (SF) crime • **las cifras de la ~** the incidence of crime ▸ **delincuencia de menores, delincuencia juvenil** juvenile delinquency ▸ **delincuencia informática** computer crime ▸ **delincuencia menor** petty crime
delincuencial (ADJ) criminal
delincuente (ADJ) delinquent
(SMF) (= *maleante*) criminal ▸ **delincuente común** common criminal ▸ **delincuente habitual** habitual offender ▸ **delincuente juvenil** juvenile delinquent
delineación (SF), **delineamiento** (SM) delineation ▸ **delineación industrial** technical drawing
delineador (SM) eyeliner
delineante (SM) draughtsman/draughtswoman, draftsman/draftswoman (*EEUU*)
delinear ▹ CONJUG 1a (VT) **1** [+ *contornos*] to outline
2 [+ *plan, propuesta*] to delineate
delinquimiento (SM) delinquency
delinquir ▹ CONJUG 3e (VI) to commit an offence *o* (*EEUU*) offense
deliquio (SM) swoon, fainting fit
delirante (ADJ) **1** (*Med*) delirious, raving
2 (= *disparatado*) [*idea*] crazy; [*chiste*] hilarious
delirantemente (ADV) deliriously
delirar ▹ CONJUG 1a (VI) **1** (*Med*) to be delirious
2 (= *desatinar*) to rave, talk nonsense • **¡tú deliras!*** you must be mad!
delirio (SM) **1** (*Med*) delirium
2 (= *frenesí*) • **cuando acabó de hablar fue el ~** when he finished speaking the place went wild • **el chocolate me gusta con ~** I absolutely adore chocolate
3 (= *manía*) ▸ **delirio de persecución** persecution mania ▸ **delirios de grandeza** delusions of grandeur
4 delirios (= *disparate*) nonsense (*sing*)
delírium (SM) ▸ **delírium tremens** delirium tremens
delito (SM) **1** (*Jur*) (= *acción criminal*) crime; (= *infracción*) offence, offense (*EEUU*) ▸ **delito común** common crime ▸ **delito contra la propiedad** crime against property ▸ **delito de empresa** corporate crime ▸ **delito de menor importancia** minor offence ▸ **delito de sangre** violent crime ▸ **delito ecológico** environmental crime ▸ **delito fiscal** tax offence ▸ **delito menor** minor offence ▸ **delito político** political crime
2 (= *fechoría*) (*lit*) felony; (*fig*) misdeed
delta (SM) (*Geog*) delta; ▹ **ala**
(SF) (= *letra*) delta
deltaplano (SM) **1** (= *aparato*) hang-glider
2 (= *deporte*) hang-gliding
deltoideo (ADJ), (SM) deltoid
deludir ▹ CONJUG 3a (VT) to delude
delusorio (ADJ) delusive
demacración (SF) emaciation
demacrado (ADJ) gaunt, haggard
demacrarse ▹ CONJUG 1a (VPR) to become emaciated
demagogia (SF) demagogy, demagoguery
demagógico (ADJ) demagogic
demagogismo (SM) demagogy, demagoguery
demagogo (SM) demagogue, demagog (*EEUU*)
demanda (SF) **1** (= *solicitud*) request (**de** for); (*exigiendo*) demand (**de** for) • **escribir en ~ de ayuda** to write asking for help • **ir en ~ de algo** to go in search of sth, go looking for sth • MODISMO: • **morir en la ~** to die in the attempt ▸ **demanda de extradición** extradition request ▸ **demanda del Santo Grial** quest for the Holy Grail ▸ **demanda de pago** demand for payment
2 (*esp LAm*) (= *pregunta*) inquiry
3 (*Com*) demand • **hay una gran ~ de profesores** teachers are in great demand • **tener ~** to be in demand • **ese producto no tiene ~** there is no demand for that product ▸ **demanda de mercado** market demand ▸ **demanda final** final demand ▸ **demanda indirecta** derived demand; ▹ **oferta**
4 (*Teat*) call
5 (*Elec*) load ▸ **demanda máxima** peak load
6 (*Jur*) action, lawsuit • **entablar ~** to bring an action, sue • **presentar ~ de divorcio a algn** to sue sb for divorce ▸ **demanda civil** private prosecution ▸ **demanda judicial** legal action
demandado/a (SM/F) defendant; (*en divorcio*) respondent
demandante (SMF) **1** (*Jur*) plaintiff
2 ▸ **demandante de empleo** job seeker
demandar ▹ CONJUG 1a (VT) **1** (= *exigir*) to demand
2 (*Jur*) to sue, file a lawsuit against • **demandó al periódico por difamación** he sued the paper for libel • **~ a algn por daños y perjuicios** to sue sb for damages
demaquillador (SM) make-up remover
demarcación (SF) **1** [*de frontera, zona*] demarcation • **línea de ~** demarcation line
2 (*Dep*) position
demarcar ▹ CONJUG 1g (VT) to demarcate
demarraje (SM) spurt, break, dash
demarrar ▹ CONJUG 1a (VI) to spurt, break away, make a dash
demás (ADJ) • **los ~ libros** the other books, the rest of the books • **y ~ gente de ese tipo** and other people of that sort
(PRON) **1** • **lo ~** the rest (of it) • **los ~** the others, the rest (of them) • **esto es lo importante y lo ~ se puede eliminar** this is the important thing, we can get rid of the rest • **todo lo ~** all the rest, everything else • **las ~ no tenían dinero** the others didn't have any money, the rest (of them) didn't have any money, no-one else had any money • **esta ropa es de Juan y lo ~ de Pedro** these clothes are Juan's and the others *o* the rest are Pedro's
2 • **por lo ~** otherwise, apart from that • **es muy larga, pero, por lo ~, es una buena novela** it's very long, but otherwise *o* apart from that it's a good novel
3 • **y ~** and so on, and so forth • **vimos la catedral, la muralla y ~** we saw the cathedral, the walls and so on *o* and so forth
4 • **por ~** (*frm*) **a** (= *a propósito*) • **una característica que, por ~, no es exclusiva suya** a characteristic which, incidentally *o* by the way, is not unique to him • **ha escrito decenas de novelas, por ~ excelentes** he has written dozens of novels, which are excellent by the way, he has written dozens of novels, excellent ones at that
b (= *en vano*) • **está por ~ presentar una queja** it is pointless to make a complaint • **nunca está por ~ solicitarlo** you have nothing to lose by asking for it, it is always worthwhile asking for it
c (= *demasiado*) excessively • **un informe extenso por ~** an excessively long report • **un político alabado por ~** a politician who has received excessive praise
demasía (SF) **1** (= *exceso*) excess • **con** *o* **en ~** too much, excessively • **habló en ~** he talked too much • **el maquillaje, en ~, es poco natural** too much make-up *o* an excess of make-up doesn't look very natural
2 (= *insolencia*) insolence
demasiado (ADJ) **1** (= *excesivo*) too much • **eso es ~** that's too much • **hace ~ calor** it's too hot • **con ~ cuidado** with excessive care • **¡esto es ~!** that's the limit! • **no tengo ~ tiempo** I don't have much time • **¡qué ~!*** wow!*; ▹ DEMASIADO
2 demasiados too many
(ADV) **1** (= *en exceso*) (*con adjetivos, adverbios*) too; (*con verbos*) too much • **es ~ pesado para levantarlo** it is too heavy to lift • **~ bien lo sé** I know it only too well • **comer ~** to eat too much
2 (*LAm*) (= *mucho*) • **lo siento ~** I'm very *o* really sorry • **es ~ sabio** he's very wise
demasié‡ (ADJ), (ADV) • **¡qué ~!** wow!*
(SM) • **es un ~** it's way over the top
demediar ▹ CONJUG 1b (VT) to divide in half
(VI) to be divided in half
demencia (SF) madness, insanity ▸ **demencia senil** senile dementia
demencial (ADJ) mad, demented
dementar ▹ CONJUG 1a (VT) to drive mad
(VPR) **dementarse** to go mad, become demented
demente (ADJ) mad, demented
(SMF) lunatic; (*Med*) mental patient
demérito (SM) **1** (*frm*) (= *falta*) demerit (*frm*), fault • **es un ~ para nuestra familia** it brings discredit on *o* to our family • **va en ~ de todos** it brings discredit to everyone, it discredits everyone
2 (= *indignidad*) unworthiness
3 (*LAm*) (= *menosprecio*) contempt
demeritorio (ADJ) undeserving, unworthy
demo* (SMF) (*Chile*) Christian Democrat
(SF) (*Inform, Mús*) demo
democracia (SF) democracy ▸ **democracia parlamentaria** parliamentary democracy ▸ **democracia popular** people's democracy
demócrata (ADJ) **1** [*valores, país*] democratic
2 (*en Estados Unidos*) Democrat
(SMF) **1** (*gen*) democrat
2 (*en Estados Unidos*) Democrat

d

DEMASIADO

¿"Too", "too much" o "too many"?

▷ **Demasiado** *se traduce por* **too** *delante de adjetivos y adverbios:*

Hace demasiado calor
It's too hot
Hace un día demasiado bueno para quedarse trabajando en casa
It's too nice a day to stay at home working
Hablas demasiado deprisa
You talk too quickly

▷ *Se traduce por* **too much** *cuando* **demasiado** *describe o se refiere a nombres incontables y como complemento de verbos:*

Le he echado demasiada agua a las patatas
I've put too much water in the potatoes
Creo que he comido demasiado
I think I've eaten too much
Habla demasiado
He talks too much

Cuando acompaña a un verbo de tiempo **demasiado** *suele traducirse como* **too long:**

Ha tardado demasiado en acabar la tesis
He's taken too long to finish his thesis

Too many

▷ *Se traduce por* **too many** *cuando* **demasiado** *precede a nombres contables en plural:*

Tiene demasiadas preocupaciones
She has too many worries

Para otros usos y ejemplos ver la entrada.

democratacristiano/a (ADJ), (SM/F) Christian Democrat
democráticamente (ADV) democratically
democrático (ADJ) democratic
democratización (SF) democratization
democratizador (ADJ) democratizing
democratizar ▷ CONJUG 1f (VT) to democratize
democristiano/a (ADJ), (SM/F) Christian Democrat
demodé (ADJ) démodé, passé
demografía (SF) demography
demográficamente (ADV) demographically
demográfico (ADJ) demographic • **la explosión demográfica** the population explosion
demógrafo/a (SM/F) demographer
demoledor (ADJ) **1** [*ataque, efecto*] shattering
2 (= *destructivo*) [*argumento*] overwhelming; [*crítica*] devastating
demoledoramente (ADV) overwhelmingly
demoler ▷ CONJUG 2h (VT) [+ *edificio*] to demolish, pull down; [+ *argumento, teoría*] to demolish
demolición (SF) demolition, disbanding
demonche (SM) (*euf*) = **demonio**
demoniaco (ADJ), **demoníaco** (ADJ) demoniacal, demonic
demonio (SM) **1** (= *diablo*) devil • **ese ~ de niño** that demon *o* little devil of a child • **ser el mismísimo ~** to be a right little devil ▸ **demonio familiar** familiar spirit
2* • MODISMOS: • **ir como el ~** to go like the devil, go hell for leather • **esto pesa como un ~** this is hellishly heavy • **¡vete al ~!** go to the devil *o* hell! • **¡que se lo lleve el ~!** to hell with it! • **un ruido de todos los** *o* **de mil ~s** a hell of a noise* • **esto sabe a ~s** this tastes awful • **tiene el ~ en el cuerpo** he can't sit still for five minutes
3* (*frases de sentido exclamativo*) • **¡qué ~s!** (*expresando ira*) hell!, damn it!; (*expresando sorpresa*) well, I'll be blowed!, what the devil? • **¡qué príncipe ni qué ~s!** prince my foot!* • **¿quién ~s será?** who the devil can that be? • **¿dónde ~s lo habré dejado?** where the devil can I have left it?
demonizar ▷ CONJUG 1f (VT) to demonize
demonología (SF) demonology
demontre (SM) (*euf*) = **demonio**
demora (SF) **1** (= *retraso*) delay • **sin ~** without delay
2 (*Náut*) bearing
demorar ▷ CONJUG 1a (VT) [+ *viaje*] to delay; [+ *llegada, terminación*] to hold up
(VI) **1** (= *detenerse*) to stay on, linger on • **¡no demores!** don't be long!
2 (= *perder tiempo*) to waste time • **~ en hacer algo** (*LAm*) to take a long time to do sth, be slow in doing sth • **no demores mucho** don't be too long
(VPR) **demorarse 1** ▷ VI
2 (= *tardar mucho*) to take a long time, be slow • **¿cuántos días se demora para ir allá?** (*LAm*) how many days does it take to get there? • **~se en hacer algo** to take a long time to do sth, be slow in doing sth
demorón (ADJ) (*LAm*) (= *lento*) slow • **ser ~ en hacer algo** to take a long time to do sth, be slow in doing sth
demoroso (ADJ) (*LAm*) **1** (= *moroso*) late, overdue
2 (= *lento*) slow • **ser ~ en hacer algo** to take a long time to do sth, be slow in doing sth
demos ▷ **dar**
demoscopia (SF) public opinion research
demoscópico (ADJ) • **sondeo ~** public opinion survey, survey of public opinion
Demóstenes (SM) Demosthenes
demostrable (ADJ) demonstrable
demostración (SF) **1** (= *comprobación*) [*de ejemplo, producto*] demonstration; [*de teorema, teoría*] proof • **hicieron una ~ del funcionamiento** they gave a demonstration of how it worked ▸ **demostración comercial** commercial exhibition, trade exhibition
2 (= *manifestación externa*) [*de cariño, fuerza*] show; [*de amistad*] gesture; [*de cólera*] display
demostrador(a) (SM/F) demonstrator
demostrar ▷ CONJUG 1l (VT) **1** (= *probar*) to prove • **usted no puede ~ nada** you can't prove anything • **demostró que Galileo tenía razón** she proved Galileo right, she proved *o* showed that Galileo was right • **demostró lo mal que hablaba francés** it proved *o* showed how badly he spoke French • **ha demostrado ser muy buena amiga** she has shown herself to be a very good friend
2 (= *enseñar*) to show, demonstrate • **nos ~on cómo funcionaba el sistema eléctrico** they showed us *o* demonstrated to us how the electrical system worked
3 (= *mostrar*) [+ *emoción, sentimiento*] to show, display • **no demostró ningún interés en mis problemas** he showed *o* displayed no interest in my problems
demostrativo (ADJ) demonstrative
(SM) demonstrative
demótico (ADJ) demotic
demudación (SF) change, alteration (*of countenance*)
demudado (ADJ) [*rostro*] upset, distraught
demudar ▷ CONJUG 1a (VT) [+ *rostro*] to change, alter
(VPR) **demudarse 1** [*expresión*] to change, alter
2 [*persona*] (= *perder color*) to turn pale; (= *alterarse*) to look upset • **se le demudó el rostro** the colour drained from her face • **continuó sin ~se** he went on without turning a hair
den ▷ **dar**
denante (ADV) (*LAm*), **denantes** (ADV) (*LAm*) (= *hace un rato*) earlier, a while ago; (= *antiguamente*) in past times
dendrocronología (SF) dendrochronology
dendrograma (SM) dendrogram, tree diagram
denegación (SF) [*de permiso, petición*] refusal; [*de derechos*] denial ▸ **denegación de auxilio** (*Jur*) failure to offer assistance (*though legally bound to do so*)
denegar ▷ CONJUG 1h, 1j (VT) **1** (= *rechazar*) [+ *permiso, petición*] to refuse; [+ *derechos*] to deny
2 (*Jur*) [+ *cargo*] to deny
dengoso (ADJ) (= *afectado*) affected; (= *coqueto*) coy
dengue (SM) **1** (= *remilgo*) prudery • **no me vengas con esos ~s** I don't want to hear your silly complaints
2 [*de persona*] (= *afectación*) affectation; (= *coquetería*) coyness
3 (*Med*) dengue fever, breakbone fever
4 (*And*) (= *contoneo*) wiggle
denguero (ADJ) = **dengoso**
denier (SM) denier
denigración (SF) denigration
denigrante (ADJ) **1** (= *difamante*) degrading
2 (= *injurioso*) insulting
denigrar ▷ CONJUG 1a (VT) (= *difamar*) to denigrate, run down; (= *injuriar*) to insult
denigratorio (ADJ) denigratory • **campaña denigratoria** campaign of denigration, smear campaign
denodadamente (ADV) boldly, dauntlessly, intrepidly • **luchar ~** to fight bravely
denodado (ADJ) bold, brave
denominación (SF) **1** (= *acto*) naming
2 (= *nombre*) name, designation ▸ **denominación social** (*Méx*) official company name
3 [*de billete*] denomination • **moneda de baja ~** (*LAm*) low value coin

DENOMINACIÓN DE ORIGEN

The **Denominación de Origen**, abbreviated to **D.O.**, is a prestigious product classification which is awarded to food products such as wines, cheeses, sausages and hams that are produced in designated Spanish regions according to stringent production criteria. **D.O.** labels serve as a guarantee of quality.

denominado (ADJ) named, called • **el ~ jet lag** so-called jet lag
denominador (SM) denominator ▸ **denominador común** (*Mat*) (*tb fig*) common denominator
denominar ▷ CONJUG 1a (VT) to name, designate
denostar ▷ CONJUG 1l (VT) (*frm*) to insult
denotación (SF) (*Ling, Fil*) denotation
denotar ▷ CONJUG 1a (VT) **1** (= *significar*) (*tb Ling*) to denote
2 (= *indicar*) to indicate, show • **eso denota un cambio en su política** that indicates a change in policy • **denotó nerviosismo en la entrevista** he showed a certain nervousness in the interview

densamente ADV densely
densidad SF **1** (= *concentración*) [*de sustancia, tráfico*] density; [*de humo, vegetación*] thickness, denseness; [*de caracteres*] (*Inform*) pitch ▸ **densidad de grabación** recording density ▸ **densidad de población** population density
2 [*de discurso, relato*] denseness
3 (*Fís*) density
denso ADJ **1** (= *concentrado*) [*sustancia*] dense; [*tráfico*] heavy; [*humo, vegetación*] thick, dense
2 [*discurso, relato*] dense
3 (*Fís*) dense
dentado ADJ [*filo*] jagged; [*sello*] perforated; (*Bot*) dentate • **rueda dentada** cog
SM [*de sello*] perforation
dentadura SF teeth (*pl*) • **tener mala ~** to have bad teeth ▸ **dentadura artificial, dentadura postiza** false teeth (*pl*), dentures (*pl*)
dental ADJ dental
SF (*Ling*) dental
dentamen* SM teeth (*pl*)
dentar ▸ CONJUG 1j VT [+ *filo*] to make jagged; [+ *superficie, sello*] to perforate • **sello sin ~** imperforate stamp, unperforated stamp
VI [*niño*] to teethe
dentellada SF **1** (= *mordisco*) bite, nip • **partir algo a ~s** to sever sth with one's teeth
2 (= *señal*) tooth mark
dentellar ▸ CONJUG 1a VI [*dientes*] to chatter • **estaba dentellando** his teeth were chattering • **el susto le hizo ~** the fright made his teeth chatter
dentellear ▸ CONJUG 1a VT to nibble
dentera SF **1** (= *grima*) • **dar ~ a algn** to set sb's teeth on edge
2 (= *envidia*) envy, jealousy • **dar ~ a algn** to make sb jealous • **le da ~ que le hagan fiestas al niño** it makes him jealous when they make a fuss of the baby
dentición SF **1** (= *acto*) teething • **estar con la ~** to be teething
2 (= *dientes*) teeth (*pl*) ▸ **dentición de leche** milk teeth
dentífrico ADJ tooth (*antes de s*) • **pasta dentífrica** toothpaste
SM toothpaste
dentilargo ADJ long-toothed
dentina SF dentine, dentin (EEUU)
dentista SMF dentist
dentistería SF (*Col, Ven*) **1** (= *ciencia*) dentistry
2 (= *clínica*) dental clinic, dental surgery, dentist's office (EEUU)
dentística SF (*Chile*) dentistry
dentón ADJ toothy
dentradera SF (*And*), **dentrera** SF (*And*) housemaid
dentro ADV **1** inside • **María está ~** María is inside • **allí ~** in there • **vamos ~** let's go in(side) • **comimos ~ porque estaba lloviendo** we ate inside *o* indoors because it was raining • **de** *o* **desde ~** from inside, from within (*frm*) • **para ~**: • **se fueron para ~** they went in(side) • **mételo para ~ para que quepa en la funda** push it in so that it fits in the cover • **por ~** inside • **el edificio es precioso por ~** the building is beautiful inside • **la sandía es roja por ~** a watermelon is red on the inside • **el vestido lleva un forro por ~** the dress is lined *o* has a lining inside • **se siente muy desgraciado por ~** he feels very unhappy inside
2 • **~ de a** (= *en el interior de*) in, inside • **~ de la casa** in(side) the house • **tenía un pañuelo ~ del bolso** she had a handkerchief in *o* inside her bag • **lo metió ~ del cajón** he put it in the drawer • **ascensos ~ de la empresa** promotions within the company
b (= *después de*) in • **~ de tres meses** in three months, in three months' time • **llegará ~ de poco** he'll be here shortly
c (= *en los límites de*) within • **esto no está ~ de mi competencia** this is not within my area of responsibility • **~ de lo posible** as far as possible • **su reacción estaba ~ de lo previsto** her reaction was what one might have expected • **~ de todo, me puedo considerar afortunado** all in all *o* all things considered, I can count myself lucky; ▸ **caber**
dentrodera SF (*And*) servant
dentudo ADJ toothy
denudación SF denudation
denudar ▸ CONJUG 1a VT to denude, lay bare
denuedo SM (*liter*) valour, valor (EEUU)
denuesto SM (*liter*) insult • **llenar a algn de ~s** to heap insults on sb
denuncia SF **1** [*de delito, infracción, accidente*] • **hizo** *o* **presentó** *o* **puso una ~ en comisaría** he made a formal complaint *o* accusation to the police, he reported it to the police • **hice** *o* **presenté** *o* **puse una ~ por el** *o* **del robo del bolso** I reported the theft of the bag • **hacer** *o* **presentar** *o* **poner una ~ contra algn** to report sb, make *o* file a formal complaint against sb ▸ **denuncia falsa** false accusation
2 (= *crítica*) condemnation, denunciation • **el artículo es una ~ de las injusticias del sistema** the article is a condemnation *o* denunciation of the unfairness of the system
denunciable ADJ [*delito*] indictable, punishable
denunciación SF denunciation
denunciador(a) SM/F, **denunciante** SMF **1** [*de delito*] accuser • **el ~ del accidente** the person who reported the accident
2 (= *delator*) informer
denunciar ▸ CONJUG 1b VT **1** [+ *delito, accidente*] to report • **el accidente fue denunciado a la policía** the accident was reported to the police • **denuncié en comisaría el robo de mi bolso** I reported the theft of my handbag to the police • **han denunciado al director por malversación de fondos** the manager has been reported for embezzlement • **denunció a su alumno por insultarle** she reported the student for insulting her
2 (= *criticar*) to condemn, denounce • **denunció la política derechista del gobierno** he condemned *o* denounced the government's right-wing policies
3 (*frm*) (= *indicar*) to reveal, indicate • **el olor denunciaba la presencia del gas** the smell revealed *o* indicated the presence of gas
4† (= *presagiar*) to foretell
denuncio SM = **denuncia**
deontología SF (= *ciencia*) deontology; (*profesional*) professional ethics (*pl*)
D.E.P. ABR (= **descanse en paz**) RIP
Dep. ABR **1** (= **Departamento**) Dept
2 (*Com*) = **Depósito**
deparar ▸ CONJUG 1a VT (= *proporcionar*) to provide with, afford (*frm*) • **nos deparó la ocasión de conocer a su familia** it provided us with *o* (*frm*) afforded us the opportunity to meet his family • **los placeres que el viaje nos deparó** the pleasures which the trip afforded us (*frm*) • **pero también nos deparó la solución** but it also furnished us with the solution • **lo que el destino nos depare** what fate has *o* holds in store for us • MODISMO: • **¡Dios te la depare buena!** and the best of luck!
departamental ADJ departmental
departamento SM **1** [*de empresa, universidad*] department • **Departamento de Lingüística Aplicada** Department of Applied Linguistics ▸ **departamento de envíos** dispatch department ▸ **departamento de visados** visa section ▸ **departamento jurídico** legal department
2 [*de caja, tren*] compartment ▸ **departamento de fumadores** smoking compartment ▸ **departamento de no fumadores** non-smoking compartment ▸ **departamento de primera** first-class compartment
3 (*Náut*) ▸ **departamento de máquinas** engine room
4 (*LAm*) (= *piso*) flat, apartment (EEUU)
5 (*And, Chile*) (= *provincia*) province
departir ▸ CONJUG 3a VI (*frm*) converse (*frm*) (**con** with, **de** about)
depauperación SF **1** (= *empobrecimiento*) impoverishment
2 (*Med*) weakening
depauperar ▸ CONJUG 1a VT **1** (= *empobrecer*) to impoverish
2 (= *debilitar*) to weaken
VPR **depauperarse 1** (= *empobrecerse*) to become impoverished
2 (= *debilitarse*) to become weak
dependencia SF **1** (= *estado*) dependence (**de** on) ▸ **dependencia psicológica** psychological dependence, psychological dependency
2 (= *parentesco*) relationship
3 (*Arquit*) (= *habitación*) room ▸ **dependencia policial** police station • **permanecer en ~s policiales** to remain in police custody
4 (*Com*) (= *sección*) section, office; (= *sucursal*) branch office; (= *empleados*) personnel, employees (*pl*)
5 (*Pol*) dependency
6 dependencias (= *anexo*) [*de edificio, castillo*] outbuildings; [*de aparato*] accessories
depender ▸ CONJUG 2a VI **1** • **—¿vas a ir? —depende** "are you going?" —"it depends"
2 • **~ de algn/algo** to depend on sb/sth • **mi futuro depende de este examen** my future depends on this exam • **depende de lo que diga mi madre** it depends (on) what my mother says • **no te eches atrás ahora, que dependo de ti** don't back out now, I'm relying *o* depending on you • **sin coche, dependes de los demás** without a car you depend on *o* you're dependent on other people, without a car you have to rely on other people • **todavía depende económicamente de sus padres** he is still financially dependent on his parents • **depende completamente de las drogas** she is completely dependent on drugs
3 • **~ de** [*empleado, institución*] to be accountable to, be answerable to • **esta oficina depende de la Generalitat** this office is accountable *o* answerable to the Generalitat
4 • **~ de algn** (= *corresponder a*): • **lo siento, su aceptación no depende de mí** I'm sorry, it's not up to me whether you are accepted or not
5 (*Pol*) • **un territorio que depende de Gran Bretaña** a British dependency
dependiente¹ ADJ dependent (**de** on)
dependiente²/a SM/F (*en tienda*) shop assistant, sales assistant, salesclerk (EEUU)
depilación SF, **depilado** SM (*con crema, con depiladora*) hair removal, depilation; (*con cera*) waxing; (*con pinzas*) plucking
depilador ADJ • **crema ~a** hair remover, depilatory cream
SM hair remover, depilatory
depiladora SF hair remover

d

depilar ▹ CONJUG 1a (VT) (*con crema, con depiladora*) to remove (unwanted) hair from; (*con cera*) to wax; (*con pinzas*) to pluck
(VPR) **depilarse** • **~se las piernas** to wax one's legs • **~se las cejas** to pluck one's eyebrows

depilatorio (ADJ) depilatory
(SM) hair remover, depilatory

deplorable (ADJ) [*conducta*] deplorable; [*estado*] appalling • **vuestro comportamiento fue ~** your behaviour was deplorable

deplorablemente (ADV) deplorably, appallingly

deplorar ▹ CONJUG 1a (VT) **1** (= *lamentar*) to deplore • **lo deploro mucho** I'm extremely sorry
2 (= *censurar*) to condemn

deponente (ADJ) **1** (*Ling*) deponent
2 (*Jur*) • **persona ~** deponent, person making a statement
(SMF) (*Jur*) deponent

deponer ▹ CONJUG 2q (VT) **1** (= *dejar*) [+ *armas*] to lay down; [+ *actitud*] to change • **no conseguirás que deponga su actitud** you won't be able to persuade him to change his attitude
2 (= *quitar*) [+ *rey*] to depose; [+ *gobernante*] to oust, overthrow; [+ *ministro*] to remove from office
(VI) **1** (*Jur*) to give evidence
2 (*CAm, Méx*) (= *vomitar*) to vomit

deportación (SF) deportation

deportar ▹ CONJUG 1a (VT) to deport

deporte (SM) sport • **es muy aficionada al ~** she is very keen on sport • **el fútbol es mi ~ favorito** football is my favourite sport • **unas zapatillas de ~** a pair of sports shoes *o* trainers *o* (*EEUU*) sneakers ▸ **deporte blanco** winter sports (*pl*); (*esp*) skiing ▸ **deporte de competición** competitive sport ▸ **deporte de exhibición** show event ▸ **deporte del remo** rowing ▸ **deporte de riesgo** extreme sport ▸ **deporte de vela** sailing ▸ **deporte hípico** horse-riding ▸ **deporte náutico** (*con lancha*) water sports (*pl*) (*in which a boat is used*); (*con velero*) yachting ▸ **deportes acuáticos** water sports ▸ **deportes de invierno** winter sports

deportista (ADJ) sports (*antes de s*), sporting • **el público ~** the sporting public • **es muy ~** she's very keen on sport(s), she's very sporty*
(SMF) sportsman/sportswoman

deportivamente (ADV) **1** (= *sin agresividad*) sportingly • **se tomó la derrota muy ~** she took the defeat very sportingly
2 (= *relacionado con el deporte*) • **hablando ~** in sporting terms • **viste ~** she wears sports clothes

deportividad (SF) sportsmanship

deportivo (ADJ) **1** [*club, periódico, zapatillas*] sports (*antes de s*); ▹ **puerto**
2 [*actitud*] sporting, sportsmanlike
3 [*ropa*] casual
(SM) **1** (*Aut*) sports car
2 deportivos (= *zapatos*) sports shoes, trainers, tennis shoes (*EEUU*)
3 (*Prensa*) sports paper

deposición (SF) **1** (= *derrocamiento*) [*de rey*] deposition; [*de gobernante*] overthrow, ousting; [*de ministro*] removal from office, sacking
2 (*Jur*) (= *testimonio*) deposition, evidence
3 (*euf*) (= *acto*) bowel movement; (= *excremento*) stool • **hacer una ~** to have a bowel movement

depositador(a) (SM/F), **depositante** (SMF) (*Com, Econ*) depositor

depositar ▹ CONJUG 1a (VT) **1** (*frm*) (= *colocar*) [+ *flor, ofrenda*] to place (**en, sobre** on); [+ *mercancías*] to put away, store • **"depositen las bolsas en información"** "please leave your bags at the information desk" • **~ la confianza en algn** to place one's trust in sb
2 (*Econ*) [+ *dinero, joyas*] to deposit
(VPR) **depositarse** [*líquido, polvo*] to settle

depositaría (SF) (*Econ*) trust

depositario/a (SM/F) [*de dinero*] depository, trustee; [*de secreto*] repository ▸ **depositario/a judicial** official receiver

depósito (SM) **1** (= *contenedor*) (*gen*) tank ▸ **depósito de agua** (= *tanque*) water tank, cistern; (= *pantano*) reservoir ▸ **depósito de combustible** fuel tank ▸ **depósito de gasolina** petrol tank, gas tank (*EEUU*)
2 (= *almacén*) [*de mercancías*] warehouse, depot; [*de animales, coches*] pound; (*Mil*) depot; [*de desechos*] dump • **mercancías en ~** bonded goods ▸ **depósito afianzado** bonded warehouse ▸ **depósito de aduana** customs warehouse ▸ **depósito de alimentación** (*Inform*) feeder bin ▸ **depósito de basura** rubbish dump, tip ▸ **depósito de cadáveres** mortuary, morgue ▸ **depósito de carbono** coal tip ▸ **depósito de equipajes** left-luggage office, checkroom (*EEUU*) ▸ **depósito de libros** book stack ▸ **depósito de locomotoras** engine shed, roundhouse (*EEUU*) ▸ **depósito de maderas** timber yard, lumber yard (*EEUU*) ▸ **depósito de municiones** ammunition dump
3 (*Com, Econ*) deposit • **dejar una cantidad en ~** to leave a sum as a deposit ▸ **depósito a la vista** sight deposit ▸ **depósito a plazo (fijo)** fixed-term deposit ▸ **depósito bancario** bank deposit
4 (*Quím*) sediment, deposit

depravación (SF) **1** (= *cualidad*) depravity
2 (= *acto*) depraved act

depravado/a (ADJ) depraved, corrupt
(SM/F) degenerate

depravar ▹ CONJUG 1a (VT) to deprave, corrupt
(VPR) **depravarse** to become depraved

depre* (SF) (= *depresión*) • **tiene la ~** she's feeling a bit low
(ADJ) • **estar ~** to be feeling down

depreciación (SF) depreciation ▸ **depreciación acelerada** accelerated depreciation ▸ **depreciación normal** wear and tear

depreciar ▹ CONJUG 1b (VT) to depreciate, reduce the value of
(VPR) **depreciarse** to depreciate

depredación (SF) **1** (= *saqueo*) pillage
2 (*Zool*) predation

depredador (ADJ) [*animal, instinto*] predatory
(SM) (*Zool*) predator

depredar ▹ CONJUG 1a (VT) **1** (= *saquear*) to pillage
2 (*Zool*) to prey on

depresión (SF) **1** (*Med*) depression ▸ **depresión nerviosa** nervous breakdown ▸ **depresión posparto** postnatal depression
2 (= *hondonada*) (*en terreno*) depression; (*en horizonte, camino*) dip
3 (= *descenso*) [*de temperatura, presión*] drop, fall (de in) • **~ del mercurio** fall in temperature
4 (*Econ*) depression, recession
5 (*Meteo*) depression

depresivo/a (ADJ) [*carácter, persona*] depressive • **es una persona depresiva** she's a depressive, she's always feeling depressed
(SM/F) depressive

deprimente (ADJ) depressing
(SM) depressant

deprimido (ADJ) depressed

deprimir ▹ CONJUG 3a (VT) **1** (*Psic*) to depress • **este tiempo me deprime** I find this weather depressing, this weather gets me down* • **la muerte de su marido la deprimió** the death of her husband sent her into a depression *o* made her depressed
2 (*Com*) [+ *mercado, economía*] to depress; [+ *consumo*] to slow (down)
3 (*Med*) [+ *sistema inmunológico*] to depress
(VPR) **deprimirse** to get depressed, become depressed

deprisa (ADV) ▹ **prisa**

depuración (SF) **1** (= *purificación*) [*de agua*] treatment, purification; [*de aguas residuales*] treatment; [*de estilo*] refinement
2 (*Pol*) purge
3 (*Inform*) debugging

depurado (ADJ) [*estilo*] pure, refined

depurador (SM) purifier

depuradora (SF) [*de agua*] water-treatment plant; (*en piscina*) filter system ▸ **depuradora de aguas residuales** sewage plant *o* farm

depurar ▹ CONJUG 1a (VT) **1** (= *purificar*) [+ *agua*] to treat, purify; [+ *aguas residuales*] to treat; [+ *sangre*] to cleanse
2 (*Pol*) to purge
3 (*Inform*) to debug
4 (*Caribe**) [+ *empleado*] to fire*

depurativo (SM) blood tonic

dequeísmo (SM) *tendency to use "de que" in place of "que" (eg "pienso de que")*

der. (ABR), **der.°** (ABR) (= **derecho**) r

derbi (SM) (PL: **derbis**), **derby** (SM) (PL: **derbys**) (local) derby

derecha (SF) **1** (= *lado derecho*) • **la ~** the right • **está prohibido adelantar por la ~** you're not allowed to overtake on the right • **se sentó a la ~ del embajador** he sat on the right *o* to the right of the ambassador • **toma el desvío de la ~** take the turning on the right • **seguir por la ~** to keep (to the) right • **torcer a la ~** to turn right • MODISMO: • **no dar *o* hacer nada a ~s** (*Esp*) not to do *o* get anything right; ▹ **conducción**
2 (*Anat*) (*tb* **mano derecha**) right hand; (*tb* **pierna derecha**) right leg • **escribe con la ~** he writes with his right hand
3 (*Esp*) (*Pol*) • **la ~** the Right • **ser de ~s** to be right-wing; ▹ **extremo**

derechamente (ADV) **1** (= *en línea recta*) straight, directly
2 (= *correctamente*) properly, rightly

derechazo (SM) **1** (*Boxeo*) right
2 (*Tenis*) forehand drive
3 (*Taur*) *pass with the cape*

derechismo (SM) right-wing outlook *o* tendencies *etc*

derechista (ADJ) right-wing
(SMF) right-winger

derechización (SF) drift towards the right

derechizar ▹ CONJUG 1f (VT) [+ *partido*] to lead towards the right
(VPR) **derechizarse** to move to the right, become right-wing

derecho (ADJ) **1** [*línea, dirección*] (= *recto*) straight; (= *vertical*) upright, straight • **traza las líneas derechas** draw the lines straight • **siéntate ~** sit upright *o* straight • **anda derecha** walk upright, stand straight when you walk • **poner algo ~** (= *no torcido*) to put sth straight, straighten sth; (= *no caído*) to stand sth upright • MODISMO: • **tener a algn más ~ que una vela** to have sb under one's thumb
2 (= *del lado derecho*) [*brazo, pierna, oreja*] right; [*lado, cajón*] right-hand • **tiene toda la parte derecha del cuerpo paralizada** he's paralysed down the right side of his body • **entre por la puerta derecha** go through the right-hand door; ▹ **brazo, ojo**
3 (= *honrado*) honest, straight
4 (*CAm*) (= *afortunado*) lucky

ADV 1 (= *en línea recta*) • **seguir ~** to carry *o* go straight on • **siga todo ~** carry *o* go straight on
2 (= *directamente*) straight • **después del cine, derechito para casa** after the cinema, straight home • **fui ~ a Londres** I went straight to London
SM 1 (*Jur*) (= *estudios, legislación*) law; (= *justicia*) justice • **estudiante de Derecho** law student • **Facultad de Derecho** Faculty of Law • **lo que manda el ~ en este caso** what justice demands in this case • **conforme a ~** in accordance with the law • **no actuó conforme a ~** he acted unlawfully • **propietario en ~** legal owner • **por ~** in law, legally • **lo que me corresponde por ~** what is legally mine, what is mine by law • **por ~ propio** in one's own right ▸ **derecho administrativo** administrative law ▸ **derecho canónico** canon law ▸ **derecho civil** civil law ▸ **derecho comunitario** Community law ▸ **derecho consuetudinario** common law ▸ **derecho de compañías** company law ▸ **derecho de familia** family law ▸ **derecho del trabajo** labour *o* (*EEUU*) labor law ▸ **derecho de sociedades** company law ▸ **derecho escrito** statute law ▸ **derecho fiscal** tax law ▸ **derecho foral** *legislation pertaining to those Spanish regions which have charters called "fueros"* ▸ **derecho internacional** international law ▸ **derecho laboral** labour law, labor law (*EEUU*) ▸ **derecho marítimo** maritime law ▸ **derecho mercantil** commercial law ▸ **derecho penal** criminal law ▸ **derecho político** constitutional law ▸ **derecho positivo** statute law ▸ **derecho privado** private law ▸ **derecho procesal** procedural law ▸ **derecho público** public law ▸ **derecho romano** Roman law ▸ **derecho tributario** tax law
2 [*de persona, entidad*] right • **"se reserva el derecho de admisión"** "the management reserve(s) the right to refuse admission" • **¿con qué ~ me hablas así?** what right have you to talk to me that way? • **es miembro de pleno ~** he's a full member • **¡no hay ~!** it's not fair! • **~ a la educación** right to education • **el ~ a la libertad** the right to be free • **~ a la intimidad** right to *o* of privacy • **lo único que nos queda es el ~ al pataleo** (*hum*) the only thing we can do is kick up a fuss* • **~ al voto** • **~ a votar** (*gen*) right to vote; (*como derecho civil*) franchise, right to vote • **con ~ a algo** entitled to sth • **declaraciones de la renta con ~ a devolución** tax returns entitled to a rebate • **entrada con ~ a consumición** *entrance ticket including one free drink* • **dar ~ a hacer algo** to give the right to do sth • **eso no te da ~ a hablarme así** that doesn't give you the right to talk to me that way • **estar en su ~** to be within one's rights • **claro, estás en tu ~ de decir lo que quieras** of course, you are perfectly entitled to say whatever you like • **tener ~ a algo** to be entitled to sth • **no tenemos ~ a vacaciones** we are not entitled to holidays • **tener ~ a hacer algo** to have a *o* the right to do sth • **no tienes ningún ~ a insultarme** you have no right to insult me ▸ **derecho de asilo** right of asylum ▸ **derecho de huelga** right to strike ▸ **derecho de paso** right of way, easement (*EEUU*) ▸ **derecho de pernada** (*Hist*) droit du seigneur ▸ **derecho de réplica** right of reply ▸ **derecho de retención** (*Com*) lien ▸ **derecho de reunión** right of assembly ▸ **derecho de tránsito** right of passage ▸ **derecho de veto** right of veto ▸ **derecho de visita** right of access ▸ **derecho divino** divine right ▸ **derecho preferente** preferential right ▸ **derechos civiles** civil rights ▸ **derechos de la mujer** women's rights
3 **derechos** (*Com*) rights • **"reservados todos los ~s"** "all rights reserved" • **tienen los ~s exclusivos para la venta del disco** they have the exclusive rights to sales of the record ▸ **derechos cinematográficos** film rights ▸ **derechos de antena** broadcasting rights ▸ **derechos de autor** copyright (*sing*) ▸ **derechos de edición** publishing rights ▸ **derechos de emisión** (*TV, Radio*) broadcasting rights ▸ **derechos de patente** patent rights ▸ **derechos editoriales** publishing rights ▸ **derechos humanos** human rights • **Declaración de los Derechos Humanos** Declaration of Human Rights
4 **derechos** (= *honorarios*) [*de arquitecto, notario*] fee(s); (= *impuestos*) duty (*sing*) • **franco de ~s** duty-free • **sujeto a ~s** subject to duty, dutiable ▸ **derechos aduaneros, derechos arancelarios, derechos de aduana** customs duty ▸ **derechos de asesoría, derechos de consulta** consulting fees, consultancy fees ▸ **derechos de autor** royalties ▸ **derechos de enganche** (*Telec*) connection charges ▸ **derechos de entrada** import duties ▸ **derechos de exportación** export duties ▸ **derechos de importación** import duties ▸ **derechos de matrícula** registration fee (*sing*) ▸ **derechos de muelle** dock dues, docking fees (*EEUU*) ▸ **derechos de peaje** (*Aut*) toll (*sing*) ▸ **derechos portuarios** harbour dues, harbor dues (*EEUU*) ▸ **derechos reales** *tax paid after the completion of an official transaction*
5 (*tb* **lado derecho**) [*de tela, papel*] right side; [*de calcetín, chaqueta*] outside • **¿cuál es el ~ de esta tela?** which is the right side of this fabric? • **puedes planchar la falda por el ~** you can iron the skirt on the outside • **poner algo al** *o* **del ~** to put sth the right side *o* way up • **pon el mantel del ~** put the tablecloth the right side *o* way up • **ponte la camiseta al ~** put your T-shirt on the right way round

derechohabiente SMF rightful claimant

derechura SF 1 (= *honestidad*) straightness • **hablar en ~** to speak plainly, talk straight • **hacer algo en ~** to do sth right away
2 (= *franqueza*) directness
3 (= *justicia*) rightness, justice
4 (*LAm*) (= *suerte*) luck, good luck

deriva SF (*Náut*) drift • **buque a la ~** ship adrift, drifting ship • **ir** *o* **estar a la ~** to drift • **el país va a la ~** the country has lost direction ▸ **deriva continental, deriva de los continentes** continental drift

derivación SF 1 (= *procedencia*) derivation
2 (*Elec*) shunt • **hacer una ~ en un alambre** to tap a wire • **en ~** shunt (*antes de s*)
3 (*Ling*) (= *etimología*) etymology, derivation; (= *composición*) word formation ▸ **derivación regresiva** back-formation
4 [*de río*] diversion

derivado ADJ derived
SM 1 (*Ling*) derivative
2 (*Industria, Quím*) by-product ▸ **derivado cárnico** meat product ▸ **derivado del petróleo** oil product ▸ **derivado lácteo** milk product • **~s lácteos** dairy products

derivar[1] ▹ CONJUG 1a VI 1 • **~ de algo** (= *provenir de*) to derive from sth • **esta palabra deriva del griego** this word derives from *o* is derived from the Greek • **esta crisis deriva de una mala política financiera** this crisis stems from *o* springs from bad financial policy • **de estos datos se deriva que ...** from this it follows that ...
2 • **~ en algo** (= *tener como resultado*) to lead to sth, result in sth • **esto derivó en la pérdida de las colonias** this led to *o* resulted in the loss of the colonies • **derivó en tragedia** it ended in tragedy
3 • **~ hacia algo** to turn to sth • **la conversación derivó hacia otros temas** the conversation moved on to *o* turned to different topics • **en su vejez su interés derivó hacia la literatura** in his old age his interest turned to literature
4 (*Náut*) to drift
VT 1 [+ *carretera, río*] to divert
2 [+ *conversación, charla*] to divert, steer • **derivó el debate hacia temas menos controvertidos** he diverted *o* steered the discussion towards less controversial subjects
3 (*Mat*) to derive
4 (*Elec*) to shunt
VPR **derivarse** • **~se de algo** [*palabra, término*] to derive from sth, be derived from sth

derivar[2] ▹ CONJUG 1a VI (*Náut*) to drift

derivativo ADJ, SM derivative

dermatología SF dermatology

dermatólogo/a SM/F dermatologist

dérmico ADJ skin (*antes de s*) • **enfermedad dérmica** skin disease

dermohidratante SM skin moisturizer

dermoprotector ADJ skin (*antes de s*) SM skin protector

derogación SF [*de ley*] repeal; [*de contrato*] revocation

derogar ▹ CONJUG 1h VT [+ *ley*] to repeal; [+ *contrato*] to revoke

derrabar ▹ CONJUG 1a VT to dock, cut off the tail of

derrabe SM [*de monte*] rock-fall; [*de techo*] cave-in

derrama SF 1 (= *reparto*) apportionment of (local) tax
2 (= *sobretasa*) special levy
3 (= *tasación*) valuation, rating
4 (= *vale*) credit voucher
5 (= *dividendo*) interim dividend payment

derramadero SM spillway ▸ **derramadero de basura** rubbish dump

derramamiento SM 1 [*de líquido*] spilling; (*al rebosar*) overflowing ▸ **derramamiento de sangre** bloodshed
2 [*de vidas, recursos*] squandering
3 (= *esparcimiento*) scattering

derramar ▹ CONJUG 1a VT 1 (*fuera de recipiente*) [+ *líquido*] to spill; [+ *sangre, lágrimas, luz*] to shed • **~ una taza de café** to spill a cup of coffee
2 (= *desaprovechar*) [+ *talento, dinero*] to squander, waste
3 (= *esparcir*) [+ *favores*] to lavish, pour out; [+ *chismes, noticias*] to spread
4 [+ *impuestos*] to apportion
VPR **derramarse** 1 (= *salirse*) [*líquido*] to spill; [*harina*] to pour out, spill out • **llenar una taza hasta ~se** to fill a cup to overflowing
2 (= *esparcirse*) to scatter • **la multitud se derramó por todos lados** the crowd scattered in all directions

derrame SM 1 (= *acto*) = **derramamiento**
2 (*Med*) • **tiene un ~ en el ojo** he's got a burst blood vessel in his eye ▸ **derrame cerebral** brain haemorrhage *o* (*EEUU*) hemorrhage ▸ **derrame sinovial** synovitis
3 (= *salida*) (*por encima del recipiente*) overflow; (*en pluma, recipiente*) leakage

derrapada SF, **derrapamiento** SM skid, skidding

derrapante ADJ • **"camino derrapante"** (*Méx*) "slippery road"

derrapar ▹ CONJUG 1a VI (*Aut*) to skid
VPR **derraparse** (*Méx*) 1 (= *patinar*) to slip

2 • **~se por algn*** to be mad about sb*
derrape (SM) **1** (*Aut*) skid
2 (*Caribe*‡) (= *alboroto*) uproar, shindy*
derredor (SM) • **al** *o* **en ~ (de)** around, about • **en su ~** round about him
derrelicto (SM) (*Náut*) derelict
derrengado (ADJ) **1** (= *torcido*) bent, twisted
2 (= *cojo*) crippled, lame
3 (= *cansado*) • **estar ~** to ache all over • **dejar ~ a algn** to wear sb out
derrengante (ADJ) exhausting, crippling
derrengar ▷ CONJUG 1h (VT) **1** (= *torcer*) to bend, twist
2 • **~ a algn** (= *deslomar*) to break sb's back; (= *agotar*) to wear sb out
(VPR) **derrengarse*** to collapse • **~se de risa** to collapse with laughter, fall about laughing
derrepente (SM) (*CAm*) • **de** *o* **en un ~** ▷ **repente**
derretido (ADJ) **1** (= *fundido*) [*mantequilla, helado*] melted; [*metal*] molten; [*nieve*] thawed
2 • **estar ~ por algn** to be crazy about sb
derretimiento (SM) **1** (= *fundido*) [*de mantequilla, helado*] melting; [*de nieve*] thawing • **se produjo el ~ del metal en el horno** the metal was melted (down) in the furnace
2 (= *derroche*) squandering
derretir ▷ CONJUG 3k (VT) (= *fundir*) [+ *mantequilla, helado*] to melt; [+ *metal*] to melt, melt down; [+ *nieve*] to melt, thaw
(VPR) **derretirse 1** (= *fundirse*) [*mantequilla, helado, metal*] to melt; [*nieve*] to thaw, melt
2* (= *sulfurarse*) to get worked up
3* (= *mostrarse sensible*) to come over all sentimental • **te derrites cada vez que te habla** whenever she speaks to you, you go all soppy *o* come over all sentimental
derribar ▷ CONJUG 1a (VT) **1** (= *derrumbar*) [+ *edificio*] to knock down, pull down; [+ *puerta*] to batter down; [+ *barrera*] to tear down • **van a ~ la fábrica** they are going to knock down *o* pull down the factory • **el huracán derribó varias casas** the hurricane blew down *o* brought down a number of houses
2 [+ *persona*] to knock down; (*Boxeo*) to floor
3 (*Aer*) to shoot down, bring down • **fue derribado sobre el lago** he was shot down over the lake
4 (*Caza*) to shoot, bag
5 [+ *gobierno*] to bring down, topple
6 [+ *pasión*] to subdue
(VPR) **derribarse 1** (= *caer al suelo*) to fall down, collapse
2 (= *tirarse al suelo*) to throw o.s. down
derribo (SM) **1** [*de edificio*] knocking down, demolition
2 (*Lucha*) throw, take-down (*EEUU*)
3 (*Aer*) shooting down
4 (*Pol*) overthrow
5 **derribos** (= *escombros*) rubble (*sing*), debris (*sing*)
derrisco (SM) (*Caribe*) gorge, ravine
derrocadero (SM) cliff, precipice, steep place
derrocamiento (SM) **1** [*de gobierno*] overthrow
2 [*de edificio*] demolition
derrocar ▷ CONJUG 1g (VT) **1** (*Pol*) [+ *gobierno*] to overthrow, topple; [+ *ministro*] to oust
2 [+ *edificio*] to knock down, demolish
3 (= *despeñar*) to hurl down
(VPR) **derrocarse** • **~se por un precipicio** to throw o.s. over a cliff
derrochador(a) (ADJ), (SM/F) spendthrift
derrochar ▷ CONJUG 1a (VT) **1** [+ *dinero, recursos*] to squander, waste
2 (= *tener*) [+ *energía, salud*] to be bursting with, be full of • **~ mal genio** to be excessively bad-tempered
derroche (SM) **1** (= *despilfarro*) waste, squandering • **regar todos los días es un ~ de agua** it's a waste of water watering the plants every day • **con un imperdonable ~ de recursos** with an unforgivable squandering of resources • **no se puede tolerar tal ~** such extravagance *o* wastefulness cannot be tolerated
2 (= *abundancia*) abundance, excess • **con un ~ de buen gusto** with a fine display of good taste
derrochón/ona (ADJ), (SM/F) = **derrochador**
derrota¹ (SF) **1** (= *camino, vereda*) route, track
2 (*Náut*) course
derrota² (SF) (*Dep, Mil*) defeat • **sufrir una grave ~** (*en batalla, partido*) to suffer a heavy defeat; (*en proyecto*) to suffer a grave setback
derrotado (ADJ) **1** (= *vencido*) [*ejército*] defeated; [*equipo*] losing, defeated
2 [*vestidos, persona*] shabby • **un actor ~** a down-and-out actor
derrotar ▷ CONJUG 1a (VT) **1** (= *vencer*) [+ *ejército*] to defeat; [+ *equipo*] to defeat, beat
2 (= *estropear*) [+ *ropa*] to tear, ruin; (*fig*) [+ *salud*] to ruin
(VPR) **derrotarse**‡ [*delincuente*] to cough‡, sing‡ • **~se de algn** to grass on sb‡
derrotero (SM) **1** (*Náut*) course • MODISMO: • **tomar otro(s) ~(s)** to adopt a different course
2 (*Caribe*) (= *tesoro*) hidden treasure
derrotismo (SM) defeatism
derrotista (ADJ), (SMF) defeatist
derruir ▷ CONJUG 3g (VT) to demolish, tear down
derrumbadero (SM) **1** (= *precipicio*) cliff, precipice, steep place
2 (= *peligro*) danger, hazard
derrumbamiento (SM) **1** [*de edificio*] (= *desplome*) collapse; (= *demolición*) demolition ▸ **derrumbamiento de piedras** rockfall ▸ **derrumbamiento de tierra** landslide
2 [*del techo*] collapse, cave-in
3 (= *descenso brusco*) [*de pacto, sistema*] collapse; [*de precios*] sharp fall
derrumbar ▷ CONJUG 1a (VT) **1** [+ *edificio*] to knock down, demolish
2 (= *despeñar*) to fling down, hurl down
3 (= *volcar*) to upset, overturn
(VPR) **derrumbarse 1** (= *hundirse*) [*edificio*] to collapse, fall down; [*techo*] to fall in, cave in
2 (= *precipitarse*) [*persona*] to fling o.s., hurl o.s. (**por** down, over)
3 [*esperanzas*] to collapse • **se han derrumbado los precios** prices have tumbled
derrumbe (SM) **1** = **derrumbamiento**
2 (= *precipicio*) cliff, precipice, steep place
3 (= *peligro*) danger, hazard
derviche (SMF) dervish
des... (PREF) de..., des..., un..., dis... • **descolonización** decolonization • **desmilitarizado** demilitarized • **desempleo** unemployment • **desfavorable** unfavourable • **desgana** unwillingness • **desalentador** discouraging
desabastecer ▷ CONJUG 2d (VT) to leave short
desabastecido (ADJ) • **estar ~ de algo** to be out of sth • **nos cogió ~s de gasolina** it caught us out of *o* without petrol
desabastecimiento (SM) shortage, scarcity
desabillé (SM) deshabille
desabolladura (SF) (*esp LAm*) (*Aut*) panel beating
desabollar ▷ CONJUG 1a (VT) to knock the dents out of
desabonarse ▷ CONJUG 1a (VPR) to stop subscribing, cancel one's subscription
desabono (SM) **1** (= *acto*) cancellation of one's subscription
2 (= *descrédito*) discredit • **hablar en ~ de algn** to say damaging things about sb, speak ill of sb
desaborido/a (ADJ) [*comida*] insipid, tasteless; [*persona*] dull
(SM/F) • **es un ~** he's so dull, he's such a bore
desabotonar ▷ CONJUG 1a (VT) to unbutton, undo
(VI) (*Bot*) to blossom
(VPR) **desabotonarse** [*camisa, pantalón*] to come undone • **él se desabotonó la camisa** he unbuttoned *o* undid his shirt
desabrido (ADJ) **1** (= *poco amable*) [*persona*] surly; [*tono*] harsh; [*respuesta*] sharp; [*debate*] bitter, acrimonious
2 [*comida*] tasteless, insipid
3 [*tiempo*] unpleasant
desabrigado (ADJ) **1** [*persona*] • **no deberías salir ~ a la calle** you shouldn't go out without warm clothes on
2 [*lugar*] exposed
desabrigar ▷ CONJUG 1h (VT) **1** (= *quitar ropa a*) to remove the clothing of • **desabrígalo un poco, que hace mucho calor** take some *o* a layer of his clothes off, it's very hot
2 (= *desproteger*) to deprive of protection
(VPR) **desabrigarse** (*quitándose ropa*) to take off one's clothes; (*en la cama*) to throw off the bedcovers, kick off the bedcovers • **no te desabrigues cuando salgas** stay well wrapped up when you're outside
desabrigo (SM) **1** (= *acto*) uncovering
2 (= *falta de protección*) lack of protection
desabrimiento (SM) **1** (= *falta de amabilidad*) [*de persona*] surliness, rudeness; [*de tono*] harshness; [*de respuesta*] sharpness; [*de debate*] acrimony • **contestar con ~** to answer sharply
2 (*en comida*) tastelessness, insipidness
3 (= *disgusto*) unpleasantness
4 (= *depresión*) depression, lowness of spirits
desabrir ▷ CONJUG 3a (VT) **1** [+ *comida*] to give a nasty taste to
2 [+ *persona*] (= *amargar*) to embitter; (= *atormentar*) to torment
desabrochado (ADJ) [*camisa*] unbuttoned; [*cremallera, bragueta, zapatos*] undone
desabrochar ▷ CONJUG 1a (VT) **1** [+ *camisa*] to unbutton, undo; [+ *cremallera, bragueta, zapatos*] to undo • **¿me puedes ~ el collar?** can you undo *o* unfasten my necklace?
2 [+ *secreto, misterio*] to penetrate
(VPR) **desabrocharse 1** [*ropa*] to come undone • **¿me ayudas a ~me el vestido?** would you help me undo my dress?
2 (= *desahogarse*) to unburden o.s.
desaburrirse ▷ CONJUG 3a (VPR) (*LAm*) to enjoy o.s., have a good time
desacatador (ADJ) disrespectful, insulting
desacatar ▷ CONJUG 1a (VT) [+ *ley*] to disobey; [+ *norma*] to fail to comply with; [+ *persona*] to be disrespectful to
desacato (SM) **1** (= *desobediencia*) (*a la norma*) failure to comply (**a** with); (*a la autoridad*) disrespect (**a** for)
2 (*Jur*) contempt, act of contempt ▸ **desacato a la autoridad, desacato a la justicia, desacato al tribunal** contempt of court
desaceleración (SF) **1** (*Aut*) deceleration, slowing down
2 (*Econ*) downturn

desacelerar ▷ CONJUG 1a VT (*Aut*) to slow down
VI **1** (*Aut*) to decelerate, slow down
2 (*Econ*) to slow down, decline
desacertadamente ADV [*diagnosticar, opinar*] mistakenly, erroneously, wrongly; [*actuar*] unwisely, injudiciously
desacertado ADJ [*diagnóstico, opinión*] mistaken; [*medida*] unwise
desacertar ▷ CONJUG 1j VI (*al diagnosticar, opinar*) to be mistaken, be wrong; (*al actuar*) to act unwisely
desachavar* ▷ CONJUG 1a VI (*Cono Sur*) to spill the beans*
desacierto SM (= *error*) mistake; (*al opinar*) unfortunate remark • **ha sido un ~ elegir este sitio** it was a mistake to choose this place • **fue uno de muchos ~s suyos** it was one of his many mistakes *o* errors
desacomedido ADJ (*And*) unhelpful, obstructive
desacomodado ADJ **1** (*euf*) (= *pobre*) badly off, hard up
2 (= *incómodo*) awkward, inconvenient
3 (= *parado*) unemployed, out of a job
desacomodar ▷ CONJUG 1a VT
1 (= *incomodar*) to put out, inconvenience
2 [+ *criado*] to discharge
VPR **desacomodarse** to lose one's post
desacompasado ADJ = **descompasado**
desaconsejable ADJ inadvisable
desaconsejado ADJ • **tengo ~ hacer ejercicio** I've been advised not to do any exercise, I've been advised against doing any exercise
desaconsejar ▷ CONJUG 1a VT [+ *persona*] to dissuade, advise against; [+ *proyecto*] to advise against • **los rigores del viaje ~on esa decisión** the rigours of the journey made that decision inadvisable
desacoplable ADJ detachable, removable
desacoplar ▷ CONJUG 1a VT (*Elec*) to disconnect; (*Mec*) to uncouple
VPR **desacoplarse** to come off
desacordar ▷ CONJUG 1l VT to put out of tune
VPR **desacordarse** **1** (*Mús*) to get out of tune
2 (= *olvidar*) to be forgetful • **~se de algo** to forget sth
desacorde ADJ **1** (*Mús*) discordant
2 (= *diverso*) [*opiniones*] conflicting; [*colores*] clashing
desacostumbradamente ADV unusually
desacostumbrado ADJ **1** • **estar ~ a algo: estamos ~s al frío** we're not used to the cold, we're unused to the cold
2 (= *insólito*) unusual
desacostumbrar ▷ CONJUG 1a VT • **~ a algn de algo** to get sb out of the habit of sth
VPR **desacostumbrarse** • **~se de algo** to get out of the habit of sth
desacralizar ▷ CONJUG 1f VT to demystify
desacreditado ADJ discredited
desacreditar ▷ CONJUG 1a VT [+ *político, gobierno*] to discredit
VPR **desacreditarse** to be discredited
desactivación SF defusing, making safe ▸ **desactivación de bombas, desactivación de explosivos** bomb disposal
desactivador SM bomb-disposal officer
desactivar ▷ CONJUG 1a VT [+ *bomba*] to defuse, deactivate; [+ *alarma*] to deactivate, neutralize
VPR **desactivarse** (*Inform*) to be disabled
desactualizado ADJ out of date
desacuerdo SM **1** (= *discrepancia*) disagreement, discord • **en ~** out of keeping (**con** with), at variance (**con** with) • **la corbata estaba en ~ con la camisa** the tie didn't go with the shirt ▸ **desacuerdo amistoso** agreement to differ
2 (= *error*) error, blunder
3 (= *falta de memoria*) forgetfulness
desadaptación SF maladjustment
desadaptado/a ADJ, SM/F = **inadaptado**
desadeudarse ▷ CONJUG 1a VPR to get out of debt
desadorno SM bareness
desadvertido ADJ careless
desadvertir ▷ CONJUG 3i VT **1** (= *no ver*) to fail to notice
2 (= *desatender*) to disregard
desafecto ADJ disaffected • **~ a algo** hostile to sth • **elementos ~s al régimen** those hostile to the régime
SM disaffection
desaferrar ▷ CONJUG 1a VT **1** (= *soltar*) to loosen, unfasten; (*Náut*) [+ *ancla*] to weigh
2 (= *disuadir*) to dissuade
VI to weigh anchor
desafiador(a) ADJ **1** [*actitud, voz*] defiant
2 [*decisión, experiencia*] challenging
SM/F challenger
desafiante ADJ **1** [*actitud, voz*] defiant
2 [*decisión, experiencia*] challenging
desafiar ▷ CONJUG 1c VT **1** to challenge, dare • **~ a algn a hacer algo** to challenge *o* dare sb to do sth
2 [+ *peligro*] to defy
3 (= *competir*) to challenge, compete with
4 (*Méx*) (= *pelear*) to fight
desaficionarse ▷ CONJUG 1a VPR • **~ de algo** to come to dislike sth
desafilado ADJ blunt
desafilar ▷ CONJUG 1a VT to blunt, dull
VPR **desafilarse** to get blunt
desafiliarse ▷ CONJUG 1b VPR to disaffiliate (**de** from)
desafinadamente ADV [*cantar, tocar*] out of tune, off key
desafinado ADJ out of tune
desafinar ▷ CONJUG 1a VI **1** (*Mús*) [*instrumento*] to be out of tune; [*cantante*] to sing out of tune; [*músico*] to play out of tune, be out of tune
2 (= *hablar inoportunamente*) to speak out of turn
desafío SM **1** (= *reto*) challenge • **es un ~ a todos nosotros** it is a challenge to us all
2 (= *combate*) duel
3 (*a peligro, muerte*) defiance
desaforadamente ADV [*comportarse*] outrageously • **gritar ~** to shout one's head off
desaforado ADJ [*comportamiento*] outrageous; [*persona*] lawless, disorderly; [*grito*] ear-splitting • **es un ~** he's a violent sort, he's dangerously excitable
desaforarse ▷ CONJUG 1l VPR to behave in an outrageous way, act violently
desafortunadamente ADV unfortunately
desafortunado ADJ **1** (= *desgraciado*) unfortunate, unlucky
2 (= *no oportuno*) [*comentario, anuncio*] inopportune, unfortunate; [*decisión, medida*] unfortunate
desafuero SM outrage, excess
desagotar ▷ CONJUG 1a VT (*Arg*) to drain
desagraciado ADJ graceless, unattractive
desagradable ADJ unpleasant, disagreeable (*más frm*) • **ser ~ con algn** to be unpleasant to sb
desagradablemente ADV unpleasantly
desagradar ▷ CONJUG 1a VT • **me desagrada ese olor** I don't like that smell • **ese estilo no me desagrada en absoluto** I don't dislike that style at all • **me desagrada tener que hacerlo** I dislike having to do it
VI to be unpleasant
desagradecido/a ADJ **1** [*persona*] ungrateful
2 [*trabajo*] thankless
SM/F • **eres un ~** you're so ungrateful
desagradecimiento SM ingratitude
desagrado SM **1** (= *disgusto*) displeasure • **hacer algo con ~** to do sth unwillingly
2 (= *descontento*) dissatisfaction
desagraviar ▷ CONJUG 1b VT **1** [+ *persona*] (*gen*) to make amends to (**de** for); (*con dinero*) to indemnify; (*con disculpas*) to apologize to
2 [+ *agravio, ofensa*] to make amends for
VPR **desagraviarse** (= *vengarse*) to get one's own back
desagravio SM apology • **hacer algo en ~ de algo** to make amends for sth by doing sth
desagregación SF disintegration
desagregar ▷ CONJUG 1h VT to disintegrate
VPR **desagregarse** to disintegrate
desaguadero SM **1** [*de agua*] drain
2 (*Méx**) loo*, john (*EEUU**)
desaguar ▷ CONJUG 1i VT **1** (= *vaciar*) [+ *líquido*] to drain; [+ *recipiente, bañera*] to empty, drain
2 [+ *dinero, fortuna*] to squander
3 (*And*) (= *enjuagar*) to rinse (out)
VI **1** [*líquido*] to drain away, drain off
2 [*río*] • **~ en algo** to flow into sth
desagüe SM **1** (= *acto*) drainage, draining
2 (= *conducto*) [*de bañera, lavadora*] wastepipe, drainpipe; [*de azotea*] drain; [*de río, pantano*] drainage channel • **tubo de ~** drainpipe, wastepipe
desaguisado ADJ illegal
SM (= *lío*) mess; (= *acto ilegal*) crime
desahogadamente ADV comfortably
desahogado/a ADJ **1** (= *amplio*) [*habitación, casa, apartamento*] spacious; [*vestido*] loose-fitting; [*espacio*] clear, free
2 [*vida, situación*] comfortable • **ahora andamos algo más ~s de tiempo** we're less pressed for time now
3 (= *con dinero*) comfortably off
4 (= *descarado*) brazen • **él, tan ~, se lo comió todo** he was brazen enough to eat it all up
SM/F brazen person
desahogar ▷ CONJUG 1h VT **1** (= *manifestar*) [+ *ira*] to vent (**en** on) • **desahogó sus penas** she unburdened herself of her woes
2 [+ *persona*] to console
VPR **desahogarse** **1** (= *desfogarse*) to let off steam* • **me desahogué diciéndole todo lo que pensaba** I got it out of my system by telling him everything I thought
2 (= *confesarse*) to get it off one's chest* • **~se con algn** to pour one's heart out to sb
3 (= *librarse*) (*de deuda*) to get out of • **~se de un problema** to get out of a difficulty
desahogo SM **1** (= *alivio*) relief • **es un ~ de tantas cosas malas** it's an outlet for so many unpleasant things
2 (= *comodidad*) comfort, ease • **vivir con ~** to be comfortably off
3 (= *libertad*) freedom • **expresarse con cierto ~** to express o.s. with a degree of freedom
4* (= *descaro*) brazenness • **le habló con mucho ~** he spoke to her very cheekily *o* (*EEUU*) freshly
desahuciado ADJ [*caso*] hopeless • **estar ~** to be beyond recovery, be hopelessly ill
desahuciar ▷ CONJUG 1b VT **1** [+ *inquilino*] to evict
2 (= *quitar esperanza a*) (*gen*) to deprive of hope; [+ *enfermo*] to declare beyond recovery; [+ *plan*] to give up as a lost cause • **con esa decisión le ~on definitivamente** with that decision they finally put an end to his hopes

d

3 (*Chile*) [+ *empleado*] to dismiss
VPR **desahuciarse** to lose all hope

desahucio SM **1** [*de inquilino*] eviction
2 (*Chile*) [*de empleado*] dismissal

desairado ADJ **1** (= *menospreciado*) disregarded • **quedar ~** to come off badly
2 (= *desgarbado*) unattractive

desairar ▹ CONJUG 1a VT **1** [+ *persona*] to slight, snub; [+ *cosa*] to disregard
2 (*Com*) to default on
VI • **lo haré por no ~** I'll do it rather than cause offence *o* (*EEUU*) offense

desaire SM **1** (= *menosprecio*) slight, snub • **fue un ~ sin precedentes** it was an unprecedented slight *o* snub • **no lo tomes como un ~** don't be offended • **dar** *o* **hacer un ~ a algn** (= *rechazar*) to slight sb, snub sb; (= *ofender*) to offend sb • **¿no me va usted a hacer ese ~?** I won't take no for an answer! • **sufrir un ~** to suffer a rebuff
2 (= *falta de garbo*) unattractiveness, gracelessness

desajustado ADJ ill-adjusted, poorly adjusted

desajustar ▹ CONJUG 1a VT **1** (= *desarreglar*) [+ *brillo, color*] to disarrange; [+ *máquina*] to put out of order
2 [+ *planes*] to upset
VPR **desajustarse 1** (= *estropearse*) [*máquina*] to break down; [*clavija, tornillo*] to come loose
2 [*persona*] (= *estar en desacuerdo*) to disagree, fall out; (= *desdecirse*) to break one's word

desajuste SM **1** (= *desarreglo*) [*de hormonas, presupuesto*] imbalance; [*de máquina*] breakdown • **el ~ entre los países ricos y pobres** the disparity *o* imbalance between rich and poor countries
2 (= *desacuerdo*) (*gen*) disagreement; [*de planes*] upsetting

desalación SF desalination

desalado¹ ADJ (= *apresurado*) hasty

desalado² ADJ desalted; [*agua salada*] desalinated

desaladora SF desalination plant

desalar¹ ▹ CONJUG 1a VT to clip the wings of
VPR **desalarse 1** (= *apresurarse*) to rush • **~se por hacer algo** to rush to do sth
2 (= *anhelar*) to long, yearn • **~se por hacer algo** to long *o* yearn to do sth

desalar² ▹ CONJUG 1a VT [+ *pescado*] to desalt; [+ *agua salada*] to desalinate

desalentador ADJ discouraging

desalentar ▹ CONJUG 1j VT **1** (= *desanimar*) to discourage
2 (= *agotar*) to make breathless
VPR **desalentarse** to get discouraged, lose heart

desaliento SM **1** (= *desánimo*) discouragement
2 (= *abatimiento*) dismay, dejection

desalinización SF desalination

desalinizador ADJ • **planta ~a** desalination plant

desalinizar ▹ CONJUG 1f VT, **desalinar** ▹ CONJUG 1a VT to desalinate

desaliñado ADJ **1** (= *descuidado*) slovenly
2 (= *desordenado*) untidy, dishevelled, disheveled (*EEUU*)
3 (= *negligente*) careless, slovenly

desaliño SM **1** (= *descuido*) slovenliness
2 (= *desorden*) untidiness
3 (= *negligencia*) carelessness

desalmado ADJ cruel, heartless

desalmarse ▹ CONJUG 1a VPR • **~ por algo** to long for sth, crave sth

desalojamiento SM **1** [*de inquilino*] eviction, ejection
2 (= *desocupación*) [*de edificio*] evacuation; [*de barco*] abandonment

desalojar ▹ CONJUG 1a VT **1** [+ *inquilino*] to evict, eject
2 (= *desocupar*) [+ *edificio*] to evacuate; [+ *barco*] to abandon • **las tropas han desalojado el pueblo** the troops have evacuated the village • **la policía desalojó el local** the police cleared the premises • **~ un tribunal de público** to clear a court
3 [+ *contenido, gas*] to dislodge, remove
4 (*Mil*) to dislodge, oust
5 (*Náut*) to displace
VI to move out

desalojo SM **1** [*de inquilino*] eviction, ejection
2 (= *desocupación*) [*de edificio*] evacuation; [*de barco*] abandonment

desalquilado ADJ vacant, untenanted

desalquilar ▹ CONJUG 1a VT to vacate, move out of
VPR **desalquilarse** to become vacant

desalterar ▹ CONJUG 1a VT to assuage, calm *o* quieten down
VPR **desalterarse** to calm down, quieten down

desamar ▹ CONJUG 1a VT to cease to love

desamarrar ▹ CONJUG 1a VT to untie; (*Náut*) to cast off

desamarre SM untying; (*Náut*) casting-off

desambiguar ▹ CONJUG 1i VT to disambiguate

desamor SM coldness, indifference

desamorado ADJ cold-hearted

desamortización SF **1** (*Jur*) disentailment
2 (*Esp*) (*Hist*) *sale of Church lands*

desamortizar ▹ CONJUG 1f VT to disentail

desamparado ADJ **1** (= *sin protección*) helpless, defenceless, defenseless (*EEUU*) • **los niños ~s de la ciudad** the city's waifs and strays • **sentirse ~** to feel defenceless *o* helpless
2 [*lugar*] (= *expuesto*) exposed; (= *desierto*) deserted

desamparar ▹ CONJUG 1a VT **1** [+ *persona*] (= *abandonar*) to desert, abandon; (= *dejar indefenso*) to leave defenceless *o* (*EEUU*) defenseless
2 [+ *lugar*] to leave, abandon
3 [+ *actividad*] to cease, abandon

desamparo SM **1** (= *acto*) desertion, abandonment
2 (= *estado*) helplessness
3 (= *cese*) cessation

desamueblado ADJ unfurnished

desamueblar ▹ CONJUG 1a VT to remove the furniture from, clear the furniture out of

desandar ▹ CONJUG 1p VT • **~ lo andado** • **~ el camino** to retrace one's steps • **no se puede ~ lo andado** what's done can't be undone

desangelado ADJ **1** [*lugar*] soulless
2 [*persona*] charmless, dull, unattractive

desangramiento SM bleeding • **morir de ~** to bleed to death

desangrar ▹ CONJUG 1a VT **1** [+ *persona*] to bleed
2 [+ *lago*] to drain
3 (= *quitar dinero a*) to bleed white
VPR **desangrarse** (= *perder sangre*) to lose a lot of blood; (= *morir*) to bleed to death

desangre SM (*LAm*) bleeding, loss of blood

desanidar ▹ CONJUG 1a VT to oust, dislodge
VI to fly, begin to fly, leave the nest

desanimado/a ADJ **1** [*persona*] downhearted, dejected
2 [*espectáculo, fiesta*] dull, lifeless • **fue una fiesta de lo más ~** it was a terribly dull party
SM/F dropout (*from the labour market*)

desanimante ADJ discouraging

desanimar ▹ CONJUG 1a VT **1** (= *desalentar*) to discourage
2 (= *deprimir*) to depress, sadden
VPR **desanimarse** to get discouraged, lose heart • **no hay que ~se** we must not lose heart, we must keep our spirits up

desánimo SM **1** [*de persona*] (= *desaliento*) despondency; (= *abatimiento*) dejection
2 [*de lugar, fiesta*] dullness

desanudar ▹ CONJUG 1a VT [+ *nudo, lazo*] to untie, undo; [+ *misterio*] to unravel • **~ la voz** to find one's voice

desapacible ADJ [*tiempo*] unpleasant; [*sabor, carácter*] surly; [*tono*] harsh; [*sonido*] sharp, jangling; [*discusión*] bitter, bad-tempered; [*persona*] unpleasant

desaparcar ▹ CONJUG 1g VI to drive off

desaparecer ▹ CONJUG 2d VI **1** [*persona, objeto*] to disappear, go missing • **han desaparecido dos niños en el bosque** two children have disappeared *o* gone missing in the wood • **me han desaparecido diez euros** ten euros of mine have disappeared *o* gone missing • **con él desapareció toda una ideología** a whole ideology died with him • **el mago hizo ~ una paloma** the magician made a dove disappear • **¡desaparece de mi vista!** get out of my sight!; ▹ **mapa**
2 [*mancha, olor, síntoma*] to disappear, go (away)
3 (*euf*) (= *morir*) to pass away
VT (*LAm*) (*Pol*) to disappear
• **desaparecieron a los disidentes** they disappeared the dissidents, the dissidents were disappeared

desaparecido/a ADJ [*persona, objeto*] missing; [*especie*] extinct; (*LAm*) (*Pol*) missing • **el libro ~** the missing book • **tres continúan ~s** three are still missing • **uno de los animales ~s** one of the extinct animals • **~ en combate** missing in action, MIA
SM/F (*LAm*) (*Pol*) missing person • **los ~s** missing persons (*pl*) • **número de muertos, heridos y ~s** number of dead, wounded and missing

> **LOS DESAPARECIDOS**
> **Los desaparecidos** is the name given to those who disappeared during the military dictatorships in the Southern Cone in the 1970s. Thousands of people were taken from their homes, schools and places of work and never seen again. Few of "the disappeared" were ever found alive, although a certain number of bodies were recovered in mass graves. Families of the victims joined forces to form pressure groups like Argentina's **Madres y Abuelas de la Plaza de Mayo**, but although some managed to identify and recover the bodies of their relatives, the perpetrators were rarely brought to justice.

desaparejar ▹ CONJUG 1a VT **1** [+ *caballo*] to unharness, unhitch
2 (*Náut*) to unrig

desaparición SF **1** [*de persona, objeto*] disappearance
2 [*de especie*] extinction

desapasionadamente ADV dispassionately, impartially

desapasionado ADJ dispassionate, impartial

desapego SM **1** (= *frialdad*) coolness, indifference (**hacia** towards)
2 (= *ecuanimidad*) detachment

desapercibido ADJ **1** (= *no visto*) unnoticed • **marcharse ~** to slip away unnoticed • **pasar ~** to go unnoticed
2 (= *desprevenido*) unprepared

desaplicación SF slackness, laziness

desaplicado ADJ slack, lazy

desapoderado ADJ [*acción, movimiento*]

headlong, precipitate; [*pasión*] wild, violent, uncontrollable; [*avidez*] excessive; [*orgullo*] overweening

desapoderar ▸ CONJUG 1a (VT) (= *quitar autoridad a*) to deprive of authority; (= *quitar posesiones a*) to dispossess

desapolillarse ▸ CONJUG 1a (VPR) (*fig*) to get rid of the cobwebs

desaprender ▸ CONJUG 2a (VT) **1** [+ *lección*] to unlearn
2 (= *olvidar*) to forget

desaprensión (SF) unscrupulousness

desaprensivamente (ADV) unscrupulously

desaprensivo/a (ADJ) unscrupulous
(SM/F) • **es un ~** he's an unscrupulous individual

desapretar ▸ CONJUG 1j (VT) to loosen

desaprobación (SF) [*de actitud, conducta, acción*] disapproval; [*de solicitud*] rejection

desaprobar ▸ CONJUG 1l (VT) **1** (= *no aprobar*) to disapprove of
2 (= *condenar*) to condemn
3 [+ *solicitud*] to reject, dismiss

desaprobatorio (ADJ) disapproving

desapropiarse ▸ CONJUG 1b (VPR) • **~ de algo** to divest o.s. of sth, surrender sth

desaprovechado (ADJ) **1** [*oportunidad, tiempo*] wasted
2 [*alumno, estudiante*] slack
3 [*terreno*] underused, unproductive

desaprovechamiento (SM) waste

desaprovechar ▸ CONJUG 1a (VT) [+ *ocasión, oportunidad*] to waste, miss; [+ *talento*] not to use to the full
(VI) (= *perder terreno*) to lose ground, slip back

desarbolado (ADJ) [*paisaje*] treeless

desarbolar ▸ CONJUG 1a (VT) to dismast

desarmable (ADJ) • **mesa ~** foldaway table

desarmadero (SM) (*Arg, Uru*) scrapyard

desarmado (ADJ) unarmed

desarmador (SM) **1** [*de fusil*] hammer
2 (*Méx*) (= *destornillador*) screwdriver

desarmante (ADJ) disarming

desarmar ▸ CONJUG 1a (VT) **1** (*Mil*) to disarm
2 (= *desmontar*) [+ *juguete*] to take apart, take to pieces; [+ *rompecabezas*] to break up; [+ *tienda de campaña*] to take down; [+ *estantería, mueble*] to dismantle, take apart; [+ *remos*] to ship; [+ *barco*] to lay up; [+ *barrera*] to remove, take down
3 (= *dejar sin argumentos*) [+ *persona*] to disarm; [+ *ira*] to calm
(VI) to disarm
(VPR) **desarmarse** [*rebeldes, terroristas*] to disarm

desarme (SM) disarmament ▸ **desarme arancelario, desarme industrial** removal of tariff barriers ▸ **desarme unilateral** unilateral disarmament

desarraigado (ADJ) [*persona*] rootless, without roots

desarraigar ▸ CONJUG 1h (VT) **1** [+ *árbol*] to uproot
2 (= *separar*) [+ *pueblo, persona*] to uproot
3 [+ *costumbre*] to root out, eradicate

desarraigo (SM) [*de árbol, persona*] uprooting; [*de vicio*] eradication

desarrajar* ▸ CONJUG 1a (VT) (*LAm*) = descerrajar

desarrapado (ADJ), (SM/F) = **desharrapado**

desarrebujar ▸ CONJUG 1a (VT) **1** (= *desenredar*) to untangle
2 (= *descubrir*) [+ *objeto oculto*] to uncover; [+ *misterio*] to clarify, elucidate

desarreglado (ADJ) **1** (= *desordenado*) untidy
2 (= *descuidado*) [*aspecto*] slovenly; [*comportamiento*] disorderly; [*hábitos*] disorganized, chaotic; (*al comer*) immoderate
3 (*Mec*) out of order

desarreglar ▸ CONJUG 1a (VT) **1** (= *desordenar*) [+ *cama, habitación*] to mess up; [+ *planes*] to upset • **los niños ~on el cuarto** the children messed up the room • **el viento le desarregló el peinado** the wind messed up her hair
2 (*Mec*) to put out of order
(VPR) **desarreglarse 1** (= *desordenarse*) [*persona*] to get untidy; [*pelo*] to get messed up
2 (*Mec*) to break down

desarreglo (SM) **1** (= *desorden*) (*gen*) disorder, confusion; [*de habitación*] mess; [*de ropa*] untidiness • **viven en el mayor ~** they live in complete chaos
2 (*Mec*) trouble
3 (*Med*) • **para evitar los ~s estomacales** in order to avoid stomach upsets

desarrimado* (SM) loner, lone wolf

desarrimar ▸ CONJUG 1a (VT) **1** (*de un lugar*) to move away, separate
2 (= *disuadir*) to dissuade

desarrollado (ADJ) developed • **bien ~** well-developed

desarrollar ▸ CONJUG 1a (VT) **1** [+ *economía, industria, mercado*] to develop
2 (= *explicar*) [+ *teoría, tema, punto*] to develop
3 (= *realizar*) [+ *trabajo, proyecto*] to carry out; [+ *técnica, método*] to develop • **aquí desarrollan un trabajo muy importante** they carry out very important work here • **han desarrollado nuevas técnicas de reciclaje de residuos** they have developed new techniques for waste recycling
4 [+ *capacidad, músculos, memoria*] to develop
5 (*Mec*) • **el motor desarrolla 200 caballos** the engine develops 200hp
6 (*Mat*) [+ *ecuación, función*] to expand • **desarolló bien el problema pero no llegó a la solución** he applied the correct method *o* working but failed to find the solution, he worked through the problem correctly but failed to find the solution
7 (= *desenrollar*) [+ *algo enrollado*] to unroll; [+ *algo plegado*] to unfold, open (out)
(VPR) **desarrollarse 1** (= *madurar*) [*adolescente*] to develop, reach puberty; [*planta, animal*] to develop, reach maturity; [*país*] to develop
2 (= *ocurrir*) [*suceso, reunión*] to take place; [*trama*] to unfold, develop • **la acción de la película se desarrolla en Roma** the action in the film takes place in Rome • **la manifestación se desarrolló sin incidentes** the demonstration passed off without incident
3 (= *desenrollarse*) [*algo enrollado*] to unroll; [*algo plegado*] to unfold, open (out)

desarrollismo (SM) policy of economic development

desarrollo (SM) **1** [*de economía, industria, mercado*] development • **la industria está en pleno ~** industry is developing rapidly • **un país en vías de ~** a developing country ▸ **desarrollo sostenible** sustainable development
2 [*de teoría, tema, punto*] development
3 (= *realización*) [*de proyecto, plan*] carrying out; [*de técnica, método*] development
4 [*de capacidad, memoria, músculos*] development
5 (*Mat*) [*de ecuación, función*] expansion; [*de problema*] working • **hizo bien el ~ del problema** he did the working correctly
6 [*de persona, animal, planta*] development • **es bueno para el ~ emocional del niño** it is good for the child's emotional development • **está en la edad del ~** she's reaching puberty, she's beginning to develop ▸ **desarrollo infantil** child development
7 [*de historia, acontecimiento*] development • **el ~ de la trama** the unfolding *o* development of the plot • **ocurrió durante el ~ del partido** it happened in the course of the match
8 [*de bicicleta*] gear ratio

desarropado (ADJ) • **estar ~** (*en la cama*) to have lost the covers; (= *sin defensa*) to be exposed

desarropar ▸ CONJUG 1a (VT) to take the covers off
(VPR) **desarroparse** to throw the covers off • **todavía no hace tiempo como para ~se** it's not yet the weather for leaving off any layers of clothing

desarrugar ▸ CONJUG 1h (VT) (= *alisar*) [+ *mantel, sábana*] to smooth out; [+ *ropa*] to remove the creases from, remove the wrinkles from (*EEUU*)

desarticulación (SF) **1** (= *desmembración*) [*de máquina, reloj*] dismantling, taking to pieces; [*de comando, pandilla*] breaking up
2 [*de codo, rodilla*] dislocation

desarticulado (ADJ) disjointed

desarticular ▸ CONJUG 1a (VT) **1** (= *desarmar*) [+ *máquina, reloj*] to take apart, take to pieces; [+ *pandilla*] to break up • **~ un grupo terrorista** to force a terrorist group out of action
2 [+ *codo, rodilla*] to dislocate

desarzonar ▸ CONJUG 1a (VT) [+ *jinete*] to throw, unsaddle

desaseado (ADJ) [*persona*] dirty, grubby; [*aspecto, pelo*] untidy, unkempt

desasear ▸ CONJUG 1a (VT) to dirty, soil

desaseo (SM) [*de persona*] dirtiness, grubbiness; [*de aspecto*] untidiness

desasimiento (SM) **1** (= *acto*) (*al soltarse uno*) undoing; (*al ser soltado*) release
2 (= *desapego*) detachment (**de** from)

desasir ▸ CONJUG 3a; *presente como* salir
(VT) (= *soltar*) to undo
(VPR) **desasirse 1** (= *soltarse*) to extricate *o* free o.s. (**de** from)
2 • **~se de algo** (= *ceder*) to let sth go, give sth up; (= *deshacerse de algo*) to rid o.s. of sth

desasistir ▸ CONJUG 3a (VT) (= *abandonar*) to desert, abandon; (= *desatender*) to neglect

desasnar ▸ CONJUG 1a (VT) (= *civilizar*) to civilize; (= *instruir*) to make less stupid

desasosegado (ADJ) uneasy, anxious

desasosegador (ADJ), **desasosegante** (ADJ) disturbing, upsetting

desasosegar ▸ CONJUG 1h, 1j (VT) to make uneasy, make anxious
(VPR) **desasosegarse** to become uneasy, become anxious

desasosiego (SM) (= *inquietud*) uneasiness, anxiety; (= *intranquilidad*) restlessness; (*Pol*) unrest

desastrado (ADJ) **1** [*persona, aspecto*] (= *sucio*) scruffy, untidy; (= *harapiento*) shabby, ragged
2 (= *desgraciado*) unlucky

desastre (SM) disaster • **¡qué ~!** how awful! • **la función fue un ~** the show was a shambles • **como pintor es un ~** he's a totally useless painter • **llegó a la fiesta hecha un ~** she arrived at the party looking a terrible sight • **soy un ~ dibujando** I'm terrible *o* hopeless at drawing • **es un ~ de hombre*** he's a dead loss*

desastrosamente (ADV) disastrously

desastroso (ADJ) disastrous, calamitous

desatado (ADJ) (= *descontrolado*) uncontrolled • **está ~** he's gone absolutely wild*

desatar ▸ CONJUG 1a (VT) **1** [+ *nudo, cuerda, cordones*] to untie, undo • **desátate los zapatos** untie *o* undo your shoelaces • **desata el paquete y saca el regalo** untie *o* undo the parcel and take out the present • **no consiguió ~ al prisionero** he couldn't

manage to untie the prisoner • **la bebida le desató la lengua** the drink loosened his tongue
2 (= *desencadenar*) [+ *guerra, crisis*] to trigger, spark (off); [+ *sentimiento, pasión*] to unleash • **las nuevas medidas han desatado una ola de atentados** the new measures have triggered *o* sparked (off) a wave of attacks • **sus palabras ~on una intensa polémica** his words sparked (off) *o* unleashed a storm of controversy
3 (= *disolver*) to dissolve
4† • **~ un compromiso** to break an agreement
VPR **desatarse 1** (= *soltarse*) [*nudo, cuerda, cordones*] to come undone *o* untied; [*perro*] to break loose • **se le ~on los zapatos** his shoelaces came untied *o* undone • **el prisionero consiguió ~se** the prisoner managed to untie himself
2 (= *desencadenarse*) [*incendio, guerra, motín*] to break out; [*crisis, polémica*] to flare up; [*tormenta, escándalo*] to break; [*desastre*] to strike • **con el gol se desató el entusiasmo de la afición** the crowd's enthusiasm spilled over at the goal • **se desató en injurias contra el ministro** (*frm*) he unleashed a torrent of abuse against the minister

desatascador SM plunger, plumber's helper (*EEUU*)

desatascar ▸ CONJUG 1g VT **1** [+ *cañería*] to clear, unblock
2 [+ *carro*] to pull out of the mud • MODISMO: • **~ a algn** to get sb out of a jam

desatención SF **1** (= *descuido*) inattention
2 (= *distracción*) inattentiveness
3 (= *descortesía*) discourtesy

desatender ▸ CONJUG 2g VT **1** (= *descuidar*) [+ *consejo, deseos*] to disregard, ignore; [+ *obligación*] to neglect
2 [+ *persona*] to neglect

desatentado ADJ **1** (= *irreflexivo*) thoughtless, rash
2 (= *desmesurado*) excessive, extreme

desatento ADJ **1** (= *descuidado*) heedless, careless
2 (= *distraído*) inattentive
3 (= *descortés*) discourteous (**con** to)

desatierre SM (*LAm*) slag heap

desatinadamente ADV foolishly

desatinado ADJ foolish

desatinar ▸ CONJUG 1a VT to perplex, bewilder
VI **1** (= *equivocarse*) (*al actuar*) to act foolishly; (*al hablar*) to talk nonsense
2 (= *ponerse nervioso*) to begin to act wildly

desatino SM **1** (= *cualidad*) (= *falta de cordura*) foolishness; (= *falta de tacto*) tactlessness
2 (= *error*) blunder, mistake; (*al actuar*) foolish act • **¡qué ~!** what rubbish! • **cometer un ~** to make a blunder
3 desatinos (= *disparates*) nonsense (*sing*) • **un libro lleno de ~s** a book stuffed with nonsense

desatochar ▸ CONJUG 1a VT (*Cono Sur*) [+ *tráfico*] to clear

desatornillador SM (*LAm*) screwdriver

desatornillar ▸ CONJUG 1a VT to unscrew
VPR **desatornillarse** to come unscrewed, unscrew

desatracar ▸ CONJUG 1g VI (*Náut*) to cast off

desatraillar ▸ CONJUG 1a VT to unleash, let off the lead

desatrancar ▸ CONJUG 1g VT **1** [+ *puerta*] to force open
2 [+ *cañería*] to unblock; [+ *pozo*] to clean out

desatraque SM casting-off

desatufarse ▸ CONJUG 1a VPR **1** (*quitarse el mal olor*) to get some fresh air
2 (= *calmarse*) to calm down

desautorización SF denial

desautorizado ADJ **1** (= *no aprobado*) (*gen*) unauthorized; [*informe*] repudiated
2 (= *no oficial*) unofficial
3 (= *no justificado*) unwarranted

desautorizar ▸ CONJUG 1f VT **1** (= *quitar autoridad a*) [+ *oficial*] to deprive of authority; [+ *palabras, declaración*] to discredit
2 [+ *noticia*] to deny

desavenencia SF (= *desacuerdo*) disagreement; (= *riña*) quarrel

desavenido ADJ **1** (= *opuesto*) contrary
2 (= *incompatible*) incompatible • **ellos están ~s** they have fallen out

desavenir ▸ CONJUG 3r VT (= *enemistar*) to make trouble between
VPR **desavenirse** to fall out (**con** with)

desaventajado ADJ disadvantageous

desavisado ADJ (= *desprevenido*) unwary; (= *desinformado*) uninformed

desayunado ADJ • **vengo ~** I've had breakfast • **estar ~** to have had breakfast

desayunar ▸ CONJUG 1a VT to have for breakfast
VI, VPR **desayunarse** to have breakfast
1 (= *tomar el desayuno*) • **~ con café** to have coffee for breakfast
2 (= *enterarse*) • **ahora me desayuno de ello** this is the first I've heard of it • **~ con algo** to get the first news of sth

desayuno SM breakfast ▸ **desayuno a la inglesa, desayuno británico** English breakfast ▸ **desayuno buffet** buffet breakfast ▸ **desayuno continental** continental breakfast ▸ **desayuno de trabajo** working breakfast

desazón SF **1** (= *desasosiego*) uneasiness
2 (= *falta de sabor*) tastelessness
3 (*Med*) discomfort

desazonante ADJ annoying, upsetting

desazonar ▸ CONJUG 1a VT **1** (= *desasosegar*) to make uneasy
2 [+ *comida*] to make tasteless
VPR **desazonarse 1** (*Med*) to be out of sorts
2 (= *irritarse*) to be annoyed
3 (= *preocuparse*) to worry

desbancar ▸ CONJUG 1g VT **1** (*de un puesto*) (= *quitar el puesto a*) to oust; (= *suplantar a*) to supplant (*in sb's affections*) • **el corredor fue desbancado por el pelotón a cinco km de la meta** the pack overtook the leader five km from the finish
2 (*en juegos*) [+ *banca*] to bust*; [+ *persona*] to take the bank from
VI (*Naipes*) to go bust*

desbandada SF rush (*to get away*) • **hubo una ~ general de turistas** there was a mass exodus of tourists • **cuando empezó a llover hubo una ~ general** when it started to rain everyone rushed for shelter • **a la ~** in disorder • **retirarse a la ~** to retreat in disorder • **salir en ~** to run off *o* scatter in all directions

desbandar* ▸ CONJUG 1a VT (*Caribe*) [+ *empleado*] to fire*

desbandarse ▸ CONJUG 1a VPR **1** (*Mil*) to disband
2 (= *huir*) to run off *o* scatter in all directions

desbande* SM (*Cono Sur*) rush (*to get away*)

desbarajustar ▸ CONJUG 1a VT **1** (= *causar confusión*) to throw into confusion
2 (= *desordenar*) to mess up

desbarajuste SM confusion, chaos • **¡qué ~!** what a mess!

desbaratamiento SM **1** (= *descomposición*) [*de planes*] thwarting; [*de teoría*] destruction; [*de empresa, grupo*] ruin • **los culpan del ~ de nuestra región** they blame them for ruining our region
2 (*Mil*) rout
3 (*Med*) ▸ **desbaratamiento de vientre** bowel upset
4 (= *derroche*) squandering

desbaratar ▸ CONJUG 1a VT **1** (= *descomponer*) [+ *plan*] to spoil, thwart; [+ *empresa, grupo*] to ruin; [+ *teoría*] to destroy; [+ *sistema*] to disrupt, cause chaos in
2 (*Mil*) to rout
3 [+ *fortuna*] to squander
4 (*Mec*) to take to pieces
VI to talk nonsense
VPR **desbaratarse 1** (*Mec*) to break down
2 [*persona*] (= *descontrolarse*) to fly off the handle*; (= *desestabilizarse*) to become unbalanced

desbarbar* ▸ CONJUG 1a VT [+ *persona*] to shave; [+ *papel*] to trim, trim the edges of; [+ *planta*] to cut back, trim
VPR **desbarbarse** to shave

desbarrancadero SM (*LAm*) precipice

desbarrancar ▸ CONJUG 1g VT **1** (*LAm*) to fling over a precipice
2 (*And, Caribe*) (= *arruinar*) to ruin
3 (*And**) (= *aplastar*) to crush
VPR **desbarrancarse 1** (*LAm*) to fall over a precipice
2* to come down in the world

desbarrar ▸ CONJUG 1a VI **1** (*al hablar*) to talk rubbish
2 (= *hacer tonterías*) to act the fool

desbastación SF = **desbaste**

desbastado ADJ planed

desbastar ▸ CONJUG 1a VT **1** (*Téc*) [+ *madera*] to plane down; [+ *piedra*] to smooth down
2 [+ *recluta, aprendiz*] to knock the corners off, lick into shape
VPR **desbastarse** [*persona*] to acquire some polish

desbaste SM **1** (*Téc*) [*de madera*] planing; [*de piedra*] smoothing
2 [*de persona*] polishing

desbeber‡ ▸ CONJUG 2a VI to piss**

desbloquear ▸ CONJUG 1a VT **1** (= *quitar un obstáculo de*) [+ *caño*] to unblock; [+ *tráfico*] to free, get moving; [+ *negociación*] to break the stalemate in
2 (*Com, Econ*) to unfreeze
3 (*Mil*) to break the blockade of

desbloqueo SM [*de negociación*] breaking of the deadlock; [*de cuenta*] unfreezing, unblocking, freeing

desbocado ADJ **1** [*caballo*] runaway
2 [*herramienta*] worn
3 [*vestido, jersey*] baggy
4 [*persona*] (= *malhablado*) foulmouthed; (= *descarado*) cheeky, sassy (*EEUU*)
5 [*cañón*] wide-mouthed
6 (*LAm*) [*líquido*] overflowing

desbocar ▸ CONJUG 1g VT [+ *vasija, taza*] to break the rim of
VI = **desembocar**
VPR **desbocarse 1** (= *descontrolarse*) [*caballo*] to bolt; [*multitud*] to run riot, get out of control
2 [*vestido, jersey*] to go baggy
3 [*persona*] (= *insultar*) to let out a stream of insults

desbolado‡ ADJ (*Cono Sur*) disorganized

desbole‡ SM (*Cono Sur*) (= *desorden*) mess, mix-up; (= *alboroto*) row, racket

desbordamiento SM **1** [*de lago, río*] overflowing • **tras el ~ del río** after the river burst its banks *o* overflowed • **el ~ de los gastos** overspending
2 (= *manifestación*) [*de cólera, fanatismo*] outburst; [*de alegría*] overflowing; [*de energía*] surge • **mi aguante está al borde del ~** my temper is about to boil over, my temper is at boiling point
3 (*Inform*) overflow

desbordante (ADJ) **1** (= *que rebosa*) • **una copa ~ de champán** a glass full to the brim with champagne • **la sala estaba ~ de gente** the room was full to bursting
2 (= *abundante*) [*alegría, entusiasmo, actividad*] overwhelming; [*humor, imaginación*] unbounded, boundless
3 • **~ de** [+ *salud, entusiasmo, energía*] brimming (over) with • **una carta ~ de felicidad** a letter brimming (over) with happiness
desbordar ▷ CONJUG 1a (VT) **1** (= *rebosar*) • **la lluvia ha desbordado el río** the rain has caused the river to burst its banks *o* to overflow • **la leche estuvo a punto de ~ el cazo** the milk nearly boiled over • **han desbordado la centralita con tantas llamadas** the switchboard has been inundated *o* overwhelmed with calls
2 (= *exceder*) [+ *límite, previsiones*] to exceed; [+ *persona, tolerancia*] to be beyond, be too much for • **los beneficios han desbordado todas nuestras previsiones** profits have exceeded all our forecasts • **su fama ha desbordado las fronteras de este país** her fame has spread far beyond this country • **el trabajo me desborda** the work is just too much for me
3 [+ *energía, entusiasmo*] to be brimming (over) with • **desborda alegría y buen humor** he's brimming (over) with happiness and good humour
4 (*Mil*) [+ *enemigo, policía*] to break through • **~on las líneas enemigas** they broke through enemy lines
5 (*Dep*) (= *aventajar*) to outplay • **~on por completo al equipo visitante** they totally outplayed the visiting team
(VPR) **desbordarse 1** (= *rebosar*) **a** [*lavabo, río*] to overflow; [*líquido*] to overflow, spill (over) • **con el deshielo se ha desbordado el cauce del río** with the thaw the river has burst its banks *o* overflowed • **se desbordó la espuma de la cerveza** the froth on the beer overflowed *o* spilled over • **~se de algo** to be overflowing with sth • **el cajón se desbordaba de cartas** the drawer was overflowing with letters
b • **~se fuera de** [*epidemia, guerra*] to spread beyond • **la guerra se ha desbordado fuera de nuestras fronteras** the war has spread beyond our borders
2 (= *desatarse*) [*ira*] to boil over • **la euforia se desbordó al final del partido** they were unable to contain their euphoria at the end of the match • **llegó un momento en que la emoción se desbordó** it got to a point when emotions got out of hand *o* control
3 (= *excederse*) to get carried away; (*pey*) to lose control • **el público se desbordó en aplausos** the audience applauded ecstatically • **~se de alegría** to be brimming (over) with happiness
desborde (SM) (*Cono Sur*) = **desbordamiento**
desbraguetado* (ADJ) • **estar ~** to be broke*
desbravador (SM) horse-breaker
desbravar ▷ CONJUG 1a (VT) (= *amansar*) [+ *caballo*] to break in; [+ *animal salvaje*] to tame
(VI), (VPR) **desbravarse 1** [*animal salvaje*] to become tamer
2 (= *perder fuerza*) [*corriente*] to lose its strength; [*viento*] to drop, become less wild; [*licor*] to lose its strength
desbrozadora (SF) weeding machine
desbrozar ▷ CONJUG 1f (VT) [+ *camino*] to clear (*of rubbish*); [+ *campo*] to clear of scrub; [+ *cosecha*] to weed
desburocratizar ▷ CONJUG 1f (VT) to make less bureaucratic
descabal (ADJ), **descabalado** (ADJ) incomplete
descabalar ▷ CONJUG 1a (VT) [+ *juego*] to leave incomplete; [+ *medias*] to lose one of a pair of; [+ *planes*] to scupper
descabalgar ▷ CONJUG 1h (VI) to dismount
(VT) to unseat, remove from office
descabellado (ADJ) [*plan, idea*] crazy, wild, preposterous
descabellar ▷ CONJUG 1a (VT) **1** [+ *pelo*] to ruffle
2 (*Taur*) *to kill with a thrust to the neck*
descabello (SM) (*Taur*) final thrust, coup de grâce
descabezado (ADJ) **1** (= *sin cabeza*) headless
2 (= *insensato*) wild
descabezar ▷ CONJUG 1f (VT) **1** (= *quitar la cabeza de*) [+ *persona*] to behead; [+ *árbol*] to lop; [+ *planta*] to top
2 [+ *dificultad*] to surmount
(VPR) **descabezarse 1** (*Bot*) to shed its grain
2 [*persona*] to rack one's brains
descachalandrado* (ADJ) (*And*) shabby, scruffy
descachalandrarse* ▷ CONJUG 1a (VPR) (*And*) to dress carelessly
descachar ▷ CONJUG 1a (VT) (*And, Caribe, Cono Sur*) to de-horn
descacharrado (ADJ) (*CAm*) dirty, slovenly
descacharrante* (ADJ) hilarious
descacharrar ▷ CONJUG 1a (VT) = escacharrar
descachimbarse* ▷ CONJUG 1a (VI) (*CAm*) to fall flat on one's face, come a cropper*
descafeinado (ADJ) **1** [*café*] decaffeinated
2 [*lenguaje, ideales*] diluted, watered-down
(SM) decaffeinated coffee
descafeinar ▷ CONJUG 1a (VT) **1** [+ *café*] to decaffeinate
2 [+ *lenguaje, ideales*] to dilute, water down
descalabrado (ADJ) • **salir ~** to come out the loser (**de** in)
descalabrar ▷ CONJUG 1a (VT) **1** (= *golpear*) [+ *objeto*] to smash, damage • **~ a algn** to split sb's head open
2 (= *perjudicar*) to harm, damage
3 (*Náut*) to cripple, disable
(VPR) **descalabrarse** to hurt one's head
descalabro (SM) **1** (= *contratiempo*) blow, setback ▸ **descalabro electoral** disaster at the polls
2 (*Mil*) defeat
descalcificación (SF) (*Med*) lack of calcium, calcium deficiency
descalcificar ▷ CONJUG 1g (VT) (*Med*) to decalcify
descalificación (SF) **1** (*Dep*) disqualification
2 (= *pérdida de crédito*) discrediting
▸ **descalificación global** widespread condemnation
descalificar ▷ CONJUG 1g (VT) **1** (*Dep*) to disqualify
2 (= *desacreditar*) to discredit
descalzar ▷ CONJUG 1f (VT) **1** • **~ a algn** to take off sb's shoes
2 (= *quitar la cuña*) [+ *rueda*] to remove the chocks from; [+ *armario, mesa*] to remove the wedge(s) from
(VPR) **descalzarse 1** to take off one's shoes • **~se los guantes** to take off one's gloves
2 [*caballo*] to cast a shoe
descalzo (ADJ) **1** (= *sin calzado*) barefoot, barefooted • **estar ~** • **estar con los pies ~s** to be barefoot(ed) • **ir ~** to go barefoot(ed)
2 (*Rel*) discalced
3 (= *indigente*) destitute • **su padre lo dejó ~** his father left him without a bean
descamarse ▷ CONJUG 1a (VPR) to flake off, scale off; (*Med*) to desquamate
descambiar* ▷ CONJUG 1b (VT)
1 (= *intercambiar*) to swap, change back
2 (*Com*) [+ *camisa, libro*] to change
descaminado (ADJ) [*proyecto*] misguided • **andar** *o* **ir ~** to be on the wrong track • **en eso no andas muy ~** you're not far wrong there • **andar ~ en algo** to be mistaken in *o* about sth
descaminar ▷ CONJUG 1a (VT) (= *hacer perderse*) (*lit*) to misdirect, put on the wrong road; (*fig*) to lead astray
(VPR) **descaminarse** (*en camino*) to go the wrong way; (*en proyecto, actividad*) to go astray
descamisado/a (ADJ) **1** (= *sin camisa*) shirtless
2 (= *con la camisa abierta*) open-shirted
3 (= *mal vestido*) ragged, shabby
(SM/F) **1** (= *desharrapado*) ragamuffin
2 (= *vagabundo*) down-and-out
3 (*Arg*) (*Hist, Pol*) Peronist
descamisar ▷ CONJUG 1a (VT) **1** [+ *persona*] (= *quitar la camisa*) to strip the shirt off; (= *arruinar*) to ruin; (*en el juego*) to fleece
2 [+ *fruta*] to peel
(VPR) **descamisarse** (*Cono Sur*) to take off one's shirt
descampado (SM) open space, area of empty ground • **comer al ~** to eat in the open air • **vivir en ~** to live in open country • **se fue a vivir en ~** he went off to live in the wilds
descansadero (SM) stopping place, resting place
descansado (ADJ) **1** [*persona*] rested, refreshed
2 [*lugar*] restful
descansapié (SM) pedal, footrest
descansar ▷ CONJUG 1a (VI) **1** (= *reposar*) to rest, have a rest • **siéntate aquí y descansa** sit down here and have a rest, sit down here and rest • **paramos en un bar a** *o* **para ~** we stopped at a bar for a rest *o* to have a rest • **necesito ~ para despejarme** I need (to have) a rest to clear my head • **no descansé en todo el día** I didn't have a moment's rest all day • **nadé diez largos sin ~** I swam ten lengths without a rest *o* break • **no ~á hasta conseguir que dimita el presidente** he will not rest until he gets the president to resign • **va al campo a ~ de las preocupaciones** she goes to the country to get away from *o* get a break from her worries
2 (= *dormir*) • **a medianoche, se retiraron a ~** at midnight they retired (to bed) • **¡hasta mañana! ¡que descanses!** see you in the morning! sleep well!
3 • **~ sobre algo** [*cúpula, tejado*] to be supported by sth, rest on sth; [*argumento, tesis*] to be based on sth
4 (= *estar enterrado*) • **aquí descansan los restos mortales de José Fernández** here lie the mortal remains of José Fernández • **tu tío, que en paz descanse** your uncle, may he rest in peace • **descanse en paz** rest in peace
5 (*Mil*) • **¡descansen!** at ease!, stand at ease!
6 (*Agr*) [*terreno, parcela*] to rest, lie fallow
(VT) **1** (= *apoyar*) to rest • **dejé de leer para ~ la vista** I stopped reading to rest my eyes
2 (*Mil*) • **¡descansen armas!** order arms!
descansillo (SM) (*en escalera*) landing
descanso (SM) **1** (= *reposo*) rest • **los niños no me dejan ni un minuto de ~** the children don't give me a moment's rest • **hoy es jornada de ~ en la competición** today is a rest day in the competition • **el silencio será bueno para el ~ del bebé** the quiet will be a good chance for the baby to get some rest *o* sleep • **tengo tres días de ~ a la semana** I get three days off every week
2 (= *pausa*) break; (*Dep*) half-time; (*Teat*)

d

interval, intermission (EEUU) • **hago un ~ cada dos horas** I have *o* take a break every two hours • **estudió sin ~ hasta aprobar** she studied constantly until she passed • **condujo toda la noche sin ~** he drove all night without a break
3 (= *alivio*) relief • **ya he aprobado, ¡qué ~!** I've passed! what a relief! • **es un ~ saber que estás tan cerca** it puts my mind at rest to know you are so close by
4 (*Rel*) • **rogamos una oración por su eterno ~** we ask you to pray for her eternal rest
5 (*en escalera*) landing
6 (*Téc*) rest, support

descañonar ▸ CONJUG 1a VT **1** [+ *gallina*] to pluck
2 [+ *cara*] to shave against the grain
3 (*Naipes**) to fleece, clean out*

descapachar ▸ CONJUG 1a VT (*And*) [+ *maíz*] to husk

descapiruzar ▸ CONJUG 1f VT (*And*) to rumple the hair of

descapitalización SF **1** (= *pérdida*) • **la empresa sufrió una ~ de 13.000 millones** the net worth of the company fell by 13 billion
2 (*intencionada*) asset-stripping

descapitalizado ADJ undercapitalized

descapitalizar ▸ CONJUG 1f VT **1** (*no intencionadamente*) • **~ una empresa** to reduce a company's net worth
2 (*intencionadamente*) to asset strip

descapotable ADJ, SM (*Aut*) convertible

descapsulador SM bottle-opener

descaradamente ADV **1** (= *sin vergüenza*) shamelessly, brazenly
2 (= *con frescura*) cheekily, saucily

descarado ADJ **1** [*persona*] (= *desvergonzado*) shameless; (= *insolente*) cheeky, sassy (EEUU)
2 (= *evidente*) [*mentira*] barefaced; [*prejuicio*] blatant
ADV* • **sí voy, ~** I'm going all right, you bet I'm going • **si supiera inglés, ~ que me iba a Londres** if I spoke English, you can bet your life I'd go to London

descararse ▸ CONJUG 1a VPR to behave impudently, be insolent, be cheeky (**con** to) • **~ a pedir algo** to have the nerve to ask for sth

descarburar ▸ CONJUG 1a VT to decarbonize

descarga SF **1** [*de camión, mercancías*] unloading • **la ~ de residuos sólidos** the unloading of solid waste ▸ **descarga de aduana** customs clearance
2 [*de adrenalina, emociones*] release • **llorar es una buena ~ emocional** crying is a good way to release your emotions *o* a good form of release
3 (*Mil*) firing, discharge (*frm*) • **recibió varias ~s en el pecho** he received several shots in his chest ▸ **descarga cerrada** volley
4 (*Elec*) discharge • **recibió una ~ eléctrica** he received an electric shock • MODISMO: • **como una ~** suddenly, unexpectedly

descargable ADJ (*Inform*) downloadable

descargadero SM wharf

descargado ADJ **1** [*arma*] unloaded
2 (*Elec*) [*pila*] run down; [*batería*] flat

descargador SM **1** (= *persona*) [*de camiones, mercancías*] unloader; [*de barcos*] docker, stevedore
2 (*Elec*) discharger

descargar ▸ CONJUG 1h VT **1** (= *quitar la carga de*) [+ *camión, contenedor, arma*] to unload; [+ *mercancías*] to unload • **están descargando los sacos del camión** they are unloading the sacks from the lorry
2 (= *disparar*) [+ *arma, tiro*] to fire
3 (= *soltar*) [+ *golpe*] to land; [+ *bomba*] to drop, release • **le descargó un puñetazo en la cara** he punched him in the face *o* landed a punch on his face • **empezó a ~ golpes sobre la mesa** he started banging (on) the table
4 (*Elec*) [+ *pila, batería*] to run down; [+ *corriente*] to discharge
5 (= *liberar*) [+ *tensión, agresividad*] to release; [+ *enfado, ira*] to vent; [+ *conciencia*] to ease; [+ *responsabilidad, sentimiento*] to offload • **siempre descarga su enfado con nosotros** he always vents his anger on us • **no descargues tu frustración sobre mí** don't take out *o* offload your frustration on me • **necesito a alguien en quien ~ mi corazón** I need to pour out my heart to somebody • **~ a algn de** [+ *obligación, responsabilidad*] to relieve sb of; [+ *deuda*] to discharge sb from; [+ *acusación*] to clear sb of, acquit sb of
6 (*euf*) [+ *vientre*] to evacuate, empty; [+ *vejiga*] to empty
7 (*Com*) [+ *letra*] to take up
8 (*Inform*) to download
VI **1** [*río*] to flow, run (**en** into)
2 [*tormenta*] to break • **la tempestad descargó sobre el barco** the storm broke over the ship • **una fuerte tromba de agua descargó sobre la ciudad** a torrential downpour fell on the city
3 (*Elec*) to discharge
VPR **descargarse 1** (= *desahogarse*) to unburden o.s. • **se descargaba con sus amigos** she unburdened herself to her friends • **~se de** [+ *carga, problema*] to unburden o.s. of; [+ *responsabilidad*] to unload • **se descargó de todas sus responsabilidades sobre un colega** he unloaded all his responsibilities on to a colleague • **se descargó con él de todas sus penas** she poured out all her troubles to him
2 (*Elec*) [*batería*] to go flat; [*pila*] to run down • **a la cámara se le han descargado las pilas** the camera batteries have run out *o* run down
3 (*Jur*) to clear o.s. (**de** of)
4 (= *dimitir*) to resign
5 • **~se algo de Internet** to download sth from the internet

descargo SM **1** [*de camión, mercancías*] unloading
2 (= *disculpa*) • **en ~ de su conciencia** to ease his conscience • **nota de ~** disclaimer
3 (*Jur*) • **en ~ de algn** in defence *o* (EEUU) defense of sb • **quisiera decir algo en mi ~** I would like to say something in my defence • **pliego de ~** evidence • **testigo de ~** witness for the defence
4 (*Com*) (= *recibo*) receipt; [*de deuda*] discharge

descargue SM unloading

descarnadamente ADV starkly, brutally

descarnado ADJ **1** [*cara, persona*] gaunt
2 [*estilo, descripción*] stark, brutal

descarnador SM [*de dientes*] dental scraper; [*de uñas*] cuticle remover

descarnar ▸ CONJUG 1a VT **1** [+ *hueso*] to remove the flesh from; [+ *piel*] to scrape the flesh from
2 (= *desgastar*) to eat away, corrode, wear down
VPR **descarnarse** to lose flesh, get thin

descaro SM (= *insolencia*) cheek*, nerve* • **tuvo el ~ de decirme que ...** he had the cheek *o* nerve to tell me that ...* • **¡qué ~!** what a cheek!*, what a nerve!*

descarozado ADJ (*Cono Sur*) [*fruta*] dried

descarriado ADJ **1** [*animal*] stray • MODISMO: • **ser una oveja descarriada** to be like a lost sheep
2 [*persona*] errant • **es el hijo ~ de una familia tradicional** he's the errant son of a respectable family

descarriar ▸ CONJUG 1c VT **1** (*en camino*) [+ *persona*] to misdirect; [+ *animal*] to separate from the herd, single out
2 (*en proyecto, vida*) to lead astray
VPR **descarriarse 1** (= *perder el camino*) [*persona*] to lose one's way; [*animal*] to stray
2 (= *desviarse de lo correcto*) to go astray

descarrilamiento SM derailment

descarrilar ▸ CONJUG 1a VI to be derailed
VPR **descarrilarse 1** (*Ferro*) to be derailed
2 (*LAm*) [*persona*] to get off the track

descarrilo SM derailment

descartable ADJ **1** (= *desechable*) dispensable
2 (*Inform*) temporary

descartar ▸ CONJUG 1a VT **1** (= *eliminar*) [+ *candidato, plan, opción*] to reject, rule out; [+ *posibilidad, hipótesis*] to dismiss, discount • **no hay que ~ la existencia de agua en el planeta** we cannot dismiss *o* discount the possibility of water on the planet • **han descartado la convocatoria de elecciones anticipadas** they've ruled out (the possibility of) an early election • **ya puedes ~ lo de hacer una fiesta en casa** you can forget about having a party at home
2 (*Naipes*) to throw away, discard
VPR **descartarse 1** (*Naipes*) • **se descartó de un as** he threw away *o* discarded an ace
2 (= *excusarse*) • **~se de algo** (*iró*) to excuse o.s. from sth

descarte SM **1** (= *rechazo*) rejection
2 (= *excusa*) excuse
3 (*Naipes*) discard

descasar ▸ CONJUG 1a VT **1** [+ *matrimonio, pareja*] to annul the marriage of
2 [+ *objetos*] (= *separar*) to separate; (= *desordenar*) to disarrange, upset the arrangement of

descascar ▸ CONJUG 1g VT [+ *nuez, huevo*] to shell; [+ *árbol*] to remove the bark from; [+ *fruta*] to peel
VPR **descascarse 1** (= *romperse*) to smash to pieces, come apart
2* (= *ponerse bravucón*) to bluster

descascarar ▸ CONJUG 1a VT **1** (= *quitar la corteza de*) [+ *naranja, limón*] to peel; [+ *nuez, huevo cocido, gamba*] to shell
2 (*And*) [+ *animal*] to flay, skin
3 (*And*) (= *deshonrar*) to dishonour, dishonor (EEUU)
VPR **descascararse** to peel, peel off

descascarillado SM [*de plato, vasija*] chipping; [*de pintura*] peeling, flaking; [*de pared*] peeling

descascarillar ▸ CONJUG 1a VT [+ *plato, vasija*] to chip; [+ *arroz*] to husk
VPR **descascarillarse** [*plato, vasija*] to get chipped; [*pintura*] to flake • **las paredes estaban descascarilladas** the paint had flaked off the walls

descastado ADJ **1** (= *indiferente*) cold, indifferent
2 [*persona*] untouchable
3 [*palabra*] improper
SM/F • **es un ~** he's a cold fish

descaste SM culling

descatalogado ADJ [*libro*] out-of-print, unlisted; [*disco*] unlisted; [*producto*] discontinued

descaudalado ADJ penniless

descelerar ▸ CONJUG 1a VT = **desacelerar**

descendedero SM ramp

descendencia SF **1** (= *descendientes*) descendants (*pl*) • **morir sin dejar ~** to leave no children behind, die without issue (*frm*)
2 (= *origen*) descent

descendente ADJ **1** (= *hacia abajo*) [*dirección, trayectoria*] downward; [*orden, escala*] descending; [*cantidad*] diminishing • **tren ~**

down train
2 (*Inform*) top-down
descender ▸ CONJUG 2g VT **1** [+ *escalera, colina*] to come down, go down, descend (*frm*) • **descendió las escaleras y se nos acercó** he came down *o* (*frm*) descended the stairs and approached us
2 (= *llevar abajo*) • **~ a algn** to lower sb • **~ algo** to lower sth • **descendieron al bombero al pozo** they lowered the fireman *o* let the fireman down into the well • **descendieron al gato del tejado** they brought *o* got the cat down from the roof • **un señor le ayudó a ~ el equipaje** a man helped her to get *o* reach her luggage down
3 (*en orden, jerarquía*) to downgrade, demote • **lo han descendido de categoría por ineficacia** he has been downgraded *o* demoted for inefficiency • **el single descendió tres puestos en las listas de éxitos** the single went down three places in the charts
VI **1** (= *disminuir*) [*fiebre*] to go down, abate; [*temperatura, precio, número, nivel*] to go down, fall, drop; [*ventas, demanda, producción*] to fall, drop (off); [*calidad*] to go down, decline • **el índice de paro descendió considerablemente** unemployment has fallen *o* gone down considerably
2 (*de un lugar a otro*) [*persona*] to come down, go down, descend (*frm*); [*avión*] to descend • **el río desciende limpio de la sierra** the river comes *o* runs down clean from the mountains
3 (*en orden, jerarquía*) to be downgraded, be demoted; (*Dep*) to be relegated • **ha descendido tras el reajuste de la plantilla** he has been downgraded *o* demoted in the staff reorganization • **el restaurante ha descendido de categoría** the restaurant has been downgraded • **su libro descendió al puesto cuarto** her book went down to fourth place
4 • **~ de** (= *provenir de*): • **esta palabra desciende del latín** this word comes from *o* derives from (the) Latin • **el hombre desciende del mono** man is descended from apes • **desciende de linaje de reyes** he is descended from *o* comes from a line of kings
descendiente SMF descendant • **murió sin ~s** he left no children behind, he died without issue (*frm*)
descendimiento SM descent • **el Descendimiento de la Cruz** the Descent from the Cross
descenso SM **1** [*de temperatura, nivel, precio, demanda*] fall, drop • **un ~ de la producción** a fall *o* drop in production • **un ~ en el número de escolares** a fall *o* drop in the number of pupils • **un ~ de la calidad del servicio** a decline in the quality of service ▸ **descenso térmico** fall *o* drop in temperature
2 (*de un lugar a otro*) descent • **inició el ~ 20 minutos antes de aterrizar** he began his descent 20 minutes before landing • **el ciclista se cayó en el ~** the cyclist fell off during the descent • **la prueba de ~** (*Dep*) the downhill event
3 (*en orden, jerarquía*) downgrading, demotion; (*Dep*) relegation • **el CD ha sufrido un ~ de tres puestos** the CD has gone down three places in the charts
4 (= *pendiente*) slope • **el ~ hacia el río** the slope down to the river
descentración SF maladjustment
descentrado ADJ **1** (*Téc*) [*pieza*] off-centre, off-center (EEUU); [*rueda*] out of true • **parece que el problema está ~** the problem seems to be out of focus, it seems that the question has not been properly stated
2 [*persona*] disorientated, disoriented (*esp* EEUU) • **todavía está algo ~** he's still rather disorientated
descentralización SF decentralization
descentralizar ▸ CONJUG 1f VT to decentralize
descentrar ▸ CONJUG 1a VT to put off-centre*, to put off-center (EEUU*), put off one's stroke
desceñir ▸ CONJUG 3h, 3k VT [+ *cinturón, ropa*] to loosen; [+ *nudo, corbata*] to undo, unfasten
descepar ▸ CONJUG 1a VT **1** (*Agr*) to uproot, pull up by the roots
2 (= *eliminar*) to extirpate, eradicate
descercar ▸ CONJUG 1g VT **1** (*Agr*) to remove the fence round, remove the wall round
2 (*Mil*) [+ *ciudad*] to relieve, raise the siege of
descerco SM (*Mil*) relief
descerebrado ADJ brainless, mindless
descerrajar ▸ CONJUG 1a VT **1** [+ *cerradura, puerta*] to break open, force
2 [+ *tiro*] to let off, fire (**a** at)
descervigar ▸ CONJUG 1h VT to break the neck of
deschachar* ▸ CONJUG 1a VT (*CAm*) to sack*, fire*
deschalar ▸ CONJUG 1a VT (*And, Cono Sur*) [+ *maíz*] to husk
deschapar ▸ CONJUG 1a VT (*LAm*) [+ *cerradura*] to break
descifrable ADJ [*código*] decipherable; [*letra*] legible
descifrador(a) SM/F • **el ~ del misterio** the man who solved the mystery
SM (= *instrumento*) decipherer
descifrar ▸ CONJUG 1a VT **1** (= *descodificar*) [+ *escritura*] to decipher, make out; [+ *mensaje*] to decode • **está muy lejos y no puedo ~ lo que pone** it's too far away for me to decipher *o* make out what it says
2 (= *resolver*) [+ *problema*] to puzzle out; [+ *misterio*] to unravel
descinchar ▸ CONJUG 1a VT [+ *caballo*] to loosen the girths of
desclasado/a ADJ *who has gone from one social class to another*
SM/F *person who has gone from one social class to another*
desclasificación SF (*Dep*) disqualification
desclasificar ▸ CONJUG 1g VT (*Dep*) to disqualify
desclavar ▸ CONJUG 1a VT to pull out the nails from, unnail
descobijar ▸ CONJUG 1a VT to uncover, leave exposed
descocado ADJ **1** (= *descarado*) cheeky, sassy (EEUU)
2 (= *atrevido*) brazen
descocarse ▸ CONJUG 1g VPR (= *descararse*) to be cheeky; (= *atreverse*) to be brazen
descochollado ADJ (*Cono Sur*)
1 (= *harapiento*) ragged, shabby
2 (= *malo*) wicked
3 (= *de mal genio*) ill-tempered
descoco SM **1** (= *descaro*) cheek, sass (EEUU)
2 (= *atrevimiento*) brazenness
descodificación SF decoding
descodificador SM decoder
descodificar ▸ CONJUG 1g VT [+ *mensaje*] to decode
descoger ▸ CONJUG 2c VT to spread out, unfold
descojonación‡ SF • **¡es la ~!** it's the absolute bloody end!‡
descojonado‡ ADJ (= *cansado*) knackered*, pooped (EEUU*)
descojonante‡ ADJ **1** (= *gracioso*) bloody hilarious‡
2 (= *impresionante*) bloody impressive‡
descojonarse‡ ▸ CONJUG 1a VPR **1** (= *reír*) to piss o.s. laughing‡
2 (= *matarse*) to do o.s. in*
descojone‡ SM **1** (= *situación graciosa*) • **¡qué ~!** what a bloody riot!‡
2 (= *caos*) • **¡esto es un ~!** what a bloody shambles!‡
descolada SF (*Méx*) snub, rebuff
descolar ▸ CONJUG 1a VT **1** [+ *animal*] to dock, cut the tail off
2 (*CAm*) (= *despedir*) to fire, sack
3 (*Méx*) (= *desairar*) to snub, slight
descolgado/a SM/F backslider
descolgar ▸ CONJUG 1h, 1l VT **1** [+ *cuadro, cortina*] to take down, get down • **descuelga el abrigo de ahí** take the coat off there *o* down from there
2 [+ *teléfono*] to pick up • **dejó el teléfono descolgado** he left the phone off the hook
3 [+ *competidor, pelotón*] to pull away from • **quedar descolgado** to be left behind
VPR **descolgarse 1** (= *bajar por una cuerda*) to let o.s. down, lower o.s. • **~se por** [+ *cuerda*] to slip down, slide down; [+ *pared*] to climb down • **~se por una montaña** (*escalando*) to climb down the face of a mountain; (*con cuerda*) to lower o.s. down the face of a mountain
2* (= *aparecer inesperadamente*) [*persona*] to turn up unexpectedly; [*nube*] set in unexpectedly; [*sol*] to come out suddenly • **~se con una cifra** to come up with a figure • **~se con una estupidez** to come out with a silly remark, blurt out something silly
3 (*Ciclismo*) • **~se del pelotón** to be left behind the group
descollante ADJ outstanding
descollar ▸ CONJUG 1l VI (= *sobresalir*) [*persona*] to stand out, be outstanding; [*montaña*] to tower • **descuella entre los demás** he stands out above the others • **la obra que más descuella de las suyas** his most outstanding work • **la iglesia descuella sobre los demás edificios** the church towers over the other buildings
descolocado ADJ [*objeto*] misplaced; [*lugar*] untidy • **sentirse ~** to feel out of place
descolocar ▸ CONJUG 1g VT [+ *papeles, libros*] to misplace; [+ *cajón, habitación*] to mess up
descolón SM (*Méx*) snub, rebuff
descolonización SF decolonization
descolonizar ▸ CONJUG 1f VT to decolonize
descoloramiento SM (*con tinte*) discoloration; (*con sol, desgaste*) fading
descolorar ▸ CONJUG 1a VT = **decolorar**
descolorido ADJ **1** (= *sin color*) (*con tinte*) discoloured, discolored (EEUU); (*por el sol*) faded
2 [*persona*] pale
descombrar ▸ CONJUG 1a VT to clear (*of obstacles*), disencumber
descomedidamente ADV
1 (= *excesivamente*) excessively
2 (= *groseramente*) rudely, insolently, disrespectfully
descomedido ADJ **1** [*tendencia, odio*] excessive, immoderate
2 [*persona*] rude, discourteous (**con** to, towards)
descomedimiento SM rudeness, discourtesy
descomedirse ▸ CONJUG 3k VPR to be rude, be disrespectful (**con** to, towards)
descompaginar ▸ CONJUG 1a VT to disarrange, disorganize, mess up
descompasadamente ADV excessively, disproportionately
descompasado ADJ **1** (= *excesivo*) excessive
2 (= *sin proporción*) out of all proportion • **de**

d

tamaño ~ disproportionately big • **a una hora descompasada** at an unearthly hour

descompasarse ▹ CONJUG 1a (VPR) = descomedirse

descompensar ▹ CONJUG 1a (VT) to unbalance

descompletar ▹ CONJUG 1a (VT) (*LAm*) (*gen*) to make incomplete; [+ *serie, conjunto*] to break, ruin

descomponer ▹ CONJUG 2q (PP: **descompuesto**) (VT) **1** (= *dividir*) [+ *palabra, frase*] to break down, break up; [+ *sustancia, molécula, número*] to break down; [+ *luz*] to break up, split up • **tienes que ~ el informe en partes** you have to break down the report into separate parts
2 (= *pudrir*) [+ *alimento*] to rot; [+ *cadáver, cuerpo*] to decompose
3* (= *alterar*) • **la mala noticia lo descompuso** the bad news really shook him • **me descompone tanto desorden** all this mess really gets to me* *o* irritates me • **las especias me descomponen el vientre** spicy food gives me diarrhoea *o* (*EEUU*) diarrhea
4* (= *romper*) to break
5 (*frm*) [+ *peinado*] to disturb, disarrange; [+ *planes*] to upset, disrupt
(VPR) **descomponerse 1** (= *pudrirse*) to decompose, rot
2* (= *alterarse*) • **me descompongo con tanto ruido** all this noise gets to me* *o* irritates me • **se le descompuso el cuerpo del frío** the cold made her feel unwell • **se me descompuso el vientre** I had an attack of diarrhoea *o* (*EEUU*) diarrhea • **se le descompuso la cara cuando se lo dije** her face fell when I told her
3 (*Cono Sur*) (= *vomitar*) to be sick; (= *llorar*) to break down
4 (*esp Méx*) (= *romperse*) to break down
5 • **~se el brazo** (*And*) to put one's arm out of joint

descomponible (ADJ) separable, detachable

descomposición (SF) **1** (= *putrefacción*) decomposition • **en avanzado estado de ~** in an advanced state of decomposition
2 (= *separación*) [*de cifra*] breakdown ▸ **descomposición estadística** statistical breakdown
3 (*Med*) ▸ **descomposición de vientre, descomposición intestinal** diarrhoea, diarrhea (EEUU)
4 (*LAm*) (*Aut*) breakdown

descompostura (SF) **1** [*de cara*] discomposure
2 (= *descaro*) brazenness
3 (= *fallo*) (*LAm*) (*Téc*) breakdown, fault; (*Elec*) fault, failure
4 (*esp Méx*) (= *desaliño*) untidiness
5 (*And*) (= *dislocación*) dislocation

descompresión (SF) decompression

descomprimir ▹ CONJUG 3a (VT) (*Inform*) to unzip

descomprometido (ADJ) lacking in commitment, uncommitted

descompuesto (PP) *de* **descomponer**
(ADJ) **1** (= *estropeado*) (*esp Méx*) [*reloj*] broken; [*motor*] broken down; [*sistema*] disorganized, chaotic; [*cuarto*] untidy; [*aspecto*] slovenly • **el coche está ~** the car has broken down
2 (*Med*) • **estar ~** to have diarrhoea *o* (*EEUU*) diarrhea
3 [*cifra*] decomposed
4 [*roca*] loose
5 (= *alterado*) [*rostro*] distorted
6 [*persona*] (= *descarado*) brazen, forward; (= *furioso*) angry • **ponerse ~** to get angry, lose one's composure
7 (*LAm**) (= *medio borracho*) tipsy

descomunal (ADJ) huge, enormous

descomunalmente (ADV) enormously

desconcentración (SF) **1** (*Pol*) decentralization, breaking-up
2 (= *defecto*) lack of concentration

desconcentrar ▹ CONJUG 1a (VT) **1** [+ *industria*] to decentralize
2 [+ *persona*] to distract
(VPR) **desconcentrarse** to lose one's concentration, get distracted

desconceptuado (ADJ) discredited

desconceptuar ▹ CONJUG 1e (VT) to discredit

desconcertado (ADJ) disconcerted • **se quedó ~ sin saber qué decir** he was disconcerted and didn't know what to say • **el final de la película te deja ~** the end of the film leaves you rather puzzled *o* disconcerted

desconcertador (ADJ) disconcerting

desconcertante (ADJ) disconcerting

desconcertar ▹ CONJUG 1j (VT) (= *desorientar*) to disconcert • **la pregunta me desconcertó** I was disconcerted by the question • **cambió de táctica para ~ al rival** she changed tactics to disconcert her opponent *o* to put her opponent off
(VPR) **desconcertarse** (= *desorientarse*) to be disconcerted • **me desconcierto con sus extrañas ideas** I find his strange ideas disconcerting

desconchabar ▹ CONJUG 1a (VT) (*LAm*) to dislocate

desconchado (SM) (*en plato, vasija*) chip

desconchar ▹ CONJUG 1a (VT) [+ *pared*] to strip off, peel off; [+ *loza*] to chip off • **las goteras han desconchado la pared** the leak has made some of the paint flake *o* peel off the wall
(VPR) **desconcharse** [*plato, vasija*] to chip • **se ha desconchado la pared** the paint has flaked *o* peeled off the wall

desconcierto (SM) **1** (= *desorden*) disorder
2 (= *desorientación*) uncertainty, confusion • **la inesperada medida ha creado un clima de ~** the unexpected measure has created a climate of uncertainty *o* confusion • **el cambio de táctica provocó ~ en el rival** his opponent was disconcerted by the change of tactics

desconectado (ADJ) **1** (*Inform*) offline
2 [*persona*] • **estar ~ de algo** to have no contact with sth

desconectar ▹ CONJUG 1a (VT) (*Elec*) [+ *gas, teléfono*] to disconnect; [+ *enchufe*] to unplug; [+ *radio, televisor*] to switch off, turn off; (*Inform*) to switch off
(VI) (*durante una conversación*) to switch off
(VPR) **desconectarse** (*de un sistema*) to log off

desconexión (SF) **1** (*Elec*) disconnection
2 (*entre personas, capítulos*) lack of connection • **hay una ~ total entre las dos cosas** there is no connection at all between the two things • **su ~ con el manejo de la empresa** her own lack of involvement in the running of the firm

desconfiado (ADJ) distrustful, suspicious (**de** of)

desconfianza (SF) distrust, mistrust • **voto de ~** vote of no confidence

desconfiar ▹ CONJUG 1c (VI) **1** [*ser desconfiado*] to be distrustful *o* mistrustful • **~ de algn/algo** (= *no fiarse*) to distrust sb/sth, mistrust sb/sth; (= *no tener confianza*) to have no faith *o* confidence in sb/sth • **"desconfíe de las imitaciones"** "beware of imitations" • **desconfía de sus posibilidades** he has no faith in his chances • **desconfío de poder hacerlo** I don't think I can do it • **desconfío de que llegue a tiempo** I'm doubtful whether *o* I'm not confident that he will get here in time
2 (= *sentirse inseguro*) to lack confidence

desconformar ▹ CONJUG 1a (VI) (= *disentir*) to disagree, dissent
(VPR) **desconformarse** • **se desconforman** they do not get on well together

desconforme (ADJ) = **disconforme**

descongelación (SF) **1** [*de alimentos*] defrosting • **para la ~ de alimentos** for defrosting food
2 [*de salarios*] freeing, unfreezing
3 (*Aer*) de-icing

descongelado (SM) defrosting

descongelar ▹ CONJUG 1a (VT) **1** (= *quitar el hielo de*) [+ *congelador*] to defrost; [+ *alimentos*] to defrost, thaw; [+ *coche*] to de-ice
2 (*Econ*) [+ *créditos, salarios*] to unfreeze
(VPR) **descongelarse** [*congelador*] to defrost; [*alimentos*] to defrost, thaw

descongestión (SF) **1** (= *alivio*) relief, relieving • **una política de ~** a policy of relieving population pressure in the cities
2 [*de pulmones, nariz*] clearing, decongestion (*frm*)

descongestionante (SM) decongestant

descongestionar ▹ CONJUG 1a (VT) **1** (= *quitar el bullicio a*) [+ *calle, ciudad*] to relieve, ease congestion in; [+ *prisión*] to relieve overcrowding in • **una política de listas de espera que ~á los hospitales** a policy aimed at cutting hospital waiting lists
2 (= *despejar*) [+ *pulmones, nariz*] to clear, decongest (*frm*); [+ *cabeza*] to clear

desconocer ▹ CONJUG 2d (VT) **1** (= *ignorar*) not to know, be ignorant of • **desconocen los principios fundamentales** they don't know the basic principles, they are ignorant of the basic principles • **no desconozco que ...** I am not unaware that ...
2 (= *no reconocer*) [+ *persona*] not to recognize; [+ *obra*] to disown • **el poeta desconoció la obra** the poet disowned the work • **~ la autoridad del gobierno** to refuse to recognize the government's authority

desconocido/a (ADJ) **1** (*gen*) unknown • **su apellido me es totalmente ~** his surname is completely unfamiliar to me • **una explosión de origen ~** an explosion of unknown origin • **por razones desconocidas** for reasons which are not known (to us *etc*) • **el triunfo de un atleta ~** the success of an unknown athlete • **tiene miedo a lo ~** he's afraid of the unknown
2 • **estar ~: con ese traje estás ~** I'd hardly recognize you *o* you're unrecognizable in that suit • **después del divorcio está ~** he's a changed person *o* he's like a different person since the divorce
(SM/F) stranger • **un ~ llamó a la puerta** a stranger knocked on the door • **unos ~s le dispararon por la espalda** some unidentified attackers shot him in the back

desconocimiento (SM) **1** (= *falta de conocimientos*) ignorance
2 (= *repudio*) disregard
3 (= *ingratitud*) ingratitude

desconsideración (SF) thoughtlessness, inconsiderateness

desconsideradamente (ADV) inconsiderately, thoughtlessly

desconsiderado (ADJ) thoughtless, inconsiderate

desconsoladamente (ADV) [*llorar*] inconsolably; [*buscar*] disconsolately

desconsolado (ADJ) disconsolate

desconsolador (ADJ) distressing, grievous

desconsolar ▹ CONJUG 1l (VT) to distress
(VPR) **desconsolarse** to despair

desconstrucción (SF) deconstruction

desconsuelo SM (= *pena*) distress, grief • **con ~** sadly, despairingly
descontable ADJ deductible
descontado ADJ • **por ~** of course • **dar algo por ~** to take sth for granted • **por ~ que …** (*como conj*) of course …
descontaminación SF decontamination
descontaminar ▷ CONJUG 1a VT to decontaminate
descontar ▷ CONJUG 1l VT **1** (= *deducir*) to deduct, take off • **tienes que ~ diez euros del total** you have to deduct ten euros from the total, you have to take ten euros off the total • **me lo descuentan de mi nómina** it gets deducted from *o* taken off my wages, it comes off my wages
2 (*Com*) (*al pagar*) • **si pagas al contado te descuentan un 10%** they give you 10% off if you pay (in) cash, there is a discount of 10% *o* a 10% discount for cash • **me ~on 100 libras del total de la factura** they gave me £100 off the total bill, they gave me a discount of £100 on the total bill
3 (= *excluir*) to exclude • **descontando los gastos de alojamiento** excluding *o* not including accommodation expenses • **son diez días si descuentas los días festivos** it's ten days excluding *o* not including public holidays • **sin ~ la hora y media de viaje** including *o* not excluding an hour and a half's travelling time • **descontándome a mí, todos están casados** apart from me, everyone is married
descontentadizo ADJ hard to please
descontentar ▷ CONJUG 1a VT to displease
descontento/a ADJ **1** (= *insatisfecho*) dissatisfied, discontented (**de** with)
2 (= *disgustado*) disgruntled (**de** about, at)
SM/F (*Méx*) malcontent
SM **1** (= *insatisfacción*) dissatisfaction
2 (= *disgusto*) disgruntlement
3 (*Pol*) discontent, unrest • **hay mucho ~** there is a lot of unrest ▸ **descontento social** social unrest
descontextualización SF decontextualization
descontextualizar ▷ CONJUG 1f VT to decontextualize, take out of context
descontinuación SF discontinuation
descontinuar ▷ CONJUG 1e VT to discontinue
descontrol SM lack of control • **hay un ~ en la oficina** the office is in chaos • **esta organización es un ~** this organization is totally chaotic
descontroladamente ADV in an uncontrolled way
descontrolado ADJ **1** (= *sin control*) uncontrolled • **desarrollo ~** uncontrolled development • **elementos ~s** wild elements; (*Pol*) rebellious factions • **estar ~** to be out of control
2 (*LAm*) (= *perturbado*) upset, irritated
descontrolarse ▷ CONJUG 1a VPR **1** (= *perder control*) to get out of control, go wild
2* (= *enojarse*) to blow one's top*, go up the wall*
desconvenir ▷ CONJUG 3s VI **1** [*personas*] to disagree (**con** with)
2 [*no corresponder*] to be incongruous
3 (= *diferir*) to differ (**con** from)
4 (= *no convenir*) to be inconvenient
desconvocación SF calling-off, cancellation
desconvocar ▷ CONJUG 1g VT [+ *huelga, reunión*] to call off, cancel
desconvocatoria SF calling-off, cancellation
descoordinación SF lack of coordination
descoque SM = **descoco**
descorazonado ADJ discouraged, disheartened
descorazonador ADJ discouraging, disheartening
descorazonamiento SM discouragement
descorazonar ▷ CONJUG 1a VT to discourage, dishearten
VPR **descorazonarse** to get discouraged, lose heart
descorbatado ADJ tieless
descorchador(a) SM/F bark stripper
SM corkscrew
descorchar ▷ CONJUG 1a VT **1** [+ *botella*] to uncork, open
2 [+ *alcornoque*] to strip the bark from
3 [+ *arca*] to force, break open
descorche SM uncorking, opening
descornar ▷ CONJUG 1l VT to de-horn, poll
VPR **descornarse*** **1** (= *trabajar*) to slog away*, work like a slave
2 (= *pensar*) to rack one's brains
3 (= *caer*) to break one's neck
descorrer ▷ CONJUG 2a VT [+ *cerrojo, cortina*] to draw back; [+ *velo*] to remove
descortés ADJ [*persona, comportamiento*] rude, impolite, discourteous (*frm*) • **no quisiera ser ~, pero tenemos que marcharnos** I don't want to be *o* seem rude, but we really must be going
descortesía SF **1** (= *acto*) discourtesy
2 (= *cualidad*) rudeness, impoliteness
descortésmente ADV discourteously, rudely, impolitely
descortezar ▷ CONJUG 1f VT **1** (= *quitar la corteza a*) [+ *árbol*] to strip the bark from; [+ *pan*] to cut the crust off; [+ *fruta*] to peel
2 [+ *estilo, técnica*] to polish up, knock the corners off
descoser ▷ CONJUG 2a VT **1** (*Cos*) [+ *costura, puntos*] to unstitch, unpick
2 (= *separar*) to separate, part; ▸ **labio**
VPR **descoserse 1** (*Cos*) [*pantalón*] to come apart at the seam(s); [*costura, manga*] to come unstitched • **se me ha descosido el bajo de la falda** the hem of my skirt has come unstitched • **llevas un botón descosido** one of your buttons is loose *o* is coming off
2* • **~se de risa** to split one's sides laughing
3‡ (= *ventosear*) to fart‡
descosido/a ADJ **1** (*Cos*) unstitched, torn
2 [*narración, historia*] disconnected, disjointed, chaotic
3 [*persona*] (= *hablador*) talkative; (= *indiscreto*) big-mouthed*, indiscreet, blabbing
SM/F • MODISMO: • **como un ~***: • **beber como un ~** to drink an awful lot • **comer como un ~** to eat to excess, stuff o.s. • **gastar como un ~** to spend money wildly • **habla como un ~** he just rattles on and on* • **obrar como un ~** to act wildly
SM (*Cos*) open seam
descotado ADJ (*LAm*) = **escotado**
descoyuntado ADJ **1** (*Anat*) dislocated, out of joint
2 [*narración, historia*] incoherent, disjointed, chaotic
descoyuntar ▷ CONJUG 1a VT **1** (*Anat*) to dislocate
2 [+ *hechos*] to twist
VPR **descoyuntarse 1** (*Anat*) • **~se un hueso** to put a bone out of joint • **el hombro se me descoyuntó** I dislocated my shoulder
2* • **~se de risa** to split one's sides laughing • **~se a cortesías** to overdo the courtesies, be over-polite
descrecer ▷ CONJUG 2d VI to decrease
descrédito SM (= *desprestigio*) discredit, disrepute • **caer en ~** to fall into disrepute • **ir en ~ de algn** to be to sb's discredit
descreencia SF unbelief
descreer ▷ CONJUG 2e VT to disbelieve, place no faith in
VI (*Rel*) to lose one's faith
descreído/a ADJ **1** (= *incrédulo*) unbelieving
2 (= *ateo*) godless
SM/F unbeliever
descreimiento SM unbelief
descremado ADJ [*leche*] skimmed, low-fat
descremar ▷ CONJUG 1a VT [+ *leche*] to skim
describir ▷ CONJUG 3a (PP: **descrito**) VT to describe
descripción SF description • **supera toda ~** it defies description
descriptible ADJ describable
descriptivo ADJ descriptive
descripto PP (*Cono Sur*) = **descrito**
descrismar* ▷ CONJUG 1a VT • **~ a algn** to bash sb on the head* • **¡o eso o te descrismo!** either that or I'll bash you!*
VPR **descrismarse 1** (= *romperse la cabeza*) (*con un golpe*) to split one's head open; (*al pensar*) to rack one's brains
2 (= *trabajar*) to slave away
3 (= *enojarse*) to blow one's top*
descrispar ▷ CONJUG 1a VT to take the tension out of
descrito PP *de* **describir**
descruzar ▷ CONJUG 1f VT [+ *piernas*] to uncross; [+ *brazos*] to unfold
descuadre SM imbalance
descuajar ▷ CONJUG 1a VT **1** [+ *masa, sólido*] to melt, dissolve
2 (= *arrancar*) [+ *árbol, planta*] to uproot; [+ *diente*] to pull out
3 (= *extirpar*) to eradicate, wipe out
4 (= *desanimar*) to dishearten
descuajaringado* ADJ (= *destartalado*) broken-down; (= *desaliñado*) scruffy, shabby • **el libro estaba todo descuajeringado** the book was falling apart
descuajaringante* ADJ side-splitting
descuajaringar* ▷ CONJUG 1h VT (= *romper*) to break to bits *o* pieces
VPR **descuajaringarse 1** (= *partirse*) [*brazo, pierna*] to come apart • **~se de risa** to split one's sides laughing • **es para ~se** it's enough to make you die laughing*
2 (= *cansarse*) to tire o.s. out
3 [*objeto*] to fall to bits
descuajeringar ▷ CONJUG 1h VT = **descuajaringar**
descuartizamiento SM [*de animal*] carving up, cutting up; [*de cuerpo, cadáver*] quartering
descuartizar ▷ CONJUG 1f VT **1** (= *despedazar*) [+ *animal*] to carve up, cut up; [+ *cuerpo, cadáver*] to quarter
2 (= *hacer pedazos*) to tear apart • **ni que me descuarticen** not even if they tear me apart
descubierta SF **1** (*Mil*) reconnoitring, patrolling
2 • MODISMO: • **a la ~** (= *sin disfraz*) openly; (= *sin protección*) in the open
descubierto PP *de* **descubrir**
ADJ **1** (= *sin cubrir*) [*cabeza, pecho*] bare; [*patio, piscina*] open-air; [*autobús, carroza*] open-top; [*cielo*] clear • **salió con el pecho ~** he went out bare-chested • **llevaba los hombros ~s** her shoulders were bare • **dame una carta boca abajo y dos descubiertas** give me one card face down and two face up
2 (= *sin protección*) [*situación*] open, exposed • **una zona descubierta del bosque** an open area of the wood
3 (= *sin sombrero*) bareheaded
4 (*Com*) [*préstamo*] unbacked
SM **1** • **al ~** (= *al aire libre*) outdoors, out in the open; (= *sin rodeos*) openly; (*Mil*) under

fire • **pasamos la noche al ~** we spent the night outdoors *o* in the open • **dejar algo al ~** to expose sth (to view) • **la humedad dejó al ~ varios murales antiguos** the damp brought some ancient murals to view, the damp exposed some ancient murals (to view) • **la falda dejaba sus rodillas al ~** the skirt left her knees bare, the skirt exposed her knees • **poner algo al ~** to expose sth • **la operación policial que puso al ~ la estafa** the police operation that exposed the fraud • **quedar al ~** to be exposed • **quedaron al ~ sus malas intenciones** her bad intentions came to light *o* were exposed
2 (*Com*) (*en cuenta corriente*) overdraft; (*en presupuesto*) shortage • **estar en ~** to be overdrawn, be in the red* • **girar al** *o* **en ~** to overdraw • **vender al ~** to sell short

descubretalentos SMF INV = **cazatalentos**

descubridero SM look-out post

descubridor(a) SM/F **1** [*de lugar, invento, deportista*] discoverer
2 (*Mil*) scout

descubrimiento SM **1** (= *hallazgo*) [*de país, invento, deportista*] discovery • **la era de los grandes ~s** the age of great discoveries • **este restaurante ha sido todo un ~** this restaurant has been a real find *o* discovery
2 [*de conspiración, estafa*] uncovering
3 [*de secreto*] revelation
4 [*de estatua, placa*] unveiling

descubrir ▷ CONJUG 3a (PP: **descubierto**) VT
1 (= *encontrar*) [+ *tesoro, tratamiento, persona oculta*] to discover, find; [+ *país, deportista*] to discover • **al revisar las cuentas ha descubierto numerosas irregularidades** when he went over the accounts he discovered *o* found numerous irregularities • **descubra Bruselas, corazón de Europa** discover Brussels, the heart of Europe • **he descubierto una tienda de ropa fantástica** I've discovered a fantastic clothes shop • **se dedica a ~ nuevos talentos** her job is to discover new talent • **los análisis han descubierto la presencia de un virus** the tests have revealed *o* shown up the presence of a virus • MODISMO: • **~ América** to reinvent the wheel
2 (= *averiguar*) [+ *verdad*] to find out, discover • **he descubierto la causa de su malhumor** I've found out *o* discovered why he's in such a bad mood • **descubrió que era alérgica a las gambas** she found out *o* discovered she was allergic to prawns
3 (= *sacar a la luz*) [+ *conspiración, estafa*] to uncover; [+ *secreto, intenciones*] to reveal • **una red de narcotraficantes descubierta en Colombia** a drug-trafficking ring uncovered in Colombia • **nunca nos ~á sus secretos** he will never tell us his secrets, he will never reveal his secrets to us • **ha descubierto su verdadera identidad** he has revealed his true identity
4 (= *delatar*) to give away • **fue la criada quien los descubrió a la policía** it was the maid who gave them away to the police • **lo descubrió su voz** his voice gave him away
5 (= *destapar*) [+ *estatua, placa*] to unveil; [+ *cacerola*] to take the lid off; [+ *naipes*] to turn over, lay up; [+ *cara*] to uncover • **descubrió la cara y su contrincante le asestó un derechazo en la mandíbula** he uncovered his face and his opponent landed a right on his jaw • **le descubrió el tobillo para ver la cicatriz** she uncovered his ankle to look at the scar • MODISMO: • **~ el juego a algn** to call sb's bluff; ▷ **pastel**
6 (= *divisar*) to make out • **apenas se podía ~ al avión entre las nubes** you could just make out the plane among the clouds
7 (*liter*) (= *transparentar*) to reveal • **la seda le descubría el escote** the silk revealed *o* exposed her cleavage
VPR **descubrirse 1** (= *quitarse el sombrero*) to take one's hat off; (*para saludar*) to raise one's hat (in greeting) • **~se ante algo/algn** to take one's hat off to sth/sb • **ante tal muestra de valor hay que ~se** you have to take your hat off to her for such bravery
2 (= *dejar ver*) [+ *cara, rostro*] to uncover; [+ *cabeza*] to bare • **descúbrase el brazo, por favor** roll up your sleeve, please
3 (= *delatarse*) to give o.s. away • **se descubrió con una falsa coartada** he gave himself away with a false alibi
4 • **~se a** *o* **con algn** to pour one's heart out to sb
5 (= *mostrarse*) to reveal o.s. • **se descubre como un compositor de gran talento** he has revealed himself to be a composer of great talent

descuelgue SM **1** (*de algo colgado*) removal, taking out
2* (*de hacer algo*) opting out

descuento SM **1** (*Com*) discount • **un ~ del 3%** a discount of 3%, a 3% discount • **acciones a ~** shares below par • **con ~** at a discount • **hacer ~** to give a discount • **me hicieron un buen ~** they gave me a good discount • **¿me podría hacer un ~?** could I have a discount? ▸ **descuento por no declaración de siniestro** no claims bonus ▸ **descuento por pago al contado** cash discount ▸ **descuento por volumen de compras** volume discount
2 (*Dep*) injury time, overtime (*EEUU*)

descuerar* ▷ CONJUG 1a VT **1** (*Chile*) to tell off*
2 (*Cono Sur*) (= *desollar*) to flay, skin
3 (*Cono Sur*) (= *infamar*) to defame

descuernar ▷ CONJUG 1a VT (*And, CAm, Caribe*) to de-horn

descueve* ADJ (*Cono Sur*) great*, fantastic*

descuidadamente ADV
1 (= *despreocupadamente*) carelessly
2 (= *desaliñadamente*) untidily

descuidado ADJ **1** [*persona*] (= *despreocupado*) careless; (= *olvidadizo*) forgetful; (= *desprevenido*) unprepared; (= *tranquilo*) easy in one's mind • **coger** *o* **pillar a algn ~** to catch sb off his guard • **puedes estar ~** you needn't worry, you can relax
2 (= *desaliñado*) [*aspecto*] untidy, slovenly; [*habitación*] untidy, messy
3 (= *abandonado*) neglected • **con aspecto de niños ~s** with the look of neglected children

descuidar ▷ CONJUG 1a VT **1** (= *desatender*) [+ *deberes*] to neglect; [+ *consejo*] to disregard • **ha descuidado mucho su negocio** he has neglected his business a lot
2 (= *olvidar*) to overlook
VI (= *no preocuparse*) not to worry • **¡descuida!** don't worry!, it's all right! • **descuida, que yo me encargo de esto** don't worry, I'll take care of this
VPR **descuidarse 1** (= *no prestar atención*) to be careless • **~se de algo** not to bother about sth • **~se de hacer algo** not to bother to do sth, neglect to do sth
2 (= *desprevenirse*) to drop one's guard • **si te descuidas** • **como te descuides** if you don't watch out • **a poco que te descuides te cobran el doble** you've got to watch them all the time or they'll charge you double • **a poco que te descuides ya no está** before you know where you are it's gone • **en cuanto me descuidé me lo robaron** the moment I dropped my guard *o* stopped watching out they stole it from me
3 (= *abandonarse*) to let o.s. go

descuidero/a SM/F sneak thief, pickpocket

descuido SM **1** (= *distracción*) • **en un ~ le robaron el bolso** her bag was stolen when she wasn't looking *o* in a moment of inattention • **al menor ~ te puedes salir de la carretera** if your attention wanders *o* if you get distracted, even for a moment, the car can go off the road • **la colisión ocurrió por un ~ del maquinista** the crash was caused by a careless mistake on the part of the driver • **se me olvidó invitarla por ~** I carelessly forgot to invite her • **dejó caer el pañuelo como por ~** she dropped her handkerchief as if by accident
2 (*frm*) (= *negligencia*) carelessness • **no toleran el ~ en el aspecto externo** they don't tolerate any carelessness in one's appearance • **con ~** carelessly

desculpabilizar ▷ CONJUG 1f VT to exonerate, free from blame

desculturización SF cultural impoverishment

desde PREP **1** (*indicando origen*) from • **lo llamaré ~ la oficina** I'll ring him from the office • **~ Burgos hay 30km** it's 30km from Burgos • **~ Ávila hasta Madrid** from Ávila to Madrid • **~ abajo** from below • **~ arriba** from above • **~ lejos** from a long way off, from afar (*liter*)
2 (*con cantidades, categorías*) from • **camisetas ~ ocho euros** T-shirts from eight euros • **los platos van ~ la pasta hasta la paella** the dishes range from pasta to paella
3 (*en el tiempo*) • **~ el martes** (= *el pasado*) since Tuesday; (= *el próximo*) after Tuesday • **~ el siglo XV en adelante** from the 15th century onward • **no existe ~ 1960** it ceased to exist in 1960 • **~ ahora** from now on • **¿~ cuándo vives aquí?** how long have you been living here? • **¿~ cuándo ocurre esto?** how long has this been happening? • **~ entonces** since then • **~ hace tres años** for three years • **está lloviendo ~ hace tres días** it's been raining for three days • **~ el 4 hasta el 16** from the 4th until *o* to the 16th • **cerramos ~ las dos hasta las cuatro** we close from two until *o* to four • **~ niño** since childhood, since I was a child • **la conozco ~ niño** I've known her since I was a child • **~ siempre** always • **—¿~ cuándo eres comunista? —~ siempre** "since when have you been a communist?" — "I've always been one"
4 • **~ luego a** (= *por supuesto*) of course • **—¿vendrás? —~ luego** "are you coming?" — "of course (I am)" • **eso, ~ luego, no es culpa mía** that, of course, is not my fault • **—¿quieres venir con nosotros? —~ luego que sí** "do you want to come with us?" — "of course I do" • **—¿no sabes nada de eso? —~ luego que no** "you don't know anything about it?" — "of course not" • **no era muy morena pero rubia ~ luego que no** she wasn't really dark-haired, but she certainly wasn't blonde
b (*como coletilla*) • **~ luego, vaya fama estamos cogiendo** we're certainly getting quite a reputation • **~ luego, ¿quién lo iba a pensar?** I ask you, who would have thought it?, well, who would have thought it? • **¡mira que olvidarte de llamar! ¡~ luego que eres despistado!** how could you forget to phone? you're so absent-minded!
5 • **~ que** since • **~ que llegó el invierno** since winter arrived • **~ que llegó no ha salido** he hasn't been out since he arrived • **~ que se ha mudado está mejor** he's been better since he moved • **~ que se inventó la televisión** (ever) since television was invented • **escribo ~ que era pequeña** I've

been writing since I was little • ~ **que puedo recordar** ever since I can remember, as long as I can remember

DESDE

Expresiones temporales

En expresiones temporales, **desde** *puede traducirse por* **since, from** *o, en combinación con* **hace/hacía,** *por* **for.**

▹ **Desde (que)** *se traduce por* **since** *siempre que se especifique a partir de cuándo comenzó una acción o un estado que sigue desarrollándose en el presente o en el momento en que se habla:*

Llevo aquí de vacaciones desde el viernes
I have been here on holiday since Friday
No come mejillones desde que sufrió aquella intoxicación alimenticia
He hasn't eaten mussels since he had that bout of food poisoning
Dijo que no la había visto desde la guerra
He said he hadn't seen her since the war

NOTA: Hay que tener en cuenta que en casos como estos cuando se trata de algo que comienza en el pasado y sigue en el presente, el inglés hace uso del pretérito perfecto (en sus formas simple o progresiva).

▹ *Traducimos* **desde** *por* **from** *cuando* **desde** *simplemente indica el momento en el que empezó la acción cuando la oración indica el final de la acción o se implica, de algún modo, que esta ya ha terminado:*

Y desde aquel día el rey no volvió a hablar del asunto
And from that day on(wards), the king never spoke about the subject again

▹ *La construcción* **desde ... hasta** *se traduce por* **from ... until** *o por* **from ... to:**

Trabajamos desde las nueve de la mañana hasta las cinco de la tarde
We work from nine in the morning until *o* to five in the afternoon
Tendrás que pagar el alquiler desde julio hasta octubre
You will have to pay rent from July until *o* to October

▹ **Desde hace** *y* **desde hacía** *se traducen por* **for** *ya que van seguidos de una cantidad de tiempo:*

Estoy esperando desde hace más de una hora
I have been waiting for over an hour
No se había sentido tan feliz desde hacía años
He hadn't felt so happy for years

▹ *En oraciones interrogativas,* **desde cuándo** *se traduce por* **how long.** *En este tipo de preguntas, el inglés utiliza el pretérito perfecto para referirse a algo que empezó en el pasado y continúa en el presente:*

¿Desde cuándo os conocéis?
How long have you known each other?

Para otros usos y ejemplos ver la entrada.

desdecir ▹ CONJUG 30 (VI) **1** (= *desmerecer*) • ~ **de algo** to be unworthy of sth • **desdice de su patria** he is unworthy of his country • **esta novela no desdice de las otras** this novel is well up to the standard of the others
2 (= *no corresponder*) • ~ **de algo** to clash with sth • **la corbata desdice del traje** the tie clashes *o* doesn't go with the suit
(VPR) **desdecirse** to go back on what one has said • **~se de algo** to go back on sth • **~se de una promesa** to go back on a promise

Desdémona (SF) Desdemona

desdén (SM) scorn, disdain • **al ~** disdainfully

desdentado (ADJ) toothless

desdeñable (ADJ) contemptible • **nada ~** far from negligible

desdeñar ▹ CONJUG 1a (VT) **1** (= *despreciar*) to scorn, disdain
2 (= *rechazar*) to turn up one's nose at
(VPR) **desdeñarse** • **~se de hacer algo** to scorn to do sth, not deign to do sth

desdeñosamente (ADV) (= *con desprecio*) scornfully, disdainfully

desdeñoso (ADJ) scornful, disdainful

desdibujado (ADJ) **1** [*contorno*] blurred
2 (= *descolorado*) faded

desdibujar ▹ CONJUG 1a (VT) to blur, blur the outlines of
(VPR) **desdibujarse** to get blurred, fade • **el recuerdo se ha desdibujado** the memory has become blurred

desdicha (SF) **1** (= *infelicidad*) unhappiness
2 (= *contratiempo*) misfortune • **tuve la ~ de ser amigo suyo** I had the misfortune to be a friend of his, I was unlucky enough to be a friend of his • **para mi ~, mi suegra vive con nosotros** unfortunately for me, my mother-in-law lives with us
3* (= *persona, cosa inútil*) dead loss*

desdichadamente (ADV) unhappily

desdichado/a (ADJ) **1** [*persona*] (= *infeliz*) unhappy; (= *desgraciado*) unlucky • **¡qué ~ soy!** how wretched I am!
2 [*día*] ill-fated • **fue un día ~** it was an ill-fated day
(SM/F) poor devil

desdicho (PP) *de* **desdecir**

desdinerar ▹ CONJUG 1a (VT) to impoverish
(VPR) **desdinerarse*** to cough up*, fork out‡

desdoblado (ADJ) **1** [*carretera*] two-lane
2 [*personalidad*] split
3 (*Escol*) • **grupo ~** group which has been split into two

desdoblamiento (SM) **1** [*de carreteras*] widening
2 ▸ **desdoblamiento de la personalidad** split personality
3 (*Escol*) [*de grupos*] splitting into two

desdoblar ▹ CONJUG 1a (VT) **1** (= *desplegar*) [+ *pañuelo*] to unfold; [+ *mantel*] to spread out; [+ *alambre*] to untwist
2 (*Quím*) to break down (**en** into)
3 (= *duplicar*) to double • ~ **un cargo** to split the functions of a post
4 [+ *carretera*] to widen
5 [+ *tema*] to expand upon, explain
(VPR) **desdoblarse** to divide, split in two

desdoble (SM) (*Econ*) reorganization of capital

desdorar ▹ CONJUG 1a (VT) to tarnish

desdoro (SM) (*en fama, reputación*) stigma, dishonour, dishonor (*EEUU*) • **consideran un ~ trabajar** they think it dishonourable to work • **es un ~ para todos** it is a blot on us all • **hablar en ~ de algn** to speak disparagingly of sb, discredit sb by what one says

desdramatizar ▹ CONJUG 1f (VT) [+ *situación*] to take the drama out of; [+ *crisis*] to defuse

deseabilidad (SF) desirability

deseable (ADJ) **1** [*situación, solución*] desirable • **sería ~ un cambio** a change would be desirable • **no** *o* **poco ~** undesirable
2 [*cuerpo, persona*] desirable

deseado (ADJ) **1** (= *anhelado*) sought-after, coveted • **uno de los premios más ~s en el mundo del cine** one of the most coveted prizes in the film world
2 [*embarazo*] planned • **un embarazo no ~** an unwanted *o* unplanned pregnancy

desear ▹ CONJUG 1a (VT) **1** (= *anhelar*) to want • **solo deseo que me dejen en paz** I just want to be left in peace • **no deseo que le pase nada malo** I wouldn't want *o* wish anything bad to happen to him • **la vida que tanto había deseado** the life she had wanted so much *o* longed for • **dejar bastante** *o* **mucho que ~** to leave a lot to be desired • **estar deseando algo:** • **estaba deseando conocerte** I've been looking forward to meeting you • **estoy deseando que esto termine** I'm really looking forward to this finishing, I can't wait for this to finish • **estoy deseando que lleguen las vacaciones** I'm really looking forward to the holidays, I can't wait for *o* till the holidays • **ser de ~:** • **sería de ~ que actualizaran su información** it would be desirable for them to update their information • **es de ~ que mejoren nuestras relaciones** an improvement in our relations would be desirable • **no hemos avanzado tanto como sería de ~** we haven't made as much progress as we would have liked • **MODISMO:** • **no se lo deseo a nadie** *o* **ni a mi peor enemigo** I wouldn't wish it on anyone *o* my worst enemy; ▹ **ver**
2 (*frm*) **a** (*en peticiones*) to wish • **~ía ver al director** I would like *o* I wish to see the manager • **el doctor desea hablar un momento con usted** the doctor wishes to speak to you for a moment • **todo se hará como tú desees** everything will be done as you wish
b (*en preguntas, sugerencias*) • **si lo desea se lo podemos enviar por correo** if you wish we can send it by post • **¿~ía el señor algún postre?** would Sir like a dessert?, do you wish a dessert? • **¿qué desean beber?** what would you like to drink? • **¿desea que le hagamos una factura?** do you wish us to make out an invoice? • **¿qué desea?** can I help you?
3 (*en fórmulas de cortesía*) [+ *éxito, suerte*] to wish • **os deseamos una Feliz Navidad** we wish you a Merry Christmas • **te deseo la mejor suerte del mundo** I wish you all the luck in the world • **le deseamos una pronta recuperación** we wish you a prompt recovery
4 (*sexualmente*) to want

desecación (SF) [*de terreno*] (*de forma artificial*) draining, drainage; (*por el sol*) drying, desiccation (*frm*)

desecado (ADJ) **1** [*fruta*] dried
2 [*lago, terreno*] (*de forma artificial*) drained; (*por el sol*) dried up

desecar ▹ CONJUG 1g (VT) **1** [+ *fruta*] to dry; [+ *coco*] to dessicate (*frm*)
2 (= *quitar la humedad*) [*persona*] to drain • **el sol ha desecado el lago** the sun has dried up the lake
(VPR) **desecarse** to dry up

desecha (SF) (*And*) = desecho

desechable (ADJ) **1** [*jeringuilla, pañal*] disposable • **envases ~s** non-returnable containers • **la oferta no es ~** the offer is not to be turned down lightly
2 [*variable*] temporary

desechar ▹ CONJUG 1a (VT) **1** (= *tirar*) [+ *basura*] to throw out; [+ *objeto inútil*] to scrap, get rid of
2 (= *rechazar*) [+ *consejo, miedo*] to cast aside; [+ *oferta*] to reject; [+ *plan*] to drop
3 (= *censurar*) to censure, reprove
4 [+ *llave*] to turn

desecho (SM) **1** (= *residuo*) • **productos de ~**

waste products • **ropa de ~** castoffs (*pl*)
▸ **desecho de hierro** scrap iron
2 desechos (= *desperdicios*) (*gen*) rubbish (*sing*), garbage (*sing*) (*EEUU*); [*de la industria*] waste (*sing*); [*de ropa*] castoffs; [*de animal*] offal (*sing*) ▸ **desechos radiactivos** radioactive waste
3* (= *persona inútil*) dead loss* • **el ~ de la sociedad** the scum *o* dregs (*pl*) of society
4 (= *desprecio*) contempt, scorn
5 (*LAm*) (= *atajo*) short cut; (= *desvío*) detour; (= *sendero*) path, temporary road

d

desegregación SF desegregation
desegregar ▸ CONJUG 1h VT to desegregate
desellar ▸ CONJUG 1a VT to unseal, open
desembalaje SM unpacking
desembalar ▸ CONJUG 1a VT to unpack
desembanastar ▸ CONJUG 1a VT **1** (= *sacar*) to unpack
2* [+ *espada*] to draw
3 [+ *secreto*] to blurt out
VPR **desembanastarse 1** [*animal*] to break out
2 (= *bajar*) to alight
desembarazado ADJ **1** (= *desenvuelto*) free and easy • **~ de trabas** free, unrestrained
2 (= *libre*) clear, free
3 (= *sin carga*) unburdened, light
desembarazar ▸ CONJUG 1f VT **1** [+ *camino, cuarto*] to clear • **~ un cuarto de trastos** to clear a room of furniture
2 • **~ a algn de algo** to rid sb of sth
3 (*And, Caribe, Cono Sur*††) (= *dar a luz a*) to give birth to
VPR **desembarazarse** • **~se de algo** to get rid of sth
desembarazo SM **1** (= *acto*) [*de camino, cuarto*] clearing; [*de carga*] unburdening
2 (= *desenfado*) ease, naturalness • **hablar con ~** to talk easily, talk freely
3 (*LAm*) (= *parto*) birth
desembarcadero SM quay, landing stage
desembarcar ▸ CONJUG 1g VT [+ *personas*] to disembark; [+ *mercancías*] to unload
VI **1** (*de barco, avión*) [*pasajeros*] to disembark; [*tropas*] to land, disembark
2 (*esp LAm*) (*de tren*) to alight (*frm*) (**de** from), get out (**de** of)
3 • **estar para ~*** to be about to give birth
desembarco SM [*de pasajeros*] disembarkation; [*de tropas*] landing, disembarkation; [*de mercancías*] unloading
desembargar ▸ CONJUG 1h VT (*Jur*) to lift the embargo on
desembargo SM lifting (*of an embargo*)
desembarque SM [*de pasajeros*] disembarkation; [*de mercancías*] unloading
desembarrancar ▸ CONJUG 1g VT [+ *barco*] to refloat
desembarrar ▸ CONJUG 1a VT to clear of mud, remove the silt from
desembaular ▸ CONJUG 1a VT **1** [+ *equipaje*] to unpack
2 (= *descargarse de*) to unburden o.s. of
desembocadero SM, **desembocadura** SF [*de río*] mouth; [*de alcantarilla*] outfall; [*de calle*] opening, end
desembocar ▸ CONJUG 1g VI **1** • **~ en** [*río*] to flow into, run into; [*calle*] to join, lead into
2 • **~ en** (= *terminar en*) to end in, result in • **esto desembocó en una tragedia** this ended in *o* led to tragedy
desembolsar ▸ CONJUG 1a VT **1** (= *pagar*) to pay out
2 (= *gastar*) to lay out
desembolso SM **1** (= *pago*) payment
▸ **desembolso de capital** capital outlay
▸ **desembolso inicial** deposit
2 (= *gastos*) outlay, expenditure • **cubrir ~s** to cover expenses

desembozar ▸ CONJUG 1f VT to unmask
desembragado ADJ disengaged
desembragar ▸ CONJUG 1h VT (*Mec*) [+ *embrague*] to release, let out; [+ *marcha*] to disengage
VI (*Aut*) to declutch, let out the clutch
desembrague SM (*Aut*) (= *acto*) declutching; (= *mecanismo*) clutch release
desembravecer ▸ CONJUG 2d VT [+ *animal*] to tame; [+ *persona*] to calm, pacify
VPR **desembravecerse** to calm down
desembriagar ▸ CONJUG 1h VT to sober up
VPR **desembriagarse** to sober up
desembrollar ▸ CONJUG 1a VT **1** [+ *madeja*] to unravel
2 [+ *asunto, malentendido*] to sort out
desembuchar ▸ CONJUG 1a VT **1** [*ave*] to regurgitate
2* [+ *conclusiones*] to come out with
VI* (= *confesar*) to spill the beans* • **¡desembucha!** out with it!, spit it out!
VPR **desembucharse** (*Chile*) to be sick
desemejante ADJ dissimilar • **su comportamiento es muy ~ al de su padre** his behaviour is very dissimilar to his father's
desemejanza SF dissimilarity
desemejar ▸ CONJUG 1a VT to alter, alter the appearance of, change (*for the worse*)
VI to be dissimilar, look different, not look alike
desempacar ▸ CONJUG 1g VT (*esp LAm*) to unpack
desempacharse ▸ CONJUG 1a VPR **1** (*Med*) • **se desempachó** his stomach settled down
2 (= *perder la timidez*) to come out of one's shell
desempacho SM (= *soltura*) ease; (= *despreocupación*) unconcern; (= *desparpajo*) forwardness
desempadronarse‡ ▸ CONJUG 1a VPR (*Méx*) to do o.s. in‡, commit suicide
desempantanar ▸ CONJUG 1a VT [+ *asunto, problema*] to clear up, resolve
desempañador SM (*Aut*) demister
desempañar ▸ CONJUG 1a VT [+ *cristal*] (*con trapo*) to wipe clean; [*dispositivo antivaho*] to demist, defog (*EEUU*)
desempapelar ▸ CONJUG 1a VT [+ *pared*] to strip; [+ *paquete*] to unwrap
desempaquetar ▸ CONJUG 1a VT to unpack, unwrap
desempatar ▸ CONJUG 1a VI • **van a jugar la prórroga para ver si desempatan** extra time will be played to try and break the deadlock *o* to get a result
desempate SM **1** (*Ftbl*) (= *partido*) • **el ~ llegó con el gol de Roque** the breakthrough came with Roque's goal • **marcó el gol del ~ en el minuto 15** he put his side ahead *o* broke the deadlock in the 15th minute ▸ **desempate a penaltis** penalty shoot-out
2 (*Tenis*) tie break
desempedrar ▸ CONJUG 1j VT [+ *calle*] to take up the paving stones of • MODISMO: • **ir desempedrando la calle** to dash along the street
desempeñar ▸ CONJUG 1a VT
1 [+ *propiedades, joyas*] to redeem, get out of pawn • **~ a algn** to get sb out of debt, pay sb's debts
2 (= *llevar a cabo*) [+ *deber, función*] to perform, carry out; [+ *papel*] (*tb Teat*) to play
3 (= *ocupar*) [+ *cargo*] to occupy, hold
VPR **desempeñarse 1** (= *quitarse deudas*) to get out of debt
2 • **~se como** (*LAm*) to act as
desempeño SM **1** [*de propiedades, joyas*] redeeming, redemption
2 [*de deber*] performance, carrying out; [*de cargo*] carrying out • **durante el ~ de sus funciones como presidente** in the course of carrying out *o* performing his duties as president
3 (*Teat*) performance • **un ~ meritorio** a worthy performance • **una mujer de mucho ~** a most active and able woman
desempleado/a ADJ unemployed, out of work
SM/F unemployed man/woman • **los ~s** the unemployed
desempleo SM **1** (= *falta de trabajo*) unemployment ▸ **desempleo de larga duración** long-term unemployment
2 (= *subsidio*) unemployment benefit • **cobrar el ~** to draw unemployment benefit
desempolvar ▸ CONJUG 1a VT **1** [+ *libros, muebles*] to dust; [+ *objeto no usado*] to dust off
2 [+ *recuerdos*] to revive
desencadenamiento SM [*de pasión, energía*] unleashing ▸ **desencadenamiento de hostilidades** outbreak of hostilities
desencadenante ADJ • **los factores ~s del accidente** the factors which triggered (off) *o* caused the accident
SM cause, trigger
desencadenar ▸ CONJUG 1a VT **1** (= *quitar las cadenas de*) [+ *prisionero*] to unchain; [+ *perro*] to unleash
2 (= *desatar*) [+ *ira*] to unleash; [+ *crisis*] to trigger, set off
VPR **desencadenarse 1** (= *soltarse*) to break loose
2 (= *estallar*) [*tormenta*] to burst; [*guerra*] to break out • **se desencadenó una violenta reacción** a violent reaction was unleashed • **se ~on los aplausos** applause broke out
desencajado ADJ [*cara*] twisted, contorted; [*mandíbula*] dislocated; [*ojos*] wild
desencajar ▸ CONJUG 1a VT **1** (*Anat*) [+ *hueso*] to throw out of joint; [+ *mandíbula*] to dislocate
2 (*Mec*) to disconnect, disengage
VPR **desencajarse** [*cara*] to become distorted *o* contorted; [*ojos*] to look wild • **se le desencajó la mandíbula** he dislocated his jaw
desencajonar ▸ CONJUG 1a VT to unpack
desencallar ▸ CONJUG 1a VT [+ *barco*] to refloat
desencaminado ADJ (*lit*) headed in the wrong direction; (*fig*) misguided • **no vas muy ~** you're not far wrong there
desencantar ▸ CONJUG 1a VT **1** (= *quitar la ilusión a*) to disillusion, disenchant
2 (= *quitar un encantamiento a*) to free from a spell
desencanto SM disillusion, disillusionment, disenchantment
desencapotarse ▸ CONJUG 1a VPR [*cielo*] to clear, clear up
desenchufar ▸ CONJUG 1a VT to disconnect, unplug
VPR **desenchufarse*** (*hum*) to unwind, switch off
desencoger ▸ CONJUG 2c VT **1** (= *extender*) to spread out
2 (= *alisar*) to smooth out, straighten out
VPR **desencogerse** to lose one's timidity
desencolarse ▸ CONJUG 1a VPR to come unstuck
desenconar ▸ CONJUG 1a VT **1** [+ *cólera*] to calm down, soothe
2 [+ *inflamación*] to soothe
VPR **desenconarse 1** (= *calmarse*) [*odio*] to die down; [*persona*] to calm down
2 [*inflamación*] to die down, go down
desencontrarse ▸ CONJUG 1n VPR (= *separarse*) to become separated, get split up; (= *no encontrarse*) to fail to meet up
desencorvar ▸ CONJUG 1a VT to unbend,

straighten, straighten out
desencuadernar ▷ CONJUG 1a VT to unbind
VPR **desencuadernarse** to come unbound
desencuadrado ADJ (*Fot*) off centre
desencuentro SM **1** (= *falta de encuentro*) failure to meet up
2 (= *falta de acuerdo*) mix-up
desendeudar ▷ CONJUG 1a VI (*LAm*) to pay one's debts, get out of the red
VPR **desendeudarse** (*LAm*) to pay one's debts, get out of the red
desenfadaderas SFPL • **tener buenas ~** (= *no alterarse*) to be unflappable, be slow to anger; (*al salir de problemas*) to be good at getting out of jams
desenfadado ADJ **1** [*aire, carácter*] free, uninhibited
2 [*persona*] (= *despreocupado*) free-and-easy, carefree; (= *desenvuelto*) self-confident; (= *descarado*) forward; (*en el vestir*) casual
3 [*espacio*] free, unencumbered
desenfadar ▷ CONJUG 1a VT to pacify, calm down
VPR **desenfadarse** to calm down
desenfado SM **1** (= *despreocupación*) free-and-easy manner
2 (= *libertad*) freedom, lack of inhibition
3 (= *descaro*) forwardness
4 (= *desenvoltura*) self-confidence
desenfocado ADJ (*por mal uso*) out of focus; (*de forma intencionada*) in soft focus
desenfocar ▷ CONJUG 1g VT **1** (*Fot*) to get out of focus
2 [+ *asunto*] to read wrongly
VPR **desenfocarse** (*Fot*) to go out of focus
desenfoque SM (*por mal uso*) lack of focus, state of being out of focus; (*de forma intencionada*) soft focus
desenfrenadamente ADV wildly, in an uncontrolled way
desenfrenado ADJ [*persona*] wild, uncontrolled; [*apetito, pasiones*] unbridled
desenfrenarse ▷ CONJUG 1a VPR
1 (= *desmandarse*) [*persona*] to lose all self-control; [*multitud*] to run riot
2 (*Meteo*) [*tempestad*] to burst; [*viento*] to rage
desenfreno SM **1** [*de pasiones*] unleashing
2 (= *libertinaje*) licentiousness
desenfundar ▷ CONJUG 1a VT [+ *pistola*] to pull out, draw
VI* to flash*
desenganchar ▷ CONJUG 1a VT **1** (= *soltar*) [+ *cortinas*] to unhook; [+ *vagones*] to uncouple; [+ *caballo*] to unhitch
2 (*Mec*) to disengage
VPR **desengancharse**‡ to kick the habit* • **~se de algo** to come off sth
desengañado ADJ **1** (= *decepcionado*) disillusioned
2 (*And, Cono Sur*) (= *feo*) terribly ugly
desengañar ▷ CONJUG 1a VT **1** (= *desilusionar*) to disillusion • **es mejor no ~la** it is best not to take away her hopes *o* not to disillusion her
2 (= *decepcionar*) to disappoint
3 (= *abrir los ojos a*) to open the eyes of
VPR **desengañarse 1** (= *desilusionarse*) to become disillusioned (**de** about)
2 (= *decepcionarse*) to be disappointed
3 (= *abrir los ojos*) to see the light, see things as they really are • **¡desengáñate!** wise up!*
desengaño SM **1** (= *desilusión*) disillusion, disillusionment • **los ~s te enseñarán** you'll learn the hard way
2 (= *decepción*) disappointment • **sufrir un ~ amoroso** to be disappointed in love
desengranar ▷ CONJUG 1a VT to disengage
desengrasado ADJ **1** [*máquina*] rusty, needing oil
2 (*Culin*) fat-free
desengrasar ▷ CONJUG 1a VT to degrease
desenhebrar ▷ CONJUG 1j VT to unthread
desenjaular ▷ CONJUG 1a VT **1** [+ *animal*] to take out of a cage
2* [+ *preso*] to let out of jail
desenlace SM [*de libro, película*] ending, dénouement (*frm*); [*de aventura*] outcome • **~ fatal** *o* **trágico** tragic ending • **el libro tiene un ~ feliz** the book has a happy ending
desenlatar ▷ CONJUG 1a VT (*LAm*) [+ *latas*] to open
desenlazar ▷ CONJUG 1f VT **1** (= *desatar*) to untie
2 (= *resolver*) [+ *problema*] to solve; [+ *asunto*] to unravel
VPR **desenlazarse 1** (= *desatarse*) to come undone
2 [*libro, película*] to end, turn out
desenmarañar ▷ CONJUG 1a VT **1** [+ *cuerda, lana, pelo*] to untangle, disentangle
2 [+ *misterio*] to unravel, clear up
VPR **desenmarañarse** [*misterio*] to unravel
desenmascarar ▷ CONJUG 1a VT (*lit*) to unmask; (*fig*) to unmask, expose
desenojar ▷ CONJUG 1a VT to soothe, appease, calm down
desenredar ▷ CONJUG 1a VT **1** [+ *pelo, lana*] to untangle, disentangle
2 [+ *dificultad, problema*] to straighten out
VPR **desenredarse** (*de un problema*) to extricate o.s. (**de** from)
desenredo SM **1** (= *acto*) unravelling, disentanglement
2 (*Literat*) dénouement
desenrollar ▷ CONJUG 1a VT [+ *alfombra*] to unroll; [+ *cable*] to unwind
VPR **desenrollarse** [*alfombra*] to unroll; [*cable*] to unwind
desenroscar ▷ CONJUG 1g VT [+ *tornillo*] to unscrew
VPR **desenroscarse** [*tornillo*] to come unscrewed, unscrew
desensibilizar ▷ CONJUG 1f VT to desensitize
desensillar ▷ CONJUG 1a VT to unsaddle
desentablar ▷ CONJUG 1a VT to break up
VPR **desentablarse** • **se desentabló una discusión** a row broke out
desentenderse ▷ CONJUG 2g VPR
1 (= *simular ignorancia*) • **~ de algo** to pretend not to know about sth
2 (= *repudiar*) • **~ de algo** to wash one's hands of sth, want nothing to do with sth • **se ha desentendido del asunto** he wants nothing to do with the matter
desentendido ADJ • **hacerse el ~** to pretend not to notice • **se hizo el ~** he didn't take the hint • **no te hagas el ~** don't pretend you haven't heard
desentendimiento SM • **su ~ sobre el asunto** his refusal to have anything to do with the matter
desenterrar ▷ CONJUG 1j VT **1** [+ *cadáver*] to disinter; [+ *tesoro*] to unearth
2 [+ *recuerdo, odio*] to rake up
desentonado ADJ **1** (*Mús*) out of tune
2 [*color*] clashing
desentonar ▷ CONJUG 1a VI **1** (= *no encajar*) [*persona, comentario*] to be out of place; [*colores*] to clash (**con** with) • **para no ~** so as to do the right thing, so as to fall into line • **el edificio desentona con el entorno** the building doesn't fit in with the surroundings
2 (*Mús*) to be out of tune
VPR **desentonarse** to raise one's voice angrily
desentono SM **1** (= *cualidad*) rudeness, disrespect
2 (= *tono*) rude tone of voice
desentorpecer ▷ CONJUG 2d VT
1 [+ *miembro*] to stretch, loosen up
2* [+ *persona*] to polish up
desentramparse* ▷ CONJUG 1a VPR to get out of the red
desentrañar ▷ CONJUG 1a VT **1** (= *resolver*) [+ *misterio*] to get to the bottom of, unravel; [+ *significado*] to puzzle out
2 (= *destripar*) to disembowel
desentrenado ADJ [*jugador*] out of training; [*soldado*] untrained
desentumecer ▷ CONJUG 2d VT [+ *miembro*] to stretch; [+ *músculos*] to loosen up
VPR **desentumecerse** to loosen up
desenvainar ▷ CONJUG 1a VT **1** (= *sacar de la vaina*) [+ *espada*] to draw, unsheathe; [+ *guisantes*] to shell; [+ *garras*] to show, put out
2 (= *mostrar*) to reveal, expose
desenvoltura SF **1** (= *facilidad*) (*al moverse*) ease; (*al hablar*) fluency
2 (= *falta de timidez*) confidence, self-confidence
3 (*pey*) (= *desparpajo*) forwardness, brazenness
desenvolver ▷ CONJUG 2h (PP: **desenvuelto**)
VT **1** (= *desliar*) [+ *paquete*] to unwrap; [+ *rollo*] to unwind, unroll; [+ *lana*] to disentangle, unravel
2 [+ *teoría*] to develop
VPR **desenvolverse 1** [*persona*] to manage, cope • **se desenvuelve muy bien en público** he comes across really well in public
2 [*acción, suceso*] (= *suceder*) to go off; (= *desarrollarse*) to develop
desenvolvimiento SM development
desenvuelto PP *de* **desenvolver**
ADJ **1** (= *falto de timidez*) confident, self-confident
2 (*al hablar*) fluent; (*pey*) forward, brazen
desenyugar ▷ CONJUG 1h VT (*LAm*),
desenyuntar ▷ CONJUG 1a VT (*LAm*) to unyoke
deseo SM **1** (= *anhelo*) desire, wish • **mi mayor ~ es encontrar un trabajo** my dearest wish *o* greatest desire is to find a job • **el ~ de poder** the lust for power • **un inacabable ~ de saber** an unquenchable thirst for knowledge • **llegó al poder con buenos ~s de mejorarlo todo** he came to power with every intention of improving things • **tengo ~s de verla** I yearn to see her, I'm longing to see her • **ardo en ~s de conocerla** (*liter*) I have a burning desire to meet her
2 (= *cosa deseada*) wish • **pedir** *o* **formular un ~** to make a wish • **su último ~ fue que la incineraran** her dying wish was to be cremated • **nuestro ~ es que seas feliz** our wish is for you to be happy • **con mis mejores ~s para el Año Nuevo** with best wishes for the New Year • **tus ~s son órdenes** your wish is my command
3 (*tb* **deseo sexual**) desire
deseoso ADJ • **estar ~ de hacer algo** to be anxious *o* eager to do sth
desequilibrado/a ADJ [*persona*] unbalanced; [*rueda*] out of balance, not properly balanced, out of true; [*distribución*] one-sided, lop-sided
SM/F unbalanced person • **es un ~ mental** he's mentally unbalanced
desequilibrador ADJ destabilizing
desequilibrar ▷ CONJUG 1a VT **1** [+ *barca, mueble*] to unbalance, make unbalanced
2 [+ *persona*] (*físicamente*) to throw off balance; (*psicológicamente*) to unbalance
3 • **~ un país/régimen** to destabilize a country/regime
VPR **desequilibrarse** [*balanza*] to get out of

d

balance; [*persona*] to become mentally unbalanced

desequilibrio SM **1** [*de mente*] unbalance
2 (*entre cantidades*) imbalance
3 (*Med*) unbalanced mental condition

deserción SF **1** (*Mil*) desertion
2 (= *abandono*) (*de un partido a otro*) defection; (*de una actividad*) giving up

desertar ▸ CONJUG 1a VI to desert • **~ de** (*Mil*) to desert • **~ del hogar** to abandon one's home • **~ de sus deberes** to neglect one's duties • **~ de una tertulia** to stop going to a gathering

desértico ADJ **1** (= *del desierto*) desert (*antes de s*)
2 (= *árido*) desert-like, barren
3 (= *despoblado*) deserted

desertificar ▸ CONJUG 1g VT = **desertizar**

desertización SF **1** [*de terreno*] desertification
2 (= *despoblación*) depopulation

desertizar ▸ CONJUG 1f VT **1** [+ *terreno*] to turn into a desert
2 (= *despoblar*) to depopulate

desertor(a) SM/F (*Mil*) deserter; (*Pol*) defector

deservicio SM disservice

desescalada SF de-escalation

desescalar ▸ CONJUG 1a VT, VI to de-escalate

desescamar ▸ CONJUG 1a VT to descale, remove the fur from (*EEUU*)

desescarchador SM (*Mec*) defroster

desescolarización SF lack of schooling

desescolarizado ADJ • **niños ~s** children deprived of schooling

descombrar ▸ CONJUG 1a VT **1** [+ *lugar*] to clear up, clear of rubbish *o* debris *etc*, clean up
2 [+ *cadáver*] to dig out, extract

descombro SM clearing-up, clean-up

desespañolizar ▸ CONJUG 1f VT [+ *costumbre*] to weaken the Spanish nature of; [+ *persona*] to cause to become less Spanish, wean away from Spanish habits *etc*

desesperación SF **1** (= *pérdida de esperanza*) despair, desperation • **mirar a algn con ~** to look at sb despairingly • **nadar con ~** to swim desperately
2 (= *resultado*) • **es una ~** it's maddening • **es una ~ tener que ...** it's infuriating to have to ...

desesperada SF • MODISMO: • **hacer algo a la ~** to do sth as a last resort *o* in desperation

desesperadamente ADV desperately, despairingly

desesperado/a ADJ **1** (= *sin esperanza*) [*persona*] desperate; [*caso, situación*] hopeless • **estar ~ de algo** to have despaired of sth, have lost hope of sth
2 [*esfuerzo*] furious, frenzied
SM/F • **como un ~** like mad • **come como una desesperada** she eats as if she were half-starved

desesperante ADJ [*situación*] infuriating; [*persona*] infuriating, hopeless

desesperanza SF despair

desesperanzar ▸ CONJUG 1f VT to drive to despair
VPR **desesperanzarse** to lose hope, despair

desesperar ▸ CONJUG 1a VT **1** (= *exasperar*) • **mi hermano me desespera** my brother drives me mad *o* crazy, my brother is infuriating *o* maddening • **me desespera que el tren llegue tarde** it's infuriating *o* maddening when the train is late
2 (= *desalentar*) • **no dejes que sus críticas te desesperen** don't let their criticism make you lose hope *o* heart, don't let their criticism get to you* • **tantos problemas la ~on y acabó dimitiendo** all these problems drove her to despair and in the end she resigned
VI (= *perder la esperanza*) to despair, lose hope • **sigue adelante, no desesperes** keep at it, don't despair *o* lose hope • **~ de hacer algo** (*frm*) to despair of doing sth, lose all hope of doing sth • REFRÁN: • **el que espera, desespera** waiting gets you down
VPR **desesperarse 1** (= *exasperarse*) • **me desespero con tanto trabajo** all this work is driving me mad *o* crazy • **me estaba desesperando porque el taxi no llegaba** the taxi still hadn't come and I was going mad *o* crazy *o* getting desperate
2 (= *desalentarse*) to despair, lose hope • **nunca se desespera aunque las cosas le vayan mal** she never loses hope *o* despairs even when things go badly for her • **no te desesperes si no apruebas a la primera** if you don't pass first time, don't despair *o* give up hope

desespero SM (*LAm*) despair, desperation

despinar ▸ CONJUG 1a VT [+ *pescado*] to fillet, bone

desestabilización SF destabilization

desestabilizador ADJ **1** [*campaña, influencia*] destabilizing
2 [*elemento, grupo*] subversive

desestabilizar ▸ CONJUG 1f VT **1** [+ *situación*] to destabilize
2 [+ *confianza, orden moral*] to undermine

desestancar ▸ CONJUG 1g VT [+ *producto*] to remove the state monopoly from, allow a free market in

desestiba SF (*Náut*) unloading

desestibar ▸ CONJUG 1a VT (*Náut*) to unload

desestimable ADJ insignificant

desestimar ▸ CONJUG 1a VT
1 (= *menospreciar*) to look down on
2 (*Jur*) [+ *demanda, moción*] to reject

desestímulo SM disincentive

desestresarse ▸ CONJUG 1a VPR to de-stress

desestructurado ADJ badly structured • **familia desestructurada** broken home

desexilio SM (*LAm*) return from exile, return home

desfachatado* ADJ brazen, impudent, barefaced

desfachatez SF **1** (= *descaro*) brazenness, cheek
2 • **una ~** a cheeky remark*, a brazen remark

desfalcador(a) SM/F embezzler

desfalcar ▸ CONJUG 1g VT to embezzle

desfalco SM embezzlement

desfallecer ▸ CONJUG 2d VI **1** (= *perder las fuerzas*) to get weak • **~ de ánimo** to lose heart
2 (= *desmayarse*) to faint

desfallecido ADJ (= *débil*) weak

desfallecimiento SM **1** (= *debilidad*) weakness
2 (= *desmayo*) fainting fit

desfasado ADJ **1** (= *anticuado*) behind the times
2 (*Téc*) out of phase
3 • **estar ~** (*Aer*) to be suffering from jetlag

desfasar ▸ CONJUG 1a VT **1** (= *dejar anticuado*) to phase out
2 (*Elec*) to change the phase of

desfase SM (= *diferencia*) gap • **hay un ~ entre las dos generaciones** there's a generation gap ▸ **desfase horario** jet lag

desfavorable ADJ unfavourable, unfavorable (*EEUU*)

desfavorablemente ADV unfavourably, unfavorably (*EEUU*)

desfavorecer ▸ CONJUG 2d VT **1** [+ *persona, causa*] • **estas medidas ~án a los pequeños agricultores** these measures will hurt small farmers *o* go against the interests of small farmers • **han desfavorecido las calles peatonales** they are opposed to the pedestrianization of the streets
2 (= *sentar mal a*) [*ropa*] not to suit

desfavorecido ADJ **1** (= *discriminado*) disadvantaged
2 (= *afeado*) • **siempre salgo ~ en las fotos** I never look good in photos

desfibradora SF shredder, shredding machine

desfibrar ▸ CONJUG 1a VT [+ *papel*] to shred

desfibrilador SM defibrillator

desfiguración SF, **desfiguramiento** SM **1** (= *transformación*) [*de persona*] disfigurement; [*de monumento*] defacement; [*de la realidad*] distortion
2 (*Fot*) blurring
3 (*Radio*) distortion

desfigurado ADJ [*persona*] disfigured; [*sonido, voz, sentido, realidad*] distorted; [*foto*] blurred

desfigurar ▸ CONJUG 1a VT **1** (= *transformar*) [+ *cara*] to disfigure; [+ *cuerpo*] to deform; [+ *cuadro, monumento*] to deface; [+ *voz, sonido*] to distort, disguise; [+ *sentido*] to twist; [+ *suceso*] to misrepresent • **una cicatriz le desfigura la cara** his face is disfigured by a scar • **la niebla lo desfigura todo** the fog makes everything look strange
2 (*Fot*) to blur

desfiladero SM defile, gorge

desfilar ▸ CONJUG 1a VI **1** (*Mil*) to parade • **~on ante el general** they marched past the general
2 (= *pasar*) to come, pass by • **por su despacho han desfilado muchos acreedores** many creditors have passed through his office • **según acababan, iban desfilando por la puerta** as they finished, they filtered out of the door
3 [*modelo*] to model • **nunca he desfilado con ropa de Armani** I've never modelled Armani clothes

desfile SM **1** (*Mil*) parade ▸ **desfile aéreo** flypast, flyover (*EEUU*) ▸ **desfile de la victoria** victory parade ▸ **desfile de promoción** passing-out parade ▸ **desfile naval** naval review
2 [*de carrozas*] procession
3 ▸ **desfile de modas, desfile de modelos** fashion show, fashion parade

desfiscalización SF exemption from tax

desfiscalizar ▸ CONJUG 1f VT to exempt from taxation

desfloración SF deflowering, defloration

desflorar ▸ CONJUG 1a VT **1** (= *aspecto, reputación*) to tarnish
2 [+ *asunto*] to touch on
3 (*liter*) [+ *mujer*] to deflower (*liter*)

desfogar ▸ CONJUG 1h VT [+ *cólera, frustración*] to vent (**con, en** on)
VI (*Náut*) [*tormenta*] to burst
VPR **desfogarse** [*persona*] to vent one's anger (**con, en on**) • **tiene que hacer deporte para ~se** he needs to do sport to let off steam

desfogue SM venting

desfondado ADJ (*Econ*) bankrupt

desfondar ▸ CONJUG 1a VT **1** (= *romper el fondo*) to knock the bottom out of, stave in (*tb Náut*)
2 (*Agr*) to plough deeply
VPR **desfondarse** to go to pieces, have the bottom fall out of one's life

desforestación SF deforestation

desforestar ▸ CONJUG 1a VT to deforest

desformatear ▸ CONJUG 1a VT to unformat

desgaire SM **1** (= *desaseo*) slovenliness, carelessness • **vestido al ~** dressed in a slovenly way
2 (= *desdén*) scornful attitude, disdain
• MODISMOS: • **hacer algo al ~** to do sth with a scornful air • **mirar a algn al ~** to sneer at sb, look scornfully at sb
desgajado ADJ separated, unconnected
desgajar ▹ CONJUG 1a VT **1** (= *desprender*) [+ *rama*] to tear off; [+ *página, capítulo*] to tear out
2 [+ *naranja*] to split into segments
3 • **~ a algn de un lugar** to tear sb away from somewhere
VPR **desgajarse 1** [*rama*] to come off, break off
2 • **~se de algn** to tear o.s. away from sb
desgalichado ADJ **1** [*movimiento*] clumsy, awkward
2 (= *poco cuidado*) [*vestido*] shabby, slovenly, sloppy; [*persona*] down-at-heel, unprepossessing
desgana SF **1** (= *falta de apetito*) lack of appetite
2 (= *apatía*) unwillingness, reluctance • **su ~ para hacerlo** his unwillingness *o* reluctance to do it • **hacer algo a** *o* **con ~** to do sth unwillingly *o* reluctantly
3 (*Med*) weakness, faintness
desganadamente ADV **1** [*comer*] in a desultory fashion
2 [*decir, hacer*] without much interest, in a desultory fashion
desganado ADJ **1** (= *sin apetito*) not hungry • **estar** *o* **sentirse ~** to have no appetite
2 (= *sin entusiasmo*) half-hearted • **estar ~** to be lethargic
desganarse ▹ CONJUG 1a VPR **1** (= *perder el apetito*) to lose one's appetite
2 (= *perder el entusiasmo*) to lose interest (**de** in), get fed up (**de** with)
desgano SM = desgana
desgañitarse* ▹ CONJUG 1a VPR to shout one's head off*
desgarbado ADJ [*movimiento*] clumsy, ungainly; [*persona*] gawky
desgarbo SM [*de movimiento*] clumsiness; [*de persona*] gracelessness; [*de aspecto*] slovenliness
desgarrado ADJ **1** [*ropa*] (= *rasgado*) torn; (= *hecho trizas*) tattered, in tatters
2 (= *descarado*) shameless, barefaced, brazen
3 (= *vicioso*) licentious
desgarrador ADJ [*escena, noticia*] heartbreaking, heartrending; [*grito*] piercing; [*emoción*] heartrending
desgarramiento SM **1** [*de tela*] tearing, ripping
2 [*de sociedad, país*] upheaval
desgarrar ▹ CONJUG 1a VT **1** [+ *vestido, papel*] to tear, rip
2 [+ *corazón*] to break
3 (*LAm*) [+ *flema*] to cough up
VPR **desgarrarse 1** [*vestido, papel*] to tear, rip
2 [*músculo*] • **se desgarró un músculo entrenando** he tore a muscle while training
desgarro SM **1** (*en tela, papel*) tear, rip
2 (*Med*) sprain
3 (= *descaro*) brazenness
4 (= *jactancia*) boastfulness
5 (*LAm*) (= *expectoración*) expectoration; (= *flema*) phlegm
desgarrón SM **1** (*en tela, papel*) big tear
2 (= *sentimiento*) agony
desgastado ADJ [*zapato, ropa*] worn-out; [*tacones*] worn down; [*moqueta, tejido*] worn; [*neumático*] bald
desgastar ▹ CONJUG 1a VT **1** [+ *ropa, zapatos, tejido, moqueta, neumático*] to wear out; [+ *tacones, suela*] to wear down; [+ *superficie*] to wear away • **las olas han desgastado las rocas** the waves have worn away the rocks • **la corrupción ha desgastado al gobierno** corruption has weakened the government
2 [+ *rival, contrincante*] to wear down
VI (= *debilitar*) • **veinte años de poder desgastan** after twenty years in power you get stale *o* run out of steam
VPR **desgastarse 1** (= *gastarse*) [*ropa, zapatos, tejido, neumático*] to wear out; [*tacones, suela, grada*] to wear down; [*superficie, roca*] to wear away • **la cuerda se desgastó con el roce** friction wore away the rope
2 (= *agotarse*) [*persona*] to wear o.s. out
desgaste SM **1** [*de ropa, zapatos, neumático*] wear; [*de superficie, roca*] wearing away, erosion
2 (= *agotamiento*) • **su larga enfermedad provocó un ~ en su organismo** her long illness exhausted her physically • **el poder produjo el ~ del gobierno** in power, the government grew stale *o* ran out of steam • **guerra de ~** war of attrition ▸ **desgaste físico** physical exhaustion
desglaciación SF thaw
desglobar ▹ CONJUG 1a VT [+ *cantidades, cifras*] to break down, analyse, split up
desglosable ADJ **1** [*cifras*] which can be broken down
2 [*impreso*] separable, detachable
desglosar ▹ CONJUG 1a VT **1** [+ *cantidades, cifras*] to break down
2 [+ *impreso*] to detach
desglose SM breakdown
desgobernado ADJ [*asunto*] uncontrollable, undisciplined; [*niño*] wild
desgobernar ▹ CONJUG 1j VT **1** (*Pol*) to misgovern, misrule
2 [+ *asunto*] to handle badly
3 (*Anat*) to dislocate
desgobierno SM **1** (*Pol*) misgovernment, misrule
2 [*de empresa*] bad handling
3 (*Anat*) dislocation
desgolletar ▹ CONJUG 1a VT [+ *botella*] to knock the neck off
desgoznar ▹ CONJUG 1a VT **1** (= *sacar de los goznes*) [+ *puerta*] to take off its hinges, unhinge
2 (= *quitar goznes de*) to take the hinges off
VPR **desgoznarse 1** [*persona*] to go wild, lose control
2 [*plan*] to be thrown out of gear
desgrabar ▹ CONJUG 1a VT [+ *cinta*] to wipe, wipe clean
desgracia SF **1** (= *mala suerte*) misfortune • **tuve la ~ de encontrármelo en el cine** I had the misfortune to *o* I was unfortunate enough to run into him at the cinema • **por ~** unfortunately • **estar en ~** (*frm*) to have constant bad luck • **en la ~ se conoce a los amigos** a friend in need is a friend indeed
2 (= *revés*) misfortune • **la familia ha sufrido una serie de ~s** the family has suffered a series of misfortunes • **ha ocurrido una ~** something terrible has happened • **ha muerto, ¡qué ~!** she has died, what a terrible thing (to happen)! • **estos niños solo me traen ~s** these children are nothing but trouble • MODISMO: • **las ~s nunca vienen solas** it never rains but it pours; ▹ colmo
3 ▸ **desgracias personales** (= *víctimas*) casualties • **no hay que lamentar ~s personales** there were no casualties
4 • **caer en ~** to lose favour *o* (EEUU) favor, fall from favour *o* (EEUU) favor
desgraciadamente ADV unfortunately, unluckily
desgraciado/a ADJ **1** [*persona*] (= *sin suerte*) unlucky; (= *infeliz*) unhappy • **~ en (sus) amores** unlucky in love • **~ en el juego** unlucky at cards • **fue ~ en su matrimonio** he was unhappy in his marriage • **¡~ de ti si lo haces!** you'd better not do that!, it'll be the worse for you if you do that!
2 [*vida, existencia*] • **¡qué desgraciada existencia la mía!** how wretched I am! • **una vida desgraciada** a wretched life, a life of misery
3 [*accidente, situación*] unfortunate • **una desgraciada elección** an unfortunate choice • **ese día ~** that ill-fated day
4 (*LAm*) (= *asqueroso*) lousy*
SM/F **1** (= *infeliz*) poor wretch • **lo tiene aquel ~** that poor wretch has got it • **la hizo una desgraciada** (*pey*) he put her in the family way, he brought shame upon her (*euf*)
2 (= *miserable*) swine*
desgraciar ▹ CONJUG 1b VT **1** (= *estropear*) to spoil
2 (= *ofender*) to displease
VPR **desgraciarse 1** (= *estropearse*) [*máquina*] to be ruined; [*plan*] to fall through • **como te caigas te vas a ~** (*hum*) you'll do yourself a permanent injury if you fall • **se le desgració el niño antes de nacer** she had a miscarriage, she lost the baby
2 • **~se con algn** to fall out with sb
desgranar ▹ CONJUG 1a VT **1** [+ *trigo*] to thresh; [+ *guisantes*] to shell • **~ un racimo de uvas** to pick the grapes from a bunch • **~ las cuentas del rosario** to tell one's beads
2 [+ *sentido*] to spell out • **~ mentiras** to come out with a string of lies • **~ imprecaciones** to let fly with a string of curses
VPR **desgranarse 1** (*Bot*) [*trigo*] to shed its grain; [*planta*] to drop its seeds
2 [*cuentas*] to come unstrung
desgrasado ADJ (*Culin*) fat-free
desgrasar ▹ CONJUG 1a VT = **desengrasar**
desgravable ADJ tax-deductible
desgravación SF ▸ **desgravación de impuestos, desgravación fiscal** tax relief ▸ **desgravación personal** tax allowance
desgravar ▹ CONJUG 1a VT **1** [+ *cantidad*] • **puede ~ hasta 400 euros por cada hijo** you can claim tax relief of up to 400 euros for each child • **tener un plan de pensiones puede ~ un 10%** you can claim 10% tax relief if you have a pension plan
2 [+ *producto*] to eliminate tax on • **la ley les desgrava estas compras** the law allows them tax relief on these purchases
VI • **esas inversiones desgravan** those investments are tax-deductible
desgreñado ADJ dishevelled, disheveled (EEUU)
desgreñar ▹ CONJUG 1a VT to dishevel
desgreño* SM (*And, Cono Sur*) **1** (= *desorden*) untidiness
2 (= *desorganización*) disorder, disarray
3 (= *descuido*) carelessness
desguace SM **1** (= *despiece*) [*de barco*] breaking-up, scrapping; [*de coche*] scrapping
2 (= *lugar*) scrapyard, breaker's yard
desguarnecer ▹ CONJUG 2d VT **1** (= *quitar los adornos de*) [+ *pared*] to strip bare; [+ *caballo*] to unharness • **~ un barco de las velas** to remove the sails from a boat
2 (*Téc*) to strip down
3 (*Mil*) [+ *pueblo*] to remove the garrison from; [+ *plaza fuerte*] to dismantle
desguarnecido ADJ **1** (= *sin adornos*) stripped, bare
2 (*Mil*) [*ciudad*] undefended, unprotected; [*flanco*] exposed

d

desguazar ▷ CONJUG 1f VT **1** (= *desmantelar*) [+ *barco*] to break up, scrap; [+ *coche, avión*] to scrap
2 [+ *madera*] to dress, rough-hew

desgubernamentalizar ▷ CONJUG 1f VT to remove from government control

deshabilitar ▷ CONJUG 1a VT (*Inform*) to disable

deshabillé SM negligee

deshabitado ADJ [*edificio*] empty, vacant; [*zona, ciudad*] uninhabited

deshabitar ▷ CONJUG 1a VT [+ *edificio*] to leave empty; [+ *zona, ciudad*] to depopulate

deshabituación SF **1** [*de costumbre*] losing the habit, breaking of the habit
2 (*Med*) treatment for drug dependency

deshabituar ▷ CONJUG 1e VT • **~ a algn de la droga** to get sb off drugs
VPR **deshabituarse 1** (*de costumbre*) to lose the habit
2 • **~se de la droga** to kick one's drug habit, conquer one's drug addiction

deshacer ▷ CONJUG 2r (PP: **deshecho**) VT
1 (= *separar*) [+ *nudo, lazo*] to untie, undo; [+ *costura*] to unpick; [+ *fila, corro*] to break up
2 (= *desarreglar*) [+ *maleta*] to unpack; [+ *rompecabezas*] to break up; [+ *paquete*] to undo, unwrap; [+ *cama*] (*al dormir*) to mess up; (*para cambiar las sábanas*) to strip • **deshacía una y otra vez su peinado** she kept redoing her hair • **era imposible ~ lo hecho** what had been done couldn't be undone • **puede hacer y ~ a su antojo** she is free to do as she wishes • **la cama estaba sin ~** the bed hadn't been slept in
3 (= *derretir*) [+ *nieve, helado*] to melt
4 (= *disolver*) [+ *pastilla, grumos*] to dissolve; (= *desmenuzar*) [+ *bizcocho, pastel, cubito de caldo*] to crumble • **~ algo en agua** to dissolve sth in water
5 (= *desgastar*) [+ *zapatos, ropa*] to wear out; [+ *metal*] to wear down, wear away
6 (= *estropear*) [+ *vista, proyecto, vida*] to ruin • **la marea deshizo los castillos de arena** the tide washed away *o* broke up our sandcastles • **este contratiempo nos ha deshecho los planes** this setback has ruined our plans
7 [+ *persona*] to shatter
8 [+ *contrato, alianza, acuerdo*] (= *romper*) to break; (= *cancelar*) to annul
9 (= *enmendar*) [+ *agravio*] to right, put right; [+ *equívoco, malentendido*] to resolve
• MODISMO: • **~ el camino** to retrace one's steps
10 (= *dispersar*) [+ *manifestación*] to break up; [+ *enemigo*] to rout
11 (= *derrotar*) [+ *contrario*] to take apart, dismantle
VPR **deshacerse 1** (= *separarse*) [*nudo*] to come undone, come untied; [*costura*] to come undone, split; [*moño, trenza*] to come undone
2 (= *romperse*) to smash, shatter • **el libro se le deshizo en las manos** the book came apart in his hands • **el jarrón se deshizo en sus manos** the vase just fell to pieces *o* came apart in his hands • **cuando lo levanté, se me deshizo todo** when I lifted it up it all fell to bits
3 (= *derretirse*) [*caramelo, hielo*] to melt • **se deshacen en la boca** they melt in your mouth • **el hielo se deshizo al subir la temperatura** the ice melted as the temperature rose
4 (= *desmembrarse*) [*organización, manifestación*] to break up; [*ejército*] to be routed • **cuando se deshizo la reunión** when the meeting broke up
5 (= *desaparecer*) to vanish • **se deshizo como el humo** it vanished into thin air
6 [*persona*] (= *afligirse*) to go to pieces; (= *impacientarse*) to be at one's wits' end • **se ha deshecho tras la tragedia** she has gone to pieces since the tragedy
7 • **~se de** (*queriendo*) to get rid of; (*sin querer*) to part with; (*Dep*) to dispose of; (*Com*) to dump • **logramos ~nos de él** we managed to get rid of him • **no quiero ~me de eso** I don't want to part with that
8 (= *esforzarse*) • **se deshace trabajando** he works incredibly hard • **~se en:** • **~se en cumplidos con algn** to be very complimentary towards sb, shower sb with compliments • **~se en elogios con algn** to be full of praise for sb, shower sb with praise • **~se en excusas** to apologize profusely • **~se en lágrimas** to burst *o* dissolve into tears • **se deshace por su familia** he bends over backwards for his family • **~se por hacer algo** to strive to do sth, do one's utmost to do sth • **~se por complacer a algn** to strive to please sb, do one's utmost to please sb
9 (*Med*) (= *debilitarse*) to get weak, grow feeble; (= *consumirse*) to waste away

desharrapado/a ADJ ragged
SM/F person dressed in rags • **los ~s de la sociedad** outcasts from society

deshebillar ▷ CONJUG 1a VT to unbuckle

deshebrar ▷ CONJUG 1a VT to unpick

deshechizar ▷ CONJUG 1f VT to remove the spell from, disenchant

deshecho PP *de* **deshacer**
ADJ **1** [*lazo, nudo*] undone
2 (= *roto*) [*objeto*] broken, smashed • **las camas están deshechas** the beds are unmade • **llegó con los nervios ~s** his nerves were shattered when he arrived • **tiene un brazo ~** he has a badly injured arm • **el pastel ha quedado ~** the cake is ruined • **estoy ~*** I'm shattered*
3 (*Med*) [*persona*] weak; [*salud*] broken
4 (*Cono Sur*) (= *desaliñado*) untidy
SM (*And, Caribe, Cono Sur*) short cut

deshelador SM (*Aer*) de-icer

deshelar ▷ CONJUG 1j VT [+ *tubería*] to thaw; [+ *congelador*] to defrost; [+ *avión, coche*] to de-ice
VI, VPR **deshelarse** [*nieve*] to thaw, melt; [*río, lago*] to thaw

desherbaje SM weeding

desherbar ▷ CONJUG 1j VT to weed

desheredado/a SM/F • **los ~s** the dispossessed

desheredar ▷ CONJUG 1a VT to disinherit

desherrarse ▷ CONJUG 1k VPR [*caballo*] to cast a shoe

deshidratación SF dehydration

deshidratado ADJ dehydrated

deshidratar ▷ CONJUG 1a VT to dehydrate
VPR **deshidratarse** to become dehydrated

deshielo SM [*de nieve*] thaw; [*de congelador*] defrosting ▸ **deshielo diplomático** diplomatic thaw

deshierbe SM weeding

deshilachado ADJ frayed

deshilachar ▷ CONJUG 1a VT to fray
VPR **deshilacharse** to fray

deshilada SF • **a la ~ 1** (*Mil*) in single file
2 (= *secretamente*) secretly, stealthily

deshilado SM (*Cos*) openwork

deshilar ▷ CONJUG 1a VT **1** (*Cos*) (= *desenmarañar*) to unravel; (= *deshilachar*) to fray
2 [+ *carne*] to shred
VI to get thin
VPR **deshilarse** to fray

deshilvanado ADJ [*historia, trama*] disjointed, incoherent

deshilvanar ▷ CONJUG 1a VT (*Cos*) to untack, take the stitches out of

deshinchar ▷ CONJUG 1a VT **1** [+ *neumático*] to let down
2 (*Med*) to reduce the swelling of
3 [+ *ira, furia*] to give vent to
VPR **deshincharse 1** [*neumático*] to go flat
2 (*Med*) to go down
3 (= *perder el orgullo*) to get down off one's high horse

deshipotecar ▷ CONJUG 1g VT [+ *propiedad*] to pay off the mortgage on

deshojado ADJ [*rama*] leafless; [*flor*] stripped of its petals

deshojar ▷ CONJUG 1a VT **1** (*Bot*) [+ *árbol*] to strip the leaves off; [+ *flor*] to pull the petals off; ▷ **margarita**
2 [+ *libro*] to tear the pages out of
3 (*LAm*) [+ *maíz*] to husk; [+ *fruta*] to peel
4 (*Quím*) to defoliate
VPR **deshojarse** [*árbol*] to lose its leaves; [*flor*] to lose its petals

deshollejar ▷ CONJUG 1a VT [+ *uvas*] to peel, skin

deshollinador(a) SM/F chimney sweep

deshollinar ▷ CONJUG 1a VT **1** [+ *chimenea*] to sweep
2 (= *mirar con atención*) to take a close look at

deshonestamente ADV **1** (= *sin honradez*) dishonestly
2 (= *indecentemente*) indecently, lewdly

deshonestidad SF **1** (= *falta de honradez*) dishonesty
2 (= *indecencia*) indecency

deshonesto ADJ **1** (= *no honrado*) dishonest
2 (= *indecente*) indecent; ▷ **proposición**

deshonor SM **1** (= *pérdida del honor*) dishonour, dishonor (*EEUU*), disgrace
2 • **un ~** an insult, an affront (**a** to) • **no es ningún ~ trabajar** it is no disgrace to work

deshonorar ▷ CONJUG 1a VT **1** (= *deshonrar*) to dishonour, dishonor (*EEUU*), disgrace
2 (= *ser indigno de*) to be unworthy of
3 (= *despedir*) to dismiss, deprive of office *o* title *etc*

deshonra SF **1** (= *deshonor*) dishonour, dishonor (*EEUU*), disgrace • **no es ninguna ~ ser pobre** it is no dishonour *o* disgrace to be poor
2 (= *vergüenza*) shame • **lo tiene a ~** he thinks it beneath him • **tienen a ~ trabajar** they think it beneath them to work
3 (= *acto vergonzoso*) shameful act

deshonrabuenos SMF INV **1** (= *calumniador*) backbiter
2 (= *oveja negra*) black sheep (*of the family*)

deshonrar ▷ CONJUG 1a VT **1** [+ *familia, compañeros*] to dishonour, dishonor (*EEUU*), disgrace
2 (= *afrentar*) to insult
3 (*euf*) [+ *mujer*] to dishonour, dishonor (*EEUU*)

deshonrosamente ADV dishonourably

deshonroso ADJ dishonourable, dishonorable (*EEUU*), disgraceful

deshora SF • **a ~** at an inconvenient time • **acostarse a ~** to go to bed at some unearthly hour • **comer a ~** to eat at odd times • **llegar a ~** to turn up unexpectedly

deshuesadero SM (*Méx*) scrapyard

deshuesado ADJ [*carne*] boned; [*fruta*] stoned; [*aceituna*] pitted, stoned

deshuesar ▷ CONJUG 1a VT [+ *carne*] to bone; [+ *fruta*] to stone; [+ *aceituna*] to pit, stone

deshuevarse** ▷ CONJUG 1a VPR = **descojonarse**

deshumanización SF dehumanization

deshumanizador ADJ, **deshumanizante** ADJ dehumanizing

deshumanizar ▷ CONJUG 1f VT to dehumanize

deshumedecerse ▸ CONJUG 2d VPR to dry up, lose its moisture
desideologizado ADJ non-ideological, free of ideological considerations
desiderátum SM (PL: **desiderátums** *o* **desiderata**) (*frm*) desideratum (*frm*), thing ideally required *o* desired
desidia SF **1** (= *pereza*) idleness
2 (*en el vestir*) slovenliness
desidioso ADJ **1** (= *perezoso*) idle
2 (= *desaseado*) slovenly
desierto ADJ **1** [*isla, región*] desert (*antes de s*); [*paisaje*] bleak, desolate; [*calle, casa*] deserted • **la calle estaba desierta** the street was deserted
2 • **declarar ~** [+ *oposiciones, premio*] to declare void
SM desert • MODISMOS: • **arar en el ~** to plough *o* (*EEUU*) plow the sands • **clamar en el ~** to preach in the wilderness
designación SF **1** (*para un cargo*) appointment
2 (= *nombre*) designation
designar ▸ CONJUG 1a VT **1** (= *nombrar*) to appoint, designate • **el dictador designó a su sucesor** the dictator appointed *o* designated his successor • **la ~on para el puesto de supervisora** they appointed her (as) supervisor, she was appointed *o* designated (as) supervisor • **me han designado candidato** they have nominated me (as a candidate) • **han designado a Sevilla sede del campeonato** Seville has been designated as the host city for the championship
2 (= *fijar*) [+ *fecha*] to fix, set
3 (*frm*) (= *denominar*) • **la palabra "rosa" designa a una flor** the word "rose" denotes a flower • **~on el plan con el nombre de "Erasmus"** the plan was given the name of "Erasmus"
designio SM plan, design • **lo haré según sus ~s** I will act in accordance with his plans • **los ~s divinos** divine intentions
desigual ADJ **1** (= *diferente*) different • **dos hermanos muy ~es** two very different brothers • **las mangas de la chaqueta me han salido ~es** the sleeves of my jacket have come out different sizes • **los ciudadanos reciben un trato ~** people are treated differently, people are not treated equally *o* the same
2 [*lucha, batalla*] unequal
3 (= *irregular*) [*terreno, calidad*] uneven; [*letra*] erratic • **es una estudiante muy ~** she is a very erratic student • **los resultados del alumno son muy ~es** the pupil's marks vary widely *o* are not at all consistent
4 (= *variable*) [*tiempo*] changeable; [*carácter*] unpredictable
desigualar ▸ CONJUG 1a VT **1** (= *nivelar*) [+ *flequillo*] to make uneven; [+ *poderes, capacidades*] to unbalance
2 (*Dep*) to alter the balance of
desigualdad SF **1** (*Econ, Pol*) inequality
2 [*de carácter, tiempo*] unpredictability
3 (= *desnivel*) [*de terreno*] roughness; [*de escritura*] unevenness
desilusión SF **1** (= *decepción*) disappointment • **me llevé una gran ~ cuando lo vi** I was very disappointed when I saw him • **caer en la ~** to get disillusioned • **sufrir una ~** to suffer a disappointment
2 (= *pérdida de ilusiones*) disillusion, disillusionment
desilusionado ADJ disillusioned • **una visión desilusionada de la realidad** a disillusioned view of reality • **te veo muy ~ con la boda** you seem very disillusioned with *o* unexcited about the wedding
desilusionante ADJ disillusioning, disappointing
desilusionar ▸ CONJUG 1a VT
1 (= *decepcionar*) to disappoint
2 (= *hacer perder las ilusiones a*) to disillusion
VPR **desilusionarse 1** (= *decepcionarse*) to be disappointed
2 (= *desengañarse*) to get disillusioned
desimantar ▸ CONJUG 1a VT to demagnetize
desincentivar ▸ CONJUG 1a VT to act as a disincentive to, discourage
desincentivo SM disincentive
desincrustante ADJ • **agente ~** descaling agent • **producto ~** descaling product
desincrustar ▸ CONJUG 1a VT to descale, remove the fur from (EEUU)
desinencia SF (*Ling*) ending
desinfección SF, **desinfectado** SM disinfection
desinfectante ADJ, SM disinfectant
desinfectar ▸ CONJUG 1a VT to disinfect
desinfestar ▸ CONJUG 1a VT to decontaminate
desinflación SF disinflation
desinflacionista ADJ disinflationary
desinflado ADJ [*neumático*] flat
desinflar ▸ CONJUG 1a VT [+ *neumático*] to deflate, let the air out of
VPR **desinflarse** [*neumático*] to go down, go flat
desinformación SF **1** (= *información engañosa*) disinformation, misleading information, black propaganda
2 (= *ignorancia*) ignorance, lack of information
desinformado ADJ uninformed
desinformador(a) ADJ [*noticia*] false, calculated to deceive
SM/F spreader of disinformation
desinformar ▸ CONJUG 1a VT to misinform
desinformativo ADJ misleading, false
desinhibición SF lack of inhibition
desinhibido ADJ uninhibited
desinhibir ▸ CONJUG 3a VT to free from inhibitions
VPR **desinhibirse** to lose one's inhibitions
desinsectación SF protection against insect pests • **la ~ de un jardín** freeing a garden of insect pests
desinsectar ▸ CONJUG 1a VT to clear of insects
desinstalar ▸ CONJUG 1a VT (*Inform*) to uninstall
desintegrable ADJ fissile
desintegración SF **1** [*de estructura*] disintegration; [*de grupo*] break-up
2 [*de átomo*] splitting ▸ **desintegración nuclear** nuclear fission
desintegrar ▸ CONJUG 1a VT **1** [+ *grupo*] to break up
2 [+ *roca, cohete*] to disintegrate
3 [+ *átomo*] to split
VPR **desintegrarse 1** [*grupo*] to break up
2 [*roca, cohete*] to disintegrate
3 [*átomo*] to split
desinterés SM **1** (= *falta de interés*) lack of interest
2 (= *altruismo*) unselfishness
3 (= *imparcialidad*) disinterestedness
desinteresadamente ADV selflessly, unselfishly
desinteresado ADJ **1** (= *altruista*) unselfish
2 (= *imparcial*) disinterested
desinteresarse ▸ CONJUG 1a VPR **1** (= *perder interés*) to lose interest (**de, por** in)
2 (= *desentenderse*) • **~ de algo** to take no interest in sth
desintoxicación SF detoxification, disintoxication • **centro de ~** detoxification centre, detoxification center (EEUU)
desintoxicar ▸ CONJUG 1g VT **1** (*Med*) to detoxify
2 (*de drogas*) to cure of drug addiction
VPR **desintoxicarse** (*de las drogas*) to undergo detoxification, undergo treatment for drug addiction; (*del alcohol*) to dry out
desinversión SF disinvestment
desinvertir ▸ CONJUG 3i VI to disinvest
desistimiento SM **1** (= *acción*) desisting
2 (*Jur*) waiver
desistir ▸ CONJUG 3a VI **1** (= *abandonar*) to cease, desist (*frm*) • **no desistió en su empeño** she did not cease in *o* (*frm*) desist from her efforts • **~ de algo** to give up sth • **desistió de su intento de convencernos** he gave up trying to convince us • **~ de hacer algo** to desist from *o* give up doing sth
2 (*Jur*) • **~ de un derecho** to waive a right
desjarretar ▸ CONJUG 1a VT **1** [+ *animal*] to hamstring
2 (*Med*) to weaken, debilitate
desjuntar ▸ CONJUG 1a VT **1** (= *separar*) to separate, take apart
2 (= *dividir*) to divide
deslavado ADJ **1** (= *medio lavado*) half-washed
2 = **deslavazado**
deslavar ▸ CONJUG 1a VT **1** (= *lavar a medias*) to half-wash, wash superficially
2 (= *desteñir*) to fade
3 (= *debilitar*) to weaken
deslavazado ADJ **1** (= *incoherente*) disjointed
2 [*tela, vestido*] (= *lacio*) limp; (= *desteñido*) faded; (= *aburrido*) colourless, colorless (EEUU)
deslave SM (*Méx*) landslide, rockfall
desleal ADJ **1** (= *infiel*) disloyal (**a, con** to)
2 (*Com*) [*competencia*] unfair
deslealmente ADV **1** (= *sin lealtad*) disloyally
2 (= *injustamente*) unfairly
deslealtad SF **1** (= *falta de lealtad*) (*gen*) disloyalty
2 (*Com*) unfairness
deslegalizar ▸ CONJUG 1f VT to outlaw, criminalize
deslegitimar ▸ CONJUG 1a VT to discredit, undermine
desleído ADJ **1** (= *disuelto*) dissolved
2 [*idea*] weak, woolly, wooly (EEUU)
desleír ▸ CONJUG 3l VT (= *disolver*) [+ *sustancia, materia*] to dissolve; [+ *líquido*] to dilute
VPR **desleírse 1** (*en un líquido*) to dissolve
2 [*líquido*] to become diluted
deslenguado ADJ (= *malhablado*) foul-mouthed
deslenguarse ▸ CONJUG 1i VPR (= *hablar demasiado*) to shoot one's mouth off; (*groseramente*) to pour out obscenities
desliar ▸ CONJUG 1c VT (= *desatar*) [+ *nudo, lazo*] to untie, undo; [+ *paquete*] to open
VPR **desliarse** to come undone
desligado ADJ **1** (= *suelto*) loose, free
2 (= *separado*) separate, detached • **vive ~ de todo** he lives in a world of his own
desligamiento SM detachment (**de** from)
desligar ▸ CONJUG 1h VT **1** (= *desatar*) to untie, undo
2 (= *separar*) to detach • **~ el primer aspecto del segundo** to separate the first aspect from the second
3 (= *absolver*) to absolve, free (**de** from) • **~ a algn de una promesa** to release sb from a promise
4 (= *aclarar*) to unravel, disentangle
VPR **desligarse 1** [*nudo, lazo*] to come undone
2 [*persona*] to extricate o.s. (**de** from)

deslindable ADJ definable
deslindar ▸ CONJUG 1a VT **1** [+ *terreno*] to mark out, mark the limits *o* boundaries of
2 (= *definir*) to define
deslinde SM **1** (= *acto*) demarcation, fixing of limits *o* boundaries
2 (= *definición*) definition
desliz SM **1** (= *equivocación*) slip • **cometer un ~** to slip up • **los deslices de la juventud** the indiscretions of youth ▸ **desliz de lengua** slip of the tongue ▸ **desliz freudiano** Freudian slip
2 (*Aut*) skid
deslizadero SM **1** (= *tobogán*) slide
2 (= *sitio*) slippery spot
3 (*Téc*) chute, slide
deslizadizo ADJ slippery
deslizador SM **1** (= *patinete*) scooter
2 (*Náut*) small speedboat
3 (*Dep*) surfboard, aquaplane, water ski
4 [*de patín*] runner, skid
deslizamiento SM **1** (= *movimiento*) [*de cosas*] sliding; [*de persona*] slipping
▸ **deslizamiento de tierra** landslide
2 (*Aut*) skid
3 ▸ **deslizamiento salarial** (upward) drift of wages
deslizante ADJ sliding
deslizar ▸ CONJUG 1f VT **1** (*frm*) (= *pasar*) • **deslicé la carta por debajo de la puerta** I slipped *o* slid the letter under the door • **deslizó el dedo por el armario y encontró polvo** she ran her finger along the cupboard and found it was dusty
2 (*frm*) (= *dar con disimulo*) to slip
3 (*frm*) (= *intercalar*) to slip in
VPR **deslizarse 1** (= *resbalarse*) to slide • **el coche se deslizó unos metros** the car slid *o* slipped forward a few metres • **los niños se deslizaban por el pasamanos** the children were sliding down the banisters • **gotas de sudor se deslizaban por su frente** beads of sweat ran *o* slid down his forehead • **el esquiador se desliza por la pista** the skier slips *o* skis down the slope • **la patinadora se deslizaba elegantemente** the skater was gliding along
2 (= *avanzar*) [*serpiente*] to slither; [*barco*] to glide, slip • **la anguila se deslizó entre mis manos** the eel slipped through my fingers • **el tren se desliza a 300km/h** the train glides along at 300km/h • **el agua se desliza mansamente** the water flows along gently
3 (*frm*) [*secreto*] to slip out; [*error*] to slip in, creep in
deslomar ▸ CONJUG 1a VT (= *romper el lomo de*) (*lit*) to break the back of; (*fig*) to wear out • **~ a algn a garrotazos** to club sb to a pulp
VPR **deslomarse*** to work one's guts out
deslucido ADJ **1** (= *sin brillo*) [*metal*] tarnished; [*mármol*] worn, faded
2 (= *aburrido*) [*actor*] dull, lacklustre; [*toro*] unimpressive; [*actuación*] undistinguished • **hizo un papel ~** he gave a lacklustre performance • **la fiesta resultó deslucida** the party was a flop • **el jugador estuvo muy ~** the player was far from his best • **quedar ~** to make a poor impression
3 (= *desgarbado*) graceless, inelegant
deslucimiento SM **1** [*de muebles, vestidos*] shabbiness
2 (= *falta de brillantez*) dullness
3 (= *falta de gracia*) gracelessness
4 (= *fracaso*) discrediting
deslucir ▸ CONJUG 3f VT **1** [+ *mármol*] to fade; [+ *metal*] to tarnish
2 (= *estropear*) to spoil, ruin • **la lluvia deslució el acto** the rain ruined the ceremony
3 [+ *persona*] to discredit
VPR **deslucirse** (= *fracasar*) to be discredited

deslumbrador ADJ, **deslumbrante** ADJ dazzling
deslumbramiento SM **1** (= *brillo*) glare, dazzle
2 (= *confusión*) confusion
deslumbrar ▸ CONJUG 1a VT **1** (*con la luz*) to dazzle
2 (= *impresionar*) to dazzle • **deslumbró a todos con su oratoria** he dazzled everyone with his oratory
deslustrado ADJ **1** (= *sin brillo*) [*vidrio*] frosted, ground; [*loza*] unglazed
2 [*actuación, papel*] dull, lacklustre, lackluster (*EEUU*)
3 [*reputación*] tarnished
deslustrar ▸ CONJUG 1a VT **1** (= *quitar lustre a*) [+ *vidrio*] to frost; [+ *loza*] to remove the glaze from
2 [+ *reputación*] to sully, tarnish
deslustre SM **1** (= *acto*) [*de vidrio*] frosting; [*de loza, paño*] removal of glaze; [*de muebles, adornos*] tarnishing
2 (*en reputación*) stigma, stain
deslustroso ADJ **1** (= *inadecuado*) unbecoming, unsuitable
2 (= *vergonzoso*) disgraceful
desmadejado ADJ (= *debilitado*) weak • **~ en un sofá delante de la televisión** slumped on a sofa in front of the TV
desmadejamiento SM enervation, weakness
desmadejar ▸ CONJUG 1a VT to enervate, weaken
VPR **desmadejarse** to weaken
desmadrado ADJ **1*** (= *desenfrenado*) • **está muy ~ últimamente** he's been pretty wild recently*
2 (= *desinhibido*) uninhibited
3 (= *confuso*) confused
desmadrarse* ▸ CONJUG 1a VPR
1 (= *descontrolarse*) to get out of control, go wild • **~ por algn** to fall madly in love with sb
2 (= *divertirse*) to let one's hair down*
3 (= *excederse*) to go over the top • **los gastos se han desmadrado** costs have gone right over the top
desmadre* SM **1** (= *exceso*) excess • **¡es el ~!** this is just too much! • **esto va de ~ total** this is really getting out of hand
2 (= *confusión*) chaos
3 (= *juerga*) rave-up*, hot party (*EEUU*)
desmalezar ▸ CONJUG 1f VT (*LAm*) to weed
desmallar ▸ CONJUG 1a VT [+ *puntos*] to pull out; [+ *media*] to make a ladder in, make a run in
VPR **desmallarse** [*media*] to ladder, run (*EEUU*)
desmamar ▸ CONJUG 1a VT to wean
desmán[1] SM **1** (= *exceso*) excess
2 (= *ultraje*) outrage • **cometer un ~** to commit an outrage (**contra** on)
desmán[2] SM (*Zool*) muskrat
desmanchar ▸ CONJUG 1a VT (*LAm*) to clean, remove the spots *o* stains from
VPR **desmancharse** (*And, CAm**) **1** (= *salir de prisa*) to bolt out
2 (= *retirarse*) to withdraw
3 (*Agr*) to stray from the herd
desmandado ADJ **1** (= *desobediente*) unruly
2 [*caballo*] runaway
desmandarse ▸ CONJUG 1a VPR
1 (= *descontrolarse*) to get out of hand
2 [*caballo*] to bolt, run away
desmano • **a ~** ADV out of the way • **me pilla a ~** it's not on my way
desmanotado ADJ clumsy, awkward
desmantelación SF dismantling
desmantelamiento SM **1** (= *desmontaje*) [*de base, fábrica*] dismantling; [*de barcos*] unrigging
2 [*de organización*] disbanding
desmantelar ▸ CONJUG 1a VT **1** (= *desmontar*) [+ *base, fábrica*] to dismantle; [+ *máquina*] to strip down; [+ *andamio*] to take down; [+ *casa*] to strip of its contents
2 [+ *organización*] to disband; [+ *pandilla*] to break up
3 (*Náut*) to unrig
VPR **desmantelarse** [*casa*] to fall into disrepair
desmaña SF (= *torpeza*) (*al actuar*) clumsiness, awkwardness; (*al pensar, reaccionar*) slowness, helplessness
desmañado ADJ **1** (= *torpe*) clumsy
2 (= *lento*) slow
desmaquillador SM, **desmaquillante** SM make-up remover
desmaquillarse ▸ CONJUG 1a VPR to remove one's make-up
desmarcado ADJ (*Dep*) unmarked
desmarcar ▸ CONJUG 1g VT to disassociate (**de** from)
VPR **desmarcarse 1** (*Dep*) to shake off one's attacker, get clear
2 (= *distanciarse*) to distance oneself (**de** from)
desmasificar ▸ CONJUG 1g VT [+ *cárceles, hospitales*] to reduce overcrowding in • **~ la universidad** to reduce student numbers
desmayado ADJ **1** (*Med*) unconscious
2 [*carácter*] dull, lacklustre, lackluster (*EEUU*)
3 [*color*] pale
desmayar ▸ CONJUG 1a VI [*persona*] to lose heart; [*esfuerzo*] to falter, flag
VPR **desmayarse 1** (*Med*) to faint
2 [*planta*] to droop low, trail
desmayo SM **1** (*Med*) (= *acto*) faint, fainting fit; (= *estado*) unconsciousness • **le dio un ~** he fainted • **sufrir un ~** to have a fainting fit, faint
2 (= *languidez*) [*de voz*] faltering; [*del cuerpo*] languidness, limpness • **hablar con ~** to talk in a small voice, speak falteringly • **las ramas caen con ~** the branches are drooping low, the branches are trailing
3 (= *depresión*) dejection, depression
desmedido ADJ **1** [*tamaño, importancia*] (= *excesivo*) excessive; (= *desproporcionado*) out of all proportion
2 [*ambición*] boundless
desmedirse ▸ CONJUG 3k VPR to go too far
desmedrado ADJ **1** (= *estropeado*) impaired
2 (= *reducido*) reduced
3 (*Med*) puny, feeble
desmedrar ▸ CONJUG 1a VT **1** (= *perjudicar*) to impair
2 (= *estropear*) to spoil, ruin, affect badly
3 (= *reducir*) to reduce
VI, VPR **desmedrarse 1** (= *decaer*) [*producción, interés*] to fall off, decline; [*conversación, país*] to go downhill
2 (= *deteriorarse*) to deteriorate
3 (*Med*) [*enfermo*] to get weak; [*niño*] to be sickly, waste away
4 (*Bot*) to grow poorly, do badly
desmedro SM **1** (= *perjuicio*) impairment
2 (= *reducción*) reduction
3 (= *decaimiento*) decline, deterioration
4 (*Med*) weakness, emaciation, thinness
desmejora SF deterioration
desmejorado ADJ • **ha quedado muy desmejorada** she's lost her looks • **está muy desmejorada** (*Med*) she's not looking at all well
desmejoramiento SM deterioration
desmejorar ▸ CONJUG 1a VT **1** (= *dañar*) to spoil
2 (*Med*) to weaken

VPR **desmejorarse 1** [*situación*] to deteriorate
2 [*persona*] (= *tener peor aspecto*) to lose one's looks; (*Med*) to get worse

desmelenado/a ADJ dishevelled, disheveled (EEUU)
SM/F long-haired lout

desmelenar ▹ CONJUG 1a VT [+ *peinado*] to dishevel
VPR **desmelenarse*** **1** (= *asearse*) to spruce o.s. up, pull one's socks up
2 (= *esforzarse*) to bend over backwards
3* (= *ir de juerga*) to let one's hair down*

desmelene* SM excess • **¡es el ~!** it's sheer chaos!, it's way over the top!*

desmembración SF, **desmembramiento** SM **1** [*de cadáver, país*] dismemberment
2 [*de partido*] break-up

desmembrar ▹ CONJUG 1j VT **1** [+ *cadáver, país*] to dismember
2 [+ *partido*] to break up
VPR **desmembrarse 1** [*país*] to break up
2 [*partido*] to fall apart

desmemoria SF poor memory, forgetfulness

desmemoriado ADJ forgetful, absent-minded

desmemoriarse ▹ CONJUG 1b VPR to grow forgetful, become absent-minded

desmentida SF denial • **dar una ~ a algo** to deny sth

desmentido SM = **desmentida**

desmentimiento SM denial

desmentir ▹ CONJUG 3i VT **1** (= *negar*) [+ *acusación*] to deny, refute; [+ *rumor*] to scotch, squelch (EEUU); [+ *teoría*] to refute; [+ *carácter, orígenes*] to belie • **~ rotundamente una acusación** to deny a charge flatly
2 (= *llevar la contraria*) [+ *persona*] to contradict
VI to be out of line • **~ de algo** to belie sth
VPR **desmentirse 1** (= *contradecirse*) to contradict o.s.
2 (= *desdecirse*) to go back on one's word

desmenuzable ADJ crumbly

desmenuzar ▹ CONJUG 1f VT **1** (*Culin*) [+ *pan*] to crumble; [+ *pescado, pollo*] to flake
2 (= *examinar*) to examine minutely
VPR **desmenuzarse** to crumble

desmerecedor(a) ADJ undeserving
SM/F undeserving person

desmerecer ▹ CONJUG 2d VT to be unworthy of
VI **1** (= *deteriorarse*) to deteriorate
2 (= *perder valor*) to lose value
3 • **~ de algo** to compare unfavourably *o* (EEUU) unfavorably with sth • **esta no desmerece de sus otras películas** this is every bit as good as his earlier films

desmesura SF **1** (= *desproporción*) disproportion
2 (= *exceso*) excess, enormity
3 (= *falta de moderación*) lack of moderation

desmesuradamente ADV disproportionately, excessively • **abrir ~ la boca** to open one's mouth extra wide

desmesurado ADJ **1** (= *desproporcionado*) disproportionate
2 (= *enorme*) [*ambición*] boundless; [*dimensiones*] enormous
3 (= *descarado*) insolent

desmesurarse ▹ CONJUG 1a VPR to become insolent, forget o.s., lose all restraint

desmigajar ▹ CONJUG 1a VT to crumble
VPR **desmigajarse** to crumble

desmigar ▹ CONJUG 1h VT = **desmigajar**

desmilitarización SF demilitarization

desmilitarizado ADJ demilitarized

desmilitarizar ▹ CONJUG 1f VT to demilitarize

desmineralizado ADJ **1** [*actuación*] lifeless, lacklustre, lackluster (EEUU)
2 [*persona*] run down

desmineralizar ▹ CONJUG 1f VT to demineralize

desmirriado ADJ weedy

desmitificación SF demythologizing

desmitificador ADJ demythologizing

desmitificar ▹ CONJUG 1g VT to demythologize

desmochar ▹ CONJUG 1a VT **1** (= *cortar la parte superior de*) [+ *árbol*] to pollard, cut the top off; [+ *cuernos*] to blunt, file down
2 [+ *texto*] to cut

desmoche SM **1** [*de árbol*] pollarding
2 • **hubo un ~ en el primer examen** there was a ruthless weeding out of candidates in the first exam

desmocho SM lopped branches, cuttings

desmodular ▹ CONJUG 1a VT (*Radio*) [+ *mensaje*] to scramble

desmolado ADJ toothless

desmoldar ▹ CONJUG 1a VT (*Culin*) to remove from its mould

desmonetizar ▹ CONJUG 1f VT **1** (*Econ*) to demonetize
2 (*Cono Sur*) (= *desvalorizar*) to devalue, devaluate (EEUU)

desmontable ADJ **1** (= *desarmable*) [*mueble, estantería*] which can be taken apart; [*pieza*] detachable
2 (= *plegable*) collapsible
SM tyre lever, tire lever (EEUU)

desmontaje SM dismantling, stripping down

desmontar ▹ CONJUG 1a VT **1** (= *desarmar*) (*gen*) to dismantle; [+ *mueble, estantería*] to take apart; [+ *motor*] to strip down; [+ *máquina*] to take apart, take to pieces; [+ *tienda de campaña*] to take down; (*Náut*) [+ *vela*] to take down
2 [+ *terreno*] (= *nivelar*) to level; (= *quitar los árboles a*) to clear
3 [+ *jinete*] to throw, unseat • **~ a algn de un vehículo** to help sb down from a vehicle
4 (*Mil*) [+ *escopeta*] to uncock; [+ *artillería*] to knock out
VI to dismount, alight (**de** from)
VPR **desmontarse** [*mueble, estantería, juguete*] to come apart

desmonte SM **1** (= *acto*) (*al allanar*) levelling, leveling (EEUU); (*al quitar los árboles*) clearing • **los trabajos exigirán el ~ de 200 metros cúbicos** the work will necessitate the removal of 200 cubic metres
2 (= *terreno*) levelled ground, leveled ground (EEUU)
3 (*Ferro*) cutting, cut (EEUU)
4 (= *madera*) felled timber

desmoralización SF demoralization

desmoralizado ADJ demoralized

desmoralizador ADJ demoralizing

desmoralizante ADJ demoralizing

desmoralizar ▹ CONJUG 1f VT **1** [+ *ejército, persona*] to demoralize
2 [+ *costumbres*] to corrupt
VPR **desmoralizarse** to lose heart, get demoralized

desmoronadizo ADJ **1** (= *que se desmigaja*) crumbling
2 (= *destartalado, maltrecho*) rickety

desmoronado ADJ [*casa, edificio*] tumbledown

desmoronamiento SM crumbling, collapse

desmoronar ▹ CONJUG 1a VT **1** (= *desgastar*) to wear away
2 (= *erosionar*) to erode • **la erosión ha desmoronado los muros** erosion has caused the walls to crumble
VPR **desmoronarse 1** (= *derrumbarse*) [*montaña, casa*] to crumble; [*ladrillos*] to fall, come down
2 (= *decaer*) to decay • **tras la muerte de su marido se desmoronó** after her husband's death she went to pieces

desmotivación SF lack of motivation

desmotivado ADJ unmotivated, lacking motivation

desmotivar ▹ CONJUG 1a VT to discourage

desmovilización SF demobilization

desmovilizado ADJ demobilized, demobbed (*Brit**)

desmovilizar ▹ CONJUG 1f VT to demobilize

desmultiplicar ▹ CONJUG 1g VT (*Mec*) to gear down

desnacionalización SF denationalization

desnacionalizado ADJ **1** [*industria*] denationalized
2 [*persona*] stateless

desnacionalizar ▹ CONJUG 1f VT to denationalize

desnarigada SF (*hum*) • **la ~** the skull

desnarigado ADJ flat-nosed

desnatado ADJ [*leche*] skimmed

desnatar ▹ CONJUG 1a VT **1** [+ *leche*] to skim • **leche sin ~** whole milk
2 (*Metal*) to remove the scum from

desnaturalizado ADJ **1** (*Quím*) denatured • **alcohol ~** methylated spirits (*sing*)
2 [*persona*] unnatural

desnaturalizar ▹ CONJUG 1f VT **1** (*Quím*) to denature
2 (= *corromper*) [+ *persona*] to pervert; [+ *significado, sucesos*] to distort
VPR **desnaturalizarse** (= *perder la nacionalidad*) to give up one's nationality

desnivel SM **1** [*de terreno*] (= *desigualdad*) drop; (= *tierra alta*) high ground; (= *tierra baja*) low ground
2 (= *diferencia*) difference (**entre** between)
3 (*Pol, Sociol*) inequality

desnivelado ADJ **1** [*terreno*] uneven
2 (= *desequilibrado*) unbalanced

desnivelar ▹ CONJUG 1a VT **1** [+ *terreno*] to make uneven
2 (= *desequilibrar*) [+ *calidad*] to make uneven; [+ *composición*] to upset, unbalance; [+ *balanza*] to tip

desnucar ▹ CONJUG 1g VT to break the neck of
VPR **desnucarse** to break one's neck

desnuclearización SF nuclear disarmament, denuclearization

desnuclearizado ADJ • **región desnuclearizada** nuclear-free area

desnuclearizar ▹ CONJUG 1f VT to denuclearize

desnudar ▹ CONJUG 1a VT **1** [+ *persona*] to undress • **él la desnudaba con la mirada** he was undressing her with his eyes
2 (*liter*) [+ *espada*] to unsheathe (*liter*)
3 (*Geol*) to denude
4* [+ *jugador*] to fleece*
VPR **desnudarse 1** [*persona*] to undress, get undressed • **~se de cintura para arriba** to strip to the waist
2 • **~se de algo** to get rid of sth • **el árbol se está desnudando de sus hojas** the tree is shedding *o* losing its leaves

desnudez SF **1** [*de persona*] nakedness, nudity
2 [*de paisaje*] bareness

desnudismo SM nudism

desnudista SMF nudist

desnudo ADJ **1** (= *sin ropa*) [*persona*] naked; [*cuerpo*] naked, bare • **cavar con las manos desnudas** to dig with one's bare hands • **iba andando con los pies ~s** she was walking along barefoot

2 (= *sin adorno*) [*árbol*] bare; [*paisaje*] bare, featureless • **en las paredes desnudas** on the bare walls
3 (= *arruinado*) ruined, bankrupt • **quedarse ~** to be ruined, be bankrupt • **~ de ideas** devoid of ideas
4 (= *puro*) [*verdad*] plain, naked; [*estilo*] unadorned
SM 1 (*Arte*) nude • **la retrató al ~** he painted her in the nude • **llevaba los hombros al ~** her shoulders were bare ▸ **desnudo integral** full-frontal nudity
2 • **poner al ~** to lay bare
desnutrición SF malnutrition, undernourishment
desnutrido ADJ undernourished
desobedecer ▹ CONJUG 2d VT, VI to disobey
desobediencia SF disobedience
▸ **desobediencia civil** civil disobedience
desobediente ADJ disobedient
desobstruir ▹ CONJUG 3g VT to unblock, unstop, clear
desocupación SF 1 (*esp LAm*) (= *desempleo*) unemployment
2 (= *ocio*) leisure
3 [*de piso, fábrica*] clearance, clearing
desocupado ADJ 1 (= *libre*) [*asiento*] empty; [*casa, piso*] unoccupied; [*mesa en restaurante*] free
2 [*tiempo*] spare, free
3 [*persona*] (= *libre*) free, not busy; (= *sin empleo*) unemployed
desocupar ▹ CONJUG 1a VT 1 (= *vaciar*) [+ *casa, piso*] to vacate, move out of; [+ *recipiente*] to empty
2 (= *desalojar*) [+ *fábrica, sala*] to clear, clear out
3 [+ *contenido*] to remove, take out
VI* (= *defecar*) to go to the toilet
VPR **desocuparse** 1 (= *quedar libre*) to be free • **cuando me desocupe, te llamo** I'll call you when I'm free • **se ha desocupado aquella mesa** that table's free now
2 • **~se de un puesto** to give up a job
3 (*Caribe, Cono Sur*) (= *dar a luz*) to give birth
desodorante SM deodorant
▸ **desodorante de ambientes** (*Arg, Uru*) air freshener
desodorizar ▹ CONJUG 1f VT to deodorize
desoír ▹ CONJUG 3p VT to ignore, disregard
desojarse ▹ CONJUG 1a VPR to strain one's eyes
desolación SF desolation
desolado ADJ 1 [*lugar*] desolate
2 [*persona*] devastated • **estoy ~ por aquello** I'm devastated about that
desolador ADJ 1 (= *entristecedor*) [*imagen*] heartbreaking, heartrending; [*noticia*] devastating, distressing; [*paisaje*] bleak, cheerless
2 [*epidemia*] devastating
desolar ▹ CONJUG 1a VT 1 [+ *ciudad, poblado*] to devastate, lay waste (to) (*liter*)
2 [+ *persona*] to devastate
VPR **desolarse** to be devastated
desolidarizarse ▹ CONJUG 1f VPR • **~ de algn/algo** to dissociate o.s. from sb/sth
desolladero SM slaughterhouse
desollado* ADJ brazen, barefaced
desollador(a) SM/F 1 [*de animal*] skinner
2 (= *extorsionista*) extortioner, robber
SM (*Orn*) shrike
desolladura SF 1 (= *herida*) graze, abrasion (*frm*)
2 (= *acto*) (*de despellejar*) skinning, flaying; (*de extorsionar*) extortion, piece of robbery
desollar ▹ CONJUG 1l VT 1 (= *quitar la piel a*) to skin, flay
2 • **~ vivo a algn** (= *hacer pagar*) to fleece sb; (= *criticar*) to tear sb to pieces
VPR **desollarse** • **me he desollado la rodilla** I've grazed my knee
desopinar ▹ CONJUG 1a VT to denigrate
desorbitado ADJ 1 (= *excesivo*) [*precio*] exorbitant; [*pretensión*] exaggerated
2 • **con los ojos ~s** popeyed
desorbitante ADJ excessive, overwhelming
desorbitar ▹ CONJUG 1a VT 1 (= *exagerar*) to exaggerate
2 (= *interpretar mal*) to get out of perspective
VPR **desorbitarse** 1 [*persona*] to lose one's sense of proportion
2 [*asunto*] to get out of hand
desorden SM 1 (= *falta de orden*) [*de objetos, ideas*] chaos; [*de casa, habitación*] mess, untidiness • **no puedo encontrar nada entre tanto ~** I can't find anything amid all this chaos • **en ~** [*gente*] in confusion; [*objetos*] in a mess, in disorder (*más frm*) • **la casa estaba en un ~ total** the house was in a complete mess • **poner las cosas en ~** to upset things
2 (= *confusión*) confusion
3 **desórdenes** (= *alborotos*) disturbances; (= *excesos*) excesses; (*Med*) disorders • **~es en las comidas** eating disorders
desordenadamente ADV 1 [*colocarse*] untidily
2 [*entrar*] in a disorderly fashion
3 [*escribir*] unmethodically
desordenado ADJ 1 (= *sin orden*) [*habitación, persona*] untidy, messy; [*objetos*] in a mess, jumbled
2 (= *asocial*) [*vida*] chaotic; [*conducta*] disorderly; [*carácter*] unmethodical; [*niño*] wild, unruly
3 [*país*] chaotic
desordenar ▹ CONJUG 1a VT 1 (= *poner en desorden*) [+ *cajón, armario*] to mess up; [+ *pelo*] to mess up, muss (up) (*EEUU**); [+ *habitación*] to make untidy, mess up; [+ *papeles*] to jumble up
2 (= *causar confusión a*) to throw into confusion
3 (*Mec*) to put out of order
VPR **desordenarse** [*casa*] to get untidy, get into a mess; [*papeles*] to get jumbled up
desorejado ADJ 1 (= *disoluto*) dissolute
2 (*And, Caribe, Cono Sur*) (= *sin mangos*) without handles
3 (*And*) (= *duro de oído*) hard of hearing; (*Mús*) tone deaf • MODISMO: • **hacerse el ~*** to turn a deaf ear
4 (*Caribe*) (= *pródigo*) lavish
5 (*CAm*) (= *tonto*) silly
desorganización SF disorganization
desorganizado ADJ disorganized
desorganizar ▹ CONJUG 1f VT to disorganize
desorientado ADJ disorientated, disoriented (*esp EEUU*); (= *sin saber qué hacer*) confused • **estoy algo ~** (= *perdido*) I've lost my bearings
desorientamiento SM, **desorientación** SF disorientation
desorientar ▹ CONJUG 1a VT 1 (= *extraviar*) • **~ a algn** to disorientate sb, disorient sb (*esp EEUU*) • **me desorientó el nuevo edificio de la esquina** the new building on the corner made me lose my bearings *o* disorientated me
2 (= *despistar*) to lead astray
3 (= *confundir*) to confuse
VPR **desorientarse** 1 (= *extraviarse*) to lose one's way, lose one's bearings
2 (= *confundirse*) to get confused
desovar ▹ CONJUG 1l VI [*pez, anfibio*] to spawn; [*insecto*] to lay eggs
desove SM [*de pez, anfibio*] spawning; [*de insecto*] egg-laying
desovillar ▹ CONJUG 1a VT 1 [+ *lana*] to unravel, unwind
2 [+ *misterio*] to unravel, clarify
desoxidar ▹ CONJUG 1a VT to deoxidize, de-rust
despabiladeras SFPL snuffers • **unas ~** a pair of snuffers
despabilado ADJ 1 (= *despierto*) wide awake
2 (= *despejado*) sharp, quick
despabilar* ▹ CONJUG 1a VT 1 (= *despertar*) to wake up • **despabila a los niños, que es tarde** wake the children up *o* wake up the children, it's late • **el café me ha despabilado** the coffee's woken me up
2 (= *avivar el ingenio de*) to buck up • **a ver si la despabilas un poco** maybe you can buck her up a bit*, maybe you can buck her ideas up a bit*
3 [+ *vela*] to snuff (out)
VI 1 (= *despertar*) to wake up • **despabila, que son las ocho** wake up, it's eight o'clock
2 (= *estar alerta*) to wake up, buck up* • **despabila o te engañarán siempre** wake up *o* buck up*, or you'll always end up being taken for a ride • **—ésta es mi última oportunidad —¡pues despabila!** "this is my last chance" — "better buck up then!* *o* better get your act together then!"*
3 (= *apresurarse*) to hurry up, get a move on* • **despabila si no quieres llegar tarde** better hurry up *o* get a move on* or you'll be late
4 (*And*) (= *pestañear*) to blink
VPR **despabilarse** 1 (= *despertarse*) to wake up • **despabílate que son ya las diez** wake up, it's ten o'clock already • **yo me despabilo con un café** one cup of coffee and I'm awake
2 (= *estar alerta*) to wake up, buck up* • **despabílate si no quieres que te tomen por tonto** you'd better wake up *o* buck up* if you don't want people to take you for a fool
3 (= *apresurarse*) to hurry up, get a move on*
4 (*CAm, Caribe, Cono Sur*) (= *marcharse*) to vanish; (= *escaparse*) to slip away, slope off*
despachaderas SFPL 1 (= *respuesta*) surly retort (*sing*), unfriendly answer (*sing*)
2 (= *inteligencia*) resourcefulness (*sing*), quickness of mind (*sing*)
3 (= *sentido práctico*) business sense (*sing*), practical know-how (*sing*) • **tener buenas ~** to be practical, be on the ball
4 (= *descaro*) brazenness (*sing*), insolence (*sing*)
despachado ADJ 1 (*Com*) • **un kilo de patatas bien ~** a good kilo of potatoes • MODISMO: • **ir ~** (*Esp**): • **coge un pedazo y vas ~** take a piece and that's your lot* • **si se cree que me va a engañar, va ~** if he thinks he can fool me, he's got another think coming* *o* he'd better think again
2 (*Esp*) (= *descarado*) brazen, insolent
3 (*Esp*) (= *ingenioso*) resourceful
despachador(a) ADJ prompt, quick
SM/F 1 (= *empleado*) quick worker
2 ▸ **despachador(a) de equipaje** baggage handler
despachante SMF (*Cono Sur*) 1 [*de oficina*] clerk
2 (*tb* **despachante de aduanas**) customs agent
despachar ▹ CONJUG 1a VT 1 (= *atender*) [+ *problema, asunto*] to deal with; [+ *correspondencia*] to deal with, see to • **el consejo despachó todos los temas pendientes** the council dealt with all the outstanding issues • **quisiera dejar despachado este asunto hoy** I would like to get this matter settled *o* out of the way today
2 (= *terminar*) **a** (*Com*) [+ *informe, negocio*] to finish

b* [+ libro, tarea] to knock off*; [+ comida] to dispose of*; [+ bebida] to knock back* • **ya llevo medio capítulo despachado** I've already knocked off half a chapter* • **despachamos el helado entre nosotros** between us we disposed of the ice cream*
3 (= vender) [+ fruta, entrada] to sell
4 (= servir) to serve • **¿le están despachando, señora?** are you being served, madam? • **en seguida le despacho** I'll be with you right away
5 (= enviar) [+ paquete, carta] to send, mail (EEUU); [+ mensajero] to send; [+ mercancías] to ship, dispatch (**a** to)
6 • **~ a algn*** (de un lugar) to send sb packing*; (de un trabajo) to sack sb*, fire sb*; (= matar) to get rid of sb, dispatch sb • **lo despaché de una patada** I kicked him out
VI **1** (Com) [dependiente] to serve; [establecimiento] to be open (for business) • **a partir de las cinco no despachan** they are not open (for business) after five
2 (Esp) (en reunión) • **~ con** (gen) to have a meeting with; [+ asesor, abogado] to consult (with) • **~ sobre algo** to discuss sth
3 (Esp*) (= darse prisa) to hurry up • **¡venga, despacha, que es tarde!** hurry up o come on, we're late!
VPR **despacharse 1** (= servirse) to serve o.s. • **usted mismo puede ~se** you can serve yourself • MODISMO: • **~se con el cucharón*** (sirviendo comida) to help o.s. to the biggest o best portion; (fig) to look after number one
2 (Esp*) (= criticar) • **~se bien o a gusto con algn** (delante de algn) to give sb a piece of one's mind; (a espaldas de algn) to really lay into sb* • **se despachó bien con ella por llegar tarde** he gave her a piece of his mind for being late* • **se han despachado a gusto con el nuevo gobierno** they really laid into the new government* • **se despachó a gusto en su crítica a la película** he didn't pull his punches in his review of the film, he really laid into the film*
3* (= terminar) [+ libro, tarea] to knock off; [+ comida] to dispose of*; [+ bebida] to knock back* • **me despaché la conferencia en media hora** I knocked off my talk in half an hour* • **en un momento se ~on dos botellas de vino** they put away o knocked back two bottles of wine in no time*
4 • **~se de algo** to get rid of sth
despachero/a SM/F (Chile) shopkeeper, storekeeper (EEUU)
despacho SM **1** (= oficina) **a** [de abogado, arquitecto] office; (en una casa) study • **una mesa de ~** an office desk • **el Despacho Oval** the Oval Office
b (= muebles) office furniture
2 (= tienda) shop; (Chile) grocer's shop
▸ **despacho de billetes, despacho de boletos** (LAm) booking office ▸ **despacho de localidades** box office ▸ **despacho de lotería** lottery ticket shop ▸ **despacho de pan** bread shop, bakery ▸ **despacho de telégrafos** telegraph office
3 (= mensaje) (Periodismo) report; (Mil) dispatch; (Pol) communiqué ▸ **despacho de oficial** (Mil) commission ▸ **despacho telegráfico** telegram, wire (EEUU)
4 (= venta) sale • **los domingos no hay ~ de billetes** there are no ticket sales on Sundays • **géneros sin ~** unsaleable goods • **tener buen ~** to find a ready sale, be in good demand
5 (= envío) dispatch, sending (out)
▸ **despacho aduanal, despacho de aduanas** customs clearance
6 (Pol) meeting, consultation
7 (= cualidad) • **tener buen ~** to be very efficient, be on top of one's job
despachurrar ▸ CONJUG 1a VT **1** [+ fruta, pastel] to crush, squash
2 [+ cuento] to mangle
3 [+ persona] to flatten
VPR **despachurrarse** [fruta, pastel] to get squashed, get crushed
despacio ADV **1** (= lentamente) slowly • **conduce muy ~** he drives very slowly • **¿puede hablar más ~?** can you speak more slowly?; ▸ **cosa**
2 (= silenciosamente) • **salí ~ para no molestar a nadie** I left quietly so as not to disturb anybody • **habla ~ que están durmiendo** speak quietly, they're asleep, keep your voice down, they're asleep
3 (= suavemente) gently • **llamó ~ a la puerta** he knocked gently at the door
despaciosamente ADV (LAm) slowly
despacioso ADJ slow, deliberate
despacito* ADV **1** (= lentamente) slowly • **¡despacito!** slowly does it! • MODISMO: • **~ y buena letra** easy does it
2 (= suavemente) softly
despampanante* ADJ [chica] stunning
despampanar ▸ CONJUG 1a VT **1** [+ vid] to prune, trim
2* (= asombrar) to shatter, stun, bowl over
VI* (= desconcertarse) to blow one's top*; (= desahogarse) to give vent to one's feelings
VPR **despampanarse*** to give o.s. a nasty knock
despancar ▸ CONJUG 1g VT (And) [+ maíz] to husk
despanzurrar ▸ CONJUG 1a VT to crush, squash
VPR **despanzurrarse 1** (= despachurrar) to get squashed, get crushed (**contra** against)
2 (= reventar) to burst
desparasitar ▸ CONJUG 1a VT **1** (de larvas) to worm; (de piojos) to delouse
2 [+ lugar] to disinfest
desparejado ADJ, **desparejo** ADJ odd • **están ~s** they're odd, they don't match
desparpajar ▸ CONJUG 1a (CAm, Méx) VT (= desparramar) to scatter
VI, VPR **desparpajarse** (= despertarse) to wake up
desparpajo SM **1** (= desenvoltura) self-confidence
2 (= descaro) (pey) nerve*, cheek*
3 (= inteligencia) savoir-faire
4 (CAm) (= confusión) muddle
5 (And) (= comentario) flippant remark
desparramado ADJ [hojas, lentejas] scattered • **la leche estaba desparramada por la mesa** the milk was spilled all over the table
desparramar ▸ CONJUG 1a VT **1** (= esparcir) [+ hojas, lentejas] to scatter (**por** over); [+ líquido] to spill
2 (= desperdiciar) [+ fortuna] to squander; [+ atención] to spread too widely
VPR **desparramarse 1** (= esparcirse) [hojas, lentejas] to scatter; [líquido] to spill, be spilt
2* (= pasarlo bomba) to have a whale of a time*
desparrame* SM confusion, disorder
desparramo SM **1** (Caribe, Cono Sur) (= esparcimiento) [de objetos] scattering, spreading; [de líquido] spilling
2 (Caribe, Cono Sur) (= fuga) rush, stampede
3 (Cono Sur) (= desorden) confusion, disorder
despatarrado ADJ • **cayó al suelo ~** he fell over on the ground and was left sprawling • **no te sientes tan despatarrada** don't sit with your legs wide apart like that
despatarrante* ADJ side-splitting
despatarrar ▸ CONJUG 1a VT **1** (= aturdir) to amaze, dumbfound
2 (= asustar) to scare to death
VPR **despatarrarse 1** (= abrir las piernas) to open one's legs wide; (en el suelo, al caer) to do the splits
2* • **~se de risa** to split one's sides laughing
despatriar ▸ CONJUG 1b VT (And, Caribe) to exile
despavorido ADJ terrified
despeado ADJ footsore, weary
despearse ▸ CONJUG 1a VPR to get footsore, get utterly weary
despechado ADJ spiteful
despechar ▸ CONJUG 1a VT **1** (= provocar) to anger, enrage
2 (= causar pena a) to spite
3 (= hacer desesperar) to drive to despair
4* [+ niño] to wean
VPR **despecharse** to get angry
despecho SM **1** (= ojeriza) spite • **por ~** out of sheer spite
2 • **a ~ de algo** in spite of sth, despite sth
3 [de niño] weaning
despechugado* ADJ [hombre] bare-chested; [mujer] bare-breasted
despechugarse* ▸ CONJUG 1h VPR [hombre] to bare one's chest; [mujer] to bare one's breasts
despectivamente ADV **1** (= con desprecio) contemptuously, scornfully
2 (Ling) pejoratively
despectivo ADJ **1** (= despreciativo) contemptuous, scornful • **hablar de algn en términos ~s** to speak disparagingly of sb
2 (Ling) pejorative
despedazar ▸ CONJUG 1f VT **1** (= hacer pedazos) [+ objeto] (con la mano) to tear apart, tear to pieces; (con cuchillo) to cut into pieces; [+ presa] to tear to pieces; [+ víctima] to chop (up) into pieces
2 (= criticar) to tear to shreds, tear to pieces
3 [+ corazón] to break
despedida SF **1** (antes de irse) goodbye, farewell; (antes de viaje) send-off • **cena/función de ~** farewell dinner/performance • **regalo de ~** parting gift
2 (= ceremonia) farewell ceremony
▸ **despedida de soltera** hen party
▸ **despedida de soltero** stag party, bachelor party (EEUU)
3 (= final) (en carta) closing formula; (Literat) envoi; (Mús) final verse
4 (Inform) log off, log out
despedir ▸ CONJUG 3k VT **1** (= decir adiós a) (gen) to say goodbye to; [+ visita] to see out; [+ cliente] to show out • **fuimos a ~lo a la estación** we went to see him off at the station • **¿cómo vais a ~ el año?** how are you going to see the new year in?
2 (= librarse de) [+ empleado] to dismiss, sack*; [+ inquilino] to evict • **~ algo de sí** to get rid of sth • **~ un pensamiento de sí** to put a thought out of one's mind
3 (= lanzar) [+ objeto] to hurl, fling; [+ flecha] to fire; [+ jinete] to throw • **salir despedido** to fly off* • MODISMO: • **~ el espíritu** to give up the ghost
4 (= desprender) [+ olor, calor] to give off
VPR **despedirse 1** (= decir adiós) to say goodbye, take one's leave (frm) • **se despidieron** they said goodbye to each other • **~se de algn** (gen) to say goodbye to sb, take one's leave of sb (frm); (en estación, aeropuerto) to see sb off • **¡ya puedes ~te de ese dinero!** you can say o kiss goodbye to that money! • **se despide atentamente** yours sincerely, sincerely yours (EEUU), yours faithfully
2 (= dejar un empleo) to give up one's job
despegado/a ADJ **1** (= separado) detached, loose • **el sobre está ~** the envelope has come unstuck • **el libro está ~** the book is

falling apart
2 [*persona*] (= *indiferente*) cold, indifferent • **es muy ~** he isn't very close to his family
SM/F • **es un ~ de la familia** he has cut himself off from his family

despegar ▷ CONJUG 1h VT **1** (= *desprender*) [+ *cosas pegadas*] to unstick; [+ *sobre*] to open • **sin ~ los labios** without uttering a word
2 (= *separar*) to detach
VI (*Aer*) [*avión*] to take off; [*cohete*] to blast off
VPR **despegarse 1** [*objeto*] to come unstuck • **se ha despegado el cartel** the poster's come unstuck
2 [*persona*] to become alienated (**de** from) • **~se de los amigos** to break with one's friends • **~se del mundo** to renounce worldly things

despego SM = **desapego**

despegue SM **1** (*Aer*) [*de avión*] takeoff; [*de cohete*] blast-off ▸ **despegue corto** short take-off ▸ **despegue vertical** vertical takeoff
2 (= *crecimiento*) boom • **en los años sesenta hubo un ~ económico** in the sixties the economy took off, there was an economic boom in the sixties ▸ **despegue industrial** industrial boom

despeinado ADJ [*pelo*] ruffled, messed up • **estoy ~** my hair's a mess
SM tousled hairstyle

despeinar ▷ CONJUG 1a VT [+ *pelo*] to ruffle • **¡me has despeinado!** look at the mess you've made of my hair!
VPR **despeinarse** to get one's hair in a mess

despejable ADJ explicable • **difícilmente ~** hard to explain

despejado ADJ **1** (= *sin obstáculos*) [*camino, mente*] clear; [*campo*] open; [*habitación, plaza*] spacious
2 [*cielo, día*] clear
3 (= *despierto*) awake, wide awake; (*Med*) free of fever
4 [*persona*] • **ser ~** to be bright, be smart

despejar ▷ CONJUG 1a VT **1** (*lugar*) to clear • **los bomberos ~on el teatro** the firemen cleared the theatre of people • **la policía obligó a ~ el tribunal** the police ordered the court to be cleared
2 (*Dep*) (*balón*) to clear
3 (= *resolver*) [+ *misterio*] to clear up; (*Mat*) [+ *incógnita*] to find
4 (*Inform*) [+ *pantalla*] to clear
5 (*Med*) [+ *nariz*] to unblock; [+ *cabeza*] to clear; [+ *persona*] to wake up
VI **1** (*de un lugar*) • **¡despejen!** (*al moverse*) move along!; (*haciendo salir*) everybody out!
2 (*Dep*) to clear, clear the ball
3 (*Meteo*) to clear
VPR **despejarse 1** (*Meteo*) [*cielo*] to clear; [*día*] to clear up • **se está despejando** the weather's clearing up
2 [*persona*] (= *despabilarse*) to brighten up • **me lavé la cara con agua fría para ~me** I washed my face with cold water to wake myself up • **voy a salir a ~me un poco** I'm going out to clear my head a bit
3 [*misterio*] to be cleared up

despeje SM **1** (*Dep*) clearance
2 [*de mente*] clarity, clearness of mind

despejo SM (*al pensar*) brightness; (*al actuar*) self-confidence, ease of manner; (*al hablar*) fluency

despellejar ▷ CONJUG 1a VT **1** [+ *animal*] to skin
2 (= *criticar*) to tear to pieces
3* (= *arruinar*) • **~ a algn** to fleece sb

despelotado* ADJ **1** (= *desnudo*) half-naked, scantily clad
2 (= *desorganizado*) (*LAm*) disorganized

despelotar* ▷ CONJUG 1a VT to strip, undress
VPR **despelotarse 1** to strip, strip off
2 • **~se de risa** to laugh fit to bust*

despelote* SM **1** (= *desnudez*) stripping off
2 • **¡vaya ~!** what a laugh!* • **se ha comprado un coche que es un ~** (*Cono Sur*) he's bought a fantastic car
3 (*LAm*) (= *lío*) mess
4 (*Caribe*) (= *juerga*) binge, great night

despeluchado ADJ dishevelled, disheveled (*EEUU*), tousled

despeluchar ▷ CONJUG 1a VT to dishevel, tousle

despeluzar, **despeluznar** ▷ CONJUG 1f VT **1** [+ *pelo*] to dishevel, tousle, rumple • **~ a algn** to horrify sb, make sb's hair stand on end
2 (*Caribe*) (= *arruinar*) to ruin, leave penniless
VPR **despeluzarse 1** [*pelo*] to stand on end
2 [*persona*] to be horrified

despenalización SF legalization, decriminalization

despenalizar ▷ CONJUG 1f VT to legalize, decriminalize

despenar ▷ CONJUG 1a VT **1** (= *consolar*) to console
2‡ (= *matar*) to do in‡, kill

despendedor ADJ extravagant

despendolado* ADJ uninhibited, wild*

despendole* SM lack of inhibitions, lack of restraint

despensa SF **1** (= *armario*) pantry, larder
2 (= *provisión de comestibles*) stock of food
3 (*Náut*) storeroom

despensero SM **1** (= *criado*) butler, steward
2 (*Náut*) storekeeper

despeñadero SM **1** (*Geog*) cliff, precipice
2 (= *riesgo*) risk, danger

despeñadizo ADJ dangerously steep, sheer, precipitous

despeñar ▷ CONJUG 1a VT (= *arrojar*) to throw over a cliff
VPR **despeñarse 1** (*por un barranco*) [*persona*] to throw o.s. over a cliff; [*coche*] to go over a cliff *o* off the side of the road
2 (= *caer*) to fall headlong

despeño SM **1** (= *caída*) fall, drop
2 (= *fracaso*) failure, collapse

despepitar ▷ CONJUG 1a VT to remove the pips from
VPR **despepitarse 1** (= *gritar*) to bawl, shriek
2 (= *obrar*) to rave, act wildly • **~se por algo** to long for sth, go overboard for sth* • **~se por hacer algo** to long to do sth • MODISMO: • **salir despepitado*** to rush out, go rushing out

despercudir ▷ CONJUG 3a VT **1** (= *limpiar*) to clean, wash
2 (*LAm*) [+ *persona*] to liven up, wake up, ginger up

desperdiciado ADJ wasteful

desperdiciador(a) ADJ, SM/F spendthrift

desperdiciar ▷ CONJUG 1b VT [+ *comida, tiempo*] to waste; [+ *oportunidad*] to waste, throw away; [+ *fortuna*] to waste, squander

desperdicio SM **1** (= *derroche*) [*de tiempo*] waste; [*de dinero*] waste, squandering • **esta carne no tiene ~** all this meat can be eaten • **el libro no tiene ~** the book is excellent from beginning to end • **el muchacho no tiene ~** (*iró*) there's very little to be said in his favour
2 desperdicios [*de comida*] scraps; (*Bio, Téc*) waste products ▸ **desperdicios de algodón** cotton waste (*sing*) ▸ **desperdicios de cocina** kitchen scraps ▸ **desperdicios de hierro** scrap iron (*sing*)

desperdigado ADJ scattered, dotted

desperdigar ▷ CONJUG 1h VT (= *esparcir*) [+ *rebaño, objetos*] to scatter; [+ *energía*] dissipate
VPR **desperdigarse** to scatter

desperezarse ▷ CONJUG 1f VPR to stretch, stretch o.s.

desperezo SM stretch

desperfecto SM flaw, imperfection • **sufrió algunos ~s en el accidente** it suffered slight damage in the accident

despernado ADJ footsore, weary

despersonalizar ▷ CONJUG 1f VT to depersonalize

despertador(a) SM/F (= *persona*) knocker-up
SM alarm clock ▸ **despertador de viaje** travelling clock, traveling clock (*EEUU*)

despertamiento SM **1** [*de persona*] awakening
2 [*de cultura, civilización*] awakening, rebirth

despertar ▷ CONJUG 1j VT **1** (*del sueño*) to wake, wake up, awaken (*liter*)
2 (= *recordar, incitar*) [+ *esperanzas*] to raise; [+ *recuerdo*] to revive; [+ *sentimiento*] to arouse • **me despertó el apetito** it whetted my appetite
VI, VPR **despertarse** to wake up, awaken • **siempre me despierto temprano** I always wake up early • **~ a la realidad** to wake up to reality
SM awakening • **el ~ religioso** the religious awakening • **el ~ de la primavera** the awakening of spring

despestañarse ▷ CONJUG 1a VPR (*Cono Sur*) **1** (= *desojarse*) to strain one's eyes
2* (= *estudiar*) to burn the midnight oil, swot*, grind (*EEUU**)

despiadadamente ADV mercilessly, relentlessly

despiadado ADJ [*persona*] heartless; [*ataque*] merciless

despicarse ▷ CONJUG 1g VPR to get even, get one's revenge

despichar ▷ CONJUG 1a VT (*And, Caribe, Cono Sur*) (= *aplastar*) (*lit*) to crush, flatten; (*fig*) to crush
VI‡ to kick the bucket‡

despido SM **1** dismissal, sacking* ▸ **despido arbitrario** wrongful dismissal, unfair dismissal ▸ **despido colectivo** wholesale redundancies (*pl*) ▸ **despido disciplinario** dismissal on disciplinary grounds ▸ **despido forzoso** compulsory redundancy ▸ **despido improcedente** wrongful dismissal, unfair dismissal ▸ **despido incentivado** voluntary redundancy ▸ **despido injustificado**, **despido injusto** wrongful dismissal, unfair dismissal ▸ **despido libre** right to hire and fire ▸ **despido voluntario** voluntary redundancy
2 (= *pago*) severance pay, redundancy payment

despiece SM **1** [*de res*] quartering, carving-up
2 (*Prensa*) comment, personal note

despierto ADJ **1** (= *no dormido*) awake
2 (= *listo*) sharp
3 (= *alerta*) alert

despiezar ▷ CONJUG 1f VT **1** [+ *res*] to quarter, carve up
2 [+ *máquina, motor*] to break up

despilfarrado ADJ **1** (= *derrochador*) extravagant, wasteful
2 (= *desaseado*) ragged, shabby

despilfarrador(a) ADJ (= *malgastador*) (*de dinero*) extravagant, wasteful; (*de recursos, esfuerzos*) wasteful

SM/F spendthrift

despilfarrar ▷ CONJUG 1a VT [+ *dinero*] to waste, squander; [+ *recursos, esfuerzos*] to waste

despilfarro SM **1** (= *derroche*) (= *acción*) waste, squandering; (= *cualidad*) extravagance, wastefulness
2 (= *desaseo*) slovenliness

despintar ▷ CONJUG 1a VT **1** (= *quitar pintura a*) to take the paint off
2 [+ *hechos*] to distort
3 (*Chile**) • **no ~ algo a algn** not to spare sb from sth
VI • **este no despinta de su casta** he is in no way different from the rest of his family
VPR **despintarse 1** [*color*] to fade; (*con la lluvia*) to wash off
2 • **~se algo** to forget sth, wipe sth from one's mind • **no se me despinta que ...** I never forget that ..., I remember vividly that ...
3 (*LAm*) [*maquillaje*] to run, get smudged
4 (*Chile**) • **no ~se de algn** *o* **algo** never to be without sb *o* sth

despiojar ▷ CONJUG 1a VT **1** (= *quitar los piojos a*) to delouse
2 (*fig*) • **~ a algn** to rescue sb from the gutter

despiole* SM (*Arg*) mess

despiporrante* ADJ killingly funny

despiporre* SM (= *caos*) mayhem • **¡fue el ~!** it was something out of this world!, it was just about the end! • **esto es el ~** this is the limit!

despique SM satisfaction, revenge

despistado/a ADJ **1** (= *distraído*) vague, absentminded
2 (= *confuso*) confused, muddled • **ando muy ~ con todo esto** I'm terribly muddled about all this
SM/F (= *distraído*) scatterbrain, absent-minded person • **es un ~** he's very absent-minded • MODISMO: • **hacerse el ~** (*para no entender*) to pretend not to understand; (*para no ver a algn*) to pretend not to be looking

despistaje SM (*Med*) early detection, early diagnosis

despistar ▷ CONJUG 1a VT **1** [+ *perro*] to throw off the scent • **lograron ~ a sus perseguidores** they managed to give the slip to *o* shake off their pursuers
2 (= *confundir*) to mislead, fox • **esa pregunta está hecha para ~** that question is designed to mislead you
3‡ (= *robar*) to nick‡; (= *timar*) rip off‡
4 (*Med*) to detect early, diagnose at an early stage
VPR **despistarse 1** (= *extraviarse*) to take the wrong route *o* road
2 (= *confundirse*) to get confused
3 (= *distraerse*) to get absent-minded • **no puedes ~te ni un momento** you can't let your attention wander for a moment

despiste SM **1** (= *error*) slip • **ha sido un ~** it was just a momentary lapse
2 (= *distracción*) absent-mindedness • **¡qué ~ tienes!** you're so absent-minded! • **tiene un terrible ~** he's terribly absent-minded

desplacer ▷ CONJUG 2w VT to displease
SM displeasure

desplanchar ▷ CONJUG 1a VT [+ *ropa*] to crease, crumple
VPR **desplancharse** to crease, crumple

desplantador SM trowel

desplantar ▷ CONJUG 1a VT **1** [+ *planta*] to pull up, uproot, take up
2 [+ *objeto*] to move out of vertical, tilt, put out of plumb

desplante SM **1** (= *dicho cortante*) rude remark • **dar** *o* **hacer un ~ a algn** to be short with sb
2 • **me hizo un ~** (*LAm**) she stood me up*
3 (*en baile*) wrong stance
4 (= *descaro*) insolence, lack of respect
5 (*LAm**) (= *disparate*) crazy idea

desplazado/a ADJ **1** [*pieza*] wrongly placed
2 • **sentirse un poco ~** to feel rather out of place
SM/F (= *inadaptado*) misfit; (*Pol*) displaced person

desplazamiento SM **1** (= *movimiento*) [*de partículas*] displacement; [*de tropas*] movement ▸ **desplazamiento continental** continental drift ▸ **desplazamiento de tierras** landslide
2 (= *viaje*) journey • **utiliza el tren para los ~s cortos** she uses the train for short journeys • **habrá más de diez millones de ~s en todo el país** over ten million journeys will be made throughout the country • **reside en Madrid aunque hace frecuentes ~s** she lives in Madrid but travels frequently
3 [*de opinión, votos*] shift, swing ▸ **desplazamiento de la demanda** (*Com*) shift in demand
4 (*Inform*) scrolling ▸ **desplazamiento hacia abajo** scrolling down ▸ **desplazamiento hacia arriba** scrolling up
5 (*Náut*) displacement

desplazar ▷ CONJUG 1f VT **1** (= *mover*) [+ *objeto*] to move; [+ *tropas*] to transfer
2 (= *suplantar*) to take the place of • **las cámaras digitales no han conseguido ~ a las convencionales** digital cameras have not taken the place of *o* superseded conventional ones • **lo ~on de su cargo** he was ousted from his position
3 (*Fís, Náut, Téc*) to displace
4 (*Inform*) to scroll
VPR **desplazarse 1** [*objeto*] to move, shift
2 [*persona, vehículo*] to go, travel • **tiene que ~se 25km todos los días** he has to travel 25km every day • **el avión se desplaza a más de 1500km/h** the aircraft travels at more than 1500km/h
3 [*votos, opinión*] to shift, swing • **se ha desplazado un 4% de los votos** there has been a swing of 4% in the voting

desplegable ADJ • **menú ~** pull-down menu
SM **1** (= *folleto*) folder, brochure
2 (*Prensa*) centrefold

desplegar ▷ CONJUG 1h, 1j VT **1** (= *extender*) [+ *mapa, mantel*] to unfold; [+ *periódico*] to open, open out; [+ *alas*] to spread; [+ *bandera, velas*] to unfurl
2 (*Mil*) [+ *misiles, tropas*] to deploy
3 (= *utilizar*) [+ *energías*] to use; [+ *recursos*] to deploy
4 [+ *misterio*] to clarify
VPR **desplegarse 1** (= *extenderse*) [*flor*] to open, open out; [*alas*] to spread, spread out
2 (*Mil*) to deploy

despliegue SM **1** (*Mil*) deployment
2 [*de fuerzas*] display, show

desplomarse ▷ CONJUG 1a VPR
1 (= *derrumbarse*) [*persona, gobierno*] to collapse; [*edificio*] to topple over; (*al vacío*) to plummet down • **se ha desplomado el techo** the ceiling has fallen in • **caer desplomado** to collapse • **el avión se desplomó** the plane fell *o* dropped out of the sky
2 (*Econ*) [*precios*] to slump, tumble

desplome SM **1** [*de edificio, sistema*] collapse • **de repente se produjo el ~ del edificio** the building suddenly collapsed
2 (*Econ*) [*de cotización, divisa*] collapse, slump
3 (*Aer*) pancake landing
4 (*Alpinismo, Arquit, Geol*) overhang

desplumar ▷ CONJUG 1a VT **1** [+ *ave*] to pluck
2* (= *estafar*) to fleece*
VPR **desplumarse** to moult, molt (EEUU)

despoblación SF depopulation ▸ **despoblación del campo, despoblación rural** rural population drift

despoblado ADJ (= *con insuficientes habitantes*) underpopulated; (= *con pocos habitantes*) depopulated; (= *sin habitantes*) unpopulated
SM deserted spot

despoblar ▷ CONJUG 1l VT **1** (*de personas*) to depopulate
2 (*de objetos*) to clear • **~ una zona de árboles** to clear an area of trees
VPR **despoblarse** to become depopulated, lose its population

despojar ▷ CONJUG 1a VT (*de bienes*) to strip; (*de honores, títulos*) to divest; (*Jur*) to dispossess • **habían despojado la casa de muebles** they had stripped the house of furniture • **verse despojado de su autoridad** to be stripped of one's authority
VPR **despojarse 1** (= *desnudarse*) to undress
2 • **~se de** [+ *ropa*] to take off; [+ *hojas*] to shed; [+ *poderes*] to relinquish, give up; [+ *prejuicios*] to get rid of, free o.s. from

despojo SM **1** (= *saqueo*) plundering
2 (*Mil*) (= *botín*) plunder, loot
3 despojos [*de comida*] left-overs; [*de animal*] offal (*sing*); [*de edificio*] rubble (*sing*); [*de mineral*] debris (*sing*) ▸ **despojos de hierro** scrap iron (*sing*) ▸ **despojos mortales** mortal remains

despolitización SF depoliticization

despolitizar ▷ CONJUG 1f VT to depoliticize

despolvorear ▷ CONJUG 1a VT to dust

desportillado ADJ **1** [*taza, plato*] chipped
2 (= *en malas condiciones*) [*coche*] battered; [*piso*] dingy

desportilladura SF chip

desportillar ▷ CONJUG 1a VT to chip
VPR **desportillarse** to get chipped

desposado ADJ recently married • **los ~s** the newly-weds

desposar ▷ CONJUG 1a VT [*sacerdote, novio*] to marry • **yo te desposo** I take you to be my lawful wedded wife/husband
VPR **desposarse 1** (= *formalizar el noviazgo*) to get engaged (**con** to)
2 (= *casarse*) to marry, get married

desposeer ▷ CONJUG 2e VT to dispossess (**de** of) • **~ a algn de su autoridad** to strip sb of his authority
VPR **desposeerse** • **~se de algo** to give sth up, relinquish sth

desposeído/a SM/F • **los ~s** the have-nots, the dispossessed

desposeimiento SM (*frm*) dispossession

desposorios SMPL **1** (= *esponsales*) betrothal (*sing*)
2 (= *ceremonia*) marriage (*sing*), marriage ceremony (*sing*)

déspota SMF despot ▸ **déspota ilustrado/a** enlightened despot

despóticamente ADV despotically

despótico ADJ despotic

despotismo SM despotism ▸ **despotismo ilustrado** enlightened despotism

despotorrarse* ▷ CONJUG 1a VPR to laugh o.s. silly*

despotricar ▷ CONJUG 1g VI to rant and rave (**contra** about)

despreciable ADJ **1** [*persona*] despicable, contemptible
2 (= *sin valor*) [*objeto*] worthless; [*cantidad*] negligible • **una suma nada ~** a not inconsiderable amount

despreciar ▷ CONJUG 1b VT **1** [+ *persona*] to despise, scorn • **desprecian a los extranjeros** they look down on foreigners
2 (= *rechazar*) [+ *oferta, regalo*] to spurn, reject

• ~ **los peligros** to scorn the dangers • **no hay que ~ tal posibilidad** one should not discount such a possibility
(VPR) **despreciarse** • **~se de hacer algo** to think it beneath o.s. to do sth, not deign to do sth
despreciativamente (ADV) scornfully, contemptuously
despreciativo (ADJ) [*observación, tono*] scornful, contemptuous; [*comentario*] derogatory
desprecintar ▷ CONJUG 1a (VT) to unseal
desprecio (SM) **1** (= *desdén*) scorn, contempt • **lo miró con ~** she looked at him contemptuously
2 (= *desaire*) slight, snub • **le hicieron el ~ de no acudir** they snubbed him by not coming
desprender ▷ CONJUG 2a (VT) **1** (= *soltar*) [+ *gas, olor*] to give off; [+ *piel, pelo*] to shed
2 (= *separar*) • **el viento desprendió unas tejas del tejado** the wind detached some tiles from the roof • **desprendió el toallero de la pared** he took the towel rail down from the wall • **tuve que ~ el botón del abrigo** I had to take the button off my coat
(VPR) **desprenderse 1** (= *soltarse*) [*pieza, botón*] to come off, become detached (*frm*); [*roca*] to come away; [*pintura, cal*] to peel, come off • **se te ha desprendido un botón del abrigo** one of the buttons has come off your coat • **se ha desprendido la cortina del salón** the living room curtain has come down
2 [*gas, olor*] to issue • **se desprendía humo de la chimenea** smoke was issuing from the chimney • **en la reacción se desprende gas** gas is given off in the reaction • **se desprendían chispas del fuego** sparks were shooting out from the fire
3 • **~se de algo** (= *deshacerse*): • **logramos ~nos de mi hermana pequeña** we managed to get rid of *o* shake off my little sister • **tuvimos que ~nos del coche** we had to part with *o* get rid of the car • **nunca se desprende de su muñequita** she never lets go of her little doll • **las serpientes se desprenden de la piel en esta época del año** snakes shed their skins at this time of year
4 (= *concluirse*) • **de esta declaración se desprende que ...** from this statement we can gather that ...
desprendido (ADJ) **1** (= *suelto*) [*pieza*] loose, detached • **uno de tus botones está ~** one of your buttons is coming off
2 (= *generoso*) generous
desprendimiento (SM) **1** [*de pieza*] loosening ▸ **desprendimiento de matriz** prolapse ▸ **desprendimiento de retina** detachment of the retina • **ha sufrido un ~ de retina** he has a detached retina ▸ **desprendimiento de tierras** landslide
2 (= *generosidad*) generosity
despreocupación (SF) **1** (= *falta de preocupación*) unconcern; (*al vestir*) sloppiness
2 (= *tranquilidad*) nonchalance
3 (= *indiferencia*) indifference
despreocupadamente (ADV) [*hablar, jugar*] nonchalantly; [*disfrutar*] in a carefree way • **se viste ~** she doesn't take much care about the way she dresses
despreocupado (ADJ) **1** (= *sin preocupación*) unworried, unconcerned • **vive ~ de todo** he has a carefree existence
2 (*al hablar, jugar*) nonchalant
3 (*en el vestir*) casual; (*pey*) careless, sloppy
4 (= *imparcial*) unbias(s)ed, impartial
5 (*Rel*) (= *indiferente*) indifferent, apathetic; (= *tolerante*) broad-minded
6† [*mujer*] loose
despreocupamiento (SM) lack of interest, apathy
despreocuparse ▷ CONJUG 1a (VPR) **1** (= *descuidarse*) • **tú despreocúpate del coche, que ya me encargo yo** don't you worry about the car, I'll take care of it
2 (= *ser indiferente*) to be unconcerned
despresar ▷ CONJUG 1a (VT) (*Cono Sur*) [+ *ave*] to cut up, carve up
desprestigiado (ADJ) discredited
desprestigiar ▷ CONJUG 1b (VT) **1** (= *criticar*) to disparage, run down
2 (= *desacreditar*) to discredit • **tus meteduras de pata desprestigian a toda la profesión** your faux pas tarnish the reputation of our whole profession
(VPR) **desprestigiarse** to lose one's prestige
desprestigio (SM) **1** (= *denigración*) disparagement
2 (= *descrédito*) discredit, loss of prestige • **campaña de ~** smear campaign • **esas cosas que van en ~ nuestro** those things which are to our discredit
despresurizar ▷ CONJUG 1f (VT) to depressurize
desprevención (SF) unreadiness, unpreparedness
desprevenido (ADJ) (= *no preparado*) unready, unprepared • **coger** *o* **pillar** *o* (*LAm*) **agarrar a algn ~** to catch sb unawares, catch sb off his guard
desprivatizar ▷ CONJUG 1f (VT) to take into public ownership
desprogramar ▷ CONJUG 1a (VT) to deprogramme, deprogram (*EEUU*)
desprolijo* (ADJ) (*Arg*) untidy, sloppy*
desproporción (SF) disproportion, lack of proportion
desproporcionadamente (ADV) disproportionately
desproporcionado (ADJ) disproportionate
despropósito (SM) **1** (= *salida de tono*) inappropriate remark
2 (= *disparate*) piece of nonsense
desprotección (SF) **1** (= *falta de protección*) vulnerability, defencelessness, defenselessness (*EEUU*)
2 (*Jur*) lack of legal protection
3 (*Inform*) deprotection
desprotegido (ADJ) unprotected, defenceless, defenseless (*EEUU*)
desproveer ▷ CONJUG 2a (PP: **desprovisto** *y* **desproveído**) (VT) • **~ a algn de algo** to deprive sb of sth
desprovisto (ADJ) • **~ de algo** devoid of sth, without sth • **un libro no ~ de méritos** a book not without merit • **estar ~ de algo** to lack sth, be lacking in sth • **estar ~ de medios** to lack means
después (ADV) **1** (*con sentido temporal*) **a** (= *más tarde*) later, later on; (*tras un hecho concreto*) afterwards, after • **nos vemos ~** I'll see you later (on) • **no me da tiempo antes de la cena, lo haré ~** I haven't got time before dinner, I'll do it after(wards) • **poco ~** soon after(wards), not long after(wards) • **lo vi en enero, pero ~ no lo he visto más** I saw him in January, but I haven't seen him since (then)
b (= *a continuación*) then, next • **¿qué pasó ~?** what happened then *o* next?
2 (*con sentido espacial*) • **primero está el bar y ~ mi casa** first there's the bar and then, next to it, my house • **gire a la derecha dos calles ~** take the second turning on the right after that
3 (*en orden, jerarquía*) then • **primero está el director y ~ el subdirector** first there's the manager, and then the assistant manager
4 • **~ de** (*con sentido temporal*) after • **lo saludé ~ del funeral** I said hello to him after the funeral • **~ de aplicarse la mascarilla, relájese** after applying the mask, relax • **nadie llamó ~ de que te fueras** nobody called after you had gone • **no debería llegar ~ de las diez** I shouldn't be any later than ten • **llegó ~ de mí** he arrived after me • **no lo he vuelto a ver ~ de Navidad** I haven't seen him since Christmas • **~ de marcharse no hemos sabido nada de él** we haven't heard anything from him since he left • **en el año 300 ~ de Cristo** in (the year) 300 AD
5 • **~ de** (*en orden, jerarquía*) after, next to • **mi nombre está ~ del tuyo** my name comes next to *o* after yours
6 • **~ de todo** after all • **~ de todo, no parece tan antipático** he doesn't seem so unpleasant, after all
7 • **~ que*** after • **me duché ~ que tú** I'll have a shower after you
despuesito* (ADV) (*Méx*) right away, in just a moment
despulgar ▷ CONJUG 1h (VT) = **espulgar**
despuntado (ADJ) blunt
despuntar ▷ CONJUG 1a (VT) [+ *lápiz, cuchillo*] to blunt
(VI) **1** (*Bot*) [*plantas*] to sprout; [*flores*] to bud
2 [*día*] to dawn • **al ~ el alba** at daybreak, at dawn
3 [*persona*] (= *destacar*) to excel, stand out • **despunta en matemáticas** he shines *o* excels at maths • **despunta por su talento** she is outstandingly talented
desquiciado (ADJ) [*persona*] deranged, unhinged • **tiene los nervios ~s** his nerves are in tatters *o* shreds
desquiciamiento (SM) **1** [*de persona*] unhinging
2 [*de orden, situación*] upsetting
desquiciante (ADJ) maddening
desquiciar ▷ CONJUG 1b (VT) **1** [+ *puerta*] to take off its hinges
2 [+ *persona*] (= *turbar*) to drive mad; (= *volver loco a*) to unhinge, drive mad
3 [+ *orden, situación*] to upset
(VPR) **desquiciarse** [*persona*] to go mad
desquicio (SM) (*CAm, Cono Sur*) confusion, disorder
desquitar ▷ CONJUG 1a (VT) [+ *pérdida*] to make good, make up
(VPR) **desquitarse 1** (= *obtener satisfacción*) to obtain satisfaction • **~se de una pérdida** to make up for a loss, compensate o.s. for a loss
2 (= *vengarse*) to get even (**con** with), get one's own back (**con** on) • **~se de una mala pasada** to get one's own back for a dirty trick
3 (*Com, Econ*) to recover a debt, get one's money back
desquite (SM) **1** (= *recompensa*) compensation
2 (= *venganza*) revenge, retaliation • **tomarse el ~** to get one's own back • **tomarse el ~ de algo** to get one's own back for sth
3 (*Dep*) (*tb* **partido de desquite**) return match, return game
desratización (SF) • **campaña de ~** anti-rat campaign
desratizador (ADJ) anti-rodent (*antes de s*)
desratizar ▷ CONJUG 1f (VT) to clear of rats
desrazonable (ADJ) unreasonable
desregulación (SF) deregulation
desregular ▷ CONJUG 1a (VT) to free, deregulate, remove controls from
desrielar ▷ CONJUG 1a (*LAm*) (VI) to derail
(VPR) **desrielarse** to be derailed
desriñonar ▷ CONJUG 1a (VT) = **deslomar**
desrizador (SM), **desrizante** (SM) hair straightener
desrizar ▷ CONJUG 1f (VT) [+ *pelo*] to straighten
Dest. (ABR) = **destinatario**

destacadamente ADV notably, outstandingly

destacado ADJ **1** (= *distinguido*) (*gen*) outstanding; [*personaje*] distinguished; [*dato*] noteworthy
2 (*Mil*) stationed • **los cascos azules ~s en la zona** the UN peacekeeping forces *o* blue helmets stationed in the area

destacamento SM (*Mil*) detachment
▸ **destacamento de desembarco** (*Náut*) landing party

destacar ▸ CONJUG 1g VT **1** (= *hacer resaltar*) to emphasize • **sirve para ~ su belleza** it serves to show off her beauty • **quiero ~ que ...** I wish to emphasize that ...
2 (*Mil*) to detach, detail
3 (*Inform*) to highlight
VI, VPR **destacarse 1** (= *verse mejor*) to stand out • **~se contra** *o* **en** *o* **sobre algo** to stand out *o* be outlined against sth • **la torre se destaca contra el cielo** the tower is silhouetted against the sky
2 [*persona*] to stand out (**por** because of)

destajar ▸ CONJUG 1a VT **1** [+ *trabajo*] to agree conditions for
2 (*Naipes*) to cut
3 (*LAm*) (= *despedazar*) [+ *reses*] to cut up

destajero/a SM/F, **destajista** SMF pieceworker

destajo SM **1** • **a ~** (= *por pieza*) by the job; (= *con afán*) eagerly; (*Cono Sur**) by guesswork • **trabajar a ~** (*lit*) to do piecework; (*fig*) to work one's fingers to the bone • **trabajo a ~** piecework • **hablar a ~*** to talk nineteen to the dozen
2 ▸ **destajo de esquí** ski-lift pass

destapado ADJ **1** (= *sin cubrir*) • **la botella está destapada** somebody left the top off the bottle • **dejó la olla destapada** he left the saucepan uncovered
2 (= *sin sábanas*) • **hoy he dormido ~** I slept without any covers last night • **durmió ~** he slept with the covers off
3 [*secreto, trama*] exposed, uncovered

destapador SM (*LAm*) bottle opener

destapamiento SM (*Méx*) (*Pol*) *announcement of official PRI presidential candidate*

destapar ▸ CONJUG 1a VT **1** (= *descubrir*) [+ *mueble*] to uncover; [+ *botella*] (*gen*) to open; (*con corcho*) to uncork; [+ *recipiente*] to take the lid off
2 (*en la cama*) to take the bedclothes off • **lo destapó** she took the covers off him
3 (= *hacer público*) [+ *secreto*] to reveal; [+ *escándalo*] to uncover
4 (*LAm*) (= *desatascar*) to unblock
VPR **destaparse 1** (= *descubrirse*) to get uncovered • **el niño se ha destapado** the bedclothes have fallen off the baby
2 (= *revelarse*) to show one's true character • **se destapó metiéndose a monja** she astounded everyone by becoming a nun
3 (= *desahogarse*) to open one's heart (**con** to)
4 (= *perder los estribos*) to let fly, lose control

destape SM **1** [*de persona*] (= *estado*) nudity; (= *acto*) undressing, stripping off ▸ **destape integral** full-frontal nudity
2 [*de costumbres*] permissiveness; (*Pol*) *process of liberalization* • **el ~ español** *the relaxation of sexual censorship (after Franco's death)*

destaponar ▸ CONJUG 1a VT [+ *conducto, tubería*] to unblock, clear

destartalado ADJ **1** [*casa*] (= *grande, mal dispuesta*) large and rambling; (= *ruinoso*) tumbledown
2 [*coche*] rickety

destazar ▸ CONJUG 1f VT to cut up

destechar ▸ CONJUG 1a VT to unroof, take the roof off

destejar ▸ CONJUG 1a VT **1** [+ *techo*] to remove the tiles from
2 (= *quitar la protección a*) to leave unprotected

destejer ▸ CONJUG 2d VT **1** (*Cos*) [+ *prenda de punto*] to undo; ▸ **tejer**
2 (= *interferir*) to interfere with the progress of

destellante ADJ sparkling

destellar ▸ CONJUG 1a VI [*diamante, ojos*] to sparkle; [*metal*] to glint; [*estrella*] to twinkle

destello SM **1** (= *brillo*) [*de diamante, ojos*] sparkle; [*de metal*] glint; [*de estrella*] twinkling
2 (*Téc*) signal light
3 (= *pizca*) glimmer, hint • **tiene a veces ~s de inteligencia** he sometimes shows a glimmer of intelligence • **no tiene un ~ de verdad** there's not an atom of truth in it

destemplado ADJ **1** (*Mús*) out of tune
2 (*Med*) (= *con fiebre*) feverish • **estar ~** to have a slight temperature *o* (*EEUU*) fever • **tienes el pulso ~** your pulse is a little irregular
3 [*carácter*] (= *malhumorado*) ill-tempered; (= *áspero*) harsh
4 (*Meteo*) unpleasant

destemplanza SF **1** (*Mús*) tunelessness
2 (*Med*) (= *fiebre*) slight temperature, slight fever (*EEUU*); (= *malestar*) indisposition
3 (= *falta de moderación*) intemperance, harshness
4 (*Meteo*) unpleasantness, inclemency

destemplar ▸ CONJUG 1a VT **1** (*Mús*) to put out of tune
2 (= *alterar*) to upset, disturb
VPR **destemplarse 1** (*Mús*) to get out of tune
2 (*Med*) [*persona*] to have a slight temperature *o* (*EEUU*) fever; [*pulso*] to become irregular
3 [*máquina*] to break down
4 (*LAm*) (= *irritarse*) to get upset • **con eso me destemplo** that sets my teeth on edge

destemple SM **1** = **destemplanza**
2 [*de metal*] lack of temper, poorly-tempered nature

destensar ▸ CONJUG 1a VT to slacken, loosen

desteñido ADJ faded, discoloured, discolored (*EEUU*)
SM discolouring, discoloring (*EEUU*)

desteñir ▸ CONJUG 3h, 3k VT (= *quitar el color a*) to fade, discolour, discolor (*EEUU*)
VI, VPR **desteñirse 1** (= *perder color*) to run • **se ha desteñido la camiseta** the T-shirt has run
2 (= *manchar*) to run • **esta tela no destiñe** this fabric won't run

desternillante* ADJ hilarious

desternillarse* ▸ CONJUG 1a VPR • **~ de risa** to split one's sides laughing

desternille* SM laughter, hilarity

desterrado/a SM/F (= *exiliado*) exile

desterrar ▸ CONJUG 1j VT **1** (= *exiliar*) to exile, banish
2 (= *desechar*) to dismiss • **~ una sospecha** to banish a suspicion from one's mind • **~ el uso de las armas de fuego** to banish firearms, prohibit the use of firearms
3 (*Agr, Min*) to remove the soil from

destetar ▸ CONJUG 1a VT to wean
VPR **destetarse 1** [*niño*] to be weaned
• MODISMO: • **~se con el vino** to have been brought up on wine
2‡ [*mujer*] to get her tits out‡

destete SM weaning

destiempo SM • **a ~** at the wrong time

destierro SM **1** (= *exilio*) exile, banishment • **vivir en el ~** to live in exile
2 (= *lugar alejado*) remote spot

destilación SF distillation

destiladera SF **1** (= *alambique*) still
2 (*LAm*) (= *filtro*) filter

destilado SM distillation

destilador(a) SM (= *alambique*) still
SM/F distiller

destilar ▸ CONJUG 1a VT **1** (*goteando*) [+ *alcohol*] to distil; [+ *pus, sangre*] to ooze
2 (= *rebosar*) to exude • **la carta destilaba odio** the letter exuded hatred • **es una orden que destila crueldad** it is an order which is steeped in cruelty
VI **1** (= *gotear*) to drip
2 (= *rezumar*) to ooze, ooze out
3 (= *filtrarse*) to filter through

destilatorio SM **1** (= *aparato*) still
2 (= *fábrica*) distillery

destilería SF distillery ▸ **destilería de petróleo** oil refinery

destinado ADJ **1** (*Correos, Transportes*) • **¿a quién va destinada la carta?** who is the letter addressed to? • **se perdieron todos los paquetes ~s a Madrid** all the parcels for *o* bound for Madrid were lost
2 (*en un trabajo*) • **está ~ en Córdoba** [*empleado*] he's based in Córdoba; [*militar*] he's stationed in Córdoba
3 • **~ a** *o* **para algo** [*dinero, fondos, material*] set aside for sth • **un camión ~ a** *o* **para el reparto** a lorry used for deliveries • **redujeron el espacio ~ al olivar** the area given over to olive trees has been reduced
4 • **~ a algo** (= *predestinado*) destined for sth • **la obra estaba destinada al fracaso** the play was destined for failure *o* to fail • **estaba ~ a morir joven** he was destined to die young
5 • **~ a algn/algo** (= *pensado para*) intended for sb/sth, aimed at sb/sth • **un libro ~ a los niños** a book intended for *o* aimed at children • **una nueva ley destinada a proteger al menor** a new law intended to protect minors, a new law aimed at protecting minors
6 • **ir ~ a** (*Náut*) to be bound for

destinar ▸ CONJUG 1a VT **1** (= *dedicar*) [+ *fondos, espacio*] to allocate; [+ *tiempo*] to devote • **destinamos el 10% del presupuesto a educación** we allocate 10% of the budget to education • **~on tres salas a la exposición** they allocated three rooms to the exhibition • **~é este dinero a pagar el viaje** I'll use this money to pay for the trip • **~on mil euros para gastos imprevistos** they set aside *o* earmarked a thousand euros for contingencies • **destina su tiempo libre a hacer obras de caridad** she devotes her free time to charity work
2 (= *enviar*) [+ *empleado, funcionario*] to assign, post; [+ *militar*] to station, post • **le han destinado a Lima** he has been assigned *o* posted to Lima
3 (*frm*) (= *dirigir*) [+ *carta*] to address
VPR **destinarse** to be allocated

destinatario/a SM/F [*de carta*] addressee; [*de giro*] payee • **los ~s de este proyecto** the project's target group

destino SM **1** (= *suerte*) destiny, fate • **es mi ~ no encontrarlo** I am fated not to find it • **el ~ lo quiso así** it was destined to happen • **rige los ~s del país** he rules the country's fate
2 [*de avión, viajero*] destination • **"a franquear en ~"** "postage will be paid by the addressee" • **van con ~ a Londres** they are going to London; (*Náut*) they are bound for London • **¿cuál es el ~ de este cuadro?** where is this picture going *o* for? • **salió con ~ al aeropuerto** she set off for the airport • **con ~ a Londres** [*avión, carta*] to London; [*pasajeros*] for London; [*barco*] bound for London
3 (= *puesto*) [*de empleado*] job, post; [*de militar*] posting; [*de funcionario*] placement • **¿qué ~**

tienes? where have you been placed? • **buscarse un ~ de sereno** to look for a job as a night watchman ▸ **destino público** public appointment
4 (= *uso*) use, purpose • **dar ~ a algo** to find a use for sth
destitución (SF) dismissal, removal
destituido (ADJ) • **~ de algo** devoid of sth, bereft of sth
destituir ▸ CONJUG 3g (VT) **1** (= *despedir*) [+ *empleado*] to dismiss (**de** from); [+ *ministro, funcionario*] to remove from office • **ha sido destituido de su cargo** he has been removed from his post • **lo destituyeron por conducta inmoral** he was dismissed for immoral conduct
2 (= *privar*) • **~ a algn de algo** to deprive sb of sth
destorcer ▸ CONJUG 2b, 2h (VT) [+ *cuerda*] to untwist, take the twists out of; [+ *alambre*] to straighten
(VPR) **destorcerse** (*Náut*) to get off course
destornillado* (ADJ) crazy, potty*
destornillador (SM) **1** (= *herramienta*) screwdriver ▸ **destornillador de estrella** Phillips screwdriver®
2* (= *bebida*) screwdriver* (*cocktail of vodka and orange juice*)
destornillar ▸ CONJUG 1a (VT) to unscrew
(VPR) **destornillarse 1** [*tornillo, tuerca*] to come unscrewed*
2 (= *enloquecer*) to go round the bend*
3 (*LAm*) = **desternillarse**
4 (*Méx*) (= *rabiar*) to burble on, rave
destrabar ▸ CONJUG 1a (VT) **1** (= *desprender*) to loosen, detach
2 [+ *prisionero*] to unfetter, take the shackles off
destral (SM) small hatchet
destreza (SF) **1** (= *habilidad*) skill ▸ **destrezas lingüísticas** linguistic skills
2 (= *agilidad*) dexterity
destripacuentos (SM INV) interrupter, person who butts in
destripador (SM) (= *asesino*) murderer • **Jack el ~** Jack the Ripper
destripar ▸ CONJUG 1a (VT) **1** (= *quitar tripas a*) [+ *animal*] to gut; [+ *persona*] to disembowel
2 [+ *chiste, cuento*] to spoil
destripaterrones (SM INV) **1** (= *campesino*) peasant, farm labourer
2* clodhopper
destrocar* ▸ CONJUG 1g, 1l (VT) to swap, change back
destronamiento (SM) [*de rey*] dethronement; [*de gobierno*] overthrow
destronar ▸ CONJUG 1a (VT) [+ *rey*] to dethrone; [+ *gobierno*] to overthrow
destroncar ▸ CONJUG 1g (VT) **1** [+ *árbol*] to chop off, lop the top off
2 [+ *persona*] (= *mutilar*) to maim, mutilate; (= *agotar*) to tire out, exhaust
3 (= *estropear*) [+ *proyecto*] to ruin; [+ *desarrollo*] to harm, damage, dislocate; [+ *discurso*] to interrupt
4 [+ *caballo*] to wear out
5 (*LAm*) [+ *planta*] to uproot
destrozado (ADJ) **1** [*cristal, cerámica*] smashed, shattered • **quedó ~** [*traje, alfombra, zapato*] it was ruined; [*coche, jardín*] it was wrecked
2 [*persona*] (= *abatido*) shattered, devastated; (= *cansado**) knackered*, pooped (*EEUU**), shattered*; [*corazón*] broken
destrozar ▸ CONJUG 1f (VT) **1** (= *romper*) [+ *cristal, cerámica*] to smash; [+ *edificio*] to destroy; [+ *ropa, zapatos*] to ruin; [+ *nervios*] to shatter • **ha destrozado el coche** he's wrecked the car • **encontraron los cuerpos destrozados** they found the mangled bodies
2 (= *dejar abatido a*) [+ *persona*] to shatter; [+ *corazón*] to break; [+ *ejército, enemigo*] to crush • **~ a algn en una discusión** to crush sb in an argument • **le ha destrozado el que no quisiera casarse con él** her refusal to marry him has devastated *o* shattered him
3 (= *arruinar*) [+ *persona, vida*] to ruin • **~ la armonía** to ruin the harmony
(VPR) **destrozarse** to disintegrate, fall apart
destrozo (SM) **1** (= *acción*) destruction
2 destrozos (= *daños*) havoc (*sing*); (= *pedazos*) debris (*sing*) • **causar** *o* **provocar ~s** to cause *o* wreak havoc (**en in**) • **los ~s causados por las inundaciones** the destruction caused by the flooding, the havoc wrought by the floods • **los manifestantes provocaron numerosos ~s** the demonstrators caused extensive damage
destrozón (ADJ) • **es muy ~** (*gen*) he's a terrible one for breaking things; (*con la ropa*) he's hard on his clothes
destrucción (SF) destruction ▸ **destrucción del empleo** job losses (*pl*)
destructible (ADJ) destructible
destructivamente (ADV) destructively
destructividad (SF) destructiveness
destructivo (ADJ) destructive
destructor (ADJ) destructive
(SM) (*Náut*) destroyer
destruible (ADJ) destructible
destruir ▸ CONJUG 3g (VT) **1** [+ *objeto, edificio*] to destroy • **el acusado había destruido todas las pruebas** the defendant had destroyed all the evidence • **el año pasado se destruyeron miles de empleos en la construcción** last year thousands of construction jobs were lost
2 (= *estropear*) [+ *amistad, matrimonio, armonía*] to wreck, destroy; [+ *argumento, teoría*] to demolish; [+ *esperanza*] to dash, shatter; [+ *proyecto, plan*] to wreck, ruin
(VPR) **destruirse** (*Mat*) to cancel out, cancel each other out
desubicado (ADJ) **1** (= *mal situado*) badly positioned
2 (*Cono Sur*) (= *falto de tacto*) tactless, silly
desubicar ▸ CONJUG 1g (VT) (*Cono Sur*) to disorientate
desudar ▸ CONJUG 1a (VT) to wipe the sweat off
desuellacaras (SM INV) **1** (= *barbero*) clumsy barber
2 (= *bribón*) rogue, villain
desuello (SM) **1** (= *acto*) skinning, flaying
2 (= *descaro*) brazenness, insolence
3* (= *robo*) extortion • **¡es un ~!** it's daylight robbery!
desuncir ▸ CONJUG 3b (VT) to unyoke
desunido (ADJ) disunited, divided
desunión (SF) **1** (= *separación*) separation
2 (= *discordia*) disunity
desunir ▸ CONJUG 3a (VT) **1** (= *separar*) to separate
2 (= *enemistar*) to cause a rift between • **el problema de la herencia ha desunido a la familia** the inheritance problem has split the family
desuñarse ▸ CONJUG 1a (VPR) **1** (= *trabajar*) to work one's fingers to the bone • **~ por hacer algo** to work one's fingers to the bone to do sth
2 (= *hacer travesuras*) to be always up to mischief • **se desuña por el juego** he's an inveterate gambler
desurbanización (SF) relief of city overcrowding, dispersal of city population (*to satellite towns*)
desusado (ADJ) **1** (= *anticuado*) obsolete, antiquated • **esa palabra está desusada de los buenos escritores** that word is no longer in use among good writers
2 (= *inusitado*) unusual
desusar ▸ CONJUG 1a (VT) to stop using, discontinue the use of, give up
(VPR) **desusarse** to go out of use, become obsolete
desuso (SM) disuse • **una expresión en ~** an obsolete expression • **caer en ~** to fall into disuse, become obsolete • **dejar algo en ~** to cease to use sth
desvaído (ADJ) **1** [*color*] pale, washed-out
2 [*contorno*] vague, blurred
3 [*persona*] characterless
4 [*personalidad*] flat, dull
desvainar ▸ CONJUG 1a (VT) to shell
desvalido (ADJ) **1** (= *sin fuerzas*) helpless
2 (= *desprotegido*) destitute • **niños ~s** waifs and strays • **los ~s** (*Pol*) the underprivileged
desvalijamiento (SM) robbing, robbery
desvalijar ▸ CONJUG 1a (VT) [+ *persona*] to rob; [+ *cajón, caja fuerte*] to rifle; [+ *casa, tienda*] to ransack
desvalimiento (SM) helplessness
desvalorar ▸ CONJUG 1a (VT) [+ *regalo, posesión*] to undervalue; [+ *moneda*] to devalue, devaluate (*EEUU*)
desvalorización (SF) [*de moneda*] devaluation
desvalorizar ▸ CONJUG 1f (VT) [+ *moneda*] to devalue, devaluate (*EEUU*); [+ *posesión*] to reduce the value of
desván (SM) loft, attic
desvanecer ▸ CONJUG 2d (VT) **1** (= *hacer desaparecer*) [+ *objeto*] to make disappear; [+ *duda*] to dispel; [+ *recuerdo, temor*] to banish
2 (*Arte*) [+ *colores*] to tone down; [+ *contorno*] to blur
3 (*Fot*) to mask
4 (= *envanecer*) to make conceited • **el dinero lo ha desvanecido** the money has gone to his head
(VPR) **desvanecerse 1** (= *desaparecer*) [*humo, niebla*] to clear, disperse; [*recuerdo, sonido*] to fade, fade away; [*duda*] to be dispelled
2 (*Med*) to faint
3 (*Quím*) to evaporate
desvanecido (ADJ) **1** (*Med*) • **caer ~** to fall in a faint
2 (= *engreído*) vain
desvanecimiento (SM) **1** (= *desaparición*) [*de colores, recuerdo, sonido*] fading; [*de contornos*] blurring; [*de dudas*] dispelling
2 (*Med*) fainting fit, fainting spell (*EEUU*)
3 (*Fot*) masking
4 (*Radio*) fading
5 (= *engreimiento*) vanity
desvarar ▸ CONJUG 1a (VT) to refloat
desvariar ▸ CONJUG 1c (VI) **1** (*Med*) to be delirious
2 (*al hablar*) to rave, talk nonsense
desvarío (SM) **1** (*Med*) delirium
2 (= *desatino*) absurdity
3 desvaríos (= *disparates*) ravings
desvede (SM) *ending of the close season*
desvelado (ADJ) **1** (= *despierto*) sleepless, wakeful • **estar ~** to be awake, be unable to get to sleep
2 (= *alerta*) watchful, vigilant
desvelar ▸ CONJUG 1a (VT) **1** (= *quitar el sueño*) to keep awake • **el café me desvela** coffee keeps me awake *o* stops me from getting to sleep
2 (= *descubrir*) [+ *algo oculto*] to reveal, unveil; [+ *misterio*] to solve, explain
(VPR) **desvelarse 1** (= *no poder dormir*) to be unable to get to sleep
2 (= *vigilar*) to be watchful, keep one's eyes open • **~se por algo** to take great care over

sth • **se desvela porque no nos falte de nada** she works hard so that we should not go short of anything • **~se por hacer algo** to do everything possible to do sth

desvelo SM **1** (= *falta de sueño*) lack of sleep, sleeplessness
2 (= *vigilancia*) watchfulness
3 desvelos (= *preocupaciones*) effort (*sing*) • **gracias a sus ~s** thanks to his efforts

desvencijado ADJ [*silla, mueble*] rickety; [*máquina*] broken-down

desvencijar ▹ CONJUG 1a VT **1** (= *romper*) to break
2 (= *agotar*) [+ *persona*] to exhaust
VPR **desvencijarse 1** (= *romperse*) to come apart, fall to pieces
2 (*Med*) to rupture o.s.

desvendar ▹ CONJUG 1a VT to unbandage, take the bandages off

desventaja SF **1** (= *perjuicio*) disadvantage • **estar en ~** to be at a disadvantage
2 (= *inconveniente*) disadvantage, drawback

desventajado ADJ disadvantaged

desventajosamente ADV disadvantageously, unfavourably, unfavorably (*EEUU*)

desventajoso ADJ disadvantageous, unfavourable, unfavorable (*EEUU*)

desventura SF misfortune

desventuradamente ADV unfortunately

desventurado/a ADJ **1** (= *desgraciado*) [*persona*] unfortunate; [*viaje, encuentro*] ill-fated
2 (= *tímido*) timid, shy
3 (= *tacaño*) mean
SM/F wretch, unfortunate • **algún ~** some poor wretch *o* unfortunate

desvergonzado/a ADJ **1** (= *sin vergüenza*) shameless
2 (= *descarado*) insolent
SM/F (= *no vergonzoso*) shameless person; (= *descarado*) insolent person

desvergonzarse ▹ CONJUG 1f, 1l VPR **1** (= *perder la vergüenza*) to lose all sense of shame
2 (= *insolentarse*) to be impertinent, be insolent (**con** to), behave in a shameless way (**con** towards)
3 • **~ a pedir algo** to have the nerve to ask for sth, dare to ask for sth

desvergüenza SF **1** (= *mala conducta*) shamelessness
2 (= *descaro*) effrontery, impudence • **esto es una ~** this is disgraceful, this is shameful • **¡qué ~!** what a nerve!* • **tener la ~ de hacer algo** to have the impudence *o* nerve* to do sth

desvertebración SF **1** (*Med*) dislocation
2 (= *trastorno*) disruption

desvertebrado ADJ lacking cohesion, disorganized

desvertebrar ▹ CONJUG 1a VT **1** to dislocate
2 (= *trastornar*) [+ *planes*] to disrupt, upset; [+ *pandilla*] to break up

desvestir ▹ CONJUG 3k VT to undress
VPR **desvestirse** to undress

desviación SF **1** (= *separación*) [*de trayectoria*] deviation (**de** from); [*de golpe, disparo*] deflection (**de** from) • **es una ~ de sus principios** it is a deviation *o* departure from his principles ▸ **desviación de columna** abnormal curvature of the spine ▸ **desviación de fondos** diversion of funds ▸ **desviación normal** standard deviation
2 (*Aut*) diversion ▸ **desviación de la circulación** traffic diversion

desviacionismo SM deviationism

desviacionista ADJ, SMF deviationist

desviadero SM (*Ferro*) siding

desviado ADJ **1** (= *apartado*) [*trayectoria*] oblique; [*bala*] deflected
2 [*prácticas, conducta*] deviant
3 [*lugar*] remote, off the beaten track • **~ de algo** remote from sth, away from sth

desviar ▹ CONJUG 1c VT **1** (= *apartar*) [+ *balón, flecha*] to deflect; [+ *golpe*] to parry; [+ *pregunta*] to evade; [+ *ojos*] to avert, turn away; [+ *tren*] to switch, switch into a siding; [+ *avión, circulación*] to divert (**por** through) • **~ el cauce de un río** to alter the course of *o* divert a river • **~ la conversación** to change the subject • **~ el balón a córner** to send the ball out for a corner
2 [+ *persona*] • **lo ~on de su propósito** they dissuaded him from his intention • **~ a algn de su vocación** to turn sb from their vocation • **~ a algn de las malas compañías** to wean sb away from bad company
• **MODISMO:** • **~ a algn del buen camino** to lead sb astray
VPR **desviarse 1** (*de camino*) [*persona*] to turn aside, turn away (**de** from); [*carretera*] to branch off • **~se de un tema** to stray off a subject • **tomamos la primera salida que se desviaba de la carretera de la costa** we took the first turning off the coastal road
2 (*Náut*) to sail off course
3 (*Aut*) to make a detour

desvincular ▹ CONJUG 1a VT to dissociate
VPR **desvincularse 1** (= *aislarse*) to be cut off
2 (= *alejarse*) to cut o.s. off (**de** from)

desvío SM **1** [*de trayectoria, orientación*] deflection (**de** from), deviation (**de** from)
2 (*Aut*) (= *rodeo*) detour; (*por obras*) diversion
3 (*Ferro*) siding

desvirgar ▹ CONJUG 1h VT **1** [+ *virgen*] to deflower (*liter*) • **se casó con el hombre que la desvirgó** she married the man to whom she lost her virginity
2* = **estrenar**

desvirtuar ▹ CONJUG 1e VT [+ *argumento, razonamiento*] to detract from; [+ *efecto*] to counteract; [+ *sentido*] to distort • **la cláusula secreta desvirtuó el objetivo del tratado** the secret clause nullified the aim of the treaty
VPR **desvirtuarse** (= *estropearse*) to go off

desvitalizado ADJ dull, lifeless

desvitalizar ▹ CONJUG 1f VT [+ *nervio*] to numb
VPR **desvitalizarse** to flag

desvivirse ▹ CONJUG 3a VPR • **~ por algo** (= *desear*) to crave sth, long for sth; (= *chiflarse por*) to be crazy about sth • **~ por los amigos** to do anything for one's friends • **~ por salir** to be dying to go out • **se desvivía por ayudarme** he used to go out of his way to help me

desyerba SF, **desyerbo** SM (*LAm*) weeding

desyerbar ▹ CONJUG 1a VT = **desherbar**

detal, detall • **al ~** ADV retail

detalladamente ADV **1** (= *con detalles*) in detail
2 (= *extensamente*) at great length

detallado ADJ [*informe, relato*] detailed; [*declaración*] circumstantial; [*conocimiento*] detailed, intimate

detallar ▹ CONJUG 1a VT **1** (= *contar con detalles*) to detail; (*en una lista, factura*) to itemize
2 [+ *cuento*] to tell in detail
3 (*Com*) to retail

detalle SM **1** (= *pormenor*) detail • **al ~** in detail • **con todo ~** • **con todos los ~s** in full detail • **para más ~s vea …** for further details see … • **hasta en sus menores ~s** down to the last detail • **no pierde ~** he doesn't miss a trick • **me observaba sin perder ~** he watched my every move
2 (= *atención*) nice gesture • **¡qué ~!** what a nice gesture, how thoughtful! • **tiene muchos ~s** he is very considerate *o* thoughtful • **lo que importa es el ~** it's the thought that counts • **es el primer ~ que te veo en mucho tiempo** it's the first sign of consideration I've had from you in a long time
3 (= *regalo*) small gift
4 (*Com*) • **al ~** retail (*antes de s*) • **vender al ~** to retail • **comercio al ~** retail trade
5 (*Econ*) (= *estado de cuenta*) statement; (= *factura*) bill

detallismo SM attention to detail, care for the details

detallista ADJ **1** (= *meticuloso*) meticulous
2 (*Com*) retail (*antes de s*) • **comercio ~** retail trade
SMF **1** (= *meticuloso*) perfectionist
2 (*Com*) retailer, retail trader

detalloso* ADJ kind, thoughtful

detección SF detection

detectable ADJ detectable

detectar ▹ CONJUG 1a VT to detect

detective SMF detective ▸ **detective privado/a** private detective

detectivesco ADJ detective (*antes de s*) • **dotes detectivescas** gifts as a detective

detector SM detector ▸ **detector de humo** smoke detector ▸ **detector de incendios** fire detector ▸ **detector de mentiras** lie detector ▸ **detector de metales** metal detector ▸ **detector de minas** mine detector

detención SF **1** (= *parada*) [*de una acción*] stoppage; (*con retraso*) holdup, delay • **una ~ de 15 minutos** a 15-minute delay ▸ **detención de juego** (*Dep*) stoppage
2 (*Jur*) (= *arresto*) arrest; (= *prisión*) detention ▸ **detención cautelar** preventive detention ▸ **detención domiciliaria** house arrest ▸ **detención en masa** mass arrest ▸ **detención ilegal** unlawful detention ▸ **detención preventiva** police custody
3 (= *cuidado*) care

detener ▹ CONJUG 2k VT **1** (= *parar*) to stop • **me detuvo en la calle** he stopped me in the street
2 (= *retrasar*) to hold up, delay • **~ el progreso de algo** to hold up the progress of sth • **no quiero ~lo** I don't want to keep *o* delay you
3 (= *retener*) [+ *objeto*] to keep
4 (*Jur*) (= *arrestar*) to arrest; (= *encarcelar*) to detain
VPR **detenerse 1** (= *pararse*) to stop • **¡no te detengas!** don't hang about! • **se detuvo a mirarlo** he stopped to look at it
2 (= *demorarse*) to waste time (**en** on) • **se detiene mucho en eso** he's taking a long time over that

detenidamente ADV **1** (= *minuciosamente*) carefully, thoroughly
2 (= *extensamente*) at great length

detenido/a ADJ **1** (*Jur*) (*por poco tiempo*) arrested, under arrest; (*por más tiempo*) in custody
2 (= *sin prisa*) [*narración, estudio*] detailed; [*análisis, examen*] thorough; [*visita*] unhurried, leisurely
3 (= *tímido*) timid
4 (= *tacaño*) mean, niggardly
SM/F (*en comisaría*) person under arrest; (*en cárcel*) prisoner

detenimiento SM care • **con ~** thoroughly

detentar ▹ CONJUG 1a VT **1** (*Dep*) [+ *récord*] to hold
2 (= *poseer*) [+ *título*] to hold unlawfully; [+ *puesto*] to occupy unlawfully

detentor(a) SM/F (*Dep*) holder • **~(a) de marca** record holder • **~(a) de trofeo** cup holder, champion

detergente ADJ, SM detergent

d

deterger ▹ CONJUG 2c VT [+ *objeto*] to clean, clean of grease; [+ *herida*] to clean; [+ *plato*] to clean with detergent

deteriorado ADJ **1** [*edificio, mueble*] dilapidated
2 [*ropa, alfombra*] worn

deteriorar ▹ CONJUG 1a VT **1** (= *estropear*) to damage • **la falta de medios puede ~ la calidad de la enseñanza** the lack of resources could harm *o* damage the quality of education
2 (*Mec*) to cause wear and tear to
VPR **deteriorarse 1** (= *estropearse*) to get damaged
2 (= *empeorarse*) • **su salud se está deteriorando** her health is getting worse *o* deteriorating • **las relaciones entre ambos países se han deteriorado** relations between the two countries have deteriorated
3 (*Mec*) to wear, get worn

deterioro SM **1** (= *daño*) damage • **en caso de ~ de las mercancías** should the goods be damaged in any way • **sin ~ de sus derechos** without affecting his rights, without impinging on his rights (*más frm*)
2 (= *empeoramiento*) deterioration
3 (*Mec*) wear and tear

determinable ADJ determinable • **fácilmente ~** easy to determine

determinación SF **1** (= *decisión*) decision • **tomar una ~** to take a decision
2 (= *valentía*) determination, resolution • **actuar con ~** to take determined action, act decisively
3 [*de fecha, precio*] fixing

determinado ADJ **1** (= *preciso*) certain • **un día ~** on a certain *o* given day • **en momentos ~s** at certain times • **hay ~s límites** there are certain limits • **no hay ningún tema ~** there is no particular theme
2 [*persona*] determined, resolute
3 (*Ling*) [*artículo*] definite
4 (*Mat*) determinate

determinante ADJ, SM determinant

determinar ▹ CONJUG 1a VT **1** (= *establecer*) to determine • **el gen que determina el color de los ojos** the gene which determines eye colour • **~on un precio tras largas negociaciones** after lengthy negotiations they determined *o* fixed a price • **"precio por ~"** "price to be agreed" • **~ el rumbo** (*Aer, Náut*) to set a course • **el reglamento determina que …** the rule lays down *o* states that …
2 (= *averiguar*) [+ *peso, volumen, causa*] to determine; [+ *daños*] to assess • **la policía logró ~ la verdad del asunto** the police succeeded in determining the truth of the matter
3 (= *motivar*) to bring about, cause • **aquello determinó la caída del gobierno** that brought about *o* caused the fall of the government
4 (= *decidir*) to decide • **~on asignarle más fondos al proyecto** they decided to allocate more funds to the project • **esto la determinó a continuar sus estudios** this decided her to continue with her studies
5 (*Ling*) to determine
VPR **determinarse** (= *decidirse*) to decide, make up one's mind • **debe ~se por un médico u otro** you must decide on one doctor or another • **~se a hacer algo** to determine to do sth, decide to do sth

determinativo ADJ determinative
SM (*Ling*) determiner

determinismo SM determinism

determinista ADJ deterministic
SMF determinist

detersión SF cleansing

detestable ADJ [*persona*] hateful; [*costumbre*] detestable; [*sabor, tiempo*] foul

detestablemente ADV detestably

detestación SF detestation, hatred, loathing

detestar ▹ CONJUG 1a VT to detest, loathe

detonación SF (= *acción*) detonation; (= *ruido*) explosion

detonador SM detonator

detonante ADJ explosive
SM **1** (= *explosivo*) explosive
2 (= *causa*) trigger (**de** for) • **eso fue el ~ de la crisis** that was what sparked off *o* triggered the crisis

detonar ▹ CONJUG 1a VI to detonate, explode

detracción SF disparagement

detractor(a) ADJ disparaging
SM/F detractor

detraer ▹ CONJUG 2o VT **1** (= *quitar*) to remove, separate, take away
2 (= *desviar*) to turn aside
3 (= *denigrar*) to disparage; (*Pol*) to knock‡

detrás ADV **1** (= *en la parte posterior*) • **el jardín está ~** the garden is at the back • **tiene una cremallera ~** it has a zip at the back • **en el coche me gusta sentarme ~** when I'm in the car I like to sit in the back • **los más altos que se pongan ~** can the tallest ones please stand at the back? • **yo estaba delante y él ~** I was in front and he was behind • **de ~**: • **el asesino salió de ~** the murderer came out from behind • **los alumnos de ~ estaban fumando** the pupils at the back were smoking • **por ~**: • **la atacaron por ~** she was attacked from behind • **siempre critica a sus amigos por ~** he's always criticizing his friends behind their backs • **la foto lleva una dedicatoria (por) ~** the photo has a dedication on the back
2 (= *a continuación*) • **primero el apellido y ~ el nombre** first the surname and then the forename • **paso yo delante y tú vienes ~** I'll go first and you follow • **entraron en el cuarto uno ~ de otro** they went into the room one after the other
3 • **~ de** behind • **~ del edificio** behind the building • **¿quién está ~ de este complot?** who's behind this plot?, who's behind all this? • **Susana anda ~ de Antonio** Susana's after Antonio • **por ~ de** behind • **dos puestos por ~ del Atlético** two places behind Atlético • **la carretera pasa por ~ del parque** the road goes behind the park
4 • **~ mío/tuyo** (*esp LAm**) behind me/you • **se colocó ~ nuestro** he stood behind us

detrasito* ADV (*LAm*) behind

detrimente ADJ detrimental

detrimento SM detriment • **lo hizo sin ~ de su dignidad** he did it without detriment to his dignity • **en ~ de algo** to the detriment of sth

detrito SM, **detritus** SM **1** (*Geol*) detritus
2 (= *desechos*) debris

detuve *etc* ▹ **detener**

deuda SF **1** (= *obligación*) debt • **una ~ de gratitud** a debt of gratitude • **estar en ~ con algn** (= *estar agradecido*) to be indebted to sb
2 (*Com*) debt • **contraer ~s** to get into debt • **estar lleno de ~s** to be heavily in debt • **estar en ~ con algn** (= *deber dinero*) to be in debt to sb ▸ **deuda a largo plazo** long-term debt ▸ **deuda exterior, deuda externa** foreign debt ▸ **deuda incobrable** bad debt ▸ **deuda morosa** bad debt ▸ **deuda pública** national debt, public borrowing ▸ **deudas activas** assets ▸ **deudas pasivas** liabilities
3 (*Rel*) • **perdónanos nuestras ~s** forgive us our trespasses *o* sins

deudo/a SM/F relative

deudor(a) ADJ **1** • **saldo ~** debit balance
2 • **le soy muy ~** I am greatly indebted to you
SM/F debtor ▸ **deudor(a) hipotecario/a** mortgager ▸ **deudor(a) moroso/a** slow payer

deuterio SM (*Quím*) deuterium

devalar ▹ CONJUG 1a VI (*Náut*) to drift off course

devaluación SF devaluation

devaluado ADJ **1** [*moneda*] devalued, devaluated (EEUU)
2 [*concurso, competición*] debased, devalued, devaluated (EEUU)

devaluar ▹ CONJUG 1e VT to devalue, devaluate (EEUU)

devaluatorio ADJ • **tendencia devaluatoria** tendency to depreciate, tendency to lose value

devanadera SF (*Cos*) reel, spool

devanado SM (*Elec*) winding

devanador SM (= *carrete*) spool, bobbin

devanar ▹ CONJUG 1a VT **1** [+ *hilo*] to wind
2 [*araña, gusano*] to spin
VPR **devanarse 1** • **~se los sesos** to rack one's brains
2 (*Méx*) • **~se de dolor** to double up with pain • **~se de risa** to double up with laughter

devanear ▹ CONJUG 1a VI to rave, talk nonsense

devaneo SM **1** (= *frusleria*) idle pursuit
2 (= *amorío*) flirtation
3 (*Med*) delirium

devastación SF devastation

devastador ADJ devastating

devastadoramente ADV devastatingly

devastar ▹ CONJUG 1a VT to devastate

devengado ADJ (*Econ*) [*intereses*] accrued; [*sueldo*] due, outstanding

devengar ▹ CONJUG 1h VT **1** [+ *intereses*] to yield, pay
2 [+ *sueldo*] (= *ganar*) to earn; (= *tener que cobrar*) to be due

devengo SM **1** (= *beneficio*) amount earned
2 devengos (= *ingresos*) income (*sing*)

devenir ▹ CONJUG 3r VI • **~ en algo** to become sth, turn into sth
SM **1** (= *movimiento progresivo*) process of development • **una nación en perpetuo ~** a nation which is changing all the time, a nation in a constant process of development
2 (= *transformación*) transformation

deveras (*Méx*) ADV ▹ **veras**
SF INV • MODISMO: • **de (a) ~**: • **un amigo de (a) ~** a true *o* real friend • **eso no es querer a alguien de (a) ~** that's not true *o* real love

devoción SF **1** (*Rel*) devotion, devoutness • **la ~ a esta imagen** the veneration of this image • **con ~** devoutly; ▹ **santo**
2 (= *admiración*) devotion (**a** to) • **sienten ~ por su madre** they are devoted to their mother • **tener gran ~ a algn** to be absolutely devoted to sb • **tener por ~ hacer algo** to be in the habit of doing sth • MODISMO: • **estar a la ~ de algn** to be completely under sb's thumb
3 (= *práctica religiosa*) devotion, religious observance

devocional ADJ devotional

devocionario SM prayer book

devolución SF **1** [*de algo prestado, robado*] return • **nos pidió por escrito la ~ de los libros** he wrote asking for the books to be returned • **consiguieron la ~ de las joyas** they managed to get the jewels back
2 (*Com*) [*de compra*] return; [*de dinero*] refund • **exigimos la ~ del dinero** we demand a refund • **"no se admiten devoluciones"** "no refunds will be given", "no goods returnable" • **sin ~** non-returnable

▸ **devolución de derechos** (*Econ*) drawback ▸ **devolución de impuestos** tax refund
3 (*Jur, Pol*) [*de poder, territorio*] devolution
4 [*de favor, visita*] return

devolver ▹ CONJUG 2h (PP: **devuelto**) (VT)
1 (= *retornar*) [+ *algo prestado, robado*] to give back, return; [+ *carta, llamada, pelota, golpe*] to return; [+ *polizón, refugiado*] to return, send back • **¿cuándo tienes que ~ esos libros?** when do you have to take back *o* return those books? • **consiguió que le devolvieran las joyas** he managed to get the jewels back • **leyó la nota y se la devolvió** she read the note and handed *o* gave it back to him • **si nos devuelve el envase le descontamos 50 céntimos** if you bring back *o* return the container you'll get a 50-cent discount • **"devuélvase al remitente"** "return to sender" • **le devolvió la bofetada** she slapped him back • **devuelve el florero a su sitio** put the vase back in its place • MODISMOS: • **~ la pelota a algn** to give sb tit for tat • **~ mal por bien** to return bad for good
2 (*Com*) **a** (= *rechazar*) [+ *producto, mercancía*] (*en mano*) to take back, return; (*por correo*) to send back, return • **devolvió el abrigo a la tienda** he took the coat back to the shop, he returned the coat to the shop • **si a su hijo no le gusta lo puede ~** if your son doesn't like it you can return it *o* bring it back • **si desea ~lo, usted se hace cargo de los gastos del envío** if you choose to send it back *o* return it you have to pay the postage
b (= *reembolsar*) [+ *dinero*] (*de una compra*) to refund, give back; (*de un préstamo*) to pay back • **si no está satisfecho con la compra le devolvemos su dinero** if you are not satisfied with your purchase we will refund your money *o* give you your money back • **¿cuándo me vas a ~ el dinero que te presté?** when are you going to pay me back *o* give me back the money I lent you? • **la máquina me devolvía las monedas** the machine rejected my coins
c [+ *cambio*] to give, give back • **me tiene que ~ cuatro euros** you have to give me back four euros, you owe me four euros • **estoy esperando que me devuelva el cambio** I'm waiting for my change • **"no devuelve cambio"** "no change given"
d (*Econ*) [+ *cheque sin fondos*] to return
3 (= *corresponder*) [+ *cumplido, favor*] to return • **¿cuándo me vais a ~ la visita?** when are you going to pay a return visit *o* to return the visit? • **¿cómo podría ~te este favor?** how can I ever return this favour?
4 (= *restituir*) **a** [+ *salud, vista*] to restore, give back • **un sueñecito te ~á la energía** a nap will give you your energy back
b (*a su estado original*) to restore • **el nuevo tratado ha devuelto la paz a la zona** the new treaty has restored peace to the area • **el sonido del teléfono me devolvió a la realidad** the sound of the telephone brought me back to reality
5 (*liter*) [+ *imagen*] to reflect • **el espejo nos devolvía una imagen distorsionada** the mirror reflected a distorted image of us
6 (= *vomitar*) to bring up
(VI) (= *vomitar*) to be sick • **creo que voy a ~** I think I'm going to be sick
(VPR) **devolverse** (*LAm*) (= *regresar*) to turn back

devónico (ADJ) Devonian
(SM) • **el ~** the Devonian

devorador (ADJ) [*pasión*] devouring; [*fuego*] all-consuming; [*hambre*] ravenous

devorar ▹ CONJUG 1a (VT) **1** (= *comer ávidamente*) [*animal*] to devour; [*persona*] to devour, wolf down* • **este coche devora los kilómetros** this car eats up the miles • **devora las novelas de amor** she laps up love stories • **la devoraba con la mirada** (*con cólera*) he looked at her as if he could kill her; (*con deseo*) he devoured her with his eyes
2 (= *destruir*) [+ *fortuna*] to run through • **todo lo devoró el fuego** the fire consumed everything • **lo devoran los celos** he is consumed with jealousy

devotamente (ADV) devoutly

devoto/a (ADJ) **1** (*Rel*) [*persona*] devout; [*obra*] devotional • **ser muy ~ de un santo** to have a special devotion to a saint • MODISMO: • **ser ~ de la Virgen del puño** (*hum*) to be tight-fisted
2 (= *apegado, fiel*) devoted (**de** to) • **su ~ amigo** your devoted friend • **su ~ servidor** (*frm*) your devoted servant • **es muy ~ de ese café** he is a big fan of that café
(SM/F) **1** (*Rel*) devout person • **los ~s** the faithful; (*en iglesia*) the congregation (*sing*)
2 (= *aficionado*) devotee • **la artista y sus ~s** the artist and her devotees *o* fans • **los ~s del ajedrez** devotees of chess

devuelto (PP) *de* **devolver**
(SM)* sick, vomit

devuelva *etc* ▹ **devolver**

dextrosa (SF) dextrose

deyección (SF) (*tb* **deyecciones**) **1** (*Med*) (= *acto*) motion; (= *heces*) excretion
2 (*Geol*) [*de avalancha*] debris; [*de erupción volcánica*] ejecta (*pl*)

deyectar ▹ CONJUG 1a (VT) (*Geol*) to deposit, leave, lay down

D.F. (ABR) (*Méx*) = **Distrito Federal**

Dg (ABR) = **decagramo(s)**

dg (ABR) (= **decigramo(s)**) dg

D.G. (ABR) **1** = **Dirección General**
2 (= **Director General**) DG

DGS (SF ABR) (*Esp*) **1** (= **Dirección General de Seguridad**) *national police headquarters*
2 (= **Dirección General de Sanidad**) ≈ Department of Health

DGT (SF ABR) **1** = **Dirección General de Tráfico**
2 = **Dirección General de Turismo**

dho. (ABR) (= **dicho**) aforesaid

di *etc* ▹ **dar, decir**

día (SM) **1** (= *período de 24 horas*) day • **pasaré un par de días en la playa** I'll spend a couple of days at the beach • **todos los días** every day • **pollitos de un día** day-old chicks • **a los pocos días** within *o* after a few days, a few days later • **día a día** day in day out, day by day • **prefiero el día a día** I prefer to do things from one day to the next *o* on a day-to-day basis • **el día a día en la gestión financiera de la empresa** the day-to-day running of the company's financial business • **siete veces al día** seven times a day • **tres horas al día** three hours a day • **al otro día** the following day • **al día siguiente** the following day • **ese problema es ya de días** that's an old problem • **menú del día** today's menu • **pan del día** fresh bread • **de día en día** from day to day • **día (de) por medio** (*LAm*) every other day, on alternate days • **ocho días** a week • **quince días** a fortnight • **un día sí y otro no** every other day • **día tras día** day after day • MODISMOS: • **a días** at times • **cuatro días** a couple of days, a few days • **todo el santo día** the whole blessed day • **no tener más que el día y la noche** not to have two pennies to rub together ▸ **día azul** (*Ferro*) *cheap ticket day* ▸ **día de asueto** day off ▸ **día de ayuno** fast day ▸ **día de boda** wedding day ▸ **día de detención** quiet day ▸ **día de diario, día de entresemana** weekday ▸ **día de fiesta** holiday, public holiday ▸ **día de inactividad** quiet day ▸ **día de la banderita** flag day ▸ **Día de la Hispanidad** Columbus Day (*12 October*) ▸ **día de la Madre** Mother's Day ▸ **Día de la Raza** = Día de la Hispanidad ▸ **día del espectador** *day each week when cinema tickets are discounted* ▸ **día del Juicio (Final)** Judgment Day • **estaremos aquí hasta el día del Juicio** (*iró*) we'll be here till Kingdom come ▸ **Día de los Difuntos** All Souls' Day, Day of the Dead ▸ **día de los enamorados** St Valentine's Day ▸ **día de los inocentes** ≈ April Fools' Day (*1 April*) ▸ **Día de (los) Muertos** (*Méx*) All Souls' Day, Day of the Dead ▸ **día de paga** pay day ▸ **Día de Reyes** Epiphany (*6 January*) ▸ **día de trabajo** working day ▸ **día de tribunales** *day on which courts are open* ▸ **día de vigilia** day of abstinence ▸ **día feriado, día festivo** holiday, public holiday ▸ **día franco** (*Mil*) day's leave ▸ **día hábil** working day ▸ **día inhábil** non-working day ▸ **día laborable** working day ▸ **día lectivo** teaching day ▸ **día libre** day off ▸ **día malo, día nulo** off day ▸ **días de gracia** (*Com*) days of grace ▸ **día señalado** (*gen*) special day; (*en calendario*) red-letter day ▸ **día útil** working day, weekday; ▹ DÍA DE LOS (SANTOS) INOCENTES, DÍA DE REYES
2 (= *no noche*) daytime • **durante el día** during the day(time) • **en pleno día** in broad daylight • **hace buen día** the weather's good today, it's a fine day • **¡buenos días!** • **¡buen día!** (*Cono Sur*) good morning! • **dar los buenos días a algn** to say good morning to sb • **de día** by day, during the day • **duerme de día y trabaja de noche** he sleeps by day and works by night, he sleeps during the day and works at night • **ya es de día** it's already light • **mientras sea de día** while it's still light • **día y noche** night and day
3 (= *fecha*) date • **¿qué día es hoy?** (*del mes*) what's the date today?; (*de la semana*) what day is it today? • **iré pronto, pero no puedo precisar el día** I'll be going soon, but I can't give an exact date • **llegará el día dos de mayo** he'll arrive on the second of May • **hoy, día cinco de agosto** today, fifth August • **día lunes/martes** *etc* (*LAm*) Monday/Tuesday *etc* • **el día de hoy** today • **el día de mañana** (*lit*) tomorrow; (*fig*) at some future date
4 (= *momento sin precisar*) • **algún día** some day • **un buen día** one fine day • **cada día es peor** it's getting worse every day *o* by the day • **un día de estos** one of these days • **el día menos pensado** when you least expect it • **en los días de la reina Victoria** in Queen Victoria's day, in Queen Victoria's times • **cualquier día (de estos)** one of these days • **cualquier día tendrá un accidente** he's going to have an accident one of these days *o* any day now • **¡cualquier día!** (*iró*) not on your life! • **cualquier día viene** (*iró*) we'll be waiting till the cows come home for him to turn up • **¡cualquier día te voy a comprar una casa!** if you think I'm going to buy you a house you've got another think coming! • **en nuestros días** nowadays • **la prensa de nuestros días** today's press, the press these days • **uno de los principales problemas de nuestros días** one of the major problems of our day *o* our times • **ha durado hasta nuestros días** it has lasted to the present day • **otro día** some other day, another day • **dejémoslo para otro día** let's leave it for the moment *o* for another day • **¡hasta otro día!** so long! • MODISMOS: • **de un día para otro** any day now • **en días de Dios** *o* **del mundo** *o* **de la vida** never • **en su día** (*referido*

al futuro) in due course; *(referido al pasado)* in its/their *etc* day • **¡tal día hará un año!*** a fat lot I care!*; ▸ **hoy**
5 *(= actualidad)* • **del día** *[estilo]* fashionable, up-to-date; *(= fresco)* • **pescado del día** fresh fish • **estar al día** *(= actualizado)* to be up to date; *(= de moda)* to be with it • **quien quiera estar al día en esta especialidad, que lea …** anyone who wishes to keep up to date with this area of study, should read … • **está al día vestir así** it's the thing to dress like that • **poner al día** *[+ texto, contabilidad]* to bring up to date; *[+ base de datos]* to update; *[+ diario]* to write up • **ponerse al día (en algo)** to get up to date (with sth) • **vivir al día** to live from one day to the next
diabetes SF INV diabetes
diabético/a ADJ, SM/F diabetic
diabla SF, **diablesa** SF she-devil
• MODISMO: • **a la ~** carelessly, any old how*
diablillo* SM little devil, little monkey
• **esta niña es un ~** this girl is a little imp
diablo SM 1 *(= demonio)* devil • **el ~ tentó a Jesús** the Devil tempted Jesus • **no le hagas caso, es un pobre ~** don't pay any attention to him, the poor devil • MODISMOS: • **como un ~***: • **esta mesa pesa como un ~** this table weighs a ton* • **del ~** *o* **de mil ~s***: • **hace un frío del ~** *o* **de mil ~s** it's hellishly cold*, it's absolutely freezing • **¡~s!** *o* **¡por todos los ~s!*** damn it!‡, oh hell!‡ • **donde el ~ perdió el poncho** *(Cono Sur*)* in some godforsaken spot*, in the back of beyond* • **irse al ~***: • **el proyecto se fue al ~** the project was a miserable failure, the project failed miserably • **¡vete al ~!** get lost!* • **mandar al ~***: • **no podía arreglarlo y lo mandé al ~** I couldn't fix it so I chucked it the hell away* • **se enfadó y nos mandó al ~** he got mad and told us to go to hell* • REFRÁN: • **más sabe el ~ por viejo que por ~** there's no substitute for experience ▸ **diablos azules** *(LAm)* DTs*, pink elephants*; ▸ **demonio**
2* *(como intensificador)* • **¿cómo ~s se le ocurrió hacer tal cosa?** what on earth *o* what the hell made him do such a thing?* • **¿quién ~s te crees que eres?** who on earth *o* who the hell do you think you are? • **¡qué ~s! ¡yo también quiero ser rico!** damn it, I want to be rich too!*
3 *(Cono Sur) (= carro)* heavy oxcart
diablura SF 1 *(= travesura)* prank
2 **diabluras** *(= maldades)* mischief *(sing)*
diabólicamente ADV diabolically, fiendishly
diabólico ADJ *[palabras, rito]* diabolic, satanic; *(= malvado)* diabolical; *(= muy difícil)* fiendishly difficult • **tiene una escritura diabólica** his writing is fiendishly hard to understand
diábolo SM diabolo
diacho* SM *(euf)* = **diablo**
diaconato SM deaconry, diaconate
diaconía SF 1 *(= distrito)* deaconry
2 *(= casa)* deacon's house
diaconisa SF deaconess
diácono SM deacon
diacrítico ADJ diacritic, diacritical • **signo ~** diacritic, diacritical mark
diacrónico ADJ diachronic
Diada SF *Catalan national day (11 September)*

diadema SF 1 *(para el pelo)* diadem
2 *(= de joyas)* tiara
diafanidad SF *[de cristal, agua]* transparency; *[de tejido]* filminess
diáfano ADJ 1 *(= translúcido)* *[agua]* crystal-clear, crystalline *(liter)*; *[cristal]* translucent; *[tela]* diaphanous
2 *[argumento, explicación]* crystal-clear • **es ~ que …** it is absolutely clear that …
3 *[espacio]* open
diafragma SM 1 *(Anat)* diaphragm
2 *(= anticonceptivo)* diaphragm, cap
3 *(Fot)* diaphragm
diagnosis SF INV diagnosis
diagnóstica SF diagnostics *(sing)*
diagnosticar ▸ CONJUG 1g VT to diagnose
diagnóstico ADJ diagnostic
SM diagnosis ▸ **diagnóstico precoz** early diagnosis
diagonal ADJ, SF diagonal • **traza una ~** draw a diagonal line
diagonalmente ADV diagonally
diagrama SM diagram ▸ **diagrama circular** pie chart ▸ **diagrama de barras** bar chart ▸ **diagrama de bloques** block diagram ▸ **diagrama de dispersión** scatter diagram ▸ **diagrama de flujo** flow chart
dial SM *(Aut, Radio)* dial
dialectal ADJ dialectal, dialect *(antes de s)*
dialectalismo SM 1 *(= carácter)* dialectal nature, dialectalism • **un texto lleno de ~** a text containing a lot of dialect
2 *(= palabra)* dialectalism, dialect word *o* phrase *etc*
dialéctica SF 1 *(= enfrentamiento)* dialectic
2 *(Fil)* dialectics *(pl)*
dialécticamente ADV dialectically
dialéctico ADJ dialectical
dialecto SM dialect
dialectología SF dialectology
dialectólogo/a SM/F dialectologist
diálisis SF INV dialysis
dialogado ADJ • **solución** *o* **salida dialogada** negotiated settlement
dialogante ADJ open to dialogue *o (EEUU)* dialog, willing to discuss
SMF participant *(in a discussion)* • **mi ~** the person I was talking to
dialogar ▸ CONJUG 1h VT to write in dialogue *o (EEUU)* dialog form
VI *(= conversar)* to have a conversation • **~ con algn** to engage in a dialogue *o (EEUU)* dialog with sb
diálogo SM 1 *(= conversación)* conversation; *(Pol)* dialogue • MODISMOS: • **~ de sordos**: • **fue un ~ de sordos** nobody listened to what anyone else had to say, it was a dialogue of the deaf • **ser un ~ para besugos** to be a fatuous exchange ▸ **diálogo norte-sur** North-South dialogue
2 *(Literat)* dialogue, dialog *(EEUU)*
diamante SM 1 *(= joya)* diamond • **una pulsera de ~s** a diamond bracelet
• MODISMO: • **ser un ~ en bruto** to be a rough diamond ▸ **diamante de imitación** imitation diamond ▸ **diamante en bruto** uncut diamond ▸ **diamante falso** paste
2 **diamantes** *(Naipes)* diamonds
diamantífero ADJ diamond-bearing
diamantina SF *(Méx)* glitter
diamantino ADJ 1 *(= de diamante)* diamond-like, adamantine
2 *(= reluciente)* glittering
diamantista SMF 1 *(Téc)* diamond cutter
2 *(Com)* diamond merchant
diametral ADJ diametrical
diametralmente ADV diametrically • **~ opuesto a algo** diametrically opposed to sth
diámetro SM diameter • **faros de gran ~** wide-angle headlights ▸ **diámetro de giro** *(Aut)* turning circle
Diana SF Diana
diana SF 1 *(= centro de blanco)* bull's-eye • **dar en la ~** *o* **hacer ~** *(lit)* to score a bull's-eye; *(fig)* to hit home
2 *[de dardos]* dartboard
3 *(Mil)* reveille • **tocar ~** to sound reveille
diantre SM • **¡diantre!*** *(euf)* dash it! • **los había como un ~** *(Cono Sur)* there were the devil of a lot of them, there were loads of them
diapasón SM *(Mús)* 1 *(= tono)* *(al afinar)* diapason range; *[de voz]* tone • **bajar el ~** to lower one's voice • **subir el ~** to raise one's voice
2 *(= instrumento)* *(para afinar)* tuning fork; *(de violín, guitarra)* fingerboard ▸ **diapasón normal** tuning fork
diapositiva SF 1 *(Fot)* slide ▸ **diapositiva en color** colour slide, color slide *(EEUU)*
2 *[de vidrio]* lantern slide
diarero SM *(Arg, Uru)* paperboy
diariamente ADV daily, every day
diariero SM *(Arg)* paperboy
diario ADJ 1 *(= todos los días)* daily • **tienen peleas diarias** they have arguments every day • **gastos ~s** everyday expenses
2 *(= cada día)* a day • **cien dólares ~s** a hundred dollars a day
ADV *(LAm)* every day, daily
SM 1 *(= periódico)* newspaper, daily ▸ **diario de la mañana** morning paper ▸ **diario dominical** Sunday paper ▸ **diario hablado** *(Radio)* news, news bulletin ▸ **diario matinal** morning paper ▸ **diario vespertino** evening paper
2 *(= libro)* diary ▸ **diario de a bordo** logbook ▸ **diario de entradas y salidas** *(Com)* daybook ▸ **diario de navegación** logbook ▸ **diario de sesiones** parliamentary report
3 *(Econ)* daily expenses *(pl)*
4 • **a ~** daily • **de** *o* **para ~** everyday • **nuestro mantel de ~** our everyday tablecloth
diarismo SM *(LAm)* journalism
diarista SMF 1 *[de libro diario]* diarist
2 *(LAm)* *[de periódico]* newspaper owner
diarrea SF diarrhoea, diarrhea *(EEUU)*
diarrucho* SM *(LAm)* rag* • **los ~s** the gutter press
diáspora SF *(= dispersión)* diaspora • **la ~** *(Hist)* the Diaspora
diatónico ADJ diatonic
diatriba SF diatribe, tirade
dibujante SMF 1 *(Arte)* *(gen)* draughtsman/draughtswoman, draftsman/draftswoman *(EEUU)*; *[de cómics, dibujos animados]* cartoonist; *[de esbozos]* sketcher; *[de moda]* designer ▸ **dibujante de publicidad** commercial artist
2 *(Téc)* draughtsman/draughtswoman, draftsman/draftswoman *(EEUU)*
dibujar ▸ CONJUG 1a VT 1 *(Arte)* to draw, sketch
2 *(Téc)* to design
3 *(= describir)* to sketch, describe
VPR **dibujarse** 1 *(= perfilarse)* to be outlined **(contra** against)
2 *[emoción]* *(de forma permanente)* to show; *(de forma temporal)* to appear • **el sufrimiento se dibujaba en su cara** suffering showed in his

DIADA NACIONAL DE CATALUNYA

The **Diada**, or Catalonia's national day, is celebrated on 11 September to commemorate the fall of Barcelona to the Bourbon Philip V in 1714 at the end of the War of the Spanish Succession. Prior to this Catalonia had enjoyed a high degree of autonomy which it lost, along with its government, the **Generalitat**. For the **Diada** streets and balconies all over Catalonia are decked out with the Catalan flag with its four red stripes on a gold background.

face • **una sonrisa se dibujó en sus labios** a smile appeared on his lips
dibujo SM **1** (= *actividad*) drawing ▸ **dibujo lineal, dibujo técnico** technical drawing
2 (= *representación gráfica*) (*Arte*) drawing; (*Téc*) design; (*en periódico*) cartoon ▸ **dibujo al carbón** charcoal drawing ▸ **dibujo a pulso** freehand drawing ▸ **dibujo del natural** drawing from life ▸ **dibujos animados** cartoons
3 (*en papel, tela*) pattern • **con ~ a rayas** with a striped pattern ▸ **dibujo escocés** tartan, tartan design
4 (= *descripción*) description, depiction
dic. ABR, **dic.**[e] ABR (= **diciembre**) Dec
dicción SF **1** (= *pronunciación*) diction
2 (= *palabra*) word
diccionario SM dictionary ▸ **diccionario bilingüe** bilingual dictionary ▸ **diccionario de bolsillo** pocket dictionary ▸ **diccionario enciclopédico** encyclop(a)edic dictionary ▸ **diccionario geográfico** gazetteer
diccionarista SMF lexicographer, dictionary maker
dicha SF **1** (= *felicidad*) happiness • **para completar su ~** to complete her happiness • **es una ~ poder** ... it is a happy thing to be able to ...
2 (= *suerte*) good luck • **por ~** fortunately
dicharachería SF wittiness, raciness
dicharachero/a ADJ **1** (= *gracioso*) witty
2 (= *parlanchín*) talkative
SM/F **1** (= *gracioso*) wit
2 (= *parlanchín*) chatterbox
dicharacho SM coarse remark
dicho VB (*pp de* **decir**) • **o ~ de otro modo** ... or, putting it another way, ..., or, in other words ... • **con esto queda todo ~** that says it all • **bueno, lo ~** OK, then • **dejar algo ~** • **le dejó ~ lo que tenía que hacer antes de irse** she gave him instructions as to what he should do before leaving • **antes de morir dejó ~ que la casa era para su hijo** before dying he gave instructions for the house to go to his son • **~ y hecho** no sooner said than done • **o mejor ~** or rather • **~ sea de paso** incidentally, by the way; ▸ **propiamente**
ADJ (= *este*) this • **quieren reformar la ley y para ~ propósito** ... they wish to reform the law and to this end ... • **y en la cuarta de dichas cartas** ... and in the fourth of these letters ... • **vamos a hablar de Cáceres: dicha ciudad fue construida en** ... and now we come to Caceres: the city was built in ... • **dicha compañía fue disuelta en 1994** this *o* the said company was dissolved in 1994
SM **1** (= *máxima popular*) saying • **como dice el ~** as the saying goes • REFRÁN: • **del ~ al hecho hay mucho trecho** saying is one thing, doing it is another
2 (= *comentario*) remark • **un ~ desafortunado** an unfortunate remark
3 dichos (*Rel*) betrothal pledge • **tomarse los ~s** to exchange promises of marriage
dichosamente ADV luckily, fortunately
dichoso ADJ **1** (= *feliz*) happy • **hacer ~ a algn** to make sb happy • **me siento ~ de hacer algo** I feel privileged to do sth
2 (= *afortunado*) lucky, fortunate • **¡~s los ojos!** how nice to see you!
3* blessed • **¡aquel ~ coche!** that blessed car!
diciembre SM December; ▸ **septiembre**
diciendo *etc* ▸ **decir**
dicotomía SF dichotomy
dictablanda SF (*hum*) kindly dictatorship, benevolent despotism
dictado SM **1** dictation • **escribir al ~** to take dictation • **escribir algo al ~** to take sth down (*as it is dictated*)
2 dictados (= *imperativos*) dictates • **los ~s de la conciencia** the dictates of (one's) conscience
3 (= *título*) honorific title
dictador(a) SM/F dictator
dictadura SF dictatorship
dictáfono SM Dictaphone®
dictamen SM **1** (= *informe*) report • **emitir un ~** to issue a report ▸ **dictamen contable** (*Méx*) auditor's report ▸ **dictamen facultativo** (*Med*) medical report ▸ **dictamen pericial** (*Jur*) expert (witness's) report
2 (= *opinión*) opinion; (*Jur*) legal opinion • **tomar ~ de algn** to consult with sb
dictaminar ▸ CONJUG 1a VT [+ *juicio*] to pass • **aún no han dictaminado la hora de la muerte** they haven't yet established the time of death
VI to pass judgment, give an opinion (en on)
dictar ▸ CONJUG 1a VT **1** [+ *carta, texto*] to dictate (a to)
2 (*Jur*) [+ *sentencia*] to pass, pronounce; [+ *decreto*] to issue
3 (= *indicar*) to suggest, dictate • **lo que dicta el sentido común** what common sense suggests *o* dictates
4 (*LAm*) [+ *clase*] to give; [+ *conferencia*] to give, deliver • **~ las noticias** (*Radio, TV*) to read the news
VI to dictate • **~ a su secretaria** to dictate to one's secretary
dictatorial ADJ dictatorial
dictatorialmente ADV dictatorially
dicterio SM taunt
didáctica SF didactics (*sing*) • **departamento de ~** (*Univ*) education department
didácticamente ADV didactically
didacticismo SM didacticism
didáctico ADJ didactic
didactismo SM = **didacticismo**
Dido SF Dido
diecinueve ADJ INV, PRON, SM (*gen*) nineteen; (*ordinal, en la fecha*) nineteenth • **le escribí el día ~** I wrote to him on the nineteenth; ▸ **seis**
dieciochesco ADJ eighteenth-century (*antes de s*)
dieciocho ADJ INV, PRON, SM (*gen*) eighteen; (*ordinal, en la fecha*) eighteenth • **le escribí el día ~** I wrote to him on the eighteenth; ▸ **seis**
dieciochoañero/a ADJ, SM/F eighteen-year-old
dieciséis ADJ INV, PRON, SM (*gen*) sixteen; (*ordinal, en la fecha*) sixteenth • **a las ~ horas** at sixteen hundred hours • **le escribí el día ~** I wrote to him on the sixteenth; ▸ **seis**
dieciseisavo ADJ, PRON sixteenth
SM • **~s de final** *in a tournament, the penultimate round before the quarter-finals*
diecisiete ADJ INV, PRON, SM (*gen*) seventeen; (*ordinal, en la fecha*) seventeenth • **le escribí el día dieciséis** I wrote to him on the seventeenth; ▸ **seis**
dieldrina SF dieldrin
diente SM **1** (*Anat*) [*de persona, caballo*] tooth; [*de elefante*] tusk; [*de reptil*] fang • **echar los ~s** to teethe • **lavarse** *o* **cepillarse los ~s** to clean *o* brush one's teeth • **le están saliendo los ~s** he's teething ▸ **diente canino** canine, canine tooth ▸ **diente cariado** decayed tooth, bad tooth ▸ **diente de leche** milk tooth ▸ **diente incisivo** incisor ▸ **diente molar** molar ▸ **dientes postizos** false teeth
2 • MODISMOS: • **estar a ~** to be ravenous • **decir algo para ~s afuera** to say one thing and mean another, say sth without meaning it • **enseñar los ~s** to show one's claws, turn nasty • **entre ~s**: • **hablar entre ~s** to mumble, mutter • **se le oía maldecir entre ~s** you could hear him cursing under his breath • **hincar el ~ en** [+ *comida*] to bite into; [+ *asunto*] to get one's teeth into • **nunca pude hincarle el ~ a ese libro** I could never get my teeth into that book • **pelar el ~** (*LAm**) to smile affectedly • **poner a algn los ~s largos** to make sb green with envy • **se me ponen los ~s largos** I get green with envy • **tener buen ~** to be a hearty eater • REFRÁN: • **más cerca están mis ~s que mis parientes** charity begins at home
3 (*Téc*) [*de máquina*] cog; [*de peine, sierra*] tooth; [*de hebilla*] tongue
4 (*Bot*) [*de ajo*] clove ▸ **diente de león** dandelion
diera *etc* ▸ **dar**
diéresis SF INV diaeresis
dieron ▸ **dar**
diesel SM **1** (*tb* **motor diesel**) diesel engine • **un (coche) ~** a diesel (car)
2 (= *combustible*) diesel
dieseléctrico ADJ diesel-electric
diestra SF right hand • **siéntate a mi ~** sit on my right
diestramente ADV **1** (= *hábilmente*) skilfully, skillfully (*EEUU*), deftly
2 (= *astutamente*) shrewdly; (*pey*) cunningly
diestro ADJ **1** (= *derecho*) right • MODISMO: • **a ~ y siniestro** left, right and centre • **repartir golpes a ~ y siniestro** to throw out punches left, right and centre
2 (= *hábil*) skilful, skillful (*EEUU*); (*con las manos*) handy
3 (= *astuto*) shrewd; (*pey*) sly
SM **1** (*Taur*) matador
2 (= *espadachín*) expert swordsman; (*en esgrima*) expert fencer
3 (= *correa*) bridle
4 (*Dep*) right-hander
dieta SF **1** (*Med*) diet • **la ~ mediterránea** the Mediterranean diet • **estar a ~** to be on a diet ▸ **dieta blanda** soft-food diet ▸ **dieta equilibrada** balanced diet ▸ **dieta láctea** milk diet
2 (*Pol*) diet, assembly
3 dietas (*de comida, viajes*) subsistence allowance (*sing*), expenses
4 (*And*) (= *guiso*) stew
dietario SM engagement book
dietética SF dietetics (*sing*)
dietético/a ADJ dietetic, dietary • **restaurante ~** restaurant for people on a diet • **alimento ~** diet food
SM/F dietician
dietista SMF dietician
diez ADJ INV, PRON, SM ten; (*ordinal, en la fecha*) tenth • **las ~** ten o'clock • **un ~ para Pérez** ten out of ten for Pérez • **le escribí el día ~** I wrote to him on the tenth • **hacer las ~ de últimas** (*Naipes*) to sweep the board; (*fig*) to queer one's own pitch, damage one's own cause; ▸ **seis**
diezmar ▸ CONJUG 1a VT to decimate
diezmillo SM (*Méx*) sirloin steak
diezmo SM tithe
difamación SF **1** (*al hablar*) slander (**de** of)
2 (*por escrito*) libel (**de** on)
difamador(a) ADJ [*palabra*] slanderous; [*escrito*] libellous, libelous (*EEUU*)
SM/F (*al hablar*) slanderer; (*por escrito*) libeller, libeler (*EEUU*)
difamar ▸ CONJUG 1a VT **1** (*Jur*) (*al hablar*) to slander; (*por escrito*) to libel
2 (= *calumniar*) to slander, malign
difamatorio ADJ [*palabras, afirmación*] slanderous, defamatory; [*artículo, escrito*] libellous, libelous (*EEUU*), defamatory
diferencia SF **1** (= *distinción*) difference • no

d

veo ~ entre el original y la copia I can't see any difference between the original and the copy • **va mucha ~ entre este libro y el anterior** there's a world of difference between this book and the previous one • **no debes hacer ~s entre tus hijos** you shouldn't discriminate between your children • **a ~ de** unlike • **a ~ de sus hermanas, ella es bajita** unlike her sisters, she's quite short • **con ~** by far • **Rosa es, con ~, la más guapa** Rosa is by far the prettiest, Rosa is the prettiest by a long way ▸ **diferencia salarial** (*Com*) wage differential, pay differential
2 (= *intervalo*) difference, gap • **hay una ~ de edad de diez años entre ellos** there's an age difference *o* age gap of ten years between them, there's ten years' difference in age between them • **llegaron con una ~ de diez minutos** they arrived ten minutes apart
3 (= *desacuerdo*) • **ya han resuelto sus ~s** they've patched up their differences • **existen ~s en el partido con respecto al aborto** there are differences of opinion within the party on the issue of abortion • **partir la ~** (*frm*) to split the difference
4 (= *resto*) difference • **pagué la ~ en efectivo** I paid the difference in cash • **halla la ~ entre las dos cantidades** find the difference between the two amounts

diferenciable ADJ distinguishable

diferenciación SF differentiation

diferenciador ADJ distinguishing

diferencial ADJ [*rasgos*] distinguishing; [*ecuación*] differential; [*impuesto*] discriminatory
SM (*Aut*) differential
SF (*Mat*) differential

diferenciar ▸ CONJUG 1b VT **1** (= *hacer diferencias*) to distinguish, differentiate • **no sabe ~ entre uno y otro** she can't distinguish *o* differentiate between the two • **no sabe ~ entre el bien y el mal** he can't distinguish between good and evil
2 (= *hacer diferente*) to make different
3 (= *variar*) to vary the use of, alter the function of
4 (*Mat*) to differentiate
VPR **diferenciarse 1** (= *ser diferente*) to differ, be different (**de** from) • **no se diferencian en nada** they do not differ at all • **se diferencian en que …** they differ in that …
2 (= *destacarse*) to stand out • **este producto se diferencia por su calidad** this product stands out because of its quality

diferendo SM difference, disagreement

diferente ADJ **1** (= *distinto*) different • **dos personas completamente ~s** two completely different people • **ser ~ de** *o* **a algn/algo** to be different to *o* from sb/sth • **mi enfoque es ~ del** *o* **al tuyo** my approach is different to *o* from yours • **eso me da igual, ~ sería que no me invitaran a la fiesta** I don't mind about that, it would be different if they didn't invite me to the party
2 • **~s** (= *varios*) various, several • **por aquí han pasado ~s personalidades** various *o* several celebrities have been here

diferentemente ADV differently

diferido ADJ • **emisión en ~** (*Radio, TV*) recorded programme, recorded program (*EEUU*) • **el partido se retransmitirá en ~ esta noche a las diez** a recording of the match will be broadcast at ten o'clock tonight

diferir (*frm*) ▸ CONJUG 3i VI **1** (= *discrepar*) to differ, disagree • **~ de algo** to disagree with sth • **difiero de todo lo que dijo** I disagree with everything he said • **~ de algn en algo** to differ with sb over sth • **difiero de mi tutor en el método a aplicar** I differ with my tutor over which method to apply
2 (= *ser diferente*) to be different, differ • **las dos declaraciones difieren en pequeños detalles** the two statements differ in some minor details, the two statements are different with regard to some minor details
VT **1** (= *aplazar*) to defer • **quieren ~ el pago hasta el año 2010** they want to defer payment until the year 2010
2 (= *enviar*) to refer • **han diferido el caso al Tribunal Supremo** the case was referred to the Supreme Court

difícil ADJ **1** (= *complicado*) [*problema*] difficult; [*tiempos, vida*] difficult, hard; [*situación*] difficult, delicate • **es ~ de hacer** it's difficult *o* hard to do • **es ~ que venga** he is unlikely to come • **me resulta muy ~ decidir** I find it very hard to decide, I have great difficulty in deciding • **creo que lo tiene ~** I think he's going to find it difficult
2 [*persona*] difficult • **es un hombre ~** he's a difficult man to get on with • **un niño ~** a difficult child
3* [*cara*] ugly

difícilmente ADV **1** (= *con dificultad*) with difficulty
2 (= *apenas*) • **~ se podrá hacer** we'll be hard-pressed to do it • **aquí ~ va a haber para todos** there's unlikely to be enough of this for everybody • **~ se alcanza eso** that is unlikely to be reached

dificultad SF **1** (= *obstáculo*) difficulty • **sin ~ alguna** without the least difficulty
2 (= *problema*) difficulty • **no hay ~ para aceptar que …** there is no difficulty about accepting that … • **tuvieron algunas ~es para llegar a casa** they had some trouble getting home • **ha tenido ~es con la policía** he's been in trouble with the police • **camina con ~** he has difficulty walking
3 (= *objeción*) objection • **poner ~es** to raise objections • **me pusieron ~es para darme el pasaporte** they made it difficult *o* awkward for me to get a passport

dificultar ▸ CONJUG 1a VT **1** (= *obstaculizar*) [+ *camino*] to obstruct; [+ *tráfico*] to hold up
2 (= *hacer difícil*) [+ *trabajo*] to make difficult; [+ *progreso*] to hinder, stand in the way of; [+ *movimientos*] to restrict • **las restricciones dificultan el comercio** the restrictions hinder trade *o* make trade difficult • **~ que suceda algo** to make it unlikely that sth will happen

dificultoso ADJ **1** (= *difícil*) difficult, hard
2 [*persona*] difficult, awkward
3* [*cara*] ugly

difracción SF diffraction

difractar ▸ CONJUG 1a VT to diffract

difteria SF diphtheria

difuminadamente ADV sketchily

difuminado ADJ vague

difuminar ▸ CONJUG 1a VT [+ *dibujo, contorno*] to blur
VPR **difuminarse 1** • **~se en algo** to fade into sth
2 (= *disiparse*) to fade away

difumino SM stump

difundir ▸ CONJUG 3a VT **1** (= *extender*) [+ *calor, luz*] to diffuse; [+ *gas*] to give off
2 (= *propagar*) [+ *programa, imagen*] to broadcast, transmit; [+ *teoría, ideología*] to spread, disseminate • **~ una noticia** to spread a piece of news
VPR **difundirse 1** [*calor, luz*] to become diffused
2 [*teoría*] to spread

difunto/a ADJ deceased • **el ~ ministro** the late minister
SM/F deceased, deceased person • **la familia del ~** the family of the deceased; ▹ **día**

difusión SF **1** [*de calor, luz*] diffusion
2 [*de noticia, teoría*] dissemination, spreading
3 (*Periodismo*) [*de programa*] broadcasting; [*de periódico*] circulation, readership figures (*pl*) • **los medios de ~** the media • **un diario de ~ nacional** a national newspaper

difuso ADJ **1** [*luz*] diffused
2 [*conocimientos*] vague, hazy
3 [*estilo, explicación*] wordy

difusor ADJ • **el medio ~** (*Radio*) the broadcasting medium
SM [*de pelo*] blow-drier

diga *etc* ▹ **decir**

digerible ADJ digestible

digerir ▹ CONJUG 3i VT **1** [+ *comida*] to digest • **no puedo ~ a ese tío*** I can't stomach that guy*
2 [+ *opinión, noticia*] to absorb, assimilate • **le ha costado ~ su fracaso** he's found it hard to take in his failure

digestible ADJ digestible

digestión SF digestion • **hacer la ~** to digest one's food, digest ▸ **digestión anaerobia** anaerobic digestion

digestivo ADJ digestive
SM digestive

digesto SM (*Jur*) digest

digitación SF (*Mús*) fingering

digital ADJ **1** [*ordenador, reloj*] digital
2 (= *dactilar*) finger (*antes de s*) • **huellas ~es** fingerprints
SF **1** (*Bot*) foxglove
2 (= *droga*) digitalis

digitalizador SM (*Inform*) digitizer

digitalizar ▹ CONJUG 1f VT to digitize

digitalmente ADV digitally

dígito SM (*Mat, Inform*) digit ▸ **dígito binario** binary digit, bit ▸ **dígito de control** check digit

diglosia SF diglossia

dignación SF condescension

dignamente ADV **1** (= *con dignidad*) with dignity, in a dignified way
2 (= *apropiadamente*) fittingly, properly
3 (= *honradamente*) honourably, honorably (EEUU)
4 (= *decentemente*) decently

dignarse ▹ CONJUG 1a VPR **1** • **~ a hacer algo** to deign to do sth, condescend to do sth
2 (*frm*) • **dígnese venir a esta oficina** please be so kind as to come to this office

dignatario/a SM/F dignitary

dignidad SF **1** (= *cualidad*) dignity
2 (*de sí mismo*) self-respect • **herir la ~ de algn** to offend sb's self-respect
3 (= *rango*) rank • **tiene ~ de ministro** he has the rank of a minister

dignificante ADJ dignifying

dignificar ▹ CONJUG 1g VT to dignify

digno ADJ **1** (= *merecedor*) • **~ de elogio** praiseworthy • **~ de mención** worth mentioning • **~ de toda alabanza** thoroughly praiseworthy, highly commendable • **es ~ de nuestra admiración** it deserves our admiration • **es ~ de verse** it is worth seeing
2 [*persona*] (= *honesto*) honourable, honorable (EEUU); (= *circunspecto*) dignified
3 (= *decoroso*) decent • **viviendas dignas para los obreros** decent homes for the workers

digresión SF digression

dije¹ ▹ **decir**

dije² SM **1** (= *relicario*) locket
2 (= *amuleto*) charm

dije³* ADJ (*Cono Sur*) **1** (= *guapo*) good-looking
2 (= *encantador*) nice, sweet

dilación SF delay • **sin ~** without delay, immediately • **esto no admite ~** we cannot

allow any delay in this matter, this matter is most urgent
dilapidación SF squandering, waste
dilapidar ▸ CONJUG 1a VT to squander, waste
dilatable ADJ expandable
dilatación SF **1** (*Med*) dilation
2 (*Fís*) expansion
dilatado ADJ **1** [*pupila*] dilated
2 (= *extenso*) [*conocimiento*] extensive; [*período*] long
dilatar ▸ CONJUG 1a VT **1** (= *extender*) [+ *pupila*] to dilate; [+ *metales*] to expand
2 [+ *fama*] to spread
3 (= *prolongar*) to protract, prolong
4 (= *retrasar*) to delay
VPR **dilatarse 1** (= *extenderse*) [*pupila*] to dilate; [*cuerpo, metal*] to expand • **la llanura se dilata hasta el horizonte** the plain stretches right to the horizon • **el valle se dilata en aquella parte** the valley spreads out *o* widens at that point
2 (*al hablar*) to be long-winded
3 (*LAm*) (= *tardar*) • **~se en hacer algo** to take a long time to do sth, be slow to do sth
4 (*CAm, Méx*) (= *retrasarse*) to be delayed, be late
dilatorias SFPL delaying tactics • **andar en ~ con algn** • **traer a algn en ~** to use delaying tactics with sb, hedge with sb • **no me vengas con ~** don't hedge with me
dilatorio ADJ delaying • **andar con ~** to drag things out
dildo SM dildo
dilección SF affection
dilema SM dilemma • **estar en un ~** to be in a dilemma
diletante SMF dilettante
diligencia SF **1** (= *cualidad*) (= *esmero*) diligence; (= *rapidez*) speed
2 (= *encargo*) errand • **hacer las ~s de costumbre** to take the usual steps • **practicar sus ~s para hacer algo** to make every possible effort to do sth, do one's utmost to do sth
3 (*Jur*) **diligencias** formalities ▸ **diligencias judiciales** judicial proceedings ▸ **diligencias policiales** police inquiries ▸ **diligencias previas** inquest (*sing*)
4 (= *carruaje*) stagecoach
diligenciado SM, **diligenciamiento** SM processing
diligenciar ▸ CONJUG 1b VT [+ *asunto*] to deal with; [+ *documento, solicitud*] to take steps to obtain
diligente ADJ **1** (= *esmerado*) diligent • **poco ~** slack
2 (= *rápido*) speedy
diligentemente ADV **1** (= *esmeradamente*) diligently
2 (= *con rapidez*) speedily
dilucidar ▸ CONJUG 1a VT **1** (= *aclarar*) [+ *asunto*] to elucidate, clarify; [+ *misterio*] to clear up
2 [+ *concurso*] to decide
dilución SF dilution
diluido ADJ [*líquido, sustancia*] diluted, dilute; [*café, té*] weak
diluir ▸ CONJUG 3g VT **1** [+ *líquido, sustancia*] to dilute
2 (= *aguar*) to water down
VPR **diluirse** to dissolve
diluvial ADJ torrential
diluviar ▸ CONJUG 1b VI to pour with rain
diluvio SM flood • **el Diluvio Universal** the Flood • **un ~ de cartas** a flood *o* deluge of letters • **¡fue el ~!** it was chaos! • **¡esto es el ~!** what a mess!
dimanar ▸ CONJUG 1a VI • **~ de algo** to arise from sth, spring from sth

dimensión SF **1** (= *magnitud*) dimension • **la cuarta ~** the fourth dimension
2 dimensiones (= *tamaño*) size (*sing*) • **de grandes dimensiones** large • **tomar las dimensiones de algo** to take sth's measurements • **las dimensiones de la tragedia** the extent of the tragedy
3 (= *importancia*) stature, standing • **un matemático de ~ universal** a mathematician of international stature *o* standing
dimensionado SM measuring
dimensionar ▸ CONJUG 1a VT to measure
dimes SMPL • **~ y diretes** (= *riñas*) bickering (*sing*), squabbling (*sing*); (= *chismes*) gossip (*sing*) • **andar en ~ y diretes con algn** to bicker with sb, squabble with sb
diminutivo ADJ, SM diminutive
diminuto ADJ tiny, diminutive
dimisión SF resignation • **presentar la ~** to hand in *o* submit one's resignation
dimisionar ▸ CONJUG 1a VI, VT = **dimitir**
dimisionario/a ADJ outgoing, resigning
SM/F person resigning, person who has resigned
dimitente ADJ resigning, outgoing, retiring • **el presidente ~** the outgoing chairman, the retiring chairman
SMF person resigning
dimitir ▸ CONJUG 3a VI to resign (**de** from) • **~ de la jefatura del partido** to resign (from) the party leadership • **lo han obligado a ~** he has been forced to resign
VT to resign
dimos ▸ **dar**
din* SM dough‡ • **el din y el don** money and rank, dough and dukedom‡
DINA SF ABR (*Chile*) (= **Dirección de Inteligencia Nacional**) *Chilean secret police (until 1977)*
Dinamarca SF Denmark
dinamarqués/esa ADJ Danish
SM/F (= *persona*) Dane
SM (= *idioma*) Danish
dinámica SF **1** (*Fís*) dynamics (*sing*)
2 (= *funcionamiento*) dynamic • **la ~ de la sociedad** the dynamic of society ▸ **dinámica de grupo** group dynamics (*pl*)
dinamicidad SF dynamism
dinámico ADJ dynamic
dinamismo SM dynamism
dinamita SF dynamite
dinamitar ▸ CONJUG 1a VT to dynamite
dinamitazo SM dynamite explosion
dinamizador ADJ revitalizing
dinamizar ▸ CONJUG 1f VT to invigorate, put new energy into
dinamo SF, **dínamo** SF, (*LAm*) SF dynamo
dinastía SF dynasty
dinástico ADJ dynastic
dinerada SF, **dineral** SM fortune • **habrá costado una ~** it must have cost a bomb *o* fortune
dinerario ADJ money (*antes de s*) • **aportación no dineraria** non-cash contribution
dinerillo* SM small amount of money • **tiene su ~ ahorrado** she's got a bit of money put by
dinero SM money • **¿cuánto es en ~ finlandés?** how much is that in Finnish money? • **andar mal de ~** to be short of money • **el negocio no da ~** the business does not pay • **es hombre de ~** he is a man of means • **el ~ lo puede todo** money can do anything, money talks • **hacer ~** to make money • **tirar el ~** to throw money away • MODISMO: • **ganar ~ a espuertas** *o* **a porrillo** to make money hand over fist • REFRÁN: • **el ~ malo echa fuera al bueno** bad money drives out good ▸ **dinero barato** cheap money, easy money ▸ **dinero caro** dear money, expensive money (*EEUU*) ▸ **dinero contante** cash ▸ **dinero contante y sonante** hard cash ▸ **dinero de bolsillo** pocket money ▸ **dinero de curso legal** legal tender ▸ **dinero electrónico** e-money ▸ **dinero en caja** cash in hand ▸ **dinero en circulación** currency, money in circulation ▸ **dinero negro** undeclared money ▸ **dinero para gastos** pocket money ▸ **dinero sucio** dirty money, money from crime ▸ **dinero suelto** loose change
dingui SM dinghy
dinosaurio SM dinosaur
dintel SM lintel
diñar* ▸ CONJUG 1a VT • **~la** to kick the bucket* • **diñársela a algn** to swindle sb
dio ▸ **dar**
diocesano ADJ diocesan
diócesis SF INV diocese
diodo SM diode
dionisiaco ADJ, **dionisíaco** ADJ Dionysian
Dionisio SM Denis; (*Mit*) Dionysius
dioptría SF dioptre, diopter (*EEUU*) • **¿cuántas ~s tienes?** what's your gradation *o* correction *o* prescription?
Dios SM **1** (*Rel*) God • **el ~ de los judíos** the Jewish God, the God of the Jews • **~ Hijo** God the Son • **~ Padre** God the Father; ▸ **bendición, temor**
2 (*en exclamaciones*) • **¡Dios!** (*con sorpresa*) God!; (*con fastidio*) for God's sake! • **¡~ mío!** • **¡~ santo!** my God!, good God! • **¡alabado sea ~!** praise be to God! • **¡~ te bendiga!** • **¡~ te lo pague!** God bless you! • **¡que ~ nos coja confesados!** God help us! • **¡con ~!** • **¡vaya usted con ~!** (may) God be with you!††, Godspeed!†† • **¡plegue a ~!** please God! • **¡válgame ~!** good God! • **¡vive ~!** by God! • **¡~ me libre!** God forbid!, Heaven forbid! • **¡líbreme ~ de que ...!** God *o* Heaven forbid that I ...! • **¡líbreme ~ de ese sufrimiento!** Heaven forbid that I should suffer so! • **¡por ~!** for heaven's sake! • **—¿puedo fumar? —¡claro, por ~!** "may I smoke?" — "of course! *o* please do!" • **una limosnita ¡por (el amor de) ~!** a few pennies, for the love of God! • **¡~ quiera que no llueva mañana!** let's hope it doesn't rain tomorrow • **¡no lo quiera ~!** God forbid! • **—ojalá te cures pronto —¡~ quiera!** "let's hope you get better soon!" — "I hope so too!" • **¡vaya por ~!** (*con compasión*) oh dear!; (*con fastidio*) oh blast!*; ▸ **bendito**
3 • MODISMOS: • **armar la de ~ (es Cristo)*** to raise hell, cause an almighty row • **a la buena de ~** (= *sin esmerarse*) any old how; (= *sin planificar*) just like that • **¡me cago en ~!**** for Christ's sake!‡, for fuck's sake!** • **costar ~ y ayuda**: • **costó ~ y ayuda convencerlo** it was a real job to persuade him • **dejado de la mano de ~**: • **una casa dejada de la mano de ~** a godforsaken house • **estos pueblos están dejados de la mano de ~** these villages have been abandoned to their fate • **estás dejado de la mano de ~** there's no hope for you • **~ dirá** time will tell • **sin encomendarse a ~ ni al diablo** without thought for the consequences • **estar de ~** to be God's will • **estaba de ~ que pasara** it was God's will that it happened • **como ~ me dio a entender** as best as I could • **a ~ gracias** • **gracias a ~** thank heaven, thank God • **como que hay (un) ~** (*esp Cono Sur*) you can bet on it • **como que hay ~ que ...** you can bet (your bottom dollar) that ... • **como ~ manda** (*con verbo*) properly; (*con sustantivo*)

proper • **¡siéntate como ~ manda!** sit properly! • **a ver si te echas una novia como ~ manda** it's time you got yourself a proper girlfriend • **~ mediante** God willing • **~ mediante nos veremos en mayo otra vez** God willing, we'll see each other again in May • **como ~ lo echó** *o* **trajo al mundo*** stark naked, in one's birthday suit‡ • **un sitio donde ~ pasó de largo** (*hum*) a godforsaken spot • **que ~ me perdone, pero ...** may God forgive me, but ... • **poner a ~ por testigo** to swear by almighty God • **pongo a ~ por testigo que no sabía la verdad** as God is my witness *o* I swear by almighty God, I did not know the truth • **ponerse a bien con ~** to make one's peace with God • **si ~ quiere** God willing • **hasta mañana si ~ quiere** good night, God bless! • **que sea lo que ~ quiera**: • **he decidido hacerlo, y que sea lo que ~ quiera** I've decided to do it, and worry about it later • **sabe ~** God knows • **sabe ~ dónde estará** God knows where he is • **solo ~ sabe lo que he sufrido** God alone knows what I've suffered • **lo vino ~ a ver** he struck lucky, he had a stroke of luck • **que venga ~ y lo vea** may God strike me dead, I'll eat my hat
• REFRANES: • **~ aprieta pero no ahoga** *o* (*Cono Sur*) **ahorca** • **~ castiga pero no a palos** (*Chile*) God shapes the back for the burden • **a ~ rogando y con el mazo dando** (*haciendo el bien*) God helps those who help themselves; (*si no se cumple lo que se dice*) practise what you preach • **~ da pan a quien no tiene dientes** it's a cruel world • **~ los cría y ellos se juntan** birds of a feather flock together; ▹ **clamar, madrugar**

dios(a) SM/F god/goddess • **los ~es paganos** the pagan gods • **comimos como ~es** we ate like kings • MODISMOS: • **no hay ~ que***: • **no hay ~ que entienda eso** no-one on earth could understand that* • **ni ~*** no one • **en el accidente no se salvó ni ~** no one survived the accident • **todo ~*** everyone • **lo sabía todo ~** the world and his wife knew about it*, everyone knew about it • **tienes que pagar como todo ~** you have to pay like everyone else

dióxido SM dioxide ▸ **dióxido de carbono** carbon dioxide ▸ **dióxido de nitrógeno** nitrogen dioxide

dioxina SF dioxin

Dip. ABR = **Diputación**

diploma SM diploma ▸ **diploma olímpico** Olympic diploma

diplomacia SF diplomacy

diplomado/a ADJ qualified
SM/F **1** (= *con diploma*) holder of a diploma
2 (*Univ*) (= *con diplomatura*) graduate

diplomarse ▹ CONJUG 1a VPR (*esp LAm*) to graduate (*from college etc*)

diplomática SF **1** (*Hist, Jur*) diplomatics (*sing*)
2 (= *cuerpo*) diplomatic corps
3 (= *carrera*) diplomatic career, career in the foreign service; ▹ **diplomático**

diplomáticamente ADV diplomatically

diplomático/a ADJ **1** [*carrera, cuerpo*] diplomatic
2 (= *que tiene tacto*) diplomatic, tactful
SM/F diplomat; ▹ **diplomática**

diplomatura SF diploma course; ▹ LICENCIATURA

dipsomanía SF dipsomania

dipsomaníaco/a SM/F, **dipsómano/a** SM/F dipsomaniac

díptero SM dipteran

díptico SM **1** (*Arte*) diptych
2 (*Com*) leaflet

diptongar ▹ CONJUG 1h VT, VI to diphthongize

diptongo SM diphthong

diputación SF **1** (= *delegación*) deputation
2 (*Pol*) ▸ **diputación permanente** standing committee ▸ **diputación provincial** (= *edificio*) ≈ county council offices (*pl*), ≈ county commission offices (*pl*) (*EEUU*); (= *personas*) ≈ county council, ≈ county commission (*EEUU*)

diputado/a SM/F **1** (= *delegado*) delegate
2 (*Pol*) ≈ member of parliament, ≈ representative (*EEUU*) • **el ~ por Guadalajara** the member for Guadalajara ▸ **diputado/a a Cortes** (*Esp*) member of the Spanish Cortes ▸ **diputado/a provincial** ≈ member of a county council, ≈ member of a county commission; ▹ CONGRESO DE LOS DIPUTADOS

diputar ▹ CONJUG 1a VT to delegate, depute

dique SM **1** (= *muro de contención*) (*en río*) dyke, dike (*esp EEUU*); (*en puerto*) dock • **entrar en ~** • **hacer ~** to dock ▸ **dique de contención** dam ▸ **dique flotante** floating dock ▸ **dique seco** dry dock
2 (= *rompeolas*) breakwater
3 (= *impedimento*) • **poner un ~ a algo** to check sth, restrain sth • **es un ~ contra la expansión** it is a barrier to expansion

diquelar‡ ▹ CONJUG 1a VT **1** (= *ver*) to see
2 (= *vigilar*) to watch over, keep an eye on
3 (= *comprender*) to twig*, catch on to

Dir. ABR **1** = **dirección**
2 (= **director**) dir

dire* SMF = director

diré *etc* ▹ **decir**

dirección SF **1** (= *sentido*) direction • **la ~ del viento** the wind direction • **¿podría indicarme la ~ de la playa?** could you show me the way to the beach? • **"dirección prohibida"** "no entry" • **salir con ~ a** to leave for • **salió con ~ desconocida** he left for an unknown destination • **el tráfico con ~ a Barcelona** traffic for Barcelona • **trenes con ~ este** eastbound trains • **ir en ~ contraria** to go the other way • **de dos direcciones** (*Esp*): • **calle de dos direcciones** two-way street • **conmutador de dos direcciones** two-way switch • **ir en ~ a** to go in the direction of, go towards, head for • **el taxi iba en ~ al aeropuerto** the taxi was going in the direction of *o* towards the airport, the taxi was heading for the airport • **el tráfico en ~ a Burgos** traffic for Burgos • **calle de ~ obligatoria** *o* **única** one-way street
2 (= *orientación*) way • **desconozco la ~ que están siguiendo los acontecimientos** I don't know which way events are going
3 (= *señas*) address • **su nombre y ~ completa** your full name and address • **la carta llevaba una ~ equivocada** the letter was wrongly addressed *o* had the wrong address • **poner la ~ a un sobre** to address an envelope ▸ **dirección absoluta** absolute address ▸ **dirección comercial** business address ▸ **dirección de correo electrónico** email address ▸ **dirección de Internet** web address ▸ **dirección del remitente** return address ▸ **dirección electrónica** email address ▸ **dirección IP** IP address ▸ **dirección particular** home address ▸ **dirección postal** postal address ▸ **dirección profesional** business address ▸ **dirección relativa** relative address
4 (= *control*) [*de empresa, hospital, centro de enseñanza*] running; [*de partido*] leadership; [*de película*] direction • **tomar la ~ de una empresa** to take over the running of a company • **le han confiado la ~ de la obra** he has been put in charge of the work • **se ha hecho cargo de la ~ de la orquesta** he's been appointed conductor of the orchestra • **con ~ de Polanski** directed by Polanski ▸ **dirección colectiva, dirección colegiada** (*Pol*) collective leadership ▸ **dirección de escena** stage management ▸ **dirección de orquesta** conducting ▸ **dirección empresarial** business management ▸ **dirección escénica** stage management
5 (= *personal directivo*) • **la ~** [*de empresa, centro escolar*] the management; [*de partido*] the leadership; [*de periódico*] the editorial board • **"prohibido fumar en este local: la dirección"** "smoking is prohibited in this building: the management" • **habrá cambios en la ~ del partido** there will be changes in the party leadership
6 (= *cargo*) (*en colegio*) headship, principalship (*EEUU*); (*en periódico, revista*) editorship; (*en partido*) leadership; [*de gerente*] post of manager; [*de alto cargo*] directorship
7 (= *despacho*) (*en colegio*) headteacher's office, principal's office (*EEUU*); (*en periódico, revista*) editor's office; [*de gerente*] manager's office; [*de alto cargo*] director's office
8 (= *oficina principal*) head office ▸ **Dirección General de Seguridad** State Security Office, State Security Service ▸ **Dirección General de Turismo** State Tourist Office ▸ **dirección provincial** *regional office of a government department*
9 (*Aut, Náut*) steering • **tiene la ~ averiada** the steering is faulty • **mecanismo de ~** steering (mechanism) ▸ **dirección asistida, dirección hidráulica** (*LAm*) power steering

direccional ADJ directional
SFPL **direccionales** (*Col, Méx*) (*Aut*) indicators, turn signals (*EEUU*)

direccionamiento SM (*Inform*) addressing

direccionar ▹ CONJUG 1a VT **1** (*Inform*) to address
2 [+ *máquina, vehículo*] to operate

directa SF (*Aut*) top gear

directamente ADV directly • **fui ~ a casa** I went straight home

directiva SF **1** (= *dirección*) [*de empresa*] board of directors; [*de partido*] executive committee, leadership
2 (*Jur*) directive
3 directivas (= *instrucciones*) guidelines

directivo(a) ADJ [*junta*] managing; [*función*] managerial, administrative; [*clase*] executive
SM/F (*Com*) manager • **un congreso de los ~s de la industria** a conference for industry executives

directo ADJ **1** [*línea*] straight
2 [*pregunta, respuesta, lenguaje*] direct, straightforward • **es muy directa hablando** she's very direct
3 [*tren*] direct, through; [*vuelo*] direct, non-stop
4 • **ir ~ a** to go straight to • **fui directa a la comisaría** I went straight *o* directly to the police station • **el balón fue ~ a portería** the ball went straight into the goal • **este tren va ~ a Granada** this is a through *o* direct train to Granada, this train goes direct to Granada
5 (= *sin intermediario*) direct • **recibo órdenes directas del sargento** I get my orders straight *o* direct from the sergeant
6 (*Ling*) [*complemento, traducción*] direct
7 (*Radio, TV*) • **en ~** live • **una entrevista en ~** a live interview • **transmitir en ~** to broadcast live
SM (*Boxeo*) straight punch; (*Tenis*) forehand drive

director(a) ADJ [*consejo, junta*] governing; [*principio*] guiding
SM/F **1** (= *responsable*) [*de centro escolar*]

headteacher, headmaster/headmistress, principal; [*de periódico, revista*] editor; (*Cine, TV*) director; [*de orquesta*] conductor; [*de hospital*] manager, administrator; [*de prisión*] governor, warden (*EEUU*) ▸ **director(a) artístico/a** artistic director ▸ **director(a) de cine** film director ▸ **director(a) de coro** choirmaster ▸ **director(a) de departamento** (*Univ*) head of department ▸ **director(a) de escena** stage manager ▸ **director(a) de funeraria** undertaker, funeral director, mortician (*EEUU*) ▸ **director(a) de interiores** (*TV*) studio director ▸ **director(a) de orquesta** orchestra conductor ▸ **director(a) de tesis** thesis supervisor, research supervisor
2 (*Com*) (= *gerente*) manager; (*de mayor responsabilidad*) director ▸ **director(a) adjunto/a** assistant manager ▸ **director(a) de empresa** company director ▸ **director(a) de exportación** export manager ▸ **director(a) de finanzas** financial director ▸ **director(a) de sucursal** branch manager ▸ **director(a) ejecutivo/a** executive director, managing director ▸ **director(a) general** general manager ▸ **director(a) gerente** managing director ▸ **director(a) técnico/a** technical manager
SM (*Rel*) ▸ **director espiritual** spiritual director

directorial ADJ (*Com*) managing, executive • **clase ~** managers (*pl*), management class

directorio SM 1 (= *norma*) directive
2 (= *junta directiva*) directors (*pl*), board of directors
3 (*Inform*) directory ▸ **directorio principal** root directory
4 ▸ **directorio de teléfonos, directorio telefónico** (*Méx*) telephone directory

directriz SF 1 (= *norma*) guideline
2 (*Mat*) directrix

dirigencia SF leadership

dirigente ADJ leading • **la clase ~** the ruling class
SMF (*Pol*) leader • **los ~s del partido** the party leaders ▸ **dirigente de la oposición** leader of the opposition

dirigible ADJ (*Aer, Náut*) steerable
SM dirigible, airship, blimp (*EEUU*)

dirigido ADJ [*misil*] guided • **~ a distancia** remote controlled

dirigir ▹ CONJUG 3c VT 1 (= *orientar*) [+ *persona*] to direct; [+ *asunto*] to advise, guide • **lo dirigió con ayuda de un mapa** she showed him the way *o* directed him with the help of a map • **¿por qué no vas tú delante y nos diriges?** why don't you go first and lead the way? • **un asesor le dirige las finanzas** a consultant advises him on his finances • **estos principios dirigen nuestra política** these are the guiding principles behind our policy • **dirigían sus pasos hacia la iglesia** they made their way *o* walked towards the church; ▹ **palabra**
2 (= *apuntar*) [+ *arma, telescopio*] to aim, point (**a, hacia** at); [+ *manguera*] to turn (**a, hacia** on), point (**a, hacia** at) • **dirigió los focos al escenario** he pointed *o* directed the lights towards the stage • **ordenó ~ el fuego hacia el enemigo** he ordered them to direct *o* aim their fire at the enemy
3 (= *destinar*) **a** [+ *carta, comentario, pregunta*] to address (**a** to) • **la carta iba dirigida al director** the letter was addressed to the editor
b [+ *libro, programa, producto*] to aim (**a** at) • **una publicación dirigida al mercado infantil** a publication aimed at the children's market
c [+ *acusación, críticas*] to make (**a, contra** against), level (**a, contra** at, against); [+ *ataques*] to make (**a, contra** against) • **dirigieron graves acusaciones contra el ministro** serious accusations were made against the minister, serious accusations were levelled at *o* against the minister • **le dirigieron fuertes críticas** he was strongly criticized, he came in for some strong criticism
d [+ *esfuerzos*] to direct (**a, hacia** to, towards) • **hay que ~ todos nuestros esfuerzos hacia este fin** we must direct all our efforts to this end
4 (= *controlar*) [+ *empresa, hospital, centro de enseñanza*] to run; [+ *periódico, revista*] to edit, run; [+ *expedición, país, sublevación*] to lead; [+ *maniobra, operación, investigación*] to direct, be in charge of; [+ *debate*] to chair; [+ *proceso judicial*] to preside over; [+ *tesis*] to supervise; [+ *juego, partido*] to referee • **dirige el Departamento de Biología** he runs the Biology Department • **el Partido Comunista dirigió los destinos del país durante siete décadas** the Communist Party controlled the fate of the country for seven decades • **el equipo de jugadores que dirige Muñoz** the team of players led by Muñoz • **dirigió la investigación desde Madrid** he directed the investigation from Madrid • **dirigió mal las negociaciones** he handled the negotiations badly, he mismanaged the negotiations; ▹ **cotarro**
5 (*Cine, Teat*) to direct
6 (*Mús*) [+ *orquesta, concierto*] to conduct; [+ *coro*] to lead • **¿quién ~á el coro?** who will be the choirmaster?, who will lead the choir?
7 (= *conducir*) [+ *coche*] to drive; [+ *barco*] to steer; [+ *caballo*] to lead • **dirigió su coche hacia la izquierda** he steered *o* drove his car towards the left
VPR **dirigirse 1** (= *ir*) • **~se a** *o* **hacia** to head for • **se dirigía a la oficina cuando lo arrestaron** he was on his way to *o* heading for the office when he was arrested • **se dirigió en su coche al aeropuerto** he drove to the airport • **se dirigió hacia él y le dio una bofetada** she went over to him and slapped him
2 (= *ponerse en contacto*) • **~se a algn** (*oralmente*) to speak to sb, address sb (*frm*); (*por escrito*) to contact sb • **el presidente se dirigió a la nación** the president spoke to *o* (*frm*) addressed the nation • **¿se dirige usted a mí?** are you speaking to me? • **"diríjase a ..."** "contact ..." • **me dirijo a usted para solicitarle su ayuda** I am writing (to you) to request your help
3 (= *estar destinado*) • **~se a algo** to be aimed at sth • **el programa se dirige a los adultos** the programme is aimed at *o* geared towards adults • **toda sus esfuerzos van dirigidos a conseguir un nuevo récord** she is concentrating all her efforts on setting a new record

dirigismo SM control ▸ **dirigismo estatal** state control

dirigista ADJ, SMF interventionist

dirimente ADJ [*argumento*] decisive; [*voto*] casting; [*opinión, decisión*] final

dirimir ▹ CONJUG 3a VT 1 [+ *contrato, matrimonio*] to dissolve, annul
2 [+ *disputa*] to settle

discada SF (*LAm*) collection of records

discado SM (*And, Cono Sur*) dialling, dialing (*EEUU*) ▸ **discado directo** direct dialling

discapacidad SF disability ▸ **discapacidad física** physical disability ▸ **discapacidad psíquica** mental disability

discapacitado/a ADJ incapacitated, disabled
SM/F disabled person ▸ **discapacitado/a psíquico/a** mentally disabled person

discapacitar ▹ CONJUG 1a VT to incapacitate, handicap

discar ▹ CONJUG 1g VT (*And, Cono Sur*) to dial

discernidor ADJ discerning, discriminating

discernimiento SM discernment

discernir ▹ CONJUG 3k VT 1 (= *distinguir*) to distinguish, discern • **~ una cosa de otra** to distinguish one thing from another
2 (*Jur*) [+ *tutor*] to appoint
3 (*esp LAm*) [+ *premio*] to award (**a** to)
VI to discern, distinguish (**entre** between)

disciplina SF 1 (= *normas*) discipline • **~ férrea** iron will ▸ **disciplina de partido, disciplina de voto** party discipline, party whip • **romper la ~ de voto** to defy the party whip ▸ **disciplina inglesa** bondage and discipline
2 (*Dep*) discipline • **ganó en la ~ de suelo** she came first in the floor exercises

disciplinado ADJ disciplined

disciplinante SMF (*Rel*) flagellant, penitent

disciplinar ▹ CONJUG 1a VT 1 (= *instruir*) [+ *persona, instintos*] to discipline; [+ *soldados*] to drill
2 (= *azotar*) to whip, scourge

disciplinario ADJ disciplinary

discipulado SM 1 (*Rel*) discipleship
2 (= *personas*) pupils (*pl*), student body

discípulo/a SM/F 1 (*Rel, Fil*) disciple
2 (= *alumno*) pupil, student

discjockey [dis'jokei] SMF disc jockey

Discman® ['disman] SM Discman®

disco[1] SM 1 (*Mús*) record • **siempre está con el mismo ~** • **no cambia de ~*** he's like a cracked record* ▸ **disco compacto** compact disc ▸ **disco de larga duración** long-playing record ▸ **disco de oro** golden disc ▸ **disco de plata** silver disc ▸ **disco de platino** platinum disc ▸ **disco microsurco** long-playing record ▸ **disco sencillo** single
2 (*Inform*) disk ▸ **disco de arranque** startup disk, boot disk ▸ **disco de cabeza fija** fixed-head disk ▸ **disco duro** hard disk ▸ **disco duro externo** external hard drive ▸ **disco fijo** hard disk ▸ **disco flexible, disco floppy** floppy disk ▸ **disco magnético** magnetic disk ▸ **disco óptico** optical disk ▸ **disco rígido** hard disk ▸ **disco virtual** virtual disk
3 (*Dep*) discus
4 (= *señal*) (*Ferro*) signal ▸ **disco rojo** red light ▸ **disco verde** green light
5 ▸ **disco de freno** (*Aut*) brake disc
6 (*Telec*) dial
7 ▸ **disco volante** flying saucer

disco[2]* SF (= *discoteca*) disco

discóbolo/a SM/F discus thrower

discografía SF 1 (= *discos publicados*) records (*pl*) • **toda la ~ de los Beatles** the Beatles' entire back catalogue, all the records released by the Beatles
2 (= *colección*) record collection

discográfica SF record company, record label

discográfico ADJ record (*antes de s*) • **casa discográfica** record company, record label • **éxito ~** chart hit • **el momento ~ actual** the present state of the record industry

díscolo ADJ 1 (= *rebelde*) unruly
2 (= *travieso*) mischievous

disconforme ADJ [*opinión*] differing • **estar ~** to be in disagreement, disagree (**con** with)

disconformidad SF disagreement • **en ~ con el espíritu olímpico** contrary to the Olympic spirit

discontinuidad SF lack of continuity,

discontinuity
discontinuo ADJ discontinuous • **línea discontinua** (*Aut*) broken line
discordancia SF discord • **eso está en ~ con lo que dijo antes** that contradicts what she said earlier
discordante ADJ **1** (*Mús*) discordant
2 [*opiniones*] clashing • **su traje fue la nota ~ en la reunión** his suit stuck out like a sore thumb in the meeting
discordar ▷ CONJUG 1l VI **1** (*Mús*) to be out of tune
2 (= *estar en desacuerdo*) [*personas*] to disagree (**de** with); [*colores, opiniones*] to clash
discorde ADJ **1** (*Mús*) [*sonido*] discordant; [*instrumento*] out of tune
2 [*opiniones*] clashing • **su actitud es ~ con la política del partido** his attitude is out of line with party policy
3 • **estar ~** [*personas*] to disagree (**de** with), be in disagreement (**de** with)
discordia SF discord, disagreement • **sembrar la ~** to sow discord
discoteca SF **1** (= *lugar de baile*) disco, club, nightclub
2 (= *colección de discos*) record collection
3 (*LAm*) (= *tienda*) record shop
discotequero/a ADJ disco (*antes de s*) • **yo no soy muy ~*** I'm not into clubbing *o* going to discos
SM/F nightclubber
discreción SF **1** (= *prudencia*) discretion • **tenemos que actuar con ~** we must act discreetly • **me callé por ~** I tactfully kept quiet
2 • **a ~**: **añadir azúcar a ~** add sugar to taste • **comer a ~** to eat as much as one likes • **con vino a ~** with as much wine as one wants • **¡a ~!** (*Mil*) stand easy! • **rendirse a ~** (*Mil*) to surrender unconditionally
3 • **a ~ de algn** at sb's discretion
discrecional ADJ **1** [*poder*] discretionary
2 (= *facultativo*) optional • **parada ~** request stop, flag stop (*EEUU*) • **servicio ~ de autobuses** private bus service
discrecionalidad SF discretional nature
discrepancia SF **1** (= *diferencia*) discrepancy
2 (= *desacuerdo*) disagreement
discrepante ADJ [*visión, opiniones*] divergent • **hubo varias voces ~s** there were some dissenting voices
discrepar ▷ CONJUG 1a VI **1** (= *estar en desacuerdo*) to disagree (**de** with) • **discrepamos en varios puntos** we disagree on a number of points • **discrepo de esa opinión** I disagree with that view
2 (= *diferenciarse*) to differ (**de** from)
discretamente ADV **1** (= *sin notarse*) discreetly
2 (= *sobriamente*) soberly
3 (= *modestamente*) unobtrusively
discretear ▷ CONJUG 1a VI to try to be clever, be frightfully witty
discreto ADJ **1** (= *poco llamativo*) [*color, vestido*] sober; [*advertencia*] discreet
2 [*persona*] (= *prudente*) discreet; (= *listo*) shrewd
3 (= *mediano*) average, middling • **de inteligencia discreta** reasonably intelligent • **le daremos un plazo ~** we'll allow him a reasonable time • **unas ganancias discretas** modest profits
4 (*Fís*) discrete
discriminación SF discrimination (**contra** against) ▸ **discriminación laboral** discrimination in the workplace ▸ **discriminación positiva** positive discrimination, affirmative action (*EEUU*) ▸ **discriminación racial** racial discrimination ▸ **discriminación sexual** sex discrimination
discriminado ADJ • **sentirse ~** to feel that one has been unfairly treated *o* has been discriminated against
discriminador SM discriminator
discriminar ▷ CONJUG 1a VT **1** [+ *persona, colectivo*] to discriminate against
2 [+ *colores, sabores*] to differentiate between
VI to discriminate (**entre** between)
discriminatoriamente ADV unfairly, in a biased way
discriminatorio ADJ discriminatory
disculpa SF **1** (= *pretexto*) excuse
2 (= *perdón*) apology • **pedir ~s a algn por algo** to apologize to sb for sth
disculpable ADJ excusable, pardonable
disculpar ▷ CONJUG 1a VT (= *perdonar*) to excuse, forgive • **disculpa que venga tarde** forgive me for coming late • **¡discúlpeme!** I'm sorry! • **le disculpan sus pocos años** his youth is an excuse, his youth provides an excuse • **te ruego me disculpes con el anfitrión** please make my apologies to the host
VPR **disculparse** to apologize (**con** to) • **se disculpó por haber llegado tarde** he apologized for arriving late
disculpativo ADJ apologetic
discurrideras* SFPL wits, brains
discurrir ▷ CONJUG 3a VT (= *inventar*) to think up • **esos chicos no discurren nada bueno** these lads are up to no good
VI **1** (= *recorrer*) to roam, wander (**por** about, along)
2 [*río*] to flow
3 [*tiempo*] to pass • **la sesión discurrió sin novedad** the meeting went off quietly • **el verano discurrió sin grandes calores** the summer passed without great heat
4 (= *meditar*) to meditate (**en** about, on) • **discurre menos que un mosquito** he just never thinks
5 (= *hablar*) to discourse (**sobre** about, on)
discursear ▷ CONJUG 1a VI to speechify
discursivo ADJ discursive
discurso SM **1** (= *alocución*) speech • **pronunciar un ~** to make a speech, give a speech • **otra vez me soltó el mismo discursito de siempre** he gave me the same old lecture as always ▸ **discurso de clausura** closing speech
2 (= *forma de hablar*) rhetoric • **su ~ nacionalista** his nationalist rhetoric
3 (= *habla*) speech, faculty of speech • **análisis del ~** discourse analysis
4 [*del tiempo*] • **en el ~ del tiempo** with the passage of time • **en el ~ de cuatro generaciones** in the space of four generations
discusión SF **1** (= *riña*) argument • **eso no admite ~** there can be no argument about that • **tener una ~** to have an argument
2 (= *debate*) discussion • **estar en ~** to be under discussion ▸ **discusión de grupo** group discussion
discutibilidad SF debatable nature
discutible ADJ debatable, arguable • **650 euros ~s** 650 euros o.n.o. • **es ~ si ...** it is debatable *o* arguable whether ... • **de mérito ~** of dubious worth
discutido ADJ **1** (= *hablado*) much-discussed
2 (= *controvertido*) controversial • **su éxito fue discutidísimo** their success was highly controversial
discutidor ADJ argumentative, disputatious
discutir ▷ CONJUG 3a VT **1** (= *debatir*) [+ *plan, proyecto, idea*] to discuss; [+ *precio*] to argue about
2 (= *contradecir*) to question, challenge • **~ a algn lo que está diciendo** to question *o* challenge what sb is saying
VI **1** (= *dialogar*) to discuss, talk
2 (= *disputar*) to argue (**de, sobre** about, over) • **¡no discutas!** don't argue! • **no le discutas porque él sabe más que tú del tema** don't argue with him because he knows more about the subject than you do • **~ de política** to argue about politics, talk politics
discutón* ADJ argumentative
disecado ADJ [*animal, planta*] stuffed; [*planta*] dried
disecar ▷ CONJUG 1g VT **1** (*Med*) to dissect
2 (*para conservar*) [+ *animal*] to stuff; [+ *planta*] to preserve, mount
disección SF **1** (*Med*) dissection
2 (= *de animal*) stuffing; (*de plantas*) preserving, mounting
diseccionar ▷ CONJUG 1a VT to dissect, analyse
diseminación SF [*de ideas*] dissemination; [*de semillas*] scattering ▸ **diseminación nuclear** spread of nuclear weapons
diseminar ▷ CONJUG 1a VT to spread, disseminate (*frm*)
disensión SF disagreement, dissension
disentería SF dysentery
disentimiento SM dissent, disagreement
disentir ▷ CONJUG 3i VI to dissent (**de** from), disagree (**de** with)
diseñador(a) SM/F designer ▸ **diseñador(a) de modas** fashion designer ▸ **diseñador(a) gráfico/a** graphic designer
diseñar ▷ CONJUG 1a VT **1** (*Téc*) to design
2 (*Arte*) to draw, sketch
3 (*con palabras*) to outline
diseño SM **1** (= *actividad*) design • **de ~ italiano** Italian-designed • **camisa de ~** designer shirt • **un asiento con ~ ergonómico** an ergonomically-designed seat ▸ **diseño asistido por ordenador**, **diseño asistido por computador** (*LAm*) computer-aided design ▸ **diseño de interiores** interior design ▸ **diseño de modas** fashion design ▸ **diseño gráfico** graphic design ▸ **diseño industrial** industrial design ▸ **diseño inteligente** intelligent design ▸ **diseño textil** textile design
2 (= *dibujo*) (*Arte*) drawing, sketch; (*Cos*) pattern
disertación SF dissertation
disertar ▷ CONJUG 1a VI to discourse (**acerca de, sobre** upon) • **~ largamente sobre algo** to speak at length about sth
disfavor SM disfavour, disfavor (*EEUU*)
disforme ADJ **1** (= *mal hecho*) ill-proportioned, badly-proportioned
2 (= *monstruoso*) monstrous
disforzado* ADJ (*And*) **1** (= *santurrón*) prim, prudish
2 (= *descarado*) cheeky*, sassy (*EEUU*)
disfraz SM **1** (= *traje*) (*para una fiesta*) fancy dress, costume (*EEUU*); (*para engañar a algn*) disguise • **yo fui a la fiesta con un ~ de pirata** I went to the party dressed as a pirate *o* in a pirate costume • **llevaba un ~ de hombre** she was disguised as a man • **baile de disfraces** fancy-dress ball
2 (= *pretexto*) facade (**de** for) • **bajo el ~ de algo** under the cloak of sth
3 (*Mil*) camouflage
disfrazado ADJ disguised (**de** as) • **ir ~ de algo** (*para ocultar algo*) to masquerade as sth; (*para fiesta*) to dress up as sth
disfrazar ▷ CONJUG 1f VT **1** [+ *persona*] to disguise (**de** as) • **lo ~on de soldado** they disguised him as a soldier
2 (= *ocultar*) [+ *sentimiento, verdad, intención*] to disguise, conceal; [+ *sabor*] to disguise

3 (*Mil*) to camouflage
VPR **disfrazarse** [*persona*] (*para una fiesta*) to dress up (**de** as); (*para ocultarse de algo*) to disguise o.s. (**de** as)
disfrutar ▹ CONJUG 1a VT **1** (= *gozar de*) to enjoy • **espero que disfrutes tus vacaciones** I hope you enjoy your holiday
2 (*frm*) (= *poseer*) to enjoy • **disfruta una posición inmejorable en el mercado** it enjoys an excellent market position
VI **1** (= *gozar*) to enjoy o.s. • **los niños disfrutan en la piscina** the children enjoy themselves in the swimming pool • **disfruté muchísimo hablando con ella** I very much enjoyed talking to her • **¡que disfrutes!** enjoy yourself! • **~ con algo** to enjoy sth • **Juan disfruta con el buen cine** Juan enjoys good films • **~ de algo** to enjoy sth • **tú sabes ~ de la vida** you know how to enjoy life
2 • **~ de algo** (= *poseer*) to enjoy sth • **disfruta de excelente salud** he enjoys excellent health • **disfrutan de una pensión del Estado** they enjoy *o* receive a state pension
disfrute SM enjoyment • **todos tenemos derecho al ~ de unas vacaciones** we all have the right to enjoy *o* have holidays
disfuerzo SM (*And*) **1** (= *descaro*) impudence, effrontery
2 (= *remilgo*) prudishness
3 disfuerzos (= *amenazas*) threats, bravado (*sing*)
disfunción SF malfunction
disfuncionalidad SF malfunction
disgregación SF **1** [*de grupo*] disintegration, breaking up
2 [*de roca*] breaking up
disgregar ▹ CONJUG 1h VT [+ *grupo*] to break up; [+ *manifestantes*] to disperse
VPR **disgregarse** to disintegrate, break up (**en** into)
disgresión SF digression
disgustado ADJ upset • **estar ~ con algn** to be upset with sb • **estar ~ por algo** to be upset about sth
disgustar ▹ CONJUG 1a VT to upset • **comprendí que le disgustaba mi presencia** I realized that my presence upset him • **me disgusta tener que repetirlo** I don't like having to repeat it • **es un olor que me disgusta** it's a smell I don't like • **estaba muy disgustado con el asunto** he was very displeased *o* upset about the matter
VPR **disgustarse 1** (= *enfadarse*) to get upset
2 (= *molestarse*) to be displeased, be offended (**con** about)
3 [*amigos*] to fall out (**con** with)
disgusto SM **1** (= *pena*) • **la noticia me causó un gran ~** I was very upset by the news • **eso te va a costar un ~** that is going to get you into trouble • **vas a darle un ~ a mamá con tan malas notas** Mum's going to be upset about those bad marks of yours • **nunca nos dio un ~** he never caused us any worry *o* trouble • **vas a matar a tu madre a ~s*** you'll be the death of your mother*, you'll send your mother to an early grave* • **—la han despedido —¡qué ~!** "they've fired her" — "that's terrible *o* awful!"
2 (= *riña*) quarrel, row • **como sigas así, tú y yo tendremos un ~** if you carry on like that, we're going to fall out
3 • **a ~**: **hacer algo a ~** to do sth unwillingly • **estar** *o* **sentirse a ~** to be *o* feel ill at ease
disidencia SF **1** (*Pol*) dissidence
2 (*Rel*) dissent
disidente ADJ (*Pol*) dissident
SMF **1** (*Pol*) dissident
2 (*Rel*) dissenter, nonconformist
disidir ▹ CONJUG 3a VI to dissent
disílabo ADJ disyllabic
SM disyllable
disímil ADJ not alike, dissimilar
disimilación SF dissimilation
disimulación SF **1** (= *cualidad*) dissimulation
2 [*de objeto, puerta*] concealment
disimuladamente ADV **1** (= *solapadamente*) furtively
2 (= *astutamente*) cunningly, slyly
3 (= *ocultamente*) covertly
disimulado ADJ **1** (= *solapado*) furtive, underhand
2 (= *astuto*) sly
3 (= *oculto*) covert • **estaba ~ entre unos papeles** it was hidden among some papers
• MODISMO: • **hacerse el ~** to pretend not to notice
disimular ▹ CONJUG 1a VT **1** [+ *emoción, alegría, tristeza*] to hide, conceal • **no pudo ~ lo que sentía** he couldn't hide *o* conceal what he felt
2 [+ *defecto, roto*] to cover up, hide; [+ *sabor, olor*] to hide • **disimuló la mancha con un poco de pintura** she covered up *o* hid the mark with a bit of paint
3† (= *perdonar*) to excuse
VI (= *fingir*) to pretend • **lo sé todo, así que no disimules** I know everything so don't bother pretending • **has sido tú, no disimules** it was you, don't pretend it wasn't • **ahí está Juan: disimula** there's Juan: pretend you haven't seen him
disimulo SM **1** (= *fingimiento*) dissimulation • **con ~** cunningly, craftily
2 (= *tolerancia*) tolerance
disimulón* ADJ furtive, shady
disipación SF [*de costumbres*] dissipation; [*de dinero*] squandering; [*de niebla*] lifting
disipado ADJ **1** (= *libertino*) dissipated
2 (= *derrochador*) extravagant
disipador(a) SM/F spendthrift
disipar ▹ CONJUG 1a VT **1** (*Meteo*) [+ *niebla*] to drive away; [+ *nubes*] to disperse
2 (= *hacer desaparecer*) [+ *duda, temor*] to dispel, remove; [+ *esperanza*] to destroy
3 [+ *dinero*] to squander, fritter away (**en** on)
VPR **disiparse 1** (*Meteo*) [*niebla*] to lift; [*nubes*] to disperse
2 [*dudas*] to be dispelled
disjunto ADJ separate, discrete
diskette SM = **disqueta**
dislate SM **1** (= *absurdo*) absurdity • **eso es un ~** that's an absurd *o* ridiculous thing to do
2 dislates (= *disparates*) nonsense (*sing*) • **un texto cargado de ~s** a text full of nonsense *o* stupid comments
dislexia SF dyslexia
disléxico/a ADJ, SM/F dyslexic
dislocación SF **1** (*Med*) dislocation
2 [*de estado*] dismemberment
dislocado ADJ **1** (*Med*) dislocated
2 (= *alocado*) wild, unrestrained
dislocar ▹ CONJUG 1g VT (*Med*) to dislocate
VPR **dislocarse** (*Med*) • **~se el tobillo** to dislocate one's ankle • **se le ha dislocado el hombro** he has dislocated his shoulder
disloque* SM **1** (= *locura*) • **al llegar la medianoche aquello fue ya el ~** when midnight came it was utter madness • **es el ~** it's the last straw
2 (= *confusión*) confusion
disminución SF **1** (= *reducción*) [*de población, cantidad*] decrease, drop, fall; [*de precios, temperaturas*] drop, fall; [*de velocidad*] decrease, reduction • **una ~ en las importaciones** a drop *o* fall in imports • **la ~ de la capa de ozono** the depletion of the ozone layer • **uno de los síntomas es la ~ de la actividad política** one of the symptoms is a decrease in political activity • **continuar sin ~** to continue unchecked *o* unabated
2 (*Med*) [*de dolor*] reduction; [*de fiebre*] drop, fall
3 (*Cos*) [*de puntos*] decreasing
disminuido/a ADJ **1** (= *achicado*) inadequate • **no me siento ~ ante nadie** there's no one that makes me feel inadequate
2 (*Med*) handicapped
3 (*Econ*) [*intervalo, valor*] diminished
SM/F (*Med*) handicapped person • **un centro para ~s** a centre for the disabled *o* the handicapped ▸ **disminuido/a físico/a** physically handicapped person ▸ **disminuido/a psíquico/a** mentally handicapped person ▸ **disminuido/a visual** visually handicapped person
disminuir ▹ CONJUG 3g VT **1** (= *reducir*) [+ *nivel, precio, gastos, intereses*] to reduce, bring down; [+ *riesgo, incidencia, dolor*] to reduce, lessen; [+ *temperatura*] to lower, bring down; [+ *prestigio, autoridad*] to diminish, lessen; [+ *fuerzas*] to sap; [+ *entusiasmo*] to dampen • **algunos bancos han disminuido en un 0,15% sus tipos de interés** some banks have reduced *o* brought down their interest rates by 0.15% • **hemos tenido que ~ la dosis** we've had to reduce the dose • **las vacunas disminuyen la resistencia a otros virus** vaccinations lower resistance to other germs • **disminuyó la velocidad para tomar la curva** she slowed down *o* reduced her speed to go round the bend • **durante el día disminuyen la vigilancia** security is not so strict during the day • **esta medicina me disminuye las fuerzas** this medicine is making me weaker *o* sapping my strength
2 (*Cos*) [+ *puntos*] to decrease
VI **1** (= *decrecer*) [*número, población*] to decrease, drop, fall; [*temperatura, precios*] to drop, fall; [*distancia, diferencia, velocidad, tensión*] to decrease; [*fuerzas, autoridad, poder*] to diminish; [*días*] to grow shorter; [*luz*] to fade; [*prestigio, entusiasmo*] to dwindle • **ha disminuido la tasa de natalidad** the birth rate has decreased *o* dropped *o* fallen • **el número de asistentes ha disminuido últimamente** attendance has decreased *o* dropped *o* fallen recently • **ya le está disminuyendo la fiebre** his temperature is dropping *o* falling now • **el paro disminuyó en un 0,3%** unemployment dropped *o* fell by 0.3% • **su poder disminuyó con el paso del tiempo** his power diminished as time went by • **con esta pastilla te ~á el dolor** this tablet will relieve *o* ease your pain
2 (= *empeorar*) [*memoria, vista*] to fail
3 (*Cos*) [*puntos*] to decrease
dismorfia SF dysmorphia
dismorfofobia SF body dysmorphic disorder
Disneylandia SF Disneyland
disociable ADJ separable
disociación SF dissociation
disociar ▹ CONJUG 1b VT to dissociate (**de** from)
VPR **disociarse** to dissociate o.s. (**de** from)
disoluble ADJ soluble
disolución SF **1** (= *acto*) dissolution
2 (*Quím*) solution ▸ **disolución de goma** rubber solution
3 (*Com*) liquidation
4 (*moral*) dissoluteness, dissipation
disoluto ADJ dissolute
disolvente SM solvent
disolver ▹ CONJUG 2h (PP: **disuelto**) VT
1 [+ *azúcar, sal*] to dissolve
2 [+ *contrato, matrimonio, parlamento*] to dissolve

3 [+ *manifestación*] to break up; (*Mil*) to disband
VPR **disolverse 1** [*azúcar, sal*] to dissolve
2 (*Com*) to go into liquidation
3 (= *deshacerse*) [*manifestación*] to break up; [*parlamento*] to dissolve

disonancia SF **1** (*Mús*) dissonance
2 (= *falta de armonía*) discord • **hacer ~ con algo** to be out of harmony with sth

disonante ADJ **1** (*Mús*) dissonant
2 (= *discordante*) discordant

disonar ▸ CONJUG 1l VI **1** (*Mús*) to be out of tune
2 (= *no armonizar*) to lack harmony • **~ con algo** to be out of keeping with sth, clash with sth

dísono ADJ discordant

dispar ADJ [*opiniones, aficiones*] different, disparate; [*rendimiento*] inconsistent

disparada SF (*LAm*) **1** (= *salida apresurada*) sudden departure • **ir a la ~** to go at full speed • **irse a la ~** to be off like a shot • **tomar la ~** (*Cono Sur**) to beat it*
2 (= *prisa*) rush

disparadero SM trigger, trigger mechanism • MODISMO: • **poner a algn en el ~** to drive sb to distraction

disparado ADJ **1** (= *con prisa*) • **entrar ~** to shoot in • **ir ~** to go like mad • **salir ~** to shoot out, be off like a shot
2 (*Caribe‡*) randy*, horny‡

disparador ADJ (*Méx**) lavish
SM **1** [*de arma*] trigger
2 (*Téc*) [*de cámara fotográfica*] release; [*de reloj*] escapement ▸ **disparador automático** delayed action release ▸ **disparador de bombas** bomb release

disparar ▸ CONJUG 1a VT **1** [+ *arma de fuego, proyectil, tiro*] to fire; [+ *flecha*] to shoot; [+ *gatillo*] to pull • **le ~on tres balazos** they fired three shots at him
2 (*Dep*) [+ *penalti, falta*] to take
3 (*Fot*) • **para ~ la cámara, aprieta el botón** to take a photograph, press the button • **los paparazzi ~on sus cámaras al verla salir** the paparazzi clicked their cameras when they saw her come out • **dispara el flash, que está oscuro** use the flash, it's dark • **"prohibido disparar el flash"** "no flash photography"
4 [+ *consumo, precio*] • **la subida del petróleo ha disparado la inflación** the rise in oil prices has caused inflation to shoot up
5 (= *hacer saltar*) [+ *alarma*] to trigger, set off; [+ *proceso, reacción*] to spark, spark off
VI **1** (*con un arma*) to shoot, fire • **¡quieto o disparo!** stop or I'll shoot *o* fire! • **los cazadores ~on al ciervo** the hunters shot *o* fired at the deer • **le ~on a la cabeza** they shot *o* fired at his head • **la policía disparó contra los manifestantes** the police fired on *o* shot at the demonstrators • **¡no dispares!** don't shoot! • **el asesino disparó a matar** the murderer shot to kill • **¡disparad!** fire! • **apuntó al blanco y disparó** he aimed at the target and fired
2 (*Dep*) to shoot • **el delantero disparó a puerta** the forward shot at *o* for goal
3 (*Fot*) to shoot • **¡enfoca y dispara!** focus the camera and shoot
4 (*Méx**) (= *gastar mucho*) to spend lavishly
5 = **disparatar**
VPR **dispararse 1** [*arma de fuego*] to go off, fire
2 [*alarma*] to go off
3 [*consumo, precios, inflación*] to shoot up, rocket
4 [*pánico, violencia*] to take hold
5 (*al hablar*) to get carried away*
6 (*LAm*) (= *marcharse*) to rush off, shoot off*

disparatadamente ADV absurdly, nonsensically

disparatado ADJ crazy, nonsensical

disparatar ▸ CONJUG 1a VI **1** (= *decir disparates*) to talk nonsense
2 (= *hacer disparates*) to behave foolishly

disparate SM **1** (= *comentario*) foolish remark • **¡no digas ~s!** don't talk nonsense! • **¡qué ~!** what rubbish!, how absurd!
2 (= *acción*) • **sacar el coche con esta niebla es un ~** taking the car out in this fog is just crazy *o* is a stupid thing to do • **está tan desesperado que es capaz de cualquier ~** he's so desperate he's capable of doing something really stupid
3 (= *error*) blunder • **hiciste un ~ protestando** it was foolish of you to complain
4* • **había un ~ de gente** there were absolutely loads of people • **costar un ~** to cost a ridiculous amount • **reírse un ~** to laugh o.s. silly
5 (*Arquit*) folly

disparejo ADJ **1** (= *diferente*) different
2 (= *desnivelado*) uneven • **los dos cuadros estaban ~s en la pared** the two pictures weren't level with each other on the wall

disparidad SF disparity

disparo SM **1** (= *tiro*) shot • **se oyeron varios ~s** some shooting was heard • **hacer ~s al aire** to fire into the air, shoot into the air ▸ **disparo de advertencia, disparo de intimidación** warning shot; (*Náut*) shot across the bows ▸ **disparo de salida** starting shot ▸ **disparo inicial** [*de cohete*] blast-off
2 (*Dep*) shot • **un buen ~ del delantero** a good shot by the striker
3 (*Mec*) release

dispendiador ADJ free-spending, big-spending

dispendio SM waste

dispendioso ADJ expensive

dispensa SF **1** (= *exención*) exemption (**de** from)
2 (*Rel*) dispensation

dispensabilidad SF dispensable nature

dispensable ADJ dispensable

dispensación SF dispensation

dispensador SM dispenser

dispensadora SF ▸ **dispensadora de monedas** change machine

dispensar ▸ CONJUG 1a VT **1** (= *conceder*) [+ *ayuda*] to give; [+ *honores*] to grant; [+ *atención*] to pay; [+ *acogida*] to give, accord; [+ *receta*] to dispense
2 (= *perdonar*) to excuse • **¡dispénseme usted!** I beg your pardon!, sorry! • **~ que algn haga algo** to excuse sb for doing sth
3 (= *eximir*) to exempt (**de** from), excuse (**de** from) • **~ a algn de una obligación** to excuse sb from an obligation • **me ~on del pago de la multa** they waived my fine, they excused me from payment of the fine • **~ a algn de hacer algo** to excuse sb from doing sth • **le han dispensado de hacer gimnasia** he's been excused from doing gymnastics • **así el cuerpo queda dispensado de ese esfuerzo** thus the body is freed from that effort *o* relieved of that effort
VPR **dispensarse** • **no puedo ~me de esa obligación** I cannot escape that duty

dispensario SM **1** (= *clínica*) community clinic
2 (*en hospital*) outpatients' department

dispepsia SF dyspepsia

dispéptico ADJ dyspeptic

dispersar ▸ CONJUG 1a VT [+ *multitud, grupo*] to disperse, scatter; [+ *manifestación*] to break up; [+ *enemigo*] to rout
VPR **dispersarse** [*multitud, grupo*] to disperse, scatter; [*manifestación*] to break up

dispersión SF **1** (= *acto*) [*de grupo, multitud*] dispersion; [*de manifestación*] breaking up; [*de energía, neutrones*] diffusion
2 (= *resultado*) dispersal

disperso ADJ **1** (= *diseminado*) scattered, dispersed • **~s en *o* por** scattered across *o* over
2 [*discurso, mente*] unfocused, unfocussed

displicencia SF **1** (= *mal humor*) peevishness
2 (= *desgana*) lack of enthusiasm • **trató a sus invitados con ~** he treated his guests in an offhand manner

displicente ADJ **1** (= *malhumorado*) peevish
2 (= *poco entusiasta*) unenthusiastic
3 (= *despreciativo*) offhand, disdainful

disponer ▸ CONJUG 2q (PP: **dispuesto**) VT
1 (= *colocar*) (*por orden*) to arrange; (*en fila*) to line up; (*de otro modo*) to set out • **dispuso los discos por orden alfabético** he arranged the records in alphabetical order • **dispuso a los niños de dos en dos** he lined up the children in twos • **dispuso los cubiertos sobre la mesa** he set out the cutlery on the table • **dispón las sillas en círculo** set out *o* arrange the chairs in a circle
2 (= *preparar*) to prepare, get ready • **dispuso la sala para el concierto** he prepared the hall *o* he got the hall ready for the concert • **~ la mesa** to lay the table
3 (= *mandar*) **a** [*persona, comisión*] to order; [*juez*] to rule, decree, order • **dispuso cerrar todas las puertas** he ordered all the doors to be shut • **el general dispuso que no saliera nadie** the general gave orders that *o* ordered that nobody was to go out • **el médico dispuso que guardara cama** the doctor ordered that she should stay in bed • **se dispuso que debía abandonar el país** it was decreed that he should leave the country • **mis padres lo han dispuesto así** my parents have decided that it should be that way • **el juez ha dispuesto que tenía que pagar la multa** the judge ruled *o* decreed *o* ordered that he must pay the fine
b (*en código, testamento*) to lay down, stipulate • **el artículo 52 dispone que ...** Article 52 lays down *o* stipulates that ... • **dispuso que su patrimonio no fuera dividido** she laid down *o* stipulated that her estate should not be divided
VI **1** • **~ de algo** (= *tener*) to have sth (at one's disposal) • **no dispongo de dinero suficiente** I don't have enough money (at my disposal) • **disponemos de muy poco tiempo** there is very little time available (to us), we have very little time (at our disposal) • **los medios de que disponemos** the means available to us, the means at our disposal • **dispone de coche propio** he has his own car • **dispone de quince días para apelar** you have fifteen days to appeal
2 • **~ de algo** (= *hacer uso de*) to make use of sth, use sth • **no puede ~ de esos bienes hasta que él muera** she cannot make use of *o* use those assets until his death • **puede ~ de mí para lo que necesites** I am at your disposal for whatever you might need
VPR **disponerse 1** • **~se a hacer algo** (= *estar a punto de*) to be about to do sth; (= *decidir*) to resolve to do sth • **en ese momento nos disponíamos a salir** at that moment we were about to go out • **me dispuse a cumplir con mi deber** I resolved to do my duty
2 (= *colocarse*) • **~se para algo** to get into position for sth • **los coches se disponían para la salida** the cars were getting into position for the start

disponibilidad SF **1** [*de persona, producto*] availability • **empleado en ~** unposted employee, employee available for posting
2 disponibilidades (*Com*) resources, liquid

assets • **~es líquidas** available liquid assets

disponible ADJ **1** (= *libre*) [*asiento, habitación, dinero*] available; [*tiempo*] spare • **quedan varias plazas ~s** there are various seats available • **no nos queda ninguna habitación ~** we don't have any vacancies *o* any rooms available • **este mes no tengo tiempo ~** I can't spare *o* I don't have the time this month
2 • **estar ~** [*persona, habitación*] to be available, be free • **si me necesitas, por las tardes estoy ~** if you need me, I'm available *o* free in the afternoons • **¿a qué hora estará ~ la habitación?** what time will the room be available *o* free? • **la casa ya está ~ para que la ocupéis** the house is now ready for you to move in
3 [*militar*] available, available for duty

disposición SF **1** (= *colocación*) [*de muebles, capítulos*] arrangement; [*de casa, habitación*] layout • **la ~ del escenario** the layout of the stage
2 (= *disponibilidad*) disposal • **a ~ de algn** at sb's disposal • **un número de teléfono a ~ del público** a telephone number for public use *o* at the public's disposal • **estamos a tu ~ para lo que haga falta** we are at your disposal for whatever you may need • **puso su cargo a ~ de la asamblea** he offered his resignation to the assembly • **pasar a ~ judicial** to be taken into custody • **tener algo a su ~** to have sth at one's disposal, have sth available
3 (= *voluntad*) willingness • **han demostrado su ~ hacia el diálogo** they have shown their willingness to enter into a dialogue • **estar en ~ de hacer algo** (= *con ánimo de*) to be ready *o* willing to do sth; (= *en condiciones de*) to be in a position to do sth ▸ **disposición de ánimo** frame of mind
4 (= *aptitud*) aptitude, talent (**para** for) • **no tenía ~ para la pintura** he had no aptitude *o* talent for painting
5 (*Jur*) (= *cláusula*) provision; (= *norma*) regulation • **según las disposiciones del código** according to the provisions of the statute • **una ~ ministerial** a ministerial order *o* regulation • **última ~** last will and testament
6 disposiciones (= *medidas*) arrangements • **adoptar** *o* **tomar las disposiciones para algo** to make arrangements for sth

dispositivo SM **1** (*Mec*) (= *aparato*) device; (= *mecanismo*) mechanism ▸ **dispositivo de alimentación** hopper ▸ **dispositivo de arranque** starting mechanism ▸ **dispositivo de seguridad** (= *mecanismo*) safety catch, safety (*EEUU*); (= *medidas*) security measures (*pl*) ▸ **dispositivo intrauterino** intrauterine device, coil ▸ **dispositivo periférico** peripheral device
2 dispositivos (*Mil*) forces ▸ **dispositivos de seguridad** security forces

dispraxia SF dyspraxia

dispuesto PP *de* **disponer**
ADJ **1** (= *preparado*) arranged, ready • **todo está ~ para las elecciones** everything is set *o* arranged *o* ready for the elections • **~ según ciertos principios** arranged according to certain principles • **los platos están ya ~s en la mesa** the plates are already laid out *o* set on the table • **¿estáis ~s para salir?** are you ready to leave?
2 (= *decidido*) willing • **es una persona muy dispuesta** she's always ready and willing • **estar ~ a:** • **estábamos ~s al diálogo** we were willing *o* prepared to discuss the matter • **estoy ~ a ir a juicio si fuera necesario** I am quite prepared to go to court if necessary • **no estoy ~ a que me insulten** I refuse to be insulted • **bien ~** well-disposed • **estaba bien ~ hacia su oferta** he was well-disposed to their offer • **mal ~** ill-disposed • **poco ~** reluctant, unwilling • **parece poco dispuesta a colaborar** she seems reluctant *o* unwilling to cooperate

disputa SF **1** (= *discusión*) dispute, argument • **los asuntos en ~** the matters in dispute *o* at issue • **sin ~** undoubtedly, beyond dispute
2 (= *controversia*) controversy

disputable ADJ disputable, debatable

disputado ADJ [*partido*] close, hard fought

disputador(a) ADJ disputatious, argumentative
SM/F (*Dep*) disputant

disputar ▷ CONJUG 1a VT **1** [+ *partido, encuentro*] to play, contest; [+ *campeonato, liga*] to play
2 (*frm*) • **~ algo a algn** to dispute sth with sb • **le disputamos a mi tío la casa** we disputed the ownership of the house with my uncle, we had a dispute with my uncle over the ownership of the house
VI • **~ por algo** to compete for sth • **cinco candidatos disputan por el puesto** five candidates are competing for the job
VPR **disputarse 1** (= *competir por*) • **ocho escritores se disputan el premio** eight writers are contending *o* competing for the prize • **los hermanos se disputan la casa familiar** the brothers are disputing *o* in dispute over the family house
2 (*Dep*) • **el Mundial se disputó en Francia** the World Cup was played *o* contested in France • **el partido se suspendió cuando se disputaba el minuto cuatro** the match was suspended in the fourth minute of play

disque‡ SM • **darse ~** (*Cono Sur*) to fancy o.s.*

disquería SF (*Caribe*) record shop

disquero ADJ record (*antes de s*)

disqueta SF (*LAm*), **disquete** SM (*Inform*) floppy disk, diskette ▸ **disquete de alta densidad** high density diskette

disquetera SF disk drive • **doble ~** dual floppy drive, double floppy drive ▸ **disquetera externa** external floppy drive

disquisición SF **1** (= *análisis*) disquisition
2 disquisiciones (= *comentarios*) asides, digressions

Dist. ABR **1** (= **distancia**) dist
2 (= **Distrito**) dist

distancia SF **1** (*en el espacio*) distance • **la ~ más corta entre dos puntos** the shortest distance between two points • **¿qué ~ hay entre Sevilla y Granada?** what's the distance between Seville and Granada? • **¿a qué ~ está Madrid de Barcelona?** how far (away) is Madrid from Barcelona?, how far is it from Madrid to Barcelona? • **la tienda está a 50 metros de ~** the shop is 50 metres away • **a tres metros de ~ del suelo** three metres from *o* off the ground • **a ~** from a distance • **el diseño se ve más claro a ~** you can see the design better from a distance • **el mando a ~** the remote control • **la Universidad a ~** ≈ the Open University • **una llamada a larga ~** a long-distance call • **acortar las ~s** to shorten the distance • **la nueva carretera acortará la ~** the new road will shorten the distance • **el Real Madrid ha acortado las ~s con el Barcelona** Real Madrid is closing in on Barcelona, Real Madrid is closing the gap with Barcelona • **ganar ~s** to get ahead, make progress • **guardar** *o* **mantener las ~s** • **mantenerse a ~** to keep one's distance • **marcar ~s:** • **el Atlético marcó ~s con el segundo clasificado** Atlético put some distance between itself and the second-placed team • **quieren marcar ~s con la dirección del partido** they want to distance themselves from *o* set themselves apart from the party leadership • **salvando las ~s:** • **es, salvando las ~s, el Picasso de nuestros días** he's the Picasso of today, give or take some obvious differences ▸ **distancia de despegue** (*Aer*) length of takeoff ▸ **distancia de detención** stopping distance ▸ **distancia de frenado** braking distance ▸ **distancia de seguridad** (*Aut*) safe distance ▸ **distancia focal** focal length
2 (*entre opiniones, creencias*) distance, gap • **hay una insalvable ~ entre los dos partidos** there's an unbridgeable distance *o* gap between the two parties

distanciado ADJ **1** (= *remoto*) remote (**de** from)
2 (= *separado*) widely separated
3 (*en relación afectiva*) • **estamos algo ~s** we are not particularly close • **está distanciada de su familia** she has grown apart from her family • **estamos ~s en nuestras ideas** our ideas are a long way *o* poles apart

distanciador ADJ • **efecto ~** distancing effect

distanciamiento SM **1** (= *acto*) spacing out
2 (= *estado*) remoteness, isolation
3 (= *distancia*) distance • **hay un ~ cada vez mayor entre ellos** they are growing further apart every day ▸ **distanciamiento generacional** generation gap
4 (*Teat, Literat*) distancing effect

distanciar ▷ CONJUG 1b VT **1** [+ *objetos*] to space out, separate
2 [+ *amigos, hermanos*] to cause a rift between
VPR **distanciarse 1** [*dos personas*] to grow apart • **~se de la familia** to grow apart from one's family
2 (*en carrera*) • **consiguió ~se del otro corredor** he managed to put some distance between himself and the other runner

distante ADJ **1** [*lugar*] (= *lejano*) distant; (= *remoto*) far-off, remote • **~ 10km** 10km away
2 [*persona, actitud*] distant

distar ▷ CONJUG 1a VI **1** (*en el espacio*) • **dista cinco kilómetros de aquí** it is five kilometres from here • **¿dista mucho?** is it far?
2 (= *diferir*) • **dista mucho de la verdad** it's very far from the truth, it's a long way off the truth • **disto mucho de aprobarlo** I am far from approving of it

distender ▷ CONJUG 2g VT to distend, stretch • **~ las relaciones entre ambos países** to ease *o* steady relations between the two countries
VPR **distenderse** [*músculos*] to relax; [*relaciones*] to ease, steady

distendido ADJ [*ambiente, charla*] relaxed

distensión SF **1** (= *relajación*) • **ambiente de ~** relaxed atmosphere
2 (*Med*) strain ▸ **distensión muscular** muscle strain
3 (*Pol*) détente

distensivo ADJ conciliatory

dístico SM distich

distinción SF **1** (= *diferencia*) distinction • **hacer una ~ entre ...** to make a distinction between ... • **a ~ de algo** unlike sth, in contrast to sth • **hacer una ~ con algn** to show special consideration to sb • **sin ~:** • **todos serán tratados sin ~** everybody will be treated without distinction • **sin ~ de edad** irrespective *o* regardless of age • **sin ~ de raza** regardless of race, without distinction of race
2 (= *privilegio*) distinction • **le acaban de otorgar una ~ al valor** he was honoured *o* (*EEUU*) honored for his bravery ▸ **distinción**

d

honorífica honour, honor (EEUU)
3 (= *elegancia*) elegance, refinement • **iba vestido con ~** he was elegantly dressed

distingo (SM) **1** (= *salvedad*) reservation • **hacer** *o* **poner ~s a algo** to raise reservations about sth
2 (= *distinción*) subtle distinction

distinguible (ADJ) distinguishable

distinguido (ADJ) **1** (= *destacado*) [*figura*] distinguished; [*artista, escritor*] celebrated; [*alumno*] outstanding • **contamos con la distinguida presencia del premio Nobel de la Paz** we are honoured to have with us the Nobel Peace Prize winner
2 (= *refinado*) [*modales, ropa*] elegant, refined; [*caballero, señora*] distinguished • **una distinguida forma de andar** an elegant *o* refined way of walking • **quisiera pedir a nuestro ~ público ...** I would like to ask our distinguished audience ... • **~ público, les vamos a presentar ...** ladies and gentlemen, allow me to present ...
3 (*frm*) (*en cartas*) • **"Distinguida Sra. Martínez"** "Dear Mrs Martinez" • **"Distinguido Señor"** (*LAm*) "Dear Sir"

distinguir ▹ CONJUG 3d (VT) **1** (= *diferenciar*) **a** (= *ver la diferencia entre*) to distinguish • **no distingo bien los colores** I can't distinguish the colours very well • **no resulta fácil ~ a los mellizos** it is not easy to tell the twins apart, it's not easy to distinguish between the twins • **he puesto una etiqueta en la maleta para ~la** I've put a label on the suitcase to be able to tell it apart from *o* distinguish it from the others • **lo sabría ~ entre un millón** I would know it *o* recognize it anywhere • **¿sabes ~ un violín de una viola?** can you tell *o* distinguish a violin from a viola? • MODISMO: • **no distingue lo blanco de lo negro** he doesn't know his right from his left
b (= *hacer diferente*) to set apart • **lo distingue su capacidad intelectual** his intellect sets him apart • **lo que nos distingue de los animales** what distinguishes us from the animals, what sets us apart from the animals
c (= *hacer una distinción entre*) to distinguish • **hay que ~ dos períodos** we need to distinguish two periods
2 (= *ver*) [+ *objeto, sonido*] to make out • **no podía ~ la matrícula** I couldn't make out the number plate • **ya distingo la costa** I can see *o* make out the coast now
3 (= *honrar*) [+ *amigo, alumno*] to honour, honor (EEUU) • **me distingue con su amistad** I am honoured to have his friendship • **lo distinguieron con el Premio Nobel** he was honoured with the Nobel Prize
4 (= *elegir*) to single out • **lo distinguieron para el ascenso** he was singled out for promotion
(VI) (= *ver la diferencia*) to tell the difference (**entre** between); (= *hacer una distinción*) to make a distinction (**entre** between) • **lo mismo le da un vino malo que uno bueno, no distingue** it's all the same to him whether it's a bad wine or a good one, he can't tell the difference • **no era capaz de ~ entre lo bueno y lo malo** he couldn't tell the difference *o* distinguish between good and bad • **es un hombre que sabe ~** he is a discerning person • **en su discurso, distinguió entre el viejo y el nuevo liberalismo** in his speech he made a distinction between the old and the new liberalism
(VPR) **distinguirse 1** (= *diferenciarse*) [*objeto*] to stand out; [*persona*] to distinguish o.s., make a name for o.s. • **nuestros productos se distinguen por su calidad** our products are distinguished by their quality, our products stand out for their quality • **se distinguió como importante investigador** he achieved renown *o* he made a name for himself as a leading researcher • **se distinguió por sus descubrimientos en física cuántica** he made a name for himself through his research into quantum physics • **no se distingue precisamente por su sutileza** subtlety is not exactly his strong point, he's not renowned for his subtlety • **nuestros muebles se distinguen del resto por calidad y diseño** our furniture stands out from the rest due to its superior quality and design
2 (= *reconocerse*) to be identified • **las cintas de cromo se distinguen por su envoltorio** chrome tapes can be identified by their packaging

distintivo (ADJ) [*rasgo, carácter*] distinctive; [*signo*] distinguishing
(SM) (= *insignia*) [*de policía*] badge, button (EEUU); [*de equipo*] emblem, badge; [*de empresa*] emblem, logo • **~ de minusválido** disabled sticker

distinto (ADJ) **1** (= *diferente*) different (**a, de** from) • **son muy ~s** they are very different • **eso es ~** that's a different matter
2 (= *definido*) [*perfil, vista*] clear, distinct
3 distintos several, various • **hay distintas opiniones sobre eso** there are several *o* various opinions about that

distorsión (SF) **1** [*de sonido, imagen*] distortion
2 [*de los hechos*] distortion, twisting
3 (*Med*) twisting

distorsionado (ADJ) **1** [*sonido, imagen*] distorted
2 [*relato, realidad*] distorted

distorsionador (ADJ), **distorsionante** (ADJ) distorting

distorsionar ▹ CONJUG 1a (VT) to distort

distracción (SF) **1** (= *entretenimiento*) entertainment • **leer es mi ~ favorita** reading is my favourite pastime *o* form of entertainment • **no faltan distracciones para los niños** there is no lack of entertainment for the children • **colecciona sellos como ~** he collects stamps as a hobby
2 [*de preocupaciones, problemas*] distraction • **el trabajo me sirve de ~** my work is a distraction for me • **este libro te servirá de ~** this book will help you take your mind off things
3 (= *despiste*) • **en un momento de ~ me robaron la cartera** my attention wandered *o* I got distracted for a moment and I had my wallet stolen • **la causa del accidente podría ser una ~ del conductor** the accident could have been caused by a lapse of concentration on the driver's part • **no te saludaría por ~** I must have been so distracted that I didn't say hello
4 (*Econ*) [*de dinero, fondos*] embezzlement
5 (= *libertinaje*) loose living, dissipation

distraer ▹ CONJUG 2o (VT) **1** (= *entretener*) to entertain, amuse • **distrajimos a los niños contándoles cuentos** we kept the children entertained *o* amused by telling them stories • **la música es lo que más me distrae** music is the thing I most enjoy • **necesito algo que me distraiga un poco** I need something to take my mind off things • **la cocina me distrae de mis problemas** cooking takes my mind off my problems • MODISMO: • **~ el hambre** to keep the wolf from the door
2 (= *despistar*) to distract (**de** from) • **no haces más que ~me** all you do is distract me • **"prohibido distraer al conductor"** "do not distract the driver's attention" • **no me distraigas de mi trabajo** don't distract me from my work
3 (*Econ*) [+ *dinero, fondos*] to embezzle
4 (*moralmente*) to lead astray
(VI) (= *entretener*) [*pesca, ejercicio*] to be relaxing, take your mind off things; [*lectura, espectáculo*] to be entertaining, take your mind off things • **salir de compras distrae mucho** going shopping takes your mind off things
(VPR) **distraerse 1** (= *entretenerse*) to keep o.s. entertained, keep o.s. amused • **me distraigo viendo la tele** I keep myself entertained *o* amused watching TV • **se distrae mucho con sus nietos** her grandchildren keep her entertained *o* amused • **deberías salir y ~te** you should get out and enjoy yourself
2 (= *despistarse*) to get distracted • **oye bien lo que digo y no te distraigas** listen carefully and don't let yourself get distracted • **se distrae mucho en clase** he gets very easily distracted in class • **me distraje un momento y se me quemó la comida** my attention wandered *o* I got distracted for a moment and the dinner got burnt • **se distrae con el vuelo de una mosca** he gets distracted by the slightest thing

distraídamente (ADV) absent-mindedly • **hojeaba ~ el periódico** she glanced absently *o* absent-mindedly through the newspaper • **se llevó ~ mis libros** she absent-mindedly took my books

distraído/a (ADJ) **1** (= *despistado*) **a** (*con estar*) • **siempre está ~ en clase** he's always daydreaming in class, he never pays attention in class • **iba yo algo ~** I was walking along with my mind on other things • **me miró distraída** she glanced absently at me, she glanced at me absent-mindedly
b (*con ser*) • **soy muy ~** I'm very absent-minded
2 (= *entretenido*) entertained, amused • **la televisión me mantenía ~** the television kept me entertained *o* amused
3 (*Esp*) (= *divertido*) entertaining, amusing • **es un juego muy ~** it's a very entertaining *o* amusing game
4 (= *disoluto*) dissolute
(SM/F) • **hacerse el ~** to pretend not to notice

distribución (SF) **1** (= *reparto*) [*de víveres, mercancías, película*] distribution; [*de correo*] delivery; [*de trabajo, tarea*] allocation; [*de folletos*] (*en buzones*) distribution; (*en mano*) handing out
2 (*Estadística*) distribution • **la ~ de los impuestos** the distribution of the tax burden
3 (*Arquit*) layout, ground plan
4 (*Aut, Téc*) distribution
5 (*Mec*) timing gears (*pl*)

distribuido (ADJ) • **una casa bien distribuida** a well laid out house

distribuidor(a) (ADJ) (*Com*) • **red ~a** distribution network • **casa ~a** distributor, distribution company
(SM/F) (= *persona*) [*de productos*] distributor; (*Correos*) sorter; (*Com*) dealer, stockist • **su ~ habitual** your regular dealer
(SM) **1** (= *máquina*) ▸ **distribuidor automático** vending machine
2 (*Aut*) distributor
3 (*LAm*) (*Aut*) motorway exit, highway exit (EEUU)

distribuidora (SF) (*Cine*) distributor

distribuir ▹ CONJUG 3g (VT) **1** (= *repartir*) [+ *víveres, mercancía, película*] to distribute; [+ *correo*] to deliver; [+ *trabajo, tarea*] to

allocate; [+ *folletos*] (*en buzones*) to distribute; (*en mano*) to hand out
2 (= *entregar*) [+ *premios*] to give out; [+ *dividendos*] to pay
3 (*Téc*) [+ *carga*] to stow, arrange; [+ *peso*] to distribute equally
4 (*Arquit*) to plan, lay out
VPR **distribuirse 1** (= *colocarse*) • **nos distribuimos en grupos de cuatro** we got into groups of four
2 (= *repartirse*) to share out

distributivo ADJ distributive

distrito SM **1** (*Admin*) district ▸ **distrito electoral** constituency, precinct (*EEUU*) ▸ **distrito postal** postal district
2 (*Jur*) circuit

distrofia SF (*Med*) dystrophy ▸ **distrofia muscular** muscular dystrophy

disturbio SM **1** (= *del orden*) (*de poca importancia*) disturbance; (*más grave*) riot • **los ~s causados por los hinchas** the disturbances caused by fans
2 (*Téc*) disturbance ▸ **disturbio aerodinámico** (*Aer*) wash, slipstream

disuadir ▹ CONJUG 3a VT to dissuade, deter • **~ a algn de hacer algo** to dissuade *o* deter sb from doing sth

disuasión SF **1** (= *convencimiento*) dissuasion • **le falta capacidad de ~** he doesn't have strong powers of persuasion
2 (*Mil*) deterrence ▸ **disuasión nuclear** nuclear deterrence; ▹ **fuerza**

disuasivo ADJ **1** [*palabras*] dissuasive
2 (*Mil*) • **arma disuasiva** deterrent
SM deterrent

disuasorio ADJ (*Mil*) deterrent; ▹ **fuerza**

disuelto PP de **disolver**

disyuntiva SF **1** (= *opción*) alternative, choice
2 (= *dilema*) dilemma

disyuntivo ADJ disjunctive

disyuntor SM (*Elec*) circuit breaker

dita¹ SF **1** (= *garantía*) surety
2 (= *fianza*) security, bond
3 (*And*) (= *empréstito*) loan at a high rate of interest; (*LAm*) (= *deuda*) small debt

dita² SF (*Caribe*) dish, cup, pot

ditirambo SM dithyramb

DIU SM ABR (= **dispositivo intrauterino**) coil, IUD, IUCD

diurético ADJ, SM diuretic

diurex SM (*Méx*) ▹ **durex**

diurno ADJ (*gen*) day (*antes de s*), daytime (*antes de s*); [*animal, planta*] diurnal

diva SF prima donna, diva; ▹ **divo**

divagación SF (= *disgresión*) digression; **divagaciones** wanderings, ramblings

divagador ADJ rambling, discursive

divagar ▹ CONJUG 1h VI **1** (= *salirse del tema*) to digress • **¡no divagues!** get on with it!, come to the point!
2 (= *hablar vagamente*) to ramble

divagatorio ADJ digressive

diván SM **1** (= *asiento*) divan
2 [*de psiquiatra*] couch

diver* ADJ, **díver*** ADJ = divertido

divergencia SF divergence ▸ **divergencia de opiniones** difference of opinion

divergente ADJ divergent

divergir ▹ CONJUG 3c VI **1** [*líneas*] to diverge
2 [*opiniones*] to differ
3 [*personas*] to differ, disagree

diversidad SF diversity

diversificación SF diversification

diversificado ADJ diversified • **ciclo ~** (*Ven*) (*Educ*) upper secondary education

diversificador ADJ diversifying

diversificar ▹ CONJUG 1g VT to diversify
VPR **diversificarse** to diversify

diversión SF **1** (= *entretenimiento*) fun • **necesita un poco de ~** he needs a bit of fun
2 (= *pasatiempo*) hobby, pastime • **diversiones de salón** parlour games, indoor games
3 (*Mil*) diversion

diverso ADJ **1** (= *variado*) diverse, varied
2 (= *diferente*) different (**de** from)
3 **diversos** several, various • **está en ~s libros** it appears in several *o* various books
SMPL **diversos** (*Com*) sundries

divertido ADJ **1** (= *entretenido*) [*libro, película*] entertaining; [*chiste, persona*] funny, amusing • **la fiesta fue muy divertida** the party was great fun *o* very enjoyable • **el viaje fue muy ~** the trip was great fun • **¡qué ~! ¿ahora me dices que no puedes ir?** (*iró*) that's just great! now you tell me you can't go?
2 • **estar ~** (*LAm**) to be tight*

> **DIVERTIDO**
>
> **¿"Funny o fun"?**
>
> ▹ **Divertido** *solo se puede traducir por* **funny** *si nos hace reír:*
>
> **Acabo de ver una obra muy divertida**
> I've just seen a very funny play
>
> ▹ *Cuando hablamos de una actividad o situación* **divertida** *(en el sentido de entretenida y agradable), a menudo se la puede describir en inglés como* **fun**:
>
> **Me gusta jugar al escondite. Es muy divertido**
> I like playing hide and seek. It's great fun
>
> *NOTA:* **Fun** *es un sustantivo incontable y por lo tanto, al contrario que* **funny**, *no puede ir acompañado de adverbios como* **very**. *Se suele acompañar de* **great**, **good** *y* **a lot of**.
>
> *Para otros usos y ejemplos ver la entrada.*

divertimento SM (*Mús*) divertimento

divertimiento SM **1** (*Mil*) diversion
2 (*Mús*) divertissement

divertir ▹ CONJUG 3i VT **1** (= *hacer reír*) • **sus imitaciones divierten mucho al público** the audience find his impressions very funny *o* amusing
2 (= *entretener*) to entertain, amuse • **divirtió a los niños con sus juegos de magia** he entertained the children with his magic tricks, he kept the children amused with his magic tricks
3 (*frm*) (= *distraer*) to distract
VPR **divertirse 1** (= *pasarlo bien*) to have a good time, enjoy o.s. • **¡que te diviertas!** have a good time!, enjoy yourself!
2 (= *distraerse*) to amuse o.s. • **le compré este juego para que se divirtiera** I bought him this game to keep him amused • **cantamos solo por** *o* **para ~nos** we sing just for fun

dividendo SM dividend ▸ **dividendo a cuenta** interim dividend ▸ **dividendo definitivo** final demand ▸ **dividendos por acción** earnings per share

dividido ADJ divided

dividir ▹ CONJUG 3a VT **1** (= *partir*) to divide • **los dividieron en tres grupos** they split them (up) *o* divided them into three groups • **las obras de Ibsen se pueden ~ en dos etapas** Ibsen's works can be divided into two periods • **dividía su tiempo entre el cargo y su familia** he divided his time between his job and his family • **la bodega del barco está dividida en cuatro secciones** the hold of the ship is divided into four sections
2 (*Mat*) to divide (**entre, por** by) • **doce dividido entre** *o* **por cuatro son tres** twelve divided by four is three
3 (= *repartir*) [+ *ganancias, posesiones*] to split up, divide up; [+ *gastos*] to split • **hemos dividido el premio entre toda la familia** we have split up *o* divided up the prize among the whole family
4 (= *separar*) to divide • **los Pirineos dividen España y Francia** the Pyrenees divide France from Spain
5 (= *enemistar*) to divide • **utilizó el chantaje para ~nos** he used blackmail to divide us • **la guerra dividió al país** the war divided the country • REFRÁN: • **divide y vencerás** divide and rule
VI (*Mat*) to divide (**entre, por** into) • **se me ha olvidado ~** I've forgotten how to do division *o* how to divide
VPR **dividirse 1** (= *partirse*) [*célula*] to divide; [*grupo, país*] to split • **el partido se dividió en dos tendencias** the party split into two factions • **me encantaría ayudarte, pero no puedo ~me** I'd love to help you, but I can't be in two places at once • **la Edad Media puede ~se en dos períodos** the Middle Ages can be divided *o* split into two periods • **la crítica estuvo muy dividida** the critics were very divided
2 (= *separarse*) [*personas*] to split up; [*camino, carretera*] to fork • **cuando llegamos al cruce nos dividimos** when we got to the crossroads, we split up • **los fundadores se dividieron porque sus ideas eran muy distintas** the founders split up because their ideas were so different • **la carretera se divide al llegar al km 28** the road forks at km 28
3 (= *repartirse*) [+ *trabajo, ganancias*] to split up, divide up • **es mucho más fácil si nos dividimos el trabajo** it is much easier if we split up *o* divide up the work

divierta* SF (*CAm*) village dance, hop*

divieso SM (*Med*) boil

divinamente ADV divinely • **lo pasamos ~** we had a wonderful time

divinidad SF **1** (= *dios*) • **una ~** a deity • **la Divinidad** God, the Godhead ▸ **divinidad marina** sea god ▸ **divinidad pagana** pagan god/goddess
2 (= *esencia divina*) divinity
3 (= *preciosidad*) • **¡qué ~!** • **¡es una ~!** it's gorgeous!, it's lovely!

divinizar ▹ CONJUG 1f VT to deify

divino ADJ **1** (*Rel*) divine
2 (= *precioso*) divine, lovely • **la casa es divina** the house is lovely *o* divine
ADV* • **pasarlo ~** to have a wonderful time

divirtiendo *etc* ▹ **divertir**

divisa SF **1** (= *distintivo*) emblem
2 (*Heráldica*) device, motto
3 (*tb* **divisas**) (*Econ*) foreign currency • **control de ~s** exchange control ▸ **divisa de reserva** reserve currency

divisar ▹ CONJUG 1a VT to make out, distinguish

divisibilidad SF divisibility

divisible ADJ divisible

división SF **1** (= *separación*) [*de célula*] division; [*de átomo*] splitting; [*de gastos, ganancias*] division • **tras la ~ del país** after the country was divided • **hay ~ de opiniones** opinions are divided ▸ **división del trabajo** division of labour ▸ **división de poderes** division of powers
2 (*Mat*) division • **hacer una ~** to divide, do a division
3 (= *desunión*) [*de partido, familia*] division, split • **no existe ~ entre nosotros** there is no division *o* split between us
4 (*Dep*) division • **primera ~** first division

• **segunda ~** second division ▸ **división de honor** top division; (*Ftbl*) premier division
5 (*Mil*) division • **general de ~** major general ▸ **división acorazada** tank division ▸ **la División Azul** the Blue Division
6 (*Com*) (= *sección*) division
7 (*Bio*) (= *categoría*) category
8 (= *zona*) ▸ **división administrativa, división territorial** administrative region

divisional ADJ divisional
divisionismo SM divisiveness
divisionista ADJ divisive
divisivo ADJ divisive
divismo SM **1** (= *sistema*) star system
2 (= *carácter*) artistic temperament, star temperament
divisor ADJ **1** [*panel, muro, línea*] dividing
2 [*cantidad, número*] dividing
SM (*Mat*) divisor • **máximo común ~** highest common factor, greatest common divisor
divisoria SF **1** (= *línea*) dividing line ▸ **divisoria de aguas** watershed
2 (*Geog*) divide ▸ **divisoria continental** continental divide
divisorio ADJ [*línea*] dividing • **línea divisoria de las aguas** watershed
divo/a SM/F star; ▹ **diva**
divorciado/a ADJ **1** [*persona, pareja*] divorced
2 [*opinión*] divided • **las opiniones están divorciadas** opinions are divided
SM/F divorcé/divorcée
divorciar ▹ CONJUG 1b VT **1** [+ *pareja*] to divorce
2 [+ *ideas, opiniones*] to divorce (**de** from), separate (**de** from)
VPR **divorciarse** to get divorced, get a divorce (**de** from)
divorcio SM **1** [*de una pareja*] divorce
2 (= *diferencia*) discrepancy • **existe un ~ entre los dos conceptos** the two ideas are divorced from each other
divorcista SMF pro-divorce campaigner
divulgación SF **1** [*de noticia, ideas*] spreading
2 [*de descubrimiento, secreto*] disclosure
• **revistas de ~ científica** popular science magazines
divulgar ▹ CONJUG 1h VT **1** [+ *noticia, ideas*] to spread
2 [+ *secreto*] to divulge, disclose
VPR **divulgarse 1** [*secreto*] to leak out
2 [*rumor*] to get about
divulgativo ADJ, **divulgatorio** ADJ informative
dizque* ADV (*LAm*) (= *al parecer*) apparently
• **~ vendrán hoy** they're supposed to be coming today
DJ SM DJ, deejay
D.J.C. ABR = **después de Jesucristo**
dl ABR = **decilitro(s)** dl
Dls ABR, **dls** ABR (*LAm*) = **dólares**
DM ABR (= **Deutschmark**) DM, D-mark
Dm ABR **1** = **decimal**
2 = **decámetro(s)**
dm ABR (= **decímetro(s)**) dm
D.m. ABR (= **Dios mediante**) DV
D.N. ABR = **Delegación Nacional**
DNI SM ABR (*Esp*) (= **documento nacional de identidad**) ID card ▸ **DNI digital, DNI electrónico** electronic ID

> **DNI**
> The Spanish **Documento Nacional de Identidad** is a laminated plastic ID card which is renewable every 5 or 10 years in most cases, depending on the age of the holder. All Spanish nationals over the age of 14 are required to carry this card bearing their photo, a microchip and personal details at all times. As a legal document it is commonly used as proof of identity and it can be used instead of a passport for travelling around the EU. In Spain it is commonly known as the **DNI**, or else the **carnet (de identidad)**. In Latin America a similar card is called the **cédula (de identidad)**.

Dña. = D.ª; ▹ **DON/DOÑA**
do SM (*Mús*) C ▸ **do de pecho** high C
• MODISMO: • **dar el do de pecho** to give one's all, do one's very best ▸ **do mayor** C major
D.O. SF ABR (= **denominación de origen**)
▹ **DENOMINACIÓN DE ORIGEN**
dóberman SM Doberman
dobladillar ▹ CONJUG 1a VT to hem
dobladillo SM **1** [*de vestido*] hem
2 (= *vuelta*) [*de pantalón*] turn-up, cuff (*EEUU*)
doblado ADJ **1** [*carta, tela*] folded
2 [*barra, rama*] bent, twisted
3 [*persona*] bent over • **iba ~ por el dolor** he was bent over with the pain
4 [*película*] dubbed
doblador¹* SM (*CAm*) roll-your-own*, hand-rolled cigarette
doblador²(a) SM/F (*Cine*) dubber
dobladura SF fold
doblaje SM (*Cine*) dubbing
doblamiento SM folding
doblar ▹ CONJUG 1a VT **1** (= *plegar*) [+ *carta, tela, periódico*] to fold; [+ *alambre, pierna*] to bend • **dobló el mapa y se lo guardó** he folded up the map and put it away
• **dóblales el bajo para afuera a tus pantalones** turn up (the hem of) your trousers • **no puedo ~ la rodilla del dolor** I can't bend my knee because of the pain
2 (= *torcer*) [+ *esquina*] to turn, go round; [+ *cabo*] (*Náut*) to round
3 (= *tener el doble de*) • **su marido le dobla el sueldo** her husband earns twice as much as her, her husband earns double what she does • **te doblo la edad** I'm twice your age
4 (= *duplicar*) [+ *cantidad, oferta*] to double
• **doblen sus apuestas, señores** double your bets, gentlemen • **en verano nos doblan el trabajo** in summer our work doubles *o* is doubled
5 (*Cine*) **a** (*en la voz*) [+ *película, actor*] to dub
• **una película doblada al francés** a film dubbed into French
b (*en la acción*) [+ *actor*] to stand in for • **en las escenas de peligro lo dobla un especialista** a stunt man stands in for him in the dangerous scenes
6* [+ *persona*] • **lo dobló de una patada** he kicked him and doubled him up from the pain • **~ a algn a palos** to beat sb up • **el sacrificio lo ha doblado** having to make this sacrifice has torn him apart
7 (*Dep*) [+ *ciclista, corredor*] to lap • **ha conseguido ~ a los últimos corredores** he has managed to lap the last runners
8 (*Teat*) • **~ dos papeles** to take two parts
9 (*Méx*) (= *matar*) to shoot down
VI **1** (= *girar*) [*persona, vehículo*] to turn • **~ a la derecha** to turn right • **~ a la izquierda** to turn left
2 [*campana*] to toll • **~ a muerto** to sound the death knell
3 (*Taur*) [*toro*] to collapse
4‡ (= *morir*) to peg out‡
VPR **doblarse 1** (= *plegarse*) [*papel, tela*] to fold (up); [*alambre, barra*] to bend • **se le ~on las rodillas** his knees buckled beneath him
2 [*persona*] (= *encorvarse*) to bend; (= *retorcerse*) to double up; (= *doblegarse*) to give up, give in
• **estaba doblándose de dolor** he was doubled up with pain • **no se doblaba ante los problemas** he didn't give up *o* in when faced by problems
3 [*cantidad*] to double • **los precios se han doblado este año** prices have doubled this year • **el número de accidentes se ha doblado** the number of accidents has doubled
doble ADJ **1** [*puerta, tela, densidad, agente*] double; [*control, nacionalidad*] dual; [*ración, café*] large; [*cuerda*] extra strong; [*ventaja*] twofold • **un whisky ~** a double whisky • **no aparcar en ~ fila** no double-parking • **lo expulsaron por ~ amonestación** he was sent off after receiving a second yellow card
• **una tela de ~ ancho** a double-width piece of fabric • **están trabajando a ~ turno** they are working double shifts • **tiene ~ motivo para quejarse** he has double reason to complain • **~ acristalamiento** (*Esp*) double glazing • **de ~ cara** [*disquete, hoja, espejo*] double-sided; [*abrigo, chaqueta*] reversible
• **impresión a ~ cara** double-sided printing
• **~ cristal** double glazing • **~ espacio** double-spacing • **diez páginas impresas a ~ espacio** ten pages printed in double-spacing
• **~ falta** (*Baloncesto, Tenis*) double fault
• **~ fondo** false bottom • **un maletín con ~ fondo** a case with a false bottom • **en todo lo que dice hay un ~ fondo** there's a double meaning in everything he says • **~ intención** double intention • **no iba con ~ intención** he did not have ulterior motives *o* double intentions • **~ juego** double-dealing • **hacer un ~ juego** to play a double game • **~ página** two-page spread, double-page spread • **una fotografía a ~ página** a two-page photograph • **~ personalidad** split personality • **de ~ sentido** [*calle*] two-way (*antes de s*); [*chiste, palabra*] with a double meaning • **todo lo que dice tiene un ~ sentido** everything he says has a double meaning • **~ tracción** four-wheel drive
• **visión ~** double vision; ▹ **imposición, moral²**
2 (= *hipócrita*) [*persona*] two-faced
3 (*Dominó*) [*ficha*] double • **el cuatro ~** the double four
ADV [*ver*] double; [*beber, comer*] twice as much • **con estas gafas veo ~** these glasses make me see double
SM **1** (= *cantidad*) • **el ~**: • **ahora gana el ~** now he earns twice as much, now he earns double • **su sueldo es el ~ del mío** his salary is twice as much as mine, his salary is double mine • **necesitamos una casa el ~ de grande** we need a house twice as big as this *o* double the size • **lleva el ~ de harina** it has twice the amount of flour, it has double the amount of flour • **¿cuál es el ~ de diez?** what's two times ten? • **apostar ~ contra sencillo** to bet two to one • **el ~ que** twice as much as • **gana el ~ que yo** he earns double what I do *o* twice as much as me • MODISMO:
• **~ o nada** double or quits
2 (= *copia*) [*de documento*] duplicate copy; [*de llave*] duplicate key
3 (*Cos*) (= *pliegue*) pleat
4 [*de campanas*] toll(ing) • **¿oyes el ~ de campanas?** can you hear the bells tolling?
5 **dobles** (*Tenis*) doubles • **un partido de ~s** a doubles match ▸ **dobles (de) caballeros** men's doubles ▸ **dobles (de) damas, dobles femeninos** ladies' doubles ▸ **dobles masculinos** men's doubles ▸ **dobles mixtos** mixed doubles
6 (*Bridge*) double ▸ **doble de castigo** penalty double ▸ **doble de llamada** asking double

7‡ [*de cárcel*] prison governor, head warden (EEUU)
(SMF) **1** (*Cine*) double, stand-in
2 (= *persona parecida*) (*gen*) double; [*de algún famoso*] lookalike • **me han dicho que tengo un ~** I've been told I have a double • **varios ~s de Elvis Presley** some Elvis Presley lookalikes
3 (= *persona falsa*) double-dealer
doblegar ▹ CONJUG 1h (VT) **1** (= *vencer*) [+ *voluntad*] to break; [+ *enemigo, oponente*] to crush, vanquish (*liter*)
2 (= *doblar*) to bend
3 [+ *arma*] to brandish
(VPR) **doblegarse** to yield, give in
doblemente (ADV) **1** (= *por dos veces*) doubly
2 (= *con hipocresía*) duplicitously
doblete (SM) • **hacer ~** (*TV, Teat*) to double (a for)
doblez (SM) (*Cos*) (= *pliegue*) fold, hem; (= *dobladillo*) turnup, cuff (EEUU)
(SF) (= *falsedad*) duplicity
doblista (SMF) doubles player
doblón (SM) (*Hist*) doubloon ▸ **doblón de a ocho** piece of eight
doc. (ABR) **1** (= **docena**) doz
2 (= **documento**) doc
doce (ADJ INV), (PRON) (*gen*) twelve; (*ordinal, en la fecha*) twelfth • **las ~** twelve o'clock • **le escribí el día ~** I wrote to him on the twelfth
(SM) (= *número*) twelve; (= *fecha*) twelfth; ▹ **seis**
doceavo (ADJ) twelfth
(SM) **1** (*numeral*) twelfth
2 (*Tip*) • **en ~** in duodecimo
docena (SF) dozen • **media ~ de huevos** half a dozen eggs • **a** *o* **por ~s** by the dozen ▸ **docena del fraile** baker's dozen
docencia (SF) teaching
doceno (ADJ) twelfth
docente (ADJ) teaching (*antes de s*) • **centro ~** educational institution • **personal ~** teaching staff • **personal no ~** non-academic staff
(SMF) teacher
dócil (ADJ) [*animal*] docile; [*persona*] submissive, meek
docilidad (SF) [*de animal*] docility; [*de persona*] submissiveness, meekness
dócilmente (ADV) meekly
doctamente (ADV) learnedly
docto/a (ADJ) learned, erudite
(SM/F) scholar, learned person
doctor(a) (SM/F) (*Med, Univ*) doctor • **fue investido ~ honoris causa** he was made an honorary doctor • **REFRÁN**: • **~es tiene la Iglesia** there are plenty of people well able to pass an opinion (on that) ▸ **doctor(a) en derecho** doctor of laws ▸ **doctor(a) en filosofía** Doctor of Philosophy
(SM) (*Rel*) father, saint
doctorado (SM) doctorate, PhD • **estudiante de ~** PhD student
doctoral (ADJ) **1** [*tesis, conferencia*] doctoral
2 [*tono*] pedantic, pompous
doctorando/a (SM/F) PhD student
doctorar ▹ CONJUG 1a (VT) to confer a doctorate on
(VPR) **doctorarse** to receive *o* get one's PhD *o* doctorate
doctrina (SF) **1** (= *ideología*) doctrine
2 (= *enseñanza*) teaching
doctrinal (ADJ) doctrinal
doctrinar ▹ CONJUG 1a (VT) to teach
doctrinario/a (ADJ) doctrinaire
(SM/F) doctrinarian
doctrinero (SM) (*LAm*) parish priest (*among Indians*)
docudrama (SM) docudrama, dramatized documentary

documentación (SF) **1** [*de vehículo*] documentation ▸ **documentación del barco** ship's papers (*pl*)
2 [*de persona*] papers (*pl*), documents (*pl*) • **la ~, por favor** your papers, please
3 (*Prensa*) reference section
documentadamente (ADV) in a well-informed way
documentado (ADJ) **1** (= *informado*) • **un libro bien ~** a well documented *o* researched book • **no estaba bien ~** I was not very well informed (about the subject)
2 (= *con documentación*) • **no voy ~** I don't have my papers with me
documental (ADJ), (SM) documentary
documentalista (SMF) **1** (*TV*) documentary maker
2 (*en biblioteca*) documentalist
documentar ▹ CONJUG 1a (VT) to document
(VPR) **documentarse** to do research, do one's homework
documento (SM) **1** (= *escrito*) document ▸ **documento adjunto** (*Inform*) attachment ▸ **documento justificativo** voucher, certificate ▸ **documento nacional de identidad** identity card; ▹ **DNI** ▸ **documentos de envío** dispatch documents ▸ **documentos del coche** car documents
2 (= *certificado*) certificate
3 (= *testimonio*) document • **es un ~ vivo de aquella época** it is a living document of that period
dodecafónico (ADJ) dodecaphonic
dodecafonismo (SM) twelve-tone system, dodecaphonism
dodecágono (SM) dodecagon
dodo (SM), **dodó** (SM) dodo
dodotis® (SM INV) nappy, diaper (EEUU)
dogal (SM) **1** (*para animal*) halter
2 (*para ahorcar*) noose • **estar con el ~ al cuello** to be in a terrible fix *o* jam
dogma (SM) dogma
dogmáticamente (ADV) dogmatically
dogmático (ADJ) dogmatic
dogmatismo (SM) dogmatism
dogmatizador(a) (SM/F) dogmatist
dogmatizar ▹ CONJUG 1f (VI) to dogmatize
dogo (SM) bull mastiff ▸ **dogo alemán** Great Dane
dola* (SF) = **pídola**
dolamas (SFPL), **dolames** (SFPL) [*de un caballo*] hidden defects; (*LAm**) chronic illness (*sing*)
dólar (SM) dollar; ▹ **montado**
dolencia (SF) ailment
doler ▹ CONJUG 2h (VI) **1** (*Med*) to hurt • **¿(te) duele?** does it hurt? • **la inyección no duele** the injection doesn't hurt • **me duele el brazo** my arm hurts • **me duele la cabeza** my head hurts; (*por migraña, resaca*) I've got a headache • **me duele el estómago** I've got (a) stomach ache • **me duelen las muelas** I've got toothache • **me duele la garganta** I've got a sore throat
2 (= *afligir*) to hurt • **ese comentario me dolió** I was hurt by that comment, that comment hurt • **no me duele gastarme el dinero en esto** I don't mind spending money on this, spending money on this doesn't bother me • **me duele no poder prestártelo** I'm very sorry I can't lend it to you • **¡ahí le duele!** so that's where the problem is!
(VPR) **dolerse** (*frm*) **1** (= *sufrir*) • **me duelo por su ausencia** I miss him terribly • **¡duélete de mí!** pity me!
2 (= *arrepentirse*) • **~se de algo** to regret sth • **se duele de su pasado egoísta** she regrets her selfish past • **~se de los pecados** to repent of one's sins

3 (= *quejarse*) to complain
dolido (ADJ) • **estar ~ con algn** to be hurt by sb
doliente (ADJ) **1** (= *dolorido*) aching
2 (= *enfermo*) ill
3 (= *triste*) sorrowful • **la familia ~** the bereaved family
(SMF) **1** (*Med*) sick person
2 (*en entierro*) mourner
dolmen (SM) dolmen
dolo (SM) fraud, deceit • **sin ~** openly, honestly
dolomía (SF), **dolomita** (SF) dolomite
dolor (SM) **1** (*físico*) pain • **estar con ~es** (*antes del parto*) to feel one's labour pains beginning ▸ **dolor de cabeza** headache ▸ **dolor de espalda** backache ▸ **dolor de estómago** stomach ache ▸ **dolor de muelas** toothache ▸ **dolor de oídos** earache ▸ **dolores de parto** labour pains, labor pains (EEUU) ▸ **dolor sordo** dull ache
2 (= *pesar*) grief, sorrow • **con ~ de mi corazón** with an ache in my heart • **le causa mucho ~** it causes him great distress
dolorido (ADJ) **1** (*Med*) sore • **la parte dolorida** the part which hurts
2 [*persona*] distressed, upset
3 [*tono*] pained
Dolorosa (SF) (*Rel*) • **la ~** the Madonna, Our Lady of Sorrow
dolorosa (SF) (*hum*) bill, check (EEUU) (*in a restaurant*)
dolorosamente (ADV) **1** (*Med*) painfully
2 (= *angustiosamente*) painfully, distressingly
doloroso (ADJ) **1** (*Med*) painful
2 (= *angustioso*) painful, distressing
doloso (ADJ) fraudulent, deceitful
dom. (ABR) (= **domingo**) Sun.
doma (SF) [*de caballo*] breaking-in; [*de animal salvaje*] taming
domable (ADJ) tamable
domador(a) (SM/F) [*de fieras*] tamer, trainer ▸ **domador(a) de caballos** horse-breaker
domadura (SF) = **doma**
domar ▹ CONJUG 1a (VT) **1** [+ *animal salvaje*] (= *amansar*) to tame; (= *adiestrar*) to train
2 [+ *caballo*] to break in
3 [+ *emoción*] to master, control
domeñar ▹ CONJUG 1a (VT) = **domar**
domesticable (ADJ) domesticable, tamable
domesticación (SF) **1** (*en costumbres*) domestication
2 [*de animal salvaje*] taming
domesticado (ADJ) tame • **un tejón ~** a tame badger, a pet badger
domesticar ▹ CONJUG 1g (VT) to tame, domesticate
(VPR) **domesticarse** to become tame, become domesticated
domesticidad (SF) **1** (= *vida de hogar*) domesticity
2 [*de animal*] captivity • **el lobo no vive bien en ~** the wolf does not take to living in captivity
doméstico/a (ADJ) **1** [*vida, servicio*] domestic (*antes de s*) • **animal ~** pet • **economía doméstica** home economy, housekeeping • **gastos ~s** household expenses • **las tareas domésticas** housework (*sing*)
2 [*vuelo*] domestic
(SM/F) servant, domestic
Domiciano (SM) Domitian
domiciliación (SF) (*Econ*) direct debiting • **la ~ de los pagos** payment by direct debit
domiciliado (ADJ) • **~ en Valencia** resident in Valencia
domiciliar ▹ CONJUG 1b (VT) **1** (*Econ*) • **~ el pago de algo** to pay sth by direct debit • **pago domiciliado** direct debit, payment by direct debit • **~ su cuenta** to give the

number of one's account, authorize direct debiting of one's account
2 (*Méx*) [+ *carta*] to address
VPR **domiciliarse** to take up residence
domiciliario ADJ • **arresto ~** house arrest • **asistencia domiciliaria** home help
domicilio SM (= *hogar*) home, residence (*frm*) • **servicio a ~** home delivery service • **ventas a ~** door-to-door selling • **sin ~ fijo** of no fixed abode ▸ **domicilio conyugal** conjugal home ▸ **domicilio particular** private residence ▸ **domicilio social** (*Com*) head office, registered office
dominación SF 1 (*Pol*) domination
2 (*Mil*) commanding position
dominador ADJ 1 [*papel, persona*] dominating
2 [*carácter*] domineering
dominante ADJ 1 (= *despótico*) domineering
2 (= *predominante*) [*viento, tendencia, opinión, ideología*] dominant, prevailing; [*grupo, cultura, rasgo, tema, color*] dominant; [*papel, rol*] dominant, leading • **el consenso ha sido la nota ~ en las negociaciones** consensus has been the keynote *o* tenor of the negotiations • **el país ~ en ingeniería genética** the leading nation in genetic engineering
3 (*Bio*) [*macho, gen*] dominant
4 (*Mús*) dominant
SF (*Mús*) dominant
dominar ▹ CONJUG 1a VT 1 (= *controlar*) [+ *población, territorio*] to dominate; [+ *países*] to rule, rule over; [+ *adversario*] to overpower; [+ *caballo*] to control • **le domina la envidia** he is ruled by envy • **el tenista español dominó todo el set** the Spanish tennis player dominated the whole set
2 (= *contener*) [+ *incendio, epidemia*] to check, bring under control; [+ *rebelión*] to put down, suppress; [+ *pasión*] to control, master; [+ *nervios, emoción*] to control; [+ *dolor*] to overcome
3 [+ *técnica, tema*] to master • **domina bien la materia** she has a good grasp of the subject • **domina cuatro idiomas** he's fluent in four languages
4 (= *estar por encima de*) • **la catedral domina toda la ciudad** the cathedral dominates *o* towers above the whole town • **desde el castillo se domina toda la vega** from the castle you can look out over the whole plain
VI 1 [*edificio*] to tower
2 (= *predominar*) [*color, rasgo*] to stand out; [*opinión, tendencia*] to predominate
VPR **dominarse** to control o.s.
dómine SM (*Hist*) schoolmaster
domingas‡ SFPL boobs‡
Domingo SM Dominic
domingo SM Sunday • **el traje de los ~s** one's Sunday best • MODISMO: • **hacer ~** to take a day off ▸ **Domingo de la Pasión** Passion Sunday ▸ **Domingo de Ramos** Palm Sunday ▸ **Domingo de Resurrección** Easter Sunday; ▹ **sábado**
dominguejo SM (*And, Cono Sur*) scarecrow
dominguero/a ADJ Sunday (*antes de s*) • **pintor ~** Sunday painter • **el traje ~** one's Sunday best
SM/F 1 (= *excursionista*) Sunday excursionist
2 (= *conductor*) Sunday driver
Dominica SF Dominica
dominical ADJ Sunday (*antes de s*) • **periódico ~** Sunday newspaper
SM Sunday supplement
dominicanismo SM *word or phrase peculiar to the Dominican Republic*
dominicano/a ADJ, SM/F (*Geog, Rel*) Dominican
dominico SM, **domínico** SM = dominicano
dominio SM 1 (= *control*) control • **tiene el ~ de la situación** he is in control of the situation ▸ **dominio de sí mismo, dominio sobre sí mismo** self-control
2 (= *conocimiento*) command • **es impresionante su ~ del inglés** his command of *o* fluency in English is impressive • **¡qué ~ tiene!** isn't he good at it? • MODISMO: • **es del ~ público** to be common knowledge
3 (= *autoridad*) authority (**sobre** over)
4 (= *territorio*) dominion
5 (*Educ*) field, domain
6 (*Inform*) domain ▸ **nombre de dominio** domain name
dominó SM 1 (= *juego*) dominoes (*pl*); (= *conjunto de fichas*) set of dominoes
2 (= *pieza*) domino
dom.º ABR (= **domingo**) Sun.
domo SM (*Méx*) skylight
domótica SF home automation
domótico ADJ automated, smart*
don¹ SM 1 (= *talento*) gift • **tiene un don especial para la música** she has a special gift for music • **tiene don con los niños** she has a way with children ▸ **don de gentes** • **tener don de gentes** to know how to handle people, be good with people ▸ **don de lenguas** gift for languages ▸ **don de mando** leadership qualities (*pl*); (*Mil*) generalship ▸ **don de palabra** gift of the gab*, gift of gab (*EEUU**)
2 (= *deseo*) wish • **el hada le concedió tres dones** the fairy gave him three wishes
3 (= *regalo*) gift
don² SM 1 (*tratamiento de cortesía*) • **Don** (*en carta, sobre*) Esquire • **Sr. Don Fernando García** (*en correspondencia*) Mr F. García, Fernando García Esq. • **¿habéis visto a don Fernando?** have you seen Mr García? • **es don perfecto, él cree que nunca se equivoca** (*iró*) he thinks he's Mr Perfect and never makes a mistake • **el rey don Pedro** King Peter; ▹ **Juan**
2 (*Arg, Col**) (*tratamiento popular*) mate*, buddy (*EEUU**)

> **DON/DOÑA**
> A courtesy title, **don/doña** placed before the first name of an older or more senior man/woman is a way of showing them your respect when talking to them or about them. E.g. **"¿Podría hablar con don César Roca?", "Buenos días doña Alicia. ¿Qué tal su viaje?"** Although now becoming rarer, in Spain **Don** and **Doña**, often abbreviated to **D.** and **Dña.**, are commonly used before full names on official documents and contracts. In formal correspondence, they are used in combination with **Sr.**, **Sra.** and **Srta.**, e.g. **Sr. D. Bernardo Esplugas Martín, Sra. Dña. Ana Rodríguez**.

dona SF 1 (*Cono Sur*) gift
2 **donas** (*Méx*) trousseau (*sing*)
donación SF 1 [*de bienes, órganos*] donation ▸ **donación de sangre** blood donation
2 (*Jur*) gift
donado/a SM/F lay brother/lay sister
donador(a) SM/F donor
donaire SM 1 (*al hablar*) wit
2 (*al moverse*) grace, elegance
3 • **un ~** a witticism • **dice muchos ~s** he's terribly witty
donante SMF donor ▸ **donante de órganos** organ donor ▸ **donante de sangre** blood donor
donar ▹ CONJUG 1a VT [+ *órganos*] to donate; [+ *sangre, propiedades, dinero*] to give, donate
donativo SM donation
doncel SM 1 (= *noble*) young nobleman, young squire
2 (*Hist*) page
doncella SF 1 (= *criada*) maidservant
2 (= *virgen*) maiden, virgin
3 (*Hist, Literat*) maid, maiden
doncellez SF 1 (= *virginidad*) virginity, maidenhood
2 (*Anat*) maidenhead
donde ADV 1 (+ *indic*) where • **la nota está ~ la dejaste** the note's where you left it • **la casa ~ nací** the house where I was born, the house I was born in • **el sitio ~ lo encontré** the place (where) I found it • **a ~**: • **ahí es a ~ vamos nosotros** that's where we're going • **fue a ~ estaban ellos** he went to (the place) where they were • **de ~**: • **el país de ~ vienen** the country they come from • **la caja de ~ lo sacó** the box he took it out of, the box from which he took it • **en ~**: • **fui a la India, en ~ nos conocimos** I went to India, (which is) where we met • **el pueblo en ~ vive** the village where *o* in which he lives • **por ~**: • **la escalera por ~ había salido** the empty staircase down which he had left • **la puerta por ~ se entra** the door you go in by • **la calle por ~ íbamos andando** the street we were walking along • **por ~ pasan lo destrozan todo** they destroy everything, wherever they go • **va siempre por ~ se le dice** she always goes wherever you tell her to
2 (+ *subjun*) wherever • **~ tú quieras** wherever you want • **quiero un trabajo ~ sea** I want a job anywhere *o* wherever • **estén ~ estén** wherever they may be • **vayas ~ vayas** wherever you go, everywhere you go • **vayas por ~ vayas** whichever way you go • REFRÁN: • **(allí) ~ fueres, haz lo que vieres** when in Rome, do as the Romans do
3 (*Cono Sur*) (= *ya que*) as, since
PREP 1 (= *al lado de*) • **es allí, ~ la catedral** it's over there by the cathedral • **lo guardamos ~ la ropa de cama** we keep it with the bed linen
2 (= *en casa de*) • **vamos ~ Ricardo** we're going to Ricardo's • **están cenando ~ mi madre** they are having dinner at my mother's
dónde ADV INTERROG 1 (*en cláusulas interrogativas*) where? • **¿~ lo dejaste?** where did you leave it? • **¿a ~ vas?** where are you going? • **¿de ~ eres?** where are you from? • **¿en ~?** where? • **¿por ~ se va al estadio?** how do I get to the stadium? • **¿por ~ queda la estación?** whereabouts is the station?
2 (*en estilo indirecto*) where • **no sé ~ lo puse** I don't know where I put it • MODISMO: • **mira por ~***: • **¡buscaban a un intérprete y mira por ~ me llamaron a mí!** they were looking for an interpreter and what do you know, they called me! • **¿así que tú has sido el vencedor? pues qué bien, mira por ~** (*iró*) so you won? well, stranger things have happened, I suppose (*iró*)
3 (*LAm*) (= *¿cómo?*) how?
dondequiera ADV anywhere • **por ~** everywhere, all over the place
CONJ wherever • **~ que lo busques** wherever you look for it
donjuan SM, **donjuán** SM casanova, womanizer
donjuanismo SM womanizing
donosamente ADV (*liter*) wittily, amusingly
donoso ADJ (*liter*) witty, amusing; (*iró*) fine • **¡donosa idea!** (*iró*) highly amusing I'm sure!
Donosti, Donostia SF San Sebastián
donostiarra ADJ of/from San Sebastián
SMF native/inhabitant of San Sebastián

• los ~s the people of San Sebastián
Don Quijote (SM) Don Quixote
donus (SM INV), **donut** (SM) (PL: **donuts**) ring doughnut, donut (*EEUU*)
doña (SF) • **Doña Alicia Pérez** Mrs Alicia Pérez • **¿está ~ Alicia?** is Mrs Pérez in?; ▹ **DON/DOÑA**
dopado (ADJ) [*caballo*] doped, doped-up*; [*persona*] on drugs • **un atleta ~** an athlete who has taken performance-enhancing drugs
(SM) [*de caballo*] doping; [*de deportista*] taking performance-enhancing drugs
dopaje (SM) = **dopado**
dopar ▹ CONJUG 1a (VT) to dope, drug
(VPR) **doparse** to take performance-enhancing drugs
doping ['dopin] (SM) doping • **han intentado acusarlo de ~** they have tried to accuse him of having taken performance-enhancing drugs
dopingar ▹ CONJUG 1h (VT) to give performance-enhancing drugs to
doquier (ADV) • **por ~** (*frm*) all over, everywhere, everyplace (*EEUU*)
dorada (SF) sea bream
doradito (ADJ) (*Culin*) golden brown
dorado (ADJ) **1** (= *parecido al oro*) gold (*antes de s*), golden (*liter*) • **los ~s sesenta** the golden sixties
2 (*Téc*) gilt, gilded
(SM) **1** (*Téc*) gilt, gilding
2 (= *pez*) dorado
doradura (SF) gilding
dorar ▹ CONJUG 1a (VT) **1** (*Téc*) to gild
2 (*Culin*) to brown • MODISMO: • **~ la píldora** to sweeten the pill
(VPR) **dorarse 1** [*cebolla, ajo*] to turn golden, brown • **rehogar la cebolla hasta que se dore** lightly fry the onion until golden brown
2 [*piel, persona*] to go brown, tan
dórico (ADJ) Doric
dorífora (SF) Colorado beetle
dormida (SF) (*LAm*) **1** (= *sueño, descanso*) sleep
2 (*por una noche*) overnight stop
dormidera (SF) **1** (*Bot*) poppy, opium poppy
2 • MODISMO: • **tener buenas ~s** to get off to sleep easily
dormidero (SM) **1** [*de ganado*] sleeping place
2 [*de gallinas*] roost
dormido (ADJ) **1** [*persona*] • **estar ~** (*durmiendo*) to be asleep; (*con sueño*) to be sleepy • **¿es que estás ~ o qué?** are you asleep or what? • **hablar ~** to talk in one's sleep • **andaba medio ~ por la calle** he walked down the street half asleep • **quedarse ~** to fall asleep • **me quedé dormida en el autocar** I fell asleep on the coach • **se está quedando ~** he's dropping off, he's falling asleep • **me quedé ~ y perdí la clase** I overslept and missed the class
2 [*pierna, brazo*] • **tengo la mano dormida** my hand has gone to sleep • **todavía tengo la cara dormida por la anestesia** my face is still numb from the anaesthetic
dormilón/ona (ADJ) fond of sleeping
(SM/F) sleepyhead
dormilona (SF) **1** (= *silla*) reclining chair
2 (*Caribe*) (= *camisón*) nightdress, nightgown
dormir ▹ CONJUG 3j (VI) **1** (= *descansar*) to sleep • **no hagas ruido, que está durmiendo** don't make a noise, he's asleep • **solo ha dormido cinco horas** she has only had five hours' sleep, she has only slept (for) five hours • **se fueron a ~ temprano** they went to bed early • **¡ahora, todos a ~!** come on, off to bed all of you *o* off to bed with you all • **la música no me dejaba ~** the music kept me awake • **es de poco ~** he doesn't need much sleep • **~ con algn** (*tb euf*) to sleep with sb • **~ de un tirón** to sleep right through (the night) • **he dormido diez horas de un tirón** I've slept ten hours right through • MODISMOS: • **~ como un bendito** *o* **un santo** to sleep like a baby • **~ como un lirón** *o* **un tronco** • **~ a pierna suelta** to sleep like a log; ▹ **saco¹**
2 (= *pasar la noche*) to spend the night, stay the night • **dormimos en una pensión** we spent *o* stayed the night in a guesthouse • **llevo una semana sin ~ en casa** I haven't slept at home for a week • **~ al raso** to sleep out in the open, sleep rough
3 (= *estar olvidado*) to lie idle • **mi solicitud ha estado durmiendo en el fondo de un cajón** my application has been lying idle at the bottom of a drawer • **no deje ~ a sus ahorros** don't let your savings lie idle
(VT) **1** (= *adormecer*) [+ *niño*] to get (off) to sleep; [+ *adulto*] (*por aburrimiento*) to send to sleep; (*con anestesia*) to put to sleep • **no podía ~lo** I couldn't get him off to sleep • **ese programa me duerme** that programme sends me to sleep
2 • **~ la siesta** to have a nap, have a siesta • MODISMOS: • **~ el sueño de los justos** to sleep the sleep of the just • **~la*** • **~ la mona*** to sleep it off*
3 (*euf*) (= *matar*) to put to sleep
(VPR) **dormirse 1** [*persona*] **a** (= *quedarse dormido*) to fall asleep, go to sleep • **no te duermas** don't fall asleep, don't go to sleep • **se me durmió en los brazos** she fell asleep *o* went to sleep in my arms • **¡duérmete!** go to sleep!
b (= *despertarse tarde*) to oversleep • **no llegué a la hora porque me dormí** I didn't arrive on time because I overslept
2 [*brazo, pierna*] to go to sleep • **se me ha dormido la mano** my hand has gone to sleep
3* (= *descuidarse*) • **si te duermes, te quedarás sin trabajo** if you don't stay on your toes, you'll lose your job • **duérmete y no conseguirás nada** if you waste time like this, you won't get anywhere • **no te duermas, respóndeme** wake up, give me an answer • MODISMO: • **~se en los laureles** to rest on one's laurels
dormirela* (SF) nap, snooze
dormirlas (SM) hide-and-seek
dormitar ▹ CONJUG 1a (VI) to doze, snooze*
dormitorio (SM) **1** (= *habitación*) bedroom ▸ **dormitorio de servicio** room for domestic staff
2 (= *muebles*) bedroom suite
3 (*en internado, cuartel*) dormitory; ▹ **ciudad**
dornillo (SM) **1** (= *recipiente*) wooden bowl
2 (*Agr*) small trough
Dorotea (SF) Dorothy
dorsal (ADJ) dorsal
(SM) (*Dep*) number (*worn on player's back*)
(SF) ridge
dorsalmente (ADV) **1** (= *por el lado*) dorsally
2 [*flotar*] on one's back
dorso (SM) back • **escribir algo al ~** to write sth on the back • **"véase al ~"** "see overleaf", "please turn over"
dos (ADJ INV), (PRON) **1** (*gen*) two; (*ordinal, en la fecha*) second • **dos a dos** two against two • **dos y dos son cuatro** two and two are four • **dos por dos son cuatro** two times two makes four • **de dos en dos** in twos, two by two • **cortar algo en dos** to cut sth into two • **los dos libros** both books • **le escribí el día dos** I wrote to him on the second • **dos piezas** two-piece • MODISMOS: • **como ese no hay dos** they don't come any better than that • **como dos y dos son cuatro** as sure as sure can be, as sure as eggs are eggs • **cada dos por tres** every five minutes • **no hay dos sin tres** these things always come in threes
2 (= *dos personas*) • **los dos** the two of them/us *etc*, both of them/us *etc* • **vosotros dos** you two • **es para los dos** it's for both of you/us *etc*
(SM) (= *número*) two; (= *fecha*) second • **estamos a dos** (*Tenis*) the score is deuce • MODISMO: • **en un dos por tres** in no time at all; ▹ **seis**

DOS

El uso de "both"

Los dos *con el sentido de* **ambos** *se traduce por* **both**, *pero el lugar que ocupa en la oración y la construcción en la que se usa depende de varios factores:*

Como sujeto de "be" o un verbo auxiliar/modal

▹ *Con nombre solo:*
Las dos hermanas son cantantes
Both (of the) sisters are singers
The sisters are both singers
Los dos castillos fueron construidos en el siglo XVIII
Both (of the) castles were built in the 18th century
The castles were both built in the 18th century

▹ *Con nombre y demostrativo/posesivo:*
Estos dos niños son huérfanos
Both (of) these children are orphans
These children are both orphans
Mis dos hijos han emigrado
Both (of) my sons have emigrated
My sons have both emigrated

▹ *Sin nombre:*
Los dos son jóvenes
Both of them are young
They're both young
Los dos sabemos esquiar
Both of us can ski
We can both ski

Como sujeto de otro verbo

▹ *Con nombre solo:*
Los dos chicos quieren estudiar medicina
Both (of the) boys want to study medicine
The boys both want to study medicine

▹ *Con nombre y demostrativo/posesivo:*
Mis dos tíos viven solos
Both (of) my uncles live alone
My uncles both live alone

▹ *Sin nombre:*
Los dos beben más de la cuenta
Both of them *o* They both drink too much

Como objeto de un verbo o preposición

Los hemos invitado a los dos
We've invited both of them *o* them both
Los dos me tenéis harta
I'm fed up with both of you *o* you both

Cuando **los dos** *no puede substituirse por* **ambos**, *se traduce por* **the two** + NOMBRE EN PLURAL *o* **the two of us/you/them**:
¿Tienes los dos libros que te dejé?
Have you got the two books (that) I lent you?

Para otros usos y ejemplos ver la entrada.

d

dos-caballos (SM INV) (*Aut*) deux-chevaux, 2 CV
doscientos/as (ADJ), (PRON), (SM) two hundred; ▸ **seiscientos**
dosel (SM) canopy
doselera (SF) valance
dosificación (SF) dosage
dosificador (SM) dispenser
dosificar ▸ CONJUG 1g (VT) **1** (*Culin, Med, Quím*) to measure out
2 (= *no derrochar*) to be sparing with • **~ las fuerzas** to save one's strength • **el ministro ha dosificado sus apariciones** the minister has chosen his appearances carefully
dosis (SF INV) **1** (*Med*) dose
2 (*Quím*) proportion
3 (= *cantidad*) dose • **una buena ~ de paciencia** a great deal of patience • **con una buena ~ de vanidad** with a good measure of vanity • **en pequeñas ~** in small doses
dossier [dosi'er] (SM) (PL: **dossiers** *o* **dossieres** [dosi'ers *o* dosi'eres]) dossier
▸ **dossier de prensa** press file
dotación (SF) **1** (= *dinero*) endowment • **han aumentado la ~ del premio** the value of the prize has been increased, the prize money has been increased
2 (= *plantilla*) staff, personnel; (*Náut*) crew • **la ~ es insuficiente** we are understaffed • **una ~ del parque de bomberos** a team of firefighters
dotacional (ADJ) • **suelo ~** non-residential land
dotado (ADJ) **1** [*persona*] gifted, exceptional (*EEUU*) • **los niños excepcionalmente ~s** exceptionally gifted children • **un hombre muy bien ~*** a well-endowed man* • **~ de algo**: • **María está dotada de talento musical** María is musically talented *o* gifted • **está ~ de una buena formación religiosa** he has received a good religious education • **~ para algo**: • **Adela no está muy dotada para el deporte** Adela does not have great sporting ability *o* a great talent for sport
2 [*máquina, edificio*] • **~ de algo: un hospital ~ de todos los adelantos técnicos** a hospital equipped with all the latest technology • **un coche ~ de cierre centralizado** a car fitted with central locking
3 [*premio, certamen*] • **un premio ~ con un millón de euros** a prize worth a million euros
dotar ▸ CONJUG 1a (VT) **1** (= *equipar*) • **~ (a) algo de** *o* **con algo** to provide sth with sth • **~on el teatro de una orquesta** the theatre was provided with an orchestra • **han dotado el laboratorio con los mejores instrumentos** the laboratory has been provided with the best equipment, the laboratory has been equipped with the best instruments • **han dotado el avión de toda la tecnología moderna** the plane has been equipped *o* fitted with all the latest technology • **intentan ~ al régimen de legitimidad** they are trying to legitimize the regime
2 • **~ a algn de algo: dotó a su hija con un millón de rupias** he provided his daughter with a million rupees as a dowry • **la naturaleza lo dotó de buenas cualidades** he was endowed *o* blessed by nature with good qualities
dote (SF) **1** [*de novia*] dowry • **con un millón de ~** with a dowry of a million ▸ **dote nupcial** dowry
2 dotes (= *cualidades*) gifts, talents • **tiene excelentes ~s para la pintura** she has a great gift *o* talent for painting ▸ **dotes de adherencia** (*Aut*) road-holding qualities ▸ **dotes de mando** leadership qualities (*pl*)
dovela (SF) keystone, voussoir
doy ▸ **dar**
dozavo (ADJ), (SM) = **doceavo**
dpdo. (ABR) (= **duplicado**) bis
Dpto. (ABR) (= **Departamento**) Dept
Dr. (ABR) (= **doctor**) Dr
Dra. (ABR) (= **doctora**) Dr
dracma (SM) (= *moneda*) drachma
(SF) (*Farm*) drachm, dram
draconiano (ADJ) draconian
DRAE (SM ABR) = **Diccionario de la Real Academia Española**
draga (SF) **1** (= *máquina*) dredge
2 (= *barco*) dredger
dragado (SM) dredging
dragaminas (SM INV) minesweeper
dragar ▸ CONJUG 1h (VT) **1** [+ *río*] to dredge
2 [+ *minas*] to sweep for
drago (SM) dragon tree
dragomán (SM) dragoman
dragón (SM) **1** (*Mit*) dragon
2 (*Mil*) dragoon
3 (*Bot*) snapdragon
4 (*Méx**) (= *tragafuegos*) flame thrower
dragona (SF) **1** (*Mil*) shoulder knot, epaulette
2 (*And, Cono Sur, Méx*) [*de espada*] guard
3 (*Méx*) (= *capa*) hooded cloak
dragoncillo (SM) (*Bot*) tarragon
dragonear ▸ CONJUG 1a (VI) **1** (*LAm*) (= *presumir*) to boast, brag
2 (*Cono Sur*) (= *fingir ser*) • **~ de algo** to pose as sth
(VT) (*Cono Sur*) (= *cortejar*) to court, woo
drama (SM) **1** (= *género*) drama
2 (= *obra*) play • **menudo ~ montó con eso she** made a great drama out of it
dramática (SF) drama, dramatic art
dramáticamente (ADV) dramatically
dramaticidad (SF) dramatic quality
dramático (ADJ) dramatic • **no seas tan ~** don't make such a drama out of it, don't be such a drama queen* (*hum*)
(SM) (= *autor*) dramatist
dramatismo (SM) drama, dramatic quality
dramatizar ▸ CONJUG 1f (VT) to dramatize
dramaturgia (SF) (*al actuar*) drama, theatre art; (*al escribir*) play-writing
dramaturgo/a (SM/F) dramatist, playwright
dramón* (SM) (*hum*) strong drama, melodrama • **¡qué ~ montaste!** you made such a big scene!, what a scene you made!
drapeado (ADJ) draped
(SM) drape
Draque (SM) Drake
drásticamente (ADV) drastically
drástico (ADJ) drastic
drenaje (SM) (*Agr, Med*) drainage
drenar ▸ CONJUG 1a (VT) **1** (*Agr, Med*) to drain
2 (*Econ*) to syphon off
Dresde (SM) Dresden
driblar ▸ CONJUG 1a = **driblear**
drible (SM) dribble
driblear ▸ CONJUG 1a (VI) (*Dep*) to dribble
(VT) • **~ a algn** to dribble past sb
dril (SM) (= *tejido*) drill ▸ **dril de algodón** denim
drive (SM) (*Golf, Tenis*) drive
driver (SM) (PL: **drivers**) (*Golf, Inform*) driver
driza (SF) halyard
droga (SF) **1** (*Med*) drug • **el problema de la ~** the problem of drugs • **cuando la ~ se convierte en adicción** when drug abuse becomes an addiction ▸ **droga blanda** soft drug ▸ **droga de diseño** designer drug ▸ **droga dura** hard drug ▸ **droga milagrosa** wonder drug
2 (*Dep*) dope
3 (*Com*) drug on the market, unsaleable article
4 (*LAm**) (*deuda*) debt • MODISMOS: • **hacer ~** (*Méx**) to refuse to pay up • **mandar a algn a la ~** (*CAm, Caribe**) to tell sb to go to hell*
drogadicción (SF) drug addiction
drogadicto/a (ADJ) addicted to drugs • **su hijo ~** her drug addict son
(SM/F) drug addict
drogado (SM) [*de caballo*] doping
drogar ▸ CONJUG 1h (VT) **1** (*Med*) to drug
2 (*Dep*) to dope
(VPR) **drogarse** to take drugs
drogata‡ (SMF) druggy‡
drogodelincuencia (SF) drug-related crime
drogodelincuente (SMF) drug addict (*who finances his habit through petty crime*)
drogodependencia (SF) drug addiction
drogodependiente (SMF) drug addict, person dependent on drugs
drogota‡ (SMF) druggy‡
droguería (SF) *store that sells household goods, paint etc*
droguero/a (SM/F) **1** [*de tienda*] shopkeeper (*of a droguería*), storekeeper (*EEUU*)
2 (*LAm**) (= *tramposo*) cheat, crook, shyster (*EEUU*); (= *moroso*) slow payer
drogui* (SM) (*Cono Sur*) **1** (= *bebida*) liquor, alcohol
2 (= *borracho*) drunkard
droguista (SMF) = **droguero**
dromedario (SM) **1** (*Zool*) dromedary
2 (*Méx**) tailor
dromeo (SM) emu
dron (SM) drone
dropar ▸ CONJUG 1a (VT) (*Golf*) to drop
druida (SM) druid
drupa (SF) drupe
DSE (SF ABR) (= **Dirección de la Seguridad del Estado**) *former national police headquarters*
Dto. (ABR), **D.to** (ABR) = **descuento**
dto. (ABR) **1** (= **departamento**) dept, dpt
2 (= **descuento**) discount
Dtor. (ABR) (= **Director**) Dir
Dtora. (ABR) (= **Directora**) Dir
dual (ADJ), (SM) (*Ling*) dual
dualidad (SF) **1** [*de aspectos, personaje*] duality
2 (*Cono Sur*) (*Pol*) tied vote, indecisive election
dualismo (SM) dualism
dualista (ADJ) dualist
dubitativamente (ADV) doubtfully, hesitantly
dubitativo (ADJ) [*persona*] hesitant; [*actitud*] uncertain, hesitant
Dublín (SM) Dublin
dublinés/esa (ADJ) Dublin (*antes de s*)
(SM/F) Dubliner
ducado (SM) **1** (= *territorio*) duchy, dukedom
2 (*Econ*) ducat
ducal (ADJ) ducal
ducentésimo (ADJ) two hundredth; ▸ **sexto**
ducha (SF) shower • **darse** *o* **tomarse** *o* **pegarse* una ~** to have a shower, take a shower (*esp EEUU*) • MODISMO: • **una ~ de agua fría**: • **el rechazo de su propuesta fue una ~ de agua fría para él** the rejection of his proposal was a real shock to the system for him • **dar una ~ de agua fría a un proyecto** to pour cold water on a plan ▸ **ducha de teléfono** detachable-head shower, hand-held shower ▸ **ducha escocesa** alternately hot and cold shower ▸ **ducha vaginal** douche
duchar ▸ CONJUG 1a (VT) to give a shower to; (*Med*) to douche • **me has duchado con la manguera** you've drenched me with the hose
(VPR) **ducharse** to have a shower, take a shower (*esp EEUU*)
duchero (SM) (*Arg, Uru*) shower unit
ducho (ADJ) • **~ en algo** (= *experimentado*)

experienced in sth; (= *hábil*) skilled at sth

duco SM lacquer • **pintar al ~** to lacquer

dúctil ADJ **1** [*metal*] ductile
2 [*persona*] easily influenced

ductilidad SF ductility

duda SF **1** (= *incertidumbre*) doubt • **yo todavía tengo mis ~s sobre él** I still have my doubts about him • **tengo la ~ de si he apagado la luz o no** I'm not sure whether I turned off the light or not • **tengo enormes ~s religiosas** I have great religious doubts • **al principio tuve muchas ~s** I had a lot of misgivings *o* doubts at first • **queda la ~ en pie sobre …** doubt remains about … • **un hecho que no admite ~** an unquestionable fact • **ante la ~, no lo hagas** if in doubt, don't • **me asaltó la ~ de si …** I was suddenly seized by a doubt as to whether … • **no cabe ~ de que …** there can be no doubt that … • **no cabe ~ de que vendrá** he'll undoubtedly come • **no me cabe la menor ~ de que vamos a ganar** I have absolutely no doubt that we will win, there is absolutely no doubt in my mind that we will win • **no te quepa ~ de que se acordarán de ti** you can be sure that they will remember you • **en caso de ~** if in doubt • **"en caso de ~, consulte a su farmacéutico"** "if in doubt, consult your pharmacist" • **para desvanecer** *o* **disipar toda ~** in order to clear up any doubts, to banish all doubts • **estar en ~**: • **aún está en ~ si él será el nuevo director** there's still some doubt as to *o* about whether he will be the new manager • **su profesionalismo no está en ~** his professionalism is not in doubt • **estoy en la ~ sobre si me iré de vacaciones o no** I'm undecided *o* in two minds about whether to go on holiday or not • **fuera de toda ~** beyond all doubt • **sin lugar a ~(s)** without doubt, undoubtedly • **dejar lugar a ~s** to leave no room for doubt • **poner algo en ~** to question sth, doubt sth • **nadie está poniendo en ~ su fidelidad** nobody is questioning *o* doubting his fidelity • **no pongo en ~ que sea verdad, pero …** I don't doubt that it's true, but … • **sacar a algn de ~s** *o* **de la ~** to clear things up for sb • **no me saca de ~s** I'm none the wiser • **salir de ~s**: • **pregúntaselo a él, así saldremos de ~s** ask him, then we'll know • **pues no salimos de ~s** we're none the wiser, then • **sin ~** undoubtedly • **esta es, sin ~ alguna, una de las mejores novelas que he leído** this is, without (any) doubt, one of the best novels I've read, this is undoubtedly one of the best novels I've read • **sin sombra de ~** without a shadow of a doubt • MODISMO: • **la ~ ofende**: • **¿cómo que si te lo voy a devolver?, por favor, la ~ ofende** what do you mean am I going to give it back to you?, how could you think otherwise?
2 (= *pregunta*) question, query • **¿queda alguna ~?** are there any queries? • **me surge una ~** there's one point I'm not quite sure about

dudar ▷ CONJUG 1a VT **1** (= *no estar seguro de*) to doubt • **espero que venga, aunque lo dudo mucho** I hope she'll come, although I doubt very much (if) she will • **—yo te ayudaré —no lo dudo, pero …** "I'll help you" — "I'm sure you will, but …" • **es lo mejor para ti, no lo dudes** it's the best thing for you, believe me • **a no ~lo** undoubtedly • **~ que**: • **dudo que sea verdad** I doubt (whether *o* if) it's true • **dudo que yo haya dicho eso** I doubt I said that • **no dudo que sea capaz de hacerlo** I don't doubt that he's capable of doing it • **~ si**: • **dudaba si había echado la carta** I wasn't sure if I had posted the letter
2 (= *vacilar sobre*) • **lo dudé mucho y al final me decidí por el azul** I thought about it *o* dithered* a lot but in the end I decided on the blue one • **si yo fuera tú, no lo ~ía** if I were you, I wouldn't hesitate
VI **1** (= *desconfiar*) to doubt, have doubts • **~ de algo** to question sth, doubt sth • **los celos le hicieron ~ de su cariño** jealousy made her question *o* doubt his affection
2 (= *vacilar*) • **no sé qué hacer, estoy dudando** I don't know what to do, I'm in two minds *o* I'm undecided • **dudamos entre ir en autobús o en taxi** we were not sure whether to go by bus or taxi • **dudaba entre los dos** she couldn't decide between the two • **~ en hacer algo** to hesitate to do sth • **dudaba en comprarlo** he hesitated to buy it • **no dudes en llamarme** don't hesitate to call me

dudosamente ADV • **un proyecto ~ legal** a scheme of dubious *o* questionable legality • **un sistema ~ eficaz** a less than effective system, a somewhat ineffective system • **un comentario ~ democrático** a somewhat anti-democratic comment

dudoso/a ADJ **1** (= *incierto*) [*diagnóstico, futuro*] doubtful, uncertain; [*resultado*] indecisive • **de origen ~** of doubtful *o* uncertain origin • **aún es dudosa su colaboración** it's still uncertain whether he will collaborate, his collaboration is still uncertain
2 (= *vacilante*) [*persona*] hesitant • **estar ~** to be undecided, be in two minds
3 (= *sospechoso*) [*actuación, dinero, reputación*] dubious • **el empleo de tácticas dudosas** the use of suspect *o* dubious tactics
SM/F • **el voto de los ~s** the "undecided" vote

duela SF stave

duele *etc* ▷ **doler**

duelista SMF duellist

duelo[1] SM (*Mil*) duel • **batirse en ~** to fight a duel • **retar a algn a ~** to challenge sb to a duel ▸ **duelo a muerte** fight to the death, duel of death

duelo[2] SM **1** (= *luto*) mourning • **toda la familia está de ~** the whole family is in mourning • **se celebrarán tres días de ~** there will be three days of mourning • **la comitiva de ~** the funeral procession
2 (= *velatorio*) wake
3 (= *dolor*) grief, sorrow
4 • MODISMO: • **sin ~** unrestrainedly • **gastar sin ~** to spend lavishly • **pegar a algn sin ~** to beat sb mercilessly

duende SM **1** (= *elfo*) goblin, elf ▸ **duende de imprenta** printer's devil
2 (= *niño travieso*) imp
3 (= *encanto*) magic • **tiene ~** it has a certain magic
4 (*Inform*) gremlin

duendecillo SM pixie

dueña SF (= *encargada*) [*de casa*] housekeeper; [*de doncellas*] duenna

dueño/a SM/F **1** (= *propietario*) [*de casa, coche, perro*] owner; [*de negocio*] owner, proprietor/proprietress; [*de pensión, taberna*] landlord/landlady • **¿quién es el ~ del caballo?** who is the owner of the horse?, who owns the horse? • **cambiar de ~** to change hands
2 • **ser ~ de**: **ser ~ de la situación** to be the master of the situation, have the situation in hand • **la marina era dueña de los mares** the navy was mistress of the seas • **ser ~ de sí mismo** to have self-control • **eres ~ de hacer lo que te parezca** you can do as you please • **hacerse ~ de algo** to take over sth, take control of sth • **hacerse ~ de una situación** to take command of a situation

duerma *etc* ▷ **dormir**

duermevela SM o SF • **pasé toda la noche en un ~** I tossed and turned all night

Duero SM Douro

dueto SM short duet

dula SF common land, common pasture

dulcamara SF nightshade

dulce ADJ **1** [*caramelo, galleta*] sweet • **este vino está muy ~** this wine is very sweet • **no me gusta lo ~** I don't like sweet things, I don't have a very sweet tooth • MODISMO: • **más ~ que la miel** sweeter than honey; ▷ **agua**
2 (= *suave*) [*metal, sonido, voz*] soft; [*carácter*] gentle; [*clima*] mild; [*música*] sweet • **un instrumento ~** a sweet-sounding instrument • **con el acento ~ del país** with the soft accent of the region
ADV softly • **habla muy ~** she speaks very softly
SM **1** (= *caramelo*) sweet, candy (*EEUU*) • **a nadie le amarga un ~** something's better than nothing ▸ **dulce de almíbar** preserved fruit ▸ **dulce de leche** (*Arg*) caramelized condensed milk ▸ **dulce de membrillo** quince jelly
2 dulces (*gen*) sweet things; (= *pasteles*) cakes and pastries • **le encantan los ~s** he loves sweet things
3 (*And, CAm, Caribe*) (= *azúcar*) sugar, brown sugar
4 (*And*) (= *paleta*) lollipop

dulcémele SM dulcimer

dulcemente ADV [*sonreír, cantar*] sweetly; [*acariciar*] gently; [*amar*] tenderly, fondly; [*contestar*] gently, softly

dulcería SF (*LAm*) confectioner's, sweetshop, candy store (*EEUU*)

dulcero ADJ • **ser ~** to have a sweet tooth

dulcificante SM sweetener

dulcificar ▷ CONJUG 1g VT **1** (*Culin*) to sweeten
2 [+ *consecuencias, carácter, noticia*] to soften
VPR **dulcificarse 1** [*carácter*] to mellow, become milder; [*consecuencias*] to become milder
2 [*clima*] to become milder

dulzaina SF *type of wind instrument, similar to a chanter*

dulzón ADJ, **dulzarrón** ADJ **1** (= *demasiado dulce*) sickly-sweet
2 (*pey*) (= *empalagoso*) cloying

dulzonería SF **1** [*de caramelo, pastel*] sickly-sweetness
2 [*de persona*] cloying nature

dulzor SM, **dulzura** SF **1** [*de caramelo, pastel*] sweetness
2 [*de carácter*] sweetness, gentleness • **con ~** sweetly, softly

dumón* SF • MODISMO: • **vivir a la gran ~** to live the life of Riley

dúmper ['dumper] SM (PL: **dúmpers**) dumper

dumping ['dumpin] SM (*Com*) dumping • **hacer ~** to dump goods

duna SF dune

dundeco* ADJ (*And, CAm*) silly, stupid

dundera* SF (*And, CAm*) silliness, stupidity

dundo* ADJ (*And, CAm*) = **dundeco**

Dunquerque SM Dunkirk

dúo SM **1** (= *composición*) duet, duo
2 [*de músicos, cantantes*] duo • **cantar a dúo** to sing a duet • **me contestaron a dúo** they answered me in unison

duodecimal ADJ duodecimal

duodécimo ADJ twelfth; ▷ **sexto**

duodenal ADJ duodenal

duodeno SM duodenum

dup. ABR, **dupdo.** ABR (= **duplicado**) bis

dupla (SF) (*Arg, Chile*) duo
dúplex (SM INV) **1** (= *piso*) duplex apartment, flat on two floors
2 (*Telec*) link-up
3 (*Inform*) duplex ▸ **dúplex integral** full duplex
duplicación (SF) duplication
duplicado (ADJ) duplicate • **número 14 ~** No. 14A
(SM) duplicate • **por ~** in duplicate
duplicar ▹ CONJUG 1g (VT) **1** [+ *documento*] to duplicate; [+ *llave*] to copy, duplicate
2 [+ *cantidad*] to double • **me duplica la edad** he's twice my age
(VPR) **duplicarse** [*cifra, ganancias*] to double
duplicidad (SF) duplicity, deceitfulness
duplo (ADJ) double
(SM) • **doce es el ~ de seis** twelve is twice six
duque(sa) (SM/F) duke/duchess
(SM) (*Orn*) (*tb* **gran duque**) eagle owl
durabilidad (SF) durability
durable (ADJ) durable, lasting
duración (SF) **1** (= *extensión*) [*de conferencia, viaje*] length; [*de llamada*] time • **la ~ del disco** the length of the record • **¿cuál es la ~ del examen?** how long does the exam last? • **de larga ~** [*parado, paro*] long-term; [*enfermedad*] lengthy • **de poca ~** short ▸ **duración media de la vida** average life expectancy
2 [*de batería, pila*] life • **baterías de larga ~** long-life batteries
duradero (ADJ) [*ropa, tela*] hard-wearing; [*paz, efecto*] lasting; [*relación*] lasting, long-term (*antes de s*)
duralex® (SM INV) Duralex®
duramente (ADV) [*atacar*] fiercely; [*castigar, criticar*] harshly; [*entrenar, trabajar*] hard
durante (PREP) (*con espacio de tiempo*) during; (*expresando la duración*) for • **¿qué hiciste ~ las vacaciones?** what did you do in *o* during the holidays? • **¿ha llovido ~ el fin de semana?** did it rain at *o* over the weekend? • **habló ~ una hora** he spoke for an hour • **~ muchos años** for many years • **~ toda la noche** all through the night, all night long

durar ▹ CONJUG 1a (VI) **1** [*aventura, programa, enfermedad*] to last • **su matrimonio duró menos de dos años** their marriage lasted (for) less than two years • **¿cuánto dura la representación?** how long is the play?, how long does the play last? • **¿cuánto dura el trayecto?** how long is the journey?, how long does the journey take? • **la película duró cinco horas** the film was five hours long • **fue hermoso mientras duró** it was wonderful while it lasted *o* for as long as it lasted • **estuvo refugiado mientras duró la guerra** he was a refugee throughout the (whole length of the) war • **no duro ni un minuto más de pie** I can't stay standing (up) a minute longer • **aún duran los efectos del terremoto** the effects of the earthquake are still being felt • **mis esperanzas ~on poco** my hopes were short-lived • **REFRÁN**: • **no hay mal ni bien que cien años dure** nothing lasts forever
2 [*comida, congelado, ropa*] to last • **a mí me duran mucho los zapatos** my shoes last me a long time • **esta camisa es mala, ~á poco** this shirt is poor quality, it won't last long • **aún me dura el aceite que traje** I've still got some of the oil that I brought back
duraznero (SM) (*esp LAm*) peach tree
durazno (SM) (*esp LAm*) (= *fruta*) peach; (= *árbol*) peach tree
Durero (SM) Dürer
durex® (SM) **1** (*Méx*) (= *cinta adhesiva*) Sellotape®, Scotch tape® (EEUU), sticky tape
2 (= *preservativo*) Durex®, sheath, condom
dureza (SF) **1** (= *resistencia*) [*de mineral, roca, agua*] hardness; [*de carne*] toughness • **la ~ de esta roca** the hardness of this rock • **el mineral de mayor ~** the hardest mineral
2 (= *agresividad*) [*de clima, régimen, crítica*] harshness, severity; [*de deporte, juego*] roughness; [*de ataque*] fierceness; [*de castigo, multa, sentencia*] severity, harshness • **la ~ extrema de la vida en la montaña** the extreme harshness of life in the mountains • **el rugby es un deporte de gran ~** rugby is a very rough sport • **la ~ negociadora del gobierno** the government's tough stance in the negotiations • **con ~: los delitos serán castigados con ~** any offence will be severely punished • **el ejército contraatacó con ~** the army counter-attacked fiercely • **arremetió con ~ contra el gobierno** he launched a fierce attack against the government
3 [*de tarea, prueba, examen*] hardness
4 (= *fortaleza*) hardiness, strength • **la ~ de las mujeres campesinas** the hardiness *o* strength of country women
5 (= *callo*) callus
durmiente (ADJ) sleeping • **la Bella Durmiente (del Bosque)** Sleeping Beauty
(SMF) (= *persona*) sleeper
(SM) (*Ferro*) sleeper, tie (EEUU)
duro/a (ADJ) **1** (= *resistente*) [*material, superficie, cama, agua*] hard; [*cable, alambre*] stiff; [*pan*] hard, stale; [*carne*] tough; [*legumbres*] hard; [*articulación, mecanismo*] stiff; [*músculo*] firm, hard • **la cerradura está muy dura** the lock is very stiff • **MODISMOS**: • **más ~ que una piedra** • **más ~ que un mendrugo** as hard as nails, as tough as old boots; ▹ **huevo**
2 (= *agresivo*) [*clima, tiempo, crítica*] harsh, severe; [*deporte, juego*] rough; [*ataque*] fierce; [*castigo, sentencia*] severe, harsh; [*carácter, actitud*] tough • **fue un ~ golpe para el partido** it was a severe *o* heavy blow to the party • **una postura dura contra la droga** a tough stance *o* hard line against drugs • **el sector ~ del partido** the hardliners in the party • **es muy ~ con sus hijos** he's very strict *o* tough with his children • **hay que tener mano dura con los estudiantes** you have to be firm *o* strict with students, students need a firm hand • **rock ~** hard rock • **MODISMO**: • **a las duras y a las maduras** through thick and thin, through good times and bad; ▹ **disco, núcleo, porno**
3 (= *difícil*) [*tarea, prueba, examen*] hard • **el slálom es una prueba muy dura** the slalom is a very hard *o* tough race • **este coche ha pasado las pruebas más duras** this car has passed the most stringent tests • **lo tienes ~ para aprobar*** it will be hard *o* difficult for you to pass • **¡qué dura es la vida!** it's a hard life! • **MODISMO**: • **ser ~ de pelar** to be a hard nut to crack; ▹ **hueso**
4* (= *torpe*) • **es muy ~ para las matemáticas** he's hopeless *o* no good at maths* • **~ de mollera** dense*, dim* • **~ de oído** (= *medio sordo*) hard of hearing; (*Mús*) tone deaf
5 (*Méx**) (= *borracho*) • **estar ~** to be drunk
(ADV) hard • **mi padre trabaja ~** my father works hard • **pégale** *o* **dale ~** hit him hard
(SM) (= *cinco pesetas*) five pesetas; (= *moneda*) five-peseta coin • **estar sin un ~*** to be broke* • **MODISMOS**: • **¡lo que faltaba para el ~!*** it's the last straw! • **¡y que te den dos ~s!*** and you can get knotted!* • **vender ~s a tres pesetas**: • **cree que en Estados Unidos venden ~s a tres pesetas** he thinks that in the States the streets are paved with gold
(SM/F) **1** (*en película, historia*) tough character • **se hizo el ~ para disimular su tristeza** he acted the tough guy *o* hard man in order to hide his sadness
2 (*Pol*) hard-liner
duvet ['duve] (SM) (= *plumón*) duvet
dux (SM) doge
DVD (SM ABR) (= **disco de vídeo digital**) DVD
DYA (SF ABR) (= **Detente y Ayuda**) *Spanish highway assistance organization*

DURANTE

Para traducir **durante** *tenemos que diferenciar si hace referencia a cuándo ocurre la acción o a cuánto dura.*

¿Cuándo ocurre la acción?

▹ *Traducimos* **durante** *por* **during** *si nos referimos al intervalo de tiempo en que ocurre la acción, cuando la referencia temporal la indica un suceso o actividad determinados:*

Se conocieron durante la guerra
They met during the war
Se puso enferma durante una visita a Madrid
She became ill during a visit to Madrid
La bomba hizo explosión durante la entrega de premios
The bomb went off during the prize-giving ceremony

▹ *También se traduce por* **during** *cuando la referencia temporal viene indicada por un periodo de tiempo concreto:*

El tráfico es peor durante el verano
The traffic is worse during the summer
Durante los años treinta la economía se hallaba en dificultades
The economy was in difficulties during the 1930s

Si se trata de una acción progresiva, o que continúa o que se repite durante todo el periodo de tiempo que se indica, es preferible traducir **durante** *por* **over**:

La situación ha empeorado durante los últimos años
The situation has worsened over the last few years
Durante el fin de semana el actor ha sido visto en varias ocasiones
There have been several sightings of the actor over the weekend

¿Cuánto dura la acción?

▹ *Si nos referimos a la duración de la acción,* **durante** *se traduce generalmente por* **for**:

Llevo sufriendo dolores de cabeza durante más de treinta años
I've been having headaches for more than 30 years
Fue periodista durante cuatro años
He was a journalist for four years

Para otros usos y ejemplos ver la entrada.

Ee

E¹, e [e] SF (*letra*) E, e
E² ABR (= **este**) E
e CONJ (*before words beginning with i and hi, but not hie*) and; ▹ **y**
-e ▹ **Aspects of Word Formation in Spanish 2**
e/ ABR (*Com*) (= **envío**) shpt
EA (*Esp*) ABR (*Mil*) = **Ejército del Aire**
SM ABR (*Pol*) (= **Eusko Alkartasuna**) *Basque political party*
ea EXCL (*llamando la atención*) hey!, say! (EEUU); (*dando ánimos*) come on! • **¡ea pues!** well then!; (= *veamos*) let's see! • **¡ea, andamos!** come on, let's go!
EAU SMPL ABR (= **Emiratos Árabes Unidos**) UAE
ebanista SMF cabinetmaker, carpenter
ebanistería SF **1** (= *oficio*) cabinetmaking
2 (= *obra*) woodwork, carpentry
3 (= *taller*) cabinetmaker's (work shop)
ébano SM ebony
ebonita SF ebonite
ebriedad SF intoxication (*frm*), drunkenness
ebrio ADJ **1** intoxicated (*frm*), drunk
2 (*fig*) blind (**de** with) • **~ de alegría** beside o.s. with joy
Ebro SM Ebro
ebullición SF **1** [*de líquidos*] boiling • **entrar en ~** to begin to boil, come to the boil • **punto de ~** boiling point
2 (*fig*) (= *movimiento*) movement, activity; (= *estado cambiante*) state of flux; (= *alboroto*) turmoil; (= *emoción*) ferment • **la juventud está en ~** young people are boiling over (with excitement) • **llevar un asunto a ~** to bring a matter to the boil
ebúrneo ADJ (*liter*) ivory, like ivory
eccehomo SM poor wretch • **estar hecho un ~** to be in a sorry state
eccema SM eczema
ECG SM ABR (= **electrocardiograma**) ECG
echacuervos SM INV **1** (= *chulo*) pimp
2 (= *tramposo*) cheat, impostor
echada SF **1** (= *acción*) throw, cast; [*de moneda*] toss
2 (*Méx*) (= *fanfarronada*) boast
echadizo/a ADJ **1** [*persona*] spying, sent to spy
2 [*propaganda*] secretly spread; [*carta*] circulated in a clandestine way
3 [*material*] waste
SM/F spy
echado ADJ (*pp de* **echar**) **1** • **estar ~** to lie, be lying (down)
2 (*CAm, Caribe*) (*económicamente*) well-placed, in a good position
3 (*CAm**) (= *perezoso*) lazy, idle
4 (*And**) (= *engreído*) stuck-up*, toffee-nosed*
5 • **MODISMOS:** • **es muy ~ pa'lante*** he's very pushy, he's very forward, he's not backward in coming forward* • **es muy ~ p'atrás*** (= *arrogante*) he's full of himself; (= *tímido*) he's very shy
echador(a) ADJ (*CAm, Méx*) boastful, bragging
SM/F **1** ▸ **echador(a) de cartas** fortune teller
2 (*CAm, Méx*) (= *presumido*) boaster, braggart
echao* ADJ = **echado**

echar

VERBO TRANSITIVO
VERBO INTRANSITIVO
VERBO PRONOMINAL

▹ CONJUG 1a

Para las expresiones **echar abajo, echar en cara, echar la culpa, echar en falta, echar de menos, echar a perder, echar raíces, echar a suertes**, *ver la otra entrada.*

VERBO TRANSITIVO
1 (= *tirar*) [+ *pelota, piedra, dados*] to throw; [+ *basura*] to throw away; [+ *ancla, red*] to cast; [+ *moneda al aire*] to toss; [+ *mirada*] to cast, give; [+ *naipe*] to deal • **échame las llaves** throw me the keys • **échalo a la basura** throw it away • **¿qué te han echado los Reyes?** ≈ what did you get for Christmas? • **MODISMO:** • **~las** (*Cono Sur**) to leg it*, scarper*; ▹ **cara**
2 (= *poner*) to put • **~ carbón a la lumbre** to put coal on the fire • **he echado otra manta en la cama** I've put another blanket on the bed • **¿te echo mantequilla en el pan?** shall I put some butter on your bread? • **échale un poco de azúcar a la mezcla** add a little sugar to the mixture • **tengo que ~ gasolina** I need to fill up (with petrol); ▹ **leña**
3 (= *verter*) to pour • **echó un poco de vino en un vaso** he poured some wine into a glass • **~ cera en un molde** to pour wax into a mould
4 (= *servir*) [+ *bebida*] to pour; [+ *comida*] to give • **échame agua** could you give *o* pour me some water? • **¿te echo más whisky?** shall I pour you some more whisky? • **no me eches tanto** don't give me so much • **tengo que ~ de comer a los animales** I have to feed the animals • **MODISMO:** • **lo que le echen:** • **resiste lo que le echen** she can take whatever they throw at her
5 (= *dejar salir*) • **la chimenea echa humo** smoke is coming out of the chimney • **¡qué peste echan tus zapatos!*** your shoes stink to high heaven!*; ▹ **chispa, espuma, hostia, leche, peste, sangre**
6 (= *expulsar*) (*de casa, bar, tienda, club*) to throw out; (*del trabajo*) to fire*, sack*; (*de colegio*) to expel • **cuando protesté me ~on** when I protested they threw me out • **me echó de su casa** he threw me out of his house • **lo han echado del colegio** he's been expelled from school • **la ~on del trabajo** she's been fired *o* sacked* • **~ algo de sí** to get rid of sth, throw sth off
7 (= *producir*) [+ *dientes*] to cut; [+ *hojas*] to sprout • **está empezando a ~ barriga** he's starting to get a bit of a belly *o* paunch • **¡vaya mal genio que has echado últimamente!** you've become *o* got really bad-tempered recently!
8 (= *cerrar*) • **~ la llave/el cerrojo** to lock/bolt the door • **~ el freno** to brake • **echa la persiana** can you draw the blinds?
9 (= *mover*) **a** [+ *parte del cuerpo*] • **~ la cabeza a un lado** to tilt *o* cock one's head to one side • **~ el cuerpo hacia atrás** to lean back
b (= *empujando*) to push • **~ a algn a un lado** to push sb aside • **~ atrás a la multitud** to push the crowd back
10 (= *enviar*) [+ *carta*] to post, mail (EEUU) • **eché la carta en el buzón** I posted the letter • **¿dónde puedo ~ esta postal?** where can I post this postcard?
11 (= *calcular*) to reckon • **¿cuántos kilos le echas?** how much do you think *o* reckon she weighs? • **¿cuántos años le echas?** how old do you think *o* reckon he is? • **échale una hora andando** you can reckon on it taking you an hour if you walk
12 (= *dar*) [+ *discurso*] to give, make • **~ maldiciones** to curse • **~ una reprimenda a algn** to tick sb off, give sb a ticking-off • **he ido a que me echen las cartas** I've had my cards read
13 (*con sustantivos que implican acciones*) [+ *trago, partida*] to have • **¿echamos un café?** shall we have a coffee? • **salió al balcón a ~ un cigarrillo** he went out onto the balcony for a smoke *o* cigarette • **~ una multa a algn** to fine sb, give sb a fine; ▹ **polvo, vistazo**
14 (+ *tiempo*) • **hay que ~le muchas horas** it takes a long time • **de jóvenes nos echábamos nuestros buenos ratos de charla** we used to spend a lot of time talking when we were younger • **esta semana he echado cuatro horas extras** I did four hours overtime this week
15* (*en cine, televisión*) to show • **~on un programa sobre Einstein** there was a programme about Einstein on, they showed a programme about Einstein • **¿qué echan en el cine?** what's on at the cinema?
16 (+ *cimientos*) to lay
17 (*Zool*) (*para procrear*) • **ha echado a su perra con un pastor alemán** he has mated his bitch with a German shepherd
18 (*Caribe, Cono Sur*) (= *azuzar*) [+ *animal*] to urge on

VERBO INTRANSITIVO
(= *tirar*) • **¡echa para adelante!** lead on! • **ahora tienes que ~ para adelante y olvidarte del pasado** you need to get on with your life and forget about the past • **es un olor que echa para atrás*** it's a smell that really knocks you back* • **echa para allá** move up • **~ por una calle** to go down a street • **echemos por aquí** let's go this way

echar a (+ *infin*) • ~ **a correr** to break into a run, start running • ~ **a reír** to burst out laughing, start laughing

VERBO PRONOMINAL **echarse**

1 (= *lanzarse*) to throw o.s. • **~se en brazos de algn** to throw o.s. into sb's arms • **los niños se ~on al agua** the children jumped into the water • **~se sobre algn** (*gen*) to hurl o.s. at sb, rush at sb; (= *atacando*) to fall on sb

2 (= *acostarse*) to lie down • **voy a ~me un rato** I'm going to lie down for a bit • **me eché en el sofá y me quedé dormido** I lay down *o* stretched out on the sofa and fell asleep • **se echó en el suelo** he lay down on the floor

3 (= *moverse*) • **échate un poco para la izquierda** move a bit to the left • **me tuve que ~ a la derecha para que adelantara** I had to pull over to the right to let him overtake • **~se atrás** (*lit*) to throw o.s. back(wards), move back(wards); (*fig*) to back out • **¡échense para atrás!** move back!

4 (= *ponerse*) • **se echó laca en el pelo** she put some hairspray on • **se echó una manta por las piernas** she put a blanket over her legs **echarse a** (+ *infin*) • **se echó a correr** she broke into a run, she started running

5 (uso enfático) • **~se una novia** to get o.s. a girlfriend • **~se un pitillo** to have a cigarette *o* smoke • **~se una siestecita** to have a nap • **~se un trago** to have a drink

6 • **echárselas de** to make o.s. out to be • **se las echa de experto** he makes himself out to be an expert

7 (Méx) • **~se algo encima** (= *asumir*) to take responsibility for sth • **~se a algn encima** to alienate sb, turn sb against one

8 (Méx)* (= *matar*) • **~se a algn** to bump sb off‡

---

echarpe SM, (*a veces*) SF (woman's) stole, scarf

echazón SF **1** (= *acto*) throwing
2 (*Náut*) jetsam

echón/ona* SM/F (*Caribe, Méx*) braggart, swank* • **¡qué ~!** isn't he full of himself!*

echona SF (*Cono Sur*) small sickle, reaping hook

eclecticismo SM eclecticism

ecléctico/a ADJ, SM/F eclectic

eclesial ADJ ecclesiastic, ecclesiastical, church (*antes de s*)

eclesiástico ADJ (*gen*) ecclesiastic, ecclesiastical; [*autoridades*] church (*antes de s*)
SM clergyman, ecclesiastic

eclesiología SF ecclesiology

eclipsamiento SM eclipse

eclipsar ▸ CONJUG 1a VT (*Astron*) to eclipse; (*fig*) to eclipse, outshine

eclipse SM eclipse ▸ **eclipse lunar** eclipse of the moon, lunar eclipse ▸ **eclipse solar** eclipse of the sun, solar eclipse

eclíptica SF ecliptic

eclíptico ADJ ecliptic

eclisa SF (*Ferro*) fishplate

eclosión SF **1** (= *aparición*) bloom, blooming • **hacer ~** [*huevos, larva*] to hatch • **el modernismo hizo ~ en Latinoamérica muy pronto** modernism burst onto the scene very early in Latin America
2 (*Entomología*) hatching, emerging • **hacer ~** to hatch, emerge

eclosionar ▸ CONJUG 1a VI (*Entomología*) to hatch, emerge

eco SM **1** (= *sonido*) echo • **hacer eco** to echo
2 (= *reacción*) echo • **despertar** *o* **encontrar eco** to produce a response (**en** from) • **la llamada no encontró eco** the call produced no response, the call had no effect • **hacer eco** to make an impression • **hacerse eco de una opinión** to echo an opinion • **tener eco** to catch on, arouse interest

eco... PREF eco...

ecoaldea SF ecovillage

ecoauditor(a) SMF environmental auditor, eco-auditor

ecoauditoría SF environmental audit, eco-audit

ecobolsa SF refill bag

ecocardiograma SM echocardiogram

ecociudad SF (*de gran tamaño*) ecocity; (*más pequeña*) ecotown

ecoclimático ADJ ecoclimatic

ecodesarrollo SM sustainable development

ecoequilibrio SM ecobalance

ecoetiqueta SF eco-label

ecografía SF (= *imagen*) ultrasound scan; (= *técnica*) ultrasound scanning

ecógrafo SM ultrasound scanner

ecolalia SF (*Psic*) echolalia

ecolecuá EXCL (*LAm*) exactly!, that's it!

ecología SF ecology

ecológicamente ADV ecologically

ecológico ADJ [*desastre, zona, equilibrio*] ecological; [*producto*] environment-friendly; [*cultivo*] organic, organically-grown

ecologismo SM conservation(ism), environmentalism

ecologista ADJ conservation (*antes de s*), environmental • **el partido ~** the Green party
SMF ecologist, environmentalist • **los ~s** the Greens

ecologizar ▸ CONJUG 1f VT to make environmentally aware

ecólogo/a SM/F ecologist, environmentalist

ecómetro SM echo sounder

economato SM (= *tienda*) cooperative store; [*de empresa*] company store; (*Mil*) ≈ NAAFI, ≈ PX (EEUU)

econometría SF econometrics (*sing*)

econométrico ADJ econometric

economía SF **1** (*gen*) economy ▸ **economía de empleo completo** full-employment economy ▸ **economía de guerra** war economy ▸ **economía de libre empresa, economía de libre mercado** free-market economy ▸ **economía de mercado** market economy ▸ **economía de pleno empleo** full-employment economy ▸ **economía de subsistencia** subsistence economy ▸ **economía dirigida** planned economy ▸ **economía doméstica** domestic service, home economics ▸ **economía mixta** mixed economy ▸ **economía negra** black economy ▸ **economía oculta** hidden economy ▸ **economía política** political economy ▸ **economías de escala** economies of scale ▸ **economía subterránea, economía sumergida** underground economy, black economy
2 (= *estudio*) economics (*sing*)
3 (= *ahorro*) economy, saving • **hacer ~s** to make economies, economize
4 (*tb* **(Ministerio de) Economía (y Hacienda)**) Ministry of Finance, Treasury Department (EEUU)

económicamente ADV economically • **los ~ débiles** (*euf*) the poor • **los ~ fuertes** (*euf*) the well-off, the wealthy

economicidad SF **1** (*gen*) *economic nature or working etc*
2 (= *rentabilidad*) economic viability, profitability

económico ADJ **1** (*gen*) economic; [*año*] fiscal, financial • **la situación económica** the economic situation
2 (= *barato*) economical, inexpensive • **edición económica** cheap edition, popular edition
3 (= *ahorrativo*) thrifty; (*pey*) miserly

> **ECONÓMICO**
>
> **¿"Economic" o "economical"?**
>
> ▸ *El adjetivo* **económico** *se traduce por* **economic** *cuando se refiere al comercio o las finanzas:*
>
> **China ha vivido cinco años de reformas económicas**
> China has lived through five years of economic reforms
> **... el ritmo del crecimiento económico ...**
> ... the pace of economic growth ...
>
> ▸ **Económico** *se traduce por* **economical** *cuando se usa para describir algo que presenta una buena relación calidad-precio:*
>
> **Resulta más económico tener un coche de gasoil**
> It is more economical to have a diesel-engined car
>
> **Economic** *se puede usar en inglés para traducir* **rentable**:
>
> **Mantendremos las tarifas altas para que el servicio resulte rentable**
> We shall keep the fares high to make the service economic
>
> *Para otros usos y ejemplos ver la entrada.*

economista SMF economist

economizar ▸ CONJUG 1f VT to economize on • ~ **tiempo** to save time
VI to economize

ecónomo/a SM/F (*gen*) trustee, guardian; (*Rel*) ecclesiastical administrator

ecopacifismo SM eco-pacifism

ecopacifista ADJ, SMF eco-pacifist

ecoproducto SM eco-friendly product, environmentally-friendly product

ecosensible ADJ ecosensitive

ecosistema SM ecosystem

ecosonda SF, **ecosondador, ecosondeador** SM echo sounder

ecotasa SF green tax, eco-tax

ecotipo SM ecotype

ecoturismo SM eco-tourism

ecoturista SMF eco-tourist

ecoturístico/a ADJ eco-tourism (*antes de s*)

ectodermo SM ectoderm

ectópico ADJ ectopic

ectoplasma SM ectoplasm

ECU SF ABR (= **Unidad de Cuenta Europea**) ECU

ecu SM ecu

ecuación SF equation ▸ **ecuación cuadrática, ecuación de segundo grado** quadratic equation ▸ **ecuación diferencial** differential equation

Ecuador SM • **el ~** Ecuador

ecuador SM **1** (*Geog*) equator
2 (= *punto medio*) mid point, half-way point, half-way mark • **estamos en el ~ de nuestra vida** we're at the mid-point in our lives

ecualizador SM equalizer

ecualizar ▸ CONJUG 1f VT to equalize, tie (EEUU)

ecuánime ADJ [*carácter*] level-headed; [*humor, ánimo*] calm; [*juicio*] impartial

ecuanimidad SF **1** (= *serenidad*) level-headedness, equanimity
2 (= *imparcialidad*) impartiality

ecuatoguineano/a ADJ of/from Equatorial Guinea

(SM/F) native/inhabitant of Equatorial Guinea
ecuatoreñismo (SM), **ecuatorianismo** (SM) *word o phrase etc peculiar to Ecuador*
ecuatorial (ADJ) equatorial
ecuatoriano/a (ADJ), (SM/F) Ecuadoran
ecuestre (ADJ) equestrian
ecuménico (ADJ) ecumenical
ecumenismo (SM) ecumenicism
eczema (SM) eczema
ed. (ABR) **1** (= **edición**) ed
2 (= **editor**) ed
3 = **editorial**
edad (SF) **1** [*de persona, animal, árbol*] age • **¿qué ~ tiene?** how old is he?, what age is he? • **tenemos la misma ~** we're the same age • **a tu ~ yo ya sabía leer** I could read when I was your age • **jóvenes de ~es comprendidas entre los 18 y los 26 años** young people aged 18 to 26, young people between the age of 18 and 26 • **no aparenta la ~ que tiene** she doesn't look her age • **su madre le dobla la ~** her mother is twice her age • **¿qué ~ le echas?** how old do you think he is? • **~ adulta** adulthood • **llegar a la ~ adulta** to become an adult, reach adulthood • **a la ~ de ocho años** at the age of eight • **murió a los 85 años de ~** she died when she was 85 *o* at the age of 85 • **una mujer de ~ avanzada** a woman of advanced years • **se casó a una ~ avanzada** she married late in life • **un señor de cierta ~** a gentleman of a certain age • **a cierta ~ ya empiezan los dolores** at a certain age the aches and pains start • **un niño de corta ~** a young child • **una persona de ~** an elderly person • **en ~ escolar** of school age • **~ de (la) jubilación** retirement age • **~ límite** age limit • **~ madura** middle age • **persona de ~ madura** middle-aged person • **mediana ~** middle age • **tener ~ de hacer algo** • **estar en (la) ~ de hacer algo** to be old enough to do sth • **ya tienes ~ de trabajar** you're old enough to work now • **no tener ~ para hacer algo** (= *ser muy joven*) not to be old enough to do sth, not to be of an age to do sth; (= *ser muy mayor*) to be too old to do sth • **ya no tengo ~ para ir a la discoteca** I'm too old now to go out clubbing • **tercera ~** (= *personas*) senior citizens (*pl*), older people (*pl*); (= *edad*) old age • **excursiones organizadas para la tercera ~** organized trips for senior citizens *o* older people • **llegar a la tercera ~ es traumático para muchas personas** for many people, reaching old age is traumatic • **MODISMOS**: • **estar en ~ de merecer†** to be of courting age† • **estar en la ~ del pavo** to be at that difficult *o* awkward age ▸ **edad mental** mental age ▸ **edad penal** age of legal responsibility, age of criminal responsibility ▸ **edad viril** manhood; ▹ **mayor, mayoría, menor**
2 (*Hist*) age ▸ **Edad Antigua** *period from the beginning of history to the decline of the Roman Empire* ▸ **Edad Contemporánea** Modern Age, Modern Period ▸ **Edad de(l) Bronce** Bronze Age ▸ **Edad de(l) Hierro** Iron Age ▸ **Edad de Oro** (*Literat*) Golden Age (*of Spanish literature*) ▸ **Edad de Piedra** Stone Age ▸ **Edad Media** Middle Ages (*pl*) ▸ **Edad Moderna** *period from the Middle Ages to the French Revolution*
edafología (SF) pedology, study of soils
edecán (SM) **1** aide-de-camp
2 (*Méx*) assistant
edema (SM) oedema, edema (*EEUU*)
Edén (SM) Eden, Paradise • **es un ~** it's an earthly paradise, it's paradise on earth
ed. física (ABR) (= **educación física**) PE
edible (ADJ) (*LAm*) edible
edición (SF) **1** (= *acto*) publication, issue; (= *industria*) publishing; (*Inform*) editing • **el mundo de la ~** the publishing world • **MODISMO**: • **ser la segunda ~ de algn** to be the very image of sb, be the spitting image of sb* ▸ **edición de sobremesa** desktop publishing ▸ **edición electrónica** (= *creación*) electronic publishing; (= *texto*) electronic edition ▸ **edición en pantalla** on-line editing
2 [*de libro*] edition • **en ~ de** edited by • **"al cerrar la ~"** (*Tip*) "stop-press" ▸ **edición aérea** airmail edition ▸ **edición de bolsillo** pocket edition ▸ **edición de la mañana** morning edition ▸ **edición económica** cheap edition, popular edition ▸ **edición extraordinaria** special edition ▸ **edición numerada** numbered edition ▸ **edición príncipe** first edition ▸ **edición semanal** weekly edition ▸ **edición viva** edition in print, available edition
3 ediciones (= *editorial*) • **Ediciones Ramírez** Ramirez Publications
4 (= *celebración*) • **es la tercera ~ de este festival** this is the third occasion on which this festival has been held
edicto (SM) edict, proclamation
edificabilidad (SF) suitability for building
edificable (ADJ) • **terreno ~** building land, land available for building
edificación (SF) **1** (*Arquit*) construction, building
2 (*moral*) edification
edificante (ADJ) edifying • **una escena poco ~** an unedifying spectacle
edificar ▹ CONJUG 1g (VT) **1** (*Arquit*) to build, construct
2 (*moralmente*) to edify
edificio (SM) **1** (*Arquit*) building, edifice (*frm*) ▸ **edificio de apartamentos** block of flats, apartment building *o* house (*EEUU*) ▸ **edificio de oficinas** office block ▸ **edificio inteligente** smart building, intelligent building
2 (*moral*) edification
edil (SMF) **1** (*Esp*) (= *concejal*) town councillor, councilman/councilwoman (*EEUU*); (= *dignatario*) civic dignitary
2 (*Hist*) aedile
Edimburgo (SM) Edinburgh
Edipo (SM) Oedipus
editable (ADJ) editable
editaje (SM) editing
editar ▹ CONJUG 1a (VT) **1** (= *publicar*) to publish
2 (= *corregir*) (*tb Inform*) to edit
editor(a) (ADJ) publishing (*antes de s*) • **casa ~a** publishing house
(SM/F) **1** [*de libros, periódicos*] publisher
2 (= *redactor*) editor, compiler; (*TV*) editor
3 (*LAm*) [*de periódico*] editor
(SM) (*Inform*) ▸ **editor de pantalla** screen editor ▸ **editor de texto** text editor
editorial (ADJ) **1** [*industria, mundo*] publishing (*antes de s*) • **casa ~** publishing house
2 [*función, política*] editorial
(SM) leading article, editorial
(SF) publishing house
editorialista (SMF) leader writer
editorializar ▹ CONJUG 1f (VI) to write editorials • **el periódico editorializa contra ...** the paper argues editorially against ... • **el diario editorializa ...** the paper says in its editorial ...
Edo. (ABR) (*Méx*) = **Estado**
edredón (SM) eiderdown ▸ **edredón nórdico** duvet, comforter (*EEUU*)
ed. religiosa (ABR) (= **educación religiosa**) RE, RI
Eduardo (SM) Edward
educabilidad (SF) educability
educable (ADJ) educable (*frm*), teachable
educación (SF) **1** (*en el colegio*) education • **han aumentado el presupuesto de ~** they've increased the education budget • **(Ministerio de) Educación y Ciencia** Ministry of Education and Science ▸ **educación a distancia** distance learning ▸ **educación compensatoria** remedial education ▸ **educación de adultos** adult education ▸ **educación especial** special education ▸ **educación física** physical education ▸ **educación infantil** infant education ▸ **educación medioambiental** environmental education ▸ **educación preescolar** pre-school education, nursery education ▸ **educación primaria** primary education ▸ **educación privada** private education ▸ **educación sanitaria** health education ▸ **educación secundaria** secondary education ▸ **Educación Secundaria Obligatoria** (*Esp*) *secondary education, for 12- to 16-year-olds* ▸ **educación sexual** sex education
2 (*en familia*) upbringing • **Rosa recibió una ~ muy estricta** Rosa had a very strict upbringing, Rosa was very strictly brought up
3 (= *modales*) manners (*pl*), good behavior (*EEUU*) • **no tiene ~** she has no manners • **buena ~** good manners (*pl*) • **con ~**: • **se lo pedí con ~** I asked her politely • **falta de ~**: • **eso es una falta de ~** that's rude • **¡qué falta de ~!** how rude! • **mala ~** bad manners (*pl*) • **es de mala ~ comportarse así** it's bad manners *o* rude to behave like that
4 [*de voz, oído, animal*] training
educacional (ADJ) educational
educacionista (SMF) educationist, educationalist
educado (ADJ) (= *de buenos modales*) well-mannered, polite; (= *instruido*) cultivated • **mal ~** (= *de malos modales*) ill-mannered; (= *grosero*) rude
educador(a) (SM/F) educator, teacher
educando/a (SM/F) pupil
educar ▹ CONJUG 1g (VT) **1** (*Educ*) to educate • **la han educado en un colegio bilingüe** she was educated at a bilingual school
2 (*en familia*) to bring up • **~on a sus hijos de una manera muy estricta** their children were brought up very strictly
3 [+ *voz, oído*] to train
4 [+ *animal*] to train
(VPR) **educarse** to be educated • **se educó en un colegio de pago** he was educated at a fee-paying school
educativo (ADJ) **1** (= *instructivo*) educational • **juguete ~** educational toy
2 (= *pedagógico*) • **política educativa** education policy • **sistema ~** education system • **reforma educativa** educational *o* school reform
edulcoración (SF) sweetening
edulcorante (SM) sweetener
edulcorar ▹ CONJUG 1a (VT) to sweeten
EE (ABR) (= **Euskadiko Ezkerra**) *Basque political party*
EEB (SF ABR) (= **encefalopatía espongiforme bovina**) BSE
EE.UU. (ABR) (= **Estados Unidos**) US, USA
efe (SF) (name of the letter) F
efectismo (SM) sensationalism • **su obra rehúye todo ~** his work rejects all sensationalism • **la escena final de la película es de un gran ~** the final scene in the film is really dramatic
efectista (ADJ), (SMF) sensationalist
efectivamente (ADV) **1** (= *verdaderamente*) really • **tengo que comprobar si ~ es así** I have to check if it really is like that
2 (*confirmando algo*) indeed • **~, el robo fue**

llevado a cabo por dos personas the theft was indeed carried out by two people • **—fue ese retraso lo que le salvó la vida —~, así es** "it was that delay that saved his life" — "yes, that's right *o* indeed it was" • **pensé que iba a llegar tarde, y, ~, así fue** I thought he would be late, and sure enough, he was

efectividad (SF) effectiveness • **exigieron que la policía actuara con una mayor ~** they demanded that the police act much more effectively

efectivo (ADJ) **1** (= *eficaz*) [*vacuna, táctica*] effective • **el tratamiento comenzará a ser ~ dentro de un mes** the treatment will begin to take effect *o* will become effective within a month
2 (= *real*) • **el poder ~ está en manos de la oposición** the real power is in the hands of the opposition • **la orden no será efectiva hasta mañana** the order will not take effect *o* become effective until tomorrow • **hacer ~** [+ *plan*] to put into effect; [+ *multa, pago*] to make payable; [+ *cheque*] to cash • **el gobierno hará efectiva la subida salarial antes de marzo** the government will put the pay rises into effect before March • **su dimisión, anunciada el martes, se hizo efectiva el jueves** his resignation, announced on Tuesday, took effect *o* became effective on Thursday
(SM) **1** (= *dinero*) cash • **en ~** in cash • **50 libras en ~** £50 (in) cash • **tres premios en ~** three cash prizes ▸ **efectivo en caja, efectivo en existencia** cash in hand
2 efectivos (*Mil*) forces • **~s de la Policía** • **~s policiales** police officers

efecto (SM) **1** (= *consecuencia*) effect • **los ~s devastadores de la crisis** the devastating effects of the crisis • **ya empiezo a notar los ~s de la anestesia** I'm starting to feel the effect of the anaesthetic now • **los cambios no produjeron ningún ~** the changes did not have *o* produce (*frm*) any effect • **la reforma tuvo por ~ el aumento de los ingresos** the reform had the effect of increasing revenue • **conducía bajo los ~s del alcohol** he was driving under the influence of alcohol • **hacer ~** to take effect • **el calmante no le ha hecho ningún ~** the sedative has had no effect on him *o* has not taken effect • **por ~ de** (= *por acción de*) by; (= *a consecuencia de*) as a result of • **nos movíamos por ~ del viento** we were being driven by the wind • **la producción de vino se estancó por ~ de la crisis** wine production came to a halt as a result of the crisis • **de ~ retardado** [*bomba*] delayed-action (*antes de s*) • **es de ~s retardados** (*hum*) he's a bit slow on the uptake* • **surtir** *o* **tener** *o* **causar ~** to have an effect • **el truco no surtió el ~ deseado** the trick did not have the desired effect • **las picaduras de avispas pueden tener ~s graves** wasp stings can have serious effects ▸ **efecto 2000** (*Inform*) millennium bug, Y2K ▸ **efecto bumerán** boomerang effect ▸ **efectos colaterales** collateral damage (*sing*) ▸ **efecto dominó** domino effect ▸ **efecto embudo** funnel effect ▸ **efecto invernadero** greenhouse effect ▸ **efecto óptico** optical illusion ▸ **efectos especiales** special effects ▸ **efectos secundarios** side effects ▸ **efectos sonoros** sound effects ▸ **efecto túnel** tunnel effect ▸ **efecto útil** (*Mec*) efficiency, output
2 • **en ~** indeed • **nos encontramos, en ~, ante un invento revolucionario** we are indeed faced with a revolutionary invention • **en ~, así es** yes, indeed *o* that's right • **y en ~, el libro estaba donde él dijo** sure enough, the book was where he had said it would be
3 (= *vigencia*) [*de ley, reforma*] • **una ley con ~ desde 1950** a law that has been in force since 1950 • **~ retroactivo**: • **esas medidas tendrán ~ retroactivo** those measures will be applied retroactively *o* retrospectively • **una subida con ~s retroactivos desde primeros de año** an increase backdated to the beginning of the year • **tener ~** to take effect, come into effect
4 (*frm*) (= *objetivo*) purpose • **a ~s fiscales/prácticos** for tax/practical purposes • **a estos ~s se convocó una nueva reunión** a new meeting was called for this purpose • **a ~s legales** for legal purposes, in legal terms • **a ~s de contrato, los dos cónyuges son copropietarios** for the purposes of the contract, husband and wife are co-owners • **a ~s de máxima seguridad** in order to ensure the tightest security • **al ~** for the purpose • **una comisión designada al ~** a specially established commission, a commission set up for the purpose • **a ~s de hacer algo** in order to do sth • **a ~s de conseguir una rebaja de su condena** in order to achieve a reduction of his sentence • **llevar a ~** [+ *acción, cambio*] to carry out; [+ *acuerdo, pacto*] to put into practice; [+ *reunión, congreso*] to hold • **llevaron a ~ sus amenazas** they carried out their threats • **la reunión se llevará a ~ en Bruselas** the meeting is to be held in Brussels • **a tal ~** to this end, for this purpose • **a tal ~, han convocado un referéndum** to this end *o* for this purpose, a referendum has been called • **una habitación habilitada a tal ~** a room fitted out for this purpose • **a todos los ~s** to all intents and purposes • **lo reconoció como hijo suyo a todos los ~s** he recognized him to all intents and purposes as his son
5 (= *impresión*) effect • **no sé qué ~ tendrán mis palabras** I don't know what effect *o* impact my words will have • **les has causado un ~ sorprendente a mis padres** you've made quite an impression on my parents • **ser de buen/mal ~** to create *o* give a good/bad impression • **es de mal ~ llegar tarde a una reunión** being late for a meeting creates *o* gives a bad impression
6 (*Dep*) (*gen*) spin; (*Ftbl*) swerve • **sacó la pelota con ~** she put some spin on her service, she served with topspin • **dar ~ a la pelota** • **lanzar la pelota con ~** (*Tenis*) to put spin on the ball; (*Ftbl*) to put a swerve on the ball
7 efectos (*Com*) (= *bienes*) stock (*sing*), goods; (= *documentos*) bills ▸ **efectos a cobrar** bills receivable ▸ **efectos a pagar** bills payable ▸ **efectos bancarios** bank bills ▸ **efectos de consumo** consumer goods ▸ **efectos de escritorio** writing materials ▸ **efectos descontados** bills discounted ▸ **efectos navales** chandlery (*sing*) ▸ **efectos personales** personal effects
8 (*Numismática*) ▸ **efecto postal** postage stamp

efectuación (SF) accomplishment

efectuar ▷ CONJUG 1e (VT) [+ *acción, reparación, investigación*] to carry out; [+ *viaje, visita, declaración, pago*] to make; [+ *disparo*] to fire; [+ *censo*] to take • **la policía efectuó un registro en la vivienda** the police searched the house, the police carried out a search of the house • **los pagos serán efectuados en metálico** the payments will be made in cash • **el tren ~á parada en todas las estaciones** the train will stop at all stations

efedrina (SF) ephedrine

efeméride (SF) event (*remembered on its anniversary*) • **"efemérides"** (*en periódico*) "list of the day's anniversaries"

efervescencia (SF) **1** [*de líquidos*] fizziness • **entrar** *o* **estar en ~** to effervesce
2 (= *alboroto*) commotion; (= *ánimo*) high spirits (*pl*)

efervescente (ADJ) **1** (= *con burbujas*) [*pastilla, sustancia*] effervescent; [*bebida*] fizzy
2 (= *animado*) high-spirited

eficacia (SF) [*de ley, remedio, producto, sanción*] effectiveness; [*de persona, método*] efficiency

eficaz (ADJ) [*ley, remedio, producto, sanción*] effective; [*persona, método, instrumento*] efficient

eficazmente (ADV) **1** (= *con efecto*) effectively
2 (= *eficientemente*) efficiently

eficiencia (SF) efficiency

eficiente (ADJ) efficient

eficientemente (ADV) efficiently

efigie (SF) **1** (= *busto, escultura*) effigy
2 (= *imagen pintada*) image • **tiene en su despacho una ~ de su abuelo** in his office he's got a portrait of his grandfather • **el euro tendrá la ~ del rey** the euro will carry a likeness of the king
3 (*liter*) (= *personificación*) • **es la ~ de la desesperación** she's despair personified

efímera (SF) mayfly

efímero (ADJ) ephemeral

eflorescente (ADJ) efflorescent

efluvio (SM) outpour, outflow • **un ~ de optimismo** a sudden burst of optimism

efugio (SM) subterfuge, evasion

efusión (SF) **1** (= *derramamiento*) [*de sentimientos*] outpouring; [*de sangre*] shedding ▸ **efusión de sangre** bloodshed, shedding of blood
2 [*de persona*] (*gen*) effusion, outpouring; (*en el trato*) warmth, effusiveness; (*pey*) gushing manner • **con ~** effusively • **efusiones amorosas** amorous excesses

efusivamente (ADV) warmly, effusively • **me saludó muy ~** he gave me a very warm greeting, he greeted me very warmly • **me felicitó muy ~ por mi cumpleaños** he congratulated me very warmly *o* effusively on my birthday

efusividad (SF) effusiveness

efusivo (ADJ) [*persona, modales*] effusive; [*gracias*] effusive, warm • **mis más efusivas gracias** my warmest thanks

EGB (SF ABR) (*Esp*) (= **Educación General Básica**) *former primary school education*

Egeo (SM) • **el mar ~** the Aegean Sea

égida (SF) aegis, protection • **bajo la ~ de** under the aegis of

egipcio/a (ADJ), (SM/F) Egyptian

Egipto (SM) Egypt

egiptología (SF) Egyptology

eglantina (SF) eglantine

eglefino (SM) haddock

égloga (SF) eclogue

ego (SM) ego

egocéntrico (ADJ) egocentric, egocentrical, self-centred, self-centered (*EEUU*)

egocentrismo (SM) egocentrism

egocentrista (SMF) egocentric, self-centred person, self-centered person (*EEUU*)

egoísmo (SM) egoism, selfishness

egoísta (ADJ) egoistical, selfish
(SMF) egoist, selfish person

egoístamente (ADV) egoistically, selfishly

egoistón* (ADJ) rather selfish

ególatra (ADJ) egomaniacal
(SMF) egomaniac

egolatría (SF) egomania

egotismo (SM) egotism

egotista (ADJ) egotistical, egotist
(SMF) egotist

egregio (ADJ) eminent, distinguished

egresado/a (SM/F) (*LAm*) (= *licenciado*)

graduate
egresar ▷ CONJUG 1a (VI) (LAm) **1** (= irse) to go out, leave • ~ **de** to go away from
2 (Univ) to graduate
egreso (SM) (LAm) **1** (= acto) departure
2 (= salida) exit
3 (Univ) graduation
4 (Econ) outgoings (pl), expenditure
eh (EXCL) **1** (llamando la atención) hey!, say! (EEUU) • **¡eh, ven aquí!** hey, come here! • **¡a mí no me repliques, eh!** hey, don't you answer me back!
2 (cuando no se ha entendido algo) eh? • **—¿quieres venir con nosotros? —¿eh?** "do you want to come with us?" — "eh?"
eider (SM) eider duck
eidético (ADJ) eidetic
Eire (SM) Eire
ej. (ABR) (= **ejemplo**) ex
eje (SM) **1** (Geog, Mat) axis • MODISMO: • **partir a algn por el eje***: • **¿que no vienes?, pues me partes por el eje** so you're not coming? well, that really upsets my plans • **me hizo una pregunta que me partió por el eje** he asked me a question which really stumped o floored me* ▸ **eje de abscisas** x-axis ▸ **eje de ordenadas** y-axis ▸ **eje de rotación** axis of rotation ▸ **eje de simetría** axis of symmetry
2 [de rueda] axle ▸ **eje delantero** front axle ▸ **eje trasero** rear axle
3 [de máquina] shaft, spindle • MODISMO: • **untar el eje a algn*** to grease sb's palm ▸ **eje de balancín** rocker shaft ▸ **eje de la hélice** propeller shaft ▸ **eje de impulsión**, **eje motor** drive shaft ▸ **eje del cigüeñal** crankshaft
4 (= centro) • **la economía fue el eje de la conversación** the economy was the main topic of conversation, the conversation centred on the economy • **el eje de la doctrina** the central point of the doctrine
5 (Hist) • **el Eje** the Axis
6 ▸ **eje vial** (Méx) (Aut) urban motorway
ejecución (SF) **1** (= ajusticiamiento) execution ▸ **ejecución sumaria** summary execution
2 (= cumplimiento) [de orden] carrying out, execution; [de deseos] fulfilment, fulfillment (EEUU) • **poner en ~** to carry out
3 (Mús) performance
4 (Jur) attachment
ejecutable (ADJ) feasible, practicable • **legalmente ~** legally enforceable
ejecutante (SMF) (Mús) performer (SM) (Jur) distrainer
ejecutar ▷ CONJUG 1a (VT) **1** (= ajusticiar) to execute
2 (= hacer cumplir) [+ orden, sentencia] to carry out, execute; [+ deseos] to perform, fulfil, fulfill (EEUU)
3 (Mús) to perform, play
4 (Inform) to run
5 (Jur) to attach, distrain on
ejecutiva (SF) (Pol) executive body, executive committee
ejecutivo/a (ADJ) **1** [función, poder] executive
2 (= urgente) [petición] pressing, insistent; [respuesta] prompt; [negocio] urgent, immediate
(SM) (Pol) executive • **el Ejecutivo** the Executive
(SM/F) (Com) executive ▸ **ejecutivo/a de cuentas** account executive ▸ **ejecutivo/a de ventas** sales executive
ejecutor(a) (SM/F) executor/executrix • **los ~es testamentarios** the executors of the will
ejecutoria (SF) **1** (= título) letters patent of nobility; (fig) pedigree
2 (Jur) final judgment
ejem (EXCL) hem! (cough)
ejemplar (ADJ) exemplary, model
(SM) **1** (= individuo) (gen) example; (Zool) specimen, example; [de libro] copy; [de revista] number, issue ▸ **ejemplar de firma** specimen signature ▸ **ejemplar de regalo** complimentary copy ▸ **ejemplar gratuito** free copy ▸ **ejemplar obsequio** complimentary copy
2 (= precedente) example, model, precedent • **sin ~** unprecedented
ejemplaridad (SF) exemplariness
ejemplarizador (ADJ), **ejemplarizante** (ADJ) exemplary
ejemplarizar ▷ CONJUG 1f (VT) (esp LAm) (= dar ejemplo) to set an example to; (= ilustrar) to exemplify, illustrate
ejemplarmente (ADV) [actuar] in exemplary fashion • **castigar ~ a algn** to make an example of sb
ejemplificar ▷ CONJUG 1g (VT) to exemplify, illustrate
ejemplo (SM) **1** (= paradigma) example • **¿puedes ponerme o darme un ~?** can you give me an example? • **por ~** for example, for instance • **poner como o de o por ~** to give as an example • **tomar algo por ~** to take sth as an example
2 (= modelo) example • **dar ~ a algn** to set sb an example • **servir de o como ~** to serve as an example • MODISMOS: • **predicar con el ~** to set a good example, lead by example • **ser el vivo ~ de algo** to be a model of sth • **es el vivo ~ de la cortesía** he's a model of politeness
ejercer ▷ CONJUG 2b (VT) **1** [+ medicina, abogacía] to practise, practice (EEUU) • **es abogado pero no ejerce su profesión** he's a lawyer by training, but he doesn't practise
2 (= hacer efectivo) [+ influencia] to exert, exercise; [+ poder] to exercise, wield • **ejerce mucha influencia sobre sus hermanos** he exerts o has a great deal of influence on his brothers
3 [+ derecho] to exercise • **~ el derecho al voto** to exercise one's right to vote
(VI) [profesional] to practise, practice (EEUU) (de as) • **es médico, pero ya no ejerce** he's a doctor, but he no longer practises
ejercicio (SM) **1** (físico) exercise • **la natación es un ~ muy completo** swimming is an all-round exercise • **hacer ~** to exercise ▸ **ejercicio de calentamiento** warm-up exercise ▸ **ejercicio de estiramiento** stretching exercise ▸ **ejercicio de mantenimiento** keep-fit exercise ▸ **ejercicios gimnásticos** gymnastic exercises
2 (Educ) exercise • **la maestra nos puso varios ~s** the teacher gave us several exercises to do ▸ **ejercicio escrito** written exercise ▸ **ejercicio práctico** practical
3 (Mil) exercise • **las tropas españolas participan en los ~s de la OTAN** Spanish troops are taking part in NATO exercises ▸ **ejercicio acrobático** (Aer) stunt ▸ **ejercicios de tiro** target practice (sing)
4 [de cargo] • **en el ~ de mi cargo** in the exercise of my duties • **abogado en ~** practising o (EEUU) practicing lawyer • **hicieron ~ de su derecho al voto** they exercised their right to vote
5 (Com, Econ) financial year, fiscal year • **durante el ~ actual** during the current financial year ▸ **ejercicio contable** year of account, accounting year ▸ **ejercicio fiscal** fiscal year, tax year ▸ **ejercicio presupuestario** budget year
6 (Rel) ▸ **ejercicios espirituales** retreat (sing)
ejerciente (ADJ) practising, practicing (EEUU)
ejercitación (SF) [de la mente, los músculos] exercising; [de un idioma] practice
ejercitar ▷ CONJUG 1a (VT) [+ músculo, memoria] to exercise; [+ profesión] to practise, practice (EEUU); [+ ejército] to drill, train; [+ alumno] to train, coach
(VPR) **ejercitarse** [+ músculos, memoria] to exercise; [+ profesión] to practise, practice (EEUU); (Mil) to drill, train
ejército (SM) **1** (Mil) army • **estar en el ~** to be in the army • **los tres ~s** the forces, the Services ▸ **ejército del aire** Air Force ▸ **ejército de ocupación** army of occupation ▸ **Ejército de Salvación** Salvation Army ▸ **ejército de tierra** Army ▸ **ejército permanente** standing army
2 (= multitud) army • **un ~ de fotógrafos** an army of photographers
ejidal (ADJ) (Méx) communal land (antes de s); [terreno] communal
ejidatario/a (SM/F) (esp Méx) holder of a share in common lands
ejido (SM) common land
-ejo, -eja ▷ **Aspects of Word Formation in Spanish 2**
ejote (SM) (CAm, Méx) string bean
el, la, los, las (ART DEF) **1** (con nombres de referente único o concreto) the • **el sol** the sun • **perdí el autobús** I missed the bus • **¿está fría el agua?** is the water cold? • **¿ha llegado ya el abogado?** has the lawyer arrived yet? • **el tío ese*** that chap
2 (en algunos casos no se traduce) **a** (con nombres propios) • **La India** India • **en el México de hoy** in present-day Mexico • **el Real Madrid ganó la liga** Real Madrid won the league • **el General Prim** General Prim • **¿qué manda la señora?** what would madam like? • **ha llamado el Sr. Sendra** Mr. Sendra called • **dáselo a la Luisa*** give it to Luisa
b (con nombres en sentido genérico) • **me gusta el baloncesto** I like basketball • **no me gusta el pescado** I don't like fish • **está en la cárcel** he's in jail
c (con infinitivo) • **el hacerlo fue un error** doing it was a mistake, it was a mistake to do it
d (con cifras, proporciones) • **la mitad de la población** half of the population • **ahora gano el 3% más** I now earn 3% more
3 (traducido por el posesivo) • **se lavó las manos** he washed his hands • **me he cortado el pelo** I've had my hair cut • **ayer me lavé la cabeza** I washed my hair yesterday • **me puse el abrigo** I put my coat on
4 (con expresiones temporales) • **a las ocho** at eight o'clock • **a los quince días** after a fortnight • **vendrá el lunes que viene** he's coming next Monday • **la reunión será el 15 de abril** the meeting's on 15 April • **en el mes de julio** in (the month of) July
5 (= uso distributivo) • **cuesta dos euros el kilo** it costs two euros a kilo
6 (en exclamaciones) • **¡el frío que hacía!** it was freezing!
7 (posesivo) • **el de**: • **mi libro y el de usted** my book and yours • **este jugador y el de la camisa azul** this player and the one in the blue shirt • **el del sombrero rojo** the one with o in the red hat • **es un traje bonito, pero prefiero el de Ana** it's a nice suit, but I prefer Ana's • **y el de todos los demás** and that of everybody else, and everybody else's • **el idiota de Pedro no me contestó al teléfono** that idiot Pedro didn't answer the phone
8 • **el que a** (+ indic) • **el que compramos no vale** the one we bought is no good • **a los que mencionamos añádase este** add this one to the ones we mentioned • **yo fui el que**

e

lo encontró I was the one who found it • **él es el que quiere** it's he who wants to, he's the one who wants to • **los que hacen eso son tontos** anyone who does that is a fool, those who do so are foolish
b (+ *subjun*) whoever • **el que quiera, que lo haga** whoever wants to can do it
él (PRON PERS MASC) **1** (*sujeto*) (= *persona*) he; (= *cosa, animal*) it • **¡es él!** it's him!
2 (*después de prep*) (= *persona*) him; (= *cosa, animal*) it • **esto es para él** this is for him • **vamos sin él** let's go without him
3 (*uso posesivo*) • **de él** (= *persona*) his; (= *cosa, animal*) its • **mis libros y los de él** my books and his • **todo eso es de él** all that is his, all that belongs to him
elaboración (SF) **1** (= *fabricación*) [*de producto*] production; [*de madera, metal*] working • **el proceso de ~ del vino** the wine-making process • **la ~ de nuestros quesos es artesanal** our cheeses are made by traditional methods
2 (= *preparación*) [*de proyecto, presupuesto, lista, candidatura*] drawing up; [*de estrategia*] devising • **la ~ del plan pasó por diversas fases** the process of drawing up the plan went through various stages
3 [*de documento, código*] writing, preparation
elaborar ▸ CONJUG 1a (VT) **1** (= *fabricar*) [+ *producto*] to produce, make; [+ *metal, madera*] to work • **elaboramos todos nuestros productos con ingredientes naturales** we make all our products from natural ingredients
2 (= *preparar*) [+ *proyecto, plan*] to draw up, prepare; [+ *estrategia*] to devise; [+ *presupuesto, lista, candidatura*] to draw up • **cómo ~ un plan de emergencia** how to draw up *o* prepare an emergency plan
3 [+ *documento, código*] to write, prepare
(VPR) **elaborarse** • **un postre que se elabora con coco y azúcar** a dessert that's made using coconut and sugar
elación (SF) **1** (= *alegría*) elation
2 (= *orgullo*) haughtiness, pride
3 (= *pomposidad*) pomposity
4 (*LAm*) (= *alegría*) elation
elasticidad (SF) **1** [*de material*] elasticity; [*de la madera*] spring
2 (= *adaptabilidad*) elasticity
elástico (ADJ) **1** [*material*] elastic; [*principio*] flexible; [*superficie etc*] springy
2 (= *adaptable*) (*gen*) elastic; (*moralmente*) resilient
(SM) (= *material*) elastic; (= *trozo*) piece of elastic; (= *goma*) elastic band
ELE (ABR) = **español como lengua extranjera**
ele (SF) (name of the letter) L
elección (SF) **1** (= *selección*) choice • **una ~ muy acertada** an excellent choice • **lo dejo a su ~** I'll leave the choice to you • **no tuve otra ~ que irme** I had no choice *o* alternative but to leave • **no queda otra ~** there is no choice *o* alternative • **su patria de ~** his chosen country ▸ **elección al azar** (*Mat*) random sampling
2 (*Pol*) election (a for) ▸ **elecciones autonómicas** regional election (*sing*) ▸ **elecciones generales** general election (*sing*) ▸ **elecciones legislativas** parliamentary election (*sing*) ▸ **elecciones municipales** local elections ▸ **elecciones primarias** primaries
eleccionario (ADJ) (*LAm*) electoral, election (*antes de s*)
electivo (ADJ) elective
electo (ADJ) elect • **el presidente ~** the president-elect
elector(a) (SM/F) elector, voter
electorado (SM) electorate, voters (*pl*)
electoral (ADJ) electoral • **potencia ~** voting power
electoralismo (SM) electioneering
electoralista (ADJ) electioneering (*antes de s*)
electoralmente (ADV) electorally
electorero* (ADJ) electioneering (*antes de s*)
electorista (ADJ) election (*antes de s*)
eléctrica (SF) electricity company; ▸ eléctrico
electricidad (SF) electricity ▸ **electricidad estática** static electricity
electricista (SMF) electrician
eléctrico (ADJ) electric, electrical; ▸ eléctrica

> **ELÉCTRICO**
>
> **¿"Electric" o "electrical"?**
>
> ▷ *El adjetivo* **eléctrico** *se traduce por* **electric** *cuando nos referimos a un aparato en particular o a la luz eléctrica:*
>
> **Siempre duermo con una manta eléctrica**
> I always sleep with an electric blanket
> **... una estufa eléctrica ...**
> ... an electric heater ...
> **... la invención de la luz eléctrica ...**
> ... the invention of electric light ...
>
> ▷ *En cambio, si hablamos de aparatos eléctricos en general o de la electricidad generada por un organismo vivo, se traduce por* **electrical**:
>
> **... aparatos eléctricos ...**
> ... electrical appliances ...
> **... componentes eléctricos ...**
> ... electrical components ...
> **... la actividad eléctrica en el cerebro ...**
> ... electrical activity in the brain ...
> **Eso ha ocurrido a consecuencia de un fallo eléctrico**
> That was caused by an electrical fault

electrificación (SF) electrification
electrificar ▸ CONJUG 1g (VT) to electrify
electrizante (ADJ) electrifying (*tb fig*)
electrizar ▸ CONJUG 1f (VT) to electrify (*tb fig*) • **su discurso electrizó al público** his speech electrified his listeners
electro... (PREF) electro...
electrocardiograma (SM) electrocardiogram
electrochapado (ADJ) electroplated
electrochoque (SM) electroshock
electroconvulsivo (ADJ) electroconvulsive
electrocución (SF) electrocution
electrocutar ▸ CONJUG 1a (VT) to electrocute
(VPR) **electrocutarse** to be electrocuted, electrocute o.s.
electrodinámica (SF) electrodynamics (*sing*)
electrodo (SM), **eléctrodo** (SM) electrode
electrodoméstico (ADJ) • **aparato ~** electrical household appliance
(SM) electrical household appliance
▸ **electrodomésticos de línea blanca** white goods, major appliances (*EEUU*)
electroencefalograma (SM) electroencephalogram
electroimán (SM) electromagnet
electrólisis (SF INV) electrolysis
electroluminiscente (ADJ) electroluminescent
electromagnético (ADJ) electromagnetic
electromagnetismo (SM) electromagnetism
electromecánico (ADJ) electromechanical
electromotor (SM) electric motor
electrón (SM) electron
electrónica (SF) electronics ▸ **electrónica de consumo** consumer electronics ▸ **electrónica de precisión** precision electronics
electrónico (ADJ) [*juego, sistema, música*] electronic; [*microscopio*] electron (*antes de s*) • **proceso ~ de datos** (*Inform*) electronic data processing
electronuclear (ADJ) • **central ~** nuclear power station • **programa ~** nuclear power programme
electroquímico (ADJ) electrochemical
electroshock (SM) = electrochoque
electrostático (ADJ) electrostatic
electrotecnia (SF) electrical engineering
electrotécnico/a (SM/F) electrical engineer
electrotermo (SM) immersion heater, immersible heater (*EEUU*)
electrotren (SM) express electric train
elefante/a (SM/F) elephant • **MODISMO**: • **como un ~ en una cacharrería** like a bull in a china shop ▸ **elefante blanco** white elephant
elefantino (ADJ) elephantine
elegancia (SF) **1** [*de persona*] (*en el hablar*) elegance; (*en los movimientos*) gracefulness; (*en el vestir*) stylishness, smartness
2 [*de decoración*] tastefulness, elegance
3 [*de estilo*] polish
elegante (ADJ) (*gen*) elegant; [*traje, fiesta, tienda*] fashionable, smart; [*sociedad*] fashionable, elegant; [*decoración*] tasteful; [*frase*] elegant, well-turned, polished
elegantemente (ADV) [*hablar*] elegantly; [*moverse*] gracefully; [*vestir*] stylishly, smartly; [*decorar*] tastefully, elegantly
elegantón (ADJ), **elegantoso** (ADJ) (*LAm*) = elegante
elegía (SF) elegy
elegiaco (ADJ), **elegíaco** (ADJ) elegiac
elegibilidad (SF) eligibility
elegible (ADJ) eligible
elegido (ADJ) **1** (= *escogido*) chosen, selected
2 (*Pol*) elect, elected
elegir ▸ CONJUG 3c, 3k (VT) **1** (= *escoger*) to choose, select • **la eligieron por su profesionalidad** she was chosen *o* selected for her professionalism • **no sabía qué color ~** I didn't know which colour to choose • **a ~ entre cinco tipos** there are five sorts to choose *o* select from • **café con bizcochos a ~** coffee with a choice of cakes • **hablará en francés o italiano, a ~** he will speak in French or Italian as you prefer • **te dan a ~ entre dos modelos** you're given a choice of two models
2 [+ *candidato*] to elect • **me eligieron delegado de curso** I was elected class representative
elementado (ADJ) (*And, Cono Sur*) (= *aturdido*) bewildered; (= *bobo*) silly, stupid
elemental (ADJ) **1** (= *básico, rudimentario*) elementary • **un curso de inglés ~** an elementary English course • **tiene nociones ~es de matemáticas** she's got a basic knowledge of maths • **eso va en contra de las reglas de cortesía más ~es** that's contrary to the most basic standards of politeness
2 [*derecho, principio*] basic
3 (= *necesario*) essential • **saber inglés es ~ para este trabajo** a knowledge of English is essential for this job
4 (= *de los elementos*) elemental • **física ~** elemental *o* elementary physics
elementarse ▸ CONJUG 1a (VPR) (*Cono Sur*) to get bewildered
elemento (SM) **1** (= *parte*) element • **la integridad es un ~ importante de su**

carácter integrity is an important element in his character • **los ~s de una máquina** the parts of a machine • **el ~ narrativo** the narrative element • **el ~ sorpresa** the element of surprise ▸ **elemento constituyente** constituent
2 (*Fís, Quím*) element ▸ **elemento radioactivo** radioactive element
3 (*Elec*) element; [*de pila*] cell
4 (= *ambiente*) • **estar en su ~** to be in one's element
5 (= *persona*) • **vino a verle un ~** (*LAm*) someone came to see you • **~s subversivos** subversive elements • **¡menudo ~ estás hecho, Pepe!** (*Esp**) you're a proper little terror Pepe! • **su marido es un ~ de cuidado** (*Esp**) her husband is a nasty piece of work*
6 (*And, Caribe, Cono Sur*) (= *imbécil*) dimwit*
7 (*Caribe*) (= *tipo raro*) odd person, eccentric
8 **elementos** (= *nociones*) elements, basic principles • **~s de geometría** elements of geometry, basic geometry (*sing*)
9 **elementos** (= *fuerzas naturales*) elements • **los cuatro ~s** the four elements • **quedó a merced de los ~s** (*liter*) she was left at the mercy of the elements
10 ▸ **elementos de juicio** data (*sing*), facts
Elena (SF) Helen
elenco (SM) 1 (= *lista*) catalogue, catalog (EEUU), list; (*Teat*) cast
2 (*And, Cono Sur*) (= *personal*) staff, team
3 (*LAm*) (*Dep*) (= *equipo*) team
elepé (SM) long-playing record, LP
elevación (SF) 1 [*de objeto, brazo*] raising
2 (= *aumento*) [*de precios, tipos*] rise, increase; [*de nivel, temperatura*] rise • **la ~ del nivel del mar** the rise in the sea level
3 (= *montículo*) hill, elevation (*frm*)
4 (= *ascenso*) elevation • **su ~ al Papado** his elevation to the Papacy
5 (*Jur*) presentation, submission • **la ~ de un recurso al Tribunal Supremo** the presentation *o* submission of an appeal to the High Court
6 (= *sublimidad*) [*de estilo*] elevation, loftiness; [*de sentimientos*] nobility
7 (*Rel*) (*en la misa*) elevation
elevadamente (ADV) loftily
elevado (ADJ) 1 (*en nivel*) [*precio, temperatura, cantidad*] high; [*velocidad*] high, great; [*ritmo*] great • **un porcentaje muy ~ de usuarios** a very high percentage of users • **debido al ~ número de accidentes** due to the large number of accidents
2 (*en altura*) [*edificio*] tall; [*montaña, terreno*] high; ▸ **paso²**
3 (= *sublime*) [*estilo*] elevated, lofty; [*pensamientos*] noble, lofty
4 [*puesto, rango*] high, important
(SM) (*Cuba*) (*Ferro*) overhead railway; (*Aut*) flyover, overpass (EEUU)
elevador (SM) elevator, hoist; (*LAm*) lift, elevator (EEUU) ▸ **elevador de granos** elevator, grain elevator ▸ **elevador de tensión, elevador de voltaje** (*Elec*) booster
elevadorista (SMF) (*LAm*) lift operator, elevator operator (EEUU)
elevalunas (SM INV) ▸ **elevalunas eléctrico** electric windows
elevar ▸ CONJUG 1a (VT) 1 (= *levantar*) [+ *objeto, brazos*] to raise • **~on el coche con la grúa** they raised the car with the crane • **elevemos nuestro pensamiento a Dios** let us raise our thoughts to God • **una sinfonía que eleva el espíritu** a symphony that is spiritually uplifting *o* that uplifts the spirit
2 (= *aumentar*) **a** [+ *precio, tipo, temperatura, calidad*] to raise • **el consumo de huevos eleva el nivel de colesterol** eating eggs increases *o* raises one's cholesterol level • **el juez le elevó la condena a dos años** the judge increased (the length of) his sentence to two years
b [+ *voz*] to raise • **~ el tono de la voz** to raise one's voice
3 [+ *muro*] to raise, make higher
4 • **~ a algn a algo** to elevate sb to sth (*frm*) • **lo ~on al pontificado** he was made Pope, he was elevated to the pontificate (*frm*) • **~on a su ídolo a la categoría de dios** they raised *o* elevated (*frm*) their idol to the level of a god • **~ a algn a los altares** to canonize sb
5 [+ *petición, solicitud*] to present, submit • **elevó una petición al Tribunal Supremo** he presented *o* submitted an appeal to the High Court, he appealed to the High Court
6 (*Mat*) • **~ al cuadrado** to square • **tres elevado al cuadrado** three squared • **~ al cubo** to cube • **~ un número a la cuarta potencia** to raise a number to the power of four
7 (*Elec*) [+ *voltaje*] to boost
8 (*Chile**) (= *reprender*) to tell off*
(VPR) **elevarse** 1 (= *erguirse*) [*montaña, edificio*] to rise • **la cordillera se eleva 2.500m sobre el nivel del mar** the mountain range rises to 2,500m above sea level • **el rascacielos se eleva por encima del parque** the skyscraper soars *o* rises above the park
2 (= *estar situado*) to stand • **en la plaza se eleva la iglesia** the church stands in the square
3 (= *ascender*) [*humo*] to rise; [*avión*] to climb • **el humo se elevaba hacia el cielo** the smoke rose into the sky • **el avión se elevó hasta 7.800 metros** the plane climbed to 7,800 metres • **el balón se elevó por encima de la portería** the ball went over the top of the goal
4 (= *aumentar*) to rise, increase • **si se le eleva la fiebre** if his temperature rises *o* increases • **en el interior de la cámara la temperatura se eleva tres grados más** inside the chamber the temperature rises *o* increases by three degrees
5 (= *alcanzar*) • **~se a** [*cifra, cantidad*] to stand at, amount to; [*temperatura*] to be, reach • **la cifra de heridos se eleva ya a 300** the number of the injured now stands at 300 *o* is now 300 • **la temperatura se elevó a 40 grados** the temperature reached 40 degrees
6 (*en estilo*) • **el tono de la obra se eleva al final** the tone of the work becomes loftier *o* more elevated at the end
7 (= *enajenarse*) to go into raptures
8 (= *envanecerse*) to get conceited
Elías (SM) Elijah
elidir ▸ CONJUG 3a (VT) to elide
(VPR) **elidirse** to elide, be elided
elija *etc* ▸ **elegir**
eliminable (ADJ) dispensable
eliminación (SF) 1 (= *de posibilidades*) elimination • **acertó la respuesta por ~** he got the right answer by (a) process of elimination
2 [*de concursante, deportista*] elimination • **protestó por su ~ del concurso** she protested against her elimination from the competition
3 (= *desaparición*) [*de mancha, obstáculo*] removal; [*de residuos*] disposal • **la ~ de la corrupción** the rooting out of corruption
4 [*de incógnita*] elimination
5 (*Fisiol*) elimination
eliminar ▸ CONJUG 1a (VT) 1 (= *hacer desaparecer*) [+ *mancha, obstáculo*] to remove, get rid of; [+ *residuos*] to dispose of; [+ *pobreza*] to eliminate, eradicate; [+ *posibilidad*] to rule out • **un detergente que elimina las manchas** a washing powder that removes the stains • **debemos ~ la desigualdad entre los sexos** we must eliminate sexual inequality • **~ un directorio** (*Inform*) to remove *o* delete a directory
2 [+ *concursante, deportista*] to knock out, eliminate • **fueron eliminados de la competición** they were knocked out of *o* eliminated from the competition
3 (*euf*) (= *matar*) to eliminate, do away with*
4 [+ *incógnita*] to eliminate
5 (*Fisiol*) to eliminate
(VPR) **eliminarse** (*Méx*) to go away
eliminatoria (SF) (*Dep*) (= *partido*) qualifying round; (= *carrera*) heat; (= *competición*) qualifying competition
eliminatorio (ADJ) [*carrera, partido, examen*] qualifying; [*fase, ronda*] qualifying, preliminary
elipse (SF) ellipse
elipsis (SF INV) ellipsis
elíptico (ADJ) elliptical, elliptic
Eliseo¹ (SM) (*Biblia*) Elisha
Elíseo² (SM) (*clásico*) Elysium • **Los Campos ~s** the Champs Elysées
elisión (SF) elision
élite ['elite] (SF), **elite** [e'lite] (SF) elite
elitismo (SM) elitism
elitista (ADJ), (SMF) elitist
elixir (SM) elixir ▸ **elixir bucal** mouthwash ▸ **elixir de la (eterna) juventud** elixir of life
ella (PRON PERS FEM) 1 (*sujeto*) (= *persona*) she; (= *cosa*) it
2 (*después de prep*) (= *persona*) her; (= *cosa*) it • **estuve con ~** I was with her • **no podemos sin ~** without her we can't
3 (*uso posesivo*) • **de ~** (= *persona*) hers; (= *cosa*) its • **nada de esto es de ~** none of this is hers • **mi sombrero y el de ~** my hat and hers
ellas (PRON PERS FPL) ▸ **ellos**
elle (SF) (name of the letter) ll
ello (PRON) 1 it • **no tiene fuerzas para ~** he's not strong enough for it • **~ no es obstáculo para que venga** that shouldn't stop him coming • **~ es difícil** it's awkward • **~ no me gusta** I don't like it • **todo ~ se acabó** the whole thing is over and done with
2 (*locuciones*) • **es por ~ por lo que …** • **es por ~ que …** that is why … • **por ~ no quiero** that's why I don't want to • **~ dirá** time will tell • **¡a por ~!** here goes!
ellos/as (PRON PERS MPL/FPL) 1 (*como sujeto*) they • **—¿quién lo sabe? —ellos** "who knows?" — "they do" *o* "them" • **ellas no lo saben** they don't know • **me dijiste que ~ no vendrían** you told me they wouldn't be coming • **ellas nunca llegan tarde, pero ellos sí** the girls never arrive late, but the boys do
2 (*después de prep*) them • **a ~: dáselo a ~** give it to them • **pregúntales a ellas** ask them • **no se lo digas a ~** don't tell them • **a ~ no les han robado** they didn't rob them • **estamos esperándolas a ellas** we're waiting for them • **con ~** with them • **entre ~** between them • **para ~** for them
3 (*en comparaciones*) • **como ~** as them • **soy tan rica como ellas** I'm just as rich as them • **no puedo comportarme como ~** I can't behave like them • **que ~** than them • **tenemos más poder que ~** we're more powerful than them
4 (*como posesivo*) • **de ~** theirs • **el libro es de ~** the book is theirs • **este dinero es de ellas** this money is theirs • **estuvimos en casa de ~** we were at their house • **fue culpa de ellas** it was their fault; ▸ **él, ella**
ELN (SM ABR) (*Bol, Col*) = **Ejército de Liberación Nacional**
elocución (SF) elocution
elocuencia (SF) eloquence
elocuente (ADJ) eloquent • **un dato ~** a fact

e

which speaks for itself
elocuentemente ADV eloquently
elogiable ADJ praiseworthy
elogiar ▷ CONJUG 1b VT to praise, eulogize (*liter*)
elogio SM (= *alabanza*) praise; (= *homenaje*) tribute • **queda por encima de todo ~** it's beyond praise • **hacer ~ de** to sing the praises of • **hizo un caluroso ~ del héroe** he paid a warm tribute to the hero
elogiosamente ADV with warm approval • **comentó ~ sus cualidades** he spoke very favourably o (EEUU) favorably of his qualities
elogioso ADJ highly favourable, highly favorable (EEUU) • **en términos ~s** in highly favourable terms
elotada SF (*CAm, Méx*) (*Agr*) ears of maize (*pl*) (*collectively*)
elote SM (*CAm, Méx*) (= *mazorca*) corncob, corn on the cob; (= *maíz*) maize, corn (EEUU), sweet corn • MODISMOS: • **coger a algn asando ~s** to catch sb red-handed • **pagar los ~s*** to carry the can*
elotear ▷ CONJUG 1a VI (*CAm, Méx*) [*maíz*] to come into ear
El Salvador SM El Salvador
elucidación SF elucidation
elucidar ▷ CONJUG 1a VT to elucidate
elucubración SF lucubration
elucubrar ▷ CONJUG 1a VI to lucubrate
eludible ADJ avoidable
eludir ▷ CONJUG 3a VT **1** (= *evitar*) [+ *problema, responsabilidad*] to evade; [+ *control, vigilancia*] to dodge; [+ *pago, impuesto*] to avoid • **no eludas mis preguntas** don't evade o avoid my questions • **eludió pagar impuestos** he avoided paying tax • **~ el servicio militar** to avoid military service
2 [+ *persona*] to avoid • **siempre me estás eludiendo** you're always avoiding me • **logró ~ a sus perseguidores** she managed to evade her pursuers
elusivo ADJ elusive, evasive
E.M. ABR (= **Estado Mayor**) GS
Em.ª ABR = **Eminencia**
email ['imeil] SM (PL: **emails**) (*gen*) email; (= *dirección*) email address • **mandar un ~ a algn** to email sb, send sb an email
emanación SF [*de gas, humo, luz*] (= *acto*) emission, emanation (*frm*); (= *olor*) smell • **emanaciones de gas** gas emissions • **emanaciones tóxicas** toxic emissions
emanar ▷ CONJUG 1a VI • **~ de** to emanate from (*frm*), come from
emancipación SF emancipation
emancipado ADJ (= *liberado*) emancipated; (= *libre*) independent, free
emancipar ▷ CONJUG 1a VT to emancipate, free
VPR **emanciparse** to become emancipated, free o.s. (**de** from)
Emanuel SM Emmanuel
emascular ▷ CONJUG 1a VT to emasculate
embadurnar ▷ CONJUG 1a VT to daub, smear (**de** with)
embaidor†† SM cheat, swindler
embaimiento†† SM trick, swindle
embaír†† ▷ CONJUG 3a; defectivo VT to cheat, swindle
embajada SF **1** (= *edificio*) embassy
2 (= *cargo*) ambassadorship
3 (= *mensaje*) mission
4 (*pey*) unwelcome proposal, silly suggestion
embajador(a) SM/F ambassador (**en** in) • **el ~ de España en Francia** the Spanish ambassador in France ▸ **embajador(a) itinerante** roving ambassador, ambassador at large ▸ **embajador(a) político/a** politically-appointed ambassador ▸ **embajador(a) volante** = embajador itinerante
embajadora SF (= *mujer de embajador*) ambassador's wife
embajatorio ADJ ambassadorial
embalado ADJ **1*** (= *rápido*) • **el coche pasó ~** the car flew past
2 (*Caribe**) (= *drogado*) high‡
SM (= *embalaje*) packing, packaging
embalador(a) SM/F packer
embaladura SF (*LAm*), **embalaje** SM packing
embalar ▷ CONJUG 1a VT **1** (= *empaquetar*) [+ *mercancías*] to pack, parcel up, wrap; [+ *mercancías pesadas*] to crate
2 (*LAm*) (*Aut*) to race along
VI (*Caribe*) (= *huir*) to run off, escape
VPR **embalarse*** **1** (*Dep*) (= *acelerar*) to sprint, make a dash; (= *tomar velocidad*) to gather speed
2 (= *apresurarse*) • **la profesora se embala hablando** the teacher gets carried away when she's speaking • **no te embales, que hay tiempo** don't rush yourself, there's time, take your time, there's no rush • **el orador se estaba embalando** the speaker was in full flow
3 (*LAm*) to run off, escape
4 (= *entusiasmarse*) to get carried away
embaldosado SM tiled floor
embaldosar ▷ CONJUG 1a VT to tile
embalsadero SM boggy place
embalsado SM (*Cono Sur*) mass of floating water weeds
embalsamado ADJ embalmed
embalsamar ▷ CONJUG 1a VT to embalm
embalsar ▷ CONJUG 1a VT **1** [+ *río*] to dam, dam up; [+ *agua*] to retain, collect • **este mes se han embalsado 1000 metros cúbicos** this month reservoir stocks have gone up by 1000 cubic metres
2 (*Náut*) to sling, hoist
VI (*And*) (= *cruzar*) to cross (*a river*)
embalse SM (= *presa*) dam; (= *lago*) reservoir
embanastar ▷ CONJUG 1a VT to put into a basket
embancarse ▷ CONJUG 1g VPR (*And, Cono Sur*) to silt up, become blocked by silt
embanderar ▷ CONJUG 1a VT to deck with flags
embanquetado SM (*LAm*) pavement(s), sidewalk(s) (EEUU)
embanquetar ▷ CONJUG 1a VT (*LAm*) to provide with pavements, provide with sidewalks (EEUU)
embarazada ADJ pregnant • **dejar ~ a una chica** to get a girl pregnant • **estar ~ de cuatro meses** to be four months pregnant
SF pregnant woman
embarazar ▷ CONJUG 1f VT **1** (= *estorbar*) to hamper, hinder
2 [+ *mujer*] to make pregnant
embarazo SM **1** [*de mujer*] pregnancy • **durante el ~** during pregnancy • **interrumpir el ~** to terminate a pregnancy • **prueba del ~** pregnancy test ▸ **embarazo ectópico, embarazo extrauterino** ectopic pregnancy ▸ **embarazo involuntario** unwanted pregnancy ▸ **embarazo múltiple** multiple pregnancy ▸ **embarazo nervioso** phantom pregnancy ▸ **embarazo no deseado** unwanted pregnancy ▸ **embarazo psicológico** phantom pregnancy
2 (= *turbación*) embarrassment • **nos miró con ~** she looked at us in embarrassment
3 (= *estorbo*) obstacle, hindrance
embarazosamente ADV (= *molestamente*) awkwardly, inconveniently; (= *violentamente*) embarrassingly
embarazoso ADJ (= *molesto*) awkward, inconvenient; (= *violento*) embarrassing
embarcación SF **1** (= *barco*) boat, craft, (small) vessel ▸ **embarcación auxiliar** tender ▸ **embarcación de arrastre** trawler ▸ **embarcación de cabotaje** coasting vessel ▸ **embarcación de recreo** pleasure boat ▸ **embarcación de vela** sailing boat, sailboat (EEUU) ▸ **embarcación fueraborda** motorboat ▸ **embarcación pesquera** fishing boat
2 (= *acto*) embarkation
embarcadero SM **1** (= *amarradero*) pier, jetty
2 (*LAm*) (*Ferro*) *cattle loading yard of a station*
embarcar ▷ CONJUG 1g VT **1** (*en barco*) [+ *personas*] to embark, put on board; [+ *carga*] to ship, stow
2 (= *implicar*) • **~ a algn en una empresa** to launch sb on an enterprise
3 (*LAm**) • **~ a algn** to set sb up*
4 (*Caribe*) (= *engañar*) to con*, trick
VPR **embarcarse 1** (*en barco*) to embark, go on board • **~ para** to sail for
2 (= *enrolarse*) [*marinero*] to sign on
3 (= *implicarse*) • **~se en un asunto** to get involved in a matter
4 (*LAm*) (*en vehículo*) to get on, get in
embarco SM embarkation
embargar ▷ CONJUG 1h VT **1** (*Jur*) to seize, impound
2 [+ *sentidos*] to overpower, overwhelm
3 (= *estorbar*) to impede, hinder
4 (= *frenar*) to restrain
embargo SM **1** (*Jur*) seizure, distraint
2 (*Pol*) ▸ **embargo comercial** trade embargo
3 • **sin ~** still, however, nonetheless • **sin ~ de** despite the fact that
4 (*Med*) indigestion
embarnizar ▷ CONJUG 1f VT to varnish
embarque SM **1** (*en barco*) [*de personas*] embarkation, boarding; [*de carga*] shipment, loading • **tarjeta de ~** boarding card
2 (*Caribe**) (= *melodrama*) melodrama; (= *amorío*) emotional affair
embarrada* SF (*LAm*) blunder
embarrado ADJ [*calle etc*] muddy
embarradura SF smear, daub
embarrancamiento SM [*de barco*] running aground; [*de ballena*] beaching, stranding
embarrancar ▷ CONJUG 1g VT, VI **1** (*Náut*) to run aground
2 (*Aut*) to run into a ditch
VPR **embarrancarse 1** (*Náut*) to run aground • **quedarse embarrancado** to be beached, be stranded
2 (*Aut*) to run into a ditch
3 (*en un asunto*) to get bogged down
embarrar ▷ CONJUG 1a VT **1** (= *enfangar*) to splash with mud
2 (*LAm*) [+ *pared*] (*con barro*) to cover with mud; (*con yeso*) to plaster
3 • **~ a algn** (*Caribe, Cono Sur*) to smear sb, damage sb's standing; (*CAm, Méx**) to set sb up* • **la embarré** (*Cono Sur**) I put my foot in it*, I spoiled things
VI (*Cono Sur*) to make a mess of things
VPR **embarrarse 1** (*con barro*) to get covered in mud
2 (*Caribe*) [*niño*] to dirty o.s.
embarrialarse ▷ CONJUG 1a VPR **1** (*CAm, Ven*) (= *enfangarse*) to get covered with mud
2 (*CAm, Caribe**) (= *enredarse*) to get o.s. in a mess
embarullador ADJ bungling
embarullar ▷ CONJUG 1a VT to bungle, mess up
embastar ▷ CONJUG 1a VT to stitch, tack

embaste SM stitching, tacking
embate SM **1** (= *golpe*) [*de mar, viento*] beating, violence; [*de olas*] dashing, breaking, beating
2 ▸ **embates de la fortuna** blows of fate
3 (*Mil*) sudden attack
embaucador(a) SM/F (= *estafador*) trickster, swindler; (= *impostor*) impostor; (= *farsante*) humbug
embaucamiento SM swindle, swindling
embaucar ▸ CONJUG 1g VT to trick, fool, lead up the garden path*
embaular ▸ CONJUG 1a VT **1** to pack (*into a trunk*)
2* [+ *comida*] to tuck away*, stuff o.s. with; [+ *bebida*] to sink*, knock back*
3 (*Caribe*) to clean out
embazar ▸ CONJUG 1f VT **1** (= *teñir*) to dye brown
2 (= *pasmar*) to astound, amaze
3 (= *estorbar*) to hinder
embebecer ▸ CONJUG 2d VT to fascinate
VPR **embebecerse** to be fascinated, be lost in wonder
embebecimiento SM **1** (= *fascinación*) absorption, fascination
2 (= *encanto*) enchantment
3 (= *asombro*) astonishment, wonderment
embeber ▸ CONJUG 2a VT **1** (= *absorber*) to absorb, soak up
2 (*Cos*) to take in, gather
3 (= *abstraer*) to absorb, distract
4 (= *meter*) to insert, introduce (*frm*) (**en** into)
5 (= *abarcar*) to contain, incorporate
VI (= *encoger*) to shrink
VPR **embeberse 1** (= *abstraerse*) to be absorbed, become engrossed (**en** in)
2 • **~se de** to imbibe, become well versed in
embelecar ▸ CONJUG 1g VT to deceive, cheat
embeleco SM, **embelequería** (*LAm*) SF deceit, fraud
embelequero ADJ **1** (*LAm*) (= *aspaventero*) highly emotional, extremely fussy
2 (*And, Caribe*) (= *tramposo*) shifty
3 (*Caribe*) (= *frívolo*) frivolous, silly
embelesado ADJ spellbound, enraptured
embelesador ADJ enchanting, entrancing
embelesar ▸ CONJUG 1a VT to enchant, entrance
VPR **embelesarse** to be enchanted, be enraptured
embeleso SM enchantment, delight
embellecedor ADJ • **productos ~es** beauty products
SM **1** (*Aut*) hub cap ▸ **embellecedores laterales** "go-faster" stripes
2 (= *adorno*) trim
embellecer ▸ CONJUG 2d VT to embellish, beautify
embellecimiento SM embellishment
embestida SF (= *ataque*) (*gen*) attack; [*de olas, viento*] onslaught; [*de toro*] charge
embestir ▸ CONJUG 3k VT **1** (= *atacar*) to assault, attack
2 (= *abalanzarse sobre*) to rush at, rush upon
3 [*toro*] to charge
VI **1** (= *atacar*) to attack
2 [*toro*] to rush, charge • **~ contra algn** to rush at sb • **el toro embistió contra la pared** the bull charged at the wall
embetunar ▸ CONJUG 1a VT [+ *zapatos*] to polish
embicar ▸ CONJUG 1g VT **1** (*Cono Sur*) (*Náut*) to head straight for land
2 (*Caribe*) (= *insertar*) to insert
3 (*Méx*) (= *invertir*) to turn upside down, upturn
embicharse ▸ CONJUG 1a VPR (*Cono Sur*) to become wormy, get maggoty
embiste SM (*Caribe*) = **embestida**
emblandecer ▸ CONJUG 2d VT **1** (= *poner blando*) to soften
2 [+ *persona*] to mollify
VPR **emblandecerse 1** (= *ponerse blando*) [*galletas, pan*] to go soggy; [*metal, plástico*] to soften, go soft
2 [*persona*] (*temporalmente*) to relent; (*en carácter*) to become more soft-hearted
emblanquecer ▸ CONJUG 2d VT to whiten, bleach
VPR **emblanquecerse** to turn white, bleach
emblema SM emblem
emblemático ADJ emblematic
embobado ADJ **1** (= *atontado*) stupefied, dazed
2 (= *fascinado*) fascinated
embobamiento SM (= *fascinación*) fascination; (= *perplejidad*) bewilderment
embobar ▸ CONJUG 1a VT **1** (= *atontar*) to stupefy, daze
2 to fascinate • **al niño le emboba la televisión** the child was addicted to *o* hooked on television • **esa niña me emboba** that girl is driving me crazy
VPR **embobarse** to be amazed (**con, de, en** at), be fascinated (**con, de, en** by) • **reírse embobado** to laugh like mad, laugh one's head off • **se quedó embobado mirando los pájaros** he was completely captivated *o* entranced by the birds
embobecer ▸ CONJUG 2d VT to make silly
VPR **embobecerse** to get silly
embocadura SF **1** (= *entrada*) [*de río*] mouth; (*Náut*) passage, narrows (*pl*)
2 (= *pieza*) [*de flauta, trompeta*] mouthpiece; [*de cigarrillo*] tip; [*de brida*] bit
3 [*de vino*] flavour, flavor (*EEUU*)
4 (*Teat*) proscenium arch
embocar ▸ CONJUG 1g VT **1** (= *insertar*) • **~ algo** to put sth into sb's mouth • **~ la comida** to cram one's food, wolf one's food • **~ algo en un agujero** to insert sth into a hole • **~ la bola** (*Golf*) to hole the ball; (*Billar*) to pocket the ball, pot the ball
2 • **~ un negocio** to undertake a piece of business
3 • **~ algo a algn** (*fig*) to put one over on sb • **~ un túnel** to go into a tunnel, enter a tunnel
VI (*Golf*) to hole out
embochinchar ▸ CONJUG 1a VT (*LAm*) to throw into confusion, create chaos in
emboinado ADJ wearing a beret
embojotar* ▸ CONJUG 1a (*Ven*) VT to wrap (up)
VPR **embojotarse** to wrap o.s. (up)
embolado SM **1** (*Teat*) bit part, minor role
2* (= *mentira*) fib*, lie
3* (= *aprieto*) jam*, fix* • **meter a algn en un ~*** to put sb in a tight spot*
4 (= *toro*) *bull with wooden balls on its horns*
embolador(a) SM/F (*And*) shoeblack, bootblack (*EEUU*)
embolar ▸ CONJUG 1a VT **1** (*Taur*) [+ *cuernos*] to tip with wooden balls
2 (*And*) [+ *zapatos*] to black
3 (*CAm, Méx**) (= *emborrachar*) to make drunk
embolia SF (*Med*) embolism ▸ **embolia cerebral** brain embolism, blood clot on the brain
embolismar* ▸ CONJUG 1a VT to gossip about
embolismo SM **1** (= *lío*) muddle, mess, confusion
2 (= *cotilleo*) gossip, backbiting
3 (= *engaño*) hoax, trick
émbolo SM plunger; (*Mec*) piston
embolsar* ▸ CONJUG 1a VT, **embolsicar** ▸ CONJUG 1g VT **1** (*LAm*) (*en bolsillo*) to pocket, put into one's pocket
2 [+ *dinero, ganancias*] to collect, take in
3 (*Billar*) to pot, pocket
embolsillar ▸ CONJUG 1a VT • **~ las manos** to put one's hands in one's pockets
embonar ▸ CONJUG 1a VT **1** (*Caribe, Cono Sur, Méx*) [+ *tierra*] to manure
2 (= *mejorar*) to improve
3 (*Náut*) to sheathe
4 (*And, Méx*) [+ *cuerda*] to join (the ends of)
5 (*And, Caribe, Méx*) • **le embona el sombrero** the hat suits him
emboque* SM (= *engaño*) trick, hoax
emboquillado ADJ [*cigarrillo*] tipped
emboquillar ▸ CONJUG 1a VT **1** [+ *cigarrillo*] to tip
2 (*Cono Sur*) (*Arquit*) to point, repoint
emborrachar ▸ CONJUG 1a VT to make drunk
VPR **emborracharse** to get drunk (**con, de** on)
emborrar ▸ CONJUG 1a VT **1** (= *rellenar*) to stuff, pad, wad (**de** with)
2* [+ *comida*] to cram, wolf
emborrascarse ▸ CONJUG 1g VPR **1** (*Meteo*) to get stormy
2 (= *irritarse*) to get cross, get angry
3 (*Com*) [*negocio*] to fail
4 (*Cono Sur, Méx*) [*mina*] to peter out
emborronado ADJ (= *manchado*) smudged; (= *garabateado*) scribbled on
emborronar ▸ CONJUG 1a VT (= *manchar*) to blot, make blots on; (= *garabatear*) to scribble on
VI (= *manchar*) to make blots; (= *garabatear*) to scribble
VPR **emborronarse** to get smudged
emboscada SF ambush • **tender una ~ a** to lay an ambush for
emboscarse ▸ CONJUG 1g VPR to lie in ambush • **estaban emboscados cerca del camino** they were in ambush near the road
embotado ADJ (*lit, fig*) dull, blunt
embotamiento SM **1** (= *acción*) dulling, blunting (*tb fig*)
2 (= *estado*) dullness, bluntness (*tb fig*)
embotar ▸ CONJUG 1a VT **1** [+ *objeto*] to blunt
2 [+ *sentidos*] to dull, blunt; (= *debilitar*) to weaken, enervate
embotellado ADJ [*líquido, bebida*] bottled; [*discurso*] prepared, prepared beforehand
SM bottling
embotellador(a) ADJ • **planta ~a** bottling plant • **compañía ~a** bottling company, bottler's
SM/F bottler
embotellamiento SM **1** (= *atasco*) traffic jam
2 (= *lugar*) bottleneck
3 [*de líquido*] bottling
embotellar ▸ CONJUG 1a VT **1** [+ *líquido*] to bottle
2 (*Mil*) to bottle up
3 (*Cono Sur, Caribe*) [+ *discurso*] to prepare beforehand, memorize
VPR **embotellarse 1** (*Aut*) [*tráfico*] to get into a jam; [*vehículo*] to get caught in a traffic jam
2 (*Caribe*) to learn a speech off by heart
emboticarse ▸ CONJUG 1g VPR (*Cono Sur, Méx*) to stuff o.s. with medicines
embotijar ▸ CONJUG 1a VT (= *enfrascar*) to put into jars, keep in jars
VPR **embotijarse 1** (= *hincharse*) to swell, swell up
2 (= *encolerizarse*) to fly into a passion
embovedar ▸ CONJUG 1a VT to arch, vault
embozadamente ADV covertly, stealthily
embozado ADJ **1** (= *cubierto*) muffled up (to the eyes)

e

2 (= *disimulado*) covert, stealthy
embozalar ▸ CONJUG 1a (VT) (*Cono Sur*) to muzzle
embozar ▸ CONJUG 1f (VT) **1** (= *cubrir*) to muffle, muffle up
2 (= *ocultar*) to cloak
(VPR) **embozarse** to muffle o.s. up (**con, de** in)
embozo (SM) **1** [*de la capa*] top of the cape, fold of the cape • MODISMO: • **quitarse el ~** to drop the mask, end the play-acting
2 [*de sábana*] turnover
3 [*de persona*] (= *astucia*) cunning; (= *disimulo*) concealment • **sin ~** frankly, openly
embragar ▸ CONJUG 1h (VT) **1** (*Aut, Mec*) [+ *motor*] to engage; [+ *piezas*] to connect, couple
2 (*Náut*) to sling
(VI) (*Aut etc*) to put the clutch in
embrague (SM) clutch • MODISMO: • **le patina el ~*** he's not right up top*, he's got a screw loose*
embravecer ▸ CONJUG 2d (VT) to enrage, infuriate
(VI) (*Bot*) to flourish
(VPR) **embravecerse 1** [*mar*] to get rough, get choppy
2 [*persona*] to get furious
embravecido (ADJ) **1** [*mar*] rough, choppy; [*viento*] wild
2 [*persona*] furious, enraged
embravecimiento (SM) rage, fury
embrear ▸ CONJUG 1a (VT) to tar, cover with tar • **~ y emplumar a algn** to tar and feather sb
embretar ▸ CONJUG 1a (VT) (*LAm*) [+ *animales*] to pen, corral
(VI) (*Cono Sur*) (= *asfixiarse*) to suffocate; (= *ahogarse*) to drown
embriagado (ADJ) **1** (= *borracho*) drunk, inebriated (*frm*)
2 (*fig*) • **~ de éxito** drunk with success • **~ de poder** power-crazed
embriagador (ADJ) [*olor, perfume*] intoxicating; [*vino*] heady
embriagar ▸ CONJUG 1h (VT) **1** (= *emborrachar*) to make drunk
2 (= *fascinar*) to delight, enrapture
(VPR) **embriagarse** (= *emborracharse*) to get drunk
embriaguez (SF) **1** (= *borrachera*) drunkenness
2 (= *entusiasmo*) rapture, delight
embridar ▸ CONJUG 1a (VT) **1** [+ *caballo*] to bridle, put a bridle on
2 (= *contener*) to check, restrain
embriología (SF) embryology
embriológico (ADJ) embryological
embriólogo/a (SM/F) embryologist
embrión (SM) [*de ser vivo*] embryo; [*de proyecto, idea*] germ • **en ~** (*lit*) in embryo; (*fig*) in its infancy, in its early stages
embrionario (ADJ) embryonic
embriónico (ADJ) embryonic
embrocación (SF) embrocation
embrocar ▸ CONJUG 1g (VT) **1** (*Cos*) [+ *hilo*] to wind (*on to a bobbin*); [+ *zapatos*] to tack
2 [+ *líquido*] to pour from one container into another
3 (= *volcar*) to turn upside down, invert
(VPR) **embrocarse** • **~se un vestido** (*Méx*) to put a dress on over one's head
embrollante (ADJ) muddling, confusing
embrollar ▸ CONJUG 1a (VT) **1** (= *confundir*) to muddle, confuse
2 (= *involucrar*) to involve, embroil (*frm*)
(VPR) **embrollarse** to get into a muddle, get into a mess • **~se en un asunto** to get involved in a matter
embrollista (SMF) (*And, CAm, Cono Sur*) = **embrollón**
embrollo (SM) (= *confusión*) muddle, confusion; (= *aprieto*) fix*, jam*; (= *fraude*) fraud, trick; (= *mentira*) lie, falsehood
embrollón(a) (SM/F) troublemaker
embromado* (ADJ) **1** (*LAm*) tricky*, difficult
2 • **estar ~** to be in a fix*; (*Med*) to be in a bad way; (*Econ*) to be in financial trouble *o* difficulties; (= *tener prisa*) to be in a hurry
embromar ▸ CONJUG 1a (VT) **1** (= *burlarse de*) to tease, make fun of
2 (= *engañar*) to hoodwink
3 (= *engatusar*) to wheedle, cajole
4 (*LAm**) (= *molestar*) to annoy; (= *perjudicar*) to harm, set back
5 (*Chile*) (= *atrasar*) to delay unnecessarily
(VPR) **embromarse** (*LAm*) (= *enojarse*) to get cross, get angry; (= *aburrirse*) to get bored
embroncar* (*esp LAm*) (VT) (= *enfadar*) to drive mad
(VPR) **embroncarse** (= *enfadarse*) to get mad
embroncarse ▸ CONJUG 1g (VPR) (*Cono Sur*) to get angry
embrujado (ADJ) [*persona*] bewitched; [*lugar*] haunted • **una casa embrujada** a haunted house
embrujar ▸ CONJUG 1a (VT) [+ *persona*] to bewitch, put a spell on; [+ *lugar*] to haunt • **la casa está embrujada** the house is haunted
embrujo (SM) **1** (= *acto*) bewitching
2 (= *maldición*) curse
3 (= *ensalmo*) spell, charm • **el ~ de la Alhambra** the enchantment *o* magic of the Alhambra
embrutecedor (ADJ) stupefying, stultifying
embrutecer ▸ CONJUG 2d (VT) to stupefy, dull the senses of
(VPR) **embrutecerse** to be stupefied
embrutecimiento (SM) • **una televisión de pésima calidad contribuye al ~ progresivo de la población** low-quality television is increasingly helping to dull people's wits *o* senses
embuchacarse ▸ CONJUG 1g (VPR) (*CAm, Méx*) • **~ algo** to pocket sth
embuchado (SM) **1** (*Culin*) sausage
2 (*Pol*) electoral fraud
3 (*Teat*) gag
embuchar ▸ CONJUG 1a (VT) **1** (*Culin*) to stuff with minced meat
2* [+ *comida*] to wolf, bolt • **estoy embuchado de cerveza*** I'm bloated with beer
embudar ▸ CONJUG 1a (VT) (*Téc*) to fit with a funnel, put a funnel into
embudo (SM) **1** (*para líquidos*) funnel • MODISMO: • **la ley del ~** one law for one and another for another • **esto es como la ley del ~** there's one law for some people and another for the rest around here
2 [*de tráfico*] bottleneck
embullar ▸ CONJUG 1a (*LAm*) (VT) **1** (= *excitar*) to excite
2 [+ *enemigo*] to put to flight
embullo (SM) (*CAm*) (= *ruido*) excitement, revelry
emburujar ▸ CONJUG 1a (VT) **1** (= *mezclar*) to jumble together, jumble up; (= *amontonar*) to pile up; [+ *hilo*] to tangle up
2 (*And*) (= *desconcertar*) to bewilder
(VPR) **emburujarse** (*And, Caribe, Méx*) to wrap o.s. up
emburujo (SM) (*Caribe*) ruse, trick
embuste (SM) **1** (= *mentira*) lie
2 embustes (= *adornos*) trinkets
embustero/a (ADJ) **1** (= *mentiroso*) lying
2 • **persona embustera** (*Cono Sur*) person who cannot spell properly
3 (*CAm*) (= *altanero*) haughty
(SM/F) (= *mentiroso*) liar
embute (SM) (*Méx*) bribe
embutido (SM) **1** (*Culin*) sausage
2 (*Téc*) inlay, inlaid work, marquetry
3 (*Cono Sur, Méx, Ven*) lace insert
4 (= *acción*) stuffing
embutir ▸ CONJUG 3a (VT) **1** (= *meter*) to stuff (en into) • **ella estaba embutida en un vestido apretadísimo** she was squeezed into a terribly close-fitting dress
2* (= *atiborrar*) to pack tight, stuff, cram (**de** with, **en** into)
3 (*Téc*) [+ *madera*] to inlay; [+ *metal*] to hammer, work
(VPR) **embutirse*** to stuff o.s. (**de** with)
eme (SF) **1** (name of the letter) M
2* (*euf*) = **mierda**
emergencia (SF) **1** (= *urgencia*) emergency • **de ~** emergency (*antes de s*)
2 (= *acción*) emergence
emergente (ADJ) **1** [*nación, ideología, mercado*] emerging, emergent
2 (= *resultante*) resultant, consequent
3 (*Inform*) pop-up (*antes de s*)
emerger ▸ CONJUG 2c (VI) (= *aparecer*) to emerge; [*submarino*] to surface
emeritense (ADJ) of/from Mérida
(SMF) native/inhabitant of Mérida • **los ~s** the people of Mérida
emérito (ADJ) emeritus
emético (ADJ), (SM) emetic
emigración (SF) [*de personas*] emigration; [*de aves*] migration ▸ **emigración golondrina** (*Méx*) seasonal migration of workers
emigrado/a (SM/F) emigrant; (*Pol etc*) émigré(e)
emigrante (ADJ), (SMF) emigrant
emigrar ▸ CONJUG 1a (VI) [*personas*] to emigrate; [*aves*] to migrate
Emilia (SF) Emily
emilianense (ADJ) of San Millán de la Cogolla
emilio* (SM) (*Inform*) (*hum*) email • **mandar un ~ a algn** to email sb
eminencia (SF) **1** (= *excelencia*) eminence
2 (*en títulos*) • **Su Eminencia** His Eminence • **Vuestra Eminencia** Your Eminence
3 (*Geog*) height, eminence
eminente (ADJ) eminent, distinguished
eminentemente (ADV) eminently, especially
emir (SM) emir
emirato (SM) emirate
emisario/a (SM/F) emissary, envoy
emisión (SF) **1** (= *acción*) emission; (*Econ etc*) issue; (*Bolsa*) share issue ▸ **emisión de acciones, emisión de valores** flotation ▸ **emisión gratuita de acciones** rights issue
2 (*Radio, TV*) (= *difusión*) broadcasting; (= *programa*) broadcast, programme, program (*EEUU*) ▸ **emisión deportiva** sports programme ▸ **emisión publicitaria** commercial, advertising spot
3 (*Inform*) output
emisor (ADJ) • **banco ~** issuing bank
(SM) **1** (*Radio, TV*) transmitter ▸ **emisor de radar** radar station
2 (*Econ*) issuing company
emisora (SF) radio station, broadcasting station ▸ **emisora comercial** commercial radio station ▸ **emisora de onda corta** shortwave radio station ▸ **emisora pirata** pirate radio station
emisor-receptor (SM) walkie-talkie
emitir ▸ CONJUG 3a (VT) **1** [+ *sonido, olor*] to emit, give off, give out
2 (*Econ*) [+ *dinero, sellos, bonos*] to issue; [+ *dinero falso*] to circulate; [+ *préstamo*] to grant, give
3 (= *expresar*) [+ *opinión*] to express; [+ *veredicto*] to return, issue, give; [+ *voto*] to cast

4 (*Radio, TV*) to broadcast; [+ *señal*] to send out
VPR **emitirse** to be broadcast

Emmo. ABR = **eminentísimo**

emoción SF **1** (= *sentimiento*) emotion • **llorar de ~** to be moved to tears • **sentir una honda ~** to feel a deep emotion • **nos comunica una ~ de nostalgia** it gives us a nostalgic feeling
2 (= *excitación*) excitement • **¡qué ~!** (*lit*) how exciting!; (*iró*) big deal! • **al abrirlo sentí gran ~** I felt very excited when I opened it • **con la ~ del momento no me di cuenta** in the heat of the moment I just didn't realise • **la ~ de la película no disminuye** the excitement *o* tension of the film does not flag

emocionado ADJ **1** (= *conmovido*) deeply moved, stirred
2 (= *entusiasmado*) excited

emocional ADJ emotional

emocionalmente ADV emotionally

emocionante ADJ **1** (= *conmovedor*) moving
2 (= *excitante*) exciting, thrilling

emocionar ▸ CONJUG 1a VT (= *excitar*) to excite, thrill; (= *conmover*) to move, touch
VPR **emocionarse** (= *entusiasmarse*) to get excited; (= *conmoverse*) to be moved, be touched • **¡no te emociones tanto!** don't get so worked up! • **me emociono con las películas románticas** I get all emotional when I watch romantic films • **cuando le gusta un tema se emociona y no para de hablar** when she's interested in a subject she gets carried away and doesn't stop talking

emoliente ADJ, SM emollient

emolumento SM emolument

emoticón SM, **emoticono** SM smiley, emoticon

emotivamente ADV emotionally

emotividad SF emotive nature

emotivo ADJ [*persona*] emotional; [*escena*] moving, touching; [*palabras*] emotive, moving

empacada SF (*LAm*) **1** [*de caballo*] balk, shy
2 (= *terquedad*) obstinacy

empacado SM baling

empacadora SF **1** (*Agr*) baler
2 (*Méx*) packing company

empacar ▸ CONJUG 1g VT **1** (*esp LAm*) (*gen*) to pack; (*And, Méx*) (= *embalar*) to package
2 (*Agr*) to bale
VI (*Méx*) (= *hacer las maletas*) to pack
VPR **empacarse 1** (= *enfadarse*) to get rattled*
2 (*LAm*) [*caballo*] to balk, shy
3 (*LAm*) (= *obstinarse*) to dig one's heels in

empachado ADJ **1** [*estómago*] upset • **estoy ~ de comer tanto chocolate** I've got indigestion from eating all that chocolate • **estoy ~ de tanto deporte en televisión** I'm fed up with all this sport on television
2 (= *avergonzado*) embarrassed

empachar ▸ CONJUG 1a VT **1** (= *causar indigestión*) to give indigestion to • **el chocolate empacha** chocolate gives you indigestion
2 (*fig*) (= *molestar*) to annoy; (= *aburrir*) to bore • **me empacha tanta música tecno** I get fed up with all this techno music
VPR **empacharse 1** (*Med*) to get indigestion
2 (= *molestarse*) to get annoyed
3 (= *aburrirse*) to get bored, get fed up*
4 (= *avergonzarse*) to get embarrassed, feel awkward

empacho SM **1** (*Med*) indigestion • **darse** *o* **coger un ~ de algo** (*fig*) to get a bellyful of sth*
2 (= *timidez*) bashfulness • **sin ~** without ceremony • **no tener ~ en hacer algo** to have no objection to doing sth

empachoso ADJ **1** [*comida*] indigestible • **la nata me resulta empachosa** cream gives me indigestion
2 [*persona*] (= *empalagoso*) cloying, over-sweet; (= *vergonzoso*) embarrassing

empadronamiento SM **1** (= *censo*) [*de habitantes*] census; [*de electores*] electoral register, list of registered voters (*EEUU*)
2 (= *acto*) [*de habitantes*] census taking; [*de electores*] registration

empadronar ▸ CONJUG 1a VT (= *censar*) (*como habitante*) to take a census of; (*como elector*) to register
VPR **empadronarse** to register

empajar ▸ CONJUG 1a VT to cover with straw, fill with straw

empalagar ▸ CONJUG 1h VT **1** [*comida*] to be too sweet for
2 • **su conversación me empalaga** I find his conversation too sickly-sweet
VI [*chocolate, tarta*] to be too sweet
VPR **empalagarse** to get sick (**de** of)

empalago SM **1** [*de comida*] cloying, palling
2 [*de persona*] sickly-sweetness

empalagosamente ADV cloyingly

empalagoso ADJ **1** (= *dulce*) cloying
2 (= *pesado*) sickly-sweet

empalar ▸ CONJUG 1a VT to impale
VPR **empalarse** (*And, Cono Sur*) to dig one's heels in

empalidecer ▸ CONJUG 2d VI = **palidecer**

empalizada SF fence; (*Mil etc*) palisade, stockade

empalmar ▸ CONJUG 1a VT (= *juntar*) [+ *tuberías, cables*] to connect, join; [+ *cuerdas, películas*] to splice • **empalma los dos cables** connect the two cables • **fueron empalmando un tema de conversación tras otro** one subject led to another as they spoke
VI **1** (*Ferro*) [*trenes*] to connect; [*vías*] to join • **el cercanías empalma con el expreso de las nueve** the local train connects with the nine o'clock express
2 [*carreteras, líneas*] to join; [*cables, piezas*] to connect (**con** with) • **esta carretera empalma con la autopista** this road links up with *o* joins the motorway
3 (= *sucederse*) to follow (on) (**con** from) • **su programa empalma con las noticias** her programme follows (on from) the news
VPR **empalmarse**** to get a hard-on**

empalme SM **1** (*Téc*) joint, connection
2 (= *conexión*) [*de vías, carreteras*] junction; [*de trenes*] connection
3** hard-on**, erection

empamparse ▸ CONJUG 1a VPR (*LAm*) **1** to get lost on the pampas; (= *desorientarse*) to lose one's way
2 (= *asombrarse*) to be amazed

empanada SF **1** (*Culin*) meat pie, patty
2 (= *fraude*) fraud, piece of shady business
3 ▸ **empanada mental*** confusion

empanadilla SF patty, small pie

empanado ADJ **1** (*Culin*) *cooked or rolled in breadcrumbs or pastry*
2 (= *atontado*) • **estar ~** to be confused

empanar ▸ CONJUG 1a VT (*Culin*) (*con masa*) *to cover in a pastry case;* (*con pan rallado*) *to cook or roll in breadcrumbs or pastry*

empantanado ADJ flooded, swampy; (*fig*) [*proyecto*] bogged down

empantanamiento SM (*fig*) stagnation

empantanar ▸ CONJUG 1a VT **1** (= *inundar*) to flood, swamp
2 [+ *negociación, proyecto*] to bog down
VPR **empantanarse 1** (= *inundarse*) to be flooded, get swamped
2 [*asunto, negociación*] to get bogged down, get held up • **~se en un asunto** to get bogged down in a matter

empañado ADJ [*cristal, espejo*] misty, steamed-up; [*superficie*] tarnished; [*voz*] faint, unsteady; [*honra*] tarnished • **con los ojos ~s en lágrimas** with her eyes moist with tears

empañar ▸ CONJUG 1a VT [+ *cristal, espejo, gafas*] to steam up, mist over; [+ *superficie, honra*] to tarnish
VPR **empañarse 1** [*cristales, gafas*] to get steamed up, mist over; [*voz*] to falter • **se le ~on los ojos de lágrimas** tears welled up in her eyes
2 [*reputación*] to get tarnished

empañetar ▸ CONJUG 1a VT (*LAm*) (= *enyesar*) to plaster; (= *encalar*) to whitewash

empapado ADJ soaked, soaking wet

empapar ▸ CONJUG 1a VT **1** (= *mojar*) to soak, drench • **cierra la ducha que me estás empapando** can you turn the shower off, you're soaking *o* drenching me • **estar empapado hasta los huesos** to be soaked to the skin
2 (= *absorber*) to soak up • **empapó toda el agua con una bayeta** she soaked up all the water with a cloth
VPR **empaparse 1** (= *mojarse*) to get soaked • **se me han empapado los zapatos** my shoes got soaked • **las patatas se ~on de aceite** the potatoes soaked up the oil
2 (= *enterarse*) • **~se de: se empapó de filosofía griega** he steeped himself in Greek philosophy • **se empapó de gramática antes del examen** he swotted up on grammar before the exam* • MODISMO: • **¡para que te empapes!*** so there! • **yo he aprobado y tú no, ¡para que te empapes!** I passed and you didn't, so there!

empapelado SM (= *acción*) papering, paperhanging; (= *papel*) wallpaper

empapelador(a) SM/F paperhanger

empapelar ▸ CONJUG 1a VT **1** [+ *cuarto, pared*] to paper; [+ *caja*] to line with paper
2 • **~ a algn** (= *abrir expediente*) to throw the book at sb;* (= *matar*) to do sb in*

empapuzar ▸ CONJUG 1f VT to stuff with food

empaque SM **1*** (= *aspecto*) look, appearance
2 (= *distinción*) presence
3 (*LAm*) (= *descaro*) nerve, effrontery, cheek*

empaquetado ADJ pre-packed
SM packaging

empaquetador(a) SM/F packer

empaquetadura SF packing; (*Mec*) gasket

empaquetamiento SM packaging

empaquetar ▸ CONJUG 1a VT **1** to pack, parcel up; (*Com*) to package
2 (= *conservar*) [+ *buque*] to mothball
3‡ [+ *soldado*] to punish

emparamarse ▸ CONJUG 1a VPR (*And, Caribe*) **1** (= *entumecerse*) to go numb with cold
2 (= *morir*) to die of cold
3 (= *mojarse*) to get soaked

emparar* ▸ CONJUG 1a (*And*) VT to catch
VPR **empararse 1** (= *sonrojarse*) to blush
2 • **~se de algo** to mock sth

emparedado SM sandwich

emparedar ▸ CONJUG 1a VT to confine

emparejamiento SM (*Bio*) pairing, mating; (*Psic*) pair bonding

emparejar ▸ CONJUG 1a VT **1** [+ *dos cosas, dos personas*] to pair, match
2 (= *nivelar*) to level, make level
VI **1** (= *alcanzar*) to catch up (**con** with)
2 (= *nivelarse*) to be even (**con** with)
VPR **emparejarse** to match

emparentado ADJ related by marriage (**con** to)

emparentar ▷ CONJUG 1j (VI) to become related by marriage (**con** to) • **~ con una familia** to marry into a family

emparrado (SM) trained vine

emparrandarse ▷ CONJUG 1a (VPR) (*LAm*) to go on a binge*

empastado (ADJ) **1** (*Tip*) clothbound
2 [*diente*] filled

empastar ▷ CONJUG 1a (VT) **1** [+ *diente*] to fill, stop
2 (= *engomar*) to paste
3 (*Tip*) to bind in stiff covers
4 (*LAm*) to convert into pasture land
(VPR) **empastarse** (*Cono Sur*) [*ganado*] to get bloated

empaste (SM) **1** [*de diente*] filling
2 (*Tip*) binding

empatado (ADJ) **1** [*partido*] • **el partido está ~ a dos** the score is two-all • **vamos ~s en segundo lugar** we're in joint second place
2 [*votación*] neck and neck

empatar ▷ CONJUG 1a (VT) **1** (*Dep*) • **han quedado vencedores tras ~ dos partidos** they eventually won after drawing two matches • **acaban de ~ el partido** they have just levelled the scores
2 (*LAm*) (= *conectar*) to connect
3 (*Caribe*) (= *acosar*) to bother, harass
4 (*Cono Sur*) [+ *tiempo*] to waste
(VI) **1** (*Dep*) (*en partido*) to draw, tie (*EEUU*); (*en carreras*) to tie, have a dead heat • **los equipos ~on a dos** the teams drew two-all • **los tres equipos quedan empatados a puntos** the three teams are level on points
2 (*en votación*) to tie

empate (SM) **1** (*en partido*) draw • **un ~ a cero** a nil-nil draw • **el gol del ~** the equalizer • **continúa el ~ en el marcador** the scores are still level
2 (*en votación*) tie
3 (*LAm*) (= *junta*) joint, connection

empatía (SF) empathy

empatizar ▷ CONJUG 1f (VI) (*tb* **empatizarse**) to empathize (**con** with)

empavado* (ADJ) (*Caribe*) unlucky, jinxed*

empavar* ▷ CONJUG 1a (VT) (*Caribe*) to put a jinx on*, bring bad luck to

empavesado (SM) bunting

empavesar ▷ CONJUG 1a (VT) (= *adornar*) to deck, adorn; [+ *barco*] to dress

empavonar ▷ CONJUG 1a (VT) **1** (*Téc*) [+ *acero*] to blue
2 (*LAm*) (*Mec*) to grease, cover with grease
(VPR) **empavonarse** (*CAm*) to dress up

empecatado* (ADJ) **1** (= *incorregible*) incorrigible
2 (= *astuto*) wily
3 (= *malhadado*) ill-fated
4 (= *maldito*) damned, cursed

empecinadamente (ADV) stubbornly, pig-headedly

empecinado (ADJ) stubborn, pig-headed

empecinamiento (SM) stubbornness, pig-headedness

empecinarse ▷ CONJUG 1a (VPR) • **~ en algo** to be stubborn about sth • **~ en hacer algo** to persist in doing sth

empedarse* ▷ CONJUG 1a (VPR) (*Méx, Cono Sur*) to get drunk, get sloshed*

empedernido (ADJ) **1** [*vicio*] hardened, inveterate • **un bebedor ~** a heavy drinker • **un fumador ~** a heavy smoker • **un pecador ~** an unregenerate sinner, a reprobate • **un soltero ~** a confirmed bachelor
2 (= *cruel*) heartless, cruel

empedernir ▷ CONJUG 3a; defectivo (VT) to harden
(VPR) **empedernirse** (*fig*) to harden one's heart

empedrado (ADJ) [*superficie*] paved; [*cara*] pockmarked; [*cielo*] cloud-flecked
(SM) paving

empedrar ▷ CONJUG 1j (VT) to pave

empegado (SM) tarpaulin, tarp (*EEUU*)

empeine (SM) **1** [*de pie, zapato*] instep
2 (= *vientre*) groin
3 empeines (*Med*) impetigo (*sing*)
4 (*Bot*) cotton flower

empella (SF) **1** [*de zapato*] upper; [*de zapatero*] vamp
2 (*LAm*) lard

empellar ▷ CONJUG 1a (VT) to push, shove, jostle

empellón (SM) push, shove • **abrirse paso a ~es** to push roughly past • **dar empellones** to shove, jostle • **lo sacaron a empellones** they shoved *o* pushed him out of the door

empelotado* (ADJ) **1** (*LAm*) (= *desnudo*) naked, starkers*
2 (*Méx*) (= *enamorado*) in love

empelotar ▷ CONJUG 1a (VT) **1** (*LAm*) (= *desvestir*) to undress, strip to the skin
2 (*LAm*) (*Mec*) to strip down, dismantle, take to pieces
(VPR) **empelotarse 1**‡ (= *emporrarse*) to get stoned*
2* (*LAm*) to strip naked, strip off
3 (*Caribe, Méx**) (= *enamorarse*) to fall head over heels in love

empelucado (ADJ) bewigged

empenachado (ADJ) **1** [*caballo*] plumed
2 [*columna*] pretentious, extravagant

empenachar ▷ CONJUG 1a (VT) to adorn with plumes

empeñado (ADJ) **1** [*objeto de valor*] pawned • MODISMO: • **estar ~ hasta los ojos** to be deeply in debt, be up to one's eyes in debt*
2 (= *empecinado*) determined • **estar ~ en hacer algo** to be determined to do sth
3 [*discusión*] bitter, heated

empeñar ▷ CONJUG 1a (VT) **1** [+ *objeto de valor*] to pawn, pledge
2 (= *comprometer*) [+ *palabra*] to give; [+ *persona*] to engage, compel
3 (= *comenzar*) to start
(VPR) **empeñarse 1** (= *endeudarse*) to get into debt
2 • **~se en algo** to insist on sth • **~se en hacer algo** to be set on doing sth • **se empeñó en irse a trabajar al extranjero** he insisted on going to work abroad • **me empeñé en que estudiara inglés** I insisted that she should study English • **~se en una discusión** to get involved in a heated argument • **se empeña en que fue así** he insists that it was so
3 • **~se por algn** to intercede for sb

empeñero/a (SM/F) (*Méx*) pawnbroker, moneylender

empeño (SM) **1** (= *resolución*) determination; (= *insistencia*) insistence • **poner ~ en algo** to put a lot of effort into sth • **poner ~ en hacer algo** to strive to do sth • **tener ~ en hacer algo** to be bent on doing sth • **con ~** (= *con insistencia*) insistently; (= *con ahínco*) eagerly, keenly
2 (= *tienda*) pawnshop
3 (= *objeto*) pledge
4 (= *empresa*) undertaking • **morir en el ~** to die in the attempt

empeñoso (ADJ) (*LAm*) persevering, diligent

empeoramiento (SM) deterioration, worsening

empeorar ▷ CONJUG 1a (VT) to make worse, worsen
(VI), (VPR) **empeorarse** to get worse, worsen

empequeñecedor (ADJ) belittling

empequeñecer ▷ CONJUG 2d (VT) **1** (= *achicar*) to dwarf, make (seem) smaller
2 (= *menoscabar*) to minimize, belittle
(VI) • **ha empequeñecido con los años** she has got smaller as she has got older

empequeñecimiento (SM) belittling

emperador (SM) **1** (= *gobernante*) emperor
2 (= *pez*) swordfish

emperatriz (SF) empress

emperejilarse ▷ CONJUG 1a (VPR) to dress up, doll o.s. up*

empericarse* ▷ CONJUG 1g (VPR) **1** (*And*) (= *emborracharse*) to get drunk
2 (*Caribe, Méx*) (= *ruborizarse*) to blush

emperifollar ▷ CONJUG 1a (VT) (*gen*) to adorn, deck; [+ *persona*] to doll up
(VPR) **emperifollarse** to dress up, doll o.s. up*

empernar ▷ CONJUG 1j (VT) to bolt, secure with a bolt

empero†† (CONJ) (*liter*) (= *pero*) but; (= *sin embargo*) yet, however • **estaba muy cansado, no se sentó ~** he was very tired, nonetheless he didn't sit down

emperramiento (SM) stubbornness, pig-headedness

emperrarse ▷ CONJUG 1a (VPR) to get stubborn, be obstinate • **~ en algo** to persist in sth

emperro (SM) (*esp And*) (= *terquedad*) stubbornness; (= *rabieta*) fit of temper

empertigar ▷ CONJUG 1h (VT) (*Chile*) [+ *caballo*] to hitch up

empezar ▷ CONJUG 1f, 1j (VI) **1** (= *comenzar*) (*gen*) to start, begin; (*en un puesto de trabajo*) to start • **el curso empieza en octubre** the course starts *o* begins in October • **el año ha empezado mal** the year got off to a bad start, the year started *o* began badly • **antes de ~, os recordaré que ...** before we start *o* begin, I'd like to remind you that ... • **al ~ el año** at the start *o* beginning of the year • **¿cuándo empieza el nuevo cocinero?** when does the new cook start? • **empecé de ayudante** I started as an assistant • **¡no empieces!*** don't you start!* • **para ~** to start with, begin with • **para ~ quisiera agradecerte tu presencia entre nosotros** I would like to start *o* begin by thanking you for being with us, to start *o* begin with, I would like to thank you for being with us • MODISMO: • **todo es (cuestión de) ~** it's all a matter of getting started; ▷ **cero**
2 • **~ a hacer algo** (*gen*) to start *o* begin to do sth, start *o* begin doing sth; (*en un trabajo*) to start to do *o* doing sth • **empezó a llover** it started *o* began to rain, it started *o* began raining • **la película me está empezando a aburrir** the film is starting *o* beginning to bore me • **ya empiezo a entrar en calor** I'm starting *o* beginning to feel warm now • **empiezo a trabajar en octubre** I start work in October
3 • **~ haciendo algo** to begin *o* start by doing sth • **~emos pidiendo ayuda** we'll start *o* begin by asking for help • **la canción empieza diciendo que ...** the song begins *o* starts by saying that ...
4 • **~ con algo** [*película, curso, año*] to start *o* begin with sth • **la novela empieza con una referencia a Sartre** the novel starts *o* begins with a reference to Sartre • **empezamos con cerveza y acabamos con vino** we started on *o* began with beer and ended up on wine • **¿cuándo empezáis con las clases de inglés?** when do you start your English classes? • **¡no empieces otra vez con lo mismo!** don't start on that again!
5 • **~ por algo/algn** to start with sth/sb, begin with sth/sb • **~é por la cocina** I'll start *o* begin with the kitchen • **"huelga" empieza por hache** "huelga" starts *o* begins with (an) h • **no sé por dónde ~** I don't know

where to start *o* begin • **la carcoma empezó por las patas del armario** the woodworm started in the legs of the wardrobe • **ya podías haber empezado por ahí** why couldn't you have said that at the beginning *o* at the start? • **~ por hacer algo** to start by doing sth, begin by doing sth
VT [+ *actividad, temporada*] to start, begin; [+ *botella, jamón*] to start • **hemos empezado mal la semana** the week got off to a bad start for us, the week started badly for us • **el queso está ya empezado** the cheese has already been started

empicotar ▸ CONJUG 1a VT to pillory

empiece* SM beginning, start

empiezo* SM (*LAm*) = **comienzo**

empilchar ▸ CONJUG 1a VT (*Cono Sur*) [+ *caballo*] to saddle; [+ *persona**] to keep in clothes
VPR **empilcharse** (*Cono Sur**) to dress up, get dolled up*

empilonar ▸ CONJUG 1a VT (*LAm*) to pile up

empinada SF (*Aer*) steep climb

empinado ADJ **1** [*cuesta*] steep; [*edificio*] high, lofty
2 (= *orgulloso*) proud

empinar ▸ CONJUG 1a VT (*gen*) to raise; [+ *botella*] to tip up • MODISMO: • **~ el codo** to booze*, prop up the bar*
VI* to drink, booze*
VPR **empinarse** [*persona*] to stand on tiptoe; [*caballo*] to rear up; (*Aer*) to zoom upwards

empingorotado* ADJ stuck-up*, toffee-nosed*

empipada* SF (*And, Cono Sur*) blow-out*, chow-down (*EEUU**)

empiparse ▸ CONJUG 1a VPR (*LAm*)
1 (= *comer*) to stuff o.s. with food
2 (= *beber*) • **se empipó una botella de vino él solito** he downed a bottle of wine all by himself

empíricamente ADV empirically

empírico/a ADJ empirical, empiric
SM/F empiricist

empirismo SM empiricism

empitonar ▸ CONJUG 1a VT (*Taur*) to gore, impale (on the horns of the bull)

empizarrado SM slate roof

empizarrar ▸ CONJUG 1a VT to roof with slates

emplantillar ▸ CONJUG 1a VT **1** (*And, Caribe, Cono Sur*) [+ *zapatos*] to put insoles into
2 (*And, Cono Sur*) [+ *pared*] to fill with rubble

emplastar ▸ CONJUG 1a VT (*Med*) to put a plaster on, put a poultice on

emplasto SM **1** (*Med*) poultice
2 (= *arreglo*) makeshift arrangement
3 (= *persona*) sickly person

emplazamiento SM **1** (*Jur*) summons; (= *llamamiento*) summoning
2 (= *sitio*) location; (*Mil*) emplacement, gun emplacement
3 (*Com*) [*de producto*] product placement

emplazar ▸ CONJUG 1f VT **1** (= *convocar*) to summon, convene; (*Jur*) to summons
2 (= *ubicar*) (*gen*) to site, place; [+ *estatua*] to erect
3 • **~ a algn a hacer algo** to call on sb to do sth

empleabilidad SF (*Econ, Pol*) employability

empleado/a SM/F (*gen*) employee; (= *oficinista*) clerk, office worker ▸ **empleada del hogar** servant, maid ▸ **empleado/a bancario/a, empleado/a de banco** bank clerk ▸ **empleado/a de correos** post-office worker ▸ **empleado/a de cuello y corbata** (*Cono Sur*) white-collar worker ▸ **empleado/a de finca urbana** porter, concierge ▸ **empleado/a de pompas fúnebres** undertaker's assistant, mortician's assistant (*EEUU*) ▸ **empleado/a de ventanilla** booking office clerk, counter clerk ▸ **empleado/a público/a** civil servant

empleador(a) SM/F employer

emplear ▸ CONJUG 1a VT **1** (= *usar*) to use • **puedes ~ cualquier jabón** you can use any soap (you like) • **se emplea para abrillantar el suelo** it is used to polish the floor • **empleó todo tipo de artimañas para convencerla** he used all sorts of tricks to convince her • **siempre emplea una terminología muy rebuscada** he always uses *o* employs very affected language • **~ mal** to misuse • **ha empleado mal el término** she has misused the term • MODISMO: • **¡le está bien empleado!** it serves him right!
2 [+ *trabajador*] to employ • **la fábrica emplea a veinte trabajadores** the factory employs twenty workers
3 [+ *tiempo, dinero*] to spend, use • **empleó toda la mañana para ordenar su despacho** he spent the whole morning tidying up his office • **ha empleado cuatro años en acabar la tesis** it's taken him four years to finish his thesis • **dinero bien empleado** money well spent • **~ mal el tiempo** to waste time
VPR **emplearse** (*frm*) • **~se haciendo algo** to occupy o.s. doing sth, spend one's time doing sth; ▸ **fondo**

empleo SM **1** (= *uso*) use; [*de tiempo*] spending; (*Com*) investment • **"modo de empleo"** "instructions for use" • **el ~ de esa palabra es censurable** the use of that word is to be condemned
2 (= *trabajo*) employment, work • **pleno ~** full employment ▸ **empleo juvenil** youth employment ▸ **oficina de empleo** ≈ employment agency
3 (= *puesto*) job, post • **buscar un ~** to look for a job, seek employment • **estar sin ~** to be unemployed • **"solicitan empleo"** "situations wanted" • **suspender a algn de ~ y sueldo** to suspend sb without pay

emplomadura SF **1** (= *cubierta*) lead covering
2 (*Cono Sur*) [*de diente*] filling

emplomar ▸ CONJUG 1a VT **1** [+ *vidrieras*] to lead
2 (*con plomo*) (= *revestir*) to cover with lead, line with lead, weight with lead; (= *precintar*) to seal with lead
3 (*Arg, Uru*) [+ *diente*] to fill

emplumar ▸ CONJUG 1a VT **1** (= *cubrir*) to adorn with feathers
2 (= *castigar*) to tar and feather • **le ~on seis meses de cárcel*** they packed him off to prison for six months*
3 (*LAm**) (= *estafar*) to swindle
4 (*Hond**) (= *zurrar*) to beat up, thrash
5 (*Chile**) • MODISMO: • **~las** to run away, leg it*
VI **1** [*pájaro*] to grow feathers
2 (*LAm**) (= *huir*) to take to one's heels
VPR **emplumarse** • MODISMO: • **emplumárselas** (*And, Cono Sur**) (= *huir*) to run away, leg it*

emplumecer ▸ CONJUG 2d VI to grow feathers

empobrecer ▸ CONJUG 2d VT to impoverish
VPR **empobrecerse** to become poor

empobrecido ADJ impoverished

empobrecimiento SM impoverishment

empoderamiento SM empowerment

empoderar VT to empower

empollada* SF • **darse** (*o* **pegarse**) **una ~** to swot*, cram

empollar ▸ CONJUG 1a VT **1** (*Zool*) to incubate, sit on
2* [+ *asignatura*] to swot up*
VI **1** [*gallina*] to sit, brood
2 [*abejas*] to breed
3* [*estudiante*] to swot*, grind away (*EEUU*), cram

empolle* SM swotting*, cramming • **¡tiene un ~!** he's been working really hard, he really knows his stuff*

empollón/ona* SM/F (= *estudiante*) swot*, grind (*EEUU**)

empolvado ADJ [*sustancia*] powdery; [*superficie*] dusty

empolvar ▸ CONJUG 1a VT [+ *cara*] to powder; [+ *superficie*] to cover with dust
VPR **empolvarse 1** [+ *cara*] to powder one's face
2 [*superficie*] to get dusty
3 (*CAm, Méx*) to get rusty, get out of practice
4 (*Caribe*) (= *huir*) to run away

emponchado ADJ **1** (*LAm*) (= *vestido de poncho*) wearing a poncho, covered with a poncho
2 (*And, Cono Sur*) (= *sospechoso*) suspicious

emponcharse ▸ CONJUG 1a VPR (*esp LAm*) to put on one's poncho

emponzoñamiento SM poisoning

emponzoñar ▸ CONJUG 1a VT to poison

emporcar ▸ CONJUG 1g, 1l VT to soil

emporio SM **1** emporium, trading centre, trading center (*EEUU*)
2 (*LAm*) large department store

emporrado‡ ADJ • **estar ~** to be high (on drugs)‡

emporrarse* ▸ CONJUG 1a VPR to get stoned*

emporroso ADJ (*CAm, Caribe*) annoying

empotrable ADJ fitted, built-in
SM fitted unit, built-in unit

empotrado ADJ [*armario*] built-in; (*Mec*) fixed, integral

empotrar ▸ CONJUG 1a VT (*gen*) to embed, fix; [+ *armario*] to build in
VPR **empotrarse** • **el coche se empotró en la tienda** the car embedded itself in the shop • **los vagones se ~on uno en otro** the carriages telescoped together

empotrerar ▸ CONJUG 1a VT **1** (*LAm*) [+ *ganado*] to pasture, put out to pasture
2 (*Caribe, Cono Sur*) [+ *tierra*] to enclose

empozarse ▸ CONJUG 1f VPR (*Méx*) to form pools

emprendedor(a) ADJ enterprising, go-ahead SM/F (*Econ*) entrepreneur

emprender ▸ CONJUG 2a VT **1** (= *empezar*) [+ *trabajo*] to undertake; [+ *viaje*] to embark on • **~ la marcha a** to set out for • **~ el regreso** to return • **~ la retirada** to retreat
2 • **~la con algn** to take it out on sb • **la emprendieron a botellazos con el árbitro** they threw bottles at the referee

emprendimiento SM **1** (*Econ*) entrepreneurship, entrepreneurial activity
2 (*Cono Sur*) undertaking

empreñador* ADJ irksome, vexatious

empreñar ▸ CONJUG 1a VT **1** (= *dejar embarazada*) [+ *mujer*] to make pregnant; [+ *animal*] to impregnate, mate with
2* (= *fastidiar*) to rile*, irk, vex
VPR **empreñarse** to become pregnant

empresa SF **1** (= *tarea*) enterprise ▸ **empresa libre** free enterprise ▸ **empresa privada** private enterprise
2 (*Com, Econ*) (= *compañía*) firm, company • **pequeñas y medianas ~s** small and medium-sized companies ▸ **empresa colectiva** joint venture ▸ **empresa de seguridad** security company ▸ **empresa de servicios públicos** public utility company ▸ **empresa de trabajo temporal** temp recruitment agency ▸ **empresa fantasma** dummy company ▸ **empresa filial** affiliated company ▸ **empresa fletadora** shipping company ▸ **empresa funeraria** undertaker's, mortician's (*EEUU*) ▸ **empresa matriz** parent company

▸ **empresa particular** private company
▸ **empresa pública** public sector company
3 (= *dirección*) management • **la ~ lamenta que ...** the management regrets that ...
empresariado (SM) (= *negocios*) business, business world; (= *gerentes*) managers (*pl*), management
empresarial (ADJ) [*función, clase*] managerial • **estudios ~es** business studies • **sector ~** business sector
empresariales (SFPL) business studies
empresario/a (SM/F) **1** (*Com*) businessman/businesswoman • **pequeño ~** small businessman ▸ **empresario/a de pompas fúnebres** undertaker, mortician (*EEUU*) ▸ **empresario/a de transporte** shipping agent
2 [*de opera, teatro*] impresario
3 (*Boxeo*) promoter
empresología (SF) business consultancy
empresólogo/a (SM/F) business consultant
emprestar* ▸ CONJUG 1a (VT) (*LAm*) (= *dar prestado*) to lend
empréstito (SM) **1** loan, public loan ▸ **empréstito de guerra** war loan
2 (*Com*) (= *cantidad prestada*) loan capital
empufado* (ADJ) • **estar ~** to be in debt, be in the red
empujada (SF) (*LAm*) push, shove
empujadora (SF) (*tb* **empujadora frontal**) bulldozer
empujadora-niveladora (SF) bulldozer
empujar ▸ CONJUG 1a (VT) (= *presionar*) (*gen*) to push; (*con fuerza*) to shove, thrust; (*Mec*) to drive • **"empujar"** (*en puertas*) "push" • **¡no empujen!** stop pushing! • **~ el botón a fondo** to press the button down hard
empujaterrones (SM INV) bulldozer
empujatierra (SF) bulldozer
empuje (SM) **1** (= *fuerza*) push, drive • **le falta ~** he lacks drive • **en un espíritu de ~** in a spirit of determination
2 (= *empujón*) push, shove
3 (= *presión*) pressure; (*Mec, Fís*) thrust
empujón (SM) **1** (*con la mano*) push, shove • **abrirse paso a empujones** to push *o* shove one's way through • **avanzar a empujones** to go forward in fits and starts
2 (= *incitación*) push, drive • **dar un ~ a algo** to push sth through, push sth forward • **trabajar a empujones** to work intermittently
empulgueras (SFPL) thumbscrew
empuntar ▸ CONJUG 1a (VT) **1** to put a point on
2 • MODISMO: • **~las** (*And*) to run away
(VPR) **empuntarse** (*Caribe*) (= *empecinarse*) to dig one's heels in; (= *caminar de puntillas*) to walk on tiptoe
empuñadura (SF) **1** [*de espada*] hilt; [*de herramienta*] handle
2 [*de cuento*] start, opening
empuñar ▸ CONJUG 1a (VT) **1** (= *coger*) to grasp, clutch • **~ las armas** to take up arms • MODISMO: • **~ el bastón** to take command
2 (*Cono Sur*) [+ *puño*] to clench
3 (*And*) (= *dar un puñetazo a*) to punch
empupar ▸ CONJUG 1a (VI) (*LAm*) to pupate
empurar‡ ▸ CONJUG 1a (VT) (*Mil*) to punish
empurrarse ▸ CONJUG 1a (VPR) (*CAm*) to get angry
E.M.T. (SF ABR) (*Esp*) = **Empresa Municipal de Transportes**
emú (SM) emu
emulación (SF) emulation
emulador(a) (ADJ) emulous (**de** of)
(SM/F) rival
emular ▸ CONJUG 1a (VT) to emulate
emulgente (SM) emulsifier
émulo/a (ADJ) emulous
(SM/F) rival, competitor
emulsión (SF) emulsion
emulsionante (SM) emulsifier
emulsionar ▸ CONJUG 1a (VT) to emulsify
en (PREP) **1** (*indicando lugar*) **a** (= *dentro de*) in • **está en el cajón/en el armario** it's in the drawer/in the wardrobe • **"curvas peligrosas en 2 kilómetros"** "dangerous bends 2 kilometres ahead"
b (= *encima de*) on • **las llaves están en la mesa** the keys are on the table • **lo encontré tirado en el suelo** I found it lying on the floor • **la oficina está en el quinto piso** the office is on the fifth floor
c (*con países, ciudades, calles*) • **está en Argentina** it's in Argentina • **viven en Granada** they live in Granada • **está en algún lugar de Murcia** it's somewhere in Murcia • **la librería está en la calle Pelayo** the bookshop is on Pelayo street • **vivía en el número 17** she lived at number 17 • **trabaja en una tienda** she works in a shop
d (*con edificios*) • **en casa** at home • **en el colegio** at school • **en la oficina** at the office • **te esperé en la estación** I waited for you at the station • **te veo en el cine** see you at the cinema
2 (*indicando movimiento*) into • **entré en el banco** I went into the bank • **me metí en la cama a las diez** I got into bed at ten o'clock • **meterse algo en el bolsillo** to put sth in(to) one's pocket • **entra en el coche** get in(to) the car • **no entra en el agujero** it won't go in(to) the hole • **ir de puerta en puerta** to go from door to door
3 (*indicando modo*) in • **en inglés** in English • **en pantalón corto** in shorts • **fotografías en color** colour photographs • **hablar en voz alta** to speak loudly • **una escultura en madera** a wooden sculpture • **una serie en diez capítulos** a ten-part series
4 (*indicando proporción*) by • **reducir algo en una tercera parte** to reduce sth by a third • **ha aumentado en un 20 por ciento** it has increased by 20 per cent
5 (*indicando tiempo*) • **en 1605** in 1605 • **en el siglo X** in the 10th century • **en invierno** in (the) winter • **en enero** in January • **lo hice en dos días** I did it in two days • **no he salido en todo el día** I haven't gone out all day • **en aquella ocasión** on that occasion • **mi cumpleaños cae en viernes** my birthday falls on a Friday • **en aquella época** at that time • **en ese momento** at that moment • **en Navidades** at Christmas • **ayer en la mañana** (*LAm*) yesterday morning • **en la mañana del accidente** (*LAm*) on the morning of the accident
6 (*indicando tema, ocupación*) • **un experto en la materia** an expert on the subject • **es bueno en dibujo** he's good at drawing • **trabaja en la construcción** he works in the building industry • **Hugo en Segismundo** (*Cine, Teat*) Hugo as Segismundo, Hugo in the role of Segismundo
7 (*con medios de transporte*) by • **en avión** by plane • **en coche** by car • **en autobús** by bus
8 (*con cantidades*) at, for • **lo vendió en cinco dólares** he sold it at *o* for five dollars • **estimaron las ganancias en unos trescientos mil euros** they estimated the profits to be around three hundred thousand euros
9 (*con infinitivo*) • **fue el último en hacerlo** he was the last to do it • **lo reconocí en el andar** I recognized him by his walk
10† (*con gerundio*) • **en viéndolo se lo dije** the moment I saw him I told him

EN

Como preposición de lugar, **en** *se traduce normalmente por* **on, in** *o* **at**. *La elección de una de estas tres preposiciones depende a menudo de cómo percibe el hablante la relación espacial. He aquí unas líneas generales:*

▸ *Se traduce por* **on** *cuando* **en** *equivale a* **encima de** *o nos referimos a algo que se percibe como una superficie o una línea, por ejemplo una mesa, una carretera etc:*
"¿Has visto mi vestido?" — "Está en la tabla de planchar"
"Have you seen my dress?" — "It's on the ironing-board"
Estaban tumbados en la playa
They were lying on the beach
Está construyendo una casa en la colina
He's building a house on the hill
... un pueblo en la costa oeste ...
... a village on the west coast ...
La gasolinera está en la carretera que va a Motril
The petrol station is on the road to Motril
Dibujó un león en la hoja de papel
He drew a lion on the piece of paper
Tiene un grano en la nariz
He has a spot on his nose
Lo vi en la tele
I saw him on TV

▸ *Se usa* **in** *cuando equivale a* **dentro de** *o cuando nos referimos a un espacio que se percibe como limitado (calle, montañas, etc):*
Tus gafas están en mi bolso
Your glasses are in my bag
Tienes una pestaña en el ojo
You've got an eyelash in your eye
Lo leí en un libro
I read it in a book
Se han comprado un chalet en la sierra
They've bought a chalet in the mountains
Viven en la calle de Serrano
They live in the Calle de Serrano

▸ *Lo traducimos por* **at** *para referirnos a un edificio cuando hablamos de la actividad que normalmente se realiza en él o cuando* **en** *indica un lugar concreto. También se traduce por* **at** *cuando en la dirección incluimos el número o el nombre de la casa:*
¿Por qué no comemos en el restaurante de tu hermano?
Why don't we have lunch at your brother's restaurant?
Voy a pasar el día en el museo
I'm going to spend the day at the museum
Te espero en la parada del autobús
I'll meet you at the bus-stop
Vivimos en la calle Dale nº 12
We live at 12 Dale Street

Para otros usos y ejemplos ver la entrada.

en.º (ABR) (= **enero**) Jan
enaceitar ▸ CONJUG 1a (VT) to oil
Enagas (SF ABR) (*Esp*) = **Empresa Nacional del Gas**
enagua (SF) (*esp LAm*), **enaguas** (SFPL) petticoat
enaguazar ▸ CONJUG 1f (VT) to flood
enajenación (SF), **enajenamiento** (SM)
1 (*Jur*) alienation ▸ **enajenación forzosa** expropriation
2 (*Psic*) alienation ▸ **enajenación mental** mental derangement

3 (= *distracción*) absentmindedness
enajenado ADJ deranged
enajenar ▹ CONJUG 1a VT 1 (*Jur*) [+ *propiedad*] to alienate, transfer; [+ *derechos*] to dispose of
2 (*Psic*) (*gen*) to alienate, estrange; (= *enloquecer*) to drive mad; (= *extasiar*) to enrapture, carry away
VPR **enajenarse 1** • **~se algo** to deprive o.s. of sth • **ha conseguido ~se la amistad de todos** he has managed to alienate himself from everybody
2 • **~se de los amigos** to become estranged from one's friends
3 (= *extasiarse*) to be enraptured, be carried away
enaltecer ▹ CONJUG 2d VT to extol
enamoradizo ADJ who easily falls in love
enamorado/a ADJ 1 [*de persona*] in love (**de** with) • **estar ~** to be in love • **estaban locamente ~s** they were madly in love • **estoy ~ de Ana** I'm in love with Ana
2 (*Caribe, Cono Sur*) = **enamoradizo**
SM/F 1 (= *amante*) lover • **el día de los ~s** St. Valentine's Day
2 (= *aficionado*) • **es un ~ del fútbol** he's a real football fan, he really loves football
enamoramiento SM falling in love
enamorar ▹ CONJUG 1a VT 1 [+ *persona*] to win the love of
2 (= *encantar*) • **me enamora este paisaje** I simply adore this scenery, I just love this scenery
VPR **enamorarse** to fall in love (**de** with)
enamoricarse* ▹ CONJUG 1g VPR, **enamoriscarse*** ▹ CONJUG 1g VPR to be infatuated (**de** with), get a crush* (**de** on)
enancar ▹ CONJUG 1g VT • **~ a algn** (*LAm*) to put sb on the crupper (of one's horse)
VI (*Cono Sur*) (= *seguir*) to follow, be a consequence (**a** of)
VPR **enancarse 1** (*LAm*) to get up on the crupper, ride behind
2 (*Méx*) [*caballo*] to rear up
enanez SF (*lit*) dwarfishness; (*fig*) stunted nature
enangostar ▹ CONJUG 1a VT to narrow
VPR **enangostarse** to narrow, get narrower
enanismo SM (*Med*) dwarfism
enanito/a SM/F dwarf
enano/a ADJ dwarf (*antes de s*)
SM/F dwarf, midget; (*pey*) runt • **MODISMO**: • **disfrutar** *o* **pasárselo como un ~** to have a brilliant time
enantes ADV (*And*) = **denante(s)**
enarbolar ▹ CONJUG 1a VT [+ *bandera*] to hoist; [+ *espada*] to flourish
VPR **enarbolarse 1** [*persona*] to get angry
2 [*caballo*] to rear up
enarcar ▹ CONJUG 1g VT 1 [+ *tonel*] to put a hoop on
2 (= *arquear*) [+ *cejas*] to raise; [+ *lomo*] to arch; [+ *pecho*] to throw out
enardecer ▹ CONJUG 2d VT 1 (= *dar fuerza a*) [+ *pasión*] to inflame; [+ *discusión*] to enliven, liven up
2 [+ *público*] (= *entusiasmar*) to fill with enthusiasm; (= *provocar*) to incite, inflame
VPR **enardecerse 1** (*Med*) to become inflamed
2 (= *entusiasmarse*) to get excited (**por** about)
enarenar ▹ CONJUG 1a VT to cover with sand
VPR **enarenarse** (*Náut*) to run aground
enastado ADJ horned
encabalgamiento SM (*Literat*) enjambement
encabestrar ▹ CONJUG 1a VT 1 [+ *caballo*] to put a halter on
2 (= *convencer*) to induce
VPR **encabestrarse** (*LAm*) to dig one's heels in
encabezado ADJ [*vino*] fortified
SM 1 (*Méx*) (*Prensa, Tip*) (= *encabezamiento*) heading; (= *titular*) headline
2 (*Caribe*) (= *capataz*) foreman
encabezamiento SM 1 (= *en periódico*) headline, caption; (= *de carta*) heading; (= *preámbulo*) foreword, preface; (*Com*) bill head, letterhead
2 (= *registro*) roll, register
encabezar ▹ CONJUG 1f VT 1 [+ *movimiento, revolución, partido, delegación*] to lead • **dirigentes sindicalistas encabezaban la manifestación** union leaders led the demonstration
2 [+ *lista, liga*] to head, be at the top of • **el Betis encabeza la clasificación de la Liga** Betis are at the top of *o* heading the League • **el ciclista español encabeza la carrera** the Spanish cyclist is in the lead
3 [+ *carta, artículo*] to head • **la cita que encabeza el artículo** the quotation heading the article
4 [+ *vino*] to fortify
5†† [+ *población*] to register (*for tax purposes*)
encabrestarse ▹ CONJUG 1a VPR (*LAm*) = **emperrarse**
encabritamiento* SM fit of bad temper
encabritar ▹ CONJUG 1a VT* to rile*, make cross
VPR **encabritarse 1** [*caballo*] to rear up
2* (= *enfadarse*) to get riled*, get cross
encabronar* ▹ CONJUG 1a VT to make angry
VPR **encabronarse** to get riled*, get cross
encabuyar ▹ CONJUG 1a VT (*And, Caribe*) to tie up
encachado ADJ (*Cono Sur*) appealing, attractive
encachar ▹ CONJUG 1a VT 1 (*Taur*) [+ *cabeza*] to lower before charging
2 (*Chile**) to make nice
VPR **encacharse** (*Chile**) to spruce o.s. up
encachilarse* ▹ CONJUG 1a VPR (*Arg*) to get furious
encachimbado* ADJ • **está ~** (*CAm*) he's livid, he's hopping mad*
encachimbarse* ▹ CONJUG 1a VPR (*CAm*) to fly off the handle*, lose one's temper
encachorrarse ▹ CONJUG 1a VPR (*And*) to get angry
encadenación SF, **encadenamiento** SM 1 [*de personas, objetos*] chaining, chaining together
2 [*de hechos, ideas*] linking, connection, concatenation (*frm*)
encadenado SM (*Cine*) fade, dissolve
encadenar ▹ CONJUG 1a VT 1 (= *atar con cadenas*) (*lit*) to chain, chain together; (*fig*) to tie down • **los negocios le encadenan al escritorio** business ties him to his desk
2 [+ *prisionero*] to fetter, shackle
3 [+ *de hechos, ideas*] to connect, link
4 (= *inmovilizar*) to shackle, paralyze, immobilize
VI (*Cine*) to fade in • **~ a** to fade to
encajable ADJ • **500 piezas ~s una dentro de la otra** 500 pieces that fit together • **esa idea no es ~ en su concepción del mundo** that idea doesn't fit into the way he sees the world
encajadura SF 1 (= *acto*) insertion
2 (*para meter algo*) (= *hueco*) socket; (= *ranura*) groove; (= *armazón*) frame
encajar ▹ CONJUG 1a VT 1 (= *acoplar*) [+ *pieza, tapón*] to fit; [+ *partes*] to fit together • **no he podido ~ las dos partes** I haven't managed to fit the two parts together • **~ algo en algo** to fit sth into sth
2 (= *aceptar*) [+ *broma, crítica*] to take; [+ *desgracia, derrota*] to handle, cope with • **hay que ~ las críticas con sentido del humor** you have to be able to take criticism and not lose your sense of humour • **el equipo no supo ~ el resultado** the team couldn't handle *o* cope with the result • **no supo ~ el golpe** he couldn't handle it
3* • **~ algo a algn** (= *endilgar*) to lumber sb with sth*, dump sth on sb*; (= *timar*) to palm sth off on *o* onto sb* • **cada vez que se van me encajan a su gato** every time they go away they lumber me with their cat* *o* they dump their cat on me* • **le encajó un billete falso** he managed to palm a fake note off onto him* • **a mí no me encajas tú esa historia** I won't be taken in by a story like that
4 (= *dar, meter*) [+ *golpe, patada*] to give • **le encajó un buen bofetón** he gave him a good slap • **no le dejó ~ ni un solo comentario** she didn't let him get a word in edgeways
5 (= *dejarse meter*) to let in • **llevamos tres partidos sin ~ un gol** we've gone three matches without letting in a goal
VI 1 (= *ajustar*) [*puerta*] to fit; [*piezas*] to fit (together) • **las dos partes ~on perfectamente** both parts fitted (together) perfectly • **~ en algo** to fit into sth
2 (= *coincidir*) [*teoría, coartada*] to fit • **aquí hay algo que no encaja** something here doesn't tally *o* fit • **ahora todo empieza a ~** it's all beginning to fall into place *o* fit together now • **~ con algo** to tie in with sth, tally with sth • **su versión no encaja con lo que he oído** his version does not tie in *o* tally with what I've heard
3 (= *integrarse*) • **~ con algn** to fit in with sb • **los nuevos alumnos ~on bien con sus compañeros** the new students fitted in well with their classmates • **~ en** [+ *serie, papel*] to be right for; [+ *ambiente*] to fit in • **un espectáculo que puede ~ bien en Broadway** a show that could be just right for Broadway • **no creo que vayas a ~ en ese papel** I don't think you'll be right for *o* suit that role • **no le costó ~ en la oficina** he had no trouble fitting in in the office • **sus ideas encajan dentro de una mentalidad conservadora** her ideas are in keeping with a conservative mentality
VPR **encajarse 1** (= *atrancarse*) • **la puerta se quedó encajada** the door got jammed *o* stuck • **se me ha encajado el dedo en la botella** my finger's got stuck in the bottle • **el coche se encajó dentro del muro** the car jammed into the wall
2 (= *ponerse*) [+ *abrigo, sombrero*] to put on • **se encajó el sombrero hasta las orejas** he pulled his hat (on) down to his ears
3 (*Méx*) (= *aprovecharse*) to take advantage • **~se con algn** to take advantage of sb
encaje SM 1 (*Cos*) lace • **una blusa de ~** a lace blouse • **se le veían los ~s de las enaguas** you could see the lace of her petticoat
▸ **encaje de bolillos** (*lit*) bobbin lace • **tengo que hacer ~ de bolillos para que el sueldo me llegue a fin de mes** I have to juggle things around constantly to make ends meet
2 [*de piezas*] fitting
3 (= *cabida*) • **una obra de difícil ~ en el concepto de teatro moderno** a work which does not fit easily into the concept of modern theatre
4 (*Téc*) (= *hueco*) socket; (= *ranura*) groove
5 (= *taracea*) inlay, mosaic ▸ **encaje de aplicación** appliqué, appliqué work
6 (*Econ*) reserve, stock ▸ **encaje de oro** gold reserve

encajero/a SM/F lacemaker
encajetillar ▸ CONJUG 1a VT to pack in boxes, box
encajonado SM cofferdam
encajonar ▸ CONJUG 1a VT **1** (= *guardar*) to box, box up, put in a box; (*Mec*) to box in
2 [+ *río*] to canalize
3 (= *meter en un sitio estrecho*) to squeeze in, squeeze through
VPR **encajonarse** [*río*] to run between steep banks
encajoso‡ SM (*LAm*) creep‡
encalabrinar* ▸ CONJUG 1a VT
1 (= *emborrachar*) to go to one's head
2 • ~ a algn (= *enojar*) to get sb worked up; (= *atraer*) to attract sb
VPR **encalabrinarse 1 • ~se de algn** to become infatuated with sb, get a crush on sb
2 (= *empeñarse*) to get an obsession, get the bit between one's teeth
encaladura SF **1** (= *blanqueo*) whitewash, whitewashing
2 (*Agr*) liming
encalambrarse ▸ CONJUG 1a VPR (*LAm*) (= *acalambrarse*) to get cramp; (= *aterirse*) to grow stiff with cold
encalamocar ▸ CONJUG 1g VT (*And, Caribe*)
1 (= *emborrachar*) to make drunk
2 (= *aturdir*) to confuse, bewilder
VPR **encalamocarse** (*And, Caribe*)
1 (= *emborracharse*) to get drunk
2 (= *aturdirse*) to get confused, get bewildered
encalar ▸ CONJUG 1a VT **1** [+ *pared*] to whitewash
2 (*Agr*) to lime
encalatarse ▸ CONJUG 1a VPR (*And*)
1 (= *desnudarse*) to strip naked
2 (= *arruinarse*) to be ruined
encalladero SM shoal, sandbank
encalladura SF stranding, running aground
encallar ▸ CONJUG 1a VI **1** (*Náut*) to run aground, get stranded (**en** on)
2 [*negociación*] (= *fracasar*) to fail; (= *estancarse*) to get bogged down
VPR **encallarse 1** (*Náut*) to run aground, get stranded (**en** on)
2 [*carne*] to go rubbery
encallecer ▸ CONJUG 2d VI, VPR **encallecerse** to harden, form corns
encallecido ADJ hardened
encalmada SF period of calm
encalmado ADJ **1** (*Náut*) becalmed
2 (*Com, Econ*) quiet, slack
encalmarse ▸ CONJUG 1a VPR to calm down
encalomarse‡ ▸ CONJUG 1a VPR to hide
encalvecer ▸ CONJUG 2d VI to go bald
encamar ▸ CONJUG 1a VT **1** (*CAm, Méx*) (= *hospitalizar*) to take to hospital, hospitalize
2 (*Caribe*) [+ *animal*] to litter, bed down; (*Méx*) [+ *niño*] to put to bed
VPR **encamarse 1** [*persona*] to take to one's bed • **estar encamado** to be confined to bed • **~se con algn** (*And, Cono Sur*) to go to bed with sb, sleep with sb
2 [*cosecha*] to be laid, be flattened
3 [*animal*] to crouch, hide
encamburarse ▸ CONJUG 1a VPR (*Caribe*) (*gen*) to make good; (*como funcionario*) to achieve public office
encame SM den, lair
encamillado/a SM/F (*CAm, Méx*) stretcher case
encaminamiento SM (*Inform*) routing
encaminar ▸ CONJUG 1a VT **1** (= *orientar*) [+ *plan, esfuerzo*] to direct; [+ *alumno, hijo*] to guide, direct • **el proyecto está encaminado a ayudarles** the plan is designed to help them, the plan is aimed at helping them • **aquel maestro lo encaminó en sus estudios** that teacher guided *o* directed him in his studies
2 (= *dirigir*) to direct • **una señora me encaminó hacia la autopista** a lady directed me towards the motorway • **encaminó sus pasos hacia el monasterio** (*liter*) he turned his steps towards the monastery (*liter*)
VPR **encaminarse 1 • ~se a** *o* **hacia** (= *dirigirse a*) to head for, set out for • **nos encaminamos hacia el pueblo** we headed *o* set out for the village
2 • ~se a (= *tener como objetivo*) to be designed to, be aimed at • **nuestros esfuerzos se encaminan a la solución del conflicto** our efforts are designed to solve the conflict, our efforts are aimed at solving the conflict
encamotado* ADJ (*LAm*) • **estar ~** to be in love (**de** with)
encamotarse* ▸ CONJUG 1a VPR (*LAm*) to fall in love (**de** with)
encampanado ADJ bell-shaped
encampanar ▸ CONJUG 1a VT **1** (= *elevar*) to raise
2 (*And, Caribe*) (= *encumbrar*) to raise, raise on high
3 (*And, Caribe, Méx**) (= *abandonar*) to leave in the lurch, leave in a jam*
4 • ~ a algn a (*Caribe*) to send sb to
5 (*Méx*) (= *agitar*) to excite, agitate
VPR **encampanarse 1** (*LAm*) (= *encumbrarse*) to rise
2 (*Col, Méx*) (= *enamorarse*) to fall in love
3 (*Méx*) (= *meterse en un lío*) to get into a jam*
4 (*Caribe*) to go off to a remote spot
5 (*And**) (= *complicarse*) to become difficult, get complicated
encanado/a* SM/F (*And*) prisoner
encanalar ▸ CONJUG 1a VT, **encanalizar** ▸ CONJUG 1f VT to pipe
encanallarse ▸ CONJUG 1a VPR (= *envilecerse*) to become a bastard‡
encanar‡ ▸ CONJUG 1a VT (*And, Cono Sur*) to throw into jail
encandecer ▸ CONJUG 2d VT to make white-hot
encandelar ▸ CONJUG 1a VT (*Caribe*) to annoy, irritate
encandelillar ▸ CONJUG 1a VT (*LAm*) to dazzle
encandellar ▸ CONJUG 1a VT (*And*) [+ *fuego*] to fan
encandiladera† SF procuress†
encandilado ADJ **1*** (= *deslumbrado*) • **estar ~ con algn** to be all taken with sb
2 (= *tieso*) high, erect
encandiladora† SF procuress†
encandilar ▸ CONJUG 1a VT **1** (= *fascinar*) to daze, bewilder
2 (= *deslumbrar*) to dazzle
3 [+ *lumbre*] to stir, poke
4 [+ *emoción*] to kindle, stimulate
VPR **encandilarse 1** [*ojos*] to light up
2 (= *quedar fascinado*) • **se encandiló con la belleza de Laura** he was taken with *o* dazzled by Laura's beauty
3 (*And, Caribe*) (= *asustarse*) to get scared
encanecer ▸ CONJUG 2d VI, **encanecerse** VPR **1** [*pelo*] to go grey, go gray (*EEUU*); [*persona*] to go grey
2 (*con moho*) to go mouldy, go moldy (*EEUU*)
encanijado ADJ weak, puny
encanijarse ▸ CONJUG 1a VPR to grow weak, become emaciated
encanillar ▸ CONJUG 1a VT to wind (on to a spool)
encantado ADJ **1** (= *muy contento*) delighted • **si te encargas tú, yo por mí encantada** I'd be only too pleased *o* I'd be delighted if you'd take care of it • **estar ~ con algo/algn** to be delighted with sth/sb • **está encantada con el piso nuevo** she's delighted with the new flat • **estar ~ de algo: estoy ~ de tu éxito** I'm delighted at your success • **estoy encantada de poder ayudarte** I'm delighted to be able to help you
2 (*en fórmulas de presentación*) • **~ de conocerlo** (I'm) delighted to meet you • **—el Sr. Martínez —¡encantado!** "let me introduce you to Mr Martínez" — "how do you do!" *o* "pleased to meet you!"
3 (= *embrujado*) enchanted
4 (= *distraído*) • **¡espabila, que parece que estés encantada!** wake up, you seem to be in a trance!
encantador(a) ADJ [*persona*] charming, delightful; [*lugar*] lovely
SM/F magician, enchanter/enchantress
▸ **encantador(a) de serpientes** snake charmer
encantadoramente ADV charmingly, delightfully
encantamiento SM enchantment
encantar ▸ CONJUG 1a VI (*con complemento personal*) to love • **me encanta tu casa** I love your house • **me encantan las flores** I adore *o* love flowers • **me ~ía que vinieras** I'd be delighted if you come, I'd love you to come
VT to cast a spell on *o* over, bewitch
encanto SM **1** (= *atractivo*) charm • **el pueblecito tiene mucho ~** the village has a lot of charm *o* is very charming • **no es guapa, pero tiene su ~** she isn't pretty, but she has charm • **se dejó seducir por sus ~s** he allowed himself to be seduced by her charms
2 (= *maravilla*) • **el niño es un ~** he's a charming *o* lovely *o* delightful little boy • **¡qué ~ de jardín!** what a lovely garden!
3 (*uso apelativo*) darling • **¡oye, ~!** hello, gorgeous!*
4 (= *encantamiento*) spell • **romper el ~** to break the spell • **el bolso desapareció como por ~** the bag disappeared as if by magic
encañada SF ravine
encañado SM pipe
encañar ▸ CONJUG 1a VT **1** [+ *agua*] to pipe
2 [+ *planta*] to stake
3 [+ *tierra*] to drain
encañizado SM wire netting fence
encañonar ▸ CONJUG 1a VT **1** [+ *agua*] to pipe
2* (= *asaltar con arma*) to stick up*, hold up; (= *amenazar*) to cover (with a gun)
VI [*ave*] to grow feathers
encapado ADJ cloaked, wearing a cloak
encapotado ADJ **1** [*cielo*] cloudy, overcast
2 (*con capa*) wearing a cloak
encapotar ▸ CONJUG 1a VT to cover with a cloak
VPR **encapotarse 1** [*cielo*] to become cloudy, cloud over, become overcast
2 (= *ponerse la capa*) to put on one's cloak
3 (= *enfurruñarse*) to frown
encaprichamiento SM whim
encapricharse ▸ CONJUG 1a VPR to take a fancy (**con, por** to)
encapuchado/a ADJ hooded
SM/F masked man/woman
encapuchar ▸ CONJUG 1a VT • **~ un pozo de petróleo** to cap an oil well
encarado ADJ • **bien ~** nice-looking • **mal ~** evil-looking
encaramar ▸ CONJUG 1a VT **1** (= *subir*) to raise, lift up
2 (= *alabar*) to praise, extol, extoll (*EEUU*)
VPR **encaramarse** (= *subirse*) to perch, sit up high • **~se a** [+ *árbol*] to climb up to, climb on to
encarapitarse ▸ CONJUG 1a VPR (*And,*

Caribe) = **encaramar**

encarar ▸ CONJUG 1a VT **1** [*+ problema*] to face, face up to, confront
2 [*+ dos cosas*] to bring face to face
3 [*+ arma*] to aim, point
VI (*Cono Sur*) to fall sick
VPR **encararse** • **~se a** *o* **con algn** to confront sb

encarcelación SF, **encarcelamiento** SM imprisonment

encarcelar ▸ CONJUG 1a VT to imprison, jail

encarecer ▸ CONJUG 2d VT **1** (*Com*) to put up the price of
2 (= *alabar*) to praise, extol, extoll (*EEUU*)
3 • **le encarezco que lo haga** I urge you to do it
VI, VPR **encarecerse** (*Com*) to get dearer

encarecidamente ADV insistently, earnestly

encarecimiento SM **1** [*de precio*] increase, rise
2 (= *alabanza*) extolling
3 (= *insistencia*) stressing, emphasizing • **con ~** insistently, strongly

encargado/a ADJ • **estar ~ de algo** to be in charge of sth, be responsible for sth • **¿puedo hablar con la persona encargada de los impuestos?** can I speak to the person in charge of *o* responsible for taxes? • **la arteria encargada de conducir la sangre** the artery responsible for directing blood flow
SM/F (= *responsable*) [*de tarea, expedición*] person in charge; [*de tienda, restaurante*] manager; [*de parque, cementerio*] groundkeeper • **quisiera hablar con el ~ de las obras** I would like to speak to the person in charge of the building work • **él era el ~ de las bebidas** he was in charge of the drinks • **el ~ de la librería** the person in charge of the bookshop, the manager of the bookshop ▸ **encargado/a de campo** (*Dep*) groundsman/groundswoman ▸ **encargado/a de curso** student representative ▸ **encargado/a de la recepción** receptionist ▸ **encargado/a de mostrador** counter clerk ▸ **encargado/a de negocios** (*Pol*) chargé d'affaires ▸ **encargado/a de obra** site manager ▸ **encargado/a de prensa** press officer ▸ **encargado/a de relaciones públicas** public relations officer ▸ **encargado/a de seguridad** security officer ▸ **encargado/a de vestuario** (*Teat*) wardrobe manager; (*Cine, TV*) costume designer

encargar ▸ CONJUG 1h VT **1** [*+ tarea, misión*] to give • **encargó el cuidado de sus hijos a un familiar** he left his children in the care of a relative • **~ a algn de algo** to give sb the job of doing sth • **lo ~on de resolver el conflicto** he was given the job of resolving the conflict
2 (*a profesional, empresa*) [*+ obra de arte, informe*] to commission • **nos ~on el diseño del folleto** they commissioned us to design the brochure
3 (= *hacer un pedido de*) to order • **hemos encargado dos pizzas** we've ordered two pizzas • **encargué los libros por correo** I ordered the books by post • **le he encargado un traje al sastre** I've ordered a suit from my tailor • MODISMOS: • **~ familia** to start a family • **~ un niño**: • **¿habéis encargado otro niño?** are you having another child?, do you have another one on the way?*
4 (= *pedir como favor*) • **le encargué dos latas de caviar ruso** I asked him to bring *o* buy me two tins of Russian caviar • **me ha encargado varias cosas del supermercado** she's asked me to get her some things from the supermarket • **~ a algn que haga algo** to ask sb to do sth • **me encargó que le regara las plantas** he asked me to water his plants
5 (= *aconsejar*) to advise • **le encargó varias veces que no dejara el tratamiento** he advised him several times not to stop the treatment
6 (*Chile*) (*Jur*) • **~ reo a algn** to submit sb to trial
VPR **encargarse** • **~se de** (= *ocuparse de*) to take care of; (= *ser responsable de*) to be in charge of; (= *tomar la responsabilidad de*) to take charge of • **¿qué empresa se va a ~ de la mudanza?** which firm is going to do *o* take care of the moving? • **ya me encargo yo de decírselo a todo el mundo** I'll make sure everyone knows, I'll take care of telling everyone • **de ese me encargo yo personalmente** (*hum*) I'll see to him myself!, I'll take care of him myself! • **yo me encargo de los asuntos culturales** I'm in charge of cultural affairs • **yo me encargo normalmente de cocinar** I normally do the cooking, I'm normally in charge of the cooking • **no irá, de eso me encargo yo** he won't go, I'll see to that *o* I'll make sure of that • **cuando ella murió, él se encargó del negocio** when she died, he took over the business *o* he took charge of the business

encargatoria SF (*Chile*) (*Jur*) (*tb* **encargatoria de reo**) committal for trial

encargo SM **1** (= *pedido*) order • **su ~ se perdió en el correo** your order got lost in the post • **de** *o* **por ~** [*traje, vestido*] tailor made, made to order; [*muebles*] made to order • **"se hacen tartas por ~"** "cakes made to order" • **ni hecho de ~ podrías ser más torpe** (*hum*) you couldn't be more clumsy if you tried
2 (*profesional*) job, commission • **todavía no me ha salido ningún ~** I haven't been given any jobs *o* commissions yet • **una exposición realizada por ~ del Ayuntamiento** an exhibition commissioned by the Council
3 (*para comprar algo*) errand • **ha salido a hacer un ~ a la tienda** he's gone to the shop on an errand • **le hice varios ~s de Nueva York** I asked him to buy a few things in New York, I asked him to bring back a few things from New York
4 • MODISMOS: • **dejar a algn con ~** (*LAm**) to leave sb in the family way* • **traer a algn de ~** (*Méx**) to give sb a hard time*

encargue SM • MODISMO: • **estar de ~** (*Cono Sur**) to be expecting, be in the family way*

encariñado ADJ • **estar ~ con** to be fond of

encariñarse ▸ CONJUG 1a VPR • **~ con** to grow fond of, get attached to; (*Psic*) to bond

Encarna SF *forma familiar de* **Encarnación**

encarnación SF (*Rel*) incarnation; (= *personificación*) embodiment, personification

encarnadino ADJ blood-red

encarnado ADJ **1** (*Rel*) incarnate • **es la sencillez encarnada** it's simplicity itself
2 (= *rojo*) [*color*] red; [*tez*] ruddy, florid (*pey*) • **ponerse ~** to blush

encarnadura SF • **tiene buena ~** his skin heals (up) well

encarnar ▸ CONJUG 1a VT **1** (= *personificar*) to personify; (*Teat*) [*+ papel*] to play, bring to life • **Iago encarna el odio** Iago is hatred personified
2 [*+ anzuelo*] to bait
VI **1** (*Rel*) to become incarnate
2 (*Med*) to heal, heal up
3 [*arma*] to enter the flesh, penetrate the body
VPR **encarnarse** (*Rel*) to become incarnate, be made flesh

encarnecer ▸ CONJUG 2d VI to put on flesh

encarnizadamente ADV bloodily, fiercely

encarnizado ADJ **1** [*batalla, lucha*] bloody, fierce
2 (= *sangrante*) [*herida*] red, inflamed; [*ojo*] bloodshot

encarnizamiento SM **1** (= *ira*) rage, fury
2 (= *crueldad*) bitterness, ferocity

encarnizar ▸ CONJUG 1f VT (= *volver cruel*) to make cruel; (= *enfadar*) to enrage
VPR **encarnizarse** to fight fiercely • **~se con algn** to attack sb viciously

encaro SM **1** (= *mirada*) stare, staring, gaze
2 (= *puntería*) aim, aiming
3 (*Hist*) blunderbuss

encarpetar ▸ CONJUG 1a VT **1** (= *guardar*) [*+ papeles*] to file away; [*+ proyecto*] to shelve, bury
2 (*LAm*) [*+ moción*] to shelve, bury

encarrilamiento SM [*de conducta*] improvement; [*de niño*] guidance

encarrilar ▸ CONJUG 1a VT **1** [*+ tren*] to put back on the rails
2 (= *dirigir*) to direct, guide • **no es fácil ~ a los niños en nuestros días** it's not easy to guide *o* provide guidance to one's children these days • **ir encarrilado** to be on the right lines; (*pey*) to be in a rut

encarrujar ▸ CONJUG 1a VT (*Cono Sur*) (*Cos*) to ruffle, frill

encartado/a SM/F (*Jur*) accused, defendant

encartar ▸ CONJUG 1a VT **1** (*Jur*) to summon
2 (= *proscribir*) to outlaw
3 (= *registrar*) to enrol, enroll (*EEUU*)
VI (*Naipes*) to lead
VPR **encartarse** (*Naipes*) *to take on one's opponent's suit*

encarte SM **1** (*Tip*) insert, inset
2 (*Naipes*) lead

encartonar ▸ CONJUG 1a VT **1** (= *cubrir*) to cover with cardboard
2 (*Tip*) to bind in boards

encartuchar ▸ CONJUG 1a VT (*LAm*) [*+ papel*] to roll up into a cone

encasar ▸ CONJUG 1a VT [*+ hueso*] to set

encasillado ADJ [*actor*] typecast
SM pigeonholes (*pl*), set of pigeonholes

encasillamiento SM **1** pigeonholing • **de difícil ~** difficult to categorize
2 (*Teat*) typecasting

encasillar ▸ CONJUG 1a VT **1** (= *poner en casillas*) to pigeonhole, categorize; (= *clasificar*) to classify • **no me gusta que me encasillen como escritor romántico** I don't like being pigeonholed *o* categorized as a romantic writer
2 (*Teat*) to typecast

encasquetar ▸ CONJUG 1a VT **1** [*+ sombrero*] to pull down tight
2* • **~ algo a algn** to foist sth on sb
3* • **~ una idea a algn** to put an idea into sb's head
4 (*Teat*) to typecast

encasquillado ADJ jammed

encasquillador SM (*LAm*) blacksmith

encasquillar ▸ CONJUG 1a VT **1** (*LAm*) [*+ caballo*] to shoe
2* (= *incriminar*) to frame*
VPR **encasquillarse 1** [*bala, revólver*] to jam
2 (*And*) (*en discurso*) to get stuck, dry up*
3 (*Caribe*) (= *asustarse*) to get scared
4 (*Caribe**) (= *vacilar*) to waver

encastillado ADJ **1** (*Arquit*) castellated
2 [*persona*] (= *soberbio*) haughty; (= *obstinado*) stubborn

encastillar ▸ CONJUG 1a VT to fortify, defend with castles
VPR **encastillarse 1** (*Mil*) to take to the hills
2 (*Hist*) to shut o.s. up in a castle

3 (= *obstinarse*) to refuse to yield • **~se en un principio** to stick to a principle, refuse to give up a principle

encastrar ▸ CONJUG 1a VT (= *encajar*) to fit

encatrado SM (*Cono Sur*) hurdle

encatrinarse ▸ CONJUG 1a VPR (*Méx*) to dress up

encauchado SM (*And, Caribe*) (= *tela*) rubberized cloth; (= *capa*) waterproof cape

encauchar ▸ CONJUG 1a VT to rubberize, waterproof

encausado/a SM/F (*Jur*) accused, defendant

encausamiento SM prosecution

encausar ▸ CONJUG 1a VT to prosecute, sue

encauzar ▸ CONJUG 1f VT 1 [+ *agua, río*] to channel
2 (= *dirigir*) to channel, direct • **las protestas se pueden ~ a fines positivos** the protests can be guided into useful channels

encefálico ADJ encephalic

encefalitis SF INV encephalitis ▸ **encefalitis letárgica** sleeping sickness, encephalitis lethargica (*frm*)

encefalograma SM encephalogram

encefalomielitis SF INV ▸ **encefalomielitis miálgica** myalgic encephalomyelitis

encefalopatía SF ▸ **encefalopatía espongiforme bovina** bovine spongiform encephalopathy

enceguecedor ADJ (*LAm*) blinding, dazzling

enceguecer ▸ CONJUG 2d (*LAm*) VT to blind
VI, VPR **enceguecerse** to go blind

encelar ▸ CONJUG 1a VT to make jealous
VPR **encelarse 1** [*persona*] to become jealous
2 (*Zool*) to rut, be on heat

encenagado ADJ 1 (= *enfangado*) muddy, mud-stained
2 (= *enviciado*) sunk in vice, depraved

encenagarse ▸ CONJUG 1h VPR
1 (= *enfangarse*) to get muddy
2 (= *enviciarse*) to become depraved

encendedor SM 1 (= *mechero*) lighter ▸ **encendedor de bolsillo** pocket lighter ▸ **encendedor de cigarrillos** cigarette lighter ▸ **encendedor de cocina** gas poker ▸ **encendedor de gas** gas lighter ▸ **encendedor del gas** gas poker
2 (= *persona*) lamplighter

encender ▸ CONJUG 2g VT 1 (= *prender*) [+ *fuego, cigarrillo*] to light; [+ *cerilla*] to strike; [+ *luz, radio*] to turn on, switch on, put on; [+ *gas*] to light, turn on; (*Inform*) to toggle on, switch on
2 (= *avivar*) [+ *pasiones*] to inflame; [+ *entusiasmo*] to arouse; [+ *celos, odio*] to awake; [+ *guerra*] to spark off
3 (*Caribe*) (= *azotar*) to beat; (= *castigar*) to punish
VPR **encenderse 1** (= *prenderse*) to light • **¿cuándo se encienden las luces?** when is lighting-up time?
2 [*cara, ojos*] to light up
3 [*persona*] (= *exaltarse*) to get excited; (= *ruborizarse*) to blush; (= *estallar*) to break out • **~se de ira** to flare up with rage, fly into a temper

encendida* SF (*Caribe*) (= *paliza*) beating; (= *reprimenda*) telling-off*

encendidamente ADV passionately, ardently

encendido ADJ 1 (*gen*) alight; [*colilla, fuego*] lighted, lit; [*luz, radio*] on, switched on; [*hilo*] live; [*color*] glowing
2 (= *rojo vivo*) bright red; [*mejillas*] glowing; [*cara*] (*por el vino*) flushed; (*por la ira*) purple; [*mirada*] fiery, passionate
SM [*de faroles*] lighting; (*Aut*) ignition ▸ **encendido eléctrico** electric lighting

encendimiento SM (= *pasión*) passion, ardour, ardor (*EEUU*); (= *ansia*) eagerness; (= *intensidad*) intensity

encenizar ▸ CONJUG 1f VT to cover with ashes

encentar ▸ CONJUG 1j VT 1 (*para el uso*) to begin to use
2 [+ *pan*] to cut the first slice from

encerado ADJ 1 [*suelo*] waxed, polished
2 (= *de color cera*) wax-coloured, wax-colored (*EEUU*)
SM 1 (= *hule*) oilcloth
2 (*Escol*) blackboard
3 (*Náut*) tarpaulin, tarp (*EEUU*)

encerador(a) SM/F (= *persona*) polisher
SF polishing machine

encerar ▸ CONJUG 1a VT [+ *suelo*] to wax, polish

encercamiento SM (*LAm*) encirclement

encercar ▸ CONJUG 1g VT (*LAm*) = **cercar**

encerotar ▸ CONJUG 1a VT [+ *hilo*] to wax

encerradero SM fold, pen

encerrado ADJ • **no soporto pasar todo el día encerrada** I can't stand being shut in all day • **el prisionero llevaba siete años ~** the prisoner had been locked up for seven years • **la puerta dio un portazo y me quedé ~** the door slammed shut and I was locked in

encerrar ▸ CONJUG 1j VT 1 (= *meter*) to shut (up); (*con llave*) to lock (up) • **encerré el gato en la cocina** I shut the cat (up) in the kitchen • **lo ~on en su celda** they locked him in his cell • **la ~on en un psiquiátrico** they locked her up in a mental hospital • **~ una frase entre paréntesis** to put a phrase in brackets
2 (= *contener*) to contain • **el libro encierra profundas verdades** the book contains profound truths • **el plan encierra graves problemas** the plan has serious problems
3 (= *implicar*) to involve • **cualquier cambio encierra ciertos riesgos** any change involves certain risks
4 (*Ajedrez, Damas*) to block
VPR **encerrarse 1** (= *meterse*) to shut o.s. (up); (*con llave*) to lock o.s. (up) • **se encerró en su cuarto** she shut herself (up) in her room • **~se en sí mismo** to withdraw into o.s. • **~se en el silencio** to maintain a total silence
2 (*como protesta*) to hold a sit-in, stage a sit-in • **los manifestantes se ~on en el ayuntamiento** the demonstrators held *o* staged a sit-in in the town hall
3 (*Méx*) (= *ser hosco*) to be stand-offish

encerrona SF 1 (= *protesta*) sit-in
2 (= *trampa*) trap • **preparar a algn una ~** (*fig*) to lay *o* set a trap for sb

encespedar ▸ CONJUG 1a VT to turf

encestar ▸ CONJUG 1a VI (*Dep*) to score (a basket)

enceste SM (*Dep*) basket

enchalecar ▸ CONJUG 1g VT to place in a strait-jacket

enchapado SM [*de metal*] plating; [*de madera*] veneer

enchapar ▸ CONJUG 1a VT 1 (*Téc*) (*con metal*) to plate, overlay (*with metal*); (*con madera*) to veneer
2 (*Méx*) [+ *puerta*] to fit locks to

enchaquetarse ▸ CONJUG 1a VPR
1 (= *vestirse elegante*) to dress up
2 (*And, Caribe*) to put one's jacket on

encharcada SF pool, puddle

encharcado ADJ [*terreno*] swamped

encharcar ▸ CONJUG 1g VT 1 (= *formar charcos en*) to cover with puddles, turn into pools
2 (= *inundar*) to swamp, flood
VPR **encharcarse 1** [*tierra*] to swamp, get flooded
2 [*agua*] (= *estancarse*) to become stagnant
3 (*Med*) [*pulmones*] to get clogged up
4 (*LAm*) (= *enfangarse*) to get muddy
5 (*Cono Sur*) (= *atascarse*) to get stuck in a puddle
6 • **~se en los vicios** to wallow in vice

encharralarse ▸ CONJUG 1a VPR (*CAm*) to make an ambush, lie in ambush

enchastrar ▸ CONJUG 1a VT (*Cono Sur*) to dirty, make dirty

enchauchado* ADJ (*Cono Sur*) well-heeled

enchicharse* ▸ CONJUG 1a VPR 1 (*LAm*) (= *emborracharse*) to get drunk on chicha
2 (*And, CAm*) (= *enojarse*) to get angry, lose control

enchilada SF (*CAm, Méx*) stuffed tortilla

enchilado ADJ 1 (*CAm, Méx*) (*Culin*) seasoned with chilli
2 (*Méx*) (= *rojo*) bright red
SM (*CAm, Méx*) stew with chilli sauce

enchilar ▸ CONJUG 1a VT 1 (*LAm*) (*Culin*) to season with chilli
2 (*Méx*) (= *molestar*) to annoy
VI (*Méx*) to sting, burn
VPR **enchilarse** (*Méx**) (= *enfadarse*) to get angry, get mad (*EEUU*); (*Méx*) (= *ruborizarse*) to go red in the face

enchiloso ADJ (*CAm, Méx*) [*sabor*] hot

enchilotarse* ▸ CONJUG 1a VPR (*Cono Sur*) to get cross

enchinar ▸ CONJUG 1a (*Méx*) VT [+ *pelo*] to curl, perm
VPR **enchinarse** • **se le enchinó el cuerpo** he got goose pimples *o* goosebumps *o* (*EEUU*) gooseflesh

enchinchar ▸ CONJUG 1a VT 1 (*LAm*) (= *molestar*) to put out, bother
2 (*Méx*) [+ *persona*] to cause to waste time; [+ *asunto*] to delay
VPR **enchincharse 1** (*LAm*) (= *infestarse*) to get infested with bugs
2 (*Arg, Méx*) (= *enfadarse*) to get bad-tempered

enchiquerar ▸ CONJUG 1a VT to pen, corral

enchironar* ▸ CONJUG 1a VT to jail, lock up, put away*

enchisparse* ▸ CONJUG 1a VPR (*LAm*) to get tight*

enchisterado ADJ top-hatted, with a top hat on

enchivarse* ▸ CONJUG 1a VPR (*And*) to fly into a rage

enchufable ADJ which plugs in, plug-in (*antes de s*)

enchufado/a* SM/F (*en escuela*) teacher's pet; (*en trabajo*) well-connected person, person with pull
ADJ • **estar ~** to have connections

enchufar ▸ CONJUG 1a VT 1 (*Elec*) to plug in
2 (*Téc*) (*gen*) to join, fit together, fit in; [+ *dos tubos*] to telescope together
3* (*en un trabajo*) • **la han enchufado para el puesto de secretaria** they have set *o* lined her up for the secretary's job (*using contacts*), they pulled strings to get her the secretary's job
VPR **enchufarse* 1** (*en el trabajo*) to wangle o.s. a job*, get a cushy job‡
2 (= *relacionarse bien*) to get in with the right people

enchufe SM 1 (*Elec*) (= *macho*) plug; (= *hembra*) socket; (*en la pared*) point, socket ▸ **enchufe múltiple** adaptor
2 (*Téc*) (= *conexión*) joint; (= *manguito*) sleeve, jacket (*EEUU*)
3* (= *puesto laboral*) cushy job*
4* (= *influencia*) useful contact • **lo consiguió por ~s** he pulled strings to do it • **tener ~s** to have connections

enchufismo* SM string-pulling*,

wirepulling (*EEUU**)
enchufista* SMF person who can pull strings, wirepuller (*EEUU**)
encía SF gum
encíclica SF encyclical
enciclopedia SF encyclopaedia, encyclopedia
enciclopédico ADJ encyclopaedic, encyclopedic
encielar ▸ CONJUG 1a VT (*CAm, Cono Sur*) to roof, put a roof on
encienda *etc* ▸ **encender**
encierra SF (*Cono Sur*) **1** (= *acto*) penning (*of cattle, for slaughter*)
2 (= *pasto*) winter pasture
encierras ▸ **encerrar**
encierre SM (*Caribe*) penning (*of cattle, for slaughter*)
encierro SM **1** (*de manifestantes*) sit-in; (*en fábrica*) sit-in, work-in
2 (= *reclusión*) • **nunca sale de su habitación, no hay quien la saque de su ~** she never leaves her room, no one can persuade her to come out
3 (*Taur*) (= *fiesta*) *running of the bulls*; (= *toril*) bull pen; ▸ SANFERMINES
4† (= *cárcel*) prison
encima ADV **1** (*en el espacio*) • **allí está el cerro y ~ el castillo** you can see the hill there and the castle on top • **le puse un libro ~** I put a book on top of it • **déjelo ahí ~** leave it up there • **el gato se me sentó ~** the cat sat on me • **me he echado el café ~** I've spilt the coffee on myself • **~ de** (*con contacto*) on top of; (*sin contacto*) above • **déjalo ~ de la mesa** leave it on top of the table • **colgó el cuadro ~ del sofá** he hung the painting above the sofa • **llevar** *o* **tener algo ~**: • **no llevaba ~ la documentación** I didn't have the papers on me • **nunca tiene dinero ~** he never has any money on him • **creo que ya tienes bastante ~** I think you've got enough on your plate • **venirse ~ de algn** [*animal, vehículo*] to come (straight) at sb, bear down on sb; [*peso, mueble*] to fall on (top of) sb • **el armario se le vino ~** the wardrobe fell on top of me • **no sabía lo que se le venía ~ cuando llegara a casa** he didn't know what was going to hit him when he got home • MODISMOS: • **echarse a algn ~** (*LAm*) to get on the wrong side of sb • **con su actitud se echó ~ a todos sus compañeros** he got on the wrong side of all his colleagues because of his attitude • **echársele ~ a algn** (= *atrapar*) to catch up with sb; (= *criticar*) to come down (hard) on sb • **el Parlamento se le echó ~** Parliament came down (hard) on him • **estar ~ de algn** (= *estar pendiente*) to stand over sb; (*pey*) to be on someone's back* • **tengo que estar siempre ~ de mis hijos para que estudien** I always have to stand over my children to make them work • **tengo a mi jefe siempre ~** my boss is always on my back* • **hacerse ~** (*LAm*) (*euf*) • **hacérselo ~** (*Esp*) (*euf*) (= *orinarse*) to wet o.s.; (= *defecar*) to mess o.s. • **poner a algn el dedo** *o* **la mano ~** to lay a finger on sb • **quitarse algo/a algn de ~** to get rid of sth/sb • **nos hemos quitado un gran problema de ~** that's a great problem out of the way for us; ▸ **mundo**
2 (*en el tiempo*) upon • **ya tenemos el invierno ~ otra vez** winter is upon us again • **tenían ya la guerra ~** war was imminent *o* upon them • **se nos echó la noche ~** it grew dark, night fell • **se nos viene ~ la fecha de la boda** the wedding is nearly upon us, the wedding is just around the corner
3 • **por ~ a** (= *por lo alto*) over • **le eché una manta por ~** I put a blanket over her • **el avión les pasó por ~** the plane passed overhead • **por ~ tiene a su jefe y al director** there's his boss and the director above him • **por ~ de** over • **el avión pasó rozando por ~ de la catedral** the plane skimmed over the top of the cathedral • **ha nevado por ~ de los 2.500m** there is snow above *o* over 2,500 metres • **estar por ~ de algo** (*en cantidad, nivel*) to be above sth; (*en preferencia*) to come before sth • **la asistencia estuvo por ~ de lo habitual** there was above average attendance • **no hay nadie por ~ de ella** there's no one above her • **estoy por ~ de él en categoría** I'm higher in rank *o* level than him • **eso está por ~ de mis posibilidades** that's beyond my means • **la felicidad está por ~ del dinero** happiness comes before money • **estar por ~ del bien y del mal** to be above the law • **por ~ de todo** above all • **quiero hacerlo por ~ de todo** I want to do it above all else • **la seguridad por ~ de todo** safety first
b (= *superficialmente*) • **hoy hemos limpiado muy por ~** we've just done a quick clean today • **hicimos una revisión por ~ del texto** we had a quick check on the text • **hojear algo por ~** to leaf through sth
4 (= *además*) on top of that • **y ~ no me dio ni las gracias** and on top of that he didn't even thank me • **te lo envían a casa y ~ te regalan un libro** they send it to your house and you get a free book too *o* as well • **le toca la lotería y ~ se queja** she wins the lottery and even then she complains • **~ de** besides, as well as • **y luego, ~ de todo lo que dijo, se fue sin disculparse** and then, as well as *o* on top of saying all that, he left without apologizing
5 (*esp Cono Sur*) • **~ mío/tuyo/***etc* above me/you/*etc* • **está siempre ~ mío vigilando lo que hago** he's always on top of me watching everything I do
encimar ▸ CONJUG 1a VT **1** (*LAm**) to add as a bonus
2 (*Dep*) to mark
VI (*Naipes*) to add a new stake
encime SM (*And*) bonus, extra
encimera SF worktop, work surface
encimero ADJ top, upper
encina SF ilex, holm oak
encinar SM holm-oak wood
encinta ADJ pregnant; (*Zool*) with young • **mujer ~** pregnant woman • **dejar a una chica ~** to get a girl pregnant
encintado SM kerb, curb (*EEUU*)
encizañar ▸ CONJUG 1a VT to sow discord among, create trouble among
VI to sow discord, cause trouble
enclaustrar ▸ CONJUG 1a VT **1** (*Rel*) to cloister
2 (= *ocultar*) to hide away
VPR **enclaustrarse** (= *encerrarse*) to shut o.s. away • **se enclaustró en su cuarto para prepararse los exámenes** he shut himself away in his room to prepare for the exams
enclavado ADJ (= *situado*) • **las ruinas están enclavadas en un valle** the ruins are set deep in a valley
enclavar ▸ CONJUG 1a VT **1** (= *situar*) to place
2 (*Téc*) (= *clavar*) to nail; (= *traspasar*) to pierce, transfix
3 (= *empotrar*) to embed, set
4* (= *engañar*) to swindle, con*
enclave SM enclave
enclavijar ▸ CONJUG 1a VT to peg, pin
enclencle ADJ (*LAm*) terribly thin
enclenco ADJ (*And, Caribe*) = **enclenque**
enclenque ADJ weak, sickly
enclítica SF enclitic
enclítico ADJ enclitic
enclocar ▸ CONJUG 1g, 1l VI, **encloquecer** ▸ CONJUG 2d VI to go broody
encobar ▸ CONJUG 1a VI, **encobarse** VPR [*gallina*] to brood
encocorante* ADJ annoying, maddening
encocorar* ▸ CONJUG 1a VT to annoy, madden
VPR **encocorarse 1** (= *enojarse*) to get cross, get mad
2 (*Caribe*) (= *sospechar*) to get suspicious
3 (*Cono Sur*) to put on airs
encofrado SM (*Téc*) form, plank mould
encofrador/a SM/F (*Constr*) shutterer
encofrar ▸ CONJUG 1a VT to plank, timber
encoger ▸ CONJUG 2c VT **1** [+ *tejidos*] to shrink
2 (= *acobardar*) to intimidate
VI [*tela*] to shrink
VPR **encogerse 1** to shrink
2 • **~se de hombros** to shrug one's shoulders
3 [*persona*] (= *acobardarse*) to cringe; (= *desanimarse*) to get discouraged
encogidamente ADV shyly, bashfully
encogido ADJ **1** [*tejido*] shrunken
2 (= *tacaño*) stingy*
3 (= *tímido*) shy, bashful
encogimiento SM **1** [*de tejidos*] shrinking
2 ▸ **encogimiento de hombros** shrug (*of the shoulders*)
3 (= *timidez*) shyness, bashfulness
encogollado* ADJ (*Cono Sur*) stuck-up*, snobbish
encogollarse* ▸ CONJUG 1a VPR (*Cono Sur*) to get conceited, be haughty
encohetarse ▸ CONJUG 1a VPR (*And, CAm*) to get furious
encojar ▸ CONJUG 1a VT to lame, cripple
VPR **encojarse 1** (= *cojear*) to go lame*
2 (= *fingir enfermedad*) to pretend to be ill
encojonarse** ▸ CONJUG 1a VPR (*CAm*) to fly off the handle*, explode
encolar ▸ CONJUG 1a VT (= *engomar*) to glue, paste; (= *pegar*) to stick down, stick together; (= *aprestar*) to size
encolerizar ▸ CONJUG 1f VT to anger, provoke
VPR **encolerizarse** to get angry
encomendar ▸ CONJUG 1j VT to entrust, commend (a to, to the charge of)
VPR **encomendarse** • **~se a** to entrust o.s. to
encomendería SF (*Perú*) grocery store, grocer's
encomendero SM **1** (*Perú*) grocer; (*Caribe*) wholesale meat supplier
2 (*LAm*) (*Hist*) *holder of an encomienda*
encomiable ADJ laudable, praiseworthy
encomiar ▸ CONJUG 1b VT to praise, pay tribute to
encomienda SF **1** (= *encargo*) charge, mission
2 (= *elogio*) praise
3 (= *protección*) protection
4 (= *patrocinio*) patronage
5 (*LAm*) (= *almacén*) warehouse
6 (*LAm*) (= *paquete postal*) parcel
▸ **encomienda contra reembolso** parcel sent cash on delivery
7 encomiendas†† regards, respects
8 (*Hist*) *colonial grant of land and native inhabitants to a settler*
9 (*Hist, Mil*) command (*of a military order*)
▸ ENCOMIENDA
encomio SM praise, eulogy
encomioso ADJ (*LAm*) laudatory, eulogistic
enconadamente ADV angrily, bitterly
enconado ADJ **1** [*discusión*] bitter
2 (*Med*) (= *inflamado*) inflamed; (= *dolorido*) sore
enconamiento SM (*Med*) inflammation, soreness

ENCOMIENDA

The **encomienda** was a repressive system fixing the Spanish conquistadors' entitlement to labour and tribute from Indian communities. Although the Indians theoretically remained free subjects of the Spanish Crown, in practice they were enslaved to the **encomenderos** (those having **encomienda** rights). One of its most celebrated opponents was the Dominican friar and former **encomendero** Fray Bartolomé de Las Casas (1474-1566). In 1542, in response to protests from the Church, and fearful of the growing power of the **encomenderos**, Charles V brought in laws aimed at phasing out the system. The Spanish settlers rebelled, but the Crown held fast to the central principle that **encomienda** rights should not be hereditary.

e

enconar ▷ CONJUG 1a (VT) **1** (= *encolerizar*) to anger, irritate
2 (= *enfervorecer*) [+ *disputa*] to inflame, embitter; [+ *odio, rencor*] to inflame
3 (*Med*) (= *inflamar*) to inflame
(VPR) **enconarse 1** (= *encolerizarse*) to get angry, get irritated
2 (= *enfervorecerse*) [*agravio*] to fester, rankle; [*disputa*] to become inflamed, become bitter; [*odio, rencor*] to become inflamed
3 (*Med*) to become inflamed

enconcharse ▷ CONJUG 1a (VPR) (*psicológicamente*) to go into one's shell; (*físicamente*) to retire into seclusion

encono (SM) **1** (= *rencor*) rancour, rancor (EEUU), spite, spitefulness
2 (= *mala voluntad*) bad blood
3 (*Col, Méx*) inflammation, soreness

enconoso (ADJ) **1** (= *malévolo*) malevolent
2 (*Med*) sensitive
3 (*LAm*) [*planta*] poisonous

encontradizo (ADJ) met by chance • **hacerse el ~** to contrive an apparently chance meeting, manage to bump into sb

encontrado (ADJ) [*situación*] conflicting; [*posiciones*] opposite • **las posiciones siguen encontradas** their positions are still poles apart • **tienen sentimientos ~s sobre el aborto** they have mixed feelings on abortion

encontrar ▷ CONJUG 1l (VT) **1** (= *hallar buscando*) to find • **al final encontré la casa** I finally found the house • **ha encontrado trabajo** he has found work *o* a job • **no encuentro las llaves** I can't find the keys • **no encontramos ningún sitio para alojarnos** we couldn't find anywhere to stay • **no encuentro mi nombre en la lista** I can't find *o* see my name on the list • **ya no vas a ~ entradas** you won't get any tickets now
2 (*por casualidad*) [+ *objeto, dinero*] to find, come across; [+ *persona*] to meet, run into • **han encontrado unos restos romanos** they have found some Roman remains • **acabo de ~ 50 euros** I've just found 50 euros • **le ~on un tumor** they found him to have a tumour, he was found to have a tumour • **encontró la muerte en un accidente de tráfico** he met his death in a road accident • **~ a algn haciendo algo** to find sb doing sth • **la encontré llamando por teléfono** I found her making a phone call • **cuando llegué a casa lo encontré durmiendo** when I got home I found him asleep
3 [+ *oposición*] to meet with, encounter; [+ *problema*] to find, encounter, come across • **hasta el momento sus actividades no han encontrado oposición** so far their activities haven't met with *o* encountered any opposition • **no encontré oposición alguna para acceder a su despacho** no one tried to stop me from getting into his office • **~ dificultades** to encounter difficulties, run into trouble • **no encontramos ninguna dificultad para llegar hasta allí** we didn't have any trouble getting there
4 (= *percibir*) to see • **no le encuentro sentido a lo que dices** I can't see the sense in what you're saying • **no le encuentro ninguna lógica a esta situación** I can't make any sense of this situation • **no sé lo que le encuentran** I don't know what they see in her
5 (= *considerar*) to find • **¿encuentras el libro fácil de leer?** do you find the book easy to read? • **yo la encuentro bastante atractiva** I find her quite attractive • **¿cómo encontraste a tus padres después del viaje?** how did you find your parents after the trip? • **encuentro muy correctos sus comentarios** I think his comments are absolutely right • **¿qué tal me encuentras?** how do I look? • **te encuentro estupendamente** you look fantastic
(VPR) **encontrarse 1** (= *descubrir*) to find • **¿qué te has encontrado?** what have you found? • **se ~on la casa llena de gente** they found the house full of people • **me los encontré llorando a los dos** I found both of them crying • **~se con:** • **al llegar nos encontramos con la puerta cerrada** when we arrived we found the door locked • **~se con algo de pura casualidad** to come across sth by pure *o* sheer chance • **~se con que:** • **me encontré con que no tenía gasolina** I found (that) I was out of petrol • **~se a sí mismo** to find oneself
2 (= *coincidir*) to meet • **se ~on en Lisboa** they met in Lisbon • **este es el punto en el que se encuentran las dos calles** this is the point where the two streets meet • **~se a algn** to run into sb, meet sb • **~se con** [+ *persona*] to run into, meet; [+ *obstáculo, dificultad*] to run into, encounter • **me encontré con Isabel en el supermercado** I ran into *o* met Isabel in the supermarket • **me lo encontré por la calle de casualidad** I ran into *o* bumped into him in the street by chance • **nos encontramos con muchos problemas en la escalada** we encountered *o* ran into *o* came up against a lot of problems during the ascent
3 (= *quedar citados*) to meet • **¿nos encontramos en el aeropuerto?** shall we meet at the airport? • **nos encontramos en un bar** we met in a bar • **quedamos en ~nos a las siete** we arranged to meet at seven
4 (= *chocar*) [*vehículos*] to crash, collide; [*opiniones*] to clash • **al tomar la curva se encontró de frente con el camión** he collided head-on with the lorry when he went round the bend
5 (= *estar*) to be • **me dijeron que no se encontraba en casa** I was told that she wasn't at home • **no se encuentra aquí en este momento** he's not here at the moment • **los dos heridos se encuentran en coma** the two injured people are in a coma • **el museo se encontraba vacío** the museum was empty • **el ayuntamiento se encuentra en el centro de la ciudad** the city hall is situated *o* is in the town centre • **este cuadro se encuentra entre los más famosos de Goya** this picture is one of Goya's most famous ones, this picture is amongst Goya's most famous ones
6 (*de salud*) (= *estar*) to be; (= *sentirse*) to feel • **su familia se encuentra perfectamente** his family are all very well • **se encuentra enferma** she is ill • **¿te encuentras mejor?** are you feeling better? • **~se bien** to be well • **ahora me encuentro bien** I'm well now • **hoy no me encuentro bien** I don't feel well today • **~se mal** to feel ill • **me encuentro mal** I feel ill, I don't feel very well

encontronazo (SM), **encontrón** (SM) collision, crash, fender-bender (*EEUU**)

encoñado‡ (ADJ) • **estar ~ con algn** to have the hots for sb* • **estar ~ con algo** to be mad keen on sth

encoñamiento‡ (SM) (= *enamoramiento*) infatuation; (= *capricho*) whim

encoñar‡ ▷ CONJUG 1a (VT) **1** (= *alentar*) to lead on, draw on, raise (false) hopes in
2 (= *enojar*) to upset
(VPR) **encoñarse** • **~se con algn** to get the hots for sb*

encopetado (ADJ) **1** (= *emperifollado*) dressed to the nines*
2 (= *señorial*) posh*, grand
3 (= *altanero*) haughty

encopetarse ▷ CONJUG 1a (VPR) **1** (= *acicalarse*) to dress to the nines*
2 (= *engreírse*) to get conceited, give o.s. airs

encorajar ▷ CONJUG 1a (VT) **1** (= *inflamar*) to inflame
2 (= *animar*) to encourage, put heart into
(VPR) **encorajarse** to fly into a rage

encorajinar ▷ CONJUG 1a (VT) **1** (*LAm*) = **encorajar**
2 (= *enfadar*) to anger, irritate
(VPR) **encorajinarse 1** (= *enfadarse*) to fly into a rage
2 (*Cono Sur*) [*trato*] to fail, go awry

encorar ▷ CONJUG 1l (VT) to cover with leather

encorbatado (ADJ) wearing a tie

encorchado (SM) **1** [*de botella*] corking
2 [*de abejas*] hiving

encorchar ▷ CONJUG 1a (VT) **1** [+ *botella*] to cork
2 [+ *abejas*] to hive

encordado (SM) **1** (*Boxeo*) ring
2 (*Cono Sur*) (*Mús*) (= *cuerdas*) strings (*pl*); (= *guitarra*) guitar

encordar ▷ CONJUG 1l (VT) **1** (*Mús*) to fit strings to
2 (= *atar*) to bind, tie (with ropes)
3 [+ *espacio, zona*] to rope off
(VPR) **encordarse** [*alpinistas*] to rope themselves together

encordelar ▷ CONJUG 1a (VT) to tie (with string)

encornado (ADJ) • **un toro bien ~** a bull with good horns

encornadura (SF) horns (*pl*)

encornar ▷ CONJUG 1l (VT) to gore

encornudar ▷ CONJUG 1a (VT) to cuckold

encorralar ▷ CONJUG 1a (VT) to pen, corral

encorsetar ▷ CONJUG 1a (VT) to confine, put into a straitjacket

encorvada (SF) stoop, bend • **hacer la ~*** to malinger, pretend to be ill

encorvado (ADJ) (= *doblado*) curved, bent; (= *inclinado*) stooping; (= *torcido*) crooked • **andar ~** to walk with a stoop

encorvadura (SF) (= *curva*) curve, curvature; (= *torcedura*) bend

encorvar ▷ CONJUG 1a (VT) (= *doblar*) to bend, curve; (= *inclinar*) to bend down, bend over; (= *torcer*) to make crooked
(VPR) **encorvarse 1** [*persona*] (= *doblarse*) to stoop; (= *inclinarse*) to bend down, bend over, stoop; (= *torcerse*) to buckle

2 (= *combarse*) to sag
encrespado ADJ [*pelo*] curly; [*mar*] choppy
encrespador SM curling tongs (*pl*)
encrespar ▷ CONJUG 1a VT **1** (= *rizar*) [+ *pelo*] to curl; [+ *plumas*] to ruffle; [+ *agua*] to ripple; [+ *mar*] to make rough
2 (= *irritar*) to anger, irritate
VPR **encresparse 1** (= *rizarse*) [*pelo*] to curl; [*agua*] to ripple; [*mar*] to get rough
2 (= *irritarse*) to get cross, get irritated
encrestado ADJ haughty
encriptado ADJ (*Inform*) encrypted
encriptar ▷ CONJUG 1a VT (*Inform*) to encrypt
encrucijada SF (= *cruce*) crossroads; (= *empalme*) intersection • **poner a algn en la ~** to put sb on the spot • **estamos en la ~** we are at a crossroads
encuadernación SF **1** binding ▸ **encuadernación en cuero** leather binding ▸ **encuadernación en pasta** hardback (binding) ▸ **encuadernación en piel** cloth binding ▸ **encuadernación en tela** cloth binding
2 (= *taller*) binder's
encuadernado SM binding
encuadernador(a) SM/F bookbinder
encuadernar ▷ CONJUG 1a VT to bind • **libro sin ~** unbound book
encuadrable ADJ • **~ en** that can be placed in, that can be included in
encuadramiento SM **1** (= *acto*) framing
2 (= *encuadre*) frame, framework
encuadrar ▷ CONJUG 1a VT **1** [+ *pintura*] to put in a frame, frame
2 (= *clasificar*) to place, classify
3 (= *abarcar*) to contain
4 (*LAm*) (= *resumir*) to summarize, give a synthesis of
5 (*Fot*) to frame • **la foto está mal encuadrada** the composition of the photo is poor
6 (= *encajar*) to fit, insert (**en** into)
VI (*Cono Sur*) to fit, square (**con** with)
encuadre SM (*Fot*) setting, background, frame; (*fig*) setting
encuartar ▷ CONJUG 1a (*Méx*) VT [+ *ganado*] to tie up, rope
VPR **encuartarse 1** [*animal*] to shy, balk
2 (= *implicarse*) to get involved, get bogged down (**en** in)
3 (= *interrumpir*) to butt in
encuartelar ▷ CONJUG 1a VT (*LAm*) to billet, put in barracks
encubierta SF fraud
encubiertamente ADV secretly
encubierto PP *de* **encubrir**
ADJ (= *oculto*) hidden; (= *turbio*) underhand; (= *secreto*) undercover; [*crítica*] veiled
encubridor(a) ADJ concealing
SM/F [*de delito*] accessory (after the fact); [*de objeto robado*] receiver, fence* • **lo acusaron de ~ del homicidio** he was accused of helping to cover up the murder
encubrimiento SM [*de delito*] covering up; [*de objeto robado*] receiving • **se le acusó de ~** he was accused of being part of the cover-up operation, he was charged with being an accessory after the fact (*frm*)
encubrir ▷ CONJUG 3a (PP: **encubierto**) VT
1 (*gen*) (= *ocultar*) to hide
2 (*Jur*) [+ *delincuente*] to harbour, harbor (EEUU); [+ *delito*] to cover up
3 (= *ayudar*) to be an accomplice in
encucurucharse* ▷ CONJUG 1a VPR (*And, CAm*) to get up on top, reach the top
encuentro SM **1** (= *reunión*) meeting • **un ~ fortuito** a chance meeting • **su primer ~ con la policía** his first encounter with the police ▸ **encuentro cumbre** summit meeting ▸ **encuentro de escritores** (small) congress of writers ▸ **encuentro en la cumbre** summit meeting
2 • **ir o salir al ~ de algn** to go to meet sb • **ir al ~ de lo desconocido** to go out to face the unknown
3 (*Mil*) (= *enfrentamiento*) encounter; (= *escaramuza*) skirmish
4 (*Dep*) (= *partido*) match ▸ **encuentro de ida** first leg ▸ **encuentro de vuelta** return leg
5 (*Aut*) collision, crash
6 [*de opiniones*] clash
7 • MODISMOS: • **llevarse a algn de ~** (*Caribe, Méx**) (= *arruinar*) to drag sb down, ruin sb • **llevarse todo de ~** (*Caribe**) to ride roughshod over everyone
encuerada* SF (*Caribe, Méx*) = **encuerista**
encuerado* ADJ (*Caribe, Méx*) (= *harapiento*) ragged; (= *desnudo*) nude, naked, starkers*
encuerar* ▷ CONJUG 1a VT (*LAm*)
1 (= *desnudar*) to strip, strip naked
2 (= *dejar sin dinero*) to skin, fleece
VPR **encuerarse 1** (*LAm*) (= *desnudarse*) to strip off, get undressed
2 (*Caribe*) (= *vivir juntos*) to live together
encueratriz* SF (*Méx*) = **encuerista**
encuerista* SF (*Caribe, Méx*) striptease artiste, stripper
encuesta SF **1** (= *sondeo*) opinion poll, survey ▸ **encuesta de opinión** opinion poll ▸ **encuesta de población activa** (*Esp*) *quarterly survey of the labour market, carried out by national statistics office* ▸ **Encuesta Gallup** Gallup Poll ▸ **encuesta por teléfono** telephone poll
2 (= *pesquisa*) inquiry, investigation (**de** into) ▸ **encuesta judicial** post mortem
encuestador(a) SM/F pollster
encuestar ▷ CONJUG 1a VT to poll, take a poll of • **el 69 por 100 de los encuestados** 69% of those polled
encuetarse‡ ▷ CONJUG 1a VPR (*CAm*) to fly off the handle*, lose one's temper
encuitarse ▷ CONJUG 1a VPR **1** (*liter*) (= *afligirse*) to grieve
2 (*And*) (= *endeudarse*) to get into debt
encujado SM (*Caribe*) framework, lattice
enculebrarse‡ ▷ CONJUG 1a VPR (*CAm*) to fly off the handle*, lose one's temper
enculecarse ▷ CONJUG 1g VPR (*LAm*) to go broody
encumbrado ADJ **1** [*persona*] exalted, haughty (*pey*)
2 [*edificio*] towering, high
encumbramiento SM **1** (= *acción*) raising, elevation
2 (= *exaltación*) exaltation, eminence; (= *altanería*) haughtiness
3 (= *altura*) height, loftiness
encumbrar ▷ CONJUG 1a VT **1** (= *alzar*) to raise, elevate
2 (= *ensalzar*) to extol, exalt
VPR **encumbrarse 1** [*edificio*] to rise, tower
2 (= *engreírse*) to be proud, be haughty • **~se sobre algn** to be far superior to sb
encurdelarse‡ ▷ CONJUG 1a VPR (*Cono Sur*) to get sloshed*
encurrucarse* ▷ CONJUG 1g VPR (*LAm*) (*en cuclillas*) to squat, crouch; (*formando un ovillo*) to curl up (*in a ball*)
encurtidos SMPL pickles
encurtir ▷ CONJUG 3a VT to pickle
ende ADV • **por ~** (*frm*) hence (*frm*), therefore
endeble ADJ [*persona*] feeble, weak; [*argumento, excusa*] feeble, flimsy
endeblez SF [*de persona*] weakness, frailty; [*de argumento, excusa*] flimsiness
endecasílabo ADJ hendecasyllabic
SM hendecasyllable
endecha SF lament, dirge
endecharse ▷ CONJUG 1a VPR to grieve, mourn
endémico ADJ [*enfermedad*] endemic; [*mal*] rife, chronic
endemoniado ADJ **1** (= *poseído*) possessed (of the devil)
2 (= *travieso*) devilish, fiendish; (= *perverso*) perverse; (= *furioso*) furious, wild
endemoniar ▷ CONJUG 1b VT **1** (= *endiablar*) to bedevil
2 (= *provocar*) to provoke
VPR **endemoniarse*** to get angry
endenantes* ADV (*LAm*) (= *hace algún tiempo*) a short time back; (= *antes*) earlier, before
endentar ▷ CONJUG 1j VT, VI (*Mec*) to engage, mesh (**con** with)
endentecer ▷ CONJUG 2d VI to teethe, cut one's teeth
enderezado ADJ (= *adecuado*) appropriate; (= *propicio*) favourable, favorable (EEUU)
enderezar ▷ CONJUG 1f VT **1** [+ *cable, alambre*] (= *poner derecho*) to straighten out, straighten up; (= *destorcer*) to unbend
2 (= *poner vertical*) (*gen*) to set upright, stand vertically; (*Náut*) to right; [+ *vehículo*] to stand the right way up, put back on its wheels, straighten up
3 (= *arreglar*) to put in order
4 (= *dirigir*) to direct • **las medidas están enderezadas a o para corregirlo** the measures are designed to correct it
5 (*en conducta*) • **~ a algn** to correct sb's faults
VPR **enderezarse 1** (= *ponerse recto*) to straighten up, draw o.s. up; (*Náut*) to right itself; (*Aer*) to flatten out
2 • **~se a un lugar** to set out for a place
3 • **~se a hacer algo** to take steps to do sth
Endesa SF ABR (*Esp*) = **Empresa Nacional de Electricidad, Sociedad Anónima**
endespués ADV (*And, Caribe*) = **después**
endeudado ADJ in debt
endeudamiento SM indebtedness, (extent of) debt
endeudarse ▷ CONJUG 1a VPR to get into debt (**con** with) • **~ con algn** (*fig*) to become indebted to sb
endeveras ADV (*LAm*) = **veras**
endiabladamente* ADV • **~ difícil** devilish(ly) difficult
endiablado ADJ **1** (= *diabólico*) devilish, diabolical
2 (= *travieso*) impish, mischievous
3 (= *feo*) ugly
4 (= *enfadado*) furious
5 (= *difícil*) [*problema*] tricky; [*carretera*] difficult, dangerous
endiablar ▷ CONJUG 1a VT **1** (= *endemoniar*) to bedevil, bewitch
2 (= *corromper*) to pervert, corrupt
VPR **endiablarse** to get furious
endibia SF endive, chicory (EEUU)
endija SF (*LAm*) = **rendija**
endilgar* ▷ CONJUG 1h VT • **~ algo a algn: le endilgó una patada en el vientre** she kicked him in the stomach • **papá nos endilgó una insoportable disertación política** Dad gave us an unbearable lecture on politics • **siempre me endilgan los peores trabajos** I always get landed *o* saddled with the worst jobs* • **le han endilgado el sambenito de holgazán** they've labelled him as lazy
endiñar* ▷ CONJUG 1a VT **1** [+ *golpe*] • **le endiñó un puñetazo** he thumped him one* • **le endiñó una patada en el culo** she booted him up the backside*
2 = **endilgar**
endiosado ADJ stuck-up*, conceited
endiosamiento SM (= *engreimiento*) vanity, conceit; (= *altanería*) haughtiness

endiosar ▸ CONJUG 1a VT to deify; (*fig*) to make a god out of
VPR **endiosarse 1** (= *engreírse*) to get conceited, give o.s. airs
2 • **~se en algo** to become absorbed in sth
enditarse ▸ CONJUG 1a VPR (*LAm*) to get into debt
endocrina SF (*tb* **glándula endocrina**) endocrine, endocrine gland
endocrino ADJ endocrine (*antes de s*)
endodoncia SF endodontics (*sing*)
endogamia SF inbreeding • **engendrado por ~** inbred
endógeno ADJ endogenous
endometriosis SF (*Med*) endometriosis
endomingado ADJ in one's Sunday best
endomingarse ▸ CONJUG 1h VPR to put on one's Sunday best
endomorfina SF endomorphine
endomorfo SM endomorph
endorfina SF endorphin
endorsar ▸ CONJUG 1a = **endosar**
endosante SMF endorser
endosar ▸ CONJUG 1a VT **1** [+ *cheque*] to endorse, back
2 (= *confirmar*) to confirm
3* • **~ algo a algn** to lumber sb with sth*
endosatario/a SM/F endorsee
endoso SM endorsement • **sin ~** unendorsed
endriago SM fabulous monster, dragon
endrina SF sloe
endrino SM blackthorn, sloe
endrogarse ▸ CONJUG 1h VPR (*And, Méx*) to get into debt
endulzante SM sweetener
endulzar ▸ CONJUG 1f VT to sweeten
endurecer ▸ CONJUG 2d VT **1** [+ *material, sustancia*] (= *poner duro*) to harden; (= *hacer más resistente*) to toughen • **un barniz que endurece las uñas** a varnish that hardens your nails • **el proceso de estiramiento endurece el metal** the drawing process toughens the metal • **ejercicios para ~ los músculos** exercises to strengthen the muscles
2 [+ *persona*] (= *curtir*) to toughen up; (= *volver insensible*) to harden • **la vida del campo lo ~á** life in the country will toughen him up • **los años que pasó en la cárcel lo endurecieron** the years he spent in prison hardened him
3 (*Jur*) [+ *ley*] to tighten, tighten up; [+ *pena, castigo*] to make more severe • **han endurecido la política antiterrorista** they've taken a tougher anti-terrorist line, they're toughening up on terrorism • **los sindicatos han endurecido su postura** the unions have taken a tougher stance • **proponen ~ las medidas contra el fraude** they're proposing to take tougher *o* firmer measures against fraud • **el gobierno ha endurecido los controles** the government has tightened (up) controls
VPR **endurecerse 1** [*material, sustancia*] (= *ponerse duro*) to harden, get hard; (= *hacerse más resistente*) to toughen
2 [*persona*] (= *curtirse*) to toughen up; (= *volverse insensible*) to harden, become hardened • **se le ha endurecido el corazón** he's become hardened *o* hard-hearted
endurecido ADJ **1** [*material, sustancia*] hardened, caked
2 [*persona*] (= *curtido*) toughened; (= *insensible*) hardened
endurecimiento SM **1** (= *acto*) hardening • **el ~ de las arterias** the hardening of the arteries
2 [*de persona*] (*por curtirse*) toughening up; (*por insensibilidad*) hardening

ENE ABR (= **estenordeste**) ENE
ene SF (name of the letter) N • **supongamos que hay ene objetos** let us suppose there are X (number of) objects
ene. ABR (= **enero**) Jan
enea SF = **anea**
Eneas SM Aeneas
enebro SM juniper
Eneida SF Aeneid
eneldo SM dill
enema SF enema
enemiga SF (= *enemistad*) enmity, hostility; (= *mala voluntad*) ill-will
enemigo/a ADJ enemy, hostile; (= *poco amistoso*) unfriendly • **ser ~ de algo** to be inimical to sth • **una actitud enemiga de todo progreso** an attitude inimical to all progress
SM/F (*gen*) enemy; (= *adversario*) foe, opponent • **pasarse al ~** to go over to the enemy ▸ **enemigo infiltrado, enemigo interior** enemy within
enemistad SF enmity
enemistar ▸ CONJUG 1a VT to make enemies of, cause a rift between
VPR **enemistarse** to become enemies • **~se con algn** to fall out with sb, have a falling out with sb (*EEUU*)
energético ADJ **1** [*política*] energy (*antes de s*) • **la crisis energética** the energy crisis
2 (= *vigorizante*) [*bebida, comida*] energy (*antes de s*); [*componente*] energy-giving
3 (= *vigoroso*) energetic
4 (*LAm*) = **enérgico**
energía SF **1** (= *fuerza*) energy, drive • **obrar con ~** to act energetically • **reaccionar con ~** to react vigorously
2 (*Téc*) power, energy ▸ **energía(s) alternativa(s)** alternative energy (*sing*) ▸ **energía atómica** atomic power ▸ **energía eléctrica** electric power, electricity ▸ **energía eólica** wind power ▸ **energía hidráulica** hydraulic power ▸ **energía nuclear** nuclear power ▸ **energía renovable** renewable energy ▸ **energía solar** solar power
enérgicamente ADV [*condenar, defender*] forcefully, vigorously; [*desmentir*] emphatically, vigorously; [*resistir*] strenuously; [*actuar*] boldly • **un proceso rentable energéticamente** an energy-efficient process
enérgico ADJ [*persona*] energetic, vigorous; [*gesto, habla, tono*] emphatic; [*esfuerzo*] determined; [*ejercicio*] strenuous; [*campaña*] vigorous, high-pressure; [*medida, golpe*] bold, drastic; [*ataque*] vigorous, strong; [*protesta*] forceful • **realizó su protesta de manera enérgica** he made his protest forcefully • **ponerse ~ con algn** to get tough with sb
energizar ▸ CONJUG 1f VT to energize
energúmeno/a SM/F **1** (= *loco*) madman/ madwoman • **ponerse como un ~*** to get mad
2 (= *gritón*) loud and irascible person
3 (*Pol*) fanatic, extremist
4 (= *poseso*) person possessed of the devil
enero SM January; ▸ **septiembre**
enervador ADJ, **enervante** ADJ enervating
enervar ▸ CONJUG 1a VT (= *debilitar*) to enervate, weaken; (= *poner nervioso a*) to get on sb's nerves
enésimo ADJ **1** (*Mat*) n^{th} • **elevado a la enésima potencia** (*lit*) raised to the nth power; (*fig*) to the nth degree
2 (*fig*) • **por enésima vez** for the umpteenth time, for the nth time
enfadadizo ADJ irritable, crotchety
enfadado ADJ angry, cross • **estar ~ con alguien** to be angry *o* annoyed *o* cross with sb • **estar ~ por algo** to be angry *o* annoyed *o* cross about sth • **dijo, ~** he said, angrily *o* crossly
enfadar ▸ CONJUG 1a VT **1** (= *irritar*) to anger, irritate
2 (= *ofender*) to offend • **enfadé a mi madre porque no me gustó su comida** I offended my mother because I didn't like her cooking
3 (*LAm*) (= *aburrir*) to bore
VPR **enfadarse 1** (= *irritarse*) to get annoyed, get angry, get cross (**con** with, **por, de** about, at) • **no te enfades con él, lo ha hecho sin intención** don't be cross *o* angry with him, he didn't mean to do it • **no te enfades, pero creo que lo has hecho mal** don't get offended, but I think you've done it wrong • **de nada sirve ~te** it's no good getting cross • **se enfadó con su novio** she fell out with her boyfriend • **se enfada por nada** he gets angry at the slightest thing
2 (*LAm*) (= *aburrirse*) to be bored, get bored
enfado SM annoyance, anger
enfadoso ADJ (= *molesto*) annoying; (= *pesado*) tedious
enfajillar ▸ CONJUG 1a VT (*CAm, Méx*) (*Correos*) to put a wrapper on
enfangado ADJ **1** [*terreno, persona*] muddy
2 (*fig*) [*ideal*] muddied
enfangar ▸ CONJUG 1h VT to cover with mud
VPR **enfangarse 1** (= *enlodarse*) to get muddy, get covered in mud
2 (= *implicarse*) to dirty one's hands • **~se en el vicio** to wallow in vice
enfardado SM baling
enfardadora SF (*Agr*) baler, baling machine
enfardar ▸ CONJUG 1a VT to bale
énfasis SM **1** (*en la entonación*) emphasis • **hablar con ~** to speak emphatically • **poner el ~ en** to stress
2 (= *insistencia*) stress
enfáticamente ADV emphatically
enfático ADJ emphatic • **dijo, ~** he said emphatically
enfatizar ▸ CONJUG 1f VT to emphasize, stress
enfebrecidamente ADV feverishly
enfebrecido ADJ feverish
enfermante ADJ (*Cono Sur*) irritating, annoying
enfermar ▸ CONJUG 1a VT (*Med*) to make ill • **su actitud me enferma** her attitude makes me sick
VI to fall ill, be taken ill (**de** with) • **~ del corazón** to develop heart trouble
VPR **enfermarse** (*esp LAm*) to fall ill, be taken ill (**de** with)
enfermedad SF **1** (= *estado*) illness, sickness • **durante esta ~** during this illness • **ausentarse por ~** to be off sick; ▸ **baja**
2 (*en concreto*) (*gen*) illness, disease; (= *mal*) complaint, malady • **una ~ muy peligrosa** a very dangerous disease • **pegar*** *o* **contagiar una ~ a algn** to give sb a disease ▸ **enfermedad contagiosa** contagious disease ▸ **enfermedad de Alzheimer** Alzheimer's (disease) ▸ **enfermedad de declaración obligatoria** notifiable disease ▸ **enfermedad degenerativa** degenerative disease ▸ **enfermedad de la descompresión** decompression sickness ▸ **enfermedad de la piel** skin disease ▸ **enfermedad del legionario** legionnaire's disease ▸ **enfermedad del sueño** sleeping sickness ▸ **enfermedad de transmisión sexual** sexually transmitted disease ▸ **enfermedad diverticular** diverticular disease

▸ **enfermedad hereditaria** hereditary disease ▸ **enfermedad holandesa del olmo** Dutch elm disease ▸ **enfermedad profesional** occupational disease ▸ **enfermedad terminal** terminal illness ▸ **enfermedad transmisible** contagious disease ▸ **enfermedad transmitida por virus** viral infection ▸ **enfermedad venérea** venereal disease

ENFERMEDAD

¿"Illness" o "disease"?

Enfermedad *tiene dos traducciones principales en inglés:* **illness** *y* **disease**.

▹ *Lo traducimos por* **illness** *cuando no concretamos la enfermedad de la que se trata, y también cuando se refiere al tiempo que una persona está enferma:*

Su enfermedad no le permite llevar una vida normal
Her illness prevents her from living a normal life
Adelgazó mucho durante su enfermedad
She lost a lot of weight during her illness

▹ *Lo traducimos por* **disease** *cuando nos referimos a una enfermedad infecciosa, a una enfermedad en concreto o a un tipo específico de enfermedad:*

Este tipo de enfermedad venérea es muy común
This type of venereal disease is very common
... mineros que sufren de enfermedades de pulmón ...
... miners suffering from lung diseases ...

Para otros usos y ejemplos ver la entrada.

enfermería (SF) **1** (= *hospital*) infirmary
2 (= *estudios*) nursing
3 (*en centro escolar*) sick bay

enfermero/a (SM/F) (*en hospital*) male nurse/nurse; (*Mil*) medical orderly ▸ **enfermero/a ambulante** visiting nurse ▸ **enfermero/a jefe/a** head nurse

enfermizo (ADJ) [*persona*] sickly; [*mente*] morbid; [*pasión*] morbid, unhealthy

enfermo/a (ADJ) **1** ill, sick, unwell • **~ de amor** lovesick • **estar ~ de gravedad** *o* **peligro** to be seriously *o* dangerously ill • **caer** *o* **ponerse ~** to fall ill (**de** with) • MODISMO: • **~ del chape** *o* **mate** (*Cono Sur*) crazy
2 • **estar ~** (= *encarcelado*) (*Cono Sur‡*) to be in jail
3 (*Cono Sur**) • **es ~ de malo** it's terribly bad • **es enferma de loca** she's clean crazy*
(SM/F) (*gen*) sick person; (*en hospital*) patient ▸ **enfermo/a terminal** terminal patient, terminally ill person

enfermoso (ADJ) (*LAm*) = **enfermizo**

enfervorizado (ADJ) ecstatic

enfervorizar ▹ CONJUG 1f (VT) to arouse, arouse fervour *o* (*EEUU*) fervor in

enfeudar ▹ CONJUG 1a (VT) (*Hist*) to enfeoff • **~ a algn de una propiedad** to grant sb (the freehold of) a property

enfiestado (ADJ) (*LAm*) • **estar ~** to be partying*

enfiestarse ▹ CONJUG 1a (VPR) (*LAm*) to party*, have a good time

enfilada (SF) enfilade

enfilar ▹ CONJUG 1a (VT) **1** (*Mil*) to rake with fire
2 (= *colocar en fila*) to line up, put in a row
3 (= *ensartar*) to thread
4 [+ *calle*] to go straight along, go straight down • **el piloto trató de ~ la pista** the pilot tried to line up with the runway
5 (= *apuntar*) [+ *pistola, cañón*] to aim, train on
6* (= *dirigir*) [+ *tema, asunto*] to direct • **el gobierno ya tiene enfilada la nueva ley de televisión digital** the government has already got the new act on digital TV ready
7* (= *coger manía a*) • **tener enfilado a algn** to have it in for sb*

enfisema (SM) emphysema

enflaquecer ▹ CONJUG 2d (VT) (= *adelgazar*) to make thin; (= *debilitar*) to weaken, sap the strength of
(VI), (VPR) **enflaquecerse 1** (= *adelgazar*) to get thin, lose weight
2 [*esfuerzo*] to flag
3 (= *desanimarse*) to lose heart

enflaquecido (ADJ) thin

enflaquecimiento (SM) **1** (= *adelgazamiento*) loss of weight
2 (= *debilitamiento*) weakening

enflatarse ▹ CONJUG 1a (VPR) **1** (*LAm*) (= *entristecerse*) to become depressed
2 (*Caribe, Méx*) (= *enfadarse*) to become bad tempered

enflautada* (SF) (*And, CAm*) blunder

enflautado (ADJ) pompous

enflautar* ▹ CONJUG 1a (VT) (*LAm*) • **~ algo a algn** to unload sth on to sb

enfocar ▹ CONJUG 1g (VT) **1** (*Fot*) to focus (**a, sobre** on)
2 [+ *cuestión, problema*] to consider, look at • **podemos ~ este problema de tres maneras** we can approach this problem in three ways • **no me gusta su modo de ~ la cuestión** I don't like his approach to the question
(VI), (VPR) **enfocarse** to focus (**a, sobre** on)

enfollonado* (ADJ) (= *confuso*) muddled, confused

enfollonarse* ▹ CONJUG 1a (VPR) to get muddled, get confused

enfoque (SM) **1** (*Fot*) (= *acción*) focusing; (= *resultado*) focus
2 [*de tema*] approach
3 • **potencia de ~** magnifying power

enfoscar ▹ CONJUG 1g (VT) [+ *pared*] to fill with mortar
(VPR) **enfoscarse 1** (= *malhumorarse*) to sulk, be sullen
2 • **~se en** to get absorbed in, get up to one's eyes in
3 [*cielo*] to cloud over, become overcast

enfrascar ▹ CONJUG 1g (VT) to bottle
(VPR) **enfrascarse** • **~se en un libro** to bury o.s. in a book • **~se en un problema** to get deeply involved in a problem • **se enfrascó en su laboratorio** he buried *o* hid himself away in his laboratory

enfrenar ▹ CONJUG 1a (VT) **1** (= *frenar*) [+ *caballo*] to bridle; (*Mec*) to brake
2 (= *reprimir*) to curb, restrain

enfrentado (ADJ) [*posiciones*] conflicting; [*opiniones*] opposing

enfrentamiento (SM) (= *conflicto*) confrontation; (= *encuentro*) (face to face) encounter, (face to face) meeting; (*Dep*) encounter

enfrentar ▹ CONJUG 1a (VT) **1** (= *enemistar*) to set against • **la herencia enfrentó a los dos hermanos** the inheritance set the two brothers against each other *o* at loggerheads
2 (= *afrontar*) [+ *dificultad*] to face (up to), confront; [+ *realidad*] to face (up to) • **tienes que ~ el problema** you have to face (up to) *o* confront the problem
3 (= *encarar*) • **este partido ~á a los dos mejores tenistas** this match will bring together the two best tennis players, this match will bring the two best tennis players face to face
(VPR) **enfrentarse 1** (= *pelear*) [*personas*] to have a confrontation; [*equipos*] to face each other • **Juan y su padre se ~on durante la comida** Juan and his father had a confrontation over lunch • **hoy se enfrentan el Madrid y el Barcelona** today Madrid and Barcelona are facing each other
2 • **~se a** *o* **con a** [+ *persona*] to confront • **se enfrentó a sus secuestradores** he confronted his kidnappers • **se ~on al enemigo** they faced *o* confronted the enemy • **la selección de España se enfrentó a la de Italia** the Spanish team came up against *o* faced the Italian team
b [+ *problema, dificultad*] to face (up to), confront • **se niega a ~se a la realidad** he refuses to face (up to) reality • **hay que ~se con el peligro** we have to face up to the danger

enfrente (ADV) **1** (= *en el lado opuesto*) opposite • **Luisa estaba sentada ~** Luisa was sitting opposite • **de ~** opposite • **la casa de ~** the house opposite, the house across the road • **~ de** opposite (to) • **mi casa está ~ del colegio** my house is opposite the school, my house is across the road from the school • **se sentó ~ mío/tuyo** (*esp LAm**) he sat down opposite *o* facing me/you
2 (= *delante*) in front • **te espero ~ del cine** I'll wait for you in front of the cinema

enfriadera (SF) cooling jar

enfriadero (SM) cold storage, cold room

enfriado (SM) cooling, chilling

enfriador (SM) cooler, cooling plant

enfriamiento (SM) **1** (= *acción*) [*de líquido*] (*gen*) cooling; (*en nevera*) refrigeration
2 [*de pasión, entusiasmo, relaciones*] cooling
3 (*Econ*) cooling-down
4 (= *catarro*) cold, chill

enfriar ▹ CONJUG 1c (VT) **1** (= *refrescar*) [+ *vino, refresco*] to cool, chill; [+ *sopa, motor*] to cool down
2 (= *quitar fuerza a*) [+ *pasión, economía*] to cool down; [+ *entusiasmo*] to dampen, cool
3 (*LAm**) (= *matar*) to kill, bump off*
(VPR) **enfriarse 1** (= *refrescarse*) [*alimentos*] (*lo suficiente*) to cool down, cool off; (*demasiado*) to get cold • **déjalo que se enfríe** leave it to cool (down) • **se te va a ~ el café** your coffee's going to get cold
2 (= *perder fuerza*) [*pasión*] to cool off; [*entusiasmo, relaciones*] to cool
3 (*Med*) to catch a chill

enfrijolarse ▹ CONJUG 1a (VPR) (*Méx*) [*negocio*] to get messed up, fall through

enfullinarse ▹ CONJUG 1a (VPR) (*Cono Sur*) to get angry

enfundar ▹ CONJUG 1a (VT) **1** (= *guardar*) [+ *espada*] to sheathe; [+ *gafas, violín*] to put in its case; [+ *diente*] to cap
2 (= *llenar*) to fill, stuff (**de** with)
3* [+ *comida*] to scoff*, wolf*
(VPR) **enfundarse** • **se enfundó la capa** he wrapped himself (up) in his cape • **una señora enfundada en visón** a lady swathed in mink

enfurecer ▹ CONJUG 2d (VT) to enrage, madden
(VPR) **enfurecerse 1** [*persona*] to get furious, fly into a rage
2 [*mar*] to get rough

enfurecido (ADJ) enraged, furious

enfurruñado (ADJ) sulky

enfurruñarse* ▹ CONJUG 1a (VPR)
1 (= *enfadarse*) to get angry, get cross
2 (= *ponerse mohíno*) to sulk
3 [*cielo*] to cloud over

engaitar* ▹ CONJUG 1a (VT) • **~ a algn** to talk sb round

engajado ADJ (*And*) curly
engalanar ▷ CONJUG 1a VT to adorn, deck (**de** with)
VPR **engalanarse** to adorn o.s., dress up
engallado ADJ (= *arrogante*) arrogant, haughty; (= *confiado*) confident; (= *jactancioso*) boastful
engallinar ▷ CONJUG 1a VT (*LAm*) to cow, intimidate
enganchado* ADJ • **estar ~ a la droga** to be hooked on drugs*
enganchar ▷ CONJUG 1a VT **1** (= *conectar con gancho*) (*gen*) to hook; [+ *caballo*] to harness; [+ *carro, remolque*] to hitch up; (*Mec*) to couple, connect; [+ *dos vagones*] to couple up
2‡ (= *atrapar*) to nab* • **lo enganchó la policía robando en la joyería** the police nabbed him robbing the jeweller's*
3* (= *atraer*) [+ *persona*] to rope in; [+ *marido*] to land • **a mí no me enganchan para cuidar a los niños** they're not going to rope me into looking after the children • **los programas que más enganchan** the programmes which get most people hooked
4 (*Mil*) to recruit
5 (*Méx*) [+ *trabajadores*] to contract
VPR **engancharse 1** (= *quedarse prendido*) to get hooked up, catch (**en** on); (*Mec*) to engage (**en** with) • **el vestido se enganchó en un clavo** the dress got caught on a nail • **~se a la droga*** to get hooked on drugs*, become addicted to drugs
2 (*Mil*) to enlist, join up
enganche SM **1** (= *acto*) (*gen*) hooking, hooking up; [*de remolque*] hitching; (*Mec*) coupling, connection; (*Ferro*) coupling
2 (= *mecanismo*) hook
3 (*Mil*) (= *reclutamiento*) recruitment, enlistment; (= *pago*) bounty
4 (*Méx*) (*Com*) (= *depósito*) deposit, initial payment
5 (*Telec*) connection
6 (*Caribe*) (= *trabajo*) job
enganchón SM tear
engañabobos SMF INV (= *persona*) trickster
SM (= *trampa*) trick, trap
engañadizo ADJ gullible
engañado ADJ • **sentirse ~** to feel cheated
engañador(a) ADJ [*persona*] deceiving, cheating; [*cosa*] deceptive
SM/F (= *impostor*) impostor
engañapichanga* SF (*Arg*) swindle, hoax, fraud
engañar ▷ CONJUG 1a VT **1** [+ *persona*] (= *embaucar*) to deceive, trick; (= *despistar*) to mislead; (*con promesas, esperanzas*) to delude; (= *estafar*) to cheat, swindle • **engaña a su mujer** he's unfaithful to his wife, he's cheating on his wife • **a mí no me engaña nadie** you can't fool me • **no te dejes ~** don't let yourself be taken in • **logró ~ al inspector** he managed to trick the inspector
2 • **necesito picar algo para ~ el hambre** I need to nibble at sth to stop me feeling hungry • **~ el tiempo** to kill time
VI to be deceptive • REFRÁN: • **las apariencias engañan** appearances are misleading
VPR **engañarse 1** (= *equivocarse*) to be wrong, be mistaken • **en eso te engañas** you're wrong there
2 (= *ocultarse la verdad*) to delude o.s., fool o.s. • **no te engañes** don't kid yourself
engañifa* SF trick, swindle
engañito SM (*Cono Sur*) small gift, token
engaño SM **1** (= *acto*) (*gen*) deception; (= *ilusión*) delusion • **todo es ~** it's all a sham • **llamarse a ~** to protest that one has been cheated • **que nadie se llame a ~** let nobody say he wasn't warned • **aquí no hay ~** there is no attempt to deceive anybody here, it's all on the level*
2 (= *trampa*) trick, swindle
3 (= *malentendido*) mistake, misunderstanding • **padecer ~** to labour under a misunderstanding, labor under a misunderstanding (*EEUU*) • **no haya ~** let there be no mistake about it
4 engaños (= *astucia*) wiles, tricks
5 [*de pesca*] lure
6 (*Cono Sur*) (= *regalo*) small gift, token
engañosamente ADV **1** [*comportarse*] deceitfully, dishonestly
2 (= *en apariencia*) deceptively
engañoso ADJ (= *persona*) deceitful, dishonest; (= *apariencia*) deceptive; (= *consejo*) misleading
engañufla* SF trick*, swindle
engarabitarse ▷ CONJUG 1a VPR **1** (= *subir*) to climb, shin up
2 (= *padecer frío*) to get stiff with cold
3 (*And*) (= *debilitarse*) to grow weak, get thin
engaratusar ▷ CONJUG 1a VT (*And, CAm, Méx*) = **engatusar**
engarce SM **1** [*de piedra, joyas*] setting, mount
2 (= *inserción*) linking, connection
3 (*And**) (= *jaleo*) row, shindy*
engaripolarse* ▷ CONJUG 1a VPR (*Caribe*) to doll o.s. up*
engarrotarse ▷ CONJUG 1a VPR [*miembros*] to get stiff
engarruñarse* ▷ CONJUG 1a VPR (*And, CAm, Méx*) = **engurruñarse**
engarzar ▷ CONJUG 1f VT **1** [+ *joya*] to set, mount; [+ *cuentas*] to thread
2 [+ *ideas, tendencias*] to link, connect
3 [+ *pelo*] to curl
VPR **engarzarse** (*Cono Sur*) to get tangled, get stuck
engastar ▷ CONJUG 1a VT [+ *joya*] to set, mount
engaste SM setting, mount
engatado ADJ thievish
engatusar ▷ CONJUG 1a VT to coax, wheedle • **~ a algn para que haga algo** to coax sb into doing sth • **no me vas a ~** you're not going to get round me
engavetado ADJ (*Ven*) • **estar ~** to be gathering dust
engavetar ▷ CONJUG 1a VT (*Ven*) [+ *proyecto, documento*] to allow to gather dust
engendrar ▷ CONJUG 1a VT **1** (*Bio*) to beget, breed
2 (*Mat*) to generate
3 [+ *problemas, situación*] to cause
engendro SM **1*** (= *ser deforme*) freak • **¡mal ~!** • **¡~ del diablo!** little monster!
2 (= *feto*) foetus, fetus (*EEUU*)
3 (= *invención*) idiotic scheme, impossible plan • **el proyecto es el ~ del ministro** the plan is the brainchild of the minister
engerido* ADJ (*And*) (= *alicaído*) down, glum
engerirse* ▷ CONJUG 3k VPR (*And*) to grow sad
engestarse* ▷ CONJUG 1a VPR (*Méx*) to scowl
englobar ▷ CONJUG 1a VT to include, comprise
engodo SM (*Caribe*) bait
engolado ADJ (*fig*) haughty
engolfarse ▷ CONJUG 1a VPR **1** (*Náut*) to sail out to sea
2 • **~ en** [+ *política*] to get deeply involved in; [+ *estudio*] to bury o.s. in
engolletarse ▷ CONJUG 1a VPR to give o.s. airs
engolondrinarse ▷ CONJUG 1a VPR
1 (= *envanecerse*) to get conceited
2 (= *enamoriscarse*) to become infatuated
engolosinar ▷ CONJUG 1a VT to tempt, entice
VPR **engolosinarse** (= *encariñarse*) to grow fond (**con** of)
engomado ADJ gummed
engomar ▷ CONJUG 1a VT to gum, glue
engominar ▷ CONJUG 1a VT [+ *pelo*] to put hair cream on • **iba todo engominado** his hair was all smarmed down
engorda SF **1** (*LAm*) (= *cebadura*) fattening (up)
2 (*Cono Sur*) (= *ganado*) fattened animals (*pl*)
engordante ADJ fattening
engordar ▷ CONJUG 1a VT **1** [+ *animal, persona*] to fatten (up)
2 [+ *número*] to swell, increase
VI **1** (= *ponerse gordo*) to get fat; (= *aumentar de peso*) to put on weight; (*Agr*) to fatten
2 [*comida*] to be fattening
3* (= *enriquecerse*) to get rich
engorde SM fattening (up)
engorrar ▷ CONJUG 1a VT (*LAm*) to annoy
engorro* SM hassle*, bother, nuisance
engorroso ADJ [*asunto*] bothersome, trying; [*situación, problema*] awkward
engrampador SM (*LAm*) stapler
engrampar ▷ CONJUG 1a VT (*LAm*) to clip together, staple
engranaje SM **1** (*Mec*) (= *rueda dentada*) [*de reloj*] cogs (*pl*); [*de máquina*] gear teeth (*pl*); (= *conjunto de engranajes*) gears (*pl*), gear assembly • **el ~ transmite la fuerza a la muela** the gearwheels convey the power to the grindstone ▸ **engranaje cónico** bevel gears (*pl*) ▸ **engranaje de distribución** timing gear ▸ **engranaje de inversión de marcha** reverse gear assembly ▸ **engranaje diferencial** differential gear assembly ▸ **engranaje helicoidal** helicoidal gear assembly
2 (= *sistema*) mechanism • **el delicado ~ de la justicia** the delicate mechanism of the judicial system • **el ~ de la dictadura** the machinery of the dictatorship • **una pieza básica del ~ de poder comunista** a fundamental part of the apparatus of communist power
engranar ▷ CONJUG 1a VT **1** (*Téc*) to gear • **~ algo con algo** to engage sth with sth
2 [+ *ideas*] to link together, link up
VI to interlock; (*Mec*) to engage (**con** with) • **A engrana con B** A is in gear with B • **A y B están engranados** A and B are in mesh
VPR **engranarse** (*Cono Sur, Méx*) (*Mec*) to seize up, get locked, jam
engrandecer ▷ CONJUG 2d VT **1** (= *aumentar*) to enlarge, magnify
2 (= *ensalzar*) to speak highly of
3 (= *exagerar*) to exaggerate
engrandecimiento SM **1** (= *aumento*) enlargement
2 (= *exaltación*) exaltation
3 (= *exageración*) exaggeration
engrane SM **1** (*Mec*) mesh, meshing
2 (*Cono Sur, Méx*) (*Mec*) seizing, jamming
engrapadora SF (*LAm*) stapler
engrapar ▷ CONJUG 1a VT (*LAm*) to staple
engrasación SF, **engrasado** SM greasing, lubrication
engrasador SM **1** (= *recipiente*) grease cup ▸ **engrasador de compresión**, **engrasador de pistón** grease gun
2 (= *punto de engrase*) grease point; (*Aut*) grease nipple
engrasamiento SM greasing, lubrication
engrasar ▷ CONJUG 1a VT **1** (*Mec*) to grease, oil
2 (= *manchar*) to stain with grease
3 (*Agr*) to manure
4 (*Méx*) (*Med*) to contract

5* (= *sobornar*) to bribe
engrase SM 1 (*Mec*) greasing, lubrication
2* (= *soborno*) bribe, sweetener (*EEUU*)
engreído/a ADJ 1 (= *vanidoso*) vain, stuck-up*
2 (*LAm*) (= *afectuoso*) affectionate; (= *mimado*) spoiled, spoilt
SM/F bighead*, spoiled brat
engreimiento SM (= *vanidad*) vanity, conceit
engreír ▸ CONJUG 3l VT 1 (= *envanecer*) to make vain, make conceited
2 (*LAm*) [+ *niño*] to spoil, pamper
VPR **engreírse** 1 (= *envanecerse*) to get conceited
2 (*LAm*) (= *encariñarse*) to grow fond (**a, con** of)
3 (*LAm*) [*niño*] to get spoiled, be pampered
engrifarse* ▸ CONJUG 1a VPR 1 (*And*) to get haughty
2 (*Méx*) to get cross, get angry
3‡ (= *colocarse*) to get high on drugs, get wasted‡
engrillar ▸ CONJUG 1a VT 1 (= *poner grilletes a*) to shackle
2 (*And, Caribe*) to trick
VPR **engrillarse** 1 (*Caribe*) [*caballo*] to lower its head
2 (*Caribe*) (= *engreírse*) to get conceited
3 (*And, CAm*) (= *endeudarse*) to get into debt
engringolarse ▸ CONJUG 1a VPR (*Caribe*) to doll o.s. up
engriparse ▸ CONJUG 1a VPR to catch the flu
engrosar ▸ CONJUG 1l VT 1 [+ *cantidad*] to increase
2 (= *espesar*) to thicken
VI (= *engordar*) to get fat
VPR **engrosarse** (= *aumentar*) to increase, swell
engrudar ▸ CONJUG 1a VT to paste
engrudo SM paste
engrupido/a* (*Cono Sur*) ADJ 1 (= *engreído*) stuck-up*, conceited
2 (= *zalamero*) smooth-talking
SM/F (= *zalamero*) smooth talker; (= *embustero*) con*
engrupir* ▸ CONJUG 3a (*Cono Sur*) VT (= *engañar*) to con*
VI to blarney one's way in
VPR **engrupirse** (= *engañarse*) to be conned*; (= *engreírse*) to get conceited, put on airs
enguacharse ▸ CONJUG 1a VPR (*And*) to coarsen, get coarse
enguadar ▸ CONJUG 1a VT (*Caribe*) = **engatusar**
engualichar ▸ CONJUG 1a VT (*Cono Sur*)
1 (= *embrujar*) to bewitch (with a potion)
2 [+ *amante*] to rule, tyrannize
enguandos* SMPL (*And*) knick-knacks
enguantado ADJ [*mano*] gloved
enguantarse ▸ CONJUG 1a VPR to put one's gloves on
enguaracarse ▸ CONJUG 1g VPR (*CAm*) to hide o.s. away
enguaraparse ▸ CONJUG 1a VPR (*CAm*) to ferment
enguarrado* ADJ filthy, dirty
enguarrar* ▸ CONJUG 1a VT to make filthy, make dirty
enguasimar ▸ CONJUG 1a VT (*Caribe*) to hang
enguayabado* ADJ • **está ~** (*And, Caribe*) he's got a hangover*, he's hung over*
enguijarrado SM cobbles (*pl*)
enguijarrar ▸ CONJUG 1a VT to cobble
enguirnaldar ▸ CONJUG 1a VT to garland, wreathe (**de, con** with)
engullir ▸ CONJUG 3h VT to guzzle, gobble, gulp down
VPR **engullirse** to guzzle
engurrioso* ADJ jealous, envious
engurruñarse ▸ CONJUG 1a VPR to get sad, grow gloomy
enharinar ▸ CONJUG 1a VT to flour
enhebrado SM threading
enhebrar ▸ CONJUG 1a VT to thread
enhestar ▸ CONJUG 1j VT (= *poner vertical*) to set upright
enhiesto ADJ (= *derecho*) erect, upright
enhilar ▸ CONJUG 1a VT 1 [+ *aguja*] to thread
2 (= *ordenar*) to arrange, put in order
enhorabuena SF 1 congratulations (*pl*)
• **¡enhorabuena!** congratulations! • **dar la ~ a algn** to congratulate sb • **estar de ~** to be in luck, be on to a good thing
2 • **~ que ...** thank heavens that ...
enhoramala EXCL good riddance! • **¡vete ~!** go to hell!
enhorquetarse ▸ CONJUG 1a VPR (*Caribe, Cono Sur, Méx*) to sit astride
enhuerar ▸ CONJUG 1a VT to addle
enigma SM enigma
enigmáticamente ADV enigmatically
enigmático ADJ enigmatic
enjabonado ADJ soapy
SM soaping, lathering
enjabonadura SF = **enjabonado**
enjabonar ▸ CONJUG 1a VT 1 (= *lavar*) [+ *manos, ropa*] to soap, wash; [+ *barba*] to lather
2* [+ *persona*] (= *adular*) to soft-soap; (= *reprender*) to give sb a dressing-down
VPR **enjabonarse** [+ *cara*] to soap, wash; [+ *barba*] to lather • **enjabónate bien** to have a good *o* thorough wash, wash thoroughly
enjaezar ▸ CONJUG 1f VT to harness, saddle up
enjalbegado SM, **enjalbegadura** SF whitewashing
enjalbegar ▸ CONJUG 1h VT [+ *pared*] to whitewash; [+ *cara*] to make up
enjambrar ▸ CONJUG 1a VT to hive
VI to swarm
enjambre SM swarm
enjaranarse ▸ CONJUG 1a VPR (*CAm*) to get into debt
enjarciar ▸ CONJUG 1b VT (*Náut*) to rig
enjaretado SM grating, grille
enjaretar ▸ CONJUG 1a VT 1* (= *recitar*) to reel off, spout
2* (= *endilgar*) • **me enjaretó la tarea de ...** he lumbered me with the task of ...
3 (= *hacer deprisa*) to rush, rush through
4 (*Cono Sur, Méx*) to slip in
VPR **enjaretarse** • **~se la carrera** to shape one's career, mould one's career
enjaular ▸ CONJUG 1a VT 1 (= *guardar*) to cage, put in a cage • **he estado todo el día enjaulado en mi habitación** I've been cooped up in my room all day*
2* (= *encarcelar*) to jail, lock up, bang up*
enjertar ▸ CONJUG 1a VT = **injertar**
enjetado‡ ADJ (*Cono Sur, Méx*) cross-looking, scowling
enjetarse‡ ▸ CONJUG 1a VPR (*Cono Sur, Méx*) (= *enojarse*) to get cross; (= *hacer muecas*) to scowl
enjoyado ADJ 1 [*corona*] bejewelled, set with jewels
2 [*persona*] • **todas las señoras iban enjoyadas al teatro** all the ladies wore jewels to the theatre • **iba demasiado enjoyada** she was dripping with jewellery
enjoyar ▸ CONJUG 1a VT to adorn with jewels, set with precious stones
VPR **enjoyarse** to get all dressed up in jewels
enjuagadientes SM INV mouthwash
enjuagado SM rinsing
enjuagar ▸ CONJUG 1h VT [+ *ropa*] to rinse, rinse out; [+ *boca*] to wash out
VPR **enjuagarse** to rinse • **enjuágate la boca** rinse your mouth
enjuague SM 1 (= *líquido*) (*tb* **enjuague bucal**) mouthwash
2 (= *acto*) [*de ropa*] rinsing; [*de boca*] washing, rinsing
3 (= *intriga*) scheme
enjugamanos SM INV (*LAm*) towel
enjugar ▸ CONJUG 1h VT 1 (= *secar*) [+ *sudor*] to wipe, wipe off; [+ *lágrimas*] to wipe away; [+ *platos*] to wipe, wipe up, dry; [+ *agua*] to wipe up, mop up
2 [+ *deuda*] to wipe out
VPR **enjugarse** • **~se la frente** to wipe one's brow, mop one's brow
enjuiciamiento SM 1 (= *acción*) judgment
2 (*Jur*) ▸ **enjuiciamiento civil** lawsuit
▸ **enjuiciamiento criminal** trial
enjuiciar ▸ CONJUG 1b VT 1 (= *juzgar*) to judge, pass judgment on
2 (*Jur*) (= *acusar*) to indict; (= *procesar*) to prosecute; (= *sentenciar*) to sentence
enjundia SF 1 (= *sustancia*) substance
2 (= *fuerza*) strength • **una novela con mucha ~** a very weighty novel
3 (= *grasa*) animal fat
enjundioso ADJ 1 [*libro, tema*] substantial, meaty
2 (= *grasiento*) fat
enjuto ADJ 1 (= *flaco*) lean, skinny
2 [*economía*] lean, lean and fit
3 (= *seco*) dry, dried
enlabiar* ▸ CONJUG 1b VT to blarney*, bamboozle*, take in
enlabio* SM blarney*, plausible talk
enlace SM 1 (= *relación*) connection, relationship
2 (= *conexión*) (*Elec*) linkage; (*Quím*) bond; (*Ferro*) connection; [*de vías*] crossover; (*en autopista*) motorway junction; (*Mil*) liaison • **los buques no lograron efectuar el ~ en el punto indicado** the ships did not manage to rendezvous at the spot indicated • **estación de ~** junction ▸ **enlace fijo** fixed link ▸ **enlace telefónico** telephone link-up
3 (= *matrimonio*) (*tb* **enlace matrimonial**) marriage • **el ~ de las dos familias** the linking of the two families by marriage
4 (= *mediador*) link, go-between ▸ **enlace sindical** shop steward
5 (*Internet*) link ▸ **enlace de datos** (*Inform*) data link
enladrillado SM brick paving
enladrillar ▸ CONJUG 1a VT to pave with bricks
enlardar ▸ CONJUG 1a VT (*Culin*) to baste
enlatado ADJ 1 [*alimentos, conservas*] canned, tinned
2 [*música*] canned
SM canning, tinning
enlatar ▸ CONJUG 1a VT 1 to can, tin
2 (= *grabar*) to record; (*TV*) to pre-record
enlazar ▸ CONJUG 1f VT 1 (= *unir con lazos*) to bind together; (= *atar*) to tie
2 [+ *ideas*] to link, connect
3 (*LAm*) to lasso
VI [*tren, vuelo*] to connect; [*carretera*] to link (up); [*idea, movimiento*] to meet, link (up) (**con** with)
VPR **enlazarse** [*ciudades*] to become linked; [*ideas*] to be connected; [*novios*] to get married; [*dos familias*] to become related by marriage
enlentecer ▸ CONJUG 2d VT to slow down
enlentecimiento SM slowing-down
enlistado SM (*Méx*) list
enlistar ▸ CONJUG 1a VT (*CAm, Caribe, Méx*) = **alistar**

VPR **enlistarse** (*CAm, Caribe, Méx*) (*Mil*) to enlist, join up

enllavar ▹ CONJUG 1a VT (*CAm*) to lock up

enlodar ▹ CONJUG 1a VT **1** (= *embarrar*) to cover in mud
2 (*fig*) (= *manchar*) to stain
VPR **enlodarse 1** (= *embarrarse*) to get muddy
2 (= *mancharse*) to become stained

enlodarzar ▹ CONJUG 1f VT = **enlodar**

enloquecedor ADJ [*ruido, trabajo, experiencia*] maddening; [*dolor de cabeza*] splitting; [*dolor*] excruciating

enloquecedoramente ADV maddeningly • **gritar ~** to shout excruciatingly loudly

enloquecer ▹ CONJUG 2d VT (= *volver loco*) to drive mad; (= *enfurecer*) to madden, drive crazy
VI • **le enloquece la música pop** she's mad about pop music
VPR **enloquecerse** to go mad, go out of one's mind

enloquecido ADJ crazed, frenzied

enloquecimiento SM madness

enlosado SM flagstone pavement

enlosar ▹ CONJUG 1a VT to pave (with flagstones)

enlozado ADJ (*LAm*) enamelled, enameled (*EEUU*), glazed

enlozar ▹ CONJUG 1f VT (*LAm*) to enamel, glaze

enlucido SM plaster

enlucidor(a) SM/F plasterer

enlucir ▹ CONJUG 3f VT [+ *pared*] to plaster; [+ *metal*] to polish

enlutado ADJ [*persona*] in mourning, wearing mourning; [*ciudad*] stricken

enlutar ▹ CONJUG 1a VT **1** [+ *persona*] to put into mourning
2 [+ *ciudad, país*] to plunge into mourning; (= *entristecer*) to sadden, grieve • **el accidente enlutó a la ciudad entera** the accident plunged the whole town into mourning
3 [+ *vestido*] to put crêpe on
4 (= *oscurecer*) to darken
VPR **enlutarse** to dress in mourning

enmacetar ▹ CONJUG 1a VT [+ *planta*] to pot (up), put in a pot

enmaderado ADJ [*pared, habitación*] timbered; [*suelo*] boarded

enmaderamiento SM [*de pared, habitación*] timbering; [*de suelo*] boarding

enmaderar ▹ CONJUG 1a VT [+ *pared, habitación*] to timber; [+ *suelo*] to put down floorboards on

enmadrado* ADJ • **está ~** he's a mummy's boy, he's tied to his mother's apron strings

enmalezarse ▹ CONJUG 1f VPR (*And, Caribe, Cono Sur*) to get overgrown, get covered in scrub

enmaniguarse ▹ CONJUG 1i VPR (*LAm*) to get overgrown with trees

enmantecar ▹ CONJUG 1g VT (*Culin*) to grease, butter

enmarañado ADJ **1** [*pelo*] tousled, tangled
2 [*asunto*] messy, complicated

enmarañar ▹ CONJUG 1a VT **1** [+ *madeja, hilo*] to tangle, tangle up
2 (= *complicar*) to complicate • **sólo logró ~ más el asunto** he only managed to make matters worse
3 [+ *persona*] to confuse, perplex
VPR **enmarañarse 1** (= *enredarse*) to get tangled (up), become entangled
2 (= *complicarse*) to become involved, become complicated
3 (= *confundirse*) to get confused
4 (= *implicarse*) to get involved
5 [*cielo*] to darken, cloud over

enmarcado SM **1** (= *marco*) frame
2 (= *acto*) framing

enmarcar ▹ CONJUG 1g VT [+ *cuadro*] to frame • **la catedral enmarcaba perfectamente la ceremonia** the cathedral was the perfect setting for the ceremony
VPR **enmarcarse** • **el acuerdo se enmarca dentro del proceso de paz** the agreement is part of the peace process • **su obra se enmarca en las corrientes vanguardistas** his work forms part of the avant-garde movements

enmarillecerse ▹ CONJUG 2d VPR (= *amarillear*) to turn yellow; (= *empalidecer*) to turn pale

enmascarado/a SM/F masked man/woman

enmascaramiento SM masking, disguising

enmascarar ▹ CONJUG 1a VT **1** [+ *cara*] to mask
2 [+ *intenciones*] to disguise
VPR **enmascararse 1** (*lit*) to put on a mask
2 (*fig*) • **~se de** to masquerade as

enmedallado ADJ bemedalled

enmedio ADV = **medio**

enmendación SF emendation, correction

enmendar ▹ CONJUG 1j VT **1** (= *corregir*) [+ *texto*] to emend, correct; [+ *ley, conducta*] to amend
2 [+ *moral*] to reform
3 [+ *pérdida*] to make good, compensate for
VPR **enmendarse** [*persona*] to mend one's ways

enmicado SM (*Méx*) plastic cover(ing)

enmicar ▹ CONJUG 1g VT (*Méx*) (*Téc*) [+ *documento*] to cover in plastic, laminate

enmienda SF **1** (= *corrección*) (*gen*) emendation, correction; (*Jur, Pol*) amendment ▸ **enmienda a la totalidad** motion for the rejection of a bill
2 [*de comportamiento*] reform
3 (= *compensación*) compensation, indemnity

enmohecer ▹ CONJUG 2d VT **1** [+ *metal*] to rust
2 (*Bot*) to make mouldy, make moldy (*EEUU*)
VPR **enmohecerse** [*metal*] to rust, get rusty; [*planta*] to get mouldy, get moldy (*EEUU*)

enmohecido ADJ **1** [*metal*] rusty, rust-covered
2 [*planta*] mouldy, moldy (*EEUU*), mildewed

enmonarse* ▹ CONJUG 1a VPR **1** (*con droga*) to go cold turkey‡, suffer withdrawal symptoms
2 (*LAm*) to get tight*

enmontarse ▹ CONJUG 1a VPR (*CAm, Col, Méx*) to get overgrown

enmoquetado ADJ carpeted

enmoquetador(a) SM/F carpet layer

enmoquetar ▹ CONJUG 1a VT to carpet

enmudecer ▹ CONJUG 2d VT to silence
VI (= *perder el habla*) (*gen*) to go dumb; (*por miedo, sorpresa*) to be dumbstruck
VPR **enmudecerse** (= *callarse*) to remain silent, say nothing; (*por miedo*) to be struck dumb

enmugrar* ▹ CONJUG 1a VT (*LAm*), **enmugrecer*** ▹ CONJUG 2d VT, **enmugrentar*** ▹ CONJUG 1a VT (*Chile*) (= *ensuciar*) to soil, dirty

ennegrecer ▹ CONJUG 2d VT (= *poner negro*) to blacken; (= *oscurecer*) to darken; (= *teñir*) to dye black
VI, VPR **ennegrecerse** (= *ponerse negro*) to turn black; (= *oscurecerse*) to get dark, darken

ennegrecido ADJ (= *negro*) blackened; (= *oscurecido*) darkened

ennoblecer ▹ CONJUG 2d VT **1** (= *hacer noble*) to ennoble
2 (= *adornar*) to embellish

ennoblecimiento SM ennoblement

ennoviarse* ▹ CONJUG 1b VPR to start courting

enofilia SF (= *afición*) oenophilia, liking for wines; (= *conocimiento*) expertness in wines

enófilo/a SM/F (= *aficionado*) oenophile, lover of wines; (= *conocedor*) wine expert

enojada SF (*Caribe, Méx*) anger, fit of anger

enojadizo ADJ (*esp LAm*) irritable, short-tempered

enojado ADJ angry, cross, mad (*EEUU*) • **dijo, ~** he said angrily

enojar ▹ CONJUG 1a (*esp LAm*) VT (= *encolerizar*) to anger; (= *molestar*) to upset, annoy
VPR **enojarse** (= *enfadarse*) to get angry, lose one's temper; (= *irritarse*) to get annoyed, get cross, get mad (*EEUU*) (**con, contra** with, **por** at, about)

enojo SM **1** (= *enfado*) anger; (= *irritación*) annoyance • **decir con ~** to say angrily
2 • **tener repentinos ~s** to be quick to anger, be easily upset • **de prontos** *o* **repentinos ~s** quick-tempered
3 enojos (= *problemas*) troubles, trials

enojón ADJ (*Chile, Col, Méx*) = **enojadizo**

enojoso ADJ irritating, annoying

enología SF oenology (*frm*), enology (*EEUU*) (*frm*), study of wine(-making)

enólogo/a SM/F oenologist, wine expert

enorgullecer ▹ CONJUG 2d VT to fill with pride
VPR **enorgullecerse** to be proud (**de** of), pride o.s. (**de** on)

enorme ADJ **1** (= *muy grande*) enormous, huge
2* (= *estupendo*) killing*, marvellous • **cuando imita al profe es ~** when he takes off the teacher he's killing*

enormemente ADV enormously • **me gustó ~** I enjoyed it enormously *o* tremendously • **estaba ~ sobrevalorado** it was vastly *o* enormously overrated

enormidad SF **1** (= *inmensidad*) enormousness, hugeness
2 [*de crimen*] enormity
3 (= *desatino*) wicked thing, monstrous thing
4* • **me gustó una ~** I liked it enormously *o* tremendously

enoteca SF wine cellar, collection of wines

enqué* SM (*And*) • **lo traeré si encuentro ~** I'll bring it if I can find something to put it in *o* a bag for it

enquistamiento SM **1** (*Med*) • **cuando se produjo el ~ del grano** when the pimple turned into a cyst
2 (= *atranque*) deadlock • **dado el ~ de la situación** given the current deadlock • **su actitud provocó el ~ de las conversaciones** their attitude caused the negotiations to break down

enquistar ▹ CONJUG 1a VT [+ *conversaciones*] to seal off, shut off, enclose
VPR **enquistarse 1** (*Med*) to turn into a cyst
2 [*mal social*] to take hold, fester within

enrabiar ▹ CONJUG 1b VT to enrage
VPR **enrabiarse** to get enraged

enrabietarse ▹ CONJUG 1a VPR to throw a tantrum, get very cross

enrachado ADJ enjoying a run of luck

enraizado ADJ [*tradición*] well established, long-standing; [*idea, prejuicio*] deep-seated, deeply rooted

enraizar ▹ CONJUG 1f VI to take root

enramada SF **1** (= *follaje*) leafy foliage
2 (*Cono Sur*) (= *cobertizo*) arbour, arbor (*EEUU*), cover made of branches

enramar ▹ CONJUG 1a VT (= *cubrir*) to cover with branches

VI (*Cono Sur*) (= *enverdecer*) to come into leaf
enranciarse ▹ CONJUG 1b VPR to go rancid, get stale
enrarecer ▹ CONJUG 2d VT **1** (= *viciar*) [+ *aire*] to rarefy; [+ *ambiente*] to strain
2 (= *hacer escasear*) to make scarce
VPR **enrarecerse 1** [*aire*] to become rarefied, get thin
2 [*relaciones, ambiente*] to become strained, become tense
3 (= *escasear*) to become scarce
enrarecido ADJ [*aire*] rarefied; [*relaciones, ambiente*] strained, tense
enrarecimiento SM **1** [*del aire*] rarefaction
2 [*de relaciones, ambiente*] straining
3 (= *escasez*) scarceness, rareness
enrastrojarse ▹ CONJUG 1a VPR (*Méx*) to get covered in scrub
enratonado* ADJ (*Ven*) hung over*
enrazado ADJ (*And*) [*persona*] half-breed; [*animal*] crossbred
enrazar ▹ CONJUG 1f VT (*And*) [+ *personas*] to mix (racially); [+ *animales*] to crossbreed
enredadera SF (*Bot*) climbing plant, creeper ▸ **enredadera de campo** bindweed
enredado ADJ [*hilos, cuerdas*] tangled (up)
enredador(a) ADJ **1** (= *chismoso*) • **es muy ~** he's a stirrer
2 (= *alborotador*) troublemaking
3 (= *travieso*) naughty, mischievous
SM/F **1** (= *chismoso*) gossip
2 (= *alborotador*) troublemaker
3 (= *travieso*) naughty child
enredar ▹ CONJUG 1a VT **1** [+ *hilos, cuerda*] to tangle up • **este viento te enreda el pelo** your hair gets tangled up in this wind, this wind tangles your hair up
2 [+ *situación, asunto*] to make complicated, complicate • **con tanta mentira enredó las cosas aún más** with all his lies he made matters even more complicated, with all his lies he complicated matters even more
3* (= *desordenar*) to get into a mess, mess up • **estos niños lo han enredado todo** these children have got everything into a mess, these children have messed everything up
4* (= *involucrar*) to get mixed *o* caught up (**en** in) • **la han enredado en un asunto turbio** they've got her mixed *o* caught up in some shady deal
5* (= *entretener*) • **no me enredes, que llego tarde** don't hold me back, or I'll be late
6* (= *engañar*) to trick • **le ~on unos timadores** some conmen tricked him
7 (= *enemistar*) to cause trouble among *o* between
8 (*Caza*) [+ *animal*] to net; [+ *trampa*] to set
VI* (= *juguetear*) to play around, monkey around* • **¡no enredes!** stop playing around! • **~ con algo** to fiddle with sth • **¡deja ya de ~ con los lápices!** stop fiddling (around) with the pencils, will you?
VPR **enredarse 1** [*hilos, cuerda*] to get tangled up • **se me ha enredado el pelo** my hair's got all tangled up • **la cinta se enredó en el ventilador** the ribbon got tangled up *o* caught in the fan • **el sedal se enredó en la hélice** the fishing line fouled the propeller
2 [*situación, asunto*] to get complicated
3* (= *involucrarse*) to get mixed up, get involved (**con, en** with) • **se enredó en un asunto de drogas** he got mixed up *o* involved in some business to do with drugs
4* (= *liarse*) to get into a tangle*, get into a muddle* • **me enredé haciendo las cuentas** I got into a tangle *o* muddle with the accounts* • **me enredé al pronunciar su nombre** I got tongue-tied when I tried to say his name
5* (*sentimentalmente*) to get involved, get embroiled • **se enredó con una estudiante** he got involved *o* embroiled with a student
enredista* ADJ, SMF (*LAm*) = **enredador**
enredo SM **1** [*de hilos, cuerda*] tangle • **un ~ de pelos** a tangle of hair
2 [*de datos*] (*gen*) maze, tangle; (= *confusión*) mix-up
3 (= *laberinto*) maze
4 (= *asunto turbio*) shady business
5 (= *amorío*) love affair
6 (= *implicación*) embroilment, involvement
7 (*en novela*) complicated situation
8 enredos (= *intrigas*) intrigues; (= *mentiras*) mischief (*sing*), mischievous lies • **comedia de ~(s)** comedy of intrigue
enredoso/a ADJ **1** (= *complicado*) complicated; (= *tramposo*) tricky
2 (*Méx*) = **enredador**
SM/F (*Méx*) = **enredador**
enrejado SM **1** (= *rejas*) grating; [*de ventana*] lattice; (*en jardín*) trellis; (*de jaula*) bars (*pl*) • **~ de alambre** wire netting, wire netting fence
2 (*Cos*) openwork
enrejar ▹ CONJUG 1a VT **1** (= *poner rejilla*) to put a grating on; (= *cercar*) to fence
2 (*LAm*) (= *poner el ronzal*) to put a halter on
3 (*Méx*) (= *zurcir*) to darn, patch
enrejillado SM small-mesh grille
Enresa SF ABR (*Esp*) = **Empresa Nacional de Residuos Radiactivos**
enrevesado ADJ [*asunto*] difficult, complex; [*mente, carácter*] twisted
enrielar ▹ CONJUG 1a VT **1** (= *poner rieles a*) to lay rails on
2 (*LAm*) [+ *asunto*] to put on the right track
Enrique SM Henry
enriquecedor ADJ enriching
enriquecer ▹ CONJUG 2d VT to make rich, enrich
VPR **enriquecerse** to get rich; (= *prosperar*) to prosper • **~se a costa ajena** to do well at other people's expense
enriquecido ADJ [*producto*] enriched
enriquecimiento SM enrichment
enriscado ADJ craggy, rocky
enristrar ▹ CONJUG 1a VT **1** [+ *cebollas, ajos*] to (put on a) string
2 [+ *lanza*] to take up
3 [+ *lugar*] to go straight to
enrizar ▹ CONJUG 1f VT to curl
VPR **enrizarse** to curl
enrocar ▹ CONJUG 1g VI (*Ajedrez*) to castle
enrojecer ▹ CONJUG 2d VT (= *poner rojo*) to redden, turn red; (= *ruborizar*) to make blush; [+ *metal*] to make red-hot
VI, VPR **enrojecerse** (= *ruborizarse*) to blush; (*de ira*) to go red (with anger), go red in the face; [*hierro*] to get red-hot
enrojecido ADJ red
enrojecimiento SM (*gen*) reddening; (= *de rubor*) blushing, blush
enrolar ▹ CONJUG 1a (*esp LAm*) VT (= *reclutar*) to enrol, enroll (*EEUU*), sign on *o* up; (*Mil*) to enlist
VPR **enrolarse** to enrol, enroll (*EEUU*), sign on; (*Mil*) to enlist, join up; (*Dep*) to enter (**en** for)
enrollable ADJ [*colchón, pantalla, persiana*] roll-up (*antes de s*) • **cinturón ~** inertia-reel seat belt
enrollado ADJ **1** (= *liado*) [*alfombra, pergamino*] rolled (up); [*cuerda, cable*] (*en sí mismo*) coiled (up); (*alrededor de algo*) wound (up) • **llevaba el periódico ~ bajo el brazo** he was carrying the newspaper rolled up under his arm • **un hilo ~ en el cable** a wire wound around the cable
2 (*Esp*‡) (= *simpático*) [*persona, música*] cool‡ • **es un tío muy ~** he's a really cool guy‡
3 (*Esp*‡) (*en relación amorosa*) • **llevan varios meses ~s** they've been going out *o* (*EEUU*) they've been dating for several months • **estar ~ con algn** to be going out with sb, be dating sb (*EEUU*)
4 (*Esp*‡) (*con una actividad*) involved, busy • **parecían muy enrolladas hablando de sus cosas** they seemed very involved *o* busy talking about their own things • **estar ~ con algo** to be busy with sth • **¿todavía estás ~ con los exámenes?** are you still busy with exams? • **siempre te veo ~ con las plantas** you're always busy with your plants • **estar ~ en algo** to be involved in sth • **ahora estoy ~ en política** I'm involved in politics now
enrollamiento SM [*de alfombra, papel*] rolling (up); [*de cuerda, cable*] (*en sí mismo*) coiling (up); (*alrededor de algo*) winding (up)
enrollante ADJ **1*** (= *confuso*) confusing
2 (*Esp*‡) (= *atractivo*) smashing*, super*
enrollar ▹ CONJUG 1a VT **1** (= *liar*) [+ *papel, persiana, filete*] to roll (up); [+ *cuerda, cable*] (*en sí mismo*) to coil (up); (*alrededor de algo*) to wind (up)
2 (*Esp*‡) (= *atraer*) • **esa tía me enrolla mucho** I'm really into that girl* • **a mí la droga no me enrolla nada** drugs don't do anything for me, I'm not into drugs*
3 (*Esp*‡) (= *enredar*) • **no me enrolles más, así no me vas a convencer** don't give me that, you're not going to convince me* • **~ a algn en algo** to get sb involved in sth • **no dejes que te enrolle en sus movidas** don't let him get you involved in his dealings
VPR **enrollarse 1** (= *liarse*) [*papel*] to roll up; [*cuerda, cable*] (*en sí mismo*) to coil up; (*alrededor de algo*) to wind up • **el cable se le enrolló en la pierna** the cable wound (itself) *o* got wound around his leg
2 (*Esp*‡) (= *extenderse demasiado*) (*al hablar*) to go on*; (*sin decir nada*) to waffle on* • **no veas como se enrolla en las cartas** he certainly goes on a bit in his letters* • **nos enrollamos hablando hasta muy tarde** we were chattering away till very late • **por favor, no te enrolles, que tenemos prisa** please, don't get talking, we've got to hurry • **creo que me he enrollado demasiado en el examen** I think I waffled too much in the exam* • **~se con algo**: • **si os enrolláis con el fútbol, será mejor que me vaya** if you get onto football, I'm going to leave • MODISMO: • **~se como una persiana** to go on and on
3 (*Esp*‡) (= *ser simpático*) • **venga, enróllate y échanos una mano** come on, be a sport and give us a hand* • **~se bien** to be cool‡ • **el camarero se enrolló muy bien y nos puso una copa gratis** the waiter was really nice to us *o* really cool‡ and gave us a free drink • **~se mal** to be uncool‡ • **tu madre se enrolla fatal** your mum is so uncool‡
4 (*Esp*‡) [*dos personas*] (= *tener una relación sexual*) to have it off‡, make out (*EEUU**); (= *empezar una relación amorosa*) to get off (together)*, get it on (together) (*EEUU**) • **~se con algn** (= *tener una relación sexual*) to have it off with sb‡; (= *empezar una relación amorosa*) to get off with sb*
5 (*Esp*‡) (= *involucrarse*) • **~se en algo** to get into sth*, get involved in sth • **se enrolló en el mundo del cine** he got into* *o* got involved in the movie world
6 (*Ven**) (= *confundirse*) to get mixed up; (= *preocuparse*) to get worked up*
enrolle‡ SM bad scene*, pain*
enronquecer ▹ CONJUG 2d VT to make hoarse
VI, VPR **enronquecerse** to grow hoarse
enronquecido ADJ hoarse
enroque SM (*Ajedrez*) castling

enroscado ADJ **1** (= *enrollado*) [*serpiente, cuerda*] coiled
2 (*And*) angry

enroscadura SF coil

enroscar ▹ CONJUG 1g VT **1** (= *poner*) [+ *tapón*] to screw on; [+ *tornillo*] to screw in
2 [+ *cable, manguera*] to coil
VPR **enroscarse** [*serpiente*] to coil up; [*gato*] to curl up • **la manguera se le enroscó en la pierna** the hose coiled round his leg • **la serpiente se enroscaba alrededor del árbol** the snake coiled round the tree

enrostrar ▹ CONJUG 1a VT (*LAm*) to reproach

enrulado ADJ (*Cono Sur*) curly

enrular ▹ CONJUG 1a VT (*And, Cono Sur*) to curl

enrumbar ▹ CONJUG 1a VI (*And, Cono Sur*) to set off

enrutador SM (*Telec*) router

ensacar ▹ CONJUG 1g VT to sack, bag, put into bags

ensaimada SF *light, spiral-shaped pastry typical of Mallorca*

ensalada SF **1** (*Culin*) salad ▸ **ensalada de col** coleslaw ▸ **ensalada de frutas** fruit salad ▸ **ensalada de patatas** potato salad
2 (= *mescolanza*) hotchpotch, hodgepodge (*EEUU*)
3 (= *lío*) mix-up ▸ **ensalada de tiros*** wild shoot-out

ensaladera SF salad bowl

ensaladilla SF diced vegetable salad ▸ **ensaladilla rusa** Russian salad

ensalmado ADJ (*LAm*) magic

ensalmador(a) SM/F quack, bonesetter

ensalmar ▹ CONJUG 1a VT [+ *hueso*] to set; [+ *enfermedad*] to treat by quack remedies

ensalme SM (*And*) spell, incantation

ensalmo SM (= *encantamiento*) spell, charm; (*Med*) quack remedy, quack treatment • **(como) por ~** as if by magic

ensalzable ADJ praiseworthy, meritorious

ensalzamiento SM [*de persona*] praise; [*de virtudes*] extolling

ensalzar ▹ CONJUG 1f VT [+ *persona*] to praise; [+ *virtudes*] to extol

ensamblado SM (*Aut*) assembly

ensamblador(a) SM/F (= *carpintero*) joiner; (= *ajustador*) fitter; (*Inform*) assembler

ensambladura SF (= *acción*) assembly; (= *juntura*) joint

ensamblaje SM **1** (*Téc*) assembly; [*de astronaves*] docking, link-up; [*de madera*] joint • **planta de ~** assembly plant
2 (*Inform*) assembly language

ensamblar ▹ CONJUG 1a VT (= *montar*) to assemble; [+ *madera*] to joint; [+ *astronaves*] to dock, link up

ensanchador SM (*Téc*) stretcher

ensanchar ▹ CONJUG 1a VT (= *agrandar*) to enlarge, widen; (= *aumentar*) to expand; (*Cos*) to let out
VPR **ensancharse 1** (= *ampliarse*) [*carretera, río*] to get wider, widen; [*vestido, ropa*] to stretch, get stretched out
2 (= *enorgullecerse*) to be pleased with o.s. • **cada vez que habla de sus hijos se ensancha de orgullo** whenever she talks about her children she fills up with pride

ensanche SM **1** (= *extensión*) [*de ciudad*] enlargement; [*de calle*] widening, expansion; [*de elástico*] stretch, stretching
2 (= *barrio*) suburban development
3 (*Cos*) room to let out

ensangrentado ADJ bloodstained

ensangrentar ▹ CONJUG 1j VT to stain with blood, cover in blood
VPR **ensangrentarse** to become stained with blood • **~se con** *o* **contra** to be cruel to, treat cruelly

ensañado ADJ (= *colérico*) furious; (= *cruel*) cruel, merciless

ensañamiento SM (= *cólera*) rage; (= *crueldad*) cruelty

ensañar ▹ CONJUG 1a VT to enrage
VPR **ensañarse** • **~se con** *o* **en** to treat brutally

ensarnarse ▹ CONJUG 1a VPR (*Méx*) to get mangy

ensartada* SF • **pegarse una ~** (*And*) to be very disappointed, feel let down

ensartador SM (*Cono Sur*) roasting spit

ensartar ▹ CONJUG 1a VT **1** (= *pinchar*) [+ *cuentas*] to string; [+ *aguja*] to thread; [+ *carne*] to spit
2 [+ *ideas*] to string together; [+ *disculpas*] to reel off
3 (*Chile, Méx*) (= *engañar*) to deceive
VPR **ensartarse 1** (= *implicarse*) to get involved
2 (*And, Caribe*) (= *meterse en un aprieto*) to get into a jam*, fall into a trap
3 (*Cono Sur*) (= *salir mal*) to mess things up

ensarte* SM (*And*) disappointment, let-down

ensayar ▹ CONJUG 1a VT **1** (= *probar*) to test, try (out)
2 [+ *metal*] to assay
3 (*Mús, Teat*) to rehearse
VPR **ensayarse 1** (= *practicar*) to practice, practise (*EEUU*)
2 (*Mús, Teat*) to rehearse • **~se a hacer algo** to practise doing sth, practice doing sth (*EEUU*)

ensaye SM assay

ensayista SMF essayist

ensayística SF (= *género literario*) genre of the essay

ensayístico ADJ essay (*antes de s*) • **obra ensayística** essays (*pl*), work in essay form

ensayo SM **1** (= *prueba*) test, trial; (= *experimento*) experiment; (= *intento*) attempt • **de ~** experimental • **pedido de ~** (*Com*) trial order • **viaje de ~** trial run • **vuelo de ~** test flight • **hicimos un ~ de la obra** we rehearsed the play • **hacer algo a modo de ~** to do sth as an experiment ▸ **ensayo clínico** clinical trial ▸ **ensayo nuclear** nuclear test
2 [*de metal*] assay
3 (*Literat, Escol etc*) essay
4 (*Mús, Teat*) rehearsal ▸ **ensayo general** dress rehearsal
5 (*Rugby*) try

ensebado ADJ greased, greasy

enseguida ADV ▹ **seguida**

enselvado ADJ wooded

ensenada SF **1** (*Geog*) inlet, cove
2 (*Cono Sur*) small fenced pasture

enseña SF ensign, standard

enseñado ADJ trained, educated • **bien ~** [*perro*] house-trained

enseñante ADJ teaching
SMF teacher

enseñanza SF **1** (= *educación*) education; (= *acción, profesión*) teaching • **primera ~** elementary education • **segunda ~** secondary education ▸ **enseñanza a distancia** distance learning ▸ **enseñanza asistida por ordenador** computer-assisted learning ▸ **enseñanza de niños con dificultades de aprendizaje** remedial teaching, special needs teaching ▸ **enseñanza general básica** *education course in Spain from 6 to 14* ▸ **enseñanza primaria** elementary education ▸ **enseñanza programada** programmed learning, programed learning (*EEUU*) ▸ **enseñanza secundaria** secondary education ▸ **enseñanza superior** higher education ▸ **enseñanza universitaria** university education
2 (= *entrenamiento*) training
3 (= *doctrina*) teaching, doctrine • **la ~ de la Iglesia** the teaching of the Church

enseñar ▹ CONJUG 1a VT **1** (*Educ*) to teach, educate • **~ a algn a hacer algo** to teach sb (how) to do sth • **enseña francés** he teaches French
2 (= *mostrar*) to show; (= *señalar*) to point out • **estás enseñando el sujetador** your bra's showing • **~ algo con el dedo** to point to sth • **nos enseñó el museo** he showed us over *o* around the museum • **te ~é mis pinturas** I'll show you my paintings • **esto nos enseña las dificultades** this reveals the difficulties to us
3 (= *entrenar*) to train
VI to teach, be a teacher
VPR **enseñarse** (*esp LAm*) (= *acostumbrarse*) to become accustomed (**a** to) • **no me enseño aquí** I can't settle down here

enseñorearse ▹ CONJUG 1a VPR • **~ de** to take possession of, take over

enseres SMPL **1** (= *avíos*) equipment (*sing*) • **~ domésticos** household goods • **~ eléctricos** electrical appliances
2 (= *efectos personales*) goods and chattels

enseriarse ▹ CONJUG 1b VPR (*And, CAm, Caribe*) to look serious

Ensidesa SF ABR (*Esp*) = **Empresa Nacional Siderúrgica, Sociedad Anónima**

ensilado SM ensilage ▸ **ensilado de patatas** potato clamp

ensiladora SF silo

ensilar ▹ CONJUG 1a VT to store in a silo

ensillado ADJ [*caballo*] saddled (up)

ensillar ▹ CONJUG 1a VT to saddle (up)

ensimismado ADJ (*en uno mismo*) engrossed

ensimismamiento SM **1** (*en uno mismo*) absorption
2 (*LAm*) (= *vanidad*) conceit

ensimismarse ▹ CONJUG 1a VPR **1** (*en uno mismo*) to become engrossed, lose o.s.
2 (*LAm*) (= *envanecerse*) to get conceited

ensoberbecer ▹ CONJUG 2d VT to make proud
VPR **ensoberbecerse 1** [*persona*] to become proud, become arrogant
2 [*mar*] to get rough

ensobrar ▹ CONJUG 1a VT [+ *carta*] to put in an envelope; (*Inform*) [+ *fichero*] to attach

ensombrecer ▹ CONJUG 2d VT **1** [+ *cielo*] to darken, cast a shadow over
2 (= *cubrir de sombra*) to overshadow, cast a shadow over
VPR **ensombrecerse 1** [*cielo*] to darken, grow dark
2 (*fig*) to become gloomy

ensombrerado ADJ with a hat, wearing a hat

ensoñación SF fantasy, fancy, dream • **¡ni por ~!** not a bit of it!, never!

ensoñador(a) ADJ dreamy
SM/F dreamer

ensopar ▹ CONJUG 1a (*LAm*) VT **1** (= *empapar*) to soak, drench
2 [+ *galleta, bizcocho*] to dip, dunk
VPR **ensoparse** [*persona*] to get soaked

ensordecedor ADJ deafening

ensordecer ▹ CONJUG 2d VT [+ *persona*] to deafen; [+ *ruido*] to muffle
VI to go deaf

ensortijado ADJ [*pelo*] in ringlets

ensortijar ▹ CONJUG 1a VT **1** [+ *pelo*] to curl
2 [+ *nariz*] to fix a ring in
VPR **ensortijarse** [*pelo*] to curl

ensuciamiento SM soiling, dirtying

ensuciar ▹ CONJUG 1b VT **1** (= *manchar*) to get dirty, dirty • **no me ensuciéis el suelo al**

entrar don't get the floor dirty when you come in, don't dirty the floor when you come in
2 (*liter*) [+ *reputación, nombre*] to sully, soil (*liter*)
VPR **ensuciarse 1** (= *mancharse*) to get dirty • **no te ensucies el vestido** don't get your dress dirty • **me he ensuciado las manos** I've got my hands dirty • **te has ensuciado de barro los pantalones** you've got mud on your trousers
2 [*bebé*] to dirty *o* soil one's nappy
ensueño SM **1** (= *ensoñación*) dream, fantasy
2 (= *ilusión*) reverie • **de ~** dream-like • **una cocina de ~** a dream kitchen • **mundo de ~** dream world, world of fantasy
3 ensueños (= *fantasías*) visions, fantasies • **¡ni por ~s!** never!
entabicar ▸ CONJUG 1g VT to partition off
entablado SM (= *tablas*) boarding, planking; (= *suelo*) floorboards (*pl*)
entabladura SF boarding, planking
entablar ▸ CONJUG 1a VT **1** [+ *suelo*] to board (in), board (up)
2 (= *empezar*) [+ *conversación*] to strike up; [+ *negocio*] to enter into, embark upon; [+ *proceso*] to file; [+ *reclamación*] to put in
3 (*Ajedrez*) to set up
4 (*Med*) to splint, put in a splint
VI (*Ajedrez*) to draw
VPR **entablarse** [*viento*] to settle
entable SM **1** (= *tablas*) boarding, planking
2 (*Ajedrez*) position
3 (*LAm*) (= *organización*) order, arrangement, disposition
4 (*And*) (= *empresa nueva*) new business
5 (*And*) [*de terrenos vírgenes*] breaking, opening up
entablillar ▸ CONJUG 1a VT (*Med*) to (put in a) splint • **con el brazo entablillado** with his arm in a splint
entalegar ▸ CONJUG 1h VT **1** to bag, put in a bag
2 (= *acumular*) to hoard, stash away
3‡ (= *enchironar*) to jail
entallado ADJ (*Cos*) waisted, with a waist
entallador(a) SM/F [*de figuras*] sculptor; [*de grabados*] engraver
entalladura SF **1** (= *arte, objeto*) sculpture, carving; (= *grabado*) engraving
2 (= *corte*) slot, notch, groove
entallar ▸ CONJUG 1a VT **1** (*Cos*) to cut, tailor; (= *ceñir*) to bring in
2 (*Arte*) (= *esculpir*) to sculpt, carve; (= *grabar*) to engrave • **~ el nombre en un árbol** to carve one's name on a tree
3 (= *hacer un corte en*) to notch, cut a slot in, cut a groove in
VI to fit (well) • **un traje que entalla bien** a well-cut suit
entallecer ▸ CONJUG 2d VI, VPR **entallecerse** to shoot, sprout
entapizado ADJ **1** (= *forrado*) [*mueble*] upholstered (**de** with); [*pared*] lined (**de** with); [*butaca*] covered, upholstered (**de** with)
2 (*Bot*) overgrown (**de** with)
SM **1** (= *material*) upholstery
2 (*Méx*) wall-coverings (*pl*), tapestries (*pl*)
entapizar ▸ CONJUG 1f VT **1** (= *forrar*) [+ *mueble*] to upholster (**de** with, in); [+ *pared*] to hang with tapestries; [+ *butaca*] to cover with fabric; (*Cono Sur*) [+ *suelo*] to carpet
2 (*Bot*) to grow over, cover, spread over
entarascar ▸ CONJUG 1g VT to dress up, doll up
VPR **entarascarse** to dress up, doll up
entarimado SM **1** (= *suelo*) parquet floor
2 (*de madera*) (= *tablas*) floorboarding, roof boarding; (= *taracea*) inlaid floor
3 (= *estrado*) dais, stage, platform
entarimar ▸ CONJUG 1a VT to parquet
entarugado SM block flooring
ente SM **1** (= *organización oficial*) body, organization • **el Ente** (*Esp**) *the Spanish state television and radio* ▸ **ente moral** (*Méx*) non-profit-making organization ▸ **ente público** public body, public corporation
2 (*Fil*) entity, being
3* (= *sujeto*) oddball*
entecarse ▸ CONJUG 1g VPR (*Cono Sur*) to be stubborn
entechar ▸ CONJUG 1a VT (*LAm*) to roof
enteco ADJ weak, sickly, frail
entediarse ▸ CONJUG 1b VPR to get bored
entejar ▸ CONJUG 1a VT (*LAm*) to tile
enteje SM (*LAm*) tiling
Entel SF ABR = **Empresa Nacional de Telecomunicaciones**
entelar ▸ CONJUG 1a VT [+ *pared*] to cover with hangings
entelequia SF **1** (*Fil*) entelechy
2 (= *plan irrealizable*) pipe dream, pie in the sky
entelerido ADJ **1** (= *temblando*) (*de frío*) shivering with cold; (*de miedo*) shaking with fright, trembling with fear
2 (*LAm*) (= *débil*) weak
3 (*LAm*) (= *acongojado*) distressed, upset
entenado/a SM/F stepson/stepdaughter, stepchild
entendederas* SFPL brains • **ser corto de** *o* **tener pocas ~** to be pretty dim • **sus ~ no llegan a más** he has a brain the size of a pea*, he's bird-brained*
entendedor(a) SM/F understanding person • REFRÁN: • **a buen ~, pocas palabras bastan** a word to the wise is sufficient
entender¹ ▸ CONJUG 2g VT **1** (= *comprender*) to understand • **no he entendido la pregunta** I didn't understand the question • **ahora lo entiendo todo** now I understand everything • **entiendo un poco de francés** I (can) understand a little French • **la verdad es que no entiendo el chiste** I don't really get *o* understand the joke • **lo has entendido todo al revés** you've got it all wrong • **no entiendo tu letra** I can't read your writing • **no entiendo cómo has podido hacer eso** I don't understand *o* know how you could do that • **¡a ti no hay quien te entienda!** you're impossible to understand! • **que no te vuelva a ver fumando ¿me has entendido?** don't let me catch you smoking again, do you understand? • **¿entiendes lo que te quiero decir?** do you know what I mean?, do you know what I'm trying to say? • **es un poco rarito, tú ya me entiendes** he's a bit odd, if you know what I mean • **dar algo a ~** to imply sth • **dio a ~ que no le gustaba** he implied that he didn't like it • **nos dieron a ~ que querían marcharse** they gave us to understand *o* led us to believe that they wanted to leave • **según él me dio a ~, no está contento en su trabajo** from what he said to me, he is not happy in his job, he gave me to understand that he is not happy in his job • **hacer ~ algo a algn** to make sb understand sth • **hacerse ~** to make o.s. understood • **~ mal** to misunderstand • **si no he entendido mal, esto es lo que queréis decir** unless I've misunderstood what you're saying, this is what you mean • **no quiero que me entiendas mal** don't get me wrong • **no entendió ni una palabra** he didn't understand a word of it • **no entendí una palabra de lo que dijo** I didn't understand a word he said • **no entiendo ni una palabra de ordenadores** I don't understand a thing about computers
• MODISMO: • **no ~ ni jota** *o* **ni patata***: • **no entendí ni jota** *o* **ni una patata de lo que decían** I didn't have a clue what they were on about • **no entiendo ni jota de alemán*** I don't understand a single word of German
2 (= *opinar*) to think, believe • **entiendo que sería mejor decírselo** I think *o* believe it would be better to tell him • **yo entiendo que no es correcto hacerlo así** I don't think *o* believe that that's the right way to do it
3 (= *interpretar*) to understand • **¿tú qué entiendes por libertad?** what do you understand by freedom? • **¿debo ~ que lo niegas?** am I to understand that you deny it? • **me ha parecido ~ que estaban en contra** I understood that they were against it, as I understand it they were against it • **cada uno entiende el amor a su manera** everyone sees love differently, everyone understands something different by love
4* (= *saber manejar*) to know how to use, know how to work • **¿tú entiendes esta lavadora?** do you know how this washing machine works?, do you know how to use this washing machine?
5 (= *oír*) to hear • **no se entiende nada** I can't make out *o* hear a thing
VI **1** (= *comprender*) to understand • **¡ya entiendo!** now I understand!, now I get it! • **la vida es así ¿entiendes?** that's life, you know • **~ de algo** to know about sth • **no entiendo de vinos** I don't know much about wine • **Luis sí que entiende de mujeres** Luis certainly knows a thing or two about women • MODISMO: • **no ~ de barcos**: • **si le preguntas cualquier cosa, él no entiende de barcos** if you ask him something, he makes out he doesn't know anything about anything
2 (*Jur*) (= *tener competencia*) • **entiende en divorcios** he hears divorce cases • **~ en un asunto** to be in charge of an affair
3 [*perro, gato*] • **entiende por Moncho** he answers to the name of Moncho
4‡ (= *ser homosexual*) to be one of them*
VPR **entenderse 1** (*uso reflexivo*) to understand o.s. • **si no te entiendes ni tú, ¿quién te va a ~?** if you don't even understand yourself, then how is anyone else going to understand you? • **déjame, que yo me entiendo** leave me alone, I know what I mean • MODISMOS: • **entendérselas**: • **que ella se las entienda como pueda** well that's her problem • **allá tú te las entiendas con tus asuntos** you go and sort out your own affairs • **entendérselas con algn**: • **van a tener que entendérselas conmigo** they're going to have to deal with me
2 (*uso recíproco*) • **nosotras nos entendemos** we understand each other • **nos entendimos por señas** we communicated using sign language, we used sign language to communicate • **a ver si nos entendemos ¿quién de los dos tiene el dinero?** now let's get this straight, which of the two has got the money? • **ya nos ~emos en el precio** we'll work out a price that we're both happy with • **digamos, para ~nos, que …** let's say, to avoid any misunderstanding, that … • **~se con algn** (= *llevarse bien*) to get on *o* along with sb; (= *tener una relación amorosa*) to have an affair with sb • **eso no se entiende conmigo** that doesn't concern me, that has nothing to do with me • **~se con algo** to know how to deal with sth
3 (*uso impersonal*) • **se entiende que …** it is understood that … • **se entiende que no quiera salir con ellos** it's understandable that she doesn't want to go out with them

• **¿qué se entiende por estas palabras?** what is meant by these words? • **¿cómo se entiende que no nos llamaras antes?** why didn't you call us first?
4 (= *tratar*) • **en caso de duda entiéndase con el cajero** in case of doubt please contact the cashier

entender² SM (= *opinión*) opinion • **a mi ~** in my opinion; ▹ **saber**

entendido/a ADJ **1** (= *comprendido*) understood • **¡entendido!** (= *convenido*) agreed! • **bien ~ que** on the understanding that • **no darse por ~** to pretend not to understand • **tenemos ~ que ...** we understand that ... • **según tenemos ~** as far as we can gather
2 [*persona*] (= *experto*) expert; (= *cualificado*) skilled; (= *sabio*) wise; (= *informado*) well-informed • **ser ~ en** to be well up on
SM/F expert • **según el juicio de los ~s** according to the experts • **el whiskey de los ~s** the connoisseur's whisky

entendimiento SM **1** (= *inteligencia*) understanding, mind • **el ~ humano no tiene límites** human understanding *o* the human mind has no limits • **un hombre de mucho ~** a man of great understanding, a very wise man • **¡este chico no tiene ~!** this boy has no brains!
2 (= *comprensión*) understanding • **medidas para fomentar un mejor ~ de las leyes** measures to foster a better understanding of the laws
3 (= *acuerdo*) understanding • **llegar a un ~** to reach an understanding

entenebrecer ▹ CONJUG 2d VT **1** (= *oscurecer*) to darken, obscure
2 [+ *asunto*] to cloud, obscure • **esto entenebrece más el asunto** this fogs the issue still more
VPR **entenebrecerse** to get dark

entente SF entente

enteradillo/a* SM/F little know-all, smarty*

enterado/a ADJ **1** (= *informado*) (*de una especialidad*) knowledgeable; (*sobre un asunto concreto*) well-informed • **esta muy ~ de política** he's very knowledgeable about politics • **—¿sabes lo que pasó? —sí, estoy ~** "do you know what happened?" — "yes, I know *o* I've heard" • **estar ~ de algo** to know sth • **no estaba ~ de que os fuerais a casar** I didn't know you were getting married • **quedo ~ de que ...** I am now aware that ... • **darse por ~** to get the message
2 (*Chile**) (= *engreído*) snooty*, stuck-up*
SM/F (= *conocedor*) [*de materia*] expert; (*pey*) know-all*, bighead* • **no fue una gran sorpresa para los ~s** it wasn't a great surprise for those in the know* • **ese tío es un ~** that guy is a real know-all *o* bighead*

enteramente ADV entirely, completely

enterar ▹ CONJUG 1a VT **1** (= *informar*) • **~ a algn de algo** to inform sb of sth, notify sb of sth, let sb know of sth
2 (*Chile, Méx*) (= *pagar*) [+ *dinero, deuda*] to pay
3 (*Chile*) (= *completar*) [+ *cantidad*] to make up, complete • **hoy entero dos meses sin fumar** it's two months today since I last smoked
VPR **enterarse 1** (*de noticia, secreto*) **a** (*por casualidad*) to hear, find out • **nos enteramos a través de la radio** we heard it on the radio, we found out from the radio • **¿sí? no me había enterado** really? I hadn't heard • **no sabía nada, ahora mismo me entero** I had no idea, this is the first I've heard • **~se de algo** to hear about sth, find out about sth • **no quiero que nadie se entere de esto** I don't want anyone to hear about *o* find out about this • **me enteré de tu accidente por Juan** I heard about *o* found out about your accident from Juan • **me enteré del secuestro a través de la prensa** I read about the kidnapping in the paper • **nos enteramos de que se había ido ayer** we heard *o* found out that he'd gone yesterday
b (*haciendo averiguaciones*) to find out • **entérate y me lo cuentas** find out and let me know • **~se de algo** to find out about sth • **tenemos que ~nos bien de la oferta** we must find out about the details of the offer • **entérate de lo que cuesta** find out what it costs
2 (= *darse cuenta*) to notice • **estaba tan dormido que no se enteró** he was so fast asleep that he didn't notice • **oye, que es a ti, que no te enteras*** hey, you, are you deaf or something?* • **~se de algo** to notice sth • **no se enteró de que le habían quitado la cartera** he didn't notice that his wallet had been stolen • **tú es que no te enteras de nada** you never know what's going on • **todavía no se han enterado de qué tipo de persona es** they still don't know what kind of person he is • MODISMOS: • **te vas a ~ (de quien soy yo *o* de lo que vale un peine)** you'll find out what's what* • **para que te enteres** for your information • **he aprobado el examen, para que os enteréis** I've passed the exam, for your information!*
3 (*Esp*) (= *comprender, oír*) to understand • **si hablas tan flojo no me entero** if you talk so quietly I can't understand • **no quiero que vuelvas por aquí ¿te enteras?** I don't want you coming back here, do you understand *o* do you get it?* • **¡a ver si te enteras!** wise up!* • **~se de algo** to understand sth • **no se enteraba de lo que leía** he didn't take in *o* understand what he was reading

entercado* ADJ • **~ en hacer algo** (*LAm*) determined to do sth, dead set on doing sth

entereza SF **1** (= *integridad*) integrity
2 (= *firmeza*) firmness ▸ **entereza de carácter** strength of character

entérico ADJ enteric

enteritis SF INV enteritis

enterito SM (*Arg*) boilersuit

enterizo ADJ in one piece, one-piece (*antes de s*)

enternecedor ADJ touching

enternecer ▹ CONJUG 2d VT (= *ablandar*) to soften; (= *conmover*) to affect, move (to pity)
VPR **enternecerse 1** (= *conmoverse*) to be affected, be moved (to pity)
2 (= *ceder*) to relent, give in

entero ADJ **1** (= *completo*) whole, entire • **se comió el paquete ~ de galletas** he ate the whole *o* entire packet of biscuits • **se pasa el día ~ quejándose** he spends the whole *o* entire day complaining • **es famoso en el mundo ~** he's famous the whole world over, he's famous all over the world
2 • **por ~** wholly, fully • **me dediqué por ~ a la investigación** I devoted myself wholly *o* fully to research
3 (*Mat*) whole, integral
4 [*persona*] (= *íntegro*) upright; (= *sereno*) composed • **un hombre muy ~** a man of great integrity, a very upright man • **estuvo muy entera durante el funeral** she was very composed *o* she kept her composure during the funeral
5 (*And, CAm, Caribe**) (= *idéntico*) identical, similar • **está ~ a su papá** he's just like his dad, he's the spitting image of his dad
6 (= *no castrado*) entire
SM **1** (*Mat*) integer, whole number
2 (*Com, Econ*) point • **las acciones han subido dos ~s** the shares have gone up two points
3 (*LAm*) (= *pago*) payment
4 (*Cono Sur*) (*Econ*) balance
5 (*Arg*) boilersuit

enteropostal SM air letter, aerogram

enterradero SM (*Cono Sur*) burial ground

enterrado ADJ [*tesoro, persona*] buried; [*uña*] ingrowing

enterrador(a) SM/F gravedigger

enterramiento SM burial, interment (*frm*)

enterrar ▹ CONJUG 1j VT **1** (= *ocultar en tierra*) to bury
2 (= *olvidarse de*) to bury, forget
3 (*LAm*) [+ *arma*] to thrust (**en** into), bury (**en** in)

enterratorio SM (*Cono Sur*) (= *cementerio*) Indian burial ground; (= *restos*) archaeological remains (*pl*), site of archaeological interest

entesar ▹ CONJUG 1j VT to stretch, tauten

entibiar ▹ CONJUG 1b VT **1** [+ *lo caliente*] to cool, cool down
2 [+ *ira*] to cool, cool down
VPR **entibiarse 1** [*lo caliente*] to become lukewarm
2 [*ira, amistad*] to cool off

entibo SM **1** (*Arquit*) buttress
2 (*Min*) prop

entidad SF **1** (= *esencia*) entity
2 (= *colectividad*) (*Admin, Pol*) body, organization; (*Com, Econ*) firm, company ▸ **entidad bancaria** bank ▸ **entidad comercial** company, business ▸ **entidad crediticia** credit company ▸ **entidad financiera** financial institution
3 • **de ~** of importance

entienda *etc* ▹ **entender**

entierrar* ▹ CONJUG 1a VT (*Chile*) [+ *zapatos*] to dirty, make dirty

entierro SM **1** (= *acto*) burial, interment
2 (= *funeral*) funeral • **asistir al ~** to go to the funeral; ▹ CARNAVAL
3 (= *tumba*) grave
4 (*LAm*) (*Arqueología*) (buried) treasure

entintar ▹ CONJUG 1a VT **1** (= *llenar de tinta*) [+ *tampón*] to ink; [+ *blanco*] to ink in
2 (= *manchar*) to stain with ink

entizar ▹ CONJUG 1f VT (*LAm*) (*Billar*) to chalk

entlo. SM ABR (= **entresuelo**) mezzanine

entoldado SM awning

entoldar ▹ CONJUG 1a VT **1** [+ *patio, terraza*] to put an awning over, fit with an awning
2 (= *decorar*) to decorate (*with hangings*)
VPR **entoldarse 1** (*Meteo*) to become overcast, cloud over
2 [*emoción, alegría*] to be dimmed
3 [*persona*] to give o.s. airs

entomología SF entomology

entomólogo/a SM/F entomologist

entonación SF **1** (*Ling*) intonation
2 (= *arrogancia*) haughtiness

entonado ADJ **1** (*Mús*) in tune
2 (= *arrogante*) haughty, arrogant
3* (= *en forma*) lively, in good form

entonar ▹ CONJUG 1a VT **1** (*Mús*) [+ *canción*] to intone, sing; (*afinando*) to sing in tune; [+ *voz*] to modulate; [+ *nota*] to give, set; [+ *órgano*] to blow
2 [+ *alabanzas*] to sound
3 (*Med*) to tone up
4 (*Arte, Fot*) to tone
5 (= *vigorizar*) to liven up, enliven, invigorate
VI **1** (*Mús*) (= *cantar*) to intone (*frm*), sing; (= *cantar afinadamente*) to be in tune (**con** with)
2 [*colores*] to match
VPR **entonarse 1** (= *mejorarse*) • **toma, un cafecito para ~te** here's a nice cup of coffee to pick *o* perk you up
2* (= *animarse*) to perk up
3 (= *engreírse*) to get arrogant, give o.s. airs

entonces (ADV) **1** (*uso temporal*) then, at that time • **desde ~** since then • **en aquel ~** at that time • **hasta ~** up till then • **las costumbres de ~** the customs of the time • **el ~ embajador de España** the then Spanish ambassador • **fue ~ que** ... it was then that ..., that was when ...
2 (*uso concesivo*) so, then • **~, ¿qué hacemos?** so, what shall we do?, what shall we do then? • **¿~ cómo que no viniste?** then *o* so why didn't you come? • **pues ~** well then • **¡y ~!** (*Caribe, Cono Sur*) why of course!
entonelar ▹ CONJUG 1a (VT) to put into barrels, put into casks
entongado* (ADJ) (*And*) cross, riled*
entongar ▹ CONJUG 1h (VT) **1** (= *apilar*) to pile up, pile in layers
2 (*And**) (= *enojar*) to anger
entono (SM) **1** (*Mús*) intoning, intonation; (*afinando*) being in tune, singing in tune
2 (= *arrogancia*) haughtiness
entontecedor (ADJ) stupefying
entontecer ▹ CONJUG 2d (VT) to make silly
(VPR) **entontecerse** to get silly
entorchado (SM) **1** (*en uniforme*) gold braid, silver braid
2 (*Mús*) bass string
entorchar ▹ CONJUG 1a (VT) **1** (= *retorcer*) to twist, twist up
2 [+ *uniforme*] to braid
entornacional (ADJ) environmental
entornado (ADJ) [*ojos*] half-closed; [*puerta*] ajar
entornar ▹ CONJUG 1a (VT) **1** [+ *ojos*] to half-close; (*por el sol*) to screw up; [+ *puerta*] to leave ajar, half-close
2 (= *volcar*) to upset, tip over
entorno (SM) **1** (= *medioambiente*) environment; (*Literat*) setting, milieu; (= *clima*) climate; (= *escenario*) scene • **las personas de su ~** the people around him • **sacar a algn de su ~** to take sb away from/out of their normal environment • **el ~ cultural** the cultural scene ▸ **entorno natural** natural environment ▸ **entorno social** social setting
2 (*Inform*) environment ▸ **entorno de programación** programming environment ▸ **entorno de red(es)** network environment ▸ **entorno de trabajo** work(ing) environment ▸ **entorno gráfico** graphics environment
entorpecer ▹ CONJUG 2d (VT) **1** (= *estorbar*) (*gen*) to obstruct, hinder; [+ *proyectos*] to set back; [+ *tráfico*] to slow down, slow up; [+ *trabajo*] to delay, hinder
2 (= *aletargar*) [+ *entendimiento*] to dull, stupefy; [+ *miembro*] to make numb
entorpecimiento (SM) **1** (= *estorbo*) obstruction; (= *problema*) obstacle; (= *retraso*) delay, slowing-up
2 (= *aletargamiento*) [*del entendimiento*] dullness, stupefaction; [*de un miembro*] numbness
entrabamiento (SM) (*Chile*) obstruction
entrabar ▹ CONJUG 1a (VT) (*Chile*) to obstruct
entrada (SF) **1** (= *lugar de acceso*) entrance • **"entrada"** "way in", "entrance" • **a la ~ del metro** at the entrance to the underground • **le pidieron la identificación a la ~** they asked for some identification at the door • **las ~s a Madrid** roads into Madrid ▸ **entrada de artistas** stage door ▸ **entrada de servicio** tradesman's entrance ▸ **entrada lateral** side entrance ▸ **entrada principal** main entrance
2 (= *vestíbulo*) [*de casa*] hall, entrance hall; [*de hotel*] foyer
3 (= *llegada*) **a** (*a un lugar*) • **no advirtió la ~ de su padre** she didn't notice her father come in • **sus ~s y salidas de prisión fueron constantes** he was constantly in and out of jail • **hicieron una ~ triunfal en Egipto** they made a triumphal entry into Egypt • **dar ~ a un lugar** to give access to a place • MODISMO: • **de ~ por salida** (*Méx*): • **nunca podemos platicar, tus visitas son siempre de ~ por salida** we never have time to chat, you're always in and out • **una muchacha de ~ por salida** a non-live-in maid, a daily maid
b [*de correspondencia*] arrival • **bandeja de ~s** in-tray
c (*Teat*) (*tb* **entrada en escena**) entrance (on stage) • **tropezó a la ~** he tripped as he made his entrance
d (*Mús*) [*de instrumento, voz*] entry • **la soprano hizo una ~ muy brusca** the soprano came in very abruptly, the soprano's entry was very abrupt • **el director dio ~ a los vientos** the conductor brought in the wind section
e (*Jur*) (*en un domicilio*) entry • **~ a viva fuerza** forced entry ▸ **entrada en vigor** • **tras la ~ en vigor de la ley** after the law came into effect *o* force • **la ~ en vigor del nuevo presupuesto tendrá lugar en enero** the new budget will take effect from January, the new budget will come into effect *o* force from January
4 (= *invasión*) [*de militares*] entry; [*de turistas, divisas*] influx • **la ~ de las tropas en 1940** the entry of the troops in 1940 • **la ~ masiva de turistas** the huge influx of tourists
5 (= *acceso*) (*a espectáculo*) admission, entry; (*a país*) entry; (*a club, institución, carrera*) admission • **"entrada gratuita"** "admission free" • **la ~ de España en la Comunidad Europea** the entry of Spain into the European Community • **en su discurso de ~ a la Academia** in his introductory *o* opening speech to the Academy • **sus buenas notas le facilitaron la ~ en Medicina** his good marks enabled him to study Medicine • **dar ~ a algn** (*en un lugar*) to allow sb in; (*en club, sociedad*) to admit sb • **no le dimos ~ en nuestra sociedad** he was refused entry to our society, we did not admit him to our society • **prohibir la ~ a algn** to ban sb from entering • **"prohibida la entrada"** "no entry"
6 (= *billete*) ticket • **"no hay entradas"** "sold out" • **media ~** half price • **sacar una ~** to buy a ticket ▸ **entrada de abono** season ticket ▸ **entrada de protocolo** complimentary ticket
7 (= *público*) (*Teat*) audience; (*Dep*) crowd, turnout • **la segunda función contó con una buena ~** there was a good audience for the second performance • **la plaza registró más de media ~** the bullring was over half full • **el sábado hubo una gran ~** there was a big crowd *o* turnout on Saturday
8 (= *recaudación*) (*Teat*) receipts (*pl*), takings (*pl*); (*Dep*) gate money, receipts (*pl*)
9 (= *principio*) start • **os deseamos una feliz ~ de año** we wish you all the best for the new year • **de ~** (*desde el principio*) from the start, from the outset; (*al principio*) at first • **de ~ ya nos dijo que no** he said no from the outset, he said no right from the start • **de ~ no se lo quiso creer** at first he refused to believe it • **~ en materia** introduction
10 (*Esp*) (= *primer pago*) (*al comprar una vivienda, coche*) down payment, deposit • **hay que dar un 20% de ~** you have to put down a 20% deposit, you have to make a down payment of 20% • **"compre sin ~"** "no down payment", "no deposit"
11 (*Com*) (*en libro mayor*) entry
12 (= *vía de acceso*) (*Mec*) inlet, intake; (*Elec*) input ▸ **entrada de aire** air intake
13 (*Inform*) input ▸ **entrada de datos** data entry, data input ▸ **entrada de trabajos a distancia** remote job entry ▸ **entrada inmediata** immediate access
14 (*Ftbl*) tackle • **hacer una ~** to tackle sb
15 (*Culin*) starter • **de ~ tomaremos una sopa de verduras** we'll have vegetable soup as a starter
16 [*de diccionario*] entry
17 entradas: **a** (*en el pelo*) receding hairline (*sing*) • **tener ~s** to have a receding hairline
b (*Econ*) income (*sing*) • **el total de sus ~s** his total income ▸ **entradas familiares** family income (*sing*) ▸ **entradas y salidas** income and expenditure (*sing*)
18 (*Caribe*) (= *ataque*) attack, onslaught; (= *asalto*) assault; (= *paliza*) beating
entradilla (SF) (*Prensa*) lead-in, opening paragraph
entrado (ADJ) **1** (= *abundante*) • **~ en años** (*euf*) elderly • **~ en carnes** (*euf*) overweight
2 (= *avanzado*) • **hasta bien ~ el siglo XIX** until well into the 19th century • **hasta muy entrada la noche** (*antes de medianoche*) until late at night; (*de madrugada*) until the small hours
entrador (ADJ) **1** (*LAm**) (= *atrevido*) daring, forward
2 (*Cono Sur**) (= *simpático*) charming, likeable
3 (*And, Caribe, Méx*) (= *mujeriego*) amorously inclined
4 (*CAm*) (= *coqueto*) flirtatious
entramado (SM) **1** (*Arquit*) (= *estructura*) framework, timber, lumber (*EEUU*); [*de puente*] framework
2 (= *red*) network
entrambos (ADJ PL) (*liter*) both
entrampar ▹ CONJUG 1a (VT) **1** [+ *animal*] to trap, snare
2 (= *engañar*) to snare, trick
3 (= *endeudar*) to burden with debts
4 (= *enredar*) to tangle up
(VPR) **entramparse 1** (= *endeudarse*) to get into debt
2 (= *enredarse*) to get tangled up
entrante (ADJ) **1** [*mes, semana*] next • **la semana ~** next week
2 [*ministro, presidente*] new, incoming; [*correo*] incoming • **correo ~ y saliente** incoming and outgoing mail
(SM) **1** (*Culin*) starter
2 (*Geog*) inlet
3 (*Arquit*) recess
4 ▸ **entrantes y salientes**† people coming to and leaving a house *etc*
entraña (SF) **1 entrañas** (*Anat*) entrails, bowels • **en las ~s de la Tierra** in the bowels of the Earth • MODISMOS: • **arrancar las ~s a algn** to break sb's heart, tear sb's heart out • **dar hasta las ~s** to give one's all • **echar las ~s*** to puke (up)*
2 (= *lo esencial*) core
3 entrañas (= *sentimientos*) heart (*sing*), feelings; (= *temperamento*) disposition (*sing*) • **no tener ~s** to be heartless • **¡hijo de mis ~s!** my precious child!, my beloved son! • **de malas ~s** malicious, evil-minded • **de buenas ~s** well-intentioned, kind-hearted
entrañabilidad (SF) **1** (= *intimidad*) closeness, intimacy
2 (= *afabilidad*) loveable nature
3 (= *encanto*) charm, winning nature
entrañable (ADJ) **1** (= *querido*) [*amigo*] dear, close; [*amistad*] deep; [*paisaje*] beloved, dearly loved; [*recuerdo*] fond
2 (= *afectuoso*) affectionate
3 (= *simpático*) charming, winning
entrañablemente (ADV) [*amar etc*] dearly, deeply
entrañar ▹ CONJUG 1a (VT) (= *contener*) to contain; (= *acarrear*) to entail
(VPR) **entrañarse** to become deeply

attached (**con** to)

entrañudo ADJ (*Cono Sur*) **1** (= *valiente*) brave, daring
2 (= *cruel*) cruel, heartless

entrar ▷ CONJUG 1a VI **1** (*en un lugar*) (*acercándose al hablante*) to come in, enter (*más frm*); (*alejándose del hablante*) to go in, enter (*más frm*) • **—¿se puede? —sí, entra** "may I?" — "yes, come in" • **hágalo ~** show him in • **entré en** *o* (*LAm*) **a la casa** I went into the house • **~on en mi cuarto mientras yo dormía** they came into my room while I was asleep • **la ayudó a ~ en el coche** he helped her (get) into the car • **no me dejaron ~ en la discoteca** I wasn't allowed into the club • **entró en la habitación dando saltos** she bounced into the room • **entró corriendo en la habitación** she ran into the room • **entró tercero en la meta** he crossed the line in third place • **entra frío por la puerta** there's a draught coming in through the door • **el río entra en el lago** the river flows into the lake • **me ha entrado algo en el ojo** I've got something in my eye • **espera un momento, es solo ~ y salir** wait for me a minute, I won't be long • MODISMOS: • **yo por ahí no entro** that's one thing I won't accept *o* have • **~ en detalles** to go into detail • **no ~ ni salir en un asunto** to play no part in a matter
2 (= *encajar*) • **la maleta no entra en el maletero** the case won't go *o* fit in the boot • **el sofá no entraba por la puerta** the sofa wouldn't go *o* fit through the door • **¿entra uno más?** is there room for one more?, will one more fit? • **estoy lleno, ya no me entra nada más** I'm full, I couldn't eat another thing • **este pantalón no me entra** these trousers don't fit (me) • **las historias de este libro entran de lleno en el surrealismo** the stories in this book are genuinely surrealist, the stories in this book come right into the category of surrealism
3 (= *estar incluido*) • **el vino no entra en el precio** the wine is not included (in the price) • **eso no entraba en nuestros planes** that wasn't part of our plans • **ese partido entra dentro de la segunda ronda** that is a second-round match • **en un kilo entran cuatro manzanas** you get four apples to the kilo
4 (= *comenzar*) **a** [*persona*] • **¿a qué hora entras a clase?** what time do you start school? • **entra a trabajar a las ocho** she starts work at eight o'clock • **~ en una profesión** to take up a profession • **~ en una asociación** to join a society • **al ~ en la madurez** on reaching middle age • **entró de mensajero** he started out as a courier • **entró en la revista como director** he joined the magazine as editor • **entró a formar parte del comité central** he became a member of the central committee
b • **~ en calor** to warm up • **~ en coma** to go into a coma • **~ en contacto con algn** to contact sb
c [*época, estación*] • **en el milenio que entra** in the new millennium • **el mes que entra** the coming month, next month
5 (*con sensaciones*) • **me entró sed** I started to feel thirsty • **me entró sueño** I started to feel sleepy • **me ha entrado hambre al verte comer** watching you eat has made me hungry • **me ~on ganas de reír** I felt like laughing
6 [*conocimientos, idea*] • **no hay forma de que le entre el álgebra** he just can't seem to get the hang of algebra • **no les entra en la cabeza que eso no puede ser así** they can't seem to get it into their heads that this isn't on
7* (= *soportar*) to bear, stand • **ese tío no me entra** I can't bear *o* stand that fellow
8 (*Inform*) to access • **~ en el sistema** to access the system
9 (*Mús*) [*instrumento, voz*] to come in
10 (*Teat*) to enter
VT **1*** [+ *objeto*] (*acercándose al hablante*) to bring in; (*alejándose del hablante*) to take in • **entra las sillas para que no se mojen** bring the chairs in so they don't get wet • **la maestra entró a los niños a clase** the teacher took the children into the classroom • **no podrás ~ el sillón por esa puerta** you won't be able to get the armchair in through that door • **necesitó ayuda para ~ el coche en el garaje** he needed some help getting the car into the garage
2* (= *abordar a*) to deal with, approach • **sabe ~ a la gente** he knows how to deal with *o* approach people
3 [+ *futbolista*] to tackle
4 (*Mil*) to attack

> **ENTRAR**
>
> **Para precisar la manera de entrar**
>
> **Entrar (en)** *por regla general se suele traducir por* **come in (to)** *o por* **go in (to)**, *según la dirección del movimiento (hacia o en dirección contraria al hablante), pero,* **come** *y* **go** *se pueden substituir por otros verbos de movimiento si la frase en español explica la forma en que se entra:*
>
> **Entró cojeando en Urgencias**
> He limped into Casualty
> **Acabo de ver a un ratón entrar corriendo en ese agujero**
> I've just seen a mouse running into that hole
>
> *Para otros usos y ejemplos ver la entrada.*

entrazado* ADJ (*Cono Sur*) **1** [*persona*] [*vestido*] • **mal ~** shabby, ragged • **bien ~** well-dressed, natty*
2 [*persona*] [*expresión*] • **mal ~** nasty-looking • **bien ~** pleasant-looking

entre PREP **1** (= *en medio de*) **a** (*dos elementos*) between • **~ las montañas y el mar** between the mountains and the sea • **vendrá ~ las diez y las once** he'll be coming between ten and eleven • **nos veíamos ~ clase y clase** we saw each other between lessons • **~ azul y verde** somewhere between blue and green • **un líquido ~ dulce y amargo** a liquid which is half-sweet, half-sour • **dudo ~ comprar este o aquel** I'm not sure whether to buy this one or that one • **lo cogió ~ sus manos** she took it in her hands • MODISMO: • **estar ~ la vida y la muerte** to be fighting for one's life; ▷ **paréntesis, semana**
b (*más de dos elementos*) among, amongst • **había un baúl ~ las maletas** there was a trunk in among(st) the cases • **¿has buscado ~ las fotografías?** have you looked among(st) the photographs? • **una costumbre muy extendida ~ los romanos** a widespread custom among(st) the Romans • **puedes hablar, estamos ~ amigos** you can speak freely, we're among(st) friends • **paso el día ~ estas cuatro paredes** I spend the whole day within these four walls • **se abrieron paso ~ la multitud** they forced their way through the crowd • **lo vi ~ el público** I saw him in the audience • **~ los que conozco es el mejor** it's the best of those that I know • **empezó a trabajar como mensajero, ~ otras cosas** he started work as a courier, among(st) other things
2 (*indicando colaboración, participación*) • **lo terminamos ~ los dos** between the two of us we finished it • **le compraremos un regalo ~ todos** we'll buy her a present between all of us, we'll all club together to buy her a present • **¿~ cuántos habéis hecho el trabajo?** how many of you did it take to do the work? • **esto lo solucionaremos ~ nosotros** we'll sort that out among(st) *o* between ourselves • **la cuento ~ mis mejores amigas** I count her as one of my best friends • **~ sí: las mujeres hablaban ~ sí** the women were talking among(st) themselves • **los tres hermanos están muy unidos ~ sí** the three brothers are very close to each other
3 (*uso aditivo*) • **~ viaje y alojamiento nos gastamos 80 euros** we spent 80 euros between the travel and the accommodation, the travel and the accommodation came to 80 euros between them • **~ niños y niñas habrá unos veinte en total** there are about twenty in total, if you count boys and girls • **~ que era tarde y hacía frío, decidimos no salir** what with it being late and cold, we decided not to go out • **~ unas cosas y otras no conseguía dormir** what with one thing and another I couldn't sleep • **~ unas cosas y otras se nos hizo de noche** before we knew it, it was night
4 (*Mat*) • **20 ~ 4** 20 divided by 4 • **20 ~ 4 es igual a 5** 4 into 20 goes 5 (times)
5 (*esp LAm**) • **~ más estudia más aprende** the more he studies the more he learns
6 • **~ tanto** ▷ **entretanto**

entre... PREF inter...

entreabierto PP *de* **entreabrir**
ADJ (*gen*) half-open; [*puerta*] ajar

entreabrir ▷ CONJUG 3a (PP: **entreabierto**) VT (*gen*) to half-open, open halfway; [+ *puerta*] to leave ajar

entreacto SM interval, intermission (*EEUU*), entr'acte (*frm*)

entreayudarse ▷ CONJUG 1a VPR to help one another, be of mutual assistance

entrecano ADJ [*pelo*] greyish, grayish (*EEUU*), greying, graying (*EEUU*); [*persona*] going grey *o* (*EEUU*) gray

entrecejo SM space between the eyebrows • **arrugar el ~, fruncir el ~** to frown, wrinkle one's brow

entrecerrar ▷ CONJUG 1j VT (*esp LAm*) (*gen*) to half-close, close halfway; [+ *puerta*] to leave ajar
VPR **entrecerrarse** [*puerta, ventana*] to half-close

entrechocar ▷ CONJUG 1g VI [*dientes*] to chatter
VPR **entrechocarse** **1** (= *chocar*) to collide, crash
2 [*opiniones*] to clash

entrecó SM entrecote, sirloin steak

entrecoger ▷ CONJUG 2c VT **1** to catch, intercept
2 (= *obligar*) to press, compel

entrecomillado ADJ in inverted commas, in quotes (*EEUU*)
SM inverted commas (*pl*), quotes (*pl*)

entrecomillar ▷ CONJUG 1a VT to place in inverted commas, put inverted commas round

entrecoro SM chancel

entrecortadamente ADV [*respirar*] in a laboured way; [*hablar*] falteringly, hesitatingly

entrecortado ADJ [*respiración*] laboured, labored (*EEUU*), difficult; [*habla*] faltering, hesitant • **con la voz entrecortada** in a faltering voice, in a voice choked with emotion

entrecortar ▷ CONJUG 1a (VT) **1** [+ *objeto*] to cut halfway through, partially cut
2 (= *interrumpir*) to cut off, interrupt; [+ *voz*] to cause to falter
(VPR) **entrecortarse** [*voz*] to falter; [*señal*] to cut out • **se le entrecortaba la voz** he had a catch in his voice
entrecot (SM) entrecote, sirloin steak
entrecruzado (ADJ) interwoven
entrecruzar ▷ CONJUG 1f (VT) **1** (= *entrelazar*) to interlace, interweave, intertwine
2 (*Bio*) to cross, interbreed
(VPR) **entrecruzarse 1** [*hilos, cintas*] to interweave, intertwine
2 (*Bio*) to interbreed
entrecubierta (SF), **entrecubiertas** (SFPL) between decks
entredicho (SM) **1** • **estar en ~** (= *ser discutible*) to be questionable, be debatable • **su profesionalidad está** *o* **ha quedado en ~** grave doubts have been cast on his professionalism • **poner algo en ~** (= *cuestionar*) to raise doubts about sth, call sth into question; (= *comprometer*) to jeopardize sth, endanger sth
2 (= *prohibición*) prohibition, ban; (*Jur*) injunction • **estar en ~** to be under a ban, be banned • **levantar el ~ a** to raise the ban on • **poner algo en ~** (= *prohibir*) to place a ban on sth
3 (*Cono Sur*) (= *ruptura*) break-up, split
4 (*And*) (= *alarma*) alarm bell
entredós (SM) **1** (*Cos*) insertion, panel
2 (= *mueble*) cabinet, dresser
entrefino (ADJ) [*tela*] medium, medium-quality
entrefuerte (ADJ) (*LAm*) [*tabaco*] medium strong
entrega (SF) **1** (= *acto*) [*de documento, solicitud*] submission • **esta noche es la ~ de premios** tonight is the awards ceremony • **mañana será la ~ de notas** the marks will be given out tomorrow • **tienen que pagar un millón a la ~ de llaves** they have to pay a million on handing over the keys *o* when the keys are handed over • **"entrega de llaves inmediata"** "ready for immediate occupancy" • **hacer ~ de** [+ *regalo, premio, cheque*] to present • **le hizo ~ de la medalla al valor** he presented him with an award for bravery
2 (*Com*) [*de cartas, mercancías*] delivery • **pagadero a la ~** payable on delivery • **los gastos de ~ no están incluidos** delivery is not included • **si no se efectúa la ~, devuélvase a ...** if undelivered, please return to ... • **la ~ se hará en un plazo de 15 días** it will be delivered within 15 days, delivery within 15 days • **"entrega a domicilio"** "we deliver" • **orden de ~** delivery order ▸ **entrega contra pago, entrega contra reembolso** cash on delivery
3 (*al rendirse*) [*de rehenes*] handover; [*de armas*] surrender, handover
4 (= *sección*) [*de enciclopedia, novela*] instalment, installment (*EEUU*); [*de revista*] issue; [*de serie televisiva*] series • **una novela por ~s** a novel published in instalments, a serialized novel
5 (= *dedicación*) dedication, devotion • **su ~ a la causa de los indígenas** her dedication to the cause of the native people
6 (*Dep*) pass
entregado (ADJ) **1** (= *dedicado*) • **estar ~ a** [+ *causa, creencia, actividad, trabajo*] to be dedicated to, be devoted to • **una vida entregada a ayudar a los más necesitados** a life dedicated *o* devoted to helping those most in need • **vive totalmente ~ a la música** his life is totally dedicated *o* devoted to music
2 (= *sacrificado*) selfless • **es una persona muy entregada** she's a very selfless person
entregar ▷ CONJUG 1h (VT) **1** (= *dar*) **a** [+ *impreso, documento, trabajo*] to hand in, give in, submit (*frm*) • **hay que ~ la redacción mañana** the essay has to be handed in *o* given in tomorrow • **el proyecto se ~á a la comisión para que lo estudie** the plan will be put before the commission for them to study • **entregó su alma a Dios** he departed this life • MODISMO: • **~las** (*Chile*‡) to kick the bucket‡
b (*en mano*) (*gen*) to hand over; [+ *regalo*] to give • **me entregó la carta esta mañana** she gave me the letter this morning, she handed over the letter to me this morning
c [+ *premio, cheque*] to present • **hoy entregan los premios** they are presenting the awards today, the awards ceremony is today
2 (= *distribuir*) (*gen*) to give out; [+ *correo, pedido*] to deliver • **mañana ~emos las notas del examen** we'll give out the exam marks tomorrow • **"entregamos sus pedidos al día siguiente"** "next day delivery" • **"para entregar a"** (*Com*) (*en envíos*) "for the attention of"
3 (= *ceder*) [+ *poderes, botín, rehenes*] to hand over; [+ *armas, país*] to hand over, surrender • **~on las joyas a la policía** they handed over the jewels to the police • **el enemigo acabó por ~ las armas** the enemy finally handed over *o* surrendered their weapons • **el juez entregó la custodia del niño a su abuela** the judge gave *o* awarded *o* granted custody of the boy to his grandmother
4 (*en boda*) [+ *novia*] to give away
(VPR) **entregarse 1** (= *rendirse*) to give o.s. up, surrender • **los secuestradores se ~on a la policía** the hijackers gave themselves up *o* surrendered to the police
2 (= *dejarse dominar*) • **~se a** [+ *sueño, tentación*] to succumb to • **se entregó a la desesperación** she gave in to despair • **~se a la bebida** to take to drink
3 (= *dedicarse*) • **~se a algo** to devote o.s. to sth • **se ha entregado por completo al cuidado de su padre** she has devoted herself entirely to looking after her father • **todas las noches me entrego a la lectura de la Biblia** I devote all my evenings to reading the Bible • **~se a algn** (*sexualmente*) to give o.s. to sb • **me entregué a ella sin condiciones** I gave her my unconditional love
4 (= *adueñarse*) • **~se de algo** to take possession of sth
entreguerras • **el período de ~** the inter-war period, the period between the wars (*i.e.* 1918-39)
entreguismo (SM) (*Pol*) (= *apaciguamiento*) appeasement, policy of appeasement; (= *derrotismo*) defeatism; (= *oportunismo*) opportunism; (= *traición*) betrayal, selling-out
entrelazado (ADJ) intertwined, interlaced, interwoven (**de** with)
entrelazar ▷ CONJUG 1f (VT), **entrelazarse** (VPR) to intertwine, interlace, interweave
entrelistado (ADJ) striped
entrelucir ▷ CONJUG 3f (VI) **1** (= *verse*) to show through
2 (= *relucir*) to gleam, shine dimly
entremás (ADV) (*And, Méx*) (= *además*) moreover; (= *especialmente*) especially
(CONJ) • **~ lo pienso, más convencido estoy** the more I think about it the more convinced I am
entremedias (ADV) **1** (= *en medio*) in between, halfway; (= *entretanto*) in the meantime
2 • **~ de** between, among
entremedio (SM) (*LAm*) interval, intermission (*EEUU*)
entremés (SM) **1** (*Teat, Hist*) interlude, short farce
2 (*Culin*) side dish • **"entremeses"** "hors d'oeuvres" ▸ **entremés salado** savoury, savory (*EEUU*)

ENTREMÉS

An **entremés** is a short farce used as an entertaining interval between the first and second acts of a **comedia**. It is thought that the **entremés** (derived from the Italian **intermezzo**) was first performed on the Spanish stage in the 16th century and derives from the influential Italian **Commedia dell'Arte**. Often using slapstick, stock characters and situations, **entremeses** had enormous audience appeal and were written by such distinguished writers as Miguel de Cervantes.

entremesera (SF) tray for hors d'oeuvres
entremeter ▷ CONJUG 2a (VT) (= *insertar*) to insert; (= *poner entre*) to put between
entremeterse *etc* ▷ **entrometerse** *etc*
entremezclar ▷ CONJUG 1a (VT), **entremezclarse** (VPR) to intermingle • **entremezclado de** interspersed with
entrenador(a) (SM/F) trainer, coach ▸ **entrenador(a) personal** personal trainer
(SM) (*Aer*) trainer, training plane ▸ **entrenador de pilotaje** flight simulator
entrenamiento (SM) (= *ejercicios*) training; (= *sesión*) training session; (*por el entrenador*) coaching
entrenar ▷ CONJUG 1a (VT) (*Dep*) to train, coach; [+ *caballo*] to exercise • **estar entrenado** [+ *futbolista, atleta*] to be in training, be fit
(VI) to train
(VPR) **entrenarse** to train
entreno (SM) = **entrenamiento**
entreoír ▷ CONJUG 3p (VT) to half-hear, hear indistinctly
entrepágina (SF) centrefold
entrepaño (SM) **1** (= *muro*) wall, stretch of wall
2 (= *panel*) door panel
3 (= *anaquel*) shelf
entrepierna (SF), **entrepiernas** (SFPL) **1** (*Anat*) crotch, crutch
2 (= *medida*) inside leg (measurement)
• MODISMO: • **pasarse algo por la ~**‡ (= *rechazar*) to reject sth totally, throw sth out of the window*; (= *despreciar*) to feel utter contempt for sth
entreplanta (SF) mezzanine
entrepuente (SM) between-decks
entrerrejado (ADJ) interwoven, criss-crossed
entrerrenglonar ▷ CONJUG 1a (VT) to interline, write between the lines of
entresacar ▷ CONJUG 1g (VT) **1** [+ *información, datos*] (= *seleccionar*) to pick out, select; (= *cribar*) to sift
2 [+ *pelo, plantas*] to thin out
entresemana (SF) midweek; (= *días laborables*) working days of the week • **de ~** midweek (*antes de s*); (*LAm*) midweek • **cualquier día de ~** any day midweek, any day in the middle of the week
entresijo (SM) **1** (= *secreto*) secret, mystery; (= *parte oculta*) hidden aspect; (= *dificultad*) difficulty, snag • **este asunto tiene muchos ~s** this business has many ins and outs • **él tiene sus ~s** he's hard to fathom • **se conoce todos los ~s de la justicia** he knows all the ins and outs of the law, he knows the law inside-out
2 (*Anat*) mesentery

e

entresuelo SM mezzanine, entresol; (*Teat*) dress circle

entretanto ADV meanwhile, meantime
CONJ • **~ esto se produce** until this happens
SM meantime • **en el ~** in the meantime

entretecho SM (*Chile, Col*) attic, garret

entretejer ▸ CONJUG 2a VT **1** [+ *hilos*] to interweave, intertwine
2 (= *entremezclar*) to interweave

entretejido SM interweaving

entretela SF **1** (*Cos*) interlining
2 entretelas (= *entrañas*) • **¡hijo de mis ~s!** my beloved son!, my beloved child! • **confesó sentirse feliz en sus ~s** he admitted feeling really happy deep down • **conozco las ~s del partido** I know the ins and outs of the party, I know the party inside-out

entretelar ▸ CONJUG 1a VT to interline

entretelón SM thick curtain, heavy curtain

entretención SF (*LAm*) (= *entretenimiento*) entertainment

entretener ▸ CONJUG 2k VT **1** (= *divertir*) to entertain, amuse • **nos entretuvo con sus chistes mientras esperábamos** he kept us entertained *o* amused with his jokes while we were waiting • **hacer punto la entretiene** she amuses herself by knitting
2 (= *retener*) to keep, detain (*más frm*) • **pues no le entretengo más** then I won't keep *o* (*más frm*) detain you any longer • **una vecina me entretuvo hablando en las escaleras** a neighbour kept me talking on the stairs
3 (= *distraer*) • **~ a algn** to distract sb's attention • **uno de los ladrones entretuvo a la dependienta** one of the thieves distracted the shop assistant's attention • **~ algo: entretuvieron la espera leyendo** they whiled away the time by reading • **me tomé una tapa para ~ el hambre** I had a snack to take the edge off my hunger
4 (= *dar largas a*) • **me está entreteniendo con mentiras para no pagarme** he's putting me off with lies so as not to pay me
5 (= *mantener*) [+ *ilusiones*] to nourish; [+ *fuego*] to maintain
VI • **la tele entretiene mucho** TV is very entertaining
VPR **entretenerse 1** (= *divertirse*) to amuse o.s. • **se entretenían contando historias** they amused themselves by telling stories, they kept themselves amused by telling stories
2 (= *tardar*) to hang about • **¡no te entretengas!** don't hang about!

entretenida SF **1** (= *querida*) mistress; (= *mantenida*) kept woman
2 • **dar (con) la ~ a algn** (*con promesas*) to hold sb off with vague promises, stall sb; (*hablando*) to keep sb talking

entretenido ADJ [*libro, obra de teatro*] entertaining, amusing; [*trabajo*] demanding
SM* gigolo, toyboy*

entretenimiento SM **1** (= *diversión*) entertainment, amusement • **hace crucigramas como ~** he does crosswords for entertainment *o* amusement • **es solo un ~** it's just for amusement • **programa de ~** an entertainment programme
2†† (= *mantenimiento*) upkeep, maintenance • **sólo necesita un ~ mínimo** it only needs minimum maintenance

entretiempo SM (= *primavera*) spring; (= *otoño*) autumn, fall (*EEUU*) • **un abrigo de ~** a light coat, a lightweight coat

entrever ▸ CONJUG 2u VT **1** (= *vislumbrar*) to make out • **podía ~ una luz a lo lejos** I could just make out a light in the distance • **dejar ~ algo** to suggest sth, hint at sth • **dejó ~ la posibilidad de que me renovaran el contrato** he suggested that my contract might be renewed, he hinted at the possibility of my contract being renewed • **dejó ~ sus reservas sobre la moneda única** he let it be seen *o* known that he had reservations over the single currency • **estas manifestaciones dejan ~ fisuras en el partido** these demonstrations seem to suggest divisions within the party
2 (= *adivinar*) to guess • **supo ~ sus verdaderas intenciones** she guessed his true intentions
3 (= *presentir*) to glimpse • **podemos ~ una solución** we can glimpse a solution

entreverado ADJ **1** [*tocino*] streaky
2 (= *intercalado*) mixed, interspersed, intermingled (**de** with)
3 (= *poco uniforme*) patchy

entreverar ▸ CONJUG 1a VT (= *intercalar*) to mix, intermingle
VPR **entreverarse 1** to be intermingled, be intermixed
2 (*Cono Sur*) (= *implicarse*) to become mixed up in, get involved in

entrevero SM **1** (*LAm*) mix-up
2 (*Cono Sur*) (= *desorden*) confusion, disorder; (= *riña*) brawl; (*Mil*) confused cavalry skirmish

entrevía SF (*Ferro*) gauge, gage (*EEUU*) • **de ~ angosta** narrow-gauge (*antes de s*)
▸ **entrevía angosta** narrow gauge
▸ **entrevía normal** standard gauge

entrevista SF **1** (= *conversación*) interview • **hacer una ~ a algn** to interview sb
▸ **entrevista de trabajo** job interview
2 (= *reunión*) meeting, conference • **celebrar una ~ con algn** to hold a meeting with sb

entrevistado/a SM/F interviewee, person being interviewed

entrevistador(a) SM/F interviewer

entrevistar ▸ CONJUG 1a VT to interview
VPR **entrevistarse** to meet • **~se con algn** to have a meeting with sb, meet with sb • **el ministro se entrevistó con la reina ayer** the minister had a meeting with *o* met with the queen yesterday • **los vecinos se ~on con el alcalde** the residents were received by the Mayor yesterday

entripado SM (= *secreto*) ghastly secret; (= *resentimiento*) concealed anger, suppressed rage

entripar ▸ CONJUG 1a VT **1** (*And**) (= *enfurecer*) to enrage, madden
2 (*Caribe, Méx*) (= *mojar*) to soak
3 (*Méx*‡) (= *embarazar*) to put in the family way, put in the club
VPR **entriparse 1** (*And**) (= *enfadarse*) to get cross, get upset
2 (*Caribe, Méx*) (= *mojarse*) to get soaked

entristecer ▸ CONJUG 2d VT to sadden, make sad
VPR **entristecerse** to grow sad

entristecido ADJ sad

entrometerse ▸ CONJUG 2a VPR (= *interferir*) to meddle, interfere (**en** in, with); (= *molestar*) to intrude

entrometido/a ADJ meddlesome, interfering
SM/F busybody, meddler

entromparse* ▸ CONJUG 1a VPR
1 (= *emborracharse*) to get drunk, get sozzled*
2 (*LAm*) (= *enfadarse*) to get cross, get mad (*EEUU*)

entrón ADJ **1** (*And*) (= *entrometido*) meddlesome
2 (*Méx*) (= *animoso*) spirited, daring
3 (*Méx*) (= *coqueto*) flirtatious

entroncar ▸ CONJUG 1g VT to connect, establish a relationship between
VI **1** [*familia*] to be related, be connected (**con** to)
2 (= *estar relacionado*) to be linked, be related (**con** to)
3 (*Ferro*) to join, connect (**con** to)

entronización SF **1** [*de rey*] enthronement
2 (= *ensalzamiento*) exaltation

entronizar ▸ CONJUG 1f VT **1** [+ *rey*] to enthrone
2 (*fig*) (= *ensalzar*) to exalt

entronque SM **1** (= *parentesco*) relationship, link
2 (= *enlace*) connexion, link
3 (*LAm*) (*Ferro*) junction

entropía SF entropy

entruchada* SF **1** (= *trampa*) trap, trick
2 (*Cono Sur*) (= *discusión*) slanging match*; (= *conversación*) intimate conversation

entruchar* ▸ CONJUG 1a VT to lure, decoy, lead by the nose
VPR **entrucharse** (*Méx*) (= *entrometerse*) to stick one's nose into other people's affairs

entubar ▸ CONJUG 1a VT (*Med*) to intubate

entuerto SM **1** (= *injusticia*) wrong, injustice
2 entuertos (*Med*) afterpains

entumecer ▸ CONJUG 2d VT to numb
VPR **entumecerse 1** [*miembro*] to go numb, go to sleep
2 [*río*] to swell, rise; [*mar*] to surge

entumecido ADJ numb

entumecimiento SM numbness

entumido ADJ **1** (*LAm*) (= *entumecido*) numb
2 (*And, Méx*) (= *tímido*) timid

enturbiar ▸ CONJUG 1b VT **1** [+ *líquido*] to muddy, make cloudy
2 (= *complicar*) [+ *asunto*] to confuse, fog; [+ *mente, persona*] to confuse
VPR **enturbiarse 1** [*líquido*] to get muddy, become cloudy
2 (= *complicarse*) [*asunto*] to become obscured; [*mente, persona*] to get confused
3 [*relaciones*] to be marred

enturcado‡ ADJ (*CAm*) [*persona*] hopping mad*, livid • **un problema ~** a knotty problem

entusiasmado ADJ excited, enthusiastic • **están muy ~s con el nuevo bebé** they're very excited or enthusiastic about the new baby • **el público recibió ~ a los campeones** the audience welcomed the champions enthusiastically

entusiasmante ADJ thrilling, exciting

entusiasmar ▸ CONJUG 1a VT (= *apasionar*) to fire with enthusiasm, excite; (= *encantar*) to delight • **me entusiasma el trabajo** I love my work • **no le entusiasma mucho la idea** he's not very keen on the idea
VPR **entusiasmarse** to get enthusiastic, get excited (**con, por** about) • **se ha quedado entusiasmada con el vestido** she loves the dress, she is delighted with the dress

entusiasmo SM enthusiasm (**por** for) • **con ~** (= *con apasionamiento*) enthusiastically; (= *con interés*) keenly

entusiasta ADJ (= *apasionado*) enthusiastic (**de** about); (= *interesado*) keen (**de** on)
SMF (= *aficionado*) enthusiast, fan*; (= *admirador*) admirer

entusiástico ADJ enthusiastic

enumeración SF (= *listado*) enumeration; (= *cuenta*) count, reckoning

enumerar ▸ CONJUG 1a VT (= *nombrar*) to enumerate; (= *contar*) to count, reckon up

enunciación SF **1** [*de teoría*] enunciation
2 (= *declaración*) declaration

enunciado SM **1** (= *principio*) principle
2 (*Prensa*) heading

enunciar ▸ CONJUG 1b VT [+ *teoría*] to enunciate, state; [+ *idea*] to put forward

enuresis SF INV enuresis

envagonar ▸ CONJUG 1a VT (*LAm*) [+ *mercancías*] to load onto a railway truck

envainar ▸ CONJUG 1a VT **1** [+ *arma*] to sheathe, put in a sheath • **¡enváinala!‡** shut your trap!‡, shut it!‡
2 (*And*) (= *molestar*) to vex, annoy
VI (*And*) (= *sucumbir*) to succumb
VPR **envainarse 1** (*And, Caribe**) (*en líos*) to get into trouble • **estar envainado** to be in a jam *o* fix*, be in trouble
2 • **envainársela*** to take back what one has said, back down

envalentonamiento SM (= *valor*) boldness; (*pey*) Dutch courage, bravado

envalentonar ▸ CONJUG 1a VT to make bold, embolden
VPR **envalentonarse** (= *cobrar valor*) to pluck up courage; (*pey*) (= *insolentarse*) to become defiant; (= *jactarse*) to brag

envanecer ▸ CONJUG 2d VT to make conceited
VPR **envanecerse** to become conceited, grow vain

envanecido ADJ conceited, stuck-up*

envanecimiento SM conceit, vanity

envarado ADJ rigid, stiff

envaramiento SM (*Méx*) numbness, stiffness

envarar ▸ CONJUG 1a VT to stiffen, make stiff
VPR **envararse** [*pierna, brazo*] to become stiff; [*persona*] to stiffen

envasado SM (*en cajas*) packing; (*en paquetes*) packaging; (*en latas*) canning; (*en botellas, tarros*) bottling

envasador(a) SM/F (*en cajas, paquetes*) packer; (*en latas*) canner; (*en botellas, tarros*) bottler

envasar ▸ CONJUG 1a VT **1** (= *guardar*) (*en cajas*) to pack; (*en paquetes*) to package; (*en botellas, tarros*) to bottle; (*en latas*) to can, tin; (*en tonel*) to barrel; (*en saco*) to sack, bag
2* [+ *vino*] to knock back*
3 (*esp LAm*) • **~ un puñal en algn** to plunge a dagger into sb, bury a dagger in sb
VI* to tipple, knock it back*

envase SM **1** (= *acto*) (= *empaquetado*) packing, wrapping; (= *embotellado*) bottling; (= *enlatado*) canning
2 (= *recipiente*) container • **precio con ~** price including packing • **~ retornable** returnable container • **géneros sin ~** loose goods, unpackaged *o* unwrapped goods • **~ de vidrio** glass container
3 (= *botella*) (*llena*) bottle; (*vacía*) empty • **~s a devolver** returnable empties
4 (= *lata*) can, tin

envasijar ▸ CONJUG 1a VT (*LAm*) = **envasar**

envedijarse ▸ CONJUG 1a VPR **1** (= *enredarse*) [*pelo*] to get tangled; [*ovillo*] to get tangled, become entangled
2 [*personas*] to come to blows

envegarse ▸ CONJUG 1h VPR (*Cono Sur*) to get swampy, turn into a swamp

envejecer ▸ CONJUG 2d VT to age, make look old
VI, VPR **envejecerse 1** [*persona*] (= *volverse viejo*) to age, get old, grow old; (= *parecer viejo*) to look old • **en dos años se ha envejecido mucho** he's aged a lot these last two years
2 [*ropa, muebles*] to become old-fashioned
3 [*vino*] to mature, age

envejecido ADJ **1** [*persona*] old, aged; (*de aspecto*) old-looking • **está muy ~** he's aged a lot
2 [*piel, madera, tela*] distressed

envejecimiento SM ageing

envelar ▸ CONJUG 1a VI (*Cono Sur*) (*Náut*) to hoist the sails • **~las** to run away

envenenador(a) SM/F poisoner

envenenamiento SM poisoning

envenenar ▸ CONJUG 1a VT **1** (*con veneno*) to poison
2 (= *amargar*) to embitter
VPR **envenenarse 1** (*voluntariamente*) to poison o.s., take poison
2 (*por accidente*) to be poisoned

enverdecer ▸ CONJUG 2r VI to turn green

enveredar ▸ CONJUG 1a VI • **~ hacia** to head for, make a beeline for

envergadura SF **1** (= *importancia*) importance • **el edificio sufrió daños de cierta ~** the building suffered considerable *o* substantial damage • **un programa de gran ~** a wide-ranging programme, a programme of considerable scope • **una operación de cierta ~** an operation of some magnitude *o* size • **la obra es de ~** the plan is ambitious
2 (= *tamaño*) scope, magnitude
3 (= *extensión*) (*gen*) expanse, spread; (*Náut*) breadth, beam; (*Aer, Orn*) wingspan; [*de boxeador*] reach

envés SM **1** (= *parte trasera*) [*de tela*] back, wrong side; [*de hoja de planta*] underside; [*de espada*] flat
2 (*Anat**) back

enviado/a SM/F (*Pol*) envoy ▸ **enviado/a especial** [*de periódico, TV*] special correspondent

enviar ▸ CONJUG 1c VT to send • **~ un mensaje a algn** (*por móvil*) to text sb, send sb a text message • **~ a algn a hacer algo** to send sb to do sth • **~ a algn a una misión** to send sb on a mission • **~ por el médico** to send for the doctor, fetch the doctor

enviciador(a) SM/F (*LAm*) drug-pusher

enviciar ▸ CONJUG 1b VT to corrupt
VPR **enviciarse** (= *corromperse*) to get corrupted • **~se con** *o* **en** to become addicted to

envidar ▸ CONJUG 1a VT, VI (*Naipes*) to bid • **~ en falso** to bluff

envidia SF envy, jealousy • **es pura ~** it's sheer *o* pure envy *o* jealousy, he's just jealous • **con este vestido serás la ~ de todas tus amigas** with that dress you'll be the envy of all your friends • **¡qué ~ me da verte tan contenta!** I'm so envious *o* jealous seeing you so happy! • **dar ~ a algn** to make sb envious *o* jealous • **tener ~ a algn** to envy sb, be jealous of sb • MODISMOS: • **carcomerle** *o* **corroerle a algn la ~** to be eaten up with envy *o* jealousy • **estar muerto de ~** to be green with envy • REFRÁN: • **si la ~ fuera tiña (cuántos tiñosos habría)** the world's full of envious people

envidiable ADJ enviable

envidiar ▸ CONJUG 1b VT **1** [+ *persona*] to envy
2 (= *codiciar*) to desire, covet • **~ algo a algn** to envy sb sth, begrudge sb sth • **su casa no tiene nada que ~ a la tuya** her house is at least as good as yours, her house is quite up to the standard of yours

envidioso ADJ **1** [*de persona*] envious, jealous
2 (= *codicioso*) covetous

envilecer ▸ CONJUG 2d VT to debase, degrade
VPR **envilecerse** to degrade o.s., lower o.s.; (*implorando*) to grovel, crawl

envilecimiento SM degradation, debasement

envinado ADJ (*Cono Sur*) drunk

envío SM **1** (= *acción*) (*gen*) sending; (*Com*) dispatch; (*en barco*) shipment • **proponen el ~ de fuerzas de paz** they propose sending peace-keeping forces • **gastos de ~** (cost of) postage and packing, postage and handling (*EEUU*) ▸ **envío a domicilio** home delivery (service) ▸ **envío contra reembolso** cash on delivery ▸ **envío de datos** data transmission ▸ **envío de fotos por MMS** picture messaging ▸ **envío de segundo curso** second-class mail
2 (= *mercancías*) (*gen*) consignment, lot; (*Náut*) shipment
3 (= *dinero*) remittance

envión SM push, shove

envite SM **1** (= *apuesta*) stake
2 (= *ofrecimiento*) offer, bid; (= *invitación*) invitation
3 (= *empujón*) push, shove • **al primer ~** from the very start, right away

enviudar ▸ CONJUG 1d VI [*mujer*] to become a widow, be widowed; [*hombre*] to become a widower, be widowed • **~ de la primera mujer** to lose one's first wife • **enviudó tres veces** she lost three husbands

envoltorio SM, **envoltijo** SM bundle, package; ▸ **envoltura**

envoltura SF **1** (*gen*) cover; [*de papel*] wrapper, wrapping; (*Bot, Aer*) envelope; (*Mec*) case, casing; (= *vaina*) sheath
2 envolturas [*de bebé*] baby clothes

envolvedero SM, **envolvedor** SM (= *cubierta*) cover; (= *papel*) wrapper, wrapping; (= *sobre*) envelope

envolvente ADJ **1** (= *circundante*) [*ambiente*] surrounding; [*música*] all-enveloping; [*atmósfera*] absorbing; (*Mil*) [*movimiento, maniobra*] encircling, enveloping • **asiento ~** bucket seat • **gafas de sol ~s** wraparound sunglasses *o* shades • **falda ~** wraparound skirt • **parachoques ~** wraparound bumper • **sonido ~** surround sound®
2 (= *completo*) comprehensive
3 (*Caribe, Cono Sur*) (= *interesante*) fascinating, intriguing

envolver ▸ CONJUG 2h (PP: **envuelto**) VT
1 (= *cubrir*) (*con papel*) to wrap (up); (*con ropa*) to wrap (up), cover (up) • **¿quiere que se lo envuelva?** shall I wrap it (up) for you? • **dos paquetes envueltos en papel** two parcels wrapped in paper • **llevaba al niño envuelto en una manta** she was carrying the baby wrapped up in a blanket
2 (= *rodear*) to surround, shroud • **una niebla espesa envolvía el castillo** the castle was surrounded *o* shrouded in thick fog • **su muerte está envuelta en misterio** her death is shrouded in mystery
3 (= *involucrar*) to involve (**en** in) • **lo han envuelto en el tráfico de drogas** they've got him involved in drug trafficking
4 (*frm*) (= *contener*) to contain • **sus elogios envuelven una censura** there is criticism contained in his praise
VPR **envolverse 1** (*con ropa*) to wrap o.s. up (**en** in)
2 (= *involucrarse*) to become involved (**en** in)

envolvimiento SM **1** [*de paquete*] wrapping
2 (*Mil*) encirclement
3 (*en asunto, escándalo*) involvement

envuelto PP *de* **envolver**

enyerbar ▸ CONJUG 1a VT (*And, Cono Sur, Méx*) (= *hechizar*) to bewitch
VPR **enyerbarse 1** (*LAm*) [*campo*] to get covered with grass
2 (*Caribe*) [*trato*] to fail
3 (*CAm, Méx*) (= *envenenarse*) to poison o.s.
4 (*Méx*) (= *enamorarse*) to fall madly in love
5 (*Caribe**) (= *complicarse*) to get complicated

enyesado SM, **enyesadura** SF **1** [*de pared*] plastering
2 (*Med*) (= *escayola*) plaster cast

enyesar ▸ CONJUG 1a VT **1** [+ *pared*] to plaster
2 (*Med*) to put in a plaster cast, put in plaster • **le ~on el brazo** his arm was put in a (plaster) cast *o* in plaster • **tener una pierna**

enyesada to have one's leg in a (plaster) cast, have a leg in plaster
enyeyado* ADJ (*Caribe*) gloomy, depressed
enyugar ▹ CONJUG 1h VT to yoke
enyuntar ▹ CONJUG 1a VT (*LAm*) to put together, join
enzacatarse ▹ CONJUG 1a VPR (*CAm, Méx*) to get covered with grass
enzarzar ▹ CONJUG 1f VT (*en una disputa*) to involve, entangle, embroil
VPR **enzarzarse** (*en una disputa*) to get involved; (*en problemas*) to get o.s. into trouble • **~se a golpes** to come to blows • **~se en una discusión** to get involved in an argument
enzima SF enzyme
enzocar ▹ CONJUG 1g VT (*Cono Sur*) to insert, put in, fit in
-eo ▹ **Aspects of Word Formation in Spanish 2**
eoceno SM (*Geol*) Eocene
EOI SF ABR (*Esp*) (= **Escuela Oficial de Idiomas**) ▹ **ESCUELA OFICIAL DE IDIOMAS**
eólico ADJ wind (*antes de s*) • **energía eólica** wind power
eón SM aeon, eon (*esp EEUU*)
EP SF ABR (*Esp*) = **Educación Primaria, Enseñanza Primaria**

EP — EDUCACIÓN PRIMARIA
Following the implementation of the 1990 Spanish education reform law, **LOGSE**, primary education was renamed **Educación Primaria** and divided into two **ciclos** or stages: **primer ciclo** for 6- to 9-year-olds, and **segundo ciclo** for 9- to 12-year-olds.
▹ **ESO, LOGSE**

EPA SF ABR (*Esp*) = **Encuesta de Población Activa**
epa* EXCL, **épale*** EXCL (*LAm*) hey!, wow!, say! (EEUU)
epatante* ADJ (= *asombroso*) amazing, astonishing; (= *deslumbrante*) startling, dazzling
epatar* ▹ CONJUG 1a VT (= *asombrar*) to amaze, astonish; (= *deslumbrar*) to startle, dazzle; (= *escandalizar*) to shock • **~ al burgués** to shock the bourgeoisie
epazote SM (*Méx*) herb tea
E.P.D. ABR (= **en paz descanse**) RIP
epi... PREF epi...
épica SF epic poetry
epiceno ADJ (*Ling*) epicene
epicentro SM epicentre, epicenter (*EEUU*)
épico ADJ epic
epicureísmo SM, **epicurismo** SM epicureanism
epicúreo/a ADJ, SM/F epicurean
epidemia SF epidemic
epidémico ADJ epidemic
epidérmico ADJ **1** (= *de la piel*) skin (*antes de s*)
2 (= *superficial*) superficial, skin-deep
epidermis SF INV epidermis
epidural (*Med*) ADJ epidural
SF epidural
Epifanía SF Epiphany, Twelfth Night
epiglotis SF INV epiglottis
epígrafe SM **1** (*en libro, artículo*) epigraph
2 (*en piedra, metal*) epigraph, inscription
epigrafía SF epigraphy
epigrama SM epigram
epigramático ADJ epigrammatic(al)
epilepsia SF epilepsy
epiléptico/a ADJ epileptic • **ataque ~** epileptic fit, epileptic seizure (*frm*)
SM/F epileptic
epilogar ▹ CONJUG 1h VT (= *resumir*) to sum up; (= *rematar*) to round off, provide a conclusion to
epílogo SM epilogue
episcopado SM **1** (= *cargo*) bishopric
2 (= *obispos*) bishops (*pl*), episcopacy (*frm*)
3 (= *período*) episcopate (*frm*)
episcopal ADJ [*autoridad, iglesia*] episcopal; [*cargo*] bishopric • **palacio ~** bishop's palace • **sede ~** (= *ciudad*) see • **la Conferencia Episcopal Española** the Synod of Spanish bishops
episcopalista ADJ, SMF Episcopalian
episódico ADJ episodic
episodio SM [*de aventura, suceso*] episode, incident; [*de serie, novela*] episode, part
epistemología SF epistemology
epistemológico ADJ epistemological
epístola SF epistle, letter
epistolar ADJ epistolary
epistolario SM collected letters (*pl*)
epitafio SM epitaph
epitelial ADJ epithelial
epíteto SM epithet
epitomar ▹ CONJUG 1a VT to summarize
epítome SM summary, epitome (*frm*)
EPL SM ABR (*Col*) = **Ejército Popular de Liberación**
época SF **1** (= *momento histórico*) age, period, epoch (*frm*) • **la ~ de Carlos III** the age of Charles III • **durante la ~ isabelina** in Elizabethan times, in the Elizabethan era *o* age • **en aquella ~** at that time, in that period • **muebles de ~** period furniture • **coche de ~** vintage car • **drama de ~** costume drama • **con decoraciones de ~** with period set • **un Picasso de primera ~** an early (period) Picasso • **la ~ azul del artista** the artist's blue period • **anticiparse a su ~** to be ahead of one's time • **todos tenemos ~s así** we all go through spells like that • **estoy pasando una mala ~** I'm going through a bad patch • **hacer ~** to be epoch-making, be a landmark • **el invento hizo ~** it was an epoch-making invention • **eso hizo ~ en nuestra historia** that was a landmark in our history ▸ **época de la serpiente de mar** (*hum*) silly season ▸ **época dorada** golden age ▸ **época glacial** ice age
2 (*tb* **época del año**) (= *temporada*) season, time of year ▸ **época de celo** (*Zool*) mating season, rutting season ▸ **época de lluvias** rainy season ▸ **época de sequía** dry season ▸ **época monzónica** monsoon season
epónimo (*Ling*) ADJ eponymous
SM eponym
epopeya SF epic
epopéyico ADJ epic
EPS SM ABR (*Nic*) = **Ejército Popular Sandinista**
equi... PREF equi...
equidad SF (= *justicia*) fairness, equity (*frm*); [*de precio*] reasonableness
equidistante ADJ equidistant
equilátero ADJ equilateral
equilibradamente ADV in a balanced way
equilibrado ADJ **1** [*persona*] (= *sensato*) level-headed, sensible; (= *ecuánime*) well-balanced
2 [*dieta*] balanced
3 [*partido*] close
SM ▸ **equilibrado de ruedas** wheel-balancing
equilibrar ▹ CONJUG 1a VT (*gen*) to balance; [+ *una cosa con otra*] to counterbalance • **~ gastos e ingresos** to balance outgoings and income • **~ la balanza de pagos** to restore the balance of payments • **~ el marcador** to level the score
VPR **equilibrarse** [*persona*] to balance o.s. (en on); [*fuerzas*] to counterbalance each other
equilibrio SM **1** (= *estabilidad*) balance • **perturbó el ~ de la balanza** he threw the scales out of balance • **ahora las pesas están en ~** now the weights are evenly balanced • **intentó mantener el ~ sobre la cuerda** he tried to keep his balance on the rope • **mantuvo en ~ el palo sobre su dedo** he balanced the stick on his finger • **perder el ~** to lose one's balance • MODISMO: • **hacer ~s** to do a balancing act ▸ **equilibrio ecológico** ecological balance ▸ **equilibrio estable** stable equilibrium ▸ **equilibrio inestable** unstable equilibrium ▸ **equilibrio presupuestario** balanced budget
2 (= *armonía*) balance, equilibrium • **existe un ~ estable entre las dos potencias mundiales** there is a stable balance between the two superpowers ▸ **equilibrio de fuerzas, equilibrio de poderes** balance of power
3 (= *serenidad*) level-headedness
equilibrista SMF **1** (*en circo*) (= *funámbulo*) tightrope walker; (= *acróbata*) acrobat
2 (*LAm*) *politician of shifting allegiance*
equino ADJ equine, horse (*antes de s*)
SM **1** (= *caballo*) horse • **(carne de) ~** horsemeat
2 [*de mar*] sea urchin
equinoccial ADJ equinoctial
equinoccio SM equinox ▸ **equinoccio otoñal** autumnal equinox ▸ **equinoccio vernal** vernal equinox
equipaje SM **1** (*para viajar*) (= *conjunto de maletas*) luggage, baggage (*EEUU*); (= *avíos*) equipment, kit • **facturar el ~** to register one's luggage • **hacer el ~** to pack, do the packing • **pagar exceso de ~** to pay excess baggage • **compartimento de ~s** luggage compartment, baggage compartment (*esp EEUU*) • **zona de recogida de ~s** luggage *o* (*esp EEUU*) baggage collection point ▸ **equipaje de mano** hand luggage
2 (*Náut*) crew
equipal SM (*Méx*) *wicker chair with seat and back of leather or palm leaves*
equipamiento SM equipment ▸ **equipamiento de serie** standard equipment
equipar ▹ CONJUG 1a VT **1** [+ *casa, coche*] to fit, equip (**con, de** with); (*Náut*) to fit out • **~on la cocina con los electrodomésticos más modernos** they fitted *o* equipped the kitchen with the most modern appliances • **el nuevo modelo viene equipado con elevalunas eléctrico** the new model is fitted with electric windows • **un gimnasio muy bien equipado** a very well-equipped gymnasium
2 [+ *persona*] (*con armas, útiles*) to equip (**con, de** with); (*con ropa*) to kit out (**con, de** with) • **cuesta mucho dinero ~ a un colegial** it costs a lot of money to get a child kitted out for school • **~on a los obreros con armas** they equipped the workers with weapons • **iban equipados con uniforme de campaña** they were kitted out with battledress
VPR **equiparse** (= *pertrecharse*) to equip o.s. (**con, de** with) • **se ~on con cuerdas y linternas** they equipped themselves with ropes and torches
equiparable ADJ comparable (**con** to, with)
equiparación SF comparison
equiparar ▹ CONJUG 1a VT (= *igualar*) to put on the same level, consider equal; (= *comparar*) to compare (**con** with)
VPR **equipararse** • **~se con** to be on a level with, rank equally with
equipazo* SM crack team
equipo SM **1** (*Dep*) team ▸ **equipo de casa** home team ▸ **equipo de fuera** away team ▸ **equipo de fútbol** football team ▸ **equipo de relevos** relay team ▸ **equipo local** home

team ▸ **equipo titular** A team, first team ▸ **equipo visitante** visiting team
2 [*de personas*] team • **trabajar en ~** to work as a team ▸ **equipo cinematográfico móvil** mobile film unit ▸ **equipo de cámara** camera crew ▸ **equipo de desactivación de explosivos** bomb-disposal unit ▸ **equipo de gobierno** government team ▸ **equipo de rescate, equipo de salvamento, equipo de socorro** (*civil*) rescue team; (*militar*) rescue squad, rescue unit ▸ **equipo directivo** management team ▸ **equipo médico** medical team, medical unit
3 (= *utensilios, accesorios*) (*gen*) equipment; (*para deportes*) equipment, kit • **me robaron todo el ~ de esquí** they stole all my skiing equipment *o* gear* • **MODISMO**: • **caerse con todo el ~*** to make a right mess of things* ▸ **equipo de alpinismo** climbing gear ▸ **equipo de alta fidelidad** hi-fi system ▸ **equipo de caza** hunting gear ▸ **equipo de fumador** smoker's outfit, smoker's accessories ▸ **equipo de música** stereo system ▸ **equipo de novia** trousseau ▸ **equipo de oficina** office furniture ▸ **equipo de primeros auxilios** first-aid kit ▸ **equipo de reparaciones** repair kit ▸ **equipo físico** (*Inform*) hardware ▸ **equipo industrial** plant ▸ **equipo lógico** (*Inform*) software ▸ **equipo rodante** (*Ferro*) rolling stock

equis (SF INV) **1** (= *letra*) (name of the letter) X • **rayos ~** X-rays • **cada ~ años** every so many years • **durante ~ años** for X number of years • **pongamos que cuesta ~ dólares** let's suppose it costs X dollars • **averiguar la ~** to find the value of X • **marcar con una ~ la respuesta correcta** put a cross by the correct answer • **tenía que hacer ~ cosas*** I had to do any amount of things
2 (*And, CAm**) • **MODISMO**: • **estar en la ~** (= *flaco*) to be all skin and bones; (= *sin dinero*) to be broke*, be skint*

equitación (SF) **1** (= *acto*) riding • **escuela de ~** riding school
2 (= *arte*) horsemanship

equitativamente (ADV) (= *con justicia*) equitably, fairly; (= *razonablemente*) reasonably

equitativo (ADJ) [*distribución, división*] fair; [*precio*] reasonable; [*reparto*] fair, equitable (*frm*) • **trato ~** fair deal, square deal

equivalencia (SF) equivalence

equivalente (ADJ) equivalent (a to)
(SM) equivalent

equivaler ▹ CONJUG 2p (VI) • **~ a** to be equivalent to, be equal to; (*en grado, nivel*) to rank as, rank with

equivocación (SF) (= *error*) mistake, error; (= *descuido*) oversight; (= *malentendido*) misunderstanding • **por ~** by mistake, in error • **ha sido por ~** it was a mistake

equivocadamente (ADV) mistakenly, wrongly

equivocado (ADJ) **1** [*número, dirección*] wrong; [*persona*] mistaken, wrong • **estás ~** you are wrong, you are mistaken (*más frm*)
2 [*afecto, confianza*] misplaced

equivocar ▹ CONJUG 1g (VT) **1** (= *confundir*) to get mixed up, mix up • **he equivocado las direcciones de los sobres** I've got the addresses mixed up on the envelopes, I've mixed up the addresses on the envelopes
2 • **~ a algn** to make sb make a mistake • **si me hablas mientras escribo me equivocas** if you talk to me while I'm writing, you'll make me make a mistake *o* you'll make me go wrong
3 (= *errar*) • **~ el camino** (*lit*) to go the wrong way; (*fig*) to make the wrong choice
(VPR) **equivocarse** (= *no tener razón*) to be wrong, be mistaken; (= *cometer un error*) to make a mistake • **te equivocas, eso no es así** you're wrong *o* mistaken, it isn't like that • **si crees que voy a dejarte ir, te equivocas** if you think I'm going to let you go, you're wrong *o* mistaken • **me equivoqué muchas veces en el examen** I made a lot of mistakes in the exam • **~se con algn** to be wrong about sb • **la consideraba honesta, pero me equivoqué con ella** I thought she was honest, but I was wrong about her • **~se de algo**: • **nos equivocamos de hora y llegamos tarde** we got the time wrong, and we arrived late • **se ~on de tren** they caught the wrong train • **se ~on de casa** they went to the wrong house • **perdone, me he equivocado de número** sorry, (I've got the) wrong number

equívoco (ADJ) **1** (= *confuso*) equivocal, ambiguous
2 (*LAm*) (= *equivocado*) mistaken
(SM) **1** (= *malentendido*) misunderstanding
2 (*al hablar*) (= *juego de palabras*) pun, play on words; (= *doble sentido*) double meaning • **este tipo de ~s es característico de sus escritos** this kind of wordplay is a characteristic of his writing
3 (*Méx**) mistake

era¹ ▹ **ser**

era² (SF) (*Hist*) era, age ▸ **era atómica** atomic age ▸ **era cristiana, era de Cristo** Christian era ▸ **era espacial** space age ▸ **era española, era hispánica** Spanish Era (*from 38 B.C.*) ▸ **era glacial** ice age

era³ (SF) (*Agr*) (*para cereales*) threshing floor; (*para flores*) bed, plot; (*para hortalizas*) patch

erais, éramos ▹ **ser**

erario (SM) (= *Hacienda*) treasury, exchequer; (= *fondos*) public funds (*pl*), public finance • **~ municipal** municipal funds (*pl*), council funds (*pl*) • **con cargo al ~ público** with *o* from public funds

-eras ▹ Aspects of Word Formation in Spanish 2

erasmismo (SM) Erasmism

erasmista (ADJ), (SMF) Erasmist

Erasmo (SM) Erasmus

ERC (SF ABR) (= **Esquerra Republicana de Catalunya**) *Catalan left-wing party*

ERE (SM ABR) (= **Expediente de Regulación de Empleo**) labour *o* (*EEUU*) labor force adjustment plan

erección (SF) **1** (*Anat*) erection
2 (*Arquit*) [*de edificio*] erection; [*de monumento*] raising

ereccionarse ▹ CONJUG 1a (VPR) to become erect

eréctil (ADJ) erectile

erecto (ADJ) erect

eremita (SM) (= *ermitaño*) hermit; (= *solitario*) recluse

eremitismo (SM) living like a hermit, hermit's way of life

eres ▹ **ser**

ergio (SM) erg

ergo (CONJ) ergo

ergonomía (SF) ergonomics (*sing*)

ergonómico (ADJ) ergonomic

ergonomista (SMF) ergonomist

erguido (ADJ) **1** [*cuerpo*] erect, straight
2 (= *orgulloso*) proud

erguir ▹ CONJUG 3m (VT) **1** (= *levantar*) to raise, lift • **~ la cabeza** (*lit*) to hold one's head up; (*fig*) to hold one's head high
2 (= *enderezar*) to straighten
(VPR) **erguirse 1** (= *enderezarse*) (*al ponerse en pie*) to straighten up, stand up straight; (*estando sentado*) to sit up straight
2 (= *envanecerse*) to swell with pride

-ería ▹ Aspects of Word Formation in Spanish 2

erial (ADJ) uncultivated, untilled
(SM) (*en campo*) uncultivated land; (*en ciudad*) area of wasteland, piece of waste ground

erigir ▹ CONJUG 3c (VT) **1** (*Arquit*) [+ *monumento*] to erect; [+ *edificio*] to build
2 (= *fundar*) to establish, found
3 • **~ a algn en algo** to set sb up as sth
(VPR) **erigirse** • **~ en algo** to set o.s. up as sth

erisipela (SF) erysipelas (*pl*)

eritreo/a (ADJ) Eritrean
(SM/F) Eritrean

erizado (ADJ) **1** (= *de punta*) [*cepillo, cola*] bristly; [*pelo*] spiky • **~ de espinas** covered with thorns
2 • **~ de problemas** bristling with problems

erizar ▹ CONJUG 1f (VT) **1** • **el gato erizó el pelo** the cat bristled, the cat's hair stood on end
2 [+ *asunto*] to complicate, surround with difficulties
(VPR) **erizarse** (= *levantar*) [*pelo de animal*] to bristle; [*pelo de persona*] to stand on end • **se me erizó el pelo** my hair stood on end

erizo (SM) **1** (*Zool*) hedgehog ▸ **erizo de mar, erizo marino** sea urchin
2 (*Bot*) burr
3* (= *persona*) grumpy sort, prickly person*

ermita (SF) **1** (= *capilla*) chapel, shrine
2 [*de un ermitaño*] hermitage

ermitaño/a (SM/F) **1** (= *persona*) hermit
2 (*Zool*) hermit crab

Ernesto (SM) Ernest

-ero ▹ Aspects of Word Formation in Spanish 2

erogación (SF) **1** [*de bienes*] distribution
2 (*LAm*) (= *gasto*) expenditure, outlay
3 (*And, Caribe*) (= *contribución*) contribution, donation

erogar ▹ CONJUG 1h (VT) **1** [+ *propiedad*] to distribute
2 (*LAm*) (= *pagar*) to pay; [+ *deuda*] to settle
3 (*And, Cono Sur*) (= *contribuir*) to contribute
4 (*Méx*) (= *gastar*) to spend, lay out

erógeno (ADJ) erogenous • **zonas erógenas** erogenous zones

Eros (SM) Eros

erosión (SF) (*Geol*) erosion; (*Med*) graze • **causar ~ en** to erode

erosionable (ADJ) subject to erosion • **un suelo fácilmente ~** a soil which is easily eroded

erosionante (ADJ) erosive

erosionar ▹ CONJUG 1a (VT) to erode
(VPR) **erosionarse** to erode, be eroded

erosivo (ADJ) erosive

erótica (SF) • **la ~ del poder** the thrill of power

erótico (ADJ) (*gen*) erotic; [*versos*] love (*antes de s*) • **el género ~** the genre of love poetry

erotismo (SM) eroticism

erotizar ▹ CONJUG 1a (VT) to eroticize
(VPR) **erotizarse** to be (sexually) stimulated

erotomanía (SF) eroticism, pathological eroticism

erotómano (ADJ) erotic, pathologically erotic

ERP (SM ABR) (*Arg, El Salvador*) = **Ejército Revolucionario del Pueblo**

errabundear ▹ CONJUG 1a (VI) to wander, rove

errabundeo (SM) wanderings (*pl*)

errabundo (ADJ) wandering, roving

erradamente (ADV) mistakenly

erradicación (SF) eradication

erradicar ▹ CONJUG 1g (VT) to eradicate

erradizo (ADJ) wandering, roving

errado (ADJ) **1** (= *equivocado*) mistaken, wrong • **estás ~ si piensas que te voy a ayudar** you're mistaken if you think I'm going to help you • **no andas ~ al decir que ...** you're not mistaken when you say that ...

2 [*tiro*] wide of the mark
errante (ADJ) **1** (= *ambulante*) [*trovador*] wandering; [*reportero*] roving; [*vida*] nomadic; [*animal*] stray, lost • **el judío ~** the wandering Jew • **el holandés ~** the flying Dutchman
2 (= *infiel*) errant • **el marido ~** the errant husband
errar ▷ CONJUG 1k (VT) **1** (= *equivocar*) [+ *tiro*] to miss with, aim badly; [+ *blanco*] to miss; [+ *vocación*] to miss, mistake • **~ el camino** to lose one's way
2 (*en obligación*) to fail (*in one's duty to*)
(VI) **1** (= *vagar*) to wander, rove
2 (= *equivocarse*) to be mistaken • **~ es cosa humana • de los hombres es ~** to err is human
(VPR) **errarse** to err, be mistaken
errata (SF) misprint, printer's error • **fe de ~s** errata • **es ~ por "poder"** it's a misprint for "poder"
errático (ADJ) erratic
erratismo (SM) (= *tendencia*) wandering tendencies (*pl*), tendency to wander; (= *movimiento*) erratic movement
erre (SF) (name of the letter) R • MODISMO: • **~ que ~** stubbornly, pigheadedly • **y él, ~ que ~, seguía negándolo** he stubbornly went on denying it
erróneamente (ADV) (= *por equivocación*) mistakenly, erroneously; (= *falsamente*) falsely
erróneo (ADJ) (= *equivocado*) mistaken, erroneous; (= *falso*) untrue, false
error (SM) mistake, error (*más frm*) • **fue un ~ contárselo a Luisa** it was a mistake to tell Luisa • **salvo ~ u omisión** errors and omissions excepted • **caer en un ~** to make a mistake • **si piensas que lo hizo por tu bien, estás cayendo en un ~** if you think that he did it for your good you're making a mistake • **cometer un ~** to make a mistake • **cometí muchos ~es en el examen** I made a lot of mistakes in the exam • **estar en un ~** to be mistaken, be wrong • **estás en un ~ si piensas que voy a transigir** you're mistaken *o* wrong if you think that I'll give in • **inducir a ~** to be misleading • **estas cifras pueden inducir a ~** these figures could be misleading • **por ~** by mistake ▸ **error de cálculo** miscalculation ▸ **error de copia** clerical error ▸ **error de derecho** legal error ▸ **error de hecho** factual error, error of fact ▸ **error de imprenta** misprint ▸ **error judicial** miscarriage of justice ▸ **error tipográfico** misprint
ERT (ABR) **1** (*Esp*) = **Explosivos Río Tinto**
2 (*Arg*) = **Ente de Radiotelevisión**
ertzaina [er'tʃaina] (SMF) policeman/policewoman, *member of the autonomous Basque police force*
Ertzaintza [er'tʃaintʃa] (SF) *autonomous Basque police (force)*

ERTZAINTZA
The **Ertzaintza** is the Basque autonomous police force, recognizable by its distinctive uniform of red sweater, red beret and white truncheon. Madrid has devolved certain policing responsibilities to the Basque government (as well as to Catalonia) but the national police forces, the **Policía Nacional** and the **Guardia Civil**, continue to have a role as well.

eructación (SF) belch
eructar ▷ CONJUG 1a (VI) to belch
eructo (SM) belch
erudición (SF) learning, scholarship, erudition (*frm*)
eruditamente (ADV) learnedly
erudito/a (ADJ) learned, scholarly, erudite (*frm*)
(SM/F) scholar, learned person • **los ~s en esta materia** those who are expert in this subject, those who really know about this subject • **un ~ a la violeta** (*pey*) a pseudo-intellectual
erupción (SF) **1** (*Geol*) eruption • **estar en ~** to be erupting • **entrar en ~** to (begin to) erupt ▸ **erupción solar** solar flare
2 (*Med*) ▸ **erupción cutánea** rash, eruption (*frm*)
3 (= *estallido*) [*de violencia*] outbreak, explosion; [*de ira*] outburst
eruptivo (ADJ) eruptive
E/S (ABR) (*Inform*) (= **entrada/salida**) I/O
es ▷ **ser**
esa[1] (ADJ DEM) ▷ **ese**[2]
esa[2] (PRON DEM), **ésa** (PRON DEM) ▷ **ese**[3]
Esaú (SM) Esau
esbeltez (SF) (= *delgadez*) slimness, slenderness; (= *gracilidad*) gracefulness
esbelto (ADJ) (= *delgado*) slim, slender; (= *grácil*) graceful
esbirro (SM) **1** (= *ayudante*) henchman, minion; (= *sicario*) killer
2 (*Caribe*‡) (= *soplón*) grass‡, fink (*EEUU*‡), informer
3 (*Hist*) (= *alguacil*) bailiff, constable
esbozar ▷ CONJUG 1f (VT) **1** (*Arte*) to sketch, outline
2 [+ *plan*] to outline • **~ una sonrisa** to smile a faint smile, force a smile
esbozo (SM) **1** (*Arte*) sketch
2 [*de plan*] outline • **con un ~ de sonrisa** with a hint of a smile
escabechado (SM) pickling, marinating
escabechar ▷ CONJUG 1a (VT) **1** (*Culin*) to pickle, souse
2 [+ *canas*] to dye
3* (= *matar*) to do in*, do away with*
4 (*Univ**) (= *suspender*) to plough*, to plow (*EEUU**)
escabeche (SM) **1** (= *salsa*) pickle, brine
2 (= *pescado*) soused fish
escabechina (SF) **1** (= *matanza*) slaughter
2 (*fig*) (= *desastre*) destruction, slaughter • **hacer una ~*** to wreak havoc; (*Univ*) to fail a pile of students
escabel (SM) footstool, footrest
escabinado (SM) jury of lay people and judges
escabiosa (SF) scabious
escabioso (ADJ) (*Med*) scabious; (*Vet*) scabby, mangy
escabro (SM) **1** (*Vet*) sheep scab, scabs
2 (*Bot*) scab
escabrosamente (ADV) riskily, salaciously
escabrosidad (SF) **1** [*de terreno*] roughness, ruggedness; [*de superficie*] unevenness
2 [*de sonido*] harshness
3 [*de problema*] difficulty, toughness
4 [*de chiste*] riskiness, salaciousness (*frm*)
escabroso (ADJ) **1** (= *irregular*) [*terreno*] rough, rugged; [*superficie*] uneven
2 [*sonido*] harsh
3 [*problema*] difficult, tough, thorny
4 [*chiste*] risqué, blue, salacious (*frm*)
escabuche (SM) weeding hoe
escabullarse ▷ CONJUG 1a (VPR) (*LAm*), **escabullirse** ▷ CONJUG 3a (VPR) to slip away *o* off • **~ por** to slip through
escachalandrado* (ADJ) (*And, CAm*) slovenly
escacharrar* ▷ CONJUG 1a (VT) to bust*
(VPR) **escacharrarse** to break
escachifollarse* ▷ CONJUG 1a (VPR) to break, smash
escafandra (SF) diving suit ▸ **escafandra autónoma** scuba suit ▸ **escafandra espacial** spacesuit
escafandrismo (SM) (= *pesca*) underwater fishing; (= *submarinismo*) deep-sea diving
escafandrista (SMF) (= *pescador*) underwater fisherman; (= *buzo*) deep-sea diver
escala (SF) **1** (*en medición, gradación*) scale • **a ~** [*dibujo, mapa, maqueta*] scale (*antes de s*) • **un mapa hecho a ~** a map drawn to scale, a scale map • **una imitación a ~ reducida de un objeto real** a scaled-down version of a real object • **a ~ real** life-size (*antes de s*) • **reproducir algo a ~** to reproduce sth to scale ▸ **escala (abierta de) Richter** Richter scale ▸ **escala (de) Beaufort** Beaufort scale ▸ **escala (de) Celsius** Celsius scale ▸ **escala de colores** colour spectrum, color spectrum (*EEUU*) ▸ **escala (de) Fahrenheit** Fahrenheit scale ▸ **escala (de) Kelvin** Kelvin scale ▸ **escala (de) Mercalli** Mercalli scale ▸ **escala de salarios** salary scale ▸ **escala de tiempo** (*Geol*) time scale ▸ **escala de valores** set of values, scale of values ▸ **escala graduada** graduated scale ▸ **escala móvil** (*Téc*) sliding scale; (*Econ*) sliding salary scale ▸ **escala salarial** salary scale ▸ **escala social** social ladder, social scale
2 [*de importancia, extensión*] • **la producción a ~ industrial** production on an industrial scale • **un problema a ~ mundial** a global problem, a problem on a worldwide scale • **a *o* en gran ~** on a large scale • **a *o* en pequeña ~** on a small scale • **un caso de corrupción a pequeña ~** a case of small-scale corruption, a case of corruption on a small scale
3 (= *parada en ruta*) **a** (*Aer*) stopover • **una ~ de dos horas en París** a two-hour stopover in Paris • **un vuelo sin ~s** a non-stop flight • **hacer ~** to stop over • **el vuelo hizo ~ en Brasil** the flight stopped over in Brazil • **hizo dos ~s para repostar** it made two stopovers for refuelling
b (*Náut*) port of call • **la siguiente ~ es Barcelona** the next port of call is Barcelona • **el buque hizo ~ en Cádiz** the ship put in at Cádiz ▸ **escala técnica** refuelling *o* (*EEUU*) refueling stop
4 (= *escalera de mano*) ladder ▸ **escala de cuerda, escala de viento** rope ladder
5 (*Mús*) scale ▸ **escala cromática** chromatic scale ▸ **escala diatónica** diatonic scale ▸ **escala musical** musical scale
escalabrar ▷ CONJUG 1a (VT) = **descalabrar**
escalación (SF) (*Mil, Pol*) escalation
escalada (SF) **1** [*de montaña*] climb, ascent • **es una ~ fácil** it's an easy climb *o* ascent • **su rápida ~ al poder** his rapid rise to power ▸ **escalada artificial** artificial climbing ▸ **escalada en rocas** rock climbing ▸ **escalada libre** free climbing
2 (= *aumento*) escalation • **una ~ de la violencia** an escalation of violence • **últimamente ha habido una ~ del/en el conflicto** lately there has been an escalation of/in the conflict, lately the conflict has escalated • **se ha producido una ~ en los precios** prices have escalated
escalador(a) (SM/F) **1** (*Dep*) (*en alpinismo*) climber, mountaineer; (*en ciclismo*) climber, mountain rider ▸ **escalador(a) en roca(s)** rock climber
2 (= *ladrón*) burglar, housebreaker
escalafón (SM) **1** [*de promoción*] promotion ladder • **ascender en el ~** to go up the ladder, work one's way up
2 [*de salarios*] salary scale, wage scale
3 (= *ránking*) table, chart • **en esta industria España ocupa el tercer lugar en el ~ mundial** Spain occupies third place in the world

table for this industry
escalamiento SM = **escalada**
escálamo SM thole, tholepin
escalante ADJ escalating • **la crisis ~** the escalating crisis
escalar ▸ CONJUG 1a VT **1** [+ *montaña*] to climb, scale
2 [+ *casa*] to burgle, burglarize (*EEUU*), break into
3 (*en la escala social*) to scale, rise to
• **~ puestos** to move up
4 (*Inform*) (= *reducir*) to scale down; (= *aumentar*) to scale up
VI **1** [*alpinista*] to climb
2 (*en la escala social*) to climb the social ladder, get on, go up in the world*
3 (*Náut*) to call, put in (**en** at)
4 (*Mil, Pol*) to escalate
Escalda SM Scheldt
escaldado ADJ **1** (= *escarmentado*) • **salir ~**: • **salió ~ del negocio** he got his fingers burned in the deal • **salió escaldada de su matrimonio** she came out of the marriage feeling sadder and wiser • **salió ~ de la experiencia** he was chastened by the experience; ▸ **gato**
2 (= *receloso*) wary, cautious
3 [*mujer*] loose
escaldadura SF **1** (= *quemadura*) scald, scalding
2 (= *irritación*) chafing
escaldar ▸ CONJUG 1a VT **1** (= *quemar*) to scald; (*Culin*) to blanch
2 (= *rozar*) to chafe, rub
3 (= *escarmentar*) to teach a lesson
4 [+ *metal*] to make red-hot
VPR **escaldarse 1** (= *quemarse*) to scald o.s., get scalded
2 (= *rozarse*) to chafe; [*bebé*] to get nappy rash
escalera SF **1** [*de edificio*] stairs (*pl*), staircase • **corrió ~s abajo** she ran downstairs *o* down the stairs • **se cayó por las ~s** she fell downstairs *o* down the stairs • **han pintado la ~** they've painted the staircase • **una ~ de mármol** a marble staircase ▸ **escalera de caracol** spiral staircase ▸ **escalera de incendios** fire escape ▸ **escalera de servicio** backstairs (*pl*) ▸ **escalera mecánica, escalera móvil** escalator
2 (*portátil*) ladder ▸ **escalera de cuerda** rope ladder ▸ **escalera de mano** ladder ▸ **escalera de nudos** rope ladder ▸ **escalera de pintor, escalera de tijera, escalera doble** stepladder, steps (*pl*) ▸ **escalera extensible** extension ladder
3 (*Naipes*) run, sequence; (*en póquer*) straight ▸ **escalera de color** straight flush
escalerilla SF (*en bricolaje, piscina*) ladder; (*en barco*) gangway, companionway; (*Aer*) steps (*pl*)
escalfado ADJ [*huevo*] poached
escalfador SM chafing dish
escalfar ▸ CONJUG 1a VT **1** [+ *huevo*] to poach
2 (*Méx*) (= *desfalcar*) to embezzle
escalilla SF **1** (*Téc*) calibrated scale
2 [*de ascenso*] promotion ladder
escalinata SF (*interior*) flight of stairs (*pl*); (*exterior*) flight of steps, steps (*pl*)
escalofriado ADJ • **estar ~** to feel chilly, feel shivery, feel hot-and-cold
escalofriante ADJ (= *espeluznante*) bloodcurdling, hair-raising; (= *aterrador*) frightening, chilling
escalofriantemente ADV (= *espeluznantemente*) outrageously, hair-raisingly; (= *aterradoramente*) frighteningly, chillingly
escalofriarse ▸ CONJUG 1c VPR **1** (*por fiebre*) to feel chilly, get the shivers, feel hot and cold by turns
2 (*por miedo*) to shiver with fright, get a cold shiver of fright
escalofrío SM **1** (*Med*) chill, feverish chill
2 (= *temblor*) shiver • **aquello me produjo un ~ de terror** it made me shiver with fear, it sent a shiver down my spine
escalón SM **1** (= *peldaño*) (*gen*) step, stair; [*de escalera de mano*] rung; (= *nivel*) level; [*de cohete*] stage ▸ **escalón de hielo** ice step
2 (*al avanzar*) (= *paso*) step; (*al éxito*) stepping stone
3 (*Mil*) echelon
escalonadamente ADV step by step, in a series of steps
escalonado ADJ (= *gradual*) staggered
escalonar ▸ CONJUG 1a VT **1** (= *distribuir*) (*gen*) to spread out at intervals; [+ *tierra*] to terrace; [+ *horas de trabajo*] to stagger; [+ *novedad*] to phase in
2 (*Mil*) to echelon
3 (*Med*) [+ *dosis*] to regulate
escalopa SF (*Chile*) escalope, cutlet (*EEUU*)
escalope SM escalope, cutlet (*EEUU*) ▸ **escalope de ternera** escalope of veal, veal cutlet (*EEUU*)
escalopín SM fillet
escalpar ▸ CONJUG 1a VT to scalp
escalpelo SM scalpel
escama SF **1** (*Bot, Zool*) scale
2 [*de jabón, pintura*] flake • **jabón en ~s** soapflakes
3 (= *resentimiento*) resentment; (= *sospecha*) suspicion
4 (*Méx**) cocaine, coke*
escamado ADJ **1** (= *desconfiado*) wary, cautious
2 (*Cono Sur*) (= *harto*) wearied
escamar ▸ CONJUG 1a VT **1** [+ *pez*] to scale, remove the scales from
2 (= *producir recelo*) to make wary, create distrust in • **eso me escama** that makes me suspicious, that sounds ominous to me
VPR **escamarse 1** (= *perder escamas*) to scale, scale off, flake off
2 (= *sospechar*) to get wary, become suspicious; (= *olerse algo*) to smell a rat • **y luego se escamó** and after that he was on his guard
escamocha* SF (*Méx*) leftovers
escamón ADJ (= *que sospecha*) wary, distrustful; (= *nervioso*) apprehensive
escamondar ▸ CONJUG 1a VT **1** [+ *árbol*] to prune
2 (= *limpiar*) to prune, trim
escamoso ADJ [*pez*] scaly; [*sustancia*] flaky
escamotar ▸ CONJUG 1a VT = **escamotear**
escamoteable ADJ retractable
escamoteador(a) SM/F (= *prestidigitador*) conjurer; (= *estafador*) swindler
escamotear ▸ CONJUG 1a VT **1** (= *hacer desaparecer*) to make vanish, whisk away; [+ *naipe*] to palm; (*Téc*) to retract
2* (= *robar*) to lift*, pinch*
3 [+ *hechos, verdad*] to hide, cover up
4 (= *esquivar*) [+ *responsabilidad*] to shirk
escamoteo SM **1** (= *ilusionismo*) conjuring; (= *truco*) conjuring trick; (= *destreza*) sleight of hand
2* (= *robo*) lifting*; (= *estafa*) swindling, swindle
3 (= *ocultación*) concealment
4 [*de responsabilidad*] shirking
escampar ▸ CONJUG 1a VI **1** (*Meteo*) [*cielo*] to clear; [*lluvia*] to stop; [*tiempo*] to clear up
2 (*Caribe, Méx*) (*de la lluvia*) to shelter
3 (*LAm**) (= *largarse*) to clear off*, scarper*
VT [+ *sitio*] to clear out
escampavía SF revenue cutter
escanciador(a) SM/F **1** wine waiter
2 (*Hist*) cupbearer
escanciar ▸ CONJUG 1b VT [+ *vino*] to pour, pour out, serve; [+ *copa*] to drain
VI to drink (a lot of) wine
escandalera* SF row, uproar
escandalizante ADJ scandalous, shocking
escandalizar ▸ CONJUG 1f VT to scandalize, shock
VI to make a fuss, create a scene
VPR **escandalizarse** to be shocked, be scandalized (**de** at, by) • **se escandalizó ante la pintura** he was horrified at the picture, he threw up his hands in horror at the picture
escandallo SM **1** (*Náut*) lead
2 (*Com*) (= *etiqueta*) price tag; (= *acto*) pricing
3 (= *prueba*) sampling
escándalo SM **1** (= *tumulto*) scandal, outrage • **¡qué ~!** what a scandal! • **¡es un ~!** it's outrageous *o* shocking! • **precios de ~** (= *caros*) outrageous prices; (= *baratos*) amazing prices • **comportamiento de ~** scandalous behaviour • **un resultado de ~** (= *malo*) a scandalous result; (= *bueno*) a great result, an outstanding result
2 (= *ruido*) row, uproar • **armar un ~** to make a scene, cause a row *o* an uproar
3 (= *asombro*) astonishment • **llamar a ~** to cause astonishment, be a shock
escandalosa SF **1** (*Náut*) topsail
2 (*And*) (= *tulipán*) tulip
3 • MODISMO: • **echar la ~** to fly off the handle, curse and swear
escandalosamente ADV
1 (= *sorprendentemente*) [*actuar, hablar*] scandalously, outrageously; [*delinquir*] flagrantly • **~ caro** outrageously expensive
2 (= *con ruido*) [*romper*] noisily; [*reírse*] loudly, heartily
escandaloso ADJ **1** (= *sorprendente*) [*actuación*] scandalous, shocking; [*delito*] flagrant; [*vida*] scandalous
2 (= *ruidoso*) [*risa*] hearty, uproarious; [*niño*] noisy
3 [*color*] loud
Escandinavia SF Scandinavia
escandinavo/a ADJ, SM/F Scandinavian
escandir ▸ CONJUG 3a VT [+ *versos*] to scan
escaneado SM scanning
escanear ▸ CONJUG 1a VT to scan
escaneo SM scanning
escáner SM **1** (= *aparato*) scanner
2 (= *imagen*) scan • **hacerse un ~** to have a scan
escansión SF scansion
escantillón SM pattern, template
escaño SM (= *banco*) bench; (*Pol*) seat
escapada SF **1** (= *huida*) escape, breakout • MODISMO: • **en una ~** in a spare moment • **¿puedes comprarme tabaco en una ~?** have you got a spare moment to buy me some cigarettes?
2 (= *viaje, salida*) • **conseguí hacer una ~ rápida a Bruselas** I managed to get away to Brussels, I managed a quick getaway to Brussels • **las ~s nocturnas del heredero al trono** the heir to the throne's nocturnal jaunts
3 (*Ciclismo*) breakaway
escapado/a ADJ (= *rápido*) • **lo harán ~s** they'll do it like a shot • **irse ~** to rush off • **salió escapada de aquella casa** she rushed out of the house • **tengo que volverme ~ a la tienda** I must get back to the shop double-quick, I have to rush back to the shop
SM/F **1** (= *fugitivo*) fugitive, runaway
2 (*Ciclismo*) • **los ~s** the breakaway group
escapar ▸ CONJUG 1a VI **1** (= *huir*) to escape • **sintió una gran necesidad de ~** he felt a great need to get away *o* escape • **~ a algo**: • **no pude ~ a sus encantos** I could not

escape her charms • **hay cosas que escapan a nuestro control** some things are beyond our control • **este caso escapa a mi responsabilidad** this case is not my responsibility • **~ de** [*+ cárcel, peligro*] to escape from; [*+ jaula*] to get out of; [*+ situación opresiva*] to escape from, get away from • **logramos ~ de una muerte cierta** we managed to escape certain death • **necesitaba ~ de todo aquello** I needed to escape from *o* get away from all that • **dejar ~** [*+ grito, risa, suspiro*] to let out; [*+ oportunidad*] to let slip • **dejar ~ a algn** to let sb get away • **han dejado ~ al perro** they let the dog get away
2 (*Dep*) (*en carreras*) to break away • **el ciclista escapó del pelotón** the cyclist broke away from the pack
VT [*+ caballo*] to drive hard
VPR **escaparse 1** (= *huir*) [*preso*] to escape; [*niño, adolescente*] to run away • **se escapó por la puerta de atrás** he escaped through the back door • **se me ha escapado la paloma** my pigeon has escaped • **me escapé porque no podía aguantar más a mis padres** I ran away because I couldn't stand my parents any longer • **ven aquí, no te me escapes** come here, don't run away • **~se de** [*+ cárcel, peligro*] to escape from; [*+ jaula*] to get out of; [*+ situación opresiva*] to escape from, get away from • **el león se ha escapado del zoológico** the lion has escaped from the zoo • **de esta no te escapas** you can't get away this time; ▹ **pelo**
2 (= *filtrarse*) [*gas, líquido*] to leak, leak out (**por** from)
3 (= *dejar pasar*) • **me voy, que se me escapa el tren** I'm going, or I'll miss my train • **se me había escapado ese detalle** that detail had escaped my notice, I had overlooked *o* missed that detail • **a nadie se le escapa la importancia de esta visita** everybody is aware of *o* realizes the importance of this visit • **no se me escapa que ...** I am aware that ..., I realize that ... • MODISMO: • **~se de las manos**: • **la realidad se me escapa de las manos** I'm losing touch with reality, I'm losing my grip on reality • **la situación se les escapó de las manos** they lost control of the situation
4 (= *dejar salir*) **a** [*grito, eructo*] • **se me escapó un eructo sin darme cuenta** I accidentally burped *o* let out a burp • **se le escapó un suspiro de alivio** she breathed *o* let out a sigh of relief • **no pude evitar que se me ~a una carcajada** I couldn't help bursting out laughing • **se me escapó una lágrima** a tear came to my eye
b [*dato, noticia*] • **se le escapó la fecha de la reunión** he let slip the date of the meeting
5 (= *soltarse*) **a** [*globo, cometa*] to fly away
b [*punto de sutura*] to come undone
c (*Cos*) • **se le escapó un punto en la manga** she dropped a stitch in the sleeve
6 (= *hacerse público*) [*información*] to leak, leak out • **se escapó la noticia de que iban a vender la compañía** the news leaked that they were going to sell the firm
7 (= *olvidarse*) to slip one's mind • **ahora mismo se me escapa su nombre** his name escapes me *o* slips my mind right now

escaparate SM **1** (*de tienda*) window, shop window • **ir de** *o* **mirar ~s** to go window-shopping
2 [*de promoción*] showcase
3 (*LAm*) (= *armario*) wardrobe
4‡ (= *pecho*) tits‡ (*pl*), bosom (*hum*), chest

escaparatismo SM window dressing

escaparatista SMF window dresser

escapatoria SF **1** (= *huida*) [*de lugar*] escape, way out; [*de situación*] way out • **un sitio de donde no había ~ posible** a place from which there was no possible escape *o* way out • **no tienes ~** there is no way out for you • **me temo que eso no te va servir como ~** I'm afraid that excuse isn't going to work
2* ▹ **escapada**

escape SM **1** [*de situación opresiva*] escape • **la lectura es mi única forma de ~** reading is my only form of escape • **vía de ~** (*lit*) escape route; (*fig*) (form of) escape • **la televisión es mi única vía de ~** the television is my only (form of) escape • **utilizan el fútbol como una vía de ~ de sus problemas** they use football as an escape from *o* as a way of escaping from their problems • MODISMO: • **a ~** at full speed • **salir a ~** to rush out
2 (= *fuga*) [*de gas*] leak; [*de líquido, radiación*] leak, leakage • **un ~ de gas** a gas leak
3 (*Mec*) (*tb* **tubo de escape**) exhaust • **gases de ~** exhaust, exhaust fumes; ▹ **válvula**, **vía**

escapismo SM escapism

escapista ADJ, SMF escapist

escápula SF scapula (*pl*), shoulder blade

escapulario SM scapular, scapulary

escaque SM **1** [*de tablero*] square
2 escaques (*Hist*) (= *ajedrez*) chess (*sing*)

escaqueado ADJ checked, chequered, checkered (*EEUU*)

escaquearse‡ ▹ CONJUG 1a VPR (= *irse*) to slope off*; (= *gandulear*) to shirk, skive‡; (= *negar la responsabilidad*) to pass the buck*; (= *rajarse*) to duck out

escara SF (*Med*) crust, slough

escarabajas SFPL firewood (*sing*), kindling (*sing*)

escarabajear ▹ CONJUG 1a VT* (= *preocupar*) to bother, worry
VI **1** (*al moverse*) (= *agitarse*) to wriggle, squirm; (= *arrastrarse*) to crawl
2 (= *garabatear*) to scribble, scrawl

escarabajo SM **1** (= *insecto*) beetle ▸ **escarabajo de Colorado, escarabajo de la patata** Colorado beetle
2 (*Téc*) flaw
3* (= *persona*) dwarf, runt
4 (*Aut*) Beetle
5 escarabajos* (= *garabatos*) scribble (*sing*)

escaramujo SM **1** (*Bot*) (= *planta*) wild rose, briar; (= *fruto*) hip, rosehip
2 (*Zool*) goose barnacle
3 (*Caribe*) (= *mal de ojo*) spell, curse

escaramuza SF **1** (*Mil*) skirmish, brush
2 (= *enfrentamiento*) brush

escaramuzar ▹ CONJUG 1f VI to skirmish

escarapela SF **1** (= *insignia*) rosette, cockade
2* (= *riña*) brawl, shindy*

escarapelar ▹ CONJUG 1a VT **1** (*LAm*) (= *descascarar*) to scrape off, scale off, chip off
2 (*And*) (= *arrugar*) to crumple, rumple
VI **1** (= *reñir*) to wrangle, quarrel
2 ▹ VPR
VPR **escarapelarse 1** (*LAm*) (= *descascararse*) to peel off, flake off
2 (*And, Méx*) (= *temblar*) to go weak at the knees, tremble all over

escarbadientes SM INV toothpick

escarbador SM scraper

escarbar ▹ CONJUG 1a VT **1** (= *remover*) [*+ tierra*] to scratch; [*+ fuego*] to poke; [*+ dientes*] to pick
2 (= *investigar*) to investigate, delve into; (= *curiosear*) to pry into
VI **1** to scratch
2 • **~ en** to investigate, delve into; (= *curiosear*) to pry into

escarcear ▹ CONJUG 1a VI (*Cono Sur*) to prance

escarcela SF (*Caza*) pouch, bag

escarceo SM, **escarceos** SMPL **1** [*de caballo*] nervous movement, prance
2 (= *flirteo*) amateur effort • **en mis ~s con la política** in my occasional dealings with politics ▸ **escarceos amorosos** romantic flings, love affairs
3 (= *olas*) small waves (*pl*)

escarcha SF frost

escarchado ADJ **1** covered in hoarfrost, frosted
2 [*fruta*] crystallized

escarchar ▹ CONJUG 1a VT **1** (*Culin*) [*+ tarta*] to ice; [*+ fruta*] to crystallize
2 (= *helar*) (*gen*) to frost, cover in hoarfrost; [*+ vaso*] to frost
3 (*Cos*) *to embroider with silver or gold*
VI • **escarcha** it's frosty, it's freezing

escarchilla SF (*And, Caribe*) hail

escarcho SM (red) gurnard

escarda SF **1** (= *acción*) (*lit*) hoeing; (*fig*) weeding out
2 (= *herramienta*) weeding hoe

escardador SM weeding hoe

escardadura SF weeding, hoeing

escardar ▹ CONJUG 1a VT to weed, weed out

escardillo SM weeding hoe

escariador SM reamer

escariar ▹ CONJUG 1b VT to ream

escarificación SF (*Agr, Med*) scarification

escarificador SM scarifier

escarificar ▹ CONJUG 1g VT to scarify

escarlata ADJ INV scarlet
SM (= *color*) scarlet
SF **1** (= *tela*) scarlet cloth
2 (*Med*) scarlet fever

escarlatina SF scarlet fever

escarmenar ▹ CONJUG 1a VT **1** [*+ lana*] to comb
2 (= *castigar*) to punish • **~ algo a algn*** to swindle sb out of sth

escarmentado ADJ wary, cautious • **estoy escarmentada** I've learned my lesson

escarmentar ▹ CONJUG 1j VT to teach a lesson to
VI to learn one's lesson • **¡para que escarmientes!** that'll teach you! • **no escarmientan** they never learn • **escarmenté y no lo volví a hacer** I learned my lesson and never did it again • **~ en cabeza ajena** to learn from someone else's mistakes

escarmiento SM (= *castigo*) punishment; (= *aviso*) lesson, warning • **que esto te sirva de ~** let this be a lesson *o* warning to you • **para ~ de los malhechores** as a lesson *o* warning to wrongdoers

escarnecedor/a ADJ mocking
SM/F scoffer, mocker

escarnecer ▹ CONJUG 2d VT to scoff at, mock, ridicule

escarnio SM (= *insulto*) jibe, taunt; (= *burla*) ridicule • **para mayor ~** to add insult to injury

escarola SF **1** (*Bot*) curly endive, escarole (*EEUU*)
2 (*Méx*) (*Cos*) ruff, flounce

escarolar ▹ CONJUG 1a VT (*Méx*) (*Cos*) to frill, flounce

escarpa SF **1** (= *cuesta*) slope; (*Geog, Mil*) scarp, escarpment
2 (*Méx*) (= *acera*) pavement, sidewalk (*EEUU*)

escarpado ADJ (= *empinado*) steep, sheer; (= *abrupto*) craggy

escarpadura SF = **escarpa**

escarpar ▹ CONJUG 1a VT **1** (*Geog*) to escarp
2 (*Téc*) to rasp

escarpia SF (*gen*) hook; (*para carne*) meat hook; (*Téc*) tenterhook

escarpín SM **1** (= *zapato*) pump; (= *zapatilla*) slipper
2 (= *calcetín*) (*de sobra*) extra sock, outer sock;

[*de niña*] ankle sock, anklet (EEUU)
escarrancharse* ▹ CONJUG 1a (VPR) to do the splits
escasamente (ADV) **1** (= *insuficientemente*) scantily, sparingly
2 (= *apenas*) scarcely, hardly
escasear ▹ CONJUG 1a (VI) to be scarce
(VT) (= *escatimar*) to be sparing with, skimp
escasez (SF) **1** (= *insuficiencia*) shortage, scarcity (*más frm*) • **~ de agua** shortage *o* scarcity (*más frm*) of water • **~ de fondos** shortage of funds • **hay ~ de medicamentos** there is a shortage of medicine, medicine is in short supply • **~ de mano de obra/ viviendas** labour/housing shortage
2 (= *pobreza*) poverty • **viven en la ~** they live in poverty
3 escaseces (= *apuros*) • **han pasado muchas escaseces** they suffered great hardships
4†† (= *tacañería*) meanness, stinginess
escaso (ADJ) **1** (= *limitado*) • **los alimentos están muy ~s** food is very scarce • **las posibilidades de encontrarlo vivo son muy escasas** the chances of finding him alive are very slim • **habrá escasa visibilidad en las carreteras** visibility on the roads will be poor • **el recital tuvo ~ público** the recital was poorly *o* sparsely attended • **tenemos escasa información del asunto** we have very little information on the subject • **un programa de ~ interés** a programme of limited interest • **un motor de escasa potencia** a not very powerful engine • **iba a escasa distancia del otro coche** he was a short distance behind the other car
2 • **~ de algo** short of sth • **anda ~ de dinero** he's short of money • **estar ~ de víveres** to be short of food • **~ de recursos naturales** poor in natural resources • **una región escasa de población** a thinly populated region • **la fábrica está escasa de personal** the factory is short-staffed
3 (= *muy justo*) • **hay dos toneladas escasas** there are barely *o* scarcely two tons • **duró una hora escasa** it lasted barely *o* scarcely an hour • **tiene 15 años ~s** he's barely *o* hardly 15 • **ganar por una cabeza escasa** to win by a short head
4†† (= *tacaño*) mean, stingy
escatimar ▹ CONJUG 1a (VT) (= *dar poco*) to skimp, be sparing with, stint; (= *reducir*) to curtail, cut down • **no ~ esfuerzos (para)** to spare no effort (to) • **no ~ gastos** to spare no expense • **no escatimaba sus alabanzas de ...** he was unstinting in his praise of ..., he did not stint his praise of ...
escatimoso (ADJ) **1** (= *tacaño*) sparing, scrimpy, mean
2 (= *taimado*) sly
escatología (SF) **1** (*de los excrementos*) scatology
2 (*Fil, Rel*) eschatology
escatológico (ADJ) **1** (= *de los excrementos*) scatological
2 (*Fil, Rel*) eschatological
escay (SM) imitation leather
escayola (SF) **1** (*Arte*) plaster of Paris
2 (*Constr*) plaster, plaster of Paris
3 (*Med*) (= *material*) plaster; (= *férula*) plaster cast, cast
escayolado (SM) plastering
escayolar ▹ CONJUG 1a (VT) to put in a plaster cast, put in plaster • **le ~on la pierna** his leg was put in a (plaster) cast *o* in plaster
escena (SF) **1** (= *escenario*) stage • **¡todo el mundo a ~!** everyone on stage! • **entrar en ~** • **salir a ~** to come on stage, go on stage • **poner en ~** to stage
2 (= *parte de obra, película*) scene • **la primera ~ del segundo acto** the first scene of the second act ▸ **escena retrospectiva** flashback
3 (= *suceso*) scene • **presenciamos ~s terribles** we witnessed terrible scenes • **hacer** *o* **montar una ~** to make a scene
4 (= *ámbito*) scene • **la ~ internacional** the international scene
5 • **la ~** (= *el teatro*) the stage • **se retiró después de toda una vida dedicada a la ~** she retired after a lifetime in theatre *o* on the stage
escenario (SM) **1** (*Teat*) stage • **en el ~** on (the) stage
2 (*Cine*) setting
3 (*uso figurado*) scene • **el ~ del crimen** the scene of the crime • **el ~ político** the political scene • **la ceremonia tuvo por ~ el auditorio** the ceremony took place in the auditorium
escénico (ADJ) stage (*antes de s*)
escenificación (SF) [*de comedia*] staging; [*de novela*] dramatization; [*de suceso histórico*] re-enactment, reproduction
escenificar ▹ CONJUG 1g (VT) [+ *comedia*] to stage; [+ *novela*] to dramatize, make a stage version of; [+ *suceso histórico*] to re-enact, reproduce
escenografía (SF) scenography, stage design
escenógrafo/a (SM/F) (= *diseñador*) stage designer, theatrical designer; (= *pintor*) scene painter
escenotecnia (SF) staging, stagecraft
escepticismo (SM) scepticism, skepticism (EEUU)
escéptico/a (ADJ) sceptical, skeptical (EEUU)
(SM/F) sceptic, skeptic (EEUU)
Escila (SF) Scylla • **~ y Caribdis** Scylla and Charybdis
escindible (ADJ) fissionable
escindir ▹ CONJUG 3a (VT) to split, divide • **el partido está escindido** the party is split *o* divided
(VPR) **escindirse** (= *dividirse*) to split, divide (**en** into); [*facción*] to split off
Escipión (SM) Scipio
escisión (SF) **1** (= *división*) split, division • **la ~ del partido** the split in the party
2 (*Med*) excision (*frm*), surgical removal
escisionismo (SM) (*Pol*) tendency to split into factions
escisionista (ADJ) • **facción ~** breakaway faction • **tendencia ~** breakaway tendency
esclarecedor (ADJ) illuminating
esclarecer ▹ CONJUG 2d (VT) **1** (= *explicar*) [+ *duda, misterio*] to explain, clear up, elucidate; [+ *misterio*] to shed light on; [+ *crimen*] to clear up; [+ *situación*] to clarify
2 (= *instruir*) to enlighten
3 (= *ennoblecer*) to ennoble
4 (= *dar luz*) to light up, illuminate
(VI) to dawn
esclarecido (ADJ) illustrious, distinguished
esclarecimiento (SM) **1** (= *explicación*) explanation, elucidation, clarification
2 [*de persona*] (= *instrucción*) enlightenment
3 (= *ennoblecimiento*) ennoblement
4 (= *iluminación*) illumination
esclava (SF) bangle, bracelet; ▹ **esclavo**
esclavatura (SF) (*LAm*) (*Hist*) **1** (= *esclavos*) slaves (*pl*)
2 (= *período*) period of slavery
3 (= *esclavitud*) slavery
esclavina (SF) short cloak, cape
esclavismo (SM) = **esclavitud**
esclavitud (SF) (*lit, fig*) slavery, servitude, bondage
esclavización (SF) enslavement
esclavizar ▹ CONJUG 1f (VT) to enslave
esclavo/a (SM/F) slave • **vender a algn como ~** to sell sb into slavery • **ser ~ del tabaco** to be a slave to tobacco ▸ **esclavo/a blanco/a** white slave ▸ **esclavo/a sexual** sex slave; ▹ **esclava**
esclerosis (SF INV) **1** (*Med*) sclerosis ▸ **esclerosis múltiple** multiple sclerosis
2 (= *fosilización*) fossilization, stagnation
esclerotizado (ADJ) fossilized, stagnant
esclerotizar ▹ CONJUG 1f (VT) (*fig*) to make stagnant
esclusa (SF) [*de canal*] (= *cierre*) lock, sluice; (= *compuerta*) floodgate ▸ **esclusa de aire** airlock
esclusero/a (SM/F) lock keeper
-esco ▹ **Aspects of Word Formation in Spanish 2**
escoba (SF) **1** (*para barrer*) broom, brush • **pasar la ~** to sweep up • MODISMO: • **esto no vende una ~** this is a dead loss ▸ **escoba mecánica** carpet sweeper
2 (*Bot*) broom
(SMF) (*Dep*) sweeper
escobada (SF) brush, sweep
escobar ▹ CONJUG 1a (VT) to sweep, sweep out
escobazo (SM) **1** (= *golpe*) blow with a broom • **echar a algn a ~s** to kick sb out
2 (= *barrido*) quick sweep • **dar un ~** to have a quick sweep-up
escobilla (SF) **1** (= *escoba*) small broom; (*esp LAm*) (= *cepillo*) brush; [*de wáter*] toilet brush ▸ **escobilla de dientes** (*And*) toothbrush
2 (*Aut*) (= *limpiaparabrisas*) windscreen wiper
3 (*Aut, Elec*) dynamo brush
4 (*Bot*) teasel
escobillar ▹ CONJUG 1a (VI) (*LAm*) to tap one's feet on the floor
(VT) (*And*) (= *cepillar*) to brush; (= *restregar*) to scrub
escobillón (SM) swab
escobón (SM) (= *escoba*) large broom, long-handled broom; (= *cepillo*) scrubbing brush; (*de algodón*) swab
escocedor (ADJ) painful, hurtful
escocedura (SF) = **escozor**
escocer ▹ CONJUG 2b, 2h (VI) to sting, smart • **el alcohol te va a ~ un poco** the alcohol will sting *o* smart a little • **me escuece el labio/la herida** my lip/the cut stings *o* is smarting
(VT) (= *irritar*) to annoy, upset
(VPR) **escocerse** to chafe, get sore
escocés/esa (ADJ) [*persona*] Scottish, Scots; [*whisky*] Scotch • **falda escocesa** kilt • **tela escocesa** tartan, plaid
(SM/F) (= *persona*) Scot, Scotsman/ Scotswoman • **los escoceses** the Scots
(SM) **1** (*Ling*) Scots
2 (= *whisky*) Scotch ▸ **escocés de malta** malt whisky
Escocia (SF) Scotland
escocido (ADJ) • **el niño está ~** • **el niño tiene el culito ~** the baby has a nappy rash
escoda (SF) stonecutter's hammer
escofina (SF) rasp, file
escofinar ▹ CONJUG 1a (VT) to rasp, file
escogedor (SM) (*Agr*) riddle
escogencia (SF) (*And, Caribe*) choice
escoger ▹ CONJUG 2c (VT) to choose, pick; (*por votación*) to elect • **yo escogí el azul** I chose *o* picked the blue one • **escogió los mejores vinos para la cena** he picked out *o* chose *o* selected the best wines to go with the meal
(VI) to choose • **no hay mucho donde ~** there isn't much to choose from, there isn't much choice • **hay que ~ entre los dos** you must choose between the two • **puestos a ~, me quedo con estos** faced with the choice, I'll keep these • **tener donde ~** to have plenty to choose from, have plenty of choice

escogido ADJ **1** (= *seleccionado*) (*gen*) chosen, selected; [*mercancías*] choice, select; [*obras*] selected
2 [*persona*] • **ser muy ~** to be choosy • **ser muy ~ para** *o* **con algo** to be fussy about sth

escogimiento SM choice, selection

escolanía SF (= *centro*) schola cantorum; (= *niños*) choirboys (*pl*)

escolano SM choirboy

escolar ADJ [*edad, vacaciones*] school (*antes de s*) • **año** *o* **curso ~** school year; ▹ **libro**
SMF schoolboy/schoolgirl, schoolchild

escolaridad SF schooling, education • **el porcentaje de ~ es elevado** the proportion of those in school is high ▸ **escolaridad obligatoria** compulsory schooling, compulsory attendance at school

escolarización SF schooling, education; (= *asistencia*) school attendance; (= *alumnos matriculados*) enrolment in school

escolarizar ▹ CONJUG 1f VT (= *educar*) to provide with schooling, educate; (= *matricular*) to enrol in school; (= *mandar*) to send to school • **niños sin ~** children not in school, children receiving no schooling *o* education

escolástica SF, **escolasticismo** SM scholasticism

escolástico ADJ scholastic
SM scholastic, schoolman

escoleta SF (*Méx*) **1** (= *banda*) amateur band
2 (= *ensayo*) rehearsal, practice (*of an amateur band*)
3 (= *lección de baile*) dancing lesson

escollar ▹ CONJUG 1a VI **1** (*And, Cono Sur*) (*Náut*) to hit a reef, strike a rock
2 (*Cono Sur*) [*empresa*] to fail, come unstuck

escollera SF breakwater, jetty

escollo SM **1** (= *arrecife*) reef, rock
2 (= *obstáculo oculto*) (*en el camino*) pitfall, stumbling block; (*en actividad*) hidden danger • **los muchos ~s del inglés** the many pitfalls of English

escolopendra SF (*Zool*) centipede

escolta SMF (= *acompañante*) escort; (= *guardaespaldas*) bodyguard; [*de ministro*] minder*
SF escort • **dar ~ a** to escort, accompany

escoltar ▹ CONJUG 1a VT **1** (= *acompañar*) (*gen*) to escort; (*dando protección*) to guard, protect
2 (*Náut*) to escort, convoy

escombrar ▹ CONJUG 1a VT to clear out, clean out, clear of rubbish

escombrera SF **1** (= *vertedero*) dump, tip
2 (*Min*) slag heap

escombro[1] SM (= *pez*) mackerel

escombro[2]* SM • **armar** *o* **hacer ~** (*Arg*) to kick up a fuss

escombros SMPL (= *basura*) rubbish (*sing*), garbage (*EEUU*) (*sing*); [*de obra, edificio*] debris (*sing*), rubble (*sing*); (*Min*) slag (*sing*)

escondedero SM hiding place

escondeloro SM (*CAm*) hide-and-seek

esconder ▹ CONJUG 2a VT to hide, conceal (**de** from)
VPR **esconderse** (= *ocultarse*) to hide, hide o.s., conceal o.s.; (= *estar escondido*) to be hidden, lurk

escondidas SFPL **1** • **a ~** secretly, by stealth • **hacer algo a ~ de algn** to do sth behind sb's back
2 (*LAm*) hide-and-seek • **jugar a (las) escondida(s)** to play hide-and-seek

escondido SM (*LAm*), **escondidos** SMPL (*LAm*) hide-and-seek

escondite SM **1** (= *escondrijo*) hiding place; (*Caza, Orn*) hide, blind (*EEUU*)
2 (= *juego*) hide-and-seek • **jugar al ~ con algn** (*lit, fig*) to play hide-and-seek with sb

escondrijo SM (= *escondite*) hiding place, hideout; (= *rincón poco visible*) nook

escoñado/a‡ SM/F has-been*

escoñar‡ ▹ CONJUG 1a VT to smash up, break, shatter
VPR **escoñarse 1** [*persona*] to hurt o.s. • **estoy escoñado** I'm knackered*
2 [*máquina*] to break, get broken

escopeta SF **1** (= *arma*) shotgun ▸ **escopeta de aire comprimido** airgun, air rifle ▸ **escopeta de cañones recortados** sawn-off shotgun ▸ **escopeta de dos cañones** double-barrelled gun ▸ **escopeta de perdigones, escopeta de postas** shotgun ▸ **escopeta de tiro doble** double-barrelled gun ▸ **escopeta de viento** airgun, air rifle ▸ **escopeta paralela** double-barrelled gun ▸ **escopeta recortada** sawn-off shotgun
2‡ prick**

escopetado* ADJ, **escopeteado*** ADJ • **salir ~** to be off like a shot • **voy ~** I'm in a terrible rush, I must shoot off • **ella hablaba escopetada** her words came in a torrent, her words came pouring out

escopetazo SM **1** (= *disparo*) gunshot
2 (= *herida*) gunshot wound
3 (= *noticia*) blow, bombshell

escopetear ▹ CONJUG 1a VT **1** (= *disparar*) to shoot at (with a shotgun)
2 (*Méx**) to get at, have a dig at*
VI (*Caribe*) (= *contestar*) to answer irritably
VPR **escopetearse** • **se ~on en el bosque** they shot at each other in the wood • **se escopetean a injurias** they shower one another with insults, they heap insults upon each other

escopeteo SM **1** (= *disparos*) shooting, volley of shots
2 [*de injurias, cumplimientos*] shower, lively exchange

escopetero SM gunsmith; (*Mil*) rifleman

escoplear ▹ CONJUG 1a VT to chisel

escoplo SM chisel

escor SM (*LAm*) score

escora SF (*Náut*) **1** (= *línea*) level line, load line
2 (= *apoyo*) prop, shore
3 (= *inclinación*) list • **con una ~ de 30 grados** with a thirty-degree list

escoración SF, **escorada** SF **1** (*Náut*) list (**a, hacia** to)
2 (*fig*) leaning, inclination

escorar ▹ CONJUG 1a (*Náut*) VT to shore up
VI **1** (*Náut*) to list, heel, heel over • **~ a babor** to list to port
2 (= *inclinarse*) • **~ a** *o* **hacia** to lean towards, be inclined towards

escorbútico ADJ scorbutic

escorbuto SM scurvy

escorchar ▹ CONJUG 1a VT **1** to flay, skin
2 (*Cono Sur*) (= *fastidiar*) to bother, annoy

escoria SF **1** [*de alto horno*] slag, dross ▸ **escoria básica** basic slag
2 (= *lo más miserable*) scum, dregs (*pl*) • **la ~ de la humanidad** the scum *o* dregs of humanity

Escorial SM • **el ~** *monastery and palace north of Madrid built by Philip II*

escorpena SF, **escorpina** SF scorpion fish

Escorpio SM (*Astron, Astrol*) Scorpio • **es de ~** (*LAm*) she's (a) Scorpio

escorpio (*Astrol*) SMF INV Scorpio • **los ~ son así** that's what Scorpios are like
ADJ INV Scorpio • **soy ~** I'm (a) Scorpio

Escorpión SM (*Astron, Astrol*) Scorpio

escorpión SM (= *alacrán*) scorpion
SMF INV (*Astrol*) Scorpio

escorrentía SF **1** (= *torrente*) rush, torrent
2 (= *derrame*) overflow
3 (*Agr*) run-off (*of chemicals*) ▸ **escorrentía superficial** surface run-off

escorzar ▹ CONJUG 1f VT to foreshorten

escorzo SM foreshortening

escota SF sheet

escotado ADJ [*vestido*] low-cut

escotadura SF **1** (*Cos*) low neck, low neckline
2 (*Teat*) large trap door

escotar ▹ CONJUG 1a VT **1** (*Cos*) [+ *vestido*] to cut low in front; [+ *cuello*] to cut low
2 [+ *río*] to draw water from
VI (= *pagar su parte*) to pay one's share, chip in

escotch SM (*LAm*) sticky tape

escote SM **1** [*de vestido*] neck, neckline • **un ~ profundo** a plunging neckline • MODISMO: • **ir** *o* **pagar a ~** (*entre varios*) to share the expenses; (*entre dos*) to go Dutch, go fifty-fifty ▸ **escote a la caja** round neck ▸ **escote de bañera** off-the shoulder neckline ▸ **escote en pico, escote en V** V-neck ▸ **escote redondo** round neck
2 [*de mujer*] cleavage

escotilla SF (*Náut*) hatchway, hatch • MODISMO: • **atrancar las ~s** to batten down the hatches

escotillón SM trap door

escozor SM **1** (= *picor*) stinging, burning
2 (= *sentimiento*) grief, heartache

escrachar VT to stage a noisy protest against • **escracharon al ministro en su casa** they staged a noisy protest against the minister outside his house

escrache SM noisy protest • **hacer un ~ a algn** to stage a noisy protest against sb

escriba SM scribe

escribanía SF **1** (= *mueble*) writing desk
2 (= *estuche*) writing case
3 (= *enseres*) (*para escribir*) writing materials (*pl*); (*para tintero*) inkstand
4 (*Jur*) (= *cargo*) clerkship; (= *secretaría judicial*) clerk's office; (*LAm*) (= *notaría*) notary's office

escribano/a SM/F (= *secretario judicial*) court clerk, lawyer's clerk; (*LAm*) (= *notario*) notary, notary public ▸ **escribano/a municipal** town clerk
SM (*Orn*) bunting ▸ **escribano cerillo** yellowhammer

escribible ADJ writable

escribiente SMF (= *administrador*) clerk; (= *copista*) copyist

escribir ▹ CONJUG 3a (PP: **escrito**) VT, VI
1 [+ *palabra, texto*] to write • **~ a mano** to write in longhand • **~ a máquina** to type • **el que esto escribe** (*gen*) the present writer; (*Prensa*) this correspondent
2 (*en ortografía*) to spell • **"voy" se escribe con "v"** "voy" is spelled with a "v" • **¿cómo se escribe eso?** how is that spelled?, how do you spell that?
3 [+ *cheque*] to write out, make out
4 [+ *música*] to compose, write
VPR **escribirse 1** [*dos personas*] to write to each other, correspond
2 • **~se con algn** to correspond with sb, write to sb

escrito PP *de* **escribir**
ADJ written, in writing • **examen ~** written exam • **lo ~ arriba** what has been said above
SM **1** (*tb* **texto escrito**) writing; (= *documento*) document; (= *original*) manuscript • **por ~** in writing • **acuerdo por ~** written agreement, agreement in writing • **poner por ~** to write down, get down in writing, commit to paper • **tomar algo por ~** to write sth down, take sth down in writing • **no lo creeré hasta que no lo vea por ~** I won't believe it until I see it in black and white *o* in writing
2 (*Jur*) brief
3 escritos (*Literat*) writings, works

escritor(a) SM/F writer • **es un ~ consolidado** he's an established writer ▸ **escritor(a) de material publicitario** copywriter ▸ **escritor(a) satírico/a** satirist, satirical writer
escritorio SM (= *mueble*) desk, bureau; (= *despacho*) office • **de ~** desktop (*antes de s*) ▸ **escritorio público** (*Méx*) *stall or kiosk offering help writing letters and filling in forms*
escritorzuelo/a SM/F hack, hack writer, scribbler
escritura SF **1** (= *sistema de comunicación*) writing; [*de individuo*] writing, handwriting • **tiene malísima ~** her writing *o* handwriting is terrible • **no acierto a leer su ~** I can't read his writing *o* handwriting • **~ a máquina** typing ▸ **escritura aérea** skywriting ▸ **escritura automática** automatic writing ▸ **escritura corrida** longhand ▸ **escritura fonética** phonetic script ▸ **escritura normal** longhand
2 (= *tipo de código*) writing, script ▸ **escritura china** Chinese writing, Chinese script
3 • **Sagrada Escritura** Scripture, Holy Scripture
4 (*Jur*) deed ▸ **escritura de aprendizaje** indenture ▸ **escritura de propiedad** title deed ▸ **escritura de seguro** insurance certificate ▸ **escritura de traspaso** conveyance, deed of transfer
escriturado ADJ [*capital*] registered
escriturar ▹ CONJUG 1a VT **1** (*Jur*) [+ *documentos*] to formalize legally; [+ *propiedad, casa*] to register (legally)
2 (*Teat*) to book, engage, sign up
escriturario ADJ, **escriturístico** ADJ scriptural
escrófula SF scrofula
escrofuloso ADJ scrofulous
escroto SM scrotum
escrupulizar ▹ CONJUG 1f VT to scruple, hesitate • **no ~ en hacer algo** not to scruple to do sth
escrúpulo SM **1** (= *recelo*) scruple • **falta de ~s** unscrupulousness, lack of scruples • **sin ~** unscrupulous • **no tuvo ~s en hacerlo** he had no qualms about doing it
2 (*con la comida*) fussiness, pernicketiness • **me da ~ beber de ahí** I'm wary about drinking from there
3 (*Farm*) scruple
escrupulosamente ADV scrupulously
escrupulosidad SF scrupulousness
escrupuloso ADJ **1** (= *minucioso*) (*al elegir algo*) particular; (*al hacer algo*) precise
2 (*con la comida*) fussy, pernickety, persnickety (EEUU)
3 (= *honesto*) scrupulous
escrushante* SMF (*Arg*) burglar, housebreaker
escrutador(a) ADJ [*mirada*] searching, penetrating
SM/F **1** [*de votos*] returning officer, scrutineer
2 (*Parl*) teller
escrutar ▹ CONJUG 1a VT **1** (= *examinar*) to scrutinize, examine • **parecía que me estaba escrutando con la mirada** he seemed to be scrutinizing *o* examining me with his eyes
2 [+ *votos*] to count
escrutinio SM **1** (= *examen atento*) scrutiny, examination
2 [*de votos*] count, counting
escuadra SF **1** (= *instrumento*) (*para dibujar*) square; (*de carpintero*) carpenter's square • **a ~** square, at right angles • **fuera de ~** out of true ▸ **escuadra de delineante** set square
2 [*de hombres*] (*Mil*) squad; (*Náut*) squadron ▸ **escuadra de demolición** demolition squad ▸ **escuadra de fusilamiento** firing squad
3 (*Aut*) [*de coches*] fleet
4 (*LAm*) (*Dep*) team, squad
5 (*And*) (= *pistola*) pistol
escuadrar ▹ CONJUG 1a VT (*Téc*) to square
escuadrilla SF (*Aer*) wing, squadron
escuadrón SM (*Mil, Aer*) squadron ▸ **escuadrón de la muerte** death squad, murder squad ▸ **escuadrón volante** flying squad
escualidez SF **1** (= *delgadez*) skinniness, scragginess
2 (= *miseria*) squalor, filth
escuálido ADJ **1** (= *delgado*) skinny, scraggy
2 (= *sucio*) squalid, filthy
escualo SM dogfish
escucha SF **1** (= *acción*) listening; (*Radio*) monitoring • **rogamos a nuestros oyentes que permanezcan a la ~** please stay tuned • **estar a la ~** to listen in • **estar de ~** to eavesdrop ▸ **escucha telefónica** phone tap, wire tap (EEUU) ▸ **escuchas telefónicas** phone tapping, wire tapping (EEUU)
2 (*Rel*) chaperon
SMF **1** (*Mil*) scout
2 (*Radio*) monitor
escuchar ▹ CONJUG 1a VT **1** (*con atención*) [+ *música, palabras*] to listen to; [+ *consejo*] to listen to, pay attention to, heed
2 (*esp LAm*) (= *oír*) to hear • **se escucha muy mal** (*Telec*) it's a very bad line *o* (EEUU) connection
VI to listen
VPR **escucharse** • **le gusta ~se** he likes the sound of his own voice • **se escucha mucho las enfermedades** she's always complaining about her illnesses
escuchimizado* ADJ • **estar ~** to be all skin and bones • **es un chico ~** he's a skinny boy
escucho SM (*And*) whispered secret
escuchón ADJ (*And*) prying, inquisitive
escudar ▹ CONJUG 1a VT to shield
VPR **escudarse** to shield o.s.
escudería SF motor-racing team
escudero SM squire
escudete SM **1** (*Heráldica, Hist*) escutcheon
2 (*Cos*) gusset
3 (*Bot*) white water lily
escudilla SF bowl, basin
escudo SM **1** [*de protección*] shield ▸ **escudo humano** human shield ▸ **escudo térmico** heat shield
2 (*Heráldica*) ▸ **escudo de armas** coat of arms
3 (= *moneda*) escudo
escudriñar ▹ CONJUG 1a VT **1** (= *investigar*) to inquire into, investigate
2 (= *examinar*) to scrutinize
escuela SF **1** (= *colegio*) school • **dejé la ~ a los catorce años** I left school at fourteen • **recuerdo los tiempos de la ~** I remember my schooldays • **ir a la ~** [*alumno, maestro*] to go to school • **fue a la ~ a hablar con el director** he went to the school to speak to the headmaster ▸ **escuela de párvulos** nursery school, kindergarten ▸ **escuela de primera enseñanza, escuela elemental** primary school ▸ **escuela infantil** nursery school ▸ **escuela primaria** primary school ▸ **escuela privada** private school, independent school ▸ **escuela pública** state school, public school (EEUU) ▸ **escuela secundaria** secondary school, high school (EEUU)
2 (= *centro de enseñanza*) (*gen*) school; (*Chile*) (= *facultad*) faculty, school ▸ **escuela de artes y oficios** school of arts and crafts ▸ **escuela de baile** school of dancing, dance school ▸ **escuela de ballet** ballet school ▸ **Escuela de Bellas Artes** art school, art college ▸ **escuela de chóferes** (*LAm*) driving school ▸ **escuela de cine** film school ▸ **escuela de comercio** business school, school of business studies ▸ **escuela de conducir** (*Col*), **escuela de conductores** (*LAm*) driving school ▸ **escuela de enfermería** nursing college ▸ **escuela de equitación** riding school ▸ **escuela de manejo** (*Méx*) driving school ▸ **escuela de verano** summer school ▸ **escuela laboral** technical school, trade school ▸ **escuela militar** military academy ▸ **escuela naval** naval academy ▸ **escuela nocturna** night school ▸ **escuela normal** teacher training college ▸ **escuela taller** *vocational training centre* ▸ **escuela universitaria** *university college offering diploma rather than degree courses*; ▹ **buque, granja**
3* (= *clases*) school • **mañana no hay *o* no tenemos ~** there's no school tomorrow • MODISMO: • **soplarse la ~** (*Esp*) to play truant, skive off*, play hooky (EEUU*)
4 (= *formación*) experience • **es buen actor pero le falta ~** he's a good actor but he lacks experience • MODISMO: • **la ~ de la vida** the university of life, the school of life
5 (= *movimiento*) school • **la ~ flamenca** the Flemish school • **la ~ romántica** the Romantic school • **la ~ veneciana** the Venetian school • **un catedrático de la vieja ~** a professor of the old school • **un escritor que ha creado ~** a writer with a great following; ▹ COLEGIO

ESCUELA OFICIAL DE IDIOMAS
The **Escuelas Oficiales de Idiomas** are state-run language schools which offer tuition in a wide range of foreign languages. Examinations are also open to external candidates and the **Certificado de la Escuela Oficial de Idiomas**, the final qualification, is recognized all over Spain.

escuelante SMF (*Col, Méx, Ven*) (= *alumno*) pupil
escuelero/a ADJ (*LAm*) school (*antes de s*)
SM/F **1** (*And, Caribe, Cono Sur*) (*pey*) (= *maestro*) schoolmaster/schoolmistress
2 (*And*) (= *alumno*) schoolboy/schoolgirl; (= *empollón**) swot*, grind (EEUU*)
escuerzo SM **1** (*Zool*) toad
2 (= *persona*) runt
escuetamente ADV plainly, baldly
escueto ADJ [*verdad*] plain, naked; [*estilo*] simple; [*explicación, presentación*] concise, succinct
escuincle/a* SM/F (*Méx*), **escuintle/a*** SM/F (*Méx*) **1** (= *niño*) child, kid*
2 (= *animal*) runt
esculcar ▹ CONJUG 1g VT (*Méx*) to search
esculpir ▹ CONJUG 3a VT [+ *estatua, piedra*] to sculpt; [+ *madera*] to carve; [+ *inscripción*] to cut
esculque SM (*LAm*) body search
escultismo SM = **escutismo**
escultor(a) SM/F sculptor/sculptress
escultórico ADJ sculptural
escultura SF sculpture, carving ▸ **escultura en madera** wood carving
escultural ADJ **1** (*Arte*) sculptural
2 [*cuerpo, mujer*] statuesque
escupe* SM (*Prensa*) scoop
escupidera SF **1** (*para escupir*) spittoon, cuspidor (EEUU)
2 (*esp And, Cono Sur*) (= *orinal*) chamberpot • MODISMO: • **pedir la ~** to get scared, get the wind up*
escupidor SM **1** (*And, Caribe*) (= *recipiente*) spittoon
2 (*And*) (= *estera*) round mat, doormat
escupir ▹ CONJUG 3a VI to spit • **~ a algn** to

spit at sb • ~ **a la cara de algn** to spit in sb's face • ~ **en el suelo** to spit on the ground • MODISMO: • **ser de medio ~*** to be as common as muck*

VT **1** *[persona]* [+ *sangre*] to spit; [+ *comida*] to spit out; [+ *palabra*] to spit, spit out

2 (= *arrojar*) [+ *llamas*] to belch out, spew

3* (= *confesar*) to cough*, sing*

escupitajo* SM gob of spit

escurana SF (*LAm*) **1** (= *oscuridad*) darkness

2 (= *cielo*) overcast sky, threatening sky

escurialense ADJ of/from El Escorial

escurreplatos SM INV plate rack

e

escurreverduras SM INV colander, strainer

escurribanda SF **1** (*Med*) *[de vientre]* looseness, diarrhoea, diarrhea (*EEUU*); *[de úlcera]* running

2 (= *fuga*) escape

3 (= *paliza*) thrashing

escurridera SF draining board

escurrideras SFPL (*Méx, CAm*) = **escurriduras**

escurridero SM draining board, drainboard (*EEUU*)

escurridizo ADJ **1** (= *resbaladizo*) *[superficie, objeto]* slippery; *[nudo]* running

2 (= *evasivo*) *[carácter]* slippery; *[idea]* elusive

escurrido ADJ **1** (= *delgado*) narrow-hipped, slightly built

2 (*And, Caribe, Méx*) (= *avergonzado*) abashed, ashamed; (= *tímido*) shy

escurridor SM **1** (*Culin*) (= *escurreplatos*) plate rack; (= *colador*) colander

2 (*Fot*) drying rack

escurriduras SFPL **1** (= *gotas*) drops

2 (= *heces*) dregs

escurrir ▹ CONJUG 3a VT [+ *ropa*] to wring, wring out; [+ *platos, líquido, botella*] to drain; [+ *verduras*] to strain

VI *[líquido]* to drip

VPR **escurrirse 1** *[líquido]* to drip

2 (= *resbalarse*) *[objeto]* to slip, slide • **se me escurrió de entre las manos** it slipped out of my hands

3 *[comentario]* to slip out

4 *[persona]* to slip away, sneak off

escúter SM scooter, motor scooter

escutismo SM scouting movement, scouting

esdrújulo ADJ proparoxytone (*frm*), *stressed on the antepenultimate syllable*

ESE ABR (= **estesudeste**) ESE

ese¹ SF name of the letter S • **en forma de ese** S-shaped • MODISMO: • **hacer eses** *[carretera]* to zigzag, twist and turn; *[coche]* to zigzag; *[borracho]* to reel about

ese²/a ADJ DEM that • **esa casa** that house • **esos/as** those • **esos dibujos** those drawings • **no conozco al tío ese** I don't know that guy*

ese³/a PRON DEM, **ése/a** PRON DEM **1** that one • **ese es el mío** that one is mine • **esos/as** those, those ones • **prefiero esos** I prefer those ones • **esos que te compré yo** the ones I bought you

2 (*en locuciones*) • **¡no me vengas con esas!** don't give me any more of that nonsense! • **y cosas de esas** and suchlike • **¡no me salgas ahora con esas!** don't bring all that up again! • **no es una chica de esas** she's not that kind of girl • **ni por esas** (= *de ningún modo*) on no account; (= *aun así*) even so

*In the past the standard spelling for these demonstrative pronouns was with an accent (ése, ésa, ésos and ésas). Nowadays the **Real Academia Española** advises that the accented forms are only required where there might otherwise be confusion with the adjective.*

esencia SF **1** (= *base*) *[de teoría]* essence; *[de asunto, problema]* heart • **en ~** essentially, in essence • **quinta ~** quintessence

2 *[de perfume]* essence

esencial ADJ **1** (= *imprescindible*) essential • **es ~ traer ropa de abrigo** it's essential to bring warm clothing

2 (= *principal*) essential, main • **lo ~ es que ...** the main *o* essential *o* most important thing is to ... • **he entendido lo ~ de la conversación** I understood the main *o* the most important points of the conversation • **en lo ~: pese a las diferencias, estamos de acuerdo en lo ~** essentially, despite our differences, we are in agreement, despite our differences, we are in agreement on the essentials

3 *[aceite]* essential

esfagno SM sphagnum

esfera SF **1** (*Geog, Mat*) sphere • **en forma de ~** spherical ▸ **esfera celeste** celestial sphere ▸ **esfera terrestre** globe

2 (*Téc*) *[de reloj]* face ▸ **esfera impresora** (*Tip*) golf ball

3 (= *campo*) sphere, field • **el proyecto ha sido autorizado por las altas ~s** the project has had the go-ahead from the top authorities *o* the upper echelons ▸ **esfera de acción** scope, range ▸ **esfera de actividad** sphere of activity ▸ **esfera de influencia** sphere of influence

esférico ADJ spherical

SM (*Dep*) football, soccer ball (*EEUU*)

esfero SM (*Col*) ballpoint pen

esferográfico SM (*Col*) ballpoint pen

esferógrafo SM (*Col*) ballpoint pen

esferoide SM spheroid

esfinge SF **1** (= *figura*) sphinx • MODISMO: • **ser como una ~** to be expressionless, have a face like a poker

2 (*Entomología*) hawk moth

esfínter SM sphincter

esforzadamente ADV vigorously, energetically

esforzado ADJ **1** (= *enérgico*) vigorous, energetic

2 (= *fuerte*) strong, tough

3 (= *emprendedor*) enterprising

4 (= *valiente*) brave

5 (= *trabajador*) hardworking

esforzar ▹ CONJUG 1f, 1l VT *[voz]* to strain • **no esfuerces la vista** don't strain your eyes

VPR **esforzarse** to exert o.s., make an effort • **hay que ~se más** you must try harder, you must make more effort • **~se en** *o* **por conseguir algo** to struggle *o* strive to achieve sth

esfuerzo SM **1** (*de fuerza física, intelectual*) effort • **sin ~** effortlessly, without strain • **hacer un ~** to make an effort • **no perdonar ~s para conseguir algo** to spare no effort to achieve sth • **no hizo el más mínimo ~ por agradar** he made absolutely no effort at all to be nice, he didn't make the slightest effort to be nice • **bien vale la pena el ~** it's well worth the effort

2 (= *vigor*) spirit, vigour, vigor (*EEUU*) • **con ~** with spirit

3 (*Mec*) stress

esfumar ▹ CONJUG 1a VT (*Arte*) to tone down, soften

VPR **esfumarse 1** *[apoyo, esperanzas]* to fade away, melt away

2 *[persona]* to vanish, make o.s. scarce • **¡esfúmate!*** get lost!*

esfumino SM (*Arte*) stump

esgrima SF **1** (*Dep*) fencing

2 (= *arte*) swordsmanship

esgrimidor(a) SM/F (*Dep*) fencer

esgrimir ▹ CONJUG 3a VT **1** [+ *espada*] to wield

2 [+ *argumento*] to use • **~ que** to argue that, maintain that

VI to fence

esgrimista SMF (*LAm*) fencer

esguazar ▹ CONJUG 1f VT to ford

esguince SM **1** (*Med*) sprain

2 (= *movimiento*) swerve, dodge • **dar un ~** to swerve, dodge

eskay SM imitation leather

eslabón SM **1** *[de cadena]* link ▸ **eslabón giratorio** swivel ▸ **eslabón perdido** (*Bio*) missing link

2 (*para afilar*) steel

eslabonar ▹ CONJUG 1a VT **1** [+ *eslabones, piezas*] to link, link together

2 [+ *ideas*] to link, connect

eslálom SM, **eslalon** SM = **slalom**

eslavo/a ADJ Slav, Slavonic

SM/F Slav

SM (*Ling*) Slavonic

eslinga SF (*Náut*) sling

eslingar ▹ CONJUG 1h VT (*Náut*) to sling

eslip SM (PL: **eslips**) = **slip**

eslogan SM (PL: **eslogans**) = **slogan**

eslomar ▹ CONJUG 1a VT = **deslomar**

eslora SF (*Náut*) length • **tiene 250m de ~** she is 250m in length

eslovaco/a ADJ Slovak, Slovakian

SM/F Slovak

Eslovaquia SF Slovakia

Eslovenia SF Slovenia

esloveno/a ADJ, SM/F Slovene, Slovenian

esmaltado ADJ enamelled

SM enamelling

esmaltar ▹ CONJUG 1a VT **1** (= *cubrir con esmalte*) [+ *metal*] to enamel; [+ *cerámica, porcelana*] to glaze; [+ *uñas*] to varnish, paint

2 (= *adornar*) to adorn (**con, de** with)

esmalte SM **1** (*para metal, diente*) enamel; (*para cerámica, porcelana*) glaze ▸ **esmalte de uñas** nail varnish, nail polish

2 (= *objeto*) enamelwork

3 (= *adorno*) lustre, luster (*EEUU*)

esmeradamente ADV carefully, neatly

esmerado ADJ **1** *[trabajo]* careful, neat

2 *[persona]* careful, painstaking

esmeralda SF emerald

esmerar ▹ CONJUG 1a VT to polish

VPR **esmerarse 1** (= *aplicarse*) to take great pains (**en** over) • **no se esmera nada en su trabajo** she doesn't take any care over her work • **~se en hacer algo** to take great pains to do sth

2 (= *hacer lo mejor*) to do one's best

esmerejón SM merlin

esmeril SM emery

esmeriladora SF lapping machine, emery wheel

esmerilar ▹ CONJUG 1a VT to polish with emery

esmero SM **1** (= *cuidado*) care, carefulness • **con el mayor ~** with the greatest care • **poner ~ en algo** to take great care *o* trouble *o* pains over sth

2 (= *aseo*) neatness

Esmirna SF Smyrna

esmirriado ADJ puny

esmoladera SF grindstone

esmoquin SM dinner jacket, tuxedo (*EEUU*)

esnifada* SF *[de cola]* sniff; *[de cocaína]* snort*

esnifar* ▹ CONJUG 1a VT [+ *cola*] to sniff; [+ *cocaína*] to snort*

esnife* SM *[de cola]* sniff; *[de cocaína]* snort*

esnob ADJ INV *[persona]* snobbish, stuck-up*;

[*coche, restaurante*] posh*, swish*, de luxe
(SMF) (PL: **esnobs** [ez'noβ]) snob
esnobear* ▹ CONJUG 1a (VT) to snub, cold-shoulder
esnobismo (SM) snobbery, snobbishness
esnobista (ADJ) snobbish
ESO (SF ABR) (*Esp*) (= **Enseñanza Secundaria obligatoria**) *compulsory secondary education for 12 to 16 year-olds*

ESO
As a consequence of the 1990 education reform law, **LOGSE**, secondary education in Spain is now divided into two stages. The first stage, **ESO**, or **Educación Secundaria Obligatoria**, is for 12- to 16-year-olds. It is free and compulsory and includes both vocational and academic subjects. Students are awarded the **Título de Graduado en Educación Secundaria** on successful completion at age 16 and can leave school at this point. If they choose to continue their education they go on to the second stage, which consists of either the academically orientated **Bachillerato** or the vocational **Formación Profesional Específica**.
▹ LOGSE

eso (PRON DEM) that • **eso no me gusta** I don't like that • **¿qué es eso?** what's that? • **eso de su coche** that business about his car • **¿es verdad eso que me han contado?** is it true what I've been told? • **¿qué es eso de que ...?** what's all this about ...? • **¡eso!** that's right! • **eso es** that's it, that's right • **eso sí** yes, of course • **el coche es viejo, eso sí** the car is certainly old • **eso digo yo** (*indicando acuerdo*) I quite agree; (*respondiendo a pregunta*) that's what I'd like to know • **¡eso no!, ¡eso sí que no!** no way! • **eso creo** I think so • **eso espero** I hope so • **a eso de las dos** at about two o'clock, round about two • **en eso llegó el cartero** at that point the postman arrived • **nada de eso** nothing of the kind, far from it • **¡nada de eso!** not a bit of it! • **¿no es eso?** isn't that so? • **por eso** therefore, and so • **por eso no vine** that's why I didn't come • **no es por eso** that's not the reason, that's not why, it's not because of that • **¿y eso?** why?, how so?* • **y eso que llovía** in spite of the fact that it was raining
esófago (SM) oesophagus (*frm*), esophagus (*EEUU*) (*frm*), gullet
Esopo (SM) Aesop
esotérico (ADJ) esoteric
esoterismo (SM) **1** (= *culto*) esotericism, cult of the esoteric
2 (*como género*) esotericism, esoterics (*sing*)
3 (= *carácter*) esotericism, esoteric nature
esp. (ABR) (= **español**) Sp, Span
espabilada* (SF) (*And*) blink • **en una ~** in a jiffy*
espabilado ▹ **despabilado**
espabilar ▹ CONJUG 1a ▹ **despabilar**
espachurrar ▹ CONJUG 1a (VT) to squash, flatten
(VPR) **espachurrarse** to get squashed, get flattened
espaciadamente (ADV) • **la revista saldrá más ~** the journal will come out less frequently *o* at longer intervals
espaciado (SM) (*Inform*) spacing
espaciador (SM) space bar
espacial (ADJ INV) **1** (*Aer*) space (*antes de s*) • **programa ~** space programme • **viajes ~es** space travel
2 (*Mat*) spatial
espaciar ▹ CONJUG 1b (VT) **1** [+ *palabras, párrafos*] to space, space out
2 (*en el tiempo*) [+ *noticia*] to spread; [+ *pagos*] to spread out, stagger • **empezó a ~ más sus visitas** his visits became less frequent, there were longer intervals between his visits
(VPR) **espaciarse 1** (*al hablar*) spread o.s., to expatiate (*frm*) • **~se en un tema** to enlarge on a subject, expatiate on a subject (*frm*)
2 (= *relajarse*) to relax, take one's ease
espacio (SM) **1** (*Astron, Fís, Aer*) space • **exploración del ~** space exploration • **viajar por el ~** to travel in space ▸ **espacio aéreo** air space ▸ **espacio exterior, espacio extraterrestre** outer space ▸ **espacio interestelar** interstellar space ▸ **espacio sideral** outer space ▸ **espacio-tiempo** space-time
2 (= *sitio*) room, space • **no hay ~ para tantas sillas** there isn't room *o* space for so many chairs • **¿me haces un ~ para que me siente?** can you make a bit of room *o* space for me to sit down? • **ocupa mucho ~** it takes up a lot of room • **aquí hay mucho ~ para aparcar** there's lots of room *o* space to park here ▸ **espacio de maniobra** room for manoeuvre ▸ **espacio libre** room ▸ **espacio muerto** clearance
3 (= *superficie*) space ▸ **espacio natural** open space ▸ **espacios verdes** green spaces ▸ **espacio vital** (*Pol*) living space; [*de persona*] living space
4 (*en un escrito*) space • **deja más ~ entre las líneas** leave more space between the lines • **un texto mecanografiado a un ~/a doble ~** a single-spaced/double-spaced typescript • **escríbelo a un ~/a doble ~** type it with single spacing/double spacing ▸ **espacio en blanco** blank space ▸ **espacio interlineal** interlinear spacing, inter-line spacing
5 [*de tiempo*] space • **en el ~ de una hora** in the space of an hour • **en el ~ de tres generaciones** in the space of three generations • **por ~ de** for
6 (*Radio, TV*) (*en la programación*) slot; (= *programa*) programme, program (*EEUU*) ▸ **espacio electoral** ≈ party political broadcast ▸ **espacio informativo** news programme ▸ **espacio publicitario** advertising spot, commercial
7 (*Mús*) interval
8†† (= *tardanza*) delay, slowness
espacioso (ADJ) **1** [*cuarto, casa*] spacious, roomy
2 [*movimiento*] slow, deliberate
espaciotemporal (ADJ) spatio-temporal
espada (SF) **1** (= *arma*) sword • **poner a algn a ~** to put sb to the sword • MODISMOS: • **estar hecho una ~** to be as thin as a rake *o* (*EEUU*) rail • **estar entre la ~ y la pared** to be between the devil and the deep blue sea • **la ~ de Damocles** the Sword of Damocles
2 espadas (*Naipes*) *one of the suits in the Spanish card deck, represented by a sword*; ▹ **BARAJA ESPAÑOLA**
(SMF) (*Taur*) matador, bullfighter
espadachín (SM) **1** (*Esgrima*) skilled swordsman
2 (*pey*) bully, thug
espadaña (SF) **1** (*Bot*) bulrush
2 (*Arquit*) steeple, belfry
espadarte (SM) swordfish
espadazo (SM) sword thrust, slash with a sword
espadero (SM) swordsmith
espadilla (SF) (= *remo*) scull (oar)
espadín (SM) **1** (= *espada pequeña*) dress sword, ceremonial sword
2 [*de espadachín*] picklock
3 espadines (= *pez*) sprats
espadista‡ (SMF) burglar, lock-picker
espadón (SM) **1** (= *arma*) broadsword
2 (*hum**) big shot*, top person; (*Mil*) brass hat*
espaguetis (SMPL) spaghetti (*sing*)
espalda (SF) **1** (*Anat*) back • **de ~s a algo** with one's back to sth • **de ~s al sentido de la marcha** facing backwards, with one's back to the engine • **lo mataron por la ~** he was killed from behind • **atar las manos a la ~** to tie sb's hands behind his back • **caer de ~s** to fall on one's back • **estar de ~s** to have one's back turned • **volver la ~** to turn away; (*pey*) to turn tail • **volver la ~ a algn** to cold-shoulder sb, turn one's back on sb • **volverse de ~s** to turn one's back
• MODISMOS: • **cubrirse las ~s** to cover o.s., cover one's own back • **dar la ~ a algo/algn** to turn away from sth/sb, face away from sth/sb • **echar algo sobre las ~s** to take sth on, take charge of sth • **hacer algo a ~s de algn** to do sth behind sb's back • **tener las ~s cubiertas** to make sure, be on the safe side; ▹ **ancho**
2 (*Dep*) backstroke • **la prueba de 200 metros ~s** the 200 metres backstroke
3 (*And*) (= *destino*) fate, destiny
(SMF) ▸ **espalda mojada** (*Méx**) wetback
espaldar (SM) **1** (*de silla*) back
2 (*para plantas*) trellis, espalier
3 espaldares (*Dep*) wall bars
espaldarazo (SM) recognition • **ese concierto supuso su ~ definitivo** that concert finally earned him recognition • **su apoyo ha dado el ~ decisivo al proyecto** his backing has been decisive in setting up the project
espaldera (SF) **1** (*para plantas*) trellis, espalier
2 (*para la espalda*) surgical corset
3 espalderas (*Dep*) wall bars
espaldero (SM) (*Caribe*) bodyguard, henchman
espaldilla (SF) **1** (*Anat*) shoulder blade
2 (*Méx*) (*Culin*) shoulder of pork
espantá* (SF) = **espantada**
espantable (ADJ) = **espantoso**
espantada (SF) stampede • **dar la ~** to bolt
espantadizo (ADJ) timid, easily scared
espantado (ADJ) **1** (= *asustado*) frightened, scared, terrified • **me quedé espantada cuando lo vi con esos pelos** I was horrified when I saw him with that hair
2 (*LAm*) (= *muy asustado*) sick with fear
espantador (ADJ) **1** (= *espantoso*) frightening
2 (*And, CAm, Cono Sur*) = **espantadizo**
espantajo (SM) **1** (= *espantapájaros*) scarecrow
2 (= *persona*) sight*, fright*
espantamoscas (SM INV) fly swat
espantapájaros (SM INV) scarecrow
espantar ▹ CONJUG 1a (VT) **1** (= *asustar*) (*gen*) to frighten, scare; (*haciendo huir*) to frighten off *o* away, scare off *o* away • **el ruido espantó a las reses** the noise frightened *o* scared the cattle • **espantó a los perros con una escoba** she frightened the dogs off *o* away with a broom • **con ese genio espanta a todas las chicas** with that temper of his he frightens *o* scares all the girls (off *o* away)
2 (= *horrorizar*) to horrify, appal • **le espantaba la idea de tener que ir solo** he was horrified *o* appalled at the thought of having to go on his own
(VPR) **espantarse 1** (= *asustarse*) to get frightened, get scared
2 (= *horrorizarse*) to be horrified, be appalled (**de** at) • **se espantó de verla tan cambiada** he was horrified *o* appalled to see her so changed
3 (*Caribe*) (= *sospechar*) to get suspicious
espanto (SM) **1** (= *susto*) fright; ▹ **curado**
2 (= *amenaza*) threat, menace

3 (*LAm*) (= *fantasma*) ghost
4* (*para exagerar*) • **¡qué ~!** how awful! • **hace un frío de ~** it's terribly cold • **es un coche de ~** it's a fabulous *o* tremendous car*

espantosamente ADV **1** (= *con miedo*) frightfully
2 (*para exagerar*) amazingly

espantosidad SF (*And*) terror, fear

espantoso ADJ **1** (= *aterrador*) frightening
2 (*para exagerar*) • **hizo un frío ~** it was absolutely freezing • **llevaba un traje ~** she was wearing an awful *o* a hideous *o* a frightful *o* ghastly* hat • **había un ruido ~** there was a terrible *o* dreadful noise

España SF Spain • **Nueva ~** (*Hist*) New Spain (*Mexico*) • **la ~ de charanga y pandereta** touristy Spain

español(a) ADJ Spanish
SM/F Spaniard • **los ~es** the Spaniards, the Spanish
SM (*Ling*) Spanish ▸ **español antiguo** Old Spanish ▸ **español medieval** Medieval Spanish ▸ **español moderno** Modern Spanish

española SF (*Méx*) spanner

españolada SF (*pey*) *film, show etc giving a clichéd, stereotypical image of Spain*

españolidad SF **1** (= *carácter español*) Spanishness
2 (= *patriotismo*) Spanish patriotism

españolísimo ADJ typically Spanish, unmistakably Spanish, Spanish to the core

españolismo SM **1** (= *amor a lo español*) love of Spain
2 (= *carácter español*) Spanishness
3 (*Ling*) Hispanicism

españolista ADJ centralist, unionist (*as opposed to regionalist*)
SMF pro-centralist

españolito* SM ordinary Spaniard, Spanish man in the street • **algún ~** some poor little Spaniard • **cada ~ de a pie** each poor little Spaniard that there is • **no quiero que llegue cualquier ~ y me diga lo que he de hacer** I don't want any old Spaniard to come along and start telling me what to do

españolizar ▹ CONJUG 1f VT to make Spanish, Hispanicize
VPR **españolizarse** to adopt Spanish ways • **se españolizó por completo** he became completely Spanish

esparadrapo SM plaster, sticking plaster, Band-Aid® (EEUU)

esparaván SM **1** (*Orn*) sparrowhawk
2 (*Vet*) spavin

esparavel SM net, casting net

esparceta SF sainfoin

esparcido ADJ **1** (= *desparramado*) scattered
2 (= *extendido*) widespread
3 (= *alegre*) cheerful

esparcimiento SM **1** (= *dispersión*) spreading
2 (= *descanso*) relaxation
3 (= *diversión*) amusement

esparcir ▹ CONJUG 3b VT **1** (= *desparramar*) to spread, scatter
2 (= *divulgar*) to disseminate
3 (= *distraer*) to amuse, divert
VPR **esparcirse 1** (= *desparramarse*) to spread, spread out, scatter
2 (= *descansar*) to relax
3 (= *divertirse*) to amuse o.s.

espárrago SM asparagus • MODISMOS: • **estar hecho un ~** to be as thin as a rake *o* (EEUU) rail • **mandar a algn a freír ~s** to tell sb to get lost, tell sb to go jump in a lake*, tell sb to get stuffed‡, tell sb where to get off* • **¡vete a freír ~s!*** get lost!, go jump in a lake!*, get stuffed!‡ ▸ **espárrago triguero** wild asparagus

esparraguera SF asparagus plant

esparrancado ADJ [*piernas*] wide apart, spread far apart; [*persona*] with legs wide apart, with legs spread far apart

esparrancarse ▹ CONJUG 1g VPR to spread one's legs, spread one's legs wide apart • **~ sobre algo** to straddle sth

Esparta SF Sparta

Espartaco SM Spartacus

espartal SM esparto field

espartano/a ADJ **1** (= *de Esparta*) Spartan
2 (= *austero*) spartan
SM/F Spartan

esparteña SF = **alpargata**

espartillo SM (*LAm*) esparto, esparto grass

espartizal SM esparto field

esparto SM esparto, esparto grass • MODISMO: • **estar como el ~** to be all dried up

Espasa SM • MODISMO: • **ser el ~*** to be a walking encyclopedia

espasmo SM spasm

espasmódicamente ADV spasmodically

espasmódico ADJ spasmodic

espasticidad SF spasticity

espástico/a ADJ, SM/F spastic

espatarrarse* ▹ CONJUG 1a VPR **1** (*al sentarse*) to sprawl
2 = **esparrancarse**

espato SM (*Geol*) spar ▸ **espato de Islandia** Iceland spar

espátula SF **1** (*Constr*) putty knife • MODISMO: • **estar hecho una ~** to be as thin as a rake *o* (EEUU) rail
2 (*Arte*) palette knife
3 (*Culin*) fish slice, spatula
4 (*Med*) spatula
5 (*Orn*) spoonbill

especia SF spice

especiado ADJ spiced, spicy

especial ADJ **1** (*para un fin concreto*) [*dieta, permiso*] special • **papel ~ para regalo** gift paper; ▹ **educación, enviado**
2 (= *extraordinario*) special • **un saludo muy ~ para nuestros compañeros** a special hello to all our colleagues • **de ~ interés es el trabajo de este novelista** the work of this novelist is especially interesting *o* of special interest • **precios ~es para niños** special prices for children
3 • **en ~** especially, particularly • **pedimos disculpas a todos, y en ~ a ...** we apologize to everyone, and especially *o* particularly to ... • **¿desea ver a alguien en ~?** is there anybody in particular you want to see?
4 (= *quisquilloso*) fussy • **soy muy ~ con la ropa** I'm very fussy about my clothes • **¡qué ~ eres con la comida!** you're such a fussy eater!
5 (= *extraño*) peculiar • **le encuentro un sabor muy ~ a este café** this coffee has a very peculiar flavour
SM **1** (*TV*) (*tb* **programa especial**) special • **un ~ sobre los Juegos Olímpicos** an Olympic special ▸ **especial (de) deportes** sports special ▸ **especial informativo** news special
2 (*Méx*) (*Teat*) show
3 (*para comer*) (*Cono Sur*) baguette, sub sandwich (EEUU); (*Chile*) hot dog

especialidad SF **1** (= *ramo*) speciality, specialty (EEUU) • **ha elegido la ~ de cirugía** he has chosen to specialize in surgery, he has chosen surgery as his speciality • **hizo dos años de ~** he did a two year specialization • **las matemáticas no son precisamente mi ~** maths is not exactly my speciality *o* strong point
2 (*Culin*) speciality, specialty (EEUU) • **"especialidad de la casa"** "speciality of the house" • **las carnes son nuestra ~** the meat dishes are our speciality
3 (*Farm*) (= *preparado*) medicine

especialista ADJ [*técnico, enfermera*] specialist • **un delantero ~ en tiros libres** a forward who specializes in free kicks • **médico ~** specialist
SMF **1** (*en estudio, profesión*) specialist, expert • **un libro útil tanto para el ~ como para el lector en general** a useful book for both the specialist and the general reader • **es el máximo ~ en biología marina** he is the top authority on marine biology
2 (*Med, Dep*) specialist • **~ de la piel** skin specialist • **un ~ en 100 metros mariposa** a specialist in the 100 metres butterfly
3 (*Cine, TV*) stuntman/stuntwoman

especialización SF specialization

especializado ADJ **1** [*personal, público*] specialized • **la creación del periodismo ~** the creation of specialized journalism • **un artículo destinado al lector no ~** an article aimed at the general reader • **una cadena especializada en programas culturales** a channel specializing in cultural programmes
2 [*obrero*] skilled, trained
3 [*lenguaje*] technical, specialized

especializarse ▹ CONJUG 1f VPR to specialize (**en** in) • **se especializó en Derecho Internacional** he specialized in International Law

especialmente ADV **1** (= *en especial*) especially, particularly • **este problema afecta ~ a los jóvenes** this problem especially *o* particularly affects young people
2 (= *para un fin concreto*) specially • **un puente ~ construido al efecto** a bridge specially built for the purpose • **un plato ~ recomendado para diabéticos** a dish specially recommended for diabetics

especiar ▹ CONJUG 1b VT to spice

especie SF **1** (*Bio*) species • **la ~ humana** the human race ▸ **especie amenazada, especie en peligro** endangered species ▸ **especie protegida** protected species
2 (= *clase*) kind, sort • **una ~ de ...** a kind *o* sort of ...
3 • **en ~** in kind • **pagar en ~** to pay in kind
4 (= *noticia*) piece of news • **con la ~ de que ...** on the pretext that ... • **corre la ~ de que ha dimitido** there is a rumour that she has resigned, it is rumoured that she has resigned

especiero SM spice rack

especificación SF specification

específicamente ADV specifically

especificar ▹ CONJUG 1g VT [+ *cantidad, modelo*] to specify; (*en una lista*) to list, itemize

específico ADJ specific
SM (*Med*) specific

especifidad SF specific nature, specificity

espécimen SM (PL: **especímenes**) specimen

especioso ADJ specious, plausible

espectacular ADJ spectacular

espectacularidad SF spectacular nature • **de gran ~** very spectacular

espectacularmente ADV spectacularly, in spectacular fashion

espectáculo SM **1** (*Teat*) (= *representación*) show; (= *función*) performance • **sección de ~s** entertainment guide, entertainments section • **el deporte como ~** sport presented as show business • MODISMO: • **dar un ~** to make a scene ▸ **espectáculo de luz y sonido** sound and light show, son et lumière show

▸ **espectáculo de variedades** variety show
2 (= *visión asombrosa*) spectacle • **el ~ de las cataratas** the amazing spectacle *o* sight of the waterfalls, the spectacular waterfalls • **fue un ~ bochornoso** it was an embarrassing spectacle *o* sight
(ADJ INV) • **atletismo ~** athletics on the grand scale • **cine ~** epic films (*pl*) • **fútbol ~** soccer presented as show-biz • **programa ~** TV variety show • **restaurante ~** restaurant with a floor-show

espectador(a) (SM/F) **1** (*Cine, Dep, Teat*) spectator • **los ~es** (*Dep*) the spectators; (*Teat*) the audience (*sing*)
2 [*de acontecimiento, accidente*] onlooker

espectral (ADJ) **1** (*Fís*) spectral
2 (= *fantasmagórico*) ghostly

espectro (SM) **1** (*Fís*) spectrum • **de amplio ~** wide-ranging, covering a broad spectrum
2 (= *fantasma*) spectre, specter (*EEUU*), ghost • **el ~ del hambre** the spectre of famine

espectrógrafo (SM) spectrograph

espectrograma (SM) spectrogram

espectrometría (SF) spectrometry

espectrómetro (SM) spectrometer

espectroscopia (SF) spectroscopy

espectroscopio (SM) spectroscope

especulación (SF) **1** (= *suposición*) speculation
2 (*Com, Econ*) speculation ▸ **especulación bursátil** speculation on the stock exchange ▸ **especulación inmobiliaria** property speculation

especulador(a) (SM/F) speculator

especular[1] ▹ CONJUG 1a (VI) **1** (= *hacer cábalas*) to speculate (**sobre** about, on)
2 (*Com, Econ*) to speculate (**en, con** with)

especular[2] ▹ CONJUG 1a (VT) (*LAm*) to ruffle the hair of

especular[3] (ADJ) specular

especulativo (ADJ) speculative

espéculo (SM) (*Med*) speculum

espejado (ADJ) glossy, shining

espejeante (ADJ) gleaming, glistening

espejear ▹ CONJUG 1a (VI) to glint

espejeras (SFPL) (*Caribe*) chafing, chafed patch

espejismo (SM) **1** (*Ópt*) mirage
2 (= *ilusión*) mirage, illusion

espejito (SM) (= *espejo pequeño*) small mirror; [*de bolso*] handbag mirror

espejo (SM) **1** (= *para mirarse*) mirror • **mirarse al ~** to look at o.s. in the mirror ▸ **espejo de cuerpo entero** full-length mirror ▸ **espejo retrovisor** rear-view mirror
2 (= *reflejo*) mirror, reflection • **un ~ de caballerosidad** a model of chivalry • **la cara es el ~ del alma** the eyes are the windows of the soul
3 (*Zool*) white patch

espejoso (ADJ) = **espejado**

espejuelo (SM) **1** (= *espejo pequeño*) small looking-glass
2 espejuelos lenses, spectacles

espeleoarqueología (SF) cave archaeology

espeleobuceo (SM) cave diving

espeleología (SF) potholing, spelunking (*esp EEUU*), speleology (*frm*)

espeleólogo/a (SM/F) potholer, spelunker (*esp EEUU*), speleologist (*frm*)

espelta (SF) (*Bot*) spelt

espelunca (SF) (*liter*) cave

espeluznante (ADJ) hair-raising, horrifying

espeluzno (SM) (*Méx*) = **escalofrío**

espera (SF) **1** (= *acción*) wait • **la ~ fue interminable** it was an endless wait • **tras una ~ de tres horas** after a three-hour wait • **el asunto no tiene ~** the matter is most urgent • **en ~ de su contestación** awaiting your reply • **en ~ de que llegue** waiting for him to arrive • **estar a la ~ de algo** to be expecting sth • **quedo a la ~ de su respuesta** (*en correspondencia*) I look forward to hearing from you
2 (= *paciencia*) patience • **es que no tienes ~** you have no patience
3 (*Jur*) stay, respite

esperable (ADJ) • **ser ~** to be hoped for

esperado (ADJ) **1** (= *previsto*) [*resultados*] expected
2 (= *deseado*) • **el acontecimiento más ~ del año** the most keenly anticipated event of the year

esperantista (SMF) Esperantist

esperanto (SM) Esperanto

esperanza (SF) hope • **acudimos a ti como última ~** we're turning to you as our last hope • **la nueva ~ del cine español** the bright young hope of Spanish cinema • **hay pocas ~s de que venga** there is little hope that he'll come • **abrigar** *o* **albergar ~s de hacer algo** to cherish hopes of doing sth • **ya no abrigamos ~s de encontrarlo con vida** we no longer hold out any hope of finding him alive • **ser la gran ~ blanca** to be the great white hope • **con la ~ de que ...** in the hope that ... • **dar ~(s) a algn** to give sb hope • **perder la ~** to lose hope • **poner la ~ en algn/algo** to pin one's hopes on sb/sth • **tenemos todas nuestras ~s puestas en él** we have pinned all our hopes on him • **tener ~ en algo** to have hope for sth • **tener ~(s) de hacer algo** to have hope(s) of doing sth • **todavía tengo ~s de que llegue a tiempo** I still hope it will arrive on time • MODISMOS: • **alimentarse** *o* **vivir de ~s** to live on hopes • **¡qué ~!** (*LAm*) some hope!, not on your life!* • **la ~ es lo último que se pierde** there's always hope • **mientras haya vida hay ~** while there's life there's hope ▸ **esperanza de vida** life expectancy

esperanzado (ADJ) hopeful • **estar ~ con** *o* **en algo** to be hopeful of sth

esperanzador (ADJ) [*perspectiva, futuro*] hopeful; [*noticia, resultado, tratamiento*] encouraging, hopeful, promising • **los resultados de la encuesta no pueden ser más ~es** the results of the survey could not be more encouraging *o* hopeful *o* promising

esperanzadoramente (ADV) encouragingly, promisingly • **los resultados de este año han mejorado ~** there has been an encouraging improvement *o* a promising improvement in this year's results, this year's results have improved encouragingly *o* promisingly

esperanzar ▹ CONJUG 1f (VT) • **~ a algn** to give hope to sb • **las mejoras laborales han esperanzado a los trabajadores** improvements in working conditions have given hope to the workers • **los abogados no quisieron ~lo** the lawyers did not want to raise his hopes *o* get his hopes up

esperar ▹ CONJUG 1a (VT) **1** (= *aguardar*) [+ *tren, persona*] to wait for • **estaba esperando el avión** I was waiting for the plane • **esperaban noticias de los rehenes** they were waiting for *o* awaiting news of the hostages • **fuimos a ~la a la estación** we went to meet her at the station • **nos espera un duro invierno** we've got a hard winter ahead of us • **¡la que te espera cuando llegues a casa!** you're (in) for it when you get home! • MODISMO: • **de aquí te espero***: • **un lío de aquí te espero*** a tremendous row* • **dijo unas tonterías de aquí te espero** he said some really stupid things
2 (= *desear*) to hope • **espero llegar a tiempo** I hope to arrive on time • **eso espero** I hope so • **han prometido castigar a los culpables y espero que sea así** they've promised to punish those responsible and I hope they will • **—ya nos pagará —espero que sea así** "he'll pay us, you'll see" — "I hope you're right *o* I hope so" • **espero que te haya gustado** I hope you liked it • **espero que vengas** I hope you'll come • **espero que no sea nada grave** I hope it isn't anything serious • **—¿vienen a la fiesta? —espero que sí** "are they coming to the party?" — "I hope so" • **—¿crees que se enfadará? —espero que no** "do you think she will be angry?" — "I hope not"
3 (= *contar con*) to expect • **¿esperas visita?** are you expecting someone? • **espero su llamada en cualquier momento** I expect his call at any moment • **no me esperes antes de las siete** don't expect me before seven • **¿acaso esperas que pague yo?** you're not expecting me to pay, are you? • **llegaron antes de lo que yo esperaba** they arrived sooner than I expected • **esperaban que les pidiera perdón** they were expecting him to apologize • **¿qué esperas, que encima te lo agradezca?** don't expect me to thank you for it as well • **¿qué puedes ~ de él, después de cómo se ha comportado?** what do you expect from him, after the way he has behaved? • **era de ~** it was to be expected • **era de ~ que eso sucediera** it was to be expected that that would happen • **era de ~ que no viniera** it was to be expected that he wouldn't come • **no esperaba menos de ti** I expected nothing *o* no less of you • **llamará cuando menos te lo esperes** he'll call when you least expect it • MODISMO: • **~ algo como agua de mayo** to await sth with eager anticipation
4 [+ *bebé*] • **está esperando un hijo** she's expecting (a baby) • **está esperando su primer hijo** she's expecting her first child
(VI) **1** (= *aguardar*) to wait • **-é aquí** I'll wait here • **¡espera un momento, este no es mi libro!** hold on *o* wait a minute, this isn't my book! • **espera en la puerta, ahora mismo voy** wait at the door, I'm just coming • **~ a** *o* **hasta que algn haga algo** to wait for sb to do sth • **hacer ~ a algn** keep sb waiting • **su respuesta no se hizo ~** his answer wasn't long in coming • MODISMOS: • **~ desesperando** to hope against hope • **espera y verás** wait and see • **puedes ~ sentado** you've got another think coming • REFRÁN: • **el que espera desespera** a watched pot never boils
2 • **~ en algn** to put one's hopes *o* trust in sb • **~ en Dios** to trust in God
(VPR) **esperarse 1** (*uso impersonal*) to be expected • **como podía ~se** as was to be expected • **no fue tan bueno como se esperaba** it was not as good as expected • **se espera que asistan más de mil personas** more than a thousand people are expected to attend
2* (= *uso enfático*) • **¡espérate un momento!** wait a minute!, hold on a minute! • **espérate a que deje de llover** wait until it stops raining • **¡no es lo que me esperaba!** it's not what I was expecting! • **¡me lo esperaba!** I was expecting this!

esperma (SM o SF) **1** (*Bio*) sperm • **~ de ballena** spermaceti
2 (*Caribe, Col*) (= *vela*) candle

espermaceti (SM) spermaceti

espermatozoide (SM), **espermatozoo** (SM) spermatozoon

ESPERAR

Esperar *tiene en inglés varias traducciones, entre las que se encuentran* **wait (for)**, **await**, **hope** *y* **expect**.

▸ *Se traduce por* **wait (for)** *cuando* **esperar** *se refiere al hecho de aguardar la llegada de alguien o de un suceso:*

Hice el examen hace dos meses y todavía estoy esperando los resultados
I took the exam two months ago and I'm still waiting for the results
La esperó media hora y después se fue a casa
He waited half an hour for her and then went home

▸ *El verbo* **await** *es un verbo de uso similar a* **wait for**, *aunque no requiere el uso de la preposición y no es muy corriente en inglés moderno:*

Esperaban ansiosamente la llegada del Rey
They eagerly awaited the arrival of the King

▸ *Se traduce por* **hope** *cuando deseamos que algo suceda, pero no estamos seguros de si ocurrirá o no:*

Espero que no se enfade mucho conmigo
I hope (that) she won't be very annoyed with me
Después de terminar la carrera espero conseguir un buen trabajo
I hope to get a good job when I finish university

▸ *Traducimos* **esperar** *por* **expect** *cuando estamos muy seguros de que algo va a suceder o cuando hay una razón lógica para que algo suceda:*

Espero aprobar porque el examen me salió muy bien
I expect to pass *o* I expect I'll pass because the exam went very well
Ha resultado mejor de lo que esperábamos
It was better than we expected
Está esperando un niño
She's expecting (a baby)

Para otros usos y ejemplos ver la entrada.

espermicida SM spermicide
espermio SM sperm
espernancarse ▹ CONJUG 1g VPR (*LAm*) = **esparrancarse**
esperón SM (*Caribe*) long wait
esperpéntico ADJ **1** (= *absurdo*) absurd, nonsensical
2 (= *grotesco*) grotesque, exaggerated
esperpentización SF presentation in an absurd *o* grotesque *etc* manner, caricaturing
esperpentizar ▹ CONJUG 1f VT to present in an absurd *o* grotesque *etc* way, caricature
esperpento SM **1** (= *persona fea*) fright*, sight*
2 (= *disparate*) nonsense • **lo que dijo no eran más que ~s** what he said was absolute nonsense
3 (*Teat*) *play which focuses on the grotesque*
4 (= *cuento*) macabre story, grotesque tale

ESPERPENTO

Esperpento is a type of theatre developed by Ramón del Valle-Inclán (1869-1936) focusing on characters whose physical and psychological characteristics have been deliberately deformed and warped to the point where they become grotesque caricatures. Valle-Inclán used this **esperpento** as a vehicle for social and political satire.

espesante SM thickener, thickening agent
espesar ▹ CONJUG 1a VT **1** (= *hacer más espeso*) [+ *líquido, chocolate*] to thicken; [+ *sustancia*] to make dense, make denser
2 (= *hacer más tupido*) [+ *tapiz*] to weave tighter; [+ *jersey, chaqueta*] to knit tighter
VPR **espesarse** [*líquido*] to thicken, get thicker; [*bosque, niebla, humo*] to get denser, get thicker; [*sangre*] to coagulate, solidify
espeso ADJ **1** (*gen*) thick; [*bosque*] dense; [*pasta*] stiff; [*líquido*] thick, heavy
2 (= *sucio*) dirty, untidy
espesor SM (*gen*) thickness; [*de nieve*] depth • **tiene medio metro de ~** it is half a metre thick
espesura SF **1** (= *espesor*) thickness; (= *densidad*) density • **en la ~ de la selva** in the thick *o* heart *o* depths of the jungle
2 (*Bot*) thicket, overgrown place • **se refugiaron en las ~s de la sierra** (*liter*) they took refuge in the mountain fastnesses (*liter*)
3 (= *suciedad*) dirtiness, untidiness
espeta‡ SM cop*
espetar ▹ CONJUG 1a VT **1** (= *atravesar*) (*gen*) to transfix, pierce, run through; [+ *carne*] to skewer, spit
2 (= *realizar*) [+ *orden*] to rap out; [+ *lección, sermón*] to read; [+ *pregunta*] to fire • **~ algo a algn** to spring sth on sb, broach a subject (unexpectedly) with sb
VPR **espetarse 1** (= *ponerse cómodo*) to steady o.s., settle o.s.
2 (= *envanecerse*) to get on one's high horse
espetera‡ SF tits*‡ (*pl*)
espetón SM **1** (*Culin*) (= *broqueta*) skewer; (= *asador*) spit; (= *clavija*) large pin, iron pin; (= *atizador*) poker
2 (= *pinchazo*) jab, poke
espía SMF spy
ADJ • **avión ~** spy plane • **buque ~** spy ship • **satélite ~** spy satellite
espiantar* ▹ CONJUG 1a VT (*Cono Sur*) (= *robar*) to pinch*
VI, VPR **espiantarse** (*Cono Sur*) to scram*, beat it*
espiar ▹ CONJUG 1c VT **1** (= *vigilar*) to spy on, keep (a) watch on
2 (*LAm*) (= *mirar*) to look at, watch
VI to spy
espich* SM (*LAm*) = **espiche**¹
espicha SF (*Asturias*) cider party
espichar¹ ▹ CONJUG 1a VT **1** • **MODISMO:** • **~la(s)**‡ to kick the bucket*, peg out‡
2 (= *pinchar*) to prick
3 (*Cono Sur*) (= *entregar*) to hand over reluctantly, relinquish
4 (*And, Cono Sur*) (*Téc*) to put a tap on
VI ‡ to kick the bucket*, peg out‡
VPR **espicharse 1** (*LAm*) (= *enflaquecerse*) to get thin
2 (*And*) [*neumático*] to go flat
3 (*CAm*) (= *asustarse*) to get scared, get frightened
espichar²* ▹ CONJUG 1a VI (*LAm*) (= *pronunciar un discurso*) to make a speech, speechify*
espiche¹* SM (*LAm*) speech
espiche² SM spike
espidómetro SM (*LAm*) speedometer
espiedo SM (*Cono Sur*) spit
espiga SF **1** (*Bot*) [*de trigo*] ear; [*de flores*] spike
2 (*Téc*) (*gen*) spigot; [*de pestillo*] shaft; [*de cuchillo, herramienta*] tang
3 (= *badajo*) clapper
4 (*Mil*) fuse
5 (*Náut*) masthead
espigadera SF gleaner
espigado ADJ **1** (*Bot*) (= *maduro*) ripe; (= *con grano*) ready to seed
2 [*persona*] tall and slim, willowy
espigador(a) SM/F gleaner
espigar ▹ CONJUG 1h VT **1** [+ *fruta*] to look closely at, scrutinize
2 [+ *libro*] to consult
3 (*Téc*) to pin, peg
VI **1** [*cereales*] to come into ear, form ears; [*flor*] to run to seed
2 [*persona joven*] to shoot up, get very tall
VPR **espigarse** [*persona joven*] to shoot up, get very tall
espigón SM **1** (*Bot*) ear, spike
2 (*Zool*) sting
3 [*de herramienta*] sharp point, spike
4 (= *malecón*) breakwater
espigueo SM gleaning
espiguero SM (*Méx*) granary
espiguilla SF herring-bone pattern
espín SM porcupine
espina SF **1** (*Bot*) [*de rosal*] thorn; [*de chumbera*] prickle • **MODISMOS:** • **mala ~** spite, resentment, ill-will • **me da mala ~** it makes me suspicious • **estar en ~s** to be on tenterhooks, be all on edge • **sacarse la ~** to get even, pay off an old score
2 [*de pez*] bone
3 (*Anat*) (*tb* **espina dorsal**) spine • **doblar la ~** to bend over ▸ **espina bífida** spina bifida
4 (= *problema*) worry, suspicion
espinaca SF (*Bot*) spinach • **~s** (*Culin*) spinach (*pl*) • **no me gustan las ~s** I don't like spinach
espinal ADJ spinal
espinaquer SM spinnaker
espinar ▹ CONJUG 1a VT **1** (= *punzar*) to prick
2 (= *ofender*) to sting, hurt, nettle
VPR **espinarse** to prick o.s.
SM **1** (*Bot*) thicket, thornbrake, thorny place
2 (= *dificultad*) difficulty
espinazo SM spine, backbone • **MODISMO:** • **doblar el ~*** to knuckle under*
espineta SF (*Mús*) spinet
espingarda SF **1** (*Hist*) (= *cañón*) *kind of cannon*; (= *mosquete*) Moorish musket
2* (= *chica*) lanky girl
espinglés SM (*hum*) Spanglish
espinilla SF **1** (= *tibia*) shin, shinbone, shank (EEUU)
2 (*en la piel*) blackhead
espinillera SF shinpad, shinguard
espinita SF irritation
espino SM ▸ **espino albar, espino blanco** hawthorn ▸ **espino cerval** buckthorn ▸ **espino negro** blackthorn, sloe
espinoso ADJ **1** (= *con espinas*) [*rosal*] thorny; [*chumbera*] prickly; [*pez*] bony
2 [*problema*] knotty, thorny
SM stickleback
espinudo ADJ (*LAm*) = **espinoso**
espión SM spy
espionaje SM espionage, spying • **novela de ~** spy story ▸ **espionaje industrial** industrial espionage
espíquer SM (*Téc*) speaker
espira SF **1** (*Mat*) spire
2 (*Zool*) whorl, ring
3 (*Elec*) turn
espiráculo SM blow hole, spiracle (*frm*)

espiral ADJ (*gen*) spiral; [*movimiento, línea*] spiral; (*Téc*) helical
SM [*de reloj*] hairspring
SF (= *forma*) (*gen*) spiral; (*anticonceptiva*) coil; (*Téc*) whorl; [*de humo*] spiral; (*Dep*) corkscrew dive • **la ~ inflacionista** the inflationary spiral • **el humo subía en ~** the smoke went spiralling up • **dar vueltas en ~** to spiral

espiralado ADJ spiral

espirar ▸ CONJUG 1a VT [+ *aire, humo*] to breathe out, exhale; [+ *olor*] to give off, give out
VI to breathe out, exhale

espirea SF spiraea

espiritado ADJ like a wraith, ghost-like

espiritismo SM spiritualism

espiritista ADJ spiritualist, spiritualistic
SMF spiritualist, spiritualistic

espiritoso ADJ **1** [*bebida*] alcoholic, spirituous (*frm*) • **licores espirituosos** spirits
2 [*persona*] spirited, lively

espíritu SM **1** (= *lo inmaterial*) spirit • **pobre de ~** poor in spirit • **levantar el ~ de algn** to raise sb's spirits • **en la letra y en el ~** in the letter and in the spirit ▸ **espíritu de cuerpo** esprit de corps ▸ **espíritu de equipo** team spirit ▸ **espíritu de lucha** fighting spirit ▸ **espíritu guerrero** fighting spirit
2 [*de persona*] (= *mente*) mind • **con ~ amplio** with an open mind • **de ~ crítico** of a critical turn of mind • **edificar el ~ de algn** to improve sb's mind
3 (*Rel*) spirit • MODISMO: • **dar** *o* **rendir el ~** to give up the ghost ▸ **Espíritu Santo** Holy Ghost, Holy Spirit
4 (= *aparecido*) spirit, ghost ▸ **espíritu maligno** evil spirit
5 (= *alcohol*) spirits (*pl*), liquor ▸ **espíritu de vino** spirits of wine (*pl*)

espiritual ADJ **1** [*vida, patria, poderes*] spiritual
2 (= *fantasmal*) unworldly, ghostly
3 (*And, Cono Sur*) (= *gracioso*) funny, witty
SM spiritual, Negro spiritual

espiritualidad SF spirituality

espiritualismo SM spiritualism

espiritualista ADJ spiritualistic
SMF spiritualist

espiritualización SF spiritualization

espiritualizar ▸ CONJUG 1f VT to spiritualize

espiritualmente ADV spiritually

espirituoso = espiritoso

espita SF **1** (*Téc*) (= *grifo*) tap, spigot (EEUU) • MODISMO: • **abrir la ~ de las lágrimas** (*hum*) to weep buckets* ▸ **espita de entrada del gas** gas tap
2* (= *borracho*) drunkard, boozer*, lush (EEUU‡)
3‡ [*de hombre*] prick**

espitar ▸ CONJUG 1a VT to tap, broach

espitoso‡ ADJ (= *eufórico*) hyper*

espléndidamente ADV **1** (= *magníficamente*) splendidly, magnificently
2 (= *generosamente*) lavishly, generously • **se gratificará** ~ there will be a generous reward

esplendidez SF **1** (= *magnificencia*) splendour, splendor (EEUU), magnificence
2 (= *generosidad*) lavishness, generosity
3 (= *pompa*) pomp

espléndido ADJ **1** (= *magnífico*) splendid, magnificent
2 (= *generoso*) lavish, generous

esplendor SM **1** (= *magnificencia*) splendour, splendor (EEUU), magnificence
2 (= *resplandor*) brilliance, radiance

esplendoroso ADJ **1** (= *magnífico*) magnificent
2 (= *resplandeciente*) brilliant, radiant

esplénico ADJ splenetic

espliego SM lavender

esplín SM melancholy, depression, the blues

espolada SF **1** (= *espolazo*) prick with a spur
2 ▸ **espolada de vino*** swig of wine*

espolazo SM prick with a spur

espolear ▸ CONJUG 1a VT **1** [+ *caballo*] to spur, spur on
2 (*para estudiar, ganar*) to spur on

espoleta SF **1** (*Mil*) fuse ▸ **espoleta de tiempo** time-fuse
2 (*Anat*) wishbone

espolón SM **1** (*Zool*) [*de gallo*] spur; [*de caballo*] fetlock
2 (*Geog*) spur (*of a mountain range*)
3 (*Náut*) (= *proa*) stem; (*para atacar*) ram
4 (= *malecón*) sea wall, dike; (= *contrafuerte*) buttress; [*de puente*] cutwater
5 (= *paseo*) promenade
6 (*Med**) chilblain
ADJ (*And**) (= *astuto*) sharp, astute

espolvoreador SM dredge

espolvorear ▸ CONJUG 1a VT to dust, sprinkle (**de** with) • **espolvoree harina sobre la superficie** dust the surface with flour

espondeo SM spondee

espongiforme ADJ (*Med*) spongiform

esponja SF **1** (*para el aseo*) sponge • MODISMOS: • **arrojar la ~** to throw in the towel • **beber como una ~** to drink like a fish • **pasemos la ~ por todo aquello** let's forget all about it ▸ **esponja de baño** bath sponge
2* (= *gorrón*) sponger*
3 (*Cono Sur, Méx‡*) (= *bebedor*) drunkard, boozer*, lush (EEUU‡)

esponjado ADJ **1** [*material*] spongy; [*toalla, jersey*] fluffy
2 [*persona*] puffed up, pompous

esponjar ▸ CONJUG 1a VT to fluff up, make fluffy
VPR **esponjarse 1** (= *hacerse esponjoso*) [*lana*] to fluff up, become fluffy; [*masa*] to rise
2 (= *engreírse*) to swell with pride, be puffed up
3 (= *rebosar salud*) to glow with health
4 (= *tener aspecto próspero*) to look prosperous

esponjera SF sponge bag, make-up bag

esponjosidad SF sponginess

esponjoso ADJ [*material*] (= *blando*) spongy; (= *poroso*) porous; [*toalla, jersey*] fluffy, springy

esponsales SMPL betrothal (*sing*)

esponsor SMF, **espónsor** SMF sponsor

esponsorizar ▸ CONJUG 1f VT to sponsor

espontáneamente ADV spontaneously

espontanearse ▸ CONJUG 1a VPR (= *confesar*) to own up; (= *hablar francamente*) to speak frankly; (= *desahogarse*) to unbosom o.s., open up (**con** to)

espontaneidad SF spontaneity

espontaneísmo SM amateurish enthusiasm, enthusiasm without experience

espontáneo/a ADJ **1** (= *sin reflexión*) spontaneous
2 (= *improvisado*) [*discurso, representación*] impromptu; [*persona*] natural
SM/F **1** (*Taur*) *spectator who rushes into the ring and attempts to take part*
2† (= *bombero*) volunteer fireman/firewoman

espora SF spore

esporádicamente ADV sporadically

esporádico ADJ sporadic

esportillo SM basket, pannier

esportivo ADJ (*LAm*) sporty

esportón SM large basket • MODISMO: • **a esportones** in vast quantities, by the ton

esposar ▸ CONJUG 1a VT to handcuff

esposas SFPL handcuffs • **poner las ~ a algn** to handcuff sb, put sb in handcuffs

esposo/a SM/F husband/wife • **los ~s** husband and wife, the couple

espray SM = spray

esprín SM (*CAm*) interior sprung mattress

esprint [es'prin] SM (PL: **esprints** *o* **esprintes**) sprint

esprintar ▸ CONJUG 1a VI to sprint

esprinter SMF (PL: **esprinters**), **esprínter** SMF (PL: **esprínters**) sprinter

espuela SF **1** (*lit, fig*) spur ▸ **espuela de caballero** (*Bot*) larkspur
2 (*And*) [*de mujer*] feminine charm; (= *coquetería*) coquettishness
3 (*And*) (*Com*) skill in business, acumen

espueleado ADJ (*And, Caribe*) tested, tried

espuelear* ▸ CONJUG 1a VT **1** (*LAm*) (= *espolear*) to spur, spur on
2 (*And, Caribe*) (= *probar*) to test, try out

espuelón ADJ (*And*) sharp, astute

espuerta SF basket, pannier • MODISMO: • **a ~s** in vast quantities, by the ton

espulgar ▸ CONJUG 1h VT **1** (= *quitar la pulgas a*) to delouse, get the lice *o* fleas out of
2† [+ *obra, novela*] to scrutinize

espuma SF **1** (= *burbujas*) [*de las olas*] surf, foam; [*de jabón, champú*] foam, lather; [*de cerveza*] head; [*de cava, champán*] froth; [*de afeitar*] foam; [*del caldo*] scum • **echar ~** to foam, froth • **el perro echaba ~ por la boca** the dog was foaming *o* frothing at the mouth • **hacer ~** to foam, froth • MODISMO: • **crecer como la ~** to mushroom ▸ **espuma de afeitar** shaving foam ▸ **espuma de baño** bubble bath, foam bath ▸ **espuma de mar** (= *mineral*) meerschaum ▸ **espuma seca** carpet shampoo
2 (= *gomaespuma*) foam, foam rubber • **un colchón de ~** a foam(-rubber) mattress ▸ **espuma de caucho, espuma de látex** foam rubber
3 (= *tejido*) (*tb* **espuma de nylon**) stretch nylon • **medias de ~** stretch tights

espumadera SF, **espumador** SM skimming ladle, skimmer

espumajear ▸ CONJUG 1a VI to foam at the mouth

espumajo SM froth, foam (*at the mouth*)

espumajoso ADJ frothy, foamy

espumar ▸ CONJUG 1a VT (= *quitar espuma a*) to skim off
VI [*cerveza*] to froth, foam; [*vino*] to sparkle

espumarajo SM froth, foam (*at the mouth*) • **echar ~s (de rabia)** to splutter with rage

espumear ▸ CONJUG 1a VI to foam

espumilla SF (*LAm*) meringue

espumillón SM tinsel

espumoso ADJ [*cerveza*] frothy; [*jabón*] foamy; [*baño*] foaming; [*vino*] sparkling

espúreo ADJ, **espurio** ADJ (= *falso*) spurious; [*niño*] illegitimate, bastard

esputar ▸ CONJUG 1a VT to cough up, expectorate (*frm*)
VI to cough up sputum, expectorate (*frm*)

esputo SM (= *escupitajo*) spit, spittle; (*Med*) sputum

esqueje SM cutting

esquela SF **1** (= *anuncio*) notice, announcement ▸ **esquela de defunción, esquela mortuoria** announcement of death, death notice
2 (= *nota*) note
3† (= *carta breve*) short letter ▸ **esquela amorosa** love letter, billet doux

esquelético ADJ skeletal, skinny*

esqueleto SM **1** (*Anat*) skeleton • MODISMOS: • **menear** *o* **mover el ~*** to strut one's stuff*, dance • **tumbar el ~*** to hit the hay*, hit the sack*, go to bed
2 (= *estructura*) (*gen*) skeleton; (= *de asunto*)

bare bones (*pl*); [*de edificio*] framework; [*de conferencia, novela*] framework, structure • **en ~** unfinished, incomplete
3 (*Chile*) (*Literat*) (= *borrador*) rough draft, outline
4 (*And, CAm, Méx*) (= *formulario*) form

esquema SM **1** (*en esbozo*) (= *resumen*) outline; (= *diagrama*) diagram; (= *dibujo*) sketch • **me hice un ~ de la lección** I prepared an outline of the lesson • **un ~ de conexiones eléctricas** a wiring diagram • **le hice un ~ del centro de la ciudad** I did him a sketch map of the centre of town
2 (= *conjunto de ideas*) thinking, way of thinking • **sus ~s mentales están anclados en el pasado** his thinking *o* way of thinking is rooted in the past • **criticó los ~s ideológicos del partido** he criticized the party's ideology • MODISMOS: • **romper ~s** to break the mould • **romperle los ~s a algn***: • **no me imaginaba que fueras a hacerte monja, me has roto todos los ~s** I never imagined you'd become a nun, you've really thrown me*
3 (*Rel, Fil*) schema

esquemáticamente ADV schematically

esquemático ADJ schematic • **un resumen ~** an outline

esquematizar ▷ CONJUG 1f VT to outline

esquí SM (PL: **esquís, esquíes**) **1** (= *tabla*) ski
2 (*Dep*) skiing • **hacer ~** to go skiing ▸ **esquí acuático** water skiing ▸ **esquí alpino** alpine skiing ▸ **esquí de fondo, esquí de travesía** cross-country skiing, ski touring (*EEUU*) ▸ **esquí náutico** water skiing

esquiable ADJ • **pista ~** slope suitable for skiing, slope that can be skied on

esquiador(a) SM/F skier ▸ **esquiador(a) acuático/a, esquiador(a) náutico/a** water skier

esquiar ▷ CONJUG 1c VI to ski

esquife SM skiff

esquijama SM winter pyjamas (*pl*) *o* (*EEUU*) pajamas (*pl*)

esquila[1] SF (= *campanilla*) small bell, handbell; (= *cencerro*) cowbell

esquila[2] SF, **esquilado** SM [*de ovejas*] shearing

esquilador(a) SM/F (= *persona*) (sheep) shearer

esquiladora SF (= *máquina*) shearing machine, clipping machine

esquilar ▷ CONJUG 1a VT [+ *ovejas*] to shear; [+ *pelo*] to clip, crop

esquileo SM shearing

esquilimoso ADJ fastidious, finicky

esquilmamiento SM [*de tierra*] impoverishment; [*de recursos*] exhaustion

esquilmar ▷ CONJUG 1a VT **1** [+ *cosecha*] to harvest
2 [+ *tierra*] to impoverish, exhaust
3* [+ *jugador*] to skin*

esquilmo SM harvest, crop, yield

Esquilo SM Aeschylus

esquimal ADJ Eskimo
SMF Eskimo
SM (*Ling*) Eskimo

esquina SF **1** (= *vértice*) corner • **a la vuelta de la ~** (*lit*) around the corner; (*fig*) just around the corner • **las vacaciones están a la vuelta de la ~** the holidays are just around the corner • **sacar de ~** to take a corner kick • **doblar la ~** (*lit*) to turn the corner; (*Cono Sur**) (= *morir*) to die, kick the bucket* • **hacer ~** [*edificio*] to be on the corner; [*calles*] to meet
2 (*Dep*) corner
3 (*LAm*) (= *tienda*) corner shop, village shop
4 • **la ~*** the game*, prostitution

esquinado ADJ **1** (= *con esquinas*) sharp-cornered, having corners
2 (*Ftbl*) swerving, with a spin on it • **tiro ~** low shot into the corner of the net
3 (*LAm*) [*mueble*] standing in a corner, corner (*antes de s*)
4 [*persona*] (= *antipático*) unpleasant; (= *difícil*) awkward, prickly; (= *malévolo*) malicious
5 [*noticia*] malicious, ill-intentioned

esquinar ▷ CONJUG 1a VT **1** (*Dep*) to put in a corner
2 (= *hacer esquina con*) to form a corner with
3 (= *estar en la esquina de*) to be on the corner of
4 [+ *madera*] to square, square off
5 [+ *pelota*] to swerve, slice
6 [+ *personas*] to set at odds
VI • **~ con** (= *hacer esquina*) to form a corner with; (= *estar en la esquina*) to be on the corner of
VPR **esquinarse 1** (= *pelearse*) to quarrel, fall out (**con** with)
2 (= *estar resentido*) to get a chip on one's shoulder

esquinazo SM **1*** (= *esquina*) corner
2 (*Cono Sur*) (= *serenata*) serenade
3 • MODISMO: • **dar ~ a algn** to give sb the slip, shake sb off

esquinera SF **1*** (= *prostituta*) tart*, hooker (*EEUU**)
2 (*LAm*) (= *mueble*) corner cupboard

esquinero/a ADJ corner (*antes de s*) • **farol ~** corner lamppost, lamppost on the corner • **café ~** corner café
SM/F* (= *persona*) idler, layabout

esquirla SF splinter

esquirol SMF strikebreaker, blackleg, scab*

esquirolada SF strike-breaking action, work of a scab*

esquirolaje SM, **esquirolismo** SM strikebreaking, blacklegging, scabbing*

esquisto SM schist

esquites SMPL (*CAm, Méx*) popcorn

esquivada SF (*LAm*) evasion, dodge

esquivar ▷ CONJUG 1a VT (= *evitar*) to avoid, shun; (= *evadir*) to dodge, side-step • **~ un golpe** to dodge a blow • **~ el contacto con algn** to avoid meeting sb • **~ hacer algo** to avoid doing sth, be chary of doing sth
VPR **esquivarse** (= *retirarse*) to shy away; (= *evadirse*) to dodge

esquivez SF **1** (= *timidez*) shyness; (= *despego*) unsociability; (= *elusión*) elusiveness; (= *evasiva*) evasiveness
2 (= *desdén*) scorn

esquivo ADJ **1** [*persona*] (= *tímido*) shy; (= *huraño*) unsociable; (= *difícil de encontrar*) elusive; (= *evasivo*) evasive
2 (= *despreciativo*) scornful

esquizo* ADJ, SMF schizo*

esquizofrenia SF schizophrenia

esquizofrénico/a ADJ, SM/F schizophrenic

esquizoide ADJ, SMF schizoid

esta[1] ADJ DEM ▸ **este**[2]

esta[2] PRON DEM, **ésta** PRON DEM ▸ **este**[3]

está ▷ **estar**

estabilidad SF stability

estabilización SF stabilization

estabilizador ADJ stabilizing
SM (*gen*) stabilizer; (*Aut*) anti-roll bar ▸ **estabilizador de cola** tailplane, rudder

estabilizante ADJ stabilizing
SM stabilizer

estabilizar ▷ CONJUG 1f VT **1** [+ *objeto*] (= *dar estabilidad a*) to stabilize; (= *fijar*) to make steady
2 [+ *precios*] to stabilize
VPR **estabilizarse 1** [*objeto, precios*] to become stable, become stabilized
2 [*persona*] to settle down

estable ADJ **1** (= *permanente*) [*pareja, hogar, mercado, bolsa, paz*] stable; [*relación*] stable, steady; [*empleo*] steady; [*inquilino, cliente*] regular
2 (*Fís, Quím*) stable

establecer ▷ CONJUG 2d VT **1** [+ *relación, comunicación*] to establish • **han logrado ~ contacto con el barco** they've managed to make *o* establish contact with the boat • **una reunión para ~ el precio del petróleo** a meeting to set *o* fix oil prices • **han establecido controles policiales** they have set up police checkpoints
2 (= *fundar*) [+ *empresa*] to establish; [+ *colonia*] to settle • **ha establecido su domicilio en Lugo** he's taken up residence in Lugo
3 (= *dictaminar*) to state, lay down • **la ley establece que ...** the law states *o* lays down that ...
4 (= *expresar*) [+ *idea, principio*] to establish; [+ *norma*] to lay down; [+ *criterio*] to set • **para ~ los límites de los poderes del presidente** to establish the extent of the President's powers • **una comisión para ~ la verdad de los hechos** a commission to establish the truth about what happened
5 [+ *récord*] to set
VPR **establecerse 1** (= *fijar residencia*) to settle • **la familia se estableció en Madrid** the family settled in Madrid
2 (= *abrir un negocio*) to set up (a business), open up (a business) • **~se por cuenta propia** to set up on one's own, open up one's own business

establecido ADJ [*orden*] established

establecimiento SM **1** (= *acto*) establishment, setting-up, founding; (= *fundación*) institution; [*de colonias*] establishment ▸ **establecimiento de llamada** minimum call charge
2 (= *local*) (*gen*) establishment; (= *bar*) bar; (= *tienda*) shop; (*Cono Sur*) plant, works (*pl*) ▸ **establecimiento central** head office ▸ **establecimiento comercial** business house, commercial establishment
3 (*Jur*) statute, ordinance

establero SM stableboy, groom

establishment SM (PL: **establishments**) establishment

establo SM **1** [*de ganado*] cowshed, stall; (*esp LAm*) (= *granero*) barn; (= *lugar sucio*) pigsty ▸ **establos de Augías** Augean stables
2 (*Caribe*) (= *garaje*) garage

estaca SF **1** (= *poste*) stake, post; [*de tienda de campaña*] peg; (= *porra*) cudgel, stick • MODISMO: • **plantar la ~**** to have a crap**
2 (*Agr*) cutting
3 (*LAm*) (*Min*) large mining claim, large mining concession
4 (*And, Cono Sur*) (= *espuela*) spur
5 • MODISMO: • **arrancar la ~** (*Méx*) to champ at the bit, strain at the leash
6 (*Caribe*) (= *indirecta*) hint; (= *pulla*) taunt

estacada SF **1** (= *cerca*) fence, fencing; (*Mil*) stockade, palisade; (*LAm*) (= *malecón*) dike • MODISMOS: • **dejar a algn en la ~** to leave sb in the lurch • **estar *o* quedar en la ~** (= *estar en apuros*) to be in a jam *o* fix, be left in the lurch; (= *fracasar*) to fail disastrously, be a total disaster*
2 (*LAm*) (= *herida*) wound

estacar ▷ CONJUG 1g VT **1** (*LAm*) (= *herir*) to wound; (= *pinchar*) to prick
2 [+ *tierra, propiedad*] to stake out, stake off
3 [+ *animal*] to tie to a post
4 (*And, Caribe*) (= *engañar*) to deceive
VPR **estacarse 1** (= *quedarse inmóvil*) to stand rooted to the spot, stand stiff as a pole

2 • **~se un pie** (*And, CAm, Caribe*) to prick o.s. in the foot
estacha SF line, mooring rope
estación SF **1** (*gen*) station ▸ **estación ballenera** whaling station ▸ **estación balnearia** (*medicinal*) spa; (*de mar*) seaside resort ▸ **estación biológica** biological research station ▸ **estación carbonera** coaling station ▸ **estación clasificadora** marshalling yard ▸ **estación cósmica** space station ▸ **estación de autobuses** bus station ▸ **estación de bombeo** pumping station ▸ **estación de bomberos** (*Col*) fire station ▸ **estación de cabeza** terminus ▸ **estación de contenedores** container terminal ▸ **estación de empalme, estación de enlace** junction ▸ **estación de escucha** listening post ▸ **estación de esquí** ski resort ▸ **estación de ferrocarril** railway station ▸ **estación de fuerza** power station ▸ **estación de gasolina** petrol station, gas station (*EEUU*) ▸ **estación de invierno** winter sports resort ▸ **estación de mercancías** goods station ▸ **estación de peaje** line of toll booths, toll plaza (*EEUU*) ▸ **estación de policía** (*Col*) police station ▸ **estación depuradora** sewage works, sewage farm ▸ **estación de rastreo, estación de seguimiento** tracking station ▸ **estación de servicio** service station, petrol station, gas station (*EEUU*) ▸ **estación de televisión** television station ▸ **estación de trabajo** (*Inform*) workstation ▸ **estación de trasbordo** junction ▸ **estación de vacaciones** holiday resort ▸ **estación emisora** broadcasting station ▸ **estación espacial** space station ▸ **estación invernal** winter sports resort ▸ **estación marítima** ferry terminal ▸ **estación meteorológica** weather station ▸ **estación orbital** orbiting space station ▸ **estación purificadora de aguas residuales** sewage works, sewage farm ▸ **estación termal** spa ▸ **estación terminal** terminus ▸ **estación transformadora, estación transmisora** transmitter ▸ **estación veraniega** summer resort
2 (*Rel*) • **Estaciones del Vía Crucis** Stations of the Cross • MODISMO: • **correr las estaciones*** to go on a pub crawl*
3 (= *parte del año*) season ▸ **estación de (las) lluvias** rainy reason ▸ **estación de plantar** planting season ▸ **estación muerta** off season, dead season
4 • **hacer ~** to make a stop (**en** at, in)
estacionado ADJ parked
estacional ADJ seasonal
estacionalidad SF seasonal nature, seasonal variation
estacionalmente ADV seasonally, according to the season
estacionamiento SM **1** [*de soldados*] stationing
2 (*Aut*) (= *acción*) parking; (*esp LAm*) (= *sitio*) car park, parking lot (*EEUU*) ▸ **estacionamiento limitado** restricted parking
estacionar ▹ CONJUG 1a VT **1** [+ *soldados*] to station, place
2 (*Aut*) to park
VPR **estacionarse** (*gen*) to station o.s.; (*Aut*) to park; (= *no moverse*) to remain stationary • **la inflación/la fiebre se ha estacionado** inflation/the fever has stabilized
estacionario ADJ (*gen*) stationary; (*Med*) stable; (*Com, Econ*) slack
estacionómetro SM (*Méx*) parking meter
estacón SM (*LAm*) prick, jab
estada SF (*LAm*) stay
estadía SF **1** (*LAm*) (= *estancia*) stay; (= *duración*) length of stay
2 (*Com*) demurrage
3 (*Náut*) stay in port
estadillo SM (*gen*) survey; (= *inventario*) inventory
estadio SM **1** (= *fase*) stage, phase
2 (*Dep*) stadium
3 (*Mat*) furlong
estadista SMF **1** (*Pol*) statesman/stateswoman
2 (*Mat*) statistician
estadística SF (= *ciencia*) statistics (*sing*) • **una ~** a figure, a statistic; ▹ **estadístico**
estadísticamente ADV statistically
estadístico/a ADJ [*datos, cifras*] statistical
SM/F (= *profesional*) statistician; ▹ **estadística**
estadizo ADJ [*comida*] not quite fresh, stale, off
estado SM **1** (= *situación*) **a** [*de objeto, proceso*] state • **¿en qué ~ se encuentran las relaciones entre los dos países?** what is the state of relations between the two countries? • **estar en buen ~** [*instalación, alimentos*] to be in good condition • **el ordenador está en perfecto ~** the computer is working perfectly *o* is in perfect working order • **estar en mal ~** [*instalación*] to be in (a) poor condition, be in a bad state; [*alimentos*] to be off • **el techo se encontraba en muy mal ~** the roof was in very poor condition *o* in a very bad state • **tras comer carne en mal ~** after eating meat that was off *o* that had gone off
b [*de persona*] condition • **el ~ general del paciente** the overall condition of the patient ▸ **estado civil** marital status ▸ **estado de alarma, estado de alerta** state of alert ▸ **estado de ánimo** (*emocional*) mood; (*mental*) state of mind ▸ **estado de atención** state of alert ▸ **estado de coma** coma, state of coma ▸ **estado de cosas** state of affairs • **en este ~ de cosas, lo mejor es convocar nuevas elecciones** given the state of affairs, the best thing to do is call another election • **¿cuál es el ~ de cosas ahora?** what's the state of play now? ▸ **estado de emergencia, estado de excepción** state of emergency ▸ **estado de gracia** [*de creyente*] state of grace; [*de político, gobierno*] honeymoon period; [*de deportista*] run of good form ▸ **estado de guerra** state of war ▸ **estado de la red** (*Inform*) volume of users ▸ **estado de salud** condition, state of health ▸ **estado de sitio** state of siege
2 (*Fís*) state ▸ **estado gaseoso** gaseous state ▸ **estado líquido** solid state ▸ **estado sólido** solid state
3 • **en ~** (= *embarazada*): • **una mujer en ~** an expectant mother • **estar en ~** to be expecting • **quedarse en ~** to become pregnant • **estar en ~ de buena esperanza** to be expecting • **en avanzado ~ de gestación** heavily pregnant, in an advanced state of pregnancy • **estar en ~ interesante** (*hum*) to be expecting, be in the family way*
4 (= *nación*) state • **los intereses del ~** national *o* state interests • **el Estado español** Spain • **asuntos de ~** affairs of state, state affairs • **hombre de ~** statesman ▸ **estado asistencial, estado benefactor** welfare state ▸ **estado colchón** buffer state ▸ **estado de derecho** democracy ▸ **estado del bienestar, estado de previsión** welfare state ▸ **estado policial** police state ▸ **estado tapón** buffer state; ▹ **golpe**
5 (= *región*) (*en EE.UU., México, Brasil*) state
6 (*Hist*) (= *clase*) estate • **el ~ eclesiástico** the clergy • **~ llano** • **tercer ~** third estate, commoners (*pl*)
7 (*Mil*) ▸ **el Estado Mayor (General)** the (General) Staff
8 (*Com, Econ*) (= *informe*) report ▸ **estado de contabilidad** (*Méx*) balance sheet ▸ **estado de cuenta** bank statement, statement of account (*frm*) ▸ **estado de cuentas** [*de una empresa*] statement of account ▸ **estado de pérdidas y ganancias** profit and loss statement ▸ **estado de reconciliación** reconciliation statement ▸ **estado financiero** financial statement
estado-ciudad SM (PL: **estados-ciudad**) city state
estado-nación SM (PL: **estados-nación**) nation state
Estados Unidos SMPL United States (of America)
estadounidense ADJ American, US (*antes de s*), of/from the United States
SMF American • **los ~s** the Americans
estafa SF **1** (= *timo*) swindle, trick
2 (*Com, Econ*) racket, ramp*
estafador(a) SM/F **1** (= *timador*) swindler, trickster
2 (*Com, Econ*) racketeer
estafar ▹ CONJUG 1a VT to swindle, defraud, twist* • **~ algo a algn** to swindle sb out of sth, defraud sb of sth • **¡me han estafado!** I've been done!*
estafermo SM **1** (*Hist*) quintain, dummy target
2* (= *idiota*) twit*, idiot
estafeta SF **1** (= *oficina*) (*tb* **estafeta de Correos**) sub post office
2 (= *correo*) post ▸ **estafeta diplomática** diplomatic post
SMF courier; (*LAm*) [*de drogas*] drug courier, drug runner
estafetero SM postmaster, post-office clerk
estafilococo SM staphylococcus
estagnación SF (*CAm, Caribe*) = **estancamiento**
estaje SM (*CAm*) piecework
estajear ▹ CONJUG 1a VT (*CAm*) (= *trabajar*) to do as piecework; (= *acordar*) to discuss rates and conditions for
estajero/a SM/F (*CAm*) pieceworker
estalactita SF stalactite
estalagmita SF stalagmite
estaliniano ADJ Stalinist
estalinismo SM Stalinism
estalinista ADJ, SMF Stalinist
estallar ▹ CONJUG 1a VI **1** (= *reventar*) [*pólvora, globo*] to explode; [*bomba*] to explode, go off; [*volcán*] to erupt; [*neumático*] to burst; [*vidrio*] to shatter; [*látigo*] to crack • **~ en llanto** to burst into tears • **el parabrisas estalló en pedazos** the windscreen shattered • **hacer ~** to set off; (*fig*) to spark off, start
2 [*epidemia, guerra, conflicto, sublevación*] to break out • **cuando estalló la guerra** when the war broke out
estallido SM **1** (= *explosión*) explosion • **el gran ~** the big bang
2 [*de látigo, trueno*] crack
3 (= *comienzo*) outbreak
estambre SM **1** (*Bot*) stamen
2 (*de la lana*) worsted, woollen yarn
Estambul SM Istanbul
estamento SM **1** (*Pol*) (*social*) class; (*político*) estate
2 (= *estrato*) stratum, layer, level
estameña SF serge
estampa SF **1** (*Tip*) (= *imagen*) print; (= *grabado*) engraving; (*en libro*) picture; (*típica, pintoresca, castiza*) vignette ▸ **estampas de la vida cotidiana** vignettes of everyday life
2 (= *aspecto*) appearance, aspect • **de magnífica ~** fine-looking, fantastic-looking*

• **de ~ poco agradable** unattractive, unpleasant-looking • **ser la propia ~ de algn** to be the very *o* absolute image of sb, be the spitting image of sb*
3† (= *arte*) printing; (= *máquina*) printing press • **dar un libro a la ~** to publish a book
4† (= *huella*) imprint
estampación SF (= *acto*) printing; (= *grabado*) engraving; (= *fileteado*) tooling
estampado ADJ printed • **un vestido ~** a print dress
SM 1 (= *impresión*) (*gen*) printing; (*con sello, pie*) stamping
2 (= *diseño*) pattern
3 (= *tela*) print
estampar ▷ CONJUG 1a VT 1 (*Tip*) (= *imprimir*) to print; (= *marcar*) to stamp; (= *grabar*) to engrave; (= *filetear*) to tool
2 (*en la mente, memoria*) to stamp, imprint (en on) • **quedó estampado en su memoria** it was stamped on her memory
3* • **le estampó un beso en la mejilla** she planted a kiss on his cheek • **le estampó una buena bofetada** he gave him a good slap • **lo estampó contra la pared** she flung him against the wall
estampía • **de ~** ADV suddenly, without warning, unexpectedly
estampida SF 1 (*Agr, Zool*) stampede • **se marchó de ~** he went off like a shot
2 • **de ~** suddenly, without warning, unexpectedly
3 = estampido
estampido SM [*de pistola, fusil*] bang, report; [*de bomba*] blast, bang; [*de trueno*] boom, crash ▸ **estampido sónico** sonic boom
estampilla SF 1 (= *sello de goma*) seal, stamp, rubber stamp
2 (*LAm*) (*Correos*) stamp
estampillado SM rubber stamping
estampillar ▷ CONJUG 1a VT to rubber-stamp
estampita SF *small religious picture*
están ▷ estar
estancado ADJ 1 [*agua*] stagnant
2 [*negociaciones*] at a standstill • **quedarse ~** to get into a rut
estancamiento SM 1 [*de agua*] stagnation
2 (= *falta de actividad*) [*de asunto, comercio, suministro*] stagnation; [*de negociaciones*] deadlock
estancar ▷ CONJUG 1g VT 1 [+ *aguas*] to hold back, stem
2 (= *detener*) [+ *progreso*] to hold up, stem; [+ *negociación*] to deadlock; [+ *negocio*] to stop, suspend
3 (*Com*) to establish a monopoly in, monopolize; (*pey*) to corner
VPR **estancarse** 1 [*agua*] to stagnate, become stagnant
2 [*economía, industria, persona*] to stagnate
estancia SF 1 (= *permanencia*) stay • **durante su ~ en Londres** during his stay in London
2 (*liter*) (= *cuarto*) living room
3 (*LAm*) [*de ganado*] farm, cattle ranch; (= *hacienda*) country estate; (*Caribe*) (= *quinta pequeña*) small farm, smallholding
4 (*Literat*) stanza
estanciera SF (*Cono Sur*) station wagon
estanciero/a SM/F (*LAm*) farmer, rancher
estanco ADJ (*al agua*) watertight; (*al aire*) airtight
SM 1 (= *expendeduría*) tobacconist's, tobacconist's shop, cigar store (EEUU)
2 (*And*) (= *bodega*) liquor store; (= *monopolio*) state monopoly, government store where monopoly goods are sold

ESTANCO
In Spain, an **estanco** is a government-licensed tobacconist's, recognizable by a brown and yellow "T" sign. Cigarettes can also be bought at some bars, restaurants and **quioscos**, but at a higher price. As well as tobacco products the **estanco** sells stamps, **papel timbrado** (official forms) and coupons for the **quiniela** or football pools.
▷ QUINIELA

estand SM = stand
estándar ADJ, SM standard
estandarización SF, **estandardización** SF standardization
estandarizado ADJ, **estandardizado** ADJ standardized
estandarizar ▷ CONJUG 1f VT, **estandardizar** ▷ CONJUG 1f VT to standardize
estandarte SM banner, standard ▸ **estandarte real** royal standard
estanflación SF stagflation
estánnico ADJ stannic
estanque SM 1 (= *lago*) (*ornamental*) lake; (*pequeño*) pool, pond ▸ **estanque de juegos**, **estanque para chapotear** paddling pool
2 (= *depósito*) tank
3 (*Cono Sur*) [*de gasolina*] petrol tank, tank, gas tank (EEUU)
estanqueidad SF (*al agua*) watertightness; (*al aire*) air tightness
estanquero/a SM/F tobacconist, tobacco dealer (EEUU)
estanquillo SM 1 (*Méx*) booth, kiosk, stall
2 = estanco
estante SM 1 (= *anaquel*) shelf
2 (= *soporte*) rack, stand; (= *estantería*) bookcase
3 (*LAm*) (= *estaca*) prop
estantería SF shelving, shelves (*pl*)
estantigua SF 1 (= *aparición*) apparition
2* (= *adefesio*) fright*, sight*, scarecrow
estantillo SM (*And, Caribe*) prop, support
estañar ▷ CONJUG 1a VT (*Téc*) to tin; (= *soldar*) to solder
estaño SM tin ▸ **estaño para soldar** solder
estaquear ▷ CONJUG 1a VT (*Cono Sur*) to stretch out between stakes
estaquilla SF [*de madera*] peg; (= *clavo largo*) spike, long nail; (*para tienda*) tent peg
estaquillar ▷ CONJUG 1a VT to pin, peg down *o* out, fasten with pegs

estar

VERBO INTRANSITIVO
VERBO PRONOMINAL

▷ CONJUG 10

*Para las expresiones **estar bien**, **estar mal**, ver la otra entrada.*

VERBO INTRANSITIVO
1 (*indicando situación*) to be • **¿dónde estabas?** where were you? • **la última vez que estuve en Roma** the last time I was in Rome • **Madrid está en el centro de España** Madrid is in the centre of Spain • **el monumento está en la plaza** the monument is in the square • **eso no está en sus declaraciones** that's not in any of his statements • **—las tijeras están en el cajón —no, aquí no están** "the scissors are in the drawer" — "no, they're not in here" • **—hola, ¿está Carmen? —no, no está** "hello, is Carmen in?" — "no, I'm afraid she isn't" • **el día que estuve a verlo** the day I went to see him • **está fuera** (*de casa*) she's out; (*de la ciudad/en el extranjero*) she's away • **ya que estamos** while we are at it
2 (*indicando un estado transitorio*) **a** (+ *adj, adv*) to be • **está mucho mejor** he's much better • **~ enfermo** *o* **malo** to be ill • **estoy muy cansada** I'm very tired • **¿estás casado o soltero?** are you married or single? • **está vacío** it's empty • **estaba herido** he was injured • **¿cómo estamos?** (*gen*) how are we doing?; (*a otra persona*) how are you? • **con este frío, aquí no se puede ~** it's unbearably cold here • **¡qué bueno está este café!** this coffee's really good! • **mis padres están como siempre** my parents are the same as ever • **¿está libre el baño?** is the bathroom free? • **¿qué tal** *o* **cómo estás?** how are you? • **el récord anterior estaba en 33 segundos** the previous record was *o* stood at 33 seconds
b (+ *participio*) to be • **la radio está rota** the radio is broken • **para las seis ~á terminado** it will be finished by six o'clock • **estaba sentada en la arena** she was sitting on the sand • **está (embarazada) de dos meses** she's two months pregnant • **él no estaba implicado** he wasn't involved • **le está bien empleado por ingenuo** it serves him right for being so naïve
c (+ *gerundio*) to be • **estaba corriendo** he was running • **me está molestando** he's annoying me • **se está muriendo** she's dying • **venga, ya nos estamos yendo, que es tarde** come on, it's time to go, it's late • **está siendo preparado** it's being prepared • **nos estamos engañando** we're deceiving ourselves
3 (= *existir*) to be • **además están los gastos del viaje** then there are the travel expenses • **dejar ~**: • **déjalo ~** just leave him be • **si dejas ~ ese asunto te irán mejor las cosas** you'll do better to let the matter drop
4 (*indicando el aspecto de algo*) to look • **¡qué elegante estás!** you're looking really smart! • **estás más delgado** you've lost weight, you look slimmer • **está más viejo** he looks older • **el sofá ~á mejor al lado de la ventana** the sofa will look better next to the window • **ese tío está muy bueno*** that guy's gorgeous*, that guy's a bit of all right* • **el traje te está grande** that suit is too big for you
5 (= *estar listo*) to be ready • **~á a las cuatro** it'll be ready at four • **en seguida está** it'll be ready in a moment • **dos vueltas más y ya está** two more laps and that'll be it • **¡ya está! ya sé lo que podemos hacer** that's it! I know what we can do • **ya estoy** I'm done, that's me* • **¡ya estamos!** (*después de hacer algo*) that's it!; (*dicho con enfado*) that's enough! • **¿estamos?** (*al estar listo*) ready?; (*para pedir conformidad*) are we agreed?, right?, OK?* • **¡ya estuvo!** (*Méx*) that's it!
6 (*indicando fecha, distancia, temperatura*) • **estamos en octubre** it's October • **cuando estemos en verano** when it's summer, in the summer
7 (*en estructuras con preposición*) **estar a** • **estamos a 8 de junio** it is 8 June *or* the 8th of June, today is 8 June *o* the 8th of June • **estábamos a 40°C** it was 40°C • **¿a cuántos estamos?** what's the date? • **¿a cuánto estamos de Madrid?** how far are we from Madrid? • **las uvas están a 1,60 euros** the grapes are one euro 60 cents • **¿a cuánto está el kilo de naranjas?** how much are oranges per kilo? • **estoy a lo que se decida en la reunión** I'm waiting to see what's decided at the meeting • **~ a lo que resulte** to be waiting to see how things turn out

estar con • **está con la gripe** he's down with flu, he's got the flu • **estuvo con la enfermedad durante dos años** she had *o* suffered from the disease for two years • **ya está otra vez con el mismo tema** he's harping on about the same old subject again • **ya estoy con ganas de ir** I want to go now • **estoy con ganas de pegarle** I feel like hitting him • ~ **con algn**: • **yo estoy con él** I'm with him • **los aliados estaban con ellos** the Allies were behind them
estar de • **está de buen humor** he's in a good mood • **están de charla** they're having a chat • **está de camarero** he's working as a waiter • **está de jefe temporalmente** he is acting as boss, he is the acting boss • **está de luto** she's in mourning • **¡estoy de nervioso!** I'm so nervous! • **están de paseo** they've gone for a walk • **estaba de uniforme** he was (dressed) in uniform • **están de vacaciones** they are on holiday • **está de viaje en este momento** he's away at the moment
estar en • **en eso está el problema** that's (exactly) where the problem is • **el problema está en que ...** the problem lies in the fact that ... • **en ello estamos** we're working on it • **no está en él hacerlo** it is not in his power to do it • **creo que está usted en un error** I think you're mistaken • **no está en sí** she's not in her right mind • **yo estoy en que ...** (= *creer*) I believe that ...
estar para • **para eso estamos** (*gen*) that's why we're here, that's what we're here for; (*respondiendo a gracias*) don't mention it • **para eso están los amigos** that's what friends are for • ~ **para hacer algo** (= *a punto de*) to be about to do sth, be on the point of doing sth • **está para salir** he's about to leave • **no estoy para bromas** I'm not in the mood for joking • **si alguien llama, no estoy para nadie** if anyone calls, I'm not in
estar por (= *en favor de*) [+ *política*] to be in favour *o* (*EEUU*) favor of; [+ *persona*] to support; ▹ **hueso**
estar por (+ *infin*) • **la historia de ese hallazgo está por escribir** the story of that discovery is still to be written *o* has yet to be written • **está por ver si es verdad lo que dijeron** it remains to be seen whether what they said is true • **está todavía por hacer** it remains to be done, it is still to be done • **yo estoy por dejarlo** I'm for leaving it, I'm in favour of leaving it • **está por llover** (*LAm*) it's going to rain
estar sin (+ *infin*) • **las camas estaban sin hacer** the beds were unmade, the beds hadn't been made • **¿todavía estás sin peinar?** haven't you brushed your hair yet?
estar sobre algn/algo • **hay que ~ mucho sobre él para que estudie** you have to keep on at him to make sure he studies • **hay que ~ sobre el arroz para que no se pegue** you need to keep a close eye on the rice to make sure it doesn't stick to the pan • ~ **sobre sí** to be in control of o.s.
8 (*en oraciones ponderativas*) • **está que rabia*** he's hopping mad*, he's furious • **estoy que me caigo de sueño** I'm terribly sleepy, I can't keep my eyes open
(VERBO PRONOMINAL) **estarse**
1 (= *quedarse*) **a** (*en un lugar*) to stay • **puedes ~te con nosotros una semana, si quieres** you can stay with us for a week if you like • **se estuvo dos horas enteras en el cuarto de baño** he was in the bathroom for two whole hours • **yo prefiero ~me en casa** I prefer staying at home
b (*en un estado*) • **usted estése tranquilo, nosotros nos encargaremos de todo** don't you worry, we'll take care of everything • **se estuvo callada un buen rato** she didn't say anything for quite a while, she stayed quiet for quite a while • **¡estáte quieto!** keep *o* stay still!
2 (*uso impersonal*) • **se está bien aquí** it's nice here • **en la cama se está muy bien** it's nice in bed

---

estarcido (SM) stencil, stencilled sketch
estarcir ▹ CONJUG 3b (VT) to stencil
estaribel‡ (SM) nick‡, can (*EEUU‡*), prison
estárter (SM) = **stárter**
estás ▹ **estar**
estatal (ADJ) 1 (= *del estado*) state (*antes de s*)
2 (*Esp*) (= *nacional*) national
estatalismo (SM) state ownership
estatalista (ADJ) (*Esp*) national, nationwide
(SMF) member of a nationwide party
estatalización (SF) nationalization, taking into public ownership
estatalizar ▹ CONJUG 1f (VT) to nationalize, take into public ownership
estática (SF) statics (*sing*)
estático (ADJ) 1 (= *fijo*) static
2 = **extático**
estatificación (SF) nationalization, taking into public ownership
estatificado (ADJ) nationalized, publicly-owned
estatificar ▹ CONJUG 1g (VT) to nationalize, take into public ownership
estatismo (SM) 1 (= *inmovilidad*) stillness, motionlessness
2 (*Pol*) state control
estatización (SF) nationalization, taking into public ownership
estatizar ▹ CONJUG 1f (VT) to nationalize, take into public ownership
estator (SM) stator
estatua (SF) statue
estatuaria (SF) (*Arte*) statuary
estatuario (ADJ) statuesque
estatuilla (SF) statuette, figure
estatuir ▹ CONJUG 3g (VT) 1 (= *establecer*) to establish; (= *ordenar*) to ordain
2 (= *probar*) to prove
estatura (SF) stature, height • **un hombre de 1,80m de ~** a man 1.80m in height • **de ~ normal** of average height
estatus (SM INV) status
estatutario (ADJ) statutory
estatuto (SM) (*Jur*) (*gen*) statute; [*de ciudad*] bylaw; [*de comité*] (standing) rule ▸ **Estatuto de Autonomía** (*Esp*) (*Pol*) statute of autonomy ▸ **estatutos sociales** (*Com*) articles of association
estay (SM) stay
este¹ (ADJ INV) [*zona, área*] east • **el ala ~ del palacio** the east wing of the palace • **la costa ~** the east *o* eastern coast • **íbamos en dirección ~** we were going east *o* eastward(s), we were going in an eastward *o* an easterly direction • **trenes en dirección ~** eastbound trains
(SM) 1 (*Geog*) East, east • **el sol sale por el Este** the sun rises in the East *o* east • **vientos fuertes del Este** strong east *o* easterly winds • **la casa está orientada hacia el Este** the house is east-facing, the house faces East *o* east
2 (*Pol*) • **el Este** the East • **los países de la Europa del Este** East European countries
3 (*tb* **zona este**) east • **al ~ de Toledo** to the east of Toledo • **soy del ~ de Londres** I'm from east London
4 (*Meteo*) (*tb* **viento del este**) east wind, easterly wind
este²/a (ADJ DEM) 1 (*indicando proximidad*) **a** (*sing*) this • **esta silla** this chair • ~ **mes** this month • **¿qué habéis hecho ~ fin de semana?** what did you do at the weekend?, what did you do this weekend? • **¿dónde vais a ir ~ fin de semana?** (*dicho un viernes*) where are you going this weekend?; (*dicho un lunes*) where are you going next weekend?
b • **estos/estas** these • **estas tijeras** these scissors, this pair of scissors
2* (*con valor enfático*) • **¡a ver qué quiere ahora el tío ~!** what does that guy want now!* • **¡~ Pedro es un desastre!** that Pedro is a complete disaster!*
este³/a (PRON DEM), **éste/a** (PRON DEM)
1 (*sing*) this one • **esta me gusta más** I prefer this one • **este no es el que vi ayer** this is not the one I saw yesterday • **¡este me quiere engañar!** this guy's out to cheat me! • **pero ¿dónde está este?** where on earth is he?
2 • **estos/estas** these; (*en texto*) the latter
3 (*locuciones*) • **en esta** (*en cartas*) in this town (from where I'm writing) • **en estas**: • **en estas se acerca y dice ...** just then he went up and said ... • MODISMO: • **jurar por estas** to swear by all that is holy
4 (*esp LAm*) (*como muletilla*) • **este ...** er ..., um ...

> *In the past the standard spelling for these demonstrative pronouns was with an accent (**éste, ésta, éstos** and **éstas**). Nowadays the **Real Academia Española** advises that the accented forms are only required where there might otherwise be confusion with the adjective.*

esté ▹ **estar**
estearina (SF) 1 (*Quím*) stearin
2 (*LAm*) (= *vela*) candle
esteatita (SF) soapstone
Esteban (SM) Stephen
estecolado (SM) manuring, muck spreading
estela (SF) 1 (= *rastro*) (*Náut*) wake, wash; (*Aer*) slipstream, trail • **el discurso dejó una larga ~ de comentarios** the speech caused a great deal of comment • **dejaron tras de sí una ~ de muerte** they left a trail of slaughter behind them ▸ **estela de condensación, estela de humo** vapour trail, vapor trail (*EEUU*)
2 (= *monumento*) stele, stela
estelar (ADJ) 1 (*Astron*) stellar
2 (*Teat*) star (*antes de s*) • **papel ~** star role • **función ~** all-star show • **combate ~** (*Boxeo*) star bout, star contest
estelarizar ▹ CONJUG 1f (VT) (*Méx*) • ~ **en** to star in
estemple (SM) pit prop
estén ▹ **estar**
esténcil (SM) (*LAm*) stencil
estenografía (SF) shorthand, stenography (*frm*)
estenografiar ▹ CONJUG 1c (VT) to take down in shorthand
estenográfico (ADJ) shorthand (*antes de s*)
estenógrafo/a (SM/F) shorthand writer
estenotipia (SF) shorthand typing
estenotipista (SMF) shorthand typist, steno (*EEUU**)
estentóreamente (ADV) in a stentorian voice
estentóreo (ADJ) [*voz*] stentorian (*frm*), booming; [*sonido*] strident
estepa (SF) 1 (*Geog*) steppe • **la ~ castellana** the Castilian steppe
2 (*Bot*) rockrose
estepario (ADJ) steppe (*antes de s*)
Ester (SF) Esther
estera (SF) 1 (= *alfombra*) mat ▸ **estera de baño** bathmat

2 (= *tejido*) matting
esteral SM (*Cono Sur*) swamp, marsh
esterar ▷ CONJUG 1a VT to cover with a mat, put a mat on
VI* to put on one's winter clothes (*ahead of time*)
estercolamiento SM manuring, muck spreading
estercolar ▷ CONJUG 1a VT to manure
estercolero SM 1 (= *para estiércol*) manure heap, dunghill
2 (= *lugar sucio*) pigsty, pigpen (*EEUU*), shit hole**
estéreo ADJ, SM stereo • **una televisión en ~** a stereo TV
estéreo... PREF stereo...
estereofonía SF stereo, stereophony
estereofónico ADJ stereo, stereophonic, in stereo
estereoscópico ADJ stereoscopic
estereoscopio SM stereoscope
estereotipación SF stereotyping
estereotipado ADJ stereotyped
estereotipar ▷ CONJUG 1a VT 1 [+ *gesto, frase*] to stereotype
2 (*Tip*) to stereotype
estereotípico ADJ stereotypical
estereotipo SM 1 (= *modelo*) stereotype
2 (*Tip*) stereotype
esterero SM • MODISMO: • **quedar en el ~** (*Caribe**) to be on one's uppers*
estéril ADJ 1 (= *no fértil*) [*mujer*] barren, sterile, infertile; [*hombre*] sterile; [*terreno*] sterile, barren
2 [*esfuerzo*] vain, futile
esterilidad SF 1 (= *infertilidad*) [*de mujer*] sterility, infertility; [*de hombre*] sterility; [*de terreno*] sterility, barrenness
2 [*de esfuerzo*] futility, uselessness
esterilización SF 1 (*contra gérmenes*) sterilization
2 (*para no ser fértil*) sterilization
esterilizado ADJ [*instrumental*] sterilized, sterilize
esterilizar ▷ CONJUG 1f VT 1 (= *quitar gérmenes*) to sterilize
2 (= *hacer infértil*) [+ *persona*] to sterilize; [+ *animal*] to sterilize, neuter
esterilla SF 1 (= *alfombrilla*) mat
2 (= *tejido*) rush matting • **silla de ~** (*Arg*) wicker chair ▸ **esterilla de alambre** wire mesh
3 (*Cos*) (*dorado*) gold braid; (*plateado*) silver braid
estérilmente ADV vainly, uselessly, fruitlessly
esterlina ADJ • **libra ~** pound sterling
esternón SM breastbone, sternum (*frm*)
estero[1] SM 1 (= *estuario*) estuary
2 (*LAm*) (= *pantano*) swamp, marsh
3 (*Cono Sur, And*) (= *arroyo*) brook
4 • MODISMO: • **estar en el ~** (*Caribe**) to be in a fix*
estero[2] SM matting
esteroide SM steroid ▸ **esteroide anabólico, esteroide anabolizante** anabolic steroid
estertor SM death rattle
estertoroso ADJ stertorous
estés ▷ **estar**
esteta SMF aesthete, esthete (*EEUU*)
estética SF 1 (*Arte*) aesthetics (*sing*), esthetics (*sing*) (*EEUU*)
2 (*Med**) • **se ha hecho la ~ para quitarse las arrugas** she had cosmetic surgery to remove her wrinkles
estéticamente ADV aesthetically
esteticién SMF beautician, beauty consultant, beauty specialist
esteticismo SM aestheticism, estheticism (*EEUU*)
esteticista SMF beautician, beauty consultant, beauty specialist
estético ADJ aesthetic, esthetic (*EEUU*) • **cirugía estética** cosmetic surgery • **se ha hecho la cirugía estética** he's had cosmetic surgery
estetoscopio SM stethoscope
esteva SF plough handle, plow handle (*EEUU*)
estevado ADJ bow-legged, bandy-legged
estiaje SM 1 [*de río*] low water level
2 (*indicando duración*) low water
estiba SF 1 (*Mil, Hist*) rammer
2 (*Náut*) stowage • MODISMO: • **mudar la ~** to shift the cargo about
3 (= *acto*) loading
4‡ (= *paliza*) beating up*, bashing*
estibado SM stowage
estibador(a) ADJ • **empresa ~a** shipping company
SM/F stevedore, docker
estibar ▷ CONJUG 1a VT 1 (*Náut*) to stow
2 [+ *lana*] to pack tight, compress
estiércol SM 1 (= *abono*) manure ▸ **estiércol de caballo** horse manure ▸ **estiércol líquido** liquid manure
2 (= *excremento*) dung
Estigio SM Styx
estigio ADJ Stygian
estigma SM 1 (= *marca, deshonra*) stigma
2 (*Bot*) stigma
3 **estigmas** (*Rel*) stigmata
estigmatizado ADJ stigmatized
estigmatizar ▷ CONJUG 1f VT to stigmatize
estilar ▷ CONJUG 1a VI, **estilarse** VPR
1 (= *estar de moda*) to be in fashion, be in style • **ya no se estila la chistera** top hats aren't in fashion *o* in style anymore
2 (= *usarse*) to be used • **~ hacer algo** to be customary to do sth
estilete SM 1 (= *arma*) stiletto
2 [*de tocadiscos*] stylus
estilismo SM fashion design, fashion designing
estilista SMF 1 (*Literat*) stylist
2 (*Téc*) designer
3 (*Peluquería*) stylist
4 (*Natación*) freestyle swimmer
estilística SF stylistics (*sing*)
estilísticamente ADV stylistically
estilístico ADJ stylistic
estilización SF (*Téc*) styling
estilizado ADJ stylized • **una joven muy estilizada** a slender young woman
estilizar ▷ CONJUG 1f VT 1 (*Arte*) to stylize
2 (*Téc*) to design, style
estilo SM 1 (= *manera*) style • **el ~ del escritor** the writer's style • **un comedor ~ Luis XV** a dining-room suite in Louis XV style • **un ~ inconfundible de andar** an unmistakeable way of walking • **al ~ antiguo** in the old style • **un mosaico al ~ de los que se hacían en Roma** a mosaic in the style of those made in Rome • MODISMO: • **por el ~**: • **algo por el ~** something of the sort *o* kind, something along those lines • **no tenemos nada por el ~** we have nothing in that line • **los banqueros y gentes por el ~** bankers and people like that ▸ **estilo de vida** way of life • **no me gusta su ~ de vida** I don't like his way of life *o* his lifestyle • **el ~ de vida británico** the British way of life • **un ~ de vida similar al nuestro** a similar lifestyle to ours ▸ **estilo directo** (*Ling*) direct speech ▸ **estilo indirecto** (*Ling*) indirect speech, reported speech
2 (= *elegancia*) style • **una chica con ~** a stylish girl • **tiene mucho ~ vistiendo** he dresses very stylishly
3 (*Natación*) stroke • **~s medley** • **los 400m ~s** the 400m medley ▸ **estilo braza** breast stroke ▸ **estilo libre** freestyle ▸ **estilo mariposa** butterfly stroke
4 (= *punzón*) (*para escribir*) stylus; (*de reloj de sol*) gnomon, needle
5 (*Bot*) style
estilográfica SF fountain pen
estiloso ADJ stylish
estima SF 1 (= *aprecio*) esteem, respect • **se ganó la ~ de todos sus compañeros** he gained the respect *o* esteem of all his friends • **tener a algn en gran ~** to hold sb in high esteem, think very highly of sb
2 (*Náut*) dead reckoning • **a ~** by dead reckoning
estimable ADJ 1 (= *respetable*) [*persona*] estimable (*frm*), esteemed • **un ~ gesto en favor de la paz** an estimable *o* esteemed gesture for peace • **su ~ carta** (*Com*) your esteemed letter
2 [*cantidad*] considerable, substantial
estimación SF 1 (= *evaluación*) estimate, valuation
2 (= *aprecio*) respect • **ha conseguido ganarse la ~ de sus compañeros** he has managed to earn the respect of his colleagues
▸ **estimación propia** self-esteem
estimado ADJ esteemed, respected
• **"Estimado señor Pérez"** "Dear Mr Pérez"
estimador/a SM/F (*Com*) estimator
estimar ▷ CONJUG 1a VT 1 (*Com*) (= *evaluar*) to estimate; (= *valorar*) to value, appraise (*EEUU*) (**en** at) • **los daños se ~on en varios millones** the damage was estimated at several million • **~ algo en mil euros** to value sth at a thousand euros • **¡se estima!** thanks very much!, I appreciate it!
2 (= *respetar*) to respect • **una persona muy estimada por los que lo conocían** a person highly-respected by those who knew him
• **~ a algn en mucho** to have a high opinion *o* regard of sb • **~ a algn en poco** to have a low opinion *o* regard of sb
3 (= *juzgar*) to consider, deem • **lo que usted estime conveniente** whatever you consider *o* deem appropriate
VPR **estimarse** to have a high opinion of o.s. • **si se estima no hará tal cosa** if he has any self-respect he'll do nothing of the sort
estimativamente ADV roughly
estimativo ADJ rough, approximate
estimulación SF stimulation
estimulador ADJ (= *estimulante*) stimulating
estimulante ADJ stimulating
SM stimulant
estimular ▷ CONJUG 1a VT 1 (= *alentar*) [+ *persona*] to encourage • **hay que ~los para que respondan adecuadamente** you must encourage them to answer correctly • **~ a algn a hacer algo** to encourage sb to do sth
2 (= *favorecer*) [+ *apetito, economía, esfuerzos, ahorro*] to stimulate; [+ *debate*] to promote
3 [+ *organismo, célula*] to stimulate
estímulo SM 1 (*Psic*) stimulus
2 (= *incentivo*) incentive
estío SM (*liter*) summer
estipendiar ▷ CONJUG 1b VT to pay a stipend to
estipendiario ADJ, SM stipendiary
estipendio SM 1 (= *sueldo*) [*de empleado*] salary; [*de abogado, notario*] fee
2 (*Hist*) stipend
estíptico ADJ 1 (*Med*) styptic
2 (= *estreñido*) constipated
3 (= *miserable*) mean, miserly
SM styptic
estipulación SF stipulation, condition
estipular ▷ CONJUG 1a VT to stipulate

estirada SF (*Dep*) dive, stretch
estirado ADJ **1** (= *alargado*) stretched
2 [*persona*] (= *tieso*) stiff, starchy; (= *engreído*) stuck-up*
3 (= *tacaño*) tight-fisted
SM [*de vidrio*] drawing; [*de pelo*] straightening ▸ **estirado de piel, estirado facial** face lift
estirador SM (*Téc*) stretcher
estirajar* ▹ CONJUG 1a VT to stretch, stretch out
estiraje SM stretching
estiramiento SM = **estirado**
estirar ▹ CONJUG 1a VT **1** (= *alargar*) [+ *goma, elástico*] to stretch; [+ *brazos*] to stretch out; [+ *cuello*] to crane • **si lo estiras más se romperá** if you stretch it any more it'll break • **salir a ~ las piernas** to go out and stretch one's legs
2 (= *aplanar*) [+ *sábana, mantel*] to smooth out; [+ *piel*] to tighten, make taut
3 (*en el tiempo*) [+ *discurso*] to spin out • **no sé cómo consigue ~ el dinero hasta fin de mes** I don't know how he manages to make his money stretch to the end of the month
4 (*LAm**) (= *matar*) to bump off*, do away with* • MODISMO: • **~ la pata** to kick the bucket*
5 (*And*) (= *azotar*) to flog, whip
6 (*Cono Sur, Méx*) (= *tirar*) to pull, tug at
VPR **estirarse 1** (= *alargarse*) to stretch
2 (*Dep*) • **el equipo se estiró** the team moved upfield • **el jugador se estiró por la banda** the player ran up the touchline
estirón SM **1** (= *tirón*) pull, tug
2 • **dar** o **pegar un ~*** [*niño*] to shoot up*, take a stretch*
estironear ▹ CONJUG 1a VT (*Cono Sur*) to pull hard at, tug sharply at
estirpe SF stock, lineage • **de la ~ regia** of royal stock, of the blood royal
estítico ADJ, SM = **estíptico**
estitiquez SF (*LAm*) constipation
estival ADJ summer (*antes de s*)
esto PRON DEM this • **~ es difícil** this is difficult • **y ~ ¿qué es?** whatever is this? • **~ es** that is, that is to say • **~ de la boda es un lío*** this wedding business is a hassle* • **por ~** for this reason • **~ ...** (*vacilando*) er ..., um ... • **en ~ entró su madre** at that point his mother came in • **no tiene ni ~ de tonto** he isn't the least o slightest bit silly
estocada SF **1** (= *acción*) stab, thrust
2 (= *herida*) stab wound
3 (*Taur*) death blow
Estocolmo SM Stockholm
estofa SF **1** (= *tejido*) quilting, quilted material
2 (= *calidad*) quality • **gente de baja ~** riffraff*
estofado ADJ **1** (*Culin*) stewed
2 (*Cos*) quilted
SM (*Culin*) stew, hotpot
estofar ▹ CONJUG 1a VT **1** (*Culin*) to stew
2 (*Cos*) to quilt
estoicamente ADV stoically
estoicidad SF stoicism, **estoicismo** SM stoicism
estoico/a ADJ stoic, stoical
SM/F stoic
estola SF stole ▸ **estola de visón** mink stole
estolidez SF stupidity
estólido ADJ stupid
estomacal ADJ stomach (*antes de s*) • **trastorno ~** stomach upset
estomagante ADJ **1** [*comida*] indigestible
2* (= *molesto*) upsetting, annoying
estomagar ▹ CONJUG 1h VT **1** (*Med*) to give indigestion to
2* (= *molestar*) to annoy, bother
estómago SM stomach • **dolor de ~** stomachache • **"no tomar con el ~ vacío"** "not to be taken on an empty stomach" • **revolver el ~ a algn** to make sb's stomach turn, turn sb's stomach • **tener buen ~** (= *resistir comidas fuertes*) to have a strong stomach; (= *ser insensible*) to be thick-skinned; (= *ser poco escrupuloso*) to have an elastic conscience
estomatólogo/a SM/F stomatologist
Estonia SF Estonia
estonio/a ADJ, SM/F Estonian
SM (*Ling*) Estonian
estopa SF **1** [*del cáñamo*] tow • MODISMO: • **largar ~ a algn**‡ to bash sb*, hit sb
2 (= *tejido*) burlap ▸ **estopa de acero** steel wool
3 (*Náut*) oakum
4 (*Caribe*) cotton waste
estopero SM (*Méx*) (*Aut*) oil seal
estoperol SM **1** (= *mecha*) tow, wick
2 (*And*) (= *tachuela*) brass tack
3 (*And*) (= *sartén*) frying pan
estopilla SF cheesecloth
estoque SM **1** (= *arma*) rapier, sword • MODISMO: • **estar hecho un ~** to be as thin as a rake o (EEUU) rail
2 (*Bot*) gladiolus, gladiola, sword lily
estoquear ▹ CONJUG 1a VT to stab, run through
estor SM roller blind
estorbar ▹ CONJUG 1a VI to be in the way • **estas maletas están estorbando aquí** these cases are in the way here • **siempre estás estorbando** you're always getting in the way
VT **1** (= *obstaculizar*) [+ *paso, avance*] to get in the way of; [+ *trabajo, progreso*] to hinder; [+ *circulación*] to slow down
2 (= *molestar*) to bother
estorbo SM **1** (= *obstáculo*) hindrance, nuisance • **no eres más que un ~** you're just a hindrance o nuisance • **no hay ~ para que se haga** there is no obstacle o impediment to it being done, there's nothing to get in the way of it being done • **el mayor ~ es el director, que no quiere dar su aprobación** the biggest obstacle is the manager, who won't give his approval
2 (= *molestia*) nuisance
estornino SM starling
estornudar ▹ CONJUG 1a VI to sneeze
estornudo SM sneeze
estoy ▸ **estar**
estrábico ADJ [*persona*] wall-eyed; [*ojo*] squinting, strabismic
estrabismo SM strabismus (*frm*), squint
Estrabón SM Strabo
estrada SF **1** (= *carretera*) road, highway • **batir la ~** (*Mil*) to reconnoitre
2 (*And*) (*Agr*) section of a rubber plantation (*150 trees*)
estrado SM **1** (= *tarima*) platform; (*Mús*) bandstand ▸ **estrado del testigo** witness stand
2 estrados (*Jur*) law courts • **citar a algn para ~s** to subpoena sb
estrafalario ADJ **1** [*persona, ideas*] odd, eccentric
2 [*ropa*] outlandish
estragado ADJ **1** (= *arruinado*) ruined
2 (= *corrompido*) corrupted, spoiled, perverted
3 (= *depravado*) depraved
4 (= *descuidado*) slovenly, careless, disorderly
estragante ADJ damaging, destructive
estragar ▹ CONJUG 1h VT **1** (= *destrozar*) [+ *estómago*] to ruin; [+ *cuerpo*] to ravage • **un cuerpo estragado por la enfermedad** a body ravaged by disease
2 [+ *gusto*] to corrupt, spoil
estragón SM (*Bot, Culin*) tarragon
estragos SMPL havoc (*sing*) • **el hambre hizo ~ entre los más necesitados** hunger wreaked havoc with those most in need • **la sequía hizo ~ en el campo** the drought wreaked havoc in the countryside • **el actor que ha causado ~ entre las jovencitas** the actor who has caused a stir with the young girls • **los ~ del tiempo** the ravages of time
estramador SM (*Méx*) comb
estrambólico ADJ (*LAm*) odd, outlandish
estrambote SM (*Literat*) extra lines (*pl*), extra verses (*pl*), addition
estrambótico ADJ odd, outlandish
estrangis ADV • **de ~*** secretly, on the quiet
estrangul SM (*Mús*) mouthpiece
estrangulación SF strangulation
estrangulado ADJ (*Med*) strangulated
estrangulador(a) SM/F (= *persona*) strangler
SM **1** (*Mec*) throttle
2 (*Aut*) choke
estrangulamiento SM **1** (= *acto*) strangulation
2 (*Aut*) narrow stretch of road, bottleneck
estrangular ▹ CONJUG 1a VT **1** [+ *persona*] to strangle, throttle
2 (*Mec*) to throttle
3 (*Aut*) to choke
estranji ADV = **estrangis**
estranqui* SMF = **extranjero**
estraperlear* ▹ CONJUG 1a VI to deal in black-market goods
estraperlista SMF black marketeer
estraperlo SM black market • **comprar algo de ~** to buy sth on the black market
estrapontín SM (= *asiento extra*) side seat, extra seat; (*Aut*) back seat
Estrasburgo SM Strasbourg
estratagema SF stratagem
estratega SMF strategist; ▸ **gabinete**
estrategia SF strategy ▸ **estrategia de la tensión** destabilizing campaign ▸ **estrategia de salida** exit strategy
estratégicamente ADV strategically
estratégico ADJ strategic
estratificación SF stratification
estratificado ADJ **1** [*muestreo, sociedad*] stratified
2 [*madera*] laminated
estratificar ▹ CONJUG 1g VT to stratify
VPR **estratificarse** to be stratified
estratigrafía SF stratigraphy
estratigráfico ADJ stratigraphic
estrato SM **1** (= *capa*) stratum
2 (= *nube*) stratus
estratocúmulo SM stratocumulus
estratosfera SF stratosphere
estratosférico ADJ stratospheric
estraza SF rag • **papel de ~** brown paper
estrechamente ADV **1** (= *íntimamente*) closely, intimately
2 (= *austeramente*) austerely
estrechamiento SM **1** [*de valle, calle*] narrowing • **hay un ~ en la calzada** there is a narrowing in the road
2 (= *aumento*) [*de lazos*] tightening; [*de amistades*] strengthening
estrechar ▹ CONJUG 1a VT **1** (= *hacer estrecho*) [+ *calle*] to narrow; [+ *vestido*] to take in • **¿me puedes ~ esta falda?** can you take in this skirt for me?
2 (= *aumentar*) [+ *lazos, relaciones*] to tighten; [+ *amistad*] to strengthen
3 (= *abrazar*) to hug, embrace (*frm*) • **me estrechó entre sus brazos** he held me in his arms, he hugged me • **~ la mano a algn** to shake sb's hand, shake hands with sb
4 (= *obligar*) to compel
5 [+ *enemigo*] to press hard

VPR **estrecharse 1** [*calle*] to narrow, get narrower • **la carretera se estrecha al llegar al puente** the road narrows *o* gets narrower over the bridge
2 (= *abrazarse*) to embrace (*frm*), embrace one another (*frm*), hug • **se ~on la mano** they shook hands
3 (= *aumentar*) [*amistad*] to become stronger, become more intimate; [*lazos, relaciones*] to become closer • **~se con algn** to get very friendly with sb, grow close to sb
4 • **~se en los gastos** to economize, cut down on expenditure

e

estrechez SF **1** (= *angostura*) [*de pasillo, calle*] narrowness; [*de ropa*] tightness
2 (= *dificultad económica*) • **está acostumbrado a vivir en la ~** *o* **con ~** he is used to living in straitened circumstances • **hemos pasado muchas estrecheces** we have been through many difficulties *o* hardships ▸ **estrechez de dinero** shortage of money
3 (= *rigidez*) strictness ▸ **estrechez de conciencia** small-mindedness ▸ **estrechez de miras** narrow-mindedness
4 [*de amistad*] closeness

estrecho/a ADJ **1** (= *angosto*) [*calle, pasillo*] narrow; [*zapato, ropa*] tight • **la falda me va muy estrecha** the skirt is very tight on me • **es muy ~ de hombros** he's very narrow-shouldered, he's got very narrow shoulders • **estábamos muy ~s en el asiento trasero** it was a tight squeeze *o* we had to squeeze up tight in the back seat
2 [*amistad, relación*] close • **trabajan en estrecha colaboración con el comité** they work in close collaboration with the committee • **la sometieron a una estrecha vigilancia** they kept her under close supervision *o* a close watch
3 (*sexualmente*) prudish, prim
4 (*de mentalidad*) narrow-minded • **~ de miras** *o* **mente** narrow-minded
SM **1** (*Geog*) strait, straits (*pl*) ▸ **estrecho de Gibraltar** Strait(s) of Gibraltar
2† (= *aprieto*) predicament • **al ~** by force, under compulsion • **poner a algn en el ~ de hacer algo** to put sb in the position of having to do sth
SM/F* prude • **no te hagas la estrecha conmigo** don't act the prude with me

estrechura SF = **estrechez**

estregadera SF **1** (= *cepillo*) scrubbing brush
2 (= *fregona*) floor mop
3 [*de puerta*] door scraper, boot scraper

estregar ▹ CONJUG 1h, 1j VT to rub; (*con cepillo*) to scrub, scour

estrella SF **1** (*Astron*) star • MODISMOS: • **poner a algn sobre las ~s** to praise sb to the skies • **tener buena ~** to be lucky • **tener mala ~** to be unlucky • **ver las ~s** to see stars ▸ **estrella de Belén** star of Bethlehem ▸ **estrella de David** Star of David ▸ **estrella de guía** guiding star ▸ **estrella del norte** north star ▸ **estrella de neutrones** neutron star ▸ **estrella de rabo** comet ▸ **estrella fija** fixed star ▸ **estrella fugaz** shooting star ▸ **estrella neutrónica** neutron star ▸ **estrella polar** polar star ▸ **estrella vespertina** evening star; ▹ **nacer**
2 (*Tip*) asterisk, star • **un hotel de cinco ~s** a five-star hotel
3 (*Cine, Teat*) star • **¿quién es la ~ de la película?** who's the star of the film?, who stars in the film? ▸ **estrella de cine** film star, movie star (*EEUU*)
4 (*Mil*) star, pip
5 (*Zool*) blaze, white patch ▸ **estrella de mar** starfish
ADJ INV star (*antes de s*) • **la atracción ~ de la temporada** the star attraction of the season • **el jugador ~ del equipo** the star player in the team

estrelladera SF slice

estrellado ADJ **1** (= *en forma de estrella*) star-shaped
2 [*cielo*] starry, star-spangled
3 (= *destrozado*) smashed, shattered
4 (*Culin*) [*huevo*] fried

estrellamar SF starfish

estrellar ▹ CONJUG 1a VT **1** (= *hacer chocar*) to smash, shatter • **lo estrelló contra la pared** he smashed it against the wall • **estrelló el balón en el poste** he hammered the ball onto the goalpost • **la corriente amenazaba con ~ el barco contra las rocas** the current threatened to dash the boat on to the rocks
2 (= *decorar con estrellas*) to spangle, cover with stars
3 (*Culin*) [+ *huevo*] to fry
VPR **estrellarse 1** (= *chocar*) to smash, crash • **el coche se estrelló contra el muro** the car smashed *o* crashed into the wall
2 [*proyecto, plan*] to fail • **~se con** *o* **contra algo** to be thwarted by sth

estrellato SM stardom • **el director que la lanzó al ~** the director who propelled her to stardom

estrellón SM **1** (*esp LAm*) (*Aer*) crash; (*Aut*) crash, collision
2 (= *estrella grande*) large star
3 [*de fuegos artificiales*] star firework

estremecedor ADJ alarming, disturbing

estremecer ▹ CONJUG 2d VT to shake
VPR **estremecerse 1** [*edificio*] to shake
2 [*persona*] (*de miedo*) to tremble (**ante** at, **de** with); (*de horror*) to shudder (**de** with); (*de frío, escalofrío*) to shiver (**de** with)

estremecido ADJ shaking, trembling (**de** with)

estremecimiento SM, **estremezón** (*Col, Ven*) SM **1** (= *sacudida*) shake
2 [*de frío*] shiver, shivering
3 (= *sobresalto*) shock
4 (= *terremoto*) (*And, Caribe*) tremor

estrena SF **1** (= *regalo*) good-luck gift, token
2 estrenas (*de Navidad*) Christmas presents
3 = **estreno**

estrenar ▹ CONJUG 1a VT **1** (= *usar por primera vez*) [+ *ropa*] to wear for the first time, put on for the first time; [+ *máquina, coche*] to use for the first time • **voy estrenando zapatos** I'm wearing these shoes for the first time • **¿has estrenado ya el coche?** have you tried your new car yet? • **el piso es a ~** it's a brand new flat
2 (*Cine*) to release; (*Teat*) to premiere • **todavía no han estrenado la película** the film hasn't been released yet, the film is not on release yet • **están a punto de ~ el nuevo montaje de "Yerma"** the new production of "Yerma" is about to open
VPR **estrenarse 1** [*persona*] to make one's debut • **todavía no se ha estrenado como profesora** she still hasn't started working as a teacher • **esta noche todavía no se ha estrenado*** he hasn't pulled so far tonight*
2 (*Cine, Teat*) [*película*] to be released • **la película se estrenó en Junio** the film was released in June
3* to cough up*, pay up

estrenista SMF (*Teat*) first nighter*

estreno SM **1** (= *primer uso*) first use • **hoy voy todo de ~** I'm wearing all new clothes today • **se puso de ~ para la boda** she wore new clothes for the wedding • **fue cuando el ~ del coche nuevo** it was when we went out in the new car for the first time
2 (= *debut*) [*de artista*] debut, first appearance; [*de película*] premiere; [*de obra de teatro*] premiere, first night, first performance • **riguroso ~ mundial** world premiere ▸ **estreno general** general release
3 (*Caribe*) down payment, deposit

estrenque SM stout esparto rope

estrenuo ADJ vigorous, energetic

estreñido ADJ constipated

estreñimiento SM constipation

estreñir ▹ CONJUG 3h, 3k VT to constipate • **el queso estriñe** cheese causes constipation
VPR **estreñirse** to get constipated

estrepitarse ▹ CONJUG 1a VPR (*Caribe*) to kick up a fuss, make a scene

estrépito SM **1** (= *alboroto*) noise, racket • **reírse con ~** to laugh uproariously
2 (= *bulla*) fuss

estrepitosamente ADV **1** (= *con ruido*) noisily
2 (= *espectacularmente*) spectacularly

estrepitoso ADJ **1** (= *ruidoso*) [*risa, canto*] noisy; [*persona, fiesta*] rowdy • **con aplausos ~s** with loud *o* thunderous applause
2 [*descenso, fracaso*] spectacular

estreptococo SM streptococcus

estreptomicina SF streptomycin

estrés SM stress ▸ **estrés postraumático** post-traumatic stress

estresado ADJ [*persona*] stressed, stressed out*; [*vida, trabajo*] stressful • **ha estado muy ~ últimamente** he's been very stressed *o* under a lot of stress recently • **lleva una vida muy estresada** he leads a very stressful life

estresante ADJ stressful

estresar ▹ CONJUG 1a VT to cause stress to, put stress on

estría SF **1** (*Anat*) stretch mark
2 (*Arquit*) flute, fluting
3 (*Bio, Geol*) striation

estriado ADJ **1** (*Anat*) stretchmarked
2 (*Arquit*) fluted
3 (*Bio, Geol*) striate, striated
SM **1** (*Arquit*) fluting
2 (*Bio, Geol*) striation

estriar ▹ CONJUG 1c VT to groove, make a groove in
VPR **estriarse** [*piel*] • **se estría la piel durante el embarazo** stretch marks appear during pregnancy

estribación SF (*Geog*) spur • **en las estribaciones del Himalaya** in the foothills of the Himalayas

estribar ▹ CONJUG 1a VI • **~ en algo:** • **su felicidad estriba en ver contentos a los demás** her happiness comes from seeing other people being happy • **la dificultad estriba en el texto** the difficulty lies in the text • **su prosperidad estriba en esta industria** their prosperity is based on *o* derives from this industry

estribera SF **1** (= *estribo*) stirrup
2 [*de moto*] footrest
3 (*LAm*) saddle strap

estriberón SM stepping stone

estribillo SM **1** (*Literat*) refrain
2 (*Mús*) chorus • **¡siempre con el mismo ~!** it's always the same old story!

estribo SM **1** (= *pieza de apoyo*) [*de jinete*] stirrup; [*de moto*] footrest • MODISMO: • **perder los ~s** (= *enfadarse*) to lose one's temper, blow one's top*; (= *agitarse*) to get hot under the collar
2 (*en coche*) running board
3 (*Arquit*) [*de edificio*] buttress; [*de puente*] support
4 (*Téc*) brace
5 (*Geog*) spur

estribor SM starboard

estricnina SF strychnine

estricote SM • MODISMO: • **andar al ~**

(*Caribe**) to live a wild life
estrictamente ADV strictly
estrictez SF (*LAm*) strictness
estricto ADJ strict
estridencia SF stridency, raucousness • **iba vestida sin ~s** she was not loudly dressed
estridente ADJ **1** [*ruido*] strident, raucous
2 [*color*] loud
estridentemente ADV **1** (= *ruidosamente*) stridently, raucously
2 (= *vistosamente*) loudly
estridor SM stridency
estrillar ▷ CONJUG 1a VI (*And, Cono Sur*) to get cross
estrillo SM (*And, Cono Sur*) bad temper, annoyance
estriptís* SM, **estriptise*** SM (*And*) striptease
estriptisero/a* SM/F (*And*) stripper*, striptease artist
estriptista* SM/F stripper*
estro SM **1** (= *inspiración*) inspiration
2 (*Med, Vet*) oestrus, estrus (*EEUU*)
estrofa SF verse, strophe (*frm*)
estrófico ADJ strophic
estrógeno SM oestrogen, estrogen (*EEUU*)
estroncio SM strontium ▸ **estroncio 90** strontium 90
estropajo SM **1** (*para fregar*) scourer, scouring pad • MODISMOS: • **poner a algn como un ~** to make sb feel a heel • **servir de ~** to be exploited, be used to do the dirty work ▸ **estropajo de acero** steel wool
2 (= *objeto inútil*) worthless object; (= *persona inútil*) dead loss
estropajoso ADJ **1** (= *áspero*) [*lengua*] coated, furry; [*carne*] tough
2 [*habla*] indistinct • **cuando bebe se le pone la lengua estropajosa** when he drinks he gets tongue-tied
3 [*pelo*] straggly
estropeado ADJ **1** (= *averiado*) [*lavadora, televisor*] broken; [*ascensor, vehículo*] broken down • **tengo ~ el vídeo** the video is not working *o* has gone wrong *o* is broken
2 (= *dañado*) [*piel*] damaged; [*carne, fruta*] off • **este jersey está ya muy ~** this jumper is falling apart now • **los muebles están muy ~s** the furniture is in very poor condition
3 [*persona*] **a** (= *afeado*) • **la encontré muy estropeada después del parto** she looked the worse for wear after the birth • **lo he visto muy ~ últimamente** he's been looking a real wreck lately*
b (= *envejecido*) • **está muy estropeada para su edad** she looks much older than she is, she looks pretty worn out for her age
estropear ▷ CONJUG 1a VT **1** (= *averiar*) [+ *juguete, lavadora, ascensor*] to break; [+ *vehículo*] to damage
2 (= *dañar*) [+ *tela, ropa, zapatos*] to ruin • **te vas a ~ la vista** you'll ruin your eyesight • **esa crema le ha estropeado el cutis** that cream has damaged *o* ruined her skin
3 (= *malograr*) [+ *plan, cosecha, actuación*] to ruin, spoil • **la lluvia nos estropeó la excursión** the rain ruined *o* spoiled our day out • **el final estropeaba la película** the ending ruined *o* spoiled the film • **la luz estropea el vino** light spoils wine, light makes wine go off
4 (= *afear*) [+ *objeto, habitación*] to ruin the look of, spoil the look of; [+ *vista, panorama*] to ruin, spoil • **estropeó el escritorio pintándolo de blanco** he ruined *o* spoiled the look of the desk by painting it white • **ese sofá estropea el salón** that sofa ruins the look of the living room, that sofa spoils (the look of) the living room • **el centro comercial nos ha estropeado la vista** the shopping centre has ruined *o* spoiled our view
5 (= *envejecer*) [+ *persona*] • **los años la han estropeado** she has aged really badly
VPR **estropearse 1** (= *averiarse*) [*lavadora, televisor*] to break; [*ascensor, vehículo*] to break down • **se me ha estropeado el vídeo** my video is *o* has broken
2 (= *dañarse*) [*ropa, zapatos, vista*] to get ruined; [*carne, fruta*] to go off, spoil • **el ante se estropea con la lluvia** suede gets ruined in the rain • **si te lo lavas con este champú no se ~á el pelo** this shampoo won't damage *o* ruin your hair • **se le ha estropeado la cara con el sol** his face has aged from too much sun
3 (= *malograrse*) [*plan, vacaciones*] to be ruined • **se me ~on todos los planes cuando me quedé sin trabajo** all my plans were ruined when I lost my job • **se nos ~on las vacaciones por culpa del accidente** our holiday was ruined by the accident
4 [*persona*] (= *afearse*) to lose one's looks; (= *envejecer*) to age • **se ha estropeado mucho desde que está enfermo** he's really lost his looks since he got ill • **no te has estropeado nada con los años** you haven't aged at all
estropiciar* ▷ CONJUG 1b VT to trash*, wreck
estropicio* SM **1** (= *rotura*) breakage, smashing
2 (= *trastorno*) harmful effects (*pl*) • **espero que el retraso no le cause ningún ~** I hope the delay won't cause you any inconvenience
3 (= *jaleo*) rumpus*
estructura SF **1** [*de poema, célula, organización*] structure ▸ **estructura atómica** atomic structure ▸ **estructura del poder** power structure ▸ **estructura profunda** (*Ling*) deep structure ▸ **estructura salarial** pay structure ▸ **estructura superficial** (*Ling*) surface structure
2 [*de edificio*] frame, framework
estructuración SF **1** (= *acción*) structuring
2 (= *estructura*) structure
estructurado ADJ structured
estructural ADJ structural
estructuralismo SM structuralism
estructuralista ADJ, SMF structuralist
estructuralmente ADV structurally
estructurar ▷ CONJUG 1a VT to structure, arrange
estruendo SM **1** (= *ruido*) din
2 (= *alboroto*) uproar, turmoil
3 (= *pompa*) pomp
estruendosamente ADV **1** (= *ruidosamente*) noisily, uproariously
2 (= *aparatosamente*) loudly, obstreperously
estruendoso ADJ **1** (= *ruidoso*) thunderous
2 (= *escandaloso*) [*derrota, fracaso*] outrageous
estrujado SM [*de uvas*] pressing
estrujadura SF squeeze, press, pressing
estrujar ▷ CONJUG 1a VT **1** (= *exprimir*) to squeeze
2 (= *apretar*) to press
3 (= *escurrir*) [+ *bayeta, trapo*] to wring
4 (= *aprovecharse de*) to drain, bleed white
VPR **estrujarse** • MODISMO: • **~se la mollera*** to rack one's brains*
estrujón SM **1** (= *apretón*) squeeze, press
2* (= *abrazo*) bear hug
Estuardo SM Stuart
estuario SM estuary
estucado ADJ **1** [*papel*] coated
2 [*pared*] plastered, stuccoed
SM stucco, stucco work
estucar ▷ CONJUG 1g VT to stucco, plaster
estuche SM **1** (= *funda*) [*de gafas, instrumento*] case; [*de lápices*] pencil case; [*de espada*] sheath ▸ **estuche de afeites** vanity case ▸ **estuche de aseo** toilet case ▸ **estuche de cigarros** cigar case ▸ **estuche de costura** sewing basket ▸ **estuche de cubiertos** canteen of cutlery ▸ **estuche de herramientas** toolbox ▸ **estuche de joyas** jewel box *o* case, jewellery box, jewelry box (*EEUU*)
2 • MODISMO: • **ser un ~*** to be a handyman, be a useful person to have around
estuchero* SM (*Méx*) safebreaker
estuco SM stucco, plaster
estudiado ADJ [*sonrisa, respuesta*] studied • **una persona de gestos muy ~s** a very mannered *o* affected person
estudiantado SM students (*pl*), student body
estudiante SMF student • **~ de derecho** law student • **~ de medicina** medical student • **~ de ruso** student of Russian
estudiantil ADJ student (*antes de s*) • **vida ~** student life • **los problemas ~es** student problems
estudiantina SF student music group • **a la ~** like a student, in the manner of students; ▷ TUNA
estudiantino ADJ student (*antes de s*)
estudiar ▷ CONJUG 1b VT **1** (= *aprender*) [+ *lección, papel*] to learn • **estoy estudiando francés en una academia** I'm learning French at a language school • **se estudió el papel en media hora** she learned her part in half an hour • **tengo mucho que ~** I've got a lot of work *o* studying to do • **esta tarde tengo que ~ matemáticas** I have to do some maths this evening
2 (= *cursar*) to study • **estudió arquitectura** he studied architecture • **estoy estudiando piano** I'm studying the piano • **quería que su hijo estudiase una carrera** she wanted her son to go to university *o* to do a degree • **¿qué curso estudias?** what year are you in?
3 (= *examinar*) [*informe, experimento*] to examine, look into; [*persona*] to study, look into • **el informe estudia los efectos de la sequía** the report examines *o* looks into the effects of the drought • **están estudiando el comportamiento de los insectos** they are studying *o* looking into insect behaviour • **me estudió de pies a cabeza** he looked me up and down
4 (= *considerar*) to consider, study • **~emos su oferta y ya le contestaremos** we shall consider *o* study your offer and get back to you • **el informe está siendo estudiado** the report is being studied *o* is under consideration • **están estudiando la posibilidad de convocar una huelga** they are looking into the possibility of calling a strike, they are considering calling a strike
VI **1** (= *aprender*) to study • **tienes que ~ más** you have to work *o* study harder • **me tengo que ir a ~ ahora** I must go and do some work *o* studying now
2 (= *cursar estudios*) to study • **estudió con el Profesor García Montero** she studied under Professor García Montero • **estudia en un colegio de monjas** she goes to a convent school • **dejé de ~ a los trece años** I left school at thirteen • **~ para algo** to study to be sth • **mi hijo estudia para abogado** my son is studying to be a lawyer
estudio SM **1** (= *investigación*) study • **los últimos ~s en lingüística** the latest work *o* studies in linguistics • **en ~s de laboratorio** in laboratory tests *o* studies ▸ **estudio de campo** field study ▸ **estudio de casos (prácticos)** case study ▸ **estudio de desplazamientos y tiempos** (*Com*) time and

motion study ▸ **estudio del trabajo** work study ▸ **estudio de mercado** market research ▸ **estudio de viabilidad** feasibility study ▸ **estudios de motivación** motivational research (*sing*); ▸ **bolsa, plan**
2 (= *actividad investigadora*) study • **una vida dedicada al ~** a life devoted to study • **horas de ~** hours of study • **primero el ~ y luego el juego** work first and play later
3 (= *análisis*) [*de intención de voto, edificio*] survey • **vamos a hacer un ~ del cabello de la víctima** we are going to examine the victim's hair • **ya les hemos entregado el proyecto para su ~** we have already put forward the plan for their consideration • **estar en ~** to be under consideration
4 estudios (= *educación*) education (*sing*) • **sus padres le pagaron los ~s** her parents paid for her education • **una persona sin ~s** an uneducated person • **cursar ~s de algo** to study sth • **dejar los ~s** (*Escol*) to drop out of school; (*Univ*) to drop out of university • **tener ~s** to have an education, be educated • **tengo algunos ~s de inglés** I've studied some *o* a bit of English ▸ **estudios primarios** primary education (*sing*) ▸ **estudios secundarios** secondary education (*sing*) ▸ **estudios superiores** higher education (*sing*) • **tener ~s superiores de derecho penal** to have studied criminal law to degree level ▸ **estudios universitarios** university degree (*sing*), university studies
5 (= *erudición*) learning • **un hombre de mucho ~** a man of great learning
6 (*Arte, Mús*) study • **un ~ de piano** a study *o* étude for piano
7 (= *lugar de trabajo*) **a** (*en una casa*) study
b (*profesional*) [*de artista, arquitecto*] studio; (*Cono Sur*) [*de abogado*] office
c (*Cine, Radio, TV*) studio ▸ **estudio cinematográfico, estudio de cine** film studio ▸ **estudio de diseño** design studio ▸ **estudio de fotografía** photographer's studio, photographic studio ▸ **estudio de grabación** recording studio ▸ **estudio de registro de sonidos** sound-recording studio ▸ **estudio de televisión** television studio ▸ **estudio radiofónico** broadcasting studio
8 (= *apartamento*) studio, studio flat
estudiosamente ADV studiously
estudioso/a ADJ studious
SM/F expert, scholar • **un ~ de la literatura medieval** an expert in *o* a scholar of medieval literature
estufa SF **1** (= *para calentarse*) heater ▸ **estufa de gas** gas heater ▸ **estufa de petróleo** oil heater ▸ **estufa eléctrica** electric fire
2 (*Agr*) hothouse • MODISMO: • **criar a algn en ~** to pamper sb
3 (*Méx*) stove
estufilla SF **1** (= *brasero*) small stove, brazier
2 (*para las manos*) muff
estulticia SF (*liter*) stupidity, foolishness
estultificar ▸ CONJUG 1g (*CAm*) VT • **~ a algn** to make sb look stupid, make sb out to be a fool
estulto ADJ (*liter*) stupid, foolish
estupa* SF drug squad
SMF member of the drug squad
estupefacción SF astonishment, amazement
estupefaciente ADJ narcotic
SM narcotic, drug
estupefacto ADJ astonished • **me miró ~** he looked at me in astonishment *o* amazement • **dejar a algn ~** to leave sb speechless
estupendamente ADV marvellously, marvelously (*EEUU*), wonderfully • **estoy ~** I feel great *o* marvellous • **nos lo pasamos ~** we had a fantastic *o* great time* • **le salió ~** he did it very well
estupendo ADJ marvellous, marvelous (*EEUU*), great* • **¡estupendo!** that's great!*, splendid! • **—no te preocupes, yo lo hago —¡estupendo!** "don't worry, I'll do it" — "great!" • **tiene un coche ~** he's got a great *o* fantastic car* • **es ~ tocando la trompeta** he's great on the trumpet*
estúpidamente ADV stupidly
estupidez SF **1** (= *cualidad*) stupidity
2 (= *acto, dicho*) stupid thing • **lo que hizo fue una ~** what he did was stupid, that was a stupid thing to do • **fue una ~ mía** it was a stupid mistake of mine • **deja de decir estupideces** stop talking rubbish* *o* nonsense • **cometer una ~** to do something silly
estupidizador ADJ stupefying
estúpido/a ADJ stupid
SM/F idiot • **ese tío es un ~** that guy's an idiot
estupor SM **1** (= *sorpresa*) amazement, astonishment
2 (*Med*) stupor
estuprar ▸ CONJUG 1a VT to rape
estupro SM **1** (= *violación*) rape
2 (*con menor de edad*) sexual intercourse with a minor
estuque SM stucco
estuquería SF stuccoing, stucco work
esturión SM sturgeon
estuve *etc* ▸ **estar**
esvástica SF swastika
ET ABR (*Esp*) = **Ejército de Tierra**
ETA SF ABR (*Esp*) (*Pol*) (= **Euskadi Ta Askatasuna**) ≈ Patria Vasca y Libertad, ETA
-eta ▸ **Aspects of Word Formation in Spanish 2**
etano SM (*Quím*) ethane
etanol SM ethanol
etapa SF **1** [*de viaje*] stage • **en pequeñas ~s** in easy stages • MODISMO: • **quemar ~s** to make rapid progress
2 (= *fase*) stage, phase • **desarrollo por ~s** phased development, development in stages • **la segunda ~ del plan** the second phase of the plan • **una adquisición proyectada por ~s** a phased takeover • **lo haremos por ~s** we'll do it gradually *o* in stages
3 (*Dep*) leg, lap
4 (*Mil*) stopping place
5 [*de cohete*] stage • **cohete de tres ~s** 3-stage rocket
etario ADJ age (*antes de s*) • **grupo ~** age group
etarra ADJ of ETA
SMF member of ETA
etc. ABR (= **etcétera**) etc
etcétera ADV and so on
SM long list • **y un largo ~** and a lot more besides, and much much more • **y un largo ~ de autores** and many more authors besides
-ete ▸ **Aspects of Word Formation in Spanish 2**
éter SM ether
etéreo ADJ ethereal
eternamente ADV eternally, everlastingly
eternidad SF eternity • **la espera se me hizo una ~** I waited what felt like an eternity
eternizar ▸ CONJUG 1f VT **1** [+ *vida, personaje*] to perpetuate
2 [+ *entrevista, viaje*] to drag out
VPR **eternizarse 1** [*discurso, reunión*] to drag on (forever), go on forever
2 [*persona*] to take ages* • **se eterniza cada vez que va de compras** she takes ages every time she goes shopping • **~se en hacer algo** to take ages to do sth
eterno ADJ **1** (= *duradero*) eternal, everlasting • **el ~ problema del dinero** the eternal *o* everlasting problem of money
2 (= *interminable*) never-ending • **el viaje se me hizo ~** I thought the journey would never end, the journey seemed never-ending *o* interminable
ethos ['etos] SM ethos
ética SF ethics ▸ **ética profesional** professional ethics
éticamente ADV ethically
ético¹/a ADJ ethical
SM/F ethicist
ético² ADJ (*Med*) consumptive
eticoso* ADJ (*And*) fussy, finicky
etileno SM (*Quím*) ethylene
etílico ADJ • **alcohol ~** ethyl alcohol • **intoxicación etílica** alcohol poisoning • **en estado ~** intoxicated
etilo SM ethyl
étimo SM etymon
etimología SF etymology
etimológicamente ADV etymologically
etimológico ADJ etymological
etiología SF aetiology, etiology (*EEUU*)
etíope ADJ, SMF Ethiopian
Etiopía SF Ethiopia
etiquencia SF (*Caribe, Méx*) (*Med*) consumption
etiqueta SF **1** (*pegada*) label; (*atada, grapada*) tag • **despégale la ~ a la camisa** take the label off the shirt • **le han puesto la ~ de cobarde** they've labelled him a coward ▸ **etiqueta autoadhesiva** sticky label ▸ **etiqueta del precio** price tag
2 (= *formalismo*) etiquette • **de ~** formal • **baile de ~** gala ball • **traje de ~** formal dress • **ir de ~** to wear formal dress • **"vestir de ~"** (*en invitación*) "dress: formal"
etiquetación SF, **etiquetado** SM, **etiquetaje** SM labelling
etiquetadora SF labelling machine
etiquetar ▸ CONJUG 1a VT to label • **~ a algn de algo** to label sb (as) sth
etiquetero ADJ formal, ceremonious
etnia SF ethnic group
étnicamente ADV ethnically
etnicidad SF ethnicity
étnico ADJ ethnic
etnocéntrico ADJ ethnocentric
etnocentrismo SM ethnocentrism
etnografía SF ethnography
etnográfico ADJ ethnographic
etnología SF ethnology
etnológico ADJ ethnological
etnomusicología SF ethnomusicology
etrusco/a ADJ, SM/F Etruscan
SM (*Ling*) Etruscan
ETS SF ABR (*Med*) (= **enfermedad de transmisión sexual**) STD
SFPL ABR (*Esp*) (= **Escuelas Técnicas Superiores**) *technical colleges offering short degree courses*
ETT SF ABR (*Esp*) = **Empresa de Trabajo Temporal**
EU ABR (*esp LAm*) (= **Estados Unidos**) US
EUA ABR (*esp LAm*) (= **Estados Unidos de América**) USA
eucaliptal SM, **eucaliptar** SM eucalyptus plantation
eucalipto SM eucalyptus
eucaristía SF Eucharist
eucarístico ADJ Eucharistic
Euclides SM Euclid
euclidiano ADJ Euclidean
eufemismo SM euphemism
eufemísticamente ADV euphemistically

eufemístico ADJ euphemistic
eufonía SF euphony
eufónico ADJ euphonic, euphonious
euforia SF euphoria
eufórico ADJ euphoric
euforizante ADJ • **droga ~** drug that produces euphoria
euforizar ▹ CONJUG 1f VT to produce euphoria in, exhilarate
VPR **euforizarse** to become exhilarated
Eufrates SM Euphrates
eugenesia SF eugenics (*sing*)
eugenésico ADJ eugenic
Eugenio SM Eugene
eugenismo SM eugenics (*sing*)
eunuco SM eunuch
eurasiático/a ADJ, SM/F Eurasian
eureka EXCL eureka!
euribor SM (*Econ*) Euribor
Eurídice SF Eurydice
Eurípedes SM Euripides
eurítmica SF eurhythmics (*sing*)
euro SM **1** (= *moneda*) euro
2 (*liter*) (= *viento*) east wind
euro... PREF Euro...
eurobonos SMPL Eurobonds
eurocalculadora SF euro converter
Eurocámara SF Euro Parliament, European Parliament
eurocentrista ADJ Eurocentric
eurocheque SM Eurocheque
eurocomisario/a SM/F Euro-commissioner
eurocomunismo SM Eurocommunism
eurocomunista ADJ, SMF Eurocommunist
euroconector SM SCART connector, Euroconnector
Eurocopa SF (*Ftbl*) European Championship
eurócrata SMF Eurocrat
Eurocrédito SM Eurocredit
eurodiputado/a SM/F Euro MP, member of the European Parliament
eurodivisa SF Eurocurrency
eurodólar SM Eurodollar
euroescéptico/a ADJ, SM/F Eurosceptic
eurofanático ADJ fanatically pro-European
eurófilo/a ADJ, SM/F Europhile
eurófobo/a ADJ, SM/F Europhobe
eurofuncionario/a SM/F EU official
euromercado SM Euromarket
euromisil SM short-range nuclear missile
Europa SF Europe
europarlamentario/a SM/F member of the European Parliament
europarlamento SM European Parliament
europeidad SF Europeanness
europeísmo SM Europeanism
europeísta ADJ, SMF pro-European
europeización SF Europeanization
europeizante ADJ, SMF (*LAm*) = europeísta
europeizar ▹ CONJUG 1f VT to Europeanize
VPR **europeizarse** to become Europeanized
europeo/a ADJ, SM/F European
Eurotúnel® SM (*estructura*) Channel Tunnel
Eurovisión SF Eurovision
eurozona SF Eurozone
éuscaro ADJ, SM = **euskera**
Euskadi SF the Basque Country ▸ **Euskadi norte** Pays Basque (*France*)
euskaldún/una ADJ **1** (= *vasco*) Basque
2 (*Ling*) Basque-speaking
SM/F Basque speaker
euskaldunización SF **1** (*Pol*) conversion to Basque norms
2 (*Ling*) conversion to Basque, *process of making people Basque-speaking*
euskaldunizar ▹ CONJUG 1f VT **1** (*Pol*) to convert to Basque norms
2 (*Ling*) to convert to Basque, make Basque-speaking
euskera SM, **eusquera** SM, **eusquero** SM Basque, the Basque language
▸ **euskera batua** standard Basque

EUSKERA
Spoken by over half a million people in the Western Pyrenees, Basque, which is a non-Indo-European language, has been one of Spain's **lenguas cooficiales** (along with **catalán** and **gallego**) since 1982. Originally spoken also in Burgos and the Eastern Pyrenees, it began to lose ground to Castilian from the 13th century onwards. Under Franco its use was prohibited in the media, but it began to experience a revival in the 1950s through semi-clandestine Basque-language schools called **ikastolas**. In 1968 the Academy of the Basque Language created a standardized form called **euskera batua**, an attempt to homogenize several divergent dialects. Nowadays there is Basque-language radio and television, and under the autonomous government the teaching of the language has become a cornerstone of educational policy.
▹ LENGUAS COOFICIALES

eutanasia SF euthanasia, mercy killing
Eva SF Eve
evacuación SF **1** [*de habitantes, heridos*] evacuation
2 (*Téc*) waste
3 (*Med*) evacuation, bowel movement
evacuado/a SM/F evacuee
evacuar ▹ CONJUG 1d VT **1** (= *desocupar*) to evacuate
2 (*Med*) [+ *llaga*] to drain • **~ el vientre** to have a bowel movement
3 (*frm*) (= *realizar*) [+ *deber*] to fulfil; [+ *consulta*] to carry out, undertake; [+ *negocio*] to transact; [+ *trato*] to conclude
4 (*Jur*) [+ *dictamen*] to issue
evacuatorio SM public lavatory
evadido/a SM/F escaped prisoner, escaped convict
evadir ▹ CONJUG 3a VT **1** [+ *problema*] to evade, avoid
2 (*Econ*) [+ *impuestos*] to evade; [+ *dinero*] to pass, get away with
VPR **evadirse 1** (= *huir*) (*gen*) to escape; (*de cárcel*) to break out, escape • **~se de la realidad** to escape from reality
2 (*LAm*‡) to trip‡
evaluación SF **1** (= *valoración*) [*de datos*] evaluation; [*de daños, pérdidas*] assessment
▸ **evaluación del impacto ambiental** assessment of the impact upon the environment
2 (*Escol*) (= *acción*) assessment; (= *examen*) test
▸ **evaluación continua** continuous assessment ▸ **evaluación escolar** exam (*forming part of end-of-term or end-of-year assessment*)
evaluador(a) SM/F assessor
evaluar ▹ CONJUG 1e VT **1** (= *valorar*) [+ *datos*] to evaluate; [+ *daños, pérdidas*] to assess
2 (*Escol*) to assess
evaluativo ADJ evaluative
evanescente ADJ evanescent
evangélico ADJ evangelic, evangelical
evangelio SM gospel • **el Evangelio según San Juan** the Gospel according to St John
• MODISMOS: • **se aceptan sus ideas como el ~** his ideas are accepted as gospel truth • **lo que habla es el ~** he speaks the gospel truth
evangelismo SM evangelism
Evangelista ADJ • **San Juan ~** St John the Evangelist
evangelista SMF evangelist
evangelizador(a) SM/F evangelist
evangelizar ▹ CONJUG 1f VT to evangelize
evaporación SF evaporation
evaporar ▹ CONJUG 1a VT to evaporate
VPR **evaporarse 1** [*líquido*] to evaporate
2 (*fig*) to vanish *o* disappear into thin air
evaporizar ▹ CONJUG 1f VT to vaporize
VPR **evaporizarse** to vaporize
evasión SF (= *huida*) [*de lugar*] escape; [*de responsabilidad*] evasion • **literatura de ~** escapist literature ▸ **evasión de capitales** flight of capital ▸ **evasión de impuestos, evasión fiscal, evasión tributaria** tax evasion
evasionario ADJ (*Literat*) escapist
evasionismo SM escapism
evasiva SF **1** (= *pretexto*) excuse • **viene con sus ~s** he avoids a straight answer
• **contestar con ~s** to avoid the issue, dodge the issue
2 (= *escapatoria*) loophole, way out
evasivamente ADV (= *contestar*) evasively
evasivo ADJ [*respuesta*] evasive, noncommittal
evento SM **1** (= *acontecimiento*) event • **con motivo de este ~** to mark this event • **a todo ~** whatever happens
2 (= *incidente*) unforeseen happening
3 (*Dep*) fixture
eventual ADJ **1** (= *posible*) possible
2 (= *temporal*) [*trabajo, obrero*] temporary, casual; [*solución*] stopgap (*antes de s*)
3 (*LAm*) (= *final*) eventual
SMF temporary worker, casual worker
eventualidad SF **1** (= *posibilidad*) eventuality • **en esa ~** in that eventuality
2 (= *trabajo*) casual employment
eventualmente ADV **1** (= *posiblemente*) possibly • **algún número de la revista se publicará ~** special issues of the journal will be published from time to time
2 (= *por casualidad*) by chance
3 (*LAm*) (= *por fin*) eventually
Everest SM • **el (monte) ~** (Mount) Everest
evidencia SF **1** (= *obviedad*) evidence • **ante la ~ de los hechos, se confesó culpable** faced with the evidence, he pleaded guilty
• **negar la ~** to refuse to face (the) facts
• **rendirse ante la ~** to face (the) facts
2 (= *ridículo*) • **dejar *o* poner algo/a algn en ~** to show sth/sb up • **Carlos la puso en ~ delante de todos** Carlos showed her up in front of everyone • **ponerse en ~** to show o.s. up
evidencial ADJ tangible, visible
evidenciar ▹ CONJUG 1b VT **1** (= *probar*) to prove, demonstrate • **~ algo de modo inconfundible** to give clear proof of sth
2 (= *hacer ver*) to make evident
evidente ADJ obvious, clear, evident
• **¡evidente!** naturally!, obviously!
evidentemente ADV obviously, clearly, evidently
evitable ADJ avoidable, preventable • **un accidente fácilmente ~** an accident which could easily be avoided
evitación SF avoidance ▸ **evitación de accidentes** accident prevention
evitar ▹ CONJUG 1a VT **1** (= *eludir*) to avoid
• **quiero ~ ese riesgo** I want to avoid that risk • **intento ~ a Luisa** I'm trying to avoid Luisa • **no pude ~lo** I couldn't help it
• **~ hacer algo** to avoid doing sth • **María evita a toda costa encontrarse con él** María avoids

bumping into him at all costs
2 (= *ahorrar*) to save • **esto nos ~á muchos problemas** this will save us a lot of problems • **me evita (el) tener que ...** it saves me having to ...
VPR **evitarse 1** (= *ahorrarse*) to save o.s. • **~se trabajo** to save o.s. trouble • **así me evito tener que ir** that saves me having to go, that way I avoid having to go
2 [*dos personas*] to avoid each other

evocación SF **1** [*de recuerdos*] evocation
2 [*de espíritus*] invocation

evocador ADJ **1** (= *sugestivo*) evocative
2 (*del pasado*) reminiscent (**de** of)

evocar ▸ CONJUG 1g VT **1** (= *recordar*) to evoke, conjure up
2 [+ *espíritu*] to invoke, call up

evocativo ADJ (*LAm*) evocative

evolución SF **1** (*Bio*) evolution
2 (= *desarrollo*) evolution, development
3 (*Med*) progress
4 (*Mil*) manoeuvre, maneuver (EEUU)

evolucionar ▸ CONJUG 1a VI **1** (*Bio*) to evolve
2 (= *desarrollarse*) to evolve, develop
3 (*Med*) to progress
4 (*Mil*) to manoeuvre, maneuver (EEUU)
5 (*Aer*) to circle

evolucionista ADJ evolutionist

evolutivo ADJ evolutionary

ex PREF ex-, former • **ex secretario** ex-secretary, former secretary • **su ex amante** his former lover, his ex-lover
SMF • **mi ex*** my ex*, my ex-husband/ex-wife/ex-boyfriend, *etc* • **un ex del equipo** an ex-member of the team, a former member of the team

exabrupto SM **1** (= *ataque*) broadside
2 (= *observación*) sharp remark, cutting remark

exacción SF **1** (= *acto*) exaction
2 [*de impuestos*] demand

exacerbación SF exacerbation

exacerbante ADJ (*LAm*) **1** (= *irritante*) irritating, provoking
2 (= *agravante*) aggravating

exacerbar ▸ CONJUG 1a VT **1** (= *agravar*) to aggravate, exacerbate
2 (= *irritar*) to irritate

exactamente ADV exactly • **parecen ~ iguales** they look exactly the same • **sí, eso es, ~** yes, that's right, exactly

exactitud SF **1** (= *precisión*) accuracy • **la ~ del reloj** the accuracy of the watch • **con ~** [*saber, calcular, precisar*] exactly • **no lo sabemos con ~** we don't know exactly • **siguió las instrucciones con ~** he followed the instructions exactly *o* to the letter
2 (= *veracidad*) accuracy • **cuestionó la ~ de su declaración** he questioned the accuracy of her statement
3 (= *fidelidad*) accuracy • **reprodujo el original con increíble ~** he reproduced the original with incredible accuracy

exacto ADJ **1** (= *preciso*) exact • **el precio ~** the exact price • **no recuerdo sus palabras exactas** I can't remember her exact words • **el tren salió a la hora exacta** the train left exactly *o* bang on time • **tus cálculos no son muy ~s** your calculations are not very accurate • **para ser ~** to be exact *o* precise
2 (= *correcto*) correct • **perdone, pero lo que dice no es del todo ~** excuse me, but what you're saying is not entirely correct
3 (= *fiel*) [*copia, versión*] exact
EXCL exactly!, quite right!

exageración SF exaggeration • **dice que lleva diez horas trabajando ¡qué ~!** he says he's been working for ten hours? that's such an exaggeration! *o* what an exaggeration! • **—piden diez millones por esa casa —¡menuda ~!** "they're asking ten million for that house" — "that's way too much! *o* that's a ridiculous amount!"

exageradamente ADV • **movía los brazos ~** she was moving her arms in an exaggerated way *o* exaggeratedly • **es ~ prudente** he's excessively cautious, he's over-cautious

exagerado ADJ **1** [*persona*] (*en los gestos*) prone to exaggeration; (*en el vestir*) over-dressed, dressy • **¡qué ~ eres! • ¡no seas ~!** don't exaggerate!, you do exaggerate! • **es un ~ comiendo** he eats an incredible amount • **nos lo contó de forma muy exagerada** he told us in a very exaggerated *o* a completely over-the-top* way
2 [*gesto*] theatrical
3 (= *excesivo*) [*precio*] excessive, steep

exageradura SF (*Caribe*) exaggeration

exagerar ▸ CONJUG 1a VT to exaggerate • **creo que eso sería ~ las cosas** I think that would be going a bit far *o* overdoing it a bit
VI to exaggerate

exaltación SF **1** (= *ensalzamiento*) exaltation
2 (= *sobreexcitación*) overexcitement, elation
3 (= *fanatismo*) hot-headedness
4 (*Pol*) extremism

exaltado/a ADJ **1** (= *acalorado*) [*humor*] overexcited, elated; [*carácter*] excitable; [*discurso*] impassioned • **los ánimos estaban muy ~s** feelings were running high
2 (= *elevado*) exalted
3 (*Pol*) extreme
SM/F **1** (= *fanático*) hothead
2 (*Pol*) extremist

exaltante ADJ exciting

exaltar ▸ CONJUG 1a VT **1** (= *acalorar*) [+ *persona, manifestante*] to work up, excite; [+ *emoción*] to intensify; [+ *imaginación*] to fire
2 (= *elevar*) to exalt
3 (= *enaltecer*) to raise (**a** to)
VPR **exaltarse 1** [*persona*] (*gen*) to get excited, get worked up; (*en discusión*) to get heated • **¡no te exaltes!** don't get so worked up *o* hot up!
2 [*emoción*] to run high

exalumno/a SM/F (*esp LAm*) (*Univ*) graduate, former student

examen SM **1** (*Escol*) examination, exam • **hacer un ~** to sit *o* take an examination *o* exam • **presentarse a un ~** to enter for an examination *o* exam, go in for an examination *o* exam ▸ **examen de admisión** entrance examination *o* exam ▸ **examen de conciencia** • **hacer ~ de conciencia** to examine one's conscience ▸ **examen de conducir** driving test ▸ **examen de ingreso** entrance examination ▸ **examen de suficiencia** proficiency test ▸ **examen eliminatorio** qualifying examination ▸ **examen oral** oral examination ▸ **examen parcial** (*Univ*) *examination covering part of the course material in a particular subject* ▸ **examen tipo test** multiple-choice test
2 (= *estudio*) [*de problema*] consideration; [*de zona*] search • **tras el ~ de la situación** after studying the situation • **someter algo a ~** to subject sth to examination *o* scrutiny
3 (*Med*) examination ▸ **examen citológico** cervical smear, smear test, Pap test ▸ **examen ocular** eye test

examinado/a SM/F exam candidate

examinador(a) SM/F examiner

examinando/a SM/F exam candidate

examinar ▸ CONJUG 1a VT **1** [+ *alumno*] to examine
2 [+ *producto*] to test
3 [+ *problema*] to examine, study
4 [+ *paciente*] to examine
VPR **examinarse** to take an examination *o* exam, be examined (**de in**) • **¿cuándo se examinan de inglés?** when are they taking *o* doing their English exam? • **~se para doctor** to take one's doctoral examination

exangüe ADJ **1** (= *sin sangre*) bloodless
2 (= *débil*) weak

exánime ADJ **1** (= *sin vida*) lifeless
2 (= *agotado*) exhausted • **caer ~** to fall in a faint

exasperación SF exasperation

exasperador ADJ, **exasperante** ADJ exasperating, infuriating

exasperar ▸ CONJUG 1a VT to exasperate, infuriate
VPR **exasperarse** to get exasperated, lose patience

Exc.ª ABR = **Excelencia**

excarcelación SF release (*from prison*)

excarcelado/a SM/F ex-prisoner, former prisoner

excarcelar ▸ CONJUG 1a VT to release (*from prison*)

excavación SF **1** (= *acto*) excavation
2 (= *lugar*) excavation, dig

excavador(a) SM/F (= *persona*) excavator, digger

excavadora SF (= *máquina*) digger

excavar ▸ CONJUG 1a VT **1** (*Constr*) to dig, dig out, excavate (*frm*) • **excava su madriguera en la tierra** it digs its hole in the earth
2 (*Arqueología*) to excavate

excedencia SF leave of absence • **pedir la ~** to ask for leave of absence ▸ **excedencia por maternidad** maternity leave ▸ **excedencia primada** voluntary severance ▸ **excedencia voluntaria** unpaid leave

excedentario ADJ surplus (*antes de s*) • **países ~s** surplus-producing countries

excedente ADJ [*producción*] excess, surplus; [*trabajador*] redundant
SM excess, surplus ▸ **excedente empresarial** profit margin ▸ **excedente laboral** surplus of labour, surplus of labor (EEUU), overmanning
SMF person on leave of absence ▸ **excedente forzoso/a** person on compulsory leave of absence

exceder ▸ CONJUG 2a VT **1** (= *superar*) to exceed, surpass • **los beneficios han excedido el millón de euros** profits are in excess of *o* have exceeded a million euros
2 (= *sobrepasar*) to surpass • **las imágenes excedían cualquier cosa que pudieras imaginar** the pictures surpassed *o* were beyond anything you could imagine
3 (*en importancia*) to transcend
VI • **~ de algo** to exceed sth • **no puede ~ de diez páginas** it cannot exceed ten pages, it cannot be longer than ten pages
VPR **excederse 1** (= *sobrepasarse*) to excel o.s.
2 (= *exagerar*) • **no te excedas con la bebida** don't overdo it with the drink • **~se en sus funciones** to exceed one's duty

excelencia SF **1** (= *cualidad*) excellence • **por ~** par excellence
2 (= *fórmula de tratamiento*) • **su Excelencia** his Excellency • **sí, Excelencia** yes, your Excellency

excelente ADJ excellent

excelentemente ADV excellently

excelso ADJ lofty, exalted, sublime

excentricidad SF eccentricity

excéntrico/a ADJ, SM/F eccentric

excepción SF exception • **asistieron todos los invitados sin ~** all the guests came without exception • **un libro de ~** an exceptional book • **hacer una ~** to make an exception • **a** *o* **con ~ de** with the exception of, except for • **la ~ confirma la regla** the exception proves the rule

excepcional ADJ **1** (= *anómalo*) [*medidas, circunstancias*] exceptional • **un caso ~** an exceptional case • **aquí las nevadas son ~es** you rarely get any snow here • **de ~ importancia** exceptionally important
2 (= *muy bueno*) exceptional • **ha obtenido unos resultados ~es** she has achieved exceptional results

excepcionalidad SF exceptional nature

excepcionalmente ADV **1** (= *excelentemente*) exceptionally
2 (= *como excepción*) as an exception

excepto PREP except, except for • **todos, ~ Juan** everyone, except (for) *o* apart from Juan • **voy cada día, ~ los martes** I go every day, except Tuesdays • **se lo perdono todo, ~ que me mienta** I'll forgive him anything, except lying to me

exceptuar ▸ CONJUG 1e VT **1** (= *excluir*) to except, exclude • **exceptuando a uno de ellos** except for *o* with the exception of (*más frm*) one of them
2 (*Jur*) to exempt

excesivamente ADV excessively

excesivo ADJ excessive • **con generosidad excesiva** overgenerously

exceso SM **1** (= *demasía*) excess • **en** *o* **por ~** excessively, to excess ▸ **exceso de equipaje** excess luggage, excess baggage (*EEUU*) ▸ **exceso de mano de obra** = exceso de plantilla ▸ **exceso de peso** excess weight ▸ **exceso de plantilla** overmanning, overstaffing ▸ **exceso de velocidad** speeding, exceeding the speed limit
2 (*Com, Econ*) surplus
3 excesos (= *abusos*) (*al beber, comportarse*) excesses • **los ~s de la revolución** the excesses of the revolution • **los ~s cometidos en su juventud** the overindulgences *o* excesses of his youth • **cometer ~s con el alcohol** to drink excessively, drink to excess, overindulge in drink

excipiente SM (*Farm*) excipient

excisión SF (*Med*) excision

excitabilidad SF excitability

excitable ADJ excitable

excitación SF **1** (*Med*) excitation (*frm*) • **el café me produce ~** coffee makes me nervy ▸ **excitación sexual** sexual arousal
2 (*Elec*) excitation
3 (= *emoción*) excitement

excitado ADJ **1** (= *intranquilo*) worked up, agitated
2 (= *entusiasmado*) excited
3 (= *sexualmente*) excited, aroused
4 (*Bio, Elec, Fís*) excited

excitante ADJ **1** (*Med*) stimulating
2 (= *emocionante*) exciting
SM stimulant

excitar ▸ CONJUG 1a VT **1** (= *intranquilizar*) to get worked up, get excited • **no veas el partido porque te excita mucho** don't watch the game, it'll get you worked up *o* excited • **el café me excita** coffee makes me hyper*
2 (= *entusiasmar*) to make excited • **la buena noticia lo excitó tanto que ya no pudo dormir** the good news made him so excited he couldn't get to sleep
3 (= *provocar*) [+ *curiosidad*] to arouse, excite; [+ *sentimiento*] to arouse, provoke; [+ *apetito*] to stimulate
4 (*sexualmente*) to arouse, excite
5 (*Bio, Elec, Fís*) to excite
6† (= *incitar*) to rouse, incite • **~ al pueblo a la rebelión** to rouse the populace to rebellion
VPR **excitarse 1** (= *intranquilizarse*) to get worked up • **no te excites por esa tontería** don't get worked up about such nonsense
2 (= *entusiasmarse*) to get excited • **se excitó mucho cuando su equipo marcó el gol** she got very excited when her team scored
3 (*sexualmente*) to get aroused, get excited

exclamación SF **1** (*Ling*) exclamation
2 (= *grito*) cry

exclamar ▸ CONJUG 1a VT, VI to exclaim, cry out

exclamativo ADJ, **exclamatorio** ADJ exclamatory

exclaustración SF (*Rel*) [*de seglar*] secularization; [*de monje, monja*] expulsion

exclaustrado/a (*Rel*) ADJ **1** (= *secularizado*) secularized
2 (= *expulsado*) expelled (*from the order*)
SM/F **1** (= *secularizado*) secularized monk/nun
2 (= *expulsado*) expelled monk/nun

excluido(a) SM/F (*tb* **excluido social**) socially-excluded person • **los ~s sociales** the socially-excluded • **me siento un ~** I feel a social outcast

excluir ▸ CONJUG 3g VT **1** (= *de grupo, herencia*) to exclude (**de** from) • **lo han excluido del equipo** he's been dropped from *o* excluded from *o* left out of the team
2 (= *eliminar*) [+ *solución*] to reject; [+ *posibilidad*] to rule out

exclusión SF exclusion • **con ~ de** excluding

exclusiva SF **1** (*Com*) sole right, sole agency • **tener la ~ de un producto** to be sole agent *o* the sole agents for a product • **no te creas que vas a tener la ~ de coger al niño** don't think you're going to have an exclusive right to *o* exclusive control of the baby • **venta en ~** exclusive sale
2 (*Periodismo*) exclusive story, exclusive, scoop • **reportaje en ~** exclusive story, exclusive

exclusivamente ADV exclusively

exclusive ADV exclusively • **hasta el uno de enero ~** till the first of January exclusive

exclusividad SF **1** (= *cualidad*) exclusiveness
2 (*Com*) exclusive rights (*pl*), sole rights (*pl*)

exclusivista ADJ [*club*] exclusive, select; [*grupo*] clannish; [*actitud*] snobbish

exclusivo ADJ **1** (= *único*) sole • **derecho ~** sole right, exclusive right
2 (= *selecto*) exclusive

excluyente ADJ (*LAm*) [*clase, club*] exclusive

excluyentemente ADV exclusively

Excma. ABR = **Excelentísima**

Excmo. ABR = **Excelentísimo**

excombatiente SMF ex-serviceman/ ex-servicewoman, veteran

excomulgado/a ADJ **1** (*Rel*) excommunicated
2* (= *maldito*) blessed*, cursed
SM/F excommunicated person

excomulgar ▸ CONJUG 1h VT to excommunicate

excomunión SF excommunication

excoriación SF **1** (= *desolladura*) graze
2 (= *rozadura*) chafing

excoriar ▸ CONJUG 1b VT **1** (= *desollar*) to graze
2 (= *rozar*) to chafe
VPR **excoriarse** to graze o.s.

excrecencia SF excrescence

excreción SF excretion

excremento SM excrement

excretar ▸ CONJUG 1a VT to excrete

exculpación SF **1** [*de obligación*] exoneration
2 (*Jur*) acquittal

exculpar ▸ CONJUG 1a VT **1** (*de obligación*) to exonerate
2 (*Jur*) to exonerate (**de** of)
VPR **exculparse** to exonerate o.s.

exculpatorio ADJ • **declaración exculpatoria** statement of innocence

excursión SF **1** (*al campo*) excursion, trip, outing • **ir de ~** to go on a trip *o* an excursion *o* an outing ▸ **excursión a pie** hike ▸ **excursión campestre** picnic ▸ **excursión de caza** hunting trip
2 (= *viaje*) trip, excursion • **una ~ a las Alpujarras** a trip *o* an excursion to the Alpujarras
3 (*Mil*) raid

excursionar ▸ CONJUG 1a VI to go on a trip, go on an outing

excursionismo SM **1** (*por el campo*) hiking
2 (= *ir de viaje*) going on trips

excursionista SMF **1** (*por campo, montaña*) hiker
2 (*en un viaje*) tripper

excurso SM, **excursus** SM INV excursus

excusa SF excuse • **buscar una ~** to look for an excuse • **presentar sus ~s** to make one's excuses, excuse o.s.

excusabaraja SF hamper, basket with a lid

excusable ADJ excusable, pardonable

excusado ADJ **1** (= *innecesario*) unnecessary • **~ es decir que ...** needless to say ... • **pensar en lo ~** to think of something which is quite out of the question
2 • **estar ~ de algo** to be exempt from sth
SM† lavatory, comfort station (*EEUU*), toilet

excusar ▸ CONJUG 1a VT **1** (= *disculpar*) to excuse • **excúsame con los otros** apologize to the others for me
2 (= *evitar*) [+ *disgustos*] to avoid, prevent • **así excusamos disgustos** this way we avoid difficulties • **podemos ~ lo otro** we can forget about the rest of it, we don't have to bother with the rest • **excusamos decirle que ...** we don't have to tell you that ... • **por eso excuso escribirte más largo** so I can save myself the trouble of writing at greater length
3 (= *eximir*) to exempt (**de** from)
VPR **excusarse** (= *disculparse*) to apologize (**con** to) • **~se de haber hecho algo** to apologize for having done sth

execrable ADJ execrable

execración SF execration

execrar ▸ CONJUG 1a VT to loathe

exégesis SF INV exegesis

exención SF exemption (**de** from) ▸ **exención contributiva, exención de impuestos** tax exemption, tax allowance

exencionar ▸ CONJUG 1a VT = **exentar**

exentar ▸ CONJUG 1a VT **1** (= *eximir*) to exempt (**de** from)
2 (= *disculpar*) to excuse (**de** from)

exento ADJ **1** (= *libre*) exempt (**de** from), free (**de** from, of) • **~ del servicio militar** exempt from military service • **~ de derechos** duty free • **~ de impuestos** tax free • **un libro ~ de interés** a book devoid of interest • **una expedición no exenta de peligros** an expedition not without its dangers
2 [*lugar*] unobstructed, open
3 (*Arquit*) free-standing

exequias SFPL (*frm*) funeral rites, exequies (*frm*)

exfoliación SF (*Cos*) exfoliation (*frm*)

exfoliador SM (*Cono Sur*) tear-off pad, loose-leaf notebook

exfoliante SM exfoliant

exfoliar ▸ CONJUG 1b VT to exfoliate
VPR **exfoliarse** to exfoliate

ex-gratia ADJ ex gratia

exhalación SF **1** [*de suspiro, gemido*]

e

exhalation
2 (*Astron*) shooting star • MODISMO: • **pasar como una ~** to flash past

exhalar ▹ CONJUG 1a (VT) **1** (= *arrojar*) [+ *aire*] to exhale; [+ *gas*] to emit, give off
2 [*persona*] [+ *suspiro*] to breathe; [+ *gemido*] to utter • MODISMO: • **~ el último suspiro** (*euf*) to give up one's last breath, breathe one's last
(VPR) **exhalarse** to hurry

exhaustivamente (ADV) exhaustively, thoroughly

exhaustividad (SF) exhaustiveness, thoroughness

exhaustivo (ADJ) exhaustive, thorough

exhausto (ADJ) exhausted

exheredar ▹ CONJUG 1a (VT) to disinherit

exhibición (SF) **1** (= *demostración*) show, display • **una impresionante ~ de fuerza** an impressive show of strength • **hay varias esculturas en ~** there are various sculptures on show *o* on display • **no le gusta hacer ~ de sus sentimientos** he doesn't like to show his feelings ▸ **exhibición aérea** flying display ▸ **exhibición de escaparate** window display ▸ **exhibición folklórica** folk festival, display of folk-dancing *etc*
2 (*Cine*) showing
3 (*Dep*) exhibition, display • **partido de ~** exhibition match • **una ~ de judo** a judo exhibition *o* display
4 (*Méx*) (*Com*) payment of an instalment *o* (*EEUU*) installment

exhibicionismo (SM) **1** (= *deseo de exhibirse*) exhibitionism • **no me gusta cómo viste, es puro ~** I don't like the way he dresses, it's pure exhibitionism • **no me gusta la gente que hace tanto ~ de sus conocimientos** I don't like people who are always making a great show of their knowledge *o* who are always showing off how much they know
2 (*sexual*) exhibitionism (*frm*), indecent exposure

exhibicionista (ADJ), (SMF) exhibitionist
(SM) (*sexual*) flasher*, exhibitionist (*frm*)

exhibidor (SM) display case

exhibir ▹ CONJUG 3a (VT) **1** (= *mostrar*) [+ *cuadros*] to exhibit, put on show; [+ *artículos*] to display; [+ *pasaporte*] to show; [+ *película*] to screen • **los diseños exhibidos en la exposición** the designs on show *o* on display *o* exhibited in the exhibition
2 (= *mostrar con orgullo*) to show off
3 (*Méx*) [+ *cantidad*] to pay in cash
(VPR) **exhibirse 1** (= *mostrarse en público*) to show o.s. off
2 (*indecentemente*) to expose o.s.

exhortación (SF) exhortation

exhortar ▹ CONJUG 1a (VT) to exhort • **~ a algn a hacer algo** to exhort sb to do sth

exhumación (SF) exhumation, disinterment

exhumar ▹ CONJUG 1a (VT) to exhume, disinter

exigencia (SF) **1** (= *requerimiento*) demand, requirement, exigency (*frm*) • **según las ~s de la situación** as the situation requires *o* demands, according to the exigencies of the situation (*frm*) • **tener muchas ~s** to be very demanding
2 (*Caribe*) (= *petición*) request
3 (*CAm*) (= *escasez*) need, lack

exigente (ADJ) [*persona, trabajo*] demanding, exacting • **ser ~ con algn** to be demanding *o* exacting of sb, be hard on sb • **es muy ~ con la limpieza** she is very particular about cleanliness

exigir ▹ CONJUG 3c (VT) **1** [*persona*] (*gen*) to demand; [+ *dimisión*] to demand, call for • **exijo una compensación** I demand compensation • **exigió hablar con el encargado** he demanded to speak to the manager • **exigen al gobierno una bajada de los impuestos** they're demanding that the government lowers taxes • **la maestra nos exige demasiado** our teacher is too demanding, our teacher asks too much of us • **exigen tres años de experiencia** they're asking for *o* they require three years' experience • **exija que le den un recibo** insist on getting a receipt • **~ responsabilidades a algn** to call sb to account
2 [*situación, trabajo*] to demand, require, call for • **ese puesto exige mucha paciencia** this job demands *o* requires *o* calls for a lot of patience • **el conflicto exige una pronta solución** the conflict requires *o* calls for a quick solution
3 (*Ven*) (= *demandar*) • **~ algo** to ask for sth, request sth • **~ a algn** to beg sb, plead with sb
4† [+ *impuestos*] to exact, levy (**a** from)

exiguo (ADJ) **1** [*cantidad*] meagre, meager (*EEUU*)
2 [*objeto*] (= *pequeño*) tiny

exilado/a (ADJ), (SM/F) = **exiliado**

exilar ▹ CONJUG 1a (VT) = **exiliar**

exiliado/a (ADJ) exiled, in exile
(SM/F) exile

exiliar ▹ CONJUG 1b (VT) to exile
(VPR) **exiliarse** to go into exile

exilio (SM) exile • **estar/vivir en el ~** to be/live in exile • **gobierno en el ~** government in exile

eximente (SF) grounds for exemption (*pl*)

eximio (ADJ) [*persona*] distinguished

eximir ▹ CONJUG 3a (VT) **1** (*de impuestos, servicio militar*) to exempt (**de** from)
2 (*de obligación*) to free (**de** from) • **esto me exime de toda obligación con él** this frees me from any obligation to him
(VPR) **eximirse** to free o.s. • **~se de hacer algo** to free o.s. from doing sth

existencia (SF) **1** [*de ser humano, animal*] existence • **desconocía la ~ de ese documento** I was unaware of the existence of that document • **lucha por la ~** struggle for survival • **amargar la ~ a algn** to make sb's life a misery • **quitarse la ~** (*euf*) to do away with o.s., commit suicide
2 existencias (*Com*) stock (*sing*) • **nuestras ~s de carbón** our coal stocks • **liquidar ~s** to clear stock • **renovar ~s** to restock • **hasta que se acaben las ~s** while stocks last • **sin ~s** out of stock • **tener algo en ~s** to have sth in stock ▸ **existencias de mercancías** stock-in-trade

existencial (ADJ) existential

existencialismo (SM) existentialism

existencialista (ADJ), (SMF) existentialist

existencialmente (ADV) existentially

existente (ADJ) **1** (= *que existe*) existing, in existence • **la situación ~ en este momento** the existing *o* present situation, the situation at the moment • **el único documento ~ de la época** the only existing document of *o* from that period
2 (*Com*) in stock

existir ▹ CONJUG 3a (VI) **1** (= *ser*) to exist • **esta empresa existe desde hace 90 años** the company has been in existence for 90 years • **no existe tal cosa** there's no such thing
2 (= *vivir*) to live • **mientras yo exista** as long as I live *o* I'm alive • **dejar de ~** (*euf*) to pass away (*euf*)

exitazo (SM) **1** (= *gran éxito*) great success
2 (*Mús, Teat*) smash hit

éxito (SM) **1** (= *buen resultado*) success • **la operación resultó con ~** the operation was successful *o* was a success • **la tarta que trajiste fue un gran ~** the cake you brought was a great success • **tiene mucho ~ entre los hombres** she's very successful with men, she has a great deal of success with men • **es un hombre de ~** he's a successful man • **tener ~ en algo** to be successful in sth, make a success of sth • **no tener ~** to be unsuccessful, not succeed
2 (*Mús, Teat*) success, hit • **un ~ rotundo** (*gen*) a resounding success; (*Mús*) a smash hit • **grandes ~s** greatest hits ▸ **éxito de librería** best seller ▸ **éxito de taquilla** box-office success ▸ **éxito de ventas** best seller ▸ **éxito editorial** best seller
3† (= *resultado*) result, outcome • **buen ~** happy outcome, success • **con buen ~** successfully • **tener buen ~** to succeed, be successful, have a happy outcome • **tener mal ~** to have an unfortunate outcome, fail, be unsuccessful

exitosamente (ADV) successfully

exitoso (ADJ) (*esp LAm*) successful

éxodo (SM) exodus • **el ~ rural** the drift from the land, the rural exodus • **Éxodo** (*Rel*) Exodus

ex oficio (ADJ), (ADV) ex officio

exoneración (SF) **1** (= *libramiento*) exoneration
2 (= *despido*) dismissal

exonerar ▹ CONJUG 1a (VT) **1** (*de culpa, responsabilidad*) to exonerate (*frm*); (*de un impuesto*) to exempt • **~ a algn de un deber** to free sb from a duty, relieve sb of a duty
2 [+ *empleado*] to dismiss • **le ~on de sus condecoraciones** they stripped him of his decorations
3 • **~ el vientre** to have a bowel movement

exorbitancia (SF) exorbitance

exorbitante (ADJ) exorbitant

exorbitantemente (ADV) exorbitantly

exorcismo (SM) exorcism

exorcista (ADJ) • **prácticas ~s** rites designed to secure exorcism
(SMF) exorcist

exorcizar ▹ CONJUG 1f (VT) to exorcise

exordio (SM) preamble, exordium (*frm*)

exornar ▹ CONJUG 1a (VT) to adorn, embellish (**de** with)

exosto (SM) (*LAm*) (*Aut*) exhaust

exótica* (SF) (*Méx*) (= *mujer*) stripper*, striptease artist

exótico (ADJ) exotic

exotismo (SM) exoticism

expandible (ADJ) expansible

expandir ▹ CONJUG 3a (VT) **1** (= *extender*) (*gen*) to expand; (*Anat*) to expand; (*Com*) to expand, enlarge
2 [+ *noticia*] to spread • **~ el mercado de un producto** to expand the market for a product • **~ la afición a la lectura** to spread a love of reading
3 (*Tip, Inform*) • **en caracteres expandidos** double width
(VPR) **expandirse 1** [*gas, metal*] to expand
2 (= *extenderse*) [*empresa*] to expand; [*idioma, cultura, noticia*] to spread

expansible (ADJ) expansible

expansión (SF) **1** (= *difusión*) [*de empresa, mercado*] expansion; [*de noticia, ideas*] spread • **la ~ económica** economic growth *o* expansion
2 (= *recreo*) relaxation; (= *placer*) pleasure
3 (= *efusión*) expansiveness

expansionar ▹ CONJUG 1a (VT) [+ *mercado*] to expand
(VPR) **expansionarse 1** (= *dilatarse*) to expand
2 (= *relajarse*) to relax
3 (= *desahogarse*) to unbosom o.s., open one's heart (**con** to)

expansionismo (SM) expansionism

expansionista (ADJ) expansionist

expansividad SF expansiveness
expansivo ADJ **1** [*gas*] expansive • **onda expansiva** shock wave
2 (*Econ*) • **una fase/política expansiva** a phase/policy of expansion
3 [*persona*] expansive
expatriación SF **1** (= *emigración*) expatriation
2 (= *exilio*) exile
expatriado/a SM/F **1** (= *emigrado*) expatriate
2 (= *exilado*) exile
expatriarse ▹ CONJUG 1b VPR **1** (= *emigrar*) to emigrate
2 (= *exiliarse*) to go into exile
expectación SF (= *esperanza*) expectation; (= *ilusión*) excitement; (= *ansia*) eagerness • **crece la ~** excitement is growing, there is mounting excitement
expectante ADJ (= *esperanzador*) expectant; (= *ansioso*) eager; (= *ilusionado*) excited
expectativa SF **1** (= *esperanza*) expectation • **el resultado superó nuestras ~s** the result surpassed our expectations • **no tiene ~s de que le den el empleo** he isn't expecting to get the job ▸ **expectativa de vida** life expectancy
2 (= *espera*) • **estar a la ~ de algo** to be waiting for sth • **estaban a la ~ de una respuesta** they were waiting for a reply • **estamos a la ~ de conocer los resultados electorales** we are waiting to hear the election results
expectorante (*Med*) ADJ expectorant
SM expectorant
expectorar ▹ CONJUG 1a VT, VI to expectorate
expedición SF **1** [*de personas*] (*Geog, Mil*) expedition; (*Dep*) away fixture ▸ **expedición de salvamento** rescue expedition ▸ **expedición militar** military expedition
2 (*Com*) shipment, shipping • **gastos de ~** shipping charges
3 (= *prontitud*) speed, dispatch (*frm*)
expedicionario/a ADJ expeditionary
SM/F member of an expedition
expedidor SM shipping agent, shipper
expedientar ▹ CONJUG 1a VT **1** (= *investigar*) (*gen*) to make a file on, draw up a dossier on; (*Jur*) to start proceedings against
2 (= *censurar*) to censure, reprimand
3 (= *expulsar*) to expel
4 (= *despedir*) (*gen*) to dismiss; [+ *médico*] to strike off the register
expediente SM **1** (= *documento*) (*como historial*) record; (*como dossier*) dossier; (*en forma de ficha*) file • **alumnos con buen/mal ~** pupils with a good/poor track record • MODISMO: • **cubrir el ~** to do the minimum required • **lo haré por cubrir el ~** I'll do it to keep up appearances ▸ **expediente académico** (*Escol*) student's record, transcript (*EEUU*) ▸ **expediente policial** police dossier
2 (*Jur*) (= *acción*) action, proceedings (*pl*); (= *papeles*) records of a case (*pl*) • **abrir** *o* **incoar ~** to start proceedings ▸ **expediente de regulación de empleo** labour *o* (*EEUU*) labor force adjustment plan ▸ **expediente disciplinario** disciplinary proceedings (*pl*) ▸ **expediente judicial** legal proceedings (*pl*)
3 (= *medio*) expedient, means • **recurrir al ~ de hacer algo** to resort to the device of doing sth
expedienteo SM bureaucracy, red tape
expedir ▹ CONJUG 3k VT [+ *mercancías*] to send, ship off; [+ *documento*] to draw up; [+ *orden, billete*] to issue; [+ *negocio*] to deal with, dispatch
expeditar ▹ CONJUG 1a VT (*CAm, Méx*) (= *acelerar*) to expedite (*frm*), hurry along; (= *concluir*) to conclude
expeditivo ADJ expeditious (*frm*), prompt, efficient
expedito ADJ **1** (= *pronto*) expeditious (*frm*), prompt, speedy
2 [*camino*] clear, free • **dejar ~ el camino para** to clear the way for
3 (*LAm*) (= *fácil*) easy
expeler ▹ CONJUG 2a VT to expel, eject
expendedor(a) ADJ • **máquina ~a** vending machine
SM/F (= *persona*) (*al detalle*) dealer, retailer; (*como intermediario*) agent; (*de tabaco*) tobacconist, tobacco dealer (*EEUU*); (*de lotería*) lottery-ticket seller; (*Teat*) ticket agent ▸ **expendedor(a) de billetes** ticket clerk, booking clerk ▸ **expendedor(a) de moneda falsa** distributor of counterfeit money
SM ▸ **expendedor automático** vending machine ▸ **expendedor automático de bebidas** drinks (vending) machine
expendeduría SF [*de tabaco*] tobacconist's (shop), cigar store (*EEUU*); [*de lotería*] lottery outlet
expender ▹ CONJUG 2a VT **1** [+ *dinero*] to expend (*frm*), spend
2 [+ *moneda falsa*] (= *emitir*) to put into circulation; (= *hacer circular*) to pass, circulate
3 [+ *mercancías*] (= *vender*) to sell, retail; (= *traficar*) to deal in; (= *ser agente de*) to be an agent for, sell on commission
expendio SM **1** (= *gasto*) expense, outlay
2 (*LAm*) (= *tienda*) small shop ▸ **expendio de boletos** (*Méx*) ticket office
3 (*And, Cono Sur, Méx*) (= *venta*) retailing, retail selling
4 ▸ **expendio de moneda falsa** (*Jur*) issuing false coin, passing false coin
expensar ▹ CONJUG 1a VT (*LAm*) to defray the costs of
expensas SFPL • **a ~ de** at the expense of • **a mis ~** at my expense
experiencia SF **1** (= *acontecimientos*) experience • **una triste ~** a sad experience • **saber por ~** to know by *o* from experience • **aprender por la ~** to learn by experience • **intercambiar ~s** to swap stories ▸ **experiencia laboral** work experience
2 (= *experimento*) experiment (**en** on) ▸ **experiencia clínica** clinical trial ▸ **experiencia piloto** pilot scheme
experienciar ▹ CONJUG 1b VT = **experimentar**
experimentación SF experimentation
experimentado ADJ experienced
experimental ADJ experimental
experimentalmente ADV experimentally
experimentar ▹ CONJUG 1a VT **1** [+ *método, producto*] to test, try out • **el nuevo fármaco está siendo experimentado** the new drug is being tested
2 (= *notar*) [+ *cambio*] to experience, go through; [+ *pérdida, deterioro*] to suffer; [+ *aumento*] to show; [+ *sensación*] to feel • **las cifras han experimentado un aumento de un 5 por 100** the figures show an increase of 5% • **no experimenté ninguna sensación nueva** I felt no new sensation • **el enfermo ha experimentado una ligera mejoría** the patient has improved slightly
VI to experiment (**con** with, **en** on)
experimento SM experiment (**con** with, **en** on) • **como ~** as an experiment, by way of experiment • **hacer ~s** to experiment (**con** with, **en** on)
experticia SF (*LAm*) expertise
expertización SF expert assessment
expertizar ▹ CONJUG 1f VT to appraise as an expert, give an expert assessment of
experto/a ADJ expert • **es experta en la materia** she's an expert on the subject • **ser ~ en hacer algo** to be an expert at doing sth • **son ~s en restaurar muebles** they are experts at restoring furniture • **eres ~ en meterte en líos** you're an expert at getting into trouble
SM/F expert • **se dejó asesorar por un ~** he sought the advice of an expert, he sought expert advice • **ser un ~ en algo** to be an expert on *o* in sth ▸ **experto/a contable** auditor, chartered accountant ▸ **experto/a tributario/a** tax expert
expiación SF expiation (*frm*), atonement
expiar ▹ CONJUG 1c VT to expiate (*frm*), atone for
expiatorio ADJ expiatory
expiración SF expiry, expiration
expirar ▹ CONJUG 1a VI to expire
explanación SF **1** (*Téc*) levelling
2† (= *explicación*) explanation, elucidation
explanada SF area of level ground ▸ **explanada de ensillado** saddling enclosure
explanar ▹ CONJUG 1a VT **1** (*Ferro, Téc*) to level, grade
2† (= *explicar*) to explain, elucidate
explayar ▹ CONJUG 1a VT to extend, expand
VPR **explayarse 1** (= *esparcirse*) (*gen*) to relax, take it easy; (*en discurso*) to speak at length • **~se a su gusto** to talk one's head off*, talk to one's heart's content • **~se con algn** to confide in sb
2 (= *extenderse*) to extend, spread
expletivo ADJ (*Ling*) expletive
explicable ADJ explicable, explainable • **cosas no fácilmente ~s** things not easily explained, things not easy to explain
explicación SF **1** [*de tema, motivo*] explanation
2 (= *motivo*) reason (**de** for) • **sin dar explicaciones** without giving any reason
3 (*Univ*) lecture, class
explicaderas SFPL • **tener buenas ~** to be good at explaining things (away); (*pey*) to be plausible
explicar ▹ CONJUG 1g VT **1** (= *exponer*) [+ *motivo, tema, cuestión, problema*] to explain; [+ *teoría*] to expound
2 (*Escol*) [+ *materia*] to lecture in; [+ *curso*] to teach; [+ *clase*] to give, deliver (*frm*)
VPR **explicarse 1** (*al exponer algo*) to explain,

EXPLICAR

▹ *Cuando* **explicar** *lleva objeto directo e indirecto, el orden en inglés es normalmente* **explain** + *objeto directo* + **to** + *objeto indirecto:*
¿Puedes explicarme eso?
Can you explain that to me?
Ya se lo he explicado a mi familia
I've already explained it to my family
Os explicaré la situación
I will explain the situation to you

▹ *Sin embargo, si el objeto directo es una construcción más compleja, en inglés se sigue el mismo orden que en español, sin olvidar el uso de la preposición* **to:**
¿Puedes explicarme por qué no viniste ni llamaste ayer?
Can you explain to me why you didn't come or phone yesterday?

Para otros usos y ejemplos ver la entrada.

explain o.s. • **¡explíquese usted!** explain yourself! • **explíquese con la mayor brevedad** please be as brief as possible • **se explica con claridad** he states things *o* expresses himself clearly • **esto no se explica fácilmente** this cannot be explained (away) easily, this isn't easy to explain
2 (*al entender algo*) • **no me lo explico** I can't understand it, I can't make it out
3* (= *pagar*) to cough up*, pay

explicativo ADJ, **explicatorio** ADJ explanatory

explícitamente ADV explicitly

explicitar ▹ CONJUG 1a VT (= *declarar*) to state, assert; (= *aclarar*) to clarify • **~ que ...** to make clear that ...

explícito ADJ explicit

exploración SF **1** [*de terreno, parte del cuerpo*] exploration; (*Mil*) reconnaissance, scouting; (*con radar*) scanning ▸ **exploración submarina** underwater exploration; (*como deporte*) skin-diving
2 (*Med*) ▸ **exploración física** physical examination

explorador(a) SM/F (*Geog*) explorer; (*Mil*) scout
SM **1** (*Med*) probe
2 (*con radar*) scanner ▸ **explorador láser** laser scanner
SM/F (boy) scout/(girl) guide *o* (*EEUU*) scout

explorar ▹ CONJUG 1a VT (*Geog*) to explore; (*Mil*) to reconnoitre; (*Med*) to probe; (*con radar*) to scan
VI to explore; (*Mil*) to reconnoitre, scout

exploratorio ADJ exploratory

explosión SF **1** [*de bomba*] explosion • **15 personas murieron a consecuencia de la ~** 15 people died in the explosion *o* blast • **hacer ~** to explode • **motor de ~** internal combustion engine • **teoría de la gran ~** big bang theory ▸ **explosión controlada** controlled explosion ▸ **explosión por simpatía** secondary explosion
2 [*de cólera*] outburst, explosion
3 (= *expansión*) explosion ▸ **explosión demográfica** population explosion

explosionar ▹ CONJUG 1a VT, VI to explode, blow up

explosiva SF (*Ling*) plosive, plosive consonant

explosivo ADJ explosive
SM explosive ▸ **explosivo de gran potencia**, **explosivo de ruido** stun grenade ▸ **explosivo detonante** powerful explosive ▸ **explosivo plástico** plastic explosive

explotable ADJ exploitable, that can be exploited

explotación SF **1** (= *uso*) [*de recursos, riquezas*] exploitation; [*de planta*] running, operation; [*de mina*] working • **en ~** in operation • **gastos de ~** operating costs, operating expenses ▸ **explotación a cielo abierto** opencast working, opencast mining, strip mining (*EEUU*) ▸ **explotación agrícola** farm ▸ **explotación forestal** forestry ▸ **explotación ganadera** livestock farm ▸ **explotación minera** mine ▸ **explotación petrolífera** oil exploration
2 (= *uso excesivo*) exploitation

explotador(a) ADJ exploitative
SM/F exploiter

explotar ▹ CONJUG 1a VT **1** (= *usar*) [+ *recursos, riquezas*] to exploit; [+ *planta*] to run, operate; [+ *mina*] to work
2 (= *usar excesivamente*) [+ *obreros*] to exploit; [+ *situación*] to exploit, make capital out of
3 [+ *bomba*] to explode
VI [*bomba*] to explode, go off • **~on dos bombas** two bombs exploded *o* went off • **cayó sin ~** it fell but did not go off, it landed without going off • **juegan con bombas sin ~** they play with unexploded bombs

expoliación SF pillaging, sacking

expoliar ▹ CONJUG 1b VT **1** (= *saquear*) to pillage, sack
2 (= *desposeer*) to dispossess

expolio SM **1** (= *saqueo*) pillaging, sacking
2 • MODISMO: • **armar un ~** to cause a hullaballoo*

exponencial ADJ exponential

exponente SMF (= *persona*) exponent
SM **1** (*Mat*) index, exponent
2 (= *ejemplo*) model, prime example • **el tabaco cubano es ~ de calidad** Cuban tobacco is the best of its kind

exponer ▹ CONJUG 2q (PP: **expuesto**) VT **1** (*al público*) **a** (*Arte*) [*museo*] to exhibit, put on show; [*galería, artista*] to show
b (*Com*) (*en tienda*) to display; (*en feria*) to exhibit
2 (*a la luz, al agua*) • **no debe ~ la cicatriz al sol** he must not expose the scar to the sun
3 (= *explicar*) [+ *teoría, argumento*] to set out, expound (*frm*); [+ *hechos*] to set out, state; [+ *situación*] to set out
4 (= *arriesgar*) to risk, put at risk • **expuso su vida por salvarla** he risked his life to save her, he put his life at risk to save her
5 (*Fot*) to expose
6 (*Rel*) • **~ el Santísimo** to expose the Holy Sacrament
7†† [+ *niño*] to abandon
VI [*pintor, escultor*] to exhibit, show
VPR **exponerse 1** (= *someterse*) • **~se a algo** to expose o.s. to sth • **con ese comentario se expone a las críticas de los periodistas** with that comment she's laying herself open to *o* exposing herself to criticism from the reporters • **le gusta ~se al peligro** she likes exposing herself to danger • **no se exponga al sol durante mucho tiempo** don't go out in the sun for a long time, don't expose yourself to the sun for a long time
2 (= *arriesgarse*) • **~se a hacer algo** to risk doing sth, run the risk of doing sth • **te expones a hacer el ridículo** you're risking making a fool of yourself, you're running the risk of making a fool of yourself • **con eso te expones a que te echen del colegio** that way you're running the risk of being expelled from school

exportable ADJ exportable

exportación SF **1** (= *acto*) export, exportation ▸ **exportación en pie** live export
2 (= *artículo*) export, exported article; (= *mercancías*) exports (*pl*) • **géneros de ~** exports, exported goods • **comercio de ~** export trade

exportador(a) ADJ [*país*] exporting
SM/F exporter

exportar ▹ CONJUG 1a VT to export

exposición SF **1** (= *muestra*) (*Arte*) exhibition; (*Com*) show, fair ▸ **exposición canina** dog show ▸ **exposición de modas** fashion show ▸ **exposición estática** static display ▸ **exposición itinerante** travelling show, traveling show (*EEUU*) ▸ **exposición universal** world fair
2 (= *acto*) (*gen*) exposing, exposure; (*Fot*) exposure; (*Com*) display
3 (= *enunciado*) [*de hechos*] statement; [*de teoría*] exposition ▸ **exposición de motivos** (*Jur*) explanatory preamble

exposímetro SM (*Fot*) exposure meter

expósito/a ADJ ▹ niño
SM/F foundling

expositor(a) SM/F (*Arte*) exhibitor; [*de teoría*] exponent
SM (= *vitrina*) showcase, display case; (= *puesto*) sales stand

exprés ADJ • **café ~** espresso • **olla ~** pressure cooker
SM **1** (*LAm*) (= *tren*) express train
2 (= *café*) espresso coffee

expresado ADJ above-mentioned • **según las cifras expresadas** according to these figures, according to the figures given earlier

expresamente ADV (= *concretamente*) expressly; (= *a propósito*) on purpose, deliberately; (= *claramente*) clearly, plainly • **no lo dijo ~** he didn't say so in so many words

expresar ▹ CONJUG 1a VT **1** (*al hablar*) (= *enunciar*) to express; (= *redactar*) to phrase, put; (= *declarar*) to state, set forth; (= *citar*) to quote; [+ *opiniones, quejas*] to voice • **expresa las opiniones de todos** he is voicing the opinions of us all • **estaba expresado de otro modo** it was worded differently • **el papel no lo expresa** the paper doesn't say so • **usted deberá ~ el número del giro postal** you should quote *o* give *o* state the number of the postal order
2 [+ *sentimiento*] to show
VPR **expresarse 1** [*persona*] to express o.s. • **no se expresa bien** he doesn't express himself well
2 [*cifra, dato*] to be stated • **como abajo se expresa** as is stated below • **el número no se expresa** the number is not given *o* stated

expresión SF **1** (= *acto*) expression • **esta ~ de nuestro agradecimiento** this expression of our gratitude • **han recibido expresiones de solidaridad** they have received messages *o* expressions of solidarity ▸ **expresión corporal** self-expression through movement
2 (*Ling*) expression • **la ~ es poco clara** the expression is not very clear ▸ **expresión familiar** colloquialism, conversational *o* colloquial expression
3 expresiones†† (= *saludos*) greetings, regards

expresionismo SM expressionism

expresionista ADJ, SMF expressionist

expresivamente ADV **1** (= *con expresividad*) expressively
2 (= *cariñosamente*) tenderly, affectionately

expresividad SF expressiveness

expresivo ADJ (= *que gesticula*) expressive; (= *cariñoso*) tender, affectionate, warm

expreso ADJ **1** (= *explícito*) express; (= *exacto*) specific, clear
2 [*tren*] express, fast
3 • **café ~** espresso
SM **1** (*Ferro*) express train, fast train
2 (= *persona*) special messenger
3 (*Caribe*) (= *autobús*) long-distance coach
ADV express • **mandar algo ~** to send sth express

exprimelimones SM INV lemon squeezer

exprimidera SF squeezer

exprimidor SM (*manual*) lemon squeezer; (*eléctrico*) juice extractor, juicer

exprimir ▹ CONJUG 3a VT **1** [+ *limón, naranja*] to squeeze; [+ *jugo*] to squeeze out, express (*frm*)
2 [+ *ropa*] to wring out, squeeze dry
3 (*pey*) [+ *persona*] to exploit
VPR **exprimirse** • MODISMO: • **~se el cerebro** *o* **los sesos*** to rack one's brains

ex profeso ADV on purpose, deliberately

expropiación SF [*de casa, terreno*] expropriation; [*de vehículo*] commandeering • **orden de ~** compulsory purchase order ▸ **expropiación forzosa** compulsory purchase

expropiar ▷ CONJUG 1b (VT) [+ *casa, terreno*] (*sin indemnización*) to expropriate; (*con indemnización*) to place a compulsory purchase order on; [+ *vehículo*] to commandeer
expuesto (VB) (*pp de* **exponer**) • **según lo arriba ~** according to what has been stated *o* set out above
(ADJ) **1** [*lugar*] (= *al descubierto*) exposed; (= *peligroso*) dangerous • **partes del cuerpo expuestas al sol** parts of the body exposed to the sun
2 [*cuadro, mercancías*] on show, on display, on view • **los artículos ~s en el escaparate** the goods displayed in the window
3 • **estar ~ a un riesgo** to be exposed *o* open to a risk
expugnar ▷ CONJUG 1a (VT) to take by storm
expulsar ▷ CONJUG 1a (VT) **1** (= *hacer salir*) [+ *alumno, inmigrante*] to expel; [+ *jugador*] to send off, eject (EEUU); [+ *intruso, alborotador*] to eject, throw out (**de** from) • **la ~on del partido** she was expelled from the party, she was thrown out of the party • **el árbitro lo expulsó del terreno de juego** the referee sent him off the pitch
2 [+ *gases, humo*] to expel
expulsión (SF) **1** (= *acto*) [*de gases, humo, persona*] expulsion; [*de país*] deportation; (*Dep*) sending-off, ejection (EEUU)
2 (*Econ*) crowding out effect
expulsor (ADJ) • **asiento ~** (*Aer*) ejector seat
(SM) (*Téc*) ejector
expurgar ▷ CONJUG 1h (VT) to expurgate
expurgatorio (ADJ) expurgatory • **índice ~** (*Rel*) Index
exquisitamente (ADV) **1** (= *con refinamiento*) exquisitely; (= *deliciosamente*) deliciously, delightfully; (= *excelentemente*) excellently
2 (*pey*) affectedly
exquisitez (SF) **1** (= *cualidad*) [*de algo refinado*] exquisiteness; [*de algo excelente*] excellence
2 [*de comida*] delicacy
3 (*pey*) affectation
exquisito (ADJ) **1** (= *excelente*) excellent
2 (= *refinado*) [*belleza*] exquisite; [*comida*] delicious
3 (*pey*) (= *afectado*) affected; (= *melindroso*) choosy*, finicky
Ext. (ABR) **1** (= **Exterior**) ext
2 (= **Extensión**) ext., extn
extasiado (ADJ) in ecstasies, in raptures • **quedarse ~ ante/con** to be mesmerized by
extasiar ▷ CONJUG 1c (VT) to entrance, enrapture, captivate
(VPR) **extasiarse** to become entranced, go into ecstasies (**ante** over, about)
éxtasis (SM INV) **1** (= *estado*) (*por arrobamiento*) ecstasy, rapture; (*por trance*) trance • **estar en ~** to be in ecstasy
2 (= *droga*) ecstasy, E*
extático (ADJ) ecstatic, rapturous • **lo miró ~** he looked at it ecstatically
extemporal (ADJ), **extemporáneo** (ADJ) [*lluvia*] unseasonable; [*comentario, viaje*] untimely
extender ▷ CONJUG 2g (VT) **1** (= *desplegar*) [+ *manta, mantel*] to spread out; [+ *alas*] to spread, stretch out; [+ *brazo, pierna, tentáculo*] to stretch out • **extendió el mapa encima de la mesa** he opened out *o* spread out the map on the table • **la corriente del Golfo extiende su acción beneficiosa hasta el norte de Europa** the beneficial effects of the Gulf Stream reach as far as northern Europe • **~ la mano a algn** to hold out one's hand to sb, extend one's hand to sb (*frm*)
2 (= *esparcir*) [+ *sellos, arena*] to lay out, spread out • **extendimos el tabaco al sol** we laid *o* spread the tobacco out in the sun
3 (= *untar*) [+ *crema, mantequilla*] to spread • **la pomada se extiende con cuidado sobre la quemadura** spread the cream carefully on the burn
4 (= *difundir*) [+ *noticia, rumor*] to spread; [+ *influencia, poder*] to extend
5 (*frm*) (= *rellenar*) [+ *cheque, receta*] to make out, write out; [+ *certificado*] to issue • **extendí un cheque a su nombre** I made out *o* wrote out a cheque to him
6 (= *ampliar*) [+ *oferta, contrato*] to extend • **han extendido la oferta hasta mayo** they have extended the offer until May • **han extendido el derecho de cobrar una pensión a las amas de casa** the right to receive a pension has been extended to include housewives
7 (*Téc*) [+ *alambre*] to draw
(VPR) **extenderse 1** (= *propagarse*) [*tumor, rumor, revolución*] to spread (**a** to) • **el fuego se extendió por toda la casa** the fire spread throughout the house
2 (= *ocupar un espacio*) [*terreno, cultivo*] to stretch, extend; [*especie, raza*] to extend • **la mancha de petróleo se extendía hasta la orilla** the oil-slick stretched *o* extended as far as the shore • **la ciudad se extendía a nuestros pies** the city (lay) stretched away beneath us • **ante nosotros se extendía todo un mundo de posibilidades** a whole world of possibilities lay before us
3 (= *durar*) to last • **su reinado se extendió a lo largo de 50 años** his reign lasted a full 50 years • **el período que se extiende desde principios de siglo hasta los años veinte** the period lasting from the beginning of the century up to the 1920s
4 (= *explayarse*) • **~se en** *o* **sobre** [+ *tema, comentarios, respuestas*] to expand on • **no quisiera ~me demasiado en esta cuestión** I'd rather not expand too much on this subject • **nos extendimos demasiado en el debate** we spent too long on the debate
extendido (ADJ) **1** (= *desplegado*) [*mantel, mapa*] spread out, outspread; [*alas, brazos*] stretched out, outstretched • **con los brazos ~s** with his arms stretched out, with outstretched arms
2 (= *propagado*) widespread • **está muy ~ el uso de esa palabra** that word is very widely used, the use of that word is very widespread • **tenía el tumor muy ~** the tumour had spread all over his body
extensamente (ADV) **1** (= *mucho*) extensively, widely • **ha viajado ~ por Asia** he has travelled extensively *o* widely in Asia
2 (= *con detalle*) at length, thoroughly • **trató el tema ~** he dealt with the subject at length *o* thoroughly
extensible (ADJ) **1** [*mesa, escalera*] extending
2 (= *ampliable*) • **un período ~ a tres meses** a period which can be extended to three months • **estas críticas son ~s al resto del equipo** these criticisms can be extended to the rest of the team
extensión (SF) **1** (= *superficie*) area • **una enorme ~ de agua** an enormous area of water • **grandes extensiones del Reino Unido** large areas of the United Kingdom • **una isla con una ~ similar a la de Europa** an island similar in area to Europe
2 (= *duración*) length • **la ~ del relato** the length of the story
3 (= *amplitud*) [*de conocimientos*] extent, range; [*de programa*] scope; [*de significado*] range • **en toda la ~ de la palabra** in every sense of the word • **por ~** by extension • **esto nos afecta a nosotros y, por ~, a todo el país** this affects us and, by extension, the whole country
4 (= *ampliación*) [*de incendio*] spread; [*de plazo*] extension • **la ~ del regadío a tierras de secano** the extending of irrigation systems to dry lands
5 [*de cable, cuerda*] extension
6 (*Telec*) extension • **¿puede ponerme con la ~ 14?** can I have extension 14, please?, can you put me through to extension 14, please?
7 (*Mús*) [*de instrumento, voz*] range, compass
8 (*en instituciones*) ▸ **Extensión Agraria** agricultural advisory service ▸ **Extensión Universitaria** extramural studies (*pl*)
9 plug-in
extensivo (ADJ) extensive • **hacer ~ a** to extend to, apply to • **la crítica se hizo extensiva a toda la ciudad** the criticism extended *o* applied to the whole city
extenso (ADJ) **1** (= *amplio*) [*superficie, objeto*] extensive; [*capítulo, documento*] long, lengthy
2 (= *completo*) [*estudio, tratado*] extensive; [*conocimientos, vocabulario*] extensive, wide • **un ~ programa de conferencias** an extensive conference programme
3 (= *detallado*) full, detailed • **estuvo muy ~ en sus explicaciones** his explanations were very detailed, he gave full *o* detailed explanations • **en** *o* **por ~** in full, at length
extensor (SM) chest expander
extenuación (SF) exhaustion
extenuado (ADJ) (= *cansado*) exhausted; (= *débil*) emaciated, wasted
extenuar ▷ CONJUG 1e (VT) (= *cansar*) to exhaust; (= *debilitar*) to emaciate, weaken
(VPR) **extenuarse** (= *cansarse*) to get exhausted; (= *debilitarse*) to become emaciated, waste away
exterior (ADJ) **1** (= *externo*) [*superficie*] outer; [*pared*] external; [*mundo*] exterior, outside • **una habitación ~** a room facing onto the street
2 (= *extranjero*) [*relaciones, deuda, política*] foreign; [*comercio, ayuda*] foreign, overseas • **asuntos ~es** foreign affairs • **comercio ~** foreign trade, overseas trade; ▷ **asunto**
(SM) **1** (= *parte de fuera*) outside, exterior • **el ~ del edificio** the outside *o* exterior of the building • **con el ~ pintado de azul** with the outside painted blue • **salimos al ~ a tomar el aire** we went outside for a breath of fresh air • **el motorista alemán avanzaba por el ~** the German driver was catching up on the outside
2 • **el ~** (= *el extranjero*) abroad • **no hemos recibido noticias del ~** we haven't received any news from abroad • **tanto aquí como en el ~** both here and abroad • **comercio con el ~** foreign trade, overseas trade
3 exteriores (*Cine*) location shots • **rodar en ~es** to film on location
4 Exteriores (*Pol*) the Foreign Ministry, the Foreign Office, the State Department (EEUU)
exterioridad (SF) **1** (= *apariencia*) outward appearance, externals (*pl*)
2 exterioridades (= *pompa*) pomp (*sing*), show (*sing*); (= *formas*) formalities
exteriorización (SF) externalization, exteriorization
exteriorizar ▷ CONJUG 1f (VT) (= *expresar*) to express outwardly; (= *mostrar*) to show, reveal
exteriormente (ADV) outwardly
exterminación (SF) extermination
exterminar ▷ CONJUG 1a (VT) to exterminate
exterminio (SM) extermination
externalización (SF) [*de servicios*] outsourcing
externalizar ▷ CONJUG 1f (VT) to outsource
externamente (ADV) externally, outwardly
externo/a (ADJ) [*influencia*] outside, external; [*superficie*] outer; [*pared*] external

• **"medicamento de uso ~"** "medicine for external use only"
SM/F (= *alumno*) day pupil

extinción SF extinction

extinguido ADJ [*animal, volcán*] extinct; [*fuego*] out, extinguished

extinguidor SM (*LAm*) (*tb* **extinguidor de incendios**) fire extinguisher

extinguir ▸ CONJUG 3d VT **1** (= *exterminar*) [+ *fuego*] to extinguish, put out; [+ *sublevación*] to put down
2 [+ *deuda*] to wipe out
3 (*Bio*) to exterminate, wipe out
4 • **~ una sentencia** (*Jur*) to serve a sentence
VPR **extinguirse 1** [*fuego*] to go out
2 (*Bio*) to die out, become extinct
3 [*contrato, plazo*] to expire

extinto ADJ **1** [*especie, volcán*] extinct
2 (*Méx*) (*euf*) (= *difunto*) dead, deceased

extintor SM ▸ **extintor de incendios** fire extinguisher ▸ **extintor de espuma** foam extinguisher

extirpación SF **1** (= *eliminación*) extirpation (*frm*), eradication
2 (*Med*) removal

extirpar ▸ CONJUG 1a VT **1** [+ *problema, vicio*] to eradicate, stamp out
2 (*Med*) to remove (surgically), take out

extorno SM (*Com*) rebate

extorsión SF **1** (*Econ*) (*con intimidación*) extortion, exaction; (*haciendo chantaje*) blackmail
2 (= *molestia*) inconvenience

extorsionador(a) SM/F (= *intimidador*) extortioner; (= *chantajista*) blackmailer

extorsionar ▸ CONJUG 1a VT **1** (= *usurpar*) to extort money from • **~on a un empresario** they extorted money from a businessman
2 (= *molestar*) to pester, bother

extorsionista SMF (*Méx*) extortionist, blackmailer

extra ADJ INV [*tiempo*] extra; [*gasolina*] high-octane • **calidad ~** top-quality, best
SMF (*Cine*) extra
SM **1** (*en cuenta*) extra; (*de pago*) bonus
2 (= *periódico*) special edition, special supplement

extra... PREF extra...

extraacadémico ADJ non-university (*adj inv*), (taking place) outside the university

extracción SF **1** (*Med*) [*de diente*] extraction; [*de bala, astilla*] extraction, removal
2 (*Min*) [*de minerales*] mining, extraction; [*de petróleo*] extraction; [*de pizarra, mármol*] quarrying
3 (*en sorteo*) • **vamos a proceder a la primera ~** we shall now draw the first number
4 (= *origen*) origins (*pl*) • **de ~ humilde** of humble origins, from a humble background
5 (*Mat*) extraction

extracomunitario ADJ • **países ~s** countries outside the European Union, non-EU countries

extraconstitucional ADJ unconstitutional

extraconyugal ADJ extramarital, adulterous

extracorto ADJ ultra-short

extractar ▸ CONJUG 1a VT **1** to make extracts from
2 (= *resumir*) to abridge, summarize

extracto SM **1** (= *resumen*) summary, abstract ▸ **extracto de cuentas** (*Econ*) (bank) statement
2 (*Farm, Culin*) extract ▸ **extracto de carne** meat extract ▸ **extracto de violeta** violet extract

extractor SM extractor ▸ **extractor de humos** extractor fan

extracurricular ADJ extracurricular, outside the curriculum

extradeportivo ADJ unrelated to sport

extradición SF extradition • **delito sujeto a ~** extraditable offence

extradicionar ▸ CONJUG 1a VT to extradite

extradir ▸ CONJUG 3a VT to extradite

extraditable ADJ subject to extradition
SMF **1** (*Pol*) person subject to extradition
2 (*esp Col*) prominent drug baron (*wanted by US police*)

extraditar ▸ CONJUG 1a VT to extradite

extraer ▸ CONJUG 2o VT **1** [+ *diente, bala, astilla*] to extract
2 (*Min*) [+ *minerales*] to mine, extract; [+ *petróleo*] to extract; [+ *pizarra, mármol*] to quarry
3 [+ *conclusiones*] to draw
4 (*en sorteo*) to draw
5 (*Mat*) to extract

extraescolar ADJ • **actividad ~** out-of-school activity

extrafino ADJ superfine

extraíble ADJ removable, detachable

extrajudicial ADJ extrajudicial, out of court

extrajudicialmente ADV out of court

extrajurídico ADJ outside the law

extralargo ADJ king-size

extralimitación SF abuse (*of authority*)

extralimitarse ▸ CONJUG 1a VPR to exceed *o* abuse one's authority, overstep the mark

extramarital ADJ extramarital

extramatrimonial ADJ [*relaciones*] extramarital • **hijo ~** child born outside marriage *o* wedlock

extramuros ADV outside the city • **~ de** outside

extranet SF extranet

extranjería SF alien status, status of foreigners • **ley de ~** law on aliens

extranjerismo SM foreign word *o* phrase *etc*

extranjerizante ADJ [*ley*] tending to favour foreign ways; [*palabra*] foreign-looking, foreign-sounding

extranjero/a ADJ foreign
SM/F foreigner; (*Jur*) alien
SM • **en el ~** abroad • **estar en el ~** to be abroad, be in foreign parts • **ir al ~** to go abroad • **pasó seis años en el ~** he spent six years abroad • **cosas del ~** things from abroad, foreign things

extranjis* • **de ~** ADV secretly, on the sly

extrañamente ADV strangely, oddly

extrañamiento SM **1** (= *enajenación*) estrangement (**de** from)
2 = **extrañeza**
3 (*Jur*) banishment

extrañar ▸ CONJUG 1a VT **1** (= *sorprender*) to surprise • **eso me extraña** that surprises me, I find that odd • **¡no me ~ía!** I wouldn't be surprised!, it wouldn't surprise me! • **¡ya me extrañaba a mí!** I thought it was a bit strange! • **me extrañaba que no hubieras venido** I was surprised you hadn't come • **me ~ía que ...** I'd be surprised if ... • **no es de ~ que ...** it's hardly surprising that ..., it's no wonder that ...
2 (= *echar de menos*) to miss • **esta noche he extrañado mi cama** last night I missed sleeping in my own bed • **extraña mucho a sus padres** he misses his parents a lot
3†† (= *desterrar*) to banish
VPR **extrañarse 1** (= *sorprenderse*) to be surprised • **~se de algo** to be surprised at sth • **me extrañé de la reacción de tu hermano** I was surprised at your brother's reaction • **se extrañó de vernos juntos** he was surprised to see us together • **~se de que ...** to be surprised that ...
2†† (= *negarse*) to refuse
3†† [*amigos*] to become estranged, grow apart

extrañeza SF **1** (= *rareza*) strangeness, oddness
2 (= *asombro*) surprise, amazement • **me miró con ~** he looked at me in surprise
3 [*de amigos*] estrangement, alienation

extraño/a ADJ **1** (= *raro*) strange • **es muy ~** it's very odd *o* strange • **¡qué ~!** how odd *o* strange! • **parece ~ que ...** it seems odd *o* strange that ...
2 (= *ajeno*) • **un cuerpo ~** a foreign body • **murió en tierra extraña** he died on foreign soil • **estas son costumbres extrañas a este país** these are customs which are foreign *o* alien to this country • **este estilo no es ~ a los lectores de su poesía** this style is not unknown to readers of his poetry
SM/F **1** (= *desconocido*) stranger • **no quiero que hables con ~s** I don't want you talking to strangers
2 (= *extranjero*) foreigner
SM • **hacer un ~: el balón hizo un ~** the ball took a bad bounce • **el caballo hizo un ~** the horse shied

extrañoso ADJ (*And*) surprised

extraoficial ADJ unofficial, informal

extraoficialmente ADV unofficially, informally

extraordinaria SF (= *paga*) Christmas bonus

extraordinariamente ADV extraordinarily

extraordinario ADJ **1** (= *especial*) extraordinary • **no tiene nada de ~** there's nothing extraordinary *o* special about it
2 (= *destacado*) outstanding; [*edición, número, descuento*] special; [*cobro*] supplementary, extra • **por sus servicios ~s** for his outstanding services
3 (= *insólito*) unusual
SM **1** (*para una ocasión especial*) treat
2 (*en menú*) special dish, extra dish
3 (*de publicación*) special issue

extraparlamentario ADJ (taking place) outside parliament

extrapeninsular ADJ outside Iberia, relating to areas outside the Peninsula

extraplanetario ADJ other-worldly

extraplano ADJ super-slim

extraplomado ADJ overhanging

extraplomo SM overhang

extrapolable ADJ comparable

extrapolación SF extrapolation

extrapolar ▸ CONJUG 1a VT to extrapolate

extrarradio SM suburbs (*pl*), outlying area

extrasensorial ADJ extrasensory

extratasa SF surcharge, extra charge

extraterrenal ADJ, **extraterreno** ADJ (*LAm*) (= *sobrenatural*) supernatural; (= *extraterrestre*) extraterrestrial, from another planet

extraterrestre ADJ from outer space, extraterrestrial
SMF alien, extraterrestrial

extraterritorial ADJ extraterritorial

extravagancia SF **1** (= *cualidad*) [*de persona, aspecto, ropa*] extravagance, outlandishness
2 (= *capricho*) whim • **tiene sus ~s** he has his oddities *o* peculiarities

extravagante ADJ [*ideas, ropa, persona*] extravagant, outlandish

extravagantemente ADV extravagantly, outlandishly

extravasarse ▸ CONJUG 1a VPR [*líquido*] to leak out, flow out; [*sangre*] to ooze out

extravertido/a ADJ, SM/F

= extrovertido

extraviado ADJ [*persona, objeto*] lost, missing; [*animal*] lost, stray • **un niño ~** a missing child

extraviar ▷ CONJUG 1C VT **1** [+ *objeto*] to lose, mislay, misplace
2 (*pey*) [+ *dinero*] to embezzle
3 (= *desorientar*) [+ *persona*] to mislead, misdirect
VPR **extraviarse 1** (= *perderse*) [*persona*] to get lost, lose one's way; [*animal*] to stray; [*objeto*] to go missing, go astray; [*carta*] to go astray, get lost in the post
2 [*persona*] (*moralmente*) to go astray, err, fall into evil ways

extravío SM **1** (= *pérdida*) [*de objeto*] loss, mislaying; [*de animal*] loss
2 (*moral*) misconduct, erring, evil ways (*pl*)

extremadamente ADV extremely, exceedingly • **pesticidas ~ peligrosas** extremely *o* exceedingly dangerous pesticides • **una obra ~ original** a highly original work

extremado ADJ extreme • **paisajes de extremada belleza** landscapes of extreme beauty • **un descubrimiento de extremada importancia** an extremely important discovery, a discovery of extreme importance • **lo trató con extremada dureza** he treated him extremely harshly, he treated him with extreme harshness

Extremadura SF Extremadura

extremar ▷ CONJUG 1A VT (= *aumentar al máximo*) • **fue necesario ~ las medidas de seguridad** it was necessary to maximize security measures • **las personas alérgicas deben ~ las precauciones** allergic people should take extra precautions • **sin ~ el sentimentalismo** without overdoing the sentimentality
VPR **extremarse** to do one's best • **veo que os habéis extremado en la organización** I see that you have done your very best in the organization • **no hace falta que te extremes en la presentación** you don't need to make a special effort in the presentation

extremaunción SF extreme unction

extremeño/a ADJ, SM/F Extremaduran

extremidad SF **1** (= *punta*) tip, extremity; (= *borde*) edge, outermost part
2 extremidades (*Anat*) extremities

extremismo SM extremism

extremista ADJ, SMF extremist

extremo[1] ADJ **1** (= *máximo*) extreme • **una situación de extrema pobreza** a situation of extreme poverty • **en situaciones de calor ~** in extremely hot weather • **el nivel de polen era ~** the pollen count was extremely high • **heridas de extrema gravedad** extremely serious wounds • **en caso ~** as a last resort, if all else fails
2 (= *alejado*) furthest • **vive en el punto más ~ de la isla** she lives on the furthest *o* most extreme point of the island; ▷ **oriente**
3 (*Pol*) (= *radical*) extreme • **representa lo más ~ de la izquierda** she represents the extreme left wing • **extrema derecha** extreme right, far right • **extrema izquierda** extreme left, far left

extremo[2] SM **1** (= *punta*) end • **vive en el otro ~ de la calle** he lives at the far *o* other end of the street • **agarra la cuerda por este ~** take this end of the rope, take hold of the rope by *o* at this end • **el ~ oriental de la península** the easternmost side *o* point of the peninsula • **de ~ a ~** from one end *o* side to the other • **de un ~ a otro** (*lit*) from one end *o* side to the other; (*fig*) from one extreme to another • MODISMOS: • **ser el ~ opuesto** to be the complete opposite • **ser los dos ~s** to be complete opposites
• REFRÁN: • **los ~s se tocan** opposites attract
2 (= *límite*) extreme • **no me gustan los ~s** I don't like extremes of any kind • **su crueldad alcanzaba ~s insospechados** his cruelty plumbed unheard-of depths • **si la situación se deteriora hasta ese ~ ...** if the situation deteriorates to that extent ... • **en ~** extremely • **la situación era en ~ peligrosa** the situation was extremely dangerous *o* was dangerous in the extreme (*más frm*)
• **todavía me pesa en ~** I still feel extremely guilty • **hasta el ~** to the full • **estamos explotando los recursos hasta el ~** we are exploiting resources to the full • **es detallista hasta el ~** he pays extremely close attention to detail • **llegar a** *o* **hasta el ~ de**: • **hemos llegado al ~ de no decirnos ni hola** it's got to the point now that we don't even say hello to each other • **llegó hasta el ~ de decir que lo mataría** she went as far as to say that she would kill him • **por ahorrar ha llegado al ~ de no comer** he's so desperate to save money he's stopped eating • **en último ~** as a last resort, if all else fails
3 (= *asunto*) point • **ese ~ no se tocó en la discusión** that point was not touched on during the discussion • **pidieron una rebaja en el rescate, ~ que fue rechazado** they asked for the ransom to be reduced, a condition which was refused
4 (= *cuidado*) great care
SMF (*Dep*) ▸ **extremo derecho** right winger • **jugaba de ~ derecho** he played (on the) right wing, he played as a right winger
▸ **extremo izquierdo** left winger

Extremo Oriente SM Far East

extremoso ADJ [*persona*] (= *efusivo*) gushing, effusive; (= *vehemente*) vehement, extreme in one's attitudes *o* reactions

extrínseco ADJ extrinsic

extroversión SF extroversion

extrovertido/a ADJ extrovert, outgoing
SM/F extrovert

exuberancia SF **1** [*de persona, conducta*] exuberance
2 (*Bot*) luxuriance, lushness
3 (*en el cuerpo*) fullness, buxomness

exuberante ADJ **1** [*persona, conducta*] exuberant
2 (*Bot*) luxuriant, lush
3 [*cuerpo, formas*] full, buxom

exuberantemente ADV luxuriantly

exudación SF exudation

exudar ▷ CONJUG 1A VT to exude, ooze
VI to exude, ooze out (**de** from)

exultación SF exultation

exultante ADJ elated, overjoyed • **~ de felicidad** flushed with happiness

exultar ▷ CONJUG 1A VI to exult

exvoto SM votive offering

eyaculación SF ejaculation ▸ **eyaculación precoz** premature ejaculation

eyacular ▷ CONJUG 1A VT, VI to ejaculate

eyectable ADJ • **asiento ~** ejector seat

eyectar ▷ CONJUG 1A VT to eject
VPR **eyectarse** (*Aer*) to eject

eyector SM (*Téc*) ejector

-ez ▷ **Aspects of Word Formation in Spanish 2**

Ezequiel SM Ezekiel

EZLN SM ABR (*Méx*) = **Ejército Zapatista de Liberación Nacional**

Ff

f

F[1], **f** ['efe] SF (= *letra*) F, f
F[2] ABR **1** = **fuerza** • **un viento F8** a force eight wind
2 (= **febrero**) Feb • **el 23-F** 23 February *(date of the Tejero coup attempt, in 1981)*
f.ª ABR (*Com*) (= **factura**) inv
fa SM (*Mús*) fa, F ▸ **fa bemol** F flat ▸ **fa mayor** F major ▸ **fa menor** F minor ▸ **fa sostenido** F sharp
fab. ABR (= **fabricante**) mfr(s)
f.a.b. ABR (= **franco a bordo**) FOB, f.o.b.
fabada SF *rich stew of beans, pork etc*
fabe SF (*Asturias*) bean
fabla SF **1** (*Hist*) pseudo-archaic style
2 ▸ **fabla aragonesa** Aragonese dialect
fábrica SF **1** (= *factoría*) factory • **marca de ~** trademark • **precio de ~** price ex-works, price ex-factory ▸ **fábrica de acero** steel plant, steelworks ▸ **fábrica de algodón** cotton mill ▸ **fábrica de cerveza** brewery ▸ **fábrica de conservas** canning plant, cannery ▸ **fábrica de gas** gasworks ▸ **fábrica de moneda** mint ▸ **fábrica de montaje** assembly plant ▸ **fábrica de papel** paper mill ▸ **fábrica de vidrio** glassworks ▸ **fábrica experimental** pilot plant
2 (*Arquit*) • **de ~** stone, stonework
3 (= *proceso*) manufacture
4 (*And*) (= *alambique*) still, distillery
fabricación SF manufacture • **de ~ casera** home-made • **de ~ nacional** home-produced • **de ~ propia** our own make • **estar en ~** to be in production ▸ **fabricación asistida por ordenador** computer-aided manufacturing ▸ **fabricación de coches** car manufacture ▸ **fabricación de tejas** tile making ▸ **fabricación en serie** mass production
fabricante ADJ • **la compañía ~** the manufacturer
SMF (*en gran escala*) manufacturer, maker; (*en pequeña escala*) maker • **es ~ de violines** he's a violin-maker
fabricar ▷ CONJUG 1g VT **1** (*gen*) to manufacture, make; (= *construir*) to build, construct • **~ en serie** to mass-produce
2 [+ *mentira*] to fabricate, concoct; [+ *documento*] to fabricate, falsify
fabril ADJ manufacturing, industrial
fabriquero†† SM **1** = **fabricante**
2 (*Rel*) churchwarden
3 (*Méx*) (= *destilador*) distillery operator *(in a sugar mill)*
fábula SF **1** (*Literat*) fable; (= *historia*) tale, story
2 (= *rumor*) rumour, rumor (EEUU); (= *chisme*) (piece of) gossip; (= *mentira*) invention
3* • **es de ~** it's fabulous
4† (= *argumento*) plot, story
5† (= *persona*) talk of the town, laughing-stock
fabulación SF **1** (= *creación*) invention • **capacidad de ~** inventiveness
2 (= *historia*) invention
fabulador(a) ADJ story-telling
SM/F story-teller
fabular ▷ CONJUG 1a VT [+ *historia*] to make up
VI • **~ sobre algo** to write a story about sth
fabulario SM collection of fables
fabulista SMF writer of fables
fabulosamente ADV [*barato, bueno*] fabulously • **anoche lo pasaron ~** they had a fabulous time last night
fabuloso ADJ **1** (= *mítico*) mythical, fabulous (*liter*); (= *ficticio*) fabulous (*liter*), imaginary
2* (= *maravilloso*) fantastic, fabulous • **es francamente ~** it's just fabulous
FACA SM ABR (*Esp*) = **Futuro avión de combate y ataque**
faca SF *large, curved knife with a sharp tip*
facción SF **1** (*Pol*) faction
2 facciones (*Anat*) features • **de facciones irregulares** with *o* of irregular features
3 (*Milt*) duty • **estar de ~** to be on duty
faccioso/a ADJ [*propaganda, jefe*] rebel; [*bando*] breakaway
SM/F (= *rebelde*) rebel; (= *agitador*) agitator
faceta SF **1** (= *aspecto*) facet
2 [*de cristal, piedra preciosa*] facet
faceto* ADJ (*Méx*) cocksure, arrogant
FACH SF ABR (*Chile*) = **Fuerza Aérea de Chile**
facha[1]* SF **1** (= *aspecto*) look; (= *cara*) face • **la tarta tiene buena ~** the cake looks really good • **esos individuos tienen una mala ~** that bunch look a bit dodgy* • **¿adónde vas con esa ~?** where are you going looking like that? • **tener ~ de** to look like • **tiene ~ de poli** he looks like a copper* • **tiene ~ de buena gente** he looks OK*
2 (*pey*) • **estar hecho una ~** to look a sight*, look terrible; **fachas** (*Méx*) slovenly dress (*sing*)
3 • **ponerse en ~** (*Náut*) to lie to
facha[2]* (*pey*) ADJ (*Esp*) fascist
SMF (*Esp*) fascist
fachada SF **1** [*de edificio*] façade, front; (= *medida*) frontage • **con ~ al parque** looking towards the park, overlooking the park • **con 15 metros de ~** with a frontage of 15m
2 (= *apariencia*) façade • **tener mucha ~** to be all show and no substance • **no tiene más que ~** it's all just a façade with him, it's all just show with him • **bajo la ~ de benefactor de las artes** under the guise of a patron of the arts
3‡ (= *cara*) mug‡
4 (*Tip*) title page
fachado* ADJ • **bien ~** good-looking • **mal ~** ugly, plain
fachenda* SF conceitedness
SMF show-off*
fachendear* ▷ CONJUG 1a VI to show off*
fachendista*, **fachendoso/a***, **fachento*** a (*CAm*) ADJ stuck-up*, snooty*
SM/F show-off*
fachinal* SM (*Cono Sur*) swamp
fachista ADJ, SMF (*LAm*) fascist
facho/a* ADJ, SM/F (*Cono Sur*) fascist
fachoso* ADJ **1** (= *raro*) ridiculous-looking, odd-looking
2 (*And, Cono Sur*) (= *elegante*) elegant, smart
3 (*Méx*) (= *engreído*) conceited
facial ADJ **1** (= *del rostro*) facial, face (*antes de s*) • **crema ~** face cream • **mascarilla ~** pack *o* mask
2 (*de sello, moneda*) • **valor ~** face value
SM face value
fácil ADJ **1** (= *sencillo*) easy • **el examen fue muy ~** the exam was very easy • **no es ~ admitir que se está equivocado** it isn't easy to admit that you're wrong • **no me lo pones nada ~** you aren't making things very easy for me • **los ricos lo tienen todo más ~** rich people have it easy • **~ de hacer** easy to do • **~ de usar** (*gen*) easy to use; (*Inform*) user-friendly
2 (= *afable*) • **nunca tuvo un carácter ~** he was never very easy to get on with • **es de trato ~** he's easy to get on with, he's quite easygoing
3 (*pey*) [*respuesta*] facile, glib; [*chiste*] obvious
4 (*pey*) [*mujer*] easy
5 (= *probable*) • **es ~ que venga** he's quite likely to come, he may well come • **no veo muy ~ que acepten** I don't think they're very likely to accept
ADV* easily • **podría costarte 5.000 ~** it could easily cost you 5,000 • **te lo arreglo en dos horas ~** I'll fix it for you in two hours, no problem*
facilidad SF **1** (= *sencillez*) easiness • **la aparente ~ de los ejercicios** the apparent easiness of the exercises • **con ~** easily • **se me rompen las uñas con ~** my nails break easily • **con la mayor ~** with the greatest (of) ease
2 (= *habilidad*) • **tener ~ para algo** to have a gift for sth • **tiene ~ para las matemáticas** she has a gift for maths, maths comes easy to her • **tener ~ de palabra** to have a way with words
3 facilidades (= *condiciones favorables*) • **me dieron todas las ~es** they gave me every facility • **"facilidades de pago"** "credit facilities"
facilitar ▷ CONJUG 1a VT **1** (= *hacer fácil*) to make easier, facilitate • **un ordenador facilita mucho el trabajo** a computer makes work much easier • **Internet facilita el acceso a la información** the internet facilitates access to information • **la nueva autovía ~á la entrada a la capital** the new motorway will give easier access to the capital, the new motorway will facilitate access to the capital
2 (= *proporcionar*) • **~ algo a algn** to provide sb with sth, supply sb with sth • **el banco me facilitó la información** the bank provided me with *o* supplied me with the information • **"le agradecería me ~a ..."** "I

would be grateful if you would provide *o* supply me with …"
3 (*Cono Sur*) (= *quitar importancia a*) • **~ algo** to make sth out to be easier than it really is, play down the difficulty of sth
fácilmente ADV 1 (= *con facilidad*) easily • **hago amigos ~** I make friends easily • **este tipo de cosas no se pueden explicar ~** there's no easy *o* simple explanation for this type of thing, this type of thing cannot be easily explained
2 (= *probablemente*) • **andará ~ por los 40** he must be at least 40
facilón* ADJ 1 (= *muy fácil*) [*problema, ejercicio, test*] dead easy* • **este crucigrama es ~** this crossword is dead easy *o* a doddle *o* a cinch* • **tiene un trabajo ~** his job's dead easy *o* a cushy number*
2 (*pey*) (= *manido*) [*comentario, recurso*] trite
3 (*pey*) (= *pegadizo*) [*canción*] trashy*
4 (*hum*) (= *dócil*) [*persona, carácter*] easy*
facilongo* ADJ (*And*) • **es ~** it's dead easy*, it's a doddle *o* a cinch*
facineroso/a ADJ 1 (= *de delincuente habitual*) criminal
2 (= *malvado*) evil, wicked
SM/F 1 (= *delincuente habitual*) criminal
2 (= *malvado*) evil person, wicked person
facistol ADJ 1 (*Caribe*) (= *descarado*) insolent; (= *vanidoso*) conceited, vain; (= *pedante*) pedantic
2 (*Caribe*) (= *bromista*) • **es tan ~** he's full of tricks, he loves playing jokes on people
SM (*Rel*) lectern
facistolería SF (*And, Caribe*) (= *descaro*) insolence; (= *jactancia*) conceit, boastfulness
facochero SM warthog
facón SM (*Cono Sur*) long gaucho knife; ▹ GAUCHO
facsímil ADJ, SM, **facsímile** ADJ, SM facsimile
factibilidad SF feasibility • **estudio de ~** feasibility study
factible ADJ feasible
fácticamente (*frm*) ADV actually, in (point of) fact
facticio (*frm*) ADJ factitious (*frm*), artificial
fáctico ADJ real, actual • **los poderes ~s** the powers that be
factor(a) SM/F 1 (*Com*) (= *representante*) agent, factor
2 (*Ferro*) freight clerk
SM 1 (*Mat*) factor
2 (= *elemento*) factor, element • **el ~ suerte** the luck factor, the element of chance • **es un nuevo ~ de la situación** it is a new factor in the situation ▸ **factor de seguridad** safety factor ▸ **factor determinante** determining factor ▸ **factor humano** human factor ▸ **factor Rh** rhesus factor ▸ **factor sorpresa** element of surprise ▸ **factor tiempo** time factor
factoría SF 1 (= *fábrica*) factory ▸ **factoría de coches** car plant
2 (*And*) (= *fundición*) foundry
3 (*Hist*) trading post
factorización SF factoring
factótum SMF 1 (= *manitas*) factotum
2 (= *persona de confianza*) agent, nominee
3† (*pey*) (= *entrometido*) busybody
factual (*frm*) ADJ (= *real*) actual
factura SF 1 (*Com*) bill, invoice • **pasar** *o* **presentar ~ a algn** to bill *o* invoice sb • **según ~** as per invoice • MODISMO: • **pasar ~:** • **el escándalo ha pasado ~ a la organización** the scandal has taken its *o* a toll on the organization • **nos pasarán (la) ~ por el apoyo que nos dieron en momentos de crisis** they will call in the favour they did us by supporting us during the crisis ▸ **factura proforma, factura simulada** pro forma invoice
2 (*frm*) (= *ejecución*) • **cuadros de ~ reciente** recently painted pictures, pictures of recent execution • **un thriller psicológico de impecable ~** a perfectly put together *o* constructed psychological thriller
3 (*Cono Sur*) bun, cake
facturación SF 1 (*Com*) (= *acto*) invoicing
2 (*Com*) (= *ventas*) turnover
3 [*de mercancías, equipaje*] (*en aeropuerto*) check-in; (*en puerto, estación*) registration ▸ **facturación online** online check-in
facturar ▹ CONJUG 1a VT 1 (*Com*) [+ *géneros*] to invoice (for), bill (for); [+ *persona*] to invoice, bill
2 [+ *volumen de ventas*] to turn over, have a turnover of • **la compañía facturó 500 millones en 1997** the company turned over *o* had a turnover of 500 million in 1997
3 [+ *equipaje*] (*en aeropuerto*) to check in; (*en puerto, estación*) to register
VI to check in
facultad SF 1 (= *capacidad*) faculty • **está perdiendo sus ~es** she's losing her faculties • **firmó el testamento en pleno uso de sus ~es** he signed the will in full possession of his faculties ▸ **facultades mentales** mental faculties, mental powers • **actuó con sus ~es mentales perturbadas** he was mentally disturbed when he did it
2 (= *autoridad*) power, authority • **tener la ~ de hacer algo** to have the power *o* authority to do sth • **tener ~ para hacer algo** to be authorized to do sth
3 (*Univ*) faculty • **está en la ~** he's at the university • **se han quedado a comer en la ~** they stayed to have lunch at the university ▸ **Facultad de Derecho** Faculty of Law ▸ **Facultad de Filosofía y Letras** Faculty of Arts ▸ **Facultad de Medicina** Faculty of Medicine
facultar ▹ CONJUG 1a VT • **~ a algn para hacer algo** (= *dar autorización*) to authorize sb to do sth, empower sb to do sth; (= *dar derecho*) to entitle sb to do sth
facultativo/a ADJ 1 (= *opcional*) optional, non-compulsory
2 (*Med*) medical • **dictamen ~** medical report • **prescripción facultativa** medical prescription
3 (*Univ*) faculty (*antes de s*)
SM/F doctor, physician (*frm*)
facundia† SF eloquence; (*pey*) verbosity (*frm*)
facundo† ADJ eloquent; (*pey*) verbose (*frm*)
FAD SM ABR (*Esp*) (= **Fondo de Ayuda al Desarrollo**) *development aid fund*
faena SF 1 (*gen*) task, job, piece of work; (*en el hogar*) chore; (*Mil*) fatigue • **estar de ~** to be at work • **estar en (plena) ~** to be hard at work • **tener mucha ~** to be terribly busy ▸ **faena doméstica** housework
2* (*tb* **mala faena**) (= *mala pasada*) dirty trick • **hacer una ~ a algn** to play a dirty trick on sb • **¡menuda ~ la que me hizo!** that was a terrible thing he did to me!
3 (*CAm, Caribe, Méx*) (= *horas extraordinarias*) extra work, overtime
4 (*Taur*) set of passes with the cape • **hizo una ~ maravillosa** he gave a splendid performance (with the cape)
5 (*Cono Sur*) (= *obreros*) gang of workers; (= *local*) work place
faenar ▹ CONJUG 1a VI 1 (= *trabajar*) to work, labour, labor (*EEUU*)
2 [*pescador*] to fish
VT 1 [+ *ganado*] to slaughter
2 (*Cono Sur*) [+ *madera*] to cut
faenero/a SM/F (*Chile*) farm worker, farmhand
fafarechero* (*Col*) ADJ stuck-up*, conceited
fagocitar ▹ CONJUG 1a VT to absorb, gobble up
fagocito SM phagocyte
fagot SM (= *instrumento*) bassoon
SMF (= *músico*) bassoonist
failear ▹ CONJUG 1a VT (*CAm, Cono Sur*) to file
fain ADJ (*CAm*) fine
fainá SF (*Cono Sur*) savoury pastry
fainada SF (*Caribe*), **fainera** SF (*CAm*) silly thing, foolish act
faíno ADJ (*Caribe*) rude
faisán SM pheasant
faisanaje SM hanging (of game)
faite (*LAm*) ADJ tough, strong
SM 1 (= *luchador*) tough man, good fighter
2 (*pey*) brawler
faitear* ▹ CONJUG 1a VI (*LAm*) to brawl
faja SF 1 (= *prenda*) girdle, corset ▸ **faja pantalón** panty girdle
2 (= *cinturón*) belt; [*de tela*] sash
3 (= *tira*) [*de adorno*] strip, band; (*Med*) bandage, support
4 (*Geog*) (= *zona*) strip • **una estrecha ~ de terreno** a narrow strip of land
5 (*Arquit*) band, fascia
6 [*de periódico, impreso*] (*tb* **faja postal**) wrapper, address label
7 (*And*) (*Aut*) fanbelt
8 (*Méx*) label, title (on spine of book)
fajada SF 1 (*Caribe*) (= *ataque*) attack, rush
2 (*Cono Sur*) (= *paliza*) beating
3 (*Caribe*) (= *decepción*) disappointment
fajar ▹ CONJUG 1a VT 1 (= *envolver*) to wrap • MODISMO: • **¡que lo fajen!** (*Cono Sur, Méx*‡) tell him to wrap up!*
2 (= *vendar*) to bandage
3 (*LAm*) (= *atacar*) to attack, go for*; (= *golpear*) to beat up
4 (*Cuba*) (= *seducir*) [+ *mujer*] to try to seduce
VI (*LAm*) • **~ con algn*** to go for sb, lay into sb*
VPR **fajarse** 1 (= *ponerse una faja*) to put on one's belt
2 (*LAm*) (= *pelearse*) to come to blows, fight • **los boxeadores se ~on duro** the boxers really went for *o* laid into each other*
3 • **~se a algn**‡ to feel sb up‡
fajilla SF [*de periódicos, revistas, impresos*] wrapper, address label
fajín SM (*Mil*) sash
fajina SF 1 (*Agr*) rick
2 (= *leña*) kindling, brushwood
3 (*Cono Sur*) (= *faena*) task, job (to be done quickly) • **tenemos mucha ~** we've a lot to do, we've a tough job on here
4 (*Mil*) (*gen*) bugle call; (*para comer*) call to mess
5 (*Caribe*) (= *horas extraordinarias*) extra work, overtime
6 (*Cono Sur*) hard work • **ropa de ~** working clothes (*pl*) • **uniforme de ~** fatigues (*pl*)
fajo SM 1 (= *manojo*) [*de papeles*] bundle, sheaf; [*de billetes*] roll, wad
2 (*Méx*) (= *cinturón*) woman's belt
3 (*Méx*) (= *golpe*) blow
4 (*LAm**) (= *trago*) swig* (of liquor)
5 **fajos**† [*de bebé*] swaddling clothes
falacia SF 1 (= *engaño*) deceit, fraud; (= *error*) fallacy
2 (= *falsedad*) deceitfulness
falange SF 1 (*Anat*) phalange
2 (*Mil*) phalanx
3 • **la Falange** (*Esp*) (*Pol*) the Falange, *the Spanish Falangist movement*

FALANGE ESPAÑOLA
Founded in 1933 by José Antonio Primo de Rivera, son of the dictator Miguel Primo de Rivera, the **Falange Española** was a sort of paramilitary fascist party. It grew rapidly in the early months of the Spanish Civil War, particularly after its leader was executed by the Republicans. Franco later merged the **Falange** with the **Carlistas** to form the **Falange Española Tradicionalista de las Juntas de Ofensiva Nacional-Sindicalista**. After the Civil War, the **FET de las JONS** was the only political party legally permitted in Franco's Spain.

falangista ADJ, SMF Falangist

falaz ADJ [*individuo*] false, deceitful; [*doctrina*] false, fallacious (*frm*); [*apariencia*] deceptive, misleading

falca SF **1** (*And, Caribe, Méx*) (= *transbordador*) river ferryboat
2 (*And*) (= *alambique*) small still

falciforme ADJ sickle-shaped

falda SF **1** (= *ropa*) skirt • **MODISMOS:** • **está cosido** *o* **pegado a las ~s de su madre** he's tied to his mother's apron strings • **estar cosido a las ~s de su mujer** to be dominated by one's wife • **haberse criado bajo las ~s de mamá** to have led a very sheltered life ▸ **falda de tablas** pleated skirt ▸ **falda de tubo** straight skirt, pencil skirt ▸ **falda escocesa** (*gen*) tartan skirt; (= *traje típico escocés*) kilt ▸ **falda pantalón** culottes (*pl*), split skirt ▸ **falda tableada** pleated skirt
2 (= *regazo*) lap • **sentarse en la ~ de algn** to sit on sb's lap
3 faldas* (= *mujeres*) women, ladies • **es muy aficionado a las ~s** he's a great one for the ladies, he's fond of the ladies • **es asunto de ~s** there's a woman behind it somewhere
4 [*de montaña*] (= *ladera*) side; (= *pie*) foot
5 [*de res*] brisket, skirt
6 [*de mesa camilla*] table cover
7 [*de sombrero*] brim

faldear ▹ CONJUG 1a VT [+ *montaña*] to skirt

faldellín SM **1**† (= *falda*) short skirt; (= *enagua*) underskirt
2 (*Caribe*) [*de bautizo*] christening robe

faldeo SM (*Cono Sur*) slope, mountainside

faldero ADJ **1** (= *mujeriego*) • **hombre ~** ladies' man • **es muy ~** he's a great one for the ladies
2 (= *sumiso*) • **perro ~** lapdog

faldicorto ADJ short-skirted

faldilla SF **1** (*Aut*) skirt, apron
2 faldillas [*de abrigo*] coat tails; [*de camisa*] shirt tails

faldón SM **1** [*de vestido*] tail, skirt; (= *pliegue*) flap
2 [*de bebé*] long dress
3 (*Arquit*) gable

falena SF moth

falencia SF **1** (*Arg*) (= *bancarrota*) bankruptcy
2 (*Cono Sur*) (= *defecto*) failing, shortcoming
3† (= *error*) error, misstatement

falibilidad SF fallibility

falible ADJ fallible

fálico ADJ phallic

falla SF **1** (*Geol*) fault
2 (= *defecto*) [*de tejido*] flaw; [*de mercancías*] fault, defect; (*LAm*) [*de carácter*] failing • **géneros que tienen ~s** seconds, defective goods
3 (*Esp*) (= *figura*) *huge ornate cardboard figure burnt in Valencia at the Fallas*
4 (*LAm*) (= *error*) error, oversight ▸ **falla de tiro** (*Mil*) misfire
5 (*LAm*) (*Mec*) failure, breakdown ▸ **falla de encendido** (*Aut*) ignition fault
6 (*LAm*) (= *escasez*) lack, shortage ▸ **falla en caja** cash shortage
7 (*And*) (*Naipes*) void

fallada SF (*Naipes*) ruff, trumping

fallar ▹ CONJUG 1a VI **1** [*freno*] to fail; [*plan*] to fail, go wrong; [*cuerda*] to break, give way; [*motor*] to misfire • **le falla la memoria** his memory is failing • **si no me falla la memoria** if my memory serves me correctly *o* right *o* well • **si no me falla la vista** if my eyes don't deceive me • **le falló el corazón** his heart failed • **me ~on las piernas** my legs gave way • **algo falló en sus planes** something went wrong with his plans • **han fallado todas nuestras previsiones** all our predictions have turned out to be wrong • **si le das un caramelo se calla, no falla nunca** if you give him a sweet he'll shut up, it never fails • **no falla, ya has vuelto a llegar tarde*** I knew it, you're late again
2 (= *defraudar*) • **~ a algn** to let sb down, fail sb • **me has fallado de nuevo** you've let me down again • **mañana hay reunión, no me falles** there's a meeting tomorrow, don't let me down
3 (*Jur*) to pass judgment • **~ a favor/en contra de algn** to rule in favour of/against sb, find for/against sb
4 (*Naipes*) to trump
VT **1** (= *errar*) • **falló las cuatro preguntas** she got all four questions wrong • **fallé el tiro** I missed • **~ el blanco** to miss the target
2 (*Jur*) to deliver judgment in
3 [+ *premio*] to award
4 (*Naipes*) to trump

Fallas SFPL *Valencian celebration of the feast of St Joseph*

FALLAS
In the week of 19 March (the feast of San José), Valencia honours its patron saint with a spectacular fiesta called **las Fallas**. **Fallas** is the name given to the huge papier-mâché, cardboard and wooden sculptures depicting politicians and other well-known public figures which, amidst a deafening display of fireworks, are put on bonfires and set alight by members of competing groups, or **falleros**, who will have spent the previous year creating and building them. Only the sculpture which is voted best escapes the flames.

falleba SF door *o* window catch, espagnolette

fallecer ▹ CONJUG 2d VI to die, pass away (*euf*)

fallecido/a ADJ deceased, late
SM/F deceased

fallecimiento SM death, demise (*frm*), passing (*euf*)

fallero¹/a ADJ *of/relating to the "Fallas"*
SM/F **1** (= *constructor*) *maker of "Fallas"*
2 (= *participante*) *person who takes part in the "Fallas"* ▸ **fallera mayor** Fallas queen

fallero² ADJ (*Cono Sur*) work-shy

fallido ADJ **1** [*esfuerzo*] unsuccessful; [*esperanza*] disappointed; [*deuda*] bad, irrecoverable; (*Mec, Mil*) dud • **un tiro ~** a missed shot, a shot wide of the mark *o* target
2 (*Caribe*) (*Com*) (= *quebrado*) bankrupt

fallir ▹ CONJUG 3a VI **1** (*Caribe*) (= *quebrar*) to go bankrupt
2† (= *fallar*) to fail
3† (= *caducar*) to run out, expire

fallo SM **1** (= *mal funcionamiento*) failure; (= *defecto*) fault • **debido a un ~ de los frenos** because of brake failure ▸ **fallo cardíaco** heart failure ▸ **fallo de diseño** design fault
2 (= *error*) mistake • **ha sido un ~ decírselo** it was a mistake telling him • **¡qué ~!** what a stupid mistake! ▸ **fallo humano** human error
3 (*Jur*) [*de un tribunal*] judgment, ruling • **el ~ fue a su favor** the judgment *o* ruling was in her favour • **han apelado contra el ~ del jurado** they have appealed against the jury's verdict ▸ **fallo absolutorio** verdict of not guilty ▸ **fallo condenatorio** verdict of guilty
4 [*de concurso, premio*] decision • **hoy se anunciará el ~ del jurado** the jury's decision will be announced today • **ya se conoce el ~ del concurso de poesía** it is already known who has won the poetry prize
5 (*Naipes*) void • **tengo ~ a picas** I have a void in spades
ADJ (*Naipes*) • **estar ~ a** to have a void in

fallón* ADJ (*Ecu*) unreliable

falluca* SF (*Méx*) smuggling

falluquear* ▹ CONJUG 1a VT (*Méx*) to smuggle

falluquero/a* SM/F **1** (*Méx*) (= *contrabandista*) smuggler
2 (*Cono Sur*) (= *viajante*) travelling salesman/saleswoman

fallutería* SF (*Cono Sur*) **1** (= *hipocresía*) hypocrisy
2 (= *poca fiabilidad*) untrustworthiness

falluto* ADJ (*Cono Sur*) **1** (= *hipócrita*) hypocritical, two-faced*
2 (= *poco fiable*) untrustworthy, unreliable
3 (= *fracasado*) unsuccessful, failed

FALN SFPL ABR (*Ven*) = **Fuerzas Armadas de Liberación Nacional**

falo SM phallus

falocracia* SF male domination, male chauvinism

falócrata SM male chauvinist pig*

falocrático ADJ male chauvinist (*antes de s*) • **actitud falocrática** male chauvinist attitude

falopa‡ SF (*Cono Sur*) hard drugs (*pl*)

falopearse‡ ▹ CONJUG 1a VPR (*Cono Sur*) to take hard drugs

falopero/a‡ SM/F (*Cono Sur*) druggy‡

falsamente ADV **1** (= *erróneamente*) falsely • **lo han acusado ~** he has been falsely accused
2 (= *insinceramente*) falsely • **con un aspecto ~ inocente** with a false look of innocence

falsario/a SM/F **1** (= *mentiroso*) liar
2 (= *falseador*) forger, counterfeiter

falseable ADJ • **fácilmente ~** easy to forge, readily forged

falseador(a) SM/F forger, counterfeiter

falsear ▹ CONJUG 1a VT [+ *cifras, datos*] to falsify, doctor; [+ *verdad, hechos*] to distort; [+ *voto*] to rig*, fiddle*; [+ *firma, moneda, documento*] to forge, fake; [+ *cerrojo*] to pick; (*Téc*) to bevel
VI **1** (= *ceder*) to buckle, sag; (*fig*) to flag, slacken
2 (*Mús*) to be out of tune

falsedad SF **1** [*de acusación, teoría*] falseness, falsity; [*de persona*] falseness, insincerity
2 (= *mentira*) lie, falsehood (*frm*)

falsete SM **1** (*Mús*) falsetto
2 [*de cuba*] plug, bung
3 (*And**) hypocrite

falsía SF duplicity (*frm*), falseness

falsificación SF **1** (= *acto*) (= *creación*) forging, faking; (= *alteración*) falsification
2 (= *objeto*) forgery

falsificado ADJ [*firma, cuadro*] forged; [*billete*] counterfeit, forged; [*documento*] forged, fake

falsificador(a) SM/F forger, counterfeiter

falsificar ▸ CONJUG 1g (VT) [+ *billete, firma, cuadro*] to forge, fake, counterfeit; [+ *resultado, elección*] to rig*, fiddle*; [+ *documento*] (= *crear*) to forge, fake; (= *cambiar*) to falsify
falsilla (SF) guide (*in copying*)
falso (ADJ) **1** [*acusación, creencia, rumor*] false • **lo que dices es ~** what you're saying is false *o* untrue • **se inscribió con un nombre ~** she registered under a false name • **ha sido una falsa alarma** it was a false alarm • **~ testimonio** perjury, false testimony
2 [*firma, pasaporte, joya*] false, fake; [*techo*] false; [*cuadro*] fake; [*moneda*] counterfeit
3 (= *insincero*) [*persona*] false, insincere; [*sonrisa*] false
4 [*caballo*] vicious
5 • **en ~**: **coger a algn en ~** to catch sb in a lie • **dar un paso en ~** (*lit*) to trip; (*fig*) to take a false step • **jurar en ~** to commit perjury
(SM) (*CAm, Méx*) false evidence
falta (SF) **1** (= *carencia*) **a** [*de recursos, información, control, acuerdo*] lack • **los candidatos demostraron en el examen su absoluta ~ de preparación** in the exam the candidates revealed their total lack of preparation • **es evidente su ~ de voluntad negociadora** it is clear that they have no wish to negotiate • **~ de respeto** disrespect, lack of respect • **la ~ de respeto por las ideas de los demás** disrespect *o* lack of respect for other people's ideas • **¡qué ~ de respeto!** how rude!
b • **a ~ de** in the absence of, for want of • **a ~ de información fiable, nos limitamos a repetir los rumores** in the absence of reliable information, we can merely repeat the rumours, we can merely repeat the rumours, for want of reliable information • **a ~ de champán para celebrarlo, beberemos cerveza** as we don't have any champagne to celebrate with, we'll drink beer • **a ~ de un término/sistema mejor** for want of a better term/system • **a ~ de tres minutos para el final** three minutes from the end • **a ~ de 40kms para la meta el ciclista se retiró** the cyclist withdrew 40kms from the finish • REFRÁN: • **a ~ de pan, buenas son tortas** half a loaf is better than none
c • **por ~ de** for lack of • **se absolvió al acusado por ~ de pruebas** the defendant was acquitted for lack of evidence • **el rosal se murió por ~ de luz** the rose died due to lack of light
d • **echar algo/a algn en ~** to miss sth/sb • **echo en ~ a mis amigos** I miss my friends • **durante el festival se echaron en ~ a las grandes estrellas** the big names were missing from the festival; ▸ **educación**
2 • **hacer ~**: • **me hace mucha ~ un coche** I really *o* badly* need a car • **a este plato le hace ~ sal** this dish needs more salt • **lo que hace ~ aquí es más disciplina** what's needed here is stricter discipline • **aquí no haces ~** you're not needed here • **no nos hace ~ nada** we've got everything we need, we don't need anything else • **es el hombre que hacía ~** he is the right man for the job • **¡~ hacía!** and about time too! • **si hace ~, voy** if necessary, I'll go, if need be, I'll go • **hacer ~ hacer algo**: • **para ser enfermero hace ~ tener vocación** you have to be dedicated to be a nurse • **no hace ~ ser un experto para llegar a esa conclusión** you don't need to be an expert to reach that conclusion • **ahora lo que te hace ~ es recuperar las fuerzas** what you need now is to regain your strength • **¡hace ~ ser tonto para no darse cuenta!** you have to be pretty stupid not to realize! • **hacer ~ que** (+ *subjun*): • **hace ~ que el agua esté hirviendo** the water must be *o* needs to be boiling • **si hace ~ que os echemos una mano, llamadnos** if you need us to give you a hand, give us a call • **no hace ~ que se lo digas** there's no need for you to tell him • MODISMO: • **ni ~ que hace** (*iró*): • **—¿te han invitado al concierto? —no, ni ~ que me hace** "haven't they invited you to the concert?" — "no, and I couldn't care less"*
3 (*Escol*) (= *ausencia*) absence • **poner ~ a algn** to mark sb absent, put sb down as absent ▸ **falta de asistencia** absence • **tiene cinco ~s de asistencia** he has been absent five times
4 (= *infracción*) **a** (*Jur*) offence, offense (*EEUU*) • **~ grave** serious offence, serious offense (*EEUU*), serious misconduct • **~ leve** minor offence, minor offense (*EEUU*), misdemeanour, misdemeanor (*EEUU*)
b (*Ftbl, Balonmano*) foul; (*Tenis*) fault • **ha sido ~** it was a foul *o* fault • **va a sacar la ~** (*Ftbl*) he's going to take the free kick; (*Balonmano*) he's going to take the free throw • **cometer una ~ contra algn** to foul sb • **lanzamiento de ~** (*Ftbl*) free kick ▸ **falta personal** personal foul
5 (= *fallo*) [*de persona*] shortcoming, fault; [*de máquina, producto*] flaw, fault • **sacar ~s a algn** to point out sb's shortcomings, find fault with sb • **siempre le está sacando ~s a todo lo que hago** she's always picking holes in everything I do • **sin ~** without fail • **mañana sin ~ recibirá nuestro informe** you will get our report tomorrow without fail ▸ **falta de ortografía** spelling mistake
6 (*por estar embarazada*) missed period
faltar ▸ CONJUG 1a (VI) **1** (= *no haber suficiente*) • **faltan profesores** there aren't enough teachers • **a la sopa le falta sal** there isn't enough salt in the soup • **faltan viviendas asequibles** there is a shortage of affordable housing • **faltan dos sillas** we are two chairs short • **~ algo a algn**: • **le falta todavía un impreso** you still need another form • **¿te falta dinero?** do you need any money? • **nos falta tiempo para hacerlo** we don't have enough time to do it • **te faltan dos centímetros para poder ser policía** you're two centimetres too short to be a policeman • **no le falta valor** he doesn't lack courage • MODISMOS: • **¡lo que (me) faltaba!** that's all I needed! • **¡no faltaba** *o* **~ía más!** (= *no hay de qué*) don't mention it!; (= *naturalmente*) of course!; (= *¡ni hablar!*) certainly not!, no way!* • **¡no faltaba más que eso!** • **¡lo que faltaba!** (= *¡es el colmo!*) that's the last straw!; (= *¡ni hablar!*) certainly not!, no way!* • **es mejor que sobre que no que falte** better to have too much than too little
2 (= *no estar*) to be missing • **faltan varios libros del estante** there are several books missing from the shelf • **faltan 20 euros de la caja** there are 20 euros missing from the till • **me falta un bolígrafo** one of my pens is missing • **faltaba de su casa desde hacía un mes** he had been missing for a month • **¿quién falta?** who's missing?, who's not here? • **no podemos irnos, falta Manolo** we can't go, Manolo isn't here yet • **no ~**: • **un desayuno en el que no faltan los huevos y el beicon** a breakfast which doesn't fail to include eggs and bacon • **un partido en el que no ~on goles** a match which was not short of goals • **no falta ninguno de los ingredientes de la novela policíaca** all of the ingredients of the detective novel are present • **no falta quien opina que ...** there are those who think that ...
3 (= *no ir*) • **no he faltado ni una sola vez a las reuniones** I haven't missed a single meeting • **~on tres personas a la reunión** there were three people missing *o* absent from the meeting • **¡no ~é!** I'll be there! • **~ a una cita** (*de negocios*) to miss an appointment, not to turn up for an appointment; (*con amigo*) not to turn up for a date • **~ a clase** to miss school • **~ al trabajo** to be off work • **nunca falta al trabajo** he's never off work
4 (= *quedar*) • **falta todavía bastante por hacer** there is still quite a lot to be done, quite a lot remains to be done • **falta mucho todavía** there's plenty of time to go yet • **¿falta mucho?** is there long to go? • **¿te falta mucho?** will you be long? • **~ para algo**: • **faltan tres semanas para las elecciones** there are three weeks to go to the election, the election is three weeks off • **faltan cinco minutos para que comience la representación** the performance will begin in five minutes • **faltan cinco para las siete** (*LAm*) it's five to seven • **falta poco para las ocho** it's nearly eight o'clock, it's getting on for eight o'clock • **falta poco para que termine el partido** the match is almost over *o* finished
5 (= *estar a punto de*) • **faltó poco para que lo pillara un coche** he was very nearly run down by a car • **le faltaba poco para decírselo** she was about to tell him
6 (= *insultar*) • **¡sin ~!, ¿eh?** keep it polite, right? • **~ a algn** (= *ofender*) to offend sb; (= *ser infiel a*) to be unfaithful to sb; (= *no apoyar*) to fail sb • **~ a algn al respeto** to be rude to sb, be disrespectful to sb
7 (= *no cumplir*) • **~ en algo**: • **~ en los pagos** to default on one's payments • **no ~é en comunicárselo** I shall not fail to tell him; ▸ **decencia, palabra, promesa, respeto, verdad**
8 (*euf*) (= *estar muerto*) • **desde que falta su madre** since his mother passed away • **cuando falte yo** when I'm gone
falto (ADJ) **1** (= *carente*) • **~ de** [*recursos, información, ideas, inteligencia*] lacking in • **nos pareció un partido ~ de interés** we thought the match was uninteresting *o* lacking in interest • **un hombre ~ de carisma** a man lacking in charisma, a man with no charisma • **un hombre ~ de escrúpulos** an unscrupulous man • **un boxeador ~ de reflejos** a boxer with poor reflexes • **estar ~ de personal** to be short of staff
2† (*moralmente*) poor, wretched, mean
3 (*And*) (= *fatuo*) fatuous, vain
faltón (ADJ) **1** (= *negligente*) neglectful, unreliable (*about carrying out duties*)
2 (= *irrespetuoso*) disrespectful
3 (*LAm*) (= *vago*) slack (about work), work-shy
faltoso (ADJ) **1** (*CAm, Méx*) (= *negligente*) neglectful, unreliable (*about carrying out duties*)
2 (*CAm, Méx*) (= *irrespetuoso*) disrespectful
3 (*And*) (= *discutidor*) quarrelsome
faltriquera (SF) **1** (= *bolsillo*) pocket, pouch; [*de reloj*] fob, watch pocket • MODISMO: • **rascarse la ~** to dig into one's pocket
2 (= *bolso*) handbag, purse (*EEUU*)
falúa (SF) (*Náut*) tender
fama (SF) **1** (= *renombre*) fame • **el libro que le dio ~** the book which made him famous, the book which made his name • **llegar a la ~** to become famous • **tener ~** to be famous • **tus pasteles tienen ~** your cakes are famous • REFRÁN: • **unos tienen la ~ y otros cardan la lana** some do all the work and others take the credit
2 (= *reputación*) reputation • **tiene ~ de duro**

he has a reputation for being tough • **este restaurante tiene ~ de barato** this restaurant is (well-)known for its cheap food • **tener mala ~** to have a bad reputation • **una casa de mala ~** a house of ill repute
3 (= *rumor*) report, rumour, rumor (*EEUU*) • **corre la ~ de que ...** it is rumoured *o* (*EEUU*) rumored that ...

famélico ADJ starving, famished

familia SF **1** (= *parentela*) family • **¿cómo está la ~?** how is the family? • **es de buena ~** she comes from a good family • **sentirse como en ~** to feel thoroughly at home • **ser como de la ~** to be one of the family • **venir de ~** to run in the family • MODISMO: • **acordarse de la ~ de algn*** to curse sb, swear at sb ▸ **familia de acogida** foster family ▸ **familia monoparental** one-parent family ▸ **familia nuclear** nuclear family ▸ **familia numerosa** • **tiene una ~ numerosa** he has a large family • **las ~s numerosas quedan exentas** families with more than four children are exempt ▸ **familia política** in-laws (*pl*) ▸ **familia real** royal family
2 (= *hijos*) • **¿cuándo pensáis tener ~?** when are you thinking of starting a family? • **¿tenéis ya mucha ~?** do you already have lots of children?
3 (= *pariente*) • **Juan no es ~ mía** Juan and I aren't related • **¿sois ~?** are you related?
4 (= *comunidad*) family • **la gran ~ humana** the great human family • **la ~ socialista** the socialist community
5 (*Bot, Ling, Zool*) family ▸ **familia de lenguas** family of languages ▸ **familia de palabras** word family
6 (*Tip*) fount

familiar ADJ **1** (= *de la familia*) family (*antes de s*) • **lazos ~es** family ties • **creció en un ambiente ~ muy alegre** he grew up in a very happy family environment • **"pensión Sol, ambiente familiar"** "pensión Sol, friendly atmosphere" • **coche ~** estate car, station wagon (*EEUU*) • **dioses ~es** household gods • **envase ~** family-sized *o* family pack • **en la pensión recibes un trato ~** in the guesthouse they treat you like one of the family
2 (= *conocido*) familiar • **tu cara me resulta ~** your face looks familiar
3 [*lenguaje, término*] colloquial
SMF (= *pariente*) relative, relation

familiaridad SF **1** (*en el trato*) familiarity (**con with**) • **no le gusta que te tomes esas ~es** he doesn't like you being so familiar with him
2 [*de estilo*] familiarity, informality

familiarizar ▸ CONJUG 1f VT to familiarize, acquaint • **~ a algn con algo** to familiarize *o* acquaint sb with sth
VPR **familiarizarse** • **~se con** to familiarize o.s. with, get to know, make o.s. familiar with

famoseo SM • **una revista de ~** a celebrity magazine • **todo lo que hay que saber sobre el ~** everything you need to know about celebrities

famosillo/a* ADJ well-known in limited circles
SM/F minor celebrity

famoso/a ADJ **1** (= *célebre*) famous, well-known • **un actor ~** a famous *o* well-known actor • **el pueblo es ~ por su cerámica** the town is famous for its pottery • **es ~ por sus ocurrencias** he's renowned for his witticisms
2* (= *sonado*) • **aún recuerdo su ~ enfado** I can still remember that time she got angry
SM/F celebrity, famous person • **los ~s** celebrities

fan SMF (PL: **fans**) fan

fanal SM **1** (*Náut*) (= *farol*) (*en la costa*) harbour beacon, harbor beacon (*EEUU*); (*en barco*) lantern
2 (= *campana*) bell glass
3 (= *pantalla*) [*de lámpara*] chimney
4 (*Méx*) (*Aut*) headlight

fanaticada SF (*Caribe*) fans (*pl*)

fanáticamente ADV fanatically

fanático/a ADJ fanatical
SM/F (*gen*) fanatic; (*LAm*) (*Dep*) fan • **es un ~ del aeromodelismo** he's mad about model aeroplanes • **los ~s de la estrella** the star's fans *o* admirers

fanatismo SM fanaticism

fanatizar ▸ CONJUG 1f VT to arouse fanaticism in

fancine SM = **fanzine**

fandango SM **1** (*Mús*) fandango
2* (= *jaleo*) row, rumpus* • **se armó un ~** there was a huge row
3 (*LAm**) (= *fiesta*) rowdy party, booze-up*

fandanguear* ▸ CONJUG 1a VI (*Cono Sur*) to live it up*

fané* ADJ INV **1** (*Cono Sur*) (= *cansado*) worn out, tired out
2 (*LAm*) (= *arrugado*) messed-up, crumpled
3† (= *cursi*) vulgar

faneca SF *species of flatfish*

fanega SF **1** *grain measure (in Spain 1.58 bushels, in Mexico 2.57 bushels, in the S. Cone 3.89 bushels)*
2 *land measure (in Spain 1.59 acres, in the Caribbean 1.73 acres)*

fanfarrear ▸ CONJUG 1a VI = **fanfarronear**

fanfarria SF **1** (*Mús*) fanfare
2* (= *jactancia*) boasting

fanfarrón/ona ADJ boastful
SM/F boaster, braggart

fanfarronada SF **1** (= *acción*) boasting • **no hace más que ~s** he does nothing but boast
2 (= *farol*) bluff

fanfarronear ▸ CONJUG 1a VI to boast, talk big*

fanfarronería SF = **fanfarronada**

fangal SM bog, quagmire

fango SM (= *lodo*) mud, mire; (*fig*) mire, dirt

fangoso ADJ muddy, miry

fanguero ADJ (*Cono Sur*) [*animal, jugador*] suited to heavy going
SM (*Caribe, Méx*) **1** (= *fango*) mud, mire
2 (= *fangal*) bog, quagmire

fantasear ▸ CONJUG 1a VI to dream, fantasize

fantaseo SM dreaming, fantasizing

fantasía SF **1** (= *imaginación*) imagination • **es un producto de su ~** it's a figment of his imagination
2 (= *cosa imaginada*) fantasy • **son ~s infantiles** they're just children's fantasies • **un mundo de ~** a fantasy world
3 (*Arte, Literat*) fantasy; (*Mús*) fantasia, fantasy • **tocar por ~** to improvise
4 • **de ~** (= *con adornos, colores*) fancy • **botones de ~** fancy buttons • **joyas de ~** costume jewellery

fantasioso ADJ **1** (= *soñador*) dreamy
2 (= *presuntuoso*) vain, conceited • **¡fantasiosa!** you're so vain!

fantasma SM **1** (= *aparición*) ghost, phantom (*liter*)
2 (*TV*) ghost
SMF (*Esp**) (= *fanfarrón*) boaster, braggart
ADJ INV **1** (= *abandonado*) ghost (*antes de s*) • **buque ~** ghost ship • **ciudad ~** ghost city
2 (= *inexistente*) phantom (*antes de s*) • **embarazo ~** phantom pregnancy • **miembro ~** phantom limb • **compañía ~** bogus *o* dummy company

fantasmada* SF bluster, bravado

fantasmagoría SF phantasmagoria

fantasmagórico ADJ phantasmagoric

fantasmal ADJ ghostly, phantom (*antes de s*)

fantasmear* ▸ CONJUG 1a VI to show off

fantasmón/ona* ADJ boastful
SM/F boaster

fantásticamente ADV fantastically

fantástico ADJ **1** (= *imaginario*) fantastic
2* (= *estupendo*) fantastic, great*
3 (= *fanfarrón*) boastful
EXCL* great!, fantastic!, terrific!*

fantochada* SF **1** (= *estupidez*) • **no digas ~s** don't talk rubbish, don't talk bullshit** • **no hagas ~s** stop messing around
2 (= *fanfarronada*) • **esa es otra ~ de tu hermana** that's your sister showing off again

fantoche SM **1** (= *títere*) puppet, marionette
2* (*persona*) (= *mediocre*) mediocrity, nonentity; (= *presumido*) braggart, loudmouth*
ADJ INV puppet (*antes de s*) • **régimen ~** puppet régime

fantochesco ADJ puppet-like

fantomático ADJ shadowy, mysterious

fanzine SM fanzine

FAO SF ABR **1** (= **Food and Agriculture Organization**) FAO
2 (= **Fabricación Asistida por Ordenador**) CAM

faquín SM porter

faquir SM fakir

farabute SM (*Cono Sur*) **1** (= *pícaro*) rogue
2 (= *poco cumplidor*) unreliable person
3 (= *pobre diablo*) poor wretch

faralá SM (PL: **faralaes**) **1** (= *volante*) flounce, frill
2 **faralaes** (*pey*) frills, buttons and bows

farallón SM (*Geog*) headland; (*Geol*) outcrop; (*Cono Sur*) rocky peak

faramalla* SF **1** (= *charla*) humbug, claptrap*; (*Com*) patter, spiel
2 (= *impostura*) empty show, sham
3 (*Méx, Chile**) lie
4 (*Cono Sur*) (= *jactancia*) bragging, boasting

faramallear* ▸ CONJUG 1a VI **1** (*Méx, Chile*) (= *mentir*) to lie
2 (*Cono Sur*) (= *jactarse*) to brag, boast

faramallero* ADJ (*Cono Sur*) bragging, boastful

farándula SF **1** (*Teat, Hist*) troupe of strolling players • **el mundo de la ~** the theatre *o* (*EEUU*) theater world
2* (= *charla*) humbug, claptrap*

faranduleo SM trickery

farandulero/a ADJ (*LAm**) = **farolero**
SM/F **1** (*Teat, Hist*) strolling player
2* (= *timador*) confidence trickster, con man, swindler

faraón SM Pharaoh

faraónico ADJ (*Hist*) Pharaonic; [*plan, obra*] overambitious

faraute SM **1**†† herald
2 (= *entrometido*) busybody

FARC SFPL ABR (*Col*) = **Fuerzas Armadas Revolucionarias de Colombia**

fardada* SF show, display • **pegarse una ~** to show off

fardar* ▸ CONJUG 1a VI **1** [*persona*] (= *lucirse*) to show off, put on a display; (= *jactarse*) to boast • **fardaba de sus amigas** he boasted about his girlfriends
2 [*objeto*] to be classy • **es un coche que farda mucho** it's a car with a lot of class

farde* SM (= *lucimiento*) showing-off, display; (= *jactancia*) boasting

fardel SM **1** (= *talega*) bag, knapsack
2 (= *bulto*) bundle

fardo SM **1** (= *bulto*) bundle; (= *bala*) bale, pack

2 (*fig*) burden • **MODISMO**: • **pasar el ~** (*Perú**) to pass the buck*

fardón/ona* ADJ **1** [*objeto*] (= *con clase*) classy*, posh; (= *precioso*) nice, great*
2 (= *elegante*) [*ropa*] natty*; [*persona*] nattily dressed*
3 (= *vanidoso*) stuck-up*, swanky*
SM/F show-off*

farero/a SM/F lighthouse-keeper

farfulla* SF **1** (= *balbuceo*) spluttering
2 (= *habla atropellada*) jabbering, gabble
3 (*LAm*) (= *jactancia*) bragging, boasting
SMF jabberer, gabbler

farfullador ADJ **1** (= *balbuceante*) spluttering; (= *con habla atropellada*) jabbering, gabbling
2 (*LAm*) (= *jactancioso*) bragging, boastful

farfullar ▷ CONJUG 1a VI **1** (= *balbucear*) to splutter; (= *hablar atropelladamente*) to jabber, gabble
2 (*LAm*) (= *jactarse*) to brag, boast
VT **1** (*al hablar*) to jabber, gabble
2 (*al actuar*) to do hastily, botch

farfulleo SM (= *balbuceo*) spluttering; (= *habla atropellada*) jabbering, gabbling

farfullero* ADJ **1** (= *balbuceante*) spluttering; (= *con habla atropellada*) jabbering, gabbling
2 (*LAm*) = **fanfarrón**

farináceo ADJ starchy, farinaceous (*frm*)

faringe SF pharynx

faringitis SF INV pharyngitis

fariña SF (*Perú, Cono Sur*) coarse manioc flour

fario SM • **mal ~** bad luck

farisaico ADJ **1** (*Rel*) Pharisaic(al)
2 (= *hipócrita*) hypocritical, Pharisaic(al) (*frm*)

fariseo SM **1** (*Rel*) Pharisee
2 (= *hipócrita*) hypocrite, Pharisee

farlopa‡ SF (*Esp*) blow‡, coke‡

farmaceuta SMF (*Col, Ven*) = **farmacéutico**

farmacéutico/a ADJ [*producto*] pharmaceutical • **la industria farmacéutica** the pharmaceutical *o* drug industry
SM/F (= *persona*) pharmacist, chemist, druggist (*EEUU*)

farmacia SF **1** (= *ciencia*) pharmacy
2 (= *tienda*) chemist's (shop), drugstore (*EEUU*) ▸ **farmacia de guardia** all-night chemist's

fármaco SM drug, medicine

farmacodependencia SF drug dependency, dependence on drugs

farmacología SF pharmacology

farmacológico ADJ pharmacological

farmacólogo/a SM/F pharmacologist

farmacopea SF pharmacopoeia

faro SM **1** (*Náut*) (= *edificio*) lighthouse; (= *señal*) beacon ▸ **faro aéreo** air beacon
2 (*Aut*) headlamp, headlight ▸ **faro antiniebla** fog lamp ▸ **faro de marcha atrás** reversing light ▸ **faro halógeno** halogen headlight ▸ **faro lateral** sidelight ▸ **faro piloto, faro trasero** rear light, tail light
3 faros‡ (= *ojos*) peepers*, eyes
ADJ INV* • **idea ~** bright idea, brilliant idea

farol SM **1** (= *lámpara*) (*en terraza, jardín*) lantern, lamp; (*en la calle*) street lamp; (*Ferro*) headlamp • **MODISMOS**: • **¡adelante con los ~es!** press on regardless! • **hacer de ~*** to play gooseberry, be a third wheel (*EEUU*) ▸ **farol de viento** hurricane lamp
2* (= *mentira*) (*gen*) lie, fib; (*Naipes*) bluff • **echarse** *o* **marcarse** *o* **tirarse un ~** (*gen*) to shoot a line*, brag; (*Naipes*) to bluff
3 (*Taur*) flourishing pass
4 (*Cono Sur*) (= *ventana*) bay window, glassed-in balcony
5 (= *envase*) *wrapping of tobacco packet*
6 faroles (*LAm**) (= *ojos*) peepers*, eyes

farola SF (= *lámpara*) street lamp; (= *poste*) lamppost

faroladas* SFPL boasting (*sing*)

farolazo* SM (*CAm, Méx*) swig* (*of liquor*)

farolear* ▷ CONJUG 1a VI (= *presumir*) to boast, brag; (*Naipes*) to bluff

farolero/a ADJ* boastful
SM/F **1*** (= *fanfarrón*) boaster
2* (= *mentiroso*) bullshitter**
3 (= *fabricante*) lamp-maker
4† (*del alumbrado público*) lamplighter

farolillo SM **1** (*Elec*) fairy-light; (*de papel*) Chinese lantern ▸ **farolillo rojo** (*Atletismo*) back marker; (*Ftbl*) *team in last place*
2 (*Bot*) Canterbury bell

farra¹ SF **1** (*esp LAm*) (= *juerga*) party • **ir de ~** to go out partying/drinking
2 (*Cono Sur*) (= *mofa*) mockery, teasing • **MODISMO**: • **tomar a algn para la ~** to pull sb's leg

farra² SF (= *pez*) salmon trout

fárrago SM hotchpotch, hodgepodge (*EEUU*), jumble

farragosamente ADV convolutedly

farragoso ADJ (*gen*) cumbersome; [*discurso*] convoluted, involved, dense

farrear ▷ CONJUG 1a VI (*esp Cono Sur*) to party, be out drinking
VPR **farrearse 1** (*Cono Sur*) • **~se de algn** to tease sb
2 (*Arg*) [+ *dinero*] to squander

farrero/a ADJ (*And, Cono Sur*) merry, fun-loving
SM/F reveller

farrista ADJ **1** (*Cono Sur*) (= *borracho*) hard-drinking, dissipated
2 (= *juerguista*) boisterous, rowdy

farruco* ADJ stroppy* • **estar** *o* **ponerse ~** to get stroppy*, get aggressive

farruto* ADJ (*Chile*) (*pey*) sickly, weak

farsa¹ SF **1** (*Teat*) farce; (*pey*) bad play
2 (= *engaño*) farce, sham

farsa² SF (*Culin*) stuffing

farsante* SMF fraud, phoney*, phony (*EEUU**)

farsear ▷ CONJUG 1a VI (*CAm*) to joke

farsesco ADJ farcical

FAS ABR = **Fuerzas Armadas**

fas • **por fas o por nefas** ADV rightly or wrongly

FASA SF ABR (*Esp*) = **Fábrica de Automóviles, S.A.**

fascículo SM part, instalment, installment (*EEUU*)

fascinación SF fascination

fascinador ADJ, **fascinante** ADJ fascinating

fascinar ▷ CONJUG 1a VT to fascinate, captivate

fascismo SM fascism

fascista ADJ, SMF fascist

fase SF **1** (= *etapa*) stage, phase • **el proyecto está en ~ de estudio** the project is still under consideration • **estar en ~ ascendente** [*persona*] to be on the way up; [*equipo*] to be on a winning run ▸ **fase clasificatoria** (*Dep*) qualifying stage ▸ **fase terminal** terminal phase
2 (*Astron, Bio, Elec*) phase
3 [*de cohete*] stage

fashion* ['faʃon] ADJ trendy*

faso* SM (*Cono Sur*) cigarette, fag‡

fastidiado* ADJ **1** (= *estropeado*) ruined, bust*
2 • **ando ~ del estómago** • **tengo el estómago ~** I've got a dodgy* *o* bad stomach

fastidiar ▷ CONJUG 1b VT **1** (= *molestar*) to annoy • **lo que más me fastidia es tener que decírselo** what annoys me most is having to tell him • **su actitud me fastidia mucho** I find his attitude very annoying • **me fastidia tener que ir** it's a pain having to go* • **y encima me insultó ¡no te fastidia!** and on top of that, he was rude to me, can you believe it!
2 (= *estropear*) [+ *fiesta, plan*] to spoil, ruin; [+ *aparato*] to break • **nos ha fastidiado las vacaciones** it's spoiled *o* ruined our holidays • **¡la hemos fastidiado!** drat!*
VI (= *bromear*) • **¡no fastidies!** you're kidding!
VPR **fastidiarse 1** (= *aguantarse*) • **¡a ~se!** • **¡fastídiate!** (that's) tough *o* too bad!* • **¿no le gusta la comida? ¡pues que se fastidie!** he doesn't like the food? well, that's tough!* • **¡para que te fastidies!** so there!*
2 (= *dañarse*) to hurt • **me he vuelto a ~ la rodilla** I've hurt my knee again, I've done my knee in again
3* (= *estropearse*) [*fiesta, plan*] to be spoiled, be ruined; [*aparato*] to break down
4 (*LAm*) (= *aburrirse*) to get bored

fastidio SM **1** (= *molestia*) annoyance, bother • **¡qué ~!** what a nuisance!
2 (*LAm*) (= *asco*) disgust, repugnance

fastidioso ADJ **1** (= *molesto*) annoying
2 (= *aburrido*) tedious, boring, tiresome
3 (*LAm*) (= *quisquilloso*) fastidious

fasto SM **1** (= *pompa*) pomp, pageantry
2 fastos (*Literat*) annals

fastuosamente ADV (= *espléndidamente*) magnificently, splendidly; (= *suntuosamente*) lavishly, sumptuously

fastuoso ADJ [*palacio, carroza*] magnificent, splendid; [*banquete, fiesta*] lavish, sumptuous

fatal ADJ **1** (= *mortal*) [*accidente, desenlace*] fatal
2* (= *horrible*) awful, terrible • **tiene un inglés ~** his English is awful *o* terrible • **la obra estuvo ~** the play was awful *o* terrible
3 (= *inevitable*) [*plazo, cita*] unavoidable • **ese comentario ~ firmó su sentencia** that ill-fated *o* disastrous comment sealed his sentence
ADV* terribly • **lo pasaron ~** they had an awful *o* a terrible time (of it) • **cocina ~** he's an awful *o* a terrible cook • **me encuentro ~** I feel awful *o* terrible

fatalidad SF **1** (= *destino*) fate
2 (= *desdicha*) misfortune, bad luck

fatalismo SM fatalism

fatalista ADJ fatalistic
SMF fatalist

fatalizarse ▷ CONJUG 1f VPR **1** (*And*) (= *cometer un delito*) to commit a grave crime
2 (*Cono Sur*) (= *sufrir herida*) to seriously hurt o.s.; (*And*) (= *sufrir desgracia*) to suffer a series of misfortunes (*as a punishment for a wrong committed*)

fatalmente ADV **1** (= *mortalmente*) fatally
2 (= *inevitablemente*) unavoidably, inevitably
3* (= *muy mal*) disastrously

fatídicamente ADV **1** (= *desgraciadamente*) fatefully, ominously
2 (= *proféticamente*) prophetically

fatídico ADJ **1** (= *desgraciado*) fateful, ominous
2 (= *profético*) prophetic

fatiga SF **1** (= *cansancio*) fatigue (*frm*), tiredness, weariness ▸ **fatiga cerebral** mental fatigue ▸ **fatiga muscular** muscle fatigue
2 (= *ahogo*) breathlessness • **subir las escaleras me causa ~** climbing the stairs makes me breathless, when I climb the stairs I get *o* run out of breath
3 (= *reparo*) embarrassment • **me da ~ llamar a estas horas de la noche** I'm embarrassed calling at this time of night

4 fatigas (= *penalidades*) hardship (*sing*), troubles
5 (*Téc*) fatigue ▸ **fatiga del metal** metal fatigue

fatigabilidad SF tendency to tire easily

fatigadamente ADV with difficulty, wearily

fatigado ADJ tired, weary

fatigar ▹ CONJUG 1h VT **1** (= *cansar*) to tire
2 (= *molestar*) to annoy
VPR **fatigarse 1** (= *cansarse*) to tire, get tired • **~se al andar** to wear o.s. out walking
2 (= *ahogarse*) to get out of breath, get breathless

fatigosamente ADV painfully, with difficulty

fatigoso ADJ **1** (= *cansado*) tiring, exhausting
2 (*Med*) painful, difficult • **respiración fatigosa** laboured *o* (*EEUU*) labored breathing
3 (= *fastidioso*) trying, tiresome

fato* SM (*Cono Sur*) **1** (= *negocio*) shady deal
2 (= *amorío*) love affair

fatuidad SF **1** (= *necedad*) fatuousness, fatuity
2 (= *vanidad*) conceit

fatuo ADJ **1** (= *necio*) fatuous
2 (= *vanidoso*) conceited; ▹ **fuego**

fauces SFPL **1** (*Anat*) fauces, gullet (*sing*); (*fig*) (= *boca*) jaws
2 (*LAm*) (= *colmillos*) tusks, teeth

faul SM (PL: **fauls**) (*LAm*) (*Dep*) foul

faulear ▹ CONJUG 1a VT (*LAm*) (*Dep*) to foul

fauna SF fauna • **toda la ~ del barrio*** all the weirdos in the neighbourhood*

faunístico ADJ faunal • **riqueza faunística** wealth of the fauna

fauno SM faun

Fausto SM Faust

fausto ADJ fortunate, lucky
• **~ acontecimiento** happy event • **fausta noticia** happy news • **fausta ocasión** happy occasion
SM splendour, splendor (*EEUU*), magnificence

fautor(a) SM/F (= *cómplice*) accomplice, helper; (= *instigador*) instigator

favela SF shantytown

favor SM **1** (= *ayuda*) favour, favor (*EEUU*)
• **~ de venir puntualmente** (*Méx*) please be punctual • **hacer un ~ a algn** to do sb a favour • **¿me puedes hacer un ~?** can you do me a favour? • **¡está para hacerle un ~!‡** she's really something!* • **hacer un flaco ~ a algn** to do no favours to sb • **¿me hace el ~ de bajarme la maleta?** I wonder if you could get my suitcase down for me, please?, could you possibly get my suitcase down for me, please? • **¡haced el ~ de callaros!** will you please be quiet! • **si hace el ~ de pasar** if you'd like *o* care to go in • **si hace ~** (*LAm*) if you don't mind • **pedir un ~ a algn** to ask sb (for) a favour, ask a favour of sb (*más frm*) • **por ~** please • **¿me dejan pasar, por ~?** could I get past, please? • **¡por ~! ¡qué calor hace!** goodness me, it's hot today! • REFRÁN: • **~ con ~ se paga** one good turn deserves another
2 (*locuciones*) **a** • **a favor** in favour • **hay un 50% de gente a ~** 50% of people are in favour • **votos a ~** votes in favour • **¿estás a ~ o en contra?** are you for or against it? • **tener el viento a ~** to have the wind behind one *o* in one's favour
b • **a ~ de** in favour of • **no me convencen sus argumentos a ~ de la huelga** I'm not convinced by his arguments in favour of the strike • **¿está a ~ de poner fin al bloqueo del país?** are you in favour of ending the blockade of the country? • **la balanza está a nuestro ~** the balance is in our favour • **el tiempo corre a nuestro ~** time is on our side • **lo tenía todo a su ~** she had everything going for her • **el partido ya estaba decidido a ~ de la jugadora española** the Spanish player already had the match sewn up • **ir a ~ de la corriente** to go with the flow • **a ~ de la noche** under cover of darkness • **votar a ~ de algo** to vote in favour of sth
c • **en ~ de** [*abdicar, manifestarse*] in favour of; [*intervenir*] on behalf of; [*trabajar, luchar*] for • **el director se manifestó en ~ del cine europeo** the director spoke in favour of *o* expressed his support for the European film industry • **piden a la ONU su intervención en ~ de los detenidos** the UN is being asked to intervene on behalf of those detained • **una recogida de firmas en ~ del indulto de los presos** a petition for the pardon of the prisoners • **siempre abogó en ~ de los más débiles** he always defended the underdog • **se tomarán nuevas medidas en ~ de los ganaderos** new measures are to be taken to help livestock farmers • **el sistema fue perdiendo terreno en ~ de otros métodos más modernos** the system gradually lost ground to more up-to-date methods
3 (= *apoyo*) [*del rey, dioses*] favour, favor (*EEUU*), protection; [*del público*] support • **gracias al ~ del rey** thanks to the king's protection, thanks to the favour he enjoyed with the king • **la pérdida del ~ popular** the loss of popular support • **la película nunca tuvo el ~ del gran público** the movie never found favour with the general public • **ha sabido ganarse el ~ de la audiencia** she has succeeded in winning the audience's affection • **gozar del ~ de algn** to have sb's support *o* backing, enjoy sb's favour (*frm*) • **el partido goza del ~ del 49% de la población** the party has the support *o* backing of 49% of the population; ▹ **condición**
4 • **entrada de ~** complimentary ticket
5 favores [*de mujer*] favours, favors (*EEUU*)

favorable ADJ favourable, favorable (*EEUU*) • **esperábamos una respuesta ~** we were expecting a favourable reply • **vientos ~s** favourable winds • **~ a algo** in favour of sth • **se mostró ~ al cambio político** he was in favour of political change

favorablemente ADV favourably, favorably (*EEUU*)

favorecedor ADJ [*vestido*] becoming; [*retrato*] flattering

favorecer ▹ CONJUG 2d VT **1** (= *beneficiar*) to be favourable *o* (*EEUU*) favorable to, favour, favor (*EEUU*) • **la devaluación ha favorecido a las compañías exportadoras** devaluation has been favourable to *o* has favoured exporting companies • **el sorteo favoreció al equipo canadiense** Canada did well out of the draw • **la suerte no me favoreció** luck was not on my side, fortune did not favour me (*liter*)
2 (= *ayudar a*) [+ *desarrollo, creación, crecimiento*] to contribute to • **las nuevas medidas fiscales ~án la creación de empresas** the new tax measures will contribute to *o* encourage *o* favour the creation of new companies • **puede ~ la aparición de piedras en el riñón** it can contribute to the development of kidney stones
3 (= *tratar con favores*) • **~ a algn** to help out sb, do sb favours • **utilizó sus influencias para ~ a sus amigos** she used her influence to help out her friends *o* to do favours for her friends
4 (= *sentar bien*) [*vestido*] to suit, look good on; [*peinado*] to suit • **las faldas largas no te favorecen** long skirts don't suit you *o* look good on you • **la barba no te favorece** the beard doesn't suit you • **el retrato no la favorece** the portrait is not very flattering
VI (= *sentar bien*) to be flattering, look good

favorecido/a ADJ **1** (= *beneficiado*) (*en el trato*) favoured, favored (*EEUU*); (*por la suerte, el dinero*) fortunate • **trato de nación más favorecida** most-favoured nation treatment • **las clases menos favorecidas** the less fortunate classes • **resultó ~ en la lotería con más de un millón de euros** he won over a million euros on the lottery
2 (*físicamente*) • **estás muy ~ en esta foto** you look very good in this photo, this is a very good photo of you
SM/F • **los ~s con el primer premio** the winners of the first prize, those who won the first prize

favoritismo SM favouritism, favoritism (*EEUU*)

favorito/a ADJ, SM/F favourite, favorite (*EEUU*)

fax SM **1** (= *máquina*) fax (machine) • **mandar por fax** to fax, send by fax
2 (= *mensaje*) fax • **mandar un fax** to send a fax

faxear ▹ CONJUG 1a VT to fax, send by fax

faxteléfono SM fax-telephone (machine)

fayuca* SF (*Méx*) smuggling

fayuquear* ▹ CONJUG 1a VT (*Méx*) to smuggle

fayuquero/a* SM/F **1** (*Méx*) smuggler
2 (*Cono Sur*) travelling salesman/saleswoman

fayuto ADJ (*Cono Sur*) = **falluto**

faz SF **1** (= *cara*) face • **en la faz de la tierra** on the face of the earth • **faz a faz** face to face
2 (= *aspecto*) face, landscape • **estos incendios están cambiando la faz de nuestro país** these fires are changing the face *o* landscape of our country
3 [*de moneda*] obverse

FC ABR, **f.c.** ABR (= **ferrocarril**) Rly

Fco. ABR = **Francisco**

Fdez. ABR = **Fernández**

Fdo. ABR, **fdo.** ABR (= **firmado**) signed • **Fdo.: D. Josep Pauli i Costa** Signed, Josep Pauli i Costa Esq

FE SF ABR (*Hist*) = **Falange Española** ▸ **FE de las JONS** = **Falange Española de las Juntas de Ofensiva Nacional-Sindicalista**

fe SF **1** (*Rel*) faith (en in) • **la fe católica** the Catholic faith • MODISMO: • **la fe del carbonero** blind faith • REFRÁN: • **la fe mueve montañas** faith moves mountains
2 (= *confianza*) faith • **tener fe en algn/algo** to have faith in sb/sb • **no tengo fe en los abogados** I have no faith in lawyers • **tiene una fe ciega en ella** he has absolute faith in her • **no tiene fe en la ciencia** he has no faith in science • **dar** *o* **prestar fe a algo** (*frm*) to believe sth, place reliance on sth (*frm*)
3 (= *intención*) faith • **buena fe** good faith • **mala fe** bad faith • **actuar en** *o* **de buena fe** to act in good faith
4 (= *testimonio*) • **dar fe de algo** to vouch for sth, testify to sth • **doy fe de ello** I can vouch for *o* testify to that • **en fe de lo cual** (*frm*) in witness whereof (*frm*) • **a fe††** in truth • **a fe mía††** • **por mi fe††** by my faith, upon my honour
5†† (= *fidelidad*) fidelity
6 (= *certificado*) certificate ▸ **fe de bautismo** certificate of baptism ▸ **fe de erratas, fe de errores** (*en libro*) errata; (*en periódico*) correction ▸ **fe de soltería** proof of single status ▸ **fe de vida** *certificate testifying that a*

person is still alive ▸ **fe pública** *authority to attest documents*

FEA SF ABR 1 = **Federación Española de Automovilismo**
2 = **Federación Española de Atletismo**
3 (*Hist*) = **Falange Española Auténtica**

fealdad SF ugliness

feamente ADV hideously, terribly

feb. ABR, **feb.°** ABR (= **febrero**) Feb

feble ADJ feeble, weak

Febo SM Phoebus

febrero SM February; ▹ **septiembre**

febril ADJ 1 (*Med*) fevered, feverish
2 [*actividad*] hectic, feverish

febrilmente ADV (*fig*) feverishly, hectically

fecal ADJ faecal, fecal (*EEUU*) • **aguas ~es** sewage (*sing*)

fecha SF 1 (= *día preciso*) date • **¿a qué ~ estamos?** what's the date today? • **han adelantado la ~ de las elecciones** they've brought forward the (date of the) election • **ya tengo ~ para el dentista** I've got an appointment at the dentist's • **la carta tiene ~ del 21 de enero** the letter is dated 21 January • **a partir de esa ~ no volvió a llamar** from then on *o* thereafter he never called again • **a 30 días ~** (*Com*) at 30 days' sight • **con ~ de**: • **una carta con ~ del 15 de agosto** a letter dated 15 August • **hasta la ~** to date, so far • **pasarse de ~** (*Com*) to pass the sell-by date • **este yogur está pasado de ~** this yoghurt is past its sell-by date • **poner la ~** to date • **no se olvide poner la ~ en la solicitud** don't forget to date the form • **en ~ próxima** soon • **sin ~**: • **una carta sin ~** an undated letter, a letter with no date ▸ **fecha de caducidad** [*de medicamento, tarjeta*] expiry date; [*de alimento*] sell-by date ▸ **fecha de emisión** date of issue ▸ **fecha de entrega** delivery date ▸ **fecha de nacimiento** date of birth ▸ **fecha de vencimiento** (*Com*) due date ▸ **fecha de vigencia** (*Com*) effective date ▸ **fecha futura** • **en alguna ~ futura** at some future date • **un cheque con una ~ futura** a postdated cheque ▸ **fecha límite** deadline ▸ **fecha límite de venta** sell-by date ▸ **fecha tope** [*de finalización*] deadline; [*de entrega*] closing date
2 **fechas** (= *época*) • **son ~s de escasa actividad** it's a time of year when there isn't much happening • **siempre viene por estas ~s** he always comes about this time of year • **el año pasado por estas ~s** this time last year • **para esas ~s ya eran diez las víctimas** by then the death toll was already ten • **en breves ~s** (*frm*) shortly

fechable ADJ datable (**en** to)

fechado SM dating

fechador SM date stamp

fechar ▹ CONJUG 1a VT to date

fechoría SF misdeed, misdemeanour, misdemeanor (*EEUU*)

FECOM SM ABR (= **Fondo Europeo de Cooperación Monetaria**) EMCF

fécula SF starch ▸ **fécula de papa** (*LAm*) potato flour

feculento ADJ starchy

fecundación SF fertilization ▸ **fecundación artificial** artificial insemination ▸ **fecundación in vitro** in vitro fertilization

fecundar ▹ CONJUG 1a VT 1 (= *engendrar*) to fertilize • **~ por fertilización cruzada** to cross-fertilize
2 (*liter*) (= *fertilizar*) to make fertile

fecundidad SF 1 [*de hembra*] fertility, fecundity
2 (= *productividad*) fruitfulness, productiveness

fecundizar ▹ CONJUG 1f VT to fertilize

fecundo ADJ 1 [*persona, tierra*] fertile, fecund (*frm*)
2 [*pintor, escritor*] prolific
3 (= *fructífero*) fruitful, productive • **una década fecunda de los grandes economistas** a fruitful *o* productive period for great economists • **~ de palabras** fluent, eloquent • **~ en algo: una época muy fecunda en buenos poetas** a period which produced an abundance *o* a plethora of good poets • **un libro ~ en ideas** a book full of *o* rich in ideas

FED SM ABR (= **Fondo Europeo de Desarrollo**) EDF

FEDER SM ABR (= **Fondo Europeo de Desarrollo Regional**) ERDF

federación SF federation

federado ADJ • **los atletas ~s** athletes who are members of the federation

federal ADJ federal • **Distrito Federal** (*Méx*) Mexico City
SMF **los federales** (*Méx*) the federals, the federal police

federalismo SM federalism

federalista ADJ, SMF federalist

federalizar ▹ CONJUG 1f VT to federate, federalize

federar ▹ CONJUG 1a VT to federate
VPR **federarse** 1 (*Pol*) to federate, become federated
2 (= *hacerse socio*) (*en club, asociación*) to become a member; (*en federación*) to affiliate

federativo ADJ federative

Federico SM Frederick

feérico ADJ fairy (*antes de s*)

FEF SF ABR = **Federación Española de Fútbol**

féferes SMPL (*LAm*) (*gen*) junk (*sing*), lumber (*sing*); (= *cosas*) things (in general), thingummyjigs*

fehaciente ADJ 1 (= *fidedigno*) reliable • **de fuentes ~s** from reliable sources
2 (= *irrefutable*) irrefutable

fehacientemente ADV 1 (= *fidedignamente*) reliably
2 (= *irrefutablemente*) irrefutably

feíllo* ADJ a bit plain, rather unattractive

FE-JONS [fe'xons] SF ABR (*Hist*) = **Falange Española de las Juntas de Ofensiva Nacional Sindicalista**

felación SF fellatio

feldespato SM felspar

feliciano†‡ SM • **echar un ~** to screw**‡

felicidad SF 1 (= *satisfacción*) happiness • **curva de la ~** pot belly
2 **¡felicidades!** (= *deseos*) best wishes, congratulations!; (*en cumpleaños*) happy birthday! • **¡mis ~es!** congratulations!
3† (= *suerte*) good fortune • **viajamos con toda ~** all went well on the journey

felicitación SF 1 (= *enhorabuena*) • **mi ~** *o* **mis felicitaciones al ganador** my congratulations to the winner • **he recibido muchas felicitaciones** lots of people have congratulated me
2 (= *tarjeta*) greetings card, greeting card (*EEUU*) ▸ **felicitación de Navidad** Christmas card

felicitar ▹ CONJUG 1a VT to congratulate • **~ a algn por algo** to congratulate sb on sth • **¡le felicito!** congratulations!, well done! • **~ la Navidad a algn** to wish sb a happy Christmas
VPR **felicitarse** • **~se de algo** to be glad about sth

feligrés/esa SM/F parishioner

feligresía SF (= *parroquia*) parish; (= *feligreses*) parishioners (*pl*)

felino/a ADJ feline, catlike
SM/F feline, cat

Felipe SM Philip

felipismo SM *policies and following of Felipe González, Spanish Prime Minister from 1983 to 1996*

felipista ADJ *relating to Felipe González or his policies* • **la mayoría ~** the pro-Felipe González majority
SMF supporter of Felipe González

feliz ADJ 1 [*persona, acontecimiento, idea*] happy • **se la ve muy ~** she looks very happy • **el asunto tuvo un final ~** the affair had a happy ending • **¡Feliz Año Nuevo!** Happy New Year! • **hacer ~ a algn** to make sb happy • **"y fueron** *o* **vivieron felices y comieron perdices"** "and they lived happily ever after"
2 (*frm*) (= *acertado*) [*expresión*] apt

felizmente ADV 1 (*con felicidad*) happily • **vivieron ~ el resto de sus vidas** they lived happily ever after
2 (= *afortunadamente*) luckily, fortunately • **~ nadie resultó herido** luckily no one was hurt

felón/ona ADJ wicked, treacherous
SM/F wicked person, villain

felonía SF 1 (= *traición*) disloyalty, treachery
2 (= *crimen*) felony, crime

felpa SF 1 (= *tejido*) [*de toalla, camisa, pañal*] (terry) towelling; [*de sillón, moqueta*] plush • **ositos de ~** furry teddies
2* (= *paliza*) hiding*; (= *reprimenda*) dressing-down*, ticking-off* • **echarle una ~ a algn** to give sb a dressing-down *o* ticking-off*

felpar ▹ CONJUG 1a VT 1 (= *tapizar*) to cover with plush
2 (*poét*) (*fig*) to carpet (**de** with)

felpeada* SF (*Cono Sur, Méx*) dressing-down*, ticking-off*

felpear* ▹ CONJUG 1a VT (*Cono Sur, Méx*) to tick off*, scold

felpilla SF chenille

felpudo SM (= *alfombrilla*) doormat
ADJ plush

femenil ADJ 1 (= *femenino*) feminine
2 (*CAm, Méx*) (*Dep*) women's (*antes de s*) • **equipo ~** women's team

femenino ADJ 1 (*cualidad de mujer*) feminine • **es muy femenina** she's very feminine
2 [*sexo, representante, población*] female • **el cuerpo ~** the female body
3 (*Dep*) • **deporte ~** women's sport • **equipo ~** women's team
4 (*Ling*) feminine
SM (*Ling*) feminine

fémina SF (*hum*) woman, female

feminicidio SM femicide

feminidad SF femininity

feminismo SM feminism

feminista ADJ, SMF feminist

feminizar ▹ CONJUG 1f VT to feminize

femoral ADJ [*hueso*] femur (*antes de s*); [*arteria, vena*] femoral
SF femoral artery

FEMP SF ABR = **Federación Española de Municipios y Provincias**

fémur SM femur

fenecer ▹ CONJUG 2d VI 1 [*persona*] to pass away (*euf*), die
2 [*actividad*] to come to an end, cease; [*creencia*] to die out
VT (= *terminar*) to finish, conclude

fenecimiento SM 1 [*de persona*] passing (*euf*), death
2 (= *fin*) end, conclusion

feng shui [,feŋ'ʃu:i] SM feng shui

Fenicia SF Phoenicia

fenicio/a ADJ, SM/F Phoenician

fénico ADJ carbolic • **ácido ~** phenol, carbolic acid

fénix SM phoenix • **el Fénix de los ingenios** the Prince of Wits, the genius of our times (*Lope de Vega, Golden Age dramatist*)

fenol SM phenol, carbolic acid

f

fenomenal ADJ **1** (= *espectacular*) phenomenal, remarkable
2* (= *estupendo*) fantastic*, brilliant*
ADV* • **lo hemos pasado ~** we've had a fantastic *o* brilliant time* • **le va ~** he's getting on fantastically well *o* brilliantly*
fenomenalmente* ADV fantastically well*, brilliantly*
fenómeno SM **1** (*atmosférico, acústico, psíquico*) phenomenon
2 (= *monstruo*) freak
3 (= *portento*) genius • **Pedro es un ~** Peter is a genius, Peter is altogether exceptional
ADJ* (= *fenomenal*) fantastic*, brilliant*
ADV* • **lo hemos pasado ~** we had a fantastic *o* brilliant time* • **le va ~** he's getting on fantastically well *o* brilliantly*
fenomenológico ADJ phenomenological
feo ADJ **1** (= *sin belleza*) [*persona, casa, ropa*] ugly • **un edificio muy feo** a very ugly building • **MODISMOS:** • **más feo que Picio** *o* **un grajo** as ugly as sin • **bailar con la más fea:** • **me tocó bailar con la más fea** I drew the short straw
2 (= *desagradable*) [*asunto, tiempo*] nasty, unpleasant; [*jugada*] dirty • **tiene la fea costumbre de irse sin despedirse** he has a nasty habit of leaving without saying goodbye • **esto se está poniendo feo** things are getting nasty
3 (= *de mala educación*) • **está muy feo contestarle así a tu madre** it's very rude *o* it's not nice to answer your mother like that • **está** *o* **queda feo comerse las uñas en público** it's bad manners to bite your nails in public
4 (*LAm*) [*olor, comida*] nasty, unpleasant
SM **1** (= *desaire*) • **hacer un feo a algn** to snub sb • **le hizo el feo de no devolverle la llamada** she snubbed him by not returning his call • **—no puedo ir a tu boda —¿me vas a hacer ese feo?** "I can't come to your wedding" — "but you can't refuse!" *o* "how can you refuse!"
2* (= *fealdad*) • **hoy está con el feo** *o* **de feo subido** he's looking really ugly today
ADV (*LAm**) bad, badly • **cantar feo** to sing badly • **oler feo** to smell bad, have a nasty smell
FEOGA SM ABR (= **Fondo Europeo de Orientación y de Garantía Agrícola**) EAGGF
feón* ADJ (*LAm*) ugly • **medio ~** rather ugly
feote* ADJ plug-ugly*
feracidad SF fertility, productivity
feralla SF scrap metal
feraz ADJ fertile, productive
féretro SM coffin, casket (EEUU)
feri SM (*LAm*) = ferry
feria SF **1** (= *muestra comercial*) fair ▸ **feria comercial** trade fair ▸ **feria del libro** book fair ▸ **feria de muestras** trade show, trade exhibition ▸ **feria de vanidades** empty show, inane spectacle
2 (= *mercado al aire libre*) market; (*Agr*) show ▸ **feria agrícola** agricultural show ▸ **feria de ganado** cattle show
3 [*de atracciones*] fair, funfair
4 (= *fiesta*) festival • **durante la ~ habrá corridas de toros todos los días** during the festival there will be bullfights every day • **la Feria de Sevilla** the Seville Fair • **MODISMO:** • **irle a algn como en ~** (*Méx**) to go very badly for sb
5 (= *descanso*) holiday
6 (*Méx**) (= *cambio*) change, small change
7 (*CAm*) (= *propina*) tip
feriado ADJ • **día ~** holiday
SM (*LAm*) public holiday, bank holiday
ferial ADJ fair (*antes de s*), fairground (*antes de s*) • **recinto ~** fairground, showground
SM fairground, showground
feriante SMF **1** (= *vendedor*) (*en mercado*) stallholder, trader; (*en feria de muestras*) exhibitor
2 (= *asistente a feria*) fair-goers
feriar ▷ CONJUG 1b VT **1** (= *comerciar*) to deal in (*in a market, at a fair*)
2 (= *permutar*) to trade, exchange
3 (*Méx*) [+ *dinero*] to exchange
4 (*And*) (= *vender barato*) to sell cheap
VI (= *descansar*) to take time off, take a break
ferino ADJ savage, wild • **tos ferina** whooping cough
fermata SF (*Mús*) run
fermentación SF fermentation
fermentado ADJ fermented
SM fermentation
fermentar ▷ CONJUG 1a VI **1** [*vino, queso, compost*] to ferment • **hacer ~** to ferment, cause fermentation in
2 [*crisis, violencia*] to ferment
VT to ferment
fermento SM **1** [*de queso, cerveza*] ferment
2 [*de crisis, cambio*] ferment
fermio SM (*Quím*) fermium
Fernando SM, **Fernán**†† SM Ferdinand • **MODISMO:** • **te lo han puesto como a ~ VII** they've handed it to you on a plate
ferocidad SF ferocity, ferociousness
ferocísimo ADJ SUPERL *de* **feroz**
Feroe • **las islas ~** SFPL the Faroe Islands, the Faroes
feromona SF pheromone
feroz ADJ **1** (= *salvaje*) fierce, ferocious • **tengo un hambre ~** I'm starving, I'm famished
2 (= *cruel*) cruel
3 (*LAm*) (= *feo*) ugly
ferozmente ADV **1** (= *salvajemente*) fiercely, ferociously
2 (= *cruelmente*) cruelly
férreo ADJ **1** (= *de hierro*) iron (*antes de s*); (*Quím*) ferrous • **metal no ~** non-ferrous metal
2 (*Ferro*) rail (*antes de s*) • **vía férrea** railway track *o* line, railroad (EEUU)
3 (= *tenaz*) [*acoso*] fierce, determined; [*cerco, marcaje*] very close, tight • **una voluntad férrea** an iron will
4 (= *estricto*) [*disciplina, control, embargo*] strict, tight; [*horario*] strict, rigid; [*secreto*] strict; [*silencio*] steely
ferrería SF ironworks, foundry
ferretería SF **1** (= *objetos*) ironmongery, hardware
2 (= *tienda*) ironmonger's (shop), hardware store (EEUU)
3 = ferrería
ferretero/a SM/F ironmonger, hardware dealer (EEUU)
férrico ADJ ferric
ferroaleación SF ferro-alloy
ferrobús SM (*Ferro*) diesel car
ferrocarril SM railway, railroad (EEUU) • **por ~** by rail, by train ▸ **ferrocarril de cercanías** suburban rail network ▸ **ferrocarril de cremallera** rack railway ▸ **ferrocarril de trocha angosta** (*Cono Sur*) narrow-gauge railway, narrow-gauge railroad (EEUU) ▸ **ferrocarril de vía estrecha** narrow-gauge railway, narrow-gauge railroad (EEUU) ▸ **ferrocarril de vía única** single-track railway, single-track railroad (EEUU) ▸ **ferrocarril elevado** overhead railway, elevated railway, elevated railroad (EEUU), el (EEUU*) ▸ **ferrocarril funicular** funicular, funicular railway ▸ **ferrocarril metropolitano** metropolitan railway ▸ **ferrocarril subterráneo** underground railway, subway (EEUU)
ferrocarrilero/a (*LAm*) ADJ, SM/F = **ferroviario**
ferroprusiato SM (*Arquit, Téc*) blueprint
ferroso ADJ ferrous • **metal no ~** non-ferrous metal
ferrotipo SM (*Fot*) tintype
ferroviario/a ADJ [*red, sistema*] railway (*antes de s*), rail (*antes de s*), railroad (*antes de s*) (EEUU)
SM/F (= *trabajador*) railwayman/ railwaywoman, railway worker, railroad worker (EEUU)
ferry ['feri] (PL: **ferries**) SM ferry
ferry-boat [feri'βot] SM (*LAm*) ferry
fértil ADJ **1** [*tierra, campo*] fertile, rich
2 [*persona, animal*] fertile
3 (= *productivo*) [*idioma*] rich, expressive; [*discusión*] fertile, fruitful; [*imaginación*] fertile
fertilidad SF **1** [*del campo*] fertility, richness
2 [*de persona, animal*] fertility
3 (= *productividad*) [*de idioma*] richness, expressiveness; [*de periodo*] productivity, richness
fertilización SF fertilization ▸ **fertilización cruzada** cross-fertilization ▸ **fertilización in vitro** in vitro fertilization
fertilizante ADJ fertilizing
SM fertilizer
fertilizar ▷ CONJUG 1f VT to fertilize
férula SF **1** (= *vara*) birch, rod
2 (*Med*) splint
3 (= *dominio*) rule, domination • **vivir bajo la ~ de un tirano** to live under the iron rule of a tyrant
férvido ADJ fervid, ardent
ferviente ADJ [*devoto, partidario*] fervent; [*deseo, amor, ambición*] burning
fervientemente ADV **1** [*desear, apoyar*] fervently
2 [*defender*] passionately
fervor SM **1** (*religioso, nacionalista, popular*) fervour, fervor (EEUU)
2 (= *dedicación*) fervour, fervor (EEUU), enthusiasm • **estudia con ~** he studies enthusiastically
fervorosamente ADV fervently, passionately
fervoroso ADJ fervent, passionate
festejar ▷ CONJUG 1a VT **1** [+ *persona*] to wine and dine, entertain
2 (= *celebrar*) to celebrate
3† (= *cortejar*) to woo, court
4 (*Méx**) (= *azotar*) to thrash
festejo SM **1** (= *celebración*) celebration; (*And*) party; **festejos** (= *fiestas*) festivities
2 [*de huésped*] wining and dining, entertainment • **hacer ~s a algn** to make a great fuss of sb
3† (= *cortejo*) wooing, courtship
festín SM feast, banquet
festinar ▷ CONJUG 1a VT **1** (*CAm*) (= *agasajar*) to wine and dine, entertain
2 (*LAm*) (= *arruinar*) to mess up, ruin (*by being overhasty*)
3 (*LAm*) (= *acelerar*) to hurry along, speed up
festival SM festival
festivalero/a ADJ festival (*antes de s*)
SM/F festival-goer
festivamente ADV humorously, jovially
festividad SF **1** (*Rel*) feast, holiday
2 (*tb* **festividades**) (= *celebraciones*) festivities, celebrations
3 (= *alegría*) gaiety, merrymaking
4 (= *ingenio*) wit
festivo ADJ **1** (= *no laborable*) • **día ~** holiday
2 (= *alegre*) festive, merry
3 (= *gracioso*) witty, humorous
4 (*Literat*) burlesque, comic

festón (SM) (*Cos*) festoon, scallop; [*de flores*] garland
festonear ▷ CONJUG 1a (VT) (*Cos*) to festoon, scallop; (*con flores*) to garland
FET (SF ABR) **1** (*Dep*) = **Federación Española de Tenis**
2 (*Hist*) (*tb* **FET de las JONS**) = **Falange Española tradicionalista de las Juventudes de Ofensiva Nacional-Sindicalista**
feta (SF) (*Arg, Uru*) slice
fetal (ADJ) foetal, fetal (*EEUU*)
fetén†* (*Esp*) (ADJ INV) **1** (= *estupendo*) smashing*, super* • **una chica ~** a smashing *o* super girl* • **de ~** (= *estupendo*) smashing*, super*
2 (= *auténtico*) real, authentic
(ADV) splendidly, marvellously
(SF) (= *verdad*) truth • **ser la ~** to be gospel truth
fetiche (SM) fetish
fetichismo (SM) fetishism
fetichista (ADJ) fetishistic
(SMF) fetishist
fetidez (SF) smelliness, fetidness (*frm*)
fétido (ADJ) fetid, foul-smelling, stinking
feto (SM) **1** (*Bio*) foetus, fetus (*EEUU*)
2* (= *persona fea*) • **vaya tío feo, parece un ~** that guy's as ugly as sin*
feúcho* (ADJ) plain, homely (*EEUU*)
feudal (ADJ) feudal
feudalismo (SM) feudalism
feudo (SM) **1** (*Hist*) fief
2 (*Dep*) • **resultaron ganadores en su ~** they won on their own ground • **el Sevilla no ha perdido ni un punto en su ~** Sevilla haven't lost a single point at home
3 ▸ **feudo franco** (*Jur*) freehold
feúra (SF) (*LAm*) **1** (= *fealdad*) ugliness
2 • **una ~** (= *persona*) an ugly person; (= *cosa*) an ugly thing
FEVE (SF ABR) = **Ferrocarriles Españoles de Vía Estrecha**
fez (SM) fez
FF (ABR), **f.f.** (ABR) = **franco (en) fábrica** • **precio FF** price ex-factory
FF.AA. (ABR) = **Fuerzas Armadas**
FF. CC. (ABR), **FFCC** (ABR) = **Ferrocarriles**
FGD (SM ABR) (= **Fondo de Garantía de Depósitos**) *supervisory financial body*
fha. (ABR) (= **fecha**) d
fiabilidad (SF) reliability, trustworthiness
fiable (ADJ) reliable, trustworthy
fiaca‡ (SF) (*Arg*) laziness, apathy
fiado (SM) **1** • **al ~** on credit
2 (*Jur*) • **en ~** on bail
fiador(a) (SM/F) (*Jur*) (= *persona*) guarantor, bondsman (*EEUU*) • **salir ~ por algn** to stand security for sb; (*Jur*) to stand bail for sb
(SM) **1** (*Mec*) catch; [*de revólver*] safety catch, safety (*EEUU*); [*de cerradura*] tumbler; [*de ventana*] bolt, catch
2†* (= *trasero*) bottom, backside, butt (*esp EEUU**)
3 (*And, Cono Sur*) [*de perro*] muzzle; [*de casco*] chinstrap
fiambre (ADJ) **1** (*Culin*) cold, served cold
2* [*noticia*] old, stale
(SM) **1** (*Culin*) cold meat, cold cut (*EEUU*) • **~s** cold meats, cold cuts (*EEUU*)
2* (= *cadáver*) corpse, stiff* • **el pobre está ~** the poor guy's stone dead*, the poor guy's cold meat*
3 (*Cono Sur**) (= *fiesta*) dead party
4 (*Méx*) (*Culin*) *pork, avocado and chilli dish*
fiambrera (SF) **1** (*para almuerzo*) lunch box, dinner pail (*EEUU*)
2 (*Cono Sur*) (= *nevera*) meat safe, meat store
fiambrería (SF) (*And, Cono Sur*) delicatessen
fianza (SF) **1** (*Jur*) bail • **bajo ~** on bail ▸ **fianza carcelera** bail
2 (*Com*) (= *anticipo*) deposit; (= *garantía*) surety, security, bond ▸ **fianza de aduana** customs bond ▸ **fianza de averías** average bond
3 (= *persona*) surety, guarantor
fiar ▷ CONJUG 1c (VT) **1** (*Com*) (= *vender*) to sell on credit; (*LAm*) (= *comprar*) to buy on credit • **me fió la comida** he let me have the food on tick* *o* credit
2 (*frm*) (= *confiar*) • **le fié mi secreto** I confided my secret to him
(VI) **1** (*Com*) to give credit • **"no se fía"** (*en tienda*) "no credit given" • **dejaron de ~le en la tienda** they wouldn't let her have anything on credit anymore
2 • **ser de ~** to be trustworthy, be reliable
(VPR) **fiarse 1** (= *confiar*) • **~se de algn** to trust sb • **no me fío de él** I don't trust him • **ya no puede uno ~se de nadie** you can't trust anyone any more • **~se de algo** to believe in sth • **no te fíes de lo que digan los periódicos** don't believe what the papers say • **no me fío de su habilidad para resolver el problema** I don't believe in his ability to solve the problem • **no te fíes de las apariencias** don't go *o* judge by appearances • **¡para que te fíes de los amigos!** with friends like that, who needs enemies? • MODISMO: • **¡(cuán *o* tan) largo me lo fiáis!** (*liter, hum*) I'll believe it when I see it!; ▷ **pelo**
2 (*frm*) (= *depender*) to rely on • **nos fiamos de usted para conseguirlo** we are relying on you to get it
fiasco (SM) fiasco
fíat (SM) (PL: **fíats**) **1** (= *mandato*) official sanction, fiat
2 (= *consentimiento*) consent, blessing
fibra (SF) **1** (*gen*) fibre, fiber (*EEUU*) ▸ **fibra acrílica** acrylic fibre ▸ **fibra artificial** man-made fibre ▸ **fibra de amianto** asbestos fibre ▸ **fibra de carbono** carbon fibre ▸ **fibra de coco** coconut fibre ▸ **fibra de vidrio** fibre glass ▸ **fibra dietética** dietary fibre ▸ **fibra ocular** ocular fibre ▸ **fibra óptica** optical fibre ▸ **fibra sintética** synthetic fibre
2 (*en madera*) grain
3 (*Min*) vein
4 (= *vigor*) vigour, vigor (*EEUU*) • MODISMO: • **despertar la ~ sensible** to strike a chord, evoke ▸ **fibras del corazón** heartstrings
fibravidrio (SM) fibreglass
fibrina (SF) fibrin
fibroóptica (SF) fibre optics
fibrosis (SF INV) fibrosis ▸ **fibrosis cística** cystic fibrosis ▸ **fibrosis pulmonar** fibrosis of the lungs, pulmonary fibrosis ▸ **fibrosis quística** cystic fibrosis
fibrositis (SF INV) fibrositis
fibroso (ADJ) fibrous
fíbula (SF) **1** (*Med*) fibula
2 (*Hist*) fibula, brooch
ficción (SF) **1** (*Literat*) fiction • **obras de no ~** non-fiction books ▸ **ficción científica** science fiction
2 (= *invención*) fiction
3 (= *mentira*) fabrication
(ADJ INV) fictitious, make-believe • **historia ~** (piece of) historical fiction, fictionalized history • **reportaje ~** dramatized documentary
ficcioso/a (*Cono Sur*) (ADJ) (= *simulado*) bluffing; (= *falso*) false, double-dealing
(SM/F) (= *simulador*) bluffer; (= *falso*) double-dealer
ficha (SF) **1** (*en juegos*) counter; (*en casino*) chip; (*Telec*) token • MODISMO: • **mover ~** to make a move ▸ **ficha del dominó** domino ▸ **ficha de silicio** silicon chip
2 (= *tarjeta*) card; [*de archivo*] index card, record card; (*en hotel*) registration form ▸ **ficha antropométrica** anthropometric chart ▸ **ficha perforada** punched card ▸ **ficha policial** police dossier, police record ▸ **ficha técnica** (*TV*) (list of) credits
3 (*CAm, Caribe*) five-cent piece; (*CAm**) (= *moneda*) coin
4 (*Méx*) [*de botella*] flat bottle cap
5 (*And*) (*tb* **mala ficha**) rogue, villain
6 (*Dep*) signing-on fee
fichaje (SM) **1** (*Dep*) (= *acción*) signing, signing-up; (= *dinero*) signing-on fee
2 (*Dep*) (= *jugador*) signing
fichar ▷ CONJUG 1a (VT) **1** (= *registrar*) [+ *detenido, trabajador*] to put on file; [+ *dato*] to record, enter (*on a card etc*) • **~ a algn** to put sb on file • **está fichado** he's got a record • **lo tenemos fichado** we've got our eye on him
2 (*Dep*) [+ *jugador*] to sign, sign up
3 (*Pol*) [+ *nuevos miembros*] to sign up, recruit
4 (*Caribe*) (= *engañar*) to swindle
(VI) **1** (*Dep*) [*jugador*] to sign, sign up
2 [*trabajador*] (*al entrar*) to clock in, clock on; (*al salir*) to clock out, clock off
3 (*And*) (= *morir*) to die
fichero (SM) **1** (= *archivo*) card index
2 (= *mueble*) filing cabinet
3 [*de policía*] records (*pl*) ▸ **fichero fotográfico de delincuentes** photographic records of criminals, rogues' gallery* (*hum*)
4 (*Inform*) file ▸ **fichero activo** active file ▸ **fichero archivado** archive file ▸ **fichero de datos** datafile ▸ **fichero de reserva** back-up file ▸ **fichero de trabajo** work-file ▸ **fichero indexado** index file ▸ **fichero informático** computer file
ficticio (ADJ) [*nombre, carácter*] fictitious; [*historia, prueba*] fabricated
ficus (SM INV) rubber plant
FIDA (SM ABR) (= **Fondo Internacional de Desarrollo Agrícola**) IFAD
fidedigno (ADJ) reliable, trustworthy • **fuentes fidedignas** reliable sources
fideería (SF) (*LAm*) pasta factory
fideicomisario/a (ADJ) trust (*antes de s*) • **banco ~** trust company
(SM/F) trustee
fideicomiso (SM) trust
fidelería (SF) (*LAm*) pasta factory
fidelidad (SF) **1** (= *lealtad*) (*gen*) faithfulness, loyalty; (*sexual*) faithfulness • **~ a una marca** (*Com*) brand loyalty • **jurar ~ a la República** to swear allegiance to the Republic • **renuncia al cargo por ~ a sus convicciones** he resigned in order to stay true to his principles, he resigned rather than betray his principles
2 (= *exactitud*) [*de dato*] accuracy
3 • **alta ~** hi-fi
fidelísimo (ADJ SUPERL) *de* **fiel**
fidelización (SF) loyalty
fidelizar ▷ CONJUG 1f (VT) (*Com*) • **~ a los clientes** to gain *o* create customer loyalty
fideo (SM) **1** (*Culin*) noodle; **fideos** noodles
2* (= *delgado*) beanpole*, string bean (*EEUU**)
fiduciario/a (ADJ) fiduciary
(SM/F) fiduciary, trustee
fiebre (SF) **1** (= *síntoma*) temperature, fever • **tener ~** to have a temperature • **está a** *o* **tiene 39 de ~** she has a temperature of 39
2 (= *enfermedad*) fever ▸ **fiebre aftosa** foot-and-mouth disease ▸ **fiebre amarilla** yellow fever ▸ **fiebre del heno** hay fever ▸ **fiebre de los labios** cold sore ▸ **fiebre entérica** enteric fever ▸ **fiebre de Malta** brucellosis ▸ **fiebre glandular** glandular fever ▸ **fiebre palúdica** malaria ▸ **fiebre porcina** swine fever, hog cholera (*EEUU*) ▸ **fiebre recurrente** relapsing fever ▸ **fiebre reumática** rheumatic fever ▸ **fiebre tifoidea** typhoid fever
3 (= *agitación*) fever • **la ~ del juego** the

f

gambling fever • **la ~ de oro** gold fever
4 (*Cono Sur*) (= *taimado*) slippery customer*

fiel ADJ **1** (*gen*) faithful, loyal; (*sexualmente*) faithful • **un ~ servidor del partido** a loyal *o* faithful servant of the Party • **seguir siendo ~ a** to remain faithful to, stay true to
2 [*traducción, relación*] faithful, accurate
SMF (*Rel*) believer • **los ~es** the faithful
SM (*Téc*) [*de balanza*] needle, pointer

fielmente ADV **1** [*servir, apoyar*] faithfully, loyally • **continuó apoyando ~ a su marido** she continued to support her husband faithfully *o* loyally
2 (= *exactamente*) [*reflejar, describir*] faithfully, accurately

fieltro SM felt • **sombrero de ~** felt hat

fiera SF **1** (*Zool*) wild beast, wild animal • **como una ~ enjaulada** like a caged animal • MODISMO: • **hecho una ~**: • **entró hecha una ~** she came in absolutely furious • **ponerse hecho una ~** to be furious, be beside o.s. with rage
2 (*Taur*) bull
3 ▸ **fiera sarda** (*And*) expert, top man
SMF fiend • **es una ~ para el deporte** he's a sports fiend • **es un ~ para el trabajo** he's a demon for work

fierecilla SF (*fig*) shrew

fiereza SF **1** (= *ferocidad*) fierceness, ferocity; (*Zool*) wildness
2 (= *crueldad*) cruelty
3† (= *fealdad*) deformity, ugliness

fiero ADJ **1** (= *feroz*) fierce, ferocious; (*Zool*) wild • MODISMO: • **no es tan ~ el león como lo pintan** (= *persona*) he's not as bad as he's made out to be; (= *situación*) it's not as bad as it's made out to be
2 (= *cruel*) cruel
3† (= *feo*) ugly
SMPL **fieros**† (= *amenazas*) threats; (= *bravatas*) boasts, bragging (*sing*) • **echar** *o* **hacer ~s** (= *amenazas*) to utter threats; (= *bravatas*) to boast, brag

fierro SM (*LAm*) **1** (= *hierro*) iron
2 (= *cuchillo*) knife
3 (*Agr*) branding iron, brand
4 (*Aut*) accelerator
5* (= *arma*) gun, weapon
6 fierros (*Méx*) (= *dinero*) money (*sing*); (*LAm*) (= *resortes*) springs

fiesta SF **1** (= *reunión*) party • **dar** *u* **organizar una ~** to give *o* throw a party • **un ambiente de ~** a party atmosphere • **el país entero está de ~ ante la buena noticia** the whole country is celebrating the good news • MODISMOS: • **no estar para ~s** to be in no mood for jokes • **no sabe de qué va la ~** he hasn't a clue • **para coronar la ~** to round it all off, as a finishing touch • **tener la ~ en paz**: • **no os peleéis, ¡tengamos la ~ en paz!** behave yourselves, don't fight! ▸ **fiesta de caridad** charity event ▸ **fiesta de cumpleaños** birthday party ▸ **fiesta de disfraces** fancy-dress party ▸ **fiesta familiar** family celebration; ▸ **aguar**
2 (= *día festivo*) holiday • **mañana es ~** it's a holiday tomorrow • **hacer ~** to take a day off ▸ **fiesta de la banderita** flag day ▸ **Fiesta de la Hispanidad** Columbus day ▸ **Fiesta del Trabajo** Labour day, Labor day (*EEUU*) ▸ **fiesta fija** immovable feast ▸ **fiesta nacional** public holiday, bank holiday ▸ **fiesta movible, fiesta móvil** movable feast ▸ **fiesta patria** (*LAm*) independence day
3 (*Rel*) feast day • **guardar** *o* **santificar las ~s** to observe feast days ▸ **fiesta de guardar, fiesta de precepto** day of obligation
4 (= *festejo*) fiesta, festival • **el pueblo está en ~s** *o* **de ~** the town's having its local fiesta • **la ~ nacional** (*Taur*) bullfighting ▸ **fiesta de armas** (*Hist*) tournament ▸ **fiesta mayor** annual festival
5 fiestas (= *vacaciones*) holiday, vacation (*EEUU*) • **las ~s de Navidad** the Christmas holiday(s) • **¡Felices Fiestas!** (*en navidad*) Happy Christmas • **te llamaré después de estas ~s** I'll call you after the holidays
6 fiestas (= *carantoñas*) • **su perro siempre le hace ~s cuando la ve** the dog is all over her whenever he sees her

> **FIESTAS**
> There are a fixed number of public holidays in the Spanish calendar but some dates vary locally. National public holidays include **Navidad** (25 December), **Reyes** (6 January), the **Día de los Trabajadores** (1 May), the **Día de la Hispanidad/del Pilar** (12 October) and the **Día de la Constitución** (6 December). Additionally, each autonomous region and town has at its discretion a small number of public holidays that usually coincide with local traditions like a patron saint's day or other celebrations such as **Carnaval**. Thus there is a holiday in Madrid for **San Isidro**, the city's patron saint, and one in Catalonia for **Sant Jordi**, who is the patron saint of the region.

fiestero ADJ (= *alegre*) happy; (= *juerguista*) fun-loving, party-loving

fiestón* SM, **fiestorro*** SM big party

FIFA SF ABR (= **Féderation Internationale de Football Association**) FIFA

fifar** ▸ CONJUG 1a VT (*Arg*) to fuck**, screw**

fifí* SM (*Méx*) playboy

fifiriche* SM **1** (*C. Rica, Méx*) (= *lechuguino*) dandy, toff*
2 (*CAm, Méx*) (= *enclenque*) weed*

figón SM cheap restaurant

figulino ADJ clay (*antes de s*) • **arcilla figulina** potter's clay

figura SF **1** (= *estatua*) figure • **una ~ de porcelana** a porcelain figure ▸ **figura decorativa** (*lit*) decorative motif; (*fig*) figurehead ▸ **figura de nieve** snowman
2 (= *forma*) shape, form • **una chocolatina con ~ de pez** a fish-shaped chocolate, a chocolate in the shape of a fish
3 (= *silueta*) figure • **tener buena ~** to have a good figure
4 (= *personaje*) figure • **una ~ destacada** an outstanding figure • **es una ~ del toreo** he's a big name in bullfighting, he's a famous bullfighter • **la ~ del partido de hoy** (*Dep*) today's man of the match ▸ **figura de culto** cult figure ▸ **figura paterna** father figure
5 (*Geom*) figure ▸ **figura geométrica** geometric figure
6 (= *ademán*) • **hacer ~s** to make faces
7 (*Naipes*) face card; (*Ajedrez*) piece, man
8 (*Ling*) figure ▸ **figura de dicción, figura retórica** figure of speech
9 (*Teat*) character, role • **en la ~ de** in the role of
10 (*Baile, Patinaje*) figure
11 (*Mús*) note
12 (*Astron*) ▸ **figura celeste** horoscope
13†† (= *rostro*) countenance
SM • **ser un ~** to be a big name, be somebody

figuración SF **1** (*Cine*) extras (*pl*)
2 figuraciones (= *imaginación*) • **eso son figuraciones tuyas** it's just your imagination, you're imagining things

figuradamente ADV figuratively

figurado ADJ figurative

figurante SMF, **figuranta** SF **1** (*Teat*) extra
2 (*fig*) figurehead

figurar ▸ CONJUG 1a VI **1** (= *aparecer*) to figure, appear (**como** as, **entre** among) • **tu nombre no figura en la lista** your name doesn't figure *o* appear on the list
2 (= *destacar*) • **es un don nadie, pero le encanta ~** he's a nobody, but he likes to show off • **una joven que figura mucho en la alta sociedad** a young lady who is prominent in high society
VT (*frm*) **1** (= *representar*) to represent • **cada círculo figura un planeta** each circle represents a planet
2 (= *fingir*) to feign • **figuró una retirada** he feigned a retreat
VPR **figurarse** to imagine • **me figuro que Ana ya habrá llegado** I imagine that Ana will have arrived by now • **¡figúrate lo que sería con un solo coche!** imagine what it would be like with just one car! • **¿qué te figuras que me preguntó ayer?** what do you think he asked me yesterday? • **no te vayas a ~ que …** don't go thinking that … • **—¿te dio vergüenza decírselo? —¡pues, figúrate!** "were you embarrassed to tell him?" — "well, what do you think?" • **ya me lo figuraba** I thought as much

figurativismo SM figurative art

figurativo ADJ figurative

figurilla SF figurine

figurín SM **1** (= *dibujo*) design
2 (= *revista*) fashion magazine
3 (= *persona elegante*) smart dresser

figurinismo SM costume design

figurinista SMF costume designer

figurita SF (*Arg, Uru*) picture card

figurón SM **1** ▸ **figurón de proa** (*Náut*) figurehead
2* (= *presuntuoso*) pompous ass*

figuroso ADJ (*Méx*) showy, loud

fija SF **1** (*And, Cono Sur*) (*Equitación*) favourite, favorite (*EEUU*) • **es una ~** it's a cert* • **esa es la ~** that's for sure
2† (*Téc*) hinge
3† (*Arquit*) trowel

fijación SF **1** (*Psic*) fixation • **tener (una) ~ con** *o* **por algo/algn** to have a fixation about sth/sb, be fixated on sth/sb • **¡qué ~ tiene con su madre!** he's got a real mother fixation!
2 (= *acto*) (*gen*) fixing; (*con clavos*) securing • **se responsabiliza al grupo de la ~ de carteles** the group is believed to be responsible for putting up posters • **gel de ~ fuerte** extra hold gel ▸ **fijación de precios** price-fixing
3 fijaciones (*Esquí*) (safety) bindings

fijador SM **1** (*Fot*) fixative
2 (= *gomina*) setting lotion

fijamente ADV intently, fixedly • **mirar ~ a algn** to stare at sb, look at sb intently *o* fixedly

fijapelo SM setting lotion

fijar ▸ CONJUG 1a VT **1** (= *sujetar*) (*tb Fot*) to fix; (*con clavos*) to secure; (*con pegamento*) to glue; (*con chinchetas*) to pin up; [+ *pelo*] to set • **un gel para ~ el peinado** a gel to hold your hairstyle in place • **"prohibido fijar carteles"** "stick no bills"
2 (= *centrar*) [+ *atención*] to focus (**en** on); [+ *ojos*] to fix (**en** on) • **pero fijemos nuestra atención en otros aspectos del asunto** but let us focus our attention on other aspects of the matter • **le contestó sin vacilar, fijando la mirada en sus ojos** she answered him directly, looking him straight in the eye
3 (= *determinar*) [+ *fecha, hora, precio, plazo*] to fix, set; [+ *límites, servicios mínimos*] to establish; [+ *condiciones*] to lay down • **no**

hemos fijado aún la fecha de la boda we haven't fixed *o* set a date for the wedding yet • **~on un plazo de dos meses para llegar a un acuerdo** they set a two-month deadline for an agreement to be reached • **aún no se ha fijado el precio de las acciones** the price of the shares has not yet been fixed • **el Tratado de 1942 fijó los límites entre Perú y Ecuador** the 1942 Treaty established the border between Peru and Ecuador • **la organización ha fijado tres condiciones para volver a la mesa de negociaciones** the organization laid down three conditions for their return to the negotiating table • **el plazo fijado por la ley** the time period established *o* laid down by law
4 [+ *residencia*] to take up • **durante la guerra fijó su residencia en Suiza** during the war he took up residence in Switzerland
(VPR) **fijarse 1** (= *prestar atención*) to pay attention; (= *darse cuenta*) to notice • **¿no ves que lo has escrito mal? ¡es que no te fijas!** can't you see you've spelled it wrong? don't you ever pay any attention to what you're doing? • **voy a hacerlo yo primero, fíjate bien** I'll do it first, watch carefully • **¿han pintado la puerta? no me había fijado** has the door been painted? I hadn't noticed • **~se en algo** (= *prestar atención*) to pay attention to sth; (= *darse cuenta*) to notice sth • **no se fija en lo que hace** he doesn't pay attention to what he is doing • **debería ~se más en lo que dice** he ought to be more careful about *o* think more about what he says • **entre tantos candidatos, es muy difícil que se fijen en mí** out of so many candidates, they're hardly likely to notice me • **¿te has fijado en los colores?** have you noticed the colours?
2 (*uso enfático*) • **¡fíjate cómo corre!** (just) look at him run! • **¡fíjate qué precios!** (just) look at these prices! • **¡fíjate lo que me ha dicho!** guess what he just said to me! • **fíjate si será tacaño que ni siquiera les hace un regalo en Navidad** he is so mean he doesn't even give them a present for Christmas • **¿te fijas?** (*esp LAm*) see what I mean?
3 • **~se un objetivo** to set (o.s.) a goal • **nos hemos fijado el objetivo de llegar a las próximas Olimpiadas** we've set (ourselves) the goal of getting to the next Olympics • **~se algo como objetivo** to set one's sights on sth
4 (= *establecerse*) • **el dolor se me ha fijado en la pierna** the pain has settled in my leg
fijasellos (SM INV) stamp hinge
fijativo (SM) fixative
fijeza (SF) (*gen*) firmness, stability; (= *constancia*) constancy • **mirar con ~ a algn** to stare at sb, look hard at sb
fijo (ADJ) **1** (= *sujeto*) fixed • **la mesa está fija a la pared** the table is fixed to the wall; ▸ **barra, foto, piñón²**
2 (= *inmóvil*) [*mirada*] fixed, steady; [*punto*] fixed • **sentí sus ojos ~s en mí** I felt his eyes fixed on me • **estaba de pie, con la vista fija en el horizonte** he was standing staring at the horizon, he was standing with his gaze fixed on the horizon
3 (= *no variable*) [*fecha, precio*] fixed • **fiestas fijas, como el día de Navidad** fixed holidays, like Christmas Day • **no hay una fecha fija de apertura** there's no definite *o* fixed *o* set date for the opening • **no tengo hora fija para ir al gimnasio** I don't go to the gym at any particular time, I don't have a fixed time for going to the gym • **como soy fotógrafo, no tengo horario ~ de trabajo** being a photographer, I don't have fixed *o* regular work hours • **le ofrecieron una cantidad fija al mes por sus servicios** they offered him a fixed monthly sum for his services • **"sin domicilio ~"** "of no fixed abode" • **imposición a plazo ~** fixed term deposit • **fondos de renta fija** fixed-interest funds
4 (= *regular*) [*sueldo, novio*] steady; [*cliente*] regular • **el padre no tenía trabajo ~** the father didn't have a steady job, the father was not in regular employment (*frm*)
5 (= *permanente*) [*plantilla, contrato, empleado*] permanent • **estoy ~ en la empresa** I have a permanent job in the company • **¿cuándo os van a hacer ~s?** when will you get a permanent contract?
6 [*propósito*] fixed, firm; ▸ **idea, rumbo¹**
7 • **de ~*** for sure* • **sé de ~ que no va a estar en casa** I know for sure that he won't be at home* • **de ~ que llueve esta noche** it's definitely going to rain tonight, it's going to rain tonight, that's for sure*
(ADV) **1*** (= *con certeza*) for sure* • **ya sé que no voy a ganar, eso ~** I know I'm not going to win, that's for sure*
2 (= *con fijeza*) fixedly • **miraba muy ~ a su padre** she stared fixedly at her father
fil (SM) • **fil derecho** leapfrog
fila (SF) **1** (= *hilera*) [*de personas, cosas*] **a** (*una tras de otra*) line • **una ~ de coches** a line of cars • **nos colocaron en ~** they lined us up, they put us in a row • **ponerse en ~** to line up, get into line • **salirse de la ~** to step out of line • **una chaqueta de dos ~s de botones** a double-breasted jacket
b (*una al lado de otra*) • **había cuatro coches en ~** there were four cars in a row • **aparcar en doble ~** to double-park • **iban andando en ~s de tres** they were walking three abreast
c (*Mil*) • **¡en ~!** fall in! • **formar ~s** to form up, fall in • **romper ~s** to fall out, break ranks • **¡rompan ~s!** fall out!, dismiss! ▸ **fila india** • **en ~ india** in single file
2 [*de asientos*] row • **en primera/segunda ~** in the front/second row ▸ **fila cero** VIP row
3 filas: **a** (*Mil*) (= *servicio*) • **estar en ~s** to be on active service • **incorporarse a ~s** to join up • **llamar a algn a ~s** to call sb up, draft sb (*EEUU*)
b (*Pol*) ranks • **en las ~s del partido** in the ranks of the party • **MODISMO**: • **cerrar ~s** to close ranks
4* (= *antipatía*) • **tener ~ a algn** to have it in for sb* • **el jefe le tiene ~** the boss has it in for him*
5 (*CAm*) (= *cumbre*) peak, summit
filacteria (SF) phylactery
Filadelfia (SF) Philadelphia
filamento (SM) filament
filamentoso (ADJ) filamentous
filantropía (SF) philanthropy
filantrópico (ADJ) philanthropic
filantropismo (SM) philanthropy
filántropo/a (SM/F) philanthropist
filar‡ ▸ CONJUG 1a (VT) **1** (= *calar*) to size up, rumble*
2 (= *observar*) to notice, spot
filarmónica (SF) philharmonic (orchestra)
filarmónico (ADJ) philharmonic • **orquesta filarmónica** philharmonic (orchestra)
filatelia (SF) **1** (= *afición*) philately, stamp collecting
2 (= *tienda*) stamp shop, stamp dealer's
filatélico/a (ADJ) philatelic
(SM/F) = **filatelista**
filatelista (SMF) philatelist, stamp collector
filático (ADJ) (*And*) **1** [*caballo*] vicious
2 [*persona*] (= *travieso*) mischievous; (= *taimado*) crafty; (= *grosero*) rude
filete (SM) **1** (*Culin*) [*de ternera, cerdo*] steak; [*de pescado*] fillet, filet (*EEUU*) • **MODISMO**: • **darse el ~*** to neck*, pet* • **darse el ~ con algn*** to feel sb*, touch sb up*
2 (*Mec*) [*de tornillo*] worm; (= *rosca*) thread
3 [*de caballo*] snaffle bit
4 (*Cos*) narrow hem
5 (*Tip*) ornamental bar, ornamental line
6 (*Arquit*) fillet
fileteado (SM) filleting
filetear ▸ CONJUG 1a (VT) to fillet
filfa* (SF) **1** (= *fraude*) fraud, hoax
2 (= *falsificación*) fake
3 (= *rumor*) rumour, rumor (*EEUU*)
fili‡ (SM) pocket • **~ de la buena** breast pocket
filiación (SF) **1** (*a partido*) affiliation
2 [*de ideas*] connection, relationship
3 (= *señas*) particulars (*pl*)
4 [*de policía*] records (*pl*)
filial (ADJ) **1** (= *de hijo*) filial
2 (*Com*) subsidiary (*antes de s*), affiliated
(SF) (*Com*) subsidiary
filibusterismo (SM) **1** (*Pol*) filibustering
2 (= *piratería*) buccaneering
filibustero (SM) pirate, freebooter
filiforme (ADJ) **1** (*Bot*) thread-like
2 (*hum*) [*persona*] skinny
filigrana (SF) **1** (*Téc*) filigree (work)
2 (*Tip*) watermark
3 filigranas (*fig*) delicate work (*sing*); (*Dep*) elegant play (*sing*), fancy footwork (*sing*)
filípica (SF) harangue, philippic
Filipinas (SFPL) • **las (islas) ~** the Philippines
filipino/a (ADJ) Philippine, Filipino
(SM/F) Filipino
filisteísmo (SM) Philistinism
filisteo/a (ADJ), (SM/F) Philistine
film (SM) (PL: **films, filmes**) film, picture, movie (*EEUU*) ▸ **film transparente** (*Culin*) cling film
filmación (SF) **1** (= *rodaje*) filming, shooting
2 filmaciones footage (*sing*)
filmador(a) (SM/F) film maker, moviemaker (*EEUU*)
filmadora (SF) (= *estudio*) film studio; (= *aparato*) film camera
filmar ▸ CONJUG 1a (VT) to film, shoot
filme (SM) = film
fílmico (ADJ) film (*antes de s*), movie (*antes de s*) (*EEUU*) • **su carrera fílmica** her film career, her career in films • **obras teatrales y fílmicas** theatrical and screen works, works for stage and screen
filmina (SF) slide, transparency
filmografía (SF) filmography • **la ~ de Buñuel** Buñuel's films • **la ~ de la estrella** the star's screen career
filmología (SF) science of film-making, art of film-making
filmoteca (SF) film library, film archive
filo¹ (SM) **1** [*de navaja, espada*] cutting edge, blade • **un arma de doble ~** a double-edged sword • **MODISMOS**: • **dar ~ a algn** (*Caribe*) to wound sb with a knife • **herir a algn por los mismos ~s††** to pay sb back in his own coin • **pasar al ~ de la espada††** to put to the sword • **vivir en el ~ de la navaja** to live on a knife edge
2 (*con horas*) • **al ~ de las doce** just before twelve o'clock • **por ~††** exactly
3 (*Náut*) ▸ **filo del viento** direction of the wind
4 (*LAm*) (= *de montaña*) ridge
5 (*And*) • **de ~** resolutely
6 (*Méx**) (= *hambre*) • **MODISMO**: • **tener ~** to be starving
7 (*Cono Sur*) (= *cuento*) tale, tall story
8 (*Cono Sur*) (= *pretendiente*) suitor; (= *novia*) girlfriend; (= *cortejo*) courtship
filo² (SM) (*Bio*) phylum
filo³‡ (SM) con-man's accomplice*
...filo (SUF) ...phile • **francófilo** Francophile

filo... PREF philo..., pro- • **filocomunista** pro-communist
filocomunismo SM pro-communist feeling(s)
filocomunista ADJ pro-communist, with communist leanings
SMF pro-communist
filología SF philology ▸ **Filología Francesa** (= *carrera*) French Studies
filológico ADJ philological
filólogo/a SM/F (= *estudioso*) philologist; (= *estudiante*) language graduate
filomela SF, **filomena** SF (*poét*) nightingale
filón SM (*Min*) vein, lode, seam; (*fig*) gold mine
filongo SM (*Cono Sur*) girlfriend (*of inferior social status*)
filosa‡ SF **1** (= *navaja*) chiv‡, knife
2 (= *cara*) mug‡, face
filoso ADJ **1** (*LAm*) (= *afilado*) sharp
2 (*Cono Sur**) (= *agudo*) • **él es ~** he's sharp, he's really on the ball* • **estar ~ en algo** to be well up on sth
3 (*CAm*) (= *hambriento*) starving
filosofal ADJ • **piedra ~** philosopher's stone
filosofar ▹ CONJUG 1a VI to philosophize
filosofía SF philosophy • **tomarse las cosas con ~** to take things philosophically
▸ **filosofía de la ciencia** philosophy of science ▸ **filosofía de la vida** philosophy of life ▸ **filosofía moral** moral philosophy
▸ **filosofía natural** natural philosophy; ▹ **facultad**
filosóficamente ADV philosophically
filosófico ADJ philosophic, philosophical
filósofo/a SM/F philosopher
filosoviético ADJ pro-Soviet
filote SM (*And*) **1** (= *maíz*) ear of green maize, maize silk
2 • **estar en ~** [*niño*] to begin to grow hair
filotear ▹ CONJUG 1a VI (*And*) **1** [*maíz*] to come into ear, begin to ripen
2 [*niño*] to grow hair
filoxera SF phylloxera
filtración SF **1** (*Téc*) (= *proceso*) filtration
2 (= *fuga*) seepage, leakage, loss
3 [*de datos*] leak; [*de fondos*] misappropriation
filtrado ADJ **1** [*información*] leaked
2 • **estoy ~** (*Cono Sur**) I'm whacked*
SM filtering
filtrador ADJ filtering
SM filter
filtraje SM filtering
filtrar ▹ CONJUG 1a VT **1** [+ *líquido, luz*] to filter • **hay que ~ el agua** the water needs filtering
2 [+ *llamadas, visitantes*] to screen
3 [+ *información, documento, grabación*] to leak
VPR **filtrarse 1** [*líquido*] to seep, leak; [*luz, sonido*] to filter • **el agua se filtraba por las paredes** water was seeping *o* leaking in through the walls • **el sol se filtraba a través de las cortinas** the sun filtered through the curtains
2 (= *desaparecer*) [*dinero, bienes*] to disappear
filtro SM **1** (*Téc*) filter • **cigarrillo con ~** filter-tipped cigarette ▸ **filtro de aire** air filter ▸ **filtro del aceite** oil filter
2 (= *selección*) screening ▸ **filtro de llamadas** call-screening
3 (*en carretera, de policía*) checkpoint, roadblock
4 (*Hist*) (= *poción*) love-potion, philtre, philter (EEUU)
filudo ADJ (*LAm*) sharp
filván SM (*gen*) feather edge; [*de papel*] deckle edge; [*de cuchillo*] burr
fimbria SF (*Cos*) border, hem
fin SM **1** (= *final*) end • **el fin del mundo** the end of the world • **antes de fin de mes** before the end of the month • **en la noche de fin de año** on New Year's Eve • **fin de la cita** end of quote, unquote • **fin de curso** end of the school year • **fiesta de fin de curso** end-of-year party • **dar fin a** [+ *ceremonia, actuación*] to bring to a close; [+ *obra, libro*] to finish; [+ *guerra, conflicto*] to bring to an end • **estas palabras dieron fin a tres años de conflicto** these words brought three years of conflict to an end • **llegar a buen fin** [*aventura*] to have a happy ending; [*plan*] to turn out well • **llevar algo a buen fin** to bring sth to a successful conclusion • **poner fin a algo** to end sth, put an end to sth • **esta ley pondrá fin a la discriminación sexual en el trabajo** this law will end *o* will put an end to sexual discrimination in the workplace • **los acuerdos pusieron fin a doce años de guerra** the agreements ended *o* put an end to twelve years of war • **deseaban poner fin a sus vidas** they wished to end their lives • **sin fin** endless • **correa sin fin** endless belt • MODISMO: • **llegar a fin de mes** to make ends meet • **un sueldo que apenas les permite llegar a fin de mes** a salary that barely enables them to make ends meet ▸ **fin de fiesta** (*Teat*) grand finale ▸ **fin de semana** weekend
2 • **a fines de** at the end of • **a fines de abril** at the end of April • **la crisis de fines del XIX** the crisis at the end of the 19th century, the late 19th century crisis
3 (*otras locuciones*) **a** • **al fin** • **por fin** (*gen*) finally; (*con más énfasis*) at last • **al fin se ha premiado su esfuerzo** her efforts have finally been rewarded • **tras varios días de marcha, por fin llegamos a la primera aldea** after several days' walk, we finally came to the first village • **¡al fin solos!** alone at last! • **¡por fin te decides a hacer algo!** at last you've decided to do something! • **al fin y al cabo** after all • **tengo derecho a estar aquí: al fin y al cabo, soy parte de la familia** I have a right to stay here: after all, I am part of the family • **al fin y al cabo, lo que importa es que seguimos juntos** at the end of the day, what matters is that we're still together • **a fin de cuentas** at the end of the day
b • **en fin** (*quitando importancia*) anyway, oh, well; (*para resumir*) in short • **en fin, otro día seguiremos hablando del tema** anyway *o* oh, well, we will carry on discussing this another day • **¡en fin, qué se le va a hacer!** anyway *o* oh, well, there's nothing we can do about it! • **hemos tenido bastantes problemas este año, pero en fin, seguimos adelante** we've had quite a few problems this year, but still *o* anyway, we're still going • **en fin, que no he tenido un momento de descanso** in short, I haven't had a moment's rest
4 (= *intención*) aim • **se desconocen los fines de esa organización** the aims of that organization are unknown • **¿con qué fin se ha organizado esto?** what has been the aim in organizing this? • **a fin de hacer algo** in order to do sth • **a fin de que** (+ *subjun*) so that, in order that (*frm*) • **se le ha citado como testigo a fin de que explique sus relaciones con el acusado** he has been called as a witness in order to explain *o* in order that he explain (*frm*) *o* so that he can explain his relationship with the defendant • **con el fin de hacer algo** in order to do sth • **a tal fin** with this aim in mind, to this end • REFRÁN: • **el fin justifica los medios** the end justifies the means
5 (= *propósito*) purpose • **un millón de dólares será destinado a fines benéficos** a million dollars is to go to charity • **el dinero había sido destinado a otros fines** the money had been put aside for other purposes • **con fines experimentales/militares/políticos** for experimental/military/political purposes • **planean intervenir con fines humanitarios** they are planning to intervene for humanitarian reasons
Fina SF *forma familiar de* **Josefina**
finado/a ADJ late, deceased • **el ~ presidente** the late president
SM/F deceased
SM (*Téc*) finishing
final ADJ (= *último*) [*momento, capítulo, resultado, decisión*] final; [*objetivo*] ultimate • **los años ~es de la dictadura** the final years of the dictatorship • **estaban deseando ver el producto ~** they were looking forward to seeing the end product; ▹ **juicio, recta, punto**
SM **1** (= *fin*) [*de ceremonia, vida, aventura, guerra*] end; [*de obra musical*] finale • **hasta el ~ de sus días** till the end of her days • **no vi el ~ de la película** I didn't see the end of the film • **al ~** in the end • **al ~ tuve que darle la razón** in the end I had to admit that he was right • **al ~ de algo** at the end of sth • **el anuncio se realizó ayer al ~ de la reunión** the announcement was made yesterday at the end of the meeting • **al ~ de la calle** at the end of the street • **estamos al ~ de la lista** we are at the bottom of the list
2 (= *desenlace*) [*de película, libro*] ending • **la novela tiene un ~ inesperado** the novel has an unexpected ending • **un ~ feliz** a happy ending
3 • **a finales de** at the end of • **a ~es del siglo XIX** at the end of the 19th century
SF (*Dep*) final • **consiguieron pasar a la ~** they managed to get through to the final • **cuartos de ~** quarter-finals ▸ **final de consolación** third-place play-off
finalidad SF **1** (= *propósito*) purpose • **¿qué ~ tendrá todo esto?** what can the purpose of all this be? • **el congreso tuvo como ~ debatir el desarrollo social** the purpose *o* aim of the conference was to discuss social development
2 (*Fil*) finality
finalista ADJ • **los relatos ~s** the short-listed stories • **quedó ~ en dos ocasiones** he was short-listed twice *o* on two occasions
SMF finalist
finalización SF ending, conclusion
finalizar ▹ CONJUG 1f VT to finish • **muchos universitarios no finalizan la carrera** many university students do not finish their degree • **~ la sesión** (*Inform*) to log out, log off • **con el himno se dio por finalizada la ceremonia** the ceremony came to an end *o* ended with the national anthem
VI to end • **aún no ha finalizado la sesión** the session has not ended yet • **su contrato finaliza el próximo verano** his contract ends *o* comes to an end next summer • **hoy finaliza el plazo para presentar las solicitudes** today is the deadline for submitting applications • **~ con algo** to end with sth • **la jornada finalizó con la prueba de atletismo femenino** the day ended with the women's athletics trials
finalmente ADV **1** (= *al final*) finally, in the end • **~ decidimos ir a Mallorca** finally *o* in the end we decided to go to Majorca • **insistió hasta que, ~, consiguió convencerla** he went on until finally *o* in the end *o* eventually he managed to persuade her
2 (= *por último*) lastly • **50% están a favor, 30%**

en contra y, ~, un 20% se muestra indeciso 50% are in favour, 30% are against and lastly, 20% don't know
finamente (ADV) **1** (= *elegantemente*) elegantly; (= *educadamente*) politely; (= *delicadamente*) delicately
2 (= *inteligentemente*) acutely, shrewdly; (= *sutilmente*) subtly
finamiento (SM) passing*, death
financiación (SF) financing, funding
financiador(a) (SM/F) financial backer
financiamiento (SM) financing, funding
financiar ▷ CONJUG 1b (VT) to finance, fund
financiera (SF) finance company, finance house
financiero/a (ADJ) financial • **el mundo ~** the world of finance, the financial world • **los medios ~s** the financial means
(SM/F) (= *banquero*) financier
financista (ADJ) (= *financiero*) financial
(SMF) (*LAm*) (= *bolsista*) financier; (= *consejero*) financial expert
finanzas (SFPL) finances
finar ▷ CONJUG 1a (VI) (= *morir*) to pass away (*euf*), die
(VPR) **finarse** (= *desear*) to long, yearn (**por** for)
finca (SF) **1** (= *bien inmueble*) property, land, real estate • **cazar en ~ ajena** to poach (*on sb else's property*) • **penetrar en ~ ajena** to trespass (*on sb else's property*) ▸ **finca raíz** (*And*) real estate ▸ **finca urbana** town property
2 (= *casa de recreo*) country house, country estate • **pasan un mes en su ~** they're spending a month at their country place • **tienen una ~ en Guadalajara** they have a country house *o* country estate in Guadalajara
3 (= *granja*) farm; (= *minifundio*) small holding; [*de ganado*] ranch ▸ **finca azucarera** sugar plantation ▸ **finca cafetera** coffee plantation
fincar ▷ CONJUG 1g (VT) (*Caribe*) (= *cultivar*) to till, cultivate
(VI) (*And, Méx*) • **~ en** (= *consistir*) to consist of, comprise
finchado* (ADJ) stuck-up*, conceited
fincharse* ▷ CONJUG 1a (VPR) to become stuck-up*, get conceited
finde* (SM ABR) (= **fin de semana**) weekend
finés/esa (ADJ) Finnish
(SM/F) Finn
(SM) (*Ling*) Finnish
fineza (SF) **1** (= *cualidad*) fineness, excellence
2 [*de modales*] refinement; (= *elegancia*) elegance
3 (= *acto*) kindness; (= *dádiva*) small gift, token
4 (= *cumplido*) compliment
fingar‡ ▷ CONJUG 1h (VT) to nick‡, swipe‡
finger ['finger] (SM) (PL: **fingers**) (*Aer*) (telescopic) passenger walkway
fingidamente (ADV) feignedly
fingido (ADJ) feigned, false • **con ~ enojo** with feigned annoyance • **nombre ~** assumed name, false name
fingimiento (SM) pretence, pretense (*EEUU*), feigning
fingir ▷ CONJUG 3c (VT) to feign • **intenté ~ indiferencia** I tried to feign indifference *o* to appear indifferent • **fingió interés** he pretended to be interested • **~ hacer algo** to pretend to do sth • **finge dormir** *o* **que duerme** he's pretending to be asleep
(VI) to pretend • **¡no finjas más!** stop pretending!
(VPR) **fingirse** (*frm*) • **~se dormido** to pretend to be asleep • **~se muerto** to play dead, act dead • **~se un sabio** to pretend to be an expert

finiquitar ▷ CONJUG 1a (VT) **1** (*Econ*) [+ *cuenta*] to settle and close, balance up
2* [+ *asunto*] to conclude, wind up
finiquito (SM) (*Com, Econ*) settlement • **dar el ~ a una cuenta** to settle an account • **dar el ~ a algn** to dismiss sb
finisecular (ADJ) fin-de-siècle (*antes de s*), turn-of-the-century (*antes de s*)
Finisterre (SM) (*tb* **el cabo de Finisterre**) Cape Finisterre
finito (ADJ) finite
finlandés/esa (ADJ) Finnish
(SM/F) Finn
(SM) (*Ling*) Finnish
Finlandia (SF) Finland
finlandización (SF) Finlandization, neutralization and subordination (*of one country to another*)
finlandizar ▷ CONJUG 1f (VT) [+ *país*] to Finlandize, neutralize and subordinate
fino (ADJ) **1** (= *no grueso*) [*arena, punta, pelo*] fine; [*papel, capa*] thin; [*dedos, cuello*] slender; [*cutis, piel*] smooth • **bolígrafo de punta fina** fine-tipped ballpoint pen
2 (= *de buena calidad*) [*cristal, porcelana, papel*] fine; [*tabaco*] select • **oro ~** fine gold; ▷ **lencería**
3 (= *cortés*) polite, well-bred; (= *refinado*) refined • **no te hagas la fina** you needn't start putting on airs
4 (= *agudo*) [*vista*] sharp; [*oído*] acute • **su fina inteligencia analítica** her fine *o* acute analytical intelligence
5 (= *sutil*) subtle, fine • **me sorprendió su fina ironía** her subtle irony surprised me
6 [*jerez*] fino, dry
(SM) (= *jerez*) dry sherry, fino sherry
finolis* (ADJ INV) affected
finquero (SM) (*LAm*) farmer
finta (SF) feint • **hacer ~s** to feint, spar
fintar ▷ CONJUG 1a (VI), **fintear** ▷ CONJUG 1a (VI) (*LAm*) to feint, spar
finura (SF) **1** (= *buena calidad*) fineness, excellence
2 (= *cortesía*) politeness, courtesy; (= *refinamiento*) refinement • **¡qué ~!** how refined!, how charming!
3 (= *sutileza*) subtlety
4 (= *poco grosor*) fineness
fiñe (ADJ) (*Caribe*) small, weak, sickly
fiordo (SM) fiord
fique (SM) (*Col, Méx, Ven*) **1** (= *fibra*) vegetable fibre *o* (*EEUU*) fiber
2 (= *cuerda*) rope, cord
firma (SF) **1** (= *nombre*) signature; (= *acto*) signing • **es de mi ~** I signed that • **seis novelas de su ~** six novels of his, six novels which he has written • **me presentó varios documentos a la ~** he handed me several documents to sign ▸ **firma de libros** book-signing session ▸ **firma digitalizada** digital signature ▸ **firma electrónica** electronic signature
2 (= *empresa*) firm, company
firmamento (SM) firmament
firmante (ADJ) signatory (**de** to)
(SMF) signatory • **los abajo ~s** the undersigned • **el último ~** the last person signing *o* to sign
firmar ▷ CONJUG 1a (VT) to sign • **~ un cheque en blanco** to write *o* sign a blank cheque • **~ un contrato** to sign a contract • **firmado y sellado** signed and sealed
(VI) to sign • **firme aquí** sign here • **no te quejes, si me dieran tu trabajo ~ía ahora mismo** stop complaining, if I was offered your job I'd take it straight away
firme (ADJ) **1** [*mesa, andamio*] steady; [*terreno*] firm, solid • **mantén la escalera ~** can you hold the ladder steady?

2 [*paso*] firm, steady; [*voz*] firm; [*mercado, moneda*] steady; [*candidato*] strong • **la libra se ha mantenido ~** the pound has remained steady • **oferta en ~** firm offer • **pedido en ~** firm order
3 [*amistad, apoyo*] firm, strong; [*decisión, convicción*] firm • **mantenerse ~** to hold one's ground • **se mostró muy ~ con ella** he was very firm with her • **de ~** hard • **trabajar de ~** to work hard • **estar en lo ~†** to be in the right
4 [*sentencia*] final
5 (*Mil*) • **¡~s!** attention! • **estar en posición de ~s** to stand to attention • **ponerse ~s** to come *o* stand to attention
(ADV) hard • **trabajar ~** to work hard
(SM) (*Aut*) road surface • **"firme provisional"** "temporary surface" ▸ **firme del suelo** (*Arquit*) rubble base (of floor)
firmemente (ADV) (= *con firmeza*) firmly; (= *bien sujeto*) securely
firmeza (SF) **1** [*del terreno*] firmness
2 [*de carácter, convicciones*] strength, firmness • **con ~** firmly • **se negó con ~ a delatarlos** he firmly refused to inform on them
firmita* (SF) (mere) signature • **echar una ~** to sign on the dotted line (*tb fig*) • **¿me echas una ~?** would you sign here please?
firuletes* (SMPL) (*LAm*) **1** (= *objetos*) knick-knacks
2 (*al bailar*) gyrations, contortions
fiscal (ADJ) (= *relativo a impuestos*) fiscal, tax (*antes de s*); (= *económico*) fiscal, financial • **año ~** fiscal year, financial year
(SMF) **1** (*Jur*) public prosecutor, district attorney (*EEUU*) ▸ **fiscal general del Estado** Director of Public Prosecutions, Attorney General (*EEUU*)
2* (= *entrometido*) busybody, meddler
fiscala (SF) ▷ **fiscal**
fiscalía (SF) office of the public prosecutor, District Attorney's office (*EEUU*)
fiscalidad (SF) (*gen*) taxation; (= *sistema*) tax system; (= *normas*) tax regulations (*pl*)
fiscalista (ADJ) • **abogado ~** lawyer specializing in tax affairs
fiscalizar ▷ CONJUG 1f (VT) **1** (= *controlar*) to control; (= *supervisar*) to oversee; (= *registrar*) to inspect (officially)
2 (= *criticar*) to criticize, find fault with
3* (= *hurgar*) to pry into
fiscalmente (ADV) from a tax point of view, taxation-wise
fisco (SM) treasury, exchequer • **declarar algo al ~** to declare sth to the Inland Revenue *o* (*EEUU*) Internal Revenue Service
fisga (SF) **1** [*de pesca*] fish spear
2 (*Guat, Méx*) (*Taur*) banderilla
3 (= *bromas*) banter • **hacer ~ a algn** to tease sb, make fun of sb
fisgar* ▷ CONJUG 1h (VT) **1** (= *curiosear*) to snoop on*
2 [+ *pez*] to spear, harpoon
(VI) **1*** (= *curiosear*) to snoop* (**en** on)
2 (= *mofarse*) to mock
fisgón/ona* (ADJ) **1** (= *curioso*) nosey*
2 (= *guasón*) bantering, teasing; (= *mofador*) mocking
(SM/F) **1** snooper*
2 (= *guasón*) tease
fisgonear* ▷ CONJUG 1a (VI) to snoop*
fisgoneo* (SM) (= *acción*) snooping*; (= *actitud*) nosiness*
física (SF) physics (*sing*) ▸ **física cuántica** quantum physics ▸ **física de alta(s) energía(s)** high-energy physics ▸ **física del estado sólido** solid-state physics ▸ **física de partículas** particle physics ▸ **física nuclear** nuclear physics ▸ **física teórica** theoretical physics; ▷ **físico**

físicamente ADV physically

físico/a ADJ **1** physical
2 (*Caribe*) (= *melindroso*) finicky; (= *afectado*) affected
SM/F **1** (= *científico*) physicist ▸ **física/o nuclear** nuclear physicist
2† (= *médico*) physician
SM (*Anat*) physique; (= *aspecto*) appearance, looks (*pl*) • **de ~ regular** ordinary-looking; ▹ **física**

fisil ADJ fissile

fisiología SF physiology

fisiológicamente ADV physiologically

fisiológico ADJ physiological

fisiólogo/a SM/F physiologist

fisión SF fission ▸ **fisión nuclear** nuclear fission

fisionable ADJ fissionable

fisionarse ▹ CONJUG 1a VPR to undergo fission, split

fisionomía SF = **fisonomía**

fisioterapeuta SMF physiotherapist, physical therapist (*EEUU*)

fisioterapia SF physiotherapy, physical therapy (*EEUU*)

fisioterapista SMF (*esp LAm*) physiotherapist, physical therapist (*EEUU*)

fiso‡ SM (*LAm*) mug‡

fisonomía SF **1** (= *cara*) physiognomy, features (*pl*)
2 [*de objeto, lugar*] appearance • **la ~ de la ciudad** the appearance of the city

fisonomista SMF • **ser buen ~** to have a good memory for faces

fisoterapeuta SMF physiotherapist

fistol SM (*Méx*) tiepin

fístula SF fistula

fisura SF **1** (*en roca*) crack, fissure (*frm*); (*en órgano*) fissure (*frm*); (*en hueso*) crack ▸ **fisura del paladar, fisura palatina** cleft palate
2 • **sin ~s** [*apoyo, fe, convencimiento*] solid

fitobiología SF phytobiology, plant breeding

fitocultura SF plant breeding

fitófago/a ADJ plant-eating
SM/F plant eater

fitopatología SF phytopathology, plant pathology

fitoplancton SM phytoplankton

fitoquímica SF phytochemistry

fitosanitario ADJ [*productos, industria, problemas, tratamiento*] phytosanitary
SM pesticide

FIV SF ABR (= **fecundación in vitro**) IVF

flaccidez SF flaccidity (*frm*), softness, flabbiness

fláccido ADJ flaccid (*frm*), flabby

flacidez SF = **flaccidez**

flácido ADJ = **fláccido**

flaco ADJ **1** (= *delgado*) thin, skinny* • **años ~s** (*LAm*) lean years • **ponerse ~** (*LAm*) to get thin
2 (= *débil*) weak, feeble; [*memoria*] bad, short; (*LAm*) [*tierra*] barren • **su punto ~** his weak point, his weakness
SM (= *defecto*) failing; (= *punto débil*) weakness, weak point

flacón* ADJ (*Caribe, Cono Sur*) very thin

flacuchento* ADJ (*LAm*) very thin

flacucho* ADV skinny*

flacura SF **1** (= *delgadez*) thinness, skinniness*
2 (= *debilidad*) weakness, feebleness

flagelación SF flagellation (*frm*), whipping

flagelar ▹ CONJUG 1a VT **1** (= *azotar*) to flagellate (*frm*), whip
2 (= *criticar*) to flay, criticize severely

flagelo SM **1** (= *azote*) whip, scourge
2 (= *calamidad*) scourge, calamity

flagrante ADJ flagrant • **pillar** *o* **sorprender a algn en ~ delito** to catch sb in the act, catch sb redhanded, catch sb in flagrante delicto (*frm*)

flama SF **1** (*Méx*) (= *llama*) flame
2 (= *destello*) glitter
3 (= *calor*) stifling heat

flamable ADJ (*Méx*) flammable

flamante ADJ **1** (= *nuevo*) [*automóvil, traje*] brand-new; [*campeón, director*] new
2 (= *estupendo*) brilliant, fabulous; (= *lujoso*) luxurious, high-class
3 (= *resplandeciente*) brilliant, flaming

flambeado ADJ flambé

flambear ▹ CONJUG 1a VT to flambé

flamear ▹ CONJUG 1a VI **1** (= *llamear*) to flame, blaze (up)
2 [*vela*] to flap; [*bandera*] to flutter

flamenco¹ SM (= *ave*) flamingo

flamenco²/a ADJ **1** (*Geog*) Flemish
2 (*Mús*) flamenco • **cante ~** flamenco
3 (*pey*) flashy, vulgar, gaudy
4 • **ponerse ~*** (= *engreído*) to get cocky*
5 (*CAm*) = **flaco**
SM/F (= *persona*) Fleming • **los ~s** the Flemings, the Flemish
SM **1** (*Mús*) flamenco
2 (*Ling*) Flemish

flamencología SF *study of flamenco music and dance*

flamencólogo/a SM/F *student of flamenco music and dance*

flamenquilla SF marigold

flamígero ADJ • **estilo gótico ~** flamboyant Gothic style

flámula SF pennant

flan SM (*dulce*) creme caramel; (*salado*) mould, mold (*EEUU*) • MODISMO: • **estar hecho** *o* **estar como un ~** to shake like a jelly *o* a leaf

flanco SM **1** (= *lado*) [*de animal*] side, flank; [*de persona*] side
2 (*Mil*) flank • **coger a algn por el ~** to catch sb off guard
3 (*Geog*) flank

Flandes SM Flanders

flanear* ▹ CONJUG 1a VI to stroll, saunter

flanera SF jelly mould, jelly mold (*EEUU*)

flanquear ▹ CONJUG 1a VT **1** [+ *persona, construcción*] to flank; [+ *calle, costa, río*] to line
2 (*Mil*) (= *sobrepasar*) to outflank

flaquear ▹ CONJUG 1a VI **1** (= *debilitarse*) (*gen*) to weaken, grow weak; [*esfuerzo*] to slacken, flag; [*salud*] to decline (*frm*), get worse; [*viga*] to give way • **me flaquean las piernas** my legs are like jelly
2 (= *desanimarse*) to lose heart, become dispirited

flaquencia SF (*LAm*) = **flacura**

flaqueza SF **1** (= *delgadez*) thinness, leanness; (= *debilidad*) feebleness, frailty • **la ~ de su memoria** his poor memory • **la ~ humana** human frailty
2 • **una ~** (= *defecto*) a failing; (= *punto flaco*) a weakness • **las ~s de la carne** the weaknesses of the flesh

flaquísimo ADJ *superl de* **flaco**

flash [flas] SM (PL: **flashes** ['flases]) **1** (*Fot*) flash, flashlight
2 (*TV etc*) newsflash ▸ **flash informativo** newsflash
3‡ (= *sorpresa*) shock • **¡qué ~!** what a shock!

flashback ['flasbak] SM (PL: **flashbacks**) flashback

flato SM **1** (*Med*) • **tener ~** to have a stitch
2 (*LAm*) (= *depresión*) gloom, depression; (*CAm*) (= *temor*) fear, apprehension

flatoso ADJ **1** (*Med*) flatulent
2 (*CAm, Col, Méx*) (= *deprimido*) depressed; (*CAm*) (= *inquieto*) apprehensive

flatulencia SF flatulence

flatulento ADJ flatulent

flatuoso ADJ flatulent

flauta SF **1** (= *instrumento*) (*tb* **flauta travesera**) flute; (*tb* **flauta dulce**) recorder • **~ de Pan** panpipes • MODISMOS: • **estar hecho una ~** to be as thin as a rake • **sonó la ~ (por casualidad)** it was a fluke, it was sheer luck
2 (= *barra de pan*) French stick, baguette
3 (*LAm*) • MODISMOS: • **¡~ la ~!** gosh!* • **¡la gran ~!** my God! • **de la gran ~*** terrific*, tremendous* • **¡hijo de la gran ~!**** bastard**, son of a bitch (*EEUU***) • **¡por la ~!** oh dear!
SMF flautist, flute player, flutist (*EEUU*)

flautín SM (= *instrumento*) piccolo
SMF (= *persona*) piccolo player

flautista SMF flautist, flute player, flutist (*EEUU*) • **el ~ de Hamelin** the Pied Piper of Hamelin

flavina SF flavin

flebitis SF INV phlebitis

flecha SF **1** (= *arma*) arrow; (*en juego*) dart; (*Arquit*) spire; [*de billar*] cue rest • **como una ~** like an arrow, like a shot • **con alas en ~** swept-wing, with swept-back wings • **subida en ~** sharp rise • **subir en ~** to rise sharply ▸ **flecha de dirección** (*Aut*) indicator ▸ **flecha de mar** squid
2 (*And*) sling; (*Méx*) (*Aut*) axle
3 (*Cono Sur**) (= *coqueta*) flirt
SMF (*Hist**) *member of the Falangist youth movement*

flechado* ADV • **el médico vino ~** the doctor came in a flash* • **salir ~** to shoot off*

flechar ▹ CONJUG 1a VT **1** [+ *arco*] to draw
2 (= *herir*) to wound with an arrow; (= *matar*) to kill with an arrow; (= *disparar*) to shoot (with an arrow)
3* (= *enamorar*) • **~ a algn** to sweep off sb's feet
4 (*Arg, Méx*) (= *picar*) [*persona*] to prick (*esp with a goad*); [*sol*] to burn, scorch

flechazo SM **1** (= *acción*) bowshot; (= *herida*) arrow wound
2* (= *amor*) love at first sight • **fue el** *o* **un ~** it was love at first sight
3* (= *revelación*) revelation • **aquello fue el ~** then it hit me, that was the moment of revelation

flechero SM (= *soldado*) archer, bowman; (= *artesano*) arrow maker

fleco SM **1** (*Méx*) (= *flequillo*) fringe, bangs (*pl*) (*EEUU*)
2 flecos: a (= *adorno*) fringe (*sing*) • **una cazadora de ante con ~s** a fringed suede jacket
b (= *borde deshilachado*) frayed edge (*sing*) (*of cloth*)
c (= *detalles pendientes*) loose ends

flejadora SF strapping machine

flejar ▹ CONJUG 1a VT **1** (*esp LAm*) to strap, secure with metal strips
2 (*Méx*) [+ *paquete*] to pack

fleje SM (*Téc*) (= *tira*) hoop, metal band; (= *resorte*) spring clip

flema SF **1** (*Med*) phlegm
2 (= *impasibilidad*) phlegm

flemático ADJ (= *imperturbable*) [*persona*] phlegmatic; [*tono, comportamiento*] matter-of-fact, unruffled

flemón SM gumboil

flemudo ADJ slow, sluggish

flequetería SF (*And*) cheating, swindling

flequetero ADJ (*And*) tricky, dishonest

flequillo SM fringe, bangs (*pl*) (*EEUU*)

Flesinga SM Flushing

fleta SF (*And, Caribe*) **1** (= *fricción*) rub, rubbing

2 (= *paliza*) thrashing
fletado* ADJ 1 (*CAm*) sharp, clever
2 (*Caribe, Méx*) • **salir ~*** to be off like a shot
fletador ADJ shipping (*antes de s*), freighting (*antes de s*)
SM [*de avión, barco*] charterer; [*de pasajeros, mercancías*] carrier
fletamiento SM, **fletamento** SM chartering • **contrato de ~** charter
fletán SM • **~ negro** Greenland halibut
fletar ▷ CONJUG 1a VT 1 [+ *avión, barco*] to charter; (= *cargar*) to load, freight
2 (*LAm*) [*autobús*] to hire
3 (*Cono Sur**) (= *despedir*) to get rid of, fire*; (= *expulsar*) to chuck out*
4 (*And, Cono Sur*) [+ *insultos*] to let fly*; [+ *golpe*] to deal
VPR **fletarse** 1 (*And, Caribe, Méx**) (= *largarse*) to get out, beat it*; (*con sigilo*) to slip away, get away unseen; (*Arg*) (= *colarse*) to gatecrash
2 (*CAm*) (= *enojarse*) to be annoyed, get cross
3 (*Cono Sur*) • **"se fleta"** "for hire"
flete SM 1 (= *alquiler*) **a** [*de avión, barco*] charter • **vuelo ~** charter flight
b (*LAm*) [*de autobús, camión*] hire; (= *precio*) hire charge, hiring fee
2 (= *carga*) freight; (*Náut, Aer*) cargo
• MODISMO: • **salir sin ~s** (*And*) to leave in a hurry, be off like a shot
3 (= *precio del transporte*) freightage, carriage ▸ **flete debido** freight forward ▸ **flete pagado** advance freight, prepaid freight ▸ **flete por cobrar** freight forward ▸ **flete sobre compras** inward freight
4 (*LAm*) (= *caballo*) fast horse; [*de carreras*] racehorse; (*Cono Sur*) (= *rocín*) old nag
5 (*And*) (= *amante*) lover, companion
6* (= *prostitución*) prostitution, the game*
7 • **echarse un ~**‡ to have a screw**‡
fletera* SF (*Caribe*) prostitute
fletero/a ADJ (*LAm*) 1 (= *de alquiler*) [*avión*] charter (*antes de s*); [*camión*] for hire, for rent (EEUU)
2 (= *de carga*) freight (*antes de s*)
SM/F 1 (*LAm*) (= *transportista*) haulier; (= *recaudador*) collector of transport charges
2 (*And, Guat*) (= *mozo*) porter
flexibilidad SF (*gen*) flexibility; [*del cuerpo*] suppleness; (*Téc*) pliability; [*de carácter*] flexibility, adaptability ▸ **flexibilidad laboral, flexibilidad de plantillas** freedom to "restructure", freedom to hire and fire
flexibilización SF [*de control, sanción*] relaxation; [*de horario, programa*] adjusting, adapting ▸ **flexibilización del mercado laboral, flexibilización del trabajo** *relaxation of laws relating to terms of employment*
flexibilizar ▷ CONJUG 1f VT [+ *control, sanción*] to relax; [+ *horario, programa*] to make (more) flexible, adjust, adapt; [+ *plantilla*] to downsize
flexible ADJ 1 [*material, actitud*] flexible; [*cuerpo*] supple; (*Téc*) pliable; [*sombrero*] soft • **horario ~** flexitime
2 [*persona*] flexible, open-minded; (*pey*) compliant
SM 1 soft hat
2 (*Elec*) flex, cord
flexión SF 1 • **hacer flexiones (de brazos)** to do press-ups *o* push-ups • **hacer flexiones de cintura** to touch one's toes • **flexiones de piernas** squats
2 (*Ling*) inflection ▸ **flexión nominal** noun inflection ▸ **flexión verbal** verb inflection
3 (*Med, Téc*) flexion
flexional ADJ flexional, inflected
flexionar ▷ CONJUG 1a VT (*gen*) to bend; [+ *músculo*] to flex
VPR **flexionarse** to bend

flexivo ADJ (*Ling*) inflected
flexo SM adjustable table-lamp
flexor (*Anat*) ADJ flexor
SM flexor
flipado‡ ADJ 1 (= *drogado*) stoned*
2 (= *pasmado*) gobsmacked‡ • **me quedé ~** I was gobsmacked‡
flipante‡ ADJ 1 (= *estupendo*) great*, smashing*, cool‡
2 (= *pasmoso*) amazing
flipar‡ ▷ CONJUG 1a VT 1 (= *gustar*) • **esto me flipa** I really love this
2 (= *pasmar*) • **me flipó lo que pasó** I was gobsmacked at what happened‡
VI 1 (= *pasmarse*) • **yo flipaba al ver tanta cosa** I was gobsmacked at all the things I saw‡ • **¡este tío flipa!** this guy must be kidding!*
2 (= *pasarlo bien*) to have a great time • **~ con algo** (= *disfrutar*) to really love sth • **yo flipo con esa canción** I really love that song
3 (= *drogarse*) to get stoned*
VPR **fliparse** 1 • **~se por algo** to be mad keen on sth
2 (= *drogarse*) to get stoned*
flipe‡ SM 1 (= *experiencia*) amazing experience, startling revelation
2 (*por drogas*) (= *viaje*) trip‡; (= *subida*) high*
flipper* ['fliper] SM pinball machine • **jugar al ~** to play pinball
flirt [flir, fler] SM (PL: **flirts**) 1 (= *amorío*) fling*
2 (= *persona*) boyfriend/girlfriend • **la estrella vino con su ~ del momento** the star came with her latest boyfriend
flirteador(a) SM/F flirt
flirtear ▷ CONJUG 1a VI to flirt (**con** with)
flirteo SM 1 (= *coqueteo*) flirting
2 • **un ~** a flirtation
FLN SM ABR (*Pol*) = **Frente de Liberación Nacional**
flojamente ADV weakly, feebly
flojear ▷ CONJUG 1a VI 1 (= *debilitarse*) • **me flojean las piernas** my legs are tired
2 (= *flaquear*) • **flojeó en el último examen** she did less well in the last exam • **el ritmo flojea hacia el final** the pace slackens towards the end
flojedad SF = **flojera**
flojel SM [*de tela*] nap; [*de ave*] down
flojera SF 1 (= *debilidad*) weakness, feebleness
2 (*esp LAm**) (= *pereza*) • **me da ~** I can't be bothered
flojo ADJ 1 [*nudo, tuerca*] loose; [*cable, cuerda*] slack • MODISMO: • **me la trae floja****‡ I don't give a fuck *o* bugger**‡; ▷ **cuerda**
2 (= *débil*) [*persona*] weak; [*viento*] light • **está muy ~ después de su enfermedad** he's very weak after his illness • **todavía tengo las piernas muy flojas** my legs are still very weak
3 (= *mediocre*) [*trabajo, actuación*] poor, feeble; [*estudiante, equipo*] weak, poor • **ha escrito una redacción muy floja** he's written a very poor *o* feeble essay • **el guión era muy ~** the script was very weak • **está ~ en matemáticas** he's weak in maths
4 [*té, vino*] weak
5 [*demanda, mercado*] slack
6 (= *holgazán*) lazy, idle
7 (*LAm*) (= *cobarde*) cowardly
floppy ['flopi] SM (PL: **floppys**) floppy disk
flor SF 1 (*Bot*) flower • **un ramo de ~es** a bunch of flowers • **un vestido de ~es** a floral dress • **~es artificiales** artificial flowers • **~ cortada** (*Com*) cut flowers (*pl*) • **~es secas** dried flowers • MODISMOS: • **a ~ de labios** (*LAm*): • **siempre anda con una sonrisa a ~ de labios** he always has a slight grin on his face • **de ~** (*Cono Sur*) very good, splendid • **ir de ~ en ~** (*gen*) to flit from flower to flower; (*en cuestiones amorosas*) to flit from one lover to the next • **¡ni ~es!***: • **—¿has oído alguna noticia? —¡ni ~es!** "have you heard any news?" — "not a thing" • **de libros sé mucho, pero de cocina ni ~es** I know a lot about books, but I don't know the first thing about cooking* • **de lo prometido, ni ~es** as for what they promised, not a word was mentioned* • **ser ~ de un día**: • **su amor fue ~ de un día** their love was short-lived • **su triunfo no fue ~ de un día** his win was no mere flash in the pan • **ser ~ de estufa** to be very delicate ▸ **flor de lis** fleur-de-lis, fleur-de-lys ▸ **flor de mano**† artificial flower ▸ **flor de nieve** snowdrop ▸ **flor de Pascua** poinsettia ▸ **flor somnífera** opium poppy
2 • **en ~** [*planta, campo*] in flower, in bloom; [*árbol*] in blossom, in flower; [*muchacha*] (*liter*) in the first flower of womanhood (*liter*) • **los naranjos en ~** the orange trees in blossom *o* flower
3 • **la ~** (= *lo mejor*): • **la ~ de la harina** the finest flour • **la ~ del ejército** the elite of the army • **está en la ~ de su carrera deportiva** he is at the peak of his sporting career • **en la ~ de la edad** in the flower of one's youth • **la ~ y nata de la sociedad** the cream of society • **en la ~ de la vida** in the prime of life • MODISMO: • **ser la ~ de la canela** to be the pick of the bunch*
4 • **a ~ de agua**: • **los peces se veían a ~ de agua** you could see the fish just under the surface of the water • **a ~ de cuño** in mint condition • **a ~ de piel**: • **tenía los nervios a ~ de piel** her nerves were all on edge • **tiene la sensibilidad a ~ de piel** she is highly sensitive • **el odio le salía a ~ de piel** his hatred came out into the open, his hatred came to the surface • **a ~ de tierra** at ground level
5 (= *piropo*) compliment, flattering remark • **decir** *o* **echar ~es a algn** to pay compliments to sb, flatter sb
6 [*de ciruela, uva*] bloom
7 [*de cuero*] grain
8 (*Cono Sur**) • **~ de**: • **~ de caballo** a wonderful horse • **~ de alegre** really happy, very cheerful • **¡~ de discurso se mandó!** what a brilliant talk he gave! • **~ de reloj me regalaste, ya no funciona** (*iró*) what a great watch you bought me, it doesn't work anymore (*iró*) • **~ de marido, le pega y no le da plata** (*iró*) her husband is a real gem, he beats her up and gives her no money (*iró*)
9 • **ajustado a ~** flush
ADJ (*Cono Sur*) great • **aquí estoy ~** I feel great here • **la fiesta estuvo ~** the party was excellent *o* great
ADV (*Cono Sur**) • **hoy me siento ~** I feel great today • **lo pasamos ~** we had a whale of a time*
flora SF flora
floración SF flowering • **en plena ~** in full bloom
floral ADJ floral
florar ▷ CONJUG 1a VI to flower, bloom
florcita SF (*LAm*) little flower
floreado ADJ 1 [*tela*] flowered, floral
2 [*pan*] made with the finest flour, top-quality
3 (*Mús*) elaborate
florear ▷ CONJUG 1a VT 1 [+ *tela*] to decorate *o* pattern with flowers
2 [+ *harina*] to sift
3 [+ *naipes*] to stack
4 (= *adular*) to flatter
VI 1 (*LAm*) (= *florecer*) to flower, bloom

2 (*Mús*) to play a flourish; (*Esgrima*) to flourish
3 (= *piropear*) to flatter
VPR **florearse** (*LAm*) (= *lucirse*) to perform brilliantly; (= *presumir*) to show off
florecer ▸ CONJUG 2d VI 1 (*Bot*) to flower, bloom
2 (= *prosperar*) to flourish, thrive
VPR **florecerse** (= *enmohecer*) to go mouldy, go moldy (*EEUU*)
floreciente ADJ 1 (*Bot*) in flower, flowering, blooming
2 (= *próspero*) flourishing, thriving
florecimiento SM 1 (*Bot*) flowering, blooming
2 (= *prosperidad*) blossoming, flowering
Florencia SF Florence
florentino/a ADJ Florentine
SM/F Florentine
floreo SM 1 (*Esgrima, Mús*) flourish
2 (= *gracia*) witty but insubstantial talk; (= *cumplido*) compliment, nicely-turned phrase • **andarse con ~s** to beat about the bush
florería SF florist's (shop)
florero/a SM/F 1 (= *florista*) (*en tienda, puesto*) florist; (*en la calle*) (street) flower-seller
2 (= *halagador*) flatterer
SM 1 (= *recipiente*) vase • **MODISMO**: • **estar de ~** to be just for show *o* decoration
2 (*Arte*) (= *cuadro*) flower painting
florescencia SF florescence
floresta SF 1 (= *bosque*) wood, grove; (= *claro*) glade; (*LAm*) (= *selva*) forest, jungle
2 (= *lugar atractivo*) beauty spot; (= *escena rural*) charming rural scene
florete SM (*Esgrima*) foil
floretear ▸ CONJUG 1a VT to decorate with flowers
floretista SMF (*LAm*) fencer
florícola ADJ • **el sector ~** the flower-growing sector
floricultor(a) SM/F flower-grower
floricultura SF flower growing
florido ADJ 1 [*campo, jardín*] full of flowers; [*árbol, planta*] in blossom, in flower
2 (= *selecto*) choice, select • **lo más ~ del arte contemporáneo** the pick of contemporary art • **lo más ~ de la sociedad** the cream of society
3 [*estilo*] flowery, florid
florilegio SM anthology
florín SM 1 (*holandés*) guilder
2 (*Hist*) florin
florión/ona SM/F (*And*) = **fanfarrón**
floripón SM (*LAm*) = **floripondio**
floripondio SM 1 (*pey*) big flower
2 (*Literat*) rhetorical flourish, extravagant figure
3 (*LAm**) (= *hombre*) pansy*, poof**, fag (*EEUU*‡)
4 (*And*) (*Bot*) lily of the valley
florista SMF florist
floristería SF florist's (shop)
floristero/a ADJ florist (*antes de s*)
SM/F florist
florístico ADJ floral
floritura SF flourish
florón SM 1 (*Bot*) big flower
2 (*Arquit*) fleuron, rosette
3 (*Tip*) tailpiece
flota SF 1 [*de buques*] fleet • **la ~ española** the Spanish fleet ▸ **flota de altura** deep-sea fishing fleet ▸ **flota de bajura** inshore fishing fleet ▸ **flota mercante** merchant navy ▸ **flota pesquera** fishing fleet
2 (*Aer, Aut*) fleet
3 (*And*) (= *autobús*) long-distance bus, inter-city bus
4 (*LAm*) (= *muchedumbre*) lot, crowd, heap • **una ~ de** a lot of, a crowd of
5 (*And*) (= *jactancia*) boasting, bluster • **echar ~s** (*And, CAm, Caribe*) to brag
flotación SF 1 (*Náut*) flotation ▸ **línea de flotación** waterline
2 (*Econ*) flotation
flotador SM 1 [*de bañista*] (*para la cintura*) rubber ring, life preserver (*EEUU*); (*para los brazos*) (inflatable) armband; (*para las manos*) float
2 [*de hidroavión, para mediciones*] float; [*de cisterna*] ballcock, floater (*EEUU*)
flotante ADJ floating • **de coma ~** (*Inform*) floating-point
SM (*Col*) braggart
flotar ▸ CONJUG 1a VI 1 (*en líquido*) to float
2 [*bandera*] to flutter • **~ al viento** [*cabello*] to stream in the wind
3 (*Econ*) to float
flote SM • **a ~** afloat • **mantenerse a ~** [*barco, negocio*] to stay afloat • **poner** *o* **sacar a ~** [+ *barco*] to refloat; [+ *negocio, economía*] to get back on its feet • **salir a ~** [*negocio, economía, persona*] to get back on one's feet; [*secreto*] to come to light
flotilla SF 1 (*Náut*) flotilla, fleet; (*a remolque*) line of vessels being towed, string of barges
2 [*de aviones, taxis etc*] fleet
flou [flo] SM soft focus (effect)
flox [flos] SM phlox
FLS SM ABR (*Nic*) (*Pol*) = **Frente de Liberación Sandinista**
fluctuación SF 1 (= *cambio*) fluctuation • **las fluctuaciones de la moda** the ups and downs of fashion
2 (= *indecisión*) uncertainty, hesitation
fluctuante ADJ (*gen*) fluctuating; [*población*] floating
fluctuar ▸ CONJUG 1e VI 1 (= *cambiar*) to fluctuate
2 (= *vacilar*) to waver, hesitate
fluente ADJ fluid, flowing
fluidamente ADV • **habla ~ (el) alemán** he speaks German fluently, he speaks fluent German
fluidez SF 1 (*Téc*) fluidity
2 (*fig*) fluency
fluido ADJ (*Téc*) fluid; [*lenguaje*] fluent; [*estilo*] fluid, free-flowing • **la circulación es bastante fluida** traffic is moving quite freely
SM 1 (*Téc*) fluid ▸ **fluidos corporales** body fluids
2 (*Elec*) current, juice* • **cortar el ~** to cut off the electricity
fluir ▸ CONJUG 3g VI (= *deslizarse*) to flow, run; (= *surgir*) to spring
flujo SM 1 (= *corriente*) flow, stream • **~ de lava** lava flow ▸ **flujo axial** axial flow ▸ **flujo de conciencia** stream of consciousness
2 (*Med*) ▸ **flujo de vientre** diarrhoea, diarrhea (*EEUU*) ▸ **flujo menstrual** menstrual flow ▸ **flujo sanguíneo** flow of blood, blood flow ▸ **flujo vaginal** vaginal discharge
3 (= *marea*) incoming tide, rising tide ▸ **flujo y reflujo** (*lit, fig*) ebb and flow
4 (*Fís*) ▸ **flujo eléctrico** electric flux ▸ **flujo magnético** magnetic flux
5 (*Com*) ▸ **flujo de caja, flujo de fondos** cashflow ▸ **flujo negativo de efectivo** negative cash flow ▸ **flujo positivo de efectivo** positive cash flow
flujograma SM flow chart
fluminense ADJ of/from Rio de Janeiro
SMF native/inhabitant of Rio de Janeiro • **los ~s** the people of Rio de Janeiro
flúor SM, **fluor** SM 1 (= *gas*) fluorine
2 (*en agua, pasta de dientes*) fluoride
fluoración SF fluoridation
fluorescencia SF fluorescence
fluorescente ADJ fluorescent
SM (*tb* **tubo fluorescente**) fluorescent tube
fluorización SF fluoridation
fluorizar ▸ CONJUG 1f VT to fluoridate
fluoruro SM fluoride
flus SM (*Col, Ven*) suit of clothes
flute SF champagne glass
fluvial ADJ fluvial, river (*antes de s*)
flux [flus] SM INV 1 (*Naipes*) flush ▸ **flux real** royal flush
2 (*CAm**) (= *suerte*) stroke of luck
3 (*Méx**) • **MODISMOS**: • **estar** *o* **quedarse a ~** to be completely broke* • **hacer ~** to blow all one's money*
4 (*And, Caribe*) (= *traje*) suit of clothes
FM SF ABR (= **Frecuencia Modulada**) FM
FMI SM ABR (= **Fondo Monetario Internacional**) IMF
FMLN SM ABR (*El Salvador*) = **Frente Farabundo Martí de Liberación Nacional**
FN SM ABR = **Frente Nacional**
SF ABR (*Esp*) (*Hist*) = **Fuerza Nueva**
FNMT SF ABR (*Esp*) (= **Fábrica Nacional de Moneda y Timbre**) ≈ Royal Mint, ≈ (*US*) Mint (*EEUU*)
f.º ABR (= **folio**) fo., fol
fobia SF phobia • **yo a esos aparatos les tengo ~** I hate *o* can't stand these machines ▸ **fobia a las alturas** fear of heights ▸ **fobia escolar** fear of going to school
...fobia SUF ...phobia • **agorafobia** agoraphobia
fóbico ADJ phobic
...fobo SUF ...phobe • **francófobo** francophobe
foca SF 1 (*Zool*) seal; (= *piel*) sealskin ▸ **foca capuchina** hooded seal ▸ **foca de fraile** monk seal ▸ **foca de trompa** elephant seal, sea elephant
2* (= *persona gorda*) fat lump*
3 (= *dormilón*) lie-abed
focal ADJ focal
focalizar ▸ CONJUG 1f VT [+ *objeto*] to focus on, get into focus; [+ *atención*] to focus
focha SF coot
foche* ADJ smelly, pongy‡
foco SM 1 (*Mat, Med, Fís*) focus • **estar fuera de ~** (*LAm*) to be out of focus
2 (= *centro*) focal point, centre, center (*EEUU*); (= *fuente*) source; [*de incendio*] seat • **un ~ de infección** a source of infection
3 (*Elec*) (*en monumento, estadio*) floodlight; (*en teatro*) spotlight; (*LAm*) (= *bombilla*) light bulb; (*Aut*) headlamp
fodolí ADJ meddlesome
fodongo* ADJ (*Méx*) (= *vago*) lazy, slovenly; (= *sucio*) filthy
foete SM = **fuete**
fofadal SM (*Agr*) bog, quagmire
fofera* SF, **fofez*** SF flabbiness, podginess
fofo ADJ 1 (= *esponjoso*) soft, spongy
2* [*persona*] (= *fláccido*) flabby, podgy, pudgy (*EEUU*)
fofoscientos* ADJ umpteen • **~ mil euros** umpteen thousand euros
fogaje SM 1 (*Méx, Ven*) (= *fiebre*) fever, high temperature; (= *sarpullido*) heat rash; (= *rubor*) flush, blush; (*fig*) fluster
2 (*Col, Ven*) (= *bochorno*) sultry weather
3 (*And*) (= *fuego*) fire, blaze
fogarada SF, **fogarata** SF (*Cono Sur*) = **fogata**
fogata SF (= *hoguera*) bonfire; (= *llamas*) blaze
fogón SM 1 (*Culin*) range, stove; (*Ferro*) firebox; (*Náut*) galley
2 [*de cañón, máquina*] vent

3 (*LAm*) (= *hoguera*) bonfire; (= *hogar*) hearth
fogonazo SM **1** (= *estallido*) flash, explosion
2 (*Méx*) (= *carajillo*) coffee with brandy
fogonero SM **1** (*Náut*) stoker
2 (*Ferro*) fireman, stoker
3 (*And*) (*chófer*) chauffeur
fogosidad SF (= *temple*) spirit, mettle; (= *ímpetu*) dash, verve; [*de caballo etc*] friskiness
fogoso ADJ (= *enérgico*) spirited, mettlesome; (= *apasionado*) fiery, ardent; [*caballo etc*] frisky
fogueado ADJ **1** (*LAm*) [*persona*] expert, experienced; (*Méx*) [*animal*] trained
2 (*And*) (= *cansado*) weary
foguear ▸ CONJUG 1a (*LAm*) VT to fire on
VPR **foguearse** (*Mil*) to have one's baptism of fire; (= *acostumbrarse*) to gain experience, become hardened
fogueo SM • **bala** *o* **cartucho de ~** blank cartridge • **disparo** *o* **tiro de ~** warning shot • **pistola de ~** starting pistol
foguerear ▸ CONJUG 1a VT (*Caribe, Cono Sur*) [+ *maleza*] to burn off; [+ *fogata*] to set light to
foguista SM (*Cono Sur*) = **fogonero**
foie-gras [fwa'gras] SM INV foie gras
foil SM (*Méx*) (*Culin*) foil
foja[1] SF (*Orn*) coot
foja[2] SF (*LAm*) = **hoja**
fol. ABR (= **folio**) fo., fol
folclore SM, **folclor** SM = **folklore**
folclórico/a ADJ, SM/F = **folklórico**
folclorista ADJ, SMF = **folklorista**
folclorizar ▸ CONJUG 1f VT = **folklorizar**
folder SM, **fólder** SM (*LAm*) folder
folgo SM foot muff
foliación SF **1** (*Bot*) foliation
2 (*Tip*) [*de páginas*] numbering
foliar ▸ CONJUG 1b VT to foliate, number the pages of • **páginas sin ~** unnumbered pages
folículo SM follicle ▸ **folículo piloso** hair follicle
folio SM **1** (*Tip*) (*gen*) folio; (= *encabezamiento*) running title, page heading • **al primer ~** (*fig*) from the very start, at a glance • **en ~** in folio • **libro en ~** folio (book)
2 (= *hoja*) sheet (of paper); [*de libro, documento*] page • **un documento de diez ~s** a ten-page document
3 (*tb* **tamaño folio**) A4 size • **doble ~** A3 size • **un ~** an A4 sheet • **~s** A4 paper
4 (*And*) (= *dádiva*) tip; [*de bautismo*] money given as christening present
folk ADJ INV, SM folk
folklore SM **1** folklore
2* row, shindy* • **se armó un ~** there was a row
folklórico/a ADJ **1** folk (*antes de s*) • **es muy ~** it's very picturesque, it's full of local colour *o* (EEUU) color
2 (*pey*) frivolous, unserious
SM/F **1** (*Mús*) folk singer
2 (*pey*) clown, figure of fun
folklorista ADJ **1** folklore (*antes de s*)
2 (*pey*) frivolous, unserious
SMF folklorist, specialist in folklore, student of folklore
folklorizar ▸ CONJUG 1f VT to give a popular *o* folksy character to
VPR **folklorizarse** to acquire popular *o* folksy features
follá‡ SF • **tener mala ~** to be thoroughly nasty
follada** SF shag**, screw**
follado ADJ • **ir ~**** to go like fuck**
SM (*And*) petticoat
follador(a)** ADJ shag-happy**
follaje[1] SM **1** (*Bot*) foliage, leaves (*pl*); (*Arte*) leaf motif
2 (= *palabrería*) waffle*, verbiage; (= *adorno*) excessive ornamentation
follaje[2]** SM shagging**, screwing**
follamigo/a‡ SM/F sex buddy*, friend with benefits*
follar ▸ CONJUG 1l VT **1**** to shag**, screw**
2‡ (= *molestar*) to bother, annoy
3 (*Téc*) to blow on with the bellows
VI ** to shag**, screw**
VPR **follarse 1**** to shag**, screw** • **se la folló** he shagged *o* screwed her** • **me lo voy a ~ vivo** I'll have his guts for garters*
2* (= *ventosear*) to do a silent fart‡
folletería SF leaflets (*pl*)
folletín SM **1** (*en periódico*) newspaper serial; (*TV*) soap opera, TV serial; (*Radio*) radio serial
2 (*fig*) drama, saga

> **FOLLETÍN**
> Folletines were originally popular serialized stories that appeared in newspapers and magazines in the 19th and early 20th centuries, often before being published as novels. They usually covered familiar themes such as unrequited love, adultery and family relationships. Nowadays, the word **folletín** can refer to radio or TV serials and soaps, **radionovelas** or **telenovelas**, and people even use **folletín** figuratively to talk about any long-running story or intrigue.

folletinesco ADJ melodramatic
folletinista SMF pulp writer
folletista SMF pamphleteer
folleto SM (*Com*) brochure; (*Pol*) pamphlet; (= *volatín*) leaflet ▸ **folleto informativo** information leaflet
follín* SM (*Cono Sur*) bad-tempered person
follisca SF (*And*) (= *lío*) row; (= *riña*) brawl
follón SM **1*** (= *desorden*) mess • **¡qué ~ de papeles!** what a mess of papers!
2* (= *alboroto*) rumpus, row; (= *lío*) trouble • **armar un ~** to make a row, kick up a fuss • **hubo** *o* **se armó un ~ tremendo** there was a hell of a row
3 (*Bot*) sucker
4 (*And*) (= *prenda*) petticoat
5 (*Caribe*) (= *juerga de borrachera*) drinking bout
6 (= *cohete*) noiseless rocket
7 (*Méx**) silent fart‡
ADJ † **1** (= *perezoso*) lazy, idle
2 (= *arrogante*) arrogant, puffed-up; (= *fanfarrón*) blustering
3 (= *cobarde*) cowardly
4 (*CAm*) [*vestido*] roomy, loose
follonarse* ▸ CONJUG 1a VPR (*Méx*) to do a silent fart‡
follonero/a* ADJ [*persona*] rowdy; [*conducta*] outrageous
SM/F rowdy, troublemaker
fome* ADJ INV (*Chile*) boring, dull
fomentación SF (*Med*) fomentation, poultice
fomentar ▸ CONJUG 1a VT **1** [+ *desarrollo, investigación, ahorro, inversión, participación*] to encourage; [+ *turismo, industria*] to promote, boost; [+ *competitividad, producción*] to boost; [+ *odio, violencia*] to foment • **medidas destinadas a ~ la integración racial** measures aimed at promoting *o* encouraging racial integration
2 (*Med*) to foment, warm
3 (= *incubar*) • **la gallina fomenta sus huevos** the hen sits on *o* incubates her eggs
fomento SM **1** (= *ayuda*) promotion, encouragement; [*de ventas*] promotion
▸ **Ministerio de Fomento** *ministry responsible for public works, buildings etc*
2 (*Med*) poultice
fonador ADJ [*sistema, aparato, órgano*] speech (*antes de s*)
fonda SF (= *restaurante*) small restaurant; (= *pensión*) boarding house; (*Hist*) inn, tavern; (*Ferro*) buffet; (*Cono Sur*) refreshment stall; (*LAm*) (*pey*) cheap restaurant
fondeadero SM (*gen*) anchorage; (*en puerto*) berth
fondeado ADJ **1** (*Náut*) • **estar ~** to be anchored, be at anchor
2 (*LAm**) • **estar ~** to be in the money, be well heeled* • **quedar ~** to be in the money*
fondear ▸ CONJUG 1a VT **1** [*barco*] (= *anclar*) to anchor; (= *registrar*) to search
2 [+ *profundidad*] to sound
3 (= *examinar*) to examine
4 (*CAm*) (= *financiar*) to provide with money
5 (*Chile*) (= *ocultar*) to hide; (= *ahogar*) to drown
6 (*Caribe*) (= *violar*) to rape
VI [*barco*] to anchor, drop anchor
VPR **fondearse 1** (*LAm**) (= *enriquecerse*) to get rich; (= *ahorrar*) to save for the future
2 (*LAm**) (= *emborracharse*) to get drunk
3 (*Chile**) (= *ocultarse*) • **fondéate, que vienen los pacos** take cover, the police are coming • **anda fondeado de la policía** he's on the run from the police
fondeo SM **1** (*Náut*) anchoring
2 (*Chile*) dumping at sea, drowning at sea
fondero/a SM/F (*LAm*) innkeeper
fondillo SM (*LAm*), **fondillos** SMPL **1** [*de pantalones*] seat
2 (*LAm*) (*Anat*) seat, bottom
fondilludo/a* ADJ (*LAm*) big-bottomed
SM/F • **es un ~** he's got a big backside
fondista SMF **1** [*de restaurante*] restaurant owner; (*Hist*) innkeeper
2 (*Dep*) long-distance runner
fondo SM **1** (*parte inferior*) [*de caja, botella, lago, mar*] bottom; [*de río*] bed • **descendieron al ~ del cráter** they got down to the bottom of the crater • **los bajos ~s** the underworld • **una maletín con doble ~** a case with a false bottom, a false-bottomed case • **en todo lo que dice hay un doble ~** there's a double meaning in everything he says • **irse al ~** to sink to the bottom • **en el ~ del mar** (*gen*) at the bottom of the sea; (= *en el lecho marino*) on the sea bed • **sin ~** bottomless • MODISMO: • **tocar ~** to reach *o* hit rock bottom • **la economía tocó ~ y el gobierno tuvo que devaluar la moneda** the economy reached *o* hit rock bottom and the government had to devalue the currency • **hemos tocado ~ y todo indica que la recuperación está muy próxima** the market has bottomed out and all the indications are that a recovery is just around the corner
2 (*parte posterior*) [*de pasillo, calle, nave*] end; [*de habitación, armario*] back • **llegaron hasta el ~ de la gruta** they got to the back of the cave • **al ~**: • **su oficina está al ~ a la izquierda** her office is at the end on the left • **al ~ del pasillo** at the end of the corridor • **la barra está al ~ de la cafetería** the bar is at the (far) end of the cafe • **había unas cortinas al ~ del escenario** at the back of the stage there were some curtains
3 (= *profundidad*) [*de cajón, edificio, bañera*] depth • **¿cuánto tiene de ~ el armario?** how deep is the wardrobe? • **tener mucho ~** to be deep • **tener poco ~** [*bañera*] to be shallow; [*cajón, armario*] not to be deep enough
4 (= *lo fundamental*) • **en el ~ de esta polémica late el miedo al cambio** at the heart *o* bottom of this controversy lies a fear of change • **la cuestión de ~** the basic *o* fundamental issue • **el problema de ~** the basic *o* fundamental *o* underlying problem • **la forma y el ~** form and content • **llegar al ~ de la cuestión** to get to the bottom of the

f

matter; ▹ **artículo**
5 (= *segundo plano*) background • **verde sobre ~ rojo** green on a red background • **la historia transcurre sobre un ~ de creciente inquietud social** the story takes place against a background of growing social unrest • **música de ~** background music • **ruido de ~** background noise ▸ **fondo de escritorio, fondo de pantalla** (*Inform*) (desktop) wallpaper
6 • **a fondo a** (*como adj*) • **una investigación a ~** (*policial*) a thorough investigation; [*de estudio*] an in-depth study • **una limpieza a ~** a thorough clean • **una vez al mes hacemos una limpieza a ~** once a month we do a really thorough clean • **una limpieza a ~ de las fuerzas de seguridad** a thorough clean-up of the security forces
b (*como adv*) • **no conoce a ~ la situación del país** he does not have a thorough *o* an in-depth knowledge of the country's situation • **la policía investigará a ~ lo ocurrido** the police will conduct a thorough investigation of what happened • **he estudiado a ~ a los escritores del Siglo de Oro** I have studied Golden Age writers in great depth • **aseguró que estudiaría a ~ nuestra propuesta** he promised to look closely at our proposal • **emplearse a ~**: • **tuvo que emplearse a ~ para disuadirlos** he had to use all his skill to dissuade them • **el equipo deberá emplearse a ~ para derrotar a sus adversarios** the team will have to draw on all its resources to beat their opponents • **pisar a ~ el acelerador** to put one's foot down (*on the accelerator*)
7 • **en el fondo a** (= *en nuestro interior*) deep down • **en el ~, es buena persona** deep down he's a good person, he's a good person at heart • **en el ~ de su corazón** in his heart of hearts, deep down
b (= *en realidad*) really • **lo que se debatirá en la reunión, en el ~, es el futuro de la empresa** what is actually *o* really going to be debated in the meeting is the future of the company • **la verdad es que en el ~, no tengo ganas** to be honest, I really don't feel like it • **en el ~ no quiere irse** when it comes down to it, he doesn't want to leave
c (= *en lo fundamental*) fundamentally, essentially • **en el ~ ambos sistemas son muy parecidos** fundamentally *o* essentially, both systems are very similar
8 (*Dep*) • **carrera de ~** long-distance race • **esquí de ~** cross-country skiing • **corredor de medio ~** middle-distance runner • **pruebas de medio ~** middle-distance events ▸ **fondo en carretera** long-distance road-racing
9 (= *dinero*) (*Com, Econ*) fund; (*en póker, entre amigos*) pot, kitty • **tenemos un ~ para imprevistos** we have a contingency fund • **contamos con un ~ de 150.000 euros para becas** we have at our disposal a budget of 150,000 euros for grants • **hemos puesto un ~ para la comida** we have a kitty for the food • **a ~ perdido** [*crédito, inversión*] non-recoverable, non-refundable • **subvención a ~ perdido** capital grant • **su padre le ha prestado bastante dinero a ~ perdido** his father has given him quite a lot of money on permanent loan ▸ **fondo común** common fund ▸ **fondo consolidado** consolidated fund ▸ **fondo de amortización** sinking fund ▸ **Fondo de Ayuda al Desarrollo** Development Aid Fund ▸ **Fondo de Cohesión** Cohesion Fund ▸ **fondo de comercio** goodwill ▸ **Fondo de Compensación Interterritorial** *system of financial redistribution between the autonomous regions of Spain* ▸ **fondo de empréstitos** loan fund ▸ **fondo de inversión** investment fund ▸ **fondo de pensiones** pension fund ▸ **fondo de previsión** provident fund ▸ **fondo ético** (*Econ*) ethical investment fund ▸ **Fondo Monetario Internacional** International Monetary ▸ **fondo mutualista** mutual fund
10 fondos (= *dinero*) funds • **recaudar ~s** to raise funds • **estar sin ~s** to be out of funds, be broke* • **cheque *o* talón sin ~s** bounced cheque, rubber check (*EEUU*) • **el cheque no tenía ~s** the cheque bounced ▸ **fondos bloqueados** frozen assets ▸ **fondos públicos** public funds ▸ **fondos reservados** secret funds
11 (= *reserva*) [*de biblioteca, archivo, museo*] collection • **el ~ de arte del museo** the museum's art collection • **hay un ~ de verdad en lo que dice** there is a basis of truth in what he is saying • **tiene un buen ~ de energías** he has boundless energy ▸ **fondo de armario** basic wardrobe ▸ **fondo editorial** list of titles
12 (= *carácter*) nature, disposition • **de ~ jovial** of cheery *o* cheerful disposition, cheerful-natured • **tiene un ~ de alegría** he is irrepressibly cheerful • **tener buen ~** to be good-natured
13 (*Dep*) (= *resistencia*) stamina • **tener mucho ~** to have a lot of stamina • **tener poco ~** to have no staying power
14 (*Chile, Méx, Ven*) [*de comida, espectáculo*] • **como plato de ~ servirán pavo relleno** the main dish will be stuffed turkey • **de ~ actuó el orfeón de carabineros** the main attraction was the police choir
15 (*Méx*) • **con *o* de ~** serious • **una película de ~** a serious film
16 (*Méx, Ven*) (= *combinación*) petticoat • **medio ~** slip
17 (*And*) (= *finca*) country estate
18 (*Chile*) (*Culin*) large pot (*to feed a large number of people*)

fondón* (ADJ) big-bottomed*, broad in the beam*
fondongo (SM) (*Caribe*) bottom
fonducha (SF), **fonducho** (SM) cheap restaurant
fonema (SM) phoneme
fonémico (ADJ) phonemic
fonendoscopio (SM) phonendoscope
fonética (SF) phonetics (*sing*)
fonéticamente (ADV) phonetically
fonético (ADJ) phonetic
fonetista (SMF) phonetician
foniatra (SMF) speech therapist
foniatría (SF) speech therapy
fónico (ADJ) phonic
fono (SM) **1** (*Chile*) (*Telec*) (= *auricular*) earpiece; (= *número*) telephone number
2 (*Ling*) phone
fonobuzón (SM) voice mail
fonocaptor (SM) [*de tocadiscos*] pickup
fonógrafo (SM) (*esp LAm*) gramophone, phonograph (*EEUU*)
fonología (SF) phonology
fonológico (ADJ) phonological
fonoteca (SF) record library, sound archive
fontanal (SM), **fontanar** (SM) spring
fontanería (SF) **1** (= *oficio*) plumbing; (= *instalación*) plumbing
2 (= *tienda*) ironmonger's, hardware store
fontanero/a (SM/F) plumber
footing ['futin] (SM) jogging • **hacer ~** to jog, go jogging
F.O.P. (SFPL ABR) = **Fuerzas del Orden Público**
foque (SM) jib
foquillos (SMPL) fairy lights
foquismo (SM) (*LAm*) (*Pol*) *a theory of guerrilla warfare advocated by Che Guevara and Fidel Castro*
forajido/a (SM/F) outlaw, bandit, fugitive from justice
foral (ADJ) *relative to the fueros, pertaining to the privileges of a town or region* • **parlamento ~** regional parliament • **policía ~** autonomous police; ▹ **FUEROS**
foramen (SM) (*Méx*) hole
foráneo/a (ADJ) foreign
(SM/F) outsider, stranger
forasta* (SMF) = **forastero**
forastero/a (ADJ) alien, strange
(SM/F) stranger, outsider
forcejear ▹ CONJUG 1a (VI) (*gen*) to struggle, wrestle; (= *afanarse*) to strive
forcejeo (SM) struggle
forcejudo (ADV) tough, strong, powerful
fórceps (SM INV) forceps
forcito (SM) (*LAm*) little Ford (*vehicle*)
forense (ADJ) forensic; ▹ **médico**
(SMF) (*Med*) forensic scientist; (*Jur*) coroner
forestación (SF) afforestation
forestal (ADJ) (*gen*) forest (*antes de s*); [*industria*] timber (*antes de s*), lumber (*EEUU*) (*antes de s*) • **cobertura ~** tree cover; ▹ **guarda, repoblación**
forestalista (SMF) owner of a woodland
forestar ▹ CONJUG 1a (VT) (*LAm*) to afforest
forfait [for'fe] (SM) **1** (*Esquí*) ski pass
2 (= *precio*) flat rate, fixed price • **viajes a ~** package tours
3 (*Dep*) (= *ausencia*) absence, non-appearance; (= *retirada*) withdrawal, scratching • **declararse ~** to withdraw • **ganar por ~** to win by default • **hacer ~** to fail to show up
fori‡ (SM) hankie*, handkerchief
forito (SM) (*LAm*) = **fotingo**
forja (SF) **1** (= *fragua*) forge; (= *fundición*) foundry
2 (= *acción*) forging
forjado (ADJ) • **hierro ~** wrought iron
forjar ▹ CONJUG 1a (VT) **1** [+ *hierro*] to forge, shape
2 (= *crear*) (*gen*) to forge, shape; [+ *sueños, ilusiones*] to build up • **~ un plan** to hammer out a plan • **tratamos de ~ un estado moderno** we are trying to build a modern state
3 [+ *mentiras*] to invent, concoct
forma (SF) **1** (= *figura*) shape • **tiene ~ de pirámide** it is pyramid-shaped • **hojas de ~ triangular** triangular leaves • **una serie de elementos dispuestos de ~ circular** a series of elements arranged in a circle • **la camisa ha cogido la ~ de la percha** the shirt has been stretched out of shape by the hanger • **nubes de humo con ~ de hongo** mushroom-shaped clouds of smoke • **un pendiente con ~ de animal mitológico** an earring in the shape of a mythological animal • **dar ~ a** [+ *objeto, joya*] to shape; [+ *idea, teoría*] to give shape to • **quiso dar ~ literaria a sus teorías filosóficas** he wanted to put his philosophical theories into literary form • **en ~ de U** U-shaped • **pendientes en ~ de corazón** heart-shaped earrings • **tomar ~** to take shape • **la idea empezó a tomar ~ el año pasado** the idea began to take shape last year
2 (= *modo*) way • **me gusta más de esta ~** I like it better this way • **yo tengo otra ~ de ver las cosas** I see things in a different way • **solo conozco una ~ llegar hasta allí** I only know one way of getting there *o* one way to get there • **no estoy de acuerdo con su ~ de actuar** I don't agree with his way of doing things • **no hubo ~ de convencerlo** there was no way we could persuade him • **de ~ directa/inmediata/natural** directly/ immediately/naturally • **el plan entrará en**

vigor de ~ inmediata the plan will take immediate effect, the plan will take effect immediately • **este tema me preocupa de ~ especial** this subject is of particular concern to me • **de esta ~** *(gen)* in this way; (= *por consecuencia*) thus • **queremos controlar los costes y, de esta ~, evitar reducir la plantilla** we want to bring down costs and thus avoid having to downsize • **de todas ~s** anyway, in any case • **pero de todas ~s te agradezco que me lo hayas dicho** but thank you for letting me know anyway, but in any case thank you for letting me know ▸ **forma de pago** method of payment, form of payment ▸ **forma de ser** • **es mi ~ de ser** that's how I am, that's the way I am
3 • **de ~ que** (= *en un modo que*) in such a way as, so as; (= *por eso*) so that • **él intentó contestar la pregunta de ~ que no le comprometiese** he tried to answer the question so as *o* in such a way as not to commit himself • **el número de socios fue creciendo cada año, de ~ que en 1989 eran ya varios miles** the number of members grew every year, so that *o* such that by 1989 there were several thousand • **de tal ~ que** (= *en un modo que*) in such a way that; (= *tanto que*) so much that; (= *por eso*) so that • **la noticia se filtró de tal ~ que fueron incapaces de evitarlo** news leaked out in such a way that they were unable to stop it • **la empresa ha crecido de tal ~ que es irreconocible** the company has grown so much *o* to such an extent that it is unrecognizable • **su padre era italiano y su madre polaca, de tal ~ que él siempre se ha sentido europeo** his father was Italian and his mother Polish, so (that) he has always felt himself to be European
4 (*tb* **forma física**) fitness, form • **si no está al cien por cien de ~ no jugará** if he isn't a hundred per cent fit he won't play • **el jugador ha recuperado su ~ física** the player is fit again, the player has regained fitness *o* form • **cuida su ~ física practicando también otros deportes** he keeps fit by playing other sports too • **estar en (buena) ~** *(para hacer deporte)* to be fit, be in good shape; *(para realizar otra actividad)* to be in (good) form • **estar en baja ~** *(lit)* to be not fully fit; *(fig)* to be in bad shape • **estar bajo de ~** to be in poor shape • **mantenerse en ~** to keep fit • **ponerse en ~** to get fit
5 (= *aspecto externo*) form • **la ~ y el fondo** form and content • **es pura ~** it's just for the sake of form, it's a mere formality • **defecto de ~** *(Jur)* technicality
6 formas *(femeninas)* figure *(sing)*
7 formas *(sociales)* appearances • **guardar** *o* **mantener las ~s** to keep up appearances
8 *(Rel)* • **la Sagrada Forma** the Host
9 (= *molde*) *(Téc)* mould, mold (EEUU); [*de zapatero*] last; [*de sombrero*] hatter's block; *(Tip)* forme, form (EEUU)
10 *(Ling)* [*del verbo*] form
11 *(Tip)* (= *formato*) format
12 *(LAm*)* • **en ~**: • **una fiesta en ~** a proper party, a blowout* • **va a celebrar su cumpleaños en ~** he's going to have a proper *o* a serious* birthday party • **nos aburrimos en ~** we were seriously bored*
13 *(Méx)* form; ▷ MANERA, FORMA, MODO

formación (SF) **1** (= *creación*) *(gen)* formation • **para prevenir la ~ de hielo** to prevent ice (from) forming, to prevent the formation of ice *(frm)* • **se anunció la ~ de un nuevo partido** it was announced that a new party is to be formed • **la ~ de palabras** word formation • **la Europa que está en ~** the Europe that is taking shape *o* that is in formation
2 (= *aprendizaje*) *(en un campo concreto)* training; *(en conocimientos teóricos)* education • **tenía una ~ musical clásica** she trained as a classical musician, she had a classical musical training • **nuestro objetivo es la ~ de personal técnico** our aim is to train technical staff • **la ~ del profesorado** teacher training • **se nota que tiene ~ universitaria** you can tell he's had a university education *o* background ▸ **formación laboral, formación ocupacional** occupational training ▸ **formación profesional** vocational training
3 (= *grupo*) *(político)* party; *(militar)* group; *(musical)* group, band; [*de jugadores*] squad • **las dos principales formaciones de izquierda** the two main left-wing parties • **las grandes formaciones sinfónicas europeas** the great European symphony orchestras • **no ha anunciado todavía la ~ del equipo** he hasn't announced the squad yet ▸ **formación política** political party
4 *(Mil)* • **en ~** in formation • **en ~ de combate** in battle *o* combat formation
5 *(Geol, Bot)* formation

formado (ADJ) formed, shaped • **bien ~** nicely-shaped, well-formed • **hombre (ya) ~** grown man

formal (ADJ) **1** [*persona*] (= *de fiar*) reliable, dependable; (= *responsable*) responsible • **es un trabajador muy ~** he's a very reliable worker • **un chico muy ~** a very responsible boy • **sé ~ y pórtate bien** be good and behave yourself
2 [*invitación, protesta*] formal; [*estilo, lenguaje*] formal
3 (= *oficial*) [*petición, propuesta, compromiso*] official
4 *(Fil)* formal • **lógica ~** formal logic
5 (= *estructural*) formal • **el análisis ~ del texto** formal analysis of the text
6 *(And)* (= *afable*) affable, pleasant

formaldehído (SM) formaldehyde

formaleta (SF) **1** *(CAm, Col)* (= *construcción*) wooden framework
2 *(And, CAm, Méx)* (= *trampa*) bird trap

formalidad (SF) **1** (= *requisito*) formality • **son las ~es de costumbre** these are the usual formalities • **es pura ~** it's a pure *o* mere formality, it's just a matter of form
2 (= *fiabilidad*) reliability • **alabó la ~ de nuestra empresa** he praised our company for its reliability • **se quedó sin clientes por falta de ~** he lost all his customers because of his unreliability • **esta empresa no tiene ~ ninguna** this company is totally unreliable
3 (= *seriedad*) • **¡señores, un poco de ~!** gentlemen, let's be serious! • **¡niños, ~!** kids, behave yourselves!

formalina (SF) formalin(e)

formalismo (SM) **1** *(Arte, Literat)* formalism
2 *(pey)* (= *burocracia*) red tape, useless formalities *(pl)*; (= *convencionalismo*) conventionalism

formalista (ADJ) **1** *(Arte, Literat)* formalist
2 *(pey)* conventional, rigid
(SMF) **1** *(Arte, Literat)* formalist
2 *(pey)* stickler for the regulations

formalito* (ADJ) [*adulto*] respectable; [*niño*] well-behaved

formalizar ▷ CONJUG 1f (VT) *(Jur)* to formalize; [+ *plan*] to formulate, draw up; [+ *situación*] to put in order, regularize • **~ sus relaciones** to become formally engaged
(VPR) **formalizarse 1** (= *ponerse serio*) to grow serious
2 [*situación*] to be put in order, be regularized; [*relación*] to acquire a proper form, get on to a proper footing
3 (= *ofenderse*) to take offence

formalmente (ADV) (= *de forma oficial*) officially (= *referido a la forma*) in form • **~, su última película es más sencilla que las anteriores** his latest film is simpler in form than his previous ones

formalote* (ADJ) stiff, serious

formar ▷ CONJUG 1a (VT) **1** [+ *figura*] to form, make • **los barracones se disponen formando un cuadrado** the barrack huts are arranged forming *o* making a square • **los curiosos ~on un círculo a su alrededor** the onlookers formed *o* made a circle around him
2 (= *crear*) [+ *organización, partido, alianza*] to form • **las personas interesadas en ~ un club** people interested in forming a club • **~ gobierno** to form a government • **¿cómo se forma el subjuntivo?** how do you form the subjunctive? • **quieren casarse y ~ una familia** they want to get married and start a family
3 (= *constituir*) to make up • **los chiitas forman el 60% de la población** the Shiites make up *o* form 60% of the population • **la plantilla la forman 94 bomberos** there are 94 firefighters on the staff • **las dos juntas formaban un dúo de humoristas insuperable** the two of them together made an unbeatable comedy duo • **formamos un buen equipo** we make a good team • **~ equipo con algn** to join forces with sb • **estar formado por** to be made up of • **la asociación está formada por parados y amas de casa** the association is made up of unemployed and housewives • **~ parte de** to be part of • **nuestros soldados ~án parte de las tropas de paz** our soldiers will be part of the peace-keeping force • **el edificio forma parte del recinto de la catedral** the building is *o* forms part of the cathedral precinct • **sus obras no ~án parte de la colección** his works will not be part of the collection
4 (= *enseñar*) [+ *personal, monitor, técnico*] to train; [+ *alumno*] to educate
5 [+ *juicio, opinión*] to form
6 *(Mil)* to order to fall in • **el sargento formó a los reclutas** the sergeant had the recruits fall in, the sergeant ordered the recruits to fall in
(VI) **1** *(Mil)* to fall in • **¡a ~!** fall in!
2 *(Dep)* to line up • **los equipos ~on así: ...** the teams lined up as follows: ...
(VPR) **formarse 1** (= *crearse*) to form • **se ~án nubes por la tarde** there will be a build-up of clouds in the afternoon, clouds will form in the afternoon • **remover la salsa para evitar que se formen grumos** stir the sauce to prevent lumps forming • **los vientos que se forman en el Antártico** winds that form *o* develop in the Antarctic • **es inevitable que se formen distintos grupos de opinión** different groups of opinion will inevitably form • **se forman colas diarias en el cine** queues form daily outside the cinema • **en 1955 se formó el segundo gobierno liberal** in 1955 the second liberal government was formed
2 (= *armarse*) [*jaleo, follón*] • **no fue tanto el revuelo que se formó** there wasn't that much of a rumpus • **se formó tal follón que no llegaron a oír el final de su discurso** there was such an uproar that they didn't get to hear the end of his speech
3 (= *prepararse*) [*profesional, jugador, militar*] to train; [*estudiante*] to study • **se había formado como neurobiólogo** he had trained as a neurobiologist • **París fue la ciudad en la que se formó como pintor** Paris was the city

in which he learned the art of painting • **se formó en el mejor colegio de Inglaterra** he studied *o* was educated at the best school in England
4 (*Mil*) to fall in • **¡fórmense!** fall in! • **se ~on en grupos de a tres** they formed into groups of three
5 (*Dep*) to line up • **el equipo se formó sin González** the team lined up without Gonzalez
6 [+ *opinión, impresión*] to form • **¿qué impresión te has formado?** what impression have you formed? • **te formaste una idea equivocada de mí** you got the wrong idea about me

formateado (SM) formatting

formatear ▹ CONJUG 1a (VT) to format

formateo (SM) formatting

formativo (ADJ) formative

formato (SM) (*Tip, Inform*) format; (= *tamaño*) [*de papel*] size • **¿de qué ~ lo quiere?** what size do you want? • **papel (de) ~ holandesa** ≈ foolscap • **periódico de ~ reducido** tabloid newspaper ▸ **formato apaisado** landscape format, landscape ▸ **formato de registro** record format ▸ **formato fijo** fixed format ▸ **formato libre** free format ▸ **formato vertical** portrait format, portrait

formica® (SF) Formica®

fórmico (ADJ) • **ácido ~** formic acid

formidable (ADJ) **1** [*enemigo, problema*] formidable
2 (= *estupendo*) terrific, tremendous • **¡formidable!** that's great!*, splendid!

formol (SM) formaldehyde

formón (SM) chisel

Formosa (SF) • **la isla de ~** (*Hist*) Formosa

fórmula (SF) **1** (*Quím, Mat*) formula ▸ **fórmula magistral** magistral formula ▸ **fórmula molecular** molecular formula
2 (*Med*) ▸ **fórmula dentaria** dental profile ▸ **fórmula leucocitaria** leucocyte count
3 (= *método*) formula • **una ~ para conseguir el éxito** a formula to ensure success ▸ **fórmula mágica** magic formula
4 (= *expresión*) ▸ **fórmula de cortesía** polite set expression
5 (= *formalidad*) • **por pura ~** purely as a matter of form
6 (*Aut*) • **coches de Fórmula 1** Formula 1 cars

formulación (SF) formulation ▸ **formulación de datos** data capture

formulaico (ADJ) formulaic

formular ▹ CONJUG 1a (VT) [+ *política, teoría*] to formulate; [+ *plan*] to draw up; [+ *pregunta*] pose; [+ *protesta*] to make, lodge; [+ *demanda*] to file, put in; [+ *deseo*] to express

formulario (ADJ) routine, formulaic
(SM) **1** (= *impreso*) form • **rellenar un ~** to fill in *o* complete a form ▸ **formulario de inscripción** registration form ▸ **formulario de pedido** (*Com*) order form ▸ **formulario de solicitud** application form
2 (= *fórmulas*) (*Farm*) formulary, collection of formulae

formulismo (SM) formulism, red tape

fornicación (SF) fornication

fornicador(a), fornicario/a (ADJ) fornicating
(SM/F) fornicator; (= *adúltero*) adulterer/adulteress

fornicar ▹ CONJUG 1g (VI) to fornicate

fornicio (SM) fornication

fornido (ADJ) (= *corpulento*) strapping, hefty; (= *apuesto*) well-built

fornitura (SF) (*Téc*) movement; (*Cos*) accessories (*pl*); (*Mil*) cartridge belt; (*CAm, Caribe*) furniture

foro (SM) **1** (*Pol, Hist, Internet*) forum; (= *reunión*) forum, (open) meeting ▸ **foro de discusión** (*Internet*) discussion forum
2 (*Jur*) (= *tribunal*) court of justice; (= *abogados*) bar, legal profession • **el Foro** (*Esp*) Madrid
3 (*Teat*) upstage area • **desaparecer** *o* **marcharse por el ~** (*lit*) to exit stage left; (*fig*) to do a disappearing act; ▹ **mutis**

forofada* (SF) fans (*pl*), supporters (*pl*)

forofismo (SM) (volume of) support

forofo/a* (SM/F) fan, supporter

FORPPA (SM ABR) (*Esp*) = **Fondo de Ordenación y Regulación de Precios y Productos Agrarios**

FORPRONU (SF ABR) (= **Fuerza(s) de Protección de las Naciones Unidas**) UNPROFOR, Unprofor

forrado (ADJ) **1** (= *con forro*) lined • **~ de nilón** lined with nylon • **un libro ~ de pergamino** a book bound in parchment • **un coche ~ de ...** a car upholstered in ...
2* (= *rico*) • **estar ~** to be loaded*, be rolling in it*

forraje (SM) **1** (*Agr*) (= *alimento*) fodder, forage
2 (*Agr*) (= *acción*) foraging
3* (= *mezcla*) hotchpotch, hodgepodge (*EEUU*), mixture

forrajear ▹ CONJUG 1a (VI) to forage

forrapelotas‡ (SMF INV) **1** (= *caradura*) rotter*, berk‡
2 (= *tonto*) idiot

forrar ▹ CONJUG 1a (VT) **1** (= *poner forro a*) to line (**de** with); (= *acolchar*) to pad; [+ *coche*] to upholster
2 [+ *libro*] (*como protección*) to cover (**de** with); (= *encuadernar*) to bind (**de** in)
3 (*Téc*) (*gen*) to line; [+ *tubería, caldera*] to lag
(VPR) **forrarse 1*** (= *enriquecerse*) to line one's pockets, make a fortune, make a packet*
2* (*de comida*) to stuff o.s. (**de** with); (*Méx, Guat*) to eat a heavy meal
3 (*CAm, Méx*) (= *proveerse*) to stock up (**de** with)

forro (SM) **1** (*gen*) lining; [*de libro*] cover; (*Aut*) upholstery • **con ~ de piel** fur-lined • MODISMOS: • **ni por el ~*** not in the least, not a bit • **no nos parecemos ni por el ~** we are not in the least alike, we are not a bit alike • **limpiar el ~ a algn** (*LAm‡*) to bump sb off‡ • **pasarse algo por el ~ de las narices‡** not to give a damn about sth*, not to give a toss about sth‡ ▸ **forro acolchado** padded lining ▸ **forro polar** fleece, Polartec®
2 (*Téc*) (*gen*) lining; [*de tubería*] lagging ▸ **forro de freno** (*Aut*) brake lining
3 (*Cono Sur**) (= *preservativo*) rubber*, condom
4 (*Chile*) [*de bicicleta*] tyre, tire (*EEUU*)
5 (*LAm*) (= *fraude*) swindle, fraud
6 (*Cono Sur*) (= *talento*) aptitude

forsitia (SF) forsythia

fortacho (SM) (*Cono Sur*) strongly-built car, good car; (*pey*) old car, old crock

fortachón* (ADJ) strong, tough

fortalecer ▹ CONJUG 2d (VT) **1** (= *reforzar*) [+ *músculos, uña*] to strengthen
2 [+ *divisa, sistema, posición*] to strengthen
(VPR) **fortalecerse** [*divisa, poder, opinión*] to become stronger

fortalecimiento (SM) strengthening

fortaleza (SF) **1** (*Mil*) fortress, stronghold
2 (= *fuerza*) strength, toughness; (*moral*) fortitude, strength (of spirit)
3 (*Cono Sur, Méx‡*) (= *olor*) stench, pong‡

fortificación (SF) fortification

fortificar ▹ CONJUG 1g (VT) **1** (*Mil*) to fortify
2 (= *fortalecer*) to strengthen

fortín (SM) (= *fuerte*) (small) fort; [*de hormigón*] pillbox

fortísimo (ADJ) (*superl de* **fuerte**) (*Mús*) fortissimo

fortuitamente (ADV) (= *por casualidad*) fortuitously (*frm*), by chance; (= *por accidente*) accidentally

fortuito (ADJ) (*gen*) fortuitous (*frm*); [*encuentro*] accidental, chance (*antes de s*)

fortuna (SF) **1** (= *suerte*) fortune • **la ~ le ha sido adversa** (*liter*) fortune has been unkind to him • **tuvo la buena ~ de heredar la casa** he had the good fortune to inherit the house • **ha tenido la mala ~ de ponerse enferma** she had the misfortune to fall ill • **no tuvo ~ en el concurso** he was unlucky in the competition, he didn't have any luck in the competition • **por ~** luckily, fortunately • **probar ~** to try one's luck
2 (= *riqueza*) fortune • **heredó una inmensa ~** she inherited a vast fortune • **este piso cuesta una ~** this flat costs a fortune
3 (*Náut*) (= *tempestad*) storm • **correr ~** to ride out a storm

fortunón* (SM) huge fortune

fórum (SM) = **foro**

forúnculo (SM) boil

forzadamente (ADV) forcibly, by force • **sonreír ~** to force a smile • **reírse ~** to force a laugh

forzado (ADJ) **1** (= *obligado*) forced • **verse ~ a hacer algo** to be forced *o* obliged to do sth • **con una sonrisa forzada** with a forced smile
2 [*puerta, cerradura*] forced
3 (= *rebuscado*) [*traducción, estilo, metáfora*] forced; ▹ **trabajo, marcha**

forzar ▹ CONJUG 1f, 1l (VT) **1** (= *obligar*) to force • **~ a algn a hacer algo** to force sb to do sth, make sb do sth • **les forzó a dimitir** he forced them to resign, he made them resign
2 [+ *puerta, cerradura*] to force; (*Mil*) [+ *ciudadela, fuerte*] to storm, take
3 [+ *ojos, voz*] to strain; [+ *sonrisa*] to force • **estás forzando la vista** you're straining your eyes
4 (= *violar*) to rape

forzosamente (ADV) • **tiene ~ que ser así** this is the way it has to be • **tuvieron que cerrarlo ~** they had (no alternative but) to close it • **~ lo harás** you'll have no choice but to do it

forzoso (ADJ) (= *necesario*) necessary; (= *inevitable*) inescapable, unavoidable; (= *obligatorio*) compulsory • **aterrizaje ~** forced landing • **es ~ que** it is inevitable that • **le fue ~ hacerlo** he had no choice but to do it

forzudo/a (ADJ) (= *fuerte*) tough, brawny
(SM/F) [*de circo*] strongman/strongwoman; (*pey*) (= *matón*) thug

fosa (SF) **1** (= *hoyo*) pit; (= *sepultura*) grave ▸ **fosa atlántica** Atlantic trench ▸ **fosa común** (*para gente sin familia*) common grave; (*para soldados, prisioneros*) mass grave ▸ **fosa de reparaciones** (*Aut*) inspection pit ▸ **fosa fecal** septic tank ▸ **fosa marina** oceanic trench ▸ **fosa séptica** septic tank
2 (*Anat*) cavity ▸ **fosas nasales** nostrils

fosar ▹ CONJUG 1a (VT) to dig a ditch *o* trench round

fosco (ADJ) **1** [*pelo*] wild, disordered
2 = **hosco**

fosfatina* (SF) • MODISMO: • **estar hecho ~** to be worn out, be shattered*

fosfato (SM) phosphate

fosforecer ▹ CONJUG 2d (VI) to phosphoresce (*frm*), glow

fosforera (SF) **1** (= *fábrica*) match factory
2 (= *caja*) matchbox

fosforescencia (SF) phosphorescence

fosforescente (ADJ) phosphorescent

fosfórico (ADJ) phosphoric

fosforito* (ADJ INV) fluorescent • **amarillo ~** fluorescent yellow, luminous yellow

fósforo (SM) **1** (*Quím*) phosphorus

2 (*esp LAm*) (= *cerilla*) match
3 (*And*) (= *cápsula fulminante*) percussion cap
4 (*Méx*) (= *carajillo*) coffee laced with brandy
5 • MODISMO: • **tener ~** (*Cono Sur**) to be shrewd, be sharp
6 (*CAm*) (= *exaltado*) hothead
7 (*CAm**) (= *pelirrojo*) redhead
fosforoso (ADJ) phosphorous
fosgeno (SM) phosgene
fósil (ADJ) fossil (*antes de s*), fossilized
(SM) 1 (*Bio*) fossil
2* (= *viejo*) old crock*, old dodderer*; (= *carroza*) old square*
fosilizado (ADJ) fossilized
fosilizarse ▷ CONJUG 1f (VPR) to fossilize, become fossilized
foso (SM) 1 (= *agujero*) (*redondo*) pit, hole; (*alargado*) ditch, trench; (*en castillo*) moat ▸ **foso de agua** (*Dep*) water jump ▸ **foso de reconocimiento** (*Aut*) inspection pit ▸ **foso generacional** generation gap
2 (*Teat*) pit • MODISMO: • **irse** *o* **venirse al ~** (*Teat*) to flop* ▸ **foso de la orquesta** orchestra pit
fotingo* (SM) (*LAm*) old banger*, jalopy*, clunker (*EEUU**)
foto (SF) photo, picture • **sacar** *o* **tomar una ~** to take a photo *o* picture (**de** of) • MODISMO: • **salir en la ~** to be in the picture, play one's part ▸ **foto aérea** aerial photo ▸ **foto de carnet** passport(-size) photo ▸ **foto de conjunto** group photo ▸ **foto de familia** [*de familiares*] family photo; [*de colegas*] group photo, team photo ▸ **foto fija** still, still photo ▸ **foto robot** quick photo; (= *cabina*) photo booth
foto... (PREF) photo...
fotoacabado (SM) photo-finishing
fotocalco (SM) photoprint
fotocomponedora (SF) photocomposer
fotocomponer ▷ CONJUG 2q (VT) to typeset
fotocomposición (SF) typesetting
fotocompositora (SF) photocomposer
fotoconductor (SM) photoconductor
fotocontrol (SM) • **resultado comprobado por ~** (*Dep*) photo finish
fotocopia (SF) 1 (= *copia*) photocopy, print
2 (= *acción*) photocopying
fotocopiable (ADJ) photocopiable
fotocopiadora (SF) (= *máquina*) photocopier, photocopying machine; (= *local*) photocopying shop, photocopier's
fotocopiar ▷ CONJUG 1b (VT) to photocopy
fotocopista (SMF) photocopier
fotocopistería (SF) photocopying shop
fotocromía (SF) colour photography, color photography (EEUU)
fotodenuncia (SF) photo report
fotoeléctrico (ADJ) photoelectric • **célula fotoeléctrica** photoelectric cell
fotoenvejecimiento (SM) photo-ageing
foto-finish (SF INV), **foto finish** [foto'finis] (SF INV) photo finish
fotogenia (SF) photogenic qualities (*pl*) • **es de una ~ maravillosa** she's wonderfully photogenic
fotogénico (ADJ) photogenic
fotograbado (SM) photogravure, photoengraving
fotografía (SF) 1 (= *arte*) photography ▸ **fotografía aérea** aerial photography ▸ **fotografía en color** colour photography, color photography (EEUU)
2 (= *imagen*) photograph • **sacar** *o* **tomar una ~ de algo** to take a photograph of sth ▸ **fotografía al flash, fotografía al magnesio** flash photograph ▸ **fotografía de carnet** ≈ passport photograph ▸ **fotografía en color** colour photograph, color photograph (EEUU) ▸ **fotografía instantánea** snapshot; ▷ **foto**
fotografiar ▷ CONJUG 1c (VT) to photograph
(VPR) **fotografiarse** to have one's photograph taken
fotográficamente (ADV) photographically • **le reconocieron ~** they recognized him through photographs
fotográfico (ADJ) photographic
fotógrafo/a (SM/F) photographer ▸ **fotógrafo/a aficionado/a** amateur photographer ▸ **fotógrafo/a ambulante, fotógrafo/a callejero/a** street photographer ▸ **fotógrafo/a de estudio** portrait photographer ▸ **fotógrafo/a de prensa** press photographer
fotograma (SM) (*Cine*) still
fotogrametría (SF) photogrammetry
fotolibro (SM) photobook
fotolito (SM) photolithograph, photolitho
fotomatón (SM) 1 (= *quiosco*) photo booth • **una foto de ~** a passport photo
2* (= *foto*) passport photo
fotómetro (SM) light meter, photometer
fotomodelo (SMF) photographic model
fotomontaje (SM) photomontage
fotón (SM) photon
fotonoticia (SF) photographic reportage
fotonovela (SF) *romance or crime story illustrated with photos*
fotoperiodismo (SM) photojournalism
fotoperiodista (SMF) photojournalist
fotoprotección (SF) UV protection
fotoprotector (ADJ) UV protective
(SM) UV protectant
fotoquímico (ADJ) photochemical
foto-robot (SF) (PL: **foto-robots**) Photofit picture®
fotorreceptor (ADJ) photoreceptor
fotorreportaje (SM) photo story
fotorrobot (SF) (PL: **fotorrobots**) = foto-robot
fotosensible (ADJ) photosensitive
fotosensor (SM) photosensor
fotosíntesis (SF INV) photosynthesis
fotostatar ▷ CONJUG 1a (VT) to photostat
fotostato (SM) photostat
fototeca (SF) (= *colección*) collection of photographs; (= *archivo*) photographic library
fototopografía (SF) = **fotogrametría**
fototropismo (SM) phototropism
fotovoltaico (ADJ) photovoltaic
fotuto (SM) 1 (*LAm*) (*Mús*) wind instrument (of gourd)
2 (*Cuba*) (= *bocina*) car horn
foul [faul] (PL: **fouls**) (SM) (*LAm*) = **faul**
foulard [fu'lar] (SM) [*de mujer*] (head)scarf; [*de hombre*] cravat
fox [fos] (SM INV) foxtrot
FP (SF ABR) (*Esp*) (*Educ*) (= **Formación Profesional**) *vocational courses for 14- to 18-year-olds*
(SM ABR) (*Pol*) = **Frente Popular**
FPA (SF ABR) (*Arg, Esp*) = **Formación Profesional Acelerada**
FPLP (SM ABR) (= **Frente Popular para la Liberación de Palestina**) PFLP
FPMR (SM ABR) (*Chile*) = **Frente Patriótico Manuel Rodríguez**
Fr. (ABR) (= **Fray**) Fr
fr., frs. (ABR) (= **franco(s)**) fr
fra. (ABR) (= **factura**) inv
frac (SM) (PL: **fracs** *o* **fraques**) tailcoat, tails (*pl*) • **ir (vestido) de ~** (*para una ceremonia*) to be in morning dress
fracasado/a (ADJ) failed, unsuccessful
(SM/F) failure
fracasar ▷ CONJUG 1a (VT) (*LAm*) to mess up, make a mess of
(VI) (*gen*) to fail, be unsuccessful; [*plan*] to fail, fall through
fracaso (SM) failure • **el ~ de las negociaciones** the failure of the negotiations • **la reforma está condenada al ~** the reform is doomed to failure, the reform is destined to fail • **ir en dirección al ~** to be heading for disaster • **¡es un ~!** he's a disaster! • **es un ~ total** it's a complete disaster ▸ **fracaso escolar** academic failure ▸ **fracaso sentimental** disappointment in love
fracción (SF) 1 (*Mat*) fraction ▸ **fracción decimal** decimal fraction
2 (= *parte*) part, fragment
3 (*Pol etc*) faction, splinter group
4 (= *repartición*) division, breaking-up (**en** into)
fraccionado (ADJ) • **pago ~** payment by instalments *o* (EEUU) installments
fraccionadora (SF) (*Méx*) estate agent, realtor (EEUU)
fraccionalismo (SM) (*Pol*) factionalism, tendency to form splinter groups
fraccionamiento (SM) 1 (*gen*) division, breaking-up (**en** into) ▸ **fraccionamiento de pagos** payment by instalments *o* (EEUU) installments ▸ **fraccionamiento de tierras** land distribution
2 (*Méx*) housing estate, real estate development (*esp EEUU*)
3 (*Téc*) [*de petróleo*] cracking
fraccionar ▷ CONJUG 1a (VT) to divide, break up, split up (**en** into) • **~ los pagos** to pay by instalments
fraccionario (ADJ) fractional • **"se ruega moneda fraccionaria"** "please tender exact fare"
fracking ['frakin] (SM) fracking
fractal (SM) (*Mat*) fractal
fractura (SF) 1 (*Med*) fracture ▸ **fractura complicada** compound fracture ▸ **fractura múltiple** multiple fracture
2 (*Jur*) • **robo con ~** burglary
fracturación (SF) 1 [*de brazo, pierna*] fracture
2 ▸ **fracturación hidráulica** fracking, hydraulic fracturing (*frm*)
fracturado (ADJ) fractured
fracturar ▷ CONJUG 1a (VI) to fracture
(VPR) **fracturarse** to fracture
fragancia (SF) fragrance, perfume
fragante (ADJ) 1 (= *perfumado*) fragrant, scented
2 = **flagrante**
fraganti ▷ **in fraganti**
fragata (SF) frigate
frágil (ADJ) 1 [*construcción, material, objeto*] fragile
2 [*anciano*] frail; [*salud*] delicate; [*acuerdo, sistema*] fragile • **una mujer aparentemente ~** a seemingly fragile woman
fragilidad (SF) (*gen*) fragility; [*de anciano*] frailty
fragmentación (SF) fragmentation
fragmentadamente (ADV) • **pagar ~** to pay in instalments *o* (EEUU) installments
fragmentado (ADJ) fragmented • **solo nos han llegado informaciones fragmentadas** we have only received snippets of information *o* fragmented pieces of information
fragmentar ▷ CONJUG 1a (VT) to fragment
(VPR) **fragmentarse** to fragment • **se fragmenta en miles de partículas** it fragments into thousands of particles
fragmentariedad (SF) (*frm*) fragmentary nature
fragmentario (ADJ) fragmentary
fragmento (SM) 1 (= *trozo*) [*de escultura, hueso, bomba, roca*] fragment; [*de vasija*] fragment, shard • **fue alcanzada por ~s de cristales** she was hit by flying glass *o* fragments of glass
2 (= *extracto*) [*de novela, discurso, obra musical*] passage; (*ya aislado*) excerpt, extract • **a través del tabique se oían ~s de la**

conversación you could hear snippets *o* snatches of their conversation through the partition

fragor SM (*gen*) din, clamour, clamor (*EEUU*); [*de trueno*] crash, clash; [*de máquina*] roar

fragoroso ADJ deafening, thunderous

fragosidad SF **1** (= *cualidad*) [*de terreno*] roughness, unevenness; [*de bosque, maleza*] denseness
2 (= *lugar*) rough spot

fragoso ADJ [*terreno*] rough, uneven; [*bosque*] dense, overgrown

fragua SF forge

fraguado SM **1** [*de metal*] forging
2 [*de hormigón*] hardening, setting

fraguar ▸ CONJUG 1i VT **1** [+ *metal*] to forge
2 [+ *plan*] to hatch, concoct
VI [*hormigón*] to harden, set
VPR **fraguarse** [*tormenta*] to blow up; (*fig*) to be brewing

fraile SM **1** (*Rel*) friar, monk ▸ **fraile de misa y olla**† simple-minded friar ▸ **fraile descalzo** barefoot monk ▸ **fraile mendicante** mendicant friar (*gen Franciscan*) ▸ **fraile predicador** preaching friar, friar preacher
2 (*Caribe*) (= *bagazo*) bagasse, residue of sugar cane

frailecillo SM (= *ave*) puffin

frailería SF friars (*pl*), monks (*pl*); (*pey*) priests (*pl*)

frailesco ADJ, **frailuno** ADJ monkish

frambuesa SF raspberry

frambuesero SM, **frambueso** SM raspberry cane

francachela* SF (= *comida*) spread*; (= *juerga*) spree, binge*

francachón ADJ outspoken, forthright

francamente ADV **1** (= *abiertamente*) frankly • ~, **eso está mal** (quite) frankly, I think that's wrong
2 (= *realmente*) really • **es una obra ~ divertida** it's a really funny play
3 (= *generosamente*) generously, liberally

francés/esa ADJ French • **a la francesa** in the French manner, French style, the way the French do • MODISMO: • **despedirse a la francesa** to leave without saying goodbye, take French leave • **tortilla francesa** plain omelette, French omelette
SM/F Frenchman/Frenchwoman
SM **1** (*Ling*) French
2** (= *acto sexual*) blow job**

francesilla SF **1** (*Bot*) buttercup
2 (*Culin*) French roll

Fráncfort SM Frankfurt

franchute/a* ADJ Frog*, French
SM/F Frog*, Frenchy*
SM (*Ling*) Frog*, French

Francia SF France

fráncico ADJ Frankish
SM (*Ling*) Frankish

francio SM (*Quím*) francium

Francisca SF Frances

franciscano ADJ, SM Franciscan

Francisco SM Francis

francmasón SM freemason

francmasonería SF freemasonry

franco[1] SM (*Econ*) franc

franco[2] ADJ **1** (= *directo*) frank • **seré ~ contigo** I will be frank with you • **para serte ~** to be frank *o* honest (with you) • **si he de ser ~** frankly, to tell you the truth
2 (= *patente*) clear, evident • **estar en franca decadencia** to be in visible decline • **estar en franca rebeldía** to be in open rebellion
3 (*Com*) (= *exento*) free • **~ a bordo** free on board • **~ al costado del buque** free alongside ship • **~ de derechos** duty-free • **precio ~ (en) fábrica** price ex-factory, price ex-works • **~ de porte** carriage-free; (*Correos*) post-free • **~ puesto sobre vagón** free on rail
4 (*Com*) [*puerto*] free; [*camino*] open • **mantener mesa franca** to keep open house
5 • **~ de servicio** (*Mil*) off-duty
6 (*Cono Sur*) • **estar de ~** to be off duty, be on leave
7 (= *liberal*) generous

franco[3] (*Hist*) ADJ Frankish
SM Frank

franco... PREF franco...

franco-británico ADJ Franco-British, French-British

francocanadiense ADJ, SMF French-Canadian

francófilo/a ADJ, SM/F Francophile

francófobo/a ADJ francophobe, francophobic (*antes de s*)
SM/F Francophobe

francófono/a ADJ French-speaking
SM/F French speaker

franco-hispano ADJ Franco-Spanish

francote* ADJ outspoken, blunt

francotirador(a) SM/F **1** (= *tirador*) sniper
2 (*fig*) freelance, free agent

franela SF **1** (= *tela*) flannel
2 (*LAm*) (= *camiseta*) T-shirt; (*de ropa interior*) vest, undershirt (*EEUU*)

franelear‡ ▸ CONJUG 1a VI to pet*, make out (*EEUU*‡)

frangollar ▸ CONJUG 1a VT **1** (*And, Cono Sur*) (= *chapucear*) to bungle, botch
2 (*Cono Sur*) [+ *granos*] to grind
VI (*And*) to dissemble

frangollero ADJ (*And, Cono Sur*) bungling

frangollo SM **1** (*Culin*) (*And, Cono Sur*) corn mash; (*Cono Sur*) (= *locro*) meat and maize stew; (*Caribe*) (= *dulce*) *sweet made from mashed bananas*
2 (*Méx*) dog's dinner*
3 (*LAm*) (= *alpiste*) birdseed
4 (*Méx*) (= *lío*) muddle, mess; (= *mezcla*) mixture

frangollón/ona (*LAm*) ADJ bungling
SM/F bungler

franja SF **1** (= *banda*) strip; [*de uniforme*] stripe • **~ de tierra** strip of land • **la ~ de Gaza** the Gaza strip ▸ **franja de edad** age-group ▸ **franja horaria** time zone
2 (= *borde*) fringe, border

franjar ▸ CONJUG 1a VT, **franjear** ▸ CONJUG 1a VT to fringe, trim (**de** with)

Frankfurt SM Frankfurt

franqueadora SF (*Correos*) franking machine

franquear ▸ CONJUG 1a VT **1** [+ *camino*] to clear, open • **~ el paso a algn** to clear the way for sb • **~ la entrada a** to give free entry to
2 (= *atravesar*) [+ *río*] to cross; [+ *obstáculo*] to negotiate
3 (*Correos*) to frank, stamp • **una carta franqueada** a post-paid letter • **una carta insuficientemente franqueada** a letter with insufficient postage
4 [+ *esclavo*] to free, liberate
5 [+ *derecho*] to grant, concede (**a** to)
VPR **franquearse** (= *sincerarse*) • **~se con algn** to have a heart-to-heart talk with sb

franqueo SM (*Correos*) franking • **con ~ insuficiente** with insufficient postage

franqueza SF **1** (= *sinceridad*) frankness • **con ~** frankly • **lo digo con toda ~** I'll be quite frank with you
2 (= *confianza*) familiarity • **tengo suficiente ~ con él para discrepar** I am on close enough terms with him to disagree
3 (= *liberalidad*) generosity

franquía SF (*Náut*) room to manoeuvre *o* (*EEUU*) maneuver, searoom

franquicia SF **1** (*Com*) franchise
2 (= *exención*) exemption (**de** from) ▸ **franquicia aduanera**, **franquicia arancelaria** exemption from customs duties ▸ **franquicia de equipaje** (*Aer*) free baggage allowance ▸ **franquicia postal** Freepost®

franquiciado/a SM/F franchise holder, franchisee

franquiciador(a) SM/F franchisor

franquiciamiento SM franchising

franquiciar ▸ CONJUG 1b VT to franchise

franquismo SM • **el ~** (= *período*) the Franco years, the Franco period; (= *política*) the Franco system • **bajo el ~** under Franco • **luchó contra el ~** he fought against Franco

> **FRANQUISMO**
> **Franquismo** is the term used to refer both to the years when General Francisco Franco was the dictator of Spain (from the end of the **Guerra Civil** in 1939 to his death in 1975) and to his style of government. He was an authoritarian, right-wing dictator whose political philosophy included imposing traditional Catholic values and making Spain self-sufficient economically. In the 1960s, after a long period of isolation, Spain began to open its doors to foreign investment and influence. On Franco's death, Spain became a democratic constitutional monarchy.

franquista ADJ pro-Franco • **tendencia ~** pro-Franco tendency • **una familia muy ~** a strongly pro-Franco family
SMF supporter of Franco

FRAP SM ABR **1** (*Esp*) = **Frente Revolucionario Antifascista y Patriótico**
2 (*Chile*) = **Frente de Acción Popular**

fraques SMPL *de* frac

frasca SF **1** (= *hojas*) dry leaves (*pl*); (= *ramitas*) small twigs (*pl*)
2 (*CAm, Méx*) (= *fiesta*) riotous party
3 • MODISMO: • **pegarle a la ~*** to hit the bottle*

frasco SM **1** (= *botella*) bottle • **~ de perfume** perfume bottle • MODISMOS: • **¡chupa del ~!**‡ • **¡toma del ~ (Carrasco)!**‡ stone the crows!* ▸ **frasco de campaña** (*LAm*) water bottle, canteen
2 (= *medida*) *liquid measure: Caribe = 2.44 litres, Cono Sur = 21.37 litres*

frase SF (= *oración*) sentence; (= *locución*) phrase, expression; (= *cita*) quotation • **diccionario de ~s** dictionary of quotations ▸ **frase compleja** complex sentence ▸ **frase hecha** set phrase; (*pey*) cliché, stock phrase ▸ **frase lapidaria** axiom

fraseo SM (*Mús*) phrasing

fraseología SF **1** (= *estilo*) phraseology
2 (*pey*) verbosity, verbiage

Frasquita SF *forma familiar de* **Francisca**

Frasquito SM *forma familiar de* **Francisco**

fratás SM (plastering) trowel

fraterna* SF ticking-off*

fraternal ADJ brotherly, fraternal

fraternidad SF brotherhood, fraternity

fraternización SF fraternization

fraternizar ▸ CONJUG 1f VI to fraternize

fraterno ADJ brotherly, fraternal

fratricida ADJ fratricidal
SMF fratricide

fratricidio SM fratricide

fraude SM **1** (= *engaño*) fraud • **por ~** by fraud ▸ **fraude electoral** electoral fraud ▸ **fraude fiscal** tax evasion
2 (= *falta de honradez*) dishonesty, fraudulence

fraudulencia SF fraudulence

fraudulentamente ADV fraudulently, dishonestly

fraudulento ADJ fraudulent, dishonest

fray SM brother, friar • **Fray Juan** Brother John, Friar John

frazada SF (*LAm*) blanket

freaky* ADJ weird* • **me pasó una cosa muy ~** something really weird* happened to me • **¡qué tío más ~!** what a weirdo!* SMF weirdo*

freático ADJ ▹ **capa**

frecuencia SF frequency • **con ~** frequently, often • **alta ~** (*Elec, Radio*) high frequency • **de alta ~** high-frequency ▸ **frecuencia de onda** wavelength • **estar en la misma ~ de onda** to be on the same wavelength ▸ **frecuencia de red** mains frequency ▸ **frecuencia de reloj** clock speed ▸ **frecuencia modulada** frequency modulation

frecuentador(a) SM/F frequenter

frecuentar ▹ CONJUG 1a VT to frequent

frecuente ADJ **1** (*gen*) frequent; [*costumbre*] common, prevalent; [*vicio*] rife
2 (*Méx*) (= *familiar*) familiar, over-familiar • **andarse ~ con** to be on close terms with

frecuentemente ADV frequently, often

Fredemo SM ABR (*Perú*) = **Frente Democrático**

freelance [fri'lans] ADJ, SMF INV freelance

freeware [fri'wer] SM freeware

freezer ['friser] SM (*LAm*) freezer

fregada* SF (*CAm, Méx*) (= *embrollo*) mess; (= *problema*) snag; (= *molestia*) nuisance, pain* • MODISMOS: • **¡la ~!‡** you don't say!, never! • **¡me lleva la ~!‡** well, I'll be damned!*

fregadera* SF (*LAm*) (= *fastidio*) nuisance, pain*

fregadero SM **1** (= *pila*) (kitchen) sink
2 (= *habitación*) scullery
3 (*CAm, Méx**) (= *molestia*) pain in the neck*

fregado/a ADJ **1** (*LAm**) (= *molesto*) annoying
2 (*LAm**) (= *difícil*) [*trabajo, tarea*] tricky; [*carácter, persona*] fussy
3 (*LAm**) [*persona*] (= *en mala situación económica*) broke*; (= *deprimido*) down, in a bad way*; (= *dañado, enfermo*) in a bad way* • **le quedó la pierna fregada después del accidente** his leg was in a bad way after the accident* • **ando muy ~ del estómago** my stomach is in a really bad way*
4 (*LAm**) (= *puñetero*) damn*, lousy*, bloody‡
5 (*Col, Perú*) (= *astuto*) cunning
6 (*Chile, Col, Perú, Ven*) (= *estricto*) strict
SM/F (*LAm*) (= *persona difícil*) fussy person
SM **1** (= *acción de fregar*) (*con fregona*) mopping; (*con estropajo, cepillo*) scrubbing; (*con esponja, trapo*) washing; [*de platos*] washing-up
2* (= *lío*) mess • **está siempre metido en algún ~** he's always involved in shady business
3* (= *riña*) row

fregador SM **1** (= *fregadero*) sink
2 (= *trapo*) dishcloth; (= *estropajo*) scourer; (= *fregona*) mop

fregadura SF = **fregado**

fregancia SF (*And*) = **fregada**

fregandera SF (*Méx*) charwoman, cleaner

fregantina SF (*And, Cono Sur*) = **fregada**

fregar ▹ CONJUG 1h, 1j VT **1** (= *limpiar*) (*con fregona*) to mop, wash; (*con estropajo, cepillo*) to scrub; (*con esponja, trapo*) to wash • **~ los cacharros** *o* **los platos** to wash the dishes, do the washing up, wash up
2 (*LAm**) (= *fastidiar*) [+ *persona*] to annoy • **lo hicieron para ~ a la competencia** they did it to annoy the competition • **¡no me friegues!** (*expresando molestia*) don't be a nuisance!, stop bothering me!; (*expresando asombro*) you're kidding!* • MODISMO: • **~ la paciencia** *o* (*Chile**) **la cachimba a algn** to pester sb*
3 (*LAm**) (= *malograr*) [+ *planes*] to ruin, mess up; [+ *fiesta*] to ruin; [+ *aparato*] to wreck • **me ~on con el cambio de horario** the timetable change really messed me up • **le ~on el taxi con el choque** his taxi was wrecked in the crash
4 (*Cono Sur**‡) to fuck‡, screw‡
5 (*Caribe**) (= *pegar*) to beat up; (*Dep*) to beat, thrash
VI **1** (= *fregar los platos*) to wash the dishes, do the washing up, wash up
2 (= *fregar el suelo*) (*con fregona*) to wash the floor, mop the floor; (*con cepillo*) to scrub the floor
3 (*LAm**) (= *molestar*) to annoy • **ya viene el vecino a ~ otra vez** here comes the neighbour to annoy us again • **¡no friegues!** (*expresando asombro*) you're kidding!*
VPR **fregarse** (*LAm**) **1** (= *aguantarse*) • **unos pocos se llenan los bolsillos y nosotros nos tenemos que ~** a few line their pockets and we have to grin and bear it • **si nos descubren, nos fregamos** if they find us, we've had it *o* we're done for*
2 (= *malograrse*) [*planes*] to be ruined, be messed up; [*fiesta*] to be ruined
3 (= *dañarse*) [+ *pierna, rodilla*] to do in* • **me fregué la espalda levantando sacos** I did my back in lifting sacks*

fregasuelos SM INV mop

fregazón* SM (*Cono Sur*) = **fregada**

fregón* ADJ **1** (*LAm*) (= *molesto*) annoying
2 (*LAm*) (= *tonto*) silly, stupid
3 (*And, Caribe*) (= *fresco*) brazen, fresh

fregona SF **1** (= *utensilio*) mop
2* (= *persona*) kitchen maid, dishwasher; (*fig*) (*pey*) slave, skivvy*; (*Caribe*) (= *sinvergüenza*) shameless hussy

fregota‡ SM waiter

fregoteo* SM = **fregado**

freidera SF (*Caribe*) frying pan

freidora SF deep-fat frier

freiduría SF ▸ **freiduría (de pescado)** fried-fish shop

freír ▹ CONJUG 3l (PP: **frito**) VT **1** (*Culin*) to fry • REFRÁN: • **al ~ será el reír** he who laughs last laughs longest
2 [*sol*] to burn, fry
3* (= *molestar*) to annoy; (= *acosar*) to harass; (= *atormentar*) to torment; (= *aburrir*) to bore • **~le a algn a preguntas** to bombard sb with questions
4* (= *matar*) to do in* • **~ a algn a tiros** to riddle sb with bullets
VPR **freírse 1** (*Culin*) to fry
2 • **~se de calor*** to be roasting
3 • **~sela a algn*** to have sb on*, put sb on (*EEUU**)

frejol SM, **fréjol** SM (*esp Perú*) = **fríjol**

frenada SF, **frenaje** SM (*Aut*) (sudden) braking

frenado SM (*Aut*) braking ▸ **frenado antibloqueo** anti-lock braking

frenar ▹ CONJUG 1a VT **1** (*Aut, Mec*) to brake
2 (= *contener*) [+ *inflación, crecimiento, avance, deterioro*] to check, slow down; [+ *pasiones, entusiasmo*] to curb; [+ *enemigo, ataque*] to check, hold back • **su novia tiene que ~le para que no beba tanto** his girlfriend has to restrain him from drinking so much
VI (*Aut*) to brake • **frena, que viene una curva** brake, there's a bend coming up • **~ en seco** to brake sharply *o* suddenly
VPR **frenarse** (= *contenerse*) to restrain o.s.

frenazo SM (= *acción*) sudden braking; (= *parada*) sudden halt; (= *ruido*) squeal of brakes • **dar un ~** to brake suddenly, brake hard

frenesí SM frenzy

frenéticamente ADV (= *con desenfreno*) frantically, frenziedly; (= *con furia*) furiously, wildly

frenético ADJ (= *desenfrenado*) frantic, frenzied; (= *furioso*) furious, wild • **ponerse ~** to lose one's head

frenillo SM **1** (= *defecto*) • **tener ~** to have a speech defect
2 (*Anat*) [*del pene*] fraenum, frenum (*esp EEUU*)
3 (= *correa, cuerda*) muzzle

freno SM **1** (*Aut, Mec*) brake • **líquido de ~s** brake fluid • **el pedal del ~** the brake pedal • **echar el ~** *o* **los ~s** to apply the brake(s) • **pisé el ~** I put my foot on the brake, I applied the brake • **soltar el ~** to release the brake • MODISMO: • **¡echa el ~, Madaleno!‡** put a sock in it!* ▸ **freno de aire** air brake ▸ **freno de disco** disc brake ▸ **freno de mano** handbrake, emergency brake (*EEUU*) • **poner** *o* **echar el ~ de mano** to put on the handbrake ▸ **freno de tambor** drum brake ▸ **freno de vacío** vacuum brake ▸ **freno hidráulico** hydraulic brake ▸ **freno neumático** pneumatic brake ▸ **freno pedal** foot brake ▸ **frenos ABS** ABS (brakes), ABS (braking)
2 [*de caballo*] bit • **morder** *o* **tascar el ~** (*lit, fig*) to champ at the bit
3 (= *contención*) brake • **medidas que actúan como ~ al crecimiento económico** measures that act as a brake on economic growth, measures that slow down economic growth • **poner ~ a algo: hay que poner ~ a la especulación** we must curb speculation • **puso ~ a las malas lenguas** he stopped the gossip ▸ **frenos y contrapesos, frenos y equilibrios** (*Pol*) checks and balances
4 (*Cono Sur**) (= *hambre*) hunger

frenología SF phrenology

frenólogo/a SM/F phrenologist

frenopático ADJ psychiatric
SM (*Med*) mental home; (*hum**) loony bin‡, nuthouse‡

frentazo SM (*Méx*) disappointment, rebuff • **pegarse un ~** to come a cropper*

frente SF (*Anat*) forehead, brow (*liter*) • **arrugar la ~** to frown, knit one's brow • MODISMOS: • **adornar la ~ a algn*** to cheat on sb* • **con la ~ (muy) alta** with one's head held high • **lo lleva escrito en la ~** it's written all over his face • **~ a ~** face to face; ▹ **dedo**
SM **1** (= *parte delantera*) front • **al ~** in front • **un ejército con su capitán al ~** an army led by its captain, an army with its captain at the front • **al ~ de:** • **entró en Madrid al ~ de las tropas** he led the troops into Madrid, he entered Madrid at the head of his troops • **el Madrid sigue al ~ de la clasificación** Madrid still lead the table *o* are still top of the league • **espero seguir al ~ del festival** I hope to continue as director of the festival • **estuvo al ~ del Ministerio de Industria** he was Minister for Industry • **un concierto con Herbert Von Karajan al ~ de la Filarmónica de Berlín** a concert by the Berlin Philharmonic conducted by Herbert Von Karajan • **en ~:** • **la casa de en ~** the house opposite • **hacer ~ a** [+ *crisis, problemas*] to tackle; [+ *situación, realidad*] to face up to • **hay que hacer ~ a las dificultades** we have to tackle the problems • **tenemos que hacer ~ a grandes gastos** we are facing considerable expenses • **~ por ~:** • **vivimos ~ por ~** we live directly opposite each other • **está ~ por ~ del cine** it's directly opposite the cinema ▸ **frente de arranque, frente de trabajo** (*Min*) coalface

2 • de ~: • **atacar de ~** to make a frontal attack • **chocar de ~** to crash head-on • **ir de ~** to go forward • **mirar de ~** to look (straight) ahead • **seguir de ~** to go straight on, go straight ahead • **viene un coche de ~** there's a car heading straight for us
3 (*Mil, Pol*) front • **formar** *o* **hacer un ~ común con algn** to form a united front with sb • **han formado un ~ contra la corrupción** they have formed an alliance against corruption ▸ **frente de batalla** battle front ▸ **frente del oeste** western front ▸ **Frente Polisario** Polisario Front ▸ **frente popular** popular front ▸ **frente unido** united front
4 (*Meteo*) front ▸ **frente cálido** warm front ▸ **frente frío** cold front
5 • **frente a a** (= *enfrente de*) opposite • **~ al hotel hay un banco** there's a bank opposite the hotel • **ella está ~ a mí** she is facing *o* opposite me • **el barco encalló ~ a la costa irlandesa** the boat ran aground off the Irish coast
b (= *en presencia de*) • **~ a las cámaras** in front of the cameras • **me encontré ~ a una situación difícil** I found myself facing a difficult situation • **ceder ~ a una amenaza** to give way to *o* in the face of a threat
c (= *en oposición a*) • **el euro sigue fuerte ~ al dólar** the euro remains strong against the dollar • **logró un 39% de los votos, ~ al 49% de 1990** she got 39% of the vote, as against 49% in 1990 • **empataron ~ al Santander** they drew against *o* with Santander • **~ a lo que pensaba, eran franceses** in contrast to what I thought, they were French
6 • **~ mío/suyo** (*esp Cono Sur**) in front of me/you, opposite me/you

freo (SM) channel, strait

fresa (SF) **1** (*Bot*) (= *fruta*) strawberry; (= *planta*) strawberry plant
2 (*Téc*) milling cutter; [*de dentista*] drill
3 (*Méx**) (*pey*) snob
(ADJ INV) (*Méx**) • **la gente ~** the in crowd

fresado (SM) (*Mec*) milling

fresadora (SF) (*Mec*) milling machine ▸ **fresadora de roscar** thread cutter

fresal (SM) (= *cantero*) strawberry bed; (= *campos*) strawberry fields (*pl*)

fresar ▹ CONJUG 1a (VT) (*Mec*) to mill

fresca* (SF) **1** • **la ~: saldremos temprano, con la ~** we'll leave early, while it's still cool, we'll leave early, in the cool of the morning • **charlaban en la calle, sentados a la ~** they were sitting in the street chatting in the cool air • **salir a tomar la ~** to go out for a breath of (fresh) air
2* (= *insolencia*) • **decir** *o* **soltar cuatro ~s a algn** to give sb a lot of cheek*; ▹ **fresco**

frescachón (ADJ) **1** [*persona*] (= *saludable*) healthy, glowing with health; (= *de buen color*) ruddy
2 (*Náut*) [*viento*] fresh, stiff

frescales* (SMF INV) rascal, cheeky rascal

fresco/a (ADJ) **1** (*Culin*) **a** (= *no congelado, no cocinado*) fresh • **es mejor comer alimentos ~s** it is best to eat fresh food
b (= *no pasado*) [*carne, fruta*] fresh; [*huevo*] fresh, new-laid • **el pescado está muy ~** the fish is very fresh
c (= *no curado*) [*queso*] unripened; [*salmón*] fresh
2 (= *frío*) **a** [*brisa, viento*] cool • **salí a respirar un poco de aire ~** I went outside to get a breath of fresh air
b [*bebida*] cool, cold; [*agua*] (*para beber*) cold; (*en piscina, río*) cool • **una cerveza fresca** a cool *o* cold beer
c [*tiempo*] (*desagradable*) chilly; (*agradable*) cool • **ponte una chaqueta, que la noche está fresca** put a jacket on, it's chilly tonight • **¡qué ~ se estará ahora en la montaña!** it will be so nice and cool just now in the mountains
d [*tela, vestido*] cool
3 (= *reciente*) [*ideas*] fresh; [*pintura*] wet • **la tragedia aún está fresca en mi memoria** the tragic events are still fresh in my memory • **venía contento, con dinero ~ en el bolsillo** he came along looking happy, with fresh money in his pocket • **traigo noticias frescas** I have the latest news • **"pintura fresca"** "wet paint"
4 (= *natural*) [*piel, estilo*] fresh
5 (= *refrescante*) [*colonia, perfume*] refreshing
6 (= *persona*) (= *descansado*) fresh; (= *descarado*) cheeky, sassy (*EEUU*) • **prefiero estudiar por las mañanas, cuando aún estoy ~** I prefer studying in the morning while I'm still fresh • **¡qué ~!** what a cheek!*, what a nerve!* • **¡está** *o* **va ~, si cree que le voy a ayudar otra vez!** he couldn't be more wrong if he thinks that I'm going to help him again!, if he thinks I'm going to help him again, he's got another think coming! • **me lo dijo tan ~** he just said it to me as cool as you like • **me lo dijo y se quedó tan ~** he said it without batting an eyelid • MODISMO: • **ser más ~ que una lechuga*** to have a lot of nerve*
(SM/F)* (*sinvergüenza*) • **¡usted es un ~!** you've got a nerve!*
(SM) **1** (= *temperatura*) • **se sentó a la sombra del árbol buscando el ~** she sat down under the tree, in the cool of its shade • **voy a sentarme fuera, al ~** I'm going to sit outside where it's nice and cool • **el ~ de la mañana** the cool of the morning • **dormir al ~** to sleep in the open air, sleep outdoors • **hace ~** (*desagradable*) it's chilly; (*agradable*) it's cool • **tomar el ~** to get some fresh air • MODISMO: • **me trae al ~***: • **que te lo creas o no, me trae al ~** I couldn't care less whether you believe it or not
2 (*Arte*) fresco • **pintar al ~** to paint in fresco
3 (*Col, Perú, Ven*) (= *bebida*) (*sin gas*) fruit drink; (*con gas*) fizzy fruit drink; ▹ **fresca**

frescor (SM) [*de temperatura, alimentos*] freshness; [*de lugar, bebida*] coolness • **gozar del ~ nocturno** to enjoy the cool night air

frescote (ADJ) (= *saludable*) healthy, glowing with health, blooming; (= *de buen color*) ruddy; [*mujer*] buxom

frescura (SF) **1** [*de temperatura, alimentos*] freshness; [*de lugar, bebida*] coolness
2 (= *serenidad*) coolness, calmness • **lo dijo con la mayor ~** she said it without batting an eyelid
3* (= *descaro*) cheek, nerve* • **tiene la mar de ~** he's got the cheek of the devil* • **tuvo la ~ de pedirme dinero** she had the nerve to ask me for money*
4 (= *impertinencia*) cheeky thing (to say), impudent remark • **me dijo unas ~s** he was cheeky to me

fresia (SF) freesia

fresnada (SF) ash grove

fresno (SM) ash (tree)

fresón (SM) (*Bot*) (= *fruto*) strawberry; (= *planta*) strawberry plant

fresquera (SF) (= *armario*) meat safe, cooler (*EEUU*); (= *habitación*) cold room

fresquería (SF) (*LAm*) refreshment stall

fresquito (ADJ), (SM) ▹ **fresco**

freudiano/a (ADJ), (SM/F) Freudian

freza (SF) **1** [*de peces*] (= *huevos*) spawn; (= *acto*) spawning; (= *estación*) spawning
2 (= *excremento*) dung, droppings (*pl*)

frezadero (SM) spawning ground

frezar ▹ CONJUG 1f (VI) to spawn

friable (ADJ) friable

frialdad (SF) **1** [*de material, líquido*] coldness
2 (= *indiferencia*) (*en sentimientos, actitudes*) coolness; (*en carácter, mirada*) coldness • **se comportaban con una ~ envidiable** they behaved with enviable coolness • **la novela ha sido acogida con ~ por la crítica** the novel has been given a cool reception by the critics • **reaccionó con ~ ante la noticia** he showed no emotion when he heard the news • **hemos de actuar con ~ y analizar el problema detenidamente** we have to act dispassionately and analyze the problem at length • **ella lo miró con ~** she looked at him coldly

fríamente (ADV) **1** (= *con indiferencia, sin apasionamiento*) coolly; (= *con hostilidad*) coldly • **luego, cuando pudo pensar ~, se le ocurrió una posible respuesta** later, when she could think about it coolly, she came up with a possible answer • **la propuesta fue acogida ~** the proposal was given a cool reception • **mirado ~, tiene parte de razón en lo que dice** viewed dispassionately, he is partly right in what he says • **el reo miró ~ a los parientes de sus víctimas** the accused looked with cold detachment at the relatives of his victims
2 (= *a sangre fría*) [*matar*] in cold blood; [*torturar*] coldheartedly

frían ▹ **freír**

frica (SF) (*Cono Sur*) beating

fricandó (SM), **fricasé** (SM) fricassee

fricativa (SF) fricative

fricativo (ADJ) fricative

fricción (SF) **1** (= *frotamiento*) rub, rubbing; (*Med*) massage
2 (*Mec*) friction
3 (*Pol*) (= *enfrentamiento*) friction, trouble

friccionar ▹ CONJUG 1a (VT) (= *frotar*) to rub; (*Med*) to rub, massage

friega (SF) **1** (*gen*) rub, rubbing; (*Med*) massage; (*Dep*) rub-down
2 (*LAm**) (= *molestia*) nuisance; (= *problema*) bother; (= *lío*) fuss
3 (*And, Cono Sur**) (= *zurra*) thrashing
4 (*LAm**) (= *idiotez*) silliness, stupidity
5 (*And, Méx**) (= *reprimenda*) ticking-off*

friegaplatos (SM INV) (= *aparato*) dishwasher
(SMF INV) (= *persona*) dishwasher, washer-up

friegasuelos (SM INV) floor mop

frígano (SM) caddis fly

frigidaire† (SM) (*LAm*) refrigerator

frigidez (SF) frigidity

frígido (ADJ) frigid

frigo* (SM) (*Esp*) fridge, icebox (*EEUU*)

frigorífico (ADJ) • **camión ~** refrigerator lorry, refrigerator truck (*EEUU*) • **instalación frigorífica** cold-storage plant
(SM) **1** (= *nevera*) refrigerator, fridge, icebox (*EEUU*)
2 (= *camión*) refrigerator lorry, refrigerator truck (*EEUU*); (*para congelados*) freezer lorry *o* (*EEUU*) truck; (*Náut*) refrigerator ship
3 (*Cono Sur*) cold-storage plant, meat-packing depot

frigorífico-congelador (SM) (PL: **frigoríficos-congeladores**) fridge-freezer

frigorista (SMF) refrigeration engineer

fríjol (SM), **frijol** (SM) **1** (*esp LAm*) (*Bot*) (= *judía*) bean ▸ **frijol colorado** kidney bean ▸ **frijol de café** coffee bean ▸ **frijol de soja** soya bean
2 frijoles (*LAm**) (= *comida*) food (*sing*)
• MODISMO: • **buscarse los frijoles** (*Cuba**) to earn a crust*, earn a living
3 • MODISMOS: • **¡frijoles!** (*Caribe*) certainly not!, not on your life! • **echar frijoles** (*Méx*) to blow one's own trumpet • **ser como los frijoles que al primer hervor se arrugan** (*And, Méx*) to run at the first sign of trouble

4 (*Méx*) (= *mofa*) taunt

5 (*And, Méx*) (= *cobarde*) coward

frikada‡ SF weird thing to do • **¡menuda ~!** that's a really weird thing to do!

friki‡ SMF weirdo**

fringolear ▸ CONJUG 1a VT (*Cono Sur*) to thrash, beat

frío ADJ **1** (*en temperatura*) [*agua, aire, invierno, refresco, sopa*] cold • **el agua está muy fría** the water is very cold • **una cervecita bien fría** an ice cold beer • **el café se ha quedado ~** the coffee has got cold • **un sudor ~** a cold sweat • **tienes las manos frías** your hands are cold, you've got cold hands • **me quedé ~** I got cold • MODISMO: • **~ como el mármol** as cold as ice

2 (*en sentimientos, actitudes*) **a** [*relaciones, acogida, recibimiento*] cool • **su familia se mostró muy fría con él** his family were very cool towards him

b (= *desapasionado*) cool • **la mirada fría y penetrante del fotógrafo** the cool, penetrating eye of the photographer • **mantener la cabeza fría** to keep a cool head, keep one's cool

c (= *insensible, inexpresivo*) cold • **era ~ y calculador** he was cold and calculating • **los ingleses tienen fama de ser muy ~s** the English have a reputation for being cold • **este público es más ~ que el de otras ciudades** this audience is less responsive than those in other cities • **esos asesinos se comportan de forma fría y profesional** they are cold-blooded, professional killers

d • MODISMOS: • **dejar ~ a algn** (= *indiferente*) to leave sb cold • **todo lo que me digas me deja ~** everything you say just leaves me cold • **aquellas revelaciones me dejaron ~** I was stunned by those revelations • **quedarse ~** (= *indiferente*) to be unmoved; (= *pasmado*) to be stunned

3 [*bala*] spent

SM **1** (= *baja temperatura*) cold • **pese al ~ reinante** despite the cold • **la ola de ~ que azota el país** the cold spell which has gripped the country • **ya han llegado los ~s** the cold weather is here • **una planta resistente al ~** a hardy plant • **laminado en ~** cold-rolled • **hace (mucho) ~** it's (very) cold • **¡qué ~ hace!** it's freezing!, it's so cold! ▸ **frío industrial** industrial refrigeration ▸ **frío polar** arctic weather, arctic conditions (*pl*)

2 (= *sensación*) cold • **tiritaba de ~** she was shivering with cold • **me entró ~ viendo el partido de fútbol** I got cold at the football match • **coger ~** to catch cold • **pasar ~** to be cold • **tener ~** to be cold, feel cold

3 • **en ~ a** (= *en calma*) • **ambas partes tendrán que pactar un acuerdo en ~** the two sides will have to negotiate an agreement with cool heads • **cuando se contemplan las cifras totales en ~** when one calmly *o* coolly considers the total numbers

b (= *repentinamente*) • **me lo dijo en ~ y no supe cómo reaccionar** he sprang it on me out of the blue *o* he told me just like that and I didn't know quite what to say • MODISMO: • **no dar ni ~ ni calor a algn**: • **el hecho de que no me hayan seleccionado no me da ni ~ ni calor** I'm not at all bothered about not being selected • **sus comentarios sobre mí no me dan ni ~ ni calor** his comments about me don't bother me one way or the other, I'm not at all bothered about *o* by his comments

4 fríos (*And, CAm, Méx*) (= *fiebre*) intermittent fever (*sing*); (= *paludismo*) malaria (*sing*)

friolento ADJ (*LAm*) sensitive to cold

friolera SF trifle, mere nothing • **gastó la ~ de 1.000 euros** he spent a mere 1,000 euros

friolero ADJ sensitive to cold

friorizado ADJ deep-frozen

frisa SF **1** (= *tela*) frieze

2 (*And, Cono Sur*) (= *pelo*) nap (*on cloth*); (*Cono Sur*) (= *pelusa*) fluff; (*Caribe*) (= *manta*) blanket • MODISMOS: • **sacar a algn la ~** (*Cono Sur**) to tan sb's hide* • **sacar la ~ a algo** (*Cono Sur**) to make the most of sth

frisar ▸ CONJUG 1a VT [+ *tela*] to frizz, rub

VI • **~ en** to border on, be *o* come close to • **frisa en los 50** he's getting on for 50

Frisia SF Friesland

friso SM frieze

fritada SF fry, fry-up*

fritanga SF **1** (= *comida frita*) fry, fry-up*; (*pey*) greasy food

2 (*And, CAm*) (= *guiso*) ≈ hotpot, ≈ stew

3 (*CAm*) (= *restaurante*) cheap restaurant

4 (*Cono Sur**) (= *molestia*) pain in the neck*, nuisance

fritanguería SF (*Chile, Perú*) (= *tienda*) fried food shop; (= *puesto*) fried food stall

fritar ▸ CONJUG 1a VT (*LAm*) to fry

frito PP *de* **freír**

ADJ **1** (*gen*) fried • **patatas** *o* (*LAm*) **papas fritas** chips, French fries (*EEUU*)

2 • MODISMOS: • **dejar ~ a algn*** (= *matar*) to do sb in*, waste sb* • **estar ~*** (= *dormido*) to be kipping*, be out for the count*; (= *muerto*) to have snuffed it‡; (= *excitado*) to be really worked up; (*Caribe, Cono Sur*) (= *acabado*) to be finished, be done for* • **quedarse ~*** (= *dormirse*) to go out like a light; (= *morir*) to snuff it‡ • **tener** *o* **traer ~ a algn*** (= *enojar*) to get on sb's nerves; (= *acosar*) to worry sb to death; (= *vencer*) to trounce sb, wipe the floor with sb* • **este trabajo me tiene ~** I'm fed up with this job • **ese hombre me trae ~** I've totally had it with this guy* • **las matemáticas me traen ~** I've totally had it with maths*, I'm totally fed up with maths

3 [*pelo*] frizzy

SM **1** (= *plato*) fry, fried dish ▸ **fritos variados** mixed grill

2 • MODISMO: • **gustarle el ~ a algn** (*Cono Sur‡*): • **a esa mujer le gusta el ~** she looks like hot stuff*

3 (*en disco*) hiss, crackling

fritura SF **1** (= *plato*) fried food, fry • **~ de pescado** fried fish • **~ variada** mixed fry

2 (= *buñuelo*) fritter

3 (*Telec*) crackling, interference

frívolamente ADV frivolously

frivolidad SF frivolity, frivolousness

frivolité SM (*Cos*) tatting

frivolizar ▸ CONJUG 1f VT (= *trivializar*) to trivialize; (= *quitar importancia a*) to play down

frívolo ADJ frivolous

frivolón ADJ superficial, lightweight

frízer SM (*Cono Sur*) freezer

fronda SF **1** (= *hoja*) frond

2 frondas (= *follaje*) foliage (*sing*), leaves

frondís ADJ (*And*) dirty

frondosidad SF leafiness, luxuriance

frondoso ADJ leafy, luxuriant

frontal ADJ **1** [*parte, posición*] front; (*Inform*) front-end • **choque ~** head-on collision

2 [*enfrentamiento*] direct, frontal; [*rechazo*] outright

SM front, front part

frontalmente ADV directly • **chocar ~** to crash *o* collide head-on, have a head-on crash *o* collision • **está situado ~** it is placed on the front • **se oponen ~** they are directly opposed

frontera SF **1** (= *línea divisoria*) frontier, border; (= *zona fronteriza*) frontier zone, borderland

2 (*Arquit*) façade

fronterizo ADJ frontier (*antes de s*), border (*antes de s*) • **el río ~ con Eslobodia** the river bordering Slobodia *o* forming the border with Slobodia

frontero ADJ opposite, facing

frontis SM INV (*Arquit*) façade

frontispicio SM **1** [*de libro*] frontispiece; (*Arquit*) façade

2* (= *cara*) face

frontón SM **1** (*Arquit*) pediment

2 (*Dep*) (= *cancha*) pelota court; (= *pared*) (main) wall (*of a pelota court*)

frotación SF, **frotadura** SF, **frotamiento** SM rub, rubbing; (*Mec*) friction

frotado SM rubbing

frotar ▸ CONJUG 1a VT to rub; [+ *fósforo*] to strike • **quitar algo frotando** to rub sth off

VPR **frotarse** to rub, chafe • **~se las manos** to rub one's hands (together) • **frotársela**** to have a wank**, jerk off (*EEUU***)

frote SM (= *acción*) rub

frotis SM INV ▸ **frotis cervical** cervical smear, smear test, Pap smear ▸ **frotis vaginal** vaginal smear

fructíferamente ADV productively

fructífero ADJ fruitful, productive

fructificación SF fruition

fructificar ▸ CONJUG 1g VI **1** (*Bot*) to produce fruit, bear fruit

2 [*esfuerzos*] to bear fruit; [*plan*] to come to fruition

fructosa SF fructose

fructuosamente ADV fruitfully

fructuoso ADJ fruitful

frufrú SM rustling, rustle

frugal ADJ frugal, thrifty

frugalidad SF frugality

frugalmente ADV frugally (*frm*), thriftily

fruición SF delight • **leer con ~** to read with delight • **beber con ~** to drink with relish • **comer con ~** to eat with relish ▸ **fruición maliciosa** perverse pleasure *o* delight

frunce SM (*Cos*) gather, shirr

fruncido ADJ **1** (*Cos*) [*tela*] gathered

2 (*Cono Sur**) (= *remilgado*) prudish, demure; (= *afectado*) affected

SM = **frunce**

fruncimiento SM = **frunce**

fruncir ▸ CONJUG 3b VT **1** (*Cos*) to gather, shirr

2 [+ *labios*] to purse • **~ el ceño** *o* **entrecejo** to frown, knit one's brow • **~ las cejas** to frown

fruslería SF (= *chuchería*) trinket; (= *nimiedad*) trifle, triviality

frustración SF frustration

frustrado ADJ [*persona*] frustrated; [*intento, plan, atentado*] failed • **delito de homicidio ~** attempted murder • **intento de suicidio ~** failed suicide attempt

frustrante ADJ frustrating

frustrar ▸ CONJUG 1a VT **1** [+ *persona*] to frustrate; [+ *proyecto, aspiración, deseo, sueño*] to thwart • **no quiero ~ sus esperanzas** I don't want to frustrate *o* thwart their hopes • **le frustra no poderse comunicar** he finds it frustrating not being able to communicate

2 (= *abortar*) [+ *atentado, operación*] to foil • **los guardas ~on el intento de fuga** the guards foiled their escape attempt

VPR **frustrarse** [*persona*] to be frustrated; [*aspiración, deseo*] to be thwarted; [*proyecto*] to be thwarted, fall through • **se frustró enormemente por no poder acabar la carrera** he was terribly frustrated at not being able to finish his studies • **nuestros sueños se ~on** our dreams were dashed *o* shattered

frustre* SM = **frustración**

fruta SF fruit ▸ **fruta abrillantada** (*Arg, Uru*) glacé fruit ▸ **fruta de estación** (*Arg, Uru*) seasonal fruit ▸ **fruta de la pasión** passion fruit ▸ **fruta del tiempo** seasonal fruit

▸ **fruta de sartén** fritter ▸ **fruta escarchada** crystallized fruit ▸ **fruta prohibida** forbidden fruit ▸ **frutas confitadas** candied fruits ▸ **frutas del bosque** fruits of the forest, forest fruits ▸ **fruta(s) seca(s)** (*LAm*) nuts and dried fruit

frutal ADJ fruit-bearing, fruit (*antes de s*) • **árbol ~** fruit tree
SM fruit tree

frutar ▹ CONJUG 1a VI to fruit, bear fruit

frutera SF fruit dish, fruit bowl

frutería SF fruiterer's (shop), fruit shop, greengrocer's

frutero/a ADJ fruit (*antes de s*) • **plato ~** fruit dish
SM/F (= *persona*) fruiterer, greengrocer, grocer (*EEUU*)
SM (= *recipiente*) fruit dish, fruit bowl; (= *cesta*) fruit basket

fruticultor(a) SM/F fruit farmer, fruit grower

fruticultura SF fruit growing, fruit farming

frutilla SF (*And, Cono Sur*) strawberry

fruto SM **1** (*Bot*) fruit • **dar ~** to fruit, bear fruit ▸ **fruto del pan** breadfruit ▸ **frutos del país** (*LAm*) agricultural produce ▸ **frutos secos** nuts and dried fruit
2 (= *resultado*) result, product; (= *beneficio*) profit, benefit; [*de esfuerzo*] fruits (*pl*) • **dar ~** to bear fruit • **sacar ~ de algo** to profit from sth, derive benefit from sth
3 (= *hijo*) offspring • **el ~ de esta unión** the offspring of this marriage, the fruit *o* product of this union (*liter*) ▸ **fruto de bendición** legitimate offspring

frutosidad SF fruitiness, fruity flavour *o* (*EEUU*) flavor

FSE SM ABR (= **Fondo Social Europeo**) ESF

FSLN SM ABR (*Nic*) = **Frente Sandinista de Liberación Nacional**

FSM SF ABR (= **Federación Sindical Mundial**) WFTU

fu SM [*de gato*] spit, hiss • MODISMO: • **ni fu ni fa** (= *ni una cosa ni otra*) neither one thing or the other; (= *ni bonito ni feo*) so-so
EXCL ugh!

fuácata* SF (*Cuba, Méx*) • MODISMO: • **estar en la ~** to be broke*

fucha EXCL (*Méx*), **fuchi** EXCL (*Méx*) (*asco*) yuk!, ugh!; (*sorpresa*) phew!, wow!

fucilazo SM (flash of) sheet lightning

fuco SM (*Bot*) wrack

fucsia SF fuchsia

fudiño ADJ (*Caribe*) weak, sickly

fudre‡ SM drunk

fue ▹ ser, ir

fuego SM **1** (= *llamas*) fire • **buscamos un claro donde hacer ~** we looked for a clearing to make a fire in • **el ~ se declaró en el interior del almacén** the fire broke out inside the warehouse • **¡fuego!** fire! • **apagar el ~** to put out the fire • **atizar el ~** (*lit*) to poke the fire; (*fig*) to stir things up • **encender el ~** to light the fire • **marcar algo a ~** to brand sth • **pegar** *o* **prender ~ a algo** to set fire to sth, set sth on fire • **prendieron ~ a los vehículos** they set fire to the vehicles, they set the vehicles alight *o* on fire • **prender el ~** (*LAm*) to light the fire • **sofocar el ~** to extinguish the fire • MODISMOS: • **echar ~ por los ojos**: • **se marchó echando ~ por los ojos** he went off, his eyes blazing • **jugar con ~** to play with fire ▸ **fuego de artificio** firework • **el procedimiento ha sido solo un ~ de artificio destinado a calmar a la opinión pública** the proceedings have been mere window dressing aimed at appeasing public opinion • **ha llegado a la cima sin los ~s de artificio típicos de muchas grandes estrellas** she has got to the top without the typical blaze of publicity attached to many big stars ▸ **fuego fatuo** will-o'-the-wisp ▸ **fuegos artificiales** fireworks
2 [*de cocina*] **a** (= *quemador*) (*de gas*) burner, ring; (*eléctrico*) ring • **una cocina de gas de cuatro ~s** a four-ring gas cooker
b (= *calor*) heat, flame • **a ~ lento** on *o* over a low heat, on *o* over a low flame • **se mete en el horno a ~ lento** put in a low *o* slow oven • **se deja cocer a ~ lento 15 minutos** simmer for 15 minutes, cook on *o* over a low heat for 15 minutes • **a ~ suave** on *o* over a low heat, on *o* over a low flame • **a ~ vivo** on *o* over a high flame, on *o* over a high heat
3 (*para cigarro*) light • **¿tienes** *o* **me das ~?** have you got a light? • **le pedí ~** I asked him for a light
4 (*Mil*) fire • **¡fuego!** fire! • **abrir ~ (contra algo/algn)** to open fire (on sth/sb) • **¡alto el ~!** cease fire! • **hacer ~ (contra** *o* **sobre algo)** to fire (at sth) • **romper el ~** to open fire • MODISMO: • **estar entre dos ~s** to be caught in the crossfire ▸ **fuego a discreción** (*lit*) fire at will; (*fig*) all-out attack ▸ **fuego amigo** friendly fire ▸ **fuego artillero** artillery fire ▸ **fuego cruzado** crossfire ▸ **fuego de andanada** (*Náut*) broadside ▸ **fuego de artillería** artillery fire ▸ **fuego de mortero** mortar fire ▸ **fuego graneado**, **fuego nutrido** sustained fire ▸ **fuego real** live ammunition; ▹ **alto²**
5 (= *pasión*) passion, fire • **apagar los ~s de algn** to dampen sb's ardour *o* (*EEUU*) ardor
6 (*Náut*) beacon, signal fire
7 (*Med*) (= *erupción*) rash; (*Méx, Chile, Col*) (*en los labios*) cold sore ▸ **fuego pérsico** shingles (*pl*)
8 (= *hogar*) dwelling • **un pueblo de 50 ~s** a village of 50 dwellings

fueguear ▹ CONJUG 1a VT (*CAm*) to set fire to

fueguino/a (*Cono Sur*) ADJ of/from Tierra del Fuego
SM/F native/inhabitant of Tierra del Fuego • **los ~s** the people of Tierra del Fuego

fuel SM fuel oil

fuelle SM **1** (*para el fuego*) bellows (*pl*); [*de gaita*] bag; [*de bolso, maleta*] gusset; [*de autobús, tren*] *connecting section* • MODISMO: • **tener el ~ flojo‡** to fart‡ ▸ **fuelle de pie** foot pump
2 (*Aut*) folding top, folding hood (*EEUU*)
3 (*Fot*) bellows (*pl*) ▸ **fuelle quitasol** hood
4 (= *pulmones*) puff*, breath
5 (= *aguante*) stamina, staying power • **tener ~** to have the stamina, have the staying power • MODISMO: • **perder ~** to run out of steam
6* (= *soplón*) grass*

fuel-oil [fuel'oil] SM fuel oil

fuelóleo SM = **fuel**

fuente SF **1** (= *construcción*) fountain; (= *manantial*) spring • MODISMO: • **abrir la ~ de las lágrimas** (*hum*) to open the floodgates* ▸ **fuente de beber** drinking fountain ▸ **fuente de río** source of a river ▸ **fuente de soda** (*LAm*) *café selling ice-cream and soft drinks*, soda fountain (*EEUU*) ▸ **fuente termal** hot spring
2 (*Culin*) serving dish, platter ▸ **fuente de hornear**, **fuente de horno** ovenproof dish
3 (= *origen*) source, origin • **de ~ desconocida/fidedigna** from an unknown/a reliable source ▸ **fuente de alimentación** (*Inform*) power supply ▸ **fuente de ingresos** source of income ▸ **fuente de suministro** source of supply

fuer SM • **a ~ de** (*liter*) as a • **a ~ de caballero** as a gentleman • **a ~ de hombre honrado** as an honest man

fuera ADV **1** (*de edificio, objeto*) (*indicando posición*) outside; (*indicando dirección*) out • **los niños estaban jugando ~** the children were playing outside • **¡estamos aquí ~!** we're out here! • **el perro tenía la lengua ~** the dog had his tongue hanging out • **llevaba la camisa ~** his shirt was hanging out • **¡fuera!** get out! • **¡segundos ~!** (*Boxeo*) seconds out! • **ir** *o* **salir ~** to go out, go outside • **comer ~** (*al aire libre*) to eat outside; (*en restaurante*) to eat out • **hoy vamos a cenar ~** we're going out for dinner tonight, we're eating out tonight • **de ~** from outside • **trae una silla de ~** bring a chair in from outside • **productos que vienen de ~ de la Unión Europea** products from outside the European Union • **tenemos que traer a alguien de ~** we need to bring somebody from outside in • **desde ~** from outside • **la parte de ~** the outside, the outer part • **por ~** (on the) outside • **lo han pintado solo por ~** they've only painted it on the outside • **por ~ está duro** it's hard on the outside • **esta camisa se lleva por ~** this shirt is worn outside, this shirt is not tucked in; ▹ **lengua**
2 (*de ciudad, trabajo*) • **estar ~** to be away, be out of town • **estuvo ~ ocho semanas** he was away for eight weeks • **mis padres llevan varios días ~** my parents have been away for several days
3 (*tb* **fuera del país**) abroad, out of the country • **toda la maquinaria viene de ~** all the machinery comes from abroad • **vienen visitantes de ~ para verlo** people come from abroad to see it • **"¡invasores ~!"** "invaders go home!" • **estar ~** to be abroad • **ir** *o* **salir ~** to go abroad
4 (*Dep*) **a** (*en un partido*) • **estar ~** [*pelota*] (*Ftbl*) to be out of play; (*Rugby*) to be in touch; (*Tenis*) to be out • **~ de juego** offside • **~ de tiempo**: • **estamos ~ de tiempo** time's up • **tirar ~** to shoot wide
b (*tb* **fuera de casa**) away, away from home • **el equipo de ~** the away team • **una victoria ~ de casa** an away win • **jugar ~** to play away (from home)
5 • **~ de a** (= *en el exterior de*) outside, out of • **estaba ~ de su jaula** it was outside *o* out of its cage • **esperamos ~ de la puerta** we waited outside the door
b (= *aparte*) apart from, aside from • **pero ~ de eso** but apart *o* aside from that • **~ de que ...** apart from the fact that ...
c • **~ de alcance** out of reach • **~ de combate** (*Mil*) wounded; (*Boxeo*) K.O.ed • **dejar a algn ~ de combate** to knock sb out • **quedar ~ de combate** to be knocked out • **~ de lo común** unusual • **estar ~ de lugar** to be inappropriate, be out of place • **~ de peligro** out of danger • **~ de serie** exceptional • **se ha comprado un coche ~ de serie** he has bought an exceptional car • **es un ~ de serie** he's quite exceptional • MODISMO: • **estar ~ de sí** to be beside o.s.

fueraborda SM INV, **fuera-borda** SM INV, **fuerabordo** SM INV (= *motor*) outboard engine, outboard motor; (= *bote*) dinghy with an outboard engine

fuereño/a SM/F (*Méx*) outsider; (*pey*) rustic, provincial

fuerino/a SM/F (*Cono Sur*) stranger, non-resident

fuero SM **1** (= *carta municipal*) municipal charter; (= *ley local*) local/regional law code; (= *privilegio*) (*tb* **fueros**) privilege, exemption • **a ~** according to law • **¿con qué ~?** by what right? • **de ~** de jure, in law
2 (= *autoridad*) jurisdiction • **el ~ no alcanza a tanto** his authority does not extend that far • MODISMOS: • **en mi ~ interno ...** in my

heart of hearts ..., deep down ... • **volver por sus ~s** (= *recuperarse*) to be oneself again; (= *reincidir*) to go back to one's old ways

FUEROS

Fueros were the charters granted to villages, towns and regions by Spanish monarchs in the Middle Ages and which established their rights and obligations. The **fueros** under which the Basques and Navarrese received certain privileges (some fiscal autonomy, their own local administration system and exemption from military service outside their province) became a political football in the 19th Century, being alternately abolished and restored depending on the interests of the monarch or administration in power. Today, Navarre is recognized in the **Estado de las Autonomías** as the **Comunidad Foral de Navarra**.

fuerte ADJ **1** [*persona*] **a** (*físicamente*) (*gen*) strong; (= *robusto*) sturdy, powerfully built; (*euf*) (= *obeso*) large • MODISMO: • **~ como un roble** *o* **un toro** as strong as an ox *o* a horse
b (*emocionalmente*) strong, tough • **hemos de ser ~s ante la adversidad** we must be strong *o* tough in the face of adversity
c • **estar ~ en filosofía/historia** [*estudiante*] to be strong in philosophy/history
2 (= *intenso*) **a** [*sabor, olor, viento*] strong; [*dolor, calor*] intense; [*lluvia*] heavy; [*ejercicio*] strenuous
b [*explosión, voz, ruido*] loud; [*golpe*] heavy, hard; [*acento*] strong, thick
c [*color*] (= *no pálido*) strong; (= *llamativo*) bright • **una blusa de un rosa ~** a bright pink blouse
d [*impresión*] strong, powerful; [*deseo*] strong, deep; [*fe, objeción*] strong; [*discusión*] heated • **los vecinos tuvieron una discusión muy ~** the neighbours had a heated argument • **en la película se oyen expresiones muy ~s** the film contains strong language • **el taco más ~ que ha pronunciado** the worst swearword he has ever said
e [*abrazo, beso*] big • **un beso muy ~** (*en cartas*) lots of love • **un ~ abrazo, Carmen** best wishes, Carmen; (*más cariñoso*) love, Carmen
3 [*bebida, medicamento*] strong; [*comida*] (= *pesada*) heavy; (= *indigesta*) indigestible • **nunca toma cosas ~s, solo cerveza y vino** he never drinks spirits *o* the hard stuff*, just beer and wine
4 (= *resistente*) [*cuerda, tela*] strong; [*economía, moneda, país*] strong
5 (= *importante*) [*aumento, bajada*] sharp; [*crisis*] serious, severe; [*pérdidas*] large, substantial • **la ~ caída de ventas** the sharp drop in sales
6 (= *impactante*) [*escena*] shocking, disturbing • **me dijo cosas muy ~s que no podría repetir ahora** she said some harsh *o* nasty* things that I couldn't repeat now • **—lo llamó a la oficina y lo despidió en el acto —¡qué ~!*** "he called him at the office and fired him there and then" — "that's outrageous *o* appalling!"
7 • **hacerse ~** (= *protegerse*) to hole up; (= *volverse fuerte*) to gain strength • **un comando se hizo ~ en las montañas** a group of commandos holed up in the mountains • **el fundamentalismo se hace ~ otra vez** fundamentalism is gaining strength again
8 [*terreno*] rough, difficult
9 (*Chile*) (= *apestoso*) [*persona*] stinky • **ser** *o* **estar ~ a algo** to stink of sth
ADV **1** (= *con fuerza*) [*golpear*] hard; [*abrazar*] tight, tightly • **pegar ~ al enemigo** to hit the enemy hard • **apostar ~** to bet heavily • **la editorial ha apostado ~ por los nuevos poetas** the publishing house is backing new poets in a big way • **jugar ~** (*lit*) to gamble heavily; (*fig*) to take a gamble
2 (= *en voz alta*) [*hablar, tocar*] loud, loudly • **toca muy ~** she plays very loud *o* loudly • **¡más ~! ¡que no se le oye aquí atrás!** speak up! we can't hear at the back • **poner la radio más ~** to turn the radio up
3 (= *gran cantidad*) • **desayunar ~** to have a big breakfast • **comer ~** to have a big lunch
SM **1** (*Mil*) fort
2 (*Mús*) forte
3 (= *especialidad*) forte, strong point • **el canto no es mi ~** singing is not my forte *o* strong point
4 (*Chile*) (= *bebida*) hard liquor, hard stuff*

fuertemente ADV **1** (= *con fuerza*) [*golpear*] hard; [*abrazar, apretar*] tightly
2 (= *mucho*) [*apoyar, favorecer, contrastar*] strongly; [*aumentar, disminuir*] sharply, greatly • **la medida ha sido ~ criticada por los sindicatos** the measure has been strongly criticized by the unions • **hemos conseguido reducir ~ los costes** we have managed to reduce costs greatly
3 (+ *adj*) • **un acto ~ emotivo** a highly emotional ceremony • **grupos ~ armados** heavily armed groups • **divisas ~ vinculadas al dólar** currencies closely tied to the dollar

fuerza SF **1** [*de persona*] **a** (*física*) strength • **tienes mucha ~** you're very strong • **con ~** [*golpear*] hard; [*abrazar, agarrar, apretar*] tightly, tight; [*aplaudir*] loudly • **le golpeó con toda su ~ en la cabeza** she hit him on the head as hard as she could • **me agarré con ~ a una roca** I held on tight *o* tightly to a rock • **grita con todas tus ~s** shout with all your might • **hacer ~**: • **el médico me ha prohibido que hiciera ~** the doctor has told me not to exert myself • **vamos a intentar levantar la losa: haced ~** let's try and lift up the slab: heave! • **si somos muchos en la manifestación haremos más ~** if there are lots of us at the demonstration we'll be stronger *o* it will lend more force to it • **hacer ~ de vela** to crowd on sail
b [*de carácter*] strength • **con toda la ~ de su amor** with all the strength of his love • **la ~ creadora de Picasso** Picasso's creative energy • **restar ~s al enemigo** to reduce the enemy's strength • **sentirse con ~s para hacer algo** to have the strength to do sth • **no me siento con ~s para seguir adelante** I don't have the strength to go on • **lo haré cuando me sienta con ~s para ello** I'll do it when I feel strong enough *o* up to it* • **tener ~s para hacer algo** to be strong enough to do sth, have the strength to do sth • MODISMOS: • **se le va la ~ por la boca*** he's all talk and no action, he's all mouth* • **sacar ~s de flaqueza** to make a supreme effort, gather all one's strength ▸ **fuerza de voluntad** willpower; ▹ **medir**
2 (= *intensidad*) [*de viento*] strength, force; [*de lluvia*] intensity • **el viento empezó a soplar con ~** the wind began to blow strongly • **un viento de ~ seis** a force six wind • **a los pocos minutos rompió a llover con ~** a few minutes later it began to rain heavily • **el agua caía con ~ torrencial** the rain came down in torrents, there was torrential rainfall • **el terremoto ha golpeado con ~ el país** the earthquake has struck the country violently
3 (= *ímpetu*) • **en los setenta la mujer entró con ~ en el periodismo** in the seventies women entered journalism in force • **su nombre ha irrumpido con ~ en el mundo artístico** his name has burst onto the art scene • **la ultraderecha renace con ~** the extreme right is making a strong comeback • **la banda terrorista volvió a golpear con ~ ayer** the terrorist group struck another devastating blow yesterday
4 (= *poder*) [*de fe*] strength; [*de argumento*] strength, force, power; [*de la ley*] force • **es un argumento de poca ~** it is not a very strong *o* powerful argument • **les asistía la ~ de la razón** they were helped by the power of reason • **serán castigados con toda la ~ de la ley** they will be punished with the full weight of the law, they will feel the full force of the law • **conquistaron la región por la ~ de las armas** they took the region by force of arms • **cobrar ~** [*rumores*] to grow stronger, gain strength • **la rebelión iba cobrando ~** the rebellion gathered *o* gained strength • **la idea ha cobrado ~ últimamente** the idea has gained in popularity *o* gained momentum recently • **por la ~ de la costumbre** out of habit, from force of habit • **es la ~ de la costumbre** it's force of habit • **con ~ legal** (*Com*) legally binding ▸ **fuerza mayor** (*Jur*) force majeure • **un caso de ~ mayor** a case of force majeure • **aplazaron el partido por razones de ~ mayor** the match was postponed due to circumstances beyond their control
5 (= *violencia*) force • **recurrir a la ~** to resort to force • **por la ~**: • **quisieron impedirlo por la ~** they tried to prevent it forcibly *o* by force • **tuvieron que separarlos por la ~** they had to separate them by force • **por la ~ no se consigue nada** using force doesn't achieve anything, nothing is achieved by force • **imponer algo por la ~** to impose sth forcibly • **a viva ~**: • **abrió la maleta a viva ~** he forced open the suitcase • **lo arrancaron de allí a viva ~** they wrenched him away forcibly ▸ **fuerza bruta** brute force
6 (*locuciones*) **a** • **a ~ de** by • **a ~ de repetirlo acabó creyéndoselo él mismo** by repeating it so much he ended up believing it himself • **a ~ de autodisciplina** by exercising great self control • **bajar kilos a ~ de pedaleo** to lose weight by cycling • **conseguí aprobar a ~ de pasarme horas y horas estudiando** I managed to pass by dint of hours and hours of study • **a ~ de paciencia logró convencerlos** he succeeded in persuading them by dint of great patience
b • **a la ~**: • **hacer algo a la ~** to be forced to do sth • **yo no quería, pero tuve que hacerlo a la ~** I didn't want to, but I was forced to do it • **se lo llevaron de su casa a la ~** he was taken from his home by force, he was taken forcibly from his home • **fueron repatriados a la ~** they were forcibly repatriated • **a la ~ tuvo que oírlos: ¡estaba a su lado!** he must have heard them: he was right next to them! • **alimentar a algn a la ~** to force-feed sb • **entrar en un lugar a la ~** [*ladrón*] to break into a place, break in; [*policía, bombero*] to force one's way into a place, enter a place forcibly • MODISMO: • **a la ~ ahorcan**: • **dejará el ministerio cuando lo haga su jefe, ¡a la ~ ahorcan!** he'll leave the ministry when his boss does, not that he has any choice anyway *o* life's tough!*
c • **en ~ de** by virtue of
d • **es ~ hacer algo** it is necessary to do sth • **es ~ reconocer que ...** we must recognize that ..., it must be admitted that ...
e • **por ~** inevitably • **una región pobre como la nuestra, por ~ ha de ser más barata** in a poor region like ours prices will inevitably be *o* must be cheaper
7 (*Fís, Mec*) force ▸ **fuerza ascensional** (*Aer*) buoyancy ▸ **fuerza centrífuga** centrifugal force ▸ **fuerza centrípeta** centripetal force

▸ **fuerza de arrastre** pulling power ▸ **fuerza de (la) gravedad** force of gravity ▸ **fuerza de sustentación** (*Aer*) lift ▸ **fuerza hidráulica** hydraulic power ▸ **fuerza motriz** (*lit*) motive force; (*fig*) driving force
8 (= *conjunto de personas*) (*Mil, Pol*) force
▸ **fuerza(s) aérea(s)** air force (*sing*) ▸ **fuerza de apoyo** back-up force ▸ **fuerza de brazos** manpower ▸ **fuerza de choque** strike force ▸ **fuerza de disuasión** deterrent ▸ **fuerza de intervención rápida** rapid intervention force ▸ **fuerza de pacificación** peace-keeping force ▸ **fuerza de trabajo** workforce, labour force, labor force (*EEUU*) ▸ **fuerza de ventas** sales force ▸ **fuerza disuasoria** deterrent ▸ **fuerza expedicionaria** expeditionary force ▸ **fuerza política** political force ▸ **fuerza pública** police, police force ▸ **fuerzas aliadas** allied forces ▸ **fuerzas armadas** armed forces ▸ **fuerzas del orden (público)** forces of law and order ▸ **fuerzas de seguridad** security forces ▸ **fuerzas de tierra** land forces ▸ **las fuerzas vivas** the powers that be • **las ~s vivas locales** the local power group
9 (*Elec*) power • **han cortado la ~** they've cut off the power

fuese ▷ ser, ir

fuetazo SM (*LAm*) lash

fuete (*LAm*) SM whip • **dar ~ a** to whip

fuetear ▷ CONJUG 1a VT (*LAm*) to whip

fuga[1] SF **1** (*gen*) flight, escape; [*de enamorados*] elopement • **darse a la** *o* **ponerse en ~** to flee, take flight • **poner al enemigo en ~** to put the enemy to flight • **le aplicaron la ley de ~(s)** he was shot while trying to escape ▸ **fuga de capitales** flight of capital (abroad) ▸ **fuga de cerebros** brain drain ▸ **fuga de(l) domicilio** running away from home ▸ **fuga de la cárcel** escape from prison, jailbreak
2 [*de gas*] leak, escape
3 (= *ardor*) ardour, ardor (*EEUU*), impetuosity

fuga[2] SF (*Mús*) fugue

fugacidad SF fleetingness, transitory nature

fugado/a SM/F escapee

fugarse ▷ CONJUG 1h VPR [*preso*] to escape; [*niño, adolescente*] to run away; [*enamorados*] to elope • **se fugó de casa** he ran away from home • **~ de la ley** to abscond from justice

fugaz ADJ **1** [*momento*] fleeting, brief
2 • **estrella ~** shooting star
3 (= *esquivo*) elusive

fugazmente ADV fleetingly, briefly

fugitivo/a ADJ **1** fugitive, fleeing
2 = **fugaz**
SM/F fugitive

fuguista SMF escaper, jailbreaker

fui, fuimos *etc* ▷ **ser, ir**

fuina SF marten

ful[1] (*And*) ADJ full, full up
SM • **marchar a todo ful** to work at full capacity

ful[2]‡ ADJ = **fulastre**

ful[3]‡ SF (= *droga*) hash*

fulana‡ SF (*pey*) tart‡, slut‡; ▷ **fulano**

fulaneo* SM whoring

fulano* SM **1** (= *alguien*) so-and-so • **~ de tal** • **Don Fulano** Mr So-and-so, Joe Bloggs, John Doe (*EEUU*) • **Doña Fulana** Mrs So-and-so • **~, zutano y mengano** Tom, Dick and Harry • **me lo dijo ~** somebody or other told me • **no te vas a casar con un ~** you're not going to marry just anybody • **nombramos a ~ y ya está** we nominate some guy and that's that*
2 (= *tío*) guy*; ▷ **fulana**

fular SM = **foulard**

fulastre‡ ADJ (= *falso*) false, sham; (= *malo*) bad, rotten*

fulbito SM five-a-side football

fulcro SM fulcrum

fulero/a ADJ **1** [*objeto*] (= *inútil*) useless; (= *malo*) shoddy, cheap, poor-quality; (= *falso*) sham, bogus
2 [*persona*] (= *astuto*) sly; (= *embustero*) lying; (= *torpe*) blundering, incompetent; (= *tramposo*) cheating, deceitful
SM/F (= *astuto*) clever clogs*; (= *embustero*) liar; (= *torpe*) blunderer; (= *tramposo*) cheat

fulgente ADJ, **fúlgido** ADJ dazzling, brilliant

fulgir ▷ CONJUG 3c VI to shine, glow

fulgor SM brilliance, glow; (*fig*) splendour, splendor (*EEUU*)

fulgurante ADJ **1** (= *reluciente*) bright, shining
2 (= *tremendo*) shattering, stunning

fulgurar ▷ CONJUG 1a VI (= *brillar*) to shine, glow; (= *relampaguear*) to flash

fulguroso ADJ (= *brillante*) bright, shining, gleaming; (= *relampagueante*) flashing

fúlica SF coot

full* [ful] ADJ (*LAm*) full • **tenía los dos tanques ~ de gasolina** his two tanks were full of petrol
SM (*Cono Sur*) • **a ~: trabajan a ~ para que no quede impune** they are working flat out so he doesn't go unpunished

full contact [ful'kontat] SM full contact sports (*pl*)

fullerear* ▷ CONJUG 1a VI (*And*) to show off

fullería SF **1** (*Naipes*) (= *acción*) cheating, cardsharping; (= *cualidad*) guile, cunning
2 (= *trampa*) trick
3 (*And*) (= *ostentación*) showing-off

fullero/a ADJ **1** (= *tramposo*) cheating, deceitful
2 (= *chapucero*) blundering, incompetent • **hacer algo en plan ~** to botch sth*
SM/F **1** (= *tramposo*) (*gen*) sneak*, tattler (*EEUU*); (*con cartas*) cheat, cardsharp
2 (= *criminal*) crook*
3 (= *chapucero*) blunderer
4 (= *astuto*) clever clogs*
5 (*And*) (= *fachendón*) show-off*

fullingue ADJ (*Cono Sur*) **1** [*tabaco*] inferior, poor-quality
2 [*niño*] small, sickly

fulmicotón SM gun cotton

fulminación SF fulmination

fulminador(a) ADJ = **fulminante**
SM/F fulminator (**de** against)

fulminante ADJ **1** [*pólvora*] fulminating; [*mirada*] withering • **cápsula ~** percussion cap
2 (= *súbito*) sudden, fulminant (*frm*) • **apoplejía ~** sudden stroke
3* (= *tremendo*) terrific, tremendous • **golpe ~** terrific blow • **tiro ~** (*Ftbl etc*) sizzling shot
SM (*LAm*) percussion cap

fulminantemente ADV without warning • **despedir ~ a algn** to fire sb on the spot*

fulminar ▷ CONJUG 1a VT **1** (= *destruir*) to strike down • **murió fulminado por un rayo** he was struck dead *o* killed by lightning • MODISMO: • **~ a algn con la mirada** to look daggers at sb
2 [+ *amenazas*] to utter (**contra** against)
VI to fulminate, explode

fulo ADJ **1** (*CAm*) (= *rubio*) blond(e), fair
2 (*Cono Sur**) (= *furioso*) furious, hopping mad*

fumada SF [*de cigarro*] puff, drag*

fumadero SM smoke room • **este cuarto es un ~** this room is full of smoke ▸ **fumadero de opio** opium den

fumado ADJ • **estar ~*** to be stoned*

fumador(a) SM/F smoker • **no ~** non-smoker • **en la sección de no ~es** in the no-smoking *o* non-smoking section • **gran ~** heavy smoker ▸ **fumador(a) de pipa** pipe smoker ▸ **fumador(a) pasivo/a** passive smoker

fumar ▷ CONJUG 1a VT [+ *cigarro, pipa*] to smoke
VI to smoke • **él fuma en pipa** he smokes a pipe • **¿puedo ~?** can I smoke? • **"prohibido fumar"** "no smoking" • MODISMO: • **~ como un carretero** to smoke like a chimney
VPR **fumarse 1*** [+ *dinero*] to squander, blow*; [+ *clase*] to miss
2 (*Méx**) (= *escaparse*) to vanish, slope off*
3 • **fumárselo a algn** (*LAm**) (= *engañar*) to trick sb, swindle sb
4 • **~se a algn***‡ to screw sb*‡

fumarada SF **1** (= *humo*) puff of smoke
2 (*en pipa*) pipeful

fumata SF **1**‡ smoking session (*of drugs*)
2 ▸ **fumata blanca** (*Rel*) (puff of) white smoke; (*fig*) indication of success
SMF‡ (= *persona*) dope-smoker*
SM‡ (= *cigarrillo*) fag*

fumeta‡ SMF dope-smoker*

fumeteo* SM smoking

fumigación SF **1** [*de local, ropa*] fumigation
2 (*Agr*) crop-dusting, crop-spraying

fumigar ▷ CONJUG 1h VT **1** [+ *local, ropa*] to fumigate
2 (*Agr*) to dust, spray

fumista SMF **1** (= *de chimeneas*) chimney sweep
2 (= *gandul*) idler, shirker
3 (*Cono Sur*) (= *bromista*) joker, tease

fumo SM (*Caribe*) puff of smoke

fumosidad SF smokiness

fumoso ADJ smoky

funambulesco ADJ grotesque, wildly extravagant

funambulista SMF, **funámbulo/a** SM/F tightrope walker, funambulist (*frm*)

funcia SF (*And, CAm*) (*hum*) = **función**

función SF **1** (= *actividad*) (*física, de máquina*) function • **el desarrollo de las funciones cerebrales** the development of the brain functions • **el ordenador realiza cinco funciones básicas** the computer performs five basic functions
2 (= *papel*) function • **¿cuál es la ~ del Estado?** what is the function of the State? • **esa debería ser la ~ de la prensa** that should be the role *o* function of the press • **es una escultura que también cumple** *o* **hace la ~ de puerta** it is a sculpture which also acts as *o* serves as a door • **desempeñar la ~ de director/inspector/secretario** to have *o* hold the position of director/inspector/secretary • **el ministro desempeñará la ~ de mediador** the minister will act as (a) mediator • **la ~ de hacer algo** the task of doing sth • **la ~ de educar corresponde a la escuela** the task of educating falls to the school • **las fuerzas armadas tienen la ~ de proteger el país** the role *o* function of the armed forces is to protect the country
3 funciones: a (= *deberes*) duties • **volvió a ejercer sus funciones como alcalde** he returned to carry out his duties as mayor • **en el ejercicio de sus funciones** in the course of her duties • **excederse** *o* **extralimitarse en sus funciones** to exceed one's duties
b • **en funciones** [*ministro, alcalde, presidente*] acting (*antes de s*) • **secretario general en funciones** acting secretary general • **gobierno en funciones** interim government • **entrar en funciones** [*funcionario*] to take up one's duties *o* post; [*ministro, alcalde, presidente*] to take up office,

assume office; [*organismo*] to come into being
4 • en ~ de a (= *según*) according to **• el dinero se repartirá en ~ de las necesidades de cada país** the money will be distributed according to the needs of each country **• el punto de ebullición del agua varía en ~ de la presión atmosférica** the boiling point of water varies according to atmospheric pressure **• el desarrollo cultural está en ~ de la estructura política de un país** cultural development depends on the political structure of a country
b (= *basándose en*) on the basis of **• los consumidores realizan sus compras en ~ de la calidad y el precio** consumers make their purchases on the basis of quality and price
5 (= *espectáculo*) [*de teatro, ópera*] performance; [*de títeres, variedades, musical*] show **• ir a ver una ~ de circo** to go to the circus **▸ función benéfica** charity performance **▸ función continua** (*LAm*), **función continuada** (*Cono Sur*) continuous performance **▸ función de despedida** farewell performance **▸ función de noche** late performance, evening performance **▸ función de tarde** matinée
6 • la ~ pública the civil service
7 (*Mat*) function
8 (*Ling*) function **• ~ gramatical** grammatical function

funcional ADJ **1** [*capacidad, actividad*] functional **• analfabetismo ~** functional illiteracy
2 (= *práctico*) [*diseño, casa*] functional

funcionalidad SF functional nature

funcionalismo SM functionalism

funcionalista ADJ functionalist

funcionamiento SM **• lo lubrico cada 2.000 horas de ~** I lubricate it after every 2,000 hours of operation **• es vital para el ~ del sistema nervioso** it's vital for the functioning of the nervous system **• nos explicó el ~ de un carburador** he told us how a carburettor works **• esta máquina no está en ~** this machine is not in operation **• entrar en ~** to come into operation **• poner en ~** to bring into operation

funcionar ▹ CONJUG 1a VI **1** [*aparato, mecanismo*] to work; [*motor*] to work, run; [*sistema*] to work, function **• ¿cómo funciona el vídeo?** how does the video work?, how do you work the video? **• funciona con monedas de un euro** it works with one-euro coins **• hacer ~ una máquina** to operate a machine **• "no funciona"** "out of order"
2 [*plan, método*] to work; [*negocio, película*] to be a success **• su primer matrimonio no funcionó** her first marriage did not work out *o* was not a success **• su última novela no ha funcionado tan bien como la anterior** his latest novel hasn't been as successful *o* as much of a success as the previous one

funcionariado SM civil service, bureaucracy

funcionarial ADJ administrative; (*pey*) bureaucratic

funcionario/a SM/F **1** (*tb* **funcionario público**) civil servant **▸ funcionario/a aduanero/a** customs official **▸ funcionario/a de policía** police officer **▸ funcionario/a de prisiones, funcionario/a penitenciario/a** prison officer
2 [*de banco etc*] clerk

funda SF **1** (*gen*) case, cover; [*de disco*] sleeve **▸ funda de almohada** pillowcase, pillowslip **▸ funda de gafas** spectacles case, glasses case **▸ funda de pistola** holster **▸ funda protectora del disco** (*Inform*) disk cover **▸ funda sobaquera** shoulder holster
2 (= *bolsa*) small bag, holdall
3 [*de diente*] cap
4* (= *condón*) French letter
5 (*Col*) (= *falda*) skirt

fundación SF foundation

fundadamente ADV with good reason, on good grounds

fundado ADJ (= *justificado*) well-founded, justified **• una pretensión mal fundada** an ill-founded claim

fundador(a) SM/F founder

fundamental ADJ fundamental, basic

fundamentalismo SM fundamentalism

fundamentalista ADJ, SMF fundamentalist

fundamentalmente ADV fundamentally, basically; (= *esencialmente*) essentially

fundamentar ▹ CONJUG 1a VT **1** (= *basar*) to base, found (**en** on)
2 (= *poner las bases de*) to lay the foundations of
VPR **fundamentarse • ~se en** [*persona*] to base o.s. on; [*argumento, teoría*] to be based on

fundamento SM **1** (*Arquit*) foundations (*pl*)
2 (= *base*) foundation, basis; (= *razón*) grounds, reason **• eso carece de ~** that is completely without foundation **• creencia sin ~** groundless *o* unfounded belief
3 (= *formalidad*) reliability, trustworthiness
4 (*Téc*) weft, woof
5 fundamentos (= *principios*) fundamentals, basic essentials

fundar ▹ CONJUG 1a VT **1** (= *crear*) [+ *institución, asociación, ciudad, revista*] to found; [+ *partido*] to found, set up, establish
2 (= *basar*) to base (**en** on)
VPR **fundarse 1** [*institución, asociación, ciudad, revista*] to be founded; [+ *partido*] to be founded, be established, be set up
2 (= *basarse*) **• ~se en** [*teoría*] to be based on, be founded on; [*persona*] to base o.s. on **• me fundo en los siguientes hechos** I base my opinion on the following facts

fundente ADJ melting
SM (*Metal*) flux; (*Quím*) dissolvent

fundería SF foundry **▸ fundería de hierro** iron foundry

fundición SF **1** (= *acción*) [*de mineral*] smelting; (*en moldes*) casting; [*de lingotes, joyas*] melting down
2 (= *fábrica*) foundry
3 (= *hierro fundido*) cast iron
4 (*Tip*) font

fundido/a ADJ **1** [*metal, acero, cera*] molten **• sartén de hierro ~** cast iron frying pan
2 [*bombilla*] blown
3 [*queso*] melted
4* (= *muy cansado*) shattered*, whacked*, pooped (*EEUU**)
5 (*Perú, Cono Sur**) (= *arruinado*) ruined, bankrupt
6 (*Chile**) [*niño*] spoilt
SM/F (*Chile**) spoilt brat*
SM **1** (*Cine*) (= *resultado*) fade; (= *acción*) fading **▸ fundido a blanco** fade-to-white **▸ fundido a negro** fade-to-black **▸ fundido de cierre** fade-out **▸ fundido en negro** fade-to-black
2 ▸ fundido nuclear (*Téc*) nuclear meltdown

fundidor(a) SM/F (= *persona*) smelter, founder; (*en fábrica*) foundry worker

fundidora SF (= *fábrica*) foundry

fundillo SM (*LAm*), **fundillos** SMPL (*LAm*)
1 [*del pantalón*] seat
2* (= *culo*) bum, backside*, ass (*esp EEUU**)

fundir ▹ CONJUG 3a VT **1** (= *derretir*) **a** (*para hacer líquido*) [+ *metal, cera, nieve*] to melt; [+ *monedas, lingotes, joyas*] to melt down
b (*Min*) (*para extraer el metal*) to smelt
c (*en molde*) [+ *estatuas, cañones*] to cast
2 [+ *bombilla, fusible*] to blow
3 (= *fusionar*) [+ *organizaciones, empresas*] to merge, amalgamate; [+ *culturas, movimientos*] to fuse **• intentaba ~ los elementos andaluces con los hindúes** she aimed to fuse Andalusian and Indian elements
4 (*Cine*) [+ *imágenes*] to fade
5* [+ *dinero*] to blow* **• nos lo fundimos todo a la ruleta** we blew it all on roulette*
6 (*Perú, Cono Sur**) (= *arruinar*) ruin **• la nieve nos fundió la cosecha** the snow ruined the crop
7 (*Chile**) [+ *niño*] to spoil
VPR **fundirse 1** (= *derretirse*) [*hielo*] to melt
2 (*Elec*) [*bombilla, fusible*] to blow, go **• se fundieron los plomos** the fuses blew *o* went
3 (= *fusionarse*) **a** [*organizaciones, empresas*] to amalgamate, merge; [*partidos políticos*] to merge **• los ritmos caribeños y el flamenco se ~án durante el festival** Caribbean rhythms and flamenco will fuse together *o* merge in the festival **• ~se en algo** [*organizaciones*] to merge to form sth, amalgamate into sth; [*sonidos*] to merge into sth; [*colores, imágenes*] to merge to form sth, blend together to form sth **• ambos museos se fundieron en el Museo Nacional** both museums merged to form *o* (were) amalgamated into the National Museum **• las voces se fundieron en un solo grito** the voices merged into a single cry **• se fundieron en un abrazo** they melted into each other's arms
b • ~se con algo: el cielo se fundía con el mar the sea and the sky blended *o* merged into one **• la necesidad de ~se con la naturaleza** the need to be at one with nature
4 (*Cine*) [*imagen*] to fade
5 (*Perú, Cono Sur**) (= *arruinarse*) to be ruined

fundo SM (*Perú, Chile*) landed property, estate; (= *granja*) farm

fundón SM (*And, Caribe*) riding-habit

fúnebre ADJ **1 • coche ~** hearse **• pompas ~s** undertaker's, funeral parlor (*EEUU*)
2 (= *lúgubre*) mournful, funereal (*frm*)

funeral ADJ funeral (*antes de s*)
SMPL **funerales** (= *exequias*) funeral (*sing*); (= *oficio religioso*) funeral service (*sing*)

funerala* SF **• MODISMOS: • marchar a la ~** to march with reversed arms **• ojo a la ~** black eye

funeraria SF undertaker's, funeral parlor (*EEUU*) **• director de ~** undertaker, funeral director, mortician (*EEUU*)

funerario ADJ, **funéreo** ADJ funeral (*antes de s*)

funestamente ADV (= *desastrosamente*) fatally, disastrously; (= *perjudicialmente*) banefully

funestidad SF (*Méx*) calamity

funesto ADJ (= *maldito*) ill-fated; (= *desastroso*) fatal, disastrous; (= *nocivo*) baneful

fungible ADJ (*Jur*) **• bienes ~s** perishable goods

fungicida SM fungicide

fungiforme ADJ mushroom-shaped

fungir ▹ CONJUG 3c VI (*CAm, Méx*) (= *actuar*) to act (**de** as); (*Caribe*) to substitute, stand in (**a** for)

fungo SM (*Med*) fungus

fungoideo ADJ fungoid

fungoso ADJ fungous

funguelar‡ ▹ CONJUG 1a VI to pong‡

funicular SM **1** (= *tren*) funicular, funicular railway
2 (= *teleférico*) cable car

fuñido ADJ **1** (*Caribe*) (= *pendenciero*) quarrelsome; (= *insociable*) unsociable
2 (*Caribe*) (= *enfermizo*) sickly, feeble

fuñingue ADJ (*Cono Sur*) weak

fuñir‡ (*LAm*) ▸ CONJUG 3h VT • **~la** to make a real mess of things, mess things up

furcia‡* SF tart‡, whore* • **¡furcia!** you slut!‡

furgón SM (*Aut*) truck, van; (*Ferro*) goods van, boxcar (*EEUU*) ▸ **furgón acorazado** armoured van, armored truck (*EEUU*) ▸ **furgón blindado** armoured *o* (*EEUU*) armored truck ▸ **furgón celular** police van, prison van ▸ **furgón de cola** guard's-van, caboose (*EEUU*) ▸ **furgón de equipajes** luggage car, baggage car (*EEUU*) ▸ **furgón de mudanzas** removal van, removal truck (*EEUU*) ▸ **furgón de reparto** delivery van, delivery truck (*EEUU*) ▸ **furgón funerario** hearse ▸ **furgón postal** mail van, post office van

f

furgonada SF vanload, truckload, wagonload

furgonero SM carter, vanman

furgoneta SF (= *furgón*) (transit) van, pickup (truck) (*EEUU*); (= *coche*) estate (car), station wagon (*EEUU*) ▸ **furgoneta de reparto** delivery van, delivery truck (*EEUU*)

furia SF (= *rabia*) fury, rage; (= *violencia*) violence • MODISMOS: • **hecho una ~**: • **estar hecho una ~** to be furious • **ponerse hecho una ~** to get mad • **salió hecha una ~** she stormed out • **a la ~** • **a toda ~** (*Cono Sur*) at top speed, real fast (*EEUU**) • **trabajar a toda ~** to work like fury

furibundo ADJ (= *furioso*) furious; (= *frenético*) frenzied

furiosamente ADV (= *con rabia*) furiously; (= *con violencia*) violently; (= *frenéticamente*) frantically

furioso ADJ (= *con rabia*) furious; (= *violento*) violent; (= *frenético*) frantic • **estar ~** to be furious • **ponerse ~** to get mad, be furious

furor SM **1** (= *ira*) fury, rage; (= *pasión*) frenzy, passion • **dijo con ~** he said furiously ▸ **furor uterino** nymphomania
2 (= *afición*) rage • **hacer ~** to be all the rage*, be a sensation • **tener ~ por** (*LAm*) to have a passion for

furquina SF (*And*) short skirt

furriel SM, **furrier** SM quartermaster

furriña SF (*Méx*) anger

furrular* ▸ CONJUG 1a VI to work

furrús* SM switch, swap, change

furrusca* SF (*And*) row, brawl

furtivamente ADV furtively

furtivismo SM poaching

furtivo/a ADJ **1** (= *ilegal*) [*persona*] furtive; [*edición*] pirated • **cazador/pescador ~** poacher • **lágrima furtiva** silent tear • **avión ~** stealth bomber
2 (= *astuto*) sly, stealthy
SM/F (= *persona*) poacher

furular* ▸ CONJUG 1a VI to work

furuminga SF (*Cono Sur*) intrigue, scheme

furúnculo SM (*Med*) boil

fusa SF demisemiquaver, thirty-second note (*EEUU*)

fusca‡ SF, **fusco**‡ SM gun, rod‡

fuselado ADJ streamlined

fuselaje SM fuselage • **de ~ ancho** wide-bodied

fusible SM fuse

fusil SM rifle, gun ▸ **fusil de asalto** assault rifle

fusilamiento SM **1** (*Jur*) execution (*by firing squad*); (*irregular*) summary execution
2* (= *plagio*) pinching*, plagiarism; [*de producto*] piracy, illegal copying

fusilar ▸ CONJUG 1a VT **1** (= *ejecutar*) to shoot, execute (*by firing squad*)
2 (*Caribe*) (= *matar*) to kill; (*Dep*) [+ *gol*] to shoot
3* (= *plagiar*) (*Literat, Cine*) to pinch*, plagiarize; (*Com*) to pirate, copy illegally

fusilazo SM rifle-shot

fusilería SF gunfire, rifle-fire

fusilero SM rifleman, fusilier

fusión SF **1** (= *unión*) joining, uniting; (*Com*) merger, amalgamation
2 (*Inform*) merge
3 [*de metal*] melting
4 (*Fís*) fusion ▸ **fusión nuclear** nuclear fusion
5 (*Mús*) crossover

fusionamiento SM (*Com*) merger, amalgamation

fusionar ▸ CONJUG 1a VT (*gen*) to fuse (together); (*Com*) to merge, amalgamate; (*Inform*) to merge
VPR **fusionarse** (*gen*) to fuse; (*Com*) to merge, amalgamate

fusta SF **1** (= *látigo*) riding whip
2 (= *leña*) brushwood, twigs (*pl*)

fustán SM **1** (= *tela*) fustian
2 (*LAm*) (= *enagua*) petticoat, underskirt; (= *falda*) skirt

fuste SM **1** (= *importancia*) importance • **de ~** important, of some consequence • **de poco ~** unimportant
2 (= *madera*) timber, lumber (*EEUU*) • **de ~** wooden
3 [*de lanza*] shaft; [*de chimenea*] shaft
4 (*CAm*) (*Anat**) bottom
5 (= *silla*) saddle tree

fustigar ▸ CONJUG 1h VT **1** (= *pegar*) to whip, lash
2 (= *criticar*) to upbraid, give a tongue-lashing to*

futbito SM five-a-side football, five-a-side soccer (*EEUU*)

fútbol SM, **futbol** SM (*LAm*) football, soccer (*esp EEUU*) • **~ ofensivo** attacking football ▸ **fútbol americano** American football ▸ **fútbol asociación** association football, soccer

futbolero/a ADJ football (*antes de s*), soccer (*antes de s*)
SM/F football supporter, soccer supporter (*EEUU*)

futbolín SM **1** (= *juego*) table football, table soccer (*EEUU*)
2 (*tb* **futbolines**) (= *local*) amusement arcade, amusements (*pl*)

futbolista SMF footballer, football player, soccer player (*esp EEUU*)

futbolístico ADJ football (*antes de s*), soccer (*antes de s*)

futbolmanía SF football mania, soccer mania (*EEUU*)

fútbol-sala SM, **fútbol sala** SM indoor football, indoor soccer (*EEUU*)

futearse ▸ CONJUG 1a VPR (*And*) [*fruta*] to go bad, rot

futesa SF trifle, mere nothing; **futesas** (*en conversación*) small talk (*sing*), trivialities

fútil ADJ **1** (= *inútil*) futile
2 (= *sin importancia*) trifling, trivial

futileza SF, **futilidad** SF **1** (= *cualidad*) triviality, trifling nature
2 (*Cono Sur*) trifle, bagatelle • **una ~** a trifle

futing ['futin] SM = **footing**

futón SM futon

futre* SM (*Chile*) toff*, dude (*EEUU**)

futrería SF (*Chile*) **1** (= *conducta*) affected behaviour, affected behavior (*EEUU*)
2 (= *grupo*) group of toffs*, group of dudes (*EEUU**)
3 (= *querencia*) hang-out (*EEUU**)

futura SF (*Jur*) reversion; ▸ **futuro**

futurible ADJ (= *venidero*) forthcoming; (= *potencial*) potential; (= *probable*) likely; (= *especulativo*) speculative; (= *digno de ascenso*) promotion-worthy
SMF (*Pol*) (= *dirigente*) potential leader; (= *ministro*) potential minister
SM hot tip, good bet • **es un ~ olímpico** he's a good prospect for the Olympics

futurismo SM futurism

futurista ADJ futuristic
SMF futurist

futurístico/a ADJ futuristic
SMF futurist

futuro/a ADJ future • **futura madre** mother-to-be • **los equipos más ~s son A y B** the teams with the best prospects are A and B
SM/F* fiancé/fiancée
SM **1** future • **en el ~** in (the) future • **en lo ~** • **en un ~** some time in the future • **en un ~ próximo** in the near future • **el ~ se presenta muy oscuro** the future looks bleak • **a ~** (*Chile*) in the future
2 (*Ling*) future (tense)
3 futuros (*Com*) futures; ▸ **futura**

futurología SF futurology

futurólogo/a SM/F futurologist

Gg

G, g[1] [xe] SF (= *letra*) G, g
g[2] ABR (= **gramo(s)**) g, gm(s)
g/ ABR (= **giro**) p.o., m.o. (*EEUU*)
gabacho/a ADJ **1*** (*pey*) (= *francés*) froggy*, Frenchy*
2 (*Geog*) Pyrenean
3 • **MODISMO**: • **le salió gabacha la cosa** (*And**) it came to nothing
SM/F **1*** (*pey*) frog*, Frenchy*
2 (*Geog*) Pyrenean villager
3 (*Méx*) (= *extranjero*) foreigner, outsider; (*en Tejas*) white American, Yankee
gabán SM overcoat, topcoat; (*Caribe*) jacket
gabanear ▹ CONJUG 1a VT (*CAm*) to steal
VI (*Méx*) to flee
gabanero SM hall wardrobe
gabarda SF wild rose
gabardina SF **1** (= *abrigo*) raincoat, mackintosh† • **gambas en ~** prawns in batter, battered prawns
2 (= *tela*) gabardine
gabardino/a SM/F (*Méx*) (*pey*) white American, Yankee
gabarra SF barge, flatboat
gabarrero/a SM/F bargee, bargeman (*EEUU*)
gabarro SM **1** (*en una tela*) flaw, defect
2 (*Vet*) (= *moquillo*) distemper, pip; [*de caballo*] tumour, tumor (*EEUU*)
3 (*en las cuentas*) error, miscalculation
4 (= *obstáculo*) snag; (= *molestia*) annoyance
gabear ▹ CONJUG 1a VT (*Caribe*) to climb
gabela SF **1** (*Hist*) (= *impuesto*) tax, duty; (= *carga*) burden
2 (*And*) (= *ventaja*) advantage, profit
gabinete SM **1** (*profesional*) office ▸ **gabinete de consulta** consulting-room, doctor's office (*EEUU*) ▸ **gabinete de diseño** design consultancy ▸ **gabinete de estrategia** (*Pol*) think-tank ▸ **gabinete de imagen** public relations office ▸ **gabinete de prensa** press office ▸ **gabinete fiscal** tax advisory office ▸ **gabinete jurídico** (*en empresa*) legal department; (= *bufete*) law firm
2 (*en casa*) (= *despacho*) study, library; (= *salita*) private sitting room; (= *tocador*) boudoir; (*Arte*) studio • **estratega de ~** armchair strategist ▸ **gabinete de lectura** reading room
3 (*Pol*) cabinet ▸ **gabinete en la sombra, gabinete fantasma** shadow cabinet
4 (= *laboratorio*) laboratory
5 (= *museo*) museum
6 (= *muebles*) suite of office furniture
7 (*And*) (= *balcón*) enclosed balcony
8 ▸ **gabinete de teléfono** (*Méx*) telephone booth
gablete SM gable
Gabriel SM Gabriel
gacel SM gazelle
gacela SF gazelle
gaceta SF **1** (= *boletín*) gazette, official journal; (*LAm*) (= *diario*) newspaper
2 (*Caribe**) (= *chismoso*) gossip; (= *soplón*) telltale, tattletale (*EEUU*)
gacetero/a SM/F **1** (= *periodista*) newswriter, journalist
2 (= *vendedor*) newspaper seller
gacetilla SF **1** (= *notas sociales*) gossip column; (= *noticias generales*) miscellaneous news section; (= *noticias locales*) local news section • **"Gacetilla"** "News in Brief"
2* (= *chismoso*) gossip • **ella es una ~ con dos patas** she's a dreadful gossip
gacetillero/a SM/F (= *reportero de sociedad*) gossip columnist; (= *periodista**) hack (*pey*)
gacetista SMF gossip
gacha SF **1** thin paste, mush
2 gachas (*Culin*) pap • **MODISMO**: • **se ha hecho unas ~s** she's turned all sentimental ▸ **gachas de avena** oatmeal porridge
3 (*LAm*) (= *vasija*) earthenware bowl
gachí‡ SF (PL: **gachís**) bird‡, chick (*EEUU‡*)
gacho ADJ **1** (= *encorvado*) bent down, turned downward; [*cuerno*] down-curved; [*orejas*] drooping, floppy • **sombrero ~** slouch hat • **salió con las orejas gachas** *o* **con la cabeza gacha** he went out all down in the mouth* • **MODISMO**: • **a cabeza gacha** (*Cono Sur*) obediently
2 • **ir a gachas*** to go on all fours
3 (*Méx**) (= *feo*) nasty, ugly; (= *sin suerte*) unlucky
gachó* SM (PL: **gachós**) guy*, bloke* • **¡gachó!** brother!* • **qué terco eres, ~** man, you're so stubborn
gachón ADJ **1*** (= *encantador*) charming, sweet; [*niño*] spoilt
2‡ [*mujer*] sexy
gachumbo SM (*LAm*) hollowed-out shell
gachupín/ina SM/F (*Méx*), **gachuzo/a** SM/F (*Méx*) (*pey*) Spaniard
gacilla SF (*CAm*) (= *imperdible*) safety pin; (= *broche*) clasp
gaditano/a ADJ of/from Cadiz
SM/F native/inhabitant of Cadiz • **los ~s** the people of Cadiz
GAE SM ABR (*Esp*) (*Mil*) = **Grupo Aéreo Embarcado**
gaélico/a ADJ Gaelic
SM/F Gael
SM (*Ling*) Gaelic
gafa SF **1** (= *grapa*) grapple; (= *abrazadera*) clamp
2 gafas (*para ver*) glasses, spectacles†, eyeglasses (*EEUU*); (*Dep*) goggles ▸ **gafas bifocales** bifocals ▸ **gafas de aro** wire-rimmed glasses ▸ **gafas de baño, gafas de bucear** diving goggles ▸ **gafas de cerca** reading glasses ▸ **gafas de culo de vaso** pebble glasses ▸ **gafas de esquiar** skiing goggles ▸ **gafas de leer** reading glasses ▸ **gafas de media luna** half-moon glasses ▸ **gafas de motorista** motorcyclist's goggles ▸ **gafas de protección** safety goggles, protective goggles ▸ **gafas de sol** sunglasses ▸ **gafas graduadas** prescription glasses ▸ **gafas negras, gafas oscuras** dark glasses ▸ **gafas protectoras** safety goggles, protective goggles ▸ **gafas sin aros** rimless glasses ▸ **gafas submarinas** underwater goggles; ▹ **gafo, PANTALONES, ZAPATOS, GAFAS**
gafancia* SF (= *mala suerte*) propensity to attract bad luck; (= *tendencia*) accident-proneness
gafapasta* SMF hipster*
gafar ▹ CONJUG 1a VT **1*** (= *traer mala suerte*) to jinx*, put a jinx on*; (= *estropear*) to mess up • **la máquina parece gafada** the machine is jinxed*, the machine seems to have a jinx on it*
2 (= *arrebatar*) to hook, latch on to
gafe* ADJ • **ser ~** to have a jinx*, be jinxed* • **tener un día ~** to have a bad day, have an off day • **un número con ~** an unlucky number
SMF • **ser un ~** to have a jinx*, be jinxed*
SM (= *mala suerte*) jinx*
gafete SM clasp, hook and eye
gafo/a ADJ **1** (*LAm*) (= *cansado*) footsore
2 (*Méx*) (= *adormecido*) numb
3 • **estar ~** (*CAm**) to be broke*
4 (*Caribe*) (= *no fiable*) unreliable, erratic; (= *bruto‡*) thick*
SM/F (*Caribe*) idiot; ▹ **gafa**
gafudo ADJ who wears glasses, with glasses
gag SM (PL: **gags**) gag
gagá* ADJ • **estar ~** to be gaga*
SMF old dodderer
gago/a* (*LAm*) ADJ stammering, stuttering
SM/F stammerer, stutterer
gagoso* ADJ (*LAm*) stammering, stuttering
gaguear* ▹ CONJUG 1a VI (*LAm*) to stammer, stutter
gagueo* SM (*LAm*) stammer(ing), stutter(ing)
gaguera* SF (*LAm*) stammer, stutter
gaita SF **1** (*Mús*) bagpipes (*pl*) • **tocar la ~** to play the bagpipes • **MODISMOS**: • **ser como una ~*** to be very demanding • **estar de ~*** to be merry • **estar hecho una ~*** to be a wreck* • **templar ~s*** to pour oil on troubled waters ▸ **gaita gallega** Galician bagpipes
2 (*Mús*) (= *flauta*) flute; (= *organillo*) hurdy-gurdy
3* (= *pescuezo*) neck • **MODISMO**: • **sacar la ~** to stick one's neck out
4* (= *dificultad*) bother, nuisance • **¡qué ~!** what a pain!* • **déjame, que hoy no estoy para ~s** leave me alone, I don't need any hassle today* • **y toda esa ~*** and all that jazz*
5 (*Méx**) (= *maula*) cheat, trickster
6 (*Ven*) folk music
SMF (*LAm*) (*hum*) (= *gallego*) Galician; (= *español*) Spaniard
gaitero/a SM/F (*Mús*) (bag)piper
ADJ **1** [*color*] gaudy, flashy
2 [*persona*] buffoonish
gaje SM **1** • **en ~ de** (*LAm*) as a token of, as a sign of

g

2 gajes (= *emolumentos*) pay (*sing*), emoluments; (= *beneficios*) perquisites; (= *recompensa*) reward (*sing*), bonus (*sing*) • **~s y emolumentos** (*Com*) perquisites ▸ **gajes del oficio** (*hum*) occupational hazards, occupational risks

gajo SM **1** [*de naranja*] slice, segment
2 [*de uvas*] small cluster, bunch
3 (= *rama*) torn-off branch, torn-off bough
4 [*de horca*] point, prong
5 (*Geog*) spur
6 (*And*) curl, ringlet

GAL SMPL ABR (*Esp*) (= **Grupos Antiterroristas de Liberación**) *anti-ETA terrorist group*

gal SMF member of GAL

gala SF **1** (= *fiesta*) show ▸ **gala benéfica** charity event
2 • **de ~: cena de ~** gala dinner • **función de ~** gala • **uniforme de ~** full-dress uniform • **traje de ~** (*gen*) formal dress; (*Mil*) full dress • **estar de ~** [*ciudad*] to be in festive mood
3 galas (= *ropa*) finery (*sing*); (= *joyas*) jewels • **vestir sus mejores ~s** [*persona*] to put on one's Sunday best; [*edificio, ciudad*] to show one's best face ▸ **galas de novia** bridal attire (*sing*)
4 (= *elegancia*) elegance, gracefulness; (= *pompa*) pomp, display • **hacer ~ de algo** (= *jactarse*) to boast of sth; (= *lucirse*) to show sth off • **tener algo a ~** to be proud of sth • **tener a ~ hacer algo** to be proud to do sth
5 (= *lo más selecto*) pride • **es la ~ de la ciudad** it is the pride of the city • **llevarse las ~s** to win applause
6 (= *especialidad*) speciality, specialty (*EEUU*)
7 (*LAm*) (= *regalo*) gift; (= *propina*) tip; ▹ **galo**

galáctico ADJ galactic

galafate SM sly thief

galaico ADJ Galician

galán SM **1** (= *hombre apuesto*) handsome fellow; (= *Don Juan*) ladies' man; (*Hist*) young gentleman, courtier
2 (= *novio*) gallant, beau; (= *pretendiente*) suitor
3 (*Teat*) male lead; (= *protagonista*) hero • **primer ~** leading man • **joven ~** juvenile lead ▸ **galán de cine** screen idol
4 ▸ **galán de noche** (= *mueble*) clothes-rack and trouser press; (= *planta*) night jasmine
ADV (*LAm**) = **bien**

galanamente† ADV (= *primorosamente*) smartly, sprucely; (= *con elegancia*) elegantly, tastefully

galanas SFPL (*CAm*) • **echar ~** to boast, brag • **hacer ~** to do naughty things, be wicked

galancete† SM **1** (= *joven*) handsome young man; (*hum*) dapper little man
2 (*Teat*) juvenile lead

galancito† SM juvenile lead

galano† ADJ **1** (= *primoroso*) smart, spruce; (= *elegante*) elegant, tasteful; (= *gallardo*) smartly dressed
2 (*Cuba*) [*vaca*] mottled (*with red and white patches*)

galante ADJ **1** [*hombre*] (= *caballeroso*) gallant; (= *atento*) charming, attentive (*to women*); (= *cortés*) polite, urbane (*frm*)
2†† [*mujer*] flirtatious, flirty; (*pey*) wanton, licentious

galantear ▹ CONJUG 1a VT (= *cortejar*) to court, woo; (= *coquetear*) to flirt with

galantemente ADV (= *con caballerosidad*) gallantly; (= *con atención*) charmingly, attentively; (= *con cortesía*) politely

galanteo SM (= *corte*) courtship, wooing; (= *coqueteo*) flirting

galantería SF **1** (= *caballerosidad*) gallantry; (= *atención*) charm, attentiveness (*to women*); (= *gentileza*) politeness, urbanity (*frm*)
2 (= *cumplido*) compliment; (= *piropo*) charming thing to say, gallantry

galanto SM snowdrop

galanura SF (= *gracia*) prettiness; (= *encanto*) charm; (= *gallardía*) elegance, tastefulness

galápago SM **1** (= *tortuga*) freshwater turtle
2 (= *molde*) tile mould, tile mold (*EEUU*)
3 (*Téc*) ingot, pig
4 (= *montura*) light saddle; (*LAm*) (= *montura de lado*) sidesaddle
5 [*de bicicleta*] racing saddle

Galápagos SFPL • **las (islas) ~** the Galapagos (Islands)

galapagueño/a ADJ of/from the Galapagos (Islands)
SM/F native/inhabitant of the Galapagos (Islands)

galardón SM (= *premio*) award, prize; (= *recompensa*) reward

galardonado/a SM/F award-winner, prize-winner

galardonar ▹ CONJUG 1a VT [+ *obra, candidato*] to award a prize to, give a prize *o* an award to • **ha sido galardonado con el premio Nobel** he was awarded the Nobel prize • **obra galardonada por la Academia** work which won an Academy prize

galaxia SF galaxy

galbana SF laziness, sloth

galbanoso ADJ lazy, slothful

galdosiano ADJ *relating to Benito Pérez Galdós* • **estudios ~s** Galdós studies

galembo SM (*And, Caribe*) turkey buzzard

galena SF galena, galenite; ▹ **galeno**

galeniano ADJ Galenic

Galeno SM Galen

galeno[1]/a SM/F (*Literat*) (*hum*) physician; (*LAm*) doctor; ▹ **galena**

galeno[2] ADJ [*viento*] moderate, soft

galeón SM galleon

galeote SM galley slave

galera SF **1** (*Náut*) galley • **condenar a algn a ~s** to condemn sb to the galleys
2 (= *carro*) covered wagon
3 (*Med*) hospital ward; (*Hist*) women's prison
4 (*CAm, Méx*) (= *cobertizo*) shed
5 (*CAm*) (= *matadero*) slaughterhouse
6 (*LAm*) (= *chistera*) top hat; (= *fieltro*) felt hat, trilby, fedora (*EEUU*); (= *hongo*) bowler hat, derby (*EEUU*)
7 (*Tip*) galley

galerada SF **1** (*Tip*) galley proof
2 (= *carga*) wagonload

galería SF **1** (= *espacio*) (*interior, en mina*) gallery; (*exterior*) balcony ▸ **galería comercial** shopping mall ▸ **galería de alimentación** food hall ▸ **galería de arte** art gallery ▸ **galería de columnas** colonnade ▸ **galería de la muerte** death row ▸ **galería de popa** (*Náut*) stern gallery ▸ **galería de tiro** shooting gallery ▸ **galería de viento** (*Aer*) wind tunnel ▸ **galería secreta** secret passage
2* (= *público*) audience • MODISMO: • **hacer algo para *o* de cara a la ~** to play to the gallery • **ha sido un gesto para la ~** it was just playing to the gallery
3 (*para cortinas*) pelmet, cornice (*EEUU*)
4 (*And, Caribe*) store

galerista SMF (= *propietario*) gallery owner; (= *director*) art gallery director

galerita SF crested lark

galerna SF, **galerno** SM *violent north-west wind on North coast of Spain*

galerón SM **1** (*CAm*) (= *cobertizo*) shed; (= *tejado*) shed roof
2 (*Méx*) (= *sala*) hall
3 (*Caribe*) (= *baile*) folk dance

Gales SM Wales

galés/esa ADJ Welsh
SM/F Welshman/Welshwoman • **los galeses** the Welsh
SM (*Ling*) Welsh

galfaro SM (*Caribe*) little rascal

galga SF **1** (= *instrumento*) gauge, gage (*EEUU*)
2 (*Geol*) boulder
3 [*de molino de aceite*] millstone

galgo[1]/a SM/F greyhound • MODISMOS: • **¡échale un ~!*** catch him if you can! • **¡vete a espulgar un ~!*** go to blazes! ▸ **galgo afgano** Afghan (hound) ▸ **galgo ruso** borzoi, Russian wolfhound

galgo[2]* ADJ, **galgón*** ADJ (*And*) sweet-toothed, fond of sweets

galgódromo SM (*Méx*) dog track, greyhound track

galguear* ▹ CONJUG 1a VI (*CAm, Cono Sur*) (= *tener hambre*) to be starving, be ravenous; (= *buscar comida*) to wander about looking for food

Galia SF Gaul

gálibo SM **1** (*Téc*) gauge
2 (= *luz*) warning light, flashing light

galicano† ADJ **1** (= *galo*) Gallic
2 (*Rel*) Gallican

Galicia SF Galicia

galiciano/a ADJ, SM/F Galician

galicismo SM Gallicism

gálico ADJ Gallic
SM syphilis

galicoso/a ADJ, SM/F syphilitic

Galilea SF Galilee

galileo/a ADJ, SM/F Galilean

galillo SM uvula

galimatías SM INV (= *asunto*) rigmarole; (= *lenguaje*) gibberish, nonsense

gallada SF **1** (*LAm*) (= *acto atrevido*) bold deed, great achievement; (= *jactancia*) boast
2 • **la ~** (*Cono Sur**) (= *chicos*) the boys*, the lads*; (= *gente*) people

gallardamente ADV (= *con elegancia*) gracefully, elegantly; (= *con magnificencia*) splendidly; (= *con valentía*) bravely; (= *con caballerosidad*) gallantly, dashingly; (= *con nobleza*) nobly

gallardear ▹ CONJUG 1a VI **1** (= *actuar con gracia*) to act with ease and grace; (= *tener buen porte*) to bear o.s. well
2 (= *pavonearse*) to strut

gallardete SM pennant, streamer

gallardía SF (= *elegancia*) gracefulness; (= *magnificencia*) fineness; (= *valentía*) bravery; (= *caballerosidad*) gallantry, dash; (= *nobleza*) nobleness

gallardo ADJ (= *elegante*) graceful, elegant; (= *magnífico*) fine, splendid; (= *valiente*) brave; (= *caballeroso*) gallant, dashing; (= *noble*) noble

gallareta SF (*LAm*) South American coot

gallear ▹ CONJUG 1a VT [+ *gallina*] to tread
VI **1** (= *destacar*) to excel, stand out
2 (= *pavonearse*) to strut around; (= *jactarse*) to brag; (= *bravuconear*) to be a bully, chuck one's weight about; (= *gritar*) to bluster, bawl

gallego/a ADJ **1** (= *de Galicia*) Galician
2 (*LAm*) (*pey*) Spanish
SM/F **1** (= *de Galicia*) Galician
2 (*LAm*) (*pey*) Spaniard
SM **1** (*Ling*) Galician
2 (= *viento*) north-west wind

GALLEGO

Gallego, a romance language dating back to the 12th century and closely related to Portuguese, is spoken by most of the inhabitants of **Galicia**. During the Franco régime, the use of Galician and other minority national languages was prohibited in the media and in public institutions. It has enjoyed **lengua cooficial** status alongside **castellano** since 1981. There are several dialects of the language and formal attempts to standardize them in the 1970s were unsuccessful. However, a standard form is now beginning to emerge naturally in the larger urban areas.

▷ **LENGUAS COOFICIALES**

galleguismo SM **1** (*Ling*) Galleguism, *word or phrase peculiar to Galicia*
2 (= *sentimiento*) *sense of the differentness of Galicia*; (*Pol*) *doctrine of/belief in Galician autonomy*

galleguista ADJ, SMF pro-Galician

gallera SF **1** (*LAm*) (= *palenque*) cockpit
2 (*And, CAm*) (= *gallinero*) coop (*for gamecocks*); ▷ **gallero**

gallería SF (*Caribe*) **1** (= *palenque*) cockpit
2 (= *egoísmo*) egotism, selfishness

gallero/a ADJ (*LAm, Canarias*) fond of cockfighting
SM/F **1** (*LAm, Canarias*) (= *encargado*) *owner or trainer of fighting cocks*; (= *aficionado*) cockfighting enthusiast
2 (*Cono Sur*) pilferer; ▷ **gallera**

galleta SF **1** (*Culin*) (= *dulce*) biscuit, cookie (EEUU); (*Náut*) ship's biscuit, hardtack; (*Cono Sur*) coarse bread • **MODISMO**: • **ir a toda ~*** to go full-speed ▸ **galleta de soda** (*And*) cracker ▸ **galleta para perros** dog biscuit ▸ **galleta salada** cracker
2* (= *bofetada*) bash*, slap • **se pegó una ~ con la moto** he had a bad smash on the bike
3 (*And, Cono Sur*) *small bowl for drinking maté*
4 (*LAm**) confusion, disorder • **MODISMO**: • **hacerse una ~** (*Cono Sur*) to get muddled ▸ **galleta del tráfico** (*Ven**) (= *atasco*) traffic jam; (= *burla*) practical joke
5 (*Cono Sur*) (= *bronca*) ticking-off* • **le dieron una buena ~** they gave him a good ticking-off*
6 • **MODISMOS**: • **colgar** *o* **dar la ~ a algn** (*And, Arg**) (= *despedir*) to sack sb*, fire sb*; (= *plantar*) to jilt sb; (= *rechazar*) to give sb the brush-off*; (= *no hacer caso a*) to give sb the cold shoulder • **tener mucha ~** (*Méx**) to be very strong

galletear ▷ CONJUG 1a VT **1** (*Méx*) (= *golpear*) to belt*, punch
2 (*Cono Sur*) (= *despedir*) to sack*, fire*

galletero/a SM/F (*Cono Sur*) (= *irritable*) quick-tempered person; (= *pendenciero*) roughneck
SM (= *recipiente*) biscuit tin

gallina SF **1** (= *ave*) hen • **MODISMOS**: • **acostarse con las ~s** to go to bed early • **cantar la ~** to own up, hold up one's hands • **andar como ~ clueca** (*Méx*) to be as pleased as Punch • **estar como ~ en corral ajeno** (= *estar incómodo*) to be like a fish out of water; (= *no tener libertad*) to have no freedom of movement • **estar como ~ con huevos** to be very distrustful • **¡hasta que meen las ~s!*** pigs might fly!* • **matar la ~ de los huevos de oro** to kill the goose that lays the golden eggs • **REFRÁN**: • **las ~s de arriba ensucian a las de abajo** (*Chile*) the underdog always suffers ▸ **gallina ciega** (*CAm, Caribe*) (= *gusano*) white worm • **jugar a la ~ ciega** to play blind man's buff ▸ **gallina clueca** broody *o* (EEUU) brooding hen ▸ **gallina de agua** coot ▸ **gallina de bantam** bantam ▸ **gallina de Guinea** guinea fowl ▸ **gallina de mar** gurnard ▸ **gallina ponedora** laying hen
2 (*Culin*) chicken • **caldo de ~** chicken broth • **~ en pepitoria** *chicken in a sauce made with wine, bread, egg, almonds and pine nuts*
SMF* (= *cobarde*) chicken*, coward

gallinacera SF (*And*) (*pey*) bunch of blacks

gallinaza SF hen droppings (*pl*)

gallinazo SM (*LAm*) turkey buzzard

gallinería SF **1** (= *gallinas*) flock of hens
2 (*Com*) (= *tienda*) poultry shop; (= *mercado*) chicken market
3* (= *cobardía*) cowardice

gallinero/a SM/F **1** (= *criador*) chicken farmer
2 (= *pollero*) poulterer, poultry dealer
SM **1** (= *criadero*) henhouse, coop; (= *cesta*) poultry basket
2 (*Teat*) gods (*pl*), top gallery
3 (= *confusión*) hubbub; (= *griterío*) noisy gathering; (= *casa de locos*) madhouse

gallineta SF **1** (*Orn*) (= *chocha*) woodcock; (= *fúlica*) coot; (*LAm*) guinea fowl
2 ▸ **gallineta del Atlántico**, **gallineta nórdica** Atlantic redfish

gallinilla SF ▸ **gallinilla de bantam** bantam

gallipavo SM **1** (= *ave*) turkey
2 (*Mús*) false note, wrong note

gallito ADJ* (= *bravucón*) cocky*, cocksure • **ponerse ~** to get cocky*
SM **1** (= *ave*) cockerel
2 (= *persona*) tough guy* • **es el ~ del grupo** he's top dog* • **el ~ del mundo** the cock-o'-the-walk
3 (*Col, Méx*) (*Dep*) shuttlecock
4 (*And*) (= *flecha*) small arrow, dart

gallo¹ SM **1** (= *ave*) cock, rooster (*esp EEUU*); (*más pequeño*) cockerel • **MODISMOS**: • **alzar el ~** (*LAm*) to bawl • **comer ~** (*And, CAm**) to suffer a setback • **haber comido ~** (*Méx**) to be in a fighting mood • **como ~ en corral ajeno** like a fish out of water • **entre ~s y medianoche** (*Arg*) on the spur of the moment • **estar como ~ en gallinero** to be highly esteemed, be well thought of • **dormírsele a algn el ~** (*CAm, Méx**) to let an opportunity slip • **no me va nada en el ~** (*Méx**) it doesn't matter to me, it's no skin off my nose* • **levantar el ~** (*LAm*) to bawl; (*Caribe, Méx**) to throw in the towel *o* (EEUU) sponge • **matar el ~ a algn** to floor sb, shut sb up* • **en menos que canta un ~** in an instant, in a flash • **otro ~ cantaría** things would be very different • **pelar ~** (*Méx**) (= *salir huyendo*) to make a run for it*; (= *morirse*) to kick the bucket* • **al primer ~** (*Méx*) at midnight • **hay ~ tapado** (*Col*) I smell a rat • **tener mucho ~** to be cocky* ▸ **gallo de pelea**, **gallo de riña** gamecock, fighting cock ▸ **gallo lira** black grouse ▸ **gallo pinto** (*CAm*) (*Culin*) beans and rice ▸ **gallo silvestre** capercaillie; ▷ **pata**, **pelea**, **peso**
2 (= *pez*) john dory
3 (*en la voz*) false note • **soltó un ~** (*al cantar*) he sang a false note; (*al hablar*) his voice cracked • **tengo un ~ en la garganta** I have a frog in my throat
4* (= *bravucón*) tough guy*; (*LAm*) expert, master • **yo he sido ~ para eso** I was a great one at that
5 (*Pesca*) cork float
6‡ (= *flema*) spit; (*Méx*) (= *gargajo*) gob of spit‡
7 (*Méx*) (= *serenata*) street serenade
8 (*Méx**) (= *ropa usada*) hand-me-down, cast-off • **anda siempre de ~s** all his clothes are hand-me-downs • **lo visten con los ~s del hermano mayor** they dress him in his brother's hand-me-downs *o* cast-offs
9 (*And*) (= *flecha*) dart
10 (*Col, Méx*) (*Dep*) shuttlecock
11 (*And*) [*de bomberos*] hose truck

gallo²/a SM/F (*Chile*) guy*/girl • **conocí a un ~ estupendo** I met a great guy* • **¡qué galla tan antipática!** she is so unfriendly!

gallofero/a ADJ idle, vagabond
SM/F (= *holgazán*) idler, loafer; (= *vagabundo*) tramp, bum (EEUU), hobo (EEUU); (= *mendigo*) beggar

gallón* (*Méx*) ADJ cocky*
SM local boss

gallote* ADJ (*CAm, Méx*) cocky*
SM (*CAm*) cop*

gallumbos‡ SMPL underpants

galo/a ADJ (*Hist*) Gallic; (*moderno*) French
SM/F (*Hist*) Gaul; (*moderno*) Frenchman/Frenchwoman; ▷ **gala**

galocha SF clog

galón¹ SM (*Cos*) braid; (*Mil*) stripe, chevron • **la acción le valió dos galones** his action gained him a couple of stripes • **quitar los galones a algn** to demote sb

galón² SM (= *medida*) gallon

galonear ▷ CONJUG 1a VT to braid, trim with braid

galopada SF gallop

galopante ADJ (*gen*) galloping; [*inflación*] galloping, runaway; [*déficit*] spiralling; [*paro*] soaring, spiralling • **el número de casos aumentó a un ritmo ~** the number of cases shot up

galopar ▷ CONJUG 1a VI to gallop • **echar a ~** to break into a gallop

galope SM gallop • **a** *o* **al ~** (*lit*) at a gallop; (*fig*) in great haste, in a rush • **a ~ tendido** at full gallop • **alejarse a ~** to gallop off • **desfilar a ~** to gallop past • **llegar a ~** to gallop up • **medio ~** canter

galopín SM **1** (= *pícaro*) ragamuffin, urchin; (= *bribón*) scoundrel; (= *sabelotodo*) smart Aleck*, clever Dick*
2 (*Náut*) (= *grumete*) cabin boy

galpón SM **1** (*LAm*) (= *cobertizo*) shed, storehouse; (*Aut*) garage
2 (*And*) (= *tejar*) tileworks, pottery

galucha SF (*LAm*) short gallop; (*Caribe*) start of a gallop

galuchar ▷ CONJUG 1a VI (*LAm*) to gallop

galvánico ADJ galvanic

galvanismo SM galvanism

galvanizado ADJ galvanized

galvanizar ▷ CONJUG 1f VT **1** (*Fís*) to electroplate, galvanize
2 (= *estimular*) to galvanize

galvano SM (*Cono Sur*) commemorative plaque

galvanoplastia SF electroplating

gama¹ SF **1** (= *serie*) range • **una extensa ~ de colores** an extensive range of colours • **alto de ~** • **de ~ alta** top of the range • **bajo de ~** • **de ~ baja** bottom of the range ▸ **gama de frecuencias** frequency range ▸ **gama de ondas** wave range ▸ **gama sonora** sound range
2 (*Mús*) scale

gama² SF (= *letra*) gamma

gama³ SF (*Zool*) doe (*of fallow deer*) • **MODISMO**: • **sentársele a algn la ~** (*Cono Sur*) to get discouraged

gamarra SF (*CAm*) halter • **MODISMO**: • **llevar a algn de la ~*** to lead sb by the nose

gamba SF **1** (= *marisco*) prawn • **cóctel de ~s** prawn cocktail
2‡ (= *pierna*) leg • **MODISMO**: • **meter la ~** to put one's foot in it*
3†‡ 100 pesetas • **media ~** 50 pesetas

gambado ADJ (*Caribe*) knock-kneed

gamberrada SF (= *acto vandálico*) piece of hooliganism; (= *grosería*) loutish thing (to do); (= *broma*) lark*, rag*, piece of horseplay • **hacer ~s** = **gamberrear**

gamberrear ▹ CONJUG 1a VI **1** (= *hacer el gamberro*) to go around causing trouble, act like a hooligan; (= *hacer el tonto*) to lark about*, horse around*
2 (= *gandulear*) to loaf around

gamberrismo SM hooliganism, loutish behaviour

gamberrístico ADJ loutish, ill-bred

gamberro/a ADJ **1** (*pey*) loutish, ill-bred
2 (= *bromista*) joking, teasing
SM/F **1** (*pey*) hooligan, troublemaker • **hacer el ~** to act like a hooligan
2 (= *bromista*) joker

gambeta SF **1** [*de caballo*] prance, caper
2 (*LAm*) (= *esguince*) dodge, avoiding action
3 (*Dep*) dribble
4* (= *pretexto*) dodge, pretext

g

gambito SM gambit

gambuza SF (*Náut*) store, storeroom

gamella SF (= *abrevadero*) trough; (= *artesa*) washtub

gameto SM gamete

gamín/ina* SM/F (*Col*) street urchin

gamma SF (= *letra*) gamma • **radiación ~** gamma radiation
ADJ INV • **rayos ~** gamma rays

gamo SM buck (*of fallow deer*)

gamonal SM (*LAm*) = **cacique**

gamonalismo SM (*LAm*) = **caciquismo**

gamulán SM (*Cono Sur*) sheepskin

gamuza SF **1** (*Zool*) chamois
2 (= *piel*) chamois leather, wash leather • **una cazadora de ~** a suede jacket
3 (= *paño*) duster, dustcloth (*EEUU*)

gana SF **1** • **hacer algo con ~s** to do sth willingly *o* enthusiastically • **comer/reírse con ~s** to eat/laugh heartily • **un chico joven y con ~s de trabajar** a young lad willing to work • **jóvenes con ~s de divertirse** young people keen to enjoy themselves • **con ~s de pelea** spoiling for a fight • **dar ~s**: • **esto da ~s de comerlo** it makes you want to eat it • **dan ~s de pegarle una patada** you feel like kicking him • **le entran ~s de hacer algo** he gets the urge to do sth • **quedarse con las ~s** to be left disappointed, be left wanting • **nos quedamos con las ~s de saberlo** we never got to find out • **me quedé con las ~s de decirles lo que pensaba** I never got to tell them what I thought • **quitársele a algn las ~s de algo**: • **se me han quitado las ~s de ir** I don't feel like going now *o* any more • **hacer algo sin ~s** to do sth reluctantly *o* unwillingly • **tener ~s de hacer algo** to feel like doing sth • **tengo ~s de ir al cine** I feel like going to see a film • **tengo ~s de vomitar** I feel sick, I'm going to be sick • **tengo ~s de ir al servicio** I need (to go to) the loo • **tengo ~s de que llegue el sábado** I'm looking forward to Saturday • **hola, ¿cómo estás? tenía ~s de verte** hi, how are you? I was hoping I'd see you • **tengo unas ~s locas de verte** I can't wait to see you, I'm dying to see you • **tengo pocas ~s de ir** I don't feel like going much, I don't really want to go • **malditas las ~s que tengo de ir*** there's no way I want to go
2 • MODISMOS: • **de buena ~** gladly • **de buena ~ te ayudaría, pero no puedo** I'd gladly help you, but I can't • **con ~s** (= *de verdad*) really • **ser malo con ~s** to be thoroughly nasty • **hacer lo que le da la ~ a uno** to do as one pleases • **haz lo que te dé la ~** just do as you please • **me visto como me da la ~** I dress the way I want to, I dress as I please • **hazlo como te dé la ~** do it however you like • **¡no me da la ~!** I don't want to! • **porque (no) me da la real ~** because I (don't) damned well want to* • **me da la ~ de** (+ *infin*) I feel like (+ *ger*), I want to (+ *infin*) • **de ~** (*And*) (= *sin querer*) unintentionally; (= *en broma*) as a joke, in fun • **hasta las ~s** (*Méx*) right up to the end • **pagar hasta las ~s*** to pay over the odds • **¡las ~s!*** you'll wish you had! • **de mala ~** reluctantly, grudgingly • **no me pega la ~** (*Méx**) I don't feel like it • **siempre hace su regalada ~** (*Méx**) he always goes his own sweet way • **ser ~s de**: • **son ~s de molestar** *o* **fastidiar** they're just trying to be awkward • **es ~** (*And, Caribe, Méx*) it's a waste of time, there's no point • **tenerle ~s a algn*** to have it in for sb* • **venirle en ~ a algn**: • **hacen lo que les viene en ~** they do exactly as they please • **no me viene en ~** I don't feel like it, I can't be bothered • REFRANES: • **~ tiene de coles quien besa al hortelano** it's just cupboard love • **donde hay ~ hay maña** where there's a will, there's a way

ganadería SF **1** (= *crianza*) cattle raising, stockbreeding; (*en estancia*) ranching
2 (= *estancia*) stock farm; (= *rancho*) cattle ranch • **toros de ~ de Valdemoro** bulls from the Valdemoro ranch
3 (= *ganado*) cattle, livestock; (= *raza*) breed, race of cattle

ganadero/a ADJ cattle (*antes de s*), stock (*antes de s*); (= *de cría*) cattle-raising (*antes de s*)
SM/F **1** (= *criador*) cattle-raiser, stockbreeder (*EEUU*); (= *hacendado*) rancher
2 (= *comerciante*) cattle dealer

ganado SM **1** (= *animales*) livestock; (*esp LAm*) (*vacuno*) cattle; (= *rebaño*) herd, flock • **íbamos amontonados como ~** we were packed in like sardines ▸ **ganado asnal** donkeys (*pl*) ▸ **ganado caballar** horses (*pl*) ▸ **ganado cabrío** goats (*pl*) ▸ **ganado equino** horses (*pl*) ▸ **ganado lanar** sheep (*pl*) ▸ **ganado mayor** *cattle, horses and mules* ▸ **ganado menor** *sheep, goats and pigs* ▸ **ganado mular** mules (*pl*) ▸ **ganado ovejuno** sheep (*pl*) ▸ **ganado porcino** pigs (*pl*) ▸ **ganado vacuno** cattle
2 (*pey*) (= *gente*) • **¡ya verás qué ~ tenemos esta noche!** we've got a right bunch in here tonight!*
3 (*LAm*) • **un ~ de** a crowd *o* mob of

ganador(a) ADJ (= *vencedor*) winning, victorious • **el equipo ~** the winning team • **apostar a ~ y colocado** to back (a horse) each way, back for a win and a place
SM/F winner; (*Econ*) earner; (*que se beneficia*) gainer

ganancia SF **1** (= *beneficio*) gain; (= *aumento*) increase
2 ganancias (*Com, Econ*) (= *ingresos*) earnings; (= *beneficios*) profits • **sacar ~s de algo** to draw profit from sth • **~s y pérdidas** profit and loss • MODISMO: • **no le arriendo la ~** I don't envy him ▸ **ganancias brutas** gross profit (*sing*) ▸ **ganancias de capital** capital gains ▸ **ganancias líquidas** net profit (*sing*)
3 (*LAm*) (= *propina*) extra, bonus

ganancial ADJ profit (*antes de s*); ▹ **bien**
SMPL **gananciales** joint property (*sing*)

ganancioso/a ADJ **1** (= *lucrativo*) gainful
2 (= *triunfador*) winning • **resultar** *o* **salir ~** to be the gainer
SM/F gainer

ganapán SM **1** (*sin trabajo fijo*) casual labourer *o* (*EEUU*) laborer
2 (*que hace pequeños arreglos*) odd-job man
3 (= *palurdo*) lout
4 (= *recadero*) messenger

ganar ▹ CONJUG 1a VT **1** [+ *sueldo*] to earn • **¿cuánto ganas al mes?** how much do you earn *o* make a month? • **ha ganado mucho dinero** she has made a lot of money
2 [+ *competición, partido, premio, guerra*] to win • **le ganó cien euros a Rosa** he won a hundred euros from Rosa • **¿quién ganó la carrera?** who won the race? • **si te toca puedes ~ un millón** if you win you could get a million • **~ unas oposiciones para un puesto** to obtain a post by public examination
3 [+ *contrincante*] to beat • **¡les ganamos!** we beat them! • **ganamos al Olimpic tres a cero** we beat Olimpic three-nil • **no hay quien le gane** there's nobody who can beat him, he's unbeatable • **como orador no hay quien le gane** *o* **no le gana nadie** as a speaker there is no one to touch him, no one outdoes him at speaking
4 (= *conseguir*) [+ *tiempo, peso, terreno*] to gain • **¿qué gano yo con todo esto?** what do I gain *o* get from all this? • **con eso no ganas nada** that won't get you anywhere • **tierras ganadas al mar** land reclaimed *o* won from the sea • **~ popularidad** to win *o* earn popularity
5 (= *alcanzar*) [+ *objetivo*] to achieve, attain • **~ la orilla** to reach the shore • **~ la orilla nadando** to swim to the shore
6 (= *convencer*) to win over • **dejarse ~ por algo** to allow o.s. to be won over by sth
7 (= *aventajar*) • **te gana en inteligencia** he's more intelligent than you • **me gana en pericia** he has more expert knowledge than me • **te gana trabajando** he's a better worker than you
8 (*Mil*) [+ *plaza, pueblo*] to take, capture
VI **1** (*trabajando*) to earn • **no gano para comprar un piso** I don't earn enough to buy a flat • MODISMO: • **no ganamos para sustos** we have nothing but trouble
2 (*en competición, guerra*) to win • **~on por cuatro a dos** they won four-two • **~on por 40 votos** they won by 40 votes • **lo importante no es ~** winning isn't the most important thing • **nuestras ideas terminaron ganando** our ideas won out in the end • **dejarse ~** (*con trampas*) to lose on purpose • **se deja ~ por el niño** he lets the kid beat him
3 (= *mejorar*) to benefit, improve • **la película ~ía mucho si se cortase** the film would greatly benefit from being cut, the film would be greatly improved if it was cut • **hemos ganado con el cambio** we've greatly benefited from the change • **ha ganado mucho en salud** his health has greatly improved • **su juego ha ganado en confianza** her play has become more confident • **salir ganando** to do well • **saldrás ganando** you'll do well out of it • **salí ganando con la venta del coche** I did well out of the sale of the car
VPR **ganarse 1** [+ *afecto, confianza*] to win • **ha sabido ~se el afecto de todos** she has managed to win everyone's affection • **~se la confianza de algn** to win sb's trust • **~se las antipatías de algn** to make oneself unpopular with sb
2 [+ *sueldo*] to earn • **~se la vida** to earn a living • **se lo ha ganado** he has earned it *o* deserves it • **se ganó a pulso el título de campeón** he became champion the hard way • **¡te la vas a ~!*** you're for it!*
3 (*LAm*) (= *acercarse*) to go off • **~se a la cama** to go off to bed • **~se hasta la casa** to get to the house • **el caballo se ganó para el bosque** the horse moved off towards the wood, the horse made for the wood
4 (= *refugiarse*) to take refuge • **se ganó en la iglesia** he took refuge in the church

gancha‡ SF hash*, pot‡

ganchera SF (*Cono Sur*) matchmaker

ganchero/a SM/F (*Cono Sur*) (= *ayudante*) helper, assistant; (= *factótum*) odd-job man/odd-job woman

ganchete SM • MODISMOS: • **mirar al ~** (*Caribe**) to look out of the corner of one's eye (at) • **ir de ~** (*LAm*) to go arm-in-arm

ganchillo SM **1** (= *gancho*) crochet hook **2** (= *labor*) crochet work • **una colcha de ~** a crocheted quilt • **hacer (labores de) ~** to crochet

ganchito® SM *light cheese-flavoured snack*, ≈ Wotsit®

gancho SM **1** (= *garfio*) hook; [*de árbol*] stump; (*Agr*) shepherd's crook • MODISMOS: • **echar el ~ a algn*** to hook sb, capture sb • **estar en ~s** (*LAm*‡) to be hooked on drugs* ▸ **gancho de carnicero** butcher's hook ▸ **gancho de remolque** towing hook, trailer hitch
2 (*LAm*) (= *horquilla*) hairpin; (*para la ropa*) hanger; (*CAm*) (= *imperdible*) safety pin
3* (= *atractivo sexual*) sex appeal; (= *atractivo popular*) pulling power • **una chica con mucho ~** a girl with lots of sex appeal • **un actor con mucho ~** an actor with great pulling power • **el nuevo delantero tiene ~** the new forward is a crowd-puller • **esta música tiene ~** this music's really got something • **lo usan de ~ para atraer a la gente** they use it as an attraction to pull the crowds in
4 [*de timador*] accomplice
5 (*Boxeo*) (= *golpe*) hook • **un ~ hacia arriba** an uppercut
6 (*LAm*) (= *ayuda*) help; (= *protección*) protection • MODISMO: • **hacer ~** (*Cono Sur**) to lend a hand
7 (*And*) lady's saddle

ganchoso ADJ, **ganchudo** ADJ hooked, curved

gandalla‡ SMF (*Méx*) **1** (= *vagabundo*) tramp, bum (*EEUU**), hobo (*EEUU*) **2** (= *arribista*) upstart

gandido ADJ (*And*) greedy

gandinga SF (*Caribe*) **1** (*Culin*) thick stew **2*** (= *apatía*) sloth, apathy **3** (= *vergüenza*) • **tener poca ~** to have no sense of shame

gandola SF (*LAm*) articulated truck

gandul(a) ADJ (= *holgazán*) idle, slack; (= *inútil*) good-for-nothing
SM/F (= *holgazán*) idler, slacker; (= *inútil*) good-for-nothing

gandula* SF (*Hist*) law on vagrancy

gandulear ▹ CONJUG 1a VI to idle, loaf around

gandulería SF idleness, loafing

gandulitis SF INV (*hum*) congenital laziness

gane SM (*CAm*) (*Dep*) win, victory • **llevarse** *o* **lograr el ~** to win

gang SM (PL: **gangs**) gang

ganga SF **1** (*Com*) bargain • **¡una verdadera ~!** a genuine bargain! • **precios de ~** bargain prices, giveaway prices
2 (= *golpe de suerte*) windfall; (= *cosa fácil*) cinch*, gift* • **esto es una ~** this is a gift*
3 (*Méx**) (= *sarcasmo*) taunt, jeer

Ganges SM • **el ~** the Ganges

ganglio SM **1** (*Anat*) [*de células nerviosas*] ganglion; (*linfático*) lymph node **2 ganglios**‡ [*de mujer*] tits‡

gangosear ▹ CONJUG 1a VI (*And, Cono Sur*) **1*** (*pey*) to talk through one's nose, whine **2** = **ganguear**

gangoseo SM (*And, Cono Sur*) = **gangueo**

gangoso ADJ nasal, twanging

gangrena SF gangrene

gangrenar ▹ CONJUG 1a VT **1** (*Med*) to make gangrenous, cause gangrene in **2** (*Pol*) to infect, destroy
VPR **gangrenarse** to become gangrenous

gangrenoso ADJ gangrenous

gángster ['ganster] SM (PL: **gángsters** ['ganster]) gangster; (= *pistolero*) gunman

gangsteril ADJ gangster (*antes de s*)

gangsterismo SM gangsterism

ganguear ▹ CONJUG 1a VI to talk with a nasal accent, speak with a twang

gangueo SM nasal accent, twang

ganoso ADJ **1** (= *afanoso*) anxious, keen • **~ de hacer algo** anxious to do sth, keen to do sth **2** (*Cono Sur*) [*caballo*] spirited, fiery

gansada* SF (= *acto*) stupid thing (to do), piece of stupidity; (= *broma*) lark, caper* • **decir ~s** to talk nonsense • **hacer ~s** to play the fool, clown around

gansear* ▹ CONJUG 1a VI to play the fool, clown around

ganso/a ADJ* **1** (= *grande*) huge, hefty **2** (= *gandul*) lazy **3** (= *estúpido*) idiotic; (*pey*) (= *bromista*) play-acting • **¡no seas ~!** don't be an idiot! **4** (= *atractivo*) hunky*, dishy*; ▹ **pasta**
SM/F* (= *torpe*) idiot, dimwit*; (= *rústico*) country bumpkin, hick (*EEUU**)
SM (= *ave*) (*gen*) goose; (= *macho*) gander • MODISMO: • **hacer el ~** to play the fool, clown around ▸ **ganso salvaje** wild goose

gánster SM (PL: **gánsters**) gangster; (= *pistolero*) gunman

Gante SM Ghent

ganzúa SF (= *gancho*) picklock, skeleton key
SMF (= *ladrón*) burglar, thief; (= *sonsacador*) inquisitive person

gañán SM farmhand, labourer, laborer (*EEUU*)

gañido SM [*de perro*] yelp, howl; [*de pájaro*] croak; [*de persona*] wheeze

gañir ▹ CONJUG 3h VI [*perro*] to yelp, howl; [*pájaro*] to croak; [*persona*] to wheeze

gañón* SM, **gañote** SM throat, gullet

gapo‡ SM • **echar un ~** to gob‡, spit

GAR SM ABR (*Esp*) (= **Grupo Antiterrorista Rural**) *anti-terrorist branch of the Civil Guard*

garabatear ▹ CONJUG 1a VT to scribble, scrawl
VI **1** (*al escribir*) to scribble, scrawl **2** (= *andar con rodeos*) to beat about the bush **3** (*con gancho*) (= *utilizar*) to use a hook; (= *echar*) to throw out a hook

garabato SM **1** (= *dibujo*) doodle; (= *escritura*) scribble • **una hoja cubierta de ~s inintelegibles** a page full of unintelligible scribbles • **echar un ~** (= *firmar*) to scrawl a signature • **hacer ~s** (= *dibujar*) to doodle; (= *escribir*) to scribble
2 (= *gancho*) hook; (*Náut*) grappling iron; (*Caribe*) long forked pole ▸ **garabato de carnicero** meat hook
3 (*Caribe**) (= *flaco*) beanpole*, string bean (*EEUU**)
4 (*Cono Sur*) (= *palabrota*) swearword • **echar ~s** to swear

garabina SF **1** (*And*) (= *bagatela*) trifle, bagatelle; (= *bisutería*) cheap finery **2** (*Caribe*) (= *crisálida*) chrysalis

garabito SM **1** [*de mercado*] market stall **2** (*Cono Sur*) (= *vagabundo*) tramp, bum (*EEUU**), hobo (*EEUU*)

garabullo†‡ SM five pesetas

garaje SM garage • **"duerme en garaje"** "kept in a garage" • **una plaza de ~** a parking space • MODISMO: • **el ~ La Estrella** (*hum*) the street

garajista SMF (= *dueño*) garage owner; (= *trabajador*) garage attendant

garambaina SF **1** (= *adorno*) cheap finery, tawdry finery **2** (= *carácter chillón*) gaudiness **3 garambainas** (= *muecas*) affected grimaces; (= *ademanes afectados*) absurd mannerisms • **¡déjate de ~s!** stop your nonsense! **4 garambainas** (= *escritura*) scribbles

garambetas* SFPL (*Caribe*) **1** = **garambaina 2** • **hacer ~** to pull faces

garandumba SF (*Arg*) flatboat, flat river boat

garante ADJ responsible, guaranteeing
SMF (*Econ*) guarantor, surety

garantía SF **1** [*de producto*] guarantee, warranty • **bajo** *o* **en ~** under guarantee *o* warranty • **de máxima ~** absolutely guaranteed
2 (= *seguridad*) pledge, security; (= *compromiso*) undertaking, guarantee • **~ de trabajo** job security • **dar ~s a algn** to give sb guarantees • **suspender las ~s (ciudadanas)** to suspend civil rights ▸ **garantías constitucionales** constitutional guarantees
3 (*Jur*) warranty ▸ **garantía escrita** express warranty ▸ **garantía implícita** implied warranty

garantir ▹ CONJUG 3a; defectivo VT **1** (= *garantizar*) to guarantee **2** (*And, Caribe, Cono Sur*) (= *asegurar*) to guarantee, assure

garantizadamente ADV genuinely, authentically

garantizado ADJ guaranteed; (= *auténtico*) genuine, authentic

garantizar ▹ CONJUG 1f VT **1** (= *responder de*) [+ *producto, crédito*] to guarantee • **la lavadora está garantizada por dos años** the washing machine is guaranteed for two years, the washing machine has a two-year guarantee • **garantizamos la calidad de nuestros productos** we guarantee the quality of our products
2 (= *avalar*) [+ *persona*] to vouch for
3 (= *asegurar*) to guarantee • **le garantizo que lo recibirá antes del jueves** I guarantee you'll receive it before Thursday • **me van a oír ¡te lo garantizo!** they'll listen to me, I can guarantee it!

garañón SM **1** (*Zool*) (= *asno*) stud jackass; (*LAm*) (= *semental*) stallion **2** (*Cono Sur*) (= *persona*) brothel keeper

garapiña SF **1** (*Culin*) sugar icing, sugar coating **2** (*LAm*) (= *bebida*) iced pineapple drink **3** (*Méx*) (= *robo*) theft

garapiñado ADJ • **almendra garapiñada** sugared almond

garapiñar ▹ CONJUG 1a VT **1** [+ *granizado*] to freeze **2** [+ *pastel*] to ice, coat with sugar **3** [+ *fruta*] to candy **4** [+ *nata*] to clot

garapiñera SF ice-cream freezer

garapullo SM (= *rehilete*) dart; (*Taur*) banderilla

garata* SF (*Caribe*) fight, brawl

garatusas SFPL • **hacer ~ a algn** to coax sb, wheedle sb

garba SF sheaf

garbanzo SM **1** (= *legumbre*) chickpea • MODISMOS: • **ganarse los ~s** to earn one's living • **ser el ~ negro de la familia** to be the black sheep of the family
2 • MODISMO: • **de ~** (= *corriente*) ordinary, unpretentious • **gente de ~** humble folk, ordinary people, regular people (*EEUU*)

garbear ▹ CONJUG 1a VT* (= *robar*) to pinch*, swipe‡
VI **1** (= *afectar garbo*) to make a show, show off **2** (= *robar*) to steal (*for a living*) **3** (= *buscarse la vida*) to get along, rub along
VPR **garbearse** to get along, rub along

g

garbeo* SM • **darse** *o* **pegarse un ~** (= *dar un paseo*) to go for a stroll; (= *ir por ahí*) to go out, go out and about; (*en coche*) to go for a ride*, go for a spin*

garbera SF stook, shock

garbí SM south-west wind

garbillar ▹ CONJUG 1a VT (*Agr*) to sift, sieve; (*Min*) to sift, screen, riddle

garbillo SM (*para grano*) sieve; (*para mineral*) screen, riddle

garbo SM **1** (= *elegancia*) grace, elegance; (= *porte*) graceful bearing; (= *aire*) jauntiness; [*de mujer*] glamour, glamor (*EEUU*); [*de escrito*] style, stylishness • **hacer algo con ~** to do sth with grace and ease *o* with style • **andar con ~** to walk gracefully • **¡qué ~!** she's so graceful
2 (= *brío*) agility • **empezó a limpiar el cuarto con mucho ~** she went whizzing round the room cleaning up
3 (= *largueza*) magnanimity, generosity

garbosamente ADV **1** (= *con elegancia*) gracefully, elegantly; (*al andar*) jauntily; (= *con estilo*) stylishly
2 (= *con generosidad*) generously

garboso ADJ **1** (= *elegante*) graceful, elegant; [*andar*] jaunty; (= *encantador*) glamorous, alluring; (= *con estilo*) stylish
2 (= *desinteresado*) generous, magnanimous

garceta SF egret

garciamarquiano ADJ *of or relating to Gabriel García Márquez*

garcilla SF little egret ▸ **garcilla bueyera** cattle egret

garçon [gar'son] SM • **con pelo a lo ~** with bobbed hair, with hair in a boyish style; ▹ **garzón**

gardenia SF gardenia

garduña SF marten

garduño/a SM/F sneak thief

garete SM • **irse al ~** [*barco*] to be adrift; [*plan, proyecto etc**] to fall through, bomb (*EEUU**); [*empresa*] to go bust*

garfa SF claw

garfada SF clawing, scratching

garfil* SM (*Méx*) cop*

garfio SM **1** (= *gancho*) hook
2 (*Téc*) (= *arpeo*) grappling iron, claw
3 (*Alpinismo*) (= *pico*) climbing iron

gargajear ▹ CONJUG 1a VI to spit up phlegm, hawk

gargajo SM phlegm, sputum • **echar un ~** to spit up phlegm, hawk

garganta SF **1** (*Anat*) throat, gullet; (= *cuello*) neck • **me duele la ~** I have a sore throat • MODISMOS: • **le tengo atravesado en la ~** he sticks in my gullet • **mojar la ~** to wet one's whistle* • **tener el agua a la ~** to be in great danger
2 [*del pie*] instep
3 (*Mús*) singing voice • **tener buena ~** to have a good singing voice
4 [*de botella*] neck
5 (*Geog*) (= *barranco*) ravine, gorge; (= *desfiladero*) narrow pass
6 (*Arquit*) [*de columna*] shaft

gargantear ▹ CONJUG 1a VI to warble, quaver, trill

garganteo SM warble, quaver, trill

gargantilla SF choker, necklace

gargantuesco ADJ gargantuan

gárgara SF gargle, gargling • **hacer ~s** to gargle • MODISMO: • **mandar a algn a hacer ~s*** to tell sb to go to hell • **¡vete a hacer ~s!*** go to blazes!

gargarear ▹ CONJUG 1a VI (*And, CAm, Cono Sur*) to gargle

gargarismo SM **1** (= *acto*) gargling
2 (= *líquido*) gargle, gargling solution

gargarizar ▹ CONJUG 1f VI to gargle

gárgol SM groove

gárgola SF gargoyle

garguero SM (= *garganta*) gullet; (= *esófago*) windpipe

garifo ADJ **1**† (= *elegante*) spruce, elegant, natty*
2 (*Cono Sur*) (= *astuto*) sharp
3 (*And*) (= *engreído*) stuck-up*
4 (*CAm*) (= *hambriento*) hungry
5 • **estar ~** (*And*) to be broke*

gariga SF (*Méx*) drizzle

garita SF **1** [*de centinela*] sentry box; [*de conserje*] porter's lodge; (*LAm*) [*de policía de tráfico*] stand, box ▸ **garita de control** checkpoint ▸ **garita de señales** (*Ferro*) signal box
2 (= *caseta*) cabin, box
3 [*de camión*] cab

garitea SF (*And*) river flatboat

garitero/a SM/F (= *dueño*) keeper of a gaming house; (= *jugador*) gambler

garito SM **1** (= *club*) nightclub, nightspot; [*de juego*] gaming house, gambling den
2 (= *ganancias del juego*) gambling profits (*pl*), winnings (*pl*)

garla SF talk, chatter

garlador(a) ADJ garrulous
SM/F chatterer, great talker

garlar* ▹ CONJUG 1a VI (*Col*) to chat

garlito SM **1** (= *red*) fish trap
2 (= *celada*) snare, trap • **caer en el ~** to fall into the trap • **coger a algn en el ~** to catch sb in the act

garlopa SF jack plane

garnacha SF **1** (= *uva*) garnacha grape; (= *vino*) garnacha (*sweet wine from garnacha grape*)
2 (*Jur, Hist*) (= *vestidura*) gown, robe; (= *persona*) judge
3 (*Méx*) (*Culin*) *tortilla with meat filling*
4 • MODISMO: • **a la ~** (*CAm**) violently • **¡ni de ~!** (*Caribe**) not on your life!
5 (*Chile*) (= *ventaja*) advantage, edge

garnachear ▹ CONJUG 1a VT (*Cono Sur*) (= *llevar ventaja a*) to have the edge over

garnucho SM (*Méx*) tap, rap on the nose

Garona SM • **el (río) ~** the Garonne

garpar‡ ▹ CONJUG 1a VT (*Cono Sur*) to pay, fork out*

garra SF **1** (= *pata*) [*de animal*] claw; [*de águila*] talon; [*de persona**] hand, paw* • MODISMOS: • **echar la ~ a algn*** to nab sb*, seize sb • **estar como una ~** (*And, Cono Sur*) to be as thin as a rake*
2 garras (= *dominio*) clutches • MODISMO: • **caer en las ~s de algn** to fall into sb's clutches
3 (*Téc*) claw, hook; (*Mec*) clutch ▸ **garra de seguridad** safety clutch
4 (= *fuerza*) bite; (*Dep*) sharpness, edge • **esa canción no tiene ~** that song has no bite to it
5 (*Méx**) muscular strength
6 (*Chile**) strip of old leather
7 garras (*Méx**) bits, pieces • MODISMO: • **no hay cuero sin ~s*** nothing is ever perfect
8 (*And*) (= *bolsa*) leather bag

garrafa SF **1** (= *garrafón*) demijohn; (*para agua*) *large glass water container* • **de ~*** (*pey*) [*ginebra, vino*] cheap, dodgy*
2 (= *licorera*) decanter
3 (*Arg*) [*de gas*] cylinder

garrafal ADJ (= *enorme*) enormous, terrific; [*error*] monumental, terrible

garrafón SM carboy, demijohn

garrancha* SF **1** (= *espada*) sword
2 (*Col*) (= *gancho*) hook

garrapata SF **1** (*Zool*) tick
2 (*Mil**) disabled horse, useless horse

garrapatear ▹ CONJUG 1a VI to scribble, scrawl

garrapatero SM (= *ave*) cowbird, buffalo bird; (*LAm*) tick-eater

garrapaticida ADJ pesticidal
SM insecticide, tick-killing agent

garrapato SM = **garabato**

garrapiñada SF sugared almond

garrapiñado ADJ • **almendra garrapiñada** sugared almond

garrapiñar ▹ CONJUG 1a VT = **garapiñar**

garrear ▹ CONJUG 1a (*Cono Sur*) VT
1 [+ *animal*] to skin the feet of
2* (= *robar*) to pinch*
VI* to sponge*, live off others

garreo* SM • **es de puro ~** (*Cono Sur*) it's a piece of cake*

garrete SM (*And, CAm, Cono Sur*) [*de caballo*] hock; [*de persona*] back of the knee

garrido ADJ (*liter*) **1** (= *galano*) neat, smart
2 (= *atractivo*) [*hombre*] handsome; [*mujer*] pretty

garroba SF carob bean

garrobo SM (*CAm*) (= *lagarto*) iguana; (= *caimán*) small alligator

garrocha SF **1** (*Agr*) goad
2 (*Taur*) spear
3 (*LAm*) (*Dep*) vaulting pole

garrochista SMF (*LAm*) pole vaulter

garrón SM **1** (*Zool*) [*de ave*] spur; [*de otros animales*] paw; (= *talón*) heel
2 [*de carne*] shank
3 (*Arg*) hock • MODISMO: • **vivir de ~** to sponge*, live off others
4 (*Bot*) snag, spur

garronear* ▹ CONJUG 1a VI (*Arg*) to sponge*, live off others

garrota SF (= *palo*) stick, club; [*de pastor*] crook

garrotazo SM blow with a stick *o* club

garrote SM **1** (= *palo*) stick, club • **la política del ~ y la zanahoria** the carrot-and-stick approach
2 (*Med*) tourniquet
3 (*Jur*) (= *ejecución*) garrotte • **dar ~ a algn** to garrotte sb
4 (*Méx*) (*Aut*) brake • MODISMO: • **darse ~*** to check o.s., hold o.s. back

garrotear ▹ CONJUG 1a VT (*LAm*) to club, cudgel

garrotero/a ADJ (*Caribe, Cono Sur**) stingy*
SM/F **1** (*Méx*) (*Ferro*) guard, brakeman (*EEUU*)
2 (*And, Cono Sur*) (= *matón*) bully, tough*; (= *pendenciero*) brawler, troublemaker
3 (*Caribe*) (= *prestamista*) moneylender

garrotillo SM **1** (= *difteria*) croup
2 (*Cono Sur*) (= *granizada*) summer hail

garrucha SF pulley

garrudo ADJ **1** (*Méx*) (= *forzudo*) tough, muscular
2 (*And*) [*vaca*] terribly thin

garrulería SF chatter

garrulidad SF garrulousness

garrulo/a ADJ loutish
SM/F lout

gárrulo ADJ **1** (= *hablador*) garrulous
2 [*pájaro*] twittering; [*agua*] babbling, murmuring; [*viento*] noisy

garúa SF **1** (*LAm*) (= *llovizna*) drizzle
2 (*Caribe*) (= *alboroto*) row, din

garuar ▹ CONJUG 1e VI (*LAm*) to drizzle
• MODISMO: • **¡que le garúe fino!** I wish you luck!, I hope it keeps fine for you!

garubar ▹ CONJUG 1a VI (*Cono Sur*) = **garuar**

garufa* SF • **ir de ~** (*Cono Sur*) to go on a spree

garuga SF (*Cono Sur*) = **garúa**

garugar ▹ CONJUG 1h VI (*Cono Sur*) = **garuar**

garulla SF **1** (= *uvas*) loose grapes (*pl*)
2 (= *gentío*) mob, rabble
SMF* urchin, rascal

garullada* SF mob, rabble
garza SF **1** (*tb* **garza real**) heron ▸ **garza imperial** purple heron
2 (*Chile*) lager glass, beer glass
garzo ADJ (*liter*) [*ojos*] blue, bluish; [*persona*] blue-eyed
garzón/ona SM/F (*Chile, Uru*) waiter/ waitress
gas SM **1** (= *combustible*) gas • **una cocina de gas** a gas cooker • **esta cerveza tiene mucho gas** this beer is very gassy *o* fizzy • **asfixiar con gas a algn** to gas sb • **agua (mineral) con gas** sparkling (mineral) water • **una bebida con gas** a fizzy drink • **agua (mineral) sin gas** still (mineral) water • **una bebida sin gas** a still drink ▸ **gas butano** butane, butane gas ▸ **gas ciudad** town gas ▸ **gas de (efecto) invernadero** greenhouse gas ▸ **gas de esquisto** shale gas ▸ **gas del alumbrado** coal gas ▸ **gas de los pantanos** marsh gas ▸ **gas de lutita** shale gas ▸ **gas hilarante** laughing gas ▸ **gases lacrimógenos** tear gas (*sing*) ▸ **gas inerte** inert gas ▸ **gas licuado** liquefied gas; (*Chile*) (*para uso doméstico*) Calor gas® ▸ **gas mostaza** mustard gas ▸ **gas natural** natural gas ▸ **gas nervioso** nerve gas ▸ **gas noble** noble gas, rare gas ▸ **gas pobre** producer gas ▸ **gas propano** propane, propane gas ▸ **gas tóxico** poison gas
2 (*CAm, Méx*) (= *gasolina*) petrol, gas (*EEUU*) • **darle gas*** to step on the gas* • MODISMOS: • **a medio gas**: • **el equipo jugó a medio gas** the team played with the foot off the pedal • **estar gas** (*CAm*) (*hum*) to be head over heels in love • **a todo gas** (*Esp*) (*Aut*) full out, flat out*; [*trabajar*] flat out* • **el coche iba a todo gas** the car was going full out *o* flat out* • **tenían el aire acondicionado a todo gas** they had the air conditioning full on • **tuvimos que terminarlo a todo gas** we had to work flat out to get it finished* • **la maquinaria electoral funciona ya a todo gas** the electoral machine is now in full swing • **perder gas**: • **el equipo comenzó la temporada con fuerza pero ha ido perdiendo gas** the team began the season well but has been running out of steam • **los hinchas fueron perdiendo gas a medida que transcurría el partido** the fans gradually lost enthusiasm as the match progressed
3 gases (= *emanaciones perjudiciales*) fumes • **los gases tóxicos que se emiten a la atmósfera** the toxic *o* poisonous fumes released into the atmosphere ▸ **gases de escape** exhaust fumes • **emisiones de gases de escape** exhaust emissions
4 gases (= *flatulencias*) wind (*sing*), flatulence (*sing*), gas (*sing*) (*EEUU*) • **tener gases** to have wind, have gas (*EEUU*)
gasa SF **1** (= *tela*) gauze; [*de luto*] crêpe
2 (*Med*) gauze, lint • **una ~** a dressing
3 (= *pañal*) nappy, diaper (*EEUU*)
Gascuña SF Gascony
gaseado ADJ carbonated, aerated
gasear ▸ CONJUG 1a VT to gas, kill with gas
gaseoducto SM gas pipeline
gaseosa SF **1** (= *bebida efervescente*) lemonade
2 (= *cualquier refresco*) fizzy drink, soda (*EEUU*)
gaseoso ADJ **1** [*estado, densidad, mezcla*] gaseous
2 [*bebida*] sparkling, fizzy
gásfiter SMF (PL: **gásfiters**) (*And, Cono Sur*) plumber
gasfitería SF (*And, Cono Sur*) plumber's (shop)
gasfitero/a SM/F (*And, Cono Sur*) plumber
gasificación SF **1** (*Quím*) gasification
2 [*de ciudad*] supply of piped gas (**de** to)
gasificar ▸ CONJUG 1g VT **1** (= *volatilizar*) to gasify
2 [+ *bebida*] to carbonate
gasista ADJ gas (*antes de s*) • **industria ~** gas industry
SMF gas fitter
gasístico ADJ gas (*antes de s*)
gasoducto SM gas pipeline
gasofa‡ SF juice*, petrol, gas(oline) (*EEUU*)
gasoil SM, **gas-oil** SM [ga'soil] (*para vehículos*) diesel (oil); (*para calefacción*) (heating) oil ▸ **gasoil B** red diesel ▸ **gasoil de calefacción** central heating oil
gasóleo SM (*para vehículos*) diesel (oil); (*para calefacción*) (heating) oil ▸ **gasóleo B** red diesel ▸ **gasóleo de calefacción** central heating oil
gasolero SM diesel-powered car
gasolina SF **1** (*Aut*) petrol, gas(oline) (*EEUU*) • **echar ~** (*a un vehículo*) to put petrol in • **repostar ~** (*lit*) to fill up with petrol;‡ (*fig*) to have a drink ▸ **gasolina con plomo** leaded petrol ▸ **gasolina de alto octanaje** high octane petrol ▸ **gasolina de aviación** aviation spirit, aviation fuel ▸ **gasolina extra** four-star petrol ▸ **gasolina normal** two-star petrol ▸ **gasolina sin plomo** unleaded (petrol) ▸ **gasolina súper** four-star petrol
2 (*Caribe*) (= *gasolinera*) petrol station, gas station (*EEUU*)
gasolinera SF **1** (*Aut*) petrol station, gas station (*EEUU*)
2 (*Náut*) motorboat
gasolinero/a SM/F (= *dueño*) petrol station owner, gas station owner (*EEUU*); (= *empleado*) petrol pump attendant, gas station attendant (*EEUU*)
gasómetro SM gasometer
gásquet SM (PL: **gásquets**) (*LAm*) gasket
gastable ADJ expendable
gastado ADJ **1** (= *desgastado*) [*ropa, neumático, superficie*] worn • **tenía el uniforme ~ y sucio** his uniform was worn and dirty • **alfombras de lana muy gastadas** threadbare woollen rugs • **las páginas del libro estaban muy gastadas por el uso** the pages of the book were well-thumbed
2 (= *trillado*) [*metáfora*] stale, hackneyed; [*broma*] old, stale • **un político ~** a washed-up politician*
3 [*pilas*] dead
gastador(a) ADJ extravagant • **es muy ~a** she's very extravagant, she's a spendthrift
SM/F **1** spendthrift • **es un ~** he's a spendthrift, he's very extravagant
2 (*Mil*) sapper
gastar ▸ CONJUG 1a VT **1** [+ *dinero*] to spend (en on) • **han gastado un dineral en el arreglo del coche** they've spent a fortune on fixing the car
2 (= *consumir*) [+ *gasolina, electricidad, agua*] to use • **un radiocasete como este gasta más pilas** a radio cassette player like this goes through *o* uses more batteries • **he gastado todas las velas que tenía** I've used up all the candles I had
3 (= *desgastar*) [+ *ropa, zapato*] to wear out; [+ *tacones*] to wear down
4 (= *malgastar*) to waste • **~ palabras** to waste one's breath; ▸ **saliva**
5 (= *llevar*) [+ *ropa, gafas*] to wear; [+ *barba*] to have • **antes no gastaba gafas** he didn't use to wear glasses • **¿qué número (de zapatos) gasta?** what size (shoes) do you take? • **¿qué talla gasta?** what size are you?
6 [+ *broma*] to play (a on) • **~ una broma pesada a algn** to play a practical joke *o* a hoax on sb
7 • **gastarlas** (*Esp**): **no le repliques, que ya sabes como las gasta** don't answer him back, you know what he's like when he gets angry*
VI **1** (= *gastar dinero*) • **a todos nos gusta ~** we all like spending money
2 (= *consumir*) • **este coche gasta poco** this car uses very little petrol • **una bombilla normal apenas gasta** a normal light bulb uses hardly any electricity
VPR **gastarse 1** (= *consumirse*) [*pilas*] to run out; [*vela*] to burn down • **así se gastan antes las pilas** the batteries run out sooner that way
2 (= *desgastarse*) [*suelas, neumáticos*] to wear, wear out; [*tacones*] to wear down
3 (*Esp*) (*enfático*) [+ *dinero*] to spend • **se lo gasta todo en música** he spends all his money on music • **se gastó 400 euros solo en zapatos** she got through *o* spent 400 euros just on shoes
4 (*enfático*) (= *tener*) • **¡vaya genio que te gastas!** what a filthy temper you've got! • **es increíble la intolerancia que se gastan algunas personas** it's amazing how intolerant some people are • **¡vaya humos se gasta la señora!** she's so stuck up! • **hay que tener cuidado con las bromas que se gasta ese** you have to watch out for the jokes he plays on people
Gasteiz SM Vitoria
gasto SM **1** [*de dinero*] • **la inversión nos supondría un ~ de varios millones** the investment would involve an expense *o* expenditure of several million • **tenemos que reducir el ~** we must cut costs *o* spending • **no tenías que haberte metido en tanto ~** you needn't have spent so much ▸ **gasto militar** military spending, military expenditure ▸ **gasto público** public spending, public expenditure ▸ **gasto sanitario** health spending, health expenditure ▸ **gasto social** welfare spending, welfare expenditure
2 gastos expenses • **este dinero es para tus ~s** this money is for your expenses • **este mes he tenido muchos ~s** I have had a lot of expenses this month • **un viaje con todos los ~s pagados** an all-expenses-paid trip • **cubrir ~s** to cover (one's) costs ▸ **gastos administrativos** administrative costs ▸ **gastos bancarios** bank charges ▸ **gastos comerciales** business expenses ▸ **gastos corrientes** (*en empresa*) running costs; (*en la Administración*) revenue expenditure (*sing*) ▸ **gastos de administración** administrative costs ▸ **gastos de comunidad** service charges ▸ **gastos de conservación** maintenance costs ▸ **gastos de correo** postal charges ▸ **gastos de defensa** defence spending (*sing*), defense spending (*sing*) (*EEUU*) ▸ **gastos de desplazamiento** (*por viaje*) travelling expenses, traveling expenses (*EEUU*); (*por mudanza*) relocation allowance (*sing*) ▸ **gastos de distribución** distribution costs ▸ **gastos de entrega** delivery charge (*sing*) ▸ **gastos de envío** postage and packing (*sing*), postage and handling (*sing*) (*EEUU*) ▸ **gastos de explotación** operating costs ▸ **gastos de flete** freight charges ▸ **gastos de mantenimiento** maintenance costs ▸ **gastos de representación** entertainment allowance (*sing*) ▸ **gastos de servicio** service charge (*sing*) ▸ **gastos de tramitación** handling charge (*sing*) ▸ **gastos de transporte** [*de personal*] travelling expenses, traveling expenses (*EEUU*); [*de mercancías*] freight charges ▸ **gastos de viaje** travelling expenses, traveling expenses (*EEUU*) ▸ **gastos fijos** fixed charges ▸ **gastos generales** overheads, overhead (*sing*) (*EEUU*) ▸ **gastos menores (de caja)** petty cash

expenses ▸ **gastos operacionales** operating costs ▸ **gastos vendidos** accrued charges
3 [*de gas*] flow, rate of flow
gastón¹‡ SM (*CAm*) (= *diarrea*) the runs‡
gastón²* ADJ free-spending
gastoso ADJ extravagant, wasteful
gástrico ADJ gastric
gastritis SF INV gastritis
gastrobar SM gastro-pub
gastroenteritis SF INV gastroenteritis
gastrointestinal ADJ gastrointestinal
gastronomía SF gastronomy
gastronómico ADJ gastronomic
gastrónomo/a SM/F gastronome, gourmet
gastroplastia SF gastroplasty
gastrópodo SM gastropod
gata SF 1 (*Chile, Perú*) (*Aut*) jack
2 • **a gatas a** • **andar a ~s** to crawl • **subió las escaleras a ~s** he crawled up the stairs • **el niño entró andando a ~s** the baby crawled in • **en este juego tenéis que andar a ~s** in this game you have to crawl on all fours
b (*Cono Sur**) (= *apenas*) barely, by the skin of one's teeth
3 (*Meteo*) hill cloud
4 (= *agujetas*) • **tener ~** to ache all over
5 • MODISMOS: • **echar la ~** (*CAm**) • **soltar la ~** (*Perú**) to lift*, steal; ▹ **gato**
gatada SF 1 (= *movimiento*) *movement o act typical of a cat*
2 (= *arañazos*) scratching, clawing
3 (= *trampa*) artful dodge, sly trick
gatazo* SM • MODISMO: • **dar el ~** (*LAm*) to look younger than one is, not to show one's age
gateado ADJ 1 (= *gatuno*) catlike, feline
2 [*mármol*] striped, veined
SM 1 (= *movimiento*) (*al gatear*) crawl, crawling; (*al subir*) climb, climbing
2 (= *arañazos*) scratching, clawing
3 (*Caribe*) hard veined wood (*used in cabinet-making*)
gateamiento SM = **gateado**
gatear ▹ CONJUG 1a VI 1 (= *andar a gatas*) to crawl; (= *trepar*) to climb, clamber (**por** up)
2 (*LAm*) to be on the prowl
VT 1 (= *arañar*) to scratch, claw
2* (= *hurtar*) to pinch*, steal
3 (*CAm, Méx**) (= *ligar*) to try to pick up*; (= *seducir*) to seduce
gateo SM crawling
gatera¹ SF 1 (*para gato*) catflap
2 (*Náut*) cat hole; ▹ **gatero**
gatera² SF (*And*) (= *verdulera*) market woman, stallholder; ▹ **gatero**
gatería SF 1 (= *gatos*) cats (*pl*), collection of cats
2 (= *pandilla*) gang of louts
3 (= *cualidad*) false modesty
gatero/a ADJ fond of cats
SM/F cat lover; ▹ **gatera**
gatillar ▹ CONJUG 1a VT to cock
gatillero SM (*Méx*) hired gun(man), hitman
gatillo SM 1 [*de arma*] trigger • **apretar el ~** to pull *o* press *o* squeeze the trigger
2 (= *herramienta*) [*de dentista*] dental forceps; (*Téc*) clamp
3 (*Zool*) nape of the neck
4* (= *ratero*) young pickpocket, young thief
gatito/a SM/F (*gen*) kitten; (*como término cariñoso*) pussycat
gato¹/a SM/F 1 (*Zool*) (*gen*) cat; (*especificando el sexo*) tomcat/she-cat • **"El ~ con botas"** "Puss in Boots" • MODISMOS: • **dar a algn ~ por liebre** to con sb* • **te han dado ~ por liebre** you've been had *o* conned*, you've been done* • **cuatro ~s**: • **no había más que cuatro ~s** there was hardly anyone *o* a soul there • **este programa solo lo ven cuatro ~s** hardly anyone watches this programme, this programme is only watched by a handful of people • **no son más que cuatro ~s en la oficina** there's only a handful of people in the office • **aquí hay ~ encerrado** there's something fishy (going on) here • **jugar al ~ y al ratón con algn** to play cat and mouse with sb, play a cat-and-mouse game with sb • **lavarse como los ~s** to give o.s. a quick wash • **llevarse el ~ al agua** to win the day, pull it off* • **estar para el ~** (*Chile**) to be in a terrible state* • **esta gripe me tiene para el ~** I'm in a really terrible state with this flu* • **ser ~ viejo** to be an old hand • REFRANES: • **el ~ escaldado del agua fría huye** once bitten twice shy • **de noche todos los ~s son pardos** everything looks the same in the dark ▸ **gato callejero** stray cat, alley cat (*esp EEUU*) ▸ **gato de algalia** civet cat ▸ **gato de Angora** Angora cat ▸ **gato montés** wild cat ▸ **gato romano** tabby cat ▸ **gato siamés** Siamese cat; ▹ **defender, pie**
2 (*Esp**) (= *madrileño*) *native of Madrid*
3 (*Méx**) (= *criado*) servant
SM 1 (*Téc*) [*de coche*] jack; (= *torno*) clamp, vice, vise (*EEUU*); (= *grapa*) grab, drag (*EEUU*); (*Méx*) [*de arma*] trigger ▸ **gato de tornillo** screw jack ▸ **gato hidráulico** hydraulic jack
2* (= *ladrón*) sneak thief, petty thief
3 (= *baile*) *a popular Argentinian folk dance*
4† (*para el dinero*) money bag
5 (*CAm*) (= *músculo*) muscle
6 (*Méx*) (= *propina*) tip
7 (*Cono Sur*) (= *bolsa de agua*) hot-water bottle; ▹ **gata**
gato² SM (*And*) open-air market, market place
gatopardo SM ocelot
GATT SM ABR (= **General Agreement on Tariffs and Trade**) GATT
gatuno ADJ catlike, feline
gatuperio SM 1 (= *mezcla*) hotchpotch, hodgepodge (*EEUU*)
2 (= *chanchullo*) shady dealing; (= *fraude*) fraud
gaucano* SM (*Caribe*) *rum-based cocktail*
gaucha† SF (*Cono Sur*) mannish woman
gauchada SF (*Cono Sur*) 1 (= *favor*) kind deed, favour, favor (*EEUU*) • **hacer una ~ a algn** to do sb a favour
2 (= *conjunto*) gauchos (*pl*)
3† (= *acción*) gaucho exploit; (*pey*) gaucho trick
gauchaje SM 1 (*Cono Sur*) (= *personas*) gauchos (*pl*); (= *reunión*) gathering of gauchos
2 (*pey*) (= *gentuza*) riffraff, rabble
gauchear ▹ CONJUG 1a VI (*Cono Sur*) to live like a gaucho
gauchesco ADJ (*Cono Sur*) gaucho (*antes de s*), of the gauchos • **vida gauchesca** gaucho life
gaucho SM 1 (*LAm*) gaucho; (= *vaquero*) cowboy, herdsman, herder (*EEUU*)
2 (*Cono Sur*) (= *jinete*) good rider, expert horseman
3 (*And*) (= *sombrero*) wide-brimmed straw hat
ADJ 1 gaucho (*antes de s*), gaucho-like
2 (*Cono Sur**) (= *servicial*) helpful

GAUCHO

Gaucho is the name given to the men who rode the **Pampa**, the plains of Argentina, Uruguay and parts of southern Brazil, earning their living on cattle farms. Important parts of the **gaucho's** traditional costume include the **faja**, a sash worn around the waist, the **facón**, a sheath knife, and **boleadoras**, strips of leather weighted with stones at either end which were used somewhat like lassos to catch cattle. During the 19th century this vast **pampas** area was divided up into large ranches and the free-roaming lifestyle of the **gaucho** gradually disappeared. **Gauchos** were the inspiration for a tradition of **literatura gauchesca**, of which the most famous work is the two-part epic poem "Martín Fierro" written by the Argentine José Hernández between 1872 and 1879 and mourning the loss of the **gaucho** way of life and their persecution as outlaws.

gaudeamus* SM INV (= *fiesta*) party
gaulista ADJ, SMF Gaullist
gavera SF (*LAm*) crate
gaveta SF (= *cajón*) drawer; (*con llave*) locker • **~ de archivo** filing drawer
gavia SF 1 (*Náut*) (= *vela*) main topsail
2 (*Agr*) (= *zanja*) ditch
3 (= *cuadrilla*) squad of workmen
4 (= *ave*) seagull
gavilán SM 1 (= *ave*) sparrowhawk
2 [*de pluma*] nib
3 [*de espada*] quillon
4 (*LAm*) (= *uñero*) ingrowing toenail
gavilla SF 1 (*Agr*) sheaf
2* (= *pandilla*) gang, band
gavillero SM (*LAm*) gunman
gaviota SF 1 (= *ave*) seagull ▸ **gaviota argente, gaviota argéntea** herring gull
2 (*Méx*) (*hum*) flier
gavota SF gavotte
gay ADJ INV gay
SM (PL: **gays**) gay man, gay
gaya SF 1 (= *ave*) magpie
2 (*en tela*) coloured *o* (*EEUU*) colored stripe
gayo (*liter*) ADJ 1 (= *alegre*) merry, gay • **gaya ciencia** (*Literat, Hist*) art of poetry
2 (= *vistoso*) bright, showy
gayola SF 1 (= *jaula*) cage
2* (= *cárcel*) jail, slammer‡, can (*EEUU**)
gayumbos‡ SMPL underpants
gaza SF (= *lazo*) loop; (*Náut*) bend, bight
gazafatón* SM = **gazapatón**
gazapa* SF fib, lie
gazapatón* SM (= *error*) blunder, slip; (= *disparate*) piece of nonsense
gazapera SF 1 (= *madriguera*) rabbit hole, warren
2* [*de maleantes*] den
3 (= *riña*) brawl, shindy*
gazapo SM 1 (*Zool*) young rabbit
2* (= *disparate*) blunder*, bloomer* • **meter un ~** to make a blunder *o* bloomer* • **cazar un ~** to spot a mistake
3 (= *errata*) printing error, misprint
4 (= *hombre*) (= *taimado*) sly fellow; (= *ladrón**) cat burglar; (*LAm*) (= *mentiroso*) liar
5 (*Caribe*) (= *estafa*) trick
gazmoñería SF, **gazmoñada** SF
1 (= *mojigatería*) prudery, priggishness; (= *beatería*) sanctimoniousness
2 (= *hipocresía*) hypocrisy, cant
gazmoño/a, gazmoñero/a ADJ
1 (= *mojigato*) prudish, priggish; (= *puritano*) strait laced; (= *beato*) sanctimonious
2 (= *hipócrita*) hypocritical, canting
SM/F 1 (= *mojigato*) prude, prig; (= *beato*) sanctimonious person
2 (= *hipócrita*) hypocrite
gaznápiro/a SM/F dolt, simpleton
gaznatada‡ SF (*CAm, Caribe, Méx*) smack, slap
gaznate SM 1 (= *pescuezo*) gullet; (= *garganta*) windpipe, throttle

• MODISMO: • **refrescar el ~*** to wet one's whistle*
2 (*Méx*) (fruit) fritter
gaznetón/ona ADJ (*And, Méx*) loud-mouthed
SM/F loudmouth*
gazpacho SM **1** (*Culin*) *cold vegetable soup*
• REFRÁN: • **de ~ no hay empacho** one can never have too much of a good thing
2 (*CAm*) (*bebida*) dregs (*pl*); (*comida*) leftovers (*pl*)
gazuza* SF **1** (= *hambre*) ravenous hunger
2 (*CAm*) (= *alboroto*) din, row
3 (*CAm*) (= *chusma*) common people
4 • **es una ~** (*CAm*) she's a wily old bird
GC ABR = **Guardia Civil**
geco SM gecko
géiser SM geyser
geisha ['geisa] ['xeisa] SF geisha girl
gel SM (PL: **gels, geles**) gel • **gel de baño** bath gel • **gel de ducha** shower gel
gelatina SF (= *ingrediente*) gelatin(e); (= *postre*) jelly, Jell-O® (EEUU) ▸ **gelatina explosiva** gelignite
gelatinoso ADJ gelatinous
gelidez SF chill, iciness
gélido ADJ chill, icy
gelificarse ▹ CONJUG 1g VPR to gel, coagulate
gelignita SF gelignite
gema SF **1** (= *piedra preciosa*) gem, jewel
2 (*Bot*) (= *botón*) bud
gemelo/a ADJ (= *hermano*) (identical) twin • **torres gemelas** twin towers • **buque ~** sister ship • **es mi alma gemela** we're two of a kind
SM/F (= *hermano*) (identical) twin
SM **1** (= *músculo*) calf muscle
2 [*de camisa*] cufflink
3 (*Náut*) sister ship
4 **gemelos** (= *prismáticos*) binoculars
▸ **gemelos de campo** field glasses
▸ **gemelos de teatro** opera glasses
5 **Gemelos** [*del zodíaco*] Gemini, Twins
gemido SM (= *quejido*) groan, moan; (= *lamento*) wail, howl; [*de animal*] whine; [*del viento*] howling, wailing
gemidor ADJ (= *que se queja*) groaning, moaning; (= *que se lamenta*) wailing, howling
Géminis SM INV (*Astron, Astrol*) Gemini • **es de ~** (*LAm*) she's (a) Gemini, she's a Geminian
géminis (*Astrol*) SMF INV Gemini, Geminian • **los ~ son así** that's what Geminis *o* Geminians are like
ADJ INV Gemini, Geminian • **soy ~** I'm (a) Gemini, I'm a Geminian
gemiquear ▹ CONJUG 1a VI (*Cono Sur*) to whine
gemiqueo SM (*Cono Sur*) whining
gemir ▹ CONJUG 3k VI (= *quejarse*) to groan, moan; (= *lamentarse*) to wail, howl; [*animal*] to whine; [*viento*] to howl, wail • **—sí —dijo gimiendo** "yes," he groaned
gen SM gene ▸ **gen recesivo** recessive gene
Gen. ABR (= **General**) Gen
gen. ABR (*Ling*) **1** (= **género**) gen
2 (= **genitivo**) gen
genciana SF gentian
gendarme SMF (*esp LAm*) policeman/policewoman, gendarme
gendarmería SF (*esp LAm*) police, gendarmerie
gene SM gene
genealogía SF (= *ascendientes*) genealogy; (= *árbol*) family tree; (= *raza*) pedigree
genealógico ADJ genealogical
genealogista SMF genealogist
generación SF **1** (= *acto*) generation • **~ de empleo** employment creation • MODISMO: • **producirse** *o* **surgir por ~ espontánea** to come out of nowhere, come out of the blue
2 (= *grupo*) generation • **la ~ del 27/98** the generation of '27/'98 • **las nuevas generaciones** the rising generation
• **primera/segunda/tercera/cuarta ~** (*Inform*) first/second/third/fourth generation
3 (= *descendencia*) progeny, offspring; (= *crías*) brood; (= *sucesión*) succession

GENERACIÓN DEL 27/DEL 98

The **Generación del 27** is the collective name given to a group of writers and poets including Lorca, Alberti, Guillén, Cernuda and Aleixandre, who drew inspiration from earlier Spanish poets as well as from popular folk song and contemporary European art (Dadaism, Surrealism, Cubism). They particularly admired Góngora (1561-1627) and it was their commemoration of the anniversary of his death that earned them the title **Generación del 27**.

The **Generación del 98** was the name coined by Azorín for a group of writers (Baroja, Machado, Unamuno, Maeztu, Ganivet, and himself, amongst others) who saw Spain's defeat in the Cuban American war of 1898 as the start of a decline in values. While not all the supposed members of the group accepted their inclusion in it, their work demonstrates shared themes, ideals and concerns.

generacional ADJ generation (*antes de s*)
generacionalmente ADV in terms of generation(s)
generado ADJ • **~ por ordenador** (*Inform*) computer-generated
generador ADJ generating • **una demagogia ~a de odio** a demagogy which generates hatred
SM generator ▸ **generador de programas** (*Inform*) program generator ▸ **generador eólico** wind turbine
general ADJ **1** (= *común, no detallado*) general • **información de interés ~** information of general interest • **el estado ~ de su salud** his general state of health • **una visión ~ de los problemas del país** an overall *o* general view of the problems of the country
• **declaraciones de carácter ~** general comments • **estamos perdiendo de vista el interés ~** we are losing sight of the common interest • **la corrupción es ~ en todo el país** corruption is widespread in the whole country
2 • **en ~ a** (*con verbo*) generally, in general
• **estoy hablando en ~** I am talking generally *o* in general terms • **en ~, las críticas de la obra han sido favorables** generally (speaking) *o* in general, the play has received favourable criticism
b (*detrás de s*) in general • **literatura, música y arte en ~** literature, music and the arts in general • **el público en ~** the general public
3 • **por lo ~** generally • **iban a visitarla, por lo ~, dos o tres veces al año** they generally went to see her two or three times a year
• **los resultados son, por lo ~, bastante buenos** in general *o* on the whole, the results are pretty good
SMF (*Mil*) general ▸ **general de brigada** brigadier general ▸ **general de división** major general
SM (*Rel*) general
SF **1** (*tb* **carretera general**) (*Esp*) main road
2 (*tb* **clasificación general**) (*Ciclismo*) general classification
3 ▸ **generales de la ley** prescribed personal questions
generala SF **1**† (= *persona*) (woman) general; (= *esposa*) general's wife
2 (= *llamamiento*) call to arms, general alert
generalato SM **1** (= *arte, rango*) generalship
2 (= *personas*) generals (*pl*)
3 (*Méx**) (= *madama*) madam, brothel keeper
generalidad SF **1** generality; (= *mayoría*) mass, majority • **la ~ de los hombres** the majority of men, most men
2 (= *vaguedad*) vague answer, generalization
• **¡déjate de ~es!** stop speaking in generalities!
3 • **la Generalidad** (*Pol*) = **Generalitat**
generalísimo SM (*Mil*) supreme commander, generalissimo • **el Generalísimo Franco** General Franco
generalista ADJ [*radio, televisión*] general-interest (*antes de s*); [*formación*] general • **médico ~** general practitioner
SMF general practitioner, G.P., family practitioner (EEUU)
Generalitat SF • **la ~ (de Cataluña)** Catalan autonomous government • **la ~ Valenciana** Valencian autonomous government

GENERALITAT

The **Generalitat** is the autonomous government of Catalonia. The name originally applied to the finance committee of the Catalan parliament, or **Corts**, in the early 13th century, but in 1932 was given to the partially devolved government granted to Catalonia under the Second Republic (1931-36). When its leader, Luis Companys, went on to proclaim the "Catalan State of the Spanish Federal Republic" in 1934, Madrid sent in the troops, and imprisoned members of the breakaway **Generalitat**. Catalan autonomy was restored under the Popular Front in 1936, but was abolished by Franco after the Civil War. Since his death the **Generalitat** has risen again under the 1978 Constitution and Catalonia now enjoys a considerable degree of autonomy from Madrid.

▹ LA CONSTITUCIÓN ESPAÑOLA

generalización SF **1** (= *ampliación*) [*de práctica, tendencia*] spread; [*de conflicto*] widening, spread • **la ~ del uso de herbicidas** the increased use of herbicides
2 (= *afirmación general*) generalization • **hacer generalizaciones** to make generalizations, generalize
generalizado ADJ [*crisis, creencia, guerra*] widespread • **existe la creencia generalizada de que ...** it is commonly *o* widely believed that ..., there is a widely held belief that ...
generalizar ▹ CONJUG 1f VT (= *extender*) [+ *práctica*] to make (more) widespread; [+ *conflicto*] to widen, spread • **el uso ha generalizado una pronunciación distinta** a different pronunciation has become widespread through use • **quieren ~ la situación de Madrid a toda España** they want to apply the situation of Madrid to the whole of Spain
VI (= *hacer generalizaciones*) to generalize
• **no se puede ~** you can't generalize
VPR **generalizarse** [*crisis, plaga, costumbre*] to become (more) widespread; [*conflicto*] to widen, spread • **el descontento se está generalizando en todo el país** discontent is spreading *o* becoming more widespread throughout the country • **hoy día se ha generalizado el uso de la palabra "tío"** nowadays the use of the word "tío" has become widespread
generalmente ADV generally

g

generar ▹ CONJUG 1a VT **1** [+ *electricidad, energía*] to generate
2 [+ *empleo, interés, riqueza*] to generate, create; [+ *problemas, tensiones*] to cause; [+ *beneficios*] to generate • **el turismo ~á muchos puestos de trabajo** tourism will generate *o* create many jobs • **sus comentarios ~on numerosas quejas** his comments generated *o* raised many complaints

generativismo SM generative grammar

generativo ADJ generative

genéricamente ADV generically

genérico ADJ generic

género SM **1** (= *clase*) kind, type • **personas de ese ~** people of that kind *o* type, people like that • **este festival es el único en su ~** this festival is unique of its kind • **le deseo todo ~ de felicidades** I wish you all the happiness in the world ▸ **género humano** human race, mankind
2 (*Arte, Literat*) genre, type • **pintor de ~** genre painter • **es todo un ~ de literatura** it is a whole type of literature ▸ **género chico** (= *sainetes*) (genre of) short farces; (= *zarzuela*) Spanish operetta ▸ **género literario** literary genre ▸ **género narrativo** novel genre, fiction
3 (*Ling*) gender • **del ~ masculino** of the masculine gender
4 (*Bio*) (= *especie*) genus
5 géneros (*Com*) (= *productos*) goods; (= *mercancías*) commodities ▸ **géneros de lino** linen goods ▸ **géneros de punto** knitwear (*sing*)
6 (= *tela*) cloth, material • MODISMO: • **le conozco el ~** I know his sort, I know all about him

generosamente ADV **1** (= *con largueza*) generously
2 (= *con magnanimidad*) nobly, magnanimously

generosidad SF **1** (= *largueza*) generosity
2 (= *magnanimidad*) nobility, magnanimity
3 (*Hist*) nobility

generoso ADJ **1** (= *dadivoso*) generous • **ser ~ con algn** to be generous to sb • **ser ~ con algo** to be generous with sth
2 (= *noble*) noble, magnanimous • **de sangre generosa** of noble blood • **en pecho ~** in a noble heart
3 (*Hist*) highborn, noble
4 [*vino*] rich, full-bodied

genésico ADJ genetic

Génesis SM Genesis

génesis SF INV genesis

genética SF genetics (*sing*) ▸ **genética de poblaciones** population genetics; ▹ genético

genéticamente ADV genetically

geneticista SMF geneticist

genético/a ADJ genetic
SM/F geneticist; ▹ **genética**

genetista SMF geneticist

genial ADJ **1** (= *de talento*) brilliant, of genius • **escritor ~** brilliant writer, writer of genius • **fue una idea ~** it was a brilliant idea • **Pablo es ~** Pablo's a genius
2 (= *estupendo*) wonderful, marvellous, marvelous (*EEUU*) • **fue una película ~** it was a wonderful *o* marvellous film • **¡eso fue ~!** it was wonderful *o* marvellous!
3 (= *ocurrente*) witty
4 (= *placentero*) pleasant, genial; (= *afable*) cordial, affable

genialidad SF **1** (= *cualidad*) genius
2 (= *acto genial*) stroke of genius, master stroke • **es una ~ suya** (*iró*) it's one of his brilliant ideas

genialmente ADV in an inspired way, brilliantly, with genius

genio SM **1** (= *temperamento*) temper • **¡menudo ~ tiene!** he's got such a temper! • **es una mujer de mucho ~** she's a quick-tempered woman • **tener mal ~** to be bad tempered • **~ vivo** quick temper, hot temper • MODISMO: • **llevar el ~ a algn** (= *seguir la corriente*) to humour sb, humor sb (*EEUU*); (= *no contradecir*) not to dare contradict sb • REFRÁN: • **~ y figura hasta la sepultura** a leopard cannot change his spots
2 (= *carácter*) nature, disposition • **~ alegre** cheerful nature • **tener buen ~** to be good natured, be even tempered • **corto de ~** timid, spiritless • **de ~ franco** of an open nature
3 (= *estado de ánimo*) • **estar de buen ~** to be in a good mood • **estar de mal ~** to be in a bad temper, be in a bad mood
4 (= *talento*) genius • **¡eres un ~!** you're a genius!
5 (= *peculiaridad*) genius, peculiarities (*pl*) • **esto va en contra del ~ de la lengua** this goes against the genius of the language • **el ~ andaluz** the Andalusian spirit, the spirit of Andalucía
6 (= *ser fantástico*) genie
7 (= *divinidad*) spirit ▸ **genio del mal** evil spirit ▸ **genio tutelar** guardian spirit

genioso ADJ (*CAm*) bad-tempered

genista SF broom, genista

genital ADJ genital
SMPL **genitales** genitals, genital organs

genitalidad SF sexual activity

genitivo ADJ (= *reproductivo*) generative, reproductive
SM (*Ling*) (= *caso*) genitive ▸ **genitivo sajón** *possessive using apostrophe*

genocida SMF *person accused or guilty of genocide*

genocidio SM genocide

genoma SM, **genomio** SM genome

genómica SF genomics (*sing*)

genómico ADJ genomic

genotipo SM genotype

Génova SF Genoa

genovés/esa ADJ, SM/F Genoese

gental SM (*And*) lot, mass • **un ~ de gente** a mass of people

gente SF **1** (= *personas*) people (*pl*) • **hay muy poca ~** there are very few people • **no me gusta esa ~** I don't like those people • **España y sus ~s** Spain and its people • **son muy buena ~** they are very nice people • **Juan es buena ~*** Juan is a nice guy* • MODISMO: • **hacer ~** to make a crowd ▸ **la gente baja** the lower classes (*pl*) ▸ **gente bien** (= *los ricos*) well-off people, well-to-do people; (= *los decorosos*) decent people ▸ **gente bonita** (*Méx*) beautiful people ▸ **gente de bien** = **gente bien** ▸ **gente de capa parda**†† country folk ▸ **gente de color** coloured people, colored people (*EEUU*) ▸ **gente de la cuchilla**†† butchers (*pl*) ▸ **gente de mar** seafaring men (*pl*) ▸ **gente de medio pelo** people of limited means, common people ▸ **gente de paz** peace-loving people • **¡~ de paz!** (*Mil*) friend! ▸ **gente de pelo**†† well-to-do people ▸ **gente de pluma**†† clerks (*pl*), penpushers (*pl*) ▸ **gente de trato**†† tradespeople ▸ **gente gorda** (*Esp**) well-to-do people, rich people ▸ **gente guapa, gente linda** (*LAm*) beautiful people ▸ **gente menuda** children (*pl*) ▸ **gente natural** (*CAm*) Indians (*pl*), natives (*pl*) ▸ **gente perdida**† riff-raff ▸ **gente principal** nobility, gentry; ▹ **don¹**
2 (*Méx*) (= *persona*) person • **había dos ~s** there were two people
3* (= *parientes*) family, folks* (*pl*) • **mi ~** my family, my folks* • MODISMO: • **de ~ en ~** from generation to generation
4 (= *nación*) nation
5 (*Mil*) men (*pl*), troops (*pl*)
6 (= *séquito*) retinue • **el rey y su ~** the king and his retinue
7 (*LAm*) upper-class people (*pl*) • **ser (buena) ~** to be respectable people
ADJ • **es muy ~*** (*Chile*) he's very decent*; (*Méx*) he's very kind

gentecilla SF (= *pobre gente*) unimportant people; (*pey*) (= *gentuza*) rabble, riffraff

genterío SM (*CAm*) = **gentío**

gentil ADJ **1** (= *cortés*) courteous; (*Méx*) (= *amable*) kind, helpful
2 (= *elegante*) graceful, elegant; (= *encantador*) charming
3 (*iró*) pretty, fine • **¡~ cumplido!** a fine compliment!
4 (= *idólatra*) pagan, heathen; (= *no judío*) gentile
SMF (= *idólatra*) pagan, heathen; (= *no judío*) gentile

gentileza SF **1** (= *amabilidad*) kindness; (= *cortesía*) courtesy • **agradezco su ~** I appreciate your kindness • **tuvieron la ~ de invitarme** they were kind enough to invite me • **tenga la ~ de acompañarme** I would appreciate it if you came with me • **"por ~ de ..."** "by courtesy of ..."
2 (= *gracia*) gracefulness; (= *encanto*) charm
3 (= *pompa*) splendour, splendor (*EEUU*)
4 (= *gallardía*) dash, gallantry

gentilhombre SM (PL: **gentileshombres**) gentleman ▸ **gentilhombre de cámara** gentleman-in-waiting

gentilicio ADJ (= *de las naciones*) national, tribal; (= *de la familia*) family (*antes de s*) • **nombre ~** family name
SM *name of the inhabitants of a country or region etc*

gentilidad SF, **gentilismo** SM (= *paganos*) the pagan world; (= *creencias*) heathenism, paganism

gentilmente ADV **1** (= *con amabilidad*) kindly; (= *cortésmente*) courteously, politely • **me cedió ~ el paso** he courteously *o* politely let me past
2 (= *con elegancia*) elegantly, gracefully; (= *con encanto*) charmingly
3 (*iró*) prettily

gentío SM crowd, throng • **había un ~** there were lots of people

gentualla SF = **gentuza**

gentuza SF (*pey*) (= *populacho*) rabble, mob; (= *chusma*) riffraff • **¡qué ~!** what a rabble!*, what a shower!*

genuflexión SF genuflexion

genuflexo ADJ (*Cono Sur*) servile, slavish

genuinamente ADV genuinely

genuino ADJ **1** (= *auténtico*) genuine
2 (*And**) smashing*, super*

GEO SMPL ABR (*Esp*) (= **Grupo Especial de Operaciones**) *special police unit*

geo SMF member of GEO

geo... PREF geo...

geoambiental ADJ geoenvironmental

geobiológico ADJ geobiological

geobotánica SF geobotany

geociencia SF geoscience

geoclimático ADJ geoclimatic

geodemografía SF geodemography

geodesía SF geodesy

geodésico ADJ geodesic

geoecología SF geoecology

geoeconómico ADJ geoeconomic

geoestacionario ADJ geostationary

geoestadística SF geostatistics (*sing*)

geoestrategia SF geostrategy

geoestratégico ADJ geostrategic

geofísica SF geophysics (*sing*)

geofísico/a ADJ geophysical
SM/F geophysicist
Geofredo SM Geoffrey
geografía SF **1** geography ▸ **geografía física** physical geography ▸ **geografía humana** human geography ▸ **geografía política** political geography
2 (= *país*) country, territory • **en toda la ~ nacional** all over the country • **recorrer la ~ nacional** to travel all over the country
geográficamente ADV geographically
geográfico ADJ geographical
geógrafo/a SM/F geographer
geohistoria SF, **geo-historia** SF geohistory
geoingeniería SF geoengineering
geolingüística SF geolinguistics (*sing*)
geolocalización SF geolocation
geolocalizador SM geolocator
geolocalizar VT to geolocate
geología SF geology
geológicamente ADV geologically
geológico ADJ geological
geólogo/a SM/F geologist
geomagnético ADJ geomagnetic
geometría SF geometry • **de ~ variable** (*Aer*) variable-geometry (*antes de s*)
▸ **geometría algebraica** algebraic geometry
▸ **geometría del espacio** solid geometry
geométricamente ADV geometrically
geométrico ADJ geometric(al)
geomorfología SF geomorphology
geomorfológico ADJ geomorphological
geopolítica SF geopolitics (*sing*)
geopolítico ADJ geopolitical
geoquímico ADJ geochemical
Georgia SF Georgia • **~ del Sur** South Georgia
georgiano/a ADJ, SM/F Georgian
SM (*Ling*) Georgian
geosistema SM geosystem
geostacionario ADJ geostationary
geotermal ADJ geothermal
geotérmico ADJ geothermal
geranio SM geranium
Gerardo SM Gerard
gerencia SF **1** (= *dirección*) management
▸ **gerencia de empresas** business management
2 (= *cargo*) post of manager
3 (= *oficina*) manager's office
4 (= *personas*) management, managers (*pl*) • **alta ~** senior management • **~ intermedia** middle management
gerencial ADJ managerial
gerenciar ▹ CONJUG 1b VT to manage
gerente SMF manager/manageress
▸ **gerente de fábrica** works manager
▸ **gerente de ventas** sales manager
geriatra SMF geriatrician
geriatría SF geriatrics (*sing*)
geriátrico ADJ geriatric • **centro ~** old people's home
SM old people's home
gerifalte SM **1** (= *persona*) important person, bigwig* • **los ~s de la empresa** the company bigwigs* • **estar** *o* **vivir como un ~** to live like a king *o* lord
2 (= *ave*) gerfalcon
germanesco ADJ • **palabra germanesca** underworld slang
germanía SF criminals' slang, underworld slang
germánico ADJ Germanic
germanio SM germanium
germanista SMF Germanist
germanística SF German studies (*pl*)
germano/a ADJ Germanic, German
SM/F German
germanófilo/a ADJ, SM/F Germanophile
germanófobo/a ADJ anti-German
SM/F Germanophobe
germanófono/a ADJ German-speaking
SM/F German speaker
germanooccidental ADJ, SMF (*Hist*) West German
germanooriental ADJ, SMF (*Hist*) East German
germanoparlante ADJ German-speaking
SMF German speaker
germen SM **1** (= *microorganismo*) germ
▸ **germen plasma** germ plasma
2 (= *brote*) germ ▸ **germen de trigo** wheatgerm
3 (= *raíz*) germ, seed; (= *origen*) source • **el ~ de una idea** the germ of an idea
germicida ADJ germicidal
SM germicide, germ killer
germinación SF germination
germinar ▹ CONJUG 1a VI to germinate
Gerona SF Gerona
gerontocracia SF gerontocracy
gerontología SF gerontology
gerontólogo/a SM/F gerontologist
Gertrudis SF Gertrude
gerundense ADJ of/from Gerona
SMF native/inhabitant of Gerona • **los ~s** the people of Gerona
gerundiano ADJ bombastic
gerundiar ▹ CONJUG 1b VI (= *hablar*) to speak meaninglessly; (= *escribir*) to write meaninglessly
gerundino SM gerundive
gerundio SM (*Ling*) gerund • MODISMO: • **andando, que es ~** get a move on — now!
▸ **gerundio adjetivado** gerundive
gervasio SM (*And*) (= *hombre*) guy*; (= *astuto*) smart guy*
gesta SF **1** (= *acción heroica*) heroic deed, epic achievement
2 (*Literat, Hist*) epic poem, epic; ▹ **cantar**
gestación SF **1** (*Bio*) pregnancy, gestation • **los tres primeros meses de ~** the first three months of pregnancy • **en avanzado estado de ~** heavily pregnant • **animales en ~** gestating animals ▸ **gestación de alquiler** surrogate pregnancy
2 [*de idea, proyecto*] gestation • **un trabajo de tan larga ~** a project which has been so long in preparation *o* gestation
gestante ADJ expectant
SF expectant mother, pregnant woman
Gestapo SF • **la ~** the Gestapo
gestar ▹ CONJUG 1a VT (*Bio*) to gestate
VPR **gestarse 1** (*Bio*) to gestate
2 (*fig*) to be conceived
gestear ▹ CONJUG 1a VI = **gesticular**
gesticulación SF gesticulation
gesticular ▹ CONJUG 1a VI (*con ademanes*) to gesticulate • **~ con las manos** to wave one's hands around, gesticulate with one's hands • **~ con los brazos** to wave one's arms around, gesticulate with one's arms • **siempre habla sin ~** (= *sin ademanes*) he never gesticulates when he speaks; (= *sin gestos faciales*) he's always expressionless when he speaks
gestión SF **1** (= *administración*) management • **le despidieron por su mala ~** he was dismissed for bad management ▸ **gestión de datos** data management ▸ **gestión de ficheros** file management ▸ **gestión de personal** personnel management ▸ **gestión empresarial** business management ▸ **gestión financiera** financial management ▸ **gestión forestal** woodland management ▸ **gestión interna** (*Inform*) housekeeping ▸ **gestión presupuestaria** budget management
2 gestiones (= *trámites*) • **tenía que realizar unas gestiones in Madrid** he had some business to do in Madrid • **hacer las gestiones necesarias para algo** to take the necessary steps for sth • **hacer las gestiones preliminares** to do the groundwork • **el gobierno tendrá que hacer las primeras gestiones** the government will have to make the first move
gestionable ADJ manageable • **difícilmente ~** difficult to manage
gestionar ▹ CONJUG 1a VT **1** (= *administrar*) to manage • **se encargaba de ~ los presupuestos de la empresa** he managed the budgets for his company
2 (= *tramitar*) [+ *permiso, crédito*] to arrange • **su marido le gestionó el permiso de residencia** her husband arranged her residence permit • **gestionamos la venta de su piso** we will arrange the sale of your flat
gesto SM **1** (= *ademán*) gesture • **con un ~ de cansancio** with a weary gesture • **hacer ~s (a algn)** to make gestures (to sb) • **hacer ~s con la(s) mano(s)** to gesture with one's hand(s) • **me hizo un ~ para que me sentara** he gestured for me to sit down
2 (= *expresión*) • **hizo** *o* **puso un ~ de alivio** he looked relieved • **hizo** *o* **puso un ~ de asco** he looked disgusted • **hizo** *o* **puso un ~ de extrañeza** he looked surprised • **fruncir el ~** to scowl, look cross • MODISMO: • **poner mal ~** *o* **torcer el ~** to make a wry face
3 (= *acción*) gesture • **un ~ de buena voluntad** a goodwill gesture, a gesture of goodwill • **con un ~ generoso remitió la deuda** in a generous gesture he waived the debt
gestología SF study of body language
gestor(a) ADJ (= *que gestiona*) managing
SM/F manager/manageress; (= *promotor*) promoter; (= *agente*) business agent, representative; (*tb* **gestor(a) administrativo/a**) *agent undertaking business with government departments, insurance companies etc* ▸ **gestor(a) de carteras** portfolio manager
SM ▸ **gestor de bases de datos** database manager ▸ **gestor de ficheros** file manager
gestora SF (= *comité*) management committee
gestoría SF agency (*for undertaking business with government departments, insurance companies etc*)

GESTORÍA
In Spain **gestorías** are private agencies which specialize in dealing with legal and administrative work. For a fee they carry out the **trámites** (paperwork) involved in getting passports, work permits, car documentation etc and liaise with the **Agencia Tributaria** (Inland Revenue), thereby saving their clients much inconvenience and queueing time.

gestual ADJ gestural • **lenguaje ~** body-language
gestualidad SF body-language
Getsemaní SM Gethsemane • **el huerto de ~** the garden of Gethsemane
geyser ['ɣeiser] SM geyser
Ghana SF Ghana
ghanés/esa ADJ, SM/F Ghanaian
ghetto SM ghetto
giba SF **1** (= *joroba*) [*de camello*] hump; [*de persona*] hump, hunchback
2‡ (= *molestia*) nuisance, bother
gibado ADJ with a hump, hunchbacked
gibar‡ ▹ CONJUG 1a VT **1** (= *molestar*) to annoy, bother
2 (= *embaucar*) to put one over on*; (= *tomar la revancha*) to get one's own back on
VPR **gibarse** to put up with it • **se van a ~** they'll have to lump it*
gibón SM gibbon

g

giboso ADJ with a hump, hunchbacked
Gibraltar SM Gibraltar
gibraltareño/a ADJ of/from Gibraltar, Gibraltarian
SM/F Gibraltarian, native/inhabitant of Gibraltar • **los ~s** the Gibraltarians, the people of Gibraltar
giga SM gig
gigabyte [giga'bait] SM gigabyte
giganta SF **1** (= *persona*) giantess, giant
2 (*Bot*) sunflower
gigante ADJ giant (*antes de s*), gigantic
• **pantalla ~** giant screen • **tamaño ~** giant size
SM **1** (*Mit*) giant
2 (= *persona alta*) giant
3 (= *genio*) giant • **un ~ de la música clásica** one of the giants of classical music
4 (*en fiestas populares*) giant figure
gigantesco ADJ gigantic, giant (*antes de s*)
gigantez SF gigantic stature, vast size
gigantismo SM gigantism, giantism
gigantón/ona SM/F (= *muñeco*) giant carnival figure
gigantona SF (*CAm*) (= *baile*) *folk dance with giant masks*
gigoló [dʒigo'lo] SM gigolo
Gijón SM Gijón
gijonés/esa ADJ of/from Gijón
SM/F native/inhabitant of Gijón • **los gijoneses** the people of Gijón
Gil SM Giles
gil* (*esp Cono Sur*) ADJ stupid, silly
SMF fool, twit*
gilar‡ ▹ CONJUG 1a VT to watch, keep tabs on*
gili‡, gilí‡ ADJ **1** (= *tonto*) stupid, silly
2 (= *vanidoso*) stuck-up*; (= *presumido*) pig-headed*
SMF **1** (= *tonto*) ass‡, prat‡, jerk (*EEUU**) • **no seas ~** don't be such an ass *o* prat‡ • **hacer el ~** to make an ass *o* prat of o.s.‡
2 (= *vanidoso*) pompous ass‡
gilipollada** SF = **gilipollez**
gilipollas** ADJ INV • **no seas ~** don't be such a dickhead *o* wanker**
SMF INV **1** (= *estúpido*) dickhead**, wanker**
2 (= *vanidoso*) pompous ass‡
gilipollear** ▹ CONJUG 1a VI to piss about**, be a dickhead**, be a jerk (*EEUU**)
gilipollesco** ADJ bloody stupid‡, bloody idiotic‡
gilipollez** SF **1** (= *idiotez*) • **es una ~** it's bloody stupid‡ • **decir gilipolleces** to talk bullshit**
2 (= *vanidad*) pig-headedness*
gilipuertas‡ ADJ, SMF INV (*euf*) = **gili**
gillete® [xi'lete] SF (= *hoja*) razor blade; (= *maquinilla*) safety razor
gimnasia SF (*Dep*) gymnastics (*sing*); (*Escol*) P.E., gym; (= *entrenamiento*) exercises (*pl*)
• **una clase de ~** a P.E. *o* gym lesson • **monitor de ~** (*Escol*) P.E. *o* gym teacher • **mi madre hace ~ todas las mañanas** my mother does exercises every morning • MODISMO:
• **confundir la ~ con la magnesia*** to get things mixed up ▸ **gimnasia aeróbica** aerobics (*sing*) ▸ **gimnasia artística** artistic gymnastics ▸ **gimnasia correctiva** remedial gymnastics ▸ **gimnasia de mantenimiento** keep-fit ▸ **gimnasia deportiva** competitive gymnastics ▸ **gimnasia mental** mental gymnastics ▸ **gimnasia respiratoria** breathing exercises (*pl*) ▸ **gimnasia rítmica** rhythmic gymnastics ▸ **gimnasia sobre suelo** floor exercises (*pl*)
gimnasio SM gymnasium, gym*
• **~ múltiple** multigym
gimnasta SMF gymnast
gimnástica SF gymnastics (*sing*)
gimnástico ADJ [*ejercicio, tabla*] exercise (*antes de s*); [*club, asociación*] gymnastic, gymnastics (*antes de s*)
gimotear ▹ CONJUG 1a VI (= *gemir*) to whine; (= *lamentar*) to wail; (= *lloriquear*) to snivel
gimoteo SM (= *gemido*) whine, whining; (= *lamento*) wailing; (= *lloriqueo*) snivelling, sniveling (*EEUU*)
gincana SF gymkhana
Ginebra¹ SF (*Geog*) Geneva
Ginebra² SF (*Hist*) Guinevere
ginebra¹ SF (= *bebida*) gin
ginebra²* SF (= *confusión*) bedlam, uproar
ginebrés/esa ADJ of/from Geneva
SM/F native/inhabitant of Geneva • **los ginebreses** the people of Geneva
ginecología SF gynaecology, gynecology (*EEUU*)
ginecológico ADJ gynaecological, gynecological (*EEUU*)
ginecólogo/a SM/F gynaecologist, gynecologist (*EEUU*)
ginesta SF broom
gineta SF genet
gingival ADJ gum (*antes de s*), gingival
• **campaña de salud ~** campaign for healthy gums
gingivitis SF INV gingivitis
ginkana SF gymkhana
ginseng [jin'sen] SM ginseng
gin-tonic [jin'tonik] SM (PL: **gin-tonics**) gin and tonic
giña‡ SF (*Caribe*) hatred
Gioconda [dʒo'konda] SF • **la ~** (the) Mona Lisa
gira SF **1** (= *viaje*) tour • **estar de ~** to be on tour • **el grupo realiza una ~ por Sudamérica** the group is touring South America, the group is on a tour of South America ▸ **gira artística** artistic tour ▸ **gira de conciertos** concert tour ▸ **gira promocional** promotional tour
2 (= *excursión*) trip, excursion; (*tb* **gira campestre**) picnic • **ir de ~** to go on a trip *o* an excursion
giradiscos† SM INV record turntable
girado/a SM/F drawee
girador(a) SM/F drawer
giralda SF **1** (= *veleta*) weathercock
2 • **la Giralda** *Seville cathedral tower*
girante ADJ revolving, rotating
girar ▹ CONJUG 1a VT **1** (= *dar vueltas a*) [+ *llave, manivela, volante*] to turn; [+ *peonza, hélice, ruleta*] to spin • **gira la llave de contacto hacia la derecha** turn the ignition key to the right • **~ la cabeza** to turn one's head
2 (*Com*) [+ *dinero, facturas*] to send; [+ *letra, cheque*] (*gen*) to draw; (*a una persona concreta*) to issue • **le giró 600 euros para que pagara el alquiler** she sent him 600 euros to pay the rent
VI **1** (= *dar vueltas*) [*noria, rueda*] to go (a)round, turn, revolve; [*disco*] to revolve, go (a)round; [*planeta*] to rotate; [*hélice*] to go (a)round, rotate, turn; [*peonza*] to spin • **gira a 1600rpm** it revolves *o* goes (a)round at 1600rpm • **la tierra gira alrededor del sol** the earth revolves around *o* goes (a)round the sun • **el satélite gira alrededor de la tierra** the satellite circles *o* goes (a)round the earth
2 (= *cambiar de dirección*) to turn (a)round • **al verla giró en redondo** when he saw her he turned right (a)round • **hacer ~** [+ *llave*] to turn; [+ *sillón*] to turn (a)round • **la puerta giró sobre sus bisagras** the door swung on its hinges • **~ sobre sus talones** to turn on one's heel
3 (= *torcer*) [*vehículo*] to turn; [*camino*] to turn, bend • **el conductor giró bruscamente hacia el otro lado** the driver swerved sharply the other way • **~ a la derecha/izquierda** to turn right/left • **el camino gira a la derecha varios metros más allá** the path turns *o* bends to the right a few metres further on • **el partido ha girado a la izquierda en los últimos años** the party has moved *o* shifted to the left in recent years
4 • **~ alrededor de** *o* **sobre** *o* **en torno a** [+ *tema, ideas*] to revolve around, centre around, center around (*EEUU*); [+ *líder, centro de atención*] to revolve around • **la conversación giraba en torno a las elecciones** the conversation revolved *o* centred around the election • **su última obra gira en torno al tema del amor cortés** his latest work revolves around the subject of courtly love • **el número de asistentes giraba alrededor de 500 personas** there were about 500 people in the audience
5 • **~ en descubierto** (*Com, Econ*) to overdraw
6 (= *negociar*) to operate, do business • **la compañía gira bajo el nombre de Babel** the company operates under the name of Babel
VPR **girarse** to turn (a)round • **se giró para mirarme** she turned (a)round to look at me
girasol SM sunflower
giratorio ADJ [*movimiento*] circular; [*eje, tambor*] revolving, rotating; [*puerta, escenario*] revolving; [*puente*] swing (*antes de s*); [*silla*] swivel (*antes de s*)
girl* SF **1** (*Teat*) showgirl, chorus girl
2 (*Dep*) junior player
giro¹ SM **1** (= *vuelta*) (*gen*) turn (**sobre** around); [*de planeta*] (*sobre sí mismo*) rotation; (*alrededor de otro planeta*) revolution • **el avión realizó un ~ de 80 grados** the plane did an 80-degree turn • **con un ~ brusco de cadera** with a sudden twist of the hips • **el coche dio un ~ brusco** the car swerved suddenly • **daba ~s sobre sí misma** she spun round and round ▸ **giro copernicano** U-turn, complete turnabout ▸ **giro de 180 grados** (*lit*) U-turn; (*fig*) U-turn, complete turnabout • **la situación ha dado un ~ de 180 grados** the situation has taken a U-turn, there has been a complete turnabout in the situation
2 (= *cambio*) [*de conversación, acontecimientos*] turn • **el nuevo ~ que dieron ayer los acontecimientos** the new turn events took yesterday • **se produjo un ~ radical en arquitectura** there was a radical change *o* turnabout in architecture • **el electorado ha dado un ~ a la derecha** the electorate has shifted *o* moved to the right
3 (= *envío de dinero*) (*por correo*) money order; (*Com*) draft • **le mandó** *o* **puso un ~ de 400 euros** he sent him a money order for 400 euros ▸ **giro a la vista** sight draft ▸ **giro bancario** bank giro, bank draft ▸ **giro en descubierto** overdraft ▸ **giro postal** postal order, money order ▸ **giro postal internacional** international money order ▸ **giro telegráfico** = **giro postal**
4 (*Ling*) turn of phrase, expression
giro² ADJ (*LAm*) [*gallo*] *with some yellow feathers*
girocompás SM gyrocompass
girola SF ambulatory
Gironda SM Gironde
giroscópico ADJ gyroscopic
giroscopio SM, **giróscopo** SM gyroscope
gis SM **1** (*Méx*) (= *tiza*) chalk
2 (*And, Méx*) (= *pizarrín*) slate pencil
3 (*Méx**) (= *bebida*) pulque
gitanada SF (*pey*) **1** (= *acción*) gypsy trick, mean trick
2 (= *halago*) wheedling, cajolery
gitanear ▹ CONJUG 1a VT (*pey*) to wheedle, cajole

gitanería SF **1** (= *grupo*) band of gypsies
2 (= *vida*) gypsy (way of) life
3 (= *dicho*) gypsy saying
4 (*pey*) (= *acción*) wheedling, cajolery

gitanesco ADJ **1** (= *de gitanos*) gypsy (*antes de s*)
2 (*pey*) (= *taimado*) wily, sly

gitano/a ADJ **1** (*de gitanos*) gypsy (*antes de s*) • **las costumbres gitanas** gypsy customs
2 (*pey*) (= *camelador*) wheedling, cajoling; (= *taimado*) wily, sly
3* (= *sucio*) dirty
SM/F gypsy • **MODISMOS**: • **vivir como ~s*** to live like tramps • **volvió hecho un ~*** he came back in a right mess*

glabro ADJ hairless

glaciación SF glaciation

glacial ADJ **1** [*era*] glacial
2 [*viento*] icy, bitter
3 [*saludo, acogida*] icy, frosty

glaciar SM glacier

gladiador SM gladiator

gladiola SF (*Méx*) gladiolus

gladiolo SM, **gladíolo** SM gladiolus • **un ramo de ~s** a bouquet of gladioli

glamoroso ADJ glamorous

glamour [gla'mur] SM glamour, glamor (*EEUU*)

glamouroso [glamu'roso] ADJ glamorous

glande SM glans

glándula SF (*Anat, Bot*) gland ▸ **glándula cerrada, glándula de secreción interna** ductless gland ▸ **glándula endocrina** endocrine gland ▸ **glándula lagrimal** tear gland ▸ **glándula mamaria** mammary gland ▸ **glándula pineal** pineal gland ▸ **glándula pituitaria** pituitary (gland) ▸ **glándula prostática** prostate (gland) ▸ **glándula tiroides** thyroid (gland)

glandular ADJ glandular

glas ADJ INV • **azúcar ~** icing sugar

glaseado ADJ (= *brillante*) glazed, glossy; [*tela*] glacé
SM [*de papel, pastel*] glaze

glasear ▸ CONJUG 1a VT **1** [+ *papel*] to glaze
2 (*Culin*) to glacé, glaze

glásnost SF glasnost

glauco ADJ (*liter*) (= *verde claro*) light-green, glaucous; (*esp LAm*) (= *verde*) green

glaucoma SM (*Med*) glaucoma

gleba SF **1** (= *terrón*) clod
2 (*Hist*) glebe

glicerina SF glycerin(e)

glicina SF (*Bot*) wisteria

global ADJ **1** (*en conjunto*) [*cantidad, resultado*] overall, total; [*investigación, análisis*] comprehensive • **estas cifras nos dan una idea ~ del coste** these figures give us an overall picture of the cost
2 (= *mundial*) global • **la aldea ~** the global village

globalidad SF totality • **la ~ del problema** (*en conjunto*) the problem as a whole; (*en sentido amplio*) the problem in its widest sense • **abordar la cuestión en su ~** to tackle the issue in its entirety

globalización SF globalization • **la ~ de la economía** globalization of the economy

globalizador ADJ comprehensive

globalizante ADJ universalizing, world-wide

globalizar ▸ CONJUG 1f VT **1** (= *abarcar*) to encompass, include
2 (= *extender*) to globalize

globalmente ADV **1** [*considerar, examinar*] globally, as a whole
2 (= *en términos generales*) overall

globo SM **1** [*de aire*] balloon ▸ **globo aerostático** balloon ▸ **globo cautivo** observation balloon ▸ **globo de aire caliente** hot-air balloon ▸ **globo de barrera, globo de protección** barrage-balloon ▸ **globo dirigible** airship, dirigible ▸ **globo meteorológico** weather balloon ▸ **globo sonda** (*Pol*) • **lanzar un ~ sonda sobre la posibilidad de convocar un referéndum** to test the political waters regarding the possibility of a referendum
2 (= *esfera*) globe, sphere ▸ **globo del ojo, globo ocular** eyeball ▸ **globo de luz** spherical lamp ▸ **globo terráqueo, globo terrestre** globe
3 (*en un cómic*) balloon
4 [*de chicle*] bubble
5‡ (*con drogas*) • **cogerse un ~** to get high* • **tener un ~** to be high*
6 (*Ftbl, Tenis*) lob
7‡ (= *preservativo*) condom, rubber‡, safe (*EEUU‡*)
8 globos‡ (= *pechos*) boobs‡
9 • **en ~** = **globalmente**

globoso ADJ, **globular** ADJ globular, spherical

glóbulo SM **1** (= *esfera*) globule
2 (*Anat*) blood cell, corpuscle ▸ **glóbulo blanco** white blood cell, white corpuscle ▸ **glóbulo rojo** red blood cell, red corpuscle

gloria SF **1** (= *cielo*) glory • **ganarse la ~** to go to heaven • **¡por la ~ de mi madre!** by all that's holy! • **Dios le tenga en su santa ~** God rest his soul
2 (= *delicia*) delight; (= *éxtasis*) bliss • **esta piscina es una ~** this pool is heavenly • **MODISMOS**: • **a ~**: • **oler a ~** to smell divine • **saber a ~** to taste heavenly • **dar ~**: • **cocina que da ~** she's a wonderful cook • **está que da ~ verla** she looks wonderful • **estar en la ~** to be in heaven
3 (= *fama*) glory • **cubrirse de ~** (*iró*) to make a fine mess of sth
4 (= *personalidad*) great figure, great* • **una de las grandes ~s del cine** one of the greats* *o* great figures of the cinema • **una vieja ~** a has-been*
5 (*apelativo*) • **¡sí, ~!** yes, my love!
6‡ (= *droga*) hash*, pot‡

gloriado SM (*And*) hot toddy

gloriarse ▸ CONJUG 1b VPR • **~ de algo** to boast of sth, be proud of sth • **~ en algo** to glory in sth, rejoice in sth

glorieta SF **1** (= *pérgola*) bower, arbour, arbor (*EEUU*); (= *cenador*) summerhouse
2 (*Aut*) roundabout, traffic circle (*EEUU*); (= *plaza redonda*) circus; (= *cruce*) junction, intersection

glorificación SF glorification

glorificar ▸ CONJUG 1g VT to glorify, praise
VPR **glorificarse** • **~se de** *o* **en** to boast of, glory in

Gloriosa SF • **la ~** (*Esp*) (*Hist*) *the 1868 revolution*; (*Rel*) the Blessed Virgin

gloriosamente ADV gloriously

glorioso ADJ **1** (= *digno de gloria*) glorious • **el ~ alzamiento nacional** (*Esp*) (*Hist*) *the Spanish Civil War*
2 (*Rel*) [*santo*] blessed, in glory; [*memoria*] blessed
3 (*pey*) proud, boastful

glosa SF **1** (= *explicación*) gloss; (= *comentario*) comment, note
2 (*And*) telling-off

glosar ▸ CONJUG 1a VT (= *explicar*) to gloss; (= *comentar*) to comment on, annotate; (= *criticar*) to criticize

glosario SM glossary

glosopeda SF foot-and-mouth disease

glotal ADJ, **glótico** ADJ glottal

glotis SF INV glottis

glotón/ona ADJ greedy, gluttonous (*frm*)
SM/F glutton
SM (*tb* **glotón de América**) wolverine

glotonear ▸ CONJUG 1a VI to be greedy, be gluttonous (*frm*)

glotonería SF greediness, gluttony

GLP SM ABR (= **gas licuado de petróleo**) LPG

glub EXCL gulp!

glucosa SF glucose

gluglú SM **1** [*de agua*] gurgle, gurgling • **hacer ~** to gurgle
2 [*de pavo*] gobble, gobbling • **hacer ~** to gobble

gluglutear ▸ CONJUG 1a VI to gobble

glutamato SM glutamate ▸ **glutamato monosódico** monosodium glutamate

gluten SM gluten

glúteo ADJ gluteal
SM **1** (= *músculo*) gluteus
2 glúteos (= *nalgas*) buttocks, backside (*sing*)

glutinoso ADJ glutinous

GN ABR (*Nic, Ven*) = **Guardia Nacional**

gneis [neis] SM INV gneiss

gnómico ADJ (*Literat*) gnomic

gnomo ['nomo] SM gnome

gnóstico/a ADJ gnostic
SM/F gnostic

gobelino SM Gobelin tapestry

gobernabilidad SF governability • **llegar a un pacto de ~** to form a government with the support of minority parties

gobernable ADJ **1** (*Pol*) governable • **un pueblo difícilmente ~** an unruly people, a people hard to govern
2 (*Náut*) navigable, steerable

gobernación SF **1** (= *acto*) governing, government
2 (= *residencia*) governor's residence; (= *oficina*) governor's office
3 (*esp LAm*) (*Pol*) Ministry of the Interior • **Ministro de la Gobernación** Minister of the Interior, ≈ Home Secretary, ≈ Secretary of the Interior (*EEUU*)

gobernador(a) ADJ [*partido*] governing, ruling
SM/F governor • **el ~ del Banco de España** the governor of the Bank of Spain ▸ **gobernador(a) civil** civil governor ▸ **gobernador(a) general** governor general ▸ **gobernador(a) militar** military governor

gobernalle SM rudder, helm

gobernanta SF **1** [*de hotel*] staff manageress, housekeeper
2 (*esp LAm*) (= *niñera*) governess

gobernante ADJ ruling, governing • **la clase ~** the ruling *o* governing class
SMF (= *líder*) ruler • **nuestros ~s incumplen sus promesas** our rulers have failed to keep their promises

gobernanza SF governance

gobernar ▸ CONJUG 1j VT **1** (*Pol*) to govern, rule
2 (= *dirigir*) to govern; (= *guiar*) to guide, direct; (= *controlar*) to manage, run; (= *manejar*) to handle
3 (*Náut*) to steer, sail
VI **1** (*Pol*) to govern, rule • **~ mal** to misgovern
2 (*Náut*) to handle, steer

gobi‡ SF nick‡, slammer‡, can (*EEUU‡*)

gobierno SM **1** (*Pol*) government • **el ~ español** the Spanish government ▸ **gobierno autonómico, gobierno autónomo** autonomous government, regional government ▸ **gobierno central** central government ▸ **gobierno de coalición** coalition government ▸ **gobierno de concentración** government of national unity ▸ **gobierno de gestión** caretaker government ▸ **el Gobierno de la Nación** central Government ▸ **gobierno de transición** transition government ▸ **gobierno directo** direct rule ▸ **gobierno en funciones** caretaker government

g

▸ **gobierno fantasma** shadow cabinet ▸ **gobierno interino** interim government ▸ **gobierno militar** military government
2 (= *dirección*) guidance, direction; (= *gerencia*) management; (= *manejo*) control, handling • **para su ~** for your guidance, for your information • **servir de ~ a algn** to act as a guide to sb, serve as a norm for sb ▸ **gobierno doméstico, gobierno de la casa** housekeeping, running of the household
3 (= *puesto*) governorship; (= *edificio*) Government House ▸ **gobierno civil** (= *puesto*) civil governorship; (= *edificio*) civil governor's residence
4 (*Náut*) steering; (= *timón*) helm • **buen ~** navigability • **de buen ~** navigable, easily steerable
5 • MODISMO: • **mirar contra el ~** (*Cono Sur*‡) to squint, be boss-eyed*

gobio SM gudgeon

gob.no ABR (= **gobierno**) govt

goce SM (= *disfrute*) enjoyment; (= *posesión*) possession

gocho* SM pig, hog (*EEUU*)

godo/a ADJ (= *gótico*) Gothic
SM/F 1 (*Hist*) Goth
2 (*LAm*) (*Hist*) loyalist; (*pey*) Spaniard; (*Pol*) (= *conservador*) conservative
3 (*Canarias*) (*pey*) (Peninsular) Spaniard

Godofredo SM Godfrey

gofio SM (*Canarias, LAm*) *roasted maize meal often stirred into coffee*

gofre SM waffle

gogó, go-gó SF go-go girl, go-go dancer
ADV* • **a ~** aplenty, by the bucketful*

gol SM goal • **¡gol!** goal! • **el gol del empate** the equalizer • **el gol del honor** the consolation goal • **el gol de la victoria** the winning goal • **meter** *o* **marcar un gol** to score a goal • MODISMO: • **meter un gol a algn** to score a point against sb, put one over on sb* ▸ **gol average** goal average

gola SF 1 (*Anat*) throat, gullet
2 (*Hist*) [*de armadura*] gorget; [*de adorno*] ruff
3 (*Arquit*) cyma, ogee

golazo* SM great goal

goleada SF hammering*, thrashing* • **les ganaron por ~** they were hammered *o* thrashed*

goleador(a) ADJ • **el equipo más ~** the highest-scoring team, the team which has scored most goals • **aumentó su cuenta ~a** he improved his goal-scoring record
SM/F (goal) scorer • **el máximo ~ de la liga** the top (goal) scorer in the league

golear ▸ CONJUG 1a VT • **el Celta fue goleado por el Betis** Celta were hammered *o* thrashed by Betis* • **España goleó a Rumania por seis a cero** Spain hammered *o* thrashed Romania 6-0* • **el portero menos goleado** the keeper who has let in *o* conceded fewest goals • **el equipo más goleado** the team which has conceded most goals
VI to score (a goal)

golero/a SM/F (*Cono Sur*) goalkeeper

goleta SF schooner

golf SM 1 (= *juego*) golf • **campo de ~** golf course ▸ **golf miniatura** miniature golf
2 (= *pista*) golf course; (= *club*) golf club; (= *chalet*) clubhouse

golfa‡ SF tart‡, whore*, slut‡

golfada SF loutish behaviour *o* (*EEUU*) behavior, hooliganism

golfán SM water lily

golfante ADJ (= *gamberro*) loutish; (= *delincuente*) delinquent, criminal
SM (= *gamberro*) lout; (= *pillo*) rascal

golfear ▸ CONJUG 1a VI (= *vagabundear*) to idle around, laze around; (= *vivir a la briba*) to live like a street urchin

golferas‡ SM INV = **golfo²**

golfería SF 1 (= *golfos*) louts (*pl*); (= *golfillos*) street urchins (*pl*)
2 (= *comportamiento*) idling; (= *estilo de vida*) life of idleness; (= *vida callejera*) street life
3 (= *trampa*) dirty trick

golfillo SM urchin, street urchin

golfismo SM golfing

golfista ADJ golf (*antes de s*), golfing (*antes de s*)
SMF golfer

golfístico ADJ golf (*antes de s*), golfing (*antes de s*)

golfo[1] SM 1 (*Geog*) (= *bahía*) gulf • **la guerra del Golfo** the Gulf War • **la corriente del Golfo** the Gulf Stream ▸ **golfo de Méjico** (*Esp*), **golfo de México** (*LAm*) Gulf of Mexico ▸ **golfo de Vizcaya** Bay of Biscay ▸ **golfo Pérsico** Persian Gulf
2 (= *mar*) open sea

golfo[2] SM (= *gamberro*) lout; (= *travieso*) rascal; (= *pilluelo*) street urchin; (= *holgazán*) layabout • **¡menudo ~ estás hecho!** (*hum*) you rascal!

Gólgota SM Golgotha

Goliat SM Goliath

golilla SF 1 (= *adorno*) (*Cos, Hist*) ruff, gorget; [*de magistrado*] magistrate's collar
2 (*LAm*) (= *bufanda*) neckerchief • MODISMOS: • **alzar ~** (*Méx*) to puff out one's chest • **andar de ~** to be all dressed up • **ajustar la ~** to do one's duty
3 (*LAm*) [*de ave*] collar, ruff
4 (*Téc*) flange (*of a pipe*)
5 (*Caribe*) (= *deuda*) debt
6 (*Caribe*) (= *trampa*) trick, ruse
7 • **de ~** (*CAm*) (= *gratis*) free, for nothing; (*Caribe**) (= *por casualidad*) by chance, accidentally

gollería SF 1 (= *golosina*) dainty, delicacy
2* (= *extra*) extra, special treat • **pedir ~s** to ask too much • **es un empleo con muchas ~s** the job has a lot of perks

golleroso ADJ (= *afectado*) affected; (= *puntilloso*) pernickety, persnickety (*EEUU*)

gollete SM (= *garganta*) throat, neck; [*de botella*] neck • **beber a ~** to drink straight from the bottle • MODISMO: • **estar hasta el ~*** (= *harto*) to be up to here*, be fed up*; (= *lleno*) to be full up

golletero/a* SM/F (*LAm*) scrounger*

golondrina SF 1 (= *ave*) swallow • REFRÁN: • **una ~ no hace verano** one swallow does not make a summer ▸ **golondrina de mar** tern
2 (= *lancha*) motor launch
3 (*Cono Sur*) (= *emigrante*) migrant worker
4 (*Chile*) (*Hist*) furniture cart

golondrino SM 1 (= *vagabundo*) tramp, drifter, hobo (*EEUU*); (*Mil*) deserter
2 (*Med*) *tumour under the armpit*

golondro* SM fancy, yen*, longing • **andar en ~s** to cherish foolish hopes • MODISMO: • **campar de ~** to sponge*, live on other people

golosina SF 1 (= *manjar*) titbit, tidbit (*EEUU*), dainty; (= *dulce*) sweet, piece of candy (*EEUU*)
2 (= *incentivo*) incentive
3 (= *bagatela*) trifle; (= *cosa inútil*) useless object
4 (= *deseo*) desire, longing; (= *antojo*) fancy
5 (= *gula*) sweet tooth, liking for sweet things; (= *glotonería*) greed

goloso ADJ 1 (*de lo dulce*) sweet-toothed
2 (*pey*) greedy
3 (= *apetecible*) attractive, inviting

golpazo SM heavy thump, whack

golpe SM 1 (= *impacto*) hit, knock; (= *choque*) shock, clash; (= *encuentro*) bump; (*con un remo*) stroke; [*del corazón*] beat, throb • **oímos un ~ a la puerta** we heard a knock at the door • **en cuanto compras un coche nuevo tienes un ~** as soon as you buy a new car it gets a knock • **tras el ~ contra el muro tuvo que abandonar la carrera** after crashing into the wall he had to abandon the race • **dar un ~**: • **el coche de atrás nos dio un ~** the car behind ran into us • **dar ~s en la puerta** to hammer at the door • **darse un ~**: • **se dio un ~ en la cabeza** he got a bump on his head, he banged his head • **se dio un ~ contra la pared** he hit the wall • **darse ~s de pecho** to beat one's breast • **errar el ~** to fail in an attempt • MODISMO: • **no dar ~*** to be bone idle • REFRÁN: • **a ~ dado no hay quite** (*CAm**) what's done cannot be undone
2 (*dado por una persona a otra*) blow • **le dio un ~ con un palo** he gave him a blow with his stick, he hit him with his stick • **a ~s**: • **la emprendieron a ~s contra él** they began to beat him • **le mataron a ~s** they beat him to death • **les molieron a ~s** they beat them up • **los sacaron de la cama a ~s** they were beaten from their beds • **descargar ~s sobre algn** to rain blows on sb ▸ **golpe aplastante** crushing blow, knockout blow ▸ **golpe bien dado** hit, well-aimed blow ▸ **golpe de gracia** coup de grâce ▸ **golpe mortal** death blow
3 (*Med*) (= *cardenal*) bruise
4 (*en deportes*) (*Ftbl*) kick; (*Boxeo*) (*gen*) blow; (= *puñetazo*) punch • **con un total de 280 ~s** (*Golf*) with a total of 280 strokes • **preparar el ~** (*Golf*) to address the ball ▸ **golpe bajo** (*Boxeo*) low punch, punch below the belt • **aquello fue un ~ bajo** that was below the belt ▸ **golpe de acercamiento** (*Golf*) approach shot ▸ **golpe de castigo** (*Ftbl etc*) penalty kick ▸ **golpe de martillo** (*Tenis*) smash ▸ **golpe de penalidad** (*Golf*) penalty stroke ▸ **golpe de salida** (*Golf*) drive, drive-off ▸ **golpe franco, golpe libre** (*Ftbl*) free kick ▸ **golpe libre indirecto** indirect free kick
5 (*Téc*) stroke ▸ **golpe de émbolo** piston stroke
6 (= *desgracia*) blow • **mi ingreso en la cárcel fue un duro ~ para la familia** my imprisonment was a harsh blow to the family • **ha sufrido un duro ~** he has had a hard knock, he has suffered a severe blow • **la policía ha asestado un duro ~ al narcotráfico** the police have dealt a serious blow to drug traffickers • **acusar el ~** to suffer the consequences
7 (= *sorpresa*) surprise • **dar el ~ con algo** to cause a sensation with sth
8* (= *atraco*) job*, heist (*EEUU*) • **dieron un ~ en un banco** they did a bank job* • **preparaba su primer ~** he was planning his first job*
9 (= *salida*) witticism, sally • **¡qué ~!** how very clever!, good one! • **el libro tiene unos ~s buenísimos** the book's got some great lines in it
10 (*Pol*) coup ▸ **golpe blanco** bloodless coup ▸ **golpe de estado** coup d'état ▸ **golpe de mano** rising, sudden attack ▸ **golpe de palacio** palace coup
11 (*otras expresiones*) • **a ~ de**: • **abrir paso a ~ de machete** to hack out a path with a machete • **lo consiguieron a ~ de talonario** they got it through chequebook power • **al ~** (*Caribe*) instantly • **de ~**: • **la puerta se abrió de ~** the door flew open • **cerrar una puerta de ~** to slam a door (shut) • **la puerta se cerró de ~** the door slammed shut • **de ~ decidió dejar el trabajo** he suddenly decided to give up work • **de un ~** in one go

• **MODISMOS**: • **ir a ~ de calcetín** *o* **de alpargata*** to go on shanks's pony • **de ~ y porrazo** suddenly, unexpectedly ▸ **golpe de agua** heavy fall of rain ▸ **golpe de calor** heatstroke ▸ **golpe de efecto** coup de théâtre ▸ **golpe de fortuna** stroke of luck ▸ **golpe de gente** crowd of people ▸ **golpe de mar** heavy sea, surge ▸ **golpe de sol** sunstroke ▸ **golpe de suerte** stroke of luck ▸ **golpe de teatro** coup de théâtre ▸ **golpe de teléfono** telephone call ▸ **golpe de timón** change of direction ▸ **golpe de tos** fit of coughing ▸ **golpe de viento** gust of wind ▸ **golpe de vista** • **al primer ~ de vista** at first glance ▸ **golpe maestro** master stroke, stroke of genius
12 (*Cos*) (= *adorno*) pocket flap; (*Col*) (= *vuelta*) facing
13 (*Méx*) (= *mazo*) sledgehammer
14 (*Caribe**) (= *trago*) swig*, slug* (*of liquor*)

golpeador SM (*LAm*) door knocker

golpeadura SF = golpeo

golpear ▹ CONJUG 1a VT **1** (= *dar un golpe a*) to hit; (= *dar golpes a*) [+ *persona, alfombra*] to beat; (*para llamar la atención*) [+ *mesa, puerta, pared*] to bang on • **la ~on en la cabeza con una pistola** (*una vez*) they hit her on the head with a gun; (*varias veces*) they beat her about the head with a gun • **el maestro golpeó el pupitre con la mano** the teacher banged (on) the desk with his hand
2 [*desastre natural*] to hit, strike • **la vida le ha golpeado mucho** life has treated him badly
VI to beat • **la lluvia golpeaba contra los cristales** the rain was beating against the windows
VPR **golpearse** to hit, bang • **me golpeé la cabeza contra el armario** I hit *o* banged my head on the cupboard

golpecito SM (light) blow, tap • **dar ~s en algo** to tap (on) sth, rap (on) sth

golpeo SM (= *acción*) (*de una vez*) hitting; (*repetidamente*) beating; (*en mesa, puerta, pared*) banging

golpetazo* SM thump • **darse un ~ contra algo** to bang into sth, crash into sth

golpetear ▹ CONJUG 1a VT, VI (= *martillear*) to drum, tap; (= *traquetear*) to rattle

golpeteo SM (= *martilleo*) drumming, tapping; (= *traqueteo*) rattling

golpismo SM (= *tendencia*) *tendency to military coups*; (= *actitud*) *coup d'état mentality*

golpista ADJ • **intentona ~** coup attempt • **trama** *o* **conspiración ~** coup plot *o* conspiracy
SMF (= *participante*) *participant in a coup*; (= *partidario*) *supporter of a coup*

golpiza SF (*LAm*) (= *paliza*) beating-up, bashing* • **dar una ~ a algn** to beat sb up, bash sb*

goma SF **1** (= *sustancia*) (*Bot*) gum; (= *caucho*) rubber • **unos guantes de ~** a pair of rubber gloves ▸ **goma 2** plastic explosive ▸ **goma arábiga** gum arabic ▸ **goma de mascar** chewing gum ▸ **goma de pegar** gum, glue ▸ **goma espuma, goma espumosa** foam rubber
2 (= *banda*) (*para el pelo, papeles, paquetes*) rubber band, elastic band; (*en costura*) elastic; (= *tira*) piece of elastic, length of elastic • **jugar** *o* **saltar a la ~** to skip (*with a long elastic*)
3 (*tb* **goma de borrar**) rubber, eraser
4 (*Cono Sur*) (*Aut*) tyre, tire (*EEUU*)
5* (= *preservativo*) condom, sheath
6‡ (= *droga*) hash*, pot‡; [*de calidad*] good hash*, good pot‡
7 (*LAm*) [*de zapato*] rubber overshoe
8‡ [*de policía*] truncheon
9 (*CAm**) (= *resaca*) hangover • **estar de ~** to have a hangover

goma-espuma SF, **gomaespuma** SF foam rubber

gomal SM (*And*) rubber plantation

Gomera SF • **la ~** Gomera

gomería SF (*Cono Sur*) tyre *o* (*EEUU*) tire repair shop

gomero/a ADJ (= *de caucho*) rubber (*antes de s*)
SM/F **1** (*LAm*) (= *dueño*) rubber planter, rubber producer; (= *trabajador*) rubber-plantation worker
2 (*Cono Sur*) (*Aut*) tyre *o* (*EEUU*) tire mechanic
SM **1** (= *árbol*) rubber tree
2 (= *frasco*) glue container

gomina SF (hair) gel

gominola SF (*azucarada*) Fruit Pastille®; (*no azucarada*) wine gum

gomita SF rubber band, elastic band

Gomorra SF Gomorrah

gomosidad SF gumminess

gomoso ADJ [*líquido*] gummy; [*pan*] rubbery
SM †* toff*, dandy

gónada SF gonad

góndola SF **1** (= *vehículo*) (= *barca*) gondola; (*And, Chile*) bus ▸ **góndola de cable** (= *teleférico*) cable car; [*de esquí*] ski-lift ▸ **góndola del motor** (*Aer*) engine casing
2 (*en supermercado*) gondola

gondolero SM gondolier

gong SM (PL: **gongs**), **gongo** SM gong

gongorino ADJ *relating to Luis de Góngora* • **estilo ~** Gongoristic style • **estudios ~s** Góngora studies

gongorismo SM Gongorism (*literary style pioneered by Luis de Góngora in the 17th century*); ▹ CULTERANISMO, CONCEPTISMO

gonorrea SF gonorrhoea, gonorrhea (*EEUU*)

googlear [gugle'ar] ▹ CONJUG 1a VT, VI to google

gorda SF **1** • **MODISMO**: • **ni ~***: • **no tener ni ~** to be skint*, be broke* • **lo hice sin cobrar ni ~** I didn't get a penny for it • **no se oye ni ~** you can hear absolutely nothing • **no entiende ni ~** he doesn't understand a blind thing*
2 • **la Gorda** *the 1868 revolution in Spain*
• **MODISMOS**: • **armar la ~*** to kick up a fuss *o* a stink* • **si no me pagan voy a armar la ~** if they don't pay me I'm going to kick up a fuss *o* a stink* • **armarse la ~***: • **se armó la ~** all hell broke loose • **se armó la ~ cuando volvieron mis padres** there was a hell of a row when my parents came back*
3 (*Méx*) thick tortilla; ▹ **gordo**

gordal ADJ fat, big, thick
SM *kind of large olive*

gordinflón/ona* ADJ chubby, podgy, pudgy (*EEUU*) • **¡gordinflón!** fatty!*, fatso!*
SM/F fatty*, fatso*

gordito/a* ADJ **1** (= *gordo*) chubby, plump
2 (*Chile*) (= *querido*) darling*
SM/F fatty*, fatso*

gordo/a ADJ **1** [*persona*] (= *obeso*) fat; (= *corpulento*) stout, plump • **está más ~ que nunca** he's fatter than ever • **MODISMO**: • **caer ~ a algn***: • **ese tipo me cae ~** I can't stand that guy*
2* [*cosa, hecho*] big • **fue el desastre más ~ de su historia** it was the biggest *o* worst disaster in their history • **ha pasado algo muy ~** something major has happened • **una mentira de las gordas** a big fat lie* • **y lo más ~ fue que ...** and then to cap it all ...*
3 [*comida, sustancia*] greasy, oily • **tocino ~** fatty bacon
4 [*agua*] hard
5 [*lienzo, hilo*] coarse
6 (*Chile**) (= *querido*) darling*; ▹ **gota, perra, dedo, pez**[1]
SM/F fat man/woman • **¡gordo!** fatty!*, fatso!*
SM **1** (*Culin*) fat, suet
2 (= *premio*) jackpot, big prize • **ganar el ~** to hit the jackpot, win the big prize
• **MODISMO**: • **sacarse el ~** to bring home the bacon*; ▹ **gorda**

EL GORDO

El Gordo, "the fat one", refers to a large lottery jackpot, particularly the one offered in the Spanish **Lotería Nacional** at Christmas. The **Sorteo Extraordinario de Navidad** takes place on December 22 and the jackpot is worth several million pounds to the holder or holders of the winning number. Because of the cost of buying an entire number, people generally buy **décimos** (tenth-part shares), which means the total winnings are usually shared out between a number of people.
▹ LOTERÍA

gordolobo SM mullein

gordura SF **1** (= *obesidad*) fat, fatness; (= *corpulencia*) stoutness, plumpness
2 (*Culin*) grease, fat
3 (*Caribe, Cono Sur**) (= *crema*) cream

gorgojear ▹ CONJUG 1a VI = gorjear

gorgojeo SM = gorjeo

gorgojo SM **1** (= *insecto*) grub, weevil
2 (= *persona**) dwarf‡

gorgón SM (*And*) concrete

gorgoritear ▹ CONJUG 1a VI to trill, warble

gorgorito SM trill, warble • **hacer ~s** to trill, warble

gorgorizar ▹ CONJUG 1f VI to trill, warble

górgoro SM (*Méx*) bubble

gorgotear ▹ CONJUG 1a VI to gurgle

gorgoteo SM gurgle

gorguera SF (= *adorno*) ruff; (*Mil, Hist*) gorget

gori SM • **MODISMO**: • **armar el ~*** to make a row, kick up a fuss

gorigori* SM (= *canto*) gloomy chanting; (*en funeral*) funeral chanting; (= *gemidos*) wailing

gorila SM **1** (*Zool*) gorilla
2* (= *matón*) tough*, thug*; [*de club*] bouncer*; (= *guardaespaldas*) bodyguard, minder*
3 (*Cono Sur*) (*Pol**) right-winger; (*Mil*) senior officer
ADJ (*Cono Sur*) (*Pol**) reactionary

gorilismo SM thuggery

goriloide SM brute, thug

gorja SF throat, gorge • **MODISMO**: • **estar de ~*** to be very cheerful

gorjear ▹ CONJUG 1a VI [*ave*] to chirp, trill
VPR **gorjearse** [*niño*] to gurgle, burble

gorjeo SM **1** [*de ave*] chirping, trilling
2 [*de bebé*] gurgling, burbling

gorobeto ADJ (*And*) twisted, bent, warped

gorra SF **1** (*para la cabeza*) (*gen*) cap; [*de bebé*] bonnet; (*Mil*) bearskin, busby • **MODISMOS**: • **pasar la ~** to pass the hat round • **pegar la ~*** to be unfaithful ▸ **gorra de baño** (*Méx, Arg, Uru*) bathing cap, swimming cap ▸ **gorra de montar** riding hat ▸ **gorra de paño** cloth cap ▸ **gorra de punto** knitted cap ▸ **gorra de visera** peaked cap ▸ **gorra de yate** yachting cap
2 • **MODISMO**: • **de ~***: • **una comida de ~** a free meal • **andar** *o* **ir** *o* **vivir de ~** to sponge*, scrounge* • **comer de ~** to scrounge a meal* • **entrar de ~** to get in free • **sacar algo de ~** to scrounge sth* • **me vino de ~** (*CAm**) it was a stroke of luck, it came out of the blue
SMF * (= *gorrón*) sponger*, cadger*, parasite

g

gorrazo SM • **correr a algn a ~s** to run sb out of town

gorrear ▸ CONJUG 1a VT **1*** (= *gorronear*) to scrounge*, cadge* • **siempre me está gorreando cigarrillos** he's always scrounging *o* cadging cigarettes off me*
2 (*Cono Sur‡*) to cuckold
VI* to scrounge*, sponge* • **a ver cuándo dejas de ~ y te pagas tú las cosas** when are you going to stop scrounging *o* sponging and pay your own way?*

gorrero/a SM/F **1** cap maker
2* = **gorrón²**

gorrinada SF **1** (= *mala pasada*) dirty trick
2 (= *cerdos*) (number of) pigs (*pl*)

gorrinera SF pigsty, pigpen (*EEUU*)

gorrinería SF **1** (= *porquería*) dirt
2 (= *mala pasada*) dirty trick

gorrino/a SM/F **1** (= *cerdo*) pig, hog (*EEUU*); (= *cochinito*) piglet • **chillaba como un ~** he was squealing like a pig
2 (= *persona*) pig*

gorrión SM **1** (= *ave*) sparrow
2 • MODISMO: • **de ~** (*Caribe*) ▸ **gorra**

gorrista* SMF = **gorra**

gorro SM [*de lana*] hat; [*de bebé*] bonnet
• MODISMOS: • **estar hasta el ~*** to be fed up* • **hinchar el ~ a algn‡** to get on sb's wick‡ • **poner el ~ a algn*** (= *avergonzar*) to embarrass sb; (*Cono Sur, Méx‡*) to be unfaithful to sb, cuckold sb‡ ▸ **gorro de baño** bathing cap ▸ **gorro de caña** pith helmet ▸ **gorro de dormir** nightcap ▸ **gorro de montaña** Balaclava (helmet) ▸ **gorro de papel** paper hat ▸ **gorro de piel** fur hat ▸ **gorro frigio** Phrygian cap, revolutionary cap

gorrón¹ SM **1** (= *guijarro*) pebble; (= *adoquín*) cobblestone
2 (*Mec*) pivot, journal

gorrón²/ona* SM/F (= *aprovechado*) sponger*, cadger*, parasite

gorronear* ▸ CONJUG 1a VT to scrounge*, cadge* • **~ algo a algn** to scrounge *o* cadge sth from sb* • **le gorronean los amigos** his friends scrounge *o* cadge off him*
VI to sponge*, scrounge*

gorroneo* SM sponging*, scrounging*

gorronería* SF **1** (= *abuso*) sponging*, scrounging*
2 (*And*) (= *avaricia*) greed, avarice

gospel SM gospel music

gota SF **1** (*de líquido*) drop; (*de sudor*) drop, bead • **unas ~s de coñac** a few drops of brandy • **todo ello mezclado con algunas ~s de humor** all mixed with a few touches of humour • **se añade el aceite ~ a ~** add the oil drop by drop • **van filtrando la información ~ a ~ a la prensa** they let the news leak out to the press in dribs and drabs • **sistema de riego ~ a ~** trickle irrigation • **caer a ~s** to drip • MODISMOS: • **la ~ que colma el vaso** the straw that breaks the camel's back, the last straw • **¡ni ~!** not a bit! • **no bebo ni ~ de alcohol** I don't drink a drop of alcohol • **no corre ni ~ de aire** there isn't a breath of air • **no ver ni ~** to see nothing • **parecerse como dos ~s de agua** to be as like as two peas • **sudar la ~ gorda** to sweat blood ▸ **gotas amargas** bitters
2 (= *enfermedad*) gout ▸ **gota caduca, gota oral** epilepsy
3 (*Meteo*) ▸ **gota fría** *severe weather which brings flooding*
4 ▸ **gota de leche** (*Chile*) (*fig*) child welfare clinic, welfare food centre
5 gotas (= *medicina*) drops ▸ **gotas nasales** nose drops, nasal drops
SM ▸ **gota a gota** drip, IV (*EEUU*) • **le pusieron el ~ a ~** he was put on a drip

goteado ADJ speckled, spotted

gotear ▸ CONJUG 1a VI **1** [*líquido, grifo, vela*] to drip; [*cañería, recipiente*] to leak • **pintó el techo sin ~** he painted the ceiling without spilling a drop
2 (*Meteo*) to rain lightly

goteo SM **1** [*de líquido, grifo*] dripping; [*de cañería, recipiente*] leak; (= *chorrito*) trickle • **el ~ de cartas de protesta se convirtió en avalancha** the trickle of letters of complaint became a flood • **un constante ~ de dimisiones** a steady flow *o* stream of resignations • **riego por ~** trickle irrigation
2 (*Med*) drip, IV (*EEUU*)

gotera SF **1** (= *filtración*) leak; (= *gotas*) drip; (= *chorrito*) trickle
2 (= *mancha*) damp stain
3 (*Med*) (= *achaque*) chronic ailment • **estar lleno de ~s** to be full of aches and pains, feel a wreck*
4 [*de colgadura*] valance
5 goteras (*LAm*) (= *afueras*) outskirts, environs

gotero SM **1** (*Med*) drip, IV (*EEUU*)
2 (*LAm*) [*de laboratorio*] dropper

goterón SM big raindrop

gótico ADJ **1** [*estilo, arte, letra*] Gothic
2 (= *noble*) noble, illustrious
SM (*Ling*) Gothic

gotita SF droplet • **¡una ~ nada más!** [*de bebida*] just a drop!

gotoso ADJ gouty

gouache [gwaʃ] SM gouache

gourmet [gur'me] SMF (PL: **gourmets** [gur'mes]) gourmet, connoisseur (*of food*)

goyesco ADJ **1** (= *de Goya*) of Goya
2 [*estilo artístico*] Goy(a)esque, *in the style of Goya, after the manner of Goya*

gozada* SF • **es una ~** it's brilliant *o* fantastic* • **aquí se está de maravilla, ¡qué ~!** it's wonderful here, sheer heaven!

gozar ▸ CONJUG 1f VT **1** (= *disfrutar*) to enjoy; (= *poseer*) to have, possess
2†† [+ *mujer*] to have, seduce
VI **1** (= *disfrutar*) to enjoy o.s., have a good time (**con** with) • **~ de algo** (= *disfrutar*) to enjoy sth; (= *tener*) to have sth, possess sth • **~ de buena salud** to enjoy good health
2‡ (= *llegar al orgasmo*) to come‡
VPR **gozarse** to enjoy o.s. • **~se en hacer algo** to enjoy doing sth, take pleasure in doing sth

gozne SM hinge

gozo SM **1** (= *placer*) enjoyment, pleasure; (= *complacencia*) delight; (= *júbilo*) joy, rejoicing • **no caber (en sí) de ~** to be overjoyed • **da ~ escucharle** it's a pleasure to listen to him • **es un ~ para los ojos** it's a joy to see, it's a sight for sore eyes • MODISMO: • **¡mi ~ en un pozo!** it's gone down the drain!
2 gozos (*Literat, Mús*) *couplets in honour of the Virgin*

gozosamente ADV joyfully • **se lo comunicó ~ a los demás** he joyfully told the others • **aceptaron ~ la ofrenda** they were delighted to accept the gift

gozoso ADJ joyful

gozque SM (= *perro*) small yapping dog; (= *cachorro*) puppy

g.p. ABR, **g/p** ABR (= **giro postal**) p.o., m.o. (*EEUU*)

GPL SF ABR (*Inform*) (= **General Public License**) GPL

GPS SM ABR (= **Global Positioning System**) GPS

gr. ABR (= **gramo(s)**) gm(s)

grabable ADJ writable

grabación SF recording ▸ **grabación digital** digital recording ▸ **grabación en cinta** tape-recording ▸ **grabación en directo** live recording ▸ **grabación en vídeo** video recording ▸ **grabación magnetofónica** tape-recording

grabado ADJ • **se me quedó grabada la expresión de la niña** I'll never forget the girl's expression • **tengo grabada en la memoria su cara** her face is engraved *o* etched on my memory
SM (= *impresión*) engraving, print; (*en un libro*) illustration, print ▸ **grabado al agua fuerte** etching ▸ **grabado al agua tinta** aquatint ▸ **grabado en cobre, grabado en dulce** copperplate ▸ **grabado en madera** woodcut ▸ **grabado rupestre** rock carving

grabador¹ SM tape recorder

grabador²(a) SM/F (= *persona*) engraver

grabadora SF **1** (*tb* **grabadora de cinta**) tape recorder ▸ **grabadora de CD(s)** CD writer ▸ **grabadora de DVD(s)** (*gen*) DVD recorder; (*en ordenador*) DVD writer, DVD burner ▸ **grabadora de sonido** voice recorder ▸ **grabadora de vídeo** video (recorder)
2 (= *empresa*) recording company
3 (*Téc*) graver, cutting tool

grabadura SF engraving

grabar ▸ CONJUG 1a VT **1** (*en madera, metal*) to engrave • **grabó sus iniciales en la medalla** he engraved his initials on the medal • **~ al agua fuerte** to etch
2 [+ *sonidos, imágenes*] (*gen*) to record; (= *hacer una copia en cinta*) to tape • **están grabando su nuevo álbum** they are recording their new album • **un disco grabado en 1960** a record made in 1960 • **¿me puedes ~ este CD?** can you tape this CD for me?
3 (= *fijar*) to etch • **lo tengo grabado en la memoria** it's etched on my memory • **lleva el dolor grabado en el rostro** the pain is engraved *o* etched on her face • **~ algo en el ánimo de algn** to impress sth on sb's mind

gracejada* SF (*CAm, Méx*) stupid joke

gracejo SM **1** (= *chispa*) wit, humour, humor (*EEUU*); (*en conversación*) repartee
2 (= *encanto*) charm, grace
3 (*CAm, Méx*) (= *payaso*) clown

gracia SF **1** (= *diversión*) **a** [*de chiste, persona*] • **yo no le veo la ~** I don't see what's so funny • **si no lo cuentas bien se le va la ~** if you don't tell it well the joke is lost • **nos lo contó con mucha ~** he told it to us in a very funny *o* amusing way • **ahí está la ~** that's the whole point • **coger** *o* **pescar la ~** to see the point (*of a joke*)
b • **hacer ~ a algn**: • **a mí no me hace ~ ese humorista** I don't find that comedian funny • **me hace ~ ver a mi padre en la televisión** it's funny seeing my father on television • **me hace ~ que me llamen conservador precisamente ellos** it's funny that they of all people should call me conservative • **no me hacía ~ su aire de superioridad** I didn't like his air of superiority • **al jefe no le va a hacer ninguna ~ que nos vayamos a casa** our boss is not going to be at all happy about us going home • **no me hace mucha ~ la idea de tener que trabajar este domingo** I'm not wild about the idea of having to work this Sunday*
c • **tener ~** [*broma, chiste*] to be funny; [*persona*] (= *ser ingenioso*) to be witty; (= *ser divertido*) to be funny, be amusing • **la broma no tuvo ~** the joke wasn't funny • **¡tiene ~ la cosa!** (*iró*) isn't that (just) great! (*iró*) • **tendría ~ que se estropeara el despertador justamente hoy** (*iró*) wouldn't it be just great if the alarm didn't go off today of all days? (*iró*) • **tiene mucha ~ hablando** he's very witty, he's very funny *o* amusing

• tiene mucha ~ contando chistes his jokes are really funny
d • ¡qué ~! (*gen*) how funny!; (*iró*) it's great, isn't it? **• ¿así que tu hermano y mi hermano se conocen? ¡qué ~!** so your brother and mine know each other — how funny! **• y, ¡qué ~!, me dice el profesor: —señorita, compórtese** and the teacher said to me, it was so funny, "behave yourself, young lady" **• ¡qué ~! ¿no? tú de vacaciones y yo aquí estudiando** (*iró*) it's great, isn't it? you are on holiday while I am here studying (*iró*)
e • dar en la ~ de hacer algo to take to doing sth
2 (= *encanto*) **a** (*al moverse*) gracefulness, grace **• se mueve con ~** she moves gracefully **• sin ~** ungraceful, lacking in gracefulness *o* grace **• tener ~** to be graceful
b (*en la personalidad*) charm **• tener ~** [*persona*] to have charm; [*objeto*] to be nice **• no es guapo, pero tiene cierta ~** he's not good-looking but he has a certain charm **• no tiene ninguna ~ vistiendo** she has no dress sense
3 (= *chiste*) joke **• hacer una ~ a algn** to play a prank on sb **• hizo una de sus ~s** he showed himself up once again **• reírle las ~s a algn** to laugh along with sb
4 gracias: **a** (*para expresar agradecimiento*) thanks **• ¡~s!** thank you! **• ¡muchas ~s!** thank you very much!, thanks a lot!, many thanks! (*más frm*) **• dar las ~s a algn** to thank sb (**por** for) **• no nos dio ni las ~s** he didn't even say thank you, he didn't even thank us **• llamaba para darte las ~s por todo** I am phoning to thank you for everything **• toma eso, ¡y ~s!** take that and be thankful! **• y ~s que no llegó a más** and we *etc* were lucky to get off so lightly
b • ~s a thanks to **• hemos conseguido esta casa ~s a ellos** it's thanks to them that we got this house **• han sobrevivido ~s a la ayuda internacional** they have survived with the help of *o* thanks to international aid **• la familia se mantiene ~s a que el padre y la madre trabajan** the family manages to support itself thanks to the fact that both parents work **• ~s a Dios** thank heaven(s)
5 (*Rel*) grace **• estar en ~ (de Dios)** to be in a state of grace **• por la ~ de Dios** by the grace of God; ▷ **obra**
6 (*Jur*) mercy, pardon **• medida de ~** pardon; ▷ **tiro**
7 (= *favor*) favour, favor (EEUU) **• te concederé la ~ que me pidas** I will grant you whatever favour you request **• caer de la ~ de algn**† fall out of favour with sb **• de ~**† free, gratis
• MODISMOS: • caer en ~ a algn to warm to sb, take a liking to sb **• me cayó en ~ enseguida** I warmed to him immediately, I took an immediate liking to him **• nunca me cayó en ~ tu suegra** I never really liked your mother-in-law **• hacer a algn ~ de algo** to spare sb sth **• te hago ~ de los detalles** I'll spare you the details
8 (= *benevolencia*) graciousness
9 (*Mit*) **• las tres Gracias** the Three Graces
10 • en ~ a† on account of **• en ~ a la brevedad** for the sake of brevity
11† (= *nombre*) name **• ¿cuál es su ~?** what is your name?
graciable (ADJ) **1** [*persona*] (= *benévolo*) gracious; (= *amable*) kind
2 [*concesión*] easily-granted
3 [*pago*] discretionary
graciablemente (ADV) **1** [*comportarse*] (= *con benevolencia*) graciously; (= *con amabilidad*) kindly
2 [*pagar*] on a discretionary basis
grácil (ADJ) [*figura, líneas, movimientos*] graceful; [*talle*] slender
gracilidad (SF) gracefulness, grace
graciosamente (ADV) **1** (= *con encanto*) gracefully; (= *con elegancia*) pleasingly, elegantly
2 (= *con humor*) funnily, amusingly; (= *con agudeza*) wittily; (= *payaseando*) comically
graciosidad (SF) **1** (= *encanto*) grace, gracefulness; (= *elegancia*) elegance; (= *belleza*) beauty
2 (= *humor*) funniness, amusing qualities (*pl*); (= *agudeza*) wittiness
gracioso/a (ADJ) **1** (= *divertido*) funny, amusing **• una situación muy graciosa** a very funny *o* amusing situation **• es de lo más ~** he's really funny *o* amusing **• estás tú muy graciosillo hoy** (*iró*) you're very witty *o* funny today **• lo ~ del caso es que ...** the funny *o* amusing thing about it is that ... **• lo ~ sería que ganaran ellos, cuando van los últimos** it would be funny if they won, when they're last at the moment **• ¡qué ~!** how funny! **• has visto cómo me ha adelantado ese coche ¡qué ~!** (*iró*) did you see how that car overtook me — now that was really clever, wasn't it?
2 (= *mono*) cute **• tiene una nariz muy graciosa** she's got a cute little nose **• un sombrerito muy ~** a lovely *o* cute little hat
3 (*como título*) gracious **• su graciosa Majestad** her gracious Majesty
4 (= *gratuito*) free
(SM/F) (*iró*) joker* **• habrá sido algún ~** it must have been some joker* **• hacerse el ~** to try to be funny **• ¡no se haga el ~!** don't try to be funny!
(SM) (*Teat, Hist*) comic character, fool
grada (SF) **1** (= *asiento*) tier, row of seats **• asientos de ~** stands **• la(s) ~(s)** the stands, the terraces, the terracing **• un gol coreado en la(s) ~(s)** a goal which was hailed in the stands *o* on the terraces *o* on the terracing
2 (= *peldaño*) step, stair; (*Rel*) altar step; **gradas** (= *escalinata*) flight (*sing*) of steps; (*And, Cono Sur*) paved terrace (*sing*) (*in front of a building*)
3 (*Náut*) [*de construcción*] slip; [*de reparaciones*] slipway
4 (= *azada*) harrow ▸ **grada de disco** disk harrow ▸ **grada de mano** hoe, cultivator
gradación (SF) **1** (= *progresión*) gradation; (= *serie*) graded series
2 (*Retórica*) climax; (*Ling*) comparison
gradar ▷ CONJUG 1a (VT) (*Agr*) (= *allanar*) to harrow; (= *cultivar*) to hoe
gradería (SF), **graderío** (SM) stands (*pl*), terraces (*pl*), terracing **• ambiente crispado en el graderío *o* los graderíos** tense atmosphere in the stands *o* on the terraces *o* on the terracing ▸ **gradería cubierta** grandstand
gradiente (SF) (*LAm*) gradient
grado (SM) **1** (= *nivel*) degree **• un alto ~ de desarrollo** a high degree of development **• quemaduras de primer/segundo ~** first-/second-degree burns **• parentesco de segundo ~** second-degree kinship **• en alto ~** to a great degree **• la censura dificultó en alto ~ la investigación científica** scientific research was greatly hindered *o* was hindered to a great degree by censorship **• de ~ en ~** step by step, by degrees **• en mayor ~** to a greater degree *o* extent **• en menor ~** to a lesser degree *o* extent **• en mayor o menor ~** to a greater or lesser extent **• en sumo ~ *o* en ~ sumo: • era humillante en sumo ~** it was humiliating in the extreme **• me complace en sumo ~** it gives me the greatest pleasure **• en ~ superlativo** in the extreme **• tercer ~ (penitenciario)** (*Esp*) *lowest category within the prison system which allows day release privileges*
2 (*Geog, Mat, Fís*) degree **• la temperatura es de 40 ~s** the temperature is 40 degrees **• estamos a cinco ~s bajo cero** it is five degrees below zero **• un ángulo de 45 ~s** a 45-degree angle **• este vino tiene 12 ~s** this wine is 12 per cent alcohol **• esta cerveza no tiene muchos ~s** this beer is very low in alcohol ▸ **grado Celsius** degree Celsius ▸ **grado centígrado** degree centigrade ▸ **grado Fahrenheit** degree Fahrenheit
3 [*de escalafón*] grade; (*Mil*) rank **• tiene el ~ de teniente** he holds the rank of lieutenant **• un militar de ~ superior** a high-ranking army officer
4 (= *etapa*) stage **• está en el segundo ~ de elaboración** it is now in the second stage of production
5 (*esp LAm*) (*Educ*) (= *curso*) year, grade (EEUU); (= *título*) degree **• tiene el ~ de licenciado** he is a graduate **• colación de ~s** (*Arg*) conferment of degrees ▸ **grado universitario** university degree
6 (*Ling*) degree of comparison **• adjetivos en ~ comparativo** comparative adjectives, comparatives **• adjetivos en ~ superlativo** superlative adjectives, superlatives
7 (= *gusto*) **• de (buen) ~** willingly **• aceptó las nuevas normas de buen ~** she willingly agreed the new regulations **• de mal ~** unwillingly **• MODISMO: • de ~ o por (la) fuerza: • otros muchos países entraron en guerra, de ~ o por la fuerza** many other countries were forced willy-nilly to enter the war **• pues tendrás que ir, de ~ o por la fuerza** well you'll have to go, like it or not
8 [*de escalera*] step
9 grados (*Rel*) minor orders
graduable (ADJ) adjustable, that can be adjusted
graduación (SF) **1** [*de volumen, temperatura*] adjustment
2 [*de una bebida*] alcoholic strength, proof grading **• bebidas de baja ~** drinks with a low alcohol content ▸ **graduación octánica** octane rating
3 [*de la vista*] testing
4 (*Univ*) graduation **• baile de ~** graduation ball
5 (*Mil*) (= *rango*) rank **• de alta ~** of high rank, high-ranking
graduado/a (ADJ) **1** [*escala*] graduated **• gafas graduadas** prescription glasses, glasses with prescription lenses
2 (*Educ*) graduate (*antes de s*)
3 [*militar*] commissioned
(SM/F) (= *estudiante*) graduate
(SM) **graduado escolar** (*Esp*) *formerly, certificate of success in EGB course*
gradual (ADJ) gradual
gradualidad (SF) gradualness
gradualismo (SM) (*esp Pol*) gradualism
gradualista (ADJ), (SMF) gradualist
gradualmente (ADV) gradually
graduando/a (SM/F) graduand
graduar ▷ CONJUG 1e (VT) **1** (= *regular*) [+ *volumen, temperatura*] to adjust **• hay que ~ la salida del agua** the outflow of water has to be regulated
2 (= *medir*) to gauge, measure; (*Téc*) to calibrate; [+ *termómetro*] to graduate; [+ *vista*] to test **• tengo que ~me la vista** I've got to have my eyes tested
3 (*Univ*) to confer a degree on
4 (*Mil*) to confer a rank on **• ~ a algn de capitán** to confer the rank of captain on sb
(VPR) **graduarse 1** (*Univ*) to graduate, take one's degree **• se graduó en Derecho** he

graduated in law
2 (*Mil*) to take a commission (**de** as)

GRAE ABR = **Gramática de la Real Academia Española**

grafía SF spelling • **se inclina por la ~ "gira"** he prefers the spelling "gira"

gráfica SF **1** (= *representación*) (*Mat*) graph; (= *diagrama*) chart ▸ **gráfica de fiebre, gráfica de temperatura** (*Med*) temperature chart
2 (= *empresa*) • **"Gráficas Giménez"** "Giménez Graphics"

graficación SF **1** (*Inform*) graphics (*sing*)
2 (*Mat*) representation on a graph

gráficamente ADV graphically

gráfico ADJ **1** [*diseño, artes*] graphic • **tarjeta gráfica** graphics card • **información gráfica** photographs (*pl*), pictures (*pl*) • **reportero ~** press photographer
2 [*descripción, relato*] graphic
SM **1** (= *diagrama*) chart; (*Mat*) graph ▸ **gráfico de barras** bar chart ▸ **gráfico de sectores, gráfico de tarta** pie chart
2 gráficos (*Inform*) graphics

grafiosis SF INV Dutch elm disease

grafismo SM **1** (*Arte*) graphic art; (*Inform*) computer graphics
2 (= *logotipo*) logo
3 (= *escritura*) graphology

grafista SMF graphic artist, graphic designer

grafitero/a SM/F graffiti artist

grafiti SMPL graffiti

grafito SM graphite, black lead

grafología SF graphology

grafólogo/a SM/F graphologist

gragea SF **1** (*Med*) sugar-coated pill
2 (= *confite*) small coloured *o* (*EEUU*) colored sweet

graifrú SM (*CAm, Ven*) grapefruit

graja SF rook

grajea SF (*And*) fine shot, birdshot

grajear ▷ CONJUG 1a VI [*ave*] to caw; [*bebé*] to gurgle

grajiento ADJ (*LAm*) smelly

grajilla SF jackdaw

grajo SM **1** (= *cuervo*) rook
2 (*LAm*) (= *olor corporal*) body odour *o* (*EEUU*) odor; [*del sobaco*] underarm smell

Gral. ABR, **gral.** ABR (= **General**) Gen

grama SF (*esp LAm*) (= *hierba*) Bermuda grass; (*Caribe**) (= *césped*) lawn

gramaje SM weight (*of paper etc*)

gramática SF (= *estudio*) grammar; (= *texto*) grammar (book) ▸ **gramática de casos** case grammar ▸ **gramática generativa** generative grammar ▸ **gramática parda** native wit • **saber** *o* **tener mucha ~ parda** to be worldly-wise, know the ways of the world ▸ **gramática profunda** deep grammar ▸ **gramática transformacional** transformational grammar; ▹ **gramático**

gramatical ADJ grammatical

gramático/a ADJ grammatical
SM/F (= *persona*) grammarian; ▹ **gramática**

gramil SM gauge, gage (*EEUU*)

gramilla SF (*LAm*) grass, lawn

gramillar SM (*Cono Sur*) meadow, grassland

gramínea SF grass; (*LAm*) pulse

gramo SM gramme, gram (*EEUU*)

gramófono SM gramophone, phonograph (*EEUU*)

gramola† SF gramophone, phonograph (*EEUU*); (*en bar, cafetería*) jukebox

grampa SF (*esp LAm*) staple

gran ▹ **grande**

grana[1] SF (*Bot*) **1** (= *semilla*) small seed • **dar en ~** to go to seed, run to seed
2 (= *acto*) seeding; (= *estación*) seeding time
3 (*LAm*) (= *pasto*) grass; (*CAm, Méx*) (*Dep*) turf

grana[2] SF (*Zool*) cochineal; (= *tinte*) kermes; (= *color*) scarlet; (= *tela*) scarlet cloth • **de ~** scarlet, bright red • MODISMO: • **ponerse como la ~** to go as red as a beetroot

Granada SF (*Esp*) Granada; (*Caribe*) Grenada

granada SF **1** (*Bot*) pomegranate
2 (= *bomba*) grenade ▸ **granada anticarro** anti-tank grenade ▸ **granada de fragmentación** fragmentation grenade ▸ **granada de humo** smoke-bomb ▸ **granada de mano** hand grenade ▸ **granada de metralla** shrapnel shell ▸ **granada de mortero** mortar shell ▸ **granada detonadora** stun grenade ▸ **granada lacrimógena** teargas grenade

granadero SM **1** (*Mil*) grenadier
2 granaderos (*Méx*) (= *policía*) riot police

granadilla SF (= *pasionaria*) passionflower; (= *fruto*) passion fruit

granadino/a ADJ of/from Granada
SM/F native/inhabitant of Granada • **los ~s** the people of Granada

granado[1] SM (= *árbol*) pomegranate tree

granado[2] ADJ **1** (= *selecto*) choice, select; (= *notable*) distinguished • **lo más ~ de la sociedad** the cream of society • **lo más ~ de la prosa en lengua española** the pick of Spanish prose writing
2 (= *maduro*) mature; (= *alto*) full-grown, tall

granangular ADJ • **objetivo ~** wide-angle lens

granar ▷ CONJUG 1a VI to seed, run to seed

granate SM **1** (= *mineral*) garnet
2 (= *color*) deep red, dark crimson
ADJ INV deep red, dark crimson

granazón SF seeding

Gran Bretaña SF Great Britain

Gran Canaria SF Gran Canaria, Grand Canary

grancanario/a ADJ of/from Gran Canaria, of/from Grand Canary
SM/F native/inhabitant of Gran Canaria *o* Grand Canary • **los ~s** the people of Gran Canaria *o* Grand Canary

grande ADJ (*antes de sm sing:* **gran**) **1** (*de tamaño*) big, large; (*de estatura*) big, tall; [*número, velocidad*] high, great • **viven en una casa muy ~** they live in a very big *o* large house • **¿cómo es de ~?** how big *o* large is it?, what size is it? • **los zapatos le están muy ~s** the shoes are too big for her • **en cantidades más ~s** in larger *o* greater quantities • **grandísimo** enormous, huge • **un esfuerzo grandísimo** an enormous effort, a huge effort • **un coche grandísimo** a whacking great car* • **¡grandísimo tunante!** you old rogue! • **el gran Buenos Aires** greater Buenos Aires • MODISMOS: • **a lo ~*** in style • **hacer algo a lo ~** to do sth in style, make a splash doing sth* • **vivir a lo ~** to live in style • **quedarle algo ~ a algn** to be too much for sb, be more than sb can handle • **pasarlo en ~** to have a tremendous time*
2 (= *importante*) [*artista, hazaña*] great; [*empresa*] big • **un gran pintor** a great painter • **un gran desastre** a great disaster • **es una ventaja muy ~** it's a great advantage • **hay una diferencia no muy ~** there is not a very big *o* great difference • **los ~s bancos internacionales** the big international banks • **las ~s empresas multinacionales** the big multinationals • **la gran mayoría** the great majority
3 (= *mucho, muy*) great • **con gran placer** with great pleasure • **fueron ~s amigos** they were great friends • **he sentido una gran pena** I felt very sad • **me llevé una alegría muy ~** I felt very happy • **comer con gran apetito** to eat hungrily • **un mes de gran calor** a very hot month • **un programa de gran éxito** a very successful programme • **se estrenó con gran éxito** it was a great success, it went off very well
4 (*en edad*) (= *mayor*) • **ya eres ~, Raúl** you are a big boy now, Raúl • **¿qué piensas hacer cuando seas ~?** what do you want to do when you grow up?
5 • **¡qué ~!** (*Arg**) how funny!
SMF **1** (= *personaje importante*) • **los ~s de la industria** the major companies in the industry • **uno de los ~s de la pantalla** one of the screen greats • **los siete ~s** the Big Seven ▸ **Grande de España** grandee
2 (*LAm*) (= *adulto*) adult
SF **1** (*Arg*) [*de lotería*] first prize, big prize
2 (*And‡*) (= *cárcel*) clink‡, jail

grandemente ADV greatly, extremely • **~ equivocado** greatly mistaken

grandeza SF **1** (= *nobleza*) nobility • **la ~ de su acción humanitaria** the nobility *o* greatness of his humanitarian action • **~ de alma** *o* **espíritu** magnanimity
2 [*de artista etc*] greatness
3 (= *esplendidez*) grandness, impressiveness; (= *ostentación*) grandeur, magnificence
4 (= *personas*) grandees (*pl*) • **la Grandeza de España** the Spanish nobility
5 (= *rango*) status of grandee
6 (= *tamaño*) size; (= *gran tamaño*) bigness; (= *magnitud*) magnitude

grandilocuencia SF grandiloquence

grandilocuente ADJ, **grandílocuo** ADJ grandiloquent

grandiosidad SF = **grandeza**

grandioso ADJ (= *magnífico*) grand, magnificent; (*pey*) grandiose

grandísimo ADJ *superl de* **grande**

grandón ADJ solidly-built

grandor SM size

grandote* ADJ huge

grandullón/ona*, **grandulón/ona*** (*And*)
ADJ overgrown, oversized
SM/F big kid

granear ▷ CONJUG 1a VT **1** [+ *semilla*] to sow
2 (*Téc*) to grain, stipple

granel SM **1** (*Com*) • **a ~** (= *en cantidad*) in bulk; (= *sin envasar*) loose • **vender a ~** [+ *líquidos*] to sell by the pint *o* litre; [+ *alimentos*] to sell loose • **vino a ~** wine in bulk *o* in the barrel • **olía a colonia de ~** she smelled of cheap perfume
2 (= *montón*) heap • **a ~** (= *mucho*) in abundance; (= *a montones*) by the ton; (= *con profusión*) lavishly

granelero SM bulk-carrier

granero SM **1** (= *edificio*) granary, barn
2 (= *distrito*) granary, corn-producing area • **el ~ de Europa** the breadbasket of Europe

granetario SM precision balance

granete SM punch

granguiñolesco ADJ melodramatic, exaggerated

granilla SF grain (*in cloth*)

granítico ADJ granitic, granite (*antes de s*)

granito[1] SM (*Geol*) granite

granito[2] SM **1** [*de sal, azúcar etc*] grain • **aportaremos nuestro ~ de arena** we'll do our bit*
2 (*Med*) pimple

granizada SF **1** (*Meteo*) hailstorm, hail
2 (*fig*) hail; (= *abundancia*) shower, vast number • **una ~ de balas** a hail of bullets
3 (*And*) (= *bebida*) iced drink

granizado SM (= *bebida*) iced drink; [*de hielo*] slush ▸ **granizado de café** iced coffee ▸ **granizado de limón** iced lemon drink

granizal SM (*LAm*) hailstorm

granizar ▷ CONJUG 1f VI (*Meteo*) to hail; (*fig*) to shower, rain

granizo SM hail

granja SF farm • **animales de ~** farm animals • **huevos de ~** free-range eggs • **pollo de ~** free-range eggs ▸ **granja avícola** chicken farm, poultry farm ▸ **granja colectiva** collective farm ▸ **granja de multiplicación** factory farm ▸ **granja de pollos** chicken farm ▸ **granja escuela** educational farm ▸ **granja marina** fish farm

granjear ▷ CONJUG 1a VT **1** (= *adquirir*) [+ *respeto, enemigos*] to earn • **su actitud le granjeó una fama de intolerante** his attitude earned him a reputation as a bigot
2 (*And, Cono Sur*) (= *robar*) to steal
VPR **granjearse** [+ *respeto, enemigos*] to earn

granjería SF **1** (*Com, Econ*) profit, earnings (*pl*); (*Agr*) farm earnings (*pl*)
2 (= *zootecnia*) farming, husbandry

granjero/a SM/F farmer

grano SM **1** (= *semilla*) [*de cereales*] grain; [*de mostaza*] seed • MODISMOS: • **ir (directo) al ~** to get to the point • **¡vamos al ~!** let's get to the point! • **no es ~ de anís** it's not just a small thing ▸ **grano de arroz** grain of rice ▸ **grano de cacao** cocoa bean ▸ **grano de café** coffee bean ▸ **grano de sésamo** sesame seed ▸ **grano de trigo** grain of wheat ▸ **granos panificables** bread grains
2 (= *semillas*) grain • **aquí se almacena el ~** the grain is stored here • MODISMO: • **apartar el ~ de la paja** to separate the wheat from the chaff
3 (= *partícula*) grain; (= *punto*) speck • **un ~ de arena** a grain of sand • MODISMO: • **poner su ~ de arena** to do one's bit*
4 (*en la piel*) spot, pimple
5 (*en piedra, madera, fotografía*) grain • **de ~ fino** fine-grained • **de ~ gordo** coarse-grained
6 (*Farm*) grain
7‡ [*de droga*] fix‡, shot*

granoso ADJ granular, granulated

granuja SMF (= *bribón*) rogue; (*dicho con afecto*) rascal; (= *pilluelo*) urchin, ragamuffin
SF (= *uvas*) loose grapes (*pl*); (= *semilla*) grape seed

granujada SF dirty trick • **hacer una ~ a algn** to pull a fast one on sb* • **es una ~** it's a low-down thing to do*

granujería SF (*en conjunto*) rogues (*pl*), urchins (*pl*)

granujiento ADJ, **granujoso** ADJ pimply, spotty

granulación SF granulation

granulado ADJ granulated
SM (*Farm*) • **un ~ vitamínico** a vitamin powder

granular¹ ADJ granular

granular² ▷ CONJUG 1a VT to granulate
VPR **granularse 1** (= *superficie*) to granulate, become granulated
2 (*Med*) to break out in spots, become spotty

gránulo SM granule

granuloso ADJ granular

grapa¹ SF **1** (*para papeles*) staple
2 (*para cables*) cable clip; (*Mec*) dog clamp; (*Arquit*) cramp

grapa² SF (*Cono Sur*) (= *aguardiente*) (cheap) grape liquor, grappa

grapadora SF stapler, stapling gun

grapar ▷ CONJUG 1a VT to staple

GRAPO SMPL ABR (*Esp*) (*Pol*) (= **Grupos de Resistencia Antifascista Primero de Octubre**) *terrorist group*

grapo SMF member of GRAPO

grasa SF **1** [*de alimentos*] fat • **alimentos bajos en ~s** low-fat foods • **reducir el consumo de ~s** to cut down on fatty foods • **tener mucha ~** [*carne*] to be fatty; [*guiso, plato*] to be (very) greasy ▸ **grasa de ballena** blubber ▸ **grasa de pescado** fish oil ▸ **grasa no saturada** unsaturated fat ▸ **grasa saturada** saturated fat ▸ **grasa vegetal** vegetable fat
2 (*Anat*) fat • **eliminar ~s** to get rid of fat
3 (= *suciedad*) grease • **la cocina está llena de ~** the kitchen is really greasy
4 (*Aut, Mec*) (= *lubrificante*) grease ▸ **grasa para ejes** axle grease
5 (*Méx**) (*para el calzado*) shoe polish
6 (*Arg**) working-class person
7 grasas (= *escorias*) slag (*sing*)
ADJ* **1** (*Arg*) (= *torpe*) stupid, slow
2 (*Cono Sur*) (*pey*) common
SMF • **es un ~** (*Cono Sur**) he's common

grasiento ADJ **1** [*guiso, pelo*] greasy
2 (= *sucio*) greasy

graso ADJ **1** [*alimentos, ácidos*] fatty; [*cutis*] greasy, oily; [*pelo*] greasy
2 (= *aceitoso*) [*guiso*] greasy, oily

grasoso ADJ greasy

grata SF • **su ~ del 8** your letter of the 8th

gratamente ADV pleasantly, pleasingly • **quedé ~ sorprendido** I was pleasantly surprised

gratificación SF **1** (= *recompensa*) reward, recompense; (= *propina*) tip; (= *aguinaldo*) gratuity; [*de sueldo, como prima*] bonus
2 (= *satisfacción*) gratification

gratificador ADJ gratifying

gratificante ADJ gratifying

gratificar ▷ CONJUG 1g VT **1** (= *recompensar*) to reward, recompense; (*con sueldo extra*) to give a bonus to, pay extra to; (*con propina*) to tip; (*con aguinaldo*) to give a gratuity to • **"se ~á"** "a reward is offered"
2 (= *satisfacer*) to gratify; (= *complacer*) to give pleasure to, satisfy; [+ *anhelo*] to indulge, gratify

gratinado ADJ au gratin
SM *dish cooked au gratin* • **~ de patatas** potato gratin

gratinador SM grill

gratinar ▷ CONJUG 1a VT to cook au gratin

gratis ADV free, for nothing • **te lo arreglarán ~** they'll fix it (for) free *o* for nothing • **comimos ~** we ate for free *o* nothing • **de ~** (*LAm*) gratis
ADJ free • **la entrada es ~** entry is free

gratitud SF gratitude

grato ADJ **1** (= *placentero*) pleasant, pleasing; (= *satisfactorio*) welcome • **recibir una grata impresión** to get a pleasant impression • **una decisión muy grata para todos** a very welcome decision for everybody • **guarda muy ~s recuerdos de su visita a España** he holds very fond memories of his visit to Spain • **nos es ~ informarle que ...** we are pleased to inform you that ...
2 (*And*) (= *agradecido*) grateful • **le estoy ~** I am most grateful to you

gratuidad SF **1** (= *cualidad de gratuito*) cost-free status • **debemos garantizar la ~ de la enseñanza** we must ensure that education remains free
2 (= *arbitrariedad*) gratuitousness • **no comparto la ~ de sus afirmaciones** I can't agree with such gratuitous statements

gratuitamente ADV **1** (= *gratis*) free
2 [*comentar*] gratuitously; [*acusar*] without foundation

gratuito ADJ **1** (= *gratis*) free, free of charge
2 [*comentario*] gratuitous, uncalled-for; [*acusación*] unfounded, unjustified

gratulatorio ADJ congratulatory

grava SF (= *guijos*) gravel; (= *piedra molida*) crushed stone; (*en carreteras*) road metal

gravable ADJ taxable, subject to tax

gravamen SM **1** (= *impuesto*) tax • **exento de ~** exempt from tax • **libre de ~** free of tax, tax-free
2 [*de aduanas*] duty
3 (= *carga*) burden, obligation; (*Jur*) lien, encumbrance • **libre de ~** free from encumbrances, unencumbered ▸ **gravamen bancario** banker's lien ▸ **gravamen del vendedor** vendor's lien ▸ **gravamen general** general lien

gravar ▷ CONJUG 1a VT **1** (*con impuesto*) to tax; (= *calcular impuestos*) to assess for tax • **~ un producto con un impuesto** to place a tax on a product, tax a product • **los impuestos que gravan esta vivienda** the taxes to which this dwelling is subject
2 (*con carga, hipoteca*) to burden, encumber (**de** with); (*Jur*) [+ *propiedad*] to place a lien upon • **el préstamo y el interés que se le grava** the loan and the interest charged upon it
VPR **gravarse** (*LAm*) (= *empeorar*) to get worse, become more serious

gravativo ADJ burdensome

grave ADJ **1** (*Med*) [*enfermedad, estado*] serious • **estar ~** to be seriously ill • **hubo 20 heridos ~s** there were 20 people seriously injured
2 (= *serio*) serious; (= *importante*) important, momentous • **la situación es ~** the situation is serious
3 [*carácter*] serious, dignified • **y otros hombres ~s** and other worthy men
4 (*Mús*) [*nota, tono*] low, deep; [*voz*] deep
5 (*Ling*) [*acento*] grave; [*palabra*] stressed on the penultimate syllable

gravedad SF **1** (*Fís*) gravity ▸ **gravedad nula** zero gravity
2 (*Med*) seriousness • **estar enfermo de ~** to be seriously ill • **el herido evoluciona favorablemente, dentro de la ~** the patient is progressing well, but his condition remains serious • **parece que la lesión es de poca ~** it seems that the injury is not serious
3 (= *seriedad*) seriousness
4 (= *dignidad*) seriousness, dignity
5 (*Mús*) depth

gravemente ADV **1** [*afectar, perjudicar*] seriously • **no están ~ afectados** they are not seriously affected • **estar ~ enfermo** to be seriously ill • **resultó ~ herido** he was seriously injured
2 (= *con solemnidad*) gravely • **habló ~** he spoke gravely

gravera SF gravel bed, gravel pit

gravidez SF pregnancy • **en estado de ~** pregnant • **con pocos miramientos hacia su estado de ~** with little account taken of the fact that she was pregnant

grávido ADJ **1** (= *embarazada*) pregnant; (*Zool*) carrying young, with young
2 (*liter*) (= *lleno*) full (**de** of), heavy (**de** with) • **me sentí ~ de emociones** I was weighed down with emotions, I was full of emotions

gravilla SF gravel

gravitación SF gravitation

gravitacional ADJ gravitational

gravitante ADJ menacing

gravitar ▷ CONJUG 1a VI **1** (*Fís*) to gravitate (**hacia** towards)
2 (= *girar*) to rotate • **la tierra gravita en torno al sol** the earth rotates round the sun
3 • **~ sobre algn/algo** (= *apoyarse*) to rest on sb/sth; (= *caer sobre*) to bear down on sb/sth; (*fig*) (= *pesar sobre*) to be a burden to sb/sth; (= *amenazar*) to loom over sb/sth

gravitatorio ADJ gravitational

gravoso ADJ **1** (= *caro*) costly, expensive; (= *oneroso*) burdensome; [*precio*] extortionate • **el impuesto es especialmente ~ para las pequeñas empresas** the tax is a particular burden for small businesses
2 (= *molesto*) burdensome, oppressive • **ser ~ a algn/algo** to be a burden to sb/sth, weigh on sb/sth
3 (= *insufrible*) tiresome, vexatious

graznar ▷ CONJUG 1a VI **1** [*cuervo*] to croak, caw; [*ganso*] to cackle; [*pato*] to quack
2 (*pey*) [*cantante*] to croak

graznido SM [*de cuervo*] croak; [*de ganso*] cackle; [*de pato*] quack

grébano/a‡ SM/F (*Cono Sur*) (*pey*) Italian, wop**

greca SF border

Grecia SF Greece

greco (*liter*) = **griego**

grecochipriota ADJ, SMF Greek-Cypriot

greda SF (= *arcilla*) clay; (*Téc*) fuller's earth

gredal SM claypit

gredoso ADJ clayey

green [grin] SM (PL: **greens** [grin]) (*Golf*) green

gregario ADJ **1** [*animal, persona*] gregarious • **tiene un carácter ~** he's a gregarious character • **instinto ~** herd instinct
2 (= *servil*) servile, slavish
SM (*Dep*) domestic

gregarismo SM gregariousness

gregoriano ADJ Gregorian • **canto ~** Gregorian chant

Gregorio SM Gregory

greguería SF **1** (= *ruido*) hubbub, uproar, hullabaloo
2 (*Literat*) *brief, humorous and often mildly poetic comment or aphorism about life*

grei SM (*Col*), **greifrú** SM (*CAm, Ven*) grapefruit

grelos SMPL turnip tops

gremial ADJ **1** (*Hist*) guild (*antes de s*)
2 (= *sindical*) trade-union (*antes de s*)
SM (= *miembro*) guild member

gremialista SMF (*LAm*) trade unionist

gremio SM **1** (= *profesión*) trade, profession • **la jerga del ~** trade jargon • **ser del ~** to be in the trade
2 (*Hist*) guild, corporation
3 (= *sindicato*) (trade) union; (= *asociación*) association, organization

greña SF **1** (= *enredo*) tangle, entanglement • **andar a la ~** to bicker, squabble • **estar a la ~ con algn** to be at daggers drawn with sb
2 greñas (= *cabello revuelto*) shock of hair, mat of hair, mop of hair
3 • **en ~** (*Méx*) [*seda*] raw; [*plata*] unpolished; [*azúcar*] unrefined

greñudo ADJ [*cabello*] tangled, matted; [*persona*] dishevelled, disheveled (EEUU)

gres SM (= *arcilla*) potter's clay; (= *cerámica*) earthenware, stoneware

gresca SF (= *bulla*) uproar, hubbub; (= *trifulca*) row, shindy* • **andar a la ~** to row, brawl • **armar una ~** to start a fight

grey SF **1** (*Rel*) flock, congregation
2 [*de ovejas*] flock

Grial SM • **Santo ~** Holy Grail

griego/a ADJ Greek, Grecian
SM/F **1** (= *persona*) Greek
2†† (= *tramposo*) cheat
SM **1** (*Ling*) Greek ▸ **griego antiguo** ancient Greek
2 (= *lenguaje ininteligible*) gibberish, double Dutch • **hablar en ~** to talk double Dutch • **para mí es ~** it's all Greek to me

grieta SF **1** (= *fisura*) fissure, crack; (= *hendidura*) chink; (= *quiebra*) crevice; (*en la piel*) chap, crack
2 (*Pol*) rift

grietarse ▷ CONJUG 1a VPR = **agrietar**

grifa‡ SF (= *droga*) dope*; ▷ **grifo**

grifear‡ ▷ CONJUG 1a VI to smoke dope*

grifería¹ SF taps (*pl*), faucets (*pl*) (EEUU)

grifería² SF (*Caribe*‡) blacks (*pl*)

grifero/a SM/F (*And*) petrol pump attendant, gas pump attendant (EEUU)

grifo¹ SM **1** [*de agua*] tap, faucet (EEUU); (*a presión*) cock • **agua del ~** tap water • **cerveza (servida) al ~** draught *o* (EEUU) draft beer • MODISMO: • **cerrar el ~** to turn off the tap, cut off the funds
2 (*LAm*) (= *surtidor de gasolina*) petrol pump, gas pump (EEUU); (*And*) (= *gasolinera*) petrol station, gas station (EEUU); (= *bar*) dive*
3 (*Cono Sur*) [*de incendios*] fire hydrant

grifo²/a* ADJ **1** • **estar ~** (*Méx*) (= *borracho*) to be plastered*, be soused (EEUU*); (= *loco*) to be nuts*; (= *drogado*) to be high*, be doped up*
2 (*And*) (= *engreído*) snobbish, stuck-up*
SM/F **1** [*de drogas*] (= *fumador*) dope smoker*; (= *adicto*) dope addict*
2 (= *borracho*) drunkard; ▷ **grifa**

grifo³/a ADJ **1** [*pelo*] curly, kinky
2 (*Caribe*†) [*persona*] black
SM/F (*Caribe*†) black man/woman, black person; ▷ **grifa**

grifo⁴ SM (*Mit*) griffin

grifón SM (= *perro*) griffon; (*mítico*) griffin

grifota‡ SMF dope smoker*

grigallo SM blackcock

grill [gril] SM **1** (= *aparato*) grill • **asar al ~** to grill
2 (= *local*) grillroom

grilla SF **1** (= *insecto*) female cricket • MODISMOS: • **¡esa es ~ (y no canta)!*** that's a likely story! (*iró*) • **dice la ~ que** ... (*Méx*) there's word going round that ...
2 (*And*) (= *pleito*) row, quarrel

grillado‡ ADJ barmy*

grilladura‡ SF barminess*

grillera SF **1** (= *jaula*) cage for crickets; (= *nido*) cricket hole
2* (= *casa de locos*) madhouse, bedlam
3‡ (= *furgón*) police wagon

grillete SM fetter, shackle

grillo SM **1** (= *insecto*) cricket ▸ **grillo cebollero, grillo real** mole cricket
2 (*Bot*) (= *brote*) shoot, sprout
3 grillos (= *cadenas*) fetters, shackles; (= *esposas*) handcuffs; (= *estorbo*) shackles

grilo‡ SM **1** (= *cárcel*) nick‡, slammer‡, can (EEUU‡)
2 (= *bolsillo*) pocket ▸ **grilo bueno** right-hand pocket

grima SF **1** • **dar ~ a algn** (= *dentera*) to set sb's teeth on edge; (= *irritación*) to get on sb's nerves • **me da ~ sentarme ahí** I can't sit there, it's revolting • **un dato de ~** a bombshell
2 • **una ~ de licor** (*Cono Sur*) a drop of spirits
3 • **en ~** (*And*) alone

grimillón SM (*Cono Sur*) lot, heap

grímpola SF pennant

gringada* SF (*LAm*) **1** (= *personas*) (= *extranjeros*) foreigners (*pl*); (= *norteamericanos*) Yankees (*pl*)
2 (= *canallada*) dirty trick

gringo/a* (*LAm*) ADJ **1** (= *extranjero*) foreign; (= *norteamericano*) Yankee, North American
2 (= *rubio*) blond(e), fair
3†† [*idioma*] foreign, unintelligible
SM/F **1** (= *extranjero*) foreigner; (= *norteamericano*) Yankee, North American
2 (*Cono Sur*) (= *italiano*) Italian, wop**
3 (= *rubio*) blond(e), fair-haired person
SM †† (= *lenguaje ininteligible*) gibberish • **hablar en ~** to talk double Dutch*

> **GRINGO**
> The word **gringo** is a derogatory term used in Latin America to refer to white English-speakers, usually Americans, especially in the context of alleged economic, cultural and political interference in Latin America. One rather fanciful theory traces its origin to the Mexican-American War of 1846-48 and the song "Green Grow the Rushes-oh", supposedly sung by the American troops. According to another theory it is a corruption of **griego** or "Greek", in the sense of anything foreign and unintelligible, as in the English expression "it's all Greek to me".

gringolandia* SF (*LAm*) (*pey*) USA, Yankeedom*

gringuería* SF (*LAm*) foreigners (*pl*), gringos** (*pl*)

gripa SF (*LAm*) flu, influenza

gripaje SM seize-up

gripal ADJ flu (*antes de s*)

gripar* ▷ CONJUG 1a VI to seize up

gripazo SM attack of flu

gripe SF flu, influenza ▸ **gripe asiática** Asian flu ▸ **gripe aviar** bird flu, avian flu (*frm*) ▸ **gripe del cerdo** swine fever

griposo ADJ • **estar ~** to have flu

gris ADJ [*color*] grey, gray (EEUU); [*día, tiempo, persona*] grey, dull • **~ carbón** charcoal grey • **~ ceniza** ash-grey • **~ marengo** dark grey • **~ perla** pearl-grey; ▷ **oso**
SM **1** (= *color*) grey
2 (*Esp*†*) cop*, *member of the armed police* • **los ~es** the fuzz‡
3* (= *viento*) • **hace un ~** there's a cold wind

grisáceo ADJ greyish, grayish (EEUU)

grisalla SF (*Méx*) **1** (= *chatarra*) rusty scrap metal
2 (= *basura*) rubbish, garbage (EEUU)

grisines SMPL (*Arg*) breadsticks

grisma SF (*Cono Sur*) bit, shred

grisoso ADJ (*esp LAm*) greyish, grayish (EEUU)

grisú SM firedamp

grisura SF [*de color*] greyness, grayness (EEUU); (= *falta de interés*) dullness

grita SF (= *jaleo*) uproar, hubbub; (= *gritos*) shouting; (*Teat*) catcalls (*pl*), catcalling, booing • **dar ~ a algn/algo** to boo at sb/sth

gritadera SF (*LAm*) loud shouting, clamour, clamor (EEUU)

gritar ▷ CONJUG 1a VI **1** (= *dar voces*) to shout • **¡no grites!** don't shout! • **no sabes hablar sin ~** you can't talk without shouting • **no me grites, que no estoy sorda** don't shout, I'm not deaf • **¡no le grites a tu madre!** don't shout at your mother! • **gritaba de alegría** he shouted for joy
2 (= *chillar*) to scream • **el enfermo no podía dejar de ~** the patient couldn't stop screaming • **gritaba de dolor** he was screaming with pain
3 (= *abuchear*) to jeer • **el público gritaba al árbitro** the crowd were jeering the referee
VT [+ *instrucciones, órdenes*] to shout • **le ~on que callara** they shouted at him to be quiet

gritería SF **1** (= *gritos*) shouting, uproar
2 (*CAm*) (*Rel*) festival of the Virgin

griterío SM shouting, uproar

grito SM **1** (= *voz alta*) shout; (= *chillido*) scream; [*de animal*] cry, sound • **a ~s** at the top of one's voice • **¡no des esos ~s!** stop shouting like that! • **llorar a ~s** to weep and wail • **pegar** *o* **lanzar un ~** to cry out • **~s de protesta** shouts of protest • MODISMOS: • **poner el ~ en el cielo** to scream blue murder* • **pedir algo a ~s**: • **esa chica está pidiendo un corte de pelo a ~s** that girl

badly needs a haircut • **a ~ pelado** at the top of one's voice • **es el último ~** it's the very latest, it's the latest thing • **es el último ~ del lujo** it's the last word in luxury • **a voz en ~** at the top of one's voice
2 (= *abucheo*) jeer
3 (*LAm*) proclamation • **el ~ de Dolores** *the proclamation of Mexican independence (1810)*
▸ **grito de independencia** proclamation of independence

gritón ADJ **1** (= *que grita*) shouting
2 (*pey*) loud-mouthed • **son muy gritones** they're very loud

gro SM grosgrain

groenlandés/esa ADJ Greenland (*antes de s*)
SM/F Greenlander

Groenlandia SF Greenland

groggy‡ ADJ, **grogui**‡ ADJ (= *atontado*) groggy; (= *impresionado*) shattered, shocked, in a state of shock

groncho/a‡ SM/F (*Cono Sur*) (*pey*) worker

grosella SF redcurrant ▸ **grosella colorada** redcurrant ▸ **grosella espinosa** gooseberry ▸ **grosella negra** blackcurrant ▸ **grosella roja** redcurrant

grosellero SM currant bush ▸ **grosellero espinoso** gooseberry bush

groseramente ADV (= *descortésmente*) rudely; (= *con ordinariez*) coarsely; (= *toscamente*) roughly, loutishly

grosería SF **1** (= *mala educación*) rudeness; (= *ordinariez*) coarseness, vulgarity; (= *tosquedad*) roughness
2 (= *comentario*) rude remark, vulgar remark; (= *palabrota*) swearword

grosero ADJ (= *descortés*) rude; (= *ordinario*) coarse, vulgar; (= *tosco*) rough, loutish; (= *indecente*) indelicate

grosor SM thickness

grosso modo ADV roughly speaking

grosura SF fat, suet

grotesca SF (*Tip*) sans serif

grotescamente ADV (= *de modo ridículo*) grotesquely; (= *de modo absurdo*) bizarrely, absurdly

grotesco ADJ (= *ridículo*) grotesque; (= *absurdo*) bizarre, absurd

grúa SF **1** (*Téc*) crane; (*Náut*) derrick ▸ **grúa corredera, grúa corrediza** travelling crane ▸ **grúa de pescante** jib crane ▸ **grúa de puente** overhead crane, gantry crane ▸ **grúa de torre** tower crane ▸ **grúa horquilla** (*Chile*) forklift truck ▸ **grúa móvil** travelling crane
2 (*Aut*) tow truck, towing vehicle • **avisar** *o* **llamar a la ~** to call for a tow truck • **el coche fue retirado por la ~** the car was towed away

gruesa SF gross, twelve dozen

grueso ADJ **1** (= *obeso*) [*persona*] stout, thickset
2 [*jersey, pared, libro, tronco*] thick; [*intestino*] large; [*mar*] heavy
3 (= *basto*) [*tela, humor*] coarse
SM **1** (= *grosor*) thickness
2 (= *parte principal*) main part, major portion; [*de gente, tropa*] main body, mass • **el ~ del pelotón** (*en carrera*) the pack, the main body of the runners • **va mezclado con el ~ del pasaje** he is mingling with the mass of the passengers
3 (*Com*) • **en ~** in bulk

grujidor SM glass cutter, glazier

grulla SF (*tb* **grulla común**) crane

grullo/a ADJ **1*** (= *grosero*) uncouth, rough
2 (*Méx*) (= *aprovechado*) sponging*, cadging*
3 (*CAm, Méx*) [*caballo*] grey, gray (EEUU)
SM/F bumpkin, yokel, hick (EEUU*)
SM (*CAm, Méx*) grey horse; (*Cono Sur*) big colt, large stallion

grumete SM (*Náut*) cabin boy, ship's boy

grumo SM **1** (*en salsa*) lump • **una salsa con ~s** a lumpy sauce
2 [*de sangre*] clot ▸ **grumo de leche** curd
3 [*de uvas*] bunch, cluster

grumoso ADJ **1** [*salsa*] lumpy
2 (= *cuajado*) clotted

grunge [grunch] SM grunge

gruñido SM **1** [*de animal*] grunt, growl • **dar ~s** to grunt, growl
2 (= *queja*) grouse*, grumble • **dar ~s** to grouse*, grumble

gruñidor(a) ADJ **1** [*animal*] grunting, growling
2 [*persona*] grumbling
SM/F grumbler

gruñir ▸ CONJUG 3h VI **1** [*animal*] to grunt, growl
2 [*persona*] to grouse*, grumble

gruñón/ona ADJ grumpy, grumbling
SM/F grumbler

grupa SF crupper, hindquarters (*pl*)

grupal ADJ group (*antes de s*)

grupalmente ADV in groups

grupera SF pillion (seat) • **ir en la ~** to sit behind the rider, be carried on the horse's rump

grupi‡ SF groupie*

grupín* SM (*Cono Sur*) crook*; (= *desfalcador*) embezzler; (*en subasta*) false bidder

grupo SM **1** (*gen*) group; (= *equipo*) team; [*de árboles*] cluster, clump • **discusión en ~** group discussion • **reunirse en ~s** to gather in groups ▸ **grupo de contacto** (*Pol*) contact group ▸ **grupo de control** control group ▸ **grupo de encuentro** encounter group ▸ **grupo de estafas** (*Policía*) fraud squad ▸ **grupo de estupefacientes** (*Policía*) drug squad ▸ **grupo de homicidios** (*Policía*) murder squad ▸ **grupo de investigación** research team, team of researchers ▸ **grupo del dólar** dollar block ▸ **grupo de lectura** reading group ▸ **grupo de noticias** newsgroup ▸ **grupo de presión** pressure group, special interest group (EEUU) ▸ **grupo de riesgo** high-risk group ▸ **grupo de trabajo** working party ▸ **grupo sanguíneo** blood group ▸ **grupo testigo** control group
2 (*Elec, Téc*) unit, plant; (= *montaje*) assembly ▸ **grupo compresor** compressor unit ▸ **grupo electrógeno, grupo generador** generating set, power plant
3 (*Cono Sur*) (= *trampa*) trick, con*

grupúsculo SM small group, splinter group

gruta SF cavern, grotto

GT ABR (= **Gran Turismo**) GT

Gta. ABR (*Aut*) = **glorieta**

gua[1] EXCL (*LAm*) (= *preocupación*) oh dear!; (= *sorpresa*) well!; (= *desdén*) get away!*

gua[2] SM (= *juego*) marbles (*pl*); (= *hoyo*) hole for marbles

gua... PREF (*para diversas palabras escritas así en LAm*) ▸ **hua...**

guabiroba SF (*Cono Sur*) dugout canoe

guaca SF **1** (*LAm*) (= *sepultura*) (Indian) tomb, funeral mound
2 (= *tesoro*) buried treasure; [*de armas, droga*] cache
3 (= *riqueza*) wealth, money; (*And, CAm, Caribe, Méx*) (= *hucha*) money box • **hacer ~** (*And, Caribe*‡) to make money, make one's pile*
• MODISMO: • **hacer su ~** (*Caribe*) to make hay while the sun shines
4 (*Caribe*) (= *reprimenda*) ticking-off*
5 (*Méx*) (= *escopeta*) double-barrelled shotgun
6 (*Caribe*) large sore

guacal SM (*LAm*) (= *cajón*) wooden crate; (= *calabaza*) gourd, vessel

guacamarón SM (*Caribe*) brave man

guacamaya SF (*LAm*) macaw

guacamayo/a ADJ (*Méx**) absurdly dressed
SM/F (*Caribe*) (*pey*) Spaniard
SM (= *ave*) macaw

guacamole SM guacamole

guacamote SM (*Méx*) yucca plant

guacarear* ▸ CONJUG 1a VI (*Méx*) to throw up*

guacarnaco ADJ **1** (*And, Caribe, Cono Sur*) silly, stupid
2 (*Cono Sur*) long-legged

guachada* SF (*Arg*) dirty trick

guachafita SF (*Ven*) **1** (= *batahola*) hubbub, din; (= *desorden*) disorder
2 (= *garito*) gambling joint‡
3 (= *mofa*) mockery, jeering

guachafitero/a (*Ven*) ADJ (= *desorganizado*) chaotic, inefficient
SM/F inefficient person

guachaje SM (*Cono Sur*) (= *animal*) orphaned animal; (= *terneras*) *group of calves separated from their mothers*

guachalomo SM (*Cono Sur*) sirloin steak

guachapear ▸ CONJUG 1a VT **1** (*en agua*) to dabble in, splash about in
2 (= *estropear*) to botch, mess up
3 (*Cono Sur**) to pinch*, borrow
4 (*And*) [+ *maleza*] to clear, cut
VI (= *sonar*) to rattle, clatter

guachar ▸ CONJUG 1a VT (*Méx*) to watch

guáchara* SF (*Caribe*) lie

guácharo SM (*CAm*) nightingale

guache[1]* SM **1** (*Caribe*) (= *del campo*) rustic, peasant, hick (EEUU*)
2 (*And, Caribe*) (= *zafio*) uncouth person
3 (= *vago*) layabout, loafer

guache[2] SM (*Arte*) gouache

guachicar SM, **guachicarro** SM (*Méx*) parking attendant

guachimán SM (*LAm*) watchman

guachinanga SF (*Caribe*) wooden bar (*on door etc*)

guachinango/a ADJ* **1** (*And*) (= *zalamero*) smooth; (= *falso*) slimy
2 (*Caribe*) (= *astuto*) sharp, clever; (= *con labia*) smooth-tongued
SM/F* (*Caribe*) **1** (*pey*) Mexican
2 (= *persona astuta*) clever person
SM (*Caribe, Méx*) (= *pez*) red snapper

guacho/a ADJ **1** (*And, Cono Sur*) (= *sin casa*) homeless
2 (*And, Cono Sur*) (= *huérfano*) [*niño*] orphaned; [*animal*] motherless, abandoned
3 (*And, Cono Sur*) [*zapato etc*] odd
4 (*Méx*‡) (= *capitalino*) of/from Mexico City
SM/F **1** (*And, Cono Sur*) (= *expósito*) homeless child, abandoned child; (= *huérfano*) orphan, foundling; (= *animal*) motherless animal; (= *bastardo**) illegitimate child, bastard*
2 (*Méx*‡) (= *capitalino*) *person from Mexico City*

guaco SM (*And*) *piece of pre-Columbian tomb pottery*

guadal SM (*And, Cono Sur*) sandy bog

Guadalajara SF Guadalajara

guadalajareño/a ADJ of/from Guadalajara
SM/F native/inhabitant of Guadalajara
• **los ~s** the people of Guadalajara

guadaloso ADJ (*Cono Sur*) boggy

Guadalquivir SM • **el río ~** the Guadalquivir

guadamecí SM embossed leather

guadaña SF (*Agr*) scythe • **la Guadaña** (*fig*) the Grim Reaper

guadañadora SF mowing machine

guadañar ▸ CONJUG 1a VT to scythe, mow

guadañero SM mower

guadaño SM (*Cuba, Méx*) lighter, small harbour *o* (EEUU) harbor boat

g

Guadiana SM • **el ~** the Guadiana • MODISMO: • **aparece y desaparece como el ~** it keeps coming and going, now you see it now you don't

guadianesco ADJ (= *intermitente*) sporadic, intermittent; (= *quimérico*) will-o'-the-wisp

guágara* SF • **echar ~** (*Méx*) to gossip, chew the fat

guagua¹ SF (*Cuba, Canarias*) bus

guagua² ADJ (*And*) small, little
SF (*And, Cono Sur*) **1** (= *bebé*) baby
2 (= *bagatela*) trifle, small thing • MODISMO: • **de ~** (*Cuba, Méx*) free, for nothing

guaguarear* ▷ CONJUG 1a VI (*CAm, Méx*) to babble, chatter

guaguatear ▷ CONJUG 1a VT (*CAm, Cono Sur*) to carry in one's arms

guaguatera SF (*Cono Sur*) nurse

guagüero/a ADJ **1** (*Caribe*) (= *gorrón*) sponging*, parasitical
2 (*Cuba*) bus (*antes de s*)
SM/F (*Cuba*) (= *chófer*) bus driver

guai* ADJ, ADV = **guay**

guaica SF **1** (*Cono Sur*) (= *cuenta*) rosary bead
2 (*And*) (= *collar*) bead necklace

guaico SM (*And*) **1** (= *hondonada*) hollow, dip; (= *barranco*) ravine; (= *hoyo*) hole, pit
2 (= *estercolero*) dung heap; (= *basurero*) rubbish tip, garbage tip (EEUU)
3 (= *alud*) avalanche

guaina SF **1** (*Arg*) (= *muchacha*) girl, young woman
2 (*Bol, Chile*) (= *muchacho*) youth, young man

guaino SM (*Cono Sur*) jockey

guaipe SM (*Chile*) (= *estopa*) cotton waste; (= *trapo*) cloth, rag

guáiper SM (*CAm*) windscreen wiper, windshield wiper (EEUU)

guaira SF **1** (*CAm*) Indian flute
2 (*And, Cono Sur*) (*Min*) earthenware smelting furnace (*for silver ore*)
3 (*Náut*) triangular sail

guairana SF **1** (*And*) [*de cal*] limekiln
2 = **guaira**

guairo SM (*Cuba, Ven*) small coastal vessel

guairuro SM (*And, CAm*) dried seed

guajada* SF (*Méx*) stupid thing

guajalote ADJ, SM (*Caribe, Méx*) = **guajolote**

guaje¹ ADJ (*Méx**) (= *estúpido*) silly, stupid • MODISMO: • **hacer ~ a algn** to fool sb, take sb in*
SMF (*CAm, Méx**) (= *estúpido*) idiot, fool
SM **1** (*Méx*) (= *calabaza*) gourd, calabash
2 (*CAm**) (= *trasto*) old thing, piece of junk
3 (*CAm, Méx*) (= *acacia*) *species of acacia*

guaje²/a SM/F **1*** kid*, child
2 (*Min*) mining apprentice

guajear* ▷ CONJUG 1a VI (*Méx*) to play the fool, be silly

guajería* SF (*Méx*) **1** (= *estupidez*) idiocy, foolishness
2 (= *acto*) stupid thing, foolish act

guajiro/a SM/F **1** (*Cuba*) (white) peasant
2 (*Col, Ven*) *native/inhabitant of the Guajira region*

guajolote (*Méx*) ADJ* silly, stupid
SM **1** (= *pavo*) turkey
2* (= *tonto*) fool, idiot, turkey (EEUU)

gualda SF (= *planta*) dyer's greenweed, reseda

gualdo ADJ (= *color*) yellow, golden; ▷ **bandera**

gualdrapa SF **1** (*Hist*) [*de caballo*] horse blanket
2 gualdrapas* (= *harapos*) tatters, ragged ends
3 (*CAm**) (= *vagabundo*) down-and-out, bum (EEUU), hobo (EEUU)

gualdrapear ▷ CONJUG 1a VI **1** (*Náut*) [*velas*] to flap
2 (*Cuba*) [*caballo*] to walk slowly

gualicho SM **1** (*And, Cono Sur*) (= *maleficio*) evil spell; (= *diablo*) devil, evil spirit
2 (*Arg*) (= *talismán*) good-luck charm, talisman

guallipén SM (*Cono Sur*) fool, idiot

Gualterio SM Walter

guama* SF **1** (*And, CAm*) (= *mentira*) lie
2 (*And*) (= *pie*) big foot; (= *mano*) big hand
3 (*And*) (= *desastre*) calamity, disaster

guambito SM (*And*) kid*, boy

guambra SMF (*Ecu*) **1** (= *muchacho*) young Indian
2 (= *niño*) (*gen*) child, baby; (= *indio*) Indian child; (= *mestizo*) mestizo child
3 (= *amor*) sweetheart

guamiza* SF (*Méx*) beating-up*

guampa SF (*And, Cono Sur*) horn

guampara SF (*Caribe*) machete

guámparo SM (*Cono Sur*) (= *cuerno*) horn; (*para beber*) drinking vessel

guampudo ADJ (*And, Cono Sur*) horned

guanábana SF **1** (*LAm*) (= *fruta*) soursop, prickly custard apple
2 (*And*) (= *tonto*) fool

guanábano SM soursop (tree)

guanacada* SF (*LAm*) **1** (= *estupidez*) silly thing, foolish act
2 (= *persona*) simpleton, dimwit*; (= *campesino*) rustic

guanaco/a ADJ (*LAm**) (= *tonto*) simple, silly; (= *torpe*) slow
SM/F* **1** (*LAm*) (= *tonto*) simpleton, dimwit*; (= *campesino*) rustic, bumpkin*
2 (*CAm*) (*pey*) (= *salvadoreño*) Salvadorean
SM **1** (*Zool*) guanaco
2 (*Cono Sur*) (= *antidisturbios*) water cannon

guanajada* SF (*Caribe*) silly thing, foolish act

guanajo/a SM/F (*LAm*) **1** (= *pavo*) turkey
2* (= *tonto*) fool, idiot

guanay¹ SM (*Chile*) cormorant

guanay² SM (*Cono Sur*) (= *remero*) oarsman; (= *estibador*) longshoreman; (= *fortachón*) tough man

guanayerías* SFPL (*Caribe*) silly actions

guanche ADJ Guanche
SMF Guanche (*original inhabitant of Canary Islands*)

guando SM (*And, Chile*) stretcher

guanear ▷ CONJUG 1a VT **1** (*Perú*) (*Agr*) to fertilize with guano
2 (*Bol*) (= *ensuciar*) to dirty, soil
VI (*LAm*) [*animales*] to defecate

guanera SF (*LAm*) guano deposit

guanero ADJ (*LAm*) guano (*antes de s*)

guango* ADJ (*Méx*) (= *holgado*) loose • MODISMO: • **me viene ~** I couldn't care less*

guanín SM (*And, Caribe, Cono Sur*) (*Hist*) base gold

guano¹ SM **1** [*de aves marinas*] guano
2 (*LAm*) (= *estiércol*) dung, manure
3 (*Cuba**) money, brass*
4 • MODISMO: • **meter ~** (*Caribe**) to put one's back into it

guano² SM (*LAm*) (= *palma*) palm tree; (= *hoja*) palm leaf

guantada SF, **guantazo** SM slap • **dar** *o* **largar una ~ a algn** to give sb a slap, slap sb

guante SM **1** glove • **hacer ~s** (*Dep*) to shadow-box • MODISMOS: • **ajustarse como un ~** to fit like a glove • **arrojar el ~** to throw down the gauntlet • **de ~ blanco**: • **crimen de ~ blanco** white-collar crime • **una campaña electoral de ~ blanco** a clean election campaign • **un partido de ~ blanco** a sporting match • **tratar con ~ blanco** to treat *o* handle with kid gloves • **colgar los ~s** (*Boxeo*) to quit boxing; (= *jubilarse*) to retire • **echar el ~ a algn** to catch hold of sb, seize sb; [*policía*] to catch sb • **echar el ~ a algo** to lay hold of sth • **recoger el ~** to take up the challenge • **ser como un ~** (= *obediente*) to be very meek and mild, be submissive ▸ **guante con puño** gauntlet ▸ **guantes de boxeo** boxing gloves ▸ **guantes de cabritilla** kid gloves ▸ **guantes de cirujano** surgical gloves ▸ **guantes de goma** rubber gloves ▸ **guantes de jardinería** gardening gloves ▸ **guantes de terciopelo** (*fig*) kid gloves ▸ **guantes para uso quirúrgico** surgical gloves
2 (*Chile*) whip, cat-o'-nine-tails
3 guantes (= *gratificación*) tip (*sing*), commission (*sing*)

guantear ▷ CONJUG 1a VT (*LAm*) to slap, hit

guantelete SM gauntlet

guantera SF (*Aut*) glove compartment; ▷ **guantero**

guantería SF **1** (= *tienda*) glove shop; (= *fábrica*) glove factory
2 (= *fabricación*) glove making

guantero/a SM/F glover; ▷ **guantera**

guantón SM (*LAm*) slap, hit, blow

guañusco* ADJ (*Arg*) **1** (= *marchito*) withered, faded
2 (= *chamuscado*) burned, burned up

guapear* ▷ CONJUG 1a VI **1** (= *ostentar*) to cut a dash, dress flashily
2 (= *bravear*) to bluster, swagger
VT (*And*) to urge on

guaperas* ADJ INV gorgeous*
SM INV heart-throb*, dream-boy*

guapetón/ona ADJ **1** (= *guapo*) good-looking
2 (= *elegante*) dashing; (*pey*) flashy
SM/F (= *perdonavidas*) bully

guapeza SF **1** (= *atractivo*) good looks (*pl*), attractiveness
2 (= *elegancia*) smartness, elegance; (*pey*) (= *ostentación*) flashiness
3 (= *valentía*) boldness, dash; (*pey*) bravado

guapo ADJ **1** (= *atractivo*) [*mujer*] attractive, good-looking; [*hombre*] handsome, good-looking; [*bebé*] beautiful • **va de ~ por la vida** he thinks good looks are all he needs in life
2 (= *elegante*) smart, elegant • **ir ~** to look smart • **qué ~ estás con ese traje** you look really nice in that suit
3* (= *bonito*) great* • **qué camiseta más guapa** what a great T-shirt!* • **¿qué tal la película? —¡muy guapa!** "how was the film?" — "great!"*
4* (*como apelativo*) • **¡ven, ~!** (*a un niño*) come here, love! • **¡oye, guapa!** hey! • **¡cállate, ~!** just shut up!
5 (= *valiente*) bold, dashing; (*Cono Sur, Méx*) (= *duro*) bold, tough; (= *sin escrúpulos*) unscrupulous
SM **1*** (= *valiente*) • **¿quién es el ~ que entra primero?** who's got the guts to go in first?*, who's brave enough to go in first?
2 (*esp LAm*) (= *bravucón*) bully, tough guy; (= *fanfarrón*) braggart
3 (*CAm*) (*Cine*) male lead

guaposo ADJ (*Caribe*) bold, dashing

guapucha* SF (*And*) cheating

guapura* SF good looks (*pl*)

guaquear ▷ CONJUG 1a VI (*And, CAm*) to rob tombs *o* graves (*in search of archaeological valuables*)

guaqueo SM (*And, CAm*) grave robbing, tomb robbing

guaquero/a SM/F (*And, CAm*) grave robber, tomb robber

guara SF **1** (*And*) lot, heap
2 guaras (*Cono Sur*) tricks, wiles

guaraca SF (*And*) (= *honda*) sling, catapult, slingshot (EEUU); (*para trompo*) whip

guaracha SF **1** (*Caribe*) (= *canción*) popular song; (= *baile*) folk dance
2 (*Caribe**) (= *alboroto*) din, racket; (= *riña*) quarrel; (= *juerga*) party, shindig*
3 (*Caribe*) (= *banda*) street band
4 (*Caribe*) (= *chanza*) joke
5 (*And*) litter, rough bed
6 guarachas (*CAm*) old shoes
7 (*CAm*) = **guarache**

guarache SM (*Méx*) **1** (= *sandalia*) sandal, light shoe
2 (*Aut*) patch

guarachear* ▹ CONJUG 1a VI (*Caribe*) to revel; (*fig*) to let one's hair down

guaragua SF **1** (*CAm*) (= *mentira*) lie; (= *mentiroso*) liar, tale-teller
2 (*LAm*) (= *contoneo*) rhythmical movement (*in dancing*)
3 guaraguas (*And*) adornments, finery (*sing*)

guaral SM (*And, Caribe*) (= *cuerda*) rope, cord; [*de trompo*] whip

guarangada SF (*LAm*) rude remark

guarango ADJ **1** (*And, Cono Sur*) (= *grosero*) [*acto*] rude; [*persona*] uncouth
2 (*And*) (= *sucio*) dirty; (= *harapiento*) ragged

guaranguear ▹ CONJUG 1a VI (*And, Cono Sur*) to be rude

guarangueria SF (*And, Cono Sur*) rudeness

guaraní ADJ, SMF Guarani
SM (*Ling*) Guarani

GUARANÍ

Guaraní is an American Indian language of the **tupí-guaraní** family and is widely spoken in Paraguay, Brazil, Argentina and Bolivia. In Paraguay it is the majority language and has equal official status with Spanish, which is spoken mainly by non-Indians. In parts of southern Brazil, **tupí-guaraní** is the basis for a pidgin known as **Língua Geral**, now losing ground to Portuguese. From **guaraní** and its sister dialect **tupí** come words like "jaguar", "tapir", "toucan" and "tapioca".

guaranismo SM (*Ling*) *word or expression from the Guarani language*

guarapazo SM (*And*) **1** [*de bebida*] shot*, slug*
2 (= *golpe*) blow, knock; (= *caída*) hard fall

guarapear ▹ CONJUG 1a VI **1** (*Perú*) to drink sugar-cane liquor
2 (*Caribe*) (= *emborracharse*) to get drunk
VPR **guarapearse** (*Caribe*) to get drunk

guarapo SM (*LAm*) (= *bebida*) sugar-cane liquor; (*Ven*) [*de piña*] fermented pineapple juice • MODISMOS: • **se le enfrió el ~** (*Caribe**) he lost his nerve • **menear el ~** (*Cuba, Ven*) to get a move on • **volver ~ algo** to tear sth up

guarapón SM (*And, Cono Sur*) broad-brimmed hat

guarda SMF **1** (= *vigilante*) [*de parque, cementerio*] keeper; [*de edificio*] security guard ▸ **guarda de caza, guarda de coto** gamekeeper ▸ **guarda de dique** lock keeper ▸ **guarda de pesca** water bailiff, fish (and game) warden (*EEUU*) ▸ **guarda de seguridad** security guard ▸ **guarda fluvial** water bailiff ▸ **guarda forestal** (forest) ranger ▸ **guarda jurado** (armed) security guard
2 (*Cono Sur*) (*Ferro*) ticket inspector
SF **1** [*de libro*] flyleaf, endpaper
2 (*Téc*) [*de cerradura*] ward; [*de espada*] guard
3 (*Cono Sur*) (*Cos*) trimming, border
4 (= *custodia*) [*de lugar, costumbre*] guarding; [*de niño*] guardianship; ▹ **ángel**
5 [*de la ley*] observance

guardaagujas SMF INV (*Ferro*) pointsman/ pointswoman, switchman/switchwoman (*EEUU*)

guardaalmacén SMF storekeeper

guardabarrera SMF (= *persona*) crossing keeper
SM (*en paso*) level-crossing gate(s), grade-crossing gate(s) (*EEUU*)

guardabarros SM INV mudguard, fender (*EEUU*)

guardabosque SMF, **guardabosques** SMF INV (*en bosque, parque*) ranger, forester; (*en finca*) gamekeeper

guardabrisa SF **1** (= *parabrisas*) windscreen, windshield (*EEUU*)
2 [*de vela*] shade
3 (*Méx*) screen

guardacabo SM (*Náut*) thimble

guardacabras SMF INV goatherd

guardacalor SM cosy, cover

guardacamisa SF (*Caribe*) vest, undershirt (*EEUU*)

guardacantón SM (*en las esquinas o caminos*) kerbstone, curbstone (*EEUU*); (= *poste*) roadside post, corner post

guardacoches SMF INV parking attendant

guardacostas SMF INV (= *persona*) coastguard
SM INV (= *barco*) coastguard vessel, revenue cutter

guardador(a) ADJ **1** (= *protector*) protective
2 (*de orden, ley*) observant, watchful
3 (*pey*) mean, stingy
SM/F **1** (= *cuidador*) keeper; (= *guarda*) guardian; (= *protector*) protector
2 [*de la ley*] observer
3 (*pey*) mean person

guardaespaldas SMF INV bodyguard, minder*

guardaesquinas* SMF INV layabout

guardafango SM mudguard, fender (*EEUU*)

guardafrenos SMF INV guard, conductor (*EEUU*)

guardafuego SM **1** (= *de chimenea*) fireguard
2 (*Náut*) (= *defensa*) fender

guardagujas SMF INV pointsman/ pointswoman, switchman/switchwoman (*EEUU*)

guardajoyas SM INV jewel case

guardajurado SMF (armed) security guard

guardalado SM railing, parapet

guardalmacén SMF storekeeper

guardalodos SM INV mudguard, fender (*EEUU*)

guardamano SM guard (*of a sword*)

guardamechones SM INV locket

guardameta SMF goalkeeper

guardamontes SMPL (*Arg*) rawhide chaps

guardamuebles SM INV furniture repository • **llevar algo a un ~** to put sth in storage

guardapapeles SM INV filing cabinet

guardaparques SMF INV park ranger

guardapelo SM locket

guardapolvo SM **1** (= *cubierta*) dust cover, dust sheet
2 (= *bata*) dust coat; (= *mono*) overalls (*pl*); (= *sobretodo*) outdoor coat
3 [*de reloj*] inner lid

guardapolvos‡ SM INV **1** (= *condón*) rubber*, safe (*EEUU**)
2 (*Anat*) pussy**, beaver (*EEUU***)

guardapuerta SF (= *puerta*) outer door, storm door; (= *cortina*) door curtain, draught excluder, draft excluder (*EEUU*)

guardapuntas SM INV top (*of pencil etc*)

guardar ▹ CONJUG 1a VT **1** [+ *objetos*] **a** (= *meter*) (*en un lugar*) to put; (*en su sitio*) to put away • **lo guardó en el bolsillo** he put it in his pocket • **no sé dónde he guardado el bolso** I don't know where I've put the bag • **si no vas a jugar más, guarda los juguetes** if you're not going to play any more, put the toys away • **guardó los documentos en el cajón** he put the documents away in the drawer
b (= *conservar*) to keep • **guardaba el dinero en una caja de seguridad** she kept the money in a safe • **no tira nunca nada, todo lo guarda** he never throws anything away, he hangs on to *o* keeps everything • **guarda tú las entradas del concierto** you hold on to *o* keep the concert tickets • **el grano que se guarda en el almacén** the grain that is stored in the warehouse • **~ algo para sí** to keep sth for o.s.
c (= *reservar*) to save • **guardo los sellos para mi hermano** I save the stamps for my brother • **te ~é un poco de tarta para cuando vengas** I'll save *o* keep you a bit of cake for when you come • **guárdame un par de entradas** hold *o* save me a couple of tickets, put aside a couple of tickets for me • **guárdame un asiento** keep me a place • **¿puedes ~me el sitio en la cola?** can you keep my place in the queue? • **puedo ~le la habitación solo hasta mañana** I can only keep *o* hold the room for you till tomorrow
d (*Inform*) [+ *archivo*] to save
2 (= *mantener*) [+ *promesa, secreto*] to keep; [+ *recuerdo*] to have • **guardo muy buenos recuerdos de esa época** I have fond memories of that time • **~ el anonimato** to remain anonymous • **~ las apariencias** to keep up appearances • **~ la calma** (*en crisis, desastre*) to keep calm; (*ante una provocación*) to remain composed • **~ las distancias** to keep one's distance • **~ las formas** to keep up appearances • **~ la línea** (= *mantenerla*) to keep one's figure; (= *cuidarla*) to watch one's figure • **~ en secreto** [+ *objeto, documento*] to keep in secret, keep secretly; [+ *actividad, información*] to keep secret; ▹ **cama, silencio**
3 (= *tener*) [+ *relación*] to bear; [+ *semejanza*] to have • **su teoría guarda cierto paralelismo con la de Freud** his theory has a certain parallel with that of Freud
4 (= *sentir*) [+ *rencor*] to bear, have; [+ *respeto*] to have, show • **no le guardo rencor** I have no ill feeling towards him, I bear him no resentment • **los jóvenes de hoy no guardan ningún respeto a sus mayores** young people today have *o* show no respect for their elders
5 (= *cumplir*) [+ *ley*] to observe • **~ los Diez Mandamientos** to follow the Ten Commandments
6 (= *cuidar*) to guard • **un mastín guardaba la entrada** a mastiff guarded the entrance • **los soldados del rey guardan la fortaleza** the king's soldiers are guarding the fortress • **~ a algn de algo** to protect sb from sth • **¡Dios guarde a la Reina!** God save the Queen! • **¡Dios os guarde!††** may God be with you!
VI • **¡guarda!** (*Arg, Chile**) look out!, watch out!
VPR **guardarse 1** (= *meter*) • **me guardé en el bolsillo la foto que me dio** I put the photo he gave me (away) in my pocket • **se guardó rápidamente el paquete de tabaco** he quickly put his cigarettes away
2 (= *conservar*) to keep • **se guardó el dinero del grupo** he kept the group's money for himself, he kept the money that belonged to the group • **¡puedes ~te tus consejos!** you can keep your advice to yourself!
3 • **~se de algo** to guard against sth • **debes ~te de las malas compañías** you should guard against bad company • **~se de hacer**

algo to be careful not to do sth • **se guardó mucho de reconocer su participación en el asunto** he was careful not to admit his involvement in the affair • **guárdate de no ofenderlo** take care not to upset him • **¡guárdate mucho de hacerlo!** don't you dare!, you'd better not do that!
4 (= *recelar*) to be on one's guard
5 (= *precaverse*) to take care, look out for o.s.*
6 • MODISMO: • **guardársela a algn** to have it in for sb* • **se la guarda desde hace muchos años** she's had it in for him for years • **¡esta te la guardo!** I won't forget this!, you haven't heard the end *o* last of this!

guardarraya SF **1** (*Cuba, Puerto Rico*) *path between rows of coffee bushes*
2 (*And, CAm, Caribe*) boundary

guardarropa SM **1** (*en teatro, discoteca*) cloakroom, checkroom (EEUU)
2 (= *armario*) wardrobe
3 (= *ropa*) wardrobe
SMF (= *persona*) cloakroom attendant

guardarropía SF (*Teat*) (= *trajes*) wardrobe; (= *accesorios*) properties (*pl*), props* (*pl*)
• MODISMO: • **de ~** make-believe; (*pey*) sham, fake

guardatiempo SM, **guardatiempos** SM INV timekeeper

guardatrén SMF (*Cono Sur*) guard, conductor (EEUU)

guardavalla SMF, **guardavallas** SMF INV (*LAm*) goalkeeper

guardavía SMF (*Ferro*) linesman/ lineswoman

guardavidas SMF INV (*Arg*) lifeguard

guardavista SM visor, sunshade

guardería SF (*tb* **guardería infantil**) nursery, day nursery, day-care centre *o* (EEUU) center; (*en empresa, tienda*) crèche ▸ **guardería canina** kennels (*pl*)

guardés/esa SM/F (*gen*) guard; [*de puerta*] doorkeeper; [*de casa de campo*] gatekeeper

guardia SMF (= *policía*) policeman/policewoman; (*Mil*) guardsman ▸ **guardia civil** civil guard, *police corps with responsibilities outside towns or cities* ▸ **guardia de tráfico** traffic policeman/policewoman ▸ **guardia forestal** (forest) ranger, warden ▸ **guardia jurado** (armed) security guard ▸ **guardia marina** midshipman ▸ **guardia municipal, guardia urbano/a** police officer (*of the city or town police*) ▸ **guardias de asalto** riot police; (*Mil*) shock troops
SF **1** (= *vigilancia*) • **estar de ~** [*empleado, enfermero, médico*] to be on duty; [*soldado*] to be on sentry duty, be on guard duty; (*Náut*) to be on watch • **médico de ~** doctor on duty, duty doctor • **oficial de ~** officer on duty, duty officer • **puesto de ~** (*Mil*) guard post, sentry box • **hacer ~** [*médico, empleado*] to be on duty; [*soldado*] to do guard duty, do sentry duty • **el soldado que hacía ~** the soldier (who was) on duty • **los fotógrafos hacían ~ junto al juzgado** the photographers were keeping guard outside the court • **montar ~** to stand guard • **los periodistas montaban ~ en la puerta** the journalists were standing guard at the door • **montar la ~** (= *empezarla*) to mount guard • **relevar la ~** to change guard • MODISMOS: • **bajar la ~** to lower one's guard • **estar en ~** to be on (one's) guard • **poner a algn en ~ (contra algo)** to put sb on one's guard (against sth) • **su alusión a mi familia me puso en ~** his reference to my family put me on my guard • **se enciende una luz amarilla para poner en ~ al conductor** a yellow light appears to alert the driver • **ponerse en ~** to be on one's guard; ▸ **farmacia, juzgado**
2 (*tb* **turno de guardia**) [*de médico, enfermera*] shift; [*de soldado*] duty session
3 (*Esgrima*) (= *posición*) guard, garde • **estar en ~** to be on guard, be en garde
4 (= *cuerpo*) (*Mil*) guard • MODISMO: • **la vieja ~** the old guard ▸ **Guardia Civil** Civil Guard ▸ **guardia costera** coastguard service ▸ **guardia de asalto** riot police ▸ **guardia de honor** guard of honour, guard of honor (EEUU) ▸ **guardia montada** horse guards (*pl*) ▸ **guardia municipal** city police, town police ▸ **Guardia Nacional** (*Nic, Pan*) National Guard, Army ▸ **guardia pretoriana** (*Hist*) Praetorian Guard; (*pey*) corps of bodyguards ▸ **Guardia Suiza** Swiss Guard ▸ **guardia urbana** city police, town police

GUARDIA CIVIL

The **Guardia Civil**, commonly referred to as **la Benemérita**, is the oldest of Spain's various police forces. A paramilitary force like the French **Gendarmerie**, it was set up in 1844 to combat banditry in rural areas, but was also used as an instrument of repression in the cities. Under Franco it was resented by many as an oppressive, reactionary force, and was especially hated in the Basque Country. With the return of democracy, Franco's despised **Policía Armada** were reformed as the **Policía Nacional**, and the present-day role of the **Guardia Civil** was redefined. They are mainly stationed in rural areas, and their duties include policing highways and frontiers and taking part in anti-terrorist operations. Their traditional tunics and capes have been replaced by a green uniform, and the famous black patent-leather three-cornered hats are now reserved for ceremonial occasions.
▸ POLICÍA

guardián/ana SM/F **1** (= *defensor*) guardian
2 (= *guarda*) warden, keeper (EEUU); (*Zool*) keeper; (= *vigilante*) watchman; ▸ **perro**

guardiero SM (*Caribe*) watchman (*on an estate*)

guardilla SF (= *desván*) attic, garret; (= *cuarto*) attic room

guardiola* SF piggy bank, money box

guardoso ADJ careful, thrifty; (*pey*) mean

guare SM (*And*) punt pole

guarearse* ▸ CONJUG 1a VPR (*CAm*) to get tight*

guarecer ▸ CONJUG 2d VT (= *cobijar*) to protect, give shelter to; (= *preservar*) to preserve
VPR **guarecerse** to shelter, take refuge (**de** from)

guargüero SM (*LAm*) throat, throttle

guari SM (*Cono Sur*) throat, throttle

guaricha SF **1** (*Ven*) (= *joven*) *young unmarried Indian girl*
2 (*And, CAm, Caribe*) (= *mujer*) woman; (*vieja*) old bag*
3 (*And, CAm, Caribe**) (= *prostituta*) whore

guariche SM (*And*) = **guaricha**

guaricho SM (*Caribe*) young farm labourer, young farmhand

guarida SF **1** [*de animales*] den, hideout; [*de persona*] haunt, hideout
2 (*fig*) refuge, shelter; (= *amparo*) cover

guarismo SM figure, numeral • **en ~ y por extenso** in figures and in words

guarnecer ▸ CONJUG 2d VT **1** (= *proveer*) to equip, provide; (= *adornar*) to adorn, garnish; (*Cos*) to trim; (*Téc*) to cover, protect, reinforce; [+ *frenos*] to line; [+ *joya*] to set, mount; [+ *caballo*] to harness
2 (*Culin*) to garnish • **carne guarnecida con cebolla y zanahoria** meat garnished with onion and carrot
3 (*Mil*) to man, garrison
4 (*Arquit*) [+ *pared*] to plaster, stucco

guarnecido SM **1** [*de pared*] plaster, plastering
2 (*Aut*) upholstery

guarnés SM (*Méx*) harness room

guarnición SF **1** (= *acto*) (*de proveer*) equipment, provision; (*de adornar*) adorning; (*Culin*) garnishing
2 (= *adorno*) (*gen*) adornment; (*Cos*) trimming; (*Culin*) garnish; [*de frenos*] lining; [*de joya*] setting, mount; [*de espada*] guard • **ganso con ~ de lombarda y patata** goose with a red cabbage and potato garnish
3 guarniciones [*de caballo*] harness (*sing*); (= *equipo*) gear (*sing*); [*de casa*] fittings, fixtures • **guarniciones del alumbrado** light fittings
4 (*Mil*) garrison
5 [*de pared*] plastering

guarnicionar ▸ CONJUG 1a VT (*Mil*) to garrison, man

guarnicionero/a SM/F leather worker, leather craftsman/craftswoman; (*para caballos*) harness maker

guaro SM **1** (*CAm*) (= *ron*) liquor, spirits (*pl*)
2 (= *ave*) small parrot

guarola* SF (*CAm*) old crock, old banger‡, jalopy (EEUU)

guarolo ADJ (*Caribe*) stubborn

guarra SF **1** (*Zool*) sow
2** (*pey*) (= *mujer*) slut‡
3‡ (= *golpe*) punch, bash*; ▸ **guarro**

guarrada* SF **1** (= *porquería*) dirty mess, disgusting mess • **hacer una ~** to make a dirty *o* disgusting mess
2 (= *indecencia*) (= *dicho*) filthy thing (to say), disgusting thing (to say) • **ese libro es una ~** that book is a piece of filth* • **decir ~s** to talk filth* • **hacer ~s** to do dirty *o* filthy things
3 (= *mala pasada*) dirty trick

guarrazo* SM (= *golpe*) • **darse** *o* **pegarse un ~** (*gen*) to take a thump*; (*en coche*) to have a smash

guarrear* ▸ CONJUG 1a VT to dirty, mess up

guarrería* SF = **guarrada**

guarrindongo/a* ADJ, SM/F = **guarro**

guarro/a ADJ* **1** (= *sucio*) dirty, filthy
2 (= *indecente*) dirty, filthy • **un chiste ~** a dirty *o* filthy joke
SM/F* (= *persona*) (= *sucio*) dirty person; (= *descuidado*) slovenly person; (= *indecente*) filthy person, disgusting person
SM (= *animal*) pig, hog (EEUU); ▸ **guarra**

guarrusca SF (*And*) machete, big knife

guarte†† EXCL look out!, take care!

guarura* SMF (*Méx*) **1** (= *guardaespaldas*) bodyguard, minder*
2 (= *policía*) cop*

guasa SF **1** (= *chanza*) joking, teasing, kidding* • **con** *o* **de ~** jokingly, in fun • **estar de ~** to be joking *o* kidding • **sonreírse con ~** to smile jokingly • **tomarse algo a ~** to take sth as a joke • **no tengo ganas de ~** I'm not in the mood for jokes
2 (= *sosería*) dullness, insipidness
3 (*CAm*) (= *suerte*) luck; ▸ **guaso**

guasábara SF (*And, Caribe*) **1** (*Hist*) [*de esclavos*] uprising
2†† (= *clamor*) clamour, clamor (EEUU), uproar

guasada‡ SF (*Cono Sur*) obscenity

guasamaco ADJ (*Cono Sur*) rough, coarse

guasanga SF **1** (*CAm, Cuba, Méx*) (= *bulla*) din, uproar
2 (*CAm*) (= *chiste*) joke

guasca[1] SF **1** (*LAm*) (= *correa*) leather strap, rawhide thong; (*And*) (= *látigo*) riding whip, crop • **dar ~** (= *azotar*) to whip, flog
• MODISMOS: • **dar ~ a algo** (*Cono Sur*) to insist

stubbornly on sth • **¡déle ~ no más!** (*Cono Sur*) keep at it! • **dar ~ a algn** (*And*) to wind sb up* • **pisarse la ~** (*And, Cono Sur*‡) to fall into the trap • **volverse ~** (*And*) to be full of longing
2 (*Cono Sur***) prick**
guasca² SF (*And*) mountain peak
guascaro ADJ (*And*) impulsive
guascazo SM (*LAm*) (= *latigazo*) lash; (= *golpe*) blow, punch
guasch [gwaʃ] SM gouache
guasearse ▷ CONJUG 1a VPR to joke, tease, kid* • **~ de algo/algn** to poke fun at sth/sb
guasería* SF (*And, Cono Sur*) rudeness
guaserío SM (*Cono Sur*) rabble
guaso/a* (*And, Caribe, Cono Sur*) ADJ
1 (= *grosero*) coarse, rough
2 (*Cono Sur*) (= *tímido*) shy
3 (= *sencillo*) simple, unsophisticated
SM/F **1** (*Chile*) (= *campesino*) peasant, countryman/woman, hick (*EEUU**); (= *vaquero*) cowboy/cowgirl
2 (*Cono Sur*) (= *grosero*) uncouth person
SM (*Cuba*) (= *bulla*) merry din; (= *parranda*) merrymaking, revelry; ▷ **guasa**
guasón/ona ADJ **1** (= *bromista*) joking, teasing • **se pusieron en plan ~** they started joking around *o* teasing
2 (= *burlón*) mocking • **en tono ~** in a mocking tone
SM/F (= *bromista*) joker, tease; (= *ocurrente*) wag, wit
guasqueada* SF (*LAm*) (= *latigazo*) lash; (= *azotaina*) whipping, flogging
guasquear ▷ CONJUG 1a VT (*LAm**) (= *azotar*) to whip, flog
VI (*Chile*) to crack
guata¹ SF **1** (= *algodón*) raw cotton; (= *relleno*) padding
2 (*And*) (= *cuerda*) twine, cord
3 (*Cuba*) (= *mentira*) lie, fib
4 (*And**) (= *amigo*) inseparable friend, bosom pal
guata² SF **1** (*And, Cono Sur*) (= *panza*) paunch, belly • **echar ~** (*Chile**) to get fat
2 guatas (*Cono Sur*) (*Culin*) tripe (*sing*)
3 (*Cono Sur*) warping, bulging
guata³ SMF (*And*) *inhabitant of the interior*
guataca SF (*Caribe*) **1** (= *azada*) small hoe; (= *pala de madera*) wooden shovel
2 (*Anat*) big ear
SMF (= *lameculos*) crawler*, creep‡, brown-nose (*EEUU*‡)
guataco ADJ **1** (*And*) (*pey*) (= *indio*) Indian, native
2 (*CAm, Méx**) (= *gordito*) chubby, plump
guatal SM (*CAm*) hillock
guate SM **1** (*CAm*) [*de maíz*] maize plantation
2* (*Ven*) (= *serrano*) highlander; (*Caribe*) (= *colombiano*) Colombian
3 (*And**) (= *amigo*) bosom pal
guateado ADJ quilted
guatearse ▷ CONJUG 1a VPR (*Chile*) to warp, bulge
Guatemala SF Guatemala • **MODISMO:** • **salir de ~ y entrar en Guatepeor** to jump out of the frying pan into the fire
guatemalteco/a ADJ Guatemalan, of/from Guatemala
SM/F Guatemalan • **los ~s** the people of Guatemala
guatemaltequismo SM *word or phrase peculiar to Guatemala*
guateque SM party, binge*
guatero SM (*Chile*) hot water bottle
guatitas SFPL (*Chile*) tripe (*sing*)
guato‡ SM (*LAm*) joint‡, reefer‡
guatón* ADJ (*Chile*) (= *barrigón*) fat, pot-bellied; (= *regordete*) plump • **sí, ~** yes, darling

guatuso ADJ (*CAm*) blond(e), fair
guau EXCL **1** (*de perro*) woof!, bow-wow!
2 (*de sorpresa*) wow!*
SM (= *ladrido*) bark
guay* ADJ super*, smashing*
ADV • **pasarlo ~** to have a super *o* smashing time*
guaya SF (*Ven*) steel cable
guayaba SF **1** (*LAm*) (*Bot*) guava; (= *jalea*) guava jelly
2 (*LAm**) (= *mentira*) fib, lie
3 (*LAm*) (= *tobillo*) ankle
4 (*CAm*) (= *beso*) kiss; (= *boca*‡) gob‡
5 • **la ~** (*CAm*) power
guayabal SM grove of guava trees
guayabear* ▷ CONJUG 1a VT (*CAm*) (= *besar*) to kiss
VI (*LAm*) (= *mentir*) to lie, tell fibs
guayabera SF (*LAm*) (= *camisa*) *loose shirt with large pockets*; (= *chaqueta*) lightweight jacket
guayabero* ADJ (*LAm*) lying, deceitful
guayabo SM **1** (*Bot*) guava tree
2 (*And*) (= *pena*) grief, sorrow
3 (*Ven*) (= *murria*) nostalgia
4 (*And, Cono Sur**) (= *resaca*) hangover
5* (= *guapa*) pretty girl, smasher* • **está hecha un ~** (= *atractiva*) she looks marvellous; (= *joven*) she looks very young
6 (*Méx***) pussy**, beaver (*EEUU***)
guayaca ADJ (*Cono Sur*) (= *torpe*) slow, dull; (= *corto*) simple-minded
SF (*LAm*) (= *bolso*) bag, purse (*EEUU*)
guayacán SM lignum vitae
Guayana SF Guyana, Guiana ▸ **Guayana Británica** British Guiana ▸ **Guayana Francesa** French Guiana ▸ **Guayana Holandesa** Dutch Guiana
guayanés/esa ADJ, SM/F Guyanese
guayar ▷ CONJUG 1a VT (*Caribe*) to grate
guayo SM (*Caribe*) **1** (*Culin*) grater
2 (*Mús**) bad street band
guayuco SM (*Col, Ven*) loincloth
guayunga SF (*And*) lot, heap
gubernamental ADJ (*gen*) governmental, government (*antes de s*); [*facción*] loyalist • **organización no ~** non-governmental organization
SMF (*leal*) loyalist, government supporter; (*Mil*) government soldier
gubernamentalización SF (increase in) government intervention *o* control
gubernativo ADJ government (*antes de s*), governmental • **los delegados ~s** the government delegates • **la decisión gubernativa** the government's decision • **por orden gubernativa** by order of the government
gubia SF gouge
güe... (*para diversas palabras escritas así esp en LAm*) ▷ **hue...**
guedeja SF **1** (= *mechón*) lock
2 (= *cabellera*) long hair
3 [*de león*] mane
güegüecho ADJ **1** (*And, CAm**) (= *tonto*) silly, stupid
2 (*CAm, Méx*) (*Med*) suffering from goitre *o* (*EEUU*) goiter
SM **1** (*CAm, Méx*) (*Med*) goitre, goiter (*EEUU*)
2 (*CAm*) (= *ave*) turkey
3 (*CAm**) (= *bohío*) hovel
güeñi SM (*Cono Sur*) (= *chico*) boy; (= *criado*) servant
guepardo SM cheetah
güerequeque SM (*And*) plover
Guernesey SM Guernsey
güero ADJ (*CAm, Méx*) (= *rubio*) blond(e), fair; (*de tez*) fair, light-skinned
guerra SF **1** (*Mil, Pol*) war; (= *arte*) warfare • **Primera Guerra Mundial** First World War • **Segunda Guerra Mundial** Second World War • **de ~** military, war (*antes de s*) • **Ministerio de Guerra** Ministry of War, War Office, War Department (*EEUU*) • **declarar la ~** to declare war (**a** on) • **estar en ~** to be at war (**con** with) • **hacer la ~** to wage war (a on) ▸ **guerra a muerte** war to the bitter end ▸ **guerra atómica** atomic war(fare) ▸ **guerra bacteriana, guerra bacteriológica** germ warfare ▸ **guerra biológica** biological warfare ▸ **guerra caliente** hot war, shooting war ▸ **guerra civil** civil war ▸ **guerra comercial** trade war ▸ **guerra convencional** conventional warfare ▸ **guerra de agotamiento, guerra de desgaste** war of attrition ▸ **guerra de bandas** gang warfare ▸ **guerra de guerrillas** guerrilla warfare ▸ **Guerra de la Independencia** (*LAm*) War of Independence; (*Esp*) Peninsular War ▸ **guerra de las galaxias** Star Wars ▸ **Guerra de los Cien Años** Hundred Years' War ▸ **Guerra de los Treinta Años** Thirty Years' War ▸ **Guerra del Transvaal** Boer War ▸ **guerra de nervios** war of nerves ▸ **guerra de precios** price war ▸ **Guerra de Sucesión** War of Spanish Succession ▸ **guerra de trincheras** trench warfare ▸ **guerra económica** economic warfare ▸ **guerra nuclear** nuclear war(fare) ▸ **guerra psicológica** psychological warfare ▸ **guerra química** chemical warfare ▸ **guerra relámpago** blitzkrieg, lightning war (*EEUU*) ▸ **guerra santa** holy war, crusade ▸ **guerra sin cuartel** all-out war ▸ **guerra sucia** dirty war; ▷ **declarar**
2 (= *problemas*) • **dar ~** (*gen*) to be a nuisance (**a** to), make trouble (**a** for); [*niño*] to carry on • **pedir** *o* **querer ~** (*gen*) to look for trouble; (*sexualmente**) to feel randy *o* horny*
3 (= *juego*) billiards

GUERRA CIVIL ESPAÑOLA
Spain's political climate was extremely volatile in the 1930s. The elections of February 1936 were won by a coalition of socialist and anarchist groups known as the **Frente Popular** or **FP**, and were followed by a period of social disorder. On July 18 of that year, General Francisco Franco led a military coup. In the ensuing war Franco's side was known as the **Nacionales** and the government forces as the **Republicanos**. Neither army was well-equipped, so foreign support was a decisive factor: the USSR sent aid to the Republicans and volunteers from all over Europe formed **Brigadas Internacionales** (International Brigades) to fight for the Republican side. Fascist Italy and Germany sent troops and weapons to Franco. The fighting was bitter and protracted, and the Nationalists' superior firepower finally triumphed. The war ended officially on April 1, 1939, when Franco proclaimed himself **Jefe del Estado**, a position he held for the next 36 years.
▷ **FRANQUISMO**

guerrear ▷ CONJUG 1a VI (= *pelear*) to wage war, fight; (*fig*) to put up a fight, resist
guerrera SF (= *chaqueta*) combat jacket; (*Mil*) military jacket; (= *abrigo*) trench coat
guerrero/a ADJ **1** (= *belicoso*) war (*antes de s*) • **espíritu ~** fighting spirit • **hazañas guerreras** fighting exploits
2 (*de carácter*) warlike • **un pueblo ~** a warlike people • **virtudes guerreras** warlike virtues
3 (= *en guerra*) warring • **tribus guerreras** warring tribes
SM/F (= *soldado*) warrior, soldier
SM (*Caribe**) *rum and vodka-based cocktail*

g

guerrilla SF **1** (= *grupo*) guerrillas (*pl*); (= *fuerzas*) guerrilla forces (*pl*)
2 (= *guerra*) guerrilla warfare

guerrillear ▸ CONJUG 1a VI to wage guerrilla warfare

guerrillero/a ADJ guerrilla (*antes de s*) • **líder ~** guerrilla leader
SM/F guerrilla (fighter); (= *maqui*) partisan ▸ **guerrillero/a urbano/a** urban guerrilla

guerrista ADJ (= *luchador*) combative, fighting
SMF (*Esp*) (*Pol*) *supporter of Alfonso Guerra*

güesear‡ ▸ CONJUG 1a VT (*CAm*) to wash

gueto SM ghetto

güevo SM • MODISMO: • **a** *o* **de ~** (*Méx*) by hook or by crook

güevón/ona* (*LAm*) ADJ, SM/F = **huevón**

güi... (*para diversas palabras escritas así en LAm*) ▸ **hui...**

guía SF **1** (= *libro*) guidebook (**de** to); (= *manual*) handbook; [*de teléfono*] directory ▸ **guía de campo** (*Bio*) field guide ▸ **guía de carga** (*Ferro*) waybill ▸ **guía de datos** data directory ▸ **guía del ocio** "what's on" guide ▸ **guía del turista** tourist guide ▸ **guía de teléfonos** telephone directory ▸ **guía del viajero** traveller's *o* (*EEUU*) traveler's guide ▸ **guía gastronómica** food guide ▸ **guía oficial de ferrocarriles** (*Ferro*) official timetable ▸ **guía telefónica** telephone directory ▸ **guía turística** tourist guide
2 (= *orientación*) guidance; (= *acto*) guiding • **para que le sirva de ~** for your guidance ▸ **guía vocacional** vocational guidance
3 (*Inform*) prompt
4 (*Mec*) guide; [*de bicicleta*] handlebars (*pl*); (= *caballo*) leader, front horse; **guías** (= *riendas*) reins ▸ **guía sonora** (*Cine*) soundtrack
SMF (= *persona*) guide; (= *dirigente*) leader; (= *consejero*) adviser ▸ **guía de turismo** tourist guide
ADJ INV guide (*antes de s*), guiding • **manual ~** guidebook • **cable ~** guiding wire, guide rope

guiado SM guiding, guidance; [*de misil*] guiding

guiar ▸ CONJUG 1c VT **1** (*gen*) to guide; (= *dirigir*) to lead, direct; (= *controlar*) to manage; (= *orientar*) to advise • **no te dejes ~ por la propaganda** don't be influenced *o* led by propaganda
2 (*Aut*) to drive; (*Náut*) to steer; (*Aer*) to pilot
3 (*Bot*) to train
VPR **guiarse** • **~se por algo** to be guided by sth, be ruled by sth, go by sth • **no hay que ~se por lo que dice la televisión** you don't have to be guided *o* ruled *o* go by what's on television • **~se por el sentido común** to follow common sense

güicoy SM (*CAm*) (*Bot*) courgette, zucchini (*EEUU*)

Guido SM Guy

guija¹ SF (= *piedra*) pebble; (*en camino*) cobble, cobblestone

guija² SF (*Bot*) vetch

guijarral SM (= *terreno*) stony place; (= *playa*) shingle, pebbles (*pl*)

guijarro SM (= *piedra*) pebble; (*en camino*) cobblestone, cobble

guijarroso ADJ [*terreno*] stony; [*camino*] cobbled; [*playa*] pebbly, shingly

guijo SM **1** (= *grava*) gravel; (*para caminos*) granite chips (*pl*); (*en la playa*) shingle
2 (*Mec*) (= *gorrón*) shaft of wheel

güila¹ SF **1** (*Méx*‡) (= *prostituta*) whore, tart‡, slut‡
2 (*Chile**) (= *andrajos*) rags (*pl*), tatters (*pl*)
3 (*CAm*) (= *trompito*) small spinning top

güila²* SMF (*CAm*) kid*

güiliento ADJ (*Cono Sur*) ragged, tattered

guillado* ADJ cracked*, crazy • **estar ~** to be off one's trolley*

guillame SM (*Téc*) rabbet plane

guillarse* ▸ CONJUG 1a VPR **1** to go crazy, go round the twist*
2 • **guillárselas** (= *irse*) to beat it*; (= *morir*) to kick the bucket‡

Guillermo SM William

guillotina SF guillotine; (*para papel*) paper cutter • **ventana de ~** sash window

guillotinado SM guillotining

guillotinar ▸ CONJUG 1a VT to guillotine

güilo ADJ (*Méx*) (= *tullido*) maimed, crippled; (*fig*) weak, sickly

güincha SF (*And, Cono Sur*) **1** (= *ribete*) narrow strip of cloth; (= *cinta*) ribbon; (= *para pelo*) hair ribbon
2 (*Dep*) (= *meta*) tape, finishing line; (= *salida*) starting line
3 (= *cinta métrica*) measuring tape, tape measure
4 • **¡las ~s!** rubbish!, forget it!

güinche SM (*Arg*) (= *torno*) winch, hoist; (= *grúa*) crane

güinchero SM (*LAm*) winch operator; [*de grúa*] crane operator

guinda SF **1** (= *fruta*) morello cherry, mazzard cherry, sour cherry (*EEUU*) • MODISMOS: • **ponerse como una ~** to turn scarlet • **échale ~s al pavo** would you believe it!
2 (= *remate*) • **la ~ (del pastel)** the icing on the cake • **como ~** to cap *o* top it all • **y como ~ la actuación de Madonna** and to cap *o* top it all we had Madonna's performance • **poner la ~** (= *rematar bien*) to put the icing on the cake; (= *terminar*) to add the finishing touches • **puso la ~ con un gol en el último minuto** his goal in the last minute was the icing on the cake • **poner la ~ a la oferta** to top off the offer, add a final attraction to the offer • **aquello puso la ~ final** (*iró*) that was the last straw
3 (*Náut*) height of masts
4 (*Caribe*) guttering, spout
5 • **eso es una ~** (*Cono Sur*‡) that's simple, it's a cinch‡
6 guindas (*Cono Sur***) balls**, bollocks**

guindalejo SM (*And, Caribe*) (= *ropa vieja*) old clothes (*pl*); (= *trastos*) junk, lumber

guindaleza SF (*Náut*) hawser

guindar ▸ CONJUG 1a VT **1**‡ (= *robar*) to pinch*, swipe*
2‡ [+ *contrato, trabajo*] to win (*against competition*), land
3 (*Caribe*) (= *colgar*) to hang up
VPR **guindarse 1** (= *descolgarse*) to hang (down)
2* (= *ahorcarse*) to hang o.s.; (= *morirse*) to kick the bucket*

guindaste SM (*Náut*) jib crane

guinde‡ SM nicking‡, thieving • **un ~** a job*

guindilla SF (= *pimiento*) chilli, hot pepper • **~ roja** red chilli • **~ verde** green chilli
SMF (*Esp**) (= *policía*) cop*

guindo¹ SM mazzard cherry tree, morello cherry tree • MODISMO: • **caer del ~*** to twig*, to cotton on*

guindo² SM (*CAm*) ravine

guindola SF (*Náut*) lifebuoy

guindón‡ SM thief

Guinea SF Guinea ▸ **Guinea Ecuatorial** Equatorial Guinea ▸ **Guinea Española** Spanish Guinea

guinea SF (= *moneda*) guinea; ▸ **guineo**

Guinea-Bissau SF Guinea-Bissau

guineano/a ADJ Guinean
SM/F Guinean

guineo¹/a ADJ Guinea(n), of/from Guinea
SM/F Guinea(n); ▸ **guinea**

guineo² SM (*LAm*) banana

guiña SF **1** (*And, Caribe*) bad luck
2 (*And*) witchcraft

guiñada SF **1** (= *guiño*) wink
2 (*Aer, Náut*) yaw

guiñapo SM **1** (= *andrajo*) rag, tatter • MODISMO: • **poner a algn como un ~** to shower sb with insults
2 (= *dejado*) slovenly person; (= *granuja*) ragamuffin; (= *réprobo*) rogue, reprobate

guiñar ▸ CONJUG 1a VT to wink • **~ el ojo a algn** to wink at sb
VI **1** (*con un ojo*) to wink
2 (*Aer, Náut*) to yaw

guiño SM **1** (*con un ojo*) wink • **hacer ~s a algn** to wink at sb; (*amantes*) to make eyes at sb • **~ cómplice** (*lit*) knowing wink; (= *apoyo*) tacit support
2 (*Aer, Náut*) yaw

guiñol SM (*Teat*) puppet theatre *o* (*EEUU*) theater, Punch and Judy show

guiñolista SMF puppeteer

guión SM **1** (*Radio, TV*) script; (*Cine*) (*como transcripción*) script; (*como obra*) screenplay • **salirse del ~** to depart from the script, improvise • **el premio al mejor ~** the prize for the best screenplay
2 (*Literat*) (= *resumen*) summary, outline; (= *aclaración*) explanatory text
3 (*Tip*) hyphen, dash
4 (= *pendón*) royal standard; (*Rel*) processional cross, processional banner
5 (*Orn*) ▸ **guión de codornices** corncrake

guionista SMF scriptwriter

guionizar ▸ CONJUG 1f VT to script, write the script for

guipar‡ ▸ CONJUG 1a VT **1** (= *ver*) to see
2 (= *entender*) to cotton on to*, catch on to
3 (= *percibir*) to spot, catch sight of

güipil SM (*CAm, Méx*) *Indian regional dress or blouse*

Guipúzcoa SF Guipúzcoa

guipuzcoano/a ADJ of/from Guipúzcoa
SM/F native/inhabitant of Guipúzcoa • **los ~s** the people of Guipúzcoa

guiri SMF* (= *extranjero*) foreigner; (= *turista*) tourist
SM **1*** (= *policía*) policeman; (= *guardia civil*) civil guard
2 (*Hist*) Carlist soldier
3 • **en el ~**‡ abroad, in foreign parts

guirigay SM **1** (= *griterío*) hubbub, uproar; (= *confusión*) chaos, confusion • **¡esto es un ~!** the place is like a bear garden!
2 (= *lenguaje confuso*) gibberish, jargon

guirizapa SF (*Caribe*) quarrel, squabble

guirlache SM *type of nougat*

guirnalda SF (= *tira, collar*) garland; (*en entierro*) wreath; (*Arte*) garland, floral motif

güiro* SM **1** (*Caribe*) (= *calabaza*) gourd
2 (*Mús*) musical instrument
3 (*Caribe*) (= *cabeza*) head, nut‡, noggin (*EEUU*‡)
4 (*CAm*) (= *bebé*) small baby
5 (*Caribe*) (= *mujerzuela*) loose woman
6 (*And*) (= *brote de maíz*) maize shoot

güirro ADJ (*LAm*) weak, sickly
SM (*CAm*) small baby

guisa SF **1** • **a ~ de: se puso una cinta a ~ de pulsera** she wore a strap like a bracelet • **usando el bastón a ~ de batuta** using his walking stick like *o* as a baton
2 • **de tal ~** in such a way (**que** that)

guisado ADJ • **carne guisada** beef stew, beef casserole
SM stew • **~ de alubias** bean casserole

guisador(a) SM/F, **guisandero/a** SM/F cook

guisante (SM) pea ▸ **guisante de olor** sweet pea
guisar ▹ CONJUG 1a (VT) **1** (*Culin*) (= *cocinar*) to cook; (= *en salsa*) to stew • **REFRÁN**: • **él se lo guisa, él se lo come** he's made his bed, so he can lie in it
2* (= *tramar*) to cook up* • **¿qué estarán guisando?** what can they be cooking up?*
(VI) to cook • **me paso el día guisando** I spend the day cooking
(VPR) **guisarse*** (= *tramarse*) • **¿qué se estará guisando en la asamblea?** what are they cooking up in the meeting, I wonder?*
güisingue (SM) (*And*) whip
güisinguear ▹ CONJUG 1a (VT) (*And*) to whip
guiso (SM) **1** (= *guisado*) stew
2 (= *aliño*) seasoning
guisote (SM) (*pey*) (= *guiso*) hash, poor-quality stew; (= *mezcla*) concoction; (= *comida*) grub*, nosh‡, chow (EEUU‡)
güisquería (SF) night club
güisqui (SM) whisky
guita (SF) **1** (= *cuerda*) twine; (= *bramante*) packthread
2‡ (= *dinero*) dough*, cash • **¿cuánta ~?** how much dough* *o* cash? • **aflojar** *o* **soltar la ~** to cough up*, stump up*, fork out*
güita‡ (SF) (*Méx*) dough*
guitarra (SF) (= *instrumento*) guitar • **MODISMOS**: • **chafar la ~ a algn** to queer sb's pitch • **ser como ~ en un entierro** to be quite out of place, strike the wrong note • **estar con la ~ bien/mal templada** to be in a good/bad mood ▸ **guitarra baja** bass guitar ▸ **guitarra clásica** classical guitar ▸ **guitarra eléctrica** electrical guitar
(SMF) guitarist ▸ **guitarra solista** (*en concierto*) solo guitarist; (*en grupo*) lead guitar
guitarrear ▹ CONJUG 1a (VI) to play the guitar, strum a guitar
guitarreo (SM) strum(ming)
guitarrero/a (SM/F) (electric) guitarist
guitarrista (SMF) guitarist
guitarrón (SM) **1** (*Méx*) (*Mús*) large guitar
2 (*CAm*) (= *abeja*) bee
güito (SM) **1** (= *hueso*) stone
2 güitos*‡ balls*‡
güizcal (SM) (*CAm*) (*Bot*) chayote
gula (SF) gluttony, greed
gulag (SM) (PL: **gulags**) gulag
gulash [gu'laʃ] (SM INV) goulash
guloso (ADJ) gluttonous (*frm*), greedy
gulusmear ▹ CONJUG 1a (VI) **1** (= *comer*) to nibble titbits
2 (= *oler*) to sniff the cooking
3 (= *curiosear*) to snoop
guma‡ (SF) hen
gumarra* (SM) (*Méx*) cop*
gurguciar ▹ CONJUG 1b (VT) (*CAm*) to sniff at, sniff out
(VI) (*Méx**) (= *gruñir*) to grunt, snort
guri‡ (SM) (= *policía*) cop*; (*Mil*) soldier
gurí* (SM) (*Cono Sur*) (PL: **gurís, guríes** *o* **gurises**) **1†** (= *mestizo*) mestizo, Indian child, child of mixed race
2 (= *muchacho*) boy, kid*
guripa* (SM) **1** (*Mil*) soldier; (= *policía*) cop*
2 (= *pillo*) rascal, rogue; (= *tonto*) berk‡
3 (= *sujeto*) bloke*, guy*
gurisa* (SF) (*Cono Sur*) **1†** (= *mestiza*) Indian child, child of mixed race
2 (= *chica*) girl, bird*, chick (EEUU*); (= *esposa*) young wife
gurrí (SM) (*Col, Ecu*) wild duck
gurrumina* (SF) **1** (*And*) (= *molestia*) bother, nuisance; (= *tristeza*) sadness
2 (*Méx*) (= *fruslería*) trifle, mere nothing
gurrumino/a* (ADJ) **1** (= *débil*) weak, sickly; (= *insignificante*) small, puny
2 [*marido*] complaisant, indulgent
3 (*And*) (= *cobarde*) cowardly
4 (*CAm*) (= *listo*) clever, sharp
(SM/F) **1** (*Méx*) (= *chiquillo*) child
2 (*LAm*) (= *persona astuta*) sharp customer*
(SM) (= *cornudo*) cuckold; (= *marido complaciente*) complaisant husband, indulgent husband
gurrupié (SM) **1** (*Méx*) (*en los garitos*) croupier
2 (*Caribe, And*) (= *falso postor*) false bidder
3 (*Caribe**) (= *amigo*) pal*, buddy (*esp* EEUU)
gurú (SMF) (PL: **gurús**) guru
gurupié (SM) = **gurrupié**
gus (SM) (*And*) turkey buzzard
gusa* (SF) hunger • **tener ~** to be hungry
gusanera (SF) **1** (= *nido*) nest of maggots; (= *lugar*) breeding ground for maggots
2 (*Cuba‡*) (*pey*) • **la ~ Miami** *home of refugee Cubans since 1959*
3 (= *montón*) bunch, lot • **una ~ de chiquillos** a bunch of kids
gusaniento (ADJ) worm-eaten
gusanillo (SM) **1*** (= *hambre*) • **me anda el ~** I feel peckish • **cómete una manzana para matar el ~** have an apple to keep you going
2* (= *interés*) bug* • **le entró el ~ de la gimnasia** he caught the keep-fit bug*, he got hooked on keep-fit*
3 (= *espiral*) spiral binding • **encuadernado en ~** spiral bound
4 • **el ~ de la conciencia*** the prickings of conscience
gusano (SM) **1** (*gen*) worm; [*de tierra*] earthworm; [*de mosca*] maggot; [*de mariposa, polilla*] caterpillar • **MODISMO**: • **criar ~s** to be dead and buried, be pushing up the daisies* ▸ **gusano de la carne** maggot ▸ **gusano de la conciencia** remorse ▸ **gusano de luz** glow worm ▸ **gusano de seda** silkworm
2 (= *persona*) worm; (= *ser despreciable*) contemptible person; (= *persona dócil*) meek creature
3 (*Inform*) worm
4 (*Cuba‡*) (*pey*) *nickname for Cuban refugees post-1959*
(ADJ) (*Cuba‡*) (*pey*) Cuban-refugee (*antes de s*)
gusanoso (ADJ) worm-eaten
gusarapo (SM) **1** (= *renacuajo*) tadpole
2* (= *bicho*) bug, creature
3* (= *persona*) worm*
gusgo (ADJ) (*Méx*) sweet-toothed
gustación (SF) tasting, trying
gustado (ADJ) (*LAm*) popular • **un plato muy ~** a very popular dish
gustar ▹ CONJUG 1a (VI) **1** (*con complemento personal*) **a** (*con sustantivo*) • **me gusta el té** I like tea • **¿te gustó México?** did you like Mexico? • **no me gusta mucho** I don't like it very much • **le gustan mucho los niños** she loves children, she's very fond of children, she likes children a lot • **¿te ha gustado la película?** did you enjoy the film? • **el rojo es el que más me gusta** I like the red one best • **eso es, así me gusta** that's right, that's the way I like it • **me gusta como canta** I like the way she sings
b (+ *infin*) • **¿te gusta jugar a las cartas?** do you like playing cards? • **no me gusta nada levantarme temprano** I hate getting up early, I don't like getting up early at all • **no me ~ía nada estar en su lugar** I'd hate to be *o* I really wouldn't like to be in his place *o* shoes • **le gusta mucho jugar al fútbol** he's a keen footballer, he likes playing *o* to play football • **le gusta llegar con tiempo de sobra a una cita** she likes to get to her appointments with time to spare
c • **~ que** (+ *subjun*): • **no le gusta que lo llamen Pepe** he doesn't like being *o* to be called Pepe • **le gusta que la cena esté en la mesa cuando llega a casa** he likes his supper to be on the table when he gets home • **no me gustó que no invitaran a mi hija a la boda** I didn't like the fact that *o* I was annoyed that my daughter wasn't invited to the wedding • **me gusta mucho que me den masajes** I love having massages • **¿te ~ía que te llevara al cine?** would you like me to take you to the cinema?, would you like it if I took you to the cinema?
d (= *sentir atracción por*) • **a mi amiga le gusta Carlos** my friend fancies* *o* likes *o* is keen on Carlos
2 (*sin complemento explícito*) • **es una película que siempre gusta** it's a film that never fails to please • **la obra no gustó** the play was not a success • **mi número ya no gusta** my act isn't popular any more
3 (*en frases de cortesía*) • **¿gusta usted?** would you like some?, may I offer you some? • **si usted gusta** if you please, if you don't mind • **como usted guste** as you wish, as you please† • **cuando gusten** (*invitando a pasar*) when you're ready • **puede venir por aquí cuando guste** you can come here whenever you like *o* wish
4 • **~ de algo** to like sth • **vivía recluido y no gustaba de compañía** he was a recluse and did not like company • **la novela ideal para quienes no gusten de obras largas** the ideal novel for people who don't like *o* enjoy long books • **~ de hacer algo** to like to do sth • **Josechu, como gustan de llamarlo en su familia** Josechu, as his family like to call him • **una expresión que gustan de repetir los escritores del XVIII** an expression that 18th century writers like to use *o* are fond of using frequently
(VT) **1** (= *probar*) to taste, sample • **después de ~ la buena vida** after tasting the good life
2 (*LAm*) • **gusto un café** I'd like a coffee • **¿~ía un poco de vino?** would you like some wine? • **si gustan pasar a la sala de espera** would you like to go through to the waiting room?
gustativo (ADJ) taste (*antes de s*)
gustazo* (SM) great pleasure • **me di el ~ de levantarme a las doce** I treated myself to a lie-in till twelve
gustillo (SM) • **coger el ~ a algo** to get *o* grow to like sth
gustirrinín* (SM) = gusto
gusto (SM) **1** (= *sentido*) taste • **agregue azúcar a ~** add sugar to taste
2 [*de comida*] taste, flavour, flavor (EEUU) • **tiene un ~ amargo** it has a bitter taste *o* flavour, it tastes bitter • **le noto un ~ a almendras** it tastes of almonds • **helado de tres ~s** Neapolitan ice cream
3 (= *sentido estético*) taste • **tenemos los mismos ~s** we have the same tastes • **es demasiado grande para mi ~** it's too big for my taste • **he decorado la habitación a mi ~** I've decorated the room to my taste • **al ~ de hoy** • **según el ~ de hoy** in the taste of today • **ser persona de ~** to be a person of taste • **tiene ~ para vestir** she dresses with taste, she has taste in clothes • **una habitación decorada con ~** a tastefully decorated room • **buen ~** good taste • **no es de buen ~ decir eso** it's not in good taste to say that • **tiene buen ~ para combinar colores** she has good taste in combining colours • **un decorado de buen ~** tasteful décor • **mal ~** bad taste • **es de un mal ~ extraordinario** it is in extraordinarily bad taste • **una broma de muy mal ~** a joke in very poor taste • **un comentario de mal ~** a tasteless remark • **REFRANES**: • **sobre ~s no hay disputa** • **de ~s no hay nada escrito** there's no accounting for tastes

g

4 (= *placer*) pleasure • **a ~**: • **aquí me encuentro** *o* **siento a ~** I feel at home *o* ease here • **tengo los pies a ~ y calientes** my feet are nice and warm • **acomodarse a su ~** to make o.s. at home, make o.s. comfortable • **con mucho ~** with pleasure • **lo haré con mucho ~** I'll be glad to do it, I'll be only too happy to do it • **con sumo ~** with great pleasure • **comer con ~** to eat heartily • **dar ~ a algn** to please sb, give pleasure to sb • **lo compré para dar ~ a los chiquillos** I bought it to please the kids • **da ~ hacerlo** it's nice to do it • **da ~ trabajar contigo** it's a pleasure to work with you • **da ~ verlos tan contentos** it's lovely to see them so happy • **tienen un entusiasmo que da ~** they show a wonderful enthusiasm • **leo por ~** I read for pleasure • **no lo hago por ~** I don't do it out of choice • **es por ~ que siga allí** (*LAm*) you'll wait there in vain • **tener el ~ de hacer algo** to have the pleasure of doing sth

5 (= *agrado*) liking • **al ~ de** to the liking of • **ser del ~ de algn** to be to sb's liking • **coger el ~ a algo** • **tomar ~ a algo** to take a liking to sth • **tener ~ por algo** to have a liking for sth

6 (*en presentaciones*) • **¡mucho ~!** • **¡tanto ~!** • **¡~ verlo!** (*LAm**) how do you do?, pleased to meet you • **el ~ es mío** how do you do?, the pleasure is (all) mine • **(tengo) mucho ~ en conocerle** I'm very pleased to meet you • **tengo mucho ~ en presentar al Sr Peláez** allow me to introduce Mr Peláez

7 (= *antojo*) whim, fancy • **a ~** at will, according to one's fancy

8 (*Cono Sur*) (= *estilo*) style, design, colour; (= *gama*) range, assortment

gustosamente (ADV) gladly, willingly • **accedí ~ a su petición** I gladly *o* willingly agreed to their request • **se sometió ~ a las preguntas de los periodistas** she gladly *o* willingly answered the journalists' questions • **aprovecho ~ esta oportunidad para desearle lo mejor** I am delighted to have this opportunity to wish you the best

gustoso (ADJ) **1** (= *complacido*) gladly • **lo hizo ~** he did it gladly • **acepto ~ su ofrecimiento** I gladly accept your offer

2 (= *sabroso*) tasty

3 (= *agradable*) [*lectura*] enjoyable; [*sensación*] pleasant, pleasing

gutapercha (SF) gutta-percha

gutifarra (SF) (*LAm*) = **butifarra**

gutural (ADJ) (*Ling*) guttural; (= *de la garganta*) throaty

Guyana (SF) Guyana

guyanés/esa (ADJ), (SM/F) Guyanese, Guyanan

Gzlez. (ABR) = **González**

g

Hh

H[1], **h**[1] ['atʃe] SF (= *letra*) H, h
H[2] ABR **1** = **hectárea(s)**
2 (*Quím*) (= **hidrógeno**) H
h[2] ABR (= **hora**) h., hr.
H. ABR **1** (*Econ*) (= **haber**) Cr
2 (*Rel*) (= **Hermano**) Br., Bro.
h. ABR **1** (= **hacia**) c
2 (= **habitantes**) pop
Ha ABR = **hectárea(s)**
ha[1] EXCL oh!
ha[2] ▹ **haber**
haba SF **1** (= *legumbre*) broad bean; [*de café*] coffee bean • **MODISMOS**: • **en todas partes cuecen ~s** it's the same the whole world over • **son ~s contadas** (*para expresar escasez*) they are few and far between; (= *es seguro*) it's a sure thing, it's a dead cert* ▸ **haba de las Indias** sweet pea ▸ **haba de soja** soya bean ▸ **haba verde** young broad bean
2 (*Vet*) tumour, tumor (*EEUU*)
3** (= *pene*) prick**
Habana SF • **La ~** Havana
habanera SF (*Mús*) habanera
habanero/a ADJ of/from Havana
SM/F native/inhabitant of Havana • **los ~s** the people of Havana
habano/a ADJ, SM/F = **habanero**
SM (= *puro*) Havana cigar
hábeas corpus SM habeas corpus
haber ▹ CONJUG 2j V AUX **1** (*en tiempos compuestos*) to have • **he comido** I have *o* I've eaten • **había ido al cine** he had gone *o* he'd gone to the cinema • **lo hubiéramos hecho** we would have done it • **¡~lo dicho!** you should have said! • **¡hubieran visto la casa!** (*esp LAm**) you should have seen the house! • **pero, ¿habráse visto (cosa igual)?** well, have you ever seen anything like it? • **de ~lo sabido** if I had known, if I'd known
2 • **~ de a** (*indicando obligación*) • **he de hacerlo** I have to do it, I must do it • **hemos de tener paciencia** we must be patient • **has de saber que ...** you should know that ... • **¿qué he de hacer?** what am I to do? • **los has de ver** (*LAm*) you'll see them
b (*indicando suposición*) • **han de ser las nueve** it must be about nine o'clock • **ha de llegar hoy** (*esp LAm*) he should get here today • **has de estar equivocado** (*esp LAm*) you must be mistaken
V IMPERS **1** • **hay** (*con sustantivo en singular*) there is; (*con sustantivo en plural*) there are • **hay un hombre en la calle** there is a man in the street • **hay mucho que hacer** there is so much to be done • **hubo una guerra** there was a war • **no hubo discusión** there was no discussion • **¿habrá tiempo?** will there be time? • **tomará lo que haya** he'll take whatever there is • **lo que hay es que ...** it's like this ..., the thing is ... • **algo debe de ~ para que se comporte así** there must be some reason for him acting like that • **hay sol** the sun is shining, it's sunny • **hay dos hombres en la calle** there are two men in the street • **no hay plátanos** there are no bananas • **ha habido problemas** there have been problems • **habían muchas personas** (*LAm*) there were many people there • **¿cuánto hay de aquí a Cuzco?** how far is it from here to Cuzco? • **los hay excelentes** some are excellent • **los hay buenos y malos** some are good and some are bad • **los hay que están confusos y asustados** some (people) are confused and afraid • **las hay en negro y blanco** they are available in black and white • **oportunistas los hay en todas partes** you'll find opportunists everywhere, there are always opportunists, wherever you go • **no hay**: • **no hay nada mejor que ...** there's nothing better than ... • **no hay como esta playa para disfrutar del surf** there's nothing like this beach for surfing • **no hay más que hablar** there's no more to be said, there's nothing more to say • **no hay quien te entienda** there's no understanding you • **¡aquí no hay quien duerma!** it's impossible to get any sleep round here! • **¡no hay de qué!** don't mention it!, not at all! • **¿qué hay?** (= *¿qué pasa?*) what's up?; (= *¿qué tal?*) how's it going?, how are things? • **¡qué hubo!** (*Chile, Méx, Ven**) how's it going?, how are things? • **MODISMOS**: • **como hay pocos** • **donde los haya**: • **un amigo como hay pocos** *o* **donde los haya** a friend in a million • **de lo que no hay**: • **¡eres de lo que no hay!** you're unbelievable! • **si los hay**: • **buen chico si los hay** a good lad if ever there was one
2 (*Com*) • **"¡mejores no hay!"** "there's none better!" • **¡hay helado!** (*dicho a voces*) ice cream!; (*en cartel*) ice cream sold • **¿hay puros?** do you have any cigars? • **"no hay entradas** *o* **localidades"** "sold out"
3 • **hay que**: • **hay que trabajar** one has to work, everyone must work • **hay que hacer algo** something has to be done • **hay que hacerlo** it has to be done • **no hay que hacer nada** you don't have to do anything • **hay que ser fuertes** we must be strong • **hay que trabajar más** (*como mandato*) you must work harder • **no hay que olvidar que ...** we mustn't forget that ... • **no hay que tomarlo a mal** there's no reason to take it badly, you mustn't get upset about it • **¡había que decírselo!** we'll have to tell him! • **¡había que verlo!** you should have seen it! • **no hay más que**: • **no hay más que leer las normas** all you have to do is read the rules • **no hay más que haber viajado un poco para saberlo** anyone who has done a bit of travelling would know • **MODISMO**: • **¡hay que ver!** (*sorpresa*) well I never!
4 (*indicando tiempo*) • **tres años ha** (*frm*) three years ago • **años ha que no les veo** (*frm, hum*) I haven't seen them for years
VT **1** (= *ocurrir*) • **en el encuentro habido ayer** in yesterday's game • **el descenso de temperatura habida ayer** the fall in temperature recorded yesterday • **la lista de las víctimas habidas** the list of casualties • **MODISMO**: • **habidos y por ~**: • **se trataron todos los temas habidos y por ~** they discussed every subject under the sun
2 (= *tener*) • **un hijo habido fuera del matrimonio** a child born out of wedlock • **los dos hijos habidos en su primer matrimonio** the two children from her first marriage • **Pepe, que Dios haya en su gloria** Pepe, God rest his soul • **bien haya ...** (*Rel*) blessed be ...
3 (*liter*) (= *obtener*) • **lee cuantos libros puede ~** he reads all the books he can lay his hands on
VPR **haberse 1** • **habérselas con algn** (= *tener delante*) to be up against sb; (= *enfrentarse*) to have it out with sb • **tenemos que habérnoslas con un enemigo despiadado** we are up against a ruthless enemy
2†† (= *comportarse*) to comport o.s. (*frm*) • **se ha habido con honradez** he has comported himself honourably
SM **1** (*en balance*) credit side • **¿cuánto tengo en el ~?** how much do I have in my account? • **la autora tiene seis libros en su ~** the author has six books to her credit • **asentar** *o* **pasar algo al ~ de algn** to credit sth to sb
2 haberes (= *ingresos*) salary (*sing*); (= *bienes*) assets • **no percibieron sus ~es** they weren't paid
habichuela SF kidney bean • **MODISMO**: • **ganarse las ~s** to earn one's living
hábil ADJ **1** (= *diestro*) skilful, skillful (*EEUU*) • **un político ~** a skilful politician • **fue una ~ estrategia diplomática** it was a skilful piece of diplomacy • **es muy ~ con la aguja** he's very handy *o* good with a needle • **¡muy ~! ya me has vuelto a endilgar el trabajo** (*hum*) very clever! you've landed me with the job again • **ser ~ para algo** to be good at sth • **es muy ~ para la carpintería** he's very good at carpentry • **Juan es muy ~ aparcando el coche** Juan is very good at parking the car • **es muy ~ para solucionar conflictos** he has a real knack for resolving conflicts
2 (*Jur*) competent; ▹ **día**
habilidad SF **1** (= *capacidad*) ability; (= *destreza*) skill • **tiene mucha ~ para la pintura** she's a very able painter • **un hombre de gran ~ política** a man of great political skill • **su ~ con el balón era de leyenda** his ball skills were legendary • **tiene una gran ~ para evitar enfrentamientos** he's very skilful *o* clever at avoiding confrontation • **tiene ~ manual** he's good *o* clever with his hands • **con ~: le sacó el secreto con ~** he cleverly *o* skilfully got the secret out of him • **defendió su argumento con ~** he defended his argument skilfully *o* cleverly ▸ **habilidades sociales** social skills
2 (*Jur*) competence

h

habilidoso ADJ handy, good with one's hands
habilitación SF **1** (= *título*) qualification, entitlement
2 [*de casa*] fitting out
3 (*Econ*) (*con dinero*) financing; (*Cono Sur*) (= *crédito*) credit in kind; (*CAm, Méx*) (= *anticipo*) advance, sub*
4 (= *oficina*) paymaster's, payroll office (EEUU)
5 (*Cono Sur*) (= *sociedad*) *offer of a partnership to an employee*
habilitado/a SMF paymaster
habilitar ▷ CONJUG 1a VT **1** [+ *persona*] (= *dar derecho a*) to qualify, entitle; (= *permitir*) to enable; (= *autorizar*) to empower, authorize
2 (= *preparar*) to equip, fit out • **las aulas están habilitadas con televisores** the rooms are equipped with TVs
3 (*Econ*) (*con dinero*) to finance • **~ a algn** (*Cono Sur*) (*Agr*) to make sb a loan in kind (*with the next crop as security*), give sb credit facilities; (*CAm, Méx**) (= *dar un anticipo*) to give sb an advance, sub sb*
4 (*Cono Sur*) (*Com*) to take into partnership
5 (*CAm*) (*Agr*) to cover, serve
6 (*Caribe*) (= *fastidiar*) to annoy, bother
hábilmente ADV **1** (= *diestramente*) skilfully, skillfully (EEUU)
2 (= *capazmente*) ably, expertly
3 (= *inteligentemente*) cleverly, smartly
4 (*pey*) (= *con argucias*) cunningly
habiloso* ADJ (*Cono Sur*) clever, skilful, skillful (EEUU)
habitabilidad SF (*gen*) habitability
habitable ADJ inhabitable
habitación SF **1** (= *cuarto*) room
▸ **habitación de matrimonio, habitación doble** double room ▸ **habitación individual** single room ▸ **habitación para invitados** guest room
2 (*Bio*) habitat, habitation
habitacional ADJ (*Cono Sur*) housing (*antes de s*)
habitáculo SM (*para vivir*) living space; (*en vehículo*) inside, interior
habitado ADJ [*isla, pueblo*] inhabited; [*casa, habitación*] lived-in; [*satélite, cohete*] manned
habitante SMF **1** (*gen*) inhabitant • **una ciudad de 10.000 ~s** a town of 10,000 inhabitants *o* people, a town with a population of 10,000
2 (= *vecino*) resident
3 (= *inquilino*) occupant, tenant
SM (*hum*) (= *piojo*) louse • **tener ~s** to have lice, have nits*
habitar ▷ CONJUG 1a VT [+ *zona, territorio*] to inhabit, live in; [+ *casa*] to live in, occupy, be the occupant of
VI (= *vivir*) to live
hábitat SM (PL: **hábitats** ['aβitas]) habitat
hábito SM **1** (= *costumbre*) habit • **una droga que crea ~** a habit-forming drug • **tener el ~ de hacer algo** to be in the habit of doing sth ▸ **hábitos de consumo** buying habits
2 (*Rel*) habit • MODISMOS: • **colgar los ~s** to leave the priesthood • **tomar el ~** [*hombre*] to take holy orders, become a monk; [*mujer*] to take the veil, become a nun ▸ **hábito monástico** monastic habit
habituado/a SM/F habitué
habitual ADJ (= *acostumbrado*) habitual, customary, usual; [*cliente, lector*] regular; [*criminal*] hardened • **mi restaurante ~** my usual restaurant • **como lector ~ de su revista** as a regular reader of your magazine
SMF [*de bar, tienda*] regular
habituar ▷ CONJUG 1e VT to accustom (**a** to)
VPR **habituarse** • **~se a** to become accustomed to, get used to

habla SF **1** (= *facultad*) speech • **dejar a algn sin ~** to leave sb speechless • **perder el ~** to lose the power of speech
2 (*Ling*) (= *idioma*) language; (= *dialecto*) dialect, speech • **de ~ francesa** French-speaking
3 (= *acción*) • **¡Benjamín al ~!** (*Telec*) Benjamín speaking! • **estar al ~** (*Telec*) to be on the line, be speaking; (*Náut*) to be within hailing distance • **ponerse al ~ con algn** to get in touch with sb • MODISMO: • **negar** *o* **quitar el ~ a algn** to stop speaking to sb, not be on speaking terms with sb
hablachento ADJ (*Caribe*) talkative
hablada SF **1** (*Cono Sur*) (= *charla*) speech
2 (*Méx*) **habladas** (= *fanfarronada*) boast
3 (*And**) (= *bronca*) scolding, telling-off*
4 (*CAm, Cono Sur, Méx*) (= *indirecta*) hint, innuendo; (= *chisme*) rumour, piece of gossip • MODISMO: • **echar ~s** to drop hints, make innuendoes
habladera SF **1** (*LAm*) talking, noise of talking
2 (*Cono Sur, Méx*) = **habladuría**
habladero SM (*Caribe**) piece of gossip
hablado ADJ **1** (= *dicho*) spoken • **la palabra hablada** the spoken word
2 • **bien ~** well-spoken • **mal ~** coarse, foul-mouthed
hablador(a) ADJ **1** (= *parlanchín*) talkative, chatty*
2 (= *chismoso*) gossipy, given to gossip
3 (*Méx*) (= *jactancioso*) boastful; (= *amenazador*) bullying
4 (*Caribe, Méx**) (= *mentiroso*) lying; (= *gritón*) loud-mouthed
SM/F **1** (= *locuaz*) great talker, chatterbox*
2 (= *chismoso*) gossip
habladuría SF **1** (= *rumor*) rumour, rumor (EEUU)
2 (= *injuria*) nasty remark
3 (= *chisme*) piece of gossip
4 habladurías gossip (*sing*), scandal (*sing*), tittle-tattle* (*sing*)
hablanchín ADJ talkative, garrulous
hablante ADJ speaking
SMF speaker
...hablante SUF • **castellanohablante** (*adj*) Castilian-speaking; (*smf*) Castilian speaker
hablantín ADJ = **hablanchín**
hablantina SF **1** (*And*) (*sin sentido*) gibberish, meaningless torrent
2 (*And, Caribe*) (= *cháchara*) empty talk, idle chatter
3 (*Caribe*) (= *algarabía*) hubbub, din
hablantino ADJ (*And, Caribe*),
hablantinoso ADJ (*And, Caribe*) = **hablador**
hablar ▷ CONJUG 1a VI to speak, talk (**a, con** to, **de** about, of) • **necesito ~ contigo** I need to talk *o* speak to you • **acabamos de ~ del premio** we were just talking *o* speaking about the prize • **¡mira quién fue a ~!** look who's talking! • **los datos hablan por sí solos** the facts speak for themselves • **que hable él** let him speak, let him have his say • **¡hable!** • **¡puede ~!** (*Telec*) you're through!, go ahead! (EEUU) • **¿quién habla?** (*Telec*) who's calling?, who is it? • **~ alto** to speak *o* talk loudly • **~ bajo** to speak *o* talk quietly, speak *o* talk in a low voice • **~ claro** (*fig*) to speak plainly *o* bluntly • **dar que ~ a la gente** to make people talk, cause tongues to wag • **hablaba en broma** she was joking • **vamos a ~ en confianza** this is between you and me • **¿hablas en serio?** are you serious? • **hacer ~ a algn** to make sb talk • **el vino hace ~** wine loosens people's tongues • **~ por ~** to talk for talking's sake, talk for the sake of it • **~ por teléfono** to speak on the phone • **hablamos por teléfono todos los días** we speak on the phone every day, we phone each other every day • **acabo de ~ por teléfono con ella** I was just on the phone to her • **~ solo** to talk *o* speak to o.s. • MODISMOS: • **¡ni ~!** • —**¿vas a ayudarle en la mudanza?** —**¡ni ~!** "are you going to help him with the move?" — "no way!" *o* — "you must be joking!" • **de eso ni ~** that's out of the question • **hablando del rey de Roma ...** talk of the devil ...;
▷ **cristiano, plata**
VT **1** [+ *idioma*] to speak • **habla bien el portugués** he speaks good Portuguese, he speaks Portuguese well • **"se habla inglés"** "English spoken" • **en el Brasil se habla portugués** they speak Portuguese in Brazil
2 (= *tratar de*) • **hay que ~lo todo** we need to discuss everything • **eso habrá que ~lo con tu padre** you'll have to discuss that with your father • **no hay más que ~** there's nothing more to be said about it • **exijo que se haga lo que yo digo y no hay más que ~** you will do what I say and that's that • **me gustan las películas de vaqueros y no hay más que ~** I happen to like westerns and I

HABLAR

¿"Speak" o "talk"?

▷ *Se traduce por* **speak** *cuando* **hablar** *tiene un sentido general, es decir, hace referencia a la emisión de sonidos articulados:*

Estaba tan conmocionado que no podía hablar
He was so shocked that he was unable to speak
Su padre antes tartamudeaba al hablar
Her father used to stutter when he spoke

▷ *También se emplea* **speak** *cuando nos referimos a la capacidad de* **hablar** *un idioma:*

Habla francés y alemán
She speaks French and German

▷ *Cuando* **hablar** *implica la participación de más de una persona, es decir, se trata de una conversación, una charla, o un comentario, entonces se traduce por* **talk.**

Es una de esas personas que no para de hablar
He's one of those people who won't stop talking

▷ *Para traducir la construcción* **hablar con alguien** *podemos utilizar* **talk to** (**talk with** *en el inglés de EE.UU.*) *o, si el uso es más formal, se puede emplear* **speak to** (**speak with** *en el inglés de EE.UU.*):

Vi a Manolo hablando animadamente con un grupo de turistas
I saw Manolo talking *o* speaking animatedly to *o* with a group of tourists

▷ *Si queremos especificar el idioma en que se desarrolla la conversación, se puede emplear tanto* **talk** *como* **speak**, *aunque este último se usa en un lenguaje más formal:*

Me sorprendió bastante verla hablar en francés con tanta soltura
I was surprised to see her talking *o* speaking (in) French so fluently

Para otros usos y ejemplos ver la entrada.

don't see why I should have to justify it
3 (*Méx*) (*Telec*) to (tele)phone
VPR **hablarse 1** (*uso impersonal*) • **se habla de que van a comprarlo** there is talk of their buying it • **pagaremos los cinco millones y no se hable más** we'll pay the five million and that'll be an end to it • **si es su deber que lo hagan y no se hable más** if it's their duty then they should do it and there's nothing more to be said
2 (*uso recíproco*) • **no se hablan** they are not on speaking terms, they are not speaking (to each other) • **no me hablo con él** I'm not speaking to him, I'm not on speaking terms with him

hablilla SF (= *rumor*) rumour, rumor (EEUU), story; (= *habladuría*) piece of gossip

hablista SMF good speaker, elegant user of language

habloteo SM incomprehensible talk

habré *etc* ▷ **haber**

Habsburgo SM Hapsburg

hacedero† ADJ practicable, feasible

hacedor(a) SM/F (*gen*) maker; (*Literat*) poet • **el (Supremo) Hacedor** the Creator, the Maker

hacendado/a ADJ landed, property-owning
SM/F (= *propietario*) (*de tierras*) landowner; (*LAm*) (*de ganado*) rancher; (*Caribe*) (*de ingenio*) sugar-plantation owner

hacendario ADJ (*Méx*) treasury (*antes de s*), budgetary

hacendista SMF economist, financial expert

hacendoso ADJ **1** (= *trabajador*) industrious, hard-working
2 (= *ocupado*) busy, bustling

hacer

VERBO TRANSITIVO
VERBO INTRANSITIVO
VERBO IMPERSONAL
VERBO PRONOMINAL

▷ CONJUG 2r

*Para las expresiones **hacer añicos, hacer gracia, hacerse ilusiones, hacer pedazos, hacerse de rogar, hacer el tonto, hacer las veces de** ver la otra entrada.*

VERBO TRANSITIVO
1 (*indicando actividad en general*) to do • **¿qué haces?** what are you doing? • **¿qué haces ahí?** what are you doing there? • **no sé qué ~** I don't know what to do • **hace y deshace las cosas a su antojo** she does as she pleases • **¡eso no se hace!** that's not done! • **no hizo nada por ayudarnos** she didn't do anything to help us • **haz todo lo posible por llegar a tiempo** do everything possible to arrive on time • **~ el amor** to make love • **~ la guerra** to wage war • MODISMOS: • **¡qué le vamos a ~!** what can you do?, there's nothing you can do • **~ algo por hacer:** • **no tiene sentido ~ las cosas por ~las** there's no point doing things just for the sake of it • **¡la hemos hecho buena!** (*iró*) we've really gone and done it now!* • **ya ha hecho otra de las suyas** he's been up to his old tricks again
2 (*en lugar de otro verbo*) to do • **él protestó y yo hice lo mismo** he protested and I did the same • **no viene tanto como lo solía ~** he doesn't come as much as he used to
3 (= *crear*) [+ *coche, escultura, juguete, ropa, pastel*] to make; [+ *casa*] to build; [+ *dibujo*] to do; [+ *novela, sinfonía*] to write • **~ dinero** to make money • **le cuesta trabajo ~ amigos** he finds it hard to make friends
4 (= *realizar*) [+ *apuesta, discurso, objeción*] to make; [+ *deporte, deberes*] to do; [+ *caca, pipí*] to do; [+ *nudo*] to tie; [+ *pregunta*] to ask; [+ *visita*] to pay; [+ *milagros*] to do, work • **el gato hizo miau** the cat went miaow, the cat miaowed • **el árbol no hace mucha sombra** the tree isn't very shady, the tree doesn't provide a lot of shade • **¿me puedes ~ el nudo de la corbata?** could you knot my tie for me? • **~ un favor a algn** to do sb a favour • **~ un gesto** (*con la cara*) to make *o* pull a face; (*con la mano*) to make a sign • **~ un recado** to do *o* run an errand • **~ ruido** to make a noise • **~ sitio** to make room • **~ tiempo** to kill time
5 (= *preparar*) [+ *cama, comida*] to make • **~ el pelo/las uñas a algn** to do sb's hair/nails • **~ la barba a algn** to trim sb's beard • **~ las maletas** to pack one's bags
6 (= *dedicarse a*) • **¿qué hace tu padre?** what does your father do? • **está haciendo turismo en África** he's gone touring in Africa • **~ cine** to make films • **~ teatro** to act
7 (= *actuar*) • **~ un papel** to play a role *o* part • **~ el papel de malo** to play the (part of the) villain
8 (= *sumar*) to make • **6 y 3 hacen 9** 6 and 3 make 9 • **este hace 100** this one makes 100 • **y cincuenta céntimos, hacen diez euros** and fifty cents change, which makes ten euros • **este hace el corredor número 100 en atravesar la meta** he's the 100th runner to cross the finishing line
9 (= *cumplir*) • **voy a ~ 30 años la próxima semana** I'm going to be 30 next week, it's my 30th birthday next week
10 (= *obligar*) (+ *infin*) to make • **les hice venir** I made them come • **siempre consigue ~me reír** she always manages to make me laugh • **le gustaba ~me rabiar** he enjoyed making me mad • **hágale entrar** show him in, have him come in • **me lo hizo saber** he told me about it, he informed me of it • **~ que** (+ *subjun*): • **yo haré que vengan** I'll make sure they come
11 (= *mandar*) (+ *infin*) • **hizo construirse un palacio** she had a palace built • **hicieron pintar la fachada del colegio** they had the front of the school painted
12 (= *transformar*) (+ *adj*) to make • **esto lo hará más difícil** this will make it more difficult • **~ feliz a algn** to make sb happy • **te hace más delgado** it makes you look slimmer • **has hecho de mí un hombre muy feliz** you've made me a very happy man
13 (= *pensar*) to think • **yo le hacía más viejo** I thought he was older, I had him down as being older • **te hacíamos en el Perú** we thought you were in Peru
14 (= *acostumbrar*) • **~ el cuerpo al frío** to get one's body used to the cold
15 (= *ejercitar*) • **~ dedos** to do finger exercises • **~ piernas** to stretch one's legs
16 • **~ a algn con** (= *proveer*): • **me hizo con dinero** he provided me with money

VERBO INTRANSITIVO
1 (= *comportarse*) • **haces bien en esperar** you're right to wait • **haces mal no contestando a sus llamadas** it's wrong of you not to answer his calls
• **~ como que** *o* **como si** to make as if • **hizo como que no se daba cuenta** *o* **como si no se diera cuenta** he made as if he hadn't noticed, he pretended not to have noticed • **hizo como si me fuera a pegar** he made as if to strike me
2 • **dar que ~** to cause trouble • **dieron que ~ a la policía** they caused *o* gave the police quite a bit of trouble
3 (= *importar*) • **no le hace** (*LAm*) it doesn't matter, never mind • MODISMO: • **¡no le hagas!** (*Méx**) don't give me that!*
4 (= *ser apropiado*) • **¿hace?** will it do?, is it all right?; (= *¿de acuerdo?*) is it a deal? • **la llave hace a todas las puertas** the key fits all the doors • **hace a todo** he's good for anything
5 (= *apetecer*) • **¿te hace que vayamos a tomar unas copas?** how about going for a drink?, what do you say we go for a drink? • **¿te hace un cigarrillo?** how about a cigarette?, do you fancy a cigarette?
6 (*seguido de preposición*) **hacer de** (*Teat*) to play the part of • **~ de malo** to play the villain
hacer por (= *intentar*) • **haz por verlo si puedes** try to get round to seeing him if you can • **~ por hacer algo** to try to do sth, make an effort to do sth

VERBO IMPERSONAL
1 (*con expresiones de tiempo atmosférico*) to be • **hace calor/frío** it's hot/cold • **hizo dos grados bajo cero** it was two degrees below zero • **¿qué tiempo hace?** what's the weather like? • **ojalá haga buen tiempo** I hope the weather's nice
2 (*con expresiones temporales*) • **hace tres años que se fue** he left three years ago, it's three years since he left • **hace tres años que no lo veo** I haven't seen him for three years, it's three years since I (last) saw him • **ha estado aquí hasta hace poco** he was here only a short while ago • **no hace mucho** not long ago • **hace un mes que voy** I've been going for a month • **¿hace mucho que esperas?** have you been waiting long? • **hace de esto varios años** it is some years since this happened • **desde hace cuatro años** for four years • **está perdido desde hace 15 días** it's been missing for a fortnight
3 (*LAm*) (= *haber, tener*) • **hace sed** I'm thirsty • **hace sueño** I'm sleepy

VERBO PRONOMINAL **hacerse**
1 (= *realizar, crear*) • **~se algo** [*uno mismo*] to make o.s. sth; [*otra persona*] to have sth made • **se hizo un jersey** he made himself a jumper • **¿os hicisteis muchas fotos?** did you take a lot of photos? • **todos los días me hago 3km andando** I walk 3km every day • **~se un retrato** to have one's portrait painted • **se hizo la cirugía estética** she had plastic surgery • **~se caca** to soil one's pants • **~se pipí** to wet o.s.; ▷ **idea, nudo²**
2 (= *cocinarse*) • **todavía se está haciendo la comida** the meal's still cooking • **deja que se haga bien la carne** make sure the meat is well done
3 (+ *infin*) **a** (= *conseguir*) • **deberías ~te oír** you should make your voice heard • **la respuesta no se hizo esperar** the answer was not long in coming
b (= *mandar*) • **se hizo traer caviar directamente de Rusia** she had caviar sent over from Russia • **se hizo cortar el pelo** she had her hair cut • **~se afeitar la barba** to have one's beard trimmed • **me estoy haciendo confeccionar un traje** I'm having a suit made
4 (= *reflexivo*) • **se hizo a sí mismo** he's a self-made man
5 (*recíproco*) • **se hacían caricias** they were caressing each other • **~se cortesías mutuamente** to exchange courtesies
6 (= *llegar a ser*) **a** (+ *sustantivo*) to become • **se hicieron amigos** they became friends • **~se enfermera** to become a nurse • **el sofá se hace cama** the sofa can be turned into a bed
b (+ *adj*) • **~se cristiano** to become a Christian • **quiere ~se famoso** he wants to be famous • **esto se está haciendo pesado**

this is getting *o* becoming tedious • **se está haciendo viejo** he's getting old • **se hace tarde** it's getting late • **~se grande** to grow tall • **con tanto ruido se me hace imposible trabajar** I can't work with all this noise

7 (*= parecer*) • **se me hizo largo/pesado el viaje** the journey felt long/boring • **se me hace que ...** (*esp LAm*) it seems to me that ..., I get the impression that ... • **se me hace que nos están engañando** it seems to me that *o* I get the impression that we're being deceived

8* (*= fingirse*) • **~se el interesante** to act all high and mighty • **~se de nuevas** to act all innocent • **~se el sordo** to pretend not to hear

9 (*= moverse*) • **~se atrás** to move back • **~se a un lado** (*de pie*) to move to one side; (*sentado*) to move over • **hazte para allá, que me siente** move up that way a bit so I can sit down

10 (*seguido de preposición*) **hacerse a** (*= acostumbrarse*) to get used to • **~se a una idea** to get used to an idea • **~se a hacer algo** to get used to doing sth • **¿te has hecho ya a levantarte temprano?** have you got used to getting up early yet?

hacerse con [*+ información*] to get hold of; [*+ ciudad, fortaleza*] to take • **logró ~se con una copia** he managed to get hold of a copy • **se hizo con una importante fortuna** he amassed a large fortune • **~se con el control de algo** to gain control of sth • **finalmente se hicieron con la victoria** they eventually managed to win

hacha¹ SF **1** (*= herramienta*) axe, ax (*EEUU*); (*pequeña*) hatchet • **MODISMOS**: • **desenterrar el ~ de guerra** to renew hostilities • **enterrar el ~ de guerra** to bury the hatchet ▸ **hacha de armas** battle-axe
2 • **MODISMOS**: • **dar con el ~ a algn** (*Cono Sur**) to tear sb off a strip* • **de ~** (*Chile*) unexpectedly, without warning • **estar con el ~** (*Cono Sur**) to have a hangover* • **de ~ y tiza** (*Cono Sur**) tough, virile; (*pey*) brawling • **ser un ~***: • **María es un ~** María is a real star • **es un ~ para el fútbol** he's brilliant at football, he's a brilliant footballer

hacha² SF **1** (*= vela*) large candle
2 (*= haz de paja*) bundle of straw

hacha³ ADJ (*Méx*) • **MODISMOS**: • **estar ~** to be ready • **ser ~ para la ropa** to be hard on one's clothes

hachador(a) SM/F (*CAm*) lumberjack

hachar ▹ CONJUG 1a VT (*LAm*) = **hachear**

hachazo SM **1** (*= golpe*) blow with an axe, blow with an ax (*EEUU*)
2 (*LAm*) (*= herida*) gash, axe wound, ax wound (*EEUU*)
3 (*And*) [*de caballo*] bolt, dash

hache SF (name of the letter) H • **MODISMOS**: • **por ~ o por be** for one reason or another • **llámalo ~** call it what you will • **volverse ~s y erres** (*And*) • **volverse ~s y cúes** (*Cono Sur*) to come to nothing, fall through

hachear ▹ CONJUG 1a VT (*= partir*) to hew, cut, cut down
VI (*= empuñar*) to wield an axe

hachemita ADJ Hashemite, Jordanian

hachero¹/a SM/F **1** (*= leñador*) lumberjack
2 (*Mil*) sapper

hachero² SM torch stand, sconce

hacheta SF (*gen*) adze; (*pequeña*) small axe, hatchet

hachís SM, **hachich** SM hashish, hash

hacho SM (*= fuego*) beacon; (*= colina*) beacon hill

hachón SM large torch, firebrand

hachuela SF = **hacheta**

hacia PREP **1** (*indicando dirección*) towards, in the direction of • **ir ~ las montañas** to go towards the mountains • **eso está más ~ el este** that's further (over) to the east, that's more in an easterly direction • **vamos ~ allá** let's go in that direction, let's go over that way • **¿~ dónde vamos?** where are we going? • **~ abajo** down, downwards • **~ adelante** forwards • **~ arriba** up, upwards • **~ atrás** backwards
2 (*con expresiones temporales*) about, near • **~ las cinco** about five, around five • **~ mediodía** about noon, around noon
3 (*= ante*) towards • **su hostilidad ~ la empresa** his hostility towards the firm

hacienda SF **1** (*= finca*) country estate; (*LAm*) ranch; (*Caribe*) sugar plantation
2 (*= bienes*) property
3 (*Cono Sur*) (*= ganado*) cattle, livestock
4 (*Econ*) **a** (*tb* **Ministerio de Hacienda**) ≈ Treasury, ≈ Exchequer, ≈ Treasury Department (*EEUU*) • **Hacienda me debe mucho dinero** the Inland Revenue owes me a lot of money
b (*tb* **delegación de Hacienda**) tax office
c (*tb* **hacienda pública**) • **supondría un desembolso enorme para la ~ pública** it would involve a massive outlay of public funds *o* money • **ha defraudado a la ~ pública** he has defrauded the public purse
5 haciendas† (*domésticas*) household chores

hacina SF (*= montón*) pile, heap; (*Agr*) stack, rick

hacinado ADJ **1** (*= amontonado*) [*cosas*] heaped(-up), piled(-up); (*Agr*) stacked(-up); [*gente, animales*] crowded together, packed together • **vivían ~s** they lived on top of each other • **la gente estaba hacinada** people were crowded *o* packed together
2 (*= acumulado*) accumulated

hacinamiento SM **1** (*= amontonamiento*) [*de cosas*] heaping (up), piling (up); (*Agr*) stacking; [*de gente, animales*] crowding, overcrowding
2 (*= acumulación*) accumulation

hacinar ▹ CONJUG 1a VT **1** (*= amontonar*) [*+ cosas, objetos*] to heap (up), pile (up); (*Agr*) to stack, put into a stack, put into a rick; [*+ gente, animales*] to cram
2 (*= acumular*) to accumulate, amass
3† (*= ahorrar*) to hoard
VPR **hacinarse** • **~se en** [*gente, animales*] to pack into, cram into

hada SF fairy • **cuento de ~s** fairy tale ▸ **hada buena** good fairy ▸ **hada madrina** fairy godmother

hado SM (*frm*) fate, destiny

haga ▹ **hacer**

hágalo usted mismo SM do-it-yourself

hagiografía SF hagiography

hagiógrafo/a SM/F hagiographer

hago ▹ **hacer**

haiga†* SM (*Esp*) big car, posh car*

haiku ['haiku] SM haiku

Haití SM Haiti

haitiano/a ADJ of/from Haiti
SM/F native/inhabitant of Haiti • **los ~s** the people of Haiti

hala EXCL **1** (*mostrando sorpresa*) (*gen*) wow!; (*= qué exageración*) come off it!*
2 (*= vamos*) come on!, let's go!
3 (*= deprisa*) get on with it!*, hurry up!
4 • **no quiero, ¡hala!** I don't want to, so there!
5 (*Náut*) heave!

halaco SM (*CAm*) piece of junk, useless object

halagador(a) ADJ **1** (*= adulador*) [*retrato, opinión*] flattering
2 (*= agradable*) [*propuesta*] pleasing, gratifying
SM/F (*= persona*) flatterer

halagar ▹ CONJUG 1h VT **1** (*= adular*) to flatter
2 (*= agradar*) to please, gratify • **es una perspectiva que me halaga** it's a pleasant prospect
3† (*= mostrar afecto*) to show affection to

halago SM **1** (*= adulación*) flattery
2 (*= gusto*) pleasure, delight; (*= satisfacción*) gratification
3† (*= atracción*) attraction • **los ~s de la vida en el campo** the attractions of country life

halagüeño ADJ **1** (*= prometedor*) [*perspectiva*] promising, rosy
2 (*= adulador*) [*opinión, observación*] flattering
3 (*= agradable*) pleasing; (*= atractivo*) attractive, alluring

halar ▹ CONJUG 1a VT, VI (*LAm*) = **jalar**

halcón SM **1** (*Zool*) falcon ▸ **halcón abejero** honey buzzard ▸ **halcón común, halcón peregrino** peregrine falcon
2 (*Pol*) hawk, hardliner • **los halcones y las palomas** the hawks and the doves
3 (*Méx*) (*= matón a sueldo*) young government-sponsored thug

halconería SF falconry

halconero/a SM/F falconer

halda SF **1** (*= falda*) skirt • **MODISMO**: • **de ~s o de mangas** at all costs, by hook or by crook
2 (*= arpillera*) sackcloth, coarse wrapping material

hale EXCL = **hala**

haleche SM anchovy

halibut [ali'βu] SM (PL: **halibuts** [ali'βu]) halibut

hálito SM (*frm*) **1** (*= aliento*) breath
2 (*= vapor*) vapour, vapor (*EEUU*), exhalation
3 (*poét*) gentle breeze

halitosis SF INV halitosis (*frm*), bad breath

hall [xol] SM (PL: **halls, halles** [xol]) [*de casa*] hall; [*de teatro, cine*] foyer; [*de hotel*] lounge, foyer

hallaca SF (*Ven*) tamale

hallador(a) SM/F finder

hallar ▹ CONJUG 1a VT **1** (*= encontrar*) **a** [*+ objeto, persona, respuesta, solución*] to find • **~án a los otros invitados en el salón** you will find the other guests in the living room • **el cadáver fue hallado ayer** the body was found yesterday • **tenemos que ~ una salida a la crisis** we have to find a way out of the crisis • **hallé a tu hermano muy cambiado** (*frm*) I thought your brother had changed a lot
b (*frm*) [*+ apoyo, oposición*] to meet with • **halló la oposición de todos los vecinos** he met with opposition from all the neighbours • **no halló la aprobación que esperaba para su proyecto** his plan did not meet with the approval he had hoped for • **halló la muerte en la montaña** he met his death on the mountain
2 (*= descubrir*) [*+ método*] to find, discover • **halló el modo de producirlo sintéticamente** he found *o* discovered a way to produce it synthetically • **~on que el estado del enfermo era peor de lo que creían** they found *o* discovered that the patient's condition was worse than they had thought
3 (*= averiguar*) [*+ motivo, razón*] to find out; [*+ información*] to obtain • **halló el motivo por el que no vinieron** he found out the reason why they hadn't come
4 (*Jur*) • **ser hallado culpable de algo** to be found guilty of sth
VPR **hallarse 1** (*= estar*) **a** (*indicando posición*) to be • **nos hallamos en Sevilla** we are in Seville • **la plaza en la que se halla la**

catedral the square which the cathedral is in, the square in which the cathedral stands • **se hallan entre las cien personas más ricas del mundo** they are among the hundred richest people in the world
b (*indicando estado*) to be • **solo ocho de las islas se hallan habitadas** only eight of the islands are inhabited • **en la reunión se hallaban presentes todos los directivos** all the directors were present at the meeting
2 (= *encontrarse*) to find o.s. • **de repente me hallé en medio de un grupo de desconocidos** I suddenly found myself in the middle of a group of strangers • **nos hallamos ante un ensayo excepcional** we're talking about *o* this is an exceptional essay • **~se con: se halló con numerosos obstáculos** she found herself up against numerous obstacles • **me hallé con que tenía más dinero del que pensaba** I realized that I had more money than I had thought
3 (= *sentirse*) to feel • **sentado aquí me hallo a gusto** it's so nice sitting here, I feel very relaxed *o* good sitting here • **es muy tímido, no se halla en las fiestas** he's very shy, he feels uncomfortable *o* awkward at parties • **no me hallo en una casa tan grande** I don't feel comfortable *o* right in such a big house

hallazgo SM **1** (= *acto*) discovery • **fue detenido tras el ~ de unos documentos que le incriminaban** he was arrested following the discovery of incriminating documents
2 (= *descubrimiento*) [*de la ciencia*] discovery; (*por investigador, institución*) finding • **los últimos ~s científicos** the latest scientific discoveries • **la revista en la que el investigador ha difundido sus ~s** the journal in which the researcher published his findings
3 (= *cosa hallada*) find • **el nuevo guitarra del grupo ha sido un ~** the band's new guitarist was a real find
4 (= *recompensa*) reward • **"500 pesos de hallazgo"** "500 pesos reward"

halo SM **1** [*de luna, sol*] halo
2 [*de santo*] halo
3 (= *fama*) aura

halogenado ADJ halogenated

halógeno ADJ halogenous, halogen (*antes de s*) • **lámpara halógena** halogen lamp
SM halogen

halón SM (*LAm*) = **jalón**

haltera SF (*Dep*) **1** (= *barra*) dumb-bell, bar-bell
2 halteras (= *pesos*) weights
SMF [*persona*] weight-lifter

halterofilia SF weight-lifting

halterófilo/a SM/F weight-lifter

hamaca SF **1** (= *cama*) hammock
2 (*Cono Sur*) (= *mecedora*) rocking chair; (= *columpio*) swing ▸ **hamaca plegable** deckchair

hamacar ▷ CONJUG 1g (*LAm*), **hamaquear** ▷ CONJUG 1a (*LAm*) VT **1** (= *mecer*) to rock
2 (= *columpiar*) to swing
3 (*Méx**) • **~ a algn** to keep sb on tenterhooks
4 (*Caribe*) (= *golpear*) to beat
VPR **hamacarse** (*LAm*) **1** (= *mecerse*) to rock
2 (= *columpiarse*) to swing

hambre SF **1** (= *necesidad de comer*) hunger • **una huelga de ~** a hunger strike • **estar con ~** to be hungry • **vengo con mucha ~** I'm terribly hungry, I'm starving* • **dar ~ a algn** to make sb hungry • **entrar ~: me está entrando ~** I'm starting to feel hungry, I'm getting hungry • **matar de ~ a algn** to starve sb to death • **en el colegio nos mataban de ~** they starved us at school • **morir de ~** to die of hunger, starve to death • **padecer** *o* **pasar ~** to go hungry • **quedarse con ~: se han quedado con ~** they are still hungry • **tener ~** to be hungry • MODISMOS: • **engañar** *o* **entretener el ~** to stave off hunger • **tengo un ~ que no veo*** I'm absolutely starving* • **tener un ~ canina** *o* **de lobo** to be ravenous, be ravenously hungry • **se ha juntado el ~ con las ganas de comer** what an explosive combination they are!, they're a right pair! • **ser más listo que el ~*** to be razor sharp*, be as sharp as a needle • **matar el ~** to keep one going, take the edge off one's appetite • REFRÁN: • **a buen ~ no hay pan duro** beggars can't be choosers; ▷ **muerto, salario**
2 (= *escasez general*) famine • **la guerra ha traído muerte y ~ al país** the war has brought death and famine to the country
3 (= *deseo*) • **~ de algo** hunger for sth • **políticos con ~ de poder** politicians with a hunger for power • **el ~ de gloria del protagonista** the hero's hunger for glory • **tener ~ de justicia/triunfos** to be hungry for justice/victory

hambreado ADJ (*LAm*) = **hambriento**

hambreador(a) SM/F (*Chile, Perú*) [*de personas*] exploiter

hambrear ▷ CONJUG 1a VT (*Chile*)
1 (= *explotar*) [+ *personas*] to exploit
2 (= *hacer pasar hambre*) to starve
VI to starve, be hungry

hambriento/a ADJ **1** (= *con hambre*) hungry; (= *famélico*) starving • **venimos ~s** we're starving*, we're very hungry • **unas tristes imágenes de niños ~s** very sad pictures of hungry *o* starving children
2 • **~ de** hungry for • **políticos ~s de poder** politicians hungry for power • **están ~s de afecto** they are starved of affection
SM/F (*con hambre*) hungry person; (*en situación desesperada*) starving person • **los ~s** the hungry • **dar de comer al ~** to feed the hungry

hambrón* ADJ (*Esp*) greedy

hambruna SF **1** famine
2 (*And, Cono Sur*) = **hambrusia**

hambrusia SF (*Col, Méx*) ravenous hunger • **tener ~** to be famished

Hamburgo SM Hamburg

hamburgués/esa ADJ of/from Hamburg
SM/F native/inhabitant of Hamburg • **los hamburgueses** the people of Hamburg

hamburguesa SF hamburger, burger

hamburguesera SF hamburger-maker

hamburguesería SF burger bar, burger joint*

hamo SM fish-hook

hampa SF (*gen*) criminal underworld • **gente del ~** criminals, riffraff; (*Hist*) rogue's life, vagrancy

hampesco ADJ underworld (*antes de s*), criminal

hampón/ona SM/F thug

hámster SM (PL: **hámsters**) hamster

han ▷ **haber**

hand [xan] SM (*CAm*) (*Dep*) handball

handbol ['xandbol] SM handball

handbolista SMF handball player

handicap SM, **hándicap** SM (PL: **handicaps, hándicaps**) handicap

handling ['xanlin] SM (*Aer*) baggage handling

hangar SM (*Aer*) hangar

Hannover SM, **Hannóver** SM Hanover

Hanovre SM Hanover

hápax SM INV hapax, nonce-word

happening ['xapenin] SM (PL: **happenings**) (*Arte*) happening

haragán/ana ADJ (= *vago*) idle, lazy
SM/F (= *holgazán*) layabout, idler
SM (*Caribe*) (= *fregona*) mop

haragana* SF (*CAm*) (= *silla reclinable*) reclining chair

haraganear ▷ CONJUG 1a VI to idle, loaf about, laze around

haraganería SF idleness, laziness

harakiri SM hara-kiri • **hacerse el ~** to commit hara-kiri

harapiento ADJ tattered, in rags

harapo SM **1** (= *andrajo*) rag • MODISMO: • **estar hecho un ~** to go about dressed in rags
2 harapos (*Méx‡*) clothes, clobber‡, threads (*EEUU**)

haraposo ADJ = **harapiento**

haraquiri SM = **harakiri**

haras SM INV (*Cono Sur, Perú, Ven*) stud farm

hard [xar] SM hardware

hardware ['xarwer] SM hardware, computer hardware

haré ▷ **hacer**

harén SM harem

harina SF **1** flour • MODISMOS: • **eso es ~ de otro costal** that's a different kettle of fish, that's another story • **estar en ~s** (*And**) to be broke* • **meterse en ~** to get down to it ▸ **harina animal, harina cárnica** meat and bone meal ▸ **harina con levadura** self-raising flour ▸ **harina de arroz** ground rice ▸ **harina de avena** oatmeal ▸ **harina de flor** extra fine flour ▸ **harina de huesos** bonemeal ▸ **harina de maíz** cornflour, corn starch (*EEUU*) ▸ **harina de patata** potato flour ▸ **harina de pescado** fish-meal ▸ **harina de soja** soya flour ▸ **harina de trigo** wheat flour ▸ **harina integral** wholemeal flour ▸ **harina lacteada** malted milk ▸ **harina leudante** (*Cono Sur*) ▷ **harina con levadura**
2 (*And*) (= *pedacito*) small piece • **una ~ de pan** a bit of bread
3 (*Caribe‡*) (= *dinero*) money, dough‡

harinear ▷ CONJUG 1a VI (*Caribe*) to drizzle

harineo SM (*Caribe*) drizzle

harinero/a ADJ flour (*antes de s*)
SM/F (= *comerciante*) flour merchant
SM (= *recipiente*) flour bin

harinoso ADJ floury

harnear ▷ CONJUG 1a VT (*LAm*) to sieve, sift

harnero SM sieve

harpagón‡ ADJ (*And*) very thin, skinny

harpillera SF sacking, sackcloth

hartar ▷ CONJUG 1a VT **1** (= *cansar*) • **me harta tanta televisión** I get tired of *o* fed up with* *o* sick of* watching so much television • **los estás hartando con tantas bobadas** they're getting tired of *o* fed up with* *o* sick of* your fooling around • **ya me está hartando que siempre me hable de lo mismo** I'm getting tired of *o* fed up with* *o* sick of* him always talking about the same thing
2 (= *atiborrar*) • **~ a algn a** *o* **de** [+ *comida, alcohol*] to fill sb full of • **nos hartan a chistes malos** we get fed up with* *o* sick of* *o* tired of their bad jokes • **el maestro los harta a deberes** their teacher overloads them with homework • **lo ~on a palos** they gave him a real beating
3 (*CAm*) (= *maldecir de*) to malign, slander
VI (= *cansar*) • **todos estos tópicos manidos ya hartan** all these worn-out clichés get so boring, you get tired of *o* get fed up with* *o* sick of* all these worn-out clichés
VPR **hartarse 1** (= *cansarse*) to get fed up* • **un día se ~á y se marchará** one of these days she'll get tired *o* get fed up* of it all and leave • **~se de algo/algn** to get tired of sth/sb, get fed up with sth/sb*, get sick of sth/sb* • **me estoy hartando de todo esto** I'm getting tired of *o* fed up with* *o* sick of* all this • **ya me he hartado de esperar** I've had enough of waiting, I'm tired of *o* fed up with* *o* sick of* waiting • **se hartó de que siempre lo hicieran blanco de sus burlas** he

got fed up with* *o* sick of* *o* tired of always being the butt of their jokes
2 (= *atiborrarse*) • **~se de** [+ *comida*] to gorge o.s. on, stuff o.s. with* • **se ~on de uvas** they gorged themselves on grapes, they stuffed themselves with grapes* • **le gustaría poder ~se de marisco** he'd like to be able to have a real blowout on seafood • **me harté de agua** I drank gallons *o* loads of water*
3 (= *saciarse*) • **~se a** *o* **de algo**: • **en esa exposición puedes ~te de cultura griega** in that exhibition you can get your fill of Greek culture • **fui al museo para ~me de buena pintura** I went to the museum to see plenty of good paintings • **~se a** *o* **de hacer algo**: • **en vacaciones me harté a** *o* **de tomar el sol** I sunbathed all day on holiday • **nos hartamos de reír** we laughed till we were fit to burst • **comieron hasta ~se** they gorged *o* stuffed* themselves • **bebieron champán hasta ~se** they drank their fill of champagne • **dormimos hasta ~nos** we slept as long as we wanted

hartazgo (SM) [*de comida*] surfeit, glut • **darse un ~** [*de comida*] to eat too much, overeat; [*de noticias, televisión*] to have too much

harto (ADJ) **1** (= *cansado*) fed up* • **¡ya estamos ~s!** we've had enough!, we're fed up!* • **¡me tienes ~!** I'm fed up with you!* • **estar ~ de algo/algn** to be tired of sth/sb, be fed up with sth/sb*, be sick of sth/sb* • **estaban un poco ~s de tanta publicidad** they were a bit tired of all the publicity, they were a bit fed up with *o* sick of all the publicity* • **está ~ de su jefe** he's fed up with *o* sick of his boss* • **estar ~ de hacer algo** to be tired of doing sth, be fed up of doing sth*, be sick of doing sth* • **está ~ de no tener dinero** he's tired *o* fed up* *o* sick of* not having any money • **estar ~ de que** (+ *subjun*) to be fed up with* (+ *ger*), be sick of* (+ *ger*) • **estamos ~s de que lleguen siempre tarde** we're tired of *o* fed up with* *o* sick of* them arriving late
2 (= *lleno*) • **~ de algo** stuffed with sth*
3 (= *mucho*) **a** (*frm*) • **ocurre con harta frecuencia** it happens very often *o* very frequently • **tienen hartas razones para sentirse ofendidos** they have plenty of reasons to feel offended
b (*LAm*) plenty of, a lot of • **usaste harta harina** you used plenty of *o* a lot of flour • **~s chilenos** plenty of *o* a lot of Chileans • **ha habido ~s accidentes** there have been a lot of *o* plenty of accidents
(ADV) **1** (*con adjetivo*) **a** (*frm*) very, extremely • **una tarea ~ difícil** a very difficult task, an extremely difficult task
b (*LAm*) very • **llegaron ~ cansados** they were very tired when they arrived
2 (*LAm*) (*con adverbio*) very • **lo sé ~ bien** I know that very well *o* all too well
3 (*LAm*) (*con verbo*) a lot • **te quiero ~** I love you a lot • **dormí ~ anoche** I slept a lot last night
(PRON) (*LAm*) • **hace ~ que no lo veo** it's been a long time since I saw him • **—¿queda leche? —sí, harta** "is there any milk left?" — "yes, lots" • **falta ~ para llegar** there's still a long way to go

hartón* (SM) **1** • **darse un ~ de algo** to stuff oneself with sth* • **me di un ~ de pasteles** I stuffed myself with cakes • **se dio un ~ de leer novelas policíacas** he had a binge of reading crime novels • **nos dimos un ~ de reír** we killed ourselves laughing • **me di un ~ de llorar en el cine** I cried my eyes out in the cinema
2 (*LAm*) (= *banana*) large banana
(ADJ) (*CAm, Méx, Ven*) gluttonous

hartura (SF) **1** (= *cansancio*) • **otra vez fútbol, ¡qué ~!** football again, I'm fed up with it! *o* I'm sick of it!* • **muchos votaron a la oposición por ~ hacia el gobierno** many people voted for the opposition because they had had enough of *o* they were tired of the government
2 (= *hartazgo*) • **la comida picante da sensación de ~** spicy food leaves you feeling full
3 (*frm*) (= *abundancia*) abundance, plenty • **con ~** in abundance, in plenty

has ▷ **haber**

has (ABR) = **hectáreas**

hashtag ['xastag] (SM) (PL: **hashtags**) (*en Twitter*) hashtag

hasídico (ADJ) Hassidic

hasidita (SMF) Hassid

hasta (PREP) **1** (*en el espacio*) (*gen*) to, as far as; (= *hacia arriba*) up to; (= *hacia abajo*) down to • **fuimos juntos ~ el primer pueblo, luego nos separamos** we went to *o* as far as the first village together, then we split up • **sus tierras llegan ~ las montañas** their lands stretch to *o* as far as the mountains • **te acompaño, pero solo ~ el final de la calle** I'll go with you, but only to *o* up to *o* down to the end of the street • **con las lluvias el agua subió ~ aquí** with all the rain the water came up to here • **el vestido me llega ~ las rodillas** the dress comes down to my knees • **¿~ dónde ...?** how far ...? • **¿~ dónde vais?** how far are you going? • **~ tan lejos** that far, as far as that • **—fuimos andando ~ la ermita —¿~ tan lejos?** "we walked to *o* as far as the chapel" — "that far?" *o* "as far as that?" • **no creía que íbamos a llegar ~ tan lejos** I didn't think we'd get this far
2 (*en el tiempo*) until, till • **se va a quedar ~ el martes** she's staying until *o* till Tuesday • **no me levanto ~ las nueve** I don't get up until *o* till nine o'clock • **no iré ~ después de la reunión** I won't go until *o* till after the meeting • **falta una semana ~ los exámenes** there's a week to go to *o* until *o* till the exams • **¿siempre escuchas música ~ tan tarde?** do you always listen to music so late (at night)? • **el ~ ayer presidente de nuestro club** the hitherto president of our club (*frm*) • **~ ahora** so far, up to now • **~ ahora nadie se ha quejado** so far no one has complained, no one has complained up to now • **~ ahora no se había quejado nadie** no one had complained before *o* until now *o* till now • **tuve problemas al principio, pero luego las cosas se tranquilizaron y ~ ahora** I had problems at the beginning but then things calmed down and since then it's been OK • **¿~ cuándo ...?** how long ... for? • **¿~ cuándo podemos seguir así?** how long can we carry on like this for? • **¿~ cuándo os quedáis?** how long are you staying (for)? • **~ entonces** until then, (up) till then • **~ la fecha** to date • **~ el momento** so far, up to now, thus far (*frm*) • **~ nueva orden** until further notice
3 (*con cantidades*) (*gen*) up to; (*con valor enfático*) as much as/as many as • **puedes gastar ~ 200 euros** you can spend up to 200 euros • **duerme ~ diez horas diarias** he sleeps up to ten hours a day • **podemos llegar a producir ~ 50 toneladas** we can produce as much as 50 tons • **llegó a haber ~ 500 invitados** there were as many as 500 guests
4 (*en expresiones de despedida*) • **~ ahora** see you in a minute • **~ la vista** see you, so long • **~ luego** see you, bye* • **~ más ver** see you again • **~ nunca** I hope I never see you again • **~ otra** see you again • **~ pronto** see you soon • **~ siempre*** goodbye, farewell (*frm*)
5 (*CAm, Col, Méx*) not ... until, not ... till • **~ mañana viene** he's not coming until *o* till tomorrow • **lo hizo ~ el martes** he didn't do it until *o* till Tuesday • **~ hoy lo conocí** I only met him today, I hadn't met him until *o* till today
(CONJ) **1** • **~ que** until, till • **vivió aquí ~ que murió su mujer** he lived here until *o* till his wife died • **no me iré ~ que (no) me lo des** I won't go until *o* till you give it to me
2 (+ *infin*) until, till • **no se fueron ~ acabar** they didn't leave until *o* till they were finished
(ADV) (= *incluso*) even • **~ en Valencia hiela a veces** even in Valencia it freezes sometimes • **la música estaba tan alta que se oía ~ desde la calle** the music was so loud that you could even hear it from the street

> **HASTA**
>
> *La preposición* **hasta** *tiene varias traducciones posibles, dependiendo de si se emplea en expresiones de tiempo o de lugar.*
>
> **En expresiones de tiempo**
>
> ▷ *Generalmente se traduce por* **till** *o* **until. Till** *tiene un uso más informal que* **until** *y no suele ir al principio de la frase.*
>
> **El paquete no me llegó hasta dos semanas después**
> The parcel did not arrive until *o* till two weeks later
> **Hasta entonces las cosas nos iban bien**
> Until then things were going well for us
>
> ▷ *Además,* **hasta** *también se puede traducir por* **to** *en la construcción* **desde ... hasta ...**:
>
> **Estoy aquí todos los días desde las ocho hasta las tres**
> I'm here every day from eight until *o* till *o* to three
> **Te estuve esperando desde las once de la mañana hasta la una de la tarde**
> I was waiting for you from eleven in the morning until *o* till *o* to one in the afternoon
>
> **En expresiones de lugar**
>
> ▷ *Cuando usamos* **hasta** *en expresiones de lugar, podemos traducirlo por* **(up/down) to** *o por* **as far as**:
>
> **Caminó hasta el borde del acantilado**
> He walked (up) to *o* as far as the edge of the cliff
> **¿Vamos hasta la orilla?**
> Shall we go down to the shore?
> **Ya anda solo hasta el sofá**
> He can already walk on his own as far as *o* (up) to the sofa
>
> *Para otros usos y ejemplos ver la entrada.*

hastiador (ADJ) = hastiante

hastial (SM) (*Arquit*) gable end

hastiante (ADJ) **1** (= *que cansa*) wearisome
2 (= *que aburre*) boring
3 (= *asqueante*) sickening

hastiar ▷ CONJUG 1C (VT) **1** (= *cansar*) to weary
2 (= *aburrir*) to bore
3 (= *asquear*) to sicken, disgust
(VPR) **hastiarse** • **~se de** to tire of, get fed up with*

hastío (SM) **1** (= *cansancio*) weariness
2 (= *aburrimiento*) boredom
3 (= *asco*) disgust

hatajo (SM) lot, collection • **un ~ de sinvergüenzas** a bunch of crooks

hatillo (SM) = hato

hato (SM) **1** [*de ropa*] bundle • **MODISMOS**: • **echarse el ~ a cuestas** • **liar el ~** to pack up

• ~ y garabato (*And, Caribe**) all that one has • **menear el ~ a algn** to beat sb up* • **revolver el ~** to stir up trouble
2 (*Agr*) [*de ganado*] herd; [*de ovejas*] flock
3 [*de gente*] group, crowd; (*pey*) bunch, gang
4 [*de objetos, observaciones*] lot, heap
5 (*LAm*) (= *rancho*) cattle ranch
6 (= *víveres*) provisions (*pl*)
7 (= *choza*) shepherd's hut
8 (= *parada*) stopping place (*of migratory flocks*)
Hawai SM (*tb* **islas Hawai**) Hawaii
hawaianas SFPL (*esp LAm*) (= *chanclas*) flip flops, thongs
hawaiano/a ADJ of/from Hawaii
SM/F native/inhabitant of Hawaii • **los ~s** the people of Hawaii
hay ▹ haber
haya¹ ▹ haber
haya² SF beech, beech tree
Haya SF • **La ~** The Hague
hayaca SF (*And*) tamale; (*Caribe*) *stuffed cornmeal pasty*
hayal SM, **hayedo** SM beechwood
hayo SM (*Bot*) coca, coca leaves
hayuco SM beechnut; **hayucos** beechnuts, beechmast (*sing*)
haz¹ SM **1** (= *manojo*) bundle, bunch; [*de trigo*] sheaf; [*de paja*] truss
2 (= *rayo*) beam ▸ **haz de electrones** electron beam ▸ **haz de luz** beam of light ▸ **haz de partículas** particle beam ▸ **haz láser** laser beam
3 **haces** (*Hist, Pol*) fasces
haz² SF **1** (= *lado derecho*) right side
2 (= *superficie*) face, surface • **de dos haces** two-faced ▸ **haz de la tierra** face of the earth
haz³ ▹ hacer
haza SF small field, plot of arable land
hazaña SF feat, exploit, deed • **las ~s del héroe** the hero's exploits, the hero's great deeds • **sería una ~** it would be a great achievement, it would be a great thing to do
hazañería SF fuss, exaggerated show, histrionics (*pl*)
hazañero ADJ [*persona*] dramatic, histrionic, given to making a great fuss; [*acción*] histrionic, exaggerated
hazañoso ADJ [*persona*] heroic, gallant, dauntless; [*acción*] heroic, doughty
hazmerreír SMF INV laughing stock
HB SM ABR (*Esp*) (*Pol*) = **Herri Batasuna**
he¹ ▹ haber
he² ADV (*frm*) • **he aquí** here is, here are • **¡heme aquí!** here I am! • **¡helo aquí!** here it is! • **¡helos allí!** there they are! • **he aquí la razón de que ...** • **he aquí por qué ...** that is why ... • **he aquí los resultados** these are the results, here you have the results
heavy ['xeβi] (PL: **heavies, heavys**) ADJ
1 [*música, grupo*] heavy metal
2‡ (= *duro*) heavy‡
SMF heavy metal fan
SM (= *música*) heavy metal
hebdomadario (*frm*) ADJ weekly
SM weekly
hebilla SF buckle, clasp
hebra SF **1** [*de hilo*] thread
2 (*Bot*) (= *fibra*) fibre, fiber (*EEUU*); [*de madera*] grain; [*de gusano de seda*] thread • **tabaco de ~** loose tobacco
3 [*de metal*] vein, streak
4 **hebras** (*poét*) hair
5 • MODISMOS: • **de una ~** (*Cono Sur, Méx**) all at once • **pegar la ~** (= *entablar conversación*) to start *o* strike up a conversation; (= *hablar mucho*) to chatter, talk nineteen to the dozen • **no quedar ni ~** (*And**): • **no quedó ni ~ de comida** there wasn't a scrap of food left • **romperse la ~** (*Méx**): • **se rompió la ~ entre los dos amigos** the two friends fell out

hebraico ADJ Hebraic
hebraísta SMF Hebraist
hebreo/a ADJ Hebrew
SM/F Hebrew • **los ~s** the Hebrews
SM (*Ling*) Hebrew • MODISMO: • **jurar en ~†** to blow one's top*
Hébridas SFPL Hebrides
hebroso ADJ (= *fibroso*) fibrous; [*carne*] stringy
hecatombe SF **1** (= *catástrofe*) disaster • **¡aquello fue la ~!** what a disaster that was!
2 (= *carnicería*) slaughter, butchery
3 (*Hist*) hecatomb
heces SFPL ▹ hez
hechicería SF **1** (= *brujería*) sorcery, witchcraft
2 (= *maleficio*) spell
3 (= *encantamiento*) spell, charm
hechicero/a ADJ **1** [*rito, poder*] magic, magical
2 [*labios, ojos*] enchanting, bewitching
SM/F (= *brujo*) sorcerer/sorceress, wizard/witch; [*de tribu*] witch doctor
hechizado ADJ **1** (= *víctima de un hechizo*) under a spell
2 (= *cautivado*) captivated
hechizante ADJ enchanting, bewitching
hechizar ▹ CONJUG 1f VT **1** (= *embrujar*) to bewitch, cast a spell on
2 (= *cautivar*) to fascinate, charm, enchant
hechizo ADJ (*And, Cono Sur, Méx*) home-made, locally produced, craft (*antes de s*)
SM **1** (= *brujería*) sorcery, witchcraft
2 (= *encantamiento*) enchantment; (= *maleficio*) spell • **un ~** a magic spell, a charm
3 (= *atracción*) fascination
4 • **~s** (= *encantos*) charms
hecho PP *de* **hacer**
ADJ **1** (= *realizado*) done • **bien ~** well done • **mal ~** badly done • **si le dijiste que no fuera, mal ~** if you told him not to go, then you were wrong *o* you shouldn't have • **¡hecho!** (= *de acuerdo*) agreed!, it's a deal! • MODISMO: • **lo ~, ~ está** what's done cannot be undone • REFRÁN: • **a lo ~ pecho** it's no use crying over spilt milk
2 (= *manufacturado*) made • **¿de qué está ~?** what's it made of? • **bien ~** well made • **mal ~** poorly made • **~ a mano** handmade • **~ a máquina** machine-made • **~ a la medida** made-to-measure • **se compra la ropa hecha** he buys his clothes off-the-peg
3 (= *acabado*) done, finished; (= *listo*) ready • **el trabajo ya está ~** the work is done *o* finished • **¿está hecha la comida?** is dinner ready?
4 (*Culin*) **a** (= *maduro*) [*queso, vino*] mature; [*fruta*] ripe
b (= *cocinado*) • **muy ~** (= *bien*) well-cooked; (= *demasiado*) overdone • **no muy ~** • **poco ~** underdone, undercooked • **un filete poco** *o* **no muy ~** a rare steak
5 (= *convertido en*) • **el baño está ~ un asco** the bathroom is disgusting • **usted está ~ un chaval** you look so young! • **ella, hecha una furia, se lanzó** she hurled herself furiously • **estará hecha una mujercita** she must be quite grown up now
6 [*persona*] • **bien ~** well-proportioned • **mal ~** ill-proportioned • MODISMO: • **~ y derecho**: • **un hombre ~ y derecho** a (fully) grown man • **soldados ~s y derechos** proper soldiers
7 (= *acostumbrado*) • **estar ~ a** to be used to
SM **1** (= *acto*) • **los vecinos quieren ~s** the residents want action • **~s, y** *o* **que no palabras** actions speak louder than words ▸ **hecho consumado** fait accompli ▸ **hecho de armas** feat of arms ▸ **Hechos de los Apóstoles** Acts of the Apostles

2 (= *realidad*) fact; (= *suceso*) event • **es un ~** it's a fact • **es un ~ conocido** it's a well-known fact • **el ~ es que ...** the fact is that ... • **volvamos a los ~s** let's get back to the facts • **hay que clarificar los ~s** the facts must be clarified • **un ~ histórico** (= *acontecimiento*) an historic event; (= *dato*) a historical fact • **los ~s acaecidos ayer** yesterday's events • **el lugar de los ~s** the scene of the incident ▸ **hecho imponible** (*Econ*) taxable source of income
3 • **de ~** in fact, as a matter of fact • **de ~, yo no sé nada de eso** in fact *o* as a matter of fact, I don't know anything about that
4 (*Jur*) • **de ~ y de derecho** de facto and de jure
hechor¹(a) SM/F **1** (*Jur*) perpetrator
2 (*Cono Sur*) = **malhechor**
hechor² SM (*LAm*) (= *semental*) stud donkey
hechura SF **1** (*Cos*) (= *confección*) making-up, confection (*frm*); (= *corte*) cut • **de ~ sastre** tailor-made • **las ~s** the cost of making up
2 (= *forma*) form, shape • **a ~ de** like, after the manner of • MODISMOS: • **no tener una ~** (*LAm*) to be a dead loss • **tener ~s de algo** to show an aptitude for sth
3 [*cuadro, escultura*] craftsmanship, workmanship • **de exquisita ~** of exquisite workmanship
4 (= *creación*) (*gen*) making, creation, product; [*persona*] creature, puppet • **él es una ~ del ministro** he is a creature *o* puppet of the minister • **no tiene ~** it can't be done • **somos ~ de Dios** we are God's handiwork
hectárea SF hectare (= *2.471 acres*)
héctico ADJ (*frm*) consumptive
hectogramo SM hectogramme, hectogram (EEUU)
hectolitro SM hectolitre, hectoliter (*EEUU*)
Héctor SM Hector
heder ▹ CONJUG 2g VI **1** (= *apestar*) to stink (**a** of), reek (**a** of)
2 (= *molestar*) to be annoying
hediondez SF **1** (= *olor*) stink, stench
2 (= *cosa*) stinking thing
hediondo ADJ **1** (= *maloliente*) stinking, foul-smelling
2 (= *asqueroso*) repulsive
3 (= *sucio*) filthy
4 (= *obsceno*) obscene
5 (= *inaguantable*) annoying, unbearable
hedonismo SM hedonism
hedonista ADJ hedonistic
SMF hedonist
hedor SM stink (**a** of), stench (**a** of)
hegemonía SF hegemony
hégira SF Hegira
helada SF frost ▸ **helada blanca** hoarfrost ▸ **helada de madrugada** early-morning frost
heladamente ADV icily
heladera SF (*Cono Sur*) refrigerator, fridge*, icebox (EEUU); ▹ **heladero**
heladería SF ice-cream parlour, ice-cream parlor (EEUU)
heladero/a ADJ ice-cream (*antes de s*)
SM/F ice-cream seller; ▹ **heladera**
helado ADJ **1** (= *congelado*) [*lago, río*] frozen; [*carretera*] icy
2 (= *muy frío*) [*bebida, comida*] ice-cold; [*mirada*] frosty, icy • **¡estoy ~!** I'm frozen!, I'm freezing! • **¡tengo las manos heladas!** my hands are frozen *o* freezing *o* like ice! • **me quedé ~ de frío** I was frozen
3 (= *pasmado*) • **dejar ~ a algn** to dumbfound sb • **¡me deja usted ~!** you amaze me! • **¡me quedé ~!** (*de sorpresa*) I couldn't believe it!; (*de miedo*) I was scared stiff!
4 (*Caribe*) (*Culin*) iced, frosted

(SM) ice cream ▸ **helado de agua** (*Cono Sur*) sorbet; (*con palo*) ice lolly (*Brit*), Popsicle® (*EEUU*)
helador (ADJ) [*viento*] icy, freezing • **hace un frío ~** it's icy cold, it's perishing cold, it's freezing cold
heladora (SF) **1** (= *máquina*) ice-cream maker **2** [*de nevera*] freezer unit, freezing compartment, freezer; (*esp Cono Sur*) refrigerator, fridge*, icebox (*EEUU*)
helaje (SM) (*And*) (= *frío intenso*) intense cold; (= *sensación*) chill
helar ▸ CONJUG 1j (VT) **1** (*Meteo*) to freeze, ice up **2** (= *congelar*) [+ *líquido*] to freeze; [+ *bebidas*] to ice, chill **3** (= *pasmar*) to dumbfound, amaze **4** (= *aterrar*) to scare to death
(VI) (= *hacer frío*) (*Meteo*) to freeze
(VPR) **helarse 1** (*Aer, Ferro*) to ice up, freeze up **2** (= *congelarse*) [*líquido*] to freeze; [*plantas*] to be killed by frost; [*lago, río*] to freeze over **3** [*persona*] • **¡me estoy helando!** I'm freezing! • MODISMO: • **se me heló la sangre (en las venas)** my blood ran cold
helecho (SM) bracken, fern
Helena (SF) Helen
helénico (ADJ) Hellenic, Ancient Greek
heleno/a (SM/F) Hellene, Ancient Greek
Helesponto (SM) Hellespont
hélice (SF) **1** (= *espiral*) (*figura*) spiral; (*Anat, Elec, Mat*) helix ▸ **hélice doble** double helix **2** (*Aer*) propeller, airscrew **3** (*Náut*) propeller, screw
helicoidal (ADJ) spiral, helicoidal, helical
helicóptero (SM) helicopter ▸ **helicóptero artillado, helicóptero de ataque, helicóptero de combate** helicopter gunship ▸ **helicóptero de salvamento** rescue helicopter ▸ **helicóptero fumigador** crop-spraying helicopter
heliesquí (SM) heli-skiing
helio (SM) helium
helio... (PREF) helio...
helioesquí (SM) heli-skiing
heliógrafo (SM) heliograph
heliosfera (SF) heliosphere
heliosismología (SF) helioseismology
helioterapia (SF) heliotherapy (*frm*), sunray treatment
heliotipia (SF) heliotype
heliotropo (SM) heliotrope
helipuerto (SM) heliport
helitransportar ▸ CONJUG 1a (VT) (*gen*) to transport by helicopter; (*Mil*) to helicopter (in)
helmántico/a (ADJ) of/from Salamanca
(SM/F) native/inhabitant of Salamanca • **los ~s** the people of Salamanca
Helsinki (SM) Helsinki
helvético/a (ADJ) of/from Switzerland
(SM/F) native/inhabitant of Switzerland • **los ~s** the people of Switzerland
hematíe (SM) red (blood) corpuscle
hematología (SF) haematology, hematology (*EEUU*)
hematológico (ADJ) **1** [*sistema*] haematological, hematological (*EEUU*) **2** [*cáncer, enfermedad*] of the blood
hematoma (SM) bruise
hembra (SF) **1** (*Bot, Zool*) female • **el pájaro ~** the hen, the female bird • **el armiño ~** the female stoat, the she-stoat **2** (= *mujer*) woman, female • **"hembra"** "female" • **cinco hijos: dos varones y tres ~s** five children: two boys and three girls **3** (*Mec*) nut ▸ **hembra de terraja** die **4** (*Cos*) eye • **macho y ~** hook and eye
hembraje (SM) (*LAm*) female flock, female herd; (*hum*) womenfolk
hembrería* (SF) (*Caribe, Méx*), **hembrerío*** (SM) gaggle of women, crowd of women
hembrilla (SF) (*Mec*) nut, eyebolt
hembrista (SMF) (*hum*) feminist
hemerográfico (ADJ) newspaper (*antes de s*)
hemeroteca (SF) newspaper library
hemiciclo (SM) **1** (= *anfiteatro*) semicircular theatre, semicircular theater (*EEUU*) **2** (*Pol*) (= *sala*) chamber; (= *zona central*) floor
hemiplejía (SF) hemiplegia (*frm*), stroke
hemipléjico (ADJ) hemiplegic
hemisférico (ADJ) hemispheric
hemisferio (SM) hemisphere
hemistiquio (SM) hemistich
hemo... (PREF) haemo..., hemo... (*EEUU*)
hemodiálisis (SF INV) haemodialysis, hemodialysis (*EEUU*)
hemodinámica (SF) haemodynamics (*sing*)
hemodinámico (ADJ) haemodynamic
hemodonación (SF) donation of blood
hemofilia (SF) haemophilia, hemophilia (*EEUU*)
hemofílico/a (ADJ), (SM/F) haemophiliac, hemophiliac (*EEUU*)
hemoglobina (SF) haemoglobin, hemoglobin (*EEUU*)
hemograma (SM) haemogram, hemogram (*EEUU*)
hemorragia (SF) **1** (*Med*) haemorrhage, hemorrhage (*EEUU*), bleeding • **cortar una ~** to stop the bleeding • **morir por ~** to bleed to death ▸ **hemorragia cerebral** cerebral haemorrhage, brain haemorrhage ▸ **hemorragia nasal** nosebleed **2** [*de científicos, técnicos*] drain
hemorroides (SFPL) haemorrhoids, hemorrhoids (*EEUU*), piles
hemos ▸ **haber**
henal (SM) hayloft
henar (SM) meadow, hayfield
henchir ▸ CONJUG 3h (VT) to fill (up) (**de** with), stuff* (**de** with)
(VPR) **henchirse 1** (*gen*) to swell • **~se de comida** to stuff o.s. with food* **2** (*de orgullo*) to swell with pride
Hendaya (SF) Hendaye
hendedura (SF) = **hendidura**
hender ▸ CONJUG 2g (VT) **1** (= *resquebrajar*) to crack **2** (= *cortar*) to cleave, split **3** (= *surcar*) [+ *olas*] to cleave, breast
hendido (ADJ) [*paladar, labio*] cleft
hendidura (SF) **1** (= *grieta*) (*en pared, superficie*) crack **2** (= *corte*) cleft, split **3** (*Geol*) rift, fissure
hendija (SF) (*LAm*) crack, crevice
hendir ▸ CONJUG 3i (VT) = **hender**
henequén (SM) (*LAm*) **1** (= *planta*) agave, henequen **2** (= *fibra*) agave fibre, agave fiber (*EEUU*), henequen
henificación (SF) haymaking, tedding
henificar ▸ CONJUG 1g (VT) to ted
henil (SM) hayloft
heniquén (SM) (*Caribe, Méx*) = **henequén**
heno (SM) hay
heñir ▸ CONJUG 3h, 3k (VT) to knead
hepático (ADJ) hepatic (*frm*), liver (*antes de s*) • **trasplante ~** liver transplant
hepatitis (SF INV) hepatitis
hepato... (PREF) hepato..., hepat...
heptagonal (ADJ) heptagonal
heptágono (SM) heptagon
heptámetro (SM) heptameter
heptatlón (SM) heptathlon
Heracles (SM) Heracles
Heráclito (SM) Heraclitus
heráldica (SF) heraldry
heráldico (ADJ) heraldic
heraldo (SM) herald
herales† (SMPL) trousers, pants (*EEUU*)
herbáceo (ADJ) herbaceous
herbajar ▸ CONJUG 1a, **herbajear** ▸ CONJUG 1a (VT) to graze, put out to pasture
(VI) to graze
herbaje (SM) **1** (*gen*) herbage; (= *pasto*) grass, pasture **2** (*Náut*) coarse woollen cloth
herbario[1] (ADJ) herbal
(SM) (= *colección*) herbarium (*frm*), plant collection
herbario[2]**/a** (SM/F) (*gen*) herbalist; (= *botánico*) botanist
herbazal (SM) grassland, pasture
herbicida (SM) weed-killer ▸ **herbicida selectivo** selective weed-killer
herbívoro/a (ADJ) herbivorous
(SM/F) herbivore
herbodietética (SF) **1** • **productos de ~** health food products **2** (= *tienda*) health food shop
herbodietético (ADJ) health food (*antes de s*)
herbolario[1] (SM) **1** (= *tienda*) herbalist's (shop), health food shop **2** (= *colección*) herbarium (*frm*), plant collection
herbolario[2]**/a** (ADJ) † (= *alocado*) crazy, cracked*
(SM/F) (= *persona*) herbalist
herboristería (SF) herbalist's, herbalist's shop
herborizar ▸ CONJUG 1f (VI) (= *recoger hierbas*) to gather herbs, pick herbs; (*como coleccionista*) to botanize, collect plants
herboso (ADJ) grassy
hercio (SM) hertz
hercúleo (ADJ) Herculean
Hércules (SM) **1** (*Mit*) Hercules **2** [*de circo*] strong man • **es un ~** he's awfully strong
heredabilidad (SF) inheritability
heredable (ADJ) inheritable, that can be inherited
heredad (SF) **1** (= *hacienda*) country estate, farm **2** (= *terreno cultivado*) landed property
heredar ▸ CONJUG 1a (VT) **1** [+ *dinero, tradición, problema*] to inherit • **heredó un título nobiliario** he inherited a title • **ha heredado las deudas de su padre** he has inherited his father's debts • **el rey heredó el trono en 1865** the king succeeded to the throne in 1865 **2** [+ *rasgo*] to inherit • **ha heredado el pelo rubio de su madre** he's inherited his mother's blond hair, he gets his blond hair from his mother **3** [+ *ropa, libros*] to inherit • **los libros de texto que he heredado de mi hermano** the textbooks I inherited from my brother • **siempre hereda la ropa de su hermana mayor** her clothes are always handed down from her elder sister **4** [+ *persona*†] to name as one's heir **5** (*LAm*) (= *legar*) to leave, bequeath
heredero/a (SM/F) heir/heiress (**de** to), inheritor (**de** of) • **príncipe ~** crown prince ▸ **heredero/a de la corona** heir to the crown ▸ **heredero/a del trono** heir to the throne ▸ **heredero/a forzoso/a** heir apparent ▸ **heredero/a presunto/a** heir presumptive
hereditario (ADJ) hereditary
hereje (ADJ) **1** (*Cono Sur**) (= *irrespetuoso*) disrespectful **2** (*And, Caribe*) (= *excesivo*) excessive • **un trabajo ~*** a heavy task
(SMF) heretic
herejía (SF) **1** (*Rel*) heresy **2** (= *trampa*) dirty trick

3 (= *injuria*) insult
4 (*And, Méx*) silly remark, gaffe

herencia SF **1** [*de propiedad, valores*] inheritance, legacy • **malgastó la ~ del padre** he squandered his father's legacy, he squandered the inheritance he had from his father • **me dejó las joyas en ~** she left *o* bequeathed me her jewels • **recibieron la finca en ~** they inherited the estate • **es parte de la ~ cultural de los españoles** it's part of the cultural heritage of the Spanish, it's part of Spanish heritage • **la ~ cultural que recibimos de los romanos** the cultural legacy of the Romans ▸ **herencia yacente** unsettled estate
2 (*Bio*) heredity ▸ **herencia genética** genetic inheritance

hereque (*Caribe*) SM **1** (*Med*) skin disease
2 (*Bot*) *disease of coffee*

heresiarca SMF heresiarch, arch-heretic

herético ADJ heretical

herida SF **1** (*física*) (*por arma*) wound; (*por accidente*) injury • **una ~ de bala** a bullet wound • **me sangraba la ~ del brazo** (*de arma*) the wound in my arm was bleeding; (*por caída, golpe*) the cut on my arm was bleeding • **me he hecho una ~ en la frente** I've got a cut on my forehead • **murió a causa de las ~s del accidente** he died from injuries received in the accident • **sufrió ~s graves** he was seriously injured • **las ~s internas en el seno del partido** the rifts *o* splits within the party ▸ **herida abierta** open wound • **una ~ abierta en la conciencia española** an open wound *o* running sore on the Spanish conscience ▸ **herida contusa** bruise ▸ **herida de bala** bullet wound
2 (= *ofensa*) insult • MODISMOS: • **hurgar en la ~**: • **evitó mencionar el divorcio para no hurgar en la ~** he avoided mentioning the divorce so as to let sleeping dogs lie • **lamerse las ~s** to lick one's wounds

herido/a ADJ **1** (*físicamente*) (*gen*) injured; (*en tiroteo, atentado, guerra*) wounded • **había un hombre ~ en el suelo** there was an injured man lying on the ground • **un soldado ~** a wounded soldier • **un policía resultó ~ en el tiroteo** a policeman was injured *o* wounded in the shooting • **estaba ~ de muerte** • **estaba mortalmente ~** he was fatally injured
2 (*emocionalmente*) hurt • **Susana se sintió herida por lo que le dijiste** Susana was hurt by what you said to her • **me sentí herida en mi amor propio** it was a blow to my self-esteem • **tiene el orgullo ~** his pride has been hurt *o* wounded
SM/F (= *lesionado*) (*gen*) injured person; (*en tiroteo, atentado, guerra*) wounded person • **había un ~ en el parque** there was an injured man in the park • **hubo dos ~s en el accidente** two people were injured *o* hurt in the accident • **hubo cinco ~s leves** five people were slightly injured *o* hurt • **se llevaron a los ~s al hospital** they took the casualties *o* injured (people) to hospital • **el número de los ~s en el accidente** the number of casualties *o* people injured in the accident • **asistieron a los ~s en las trincheras** they helped the wounded in the trenches • **los ~s de guerra** the war wounded
SM (*Cono Sur*) ditch, channel

herir ▹ CONJUG 3i VT **1** (= *lesionar*) (*gen*) to injure, hurt; (*con arma*) to wound • **~ a algn en el brazo** to wound sb in the arm
2 (= *ofender*) to hurt • **me hirió en lo más hondo** it really hurt me deep down
3 (= *irritar*) [*sol, luz*] to beat down on • **un color que hiere la vista** a colour which offends the eye
4 (*liter*) (= *golpear*) to beat, strike, hit
5 (*Mús*) to pluck, play

hermafrodita ADJ, SMF hermaphrodite

hermanable ADJ **1** (*de hermano*) fraternal
2 (= *compatible*) compatible
3 (= *a tono*) matching, that can be matched

hermanamiento SM • **~ de ciudades** town-twinning

hermanar ▹ CONJUG 1a VT **1** (= *hacer juego*) to match
2 (= *unir*) [+ *ciudades*] to twin, make sister cities (*EEUU*)
3 (= *armonizar*) to harmonize, bring into harmony
4 (*Cono Sur*) (= *hacer pares*) to pair

hermanastro/a SMF (*con padre o madre común*) half brother/sister; (*sin vínculo sanguíneo*) stepbrother/stepsister

hermandad SF **1** (= *grupo*) [*de hombres*] brotherhood, fraternity; [*de mujeres*] sisterhood • **Santa Hermandad** (*Hist*) rural police (*15th to 19th centuries*)
2 (= *sindicato*) association

hermanita SF little sister ▸ **hermanitas de la caridad** Little Sisters of Charity, Sisters of Mercy

hermano/a ADJ [*barco*] sister (*antes de s*) • **ciudades hermanas** twin towns
SMF **1** brother/sister • **por favor, indique el número de ~s/as** please state number of siblings • **somos ~s de madre** we have the same mother • **medio ~** half-brother/sister • **primo ~** first cousin • **mis ~s** (= *solo chicos*) my brothers; (= *chicos y chicas*) my brothers and sisters • **Gonzalo y Luís son como ~s** Gonzalo and Luís are like brothers • **Rosa y Fernando son como ~s** Rosa and Fernando are like brother and sister ▸ **hermano/a carnal** full brother/sister ▸ **hermano de armas** brother-in-arms ▸ **hermano/a de leche** foster brother/sister ▸ **hermano/a de sangre** blood brother/sister ▸ **hermano/a gemelo/a** twin brother/sister ▸ **hermano/a mayor** elder brother/sister, big brother/sister* ▸ **hermano/a político/a** brother-in-law/sister-in-law ▸ **hermanos/as siameses/as** Siamese twins
2 (*Rel*) brother/sister; **hermanos** brethren ▸ **hermano/a lego/a** lay brother/sister
3 [*de un par*] pair • **no encuentro el ~ de este calcetín** I can't find the pair for this sock
4 (*LAm*) (= *espectro*) ghost

hermenéutica SF hermeneutics (*sing*)

hermética SF hermetic philosophy, hermetics (*sing*)

herméticamente ADV hermetically

hermeticidad SF hermetic nature, hermeticism

hermético ADJ **1** (= *cerrado*) (*gen*) hermetic; (*al aire*) airtight; (*al agua*) watertight
2 (= *inescrutable*) [*teoría*] watertight; [*misterio*] impenetrable; [*persona*] reserved, secretive

hermetismo SM (= *inescrutabilidad*) [*de teoría, misterio*] tight secrecy, close secrecy; [*de persona*] silence, reserve • **acordaron la paz con gran ~** they agreed the peace in the utmost secrecy

hermetizar ▹ CONJUG 1f VT to seal off, close off

hermosamente ADV beautifully, handsomely

hermosear ▹ CONJUG 1a VT (*frm*) to beautify, embellish

hermoso ADJ **1** (= *bello*) beautiful, lovely • **la casa tiene un ~ jardín** the house has a beautiful *o* lovely garden • **un día ~** a beautiful *o* lovely day
2 (= *robusto, saludable*) • **¡qué niño tan ~!** what a fine-looking boy! • **seis ~s toros** six magnificent bulls
3 (= *grande*) nice and big • **el coche tiene un maletero muy ~** the car has a nice big boot, the car's boot is nice and big • **me sirvió una hermosa porción de queso** she gave me a nice big chunk of cheese
4 (= *noble*) • **un ~ gesto** a noble gesture

hermosura SF **1** (= *cualidad*) beauty
2 (= *persona, cosa hermosa*) • **esta modelo es una ~** this model is a beauty, this model is beautiful • **¡qué ~ de niño!** what a lovely *o* beautiful child!

hernia SF rupture, hernia ▸ **hernia de disco, hernia discal** slipped disc ▸ **hernia estrangulada** strangulated hernia ▸ **hernia hiatal** hiatus hernia

herniarse ▹ CONJUG 1b VPR (*Med*) to rupture o.s. • **no trabajes tanto que te vas a herniar** (*iró*) don't work so hard, you're going to give yourself a hernia (*iró*)

Herodes SM Herod • MODISMOS: • **hacer lo de ~*** to put up with it • **ir de ~ a Pilatos** to be driven from pillar to post

héroe SM hero

heroicamente ADV heroically

heroicidad SF **1** (= *cualidad*) heroism
2 (= *proeza*) heroic deed

heroico ADJ heroic

heroicocómico ADJ mock-heroic

heroína¹ SF (= *mujer*) heroine

heroína² SF (= *droga*) heroin

heroinomanía SF heroin addiction

heroinómano/a SM/F heroin addict

heroísmo SM heroism

herpes SM INV (*Med*) (*en los labios, genitales*) herpes; (= *culebrilla*) shingles ▸ **herpes genital** genital herpes ▸ **herpes labial** cold sore, labial herpes (*frm*)

herrada SF **1** (*Col*) [*de caballo*] shoeing
2 (= *cubo*) bucket
3 (*And*) (*Agr*) branding

herrador SM farrier, blacksmith

herradura SF horseshoe • **camino de ~** bridle path • **curva en ~** (*Aut*) hairpin bend • MODISMO: • **mostrar las ~s** to bolt, show a clean pair of heels

herraje SM **1** (*en puerta, mueble*) ironwork, iron fittings (*pl*)
2 (*Méx*) silver harness fittings (*pl*)
3 (*Cono Sur*) (= *herradura*) horseshoe

herramental SM toolkit, toolbag

herramienta SF **1** (*gen*) tool; **herramientas** set of tools ▸ **herramienta de filo** edge tool ▸ **herramienta de mano** hand tool ▸ **herramienta mecánica** power tool
2 (*hum*) [*de toro*] horns (*pl*); (= *dientes*) teeth (*pl*)

herranza SF (*And*) branding

herrar ▹ CONJUG 1j VT **1** (*Agr*) [+ *caballo*] to shoe; [+ *ganado*] to brand
2 (*Téc*) to bind with iron, trim with ironwork

herrería SF **1** (= *taller*) smithy, blacksmith's, blacksmith's workshop (*EEUU*)
2 (= *oficio*) blacksmith's trade
3† (= *fábrica*) ironworks
4†† (= *alboroto*) uproar, tumult

herrerillo SM (*Orn*) tit

herrero/a SM/F blacksmith, smith • REFRÁN: • **en casa del ~ (cuchillo de palo)** there's none worse shod than the shoemaker's wife ▸ **herrero/a de grueso** foundry worker

herrete SM (= *cabo*) metal tip, ferrule; (*LAm*) branding-iron, brand

Herri Batasuna SM *Basque pro-independence political party*

herribatasuno/a ADJ of Herri Batasuna
SM/F (= *miembro*) member of Herri Batasuna; (= *simpatizante*) supporter of Herri Batasuna

herrumbre SF **1** (= *óxido*) rust
2 (*Bot*) rust
3 (= *gusto*) iron taste
herrumbroso ADJ rusty
hertzio SM hertz
hervederas* SFPL (*Caribe*) heartburn, indigestion
hervidero SM **1** [*de gente*] swarm, throng, crowd • **un ~ de gente** a swarm of people
2 (*Pol*) hotbed • **un ~ de disturbios** a hotbed of unrest
3 (= *manantial*) hot spring
hervido ADJ (*gen*) boiled
SM (*LAm*) (= *guiso*) stew
hervidor SM kettle
hervidora SF ▸ **hervidora de agua** water heater
hervir ▹ CONJUG 3i VT to boil
VI **1** [*agua, leche*] to boil • **~ a fuego lento** to simmer • **dejar de ~** to go off the boil, stop boiling • **empezar** *o* **romper a ~** to come to the boil, begin to boil • **MODISMO:** • **¡me hierve la sangre!** it makes my blood boil!
2 (= *burbujear*) [*líquido*] to bubble, seethe; [*mar*] to seethe, surge
3 (= *persona*) • **hiervo en deseos de ...** I'm just itching to ... • **el público hervía de emoción** the audience was carried away with *o* bubbling with excitement
4 • **~ de** *o* **en** (= *estar lleno de*) to swarm with • **la cama hervía de pulgas** the bed was swarming *o* alive with fleas
hervor SM **1** [*de agua, leche*] boiling • **dar un ~ a algo** to boil sth once • **alzar el ~** *o* **levantar el ~** to come to the boil
2 (*popular, emocional*) ardour, ardor (*EEUU*)
hervoroso ADJ **1** [*líquido*] boiling, seething; [*sol*] burning
2 = **fervoroso**
heteo/a (*Hist*) ADJ of/from Anatolia
SM/F native/inhabitant of Anatolia • **los ~s** the people of Anatolia
hetero* ADJ, SMF = **heterosexual**
heterodoxia SF heterodoxy
heterodoxo ADJ heterodox, unorthodox
heterogeneidad SF heterogeneous nature, heterogeneity (*frm*)
heterogéneo ADJ heterogeneous
heteronimia SF heteronomy
heterónimo SM heteronym
heterónomo ADJ heteronomous
heterosexual ADJ, SMF heterosexual
heterosexualidad SF heterosexuality
heticarse ▹ CONJUG 1g VPR (*Caribe*) to contract tuberculosis
hético ADJ consumptive
hetiquencia SF (*Caribe*) tuberculosis
heurístico ADJ heuristic
hexadecimal ADJ hexadecimal
hexagonal ADJ hexagonal
hexágono SM hexagon
hexámetro SM hexameter
hez SF **1 heces** (*Med*) faeces, feces (*EEUU*); [*de vino*] lees
2 (*frm*) (= *escoria*) dregs, scum • **la hez de la sociedad** the dregs *o* scum of society
hg ABR (= **hectogramo(s)**) hg
hiatal ADJ [+ *hernia*] hiatus (*antes de s*), hiatal
hiato SM (*Ling*) hiatus
hibernación SF hibernation • **estar en ~** to be in hibernation
hibernal ADJ (*frm*) wintry, winter (*antes de s*)
hibernar ▹ CONJUG 1a VI to hibernate
hibisco SM hibiscus
hibridación SF, **hibridaje** SM hybridization
hibridar ▹ CONJUG 1a VT, VI to hybridize
hibridismo SM hybridism
hibridizar ▹ CONJUG 1f VT **1** (*Bio*) to hybridize
2 [+ *paisaje*] to lend a mixed appearance to, produce a hybrid appearance in
híbrido ADJ hybrid
SM hybrid
hice *etc* ▹ **hacer**
hidalgo/a ADJ **1** (= *caballeroso*) noble
2 (= *honrado*) honourable, honorable (*EEUU*)
3 (= *generoso*) generous
SM/F nobleman/noblewoman
SM (*Méx*) (*Hist*) *10-peso gold coin*
hidalguía SF **1** (= *nobleza*) nobility
2 (= *honradez*) nobility, honourableness, honorableness (*EEUU*)
3 (= *generosidad*) generosity
hideputa** SM = **hijodeputa**
Hidra SF (*Mit*) Hydra
hidra SF hydra
hidrante SM (*CAm, Col*) hydrant ▸ **hidrante de incendios** (fire) hydrant
hidratación SF [*de la piel*] moisturizing
hidratante ADJ moisturizing • **crema ~** moisturizing cream
SF moisturizing cream, moisturizer
hidratar ▹ CONJUG 1a VT **1** [+ *piel*] to moisturize
2 (*Quím*) to hydrate
VPR **hidratarse** to put on moisturizing cream
hidrato SM hydrate ▸ **hidrato de carbono** carbohydrate
hidráulica SF hydraulics (*sing*)
hidráulico ADJ hydraulic (*frm*), water (*antes de s*) • **fuerza hidráulica** water power, hydraulic power
hídrico ADJ water (*antes de s*)
hidro... PREF hydro..., water-
hidroala SM hydrofoil
hidroavión SM seaplane, flying boat
hidrocarburo SM hydrocarbon
hidrocefalia SF (*Med*) hydrocephalus, water on the brain
hidrodeslizador SM hovercraft
hidrodinámica SF hydrodynamics (*sing*)
hidroeléctrica SF hydroelectric power station
hidroeléctrico ADJ hydroelectric • **central hidroeléctrica** hydro(electricity) station
hidroesfera SF hydrosphere
hidrófilo ADJ absorbent • **algodón ~** cotton wool, absorbent cotton (*EEUU*)
hidrofobia SF hydrophobia (*frm*), rabies
hidrofóbico ADJ, **hidrófobo** ADJ hydrophobic
hidrofoil SM hydrofoil
hidrofuerza SF hydropower
hidrófugo ADJ water-repellent, damp-proof
SM water repellant
hidrógeno SM hydrogen
hidrografía SF hydrography
hidrólisis SF INV hydrolysis
hidrolizar ▹ CONJUG 1f VT to hydrolyze
VPR **hidrolizarse** to hydrolyze
hidrológico ADJ water (*antes de s*) • **recursos ~s** water resources
hidromasaje SM hydromassage
hidropesía SF dropsy
hidrópico ADJ dropsical
hidroplano SM hydroplane
hidroponia SF hydroponics (*sing*), aquiculture
hidropónico ADJ hydroponic
hidrosfera SF hydrosphere
hidrosoluble ADJ soluble in water, water-soluble
hidroterapia SF hydrotherapy
▸ **hidroterapia del colon** colonic irrigation
hidrovía SF waterway
hidróxido SM hydroxide ▸ **hidróxido amónico** ammonium hydroxide
hiedra SF ivy
hiel SF **1** (*Anat*) gall, bile • **MODISMO:** • **echar la ~*** to sweat blood*, slog away*
2 (= *amargura*) bitterness • **no tener ~** to be very sweet-tempered
3 hieles (= *adversidades*) troubles, upsets
hiela ▹ **helar**
hielera SF (*Chile, Méx*) (= *nevera*) refrigerator, fridge*; (= *bandeja*) ice tray
hielo SM **1** (= *agua helada*) ice • **con ~** (*bebida*) with ice, on the rocks* • **MODISMOS:** • **ser más frío que el ~** to be as cold as ice • **romper el ~** to break the ice ▸ **hielo a la deriva, hielo flotante, hielo frappé** (*Méx*) crushed ice ▸ **hielo movedizo** drift ice ▸ **hielo picado** crushed ice ▸ **hielo seco** dry ice
2 (= *helada*) frost
hiena SF **1** (= *animal*) hyena
2 (= *persona cruel*) vulture • **MODISMOS:** • **hecho una ~** furious • **ponerse como una ~** to get furious, hit the roof*
hierático ADJ (*frm*) [*figura, postura*] hieratic, hieratical; [*aspecto*] stern, severe
hieratismo SM (*frm*) **1** [*de figura, postura*] hieratic attitude
2 (= *solemnidad*) solemnity, stateliness
hierba SF **1** (= *pasto*) grass • **mala ~** weed • **MODISMOS:** • **oír** *o* **sentir** *o* **ver crecer la ~** to be pretty smart • **pisar mala ~** to have bad luck • **y otras ~s** and so forth, and suchlike • **REFRÁN:** • **mala ~ nunca muere** it's a case of the proverbial bad penny ▸ **hierba artificial** artificial playing surface, Astroturf® ▸ **hierba cana** groundsel ▸ **hierba de San Juan** St John's-wort ▸ **hierba gatera** catmint ▸ **hierba lombriguera** ragwort ▸ **hierba mate** (*esp Cono Sur*) maté ▸ **hierba mora** nightshade ▸ **hierba rastrera** cotton grass
2 (*Med*) herb, medicinal plant • **cura de ~s** herbal cure • **infusión de ~s** herbal tea
3 (*Culin*) herb • **a las finas ~s** cooked with herbs
4* (= *droga*) grass*, pot*
hierbabuena SF mint
hierbajo SM weed
hierbajoso ADJ weedy, weed-infested
hierbaluisa SF lemon verbena, aloysia (*frm*)
hierbatero/a SM/F (*Chile*), **hierbero/a** SM/F (*Méx*) herbalist
hierra SF (*LAm*) branding
hierro SM **1** (= *metal*) iron • **de ~** iron (*antes de s*) • **MODISMOS:** • **fuerte como el ~** like iron, tough • **llevar ~ a Vizcaya** to carry coals to Newcastle • **machacar en ~ frío** to flog a dead horse, beat one's head against a brick wall • **quitar ~ a algo** to play sth down ▸ **hierro acanalado** corrugated iron ▸ **hierro batido** wrought iron ▸ **hierro bruto** crude iron, pig iron ▸ **hierro colado** cast iron ▸ **hierro de fundición** cast iron ▸ **hierro en lingotes** pig iron ▸ **hierro forjado** wrought iron ▸ **hierro fundido** cast iron ▸ **hierro ondulado** corrugated iron ▸ **hierro viejo** scrap iron, old iron; ▹ **fierro**
2 (= *objeto*) iron object; (= *herramienta*) tool; [*de flecha, lanza*] head • **REFRÁN:** • **quien a ~ mata, a ~ muere** those that live by the sword die by the sword
3 (*Agr*) branding-iron
4 (*Golf*) iron; **hierros** irons
hi-fi [ˈifi] SM (PL: **hi-fis**) hi-fi
higa SF **1** (= *gesto*) rude sign, obscene gesture
2 (= *burla*) • **dar ~ a** to jeer at, mock • **MODISMO:** • **no le importa una ~*** he doesn't give a damn*, he doesn't give a toss*
hígado SM **1** (*Anat*) liver • **MODISMOS:** • **castigar el ~*** to knock it back* • **ser un ~** (*CAm, Méx**) to be a pain in the neck* • **tener ~ de indio** (*CAm, Méx*) to be a disagreeable sort

2 hígados (*fig*) guts, pluck (*sing*) • **MODISMO**: • **echar los ~s** to sweat one's guts out*

higadoso ADJ • **ser ~** (*CAm, Méx‡*) to be a pain in the neck*

highball SM (*LAm*) (= *cóctel*) cocktail, highball (*EEUU*)

higiene SF hygiene ▸ **higiene íntima** personal hygiene

higiénico ADJ hygienic • **papel ~** toilet paper

higienización SF cleaning, cleansing

higienizado ADJ sterilized

higienizar ▹ CONJUG 1f VT **1** (= *limpiar*) to clean, cleanse
2 (= *desinfectar*) to sterilize
VPR **higienizarse** (*Cono Sur*) (= *lavarse*) to wash oneself

higo SM **1** (*Bot*) fig, green fig • **MODISMOS**: • **de ~s a brevas** once in a blue moon • **estar hecho un ~** to be all crumpled up • **(no) me importa un ~** I couldn't care less • **ser un ~ mustio** to be weakly ▸ **higo chumbo, higo de tuna** prickly pear ▸ **higo paso, higo seco** dried fig
2 (*Vet*) thrush
3‡‡ (= *coño*) cunt‡‡

higuera SF fig tree • **MODISMOS**: • **caer de una ~** to come down to earth with a bump • **estar en la ~** to be daydreaming, be up in the clouds ▸ **higuera chumba, higuera de tuna** prickly pear cactus, Indian fig tree ▸ **higuera del infierno, higuera infernal** castor-oil plant

higuerilla SF (*Méx*) castor-oil plant

hijadeputa‡‡ SF, **hijaputa**‡‡ SF bitch‡, cow‡

hijastro/a SMF stepson/stepdaughter

hijo/a SMF **1** son/daughter • **una pareja sin ~s** a childless couple • **¿cuántos ~s tiene Amelia?** how many children does Amelia have? • **¿cuántos ~s tiene a su cargo?** how many dependent children do you have? • **Pedro Gutiérrez, ~** Pedro Gutiérrez Junior • **su novio le hizo un ~*** her boyfriend got her pregnant • **nombrar a algn ~ predilecto de la ciudad** to name sb a favourite son of the city • **ser ~ único** to be an only child • **el Hijo de Dios** the Son of God • **MODISMOS**: • **cada** *o* **todo ~ de vecino** any Tom, Dick or Harry* • **como todo ~ de vecino** like everyone else, like the next man • **hacer a algn un ~ macho** (*LAm*) to do sb harm • **soy ~ de mis obras** I'm a self-made man ▸ **hijo/a adoptivo/a** adopted child ▸ **hijo/a biológico/a** natural child, biological child ▸ **hijo de la chingada** (*Méx*‡‡) bastard‡‡, son of a bitch‡‡ ▸ **hijo/a de leche** foster child ▸ **hijo/a de papá** rich kid* ▸ **hijo/a de puta**‡‡ (= *hombre*) bastard‡‡, son of a bitch‡‡; (= *mujer*) bitch‡, cow‡ ▸ **hijo/a natural** illegitimate child ▸ **hijo/a político/a** son-in-law/daughter-in-law ▸ **hijo pródigo** prodigal son
2 [*de un pueblo, un país*] son • **es ~ de Madrid** he hails from Madrid, he is from Madrid
3 hijos (= *descendientes*) • **todos somos ~s de Dios** we are all God's children
4 (*uso vocativo*) • **¡~ de mi alma!** my precious child! • **¡ay ~, qué pesado eres!** you're such a pain! • **¡hijo(s)!** • **¡híjole!** (*Méx**) Christ!‡, good God!*

hijodeputa‡‡ SM, **hijoputa**‡‡ SM bastard‡‡, son of a bitch (*EEUU*‡‡)

hijoputada‡‡ SF dirty trick

hijoputesco‡‡ ADJ rotten*, dirty

hijoputez‡‡ SF dirty trick

hijuela SF **1** (= *filial*) offshoot, branch
2 (*Jur*) (= *propiedades*) *estate of a deceased person*; (= *parte*) share, portion, inheritance; (= *legado*) list of bequests
3 (*And, Cono Sur*) plot of land
4 (*Cos*) piece of material (*for widening a garment*)
5 (*Agr*) small irrigation channel
6 (*Méx*) (*Min*) seam of ore
7 (*And, Cono Sur*) rural property

hijuelo SM **1** (*Zool*) young
2 (*Bot*) shoot
3 (*And*) (= *camino*) side road, minor road

hijuemadre‡‡ EXCL (*CAm*) bloody hell!‡‡, goddammit (*EEUU*‡), Jesus Christ!‡‡

hijueputa‡‡ SM (*LAm*) bastard‡‡, son of a bitch (*EEUU*‡‡)

hijuna‡‡ EXCL (*LAm*) you bastard!‡‡, you son of a bitch! (*EEUU*‡‡)

hila† SF **1** (= *fila*) row, line • **a la ~** in a row, in single file
2 (= *cuerda*) thin gut
3 hilas (*Med*) lint

hilacha SF **1** (= *hilo*) ravelled thread, loose thread ▸ **hilacha de vidrio** spun glass
2 hilachas (*Méx*) (= *andrajos*) rags
3 • **MODISMO**: • **mostrar la ~** (*Cono Sur*) to show o.s. in one's true colours *o* (*EEUU*) colors

hilachento ADJ (*LAm*) **1** (= *persona*) ragged
2 [*ropa*] (= *deshilachado*) frayed; (= *raído*) shabby

hilacho SM **1** (= *hilo*) = **hilacha**
2 hilachos = **hilacha**
3 • **MODISMO**: • **dar vuelo al ~** (*Méx**) to have a wild time

hilachudo ADJ (*Méx*) = **hilachento**

hilada SF **1** (= *fila*) row, line
2 (*Arquit*) course

hilado ADJ spun • **seda hilada** spun silk
SM **1** (= *acto*) spinning
2 (= *hilo*) thread, yarn

hilador(a) SM/F (= *persona*) spinner
SF (*Téc*) spinning jenny

hilandería SF **1** (= *oficio*) spinning
2 (= *fábrica*) spinning mill ▸ **hilandería de algodón** cotton mill

hilandero/a SM/F spinner

hilangos SMPL (*And*) rags, tatters

hilar ▹ CONJUG 1a VT **1** (*Cos*) to spin
2 (= *relacionar*) to reason, infer • **MODISMOS**: • **~ (muy) delgado** • **~ fino** to split hairs • **~ delgado** (*Cono Sur*) to be dying, be on one's last legs*

hilaracha SF = **hilacha**

hilarante ADJ hilarious • **gas ~** laughing gas

hilaridad SF hilarity

hilatura SF spinning

hilaza SF yarn, coarse thread • **MODISMO**: • **descubrir la ~** to show o.s. in one's true colours *o* (*EEUU*) colors

hilazón SF connection

hilera SF **1** (= *fila*) (*gen*) row, line; (*Mil*) rank, file; (*Arquit*) course; (*Agr*) row, drill
2 (*Cos*) fine thread

hilo SM **1** (*Cos*) thread, yarn • **tela de ~** (*Méx*) linen cloth • **coser al ~** to sew on the straight, sew with the weave • **MODISMOS**: • **a ~** continuously, uninterruptedly • **al ~** in a row, on the trot, running • **contar algo del ~ al ovillo** to tell sth without omitting a single detail • **dar mucho ~ que torcer** to cause a lot of trouble • **escapar con el ~ en una pata** (*Caribe, Cono Sur**) to get out of a tight corner, wriggle out of a jam* • **estar al ~** to be watchful, be on the look-out • **estar hecho un ~** to be as thin as a rake • **mover los ~s** to pull strings • **pender de un ~** to hang by a thread ▸ **hilo dental** dental floss ▸ **hilo de perlas** string of pearls ▸ **hilo de zurcir** darning wool
2 (= *cable*) [*de metal*] thin wire; [*de electricidad*] wire, flex; [*de teléfono*] line ▸ **hilo de tierra** earth wire, ground wire (*EEUU*) ▸ **hilo directo** direct line, hot line ▸ **hilo musical** piped music
3 (= *chorro*) [*de líquido*] thin stream, trickle; [*de gente*] thin line • **MODISMOS**: • **decir algo con un ~ de voz** to say sth in a thin *o* barely audible voice • **irse tras el ~ de la gente** to follow the crowd ▸ **hilo de humo** thin line of smoke, plume of smoke
4 (*Bot*) fibre, fiber (*EEUU*), filament
5 (= *lino*) linen • **traje de ~** linen dress *o* suit ▸ **hilo de bramante** twine ▸ **hilo de Escocia** lisle, strong cotton
6 (= *curso*) [*de conversación*] thread; [*de vida*] course; [*de pensamientos*] train • **el ~ conductor** the theme *o* leitmotiv • **coger el ~** to pick up the thread • **perder el ~** to lose the thread • **seguir el ~** [*de razonamiento*] to follow, understand ▸ **hilo argumental** story line, plot

hilván SM **1** (*Cos*) (= *hilo suelto*) tacking, basting (*EEUU*)
2 (*Cono Sur*) (= *hilo*) tacking thread, basting thread (*EEUU*)
3 (*Caribe*) (= *dobladillo*) hem

hilvanar ▹ CONJUG 1a VT **1** (*Cos*) to tack, baste (*EEUU*)
2 (= *preparar*) [+ *trabajo, discurso*] to cobble together • **bien hilvanado** well put together, well constructed
3 (= *relacionar*) to string together

Himalaya SM • **el ~** the Himalayas

himalayo ADJ Himalayan

himen SM hymen, maidenhead (*liter*)

himeneo SM **1** (*liter*) nuptials (*pl*), wedding
2 (*poét*) epithalamium

himnario SM hymnal, hymnbook

himno SM hymn ▸ **himno nacional** national anthem

hincada SF **1** (*Chile, Ecu*) (*de rodillas*) genuflection (*frm*)
2 (*Caribe*) (= *hincadura*) thrust
3 (*Caribe*) (= *dolor*) sharp pain, stabbing pain

hincadura SF thrust, thrusting, driving

hincapié SM • **hacer ~ en** (= *recalcar*) to emphasize, stress; (= *insistir en*) to insist on, demand • **hizo ~ en la necesidad de revisar el reglamento** she emphasized *o* stressed the need to revise the regulations

hincapilotes SM INV (*Cono Sur*) pile-driver

hincar ▹ CONJUG 1g VT (= *meter*) [+ *objeto punzante*] to thrust, drive (**en** into); [+ *pie*] to set (firmly) (**en** on) • **hincó el bastón en el suelo** he stuck his stick in the ground, he thrust his stick into the ground • **hincó la mirada en ella** he fixed his gaze on her, he stared at her fixedly • **MODISMO**: • **~la*** (= *trabajar mucho*) to slog*, work hard; ▹ **diente, rodilla**
VPR **hincarse** • **~se de rodillas** (*esp LAm*) to kneel, kneel down

hincha[1] SF **1** (= *antipatía*) • **tener ~ a algn** to have a grudge against sb • **tomar ~ a algn** to take a dislike to sb
2 (*Cono Sur**) (= *aburrimiento*) • **¡qué ~!** what a bore!

hincha[2] SMF **1** (*Dep*) fan, supporter • **los ~s del Madrid** the Madrid supporters
2 (*Perú**) (= *amigo*) pal*, mate*, buddy (*esp EEUU**)

hinchable ADJ inflatable

hinchabolas‡‡ SMF INV (*Cono Sur*) = **hinchapelotas**

hinchada SF supporters (*pl*), fans (*pl*)

hinchado ADJ **1** (= *inflamado*) swollen
2 (= *vanidoso*) [*persona*] swollen-headed, conceited; [*estilo*] pompous, high-flown

hinchador SM **1** ▸ **hinchador de ruedas** tyre inflator
2 (*Cono Sur*‡) pest, bloody nuisance‡

hinchante‡ ADJ **1** (= *molesto*) annoying, tiresome
2 (= *gracioso*) funny

hinchapelotas** SM INV (*Cono Sur*) • **es un ~** he's a pain in the arse**, he's a pain in the ass (*EEUU***)
hinchar ▷ CONJUG 1a VT **1** [+ *vientre*] to distend, enlarge; [+ *globo*] to blow up, inflate, pump up
2 (= *exagerar*) to exaggerate
3 (*Cono Sur*‡) (= *molestar*) to annoy, upset • **me hincha todo el tiempo** he keeps on at me all the time
VPR **hincharse 1** (= *inflamarse*) [*herida, tobillo*] to swell, swell up; [*vientre*] to get distended (*frm*), get bloated
2 (= *hartarse*) • **~se de** [+ *comida*] to stuff o.s. with* • **se ~on de gambas** they stuffed themselves with prawns* • **me hinché de agua** I drank gallons *o* loads of water* • **~se a** *o* **de hacer algo: ~se a** *o* **de correr** to run like mad • **~se de reír** to have a good laugh, split one's sides laughing
3 (= *engreírse*) to get conceited, become vain, get swollen-headed
4* (= *enriquecerse*) to make a pile*, make a mint*
hinchazón SF **1** (*Med*) [*de herida, tobillo*] swelling; (= *bulto*) bump, lump
2 (*frm*) (= *arrogancia*) conceit
3 (*frm*) [*de estilo*] pomposity
hinco SM (*Cono Sur*) post, stake
hindi SM Hindi
hindú ADJ, SMF **1** (*Rel*) Hindu
2 (= *de la India*) Indian
hinduismo SM Hinduism
hiniesta SF (*Bot*) broom
hinojo[1] SM (*Bot, Culin*) fennel
hinojo[2] SM †† • **de ~s** on bended knee • **postrarse de ~s** to kneel (down), go down on one's knees
hip EXCL hic
hipar ▷ CONJUG 1a VI **1** (= *tener hipo*) to hiccup, hiccough
2 [*perro*] to pant
3 • **~ por algo** to long for sth, yearn for sth • **~ por hacer algo** to long to do sth, yearn to do sth
4 (= *gimotear*) to whine
5 (= *estar exhausto*) to be worn out, be exhausted
hipato* ADJ **1** (*And*) (= *repleto*) full, swollen
2 (*And, Caribe*) (= *pálido*) pale, anaemic, anemic (*EEUU*); (= *soso*) tasteless
hipear ▷ CONJUG 1a VI (*Méx*) = **hipar**
hiper* ADJ (= *muy*) mega‡
hiper... PREF hyper...
híper SM INV (= *hipermercado*) hypermarket
hiperacidez SF hyperacidity
hiperactividad SF hyperactivity
hiperactivo ADJ hyperactive
hiperagudo ADJ abnormally acute
hipérbaton SM (PL: **hipérbatos**) hyperbaton
hipérbola SF hyperbola
hipérbole SF hyperbole
hiperbólico ADJ hyperbolic (*frm*), hyperbolical (*frm*), exaggerated
hiperconectividad SF hyperconnectivity
hipercorrección SF hypercorrection
hipercrítico ADJ hypercritical
hiperenlace SM (*Internet*) hyperlink
hiperexcitación SF hyperexcitement
hiperexcitado ADJ over-excited
hiperfagia SF (*Med*) binge eating
hiperglucemia SF hyperglycaemia, hyperglycemia (*EEUU*)
hiperhidrosis SF hyperhidrosis, hyperhydrosis
hiperinflación SF runaway inflation, hyperinflation
hipermedia SM INV hypermedia
hipermercado SM hypermarket
hipermétrope ADJ long-sighted, far-sighted (*EEUU*)
SMF long-sighted person, far-sighted person (*EEUU*)
hipermetropía SF, **hiperopía** SF long-sightedness, far-sightedness (*EEUU*), long-sight • **tener ~** to be long-sighted
hipermillonario ADJ [*acuerdo, ganancias*] multi-million pound/dollar *etc* (*antes de s*)
hipernervioso ADJ excessively nervous, highly strung
hiperrealismo SM hyper-realism
hipersensibilidad SF hypersensitivity (*frm*), over-sensitiveness, touchiness
hipersensible ADJ hypersensitive, over-sensitive, touchy
hipersensitivo ADJ hypersensitive
hipersónico ADJ supersonic
hipertensión SF hypertension, high blood pressure
hipertenso ADJ having high blood pressure, with high blood pressure • **ser ~** to have high blood pressure
hipertexto SM hypertext
hipertrofia SF hypertrophy
hipertrofiado ADJ (*Med*) enlarged
hipertrofiarse ▷ CONJUG 1b VPR (*Med*) to become enlarged, hypertrophy (*frm*)
hiperventilación SF (*Med*) hyperventilation, hyperventilating
hipervínculo SM hyperlink
hipervitaminosis SF INV hypervitaminosis
hip hop [xipxop] SM hip-hop
hiphopero [xipxo'pero] ADJ hip-hop
hipiar ▷ CONJUG 1b VI (*Méx*) = **hipar**
hípica SF **1** (= *deporte*) equestrianism
2 (= *local*) riding club
hípico ADJ horse (*antes de s*), equine (*frm*) • **club ~** riding club
hipido SM whine, whimper
hipismo SM horse-racing
hipnosis SF INV hypnosis
hipnoterapia SF hypnotherapy
hipnótico ADJ, SM hypnotic
hipnotismo SM hypnotism
hipnotista SMF hypnotist
hipnotizable ADJ susceptible to hypnosis
hipnotizador(a) ADJ hypnotizing
SM/F hypnotist
hipnotizante SMF hypnotist
hipnotizar ▷ CONJUG 1f VT **1** (*Psic*) to hypnotize
2 (= *hechizar*) to mesmerize
hipo SM **1** (*gen*) hiccups (*pl*), hiccoughs (*pl*) • **quitar el ~ a algn** to cure sb's hiccups • **tener ~** to have hiccups • MODISMO: • **que quita el ~** breathtaking
2†† (= *deseo*) longing, yearning • **tener ~ por** to long for, crave
hipo... PREF hypo...
hipoalergénico ADJ hypoallergenic
hipocalórico ADJ low-calorie (*antes de s*)
hipocampo SM sea horse
hipocondria SF, **hipocondría** SF hypochondria
hipocondriaco, hipocondríaco/a ADJ hypochondriac, hypochondriacal
SM/F hypochondriac
hipocorístico ADJ • **nombre ~** pet name, *affectionate form of a name, e.g. Merche = Mercedes, Jim = James*
Hipócrates SM Hippocrates
hipocrático ADJ • **juramento ~** Hippocratic oath
hipocresía SF hypocrisy
hipócrita ADJ hypocritical
SMF hypocrite
hipócritamente ADV hypocritically
hipodérmico ADJ hypodermic • **aguja hipodérmica** hypodermic needle
hipódromo SM [*de caballos*] racecourse, racetrack (*EEUU*); (*Hist*) hippodrome
hipoglucemia SF hypoglycaemia, hypoglycemia (*EEUU*)
hipoglucémico ADJ (*Med*) hypoglycaemic, hypoglycemic (*EEUU*)
hipónimo SM hyponym
hipopótamo SM hippopotamus, hippo
hiposulfito SM ▸ **hiposulfito sódico** (*Fot*) hypo, sodium thiosulphate
hipoteca SF mortgage • **segunda ~** second mortgage, remortgage • **levantar una ~** to raise a mortgage • **redimir una ~** to pay off a mortgage ▸ **hipoteca dotal** endowment mortgage
hipotecable ADJ mortgageable
hipotecar ▷ CONJUG 1g VT [+ *propiedades*] to mortgage; [+ *futuro*] to jeopardize
VPR **hipotecarse** (= *comprometerse*) to commit o.s.
hipotecario ADJ mortgage (*antes de s*)
hipotensión SF low blood pressure
hipotenso/a ADJ • **ser ~** to have low blood pressure
SM/F person with low blood pressure
hipotensor ADJ hypotensive
hipotenusa SF hypotenuse
hipotermia SF hypothermia
hipótesis SF INV **1** (= *suposición*) hypothesis, supposition
2 (= *teoría*) theory, idea • **es solo una ~** it's just an idea *o* a theory
hipotéticamente ADV hypothetically
hipotético ADJ hypothetic, hypothetical
hipotetizar ▷ CONJUG 1f VI to hypothesize
hippie ['xipi] ADJ, SMF, **hippy** ['xipi] ADJ, SMF (PL: **hippies**) hippy
hippioso/a* [xi'pjoso] ADJ hippyish
SM/F hippy type
hippismo [xi'pismo] SM hippy movement • **los años del ~** the hippy years
hiriente ADJ **1** [*observación, tono*] wounding, cutting
2 [*contraste*] striking
hirsutez SF hairiness
hirsuto ADJ **1** [*persona*] hairy, hirsute (*frm*); [*barba*] bristly
2 (= *brusco*) brusque, gruff
hirvición* SF (*And*) abundance, multitude
hirviendo ▷ **hervir**
hirviente ADJ boiling, seething
hisca SF birdlime
hisopear ▷ CONJUG 1a VT (*Rel*) to sprinkle with holy water, asperse (*frm*)
hisopo SM **1** (*Rel*) sprinkler, aspergillum (*frm*)
2 (*Bot*) hyssop
3 (*LAm*) (= *brocha*) paintbrush
4 (*Cono Sur*) [*de algodón*] cotton bud, Q-tip® (*EEUU*)
5 (*Cono Sur*) (= *trapo*) dishcloth
hispalense (*liter*) ADJ of/from Sevilla
SMF native/inhabitant of Sevilla • **los ~s** the people of Sevilla
Híspalis SF (*liter*) Seville
Hispania SF (*Hist*) Hispania, Roman Spain
hispánico ADJ Hispanic (*frm*), Spanish
hispanidad SF **1** (*gen*) Spanishness, Spanish characteristics (*pl*)
2 (*Pol*) Spanish world, Hispanic world (*frm*) • **Día de la Hispanidad** Columbus Day (*12 October*)

DÍA DE LA HISPANIDAD
El Día de la Hispanidad, on October 12, is a national holiday in Spain in honour of Columbus's arrival in the Americas. It is also a holiday in other Spanish-speaking countries, where it is called the **Día de la Raza**.

hispanismo SM **1** *word etc borrowed from Spanish*, hispanicism (*frm*)

2 (*Univ*) Hispanism, Hispanic studies (*pl*) • **el ~ holandés** Hispanic studies in Holland
hispanista SMF (*Univ*) hispanist, hispanicist
hispanística SF Hispanic studies (*pl*)
hispanizar ▷ CONJUG 1f VT to Hispanicize
hispano/a ADJ **1** (= *español*) Spanish, Hispanic (*frm*)
2 (= *latinoamericano*) Hispanic
SM/F **1** (= *español*) Spaniard
2 (= *latinoamericano*) Spanish-speaking American (*EEUU*), Hispanic
hispano-... PREF Hispano-..., Spanish-... • **pacto hispano-italiano** Hispano-Italian pact
hispano... PREF Hispano..., Spanish...
Hispanoamérica SF Spanish America, Hispanic America
hispanoamericano/a ADJ, SM/F Spanish American, Hispanic American, Latin American
hispanoárabe ADJ Hispano-Arabic
hispanófilo/a SM/F Hispanophile
hispanófobo/a SM/F hispanophobe
hispanohablante ADJ Spanish-speaking
SMF Spanish speaker
hispanomarroquí ADJ Spanish-Moroccan
hispanoparlante ADJ, SMF = **hispanohablante**
hispinglés SM (*hum*) Spanglish
histamínico ADJ histamine (*antes de s*)
histerectomía SF hysterectomy
histeria SF hysteria ▸ **histeria colectiva** mass hysteria
histéricamente ADV hysterically
histérico/a ADJ **1** (*Med*) hysterical • **paroxismo ~** hysterics (*pl*)
2 (= *nervioso*) • **no seas tan ~** don't get so worked up • **¡me pone ~!*** it drives me mad!, it drives me up the wall*
SM/F **1** (*Med*) hysteric
2 (= *nervioso*) • **no hagas caso, son unos ~s** pay no attention, they're always having hysterics
histerismo SM **1** (*Med*) hysteria
2 (= *nerviosismo*) hysterics (*pl*)
histerizarse ▷ CONJUG 1f VPR to get hysterical
histograma SM histogram
histología SF histology
historia SF **1** [*de país, institución*] history • **la ~ del cine** the history of film *o* cinema • **es licenciado en ~** he has a degree in history, he has a history degree • **es un récord absoluto en la ~ del torneo** it is a tournament record • **nuestros problemas ya son ~** the problems we had are history now • MODISMOS: • **hacer ~** to make history • **un acuerdo que hará ~** an agreement that will make history • **un atleta que ha hecho ~ en el mundo del deporte** an athlete who has made sporting history • **pasar a la ~**: • **pasará a la ~ como la primera mujer en el espacio** she will go down in history as the first woman in space • **ese modelo de coche ya ha pasado a la ~** that model of car is a thing of the past • **nuestro problema ya pasó a la ~** our problem is a thing of the past *o* has long since disappeared • **picar en ~†** to be a serious matter • **ser de ~†** to be famous; (*pey*) to be notorious • **tener ~** [*objeto*] to have an interesting history; [*suceso*] to be interesting • **tiene ~ cómo conseguimos este libro** how we got hold of this book is an interesting story, there's an interesting story behind how we got hold of this book ▸ **historia antigua** ancient history ▸ **historia clínica** medical history ▸ **historia del arte** history of art, art history ▸ **historia moderna** modern history ▸ **historia natural** natural history ▸ **Historia Sagrada** Biblical history; (*en la escuela†*) Scripture ▸ **historia universal** world history
2 (= *relato*) story • **esta ~ es larga de contar** it's a long story • **cuéntame con detalles toda la ~** tell me the whole story in detail • **esta es la ~ de una princesita** this is the story of a little princess • **la ~ de siempre** *o* **la misma ~** *o* **la ~ de todos los días** the same old story • **una ~ de amor** a love story
3 (= *enredo*) story • **¡ahora no me cuentes la ~ de tu vida!** don't tell me your whole life story now! • **tu vecina siempre viene con ~s** your neighbour is always gossiping
4 (= *excusa*) (*sobre algo pasado*) excuse, story; (*sobre algo presente o futuro*) excuse • **seguro que te viene con alguna ~** she's sure to give you some excuse *o* tell you some story • **¿así que has estado trabajando hasta ahora? ¡no me vengas con ~s** *o* **déjate de ~s!** so you've been working right up to now, have you? don't give me any of your stories! • **dijo que llegaba tarde por no sé qué ~** he said he was going to be late for some reason or other
5* (= *lío*) business* • **andan metidos en una ~ un poco rara** they're mixed up in a rather funny business*
6* (= *romance*) fling* • **tener una ~ con algn** to have a fling with sb*
historiado ADJ **1** (*Arte*) historiated (*frm*), storiated (*frm*)
2 (= *con exceso de adorno*) over-elaborate, fussy
historiador(a) SM/F **1** (= *estudioso*) historian ▸ **historiador(a) de arte** art historian
2 (= *cronista*) chronicler, recorder
historia-ficción SF historical novels (*pl*)
historial ADJ historical
SM **1** (*en archivo*) [*de acontecimiento*] record; [*de persona*] curriculum vitae, CV, résumé (*EEUU*)
2 (*Med*) case history
3 (*tb* **historial de ventas**) sales history
historiar ▷ CONJUG 1b VT **1** [*escritor*] to write the history of; [*libro*] to tell the history of, recount the history of • **este desarrollo cultural es historiado en una nueva obra** the history of this cultural development is recorded in a new book
2 (*Arte*) to depict
históricamente ADV historically
historicismo SM historicism
historicista ADJ historicist
histórico/a ADJ **1** (= *de la historia*) [*perspectiva, contexto, investigación*] historical • **una película basada en hechos ~s** a film based on historical facts • **las novelas históricas son mis preferidas** I'm particularly keen on historical novels • **el patrimonio ~ del país** the country's heritage
2 (= *importante*) [*acontecimiento, encuentro*] historic; [*récord*] all-time • **este es un momento ~** this is a historic moment • **el centro** *o* **casco ~ de la ciudad** the historic city centre • **el dólar marcó un nuevo mínimo ~ frente al yen** the dollar hit an all-time low against the yen
3 [*miembro, socio*] (*de hace tiempo*) long-serving; (*desde el principio*) founder • **los ~s fundadores del partido** the founding fathers of the party • **miembro ~** (= *de hace tiempo*) long-serving member; (= *desde el principio*) founder member
SM/F • **el Atlético, uno de los ~s del fútbol español** Atlético, one of the oldest teams in Spanish football
historiero ADJ (*Cono Sur*) gossipy
historieta SF **1** (*con viñetas*) strip cartoon, comic strip
2 (= *anécdota*) tale
historietista SMF strip cartoonist
historificar ▷ CONJUG 1g VT to consign to the history books
historiografía SF historiography (*frm*), writing of history
historiógrafo/a SM/F historiographer
histrión SM (*liter*) **1** (= *actor*) actor, player; (= *farsante*) playactor
2 (= *bufón*) buffoon
histriónico ADJ histrionic
histrionismo SM **1** (*Teat*) acting, art of acting
2 (= *oratoria*) histrionics (*pl*)
3 (= *actores*) actors (*pl*), theatre people (*pl*)
hita SF **1** (*Téc*) brad, headless nail
2 = **hito**
hitita ADJ (*Hist*) Hittite, of/from Anatolia
SMF (*Hist*) Hittite, native/inhabitant of Anatolia • **los ~s** the Hittites, the people of Anatolia
SM (*Ling*) Hittite
hitleriano ADJ Hitlerian
hito SM **1** (= *acontecimiento*) landmark, milestone • **es un ~ en nuestra historia** it is a landmark in our history • **esto marca un ~ histórico** this marks a historical milestone
2 (= *señal*) (*para límites*) boundary post; (*para distancias*) milestone; (*Aut*) (= *cono*) cone, traffic cone • MODISMO: • **mirar a algn de ~ en ~** to stare at sb ▸ **hito kilométrico** kilometre stone
3 (*Dep*) quoits
4 (*Mil*) (*lit*) target; (*fig*) aim, goal • MODISMOS: • **a ~** fixedly • **dar en el ~** to hit the nail on the head • **mudar de ~** to change one's tactics
hizo ▷ **hacer**
hl ABR (= **hectolitro(s)**) hl
hm ABR (= **hectómetro(s)**) hm
Hna., Hnas. ABR (= **Hermana(s)**) Sr(s)
Hno., Hnos. ABR (= **Hermano(s)**) Bro(s)
hobby ['xobi] SM (PL: **hobbys** ['xobis]) hobby
hocicada* SF • **darse una ~ con la puerta** to bash one's face against the door* • **darse una ~ en el suelo** to fall flat on one's face
hocicar ▷ CONJUG 1g VT [*cerdo*] to root among; [*persona*] to nuzzle
VI **1** [*cerdo*] to root; [*persona*] to nuzzle
2 (*Náut*) to pitch
3 (= *caer*) to fall on one's face
4 (= *enfrentarse*) to run into trouble, come up against it
5† [*amantes*] to pet • **~ con** *o* **en** to put one's nose against, put one's nose into
hocico SM **1** [*de animal*] snout, nose
2 [*de persona*] (= *cara*) mug*; (= *nariz*) snout* • **caer de ~s** to fall (flat) on one's face • **cerrar el ~‡** to shut one's trap‡, belt up‡ • **dar de ~s contra algo** to bump *o* walk into sth • MODISMOS: • **estar de ~s** to be in a bad mood • **meter el ~** to meddle, poke one's nose in • **poner ~** to scowl • **torcer el ~** to make a (wry) face, look cross
hocicón* ADJ (*And*) angry, cross
hocicudo* ADJ (*And, Caribe*) (= *con mala cara*) scowling; (= *de mal humor*) grumpy*
hociquear ▷ CONJUG 1a VT, VI = **hocicar**
hociquera SF (*And, Caribe*) muzzle
hockey ['oki, 'xoki] SM hockey, field hockey (*EEUU*) ▸ **hockey sobre hielo** ice hockey, hockey (*EEUU*) ▸ **hockey sobre hierba** hockey ▸ **hockey sobre patines** roller hockey
hodierno†† ADJ (= *diariamente*) daily; (= *frecuente*) frequent
hogaño†† ADV (= *este año*) this year; (= *actualmente*) these days, nowadays
hogar SM **1** (= *casa*) home • **dejó el ~ familiar a los veinte años** he left home at the age of

twenty • **artículos del** *o* **para el ~** household goods • **labores del ~** housework • **se han quedado sin ~** they have become homeless • **~, dulce ~** home, sweet home ▸ **hogar conyugal** conjugal home ▸ **hogar de acogida** (*para huérfanos, refugiados*) home ▸ **hogar de ancianos** old folk's home, old people's home ▸ **hogar del pensionista** senior citizens' social club
2 (= *chimenea*) hearth (*liter*) • **se sentaron al calor del ~** they sat around the fire • **se recuperó al calor del ~** he recuperated in the comfort of his own home
3 (*Téc*) furnace; (*Ferro*) firebox
4 (*Esp*) (*Educ*) home economics

hogareño ADJ [*cocina*] home (*antes de s*); [*ambiente*] homely; [*persona*] home-loving

hogaza SF large loaf

hoguera SF **1** (= *fogata*) bonfire • **la casa estaba hecha una ~** the house was ablaze, the house was an inferno; ▷ SAN JUAN
2 (*Hist*) stake • **murió en la ~** he was burned at the stake

hoja SF **1** (*Bot*) [*de árbol, planta*] leaf; [*de hierba*] blade • **de ~ ancha** broad-leaved • **de ~ caduca** deciduous • **de ~ perenne** evergreen • **la ~** (*LAm‡*) pot*, hash* ▸ **hoja de parra** fig leaf
2 [*de papel*] leaf, sheet; (= *página*) page; (= *formulario*) form, document • **~s sueltas** loose sheets, loose-leaf paper (*sing*) • **volver la ~** (*lit*) to turn the page; (= *cambiar de tema*) to change the subject; (= *cambiar de actividad*) to turn over a new leaf • MODISMO: • **doblar la ~** to change the subject ▸ **hoja de cálculo** spreadsheet ▸ **hoja de cumplido** compliments slip ▸ **hoja de embalaje** packing-slip ▸ **hoja de guarda** flyleaf ▸ **hoja de inscripción** registration form ▸ **hoja de pedido** order form ▸ **hoja de reclamación** complaint form ▸ **hoja de ruta** waybill; (*fig*) road map ▸ **hoja de servicio(s)** record (of service) ▸ **hoja de trabajo** (*Inform*) worksheet ▸ **hoja de vida** (*And*) curriculum vitae, résumé (*EEUU*), CV ▸ **hoja electrónica** spreadsheet ▸ **hoja informativa** leaflet, handout ▸ **hoja parroquial** parish magazine ▸ **hoja volante, hoja volandera** leaflet, handbill
3 (*Téc*) [*de metal*] sheet; [*de espada, patín*] blade ▸ **hoja de afeitar** razor blade ▸ **hoja de estaño** tinfoil ▸ **hoja de lata** tin, tinplate ▸ **hoja plegadiza** flap (*of table etc*)
4 [*de puerta*] [*de madera*] leaf; [*de cristal*] sheet, pane
5 ▸ **hoja de tocino** side of bacon, flitch

hojalata SF tin, tinplate; (*LAm*) corrugated iron

hojalatada SF (*Méx*) (*Aut*) panel beating

hojalatería SF **1** (= *obra*) tinwork
2 (= *establecimiento*) tinsmith's, tinsmith's shop
3 (*LAm*) (= *objetos*) tinware

hojalaterío SM (*And, CAm, Méx*) tinware

hojalatero/a SM/F tinsmith

hojaldre SM, **hojalda** SF (*LAm*), **hojaldra** SF (*LAm*) puff pastry

hojarasca SF **1** (= *hojas*) dead leaves (*pl*), fallen leaves (*pl*)
2 (*frm*) (*al hablar*) empty verbiage, waffle*

hojear ▷ CONJUG 1a VT **1** (= *pasar las hojas de*) to turn the pages of, leaf through
2 (= *leer rápidamente*) to skim through, glance through
VI **1** (*Méx*) (*Bot*) to put out leaves
2 (*CAm, Méx*) (*Agr*) to eat leaves
3 [*superficie*] to scale off, flake off

hojerío SM (*CAm*) leaves, foliage

hojilla SF (*Ven*) (*tb* **hojilla de afeitar**) razor blade

hojoso ADJ leafy

hojuela SF **1** (*Bot*) leaflet, little leaf
2 (= *lámina*) [*de cereal, pintura*] flake; [*de metal*] foil, thin sheet ▸ **hojuela de estaño** tinfoil ▸ **hojuelas de maíz** (*LAm*) cornflakes
3 (*Culin*) pancake; (*Caribe, Méx*) puff pastry

hola EXCL hello!, hullo!, hi!*

holán SM **1** (= *tejido*) cambric, fine linen
2 (*Méx*) (= *volante*) flounce, frill

Holanda SF Holland

holandés/esa ADJ Dutch, of/from Holland
SM/F native/inhabitant of Holland • **los holandeses** the people of Holland, the Dutch • **el ~ errante** the Flying Dutchman
SM (*Ling*) Dutch

holandesa SF (*Tip*) quarto sheet

holding ['xoldin] SM (PL: **holdings** ['xoldin]) holding company

holgadamente ADV **1** (= *ampliamente*) loosely, comfortably • **caben ~** they fit in easily, they go in with room to spare • **ganaron las elecciones ~** they won the elections easily *o* comfortably
2 (= *cómodamente*) • **vivir ~** to live comfortably, be comfortably off

holgado ADJ **1** [*ropa*] (= *suelto*) loose, comfortable, baggy • **demasiado ~** too big
2 (= *amplio*) roomy • **así quedará el cuarto más ~** this will make more space in the room • **consiguieron una victoria holgada** they won easily *o* comfortably
3 (= *cómodo*) comfortably off, well-to-do • **vida holgada** comfortable life, life of ease

holganza SF (*frm*) **1** (= *inactividad*) idleness; (= *descanso*) rest; (= *ocio*) leisure, ease
2 (= *diversión*) amusement, enjoyment

holgar ▷ CONJUG 1h, 1l VI **1** (= *descansar*) to rest, take one's ease
2 (= *no trabajar*) to be idle, be out of work
3 (*frm*) [*objeto*] to lie unused
4 (*frm*) (= *sobrar*) to be unnecessary, be superfluous • **huelga decir que ...** it goes without saying that ... • **huelga toda protesta** no protest is necessary, it is not necessary to protest
5 (= *estar contento*) • **huelgo de saberlo** I'm delighted to hear it
VPR **holgarse** (*frm*) to amuse o.s., enjoy o.s. • **~se con algo** to take pleasure in sth • **~se con una noticia** to be pleased about a piece of news • **~se de que ...** to be pleased that ..., be glad that ...

holgazán/ana ADJ idle, lazy
SM/F idler, loafer, layabout*

holgazanear ▷ CONJUG 1a VI to laze around, loaf about

holgazanería SF laziness, loafing

holgazanitis SF INV (*hum*) congenital laziness, work-shyness

holgorio SM = **jolgorio**

holgura SF **1** (= *anchura*) (*Cos*) looseness, fullness; (*Mec*) play, free movement
2 (= *bienestar*) comfortable living • **vivir con ~** to live comfortably
3† (= *goce*) enjoyment; (= *alegría*) merriment, merrymaking

holismo SM holism

holístico ADJ holistic

hollar ▷ CONJUG 1l VT (*frm*) **1** (= *pisar*) to tread, tread on
2 (= *pisotear*) to trample down
3 (= *humillar*) to humiliate

hollejo SM (*Bot*) skin, peel

hollín SM soot

holliniento ADJ, **hollinoso** ADJ sooty, covered in soot

holocausto SM **1** (*Hist*) • **el Holocausto** the Holocaust
2 (= *desastre*) ▸ **holocausto nuclear** nuclear holocaust
3 (*Rel*) (= *sacrificio*) burnt offering, sacrifice

holografía SF holograph

holograma SM hologram

hombracho SM, **hombrachón** SM hulking great brute, big tough fellow

hombrada SF manly deed, brave act • **¡vaya ~!** (*iró*) how brave!

hombradía SF manliness, courage, guts*

hombre SM **1** (= *varón adulto*) man; (= *especie humana*) mankind • **¡ven aquí si eres ~!** come over here if you're a real man! • **ayúdale, que el ~ ya no puede más** help him, the poor man's exhausted • **es otro ~ desde que se casó** he's been a different man since he got married • **es ~ de pocas palabras** he is a man of few words • **¡~ al agua!** man overboard! • **el abominable ~ de las nieves** the abominable snowman • **creerse muy ~**: • **se cree muy ~** he thinks he's a real hard man • **pobre ~**: • **el pobre ~ se quedó sin nadie** the poor man *o* poor devil ended up all alone • **no le hagas caso, es un pobre ~** don't take any notice, he's just a sad little man* • MODISMOS: • **como un solo ~**: • **contestaron como un solo ~** they answered with one voice • **desde que el ~ es ~** always, since the year dot • **hablar de ~ a ~** to talk man to man • **ser un ~ de pelo en pecho** to be a real man, be a he-man • **ser un ~ hecho y derecho** to be a grown man • **si lo compras, me haces un ~*** if you buy it, you'll be doing me a big favour • REFRÁN: • **el ~ propone y Dios dispone** man proposes, God disposes ▸ **hombre blanco** white man ▸ **hombre bueno** honest man, good man ▸ **hombre de armas** man-at-arms ▸ **hombre de bien** honest man, good man ▸ **hombre de confianza** right-hand man ▸ **hombre de estado** statesman ▸ **hombre de la calle** • **el ~ de la calle no entiende el problema** the average person can't understand the problem ▸ **hombre de las cavernas** caveman ▸ **hombre del día** man of the moment ▸ **hombre de letras** man of letters ▸ **hombre de leyes** lawyer, attorney(-at-law) (*EEUU*) ▸ **hombre del saco** bogeyman ▸ **hombre del tiempo** weatherman ▸ **hombre de mar** seafaring man, seaman ▸ **hombre de mundo** man of the world ▸ **hombre de negocios** businessman ▸ **hombre de paja** stooge* ▸ **hombre de pro, hombre de provecho** worthy *o* good man ▸ **hombre fuerte** • **el ~ fuerte del partido** the strong man of the party ▸ **hombre lobo** werewolf ▸ **hombre medio** • **el ~ medio** the man in the street, the average person ▸ **hombre mosca** trapeze artist ▸ **hombre muerto** • **¡si no te rindes eres ~ muerto!** surrender or you're a dead man! ▸ **hombre mundano** man-about-town ▸ **hombre orquesta** one-man band
2 (= *miembro de ejército, equipo*) man
EXCL • **—¿me haces un favor? —sí, ~** "would you do me a favour?" — "(yes) of course" • **—¿vendrás? —¡~ claro!** "are you coming?" — "you bet!" • **¡venga, ~, haz un esfuerzo!** come on, make an effort! • **¡~, no me vengas con eso!** oh please *o* oh come on, don't give me that! • **~, yo creo que ...** well, I think that ... • **¡~, Pedro! ¿qué tal?** hey, Pedro! how's things? • **¡vaya, ~, qué mala suerte has tenido!** dear oh dear, what terrible luck!

hombre-anuncio SM (PL: **hombres-anuncio**) sandwich-board man

hombrear[1] ▷ CONJUG 1a VI [*joven*] to act grown-up, play the man; [*hombre*] to act tough

hombrear[2] ▷ CONJUG 1a VT **1** (= *empujar*) to shoulder, push with one's shoulder

2 (*And, Cono Sur, Méx*) (= *ayudar*) to help, lend a hand to
VI • **~ con algn** to try to keep up with sb, strive to equal sb
VPR **hombrearse** ▷ VI

hombrecillo SM **1** (= *persona*) little man, little fellow
2 (*Bot*) hop

hombre-gol SM (PL: **hombres-gol**) striker who can score goals

hombre-lobo SM (PL: **hombres-lobo**) werewolf

hombre-masa SM (PL: **hombres-masa**) ordinary man, man in the street

hombre-mono SM (PL: **hombres-mono**) apeman

hombrera SF **1** (*Cos*) (= *almohadilla*) shoulder pad; (= *tirante*) shoulder strap
2 (*Mil*) epaulette

hombre-rana SM (PL: **hombres-rana**) frogman

hombrerío SM (*Ven*) men (*pl*)

hombretón SM big strong fellow

hombría SF manliness ▸ **hombría de bien** honesty, uprightness

hombrillo SM (*Caribe*) (*Aut*) hard shoulder, berm (*EEUU*)

hombro SM shoulder • **a ~s** on one's shoulders • **¡armas al ~!** • **¡sobre el ~ armas!** shoulder arms! • **cargar algo sobre los ~s** to shoulder sth • **echarse algo al ~** to shoulder sth, take sth upon o.s. • **en ~s**: • **sacar a algn en ~s** to carry sb out on their shoulders • **el vencedor salió en ~s** the victor was carried out shoulder-high • **encogerse de ~s** to shrug one's shoulders, shrug • **enderezar los ~s** to square one's shoulders, straighten up • MODISMOS: • **arrimar el ~** to put one's shoulder to the wheel, lend a hand • **~ con ~** shoulder to shoulder • **mirar a algn por encima del ~** to look down on sb, look down one's nose at sb • **poner el ~** to put one's shoulder to the wheel, lend a hand

hombruno ADJ mannish, butch*

homenaje SM **1** (= *tributo*) tribute • **en ~ a algn** in honour of sb • **rendir** *o* **tributar ~ a** to pay a tribute to, pay homage to • **rendir el último ~** to pay one's last respects
2 (= *celebración*) celebration, gathering (*in honour of sb*)
3 (*LAm*) (= *regalo*) gift, favour, favor (*EEUU*)
ADJ • **una cena-homenaje para don Manuel** a dinner in honour *o* (*EEUU*) honor of don Manuel • **un concierto-homenaje para el compositor** a concert in honour *o* (*EEUU*) honor of the composer • **libro-homenaje** homage volume • **partido-homenaje** benefit match, testimonial game

homenajeado/a SM/F • **el ~** the person being honoured *o* (*EEUU*) honored, the guest of honour *o* (*EEUU*) honor

homenajear ▷ CONJUG 1a VT to honour, honor (*EEUU*), pay tribute to

homeópata SMF homeopath

homeopatía SF homeopathy

homeopático ADJ homeopathic

homérico ADJ Homeric

Homero SM Homer

homicida ADJ homicidal • **el arma ~** the murder weapon
SMF murderer/murderess

homicidio SM (= *intencionado*) murder, homicide (*frm*); (= *involuntario*) manslaughter ▸ **homicidio frustrado** attempted murder

homilía SF homily

homínido SM hominid

homoerótico ADJ homo-erotic

homoerotismo SM homoeroticism

homofobia SF homophobia

homofóbico ADJ homophobic

homófobo/a ADJ homophobic
SM/F homophobe

homófono (*Ling*) ADJ homophonic
SM homophone

homogeneidad SF homogeneity

homogeneización SF levelling down, leveling down (*EEUU*), equalization

homogeneizante, homogeneizador ADJ homogenizing • **una tendencia ~ a** tendency for homogenization
SM homogenizer

homogeneizar ▷ CONJUG 1f VT, **homogenizar** ▷ CONJUG 1f VT to homogenize, level down, equalize

homogéneo ADJ homogeneous

homógrafo SM homograph

homologable ADJ equivalent (**a, con** to), comparable (**a, con** to)

homologación SF **1** (= *aprobación*) official approval • **el nuevo medicamento ha recibido la ~ de la UE** the new drug has received EU approval, the new drug has been licensed by the EU
2 (= *equiparación*) • **le han denegado la ~ del título** they refused to recognize her qualification as equivalent • **favorecía la ~ de lo popular y lo culto** he was in favour of equal status for popular and high culture
3 (*Dep*) ratification, recognition

homologado ADJ officially approved

homologar ▷ CONJUG 1h VT **1** (= *aprobar*) to approve officially, sanction
2 (= *equiparar*) to bring into line, standardize
3 (*Dep*) [+ *récord*] to ratify, recognize

homólogo/a ADJ equivalent (**de** to)
SM/F counterpart, opposite number

homónimo ADJ homonymous
SM **1** (*Ling*) homonym
2 (= *tocayo*) namesake

homoparental ADJ same-sex (*antes de s*) • **adopción ~** adoption by a same-sex couple

homosexual ADJ, SMF homosexual

homosexualidad SF, **homosexualismo** SM homosexuality

honda SF (*de cuero*) sling; (*elástica*) catapult, slingshot (*EEUU*)

hondear¹ ▷ CONJUG 1a VT (*Náut*) (= *sondear*) to sound; (= *descargar*) to unload

hondear² ▷ CONJUG 1a VT (*LAm*) to hit with a catapult *o* (*EEUU*) slingshot

hondo ADJ **1** (= *profundo*) deep • **plato ~** soup plate • **en lo más ~ de la piscina** at the deep end (of the pool) • **la hirió en lo más ~ de su ser** he wounded her to the depths of her being, she was cut to the quick
2 (= *intenso*) deep, profound • **con ~ pesar** with deep *o* profound sorrow
ADV • **respirar ~** to breathe deeply
SM • **el ~** the depth(s) (*pl*)

hondón SM **1** [*de taza, valle*] bottom
2 [*de espuela*] footrest
3 [*de aguja*] eye

hondonada SF **1** (= *valle*) hollow, dip
2 (= *barranco*) gully, ravine

hondura SF **1** (= *profundidad*) depth, profundity (*frm*)
2 (= *lugar*) depth, deep place • MODISMO: • **meterse en ~s** to get out of one's depth, get into deep water

Honduras SF Honduras ▸ **Honduras Británica** (*Hist*) British Honduras

hondureñismo SM *word or phrase peculiar to Honduras*

hondureño/a ADJ of/from Honduras
SM/F native/inhabitant of Honduras • **los ~s** the people of Honduras

honestamente ADV **1** (= *sinceramente*) honestly • **dime ~ lo que piensas** tell me honestly what you think
2 (= *honradamente*) honourably, honorably (*EEUU*) • **cumple ~ con su deber** she carries out her duty honourably • **se comportó ~ y nos devolvió lo nuestro** he did the decent thing and gave us back what was rightly ours
3 (= *decentemente*) decently

honestidad SF **1** (= *sinceridad*) honesty • **te diré con ~ lo que pienso** I'll tell you honestly what I think
2 (= *honradez*) honour, honor (*EEUU*) • **puso en duda la ~ del presidente** he called into question the president's honour
3 (= *decencia*) decency

honesto ADJ **1** (= *sincero*) honest • **sé ~ y dime lo que piensas** be honest and tell me what you think
2 (= *honrado*) honourable, honorable (*EEUU*) • **hay pocos políticos ~s** there are very few honourable politicians • **es muy ~ y sabe reconocer sus errores** he's very honest and is able to recognize his mistakes
3 (= *decente*) decent

hongkonés/esa, hongkongués/esa ADJ of/from Hong Kong
SM/F native/inhabitant of Hong Kong • **los hongkoneses** the people of Hong Kong

hongo SM **1** (*Bot*) fungus
2 (*Med*) fungal growth • **tengo ~s en los pies** I have athlete's foot, I have a fungal infection on my feet
3 (= *seta*) (*comestible*) mushroom; (*venenoso*) toadstool • **un enorme ~ de humo** an enormous mushroom cloud of smoke • MODISMO: • **crecen** *o* **proliferan como ~s** they sprout up like mushrooms
4 (= *sombrero*) bowler hat, derby (*EEUU*)

honkonés/esa ADJ, SM/F = **hongkonés**

Honolulú SM Honolulu

honor SM **1** (= *cualidad*) honour, honor (*EEUU*) • **en ~ a la verdad** to be fair • **en ~ de algn** in sb's honour • **hacer ~ a** to honour • **hacer ~ a su fama** to live up to its *etc* reputation • **hacer ~ a un compromiso** to honour a pledge • **hacer ~ a su firma** to honour one's signature • **tener el ~ de hacer algo** to have the honour of doing sth, be proud to do sth ▸ **honor profesional** professional etiquette
2 honores honours, honors (*EEUU*) • **sepultar a algn con todos los ~es militares** to bury sb with full military honours • **hacer los ~es de la casa** to do the honours of the house • **hacer los debidos ~es a una comida** to do full justice to a meal
3 (= *gloria*) glory • **Antonio Machado, ~ de esta ciudad** Antonio Machado, who is this city's claim to fame
4 [*de mujer*] honour, honor (*EEUU*), virtue

honorabilidad SF **1** (= *cualidad*) honourableness (*frm*), honour, honor (*EEUU*), worthiness
2 (= *persona*) distinguished person

honorable ADJ honourable, honorable (*EEUU*), worthy

honorario ADJ honorary, honorific

honorarios SMPL fees, professional fees, charges

honorífico ADJ honourable, honorable (*EEUU*) • **cargo ~** honorary post • **mención honorífica** honourable mention

honra SF **1** (= *orgullo*) honour, honor (*EEUU*), pride • **tener algo a mucha ~** to be proud of sth, consider sth an honour • **tener a mucha ~ hacer algo** to be proud to do sth, consider it an honour to do sth • **¡y a mucha ~!** and proud of it! ▸ **honra personal** personal honour
2† (= *virginidad*) honour, honor (*EEUU*), virtue
3 ▸ **honras fúnebres** funeral rites, last honours; ▷ **atentado**

h

honradamente ADV **1** (= *honestamente*) honestly
2 (= *honorablemente*) honourably, honorably (*EEUU*), uprightly

honradez SF **1** (= *honestidad*) honesty
2 (= *integridad*) uprightness, integrity, honourableness (*frm*)

honrado ADJ **1** (= *honesto*) honest • **hombre ~** honest man, decent man
2 (= *honorable*) honourable, honorable (*EEUU*), upright

honrar ▸ CONJUG 1a VT **1** (= *enorgullecer*) to honour, honor (*EEUU*) • **un gesto que le honra** a gesture to be proud of
2 (= *respetar*) to honour, honor (*EEUU*), revere (*frm*)
3 (*Com*) to honour, honor (*EEUU*)
VPR **honrarse** • **~se con algo** to be honoured *o* (*EEUU*) honored by sth • **me honro con su amistad** I am honoured by his friendship, I am privileged to be his friend • **~se de hacer algo** to be honoured to do sth, consider it an honour to do sth

honrilla SF • MODISMO: • **por la negra ~** out of concern for what people will say, for the sake of appearances

honrosamente ADV honourably, honorably (*EEUU*)

honroso ADJ **1** (= *honorable*) honourable, honorable (*EEUU*)
2 (= *respetable*) respectable • **es una profesión honrosa** it is a respectable profession

hontanar SM spring, group of springs

hopa¹ SF cassock

hopa² EXCL **1** (*Cono Sur*) (= *¡deja!*) stop it!, that hurts!
2 (*And, CAm, Méx*) (= *saludo*) hullo!
3 (*Arg*) (*a animales*) whoa!

hopo¹ ['xopo] SM (fox's) brush, tail

hopo² EXCL out!, get out!

hora SF **1** (= *periodo de tiempo*) hour • **el viaje dura una ~** the journey lasts an hour • **durante dos ~s** for two hours • **dos ~s de reloj** two hours exactly • **esperamos ~s** we waited for hours • **ocho euros la ~** eight euros an hour • **echar ~s** to put the hours in • **media ~** half an hour • **la media ~ del bocadillo** half-hour break at work, ≈ tea break • **por ~s** by the hour • **trabajar por ~s** to work on an hourly basis *o* by the hour • **sueldo por ~** hourly wage • **asistenta por ~s** daily (help) ▸ **hora puente** (*Arg, Uru*) hour off ▸ **horas de comercio** business hours ▸ **horas de consulta** opening hours (*of surgery*) ▸ **horas de mayor audiencia** (*TV*) prime time (*sing*) ▸ **horas de oficina** business hours, office hours ▸ **horas de trabajo** working hours ▸ **horas de visita** visiting hours ▸ **horas de vuelo** (*Aer*) flying time (*sing*); (*fig*) (= *experiencia*) experience (*sing*); (*fig*) (= *antigüedad*) seniority (*sing*) ▸ **horas extra, horas extraordinarias** overtime (*sing*) • **hacer ~s (extra)** to work overtime ▸ **horas libres** free time (*sing*), spare time (*sing*) ▸ **horas muertas** dead period (*sing*) • **se pasa las ~s muertas viendo la tele** he spends hour after hour watching telly
2 (= *momento*) **a** (*concreto*) time • **¿qué ~ es?** what time is it?, what's the time? • **¿tienes ~?** have you got the time? • **¿a qué ~?** (at) what time? • **¿a qué ~ llega?** what time is he arriving? • **¡la ~!** • **¡es la ~!** time's up! • **llegar a la ~** to arrive on time • **a la ~ en punto** on the dot • **a la ~ justa** in the nick of time • **a la ~ de pagar ...** when it comes to paying ... • **a altas ~s (de la madrugada)** in the small hours • **a una ~ avanzada** at a late hour • **dar la ~** [*reloj*] to strike (the hour) • **poner el reloj en ~** to set one's watch • **no comer entre ~s** not to eat between meals • **a estas ~s:** • **a estas ~s ya deben de estar en París** they must be in Paris by now • **ayer a estas ~s** at this time yesterday
b (*oportuno*) • **buena ~:** • **es buena ~ para empezar** it's a good time to start • **llegas a buena ~** you've arrived just in time • **en buena ~** at just the right time • **es ~ de hacer algo** it is time to do sth • **es ~ de irnos** it's time we went, it's time for us to go • **estas no son ~s de llegar a casa** this is no time to get home, what sort of a time is this to get home? • **le ha llegado la ~** her time has come • **mala ~:** • **es mala ~** it's a bad time • **en mala ~ se lo dije** I shouldn't have told her • **en la ~ de su muerte** at the moment of his death • **a primera ~** first thing in the morning • **a última ~** at the last moment, at the last minute • **dejar las cosas hasta última ~** to leave things until the last moment *o* minute • **cambios de última ~** last-minute changes • **noticias de última ~** last-minute news • **"última hora"** (*noticias*) "stop press" • **la ~ de la verdad** the moment of truth • **¡ya era ~!** and about time too! • **ya es *o* va siendo ~ de que te vayas** it is high time (that) you went, it is about time (that) you went • MODISMOS: • **¡a buena(s) ~(s) (mangas verdes)!** it's too late now! • **¡a buenas ~s llegas!** this is a fine time for you to arrive! • **a buena ~(s) te vuelvo a prestar nada** that's the last time I lend you anything • **no ver la ~ de algo** to be hardly able to wait for sth, look forward impatiently to sth ▸ **hora bruja** witching hour ▸ **hora cero** zero hour • **desde las cero ~s** from midnight ▸ **hora de apertura** opening time ▸ **hora de cenar** dinnertime ▸ **hora de comer** (*gen*) mealtime; (*a mediodía*) lunchtime ▸ **hora de entrada** • **la ~ de entrada a la oficina** the time when we start work at the office ▸ **hora de las brujas** witching hour ▸ **hora de recreo** playtime, recess (*EEUU*) ▸ **hora de salida** [*de tren, avión, bus*] time of departure; [*de carrera*] starting time; [*de escuela, trabajo*] finishing time ▸ **hora estimada de llegada** estimated time of arrival ▸ **hora insular canaria** *local time in the Canary Islands* ▸ **hora judicial** *time when the courts start hearing cases* ▸ **hora local** local time ▸ **hora media de Greenwich** Greenwich mean time ▸ **hora oficial** official time, standard time ▸ **hora peninsular** *local time in mainland Spain* ▸ **hora pico** (*Méx*) rush hour ▸ **hora punta** [*del tráfico*] rush hour ▸ **horas punta** [*de electricidad, teléfono*] peak hours ▸ **hora suprema** one's last hour, hour of death ▸ **horas valle** off-peak times ▸ **hora universal** universal time
3 (*Educ*) period • **después de inglés tenemos una ~ libre** after English we have a free period ▸ **horas de clase** (= *horas lectivas*) teaching hours; (= *horas de colegio*) school hours • **van a reducir las ~s de clase** teaching hours are going to be cut • **doy ocho ~s de clase** [*profesor*] I teach for eight hours • **en ~s de clase** during school hours
4 (= *cita*) appointment • **dar ~ a algn** to give sb an appointment • **pedir ~** to ask for an appointment • **tener ~** to have an appointment • **tengo ~ para el dentista** I've got an appointment at the dentist's
5 (*Rel*) • **libro de ~s** book of hours ▸ **horas canónicas** canonical hours

horaciano ADJ Horatian

Horacio SM Horace

horadar ▸ CONJUG 1a VT (= *perforar*) drill, perforate (*frm*); [+ *túnel*] to make

hora-hombre SF (PL: **horas-hombre**) man-hour

horario SM **1** [*de trabajo, trenes*] timetable • **el ~ de verano empieza hoy** summer time starts today, the clocks go forward today • **"horario de invierno: abierto solo mañanas"** "winter hours: open mornings only" • **llegar a ~** (*LAm*) to arrive on time, be on schedule ▸ **horario comercial** business hours (*pl*) ▸ **horario continuo, horario corrido** (*LAm*) continuous working day ▸ **horario de atención al público** public opening hours (*pl*) ▸ **horario de máxima audiencia** (*TV*) peak viewing time, prime time ▸ **horario de oficina** office hours (*pl*) ▸ **horario de visitas** [*de hospital*] visiting hours (*pl*); [*de médico*] surgery hours (*pl*) ▸ **horario estelar** (*Ven*) (*TV*) peak viewing time, prime time ▸ **horario flexible** flexitime ▸ **horario intensivo** continuous working day ▸ **horario partido** split shift(s)
2 [*de reloj*] hour hand
ADJ (= *cada hora*) hourly; ▸ **huso, señal**

horca SF **1** [*de ejecución*] gallows, gibbet • **condenar a algn a la ~** to condemn sb *o* send sb to the gallows
2 (*Agr*) pitchfork
3 [*de ajos*] string
4 (*Caribe*) (= *regalo*) birthday present, *present given on one's saint's day*

horcadura SF fork (*of a tree*)

horcajadas SFPL • **a ~** astride

horcajadura SF (*Anat*) crotch

horcajo SM **1** (*Agr*) yoke
2 [*de árbol, río*] fork

horcar ▸ CONJUG 1g VT (*LAm*) = **ahorcar**

horchata SF [*de chufas*] tiger nut milk; [*de almendras*] almond milk

horchatería SF refreshment stall

horcón SM **1** (= *horca*) pitchfork
2 (*para frutales*) forked prop
3 (*LAm*) (*para techo*) prop, support

horda SF horde

hordiate SM barley water

horero SM (*And, Méx*) hour hand

horita* ADV (*esp Méx*) = **ahorita**

horizontal ADJ horizontal
SF horizontal position • **se desplaza en ~** it moves horizontally • **lleva una raya en ~ sobre el logotipo** it has a horizontal line on the logo • MODISMO: • **coger *o* tomar la ~*** to crash out*

horizontalmente ADV horizontally

horizonte SM **1** (= *línea*) horizon • **la línea del ~** the horizon • **en el ~ del año 2000** around the year 2000
2 horizontes (= *perspectivas*) • **este descubrimiento abrirá nuevos ~s** this discovery will open up new horizons • **el partido tiene unos ~s muy estrechos** the party has limited horizons *o* ambitions

horma SF **1** (*Téc*) form, mould, mold (*EEUU*); [*de calzado*] last, shoetree • MODISMO: • **encontrar(se) con la ~ de su zapato** to meet one's match ▸ **horma de sombrero** hat block
2 (= *muro*) dry-stone wall

hormadoras SFPL (*And*) petticoat (*sing*)

hormiga SF **1** (*Entomología*) ant • MODISMO: • **ser una ~*** (= *trabajador*) to be hard-working; (= *ahorrativo*) to be thrifty ▸ **hormiga blanca** white ant ▸ **hormiga león** antlion, antlion fly ▸ **hormiga obrera** worker ant ▸ **hormiga roja** red ant
2 hormigas (*Med*) (= *picor*) itch (*sing*); (= *hormigueo*) pins and needles

hormigón SM concrete ▸ **hormigón armado** reinforced concrete ▸ **hormigón pretensado** pre-stressed concrete

hormigonera SF concrete mixer

hormigonero ADJ concrete (*antes de s*)

hormiguear ▸ CONJUG 1a VI **1** [*parte del cuerpo*] (*al quedarse insensible*) to tingle; (= *hacer cosquillas*) to tickle; (= *picar*) to itch • **me**

hormiguea el pie I've got pins and needles in my foot
2 *[gente, animales]* to swarm, teem
hormigueo SM **1** *(en el cuerpo) (al quedarse insensible)* tingling; *(= cosquilleo)* ticklish feeling, pins and needles; *(al picar)* itch, itching
2 *(= inquietud)* anxiety, uneasiness
3 *[de gente, animales]* swarming
hormiguero ADJ ant-eating • **oso ~** anteater
SM **1** *(Entomología)* ants' nest, ant hill
2 *[de gente]* • **aquello era un ~** it was swarming with people
hormiguillo SM = **hormigueo**
hormiguita* SF • **ser una ~** *(= muy trabajador)* to be hard-working, be always beavering away; *(= ahorrativo)* to be thrifty
hormona SF hormone ▸ **hormona de(l) crecimiento** growth hormone
hormonal ADJ hormonal
hormonarse ▸ CONJUG 1a VPR to have hormone treatment
hornacina SF niche, vaulted niche
hornada SF **1** *[de pan]* batch
2 *[de estudiantes, políticos]* collection, crop
hornalla SF *(Cono Sur) (= horno)* oven; *[de estufa]* hotplate, burner (EEUU), ring
hornazo SM **1** *(= pastel)* Easter pie *(decorated with eggs)*
2 *[de pasteles, pan]* batch
horneado SM cooking (time), baking (time)
hornear ▸ CONJUG 1a VT to cook, bake
VI to bake
hornero/a SM/F baker
hornillo SM **1** *(Culin) (gen)* cooker, stove; *(portátil)* portable stove ▸ **hornillo de gas** gas ring ▸ **hornillo eléctrico** hotplate, burner (EEUU)
2 *(Téc)* small furnace
3 *[de pipa]* bowl
4 *(Mil, Hist)* mine
horno SM **1** *(Culin)* oven, stove • **¡esta casa es un ~!** it's like an oven in here! • **al ~** baked • **asar al ~** to bake • **meter un plato al ~ fuerte** to put a dish into a high oven • **resistente al ~** ovenproof • MODISMO: • **no está el ~ para bollos** this is the wrong moment ▸ **horno de leña** wood-fired oven ▸ **horno microondas** microwave oven
2 *(Téc)* furnace; *(para cerámica)* kiln • **alto(s) ~(s)** blast furnace *(sing)* ▸ **horno crematorio** crematorium ▸ **horno de cal** lime kiln ▸ **horno de fundición** smelting furnace ▸ **horno de ladrillos** brick kiln
3 *[de pipa]* bowl
horóscopo SM horoscope • **leer el ~** to read one's stars *o* horoscope
horqueta SF **1** *(Agr)* pitchfork
2 *(Bot)* fork of a tree
3 *(LAm) [de camino]* fork
horquetear ▸ CONJUG 1a VT *(Cono Sur)* *[+ oído]* to prick up; *[+ persona]* to listen suspiciously to
VI **1** *(Méx) (= ahorcajarse)* to sit astride, straddle
2 *(LAm) (= enramar)* to grow branches, put out branches
horquetilla SF *(Ven)* = **horquilla**
horquilla SF **1** *(para pelo)* hairpin, hairclip
2 *(Agr) (para heno)* pitchfork; *(para cavar)* garden fork
3 *(Mec) (en bicicleta)* fork; *(para carga)* yoke
4 *(Telec)* rest, cradle
5 *[de zanco]* footrest
6 *(Com) [de salarios]* wage levels *(pl)*; *[de inflación]* bracket
horrarse ▸ CONJUG 1a VPR *(LAm) (Agr)* to abort
horrendo ADJ **1** *(= aterrador) [crimen]* horrific, ghastly*
2 *(= horrible) [ropa, zapatos]* hideous, ghastly*; *[película, libro]* dreadful; *[frío, calor]* terrible, dreadful, awful • **tengo un hambre ~** I'm terribly hungry
hórreo SM raised granary
horrible ADJ **1** *(= espantoso) [accidente, crimen, matanza]* horrific • **una pesadilla ~** a horrible nightmare
2 *(= feo) [persona, objeto, ropa, cuadro]* hideous • **ella es guapa pero su novio es ~** she's pretty but her boyfriend's hideous • **hizo un tiempo ~** the weather was horrible • **tienes una letra ~** your handwriting is terrible
3 *(= malo, perverso)* horrible • **¡qué hombre tan ~!** what a horrible man!
4 *(= insoportable)* terrible • **tengo un dolor de cabeza ~** I've got a terrible headache • **hizo un calor ~** it was terribly hot, the heat was terrible • **la conferencia fue un rollo ~*** the lecture was a real drag*
horriblemente ADV horribly, dreadfully
horripilante ADJ *(= espeluznante) [escena]* hair-raising, horrifying; *[persona]* creepy*, terrifying
horripilar ▸ CONJUG 1a VT • **~ a algn** to make sb's hair stand on end, horrify sb, give sb the creeps*
VPR **horripilarse** to be horrified, be terrified • **era para ~se** it was enough to make your hair stand on end
horro ADJ *(frm)* **1** *(= exento)* free, exempt, enfranchised • **~ de** bereft of, devoid of
2 *(Bio)* sterile
horror SM **1** *(= miedo)* horror **(a** of**)**, dread **(a** of**)** • **¡qué ~!** how awful *o* dreadful!, how ghastly!* • **tener ~ a algo** to have a horror of sth • **la fiesta fue un ~*** the party was ghastly*, the party was dreadful • **se dicen ~es de la cocina inglesa*** awful things are said about English cooking • **tener algo en ~** *(frm)* to detest sth, loathe sth
2 *(= acto)* atrocity, terrible thing • **los ~es de la guerra** the horrors of war
3* *(= mucho)* • **me gusta ~es** *o* **un ~** I love it • **hoy he trabajado un ~** today I worked awfully hard • **me duele ~es** it's really painful, it hurts like mad *o* like hell* • **se divirtieron ~es** they had a tremendous *o* fantastic time* • **ella sabe ~es** she knows a hell of a lot*
horrorizado ADJ horrified, appalled
horrorizar ▸ CONJUG 1f VT **1** *(= indignar)* to horrify, appal, appall (EEUU)
2 *(= dar miedo)* to terrify
VPR **horrorizarse 1** *(= indignarse)* to be horrified, be appalled
2 *(= tener miedo)* to be terrified
horrorosamente ADV **1** *(= aterradoramente)* horrifyingly
2 *[sufrir, doler]* horribly, frightfully
3 *[vestir, peinarse]* dreadfully, awfully
horroroso ADJ **1** *(= aterrador)* dreadful, ghastly*
2 *(= horrible) [ropa, peinado]* hideous, horrific; *[dolor]* terrible; *[película, libro]* dreadful • **tengo un sueño ~** I feel really sleepy
horrura SF **1** *(= suciedad)* filth, dirt
2 *(= basura)* rubbish, garbage (EEUU)
hortaliza SF **1** *(= verdura)* vegetable; **hortalizas** vegetables, garden produce
2 *(Méx) (= huerto)* vegetable garden
hortelano/a SMF **1** *(= jardinero)* gardener
2 *(Com)* market gardener, truck farmer (EEUU)
hortensia SF hydrangea
hortera[1]* *(Esp)* ADJ INV **1** *(= de mal gusto) [decoración]* tacky*, tasteless, vulgar; *[persona]* lacking in taste; *[gustos]* terrible, crude
2† *(= fingido)* fraud, sham
SMF • **es un ~** his taste stinks*, he has lousy taste*
hortera[2]† SF wooden bowl
hortera[3]† SM shop-assistant, grocer's boy
horterada* SF *(Esp)* vulgarity • **ese vestido es una ~** that dress is a sight*
horterez* SF *(Esp)*, **horterismo*** SM *(Esp)* coarseness, vulgarity
horterizar* ▸ CONJUG 1f *(Esp)* VT to coarsen, cheapen, make vulgar
hortícola ADJ horticultural, garden *(antes de s)*
SMF = **horticultor**
horticultor(a) SM/F **1** horticulturist, gardener
2 *(en vivero)* nurseryman
horticultura SF horticulture, gardening
horticulturista SMF horticulturalist, horticulturist
hortofrutícola ADJ fruit and vegetable *(antes de s)*
hortofruticultura SF fruit and vegetable growing
hosco ADJ **1** *[persona]* sullen, grim *(liter)*
2 *[tiempo, lugar, ambiente]* gloomy
hospedador SM *(Bio)* host
hospedaje SM (cost of) board and lodging
hospedar ▸ CONJUG 1a VT **1** *(= alojar)* to lodge, give a room to
2 *(= recibir)* to receive as a guest, entertain
VPR **hospedarse** to stay, lodge **(en** at**)**
hospedería SF **1** *(= posada)* hostelry, inn
2 *(en convento)* guest quarters *(pl)*
hospedero/a SM/F **1** *(= posadero)* landlord/landlady, innkeeper
2 *(= anfitrión)* host/hostess
hospiciano/a SM/F, **hospiciante** SMF *(LAm)* orphan *(living in an orphanage)*
hospicio SM **1** *(para niños)* orphanage
2 *(para pobres) (Hist)* poorhouse; *(Rel)* hospice
3 *(Cono Sur) (para ancianos)* old people's home
hospital SM hospital, infirmary ▸ **hospital de aislamiento** isolation hospital ▸ **hospital de campaña** field hospital ▸ **hospital de contagiosos** isolation hospital ▸ **hospital de día** day hospital ▸ **hospital de sangre** field dressing station

HOSPITAL

Uso del artículo

En inglés el uso del artículo delante de **hospital** *depende del motivo por el que alguien haya acudido al centro hospitalario:*

▸ *Se traduce* **al hospital** *por* **to hospital, en el hospital** *por* **in hospital** *y* **desde el hospital** *por* **from hospital** *cuando alguien está o va a ser ingresado allí:*
La llevaron con urgencia al hospital como consecuencia de un infarto
She was rushed to hospital following a heart attack
Después del accidente estuvo tres meses en el hospital
Following the accident, she was in hospital for three months

▸ *Se traduce* **al hospital** *por* **to the hospital, en el hospital** *por* **at the hospital** *y* **desde el hospital** *por* **from the hospital** *cuando alguien va o está allí por otros motivos. También se emplea el artículo cuando se trata de consultas externas:*
Este lunes tengo que ir al hospital a una revisión
I've got to go to the hospital on Monday for a check-up
Mi hermana trabaja en el hospital
My sister works at the hospital

Para otros usos y ejemplos ver la entrada.

hospitalariamente (ADV) hospitably
hospitalario (ADJ) **1** (= *acogedor*) hospitable
2 (*Med*) hospital (*antes de s*) • **estancia hospitalaria** stay in hospital • **atención hospitalaria** hospital treatment
hospitalidad (SF) hospitality
hospitalización (SF) hospitalization
hospitalizar ▹ CONJUG 1f (VT) to send to hospital, take to hospital, hospitalize (*frm*) • **estuvo hospitalizado tres meses** he spent three months in hospital
(VPR) **hospitalizarse** (*LAm*) to go into hospital
hosquedad (SF) **1** [*de persona*] sullenness, grimness (*liter*)
2 [*del tiempo, lugar*] gloominess
hostal (SM) cheap hotel, boarding house
hostelería (SF) **1** (= *industria*) hotel trade, hotel business • **empresa de ~** catering company
2 (= *gerencia*) hotel management
hostelero/a (ADJ) catering (*antes de s*) • **sector ~** hotel and catering industry
(SM/F) innkeeper, landlord/landlady
hostería (SF) **1** (= *posada*) inn, hostelry
2 (*Cono Sur*) (= *hotel*) hotel
hostia (SF) **1** (*Rel*) host, consecrated wafer
2** (= *golpe*) punch, bash*; (= *choque*) bang, bash*, smash • **dar de ~s a algn** to kick the shit out of sb** • **liarse a ~s** to get into a scrap* • **le pegué dos ~s** I walloped him a couple of times*
3** (*como exclamación*) • **¡hostia!** (*indicando sorpresa*) Christ almighty!‡, bloody hell!‡; (*indicando fastidio*) damn it all!
4** (*como intensificador*) • **de la ~**: • **ese inspector de la ~** that bloody inspector‡ • **había un tráfico de la ~** the traffic was bloody awful‡ • **una tormenta de la ~** a storm and a half* • **ni ~**: • **no entiendo ni ~** I don't understand a damn *o* bloody word of it* • **¡qué ~(s)!** (*para negar*) get away!, never!, no way!*; (*indicando rechazo*) bollocks!** • **¿qué ~s quieres?** what the hell do you want?* • **¡qué libros ni qué ~s!** books, my foot!* *o* my arse!**
5** • **mala ~**: • **estar de mala ~** to be in a filthy* *o* shitty** mood • **tener mala ~** (= *mal carácter*) to have a nasty streak; (= *mala suerte*) to have rotten luck
6** • MODISMOS: • **déjate de ~s** stop pissing around**, stop faffing around* • **echar ~s** to shout blue murder*, go up the wall* • **hacer un par como unas ~s** to muck it all up* • **ir a toda ~** to go like the clappers* • **no tiene media ~** he's no use at all, he's a dead loss* • **salió cagando *o* echando ~s** he shot out like a bat out of hell • **ser la ~**: • **¡ese tío es la ~!** (*con admiración*) he's a hell of a guy!*; (*con enfado*) what a shit he is!** • **y toda la ~** and all the rest
hostiar** ▹ CONJUG 1b (VT) to wallop*, sock*, bash*
hostiazo** (SM) bash*, sock*
hostigamiento (SM) **1** (= *acoso*) harassment
2 (*con vara, látigo*) lashing, whipping
hostigar ▹ CONJUG 1h (VT) **1** (= *molestar*) to harass, plague, pester
2 (= *dar latigazos*) to lash, whip
3 (*LAm*) [+ *comida*] to surfeit, cloy
hostigoso (ADJ) (*And, Cono Sur*) [*comida*] sickly, cloying; [*persona*] annoying, tedious
hostil (ADJ) hostile
hostilidad (SF) **1** (= *cualidad*) hostility
2 (= *acto*) hostile act • **iniciar las ~es** to start hostilities
hostilizar ▹ CONJUG 1f (VT) (*Mil*) to harry, harass, worry
hostión** (SM) (= *golpe, choque*) bash* • **su padre le dio *o* pegó un buen ~** her father gave her a good walloping • **se dio *o* pegó un ~ contra el árbol** he smashed into a tree
hotel (SM) **1** (*Com*) hotel ▸ **hotel alojamiento** (*Cono Sur*), **hotel garaje** (*Méx*) *hotel where one pays by the hour* ▸ **hotel boutique** boutique hotel
2‡ (= *cárcel*) (*tb* **hotel del Estado, hotel rejas**) nick‡, prison
3 (*Mil*) glasshouse‡
hotelería (SF) = **hostelería**
hotelero/a (ADJ) hotel (*antes de s*) • **la industria hotelera** the hotel trade
(SM/F) hotelkeeper, hotel manager/manageress, hotelier
hotelito (SM) (*gen*) small house; (*de vacaciones*) cottage, vacation retreat, second home
hotentote (ADJ) Hottentot
(SMF) Hottentot
hoy (ADV) **1** (= *en este día*) today • **¿a qué día estamos hoy?** what day is it today? • **hoy hace un mes de su boda** their wedding was a month ago today • **de hoy**: • **en el correo de hoy** in today's post • **el día de hoy** (*Esp*) this very day • **de hoy en adelante** from now on • **de hoy no pasa que le escriba** I'll write to him this very day • **está para llegar de hoy a mañana** he could arrive any day now • **desde hoy** from now on • **de hoy en ocho días** a week today • **de hoy en quince días** today fortnight, a fortnight today • **hasta hoy**: • **eso me prometió, ¡y hasta hoy!** that's what he promised me, and I've heard no more about it! • **hoy mismo**: • —**¿cuándo quieres empezar?** —**hoy mismo** "when do you want to start?" — "today" • **por hoy**: • **por hoy hemos terminado** that's all for today • MODISMO: • **hoy por ti, mañana por mí** you can do the same for me some time
2 (= *en la actualidad*) today, nowadays • **hoy todo es mejor que antes** things are better today *o* nowadays than before • **la juventud de hoy** the youth of today • **hoy (en) día** nowadays • **hoy por hoy** at the present time, right now
hoya (SF) **1** (= *agujero*) pit, hole ▸ **hoya de arena** (*Golf*) bunker, sand trap (*EEUU*)
2 (= *tumba*) grave
3 (*Geog*) vale, valley; (*LAm*) [*de río*] riverbed, river basin
4 (*Agr*) seedbed
hoyada (SF) hollow, depression
hoyador (SM) (*LAm*) dibber, seed drill
hoyanco (SM) (*Méx*) (*Aut*) pothole, hole in the road
hoyar ▹ CONJUG 1a (VT) (*CAm, Caribe, Méx*) to make holes (*for sowing seeds*)
hoyito (SM) (*en la cara*) dimple
hoyo (SM) **1** (= *agujero*) hole • **en el ~ 18** (*Golf*) at the 18th hole ▸ **hoyo negro** (*CAm, Méx*) black hole
2 (= *hondura*) pit
3 (= *tumba*) grave
4 (*Med*) pockmark
5 (= *hueco*) hollow, cavity
6 • MODISMO: • **irse al ~** (*Cono Sur**) to get into an awful jam*, face ruin; ▹ **muerto**
hoyuelo (SM) dimple
hoz (SF) **1** (*Agr*) sickle • **la hoz y el martillo** the hammer and sickle
2 (*Geog*) gorge, narrow pass, defile (*frm*)
3 • MODISMO: • **de hoz y coz** wildly, recklessly
hozar ▹ CONJUG 1f (VT) [*cerdo*] to root in, root among
hros. (ABR) = **herederos**
hs (ABR) (= **horas**) h., hrs
hua... (PREF) ▹ **gua...**
huaca (SF) = **guaca**
huacalón (ADJ) (*Méx*) **1** (= *gordo*) fat
2 (= *de voz áspera*) gravel-voiced
huacarear‡ ▹ CONJUG 1a (VI) (*LAm*) to throw up*
huacha (SF) (*And*) washer
huachafería (SF) (*And*) **1** (= *gente*) middle-class snobs (*pl*), social climbers (*pl*)
2 (= *actitud*) snobbery, airs and graces
huachafo/a (*And*) (ADJ) = **cursi**
(SM/F) middle-class snob, social climber
(SM) (*Caribe*) funny man, comic
huachinango (SM) (*Caribe, Méx*) red snapper
huacho (SM) **1** (*And*) *section of a lottery ticket*
2 (*Méx**) *common soldier*
(ADJ) (*Méx*) = **guacho**
huaco (SM) (*And*) (*Hist*) *ancient Peruvian pottery artefact*
(ADJ) (*LAm*) (= *sin dientes*) toothless
huahua (SF) (*LAm*) = **guagua**
huaica (SF) (*And*) bargain sale
huaico (SM) (*And*) alluvium
huaipe (SM) (*Chile*) cotton waste
huáncar (SM), **huáncara** (*And*) (SF) (*And*) Indian drum
huaquero/a (SM/F) (*And*) = **guaquero**
huaraca (SF) (*And*) = **guaraca**
huarache (SM) (*Méx*) (= *sandalia*) sandal
huáscar* (SM) (*Chile*) water cannon truck (*used by police*)
huasicama (SMF) (*And*) Indian servant
huasipungo (SM) (*And*) (*Agr*) (Indian's) tied plot of land
huaso/a (SM/F) (*Chile*) = **guaso**
huasteca (SF) • **la Huasteca** *the region round the Gulf of Mexico*
huatal (SM) (*LAm*) = **guatal**
huave (SMF) (*Méx*) Huave Indian
huayco (SM) **1** (*And, Chile*) (= *alud*) landslide of mud and rock; ▹ **guaico**
2 (*And*) (= *matón a sueldo*) paid thug
huayno (SM) (*And, Chile*) *folk song and dance*; ▹ CHICHA
hube *etc* ▹ **haber**
hucha (SF) **1** (*para ahorrar*) money box; (*para caridad*) collecting tin
2 (= *ahorros*) savings (*pl*) • **tener una buena ~** to have a nice little nest egg, have money laid by
3† (= *arca*) chest
hueca‡ (SF) pansy‡, queer‡, fag (*EEUU*‡)
hueco (ADJ) **1** [*árbol, tubo*] hollow • **una nuez hueca** an empty walnut shell • MODISMO: • **tener la cabeza hueca** to be empty-headed
2 [*lana, tierra*] soft
3 [*blusa, chaqueta*] loose
4 [*sonido*] hollow; [*voz*] booming, resonant
5 (= *insustancial*) [*palabras, promesas, retórica*] empty • **un discurso retórico y ~** a speech full of empty rhetoric
6 (= *pedante*) [*estilo, lenguaje*] pompous
7 [*persona*] (= *orgulloso*) proud; (= *engreído*) conceited, smug • **el niño se puso muy ~ cuando lo nombraron ganador** the boy was very proud when he was declared the winner • **la típica rubia hueca** (*pey*) the usual blonde bimbo*
(SM) **1** (= *agujero*) (*en valla, muro*) hole • **se ha caído un pájaro por el ~ de la chimenea** a bird has fallen down the chimney • **el ~ del ascensor** the lift *o* (*EEUU*) elevator shaft • **el ~ de la escalera** the stairwell • **el ~ de la puerta** the doorway
2 (= *espacio libre*) space; (*entre árboles*) gap, opening • **en este ~ voy a poner la lavadora** I'm going to put the washing machine in this (empty) space • **no hay ni un ~ para aparcar** there isn't a single parking space • **el ~ que quedaba entre las dos mesas** the gap *o* space between the two tables • **solo hay ~s en la primera fila** the only places *o* spaces are in the front row • **en su corazón**

no hay ~ para el rencor there is no room in his heart for rancour • **hacer (un) ~ a algn** to make space for sb • **¿me haces un ~?** can you make some room for me?
3 (*en texto*) gap, blank
4 (*en mercado, organización*) gap • **en el mercado hay un ~ para una revista de este tipo** there is a gap in the market for this type of magazine • **abrirse** *o* **hacerse un ~** to carve *o* create a niche for oneself • **aspiran a abrirse un ~ en el mundo de la música pop** they are hoping to carve *o* create a niche for themselves in the pop world • **llenar** *u* **ocupar un ~** to fill a gap • **deja un ~ que será difícil llenar** he leaves a gap which will be hard to fill
5 (= *cavidad*) hollow • **el ~ de la mano** the hollow of the *o* one's hand • **suena a ~** it sounds hollow
6 (= *nicho*) recess, alcove
7 (= *en una empresa*) vacancy
8 [*de tiempo*] • **en cuanto tenga un ~ hablará contigo** he will talk to you as soon as he has a gap in his schedule *o* as soon as he can fit you in • **hizo un ~ en su programa para recibirlos** he made space in his schedule to see them, he managed to fit them into his schedule
9 (*Méx‡*) (= *homosexual*) queer‡, faggot (EEUU‡)
10 (*Tip*) = huecograbado

huecograbado SM (*Tip*) photogravure

huela *etc* ▹ oler

huelán (*Cono Sur*) ADJ **1** (= *inmaduro*) (*gen*) immature, not fully developed; [*madera*] unseasoned; [*hierba*] withered; [*trigo*] unripe
2 • **una persona huelana** a person who has come down in the world

huelebraguetas‡ SMF INV private eye*

hueleguisos* SMF INV (*And*) sponger*, scrounger*

huelehuele* SMF (*Caribe*) idiot

huelga SF **1** [*de trabajo*] strike, stoppage, walkout • **los obreros en ~** the workers on strike, the striking workers • **estar en ~** to be on strike • **declarar la ~** • **declararse en ~** • **hacer ~** • **ir a la ~** • **ponerse en ~** to go on strike, come out on strike ▸ **huelga (a la) japonesa** *industrial action characterized by overproduction by the workforce* ▸ **huelga de brazos caídos** sit-down strike ▸ **huelga de celo** work-to-rule, go-slow, slowdown (strike) (EEUU) ▸ **huelga de hambre** hunger strike ▸ **huelga de hostigamiento** guerrilla strike ▸ **huelga de pago de alquiler** rent strike ▸ **huelga de reglamento** work-to-rule, go-slow, slowdown (strike) (EEUU) ▸ **huelga general** general strike ▸ **huelga oficial** official strike ▸ **huelga patronal** lock-out ▸ **huelga por solidaridad** sympathy strike ▸ **huelga rotatoria** rotating strike ▸ **huelga salvaje** wildcat strike
2 (= *descanso*) rest, repose (*frm*)
3 (*Mec*) play, free movement

huelgo SM (*frm*) **1** (= *aliento*) breath • **tomar ~** to take breath, pause
2 (= *espacio*) room, space • **entra con ~** it goes in easily, it goes in with room to spare
3 (*Mec*) play, free movement

huelguear ▹ CONJUG 1a VI (*And*) to strike, be on strike

huelguismo SM strike mentality, readiness to strike

huelguista SMF striker

huelguístico ADJ strike (*antes de s*) • **movimiento ~** wave of strikes • **el panorama ~** the strike scene

huella SF **1** (*en el suelo*) (= *pisada*) footprint, footstep; [*de coche, animal*] track • **seguir las ~s de algn** to follow in sb's footsteps ▸ **huella dactilar, huella digital** fingerprint ▸ **huella de carbono** carbon footprint ▸ **huella ecológica** carbon footprint ▸ **huella genética** genetic fingerprint
2 (= *rastro*) trace • **sin dejar ~** without leaving a trace, leaving no sign • **se le notaban las ~s del sufrimiento** you could see the signs of her suffering
3 (= *impronta*) • **el presidente dejó una ~ inconfundible en el partido** the president left his unmistakable mark *o* stamp on the party • **aquello dejó una ~ imborrable** it left an indelible memory
4 (= *acto*) tread, treading
5 [*de escalera*] tread

huellear ▹ CONJUG 1a VT (*And*) to track, follow the trail of

huellero ADJ • **perro ~** (*And*) tracker dog

huello†† SM *condition of the ground etc (for walking)* • **camino de buen ~** good road for walking • **camino de mal ~** bad road for walking, badly-surfaced road

Huelva SF Huelva

huemul SM (*Cono Sur*) southern Andean deer

huérfano/a ADJ **1** [*niño*] orphaned • **una niña huérfana de madre** a motherless child, a child that has lost her mother
2 (= *desprovisto*) • **~ de** [+ *seguridad, protección*] devoid of; [+ *cariño, amor*] bereft of (*frm*), starved of
SM/F orphan

huero ADJ **1** [*palabras, acciones*] empty, sterile • **un discurso ~** an empty speech
2 [*huevo*] rotten
3 (*CAm, Méx*) = güero

huerta SF **1** (= *huerto*) vegetable garden, kitchen garden (EEUU)
2 (*Esp*) • **la ~ murciana/valenciana** the fertile, irrigated region of Murcia/Valencia
3 (*And*) [*de cacao*] cocoa plantation

huertano/a ADJ (*Esp*) of/from "la huerta"
SM/F **1** (= *hortelano*) market gardener, truck farmer (EEUU)
2 (*Esp*) (= *habitante*) inhabitant of the "huerta"; (= *hortelano*) farmer (of the "huerta")

huertero/a SM/F (*LAm*) gardener

huerto SM [*de verduras*] kitchen garden; (*comercial*) (small) market garden, truck garden (EEUU); [*de árboles frutales*] orchard; (*en casa pequeña*) back garden • **el Huerto de los Olivos** the Mount of Olives • **MODISMO**: • **llevarse a algn al ~*** (= *engañar*) to put one over on sb*, lead sb up the garden path*; (*a la cama*) to go to bed with sb, sleep with sb, go for a roll in the hay with sb*

huesa SF grave

huesear‡ ▹ CONJUG 1a VI (*LAm*) to beg

huesecillo SM small bone

huesería SM (*And*) unsaleable merchandise

huesillo SM (*And, Cono Sur*) sun-dried peach

huesista* SMF (*Méx*) *person with a soft job*

hueso SM **1** (*Anat*) bone • **sin ~** boneless • **una blusa de color ~** an off-white blouse • **MODISMOS**: • **dar con los ~s en**: • **dio con sus ~s en la cárcel** he landed *o* ended up in jail • **estar calado** *o* **empapado hasta los ~s** to be soaked to the skin • **estar en los ~s** to be nothing but skin and bone • **estar por los ~s de algn*** to be crazy about sb* • **no dejar ~ sano a algn** to pull sb to pieces • **pinchar en ~*** to come up against a brick wall • **ser un saco de ~s*** to be a bag of bones* • **la sin ~*** the tongue • **darle a la sin ~*** to talk a lot • **irse de la sin ~** • **soltar la sin ~*** to shoot one's mouth off* • **tener los ~s molidos** to be dog-tired ▸ **hueso de santo** *filled roll of marzipan*
2 (*Bot*) stone, pit (EEUU) • **aceitunas sin ~** pitted olives • **MODISMOS**: • **ser un ~***: • **las matemáticas son un ~** maths is a nightmare • **su profesor es un ~** her teacher is terribly strict • **ser un ~ duro de roer*** to be a hard nut to crack
3 (*CAm, Méx*) (= *sinecura*) government job, sinecure; (= *puesto cómodo*) soft job
4 (*And*) mule • **MODISMO**: • **ser ~** to be stingy
5 ▸ **hueso colorado** (*Méx*) strong northerly wind

huesoso ADJ (*esp LAm*) bony, bone (*antes de s*)

huésped SMF **1** (= *invitado*) (*en casa, hotel*) guest; (*en pensión*) lodger, roomer (EEUU), boarder • **MODISMO**: • **hacerse los dedos ~es**: • **se le hacen los dedos ~es cada vez que oye hablar de dinero** he rubs his hands at the first mention of money
2 (= *anfitrión*) host/hostess
3†† (= *posadero*) innkeeper, landlord/landlady • **MODISMO**: • **no contar con la ~** to reckon without one's host
ADJ • **ordenador ~** host computer • **hembra ~** host female

huestes SFPL (*liter*) **1** (= *ejército*) host (*sing*) (*liter*), army (*sing*)
2 (= *partidarios*) followers

huesudo ADJ bony, big-boned

hueva SF **1** (*tb* **huevas**) (*Culin*) roe; (*Zool*) eggs, spawn (*sing*) ▸ **hueva de lisa** (*Méx*) cod roe ▸ **huevas de lumpo** German caviar (*sing*)
2 **huevas** (*Chile***) (= *testículos*) balls**

huevada SF **1** (*And, Cono Sur‡*) (= *comentario*) stupid remark; (= *acto*) stupid thing (to do); (= *idea*) crazy idea; **huevadas** (= *tonterías*) nonsense, rubbish*, crap**
2 (*LAm*) [*de huevos*] nest of eggs, clutch of eggs
3 • **una ~‡** (*como adv*) a hell of a lot* • **se divirtió una ~** he had a tremendous *o* fantastic time*

huevear* ▹ CONJUG 1a VI (*Chile*) to mess about*

huevera SF **1** (*para guardar huevos*) egg box
2‡ (= *suspensorio*) jockstrap

huevería SF *shop that specializes in selling eggs*

huevero ADJ egg (*antes de s*) • **industria huevera** egg industry

huevo SM **1** (*Bio, Culin*) egg • **MODISMOS**: • **andar sobre ~s** to go very gingerly • **hacerle ~ a algo** (*CAm‡*) to face up to sth • **parecerse como un ~ a una castaña*** to be like chalk and cheese • **pensar en los ~s del gallo** (*And, CAm*) to be in a daydream • **poner algo a ~**: • **nos lo han puesto a ~*** they've made it easy for us • **¡que te frían un ~!‡** get knotted!‡ • **ser como el ~ de Colón** to be simple, be easy ▸ **huevo a la copa** (*And, Chile*) boiled egg ▸ **huevo amelcochado** (*CAm*) (soft-)boiled egg ▸ **huevo cocido** hard-boiled egg ▸ **huevo crudo** raw egg ▸ **huevo de color** (*LAm*) brown egg ▸ **huevo de corral** free-range egg ▸ **huevo de Pascua** Easter egg ▸ **huevo de Paslama** (*CAm*) turtle's egg ▸ **huevo duro** hard-boiled egg ▸ **huevo en cáscara** (soft-)boiled egg ▸ **huevo escalfado** poached egg ▸ **huevo estrellado** fried egg ▸ **huevo fresco** freshly-laid egg, new-laid egg ▸ **huevo frito** fried egg ▸ **huevo moreno** brown egg ▸ **huevo pasado por agua** soft-boiled egg ▸ **huevos al plato** *fried egg in tomato sauce served with ham and peas* ▸ **huevos pericos, huevos revueltos** scrambled eggs ▸ **huevo tibio** (*And, CAm, Méx*) soft-boiled egg
2** (= *testículo*) ball** • —**me debes diez euros** —**¡un ~!** "you owe me ten euros" — "bollocks!"** • **MODISMOS**: • **estar hasta los ~s de algo** *o* **algn**: • **estoy hasta los ~s de este niño** I've had a fucking bellyful of this kid** • **estar hasta los ~s de hacer algo**: • **estoy hasta los ~s de estudiar** I'm fucking fed up

h

with studying** • **se necesitan ~s para hacer eso** you need balls to do that** • **se me pusieron los ~s de corbata** it put the fear of God into me* • **no tuve ~s de contestarle** I didn't have the balls to answer back** • **tuve que hacerlo por ~s** I had to do it, I had no fucking choice**
3 • **un ~**** (*como adv*) (= *mucho*) a hell of a lot‡ • **le queremos un ~** we like him a hell of a lot‡ • **sufrí un ~** I suffered like hell‡ • **nos costó un ~ terminarlo** it was one hell of a job to finish it‡ • **el ordenador me costó un ~** the computer cost me an arm and a leg*, the computer cost me a bomb*
4 (*Cos*) darning egg
5 (*LAm*) (= *vago*) idler, loafer; (= *imbécil*) idiot; (= *cobarde*) coward

huevón/ona‡ ADJ **1** (= *flojo*) lazy, idle
2 (*LAm*) (= *estúpido*) stupid, thick*
3 (= *lento*) slow
4 (*Chile*) (= *cobarde*) cowardly, chicken*, yellow*
SM/F (= *holgazán*) lazy sod**, skiver*, layabout*; (= *imbécil*) stupid idiot*, bloody fool‡

Hugo SM Hugh, Hugo

hugonote/a ADJ, SM/F Huguenot

hui... (*para palabras que en LAm se escriben así*) ▸ **gui..., güi...** *p.ej.* **huinche, güinche**

huida SF **1** (= *fuga*) escape, flight (*liter*) • **tras la ~ del general** following the general's escape • **la ~ de Egipto** (*Biblia*) the flight from Egypt • **los refugiados abandonaron muchas de sus posesiones en la ~** the refugees abandoned many of their possessions when they fled • **no consiguieron evitar la ~ de los prisioneros** they were unable to prevent the prisoners from getting away *o* escaping, they were unable to prevent the prisoners' escape • **el plan es una ~ hacia adelante** the plan is a bit of a leap in the dark • **emprender la ~** to take flight
2 [*de capital, inversores*] flight
3 [*de un caballo*] bolt; ▸ **huido**

huidizo ADJ **1** (= *esquivo*) [*persona*] elusive; [*mirada*] evasive
2 (= *tímido*) shy, timid
3 (= *fugaz*) [*impresión, luz*] fleeting
4 (*Anat*) [*barbilla*] wispy; [*frente*] receding

huido/a ADJ **1** (= *escapado*) [*criminal*] fugitive; [*esclavo*] runaway • **los tres terroristas ~s** the three terrorists on the run, the three fugitive terrorists • **lleva más de un año ~ de la justicia** he has been a fugitive from justice *o* he has been on the run for over a year • **los rusos ~s del Palacio de Invierno** the Russians that had fled from the Winter Palace
2 (= *receloso*) elusive • **anda ~ desde que cerró el negocio** he's been rather elusive since he closed down the business • **ha estado muy ~ de la gente desde que se divorció** he's been very wary of people since he got divorced
SM/F fugitive; ▸ **huida**

huila* SF **1** (*Méx*) (= *prostituta*) hooker*
2 huilas (*Chile*) (= *andrajos*) rags

huile SM (*Méx*) roasting grill

huilón ADJ (*And*) elusive

huincha SF (*And, Cono Sur*) = **güincha**

huipil SM (*CAm, Méx*) Indian regional dress *o* blouse

huir ▸ CONJUG 3g VI **1** (= *escapar*) to run away, flee (*liter*) • **huyó despavorido cuando comenzaron los disparos** he ran away *o* (*liter*) fled in terror when the shooting started • **los ladrones huyeron en un vehículo robado** the robbers made their getaway *o* (*liter*) fled in a stolen vehicle • **huyeron a Chipre** they escaped *o* (*liter*) fled to Cyprus • **~ de** [+ *enemigo, catástrofe, pobreza*] to flee from; [+ *cárcel, peligro*] to escape from; [+ *familia*] to run away from • **los refugiados que huyeron de la guerra civil** the refugees who fled the civil war • **~ de su casa** [*refugiados, civiles*] to flee (from) one's home; [*adolescente*] to run away from home • **~ de la justicia** to fly from justice, fly from the law • **huyó del país** he fled the country
2 (= *evitar*) • **~ de** [+ *protagonismo, publicidad, tópicos*] to avoid; [+ *calor, frío*] to escape, escape from • **huye de los periodistas como de la peste** she avoids journalists like the plague • **se metió en una iglesia huyendo del calor** he went into a church to escape (from) the heat • **se drogan para ~ de la realidad** they take drugs to escape (from) reality
3 (*frm*) [*tiempo*] to fly, fly by • **los años huyen sin darse uno cuenta** the years fly by without you realizing
VT (= *esquivar*) to avoid • **parece como si tu hijo te huyera** your son seems to be avoiding you
VPR **huirse** (*Méx*) to escape • **decidieron ~se** they decided to escape • **~se con algn** to escape with sb

huira SF (*And, Cono Sur*) **1** (= *cuerda*) rope • MODISMOS: • **dar ~ a algn*** to thrash sb • **sacar las ~s a algn*** to beat sb up*
2 (= *cabestro*) halter, tether

huiro SM (*And, Cono Sur*) seaweed

huisache (*LAm*) SM (= *árbol*) species of acacia
SMF (= *leguleyo*) unqualified lawyer

huisachear ▸ CONJUG 1a VI (*CAm, Méx*) **1** (= *litigar*) to go to law, engage in litigation
2* (= *ejercer sin título*) to practise law without a qualification

huisachería SF (*CAm, Méx*) **1** (= *tretas*) lawyer's tricks (*pl*), legal intricacies (*pl*)
2 (= *ejercicio fraudulento*) *practice of law without a qualification*

huisachero SM (*CAm, Méx*) **1** (= *leguleyo*) shyster lawyer, unqualified lawyer
2 (= *plumífero*) scribbler, pen-pusher

huitlacoche SM (*CAm, Méx*) black mushroom

huizache SM (*CAm, Méx*) = **huisache**

hulado SM (*CAm*) **1** (= *tela*) oilskin, rubberized cloth
2 (= *capa*) oilskin

hula-hop [xula'xop] SM Hula-Hoop®

hular SM (*Méx*) rubber plantation

hule[1] SM **1** (= *goma*) rubber
2 (= *tela*) oilskin, oilcloth
3 (*CAm, Méx*) (= *árbol*) rubber tree
4 (*Méx**) (= *preservativo*) condom, rubber*

hule[2] SM (*Taur*) goring, row • MODISMO: • **habrá ~** someone's going to get it*

hulear ▸ CONJUG 1a VI (*CAm*) to extract rubber

hulera SF (*CAm*) catapult (*Brit*), slingshot (EEUU)

hulero/a ADJ (*CAm*) rubber (*antes de s*)
SM/F rubber tapper

hulla SF soft coal

hullera SF colliery, coalmine

hullero ADJ coal (*antes de s*)

huloso ADJ (*CAm*) rubbery, elastic

humanamente ADV **1** [*posible, comprensible*] humanly
2 (= *con humanidad*) humanely

humanar ▸ CONJUG 1a VT to humanize
VPR **humanarse 1** (= *humanizarse*) to become more human
2 • **~se a** (+ *infin*) (*LAm*) to condescend to (+ *infin*)
3 (*Rel*) [*Cristo*] to become man

humanidad SF **1** (= *género humano*) humanity, mankind
2 (= *benevolencia*) humanity, humaneness (*frm*)
3* (= *gordura*) corpulence
4 humanidades (*Educ*) humanities

humanismo SM humanism

humanista SMF humanist

humanístico ADJ humanistic

humanitario/a ADJ **1** [*ayuda, labor, misión*] humanitarian
2 (= *benévolo*) humane
SM/F humanitarian

humanitarismo SM humanitarianism

humanización SF humanization

humanizador ADJ humanizing

humanizar ▸ CONJUG 1f VT to humanize, make more human
VPR **humanizarse** to become more human

humano ADJ **1** [*vida, existencia, derechos*] human • **ser ~** human being • REFRÁN: • **equivocarse es ~** to err is human
2 (= *benévolo*) humane
3 (*Educ*) • **ciencias humanas** humanities
SM human, human being

humanoide ADJ, SMF humanoid

humarasca SF (*CAm*), **humareda** SF cloud of smoke

humazo SM dense smoke, cloud of smoke • MODISMO: • **dar ~ a algn** to get rid of sb

humeante ADJ **1** [*pipa, madera*] smoking; [*mecha, restos*] smouldering, smoldering (EEUU); [*cañón, escopeta*] smoking
2 [*caldo, sopa*] steaming

humear ▸ CONJUG 1a VI **1** (= *soltar humo*) [*fuego, chimenea*] to smoke, give out smoke
2 (= *soltar vapor*) to steam
3 [*memoria, rencor*] to be still alive, linger on
4 (= *presumir*) to give o.s. airs, be conceited
VT **1** (*And, Caribe, Méx*) (= *fumigar*) to fumigate
2 (*Méx**) (= *golpear*) to beat, thrash

humectador SM **1** [*de ambiente*] humidifier
2 [*de cigarrillos, tabaco*] humidor

humectante ADJ moisturizing

humectar ▸ CONJUG 1a VT = **humedecer**

húmeda* SF • **la ~** the tongue

humedad SF **1** (*en atmósfera*) humidity • **en Barcelona siempre hay mucha ~** in Barcelona it's always very humid
▸ **humedad absoluta** absolute humidity
▸ **humedad relativa** relative humidity
2 (*en pared, techo*) damp, dampness • **hay manchas de ~ en el techo** there are stains of damp on the ceiling • **aquí huele a ~** this place smells of damp • MODISMO: • **sentir la ~** (*And, Caribe**) to have to answer for one's actions

humedal SM wetland

humedecedor SM humidifier

humedecer ▸ CONJUG 2d VT **1** (= *mojar*) [+ *camisa, ropa*] to moisten, dampen; [+ *suelo, sello*] to wet; [+ *piel, labios*] to moisten, wet
2 [+ *ambiente*] to humidify
VPR **humedecerse** to get damp, get wet • **se le humedecieron los ojos** his eyes filled with tears, tears came into his eyes

húmedo ADJ [*clima*] damp; [*calor*] humid; [*ropa, pared*] damp; [*pelo*] damp, wet; [*labios, tierra, bizcocho*] moist

humera SF (*Caribe*) cloud of smoke

humero SM **1** (= *tubo*) [*de chimenea*] chimney, smokestack; [*de calentador, cocina*] flue
2 (*And*) (= *humareda*) cloud of smoke

húmero SM humerus

humidificador SM humidifier

humidificar ▸ CONJUG 1g VT to humidify

humildad SF **1** [*de carácter*] humbleness, humility
2 (= *docilidad*) meekness
3 [*de origen*] humbleness, lowliness

humilde ADJ **1** (= *no orgulloso*) [*carácter, opinión, comida*] humble; [*voz*] small
2 (= *pobre*) [*clase, vivienda*] low, modest; [*origen*] lowly, humble • **son gente ~** they are humble *o* poor people

humildemente ADV humbly

humillación SF **1** (= *sumisión*) humiliation

• **¡qué ~!** I'm so humiliated!, how humiliating!
2 (= *acto*) humbling

HÚMEDO

Para traducir el adjetivo **húmedo** *en inglés hay que tener en cuenta la diferencia entre:* **damp, moist, humid** *y* **wet.**

▷ *Se traduce por* **damp** *cuando* **húmedo** *se utiliza para describir cosas que han estado mojadas y que todavía no se han secado del todo:*
No salgas con el pelo húmedo
Don't go out with your hair damp
... el olor de la tierra húmeda ...
... the smell of damp earth ...
Pásele un trapo húmedo
Wipe it with a damp cloth

▷ *Se traduce por* **moist** *cuando queremos sugerir que el hecho de que esté o sea* **húmedo** *le da un carácter agradable o atractivo.*
El pastel estaba húmedo y esponjoso
The cake was moist and smooth
Hay que mantener las raíces húmedas
The roots must be kept moist

▷ *En contextos científicos se traduce por* **humid** *cuando se refiere a condiciones atmosféricas:*
... el clima caluroso y húmedo de Chipre ...
... the hot and humid climate of Cyprus ...

▷ *También referido al tiempo atmosférico, pero en un lenguaje menos científico, lo traducimos por* **wet** *cuando se refiere a un tiempo lluvioso:*
Hemos tenido un verano muy húmedo
We've had a very wet summer

humillado ADJ humiliated
humillante ADJ humiliating
humillar ▷ CONJUG 1a VT **1** (= *rebajar*) [+ *persona*] to humiliate, humble
2 (*Mil*) [+ *enemigos, rebeldes*] to crush
3 (*frm*) [+ *cabeza*] to bow, lower
VPR **humillarse** (= *doblegarse*) to humble o.s. • **~se a** *o* **ante** to bow to, bow down before
humita SF (*And, Cono Sur*) **1** (*Culin*) (= *tamal*) tamale; (= *maíz molido*) ground maize, ground corn (*EEUU*)
2 (*Chile*) bow tie
humo SM **1** (= *de fuego, cigarro*) smoke; (= *gases*) fumes (*pl*); (= *vapor*) vapour, vapor (*EEUU*), steam • **echar ~** (*lit*) to smoke; (*fig*) to be fuming • **MODISMOS:** • **convertirse en ~** to vanish without a trace • **hacerse ~** • **irse todo en ~** (*And, Cono Sur**) to disappear, clear off*, scarper* • **írsele al ~ a algn** (*LAm*) to jump sb* • **a ~ de pajas** thoughtlessly, heedlessly • **ni hablaba a ~ de pajas** nor was he talking idly • **quedó en ~ de pajas** it all came to nothing • **tomar la del ~**‡ to beat it*
• **REFRANES:** • **lo que hace ~ es porque está ardiendo** • **donde se hace ~ es porque hay fuego** there's no smoke without fire
2 humos (= *vanidad*) conceit (*sing*), airs • **tener muchos ~s** to think a lot of o.s., have a big head • **MODISMOS:** • **bajar los ~s a algn** to take sb down a peg (or two) • **darse ~s** to brag, boast • **vender ~s** to brag, talk big*
3 humos† (= *hogares*) homes, hearths
humor¹ SM **1** (= *estado de ánimo*) mood, humour, humor (*EEUU*), temper • **buen ~** good humour, good mood • **en un tono de mal ~** in an ill-tempered tone • **estar de buen/mal ~** to be in a good/bad mood, be in a good/bad temper • **me pone de mal ~** it puts me in a bad mood • **no tengo ~ para fiestas** I'm not in a party mood • **seguir el ~ a algn** to humour sb, go along with sb's mood • **MODISMO:** • **un ~ de perros** a filthy mood *o* temper
2 (= *gracia*) humour, humor (*EEUU*), humorousness (*frm*) ▸ **humor negro** black humour
humor² SM (*Med, Bio*) humour, humor (*EEUU*)
humorada SF **1** (= *broma*) witticism, joke
2 (= *capricho*) caprice, whim
humorado ADJ • **bien ~** good-humoured, good-tempered • **mal ~** bad-tempered, cross, peevish
humorismo SM **1** [*de carácter, momento*] humour, humor (*EEUU*), humorousness (*frm*)
2 (*Teat*) stand-up comedy
humorista SMF **1** (= *cómico*) stand-up comedian/comedienne; (= *dibujante*) cartoonist; (= *escritor*) humorist
2 (= *persona graciosa*) joker
humorísticamente ADV humorously
humorístico ADJ humorous, funny, facetious (*pey*)
humoso ADJ smoky
humus SM humus
hundible ADJ sinkable
hundido ADJ **1** [*barco, huellas*] sunken
2 [*ojos*] deep-set, hollow
3 (= *desmoralizado*) downcast, demoralized
hundimiento SM **1** [*de barco*] sinking
2 (= *colapso*) [*de edificio, familia, empresa*] collapse, ruin, fall; [*de terreno*] cave-in, subsidence
hundir ▷ CONJUG 3a VT **1** (*en agua*) to sink
2 (= *destruir*) [+ *edificio*] to ruin, destroy, cause the collapse of; [+ *plan*] to sink, ruin
3 (= *desmoralizar*) to demoralize • **me hundes en la miseria** you are driving me to ruin
VPR **hundirse 1** (*en agua*) [*barco*] to sink; [*nadador*] to plunge, go down • **se hundió en el estudio de la historia** he immersed himself in the study of history, he became absorbed in the study of history • **se hundió en la meditación** he became lost in thought
2 (= *derrumbarse*) [*edificio*] to collapse, fall down, tumble down; [*terreno*] to cave in, subside
3 (= *económicamente*) • **el negocio se hundió** the business failed *o* went under *o* went to the wall • **se hundieron los precios** prices slumped • **la economía se hundió** the economy collapsed
4 (= *moralmente*) to collapse, break down • **~se en la miseria** to get really low *o* depressed
húngaro/a ADJ of/from Hungary
SM/F native/inhabitant of Hungary
SM (*Ling*) Hungarian
Hungría SF Hungary
huno SM Hun
huracán SM hurricane
huracanado ADJ • **viento ~** hurricane-force wind, gale-force wind
huraco SM (*LAm*) hole
hurañía SF (*frm*) **1** (= *timidez*) shyness
2 (= *insociabilidad*) unsociableness
3 (= *esquivez*) elusiveness
huraño ADJ **1** (= *tímido*) shy
2 (= *poco sociable*) unsociable
3 (= *esquivo*) shy, elusive
hure SM (*And*) large pot
hureque SM (*And*) = **huraco**
hurgar ▷ CONJUG 1h VT **1** [+ *herida*] to poke, poke at, jab; [+ *fuego*] to poke, rake
2 (*LAm*) = **hurguetear**
3† (= *incitar*) to stir up, provoke
VI (= *curiosear*) • **~ en** to rummage in • **~ en el bolsillo** to feel in one's pocket, rummage in one's pocket
VPR **hurgarse** • **~se la nariz** to pick one's nose
hurgón SM **1** [*de fuego*] poker, fire rake
2 (= *estocada*) thrust, stab
hurgonada SF, **hurgonazo** SM poke, jab
hurgonear ▷ CONJUG 1a VT [+ *fuego*] to poke, rake, rake out; [+ *adversario*] to thrust at, jab, jab at
hurgonero SM poker, fire rake
hurguete* SM (*Cono Sur*) nosy parker*, busybody
hurguetear ▷ CONJUG 1a VT (*LAm*)
1 (= *rebuscar*) to finger, turn over, rummage inquisitively among
2 (= *fisgonear*) to poke one's nose into*, pry into
hurí SF houri
hurón ADJ **1** (= *huraño*) unsociable
2 (*Cono Sur**) (= *glotón*) greedy
SM **1** (*Zool*) ferret
2 (= *huraño*) unsociable person
3 (= *fisgón*) (*pey*) busybody, nosy parker*, snooper*
huronear ▷ CONJUG 1a VI (= *fisgar*) to pry, snoop around*
huronera SF **1** (*Zool*) [*de hurón*] ferret hole; [*de oso, león*] den, lair
2 (= *escondrijo*) hiding place
hurra EXCL hurray!, hurrah!
hurtadillas SFPL • **a ~** stealthily, on the sly*
hurtar ▷ CONJUG 1a VT **1** (= *robar*) to steal • **pretenden ~ al país las elecciones** they are trying to deprive the country of (the chance of holding) elections
2 • **~ el cuerpo** to dodge, move out of the way
3 [*mar, río*] to eat away, erode
4 (= *plagiar*) to plagiarize, pinch*, lift*
VPR **hurtarse** (*frm*) **1** (= *retirarse*) to withdraw
2 (= *irse*) to make off
3 (= *no tomar parte*) to keep out of the way
hurto SM **1** (= *robo*) robbery; (*Jur*) larceny • **cometió un ~** he committed a robbery
• **MODISMO:** • **a ~** (*frm*) stealthily, by stealth, on the sly*
2 (= *botín*) (piece of) stolen property, loot, thing stolen
húsar SM hussar
husillo SM **1** (*Mec*) spindle, shaft
2 [*de prensa*] screw, worm
3 (= *conducto*) drain
husma SF (*frm*) snooping*, prying • **andar a la ~** to go snooping around*, go prying • **andar a la ~ de algo** to go prying for *o* after sth
husmear ▷ CONJUG 1a VT **1** (= *olisquear*) to scent, get wind of
2 (= *fisgonear*) to pry into, sniff out*
VI (= *oler mal*) to smell bad
husmeo SM **1** (= *olisqueo*) scenting
2 (= *fisgoneo*) prying, snooping*
husmo SM (*frm*) high smell, strong smell, gaminess • **MODISMO:** • **estar al ~** to watch one's chance
huso SM **1** (*Téc*) (*para tejer*) spindle; [*de torno*] drum
2 ▸ **huso horario** (*Geog*) time zone
3 (*Col**) kneecap
hutu ADJ, SMF Hutu
huy EXCL (*de dolor*) ow!, ouch!; (*de asombro*) wow!; (*de sorpresa*) well!, oh!, jeez! (*EEUU*); (*de alivio*) phew! • **¡huy, perdona!** oops, sorry!
huyente ADJ (*frm*) [*frente*] receding
huyón/ona (*LAm*) ADJ **1** (= *cobarde*) cowardly
2 (= *huraño*) unsociable
SM/F **1** (= *cobarde*) coward
2 (= *huraño*) unsociable person
Hz ABR (= **hertzio, hercio**) Hz

Ii

I, i [i] SF (= *letra*) I, i ▸ **I griega** Y, y
IA SF ABR (= **inteligencia artificial**) AI
IAC SF ABR (*LAm*) (= **ingeniería asistida por computador**) CAE
IAE SM ABR (*Esp*) (= **Impuesto de** *o* **sobre Actividades Económicas**) *tax on commercial and professional activities*
-iano ▹ **Aspects of Word Formation in Spanish 2**
IAO SF ABR **1** (= **instrucción asistida por ordenador**) CAI
2 (= **ingeniería asistida por ordenador**) CAE
IB ABR = **Iberia, Líneas Aéreas de España, Sociedad Anónima**
ib. ABR (= **ibídem**) ib, ibid
iba *etc* ▹ **ir**
Iberia SF Iberia
ibérico ADJ Iberian • **la Península Ibérica** the Iberian Peninsula
ibero/a ADJ, SM/F, **íbero/a** ADJ, SM/F Iberian
Iberoamérica SF Latin America
iberoamericano/a ADJ, SM/F Latin American
ibex SM INV ibex
IBI SM ABR (*Esp*) (= **Impuesto de** *o* **sobre Bienes Inmuebles**) rates, real estate tax (*EEUU*)
íbice SM ibex
ibicenco/a ADJ of/from Ibiza
SM/F native/inhabitant of Ibiza • **los ~s** the people of Ibiza
ibíd. ABR (= **ibídem**) ib, ibid
-ibilidad ▹ **Aspects of Word Formation in Spanish 2**
ibis SF INV ibis
Ibiza SF Ibiza
-ible ▹ **Aspects of Word Formation in Spanish 2**
ibón SM Pyrenean lake, tarn
ícaro SM (*LAm*) (*Dep*) hang-glider
ICE SM ABR (*Esp*) **1** (*Educ*) = **Instituto de Ciencias de la Educación**
2 (*Com*) = **Instituto de Ciencias Económicas**
iceberg SM [ˈiθeβer] (PL: **icebergs** [ˈiθeβer]) iceberg • **la punta** *o* **cabeza del ~** the tip of the iceberg
ICEX SM ABR (*Esp*) = **Instituto de Comercio Exterior**
ICH SM ABR (*Esp*) = **Instituto de Cultura Hispánica**
ICI SM ABR (*Esp*) = **Instituto de Cooperación Iberoamericana**
ICO SM ABR (*Esp*) = **Instituto de Crédito Oficial**
-ico, -ica ▹ **Aspects of Word Formation in Spanish 2**
ICONA SM ABR, **Icona** SM ABR (*Esp*) (= **Instituto para la Conservación de la Naturaleza**) ≈ NCC
icónico ADJ iconic
icono SM (*Arte, Inform*) icon
iconoclasia SF, **iconoclastia** SF iconoclasm
iconoclasta ADJ iconoclastic
SMF iconoclast
iconografía SF iconography
iconográfico ADJ iconographic
ictericia SF jaundice
ictio- PREF ichthyo-
ictiofauna SF fish (*pl*), fishes (*pl*)
ICYT SM ABR = **Instituto de Información y Documentación sobre Ciencia y Tecnología**
id¹ SM id
id² ▹ **ir**
I+D ABR (= **Investigación y Desarrollo**) R&D
íd. ABR (= **ídem**) do
ida SF **1** (= *movimiento*) departure • **viaje de ida** outward journey • **partido de ida** away leg • **ida y vuelta** round trip • **billete de ida y vuelta** return (ticket), round trip ticket (*EEUU*) • **idas y venidas** comings and goings • MODISMOS: • **en dos idas y venidas** in an instant • **dejar las idas por las venidas** to miss the boat
2 (*Caza*) track, trail
3 (= *acto precipitado*) rash act
IDCA SM ABR = **Instituto de Desarrollo Cooperativo en América**
iddish [ˈidiʃ] SM Yiddish
IDE SF ABR (= **Iniciativa de Defensa Estratégica**) SDI
idea SF **1** (= *concepto*) idea • **tenía una ~ muy distinta de Rusia** I had a very different idea of what Russia was like • **tenía una ~ falsa de mí** he had a false impression of me, he had the wrong idea about me • **formarse una ~ de algo** to form an impression of sth • **hacerse una ~ de algo** to get an idea of sth • **no es fácil hacerse una ~ del proyecto** it's not easy to get an idea of the project • **hacerse una ~ equivocada de algn** to get a false impression of sb, get the wrong idea about sb • **hazte a la ~ de que no va a volver nunca** you'd better get used to the idea that she's never coming back; ▹ **preconcebido**
2 (= *sugerencia*) idea • **tengo una gran ~** I've had a great idea • **¡qué ~! ¿por qué no vamos a Marruecos?** I've got an idea! why don't we go to Morocco? • **necesitamos a gente con ~s** we need people with (fresh) ideas • **~s para cuidar su cabello** hair care tips • **~ brillante** • **~ genial** brilliant idea, brainwave • MODISMO: • **~s de bombero** (*Esp*) bright ideas (*iró*), harebrained schemes*
3 (= *intención*) idea, intention • **mi ~ era salir temprano** I had intended to leave early, my idea *o* intention was to leave early • **cambiar de ~** to change one's mind • **no hemos conseguido que cambiara de ~** we haven't been able to change her mind • **~ fija** fixed idea • **salió del país con una ~ fija: no volver nunca** he left the country with one fixed idea: never to return • **su ~ fija era marcharse a Francia** she had this fixed idea about going to France • **ir con la ~ de hacer algo** to mean to do sth • **no iba nunca con la ~ de perjudicar a nadie** it was never his intention to harm anybody, he never meant to harm anybody • **tiene muy mala ~** his intentions are not good, he's a nasty piece of work* • **tuvo muy mala ~ al hacer las preguntas** his questions were really malicious *o* nasty • **nos preparó una trampa a mala ~** he played a nasty trick on us • **lo hizo sin mala ~** he didn't mean any harm • **metérsele una ~ en la cabeza a algn**: • **cuando se le mete una ~ en la cabeza no hay quien se la saque** once he gets an idea into his head no one can talk him out of it • **tener ~ de hacer algo** (*en el pasado*) to mean to do sth; (*en el futuro*) to be thinking of doing sth • **tenía ~ de traerme varias botellas de vodka** I meant *o* I was meaning to bring some bottles of vodka • MODISMO: • **tener ~ a algn** (*Cono Sur*) to have it in for sb
4 (= *conocimiento*) idea • **no tengo mucha ~ de cocina** I haven't got much (of an) idea about cooking • —**¿a qué hora llega Sara?** —**no tengo ni ~** "what time is Sara arriving?" — "I've got no idea" • **¡ni ~!** no idea! • **tener ~ de algo** to have an idea of sth • **¿tienes ~ de la hora que es?** do you have any idea of the time? • **¡no tienes ~ de las ganas que tenía de verte!** you have no idea how much I wanted to see you! • **no tenía ni ~ de que te fueras a casar** I had no idea that you were getting married • **no tener la menor ~** not to have the faintest *o* the foggiest idea • **cuando me fui a Alemania no tenía la menor ~ de alemán** when I went to Germany I couldn't speak a word of German; ▹ **pajolero, remoto**
5 ideas (= *opiniones*) ideas • **lo expulsaron por sus ~s políticas** they expelled him because of his political beliefs *o* ideas • **tengo las ~s muy claras con respecto al aborto** my position on abortion is very clear • **yo soy de ~s fijas** I have very fixed ideas about things • **una persona de ~s conservadoras/liberales/radicales** a conservative/liberal/radical-minded person
ideación SF conception, thinking-out
ideal ADJ ideal • **es el marido ~** he is the ideal husband • **un mundo ~** an ideal world • **nuestra casa ~** our dream house *o* home • **lo ~ es poder hacerlo tú mismo** ideally you would be able to do it yourself, the ideal thing is to be able to do it yourself • **lo ~ sería que el aparcamiento fuera gratis** ideally the parking would be free, the ideal thing would be for the parking to be free • **lo ~ para ella sería un piso en el centro** the ideal thing for her would be a flat in the centre of town
SM **1** (= *modelo*) ideal • **el ~ de belleza masculina** the ideal of masculine beauty
2 (= *deseo*) ideal • **mi ~ es vivir junto al mar** my ideal is to live by the sea

3 ideales (= *valores*) ideals • **jóvenes sin ~es** young people with no ideals
idealismo SM idealism
idealista ADJ idealistic
SMF idealist
idealización SF idealization
idealizar ▷ CONJUG 1f VT to idealize
idealmente ADV ideally
idear ▷ CONJUG 1a VT **1** [+ *proyecto, teoría*] to devise, think up • **siempre está ideando excusas para no ayudarme** he's always thinking up excuses to avoid helping me
2 (= *diseñar*) [+ *edificio*] to design; [+ *invento, máquina*] to design, devise • **la máquina ideada por Turing** the machine that Turing designed *o* devised • **una bombilla ideada para ...** a light bulb designed to ...
ideario SM ideology • **el ~ de la organización** the thinking of the organization
ideático ADJ **1** (*LAm*) (= *excéntrico*) eccentric, odd
2 (*CAm*) (= *inventivo*) ingenious
IDEM SM ABR (*Esp*) = **Instituto de los Derechos de la Mujer**
ídem ADV (*en lengua escrita*) idem; (*en lengua hablada*) ditto • MODISMO: • **~ de ~***: • **yo dije que no, y ella ~ de ~** I said no and she said (exactly) the same
idénticamente ADV identically
idéntico ADJ identical • **estas sillas son idénticas** these chairs are identical *o* exactly the same • **este cuadro es ~ a este otro** this picture is identical to *o* exactly the same as this other one • **llevaba una falda idéntica a la mía** she was wearing an identical skirt to mine • **ser ~ a algn** to be the spitting image of sb*
identidad SF **1** (= *rasgos distintivos*) identity • **carnet de ~** identity card ▸ **identidad corporativa** corporate identity
2 (= *igualdad*) identity • **la ~ de intereses** the identity of interests
identificable ADJ identifiable
identificación SF identification ▸ **identificación errónea** mistaken identity
identificador(a) ADJ identifying
SM/F identifier
SM ▸ **identificador de llamadas** caller ID
identificar ▷ CONJUG 1g VT **1** (= *reconocer*) to identify • **han identificado al ladrón** they have identified the thief • **aún no han identificado las causas de la tragedia** the causes of the tragedy have still not been identified • **una víctima sin ~** an unidentified victim
2 (= *equiparar*) • **no identifiques violencia con juventud** don't think that young people and violence automatically go together • **siempre la identificaban con causas humanitarias** she was always identified *o* associated with humanitarian causes
VPR **identificarse 1** (= *demostrar la identidad*) to identify o.s. • **se identificó como el padre del niño** he identified himself as the child's father • **la policía les pidió que se ~an** the police asked them to show their identity cards
2 • **~se con** to identify with • **muchos jóvenes se identifican con este personaje** many young people identify with this character • **se identificaba con las víctimas del racismo** he identified with victims of racism
identificatorio ADJ identifying
ideográfico ADJ ideographic
ideograma SM ideogram
ideología SF ideology
ideológicamente ADV ideologically
ideológico ADJ ideological
ideólogo/a SM/F ideologist
ideoso ADJ (*Méx*) (= *maniático*) obsessive; (= *caprichoso*) wilful
idílico ADJ idyllic
idilio SM **1** (= *romance*) romance, love affair
2 (*Literat*) idyll
idiolecto SM idiolect
idioma SM language • **los ~s de trabajo de la UE** the working languages of the EU
idiomáticamente ADV from a language point of view
idiomaticidad SF idiomatic nature
idiomático ADJ idiomatic • **giro ~** idiom, idiomatic expression
idiosincrasia SF idiosyncrasy
idiosincrásico ADJ idiosyncratic
idiosincrático ADJ idiosyncratic
idiota ADJ idiotic, stupid
SMF idiot • **¡idiota!** you idiot!
idiotez SF idiocy • **¡eso es una ~!** that's nonsense! • **decir idioteces** to talk rubbish • **hacer idioteces** to do silly things
idiotismo SM **1** (*Ling*) idiom, idiomatic expression
2 (= *ignorancia*) ignorance
idiotizado ADJ stupefied • **al verla se quedaron como ~s** when they saw her they were stupefied • **~s por el consumo de droga** stupefied *o* zombified by drugs
idiotizar ▷ CONJUG 1f VT **1** (= *volver idiota a*) to stupefy
2 (*LAm*) (= *volver loco a*) • **~ a algn** to drive sb crazy
IDO SM ABR (*Esp*) = **Instituto de Denominaciones de Origen**
ido ADJ* **1** (= *despistado*) absent-minded • **estar ido** to be miles away
2 (= *chiflado*) crazy, nuts* • **estar ido (de la cabeza)** to be crazy
3 (*CAm, Méx*) • **estar ido** to be drunk
SMPL • **los idos** the dead, the departed
idólatra ADJ idolatrous
SMF idolator/idolatress
idolatrar ▷ CONJUG 1a VT **1** [+ *dios*] to worship
2 [+ *amado, cantante*] to idolize
idolatría SF idolatry
idolátrico ADJ idolatrous
ídolo SM idol
idoneidad SF **1** (= *conveniencia*) suitability, fitness
2 (= *capacidad*) aptitude
idoneizar ▷ CONJUG 1f VT to make suitable
idóneo ADJ **1** (= *apropiado*) suitable, fit
2 (*Méx*) (*genuino*) genuine
idus SMPL ides
i.e. ABR (= **id est**) (= *lo mismo*) i.e.
IEE SM ABR **1** (*Admin*) = **Instituto Español de Emigración**
2 (*Esp*) (*Com*) = **Instituto de Estudios Económicos**
IEI SM ABR (*Esp*) = **Instituto de Educación e Investigación**
IEM SM ABR (*Esp*) = **Instituto de Enseñanza Media**
IES SM ABR (*Esp*) (= **Instituto de Enseñanza Secundaria**) ≈ (state) secondary school (*Brit*), ≈ high school (*EEUU*)
iglesia SF church • **casarse por la ~** to get married in church, have a church wedding • MODISMOS: • **casarse por detrás de la ~** to move in together • **¡con la ~ hemos topado!** now we're really up against it! • **llevar a algn a la ~** to lead sb to the altar ▸ **Iglesia Anglicana** Church of England, Anglican Church ▸ **iglesia catedral** cathedral ▸ **Iglesia Católica** Catholic Church ▸ **iglesia colegial** collegiate church ▸ **iglesia parroquial** parish church

IGLESIA

Uso del artículo

En inglés el uso del artículo delante de **church** *depende del motivo por el que alguien se encuentre en el edificio.*

▷ *Se traduce* **a la iglesia** *por* **to church, en la iglesia** *por* **in church, desde la iglesia** *por* **from church** *etc, cuando alguien va o está allí para asistir al servicio religioso:*

Vamos a la iglesia todos los domingos
We go to church every Sunday

▷ *Se traduce* **a la iglesia** *por* **to the church, en la iglesia** *por* **at the church** *y* **desde la iglesia** *por* **from the church** *etc cuando alguien va o está allí por otros motivos:*

Mi padre ha ido a la iglesia a arreglar las ventanas
My father has gone to the church to fix the windows

Para otros usos y ejemplos ver la entrada.

iglesiero* ADJ (*LAm*) churchy*, church-going
iglú SM igloo
IGN SM ABR (*Esp, Hond*) = **Instituto Geográfico Nacional**
Ignacio SM Ignatius
ignaro ADJ (*frm*) ignorant
igneo ADJ igneous
ignición SF ignition
ignifugación SF fireproofing
ignífugo ADJ fireproof, fire-resistant
igniscible ADJ flammable, easy to ignite
ignominia SF **1** (= *deshonor*) disgrace, ignominy • **es una ~ que ...** it's a disgrace that ...
2 (= *acto*) disgraceful act
ignominiosamente ADV ignominiously
ignominioso ADJ ignominious, disgraceful
ignorado ADJ (= *desconocido*) unknown; (= *poco conocido*) obscure, little-known
ignorancia SF ignorance • **por ~** through ignorance
ignorante ADJ ignorant
SMF ignoramus
ignorar ▷ CONJUG 1a VT **1** (= *desconocer*) to not know, be ignorant of • **ignoramos su paradero** we don't know his whereabouts • **lo ignoro por completo** I've absolutely no idea • **no ignoro que ...** I am fully aware that ..., I am not unaware that ...
2 (= *no tener en cuenta*) to ignore
ignoto ADJ (*liter*) (= *desconocido*) unknown; (= *no descubierto*) undiscovered
igual ADJ **1** (= *idéntico*) • **todas las casas son ~es** all the houses are the same • **son todos ~es** they're all the same • **llevaban la corbata ~** they were wearing the same tie • **son únicamente ~es en apariencia** they are alike in appearance only • **~ a**: • **este es ~ al otro** this one is like the other one, this one is the same as the other one • **había vendido ya dos vestidos ~es a ese** I had already sold two dresses like that one • **no he visto nunca cosa ~** I never saw the like *o* anything like it • **partes ~es** equal shares • **se dividieron el dinero en partes ~es** they divided the money into equal shares • **~ que**: • **tengo una falda ~ que la tuya** I've got a skirt just like yours, I've got a skirt the same as yours • **es ~ que su madre** (*físicamente*) she looks just like her mother; (*en la personalidad*) she's

just like her mother
2 • **~ de**: • **es ~ de útil pero más barato** it's just as useful but cheaper • **estoy ~ de sorprendido que tú** I am just as surprised as you are • **las dos habitaciones son ~ de grandes** the two rooms are the same size
3 (*en rango, jerarquía*) equal • **todos somos ~es ante la ley** we are all equal in the eyes of the law • **somos ~es en derechos y en deberes** we have the same rights and obligations
4 (*Mat*) equal • **un kilómetro es ~ a 1.000 metros** a kilometre is equal to 1,000 metres, a kilometre equals 1,000 metres • **X es ~ a Y** X is equal to Y
5 (= *constante*) [*ritmo*] steady; [*presión, temperatura*] steady, constant; [*clima*] constant; [*terreno*] even
6 (*Dep*) • **ir ~es** to be level • **quince ~es** fifteen all • **cuarenta ~es** deuce
(ADV) **1** (= *de la misma forma*) • **se visten ~** they dress the same
2 (*locuciones*) **a** • **da ~** • **es ~** it makes no difference, it's all the same • **da** *o* **es ~ hoy que mañana** today or tomorrow, it doesn't matter *o* it makes no difference • **me da ~** • **me es ~** it's all the same to me, I don't mind
b • **por ~** equally • **esta norma se aplica a todos por ~** this rule applies equally to everyone
c • **~ que** (= *como*): • **~ que cualquier otro** just like anybody else • **le gusta Brahms, ~ que a mí** like me, he is fond of Brahms • **al ~ que**: • **los chilenos, al ~ que los argentinos, estiman que ...** the Chileans, (just) like the Argentinians, think that ...
3 (*Esp**) (= *quizás*) maybe • **~ no lo saben** maybe they don't know, they may not know • **~ voy al cine** I may go to the cinema
4 (*esp Cono Sur**) (= *a pesar de todo*) just the same, still • **era inocente pero me expulsaron ~** I was innocent but they threw me out just the same, I was innocent but they still threw me out
(SMF) (*en la misma escala social*) equal; (*en la misma clase, trabajo*) peer • **estaba mucho más contento entre sus ~es** he felt much happier being amongst his equals • **se sentía como una extraña entre sus ~es** she felt like a stranger among her peers • **sus ~es en edad y clase social** people of his age and social class • **tratar a algn de ~ a ~** to treat sb as an equal
(SM) **1** (*Mat*) equals sign, equal sign (EEUU)
2 (= *comparación*) • **no tener ~** to be unrivalled, have no equal • **su crueldad hacía ellos no tenía ~** their cruelty towards them was unparalleled • **sin ~** unrivalled • **el paisaje es de una belleza sin ~** the countryside is unrivalled in its beauty
3 iguales (= *lotería*) lottery tickets
iguala (SF) **1** (*Com*) (= *acuerdo*) agreement; (= *cuota*) agreed fee
2 (= *igualación*) equalization, tying (EEUU)
igualación (SF) **1** (= *nivelación*) [*de suelo, césped*] levelling, leveling (EEUU) • **la tendencia a la ~ de los precios** the tendency to balance prices, the tendency towards balancing prices • **han ofrecido la ~ de los sueldos para todos** they have offered to give everybody the same salary • **buscan la ~ de todos los ciudadanos ante la ley** they are seeking to make all citizens equal before the law
2 (*Mat*) equating
igualada (SF) (*Dep*) **1** (= *tanto*) equalizer
2 (= *igualdad de puntos*) level score • **rompió la ~** he broke the deadlock • **todavía tenemos la ~ en el marcador** the scores are still level
igualado (ADJ) **1** (= *a la misma altura*) neck and neck • **los dos atletas iban muy ~s** the two athletes were running neck and neck • **los dos partidos van ~s en las encuestas** the two parties are running neck and neck in the opinion polls • **el partido quedó ~ a dos** the match finished two all
2 (*indicando posición*) [*competidores, equipos*] evenly-matched; [*competición, partido*] even, evenly-matched • **el marcador** *o* **el partido estaba ~ a 84 puntos** the scores were level at 84-84 • **los dos equipos están ~s a puntos** both teams are level on points
3 [*suelo, césped*] levelled off, leveled off (EEUU)
4 (*CAm, Méx**) (= *irrespetuoso*) disrespectful (*to people of a higher class*)
igualar ▷ CONJUG 1a (VT) **1** (= *hacer igual*) **a** [+ *cantidades, sueldos*] to make equal, make the same; [+ *resultado*] to equal • **a final de año nos ~án el sueldo a todos** at the end of the year they are going to make all our salaries equal *o* the same • **ha conseguido ~ el número de partidos ganados** she has managed to win the same number of matches • **conseguimos ~ el número de votos** we managed to equal the number of votes • **~ algo a** *o* **con algo** to make sth the same as sth • **han igualado mi sueldo al vuestro** they've put us on the same salary, they've made my salary the same as yours • **si igualamos la x a 2** if x is equal to 2
b (*Dep*) [+ *marca, récord*] to equal • **a los tres minutos el equipo visitante igualó el marcador** three minutes later, the away team scored the equalizer *o* equalized • **~ el partido** to draw the match, equalize • **~ a puntos a** *o* **con algn** to be level on points with sb
2 [+ *suelo, superficie*] to level, level off • **quiero que me iguales el flequillo** can you just even up the fringe? • **~ algo con algo** to make sth level with sth
3 (= *poner al mismo nivel*) [+ *precios*] to match, equal; [+ *derechos, fuerzas*] to place on an equal footing • **el museo ha igualado el precio ofrecido por el coleccionista** the museum has matched *o* equalled the price offered by the collector • **la constitución iguala los derechos de todos los ciudadanos** the constitution grants equal rights to all citizens • **~ a algn en belleza** to match sb's beauty • **nadie le igualaba en sabiduría** there was none as wise as he • **a final de curso consiguió ~ a su hermano en las notas** at the end of the year she managed to get the same marks as her brother
4 (*Com*) [+ *venta*] to agree upon
(VI) **1** (= *ser igual*) • **~ con algo** to match sth • **el bolso iguala con los zapatos** the handbag matches the shoes • **~ en belleza** to be equally beautiful • **igualan en número de representantes** they have the same number *o* an equal number of representatives
2 (*Dep*) (= *empatar*) to score the equalizer, equalize
3 (*Com*) to come to an agreement
4 (*CAm, Méx**) to be too familiar, be cheeky*
(VPR) **igualarse** (= *compararse*) • **~se a** *o* **con algn** to be on the same level as sb • **su único deseo era ~se con los más ricos que él** his only desire was to be on the same level as those richer than him • **su familia no puede ~se con la nuestra** his family doesn't compare with *o* to ours
igualatorio (SM) (*Med*) insurance group
igualdad (SF) **1** (= *equivalencia*) equality • **~ de derechos** equal rights • **~ de oportunidades** equal opportunities • **~ de salario** equal pay • **en ~ de condiciones** on an equal basis, on an equal footing
2 (= *uniformidad*) [*de superficie*] evenness; [*de rasgos, formas*] similarity
igualitario (ADJ) egalitarian
igualitarismo (SM) egalitarianism
igualito (ADJ) (*diminutivo de igual*) exactly the same, identical • **los dos son ~s** they're the spitting image of each other
igualización (SF) equalization, tying (EEUU)
igualmente (ADV) **1** (= *del mismo modo*) equally • **todos mis estudiantes son ~ vagos** all my students are equally lazy, my students are all as lazy as each other • **aunque se lo prohíbas, lo hará ~** even if you tell him not to, he'll do it anyway *o* just the same
2 (= *también*) likewise • **~, los pensionistas quedan exentos** likewise, pensioners are exempt
3 (*en saludo*) likewise, the same to you • **—¡Feliz Navidad! —gracias, ~** "Happy Christmas!" — "thanks, likewise *o* the same to you" • **—muchos recuerdos a tus padres —gracias, ~** "give my regards to your parents" — "I will, and to yours too"
4 (= *uniformemente*) evenly
iguana (SF) iguana
IHS (ABR) (= **Jesús**) IHS
III (SM ABR) (*Méx*) = **Instituto Indigenista Interamericano**
ijada (SF), **ijar** (SM) **1** (= *costado*) [*de animal*] flank; [*de persona*] side
2 (= *dolor*) stitch, pain in the side • MODISMO: • **esto tiene su ~** this has its weak side
ijadear ▷ CONJUG 1a (VI) (*Zool*) to pant
ikastola (SF) *school in which Basque is the language of instruction*; ▷ EUSKERA
ikurriña (SF) *Basque national flag*
-il ▷ **Aspects of Word Formation in Spanish 2**
ilación (SF) (= *inferencia*) inference; (= *nexo*) connection, relationship
ILARI [i'lari] (SM ABR) = **Instituto Latinoamericano de Relaciones Internacionales**
ilativo (ADJ) inferential; (*Ling*) illative
ilegal (ADJ) illegal, unlawful
ilegalidad (SF) illegality, unlawfulness • **trabajar en la ~** to work illegally
ilegalización (SF) outlawing, banning
ilegalizar ▷ CONJUG 1f (VT) to outlaw, make illegal, ban
ilegalmente (ADV) illegally, unlawfully
ilegible (ADJ) illegible, unreadable
ilegítimamente (ADV) illegitimately
ilegitimar ▷ CONJUG 1a (VT) to make illegal
ilegitimidad (SF) illegitimacy
ilegitimizar ▷ CONJUG 1f (VT) = **ilegitimar**
ilegítimo (ADJ) **1** (= *no legítimo*) illegitimate
2 (= *ilegal*) unlawful
3 (= *falso*) false, spurious
ilerdense (ADJ) of/from Lérida
(SMF) native/inhabitant of Lérida • **los ~s** the people of Lérida
ileso (ADJ) **1** (= *sin lesiones*) unhurt, unharmed • **los pasajeros resultaron ~s** the passengers were unhurt *o* unharmed • **salió ~** he escaped unscathed
2 (= *sin tocar*) untouched
iletrado (ADJ) (= *analfabeto*) illiterate; (= *inculto*) uneducated
Ilíada (SF) Iliad
iliberal (ADJ) illiberal
ilícitamente (ADV) illicitly, illegally, unlawfully
ilicitano/a (ADJ) of/from Elche
(SM/F) native/inhabitant of Elche • **los ~s** the people of Elche
ilícito (ADJ) illicit, unlawful
ilimitado (ADJ) unlimited, limitless
iliterato (ADJ) illiterate

illanco SM (*And*) slow stream, quiet-flowing stream
-illo, -illa ▹ Aspects of Word Formation in Spanish 2
Ilma. ABR = **Ilustrísima**
Ilmo. ABR = **Ilustrísimo**
ilocalizable ADJ • **ayer seguía ~** he could still not be found yesterday, he was still nowhere to be found yesterday
ilógicamente ADV illogically
ilógico ADJ illogical
ILPES SM ABR = **Instituto Latinoamericano de Planificación Económica y Social**
ilu* SF = ilusión
iluminación SF **1** (= *alumbrado*) (*en casa, calle*) lighting; (*en estadio*) floodlighting • **~ indirecta** indirect lighting
2 (= *conocimiento*) enlightenment
iluminado/a ADJ **1** (= *alumbrado*) illuminated, lit
2 (= *con conocimiento*) enlightened
3 • **estar ~‡** (= *borracho*) to be lit up*; (= *drogado*) to be high*
SM/F visionary • **los Iluminados** the Illuminati
iluminador(a) ADJ illuminating
SM/F illuminator
iluminar ▹ CONJUG 1a VT **1** [+ *cuarto, calle, ciudad*] to light; [+ *estadio, edificio, monumento*] to light up • **una sola bombilla iluminaba el cuarto** the room was lit by a single bulb • **la felicidad iluminó su rostro** his face lit up with happiness
2 [+ *grabado, ilustración*] to illuminate
3 [+ *teoría, tesis*] to illustrate
4 (*Rel*) to enlighten
VPR **iluminarse** (= *alegrarse*) [*cara, expresión*] to light up • **se le iluminó el rostro al verla** his face lit up when he saw her • **el cielo se iluminó con los fuegos artificiales** the sky was lit up with fireworks, fireworks lit up the sky
iluminista SMF (*Cine, TV*) electrician, lighting engineer
ilusión SF **1** (= *imagen no real*) illusion • **todo es ~** it's all an illusion ▸ **ilusión óptica** optical illusion
2 (= *esperanza*) • **su ~ era comprarlo** her dream was to buy it • **tendió la mano con ~** she put her hand out hopefully • **hacerse ilusiones** to get one's hopes up • **no te hagas ilusiones** don't get your hopes up • **se hace la ~ de que ...** she fondly imagines that ... • **no me hago muchas ilusiones de que ...** I am not very hopeful that ... • **poner su ~ en algo** to pin one's hopes on sth
3 (= *entusiasmo*) excitement • **¡qué ~!** how exciting! • **¡qué ~ verte aquí!** it's really great to see you here! • **trabajar con ~** to work with a will • **el viaje me hace mucha ~** I am so looking forward to the trip • **tu carta me hizo mucha ~** I was thrilled to get your letter • **me hace una gran ~ que ...** it gives me a thrill that ...
ilusionadamente ADV (= *con esperanza*) with high hopes; (= *con emoción*) excitedly
ilusionado ADJ (= *esperanzado*) hopeful; (= *entusiasmado*) excited • **estaba ~ con el viaje a Francia** he was looking forward to going to France • **joven ~** young hopeful
ilusionante ADJ exciting
ilusionar ▹ CONJUG 1a VT **1** (= *entusiasmar*) to excite, thrill • **me ilusiona mucho el viaje** I'm really excited about the journey
2 (= *alentar falsamente*) • **~ a algn** to get sb's hopes up
VPR **ilusionarse 1** (= *entusiasmarse*) to get excited
2 (*falsamente*) to get one's hopes up • **no te ilusiones** don't get your hopes up
ilusionismo SM conjuring
ilusionista SMF conjurer, illusionist
iluso/a ADJ (= *crédulo*) gullible • **¡pobre ~!** poor deluded creature! • **¡~ de mí!** silly me!
SM/F (= *soñador*) dreamer • **¡iluso!** you're hopeful!
ilusorio ADJ (= *irreal*) illusory; (= *sin valor*) empty; (= *sin efecto*) ineffective
ilustración SF **1** (= *ejemplo*) illustration
2 [*de libro*] picture, illustration
3 (= *instrucción*) learning, erudition • **la Ilustración** the Enlightenment, the Age of Enlightenment
ilustrado ADJ **1** [*libro*] illustrated
2 [*persona*] (= *culto*) learned, erudite; (= *progresista*) enlightened
ilustrador(a) ADJ **1** (= *que aclara*) illustrative
2 (= *instructivo*) enlightening
SM/F illustrator
ilustrar ▹ CONJUG 1a VT **1** [+ *libro*] to illustrate
2 [+ *tema*] to explain, illustrate
3 (= *instruir*) to instruct, enlighten
4† (= *hacer ilustre*) to make illustrious, make famous
VPR **ilustrarse 1** (= *instruirse*) to acquire knowledge
2† (= *hacerse ilustre*) to become illustrious, become famous
ilustrativo ADJ illustrative
ilustre ADJ illustrious, famous
ilustrísimo ADJ most illustrious • **Su Ilustrísima†** (*al referirse a un obispo*) His Grace • **Vuestra Ilustrísima†** (*al dirigirse a un obispo*) Your Grace, Your Lordship
IM SM ABR = **Instituto de la Mujer**
IMAC SM ABR (= **Instituto de Mediación, Arbitraje y Conciliación**) ≈ ACAS
imagen SF **1** (*Fot, Ópt*) image; (= *en foto, dibujo, TV*) picture • **las imágenes del accidente** the pictures *o* images of the accident • **es una ~ muy hermosa de tu madre** it's a beautiful picture of your mother • **~ en movimiento** moving image • REFRÁN: • **una ~ vale más que mil palabras** a picture is worth a thousand words ▸ **imágenes de archivo** library pictures ▸ **imagen especular** mirror image ▸ **imagen fija** still ▸ **imagen virtual** virtual image
2 (= *reflejo*) reflection • **vio su ~ reflejada en el lago** she saw her reflection in the lake • **le gustaba contemplar su ~ en el espejo** he liked looking at himself *o* at his reflection in the mirror • MODISMOS: • **a (la) ~ y semejanza de uno** in one's own image • **Dios creó al hombre a su ~ y semejanza** God created man in his own image • **los ha educado a su ~ y semejanza** she has brought them up to be just like her • **un campeonato a ~ y semejanza de los que se celebran en Francia** a championship of exactly the same kind as those held in France • **ser la misma** *o* **la viva ~ de algn** to be the living *o* spitting* image of sb • **ser la viva ~ de algo** to be the picture of sth • **era la viva ~ de la desesperación** he was the picture of despair • **es la viva ~ de la felicidad** she is happiness personified, she is the picture of happiness
3 (= *representación mental*) image, picture • **tenía otra ~ de ti** I had a different image *o* picture of you • **guardo una ~ borrosa del accidente** I only have a vague picture of the accident in my mind
4 (= *aspecto*) image • **Luis cuida mucho su ~** Luis takes great care over his appearance *o* image • **eso contrasta con su ~ de tipo duro** that contradicts with his tough guy image • **la ~ del partido** the party's image • **un cambio de ~** a change of image ▸ **imagen de marca** brand image ▸ **imagen pública** public image
5 (*Rel*) [*de madera, pintura*] image; [*de piedra*] statue • MODISMO: • **quedar para vestir imágenes** to be an old maid
6 (*Literat*) (= *metáfora*) image • **un texto con gran abundancia de imágenes** a text full of images *o* imagery ▸ **imágenes poéticas** poetic imagery (*sing*)
imaginable ADJ imaginable, conceivable • **una hermosura más allá de lo ~** a beauty beyond all belief (*liter*) • **su descaro va más allá de lo ~** he has an unbelievable cheek • **no es ~ que ...** it is difficult to imagine *o* conceive that ...
imaginación SF **1** imagination • **tiene mucha ~** he's got a great imagination • **eso es todo obra de tu ~** it's all a figment of your imagination • **no te dejes llevar por la ~** don't let your imagination run away with you • **no se me pasó por la ~ que ...** it never even occurred to me that ... • **ni por ~** on no account ▸ **imaginación creativa** creative imagination ▸ **imaginación poética** poetic imagination
2 imaginaciones (= *lo imaginado*) • **eso son imaginaciones tuyas** you're imagining things
imaginar ▹ CONJUG 1a VT **1** (= *suponer*) to imagine • **no puedes ~ cuánto he deseado que llegara este momento** you can't imagine how much I've been looking forward to this moment • **imagino que necesitaréis unas vacaciones** I imagine *o* suppose *o* guess* that you'll need a holiday • **imagina que tuvieras mucho dinero, ¿qué harías?** suppose *o* imagine that you had a lot of money — what would you do? • **ya estás imaginando cosas** you're just imagining things
2 (= *visualizar*) to imagine • **imaginad un mundo sin guerras** imagine a world without war
3 (= *inventar*) [+ *plan, método*] to think up
VPR **imaginarse 1** (= *suponer*) to imagine • **no te puedes ~ lo mal que iba todo** you can't imagine how bad things were • **—no sabes lo cansados que estamos —sí, ya me imagino** "you've no idea how tired we are" — "yes, I can imagine" • **¡pues, imagínate, se nos averió el coche en plena montaña!** just imagine, the car broke down right up in the mountains! • **—¿lo habéis pasado bien? —imagínate** "did you have a good time?" — "what do you think? *o* we sure did" • **~se que** (*en suposiciones*) to imagine that, suppose that, guess that*; (*en oraciones condicionales*) to imagine that, suppose that • **me imagino que tendrás ganas de descansar** I imagine *o* suppose *o* guess* you'll need a rest • **no me imaginaba que tuvieras un hermano** I never imagined *o* guessed* you had a brother • **imagínate que os pasa algo** suppose something happens to you • **me imagino que sí** I should think so, I (would) imagine so
2 (= *visualizar*) to imagine, picture • **imagínatela cubierta de nieve** imagine *o* picture it covered in snow • **me la imaginaba más joven** I had imagined *o* pictured her as being younger
imaginaria SF (*Mil*) reserve, nightguard
imaginario ADJ imaginary • **el mundo de lo ~** the imaginary world
SM **1** (*Literat*) imagery
2 (= *imaginación*) imagination • **el ~ de un niño** a child's imagination
imaginativa SF **1** (= *imaginación*) imagination, imaginativeness

2 (= *sentido común*) common sense
imaginativo ADJ imaginative • **una sátira nada imaginativa** a very unimaginative satire • **el mundo de lo ~** the imaginary world
imaginería SF **1** (*Rel*) images (*pl*), statues (*pl*)
2 (*Literat*) imagery
imaginero/a SM/F maker/painter of religious images
imam SM, **imán[1]** SM (*Rel*) imam
imán[2] SM magnet ▸ **imán de herradura** horseshoe magnet
imantación SF, **imanación** SF magnetization
imantar ▹ CONJUG 1a VT, **imanar** ▹ CONJUG 1a VT to magnetize
imbatibilidad SF unbeatable character; (*Dep*) unbeaten record
imbatible ADJ unbeatable
imbatido ADJ unbeaten
imbebible ADJ undrinkable
imbécil ADJ **1** (= *idiota*) silly, stupid
2 (*Med*) imbecile
SMF **1** (= *idiota*) imbecile, idiot • **¡imbécil!** you idiot!
2 (*Med*) imbecile
imbecilidad SF **1** (= *idiotez*) stupidity, idiocy • **decir ~es** to say silly things
2 (*Med*) imbecility
imbecilizar ▹ CONJUG 1f VT (= *idiotizar*) to reduce to a state of idiocy; (*por alcohol, drogas*) to stupefy
imberbe ADJ beardless
imbíbito ADJ (*CAm, Méx*) included (*in the bill*)
imbombera SF (*Ven*) (*Med*) pernicious anaemia, pernicious anemia (*EEUU*)
imbombo ADJ (*Ven*) anaemic, anemic (*EEUU*)
imbornal SM **1** (*Náut*) scupper
2 (*Arquit*) gutter
3 • MODISMO: • **irse por los ~es** (*LAm**) to go off at a tangent
imborrable ADJ [*tinta*] indelible; [*recuerdo*] indelible, unforgettable
imbricación SF **1** [*de placas*] overlapping
2 [*de aspectos, asuntos*] interweaving, interdependence
imbricado ADJ **1** [*placa*] overlapping
2 [*asunto*] interwoven
imbricar ▹ CONJUG 1g VT **1** (= *superponer*) to overlap
2 (= *entrelazar*) to interweave
VPR **imbricarse 1** [*placas*] to overlap
2 [*asuntos, problemas*] to be interwoven
imbuir ▹ CONJUG 3g VT to imbue, infuse (**de, en** with) • **imbuido de la cultura de** imbued with the culture of • **una tradición imbuida de cierto romanticismo** a tradition imbued with a certain romanticism
imbunchar ▹ CONJUG 1a VT (*Chile*)
1 (= *encantar*) to bewitch
2 (= *estafar*) to swindle, cheat
imbunche SM (*Cono Sur*) **1** (= *hechizo*) spell, piece of witchcraft
2 (= *brujo*) sorcerer, wizard
3 (= *confusión*) mess
IMC SM ABR (= **índice de masa corporal**) BMI
IMCE SM ABR = **Instituto Mejicano de Comercio Exterior**
IMEC SF ABR (*Esp*) = **Instrucción Militar de la Escala de Complemento**
imitable ADJ **1** (= *copiable*) imitable
2 (= *digno de imitación*) worthy of imitation
imitación SF **1** (= *copia*) imitation • **a ~ de** in imitation of • **desconfíe de las imitaciones** beware of imitations • **de ~** imitation (*antes de s*) • **joyas de ~** imitation jewellery *o* (*EEUU*) jewelry • **un bolso de ~ piel** an imitation leather bag • **una pistola de ~** a fake gun
2 (*Teat*) impression, impersonation
imitador(a) ADJ imitative
SM/F **1** (= *plagiario*) imitator
2 (= *seguidor*) follower
3 (*Teat*) impressionist, impersonator
imitar ▹ CONJUG 1a VT **1** (= *emular*) to imitate • **Susana imita a sus padres en todo** Susana copies everything her parents do • **se limita a ~ a los mejores autores** he confines himself to aping the best authors
2 (= *por diversión*) to imitate, mimic • **¡deja ya de ~me!** stop imitating *o* mimicking me! • **sabe ~ muy bien mi firma** he can imitate *o* copy my signature really well • **sabe ~ todos los acentos** he can imitate any accent • **el humorista imitó al rey** the comedian did an impression of the king
3 (= *parecerse a*) • **imita el tacto de la seda** it simulates the feel of silk • **estos pendientes imitan el oro** these earrings are meant to look like gold
imitativo ADJ imitative
impaciencia SF impatience
impacientar ▹ CONJUG 1a VT **1** [*lentitud, retraso*] to make impatient
2 (= *exasperar*) to exasperate
VPR **impacientarse 1** (*por falta de tiempo*) to get impatient (**ante, por** about, at, **con** with)
2 (= *exasperarse*) to lose patience, get worked up
impaciente ADJ **1** (= *sin paciencia*) impatient (**por** to) • **~ por empezar** impatient to start • **¡estoy ~!** I can't wait!
2 (= *irritable*) impatient
impacientemente ADV **1** (= *sin paciencia*) impatiently
2 (= *con exasperación*) impatiently
impactante ADJ (= *impresionante*) striking, impressive; (= *contundente*) shattering; (= *abrumador*) crushing, overwhelming
impactar ▹ CONJUG 1a VT to impress, have an impact on
VI **1** (= *chocar*) to crash (**contra** against, **en** into)
2 (= *afectar*) • **~ en** to affect
VPR **impactarse** • **~se ante** *o* **por algo** to be overawed by sth
impacto SM **1** (= *golpe*) [*de vehículo, disparo*] impact; (*LAm*) punch, blow ▸ **impacto de bala** bullethole
2 (= *efecto*) [*de noticia, cambios, leyes*] impact • **~ ambiental** environmental impact • **~ político** political impact
impagable ADJ (*lit*) unpayable; (*fig*) priceless
impagado ADJ unpaid
impagador(a) SM/F defaulter, non-payer
impago ADJ (*Cono Sur*) unpaid
SM non-payment, failure to pay
impajaritable* ADJ (*Cono Sur*) necessary, imperative
impalpable ADJ impalpable
impar ADJ **1** (*Mat*) odd • **los números ~es** the odd numbers
2 (= *único*) unique
SM odd number
imparable ADJ unstoppable
imparablemente ADV unstoppably
imparcial ADJ impartial, fair
imparcialidad SF impartiality
imparcialmente ADV impartially
impartible ADJ indivisible
impartición SF teaching
impartir ▹ CONJUG 3a VT [+ *instrucción*] to impart (*frm*), give; [+ *orden*] to give
impasibilidad SF impassiveness, impassivity • **le golpeó en el rostro ante la ~ de todos los que pasaban por allí** he hit her in the face and no-one passing by took any notice • **los precios siguen bajando ante la ~ del gobierno** the government remains unmoved *o* impassive despite the continual fall in prices
impasible ADJ impassive
impasse [im'pas] SM o SF **1** (= *estancamiento*) impasse
2 (*Bridge*) finesse • **hacer el ~ a algn** to finesse against sb
impávidamente ADV **1** (= *intrépidamente*) intrepidly; (= *impasiblemente*) dauntlessly
2 (*LAm*) (= *con insolencia*) cheekily
impavidez SF **1** (= *valor*) intrepidity; (= *impasibilidad*) dauntlessness
2 (*LAm*) (= *insolencia*) cheek, cheekiness, sass (*EEUU**)
impávido ADJ **1** (= *valiente*) intrepid; (= *impasible*) dauntless, undaunted
2 (*LAm*) (= *insolente*) cheeky, sassy (*EEUU**)
IMPE SM ABR (*Esp*) = **Instituto de la Mediana y Pequeña Empresa**
impecable ADJ impeccable, faultless
impecablemente ADV impeccably, faultlessly
impedido/a ADJ disabled • **estar ~ para algo** to be unfit for sth • **me veo ~ para ayudar** I am not in a position to help
SM/F disabled person
impedimenta SF (*Mil*) impedimenta (*pl*)
impedimento SM **1** (= *dificultad*) impediment, hindrance • **pidieron a los republicanos que no pusieran ~s al nombramiento** they asked the republicans not to block the appointment • **nos ponen ~s para evitar que lo hagamos** they are putting obstacles in our way to prevent us doing it
2 (*Med*) disability, handicap • **~ del habla** speech impediment
impedir ▹ CONJUG 3k VT **1** (= *parar*) to prevent, stop • **trataron de ~ la huida de los presos** they tried to prevent the prisoners escaping *o* the prisoners escape • **~ a algn el acceso al edificio** to prevent sb from entering the building • **lo que no se puede ~** what cannot be prevented • **a mí nadie me lo va a ~** nobody's going to stop me • **~ a algn hacer algo** • **~ que algn haga algo** to prevent sb (from) doing sth, stop sb doing sth • **esto no impide que ...** this does not alter the fact that ... • **~ el paso** to block the way • **un camión nos impedía el paso** a lorry was blocking our way
2 (= *dificultar*) (*con obstáculos*) to impede, obstruct; (*con problemas*) to hinder, hamper
impeditivo ADJ preventive
impeler ▹ CONJUG 2a VT **1** (= *empujar*) to drive, propel
2 (= *incitar*) to drive, urge, impel • **~ a algn a hacer algo** to drive *o* impel sb to do sth • **impelido por la necesidad** driven by need
impenetrabilidad SF impenetrability
impenetrable ADJ **1** (= *no atravesable*) [*bosque*] impenetrable
2 (= *impermeable*) impervious
3 (= *incomprensible*) obscure, impenetrable
impenitencia SF impenitence
impenitente ADJ unrepentant, impenitent
impensable ADJ unthinkable
impensadamente ADV
1 (= *inesperadamente*) unexpectedly
2 (= *por casualidad*) at random, by chance
impensado ADJ **1** (= *inesperado*) unexpected, unforeseen
2 (= *casual*) random, chance (*antes de s*)
impepinable* ADJ certain
impepinablemente* ADV inevitably • **~ se**

le olvida he's sure to forget, he always forgets
imperante (ADJ) ruling, prevailing
imperar ▹ CONJUG 1a (VI) **1** (= *prevalecer*) [*condiciones*] to prevail; [*precio*] to be in force, be current
2 (= *mandar*) [*rey*] to rule, reign; [*jefe, capitán*] to be in command
imperativamente (ADV)
1 (= *obligatoriamente*) imperatively
2 [*decir*] imperiously, in a commanding tone
imperatividad (SF) imperative nature, imperativeness
imperativo (ADJ) (*gen*) imperative; [*tono*] commanding, imperative
(SM) **1** (= *necesidad*) imperative ▸ **imperativo categórico** moral imperative
2 (*Ling*) imperative, imperative mood
imperceptibilidad (SF) imperceptibility
imperceptible (ADJ) imperceptible
imperceptiblemente (ADV) imperceptibly
imperdible (SM) safety pin
imperdonable (ADJ) unforgivable, unpardonable, inexcusable
imperdonablemente (ADV) unforgivably, unpardonably, inexcusably
imperecedero (ADJ) [*recuerdo*] immortal, undying; [*legado*] eternal; [*fama*] eternal, everlasting
imperfección (SF) **1** (= *cualidad*) imperfection
2 (= *fallo*) flaw, fault
imperfeccionar ▹ CONJUG 1a (VT) (*Cono Sur*) to spoil
imperfectamente (ADV) imperfectly
imperfecto (ADJ) **1** [*producto, método*] imperfect, flawed
2 (*Ling*) imperfect
(SM) (*Ling*) imperfect, imperfect tense
imperial (ADJ) imperial
(SF) (*en carruaje*) imperial
imperialismo (SM) imperialism
imperialista (ADJ) imperialist, imperialistic
(SMF) imperialist
imperialmente (ADV) imperially
impericia (SF) **1** (= *torpeza*) unskilfulness, unskillfulness (EEUU)
2 (= *inexperiencia*) inexperience • **a prueba de ~** foolproof
imperio (SM) **1** (*Pol*) empire • **Imperio Español** Spanish Empire • MODISMOS: • **vale un ~** • **vale siete ~s** it's worth a fortune
2 (= *autoridad*) rule • **el ~ de la ley** the rule of law
3 (= *orgullo*) haughtiness, pride
imperiosamente (ADV) **1** (= *con autoritarismo*) imperiously
2 (= *urgentemente*) urgently
imperiosidad (SF) **1** (= *autoritarismo*) imperiousness
2 (= *urgencia*) pressing necessity, overriding need
imperioso (ADJ) **1** (= *autoritario*) imperious
2 (= *urgente*) pressing, urgent • **necesidad imperiosa** pressing need, absolute necessity
imperito (ADJ) (= *inhábil*) inexpert, unskilled; (= *inexperto*) inexperienced; (= *torpe*) clumsy
impermanente (ADJ) impermanent
impermeabilidad (SF) impermeability, imperviousness
impermeabilización (SF) **1** (*Téc*) waterproofing
2 (*Aut*) undersealing
3 [*de frontera*] sealing
impermeabilizado (ADJ) waterproofed
impermeabilizar ▹ CONJUG 1f (VT) **1** (*Téc*) to waterproof, make watertight
2 (*Aut*) to underseal
3 [+ *frontera*] to seal off
impermeable (ADJ) **1** (*al agua*) waterproof
2 (= *impenetrable*) impermeable (**a** to), impervious
(SM) **1** (*prenda*) raincoat, mac*
2‡ (= *preservativo*) French letter*
impersonador(a) (SM/F) (*Méx*) impersonator
impersonal (ADJ) impersonal
impersonalidad (SF) impersonality, impersonal nature
impersonalismo (SM) **1** (= *cualidad*) impersonality, impersonal nature
2 (*LAm*) disinterestedness
impersonalmente (ADV) impersonally
impersonar ▹ CONJUG 1a (VT) (*Méx*) to impersonate
impertérrito (ADJ) **1** (= *sin miedo*) unafraid
2 (= *impávido*) unshaken, unmoved
impertinencia (SF) **1** (= *insolencia*) impertinence
2 (= *comentario*) impertinent remark
3 (*frm*) (= *irrelevancia*) irrelevance
impertinente (ADJ) **1** (= *insolente*) impertinent
2 (*frm*) (= *irrelevante*) irrelevant, not pertinent
(SMPL) **impertinentes** lorgnette (*sing*)
impertinentemente (ADV)
1 (= *insolentemente*) impertinently
2 (*frm*) (= *irrelevantemente*) irrelevantly
imperturbable (ADJ) (= *no cambiable*) imperturbable; (= *sereno*) unruffled; (= *impasible*) impassive
imperturbablemente (ADV) (= *sin cambios*) imperturbably; (= *impasiblemente*) impassively
imperturbado (ADJ) unperturbed
impétigo (SM) impetigo
impetrar ▹ CONJUG 1a (VT) **1** (= *rogar*) to beg for, beseech
2 (= *obtener*) to obtain, win
ímpetu (SM) **1** (= *impulso*) impetus; (*Mec*) momentum
2 (= *acometida*) rush, onrush
3 (*al hacer algo*) (= *impulsividad*) impetuousness, impetuosity; (= *violencia*) violence
impetuosamente (ADV) (= *con impulsividad*) impetuously, impulsively; (= *con violencia*) violently
impetuosidad (SF) impetuosity, impetuousness
impetuoso (ADJ) **1** [*persona*] impetuous, impulsive
2 [*acto*] hasty, impetuous
3 [*corriente*] rushing, violent
impiadoso (ADJ) (*LAm*) impious
impiedad (SF) **1** (*Rel*) impiety, ungodliness
2 (= *crueldad*) cruelty, pitilessness
impío (ADJ) **1** (*Rel*) impious, ungodly
2 (= *cruel*) cruel, pitiless
implacable (ADJ) implacable, relentless
implacablemente (ADV) implacably, relentlessly
implantable (ADJ) that can be implanted
implantación (SF) **1** [*de modelo, ley*] implementation • **la ~ del nuevo sistema educativo** the implementation of the new education system • **la ~ de la dictadura** the installing of the dictatorship
2 [*de costumbre, ideología*] • **una costumbre de reciente ~** a custom that has only recently become established *o* taken root • **tras la ~ del capitalismo** since capitalism became established *o* took root • **esta moda no tuvo ~ en España** this fashion never caught on in Spain
3 [*de empresa*] establishment, setting up
4 (= *popularidad*) • **un partido con escasa ~ en las ciudades** a party with little support in the cities • **un idioma de fuerte ~ en Nueva York** a language which is firmly established in New York
5 (*Med*) [*de miembro*] implantation
implantar ▹ CONJUG 1a (VT) **1** [+ *reforma, sistema, modelo*] to implement; [+ *castigo, medidas*] to bring in; [+ *toque de queda*] to impose • **hemos implantado el uso obligatorio del gallego** we have brought in *o* implemented compulsory Galician • **cuando ~on la dictadura** when the dictatorship was installed • **han vuelto a ~ la pena de muerte** they have brought back the death penalty
2 [+ *costumbre, ideas*] to introduce • **los americanos han implantado sus costumbres en Europa** the Americans have introduced their customs to Europe
3 [+ *empresa*] to establish, set up
4 (*Med*) to implant
(VPR) **implantarse** to become established • **se ha implantado el uso del catalán en la vida diaria** Catalan has become established in everyday life • **la nueva moda se ha implantado entre los jóvenes** the new fashion has caught on among young people
implante (SM) implant
implementar ▹ CONJUG 1a (VT) to implement
(VI) to help, give aid
implemento (SM) **1** (= *herramienta*) implement, tool
2 (*LAm*) means
implicación (SF) **1** (= *complicidad*) involvement
2 (= *significado*) implication
3 (= *contradicción*) contradiction (in terms)
implicancia (SF) (*LAm*) implication
implicar ▹ CONJUG 1g (VT) **1** (= *involucrar*) to involve • **las partes implicadas** the interested parties, the parties concerned
2 (= *significar*) to imply • **esto no implica que …** this does not mean that …
implícitamente (ADV) implicitly
implícito (ADJ) implicit
imploración (SF) supplication, entreaty
implorante (ADJ) [*mirada, mano*] imploring
implorar ▹ CONJUG 1a (VT) to implore, beg, beseech (*liter*) • **~ a algn que haga algo** to implore *o* beg sb to do sth, beseech sb to do sth (*liter*)
implosionar ▹ CONJUG 1a (VI), **implotar** ▹ CONJUG 1a (VI) to implode
implume (ADJ) **1** (= *sin plumas*) featherless, unfledged
2 (= *sin vello*) unfledged
impolítico (ADJ) **1** (= *imprudente*) impolitic, imprudent
2 (= *no diplomático*) tactless, undiplomatic
3 (= *descortés*) impolite
impoluto (ADJ) unpolluted, pure
imponderable (ADJ) imponderable
(SMPL) **imponderables** imponderables
imponencia (SF) **1** (*LAm*) (= *lo impresionante*) impressiveness
2 (= *majestuosidad*) stateliness, grandness
imponente (ADJ) **1** (= *que asusta*) [*persona, castillo, montaña*] imposing
2 (= *magnífico*) [*aspecto*] stunning; [*edificio, fachada*] impressive; [*paisaje, representación*] stunning, impressive • **ibas ~ con ese vestido** you looked stunning in that dress • **vivía en una ~ mansión** she lived in an imposing *o* impressive mansion
(SMF) **1** (*Econ*) depositor
2 (*Chile*) Social Security contributor
imponer ▹ CONJUG 2q (PP: **impuesto**) (VT)
1 (= *poner*) [+ *castigo, obligación*] to impose; [+ *tarea*] to set • **~ sanciones comerciales a un país** to impose trade sanctions against *o* on a country • **no quiero ~te nada, solo darte un buen consejo** I don't want to force you to

do anything *o* I don't want to impose anything on you, just to give you some good advice • **el juez le impuso una pena de tres años de prisión** the judge gave him a three-year prison sentence • **no le impusieron ningún castigo al portero** the goalkeeper was not penalized
2 (*frm*) (= *conceder*) [+ *medalla*] to award • **a la princesa le impusieron el nombre de Mercedes** the princess was given the name Mercedes, the princess was named Mercedes
3 (= *hacer prevalecer*) [+ *voluntad, costumbre*] to impose; [+ *norma*] to enforce; [+ *miedo*] to instil; [+ *condición*] to lay down, impose; [+ *enseñanza, uso*] to make compulsory • **trató de ~ su punto de vista** he tried to impose his viewpoint • **su trabajo le impone un ritmo de vida muy acelerado** her work forces her to lead a very fast lifestyle • **quieren ~ la enseñanza del catalán** they want to make the teaching of Catalan compulsory • **han impuesto por la fuerza el velo a las mujeres** women have been forced to wear the veil • **han impuesto a la fuerza la enseñanza religiosa** they have enforced religious education • **~ la moda** to set the trend • **este año han impuesto la moda del acid jazz** this year acid jazz is the trend • **algunos creadores japoneses imponen su moda en Occidente** some Japanese designers have successfully brought their fashions over to the West • **~ respeto** to command respect • **la autoridad siempre impone respeto** authority always commands respect • **tu padre me impone mucho respeto** I find your father very intimidating • **~ el ritmo** to set the pace
4 (*Com, Econ*) [+ *dinero*] to deposit; [+ *impuesto*] to put (**a, sobre** on), levy (**a, sobre** on) • **hemos impuesto tres millones a plazo fijo** we have deposited three million for a fixed term • **han impuesto nuevas tasas sobre los servicios básicos** they have put *o* levied new taxes on essential services
5 (= *instruir*) • **~ a algn en algo** to instruct sb in sth
6 (*Rel*) • **~ las manos sobre algn** to lay hands on sb
7 (*Chile*) to pay (in contributions), pay (in Social Security)
(VI) **1** (= *intimidar*) [*persona*] to command respect; [*edificio*] to be imposing; [*arma*] to be intimidating • **su forma de hablar en público impone** his style of public speaking commands respect • **el castillo imponía un poco al entrar** the castle was rather imposing as you went in • **¿no te impone dormir solo?** don't you find it rather scary sleeping on your own?
2 (*Chile*) to pay contributions, pay one's Social Security
(VPR) **imponerse 1** (= *obligarse*) [+ *horario, tarea*] to set o.s. • **nos hemos impuesto un horario de trabajo muy duro** we've set ourselves a very heavy work schedule
2 (= *hacerse respetar*) to assert one's authority, assert o.s. • **sabe ~se cuando hace falta** he knows how to assert his authority *o* himself when necessary • **~se a *o* sobre algn** to assert one's authority over sb • **el clero consiguió ~se al Gobierno** the clergy managed to assert its authority over the government • **siempre acaba imponiéndose sobre sus hermanas** he always ends up getting his own way with his sisters
3 (= *prevalecer*) [*criterio*] to prevail; [*moda*] to become fashionable • **al final se impuso un criterio de sabiduría** wisdom prevailed in the end • **se está imponiendo otra vez la ropa deportiva** sportswear is coming into fashion again • **la minifalda no ha llegado a ~se esta temporada** the mini-skirt hasn't caught on this season
4 (*frm*) (= *ser necesario*) [*cambio*] to be needed; [*conclusión*] to be inescapable • **se impone la necesidad de una gran reforma** there is an urgent need for extensive reform • **la conclusión se impone** the conclusion is inescapable
5 (*Dep*) (= *vencer*) to win • **el Barcelona se impuso en el último minuto** Barcelona won (the match) in the last minute • **el Valencia se impuso por tres a cero al Oviedo** Valencia defeated *o* beat Oviedo three nil; ▹ **sprint**
6 (= *instruirse*) • **~se en algo** to acquaint o.s. with sth
7 (*Méx**) (= *acostumbrarse*) • **~se a algo** to become accustomed to sth • **~se a hacer algo** to become accustomed to doing sth

imponible (ADJ) **1** (*Econ*) [*riqueza, hecho*] taxable, subject to tax; [*importación*] dutiable, subject to duty • **no ~** tax-free, tax-exempt (EEUU); ▹ **base**
2* [*ropa*] unwearable

impopular (ADJ) unpopular

impopularidad (SF) unpopularity

importación (SF) **1** (= *acto*) importation • **la ~ de coches** the importation of cars • **de ~** [*producto, artículo*] imported; [*comercio, permiso*] import (*antes de s*) • **whisky de ~** imported whisky
2 importaciones (= *mercancías*) imports

importador(a) (ADJ) importing
(SM/F) importer

importancia (SF) importance • **tu ayuda ha sido de gran ~** your help has been very important *o* of great importance • **un autor de ~ universal** an author of worldwide renown • **¿y eso qué ~ tiene?** and how is that important *o* significant?, and what significance does that have? • **no te preocupes, no tiene ~** don't worry, it's not important • **carecer de ~** to be unimportant • **de cierta ~** [*empresa, asunto*] of some importance, important; [*herida*] serious • **conceder *o* dar mucha ~ a algo** to attach great importance to sth • **no quiero darle más ~ de la que tiene, pero ...** I don't want to make an issue of this but ... • **darse ~** to give o.s. airs • **quitar *o* restar ~ a algo** to make light of sth, play down the importance of sth • **sin ~** [*herida, comentario*] minor • **son detalles sin ~** these are minor details

importante (ADJ) **1** (= *trascendental*) [*información, persona*] important; [*acontecimiento*] significant, important; [*papel, factor, parte*] important, major; [*cambio*] significant, major • **se trata de algo ~** it's important • **tu padre es un hombre ~** your father's an important man • **uno de los momentos más ~s de mi vida** one of the most significant *o* important moments in my life • **un paso ~ para la democracia** an important *o* a big *o* a major step for democracy • **dárselas de ~** to give o.s. airs • **lo ~ es ...** the main thing is ... • **lo ~ es participar** the main thing is taking part • **lo más ~ en la vida** the most important thing in life • **poco ~** unimportant • **es ~ que** it is important that • **es ~ que expreses tu opinión** it's important for you to express your opinion
2 (*como intensificador*) [*cantidad, pérdida*] considerable; [*herida*] serious; [*retraso*] considerable, serious • **una ~ suma de dinero** a considerable amount of money

importantizarse* ▹ CONJUG 1f (VPR) (*Caribe*) to give o.s. airs

importar[1] ▹ CONJUG 1a (VT) (*Com*) to import (**de** from)

importar[2] ▹ CONJUG 1a (VI) **1** (= *ser importante*) to matter • **¿qué importa que no seamos ricos?** what does it matter if *o* that we're not rich? • **—llegaremos allí un poco tarde —no importa** "we'll be there a bit late" — "never mind *o* it doesn't matter" • **lo que importa es la calidad** the important thing is the quality, what matters is the quality • **¿y eso qué importa?** what does that matter? • **el color importa mucho en su pintura** colour is important in her painting, colour plays an important part in her painting • **lo comprará a no importa qué precio** he'll buy it at any price • **no importa el tiempo que haga, allí estaremos** we'll be there whatever the weather
2 (*con complemento de persona*) **a** (= *interesar*) • **sí que me importa tu opinión** your opinion does matter to me, I do care about your opinion • **¿a quién le importa lo que yo diga?** who cares (about) what I say? • **no le importa nada de lo que pase** he doesn't care about anything that happens, he's not bothered about anything • **tú me importas más que nada** I care about you more than anything, you mean more to me than anything • **¿y a ti qué te importa?** what business is it of yours? • **¡a ti eso no te importa!** it's nothing to do with you!, it's none of your business! • **meterse en lo que a uno no le importa** to poke one's nose into other people's business • **deja ya de meterte en lo que no te importa** stop poking your nose into other people's business • **no quisiera meterme en lo que no me importa, pero ...** I know it's none of my business, but ... • MODISMOS: • **(no) me importa un bledo *o* un comino *o* un pito *o* un rábano*** I couldn't care less*, I don't give a damn‡ • **(no) me importa un carajo *o* un huevo**** I don't give a shit** *o* a toss‡ • **tú no le importas un carajo** he doesn't give a shit** *o* a toss‡ about you
b (= *molestar*) • **¿te ~ía prestarme este libro?** would you mind lending me this book?, could you lend me this book? • **si no le importa, me gustaría que me enviaran la factura** if it's not too much trouble, I'd like you to send me the bill • **—¿quieres venir al concierto? —pues no me ~ía** "do you want to come to the concert?" — "I wouldn't mind" • **¿te importa si fumo?** do you mind if I smoke? • **no ~ a algn hacer algo**: • **no me importa esperar** I don't mind waiting • **si os hace falta alguien, a mí no me ~ía ayudaros** if you need somebody, I'd be happy to help *o* I don't mind helping • **no me importa que llegues un poco tarde** I don't mind if you're a bit late, I don't mind you being a bit late
(VT) (*frm*) [*artículo, producto*] to cost; [*gastos, beneficios*] to amount to • **¿cuánto importa esta lámpara?** how much does this lamp cost? • **los gastos de transporte ~on 2.000 euros** transport costs amounted to 2,000 euros

importe (SM) **1** (= *valor*) [*de compra, gastos, cheque*] amount • **el ~ de esta factura** the amount of this bill • **¿a cuánto asciende el ~ de los gastos?** how much do the expenses amount to *o* come to? • **el ~ de la recaudación** (*Cine, Teat*) box office takings (*pl*); (*Dep*) gate receipts (*pl*) • **por ~ de** to the value of • **un préstamo por ~ de 10.000 euros** a loan to the value of 10,000 euros • **cheques por un ~ total de 20 millones** cheques to the total value of 20 million
▸ **importe global** grand total
2 (= *coste*) cost • **el ~ de la mano de obra** the

cost of labour

importunación SF pestering
▸ **importunación sexual** sexual harassment

importunar ▹ CONJUG 1a VT to bother, pester

importunidad SF (= *acción*) pestering; (= *efecto*) annoyance, nuisance

importuno ADJ **1** (= *fastidioso*) annoying
2 (= *inoportuno*) inopportune, inappropriate

imposibilidad SF **1** [*de suceso, acción*] impossibility
2 (= *incapacidad*) • **mi ~ para hacerlo** my inability to do it

imposibilitado ADJ **1** (*Med*) disabled • **estar** *o* **verse ~ para hacer algo** to be unable to do sth, be prevented from doing sth
2 (*Econ*) without means

imposibilitar ▹ CONJUG 1a VT **1** (*Med*) to disable
2 (= *impedir*) to make impossible, prevent • **esto me imposibilita hacerlo** this makes it impossible for me to do it, this prevents me from doing it

imposible ADJ **1** (= *no posible*) impossible • **es ~** it's impossible, it's out of the question • **es ~ de predecir** it's impossible to predict • **hacer lo ~ por hacer algo** to do one's utmost to do sth • **¡parece ~!** you'd never believe it!
2 (= *inaguantable*) impossible
3 (= *difícil*) impossible
4 (*LAm*) (= *descuidado*) slovenly, dirty; (= *repugnante*) repulsive
SM • **un ~** (*tarea*) an impossible task; (*objetivo*) an impossible goal • **lo que voy a pedir es un ~** what I'm about to ask is impossible, I'm about to ask for the impossible • **perseguía un ~** he was pursuing an impossible dream *o* aim

imposición SF **1** (= *introducción*) [*de obligación, multa*] imposition; [*de ley, moda*] introduction • **la ~ de la moneda única** the introduction of the single currency • **ante todo tenía que conseguir la ~ de su voluntad** above all he had to impose his will • **no me gustan las imposiciones** I don't like people making demands on me
2 [*de medallas*] • **la ceremonia de ~ de medallas** the medal ceremony
3 (= *impuesto*) taxation • **doble ~** double taxation ▸ **imposición directa** direct taxation ▸ **imposición indirecta** indirect taxation
4 (= *ingreso*) deposit • **efectuar una ~** to make a deposit ▸ **imposición a plazo (fijo)** fixed-term deposit
5 (*Tip*) imposition
6 (*Rel*) ▸ **imposición de manos** laying on of hands
7 (*Chile*) Social Security contribution

impositiva SF (*LAm*) tax office

impositivamente ADV for tax purposes, with regard to taxation

impositivo ADJ **1** (*Econ*) tax (*antes de s*) • **sistema ~** tax system
2 (*And, Cono Sur*) (= *autoritario*) domineering; (= *imperativo*) imperative

impositor(a) SM/F (*Econ*) depositor

impostar ▹ CONJUG 1a VT • **~ la voz** to project one's voice

impostergable ADJ • **una cita ~** an appointment that cannot be put off

impostor(a) SM/F **1** (= *charlatán*) impostor
2 (= *calumniador*) slanderer

impostura SF **1** (= *fraude*) imposture
2 (= *calumnia*) slur, slander

impotable ADJ undrinkable

impotencia SF **1** (*para hacer algo*) impotence, helplessness
2 (*Med*) impotence

impotente ADJ **1** (*para hacer algo*) impotent, helpless
2 (*Med*) impotent

impracticabilidad SF impracticability

impracticable ADJ **1** (= *irrealizable*) impracticable, unworkable
2 [*carretera*] impassable

imprecación SF imprecation, curse

imprecar ▹ CONJUG 1g VT to curse

imprecisable ADJ indeterminable

imprecisión SF lack of precision, vagueness

impreciso ADJ imprecise, vague

impredecibilidad SF unpredictability

impredecible ADJ, **impredictible** ADJ (*LAm*) unpredictable

impregnación SF impregnation

impregnar ▹ CONJUG 1a VT **1** (= *humedecer*) to impregnate
2 (= *saturar*) to soak
3 [*olor, sentimiento*] to pervade

impremeditado ADJ unpremeditated

imprenta SF **1** (= *acto*) printing • **dar** *o* **entregar a la ~** to send for printing
2 (= *máquina*) press
3 (= *taller*) printer's
4 (= *impresos*) printed matter; ▹ **letra**

imprentar ▹ CONJUG 1a VT **1** (*Cono Sur*) to put a permanent crease into
2 (*LAm*) to mark

impreparado ADJ unprepared

imprescindible ADJ essential, indispensable • **cosas ~s** essentials • **es ~ que ...** it is essential that ... • **lo más ~** the bare essentials

impresentable ADJ (= *no presentable*) unpresentable; [*acto*] disgraceful • **estás ~** you look a state • **Juan es ~** you can't take Juan anywhere

impresión SF **1** (= *sensación*) impression • **¿qué ~ te produjo?** what was your impression of it? • **cambiar impresiones** to exchange views • **causar (una) buena ~ a algn** • **hacer buena ~ a algn** [*persona*] to make a good impression on sb; [*actividad, ciudad*] to impress sb • **dar la ~ de:** • **da la ~ de ser un autor maduro** he appears to be a mature author • **daba la ~ de no caber en la caja** it looked as if it wouldn't fit in the box • **me da la ~ de que ...** I get the impression that ... • **de ~** (*Esp**) fabulous* • **¡estabas de ~ con ese vestido!** you looked fabulous in that dress!* • **intercambiar impresiones** to exchange views • **primera ~** first impression • **se deja llevar por las primeras impresiones** he's easily swayed by first impressions • **la primera ~ es la que vale** it's the first impression that counts • **tener la ~ de que ...** to have the impression that ...
2 (= *susto*) shock • **el agua fría da ~ al principio** the cold water is a bit of a shock at first • **su muerte me causó una gran ~** her death was a great shock to me • **me llevé una fuerte ~ cuando me enteré** I got a terrible shock when I found out
3 (= *huella*) imprint ▸ **impresión dactilar, impresión digital** fingerprint
4 (*Tip*) (= *acción*) printing; (= *resultado*) print; (= *tirada*) print run • **un error de ~** a printing error • **la ~ es tan mala que resulta difícil de leer** the print is so bad that it's difficult to read • **una ~ de 5.000 ejemplares** a print run of 5,000 copies ▸ **impresión en color(es)** colour printing, color printing (*EEUU*)
5 (*Inform*) (= *acción*) printing; (= *resultado*) printout
6 (*Fot*) print
7 (*Bio, Psic*) imprinting

impresionable ADJ impressionable

impresionado ADJ **1** (= *sorprendido, asustado*) affected
2 (*Fot*) exposed • **excesivamente ~** overexposed

impresionante ADJ **1** (= *maravilloso*) [*edificio, acto*] impressive; [*espectáculo*] striking
2 (= *conmovedor*) moving, affecting
3 (= *espantoso*) shocking

impresionar ▹ CONJUG 1a VT **1** (*Téc*) [+ *disco*] to cut; [+ *foto*] to expose • **película sin ~** unexposed film
2 [+ *persona*] (= *causar impresión a*) to impress, strike; (= *conmover*) to move, affect; (= *horrorizar*) to shock • **no se deja ~ fácilmente** he is not easily impressed • **la noticia de su muerte me impresionó mucho** the news of his death had a profound effect on me
VI (= *causar impresión*) to make an impression • **lo hace sólo para ~** he does it just to impress
VPR **impresionarse 1** (= *sorprenderse, asustarse*) to be affected
2 (= *conmoverse*) to be moved, be affected

impresionismo SM impressionism

impresionista ADJ impressionist, impressionistic
SMF impressionist

impreso PP *de* **imprimir**
ADJ [*papel, libro, material*] printed
SM **1** (= *formulario*) form • **un ~ de beca** a grant application form • **cumplimentar** (*frm*) *o* **rellenar un ~** to fill in a form, fill out a form ▸ **impreso de solicitud** application form
2 **"impresos"** (*en sobre*) printed matter (*sing*)

impresor(a) SM/F printer

impresora SF (*Inform*) printer ▸ **impresora (de) calidad carta** letter-quality printer ▸ **impresora de chorro de tinta** ink-jet printer ▸ **impresora de impacto** impact printer ▸ **impresora de inyección de burbujas** bubble-jet printer ▸ **impresora (de) láser** laser printer ▸ **impresora de línea** line-printer ▸ **impresora de margarita** daisy-wheel printer ▸ **impresora de matriz de puntos** dot-matrix printer ▸ **impresora de no impacto** non-impact printer ▸ **impresora en paralelo** parallel printer ▸ **impresora matricial** dot-matrix printer

imprevisibilidad SF [*de suceso, problema*] unforeseeable nature; [*de persona*] unpredictability

imprevisible ADJ [*suceso, problema*] unforeseeable; [*persona*] unpredictable

imprevisión SF lack of foresight

imprevisor ADJ lacking foresight, improvident (*frm*)

imprevisto ADJ unforeseen, unexpected
SM (= *suceso*) contingency • **~s** (= *gastos*) incidentals, unforeseen expenses; (= *emergencias*) contingencies • **si no surgen ~s** if nothing unexpected occurs

imprimar ▹ CONJUG 1a VT (*Arte*) to prime

imprimátur SM imprimatur

imprimible ADJ printable

imprimir ▹ CONJUG 3a (PP (EN TIEMPOS COMPUESTOS): **imprimido**, PP (COMO ADJ): **impreso**) VT **1** (*Tip*) [+ *libro, folleto, billetes*] to print • **"impreso en Montevideo"** "printed in Montevideo"
2 (*Inform*) [+ *documento, página*] to print out
3 (= *marcar*) [+ *nombre, número*] to print • **dejó sus huellas impresas en el jarrón** he left his fingerprints on the vase • **estar impreso en algo** to be engraved on sth • **el accidente quedó impreso en su memoria** the accident was imprinted on his memory • **el dolor estaba impreso en su rostro** pain was written all over his face
4 (= *transmitir*) [+ *estilo*] to stamp; [+ *ritmo*] to

set; [+ *velocidad*] to introduce • **el director imprimió su sello a la orquesta** the conductor put his own stamp on the orchestra • **imprime a sus escritos un particular encanto** she brings a special charm to her writing • **el equipo no ha encontrado la forma de ~ velocidad a su juego** the team have not found a way to speed up their game • **~ carácter** to be character-building • **haber vivido en Madrid le ha imprimido carácter** living in Madrid has been a character-building experience (for him) *o* has been character-building for him • **sus lecturas infantiles han imprimido carácter en su obra** his childhood reading has given character to his work
5 (*Bio*) to imprint (**a** on)

improbabilidad SF improbability, unlikelihood

improbable ADJ improbable, unlikely

improbar ▷ CONJUG 1l VT (*Caribe*) to fail to approve, not approve

improbidad SF dishonesty

ímprobo ADJ **1** (= *persona*) dishonest, corrupt
2 (= *enorme*) [*tarea, esfuerzo*] enormous

improcedencia SF **1** (= *no idoneidad*) unsuitability, inappropriateness
2 (*Jur*) inadmissibility

improcedente ADJ **1** (= *inadecuado*) unsuitable, inappropriate
2 (*Jur*) inadmissible • **despido ~** unfair dismissal

improductividad SF unproductiveness

improductivo ADJ unproductive

impronta SF **1** (*Arte*) (= *marca*) stamp, impression; [*de relieve*] rubbing; [*de hueco*] cast, mould, mold (EEUU)
2 (= *rastro*) stamp, mark

impronunciable ADJ unpronounceable

improperio SM insult • **soltar ~s** to curse

impropiamente ADV **1** (= *inadecuadamente*) inappropriately, unsuitably
2 (= *incorrectamente*) improperly

impropicio ADJ inauspicious, unpropitious

impropiedad SF **1** (= *inadecuación*) inappropriateness, unsuitability
2 (= *incorrección*) [*de estilo, palabras*] impropriety, infelicity (*frm*)

impropio ADJ **1** (= *inadecuado*) inappropriate, unsuitable • **~ de** *o* **para** inappropriate for
2 (= *incorrecto*) [*estilo, palabras*] improper, incorrect

improrrogable ADJ [*fecha, plazo*] that cannot be extended

impróvidamente ADV improvidently

impróvido ADJ improvident

improvisación SF [*de acción*] improvisation; (*Mús*) extemporization; (*Teat*) ad-lib

improvisadamente ADV **1** (= *de repente*) unexpectedly, suddenly
2 (= *sin preparación*) at the drop of a hat

improvisado ADJ [*discurso*] improvised; [*reparación*] makeshift; [*música*] impromptu

improvisamente ADV unexpectedly, suddenly

improvisar ▷ CONJUG 1a VT [+ *discurso*] to improvise; [+ *comida*] to rustle up*; [+ *música*] to extemporize; [+ *representación*] to ad-lib

improviso ADJ **1** (= *imprevisto*) unexpected, unforeseen
2 • **de ~** unexpectedly, suddenly; [*dicho*] off the cuff; [*hecho*] on the spur of the moment • **coger** *o* **pillar de ~** to catch unawares • **hablar de ~** to speak off the cuff • **tocar de ~** to play impromptu
SM • **en un ~** (*And**) suddenly, without warning

improvisto ADJ unexpected, unforeseen • **de ~** unexpectedly, suddenly

imprudencia SF **1** (= *cualidad*) (*al hacer algo*) imprudence, rashness; (*al averiguar algo*) indiscretion
2 (= *acción*) • **fue una ~ del conductor** it was the driver's carelessness ▸ **imprudencia temeraria** criminal negligence • **ser acusado de conducir con ~ temeraria** to be charged with dangerous driving

imprudente ADJ **1** (= *irreflexivo*) imprudent, rash
2 (= *indiscreto*) indiscreet
3 [*conductor*] careless

imprudentemente ADV **1** (= *sin reflexionar*) unwisely, imprudently
2 (= *indiscretamente*) indiscreetly
3 [*conducir*] carelessly

Impte. ABR (= **Importe**) amt

impúber ADJ prepubescent, immature

impublicable ADJ unprintable

impudencia SF shamelessness, brazenness

impudente ADJ shameless, brazen

impúdicamente ADV (= *sin vergüenza*) immodestly, shamelessly; (= *obscenamente*) lewdly; (= *con lascivia*) lecherously

impudicia SF (= *desvergüenza*) immodesty, shamelessness; (= *obscenidad*) lewdness; (= *lascivia*) lechery

impúdico ADJ (= *desvergonzado*) immodest, shameless; (= *obsceno*) lewd; (= *lascivo*) lecherous

impudor SM = **impudicia**

impuesto PP *de* **imponer**
ADJ • **estar ~ en** to be well versed in • **estar** *o* **quedar ~ de** to be informed about
SM (*al estado*) tax (**sobre** on); (*en operaciones de compraventa*) duty (**sobre** on), levy (**sobre** on) • **~s** taxes, taxation (*sing*) • **antes de ~s** pre-tax • **beneficios antes de ~s** pre-tax profits • **¿cuánto ganas antes de ~s?** how much do you earn before tax? • **libre de ~s** [*inversión, mercancías*] tax-free; [*bebida, perfume, tabaco*] duty-free • **sujeto a ~** taxable ▸ **impuesto al valor agregado** value added tax ▸ **impuesto comunitario** community tax ▸ **impuesto de actividades económicas** business tax ▸ **impuesto de bienes inmuebles** property tax ▸ **impuesto de circulación** road tax ▸ **impuesto del timbre** stamp duty ▸ **impuesto de lujo** luxury tax ▸ **impuesto de plusvalía** capital gains tax ▸ **impuesto de radicación** property tax ▸ **impuesto de sociedades** corporation tax ▸ **impuesto de transferencia de capital** capital transfer tax ▸ **impuesto de venta** sales tax ▸ **impuesto directo** direct tax ▸ **impuesto ecológico** eco-tax, green tax ▸ **impuesto revolucionario** *protection money paid to terrorists* ▸ **impuesto sobre apuestas** betting tax ▸ **impuesto sobre bienes inmuebles** property tax ▸ **impuesto sobre el capital** capital levy ▸ **Impuesto sobre (el) Valor Añadido, Impuesto sobre (el) Valor Agregado** (*LAm*) Value Added Tax ▸ **impuesto sobre espectáculos** entertainment tax ▸ **impuesto sobre la propiedad** property tax, rate (EEUU) ▸ **impuesto sobre la renta de las personas físicas** income tax ▸ **impuesto sobre la riqueza** wealth tax ▸ **impuesto sobre los bienes heredados** inheritance tax, estate duty ▸ **impuesto verde** green tax

impugnable ADJ contestable

impugnación SF challenge, contestation

impugnar ▷ CONJUG 1a VT [+ *decisión, fallo*] to contest, challenge; [+ *teoría*] to refute; [+ *motivos, testimonio*] to impeach

impulsador SM (*Aer*) booster

impulsar ▷ CONJUG 1a VT **1** (*Mec*) to drive, propel
2 [+ *persona*] to drive, impel • **impulsado por el miedo** driven (on) by fear
3 [+ *deporte, inversión*] to promote

impulsión SF impulsion

impulsivamente ADV impulsively

impulsividad SF impulsiveness

impulsivo ADJ impulsive • **compra impulsiva** impulse buying

impulso SM **1** (= *empuje*) • **le dio tanto ~ que la tiró del columpio** he gave her such a push that she fell off the swing • **llevaba tanto ~ que no pudo parar a tiempo** she was going so fast she couldn't stop in time • **coger** *o* **tomar ~** to gather momentum
2 (= *estímulo*) boost • **un ~ a la economía** a boost to the economy • **esto dará un ~ a las negociaciones** this will give the negotiations a boost • **este director ha dado un ~ a la empresa** this director has given the company fresh impetus *o* a boost
3 (= *deseo instintivo*) impulse • **un ~ repentino** a sudden impulse • **mi primer ~ fue salir corriendo** my first instinct was to run away • **no pude resistir el ~ de abrazarla** I couldn't resist the impulse *o* urge to embrace her • **a ~s del miedo** driven (on) by fear ▸ **impulso sexual** sexual urge, sex drive
4 (*Fís, Fisiol*) impulse ▸ **impulso eléctrico** electrical impulse ▸ **impulso nervioso** nerve impulse

impulsor(a) ADJ drive (*antes de s*), driving
SM/F (= *persona*) promoter, instigator
SM (*Mec*) drive; (*Aer*) booster

impune ADJ unpunished

impunemente ADV with impunity

impunidad SF impunity

impuntual ADJ unpunctual

impuntualidad SF unpunctuality

impureza SF **1** [*de sustancia, agua*] impurity
2 [*de persona, pensamiento*] impurity

impurificar ▷ CONJUG 1g VT **1** (= *adulterar*) to adulterate, make impure
2 (= *corromper*) to corrupt, defile

impuro ADJ **1** [*sustancia, agua*] impure
2 [*persona, pensamiento*] impure

imputable ADJ • **fracasos que son ~s a** failures which can be attributed to, failures which are attributable to

imputación SF accusation, imputation

imputar ▷ CONJUG 1a VT • **~ a** to impute to, attribute to • **los hechos que se les imputan** the acts with which they are charged

imputrescible ADJ (*frm*) (*gen*) rot-proof; (*pey*) non-biodegradable

in* ADJ INV in* • **es el estilo más in** this is the really in style* • **lo in es hablar de ...** the in thing is to talk about ... • **lo que llevan los más in** what people who are really with it are wearing*

-ín, -ina ▷ **Aspects of Word Formation in Spanish 2**

inabarcable ADJ vast, extensive

inabordable ADJ unapproachable

inacabable ADJ endless, interminable

inacabablemente ADV endlessly, interminably

inacabado ADJ [*trabajo, libro*] unfinished; [*problema*] unresolved

inaccesibilidad SF inaccessibility

inaccesible ADJ [*torre, montaña*] inaccessible; [*precio*] prohibitive; [*persona*] aloof

inacción SF (= *falta de actividad*) inactivity; (= *ociosidad*) inactivity, idleness

inacentuado ADJ unaccented, unstressed

inaceptabilidad SF unacceptability

inaceptable ADJ unacceptable

inaceptablemente ADV unacceptably
inactividad SF **1** [*de persona*] (= *falta de actividad*) inactivity; (= *pereza*) idleness
2 (*Com, Econ*) [*de mercado*] sluggishness
inactivo/a ADJ **1** [*persona*] (= *sin actividad*) inactive; (= *perezoso*) idle
2 [*volcán*] dormant, inactive
3 (*Com, Econ*) [*mercado*] sluggish; [*población*] non-working
SM/F • **los ~s** the non-working population
inactual ADJ (= *no válido*) lacking present validity, no longer applicable; (= *caduco*) old-fashioned, out-of-date
inadaptable ADJ unadaptable
inadaptación SF **1** (= *falta de adaptación*) inability to adapt • **~ social** maladjustment
2 (*Med*) rejection
inadaptado/a ADJ maladjusted (**a** to)
SM/F misfit, maladjusted person
▸ **inadaptado/a social** social misfit
inadecuación SF [*de recursos, medidas*] inadequacy; [*de película, momento*] unsuitability, inappropriateness
inadecuado ADJ [*recurso, medida*] inadequate; [*película, momento*] unsuitable, inappropriate
inadmisibilidad SF unacceptable nature
inadmisible ADJ unacceptable
inadvertencia SF **1** (= *cualidad*) inadvertence • **por ~** inadvertently
2 • **una ~** an oversight, a slip
inadvertidamente ADV inadvertently
inadvertido ADJ **1** (= *no notado*) unnoticed, unobserved • **pasar ~** to go unnoticed, escape notice
2 (= *despistado*) inattentive
inafectado ADJ unaffected
inagotabilidad SF [*de recursos*] inexhaustibility; (= *resistencia*) tireless nature
inagotable ADJ [*recursos*] inexhaustible; [*persona, paciencia*] tireless
inaguantable ADJ intolerable, unbearable
inaguantablemente ADV intolerably, unbearably
inajenable ADJ **1** [*billete*] non-transferable
2 (*Jur*) inalienable
inalámbrico ADJ wireless; (*Telec*) cordless
SM (= *micrófono*) wireless mike; (= *teléfono*) cordless telephone
in albis ADV • **quedarse ~** (= *no saber*) to be left in the dark; (= *fracasar*) to get nothing for one's trouble
inalcanzable ADJ unattainable
inalienable ADJ inalienable
inalterabilidad SF [*de materia*] inalterability, unchanging nature; [*de persona, cualidad*] immutability
inalterable ADJ [*materia*] inalterable, unchanging; [*persona, cualidad*] immutable; [*cara*] impassive; [*color*] permanent, fast; [*lustre*] permanent
inalterado ADJ unchanged, unaltered
inamistoso ADJ unfriendly
inamovible ADJ **1** (= *fijo*) fixed, immovable
2 (*Téc*) undetachable
inanición SF **1** (= *hambre*) starvation • **morir de ~** to die of starvation
2 (*Med*) inanition
inanidad SF inanity
inanimado ADJ inanimate
inánime ADJ lifeless
INAP SM ABR (*Esp*) = **Instituto Nacional de la Administración Pública**
inapagable ADJ [*sed*] unquenchable; [*fuego, incendio*] inextinguishable
inapeable ADJ **1** (= *oscuro*) incomprehensible
2 (= *terco*) obstinate, stubborn
inapelabilidad SF finality, unappealable nature
inapelable ADJ **1** (*Jur*) unappealable, not open to appeal • **las decisiones de los jueces serán ~s** the judges' decisions will be final
2 (= *irremediable*) irremediable, inevitable
inapercibido ADJ unperceived
inapetencia SF lack of appetite, loss of appetite
inapetente ADJ • **estar ~** to have no appetite, not to be hungry
inaplazable ADJ which cannot be put off *o* postponed, pressing
inaplicable ADJ not applicable
inaplicado ADJ slack, lazy
inapreciable ADJ **1** [*diferencia*] imperceptible
2 (*de valor*) invaluable, inestimable
inaprehensible ADJ, **inaprensible** ADJ **1** (= *complicado*) indefinite, hard to pin down
2 (= *escurridizo*) hard to grasp
inapropiadamente ADV inappropriately
inapropiado ADJ unsuitable, inappropriate
inaptitud SF unsuitability
inapto ADJ unsuited (**para** to)
inarmónico ADJ (*lit*) unharmonious; (*fig*) cacophonous
inarrugable ADJ crease-resistant
inarticulado ADJ inarticulate
inasequible ADJ (= *inalcanzable*) unattainable, out of reach; (= *indisponible*) unobtainable
inasistencia SF absence
inastillable ADJ shatterproof
inasumible ADJ unacceptable
inatacable ADJ unassailable
inatención SF inattention (**a** to), lack of attention (**a** to)
inatento ADJ inattentive
inaudible ADJ inaudible
inaudito ADJ (*gen*) unheard-of; (= *sin precedente*) unprecedented; (= *increíble*) outrageous
inauguración SF [*de teatro, exposición*] opening, inauguration (*frm*); [*de monumento*] unveiling; [*de casa*] house-warming party; [*de curso*] start; (*Com*) setting up • **ceremonia de ~** inauguration ceremony, opening ceremony ▸ **inauguración privada** (*Arte*) private viewing
inaugural ADJ [*ceremonia, competición, discurso*] opening, inaugural; [*concierto*] opening; [*viaje*] maiden (*antes de s*)
inaugurar ▸ CONJUG 1a VT [+ *edificio*] to inaugurate; [+ *exposición*] to open (formally); [+ *estatua*] to unveil
inautenticidad SF lack of authenticity
inauténtico ADJ inauthentic, not genuine, false
INB SM ABR (*Esp*) (*Escol*) = **Instituto Nacional de Bachillerato**
INBA SM ABR (*Méx*) = **Instituto Nacional de Bellas Artes**
INBAD SM ABR (*Esp*) = **Instituto Nacional de Bachillerato a Distancia**
INC SM ABR (*Esp*) **1** = **Instituto Nacional de Colonización**
2 (*Com*) = **Instituto Nacional de Consumo**
inc. ABR (= **inclusive**) inc.
inca SMF Inca
incachable* ADJ (*LAm*) useless
INCAE SM ABR = **Instituto Centroamericano de Administración de Empresas**
incaico ADJ Inca (*antes de s*)
incalculable ADJ incalculable
incalificable ADJ indescribable, unspeakable
incalificablemente ADV indescribably, unspeakably
incanato SM (*Perú*) (= *época*) Inca period; (= *reinado*) reign (*of an Inca*)
incandescencia SF incandescence (*frm*), white heat
incandescente ADJ **1** [*hierro, bombilla*] incandescent (*frm*), white hot
2 [*mirada*] burning, passionate
incansable ADJ tireless, untiring
incansablemente ADV tirelessly, untiringly
incapacidad SF **1** (= *falta de capacidad*) (*para una actividad*) inability; (*para una profesión*) incompetence • **~ de concentración** inability to concentrate • **su ~ de respuesta** his failure to reply • **~ de** *o* **para hacer algo** inability to do sth ▸ **incapacidad laboral permanente** invalidity ▸ **incapacidad laboral transitoria, incapacidad temporal** temporary disability
2 (= *discapacidad*) (*física*) physical handicap, disability; (*mental*) mental handicap
3 (*Jur*) (*tb* **incapacidad legal**) legal incapacity
incapacitación SF • **proceso de ~ presidencial** impeachment of a president
incapacitado ADJ **1** (= *inadecuado*) unfit (**para** for)
2 (= *descalificado*) disqualified
3 (= *minusválido*) handicapped, disabled
incapacitante ADJ incapacitating
incapacitar ▸ CONJUG 1a VT **1** (= *invalidar*) to incapacitate, handicap
2 (*Jur*) to disqualify (**para** for)
incapaz ADJ **1** • **ser ~: no es que sea ~, es que no tengo fuerzas** it's not that I can't do it, I just haven't got the strength • **no sé cómo puedes engañarlo, yo sería ~** I don't know how you can deceive him, I could never do a thing like that • **ser ~ de hacer algo** (= *no atreverse, no querer*) to never do sth, be incapable of doing sth (*frm*); (= *no poder*) to be unable to do sth • **¿es que eres ~ de hablar en serio?** can't you ever talk seriously?, aren't you capable of talking seriously? (*frm*) • **la policía se mostró ~ de prevenir la tragedia** the police proved unable to prevent the tragedy • **ser ~ para algo** to be useless at sth • **soy ~ para la física** I'm useless at physics
2 (= *incompetente*) incompetent
3 (*Jur*) unfit • **fue declarado ~ de administrar sus bienes** he was declared unfit to manage his property
4 (*CAm*) [*niño*] trying, difficult
SMF incompetent, incompetent fool
incapturable ADJ unattainable
incardinar ▸ CONJUG 1a VT (*frm*) to include (*as an integral part*)
incario SM (*Perú*) Inca period
incasable ADJ unmarriageable
incásico ADJ (*LAm*) Inca (*antes de s*)
incatalogable ADJ (= *indefinible*) indefinable; (= *poco convencional*) off-beat • **persona ~** person who refuses to be pigeon-holed
incautación SF seizure, confiscation
incautamente ADV unwarily, incautiously
incautar ▸ CONJUG 1a VT to seize, confiscate
VPR **incautarse** • **~se de** (*Jur*) to seize, confiscate; (= *intervenir*) to take possession of
incauto ADJ **1** (= *crédulo*) gullible
2 (= *imprevisor*) unwary, incautious
incendiar ▸ CONJUG 1b VT to set fire to, set alight
VPR **incendiarse** (= *empezar a arder*) to catch fire; (= *quemarse*) to burn down
incendiario/a ADJ **1** [*bomba, mecanismo*] incendiary
2 [*discurso, escrito*] inflammatory

SM/F fire-raiser, arsonist ▸ **incendiario/a de la guerra** warmonger

incendiarismo SM arson

incendio SM fire • MODISMO: • **echar** *o* **hablar ~s de algn** (*And, Cono Sur*) to sling mud at sb ▸ **incendio forestal** forest fire ▸ **incendio intencionado, incendio provocado** arson attack

incensar ▹ CONJUG 1j VT **1** (*Rel*) to cense, incense
2 (= *halagar*) to flatter

incensario SM censer

incentivación SF **1** (= *motivación*) motivation
2 (*Econ*) (= *sistema*) incentive scheme; (= *prima*) productivity bonus

incentivar ▹ CONJUG 1a VT to encourage • **baja incentivada** voluntary redundancy

incentivo SM incentive • **baja por ~** voluntary redundancy ▸ **incentivo fiscal** tax incentive

incertidumbre SF uncertainty

incesante ADJ incessant, unceasing

incesantemente ADV incessantly, unceasingly

incesto SM incest

incestuoso ADJ incestuous

incidencia SF **1** (*Mat*) incidence
2 (= *suceso*) incident
3 (= *impacto*) impact, effect • **la huelga tuvo escasa ~** the strike had little impact

incidentado ADJ **1** (= *con percances*) eventful
2 (= *descontrolado*) unruly, riotous, turbulent

incidental ADJ incidental

incidente SM **1** (= *contratiempo*) hitch • **la manifestación transcurrió sin ~s** the demonstration passed off without incident • **un viaje sin ~s** a trouble-free journey
2 (= *disputa*) incident • **un desagradable ~ entre los dos jugadores** an unpleasant incident between the two players ▸ **~ diplomático** diplomatic incident
ADJ incidental

incidentemente ADV incidentally

incidir ▹ CONJUG 3a VI **1** • **~ en** (= *afectar*) to influence, affect; (= *recaer sobre*) to have a bearing on • **~ en un error** to make a mistake • **el impuesto incide más en ellos** the tax affects them most, the tax hits them hardest • **la familia ha incidido fuertemente en la historia** the family has influenced history a lot
2 (= *hacer hincapié*) • **~ en un tema** to stress a subject
VT (*Med*) to incise

incienso SM **1** (*Rel*) incense
2 (= *halagos*) flattery

inciertamente ADV uncertainly

incierto ADJ (= *dudoso*) uncertain; (= *inconstante*) inconstant; (= *inseguro*) insecure

incineración SF [*de basuras*] incineration; [*de cadáveres*] cremation

incinerador SM, **incineradora** SF incinerator ▸ **incinerador de residuos sólidos** solid-waste incinerator

incinerar ▹ CONJUG 1a VT [+ *basuras*] to incinerate, burn; [+ *cadáver*] to cremate

incipiente ADJ incipient

incircunciso ADJ uncircumcised

incisión SF incision

incisividad SF incisiveness

incisivo ADJ **1** (= *cortante*) sharp, cutting
2 (= *mordaz*) incisive
SM incisor

inciso SM **1** (= *observación*) digression, aside • **hacer un ~** to make an aside
2 (= *interrupción*) interjection, interruption
3 (*Ling*) (= *oración*) interpolated clause; (= *coma*) comma
4 (*Jur*) subsection

incitación SF incitement (a to)

incitante ADJ provocative

incitar ▹ CONJUG 1a VT to incite • **~ a algn a hacer algo** to urge sb to do sth • **~ a algn contra otro** to incite sb against another person

incívico/a ADJ antisocial
SM/F antisocial person

incivil ADJ uncivil, rude

incivilidad SF **1** (= *cualidad*) incivility, rudeness
2 • **una ~** an incivility, a piece of rudeness

incivilizado ADJ uncivilized

incivismo SM *antisocial behaviour or outlook etc*

inclasificable ADJ unclassifiable

inclemencia SF (*Meteo*) harshness, inclemency • **la ~ del tiempo** the inclemency of the weather • **dejar algo a la ~** to leave sth exposed to the weather *o* the elements

inclemente ADJ (*Meteo*) harsh, inclement

inclinación SF **1** [*de terreno*] slope, gradient; [*de objeto*] lean, list • **la ~ del terreno** the slope of the ground, the gradient (of the ground) • **la ~ de la Torre de Pisa** the lean of the Tower of Pisa • **un poste con una ~ de siete grados** a post with a seven-degree lean *o* list ▸ **inclinación lateral** (*Aer*) bank ▸ **inclinación magnética** magnetic dip, magnetic inclination
2 (= *reverencia*) bow • **hizo una profunda ~ ante el rey** he made a deep bow before the king • **María me saludó con una ~ de cabeza** María greeted me with a nod • **el presidente dio su aprobación con una ~ de cabeza** the president nodded (his) approval
3 (= *tendencia*) inclination • **su ~ natural es conservadora** his natural inclination is conservative, he's conservative by inclination • **no tengo ~ política concreta** I have no particular political inclinations *o* leanings • **tiene inclinaciones artísticas** she has artistic inclinations, she's artistically inclined • **tiene ~ a tomárselo todo a risa** he's inclined to treat everything as a joke • **tener ~ hacia la poesía** to have a penchant for poetry, have poetic leanings ▸ **inclinación sexual** sexual preferences (*pl*)

inclinado ADJ **1** (*en ángulo*) [*terreno, línea*] sloping; [*plano*] inclined • **la torre inclinada de Pisa** the leaning tower of Pisa
2 • **estar ~ a hacer algo** to be inclined to do sth • **sentirse ~ a hacer algo** to feel inclined to do sth

inclinar ▹ CONJUG 1a VT **1** (= *ladear*) [+ *objeto vertical*] to tilt, lean • **el peso de los abrigos inclinó el perchero** the hatstand was tilting *o* leaning under the weight of the coats • **inclinó el plato para acabarse la sopa** he tilted his plate to finish off his soup • **inclinó el respaldo del asiento** he reclined his seat • **inclina el cuadro hacia la derecha** slope *o* tilt the picture to the right
2 [+ *cabeza*] to lean • **inclinó la cabeza para olerle el cabello** she leant her head forward to smell his hair • **para afirmar inclinó la cabeza** he nodded (his) agreement • **~on la cabeza ante el altar** they bowed their heads before the altar
3 (= *resolver*) [+ *balanza*] to tip • **los indecisos ~on la balanza hacia la izquierda** the floating voters tipped the balance in favour of the left • **este gol inclinó el marcador a su favor** this goal tipped the balance in their favour
4 (= *predisponer*) to incline • **la crisis inclina a los consumidores hacia el ahorro** the recession inclines consumers to save their money
5 (= *decidir*) • **eso la inclinó a pensar que yo era el culpable** that led her to think that I was guilty • **el informe lo inclinó a cambiar de estrategia** the report swayed him in favour of changing his strategy
VPR **inclinarse 1** [*objeto vertical*] to lean, tilt
2 (= *encorvarse*) to stoop, bend • **Balbino se inclinó sobre el muro** Balbino leant over the wall • **Amelia se inclinó hacia delante para coger el bolso** Amelia leant forward to pick up the bag • **me incliné hacia atrás para ponerme cómodo** I leant back to make myself comfortable • **nos inclinamos ante el rey** we bowed to the king
3 (= *tender*) • **me inclino a favor de la moneda única** I'm inclined to be in favour of the single currency • **me inclino a pensar que no es verdad** I am inclined to *o* I tend to think that it's not true • **entre los dos, me inclino por el segundo** of the two, I'm inclined to go for the second *o* I tend to prefer the second

ínclito ADJ (*frm, liter*) illustrious, renowned

incluir ▹ CONJUG 3g VT **1** (= *comprender*) to include, contain • **todo incluido** (*Com*) inclusive, all-in
2 (= *agregar*) to include; (*en carta*) to enclose

inclusa SF foundling hospital

inclusero/a SM/F foundling

inclusión SF inclusion • **con ~ de** including

inclusivamente ADV inclusive, inclusively

inclusive ADV inclusive • **del 1 al 10, ambos ~** from the 1st to the 10th inclusive • **hasta el próximo domingo ~** up to and including next Sunday

inclusivo ADJ inclusive

incluso ADV **1** (= *aun*) even • **~ le pegó** he even hit her • **no resulta sencillo ni ~ para nosotros** it isn't simple, (not) even for us • **estaba sonriente e ~ alegre** she was smiling and happy even
2 (= *incluyendo*) including • **nos gustó a todos, ~ a los más testarudos** we all liked it, even *o* including the most stubborn of us
ADJ enclosed

incoación SF inception

incoar ▹ CONJUG 1a VT to start, initiate

incoativo ADJ (*Ling*) inchoative

incobrable ADJ irrecoverable
SMPL **incobrables** irrecoverable debts, bad debts

incógnita SF **1** (*Mat*) unknown quantity • **despejar la ~** to find the unknown quantity
2 (*por averiguar*) (= *misterio*) mystery; (= *razón oculta*) hidden motive • **queda en pie la ~ sobre su influencia** there is still a question mark over his influence

incógnito ADJ unknown
SM incognito • **viajar de ~** to travel incognito

incognoscible ADJ unknowable

incoherencia SF **1** (= *falta de sentido*) (*en pensamiento, ideas*) incoherence; (*en comportamiento, respuestas*) inconsistency
2 (= *falta de conexión*) disconnectedness
3 incoherencias nonsense (*sing*)

incoherente ADJ **1** (= *sin sentido*) [*pensamiento, ideas*] incoherent; [*comportamiento, respuestas*] inconsistent • **es ~ con sus ideas** he's inconsistent in his thinking
2 (= *inconexo*) disconnected

incoherentemente ADV (= *inconsecuentemente*) inconsistently

incoloro ADJ [*líquido, luz*] colourless, colorless (*EEUU*); [*barniz*] clear

incólume ADJ (= *ileso*) unhurt, unharmed • **salió ~ del accidente** he emerged unharmed *o* unscathed from the accident

incombustible ADJ [*mueble, ropa*] fire-resistant; [*tela*] fireproof
incomible ADJ inedible, uneatable
incómodamente ADV (= *sin comodidad*) uncomfortably; (= *con molestias*) inconveniently
incomodar ▷ CONJUG 1a VT **1** (= *causar molestia*) to inconvenience, trouble
2 (= *causar vergüenza*) to make feel uncomfortable, embarrass
3 (= *enfadar*) to annoy
VPR **incomodarse 1** (= *tomarse molestia*) to put o.s. out • **¡no se incomode!** don't bother!, don't trouble yourself!
2 (= *avergonzarse*) to feel uncomfortable, feel embarrassed
3 (= *enfadarse*) to get annoyed (**con** with)
incomodidad SF **1** (= *falta de comodidad*) discomfort
2 (= *inoportunidad*) inconvenience
3 (= *fastidio*) annoyance, irritation
incomodo SM = **incomodidad**
incómodo ADJ **1** [*sofá, situación*] uncomfortable • **un paquete ~ de llevar** an awkward *o* cumbersome package to carry • **sentirse ~** to feel ill at ease, feel uncomfortable • **me resultaba ~ estar con los dos a la vez** I felt ill at ease *o* uncomfortable being with both of them together
2 [*persona*] tiresome, annoying
3 • **estar ~ con algn** (*Cono Sur*) to be angry with sb, be fed up with sb*
SM (*LAm*) = **incomodidad**
incomparable ADJ incomparable
incomparablemente ADV incomparably
incomparecencia SF failure to appear (*in court etc*), non-appearance
incomparecimiento SM • **pleito perdido por ~** suit lost by default *o* failure to appear • **pleito ganado por ~** undefended suit
incompasivo ADJ (= *indiferente*) unsympathetic; (= *despiadado*) pitiless
incompatibilidad SF incompatibility • **~ de caracteres** mutual incompatibility • **~ de intereses** conflict of interests • **ley de ~es** *law regulating the holding of multiple posts*
incompatibilizar ▷ CONJUG 1f VT to make incompatible, render incompatible
incompatible ADJ incompatible
incompetencia SF incompetence
incompetente ADJ incompetent
incompletamente ADV incompletely
incompleto ADJ incomplete
incomprendido/a ADJ [*persona*] misunderstood; [*genio*] not appreciated
SM/F (= *persona*) misunderstood person
incomprensibilidad SF incomprehensibility
incomprensible ADJ incomprehensible
incomprensiblemente ADV incomprehensibly
incomprensión SF **1** [*de padres, mayores*] incomprehension, lack of understanding
2 (= *subestimación*) lack of appreciation
incomprensivo ADJ unsympathetic
incomprobable ADJ unprovable
incomunicación SF **1** (= *aislamiento*) (*gen*) isolation; (*para presos*) solitary confinement • **ello permite la ~ de los detenidos** it allows those detained to be held incommunicado
2 (= *falta de comunicación*) lack of communication
incomunicado ADJ **1** (= *aislado*) isolated, cut off
2 [*preso*] in solitary confinement
incomunicar ▷ CONJUG 1g VT **1** (= *aislar*) to cut off, isolate
2 [+ *preso*] to put in solitary confinement • **~ a un detenido** to refuse a prisoner access to a lawyer
VPR **incomunicarse** to isolate o.s., cut o.s. off
inconcebible ADJ inconceivable
inconcebiblemente ADV inconceivably
inconciliable ADJ irreconcilable
inconcluso ADJ unfinished, incomplete
inconcluyente ADJ inconclusive
inconcreción SF vagueness
inconcreto ADJ vague
inconcuso ADJ indisputable, incontrovertible
incondicional ADJ **1** (= *sin condiciones*) [*retirada, fianza, amor, garantía*] unconditional; [*fe*] complete, unquestioning; [*apoyo*] wholehearted, unconditional; [*afirmación*] unqualified; [*partidario*] staunch, stalwart
2 (*LAm*) (*pey*) servile, fawning
SMF **1** (= *partidario*) stalwart, staunch supporter
2 (*pey*) (= *intransigente*) diehard, hardliner
3 (*LAm*) yes man*
incondicionalidad SF **1** (= *apoyo*) unconditional support
2 (= *lealtad*) unquestioning loyalty
incondicionalismo SM (*LAm*) toadyism, servility
incondicionalmente ADV (= *sin condiciones*) unconditionally, unreservedly; (= *sin reservas*) implicitly, unquestioningly; (= *totalmente*) wholeheartedly; (= *con devoción*) staunchly
inconexión SF [*de datos*] unconnectedness; [*de ideas*] disconnectedness; [*de lenguaje, palabras*] incoherence
inconexo ADJ [*datos*] unrelated, unconnected; [*ideas*] disconnected, disjointed; [*texto*] disjointed; [*lenguaje, palabras*] incoherent
inconfesable ADJ shameful, disgraceful
inconfeso ADJ [*reo*] who refuses to confess • **homosexual ~** closet homosexual
inconforme ADJ nonconformist • **estar *o* mostrarse ~ con algo** (*CAm*) to disagree with sth
inconformismo SM non-conformism
inconformista ADJ, SMF non-conformist
inconfundible ADJ unmistakable
inconfundiblemente ADV unmistakably
incongruencia SF **1** (= *falta de coherencia*) inconsistency, contradiction • **notó la ~ de su razonamiento** he spotted the inconsistency *o* contradiction in his argument
2 (= *cosa incoherente*) • **el paciente decía ~s** the patient was talking incoherently • **¡deja de decir ~s!** stop talking nonsense!
incongruente ADJ, **incongruo** ADJ incongruous
inconmensurable ADJ **1** (= *enorme*) immeasurable, vast
2 (= *fantástico*) fantastic
3 (*Mat*) incommensurate
inconmovible ADJ [*persona*] unmoved; [*creencia, fe*] unshakeable
inconmutable ADJ immutable
inconocible ADJ **1** (= *que no se puede conocer*) unknowable • **lo ~** the unknowable
2 (*LAm**) (= *irreconocible*) unrecognizable
inconquistable ADJ [*reino*] unconquerable; [*espíritu, fuerza*] unconquerable, unyielding
inconsciencia SF **1** (*Med*) unconsciousness
2 (= *ignorancia*) unawareness
3 (= *irreflexión*) thoughtlessness
inconsciente ADJ **1** (*Med*) unconscious • **lo ~** the unconscious • **lo encontraron ~** they found him unconscious
2 (= *ignorante*) unaware (**de** of), oblivious (**de** to)
3 (= *involuntario*) unwitting
4 (= *irresponsable*) thoughtless • **es más ~ que malo** he's thoughtless rather than wicked • **son gente ~** they're thoughtless people
SM unconscious • **el ~ colectivo** the collective unconscious
inconscientemente ADV **1** (= *sin saber*) unconsciously
2 (= *sin querer*) unwittingly
3 (= *sin pensar*) thoughtlessly
inconsecuencia SF inconsistency
inconsecuente ADJ inconsistent
inconsideración SF **1** (= *desconsideración*) inconsiderateness, thoughtlessness
2 (= *precipitación*) rashness, haste
inconsideradamente ADV **1** (= *sin consideración*) inconsiderately, thoughtlessly
2 (= *precipitadamente*) rashly, hastily
inconsiderado ADJ **1** (= *desconsiderado*) inconsiderate, thoughtless
2 (= *precipitado*) rash, hasty
inconsistencia SF [*de superficie*] unevenness; [*de argumento*] weakness; [*de tierra*] looseness; [*de tela*] flimsiness; [*de masa*] lumpiness
inconsistente ADJ (= *irregular*) [*de superficie*] uneven; [*argumento*] weak; [*tierra*] loose; [*tela*] flimsy; [*masa*] lumpy
inconsolable ADJ inconsolable
inconsolablemente ADV inconsolably
inconstancia SF **1** [*de equipo, sistema*] inconstancy
2 [*de tiempo*] changeability
3 (= *veleidad*) fickleness
inconstante ADJ **1** [*equipo, sistema*] inconstant
2 [*tiempo*] changeable
3 [*persona*] (= *veleidoso*) fickle; (= *poco firme*) unsteady • **un amigo ~** a fairweather friend
inconstantemente ADV (= *sin regularidad*) inconstantly; (= *caprichosamente*) in a fickle way
inconstitucional ADJ unconstitutional
inconstitucionalidad SF unconstitutional nature
inconstitucionalmente ADV unconstitutionally
inconsumible ADJ unfit for consumption
incontable ADJ countless, innumerable
incontaminante ADJ non-polluting
incontenible ADJ uncontrollable, unstoppable
incontestable ADJ **1** (= *innegable*) [*argumento*] undeniable, indisputable; [*evidencia, prueba*] irrefutable
2 [*pregunta*] unanswerable
incontestablemente ADV undeniably, indisputably
incontestado ADJ (= *sin respuesta*) unanswered; (= *sin objeciones*) unchallenged, unquestioned; (= *indiscutible*) undisputed
incontinencia SF (*tb Med*) incontinence
▸ **incontinencia verbal** verbal diarrhoea
incontinente ADJ (*tb Med*) incontinent
ADV = **incontinenti**
incontinenti adv at once, instantly, forthwith (*frm o liter*)
incontrastable adj [*dificultad*] insuperable; [*argumento*] unanswerable; [*persona*] unshakeable, unyielding
incontrolable adj uncontrollable
incontrolablemente adv uncontrollably
incontroladamente adv **1** [*temblar*] uncontrollably
2 [*extenderse*] in an uncontrolled way
incontrolado/a adj (= *sin control*) uncontrolled; (= *sin permiso*) unauthorized; (= *violento*) violent, wild
sm/f **1** (= *persona violenta*) violent person (*esp policeman etc who acts outside the law*)
2 (*Pol*) strong-arm man, bully-boy

incontrovertible ADJ incontrovertible, indisputable
incontrovertido ADJ undisputed
inconveniencia SF **1** (= *inoportunidad*) inappropriateness
2 (= *comentario*) tactless remark
3 (= *acto*) improper thing to do, wrong thing to do
inconveniente ADJ inappropriate
• **protestar ahora sería del todo ~** it would be inappropriate to complain now • **es ~ hacer públicos esos temas** it is not appropriate to make these matters public
SM **1** (= *problema*) problem • **surgieron muchos ~s y finalmente desistí** a lot of problems arose and in the end I gave up • **el ~ es que es muy caro** the problem *o* trouble is that it's very expensive
2 (= *desventaja*) disadvantage • **tiene el ~ de que consume mucha gasolina** it has the disadvantage of using a lot of petrol • **ventajas e ~s** advantages and disadvantages
3 (= *objeción*) objection • **no hay ~ en pagar a plazos** there is no objection to you paying in instalments • **¿hay ~ en pagar con tarjeta?** is it all right to pay by card? • **¿tienes algún ~ en venir?** do you mind coming? • **preferiría que se fuera, si no tiene ~** I'd rather you went, if you don't mind • **no tengo ningún ~** I don't mind • **no veo ~ en que llames desde aquí** there's no reason why you shouldn't phone from here • **poner (un) ~** to object • **mi madre pone ~s a todo lo que hago** my mother objects to everything I do
inconvertibilidad SF inconvertibility
inconvertible ADJ inconvertible
incordiante* ADJ annoying
SMF troublemaker
incordiar* ▷ CONJUG 1b VT to annoy, pester, bug* • **siempre me está incordiando con preguntas tontas** he's always pestering *o* annoying me with silly questions
VI • **¡no incordies!** stop it!, behave yourself! • **tus hijos nunca incordian** your children are never a nuisance
incordio* SM pain*, nuisance
incorporación SF (*gen*) incorporation; (*a filas*) enlisting, enlistment • **la ~ del ejército al gabinete** the inclusion of the Army in the Cabinet • **"sueldo a convenir, ~ inmediata"** "salary negotiable, start immediately"
incorporado ADJ (*Téc*) built-in • **con antena incorporada** with built-in aerial
incorporal ADJ = **incorpóreo**
incorporar ▷ CONJUG 1a VT **1** (= *añadir*) (*gen*) to incorporate (**a, en** into, in); (*Culin*) to mix in, add • **~ a filas** (*Mil*) to call up, enlist
2 (= *involucrar*) to involve (**a** in, with)
3 (= *abarcar*) to embody
4 (= *levantar*) • **~ a algn** to sit sb up (*in bed*)
5 (*Teat*) • **Rosana incorpora al personaje de Julieta** Rosana plays the part of Julieta
VPR **incorporarse 1** [*persona acostada*] to sit up • **~se en la cama** to sit up in bed
2 • **~se a** [+ *regimiento, asociación*] to join • **~se a una empresa** to join a company • **~se a filas** to join up, enlist • **~se al trabajo** to start work, report for work
incorpóreo ADJ **1** (= *sin cuerpo*) incorporeal
2 (= *inmaterial*) intangible
incorrección SF **1** [*de datos*] incorrectness, inaccuracy
2 (= *descortesía*) discourtesy • **fue una incorreción no informarles** it was bad manners *o* impolite not to inform them • **cometer una ~** to commit a faux pas
3 (*Ling*) mistake
incorrectamente ADV **1** (= *equivocadamente*) incorrectly
2 (= *con descortesía*) discourteously
incorrecto ADJ **1** [*dato*] incorrect, wrong
2 [*conducta*] (= *descortés*) discourteous, bad-mannered; (= *irregular*) improper • **ser ~ con algn** to take liberties with sb
3 [*facciones*] irregular, odd
incorregible ADJ incorrigible
incorregiblemente ADV incorrigibly
incorrosible ADJ rustproof
incorruptible ADJ incorruptible
incorrupto ADJ **1** (= *no descompuesto*) incorrupt
2 (= *no pervertido*) uncorrupted
incredibilidad SF incredibility
incredulidad SF (= *desconfianza*) incredulity; (= *escepticismo*) scepticism, skepticism (EEUU)
incrédulo/a ADJ (= *desconfiado*) incredulous; (= *escéptico*) sceptical, skeptical (EEUU)
SM/F sceptic, skeptic (EEUU)
increíble ADJ incredible, unbelievable • **es ~ que ...** it is incredible *o* unbelievable that ...
increíblemente ADV incredibly, unbelievably
incremental ADJ incremental
incrementar ▷ CONJUG 1a VT to increase
VPR **incrementarse** to increase
incremento SM [*de conocimiento*] increase, gain; [*de precio, sueldo, productividad*] increase, rise • **tomar ~** to increase ▸ **incremento de temperatura** rise in temperature ▸ **incremento salarial** pay rise
increpación SF reprimand, rebuke
increpar ▷ CONJUG 1a VT to reprimand, rebuke
in crescendo ADV • **ir ~** to increase, spiral upwards
incriminación SF incrimination
incriminar ▷ CONJUG 1a VT **1** (*Jur*) (= *sugerir culpa de*) to incriminate; (= *acusar*) to accuse • **las pruebas los incriminan** the evidence incriminates them • **varios testigos la incriminan** several witnesses accuse her
2 (= *criminalizar*) to make a crime of, consider criminal
3 (= *exagerar*) to magnify
incriminatorio ADJ incriminating
incruento ADJ bloodless
incrúspido* ADJ (*LAm*) (= *torpe*) clumsy; (= *desmañado*) ham-fisted
incrustación SF **1** (= *acto*) (*lit*) incrustation; (*fig*) grafting
2 (*Arte*) inlay, inlaid work
3 (*Téc*) scale
incrustar ▷ CONJUG 1a VT **1** (= *introducir*) (*lit*) to incrust; (*fig*) to graft
2 [+ *joyas*] to inlay • **una espada incrustada de pedrería** a sword encrusted with precious stones
3 (*Téc*) to set (**en** into)
VPR **incrustarse** • **~se en** [*bala*] to lodge in, embed itself in • **se le ha incrustado esta idea en la mente** he's got this idea firmly fixed in his head
incuantificable ADJ unquantifiable
incubación SF incubation
incubadora SF incubator
incubar ▷ CONJUG 1a VT to incubate
VPR **incubarse** to incubate
íncubo SM (*frm*) **1** (= *diablo*) incubus
2 (= *pesadilla*) nightmare
incuestionable ADJ unquestionable, unchallengeable
incuestionablemente ADV unquestionably
inculcar ▷ CONJUG 1g VT to instil, instill (EEUU), inculcate (**en** in, into)
VPR **inculcarse** (= *obstinarse*) to be obstinate
inculpable ADJ blameless, guiltless
inculpación SF (*gen*) accusation; (*Jur*) charge
inculpado/a SM/F accused person • **el ~** the accused, the defendant
inculpar ▷ CONJUG 1a VT (*gen*) to accuse (**de** of); (*Jur*) to charge (**de** with) • **los crímenes que se le inculpan** the crimes with which he is charged
incultamente ADV (= *iletradamente*) in an uncultured way; (= *groseramente*) uncouthly
incultivable ADJ uncultivable
inculto ADJ **1** [*persona*] (= *iletrado*) uncultured, uneducated; (= *incivilizado*) uncivilized; (= *grosero*) uncouth
2 (*Agr*) uncultivated • **dejar un terreno ~** to leave land uncultivated
incultura SF (= *ignorancia*) lack of culture; (= *grosería*) uncouthness
incumbencia SF (= *obligación*) obligation, duty; (= *competencia*) concern • **no es de mi ~** it is no concern of mine, it is not my job
incumbir ▷ CONJUG 3a VI • **esto solo incumbe a los implicados** this only concerns those involved • **no me incumbe a mí** it is no concern of mine, it is not my job • **le incumbe hacerlo** that is his job, it is his duty to do it
incumplible ADJ unattainable
incumplido ADJ unfulfilled
incumplimiento SM • **~ de las promesas electorales** failure to keep electoral promises • **~ de una orden** failure to comply with an order • **~ de contrato** breach of contract • **lo expulsaron por ~ del deber** he was expelled for failing to carry out his duties
incumplir ▷ CONJUG 3a VT [+ *regla*] to break, fail to observe; [+ *promesa*] to break, fail to keep; [+ *contrato*] to breach
incunable SM incunable, incunabulum • **~s** incunabula
incurable ADJ **1** (*Med*) incurable
2 (= *incorregible*) hopeless, irremediable
SMF incurable
incuria SF **1** (= *negligencia*) negligence • **por ~** through negligence
2 (= *dejadez*) carelessness, shiftlessness
incurrir ▷ CONJUG 3a VI • **~ en** [+ *error*] to make; [+ *crimen*] to commit; [+ *deuda, odio*] to incur; [+ *desastre*] to fall victim to
incursión SF raid, incursion ▸ **incursión aérea** air raid
incursionar ▷ CONJUG 1a VI • **~ en** to make a raid into, penetrate into • **~ en un tema** to tackle a subject, broach a subject
indagación SF investigation, inquiry
indagador(a) SM/F investigator (**de** into, of), inquirer (**de** into)
indagar ▷ CONJUG 1h VT (= *investigar*) to investigate, inquire into; (= *averiguar*) to find out, ascertain
indagatoria SF (*Méx*) investigation, inquiry
indagatorio ADJ investigatory
indebidamente ADV (= *injustificadamente*) unduly; (= *incorrectamente*) improperly; (= *injustamente*) illegally, wrongfully
indebido ADJ (= *injustificado*) undue; (= *incorrecto*) improper; (= *injusto*) illegal, wrongful
INDEC SM ABR (*Arg*) = **Instituto Nacional de Estadísticas y Censos**
indecencia SF **1** (= *cualidad*) (= *falta de decencia*) indecency; (= *obscenidad*) obscenity
2 (= *acto*) indecent act; (= *palabra*) indecent thing
3 (= *porquería*) filth
indecente ADJ **1** [*persona*] (= *falto de decencia*) indecent; (= *obsceno*) obscene • **algún**

empleadillo ~ some wretched clerk • **es una persona ~** he's shameless • **¡indecente!** you brute!
2 (= *asqueroso*) filthy • **la calle está ~ de lodo** the street is terribly muddy • **un cuchitril ~** a filthy pigsty of a place
indecentemente ADV 1 (= *sin decencia*) indecently
2 (= *obscenamente*) obscenely
indecible ADJ unspeakable, indescribable • **sufrir lo ~** to suffer terribly
indeciblemente ADV unspeakably, indescribably
indecisión SF indecision
indeciso/a ADJ 1 [*persona*] indecisive • **estoy ~** I'm undecided • **¡soy tan ~!** I can never make up my mind!
2 [*tema*] (= *por decidir*) undecided; (= *indefinido*) vague
3 [*resultado*] indecisive
SM/F (*Pol*) (*en votación*) undecided voter; (*en encuesta*) don't know
indeclarable ADJ undeclarable
indeclinable ADJ 1 (*Ling*) indeclinable
2 (= *inevitable*) unavoidable
indecoro SM indecorum, unseemliness
indecorosamente ADV indecorously
indecoroso ADJ unseemly, indecorous
indefectible ADJ unfailing
indefectiblemente ADV unfailingly
indefendible ADJ indefensible
indefensión SF defencelessness, defenselessness (EEUU)
indefenso ADJ defenceless, defenseless (EEUU)
indefinible ADJ indefinable
indefinición SF 1 (= *falta de definición*) lack of definition
2 (= *vaguedad*) absence of clarity, vagueness
indefinidamente ADV indefinitely
indefinido ADJ 1 (= *ilimitado*) indefinite • **por tiempo ~** indefinitely
2 (= *vago*) undefined, vague
3 (*Ling*) indefinite
indeformabilidad SF ability to keep its shape
indeformable ADJ that keeps its shape
indeleble ADJ indelible
indeleblemente ADV indelibly
indelicadeza SF indelicacy • **cometió** *o* **tuvo la ~ de preguntarle la edad** he was tactless enough to ask her age
indelicado ADJ indelicate
indemallable ADJ (*Cono Sur*) ladderproof (*Brit*), run-resist (EEUU)
indemne ADJ [*persona*] unharmed, unhurt; [*objeto*] undamaged
indemnidad SF indemnity
indemnizable ADJ that can be indemnified, recoverable
indemnización SF 1 (= *acto*) indemnification
2 (= *suma*) compensation, indemnity • **pagó mil dólares de ~** he paid one thousand dollars in damages *o* in compensation
▸ **indemnización compensatoria** financial compensation ▸ **indemnización por daños y perjuicios** damages (*pl*) ▸ **indemnización por despido** redundancy pay
▸ **indemnización por enfermedad** statutory sick pay
3 **indemnizaciones** (*Mil, Pol*) reparations
indemnizar ▷ CONJUG 1f VT to compensate, indemnify (**de** against, for)
indemnizatorio ADJ compensatory
indemostrable ADJ indemonstrable
independencia SF independence • **con ~ de (que)** irrespective of (whether)
independentismo SM independence movement
independentista ADJ pro-independence (*antes de s*)
SMF pro-independence campaigner
independiente ADJ 1 (*gen*) independent • **hacerse ~** to become independent
2 [*piso etc*] self-contained
3 (*Inform*) stand-alone
SMF independent
independientemente ADV independently • **~ de que** irrespective *o* regardless of whether
independista ADJ pro-independence (*antes de s*)
SMF pro-independent
independizar ▷ CONJUG 1f VT to make independent
VPR **independizarse** to become independent (**de** of), gain independence (**de** from) • **el país se independizó en 1962** the country became independent in 1962, the country gained independence in 1962 • **~se económicamente** to become economically independent • **~se de los padres** to become independent from one's parents
indesarraigable ADJ ineradicable
indescifrable ADJ [*código*] indecipherable, undecipherable; [*misterio*] impenetrable
indescriptible ADJ indescribable
indescriptiblemente ADV indescribably
indeseable ADJ undesirable
SMF undesirable
indeseado ADJ unwanted
indesligable ADJ inseparable (**de** from)
indesmallable ADJ [*medias*] ladder-proof, run-resist
indesmayable ADJ unfaltering
indesmentible ADJ undeniable
indespegable ADJ that will not come unstuck
indestructible ADJ indestructible
indetectable ADJ undetectable
indeterminación SF (*al hablar*) indeterminacy, vagueness; (= *sobre el futuro*) indeterminancy, uncertainty • **principio de ~** uncertainty principle, indeterminacy principle
indeterminado ADJ 1 (= *impreciso*) indeterminate; [*resultado*] inconclusive • **un número ~ de personas** an indeterminate number of people
2 (= *indefinido*) indefinite • **por (un) tiempo ~** indefinitely
3 [*persona*] irresolute
4 (*Ling*) indefinite
indexación SF (*Econ*) indexation, index-linking; (*Inform*) indexing
indexado ADJ (*Econ*) index-linked
indexar ▷ CONJUG 1a VT (*Econ*) to index-link
India SF • **la ~** India • **las ~s** the Indies
▸ **Indias Occidentales** West Indies ▸ **Indias Orientales** East Indies
indiada SF 1 (*LAm*) (= *grupo*) group of Indians; (*Cono Sur*) (*pey*) mob
2 (*LAm*) (= *acto*) *typically Indian thing to do or say*
indiana SF printed calico
indiano/a ADJ American, Spanish-American
SM/F *Spaniard who has made good in America*
• MODISMO: • **~ de hilo negro** miser
indicación SF 1 (= *señal*) sign • **me hizo una ~ con la mano** he gestured *o* signalled to me with his hand, he made a sign to me with his hand • **~ al margen** note in the margin, margin note
2 (= *consejo*) hint, suggestion • **aprovechó la ~** he took the hint • **por ~ de algn** at the suggestion of sb • **me pongo en contacto con usted por ~ del Sr. Gómez** I'm writing to you at the suggestion of Sr Gómez • **he dejado de fumar por ~ del médico** I've stopped smoking on medical advice *o* on the doctor's advice
3 [*de termómetro*] reading
4 (*Med*) sign, symptom
5 **indicaciones** (= *instrucciones*) instructions, directions • **me dio algunas indicaciones sobre el manejo del aparato** he gave me instructions *o* directions about how to use the machine • **seguiré sus indicaciones** I will follow your instructions *o* directions • **"indicaciones de uso"** "instructions for use"
indicado ADJ 1 (= *adecuado*) suitable • **un comentario muy poco ~** a highly inappropriate remark • **eres la persona indicada para este puesto** you are the right person for this job • **no es el momento más ~ para hablar de eso** it isn't the best *o* right moment to talk about this • **tú eres la menos indicada para protestar** you're the last person who should complain • **ser lo más/menos ~** to be the best/worst thing (para for) • **eso es lo más ~ en este caso** that's the best thing to do in this case
2 (= *señalado*) [*fecha, hora*] specified
indicador ADJ • **luces ~as** indicator lights • **sigue los carteles ~es** follow the road signs; ▷ **papel**
SM 1 (= *señal*) sign • **es ~ de su mala salud** it is a sign of his ill health • **el que la novela tenga un premio no es un ~ de su calidad** the fact that it has won a prize doesn't mean it's a quality novel ▸ **indicador de carretera** road sign
2 (*Téc*) (= *aparato*) gauge, gage (EEUU); (= *aguja*) pointer ▸ **indicador de dirección** (*Aut*) indicator ▸ **indicador de encendido** power-on indicator ▸ **indicador del nivel de gasolina** (*Aut*) fuel gauge ▸ **indicador del nivel del aceite** (*Aut*) oil gauge ▸ **indicador de velocidad** (*Aut*) speedometer
3 (*Econ*) indicator; (*Bolsa*) index ▸ **indicador económico** economic indicator
4 (*Inform*) flag
indicar ▷ CONJUG 1g VT 1 (= *señalar*) to show • **me indicó el camino** he showed me the way • **¿me puede usted ~ dónde está el museo?** can you tell me *o* show me where the museum is? • **indica con un rotulador rojo dónde están los errores** use a red felt-tip pen to indicate *o* show where the mistakes are • **me indicó un punto en el mapa** he showed me *o* pointed out a point on the map
2 (= *decir*) [*señal, policía*] to indicate; [*portavoz, fuentes*] to state, point out, indicate • **esta señal indica que tenemos que detenernos** this sign indicates that we have to stop • **el policía nos indicó que parásemos** the policeman gestured *o* indicated to us to stop • **según me indicaba en su carta** as you indicated in your letter • **hice lo que usted me indicó** I did as you instructed • **me indicó con el dedo que me callase** he gestured to me to be quiet • **según ~on fuentes policiales** as police sources have stated *o* pointed out *o* indicated
3 (= *mostrar*) [+ *cantidad, temperatura*] to show; [+ *subida, victoria*] to point to • **el precio viene indicado en la etiqueta** the price is shown on the label • **su actitud indicaba una enorme falta de interés** her attitude showed an enormous lack of interest • **las previsiones del tiempo indican una subida de las temperaturas** the weather forecast points to a rise in temperatures • **no hay nada que indique lo contrario** there's nothing to suggest otherwise, there is no indication to the contrary • **como indica el informe** as shown in the report • **todo**

parece ~ que van a ganar las elecciones there is every indication *o* sign that they will win the election, everything points to them winning the election • **como su (propio) nombre indica: la otitis, como su propio nombre indica, es una inflamación del oído** otitis, as its name suggests, is an inflammation of the ear
4 (*frm*) (= *recomendar*) [*abogado, médico*] to tell, say • **haz lo que te indique el médico** do as the doctor tells you, do as the doctor says
indicativo (ADJ) **1** (= *sintomático*) • **ser ~ de algo** to be indicative of sth • **esto es ~ del nuevo rumbo de la empresa** this is indicative of the company's new direction • **es un síntoma ~ de que la situación está mejorando** this is indicative of the fact that the situation is improving
2 (= *recomendado*) [*horario, precio*] recommended • **el precio ~ de la leche** the recommended price of milk
(SM) **1** (*Ling*) indicative • **presente de ~** present indicative
2 (*Radio*) call sign, call letters (*pl*) (*EEUU*)
3 (*Aut*) ▸ **indicativo de nacionalidad** national identification plate
índice (SM) **1** [*de libro, publicación*] index ▸ **índice alfabético** alphabetical index ▸ **índice de materias, índice temático** table of contents ▸ **índice toponímico** place index
2 (= *catálogo*) (library) catalogue, (library) catalog (*EEUU*)
3 (*Estadística*) rate • **por debajo del ~ de pobreza** below the poverty line ▸ **índice de audiencia** (*TV*) audience ratings (*pl*) ▸ **índice de mortalidad** death rate, mortality rate ▸ **índice de natalidad** birth rate ▸ **índice de ocupación** occupancy rate ▸ **índice de participación electoral** electoral turnout ▸ **índice de vida** life expectancy
4 (*Econ*) index ▸ **índice al por menor** retail price index ▸ **índice de deuda** debt ratio ▸ **índice del coste de (la) vida** cost-of-living index ▸ **índice de precios al consumo** retail price index ▸ **índice Dow Jones** Dow Jones Average
5 (*Mec*) ▸ **índice de compresión** compression ratio
6 (= *prueba*) sign, indication • **es un ~ claro de que el plan ha fracasado** it's a clear sign *o* indication that the plan has failed
7 (*Téc*) (= *aguja*) pointer, needle; (= *manecilla*) hand
8 (*Anat*) (*tb* **dedo índice**) index finger, forefinger
9 (*Rel*) • **el Índice** the Index ▸ **Índice expurgatorio** Index
indiciación (SF) indexing; (*Econ*) index-linking
indiciario (ADJ) • **prueba indiciaria** circumstantial proof
indicio (SM) **1** (= *señal*) (*gen*) indication, sign; [*de gratitud*] token; [*de droga*] trace; (*Inform*) marker, mark • **es ~ de** it is an indication of, it is a sign of • **no hay el menor ~ de él** there isn't the faintest sign of him, there isn't the least trace of him • **dar ~s de sorpresa** to show some surprise
2 indicios (*Jur*) evidence (*sing*), circumstantial evidence (*sing*) (**de** to) ▸ **indicios de culpabilidad** evidence of guilt ▸ **indicios de delito** evidence of a crime
indiferencia (SF) lack of interest (**hacia** in, towards), indifference (*frm*) (**hacia** towards) • **sentía una terrible ~ ante todo** she felt a terrible lack of interest in everything • **ella aparentaba ~** she pretended to be indifferent, she feigned indifference • **nos trató con ~** he treated us with indifference • **ante la ~ de los políticos** faced by the indifference of politicians
indiferente (ADJ) **1** (= *impasible*) [*actitud, mirada*] indifferent • **un grupo de transeúntes ~s** a group of unconcerned passers-by • **dejar ~ a algn: esas imágenes no pueden dejarnos ~s** those images cannot fail to move us • **todo lo deja ~** he's so indifferent to everything • **permanecer** *o* **quedarse ~** to remain indifferent (**a, ante** to) • **no podemos permanecer ~s ante esta terrible situación** we cannot remain indifferent to this terrible situation • **se mostró ~ a sus encantos** he remained indifferent to her charms • **se mostró ~ a la hora de decidir** when it came to making a decision he showed no interest • **ser ~ a algo** to be indifferent to sth
2 (= *que da igual*) • **a mí la política me es ~** politics doesn't interest me • —**¿desea salir por la mañana o por la tarde?** —**me es ~** "do you want to leave in the morning or the afternoon?"—"it makes no difference to me *o* I don't mind" • **es ~ que vengáis hoy o mañana** it makes no difference *o* it doesn't matter whether you come today or tomorrow • **hablar de cosas ~s** to talk about trivialities
indiferentemente (ADV) **1** (= *sin diferencia*) indistinctly • **sinónimos usados ~ en el texto** synonyms used indistinctly in the text • **~ de algo** regardless of sth
2 (= *sin interés*) indifferently • **la miró ~** he looked at her with indifference, he looked at her indifferently
indiferentismo (SM) (*Rel*) scepticism, indifferentism
indígena (ADJ) **1** (= *nativo*) indigenous (**de** to), native (**de** to)
2 (*LAm*) Indian
(SMF) **1** (= *nativo*) native
2 (*LAm*) Indian
indigencia (SF) poverty, destitution
indigenismo (SM) **1** (= *movimiento*) indigenism, pro-Indian political movement; (= *estudio*) study of Indian societies and cultures
2 (*Ling*) *word/phrase borrowed from a native language*
indigenista (ADJ) pro-Indian • **propaganda ~** pro-Indian propaganda
(SMF) (= *estudiante*) student of Indian cultures; (*Pol*) supporter *o* promoter of Indian cultures
indigente (ADJ) destitute
(SMF) destitute person
indigerible (ADJ) indigestible, undigestible
indigestar ▸ CONJUG 1a (VT) to give indigestion
(VPR) **indigestarse 1** [*persona*] to get indigestion
2 [*comida*] to cause indigestion • **esa carne se me indigestó** that meat gave me indigestion
3 (= *ser insoportable*) • **ese tío se me indigesta** I can't stand that guy*
4 (*LAm*) (= *inquietarse*) to get worried, get alarmed
indigestible (ADJ) indigestible
indigestión (SF) indigestion
indigesto (ADJ) **1** [*alimento*] indigestible, hard to digest; [*artículo, libro*] indigestible, difficult to get through
2 (= *confuso*) muddled, badly thought-out
indignación (SF) indignation, anger • **descargar la ~ sobre algn** to vent one's spleen on sb, take out one's anger on sb
indignado (ADJ) indignant, angry (**con, contra** with, **por** at, about)
indignamente (ADV) **1** (= *sin mérito*) unworthily
2 (= *despreciablemente*) contemptibly, meanly
indignante (ADJ) outrageous, infuriating
indignar ▸ CONJUG 1a (VT) (= *enfadar*) to anger, make indignant; (= *provocar*) to provoke, stir up
(VPR) **indignarse** to get angry • **¡es para ~se!** it's infuriating! • **~se con algn** to get angry with sb • **~se por algo** to get indignant about sth, get angry about sth
indignidad (SF) **1** (= *falta de mérito*) unworthiness
2 (= *vileza*) unworthy act • **sufrir la ~ de hacer algo** to suffer the indignity of doing sth
3 (= *insulto*) indignity, insult
indigno (ADJ) **1** (= *impropio*) unworthy • **tales comentarios son ~s de un ministro** such comments are unworthy of a minister
2 (= *desmerecedor*) unworthy • **ser ~ de algo** to be unworthy of sth • **eres indigna de nuestra confianza** you are unworthy *o* not worthy of our trust
3 (= *despreciable*) despicable • **el más ~ de los delitos** the most despicable of crimes
índigo (SM) indigo
indino* (ADJ) **1** (= *insolente*) cheeky*, sassy (*EEUU**)
2 (*And, Caribe*) (= *tacaño*) mean, stingy
indio/a (ADJ) **1** [*persona*] Indian
2 (= *azul*) blue
(SM/F) **1** Indian
2 • MODISMOS: • **hacer el ~*** to play the fool • **salirle el ~ a algn** (*CAm, Cono Sur**): • **le salió el ~** he behaved like a boor • **ser el ~ gorrón*** to live by scrounging* • **subírsele el ~ a algn** (*Cono Sur*): • **se le subió el ~*** he got over-excited
(SM) ▸ **indio viejo** (*CAm, Méx*) (*Culin*) *stewed meat with maize and herbs*
indirecta (SF) hint • **lanzar** *o* **soltar una ~** to drop a hint • **(re)coger la ~** to take the hint • MODISMO: • **~ del padre Cobos†** broad hint
indirectamente (ADV) indirectly
indirecto (ADJ) **1** [*apoyo, control, causa, respuesta*] indirect; [*referencia*] oblique; [*amenaza, crítica*] veiled • **estaba ayudando a los opresores de modo ~** he was indirectly helping the oppressors, in a roundabout way he was helping the oppressors • **de modo ~ me dijo que me fuera** he hinted that I should go • **fue una manera indirecta de pedir dinero** it was a indirect *o* roundabout way of asking for money
2 [*impuesto, coste*] indirect
3 [*iluminación, luz*] indirect
4 (*Gram*) [*complemento, estilo*] indirect
indiscernible (ADJ) indiscernible
indisciplina (SF) **1** (= *falta de disciplina*) indiscipline, lack of discipline
2 (*Mil*) insubordination
indisciplinado (ADJ) **1** [*niño, alumno*] undisciplined
2 [*soldado*] insubordinate
indisciplinarse ▸ CONJUG 1a (VPR) **1** [*niño, alumno*] to get out of control
2 [*soldado*] to be insubordinate
indiscreción (SF) **1** (= *falta de discreción*) indiscretion
2 (= *acto, dicho*) gaffe, faux pas • **si no es ~** if I may say so • **cometió la ~ de decírmelo** he was tactless enough to tell me
indiscretamente (ADV) (= *sin discreción*) indiscreetly; (= *sin tacto*) tactlessly
indiscreto (ADJ) (= *falto de discreción*) indiscreet; (= *falto de tacto*) tactless
indiscriminadamente (ADV) indiscriminately
indiscriminado (ADJ) indiscriminate
indisculpable (ADJ) inexcusable, unforgivable
indiscutible (ADJ) indisputable, unquestionable

indiscutiblemente ADV indisputably, unquestionably

indisimulable ADJ that cannot be disguised

indisimulado ADJ undisguised

indisociable ADJ inseparable (**de** from)

indisolubilidad SF indissolubility

indisoluble ADJ **1** [*matrimonio*] indissoluble
2 [*sustancia*] insoluble

indisolublemente ADV indissolubly

indispensable ADJ indispensable, essential

indisponer ▹ CONJUG 2q VT **1** (*Med*) to upset, make ill
2 (= *ofender*) to upset
3 (= *enemistar*) • **~ a algn con otro** to set sb against another person
4 [+ *plan*] to spoil, upset
VPR **indisponerse 1** (*Med*) to become ill, fall ill
2 • **~se con algn** to fall out with sb

indisponible ADJ not available, unavailable

indisposición SF **1** (*Med*) indisposition
2 (= *desgana*) disinclination, unwillingness

indispuesto ADJ **1** (*Med*) indisposed, unwell • **sentirse ~** to feel unwell
2 (= *sin ganas*) disinclined, unwilling

indisputable ADJ (= *indiscutible*) indisputable, unquestioned; (= *incontestado*) unchallenged

indistinción SF **1** (= *falta de distinción*) (*en colores*) indistinctness; (*en conceptos*) vagueness
2 (= *falta de discriminación*) lack of discrimination

indistinguible ADJ indistinguishable (**de** from)

indistintamente ADV **1** (= *sin distinción*) without distinction; (= *sin discriminación*) indiscriminately • **pueden firmar ~** either may sign (*joint holder of the account etc*)
2 (= *no claramente*) vaguely, indistinctly

indistinto ADJ **1** (= *poco claro*) indistinct, vague; (= *borroso*) faint, dim
2 (= *indiscriminado*) indiscriminate • **permiten el uso ~ del inglés y el español** they allow indiscriminate use of Spanish and English
3 (= *indiferente*) • **es ~** it makes no difference, it doesn't matter

individua SF (*pey*) woman

individual ADJ **1** [*trabajo, necesidades, características*] individual
2 [*cama, cuarto*] single
3 (*And, Cono Sur**) (= *idéntico*) identical • **es ~ a su padre** he is the spitting image of his father
SM (*Dep*) singles (*pl*), singles match • **~ femenino/masculino** women's/men's singles (*pl*)

individualidad SF individuality

individualismo SM individualism

individualista ADJ individualistic
SMF individualist

individualizado ADJ personalized, individual

individualizar ▹ CONJUG 1f VT **1** (= *diferenciar*) • **le resultaba difícil ~ con precisión a unos de otros** it was difficult for him to pick out one individual from another • **este método está basado en la capacidad de ~ genes diferentes** this method is based on the ability to pick out individual genes
2 [+ *tratamiento, situación*] to individualize • **estos importantes hallazgos permitirán ~ el tratamiento** these important discoveries will allow us to individualize the treatment *o* tailor the treatment to the individual • **~ la enseñanza** to tailor *o* target teaching to each individual's needs
VI • **prefiero no ~** I prefer not to pick out any individuals *o* single anyone out

individualmente ADV individually

individuar ▹ CONJUG 1e VT, VI = **individualizar**

individuo ADJ individual
SM **1** (= *persona*) (*gen*) individual; (*pey*) individual, character • **el ~ en cuestión** the person in question
2 (= *socio*) member, fellow

indivisibilidad SF indivisibility

indivisible ADJ indivisible

indivisiblemente ADV inextricably

indiviso ADJ undivided

indización SF (*Econ*) index-linking; (*Inform*) indexing

indizado ADJ (*Econ*) index-linked; (*Inform*) indexed
SM indexing

indizar ▹ CONJUG 1f VT (*Econ*) to index-link; (*Inform*) to index

INDO SM ABR (*Com*) = **Instituto Nacional de Denominaciones de Origen**

Indo SM (*Geog*) Indus

indo/a ADJ, SM/F Indian, Hindu

indo... PREF Indo...

Indochina SF Indochina

indócil ADJ (= *difícil*) unmanageable; (= *testarudo*) headstrong; (= *rebelde*) disobedient

indocilidad SF (= *carácter difícil*) unmanageability; (= *testarudez*) headstrong character; (= *rebeldía*) disobedience

indocto ADJ ignorant, unlearned

indoctrinar ▹ CONJUG 1a VT (= *enseñar*) to indoctrinate; (*pey*) to brainwash

indocumentado/a ADJ not carrying identity papers
SM/F person who carries no identity papers; (*Méx*) illegal immigrant

indoeuropeo/a ADJ, SM/F Indo-European
SM (*Ling*) Indo-European

índole SF **1** (= *naturaleza*) nature
2 (= *tipo*) kind, sort • **cosas de esta ~** things of this kind

indolencia SF (= *pereza*) indolence, laziness; (= *abulia*) apathy; (= *languidez*) listlessness

indolente ADJ (= *perezoso*) indolent, lazy; (= *abúlico*) apathetic; (= *lánguido*) listless

indoloro ADJ painless

indomable ADJ [*espíritu*] indomitable; [*animal*] untameable; [*pelo*] unmanageable; [*energía*] boundless

indomado ADJ wild, untamed

indomesticable ADJ untameable

indomiciliado ADJ homeless

indómito ADJ = **indomable**

Indonesia SF Indonesia

indonesio/a ADJ, SM/F Indonesian

indormia* SF (*And, Caribe*) trick, wangle*, wheeze*

Indostán SM Hindustan

indostanés/esa ADJ, SM/F Hindustani

indostaní SM (*Ling*) Hindustani

indostánico ADJ Hindustani
SM (*Ling*) Hindustani

indotado ADJ without a dowry

indte. ABR = **indistintamente**

Indubán SM ABR (*Esp*) (*Econ*) = **Banco de Financiación Industrial**

indubitable ADJ indubitable, undoubted

indubitablemente ADV indubitably, undoubtedly

inducción SF **1** (*Fil, Elec*) induction • **por ~** by induction, inductively
2 (= *persuasión*) inducement

inducido SM (*Elec*) armature

inducir ▹ CONJUG 3n VT **1** (*Fil*) to infer
2 (*Elec*) to induce
3 (= *empujar, llevar*) to induce • **~ a algn a hacer algo** to induce sb to do sth • **~ a algn a error** to lead sb into error

inductivo ADJ inductive • **pregunta inductiva** leading question

inductor(a) SM/F instigator
SM (*Elec, Bio*) inductor

indudable ADJ [*talento, encanto, lealtad*] undoubted, unquestionable • **de ~ importancia** of undoubted *o* unquestionable importance • **su inteligencia es ~** his intelligence is not in doubt, his intelligence is undeniable • **es ~ que es de Picasso** there is no doubt that it is by Picasso • **es el mejor, eso es ~** he's the best, there's no doubt about that

indudablemente ADV undoubtedly, unquestionably

indulgencia SF **1** (= *tolerancia*) (*tb Rel*) indulgence • **proceder sin ~ contra algn** to proceed ruthlessly against sb ▸ **indulgencia plenaria** plenary indulgence
2 (*para perdonar*) leniency

indulgente ADJ (= *tolerante*) indulgent; (*para perdonar*) lenient (**con** towards)

indulgentemente ADV (= *con tolerancia*) indulgently; (*para perdonar*) leniently

indultar ▹ CONJUG 1a VT **1** (= *perdonar*) to pardon, reprieve
2 (= *eximir*) to exempt (**de** from), excuse (**de** from)
VPR **indultarse 1** (*And*) (= *entrometerse*) to meddle, pry
2 (*Caribe**) to get o.s. out of a jam*

indulto SM **1** (= *perdón*) pardon, reprieve
2 (= *exención*) exemption

indumentaria SF **1** (= *ropa*) clothing, dress
2 (= *estudio*) costume, history of costume

indumentario ADJ clothing (*antes de s*) • **elegancia indumentaria** elegance of dress, sartorial elegance

indumento SM clothing, apparel, dress

industria SF **1** (*Com*) industry • **la zona con más ~ del país** the most industrialized area of the country ▸ **industria agropecuaria** farming and fishing ▸ **industria artesanal** cottage industry ▸ **industria automovilística** car industry, auto industry (*EEUU*) ▸ **industria básica** basic industry ▸ **industria casera** cottage industry ▸ **industria del automóvil** car industry, automobile industry (*EEUU*) ▸ **industria del ocio** leisure industry ▸ **industria ligera** light industry ▸ **industria militar** weapons industry, defence industry ▸ **industria pesada** heavy industry ▸ **industria petrolífera** oil industry ▸ **industria siderúrgica** iron and steel industry
2 (= *fábrica*) factory
3 (= *dedicación*) industry, industriousness
4† (= *maña*) ingenuity, skill, expertise • **de ~** on purpose

industrial ADJ **1** (= *de la industria*) industrial
2 (= *no casero*) factory-made, industrially produced
3* (= *enorme*) huge, massive • **en cantidades ~es** in huge amounts • **hay basura acumulada en cantidades ~es** there's a huge amount of rubbish piled up
SMF industrialist

industrialismo SM industrialism

industrialista SMF (*LAm*) industrialist

industrialización SF industrialization

industrializado ADJ industrialized

industrializar ▹ CONJUG 1f VT to industrialize
VPR **industrializarse** to become industrialized

industrialmente ADV industrially
industriarse ▸ CONJUG 1b VPR to manage, find a way • **industriárselas para hacer algo** to manage to do sth
industriosamente ADV **1** (= *con diligencia*) industriously
2 (= *con maña*) skilfully, skillfully (EEUU), resourcefully
industrioso ADJ **1** (= *diligente*) industrious
2 (= *mañoso*) resourceful
INE SM ABR (*Esp*) = **Instituto Nacional de Estadística**
inédito ADJ **1** [*texto*] unpublished • **un texto rigurosamente ~** a text never published previously in any form
2 (= *nuevo*) new • **una experiencia inédita** a completely new experience
3 (= *nunca visto*) hitherto unheard-of
ineducable ADJ ineducable
ineducado ADJ **1** (= *sin instrucción*) uneducated
2 (= *maleducado*) ill-bred, bad-mannered
INEF SM ABR = **Instituto Nacional de Educación Física**
inefable ADJ indescribable, ineffable
inefectivo ADJ (*LAm*) ineffective
ineficacia SF **1** [*de medida*] ineffectiveness
2 [*de proceso*] inefficiency; [*de gobierno, persona*] inefficiency, incompetence
ineficaz ADJ **1** [*medida*] ineffective
2 (= *inútil*) [*proceso*] inefficient; [*gobierno, persona*] inefficient, incompetent
ineficazmente ADV **1** (= *sin resultado*) ineffectively, ineffectually
2 (= *sin eficiencia*) inefficiently
ineficiencia SF inefficiency
ineficiente ADJ inefficient
inelástico ADJ inelastic, rigid
inelegancia SF inelegance, lack of elegance
inelegante ADJ inelegant
inelegantemente ADV inelegantly
inelegibilidad SF ineligibility
inelegible ADJ ineligible
ineluctable ADJ (*liter*) ineluctable (*liter*)
ineludible ADJ unavoidable, inescapable
ineludiblemente ADV unavoidably, inevitably
INEM SM ABR (*Esp*) **1** (= **Instituto Nacional de Empleo**) *employment organization*
2 = **Instituto Nacional de Enseñanza Media**
INEN SM ABR (*Méx*) = **Instituto Nacional de Energía Nuclear**
inenarrable ADJ inexpressible
inencogible ADJ shrink-resistant
inencontrable ADJ unobtainable
inepcia SF **1** (= *ineptitud*) ineptitude, incompetence
2 (= *necedad*) stupidity
3 (= *impropiedad*) unsuitability
4 (= *dicho*) silly thing to say; (= *acto*) silly thing to do • **decir ~s** to talk rubbish
ineptitud SF ineptitude, incompetence
inepto ADJ inept, incompetent • **~ de toda ineptitud** utterly incompetent
inequívocamente ADV unequivocally
inequívoco ADJ (= *sin ambigüedad*) unequivocal, unambiguous; (= *inconfundible*) unmistakable
inercia SF **1** (*Fís*) inertia
2 (= *indolencia*) inertia • **por ~** through force of habit, out of habit
inerme ADJ (= *sin armas*) unarmed; (= *indefenso*) defenceless, defenseless (EEUU)
inerte ADJ **1** (*Fís*) inert
2 (= *sin vida*) lifeless; (= *inmóvil*) inert, motionless
Inés SF Agnes
inescrupuloso ADJ unscrupulous
inescrutabilidad SF inscrutability
inescrutable ADJ inscrutable
inespecífico ADJ unspecific, non-specific
inesperadamente ADV (= *por sorpresa*) unexpectedly; (= *de repente*) without warning, suddenly
inesperado ADJ (= *imprevisto*) unexpected; (= *repentino*) sudden
inesquivable ADJ unavoidable
inestabilidad SF instability, unsteadiness ▸ **inestabilidad laboral** lack of job security
inestabilizar ▸ CONJUG 1f VT to destabilize
VPR **inestabilizarse** to become unstable
inestable ADJ unstable, unsteady
inestimable ADJ inestimable, invaluable
inevitabilidad SF inevitability
inevitable ADJ inevitable
inevitablemente ADV inevitably, unavoidably
inexactitud SF (= *imprecisión*) inaccuracy; (= *falsedad*) incorrectness, wrongness
inexacto ADJ (= *no preciso*) inaccurate; (= *no cierto*) incorrect, untrue
inexcusable ADJ **1** [*conducta*] inexcusable, unforgivable
2 [*conclusión*] inevitable, unavoidable • **una visita ~** a trip not to be missed
inexcusablemente ADV
1 (= *imperdonablemente*) inexcusably, unforgivably
2 (= *ineludiblemente*) inevitably, unavoidably • **el depósito será devuelto ~ si ...** the deposit will be returned as a matter of obligation if ...
inexhausto ADJ inexhaustible, unending
inexistencia SF non-existence
inexistente ADJ non-existent
inexorabilidad SF inexorability
inexorable ADJ inexorable
inexorablemente ADV inexorably
inexperiencia SF (= *falta de experiencia*) inexperience, lack of experience; (= *torpeza*) lack of skill
inexperimentado ADJ inexperienced
inexperto ADJ (= *novato*) inexperienced; (= *torpe*) unskilled, inexpert
inexplicable ADJ inexplicable
inexplicablemente ADV inexplicably
inexplicado ADJ unexplained
inexplorado ADJ [*terreno, campo, tema*] unexplored; [*ruta*] uncharted
inexplotado ADJ unexploited, unused
inexportable ADJ that cannot be exported
inexpresable ADJ inexpressible
inexpresividad SF inexpressiveness, expressionlessness
inexpresivo ADJ expressionless, inexpressive
inexpuesto ADJ (*Fot*) unexposed
inexpugnabilidad SF impregnability
inexpugnable ADJ impregnable
inextinguible ADJ eternal, inextinguishable
inextirpable ADJ ineradicable
in extremis ADV **1** (= *en el último momento*) at the very last moment
2 (= *como último recurso*) as a last resort
3 (= *moribundo*) • **estar ~** to be at death's door
inextricable ADJ [*relación, lío*] inextricable; [*bosque*] impenetrable
inextricablemente ADV inextricably
infalibilidad SF infallibility • **~ pontificia** papal infallibility
infalible ADJ **1** [*persona*] infallible
2 [*aparato, plan*] foolproof
3 [*puntería*] unerring
4 (= *inevitable*) certain, sure
infaliblemente ADV **1** (= *sin equivocarse*) infallibly
2 (= *siempre*) unfailingly
3 (= *de modo certero*) unerringly, unfailingly, without fail
infaltable ADJ (*LAm*) not to be missed
infamación SF defamation
infamador(a) ADJ defamatory, slanderous
SM/F slanderer
infamante ADJ shameful, degrading
infamar ▸ CONJUG 1a VT (= *difamar*) to defame, slander; (= *deshonrar*) to dishonour, dishonor (EEUU)
infamatorio ADJ defamatory, slanderous
infame ADJ (= *odioso*) [*persona*] odious; [*tarea*] thankless • **esto es ~** this is monstrous
SMF vile person, villain
infamia SF **1** (= *calumnia*) calumny, slur
2 (= *deshonra*) disgrace, ignominy • **sufrió la ~ de ser declarado culpable** he suffered the disgrace *o* ignominy of being found guilty
3 (= *canallada*) despicable act • **engañar a un amigo es una ~** it's despicable to deceive a friend • **recalentar el café es una ~** (*hum*) reheating coffee is a crime
4 (= *carácter infame*) infamy • **la ~ de sus actos** the infamy of his acts
infancia SF **1** [*de una persona*] childhood; [*de proyecto, teoría*] infancy • **es un amigo de la ~** he's a childhood friend • **en mi ~ nunca tuve juguetes** as a child I never had toys • **en su más tierna ~** in his tenderest youth (*liter o hum*) • **la investigación genética se halla todavía en su ~** genetic research is still in its infancy • **durante la ~ de la humanidad** in mankind's infancy; ▸ **jardín**
2 (= *niños*) children • **Día Internacional de la Infancia** International Children's Day
infante/a SM/F (*Hist*) infante/infanta, prince/princess
SM **1** (*Mil, Hist*) infantryman ▸ **infante de marina** marine
2 (= *niño*) infant • **tierno ~** young child
infantería SF infantry ▸ **infantería de marina** marines (*pl*)
infanticida SMF infanticide, child killer
infanticidio SM infanticide
infantil ADJ **1** [*educación, población, prostitución, psicología*] child (*antes de s*); [*sonrisa, mirada*] childish, childlike; [*enfermedad*] children's, childhood (*antes de s*); [*hospital, libro, programa*] children's; [*mortalidad*] infant, child (*antes de s*)
2 (*pey*) childish, infantile
3 (*Dep*) ≈ youth
infantilada* SF • **es una ~** it's such a childish thing to do
infantilismo SM infantilism
infantiloide ADJ childish, puerile
infanzón/a SM/F (*Hist*) *member of the lowest rank of the nobility*
infartante* ADJ heart-stopping
infarto SM **1** (*tb* **infarto de miocardio**) heart attack
2 • **de ~*** heart-stopping
infatigable ADJ tireless, untiring
infatigablemente ADV tirelessly, untiringly
infatuación SF vanity, conceit
infatuar ▸ CONJUG 1d VT to make conceited
VPR **infatuarse** to get conceited (**con** about)
infausto ADJ (= *infortunado*) unlucky; (= *funesto*) ill-starred, ill-fated
INFE SM ABR = **Instituto de Fomento de las Exportaciones**
infección SF infection
infecciosidad SF infectiousness
infeccioso ADJ infectious
infectado ADJ infected
infectar ▸ CONJUG 1a VT **1** (*Med*) to infect
2 (= *pervertir*) to pervert, corrupt
VPR **infectarse 1** (*Med*) to become infected (**de** with)

2 (= *pervertirse*) to become perverted, become corrupted
infecto ADJ **1** (*Med*) infected (**de** with)
2 (= *repugnante*) disgusting
infectocontagioso ADJ infectious, transmittable
infecundidad SF **1** [*de mujer*] infertility, sterility
2 [*de tierra*] infertility, barrenness
infecundo ADJ **1** [*mujer*] infertile, sterile • **la época infecunda de la mujer** woman's infertile period
2 [*tierra*] infertile, barren
3 [*esfuerzo*] fruitless
infelicidad SF unhappiness
infeliz ADJ **1** (= *desgraciado*) [*persona*] unhappy; [*vida*] unhappy, wretched; [*tentativa*] unsuccessful
2 (= *bonachón*) kind-hearted, good-natured; (*pey*) gullible
SMF **1** (= *desgraciado*) poor unfortunate, poor wretch • **vi cómo golpeaban a un ~** I saw them hitting some poor unfortunate *o* wretch
2 (= *bonachón*) kind-hearted person, good-natured person; (*pey*) gullible fool
infelizmente ADV unhappily, unfortunately
infelizón* SM, **infelizote*** SM = **infeliz**
inferencia SF inference • **por ~** by inference
inferible ADJ inferable
inferior ADJ **1** (*en el espacio*) lower • **la parte ~** the lower part • **las extremidades ~es** the lower limbs • **labio ~** bottom *o* lower lip • **el piso ~ del edificio** the ground floor of the building • **el apartamento ~ al mío** the flat below mine
2 (*en categoría, jerarquía*) inferior • **de calidad ~** of inferior quality, inferior • **los organismos ~es de la creación** the lower forms of life • **están en un puesto ~ al nuestro en la liga** they're just below us in the league • **en una posición ~ en la lista** further down the list • **le es ~ en talento** he is inferior to him in talent • **tú no eres ~ a nadie** you're as good as anyone else
3 (*con cantidades, números*) lower • **sacó una nota ~ a la esperada** he got a lower mark than expected • **temperaturas ~es a los 20°** temperatures lower than 20°, temperatures below 20° • **renta per cápita ~ a la media** per capita income lower than *o* below the average • **cualquier número ~ a nueve** any number under *o* below *o* less than nine • **ingresos ~es a los dos millones** income below two million • **la cantidad de personas fue ~ a la del año pasado** there were fewer people than last year
SMF subordinate • **habla con mucho respeto a sus ~es** he's very respectful to his subordinates
inferioridad SF inferiority • **complejo de ~** inferiority complex • **estar** *o* **encontrarse en ~ de condiciones** to be at a disadvantage
inferir ▷ CONJUG 3i VT **1** (= *deducir*) to infer, deduce • **~ una cosa de otra** to infer one thing from another
2 (= *causar*) [+ *herida*] to inflict (**a, en** on); [+ *insulto*] to offer (**a** to)
infernáculo SM hopscotch
infernal ADJ infernal, hellish • **un ruido ~** a dreadful racket*
infernillo SM = **infiernillo**
infértil ADJ infertile
infestación SF infestation
infestado ADJ • **~ de** [+ *parásitos, gérmenes*] infested with • **~ de cucarachas** cockroach-infested • **~ de turistas/mendigos** crawling with tourists/beggars
infestante ADJ invasive, pervasive
infestar ▷ CONJUG 1a VT **1** (= *infectar*) to infect
2 (= *invadir*) to overrun, invade
3 [*insectos*] to infest
infibulación SF infibulation
infibulado ADJ infibulated
infición SF (*Méx*) pollution
inficionar ▷ CONJUG 1a VT = **infectar**
infidelidad SF **1** (*en pareja*) infidelity, unfaithfulness ▸ **infidelidad conyugal** marital infidelity
2 (*Rel*) unbelief, lack of faith
3† (= *conjunto de infieles*) unbelievers (*pl*), infidels (*pl*)
infidencia SF **1** (= *deslealtad*) disloyalty, faithlessness; (= *traición*) treason
2 (= *acto*) disloyal act
3 (*Jur*) breach of trust
infiel ADJ **1** (= *desleal*) unfaithful (**a, para, con** to) • **fue ~ a su mujer** he was unfaithful to his wife
2 (*Rel*) unbelieving, infidel
3 (= *erróneo*) unfaithful, inaccurate • **la memoria le fue ~** his memory failed him
SMF (*Rel*) unbeliever, infidel
infielmente ADV **1** (= *con deslealtad*) unfaithfully, disloyally
2 (= *con error*) inaccurately
infiernillo SM (*tb* **infiernillo de alcohol**) spirit lamp, spirit stove ▸ **infiernillo campestre** camp stove ▸ **infiernillo de gasolina** petrol stove
infierno SM **1** (*Rel*) hell • **la ciudad era un ~ (de llamas)** the city was a blazing inferno • **vivieron un ~** they went through hell
• MODISMOS: • **está en el quinto ~*** it's at the back of beyond • **mandar a algn al quinto ~*** to tell sb to go to hell* • **¡vete al ~!*** go to hell!*
2 (= *lugar*) (*horrible*) hellhole*; (*ruidoso*) madhouse*
infijo SM infix
infiltración SF infiltration
infiltrado/a SM/F infiltrator
infiltrar ▷ CONJUG 1a VT **1** [+ *espía, policía*] to infiltrate • **han infiltrado un agente en la organización** they have infiltrated an agent into the organization
2 (*Med*) to infiltrate
VPR **infiltrarse 1** [*espía, agente*] to infiltrate • **el detective se infiltró en la banda de mafiosos** the detective infiltrated the mafia ring • **consiguieron ~se en territorio rumano** they succeeded in infiltrating into Romanian territory • **se infiltró en la red informática de la NASA** he hacked into NASA's computer network
2 [*ideas, costumbres*] to permeate • **el liberalismo se fue infiltrando entre los intelectuales** liberalism gradually permeated the intelligentsia
3 [*líquido*] to seep; [*luz*] to filter • **la humedad se había ido infiltrando en el techo** the damp had seeped through the ceiling
ínfimo ADJ [*calidad, grado*] very poor; [*cantidad, participación, porcentaje, nivel*] very small, tiny • **de ínfima calidad** very poor quality (*antes de s*) • **la ayuda que le dieron fue ínfima** the help they afforded him was next to nothing • **viven en ínfimas condiciones** they live in dreadful *o* appalling conditions • **precios ~s** knockdown prices
infinidad SF **1** (*Mat*) infinity
2 (= *gran cantidad*) • **~ de veces** countless times, innumerable times • **hay ~ de personas que creen ...** any number of people believe ..., there's no end of people who believe ... • **hablan una ~ de lenguas** they speak a huge number of languages • **durante una ~ de días** for days on end
infinitamente ADV infinitely • **te lo agradeceré ~** I'd be deeply *o* immensely grateful to you • **lo sintió ~** he was deeply sorry
infinitesimal ADJ infinitesimal
infinitivo ADJ infinitive
SM infinitive
infinito ADJ [*universo, variedad*] infinite; [*entusiasmo, posibilidades*] boundless • **con paciencia infinita** with infinite patience • **sonrió con infinita tristeza** she smiled with immense sadness • **tuve que copiarlo infinitas veces** I had to copy it out countless times *o* over and over again • **hasta lo ~** ad infinitum
ADV infinitely, immensely • **se lo agradezco ~** I'm deeply *o* immensely grateful to you
SM (*Mat*) infinity • **el ~** (*Fil*) the infinite • **así podríamos seguir hasta el ~** we could go on like this for ever *o* indefinitely
infinitud SF = **infinidad**
inflable ADJ inflatable
inflación SF **1** (*tb Econ*) inflation ▸ **inflación subyacente** underlying inflation
2 (= *hinchazón*) swelling
3 (= *vanidad*) pride, conceit
inflacionario ADJ inflationary • **una política económica inflacionaria** an inflationary economic policy
inflacionismo SM inflation
inflacionista ADJ inflationary
inflado SM inflating, pumping up
inflador SM (*LAm*) bicycle pump
inflagaitas* SMF INV twit*
inflamabilidad SF inflammability
inflamable ADJ inflammable
inflamación SF **1** (*Med*) inflammation
2 (*Fís*) ignition, combustion
inflamado ADJ (*Med*) **1** (*con dolor, enrojecido*) inflamed
2 (*con fluido*) swollen
inflamar ▷ CONJUG 1a VT **1** (*Med*) to inflame
2 (= *enardecer*) to inflame, arouse
3 (= *prender fuego a*) to set on fire, ignite
VPR **inflamarse 1** (*Med*) to become inflamed
2 (= *enardecerse*) to become inflamed (**de** with), become aroused
3 (= *encenderse*) to catch fire, ignite • **se inflama fácilmente** it is highly inflammable
inflamatorio ADJ inflammatory
inflapollas‡ SM INV berk‡, wimp‡
inflar ▷ CONJUG 1a VT **1** [+ *neumático, globo*] to inflate, blow up
2 (= *exagerar*) (*gen*) to exaggerate; [+ *precios*] to inflate
3 (= *engreír*) to make conceited
4 (*Econ*) to reinflate
5 (*Cono Sur*) to heed, pay attention to
VI (*Méx**) to booze*, drink
VPR **inflarse 1** (= *hincharse*) to swell
2 (= *engreírse*) to get conceited • **~se de orgullo** to swell with pride
inflatorio ADJ inflationary
inflexibilidad SF inflexibility
inflexible ADJ (= *rígido*) inflexible; (= *inconmovible*) unbending, unyielding • **~ a los ruegos** unmoved by appeals, unresponsive to appeals • **regla ~** strict rule, hard-and-fast rule
inflexiblemente ADV **1** (= *rígidamente*) inflexibly
2 (= *inconmoviblemente*) strictly
inflexión SF inflection
infligir ▷ CONJUG 3c VT to inflict (**a** on)
influencia SF **1** (= *influjo*) influence

i

• **Cervantes ejerció gran ~ en su poesía** Cervantes had a great influence on his poetry • **sus pinturas tienen ~ modernista** his pictures show a modernist influence • **la tele tiene ~ negativa sobre mis hijos** telly has *o* is a bad influence on my children • **ya no tiene ~ dentro del gobierno** he now has no influence in the government • **tiene ~ con el jefe** she has influence with the boss • **actuó bajo la ~ de las drogas** he acted under the influence of drugs
2 influencias (= *contactos*) contacts • **siempre se vale de sus ~s** he always uses his contacts; ▹ **tráfico**

influenciable (ADJ) impressionable, easily influenced

influenciar ▹ CONJUG 1b (VT) to influence

influenza (SF) (*esp LAm*) influenza, flu

influir ▹ CONJUG 3g (VT) to influence • **A, influido por B ...** A, influenced by B ...
(VI) **1** to have influence, carry weight • **es hombre que influye** he's a man of influence, he carries a lot of weight
2 • **~ en** *o* **sobre** (*gen*) to influence; (= *contribuir a*) to have a hand in

influjo (SM) influence (**sobre** on)

influyente (ADJ) influential

infografía (SF) computer graphics

infopista (SF) information superhighway

información (SF) **1** (= *datos*) information; (= *oficina*) information desk; (*Telec*) Directory Enquiries, Directory Assistance (*EEUU*) • **¿dónde podría obtener más ~?** where could I get more information? • **si desean más** *o* **mayor ~** if you require further information • **pasaron toda la ~ a la policía** they passed on all the information *o* the details to the police • **pregunte en ~** ask at information *o* at the information desk • **~ internacional ¿dígame?** international enquiries, can I help you? • **le han dado una ~ falsa** you've been given false information • **"Información"** "Information", "Enquiries" ▸ **información genética** genetic information
2 (= *noticias*) news • **según las últimas informaciones** according to the latest reports *o* news • **les daremos más ~ dentro de unos minutos** we will give you some more information in a few minutes ▸ **información caliente** hot tip ▸ **información deportiva** (*en prensa, radio*) sports section; (*en TV*) sports news ▸ **información financiera** (*en prensa, radio*) financial section; (*en TV*) financial news ▸ **información internacional** foreign news
3 (*Jur*) judicial inquiry, investigation • **abrir una ~** to begin proceedings
4 (*Inform*) (= *datos*) data (*pl*); ▹ **tratamiento**
5 (*Mil*) intelligence

informado (ADJ) **1** (= *enterado*) • **estar ~** to be informed (**de, sobre** about) • **estaba ~ de todo** he was informed about everything • **tenemos derecho a estar ~s** we have a right to know, we have a right to information • **bien ~** well-informed • **según fuentes bien informadas** according to well-informed sources • **mal ~** misinformed, badly informed • **si eso es lo que crees, estás muy mal informada** if that's what you think you're misinformed *o* you've been badly informed • **mantener ~ a algn** to keep sb informed
2 [*trabajador*] • **bien ~** with good references

informador(a) (ADJ) • **la comisión ~a** the inquiry commission, the commission of inquiry • **una charla ~a** an informative talk • **el equipo ~ de esta cadena** this channel's team of reporters
(SM/F) **1** [*de una noticia*] informant; [*de la policía*] informer ▸ **informador(a) turístico/a** tourist guide
2 (= *periodista*) journalist • **los ~es de la prensa** the media, the representatives of the media ▸ **informador(a) gráfico/a** press photographer

informal (ADJ) **1** [*persona*] unreliable
2 [*charla, lenguaje, cena*] informal; [*ropa*] casual, informal • **reunión ~** informal meeting
3 (*LAm*) (= *no oficial*) • **el sector ~ de la economía** the unofficial sector of the economy, the black economy

informalidad (SF) **1** [*de persona*] unreliability
2 [*de lenguaje, reunión*] informality; (*en el vestir*) casualness

informalmente (ADV) informally • **vestir ~** to dress informally, dress casually

informante (SMF) [*de una noticia*] informant; [*de la policía*] informer

informar ▹ CONJUG 1a (VT) **1** (= *dar información a*) • **¿dónde te han informado?** where did you get your information? • **le han informado mal** you've been misinformed, you've been badly informed • **~ a algn de algo** to inform sb of sth, tell sb about sth • **nadie me informó del cambio de planes** no one informed me of *o* told me about the change of plan • **le informé de lo que pasaba** I informed him of what was happening, I told him what was happening • **el portavoz informó a la prensa de los cambios en el gobierno** the spokesman briefed the press on the changes in the government, the spokesman informed the press about the changes in the government • **~ a algn sobre algo** to inform sb about sth, give sb information on sth • **¿me puede usted ~ sobre las becas al extranjero?** can you tell me about overseas grants here?, can you give me information on overseas grants here?
2 (= *comunicar*) • **~ que** to report that • **la policía informó que las causas del accidente no estaban claras** the police reported that the cause of the accident was not clear • **~ a algn que** to tell sb that, inform sb that • **nadie me informó que se hubiera pasado la reunión a otro día** no one told *o* informed me that the meeting had been changed to another day • **nos complace ~le que ha resultado ganadora** we are pleased to inform you that you are the winner
3 (*frm*) (= *caracterizar*) • **la seriedad informa su carácter** she's extremely serious by nature • **la preocupación por el bien general debe ~ sus actuaciones** their actions should be guided *o* governed by concern for the common good
(VI) **1** (= *dar noticias*) [*portavoz, fuentes*] to state, point out, indicate • **se ha producido un nuevo atentado terrorista, ~on fuentes policiales** police sources have reported a new terrorist attack • **el criminal había sido detenido, según ~on fuentes oficiales** according to official sources, the criminal had been arrested • **nuestros representantes ~án de los motivos de la huelga** our representatives will announce the reasons for the strike • **~ de que** to report that • **acaban de ~ de que se ha cometido un atentado** a terrorist attack has just been reported, we have just received reports of a terrorist attack • **~ sobre algo** to report on sth • **una rueda de prensa para ~ sobre el incendio** a press conference to report on the fire • **no informó sobre el traspaso del jugador** he gave no information on the player's transfer
2 (*Jur*) [*delator*] to inform (**contra** against); [*abogado*] to sum up
(VPR) **informarse** (= *obtener información*) to find out, get information • **te puedes ~ en la oficina de turismo** you can find out in the tourist office, you can get some information from the tourist office • **¿te has informado bien?** are you sure your information is correct? • **~se de** *o* **sobre algo** to find out about sth • **antes de comprar nada, infórmate de las condiciones de pago** before you buy anything find out about the terms of payment • **he estado informándome sobre los cursos de verano** I've been enquiring about *o* finding out about summer courses

informática (SF) computing ▸ **informática gráfica** computer graphics; ▹ **informático**

informáticamente (ADV) computationally • **controlado ~** controlled by computer, computer-controlled

informático/a (ADJ) computer (*antes de s*) • **centro ~** computer centre • **servicios ~s** computer services
(SM/F) (= *técnico*) computer expert; (= *programador*) computer programmer
(SM) computer equipment; ▹ **informática**

informatividad (SF) informative nature

informativo (ADJ) **1** (= *que informa*) informative • **un libro muy ~** a very informative book • **un folleto ~** an information leaflet • **boletín ~** news bulletin
2 [*comité*] consultative, advisory
(SM) (*Radio, TV*) news programme, news program (*EEUU*)

informatización (SF) computerization

informatizado (ADJ) computerized

informatizar ▹ CONJUG 1f (VT) to computerize

informe[1] (ADJ) [*bulto, figura*] shapeless

informe[2] (SM) **1** (= *escrito*) report (**sobre** on) • **el ~ de la comisión** the committee's report • **han redactado un ~ sobre la corrupción** they have drafted a report on corruption • **~ médico/policial/técnico** medical/police/technical report ▸ **informe de prensa** press release
2 informes (= *datos*) information (*sing*); [*de trabajador*] references • **según mis ~s** according to my information • **dar ~s sobre algn/algo** to give information about sb/sth • **pedir ~s de** *o* **sobre algo** to ask for information about sth • **pedir ~s de** *o* **sobre algn** (*para trabajo*) to follow up sb's references • **tomar ~s** to gather information
3 (*Jur*) report • **según el ~ del forense** according to the forensic report ▸ **informe del juez** summing-up, summation (*EEUU*) ▸ **informe jurídico** pleadings (*pl*)
4 (*Com*) report ▸ **informe anual** annual report ▸ **informe de gestión** chairman's report
5 (*Pol*) White Paper

infortunado (ADJ) unfortunate, unlucky

infortunio (SM) (= *mala suerte*) misfortune, ill luck; (= *accidente*) mishap

infra... (PREF) infra..., under...

infraalimentación (SF), **infralimentación** (SF) undernourishment

infraalimentado (ADJ), **infralimentado** (ADJ) underfed, undernourished

infracción (SF) [*de ley*] infringement (**de** of); [*de acuerdo*] breach (**de** of); [*de norma*] offence (**de** against), violation (*EEUU*) (**de** of) ▸ **infracción de contrato** breach of contract ▸ **infracción de tráfico** traffic offence, driving offence, traffic violation (*EEUU*)

infraccionar ▹ CONJUG 1a (*Chile, Méx*) (*frm*)
(VT) to fine
(VI) to commit a traffic offence *o* (*EEUU*) violation

infractor(a) SM/F offender (**de** against)

infradesarrollado ADJ under-developed

infradesarrollo SM under-development

infradotado/a ADJ **1** (= *falto de recursos*) undersupplied, short of resources; (= *falto de personal*) understaffed
2 (*pey*) [*persona*] subnormal
SM/F (*pey*) moron‡

infraestimación SF underestimate

infraestimar ▷ CONJUG 1a VT to underestimate

infraestructura SF infrastructure

in fraganti ADV • **coger** *o* **pillar** *o* **sorprender ~ a algn** to catch sb redhanded

infrahumano ADJ subhuman

infraliteratura SF pulp fiction

inframundo SM underworld

infrangible ADJ unbreakable

infranqueable ADJ [*obstáculo físico*] impassable; [*abismo, distancia*] unbridgeable; [*dificultad*] insurmountable, insuperable

infrarrojo ADJ infrared

infrarrojos SM INV infrared

infrascrito/a, infraescrito/a ADJ (= *que firma*) undersigned; (= *mencionado*) undermentioned
SM/F • **el ~** the undersigned; (*LAm*) (*hum*) the present speaker, I myself

infrautilización SF under-use

infrautilizado ADJ [*servicios, músculos*] underused; [*recursos*] untapped

infrautilizar ▷ CONJUG 1f VT to under-use

infravaloración SF **1** (= *subvaloración*) undervaluing
2 (= *subestimación*) underestimate

infravalorado ADJ underrated

infravalorar ▷ CONJUG 1a VT **1** (= *subvalorar*) to undervalue
2 (= *subestimar*) to underestimate
VPR **infravalorarse** to undervalue o.s., underrate o.s. • **no te infravalores** don't run yourself down, don't undervalue *o* underrate yourself

infravaluar ▷ CONJUG 1e VT **1** (= *subestimar*) to underestimate
2 (= *quitar importancia a*) to play down

infravivienda SF sub-standard housing

infrecuencia SF infrequency

infrecuente ADJ infrequent

infringir ▷ CONJUG 3c VT to infringe, contravene

infructuosamente ADV (= *sin resultado*) fruitlessly; (= *sin éxito*) unsuccessfully; (= *sin beneficio*) unprofitably

infructuoso ADJ [*búsqueda, esfuerzo, negociación*] fruitless; [*intento*] unsuccessful; [*empresa, operación*] unprofitable

ínfulas SFPL (= *vanidad*) conceit (*sing*); (= *disparates*) pretentious nonsense (*sing*) • **darse ~** to get all high and mighty • **tener (muchas) ~ de algo** to fancy o.s. as sth • **un joven con ~ de escritor** a young man who fancies himself as a writer

infumable ADJ **1** [*cigarro, tabaco*] unsmokable
2* (= *insoportable*) [*persona*] unbearable, intolerable; [*espectáculo, película*] unwatchable; [*libro*] unreadable

infundado ADJ unfounded, groundless

infundia* SF (*LAm*) fat

infundio SM (= *mentira*) fib; (= *cuento malicioso*) malicious story

infundir ▷ CONJUG 3a VT to instil, instill (*EEUU*) (**a, en** into) • **~ ánimo a algn** to encourage sb • **~ confianza/respeto** to inspire confidence/respect • **~ miedo a algn** to fill sb with fear, scare sb • **~ sospechas** to arouse suspicion • **~ un espíritu nuevo a un club** to inject new life into a club

infusión SF infusion ▸ **infusión de hierbas** herbal tea ▸ **infusión de manzanilla** camomile tea

infuso ADJ ▷ ciencia

Ing. ABR = **ingeniero/ingeniera**

ingeniar ▷ CONJUG 1a VT to devise, think up
VPR **ingeniarse** • **~se con algo** to manage with sth, make do with sth • **ingeniárselas para hacer algo** to manage to do sth

ingeniería SF engineering ▸ **ingeniería civil** civil engineering ▸ **ingeniería de control** control engineering ▸ **ingeniería de sistemas** (*Inform*) systems engineering ▸ **ingeniería eléctrica** electrical engineering ▸ **ingeniería financiera** financial engineering ▸ **ingeniería genética** genetic engineering ▸ **ingeniería química** chemical engineering ▸ **ingeniería social** social engineering

Ingeniero SM (*esp Méx*) graduate; (*título*) sir • **Ing. Quintanilla** ≈ Dr. Quintanilla

ingeniero/a SM/F (SF A VECES: **ingeniero**) engineer • **mi hermana es ingeniera** *o* **~** my sister's an engineer ▸ **ingeniero/a aeronáutico/a** aeronautical engineer ▸ **ingeniero/a agrónomo/a** agronomist, agricultural expert ▸ **ingeniero/a de caminos, canales y puertos** civil engineer ▸ **ingeniero/a de mantenimiento** maintenance engineer ▸ **ingeniero/a de minas** mining engineer ▸ **ingeniero/a de montes** forestry expert ▸ **ingeniero/a de sonido** sound engineer ▸ **ingeniero/a de telecomunicaciones** telecommunications engineer ▸ **ingeniero/a de vuelo** flight engineer ▸ **ingeniero/a forestal** forestry expert ▸ **ingeniero/a industrial** industrial engineer ▸ **ingeniero/a naval** naval architect ▸ **ingeniero/a químico/a** chemical engineer

ingenio SM **1** (= *inventiva*) ingenuity, inventiveness; (= *talento*) talent; (= *gracia*) wit • **aguzar el ~** to sharpen one's wits
2 (= *persona*) wit
3 (*Mec*) apparatus, device; (*Mil*) device ▸ **ingenio nuclear** nuclear device
4 (= *fábrica*) mill, plant ▸ **ingenio azucarero, ingenio de azúcar** sugar mill, sugar refinery
5 (*And*) [*de acero*] steel works; (= *fundición*) foundry

ingeniosamente ADV **1** (= *inteligentemente*) ingeniously, cleverly
2 (= *con gracia*) wittily

ingeniosidad SF **1** (= *maña*) ingenuity, ingeniousness
2 (= *idea*) clever idea
3 (= *agudeza*) wittiness

ingenioso ADJ **1** (= *mañoso*) clever, resourceful; [*invento, sistema*] ingenious
2 (= *agudo*) witty

ingénito ADJ innate, inborn

ingente ADJ huge, enormous

ingenuamente ADV naïvely, ingenuously

ingenuidad SF naïveté, ingenuousness

ingenuo ADJ naïve, ingenuous

ingerido* ADJ (*Méx*) (= *enfermo*) ill, under the weather; (= *abatido*) downcast

ingerir ▷ CONJUG 3i VT (= *tragar*) to swallow; (= *tomar*) to consume, ingest (*frm*) • **el automovilista había ingerido tres litros de alcohol** the motorist had drunk *o* consumed three litres of alcohol

ingesta SF consumption, ingestion (*frm*), intake • **la ~ de alcohol** alcohol consumption • **la ~ diaria de hierro** the daily intake of iron ▸ **ingesta compulsiva** compulsive eating

ingestión SF consumption, ingestion (*frm*) • **~ de fruta** fruit consumption • **~ máxima al día** maximum daily intake • **la ~ de vitamina C parece ser beneficiosa** taking vitamin C seems to be beneficial

Inglaterra SF England • **la batalla de ~** the Battle of Britain (1940)

ingle SF groin

inglés/esa ADJ English • **montar a la inglesa** to ride sidesaddle
SM/F Englishman/Englishwoman • **los ingleses** the English, English people
SM (*Ling*) English

inglesismo SM anglicism

inglete SM (= *ángulo*) angle of 45°; (= *ensambladura*) mitre joint

ingobernabilidad SF [*de aparato*] uncontrollable nature; [*de país, ciudad*] ungovernable nature; [*de embarcación*] unsteerability

ingobernable ADJ [*aparato*] uncontrollable; [*país, ciudad*] ungovernable; [*embarcación*] unsteerable, impossible to steer

ingratitud SF ingratitude

ingrato/a ADJ [*persona*] ungrateful; [*tarea*] thankless, unrewarding; [*sabor*] unpleasant, disagreeable • **¡ingrato!** you're so ungrateful!
SM/F ungrateful person • **¡eres un ~!** you're so ungrateful!

ingravidez SF weightlessness

ingrávido ADJ (= *sin peso*) weightless; (*liter*) (= *ligero*) very light

ingrediente SM **1** [*de comida, compuesto*] ingredient
2 ingredientes (*Arg*) (= *tapas*) appetizers

ingresado/a SM/F **1** (= *enfermo*) patient
2 (= *preso*) prisoner
3 (*Univ*) entrant, new student

ingresar ▷ CONJUG 1a VT **1** (*Esp*) (*Econ*) [+ *dinero, cheque*] to pay in, deposit; [+ *ganancias*] to take • **quería ~ este cheque** I'd like to pay in this cheque *o* to deposit this cheque • **he ingresado 500 euros en mi cuenta/en el banco** I've paid 500 euros into my account/the bank, I've deposited 500 euros in my account/the bank • **se han ingresado 200 dólares en su cuenta** 200 dollars have been credited to your account • **ingresamos unas tres mil libras en las rebajas** we took about three thousand pounds in the sales • **ingresa 2.500 euros al mes** he earns 2,500 euros a month
2 (= *internar*) **a** (*en institución*) • **la ~on en la cárcel hace dos días** she was put in prison *o* sent to prison two days ago • **la cárcel donde están ingresados los terroristas** the prison where the terrorists are being held • **~ a algn en un colegio** to enrol sb in a school, send sb to a school
b (*en hospital*) to admit (**en** to) • **lo ~on en la unidad de cuidados intensivos** he was admitted to the intensive care unit • **un paciente ingresado a consecuencia de una intoxicación** a patient admitted to hospital *o* (*EEUU*) to the hospital as a result of food poisoning • **María continúa ingresada** María is still in hospital
VI **1** (= *entrar*) **a** (*en institución*) to join • **han ingresado 500 nuevos socios en el club** 500 new members have joined the club • **fue la primera mujer que ingresó en** *o* (*LAm*) **a la Academia** she was the first woman to be elected to the Academy *o* to become a member of the Academy • **~ en** *o* (*LAm*) **a la cárcel** to go to prison, be sent to prison • **~ en** *o* (*LAm*) **a un colegio** to enter a school • **~ en el** *o* (*LAm*) **al ejército** to join the army, join up • **ingresó en el ejército británico a los 20 años** he joined the British army at the age of 20 • **~ en** *o* (*LAm*) **a una sociedad** to become a member of a club, join a club

• **~ en** *o* (*LAm*) **a la universidad** to start university, begin one's university studies **b** (*Med*) • **~ cadáver** to be dead on arrival • **~ en el hospital** to be admitted to hospital, be admitted to the hospital (*EEUU*), go into hospital, go into the hospital (*EEUU*) • **falleció poco después de ~ en el hospital** she died shortly after being admitted to hospital, she died shortly after she went into hospital • **el agente se encuentra ingresado en el hospital universitario** the police officer is a patient in the university hospital
2 (*Econ*) [*dinero*] to come in • **el dinero que ingresa en Hacienda** the money which comes into the Treasury • **hoy no ha ingresado mucho en caja** we haven't taken much today
VPR **ingresarse** (*Méx*) (*en club, institución*) to join, become a member; (*en el ejército*) to join up

ingreso SM **1** (= *entrada*) **a** (*en institución*) admission (**en** into) • **el ~ de España en la OTAN** Spain's admission into NATO • **tras su ~ en la Academia** after he joined the Academy, after his admission to the Academy • **después de su ~ en la marina** after he joined the navy • **examen de ~** (*Univ*) entrance examination • **~ en prisión** imprisonment • **el juez ordenó su ~ en prisión** the judge ordered him to be sent to prison, the judge ordered his imprisonment
b (*en hospital*) admission (**en** to) • **ha habido un aumento en el número de ~s** there has been an increase in the number of admissions • **tras su ~ en el hospital** after being admitted to hospital, after his admission to hospital • **¿a qué hora se produjo el ~?** what time was he admitted?
2 (*Econ*) **a** (*Esp*) (= *depósito*) deposit • **¿de cuánto es el ~?** how much are you paying in?, how much are you depositing? • **hacer un ~** to pay in some money, make a deposit
b ingresos [*de persona, empresa*] income (*sing*); [*de país, multinacional*] revenue (*sing*) • **el trabajo es mi única fuente de ~s** work is my only source of income • **las personas con ~s inferiores a 1.000 euros** people with incomes below 1,000 euros • **los ~s del Estado han disminuido este año** State revenue has gone down this year • **~s y gastos** [*de persona, empresa*] income and outgoings, income and expenditure; [*de país, multinacional*] income and expenditure • **~s por algo** revenue from sth • **los ~s por publicidad** advertising revenue, revenue from advertising • **~s por impuestos** tax revenue • **vivir con arreglo a los ~s** to live within one's income ▸ **ingresos anuales** [*de persona, empresa*] annual income (*sing*); [*de país, multinacional*] annual revenue (*sing*) ▸ **ingresos brutos** gross income (*sing*) ▸ **ingresos de taquilla** (*Cine, Teat*) box-office takings; (*Dep*) ticket sales ▸ **ingresos devengados** earned income (*sing*) ▸ **ingresos exentos de impuestos** non-taxable income (*sing*) ▸ **ingresos gravables** taxable income (*sing*) ▸ **ingresos netos** net income (*sing*) ▸ **ingresos personales disponibles** disposable personal income (*sing*)
3 (= *lugar de acceso*) entrance

íngrimo* ADJ • **~ y solo** (*esp LAm*) all alone, completely alone

inguandia SF (*And*) fib, tale

inguinal ADJ inguinal (*frm*), groin (*antes de s*)

INH SM ABR = **Instituto Nacional de Hidrocarburos**

inhábil ADJ **1** [*persona*] (= *torpe*) unskilful, unskillful (*EEUU*), clumsy; (= *incompetente*) incompetent; (= *no apto*) unfit (**para** for, **para hacer algo** to do sth)
2 • **día ~** non-working day • **ese día ha sido declarado ~** that day has been declared a holiday • **en horas ~es** outside office hours • **un mes parlamentariamente ~** a month when parliament is not in session
3 [*testigo*] ineligible

inhabilidad SF (= *torpeza*) unskilfulness, unskillfulness (*EEUU*), clumsiness; (= *incompetencia*) incompetence; (= *incapacidad*) unfitness (**para** for); (*para un cargo*) ineligibility; [*de testigo*] ineligibility

inhabilitación SF **1** (*Pol, Jur*) disqualification
2 (*Med*) disablement; ▹ **nota**

inhabilitar ▹ CONJUG 1a VT **1** (*Pol, Jur*) to disqualify • **el alcalde fue inhabilitado por seis años** the mayor was disqualified *o* barred from holding office for six years • **los funcionarios responsables han sido inhabilitados** the civil servants responsible have been suspended • **~ a algn para algo/hacer algo** to disqualify sb from sth/doing sth
2 (*Med*) to disable, render unfit

inhabitable ADJ uninhabitable

inhabitado ADJ uninhabited

inhabituado ADJ unaccustomed (**a** to)

inhabitual ADJ unusual, out of the ordinary, exceptional

inhalación SF **1** [*de gases*] inhalation • **~ de colas/pegamento** glue-sniffing ▸ **inhalación de humo** smoke inhalation
2 inhalaciones (*Med*) inhalations

inhalador SM inhaler

inhalante SM inhalant

inhalar ▹ CONJUG 1a VT [+ *gases*] to inhale; [+ *cola, pegamento*] to sniff

inherente ADJ inherent (**a** in) • **la función ~ a un oficio** the duties attached to an office

inhibición SF inhibition

inhibidor ADJ inhibiting
SM inhibitor ▸ **inhibidor del apetito** appetite depressant ▸ **inhibidor del crecimiento** growth inhibitor

inhibir ▹ CONJUG 3a VT **1** (= *reprimir*) to inhibit
2 (*Jur*) to restrain, stay
VPR **inhibirse 1** (= *no actuar*) to keep out (**de** of), stay away (**de** from)
2 (= *abstenerse*) to refrain (**de** from)
3 (*Bio, Quím*) to be inhibited

inhibitorio ADJ inhibitory

inhospitalario ADJ inhospitable

inhospitalidad SF inhospitality

inhóspito ADJ inhospitable

inhumación SF burial, interment (*frm*)

inhumanamente ADV (= *de forma no humana*) inhumanly; (= *sin compasión*) uncompassionately

inhumanidad SF inhumanity

inhumano ADJ **1** (= *no humano*) inhuman
2 (= *falto de compasión*) inhumane
3 (*Cono Sur*) dirty, disgusting

inhumar ▹ CONJUG 1a VT to bury, inter (*frm*)

INI SM ABR **1** (*Esp*) (= **Instituto Nacional de Industria**) ≈ National Enterprise Board
2 (*Chile*) = **Instituto Nacional de Investigaciones**

INIA SM ABR **1** (*Esp*) (*Agr*) = **Instituto Nacional de Investigación Agraria**
2 (*Méx*) = **Instituto Nacional de Investigaciones Agrícolas**

iniciación SF **1** (= *comienzo*) beginning
2 (= *introducción*) introduction • **curso de ~** introductory course
3 (*Rel*) initiation • **ceremonia de ~** initiation ceremony • **rito de ~** initiation rite

iniciado/a ADJ initiated
SM/F initiate (*frm*) • **para los ~s/no ~s** for the initiated/the uninitiated

iniciador(a) SM/F [*de plan*] initiator; [*de técnica, práctica*] pioneer
SM [*de bomba*] primer, priming device

inicial ADJ [*posición, velocidad, respuesta*] initial; [*sueldo, alineación*] starting • **capital ~** initial capital, starting capital • **salió a la venta con un precio ~ de tres millones** it went on sale at a starting price of three million
SF **1** (= *letra*) initial
2 (*Caribe*) deposit, down payment

inicialar ▹ CONJUG 1a VT to initial

inicializar ▹ CONJUG 1f VT **1** (= *poner iniciales a*) to initial
2 (*Inform*) to initialize

iniciar ▹ CONJUG 1b VT **1** [+ *actividad*] (= *comenzar*) to begin, start, initiate (*frm*); (= *dar origen a*) to originate; (= *fundar*) to pioneer • **~ la sesión** (*Inform*) to log in, log on
2 (*en conocimientos, secta*) to initiate (**en** into) • **~ a algn en un secreto** to let sb into a secret
VPR **iniciarse 1** (= *comenzar*) to begin, start
2 • **~se como actor/escritor** to start out as an actor/writer, take one's first steps as an actor/writer • **~se como fumador** to start smoking, take up smoking • **~se en política** to start out in politics • **~se en un deporte** to start a new sport

iniciático ADJ • **ritos ~s** initiation rites

iniciativa SF **1** (= *capacidad emprendedora*) initiative • **~ de paz** peace initiative • **bajo su ~** on his initiative • **por ~ propia** on one's own initiative • **carecer de ~** to lack initiative • **tomar la ~** to take the initiative ▸ **iniciativa privada** private enterprise
2 (= *liderazgo*) leadership

inicio SM start, beginning

inicuamente (*frm*) ADV wickedly, iniquitously (*frm*)

inicuo (*frm*) ADJ wicked, iniquitous (*frm*)

inidentificable ADJ unidentifiable

inidentificado ADJ unidentified

inigualable ADJ [*calidad*] unsurpassable; [*belleza, reputación*] matchless; [*oferta, precio*] unbeatable

inigualado ADJ [*fama, récord, duración*] unequalled, unequaled (*EEUU*); [*belleza, encanto*] unparalleled, unrivalled, unrivaled (*EEUU*)

inimaginable ADJ unimaginable, inconceivable

inimaginablemente ADV unimaginably

inimitable ADJ inimitable

inimitablemente ADV inimitably

ininflamable ADJ non-flammable, fire-resistant

ininteligente ADJ unintelligent

ininteligibilidad SF unintelligibility

ininteligible ADJ unintelligible

ininterrumpidamente ADV (= *continuamente*) continuously, without a break; (= *a un ritmo constante*) steadily; (= *sin interrupción*) uninterruptedly • **la canción suena ~ en la radio** the song is played continuously *o* non-stop on the radio • **dos coleccionistas pujaron ~** two collectors bid continuously • **los salarios han crecido ~** salaries have risen steadily • **continúan ~ las tareas de búsqueda** the search continues uninterrupted

ininterrumpido ADJ (= *sin interrupción*) (*gen*) uninterrupted; [*proceso*] continuous; [*progreso*] steady, sustained • **20 horas de música ininterrumpida** 20 hours of non-stop *o* uninterrupted music • **llovió de forma ininterrumpida** it rained continuously *o* non-stop • **la película se**

proyecta de manera ininterrumpida the film is shown uninterrupted *o* without a break
iniquidad SF (= *maldad*) wickedness, iniquity (*frm*); (= *injusticia*) injustice
in itinere ADV (*frm*) • **siniestros ~** accidents which happen on one's way to or from work
injerencia SF interference (**en** in), meddling (**en** in)
injerir ▷ CONJUG 3i VT **1** (= *introducir*) to insert (**en** into), introduce (**en** into)
2 (*Agr*) to graft (**en** on, on to)
VPR **injerirse** to interfere (**en** in), meddle (**en** in)
injertar ▷ CONJUG 1a VT **1** (*Agr, Med*) to graft (**en** on, on to)
2 [+ *vida*] to inject (**en** into)
injerto SM **1** (= *acción*) grafting
2 (*Agr, Med*) graft • **~ de piel** skin graft • **~ de médula ósea** bone marrow transplant • **~ de genes** gene implant
injuria SF **1** (= *insulto*) insult; (*Jur*) slander • **~s** abuse (*sing*), insults • **cubrir/llenar a algn de ~s** to heap abuse on sb • **demandar a algn por ~s** • **presentar una querella por ~s contra algn** to sue sb for slander
2†† (*liter*) (= *daño*) • **las ~s del tiempo** the ravages of time
injuriar ▷ CONJUG 1b VT **1** (= *insultar*) (*gen*) to insult, abuse; (*Jur*) to slander
2†† (*liter*) (= *dañar*) to damage, harm
injuriosamente ADV **1** (= *insultantemente*) insultingly, offensively; (*Jur*) slanderously
2†† (*liter*) (= *de modo dañino*) harmfully
injurioso ADJ **1** (= *insultante*) insulting, offensive; (*Jur*) slanderous
2†† (*liter*) (= *dañino*) harmful, damaging
injustamente ADV (= *con injusticia*) unjustly, unfairly; (= *indebidamente*) wrongfully
injusticia SF (= *falta de justicia*) injustice; (= *falta de equidad*) unfairness • **es una ~** (= *inmerecido*) it's unjust, it's an injustice; (= *no equitativo*) it's unfair • **una solemne ~** a terrible injustice • **con ~** unjustly
injustificable ADJ unjustifiable
injustificadamente ADV unjustifiably
injustificado ADJ unjustified
injusto ADJ [*castigo, crítica*] unjust, unfair; [*detención*] wrongful; [*despido, norma, persona, reparto*] unfair • **ser ~ con algn** to be unfair to sb
INLE SM ABR = **Instituto Nacional del Libro Español**
inllevable ADJ unbearable, intolerable
inmaculado ADJ **1** (= *limpio*) [*baño, cocina*] immaculate, spotless; [*persona, ropa*] immaculate; [*honradez, reputación*] impeccable
2 (*Rel*) • **la Inmaculada (Concepción)** the Immaculate Conception • **María Inmaculada** Immaculate Mary
inmadurez SF immaturity
inmaduro ADJ [*persona*] immature; [*fruta*] unripe
inmancable ADJ (*And, Caribe*) unfailing, infallible
inmanejable ADJ unmanageable
inmanencia SF immanence
inmanente ADJ immanent
inmarchitable ADJ, **inmarcesible** ADJ undying, unfading
inmaterial ADJ immaterial
INME SM ABR = **Instituto Nacional de Moneda Extranjera**
inmediaciones SFPL surrounding area (*sing*), vicinity (*sing*) • **en las ~ del bosque** in the area around the forest, in the vicinity of the forest
inmediata* SF • **la ~** the natural thing, the first thing
inmediatamente ADV **1** (= *al momento*) immediately, at once
2 • **~ de su llegada** immediately after they arrive • **desmoldar ~ de sacarlo del horno** turn out immediately after removing from the oven • **~ de recibido** immediately on receipt
inmediatez SF immediacy
inmediato ADJ **1** (= *sin mediar intervalo*) immediate
2 (= *rápido*) prompt • **de ~** immediately • **en lo ~** • **en el futuro ~** in the immediate future
3 [*lugar*] (= *contiguo*) adjoining; (= *próximo*) neighbouring, neighboring (*EEUU*) • **~ a** close to, next to
inmejorable ADJ (= *excelente*) (*gen*) excellent, superb; [*precio, récord*] unbeatable • **~s recomendaciones** excellent references • **de calidad ~** top-quality
inmejorablemente ADV excellently, superbly • **portarse ~** to behave perfectly
inmemorial ADJ, **inmemorable** ADJ immemorial • **desde tiempo ~** from time immemorial
inmensamente ADV immensely, vastly • **~ rico** immensely rich, enormously wealthy
inmensidad SF immensity, vastness
inmenso ADJ [*llanura, océano, fortuna*] vast, immense; [*objeto, ciudad, número*] enormous; [*alegría, tristeza, esfuerzo*] tremendous, immense; [*talento*] enormous, immense • **la inmensa mayoría** the vast majority • **sentí un ~ vacío tras su muerte** I felt a vast emptiness after his death • **Leonor tiene un corazón ~** Leonor is enormously big-hearted
inmensurable ADJ immeasurable
inmerecidamente ADV undeservedly
inmerecido ADJ, **inmérito** ADJ undeserved
inmergir ▷ CONJUG 3c VT to immerse
inmersión SF **1** (= *sumergimiento*) (*gen*) immersion; [*de buzo*] dive; (*en pesca submarina*) skin-diving, underwater fishing
2 (*Téc, Fot*) • **tanque de ~** immersion tank
3 (*en tema, idioma*) immersion • **periodos de ~ en el extranjero** periods of intensive exposure abroad ▸ **inmersión lingüística** language immersion
inmerso ADJ **1** (= *sumergido*) immersed
2 (*en actividades, ideas*) immersed (**en** in) • **~ en sus meditaciones** deep in thought
inmigración SF immigration
inmigrado/a SM/F immigrant
inmigrante ADJ, SMF immigrant
inmigrar ▷ CONJUG 1a VI to immigrate
inminencia SF imminence
inminente ADJ imminent
inmiscuirse ▷ CONJUG 3g VPR to interfere, meddle (**en** in)
inmisericorde ADJ merciless, pitiless
inmisericordemente ADV mercilessly, pitilessly
inmisericordioso ADJ merciless, pitiless
inmobiliaria SF **1** (= *agencia de venta*) estate agent's, real estate agency (*EEUU*)
2 (= *constructora*) property developer
inmobiliario ADJ real estate (*antes de s*), property (*antes de s*) • **agente ~** estate agent, real estate agent (*EEUU*), realtor (*EEUU*) • **venta inmobiliaria** sale of property
inmobilizador SM immobilizer
inmoderación SF lack of moderation
inmoderadamente ADV immoderately
inmoderado ADJ immoderate
inmodestamente ADV immodestly
inmodestia SF immodesty
inmodesto ADJ immodest
inmodificable ADJ that cannot be modified
inmolación SF sacrifice, immolation (*frm*)
inmolar ▷ CONJUG 1a VT sacrifice, to immolate (*frm*)
inmoral ADJ immoral
inmoralidad SF **1** (= *cualidad*) immorality
2 (= *acto*) immoral act • **es una ~** it's immoral
inmortal ADJ, SMF immortal
inmortalidad SF immortality
inmortalizar ▷ CONJUG 1f VT to immortalize
inmotivación SF lack of motivation
inmotivado ADJ [*acción, asesinato*] motiveless; [*sospecha*] groundless
inmoto ADJ (*frm*) unmoved
inmovible ADJ immovable
inmóvil ADJ (= *quieto*) still, motionless; (= *inamovible*) immovable • **quedar ~** (*gen*) to stand still *o* motionless; (*Aut*) to remain stationary
inmovilidad SF **1** [*de persona*] (= *inamovilidad*) immovability; (= *inactividad*) immobility
2 [*del mar*] stillness
inmovilismo SM (= *estancamiento*) stagnation; (= *oposición al cambio*) resistance to change; (*Pol*) (= *ideología*) ultraconservatism; (= *política*) do-nothing policy
inmovilista ADJ (= *estancado*) stagnant; (= *opuesto al cambio*) resistant to change; (*Pol*) ultraconservative
inmovilización SF **1** [*de persona, vehículo*] immobilization • **~ de vehículos con cepo** vehicle clamping • **~ de coches *o* carros** (*Méx*) traffic jam
2 (= *paralización*) paralysing
inmovilizado SM capital assets (*pl*), fixed assets (*pl*)
inmovilizar ▷ CONJUG 1f VT **1** [+ *persona, vehículo*] to immobilize
2 (= *paralizar*) to paralyse, bring to a standstill
3 (*Econ*) [+ *capital*] to tie up
inmueble ADJ • **bienes ~s** real estate (*sing*), real property (*sing*) (*EEUU*)
SM **1** (= *edificio*) property, building
2 inmuebles (= *bienes*) real estate (*sing*), real property (*sing*) (*EEUU*); (= *edificios*) buildings, properties
inmundicia SF **1** (= *inmoralidad*) filth, dirt • **esto es una ~** this is absolutely disgusting
2 inmundicias (= *basura*) rubbish (*sing*), garbage (*sing*) (*EEUU*)
inmundo ADJ filthy, dirty
inmune ADJ **1** (*Med*) immune (**a** against, to)
2 (= *no afectado*) immune (**a** to) • **~ a las críticas** immune to criticism
3 (= *exento*) exempt (**de** from)
inmunidad SF **1** (*Pol, Med*) immunity ▸ **inmunidad diplomática** diplomatic immunity ▸ **inmunidad parlamentaria** parliamentary immunity
2 (= *exención*) exemption
inmunitario ADJ immune • **respuesta inmunitaria** immune response • **sistema ~** immune system
inmunización SF immunization
inmunizar ▷ CONJUG 1f VT to immunize
inmunocomprometido ADJ immunocompromised
inmunodefensivo ADJ • **sistema ~** immune defence system
inmunodeficiencia SF immunodeficiency
inmunodeficiente ADJ immunodeficient
inmunodepresor (*Med*) ADJ immunosuppressive, immunodepressive
SM immunosuppressant, immunodepressant

inmunodeprimido (ADJ) immunodeficient
inmunología (SF) immunology
inmunológico (ADJ) immune • **sistema ~** immune system • **tolerancia inmunológica** immunological tolerance • **instituto ~** immunology institute
inmunólogo/a (SM/F) immunologist
inmunorreacción (SF) immune reaction
inmunorrespuesta (SF) immune response
inmunosupresivo (ADJ), (SM) immunosuppressive
inmunosupresor (ADJ) immunosuppressive
(SM) immunosuppressant
inmunoterapia (SF) immunotherapy
inmutabilidad (SF) immutability
inmutable (ADJ) [*principio, sociedad*] unchanging; [*persona*] impassive • **aguantó ~ los insultos** she took the insults impassively
inmutablemente (ADV) (= *sin variar*) unchangingly
inmutarse ▸ CONJUG 1a (VPR) to get perturbed, get worked up • **ni se inmutó** he didn't bat an eyelid, he didn't turn a hair • **siguió sin ~** he carried on unperturbed • **las cosas van mal, pero ¿quién se inmuta?** things are going badly, but who's worrying o bothered?
innato (ADJ) innate, inborn
innatural (ADJ) unnatural
innavegable (ADJ) [*río, canal*] unnavigable; [*barco*] unseaworthy
innecesariamente (ADV) unnecessarily
innecesario (ADJ) unnecessary
innegable (ADJ) undeniable
innegablemente (ADV) undeniably
innegociable (ADJ) non-negotiable
innoble (ADJ) ignoble
innocuo (ADJ) = **inocuo**
innombrable (ADJ) unmentionable
innominado (ADJ) nameless, unnamed
innovación (SF) innovation
innovador(a) (ADJ) innovative
(SM/F) innovator
innovar ▸ CONJUG 1a (VT) to introduce
(VI) to innovate
innovativo (ADJ) innovative, innovatory
innumerable (ADJ), **innúmero** (ADJ) countless, innumerable
inobediencia (SF) disobedience
inobediente (ADJ) disobedient
inobjetable (ADJ) [*declaración, victoria*] indisputable; [*método, trabajo*] unobjectionable; [*origen*] undisputed; [*liderazgo*] unassailable; [*fuente, honradez*] unimpeachable; [*comportamiento*] impeccable
inobservado (ADJ) unobserved
inobservancia (SF) [*de norma*] non-observance; [*de obligaciones*] neglect; [*de ley*] violation, breaking
inocencia (SF) [*de acusado*] innocence; (= *ingenuidad*) innocence, naïveté
Inocencio (SM) Innocent
inocentada (SF) **1** practical joke, April Fool joke; ▸ DÍA DE LOS (SANTOS) INOCENTES
2 (= *simpleza*) (= *dicho*) naïve remark; (= *error*) blunder
inocente¹ (ADJ) **1** (= *sin culpa*) innocent (**de** of); (*Jur*) not guilty, innocent • **fueron declarados ~s** they were found not guilty • **siempre se ha declarado ~** he has always pleaded his innocence
2 (= *ingenuo*) naïve
3 (= *inofensivo*) harmless
(SMF) **1** (= *ingenuo*) innocent person
2 (= *bobo*) simpleton • **el día de los (Santos) Inocentes** ≈ April Fools' Day, ≈ All Fools' Day

> **DÍA DE LOS (SANTOS) INOCENTES**
> 28 December, **el día de los (Santos) Inocentes**, is when the Catholic Church in Spain commemorates the New Testament story of King Herod's slaughter of the innocent children of Judaea. On this day Spaniards play practical jokes or **inocentadas** on each other, much as we do on April Fools' Day. A typical example is sticking a **monigote**, a cut-out paper figure, on someone's back. Whenever someone falls for a trick, the practical joker cries out **"¡Inocente!"**

inocente² (SM) **1** (*And, Cono Sur*) avocado pear
2 (*And*) masquerade
inocentemente (ADV) innocently
inocentón/ona* (ADJ) gullible, naïve
(SM/F) simpleton
inocuidad (SF) harmlessness, innocuousness (*frm*)
inoculación (SF) inoculation
inocular ▸ CONJUG 1a (VT) **1** (*Med*) to inoculate (**contra** against, **de** with)
2 [+ *idea, característica*] to inject • **inocula a sus personajes una gran profundidad** he injects a great deal of depth into his characters • **inoculó a los franceses la doctrina de la soberanía del pueblo** he infused the French with the doctrine of the sovereignty of the people
3 (= *pervertir*) to corrupt (**de** with), contaminate (**de** with)
inocuo (ADJ) innocuous, harmless
inodoro (ADJ) odourless, odorless (*EEUU*)
(SM) toilet, lavatory ▸ **inodoro químico** chemical toilet
inofensivamente (ADV) harmlessly
inofensivo (ADJ) inoffensive, harmless
inoficioso* (ADJ) (*LAm*) useless
inolvidable (ADJ) unforgettable
inolvidablemente (ADV) unforgettably
inope† (ADJ) impecunious, indigent
inoperable (ADJ) **1** (*Med*) inoperable
2 [*aparato, vehículo*] inoperative
3 [*plan, sistema*] unworkable
inoperancia (SF) **1** [*de plan*] inoperative character
2 [*de autoridades, policía*] ineffectiveness
3 (*LAm*) (= *inutilidad*) uselessness, fruitlessness
inoperante (ADJ) **1** (= *inviable*) [*plan*] inoperative; [*decisión*] ineffective
2 (*LAm*) (= *inútil*) useless, fruitless; (= *inactivo*) inactive, out of use
inopia (SF) indigence, poverty • MODISMO: • **estar en la ~** (= *no saber*) to be in the dark, have no idea; (= *estar despistado*) to be dreaming, be far away
inopinadamente (ADV) unexpectedly
inopinado (ADJ) unexpected
inoportunamente (ADV) **1** (= *a destiempo*) inopportunely, at a bad time
2 (= *causando molestia*) inconveniently
3 (= *de modo impropio*) inappropriately
inoportunidad (SF) **1** [*de momento*] inopportuneness, untimeliness
2 (= *molestia*) inconvenience
3 [*de comportamiento, comentario*] inappropriateness
inoportuno (ADJ) **1** [*momento*] inopportune, untimely
2 (= *molesto*) inconvenient
3 [*comportamiento, comentario*] inappropriate
inorgánico (ADJ) inorganic
inoxidable (ADJ) (*gen*) rustproof; [*acero*] stainless
inquebrantable (ADJ) [*fe*] unshakeable, unyielding; [*fidelidad, lealtad*] unswerving; [*entusiasmo*] undying; [*unidad, voluntad*] unbreakable; [*salud*] robust, stout
inquietador (ADJ) = **inquietante**
inquietamente (ADV) **1** (= *con preocupación*) anxiously, worriedly
2 (= *agitadamente*) restlessly
inquietante (ADJ) worrying, disturbing
inquietantemente (ADV) worryingly, disturbingly
inquietar ▸ CONJUG 1a (VT) to worry
(VPR) **inquietarse** to worry • **¡no te inquietes!** don't worry!
inquieto (ADJ) **1** (= *preocupado*) anxious, worried • **estar ~ por algo** to be anxious about sth, be worried about sth
2 (= *agitado*) restless, unsettled
inquietud (SF) **1** (= *preocupación*) concern • **expresaron su ~ por el futuro de sus hijos** they expressed their concern for their children's future • **los rumores han provocado ~ entre los inversores** the rumours have aroused concern among investors • **aumenta la ~ por la proliferación de armas nucleares** concern is growing over the proliferation of nuclear weapons • **esperaban su llamada con ~** they anxiously awaited her call
2 (= *interés*) interest • **mi hijo no tiene ninguna ~** my son isn't interested in anything, my son has no interest in anything • **es persona de ~es culturales** she has an interest in culture, she has cultural interests
inquilinaje (SM) **1** (*Cono Sur*) = **inquilinato**
2 (*Méx*) tenants (*pl*)
inquilinato (SM) **1** (= *arrendamiento*) tenancy; (*Jur*) lease, leasehold • **contrato de ~** tenancy agreement
2 (= *alquiler*) rent • **impuesto de ~** rates (*pl*)
3 (*Arg, Col, Uru*) (= *edificio*) tenement house; (*pey*) slum
inquilino/a (SM/F) (= *arrendatario*) tenant; (*Com*) lessee; (*Chile*) (*Agr*) tenant farmer • **~ de renta antigua** long-standing tenant, protected tenant
inquina (SF) (= *aversión*) dislike, aversion; (= *rencor*) ill will • **tener ~ a algn** to have a grudge against sb, have it in for sb*
inquiridor(a) (ADJ) inquiring
(SM/F) (= *que pregunta*) inquirer; (= *investigador*) investigator
inquiriente (SMF) inquirer
inquirir ▸ CONJUG 3i (VT) to investigate, look into
(VI) to inquire • **~ sobre algo** to make inquiries about sth, inquire into sth
inquisición (SF) **1** (= *indagación*) inquiry, investigation
2 (*Hist*) ▸ **la (Santa) Inquisición** the (Spanish) Inquisition
inquisidor (SM) inquisitor
inquisitivamente (ADV) inquisitively
inquisitivo (ADJ) inquisitive, curious
inquisitorial (ADJ) inquisitorial
inrayable (ADJ) scratch-proof
INRI (ABR) INRI
inri (SM) • **para más ~*** to make matters worse
insaciable (ADJ) insatiable
insaciablemente (ADV) insatiably
insalubre (ADJ) (= *insano*) (*gen*) unhealthy, insalubrious (*frm*); [*condiciones*] insanitary
insalubridad (SF) unhealthiness
INSALUD (SM ABR) (*Esp*), **Insalud** (SM ABR) (*Esp*) = **Instituto Nacional de la Salud**
insalvable (ADJ) insuperable
insanable (ADJ) incurable
insania (SF) insanity
insano (ADJ) **1** (= *loco*) insane, mad
2 (= *malsano*) unhealthy

insatisfacción SF dissatisfaction

insatisfactorio ADJ unsatisfactory

insatisfecho ADJ [*condición, deseo*] unsatisfied; [*persona*] dissatisfied

insaturado ADJ unsaturated

inscribir ▸ CONJUG 3a (PP: **inscrito**) VT
1 (= *grabar*) [+ *nombre, iniciales*] to inscribe (**en** on) • **el anillo tenía inscrita la fecha de su boda** the ring had the date of the wedding inscribed on it
2 (= *apuntar*) **a** [+ *persona*] (*en lista*) to put down; (*en colegio, curso*) to enrol, enroll (*EEUU*) • **he inscrito mi nombre en la lista** I've put my name down on the list
b (*Jur*) [+ *contrato, nacimiento*] to register • **~ en el registro** to enter in the register, register • **todos los nacimientos están inscritos en el registro** all births are entered in the register, all births are registered • **hemos inscrito la casa en el registro de la propiedad** we've had the house registered
c • **~ algo en el orden del día** to put sth on the agenda
3 (*Mat*) [+ *figura, polígono*] to inscribe
VPR **inscribirse 1** (= *apuntarse*) (*en colegio, curso*) to enrol, enroll (EEUU), register; (*en partido político*) to join; (*en concurso, competición*) to enter; (*en lista*) to put one's name down, register • **todos los participantes deben ~se antes del 1 de mayo** all participants should enrol *o* register before 1 May • **me he inscrito en el concurso de cuentos** I've entered the story-writing competition • **de los 25 equipos inscritos, solo se presentaron 14** of the 25 teams on the list, only 14 turned up • **~se en el censo electoral** to register o.s. on the electoral roll • **me he inscrito en el censo de residentes extranjeros** I've registered (myself) as a foreign resident • **~se en el registro** [*pareja*] to sign the marriage register
2 (= *incluirse*) • **~se dentro de** *o* **en** [+ *movimiento, tradición*] to fall within; [+ *clasificación*] to be classed among • **la novela se inscribe dentro de la tradición del realismo mágico** the novel falls within the tradition of magic realism • **esta pieza se inscribe en la línea de los grandes oratorios de la época** this piece can be classed among the great oratorios of the period • **esta reunión se inscribe en el marco de un ciclo de conferencias** this meeting forms part of a series of lectures • **la política del gobierno se inscribe dentro de un marco europeo** the government's policy follows the European framework

inscripción SF **1** (= *texto grabado*) (*gen*) inscription; (*Tip*) lettering
2 (= *acto*) (*en concurso*) entry; (*en curso*) enrolment, enrollment (EEUU); (*en congreso*) registration • **las inscripciones deberán realizarse entre el 1 y el 5 de marzo** those interested should enrol *o* (EEUU) enroll between 1 and 5 March, enrolment will take place from 1 to 5 March • **el plazo de ~ en el curso finaliza el día 3 de mayo** course applications will be accepted until 3 May, the closing date *o* deadline for enrolment on the course is 3 May • **~ en el censo electoral** registration on the electoral roll • **~ en el registro** registration; ▸ **boletín**

inscripto (*Arg*) PP *de* **inscribir**

inscrito/a PP *de* **inscribir**
ADJ (*Mat*) inscribed • **el triángulo queda ~ dentro de la circunferencia** the triangle is inscribed within the circumference
SM/F (= *persona registrada*) • **el 25% de los ~s en el censo** 25% of those registered on the census • **hemos alcanzado la cifra de doscientos ~s para el concurso** more than two hundred entries have been received for the competition

insecticida SM insecticide

insectívoro ADJ insectivorous

insecto SM insect

inseguridad SF **1** (= *peligro*) lack of safety ▸ **inseguridad ciudadana** lack of safety in the streets, decline in law and order
2 (= *falta de confianza*) insecurity
3 (= *falta de estabilidad*) unsteadiness
4 (= *incertidumbre*) uncertainty ▸ **inseguridad laboral** lack of job security

inseguro ADJ **1** (= *peligroso*) [*zona, negocio, conducción*] unsafe
2 (= *sin confianza*) insecure • **se sienten ~s** they feel insecure
3 (= *sin estabilidad*) [*paso, estructura*] unsteady
4 (= *incierto*) [*clima*] unpredictable; [*persona*] uncertain, unsure (**de** about, of); [*futuro*] insecure

inseminación SF insemination ▸ **inseminación artificial** artificial insemination

inseminar ▸ CONJUG 1a VT to inseminate

insensatez SF foolishness, stupidity • **cometieron la ~ de no negociar** they were foolish *o* stupid enough not to negotiate • **lo que propones es una ~** what you are proposing is foolish *o* stupid • **dice unas insensateces increíbles** he says such foolish *o* stupid things

insensato ADJ foolish, stupid

insensibilidad SF **1** (= *indiferencia*) insensitivity, unfeeling nature
2 (*Med*) (= *falta de conocimiento*) insensibility, unconsciousness; (= *entumecimiento*) numbness

insensibilizar ▸ CONJUG 1f VT **1** [+ *persona*] (*ante emociones, problemas*) to render insensitive; (*ante sufrimiento*) to render unfeeling
2 (*Med*) (= *anestesiar*) to anaesthetize, anesthetize (EEUU); (*a alérgenos*) to desensitize

insensible ADJ **1** [*persona*] (= *indiferente*) insensitive (**a** to); (= *no afectado*) unaffected (**a** by)
2 [*cambio*] imperceptible
3 (*Med*) (= *inconsciente*) insensible, unconscious; (= *entumecido*) numb

insensiblemente ADV imperceptibly

inseparable ADJ inseparable

inseparablemente ADV inseparably

insepulto ADJ unburied • **funeral** *o* **misa (de) corpore ~** funeral mass

inserción SF insertion

INSERSO SM ABR (*Esp*), **Inserso** SM ABR (*Esp*) = **Instituto Nacional de Servicios Sociales**

insertable ADJ plug-in

insertar ▸ CONJUG 1a VT to insert

inserto ADJ • **problemas en los que está ~ el gobierno** problems with which the government finds itself involved
SM insert

inservible ADJ (= *inútil*) useless; (= *averiado*) out of order

insidia SF **1** (= *trampa*) snare, trap
2 (= *acto*) malicious act
3 (= *mala intención*) maliciousness

insidiosamente ADV (= *engañando*) insidiously; (= *a traición*) treacherously

insidioso ADJ (= *engañoso*) insidious, deceptive; (= *traicionero*) treacherous

insigne ADJ (= *distinguido*) distinguished; (= *famoso*) famous

insignia SF **1** (= *distintivo*) badge, button (EEUU), emblem • **luce la ~ del club** he is sporting the club's badge *o* emblem
2 (= *estandarte*) flag, banner; (*Náut*) pennant
3 insignias [*de dignidad, poder*] insignia

insignificancia SF **1** (*cualidad*) insignificance
2 (= *cosa insignificante*) trifle

insignificante ADJ [*asunto, cantidad, detalle, accidente*] insignificant, trivial; [*persona*] insignificant

insinceridad SF insincerity

insincero ADJ insincere

insinuación SF insinuation • **hacer insinuaciones sobre algo** to make insinuations about sth, drop hints about sth • **insinuaciones eróticas/amorosas** sexual/amorous advances

insinuador ADJ insinuating

insinuante ADJ **1** (= *sugerente*) [*tono, movimiento*] insinuating; [*mirada, insinuación, ropa*] suggestive
2 (= *zalamero*) ingratiating
3 (= *taimado*) cunning, crafty

insinuar ▸ CONJUG 1e VT **1** (= *sugerir*) to insinuate, hint at • **~ que ...** to insinuate *o* imply that ...
2 • **~ una observación** to slip in a comment
3 • **~ una sonrisa** to give the hint of a smile
VPR **insinuarse 1** (= *entreverse*) to begin to appear
2 • **~se a algn** to make advances to sb
3 • **~se con algn** to ingratiate o.s. with sb
4 • **~se en algo** (= *introducirse*) to worm one's way into sth • **~se en el ánimo de algn** to work one's way gradually into sb's mind

insipidez SF [*de comida*] insipidness, tastelessness; [*de espectáculo, persona*] dullness, tediousness

insípido ADJ [*comida*] insipid, tasteless; [*espectáculo, persona*] dull, tedious

insistencia SF [*de persona*] insistence (**en** on); [*de quejas*] persistence • **a ~ de** at the insistence of • **se repite con ~ machacona** it is repeated with wearisome insistence

insistente ADJ [*persona*] insistent; [*quejas*] persistent

insistentemente ADV (*gen*) insistently; [*pedir, quejarse*] persistently

insistir ▸ CONJUG 3a VI **1** (= *perseverar*) • **bueno, si insistes** all right, if you insist • **insistió en que se trataba de un error** she insisted that it was a mistake, she was adamant that it was a mistake • **insistió en que nos quedásemos a cenar** she insisted that we should stay to supper • **insisto en que todos abandonen la sala** I insist that everyone leave *o* leaves the room • **no insistas, que no pienso ir** don't keep on about it because I'm not going • **yo le decía que no, pero él insistía** I said no, but he kept on and on about it • **insiste y al final lo conseguirás** keep at it and you'll get there in the end • **si no te contestan, insiste** if they don't answer, keep trying • **insistieron en casarse en junio** they were adamant that they should get married in June
2 (= *enfatizar*) • **~ en** *o* **sobre algo** to stress *o* emphasize sth

in situ ADV on the spot, in situ (*frm*)

insobornable ADJ incorruptible

insociabilidad SF unsociability

insociable ADJ unsociable

insolación SF **1** (*Med*) sunstroke • **coger una ~** to get sunstroke
2 (*Meteo*) sunshine • **horas de ~** hours of sunshine • **la ~ media diaria es de ...** the average hours of daily sunshine is ...

insolar ▸ CONJUG 1a VT to expose to the sun, put in the sun
VPR **insolarse** to get sunstroke

insolencia SF insolence • **lo que han hecho me parece una ~** I think what they did was really rude

insolentarse ▷ CONJUG 1a VPR to become insolent, become rude • ~ **con algn** to be insolent to sb, be rude to sb

insolente ADJ **1** (= *descarado*) insolent, rude
2 (= *altivo*) haughty, contemptuous

insolentemente ADV **1** (= *con descaro*) insolently, rudely
2 (= *con altivez*) haughtily, contemptuously

insolidaridad SF lack of solidarity

insolidario ADJ unsupportive • **hacerse ~ de algo** to dissociate o.s. from sth

insolidarizarse ▷ CONJUG 1f VPR • ~ **con algo** to dissociate oneself from sth

insólitamente ADV unusually, unwontedly (*frm*)

insólito ADJ unusual, unwonted (*frm*)

insolubilidad SF insolubility

insoluble ADJ insoluble

insolvencia SF insolvency, bankruptcy

insolvente ADJ insolvent, bankrupt

insomne ADJ sleepless, insomniac
SMF insomniac

insomnio SM sleeplessness, insomnia

insondable ADJ [*abismo, mar*] bottomless; [*misterio*] unfathomable (*liter*), impenetrable

insonorización SF soundproofing

insonorizado ADJ soundproof • **estar ~** to be soundproofed

insonorizar ▷ CONJUG 1f VT to soundproof

insonoro ADJ noiseless, soundless

insoportable ADJ unbearable, intolerable

insoportablemente ADV unbearably, intolerably

insoria SF (*Caribe*) insignificant thing • **una ~** a minimal amount

insoslayable ADJ unavoidable

insoslayablemente ADV unavoidably

insospechable ADJ beyond suspicion

insospechado ADJ unsuspected

insostenible ADJ untenable

inspección SF (= *revisión*) inspection, examination; (= *control*) check ▸ **la Inspección de Hacienda** ≈ Inland Revenue, ≈ Internal Revenue Service (*EEUU*) • **nos amenazan con una ~ de Hacienda** we have been threatened with a tax inspection, they have threatened us with an Inland Revenue inspection ▸ **Inspección de Trabajo** ≈ Industrial Relations Commission ▸ **inspección médica** medical examination ▸ **inspección ocular** visual inspection *o* examination ▸ **inspección técnica de vehículos** roadworthiness test, ≈ MOT test

inspeccionar ▷ CONJUG 1a VT (= *examinar*) to inspect; (= *controlar*) to check; (= *supervisar*) to supervise; (*Inform*) to peek

inspector(a) SM/F **1** (*gen*) inspector; (= *supervisor*) supervisor ▸ **inspector(a) de aduanas** customs officer ▸ **inspector(a) de enseñanza** school inspector ▸ **inspector(a) de Hacienda** tax inspector ▸ **inspector(a) de policía** police inspector
2 (*Cono Sur*) [*de autobús*] conductor

inspectorado SM inspectorate

inspiración SF **1** [*de artista*] inspiration • **le vino la ~ para componer la canción** she got the inspiration to compose the song • **ballets de ~ española** Spanish-inspired ballets • **chaqueta de ~ náutica** a sailor-style jacket
2 (*Med*) inhalation

inspirado ADJ inspired • **el poeta estaba poco ~** the poet was not very inspired, the poet was uninspired

inspirador/a ADJ inspiring, inspirational
SM/F (= *que da idea*) inspirer; (= *creador*) creator, originator

inspirar ▷ CONJUG 1a VT **1** [+ *artista*] to inspire • **eso no inspira confianza al consumidor** that does not inspire confidence in the consumer • **prefiero ~ respeto a ~ miedo** I prefer to inspire respect rather than instill fear
2 (*Med*) to inhale, breathe in
VPR **inspirarse** • ~**se en algo** to be inspired by sth, find inspiration in sth

inspirativo ADJ [*discurso*] inspirational

INSS SM ABR (*Esp*) = **Instituto Nacional de Seguridad Social**

Inst. ABR, **Instº** ABR = **Instituto**

instalación SF **1** (= *conexión*) [*de equipo, luz*] installation • **el técnico se encargará de hacer la ~ eléctrica** the technician will put in the electrics *o* (*frm*) take care of the electrical installation
2 (= *montaje*) [*de oficina, fábrica*] setting up; [*de tienda de campaña*] pitching
3 (= *equipo*) [*de luz, gas*] system • **han venido a arreglar la ~ de la luz** they've come to mend the electrical system *o* the wiring ▸ **instalación de fuerza** power plant ▸ **instalación eléctrica** electricity system, wiring ▸ **instalación sanitaria** sanitation facilities (*pl*)
4 instalaciones: a (= *recinto*) installations • **durante su recorrido por las instalaciones del museo** during her visit round the museum
b (= *servicios*) facilities • **el centro deportivo cuenta con excelentes instalaciones** the sports centre has excellent facilities ▸ **instalaciones deportivas** (= *recinto*) sports grounds; (= *servicios*) sports facilities ▸ **instalaciones portuarias** harbour installations ▸ **instalaciones recreativas** (= *recinto*) recreational areas; (= *servicios*) recreational facilities
5 (*Arte*) installation

instalador(a) ADJ [*empresa, persona*] installation (*antes de s*) • **el técnico ~** the installation engineer
SM/F fitter ▸ **instalador(a) electricista, instalador(a) eléctrico/a** electrician ▸ **instalador(a) sanitario/a** plumber

instalar ▷ CONJUG 1a VT **1** (= *conectar*) [+ *calefacción, teléfono*] to install, instal (*EEUU*); [+ *luz, gas*] to connect, connect up, put in; [+ *antena*] to put up, erect (*frm*); [+ *lavadora, lavaplatos*] to install, instal (*EEUU*), plumb in; [+ *ordenador, vídeo*] to set up; [+ *sistema de control*] to install, instal (*EEUU*), put into operation; [+ *sistema operativo*] to install, instal (*EEUU*) • **¿te han instalado ya el teléfono?** have you had the phone put in yet?, are you on the phone yet? • **hemos instalado un nuevo sistema de vigilancia** we've installed a new security system, we've put a new security system into operation • **ya tenemos instalado el lavaplatos** the dishwasher is in now • **he tenido que ~ una batería nueva en el coche** I've had to put a new battery in the car
2 (= *montar*) [+ *consulta, oficina*] to set up, open; [+ *campamento, fábrica, espectáculo, exposición*] to set up; [+ *tienda de campaña*] to pitch • **la primera galería de arte que se instala en la ciudad** the first art gallery to be opened in town • **la escultura fue instalada en el centro del escenario** the sculpture was erected in the middle of the stage
3 [+ *persona*] to put, install • **lo instaló en el cuarto de invitados** she put *o* installed him in the guest room • **el ejército lo instaló en el poder** the army put him into power
VPR **instalarse** • ~**se en** [+ *casa, oficina*] to settle into; [+ *ciudad*] to set up home in, settle in; [+ *país*] to settle in • **cuando estemos ya instalados os invitaremos a cenar** when we're settled in, we'll invite you round for dinner • **¿cuándo os ~éis en las nuevas oficinas?** when are you moving to the new offices? • **en 1940 me instalé definitivamente en España** in 1940 I settled in Spain for good • **me instalé en el sofá y de allí no me moví** I sat *o* settled myself down on the sofa and didn't move from there • ~**se en el poder** to take power, get into power • **el partido ha conseguido ~se en el poder** the party has managed to take power *o* get into power • **el general se instaló en el poder tras el golpe de estado** the general took power after the coup d'état

instancia SF **1** (= *solicitud*) application, request; (*Jur*) petition • **a ~(s) de algn** at the request of sb, at sb's request • **pedir algo con ~** to demand sth insistently, demand sth urgently
2 (= *formulario*) application form
3 (= *momento*) • **de primera ~** first of all • **en última ~** (= *como último recurso*) as a last resort; (= *en definitiva*) in the last analysis
4 (*Pol*) (= *autoridad*) authority; (= *organismo*) agency • **altas ~s** high authorities ▸ **instancias del poder** corridors of power ▸ **instancias internacionales** international authorities

instantánea SF **1** (*Fot*) snap, snapshot
2‡ tart‡, whore

instantáneamente ADV instantaneously, instantly

instantáneo ADJ [*respuesta, comunicación*] instantaneous; [*acceso, éxito, fracaso*] instant (*antes de s*) • **café ~** instant coffee • **la bala le produjo la muerte instantánea** the bullet killed him instantly

instante SM moment, instant • **se detuvo un ~** he stopped for a moment • **al ~** right now, at once • **(a) cada ~** all the time, every single moment • **en un ~** in a flash • **en ese** *o* **aquel mismo ~** at that precise moment • **hace un ~** a moment ago • **por ~s** incessantly

instantemente ADV insistently, urgently

instar ▷ CONJUG 1a VT to urge, press • ~ **a algn a hacer algo** • ~ **a algn para que haga algo** to urge sb to do sth • **me instó a que hablase** he urged me to speak
VI to be urgent, be pressing

instauración SF **1** (= *establecimiento*) establishment, setting-up
2 (= *renovación*) restoration, renewal

instaurar ▷ CONJUG 1a VT **1** (= *establecer*) to establish, set up
2 (= *renovar*) to restore, renew

insti* SM (= *instituto*) ≈ secondary school (*Brit*), ≈ high school (*EEUU*)

instigación SF instigation • **a ~ de algn** at the instigation of sb, at sb's instigation

instigador(a) SM/F instigator ▸ **instigador(a) de un delito** instigator of a crime; (*Jur*) accessory before the fact

instigar ▷ CONJUG 1h VT to incite • ~ **a algn a hacer algo** to incite *o* induce sb to do sth • ~ **a la sublevación** to incite to riot

instilar ▷ CONJUG 1a VT to instil, instill (*EEUU*) (**en** into)

instintivamente ADV instinctively

instintivo ADJ instinctive

instinto SM **1** (*de conducta*) (*gen*) instinct • **por ~** instinctively ▸ **instinto asesino, instinto de matar** killer instinct ▸ **instinto de supervivencia** survival instinct ▸ **instinto maternal** maternal instinct ▸ **instinto sexual** sexual urge
2 (= *impulso*) impulse, urge

institución SF **1** (= *organismo*) institution • **instituciones hospitalarias** hospitals • **un inspector de instituciones penitenciarias** an inspector of prisons • **esa tienda es toda una ~ en la ciudad** that shop is something of an institution in the city ▸ **institución**

benéfica, institución de beneficencia charitable foundation, charitable organization ▸ **institución pública** public institution, public body
2 (= *acción*) establishment
3 instituciones (*en nación, sociedad*) institutions

institucional ADJ institutional

institucionalizado ADJ institutionalized

institucionalizar ▷ CONJUG 1f VT to institutionalize
VPR **institucionalizarse** to become institutionalized

institucionalmente ADV institutionally

instituir ▷ CONJUG 3g VT **1** (= *establecer*) [+ *ley, reforma*] to institute, establish; [+ *costumbre, norma, premio*] to establish
2 (= *fundar*) to found, set up

instituto SM **1** (= *organismo*) institute, institution • **~ financiero** financial institution • **los ~s armados** the army, the military • **el benemérito ~** the Civil Guard ▸ **instituto de belleza** (*Esp*) beauty parlour, beauty parlor (*EEUU*) ▸ **Instituto de la Mujer** Institute of Women's Affairs ▸ **Instituto Nacional de Empleo** ≈ Department of Employment ▸ **Instituto Nacional de Industria** (*Esp*) (*Hist*) ≈ Board of Trade
2 (*Esp*) (*Educ*) ≈ secondary school (*Brit*), ≈ high school (*EEUU*) • **nos conocemos desde que íbamos al ~** we've known each other since we were at secondary school together ▸ **Instituto de Enseñanza Secundaria** (*Hist*) ≈ (state) secondary school (*Brit*), ≈ high school (*EEUU*) ▸ **Instituto Nacional de Bachillerato** ≈ (state) secondary school (*Brit*), ≈ high school (*EEUU*)
3 (= *regla*) (*gen*) principle, rule; (*Rel*) rule

institutriz SF governess

instrucción SF **1** (*Educ*) education • **recibió su ~ musical en Viena** he received his musical education in Vienna • **una persona de vasta ~** a highly educated person • **tener poca ~ en algo** to have a limited knowledge of sth ▸ **instrucción primaria** primary education ▸ **instrucción programada** programmed teaching ▸ **instrucción pública** state education
2 (*Mil*) (= *período*) training; (= *ejercicio*) drill • **hizo la ~ en Almería** he did his military training in Almería • **los soldados estaban haciendo la ~ en el patio** the soldiers were being drilled in the courtyard • **un vuelo de ~** a training flight ▸ **instrucción militar** military training
3 (*Dep*) coaching, training
4 (*Jur*) (*tb* **instrucción del sumario**) preliminary investigation; ▷ **juez, juzgado**
5 (*Inform*) statement
6 instrucciones (= *indicaciones*) instructions • **de acuerdo con tus instrucciones** in accordance with your instructions • **seguí sus instrucciones al pie de la letra** I followed her instructions to the letter • **recibir instrucciones** to receive instructions *o* orders; (*Mil*) to be briefed • **hemos recibido instrucciones de no decir nada** we've received instructions *o* orders to say nothing ▸ **instrucciones de funcionamiento** operating instructions ▸ **instrucciones de uso, instrucciones para el uso** directions for use

instructivo ADJ **1** (= *educativo*) educational
2 (= *revelador*) [*conclusión, reunión*] enlightening; [*ejemplo*] instructive

instructor(a) ADJ [*cabo, sargento*] training; [*fiscal, juez*] examining
SM/F **1** (*Dep*) coach, trainer ▸ **instructor(a) de vuelo** flight instructor
2 (*Mil*) instructor
3 (*Jur*) examining magistrate ▸ **instructor(a) de diligencias** *judge appointed to look into a case*

instruido ADJ **1** (= *educado*) well-educated • **estar ~ en algo** to be educated in sth
2 (= *informado*) well-informed

instruir ▷ CONJUG 3g VT **1** (= *formar*) **a** (*Educ*) [+ *estudiante*] to instruct; [+ *profesional*] to train • **he sido instruido para ejercer como abogado** I have been trained as a lawyer • **~ a algn en algo** to instruct sb in sth, train sb in sth • **me instruyeron en el manejo del fusil** I was taught how to use a gun • **fuimos instruidos en el arte del engaño** we were taught the art of deception, we were instructed *o* trained in the art of deception
b (*Dep*) to coach, train
c (*Mil*) to train
2 (*Jur*) (= *tramitar*) [+ *caso, causa*] to try, hear • **el juez que instruye la causa** the judge who is trying *o* hearing the case • **~ las diligencias** *o* **el sumario** to institute proceedings
VI (= *enseñar*) • **la experiencia instruye mucho** experience is a great teacher • **juegos que instruyen** educational games • **el viajar instruye mucho** travel broadens the mind • **ya lo he instruido de nuestros proyectos** I've already explained our plans to him • **este libro los ~á con detalle sobre el modo de hacerlo** this book will give you detailed information *o* instructions (on *o* about) how to do it
VPR **instruirse** to learn, teach o.s. (**de** about)

instrumentación SF orchestration, scoring

instrumental ADJ **1** (*Mús*) instrumental
2 (*Jur*) • **prueba ~** documentary evidence
SM **1** (= *conjunto de instrumentos*) instruments (*pl*), set of instruments • **el ~ de laboratorio** the laboratory instruments • **el ~ quirúrgico** the surgical instruments
2 (*Ling*) instrumental, instrumental case

instrumentalista SMF instrumentalist

instrumentalización SF exploitation

instrumentalizar ▷ CONJUG 1f VT **1** (= *llevar a cabo*) to carry out
2 • **~ a algn** (= *utilizar*) to use sb as a tool, make cynical use of sb; (= *explotar*) to exploit sb, manipulate sb

instrumentar ▷ CONJUG 1a VT **1** (*Mús*) to score, orchestrate • **está instrumentado para ...** it is scored for ...
2 [+ *medidas, plan*] to implement, bring in
3 [+ *campaña*] to orchestrate
4 (= *manipular*) to manipulate

instrumentista SMF **1** (*Mús*) (= *músico*) instrumentalist; (= *fabricante*) instrument maker • **~ de cuerda** string player
2 (*Med*) theatre nurse
3 (*Mec*) machinist

instrumento SM **1** (*Mús*) instrument ▸ **instrumento de cuerda** string instrument ▸ **instrumento de época** period instrument ▸ **instrumento de percusión** percussion instrument ▸ **instrumento de tecla** keyboard instrument ▸ **instrumento de viento** wind instrument ▸ **instrumento musical, instrumento músico** musical instrument
2 (*Téc*) (= *aparato*) instrument; (= *herramienta*) tool, implement • **volar por ~s** to fly on instruments ▸ **instrumento auditivo** listening device ▸ **instrumento de precisión** precision instrument ▸ **instrumentos científicos** scientific instruments ▸ **instrumentos de mando** (*Aer*) controls ▸ **instrumentos quirúrgicos** surgical instruments ▸ **instrumentos topográficos** surveying instruments
3 (= *medio*) instrument, tool • **fue solamente el ~ del dictador** he was just a tool in the dictator's hands
4 (*Jur*) deed, legal document ▸ **instrumento de venta** bill of sale
5** (= *pene*) tool**

insubordinación SF (= *desobediencia*) insubordination; (= *falta de disciplina*) unruliness, rebelliousness

insubordinado ADJ (= *desobediente*) insubordinate; (= *indisciplinado*) unruly, rebellious

insubordinar ▷ CONJUG 1a VT to stir up, rouse to rebellion
VPR **insubordinarse** to rebel • **~se contra el gobierno** to rise up *o* rebel against the government

insubsanable ADJ [*error*] irreparable; [*problema*] insoluble

insustituible ADJ = **insustituible**

insuceso SM (*Col*) (*frm*) unfortunate event

insudar ▷ CONJUG 1a VI (*liter*) to toil away

insuficiencia SF **1** (= *escasez*) insufficiency • **~ de franqueo** underpaid postage
2 (= *carencia*) lack, shortage • **~ de recursos** lack of resources • **debido a la ~ de personal** due to shortage of staff
3 (= *incompetencia*) incompetence
4 (*Med*) ▸ **insuficiencia cardíaca** heart failure ▸ **insuficiencia renal** kidney failure ▸ **insuficiencia respiratoria** shortage of breath
5 insuficiencias (= *fallos*) inadequacies; (= *carencias*) deficiencies • **existen muchas ~s en el sistema judicial** there are many inadequacies in the judicial system • **~s en la dieta alimenticia** deficiencies in the diet

insuficiente ADJ inadequate • **la explicación dada es ~** the explanation given is inadequate • **estos cambios son claramente ~s** these changes are clearly inadequate *o* insufficient • **el dinero recolectado es ~ para hacer la obra** the money collected is insufficient *o* not sufficient to do the work • **tu nota es ~ para hacer derecho** this mark is not good enough for you to do law
SM fail • **me han puesto tres ~s** I've had three fails

insuficientemente ADV insufficiently, inadequately

insuflar ▷ CONJUG 1a VT **1** (*Med*) • **~ aire a algo** to blow air into something
2 (*liter*) • **sus palabras ~on vida al proyecto** his words breathed life into the project • **insufló aires de esperanza a la vida política** he breathed new hope into politics

insufrible ADJ unbearable, insufferable

insufriblemente ADV unbearably, insufferably

insular ADJ island (*antes de s*)

insularidad SF insularity

insulina SF insulin

insulinodependiente ADJ insulin-dependent

insulsez SF **1** [*de comida*] tastelessness
2 [*de charla, persona*] dullness

insulso ADJ **1** [*comida*] tasteless, insipid
2 [*charla, persona*] dull

insultante ADJ insulting

insultar ▷ CONJUG 1a VT to insult

insulto SM **1** (= *ofensa*) insult (**para** to)
2 (*Méx**) (= *indigestión*) bellyache*, stomachache

insumergible ADJ unsinkable

insumisión SF **1** (= *rebeldía*) rebelliousness
2 (*Esp*) (*Mil*) *refusal to do military service or community service*

insumiso ADJ rebellious
SM **1** (*Esp*) (*Mil*) *man who refuses to do military*

service or community service
2 insumisos (*Méx*) (*Econ*) (= *entradas*) input (*sing*), input materials
insumo SM **1** (*Cono Sur*) (= *componente*) component, ingredient
2 (*esp LAm*) **insumos** (*Econ*) supplies, input, materials
insuperable ADJ [*problema*] insurmountable; [*precio*] unbeatable; [*calidad*] unsurpassable
insuperado ADJ unsurpassed
insurgencia SF **1** (= *acto*) rebellion, uprising
2 (= *fuerzas*) insurgent forces (*pl*)
insurgente ADJ, SMF insurgent
insurrección SF revolt, insurrection
insurreccional ADJ insurrectionary
insurreccionar ▷ CONJUG 1a VT to incite to rebel
VPR **insurreccionarse** to rebel, revolt
insurrecto/a ADJ, SM/F rebel, insurgent
insustancial ADJ insubstantial
insustituible ADJ irreplaceable
INTA SM ABR **1** (*Esp*) (*Aer*) = **Instituto Nacional de Técnica Aeroespacial**
2 (*Arg*) (*Agr*) = **Instituto Nacional de Tecnología Agropecuaria**
3 (*Guat*) = **Instituto Nacional de Transformación Agraria**
intachable ADJ **1** (= *perfecto*) faultless, perfect
2 [*conducta*] irreproachable
intacto ADJ **1** (= *sin tocar*) untouched • **dejó el desayuno casi ~** she left her breakfast almost untouched
2 (= *no dañado*) intact, undamaged • **el vehículo estaba ~** the vehicle was intact *o* undamaged • **conserva ~ su sentido del humor** his sense of humor is intact *o* unaffected • **su prestigio sigue ~** his reputation remains intact
intangible ADJ intangible
SM intangible, intangible asset
integérrimo ADJ *superl de* **íntegro**
integración SF **1** (= *incorporación*) integration • **la ~ de España en la UE** Spain's integration into the EU • **~ racial** racial integration
2 (*Elec*) integration • **~ a muy gran escala** very large-scale integration • **~ a pequeña escala** small-scale integration
integrado ADJ **1** (*Elec*) [*circuito*] integrated
2 (*Inform*) [*software*] integrated
integrador ADJ • **política ~a** policy of integration, integrationist policy • **proceso ~** process of integration
integral ADJ **1** (= *entero*) [*cereal*] wholegrain; [*arroz*] brown; [*pan, harina*] wholemeal
2 (= *total*) [*plan, reforma, servicio*] comprehensive, all-round • **para el cuidado ~ de la salud** for comprehensive *o* all-round health care • **educación ~** all-round education • **un desnudo ~** a full frontal
3 (= *integrante*) integral, built-in • **una parte ~ de** an integral part of
4 (= *redomado*) total, complete • **un idiota ~** a total *o* complete fool
5 (*Mat*) integral
SF (*Mat*) integral
íntegramente ADV **1** (= *completamente*) entirely • **un concierto ~ dedicado a Mozart** a concert entirely devoted to Mozart • **el periódico reprodujo ~ la carta** the newspaper published the letter in full
2 (= *con integridad*) uprightly, with integrity
integrante ADJ [*parte, elemento*] integral; [*país*] member (*antes de s*) • **es parte ~ de nuestra existencia** it is an integral part of our existence • **los estados ~s de la Unión Europea** the member states of the European Union
SMF member
integrar ▷ CONJUG 1a VT **1** (= *componer*) to make up • **la exposición la integran 150 fotografías** the exhibition is made up of 150 photographs • **una enciclopedia integrada por 12 volúmenes** an encyclopaedia consisting of 12 volumes
2 (= *incorporar*) [+ *funciones, servicios*] to incorporate, include • **este programa integra diversas funciones** this program incorporates *o* includes various functions • **han integrado bien los muebles en el resto de la decoración** they have integrated *o* incorporated the furniture very well into the rest of the decor • **~ a algn en algo** to integrate sb into sth • **un programa para ~ a los presos en el mercado laboral** a programme to integrate prisoners into the labour market • **quieren ~ a su club en la federación deportiva** they want their club to become a member of *o* join the sports federation
3 (*Mat*) to integrate
4 (*Econ*) (= *reembolsar*) to repay, reimburse; (*Cono Sur*) (= *pagar*) to pay up
VPR **integrarse 1** (= *adaptarse*) • **~se en** [+ *grupo*] to fit into, integrate into; [+ *conjunto, entorno*] to blend with • **no le costó nada ~se en la clase** he had no difficulty fitting *o* integrating into the class • **la casa se integra perfectamente en el paisaje** the house blends perfectly with *o* into the landscape
2 (= *unirse*) • **~se en** [+ *asociación, conjunto*] to join • **el año en que España se integró plenamente en la Alianza Atlántica** the year Spain became a full member of the Atlantic Alliance • **el significante y el significado se integran en un solo elemento lingüístico** the signifier and the meaning join to form a single linguistic element
integridad SF **1** (= *totalidad*) wholeness, completeness • **en su ~** completely, as a whole • **publicaron el texto en su ~** they published the text in full *o* in its entirety • **~ física** personal safety, physical well being • **peligró su ~ física** she put her personal safety at risk • **delito contra la ~ de la persona** crime against the person
2 (= *honradez*) integrity
3 (*Inform*) integrity
4† (= *virginidad*) virginity
integrismo SM **1** (= *conservadurismo*) entrenched traditionalism
2 (*Rel*) fundamentalism • **el ~ islámico** Islamic fundamentalism
integrista ADJ **1** (= *conservador*) traditionalist
2 (*Rel*) fundamentalist
SMF **1** (= *conservador*) traditionalist
2 (*Rel*) fundamentalist ▸ **integrista islámico** Islamic fundamentalist
íntegro ADJ **1** (= *completo*) [*cantidad, pago*] whole; [*condena*] full; [*grabación, texto*] unabridged • **dedica su sueldo ~ a la hipoteca** his whole salary goes towards the mortgage • **cumplió la pena íntegra** he served his sentence in full, he served his full sentence • **han publicado la versión íntegra del texto** they've published an unabridged version of the text • **el libro jamás se publicó ~** the book was never published in full • **en versión íntegra** [*película*] uncut; [*novela*] unabridged
2 (= *honrado*) upright
integumento SM integument
intelecto SM, **intelectiva** SF intellect
intelectual ADJ, SMF intellectual
intelectuala* SF (*hum*) bluestocking
intelectualidad SF **1** (= *personas*) intelligentsia, intellectuals (*pl*)
2 (*cualidad*) intellectuality, intellectual character
intelectualmente ADV intellectually
intelectualoide ADJ, SMF pseudo-intellectual
inteligencia SF **1** (= *capacidad*) intelligence ▸ **inteligencia artificial** artificial intelligence ▸ **inteligencia máquina** machine intelligence ▸ **inteligencia verbal** verbal skills (*pl*), verbal ability
2 (= *persona inteligente*) mind, intellect • **es una de las grandes ~s del partido** he is one of the great minds *o* intellects of the party
3 (*Mil*) intelligence • **servicio de ~** intelligence service
4 • **la ~** (= *intelectuales*) the intelligentsia
5 (= *comprensión*) understanding
6 (= *acuerdo*) agreement
inteligente ADJ **1** [*persona, animal, pregunta, comentario*] intelligent • **¿hay vida ~ en Marte?** is there intelligent life on Mars?
2 (*Inform*) intelligent; [*misil, edificio, tarjeta*] smart
inteligentemente ADV intelligently
inteligibilidad SF intelligibility
inteligible ADJ intelligible
inteligiblemente ADV intelligibly
intemperancia SF intemperance
intemperante ADJ intemperate
intemperie SF • **la ~** the elements (*pl*) • **estar a la ~** to be out in the open, be at the mercy of the elements • **crema para proteger la piel de la ~** cream to protect the skin against the elements • **aguantar la ~** to put up with the elements, put up with wind and weather • **una cara curtida a la ~** a weatherbeaten face, a face tanned by wind and weather • **dejar a algn a la ~** to leave sb unprotected
intempestivamente ADV in an untimely way, at a bad time
intempestivo ADJ untimely • **regresar a casa a horas intempestivas** to return home at an ungodly hour
intemporal ADJ timeless
intención SF **1** (= *propósito*) intention • **causar daño no era la ~ de mi cliente** it was not my client's intention to cause any damage (*frm*) • **perdona, no ha sido mi ~ despertarte** sorry, I didn't mean to wake you • **lo hizo con la mejor ~ del mundo** he did it with the best (of) intentions • **la ~ desestabilizadora de sus palabras** the disruptive intent of his words • **su ~ era que yo le pagara la entrada** he meant me to pay for his ticket • **su ~ era muy otra** he had something very different in mind • **no, gracias, pero se agradece la ~** no, but thanks for thinking of me, no thanks, but it was a kind thought • **la ~ es lo que cuenta** it's the thought that counts • **con ~** (= *a propósito*) deliberately, intentionally • **esto está hecho con ~** this was deliberate, this was no accident • **mencionó lo del divorcio con mala *o* mucha ~** he spitefully mentioned the divorce • **la ~ de hacer algo**: • **ha dejado clara su ~ de venir** he has made it clear that he intends to come • **no lo dijo con la ~ de ofenderla** he didn't say it with the intention of offending her, he didn't say it to offend her • **sonrió con la ~ de animarme** he smiled to try to cheer me up • **sin la menor ~ de generalizar** without wishing to generalize • **tenemos la ~ de salir temprano** we intend *o* plan to start out early • **no tengo la menor *o* más mínima ~ de pedir perdón** I haven't got the slightest intention of apologizing, I have no

intention of apologizing • **sin ~** without meaning to • **aunque lo haya hecho sin ~** even if he did it without meaning to, even if he didn't mean to do it ▸ **intención de voto** voting intention
2 intenciones (= *planes*) intentions, plans • **no te fíes, no sabes sus intenciones** don't trust him, you don't know what he has in mind • **¿cuáles son tus intenciones para el año próximo?** what are your plans for next year? • **tener buenas intenciones** to mean well, have good intentions • **tener malas intenciones** to be up to no good • REFRÁN: • **de buenas intenciones está el infierno lleno** the road to hell is paved with good intentions
3 • **doble** *o* **segunda ~** double meaning • **lo dijo con segunda** *o* **doble ~** there was a double meaning to what he said

intencionadamente ADV **1** (= *a propósito*) deliberately, on purpose
2 (= *con mala intención*) nastily

intencionado ADJ **1** (= *deliberado*) deliberate, intentional
2 • **bien ~** [*persona*] well-meaning, well-intentioned; [*acto*] well-meant, well-intentioned
3 • **mal ~** [*persona*] ill-meaning, hostile; [*acto*] ill-meant, ill-intentioned

intencional ADJ intentional

intencionalidad SF **1** (= *propósito*) purpose, intention • **la ~ del incendio** the fact that the fire was deliberately started
2 • **una pregunta cargada de ~** a loaded question

intencionalmente ADV intentionally

intendencia SF **1** (= *dirección*) management, administration
2 (= *oficina*) manager's office
3 (*Mil*) (*tb* **cuerpo de intendencia**) ≈ service corps, ≈ quartermaster corps (*EEUU*)
4 (*Arg*) (= *alcaldía*) mayoralty; (= *cargo de gobernador*) governorship

intendente SMF **1** (= *director*) manager
2 (*Mil*) ▸ **intendente de ejército** quartermaster general
3 (*LAm*) (*Hist*) governor
4 (*Arg*) (= *alcalde*) mayor; (*Arg, Chile*) (= *gobernador*) provincial governor
5 (*Méx, Ecu*) (= *policía*) police inspector

intensamente ADV **1** (= *con intensidad*) intensely
2 (= *con fuerza, vehemencia*) powerfully, strongly
3 (= *vivamente*) vividly, profoundly

intensar ▹ CONJUG 1a VT to intensify
VPR **intensarse** to intensify

intensidad SF **1** (*Elec, Téc*) strength; [*de terremoto, sonido*] intensity ▸ **intensidad luminosa** luminous intensity
2 [*de color, olor, dolor*] intensity; [*de recuerdo*] vividness; [*de emoción, sentimiento*] strength • **la ~ de su mirada la atemorizó** the intensity of his gaze frightened her • **Manuel vivió con ~** Manuel lived life to the full • **ha aumentado la ~ del tráfico** the volume of traffic has increased • **nevaba con gran ~** it was snowing heavily *o* hard

intensificación SF intensification

intensificar ▹ CONJUG 1g VT to intensify
VPR **intensificarse** to intensify

intensión SF intensity, intenseness

intensivamente ADV intensively

intensivo ADJ [*búsqueda, tratamiento*] intensive; [*curso*] intensive, crash (*antes de s*)

intenso ADJ [*frío, dolor, actividad*] intense; [*emoción*] powerful, strong; [*recuerdo*] vivid; [*color*] deep, intense; [*bronceado*] deep; [*corriente eléctrica*] strong

intentar ▹ CONJUG 1a VT to try, attempt (*frm*) • **hemos intentado un acuerdo** we've tried *o* attempted (*frm*) to reach an agreement • **¿por qué no lo intentas otra vez?** why don't you try again? • **¡venga, inténtalo!** come on, have a go *o* have a try! • **lo he intentado con regalos, pero no consigo animarla** I've tried (giving her) presents, but I just can't cheer her up • **lo ha intentado con todo** he has tried everything • **con ~ lo nada se pierde** • **por ~ lo que no quede** there's no harm in trying • **~ hacer algo** to try to do sth, attempt to do sth (*frm*) • **~emos llegar a la cima** we shall try *o* attempt (*frm*) to reach the summit • **llevo todo el día intentando hablar contigo** I've been trying to talk to you all day • **intente no fumar** try not to smoke • **~ que** (+ *subjun*): • **llevan años intentando que se celebre el juicio** they've spent years trying to bring the case to trial • **intenta que te lo dejen más barato** try and get to *o* try to get them to reduce the price • **intenta que no se enteren tus padres** try not to let your parents find out

intento SM **1** (= *tentativa*) attempt • **al primer ~** at the first attempt • **fracasó en su ~ de batir el récord mundial** he failed in his attempt to beat the world record • **~ fallido** *o* **fracasado** failed attempt ▸ **intento de asesinato** (= *acción*) murder attempt; (= *cargo*) attempted murder ▸ **intento de soborno** attempted bribe ▸ **intento de suicidio** suicide attempt ▸ **intento de violación** attempted rape
2 (= *propósito*) (*Méx*) intention • **de ~**† (*Méx, Col*) by design

intentona SF **1** (= *tentativa*) foolhardy attempt, wild attempt
2 (*Pol*) putsch, rising ▸ **intentona golpista** failed coup (d'état), attempted coup (d'état)

ínter SM (*And, Cono Sur*) (*Rel*) curate

inter... PREF inter...

interacción SF interaction • **"interacciones"** (*Farm*) "not to be taken with ..."

interaccionar ▹ CONJUG 1a VI to interact (con with)

interactivamente ADV interactively

interactividad SF interactivity

interactivo ADJ interactive • **computación interactiva** (*Inform*) interactive computing

interactuación SF interaction

interactuar ▹ CONJUG 1e VI to interact (con with)

interamericano ADJ inter-American

interandino ADJ inter-Andean, concerning areas on both sides of the Andes

interanual ADJ • **promedio ~** year-on-year average • **variación ~** variation from year to year

interbancario ADJ inter-bank (*antes de s*)

interbibliotecario ADJ inter-library (*antes de s*) • **préstamo ~** inter-library loan

intercalación SF **1** (= *inserción*) [*de comentarios, imágenes*] insertion, interspersing; [*de cultivos*] insertion, alternating
2 (*Inform*) merging

intercalar ▹ CONJUG 1a VT **1** (= *insertar*) [+ *pausa, ejemplo*] to put in, include; [+ *comentarios, cultivos*] to intersperse, alternate; [+ *actividad*] to fit in, combine • **deberías ~ algún ejemplo** you should put in *o* include the odd example • **hemos intercalado unas imágenes con otras** we have interspersed *o* alternated some images with others • **una gira mundial que ~á con el rodaje** a world tour which he will fit in with the filming • **intercala en su obra ideas innovadoras con recuerdos de su pasado** in her work she alternates innovative ideas with memories of her past • **~ algo en algo** to insert sth into sth • **en el texto se han intercalado bastantes fotografías** a number of photographs have been inserted into the text • **intercaló unas palabras de agradecimiento en su discurso** he incorporated a few words of thanks into his speech • **~ algo entre** [+ *imágenes, objetos*] to insert sth between; [+ *cultivos*] to intersperse sth between, alternate sth with • **intercalaba pétalos entre las páginas de los libros** he inserted *o* put petals between the pages of the books • **daban unos aperitivos intercalados entre los platos** they served aperitifs between courses
2 (*Inform*) [+ *archivos, texto*] to merge

intercambiable ADJ interchangeable

intercambiar ▹ CONJUG 1b VT [+ *impresiones, presos, ideas, dinero*] to exchange; [+ *sellos, fotos*] to swap, exchange

intercambio SM [*de impresiones, de presos, ideas, dinero*] exchange; [*de sellos, fotos*] swap, exchange • **hice ~ con una chica inglesa** I went *o* did an exchange with an English girl • **me junto con un estudiante de español y hacemos ~ de conversación** I get together with a Spanish student to exchange conversation

interceder ▹ CONJUG 2a VI to intercede • **~ con el juez por el acusado** to intercede with the judge on the defendant's behalf, plead with the judge for the defendant

intercentros ADJ INV • **comité ~** joint committee (*with representatives from all the different workplaces*)

interceptación SF **1** [*de correspondencia, misil*] interception
2 (*Aut*) stoppage, holdup

interceptar ▹ CONJUG 1a VT
1 [+ *correspondencia, misil, balón*] to intercept
2 (*Aut*) [+ *tráfico*] to stop, hold up; [+ *carretera*] to block, cut off

interceptor SM **1** (= *persona*) interceptor
2 (*Mec*) trap, separator

intercesión SF **1** (= *mediación*) mediation • **la ~ del alcalde no sirvió de nada** the mayor's mediation served no purpose
2 (*Rel*) intercession • **un milagro atribuido a la ~ del santo** a miracle attributed to the intercession of the saint

intercesor(a) SM/F **1** (= *mediador*) mediator
2 (*Rel*) intercessor

interclasista ADJ **1** (= *entre clases*) inter-class, which crosses class barriers
2 (= *sin clases*) classless

inter-club ADJ inter-club, between two clubs

intercomunicación SF intercommunication

intercomunicador SM intercom

intercomunicar ▹ CONJUG 1g VT to link

intercomunión SF intercommunion

interconectar ▹ CONJUG 1a VT to interconnect

interconectividad SF interconnectivity

interconexión SF interconnection

interconfesional ADJ interdenominational

interconsonántico ADJ interconsonantal

intercontinental ADJ intercontinental

intercostal ADJ (*Med*) intercostal

intercultural ADJ intercultural

interdecir ▹ CONJUG 3o VT (*frm*) to forbid, prohibit

interdepartamental ADJ interdepartmental

interdependencia SF interdependence

interdependiente ADJ interdependent

interdicción SF prohibition, interdiction

interdicto (SM) prohibition, ban; (*Jur, Rel*) interdict
interdisciplinar (ADJ), **interdisciplinario** (ADJ) interdisciplinary
interdisciplinariedad (SF) interdisciplinary nature
interés (SM) **1** (= *valor*) interest • **una cuestión de ~ general** a question of general interest • **un edificio de ~ histórico** a building of historic interest • **ese asunto no tiene ~ para nosotros** this matter is of no interest to us
2 (= *curiosidad*) interest • **el tema despertó** *o* **suscitó el ~ del público** the topic aroused public interest • **ha seguido con gran ~ la campaña electoral** he has followed the electoral campaign with great interest • **esperar algo con ~** to await sth with interest • **mostrar ~ en** *o* **por algo** to show (an) interest in sth • **poner ~ en algo** to take an interest in sth • **puse verdadero ~ en aprender inglés** I took a real interest in learning English • **sentir** *o* **tener ~ por algo** to be interested in sth • **si tienes ~ por el piso, todavía está a la venta** if you're interested in the flat, it's still for sale • **siento auténtico ~ por los idiomas** I have a real interest *o* I am really interested in languages • **sentir** *o* **tener ~ por hacer algo** to be interested in doing sth
3 (= *beneficio*) **a** [*de persona, país*] interest • **no deberías dejarte llevar por el ~** you shouldn't let yourself be swayed by personal interest • **¿qué ~ tienes tú en que pierdan el partido?** what's your interest in their losing the match? • **te lo digo por tu propio ~** I'm telling you for your own benefit *o* in your own interest • **en ~ del país ha renunciado a la reelección** in the interest(s) of the country he is not standing for re-election
b (*Econ*) interest • **un préstamo a** *o* **con un ~ del 9 por ciento** a loan at 9 per cent interest • **los intereses de mi cuenta** the interest on my account • **dar ~** [*capital, inversión*] to yield interest; [*banco, cuenta*] to pay interest • **mi capital me da un ~ del 5,3 por ciento** my capital yields an interest of 5.3 per cent • **devengar ~** to accrue interest, earn interest • **tasa** (*LAm*) *o* **tipo de ~** interest rate ▸ **intereses acumulados** accrued interest (*sing*) ▸ **interés compuesto** compound interest ▸ **interés controlador** controlling interest ▸ **interés devengado** accrued interest, earned interest ▸ **intereses por cobrar** interest receivable (*sing*) ▸ **intereses por pagar** interest payable (*sing*) ▸ **interés simple** simple interest
4 intereses: **a** (*Com*) interests • **hay intereses económicos por medio** there are financial interests involved • **tengo que defender mis intereses** I have to look after my own interests • **los intereses españoles en África** Spanish interests in Africa • **un conflicto de intereses** a conflict of interests • **tener intereses en algo** to have interests *o* a stake in sth • **tiene intereses en varias compañías extranjeras** he has interests *o* a stake in several foreign companies
b (= *aficiones*) interests • **¿qué intereses tienes?** what are your interests? • **fomentar los intereses de algn** to foster sb's interest in sth ▸ **intereses creados** vested interests
interesadamente (ADV) • **mintieron ~** they lied to protect their own interests *o* in their own interests • **actuaron ~** they had ulterior motives in acting as they did, they acted to protect their own interests • **he dejado de actuar ~** I've stopped acting purely in my own interest
interesado/a (ADJ) **1** (= *con interés*) interested • **las partes interesadas tendrán que firmar el contrato mañana** the interested parties will have to sign the contract tomorrow • **las personas interesadas pueden llamar al 900 100 100** anyone interested can phone 900 100 100 • **estar ~ en** *o* **por algo** to be interested in sth • **nadie estaba ~ por la casa** nobody was interested in the house • **estoy ~ en recibir más información** I'm interested in receiving some more information • **estamos muy ~s en el proyecto** we have a great interest in the project, we are very interested in the project
2 (= *egoísta*) self-interested, selfish • **lo veo muy ~** he seems really self-interested *o* selfish to me • **su ayuda era muy interesada** she had her own interests at heart in helping us • **actuar de forma interesada** to act selfishly
(SM/F) **1** (= *persona interesada*) • **los ~s pueden escribir una postal con sus datos** anyone interested *o* those interested should send a postcard with their personal details • **hace falta el consentimiento de los ~s** we need the consent of those concerned • **~ en algo**: • **una cita indispensable para todos los ~s en el jazz** a must for all those interested in jazz *o* for all jazz fans • **soy el primer ~ en ganar** I have the greatest interest in winning
2 (= *persona egoísta*) • **eres un ~** you always act out of self-interest, you're always on the lookout for yourself
interesante (ADJ) [*persona, película*] interesting; [*precio, sueldo*] attractive • **hacerse el/la ~** to try to attract attention
interesar ▷ CONJUG 1a (VI) **1** (= *despertar interés*) **a** [*tema, propuesta*] to be of interest, interest • **un tema que interesa a los jóvenes** a subject of interest to young people, a subject which interests young people • **esa propuesta no nos interesa** we're not interested in that proposal, that proposal is of no interest to us
b [*actividad, persona*] • **no me interesan los toros** I'm not interested in bullfighting • **solo le interesa el dinero** his only interest is money, all he's interested in is money • **no me interesa en absoluto como persona** I'm not the slightest bit interested in him as a person
2 (= *concernir*) • **~ a algn** to concern sb • **el asunto interesa a todos** the matter concerns everybody • **a ti no te interesa lo que yo esté haciendo** what I'm doing is no concern of yours • **a quien pueda ~** (*frm*) to whom it may concern (*frm*)
3 (= *convenir*) • **ese tipo de negocios no interesa** that sort of business is not worth our while • **no dice nada porque no le interesa desde el punto de vista judicial** he doesn't say anything because, from a legal point of view, it's not in his interest • **este coche podría ~te** this car could be of interest (to you), this car might interest you • **cuando algo no le interesa, cambia de tema** whenever he feels uncomfortable about something, he changes the subject • **~ía conocer más datos antes de decidirnos** it would be useful to have more details before making a decision • **te podría ~ invertir en bolsa** it could be interesting for you to invest on the stock market • **me interesa más este hotel** this hotel suits me better
(VT) **1** • **~ a algn en algo** to interest sb in sth • **no logré ~lo en mi trabajo** I failed to get him interested in my work
2 (*Med*) [+ *órgano, nervio*] to affect • **la herida interesa la región lumbar** the injury affects the lumbar region
3 (*Com*) • **el portador interesa cinco euros en …** the bearer has a stake of five euros in …
(VPR) **interesarse 1** • **~se por algo** to show an interest in sth, take an interest in sth, be interested in sth • **no se interesa por nada** he shows *o* takes no interest in anything, he's not interested in anything • **se interesó por el trabajo de los campesinos** he showed *o* took an interest in the work of the country people
2 • **~se por algn** (= *preocuparse*) to show concern for sb; (= *preguntar*) to inquire about sb, ask after sb • **si tú no haces un esfuerzo nadie se va a ~ por ti** if you don't make an effort no one will show any concern for *o* interest in you • **en la fiesta nadie se interesaba por ella** nobody paid any attention to her at the party • **llamó para ~se por su salud** she called to inquire about *o* ask after his health
3 (*Com*) • **~se en una empresa** to have an interest *o* a stake in an company
interestatal (ADJ) inter-state
interestelar (ADJ) interstellar
interétnico (ADJ) interracial
interface (SM o SF), **interfaz** (SM o SF) (*Inform*) interface ▸ **interface de serie** serial interface ▸ **interface de usuario** user interface ▸ **interface gráfica** graphical interface
interfase (SF) (*Inform*) = interface
interfecto/a (ADJ) killed, murdered
(SM/F) **1** (= *víctima*) murder victim
2* (= *individuo*) your man/woman*
interferencia (SF) **1** (*Radio, Telec*) interference; (*deliberada*) jamming; (= *escucha telefónica*) tapping
2 (*Inform*) glitch
3 (*Ling*) interference
4 (= *injerencia*) interference (**en** in) • **no ~** non-interference
interferir ▷ CONJUG 3i (VT) **1** (= *obstaculizar*) to interfere with, get in the way of
2 (*Radio, Telec*) to interfere with; (*con intención*) to jam; [+ *teléfono*] to tap
3 (= *injerirse en*) to interfere in, meddle in • **interfieren la vida privada de los ciudadanos** they interfere *o* meddle in people's private lives
(VI) to interfere (**en** in, with)
(VPR) **interferirse** to interfere (**en** in, with) • **no está en posición de ~se en el conflicto** he is in no position to interfere in the conflict
interferón (SM) interferon
interfijo (SM) infix
interfono (SM) intercom, entryphone
intergaláctico (ADJ) intergalactic
intergeneracional (ADJ) intergenerational, between generations
intergubernamental (ADJ) intergovernmental
interín, ínterin (SM) **1** (= *intervalo*) interim • **en el ~** in the meantime, in the interim (*frm*) • **en el ~ se ha producido otro caso similar** in the meantime another similar case has appeared
2 (= *período vacante*) short period • **el ~ en que el secretario sustituyó a la ministra** the (short) period during which the secretary stood in for the minister • **desempeña las funciones del director durante el ~** he deputizes for his manager in his absence
(CONJ) while, until
interinamente (ADV) **1** (= *temporalmente*) temporarily • **el Presidente ha sido sustituido ~ por el ministro del Interior** the President has temporarily been replaced by

the Interior Minister
2 (= *entretanto*) in the interim, meanwhile
interinar ▹ CONJUG 1a VT [+ *puesto*] to occupy temporarily, occupy in an acting capacity
interinato SM **1** (*Cono Sur*) (= *temporalidad*) temporary nature
2 (*Cono Sur*) (= *período*) period in a temporary post *o* position
3 (*CAm*) (*Med*) residence, internship (EEUU)
interinidad SF (= *estado*) temporary nature; (= *estatus*) provisional status; (= *empleo*) temporary work • **situación de ~** temporary state (of affairs); (*en puesto*) temporary status
interino/a ADJ [*empleo, empleado*] temporary; [*alcalde, director*] acting (*antes de s*); [*medida*] stopgap, interim • **acuerdo ~** interim accord, interim agreement • **gobierno ~** interim government • **informe ~** interim report, progress report • **profesor(a) ~/a** supply teacher, substitute teacher (EEUU)
SM/F temporary holder of a post, acting official; (*Teat*) stand-in; (*Med*) locum, on-call doctor (EEUU)
SF (= *asistenta*) non-resident maid
interior ADJ **1** [*espacio*] interior; [*patio*] inner, interior; [*escalera*] internal, interior; [*bolsillo*] inside; [*paz, fuerza*] inner • **la parte ~ de la casa** the inside *o* interior of the house • **en la parte ~** inside, on the inside • **habitación/piso ~** room/flat without a view onto the street • **pista ~** (*Dep*) inside lane • **un joven con mucha vida ~** a reflective young man; ▹ **ropa**
2 (= *nacional*) [*comercio, política, mercado*] domestic
3 (*Geog*) inland
SM **1** (= *parte interna*) inside, interior • **el ~ quedó destrozado por el fuego** the inside *o* interior was destroyed by the fire • **el ~ de la cueva** the inside *o* interior of the cave • **se dirigieron al ~ del edificio** they went inside the building • **el cuerpo fue hallado en el ~ de un vehículo** the body was found inside a vehicle • **busque su regalo en el ~ del paquete** look for your free gift inside the packet • **plantas de ~** house plants • **diseño de ~es** interior design • **decoración de ~es** interior decoration
2 (= *alma*) soul • **esto refleja un ~ atormentado** that reflects a soul in torment • **en mi ~ seguía amándola** in my heart I loved her still • **dije para mi ~** I said to myself
3 (*Geog*) interior • **una tribu del ~ del Brasil** a tribe from the Brazilian interior • **no soy de la costa, soy del ~** I'm not from the coast, I'm from inland • **mañana lloverá en las zonas del ~** tomorrow there will be rain in inland areas
4 ▸ **(Ministerio del) Interior** (*Pol*) ≈ Home Office, ≈ Justice Department (EEUU)
5 (*Dep*) inside-forward ▸ **interior derecho** inside-right ▸ **interior izquierdo** inside-left
6 interiores (*Cine*) interiors • **el estudio donde ruedan los ~es** the studio where they shoot the interiors
7 interiores (*Col, Ven*) (= *calzoncillos*) (under)pants, shorts (EEUU)
interioridad SF **1** [*de persona*] inner being • **en su ~, sabe que ...** (*CAm*) in his heart he knows that ..., deep down he knows that ...
2 interioridades (= *intimidades*) private *o* personal matters; (= *detalles*) ins and outs • **desconocen las ~es del mercado** they don't know all the ins and outs of the market • **vivió de cerca las ~es de la reforma** he was intimately acquainted with the ins and outs of the reform
interiorismo SM interior decoration, interior design
interiorista SMF interior decorator, interior designer
interiorizar ▹ CONJUG 1f VT **1** (*Psic*) to internalize
2 (*Chile*) to inform (**de, sobre** about)
VPR **interiorizarse** • **~se de/sobre algo** to familiarize o.s. with sth
interiormente ADV (= *internamente*) internally; (*de persona*) inwardly • **han remodelado el edificio ~** the building has been redesigned internally • **~ me siento estremecido** inwardly I'm shaking
interjección SF interjection
interlínea SF (*Inform*) line feed
interlineado SM space/writing between the lines
interlineal ADJ interlinear
interlinear ▹ CONJUG 1a VT **1** (*al escribir*) to interline, write between the lines
2 (*Tip*) to space, lead
interlocutor(a) SM/F (*gen*) speaker, interlocutor (*frm*); (*al teléfono*) person at the other end of the line • **mi ~** the person I was speaking to, the person who spoke to me ▸ **interlocutor(a) válido/a** (*Pol*) official negotiator, official spokesman ▸ **interlocutores sociales** social partners
intérlope ADJ (*Méx*) (= *fraudulento*) fraudulent
SM (*Com*) interloper, unauthorized trader
interludio SM interlude, intermission (EEUU)
intermediación SF (*gen*) mediation; (*Econ*) brokerage
intermediario/a ADJ intermediary
SM/F **1** (= *mediador*) (*gen*) intermediary, go-between; (*Com*) middle-man
2 (*en disputa*) mediator
intermedio ADJ **1** [*etapa, grupo, nivel*] intermediate; [*periodo*] intervening • **omitió un paso ~ del razonamiento** he missed out an intermediate stage in the reasoning • **los estratos sociales ~s** the middle classes • **un punto ~ entre colonialismo e independencia** a halfway house between colonialism and independence • **en un punto ~ entre Córdoba y Montoro** halfway between Córdoba and Montoro • **un tono ~ entre gris y negro** a shade halfway between grey and black
2 [*tamaño, talla*] medium • **de tamaño ~** medium-sized
SM **1** (*Teat*) interval; (*TV*) break; (*Cine*) intermission
2 • **por ~ de** by means of, through the intermediary of
intermezzo [inter'metso] SM intermezzo
interminable ADJ endless, interminable
interminablemente ADV endlessly, interminably
interministerial ADJ interdepartmental, interministerial • **comité/comisión ~** interdepartmental committee/commission, interministerial committee/commission
intermisión SF intermission, interval
intermitencia SF intermittence
intermitente ADJ (*gen*) intermittent; [*guerra*] sporadic; [*huelga, negociaciones*] on-off; [*luz*] flashing; [*lluvia, nieve*] sporadic, intermittent • **se escuchan disparos de forma ~** shots can be heard now and again *o* intermittently
SM **1** (*Aut*) indicator, turn signal (EEUU)
2 (*Inform*) indicator light
internación SF internment
internacional ADJ international
SMF international • **la Internacional** (= *himno*) the Internationale • **la Internacional Socialista** the Socialist International
internacionalidad SF international nature
internacionalismo SM internationalism
internacionalista ADJ internationalist
SMF **1** (= *partidario*) internationalist
2 (*Jur*) internationalist
internacionalización SF internationalization
internacionalizar ▹ CONJUG 1f VT to internationalize
VPR **internacionalizarse** to become international
internacionalmente ADV internationally
internada SF (*Dep*) run
internado/a ADJ • **estar ~ en** to be (a patient) in
SM/F (*Mil*) internee; (*Escol*) boarder; (*Med*) patient
SM **1** (= *colegio*) boarding school; (= *acto*) boarding
2 (= *alumnos*) boarders (*pl*)
internalización SF internalization
internalizar ▹ CONJUG 1f VT to internalize
internamente ADV (*gen*) internally; (*de persona*) inside, deep down • **parece frío, pero ~ es muy emotivo** he seems cold, but inside *o* deep down he's very emotional
internamiento SM (*Pol*) internment; (*Med*) admission (*to hospital*)
internar ▹ CONJUG 1a VT **1** (= *ingresar*) (*Mil*) to intern; (*Med*) to admit (**en** to) • **~ a algn en un manicomio** to commit sb to a psychiatric hospital
2 (= *enviar tierra adentro*) to send inland
VPR **internarse 1** (= *avanzar*) to advance deep, penetrate • **el jugador se internó por la derecha** the player cut inside from the right • **~se en algo** to go into *o* right inside sth • **se internó en el edificio** he disappeared into the building • **~se en un país** to go into the interior of a country • **se ~on por los pasillos** they went deep into the corridors
2 • **~se en un tema** to study a subject in depth, go deeply into a subject
internauta SMF internet user, web surfer
Internet SM o SF, **internet** SM o SF Internet
interno/a ADJ internal • **la política interna** internal politics, domestic politics • **por vía interna** (*Med*) internally • **paredes internas** interior walls • **criada interna** live-in servant
SM/F **1** (*Escol*) boarder
2 (*Med*) houseman, intern (EEUU)
3 (= *preso*) inmate, prisoner
SM (*Cono Sur*) (*Telec*) extension, telephone extension
interparlamentario ADJ interparliamentary
interpelación SF (*frm*) appeal, plea
interpelante SMF (*frm*) questioner
interpelar ▹ CONJUG 1a VT (*frm*) **1** (= *dirigirse a*) to address, speak to; (*Pol*) to ask for explanations, question
2† (= *implorar*) to implore, beseech
interpenetrarse ▹ CONJUG 1a VPR to overlap
interpersonal ADJ interpersonal • **relaciones ~es** interpersonal relationships
interplanetario ADJ interplanetary
Interpol SF ABR (= **International Criminal Police Organisation**) Interpol
interpolación SF interpolation
interpolar ▹ CONJUG 1a VT (= *intercalar*) to interpolate; (= *interrumpir*) to interrupt briefly

interponer ▷ CONJUG 2q VT **1** (= *insertar*) to interpose (*frm*), insert
2 (*Jur*) [+ *apelación*] to lodge
3 (*en discurso*) to interpose, interject
VPR **interponerse** [*persona*] to intervene; [*obstáculo*] to stand in the way • **no pensamos ~nos** we do not intend to intervene • **se interpuso en su camino** he blocked his path, he stood in his way • **se interpuso entre los dos para que no riñeran** he came between the two of them to stop them fighting • **grandes obstáculos se interponen en la solución del conflicto** there are great obstacles standing in the way of a solution to the conflict

interposición SF **1** (= *inserción*) insertion
2 (*Jur*) lodging, formulation
3 (*en discurso*) interjection

interpretable ADJ interpretable

interpretación SF **1** [*de texto, mensaje*] interpretation • **mala ~** misinterpretation, misunderstanding • **admite diversas interpretaciones** it can be interpreted in several different ways
2 (= *traducción hablada*) interpreting • **~ simultánea** simultaneous interpreting
3 (*Mús, Teat*) performance • **~ en directo** live performance

interpretar ▷ CONJUG 1a VT **1** [+ *texto, mensaje*] to interpret • **~ mal** to misinterpret, misunderstand
2 (*Ling*) to interpret • **~ del chino al ruso** to interpret from Chinese into Russian
3 (*Mús*) [+ *pieza*] to play, perform; [+ *canción*] to sing; (*Teat*) [+ *papel*] to play

interpretativo ADJ interpretative

intérprete SMF **1** (*Ling*) interpreter ▸ **intérprete de conferencias** conference interpreter ▸ **intérprete de enlace** liaison interpreter
2 (*Mús*) (= *músico*) performer; (= *cantante*) singer
SM (*Inform*) interpreter

interprofesional ADJ • **acuerdo ~** inter-trade agreement • **salario mínimo ~** minimum wage

interprovincial SM (*And*) long-distance bus, coach

interracial ADJ interracial

interregno SM (*Hist, Pol*) interregnum; (*LAm*) interval, intervening period • **en el ~** in the meantime

interrelación SF interrelation

interrelacionado ADJ interrelated

interrelacionar ▷ CONJUG 1a VT to interrelate
VPR **interrelacionarse** to be interrelated • **~se con algo** to interrelate with sth

interreligioso ADJ interfaith

interrogación SF **1** (= *interrogatorio*) questioning, interrogation
2 (= *pregunta*) question; (*Inform*) inquiry
3 (*Tip*) (= *signo de interrogación*) question mark

interrogador(a) SM/F interrogator, questioner

interrogante ADJ questioning
SMF (= *persona*) interrogator, questioner
SM o SF (= *signo*) question mark; (= *incógnita*) question mark, query; (= *pregunta*) question, query

interrogar ▷ CONJUG 1h VT to interrogate, question; (*Jur*) [+ *testigo, detenido*] to question, examine

interrogativo ADJ interrogative
SM interrogative

interrogatorio SM **1** (= *preguntas*) interrogation, questioning; (*tras una misión*) debriefing
2 (*Jur*) questioning, examination
3 (= *cuestionario*) questionnaire

interrumpir ▷ CONJUG 3a VT **1** (= *cesar*) (*gen*) to interrupt; [+ *vacaciones*] to cut short; [+ *tráfico*] to block, hold up; [+ *embarazo*] to terminate
2 (*Elec*) [+ *luz*] to switch off; [+ *suministro*] to cut off
3 (*Inform*) to abort
VI to interrupt

interrupción SF (*gen*) interruption; [*de trabajo*] holdup ▸ **interrupción de emisión** break in transmission ▸ **interrupción (voluntaria) del embarazo** termination ▸ **interrupción del fluido eléctrico** power cut, power failure

interruptor SM (*Elec*) switch ▸ **interruptor con regulador de intensidad** dimmer switch ▸ **interruptor de dos direcciones** two-way switch ▸ **interruptor de seguridad** safety switch

intersecarse ▷ CONJUG 1g VPR to intersect

intersección SF intersection; (*Aut*) junction

intersexual ADJ [*animal, persona*] sexually ambiguous; [*acercamiento, enfrentamiento*] between the sexes

intersexualidad SF sexual ambiguity

intersticio SM (= *espacio*) interstice (*frm*); (= *grieta*) crack; (= *intervalo*) interval, gap

intertanto (*LAm*) ADV meanwhile
CONJ • **~ que él llegue** until he comes, while we wait for him to come
SM • **en el ~** in the meantime

intertextualidad SF intertextuality

intertítulo SM caption, subtitle

interurbano ADJ [*autobús, transporte, llamada*] long-distance; [*tren*] inter-city
SM (*CAm*) inter-city taxi

intervalo SM **1** [*de tiempo*] (*tb Mús*) interval; (= *descanso*) break • **a ~s** (*gen*) at intervals; (= *de vez en cuando*) every now and then • **a ~s de dos horas** at two hour intervals
2 (= *espacio libre*) gap • **situados a ~s de dos metros** placed at two metre intervals • **~s de nubes** cloudy spells *o* intervals • **mantener el ~ de seguridad** (*Aut*) to keep one's distance

intervención SF **1** (= *actuación*) intervention (**en** in) • **fue necesaria la ~ de la policía** police intervention was necessary • **su ~ en la discusión** his contribution to the discussion • **política de no ~** policy of non-intervention
2 (= *discurso*) speech
3 (*Mús, Teat*) performance
4 (*Med*) (*tb* **intervención quirúrgica**) operation
5 (= *control*) (*en producción*) supervision, control; (*en empresa*) intervention; (*LAm*) [*de sindicatos*] government takeover
6 [*de contrabando, droga*] seizure, confiscation
7 (= *auditoría*) audit, auditing
8 (*Telec*) tapping

intervencionismo SM interventionism

intervencionista ADJ interventionist • **no ~** (*Com*) non-interventionist, laissez-faire
SMF interventionist

intervenir ▷ CONJUG 3r VI **1** (= *tomar parte*) to take part • **no intervino en el debate** he did not take part in the debate • **la reyerta en la que intervino el acusado** the brawl in which the defendant took part *o* was involved
2 (= *injerirse*) to intervene • **España rehusó ~ militarmente** Spain refused to intervene militarily • **la policía intervino para separar a las dos pandillas** the police intervened to separate the two gangs
3 (= *mediar*) • **el presidente intervino para que se pudiera llegar a un acuerdo** the president mediated *o* interceded so that an agreement could be reached • **intervino para que los sacaran de la cárcel** he used his influence to get them out of prison • **las circunstancias que intervinieron en mi dimisión** the circumstances that influenced my resignation • **él no intervino en la decisión** he did not have a hand in the decision
VT **1** (= *controlar*) to take over, take control of • **la junta militar intervino todas las cadenas estatales** the junta took over *o* took control of all the state-run channels • **el gobierno intervino a los ferroviarios** the government took over *o* took control of the railworkers' union
2 (*Com*) [+ *cuenta*] to audit; [+ *banco, empresa*] to take into administration; [+ *cuenta, bienes*] to freeze
3 (*Med*) to operate on • **lo intervinieron quirúrgicamente** he was operated on
4 [+ *droga, armas, patrimonio, bienes*] to confiscate, seize
5 [+ *teléfono*] to tap

interventor(a) SM/F **1** (= *inspector*) inspector, supervisor; (*en elecciones*) scrutineer, canvasser (*EEUU*) ▸ **interventor(a) de cuentas** auditor
2 ▸ **interventor(a) judicial** receiver, official receiver; (*LAm*) government-appointed manager

interviniente SMF participant

interviú SF, (*a veces*) SM, **interview** SF, (*a veces*) SM interview • **hacer una ~ a algn** to interview sb

interviuvar ▷ CONJUG 1a VT to interview, have an interview with

intestado/a ADJ, SM/F intestate

intestinal ADJ intestinal

intestino ADJ (*frm*) (= *interno*) internal; [*lucha*] internecine
SM intestine, gut • **cáncer de ~** intestinal cancer • **síndrome de ~ irritable** irritable bowel syndrome ▸ **intestino ciego** caecum ▸ **intestino delgado** small intestine ▸ **intestino grueso** large intestine

inti SM (*Perú*) *former Peruvian monetary unit*

Intifada SF, **intifada** SF Intifada

intimación SF announcement, notification

íntimamente ADV intimately • **estar ~ ligado/relacionado a algn/algo** to be closely linked/related to sb/sth

intimar ▷ CONJUG 1a VT **1** (= *notificar*) to announce, notify
2 (= *mandar*) to order, require
VI • **ahora intiman mucho** they're very friendly now • **~ con algn** to be friends with sb
VPR **intimarse 1** ▷ VI
2 (= *hacer amistad*) to become friendly (**con** with)

intimidación SF intimidation; ▷ **disparo**

intimidad SF **1** (= *amistad*) intimacy, familiarity • **disfrutar de la ~ de algn** to be on close terms with sb • **entrar en ~ con algn** to become friendly with sb
2 (= *ámbito privado*) privacy • **celebró su cumpleaños en la ~ familiar** he celebrated his birthday in the privacy of his family • **conocido en la ~ como Josemari** known in private life as Josemari • **la ceremonia se celebró en la ~** the wedding was a private affair
3 intimidades (= *cosas personales*) personal matters, private matters; (*euf*) (= *genitales*) private parts (*euf*), privates (*euf*) (*hum*)

intimidado ADJ intimidated

intimidador ADJ intimidating

intimidar ▷ CONJUG 1a VT to intimidate, scare

VPR **intimidarse** (= *temer*) to be intimidated; (= *asustarse*) to get scared
intimidatorio ADJ intimidating
intimista ADJ intimate, private
íntimo/a ADJ [*secreto, confesión*] intimate; [*amigo, relación*] close, intimate; [*pensamientos, sentimientos*] innermost; [*vida*] personal, private • **una boda íntima** a quiet wedding, a private wedding • **una cena íntima** a romantic meal • **una fiesta íntima** a private party • **es ~ amigo mío** he is a very close friend of mine • **en lo más ~ de mi corazón** in my heart of hearts
SM/F close friend • **solo lo saben sus ~s** only her close friends know
intitular ▸ CONJUG 1a VT to entitle
intocable ADJ **1** (= *sagrado*) sacred, sacrosanct • **la Constitución es ~** the Constitution is sacred *o* sacrosanct • **sigue líder ~ en los Campeonatos del Mundo** he is still the runaway leader in the World Championships
2 [*tema*] taboo
SMF (*en la India*) untouchable
intolerable ADJ intolerable, unbearable
intolerancia SF **1** (*cualidad*) intolerance
2 (*Med*) intolerance • **~ a la lactosa** intolerance to lactose • **tiene ~ al sol** he's allergic to direct sunlight
intolerante ADJ intolerant (**con** of)
SMF intolerant person
intonso ADJ **1** (= *con pelo largo*) [*persona*] with long hair; [*barba*] unshorn, shaggy
2 [*libro*] untrimmed, with edges untrimmed
3 (= *grosero*) boorish
intoxicación SF **1** (*Med*) poisoning
▸ **intoxicación alimenticia** food poisoning
▸ **intoxicación etílica** alcohol poisoning; (*euf*) drunkenness
2 (*Pol*) indoctrination • **campaña de ~ informativa** campaign of media indoctrination
intoxicador(a) ADJ **1** intoxicating
2 (*Pol*) misleading, deceptive
SM/F indoctrinator
intoxicar ▸ CONJUG 1g VT **1** (*Med*) to poison
2 (*Pol*) to indoctrinate
VPR **intoxicarse 1** (*Med*) (*con sustancia tóxica*) to be poisoned; (*con alimentos*) to get food poisoning
2 (*con drogas*) to drug o.s.; (*con alcohol*) to get intoxicated
intra... PREF intra...
intracomunitario ADJ within the EC
intraducible ADJ untranslatable
intragable ADJ (= *desagradable*) unpalatable; (= *insoportable*) intolerable; (= *no aceptable*) unacceptable
intramatrimonial ADJ • **agresión ~** domestic violence, marital violence
intramuros ADV within the city, within the walls
intramuscular ADJ (*Med*) intramuscular
intranet [intra'net] SF intranet
intranquilidad SF (= *preocupación*) worry, anxiety; (= *desasosiego*) restlessness
intranquilizar ▸ CONJUG 1f VT to worry, make uneasy
VPR **intranquilizarse** to get worried, feel uneasy
intranquilo ADJ (= *preocupado*) worried, anxious; (= *desasosegado*) restless • **estaban ~s por nuestra tardanza** they were worried *o* anxious because we were late
intranscendencia SF = **intrascendencia**
intranscendente ADJ = **intrascendente**
intranscribible ADJ unprintable
intransferible ADJ not transferable
intransigencia SF intransigence
intransigente ADJ (*gen*) intransigent; (= *que no cede*) unyielding; (= *fanático*) diehard
SMF diehard
intransitable ADJ impassable
intransitivo ADJ, SM intransitive
intrascendencia SF unimportance, insignificance
intrascendente ADJ unimportant, insignificant
intratable ADJ **1** [*persona*] difficult • **¡son ~s!** they're impossible!
2 (*Med*) untreatable
intrauterino ADJ intrauterine
intravenoso ADJ intravenous
intrépidamente ADV intrepidly
intrepidez SF intrepidness, intrepidity
intrépido ADJ intrepid
intricado ADJ = **intrincado**
intriga SF (= *maquinación*) intrigue; (= *ardid*) plot, scheme; (*Teat*) plot • **novela de ~** thriller • **película de ~** thriller ▸ **intriga secundaria** subplot
intrigante ADJ **1** (= *enredador*) scheming
2 (= *interesante*) intriguing
SMF schemer
intrigar ▸ CONJUG 1h VT **1** (= *interesar*) to intrigue • **lo que más me intriga del caso es ...** the most intriguing aspect of the case is ... • **me tienes intrigada** you've got me intrigued
2 (*LAm*) [+ *asunto*] to conduct in a surprising way
VI to scheme, plot
VPR **intrigarse** (*LAm*) to be intrigued
intrincadamente ADV **1** (= *complejamente*) intricately • **los dos asuntos están ~ vinculados** the two matters are intricately linked
2 (= *formando una trama*) densely, impenetrably
intrincado ADJ **1** (= *complejo*) complicated; (= *enmarañado*) intricate • **un laberinto ~** an intricate maze • **explorábamos los ~s recovecos** we explored the hidden corners • **un hombre de carácter ~** a man with a complex character
2 [*bosque*] dense
intrincar ▸ CONJUG 1g VT (= *complicar*) to confuse, complicate; (= *enredar*) to entangle
intríngulis* SM INV (= *pega*) hidden snag, catch*; (= *misterio*) puzzle, mystery; (= *secreto*) (hidden) secret; (= *motivo*) ulterior motive • **ahí está el ~** that's the secret • **tiene su ~** it's quite tricky*, it's not as easy as it looks
intrínsecamente ADV intrinsically, inherently
intrínseco ADJ intrinsic, inherent
intro... PREF intro...
introducción SF **1** [*de texto*] introduction • **"Introducción a la gramática española"** "Introduction to Spanish Grammar" • **un curso de ~ al psicoanálisis** an introductory course in psychoanalysis
2 (= *inserción*) insertion • **la ~ del tubo puede causar heridas** inserting the tube *o* the insertion of the tube can cause injury, the tube's insertion could cause injury
3 (= *llegada*) [*de mercancías, cambios*] introduction • **la ~ de la moneda única** the introduction of a single currency • **la revolución que supuso la ~ del vídeo en los hogares** the revolution caused by the arrival of the video in the home • **se dedicaba a la ~ de heroína en España** he was involved in smuggling heroin into Spain • **~ de contrabando** smuggling
4 (*Inform*) [*de datos*] input
introducir ▸ CONJUG 3n VT **1** (= *meter*) **a** [+ *mano, pie*] to put, place (**en** in(to)); [+ *moneda, llave*] to put, insert (**en** in(to)) • **introdujo los pies en el agua** he put *o* placed his feet in(to) the water • **no podía ~ la llave en la cerradura** he couldn't get the key in(to) the lock • **introduzca la moneda/el disquete en la ranura** insert the coin/the diskette in(to) the slot • **introdujo la carta por debajo de la puerta** he slipped the letter under the door
b [+ *enfermedad, mercancías*] to bring (**en** into), introduce (**en** into); [+ *contrabando, droga*] to bring (**en** in(to)) • **cualquier animal puede ~ la rabia en el país** any animal could bring *o* introduce rabies into the country • **el tabaco introducido ilegalmente en Europa** the tobacco brought into Europe illegally • **esa bebida hace ya años que se introdujo en España** that drink was introduced in Spain *o* was brought onto the Spanish market years ago • **~ algo de contrabando** to smuggle sth (**en** into) • **~ algo en el mercado** to bring sth onto the market, introduce sth into the market
c • **~ a algn en** [+ *habitación*] to show sb into; [+ *situación real*] to introduce sb to; [+ *situación irreal*] to transport sb to • **el mayordomo nos introdujo hasta el salón** the butler showed us into the drawing room • **quería ~la en la alta sociedad** he wanted to introduce her to high society • **su poesía nos introduce en un mundo de felicidad** his poetry transports us to a world of happiness • **la novela nos introduce en el Egipto de Cleopatra** the novel takes us back to the Egypt of Cleopatra
2 (= *empezar*) [+ *cultivo, ley, método*] to introduce • **poco a poco se fueron introduciendo las tradiciones árabes** Arab traditions were gradually introduced • **para ~ el tema, empezaré hablando de política exterior** to introduce the subject, I'll begin by discussing foreign policy • **~ la ley del divorcio causó muchos problemas** the introduction of the divorce law caused many problems, introducing the divorce law was very problematic
3 (= *realizar*) [+ *medidas, reformas*] to bring in, introduce • **quieren ~ cambios en la legislación** they want to make changes to the current legislation, they want to introduce changes into the current legislation • **las reformas se ~án gradualmente a lo largo de los próximos tres años** the reforms will be phased in over the next three years, the reforms will be brought in *o* introduced gradually over the next three years • **se deben ~ mejoras en el diseño del folleto** improvements need to be made to the pamphlet design
4 (*Inform*) [+ *datos*] to input, enter
VPR **introducirse 1** (= *meterse*) [*astilla, cristal*] to lodge • **la espina se me introdujo por debajo de la uña** the thorn lodged under my nail • **el balón se introdujo a través de los palos** the ball went in through the goalposts • **~se en algo** to get into sth, enter sth • **cuando el virus se introduce en el organismo** when the virus gets into *o* enters the organism • **se introdujo en el sótano a través de un agujero** he got into the basement through a hole • **el coche se introdujo despacio en el garaje** the car entered the garage slowly • **hemos logrado ~nos en el mercado europeo** we've managed to break *o* get into the European market • **muchas palabras se introducen en nuestro idioma procedentes del inglés** many words pass into our language from English
2 (= *entrometerse*) to interfere, meddle
introductor(a) ADJ introductory
SM/F • **el ~ de la música atonal en España**

the man who introduced atonal music in Spain • **fue la ~a de esa técnica en Latinoamérica** she was the one who introduced that technique in Latin America
▸ **introductor(a) de datos** data inputter
▸ **introductor(a) de embajadores** *head of Protocol in the Foreign Affairs Department*

introductorio ADJ **1** (*Literat*) [*curso, discurso*] introductory; [*poema, relato*] opening
2 (*Mús*) [*movimiento*] opening

introito SM **1** (*Teat*) prologue, prolog (*EEUU*)
2 (*Rel*) introit

intromisión SF **1** (= *injerencia*) interference
2 (= *inserción*) introduction, insertion

introspección SF introspection

introspectivo ADJ introspective

introversión SF introversion

introvertido/a ADJ introverted
SM/F introvert

intrusión SF (= *intromisión*) intrusion; (*Jur*) trespass ▸ **intrusión informática** hacking

intrusismo SM infiltration

intruso/a ADJ intrusive
SM/F (*gen*) intruder; (= *extraño*) outsider; (*en fiesta*) gatecrasher; (*Jur*) trespasser; (*Mil, Pol*) infiltrator ▸ **intruso/a informático/a** hacker

intuible ADJ that can be intuited

intuición SF intuition • **por ~** intuitively

intuir ▸ CONJUG 3g VT (= *saber*) to know intuitively; (= *sentir*) to sense, feel • **intuyo que alguien me sigue** I have a feeling I'm being followed
VPR **intuirse** • **eso se intuye** that can be guessed • **se intuye que ...** one can tell intuitively that ..., one can guess that ... • **el hombre se intuye observado** the man has a feeling he is under observation

intuitivamente ADV intuitively

intuitivo ADJ intuitive

intumescencia SF intumescence (*frm*), swelling

intumescente ADJ intumescent (*frm*), swollen

inuit ADJ, SMF Inuit

inundación SF (*acción*) flooding; (*efecto*) flood

inundadizo ADJ (*LAm*) liable to flooding

inundado ADJ flooded

inundar ▸ CONJUG 1a VT **1** (*con agua*) to flood • **la lluvia inundó la campiña** the rain flooded the countryside, the rain left the countryside under water
2 (*con productos*) to flood (**de, en** with), swamp (**de, en** with) • **~ el mercado de un producto** to flood the market with a product • **quedamos inundados de ofertas** offers rained in on us, we were flooded *o* swamped with offers
3 [*gente*] to flood, swamp
4 [*pena, sensación*] to overwhelm, sweep over
VPR **inundarse 1** (*con agua*) to flood • **se inundó la bodega** the cellar flooded
2 (*con productos*) to be flooded, be inundated
3 (*con personas*) to be inundated • **~se de** to be inundated with

inusitado ADJ unusual, rare

inusual ADJ unusual

inusualmente ADV unusually

inútil ADJ **1** (= *vano*) [*intento, esfuerzo*] unsuccessful, fruitless • **lo intenté todo, pero fue ~** I tried everything, but it was no use *o* useless • **es ~ que usted proteste** it's no good *o* use you protesting, there's no point in protesting • **es ~ seguir intentándolo** there's no point in keeping on trying
2 (= *inepto*) useless*, hopeless*
3 (= *inválido*) disabled • **ha quedado ~ a causa de la artritis** she is completely disabled by arthritis
4 (= *inservible*) useless • **tira todos los trastos ~es** throw away all that useless junk
5 (*Mil*) unfit • **lo han declarado ~ para el servicio militar** he has been declared unfit for military service
SMF • **¡tu hermana es una ~!** your sister is useless *o* hopeless!*

inutilidad SF uselessness • **constituir ~** to render ineligible, bar

inutilizable ADJ unusable, unfit for use

inutilización SF [*de mecanismo*] disablement; [*de sello*] cancellation

inutilizado ADJ unusable, useless

inutilizar ▸ CONJUG 1f VT (= *hacer inútil*) (*gen*) to make useless, render useless; [+ *mecanismo*] to disable, put out of action; [+ *sello*] to cancel • **el cañón quedó inutilizado** the cannon was put out of action • **las carreteras han quedado inutilizadas** the roads have become unuseable • **la mano derecha le quedó inutilizada** he lost the use of his right hand
VPR **inutilizarse** to become useless; [*mecanismo*] to be disabled

inútilmente ADV (= *sin utilidad*) uselessly; (= *en vano*) vainly, fruitlessly

INV SM ABR (*Esp*) = **Instituto Nacional de la Vivienda**

invadeable ADJ [*carretera, puente*] impassable; [*situación, problema*] unsurmountable

invadir ▸ CONJUG 3a VT **1** (= *atacar*) [+ *célula, país*] to invade; [+ *espacio aéreo, aguas jurisdiccionales*] to violate, enter • **los turistas invaden nuestras costas** tourists descend upon *o* invade our coasts • **las malas hierbas/los insectos invadieron el trigal** the wheatfield was overrun with weeds/insects • **los pájaros invadieron la plantación** birds swooped down onto the field • **~ la intimidad de algn** to invade sb's privacy
2 (= *ocupar*) **a** [*multitud*] (*gen*) to pour into/onto; (*protestando*) to storm into/onto • **los fans invadieron el estadio/el escenario** the fans poured into the stadium/onto the stage • **los manifestantes invadieron la ciudad/las calles** the protesters stormed into the city/onto the streets
b [*vehículo*] to go into/onto • **el camión invadió el carril contrario/la pista de despegue** the lorry went into the wrong lane/onto the runway
3 • **~ a algn** [*sentimiento*] to overcome sb • **la invadió una gran tristeza** she was filled with great sadness, a great sadness overcame her • **el miedo había invadido su cuerpo** she was overcome by fear, she was filled with fear, fear overcame her
4 (*Com*) [*producto*] to encroach on • **los vinos franceses invaden los mercados europeos** French wines are encroaching on European markets • **la televisión invadió nuestros hogares** television invaded our homes
5 (*Jur*) to encroach upon • **el abogado intentó ~ las funciones del juez** the solicitor attempted to encroach upon the judge's prerogatives • **el delegado invadió atribuciones que no le correspondían** the delegate went beyond the powers vested in him

invalidación SF [*de certificado, resultado*] invalidation, nullification; [*de una decisión*] reversal

invalidante ADJ disabling, incapacitating

invalidar ▸ CONJUG 1a VT [+ *certificado, resultado*] to invalidate, nullify; [+ *decisión*] to reverse; [+ *leyes*] to repeal

invalidez SF **1** (*Med*) disability, disablement • **solicitar la ~ (laboral)** to apply for disability benefit ▸ **invalidez permanente** permanent disability
2 (*Jur*) invalidity

inválido/a ADJ **1** (*Med*) disabled
2 (*Jur*) invalid, null and void • **declarar inválida una elección** to declare an election void
SM/F (*Med*) disabled person • **~ de guerra** disabled ex-serviceman

invalorable ADJ (*LAm*) invaluable

invaluable ADJ (*LAm*) invaluable

invariable ADJ invariable

invariablemente ADV invariably

invariancia SF invariability, lack of variation

invasión SF **1** [*de país, cultivos*] invasion • **la ~ aliada de Italia** the allied invasion of Italy • **una ~ de películas norteamericanas** an invasion of American films
2 [*de pista, calzada*] presence • **la ~ de la pista por un avión de carga causó el accidente** the accident was caused by the presence of a cargo plane on the runway
3 (*Jur*) [*de derechos*] encroachment; [*de funciones, poderes*] usurpation
4 (*Col*) (= *chabolas*) shantytown

invasivo ADJ invasive

invasor(a) ADJ [*ejército, pueblo*] invading; [*tumor*] invasive
SM/F invader • **la resistencia contra el ~ extranjero** resistance against the foreign invader

invectiva SF (*frm*) invective • **una ~** a tirade

invectivar ▸ CONJUG 1a VT (*frm*) (= *arremeter*) to inveigh against (*frm*); (= *insultar*) to heap abuse upon

invencibilidad SF invincibility

invencible ADJ [*enemigo, rival*] invincible, unbeatable; [*obstáculo*] insurmountable, insuperable • **La (Armada) Invencible** the (Spanish Armada) (*1588*)

invenciblemente ADV invincibly, unbeatably

invención SF **1** (= *invento*) invention • **la ~ de la imprenta** the invention of printing
2 (= *mentira*) invention, fabrication; (*Literat*) invention, fiction

invendible ADJ unsaleable, unsellable

invendido ADJ unsold
SM unsold item

inventado ADJ (= *falso*) made-up

inventar ▸ CONJUG 1a VT (*gen*) to invent; [+ *plan*] to devise; [+ *historia, excusa*] to invent, make up, concoct
VPR **inventarse** [+ *historia, excusa*] to invent, make up, concoct

inventariado SM detailed account

inventariar ▸ CONJUG 1b VT to inventory, make an inventory of

inventario SM inventory • **~ continuo** continuous inventory • **hacer el ~** (*Com*) to do the stocktaking, take inventory (*EEUU*) • **"cerrado por ~"** "closed for stocktaking", "closed for inventory" (*EEUU*)

inventiva SF (= *imaginación*) inventiveness; (= *ingenio*) ingenuity, resourcefulness

inventivo ADJ (= *imaginativo*) inventive; (= *ingenioso*) ingenious, resourceful

invento SM invention • MODISMO: • **~ del tebeo*** silly idea

inventor(a) SM/F inventor

inverificable ADJ unverifiable

invernáculo SM greenhouse

invernada SF **1** (= *estación*) winter season
2 (= *hibernación*) hibernation
3 (*And, Cono Sur*) (= *pasto*) winter pasture
4 (*Caribe*) (= *tempestad*) heavy rainstorm

invernadero SM **1** (*para plantas*) greenhouse; (*con temperatura elevada*) hothouse

2 (*LAm*) (= *pasto*) winter pasture
3 (= *lugar de recreo*) winter resort
ADJ INV • **efecto ~** greenhouse effect • **gases ~** greenhouse gases

invernal ADJ winter (*antes de s*); [*clima, frío*] wintry

invernante ADJ over-wintering
SM (*Orn*) over-wintering species, winter visitor

invernar ▸ CONJUG 1j VI **1** (= *pasar el invierno*) to winter, spend the winter; (*Zool*) to hibernate
2 (*Cono Sur*) [*ganado*] to pasture (and fatten) in winter
VT (*Cono Sur*) [+ *ganado*] to pasture (and fatten) in winter

invernazo* SM (*Caribe*) rainy season (*July to September*)

inverne SM (*LAm*) (= *pasto*) winter pasturing; (= *engorde*) winter fattening

invernizo ADJ wintry

inverosímil ADJ (= *improbable*) unlikely, improbable; (= *increíble*) implausible

inverosimilitud SF (= *improbabilidad*) unlikeliness, improbability; (= *incredibilidad*) implausibility

inversamente ADV inversely • **e ~** and vice versa

inversión SF **1** (*Com, Econ*) investment (**en** in) ▸ **inversión de capital(es)** capital investment ▸ **inversiones extranjeras** foreign investment (*sing*)
2 [*de esfuerzo, tiempo*] investment
3 [*de orden, dirección*] inversion; (*Elec*) reversal; (*Aut, Mec*) reversing ▸ **inversión de marcha** reversing, backing ▸ **inversión sexual** homosexuality ▸ **inversión térmica** temperature inversion

inversionista SMF (*Com, Econ*) investor

inverso ADJ **1** (= *contrario*) opposite • **en sentido ~** in the opposite direction • **en orden ~** in reverse order • **por orden ~ de antigüedad** in reverse order of seniority • **a la inversa** the other way round; (*al contrario*) on the contrary
2 [*cara*] reverse
3 (*Mat*) inverse

inversor(a) ADJ investment (*antes de s*)
SM/F (*Com, Econ*) investor ▸ **inversor(a) financiero/a** investments manager ▸ **inversor(a) inmobiliario/a** property investor ▸ **inversor(a) institucional** institutional investor

invertebrado ADJ, SM invertebrate

invertido/a ADJ **1** (= *al revés*) [*imagen, objeto*] inverted, upside-down; [*orden*] reversed • **escritura invertida** mirror writing • **la pirámide invertida** the inverted pyramid
2† (= *homosexual*) homosexual
SM/F† invert†, homosexual

invertir ▸ CONJUG 3i VT **1** (*Com, Econ*) to invest (**en** in)
2 [+ *esfuerzo, tiempo*] to invest (**en** on), put in (**en** on) • **invirtieron una hora en recorrer diez kilómetros** they spent an hour covering ten kilometres
3 [+ *figura, objeto*] (= *volcar*) to invert, turn upside down; (= *poner al revés*) to put the other way round, reverse
4 (= *cambiar*) [+ *orden*] to change, invert; [+ *dirección*] to reverse
5 (*Mat*) to invert
VI • **~ en algo** to invest in sth
VPR [*papeles, relación de fuerzas, tendencia*] to be reversed

investidura SF investiture • **discurso de ~** investiture speech • **votación de ~** (*Pol*) vote of confidence (*in the new prime minister*)

investigación SF **1** [*de accidente, delito*] (*por la policía*) investigation; (*por un comité*) inquiry • **la ~ policial del robo** the police investigation of the robbery • **la ~ de los dos casos de corrupción** the inquiry into the two cases of corruption • **ha ordenado la ~ de las cuentas bancarias** he has ordered their bank accounts to be investigated • **una comisión de ~** a committee of inquiry
2 (*científica, académica*) research • **están realizando una ~ sobre el ADN** they're doing research into *o* on DNA • **hace trabajo de ~** he's doing research work • **un trabajo de ~ sobre el barroco** a research project on the baroque, a piece of research on the baroque ▸ **investigación de mercado** market research ▸ **investigación operativa** operational research, operations research ▸ **investigación y desarrollo** research and development

investigador(a) ADJ (*gen*) investigative; (*en ciencia*) research (*antes de s*) • **equipo ~** (*en periodismo, policía*) team of investigators; (*en ciencia*) research team • **labor ~a** (*de periodista, policía*) investigative work; (*en ciencia*) research • **capacidad ~a** research ability • **han nombrado una comisión ~a sobre el caso** a commission of enquiry has been appointed to the case
SM/F **1** (= *periodista, policía*) investigator ▸ **investigador(a) privado/a** private investigator *o* detective
2 (= *científico*) research worker, researcher; [*de doctorado*] research student

investigar ▸ CONJUG 1h VT **1** [+ *accidente, crimen, queja, hechos*] to investigate; [+ *cuentas, patrimonio*] to audit • **el juez ordenó ~ sus actividades financieras** the judge ordered an investigation of their financial activities
2 (*Univ*) to research, do research into
3 (= *tantear*) to check out • **quédate aquí y yo ~é el terreno** stay here and I'll check out the lie of the land*
VI **1** [*policía, comité*] to investigate
2 (*Univ*) to do research • **una beca para ~ sobre el SIDA** a grant to do research into AIDS

investigativo ADJ investigative

investir ▸ CONJUG 3k VT • **fue investido doctor honoris causa** he was granted an honorary doctorate • **será investido presidente** he will be sworn in as president • **fue investido como Príncipe de Gales** the title of Prince of Wales was conferred on him • **~ a algn con *o* de algo** to confer sth on sb

inveterado ADJ [*fumador, pecador*] inveterate; [*criminal*] hardened; [*hábito*] deep-seated, well-established

inviabilidad SF (= *imposibilidad*) unfeasibility, unviability; [*de reclamación*] invalidity

inviable ADJ (= *imposible*) unfeasible, unviable, non-viable; [*reclamación*] invalid

invicto ADJ [*pueblo*] unconquered; [*equipo*] unbeaten

invidencia SF blindness

invidente ADJ blind
SMF blind person

invierno SM **1** (= *estación*) winter • **deportes de ~** winter sports ▸ **invierno nuclear** nuclear winter
2 (*And, CAm, Caribe*) (= *meses de lluvia*) rainy season
3 (*Caribe*) (= *aguacero*) heavy shower

inviolabilidad SF inviolability ▸ **inviolabilidad parlamentaria** parliamentary immunity

inviolable ADJ inviolable

inviolado ADJ inviolate

invisibilidad SF invisibility

invisible ADJ invisible • **importaciones ~s** invisible imports • **exportaciones ~s** invisible exports
SM (*Arg*) hairpin

invitación SF invitation (a to) • **a ~ de algn** at sb's invitation

invitado/a ADJ invited • **estrella invitada** guest star
SM/F guest ▸ **invitado/a de honor** guest of honour ▸ **invitado/a de piedra** unwanted guest ▸ **invitado/a estelar** star guest

invitar ▸ CONJUG 1a VT **1** (*gen*) to invite • **me invitó al cine** she invited me to the cinema • **me invitó a Marbella** she invited me to go to Marbella • **invito yo** it's on me • **os invito a una cerveza** I'll buy *o* stand you all a beer • **nos invitó a cenar (fuera)** she took us out for a meal • **dio las gracias a los que lo habían invitado** he thanked his hosts
2 (= *incitar*) to invite • **~ a algn a hacer algo** to invite sb to do sth; (*exhortando*) to call on sb to do sth • **~ a algn a la violencia** to incite sb to violence
3 (= *atraer*) to entice • **una frase que invita a comprar** a slogan which entices you to buy

in vitro ADJ, ADV in vitro • **fecundación *o* fertilización ~** in vitro fertilization

invocación SF invocation • **una ~ a la Virgen** an invocation of *o* to the Virgin • **una ~ de auxilio** a plea for help

invocar ▸ CONJUG 1g VT **1** (= *citar*) to cite, invoke
2 [+ *derecho, principio*] to cite, invoke • **~ la ley** to invoke the law
3 (= *rogar*) (*gen*) to invoke, appeal for; [+ *divinidad, santo*] to invoke, call on • **~ la ayuda de algn** to appeal for *o* invoke sb's help
4 (*Inform*) to call

involución SF (*Pol*) regression ▸ **involución demográfica** demographic regression

involucionismo SM (*Pol*) reaction; (*en sentido amplio*) reactionary forces (*pl*)

involucionista (*Pol*) ADJ regressive, reactionary
SMF reactionary

involucración SF, **involucramiento** SM involvement

involucrar ▸ CONJUG 1a VT **1** (= *implicar*) to involve • **~ a algn en algo** to involve sb in sth, mix sb up in sth • **andar involucrado en** to be mixed up in • **las personas involucradas en el caso** the people involved in the affair
2 (= *mezclar*) to jumble up, mix up • **lo tiene todo involucrado** he's got it all mixed up • **~ algo en un discurso** to bring sth irrelevant into a speech
VPR **involucrarse 1** (= *participar*) to get involved (**en** in)
2 (= *entrometerse*) to meddle, interfere (**en** in)

involuntariamente ADV (= *sin voluntad*) involuntarily; (= *sin intención*) unintentionally

involuntario ADJ [*gesto, movimiento*] involuntary; [*ofensa*] unintentional; [*agente, causante*] unwitting • **homicidio ~** involuntary manslaughter

involutivo ADJ (*Pol*) reactionary

invulnerabilidad SF invulnerability

invulnerable ADJ invulnerable

inyección SF **1** (*Med*) (= *acción, sustancia*) injection • **una ~ de morfina** an injection of morphine, a morphine injection • **ha venido a ponerme una ~** he's come to give me an injection • **se pone una ~ diaria** she gives herself an injection every day ▸ **inyección intramuscular** intramuscular injection ▸ **inyección intravenosa** intravenous injection ▸ **inyección letal**

lethal injection ▸ **inyección subcutánea** subcutaneous injection
2 [*de dinero, fondos*] injection • **una ~ financiera de 300 millones de euros** a cash injection of 300 million euros
3 [*de optimismo, energía*] injection • **una ~ de moral para el equipo** a shot in the arm for the team
4 (*Mec*) injection • **motor de ~** fuel injection engine • **impresión por ~ de burbujas** bubble-jet printing ▸ **inyección electrónica** electronic fuel injection

inyectable ADJ injectable • **"administración por vía oral o ~"** "to be taken orally or by injection"
SM (= *inyección*) injection; (= *vacuna*) vaccine

inyectado ADJ • **ojos ~s en sangre** bloodshot eyes

inyectar ▹ CONJUG 1a VT **1** (*Med*) to inject (en into) • **~ algo en algn** to inject sb with sth • **le ~on un antibiótico** he had an antibiotic injection
2 [+ *optimismo, dinero*] to inject • **~on optimismo al mercado** they injected optimism into the market
3 (*Mec*) to inject
VPR **inyectarse** to give o.s. an injection, inject o.s.

inyector SM (*en motor*) injector; (*en horno, fragua*) nozzle

ion SM ion

iónico ADJ ionic

ionizador SM ionizer, negative ionizer

ionizar ▹ CONJUG 1f VT to ionize

ionosfera SF ionosphere

IORTV ABR = **Instituto Oficial de Radiodifusión y Televisión**

iota SF iota

IPC SM ABR (= **índice de precios al consumo**) RPI, CPI (*esp EEUU*)

ipecacuana SF ipecacuanha, ipecac (*EEUU*)

IPM SM ABR (= **índice de precios al por menor**) RPI

iPod® SM iPod®

ipomea SF (*Bot*) morning glory

IPPV SM ABR = **Instituto para la Promoción Pública de la Vivienda**

ipso facto ADV right away, straightaway

ir

VERBO INTRANSITIVO
VERBO AUXILIAR
VERBO PRONOMINAL

▹ CONJUG 3S

Para las expresiones ***ir de vacaciones, ir de veras, ir dado, irse de la lengua,*** *ver la otra entrada.*

VERBO INTRANSITIVO

1 (= *marchar*) **a** (*indicando movimiento, acción*) to go • **anoche fuimos al cine** we went to the cinema last night • **¿has ido alguna vez a Quito?** have you ever been to Quito? • **¿a qué colegio vas?** what school do you go to? • **esta carretera va a Huesca** this road goes to Huesca, this is the road to Huesca • **íbamos hacia Sevilla** we were going towards Seville • **ir hasta León** to go as far as León • **ir despacio** to go slow(ly) • **ir con tiento** to go carefully *o* cautiously • **¡ya voy! • ¡ahora voy!** coming!, I'll be right there! • **vamos a casa** let's go home • **¿quién va?** (*Mil*) who goes there?
b (*indicando la forma de transporte*) • **ir andando** to walk, go on foot • **tuvimos que ir andando** we had to walk *o* go on foot • **¿vas a ir andando o en autobús?** are you walking or going by bus? • **ir en avión** to fly • **ir en bicicleta** to ride • **ir a caballo** to ride • **fui en coche** I went by car, I drove • **ir a pie** to walk, go on foot • **fui en tren** I went by train *o* rail
c (*con complemento*) • **iba muy bien vestido** he was very well dressed • **este reloj va atrasado** this clock is slow • **iban muertos de risa por la calle** they were killing themselves laughing as they went down the street
d • **ir (a) por** to go and get • **voy (a) por el paraguas** I'll go and get the umbrella • **voy por el médico** I'll go and fetch *o* get the doctor • **voy a por él** (*a buscarle*) I'll go and get him; (*a atacarle*) I'm going to get him • **solo van a por las pelas*** they're only in it for the money

2 (*indicando proceso*) **a** [*persona*] • **¿cómo va el paciente?** how's the patient doing? • **el enfermo va mejor** the patient is improving *o* doing better • **el enfermo va peor** the patient has got worse
b [*acción, obra*] to go • **¿cómo va el ensayo?** how's the essay going?, how are you getting on with the essay? • **¿cómo va el partido?** what's the score? • **¿cómo va eso?** how are things (going)? • **todo va bien** everything's fine, everything's going well • **los resultados van a mejor** the results are improving *o* getting better
c • **ir por**: • **¿te has leído ya el libro? ¿por dónde vas?** have you read the book yet? whereabouts are you? *o* how far have you got? • **ir por la mitad de algo** to be halfway through sth • **la película ya va por la mitad** it's already half way through the film • **íbamos por la mitad de nuestro viaje** we were half way there

3 (*indicando manera, posición*) • **ese cuadro debería ir encima del sofá** that picture should go over the sofa • **lo que te dijo iba en serio** he meant what he said (to you)

4 (= *extenderse*) to go, stretch • **la pradera va desde la montaña hasta el mar** the grasslands go *o* stretch from the mountains to the sea • **en lo que va de año** so far this year • **en lo que va de semana hemos recibido cientos de llamadas** we've had hundreds of calls so far this week • **en lo que va desde 1950 hasta nuestros días** from 1950 up until now

5 (*indicando distancia, diferencia*) • **va mucho de uno a otro** there's a lot of difference between them • **¡lo que va del padre al hijo!** what a difference there is between father and son!, father and son are nothing like each other! • **de 7 a 9 van 2** the difference between 7 and 9 is 2; (*en resta*) 7 from 9 leaves 2

6 (*indicando acumulación*) • **con este van 30** that makes 30 (with this one) • **van ya tres llamadas y no contesta** we've called him three times and he doesn't answer

7 (*en apuestas*) • **van cinco pesos a que no lo haces** I bet you five pesos you won't do it • **¿cuánto va?** how much do you bet?

8 (= *vestir*) • **ir con pantalones** to be wearing trousers • **¿con qué ropa** *o* **cómo fuiste a la boda?** what did you wear to the wedding? • **iba de rojo** she was dressed in red, she was wearing red • **la que va de negro** the girl in black; ▹ **etiqueta**

9 • **irle a algn a** (*indicando importancia*) • **nos va mucho en esto** we have a lot riding on this • **le va la vida en ello** his life depends on it • MODISMO: • **ni me va ni me viene** it's nothing to do with me
b (*indicando situación*) • **¿cómo te va?** how are things?, how are you doing? • **¿cómo te va en los estudios?** how are you getting on with your studies? • **¡que te vaya bien!** take care!
c (= *sentar*) to suit • **¿me va bien esto?** does this suit me? • **no le va bien el sombrero** the hat doesn't suit her
d* (= *gustar*) • **no me va nada ese rollo** I'm not into that sort of thing* • **ese tipo de gente no me va** I don't get on with that type of people • **le va al Cruz Azul** (*Méx*) (*Dep*) he supports Cruz Azul

10 (*seguido de preposición*) **ir con** (= *acompañar, combinar*) to go with • **no quería ir con ella a ninguna parte** I didn't want to go anywhere with her • **iba con su madre** he was with his mother • **esta fotocopia debe ir con la carta** this photocopy has to go (in) with the letter • **yo voy con el Real Madrid** I support Real Madrid • **el marrón no va bien con el azul** brown and blue don't go together • **eso de ser famosa no va con ella** being famous doesn't agree with her
ir de • **¿de qué va la película?** what's the film about? • **la película va nada más que de sexo** the film is all sex • **no sabe de qué va el rollo*** he doesn't know what it's all about • **va de intelectual por la vida*** he acts the intellectual all the time • **¿de qué vas?*** what are you on about?*
ir para • **va para los 40** he's getting on for 40, he's knocking on 40 • **va para viejo** he's getting old • **va para arquitecto** he's going to be an architect • **va para cinco años que entré en la Universidad** it's getting on for five years since I started University
ir por (*indicando intención*) • **eso no va por usted** I wasn't referring to you, that wasn't meant for you • **¡va por los novios!** (here's) to the bride and groom!
ir tras to go after • **se dio cuenta de que iban tras él** he realized they were after him • **ir tras una chica** to chase (after) a girl

11 (*otras locuciones*) • **a lo que iba** as I was saying • **ir a algn con algo**: • **siempre le iba con sus problemas** he always went to her with his problems • **¿dónde vas?**: • **—¿le regalamos un equipo de música? —¿dónde vas? con un libro tiene bastante** "shall we give him a stereo?" — "what do you mean? a book is fine" • **—¿le pido disculpas? —¿dónde vas? deja que sea él quien se disculpe** "shall I apologize?" — "what are you talking about? let him be the one to apologize" • **si vamos a eso** for that matter • **a eso voy** I'm coming to that • **pues, a eso voy** that's what I mean, that's what I'm getting at • **es el no va más*** it's the ultimate • **ir de mal en peor** to go from bad to worse • **ir a lo suyo** to do one's own thing; (*pey*) to look after Number One • **aquí cada uno va a lo suyo** everyone does their own thing here • **ir y venir**: • **era un constante ir y venir de ambulancias** ambulances were constantly coming and going • **llevo todo el día yendo y viniendo de un lado al otro de la ciudad** I've spent all day going from one end of town to the other • **cuando tú vas, yo ya he venido** I've been there before, I've seen it all before • **ir y**: • **ahora va y me dice que no viene** now he goes and tells me he's not coming • **fue y se marchó** (*Méx**) he just upped and left*; ▹ **lejos**

12 (*exclamaciones*) **¡vaya!** (*indicando sorpresa*) well!; (*indicando enfado*) damn! • **¡vaya! ¿qué haces tú por aquí?** well, what a surprise! what are you doing here? • **¡vaya, vaya!** well I'm blowed!* • **¡vaya coche!** what a car!, that's some car! • **¡vaya susto que me pegué!** I got such a fright!, what a fright I got! • **¡vaya con el niño!** that damn kid!*

¡vamos! (*dando ánimos*) come on!; (*para ponerse en marcha*) let's go! • **¡vamos! ¡di algo!** come on! say something! • **vamos, no es difícil** come on, it's not difficult • **una chica, vamos, una mujer** a girl, well, a woman • **es molesto, pero ¡vamos!** it's a nuisance, but there it is
¡qué va! • **—¿no me vas a echar la bronca? —no, qué va** "you're not going to tell me off, are you?" — "of course I'm not" • **¿perder la liga? ¡qué va, hombre!** lose the league? you must be joking!

VERBO AUXILIAR
ir a (+ *infin*) to go • **fui a verle** I went to see him • **vamos a hacerlo** (*afirmando*) we are going to do it; (*exhortando*) let's do it • **tras muchas vueltas fuimos a dar con la calle Serrano** after driving round for ages we eventually found Serrano Street • **¿cómo lo iba a tener?** how could he have had it? • **¡no lo va a saber!** of course he knows! • **¿no irás a decirme que no lo sabías?** you're not going to tell me you didn't know? • **¿no irá a soplar?‡** I hope he's not going to split on us* • **no vaya a ser que ...:** • **no salgas no vaya a ser que venga** don't go out in case she comes
ir (+ *gerund*) • **iba anocheciendo** it was getting dark • **iban fumando** they were smoking • **¿quién va ganando?** who's winning? • **fueron hablando todo el camino** they talked the whole way there • **como iba diciendo** as I was saying • **¡voy corriendo!** I'll be right there! • **id pensando en el tema que queréis tratar** be *o* start thinking about the subject you want to deal with • **hemos ido consiguiendo lo que queríamos** we found what we wanted eventually • **voy comprendiendo que ...** I am beginning to see that ...
ir (+ *participio*) • **van escritas tres cartas** that's three letters I've written • **va vendido todo** everything has been sold

VERBO PRONOMINAL **irse**
1 (*uso impersonal*) • **por aquí se va a Toledo** this is the way to Toledo • **¿por dónde se va al aeropuerto?** which is the way *o* which way is it to the airport?
2 (*= marcharse*) to go, leave • **se fueron** they went, they left • **se fue de la reunión sin decir nada** she left the meeting without saying anything • **es hora de irnos** it's time we were going • **me voy, ¡hasta luego!** I'm off, see you! • **vete a hacer los deberes** go and do your homework • **se le fue un hijo a Alemania** one of her sons went to Germany • **¡vete!** go away!, get out! • **¡no te vayas!** don't go! • **¡vámonos!** let's go!; (*antes de subirse al tren, barco*) all aboard! • **¡nos fuimos!** (*LAm**) let's go!, off we go!* • **me voy de con usted** (*CAm*) I'm leaving you
3 (*= actuar*) • **vete con cuidado cuando habléis de este tema** you should tread carefully when you mention that subject
4 (*= salirse*) (*por agujero*) to leak out; (*por el borde*) to overflow • **se fue el vino** the wine leaked out • **el líquido se fue por una ranura** the liquid ran out along a groove • **se me fue la leche** the milk boiled over • **a la cerveza se le ha ido el gas** the beer has gone flat
5 (*= vaciarse*) (*por agujero*) to leak; (*por el borde*) to overflow • **el neumático se va** the tyre is losing air
6 (*= desaparecer*) [*luz*] to go out • **se fue la luz** the lights went out • **la mancha se va solo con agua** you can only get the stain out with water
7 (*= terminarse*) • **írsele a algn: se me va el sueldo en autobuses** all my wages go on bus fares • **rápido, que se nos va el tiempo** be quick, we're running out of time • **no se me va este dolor de espalda** I can't seem to get rid of this backache • **hoy no se me va la mala leche** I can't seem to get out of my bad mood today • **no se le va el enfado** he's still angry
8 (*= perder el equilibrio*) • **parecía que me iba para atrás cuando andaba** I felt as if I were falling over backwards when I walked • **se le fue la pierna y tropezó** her leg went (from under her) and she tripped; ▸ **mano, pie**
9 (*euf*) (*= morirse*) (*en presente*) to be dying; (*en pasado*) to pass away • **se nos va el amo** the master is dying • **se nos fue hace tres años** he passed away three years ago
10 (*euf*) (*= ventosear*) to break wind; (*= orinar*) to wet o.s.; (*= defecar*) to soil o.s.
11‡ (*= eyacular*) to come‡

---

ira SF [*de persona*] anger, rage; [*de elementos*] fury, violence • **ha provocado la ira de los críticos** he has incurred the wrath of the critics • **las uvas de la ira** the grapes of wrath
iracundia SF (*= propensión*) irascibility (*frm*); (*= cólera*) rage, ire (*liter*)
iracundo ADJ (*= propenso a la ira*) irascible (*frm*); (*= colérico*) irate
Irak SM Iraq
irakí ADJ, SMF = **iraquí**
Irán SM Iran
iranés/esa ADJ, SM/F = **iraní**
iraní ADJ, SMF Iranian
SM (*Ling*) Iranian
iranio ADJ (*Hist*) = **iraní**
Iraq SM Iraq
iraquí ADJ, SMF Iraqi
irascibilidad SF irascibility (*frm*)
irascible ADJ irascible (*frm*)
irguiendo *etc* ▸ **erguir**
iribú SM (*Arg*) (*Orn*) turkey buzzard
iridiscente ADJ iridescent
iridología SF iridology
iris SM INV **1** (*Anat*) iris • MODISMO: • **hacer un ~** (*LAm**) to wink
2 (*Meteo*) rainbow
irisación SF iridescence
irisado ADJ iridescent
irisar ▸ CONJUG 1a VI to be iridescent
Irlanda SF Ireland • **la República de ~** the Republic of Ireland ▸ **Irlanda del Norte** Northern Ireland
irlandés/esa ADJ Irish • **café ~** Irish coffee
SM/F Irishman/Irishwoman • **los irlandeses** the Irish
SM (*Ling*) Irish
ironía SF **1** (*gen*) irony • **con ~** ironically; (*= con burla*) sarcastically
2 (*= comentario*) sarcastic remark
irónicamente ADV ironically
irónico ADJ (*gen*) ironic, ironical; (*= mordaz*) sarcastic
ironizar ▸ CONJUG 1f VT to ridicule
VI to speak ironically • **~ sobre algo** to be sarcastic about sth • **ironizó ella** she said ironically
IRPF SM ABR (*Esp*) (*=* **impuesto sobre la renta de las personas físicas**) ≈ personal income tax
irracional ADJ irrational • **un ser ~** an irrational being
SMF irrational person
irracionalidad SF irrationality
irracionalmente ADV irrationally
irradiación SF irradiation
irradiar ▸ CONJUG 1b VT **1** (*= emanar*) to irradiate, radiate
2 (*Med*) to irradiate
irrayable ADJ scratch-proof
irrazonable ADJ unreasonable
irreal ADJ unreal
irrealidad SF unreality
irrealista ADJ unrealistic
irrealizable ADJ (*gen*) unrealizable; [*meta*] unrealistic, impossible; [*plan*] unworkable
irrebatible ADJ irrefutable, unanswerable
irrechazable ADJ irresistible
irrecomendable ADJ inadvisable
irreconciliable ADJ irreconcilable
irreconocible ADJ unrecognizable
irrecuperable ADJ irrecoverable, irretrievable
irrecurrible ADJ • **la decisión es ~** there is no appeal against this decision
irrecusable ADJ unimpeachable
irredentismo SM irredentism
irredentista ADJ, SMF irredentist
irredento ADJ unrepentant, inveterate • **un machista ~** a dyed-in-the-wool chauvinist • **el sur ~** the godforsaken south
irredimible ADJ irredeemable
irreducible ADJ **1** (*= mínimo*) irreducible
2 [*diferencias*] irreconcilable
irreductible ADJ **1** (*= invencible*) [*enemigo, oposición, voluntad*] implacable, unyielding; [*obstáculo*] insurmountable • **el sector ~ de los terroristas** the hardline faction of the terrorists
2 [*espíritu, optimismo*] irrepressible
irreembolsable ADJ non-returnable
irreemplazable ADJ irreplaceable
irreflexión SF (*= falta de reflexión*) thoughtlessness; (*= ímpetu*) rashness, impetuosity
irreflexivamente ADV (*= sin reflexionar*) thoughtlessly, unthinkingly; (*= impetuosamente*) rashly
irreflexivo ADJ **1** [*persona*] (*= inconsciente*) thoughtless, unthinking; (*= impetuoso*) rash, impetuous
2 [*acto*] rash, ill-considered
irreformable ADJ unreformable
irrefrenable ADJ [*violencia*] unrestrained, uncontrollable; [*persona*] irrepressible; [*deseo*] unstoppable
irrefutable ADJ irrefutable, unanswerable
irregular ADJ **1** (*= desigual*) **a** [*superficie, terreno*] uneven; [*contorno, línea*] crooked; [*rasgos*] irregular; [*filo*] jagged
b [*latido, ritmo*] irregular; [*rendimiento*] irregular, erratic; [*jugador, equipo*] inconsistent; [*año, vida*] chaotic • **tiene el sueño ~** he has an irregular sleep pattern • **el corazón le latía de forma ~** his heart was beating irregularly • **el índice de asistencia ha sido bastante ~ este año** attendance has been quite irregular *o* erratic this year • **el comportamiento ~ de la Bolsa** the erratic behaviour of the stock market • **he tenido un año muy ~** I've had quite a chaotic year • **a intervalos ~es** at irregular intervals
2 (*= no legal*) • **la situación de la pareja es algo ~** the couple's situation is somewhat irregular • **han cometido ciertas acciones ~es** they have been involved in certain irregularities • **extranjeros en situación ~** foreigners registered illegally • **Hans admitió su comportamiento ~** Hans admitted his unlawful behaviour
3 (*Ling*) [*verbo*] irregular
4 (*Mat*) [*polígono, figura*] irregular
irregularidad SF **1** (*= desigualdad*) **a** [*de superficie, terreno*] irregularity, unevenness • **las ~es del terreno** the unevenness of the terrain
b [*de latido, ritmo, lluvias*] irregularity; [*de jugador, equipo*] inconsistency, erratic performance • **noté la ~ de su pulso** I noticed that his pulse was erratic • **la ~ del equipo se**

i

demostró una vez más en el último partido the team's inconsistency *o* erratic performance was noticeable again in their last match
2 (= *ilegalidad*) irregularity • **~es administrativas** administrative irregularities • **~es contables** irregularities in the accounts • **~es fiscales** tax irregularities • **~es urbanísticas** irregularities in town planning procedures
3 (*Ling*) irregularity

irregularmente ADV **1** (= *desigualmente*) irregularly
2 (= *ilegalmente*) illegally

irrelevante ADJ irrelevant

irreligioso ADJ irreligious (*frm*), ungodly (*pey*)

irrellenable ADJ [*botella, encendedor*] disposable

irremediable ADJ [*daño, decadencia*] irremediable; [*pérdida*] irreparable, irretrievable; [*vicio*] incurable

irremediablemente ADV
1 (= *inevitablemente*) inevitably • **~ habrá una inclinación hacia la izquierda** inevitably there will be a swing to the left
2 (= *irreparablemente*) irremediably • **una oportunidad ~ perdida** an opportunity irremediably lost, an opportunity lost forever • **el matrimonio estaba ~ roto** the marriage had broken down hopelessly *o* irretrievably

irremisible ADJ irremissible

irremisiblemente ADV irremissibly • **~ perdido** irretrievably lost, lost beyond hope of recovery

irremontable ADJ insurmountable

irremplazable ADJ irreplaceable

irremunerado ADJ unremunerated

irrentable ADJ unprofitable

irrenunciable ADJ [*derecho*] inalienable; [*condición*] absolute; [*deber*] unavoidable, inescapable • **una aspiración ~** an aspiration which can never be given up

irreparable ADJ irreparable

irreparablemente ADV irreparably

irrepetible ADJ unrepeatable

irreprensible ADJ irreproachable

irreprimible ADJ irrepressible

irreprimiblemente ADV irrepressibly

irreprochable ADJ irreproachable

irreproducible ADJ unrepeatable

irresistible ADJ irresistible; (*pey*) unbearable, insufferable

irresistiblemente ADV irresistibly

irresoluble ADJ (= *insoluble*) unsolvable; (= *sin resolver*) unresolved

irresolución SF hesitation, indecision

irresoluto ADJ **1** (= *perplejo*) indecisive
2 (= *sin resolver*) unresolved

irrespetar ▹ CONJUG 1a VT (*LAm*) to show disrespect to *o* for

irrespeto SM disrespect

irrespetuosamente ADV disrespectfully

irrespetuoso ADJ disrespectful

irrespirable ADJ unbreathable

irresponsabilidad SF irresponsibility

irresponsable ADJ irresponsible

irresponsablemente ADV irresponsibly

irrestricto ADJ (*LAm*) • **apoyo ~** unconditional support

irresuelto ADJ = **irresoluto**

irreverencia SF irreverence

irreverente ADJ irreverent • **un chiste ~** an irreverent joke

irreversible ADJ irreversible

irreversiblemente ADV irreversibly

irrevocable ADJ irrevocable

irrevocablemente ADV irrevocably

irrigación SF irrigation • **~ por aspersión** irrigation using sprinkler (system) • **~ por goteo** trickle irrigation

irrigador SM sprinkler

irrigar ▹ CONJUG 1h VT **1** (= *regar*) to irrigate
2 [+ *cerebro, músculo*] to feed, supply with blood

irrisible ADJ laughable, absurd

irrisión SF **1** (= *mofa*) derision, ridicule
2 (= *hazmerreír*) laughing stock

irrisorio ADJ (= *ridículo*) derisory, ridiculous; [*precio*] absurdly low

irritabilidad SF irritability

irritable ADJ irritable

irritación SF irritation

irritado ADJ **1** (= *enfadado*) irritated
2 [*piel*] irritated • **tengo la garganta irritada** I've got a sore throat

irritador ADJ irritating

irritante ADJ irritating
SM irritant

irritar ▹ CONJUG 1a VT **1** (= *enfadar*) to irritate
2 (*Med*) to irritate
3 [+ *celos, pasiones*] to stir up, inflame
VPR **irritarse** to get irritated • **~se por algo** to get irritated about *o* at sth, get annoyed about *o* at sth • **~se con algn** to get irritated with sb, get annoyed with sb

irrogar ▹ CONJUG 1h VT (*Jur*) to occasion

irrompible ADJ unbreakable

irrumpir ▹ CONJUG 3a VI • **~ en** to burst into • **los agentes irrumpieron en el bar** the policemen burst into the bar • **los tanques irrumpieron en la plaza** the tanks burst onto the square

irrupción SF • **la mujer está haciendo su ~ en el mundo laboral** women are breaking into the world of employment • **acaba de hacer su ~ en el mundo de la música country** she has just burst onto the country music scene

IRTP SM ABR (*Esp*) (= **impuesto sobre el rendimiento del trabajo personal**) ≈ PAYE

IRYDA SM ABR = **Instituto para la Reforma y el Desarrollo Agrario**

Isaac SM Isaac

Isabel SF Isabel, Elizabeth • **la reina ~ II** Queen Elizabeth II

isabelino ADJ • **la España isabelina** Isabelline Spain, the Spain of Isabel II • **la Inglaterra isabelina** Elizabethan England, the England of Elizabeth I

Isabelita SF *forma familiar de* **Isabel**

Isaías SM Isaiah

iscocoro‡ SM (*CAm*) (*pey*) Indian

ISDE SM ABR (*Esp*) = **Instituto Superior de Dirección de Empresas**

Iseo SF Iseult, Isolde

isidrada SF, **isidros** SMPL celebration of St Isidore (*patron saint of Madrid*)

-ísimo ▹ **Aspects of Word Formation in Spanish 2**

isla SF **1**

Para otros nombres, ver el segundo elemento.

(*Geog*) island • **una ~ desierta** a desert island ▸ **islas Baleares** Balearic Islands ▸ **islas Británicas** British Isles ▸ **islas Canarias** Canary Islands ▸ **islas Filipinas** Philippine Islands, Philippines ▸ **islas Malvinas** Falkland Islands
2 (*Arquit*) block
3 (*Aut*) (traffic) island, safety island (*EEUU*) ▸ **isla peatonal** traffic island, safety island (*EEUU*)

Islam SM Islam

islámico ADJ Islamic

islamismo SM (*Rel*) Islam; (= *integrismo*) Islamic fundamentalism

islamista ADJ, SMF (*Rel*) Islamist; (= *integrista*) Islamic fundamentalist

islamización SF Islamization

islamizante ADJ Islamicizing

islamizar ▹ CONJUG 1f VT to Islamize, convert to Islam

islamofobia SF Islamophobia

islamófobo/a ADJ Islamophobic
SM/F Islamophobe

islandés/esa ADJ Icelandic
SM/F Icelander
SM (*Ling*) Icelandic

Islandia SF Iceland

islándico ADJ Icelandic

isleño/a ADJ island (*antes de s*)
SM/F islander

isleta SF islet

islote SM small island

ismo SM ism

-ismo ▹ **Aspects of Word Formation in Spanish 2**

iso... PREF iso...

isobara SF, **isóbara** SF isobar

isoca SF (*Cono Sur*) caterpillar, grub

isoflavona SF isoflavone

isohispa SF contour line

Isolde SF Iseult, Isolde

isométrica SF isometrics (*sing*), isometric exercises (*pl*)

isométrico ADJ isometric

isomorfo ADJ (*Geol*) isomorphic

isósceles ADJ • **triángulo ~** isosceles triangle

isoterma SF isotherm

isotérmico ADJ **1** (= *con aislamiento*) [*ropa*] thermal; [*recipiente*] insulated; [*vehículo*] refrigerated
2 (*Geog*) isothermal

isotónico ADJ isotonic

isótopo SM isotope

Israel SM Israel

israelí ADJ, SMF Israeli

israelita ADJ, SMF Israelite

-ista ▹ **Aspects of Word Formation in Spanish 2**

istmeño/a ADJ of/from the Isthmus (*often Panamanian*)
SM/F native/inhabitant of the Isthmus (*often Panamanian*)

istmo SM isthmus • **el Istmo** (*Méx*) the isthmus of Tehuantepec ▸ **istmo de Panamá** Isthmus of Panama

itacate SM (*Méx*) provisions (*pl*) (*for journey*), food

Italia SF Italy

italianismo SM italianism, *word/phrase etc borrowed from Italian*

italiano/a ADJ, SM/F Italian
SM (*Ling*) Italian

itálica SF italic • **en ~** in italics

ítem SM item
ADV also, likewise

itemizar ▹ CONJUG 1f VT (*Chile*) (= *enumerar*) to itemize, list; (= *dividir*) to divide into sections

iterar ▹ CONJUG 1a VT to repeat

iterativo ADJ iterative

itinerante ADJ [*biblioteca, exposición*] travelling, traveling (*EEUU*); [*compañía de teatro*] touring • **comando ~** mobile terrorist unit • **embajador ~** roving ambassador, ambassador at large

itinerario SM **1** (= *ruta*) itinerary, route
2 (*Méx*) (*Ferro*) timetable

-itis ▹ **Aspects of Word Formation in Spanish 2**

-ito, -ita ▹ **Aspects of Word Formation in Spanish 2**

ITV SF ABR (*Esp*) (= **Inspección Técnica de Vehículos**) ≈ MOT

IU SF ABR (*Esp*) (*Pol*) (= **Izquierda Unida**) *Spanish coalition of left-wing parties*

i/v ABR = **ida y vuelta**

IVA SM ABR (= **impuesto sobre el valor añadido** *o* (*LAm*) **agregado**) VAT

Ivan (SM) Ivan • **~ el Terrible** Ivan the Terrible
IVP (SM ABR) = **Instituto Venezolano de Petroquímica**
ixtle (SM) (*Méx*) fibre, fiber (*EEUU*)
iza‡ (SF) whore
izada (SF) (*LAm*) lifting, raising
izado (SM) • **~ de la bandera** raising *o* hoisting the flag
izamiento (SM) raising, hoisting
-izante ▹ **Aspects of Word Formation in Spanish 2**
izar ▹ CONJUG 1f (VT) [+ *bandera*] to hoist, raise; [+ *velas*] to hoist, run up • **la bandera está izada** the flag is flying
izcuinche (SM) (*Méx*), **izcuintle** (SM) (*Méx*)
1 (= *perro*) mangy dog, mongrel
2* (= *chiquillo*) kid*; (= *pilluelo*) urchin
izda. (ABR) (= **izquierda**) L, l
izdo. (ABR) (= **izquierdo**) L, l
-izo ▹ **Aspects of Word Formation in Spanish 2**
izq. (ABR), **izq.º** (ABR), **izqdo.** (ABR) (= **izquierdo**) L, l
izq.ª (ABR), **izqda.** (ABR) (= **izquierda**) L, l
izquierda (SF) **1** (= *mano*) left hand; (= *lado*) left, left-hand side • **solo sabe escribir con la ~** he can only write with his left hand • **mi casa está a la ~** my house is on the left *o* on the left-hand side • **está a la ~ de tu hermano** he's to the left of your brother • **el árbol de la ~** the tree on the left *o* on the left-hand side • **tuerza por la tercera a la ~** take the third turn on the left *o* on the left-hand side • **conducen por la ~** they drive on the left *o* on the left-hand side; ▹ **cero**
2 (*Pol*) • **la ~** the left (wing) • **la extrema ~** the extreme left (wing) • **ser de ~s** to be on the left ▸ **Izquierda Unida** *Spanish coalition of left-wing parties*
izquierdismo (SM) leftism, *left-wing outlook or tendencies etc*
izquierdista (ADJ) left-wing
(SMF) left-winger
izquierdo (ADJ) **1** (*gen*) left • **metió el balón por el lado ~ del portero** he placed the ball to the goalkeeper's left, he placed the ball left of the goalkeeper • **el lateral ~ del Barcelona** the Barcelona left-winger • **las dos ruedas del lado ~** the two wheels on the left-hand side
2 (= *zurdo*) left-handed
izquierdoso/a* (*pey*) (ADJ) leftish
(SM/F) lefty*

i

Jj

J, j ['xota] SF (= *letra*) J, j
ja¹ EXCL ha!
ja²‡ SF (= *mujer*) wife; (= *novia*) bird‡, chick (EEUU‡)
jaba SF **1** (*Cuba*) (= *cesto*) straw basket
2 (*CAm, Méx*) (= *caja*) crate
3 (*Caribe*) (= *bolsa*) beggar's bag, poverty
• **MODISMOS**: • **llevar** *o* **tener algo en ~*** to have sth up one's sleeve • **no poder ver a otro con ~ grande*** to envy sb • **soltar la ~** to go up in the world • **tomar la ~** to be reduced to begging
4 (*LAm*) (*Bot*) = **haba**
jabado ADJ **1** (*Caribe, Méx*) white with brown patches
2 (= *indeciso*) hesitant, undecided
jabalí SM wild boar ▸ **jabalí verrugoso** warthog
jabalina SF **1** (*Dep*) javelin
2 (*Zool*) wild sow
jabato ADJ **1** (= *valiente*) brave, bold
2 (*Caribe, Méx*) (= *grosero*) rude, gruff; (= *malhumorado*) ill-tempered
SM **1** (*Zool*) young wild boar • **portarse como un ~** to be very brave
2* (= *persona*) tough guy*
jábega SF **1** (= *red*) sweep net, dragnet
2 (= *barca*) fishing smack
jabón SM **1** (*para lavar*) soap • **una pastilla de ~** a bar of soap • **MODISMO**: • **no es lo mismo ~ que hilo negro** (*And, Caribe*) they're as different as chalk and cheese ▸ **jabón de afeitar** shaving soap ▸ **jabón de olor** toilet soap ▸ **jabón de sastre** tailor's chalk, French chalk ▸ **jabón de tocador** toilet soap ▸ **jabón en escamas** soapflakes ▸ **jabón en polvo** soap powder, washing powder, (powdered) laundry detergent (EEUU) ▸ **jabón líquido** liquid soap
2* (= *adulación*) flattery • **dar ~ a algn** to soft-soap sb
3† (= *reprimenda*) • **dar un ~ a algn** to tell sb off
4 (*Caribe, Cono Sur, Méx*) (= *susto*) fright, scare • **agarrarse un ~** to get a fright
jabonada SF **1** = **jabonadura**
2 (*LAm*) (= *bronca*) telling-off
jabonado SM **1** (= *acción*) soaping
2 (= *ropa*) wash, laundry
3 (= *bronca*) telling-off
jabonadura SF **1** (= *acción*) soaping
2 jabonaduras (= *espuma*) lather (*sing*), soapsuds
3* (= *al regañar*) telling-off • **dar una ~ a algn** to tell sb off
jabonar ▷ CONJUG 1a VT **1** (*con jabón*) (*gen*) to soap; [+ *barba*] to lather
2* (= *reprender*) to tell off
jaboncillo SM **1** (*para lavar*) small bar of soap
2 (*tb* **jaboncillo de sastre**) tailor's chalk, French chalk
jabonera SF soapdish
jabonería SF soap factory
jabonete SM small bar of soap
jabonoso ADJ soapy
jabuco SM (*Caribe*) (= *caja*) large basket, big crate; (= *bolsa*) bag • **MODISMO**: • **dar ~ a algn** to snub sb, give sb the cold shoulder
jaca SF (= *caballo pequeño*) pony, small horse; (= *yegua*) mare; (*en lenguaje infantil*) horse; (*Caribe*) gelding
jacal SM (*CAm, Caribe, Méx*) shack, hut
• **MODISMO**: • **no tiene ~ donde meterse** he's without a roof over his head • **REFRÁN**: • **al ~ viejo no le faltan goteras** old age is bound to have its problems
jacalear* ▷ CONJUG 1a VI (*Méx*) to go around gossiping
jacalón SM (*Méx*) (= *cobertizo*) shed; (= *casucha*) shack, hovel; (*Teat**) fleapit*
jácara†† SF **1** (*Literat*) *comic ballad of low life*
2 (*Mús*) *a merry dance*
3 (= *personas*) *band of night revellers* • **estar de ~** to be very merry
4 (= *molestia*) pain*, nuisance
5 (= *cuento*) fib, story
jacarandá SM o SF (PL: **jacarandaes, jacarandás**) jacaranda, jacaranda tree
jacarandoso ADJ (= *alegre*) merry, jolly; (= *airoso*) spirited, lively
jacaré SM (*LAm*) alligator
jacarear†† ▷ CONJUG 1a VI **1** (*Mús*) (= *cantar*) to sing in the streets at nights; (= *dar serenatas*) to go serenading
2 (= *armar un escándalo*) to cause a commotion
3 (= *insultar*) to be rude, make offensive remarks
jacarero/a†† ADJ merry, fun-loving
SM/F amusing person, wag
jácena SF girder, main beam
jachís SM = **hachís**
jachudo ADJ (*And*) (= *fuerte*) strong, tough; (= *terco*) obstinate
jacinto SM **1** (*Bot*) hyacinth
2 (*Min*) jacinth
jaco SM **1** (= *caballo*) small horse, young horse; (*pey*) nag, hack
2‡ (= *heroína*) horse‡, heroin
Jacob SM Jacob
jacobeo ADJ (*Rel*) of St James • **la devoción jacobea** the devotion to St James, the cult of St James • **la ruta jacobea** the pilgrims' road to Santiago de Compostela
jacobino/a (*Hist*) ADJ Jacobin
SM/F Jacobin
jacobita (*Hist*) ADJ Jacobite
SMF Jacobite
Jacobo SM Jacob
jactancia SF (= *autoalabanzas*) boasting; (= *orgullo*) boastfulness
jactanciosamente ADV boastfully
jactancioso ADJ boastful
jactarse ▷ CONJUG 1a VPR to boast, brag
• **~ de algo** to boast about *o* of sth • **~ de hacer algo** to boast of doing sth
jacuzzi® [ja'kuzi] SM (PL: **jacuzzis**) Jacuzzi®
jade SM jade
jadeante ADJ panting, gasping
jadear ▷ CONJUG 1a VI to pant, gasp for breath
jadeo SM panting, gasping
Jaén SM Jaen
jaez SM **1** (*para el caballo*) harness • **jaeces** trappings
2 (= *ralea*) kind, sort • **y gente de ese ~** and people of that sort
jaguar SM jaguar
jagüel SM (*LAm*), **jagüey** SM (*LAm*) pool
jai‡ SF bird‡, chick (EEUU‡), dame*
jai alai SM pelota
jaiba SF **1** (*LAm*) (= *cangrejo*) crab
2 (*And*) (= *boca*) mouth • **MODISMO**: • **abrir la ~** to show o.s. greedy for money
SMF (*Caribe, Méx**) sharp customer*
jaibol SM (*LAm*) highball (EEUU)
jaibón* ADJ (*CAm*) stuck-up*, pretentious, snobbish
jáilaif* (*LAm*) ADJ high-life (*antes de s*)
SF high life
jailoso ADJ (*And*) (*gen*) well-bred; (*pey*) stuck-up*, pretentious, snobbish
Jaime SM James • **MODISMO**: • **hacer el Jaimito*** to horse around*
jalada SF (*Méx*) **1** (= *tirón*) pull, tug, heave
2 (= *reprimenda*) ticking-off*
3 (*And**) (*Univ*) failure
jaladera SF (*Méx*) handle
jalador SM (*LAm*) door-handle
jalamecate* SM (*LAm*) toady, creep‡
jalapeño SM (*Méx*) jalapeno pepper
jalar ▷ CONJUG 1a VT **1** (*LAm*) (= *tirar de*) to pull; (= *arrastrar*) (*tb Náut*) to haul • **no le jales el pelo** don't pull his hair
2 (*Méx**) (= *llevar*) to pick up, give a lift to
3 (*LAm*) (*Pol*) to draw, attract, win
4 (*LAm*) (= *trabajar*) to work hard at
5 (*And, Caribe**) (= *hacer*) to make, do, perform
6 (*Esp**) (= *comer*) to eat
VI **1** (*LAm*) (= *tirar*) to pull • **~ de** to pull at, tug at
2 (*Méx**) • **eso le jala** she's big on that*, she's a fan of that
3 (*LAm*) (= *irse*) to go off • **~ para su casa** to go off home
4 (*CAm, Méx*) [*novios*] to be courting
5 (*LAm*) (= *trabajar*) to work hard
6 (*And‡*) [*estudiante*] to flunk*, fail
7 (*Méx*) (= *exagerar*) to exaggerate
8‡ (= *correr*) to run
9 (*Méx*) (= *tener influencia*) to have pull*
10 (*And‡*) (= *fumar*) to smoke dope*
VPR **jalarse 1** (*LAm*) (= *irse*) to go off
2 (*LAm*) (= *emborracharse*) to get drunk
3 (*CAm**) [*novios*] to be courting
4‡* (= *masturbarse*) to wank**
jalbegar ▷ CONJUG 1h VT to whitewash
jalbegue SM (= *pintura*) whitewash; (= *acción*) whitewashing
jalde ADJ, **jaldo** ADJ bright yellow
jalea SF jelly • **MODISMO**: • **hacerse una ~†** (= *enamorado*) to be madly in love; (= *amable*)

to be a creep‡ ▸ **jalea de guayaba** guava jelly ▸ **jalea real** royal jelly

jalear ▹ CONJUG 1a VT **1** (*haciendo ruido*) [*+ bailaor*] to cheer on; [*+ perros*] to urge on
2 (*Méx*) (= *burlarse*) to jeer at
VI (*Méx*) to amuse o.s. noisily

jaleo SM **1*** (= *ruido*) row, racket • **armar un ~** to kick up a row
2* (= *confusión*) mess, muddle; (= *problema*) hassle • **es un ~ acordarse de tantos nombres** it's such a hassle having to remember all those names • **con tanto botón me armo unos ~s** I get into such a mess *o* muddle with all these buttons • **se armó un ~ tremendo** all hell broke loose*
3* (= *juerga*) binge* • **estar de ~** to be having a good time
4 (*Mús*) shouting and clapping (*to encourage dancers*)
5 (*Caza*) hallooing

jaleoso ADJ noisy, rowdy, boisterous

jalisciense ADJ of/from Jalisco

jalisco[1]‡ ADJ (*CAm, Méx*) plastered‡, stoned (*EEUU*‡)

jalisco[2] SM (*CAm, Méx*) straw hat

jallo ADJ (*Méx*) (= *ostentoso*) showy, flashy; (= *quisquilloso*) touchy

jalón SM **1** (= *poste*) (*gen*) stake, pole; [*de agrimensor*] surveying rod
2 (= *hito*) milestone, watershed • **esto marca un ~ en ...** this is a milestone in ...
3 (*LAm*) (= *tirón*) pull, tug; (= *robo*) snatch* • **hacer algo de un ~** (*Col, Méx*) to do sth in one go
4 (*LAm*) (= *distancia*) distance, stretch • **hay un buen ~** it's a good *o* fair way
5 (*CAm, Méx**) (= *trago*) swig*, drink
6 (*CAm*) (= *amante*) lover, sweetheart; (= *pretendiente*) suitor

jalona SF (*CAm*) flirt, flighty girl

jalonamiento SM staking out, marking out

jalonar ▹ CONJUG 1a VT to stake out, mark out • **el camino está jalonado por plazas fuertes** the route is marked out by a series of strongholds, a line of strongholds marks the route

jalonazo SM (*CAm, Méx*) pull, tug

jalonear ▹ CONJUG 1a VT (*Méx*) to pull, tug
VI **1** (*CAm, Méx*) (= *tirar*) to pull, tug
2 (*Méx*) (= *regatear*) to haggle

jalonero‡ SM bag-snatcher

jalufa‡ SF hunger • **pasar** *o* **tener ~** to be hungry

jam [jam] SF, **jam session** [jam 'sesion] SF [*de música*] jam session; (*para adolescentes*) fun day (*with concerts, skateboarding and other activities*)

Jamaica SF Jamaica

jamaica[1] SF (*CAm, Méx*) jumble sale, charity sale (EEUU)

jamaica[2] SF (*Caribe, Méx*) (*Bot*) hibiscus

jamaicano/a ADJ, SM/F, **jamaiquino/a** (*LAm*) ADJ, SM/F Jamaican

jamancia‡ SF **1** (= *comida*) grub‡, chow (*EEUU*‡)
2 (= *hambre*) hunger • **pasar** *o* **tener ~** to be hungry

jamar* ▹ CONJUG 1a VT to stuff o.s. with*
VI to eat, stuff o.s.*
VPR **jamarse** • **se lo jamó todo** he scoffed the lot*

jamás ADV never; (*con negación, en interrogación*) ever • **¡jamás!** never! • **¿se vio ~ tal cosa?** did you ever see such a thing? • **el mejor amigo que ~ ha existido** the best friend ever • **¡~ de los jamases!** never in your life!

jamba SF jamb ▸ **jamba de puerta** doorjamb, doorpost (*EEUU*); ▹ **jambo**

jambado* ADJ (*Méx*) greedy, gluttonous • **estar ~** to be feeling over-full

jambarse ▹ CONJUG 1a VPR (*CAm, Méx*) to overeat

jambo/a‡ SM/F (= *hombre*) bloke‡, geezer‡; (= *mujer*) bird‡, dame*; ▹ **jamba**

jamelgo SM nag, old hack

jamón SM **1** [*de cerdo*] ham • MODISMO: • **¡y un ~ (con chorreras)!*** get away!*, my foot!* ▸ **jamón cocido** boiled ham ▸ **jamón crudo** (*Arg, Uru*) cured ham ▸ **jamón de pata negra** *type of top-quality Parma ham made from a special breed of pig that has black legs* ▸ **jamón dulce** boiled ham ▸ **jamón serrano** ≈ Parma ham ▸ **jamón (de) York** boiled ham
2* [*de persona*] thigh, ham*
3 (*Caribe*) (= *ganga*) bargain
4 (*Caribe*) (= *conflicto*) difficulty
ADJ * [*persona*] dishy* • **un plato que está ~** a delicious meal

jamona* SF buxom woman

jampa SF (*And, Méx*) (= *umbral*) threshold; (= *puerta*) doorway

jámparo SM (*And*) canoe, small boat

jamurar* ▹ CONJUG 1a VT (*And*) to rinse

jan SM (*Caribe*) (*Agr*) seed drill • MODISMO: • **ensartarse en los janes** to get involved in an unprofitable piece of business

jandinga‡ SF (*Caribe*) grub‡, chow (*EEUU*‡)

janearse ▹ CONJUG 1a VPR (*Caribe*) **1** (= *saltar*) to leap into the saddle
2* (= *pararse*) to come to a complete stop

jangada[1] SF (*Náut*) raft

jangada[2] SF (= *disparate*) stupid remark; (= *trampa*) dirty trick

Jano SM Janus

janpa SF = **jampa**

jansenista (*Hist*) ADJ Jansenist
SMF Jansenist

Japón SM Japan

japonés/esa ADJ, SM/F Japanese
SM (*Ling*) Japanese

japuta SF pomfret

jaque SM **1** (*Ajedrez*) check • **dar ~ a algn** to put sb in check • **¡~ (al rey)!** check! • **~ continuo** continuous check • MODISMO: • **tener en ~ a algn** to hold a sword over sb's head ▸ **jaque mate** checkmate • **dar ~ mate a algn** to checkmate sb, mate sb
2* (= *matón*) bully

jaquear ▹ CONJUG 1a VT **1** (*Ajedrez*) to check
2 (*Mil*) (*tb fig*) to harass • **quedar jaqueado** to be rendered powerless

jaqueca SF **1** (= *dolor*) (severe) headache, migraine • MODISMO: • **dar ~ a algn** (= *aburrir*) to bore sb; (= *acosar*) to bother sb, pester sb
2 (*Cono Sur*) (= *resaca*) hangover

jaquet SM (*Cono Sur, Méx*) morning coat

jaquetón* SM bully, braggart

jáquima SF **1** (*LAm*) [*de caballo*] headstall
2 (*CAm, Méx**) (= *borrachera*) drunkenness, drunken state

jaquimón SM (*LAm*) headstall, halter

jara[1] SF **1** (*Bot*) rockrose, cistus
2 (= *mata*) clump, thicket
3 (= *dardo*) dart
4 • **la ~** (*Méx**) the cops* (*pl*)

jara[2] SF (*And*) halt, rest

jarabe SM **1** (= *líquido*) syrup • **~ contra** *o* **para la tos** cough syrup *o* mixture • MODISMO: • **dar ~ a algn*** to butter sb up* ▸ **jarabe de arce** maple syrup ▸ **jarabe de glucosa** glucose syrup ▸ **jarabe de palo*** beating ▸ **jarabe de pico** mere words, blarney
2 ▸ **jarabe tapatío** Mexican hat dance

jaral SM **1** (= *terreno*) thicket
2 (= *asunto espinoso*) thorny question

jaramago SM hedge mustard

jarana SF **1*** (= *juerga*) binge* • **andar/ir de ~** to be/go out on the town
2 (*Méx*) (*Mús*) small guitar
3 (*Perú*) (= *baile*) dance
4 (*Caribe*) (= *banda*) dance band
5 (*CAm*) (= *deuda*) debt
6 (*And*) (= *embuste*) fib
7 (*LAm*) (= *broma*) practical joke, hoax • **la ~ sale a la cara** (*CAm*) a joke can come back on you

jaranear ▹ CONJUG 1a VI **1*** (= *divertirse*) to be out on the town
2 (*CAm*) (= *endeudarse*) to get into debt
VT (*And, CAm*) to cheat, swindle

jaranero ADJ **1*** (= *juerguista*) merry, roistering
2 (*CAm*) (= *tramposo*) deceitful, tricky
3 (*Méx*) (*Mús*) jarana player

jaranista ADJ (*LAm*) = **jaranero**

jarano SM (*Méx*) broad hat, sombrero

jarcha SF kharja

jarcia SF **1** (*Náut*) (*tb* **jarcias**) rigging
2 [*de pesca*] fishing tackle
3 (*Cuba, Méx*) (= *cuerda*) rope (*made from agave fibre*)
4 (*CAm*) agave
5 (= *montón*) heap, mess

jardín SM garden, flower garden • MODISMO: • **ser un ~ de rosas** to be a bed of roses ▸ **jardín alpestre** rock garden ▸ **jardín botánico** botanical garden ▸ **jardín de infancia, jardín de infantes** (*LAm*) kindergarten, nursery school ▸ **jardín rocoso** rock garden ▸ **jardín zoológico** zoo

jardinaje SM (*LAm*) gardening

jardinear ▹ CONJUG 1a VI (*Chile*) to garden

jardinera SF **1** (*para plantas*) (*en ventana, balcón*) window box; (*en la calle*) flower bed
2 • **a la ~** (*Culin*) jardiniere
3 (*Cono Sur*) (= *carrito*) barrow, cart
4 (*Chile*) (= *pantalón*) overalls (*pl*), dungarees (*pl*)
5 (*And*) (= *abrigo*) jacket; ▹ **jardinero**

jardinería SF gardening

jardinero/a SM/F gardener
SM (*Cono Sur*) (= *pantalón*) overalls (*pl*), dungarees (*pl*); [*de niño*] romper suit; ▹ **jardinera**

jarea* SF (*Méx*) hunger

jarear ▹ CONJUG 1a VI (*And*) to halt, stop for a rest

jarearse* ▹ CONJUG 1a VPR (*Méx*) **1** (*de hambre*) to be starving*
2 (= *huir*) to flee

jareta SF **1** (*Cos*) (= *dobladillo*) casing; (= *adorno*) tuck
2 (*Náut*) (= *cabo*) cable, rope; (= *red*) netting
3 (*CAm, Cono Sur*) (= *bragueta*) fly, flies (*pl*)
4 (*Caribe*) (= *contratiempo*) snag, setback

jarete SM (*Caribe*) paddle

jari* SM row, racket

jarifo ADJ (*liter*) elegant, showy, spruce

jaripeo* SM (*Méx*) horse show

jaro SM arum lily

jarocho/a ADJ of/from Veracruz
SM/F native/inhabitant of Veracruz • **los ~s** the people of Veracruz

jarope SM **1** (= *jarabe*) syrup
2* brew, concoction, nasty drink • **resultó un ~ poco agradable** it was a bitter pill to swallow

jarra SF [*de leche*] jug, pitcher (*EEUU*); [*de cerveza*] mug, tankard • **de** *o* **en ~s** with arms akimbo

jarrada SF (*LAm*) jugful, pitcherful (*EEUU*)

jarrete SM **1** (*Anat*) back of the knee; (*Zool*) hock
2 (*And*) (= *talón*) heel

jarro SM jug, pitcher (*EEUU*) • MODISMOS: • **caer como un ~ de agua fría** to come as a complete shock • **echar un ~ de agua fría a una idea** to pour cold water on an idea

jarrón SM **1** (*para flores*) vase
2 (*Arqueología*) urn

J

jartón* ADJ (*CAm, Méx*) greedy, gluttonous

Jartum SM, **Jartún** SM Khartoum

jaspe SM jasper

jaspeado ADJ speckled, mottled

jaspear ▸ CONJUG 1a VT to speckle, marble to streak
VPR **jaspearse** (*Caribe**) to get cross

jato SM **1** (= *ternero*) calf
2 (*Caribe*) (= *perro*) stray dog, mongrel
3 (*Méx*) (= *carga*) load
4 (*And*) (= *silla de montar*) saddle
5 (*LAm*) = **hato**

Jauja SF, **jauja** SF **1** • **¡esto es ~!** this is the life! • **vivir en ~** to live in luxury • **¿estamos aquí o en ~?** where do you think you are?
2 (*Cono Sur**) (= *chisme*) rumour, tale

jaula SF **1** (*para animales*) (*tb Min*) cage
2 [*de embalaje*] crate
3 [*de demente*] cell
4 (*Aut*) lock-up garage
5 (*Caribe**) Black Maria*, paddy wagon (EEUU*)
6 (*Méx*) (*Ferro**) open truck
7 • MODISMO: • **hacer ~** (*Méx*) to dig one's heels in

jauría SF pack of hounds

Java SF Java

java* SF (*Caribe*) trick

javanés/esa ADJ Javanese
SM/F Javanese

jay‡ SF = **jai**

jayán SM **1** (= *forzudo*) big strong man; (*pey*) hulking great brute, tough guy*
2 (*CAm‡*) (= *grosero*) foul-mouthed person

jayares‡ SMPL bread‡, money

jáyaro* ADJ (*And*) rough, uncouth

jazmín SM jasmine ▸ **jazmín de la India**, **jazmín del Cabo** gardenia

jazz [jaθ, jas] SM jazz

jazzista ADJ jazz (*antes de s*), jazzy
SMF jazz player

jazzístico ADJ jazz (*antes de s*)

J.C. ABR (= **Jesucristo**) J.C.

jeans [jins, dʒins] SMPL jeans

jebe SM **1** (*LAm*) (= *planta*) rubber plant; (= *goma*) rubber
2 (*Cono Sur*) (= *elástico*) elastic
3 (= *porra*) club, cudgel • MODISMO: • **llevar ~** to suffer a lot
4** (= *trasero*) arse**, ass (EEUU**)
5 (*And‡*) (= *preservativo*) French letter, rubber*

jebero SM (*LAm*) rubber-plantation worker

jeep [jip] SM jeep

jefatura SF **1** (= *liderato*) leadership • **bajo la ~ de** under the leadership of • **ha dimitido de la ~ del partido** she has resigned the party leadership
2 (= *sede*) headquarters (*pl*) ▸ **Jefatura de la aviación civil** ≈ Civil Aviation Authority, ≈ Federal Aviation Administration (EEUU) ▸ **jefatura de policía** police headquarters (*pl*)
3 (*Caribe*) (= *registro*) registry office

jefazo* SM big shot*, big noise*

jefe/a SM/F **1** (= *superior*) boss; (= *director*) head; (*Pol*) leader; (*Com*) manager; (*Mil*) officer in command; [*de tribu*] chief • **comandante en ~** commander-in-chief • **¿quién es el ~ aquí?** who's in charge around here? ▸ **jefe/a civil** (*Caribe*) registrar ▸ **jefe/a de almacén** warehouse manager/manageress ▸ **jefe/a de bomberos** fire chief, chief fire officer ▸ **jefe/a de cabina** (*Aer*) chief steward/stewardess ▸ **jefe/a de camareros** head waiter/waitress ▸ **jefe/a de cocina** head chef ▸ **jefe/a de equipo** team leader ▸ **jefe/a de estación** station master, station manager ▸ **jefe/a de estado** head of state ▸ **jefe/a de estado mayor** chief of staff ▸ **jefe/a de estudios** (*Escol*) director of studies ▸ **jefe/a de filas** (*Pol*) party leader ▸ **jefe/a de máquinas** (*Náut*) chief engineer ▸ **jefe/a de márketing** marketing manager ▸ **jefe/a de obras** site manager ▸ **jefe/a de oficina** office manager/manageress ▸ **jefe/a de personal** personnel manager ▸ **jefe/a de pista** ringmaster ▸ **jefe/a de plató** (*Cine, TV*) floor manager ▸ **jefe/a de producción** production manager ▸ **jefe/a de protocolo** chief of protocol ▸ **jefe/a de realización** (*Cine, TV*) production manager ▸ **jefe/a de redacción** editor-in-chief ▸ **jefe/a de sala** head waiter/waitress ▸ **jefe/a de taller** foreman ▸ **jefe/a de tren** guard, conductor (EEUU) ▸ **jefe/a de ventas** sales manager ▸ **jefe/a ejecutivo/a** chief executive ▸ **jefe/a supremo/a** commander-in-chief
2 (*como apelativo*) • **¡oiga ~!** hey!, mate!* • **sí, mi ~** (*esp LAm*) yes, sir *o* boss

Jehová SM Jehovah

jején SM **1** (*LAm*) (*Zool*) gnat • MODISMO: • **sabe donde el ~ puso el huevo** (*Caribe*) he's pretty smart
2 (*And, Méx**) (= *montón*) loads*, masses • **un ~ de** loads of*
3 (*Méx**) (= *multitud*) mob

jelenque* SM (*Méx*) din, racket

jemer SMF Khmer • **los ~es rojos** the Khmer Rouge

jemiquear ▸ CONJUG 1a VI (*Cono Sur*) = **jeremiquear**

JEN [xen] SF ABR (*Esp*) (= **Junta de Energía Nuclear**) ≈ AEA, ≈ AEC (EEUU)

jengibre SM ginger

jenízaro ADJ mixed, hybrid
SM (*Hist*) janissary

Jenofonte SM Xenophon

jeque SM sheik(h)

jerarca SM leader, chief, heirarch (*frm*)

jerarquía SF hierarchy • **una persona de ~** a high-ranking person

jerárquicamente ADV hierarchically

jerárquico ADJ hierarchic, hierarchical

jerarquización SF [*de organismo*] hierarchical structuring; [*de elementos*] arranging in order (of importance)

jerarquizado ADJ hierarchical

jerarquizar ▸ CONJUG 1f VT [+ *organismo*] to give a hierarchical structure to; [+ *elementos*] to arrange in order (of importance)

jeremiada SF jeremiad

Jeremías SM Jeremy; (*Biblia*) Jeremiah

jeremías* SMF INV moaner*, whinger*

jeremiquear ▸ CONJUG 1a VI (*LAm*) (= *lloriquear*) to snivel, whimper; (= *regañar*) to nag

Jerez SF ▸ **Jerez de la Frontera** Jerez

jerez SM sherry

JEREZ

Jerez is a specific term for the fortified white wine from the **denominación de origen** area around Jerez de la Frontera in Andalusia. There are many varieties, which are not always equivalent to the sherries sold in Britain. The name given to each variety depends on the exact conditions of manufacture, such as the amount of yeast mould which is allowed to grow on the surface of the wine, and the blending process. The main types are: **fino** (very dry and pale), **amontillado** (dry, with a nutty flavour) and **oloroso** (darker colour, full flavour). A special type of **fino** called **manzanilla** (literally, "camomile tea") is produced only in the town of Sanlúcar de Barrameda, where the sea air is supposed to give it a salty tang.

▸ **DENOMINACIÓN DE ORIGEN, SOLERA**

jerezano/a ADJ of/from Jerez
SM/F native/inhabitant of Jerez • **los ~s** the people of Jerez

jerga[1] SF **1** (= *lenguaje*) jargon ▸ **jerga de germanía** criminal slang ▸ **jerga informática** computer jargon ▸ **jerga publicitaria** sales jargon
2 (= *galimatías*) gibberish

jerga[2] SF **1** (= *tela*) coarse cloth, sackcloth
2 (*Méx*) floor cloth
3 (*LAm*) (= *manta*) horse blanket
4 (*And*) coarse cloak

jergal ADJ jargon (*antes de s*)

jergón SM **1** (= *colchón*) palliasse, straw mattress
2 (= *vestido*) sack* (*ill-fitting garment*)
3* (= *persona*) awkward-looking person, oaf

jeribeque SM • **hacer ~s** to make faces, grimace

Jericó SM Jericho

jerigonza SF **1** (= *galimatías*) gibberish
2 (= *lenguaje*) jargon
3 (= *estupidez*) silly thing

jeringa SF **1** (*Med*) syringe ▸ **jeringa de engrase** grease gun ▸ **jeringa de un solo uso** disposable syringe
2* (= *molestia*) nuisance

jeringador* ADJ annoying

jeringar ▸ CONJUG 1h VT **1*** (= *fastidiar*) to annoy, plague • **¡nos ha jeringado!** he's pulled a sly one on us!*; (*con menosprecio*) wouldn't we all!
2 (= *inyectar*) to syringe
VPR **jeringarse*** to put up with it • **¡que se jeringue!** he can lump it!*

jeringazo SM (= *acción*) syringing; (= *chorro*) squirt

jeringón/ona* (*LAm*) ADJ annoying
SM/F pest, pain*

jeringuear* ▸ CONJUG 1a VT (*LAm*) = **jeringar**

jeringuilla[1] SF syringe ▸ **jeringuilla desechable** disposable syringe

jeringuilla[2] SF (*Bot*) mock orange, syringa

Jerjes SM Xerxes

jeró‡ SM clock‡, mug‡

jeroglífico ADJ hieroglyphic
SM **1** (= *escritura*) hieroglyph, hieroglyphic
2 (= *situación, juego*) puzzle

jerónimo[1] ADJ, SM (*Rel*) Hieronymite

jerónimo[2] SM • MODISMO: • **sin ~ de duda** (*LAm*) (*hum*) without a shadow of doubt

Jerónimo SM Jerome

jersei SM (PL: **jerseis** *o* **jerséis**), **jersey** SM (PL: **jerseys**) sweater, pullover, jumper, jersey ▸ **jersey amarillo** (*Ciclismo*) yellow jersey

Jerusalén SF Jerusalem

jeruza‡ SF (*CAm*) clink‡, jail, can (EEUU*)

Jesucristo SM Jesus Christ

jesuita ADJ **1** (*Rel*) Jesuit
2 (= *hipócrita*) Jesuitic, Jesuitical
SM **1** (*Rel*) Jesuit
2 (= *hipócrita*) hypocrite

jesuítico ADJ Jesuitic, Jesuitical

Jesús SM Jesus • **¡Jesús!** (*indicando sorpresa*) good heavens!; (*al estornudar*) bless you! • MODISMO: • **en un decir ~** before you could say Jack Robinson

jet [jet] (PL: **jets**) SM (*Aer*) jet, jet plane
SF • **la jet** the jet-set

jeta SF **1*** (= *cara*) face, mug*, dial* • **te romperé la ~** I'll smash your face in‡ • MODISMO: • **estirar la ~** (*Cono Sur‡*) to kick the bucket*
2 (= *hocico*) [*de animal*] snout; [*de persona**] gob*
3* (= *ceño*) frown, scowl • **poner ~** to frown, scowl
4* (= *descaro*) cheek*, nerve* • **¡qué ~ tienes!** you've got a nerve!* • **se quedó con mi libro**

por la ~ the cheeky thing kept my book SMF • **ser un(a) ~*** to have a nerve*, have a cheek*

jetazo* SM bash*, punch

jetear ▷ CONJUG 1a VI (*Cono Sur*) to eat at someone else's expense

jet lag SM INV jet lag • **tener ~** to be jet-lagged

jetón ADJ, **jetudo** ADJ **1** (= *de labios gruesos*) thick-lipped
2 (*Cono Sur*) stupid

jet ski ['jeteski] SM jet ski

Jezabel SF Jezebel

ji EXCL • **¡ji, ji, ji!** (*imitando la risa*) hee, hee, hee!; (*iró*) tee hee!

jibarear ▷ CONJUG 1a VI (*Caribe*) to flirt

jíbaro/a ADJ **1** [*pueblo*] Jivaro
2 (*Caribe, Méx*) (= *rústico*) country (*antes de s*), rustic; (= *huraño*) sullen
SM/F **1** (= *indígena*) Jivaro
2 (*Caribe, Méx*) peasant
3 (*CAm*‡) (= *traficante*) dealer, drug dealer
SM (*Caribe*) (= *animal*) wild animal

jibia SF (*Zool*) cuttlefish
SM‡ (= *homosexual*) queer‡, poof (*pey*‡), fag (EEUU) (*pey*‡)

jícama SF (*CAm, Méx*) edible tuber

jícara SF **1** (= *taza*) chocolate cup
2 (*CAm, Méx*) (= *vasija*) gourd • MODISMOS: • **bailar la ~ a algn*** to soft-soap sb* • **sacar la ~ a algn** to dance attendance on sb
3 (*CAm**) (= *cabeza*) head

jicarazo SM **1** (= *veneno*) (cup of) poison, poisonous drink
2 (*CAm, Méx*) (= *taza*) cupful

jícaro SM (*CAm, Méx*) **1** (*Bot*) calabash tree
2 (= *plato*) bowl

jicarón ADJ (*CAm*) big-headed

jicarudo ADJ (*Méx**) broad-faced, broad-browed

jiche SM (*CAm, Méx*) tendon, sinew

jicote SM (*CAm, Méx*) wasp

jicotera SF (*CAm, Méx*) (= *nido*) wasps' nest; (= *zumbido*) buzzing of wasps • MODISMO: • **armar una ~** to kick up a row

jienense, jiennense ADJ of/from Jaén
SMF native/inhabitant of Jaén • **los jien(n)enses** the people of Jaén

jifero ADJ* filthy
SM **1** (= *matarife*) slaughterer, butcher
2 (= *cuchillo*) butcher's knife

jifia SF swordfish

jijona SM soft nougat (*made in Jijona*); ▷ TURRÓN

jilguero SM goldfinch • **¡mi ~!*** my angel!

jilibioso* ADJ (*Cono Sur*) (= *lloroso*) weepy, tearful; (= *delicado*) finicky, hard to please; [*caballo*] nervous

jilipollas⁑ SMF INV asshole⁑

jilote SM (*CAm, Méx*) (= *elote*) green ear of maize *o* (EEUU) corn; (= *maíz verde*) young maize, young corn (EEUU)

jilotear ▷ CONJUG 1a VI (*CAm, Méx*) to come into ear

jimagua (*Caribe*) ADJ identical
SMF twin

jimba SF **1** (*And*) (= *trenza*) pigtail, plait, braid (EEUU)
2 (*Méx*) (= *bambú*) bamboo
3 (*Méx**) (= *borrachera*) drunkenness

jimbal SM (*Méx*) bamboo thicket

jimbito SM (*CAm*) (= *avispa*) small wasp; (= *nido*) wasps' nest

jimbo ADJ (*Méx*) drunk

jimeno‡ SM (*Méx*) cop*

jimio SM = **simio**

jinaiste* SM (*Méx*) bunch of kids

jincar* ▷ CONJUG 1g VT (*CAm*) to spike

jindama* SF fear, funk*

jindarse* ▷ CONJUG 1a VPR • **se lo jindó todo** he scoffed the lot*

jineta¹ SF (*esp LAm*) horsewoman, rider • **a la ~** with short stirrups

jineta² SF (*Zool*) genet

jinete SM horseman, rider; (*Mil*) cavalryman

jinetear ▷ CONJUG 1a VT **1** (*LAm*) (= *montar*) to ride; (= *domar*) to break in • MODISMO: • **~ la burra** (*CAm*) to go the whole hog, stake everything
2 (*Méx**) [+ *fondos*] to misappropriate
VI to ride around
VPR **jinetearse 1** (*And, Méx*) (= *no caerse*) to stay in the saddle; (*fig**) to hang on, keep going
2 (*And*) (= *ser presumido*) to be vain

jinetera* (*Cuba*) SF prostitute

jingoísmo SM jingoism

jingoísta ADJ jingoistic
SMF jingoist, jingo

jiote SM (*Méx*) rash, impetigo

jipa SF (*And*) Panama hat, straw hat

jipar* ▷ CONJUG 1a VT • **le tengo jipado** I've got him taped*, I've got him all sized up

jipatera SF (*And, Caribe, Méx*), **jipatez** SF (*Caribe, Méx*) paleness, wanness

jipato ADJ (*LAm*) (= *pálido*) pale, wan; (= *enclenque*) sickly, frail; (= *soso*) tasteless

jipe SM (*And, Méx*), **jipi¹** SM Panama hat, straw hat

jipi² SMF hippy

jipijapa (*LAm*) SF (= *paja*) fine woven straw
SM (*esp LAm*) (= *sombrero*) Panama hat, straw hat

jipioso/a* ADJ hippyish
SM/F hippy type

jipismo SM hippy movement

jira¹ SF [*de tela*] strip

jira² SF (= *excursión*) excursion, outing; (*tb* **jira campestre**) picnic

jirafa SF **1** (*Zool*) giraffe
2 (*TV, Cine*) boom

jiribilla SF (*Méx*) spin, turn • MODISMO: • **tener ~** (*Caribe*) (*gen*) to have its awkward points; [*persona*] to be anxious

jirimiquear ▷ CONJUG 1a VI (*LAm*) = **jeremiquear**

jirón SM **1** (= *andrajo*) rag, shred • **hacer algo jirones** to tear sth to shreds • **hecho jirones** in shreds *o* tatters
2 (= *parte*) bit, shred
3 (*Perú*) (= *calle*) street

jit* [xit] SM (PL: **jits** [xit]) (*LAm*) hit

jitazo SM (*Méx*) hit, blow; (*Dep*) hit, stroke

jitomate SM (*Méx*) tomato

jiu-jitsu SM jiu-jitsu

JJ.OO. ABR = **Juegos Olímpicos**

jo* EXCL (*para expresar disgusto*) oh!, aw!; (*para expresar sorpresa*) wow!, blimey!*, jeez! (EEUU*) • **¡jo, otra vez!** oh no, not again!, aw no, not again! • **¡jo, jo!** (*al reír*) ho ho!, ha ha!

Job SM Job

jobar* EXCL (*para expresar disgusto*) oh!, aw!; (*para expresar sorpresa*) wow!, blimey!*, jeez! (EEUU*)

jobo SM **1** (*CAm, Méx*) (*Bot*) cedar, cedar tree
2 (*CAm**) (= *aguardiente*) spirits

jockey ['joki] SM (PL: **jockeys** ['jokis]) jockey

joco ADJ **1** (*CAm, Méx*) (= *amargo*) sharp, bitter
2 (*And*) (= *hueco*) hollow

jocolote* SM (*CAm*) hut, shack

jocoque SM (*Méx*), **jocoqui** SM (*Méx*) sour milk, sour cream

jocosamente ADV humorously, comically

jocoserio ADJ seriocomic

jocosidad SF **1** (= *cualidad*) humour, humor (EEUU), jocularity (*frm*)
2 (= *chiste*) joke

jocoso ADJ humorous, jocular

joda⁑ SF (*esp LAm*) **1** (= *molestia*) bloody nuisance‡
2 (= *broma*) joke • **lo dijo en ~** he said it as a joke

jodedera⁑ SF screwing⁑

joder⁑ ▷ CONJUG 2a VT **1** (= *copular*) to fuck⁑, screw⁑
2 (= *fastidiar*) to piss off⁑ • **me jode que crea que he sido yo** it pisses me off that he thinks it was me⁑ • **me jodió mucho que perdiera Colombia** I was really pissed off when Colombia lost⁑ • **me jode tener que pagarlo yo todo** it's a bugger having to pay for it all myself⁑, it pisses me off having to pay for it all myself⁑ • **¡deja ya de ~me de una vez!** stop bugging me!*, stop being such a pain in the arse!‡ • **si te deniegan la prórroga esta vez, te han jodido** if they refuse you an extension this time, you've had it* *o* you're fucked⁑ • MODISMO: • **no te jode** (*Esp*): • **¡no te jode! ¡ahora dice que es amigo nuestro!** can you believe it! — now he's calling himself a friend of ours • **si yo tuviera un coche así también podría ir a esa velocidad, ¡no te jode!** if I had a car like that I could go that fast as well, no problem *o* (EEUU*) no sweat • **a mí también me gustaría ser rico, ¡no te jode!** I'd like to be rich too, wouldn't we all!
3 (= *estropear*) [+ *aparato*] to bust*, bugger up⁑; [+ *planes*] to screw up‡, bugger up⁑ • **¡me has jodido el reloj!** you've bust* *o* buggered up⁑ my watch!, you've busted my watch (EEUU*) • **lo que hacen es ~nos la vida al resto** what they do is fuck⁑ *o* screw* *o* bugger⁑ things up for the rest of us • MODISMO: • **~la** to mess things up*, screw things up* • **en cuanto abres la boca la jodes** as soon as you open your mouth you mess *o* screw* things up • **¡la jodimos!** now we've blown it!*
VI **1** (= *copular*) to fuck⁑, screw⁑
2 (= *fastidiar*) • **ya sé que jode tener que levantarse tan temprano** I know it's a drag* *o* a pain in the arse⁑ *o* ass (EEUU⁑) having to get up so early • **son ganas de ~** they're just trying to be awkward • MODISMO: • **¡no jodas!** (*indicando sorpresa*) bloody hell!‡, you're kidding!*; (*indicando rechazo*) you must be joking!*
VPR **joderse 1** (= *fastidiarse*) • **ellos a hacerse ricos y los demás a ~se** they get rich and the rest of us can go to hell‡ *o* can go screw ourselves⁑ • **¡(es que) hay que ~se!** for fuck's sake!⁑ • **¡que se joda!** screw him!⁑ • **si no les gusta ¡que se jodan!** if they don't like it, tough shit!⁑ • **¡te jodes!** tough shit!⁑
2 (= *estropearse*) • **se me ha jodido el coche** the car's had it*, the car's buggered‡ • **cuando llegó él se jodió todo** when he arrived it messed* *o* screwed⁑ everything up
3 • **~se la espalda/una pierna** to do one's back/leg in* • **se jodió el pie jugando al fútbol** he did his foot in playing football*
EXCL (*Esp*) shit!‡, bloody hell!‡ • **¡joder! no me esperaba este regalo** shit!‡ *o* bloody hell!‡, I didn't expect a present like this • **cállate ya ¡joder!** for Christ's sake, shut up!*, shut the fuck up!⁑, shut up for fuck's sake!⁑ • **esto hay que celebrarlo, ¡joder!** come on, this calls for a celebration!, hell, this we have to celebrate!‡ • **pero ¿cómo no iba a asustarme, ~?** well, of course I was frightened, for Christ's sake, who wouldn't be?* • **~ con: ¡~ con el pesado ese! ¡no se va a callar nunca!** God* *o* Christ*, isn't that pain in the arse ever going to shut up! • **¡~ con tu hermanito! ¡matrícula de honor!** shit⁑ *o* God* *o* Christ‡, I can't believe your brother

J

got a distinction!

jodido** ADJ **1** (*con ser*) [*situación*] bloody awkward‡ • **va a ser ~ tener que enfrentarse a él** it'll be bloody‡ *o* damn‡ awkward having to confront him • **la cárcel es muy jodida** it's bloody‡ *o* damn‡ hard being in jail • **es un libro ~** it's a bloody difficult book‡, it's a helluva difficult book*
2 (*con estar*) **a** [*persona*] (= *en mal estado*) in a bad way, fucked**, buggered**; (= *desanimado*) pissed off**
b (= *estropeado*) (= *aparato, vehículo*) bust*, busted (EEUU*)
3 (= *maldito*) damn‡, bloody‡ • **¡qué guapo es el muy ~!** he's damn‡ *o* bloody‡ good-looking! • **ni un ~ euro** not one bloody euro‡ • **¡el ~ coche no arranca otra vez!** the damn‡ *o* bloody‡ *o* fucking** car won't start again!
4 (*LAm**) (= *molesto*) damned annoying‡, bloody annoying‡ • **esa clienta es muy jodida** she's a bloody annoying customer‡
5 (*LAm*) [*persona*] (= *egoísta*) selfish; (= *malo*) evil, wicked; (= *exigente*) awkward; (= *zalamero*) smarmy, greasy

jodienda** SF **1** (= *acto sexual*) fucking**
2 (= *fastidio*) fucking nuisance**

jodón** ADJ (*LAm*) **1** (= *molesto*) bloody annoying‡ • **es tan ~** he loves arsing about**
2 (= *tramposo*) slippery

jodontón** ADJ randy*, oversexed

jofaina SF washbasin, bathroom sink (EEUU)

jogging ['joɣin] SM **1** (*Dep*) jogging • **hacer ~** to jog
2 (*Arg*) (= *ropa*) jogging suit

jojoba SF jojoba

jojoto ADJ (*Caribe*) [*fruta*] (= *manchado*) bruised; (= *inmaduro*) green, underripe; [*maíz*] tender
SM (*Ven*) (ear of) corn *o* maize

jol SM hall, lobby

jolgórico ADJ riotous, hilarious

jolgorio SM fun, revelry • **ir de ~** to go on a binge

jolín* EXCL, **jolines*** EXCL flip!*

jolinche ADJ, **jolino** ADJ (*Méx*) short-tailed, bob-tailed

jolón SM (*Méx*) (= *avispa*) wasp; (= *avispero*) wasps' nest

jolongo SM **1** (*Caribe*) (= *bolsa*) shoulder-bag
2* (= *problema*) problem

jolote SM (*CAm, Méx*) turkey

joma SF (*Méx*) hump

jombado ADJ (*Méx*), **jombeado** ADJ (*Méx*) hunchbacked

Jonás SM Jonah

Jonatás SM Jonathan

jónico ADJ Ionic

jonja SF (*Cono Sur*) mimicry

jonjear ▸ CONJUG 1a VT (*Cono Sur*) to tease, make fun of

jonjolear* ▸ CONJUG 1a VT (*And*) to spoil

jonrón SM (*esp LAm*) (= *béisbol*) home run

jonronear ▸ CONJUG 1a VI (*LAm*) (*Dep*) to make a home run

JONS [xons] SFPL ABR (*Esp*) (*Hist*) = **Juntas de Ofensiva Nacional Sindicalista**

jopé‡ EXCL (*para expresar disgusto*) oh!, aw!; (*para expresar sorpresa*) wow!, blimey!*, jeez! (EEUU*)

jopo[1] SM brush, tail

jopo[2] EXCL out!, get out!

jora SF (*LAm*) *maize specially prepared for making high-grade chicha*

Jordán SM Jordan, Jordan river • **MODISMO**: • **ir al ~** to be rejuvenated

Jordania SF Jordan

jordano/a ADJ, SM/F Jordanian

jorga* SF (*And*) gang

Jorge SM George

jorgón SM (*And*) lot, abundance

jorguín/ina SM/F sorcerer/sorceress

jorguinería SF sorcery, witchcraft

jornada SF **1** (= *tiempo de trabajo*) • **media ~** half day ▸ **jornada anual** working days in the year ▸ **jornada completa** full (working) day ▸ **jornada continua** = **jornada intensiva** ▸ **jornada de ocho horas** eight-hour day ▸ **jornada inglesa** five-day week ▸ **jornada intensiva** *full day's work with no lunch break* ▸ **jornada laboral** (*al día*) working day; (*a la semana*) working week; (*al año*) working year ▸ **jornada legal** maximum legal working hours ▸ **jornada partida** split shift ▸ **jornada semanal** working week
2 (= *día*) day ▸ **jornada de huelga** day of industrial action ▸ **jornada de lucha** day of action ▸ **jornada de movilización** day of action, day of protest ▸ **jornada de reflexión** (*Pol*) day before the election (*on which campaigning is banned*) ▸ **jornada informativa** open day, open house (EEUU)
3 [*de viaje*] day's journey; (= *etapa*) stage (of a journey) • **a largas ~s** (*Mil*) by forced marches
4 (*Mil*) expedition • **la ~ de Orán** the expedition against Oran
5 jornadas (*Univ*) congress, conference • **"Jornadas Cervantinas"** "Conference on Cervantes"
6 (= *vida*) lifetime, life span
7 (*Teat, Hist*) act
8 (*Cono Sur*) (= *sueldo*) day's wage

jornadista SMF (*Univ*) conference member, delegate

jornal SM (= *sueldo*) (day's) wage; (= *trabajo*) day's work • **política de ~es y precios** prices and incomes policy • **trabajar a ~** to be paid by the day ▸ **jornal mínimo** minimum wage

jornalero/a SM/F (day) labourer, (day) laborer (EEUU)

joro SM (*Caribe*) small basket

joroba SF **1** [*de persona, camello*] hump
2* (= *fastidio*) pain*, drag*

jorobado/a ADJ **1** (= *con chepa*) hunchbacked
2* (= *fastidiado*) • **ando algo ~ con la espalda** my back's giving me a bit of trouble, my back's playing up a bit* • **la artritis lo tiene ~** arthritis makes his life a misery
3* [*tema, asunto, decisión*] tricky
SM/F (= *con chepa*) hunchback

jorobar* ▸ CONJUG 1a VT **1** (= *fastidiar*) to annoy • **lo que más me joroba es que no reconozcan mi trabajo** what annoys me most is that they don't acknowledge the work I do • **esa música me está empezando a ~** that music is beginning to get on my nerves • **¡no me jorobes!** get off my back!
2 (= *estropear*) [+ *aparato*] to mess up, wreck; [+ *planes, fiesta*] to bust*, ruin, screw up‡
VI • **solo lo hace por ~** he only does it to be annoying
VPR **jorobarse 1** (= *aguantarse*) • **no puedo hacer nada, así que tendré que ~me** there's nothing I can do, so I'll just have to grin and bear it • **pues ¡que se jorobe!** well, he can lump it!* • **¡hay que ~se!** for God's sake!*, bloody hell!‡
2 (= *estropearse*) [*aparato*] to be wrecked, be bust*; [*planes*] to be ruined; [*fiesta*] to be ruined
3 • **~se una pierna/una rodilla** to do one's leg/a knee in*

jorobeta SF (*Cono Sur*) nuisance

jorobón ADJ (*LAm*) annoying

joronche* SM (*Méx*) hunchback

jorongo SM (*Méx*) poncho, sleeveless poncho

joropo SM (*Ven*) (*Mús*) (*national*) *Venezuelan dance*

jorro SM (*Caribe*) poor-quality cigarette

jorungo* ADJ (*Caribe*) (= *molesto*) annoying, irritating

José SM Joseph

Josefina SF Josephine

Josué SM Joshua

jota[1] SF **1** name of the letter J • **MODISMO**: • **sin faltar una ~** to a T
2 • **MODISMO**: • **ni ~**: • **no entendió ni ~** he didn't understand a word of it • **no saber ni ~** to have no idea
3 (*Mús*) *Spanish dance and tune, esp Aragonese*
4 (*Naipes*) knave, jack

jota[2] SF (*And, Cono Sur*) (*Orn*) vulture

jote SM (*Cono Sur*) **1** (= *buitre*) buzzard
2 (= *cometa*) large kite
3 (= *desagradecido*) ungrateful person
4 (= *cura*) priest

joto ADJ (*Méx‡*) effeminate
SM **1** (*Méx‡*) effeminate person, queer‡, fag (EEUU‡)
2 (*And**) bundle

jovato/a* SM/F (*Cono Sur*) old man/old woman

joven ADJ [*persona, animal*] young; [*aspecto*] youthful
SMF young man/young woman; (*como apelativo*) young man/young lady • **los jóvenes** young people, youth, the young • **¡joven!** (*Méx*) (*al cliente*) (yes), sir?; (*al empleado*) excuse me!

jovencito/a SM/F youngster

jovial ADJ jolly, cheerful

jovialidad SF jolliness, cheerfulness

jovialmente ADV in a jolly way, cheerfully

joya SF **1** (= *adorno*) jewel, gem • **~s** jewels, jewellery, jewelry (EEUU) ▸ **joyas de fantasía** costume jewellery, imitation jewellery
2 (= *objeto preciado*) gem, treasure
3 [*de novia*] trousseau

joyería SF **1** (= *tienda*) jeweller's *o* (EEUU) jeweler's (shop)
2 (= *joyas*) jewellery, jewelry (EEUU), jewels

joyero/a SM/F jeweller, jeweler (EEUU)
SM (= *estuche*) jewel case

joystick ['joiestik] (PL: **joysticks**) SM joystick

JPEG SM ABR (= **Joint Photographic Experts Group**) (*Inform*) JPEG

Jruschov SM Khrushchev

juagar ▸ CONJUG 1h VT (*And*) = **enjuagar**

Juan SM John • **San ~ Bautista** St John the Baptist • **San ~ Evangelista** St John the Evangelist • **San ~ de la Cruz** St John of the Cross • **un buen ~** a good-natured fool • **ser un Don ~** to be a Romeo ▸ **Juan Lanas** (*CAm*) (*pey*) simpleton; (= *marido*) henpecked husband ▸ **Juan Palomo** (= *solitario*) lone wolf, loner; (= *egoísta*) *person who looks after Number One* ▸ **Juan Vainas** = **Juan Lanas** ▸ **Juan Zoquete** country bumpkin

juan* SM (*Méx*) common soldier

Juana SF Joan, Jean, Jane • **~ de Arco** Joan of Arc

juana SF **1** (*And*) (= *prostituta*) whore
2 (*Méx**) marijuana
3 (*CAm**) cop*

juancarlismo SM *support for King Juan Carlos I*

juancarlista ADJ *of or relating to King Juan Carlos I* • **ser ~** to be a supporter of King Juan Carlos I
SMF supporter of King Juan Carlos I

juancho SM (*And*) boyfriend, lover

juanete SM **1** (*en el pie*) bunion
2 (*Náut*) topgallant sail
3 (*And, CAm*) (= *cadera*) hip

juanillo* SM (*And, Cono Sur*) bribe

juapao SM (*Caribe*) beating, thrashing
jubilación SF **1** (= *acción*) retirement ▸ **jubilación anticipada** early retirement ▸ **jubilación forzosa** compulsory retirement ▸ **jubilación voluntaria** voluntary retirement
2 (= *pensión*) retirement pension
jubilado/a ADJ **1** [*trabajador*] retired • **vivir ~** to live in retirement
2 (*And, Caribe**) (= *sagaz*) wise
3 (*And**) (= *lerdo*) thick*, slow-witted
SM/F retired person, pensioner
jubilar ▹ CONJUG 1a VT **1** [+ *trabajador*] to pension off, retire
2 (*hum**) (= *desechar*) [+ *objeto*] to discard; [+ *persona*] to put out to grass
VPR **jubilarse 1** [*trabajador*] to retire • **~se anticipadamente** to take early retirement, retire early
2 (*CAm*) (= *hacer novillos*) to play truant
3 (*Caribe**) (= *instruirse*) to gain experience
4 (*And**) (= *deteriorarse*) to deteriorate, go downhill; (= *enloquecer*) to lose one's head
jubileo SM (*Rel*) jubilee
júbilo SM joy, rejoicing, jubilation • **con ~** joyfully
jubiloso ADJ jubilant
jubón SM [*de hombre*] doublet, jerkin; [*de mujer*] bodice
jud SM (*CAm*) (*Aut*) bonnet, hood (*EEUU*)
Judá SM Judah
judaico ADJ Jewish, Judaic
judaísmo SM Judaism
judaizante ADJ Judaizing
SMF Judaizer
Judas SM **1** (= *nombre*) Judas
2 (= *muñeco*) Easter effigy
judas SM INV **1** (= *traidor*) traitor, betrayer
2 (= *muñeco*) Easter effigy
3 (= *mirilla*) peephole
4 (*Cono Sur**) snooper*
Judea SF Judea
judeocristiano ADJ Judaeo-Christian, Judeo-Christian (*EEUU*)
judeoespañol ADJ, SM Judeo-Spanish
judería SF **1** (= *barrio*) Jewish quarter
2 (= *judíos*) Jewry
3 (*CAm, Méx**) (= *travesura*) prank
judía SF bean ▸ **judía blanca** haricot bean ▸ **judía colorada** runner bean ▸ **judía de la peladilla, judía de Lima** Lima bean ▸ **judía escarlata** runner bean ▸ **judía pinta** pinto bean ▸ **judía verde** green bean; ▹ **judío**
judiada SF **1** (= *acto cruel*) cruel thing
2 (*Econ*) extortion
judicatura SF **1** (= *jueces*) judiciary
2 (= *cargo*) office of judge
judicial ADJ judicial • **recurrir a la vía ~** to go to law, have recourse to law
judicialmente ADV judicially, in the courts
judío/a ADJ **1** [*pueblo, religión*] Jewish
2 (*pey*) (= *tacaño*) mean, miserly
SM/F Jew/Jewess, Jewish man/woman; ▹ **judía**
Judit SF Judith
judo SM judo
judoca SMF, **judoka** SMF judoist, judoka
jue. ABR (= **jueves**) Thurs.
juego¹ ▹ **jugar**
juego² SM **1** (= *acto*) play • **se acabó el tiempo de ~** it's time to stop playing • **el balón está en ~** the ball is in play • **estar fuera de ~** [*jugador*] to be offside; [*balón*] to be out of play • **por ~** for fun ▸ **juego duro** rough play ▸ **juego limpio** fair play ▸ **juego sucio** (*Ftbl*) foul play, dirty play; (*fig*) dirty tricks (*pl*)
2 (*como entretenimiento*) game • **es solamente un ~** it's only a game • **el ~ del ajedrez** the game of chess • **"~ terminado"** "game over" • MODISMO: • **ser un ~ de niños** to be child's play ▸ **juego de azar** game of chance ▸ **juego de cartas** card game ▸ **juego de computadora** (*LAm*) computer game ▸ **juego de destreza** game of skill ▸ **juego de la cuna** cat's cradle ▸ **el juego de la oca** ≈ snakes and ladders ▸ **juego de manos** conjuring trick ▸ **juego de mesa** board game ▸ **juego de ordenador** computer game ▸ **juego de palabras** pun, play on words ▸ **juego de rol** role-playing game ▸ **juego de salón, juego de sociedad** parlour game ▸ **juego educativo** educational game ▸ **juego infantil** children's game, game for children ▸ **juego interactivo** interactive game ▸ **juegos malabares** juggling • **hacer ~s malabares con algo** to juggle sth
3 juegos (*Dep*) (= *competición*) ▸ **juegos atléticos** (*LAm*) athletics championships ▸ **Juegos Olímpicos** Olympic Games ▸ **Juegos Olímpicos de Invierno** Winter Olympics
4 (= *jugada*) (*en tenis*) game; (*de cartas*) hand; (*en bridge*) rubber • **~, set y partido** game, set and match
5 (*con apuestas*) gambling • **el ~ es un vicio** gambling is a vice • **lo perdió todo en el ~** he gambled everything away, he lost everything through gambling • **¡hagan ~!** place your bets! • MODISMOS: • **estar en ~** to be at stake • **lo que está en ~** what is at stake • **hay diversos intereses en ~** there are various interests at stake • **los factores que entran en ~** the factors that come into play • **poner algo en ~** (= *arriesgar*) to place sth at risk; (= *recurrir a*) to bring sth to bear
6 (= *estrategia*) game • **le conozco** *o* **veo el ~** I know his little game, I know what he's up to • MODISMOS: • **seguir el ~ a algn** to play along with sb • **hacer un ~ doble** to be playing a double game
7 (= *conjunto*) [*de vajilla*] set, service; [*de muebles*] suite; [*de herramientas*] kit • **con falda a ~** with skirt to match, with matching skirt • **las cortinas hacen ~ con el sofá** the curtains match the sofa, the curtains go with the sofa ▸ **juego de bolas** (*Mec*) ball bearing, set of ball bearings ▸ **juego de café** coffee set, coffee service ▸ **juego de cama** set of matching bedlinen ▸ **juego de campanas** peal of bells ▸ **juego de caracteres** character set ▸ **juego de comedor** dining-room suite ▸ **juego de luces** (*de árbol de Navidad*) fairy lights (*pl*); (*en fiesta, espectáculo*) decorative lights (*pl*) ▸ **juego de mesa** dinner service ▸ **juego de programas** (*Inform*) suite, suite of programmes ▸ **juego de té** tea set, tea service
8 [*de mecanismo*] play, movement • **el ~ de la rodilla** the movement of the knee • **estar en ~** to be in gear
9 (= *efecto*) play • **el ~ de las luces sobre el agua** the play of light on the water • **el ~ de los colores** the interplay of the colours
10 (*Pelota*) (= *pista*) court • **en el ~ de pelota** on the pelota court
juepucha‡ EXCL (*Cono Sur*) well I'm damned!
juerga* SF binge* • **ir de ~** to go out for a good time • **correr grandes ~s** to live it up* • **¡vaya ~ que nos vamos a correr!** we'll have a great time!
juergata‡ SF = **juerga**
juerguearse* ▹ CONJUG 1a VPR to live it up*
juerguista SMF reveller
juev. ABR (= **jueves**) Thurs.
jueves SM INV Thursday • MODISMO: • **no es nada del otro ~** it's nothing to write home about ▸ **Jueves Santo** Maundy Thursday; ▹ **sábado**
juez SMF, **jueza** SF **1** (*Jur*) judge • MODISMO: • **ser ~ y parte** to be an interested party ▸ **juez árbitro** arbitrator, referee ▸ **juez de diligencias, juez de instrucción** examining magistrate ▸ **juez de paz** justice of the peace, magistrate ▸ **juez de primera instancia, juez instructor** examining magistrate ▸ **juez municipal** magistrate
2 (*Dep*) judge ▸ **juez de banda, juez de línea** (*Ftbl*) linesman; (*Rugby*) touch judge; (*Tenis*) umpire ▸ **juez de raya** (*Arg, Uru*) (*Ftbl*) linesman ▸ **juez de salida** starter ▸ **juez de silla** umpire
jugable ADJ playable
jugada SF **1** (*Dep*) piece of play; (*Ftbl, Ajedrez*) move • **una bonita ~** a lovely piece of play, a lovely move • **hacer una ~** to make a move ▸ **jugada a balón parado** (*Ftbl*) set piece ▸ **jugada de pizarra** textbook move
2 (*Golf*) stroke, shot
3 • **(mala) ~** dirty trick • **hacer** *o* **gastar una mala ~ a algn** to play a dirty trick on sb
4 (*Méx*) dodge
jugado ADJ (*And*) expert, skilled
jugador(a) SM/F **1** [*de deporte, juegos de mesa*] player ▸ **jugador(a) de ajedrez** chess player ▸ **jugador(a) de baloncesto** basketball player ▸ **jugador(a) de fútbol** footballer, football player ▸ **jugador(a) de manos†** conjurer
2 [*de apuestas*] gambler ▸ **jugador(a) de bolsa** stock market speculator
jugar ▹ CONJUG 1h, 1n VI **1** [*niño, deportista*] to play • **¡si seguís así yo no juego!** if you carry on like that I'm not playing! • **~ a algo** to play sth • **~ al ajedrez** to play chess • **~ al tenis** to play tennis • **~ a la lotería** to play the lottery • **~ a la ruleta** to play roulette • **~ a los dados** to play dice • **~ al escondite** to play hide-and-seek • **~ con algo** to play with sth • **no le gusta ~ con muñecas** he doesn't like playing with dolls • **está jugando con el ordenador** she's playing on the computer • **~ contra algn** to play (against) sb • **hoy juegan contra el Celtic** today they're playing (against) Celtic • MODISMOS: • **~ con fuego** to play with fire • **~ con ventaja** to be at an advantage, have the advantage • **~ limpio** to play fair • **~ sucio** to play dirty • **de jugando** (*Caribe**) in fun, for fun
2 (= *hacer una jugada*) **a** (*en ajedrez, parchís*) to move • **¿quién juega?** whose move *o* turn *o* go is it?
b (*con cartas*) to play • **¿quién juega?** whose turn *o* go is it?
3 (= *pretender ser*) • **~ a algo** to play at being sth • **solo está jugando a detective** he's only playing at being a detective • **yo no juego a ser estrella de Hollywood** I'm not playing at being a Hollywood star • **vamos a ~ a que yo soy la madre y tú el hijo** let's pretend that I'm the mother and you the son
4 • **~ con a** (= *manosear*) (*gen*) to play around with, mess around with; (*distraídamente*) to toy with, fiddle with • **no juegues con el enchufe, que es peligroso** don't play *o* mess around with the plug - it's dangerous • **estaba jugando con un bolígrafo mientras hablaba** he was toying *o* fiddling with a pen while he spoke
b (= *no tomar en serio*) [+ *sentimientos*] to play with • **solamente está jugando contigo** he's just leading you on • **es importante permanecer en el poder, pero no a costa de ~ con la opinión pública** it is important to stay in power, but not if it means gambling with public opinion • **con la salud no se**

juega you can't put your health at risk
c (= *utilizar*) to play with • **esta obra juega con el tema del teatro dentro del teatro** this work plays with the idea of a play within a play
5 (= *influir*) • **~ en contra de algo/algn** to work against sth/sb • **su inexperiencia jugaba en contra suya** his inexperience worked against him • **la posición del sol jugaba en contra de nuestro equipo** the position of the sun put our team at a disadvantage • **~ a favor de algo/algn** [*situación*] to work in sth/sb's favour *o* (EEUU) favor; [*tiempo, destino*] to be on sb's side • **las ventajas de una moneda débil siguen jugando a su favor** the advantages of a weak currency continue to work in their favour • **existe otro elemento que juega a favor del acusado** there is another factor that should go *o* work in favour of the defendant • **has estudiado mucho y eso juega a tu favor** you have studied a lot and that should work in your favour
6 (= *apostar*) to gamble
7 (*Bolsa*) to speculate • **~ al alza** to bet on a bull market • **~ a la baja** to bet on a bear market • **~ a la bolsa** to play the stock market
8 (*LAm*) (*Mec*) to move about
VT **1** [+ *partida, partido*] to play • **el partido se juega hoy** the match will be played today
• MODISMOS: • **~ la baza de algo**: • **la oposición ~á la baza de la moción de censura** the opposition will play its trump card and move a motion of censure
• **jugársela a algn*** to do the dirty on sb* • **su hermano se la jugó** his brother did the dirty on him* • **¡me la han jugado!** I've been had!*
• **su mujer se la jugaba con otro** (*LAm*) his wife was two-timing him*; ▸ **baza**
2 [+ *papel*] to play • **juegan un papel fundamental en el desarrollo del país** they play a fundamental role in the country's development
3 (= *apostar*) to bet • **~ cinco dólares a una carta** to bet *o* put five dollars on a card
4 (*LAm*) [+ *fútbol, tenis, ajedrez, póker*] to play
5†† [+ *espada, florete*] to handle, wield
VPR **jugarse 1** [+ *dinero*] (= *apostar*) to bet, stake; (= *perder*) to gamble away • **se jugó 500 dólares** he bet *o* staked 500 dollars • **se jugó la fortuna a la ruleta** he gambled away his fortune at roulette • **jugárselo todo a una carta** (*lit*) to bet everything on one card; (*fig*) to put all one's eggs in one basket
2 (*como reto*) to bet • **me juego lo que quieras a que no te atreves** I bet you anything you won't dare • **¿qué te juegas a que tengo razón?** what do you bet I'm right?, what's the betting I'm right?
3 (= *exponerse a perder*) **a** (*en una apuesta consciente*) to stake • **nos jugamos mucho en esta operación** we're staking a lot on this operation • **jugárselo todo en algo** to stake everything on sth • **ambos equipos se lo juegan todo hoy** both teams are staking everything on today's match • MODISMOS: • **jugársela**: • **conducir más deprisa hubiera sido jugársela** to drive any faster would have been too risky • **España se la juega ante Italia esta noche** Spain is staking everything on their match with Italy tonight • **~se el todo por el todo** to take the plunge
b (= *sin darse cuenta*) • **nos estamos jugando el futuro de la democracia** the future of democracy is at stake here • **¿qué nos jugamos en las próximas elecciones?** what is at stake for us in the next election? • **esto es ~se la vida** this means risking one's life

jugarreta SF dirty trick • **hacer una ~ a algn** to play a dirty trick on sb
juglar SM minstrel, jongleur
juglaresco ADJ • **arte ~** art of the minstrel(s) • **estilo ~** minstrel style, popular style
juglaría SF minstrelsy, art of the minstrel(s)
jugo SM **1** (= *líquido*) (*gen*) juice; [*de carne*] gravy; [*de árbol*] sap ▸ **jugo de naranja** orange juice ▸ **jugos digestivos** digestive juices ▸ **jugos gástricos** gastric juices
2 (= *sustancia*) essence, substance • **sacar el ~ a algo** to get the most out of sth
jugosidad SF juiciness, succulence
jugoso ADJ **1** [*alimento*] juicy, succulent
2 (= *rentable*) [*aumento, reducción*] substantial, considerable; [*negocio*] profitable • **un discurso ~** a speech that gives/gave plenty of food for thought
jugué, juguemos *etc* ▸ **jugar**
juguera SF (*Cono Sur*) blender, liquidizer
juguete SM **1** (= *objeto*) toy • **un cañón de ~** a toy gun ▸ **juguete educativo** educational toy
2 (*uso figurado*) toy, plaything • **fue el ~ de las olas** the waves tossed it about as if it were their plaything
3 (= *chiste*) joke
4 (*Teat*) skit, sketch
juguetear ▸ CONJUG 1a VI to play, sport • **~ con** to play with, sport with
jugueteo SM playing, romping
juguetería SF **1** (= *tienda*) toyshop
2 (= *industria*) toy business
juguetero/a ADJ toy (*antes de s*)
SM/F toyshop owner
SM (= *mueble*) whatnot
juguetón ADJ playful
juguetonamente ADV playfully
juicio SM **1** (= *inteligencia*) judgment, reason
2 (= *sensatez*) good sense • **asentar el ~** to come to one's senses • **lo dejo a su ~** I leave it to your discretion • **estar en su sano ~** to be in one's right mind • **estar fuera de ~** to be out of one's mind • **perder el ~** to go mad
• **no tener ~** • **tener poco ~** to lack common sense • **tener mucho ~** to be sensible
3 (= *opinión*) opinion • **a mi ~** in my opinion
▸ **juicio de valor** value judgment
4 (*Jur*) (= *proceso*) trial; (= *veredicto*) verdict, judgment • **llevar a algn a ~** to take sb to court ▸ **juicio civil** criminal trial ▸ **juicio con jurado** trial by jury ▸ **juicio criminal** criminal trial ▸ **juicio de Dios** trial by ordeal
▸ **juicio en rebeldía** judgment by default
▸ **Juicio Final** Last Judgment ▸ **juicio sumario** summary trial
juicioso ADJ sensible, judicious
juilipío SM (*And*) sparrow
juilón‡ ADJ (*Méx*) yellow
JUJEM [xu'xem] SF ABR (*Esp*) (*Mil*) = **Junta de Jefes del Estado Mayor**
jul. ABR (= **julio**) Jul, July
julai‡ SM, **jula**‡ SM **1** (= *idiota*) twit*, berk‡
2 (= *homosexual*) poofter‡
julandra‡ SM, **julandrón**‡ SM = julai
julepe SM **1** (*Naipes*) *card game*
2* (= *reprimenda*) telling-off*, dressing-down*
3 (*LAm**) (= *susto*) scare, fright • **irse** *o* **salir de ~** (*And*) to run away in terror
4 (*Caribe, Méx**) (= *trabajo*) bind*
5 • **meter un ~** (*And*) to hurry on, speed up
6 (= *bebida*) julep
julepear* ▸ CONJUG 1a VT **1** (*Cono Sur*) (= *asustar*) to scare, frighten
2 (*Méx*) (= *cansar*) to wear out, tire out
3 (*And*) (= *apresurar*) to hurry along, speed up
VPR **julepearse** (*Cono Sur*) (= *asustarse*) to get scared; (= *estar atento*) to smell danger
julia* SF (*Méx*) Black Maria*, paddy wagon (EEUU*)
Julián SM, **Juliano** SM Julian
juliana SF (*Culin*) julienne • **cortar en ~** to cut into thin shreds, cut into julienne strips
Julieta SF Juliet
Julio SM Julius • **~ César** Julius Caesar
julio SM July; ▸ **septiembre**
juma* SF drunkenness, drunken state
jumadera* SF (*Méx*) **1** drunkenness, drunken state
2 (= *humareda*) cloud of smoke
jumado* ADJ drunk, plastered*
jumar* ▸ CONJUG 1a VI to pong‡, stink
VPR **jumarse** to get drunk
jumatán* SM (*Caribe*) drunkard
jumazo‡ SM (*Caribe*) fag‡
jumbo SM jumbo, jumbo jet
jumeado* ADJ (*And*) drunk, tight*
jumelar‡ ▸ CONJUG 1a VI to pong‡, stink
jumento SM (= *animal*) donkey; (= *insulto*) dolt
jumo* ADJ (*LAm*) drunk, plastered*
jumper ['dʒumper] SM (PL: **jumpers**) (*Cono Sur*) sleeveless sweater
jun. ABR (= **junio**) Jun
junar‡ ▸ CONJUG 1a VT (= *ver*) to see; (= *mirar*) to watch
VI (*Cono Sur*) to keep a look-out
juncal ADJ **1** (*Bot*) rushy, reedy
2 (= *esbelto*) willowy, lissom
SM reed bed
juncar SM reed bed
juncia SF sedge
junco[1] SM (= *planta*) rush, reed
junco[2] SM (= *barco*) junk
juncoso ADJ **1** (*Bot*) rushy, reedy, reed-like
2 [*lugar*] covered in rushes
jungla SF jungle ▸ **jungla de asfalto** concrete jungle
junguiano/a ADJ, SM/F Jungian
junio SM June; ▸ **septiembre**
junior ['dʒunjor], **júnior**[1] ['dʒunjor] ADJ INV junior
SMF (PL: **juniors** *o* **júniors**) junior
SM (*Cono Sur*) office boy
júnior[2] SM (PL: **juniores**) (*Rel*) novice monk, junior novice
Juno SF Juno
junquera SF rush, bulrush
junquillo SM **1** (*Bot*) jonquil
2 (= *bastón*) rattan; (= *madera*) strip of light wood
3 (*Caribe, Méx*) gold necklace
junta SF **1** (= *reunión*) meeting • **celebrar** *o* **convocar una ~** to hold a meeting ▸ **junta de acreedores** meeting of creditors ▸ **junta general de accionistas** general meeting of shareholders ▸ **junta general extraordinaria** extraordinary general meeting, special meeting (EEUU)
2 (= *comité*) (*gen*) council, committee; (*Com, Econ*) board • **la ~ de la asociación** the committee of the association ▸ **junta de gobierno** governing body ▸ **junta de portavoces** (*Parl*) House business committee ▸ **junta directiva** board of directors ▸ **junta electoral** electoral board ▸ **junta municipal** council ▸ **junta rectora** governing body
3 (*Mil*) junta ▸ **junta militar** military junta
4 (*Esp*) (*Pol*) *name given to the governments of some autonomous areas in Spain*
5 (*Téc*) (= *acoplamiento*) joint; (= *arandela*) washer, gasket ▸ **junta cardán, junta universal** universal joint
6 (*LAm*) (= *amistad*) • **las malas ~s** the wrong kind of people • **le prohibieron las ~s con esa**

gente they forbade him to go out with those people
juntadero (SM) (*Cono Sur*) meeting place
juntamente (ADV) **1** • **~ con** together with • **entregó su currículum ~ con los documentos justificativos** he handed in his CV together with the supporting documents
2 (= *conjuntamente*) together • **ella y yo ~** she and I together
3 (= *al mismo tiempo*) • **eran todos, ~, verdugos y víctimas** all of them were both executioners and victims, all of them were executioners as well as victims
juntar ▹ CONJUG 1a (VT) **1** (= *colocar juntos*) to put together • **juntó las manos en actitud de plegaria** she put her hands together as if praying • **~on varias mesas** they put several tables together • **junta el armario a la pared** put the cupboard against the wall • **~ dinero** (= *ahorrar*) to save, save up; (= *reunir fondos*) to raise funds, fundraise • **estoy juntando dinero para comprarme una bicicleta** I'm saving up to buy a bicycle
2 (= *reunir*) [+ *amigos, conocidos*] to get together; [+ *participantes, concursantes*] to bring together • **juntó a sus amigos para darles la noticia** he got his friends together to tell them the news • **¿cómo consiguió el director ~ tantas estrellas en una misma película?** how did the director manage to bring together so many stars *o* get so many stars together in one film? • **la final ha juntado a los dos mejores equipos del mundo** the final has brought together the two best teams in the world
3 (= *coleccionar*) [+ *sellos, objetos*] to collect
4 (= *entornar*) [+ *puerta, ventana*] to push to
(VPR) **juntarse 1** (= *reunirse*) **a** (*para una cita*) to get together, meet up • **por la tarde nos juntamos todos para jugar a las cartas** in the afternoons we all get together *o* meet up to play cards • **~se con algn** to get together with sb, meet up with sb • **a veces se juntan con otros matrimonios y salen por ahí** they sometimes get together *o* meet up with other couples and go out somewhere
b (*en asamblea, trabajo*) to meet • **solían ~se en ese local** they used to meet on those premises
c (*sin citarse*) to come together • **en el estadio se ~án hoy bastantes figuras del fútbol** many famous figures in football will come together in the stadium today • **en la sala apenas se ~on dos docenas de personas** less than two dozen people assembled in the hall • **se ~on más de cinco mil personas para oírlo** more than five thousand people assembled *o* came together to listen to him
2 (= *unirse*) • **se fue juntando mucha más gente por el camino** many more people joined them along the way • **se juntan un espermatozoide y un óvulo** a sperm and an egg join together • **~se a** *o* **con algn** to join up with sb • **salimos de París por la mañana y en Calais se nos juntó Pedro** we left Paris in the morning and Pedro joined up with us *o* met up with us in Calais • **se juntó a otros dos músicos para crear un nuevo grupo** he joined up with two other musicians to create a new band
3 (= *arrimarse*) [*varias personas*] to move closer together • **si te juntas un poco más cabremos todos en el banco** if you move up a bit we can all get on the bench
4 (= *relacionarse*) [*pareja*] to get together • **~se con algn** (*gen*) to mix with sb; (*en pareja*) to get together with sb • **allí se puede uno ~ con la crema de la sociedad** there you can mix with the cream of society • **no me gusta que te juntes con esa gente** I don't like you going round *o* mixing with those people
5 (= *ocurrir a la vez*) to come together • **en su poesía se juntan elementos tradicionales y renovadores** traditional and new elements come together in his poetry • **la semana pasada se me juntó todo** it was just one thing after another last week • **se ~on dos bodas el mismo día** there were two marriages on the same day • **se te va a ~ el desayuno con la comida** you'll be having breakfast at the same time as your lunch
6 [*empresas, asociaciones*] to merge • **ambas coordinadoras se ~on en una organización central** both coordinating committees merged to form a centralized organization
7 [*líneas, caminos*] to meet, join
8 (*Zool*) to mate, copulate
juntillas ▹ **pie**
junto (ADJ) **1** (= *unido, acompañado*) together • **métele todo ~ en la maleta** put it all together in the suitcase • **se pone todo ~ en un plato y se sirve** arrange it all in a dish and serve • **sinfín, como sustantivo, se escribe ~** when it is a noun, "sinfín" is written as one word • **nunca había visto tantos libros ~s** I had never seen so many books together in one place • **llevamos quince años ~s** we've been together for fifteen years • **fuimos ~s** we went together • **todos ~s** all together • **trabajar ~s** to work together • **vivir ~s** to live together
• MODISMO: • **~s pero no revueltos** (*hum*) close to each other *o* together, but not in each other's pockets
2 (= *cercano*) close together • **tenía los ojos muy ~s** his eyes were very close together • **poneos más ~s, que no cabéis en la foto** move a bit closer together, I can't get you all in (the photo)
3 (= *al mismo tiempo*) together • **las vi entrar juntas** I saw them go in together • **ocurrió todo ~** it happened all at once
(ADV) **1** • **~ a a** (= *cerca de*) close to, near • **20.000 personas seguían acampadas ~ a la frontera** 20,000 people were still camped close to *o* near the border • **tienen un chalet ~ al mar** they have a house close to *o* near the sea
b (= *al lado de*) next to, beside • **fue enterrado ~ a su padre** he was buried next to *o* beside his father • **José permanecía de pie, ~ a la puerta** José remained standing by the door
c (= *en compañía de*) with, together with • **celebró su aniversario ~ a su familia** he celebrated his anniversary (together) with his family • **expresó su deseo de volver ~ a su marido** she expressed a wish to go back to her husband
d (= *conjuntamente*) together with, along with • **nuestro equipo es, ~ al italiano, el mejor de la liga** together with the Italian team, ours is the best in the league
2 • **~ con a** (= *en compañía de*) with, together with • **fue detenido ~ con otros cuatro terroristas** he was arrested (together) with four other terrorists • **machacar los ajos en el mortero ~ con el perejil** crush the garlic in the mortar (together) with the parsley
b (= *conjuntamente*) together with • **el paro es, ~ con el terrorismo, nuestro mayor problema** together with terrorism, unemployment is our biggest problem
3 • **en ~**† in all, all together
4 • **(de) por ~**† (*Com*) wholesale
juntura (SF) (*Anat, Téc*) joint
jupa (SF) (*CAm, Méx*) **1** (= *calabaza*) gourd
2‡ (= *cabeza*) head, nut‡, noggin (*EEUU**)
jupata‡ (SF) jacket
jupiarse ▹ CONJUG 1b (VPR) (*CAm*) to get drunk
Júpiter (SM) Jupiter
jura¹ (SF) (= *juramento*) oath, pledge ▸ **jura de (la) bandera** (taking the) oath of loyalty *o* allegiance
jura²‡ (SM) (*CAm, Caribe*) cop*
(SF) • **la ~** the cops* (*pl*), the fuzz‡
juraco* (SM) (*CAm*) hole
jurado (SM) (= *tribunal*) (*Jur*) jury; (*en concurso, TV*) panel (*of judges*)
(SMF) (= *miembro*) (*Jur*) juror; (*en concurso, TV*) judge
(ADJ) [*declaración*] sworn; ▹ **guarda, guardia, traductor**
juramentar ▹ CONJUG 1a (VT) to swear in, administer the oath to
(VPR) **juramentarse** to be sworn in, take the oath
juramento (SM) **1** (= *promesa*) oath • **bajo ~** on oath • **prestar ~** to take the oath (**sobre** on) • **tomar ~ a algn** to swear sb in
▸ **juramento de fidelidad** oath of loyalty
▸ **juramento hipocrático** Hippocratic oath
2 (= *blasfemia*) oath, curse • **decir ~s** to swear
jurar ▹ CONJUG 1a (VT) **1** (*solemnemente*) to swear • **juró haberlo visto entrar** she swore she had seen him come in • **juró vengarse de ellos** he swore to avenge himself on them • **~ decir la verdad** to swear to tell the truth • **~ (la) bandera** to pledge allegiance (to the flag) • **~ el cargo** to be sworn in • **~ la Constitución** to pledge allegiance to the Constitution • **lo juro por mi honor** I swear on my honour • **lo juro por mi madre** I swear to God • MODISMO: • **tenérsela jurada a algn** (*como venganza personal*) to have it in for sb; (*a nivel político, profesional*) to be after sb's blood
2 (*uso enfático*) to swear • **no he oído nada, se lo juro** I didn't hear a thing, I swear • **te juro que fue el peor momento de mi vida** I swear it was the worst moment of my life • **~ía que estaba allí hace un momento** I could have sworn he was there a moment ago • **—yo no entiendo mucho de esto —no hace falta que lo jures, guapo** (*iró*) "I don't know much about this sort of thing" — "sure you don't, pal"*
(VI) (= *blasfemar*) to swear • **¡no jures!** don't swear! • **~ en falso** to commit perjury
• MODISMO: • **~ como un carretero** to swear like a trooper
jurásico (ADJ) Jurassic
(SM) • **el ~** the Jurassic, the Jurassic period
jurdós‡ (SM) bread‡, money
jurel (SM) **1** (= *pez*) horse mackerel
2 • **coger ~*** to get a fright
jurero/a (SM/F) (*And, Cono Sur*) perjurer, false witness
jurgo (SM) (*And*), **jurgonera** (SF) (*And*) = jorga
jurídico (ADJ) legal, juridical
• **departamento ~** (*Com*) legal department
jurisdicción (SF) **1** (= *autoridad*) jurisdiction
2 (= *distrito*) district, administrative area
jurisdiccional (ADJ) • **aguas ~es** territorial waters
jurispericia (SF) jurisprudence
jurisperito/a (SM/F) jurist, legal expert
jurisprudencia (SF) jurisprudence
jurista (SMF) jurist
juro (SM) (= *derecho*) right of perpetual ownership; (= *pago*) annuity, pension • **a ~** (*And, Caribe*) • **de ~** certainly
justa (SF) **1** (*Hist*) joust, tournament
2 (= *competición*) contest
justamente (ADV) **1** (= *exactamente*) **a** (= *coincidiendo con algo*) just • **la fábrica se instaló en los setenta, ~ cuando estalló la crisis energética** the factory was set up in the seventies, just when the energy crisis broke out • **lo sorprendente es que lo**

eligieran a él, ~ ahora que … what is surprising is that he was chosen, just when … • **ocurrió hace ~ un año** it happened exactly a year ago • **~ lo contrario** exactly the opposite
b (= *referido a cosa, lugar*) exactly, precisely • **es aquí ~ donde está la originalidad del autor** it is precisely in this where the author's originality lies • **esas son ~ las que no están en venta** those are precisely the ones which are not for sale
2 (= *con justicia*) justly • **los monumentos por los que la ciudad es ~ famosa** the monuments for which the city is justly famous
3 (= *escasamente*) frugally • **viven muy ~ con la pensión** they live very frugally on their pension

justar ▹ CONJUG 1a (VI) to joust, tilt

justicia (SF) (*gen*) justice; (= *equidad*) fairness, equity; (= *derecho*) right • **de ~** justly, deservedly • **lo estimo de ~** I think it fair • **es de ~ añadir que** it is only fair to add that • **en ~** by rights • **hacer ~ a** to do justice to • **tomarse la ~ por su mano** to take the law into one's own hands ▸ **justicia gratuita** legal aid ▸ **justicia poética** poetic justice ▸ **justicia social** social justice
(SM) †† *representative of authority* • **~s y ladrones** cops and robbers*

justiciable (ADJ) **1** (= *procesable*) actionable
2 [*decisión*] subject to review by a court

justicialismo (SM) (*Arg*) (*Hist, Pol*) *political movement founded by Perón*; ▹ PERONISMO

justicieramente (ADV) justly

justiciero (ADJ) (strictly) just, righteous

justificable (ADJ) justifiable

justificación (SF) justification
▸ **justificación automática** (*Inform*) automatic justification

justificadamente (ADV) justifiably

justificado (ADJ) justified • **no ~** unjustified

justificante (SM) [*de dinero*] receipt; [*de enfermedad*] sick note

justificar ▹ CONJUG 1g (VT) **1** (= *explicar*) to account for, explain • **tendrá que ~ su ausencia del trabajo** she will have to account for *o* explain her absence from work • **el gobierno no pudo ~ el aumento del gasto** the government was unable to account for *o* explain the increase in expenditure • **justificó las compras con facturas** he accounted for his purchases with receipts
2 (= *excusar*) [+ *decisión, comportamiento*] to justify, excuse • **nada justifica tal violencia** nothing can justify *o* excuse such violence • **siempre justifica a sus hijos ante sus amigas** she always defends her sons to her friends • **es un criminal y no pretendo ~lo** he's a criminal and I'm not trying to make excuses for him
3 (*Inform, Tip*) to justify
(VPR) **justificarse** to justify o.s., make excuses for o.s. • **no intentes ~te porque no tienes razón** don't try and justify yourself *o* make excuses for yourself because you're in the wrong • **se justificó diciendo que el tren llegó tarde** he justified himself *o* made his excuses saying the train was late

justificativo (ADJ) • **documento ~** voucher, certificate

justillo (SM) jerkin

justipreciar ▹ CONJUG 1b (VT) to evaluate, appraise

justiprecio (SM) evaluation, appraisal

justo (ADJ) **1** (= *con justicia*) [*castigo, sentencia, solución, decisión, sociedad*] fair, just; [*juicio, premio, árbitro, juez*] fair; [*causa*] just • **el pacto me pareció muy ~** the agreement seemed very fair to me • **no es ~ que ganen más los hombres que las mujeres** it's not fair that men should earn more than women • **pero seamos ~s …** but let's be fair … • **el premio ha sido ~** the prize was fairly won • **un reparto más ~ de la riqueza** a more equitable *o* just distribution of wealth
2 (= *exacto*) [*precio, medidas*] exact • **cuesta 10 euros ~s** it costs exactly 10 euros • **nació a los tres años ~s de que terminara la guerra** he was born exactly three years after the war ended • **valorar algo en su justa medida** to appreciate sth for its true worth • **tengo el tiempo ~ para tomarme un café** I've got just enough time to have a coffee • **estamos los ~s para jugar al bridge** there's just the right number of us to play bridge
3 (= *preciso*) • **encontró la palabra justa** she found exactly *o* just the right word • **vino en el momento ~** he came just at the right moment
4 (= *escaso*) • **vivimos muy ~s** we have only just enough to live on • **~ de: vamos un poco ~s de tiempo** we're a bit pushed for time • **llegaste muy ~ de tiempo** you only just made it • **el equipo ha llegado a estas alturas de la competición muy ~ de fuerzas** the team have struggled to get this far in the competition • **ando ~ de dinero** money's a bit tight at the moment • **vive con lo ~** he just manages to make ends meet
5 (= *apretado*) [*ropa*] tight • **el traje me queda** *o* **me viene** *o* **me está muy ~** the suit is very tight for *o* on me • **entramos todos en el coche, pero muy ~s** we all got into the car, but it was a real squeeze
(ADV) **1** (= *exactamente*) (*gen*) just; (*con cantidades*) exactly • **eso es ~ lo que iba a decir** that's just *o* exactly what I was going to say • **llegó ~ cuando yo salía** she arrived just *o* exactly as I was leaving • **vino ~ a tiempo** he came just in time • **su casa está ~ enfrente del cine** his house is just *o* right opposite the cinema • **¡justo!** that's it!, right!, exactly! • **me costó ~ el doble que a ti** it cost me exactly double what it cost you • **~ lo contrario** exactly the opposite
2 (= *escasamente*) • **vivir muy ~** to just manage to make ends meet, have only just enough to live on
(SMPL) • **los ~s** (*Rel*) the just • MODISMO: • **pagan ~s por pecadores** the innocent pay for the sins of the guilty

jute (SM) (*CAm*) edible snail

juvenil (ADJ) **1** [*persona*] youthful • **de aspecto ~** youthful in appearance • **en los años ~es** in one's early years, in one's youth • **obra ~** early work
2 [*equipo, torneo*] junior
(SMF) (*Dep*) junior, junior player

juventud (SF) **1** (= *época*) youth • **en mi ~ no había ordenadores** in my youth *o* when I was young there were no computers • **pecados de ~** youthful indiscretions • MODISMO: • **¡~, divino tesoro!** what it is to be young!
2 (= *los jóvenes*) young people • **la ~ de hoy** • **la ~ actual** young people today, the youth of today • **la ~ española** Spanish young people • MODISMO: • **~ no conoce virtud** boys will be boys ▸ **Juventudes Comunistas** Young Communists
3 (= *cualidad*) youth • **su cutis aún conserva su ~** her complexion is still young

juyungo/a (SM/F) (*Ecu*) black, mulatto

juzgado (SM) court ▸ **juzgado de guardia** police court • **esto es de ~ de guardia** (*fig*) this is an absolute outrage ▸ **juzgado de instrucción** examining magistrate's court ▸ **juzgado de lo penal** criminal court ▸ **juzgado de lo social** social court ▸ **juzgado de menores** juvenile court ▸ **juzgado de primera instancia** court of first instance

juzgar ▹ CONJUG 1h (VT) **1** (= *emitir un juicio*) to judge • **júzguelo usted misma** judge for yourself • **juzgue usted mi sorpresa** imagine my surprise • **~ mal** to misjudge • **a ~ por** to judge by, judging by • **a ~ por lo que hemos visto** to judge by *o* from what we have seen
2 (= *considerar*) to think, consider • **lo juzgo mi deber** I consider it my duty, I deem it my duty (*frm*)

juzgón (ADJ) (*CAm, Méx*) hypercritical, carping

Kk

K, k [ka] SF (= *letra*) K, k
K SM ABR (= **kilobyte**) K
ka SF (name of the letter) K
kabuki SM kabuki
Kadsastán SM Kazakhstan
kafkiano ADJ Kafkaesque
káiser SM Kaiser
kaki SM = **caqui**
kale borroka [,kalebo'rroka] SF *orchestrated acts of urban vandalism attributed to ETA*
kamikaze SM kamikaze
Kampuchea SF Kampuchea
kampucheano/a ADJ, SM/F Kampuchean
kantiano ADJ Kantian
kaperuj SM (*And*) embroidered shawl
kaput* [ka'pu] ADJ kaput* • **hacer ~** to go kaput*, go phut*
karaoke SM karaoke
kárate SM, **karate** SM karate
karateka SMF, **karateca** SMF karate expert
karma SM karma
karting ['kartin] SM, **kárting** ['kartin] SM go-kart racing
KAS SF ABR (= **Koordinadora Abertzale Sozialista**) *Basque nationalist umbrella group*
Katar SM Qatar
katiuska ADJ (*Esp*) • **botas ~s** wellington boots
SF wellington, wellington boot
kayac SM, **kayak** SM kayak
Kazajistán SM Kazakhstan
kazajo/a ADJ, SM/F Kazak, Kazakh
SM (*Ling*) Kazak, Kazakh
k/c ABR (= **kilociclo(s)**) kc
kebab SM (PL: **kebabs**) kebab
kedada* SF (*Internet*) gathering *o* meeting (*arranged over the internet*)
kéfir SM (*And*) *type of yoghurt*
Kenia SF Kenya
keniano/a ADJ, SM/F Kenyan
keniata ADJ, SMF Kenyan
kepis SM INV, **kepí** SM *military style round cap or hat*
kermes SM, **kermesse** SM charity fair, bazaar
kerosén SM (*LAm*), **kerosene** SM (*LAm*), **keroseno** SM, **kerosina** SF (*CAm*) kerosene, paraffin
ketchup ['ketʃap, 'ketʃup] SM ketchup, catsup (*EEUU*)
keynesiano/a ADJ, SM/F Keynesian
kg ABR (= **kilogramo(s)**) kg
KHz ABR (= **kilohertzio(s), kilohercio(s)**) KHz

kibutz [ki'βuts] SM (PL: **kibutzim, kibutz**) kibbutz
kiki‡ SM joint‡, reefer‡
kiko SM *snack of salted, toasted maize*
kikongo SM Kikongo
kilate SM = **quilate**
kilo SM **1** (= *unidad de peso*) kilo • **los ~s de más** those extra kilos • **cuarto de ~** a quarter of a kilo, 250 grams
2* (= *un millón de pesetas*) one million pesetas • **un cuarto de ~** a quarter of a million pesetas, 250,000 pesetas
3* (*como adv*) (= *mucho*) a lot, load*

> **KILOS, METROS, AÑOS**
>
> *En inglés cuando la unidad de medida precede al nombre como adjetivo compuesto, debe escribirse en singular y unida por un guión al número correspondiente. En el resto de los casos se emplea en plural, como en español:*
>
> **Una caja de bombones de dos kilos/La caja de bombones pesa dos kilos**
> A two-kilo box of chocolates/The box of chocolates weighs two kilos
> **Una regla de 20cms/La regla mide 20cms**
> A 20-centimetre ruler/The ruler is 20 centimetres long
> **Un muchacho de quince años/El muchacho tiene quince años**
> A fifteen-year-old boy/The boy is fifteen years old

kilobyte ['kilobait] SM kilobyte
kilocaloría SF kilocalorie, Calorie
kilociclo SM kilocycle
kilogramo SM kilogramme, kilogram (*EEUU*)
kilohercio SM, **kilohertzio** SM kilohertz
kilolitro SM kilolitre, kiloliter (*EEUU*)
kilometraje SM ≈ mileage
kilometrar ▸ CONJUG 1a VT to measure, measure in kilometres
kilométrico ADJ **1** (*de kilómetro*) kilometric • **(billete) ~** (*Ferro*) ≈ mileage ticket
2* (= *muy largo*) very long • **palabra kilométrica** very long word
kilómetro SM kilometre, kilometer (*EEUU*) • **~ cero** (= *punto de partida*) starting point; (*central*) central point; ▸ **KILOS, METROS, AÑOS**
kiloocteto SM kilobyte
kilopondio SM kilogramme-force
kilotón SM kiloton

kilovatio SM kilowatt
kilovatio-hora SM kilowatt-hour • **kilovatios-hora** kilowatt-hours
kimona SF (*Cuba, Méx*), **kimono** SM kimono
kínder SM (*LAm*), **kindergarten** SM (*LAm*) kindergarten, nursery school
kinesiología SF kinesiology
kión SM (*And*) ginger
kiosco SM = **quiosco**
kiosquero/a SM/F = **quiosquero**
Kirguistán SM, **Kirguizistán** SM, **Kirguisia** SF Kyrgyzstan
kit SM (PL: **kits**) kit ▸ **kit de montaje** self-assembly kit
kitsch [kitʃ] ADJ INV, SM kitsch
kiwi SM **1** (= *ave*) kiwi
2 (= *fruta*) kiwi fruit
klaxon SM horn • **tocar el ~** to blow the horn, toot (the horn)
klínex SM INV tissue, Kleenex®
km ABR (= **kilómetro(s)**) km
km/h ABR (= **kilómetros por hora**) km/h, kmh
knock-out ['nokau] SM, **K.O.** [kaw] SM (= *acto*) knockout; (= *golpe*) knockout blow • **dejar a algn knock-out** to knock sb out; ▹ **noqueo** *etc*
kodak [ko'ðak] SF (PL: **kodaks** [ko'ðak]) small camera
kohl SM (*para ojos*) kohl
koljós SM (PL: **koljoses**), **koljoz** [kol'xos] SM (PL: **koljozi**) kolkhoz
kosher ADJ kosher
kosovar ADJ Kosovan, Kosovo (*antes de s*)
SMF Kosovar
Kosovo SM Kosovo
k.p.h. ABR (= **kilómetros por hora**) km/h, kmh
k.p.l. ABR = **kilómetros por litro**
krausismo SM *philosophy and doctrine of K.C.F. Krause*
krausista ADJ Krausist, of Krause
SMF follower of Krause
kuchen SM (*Chile*) fancy cake, fancy German-style cake
Kurdistán SM Kurdistan
kurdo/a ADJ Kurdish
SM/F Kurd
SM (*Ling*) Kurdish
Kuwait SM Kuwait
kuwaití ADJ, SMF Kuwaiti
kv ABR (= **kilovoltio(s)**) kV, kv
kv/h ABR (= **kilovoltios-hora**) kV/h, kv/h
kw ABR (= **kilovatio(s)**) kW, kw
kw/h ABR (= **kilovatios-hora**) kW/h, kw/h

Ll

L, l ['ele] SF (= *letra*) L, l
l ABR **1** (= **litro(s)**) l
2 (= **libro**) bk
3 (*Jur*) = **ley**
L/ ABR (= **Letra de Cambio**) B/E, BE
la[1] ART DEF **1** (*con sustantivos*) the • **la mujer** the woman • **La India** India
2 • **la de: mi casa y la de usted** my house and yours • **esta chica y la del sombrero verde** this girl and the one in the green hat • **la de Pedro es mejor** Peter's is better • **y la de todos los demás** and everybody else's, and that of everybody else • **ir a la de Pepe** to go to Pepe's place • **la de Rodríguez** Mrs Rodríguez • **¡la de goles que marcó!** what a lot of goals he scored! • **¡la de veces que se equivoca!** how often he's wrong!; ▹ **el**
la[2] PRON PERS (*refiriéndose a ella*) her; (*refiriéndose a usted*) you; (*refiriéndose a una cosa, un animal*) it; ▹ **lo, laísmo**
la[3] SM (*Mús*) la, A • **la menor** A minor
laberintero ADJ (*Méx*) = **laberintoso**
laberíntico ADJ (*gen*) labyrinthine; [*edificio*] rambling
laberinto SM **1** (= *enredo*) [*de corredores, calles*] labyrinth, maze; (*en parque*) maze; [*de situaciones, ideas, reglas*] labyrinth, maze
2 (*esp LAm**) (= *griterío*) row, racket
laberintoso ADJ (*Méx*) **1** (= *ruidoso*) rowdy, brawling
2 (= *chismoso*) gossipy
labia SF fluency; (*pey*) glibness, glib tongue • **tener mucha ~** to have the gift of the gab*
labial ADJ, SF labial
labihendido ADJ harelipped
labio SM (*Anat*) lip; [*de vasija*] edge, rim, lip; **labios** lips, mouth (*sing*) • **lamerse los ~s** to lick one's lips • **leer los ~s** to lip-read
• MODISMOS: • **de ~s para afuera**: • **es muy valiente de ~s para afuera** he comes over brave enough, he seems brave on the face of it • **no descoser los ~s** to keep one's mouth shut • **no morderse los ~s** to be very outspoken, pull no punches • **sin despegar los ~s** without uttering a word ▸ **labio inferior** lower lip ▸ **labios mayores** labia majora ▸ **labio leporino** harelip, cleft lip ▸ **labios menores** labia minora ▸ **labio superior** upper lip
labiodental ADJ, SF labiodental
labiolectura SF, **labiología** SF lip-reading
labiosear* ▹ CONJUG 1a VT (*CAm*) to flatter
labiosidad* SF (*And, CAm*) flattery
labioso ADJ (*LAm*) **1** (= *hablador*) talkative
2 (= *lisonjero*) flattering
3 (= *persuasivo*) persuasive, glib
4 (= *taimado*) sly
labor SF **1** (= *trabajo*) labour, labor (EEUU), work • **"profesión: sus labores"** (*en censo, formulario*) "occupation: housewife" • **una ~** job, task, piece of work ▸ **labor de chinos** tedious job ▸ **labor de equipo** teamwork ▸ **labores domésticas** household chores ▸ **labor social** work for a good cause, work in a good cause
2 (= *costura*) sewing, needlework; (= *bordado*) embroidery; (= *punto*) knitting • **una ~** a piece of sewing ▸ **labor de aguja** needlework ▸ **labor de ganchillo** crochet, crocheting ▸ **labores de punto** knitting
3 (*Agr*) (= *arada*) ploughing, plowing (EEUU); (= *cultivo*) farm work, cultivation
4 labores (*Min*) workings
5 (*CAm, Caribe*) (= *parcela*) small farm, smallholding
laborable ADJ **1** [*jornada, semana*] working • **día ~** working day
2 [*tierra, terreno*] arable
laboral ADJ (*gen*) labour (*antes de s*), labor (EEUU) (*antes de s*), work (*antes de s*); [*jornada, horario*] working
laboralista ADJ labour (*antes de s*), labor (*antes de s*) (EEUU) • **abogado ~** labour lawyer
laboralmente ADV • **~ productivo** productive in terms of work
laborar ▹ CONJUG 1a VT **1** (*frm*) (= *trabajar*) to work
2 (*Agr*) to work, till (*liter*)
VI **1** (*frm*) (= *trabajar*) to work
2 (= *intrigar*) to scheme, plot
laboratorio SM laboratory ▸ **laboratorio de idiomas** language laboratory ▸ **laboratorio espacial** space laboratory
laborear ▹ CONJUG 1a VT (= *trabajar*) to work; (*Agr*) to work, till (*liter*)
laboreo SM (= *trabajo*) working; (*Agr*) working, cultivation, tilling (*liter*)
laborero SM (*And, Cono Sur*) foreman
laboriosamente ADV **1** (= *con dedicación*) industriously
2 (= *con minuciosidad*) painstakingly
3 (= *con dificultad*) with great difficulty
laboriosidad SF **1** (= *dedicación*) industry
2 (= *minuciosidad*) painstaking skill
3 (= *dificultad*) laboriousness
laborioso ADJ **1** (= *dedicado, constante*) hard-working, industrious
2 (= *minucioso*) painstaking
3 (= *dificultoso*) [*trabajo, negociaciones*] laborious, difficult
laborismo SM Labour Movement
laborista ADJ Labour (*antes de s*) • **Partido Laborista** Labour Party
SMF **1** (*en Gran Bretaña*) (*Pol*) Labour Party member, Labour supporter
2 (*CAm*) (= *trabajador*) small farmer, smallholder
laborterapia SF work-therapy
labra SF carving, working, cutting
labradío ADJ arable
labrado ADJ (= *trabajado*) worked; [*metal*] wrought; [*madera*] carved; [*tela*] patterned, embroidered
SM cultivated field; **labrados** cultivated land (*sing*)
Labrador SM (*Geog*) Labrador
labrador(a) SM/F **1** (= *propietario*) (peasant) farmer
2 (= *labriego*) farm labourer, farmhand, farmworker; (= *campesino*) peasant
3 (= *perro*) Labrador
labrantín/ina SM/F small farmer
labrantío ADJ arable
labranza SF cultivation, farming, tilling (*liter*) • **tierras de ~** farmland
labrar ▹ CONJUG 1a VT **1** (= *trabajar*) to work; [+ *metal*] to work; [+ *madera*] to carve; [+ *tierra*] to work, farm, till (*liter*); [+ *tela*] to embroider
2 [+ *imagen*] to create; [+ *fortuna*] to amass
VPR **labrarse** • **~se un porvenir** to carve out a future for o.s.
labriego/a SM/F farmhand, labourer, peasant
laburante* SM (*Cono Sur*) worker
laburar* ▹ CONJUG 1a VI (*Cono Sur*) to work
laburno SM laburnum
laburo* SM (*Cono Sur*) (= *trabajo*) work; (= *puesto*) job • **¡qué ~!** what a job!
laca SF **1** (= *gomorresina*) shellac; (= *barniz*) lacquer; [*de pelo*] hairspray ▸ **laca de uñas, laca para uñas** nail polish, nail varnish
2 (= *color*) lake
3 (*Cono Sur*) = **lacra**
lacado SM lacquer
lacar ▹ CONJUG 1g VT to lacquer
lacayo SM **1** (= *criado*) footman
2 (*pey*) (= *adulador*) lackey
laceada SF (*Cono Sur*) whipping
lacear ▹ CONJUG 1a VT **1** (*Caza*) (= *atrapar*) to snare, trap
2 (*And*) (*Caza*) [+ *ganado*] to lasso
3 (*Arg*) (= *zurrar*) to whip
4 (= *adornar*) to beribbon, adorn with bows; (= *atar*) to tie with a bow; (*CAm, Méx*) [+ *carga*] to tie on firmly, strap securely
laceración SF **1** [*de cuerpo*] laceration
2 [*de reputación, nombre*] damage
lacerante ADJ **1** [*dolor*] excruciating
2 [*palabras, comentarios*] wounding, cutting
lacerar ▹ CONJUG 1a VT **1** (= *herir*) to lacerate
2 (= *perjudicar*) to damage
laceria SF (*frm*) **1** (= *pobreza*) poverty, want
2 (= *sufrimiento*) distress, wretchedness
lacero/a SM/F dog-catcher
lacha SF (= *honor*) sense of honour; (= *vergüenza*) sense of shame
lachear* ▹ CONJUG 1a VT (*Cono Sur*) to chat up*
lacho* SM (*Chile, Perú*) lover
laciar ▹ CONJUG 1b VT (*LAm*) [+ *pelo rizado*] to straighten
Lacio SM Latium
lacio ADJ **1** [*pelo*] lank, straight
2 [*movimiento*] limp, languid
3 (*Bot*) withered, faded
lacón SM shoulder of pork
lacónicamente ADV laconically, tersely
lacónico ADJ laconic, terse
laconismo SM laconic style, laconic manner, terseness
lacra SF **1** (*Med*) scar, trace; (*LAm*) (= *llaga*)

sore, ulcer; (= *costra*) scab
2 (*social, moral*) blot, blemish • **la prostitución es una ~ social** prostitution is a blot on society
lacrado ADJ (wax-)sealed
lacrar¹ ▷ CONJUG 1a VT **1** (*Med*) (= *dañar*) to damage the health of, harm; (= *contagiar*) to infect
2 [+ *intereses*] to be prejudicial to, be against
VPR **lacrarse** • **~se con algo** to suffer harm *o* damage *o* loss from sth • **~se con el trabajo excesivo** to harm o.s. through overwork
lacrar² ▷ CONJUG 1a VT to seal (*with sealing wax*)
lacre ADJ (*LAm*) bright red
SM **1** (= *cera*) sealing wax
2 (*Chile*) (= *color*) red colour, red color (EEUU)
lacrimógeno ADJ **1** [*humo, vapor*] tear-producing • **gas ~** tear gas
2 [*canción, historia*] highly sentimental, weepy* • **novela lacrimógena** tear-jerker
lacrimoso ADJ tearful, lachrymose (*frm*)
lacrosse [la'kros] SF lacrosse
lactación SF, **lactancia** SF lactation; [*de niño*] breast-feeding ▸ **lactancia artificial** bottle-feeding
lactante ADJ • **mujer ~** nursing mother
SMF breast-fed baby
lactar ▷ CONJUG 1a VT to breast-feed, nurse; (*Zool*) feed on milk
VI to suckle, breast-feed
lácteo ADJ milk (*antes de s*), lacteal (*frm*) • **productos ~s** dairy products
láctico ADJ lactic
lacto-ovo-vegetariano/a ADJ, SM/F lacto-ovo-vegetarian
lactosa SF lactose
lactosuero SM whey, buttermilk
lacustre ADJ (*frm*) (*gen*) lake (*antes de s*), lacustrine (*frm*); (*LAm*) marshy
ladeado ADJ **1** (= *inclinado*) tilted, leaning, inclined
2 (*Arg*) (= *descuidado*) slovenly
3 (*Cono Sur*‡) (= *taimado*) crooked*
4 (*Cono Sur**) (= *enfadado*) • **andar ~** to be in a bad temper • **andar ~ con algn** to be in a huff with sb
ladear ▷ CONJUG 1a VT **1** (= *inclinar*) to tilt, tip; (*Aer*) to bank, turn; [+ *cabeza*] to tilt, put on one side
2 [+ *montaña*] to skirt, go round the side of
VI **1** (= *inclinarse*) to tilt, tip, lean
2 (= *apartarse*) to turn aside, turn off
VPR **ladearse 1** (= *inclinarse*) to lean (**a** towards); (= *torcerse*) to bend; (*Dep*) to swerve; (*Aer*) to bank, turn
2 (*Chile**) (= *enamorarse*) to fall in love (**con** with)
3 • **~se con** to be equal to, be even with
ladeo SM (= *inclinación*) tilt, leaning; (*Aer*) banking, turning
ladera SF hillside
ladero/a ADJ side (*antes de s*), lateral
SM/F (*Arg**) helper, backer
ladilla SF crab louse • MODISMO: • **¡qué ~!** (*Caribe**) what a pain!*
ladillento ADJ (*CAm, Méx*) lousy
ladillo SM (*Prensa*) subhead, subtitle
ladinazo ADJ (*Cono Sur*) cunning, shrewd
ladino¹/a ADJ **1** (= *astuto*) smart, shrewd; (= *taimado*) cunning, wily
2 (*LAm*) [*indio*] Spanish-speaking
3 (*CAm, Méx*) (= *mestizo*) half-breed, mestizo; (= *blanco*) non-Indian, white, of Spanish descent
4 (*LAm*) (= *adulador*) smooth-tongued, smarmy*
5 (*Méx**) [*voz*] high-pitched, fluty
SM/F **1** (*LAm*) (= *indio*) Spanish-speaking Indian
2 (*CAm, Méx*) (= *mestizo*) half-breed, mestizo; (= *blanco*) non-Indian, white
ladino² SM (*Ling*) Ladin (*Rhaeto-Romance dialect*); [*de sefardíes*] Ladino, Sephardic, Judeo-Spanish
lado SM **1** (= *lateral*) side • **~ derecho** right side, right-hand side • **~ izquierdo** left side, left-hand side • **a los dos ~s de la carretera** on both sides of the road • **al otro ~ de la calle** on the other side of the street, across the street • **llevar algo al otro ~ del río** to take sth across *o* over the river • **a un ~ y a otro** on all sides, all around • **es primo mío por el ~ de mi padre** he's a cousin on my father's side • **~ a ~** side by side • **de ~** sideways • **poner algo de ~** to put sth sideways • **lleva el sombrero de ~** she wears her hat at an angle • **duermo de ~** I sleep on my side • **echarse** *o* **hacerse a un ~** [*persona*] to move to one side, step aside; [*vehículo*] to swerve out of the way • **por su ~**: • **se fue cada uno por su ~** they went their separate ways • **salieron corriendo cada uno por su ~** they all ran off in different directions
• MODISMOS: • **dar a algn de ~** to give sb the cold shoulder • **a mí eso me da de ~** I couldn't care less about that • **dejar a un ~** to leave aside, forget • **echar a un ~** to cast aside • **mirar a algn de (medio) ~** to look down on sb • **poner a un ~** to put aside
2 (= *aspecto*) side • **todo tiene su ~ bueno** everything has its good side • **vamos a ver un ~ distinto de la cuestión** we're going to look at a different aspect of the issue • **ese es su ~ débil** that's her weak point • **por un ~ ..., por otro ~ ...** on the one hand ..., on the other hand ... • **por ese ~, creo que está bien** in that respect, I think it's all right
3 (= *lugar*) • **ponlo en cualquier ~** put it anywhere • **otro ~**: • **tiene que estar en otro ~** it must be somewhere else • **ir de un ~ a otro** to go to and fro, walk up and down • **estuvo de un ~ para otro toda la mañana** she was up and down all morning, she was running around all morning • **por todos ~s**: • **me lo encuentro por todos ~s** I bump into him everywhere I go • **rodeado de agua por todos ~s** surrounded by water on all sides, completely surrounded by water • **ir a todos ~s** to go all over
4 (*indicando proximidad*) • **no se movió del ~ de su madre** she never left her mother's side • **estar al ~** to be near • **el cine está aquí al ~** the cinema is just round the corner, the cinema is very near • **la mesa de al ~** the next table • **la casa de al ~** the house next door • **al ~ de**: • **la silla que está al ~ del armario** the chair beside the wardrobe • **viven al ~ de nosotros** they live next door to us • **al ~ de aquello, esto no es nada** compared to that, this is nothing • **al ~ de ella, tú pareces una belleza** compared to her, you seem really beautiful • **a mi/tu ~**: • **Felipe se sentó a mi ~** Felipe sat beside me • **estuvo a mi ~ todo el tiempo** she was at my side the whole time • **los buenos ratos que he pasado a su ~** the good times I've had with her
5 (= *bando*) (*Mil*) flank; (*Pol*) faction • **yo estoy de su ~** I'm on his side, I'm with him • **ponerse al ~ de algn** to side with sb
6 (*Mat*) side • **un triángulo tiene tres ~s** triangles have three sides • **un polígono de cinco ~s** a five-sided polygon
7 (*Dep*) end • **cambiar de ~** to change ends
8† (= *favor*) favour, protection • **tener buenos ~s** to have good connections
ladrar ▷ CONJUG 1a VI [*perro*] to bark; [*persona*] to yell; [*tripas*] to rumble • MODISMOS: • **está que ladra*** he's hopping mad* • **esta semana estoy ladrando** (*Caribe**) I'm flat broke this week* • **ladran, luego andamos** you can tell it's having some effect
ladrería SF (*And, Caribe*), **ladrerío** SM (*Méx*) barking
ladrido SM **1** [*de perro*] bark, barking
2 (= *grito*) yell • **se enfadó y nos dio unos ~s** he got angry and yelled at us
3† (= *calumnia*) slander
ladrillado SM [*de ladrillos*] brick floor; [*de azulejos*] tile floor
ladrillar ▷ CONJUG 1a VT to brick, pave with bricks
SM brickworks
ladrillazo SM • **dar un ~ a algn** to throw a brick at sb
ladrillera SF, **ladrillería** SF brickworks
ladrillo SM **1** (*Constr*) brick • MODISMO: • **ser un ~***: • **este libro es un ~** this book is really hard going* ▸ **ladrillo de fuego, ladrillo refractario** firebrick ▸ **ladrillo ventilador** air-brick
2 (= *azulejo*) tile
3 [*de chocolate*] block
ladrón/ona ADJ thieving
SM/F thief • **¡al ~!** stop thief! ▸ **ladrón de corazones** ladykiller ▸ **ladrón/ona de guante blanco** white-collar criminal ▸ **ladrón/ona de identidades** identity thief
SM (*Elec*) adaptor
ladronera SF **1** (= *guarida*) den of thieves
2† (*acto*) robbery, theft
lagaña SF = **legaña**
lagar SM [*de vino*] winepress; (= *edificio*) winery; [*de aceite*] oil press
lagarta SF **1**‡ (= *zorra*) bitch‡ • **¡lagarta!** you bitch!‡
2 (*Entomología*) gipsy moth ▸ **lagarta falsa** lackey moth; ▷ **lagarto**
lagartear* ▷ CONJUG 1a VT **1** (*Cono Sur*) (= *inmovilizar*) to pinion, pin down
2 (*And*) (= *falsear*) to fiddle*, wangle*
lagartera SF lizard hole
lagartija SF **1** (*Zool*) (small) lizard, wall lizard
2 (*Méx**) (= *salvavidas*) lifeguard
3 (= *ejercicio*) press-up
lagarto SM **1** (*Zool*) lizard; (*LAm*) (= *caimán*) alligator • MODISMO: • **¡lagarto, lagarto!** (= *cuidado*) look out!; (= *toca madera*) touch wood!; (*And, Méx*) (= *Dios nos libre*) God forbid!
▸ **lagarto de Indias** alligator ▸ **lagarto verde** green lizard
2 (= *taimado*) devious person, sly person, fox
3 (*CAm, Méx**) (= *codicioso*) get-rich-quick type*; (*And**) (= *sableador*) scrounger*, sponger*; (*And**) (= *especulador*) profiteer
4 (*Méx**) (= *astuto*) sharp customer, smart operator; ▷ **lagarta**
lagartón ADJ **1** (= *listo*) sharp, shrewd; (= *taimado*) sly
2 (*CAm, Méx*) (= *codicioso*) greedy
lagartona‡ SF (= *zorra*) bitch‡
lago SM lake; (*escocés*) loch • **los Grandes Lagos** the Great Lakes
Lagos SM Lagos
lágrima SF (*gen*) tear; (= *gota*) drop
• **beberse las ~s** to hold back one's tears
• **derramar una lagrimita** (*iró*) to shed a tear
• **deshacerse en ~s** to dissolve into tears
• **echar una ~** to shed a tear • **llorar a ~ viva** to cry one's heart out • **nadie soltará una ~ por eso** nobody is going to shed a tear over that • **se me saltaron las ~s** tears came to my eyes ▸ **lágrimas de cocodrilo** crocodile tears
▸ **lágrimas de don Pedro** (*Cono Sur*) June rains
lagrimal SM corner of the eye
lagrimar ▷ CONJUG 1a VI to cry
lagrimea SF • **tener ~** to have streaming eyes

l

lagrimear ▸ CONJUG 1a VI **1** [*persona*] (= *ser llorica*) to shed tears easily; (= *estar lloroso*) to be tearful
2 [*ojos*] to water, fill with tears
lagrimilla SF (*Cono Sur*) unfermented grape juice
lagrimoso ADJ [*persona*] tearful, lachrymose (*frm*); [*ojos*] watery
laguna SF **1** (*Geog*) (*en el interior*) pool; (*en la costa*) lagoon
2 (*en conocimientos*) gap • **sabe bien el inglés, pero tiene muchas ~s** he knows English well but has many gaps ▸ **laguna legal** (legal) loophole, loophole in the law
3 (*en libro, manuscrito*) gap, lacuna (*frm*)
4 (*en proceso*) hiatus, gap, break
lagunajo (*Caribe*) SM, **lagunato** SM (*Caribe*) (*estanque*) pool, pond; (= *charco*) puddle
lagunoso ADJ marshy, swampy
laicado SM laity
laical ADJ lay
laicidad SF (*LAm*), **laicismo** SM laicism (*doctrine of the independence of the state from church interference*)
laicizar ▸ CONJUG 1f VT to laicize
laico/a ADJ **1** (= *seglar*) [*misionero, predicador*] lay
2 [*estado, educación, colegio*] secular • **educación laica** secular education
SM/F layman/laywoman
laísmo SM *use of "la" and "las" as indirect objects*; ▸ LEÍSMO, LOÍSMO, LAÍSMO
laísta ADJ *that uses "la" and "las" as indirect objects*
SMF *user of "la" and "las" as indirect objects*
laja[1] SF **1** (*LAm*) (= *piedra*) sandstone; (= *roca*) rock
2 (*And*) (= *lugar*) steep ground
laja[2] SF (*And*) fine rope
laja[3]‡ SF (= *chica*) bird‡, chick (*EEUU*‡), dame*
Lalo SM (*LAm*) *forma familiar de* **Eduardo**
lama[1] SF **1** (= *cieno*) mud, slime, ooze
2 (*LAm*) (= *moho*) mould, mold (*EEUU*), verdigris; (*Min*) crushed ore
3 (*Méx*) (= *musgo*) moss
lama[2] SM (*Rel*) lama
lama[3] SF [*de persiana*] slat
lama[4] SF (= *tejido*) lamé
lambada SF lambada
lambarear* ▸ CONJUG 1a VI (*Caribe*) to wander aimlessly about
lambeculo‡ SMF (*LAm*) creep‡, bootlicker*
lambeladrillos* SM INV (*And*) hypocrite
lambeplatos* SMF INV (*LAm*) **1** (= *lameculos*) bootlicker*
2 (= *persona desgraciada*) poor wretch
lamber ▸ CONJUG 2a VT (*LAm*) **1** = **lamer**
2 (= *adular*) to fawn on, suck up to*
lambeta‡ SMF (*Cono Sur*) creep‡, bootlicker*
lambetazo SM (*LAm*) (= *lametón*) lick
lambetear ▸ CONJUG 1a VT (*LAm*) **1** (= *lamer*) to lick
2* (= *adular*) to suck up to*
lambiche ADJ (*Méx*) = **lambiscón**
lambida SF (*LAm*) lick
lambido* ADJ **1** (*LAm*) (= *vano*) affected, vain
2 (*Méx, CAm*) (= *cínico*) shameless, cynical
3 (= *desvergonzado*) cheeky*, sassy (*EEUU**)
lambioche* ADJ (*Méx*) fawning, servile
lambiscón* (*LAm*) ADJ **1** (= *adulón*) fawning
2 (= *glotón*) greedy
lambisconear ▸ CONJUG 1a (*LAm*) VT
1* (= *adular*) to suck up to*
2 (= *lamer*) to lick
VI* (= *adular*) to creep*, crawl*
lambisconería* SF (*LAm*) **1** (= *coba*) crawling*, brown-nosing (*EEUU*‡), fawning
2 (= *gula*) greediness, gluttony

lambisquear ▸ CONJUG 1a VI (*Méx*) to look for sweets *o* (*EEUU*) candies
lambón ADJ (*LAm*) = **lambioche**
lambonear* ▸ CONJUG 1a (*Col, Méx*) VT to suck up to*
VI to creep*, crawl*
lambraña SMF (*And*) wretch
lambrijo* ADJ (*Méx*) skinny
lambrusquear ▸ CONJUG 1a VT (*Cono Sur*) to lick
lambuzo ADJ (*And, Caribe, Méx*) **1** (= *glotón*) greedy, gluttonous (*frm*)
2 (= *desvergonzado*) shameless, brazen
lamé SM lamé
lameculismo‡ SM arselicking**‡, crawling‡, brown-nosing (*EEUU*‡)
lameculos‡ SMF INV arselicker**‡, crawler‡, brown-nose (*EEUU*‡)
lamedura SF lick, licking
lamentable ADJ [*conducta*] deplorable; [*injusticia*] shameful; [*error*] regrettable; [*escena, aspecto, estado*] sorry, pitiful; [*pérdida*] sad • **es ~ que ...** it is regrettable that ...
lamentablemente ADV regrettably, unfortunately
lamentación SF sorrow, lamentation (*frm*) • **ahora no sirven lamentaciones** it's no good crying over spilt milk
lamentar ▸ CONJUG 1a VT (= *sentir*) to be sorry about, regret; [+ *pérdida*] to lament, bewail, bemoan (*frm*) • **lamentamos la muerte de su marido** we're sorry to hear of your husband's death • **no hay que ~ víctimas** fortunately there were no casualties • **lamento lo que pasó** I'm sorry about what happened • **~ que** to be sorry that, regret that • **lamentamos mucho que ...** we very much regret that ...
VPR **lamentarse 1** (= *quejarse*) to complain • **ahora de nada sirve ~se** there's no point complaining now • **~se de algo: se lamenta del tiempo malgastado** he regrets the time he wasted • **se lamenta de su mala suerte** he's cursing his bad luck
2 (*frm*) (= *llorar*) to lament • **el país entero se lamenta por la pérdida del presidente** the whole country is mourning *o* (*frm*) lamenting the loss of the president
lamento SM lament, lamentation (*frm*), moan, wail
lamentoso ADJ (*LAm*) **1** (= *penoso*) = **lamentable**
2 (= *quejoso*) plaintive
lameplatos SMF INV **1** (= *pobre*) pauper, scavenger
2 (*Méx**) (= *adulón*) toady
3 (*Méx**) (= *parásito*) scrounger*
4 (*Méx**) (= *inútil*) disaster
lamer ▸ CONJUG 2a VT **1** (*con la lengua*) to lick
2 [*olas*] to lap (against)
3 (= *pasar rozando*) to graze
VPR **lamerse** • MODISMO: • **que no se lame**‡: • **un problema que no se lame** a bloody great problem‡
lametada SF lick; [*de ola*] lap
lametazo SM lick; [*del sol*] touch, caress
lamido ADJ **1** (= *flaco*) very thin, emaciated (*frm*); (= *pálido*) pale
2 (= *afectado*) prim, affected
SM (*Téc*) lapping
lámina[1] SF (*gen*) sheet; (*Fot, Tip*) plate; (= *grabado*) engraving; (*en libro*) plate, illustration; (*Inform*) chip ▸ **lámina de queso** slice of cheese ▸ **lámina de silicio** silicon wafer ▸ **láminas de acero** sheet steel (*sing*)
lámina[2] SMF (*And*) rogue, rascal
laminado ADJ **1** (*gen*) laminate(d)
2 (*Téc*) sheet (*antes de s*), rolled • **cobre ~** sheet copper, rolled copper
SM laminate

laminador SM, **laminadora** SF rolling mill
laminar ▸ CONJUG 1a VT (*gen*) to laminate; (*Téc*) to roll
lamiscar ▸ CONJUG 1g VT to lick greedily, lick noisily
lampa SF (*Chile, Perú*) (= *azada*) hoe; (= *pico*) pick, pickax (*EEUU*)
lampacear ▸ CONJUG 1a VT (*CAm*) [+ *piso*] to mop
lampalagua SF (*Chile*) mythical snake
lampalague SF (*Cono Sur*) **1** (= *serpiente*) boa constrictor
2 (= *glotón*) glutton
lampancia* SF ravenous hunger
lampante* SMF beggar
lampar* ▸ CONJUG 1a VI to beg
lámpara SF **1** (*Elec*) lamp, light; (*Radio*) valve, tube (*EEUU*); **lámparas** (*LAm*) (= *ojos*) eyes • MODISMOS: • **atizar la ~*** to fill up the glasses • **quebrar la ~** (*Caribe**) to ruin everything, blow it‡ ▸ **lámpara bronceador** sun lamp ▸ **lámpara de Aladino** Aladdin's lamp ▸ **lámpara de alcohol** spirit lamp, alcohol lamp (*EEUU*) ▸ **lámpara de arco** arc-lamp ▸ **lámpara de bolsillo** torch, flashlight ▸ **lámpara de cuarzo** quartz lamp ▸ **lámpara de escritorio** desk-lamp ▸ **lámpara de gas** gas lamp ▸ **lámpara de lectura** reading lamp ▸ **lámpara de mesa** table lamp ▸ **lámpara de pared** wall light ▸ **lámpara de pie** standard lamp ▸ **lámpara de señales** signalling lamp ▸ **lámpara de sol artificial** sun lamp ▸ **lámpara de soldar** blowlamp, blowtorch ▸ **lámpara de techo** overhead lamp ▸ **lámpara flexo** adjustable table lamp ▸ **lámpara plegable** angle-poise lamp ▸ **lámpara solar ultravioleta** sun lamp
2 (= *mancha*) stain, dirty mark
SMF (*Caribe*) (= *ladrón*) thief; (= *estafador*) con man*
lamparazo SM (*Méx*) gulp
lamparilla SF **1** (= *lámpara*) small lamp
2 (*Bot*) aspen
lamparín SM (*Chile, Perú*) (= *quinqué*) paraffin lamp; (*Cono Sur*) (= *vela*) candle
lamparita SF (*Arg, Uru*) light bulb
lámparo ADJ (*And*) penniless, broke*
lamparón SM **1** (*Med*) scrofula
2 (= *mancha*) large grease spot
lampazo[1] SM (*Bot*) burdock
lampazo[2] SM **1** (*LAm*) (= *escobilla*) floor mop
2 (*And, Caribe*) (= *azotamiento*) whipping
3 (*Náut*) swab
lampear ▸ CONJUG 1a VT (*And*) (*con pala*) to shovel; (*con azada*) to hoe
lampiño ADJ (= *sin pelo*) hairless; (= *sin barba*) beardless
lampión SM lantern
lampista SMF plumber
lampistería SF electrical shop
lampón[1] ADJ (*And*) starving, hungry
lampón[2] SM (*And*) (= *pala*) spade; (= *azada*) hoe
lamprea SF **1** (= *pez*) lamprey
2 (*Med*) sore, ulcer
lamprear ▸ CONJUG 1a VT (*CAm*) to whip
lana[1] SF **1** (*gen*) wool; (= *vellón*) fleece; (= *tela*) woollen cloth, woolen cloth (*EEUU*); (*para labores*) knitting wool • **de ~** • **hecho de ~** wool (*antes de s*), woollen, woolen (*EEUU*) • REFRÁN: • **ir por ~ y volver trasquilado** to get more than one bargained for ▸ **lana de acero** steel wool ▸ **lana para labores** knitting wool ▸ **lana virgen** pure new wool
2 lanas* (*hum*) long hair (*sing*), locks
3 (*And, Méx**) (= *dinero*) money, dough*
4 (*And, Méx*) (= *mentira*) lie
5 (*CAm*) (= *estafador*) swindler

lana² (SF) (*CAm*) = **lama¹**
lanar (ADJ) wool-bearing, wool (*antes de s*)
• **ganado ~** sheep
lance (SM) **1** (= *episodio*) incident, event
▸ **lance de fortuna** stroke of luck
2 (= *momento difícil*) critical moment, difficult moment
3 (= *riña*) row, quarrel ▸ **lance de honor** affair of honour, affair of honor (*EEUU*), duel
4 [*de red*] throw, cast
5 (*Pesca*) catch
6 (*Dep*) move, piece of play
7 (= *accidente*) chance, accident
8 • **tirarse (a) un ~** (*Cono Sur*) to take a chance
9 (*Com*) • **de ~** secondhand, cheap • **libros de ~** secondhand books • **comprar algo de ~** to buy sth secondhand, buy sth cheap
10 (*Cono Sur*) (= *agachada*) duck, dodge • **sacar ~** to dodge, duck away
11 (*Cono Sur*) (= *parte*) section, range • **casa de tres ~s** house in three sections
lancear ▹ CONJUG 1a (VT) to spear
lancero (SM) **1** (*Mil*) lancer
2 lanceros (*Mús*) lancers
(SMF) (*Cono Sur*) (= *soñador*) dreamer, blind optimist
lanceta (SF) **1** (*Med*) lancet • **abrir con ~** to lance
2 (*LAm*) (= *aguijada*) goad; [*de insecto*] sting
lancha¹ (SF) **1** (= *barca*) (small) boat; [*de motor*] launch ▸ **lancha cañonera** gunboat
▸ **lancha de carga** lighter, barge ▸ **lancha de carreras** speedboat ▸ **lancha de desembarco, lancha de desembarque** landing craft ▸ **lancha de pesca** fishing boat ▸ **lancha de salvamento, lancha de socorro** lifeboat ▸ **lancha fuera borda** outboard dinghy ▸ **lancha hinchable, lancha inflable** inflatable dinghy ▸ **lancha motora** motorboat, speedboat ▸ **lancha neumática** rubber dinghy, raft (*EEUU*)
▸ **lancha patrullera** patrol boat ▸ **lancha rápida** speedboat ▸ **lancha salvavidas** lifeboat ▸ **lancha torpedera** torpedo boat
2 (*Cono Sur**) police car
lancha² (SF) (*And*) **1** (= *niebla*) mist, fog
2 (= *helada*) (hoar)frost
lanchaje (SM) (*Méx*) freight charge
lanchar ▹ CONJUG 1a (VI) (*And*) **1** (= *encapotarse*) to become overcast
2 (= *helar*) to freeze
lanchero/a (SM/F) **1** (= *barquero*) boatman/boatwoman; [*de lancha de carga*] lighterman/lighterwoman, bargee, bargeman/bargewoman (*EEUU*)
2 (*Caribe*) *Cuban refugee*
lanchón (SM) lighter, barge ▸ **lanchón de desembarco** landing craft
lancinante (ADJ) (*frm*) [*dolor*] piercing
lancinar ▹ CONJUG 1a (VT) (*frm*) to lance, pierce
Landas (SFPL) • **las ~** the Landes
landó (SM) **1** (= *carruaje*) landau
2 (*And*) (*Mús*) Peruvian folk music
landre (SF) • MODISMO: • **¡mala ~ te coma!** curse you!
lanería (SF) **1** (= *géneros*) woollen goods, woolen goods (*EEUU*)
2 (= *tienda*) wool shop
lanero/a (ADJ) wool (*antes de s*), woollen, woolen (*EEUU*) • **la industria lanera** the wool industry
(SM/F) (= *persona*) wool dealer
(SM) (= *almacén*) wool warehouse
lángara‡ (SMF) (*Méx*) slippery individual*
lángaro (ADJ) **1** (*CAm*) (= *vago*) vagrant, wandering, idle
2 (*And, Méx*) (= *hambriento*) starving, poverty-stricken
3 (*Méx*) (= *malo*) wicked; (= *taimado*) sly, untrustworthy
4 (*CAm*) (= *larguirucho*) lanky
langarucho (ADJ) (*CAm, Méx*), **langarote** (ADJ) (*And*) lanky
langosta (SF) **1** [*de mar*] lobster; [*de río*] crayfish
2 (= *insecto*) locust
langostera (SF) lobster pot
langostinero (ADJ) • **barco ~** prawn-fishing boat
langostino (SM), **langostín** (SM) prawn; (*grande*) king prawn
languceta (ADJ) (*Cono Sur*), **languciento** (ADJ) (*Cono Sur, Méx*), **langucio** (ADJ) (*Cono Sur*) **1** (= *hambriento*) starving
2 (= *enclenque*) sickly
langüetear ▹ CONJUG 1a (VT) (*Chile*) to lick
lánguidamente (ADV) (= *sin espíritu*) languidly; (= *débilmente*) weakly, listlessly
languidecer ▹ CONJUG 2d (VI) to languish
languidez (SF) (= *falta de espíritu*) languor (*liter*), lassitude (*frm*); (= *debilidad*) listlessness
lánguido (ADJ) (*gen*) languid (*liter*); (= *débil*) weak, listless
languso (ADJ) (*Méx*) **1** (= *taimado*) sly, shrewd
2 (= *larguirucho*) lanky
lanilla (SF) **1** (= *flojel*) nap
2 (= *tela*) thin flannel cloth
lanolina (SF) lanolin(e)
lanoso (ADJ) woolly, wooly (*EEUU*), fleecy
lanudo (ADJ) **1** (= *lanoso*) woolly, wooly (*EEUU*), fleecy
2 (*Méx**) (= *rico*) well off
3 (*And, Caribe*) (= *maleducado*) rustic, uncouth
lanza (SF) **1** (*Mil*) lance, spear • MODISMOS:
• **estar ~ en ristre** to be ready for action
• **medir ~s** to cross swords • **romper una ~ por algn** to back sb to the hilt • **ser una ~** (= *ser hábil*) to be pretty sharp; (*Méx*) to be sly, be a rogue
2 (*en carruajes*) shaft
3 [*de manguera*] nozzle
(SMF) **1** (*LAm**) (= *estafador*) cheat, shark*
2 (*Chile**) (= *ratero*) pickpocket, thief; (*Cono Sur*) (= *tironista*) bag-snatcher
lanzabengalas (SM INV) flare
lanzabombas (SM INV) (*Aer*) bomb release; (*Mil*) mortar
lanzacohetes (SM INV) rocket launcher
▸ **lanzacohetes múltiple** multiple rocket launcher
lanzada (SF) (= *golpe*) spear thrust; (= *herida*) spear wound
lanzadera (SF) shuttle ▸ **lanzadera de misiles** missile launcher ▸ **lanzadera espacial** space shuttle
lanzadestellos (SM INV) (*Aut*) flashing light
lanzado/a (ADJ) **1** • **ser ~* a** (*al hacer algo*) • **es un tío muy ~** he's very full of confidence, he's really single-minded
b (*en las relaciones*) to be forward • **¡qué ~ es!** he's so forward! • **es muy lanzada con los hombres** she's very forward with men
2* (*al moverse*) • **salió ~ de la casa** he rushed out of the house • **ir ~** [*coche, moto*] to tear along • **el coche iba ~** the car was tearing along • **¿dónde va tan ~?** where's he going in such a rush? • **no deberías ir tan ~ en los negocios** you shouldn't rush into things in business matters
3 (*sexualmente*) • **estar ~‡** to be horny‡
(SM/F)* • **ese tío es un ~** that guy is full of confidence*
(SM) (*Pesca*) spinning
lanzador(a) (ADJ) [*avión, cohete*] launch (*antes de s*)
(SM/F) **1** (= *persona*) (*Cricket*) bowler; (*Béisbol*) pitcher • **es un experto ~ de faltas** (*Ftbl*) he's an expert at free kicks ▸ **lanzador(a) de bala** (*LAm*) shot-putter ▸ **lanzador(a) de cuchillos** knife thrower ▸ **lanzador(a) de jabalina** javelin thrower ▸ **lanzador(a) de martillo** hammer thrower ▸ **lanzador(a) de peso** shot-putter
2 [*de cohetes, misiles*] launcher
3 [*de producto, moda*] promoter
lanzaespumas (SM INV) foam extinguisher
lanzagranadas (SM INV) grenade launcher, mortar
lanzallamas (SM INV) flamethrower
lanzamiento (SM) **1** [*de objeto*] (*gen*) throwing; (*con violencia*) hurling; (*desde el aire*) dropping • **la manifestación acabó con ~ de objetos contra la policía** the demonstration ended with people hurling things at the police • **~ en paracaídas** parachuting, parachute jumping
2 (*Dep*) (*con la pierna*) kick; (*hacia portería, canasta*) shot • **falló el ~ del penalti** he missed the penalty (kick) • **un ~ de tres puntos** a three-point field goal ▸ **lanzamiento a canasta** shot at basket ▸ **lanzamiento de bala** (*LAm*) the shot put ▸ **lanzamiento de disco** the discus ▸ **lanzamiento de falta** (*Ftbl*) free kick ▸ **lanzamiento de jabalina** the javelin ▸ **lanzamiento de martillo** the hammer ▸ **lanzamiento de penaltis** penalty shoot-out ▸ **lanzamiento de peso** the shot put
3 [*de nave espacial, misil*] launch
4 (*Com, Econ*) [*de acciones, producto*] launch; [*de disco*] release • **oferta de ~** promotional offer
• **~ publicitario** advertising campaign
5 (*Jur*) repossession
lanzaminas (SM INV) minelayer
lanzamisiles (SM INV) missile launcher
lanzar ▹ CONJUG 1f (VT) **1** [+ *objeto, piedra*] (*gen*) to throw; (*con violencia*) to hurl, fling
• **lánzame la pelota** throw me the ball • **~on botes de humo contra los manifestantes** they threw *o* hurled smoke bombs at the demonstrators • **la explosión lanzó algunas piedras al cielo** the explosion threw *o* flung stones into the sky • **~ algo/a algn al suelo** (*gen*) to throw sth/sb to the ground; (*con violencia*) to hurl sth/sb to the ground
2 (= *disparar*) [+ *flecha, proyectil*] to fire; [+ *cohete, misil*] (*hacia el aire*) to launch; (*hacia tierra*) to drop • **una bomba lanzada desde un avión enemigo** a bomb dropped from an enemy aircraft
3 (*Dep*) [+ *disco, jabalina, balón*] to throw; [+ *peso*] to put; [+ *pelota*] (*Béisbol*) to pitch; (*Cricket*) to bowl • **~ una falta** (*Ftbl*) to take a free kick • **~ un penalti** to take a penalty
4 (= *emitir*) [+ *mensaje*] to deliver; [+ *insulto, ataque*] to hurl; [+ *indirecta*] to drop; [+ *desafío*] to issue, throw down; [+ *grito, suspiro*] to let out • **lanzó un mensaje tranquilizador a la población** he delivered a reassuring message to the people • **las autoridades han lanzado un nuevo mensaje a los inversores** the authorities have issued a new message to investors • **la emisora lanzó duros ataques contra el presidente** the radio station launched harsh attacks against the president • **~on al aire la idea de reducir los impuestos** they floated the idea of reducing taxes • **~ críticas contra algn** to criticize sb, level criticism against sb (*frm*) • **se ~on algunos gritos apoyando al ejército** a few shouts went out in support of the army
• **~ una mirada** to shoot a glance *o* look;
▹ **llamamiento**
5 (*Com*) [+ *producto, moda*] to launch, bring out; [+ *disco*] to release, bring out • **han lanzado al mercado un nuevo modelo** they have brought out a new model, they have released a new model onto the market • **fue el primer banco que lanzó al mercado bonos**

hipotecarios it was the first bank to issue mortgage bonds
6 (*Mil*) [+ *campaña, ataque*] to launch
7 (= *vomitar*) to bring up
8 (*Bot*) [+ *hojas, flores*] to come out in, put out
9 (*Jur*) to dispossess • **lo ~on de sus tierras** he was dispossessed of his land
VPR **lanzarse 1** (= *arrojarse*) (*al suelo, al vacío*) to throw o.s.; (*al agua*) to throw o.s., jump • **se lanzó por el precipicio** he threw himself off the precipice • **se ~on al suelo** they threw *o* flung themselves to the ground • **de un salto se lanzó al río** he jumped into the river • **los perros se ~on sobre los restos de comida** the dogs pounced on the leftovers • **~se sobre algn** to pounce on sb, leap on sb • **el vigilante se lanzó sobre el ladrón** the guard pounced *o* leapt on the robber • **la muchedumbre se lanzó sobre él** the crowd rushed towards *o* crowded round him • **~se en paracaídas** to parachute • **~se en picado** to dive, swoop down • **el águila se lanzó en picado a por su presa** the eagle swooped towards its prey
2 (= *ir rápidamente*) to hurtle • **se ~on hacia la salida** they hurtled towards the exit • **~se a hacer algo**: • **se ~on a comprar acciones** they rushed to buy shares • **la policía se lanzó a buscar al asesino** the police launched a murder hunt
3* (= *decidirse*) to take the plunge* • **llevábamos años pensando montar un negocio hasta que nos lanzamos** after years wanting to set up a business, we finally took the plunge*
4 • **~se a** (= *dedicarse*): • **no tienen dinero para ~se a la construcción de nuevas viviendas** they don't have the funds to embark upon *o* undertake new housing projects • **se lanzó a la política en 1963** she went into *o* took up politics in 1963 • **decidió ~se a la carrera presidencial** he decided to enter the presidential race

Lanzarote SM **1** (= *isla*) Lanzarote
2 (= *personaje*) Lancelot

lanzaroteño/a ADJ of/from Lanzarote
SM/F native/inhabitant of Lanzarote • **los ~s** the people of Lanzarote

lanzatorpedos SM INV torpedo tube

laña SF clamp, rivet

lañar ▷ CONJUG 1a VT **1** (*Téc*) to clamp (together), rivet
2‡ (= *robar*) to nick‡, steal

Laos SM Laos

laosiano/a ADJ, SM/F Laotian

lapa SF **1** (*Zool*) limpet • **MODISMO**: • **pegarse a algn como una ~** to stick to sb like a limpet
2 (*And, Cono Sur*) (*Bot*) half gourd (*used as bowl*)
3 (*And*) (= *sombrero*) large flat-topped hat

lapalada SF (*Méx*) drizzle

La Palma SF (*en Canarias*) La Palma

laparoscopia SF laparoscopy

laparoscópico ADJ laparoscopic

La Paz SF La Paz

lape ADJ (*Cono Sur*) **1** (= *enredado*) matted
2 [*baile*] merry, lively

lapicera SF (*Cono Sur*) (= *pluma*) fountain pen; (= *bolígrafo*) ballpoint pen

lapicero SM **1** (= *portaminas*) propelling pencil, mechanical pencil (*EEUU*) ▸ **lapicero hemostático** styptic pencil
2 (*Esp*) (= *lápiz*) pencil; (*LAm*) (= *pluma*) fountain pen
3** (= *pene*) prick**

lápida SF gravestone, tombstone ▸ **lápida conmemorativa** commemorative stone plaque ▸ **lápida mortuoria** tombstone, gravestone ▸ **lápida mural** stone plaque let into a wall ▸ **lápida sepulcral** tombstone

lapidar ▷ CONJUG 1a VT **1** [+ *persona*] to stone
2 (*LAm*) [+ *joyas*] to cut

lapidario/a ADJ lapidary • **frase lapidaria** immortal phrase
SM/F lapidary

lapislázuli SM lapis lazuli

lápiz SM **1** (*gen*) pencil; [*de color*] crayon • **escribir algo a** *o* **con ~** to write sth in pencil • **está añadido a ~** it is added in pencil, it is pencilled in • **MODISMO**: • **meter ~ a** to sign ▸ **lápiz a pasta** (*Cono Sur*) ball-point pen ▸ **lápiz de carbón** charcoal pencil ▸ **lápiz de carmín** lipstick ▸ **lápiz de cejas** eyebrow pencil ▸ **lápiz de labios** lipstick ▸ **lápiz de luz, lápiz electrónico** light pen ▸ **lápiz de ojos** eyebrow pencil ▸ **lápiz (de) plomo** lead pencil ▸ **lápiz labial** lipstick ▸ **lápiz lector** data pen ▸ **lápiz negro** (*en la censura*) blue pencil ▸ **lápiz óptico** light pen
2 (*Min*) black lead, graphite

lapo* SM **1** (*Esp*) (= *escupitajo*) spit
2 (= *golpe*) punch, bash*, swipe • **MODISMO**: • **de un ~** (*LAm*) at one go
3 (*And, Caribe*) swig*
4 (*Caribe*) (= *inocente*) simple soul

lapón/ona ADJ of/from Lapland
SM/F native/inhabitant of Lapland • **los lapones** the people of Lapland
SM (*Ling*) Lapp

Laponia SF Lapland

lapso SM **1** (= *tiempo*) lapse • **en un ~ de cinco días** in (the space of) five days ▸ **lapso de tiempo** interval of time, space of time
2 (= *error*) mistake, error

lapsus SM INV (*frm*) lapse, mistake ▸ **lapsus calami** slip of the pen ▸ **lapsus de memoria** lapse of memory ▸ **lapsus freudiano** Freudian slip ▸ **lapsus linguae** slip of the tongue

laqueado ADJ lacquered, varnished

laquear ▷ CONJUG 1a VT (*gen*) to lacquer; [+ *uñas*] to varnish, paint

LAR SF ABR (*Esp*) (*Jur*) = **Ley de Arrendamientos Rústicos**

lardar ▷ CONJUG 1a VT, **lardear** ▷ CONJUG 1a VT to lard, baste

lardo SM lard, animal fat

lardoso ADJ (*gen*) lardy, fatty; (= *grasiento*) greasy

larga SF **1** • **MODISMOS**: • **a la ~** in the long run • **dar ~s a algo/algn** to put sth/sb off • **estamos cansados de que nos den ~s** we're tired of being put off all the time • **si te pregunta por el dinero, tú dale ~s** if he asks you about the money, just fob him off* • **saberla ~** to know what's what*
2 (*Aut*) (*tb* **luz larga**) full beam • **pon las ~s** put the headlights on full beam
3 (*Taur*) pass with the cape
4 (*Dep*) length; ▷ **largo**

largada SF (*Dep*) start

largamente ADV **1** (= *por mucho tiempo*) a long time • **el conflicto podría extenderse ~** the conflict could drag on (a long time)
2 (= *con detalle*) at length • **su libro trata ~ de este tema** his book deals with this subject at length • **habló ~ de la crisis** he spoke at length about the crisis
3 (= *abundantemente*) [*compensar*] • **esto compensa ~ el esfuerzo** this fully compensates the effort • **han rentabilizado ~ su inversión** they have received a handsome return on their investment
4 (= *cómodamente*) • **vivir ~** to live comfortably *o* at ease

largar ▷ CONJUG 1h VT **1**‡ (= *dar*) **a** [+ *discurso, regañina*] to give; [+ *exclamación, suspiro*] to let out • **le largó una bronca tremenda** she gave him a good ticking-off* • **nos largó un rollo interminable sobre los viejos tiempos** he gave us a never-ending spiel about the old days*, he rabbited on forever about the old days* • **no sabe hablar sin ~ insultos** he can't open his mouth without letting fly *o* without insulting someone
b [+ *dinero*] to give • **le largó una buena propina** he gave him a good tip • **lárgame la pasta** hand over the cash*
c [+ *golpe, mordisco*] to give • **me largó un puñetazo en la boca** he punched me in the mouth, he gave me a punch in the mouth • **le ~on una buena paliza** he was badly beaten up
2‡ (= *expulsar*) [+ *empleado*] to kick out‡, give the boot‡; [+ *alumno, huésped*] to kick out‡, chuck out‡
3‡ (= *endilgar*) • **~ a algn** [+ *tarea, trabajo*] to dump on sb*, foist (off) on sb; [+ *animal, niño*] to dump on sb* • **siempre nos larga lo que ella no quiere hacer** she always dumps* *o* foists (off) what she doesn't want to do herself on us • **me ~on a los niños** they dumped their kids on me*
4‡ (= *deshacerse de*) [+ *novio, marido*] to ditch*, dump*
5 (*Náut*) [+ *bandera, vela*] to unfurl; [+ *barca*] to put out; [+ *cuerda*] (= *soltar*) to let out, pay out; (= *aflojar*) to loosen, slacken • **~ amarras** to cast off • **~ lastre** to drop ballast
6 (*Cono Sur, Méx**) (= *lanzar*) to throw, hurl
7 (*Cono Sur, Méx*) (*Dep*) to start
VI‡ **1** (*Esp*) (= *hablar*) to go on*, rabbit on* • **hay que ver lo que largas** you don't half go on *o* rabbit on* • **~ contra algn** to bad-mouth sb‡ • **siempre estás largando contra todo el mundo** you're always bad-mouthing everybody‡
2 (= *revelar un secreto*) to spill the beans* • **venga, larga** come on, spill the beans* • **no hay forma de que largue** there's no way he'll spit it out‡
VPR **largarse 1*** (= *irse*) to be off*, leave • **yo me largo** I'm off now*, I'm leaving now • **es hora de que nos larguemos** it's time for us to leave *o* be off* • **¡larguémonos de aquí!** let's get out of here!* • **¡lárgate!** get lost!*, clear off!* • **~se de casa** to leave home • **~se del trabajo** to quit one's job
2 (*Náut*) to set sail, start out
3 (*Cono Sur*) (= *empezar*) to start, begin • **~se a hacer algo** to start *o* begin doing *o* to do sth
4 (*Cono Sur*) (= *tirarse*) • **se largó de cabeza al agua** he dived into the water • **~se un eructo** to let out a burp • **~se un pedo*** to let off a fart‡

largavistas SM INV (*Cono Sur*) (*Téc*) (= *gemelos*) binoculars (*pl*)

largo ADJ **1** (*indicando longitud*) [*pasillo, pelo, uñas*] long • **el sofá es muy ~ para esa pared** the sofa is too long for that wall • **esa chaqueta te está** *o* **te queda larga** that jacket is too long for you • **me gusta llevar el pelo ~** I like to wear my hair long • **una camiseta interior de manga larga** a long-sleeved vest • **ser ~ de piernas** to have long legs • **ponerse de ~** (= *vestirse*) to wear a long dress/skirt; (= *debutar*) to make one's début • **¿hay que ponerse de ~ para la cena?** do we have to wear evening dress to the dinner? • **MODISMO**: • **ser ~ de lengua*** to be a blabbermouth*; ▷ **diente, luz, mano, puesta, vestir**
2 (*indicando distancia*) [*distancia, camino*] long • **nos queda todavía un ~ camino** we still have a long way to go • **un misil de ~ alcance** a long-range missile • **pasar de ~** [*persona, autobús*] to go past; [*momento, oportunidad*] to go by • **pasamos de ~ por Valencia** we went straight past Valencia • **no podemos dejar pasar de ~ esta oportunidad** we can't let this opportunity go by • **de ~ recorrido**

[*vuelo*] long-haul (*antes de s*); [*tren, autobús*] long-distance (*antes de s*) • **seguir de ~*** (= *no parar*) to keep on going; (= *pasar de lado*) to pass by
3 (*indicando duración*) [*espera, viaje, sílaba, película*] long • **es muy ~ de contar** it's a long story • **murió tras una larga enfermedad** he died after a lengthy *o* long illness • **pasaron tres ~s años** three long years went by • **el resultado de ~s años de investigación** the result of many years of research • **hacerse ~**: • **no se me hizo nada larga la clase** the class didn't seem at all long to me • **esta película se está haciendo larguísima** this film is really dragging on* • **para ~**: • **la reunión va para ~** the meeting looks like being a long one, the meeting looks like going on for some time yet • **cada vez que coge el teléfono tiene para ~** every time he picks up the phone he stays on it for ages • **tengo para ~ hasta que termine** I've got a long way to go before I finish • **a ~ plazo** in the long term • **venir de ~**: • **este problema viene de ~** this problem goes back a long way, this problem started way back* • MODISMOS: • **hablar ~ y tendido sobre algo** to talk at great length about sth • **tú y yo tenemos que hablar ~ y tendido** you and I have to have a long talk • **ser más ~ que un día sin pan** to take forever
4 (= *indicando exceso*) good • **tardó media hora larga** he took a good half-hour • **un kilo ~ de uvas** just over a kilo of grapes
5* [*persona*] tall • **tú que eres tan ~, alcánzame ese tarro** you're tall, can you reach that jar for me? • **se cayó al suelo cuan ~ era**† *o* **todo lo ~ que era** he fell flat on his face, he measured his length on the floor†
6 (*locuciones*) • **a lo ~** (= *longitudinalmente*) lengthways; (= *a lo lejos*) (far away) in the distance • **corté la tabla a lo ~** I sawed the board lengthways • **échate a lo ~** stretch yourself full out • **se ve un pico a lo ~** (far away) in the distance you can see a mountain peak • **a lo ~ de** [+ *río, pared*] along; [+ *día, mes, año*] all through, throughout • **viajó a lo ~ y a lo ancho de Europa** he travelled the length and breadth of Europe • **había palmeras a lo ~ de todo el paseo marítimo** there were palm trees all along the promenade • **a lo ~ de los últimos años hemos viajado mucho** we have travelled a lot over the last few years • **trabajó mucho a lo ~ de su vida** she worked hard all through *o* throughout her life • **el tiempo mejorará a lo ~ de la semana** the weather will improve in the course of the week • **a lo más ~** at the most
7 (*Esp**) (= *astuto*) sharp • **es un tío muy ~** he's a very sharp guy
8 (*Esp*) (= *generoso*) generous • **tirar de ~** to be extravagant
9 (*Esp*) [*cuerda*] loose, slack
10 (*Esp*) (*Agr*) [*cosecha*] abundant, plentiful
SM **1** (= *longitud*) length • **¿cuánto tiene de ~?** how long is it?, what's its length? • **tiene nueve metros de ~** it is nine metres long
2 (= *unidad de medida*) [*de falda, piscina*] length; [*de cortina*] drop • **~ de pernera** leg length • **hice diez ~s seguidos** I swam ten lengths without stopping
3 (*Cine*) (*tb* **largometraje**) feature film
4 (*Mús*) largo
ADV * • **¡~ (de aquí)!** clear off!, get lost!
largometraje SM full-length film, feature film
largón/ona‡ SM/F spy, informer
largona SF **1** (*And, Cono Sur*) (= *demora*) delay
2 largonas (*And*) • **dar ~s a algo*** to keep putting sth off

3 (*Cono Sur*) (= *descanso*) • **darse una ~*** to take a rest
largor SM length
largucho ADJ (*LAm*) lanky
larguero ADJ (*Cono Sur*) **1*** (= *largo*) long, lengthy; [*discurso*] wordy, long-drawn-out
2 (*Dep*) trained for long-distance running
3 (= *lento*) slow-working, slow
4* (= *generoso*) generous, lavish; (= *copioso*) abundant, copious
SM (*Arquit*) crossbeam; [*de puerta*] jamb; (*Dep*) crossbar; (*en cama*) bolster
largueza SF generosity, largesse (*frm*)
larguirucho ADJ lanky, gangling
larguísimo ADJ *superl de* **largo**
largura SF length
largurucho ADJ (*LAm*) lanky, gangling
lárice SM larch
laringe SF larynx
laringitis SF INV laryngitis
larva SF larva, grub, maggot
larvado ADJ hidden, latent • **permanecer ~** to be latent, remain dormant
las[1] ART DEF FPL ▸ **los**[1]
las[2] PRON PERS ▸ **los**[2]
lasaña SF lasagne, lasagna
lasca SF [*de piedra*] chip; [*de comida*] slice
lascadura SF (*Méx*) **1** (= *rozadura*) graze, abrasion (*frm*)
2 (= *herida*) injury
lascar ▸ CONJUG 1g VT **1** (*Méx*) [+ *piel*] to graze, bruise; [+ *piedra*] to chip, chip off
2 (*Náut*) to slacken
VI (*Méx*) to chip off, flake off
lascivamente ADV lewdly, lasciviously
lascivia SF lust, lewdness, lasciviousness
lascivo ADJ [*gesto, mirada, comentario*] lewd, lascivious; [*persona*] lecherous, lascivious
láser SM laser • **rayo ~** laser beam
láser disc SM INV, **láserdisc** SM INV laser disc
lasérico ADJ laser (*antes de s*)
laserterapia SF laser therapy
lasitud (*liter*) SF lassitude (*liter*), weariness
laso (*liter*) ADJ **1** (= *cansado*) weary
2 (= *lánguido*) languid (*liter*), limp
3 (= *débil*) weak
Las Palmas SFPL (*en Canarias*) La Palma, Las Palmas
lástima SF **1** (= *pena*) pity, shame • **es una ~** it's a pity *o* shame • **es ~ que ...** it's a pity *o* shame that ..., it's too bad that ... • **dar ~**: • **toda esta pobreza me da mucha ~** such poverty makes me really sad • **es tan desgraciado que da ~** he's so unhappy I feel really sorry for him *o* I really pity him • **es una película tan mala que da ~** it's a pathetic film, it's an awful film, it's such a pathetically bad film • **¡qué ~!**: • **—hemos perdido —¡qué ~!** "we've lost" — "what a shame! *o* what a pity! *o* that's too bad!" • **¡qué ~ de hombre!** isn't he pitiful? • **sentir** *o* **tener ~ de algn** to feel sorry for sb
2 (= *escena lastimosa*) pitiful sight • **estar hecho una ~** to be in a sorry *o* dreadful state
3 (*frm*) (= *queja*) complaint, tale of woe
lastimada SF (*CAm, Méx*) = **lastimadura**
lastimado ADJ **1** (= *herido*) injured
2 (= *ofendido*) hurt
lastimador ADJ harmful
lastimadura SF (*LAm*) **1** (= *herida*) graze
2 (= *moretón*) bruise
lastimar ▸ CONJUG 1a VT **1** (= *hacer daño*) to hurt • **me lastimó** he hurt me
2 (= *ofender*) to hurt
VPR **lastimarse 1** (= *herirse*) to hurt o.s. • **se lastimó el brazo** he hurt his arm
2 • **~se de** (= *quejarse*) to complain about; (= *apiadarse*) to feel sorry for, pity
lastimeramente ADV piteously, pitifully, pathetically
lastimero ADJ **1** (= *dañoso*) harmful
2 (= *lastimoso*) pitiful, pathetic
lastimón SM (*LAm*) = **lastimadura**
lastimosamente ADV piteously, pitifully, pathetically
lastimoso ADJ pitiful, pathetic
lastrante ADJ burdensome
lastrar ▸ CONJUG 1a VT **1** [+ *embarcación, globo*] to ballast
2 (= *obstaculizar*) to burden, weigh down
lastre SM **1** (*Náut, Téc*) ballast • **en ~** (*Náut*) in ballast
2 (= *inconveniente*) burden
3 (= *sentido común*) good sense, good judgment
4 (*Cono Sur*‡) (= *comida*) grub*, chow (*EEUU*‡)
lata SF **1** (= *envase*) [*de comida*] tin, can; [*de bebida*] can • **sardinas en ~** tinned sardines, canned sardines • **un cuatro ~s*** (= *coche viejo*) an old banger*; (= *Renault 4L*) Renault 4L
2 (= *metal*) tinplate • **suena a ~** it sounds tinny
3 (*And*) (= *comida*) food, daily ration ▸ **lata petitoria** collecting tin (*for charity*)
4* (= *molestia*) nuisance, pain*, drag* • **es una ~ tener que ...** it's a nuisance *o* pain* *o* drag* having to ... • **¡qué ~!** • **¡vaya (una) ~!** what a nuisance! *o* drag!* *o* pain!* • **dar la ~** to be a nuisance, be a pain* • **dar la ~ a algn** to pester sb, go on at sb* • **dar ~** (*And, CAm**) (= *parlotear*) to babble on; (*And**) (= *insistir*) to nag, go on
5 (= *censura*) • **dar ~ a algn** (*Caribe*) to condemn sb, censure sb
6 (= *madera*) lath
7‡ (= *dinero*) dough‡ • MODISMOS: • **estar en la(s) ~(s)** • **estar sin ~s** (*And, CAm*) to be penniless, be broke*
latazo* SM nuisance, pain*
latear ▸ CONJUG 1a VI (*LAm*) **1** (= *dar la lata*) to be a nuisance, be annoying
2 (= *hablar*) to babble on
latente ADJ **1** (*gen*) latent
2 (*LAm*) (= *vivo*) alive, intense, vigorous
lateral ADJ **1** [*calle, puerta, salida*] side (*antes de s*)
2 (*en genealogía*) [*línea, parentesco*] indirect
3 (*Fonética, Téc*) lateral
SM **1** [*de avenida*] side street
2 laterales (*Teat*) wings
SMF (*Dep*) winger ▸ **lateral derecho** right winger ▸ **lateral izquierdo** left winger
lateralmente ADV sideways, laterally (*frm*)
latería SF **1** (*CAm*) (= *hojalata*) tin, tinplate
2 (*Caribe, Cono Sur*) (= *hojalatería*) tinsmith's, tinsmith's workshop, tinworks
laterío SM (*Méx*) tinned goods (*pl*), canned goods (*pl*)
latero SM (*LAm*) **1** (= *oficio*) tinsmith
2* (= *latoso*) bore, drag*
látex SM latex
latido SM **1** (= *palpitación*) [*de corazón*] beat, beating; [*de herida, dolor*] throb, throbbing
2 [*de perro*] bark
latifundio SM large estate
latifundista SMF *owner of a large estate*
latigazo SM **1** (*con látigo*) (= *golpe*) lash; (= *chasquido*) crack (*of the whip*)
2 [*de electricidad*] shock
3 (= *insultos*) tongue lashing
4 [*de bebida*] swig*
látigo SM **1** (= *instrumento*) whip
2 (*And*) (= *sonido*) crack (*of the whip*)
3 (*Cono Sur*) (*Dep*) finishing post, finishing line • MODISMO: • **salir al ~** to complete a task
4 (*And, Cono Sur*) (= *jinete*) horseman, rider

latigudo ADJ (*LAm*) leathery
latigueada SF (*And, CAm, Cono Sur*) whipping, thrashing
latiguear ▷ CONJUG 1a VT (*LAm*) to whip, thrash
latiguera SF (*And*) whipping, thrashing
latiguillo SM **1** (= *muletilla*) cliché, overworked phrase
2 (*Teat*) hamming
latín SM **1** (*Ling*) Latin • **bajo ~** Low Latin • **MODISMO**: • **saber (mucho) ~*** to be pretty sharp ▸ **latín clásico** Classical Latin ▸ **latín tardío** Late Latin ▸ **latín vulgar** Vulgar Latin
2 latines Latin tags
latinajo SM (= *latín macarrónico*) dog Latin, bad Latin • **~s** Latin tags • **echar ~s** to come out with learned quotations and references
latinidad SF latinity
latinismo SM Latinism
latinista SMF Latinist
latinización SF latinization
latinizar ▷ CONJUG 1f VT, VI to latinize
latino/a ADJ **1** (= *latinoamericano*) Latin American
2 (*Hist*) Latin
SM/F **1** (= *latinoamericano*) Latin American • **los ~s** Latin Americans • **MODISMO**: • **te cantan los cinco ~s†*** your feet smell
2 (*Hist*) native/inhabitant of Latium • **los ~s** the people of Latium
Latinoamérica SF Latin America
latinoamericano/a ADJ, SM/F Latin American
latir ▷ CONJUG 3a VI **1** [*corazón*] to beat; [*herida*] to throb
2 (= *estar latente*) to lie, lie hidden, lurk
3 [*perro*] to bark
4 (*And, Méx**) • **me late que todo saldrá bien** something tells me that everything will turn out all right
latitud SF **1** (*Geog*) latitude • **a 45 grados de ~ sur** 45 degrees south
2 (= *área*) area • **por estas ~es** in these parts
3 (= *extensión*) breadth
latitudinal ADJ latitudinal
LATN SF ABR (*Para*) (*Aer*) = **Líneas Aéreas de Transporte Nacional**
lato ADJ (*frm*) [*territorio*] broad, wide; [*sentido*] broad
latón SM **1** (= *metal*) brass
2 (*Cono Sur*) (= *recipiente*) large tin container; (*And*) (= *cubo*) tin bucket
latonería SF (*Col*) panel beating (*Brit*), body work (*EEUU*)
latonero/a SM/F (*Col*) panel beater (*Brit*), body shop worker (*EEUU*)
latoso/a* ADJ (= *molesto*) annoying, tiresome; (= *pesado*) boring, tedious
SM/F bore, pain*, drag*
latrocinio SM larceny
Latvia SF Latvia
latvio/a ADJ Latvian
SM/F Latvian • **los ~s** the Latvians
SM (*Ling*) Latvian, Lettish
LAU SF ABR (*Esp*) (*Jur*) = **Ley de Arrendamientos Urbanos**
lauca SF (*Cono Sur*) baldness, loss of hair
laucadura SF (*Cono Sur*) baldness
laucar ▷ CONJUG 1g VT (*Cono Sur*) to fleece, shear, remove the hair *o* wool from
laucha SF **1** (*Cono Sur*) (*Zool*) small mouse • **MODISMOS**: • **aguaitar la ~** • **catear la ~*** to bide one's time • **ser una ~** • **ser una lauchita** to be very sharp *o* quick
2 (*Arg*) (= *viejo verde*) dirty old man
3* (= *flacón*) weed*
4 (*And*) expert
lauco ADJ (*Cono Sur*) bald, hairless
laúd SM (*Mús*) lute
laudable ADJ laudable, praiseworthy
laudablemente ADV laudably
láudano SM laudanum
laudatorio ADJ (*frm*) laudatory (*frm*)
laudo SM (*Jur*) decision, finding ▸ **laudo de obligado cumplimiento** binding decision
laureado/a (*frm*) ADJ [*persona*] honoured, honored (*EEUU*), distinguished; [*obra*] prize-winning • **poeta ~** poet laureate
SM/F (= *premiado*) prizewinner
laurear ▷ CONJUG 1a VT (*frm*) **1** (= *galardonar*) to honour, honor (*EEUU*)
2 (*Hist*) (= *coronar*) to crown with laurel
laurel SM **1** (*Bot*) laurel • **hojas de ~** (*Culin*) bay leaves ▸ **laurel cerezo** cherry laurel
2 laureles (= *gloria*) laurels; (= *premio*) honour (*sing*), honor (*EEUU*) • **MODISMO**: • **descansar** *o* **dormirse en los ~es** to rest on one's laurels
laurencio SM (*Quím*) lawrencium
lauréola SF **1** (= *corona*) laurel wreath, crown of laurel; (= *auréola*) halo
2 (*Bot*) daphne
lauro SM **1** (= *árbol*) laurel
2 lauros laurels
Lausana SF Lausanne
lava[1] SF (*Geol*) lava
lava[2] SF (*Min*) washing
lavable ADJ washable
lavabo SM **1** (= *pila*) washbasin, washstand†
2 (= *cuarto de baño*) bathroom, washroom (*EEUU*), toilet; (*en lugar público*) toilet, rest room (*EEUU*) • **¿dónde está el ~ de señoras, por favor?** where is the ladies, please?
lavacara SF (*And*) washbasin
lavacaras* SMF INV toady, creep*
lavacoches SM INV car wash
lavada SF wash
lavadero SM **1** (= *lavandería*) laundry, wash house; (*en río*) washing place; [*de casa*] utility room
2 (*LAm*) (*Min*) gold-bearing sands (*in river*)
lavado SM **1** [*de ropa, vehículo*] wash, washing • **le di dos ~s al jersey** I gave the jumper two washes, I washed the jumper twice • **yo me encargaré del ~ de la ropa** I'll take care of the washing • **la furgoneta quedará como nueva después de un buen ~** the van will look like new after a good wash • **prelavado y ~** pre-wash and wash ▸ **lavado a mano** hand-wash ▸ **lavado de automóviles** carwash ▸ **lavado de cabeza** shampoo ▸ **lavado en seco** dry cleaning
2 (*Med*) ▸ **lavado de estómago, lavado gástrico** • **le hicieron un ~ de estómago** he had his stomach pumped ▸ **lavado intestinal** enema ▸ **lavado vaginal** douche
3 (*fig*) • **campaña de ~ de imagen** image campaign ▸ **lavado de bonos** bond-washing ▸ **lavado de cara** face lift ▸ **lavado de cerebro** brainwashing • **le han hecho un ~ de cerebro** he's been brainwashed ▸ **lavado de dinero** money-laundering
lavador SM **1** (*Cono Sur*) (= *fregadero*) sink
2 (*Cono Sur*) (= *aseo*) lavatory, toilet, washroom (*EEUU*)
lavadora SF **1** [*de ropa*] washing machine ▸ **lavadora de carga frontal** front-loading washing machine, front-loader ▸ **lavadora de carga superior** top-loading washing machine, top-loader ▸ **lavadora de coches** car wash ▸ **lavadora de platos** dishwasher ▸ **lavadora secadora** washer-drier
2 (*And*) (= *persona*) laundress, washerwoman
lavadura SF **1** (= *lavado*) washing
2 (= *agua sucia*) dirty water
lavafaros SM INV headlamp washer
lavafrutas SM INV finger bowl
lavagallos SM (*And, Caribe*) firewater
lavaje SM (*Cono Sur*) **1** = **lavadura**
2 (*Med*) enema
lavaluneta SM rear window washer
lavamanos SM INV washbasin
lavanda SF (*Bot*) lavender • **agua de ~** lavender water
lavandera SF **1** (= *mujer*) laundress, washerwoman
2 (*Orn*) wagtail
lavandería SF laundry ▸ **lavandería automática** launderette, laundromat (*EEUU*) ▸ **lavandería industrial** industrial laundry
lavandina SF (*Cono Sur*) bleach
lavándula SF = **lavanda**
lavaojos SM INV eye bath
lavaparabrisas SM INV windscreen washer, windshield washer (*EEUU*)
lavapiés SM INV footbath (*at the beach*)
lavaplatos SM INV **1** (= *aparato*) dishwasher
2 (*Chile, Col, Méx*) (= *fregadero*) sink
SMF INV (= *empleado*) washer-up, dishwasher
lavar ▷ CONJUG 1a VT **1** (= *limpiar*) to wash • **lávale la cabeza a la niña** wash the child's hair • **~ los platos** to wash the dishes, do the washing up • **~ en seco** to dry-clean • **~ y marcar** to shampoo and set • **tejanos lavados a la piedra** stonewashed jeans • **camisa de lava y pon** drip-dry shirt
2 [+ *dinero*] to launder
3 [+ *honor, ofensa, pecado*] to wash away
4 (*Min*) to wash
VPR **lavarse** to wash, have a wash • **tengo que ~me antes de salir** I need to wash *o* have a wash before going out • **~se los dientes** to clean one's teeth • **me lavé las manos antes de comer** I washed my hands before eating • **el gobierno se lavó las manos ante este asunto** the government washed their hands of the whole affair
lavarropas SM INV (*Arg, Uru*) washing machine
lavasecadora SF washer-dryer
lavaseco SM (*Chile*) (= *tintorería*) drycleaner's
lavativa SF **1** (*Med*) enema
2† (= *molestia*) nuisance, bother, bore
lavatorio SM **1†** (= *pila*) washstand†
2 (*LAm*) (= *cuarto de baño*) bathroom, washroom (*EEUU*)
3 (*Med*) lotion
lavavajillas SM INV (= *aparato*) dishwasher; (= *detergente*) washing-up liquid, (liquid) dish soap (*EEUU*)
lavazas SFPL dishwater (*sing*), dirty water (*sing*), slops
lavoteo* SM quick wash, cat-lick*
laxante ADJ, SM laxative
laxar ▷ CONJUG 1a VT [+ *vientre*] to loosen
laxativo ADJ laxative
laxitud SF (*frm*) laxity, laxness, slackness
laxo ADJ (*frm*) lax, slack
laya SF **1** (= *pala*) spade ▸ **laya de puntas** (garden) fork
2 (*liter*) (= *tipo*) kind, sort • **de esta ~** of this kind *o* sort
lazada SF (*decorativa*) bow; [*de zapatos*] knot
lazar ▷ CONJUG 1f VT **1** (= *atrapar con lazo*) to lasso, rope
2 (*Méx*) = **enlazar**
VI (*CAm*) [*tren*] to connect
lazareto SM (*Hist*) leper hospital, isolation hospital
lazariento ADJ (*CAm, Cono Sur, Méx*) leprous
lazarillo SM blind person's guide
lazarino/a ADJ leprous
SM/F leper
Lázaro SM Lazarus
lazo SM **1** (= *nudo*) (*para asegurar*) knot; (*decorativo*) bow ▸ **lazo corredizo** slipknot ▸ **lazo de zapato** shoelace

2 (*Agr*) lasso, lariat
3 (*Caza*) snare, trap • MODISMOS: • **caer en el ~** to fall into the trap • **tender un ~ a algn** to set *o* lay a trap for sb
4 (*Aut*) hairpin bend
5 **lazos** (= *vínculos*) ties • **~s familiares** family ties • **los ~s culturales entre los dos países** cultural ties between the two countries • **~s de parentesco** ties of blood

L/C SF ABR (= **Letra de Cambio**) B/E, BE
LCD SM ABR LCD
Lda. ABR = **Licenciada**
Ldo. ABR = **Licenciado**
le PRON PERS **1** (*directo*) (= *a él*) him; (= *a usted*) you • **no le veo** I don't see him • **¿le ayudo?** shall I help you?
2 (*indirecto*) (= *a él, ella*) (to) him, (to) her, (to) it; (= *a usted*) (to) you • **le hablé** I spoke to him, I spoke to her • **quiero darle esto** I want to give you this • **le he comprado esto** I bought this for you • **una de las mejores actuaciones que le hemos visto** one of the best performances we have seen from him • **no se le conoce otra obra** no other work of his is known; ▹ **leísmo**
lea‡ SF tart‡, slut‡, whore
leal ADJ [*persona*] loyal, faithful; [*competencia*] fair
lealmente ADV loyally, faithfully
lealtad SF loyalty, fidelity ▸ **lealtad de marca** brand loyalty, loyalty to a brand
leandra†‡ SF one peseta
Leandro SM Leander
leasing ['lizin] SM (= *operación*) leasing ▸ **leasing financiero** finance lease ▸ **leasing operativo** operational lease
lebrato SM leveret
lebrel SM greyhound
lebrillo SM earthenware bowl
lebrón* ADJ (*Méx*) **1** (= *astuto*) sharp, wide-awake
2 (= *arrogante*) boastful
3 (= *taimado*) sly
LEC SF ABR (*Esp*) (*Jur*) = **Ley de Enjuiciamiento Civil**
lección SF (= *tema*) lesson; (= *clase*) lesson, class • **dar lecciones** to teach, give lessons • MODISMOS: • **aprenderse la ~** to learn one's lesson • **dar una ~ a algn** to teach sb a lesson • **saberse la ~*** to know what the score is* • **servir de ~**: • **¡qué te sirva de ~!** let that be a lesson to you! ▸ **lección magistral** master class ▸ **lección particular** private lesson ▸ **lección práctica** object lesson (**de** in)
lecha SF milt, roe, soft roe
lechada SF **1** (*Constr*) (= *lavado*) whitewash; (*para fijar baldosas*) [*de masilla*] grout; [*de papel*] pulp
2 (*Méx*) [*de leche*] milking
3** (= *semen*) spunk**
lechal ADJ sucking, suckling • **cordero ~** baby lamb, young lamb
SM milk, milky juice
lechar ▹ CONJUG 1a VT **1** (*LAm*) (= *ordeñar*) to milk
2 (*And, CAm*) (= *amamantar*) to suckle
3 (*CAm, Méx**) (= *blanquear*) to whitewash
lechazo[1] SM young lamb
lechazo[2]‡ SM **1** (= *golpe*) bash, swipe
2 (= *choque*) bash, bang
leche SF **1** [*de mamífero*] milk • **se ha cortado la ~** the milk has gone off • **café con ~** white coffee, coffee with milk • **chocolate con ~** milk chocolate • MODISMO: • **estar con** *o* **tener la ~ en los labios** to be young and inexperienced, be wet behind the ears ▸ **leche completa** full-cream milk, whole milk ▸ **leche condensada** condensed milk ▸ **leche de larga duración, leche de larga vida** long-life milk ▸ **leche del día** fresh milk ▸ **leche descremada, leche desnatada** skimmed milk ▸ **leche en polvo** powdered milk ▸ **leche entera** full-cream milk, whole milk ▸ **leche evaporada** evaporated milk ▸ **leche frita** *dessert made of milk thickened with flour, coated with egg and fried* ▸ **leche homogeneizada** homogenized milk ▸ **leche materna** mother's milk ▸ **leche maternizada** formula (milk) ▸ **leche merengada** milkshake flavoured with cinnamon ▸ **leche pasteurizada** pasteurised milk ▸ **leche semidesnatada** semi-skimmed milk ▸ **leche sin desnatar** (*Esp*) whole milk ▸ **leche UHT** long-life milk, UHT milk
2 (*Bot*) milk, milky juice; (*Bol*) rubber; (*Caribe*) rubber tree ▸ **leche de coco** coconut milk
3 (= *loción*) ▸ **leche corporal** body lotion ▸ **leche hidratante** moisturizer, moisturizing lotion ▸ **leche limpiadora** cleanser, cleansing milk
4** (= *semen*) cum**, spunk**
5‡ (= *golpe*) • **darse una ~** to come a cropper* • **se ha dado una ~ con la moto** he came a cropper on his motorbike* • **¡te voy a dar una ~!** I'll thump you!* • **se liaron a ~s** they laid into each other*, they started swinging at each other*
6 • MODISMO: • **ser la ~**‡ (= *el colmo*): • **cantando es la ~** (= *bueno*) when he sings he's a bloody marvel‡; (= *malo*) when he sings he's bloody awful‡ • **nunca se acuerdan de llamar, ¡son la ~!** they never think to call, they're unbelievable!
7‡ (*como interjección*) • **¡leche!** hell!, shit!** • **¡leches!** (= *ni hablar*) no way!*, get away!
8‡ (*con valor enfático*) • **de la ~**‡ bloody‡ • **hace un calor de la ~** it's bloody hot • **¡este tráfico de la ~ me tiene frita!** I'm fed up with this bloody traffic! • **ni ~** *o* **~s**: • **no entiende ni ~** he doesn't understand a bloody thing‡ • **qué ~**: • **¿qué ~ quieres?** what the hell do you want?‡ • **¡qué coche ni qué ~!** car my foot!*
9 (*indicando velocidad*) • MODISMOS: • **ir a toda ~**‡ to go like the clappers* • **salió echando** *o* **cagando ~s**** he went like a bat out of hell*
10 • **mala ~**‡ bad blood, ill-feeling • **aquí hay mucha mala ~** there's a lot of bad blood *o* ill-feeling here • **un tío con muy** *o* **mucha mala ~** a nasty piece of work* • **estar de mala ~** to be in a shitty mood‡ • **poner a algn de mala ~** to piss sb off** • **tener mala ~** to be a nasty piece of work*
11‡ (= *lío*) • **tuvimos que rellenar informes, impresos y toda esa ~** we had to fill in reports, forms and all that jazz*
12 (*esp LAm*) (= *suerte*) good luck • **¡qué ~ tienes!** you lucky *o* jammy* devil!
lecheada SF (*Cono Sur*) = **lechada**
lechear ▹ CONJUG 1a VT (*LAm*) to milk
lechecillas SFPL sweetbreads
lechera SF **1** (= *recipiente*) milk can, milk churn
2 (*LAm*) (= *vaca*) cow
3* [*de policía*] police car; ▹ **lechero**
lechería SF **1** (= *establecimiento*) dairy, creamery; (*And, Cono Sur*) (= *sala de ordeño*) milking parlour
2 (*Cono Sur*) (= *vacas*) cows (*pl*), herd
3 (*LAm*) (= *tacañería*) meanness
lecherita SF milk jug
lechero/a ADJ **1** [*producción, cuota*] milk (*antes de s*); [*productos, vaca*] dairy (*antes de s*) • **ganado ~** dairy cattle
2 (*LAm**) (= *suertudo*) lucky
3 (*Méx**) (= *tacaño*) mean, stingy*
4 (*Caribe*) (= *codicioso*) greedy, grasping
SM/F (= *granjero*) dairy farmer; (= *distribuidor*) milkman/milkwoman; ▹ **lechera**
lechigada SF [*de animales*] litter, brood; [*de maleantes*] gang
lecho SM **1** (= *cama*) bed ▸ **lecho de enfermo** sickbed ▸ **lecho de muerte** deathbed ▸ **lecho de rosas** bed of roses ▸ **lecho mortuorio** deathbed
2 (*Agr*) bedding ▸ **lecho de siembra** seed-bed
3 (= *fondo*) [*de río*] bed; [*de mar, lago*] bottom; [*de océano*] bottom, floor; (*Geol*) layer ▸ **lecho del mar** seabed ▸ **lecho de roca** bedrock ▸ **lecho marino** seabed
lechón/ona SM/F **1** (= *cochinillo*) piglet; (*Culin*) sucking pig, suckling pig (*EEUU*)
2 (= *desaseado*) pig*, slob*
lechoncillo SM piglet; (*Culin*) sucking pig, suckling pig (*EEUU*)
lechosa SF (*Ven*) papaya (*fruit*)
lechosidad SF milkiness
lechoso ADJ **1** [*líquido*] milky
2 (*LAm**) (= *suertudo*) lucky, jammy*
lechucear ▹ CONJUG 1a VI (*And*) to be on night duty
lechucero/a (*And*) SM/F (= *obrero*) nightshift worker; (= *taxista*) taxi driver (*who works at night*)
SM (= *taxi*) night taxi
lechudo ADJ (*LAm*) lucky, jammy*
lechuga SF **1** (*Bot*) lettuce ▸ **lechuga Cos, lechuga francesa, lechuga orejona** (*Méx*) cos lettuce; ▹ **fresco**
2 (*Cos*) frill, flounce
3 (= *billete*) (*Esp*†‡) 1000-peseta note; (*Caribe*) banknote
4 (*euf*) = **leche**
lechuguilla SF (*Cos*) frill, flounce, ruff
lechuguino SM **1** (*Bot*) young lettuce
2† (= *persona*) dandy†
lechuza SF **1** (*Orn*) owl ▸ **lechuza común** barn owl
2 (*Cono Sur, Méx*) (= *albino*) albino
3 (*Caribe, Méx*‡) (= *puta*) whore
lechuzo/a* SM/F **1** (= *feo*) ugly devil*
2 (= *lerdo*) dimwit*
leco‡ ADJ (*Méx*) nuts*, round the bend*
lectivo ADJ school (*antes de s*) • **año ~** school year
lectoescritura SF reading and writing
lector(a) ADJ • **el público ~** the reading public
SM/F **1** (= *persona*) reader ▸ **lector(a) de cartas** fortune-teller
2 (*Escol, Univ*) (conversation) assistant
SM (= *aparato*) reader ▸ **lector de código de barras** bar code scanner ▸ **lector de discos compactos** CD player, compact disc player ▸ **lector de disco óptico** optical disc scanner ▸ **lector de fichas** card reader ▸ **lector de libros electrónicos** e-reader ▸ **lector de tarjeta magnética** magnetic card reader ▸ **lector óptico de caracteres** optical character reader, optical character scanner
lectorado SM (*Educ*) assistantship
lectura SF **1** (= *acción*) reading • **dar ~ a** to read (publicly) • **sala de ~** reading room • **segunda ~** (*Esp*) (*Pol*) second reading ▸ **lectura del pensamiento** mind-reading ▸ **lectura dramatizada** dramatization, dramatized reading ▸ **lectura labial** lip-reading
2 (= *obra*) reading matter • **lista de ~s recomendadas** reading list
3 (= *interpretación*) reading • **hay varias ~s posibles de los resultados electorales** the election results can be read in various ways, there are various possible readings of the election results
leer ▹ CONJUG 2e VT to read • **~ el pensamiento a algn** to read sb's mind *o*

l

thoughts • **~ la mano a algn** to read sb's palm • **~ los labios** to lip-read • **~ para sí** to read to oneself • MODISMO: • **~ la cartilla a algn** to tell sb off
VI to read • **"al que leyere"** "to the reader" • **~ entre líneas** to read between the lines • **~ en voz alta** to read aloud • **~ en voz baja** to read quietly
lefa** SF spunk**
lega SF lay sister
legación SF legation
legado SM **1** (= *enviado*) legate
2 (*Jur*) legacy, bequest
legajar ▹ CONJUG 1a VT (*And, Cono Sur, Méx*) to file
legajo SM file, bundle (of papers)
legal ADJ **1** (= *de ley*) legal
2 [*persona*] (= *de confianza*) trustworthy, truthful, reliable • **es un tío ~*** he's a good bloke*
3 (= *sin antecedentes*) [*archivo*] clean*; [*persona*] clean*, with no police record
4 (*And*) (= *excelente*) great*
legalidad SF legality, lawfulness
legalista ADJ legalistic
legalización SF [*de partido, droga, situación*] legalization; [*de documentos*] authentication
legalizar ▹ CONJUG 1f VT [+ *partido, situación*] to legalize; [+ *documentos*] to authenticate
legalmente ADV legally, lawfully
légamo SM (= *cieno*) slime, mud; (= *arcilla*) clay
legamoso ADJ (= *viscoso*) slimy; (= *arcilloso*) clayey
legaña SF sleep, rheum
legañoso ADJ bleary
legar ▹ CONJUG 1h VT to bequeath, leave (a to)
legatario/a SM/F legatee
legendario ADJ legendary
leggings ['leɣins] SMPL leggings
legía* SM legionnaire, *member of the Spanish Foreign Legion*
legibilidad SF legibility
legible ADJ legible • **~ por máquina** (*Inform*) machine-readable
legiblemente ADV legibly
legión SF legion • **la Legión** (*Esp*) the Spanish Legion • **son ~** they are legion ▸ **Legión de Honor** Legion of Honour, Legion of Honor (EEUU) ▸ **Legión Extranjera** Foreign Legion
legionario ADJ legionary
SM (*Hist*) legionary; (*Mil*) legionnaire
legionella SF legionnaire's disease
legislación SF legislation, laws (*pl*) • **~ antimonopolio** (*Com*) anti-trust laws, anti-trust legislation
legislador(a) SM/F legislator
legislar ▹ CONJUG 1a VI to legislate
legislativas SFPL parliamentary elections
legislativo ADJ legislative
legislatura SF (*Pol*) **1** (= *mandato*) term of office, period of office; (= *año parlamentario*) session • **agotar la ~** to serve out one's term (of office)
2 (*LAm*) (= *cuerpo*) legislature, legislative body
legista SMF (= *jurista*) jurist, legist; (= *estudiante*) law student
ADJ (*LAm*) • **médico ~** forensic expert, criminal pathologist
legítima* SF • **la ~** my better half
legitimación SF legitimation
legítimamente ADV **1** (= *legalmente*) legitimately, rightfully
2 (= *auténticamente*) genuinely
legitimar ▹ CONJUG 1a VT [+ *comportamiento*] to legitimize; [+ *documento, firma*] to authenticate; [+ *divorcio, elecciones, situación ilegal*] to legalize
VPR **legitimarse** to establish one's title, establish one's claim • **considerarse legitimado para hacer algo** to consider o.s. entitled to do sth
legitimidad SF **1** [*de petición*] legitimacy
2 [*de documento, firma*] authenticity
legitimista ADJ, SMF royalist, legitimist
legitimización SF legitimization
legitimizar ▹ CONJUG 1f VT = **legitimar**
legítimo ADJ **1** [*dueño*] legitimate, rightful; [*derecho*] legitimate; [*esposo*] lawful • **en legítima defensa** in self-defence
2 (= *auténtico*) [*firma, cuadro*] authentic, genuine; (*Aut*) [*repuestos*] genuine
lego/a ADJ **1** (*Rel*) [*hermano, predicador*] lay
2 (= *ignorante*) ignorant, uninformed
SM/F **1** (*Rel*) lay brother/lay sister • **los ~s** the laity
2 (= *desconocedor*) layman/laywoman, layperson
legón SM hoe
legración SF, **legrado** SM (*Med*) D & C, scrape*
legua SF league • MODISMO: • **eso se ve *o* se nota a la ~** you can tell it a mile away
leguaje SM **1** (*CAm*) (= *distancia*) distance in leagues
2 (*And*) (= *gastos de viaje*) travelling expenses
leguleyo/a SM/F pettifogging lawyer, shyster (EEUU)
legumbre SF (= *seca*) pulse; (= *fresca*) vegetable
leguminosa SF (*Bot*) (= *planta*) leguminous plant; (= *grano*) pulse
leguminoso ADJ leguminous
lehendakari SMF *head of the Basque autonomous government*
leíble ADJ legible
leída SF (*LAm*) reading • **dar una ~ a*** to read • MODISMO: • **de una ~** in one go
Leiden SM Leyden
leído ADJ [*persona*] well-read; [*libro*] widely read • **ser muy ~** to be well-read
leísmo SM *use of "le" instead of "lo" and "la" as direct objects*

> **LEÍSMO, LOÍSMO, LAÍSMO**
> These terms refer to the reversal of the standard distinction between direct and indirect object personal pronouns in Spanish. Normally **lo(s)** and **la(s)** are the direct object pronouns (eg: **Lo/La vi ayer** I saw him/her yesterday) and **le(s)** the indirect equivalents (eg: **Le di tu recado** I gave him/her your message). **Leísmo** involves replacing **lo(s)** and sometimes **la(s)** with **le(s)** (eg: **Le vi ayer**), while **loísmo** and **laísmo** mean using **lo(s)** and **la(s)** instead of **le(s)** (eg: **Lo/La di tu recado**). Whereas **leísmo** is relatively socially acceptable in most of Spain, though not Latin America, **loísmo** and **laísmo** tend to be frowned upon everywhere.

leísta ADJ *that uses "le" instead of "lo" and "la" as direct objects*
SMF *user of "le" instead of "lo" and "la"*
lejanía SF (= *distancia*) remoteness • **en la ~** in the distance
lejano ADJ **1** (*en el espacio, en el tiempo*) distant • **en un futuro no muy ~** in the not too distant future • **en aquellas épocas lejanas** in those distant *o* far-off times • **un país ~** a far-off country • **Lejano Oeste** Far West • **Lejano Oriente** Far East
2 [*pariente*] distant
lejas ADJ PL • **de ~ tierras** of/from some distant land
lejía¹ SF **1** (= *líquido*) bleach
2†* (= *reprensión*) dressing-down*
lejía² SM = **legía**
lejísimos ADV *superl de* **lejos**
lejos ADV **1** (*en el espacio*) far, far away • **¿está ~?** is it far (away)? • **está muy ~** it's a long way (away), it's really far (away) • **el cine queda demasiado ~ para ir andando** the cinema is too far to walk • **a lo ~** in the distance • **de *o* desde ~** at *o* from a distance, from afar (*liter*) • **los curiosos observaban la escena desde ~** bystanders observed the scene at *o* from a distance • **prefiero ver los relámpagos de bien ~** I prefer watching lightning from a good distance *o* from a long way off • **veo mal de ~** I am short-sighted • **el equipo español iba seguido de ~ por Alemania** the Spanish team was followed at a distance by Germany, the Spanish team was followed, a long way behind, by Germany • **más ~** further away • **siéntate un poco más ~** sit a bit further away • MODISMOS: • **ir demasiado ~** to go too far, overstep the mark • **llevar algo demasiado ~** to take sth too far • **llegar ~** to go far • **ese chico llegará ~** that boy will go far • **sin ir más ~**: • **Javier, sin ir más ~, tuvo el mismo problema** Javier, as it happens, had the same problem • **hoy, sin ir más ~, la he visto dos veces** in fact *o* as it happens, I've seen her twice today; ▸ **mundanal**
2 • **~ de algo** a long way from sth, far from sth • **está ~ de la oficina** it is a long way *o* far from the office • **vivo lejísimos de aquí** I live miles away from here • **~ de asustarse, los niños estaban encantados con la tormenta** far from being scared, the children really loved the storm • **estaba ~ de saber lo que iba a pasar** little did I know what would happen • **en eso no andaba él muy ~** he wasn't far off the mark on that point • **nada más ~ de mi intención que hacerte daño** harming you was the last thing on my mind • **nada más ~ de la realidad** nothing could be further from the truth
3 (*en el tiempo*) far off • **junio ya no está tan ~** June is not so far off now • **está ~ el día en que podamos comprarnos una casa** the day we can afford a house is still a long way off • **¡qué ~ me parecen las vacaciones!** the holidays seem so far off! • **venir de ~**: • **su amistad viene de ~** their friendship goes back a long way
4 (*Cono Sur*) (= *con mucho*) easily • **es ~ la más inteligente** she's the most intelligent by far, she's easily the most intelligent • **ganaron ~** they won easily
SM **1** (= *aspecto*) • **tiene buen ~** it looks good from a distance
2 (*Arte*) [*de cuadro*] background
3 (*Esp*) (*en la vista*) • **tengo mal el ~** I am short-sighted
lejura SF **1** (*And*) distance
2 lejuras (*Cono Sur*) remote place, remote area
lele* ADJ, SMF (*LAm*) = **lelo**
lelo/a* ADJ (= *tonto*) slow • **quedarse ~** to be stunned
SM/F (= *tonto*) halfwit • **parece que te ven cara de ~** they seem to think you're totally stupid, they seem to think you were born yesterday
lema SM **1** (*Pol*) slogan
2 (= *máxima*) motto
3 (*en diccionario*) headword
leming, lemming ['lemin] SM lemming
lempira SM (*Hond*) *monetary unit of Honduras*
lempo (*And*) ADJ (= *grande*) big, large
SM (= *pedazo*) bit, piece • **un ~ de caballo** a big horse
lémur SM lemur
lencería SF **1** (= *ropa interior*) lingerie • **~ fina**

fine lingerie
2 (= *ropa blanca*) linen • **~ fina** fine linen
3† (= *armario*) linen cupboard
4† (= *tienda*) draper's, draper's shop
lencero/a SM/F draper
lendakari SM = lehendakari
lendroso ADJ lousy, infested with lice
lengón ADJ (*And*) = lenguón
lengua SF **1** (*Anat*) tongue • **me he mordido la ~** I've bitten my tongue • **beber con la ~** to lap up • **mala ~** gossip • **según las malas ~s ...** according to gossip ... • **sacar la ~**: • **abra la boca y saque la ~** open your mouth and put *o* stick your tongue out • **no le saques la ~ a tu hermana** don't stick your tongue out at your sister • MODISMOS: • **andar en ~s** to be the talk of the town • **atar la ~ a algn** to silence sb • **buscar la ~ a algn** to pick a quarrel with sb • **¿te ha comido la ~ el gato?** has the cat got your tongue? • **darle a la ~** to chatter, talk too much • **darse la ~*** to french-kiss • **hacerse ~s de algn/algo** to praise sb/sth to the skies, rave about sb/sth • **irse de la ~** to let the cat out of the bag • **llegar con la ~ fuera** to arrive out of breath • **morderse la ~** to hold one's tongue, bite one's lip *o* tongue • **nacer con la ~ fuera** to be born idle • **no morderse la ~** not to mince one's words, not to pull one's punches • **no tener pelos en la ~** not to mince one's words, not to pull one's punches • **tener algo en la punta de la ~** to have sth on the tip of one's tongue • **soltar la ~*** to spill the beans* • **tener mucha ~*** to be lippy*, be cheeky* • **tirar de la ~ a algn** to draw sb out, make sb talk ▸ **lengua de trapo** baby talk ▸ **lengua larga** (*LAm*), **lengua viperina** sharp tongue, vicious tongue; ▹ **largo, trabar**
2 [*de campana*] tongue, clapper
3 (*Geog*) ▸ **lengua de tierra** spit of land, tongue of land
4 (*Ling*) language, tongue; (*Esp*) (*Escol*) Spanish language (*as a school subject*) • **hablar en ~** (*And*) to speak Quichua ▸ **lengua de destino** target language ▸ **lengua de origen** source language ▸ **lengua de trabajo** working language ▸ **lengua franca** lingua franca ▸ **lengua madre** parent language ▸ **lengua materna** mother tongue ▸ **lengua minoritaria** minority language ▸ **lengua moderna** modern language ▸ **lengua muerta** dead language ▸ **lengua oficial** official language ▸ **lengua viva** living language

LENGUAS COOFICIALES
Under the Spanish constitution **catalán**, **euskera** and **gallego** are **lenguas oficiales** and enjoy the same status as **castellano** in the autonomous regions in which they are spoken. These languages are also known as **lenguas cooficiales** to show they enjoy equal status with Spanish. The regional governments actively promote their use through the media and the education system.
▹ CATALÁN, EUSKERA, GALLEGO

lenguado SM sole
lenguaje SM **1** (*gen*) language • **en ~ llano** in plain English ▸ **lenguaje comercial** business language ▸ **lenguaje corporal** body language ▸ **lenguaje de gestos** sign language ▸ **lenguaje de las manos** sign language ▸ **lenguaje del cuerpo** body language ▸ **lenguaje de los signos** sign language ▸ **lenguaje formal** formal language ▸ **lenguaje fuente** source language ▸ **lenguaje gestual** sign language ▸ **lenguaje objeto** target language ▸ **lenguaje periodístico** journalese ▸ **lenguaje vulgar** common speech
2 (*Literat*) style
3 (*Inform*) language ▸ **lenguaje de alto nivel** high-level language ▸ **lenguaje de bajo nivel** low-level language ▸ **lenguaje de programación** program(m)ing language ▸ **lenguaje ensamblador** assembly language ▸ **lenguaje informático, lenguaje máquina** machine language
lenguaraz ADJ (= *charlatán*) garrulous, talkative; (= *mal hablado*) foul-mouthed
lenguaz ADJ garrulous
lengüeta SF **1** (*gen*) tab; [*de zapatos*] tongue; [*de balanza*] needle, pointer; [*de flecha*] barb
2 (*Mús*) reed
3 (*Anat*) epiglottis
4 (*LAm*) (= *cortapapeles*) paper knife
5 (*LAm*) (*Cos*) edging (*of a petticoat*)
SMF (*LAm*) (= *hablador*) chatterbox*; (= *chismoso*) gossip
lengüetada SF, **lengüetazo** SM lick
lengüetear ▹ CONJUG 1a (*LAm*) VT (= *lamer*) to lick
VI **1** (= *sacar la lengua*) to stick one's tongue out
2 (*Caribe*) (= *parlotear*) to jabber away, chatter away
lengüeterías SFPL (*LAm*) gossip (*sing*), tittle-tattle (*sing*)
lengüetero ADJ (*Caribe*) (= *hablador*) garrulous; (= *chismoso*) gossipy
lengüicorto* (*Caribe*) ADJ shy, timid
lengüilargo ADJ, **lengüisucio** ADJ (*Caribe*) foul-mouthed
lenguón/ona (*LAm*) ADJ **1** (= *chismoso*) gossipy; (= *hablador*) garrulous
2 (= *franco*) outspoken
SM/F gossip
lenidad SF lenience
Lenin SM Lenin
Leningrado SM Leningrad
leninismo SM Leninism
leninista ADJ, SMF Leninist
lenitivo ADJ lenitive
SM lenitive, palliative
lenocinio SM pimping, procuring • **casa de ~** brothel
lentamente ADV slowly • **bébelo ~** drink it slowly • **el tráfico circulaba muy ~** the traffic was very slow-moving *o* was going very slowly • **la libra ha subido ~ en el último año** the pound has edged upwards in the last year, the pound has risen slowly in the last year
lente SF, (*a veces*) SM **1** (*gen*) lens ▸ **lente de aumento** magnifying glass ▸ **lente de gran ángulo, lente granangular** wide-angle lens ▸ **lentes de contacto** contact lenses ▸ **lentes progresivas** varifocal lenses ▸ **lente zoom** zoom lens
2 lentes (*esp LAm*) (= *gafas*) glasses, spectacles ▸ **lentes bifocales** bifocals
lenteja SF **1** (= *grano*) lentil
2 lentejas (= *guiso*) lentil soup (*sing*)
• MODISMO: • **ganarse las ~s** to earn one's crust
lentejuela SF sequin, spangle
lentificar ▹ CONJUG 1g VT to slow down
VPR **lentificarse** to slow down
lentilla SF contact lens; **lentillas** contact lenses ▸ **lentillas blandas** soft (contact) lenses ▸ **lentillas duras** hard (contact) lenses ▸ **lentillas semirígidas** gas permeable (contact) lenses
lentitud SF slowness • **con ~** slowly
lento ADJ [*ritmo, movimiento, caída*] slow; [*tráfico, película*] slow, slow-moving • **una muerte lenta** a lingering *o* slow death • **la circulación iba muy lenta esta mañana** traffic was very slow *o* slow-moving this morning • **¡qué ~s pasan los días!** the days go so slowly! • **es muy ~ en el trabajo** he's a very slow worker • **la economía está creciendo a un ritmo ~** the economy is growing sluggishly *o* slowly • **~ pero seguro** slowly but surely; ▹ **cámara, fuego, paso²**
ADV slowly • **trabaja muy ~** he works very slowly • **habla tan ~ que casi no la entiendo** she speaks so slowly that I can hardly understand her
lentorro* ADJ sluggish, slow
leña SF **1** (*para el fuego*) firewood • **hacer ~** to gather firewood • MODISMOS: • **echar ~ al fuego** to add fuel to the fire *o* flames • **llevar ~ al monte** to carry coals to Newcastle ▸ **leña de oveja** (*Cono Sur*) sheep droppings
2* (= *golpes*) thrashing, hiding • **dar ~ a algn** • **cargar** *o* **hartar de ~ a algn** to thrash sb, give sb a good hiding • **repartir ~** to lash out • **sacudirle ~ a algn** to give sb (some) stick*, lay into sb* • **trincar ~** to sweat blood
leñador(a) SM/F woodcutter, logger
leñar ▹ CONJUG 1a VT (*Cono Sur, Méx*),
leñatear ▹ CONJUG 1a VT (*And*) (= *hacer leña*) to make into firewood; (= *cortar leña*) to cut up for firewood
leñateo SM (*And, CAm*) woodpile
leñatero/a SM/F (*Cono Sur*) woodcutter, logger
leñazo* SM **1** (= *golpe*) knock
2 (= *choque*) bash*
leñe* EXCL heck* • **¿dónde ~ ...?** where the heck ...?
leñera SF woodshed
leñero/a SM/F (= *comerciante*) timber merchant
leño SM **1** (= *tronco*) log, lumber (*EEUU*)
• MODISMOS: • **dormir como un ~** to sleep like a log • **hacer ~ del árbol caído** to kick sb when he's down
2* (= *zoquete*) dolt*, blockhead*
leñoso ADJ woody
Leo SM (*Astron, Astrol*) Leo • **es de Leo** (*LAm*) he's (a) Leo
leo (*Astrol*) SMF INV Leo • **los leo son así** that's what Leos are like
ADJ INV Leo • **soy leo** I'm (a) Leo
León SM **1** (= *nombre*) Leon, Leo
2 (*Geog*) (*en España*) León
león SM **1** (*Zool*) lion; (*LAm*) puma
• MODISMOS: • **estar hecho un ~** to be furious • **ponerse como un ~** to be furious, get mad ▸ **león marino** sea lion; ▹ **fiero**
2 leones‡ (= *dados*) loaded dice
leona SF **1** (*Zool*) (*tb fig*) lioness
2* (= *portera*) porter, concierge
3 (*Chile*) (= *confusión*) confusion, mix-up*
leonado ADJ tawny, fawn-colored (*EEUU*)
leonera SF **1** (= *jaula*) lion's cage; (= *cueva*) lion's den • **parece una ~** the place is a tip*
2 (*Cono Sur*) (= *celda*) communal prison cell
3 (*And*) (= *reunión*) noisy gathering
leonés/esa ADJ of/from León
SM/F native/inhabitant of León • **los leoneses** the people of León
SM (*Ling*) Leonese
leonino ADJ **1** (*Literat*) leonine
2 [*contrato*] unfair, one-sided
Leonor SF Eleanor
leontina SF watch chain
leopardo SM leopard ▸ **leopardo cazador** cheetah
leopoldina SF fob, short watch chain
leotardo SM **1** [*de bailarina*] leotard
2 leotardos woollen tights, woolen pantyhose (*EEUU*)
Lepe SM • MODISMOS: • **ir donde las ~** (*Cono*

Sur) to make a bloomer* (*in calculating*) • **saber más que ~*** to be pretty smart • **ser más tonto que ~*** to be a complete twit*

leperada* (SF) (*CAm, Méx*) (*en el habla*) coarse remark; (= *acto*) dirty trick, rotten thing (to do)*

lépero/a* (ADJ) **1** (*CAm, Méx*) (= *grosero*) rude, uncouth

2 (*And*) • **estar ~** to be broke*

(SM/F) **1** (*CAm, Méx*) (= *grosero*) rude person, uncouth person

2 (*Méx*) (= *plebeyo*) low-class person, guttersnipe (*pey*)

leperusco* (ADJ) (*Méx*) low-class, plebeian; (*pey*) rotten*, villainous

lepidopterólogo/a (SM/F) lepidopterist

lepidópteros (SMPL) lepidoptera, butterflies and moths

lepisma (SF) silverfish

leporino (ADJ) leporine, hare-like • **labio ~** harelip, cleft lip

lepra (SF) leprosy ▸ **lepra de montaña** (*LAm*) mountain leprosy, leishmaniasis (*frm*)

leprosario (SM) (*Méx*), **leprosería** (SF) leper colony

leproso/a (ADJ) leprous

(SM/F) leper

lerdear ▹ CONJUG 1a (VI) (*CAm, Arg*) (*sin prisa*) to do things very slowly; (*sin ganas*) to drag one's feet*

(VPR) **lerdearse** to be slow (*about doing things*), drag one's feet*

lerdera (SF) (*CAm*) = **lerdez**

lerdez (SF), **lerdeza** (SF) (*CAm*) **1** (= *lentitud*) slowness

2 (= *estupidez*) slow-wittedness

3 (= *patosería*) clumsiness

4 (= *pesadez*) heaviness, sluggishness

lerdo (ADJ) **1** (= *lento*) slow

2 (= *de pocas luces*) slow-witted

3 (= *patoso*) clumsy

4 (= *pesado*) heavy, sluggish

lerdura (SF) (*Cono Sur*) = **lerdez**

lerén* (SM) (*And*) **1** (= *tipo*) bloke*, guy*

2 (= *de baja estatura*) midget

Lérida (SF) Lerida

leridano/a (ADJ) of/from Lérida

(SM/F) native/inhabitant of Lérida • **los ~s** the people of Lérida

les (PRON PERS) **1** (*directo*) (= *a ellos, ellas*) them; (= *a ustedes*) you

2 (*indirecto*) (= *a ellos, ellas*) (to) them; (= *a ustedes*) (to) you; ▹ **le**

lesbiana (SF) lesbian

lesbianismo (SM) lesbianism

lésbico (ADJ), **lesbio** (ADJ) lesbian

lesera* (SF) (*And, Cono Sur*) (= *estupidez*) stupidity; (= *tontería*) nonsense

leseras* (SFPL) (*Cono Sur*) (= *tonterías*) nonsense (*sing*)

lesión (SF) **1** (= *herida*) wound, lesion; (*Dep*) injury ▸ **lesión cerebral** brain damage ▸ **lesión de ligamentos** injured ligament

2 (*Jur*) • **agresión con lesiones** assault and battery

3 (= *agravio*) damage

lesionado (ADJ) (= *herido*) hurt; (*Dep*) injured

lesionar ▹ CONJUG 1a (VT) (= *dañar*) to hurt; (= *herir*) to injure

(VPR) **lesionarse** to injure oneself • **~se la pierna** to injure one's leg

lesividad (SF) harmfulness

lesivo (ADJ) **1** (= *dañino*) harmful, damaging

2 (= *perjudicial*) detrimental

lesna (SF) awl

leso (ADJ) **1** (*frm*) (= *ofendido*) hurt • **crimen de lesa patria** high treason • **crimen de lesa humanidad** crime against humanity • **lesa majestad** lese-majesty • **crimen de lesa majestad** lese-majesty, treason

2 (*LAm**) (= *necio*) simple, stupid • **hacer ~ a algn** (*Cono Sur*) to play a trick on sb

• MODISMOS: • **no está para ~** (*Cono Sur*) he's not easily taken in • **hacerse el ~** to pretend not to know, pretend not to notice

Lesoto (SM) Lesotho

lesura* (SF) (*Chile*) stupidity

letal (ADJ) deadly, lethal

letalidad (SF) (*frm*) deadliness, lethal nature • **la enfermedad tiene una elevada ~** there is a high death rate from this disease

letanía (SF) **1** (*Rel*) litany

2 (= *retahíla*) long list, litany

letárgico (ADJ) lethargic

letargo (SM) lethargy

Lete, Leteo (SM) Lethe

letón/ona (ADJ) Latvian

(SM/F) Latvian • **los letones** the Latvians

(SM) (*Ling*) Latvian, Lettish

Letonia (SF) Latvia

letra (SF) **1** (*Tip*) letter • MODISMOS: • **decir a una mujer las cuatro ~s†*** to call a woman a slut • **poner unas** *o* **dos** *o* **cuatro ~s a algn** to drop sb a line • REFRÁN: • **la ~ con sangre entra** spare the rod and spoil the child ▸ **letra bastardilla, letra cursiva** italics (*pl*), italic type (*EEUU*) ▸ **letra de imprenta, letra de molde** print • **escriba su nombre en ~s de imprenta** *o* **de molde** please print your name in block letters ▸ **letra gótica** Gothic script ▸ **letra inicial** initial letter ▸ **letra mayúscula** capital letter ▸ **letra menuda** small print ▸ **letra minúscula** small letter ▸ **letra muerta** dead letter ▸ **letra negrilla, letra negrita** bold type, heavy type ▸ **letra pequeña** small print ▸ **letra redonda** roman, roman type (*EEUU*) ▸ **letras sagradas** Scripture ▸ **letra versal** capital letter ▸ **letra versalita** small capital ▸ **letra voladita** superscript (type)

2 (= *escritura*) handwriting, writing • **no le entiendo la ~** I can't read his handwriting *o* writing • MODISMO: • **despacito y buena ~** easy does it

3 (= *sentido literal*) letter, literal meaning • **a la ~** to the letter • **atarse a la ~** (*frm*) to stick to the literal meaning; ▹ **pie**

4 (*Com*) (= *pago*) instalment, installment (*EEUU*) • **le faltan cinco ~s para acabar de pagar el coche** she still has five instalments to make on the car • **pagar a ~ vista** to pay on sight ▸ **letra abierta** letter of credit ▸ **letra aceptada** accepted letter ▸ **letra a la vista** sight draft ▸ **letra bancaria** banker's draft, bank draft ▸ **letra de cambio** bill (of exchange), draft ▸ **letra de crédito** letter of credit ▸ **letra del Tesoro** Treasury bill ▸ **letra de patente** letters patent (*pl*)

5 [*de canción*] words (*pl*), lyrics (*pl*)

6 letras (= *cultura*) letters, learning (*sing*) • **un hombre de ~s** a man of letters • **primeras ~s** elementary education, the three Rs

7 letras (*Escol, Univ*) (= *humanidades*) arts • **voy a hacer dos asignaturas de ~s** I'm going to study two arts subjects • **Filosofía y Letras** humanities

letrado/a (ADJ) **1** (= *culto*) learned; (*pey*) pedantic

2 (*Jur*) legal • **derecho a la asistencia letrada** right to have a lawyer present

(SM/F) lawyer, counsel, attorney (*EEUU*) ▸ **letrado/a de oficio** court-appointed counsel

letrero (SM) **1** (*en tienda*) sign, notice; (*en carretera*) sign ▸ **letrero luminoso** neon sign

2 (*en moneda*) inscription

letrina (SF) latrine, privy • **el río es una ~** the river is an open sewer

letrista (SMF) (*Mús*) songwriter, lyricist

leucemia (SF) leukaemia, leukemia (*EEUU*)

leucémico/a (SM/F) leukaemia *o* (*EEUU*) leukemia sufferer

leucocito (SM) (*Med*) leucocyte, leukocyte (*EEUU*)

leucoma (SF) leucoma

leudante (ADJ) ▹ **harina**

leudar ▹ CONJUG 1a (VT) to leaven

(VPR) **leudarse** [*pan*] to rise

leva (SF) **1** (*Náut*) weighing anchor

2 (*Mil*) levy

3 (*Mec*) cam

4 (*And, CAm*) (= *estafa*) trick, swindle, ruse

5 • MODISMOS: • **bajar la ~ a algn** (*And, Cono Sur*) to do sb a mischief • **caer de ~** (*CAm*) to play the fool • **echar ~s** (*And, Méx**) (= *jactarse*) to boast; (*And**) (= *amenazar*) to bluster, utter threats • **encender la ~ a algn** (*Caribe**) to give sb a good hiding* • **ponerse la ~** (*And*) (= *largarse*) to beat it*; (= *hacer novillos**) to play truant; (= *faltar al trabajo*) to skive off work*

levadizo (ADJ) that can be raised • **puente ~** drawbridge

levado (SM) raising • **sistema de ~** raising mechanism

levadura (SF) **1** yeast ▸ **levadura de cerveza** brewer's yeast ▸ **levadura de panadero** baker's yeast ▸ **levadura en polvo** baking powder

2 • MODISMO: • **mala ~** (*euf*) = **mala leche** ▹ **leche**

levantada (SF) (*Perú*) (= *alzamiento*) raising

levantado (ADJ) (= *despierto*) up • **no me esperes ~** don't wait up for me

levantador(a) (SM/F) ▸ **levantador(a) de pesos** weightlifter

levantamiento (SM) **1** (= *alzado*) [*de objeto*] raising, lifting; (*con una grúa*) hoisting ▸ **levantamiento de pesas** weight-lifting

2 [*de prohibición, embargo*] lifting • **el ~ de las sanciones económicas** the lifting of economic sanctions • **el ~ de la veda de caza** the opening of the hunting season

3 (*Arquit*) [*de edificio, monumento*] construction; [*de plano*] drawing up

4 (*Jur*) • **se procedió al ~ del acta de denuncia** they proceeded to issue a formal report • **~ del cadáver** removal of the body

5 (*Pol*) uprising, revolt

6 (*Geog*) survey • **~ cartográfico** topographical survey, mapping

levantamuertos* (SM INV) (*And*) (*Culin*) vegetable broth

levantar ▹ CONJUG 1a (VT) **1** (= *alzar*) **a** [+ *peso, objeto*] to lift; (*con una grúa*) to hoist • **¿puedes ~ un poco la silla?** can you lift the chair up a bit? • **era imposible ~lo del suelo** it was impossible to lift it off the floor • **levantemos las copas por los novios** let's raise our glasses to the bride and groom • **la grúa levantó el coche hasta la plataforma** the crane hoisted the car onto the platform

b [+ *pierna, cabeza, cejas*] to raise • **levanta la pierna derecha** raise your right leg • **levantemos los corazones** let us lift up our hearts • **~ la mano** to put one's hand up, raise one's hand • **levantó la mano para pedir la vez** she put her hand up *o* raised her hand to ask for a turn • **a mí no me levanta la mano nadie** nobody raises their hand to me • **~ la mirada** *o* **los ojos** *o* **la vista** to look up • **no levantó la mirada del libro cuando entramos** she didn't raise her eyes from her book *o* she didn't look up from the book when we came in • MODISMO: • **si tu padre ~a la cabeza ...** your father must be turning in his grave • **si su mujer ~a la cabeza y lo viera casado otra vez se volvería a morir** his wife would turn in her grave to see him married again; ▹ **cabeza, tapa**

c [+ *cortina, falda*] to lift, lift up; [+ *persiana, telón*] to raise • **el viento le levantó la falda** the wind lifted her skirt (up) • **~ polvo** to raise dust
2 (= *poner de pie*) **a** • **~ a algn** (*del suelo*) to lift sb, lift sb up; (*de la cama*) to get sb up • **pesaba tanto que no pude ~la del suelo** she was so heavy that I couldn't lift her off the ground • **cuando se sienta en ese sofá no hay quien lo levante** once he sits on that sofa no one can get him off it • **su actuación levantó al público de sus asientos** her performance brought the audience to their feet
b [+ *objeto caído*] to pick up
3 (= *erigir*) [+ *edificio, pared*] to put up; [+ *monumento*] to erect, put up
4 (= *fundar*) [+ *empresa, imperio*] to found, establish • **levantó un gran imperio comercial** he founded *o* established a great commercial empire
5 (= *dar un empuje*) to build up • **todos los trabajadores ayudaron a ~ la empresa** all the workers helped to build up the company • **tenemos que ~ de nuevo la economía** we've got to get the economy back on its feet
6 [+ *ánimo, moral*] to lift, raise • **necesito algo que me levante la moral** I need something to lift *o* raise my spirits
7 [+ *tono, volumen*] to raise • **levanta la voz, que no te oigo** speak up - I can't hear you • **¡no levantes la voz!** keep your voice down! • **a mí nadie me levanta la voz** nobody raises their voice to me
8 (= *desmontar*) [+ *tienda de campaña*] to take down • **~ el campamento** to strike camp • **~ la casa** to move out • **~ la mesa** (*LAm*) to clear the table
9 (= *producir*) [+ *sospechas*] to arouse; [+ *dolor*] to give; [+ *rumor*] to spark off • **tantos gritos me levantan dolor de cabeza** all this shouting is giving me a headache • **el reportaje ha levantado rumores de un posible divorcio** the report has sparked off rumours of a possible divorce • **~ falso testimonio** (*Jur*) to give false testimony; (*Rel*) to bear false witness; ▸ **ampolla**
10 (= *terminar*) [+ *prohibición, embargo*] to lift; [+ *veda*] to end • **esta semana se levanta la veda** the close season ends this week • **se ha levantado la prohibición de la caza de la ballena** the ban on whaling has been lifted • **~ el castigo a algn** to let sb off • **se ~á el castigo a los que pidan perdón** those who apologize will be let off (their punishment)
11 (*Jur*) **a** [+ *censo*] to take; [+ *atestado*] to make; [+ *sesión*] to adjourn • **se levanta la sesión** court is adjourned; ▸ **acta**
b [+ *cadáver*] to remove
12 (*Arquit*) [+ *plano*] to make, draw up
13 (*Caza*) to flush out; ▸ **liebre, vuelo²**
14 (*Mil*) [+ *ejército*] to raise
15 (= *sublevar*) (*Pol*) • **la corrupción política levantó al pueblo contra el gobierno** political corruption turned people against the government
16 (*Naipes*) (= *coger*) to pick; (= *superar*) to beat
17* (= *ganar*) [+ *dinero*] to make, earn
18* (= *robar*) to pinch*, swipe*
19 (*Ven*‡) (= *arrestar*) to nick‡, arrest
20 (*Col, Perú, Ven**) [+ *mujer*] to pick up*
VI **1** (*hum*) [*persona*] • **no levanta del suelo más de metro y medio** she's no more than five foot from head to toe
2 (*Naipes*) to cut the pack • **levanta, es tu turno** cut the pack, it's your turn
VPR **levantarse 1** (= *alzarse*) **a** (*de la cama, del suelo*) to get up • **me levanto todos los días a las ocho** I get up at eight every day • **¡venga, levántate!** come on, get out of bed *o* get up! • **se cayó y no podía ~se** she fell down and couldn't get up • **ya se levanta y anda un poco** he's getting up and about now
• MODISMO: • **~se con** *o* (*And*) **en el pie izquierdo** to get out of bed on the wrong side
b (*de un asiento*) to get up, stand up • **se ~on todos cuando entró el obispo** everyone got up *o* stood up *o* rose to their feet (*frm*) when the bishop entered • **levántense** please stand • **nadie se levanta de la mesa hasta que no lo diga yo** no one gets up from the table until I say so
2 (= *erguirse*) [*edificio, monumento*] to stand • **en la plaza se levanta el monumento a Salazar** in the square stands the monument to Salazar • **la torre se levanta por encima de los demás edificios** the tower rises *o* stands above the other buildings
3 (= *despegarse*) **a** (*Constr*) [*pintura*] to come off, peel off; [*baldosa, suelo*] to come up • **el suelo estaba todo levantado** the floor had all come up
b [*piel*] to peel
4 (*Meteo*) **a** (= *disiparse*) [*niebla, nubes*] to lift
b (= *producirse*) [*viento*] to get up • **se está levantando un viento terrible** there's a terrible wind getting up • **se ~on olas de tres metros** ten foot waves rose up
5 (= *sublevarse*) to rise, rise up
6 (*Rel*) (= *resucitar*) to rise
7* (= *apoderarse*) • **~se con algo** to make off with sth
8 (*Col, Perú, Ven**) [+ *mujer*] (= *ligarse a*) to pick up*; (= *acostarse con*) to get off with*

levantaválvulas SM INV valve tappet

levante¹ SM (*Geog*) **1** (= *este*) east
2 (*tb* **viento de levante**) east wind

levante² SM **1** (*Caribe*) (*Pol*) uprising
2 (*Caribe*) (= *arreo*) driving of cattle
3 (*And*) (= *arrogancia*) arrogance, haughtiness
4 • **dar** *o* **pegar un ~ a algn** (*Cono Sur**) to give sb a dressing-down*
5 (*Cono Sur**) (= *encuentro*) pick-up* • **hacer un ~ a algn** to pick sb up*
6 • **hacer un ~** (*Caribe**) to fall in love

Levante SM **1** (= *este de España*) east coast
2 (= *oriente*) Levant • **el ~** the Levant, the (Near) East

levantino/a ADJ **1** (= *del Levante español*) of/from the eastern coast *o* provinces of Spain
2 (= *oriental*) Levantine
SM/F **1** (= *del Levante español*) native/inhabitant of the eastern provinces of Spain • **los ~s** the people of the east of Spain
2 (= *oriental*) Levantine

levantisco ADJ [*persona*] rebellious; [*país*] turbulent, troubled

levar ▸ CONJUG 1a VT **1** (*Mil*) to levy, recruit (by force)
2 (*Náut*) • **~ anclas** to weigh anchor
VPR **levarse** to weigh anchor, set sail

leve ADJ **1** (= *sin importancia*) minor • **cometió una falta ~** he committed a minor offence • **solo tiene heridas ~s** he only has minor injuries
2 (= *suave*) [*brisa*] light; [*sonrisa*] slight • **asintió con un ~ movimiento de cabeza** she gave a slight nod of agreement
3 (= *ligero*) [*carga, peso*] light
4 (*frm*) (= *muy fino*) light, fine • **un ~ velo** a light veil

levedad SF **1** (= *poca importancia*) • **debido a la ~ de las heridas** because the injuries were not serious
2 (*frm*) (*en peso*) lightness
3 (*frm*) (*en grosor*) fineness

levemente ADV **1** (= *superficialmente*) slightly • **ocho personas resultaron ayer ~ heridas** eight people were slightly hurt yesterday
2 (= *ligeramente*) lightly • **se le notaba ~ aturdido** he appeared to be slightly stunned
3 (= *suavemente*) • **el aire empezó a soplar ~** a light breeze stirred the air

leviatán SM leviathan

levita¹ SF frock coat

levita² SM Levite

levitación SF levitation

levitar ▸ CONJUG 1a VI to levitate

Levítico SM Leviticus

lexema SM lexeme

lexicalizador ADJ lexicalizing
SM lexicalizer

lexicalizar ▸ CONJUG 1f VT to lexicalize
VPR **lexicalizarse** to be lexicalized

léxico ADJ lexical
SM (= *lexicón*) lexicon; (= *diccionario*) dictionary; (= *vocabulario*) vocabulary; (= *lista de palabras*) word list

lexicografía SF lexicography

lexicográfico ADJ lexicographical

lexicógrafo/a SM/F lexicographer

lexicología SF lexicology

lexicólogo/a SM/F lexicologist

lexicón SM lexicon

lexicosemántico ADJ lexico-semantic

ley SF **1** (= *precepto*) law • **aprobar** *o* **votar una ley** to pass a law • **todos somos iguales ante la ley** we are all equal before the law • **está por encima de la ley** he's above the law • **está fuera de la ley** he's outside the law • **un fuera de la ley** an outlaw • **de acuerdo con la ley** • **según la ley** in accordance with the law, by law, in law
• MODISMOS: • **con todas las de la ley**: • **quieren crear una fundación con todas las de la ley** they want to set up a fully-fledged charitable trust • **va a protestar, y con todas las de la ley** he's going to complain and rightly so • **quiere celebrar su aniversario con todas las de la ley** she wants to celebrate her anniversary in style • **hecha la ley hecha la trampa** • **el que hace la ley hace la trampa** every law has a loophole ▸ **ley cambiaria** currency exchange regulations ▸ **ley de extranjería** immigration laws ▸ **ley de fugas** • **se le aplicó la ley de fugas** he was shot while trying to escape ▸ **ley fundamental** constitutional law ▸ **ley marcial** martial law ▸ **ley orgánica** constitutional law ▸ **ley seca** prohibition law
2 (= *regla no escrita*) law ▸ **ley de la calle** mob law, lynch law ▸ **ley de la selva** law of the jungle ▸ **ley del embudo** unfair law ▸ **ley del más fuerte** (principle of) might is right ▸ **ley del Talión** (*Hist*) lex talionis; (*fig*) (principle of) an eye for an eye and a tooth for a tooth
3 (= *principio científico*) law ▸ **ley de la gravedad** law of gravity ▸ **ley de la oferta y la demanda** law of supply and demand ▸ **ley natural** (*Fís*) law of nature; (*Ética*) natural law
4 (*Dep*) rule, law ▸ **ley de la ventaja** advantage rule
5 (*Rel*) • **la ley de Dios** the rule of God, God's law ▸ **ley de Moisés** the law of Moses
6 (*Metal*) • **oro de ley** pure gold, standard gold • **bajo de ley** base • **ser de (buena) ley** to be genuine • **ser de mala ley** to be a bad character
7† (= *lealtad*) loyalty, devotion • **tener/tomar ley a algn** to be/become devoted to sb

leyenda SF **1** (= *historia*) legend ▸ **leyenda negra** (= *mala fama*) bad reputation; (*Hist*) *view of the Conquest of Latin America which*

emphasized the negative side of Spanish involvement
2 (= *inscripción*) [*de moneda, medalla, lápida*] legend, inscription
3 [*de cuadro, grabado, mapa*] (= *encabezamiento*) heading; (= *pie*) caption
4 (= *eslogan*) slogan

leyendo *etc* ▷ **leer**

leyente SMF reader

leyista SM (*Caribe*) pettifogging lawyer, shyster (EEUU)

leyoso ADJ (*And*) cunning, sly

lezna SF awl

LGBT ADJ ABR (= **Lesbianas, Gays, Bisexuales y Transexuales**) LGBT

lía SF (*LAm*) plaited esparto grass

liado* ADJ (= *ocupado*) • **Pedro está muy ~, así que he venido yo en su lugar** Pedro is tied up so I've come instead

liana SF liana

liante/a* SM/F 1 (= *enredador*) mischief-maker
2 (= *persona difícil*) awkward customer*
3 (= *timador*) con man*, swindler
4 (= *chismoso*) gossip

liar ▷ CONJUG 1c VT 1 [+ *fardos, paquetes*] (= *atar*) to tie up; (= *envolver*) to wrap (up) • **lía este paquete con una cuerda** tie up this parcel with some string; ▷ **bártulos, petate**
2 [+ *cigarrillo*] to roll
3 (= *confundir*) to confuse • **me ~on con tantas explicaciones** they confused me with all their explanations • **¡no me líes!** (= *no me confundas*) don't confuse me!; (= *no me metas en problemas*) don't get me into trouble!
4 • **~la*** (= *provocar una discusión*) to stir up trouble; (= *hacer algo mal*) to make a mess of things • **¡la liamos!** we've done it now!*
5 • **~las**†‡ (= *irse*) to beat it*; (= *morir*) to peg out‡
VPR **liarse** 1 (= *confundirse*) to get muddled up • **explícalo mejor, que ya te has vuelto a ~** explain it a bit better, you've got all muddled up again
2* (*sentimentalmente*) • **~se con algn** to have an affair with sb, get involved with sb • **se ha liado con su jefe** she's having an affair with her boss
3 • **~se a*** (+ *infin*) • **nos liamos a hablar y se nos pasó la hora** we got talking and we forgot the time • **nos liamos a ver fotos y estuve allí toda la tarde** we got to looking through photos and I stayed there all evening
4 • **~se a golpes** *o* **a palos*** to lay into one another*; ▷ **manta**¹

lib. ABR (= **libro**) bk

libación SF libation; **libaciones** libations, potations

libanés/esa ADJ Lebanese
SM/F Lebanese, Lebanese man/woman • **los libaneses** the Lebanese, the people of the Lebanon

Líbano SM • **el ~** the Lebanon

libar ▷ CONJUG 1a VT 1 (= *succionar*) to suck
2 (= *sorber*) to sip
3 (= *degustar*) to taste
VI (*LAm**) (= *beber*) to booze*

libelista SMF lampoonist, writer of lampoons

libelo SM 1 (= *sátira*) lampoon (**contra** of), satire (**contra** on)
2 (*Jur*) libel

libélula SF dragonfly

liberación SF (*gen*) liberation; [*de preso*] release; [*de precios*] deregulation ▸ **liberación de la mujer** women's liberation

liberacionista* SF women's libber*

liberado/a ADJ 1 (*gen*) liberated
2 [*de partido, sindicato*] full-time, professional; [*de organización*] full-time
3 (*Com, Econ*) paid-up, paid-in (EEUU)
SM/F (*Pol*) [*de sindicato, partido, organización*] full-time official

liberador(a) ADJ liberating
SM/F liberator

liberal ADJ 1 (*Pol*) liberal
2 (= *tolerante*) liberal, open-minded
3 (= *generoso*) liberal, generous
4 [*profesión*] liberal
SMF liberal

liberalidad SF 1 (= *generosidad*) liberality (*frm*), generosity
2 [*de ideas, costumbres*] liberalism

liberalismo SM liberalism

liberalización SF liberalization

liberalizador ADJ liberalizing

liberalizar ▷ CONJUG 1f VT to liberalize; [+ *mercado*] to deregulate

liberalmente ADV (= *libremente*) freely; (= *generosamente*) liberally, generously

liberar ▷ CONJUG 1a VT 1 [+ *rehén*] to free, release; [+ *país, pueblo*] to liberate
2 • **~ a algn de** [+ *carga, obligación*] to free sb of *o* from; [+ *peligro*] to save sb from • **la han liberado de una gran responsabilidad** they have freed her of a great responsibility • **~ a algn de un pago** to exempt sb from a payment
3 (*Econ*) [+ *precios*] to deregulate; [+ *acción*] to pay in full; [+ *deuda*] to release; [+ *tipo de cambio*] to float
4 [+ *energía, oxígeno*] to release
VPR **liberarse** 1 • **~se de algo** to free o.s. from sth • **el preso se liberó de las esposas** the prisoner freed himself from *o* got free of the handcuffs • **se ha liberado de su complejo de inferioridad** he has rid himself of his inferiority complex
2 (*socialmente*) to liberate o.s. • **las mujeres empiezan a ~se** women are beginning to liberate themselves

Liberia SF Liberia

liberiano/a ADJ Liberian
SM/F Liberian • **los ~s** the Liberians, the people of Liberia

líbero SMF (*Dep*) sweeper

libérrimo ADJ entirely free, absolutely free

libertad SF 1 (*gen*) freedom • **disfrutamos de la ~ de la vida en el campo** we enjoy the freedom of life in the country • **no tengo ~ para hacer lo que quiera** I'm not free to do what I want, I don't have the freedom to do what I want • **estar en ~** to be free • **poner a algn en ~** to set sb free ▸ **libertad bajo fianza** release on bail ▸ **libertad bajo palabra** parole ▸ **libertad condicional** probation • **estar en ~ condicional** to be on probation ▸ **libertad de asociación** freedom of association ▸ **libertad de cátedra** academic freedom, freedom to teach ▸ **libertad de comercio** free trade ▸ **libertad de conciencia** freedom of conscience ▸ **libertad de cultos** freedom of worship ▸ **libertad de empresa** free enterprise ▸ **libertad de expresión** freedom of speech ▸ **libertad de imprenta, libertad de prensa** freedom of the press ▸ **libertad de voto** free vote ▸ **libertades civiles** civil liberties ▸ **libertad vigilada** probation • **estar en ~ vigilada** to be on probation
2 (= *confianza*) • **hablar con entera** *o* **total ~** to speak freely • **tomarse la ~ de hacer algo** to take the liberty of doing sth • **tomarse muchas** *o* **demasiadas ~es con algn** to take too many liberties with sb

libertador(a) ADJ liberating
SM/F liberator • **El Libertador** (*LAm*) (*Hist*) the Liberator (*Simón Bolívar*)

libertar ▷ CONJUG 1a VT 1 (= *poner en libertad*) to set free, release
2 (= *eximir*) [*de deber, obligación*] to release; [*de impuestos, ley*] to exempt
3 (= *salvar*) to save (**de** from) • **~ a algn de la muerte** to save sb from death

libertario/a ADJ, SM/F libertarian

libertinaje SM licentiousness (*frm*), profligacy (*frm*)

libertino/a ADJ 1 (= *inmoral*) loose-living, profligate (*frm*)
2 (*Rel, Hist*) freethinking
SM/F 1 (= *juerguista*) libertine
2 (*Rel, Hist*) freethinker

liberto/a ADJ [*esclavo*] freed, liberated
SM/F freedman/freedwoman

Libia SF Libya

libídine SF (*frm*) (= *lujuria*) lewdness, lasciviousness; (= *líbido*) libido

libidinosamente ADV lustfully, libidinously (*frm*)

libidinoso ADJ lustful, libidinous (*frm*)

libido SF libido

libio/a ADJ Libyan
SM/F Libyan • **los ~s** the Libyans, the people of Libya

liborio* ADJ Cuban

Libra SF (*Astron, Astrol*) Libra • **es de ~** (*LAm*) she's (a) Libra, she's a Libran

libra SF 1 (= *moneda*) pound ▸ **libra esterlina** pound sterling
2 (= *unidad de peso*) pound
3 (*Perú*) (*Hist*) 10 soles note; ▷ **KILOS, METROS, AÑOS**
SMF INV (*Astrol*) Libra, Libran • **los ~ son así** that's what Libras *o* Librans are like
ADJ INV (*Astrol*) Libra, Libran • **soy ~** I'm (a) Libra, I'm a Libran

libraco* SM (= *aburrido*) boring book, trashy book*; (= *grande*) old tome

librado/a ADJ • **salir bien/mal ~ de algo** to come out of sth well/badly
SM/F (*Com*) drawee

librador(a) SM/F (*Com*) drawer

libramiento SM 1 (*gen*) deliverance
2 (*Com*) order of payment

librante SMF (*Com*) drawer

libranza SF 1 (*Com*) order of payment ▸ **libranza de correos, libranza postal** (*LAm*) postal order, money order
2 [*de trabajador*] time off

librar ▷ CONJUG 1a VT 1 (= *liberar*) • **~ a algn de** [+ *preocupación, responsabilidad*] to free sb from *o* of; [+ *peligro*] to save sb from • **¡Dios me libre!** Heaven forbid! • **¡líbreme Dios de maldecir a nadie!** heaven forbid that I should curse anyone!
2 [+ *batalla*] to fight
3 (*Com*) to draw; [+ *cheque*] to make out • **~ a cargo de** to draw on
4 [+ *sentencia*] to pass; [+ *decreto*] to issue
5 (*frm*) [+ *secreto*] to reveal
6† [+ *esperanza, confianza*] to place (**en** en)
VI 1 (*en el trabajo*) • **libro los sábados** I have Saturdays off • **trabaja seis horas y libra dos** he works six hours and has two hours off • **libro a las tres** I'm free at three, I finish work at three
2† (= *parir*) to give birth
3† • **~ bien** to succeed • **~ mal** to fail
VPR **librarse** 1 (= *eximirse*) • **~se de algo/algn** to escape from sth/sb • **se ha librado del servicio militar** he has escaped military service • **se han librado del castigo** they have escaped punishment • **logró ~se de sus captores** he managed to escape from his captors
2 (= *deshacerse*) • **~se de algn/algo** to get rid of sb/sth • **por fin nos hemos librado de él** we've finally got rid of him

libre ADJ 1 (*gen*) free (**de** from, of) • **cada cual es ~ de hacer lo que quiera** everyone is free to do as they wish • **¿estás ~?** are you free? • **el martes estoy ~, así que podemos quedar**

I'm free on Tuesday so we can meet up
2 (= *exento*) • **~ de derechos** duty-free • **~ de franqueo** post-free • **~ de impuestos** free of tax • **estar ~ de servicio** to be off duty
3 (= *sin ocupar*) [*plaza*] vacant, unoccupied • **¿está ~ este asiento?** is this seat free? • **"libre"** [*parking*] "spaces"; [*taxi*] "for hire"
4 [*tiempo*] spare, free
5 • **al aire ~** in the open air
6 • **por ~** (= *por cuenta propia*): • **examinarse por ~** to take one's exams as an independent candidate • **trabajar por ~** to freelance • **ir** *o* **funcionar por ~** to go it alone
7 (*Dep, Natación*) • **los 200 metros ~s** the 200 metres freestyle • **estilo ~** freestyle; ▹ **saque, tiro**
8 [*traducción, adaptación, verso*] free
9 • **~ a bordo** (*Com*) free on board
10† (= *inmoral*) loose, immoral • **de vida ~** loose-living, immoral
SM **1** (*Dep*) (= *tiro*) free kick ▸ **libre directo** direct free kick ▸ **libre indirecto** indirect free kick
2 (*Méx*) taxi
SMF (*Dep*) (= *jugador*) sweeper
librea SF livery, uniform
SM (*Cono Sur*) footman
librecambio SM free trade
librecambismo SM free trade
librecambista ADJ free-trade (*antes de s*)
SMF free trader
libremente ADV freely
librepensador(a) SM/F freethinker
librepensamiento SM freethinking
librera SF (*LAm*) bookcase
librería SF **1** (= *tienda*) bookshop, bookstore (EEUU) ▸ **librería anticuaria, librería de antiguo** antiquarian bookshop ▸ **librería de ocasión, librería de viejo** secondhand bookshop
2 (= *estante*) bookcase; (= *biblioteca*) library
3 (= *comercio*) book trade
librero¹/a SM/F (= *persona*) bookseller ▸ **librero/a de viejo** secondhand bookseller
librero² SM (*LAm*) (= *estante*) bookcase
libresco ADJ bookish
libreta SF **1** (= *cuaderno*) notebook ▸ **libreta de anillas** spiral-bound notebook ▸ **libreta de direcciones** address book
2 (*Com*) (= *cartilla*) account book; (= *cuenta*) savings account ▸ **libreta de ahorros** savings book ▸ **libreta de depósitos** bank book, pass book
3 (*Aut*) (*Cono Sur*) driving licence (*Brit*), driver's license (EEUU) ▸ **libreta de manejar** (*Uru*) driving licence (*Brit*), driver's license (EEUU)
4 (*LAm*) ▸ **libreta militar** certificate of military service
5 [*de pan*] one-pound loaf
librete SM booklet
libretista SMF librettist
libreto SM **1** [*de ópera*] libretto
2 (*LAm*) (= *guión*) script, film script
libro SM **1** (= *obra impresa*) book • MODISMOS: • **ser como un ~ abierto** to be an open book • **ahorcar** *o* **arrimar** *o* **colgar los ~s** to give up studying • **hablar como un ~** (= *con precisión*) to know what one is talking about; (= *con pedantería*) to sound like a text book ▸ **libro de bolsillo** paperback ▸ **libro de cabecera** bedside book ▸ **libro de cocina** cookery book, cookbook (EEUU) ▸ **libro de consulta** reference book ▸ **libro de cuentos** storybook ▸ **libro de estilo** style book ▸ **libro de imágenes** picture-book ▸ **libro de lectura** reader ▸ **libro desplegable** pop-up book ▸ **libro de texto** textbook ▸ **libro electrónico** e-book ▸ **libro encuadernado, libro en pasta** hardback (book) ▸ **libro en rústica** paperback (book) ▸ **libro escolar** (= *informe*) school report; [*de texto*] schoolbook ▸ **libro mágico, libro móvil** pop-up book ▸ **libro sonoro** audio book ▸ **libro usado** second-hand book
2 (= *registro*) book • **llevar los ~s** (*Com*) to keep the books *o* accounts ▸ **libro de actas** minute book ▸ **libro de apuntes** notebook ▸ **libro de caja** cash book, petty cash book ▸ **libro de caja auxiliar** petty cash book ▸ **libro de contabilidad** account book ▸ **libro de cría** register of pedigrees ▸ **libro de cuentas** account book ▸ **libro de familia** *booklet containing family details (marriage, births) used for official purposes* ▸ **libro de honor** visitors' book ▸ **libro de orígenes** register of pedigrees ▸ **libro de pedidos** order book ▸ **libro de reclamaciones** complaints book ▸ **libro de ruta** itinerary ▸ **libro de visitas** visitors' book ▸ **libro de vuelos** (*Aer*) logbook ▸ **libro diario** journal ▸ **libro genealógico** (*Agr*) herd-book ▸ **libro mayor** ledger ▸ **libro parroquial** parish register ▸ **libro talonario** receipt book
3 (*Pol*) ▸ **libro blanco** white paper ▸ **libro rojo** red paper ▸ **libro verde** green paper
libro-disco SM book/CD set, book and CD set
librote SM big book, tome
Lic. ABR (*esp Méx*) = **Licenciado/Licenciada**
licencia SF **1** (= *documento*) licence, license (EEUU) ▸ **licencia de armas** gun licence, gun permit (EEUU) ▸ **licencia de caza** game licence, hunting permit ▸ **licencia de conducir, licencia de conductor** driving licence, driver's license (EEUU) ▸ **licencia de construcción** ≈ planning permission ▸ **licencia de exportación** (*Com*) export licence ▸ **licencia de manejar** (*LAm*) driving licence, driver's license (EEUU) ▸ **licencia de matrimonio** marriage licence ▸ **licencia de obras** building permit, planning permission ▸ **licencia de piloto, licencia de vuelo** pilot's licence ▸ **licencia fiscal** *registration with the Spanish Inland Revenue necessary for any commercial activity*
2 (*Mil*) leave, furlough (EEUU)
3 [*de trabajo*] leave • **estar de ~** to be on leave • **ir de ~** to go on leave ▸ **licencia absoluta** discharge ▸ **licencia de maternidad** maternity leave ▸ **licencia honrosa** honourable discharge ▸ **licencia por enfermedad** sick leave ▸ **licencia sin sueldo** unpaid leave
4 (*frm*) (= *permiso*) permission • **sin mi ~** without my permission • **dar su ~** to give one's permission, grant permission
5 (= *libertinaje*) licence
6 (*Literat*) ▸ **licencia poética** poetic licence
7 (*Univ*†) degree
licenciado/a SM/F **1** (*Univ*) graduate • **Licenciado en Filosofía y Letras** Bachelor of Arts
2 (*Méx, CAm*) (= *abogado*) lawyer, attorney(-at-law) (EEUU) • **el ~ Gutiérrez nos lleva el caso** Mr Gutiérrez is conducting the case
3 (*esp Méx*) (= *título*) ≈ Dr • **el Licenciado Papacostas nos dice que ...** Dr Papacostas tells us that ...
4 (*Mil*) *soldier having completed national service*
licenciar ▹ CONJUG 1b VT **1** (*Univ*) to confer a degree on
2 (*Mil*) to discharge
3 (*Com*) [+ *patente*] to license
4 (*frm*) (= *permitir*) to permit, allow
VPR **licenciarse 1** (*Univ*) to graduate, take one's degree • **~se en Derecho** to graduate in law, get a degree in law
2 (*Mil*) to be discharged
licenciatario/a SM/F licensee
licenciatura SF **1** (= *título*) degree
2 (= *estudios*) degree course, course of study (EEUU)
3 (= *ceremonia*) graduation

LICENCIATURA
Until recently most Spanish degree courses lasted five years. Students would be awarded a **diplomatura** (general degree) if they completed three years of study, and they would get their **licenciatura** (honours degree) after another two years. Now, under new **planes de estudio**, or curricula, **licenciaturas** take four years. The first two years are referred to as the **primer ciclo** and the final two years as the **segundo ciclo**.

licencioso ADJ licentious
liceo SM **1** (= *centro cultural*) lyceum
2 (*LAm*) (= *instituto*) secondary school, junior high school (EEUU)
licha‡ SF, **liche**‡ SF street
lichi SM lychee
líchigo SM (*And*) provisions, food
licitación SF **1** (*en contratación pública*) *bidding for a public contract*
2 (*en subasta*) bidding (*at auction*)
licitador(a) SM/F **1** (*en contratación pública*) bidder
2 (*LAm*) (= *subastador*) auctioneer
licitar ▹ CONJUG 1a VT **1** (*en contratación pública*) to tender for
2 (*en subasta*) (= *pujar*) to bid for
3 (*LAm*) (= *vender*) to sell by auction
VI to bid
lícito ADJ **1** (*Jur*) [*permiso*] legal; [*comercio*] legitimate, legal; [*conducta*] legal, lawful, licit (*frm*)
2 (*frm*) (= *justo*) right, reasonable • **no es lícita tanta desigualdad social** such levels of social inequality are not right *o* are unreasonable
3 (*frm*) (= *permisible*) permissible • **si es ~ preguntarlo** if one may ask
licitud SF **1** (= *legalidad*) legality, lawfulness • **la controversia sobre la ~ del aborto** the controversy about whether abortion should be permitted
2 (= *justicia*) rightness, fairness
licor SM **1** (= *bebida dulce*) liqueur ▸ **licor de frutas** fruit liqueur
2 licores (= *alcohol*) spirits (*pl*), liquor (EEUU) (*sing*)
3 (= *líquido*) liquid
licorera SF **1** (= *botella*) decanter
2 (= *empresa*) distillery
licorería SF (*LAm*) distillery
licorero/a ADJ • **empresa licorera** distillery • **industria licorera** alcohol *o* drinks industry
SM/F (*LAm*) distiller
licorista SMF (= *fabricante*) distiller; (= *comerciante*) liquor dealer, liquor seller
licoroso ADJ [*vino*] strong, of high alcoholic content
licra® SF Lycra®
licuación SF liquefaction (*frm*), melting
licuado SM (*tb* **licuado (de frutas)**) (*LAm*) milk shake
licuadora SF (*Culin*) blender, liquidizer
licuar ▹ CONJUG 1d VT **1** (*Culin*) to blend, liquidize
2 (*Fís, Quím*) to liquefy, turn into liquid; [+ *nieve*] to melt
VPR **licuarse** (*Fís, Quím*) to liquefy
licuefacción SF liquefaction
lid SF (*frm*) **1** (= *combate*) fight, combat
2 (= *disputa*) dispute • **en buena lid** (*lit*) in (a) fair fight; (*fig*) fair and square
líder ADJ INV top, leading, foremost • **marca ~** leading brand, brand leader

SMF (*Pol*) leader; (*Dep*) leader, league leader, top club ▸ **líder del mercado** market leader

liderar ▹ CONJUG 1a VT to lead, head

liderato SM, **liderazgo** SM (*gen*) leadership; (*Dep*) lead, leadership

lideresa SF (*Méx*) (*Pol*) leader

lidia SF **1** (*Taur*) (= *espectáculo, arte*) bullfighting; (= *corrida*) bullfight • **toro de ~** fighting bull
2 (*frm*) (= *lucha*) struggle, fight
3 (*LAm*) (= *molestia*) trouble, nuisance • **dar ~** to be trying, be a nuisance

lidiador(a) SM/F (*gen*) fighter; (*Taur*) bullfighter

lidiar ▹ CONJUG 1b VT (*Taur*) to fight
VI to fight (**con, contra** against, **por** for)

liebre SF **1** (*Zool*) hare • MODISMOS: • **coger una ~*** to come a cropper*, take a flat beating (*EEUU*) • **levantar la ~** to blow the gaff*, let the cat out of the bag • **ser ~ corrida** (*Méx**) to be an old hand; ▹ **gato¹**
2 (= *cobarde*) coward
3 (*Chile*) (= *microbús*) minibus

Liechtenstein SM Liechtenstein

Lieja SF Liège

liencillo SM (*LAm*) thick cotton material

liendre SF nit

lienzo SM **1** (= *tela*) linen • **un ~** a piece of linen
2 (*Arte*) canvas
3 (= *pañuelo*) handkerchief
4 (*Arquit*) (= *muro*) wall; (= *fachada*) face, front
5 (*LAm*) [*de valla*] section of fence
6 (*Méx*) (= *corral*) corral, pen

liftar ▹ CONJUG 1a VT (*Dep*) [+ *pelota*] to loft

lifting SM face-lift • **hacerse un ~** to get a face-lift, have a face-lift

liga SF **1** (*Pol, Dep*) league ▸ **Liga de Campeones** Champions League
2 (= *faja*) suspender, garter (*EEUU*)
3 (*para sujetar*) elastic band
4 (= *muérdago*) mistletoe
5 (= *sustancia viscosa*) birdlime
6 (*CAm, Méx*) (= *unión*) binding
7 (*Metal*) alloy
8 (*And**) (= *amigo*) bosom friend
9* (= *persona*) pick-up‡

ligado SM **1** (*Mús*) (*entre dos notas*) slur, tie; (= *pasaje*) legato passage
2 (*Tip*) ligature

ligadura SF **1** (*Med*) ligature ▸ **ligadura de trompas** tubal ligation
2 ligaduras [*de cuerda, correa*] bonds, ties; (*entre personas*) ties • **eres demasiado joven para ~s** you're too young to tie yourself down to one person • **todavía tienes las marcas de las ~s** you still have the marks from the ropes when you were tied up
3 (*Mús*) ligature, tie
4 (*Náut*) lashing

ligamento SM ligament • **romperse un ~** to tear a ligament

ligamiento SM **1** (= *atadura*) tying
2 (*familiar, comercial*) tie

ligar ▹ CONJUG 1h VT **1** (= *atar*) (*gen*) to tie, bind; (*Med*) to bind up, put a ligature on
2 (= *mezclar*) [+ *metales*] to alloy, mix; [+ *bebidas*] to mix; [+ *salsa*] to thicken
3 (= *unir*) to join, bind together • **estar ligado por contrato a** to be bound by contract to
4* (= *conquistar*) to pick up*, get off with*, pull*
5* (= *birlar*) to pinch*
6* (= *conseguir*) to get hold of, lay one's hands on
7* (= *comprar*) to buy
8* (= *detener*) to nick*
9 (*Caribe*) (= *contratar*) to contract in advance for
VI **1** (= *ir juntos*) to mix well, blend well, go well together
2* (= *conquistar*) to pull* • **salieron dispuestas a ~** they went out to try to pick up a man *o* to pull* • **Pepe y Ana han ligado** Pepe and Ana have paired up
3 (*Caribe, Méx**) (= *tener suerte*) to have a bit of luck, be lucky • **la cosa le ligó** (*And, CAm*) the affair went well for him
4 (*Caribe, Méx*) (= *mirar*) to look, stare
5 • **le ligó su deseo** (*And, Caribe**) her wish came true
VPR **ligarse 1** (= *unirse*) to unite, join together
2* (= *conquistar*) to get off with* • **~se a** *o* **con algn** to get off with sb*
3 (= *comprometerse*) to bind o.s., commit o.s.

ligazón SF **1** (*Náut*) rib
2 (= *unión*) connection, bond, link

ligeramente ADV **1** (*con adjetivos*) slightly • **la foto estaba ~ desenfocada** the photo was slightly out of focus • **me siento ~ cansada** I feel rather tired
2 (= *con verbos*) **a** (= *levemente*) [*oler, saber*] slightly; [*asar, cocer*] lightly; [*desplazarse, moverse, cambiar*] slightly • **las acciones han bajado ~ esta semana** the shares have dropped slightly *o* a little this week • **se ha recuperado ~** he's made a slight recovery
b (= *rápidamente*) [*correr, andar*] quickly; [*tocar*] lightly, gently
c (= *sin sensatez*) [*actuar*] flippantly • **no deberías actuar tan ~** you shouldn't act so flippantly • **hay decisiones que no se pueden tomar ~** there are some decisions which can't be taken lightly

ligerear ▹ CONJUG 1a VI (*Cono Sur*) to walk fast, move quickly

ligereza SF **1** [*de objeto, material, tejido*] lightness
2 (= *rapidez*) speed, swiftness
3 (= *agilidad*) agility, nimbleness • **~ mental** mental agility
4 (= *falta de sensatez*) flippancy • **actuar con ~** to act flippantly • **hablar con ~** to speak without thinking • **juzgar algo con ~** to jump to conclusions about sth, judge sth hastily ▸ **ligereza de espíritu** light-heartedness
5 (= *dicho imprudente*) flippant remark; (= *hecho imprudente*) indiscretion • **lo que dijo era solo una ~** what she said was just a flippant remark • **cometí la ~ de contárselo todo** I was foolish enough to tell him everything

ligero ADJ **1** (= *poco pesado*) [*paquete, gas, metal, comida*] light; [*tela*] light, lightweight, thin; [*material*] lightweight • **una blusa ligerita** a light *o* lightweight *o* thin blouse • **construido con materiales ~s** built from lightweight materials • **hemos cenado algo ~** we had something light for dinner • **viajar ~ de equipaje** to travel light • **~ de ropa** lightly dressed • **vas muy ~ de ropa para esta época del año** you're very lightly *o* flimsily dressed for this time of the year • **fotos de chicas ligeras de ropa** photos of scantily clad girls • **tener el sueño ~** to be a light sleeper • **~ como una pluma** as light as a feather
2 (= *leve*) [*viento, caricia*] light; [*ruido*] slight; [*perfume, fragancia*] delicate • **sopla un ~ viento** a light wind is blowing • **el más ~ ruido lo despierta** he wakes at the slightest noise
3 (= *poco importante*) [*enfermedad*] minor; [*castigo*] light
4 (= *rápido*) swift • **~ de dedos** quick-fingered • **~ de pies** light-footed, quick • MODISMO: • **~ como una bala** *o* **el viento** as quick as a flash, like the wind; ▹ **paso²**
5 (= *ágil*) agile • **después del régimen me siento mucho más ligera** after the diet I feel a lot lighter on my feet *o* a lot more agile
6 (= *superficial*) [*conocimiento*] slight; [*sospecha*] sneaking • **un ~ conocimiento de alemán** a slight knowledge *o* a smattering of German • **tengo la ligera sospecha de que nos hemos equivocado** I have a sneaking suspicion that we've made a mistake
7 (= *frívolo*) [*carácter, persona*] flippant, frivolous; [*comentario, tema*] flippant; [*mujer*] (*pey*†) loose† • **no deberías ser tan ligera con estos asuntos** you shouldn't be so flippant *o* frivolous about these things; ▹ **casco**
8 (= *sin complicaciones*) [*novela, película*] lightweight; [*conversación, contexto*] light-hearted
9 • **a la ligera** (= *irreflexivamente*) rashly; (= *rápidamente*) quickly • **no se pueden hacer las cosas a la ligera** you shouldn't act so rashly • **es obvio que lo has hecho muy a la ligera** it's obvious that you rushed it *o* did it too quickly • **no podemos juzgar su conducta a la ligera** we shouldn't jump to conclusions about his behaviour, we shouldn't judge his behaviour so hastily • **tomarse algo a la ligera** not to take sth seriously
ADV (= *rápido*) [*andar, correr*] quickly • **ella corrió ~ por el puente** she ran quickly over the bridge • **venga, ~, que nos vamos** get a move on, we're going • **de ~** rashly, thoughtlessly

light [laɪt] ADJ INV [*tabaco*] low-tar (*antes de s*); [*comida*] low-calorie; [*plan, política*] watered-down, toned-down

lignito SM lignite

ligón¹ SM hoe

ligón²/ona* ADJ **1** [*persona*] flirtatious • **es muy ~** he's a great one for the girls
2 [*prenda*] (= *bonita*) attractive; (= *sexy*) provocative, sexy
SM/F • **es una ligona** she's successful with the men, she has no problem pulling the men*

ligoteo* SM • **es un sitio de ~** it's a pick-up joint* • **ese amigo tuyo siempre está de ~** that friend of yours is always on the pull*, that friend of yours is always after the women *o* eyeing up the talent* • **el ~ electrónico** computer dating

ligue* SM **1** (= *conquista*) • **ir de ~** to look for sb to get off with*, go eyeing up the talent*
2 (= *amorío*) affair
SMF (= *persona*) pick-up*, date, boyfriend/girlfriend ▸ **ligue de una noche** one-night stand

liguero¹ SM suspender belt, garter belt (*EEUU*)

liguero² ADJ (*Dep*) league (*antes de s*) • **líder ~** league leader

liguilla SF (*Dep*) (= *torneo*) small tournament; (*para ascender*) mini-league, *group of teams which play off to determine promotion*

ligur (*Hist*) ADJ Ligurian
SMF Ligurian • **los ~os** the Ligurians, the people of Liguria

ligustro SM privet

lija SF **1** (*Zool*) dogfish
2 (*Téc*) (= *papel de lija*) sandpaper ▸ **lija esmeril** emery paper
3 • **darse ~** (*Caribe**) to give o.s. airs

lijadora SF sander, sanding machine

lijar ▹ CONJUG 1a VT to sandpaper, sand down

lijoso* ADJ (*Caribe*) vain, stuck-up*

Lila SF Lille

lila¹ SF (*Bot*) lilac

lila² (SM) **1** (= *color*) lilac
2 (= *idiota*) twit*, wimp*; (= *crédulo*) sucker*
lila³‡ (SM) (*Esp*) 5000 pesetas
lilailas* (SFPL) tricks
lile* (ADJ) (*Cono Sur*) weak, sickly
liliche* (SM) (*CAm*) piece of junk
liliputiense (ADJ), (SMF) Lilliputian
liliquear* ▷ CONJUG 1a (VI) (*Chile*) to tremble nervously, shake
Lima (SF) Lima
lima¹ (SF) (*Bot*) lime, sweet-lime tree
lima² (SF) (*Téc*) **1** (= *herramienta*) file
• MODISMO: • **comer como una ~** to eat like a horse ▸ **lima de uñas, lima para las uñas** nail file, fingernail file (*EEUU*)
2 (= *pulido*) [*de superficie*] polishing • **dar la última ~ a una obra** to put the finishing touches to a work
lima³†‡ (SF) (= *camisa*) shirt
limadura (SF) **1** (*gen*) filing
2 limaduras (= *virutas*) filings
limar ▷ CONJUG 1a (VT) **1** (*Téc*) (*con lima*) to file down, file off
2 [+ *uñas*] to file
3 (= *pulir*) [+ *artículo, obra*] to polish up; [+ *diferencias*] to iron out
limatón (SM) (*LAm*) crossbeam, roofbeam
limaza (SF) slug
limazo (SM) slime, sliminess
limbo (SM) **1** (*Bot, Mat*) limb
2 (*Rel*) limbo • **estar en el ~** (*Rel*) to be in limbo; (= *estar distraído*) to be miles away
limeño/a (ADJ) of/from Lima
(SM/F) native/inhabitant of Lima • **los ~s** the people of Lima
limero (SM) lime (tree)
limeta (SF) **1** (*Cono Sur*) (= *frente*) broad brow; (= *calva*) bald head
2 (*LAm*) (= *botella*) flagon, bottle
liminar (ADJ) preliminary, introductory
limitación (SF) **1** (= *restricción*) limitation • **exigen la ~ de los poderes del gobierno** they demand a limitation of the government's powers • **intervinieron todos los diputados sin ~ de tiempo** all the MPs took part without being subject to a time limit ▸ **limitación de armamentos** arms limitation ▸ **limitación de velocidad** speed limit
2 limitaciones (= *deficiencias*) limitations • **no lo haré porque conozco mis limitaciones** I won't do it because I know my limitations
limitado (ADJ) **1** (*gen*) limited • **sociedad limitada** (*Com*) limited company, corporation (*EEUU*)
2 (= *lerdo*) slow-witted, dim*
limitador (SM) (*Aut*) limiter ▸ **limitador de ruido** limiter ▸ **limitador de velocidad** speed limiter
limitante (SF) (*Cono Sur*) limitation
limitar ▷ CONJUG 1a (VT) (= *restringir*) to limit, restrict • **nos han limitado el número de visitas** they have limited *o* restricted the number of visits we can have • **~on el tiempo del examen a dos horas** the exam time was limited to two hours • **hay que ~ el consumo de alcohol entre los adolescentes** alcohol consumption among young people should be restricted
(VI) • **~ con** to border on • **España limita al norte con Francia** Spain borders on France to the north
(VPR) **limitarse** • **~se a hacer algo** to limit *o* confine o.s. to doing sth • **no nos limitemos a tratar los aspectos económicos** let's not limit *o* confine ourselves to the economic aspects • **me he limitado a corregir unos cuantos errores** all I've done is correct a few mistakes, I've just corrected a few mistakes, that's all • **tú limítate a escuchar** just be quiet and listen
limitativo (ADJ), **limitatorio** (ADJ) limiting, restrictive
límite (SM) **1** (*gen*) limit • **podrá presentarse cualquiera, sin ~ de edad** anyone can apply, regardless *o* irrespective of age, anyone can apply, there's no age limit • **eran exámenes larguísimos, sin ~ de tiempo** the exams were very long, there was no time limit • **como** *o* **de ~**: • **tenemos como** *o* **de ~ el sábado para presentar el trabajo** the deadline for submitting our work is Saturday • **poner (un) ~ a**: • **han puesto un ~ de participantes** they have put a limit *o* restriction on the number of participants • **nos pusieron un ~ de dinero para gastar** they put a restriction on *o* limited the amount of money we had to spend • **quieren poner ~ a sus ambiciones políticas** they want to limit his political ambitions • **pretenden poner ~ a la investigación sobre embriones** they aim to put tighter controls on research into embryos, they aim to restrict *o* curb research into embryos • **sin ~s** limitless • **no tener ~s** to know no bounds ▸ **límite de crédito** (*Com*) credit limit ▸ **límite de gastos** spending limit ▸ **límite de velocidad** speed limit
2 (*Geog, Pol*) boundary, border ▸ **límite forestal** tree line, timber line
3 (*Inform*) ▸ **límite de página** page break
4 (= *final*) end
(ADJ INV) extreme, maximum • **caso ~** extreme case • **competición ~** out-and-out contest • **concentración ~** maximum concentration • **jornada ~ semanal** maximum possible working week • **sentencia ~** definitive ruling • **situaciones ~** extreme situations • **someter una máquina a pruebas ~** to test a machine to the limit
limítrofe (ADJ) bordering, neighbouring, neighboring (*EEUU*)
limo (SM) **1** (= *barro*) slime, mud
2‡ (= *bolso*) handbag, purse (*EEUU*)
limón (SM) **1** (*Bot*) lemon; (*Caribe*) lime
2 limones‡ tits‡
limonada (SF) (*natural*) lemonade; (*artificial*) lemon squash ▸ **limonada natural** fresh lemonade, lemonade (*EEUU*); ▷ **chicha¹**
limonado (ADJ) lemon, lemon-coloured, lemon-colored (*EEUU*)
limonar (SM) lemon grove
limonero (SM) lemon tree
limosina (SF) limousine
limosna (SF) charity, alms† • **¡una ~, señor!** can you spare something, sir? • **pedir ~** to beg • **vivir de ~** to live by begging, live on charity
limosnear ▷ CONJUG 1a (VI) to beg
limosnera (SF) collecting tin (*for charity*)
limosnero/a (ADJ) (= *caritativo*) charitable
(SM/F) **1** (*Hist*) almoner
2 (*LAm*) (= *mendigo*) beggar
limoso (ADJ) slimy, muddy
limpia (SF) **1** (= *acto de limpiar*) cleaning
2 (*CAm, Méx*) (*Agr*) weeding, clearing
3 (*Pol*) (= *purga*) clean-up, purge
4 (*And, Cono Sur, Méx*) (= *azotes*) beating
(SM) **1*** (= *persona*) bootblack; (= *niño*) shoeshine boy
2 (*Aut*) windscreen wiper, windshield wiper (*EEUU*)
limpiabarros (SM INV) (= *utensilio*) scraper, boot scraper; (= *felpudo*) doormat
limpiabotas (SMF INV) bootblack
limpiacabezales (SM INV) head-cleaner
limpiachimeneas (SMF INV) chimney sweep
limpiacoches (SMF INV) (= *persona*) street car-washer
limpiacristales (SM INV) **1** (= *líquido*) window-cleaning fluid; (= *trapo*) cleaning cloth
2 (*Aut*) windscreen wiper
(SMF INV) (= *persona*) window cleaner
limpiada (SF) **1** (*LAm*) (= *acto de limpiar*) clean, clean-up
2 (*Cono Sur*) (*en bosque*) clearing
limpiadientes (SM INV) toothpick
limpiador(a) (ADJ) [*líquido, crema*] cleansing
(SM/F) (= *persona*) cleaner
limpiadura (SF) **1** (= *acto de limpiar*) cleaning, cleaning-up
2 limpiaduras dirt (*sing*), dust (*sing*), scourings
limpiafaros (SM INV) headlamp wiper
limpiahogares (SM INV) household cleaning fluid
limpiahornos (SM INV) oven cleaner
limpialuneta (SM) ▸ **limpialuneta trasero, limpialuneta posterior** rear window screen wiper, rear wiper
limpiamanos (SM INV) (*CAm, Méx*) hand towel
limpiamente (ADV) **1** (= *con pulcritud*) cleanly
2 (= *honestamente*) honestly • **nos ganaron ~** they beat us fair and square
3 (= *hábilmente*) skilfully, skillfully (*EEUU*) • **hace las jugadas muy ~** he makes the moves with great skill, he makes the moves very neatly
limpiametales (SM INV) metal polish
limpiamuebles (SM INV) furniture polish
limpiaparabrisas (SM INV) windscreen wiper, windshield wiper (*EEUU*)
limpiapiés (SM INV) (= *utensilio*) scraper, boot scraper; (*Méx*) (= *estera*) doormat
limpiapipas (SM INV) pipe cleaner
limpiaplicador (SM) (*Méx*) cotton bud, Q-tip® (*EEUU*)
limpiaplumas (SM INV) penwiper
limpiar ▷ CONJUG 1b (VT) **1** [+ *casa*] to tidy, tidy up, clean; [+ *cara, piel*] to cleanse; [+ *marca*] to wipe off, clean off; [+ *maquillaje*] to remove; [+ *zapatos*] to polish, shine • **~ en seco** to dry-clean
2 (*Culin*) [+ *conejo*] to clean; [+ *pescado*] to gut
3 (= *enjugar*) to wipe, wipe off • **~ las narices a un niño** to wipe a child's nose
4 (*Mil*) to mop up; (*Policía*) to clean up
5 (*Bot*) to prune, cut back
6* (*en el juego*) to clean out*
7‡ (= *robar*) to swipe*, nick*
8 (*Méx**) (= *pegar*) to hit, bash*, beat up
9‡ (= *matar*) to do in‡
(VPR) **limpiarse** to clean o.s., wipe o.s. • **~se las narices** to blow one's nose
limpiaventanas (SMF INV) **1** (= *persona*) window cleaner
2 (= *líquido*) window-cleaning fluid
limpiavía (SM) (*LAm*) cowcatcher
limpiavidrios (SM INV) (*LAm*) (= *líquido*) window cleaner
(SM/SF INV) (*LAm*) (= *persona*) window cleaner
(SM) (*Méx*) (= *limpiaparabrisas*) windscreen wiper (*Brit*), windshield wiper (*EEUU*)
límpido (ADJ) (*frm*) limpid
limpieza (SF) **1** (= *acción*) cleaning • **la mujer** *o* **señora de la ~** the cleaning lady • **hacer la ~** to do the cleaning ▸ **limpieza en seco** dry cleaning ▸ **limpieza general** spring cleaning
2 (*Pol*) purge; (*Mil*) mopping-up; (*Policía*) clean-up ▸ **limpieza étnica** ethnic cleansing
3 (= *estado*) cleanness ▸ **limpieza de sangre** racial purity
4 • **con ~** (= *con integridad*) fair and square • **nos ha ganado con ~** he beat us fair and square
5 (= *destreza*) skill • **hace las jugadas con mucha ~** he makes the moves with great

skill, he makes the moves very neatly

limpio ADJ 1 [casa, cuarto] clean • ~ de algo free from sth, clear of sth • MODISMO: • más ~ que los chorros del oro as clean as can be
2 (= despejado) clear • el cielo estaba ~ de nubes there was a cloudless sky, there was not a cloud in the sky
3 [líquidos] pure, clean
4 (en lo moral) pure; (= honesto) honest
5 (Dep) [jugada] fair
6 (Econ) clear, net • 50 dólares de ganancia limpia 50 dollars of clear profit
7* (= sin dinero) • estar ~ to be broke • quedar(se) ~* to be cleaned out*
8* (enfático) • MODISMOS: • a pedrada limpia: • se defendieron a pedrada limpia they defended themselves with nothing but stones • a puñetazo ~ with bare fists
SM 1 • en ~ (Econ) clear, net • copia en ~ fair copy • pasar o poner algo en ~ to make a fair o neat o clean copy of sth • poner un texto en ~ to tidy a text up, produce a final version of a text • MODISMO: • sacar algo en ~ to make sense of sth • no pude sacar nada en ~ I couldn't make anything of it
2 (Méx) (= claro de bosque) clearing (in a wood), treeless area, bare ground
ADV • jugar ~ to play fair

limpión SM 1 (= acto) wipe, (quick) clean • dar un ~ a algo to give sth a wipe
2† (= trapo) cleaning rag, cleaning cloth; (And, CAm, Caribe) dishcloth
3† (= persona) cleaner
4 (And*) (= regañina) ticking-off*

limpito ADJ nice and clean

limusina SF limousine

lina SF (Cono Sur) 1 [de lana] skein of coarse wool
2 (= trenza) pigtail, long hair

linaje SM 1 (= familia) lineage, descent • de ~ de reyes descended from royalty, of royal descent • de ~ honrado of good parentage
2 (= clase) class, kind • de otro ~ of another kind ▸ linaje humano mankind
3 linajes (= familias) (local) nobility (sing), noble families

linajudo ADJ highborn, noble, blue-blooded

linar SM flax field

linaza SF linseed

lince SM 1 (Zool) lynx; (CAm, Méx) wild cat • MODISMOS: • ser un ~ (= observador) to be very sharp-eyed; (= astuto) to be very shrewd o sharp • tener ojos de ~ to be very sharp-eyed ▸ lince ibérico pardal lynx, Spanish lynx
2 (LAm) (= agudeza) sharpness
ADJ • MODISMOS: • ojos ~s eagle eyes • es muy ~ (= observador) he's very sharp-eyed; (= astuto) he's very shrewd o sharp

linchamiento SM lynching

linchar ▹ CONJUG 1a VT to lynch

linche SM (And) (= mochila) knapsack; linches (Méx†) (= alforjas) saddlebags

lindamente ADV 1 (= con belleza) prettily; (= con delicadeza) daintily; (= con elegancia) elegantly
2 (iró) well
3 (esp LAm) (= excelentemente) excellently, marvellously

lindante ADJ bordering (con on), adjacent (con to), adjoining

lindar ▹ CONJUG 1a VI • ~ con: mis tierras lindan con las suyas my land borders on theirs • el banco linda con el ayuntamiento the bank is adjacent to the town hall • eso linda con el racismo that is bordering on racism

linde SM o SF boundary

lindero ADJ (= limítrofe) adjoining, bordering
SM (= borde) edge, border; (= linde) boundary

lindeza SF 1 (= belleza) prettiness
2 (esp LAm) (= amabilidad) niceness
3 lindezas (= cosas bonitas) pretty things; (iró) (= insultos) insults, improprieties
4 (= ocurrencia) witticism

lindo ADJ (esp LAm) 1 (= bonito) nice, lovely, pretty • un ~ coche a nice car, a fine car
2 (iró) fine, pretty
3 (= excelente) fine, excellent, first-rate • un ~ partido a first-rate game • un ~ concierto a good concert • MODISMO: • de lo ~ a lot, a great deal • jugaron de lo ~ they played fantastically, they played a first-rate game
ADV (LAm) nicely, well • baila ~ she dances beautifully
SM (Hist) fop

lindura SF 1 (esp Cono Sur) (= belleza) prettiness, loveliness • está hecha una ~* she looks really pretty o lovely
2 (Caribe, Cono Sur) (= campeón) ace, champion; (= experto) expert • ella es una ~ en el vestir she dresses beautifully
3 (LAm) (= objeto) lovely thing

línea SF 1 (= raya) line • dibujó una ~ recta he drew a straight line • primera ~ de playa sea-front • en ~ (= alineado) in (a) line, in a row • en ~ recta in a straight line • tirar una ~ (Arte) to draw a line • en toda la ~ [ganar, vencer] outright; [derrotar] totally • MODISMO: • ser de una o una sola ~ (Caribe, Cono Sur*) to be as straight as a die, be absolutely straight ▸ línea a trazos broken line ▸ línea de base (Agrimensura) base-line ▸ línea de cambio de fecha International Date Line ▸ línea de carga load-line ▸ línea de flotación (Náut) water line ▸ línea de la vida life line ▸ línea del biquini bikini line ▸ línea de montaje assembly line, production line ▸ línea de puntos dotted line ▸ línea discontinua (Aut) broken line ▸ línea divisoria dividing line
2 (en un escrito) line • leer entre ~s to read between the lines • MODISMO: • poner unas ~s a algn to drop a line to sb
3 (Com) (= género, gama) line • es único en su ~ it is unique in its line, it is the only one of its kind • en esa ~ no tenemos nada we have nothing in that line • de primera ~ first-rate, top-ranking ▸ línea blanca white goods (pl) ▸ línea marrón brown goods (pl)
4 (Elec) line, cable ▸ línea aérea overhead cable ▸ línea de alta tensión high-tension cable ▸ línea de conducción eléctrica power line
5 (Telec) line • me he quedado sin ~ I've been cut off • han cortado la ~ I've o we've been cut off ▸ línea caliente hot line ▸ línea compartida shared line ▸ línea derivada extension ▸ línea de socorro helpline, telephone helpline ▸ línea directa direct line ▸ línea erótica sex-line ▸ línea exterior outside line ▸ línea gratuita freephone ▸ línea roja hot line ▸ línea telefónica telephone line ▸ línea (telefónica) de ayuda helpline, telephone helpline
6 (Mil) line • cerrar ~s to close ranks • de ~ regular, front-line • primera ~ front line ▸ línea de alto el fuego ceasefire line ▸ línea de batalla line of battle, battle line ▸ línea de fuego firing line
7 (Aer, Ferro) • autobús de ~ service bus, regular bus ▸ línea aérea airline ▸ línea de abastecimiento supply line ▸ línea férrea railway, railroad (EEUU) ▸ línea regular scheduled service
8 (Dep) line ▸ línea de balón muerto dead-ball line ▸ línea de banda sideline, touchline ▸ línea de centro halfway line ▸ línea de fondo by-line ▸ línea de gol goal line ▸ línea delantera forward line ▸ línea de llegada finishing line ▸ línea de medio campo halfway line ▸ línea de meta (en fútbol) goal line; (en carrera) finishing line ▸ línea de puerta goal line ▸ línea de saque baseline, service line ▸ línea de toque touchline ▸ línea lateral sideline, touchline
9 (Inform) • en ~ on-line • fuera de ~ off-line ▸ línea de estado, línea de situación status line
10 (= talle) figure • guardar o conservar la ~ to keep one's figure (trim)
11 (= moda) • la ~ de 2009 the 2009 look
12 [de pensamiento, acción] line • explicar algo a grandes ~s o en sus ~s generales to set sth out in broad outline, give the broad outline of sth ▸ línea de conducta course of action ▸ línea de partido party line ▸ línea dura (Pol) hard line
13 (genealógica) line • en ~ directa in an unbroken line ▸ línea de sangre blood line ▸ línea sucesoria line of succession, order of succession
SMF (Dep) linesman, assistant referee

lineal ADJ (gen) linear; (Inform) on-line • aumento ~ de sueldos across-the-board pay increase • dibujo ~ line drawing • impuesto ~ flat-rate tax

linealidad SF linearity

lineamento SM lineament

linear ▹ CONJUG 1a VT 1 (gen) to line, draw lines on
2 (Arte) to sketch, outline

linense ADJ of/from La Línea
SMF native/inhabitant of La Línea • los ~s the people of La Línea

linfa SF lymph

linfático ADJ lymphatic

linfocito SM (Med) lymphocyte

lingotazo* SM swig*, shot*

lingote SM ingot

lingüista SMF linguist

lingüística SF linguistics (sing) ▸ lingüística aplicada applied linguistics ▸ lingüística computacional computational linguistics ▸ lingüística de contrastes contrastive linguistics

lingüístico ADJ linguistic

linier SMF (PL: liniers) (Dep) linesman, assistant referee

linimento SM liniment

lino SM 1 (Bot) flax
2 (Cono Sur) (= linaza) linseed
3 (= ropa fina) linen; (= lona) canvas • géneros de ~ linen goods

linóleo SM lino, linoleum

linón SM lawn (fabric)

linotipia SF, **linotipo** SM linotype

linotipista SMF linotype operator

linterna SF 1 (eléctrica) torch, flashlight (EEUU); (= farolillo) lantern ▸ linterna mágica magic lantern ▸ linterna roja back marker
2 (Arquit) lantern
3 linternas (Méx) (hum) (= ojos) eyes

linyera SM (Cono Sur) (= vagabundo) tramp, bum (EEUU*)

lío SM 1 (= fardo) bundle; (Cono Sur) truss
2* (= jaleo) fuss; (= confusión) muddle, mix-up • ese lío de los pasaportes that fuss about the passports • en mi mesa hay un lío enorme de papeles my desk is in a real muddle with all these bits of paper • armar un lío to make a fuss, kick up a fuss • armarse un lío: • se armó un lío tremendo there was a terrific fuss • hacerse un lío to get into a muddle, get mixed up • se hizo un lío con tantos nombres he got into a muddle with all the names

3 (= *aprieto*) • **meterse en un lío** to get into trouble
4* (= *amorío*) affair • **tener un lío con algn** to be having an affair with sb ▸ **lío de faldas** affair
5 (= *cotilleo*) tale, piece of gossip • **¡no me vengas con líos!** less of your tales!
liofilizado (ADJ) freeze-dried
liofilizar ▷ CONJUG 1f (VT) to freeze-dry
Liorna† (SF) Leghorn
lioso (ADJ) gossipy
lipa (SF) (*Caribe*) belly
lipes (SF INV) (*LAm*) (*tb* **piedra lipes**) blue vitriol
lipidia (SF) 1 (*CAm*) (= *pobreza*) poverty
2 (*Chile, Perú*) (= *diarrea*) the runs*
(SMF) (*Caribe, Méx*) nuisance, pest
lipidiar ▷ CONJUG 1b (VT) (*Caribe, Méx*) to annoy, bother, pester
lipidioso (ADJ) (*Caribe, Méx*) (= *impertinente*) cheeky; (= *molesto*) annoying
lipoaspiración (SF) liposuction
lipocito (SM) fat particle
lipoescultura (SF) liposculpture
lipólisis (SF INV) lipolysis
lipón (ADJ) (*Caribe*) fat, pot-bellied
lipoplastia (SF) liposculpture
liposoma (SM) liposome
liposucción (SF) liposuction
lipotimia (SF) faint, blackout
lique‡† (SM) kick • **dar el ~ a algn** to kick sb out • **darse el ~** to clear out*
liquen (SM) lichen
líquida (SF) (*Ling*) liquid
liquidación (SF) 1 (*Com, Econ*) [*de compañía, negocio*] liquidation, winding-up; [*de cuenta, deuda*] settlement • **entrar en ~** to go into liquidation • **vender en ~** to sell up ▸ **liquidación forzosa, liquidación obligatoria** compulsory liquidation
2 (= *rebajas*) sale • **venta de ~** (clearance) sale ▸ **liquidación por cierre del negocio** closing-down sale ▸ **liquidación por fin de temporada** end-of-season sale
3 (*por despido*) redundancy pay • **oficina** *o* **sección de ~** accounts section, payments office
4 (*Quím*) liquefaction
5 (*Pol*) liquidation
liquidador(a) (SM/F) liquidator
liquidar ▷ CONJUG 1a (VT) 1 [+ *cuenta*] to settle; [+ *empresa, negocio*] to wind up, liquidate; [+ *deuda*] to settle, pay off, clear; [+ *existencias*] to sell off, sell up
2 [+ *asunto, problema*] to deal with • **ya hemos liquidado la cuestión** we've dealt with that issue now • **le pides perdón y asunto liquidado** just say you are sorry and that'll be the end of it
3* (= *gastar*) to go through*, blow* • **ha liquidado en un mes todos sus ahorros** she went through *o* blew all her savings in one month
4* (= *matar*) to bump off*
5 (*Pol*) (= *eliminar*) to liquidate
6 (*LAm*) (= *destrozar*) to destroy, ruin
7 (*Méx*) [+ *obreros*] to pay off
8 (*Quím*) to liquefy
(VPR) **liquidarse** 1* (= *gastarse*) to blow* • **se han liquidado todos sus ahorros** they have blown all their savings
2 (*Quím*) to liquefy
liquidez (SF) 1 [*de líquido, sustancia*] liquidity, fluidity
2 (*Econ*) liquidity
líquido (ADJ) 1 [*sustancia*] liquid, fluid • **el ~ elemento** water
2 (*Econ*) net • **ganancia líquida** net profit
3 (*CAm, Méx*) (= *exacto*) exact • **cuatro varas líquidas** exactly four yards
4 (*Ling*) liquid
(SM) 1 (*gen*) liquid, fluid ▸ **líquido anticongelante** antifreeze ▸ **líquido de frenos** brake fluid ▸ **líquidos corporales** body fluids ▸ **líquido seminal** seminal fluid ▸ **líquido sinovial** synovial fluid
2 (*Econ*) (= *efectivo*) ready cash, ready money ▸ **líquido imponible** net taxable income
liquiliqui (SM) (*Caribe*) Venezuelan national dress
lira (SF) 1 (*Mús*) lyre
2 (*Literat*) *5-line stanza popular in the 16th century*
3 (= *moneda*) lira
lírica (SF) lyrical poetry
lírico/a (ADJ) 1 (*Literat*) lyric(al); (*Teat*) musical
2 (*LAm*) [*persona*] full of idealistic plans; [*plan, idea*] Utopian, fantastic
(SM/F) (*LAm*) (= *soñador*) dreamer, Utopian
lirio (SM) iris ▸ **lirio de los valles** lily of the valley
lirismo (SM) 1 (*gen*) lyricism
2 (*LAm*) (= *sueños*) dreams (*pl*), Utopia; (= *manera de ser*) fantasy, Utopianism
lirón (SM) 1 (*Zool*) dormouse
2 (= *dormilón*) sleepyhead • MODISMO: • **dormir como un ~** to sleep like a log
lirondo (ADJ) ▷ **mondo**
lis (SF) lily
lisa (SF) 1 (*Caribe**) (= *cerveza*) beer
2 (*And*) (= *pez*) mullet; ▷ **liso**
lisamente (ADV) evenly, smoothly
Lisboa (SF) Lisbon
lisboeta, lisbonense (ADJ) of/from Lisbon
(SMF) native/inhabitant of Lisbon • **los ~s** the people of Lisbon
lisérgico (ADJ) • **ácido ~** lysergic acid
lisiado/a (ADJ) crippled, lame
(SM/F) cripple • **un ~ de guerra** a wounded ex-serviceman
lisiar ▷ CONJUG 1b (VT) (*gen*) to injure (permanently), hurt (seriously); (= *tullir*) to cripple, maim
liso (ADJ) 1 [*terreno, superficie*] smooth, even; [*neumático*] bald • MODISMO: • **~ como la palma de la mano** as smooth as glass
2 [*pelo*] straight
3 [*mar*] calm
4 (*Dep*) • **los 400 metros ~s** the 400-metre flat race
5 (= *sin adornos*) plain, unadorned; (= *de un solo color*) plain • MODISMOS: • **irse ~** (*Caribe**) to leave without a word • **la tiene lisa*** he's got it made* • **lisa y llanamente** (= *en términos sencillos*) plainly, in plain language; (= *evidentemente*) quite simply • **~ y llano** plain, simple, straightforward
6 (*And, Cono Sur*) (= *grosero*) rude
7 (*LAm**) (= *descarado*) fresh*, cheeky, sassy (EEUU)
8* (= *de poco pecho*) flat-chested
(SM) (*Cono Sur*) tall beer glass; ▷ **lisa**
lisol (SM) lysol
lisonja (SF) flattery
lisonjear ▷ CONJUG 1a (VT) 1 (= *alabar*) to flatter
2 (= *agradar*) to please, delight
lisonjeramente (ADV) 1 (= *aduladoramente*) flatteringly
2 (= *agradablemente*) pleasingly, agreeably
lisonjero/a (ADJ) 1 (= *adulador*) flattering
2 (= *agradable*) pleasing, agreeable
(SM/F) flatterer
lista (SF) 1 [*de nombres, elementos*] list; (*Mil*) roll, roll call; (*en escuela*) register, school list (EEUU) • **pasar ~** (*Mil*) to call the roll; (*Escol*) to call the register • MODISMO: • **pasar ~ a algn** to call sb to account ▸ **lista cerrada** (*Pol*) closed list ▸ **lista de boda** wedding list ▸ **lista de comidas** menu ▸ **lista de correos** poste restante, general delivery (*EEUU*) ▸ **lista de direcciones** mailing list ▸ **lista de encuentros** (*Dep*) fixture list ▸ **lista de espera** waiting list ▸ **lista de éxitos** (*Mús*) charts (*pl*) ▸ **lista de pagos** payroll ▸ **lista de platos** menu ▸ **lista de precios** price list ▸ **lista de premios** honours list ▸ **lista de raya** (*Méx*) payroll ▸ **lista de tandas** duty roster, rota ▸ **lista de vinos** wine list ▸ **lista electoral** electoral roll, register of voters ▸ **lista negra** blacklist ▸ **listas de audiencia** ratings, audience rating (*sing*)
2 (= *tira*) [*de tela*] strip; [*de papel*] slip
3 (= *raya*) stripe • **tela a ~s** striped material
listadillo (SM) (*And, Caribe, Méx*) striped, (white and blue) cotton cloth
listado¹ (ADJ) striped
(SM) (*And, Caribe*) = **listadillo**
listado² (SM) (= *lista*) list, listing; (*Com, Inform*) listing, printout ▸ **listado de comprobación** checklist ▸ **listado paginado** paged listing
listar ▷ CONJUG 1a (VT) to list, enter on a list; (*Inform*) to list
listeria (SF) listeria
listero/a (SM/F) timekeeper, wages clerk
listillo/a (SM/F) know-all, smart Aleck*
listín (SM) 1 (*Telec*) ▸ **listín telefónico, listín de teléfonos** telephone directory
2 (*Caribe*) (= *periódico*) newspaper
listo (ADJ) 1 (= *dispuesto*) ready • **¿estás ~?** are you ready? • **me pongo las lentillas y ~** I'll just put my lenses in and I'll be ready • **¡preparados, ~s, ya!** ready, steady, go! • **la cena está ya lista** dinner's ready • **~ para algo** ready for sth • **todo está ~ para el concierto** everything is ready for the concert • **¿~s para el ataque?** ready to attack? • **"listo para usar"** "ready to use", "ready for use" • **ya estoy lista para salir** I'm ready to go out
2 (= *terminado*) finished • **una última lectura y ~** one last read through and that's it *o* it's finished • **la traducción tendrá que estar lista para mañana** the translation will have to be finished for tomorrow • MODISMO: • **estar** *o* **ir ~***: • **pues está lista si espera que yo la llame** well, if she expects me to call her she's got another think coming • **¿que quieres ir al cine? ¡estás ~!** so you want to go to the cinema? no way!* • **—el tren va con retraso —¡pues estamos ~s!** "the train is running late" — "well, we've had it now!*" *o* we've really had it now!*"
3 (= *inteligente*) clever, bright, smart* • **el más ~ de la clase** the cleverest *o* brightest *o* smartest* in the class • **¿te crees muy lista, verdad?** you think you're really smart, don't you? • **tú, ~, ¿a qué no sabes una cosa?** (*iró*) OK, cleverclogs *o* wise guy, I bet you don't know this* • **se las da de ~** he thinks he's so clever • **va de lista por la vida** she goes round thinking she knows it all • **pasarse de ~** to be too clever by half • MODISMO: • **ser más ~ que el hambre** to be as sharp as a needle
4 (*Chile, Col, Perú*) (= *de acuerdo*) OK • **¡listo!** OK!
(SMF) 1 (= *inteligente*) clever one, smart one*
2 (*pey*) cleverclogs*, smart arse**, smart ass (EEUU‡) • **siempre hay algún ~ que te hace una pregunta** there's always some cleverclogs* *o* smart arse** who asks you a question
listón (SM) 1 [*de madera*] strip, lath; (*Dep*) bar; [*de goma, metal*] strip; (*Arquit*) fillet
2 (= *nivel*) level • **bajar el ~** to make things too easy ▸ **listón de la pobreza** poverty line ▸ **listón de los precios** price level
3 (*Cos*) ribbon
lisura (SF) 1 [*de terreno, superficie*] evenness, smoothness; [*de pelo*] straightness; [*del mar*]

calmness
2 (= *sinceridad*) sincerity; (= *ingenuidad*) naïvety
3 (*And, Cono Sur*) (= *grosería*) rude remark, cheeky remark
4 (*LAm*) (= *descaro*) impudence, brazenness

lisurero ADJ (*Perú*), **lisuriento** ADJ (*Perú*) rude, cheeky, sassy (*EEUU*)

litera SF **1** (*en alcoba*) bunk, bunk bed; (*Náut, Ferro*) bunk, berth; (*Ferro*) couchette
2 (*Hist*) (= *carruaje*) litter

literal ADJ literal

literalmente ADV literally (*tb fig*)

literario ADJ literary

literato/a SM/F man/woman of letters

literatura SF literature ▸ **literatura comparada** (study of) comparative literature ▸ **literatura de evasión** escapist literature ▸ **literatura de kiosco** cheap literature

litigación SF litigation

litigante SMF litigant

litigar ▹ CONJUG 1h VT to dispute at law
VI **1** (*Jur*) to go to law
2 (*frm*) (= *discutir*) to argue, dispute

litigio SM **1** (*Jur*) litigation; (= *pleito*) lawsuit
2 (*frm*) (= *disputa*) dispute • **en ~** in dispute • **el asunto en ~** the matter under debate

litigioso ADJ litigious, contentious

litio SM lithium

litisexpensas SFPL (*Jur*) costs

litografía SF **1** (= *proceso*) lithography
2 (= *cuadro*) lithograph

litografiar ▹ CONJUG 1c VT to lithograph

litográfico ADJ lithographic

litoral ADJ coastal, littoral (*frm*)
SM seaboard, coast, littoral (*frm*)

litre SM (*Cono Sur*) rash

litri* ADJ affected, dandified

litro¹ SM litre, liter (*EEUU*); ▹ KILOS, METROS, AÑOS

litro² SM (*Cono Sur*) coarse woollen *o* (*EEUU*) woolen cloth

litrona* SF litre *o* (*EEUU*) liter bottle

Lituania SF Lithuania

lituano/a ADJ Lithuanian
SM/F Lithuanian • **los ~s** the Lithuanians, the people of Lithuania
SM (*Ling*) Lithuanian

liturgia SF liturgy

litúrgico ADJ liturgical

livianamente ADV **1** (= *de forma inconstante*) in a fickle way
2 (= *frívolamente*) frivolously, in a trivial way
3 (= *lascivamente*) lewdly

liviandad SF **1** (= *de poco peso*) lightness
2 (= *inconstancia*) fickleness
3 (= *frivolidad*) frivolity, triviality
4 (= *lascivia*) lewdness

liviano ADJ **1** (= *ligero*) light
2 (= *inconstante*) fickle
3 (= *frívolo*) frivolous, trivial
4 (= *lascivo*) lewd
SMPL **livianos** lights, lungs

lividez SF **1** (= *palidez*) pallor, paleness
2 (= *amoratamiento*) lividness

lívido ADJ **1** (= *pálido*) pallid, pale, livid
2 (= *amoratado*) black and blue, livid

living ['liβin] SM (PL: **livings** ['liβin]) (*LAm*) living room, lounge

lixiviar ▹ CONJUG 1b VT to leach
VPR **lixiviarse** to leach

liza SF (*Hist*) lists (*pl*); (*fig*) contest

Ll, ll ['eʎe] SF *combination of consonants forming one letter in the Spanish alphabet but treated as separate letters for alphabetization purposes*

llacsa SF (*Cono Sur*) molten metal

llaga SF **1** (= *úlcera*) ulcer, sore • MODISMO: • **¡por las ~s (de Cristo)!** damnation!
2 (= *sufrimiento*) affliction, torment • **las ~s de la guerra** the havoc of war, the afflictions of war • MODISMO: • **renovar la ~** to open up an old wound; ▹ **dedo**

llagar ▹ CONJUG 1h VT to cause a sore on, wound

llalla SF (*Cono Sur*) = **yaya**

llama¹ SF (*Zool*) llama

llama² SF **1** [*de fuego*] flame • **arder sin ~** to smoulder, smolder (*EEUU*) • **en ~s** burning, ablaze, in flames • **entregar algo a las ~s** to commit sth to the flames • **estallar en ~s** to burst into flames • MODISMO: • **salir de las ~s y caer en las brasas** to jump out of the frying pan into the fire ▸ **llama piloto** pilot light (*on stove*) ▸ **llama solar** solar flare
2 [*de amor, pasión*] flame, fire; [*de esperanza, libertad*] spark

llamada SF **1** (*Telec*) call • **gracias por su ~** thank you for your call • **ahora le paso la ~** I'll put you through now • **devolver una ~** to phone back • **hacer una ~** to make a call • **desde este teléfono no se pueden hacer ~s al extranjero** you can't make international calls from this telephone • **¿puedo hacer una ~?** can I use your phone?, can I make a call? ▸ **llamada a cobro revertido** reverse charge call, collect call (*EEUU*) ▸ **llamada a larga distancia, llamada de larga distancia** (*LAm*) long-distance call, trunk call ▸ **llamada internacional** international call ▸ **llamada interprovincial** *call made between towns in different provinces* ▸ **llamada interurbana** *call made between different towns within the same province* ▸ **llamada local, llamada metropolitana** local call ▸ **llamada nacional** national call ▸ **llamada por cobrar** (*Chile, Méx*) = **llamada a cobro revertido** ▸ **llamada provincial** = **llamada interurbana** ▸ **llamada telefónica** telephone call ▸ **llamada urbana** local call
2 (*a la puerta*) (*con el puño*) knock; (*con el timbre*) ring
3 (= *aviso*) call • **última ~ para los pasajeros con destino Bruselas** last call for passengers flying to Brussels • **la ~ del deber** the call of duty • **la ~ de la selva** the call of the wild • **acudir a la ~ de algn** to answer sb's call • **la enfermera acudió rápidamente a mi ~** the nurse came quickly when I called her, the nurse answered my call quickly ▸ **llamada al orden** call to order ▸ **llamada de alerta** (*lit*) alert; (*fig*) warning, alarm call ▸ **llamada de socorro** call for help
4 (= *gesto*) signal, gesture
5 (*Tip*) mark • **haz una ~ al margen** make a mark in the margin
6 (*Inform*) ▸ **llamada a procedimiento** procedure call
7 (*Mil*) (*tb* **llamada a las armas**) call to arms

llamado ADJ **1** (= *con el nombre de*) [*persona*] named, called; [*lugar*] called • **un chico ~ Manuel** a boy named *o* called Manuel • **un hotel ~ Miramar** a hotel called Miramar
2 (= *conocido*) so-called • **la llamada generación beat** the so-called beat generation • **ordenadores paralelos, así ~s por que funcionan simultáneamente** parallel computers, so called because they work simultaneously • **el cubo de Rubik, así ~ en honor a su inventor** Rubik's cube, named after its inventor
3 (= *destinado*) • **me sentía ~ a hacerlo** I felt destined to do it • **esta ley está llamada a desaparecer** this law is bound *o* destined to disappear • **estar ~ al fracaso** to be doomed to failure
4 (= *convocado*) • **jóvenes ~s a prestar el servicio militar** young men called up (for military service)
SM **1** (*Arg*) call, phone call
2 (*LAm*) (= *llamamiento*) appeal

llamador¹ SM (*en la puerta*) (= *aldaba*) doorknocker; (= *timbre*) bell

llamador²(a) SM/F (= *visitante*) caller

llamamiento SM call • **un ~ al diálogo** a call for dialogue • **hacer** *o* **lanzar un ~ (a algo)** to make *o* issue an appeal *o* call (for sth) • **el presidente hizo un ~ a la unidad nacional** the president called for national unity, the president made *o* issued an appeal *o* a call for national unity • **han hecho un ~ a la población pidiendo donaciones de sangre** they have appealed for blood donations, they have appealed to people to give blood ▸ **llamamiento a filas** (*Mil*) call-up, draft (*EEUU*) ▸ **llamamiento de socorro** call for help

llamar ▹ CONJUG 1a VT **1** (= *nombrar*) to call • **mis amigos me llaman Mari** my friends call me Mari • **¿cómo van a ~ al niño?** what are they going to name *o* call the baby? • **me llamó imbécil** he called me an idiot • **la llamó de todo** he called her every name under the sun; ▹ **hache**
2 (= *considerar*) to call • **eso yo lo llamo un auténtico robo** that's what I call daylight robbery* • **lo que se dio en ~ la nueva generación** what became known as the new generation, what came to be called the new generation • **el mal llamado problema** what people wrongly consider a problem
3 (= *avisar*) [+ *médico, fontanero*] to call; [+ *taxi*] (*por teléfono*) to call; (*con la mano*) to hail • **te estuve llamando a voces** I was shouting for you • **me llamó con la mano para que me acercara** he beckoned me over • **no te metas donde no te llaman*** don't poke your nose in where it's not wanted* • **~ a algn a escena** to call sb to the stage • **~ a algn al orden** to call sb to order; ▹ **mandar**
4 (*Telec*) (*tb* **llamar por teléfono**) to call, ring, phone • **que me llamen a las siete** ask them to call *o* ring *o* phone me at seven • **te llaman desde París** they're calling you *o* they're on the phone from Paris • **¿quién me llama?** who's on the phone?
5 (= *atraer*) • **el ejército llama a muchos jóvenes** the army appeals to a lot of young people • **el chocolate no me llama demasiado** I'm not all that keen on chocolate; ▹ **atención**
6 (= *convocar*) to call, summon (*frm*) • **lo ~on a palacio** he was called *o* summoned (*frm*) to the palace • **Dios lo ha llamado a su lado** (*euf*) he has been called to God • **~ a algn a filas** to call sb up • **pronto seremos llamados a las urnas** an election/a referendum will soon be called; ▹ **llamado**
VI **1** (*Telec*) [*persona*] to call, ring, phone; [*teléfono*] to ring • **¿quién llama?** who's calling? • **ha llamado Maribel** Maribel called *o* rang *o* phoned
2 (*a la puerta*) (*con el puño*) to knock; (*al timbre*) to ring • **"entren sin llamar"** "enter without knocking" • **llamé pero el timbre no sonaba** I rang the bell but it didn't work • **¿quién llama?** who's there?, who is it? • **están llamando** there's someone at the door
VPR **llamarse 1** [*persona, lugar*] to be called • **mi primo se llama Benjamín** my cousin's name is Benjamín, my cousin is called Benjamín • **¿cómo te llamas?** what's your name? • **se llama Mari Paz** her name is Mari Paz • **¿sabes cómo se llama la película?** do you know the name of the film?, do you know what the film is called? • **¡como me llamo Manuel que lo haré!** I'll do it, as sure as my name's Manuel!
2 (*Esp**) (= *costar*) • **¿cómo se llama esto?** how much is this?, what's the damage?‡

llamarada SF **1** [*de fuego*] flare-up, sudden blaze
2 (*en rostro*) flush
3 [*de indignación, ira*] blaze, outburst

llamarón SM (*And, CAm, Cono Sur*) = llamarada

llamativamente ADV strikingly • **siempre le gustó vestirse ~** she always liked to wear very striking clothes

llamativo ADJ (= *vistoso*) [*color*] loud, bright • **se viste de modo ~** she wears very striking clothes

llame SM (*Cono Sur*) bird trap

llameante ADJ blazing

llamear ▹ CONJUG 1a VI to blaze, flame

llamón‡ ADJ (*Méx*) whining, whingeing*

llampo SM (*And, Cono Sur*) ore, pulverized ore

llana SF **1** (*Geog*) plain
2 (*Arquit*) trowel

llanada SF plain

llanamente ADV **1** (= *lisamente*) smoothly, evenly
2 (= *sin ostentaciones*) plainly, simply
3 (= *sinceramente*) openly, frankly
4 (= *claramente*) clearly, straightforwardly; ▹ **liso**

llanca SF (*LAm*) copper ore

llanear ▹ CONJUG 1a VI (*Aut*) to cruise, coast along

llanero/a SM/F **1** (*esp Ven*) plainsman/plainswoman ▸ **llanero solitario** lone ranger
2 (*Caribe*) (= *vaquero*) cowboy

llaneza SF **1** (= *franqueza*) openness, frankness
2 (= *sencillez*) plainness, simplicity; (= *claridad*) clearness, straightforwardness

llanito/a* SM/F Gibraltarian

llano ADJ **1** [*superficie, terreno*] (= *sin desniveles*) flat; (= *no inclinado*) level
2 (= *sencillo*) [*persona, trato*] straightforward; [*estilo, lenguaje*] simple • **en lenguaje ~** in plain language *o* terms
3 • **palabra llana** *word with the stress on the penultimate syllable*
SM plain • **Los Llanos** (*Ven*) (*Geog*) Venezuelan Plains

llanque SM (*And*) rustic sandal

llanta SF **1** [*de rueda*] rim ▸ **llanta de oruga** caterpillar track ▸ **llantas de aleación** alloy wheels
2 (*esp LAm*) (= *neumático*) tyre, tire (EEUU) ▸ **llanta de refacción** (*Méx*) spare tyre, spare tire (EEUU)
3 (*Caribe*) (= *anillo*) large finger-ring

llantén SM plantain

llantera* SF (= *lloros*) sobbing; (= *berridos*) bawling

llantería* SF (*Cono Sur*) weeping and wailing

llantina* SF sobbing • **¡no empieces con la ~!** cut out the sob stuff!*

llanto SM **1** (= *lloro*) crying, tears (*pl*) • **se oía el ~ de un niño en la otra habitación** you could hear a child crying in the next room • **¡deja ya el ~!** stop crying! • **todo acaba en ~** everything ends in tears • **estaba al borde del ~** he was close to tears • **romper en ~** to burst into tears
2 (= *lamento*) moaning, lamentation
3 (*Literat*) dirge, lament, funeral lament

llanura SF **1** (*Geog*) plain; (= *pradera*) prairie
2 (= *lisura*) flatness, smoothness, evenness

llapa SF (*LAm*) ▹ **yapa**

llapango* ADJ (*And*) barefoot

llapingacho SM (*And*) ≈ cheese omelette

llaretá SF (*And*) dried llama dung

llauto SM (*And*) headband

llave SF **1** [*de puerta*] key • **bajo ~** under lock and key • **cerrar con ~** to lock • **cerrar una puerta con ~** to lock a door • **echar (la) ~ (a)** to lock up • **"llave en mano"** "with vacant possession" • MODISMOS: • **guardar algo bajo siete ~s** to keep sth under lock and key • **¡por las ~s de San Pedro!** by heaven! • **tener las ~s de la caja** to hold the purse strings ▸ **llave de cambio** shift key ▸ **llave de contacto** (*Aut*) ignition key ▸ **llave de memoria** (*Inform*) memory stick, USB flash drive, key drive, pen drive ▸ **llave espacial** spacing bar ▸ **llave maestra** skeleton key, master key
2 [*de gas, agua*] tap, faucet (EEUU); (*Elec*) switch ▸ **llave de bola** ballcock, floater (EEUU) ▸ **llave de cierre** stopcock ▸ **llave de flotador** ballcock, floater (EEUU) ▸ **llave de paso** [*del agua*] stopcock; [*del gas*] mains tap • **cerrar la ~ de paso del agua/gas** to turn the water/gas off at the mains ▸ **llave de riego** hydrant
3 (*Mec*) spanner ▸ **llave ajustable** adjustable spanner ▸ **llave de carraca** ratchet spanner, ratchet wrench (EEUU) ▸ **llave de ruedas (en cruz)** wheel brace ▸ **llave inglesa** monkey wrench
4 (*Mús*) stop, key
5 (*Tip*) curly bracket, brace bracket
6 (*Dep*) [*de lucha libre*] lock; [*de judo*] hold
7 [*de escopeta*] lock
8 (*Cono Sur*) (*Arquit*) beam, joist
9 llaves (*Méx*) (*Taur*) horns

llavero SM **1** (= *objeto*) key ring
2† (*persona*) (*tb* **llavero de cárcel**) turnkey

llavín SM latch key

llegada SF **1** [*de un viaje*] arrival
2 (*Dep*) (= *meta*) finishing line

llegar

VERBO INTRANSITIVO
VERBO TRANSITIVO
VERBO PRONOMINAL

▹ CONJUG 1h

Para las expresiones **llegar al alma, llegar lejos, llegar a las manos**, *ver la otra entrada.*

VERBO INTRANSITIVO

1 (*movimiento, destino, procedencia*) to arrive • **Carmen no ha llegado todavía** Carmen hasn't arrived yet • **~on cubiertos de barro** they arrived covered in mud • **avíseme cuando llegue** tell me when he arrives *o* comes • **está recién llegado de Roma** he recently arrived from Rome • **por fin hemos llegado** we're here at last • **el vuelo ~á a las 14:15** the flight gets in at 14:15 • **~á en tren/autobús** he will come by train/bus • **no llegues tarde** don't be late • **~ a:** • **cuando llegamos a Bilbao estaba lloviendo** when we got to *o* arrived in Bilbao it was raining • **¿a qué hora llegaste a casa?** what time did you get home? • **los vehículos están llegando a la línea de salida** the cars are approaching the starting line • **~le a alguien:** • **¿te ha llegado ya el paquete?** have you got the parcel yet? • **estar al ~:** • **Carlos debe de estar al ~** Carlos should be arriving any minute now • **el verano está al ~** summer is just around the corner • **hacer ~ algo a algn:** • **hacer ~ una carta a algn** to send sb a letter • **¿le puedes hacer ~ este recado?** could you give her this message? • **¿le has hecho ~ el dinero?** did you get the money to her? • MODISMOS: • **~le** (*LAm*): • **le llegó el año pasado** he died last year • **me llega** (*And**) I don't give a damn • REFRÁN: • **el que primero llegue, ese la calza** first come first served; ▹ **santo**

2 (= *alcanzar*) **a** (*con las manos*) to reach • **¿me puedes quitar la cortina? yo no llego** could you take the curtain down for me? I can't reach • **no llego al estante de arriba** I can't reach the top shelf
b (*indicando distancia, nivel*) • **esta cuerda no llega** this rope isn't long enough, this rope won't reach • **me llegó muy hondo lo que me dijo** what she said made a very deep impression on me • **el tema de la película no me llega** the subject of the film does nothing for me *o* leaves me cold • **~ a** *o* **hasta** to come up to • **el agua me llegaba hasta las rodillas** the water came up to my knees • **soy bajita y justo le llego al hombro** I'm short and I only just come up to his shoulder • **el vestido le llega hasta los pies** the dress comes *o* goes down to her feet • **los pies no le llegaban al suelo** her feet weren't touching the floor • **la cola llegaba hasta la puerta** the queue went *o* reached back as far as the door • **el tren solo llega hasta Burgos** the train only goes as far as Burgos • **me llega al corazón ver tanto sufrimiento** seeing so much suffering touches me to the heart • MODISMOS: • **¡hasta allí podíamos ~!** that's the limit!, what a nerve! • **a tanto no llego:** • **soy bastante inteligente pero a tanto no llego** I'm reasonably clever, but not enough to do that • **podría dejarle un millón, pero dos no, a tanto no llego** I might let her have a million, but not two, I'm not prepared to go as far as that; ▹ **camisa, suela**
c (*indicando duración*) to last • **el pobrecito no ~á a las Navidades** the poor thing won't make it to *o* last till Christmas • **este abrigo no te llega al próximo invierno** this coat won't last till next winter • **le falta un año para ~ a la jubilación** he has a year to go till *o* before he retires

3 llegar a (+ *sustantivo*) **a** (= *conseguir*) [+ *acuerdo, conclusión*] to reach, come to • **llegó a la felicidad completa** she attained total happiness • **¿cómo has conseguido ~ a la fama?** how did you manage to achieve fame *o* become famous? • **le costó pero llegó a arquitecto** it wasn't easy, but he eventually managed to become an architect • **por fin ha llegado a catedrático** he's finally made it to professor
b (*con cantidades*) to come to • **los gastos totales ~on a 1.000 euros** the total expenditure came to 1,000 euros • **el importe llega a 50 pesos** the total is 50 pesos • **el público no llegaba a 200 espectadores** there were fewer than 200 spectators there • **la audiencia de este programa ha llegado a cinco millones** (*Radio*) as many as five million people have listened to this programme; (*TV*) the viewing figures for this programme have been as high as five million

4 llegar a (+ *infin*) **a** (= *conseguir*) • **llegó a conocer a varios directores de cine** she met *o* got to know several film directors • **no llego a comprenderlo** I just can't understand it • **el producto puede ~ a tener éxito** the product could be a success • **si lo llego a saber** if I had known • **~ a ser famoso/el jefe** to become famous/the boss • **Julia llegó a ser presidenta** Julia became president • **~ a ver:** • **no llegó a ver la película terminada** he never saw the film finished • **el proyecto no llegó a ver la luz** the project never saw the light of day • **temí no ~ a ver el año nuevo** I feared I wouldn't live to see the new year, I feared I wouldn't

l

make it to the new year
b (*como algo extremo*) • **llegué a estar tan mal, que casi no podía moverme** I got so bad, I could hardly move • **llegamos a sospechar de él** we came to suspect him • **puede ~ a alcanzar los 300km/h** it can reach speeds of up to 300km/h • **este pez puede ~ a alcanzar los dos metros de largo** this fish can grow as long as two metres • **la popularidad que un actor puede ~ a alcanzar a través de la televisión** the popularity an actor can come to attain from being on television • **¿llegó a creer que sería campeón del mundo?** did you ever believe you'd be world champion? • **yo había llegado a creer que estábamos en el camino de superar ese problema** I had really started to believe that we were on the way to overcoming that problem • **llegué a creérmelo** I came to believe it • **llegó al punto de robarle** he even went so far as to rob her
5 (*= bastar*) to be enough • **con dos euros no me llega** two euros isn't enough • **con ese dinero no le va a ~** you won't have enough money • **no me llega para ropa nueva** I can't afford to buy new clothes • **hacer ~ el sueldo a fin de mes** to make ends meet • **hacer ~ el dinero** to make one's money last
6 (*momento, acontecimiento*) to come • **~á un día en que sea rico** the day will come when I'm rich • **cuando llegó la paz** when peace came • **se fueron cuando llegó la noche** they left at nightfall
VERBO TRANSITIVO
(*= acercar*) to bring up, bring over
VERBO PRONOMINAL **llegarse**
• **voy a ~me por el banco** I'm going down *o* over to the bank • **llégate a su casa y dile que ...** go over to his house and tell him ... • **llégate a mi casa mañana** come round tomorrow • **llégate más a mí** come closer to me

LLEGAR

Llegar a

A la hora de traducir **llegar a** *al inglés, tenemos que diferenciar entre* **arrive in** *y* **arrive at.**

▷ *Empleamos* **arrive in** *con países, ciudades, pueblos etc:*

Esperamos llegar a Italia el día 11 de junio
We expect to arrive in Italy on 11 June
Llegaremos a Córdoba dentro de dos horas
We'll be arriving in Cordoba in two hours' time

▷ *En cambio, se traduce por* **arrive at** *cuando nos referimos a lugares más pequeños, como aeropuertos, estaciones, etc. La expresión* **llegar a casa** *es una excepción, ya que se traduce por* **arrive/get home**, *es decir, sin preposición:*

Llegamos al aeropuerto con cuatro horas de retraso
We arrived at the airport four hours late
Llegué a casa completamente agotada
I arrived home completely exhausted

Para otros usos y ejemplos ver la entrada.

lleísmo SM *pronunciation of Spanish "y" as "ll"*
llenador ADJ (*Cono Sur*) [*comida*] filling, satisfying

llenar ▷ CONJUG 1a VT **1** (*= rellenar*) [*+ cubo, vaso*] to fill; [*+ bañera*] to run; [*+ cajón, maleta*] to fill • **llenó tanto la maleta que no podía cerrarla** he packed *o* filled the suitcase so full that he couldn't shut it • **no sabía cómo ~ las tardes** she didn't know how to fill her evenings • **no me llenes el vaso** don't fill my glass (up to the top) • **no me llenes mucho el plato** don't give me too much food • **¿puede ~ aquí?** (*en un bar*) the same again, please • **siempre llena los auditorios** he always gets full houses • **~ con *o* de algo** [*+ contenedor*] to fill with sth; [*+ superficie*] to cover with sth • **llenó las estanterías de libros** she filled the shelves with books • **llenó la pizarra de nombres** he covered the blackboard with names • MODISMO: • **le llenó la cabeza de pájaros** he filled her head with nonsense
2 (*= ocupar*) to fill • **los coches ~on el centro de la ciudad** the town centre was filled with cars • **las cajas llenan todo el maletero** the boxes take up *o* fill the whole boot • **~ un hueco** to fill a gap • **llena un hueco que había en el mercado** it fills a gap in the market • **no podía ~ el hueco dejado por su antecesor** he couldn't fill his predecessor's shoes
3 (*= satisfacer*) [*+ deseo*] to fulfil, fulfill (*EEUU*), satisfy • **este trabajo no me llena** I don't find this job satisfying *o* fulfilling • **mi vida no me llena** I'm not getting enough out of life • **no me termina de ~ este libro** this book doesn't really convince me • **sus nietos han llenado su vejez** his grandchildren have gladdened his old age (*liter*)
4 (*= colmar*) • **~ a algn de** [*+ inquietud, dudas*] to fill sb with • **sus hijos lo ~on de orgullo** his children filled him with pride • **su tono de voz la llenó de inquietud** his tone of voice made her feel uneasy, his tone of voice filled her with unease (*liter*) • **lo ~on de insultos** they heaped insults upon him, they hurled abuse at him • **verte nos llenó de alegría** we were delighted to see you • **lo ~on de atenciones** they showered him with attention, they made a great fuss of him • **nos ~on de elogios** they showered praise on us
5 (*= cumplimentar*) [*+ documento, impreso*] to fill in, fill out (*EEUU*)
VI [*comida*] to be filling • **esta sopa no llena nada** this soup isn't really very filling, this soup doesn't really fill you up
VPR **llenarse 1** (*= ocuparse completamente*) to fill, fill up • **la sala se fue llenando rápidamente** the hall was filling up fast • **los viernes siempre se llena el restaurante** the restaurant always gets full *o* fills up on Fridays • **~se de algo** to fill (up) with sth • **la habitación se llenó de humo** the room filled with smoke • **los ojos se les ~on de lágrimas** tears welled up in their eyes, their eyes filled with tears • MODISMO: • **~se hasta la bandera *o* hasta los topes** to be full to bursting, be packed out, be packed to the rafters
2 (*= colmarse*) • **con esa tarta me he llenado** I'm full after that cake • **lo único que quiere es ~se los bolsillos** all he wants is to line his pockets* • **aquí se llena uno bien la barriga*** you can really stuff yourself here* • **se llenó los bolsillos de caramelos** she filled her pockets with sweets, she stuffed her pockets full of sweets • **~se de** [*+ orgullo, alegría*] to be filled with; [*+ comida*] to stuff o.s. with* • **con eso se ~án de gloria** that will cover them in glory • **en un año se llenó de deudas** after a year he was up to his neck in debt • **se me llenó la espalda de ronchas** my back came out in a rash all over
3 (*= cubrirse*) to get covered • **los libros se han llenado de polvo** the books have got covered in dust • **me he llenado los dedos de tinta** I've got ink all over my fingers, my fingers are covered in ink • **el techo se llenó de humedad** damp appeared all over the ceiling
4 (*frm*) (*= enfadarse*) to get cross, get annoyed

llenazo* SM (*= entradas agotadas*) sellout; (*Teat, Dep*) (*= asientos ocupados*) full house • **ayer hubo ~ en el concierto** there was a full house for the concert yesterday, yesterday's concert was a sellout • **hubo un ~ total en el estadio** the stadium was totally packed out
llenazón SM (*Méx*) blown-out feeling, indigestion
llenito ADJ plump
lleno ADJ **1** (*= completo*) [*plato, vaso*] full; [*teatro, tren*] full • **el depósito está ~** the tank is full • **no me pongas el plato muy ~** don't give me too much food • **¡~, por favor!** (*en una gasolinera*) fill her up, please! • **no hables con la boca llena** don't talk with your mouth full • **el autobús iba ~** the bus was full (up) • **~ hasta el borde** full to the brim • MODISMO: • **~ a reventar *o* hasta la bandera *o* hasta los topes** full to bursting, packed out, packed to the rafters
2 • **~ de a** [*espacio*] full of; [*superficie*] covered in • **le gusta tener la casa llena de gente** she likes to have the house full of people • **los muebles están ~s de polvo** the furniture is covered in dust • **llevaba el traje ~ de manchas** his suit was covered in stains
b [*complejos, problemas*] full of; [*odio, esperanza*] filled with • **un viaje ~ de aventuras** a journey full of adventures • **estaba ~ de dudas** I was filled with doubt • **una mirada llena de odio** a hateful look, a look full of hate • **llegué ~ de alegría** I arrived in high spirits
3 • **de ~** directly • **los cambios nos afectarán de ~** the changes will affect us directly • **nos daba el sol de ~** the sun was (shining) directly on us • **la bala le alcanzó de ~ en el corazón** the bullet hit him straight in the heart • **está dedicado de ~ a su familia** he is entirely dedicated to his family • **el impacto le dio de ~ en la cara** he took the impact full in the face • **acertaste de ~ con ese comentario** you've hit the nail on the head (with that remark), that remark was spot on
4 (*= saciado*) full, full up*
5 (*= regordete*) plump, chubby
6 (*Astron*) [*luna*] full • **hoy es luna llena** there is a full moon today
SM **1** (*= aforo completo*) (*gen*) sellout; (*Cine, Teat*) full house • **ayer hubo ~ en el concierto** there was a full house for the concert yesterday, yesterday's concert was a sellout • **el espectáculo sigue representándose con ~s absolutos** the show continues to play to packed houses ▸ **lleno absoluto, lleno hasta la bandera, lleno total** (*Cine, Teat*) packed house; (*Dep*) capacity crowd
2 (*Astron*) full moon
llevadero ADJ bearable, tolerable

llevar

VERBO TRANSITIVO
VERBO INTRANSITIVO
VERBO PRONOMINAL

▷ CONJUG 1a

Para las expresiones ***llevar adelante, llevar la contraria, llevar las de perder, llevar a la práctica, llevar a término, llevar ventaja****, ver la otra entrada.*

VERBO TRANSITIVO

1 (= transportar) (*con los brazos*) to carry; (*indicando el punto de destino*) to take; (*en vehículo*) to transport • **yo llevaba la maleta** I was carrying the case • **es muy pesado para ~lo entre los dos** it's too heavy for the two of us to carry • **no te olvides de ~ un paraguas** make sure you take an umbrella with you • **lleva los vasos a la cocina** can you take the glasses to the kitchen? • **"comida para ~"** "food to take away", "take-away food" • **¿es para ~?** is it to take away?

2 (= llevar puesto) to wear • **¿hay que ~ corbata a la reunión?** do we have to wear a tie to the meeting? • **llevaba puesto un sombrero muy raro** she had a very odd hat on, she was wearing a very odd hat

3 (= llevar encima) • **solo llevo diez euros** I've only got ten euros on me • **no llevo dinero (encima)** I haven't got any money on me • **¡la que llevaba encima aquella noche!*** he was really smashed that night!*

4 (= tener) **a** [+ *barba, pelo*] to have • **lleva barba** he has a beard • **lleva el pelo corto** he has short hair
b [+ *adorno, ingrediente*] to have • **esta raqueta no lleva el precio** this racket doesn't have the price on it • **este pastel no lleva harina** this cake doesn't have any flour in it • **lleva un rótulo que dice …** it has a label (on it) which says … • **el tren no lleva coche-comedor** the train doesn't have a dining car • **lleva mucha sal** it's very salty • **¿qué lleva el pollo que está tan bueno?** what's in this chicken that makes it taste so good?
c [+ *armas, nombre, título*] to have, bear (*frm*) • **~á el nombre de la madre** she will be named after her mother • **el libro lleva el título de …** the book has the title of …, the book is entitled …

5 (+ persona) **a** (= *acompañar, conducir*) to take • **voy a ~ a los niños al colegio** I'm going to take the children to school • **lo llevamos al teatro** we took him to the theatre • **¿adónde me llevan?** where are you taking me? • **a ver ¿cuándo me llevas a cenar?** when are you going to take me out for a meal?
b (*en coche*) to drive • **Sofía nos llevó a casa** Sofía gave us a lift home, Sofía drove us home • **yo voy en esa dirección, ¿quieres que te lleve?** I'm going that way, do you want a lift?

6 (= conducir) **a** [+ *vehículo*] to drive • **lleva muy bien el coche** she drives the car very well • **yo llevé el coche hasta Santander** I drove the car to Santander
b [+ *persona, entidad*] • **este camino nos lleva a Bogotá** this road takes us to Bogotá • **ha llevado al país a una guerra** he has led the country into a war • **llevó a su empresa a la bancarrota** he caused his company to go bankrupt, he bankrupted his company • **dejarse ~** to get carried away • **se dejaba ~ por las olas** he allowed the waves to carry him away • **no te dejes ~ por las apariencias** don't be taken in *o* deceived by appearances • **si te dejas ~ por él, acabarás mal** if you fall in with him, you'll be in trouble

7 (= dirigir) [+ *negocio, tienda*] to run • **~ una finca** to run an estate • **lleva todos sus negocios en secreto** he conducts all his business in secret • **~ la casa** to run the household • **lleva muy bien la casa** she's a very good housewife • **¿quién lleva la cuenta?** who is keeping count? • **~ las cuentas *o* los libros** (*Com*) to keep the books • **~ una materia** (*Méx*) to study a subject; ▹ **compás**

8 (= aportar) to bring • **la madre es quien lleva el dinero a la casa** it is the mother who brings home the money • **llevó la tranquilidad a todos** he brought peace to everyone • **seguro que llevas alegría a tu familia** I'm sure you're making your family happy

9 (= adelantar en) • **mi hermana mayor me lleva ocho años** my elder sister is eight years older than me • **él me lleva una cabeza** he's a head taller than me

10 (= inducir) • **~ a algn a creer que …** to lead sb to think that …, make sb think that … • **esto me lleva a pensar que …** this leads me to think that …

11 (= tolerar) • **~ las desgracias con paciencia** to bear misfortunes patiently • **¿cómo lleva lo de su hijo?** how's she coping with what happened to her son? • **lleva muy bien sus setenta años** he's doing very well for seventy • **tiene mucho genio y hay que saber ~lo** he's very bad-tempered and you have to know how to deal with him

12 (indicando tiempo) **a** (= *haber estado*) to be • **¿cuánto tiempo llevas aquí?** how long have you been here? • **llevo horas esperando aquí** I've been waiting here for hours • **el tren lleva una hora de retraso** the train is an hour late • **llevo tres meses buscándolo** I have been looking for it for three months
b (= *tardar*) to take • **el trabajo me ~á tres días** the work will take me three days • **~á varias horas reparar la avería** it will take several hours to carry out the repairs

13 (= cobrar) to charge • **me llevó 80 euros por arreglar el televisor** he charged me 80 euros for fixing the television • **no quería ~me nada** he didn't want to charge me, he didn't want to take any money

14 (= ir por) • **¿qué dirección llevaba?** what direction was he going in?, which way was he going? • **lleva camino de ser como su padre** it looks like he's going to turn out just like his father

15 (+ vida) to lead • **~ una vida tranquila** to live *o* lead a quiet life

16 (+ participio) • **llevo estudiados tres capítulos** I have covered three chapters • **llevaba hecha la mitad** he had done half of it • **lleva conseguidas muchas victorias** he has won many victories

17 (= producir) (*Com, Econ*) to bear; (*Agr*) to bear, produce • **los bonos llevan un 8% de interés** the bonds pay *o* bear interest at 8% • **no lleva fruto este año** it has no fruit this year, it hasn't produced any fruit this year

VERBO INTRANSITIVO

[*carretera*] to go, lead • **esta carretera lleva a La Paz** this road goes *o* leads to La Paz

VERBO PRONOMINAL **llevarse**

1 (= tomar consigo) to take • **se llevó todo mi dinero** he took all my money • **puedes ~te el disco que quieras** take whichever record you want • **¿puedo ~me este libro?** can I borrow this book? • **llévatelo** take it (with you) • **—¿le gusta? —sí, me lo llevo** (*al comprar*) "do you like it?" — "yes, I'll take it" • **los ladrones se ~on la caja** the thieves took the safe (away) • **se ~on más de diez mil euros en joyas** they got away with more than ten thousand euros' worth of jewels

2 (+ persona) (= *acompañar*) • **se lo ~on al cine** they took him off to the cinema • **el padre se llevó a su hijo** the father took his son away • **~se a algn por delante** (= *atropellar*) to run sb over; (*LAm*) (= *ofender*) to offend sb; (= *maltratar*) to ride roughshod over sb • **el camión se llevó una farola por delante** the truck went off the road and took a lamppost with it • **la riada se llevó el pueblo por delante** the village was swept away by *o* in the flood, the flood took the village with it • **el viento se llevó por delante los tejados de las casas** the wind blew the roofs off the houses • **una infección en el riñón se lo llevó por delante** he died from a kidney infection • **esa ley se llevó por delante los derechos de los trabajadores** this law swept away *o* rode roughshod over the rights of the workers • MODISMO: • **¡que se lo lleve el diablo!** to hell with it!

3 (= conseguir) [+ *premio*] to win • **se llevó el primer premio** she won first prize • **siempre me llevo la peor parte** I always come off worst • MODISMOS: • **llevársela*** • **¡no lo toques o te la llevas!** don't touch it or you'll live to regret it! • **¡tú te la llevas!** (*en juegos*) you're it!

4 (= sufrir) • **me llevé una gran decepción** I was very disappointed • **me llevé una alegría** I was so happy • **se llevó un buen susto** he got a real fright

5 (= arrastrar) • **el mar se lleva la arena** the sea washes the sand away • **el viento se llevó las nubes** the wind blew the clouds away • **el viento se llevó una rama** the wind tore off a branch • **la espada se le llevó dos dedos** the sword took off two of his fingers • MODISMO: • **las palabras se las lleva el viento** words are not binding

6 (en el trato) • **~se bien** to get on well (together) • **no se lleva bien con el jefe** he doesn't get on *o* along with the boss • **me llevo bien con mi hermano** I get on well with my brother • **nos llevamos muy mal** we get on very badly; ▹ **matar, perro**

7 (= estar de moda) to be in fashion, be all the rage • **se llevan los lunares** polka dots are in fashion *o* all the rage • **se vuelven a ~ las gafas negras** dark glasses are coming back into fashion

8 (con cantidades) • **mi hermano y yo nos llevamos tres años** there are three years between my brother and me • **de doce me llevo una** (*Mat*) that makes twelve so carry one

lliclla (SF) (*And*) woollen *o* (*EEUU*) woolen shawl
llicta (SF) (*And*) quinine paste
llimo (ADJ) (*Cono Sur*) (= *de orejas pequeñas*) small-eared; (= *sin orejas*) earless
llocalla (SM) (*And*) boy
lloquena (SF) (*And*) fish spear, harpoon
llora (SF) (*Caribe*) wake
llorado (ADJ) (*frm*) [*difunto*] late lamented (*frm*); [*muerte*] lamented (*frm*) • **nuestro ~ poeta** our late lamented poet • **no ~** unlamented, unmourned
llorar ▹ CONJUG 1a (VT) **1** [+ *lágrimas*] to weep, cry • MODISMO: • **~ lágrimas de cocodrilo** to weep crocodile tears
2 (*liter*) (= *lamentar*) [+ *a difunto*] to mourn; [+ *muerte*] to mourn, lament; [+ *desgracia*] to bemoan; [+ *actitud*] to lament, regret • **nadie lo ha llorado** nobody mourned *o* lamented his death, nobody mourned him • **algún día ~ás tu ligereza** some day you will regret your flippant behaviour • **lloran la pérdida de su libertad** they long for their lost freedom
(VI) **1** to cry, weep (*liter*) • **¡no llores!** don't cry! • **me dieron *o* me entraron ganas de ~** I felt like crying • **se puso a ~ desconsoladamente** she began to cry *o* weep (*liter*) inconsolably • **Rosa lloraba en silencio** Rosa cried *o* wept (*liter*) silently • **~ de algo** to cry with sth • **estuve llorando de alegría** I was crying with happiness • **lloramos de risa** we laughed until we cried, we cried with laughter • **echarse a ~**

to start to cry • **hacer ~ a algn** to make sb cry • **no hay nada que me pueda hacer ~** nothing can make me cry • **~ por algo/algn: no llores más por ella, es una idiota** don't cry over her anymore, she's an idiot • **lloraba por cualquier cosa** she would cry at *o* over the slightest thing • **no lloréis por mí cuando me vaya** don't cry for me when I'm gone • **romper a ~** to burst into tears • **MODISMOS:** • **~ a cuajo** to sob one's heart out† • **~ a mares** *o* **a moco tendido** *o* **a rienda suelta** to cry one's eyes out • **~ a moco y baba**† to sob one's heart out† • **~ como una criatura** to cry like a baby • **ser de** *o* **para ~** (*iró*) to be enough to make you cry *o* weep • **el concierto fue como para ~** the concert was enough to make you cry *o* weep • **REFRÁN:** • **el que no llora no mama** if you don't ask you don't get
2 [*ojos*] to water • **me lloran los ojos** my eyes are watering
3 (= *rogar*) • **~ a algn** to moan to sb • **llórale un poco a tu madre y ya verás ...** if you moan a bit to your mother, you'll see ...
4 (*Chile**) (= *favorecer*) • **a este rincón le llora un sofá** a sofa would look good in that corner • **a ti te llora el rojo** you look good in red, red looks good on you
5 (*And, Caribe*) (= *favorecer poco*) to be very unbecoming

llorera* (SF) fit of crying • **una buena ~** a good cry

lloretas* (SMF INV) (*And, CAm*) crybaby

llorica* (ADJ) • **no seas ~** don't be such a crybaby*
(SMF) crybaby*

lloricón* (ADJ) [*persona*] weepy*, tearful; [*película, literatura*] tear-jerking*

lloriqueante (ADJ) snivelling, sniveling (EEUU), whimpering

lloriquear ▷ CONJUG 1a (VI) to snivel, whimper

lloriqueo (SM) snivelling, sniveling (EEUU), whimpering

llorisquear ▷ CONJUG 1a (VI) (*Caribe, Cono Sur*) = **lloriquear**

llorisqueo (SM) (*Caribe, Cono Sur*) = **lloriqueo**

lloro (SM) **1** (= *llanto*) crying, weeping, tears (*pl*); (= *berrido*) wailing
2 (*en grabación*) wow

llorón/ona (ADJ) **1** (= *que llora*) • **era muy ~ de pequeño** he was a real crybaby when he was little* • **es una mujer muy llorona** she cries very easily; ▷ **sauce**
2 (= *quejica*) • **no seas tan ~** don't be such a moaner *o* whinger*
(SM/F) **1** (= *que llora*) crybaby*
2 (= *quejica*) moaner*, whinger*

llorona (SF) **1** (= *plañidera*) hired mourner
2 (*Méx*) *spectre of a wailing woman who wanders the streets*
3 (*Cono Sur*) (= *llanto*) • **le dio la ~** she got all weepy
4 (*And, Cono Sur*) **lloronas** large spurs

lloroso (ADJ) [*tono, voz*] tearful; [*ojos*] watery • **—¿me has echado de menos? —le dijo con voz llorosa** "have you missed me?" she said tearfully *o* in a tearful voice • **tenía los ojos ~s por la alergia** her eyes were watering from hayfever, her eyes were all watery from hayfever • **se le pusieron los ojos ~s cuando le regañaron** she was close to tears when they told her off

llovedera (SF) (*And, CAm, Caribe*), **llovedero** (SM) (*Cono Sur*) (period of) continuous rain; (= *época*) rainy season; (= *tormenta*) rainstorm

llovedizo (ADJ) **1** [*techo*] leaky
2 • **agua llovediza** rainwater

llover ▷ CONJUG 2h (VI) **1** (*Meteo*) to rain • **está lloviendo** it is raining • **MODISMOS:** • **~ a cántaros** to rain cats and dogs, pour (down) • **como llovido del cielo:** • **llegar** *o* **venir (como) llovido del cielo** (*inesperado*) to come (totally) out of the blue; (*muy oportuno*) to be a godsend, come just at the right time • **~ a mares** to rain cats and dogs, pour (down) • **está llovido en la milpita** (*Méx**) we're having a run of bad luck, we're going through a bad patch • **~ sobre mojado:** • **luego llovió sobre mojado** then on top of all that something else happened • **ya ha llovido desde entonces** • **ha llovido mucho desde entonces** a lot of water has flowed under the bridge since then • **nunca llueve a gusto de todos** you can't please everybody • **¡cómo ahora llueve pepinos** *o* **uvas!** (*And*) rubbish! • **siempre que llueve escampa** (*Caribe*) every cloud has a silver lining • **llueva o truene** rain or shine, come what may
2 • **MODISMO:** • **~le algo a algn:** • **le llovieron regalos encima** he was showered with gifts

llovida (SF) (*LAm*) rain, shower

llovido (SM) stowaway

llovizna (SF) drizzle

lloviznar ▷ CONJUG 1a (VI) to drizzle

lloviznoso (ADJ) drizzly

llueca (SF) broody hen

lluqui (ADJ) (*And*) left-handed

lluvia (SF) **1** (*Meteo*) rain; (= *cantidad*) rainfall • **día de ~** rainy day • **intensa ~** heavy rain • **la ~ caída en el mes de enero** the rainfall in January, the January rainfall • **REFRÁN:** • **la ~ cae sobre los buenos como sobre los malos** it rains on the just as well as on the unjust ▸ **lluvia ácida** acid rain ▸ **lluvia artificial** cloud seeding ▸ **lluvia de estrellas fugaces, lluvia de meteoros** meteor shower ▸ **lluvia de oro** (*Bot*) laburnum ▸ **lluvia menuda** drizzle, fine rain ▸ **lluvia radiactiva** (radioactive) fallout ▸ **lluvias monzónicas** monsoon rains ▸ **lluvia torrencial** torrential rain
2 (= *abundancia*) [*de balas, misiles*] hail; [*de insultos*] stream, barrage; [*de regalos*] shower; [*de infortunios*] string
3 [*de insecticida, laca*] spray; [*de regadera*] rose
4 (*Cono Sur*) (= *ducha*) shower, shower bath

lluvioso (ADJ) rainy, wet

lo¹ (ART DEF) **1** (*con adjetivos*) **a** • **el gusto por lo bello** a taste for beautiful things • **no me gusta lo picante** I don't like spicy things • **subimos a lo más alto del edificio** we went right to the top of the building • **lo difícil fue convencerla** the difficult part was convincing her • **lo difícil es que ...** the difficult thing is that ... • **yo defiendo lo mío** I defend what is mine • **la física no es lo mío** physics isn't my thing • **en vista de lo ocurrido** in view of what has happened • **sufre lo indecible** she suffers terribly • **lo insospechado del caso** what was unsuspected about the matter • **lo totalmente inesperado del descubrimiento** the completely unexpected nature of the discovery • **ven lo más pronto posible** come as soon as you possibly can • **es de lo más divertido** it's so *o* really funny • **es de lo mejor que hay en el mercado** it's among the best you can get • **lo mejor/peor de la película** the best/worst thing about the film • **lo peor fue que no pudimos entrar** the worst thing was we couldn't get in
b (*referido a un estilo*) • **construido a lo campesino** built in the peasant style • **viste a lo americano** he dresses in the American style, he dresses like an American • **un peinado a lo afro** an afro hairstyle • **un peinado a lo mohicano** a mohican
c (*con valor enfático*) • **no saben lo aburrido que es** they don't know how boring it is • **me doy cuenta de lo amables que son** I realize how kind they are • **sabes lo mucho que me gusta** you know (just) how much I like it
2 • **lo de:** • **lo de ayer** what happened yesterday • **olvida lo de ayer** forget what happened yesterday, forget about yesterday • **lo de siempre** the usual • **lo de la boda** the business about the wedding • **lo de Rumasa** the Rumasa affair • **lo de no traer dinero ya no es una excusa** saying you don't have any money on you is no excuse • **fui (a) lo de Pablo** (*Cono Sur*) (= *a casa de*) I went to Pablo's place
3 • **lo que a** (*relativo*) what • **lo que más me gusta es nadar** what I like most is swimming • **lo que digo es ...** what I say is ... • **repito lo que he dicho antes** I repeat what I said earlier • **¡sí hombre, lo que (yo) he dicho!** yes, just like I said! • **toma lo que quieras** take what *o* whatever you want • **todo lo que puedas** as much as *o* whatever you can • **empezó a tocar, lo que le fastidió** she began to play, which annoyed him, to his annoyance, she began to play • **lo que es eso ...** as for that ... • **en lo que a mí concierne** as far as I'm concerned • **cuesta más de lo que crees** it costs more than you think • **lo que pasa es que ...** the thing is ... • **lo que sea** whatever
b (*con valor intensificador*) • **¡lo que has tardado!** how long you've taken!, you've taken so long! • **¡lo que sufre un hombre honrado!** what *o* the things an honourable man has to suffer! • **¡lo que cuesta vivir!** the cost of living is so high! • **es lo que se dice feo** he's undeniably ugly • **es lo que se dice un hombre** he's a real man
c • **a lo que** (*LAm*) (*en cuanto*) as soon as • **a lo que me vio me saludó** as soon as he saw me he said hello
d • **en lo que ...** whilst ...

lo² (PRON PERS) **1** (*refiriéndose a él*) him • **¿lo habéis invitado?** have you invited him? • **no lo conozco** I don't know him • **lo han despedido** he's been sacked
2 (*refiriéndose a usted*) you • **yo a usted lo conozco** I know you
3 (*refiriéndose a una cosa, un animal*) it • **no lo veo** I can't see it • **lo tengo aquí** I have it here • **voy a pensarlo** I'll think about it • **¿el té lo tomas con leche?** do you take milk in your tea? • **no lo sabía** I didn't know • **lo sé** I know • **ya lo creo** I should think so • **no lo hay** there isn't any • **¿te acuerdas de lo bien que lo pasamos?** do you remember what a good time we had? • **¡con lo mal que lo pasamos!** we had such an awful time!
4 (*referido a un estado, cualidad*) • **no parece lista pero lo es** she doesn't seem clever but she is • **guapa sí que lo es** she's certainly pretty • **—¿estás cansado? —sí, lo estoy** "are you tired?" — "yes, I am"

loa (SF) **1** (= *elogio*) praise
2 (*Teat, Hist*) prologue, playlet
3 (*CAm, Méx**) (= *regañada*) reproof

loable (ADV) praiseworthy, laudable, commendable

loablemente (ADV) commendably

LOAPA (SF ABR) (*Esp*) (*Jur*) = **Ley Orgánica de Armonización del Proceso Autonómico**

loar ▷ CONJUG 1a (VT) to praise

lob (SM) lob

loba (SF) **1** (*Zool*) she-wolf
2 (*Agr*) ridge (between furrows)

lobanillo (SM) wen, cyst

lobato/a (SM/F) wolf cub

lobby ['loβi] (SM) (PL: **lobbys** ['loβi]) lobby, pressure group • **hacer ~** to lobby (**a favor de** for)

lobelia SF lobelia
lobero ADJ • perro ~ wolfhound
lobezno/a SM/F wolf cub
lobito SM (*Cono Sur*) (*tb* **lobito de río**) otter
lobo SM **1** (*Zool*) wolf • **MODISMOS**: • **arrojar a algn a los ~s** to throw sb to the wolves • **gritar ¡al ~!** to cry wolf • **¡menos ~s (Caperucita)!** tell me another one! • **pillar un ~‡** to get plastered‡ • **son ~s de una camada** they're birds of a feather ▸ **lobo de mar** old salt, sea dog; (*Chile*) seal ▸ **lobo gris** grey wolf, timber wolf ▸ **lobo marino** seal ▸ **lobo rojo** red wolf
2 (*Méx**) (= *guardia*) traffic cop*
ADJ (*Chile**) (= *huraño*) shy
lobotomía SF lobotomy
lóbrego ADJ dark, gloomy
lobreguez SF darkness, gloom(iness)
lóbulo SM lobe
lobuno ADJ wolfish, wolflike
LOC SM ABR (*Inform*) (= **lector óptico de caracteres**) OCR
loca SF **1‡** (= *homosexual*) queen‡ • **es una ~** he's a real queen‡
2 (*Cono Sur‡*) (= *prostituta*) whore
3 • **MODISMO**: • **darle la ~ a algn** (*Cono Sur*) to get cross, get into a temper; ▹ **loco**
local ADJ [*cultura, producción*] local • **equipo ~** home team
SM **1** [*de negocio*] premises (*pl*) • **en el ~** on the premises ▸ **local comercial** (*gen*) business premises (*pl*); (*sin ocupar*) shop unit
2 (= *lugar*) place
localidad SF **1** (= *pueblo*) town, place, locality (*frm*)
2 (*Teat*) (= *asiento*) seat; (= *entrada*) ticket • **"no hay localidades"** "house full", "sold out" • **sacar ~es** to get tickets
3 (= *lugar*) location
localismo SM localism
localizable ADJ • **el director no estaba ~** we couldn't get hold of the director • **difícilmente/fácilmente ~** [*objeto, lugar*] hard/easy to find; [*persona*] hard/easy to get hold of
localización SF **1** [*de supervivientes*] finding • **el temporal dificultó la ~ del naufragio** the storm made it difficult to find *o* locate the wreck
2 [*de llamada*] tracing • **la ~ de la llamada fue cuestión de segundos** it took a matter of seconds to trace the call
3 [*de enfermedad, dolor*] localization
4 (*frm*) (= *ubicación*) siting, location, placing
localizado ADJ localized
localizador SM pager, beeper; [*de un vuelo*] booking reference, reservation code
localizar ▹ CONJUG 1f VT **1** (= *encontrar*) to find, locate • **¿dónde se puede ~ al Sr Gómez?** where can I find *o* get hold of Mr Gómez?
2 [+ *llamada telefónica*] to trace
3 (*Med*) to localize
4 (*frm*) (= *colocar*) to site, locate, place • **el lugar donde van a ~ la nueva industria** the place where the new industry is to be sited
VPR **1** (*Méx*) (= *situarse*) to be located
2 [*dolor*] to be localized
localmente ADV locally
locamente ADV madly, wildly • **~ enamorado** madly in love
locatario/a SM/F (*LAm*) tenant, lessee
locatis* SMF INV crackpot
locería SF **1** (*LAm*) (= *loza*) pottery; (= *loza fina*) china, chinaware
2 (*Méx*) (= *vajilla*) crockery
locero/a SM/F (*LAm*) potter
locha SF loach
loche SM (*And*) (= *bermejo*) ginger colour
locho ADJ (*And*) (= *bermejo*) ginger, reddish
loción SF lotion ▸ **loción capilar** hair restorer ▸ **loción facial** (*para limpiar*) cleanser; (*para tonificar*) toner ▸ **loción para después del afeitado** aftershave lotion ▸ **loción para el cabello** hair restorer
lock-out ['lokaut] SM (PL: **lock-outs** ['lokaut]) lockout
loco/a ADJ **1** (= *no cuerdo*) mad, crazy • **¿estás ~?** are you mad *o* crazy? • **no seas ~, eso es muy arriesgado** don't be stupid, that's very risky • **una brújula loca** *a compass whose needle no longer points north* • **estaba ~ de alegría** he was mad *o* wild with joy • **andar** *o* **estar ~ con algo** (= *preocupado*) to be worried to death about sth; (= *contento*) to be crazy about sth • **ando ~ con el examen** the exam is driving me crazy • **está loca con su moto nueva** she's crazy about her new motorbike • **está ~ por algn/algo**: • **está ~ por esa chica** he's mad *o* crazy about that girl • **anda** *o* **está loca por irse a Inglaterra** she's mad keen to go to England • **tener** *o* **traer ~ a algn**: • **este asunto me tiene** *o* **trae ~** this business is driving me crazy • **volver ~ a algn** to drive sb mad, drive sb round the bend • **el marisco me vuelve ~** I'm crazy about seafood • **volverse ~** to go insane, go mad • **estoy para volverme ~** I'm at my wits' end • **este caos es para volverse ~** this is absolute chaos • **MODISMOS**: • **estar ~ de atar** *o* **de remate** to be stark raving mad • **estar más ~ que una cabra** to be as mad as a hatter • **no lo hago ni ~*** no way will I do that* • **hacer algo a lo ~** to do sth any old how • **~ de verano** (*Cono Sur*) cracked, crazy
2 (= *frenético*) hectic • **hoy he tenido un día ~** I've had a really hectic day today
3* (= *enorme*) • **llevo una prisa loca** I'm in a tremendous *o* real rush* • **he tenido una suerte loca** I've been fantastically lucky*
SM/F lunatic, madman/madwoman • **el ~ de César se ha comprado otro coche** that lunatic *o* madman César has bought another car • **esta es una casa de ~s** this place is a madhouse • **correr como un ~** to run like mad • **gritar como un ~** to shout like a madman, shout one's head off • **hacerse el ~** to act the fool • **es un ~ perdido** he's stark raving mad • **ponerse como un ~** to start acting like a madman/madwoman • **MODISMO**: • **cada ~ con su tema** everyone has their own axe to grind
SM (*Chile*) abalone, false abalone
locomoción SF **1** (= *desplazamiento*) locomotion
2 (*LAm*) (= *transporte*) transport ▸ **locomoción colectiva** public transport
locomotividad SF power of locomotion
locomotor(a)/triz ADJ **1** [*vehículo, aparato*] locomotive
2 (*Anat*) [*sistema, aparato, conducta*] locomotor
locomotora SF **1** (*Ferro*) engine, locomotive ▸ **locomotora de maniobras** shunting engine, switch engine (*EEUU*) ▸ **locomotora de vapor** steam locomotive
2 [*de la economía, del desarrollo*] driving force
locomotriz ADJ ▹ **locomotor**
locomóvil SF traction engine
locrear ▹ CONJUG 1a VI (*LAm*) to eat, have a meal
locro SM (*LAm*) *meat and vegetable stew*
locuacidad SF (*frm*) loquacity (*frm*), talkativeness
locuaz ADJ (*frm*) loquacious (*frm*), talkative
locución SF **1** (= *giro idiomático*) expression, phrase
2 (*TV*) • **"locución"** "voice", "reader"
locuelo/a* ADJ daft, loony*
SM/F loony*, crackpot*
locumba[1]* (*Perú*), **locumbeta*** (*Perú*) ADJ INV (= *loco*) crazy*, nuts*
SMF INV nutter*
locumba[2]* (*Perú*) SF grape liquor
locura SF **1** (= *demencia*) madness, insanity • **un ataque de ~** a fit of madness
2 (= *exceso*) • **¡qué ~!** it's madness! • **me gusta con ~*** I'm crazy about it • **es una casa de ~*** it's a smashing house* • **precios de ~*** fantastic prices • **tener** *o* **sentir ~ por algn** to be crazy about sb • **tiene ~ por su sobrino** she's crazy about her nephew
3 (= *acto*) • **es capaz de hacer cualquier ~** he is capable of any madness • **no hagas ~s** don't do anything crazy • **ser una ~** to be madness • **es una ~ ir sola** it's madness to go on your own
locutor(a) SM/F (*Radio, TV*) (*entre programas, en anuncios*) announcer; (*TV*) [*de noticias*] newscaster, newsreader; (= *comentarista*) commentator ▸ **locutor(a) de continuidad** (*TV, Radio*) linkman/linkwoman ▸ **locutor(a) deportivo/a** sports commentator
locutorio SM **1** (*Telec*) telephone box, telephone booth; (*negocio*) *shop or cybercafé providing telephone services*
2 (*para visitas*) [*de cárcel*] visiting room; (*Rel*) parlour, parlor (*EEUU*)
3 ▸ **locutorio radiofónico** studio
lodacero SM (*And*), **lodazal** SM quagmire, mudhole
LODE SF ABR (*Esp*) = **Ley Orgánica Reguladora del Derecho a la Educación**
lodo SM (= *barro*) mud, mire (*liter*); **lodos** (*Med*) mudbath (*sing*); (*Min*) sludge (*sing*) ▸ **lodo de depuradora** sewage sludge
lodoso ADJ muddy
loft SM loft
log ABR (= **logaritmo**) log
loga SF **1** (*CAm*) (= *eulogía*) eulogy • **MODISMO**: • **echar una ~ a algn*** (*iró*) to tell sb off*
2 (*Cono Sur*) (= *balada*) ballad, short poem
logaritmo SM logarithm
logia SF **1** (*Mil*) [*de masones*] lodge
2 (*Arquit*) loggia
lógica SF logic • **MODISMO**: • **ser de una ~ aplastante** to be blindingly obvious ▸ **lógica booleana** Boolean logic ▸ **lógica borrosa, lógica difusa** fuzzy logic ▸ **lógica simbólica** symbolic logic; ▹ **lógico**
logical SM software
lógicamente ADV logically
logicial SM software
lógico/a ADJ **1** (*relativo a la lógica*) [*conclusión, razonamiento, planteamiento*] logical
2 (= *normal*) natural • **como es ~** naturally • **es ~ it's only natural • **es ~ que ...** it stands to reason that ..., it's understandable that ... • **—ayudaría a su hijo antes que al tuyo —¡lógico!** "I would help my son before yours" — "well, naturally!" • **lo más ~ sería ...** (+ *infin*) the most sensible thing would be to ... (+ *infin*)
3 (*Inform*) logic (*antes de s*)
SM/F logician; ▹ **lógica**
login SM login
logística SF logistics (*pl*)
logísticamente ADV logistically
logístico ADJ logistic
logo SM logo
logopeda SMF speech therapist
logopedia SF speech therapy
logoprocesadora SF word processor
logoterapeuta SMF speech therapist
logoterapia SF speech therapy
logotipo SM logo
logradamente ADV successfully
logrado ADJ successful
lograr ▹ CONJUG 1a VT [+ *trabajo*] to get, obtain (*frm*); [+ *vacaciones*] to get; [+ *éxito, victoria*] to achieve; [+ *perfección*] to attain

• **logra cuanto quiere** he gets whatever he wants • **por fin lo logró** eventually he managed it • **~ hacer algo** to manage to do sth, succeed in doing sth • **~ que algn haga algo** to (manage to) get sb to do sth

logrear ▹ CONJUG 1a (VI) to lend money at interest, be a moneylender

logrero/a (SM/F) **1** (= *prestamista*) moneylender, profiteer (*pey*)
2 (*LAm*) (= *gorrón*) sponger*, parasite

logro (SM) **1** (= *éxito*) achievement, attainment (*frm*) • **uno de sus mayores ~s** one of his greatest achievements
2 (*Com, Econ*) profit • **a ~** at (a high rate of) interest

logroñés/esa (ADJ) of/from Logroño
(SM/F) native/inhabitant of Logroño • **los logroñeses** the people of Logroño

LOGSE (SF ABR) = **Ley de Ordenación General del Sistema Educativo**

LOGSE
Spain's **Ley de Ordenación General del Sistema Educativo** (1990) provided for a new educational system which began to be implemented in the 1991-92 academic year. Amongst other things, it raised the school-leaving age from 14 to 16 and introduced compulsory vocational training for all students. Religious education became optional and special-needs provision was incorporated into mainstream education. Following the implementation of the **LOGSE**, compulsory education is divided into **Educación Primaria (EP)** and **Educación Secundaria Obligatoria (ESO)**.
▹ EP — EDUCACIÓN PRIMARIA, ESO

Loira (SM) Loire

loísmo (SM) *use of "lo" instead of "le" as indirect object;* ▹ LEÍSMO, LOÍSMO, LAÍSMO

loísta (ADJ) *that uses "lo" instead of "le" as indirect object*
(SMF) *user of "lo" instead of "le"*

Lola (SF), **Lolita** (SF) *formas familiares de* **María de los Dolores**

lolailo/a* (SM/F) (*pey*) gypsy

lolo/a* (SM/F) (*Chile*) boy/girl, teenager, teen (*EEUU**)

loma (SF) **1** (= *colina*) hillock, low ridge
2 (*Cono Sur**) • MODISMO: • **en la ~ del diablo** *o* **del quinoto** at the back of beyond*
3‡ (= *mano*) mitt*

lomada (SF) (*Cono Sur*) = **loma**

lomaje (SM) (*Cono Sur*) low ridge

lombarda (SF) (*Agr*) red cabbage; ▹ **lombardo**

Lombardía (SF) Lombardy

lombardo/a (ADJ) of/from Lombardy
(SM/F) native/inhabitant of Lombardy • **los ~s** the people of Lombardy; ▹ **lombarda**

lombriciento (ADJ) (*LAm*) suffering from worms

lombriz (SF) worm, earthworm ▸ **lombriz de mar** lugworm ▸ **lombriz intestinal, lombriz solitaria** tapeworm

lomería (SF), **lomerío** (SM) (*LAm*) low hills (*pl*), series of ridges

lometón (SM) (*Caribe, Méx*) isolated hillock

lomillería (SF) (*Cono Sur*) **1** (= *taller*) harness maker's; (= *tienda*) harness shop
2 (= *equipo*) harness, harness accessories (*pl*)

lomillero/a (SM/F) (*Cono Sur*) (= *fabricante*) harness maker; (= *vendedor*) harness seller

lomillo (SM) **1** (*Cos*) cross-stitch
2 lomillos (*LAm*) (= *almohadillas*) pads (of a pack saddle)

lomo (SM) **1** (*Anat*) back; [*de cerdo*] loin ▸ **lomo embuchado** (*Esp*) cured loin of pork
2 lomos (= *costillas*) ribs • **iba a ~s de una mula** he was riding a mule
3 [*de libro*] spine
4 [*de cuchillo*] back, blunt edge
5 (*Agr*) (= *tierra*) ridge
6 (*Aut*) ▸ **lomo de burro*** (*Arg*) speed hump, speed ramp ▸ **lomo de toro** (*Chile*) speed hump, speed ramp

lona[1] (SF) (= *tejido*) canvas; (*Náut*) sailcloth; (= *arpillera*) sackcloth • **la ~** (*Dep*) the canvas, the ring • MODISMO: • **estar en la ~** (*And, Caribe**) to be broke*

lona[2]* (ADJ INV) (*Cono Sur*) • **estar ~** to be knackered*, be worn out

loncha (SF) = **lonja[1]**

lonchar ▹ CONJUG 1a (*LAm*) (VT) to have for lunch
(VI) to have lunch, lunch

lonche (SM) (*LAm*) (= *comida*) lunch; (= *merienda*) tea, afternoon snack

lonchera (SF) (*And*) lunch box

lonchería (SF) (*LAm*) lunch counter, snack bar, diner (*EEUU*)

loncho (SM) (*And*) bit, piece, slice

londinense (ADJ) London (*antes de s*)
(SMF) Londoner • **los ~s** Londoners

Londres (SM) London

londri (SM) (*LAm*) laundry

loneta (SF) (*Cono Sur*) thin canvas

longa (SF) (*And*) Indian girl

longanimidad (SF) (*liter*) forbearance (*frm*), magnanimity

longánimo (ADJ) (*liter*) forbearing (*frm*), magnanimous

longaniza (SF) **1** (= *salchicha*) *long pork sausage*; ▹ **perro**
2 (*Cono Sur*) (= *serie*) string, series
3** (= *pene*) prick**

longevidad (SF) longevity

longevo (ADJ) long-lived • **las mujeres son más longevas que los hombres** women live longer than men

longitud (SF) **1** (= *largo*) length • **salto de ~** (*Dep*) long jump ▸ **longitud de onda** wavelength
2 (*Geog*) longitude

longitudinal (ADJ) longitudinal

longitudinalmente (ADV) longitudinally (*frm*), lengthways

longo/a (SM/F) (*Ecu*) young Indian

longui* (SM) • MODISMO: • **hacerse el ~** (= *desentenderse*) to pretend not to know; (= *fingir desinterés*) to pretend not to be interested; (= *guardar secreto*) not to let on, keep mum*

lonja[1] (SF) **1** (= *loncha*) slice; [*de tocino*] rasher
2 (*Cono Sur*) (= *cuero*) strip of leather
• MODISMO: • **sacar ~s a algn** to give sb a good thrashing

lonja[2] (SF) **1** (*Com*) market, exchange
• MODISMO: • **manipular la ~** to rig the market ▸ **lonja de granos** corn exchange ▸ **lonja de pescado** fish market
2 (= *tienda*) grocer's (shop)

lonjear ▹ CONJUG 1a (VT) (*Cono Sur*) **1** [+ *cuero*] to cut into strips
2 (= *zurrar*) to thrash

lonjista (SMF) grocer

lontananza (SF) [*de cuadro*] background • **en ~** far away, in the distance

loor (SM) (*liter*) praise

LOPJ (SF ABR) (*Esp*) (*Jur*) = **Ley Orgánica del Poder Judicial**

loquear* ▹ CONJUG 1a (VI) **1** (= *hacer locuras*) to play the fool
2 (= *divertirse*) to lark about*, have a high old time*

loqueo* (SM) (*Cono Sur*) uproar, hullaballoo

loquera* (SF) **1** (= *manicomio*) madhouse, loony bin*
2 (*LAm*) (= *locura*) madness; ▹ **loquero[1]**

loquería* (SF) (*LAm*) madhouse, lunatic asylum

loquero[1]/a* (SM/F) (= *enfermero*) psychiatric nurse; ▹ **loquera**

loquero[2]* (SM) **1** (*Arg*) (= *bullicio*) row, racket; ▹ **loquera**
2 (*Cono Sur*) (*fig*) (= *manicomio*) • **esta oficina es un ~** this office is a madhouse

loquina (SF) (*And*) foolish thing, idiocy

loquincho* (ADJ) (*Cono Sur*) crazy

lor (SM) lord

lora (SF) **1** (*LAm*) (*Orn*) (female) parrot
2 (*Cono Sur**) (= *fea*) old boot*
3 (= *habladora*) chatterbox*
4 (*And, Caribe*) (= *herida*) severe wound, open wound; ▹ **loro**

lord [lor] (SM) (PL: **lores**) lord

Lorena (SF) Lorraine

Lorenzo (SM) Laurence, Lawrence

lorna‡ (ADJ INV) (*Cono Sur*) daft*, crackpot*

loro (SM) **1** (= *ave*) parrot
2‡ (= *radio*) radio; (= *radiocasete*) radio-cassette • MODISMO: • **estar al ~‡** (= *alerta*) to be on the alert; (= *informado*) to know the score* • **hay que estar al ~** you need to be on the alert • **está al ~ de lo que pasa** he's in touch with what's going on • **¡al ~!** watch out!
3 (= *charlatán*) chatterbox* • **mi hermana es un ~, no para de hablar** my sister's a chatterbox, she never stops talking
4* (= *mujer fea*) old bag*, old bat*
5 (*Cono Sur*) (= *en robo*) thieves' lookout man
6 (*Cono Sur*) (*Med*) bedpan
7 (*Cono Sur*) (= *moco*) • **sacar los ~s*** to pick one's nose
8 (*Caribe*) (= *cuchillo*) pointed and curved knife; ▹ **lora**
(ADJ) dark brown

lorquiano (ADJ) relating to Federico García Lorca • **estudios ~s** Lorca studies • **las influencias lorquianas** Lorca's influences

los[1]/las[1] (ART DEF MPL/FPL) the • **los chicos juegan en el parque** the kids are playing in the park • **las sillas que compramos** the chairs we bought • **mis libros y los de usted** my books and yours • **las de Juan son verdes** John's are green • **una inocentada de las de niño pequeño** a practical joke typical of a small child; ▹ **el**

los[2]/las[2] (PRON PERS) (*refiriéndose a ellos, ellas*) them; (*refiriéndose a ustedes*) you • **les dije a los niños que los subiría al parque** I told the children that I would take them to the park • **no te los lleves, que aún no los he leído** don't take them away, I haven't read them yet • **señoras, yo las guiaré hasta la salida** ladies, I'll show you the way out • **¿los hay?** are there any? • **los hay y muy buenos** there are some and very good they are too

losa (SF) (stone) slab, flagstone ▸ **losa radiante** (*Arg*) underfloor heating ▸ **losa sepulcral** gravestone, tombstone

losange (SM) **1** (= *forma*) diamond (shape)
2 (*Mat*) rhombus, rhomb
3 (*Dep*) diamond
4 (*Heráldica*) lozenge

loseta (SF) [*de moqueta*] carpet tile; [*de cerámica*] floor tile

lota (SF) burbot

lote[1] (SM) **1** [*de herencia, reparto*] portion, share
2 (*en subasta*) lot • **el ~ 37 es una estantería de caoba** lot 37 is a mahogany bookcase
3 (*Inform*) batch
4 (*LAm*) (= *solar*) lot, piece of land, building site
5 (*LAm**) [*de drogas*] cache (*of drugs*)
6‡ • MODISMO: • **darse** *o* **pegarse el ~ con algn** to make it with sb‡

7 (= *medida*) (*Méx*) *about 100 hectares*; (*Cono Sur*) *about 400 hectares*
8 • MODISMO: • **al ~** (*Cono Sur*) any old how*
lote²* SM (*Cono Sur*) (= *imbécil*) idiot, clot*
lotear ▸ CONJUG 1a VT (*esp Cono Sur*) to divide into lots
loteo SM (*esp Cono Sur*) division into lots
lotería SF lottery • **jugar a la ~** to play the lottery • **le cayó** *o* **le tocó la ~** • **se sacó la ~** (*LAm*) (= *ganar*) he won the big prize in the lottery; (*fig*) he struck lucky ▸ **Lotería Nacional** National Lottery ▸ **lotería primitiva** *weekly state-run lottery*

LOTERÍA
There are two state-run lotteries in Spain: the **Lotería Primitiva** and the **Lotería Nacional**, with money raised going directly to the government. The **Primitiva** is similar to the British National Lottery in that players choose six numbers, including a bonus number (**complementario**), out of a total of 49. There are also several other similar draws each week, for which players can buy a multiple-draw ticket called a **bono-loto**. The **Lotería Nacional** works differently: people buy numbered tickets, which, if their number comes up, will entitle them to a share in the prize money with others who have the same numbered ticket. Whole numbers are quite costly, so people tend to buy either **décimos** or smaller **participaciones**. Several dozen prizes are won in each of the ordinary weekly draws, **sorteos ordinarios**. Every year there are also a number of **sorteos extraordinarios**, the most famous being the Christmas draw, or **sorteo de Navidad**, and the **sorteo del Niño** at the Epiphany.
▸ EL GORDO, ONCE

lotero/a SM/F seller of lottery tickets
lotificación SF (*CAm, Méx*) division into lots
lotificar ▸ CONJUG 1g VT (*CAm, Méx*) to divide into lots
lotización SF (*And*) division into lots
lotizar ▸ CONJUG 1f VT (*And*) to divide into lots
loto¹ SM lotus
loto²* SF lottery
Lovaina SF Louvain
loza SF 1 (= *vajilla*) crockery • **hacer la ~** to wash up
2 (= *cerámica*) pottery ▸ **loza fina** china, chinaware
lozanamente ADV 1 (*Bot*) (= *frondosamente*) luxuriantly, profusely
2 (= *vigorosamente*) vigorously
lozanear ▸ CONJUG 1a VI (*Bot*) to flourish, do well, flourish; [*persona*] to bloom
lozanía SF 1 (*Bot*) (= *frondosidad*) lushness, luxuriance; (= *frescura*) freshness
2 [*de persona*] (= *vigor*) vigour, vigor (EEUU), healthiness
3 [*del rostro, mejillas*] freshness
lozano ADJ 1 (*Bot*) (= *frondoso*) lush, luxuriant; (= *fresco*) fresh; [*persona, animal*] (= *vigoroso*) vigorous, full of life; (= *saludable*) healthy-looking
2 (= *seguro de sí*) self-assured; (= *arrogante*) arrogant
LRU SF ABR (*Esp*) (*Jur*) = **Ley de Reforma Universitaria**
LSD SM ABR (= **lysergic acid diethylamide**) LSD
lúa†‡ SF one peseta
lubina SF sea bass
lubricación SF lubrication
lubricador ADJ lubricating
SM lubricator
lubricante ADJ 1 [*aceite, sustancia*] lubricant, lubricating
2* [*persona*] greasy*
SM lubricant
lubricar ▸ CONJUG 1g VT to lubricate
lubricidad SF 1 (= *deslizamiento*) slipperiness
2 (= *lujuria*) lewdness, lubricity (*frm*)
lúbrico ADJ 1 (= *resbaladizo*) slippery
2 (= *lujurioso*) lewd, lubricious (*frm*)
lubrificación SF lubrication
lubrificante ADJ lubricant, lubricating
SM lubricant
lubrificar ▸ CONJUG 1f VT = **lubricar**
luca* SF (*Cono Sur*) 1000 pesos
Lucano SM Lucan
Lucas SM Luke, Lucas; (*Rel*) Luke
lucas* ADJ INV (*Méx*) crazy, cracked*
lucecitas SFPL fairy-lights
lucense ADJ of/from Lugo
SMF native/inhabitant of Lugo • **los ~s** the people of Lugo
lucera SF skylight
Lucerna SF Lucerne
lucerna SF chandelier
lucernario SM skylight
lucero SM 1 (*Astron*) bright star; (= *Venus*) Venus ▸ **lucero del alba, lucero de la mañana** morning star ▸ **lucero de la tarde, lucero vespertino** evening star
2 (*frm*) (= *brillo*) (= *esplendor*) brilliance, radiance
Lucha SF *forma familiar de* **Luz, Lucía**
lucha SF 1 (= *combate*) fight; (= *esfuerzo*) struggle (**por** for) • **~ a muerte** fight to the bitter end, fight to the death • **la ~ contra la droga** the fight against drugs • **la ~ por la supervivencia** the fight *o* struggle for survival • **esta vida es una ~** life is a struggle • **abandonar la ~** to give up the struggle ▸ **lucha armada** armed struggle ▸ **lucha contraincendios** fire-fighting ▸ **lucha de clases** class struggle
2 (*Dep*) ▸ **lucha grecorromana, lucha libre** wrestling
luchador(a) ADJ combative
SM/F (= *combatiente*) fighter; (*Dep*) wrestler • **~ por la libertad** freedom fighter
luchar ▸ CONJUG 1a VI 1 (= *combatir*) to fight; (= *esforzarse*) to struggle (**por algo** for sth) • **luchó en el bando republicano** he fought on the Republican side • **tuvo que ~ mucho en la vida** life was a constant struggle for her • **~ con** *o* **contra algo/algn** to fight (against) sth/sb • **~on contra la corrupción** they fought against corruption • **el enfermo luchaba con la muerte** the sick man was fighting for his life • **luchaba con los mandos** he was struggling *o* wrestling with the controls
2 (*Dep*) to wrestle (**con** with)
luche SM (*Cono Sur*) 1 (= *juego*) hopscotch
2 (*Bot*) *an edible seaweed*
Lucía SF Lucy
lucidez SF 1 (= *perspicacia*) lucidity, clarity • **demuestra gran ~ al resolver los problemas** she's very lucid *o* clear when solving problems
2 (*tb* **lucidez mental**) lucidity • **es demente, pero tiene momentos de ~ (mental)** she's insane but has moments of lucidity, she's insane but has her lucid moments
3 (*CAm, Cono Sur*) (= *brillantez*) brilliance
lucido ADJ 1 (= *espléndido*) splendid, magnificent • **fue una boda muy lucida** it was a splendid *o* magnificent wedding • **la actriz tuvo una actuación muy lucida** the actress gave a splendid *o* magnificent *o* stunning performance
2 • **estar ~** • **quedar(se) ~** (*iró*) to make a mess of things • **¡estamos ~s!** a fine mess we're in! • **~s estaríamos si ...** it would be awful if ...
lúcido ADJ 1 [*persona*] • **ser/estar ~** to be lucid
2 [*observación, comentario, análisis*] lucid
luciente ADJ bright, shining, brilliant
luciérnaga SF glow-worm
Lucifer SM Lucifer
lucimiento SM 1 (= *brillo*) brilliance, sparkle • **hacer algo con ~** to do sth outstandingly well *o* very successfully
2 (= *ostentación*) show, ostentation
lucio¹ SM (= *pez*) pike
lucio² ADJ (*frm*) = **lúcido**
lución SM slow-worm
lucir ▸ CONJUG 3f VI 1 (= *brillar*) to shine • **lucían las estrellas** the stars were shining
2 (= *destacar*) to excel • **no lucía en los estudios** he did not excel as a student
3 (= *aprovechar*) • **trabaja mucho, pero no le luce el esfuerzo** he works hard but it doesn't do him much good • MODISMO: • **así le/te/me luce el pelo**: • **nunca estudia y así le luce el pelo** he never studies and it shows
4 (*LAm*) (= *parecer*) to look, seem • **(te) luce lindo** it looks nice (on you)
VT (= *ostentar*) to show off; [+ *ropa*] to sport • **~ las habilidades** to show off one's talents • **lucía un traje nuevo** he was sporting a new suit • **siempre va luciendo escote** she always wears low-cut dresses
VPR **lucirse** 1 (= *destacar*) to excel • **Carlos se lució en el examen** Carlos excelled in the exam • **se lució con un gol** he distinguished himself with a goal
2 (= *hacer el ridículo*) (*iró*) to excel o.s. • **¡te has lucido!** you've excelled yourself!
lucrarse ▸ CONJUG 1a VPR to do well out of a deal; (*pey*) feather one's (own) nest
lucrativo ADJ lucrative, profitable • **organización no lucrativa** non-profitmaking organization, not-for-profit organization
Lucrecia SF Lucretia
Lucrecio SM Lucretius
lucro SM profit • **~s y daños** (*Econ*) profit and loss; ▸ **afán**
luctuoso ADJ (*frm*) mournful, sad
lucubración SF (*frm*) lucubration (*frm*) • **déjate de lucubraciones y vamos al grano** come down off the clouds and let's talk sense
lúcuma* SF 1 (*Chile, Perú, Bol*) (= *fruta*) *variety of eggfruit*; (= *berenjena*) aubergine, eggplant (EEUU)
2 • MODISMOS: • **coger la ~** (*Caribe**) (= *enojarse*) to get mad*; (= *afanarse*) to keep at it • **dar la ~** (*Méx**) (= *empeñarse*) to keep trying
ludibrio SM (*frm*) mockery, derision
lúdico ADJ ludic (*liter*), playful
ludir ▸ CONJUG 3a VT to rub (**con, contra** against)
ludista ADJ Luddite
ludita ADJ Luddite
ludoparque SM sports centre, sports complex
ludópata ADJ addicted to gambling
SMF compulsive gambler, gambling addict
ludopatía SF compulsive gambling, addiction to gambling
ludoteca SF children's play-centre
luego ADV 1 (*en el tiempo*) **a** (*referido al pasado*) then • **—quedamos en un bar —¿y ~ qué pasó?** "we met in a bar" — "and then what happened?" • **vimos una película y ~ fuimos a cenar** we saw a film and later (on) *o* afterwards *o* then went out for dinner
b (*referido al futuro*) later (on), afterwards • **te**

lo dejo pero ~ me lo devuelves you can borrow it but you have to give me it back later (on) *o* afterwards • **~ vuelvo** I'll be back later (on) • **te veo ~** I'll see you later (on) *o* then • **~ de after** • **~ de eso** after that • **~ de cenar se fue** he left after dinner • **¡hasta ~!** bye!, see you!, see you later! • **~ que ...** (*LAm*) (*tan pronto como*) as soon as ...; (*después que*) after ...
c (*LAm*) (= *pronto*) soon • **lo vamos a saber muy ~** we'll find out really soon • **espéralo que lueguito viene** wait for him, he's coming in a minute • **empieza siempre con entusiasmo pero lueguito se aburre** he's very enthusiastic at the beginning but he gets bored quickly • **luego luego** (*esp Méx**) straight away
d (*And, Caribe, Méx*) (= *de vez en cuando*) sometimes, from time to time
2 (*en el espacio*) then • **primero está la cocina y ~ el comedor** the kitchen is first, then the dining room • **primero va usted y ~ yo** you're first and I'm next, you're first and then it's me
3 (= *además*) then • **~ tenemos estos otros colores** then we have these other colours
4 (*Méx*) (= *muy cerca*) right here, right there
5 • **desde ~** of course; ▹ **desde**
CONJ (= *así que*) therefore • **pienso, ~ existo** I think, therefore I am • **~ x es igual a 7** therefore x equals 7

lueguito ADV **1** (*LAm*) (= *inmediatamente*) at once, right now, immediately
2 (*Chile, CAm, Méx**) (= *cerca*) near, nearby • **aquí ~** close by here, very near here

luengo†† ADJ long

lúes SF syphilis

lugar SM **1** (= *sitio*) place • **dejó las joyas en ~ seguro** she left the jewels in a safe place • **es un ~ muy bonito** it is a lovely spot *o* place • **devolver un libro a su ~** to put a book back in its place • **el concierto será en un ~ cerrado** the concert will take place indoors *o* at an indoor venue • **el ~ del crimen** the scene of the crime • **algún ~** somewhere • **una emisión desde algún ~ de Europa** a broadcast from somewhere in Europe • **lo escondió en algún ~ de la casa** she hid it somewhere around the house • **los Santos Lugares** the Holy Places • **MODISMO**: • **poner las cosas en su ~** to put things straight ▸ **lugar común** cliché, commonplace ▸ **lugar de encuentro** meeting-place ▸ **lugar geométrico** locus; ▹ **composición**
2 (= *posición*) **a** (*en lista, carrera, trabajo*) • **ocupa un buen ~ en la empresa** she has a good position *o* post at the company • **ocupar el ~ de algn** to take sb's place • **llegó en último ~** he came last • **en primer ~**: • **se han clasificado en primer ~** they have qualified in first place • **en primer ~, me gustaría agradecer la invitación** first of all *o* firstly, I would like to thank you for inviting me
b (= *situación*) • **yo, en tu ~, no iría** I wouldn't go if I were you • **usted póngase en mi ~** put yourself in my place *o* shoes • **en su ~, ¡descanso!** (*Mil*) stand easy! • **dejar a algn en buen/mal ~** [*comportamiento*] to reflect well/badly on sb; [*persona*] to make sb look good/bad • **estar fuera de ~** to be out of place • **sentirse fuera de ~** to feel out of place • **MODISMO**: • **encontrar un ~ bajo el sol** to find a place in the sun
c • **en ~ de** instead of • **vino el portavoz en ~ del ministro** the spokesman came instead of the minister, the spokesman came in the minister's place • **¿puedo asistir yo en su ~?** can I go instead? • **en ~ de escribir, me llamó por teléfono** instead of writing, he called me • **en ~ de ir a la piscina, ¿por qué no vamos a la playa?** why don't we go to the beach instead of the swimming pool?
3 (= *ocasión*) opportunity, chance • **si se me da el ~** if I have the opportunity *o* chance • **no hubo ~ para decir lo que pensaba** there was no opportunity to say what I thought • **no hay ~ para preocupaciones** there is no cause for concern • **dar ~ a algo** to give rise to sth, lead to sth • **dejar ~ a algo** to leave room for sth • **los datos no dejan ~ a dudas** the figures leave no room for doubt • **la situación no dejaba ~ al optimismo** the situation left little room for *o* gave few grounds for optimism • **sin ~ a dudas** without doubt, undoubtedly • **no ha ~**: • **una reacción tan fuerte, francamente no ha ~** there is no need for such a violent response • **—¡protesto! —no ha ~** (*Jur*) "objection!" — "overruled" • **tener ~** to take place, happen, occur • **MODISMO**: • **a como dé** *o* **diera ~** (*Méx*) (= *de cualquier manera*) somehow or other, one way or another; (= *a toda costa*) at any cost
4 (= *espacio*) room, space • **no hay ~ para escribir nada más** there's no room *o* space to write any more • **¿hay ~?** is there any room? • **hacer ~ para algo** to make room for sth
5 (= *localidad*) place • **En un ~ de la Mancha ...** Somewhere in La Mancha ... • **del ~** local • **un vino del ~** a local wine • **las gentes del ~** the local people, the locals ▸ **lugar de nacimiento** (*gen*) birthplace; (*en impreso*) place of birth ▸ **lugar de trabajo** workplace

lugareño/a ADJ **1** (= *local*) local
2 (*Méx*) (= *regional*) regional; (= *nativo*) native
SM/F local

lugarteniente SM deputy, substitute (*EEUU*)

luge SM luge

Lugo SM Lugo

lugo SM (*And*) (*Zool*) ram

lugre SM lugger

lúgubre ADJ (= *triste*) mournful, lugubrious (*frm*), dismal; [*voz, tono*] sombre, somber (*EEUU*), mournful

lúgubremente ADV (= *tristemente*) mournfully; (= *seriamente, sobriamente*) sombrely, somberly (*EEUU*)

luir ▹ CONJUG 3g VT (*Cono Sur*) **1** (= *arrugar*) to rumple, mess up
2 [+ *cerámica*] to polish

Luis SM Louis

Luisa SF Louise

Luisiana SF Louisiana

lujo SM **1** (= *fasto*) luxury • **vivir con ~** to live in luxury • **hoy en día comer carne es un ~** eating meat is a luxury these days • **de ~** luxury (*antes de s*) • **un coche de ~** a luxury car • **permitirse el ~ de hacer algo** to allow o.s. the luxury of doing sth ▸ **lujo asiático*** • **¿te vas al Caribe? ¡vaya ~ asiático!** so you're off to the Caribbean? what a life of luxury!
2 (= *abundancia*) profusion, wealth, abundance • **con todo ~ de detalles** with a wealth of detail

lujosamente ADV **1** (= *con fasto*) luxuriously
2 (= *profusamente*) profusely

lujoso ADJ **1** (= *fastuoso*) luxurious
2 (= *profuso*) profuse

lujuria SF **1** (*sexual*) lust, lechery, lewdness
2 [*de vegetación*] lushness, abundance
3 [*de poder*] excess

lujuriante ADJ (*frm*) **1** [*vegetación*] luxuriant, lush; [*aroma*] delicious, inviting
2 (= *lujurioso*) lustful, lecherous, lewd

lujuriar ▹ CONJUG 1b VI (*frm*) to lust

lujuriosamente ADV lecherously

lujurioso ADJ lustful, lecherous, lewd

lullir‡ ▹ CONJUG 3h VT (*And, CAm, Méx*) to rub (**con, contra** against, on)

lulo[1]/a (*Cono Sur*) ADJ* **1** (= *desgarbado*) lanky
2 (= *torpe*) dull, slow
SM/F (= *persona desgarbada*) lanky person

lulo[2] SM **1** (*Chile**) (= *bulto*) bundle; (= *rizo*) kiss curl
2 • **MODISMO**: • **al ~** (*Caribe**) one after another
3 ▸ **lulo del ojo** (*And*) eyeball

lulú SMF (*tb* **lulú de Pomerania**) Pomeranian, pom

luma* SF (*Cono Sur*) **1** (= *bastón*) police truncheon
2 (= *reprimenda*) ticking-off*

lumbago SM lumbago

lumbalgia SF lumbago

lumbar ADJ lumbar

lumbre SF **1** (= *fuego*) fire • **a la ~** • **cerca de la ~** near the fire, by the fireside • **MODISMO**: • **echar ~ por los ojos** to be furious
2† (*para cigarro*) light • **¿me das ~?** • **¿tienes ~?** have you got a light?
3 (= *luz*) light; (= *brillo*) brightness, brilliance ▸ **lumbre del agua** surface of the water
4† (*Arquit*) (= *claraboya*) skylight; (= *abertura*) light, opening (*in a wall*)

lumbrera SF **1** (= *genio*) leading light, luminary • **estaba rodeado de ~s literarias** he was surrounded by leading literary figures
2 (= *claraboya*) skylight
3 (= *cuerpo luminoso*) luminary (*liter*)
4 (*Mec*) vent, port ▸ **lumbrera de admisión** inlet ▸ **lumbrera de escape** exhaust vent
5 (*Méx*) (*Taur, Teat*) box

lumi‡ SF whore

luminar SM = lumbrera

luminaria SF (*Rel*) altar lamp; **luminarias** illuminations, lights

luminescencia SF luminescence

luminescente ADJ luminescent

lumínico ADJ light (*antes de s*)

luminosidad SF **1** (= *resplandor*) brightness, luminosity (*frm*)
2 [*de una ocurrencia, explicación*] brilliance

luminoso ADJ **1** (*gen*) bright, shining; [*letrero*] illuminated; [*esfera, reloj*] luminous
2 [*idea*] bright, brilliant; [*exposición*] brilliant
SM (*Com*) neon sign; (*Dep*) electronic scoreboard

luminotecnia SF lighting

luminotécnico ADJ lighting (*antes de s*) • **efectos ~s** lighting effects

lumpen ADJ INV lumpen • **el Madrid ~** the Madrid underclass
SM INV underclass, lumpen

lumpo SM lumpfish • **caviar de ~** lumpfish caviar • **huevas de ~** lumpfish roe

lun. ABR (= **lunes**) Mon.

luna SF **1** (= *astro*) moon • **claro de ~** moonlight • **media ~** half moon • **MODISMOS**: • **estar de buena/mala ~** to be in a good/bad mood • **estar en la ~** to have one's head in the clouds • **estar en la ~ de Valencia** to be in a dream world • **hablar de la ~**: • **eso es hablar de la ~** that's nonsense • **quedarse a la ~ de Valencia** to be disappointed, be left in the lurch • **quedarse en la ~ de Paita** (*And**) to be struck dumb ▸ **luna creciente** crescent moon, waxing moon ▸ **luna de miel** [*de novios*] honeymoon; (*fig*) (*Pol*) honeymoon (period) ▸ **luna llena** full moon ▸ **luna menguante** waning moon ▸ **luna nueva** new moon
2 (= *vidrio*) (= *escaparate*) plate glass; (= *espejo*) mirror; [*de gafas*] lens; (*Aut*) window; [*de ventana*] pane; [*de puerta*] panel ▸ **luna térmica** (*Aut*) heated rear window

lunar ADJ lunar
SM **1** (*Anat*) mole ▸ **lunar postizo** beauty spot
2 (*en tejido*) polka-dot, spot • **MODISMO**: • **de**

~es polka-dot • **un vestido de ~es a** polka-dot dress
3 (= *defecto*) flaw, blemish; (*moral*) stain, blot
lunarejo ADJ (*LAm*) spotty, spotty-faced
lunático/a ADJ, SM/F lunatic
lunch [lunʃ] SM (PL: **lunchs** [lunʃ]) lunch; (= *refrigerio*) midday snack; (*en celebración, fiesta*) midday reception, cold buffet
lunchería SF (*LAm*) = **lonchería**
lunes SM INV Monday • MODISMOS: • **hacer San Lunes** (*LAm**) to stay away from work on Monday • **no ocurre cada ~ y cada martes** it doesn't happen every day of the week; ▹ **sábado**
luneta SF **1** [*de gafas*] lens; (*Aut*) window ▸ **luneta trasera** rear window ▸ **luneta trasera térmica** heated rear window
2 (= *media luna*) halfmoon shape, crescent
3 (*Méx*) (*Teat†*) stall
lunfa* SM (*Cono Sur*) thief
lunfardismo SM (*Cono Sur*) (= *palabra*) slang word
lunfardo SM **1** (*Arg*) *local slang of Buenos Aires*
2 (*Cono Sur*) criminal slang, language of the underworld
lupa SF magnifying glass • **ha examinado el discurso con ~** she has gone over the speech with a fine tooth comb
lupanar†† SM brothel
Lupe SF *forma familiar de* **Guadalupe**
lupia¹ SF **1** (= *lobanillo*) wen, cyst
2 (*And*) **lupias** (= *cantidad pequeña*) small amount of money (*sing*); (= *cambio*) small change (*sing*)
lupia²* SMF (*CAm*) quack*
lúpulo SM (*Bot*) hop, hops (*pl*)
luquete SM (*Cono Sur*) **1** (*Agr*) unploughed patch of land
2 (= *calva*) bald patch
3 (= *mancha*) grease spot
lurio* (*Méx*) ADJ (= *enamorado*) in love; (= *loco*) crazy, cracked*
lusitano/a ADJ Portuguese; (*Hist*) Lusitanian
SM/F Portuguese man/woman, native/inhabitant of Portugal; (*Hist*) Lusitanian • **los ~s** the Portuguese
luso/a ADJ, SM/F = **lusitano**
lustrabotas SMF INV (*LAm*) bootblack, shoeshine boy/girl
lustrada* SM (*LAm*) (= *acto*) shine, shoeshine
lustrador¹(a) SM/F (*LAm*) (= *limpiabotas*) bootblack, shoeshine boy/girl
lustrador² SM (*Téc*) polisher
lustradora SF polishing machine
lustrar ▹ CONJUG 1a VT (*esp LAm*) to shine, polish
lustre SM **1** (= *brillo*) shine, lustre, luster (EEUU), gloss • **dar ~ a** to polish, put a shine on
2 (= *sustancia*) polish ▸ **lustre para calzado** shoe polish ▸ **lustre para metales** metal polish
3 (= *prestigio*) lustre, luster (EEUU), glory
lustrín SM (*Chile*) shoeshine box, shoeshine stand
lustrina SF **1** (*Cono Sur*) *shiny material of alpaca*
2 (*And*) (= *tela*) silk cloth
3 (*Cono Sur*) (= *betún*) shoe polish
lustro SM period of five years, five year period, lustrum (*frm*)
lustroso ADJ **1** (= *brillante*) [*zapatos*] shiny; [*pelo*] glossy, shiny
2 (= *saludable*) healthy-looking
lutencio SM (*Quím*) lutetium
luteranismo SM Lutheranism
luterano/a ADJ, SM/F Lutheran
Lutero SM Luther
lutita SF shale
luto SM mourning • **medio ~** half-mourning • **dejar el ~** to come out of mourning • **estar de ~** • **llevar ~** • **vestir(se) de ~** to be in mourning (**por** for) ▸ **luto riguroso** deep mourning
luxación SF (*Med*) dislocation
Luxemburgo SM Luxembourg
luxemburgués/esa ADJ of/from Luxembourg
SM/F native/inhabitant of Luxembourg • **los luxemburgueses** the people of Luxembourg
luz SF **1** (= *claridad*) light • **una casa con mucha luz** a very bright house, a house that gets a lot of light • **necesito más luz para leer** I can't read in this light • **a media luz**: • **la habitación estaba a media luz** the room was in half-darkness • **estábamos allí tumbados a media luz** we were lying there in the half-darkness • **poner una lámpara a media luz** to dim a light • **a primera luz** at first light • **quitar** *o* **tapar la luz a algn** to be in sb's light • **aparta de ahí, que me quitas** *o* **tapas la luz** get out of the way, you're in my light • MODISMOS: • **entre dos luces** (= *al atardecer*) at twilight; (= *al amanecer*) at dawn, at daybreak • **estar entre dos luces*** (= *borracho*) to be mellow, be tipsy • **hacer luz de gas a algn** to confuse sb • **negar la luz del día a algn** to concede absolutely nothing to sb • **ver la luz al final del túnel** to see light at the end of the tunnel ▸ **luz cenital** light from above ▸ **luz del día** • **se despierta con la luz del día** she wakes up when it gets light *o* (*liter*) at first light • **con la luz del día lo veremos de otra manera** we'll see things differently in the cold light of day • MODISMO: • **tan claro como la luz del día** as clear as daylight ▸ **luz de (la) luna** • **a la luz de la luna** by the light of the moon, by moonlight ▸ **luz de las velas** • **a la luz de las velas** by candlelight ▸ **luz del sol** sunlight • **me molesta la luz del sol** the sunlight hurts my eyes ▸ **luz eléctrica** electric light ▸ **luz natural** natural light ▸ **luz solar** sunlight ▸ **luz ultravioleta** ultraviolet light ▸ **luz y sombra** light and shade ▸ **luz y sonido** • **un espectáculo de luz y sonido** a son et lumière show; ▹ **brillar**
2 (= *lámpara, foco*) light • **me dejé la luz encendida** I left the light on • **se ha fundido la luz de la cocina** the light has gone in the kitchen • **las luces de la ciudad** the city lights • **apagar la luz** to switch *o* turn *o* put the light off • **encender** *o* (*LAm*) **prender** *o* **poner la luz** to switch *o* turn *o* put the light on • MODISMO: • **hacer algo con luz y taquígrafos** to do sth openly • **reunirse sin luz ni taquígrafos** to meet behind closed doors ▸ **luces altas** (*Chile*) full-beam headlights (*Brit*), high beams (*EEUU*) ▸ **luces bajas** (*Chile*), **luces cortas** dipped headlights, low beams (*EEUU*) • **poner las luces cortas** *o* (*Chile*) **bajas** to dip one's headlights, dim one's headlights (EEUU) ▸ **luces de aterrizaje** (*Aer*) landing lights ▸ **luces de balización** (*Aer*) runway lights ▸ **luces de carretera** full-beam headlights (*Brit*), high beams (*EEUU*) • **poner las luces de carretera** to put one's headlights on full beam *o* (*EEUU*) high beam ▸ **luces de cruce** dipped headlights • **poner las luces de cruce** to dip one's headlights, dim one's headlights (*EEUU*) ▸ **luces de detención** brake lights ▸ **luces de estacionamiento** parking lights ▸ **luces de frenado, luces de freno** brake lights ▸ **luces de gálibo** clearance lights ▸ **luces de navegación** navigation lights ▸ **luces de posición** sidelights ▸ **luces de tráfico** traffic lights ▸ **luces largas** = **luces de carretera** ▸ **luces traseras** rear lights, tail lamps ▸ **luz de Bengala** (*Mil*) flare, star-shell; (*LAm*) (= *fuego de artificio*) sparkler ▸ **luz de cortesía** courtesy light; (*CAm*) sidelight ▸ **luz de costado** sidelight ▸ **luz de giro** direction indicator ▸ **luz de lectura** reading light ▸ **luz de situación** sidelight, parking light ▸ **luz intermitente** flashing light ▸ **luz piloto** sidelight, parking light ▸ **luz relámpago** (*Fot*) flashlight ▸ **luz roja** red light ▸ **luz verde** green light • **dar luz verde a un proyecto** to give a project the go-ahead *o* the green light • **recibir luz verde** to get the go-ahead *o* the green light ▸ **luz vuelta** (*Méx*) direction indicator; ▹ **traje²**
3 (= *suministro de electricidad*) electricity • **no hay luz en todo el edificio** there's no electricity in the whole building • **les cortaron la luz** their electricity (supply) was cut off • **se ha ido la luz** the lights have gone out • **¿cuánto has pagado de luz este mes?** how much was your electricity bill this month?
4 (*tb* **luz pública**) • MODISMOS: • **sacar a la luz** [+ *secreto*] to bring to light; [+ *libro, disco*] to bring out • **salir a la luz** [*secreto*] to come to light; [*libro, disco*] to come out • **el año en que el periódico salió a la luz** the year in which the newspaper first came out • **la última vez que el periódico salió a la luz** the last time the newspaper was published • **ver la luz** [*libro, disco*] to appear, come out
5 (*Med*) • **dar a luz** [+ *niño*] to give birth • **acaba de dar a luz (a) una niña** she has just given birth to a baby girl
6 (*Cono Sur*) (= *ventaja*) • **dar luz a algn** to give sb a start • **te doy diez metros de luz** I'll give you ten metres' start
7 (= *aclaración*) light • **a la luz de lo que hemos visto** in the light of what we've seen • **a la luz de un nuevo descubrimiento** in the light of a new discovery • **arrojar luz sobre algo** to cast *o* shed *o* throw light on sth • **estudiar algo a nueva luz** to study sth in a new light • MODISMO: • **a todas luces** by any reckoning
8 (*Arquit*) [*de puerta, hueco*] span; [*de edificio*] window, opening; [*de puente*] span
9 luces (= *inteligencia*) intelligence (*sing*) • **corto de luces** • **de pocas luces** dim, stupid
10 (*Hist, Literat*) • **el Siglo de las Luces** the Age of Enlightenment
11 (*Cono Sur*) (= *distancia*) *distance between two objects* ▸ **luz al suelo** clearance (*under a vehicle*)
12 (*And‡*) dough‡, money
lycra® SF Lycra®
Lyón SM Lyons

Mm

M[1], **m**[1] ['eme] (SF) (= *letra*) M, m

M[2] (ABR) **1** (= **mediano**) M
 2 (= **marzo**) Mar • **11-M** 11 March (*date of the Madrid train bombing in 2004*)

m^2 (ABR) **1** (= **metro(s)**) m • m^2 (= **metros cuadrados**) sq. m., m^2 • m^3 (= **metros cúbicos**) cu. m., m^3
 2 (= **masculino**) masc., m

M. (ABR) **1** = **Madrid**
 2 (*Ferro*) = **Metropolitano**
 3 (*Geog*) = **Meridiano**

m. (ABR) **1** (= **murió**) d
 2 (= **mes**) m
 3 (= **monte**) Mt

M-19 (SM ABR) (*Col*) (*Pol*) = **Movimiento 19 de Abril**

M.ª (ABR) = **María**

maca[1] (SF) **1** (= *defecto*) flaw, defect
 2 (= *mancha*) (*gen*) spot; (*en fruta*) bruise, blemish

maca[2] (SF) (*Caribe*) (= *loro*) parrot

maca[3]‡ (SM) = **macarra**

macabeo/a (ADJ) Maccabean; ▹ **rollo**
 (SM/F) Maccabee

macabí (SM) **1** (*And*) shrewd person
 2 (*Caribe*) bandit

macabro (ADJ) macabre

macaco (ADJ)* **1** (*LAm*) (= *deforme*) deformed, misshapen; (= *feo*) ugly
 2 (*CAm, Caribe*) (= *tonto*) silly
 (SM) **1** (*Zool*) macaque
 2 (*Cono Sur*) (*pey*) Brazilian
 3 (*Caribe*) big shot*, bigwig
 4 (*Méx*) bogey

macadamizar ▹ CONJUG 1f (VT) to macadamize, tarmac

macadán (SM) macadam

macagua (SF) **1** (*LAm*) (= *ave*) laughing falcon
 2 (*Ven*) (= *serpiente*) poisonous snake

macana (SF) **1** (*LAm*) (= *porra*) (*gen*) club, cudgel; [*de policía*] truncheon, billy (club) (EEUU); (*Hist*) Indian club *o* cudgel
 2 (*And, Cono Sur**) (= *mentira*) lie • **¡macana!** it's all lies!; **macanas** (= *tonterías*) rubbish (*sing*), nonsense (*sing*)
 3 (*Cono Sur**) (= *contrariedad*) pain*, nuisance • **¡qué ~! el ascensor no funciona** what a pain* *o* nuisance! the lift's not working
 4 (*Cono Sur**) (= *chapuza*) bad job
 5 (*Cono Sur**) (= *charla*) long boring conversation
 6 (*Caribe*) • **de ~** undoubtedly • **es de ~ que ...** of course ...

macanazo (SM) **1** (*Caribe*) blow (*with a club, cudgel*)
 2 (*Cono Sur*) = **macana**

macaneador(a)* (*Cono Sur*) (ADJ) (= *mentiroso*) deceitful; (= *poco fiable*) unreliable
 (SM/F) charlatan

macanear* ▹ CONJUG 1a (VI) **1** (*esp And, Cono Sur*) (= *mentir*) to lie; (= *exagerar*) to exaggerate wildly, tell tall stories; (= *decir tonterías*) to talk nonsense, talk rubbish; (= *hacer tonterías*) to mess about
 2 (*LAm**) (= *trabajar*) to work hard, keep one's nose to the grindstone
 (VT) **1** (*Caribe*) (= *aporrear*) to beat, hit
 2 (*Caribe*) (*en jardín, huerta*) to weed, clear of weeds
 3 (*Caribe*) [+ *asunto*] to handle

macanero* (ADJ) (*And, Cono Sur*) (= *que dice tonterías*) given to talking nonsense, silly; (= *fantasioso*) given to telling tall stories

macanudo* (ADJ) **1** (*LAm*) (= *estupendo*) great*, fantastic*
 2 (*And*) (= *duro*) [*trabajo*] tough, difficult; [*persona*] strong, tough
 3 (*Cono Sur, Méx*) (= *abultado*) swollen, overlarge
 4 (*Cono Sur*) (= *exagerado*) disproportionate

Macao (SM) Macao

macaquear ▹ CONJUG 1a (VT) (*CAm*) (= *robar*) to steal
 (VI) (*Cono Sur*) (= *hacer gestos*) to make faces

macarra‡ (SM) (*Esp*) **1** (= *bruto*) lout, thug; (= *mal vestido*) vulgar, flashy type • **tiene aspecto de ~** he looks really vulgar and flashy
 2 (= *chulo*) pimp

macarrada‡ (SF) • **lo que hiciste fue una ~** that was a really loutish thing for you to do

macarrón[1] (SM) (*tb* **macarrón de almendras**) macaroon

macarrón[2] (SM) (*Náut*) bulwark, stanchion

macarrones (SMPL) (= *pasta*) macaroni

macarrónico (ADJ) macaronic

macarse ▹ CONJUG 1g (VPR) to go bad, rot

macear ▹ CONJUG 1a (VT) to hammer, pound
 (VI) **1** (= *insistir*) = **machacar**
 2 (*CAm**) to bet

Macedonia (SF) Macedonia

macedonia (SF) ▸ **macedonia de frutas** fruit salad

macedonio/a (ADJ), (SM/F) Macedonian
 (SM) (*Ling*) Macedonian

maceración (SF) **1** (*Culin*) [*de fruta*] soaking, maceration; [*de carne*] marinading • **dejar en ~** [+ *fruta*] to leave to soak; [+ *carne*] to marinate
 2 (= *vergüenza*) mortification

macerado (SM) maceration

macerar ▹ CONJUG 1a (VT) **1** (*Culin*) [+ *fruta*] to soak, macerate; [+ *carne*] to marinate
 2 (= *avergonzar*) to mortify
 (VPR) **macerarse 1** (*Culin*) [*fruta*] to soak, macerate; [*carne*] to marinate
 2 (= *mortificarse*) to mortify o.s.

macero (SM) macebearer

maceta (SF) **1** [*de flores*] (= *tiesto*) flowerpot, plant pot; (*Cono Sur*) (= *ramo*) bouquet, bunch of flowers
 2 (= *martillo*) (*gen*) mallet, small hammer; [*de cantero*] stonecutter's hammer
 3 (*Méx**) (= *cabeza*) nut*, noggin (*EEUU**) • **ser duro de ~** (*And, Cono Sur*) to be thick in the head*
 (ADJ)* **1** (*And, Cono Sur*) thick*, slow • **ponerse ~** to get old
 2 (*Caribe*) stingy*, tight*

macetero (SM) **1** (= *soporte*) flowerpot stand, flowerpot holder
 2 (*LAm*) (= *maceta*) flowerpot

macetón (SM) tub

macha (SF) (*And, Caribe*) mannish woman, butch woman* (*pey*)

machaca (SF) (= *aparato*) crusher, pounder
 (SMF)* (= *persona*) nag, pest

machacadora (SF) crusher, pounder

machacante (ADJ) [*publicidad*] constant; [*estribillo*] monotonous, insistent

machacar ▹ CONJUG 1g (VT) **1** (= *triturar*) to crush • **machacó los ajos en el mortero** he crushed the garlic in the mortar
 2* (= *aniquilar*) [+ *contrincante*] to thrash; (*en discusión*) to crush, flatten • **el equipo visitante los machacó** they were thrashed by the visiting team
 3 [+ *precio*] to slash
 4* [+ *lección, asignatura*] to swot (up)*
 5 (*Esp**) (= *insistir sobre*) to go on about • **deja ya de ~ siempre lo mismo** stop going on and on about the same thing
 6 (*Baloncesto**) to dunk, slam dunk
 (VI)* **1** (*Esp*) (= *insistir*) to go on • **¡no machaques!** don't go on so!, stop harping on about it! • **~ con** *o* **sobre algo** to go on about sth; ▹ **hierro**
 2 (= *empollar*) to swot*
 (VPR) **machacarse 1*** [+ *dinero, herencia, sueldo*] to blow*
 2 • **machacársela** (*Esp***) to wank** • **¡a mí me la machaca!** I couldn't give a fuck!**

machacón/ona (ADJ) (= *insistente*) insistent; (= *monótono*) monotonous, repetitive; (= *pesado*) tiresome, wearisome • **con insistencia machacona** with tiresome *o* wearisome insistence
 (SM/F) pest, bore

machaconamente (ADV) (= *con insistencia*) insistently; (= *con monotonía*) monotonously, repetitively; (= *con pesadez*) tiresomely

machaconeo (SM), **machaconería** (SF) (= *insistencia*) insistence; (= *monotonía*) monotony, repetitiveness

machada* (SF) **1** courageous act, heroic deed; (*pey*) piece of macho bravado • **fue una ~** it was a piece of macho bravado
 2 (= *dicho*) macho remark

machado (SM) hatchet

machamartillo (SM) • MODISMO: • **a ~**: **eran cristianos a ~** they were staunch Christians • **creer a ~** (= *firmemente*) to believe firmly; (= *ciegamente*) to believe blindly • **cumplir algo a ~** to carry out sth to the letter

machango (ADJ) (*Cono Sur*) tedious

machaque* (SM) dunk, slam dunk

machaquear ▹ CONJUG 1a (VT), (VI) (*Méx*) = **machacar**

machaqueo (SM) crushing, pounding

machaquería (SF) (= *insistencia*) insistence;

(= *monotonía*) monotony; (= *fastidio*) tiresomeness
macharse‡ ▸ CONJUG 1a VPR (*Cono Sur*) to get drunk
machetazo SM (*esp LAm*) **1** (= *golpe*) blow with a machete
2 (= *instrumento*) large machete
machete¹ SM machete
machete² ADJ mean, stingy
machetear ▸ CONJUG 1a VT (*LAm*) **1** [+ *caña*] to cut (*with a machete*)
2 [+ *persona*] to slash (*with a machete*)
3 (*And*) (= *vender barato*) to sell cheap
VI (*Méx*) **1** (= *obstinarse*) to keep on, persevere
2 (= *trabajar*) to slog away, hammer away
machetero SM **1** (*esp LAm*) (*Agr*) cane cutter
2 (*Méx*) (= *cargador*) porter, stevedore
3 (*Méx**) (= *estudiante*) plodder*
4 (*Caribe**) revolutionary • **~ de salón** armchair revolutionary
5 (*Caribe*) (= *soldado*) soldier
machi SM (*Cono Sur*), **machí** SM (*Cono Sur*) medicine man
machiega SF (*tb* **abeja machiega**) queen bee
machihembrado SM dovetail, dovetail joint
machihembrar ▸ CONJUG 1a VT to dovetail
machina SF **1** (*Mec*) (= *grúa*) crane, derrick; (= *mazo*) pile driver
2 (*Caribe*) (= *tiovivo*) merry-go-round, carousel (EEUU)
machirulo* (*Esp*) ADJ [*niña*] tomboyish; [*mujer*] mannish, butch* (*pey*)
SM (= *niña*) tomboy; (= *mujer*) mannish woman, butch woman* (*pey*)
machismo SM **1** (*pey*) male chauvinism, machismo
2 [*de hombre*] (= *orgullo*) male pride, maleness; (= *virilidad*) virility, masculinity
machista ADJ male chauvinist(ic), macho (*antes de s*)
SMF male chauvinist
machito¹ SM (*Méx*) fried offal
machito² SM • MODISMO: • **estar montado** *o* **subido en el ~** to be well placed, be riding high
macho ADJ **1** (*Bio*) male • **la flor ~** the male flower • **una rata ~** a male rat
2* (= *viril*) manly, brave • **mi niño es muy ~ y no llora** my kid is very manly *o* brave and doesn't cry • **se cree muy ~** he thinks he's very macho*
3 (*Mec*) male
4 (*And*) (= *fantástico*) splendid, terrific*
SM **1** (*Bio*) male ▸ **macho cabrío** he-goat, billy-goat
2* (= *hombretón*) macho man*, he-man*
3* (*uso apelativo*) mate*, buddy (*EEUU**) • **vale, ~, no te enfades*** all right, mate, no need to get mad*
4 (= *mulo*) mule ▸ **macho de varas** leading mule
5 (*Mec*) male screw • MODISMO: • **atarse** *o* **apretarse los ~s** to pluck up one's courage
6 (*Elec*) male plug
7 (*Cos*) hook
8 (= *mazo*) sledgehammer
9 (*Arquit*) buttress
10 • MODISMO: • **parar el ~ a algn** (*LAm*) to take the wind out of sb's sails
11 (*CAm*) (*Mil*) US marine
12 (*Esp†‡*) five-peseta coin
machón SM buttress
machona* SF (*And, Caribe, Cono Sur*) (= *niña*) tomboy; (= *mujer*) mannish woman, butch woman* (*pey*)
machorra*** SF dyke***, lesbian
machota SF **1*** (= *mujer*) mannish woman, butch woman* (*pey*)
2 (= *mazo*) (*gen*) hammer, mallet; (*de apisonar*) tamper
3 • MODISMO: • **a la ~** (*And, Caribe**) carelessly; (*CAm*) rudely, roughly
machote SM **1*** tough guy*, he-man*
2 (*Méx*) (= *borrador*) rough draft, sketch; (= *modelo*) model
3 (*Méx*) (= *impreso*) blank form
machucadura SF bruise
machucar ▸ CONJUG 1g VT **1** (= *aplastar*) to pound, crush; (= *golpear*) to beat; (= *abollar*) to dent; (= *dañar*) to knock about, damage
2 (*Med*) to bruise
3 (*And, Caribe, Méx*) [+ *caballo*] to tire out (*before a race*)
4 (*Caribe*) [+ *ropa*] to rinse through
machucho ADJ **1** (= *mayor*) elderly, getting on in years
2 (= *prudente*) prudent; (= *tranquilo*) sedate; (= *juicioso*) sensible
3 (*And, Méx**) (= *taimado*) cunning, sly
machucón SM (*Méx*) bruise
macia SF mace
macicez SF (= *solidez*) massiveness, solidity; (= *gordura*) stoutness
macilento ADJ (= *pálido*) wan, pale; (= *demacrado*) haggard, gaunt
macillo SM (*Mús*) hammer
macis SF INV mace
maciza SF (*LAm*) chipboard, Masonite® (EEUU)
macizar ▸ CONJUG 1f VT to fill up, fill in, pack solid
macizo ADJ **1** (= *no hueco*) solid • **una mesa de roble ~** a solid oak table • **~ de gente** solid with people
2 (= *fuerte*) [*objeto*] solidly made; [*persona*] stout, well-built
3 (= *grande*) massive
4* (= *atractivo*) gorgeous* • **está maciza** she's gorgeous*
SM **1** (*Geog*) massif
2 [*de plantas*] clump
3 (*Arquit*) [*de pared*] stretch, section (*of a wall*); [*de edificios*] group
4 (= *masa*) mass
5 (*Aut*) solid tyre, solid tire (EEUU)
ADV (*CAm, Méx*) quickly, fast
macizorro‡ ADJ [*hombre*] hunky*; [*mujer*] well-stacked*
maco‡ SM **1** (= *cárcel*) nick*, prison
2 (*Mil*) glasshouse
macollo SM bunch, cluster
macramé SM macramé
macro SF (*Inform*) macro
macró* SM (*Cono Sur*) pimp
macro... PREF macro...
macrobiótico ADJ macrobiotic
macrocefalia SF **1** (*Anat*) macrocephaly
2 [*de administración, entidad*] top-heaviness
macrocefálico ADJ **1** (*Anat*) macrocephalic
2 [*administración, entidad*] top-heavy
macrocomando SM (*Inform*) macro (command)
macroconcierto SM mega-gig*
macrocosmos SM INV, **macrocosmo** SM macrocosm
macroeconomía SF macroeconomics (*sing*)
macroeconómico ADJ macroeconomic
macroestructura SF macrostructure
macrófago SM macrophage
macrofotografía SF macrophotography
macrojuicio SM mega-trial
macromolecular ADJ macromolecular
macronivel SM macro level
macroproceso SM mega-trial
macroproyecto SM large-scale project
macroscópico ADJ macroscopic
macuache* ADJ (*Méx*) rough, coarse
macuco* ADJ **1** (*And, Cono Sur*) (= *taimado*) crafty, cunning
2 (*And*) (= *inútil*) old and useless
3 (*And, Cono Sur*) (= *grande*) big; (= *demasiado grande*) overgrown
SM (*And, Cono Sur**) (= *grandullón*) overgrown boy, big lad
macuenco ADJ **1** (*Caribe**) (= *flaco*) thin, skinny; (= *débil*) weak, feeble
2 (*Caribe*) (= *inútil*) useless
3 (*And*) (= *demasiado grande*) big; (= *muy crecido*) overgrown, extra large; (= *estupendo**) great*, fantastic*
mácula SF **1** (*liter*) (= *mancha*) blemish, stain • **sin ~** [*objeto*] immaculate; [*interpretación, actuación*] faultless; [*historial, pasado*] unblemished
2 (*Anat*) blind spot
3 (*Astron*) (*tb* **mácula solar**) sunspot
4 (= *trampa*) trick, fraud
macular ▸ CONJUG 1a VT to stain, spot
macundales SMPL (*And, Caribe*), **macundos** SMPL (*Caribe*) (= *trastos*) things, gear* (*sing*), junk* (*sing*); (= *negocios*) affairs, business (*sing*)
macutazo‡ SM (= *rumor*) rumour, rumor (EEUU); (= *bulo*) hoax
macuto SM **1** (= *mochila*) [*de soldado*] backpack; [*de colegial*] satchel
2 (*Caribe*) begging basket
Madagascar SM Madagascar
madalena SF (*Culin*) fairy cake
madaleno‡ SM secret policeman
madama SF (*LAm*), **madame** SF madam, brothel keeper
madeja SF [*de lana*] skein, hank; [*de pelo*] tangle, mop • **una ~ de nervios** a bundle of nerves • MODISMOS: • **desenredar la ~ de algo** to get to the bottom of sth • **se está enredando la ~** the plot thickens, things are getting complicated • **tirar de la ~** to put two and two together
SMF (= *persona*) layabout, idler
madera¹ SF **1** (= *material*) (*gen*) wood; (*para la construcción, carpintería*) timber • **dame esa ~** give me that piece of wood • **una silla de ~** a wooden chair • **está hecho de ~** it's made of wood • **una escultura en ~** a wooden sculpture • MODISMO: • **¡toca ~!** touch wood!, knock on wood! (EEUU) ▸ **madera contrachapada** plywood ▸ **madera de balsa** balsa wood ▸ **madera dura** hardwood ▸ **madera fósil** lignite ▸ **madera maciza** solid wood ▸ **madera (multi)laminada, madera terciada** plywood
2 • **tener ~ de algo** to have the makings of sth • **tiene ~ de futbolista** he's got the makings of a footballer
3 (*Mús*) woodwind section (*of the orchestra*)
4 (*Ftbl**) • **la ~** the woodwork
5 (*Zool*) *horny part of hoof*
madera² SM (= *vino*) Madeira
Madera SF Madeira
maderable ADJ timber-yielding
maderaje SM, **maderamen** SM (= *madera*) timber, lumber (EEUU), wood; (= *trabajo*) woodwork
maderero/a SM/F timber merchant
ADJ wood (*antes de s*), timber (*antes de s*) • **industria maderera** timber industry • **productos ~s** wood products
maderismo SM (*Méx*) (*Pol*) *reform movement led by Madero*
maderista SMF (*Méx*) (*Pol*) supporter of Madero
madero SM **1** [*de construcción*] (= *tabla*) (piece of) timber; (= *viga*) beam; (= *tronco*) log
2 (*Náut*) ship, vessel
3* (= *idiota*) blockhead*

m

4 (*Esp*‡) (= *policía*) cop*, pig‡
Madona SF Madonna
madrastra SF stepmother
madraza SF **1** (= *madre*) doting mother, devoted mother
2 (= *colegio*) madrasah, madrassa
madrazo* SM (*Méx*) hard blow
madre SF **1** (= *pariente*) mother • **ser ~** to be a mother • **futura ~** mother-to-be • **su señora ~** (*esp Méx*) your mother • **sin ~** motherless • **¡~ mía!** good heavens! ▸ **madre adoptiva** adoptive mother ▸ **madre biológica** biological mother ▸ **madre de alquiler** surrogate mother ▸ **madre de Dios** Mother of God • **¡~ de Dios!** good heavens! ▸ **madre de familia** mother ▸ **madre genética** biological mother ▸ **madre nodriza** surrogate mother ▸ **la Madre Patria** the Mother Country, the Old Country ▸ **madre política** mother-in-law ▸ **madre soltera** single mother, unmarried mother ▸ **madre trabajadora** working mother
2 (*Rel*) (*en convento*) mother; (*en asilo*) matron ▸ **madre superiora** Mother Superior
3 • MODISMOS: • **como su ~ lo echó al mundo** *o* **lo parió*** in his birthday suit*, starkers* • **ni ~*** not a dicky bird*, not a sausage* • **ciento y la ~*** hundreds of people • **ahí está la ~ del cordero*** that's just the trouble, that's the crux of the matter • **darle a algn en la ~** (*Méx**) to wallop sb*, thump sb • **mentarle la ~ a algn** to insult sb (*violently*) • **¡(me cago en) la ~ que te parió!**‡ fuck off!**‡ • **no tener ~**: • **él no tiene ~*** he's a real swine* • **esto no tiene ~*** this is the limit • **a toda ~** • **de la ~** (*LAm*‡) great*, fantastic* • **¡tu ~!**‡ up yours!**‡, get stuffed!**‡; ▸ **puto**
4 (= *origen*) origin, cradle
5 [*de río*] bed • **salirse de ~** [*río*] to burst its banks; [*persona*] to lose all self-control; [*proceso*] to go beyond its normal limits • MODISMO: • **sacar de ~ a algn** to upset sb
6 [*de vino*] dregs (*pl*), sediment
7 (*Agr*) (= *acequia*) main channel, main irrigation ditch; (= *alcantarilla*) main sewer
8 (*en juegos*) home
9 (*Anat*) womb
10 (*And*) dead skin, scab
11‡ queer‡, fag (EEUU‡)
ADJ **1** (= *de origen*) • **acequia ~** main channel • **alcantarilla ~** main sewer • **buque ~** mother ship • **lengua ~** (*Ling*) parent language
2 • **color ~** dominant colour • **la cuestión ~** the chief problem, the central problem
3 (*LAm**) • **una regañada ~** a real telling-off*, one hell of a telling-off‡
madrejón SM (*Cono Sur*) watercourse
madreperla SF (= *nácar*) mother-of-pearl; (= *ostra*) pearl oyster ▸ **madreperla de río** freshwater mussel
madreselva SF honeysuckle ▸ **madreselva siempreverde** Cape honeysuckle
Madrid SM Madrid
madridista ADJ *of or relating to Real Madrid football club*
SMF (= *jugador*) Real Madrid player; (= *hincha*) Real Madrid supporter • **los ~s** Real Madrid
madrigal SM madrigal
madriguera SF **1** (= *refugio*) [*de animales*] den, burrow; [*de conejos*] warren; [*de tejones*] set
2 [*de ladrones*] den
madrileño/a ADJ of/from Madrid • **la madrileña calle de Alcalá** (= *de Madrid*) Alcalá Street in Madrid; (= *representativa de Madrid*) Alcalá Street, the archetypical Madrid street • **la madrileñísima Cibeles** Cibeles Square which is so typical of Madrid
SM/F native/inhabitant of Madrid • **los ~s** the people of Madrid
Madriles* SMPL • **los ~** Madrid
madrina SF **1** [*de bautizo*] godmother; [*de boda*] ≈ matron of honour; [*de asociación, inauguración*] patron, patroness; ▸ **hada**
2 (*Arquit*) prop, shore
3 (*Téc*) brace
4 (*Agr*) lead mare
5 (*LAm*) (= *animal*) tame animal (*used in breaking in or catching others*)
6 (*Méx**) police informer
madriza‡ SF (*Méx*) bashing*, beating-up*
madroño SM **1** (*Bot*) strawberry tree, arbutus
2 (= *borla*) tassel
madrugada SF (= *noche*) early morning, small hours (*pl*); (= *alba*) dawn, daybreak • **de ~** in the small hours • **levantarse de ~** to get up early *o* at the crack of dawn • **a las cuatro de la ~** at four o'clock in the morning, at four a.m.
madrugador(a) ADJ • **ser ~** to be an early riser
SM/F early riser
madrugar ▸ CONJUG 1h VI **1** (= *levantarse temprano*) (*una vez*) to get up early, get up at the crack of dawn; (*por costumbre*) to be an early riser • REFRANES: • **a quien madruga, Dios le ayuda** the early bird catches the worm • **no por mucho ~ amanece más temprano** time will take its course
2 (= *anticiparse*) to be quick off the mark
3 (= *precipitarse*) to jump the gun
VT • **~ a algn** (= *adelantarse*) to get in ahead of sb; (*CAm*) (= *matar*) to bump sb off*
madrugón SM • **darse** *o* **pegarse un ~** to get up really early *o* at the crack of dawn
maduración SF [*de fruta*] ripening; [*de persona, idea*] maturing
madurar ▸ CONJUG 1a VI **1** [*fruta*] to ripen
2 [*persona*] to mature
3 [*idea, plan*] to mature
VT **1** [+ *fruta*] to ripen
2 [+ *persona*] (= *hacer mayor*) to mature; (= *hacer fuerte*) to toughen, toughen up
3 [+ *idea, plan*] to think out
VPR **madurarse** to ripen
madurez SF **1** [*de fruta*] ripeness
2 [*de carácter, edad*] maturity • **revela una ~ nada frecuente en una primera novela** she shows a maturity rarely found *o* rare in a first novel
maduro ADJ **1** [*fruta*] ripe • **poco ~** underripe
2 [*persona*] [*carácter*] mature • **de edad madura** middle-aged • **el clima no está ~ para esas negociaciones** the climate is not ripe for such negotiations • MODISMO: • **el divieso está ~** the boil is about to burst
SM (*Col*) plantain
MAE SM ABR (*Esp*) (*Pol*) = **Ministerio de Asuntos Exteriores**
maesa SF queen bee
maestra SF **1** (= *abeja*) queen bee
2 (*Arquit*) guide line; ▸ **maestro**
maestranza SF **1** (*Mil*) arsenal, armoury, armory (EEUU)
2 (*Náut*) naval dockyard
3 (= *personal*) *staff of an arsenal/a dockyard*
4 (*LAm*) machine shop
maestrazgo SM (*Hist*) office of grand master
maestre SM (*Hist*) grand master (*of a military order*)
maestrear ▸ CONJUG 1a VT **1** (= *dirigir*) to direct, manage
2 (*Agr*) to prune
maestría SF **1** [*de persona*] (= *dominio*) mastery; (= *habilidad*) skill, expertise
2 (*LAm*) (*Univ*) master's degree
3 (*Esp*) (*Educ*) *vocational qualification*
maestro/a SM/F **1** (= *profesor*) teacher • **mi tía es maestra** my aunt's a teacher ▸ **maestro/a de escuela** schoolteacher
2 (*en un arte, un oficio*) master ▸ **maestro/a albañil** master mason ▸ **maestro/a de armas** fencing master ▸ **maestro/a de ceremonias** master of ceremonies ▸ **maestro/a de cocina** head chef ▸ **maestro/a de esgrima** fencing master ▸ **maestro/a de obras** foreman ▸ **maestro sastre** master tailor
SM **1** (= *autoridad*) authority • **el ~ de todos los medievalistas españoles** the greatest authority among the Spanish medievalists, the doyen of Spanish medievalists • **beber en los grandes ~s** to absorb wisdom from the great teachers
2 (*esp LAm*) (= *oficial*) skilled workman, craftsman ▸ **maestro de caminos** skilled road-construction man
3 (*Mús*) maestro • **el ~ Falla** the great musician *o* composer Falla • **¡música, ~!** music, maestro! • **"Los ~s cantores"** "The Mastersingers" ▸ **maestro de coros** choirmaster
4 (*Ajedrez*) master • **Kasparov, uno de los grandes ~s** Kasparov, one of the grand masters
ADJ **1** (*Téc*) (= *principal*) main • **cloaca maestra** main sewer • **llave maestra** master key, pass key • **plan ~** master plan • **viga maestra** main beam; ▸ **obra**
2 (*Zool*) [*animal*] trained • **halcón ~** trained hawk; ▸ **abeja, maestra**
mafafa SF (*LAm*) marijuana
mafia SF mafia • **la Mafia** the Mafia • **ese departamento es una ~*** that department is very cliquey* *o* is a bit of a mafia
mafioso/a ADJ Mafia (*antes de s*)
SM/F (= *de la Mafia*) mafioso, member of the Mafia; (= *criminal*) gangster, mobster (EEUU)
Magallanes SM • **estrecho de ~** Magellan Strait
magancear ▸ CONJUG 1a VI (*And, Cono Sur*) to idle, laze around
maganto ADJ **1** (= *macilento*) wan, wasted
2 (= *preocupado*) worried
3 (= *soso*) lifeless, dull
maganza* SF (*And*) idleness, laziness
maganzón/ona* SM/F (*LAm*) lazy person, idler
maganzonería* SF (*LAm*) = **maganza**
magazine SM (*TV*) magazine
Magdalena SF Magdalen, Madeleine • **La ~** Mary Magdalene • MODISMO: • **llorar como una ~** to cry one's eyes out
magdalena SF (*Culin*) fairy cake
magenta SF magenta
magia SF magic • **la ~ de su música** the magic of his music • **por arte de ~** (as if) by magic ▸ **magia blanca** white magic ▸ **magia negra** black magic
magiar ADJ, SMF Magyar
mágico ADJ **1** (= *con poderes*) [*alfombra, varita, fórmula, palabras*] magic; [*poderes, propiedades*] magical
2 (= *especial*) [*momentos, cualidad*] magical • **fue una noche mágica** it was a magical evening
SM magician
magín* SM (= *fantasía*) imagination; (= *mente*) mind • **darle al ~** to have a think • **me vienen al ~ un par de frases** a couple of phrases come to mind • **todo eso salió de su ~** it all came out of his own head
magisterio SM **1** (= *enseñanza*) teaching; (= *profesión*) teaching, teaching profession; (= *formación*) teacher training, teacher

education (EEUU); (= *maestros*) teachers (*pl*) • **dedicarse al ~** to go in for teaching • **ejerció el ~ durante 40 años** she taught *o* was a teacher for 40 years
2 • **Magisterio** (*CAm*) (*Univ*) Department of Education
3 (= *maestría*) mastery
4 (= *pedantería*) pompousness, pedantry
magistrado/a SM/F 1 (*Jur*) magistrate, judge
2 (*LAm*) (*Pol*) • **Primer Magistrado** head of state, President
magistral ADJ 1 (= *genial*) [*actuación, obra*] masterly • **cantó el aria de forma ~** she gave a masterly rendition of the aria
2 [*actitud, tono*] (*gen*) magisterial; (*pey*) pompous, pedantic
SM (*tb* **reloj magistral**) master clock
magistralmente ADV masterfully
magistratura SF (= *cargo*) magistracy, judgeship; (= *jueces*) judges (*pl*), magistracy • **alta ~** highest authority ▸ **Magistratura de trabajo** industrial tribunal
magma SM magma
magnánimamente ADV magnanimously
magnanimidad SF magnanimity
magnánimo ADJ magnanimous
magnate SMF tycoon, magnate • **un ~ de la prensa** a press baron • **los ~s de la industria** industrial magnates
magnavoz SM (*Méx*) loudspeaker, loudhailer
magnesia SF magnesia • **MODISMO**: • **confundir la gimnasia con la ~** to confuse two totally different things
magnesio SM 1 (*Quím*) magnesium
2 (*Fot*) flash, flashlight
magnéticamente ADV magnetically
magnético ADJ (*lit, fig*) magnetic
magnetismo SM (*lit, fig*) magnetism ▸ **magnetismo animal** animal magnetism
magnetizable ADJ magnetizable
magnetizar ▸ CONJUG 1f VT to magnetize
magneto SF magneto
magnetofón SM, **magnetófono** SM tape recorder ▸ **magnetófono de bolsillo** personal stereo ▸ **magnetófono de cinta abierta** reel-to-reel tape recorder
magnetofónico ADJ • **cinta magnetofónica** recording tape • **grabado en cinta magnetofónica** tape-recorded
magnetómetro SM magnetometer
magnetoscopio SM video recorder
magnetosfera SF magnetosphere
magnetoterapia SF magnetic therapy
magnicida SMF assassin (*of an important person*)
magnicidio SM assassination (*of an important person*)
magníficamente ADV magnificently, splendidly
magnificar ▸ CONJUG 1g VT 1 (= *exagerar*) to exaggerate, blow up out of all proportion
2 (= *alabar*) to praise, extol
magnificencia SF 1 (= *grandeza*) magnificence, splendour, splendor (EEUU)
2 (= *generosidad*) generosity
magnífico ADJ magnificent, wonderful • **es un jugador ~** he's a magnificent *o* wonderful player • **tenemos un ~ profesor** we have a magnificent *o* wonderful teacher • **Ortega estuvo ~** Ortega was magnificent • **¡magnífico!** excellent!, splendid! • **rector ~** (*Esp*) (*Univ*) honourable Chancellor, honorable Chancellor (EEUU)
magnitud SF magnitude • **de primera ~** (*Astron*) first-magnitude; (*fig*) first-rate (*antes de s*), of the first order • **un problema de gran ~** a major problem
magno ADJ (*liter*) great; ▸ **Alejandro, aula, carta**
magnolia SF magnolia
mago/a SM/F 1 (= *prestidigitador*) magician
2 (*en cuentos*) magician, wizard/sorceress • **el Mago de Oz** the Wizard of Oz • **los Reyes Magos** the Three Wise Men, the Magi (*frm*) • **es un ~ de las finanzas** he's a financial wizard
magra SF 1 [*de carne*] lean part
2 (= *loncha*) (*gen*) slice; [*de beicon*] rasher
3 • **¡magra!‡** rubbish!*, not on your nelly!*
4 (*Esp*) (= *casa*) house
magrear‡ ▸ CONJUG 1a VT (*Esp*) to touch up*, grope*
Magreb SM Maghreb
magrebí ADJ, SMF Maghrebi
magreo‡ SM (*Esp*) touching up*, groping*
magrez SF leanness
magro ADJ 1 (= *sin grasa*) [*carne*] lean; [*porción*] meagre, meager (EEUU)
2 [*persona*] lean
3 [*resultado*] poor; [*sueldo*] meagre, meager (EEUU)
4 [*tierra*] poor
SM loin
magrura SF leanness
magua SF (*Caribe*) disappointment; (= *fracaso*) failure; (= *revés*) setback
maguarse* ▸ CONJUG 1i VPR (*Caribe*)
1 [*fiesta*] to be a failure, be spoiled
2 [*persona*] (= *decepcionarse*) to be disappointed; (= *deprimirse*) to get depressed
maguer (*liter*) PREP in spite of, despite
CONJ although
maguey SM maguey
maguillo SM wild apple tree
magullado ADJ bruised
magulladura SF bruise
magullamiento SM bruising
magullar ▸ CONJUG 1a VT (= *amoratar*) to bruise; (= *dañar*) to hurt, damage; (= *golpear*) to batter, bash*; (*And, Caribe*) to crumple, rumple
VPR **magullarse** (= *hacerse un moratón*) to get bruised; (= *hacerse daño*) to get hurt
magullón SM (*LAm*) bruise
Maguncia SF Mainz
maharajá SM maharajah • **MODISMO**: • **vivir como un ~** to live like a prince
mahdi SM Mahdi
Mahoma SM Mohammed, Mahomet
mahometano/a ADJ, SM/F Muslim
mahometismo SM Islam
mahonesa SF mayonnaise
mai‡ SM joint‡
maicena® SF cornflour, cornstarch (EEUU)
maicero ADJ maize (*antes de s*), corn (*antes de s*) (EEUU)
maicillo SM (*Chile*) gravel, road gravel
mail* SM email
mailing ['mailin] SM (PL: **mailings** ['mailin]) mailshot • **hacer un ~** to do a mailshot ▸ **mailing electoral** postal canvassing
maillot [ma'jot] SM (*Dep*) jersey • **el ~ amarillo** the yellow jersey
maitines SMPL matins
maître ['metre] SM head waiter
maíz SM maize, corn (EEUU), sweetcorn • **~ en la mazorca** corn on the cob • **MODISMOS**: • **coger a algn asando ~** (*Caribe*) to catch sb red-handed • **dar a algn ~ tostado** (*And*) to give sb their comeuppance ▸ **maíz palomero** (*Méx*) popcorn
maizal SM maize field, cornfield (EEUU)
maizena® SF cornflour, cornstarch (EEUU)
maizudo ADJ (*CAm*) rich, wealthy
maja SF pestle; ▸ **majo**
majada SF 1 (= *corral*) sheep pen
2 (= *estiércol*) dung
3 (*Cono Sur*) [*de ovejas*] flock; [*de cabras*] herd
majaderear ▸ CONJUG 1a VT (*LAm*) to annoy
majadería SF 1 (= *cualidad*) (= *tontería*) silliness; (= *sinsentido*) absurdity
2 • **una ~** a silly thing, an absurdity; **majaderías** nonsense (*sing*) • **decir ~s** to talk nonsense • **hacer ~s** to be silly
majadero/a ADJ (= *tonto*) silly, stupid
SM/F (= *tonto*) idiot, fool • **¡majadero!** you idiot!
SM 1 (*Téc*) pestle
2 (*Cos*) bobbin
majador SM pestle
majagranzas†* SMF INV = **majadero**
majagua SF (*Caribe*) 1 (*Dep*) baseball bat
2* (= *traje*) suit
majar ▸ CONJUG 1a VT 1 (= *aplastar*) to pound, crush; (*Med*) to bruise
2* (= *molestar*) to bother, pester
majara‡, majareta‡ ADJ nuts*, crackers* • **estás ~** you're nuts *o* crackers*
SMF nutter*
maje ADJ (*Méx‡*) gullible • **hacer ~ al marido** to cheat on one's husband
SMF (*Méx‡*) sucker‡
SM (*CAm**) bloke*, guy*
majestad SF majesty • **Su Majestad** His/Her Majesty • **(Vuestra) Majestad** Your Majesty
majestuosamente ADV majestically
majestuosidad SF majesty
majestuoso ADJ majestic
majete* ADJ nice
SM guy*, bloke* • **tranquilo, ~** relax, man*
majeza SF 1 (= *atractivo*) good looks (*pl*), attractiveness
2 (= *belleza*) loveliness
3 (= *elegancia*) smartness; (*pey*) flashiness
majo/a ADJ (*Esp*) 1 [*persona*] (= *agradable*) nice; (= *guapo*) attractive, good-looking
2 [*cosa*] nice • **¡qué blusa tan maja!** what a nice blouse!
3 (*uso apelativo*) • **¡hola maja! ¿qué tal te va?** hello, love! how's things? • **oye, majo, haz el favor de callarte** do me a favour, will you just shut up?
SM/F (*Hist*) *inhabitant of the working-class neighbourhoods of Madrid in the 18th and 19th centuries*; ▸ **maja**
majong [ma'xon] SM mahjong
majuela SF haw, hawthorn berry
majuelo SM 1 (= *vid*) young vine
2 (= *espino*) hawthorn
mal ADV 1 (= *imperfectamente*) badly • **el negocio les va mal** their business is doing badly • **está muy mal escrito** it's very badly written • **han escrito mal mi apellido** they've spelt my surname wrong • **me entendió mal** he misunderstood me • **creo que me expliqué mal** I don't think I explained what I meant properly • **oigo/veo mal** I can't hear/see well • **lo hice lo menos mal que pude** I did it as well as I could • **si mal no recuerdo** if my memory serves me right, if I remember correctly • **mal puedo hablar yo de este asunto** I'm hardly the right person to talk to about this
2 (= *reprobablemente*) • **se portó muy mal con su mejor amiga** she behaved very badly towards her best friend • **hacer mal**: • **hace mal en mentir** he is wrong to lie
3 (= *insuficientemente*) poorly • **la habitación estaba mal iluminada** the room was poorly lit • **este disco se vendió muy mal** this record sold very poorly, this record had very poor sales • **sus hijos estaban mal alimentados** her children were underfed • **un trabajo mal pagado** a badly paid job • **comer mal**: • **en este restaurante se come**

m

mal the food isn't very good in this restaurant • **la niña come mal** the girl isn't eating properly, the girl is off her food • **por falta de dinero comemos mal** we aren't able to eat properly because we don't have enough money
4 (= *sin salud*) ill • **su padre está bastante mal** her father's pretty ill • **encontrarse** *o* **sentirse mal** to feel ill
5 (= *desagradablemente*) • **lo pasé muy mal en la fiesta** I had a very bad time at the party • **les fue muy mal en Inglaterra** things went very badly for them in England • **¡no está mal este vino!** this wine isn't bad! • **no estaría mal ir mañana de excursión** I wouldn't mind going on a trip tomorrow • **caer mal algn**: • **me cae mal su amigo** I don't like his friend • **decir** *o* **hablar mal de algn** to speak ill of sb • **llevarse mal**: • **me llevo mal con él** I don't get on with him • **los dos hermanos se llevan muy mal** the two brothers don't get on at all • **oler mal**: • **esta habitación huele mal** this room smells (bad) • **pensar mal de algn** to think badly of sb • **saber mal**: • **sabe mal** it doesn't taste nice
6 (*otras locuciones*) • **estar a mal con algn** to be on bad terms with sb • **¡menos mal!** thank goodness! • **menos mal que ...** it's just as well (that) ..., it's a good job (that) ... • **ir de mal en peor** to go from bad to worse • **mal que bien** more or less, just about • **mal que bien lo hemos solucionado** we've more or less *o* just about managed to solve it • **mal que bien vamos tirando** we're just about managing to get by • **tomarse algo (a) mal** to take sth the wrong way
CONJ • **mal que le pese** whether he likes it or not
ADJ ▸ **malo**
SM **1** (= *maldad*) • **el mal** evil • **el bien y el mal** good and evil • **caer en el mal** to fall into evil ways • **combatir el mal** (*frm*) to fight against evil • **echar algo a mal** to despise sth
2 (= *perjuicio*) harm • **no le deseo ningún mal** I don't wish him any harm *o* ill • **hacer mal a algn** to do sb harm • **el mal ya está hecho** the harm *o* damage is done now • **no hay ningún mal** there's no harm done • **¡mal haya quien ...!** (*frm*) a curse on whoever ...! • **dar mal a algn** to make sb suffer • **darse mal** to torment o.s. • **un mal menor** the lesser of two evils • **rebajamos los precios, como mal menor** we cut the prices, as the lesser of two evils • **esa solución no me satisface, pero es un mal menor** I'm not happy with that solution, but it could have been worse • **parar en mal** to come to a bad end • **REFRANES**: • **no hay mal que por bien no venga** it's an ill wind that blows nobody any good • **mal de muchos consuelo de tontos** that's no consolation
3 (= *problema*) ill • **los males de la economía** the ills afflicting the economy
4 (*Med*) disease, illness ▸ **mal caduco** epilepsy ▸ **mal de altura** altitude sickness ▸ **mal de amores** lovesickness • **sufre mal de amores** she's lovesick ▸ **mal de Chagas** Chagas' disease ▸ **mal de la tierra** homesickness ▸ **mal de mar** seasickness ▸ **mal francés** (*Hist*) syphilis
5 ▸ **mal de ojo** evil eye • **le echaron el mal de ojo** they gave him the evil eye
6 (*LAm*) (*Med*) epileptic fit
mala[1] SF bad luck
mala[2] SF (= *saco*) mailbag; (= *correo*) mail, post
malabar ADJ • **juegos ~es** juggling (*sing*)
malabarismo SM **1** (= *juegos malabares*) juggling
2 malabarismos (= *complicaciones*) juggling (*sing*), balancing act (*sing*) • **hacer ~s** (*lit*) to juggle; (*fig*) to do a balancing act
malabarista SMF juggler
malacate SM **1** (= *torno*) winch, capstan
2 (*CAm*) (= *huso*) spindle
malaconsejado ADJ ill-advised
malaconsejar ▸ CONJUG 1a VT to give bad advice to
malacostumbrado ADJ **1** (= *de malos hábitos*) given to bad habits
2 (= *consentido*) spoiled, pampered
malacostumbrar ▸ CONJUG 1a VT • **~ a algn** (*gen*) to get sb into bad habits; (= *consentir*) to spoil sb
malacrianza SF (*LAm*) rudeness
Málaga SF Malaga
malage SM = **malaje**
malagradecido ADJ ungrateful
malagueño/a ADJ of/from Málaga
SM/F native/inhabitant of Málaga • **los ~s** the people of Málaga
Malaisia SF Malaysia
malaisio/a ADJ, SM/F Malaysian
malaje* SM **1** (= *mala sombra*) malign influence; (= *mala suerte*) bad luck • **soy un ~** I'm bad luck
2 (= *sosería*) dullness, lifelessness; (= *falta de encanto*) lack of charm
3 (= *malévolo*) nasty piece of work*; (= *soso*) bore, pain*
malaleche* ADJ nasty, horrible
SMF nasty person
malamente ADV **1*** (= *mal*) badly • **el asunto acabó ~** the affair ended badly • **estar ~ de dinero** to be badly off for money
2 (= *difícilmente*) • **~ podrán vencer** they have little chance of winning • **en el sofá ~ caben dos personas** the sofa is only just big enough for two people • **tenemos gasolina ~ para ...** we barely *o* hardly have enough petrol to ...
malandante ADJ unfortunate
malandanza SF misfortune
malandrín/ina SM/F (*hum*) scoundrel, rogue
malandro‡ SM (*Caribe*) scrounger*
malanga ADJ (*Caribe**) thick*
SF (*Caribe, Méx*) *tuber resembling a sweet potato*
malapata* SMF (= *patoso*) clumsy thing; (= *aburrido*) bore; (= *pesado*) pest, nuisance
malapropismo SM malapropism
malaria SF malaria
Malasia SF Malaysia
malasio/a ADJ, SM/F Malaysian
malasombra* SMF = **malapata**
Malaui SM, **Malawi** SM Malawi
malauiano/a ADJ, SM/F Malawian
malaúva* ADJ mean, miserable
SMF miserable creature, miserable sod**
malavenido ADJ • **estar ~s** to be in disagreement *o* in conflict • **una pareja malavenida** an unsuited *o* incompatible couple
malaventura SF misfortune
malaventurado ADJ unfortunate
Malawi SM Malawi
Malaya SF Malaya
malaya SF (*Chile*) steak
malayo/a ADJ Malay, Malayan
SM/F Malay
SM (*Ling*) Malay
Malaysia SF Malaysia
malbaratar ▸ CONJUG 1a VT (= *malvender*) to sell off cheap, sell at a loss; (= *malgastar*) to squander
malcarado ADJ (= *feo*) ugly; (= *enfadado*) grim-faced
malcasado ADJ (= *infeliz*) unhappily married; (= *infiel*) errant, unfaithful
malcasarse ▸ CONJUG 1a VPR to make an unhappy marriage
malcomer ▸ CONJUG 2a VI to eat badly
malcontento/a ADJ discontented
SM/F malcontent
malcriadez SF (*LAm*) bad manners (*pl*), rudeness
malcriado ADJ (= *grosero*) bad-mannered, rude; (= *consentido*) spoiled, pampered
malcriar ▸ CONJUG 1c VT to spoil, pamper
maldad SF **1** (= *cualidad*) evil, wickedness
2 • **una ~** a wicked thing
maldecir ▸ CONJUG 3o VT **1** (*con maldición*) to curse • **maldecía mi mala suerte** I cursed my bad luck
2 (= *odiar*) to loathe, detest
VI to curse • **~ de algn/algo** (= *hablar mal*) to speak ill of sb/sth; (= *quejarse*) to complain bitterly about sb/sth
maldiciendo *etc* ▸ **maldecir**
maldiciente ADJ (= *quejoso*) grumbling; (= *grosero*) foul-mouthed
SMF (= *quejoso*) grumbler; (= *descontento*) malcontent; (= *difamador*) slanderer
maldición SF curse • **la ~ de la bruja** the witch's curse • **¡maldición!** damn!, curse it! • **parece que ha caído una ~ sobre este programa** this programme seems to be cursed
maldiga *etc* ▸ **maldecir**
maldispuesto ADJ **1** (= *enfermo*) ill, indisposed
2 (*contra alguien*) ill-disposed
maldita SF **1** (= *lengua*) tongue • **MODISMO**: • **soltar la ~** (= *hablar mucho*) to talk too much; (= *enojarse*) to explode, blow up
2 (*Caribe*) (= *llaga*) sore, swelling; (= *picadura*) insect bite
malditismo SM aura of doom
maldito ADJ **1** (= *condenado*) damned • **poeta ~** accursed poet
2 (*Rel*) accursed
3* (*uso enfático*) damn* • **¡maldita sea!** damn it!* • **ese ~ libro** that damn book* • **ese ~ niño** that wretched child • **¡~ el día en que lo conocí!** curse the day I met him! • **¡malditas las ganas que tengo de verle!** I really don't feel like seeing him! • **no le encuentro maldita la gracia** I don't see what's so damn funny* • **no entiende maldita la cosa** he doesn't understand a damn thing* • **no le hace ~ (el) caso** he doesn't take a blind bit of notice • **~ lo que me importa** I don't give a damn*
4 (= *maligno*) wicked
5 (*Méx**) (= *taimado*) crafty
SM • **el ~** (*Rel*) the Evil One, the devil
maldormir ▸ CONJUG 3j VI to sleep badly, sleep in fits and starts
maleabilidad SF malleability
maleable ADJ malleable
maleado ADJ (*LAm*) corrupt
maleante SMF (= *malhechor*) crook, villain; (= *vago*) vagrant
ADJ (= *malo*) wicked; (= *pícaro*) villainous; (= *indeseable*) unsavoury, unsavory (EEUU)
malear ▸ CONJUG 1a VT **1** (= *corromper*) to corrupt, pervert
2 (= *dañar*) to damage, harm
3 [+ *tierra*] to sour
VPR **malearse 1** (= *corromperse*) to be corrupted
2 (= *dañarse*) to spoil, be harmed
malecón SM pier, jetty
maledicencia SF slander, scandal
maledicente ADJ slanderous, scandalous
maleducado ADJ bad-mannered, rude
maleducar ▸ CONJUG 1g VT to spoil
maleficiar ▸ CONJUG 1b VT **1** (= *hechizar*) to bewitch, cast an evil spell on
2 (= *dañar*) to harm, damage

maleficio (SM) **1** (= *hechizo*) curse, spell
2 (= *brujería*) witchcraft
maléfico (ADJ) evil
malejo* (ADJ) rather bad, pretty bad
malencarado (ADJ) sour-faced
malentendido (SM) misunderstanding
malestar (SM) **1** (= *incomodidad*) discomfort • **uno de los síntomas es un ~ generalizado** one of the symptoms is a general feeling of discomfort • **sentía un ligero ~** he felt slightly unwell • **el medicamento le produjo ~ en el estómago** the medicine upset his stomach
2 (= *inquietud*) unease • **enseguida adivinó su ~** he immediately sensed her unease • **su conducta le causó un profundo ~** his behaviour disturbed her deeply
3 (= *descontento*) discontent • **las nuevas medidas han causado ~ entre la población** the new measures have aroused discontent among the population
maleta¹ (SF) **1** (*para equipaje*) case, suitcase • **fuimos a retirar nuestras ~s de la consigna** we went to get our luggage from the left-luggage office • **hacer la(s) ~(s)** (*lit*) to pack; (*fig*) to pack one's bags • **ya puede ir preparando las ~s** he's on his way out, he can start packing his bags
2 (*Aut*) boot, trunk (EEUU)
3 (*Cono Sur*) [*de caballo*] saddlebag
4 (*CAm*) (= *fajo de ropa*) bundle of clothes
5 (*And, Caribe*) (= *joroba*) hump
(SMF) **1*** (= *persona inepta*) (*gen*) dead loss*; (*Taur*) clumsy beginner; (*Dep*) useless player
2 (*LAm*) (= *vago*) lazy person, idler
maleta² (ADJ) **1** (*LAm*) (= *travieso*) naughty, mischievous; (= *malo*) wicked
2 (*And, Cono Sur*) (= *tonto*) stupid; (= *inútil*) useless
3 (*Cono Sur*) (= *astuto*) sly
4 (*LAm*) (= *vago*) lazy
5 (*CAm, Méx*) (= *torpe*) ham-fisted
maletazo (SM) bump (*with a suitcase*)
maletera (SF) **1** (*LAm*) (*Aut*) boot, trunk (EEUU)
2 (*And, Méx*) [*de caballo*] saddlebag
3 (*Cono Sur*) (= *cortabolsas*) pickpocket
maletero (SM) **1** (*Aut*) boot, trunk (EEUU)
2 (= *mozo*) porter
3 (*Cono Sur*) (= *ladrón*) pickpocket
maletilla (SMF) (*Taur*) *aspiring bullfighter*
maletín (SM) (= *maleta*) small case; (= *portafolios*) briefcase, attaché case; [*de colegial*] satchel; [*de médico*] bag ▸ **maletín de excursiones** picnic case ▸ **maletín de grupa** saddlebag ▸ **maletín de viaje** travel bag
maletón (ADJ) (*And*) hunchbacked
maletudo/a (*And, Caribe*) (ADJ) hunchbacked
(SM/F) hunchback
malevo/a (SM/F) (*Cono Sur*) malefactor
malevolencia (SF) malevolence, spite • **por ~** out of spite • **sin ~ para nadie** without meaning to offend anyone
malévolo (ADJ), **malevolente** (ADJ) malevolent, malicious
maleza (SF) **1** (= *malas hierbas*) weeds (*pl*)
2 (= *espesura*) [*de matas*] undergrowth; [*de zarza*] thicket; [*de broza*] brushwood • **fueron abriéndose camino entre la ~** they gradually beat a path through the undergrowth
3 (*Cono Sur*) (= *pus*) pus
4 (*CAm*) (= *enfermedad*) sickness, illness
malezal (SM) **1** (*Caribe, Cono Sur*) (= *hierbas*) mass of weeds
2 (*Cono Sur*) (*Med*) pus
malfamado (ADJ) notorious
malformación (SF) malformation
malformado (ADJ) malformed
Malgache (SM) Malagasy
malgache (ADJ), (SMF) Madagascan
malgastador(a) (ADJ) spendthrift (*antes de s*), wasteful
(SM/F) spendthrift
malgastar ▹ CONJUG 1a (VT) [+ *tiempo, esfuerzo*] to waste; [+ *recursos, dinero*] to squander, waste; [+ *salud*] to ruin
malgeniado (ADJ) (*LAm*), **malgenioso** (ADJ) (*LAm*) bad-tempered
malhabido (ADJ) [*ganancia*] ill-gotten
malhablado/a (ADJ) foul-mouthed
(SM/F) • **es un ~** he has a foul mouth (on him), he's so foul-mouthed
malhadado (ADJ) ill-fated, ill-starred
malhaya (EXCL) (*LAm*) damn! • **¡~ sea!** damn him!*
malhecho (ADJ)* ugly, misshapen
(SM) misdeed
malhechor(a) (SM/F) delinquent, criminal • **banda de ~es** bunch of delinquents
malherido (ADJ) badly injured, seriously injured
malhumoradamente (ADV) irritably, grumpily
malhumorado (ADJ) bad-tempered, grumpy
mali‡ (SM) joint‡
malicia (SF) **1** (= *mala intención*) malice, spite • **lo dije sin ~** I said it without malice
2 (= *picardía*) [*de persona*] mischief; [*de mirada*] mischievousness; [*de chiste*] naughtiness • **sonrió con ~** she smiled mischievously • **contó un chiste con mucha ~** he told a very naughty joke
3 (= *astucia*) slyness, guile • **el niño tiene demasiada ~ para su edad** that child is too knowing for his age
4 malicias (= *sospechas*) suspicions • **tengo mis ~s** I have my suspicions
5 [*de animal*] viciousness
maliciar ▹ CONJUG 1b (VT) to suspect, have one's suspicions about
(VPR) **maliciarse** to suspect, have one's suspicions about • **ya me lo maliciaba** I thought as much, it's just what I suspected
maliciosamente (ADV) **1** (= *con mala intención*) maliciously, spitefully
2 (= *con picardía*) mischievously
3 (= *con astucia*) slyly
malicioso (ADJ) **1** (= *malintencionado*) malicious, spiteful
2 (= *pícaro*) mischievous • **una mirada maliciosa** a mischievous look
3 (= *astuto*) sly, crafty
4 (= *malo*) wicked, evil
malignidad (SF) **1** (*Med*) malignancy
2 [*de persona*] (= *maldad*) evil nature; (= *daño*) harmfulness; (= *rencor*) malice
malignizarse ▹ CONJUG 1f (VPR) [*célula, tumor*] to become malignant
maligno (ADJ) **1** (*Med*) malignant
2 (= *perverso*) [*persona*] evil; [*influencia*] pernicious, harmful; [*actitud, observación*] malicious
(SM) • **el ~** the Devil, the Evil One
Malinche (SF) (*Méx*) *mistress of Cortés*
malinchismo (SM) (*Méx*) *tendency to favour things foreign*
malinformar ▹ CONJUG 1a (VT) to misinform
malintencionadamente (ADV) maliciously
malintencionado (ADJ) [*persona, comentario*] malicious
malinterpretación (SF) misinterpretation
malinterpretar ▹ CONJUG 1a (VT) to misinterpret
malísimamente (ADV) very badly, dreadfully
malísimo (ADJ) very bad, dreadful
malito (ADJ) • **estar ~** to be in poor shape, be rather poorly
malla (SF) **1** [*de red*] mesh; (= *red*) network • **hacer ~** to knit • **medias de ~** fishnet stockings ▸ **malla de alambre** wire mesh, wire netting
2 (*para ballet, gimnasia*) leotard; **mallas** (= *leotardos*) tights (*pl*), pantyhose (EEUU); (*sin pie*) leggings
3 (*LAm*) (*tb* **malla de baño**) swimming costume, swimsuit
4 (*Dep*) • **las ~s** the net (*sing*) • **dio con el balón en el fondo de las ~s** he placed the ball into the back of the net
5 (*Hist*) chain mail; ▹ **cota¹**
mallo (SM) mallet
Mallorca (SF) Majorca
mallorquín/ina (ADJ), (SM/F) Majorcan
(SM) (*Ling*) Majorcan
malmandado (ADJ) (= *desobediente*) disobedient; (= *terco*) obstinate, bloody-minded*
malmirado (ADJ) **1** (= *mal considerado*) • **estar ~** to be disliked
2 (= *desconsiderado*) thoughtless, inconsiderate
malmodado‡ (ADJ) (*Caribe, Méx*) (= *hosco*) heavy-handed, rough; (= *insolente*) rude, insolent
malnacido/a* (SM/F) swine*
malnutrición (SF) malnutrition
malnutrido (ADJ) malnourished
malo/a (ADJ) (ANTES DE SM SING: **mal**)
1 (= *perjudicial*) bad • **es ~ para la salud** it's bad for your health • REFRÁN: • **más vale lo ~ conocido (que lo bueno por conocer)** better the devil you know (than the devil you don't)
2 (= *imperfecto*) bad • **esta película es bastante mala** this is a pretty bad film • **un chiste malísimo** a really bad joke, a terrible joke • **este papel es ~ para escribir** this paper is bad for writing • **mala calidad** poor quality • **es una tela muy mala** it's a very poor-quality material • **joyas malas** fake jewels • **ni un(a) mal(a) ...:** • **no hay ni un mal bar para tomar algo** there isn't a single little bar where we can get a drink
3 (= *adverso*) bad • **he tenido mala suerte** I've had bad luck, I've been unlucky • **eso es una mala señal** that's a bad sign • **—es tarde y no ha llamado —¡malo!** "it's late and she hasn't called" — "oh dear!" • **~ sería que no ganáramos** it would be a disaster if we didn't win • **lo ~ es que ...** the trouble is (that) ...; ▹ **pata**
4 (= *desagradable*) bad • **un mal día** a bad day • **el tiempo estuvo muy ~ todo el verano** we had really bad weather all summer • **un olor muy ~** a bad *o* nasty smell
5 (= *podrido*) • **esta carne está mala** this meat's off
6 (= *reprobable*) wrong • **¿qué tiene de ~?** what's wrong with that? • **¿qué tiene de ~ comer helados en invierno?** what's wrong with eating ice cream in winter? • **van por mal camino** they'll come to no good if they carry on like this • **es una mala persona** he's a bad person • **una bruja mala** a wicked witch; ▹ **arte, idea, leche, lengua, manera, pasada, trato, uva**
7 (= *travieso*) naughty • **¡no seas ~!** don't be naughty!
8 (= *enfermo*) ill • **mi hija está mala** my daughter's ill • **tienes muy mala cara** you look awful *o* really ill • **se puso ~ después de comer** he started to feel ill after lunch • **me puse ~ de reírme** I nearly died laughing • **tengo mala la garganta** I've got a sore throat
9 (= *inepto*) bad • **ser ~ para algo** to be bad at

m

sth • **soy muy mala para la física** I'm very bad at physics
10 (= *difícil*) hard, difficult • **es un animal ~ de domesticar** it's a hard *o* difficult animal to tame • **es muy ~ de vencer** he's very hard *o* difficult to beat
11 • **MODISMOS**: • **a la mala** (*LAm*) (= *a la fuerza*) by force, forcibly; (= *de forma traicionera*) treacherously • **andar a malas con algn** to be on bad terms with sb • **ponerse a malas con algn** to fall out with sb • **estar de malas** (= *de mal humor*) to be in a bad mood; (= *sin suerte*) to be out of luck • **venir de malas** to have evil intentions • **por las malas** by force, willy-nilly
SM/F (= *personaje*) (*Teat*) villain; (*Cine*) baddie*
SM • **el ~** (*Rel*) the Evil One, the Devil
maloca SF **1** (*Cono Sur*) (*Hist*) Indian raid
2 (*And*) Indian village
malogrado ADJ **1** (= *difunto*) • **el ~ ministro** the late-lamented minister
2 (= *fracasado*) [*proyecto*] abortive, ill-fated; [*esfuerzo*] wasted
malograr ▹ CONJUG 1a VT (= *arruinar*) to spoil, ruin; (= *desperdiciar*) to waste
VPR **malograrse 1** (= *fracasar*) to fail; (= *decepcionar*) to fail to come up to expectations, not fulfil its promise
2 (*esp Perú*) [*máquina*] to go wrong, break down
3 [*persona*] to die before one's time
malogro SM **1** (= *fracaso*) failure; (= *desperdicio*) waste
2 (= *muerte*) early death, untimely end
maloliente ADJ stinking, smelly
malón SM (*LAm*) **1** (*Hist*) Indian raid
2 (= *persona*) tough, thug
malpagar ▹ CONJUG 1h VT to pay badly, underpay
malparado ADJ • **salir ~** to come off badly • **salir ~ de algo** to get the worst of sth
malparar ▹ CONJUG 1a VT (= *dañar*) to damage; (= *estropear*) to harm, impair; (= *maltratar*) to ill-treat
malparido/a‡‡ SM/F son of a bitch‡‡, bastard‡‡
malparir ▹ CONJUG 3a VI to have a miscarriage, miscarry
malparto SM miscarriage
malpensado ADJ evil-minded • **¡no seas ~!** why do you always have to think the worst of people!
malpensar ▹ CONJUG 1j VI • **~ de algn** to think ill of sb
malqueda* SMF shifty sort, unreliable type
malquerencia SF dislike
malquerer ▹ CONJUG 2t VT to dislike
malquerido ADJ unloved
malquistar ▹ CONJUG 1a VT • **~ a dos personas** to cause a rift between two people
VPR **malquistarse** [*dos personas*] to fall out, become estranged • **~se con algn** to fall out with sb, become estranged from sb
malquisto ADJ • **estar ~** to be disliked, be unpopular • **los dos están ~s** they have fallen out with each other, they have become estranged
malrotar ▹ CONJUG 1a VT to squander
malsano ADJ **1** [*clima*] unhealthy
2 (= *perverso*) [*curiosidad, fascinación*] morbid; [*mente*] sick, morbid
malsín SM (= *difamador*) slanderer; (= *soplón*) informer, taleteller
malsonante ADJ rude, nasty • **usar palabras ~s** to use rude words *o* bad language
malsufrido ADJ impatient
Malta SF Malta
malta SF **1** (= *cereal*) malt • **whisky de ~** malt whisky
2 (*Chile*) dark beer
malteada SF (*LAm*) malted milk shake
malteado ADJ malted
SM malting
maltear ▹ CONJUG 1a VT to malt
maltés/esa ADJ, SM/F Maltese
SM (*Ling*) Maltese
maltirar ▹ CONJUG 1a VI to scrape by, scrape a living
maltón SM (*LAm*), **maltoncillo** SM (*LAm*) (= *animal*) young animal; (= *niño*) child
maltraer ▹ CONJUG 2o VT **1** (= *maltratar*) to ill-treat • **MODISMO**: • **llevar** *o* **traer a ~ a algn** [*persona*] to give sb nothing but trouble; [*problema*] to be the bane of sb's life
2 (= *injuriar*) to insult, abuse
maltraído ADJ (*LAm*) shabby, untidy
maltratado ADJ [*bebé, niño, mujer*] (= *pegado*) battered; (= *tratado mal*) abused
maltratador(a) SM/F abuser
maltratamiento SM = **maltrato**
maltratar ▹ CONJUG 1a VT **1** [+ *persona*] (= *tratar mal*) to ill-treat, maltreat, abuse; (= *pegar*) to batter, abuse
2 [+ *cosas*] to handle roughly
3 (*tb* **maltratar de palabra**) to abuse, insult
maltrato SM **1** (= *conducta*) (*al tratar mal*) mistreatment, ill-treatment; (*al pegar*) battering ▸ **maltrato conyugal** wife-battering ▸ **maltrato infantil** child abuse ▸ **maltrato psicológico** psychological abuse
2 [*de cosas*] rough handling
3 (= *insultos*) abuse, insults (*pl*)
maltrecho ADJ **1** [*objeto*] battered, knocked-about • **las maltrechas arcas de la organización** the organization's depleted coffers
2 [*persona*] (= *herida*) injured; (= *agotada*) worn out • **dejar ~ a algn** to leave sb in a bad way • **los ~s líderes del partido** the beleaguered party leaders
malucho* ADJ (*Med*) poorly, under the weather*
malura* SF (*Cono Sur*) (= *dolor*) pain, discomfort; (= *malestar*) sickness, indisposition ▸ **malura de estómago** stomach ache
malva ADJ INV [*color*] mauve
SF (*Bot*) mallow • **(de) color de ~** mauve • **MODISMOS**: • **criar ~s** • **estar criando ~s** (*Esp**) to be pushing up the daisies* • **estar como una ~** to be very meek and mild ▸ **malva loca, malva real, malva rósea** hollyhock
malvado/a ADJ evil, wicked
SM/F villain
malvaloca SF hollyhock
malvarrosa SF hollyhock
malvasía SF malmsey
malvavisco SM marshmallow
malvender ▹ CONJUG 2a VT to sell off cheap, sell at a loss
malversación SF embezzlement, misappropriation ▸ **malversación de fondos** embezzlement, misappropriation of funds
malversador(a) SM/F embezzler
malversar ▹ CONJUG 1a VT **1** (*Econ*) to embezzle, misappropriate • **~ fondos** to embezzle *o* misappropriate funds
2 (= *distorsionar*) to distort
Malvinas SFPL (*tb* **islas Malvinas**) Falkland Islands, Falklands
malvinés/esa ADJ of/from the Falkland Islands
SM/F Falkland islander
malviviente SMF, ADJ (*Méx*) = **maleante**
malvivir ▹ CONJUG 3a VI to live badly, live poorly • **malviven de lo que pueden** they scrape by as best they can
malvón SM (*LAm*) geranium
malware SM (*Inform*) malware
mama SF **1** (*Med*) (= *glándula*) mammary gland; (= *pecho*) breast • **cáncer de ~** breast cancer
2 = **mamá**
mamá* SF **1** (= *madre*) mum*, mummy*, mom (*EEUU**), mommy (*EEUU**) • **futura ~** mother-to-be
2 (*esp CAm, Caribe, Méx*) [*de cortesía*] mother ▸ **mamá grande** (*Col*) grandmother
mamacallos* SMF INV (*Esp*) useless person
mamacita* SF (*LAm*) **1** (= *madre*) mum*, mummy*, mom (*EEUU**), mommy (*EEUU**)
2 • **¡eh, ~!** hey, gorgeous!*
mamacona‡ SF (*And*) old lady
mamada SF **1** (= *chupada*) suck
2‡‡ blow job‡‡
3‡ (= *borrachera*) binge*
4 (*LAm**) (= *cosa fácil*) cinch*; (= *ganga*) snip*, bargain; (= *trabajo*) cushy number
mamadera SF **1** (*LAm*) (= *tetilla*) rubber teat; (= *biberón*) feeding bottle
2 mamaderas‡ boobs‡
mamado ADJ **1**‡ (= *borracho*) smashed*, sloshed*
2* (= *fácil*) dead easy*
3 (*Caribe**) (= *tonto*) silly, stupid
mamagrande SF (*LAm*) grandmother; ▹ **mamá**
mamaíta* SF = **mamá**
mamalón ADJ (*Caribe*) (= *vago*) idle; (= *gorrón*) sponging
mamamama* SF (*And*) grandma*
mamandurria* SF (= *empleo*) cushy job*; (= *sueldo*) fat salary; (= *gajes*) rich pickings (*pl*)
mamantear ▹ CONJUG 1a VT (*LAm*)
1 (= *mamar*) to nurse, feed
2 (= *mimar*) to spoil, pamper
mamaón SM (*Méx*) tipsy cake
mamar ▹ CONJUG 1a VT **1** [+ *leche, pecho*] to suck
2 (= *asimilar*) • **lo mamó desde pequeño** he grew up with it from childhood • **nació mamando el oficio** he was born to the trade • **todavía no han mamado suficiente democracia** democracy hasn't become a way of life yet
3* (= *devorar*) [+ *comida*] to wolf down, bolt; [+ *recursos*] to milk, suck dry; [+ *fondos*] to pocket (illegally) • **¡cómo la mamamos!** this is the life!, we never had it so good!
4‡‡ (= *sexualmente*) to suck off‡‡, give a blow job‡‡
VI **1** [*bebé*] to suck • **dar de ~ a un bebé** to feed a baby • **dar de ~ a una cría** to suckle a baby • **MODISMO**: • **¡no mames!** (*Méx*‡) come off it!*, don't give me that!*
2‡ (= *beber*) to booze*, drink
VPR **mamarse 1**‡ (= *emborracharse*) to get smashed‡, get sloshed*
2* [+ *puesto, ventaja*] to wangle*
3 • **~se a algn*** (*LAm*) (= *engañar*) to take sb for a ride*; (*CAm*) (= *matar*) to do sb in‡
4 • **~se un susto*** to give o.s. a fright
5 (*And**) (= *rajarse*) to go back on one's word
mamario ADJ mammary
mamarrachada* SF (= *acción*) stupid thing; (= *objeto*) monstrosity*, sight*
mamarracho/a* SM/F (= *persona*) sight* • **estaba hecho un ~** he looked a sight *o* a complete mess*
SM (= *objeto*) monstrosity*, sight*; (= *obra, trabajo*) mess, botch; (= *cuadro*) daub
mamá-señora SF (*LAm*) grandmother
mambo SM (*Mús*) mambo
mameluca‡ SF (*Cono Sur*) whore

mameluco SM **1** (*Hist*) Mameluke
2 (*LAm*) (= *mono*) overalls (*pl*); (*tb* **mamelucos de niño**) rompers (*pl*), romper suit
3 (*LAm*) (*Hist*) Brazilian mestizo, half-breed
4* (= *idiota*) chump*, idiot
mameo‡ SM • **cogerse un ~** to get plastered*, get smashed*
mamerto/a SM/F twit*, idiot
mamey SM (*LAm*) mammee apple, mamey
• MODISMO: • **ser ~ colorado** (*Caribe**) to be out of this world
mameyal SM (*LAm*) mamey plantation
mamífero ADJ mammalian, mammal (*antes de s*)
SM mammal
mamila SF **1** (*Méx*) (= *biberón*) feeding bottle (*esp Brit*), nursing bottle (*EEUU*) • **dar la ~ al niño** to give the baby his bottle
2 (*Col*) (= *chupete*) dummy (*Brit*), pacifier (*EEUU*)
Mammón SM Mammon
mamografía SF mammography
mamola SF • **dar** *o* **hacer la ~ a algn** (*lit*) to tickle *o* chuck sb under the chin; (*fig*) to take sb for a ride*
mamón SM **1** (= *bebé*) small baby, baby at the breast
2** (= *idiota*) prick**, wanker**
3‡ (= *gorrón*) scrounger*; (= *indeseable*) rotter*, swine* • **¡qué suerte tienes, ~!** you lucky sod!‡
4 (*Bot*) sucker, shoot
5 (*And, Cono Sur*) (= *árbol*) papaya tree; (= *fruta*) papaya
6 (*Cono Sur, Méx*) suck
7 (*CAm*) (= *palo*) club, stick
8 (*Méx*) (= *bizcocho*) soft sponge cake
ADJ **1** [*niño*] small, suckling
2 (*Méx**) (= *bruto*) thick*; (= *engreído*) cocky*
mamonada** SF • **eso es una ~** that's bloody stupid‡
mamoncete‡ SM (little) bastard**
mamonear ▷ CONJUG 1a VT **1** (*CAm*) (= *golpear*) to beat
2 (*Caribe*) (= *aplazar*) (*gen*) to postpone; [+ *tiempo*] to waste
mamoplastia SF mammoplasty
mamotrético* ADJ (= *enorme*) gigantic; (= *inmanejable*) unwieldy
mamotreto* SM **1** (= *libro*) hefty volume; (= *objeto*) monstrosity*, useless great object
2 (*esp LAm*) (= *aparato*) contraption; (= *bulto*) lump; (= *coche viejo*) old banger*, jalopy (*EEUU*)
3 (*Méx*) (= *inútil*) dead loss*
mampara SF screen, partition
mamparo SM (*Náut, Aer*) bulkhead
mamplora‡ SM (*CAm*) queer‡, fag (*EEUU*‡)
mamporrera* SF madam, brothel-keeper
mamporro* SM (= *golpe*) (*con la mano*) clout*, bash*; (*al caer*) bump • **atizar** *o* **sacudir un ~ a algn** to give sb a clout *o* bash* • **liarse a ~s con algn** to come to blows with sb
mampostería SF masonry
mampuesto SM **1** (= *piedra*) rough stone
2 (= *muro*) wall
3 (*LAm*) [*de fusil*] rest
4 • **de ~** spare, emergency (*antes de s*)
mamúa‡ SF (*Cono Sur*) • **agarrarse una ~** to get plastered*
mamuchi* SF mumsy*
mamut SM (PL: **mamuts**) mammoth
mana SF (*LAm*) **1** (= *manantial*) spring
2 (= *alimento*) manna
maná SM manna
manada SF **1** (*Zool*) [*de ganado*] herd; [*de lobos*] pack; [*de leones*] pride
2* [*de gente*] crowd, mob • **los periodistas llegaron en ~** a swarm *o* pack of journalists arrived
manadero SM herdsman, drover
manager, mánager ['manaʒer] SMF (PL: **managers** *o* **mánagers**) manager
Managua SF Managua
managua, managüense ADJ INV of/from Managua
SMF native/inhabitant of Managua • **los ~s** the people of Managua
manantial SM **1** (= *fuente*) spring • **agua de ~** spring water ▸ **manantial termal** hot spring
2 [*de riqueza, conflicto*] (= *origen*) source, origin; (= *causa*) cause
ADJ • **agua ~** running water, flowing water
manantío ADJ running, flowing
manar ▷ CONJUG 1a VT to run with, flow with • **la herida manaba sangre** blood gushed from the wound
VI **1** [*líquido*] (*gen*) to run, flow; (*a chorros*) to pour out, stream; (= *surgir*) to well up
2 (= *abundar*) to abound, be plentiful • **~ en algo** to abound in sth
manatí SM manatee, sea cow
manazas* SMF INV • **ser (un) ~** to be clumsy
SFPL (= *manos*) big mitts*
manazo SM (*LAm*) slap
mancar ▷ CONJUG 1g VT **1** (= *mutilar*) to maim, cripple
2 (*Cono Sur*) • **~ el tiro** to miss
VI (*And**) (= *fracasar*) to blow it*; (*Escol*) to fail
mancarrón* SM **1** (*Cono Sur*) (= *caballo*) nag
2 (*And, Cono Sur*) (= *obrero*) disabled workman
3 (*And, Cono Sur*) (= *presa*) small dam
manceba†† SF (= *amante*) lover, mistress; (= *concubina*) concubine
mancebía†† SF brothel
mancebo†† SM **1** (= *joven*) youth, young man
2 (= *soltero*) bachelor
3 (*Com*) clerk
4 (*Farm*) assistant, dispenser
mancera SF plough handle
Mancha SF • **La ~** La Mancha
mancha SF **1** (= *marca*) [*de aceite, comida, pintura, sangre*] stain; [*de óxido, bolígrafo*] mark; [*de pintura de labios*] smudge • **había ~s de sangre por el suelo** there were bloodstains on the floor • **procura que no te caigan ~s en la camisa** try not to get stains on your shirt • **me cayó una ~ de tinta en la carta** a drop of ink fell on the letter • **las ~s de grasa salen mejor con agua caliente** oil stains come out better with hot water • **han salido ~s de humedad en la pared** damp patches have appeared on the wall • **quitar una ~** to get a mark *o* stain out, get a mark *o* stain off
• MODISMO: • **extenderse como una ~ de aceite** [*enfermedad, noticia*] to spread like wildfire; [*movimiento, tendencia*] to spread far and wide
2 (= *área*) [*de hielo, vegetación*] patch; (*en el Sol, en un planeta*) spot • **~s de bosque bajo** patches of scrubland ▸ **mancha de petróleo** oil slick ▸ **mancha solar** sunspot
3 (*Zool*) (*grande*) patch; (*redonda*) spot • **un cachorro blanco con ~s marrones** a white puppy with brown patches • **los leopardos tienen la piel a ~s** leopards have spotted coats *o* spots
4 (= *deshonra*) stain • **una ~ en su honor** a stain on his honour • **la expulsión del colegio fue una ~ en su expediente** his expulsion from school was a black mark *o* a blot on his record • **esa derrota fue la única ~ en una excelente temporada** that defeat was the only blot on an otherwise excellent season • **la ~ del pecado** the taint of sin • **sin ~** [*conducta*] impeccable; [*expediente*] unblemished; [*alma*] pure
5 (*Med*) [*de sarampión, rubeola*] spot; (*en el pulmón*) shadow • **le han salido unas ~s rojizas en la cara** his face has come out in reddish spots ▸ **mancha amarilla** [*de retina*] yellow spot ▸ **mancha de nacimiento** birthmark ▸ **manchas del sarampión** measles spots
6 (*Arte*) shading, shaded area ▸ **mancha de color** (*en pintura*) splash of colour *o* (*EEUU*) color; (*en fotografía*) patch of colour *o* (*EEUU*) color
7 (*CAm, Méx*) [*de langostas*] cloud, swarm; [*de peces*] school, shoal; [*de gente*] swarm
8 (*Arg, Uru*) (= *juego*) • **la ~** tag
9 (*Perú**) [*de amigos*] gang
manchado ADJ **1** (= *sucio*) stained, dirty • **esta camisa está manchada** this shirt is stained *o* dirty • **su traje estaba completamente ~** his suit was completely covered in stains • **~ de algo: la acera estaba manchada de sangre** the pavement was stained with blood • **tenía la chaqueta manchada de café** his jacket had coffee stains on it *o* was stained with coffee • **un par de botas manchadas de barro** a pair of mud-stained boots • **tenía los dedos ~s de tinta** she had ink stains on her fingers, she had ink-stained fingers • **el folio estaba ~ de tinta** the sheet of paper was smudged with ink
2 (*Zool*) [*caballo, perro*] (*con manchas pequeñas*) spotted; (*con manchas más grandes*) dappled; [*ave*] speckled • **el caballo tiene el lomo ~** the horse has dappled markings on its back
3 (= *sin honra*) [*reputación*] tarnished • **estaba ~ por el pecado original** he bore the taint of original sin
4 (*Arte*) shaded
manchar ▷ CONJUG 1a VT **1** (= *ensuciar*) to get dirty, stain • **te has manchado el vestido** you've got your dress dirty, you've stained your dress, there's dirt on your dress • **ten cuidado de no ~me** be careful you don't get me dirty *o* stain my clothes • **~ algo de algo** (*gen*) to stain sth with sth; (*más sucio*) to get sth covered in sth • **me has manchado de pintura** you've got paint on me
2 (= *desprestigiar*) [+ *honor, imagen*] to tarnish
VI to stain • **este vino no mancha** this wine doesn't stain
VPR **mancharse 1** (= *ensuciarse*) to get dirty • **no lo toques que te puedes ~** don't touch it or you'll get dirty! • **¿cómo se te ha manchado la chaqueta?** how did you get your jacket dirty? • **~se de algo**: • **se me ~on los dedos de sangre** I got blood *o* bloodstains on my fingers • **te has manchado la boca de chocolate** you've got chocolate *o* chocolate stains round your mouth • **me he manchado el traje de barro/de tinta** I got my suit covered in mud/ink, I got mud/ink all over my suit • MODISMO: • **~se las manos** to get one's hands dirty, dirty one's hands
2 (= *deshonrarse*) to tarnish one's reputation
manchego/a ADJ of/from La Mancha
SM/F native/inhabitant of La Mancha
• **los ~s** the people of La Mancha
mancheta SF [*de libro*] blurb; [*de periódico*] masthead
manchón¹ SM **1** (= *mancha*) large stain, big spot
2 (*Bot*) patch of dense vegetation
manchón² SM (*Cono Sur*) muff
Manchuria SF Manchuria
manchuriano/a ADJ, SM/F Manchurian
mancilla SF stain, blemish • **sin ~** unblemished; (*Rel*) immaculate, pure
mancillar ▷ CONJUG 1a VT to stain, sully (*liter*)

manco/a ADJ 1 (de una mano) one-handed; (de un brazo) one-armed; (= sin brazos) armless • quedó ~ de la izquierda he lost his left hand
2 (= incompleto) half-finished
3 (= defectuoso) defective, faulty
4 • MODISMO: • no ser ~ (= astuto) to be nobody's fool; (= útil) to be useful o handy; (= sin escrúpulos) to be pretty sharp • Alarcos, jugador que tampoco es ~ Alarcos, who is a pretty useful player himself • no ser ~ en algo to be pretty good at sth
SM/F (de una mano) one-handed person; (de un brazo) one-armed person; (= sin brazos) armless person, person with no arms
SM (Cono Sur) (= caballo) nag

mancomún • de ~ ADV = mancomunadamente

mancomunadamente ADV (= en conjunto) jointly, together; (= por voluntad común) by common consent • obrar ~ con algn to act jointly with sb

mancomunado ADJ joint, jointly held

mancomunar ▷ CONJUG 1a VT 1 (= unir) [+ personas] to unite, associate; [+ intereses] to combine; [+ recursos] to pool
2 (Jur) to make jointly responsible
VPR mancomunarse to unite

mancomunidad SF 1 (= unión) union, association
2 (= comunidad) (gen) community; [de recursos] pool
3 (Jur) joint responsibility
4 (Pol) commonwealth • la Mancomunidad Británica the British Commonwealth

mancornar ▷ CONJUG 1l VT 1 [+ toro] (= agarrar) to seize by the horns; (con una cuerda) to hobble
2 (= unir) to join, couple

mancornas SFPL (LAm), **mancuernas** SFPL (Méx), **mancuernillas** SFPL (CAm, Méx) cufflinks

manda SF 1 (= legado) bequest
2 (LAm) (= voto) religious vow

mandadero/a SM/F (= recadero) errand boy/girl; (= mensajero) messenger

mandado/a SM/F 1 (pey) (= subordinado) dogsbody* • yo aquí no soy más que un ~ here I just obey instructions, I'm just a dogsbody* o a minion here
2 (Méx*) (= aprovechado) opportunist • no seas ~ don't take advantage of the situation
SM 1 (= recado) errand • hacer un ~ to do o run an errand • ir a (hacer) los ~s to do the shopping
2 (= orden) order
3 (Méx) • el ~ the shopping • ir al ~ to do the shopping

mandamás SMF INV boss*, bigwig*

mandamiento SM 1 (Rel) commandment • los Diez Mandamientos the Ten Commandments
2 (Jur) (tb mandamiento judicial) writ, warrant • notificar a algn un ~ judicial to serve a writ on sb ▸ mandamiento de ejecución warrant of execution ▸ mandamiento de entrada y registro (Esp) search warrant ▸ mandamiento de prisión warrant of commitment
3 (Esp) (Econ) ▸ mandamiento de pago banker's order
4 (= orden) order, command

mandanga SF 1* (= cachaza) slowness • ¡qué ~ tienes! you take your time, don't you!
2* (= cuento) tale, story; (= excusa) excuse; (= paparrucha) rubbish* • ¡no me vengas con ~s!* don't give me that rubbish!*, who are you trying to kid?* • hay que dejarse de ~s y decirlo bien claro you have to stop beating about the bush and say it straight out • deberían obligarle a dimitir sin más ~s he should be forced to resign, no two ways about it* • ¡tiene ~! this is too much!
3‡ (= golpe) bash*
4‡ (= droga) pot*, grass*

mandanguero/a‡ SM/F (= fumador) pot-smoker*; (= vendedor) dealer in pot o grass*

mandar ▷ CONJUG 1a VT 1 (= ordenar, encargar) to tell • haz lo que te manden do as you are told • no me gusta que me manden I don't like being told what to do • ¿hoy no te han mandado deberes? haven't they given you any homework today? • ¿qué manda usted? (esp LAm) can I help you? • ¿manda usted algo más? (esp LAm) would you like anything else? • ~ (a algn) (a) hacer algo: • lo mandé a comprar pan I sent him (out) for bread o to buy some bread • me he mandado hacer un traje I'm having a suit made • tuvimos que ~ arreglar el coche we had to put the car in for repairs, we had to have the car repaired • ¿quién diablos me ~ía a mí meterme en esto?* why on earth did I get mixed up in this?* • ¿quién te manda ser tan tonto? how could you be so stupid? • ~ callar a algn (gen) to tell sb to be quiet; (con autoridad) to order sb to be quiet • ~ llamar o venir a algn to send for sb • he mandado llamar al electricista I've sent for the electrician • mandó llamar a todas las monjas al patio she summoned all the nuns to the courtyard • ~ salir a algn to order sb out • ~ a algn (a) por algo to send sb (out) for sth o to do sth • lo mandé a por el periódico I sent him (out) for the paper o to buy the paper • ~ a algn que haga algo (gen) to tell sb to do sth; (con autoridad) to order sb to do sth • me han mandado que deje de fumar I've been advised o told to stop smoking • MODISMO: • como está mandado (Esp*): • se casará por la iglesia como está mandado she'll have a church wedding as one would expect • lo hizo como estaba mandado he did the right thing*
2 (= enviar) to send • me han mandado un paquete de Madrid I've got o I've been sent a parcel from Madrid • lo ~on como representante de la empresa he was sent to represent the company, he was sent as the company's representative • he mandado a los niños a la cama I've sent the children to bed • ~ algo por correo to post sth, mail sth (EEUU) • te ~é mi dirección por correo electrónico I'll send you my address by email, I'll email you my address • ~ recuerdos a algn to send one's love to sb, send one's regards to sb (frm); ▷ carajo, mierda, mona, paseo, porra
3 (= estar al mando de) [+ batallón] to lead, command; [+ trabajadores, policías] to be in charge of • mandaba la brigada de bomberos he was in charge of the fire brigade
4 (Dep) to send, hit • mandó la pelota fuera del campo de golf he sent o hit the ball off the golf course • mandó el balón al poste she hit the post with the ball
5 (Med) to prescribe • le han mandado antibióticos she has been prescribed antibiotics
6 (= legar) to leave, bequeath (frm)
7 (LAm) (= lanzar) to throw, hurl
8 (LAm*) • ~ un golpe a algn to hit sb • ~ una patada a algn to give sb a kick, kick sb • le mandó una bofetada she slapped him
9 (LAm) (= tirar) to throw away
10 (LAm) [+ caballo] to break in
11 (Cono Sur) (Dep) to start
VI 1 (= estar al mando) (gen) to be in charge; (Mil) to be in command • ¿quién manda aquí? who's in charge here? • aquí mando yo I'm the boss here, I'm in charge here • ~ en algo to be in charge of sth; (Mil) to be in command of sth • los que mandan en este país the people that run this country • mandaba en todo un ejército he was in command of an entire army
2 (= ordenar) • ¡mande usted! at your service!, what can I do for you? • de nada, a ~ don't mention it, (I'm) at your service! • ¿mande? (esp Méx) (= ¿cómo dice?) pardon?, what did you say?; (invitando a hablar) yes? • le gusta ~ (pey) he likes bossing people around • según manda la ley (Jur) in accordance with the law; ▷ canon, Dios
VPR **mandarse** 1 [enfermo] to get about by o.s., manage unaided
2 [habitaciones] to communicate (con with)
3 (LAm*) • mándese entrar o pasar please come in • ~se cambiar (And, Cono Sur) • ~se mudar (Arg, Uru) to up and leave* • ¡mándate cambiar! beat it!*, clear off!* • MODISMO: • ~se (guarda) abajo (Chile*) to come down, come crashing down
4 (LAm) • ~se con algn to be rude to sb, be bossy with sb
5 (Caribe, Cono Sur) (= irse) to go away, slip away; (= desaparecer) to disappear secretly
6 (LAm*) [+ comida] to scoff*, polish off*; [+ bebida, trago] to knock back*
7 (And*) [+ gol] to score; [+ mentira] to come out with • se manda cada discurso he's such an amazing speaker • se manda unas metidas de pata he's always putting his foot in his mouth*
8 (Méx*) (= aprovecharse) to take advantage (of the situation)

mandarín SM 1 (Hist, Ling) Mandarin
2 (pey) petty bureaucrat

mandarina SF 1 (Bot) mandarin, tangerine • MODISMO: • ¡chúpate esa ~! (Esp‡) get that!*, hark at him!
2 (Ling) Mandarin

mandarino SM mandarin (orange) tree

mandatario/a SM/F 1 (Jur) agent, attorney
2 (= dirigente) leader; (esp LAm) (Pol) (tb primer mandatario) Head of State • los altos ~s de la Iglesia Church leaders

mandato SM 1 (= orden) mandate • bajo ~ de la ONU under UN mandate • según un ~ constitucional according to the constitution ▸ mandato judicial court order
2 (= período de mando) term of office, mandate (frm) • se acerca el final de su ~ his term of office o his mandate (frm) is coming to an end • la duración de su ~ fue de cuatro años he was in office for four years • bajo o durante el ~ de algn during sb's term of office o mandate (frm) • territorio bajo ~ mandated territory
3 (Jur) (= estatutos) terms of reference (pl); (= poder) power of attorney • eso no forma parte de mi ~ that is not in my brief
4 (Inform) command
5 (Com) ▸ mandato internacional international money order
6 (Rel) maundy

mandíbula SF (Anat, Téc) jaw; (Zool) mandible • MODISMO: • reírse a ~ batiente to laugh one's head off

mandil SM 1 (= delantal) apron; [de albañil] (leather) apron; (= bata) pinafore dress
2 (LAm) horse blanket

mandilón SM 1 (= babi) smock, pinafore dress
2 (= overol) overalls (pl)
3* (= cobarde) coward

mandinga* SM 1 (LAm) (= diablo) devil; (= duende) goblin; (malévolo) evil spirit
2 (And, Caribe) (= negro) black

ADJ **1** (*CAm, Cono Sur*) (= *afeminado*) effeminate
2 (*Caribe, Cono Sur*) (= *pícaro*) impish, mischievous
mandioca SF cassava, manioc
mandiocal SM (*LAm*) cassava plot
mando SM **1** (= *poder*) command • **ha entregado el ~ al teniente** he's handed over command to the lieutenant • **están bajo el ~ del ejercito alemán** they are under the command of the German army • **el Mando de las Fuerzas Aéreas** the Air Force Command • **al ~ de** [+ *pelotón, flota*] in command of; [+ *asociación, expedición, país*] in charge of; [+ *capitán, jefe*] under the command *o* orders of, led by • **con ella al ~, mejorarán las cosas** with her in charge, things will get better • **lo pusieron al ~ de la campaña electoral** they put him in charge of the electoral campaign • **un grupo al ~ de las labores de rescate** a group leading the rescue operations • **estuvo al ~ del país durante muchos años** he was in power for many years, he led the country for many years • **las tropas estaban al ~ de un general extranjero** the troops were under the command *o* orders of a foreign general *o* were led by a foreign general • **alto ~** high command • **tomar el ~** (*Mil*) to take command; (*Dep*) to take the lead ▸ **mando supremo** commander-in-chief; ▹ **dote, voz**
2 [*de máquina, vehículo*] control • **no podía controlar los ~s** she couldn't operate the controls • **a los ~s de algo** at the controls of sth • **cuadro de ~s** control panel • **~ a la izquierda** left-hand drive • **palanca de ~** [*de máquina*] control lever; [*de avión*] joystick • **tablero de ~s** control panel ▸ **mando a distancia** remote control ▸ **mando de teclado** push-button control ▸ **mando selector** control knob
3 (= *período de mando*) term of office
4 mandos (= *autoridades*) (*Mil*) high-ranking officers, senior officers; (*Pol*) high-ranking members, senior members ▸ **mandos intermedios, mandos medios** (*LAm*) (*Com*) middle management ▸ **mandos militares** high-ranking officers, senior officers
mandoble SM **1** (= *golpe*) two-handed blow
2 (= *espada*) broadsword, large sword
3* (= *rapapolvo*) ticking-off*
mandolina SF mandolin
mandón/ona ADJ* bossy
SM/F* bossy-boots*
SM **1** (*Cono Sur*) (*Min*) mine foreman
2 (*Chile*) (*en carreras*) starter
mandonear* ▹ CONJUG 1a VT • **~ a algn** to boss sb around
mandrágora SF mandrake
mandria ADJ worthless
SM useless individual, weakling
mandril[1] SM (*Zool*) mandrill
mandril[2] SM (*Téc*) mandrel
manduca* SF grub*, chow (*EEUU*‡), nosh*
manducar* ▹ CONJUG 1g VT to scoff*, stuff o.s. with
manducatoria‡ SF grub*, eats* (*pl*), chow (*EEUU*‡)
manea SF hobble
maneador SM (*LAm*) hobble; (*Cono Sur*) whip; (*Méx*) halter
manear ▹ CONJUG 1a VT to hobble
VPR **manearse** (*And, Méx*) to trip over one's own feet
manecilla SF **1** (*Téc*) (*gen*) pointer; [*de reloj*] hand ▸ **manecilla grande** minute hand ▸ **manecilla pequeña** hour hand
2 [*de libro*] clasp
maneco ADJ (*Méx*) **1** (= *tullido*) (*gen*) maimed, deformed; (*de manos*) with deformed hands; (*de pies*) with deformed feet
2 (= *patizambo*) knock-kneed
manejabilidad SF [*de asunto*] manageability; [*de herramienta*] handiness, ease of use; [*de vehículo*] handling
manejable ADJ [*asunto, pelo*] manageable; [*aparato, libro*] user-friendly, easy to use; [*vehículo*] manoeuvrable, maneuvrable (*EEUU*)
manejador(a) ADJ manipulative
SM/F (*LAm*) (*Aut*) driver, motorist
manejar ▹ CONJUG 1a VT **1** (= *usar*) [+ *herramienta, arma*] to handle, use; [+ *máquina*] to operate; [+ *idioma*] to use
2 (= *dirigir*) [+ *negocio, empresa*] to run; [+ *asuntos*] to look after
3 [+ *dinero*] to handle • **manejan cifras elevadísimas** they handle huge sums (of money)
4 • **~ a algn: mi tía maneja a su marido** my aunt keeps her husband under her thumb
5 (*LAm*) (*Aut*) to drive
VI **1** • **"manejar con cuidado"** "handle with care"
2 (*LAm*) (*Aut*) to drive • **el examen de ~** the driving test
VPR **manejarse 1** (*Esp*) (= *desenvolverse*) to manage • **no te preocupes, puedo ~me** *o* **manejármelas yo sola** don't worry, I can manage on my own • **se maneja bien en inglés** he gets along fine in English • **se maneja bien con los chiquillos** she's good with the kids • **¿cómo te (las) manejas para estudiar y trabajar?** how do you manage to study and work at the same time? • **ya empieza a ~se con ayuda de las muletas** she's beginning to get about with the aid of crutches
2 (= *comportarse*) to act, behave
manejo SM **1** (= *uso*) [*de herramienta, arma*] use; [*de máquina*] operation; [*de idioma*] use • **una herramienta de fácil ~** a tool that is easy to use
2 (*Com*) [*de negocio, empresa*] running; [*de dinero, fondos*] handling • **se encarga del ~ de los asuntos de la empresa** he takes charge of looking after their business affairs • **llevar todo el ~ de algo** to be in sole charge of sth
3 • **tener buen ~ de** [+ *idioma, tema*] to have a good command of • **tiene un buen ~ del alemán** she has a good command of German • **demostró tener un gran ~ de la situación** he demonstrated a thorough command of the situation
4 manejos (= *intrigas*) dealings • **turbios ~s** shady dealings
5 (*LAm*) (*Aut*) driving
manera SF **1** (= *modo*) way • **hay varias ~s de hacerlo** there are various ways of doing it • **eso no es ~ de tratar a un animal** that's not the way to treat an animal, that's no way to treat an animal • **hazlo de la ~ que sea** do it however *o* the way you like • **de una ~ u otra** (in) one way or another • **¡llovía de una ~!** it was really pouring down! • **¡nunca he visto nevar de esta ~!** I've never seen it snow like this! • **no hubo ~ de convencerla** there was no convincing her, there was no way we could convince her • **a mi/tu** *etc* **~** my/your *etc* way • **lo hice a mi ~** I did it my way • **a mi ~ de ver, tenemos dos opciones** the way I see it, we have two options • **a la ~ de algn/algo**: • **siguen arando a la ~ de sus abuelos** they still plough as *o* in the way their grandfathers did • **una novela escrita a la ~ de Kafka** a novel written in a Kafkaesque manner *o* in the style of Kafka • **de ~ perfecta** perfectly, in a perfect way • **nos recibió de ~ cortés** he received us courteously *o* in a courteous way • **de esta ~** (in) this way, (in) this fashion • **de la misma ~** (in) the same way, (in) the same fashion ▸ **manera de ser** • **es su ~ de ser** that's the way she is • **cada uno tiene una ~ de ser** everyone has their own character
2 (*locuciones*) • **de alguna ~** (= *en cierto modo*) to some extent; (= *de cualquier modo*) somehow; (*al principio de frase*) in a way, in some ways • **en cierta ~** in a way, to a certain extent • **de cualquier ~** (= *sin cuidado*) any old how; (= *de todos modos*) anyway • **en gran ~** to a large extent • **de mala ~**: • **le pegó de mala ~** he hit her really hard • **lo estafaron de mala ~*** they really ripped him off* • **me contestó de muy mala ~** he answered me very rudely • **ese tío se enrolla de mala ~*** that guy just can't stop jabbering* • **de ninguna ~**: • **eso no lo vamos a aceptar de ninguna ~** there's no way we are going to accept that • **de ninguna ~ deben paralizarse las obras** on no account must the work stop • **no quiero de ninguna ~ implicarla en esto** I don't want to involve her in this in any way • **no se parece de ninguna ~ a lo que habíamos imaginado** it's nothing like we had imagined • **¡de ninguna ~!** certainly not!, no way! • **de otra ~** (= *de otro modo*) in a different way; (= *por otra parte*) otherwise • **los jóvenes entienden el mundo de otra ~** young people see the world in a different way • **las cosas podrían haber sido de otra ~** things could have been different • **no podía ser de otra ~** it couldn't be any other way • **de otra ~, no es posible**

MANERA, FORMA, MODO

De manera + adjetivo

▹ *Cuando* **de manera + adjetivo** *añade información sobre una acción, la traducción más frecuente al inglés es un adverbio terminado en* **-ly**. *En inglés este tipo de adverbio es mucho más común que el equivalente* **-mente** *español:*

Todos estos cambios ocurren de manera natural
All these changes happen naturally
La Constitución prohíbe de manera expresa la especulación inmobiliaria
The Constitution expressly forbids speculation in real estate

▹ **De manera + adjetivo** *también se puede traducir por* **in a** + *adjetivo* + **way** *si no existe un adverbio terminado en* **-ly** *que equivalga al adjetivo:*

Se lo dijo de manera amistosa
He said it to her in a friendly way

▹ *En los casos en que se quiere hacer hincapié en la manera de hacer algo, se puede utilizar tanto un adverbio en* **-ly** *como la construcción* **in a** + *adjetivo* + **way**, *aunque esta última posibilidad es más frecuente:*

Tienes que intentar comportarte de manera responsable
You must try to behave responsibly *o* in a responsible way
Ellos podrán ayudarte a manejar tu negocio de manera profesional
They'll be able to help you run your business professionally *o* in a professional way

Para otros usos y ejemplos ver **manera, forma, modo**

m

entender su actitud otherwise, it's impossible to understand his attitude • **dicho de otra ~** in other words, to put it another way • **sobre ~** exceedingly • **de tal ~ que ...** in such a way that ... • **de todas ~s** anyway, in any case
3 • **de ~ que** (*antes de verbo*) so; (*después de verbo*) so that • **¿de ~ que esto no te gusta?** so you don't like this? • **lo hizo de ~ que nadie se dio cuenta** he did it so that nobody noticed
4 maneras (= *modales*) manners • **buenas ~s** good manners • **se lo dije con buenas ~s** I told him politely • **malas ~s** bad manners, rudeness • **con muy malas ~s** very rudely • **tener ~s** (*LAm*) to have good manners, be well-mannered
5 (*liter*) (= *tipo*) kind • **otra ~ de valentía** another kind of courage
6 (*Arte, Literat*) (= *estilo*) style • **las diferentes ~s de Picasso** Picasso's different styles

maneta SF lever

maneto ADJ (*And, CAm, Caribe*) = **maneco**

manflor‡ SM, **manflorita‡** SM (*LAm*) pansy‡ (*pey*), queer‡ (*pey*), fag (*EEUU‡*)

manga¹ SF **1** (*en ropa*) sleeve • **estar en ~s de camisa** to be in shirtsleeves • **~ japonesa** batwing sleeve • **~ ra(n)glan** raglan sleeve • **de ~ corta/larga** short-/long-sleeved • **sin ~s** sleeveless • MODISMOS: • **andar ~ por hombro** to be a mess, be all over the place • **con el nuevo jefe todo anda ~ por hombro** with this new boss everything's in a mess *o* all over the place • **la casa está ~ por hombro** the house is a mess • **bajo ~*** under the counter • **estar de ~** to be in league • **hacer ~s y capirotes de algn** to ignore sb completely • **pegar las ~s*** to kick the bucket* • **ser de** *o* **tener ~ ancha** (= *tolerante*) to be easy-going; (= *poco severo*) to be too lenient; (*pey*) (= *sin escrúpulos*) to be unscrupulous • **sacarse algo de la ~** to come up with sth • **traer algo en la ~** to have sth up one's sleeve; ▹ **corte¹**
2 (= *manguera*) (*tb* **manga de riego**) hose, hosepipe ▸ **manga de incendios** fire hose
3 (*Culin*) (= *colador*) strainer; [*de pastelería*] piping bag ▸ **manga pastelera** piping bag
4 (*Aer*) windsock ▸ **manga de mariposas** butterfly net
5 (*Geog*) [*de agua*] stretch; [*de nubes*] cloudburst • **tormentas con espesas ~s de agua** storms with heavy squally showers ▸ **manga de viento** whirlwind ▸ **manga marina** waterspout
6 (*Náut*) beam, breadth
7 (*Dep*) [*de competición*] round, stage; (*Tenis*) set; (*Bridge*) game • **ir a ~** to go to game ▸ **manga clasificatoria** qualifying round ▸ **manga de consolación** runners-up play-off
8 (*LAm*) (= *multitud*) crowd, mob
9 (*LAm*) (*Agr*) funnel, narrow entrance
10 (*CAm*) poncho, coarse blanket ▸ **manga de agua** rain cape
11 (= *bolso*) travelling bag, traveling bag (*EEUU*)

manga² SM (= *cómic*) manga

mangal SM (*LAm*) **1** = **manglar**
2 (*Méx**) (= *trampa*) dirty trick
3 (*And*) (= *plantío*) mango plantation

mangana SF lasso, lariat

mangancia* SF **1** (= *timo*) swindle, racket
2 (= *robo*) (*gen*) thieving, pilfering; (*en tienda*) shoplifting
3 (= *gorronería*) scrounging*
4 (= *cuento*) story, fib

manganear ▹ CONJUG 1a VT **1** (*Perú*) (= *molestar*) to bother, annoy
2 (= *coger con lazo*) to lasso
3 (*CAm, Cono Sur*) (= *saquear*) to pillage, plunder; (= *robar**) to pinch*, nick*
VI (*Caribe*) to loaf, hang about

manganeso SM manganese

manganeta SF (*LAm*), **manganilla** SF
1 (= *juego de manos*) sleight of hand
2 (= *engaño*) trick, deceit
3 (= *timo*) swindle, racket

mangante* SMF **1** (= *ladrón*) (*gen*) thief; (*en tienda*) shoplifter
2 (= *mendigo*) beggar
3 (= *gorrón*) scrounger*, freeloader*
4 (= *caradura*) rotter*, villain
ADJ (= *caradura*) brazen

manganzón ADJ (= *perezoso*) lazy

mangar* ▹ CONJUG 1h VT **1** (= *robar*) to pinch*, nick*
2 (= *mendigar*) to scrounge*
VI **1** (= *robar*) (*gen*) to pilfer*; (*en tienda*) to shoplift; (*Cono Sur*) to scrounge*

mangazón* ADJ (*LAm*) lazy

manglar SM mangrove swamp

mangle SM (*Bot*) mangrove

mango¹ SM **1** (*Bot*) mango
2 (*Cono Sur‡*) dough‡, dosh‡
3 (*Méx**) good-looking lad

mango² SM **1** (= *asa*) handle ▸ **mango de escoba** (*para barrer*) broomstick; (*Aer*) joystick ▸ **mango de pluma** penholder
2 (*Arg**) (= *dinero*) dough‡, dosh‡

mangón SM (*And*) (= *prado*) pasture; (= *estancia*) cattle ranch

mangoneador* a SM/F **1** (= *entrometido*) meddler; (= *mandón*) bossyboots*
2 (*Méx*) (= *oficial corrupto*) grafter, corrupt official

mangonear* ▹ CONJUG 1a VT **1** [+ *persona*] to boss about*
2 (= *birlar*) to pinch*, nick*
3 (*LAm*) (= *saquear*) to pillage, plunder
VI **1** (= *entrometerse*) to meddle, interfere (**en** in); (= *interesarse*) to dabble (**en** in)
2 (= *ser mandón*) (*con personas*) to boss people about; (*con asuntos*) to run everything
3 (*LAm*) (= *estafar*) (*gen*) to graft, be on the fiddle*; (*Pol*) to fix things, fiddle the results*

mangoneo* SM **1** (= *entrometimiento*) meddling, interference
2 (*con personas*) (= *control*) bossing people about; (= *descaro*) brazenness
3 (*LAm*) (= *estafa*) (*gen*) graft*, fiddling*; (*Pol*) fixing (of results)

mangoneón/ona*, **mangonero/a*** ADJ (= *entrometido*) meddlesome, interfering; (= *mandón*) bossy; (= *descarado*) brazen
SM/F (= *entrometido*) busybody; (= *mandón*) bossy individual; (= *descarado*) brazen sort

mangosta SF mongoose

manguear ▹ CONJUG 1a (*LAm*) VT [+ *ganado*] to drive; [+ *caza*] to beat, put up
VI* **1** (*And, Caribe*) (= *gandulear*) to skive*
2 (*Cono Sur*) (= *sablear*) to scrounge*

mangueo* SM (= *robo*) thieving, pilfering; (= *gorroneo*) scrounging*

manguera SF **1** [*de riego*] hose, hosepipe ▸ **manguera antidisturbios** water-cannon ▸ **manguera de aspiración** suction pump ▸ **manguera de incendios** fire hose
2 (*And*) [*de bicicleta*] bicycle tyre, inner tube
3 (*Meteo*) waterspout
4 (*Cono Sur*) corral, yard

mangui‡ SMF (= *ladrón*) thief; (= *ratero*) small-time crook*; (= *canalla*) villain, rotter*

manguillo SM (*Méx*) penholder

manguito SM **1** (*para manos*) muff
2 (*Téc*) sleeve, coupling ▸ **manguito incandescente** gas mantle

mangurrina* SF bash*, wallop*

mangurrino* ADJ rotten*, worthless

manguta‡ SMF (= *ladrón*) small-time thief; (= *indeseable*) good-for-nothing

mani* SF demo*

maní SM (PL: **maníes** *o* **manises**) **1** (*esp LAm*) (= *cacahuete*) peanut; (= *planta*) groundnut plant
2 (*Caribe**) (= *dinero*) dough‡, dosh‡
3 • **¡maní!** (*Cono Sur*) never!

manía SF **1** (*Med*) mania ▸ **manía de grandezas** megalomania ▸ **manía persecutoria** persecution mania
2 [*de persona*] (= *costumbre*) odd habit; (= *rareza*) peculiarity, oddity; (= *capricho*) fad, whim • **tiene sus ~s** he has his little ways • **tiene la ~ de comerse las uñas** he has the annoying habit of biting his nails • **le ha dado la ~ de salir sin abrigo** he's taken to going out without a coat
3 [*de grupo*] (= *afición*) mania; (= *moda*) rage, craze • **la ~ del fútbol** football fever, the football craze • **la ~ de la minifalda** the craze for miniskirts • **tiene la ~ de las motos** he's obsessed with motorbikes, he's motorbike-crazy*
4 (= *antipatía*) dislike • **coger ~ a algn** to take a dislike to sb • **tener ~ a algn** to dislike sb • **tengo ~ a los bichos** I can't stand insects • **el maestro me tiene ~** the teacher's got it in for me

maniabierto ADJ (*Caribe*) lavish, generous

maníaco/a, maniaco/a ADJ maniac, maniacal
SM/F maniac ▸ **maníaco/a sexual** sex maniac

maniaco-depresivo/a ADJ, SM/F manic depressive

maniatar ▹ CONJUG 1a VT **1** • **~ a algn** (*con cuerdas*) to tie sb's hands; (*con esposas*) to handcuff sb
2 [+ *animal*] to hobble

maniático/a ADJ **1** (= *con manías*) maniac, maniacal; (= *fanático*) fanatical; (= *obsesionado*) obsessive
2 (= *loco*) crazy; (= *excéntrico*) eccentric, cranky*; (= *delicado*) fussy
3 (= *terco*) stubborn
SM/F (= *obsesionado*) maniac; (= *fanático*) fanatic; (= *excéntrico*) crank* • **solo piensa en no pisar las rayas de las aceras, es un ~** his only concern is not to step on the lines on the pavement, he's obsessed • **~ de la ecología** ecology fanatic, ecology freak* • **es un ~ de la puntuación** he is obsessive about punctuation • **es un ~ del fútbol** he's football-crazy

manicero/a SM/F (*LAm*) peanut seller

manicomio SM lunatic asylum, insane asylum (*EEUU*), mental hospital • **no quiero ir a parar a un ~** I don't want to end up in the loony bin* • **ese día la ciudad es un ~** on that day the city goes mad *o* is like a madhouse

manicura SF manicure • **hacerse la ~** (*uno mismo*) to do one's nails; (*por profesional*) to have a manicure • **se me puede estropear la ~** I could ruin my nails

manicuro/a SM/F manicurist

manida SF lair, den

manido ADJ **1** (= *trillado*) [*tema*] trite, stale; [*frase*] hackneyed
2 (= *pasado*) [*carne*] high, gamy; [*frutos secos*] stale

manierismo SM mannerism

manierista ADJ, SMF mannerist

manifa* SF demo*

manifestación SF **1** (*Pol*) (= *desfile*) demonstration; (= *concentración*) mass meeting, rally
2 (= *muestra*) [*de emoción*] display, show; (= *señal*) sign • **manifestaciones de alegría/júbilo** jubilation • **han recibido**

muchas manifestaciones de apoyo they have received a lot of support • **manifestaciones de duelo** expressions of grief • **una gran ~ de entusiasmo** a great show of enthusiasm
3 (= *declaración*) statement, declaration
4 (*Chile*) (*tb* **manifestación social**) social occasion
5 ▸ **manifestación de impuesto** (*Méx*) tax return
manifestante (SMF) demonstrator
manifestar ▸ CONJUG 1j (VT) 1 (= *declarar*) to declare • **el presidente manifestó que no firmaría el acuerdo** the president declared that he would not sign the agreement • **~on su solidaridad con los damnificados** they declared their sympathy with the victims
2 [+ *emociones*] to show • **manifiesta un sincero arrepentimiento** he shows genuine regret • **nos manifestaba un gran cariño** he showed us great affection
(VPR) **manifestarse 1** (= *declararse*) • **el presidente se ha manifestado a favor del pacto** the president came out in favour of the agreement
2 (*Pol*) to demonstrate • **los estudiantes se ~on en contra de la nueva ley** the students demonstrated against the new law
3 (= *mostrarse*) to be apparent, be evident • **su pesimismo se manifiesta en todas sus obras** his pessimism is apparent *o* evident in all his works
manifiestamente (ADV) clearly, manifestly
manifiesto (ADJ) (= *claro*) (*gen*) clear, manifest; [*error*] glaring, obvious; [*verdad*] manifest • **poner algo de ~** (= *aclarar*) to make sth clear; (= *revelar*) to reveal sth • **quiero poner de ~ que ...** I wish to state that ... • **quedar ~** to be plain, be clear
(SM) **1** (*Pol, Arte*) (= *programa*) manifesto ▸ **el Manifiesto Comunista** the Communist Manifesto
2 (*Náut*) manifest
manigua (*LAm*) (SF) **1** [*de terreno*] (= *ciénaga*) swamp; (= *maleza*) scrubland; (= *selva*) jungle; (= *campo*) countryside • **irse a la ~**†† to take to the hills (*in revolt*)
2 • **agarrar ~** (*Caribe**) to get flustered
manigual (SM) (*Caribe*) = **manigua**
manigueta (SF) **1** (= *mango*) handle; (= *manivela*) crank; (*Cono Sur*) (*Aut*) starting handle
2 (= *maniota*) hobble
manija (SF) **1** (= *mango*) (*gen*) handle; (*Arg*) [*de puerta*] door knob
2 (*Mec*) clamp, collar
3 (*Ferro*) coupling
4 (*Agr*) hobble
5 (*Cono Sur*) (= *vaso*) mug, tankard
6 (*Cono Sur*) (*Aut*) starting handle • **dar ~ a algn** to egg sb on
Manila (SF) Manila
manilargo (ADJ) **1** (= *generoso*) open-handed, generous
2 (*esp LAm**) (= *ladrón*) light-fingered
manilense (ADJ) of/from Manila
(SMF) native/inhabitant of Manila • **los ~s** the people of Manila
manileño/a (ADJ), (SM/F) = **manilense**
manilla (SF) **1** [*de puerta*] handle, door handle
2 (= *mango*) handle
3 [*de reloj*] hand
4 [*de tabaco*] bundle
5 (= *pulsera*) bracelet ▸ **manillas (de hierro)** (= *grilletes*) manacles, handcuffs
manillar (SM) handlebars (*pl*)
maniobra (SF) **1** (= *giro*) (*Aut*) manoeuvre, maneuver (EEUU); (*Ferro*) shunting, switching (EEUU) • **hacer ~s** (*Aut*) to manoeuvre, maneuver (EEUU); (*Ferro*) to shunt, switch (EEUU)
2 (*Náut*) (= *operación*) manoeuvre, maneuver (EEUU); (= *aparejo*) gear, rigging
3 **maniobras** (*Mil*) manoeuvres, maneuvers (EEUU) • **estar de ~s** to be on manoeuvres
4 (= *estratagema*) manoeuvre, maneuver (EEUU), move • **una ~ política** a political manoeuvre • **fue una hábil ~ para expulsar al jefe** it was a clever manoeuvre *o* move to get rid of the boss ▸ **maniobra dilatoria** delaying tactic
maniobrabilidad (SF) [*de vehículo*] manoeuvrability, maneuverability (EEUU); [*de aparato*] handling qualities, ease of use
maniobrable (ADJ) [*vehículo*] manoeuvrable; [*aparato*] easy to handle *o* use
maniobrar ▸ CONJUG 1a (VT) **1** [+ *aparato, vehículo*] (= *manejar*) to handle, operate; (= *mover*) to manoeuvre, maneuver (EEUU)
2 (*Ferro*) to shunt
(VI) to manoeuvre, maneuver (EEUU)
maniota (SF) hobble
manipulable (ADJ) **1** (*Téc*) operable, that can be operated • **aparatos ~s por el visitante** devices that can be operated by the visitor
2 (*Bio*) controllable
3 [*persona*] easily manipulated
manipulación (SF) **1** (= *manejo*) [*de alimentos*] handling; [*de pieza, máquina*] manipulation
2 [*de información, resultados*] manipulation ▸ **manipulación genética** genetic manipulation
3 (*Med*) manipulation
manipulado (SM) handling
manipulador(a) (ADJ) manipulative
(SM/F) **1** [*de mercancías*] handler ▸ **manipulador(a) de alimentos** person who handles food ▸ **manipulador(a) de marionetas** puppeteer
2 (= *mangoneador*) manipulator
(SM) (*Elec, Telec*) key, tapper
manipular ▸ CONJUG 1a (VT) **1** (= *manejar*) [+ *alimentos, géneros*] to handle; [+ *aparato*] to operate, use
2 (= *mangonear*) to manipulate
(VI) • **~ con** *o* **en algo** to manipulate sth
manipulativo (ADJ) manipulative
manipuleo (SM) (= *mangoneo*) manipulation; (= *trampas*) fiddling
maniqueísmo (SM) **1** (*Hist*) Manicheism, Manichaeism
2 (= *tendencia a simplificar*) *tendency to see things in black and white* • **discutir sin ~s** to discuss without taking up extreme positions
maniqueísta (ADJ) Manichean, Manichaean
maniqueo/a (ADJ) **1** (*Hist*) Manichean, Manichaean
2 (= *simplista*) black and white
3 (= *extremista*) extremist
(SM/F) **1** (*Hist*) Manichean, Manichaean
2 (= *simplista*) *person who tends to see things in black and white terms*
maniquí (SMF)* poser*
(SM) **1** (= *muñeco*) [*de sastre, escaparate*] dummy, mannequin; (*Esgrima*) dummy figure
2 (= *títere*) puppet
(SF) (= *modelo*) model
manir ▸ CONJUG 3a (VT) [+ *carne*] to hang
(VPR) **manirse** (*CAm*) to go off
manirroto/a (ADJ) extravagant, lavish
(SM/F) spendthrift
manisero (*LAm*) = **manicero**
manisuelto/a (ADJ) extravagant
(SM/F) spendthrift
manita (SF) little hand • **echar una ~ a algn** to lend sb a hand • MODISMOS: • **hacer ~s** to canoodle, make out (EEUU*) (**con** with) • **tener ~s de plata** *o* **de oro** to be very skilful ▸ **manitas de cerdo** pig's trotters
manitas* (SMF INV) handyman/handywoman • **ser (un(a) ~** to be handy, be good with one's hands
manito¹ (SM) (*Méx*) pal*, buddy (EEUU*); (*en conversación*) mate*, pal*
manito²* (SM) (*LAm*) = **manita**
manivacío (ADJ) empty-handed
manivela (SF) crank, handle ▸ **manivela de arranque** starting handle
manjar (SM) **1** (= *delicia*) delicacy • **~ exquisito** tasty morsel • **~ espiritual** food for the mind, spiritual sustenance
2 (*Cono Sur*) (= *leche condensada*) heated condensed milk ▸ **manjar blanco** blancmange ▸ **manjar dulce** (*And*) fudge
3 (*CAm, Méx*) suit

mano¹

SUSTANTIVO FEMENINO
SUSTANTIVO MASCULINO

SUSTANTIVO FEMENINO

Para las expresiones **manos arriba, al alcance de la mano, frotarse las manos**, *ver la otra entrada.*

1 (*Anat*) hand • **lo hice con mis propias ~s** I made it with my own hands, I made it myself • **el asesino salió con las ~s en alto** the murderer came out with his hands up *o* with his hands in the air • **votar a ~ alzada** to vote by a show of hands • **dar la ~ a algn** (*para saludar*) to shake hands with sb; (*para andar, apoyarse*) to take sb by the hand • **darse la ~** *o* **las ~s** to shake hands • **recibir algo de ~s de algn** to receive sth from sb • **los dos iban de la ~** the two were walking hand-in-hand, the two were walking along holding hands • **llevar a algn de la ~** to lead sb by the hand • **¡~s a la obra!** (*como orden*) to work!; (*para darse ánimo*) let's get on with it!, (let's) get down to work! • **¡las ~s quietas!** hands off!, keep your hands to yourself! • **¡venga esa ~!** shake!, put it there!
a mano (= *sin máquina*) by hand; (= *cerca*) handy, at hand; (= *asequible*) handy, to hand • **cosió los pantalones a ~** she sewed the trousers by hand, she hand-sewed the trousers • **escribir a ~** to write in longhand, write out (by hand) • **escrito a ~** handwritten • **bordado a ~** hand-embroidered • **hecho a ~** handmade • **¿tienes un bolígrafo a ~?** have you got a pen handy *o* to hand? • **la tienda me queda** *o* **me pilla* muy a ~** the shop is very handy for me, the shop is very close *o* nearby
en mano • **a entregar en ~** to deliver by hand • **se presentó en el ayuntamiento pistola en ~** he turned up at the town hall with a gun in his hand • **carta en ~** letter delivered by hand • **"piso disponible, llave en mano"** (*para alquilar*) "flat available for immediate occupancy"; (*para comprar*) "flat available for immediate possession"; ▸ **estrechar, levantar, robo**
2 • MODISMOS: • **abrir la ~** to open up, loosen up; (= *dejarse*) to let one's standards slip • **a ~ airada** violently • **bajo ~** (= *secretamente*) in secret, on the quiet • **cargar la ~** (= *exagerar*) to overdo it; (= *cobrar demasiado*) to overcharge; (= *exigir*) to press too hard, be too exacting • **en ese colegio le cargan la ~** they ask too much of her *o* put too much pressure on her at that school • **no cargues la ~ con las especias** don't put too much spice in • **coger a algn con las ~s en la masa**

to catch sb red-handed • **dar de ~** to knock off*, stop working • **le das la ~ y se toma el codo** give him an inch and he'll take a mile • **dar una ~ a algn** (*LAm*) to lend *o* give sb a hand • **de ~s a boca** unexpectedly, suddenly • **estar con una ~ adelante y otra atrás** to be broke* • **estar ~ sobre ~** to be idle, be out of work • **echar ~ a** to lay hands on • **echar ~ de** to make use of, resort to • **echar una ~ a algn** to lend *o* give sb a hand • **ganar a algn por la ~** to beat sb to it • **llegar a las ~s** to come to blows • **a ~s llenas** lavishly, generously • **~ a ~**: • **se bebieron la botella ~ a ~** they drank the bottle between (the two of) them • **meter ~ a algn*** to touch sb up* • **meter ~ a algo**: • **hay que meterle ~ a la corrupción** we have to deal with *o* tackle corruption • **tengo que meterle ~ a las matemáticas** I need to get stuck into my maths* • **pasar la ~ a algn** (= *ser permisivo*) to be lenient with sb; (*LAm*) (= *adular*) to flatter sb, suck up to sb* • **ponerle a algn la ~ encima**: • **¡como me pongas la ~ encima ...!** if you lay one finger on me ...! • **poner la ~ en el fuego**: • **yo no pondría la ~ en el fuego por Juan** I wouldn't risk my neck for Juan, I wouldn't put myself on the line for Juan • **yo pondría la ~ en el fuego por su inocencia** I'd stake my life on his being innocent • **¡qué ~!** (*Ven*) not likely! • **sentar la ~ a algn** (= *pegar*) to beat sb • **tener las ~s largas** (= *ser propenso a robar*) to be light-fingered; (= *ser propenso a pegar*) to be apt to hit out • **tener las ~s libres** to have full *o* free rein, be given full *o* free rein, be free (to do sth) • **traerse algo entre ~s**: • **¿qué os traéis entre ~s?** what are you up to? • **se trae entre ~s varios asuntos a la vez** he's dealing with several matters at once • **untar la ~ a algn** to grease sb's palm • **con las ~s vacías** empty-handed • **se fue de las negociaciones con las ~s vacías** he left the negotiations empty-handed • **vivir de la ~ a la boca** to live from hand to mouth ▸ **mano derecha** right-hand man • **Pedro es mi ~ derecha** Pedro is my right-hand man ▸ **mano de santo** sure remedy • **fue ~ de santo** it came just right, it was just what the doctor ordered ▸ **mano dura** harsh treatment; (*Pol*) firm hand ▸ **manos de mantequilla** butterfingers

3 (= *posesión*) hand • **cambiar de ~s** to change hands • **la casa ha cambiado varias veces de ~** the house has changed hands several times, the house has had several owners • **de primera ~** (at) first-hand • **conocemos la noticia de primera ~** we got the news first-hand • **se ha comprado un coche de primera ~** he has bought a (brand) new car • **de segunda ~** second-hand • **ropa de segunda ~** second-hand *o* used clothes

4 (= *control*) • **está en tus ~s** it's up to you • **ha hecho cuanto ha estado en su ~** he has done all *o* everything in his power • **de buena ~** on good authority • **en buenas ~s** in good hands

a manos de at the hands of • **murió a ~s de los mafiosos** he died at the hands of the mafia • **la carta nunca llegó a ~s del jefe** the letter never reached the boss, the letter never came into the hands of the boss

en manos de in the hands of • **hemos puesto el asunto en ~s del abogado** we have placed the matter in the hands of our lawyer • **me pongo en tus ~s** I place myself entirely in your hands • **el armamento cayó en ~s de los traficantes** the weapons fell into the hands of arms dealers • MODISMOS: • **írsele a algn la ~ con algo**: • **se te ha ido la ~ con la sal** you overdid it with the salt • **írsele algo de las ~s a algn**: • **el asunto se le fue de las ~s** he lost all control of the affair • **dejado de la ~ de Dios** godforsaken • **tomarse la justicia por su ~** to take the law into one's own hands

5 (= *habilidad*) • **¡qué ~s tiene!** he's so clever with his hands! • **tener buena ~**: • **tiene buena ~ para aparcar** she's good at parking • **tener buena ~ para la cocina** to be a good cook • **tiene buena ~ con los niños** she's good with children • **tener (buena) ~ para las plantas** to have green fingers • **tener mala ~** to be clumsy, be awkward ▸ **mano izquierda** • **tiene ~ izquierda con los animales** he's got a way with animals

6 (= *lado*) side • **a ~ derecha** on the right-hand side • **a ~ izquierda** on the left-hand side

7 (= *trabajadores*) **manos** hands, workers • **contratar ~s** to sign up *o* take on workers ▸ **mano de obra** labour, labor (*EEUU*), manpower ▸ **mano de obra directa** direct labour ▸ **mano de obra especializada** skilled labour

8 (*Dep*) handling, handball • **¡mano!** handball!

9 (*Zool*) [*de mono*] hand; [*de perro, gato, oso, león*] front paw; [*de caballo*] forefoot, front hoof; [*de ave*] foot; (= *trompa*) trunk ▸ **manos de cerdo** (*Culin*) pig's trotters

10 (= *instrumento*) [*de reloj*] hand ▸ **mano de almirez, mano de mortero** pestle

11 (= *capa*) [*de pintura*] coat; [*de jabón*] wash, soaping • **dar una ~ de jabón a la ropa** to give the clothes a wash *o* soaping

12 (*Juegos, Naipes*) (= *partida*) round, game; (= *conjunto de cartas*) hand • **echar una ~ de mus** to have a game *o* round of mus • **ser *o* tener la ~** to lead • **soy ~** it's my lead

13 (= *lote*) lot, series; (*And, CAm, Cono Sur, Méx*) *group of things of the same kind*; (*LAm*) [*de plátanos*] bunch, hand • **le dio una ~ de bofetadas** he punched him several times • **una ~ de papel** a quire of paper (*24 or 25 sheets*)

14 (*Mús*) scale

15 (*LAm*) (= *desgracia*) misfortune, mishap; (= *suceso imprevisto*) unexpected event

16 (*LAm*) (= *suerte*) • **¡qué ~!** what a stroke of luck!

17 (*LAm*) (*Aut*) direction ▸ **mano única** one-way street

SUSTANTIVO MASCULINO

▸ **mano a mano** • **hubo un ~ a ~ entre los dos políticos en el parlamento** the two politicians slogged it out between them in parliament • **la corrida será un ~ a ~ entre los dos toreros** the bullfight will be a two-way contest with the two bullfighters

mano² SM (*Méx*) (*en conversación*) mate*, pal*

manoizquierdoso ADJ (= *astuto*) knowing, cunning; (= *sofisticado*) sophisticated

manojo SM **1** (= *conjunto*) handful, bunch • **un ~ de llaves** a bunch of keys • **un ~ de hierba** a tuft of grass • **un ~ de pillos** a bunch of rogues • MODISMO: • **estar hecho *o* ser un ~ de nervios** to be a bundle *o* bag of nerves

2 (*Caribe*) bundle of raw tobacco (*about 2lbs*)

manola‡ SF **1** (= *jeringuilla*) needle, syringe

2† *Madrid woman of the people, characterized by flamboyant zarzuela-type costume*

manoletina SF (*Taur*) *a kind of pass with the cape*

Manolo SM *forma familiar de* **Manuel**

manolo SM toff*; (*esp Madrid*) *Madrid man of the people, characterized by flamboyant zarzuela-type costume*

manómetro SM pressure gauge, manometer (*frm*)

manopla SF **1** (= *guante*) (*gen*) mitten; [*de cocina*] oven glove; [*de baño*] bath mitt

2 (*Hist, Téc*) gauntlet

3 (*LAm*) (= *puño de hierro*) knuckle-duster

4 (*Cono Sur*) (= *llave inglesa*) spanner

manoseado ADJ [*libro*] well-thumbed; [*tema*] hackneyed, well-worn

manosear ▹ CONJUG 1a VT **1** [+ *objeto*] (= *tocar*) to handle, paw*; (= *desordenar*) to rumple; (= *jugar con*) to fiddle with, mess about with

2 (*LAm*) [+ *persona*] to touch up*, grope*

3 [+ *tema*] to overwork, repeat

manoseo SM **1** [*de objetos*] (*gen*) handling, pawing*; (*desordenando*) rumpling

2 (*LAm*) [*de persona*] touching up*, groping*

3 [*de tema*] overworking, repetition

manos libres ADJ INV [*teléfono, dispositivo*] hands-free

SM INV hands-free kit, hands-free set

manotada SF **1** (= *golpe*) slap, smack

2 (*LAm*) (= *puñado*) handful, fistful

manotazo SM slap, smack • **dar un ~ a algn** to give sb a slap, slap sb • **le partió el labio de un ~** she split his lip with a smack in the mouth • **se lo quité de un ~** I swiped it off him

manoteador SM (*Cono Sur, Méx*) **1** (= *ladrón*) (*gen*) thief; [*de bolsos*] bag-snatcher

2 (= *estafador*) fiddler*

3 (= *aspaventero*) gesticulator

manotear ▹ CONJUG 1a VT (= *dar palmadas*) to slap, smack

VI **1** (= *gesticular*) to gesticulate

2 (*Cono Sur, Méx**) (= *arrancar*) to bag-snatch; (= *robar*) to steal

manoteo SM **1** (= *gestos*) gesticulation

2 (*Cono Sur, Méx**) (= *robo*) theft, robbery; (= *estafa*) fiddling*

manque* CONJ (*esp LAm*) = **aunque**

manquear ▹ CONJUG 1a VI **1** (= *estar lisiado*) to be maimed, be crippled

2 (= *fingir*) to pretend to be crippled

3 (*Cono Sur, Méx*) (= *cojear*) to limp

manquedad SF, **manquera** SF

1 (= *incapacidad*) disablement

2 (= *defecto*) defect

mansalino ADJ (*Cono Sur*) (= *enorme*) huge; (= *extraordinario*) extraordinary; (= *excelente*) excellent

mansalva SF • **a ~** (= *mucho*) in abundance; (= *a gran escala*) on a large scale; (= *sin riesgo*) without risk • **gastan dinero a ~** they spend money as if there were no tomorrow • **ese profesor suspende a ~** that teacher fails pupils left, right and centre • **le dispararon a ~** they shot him before he could defend himself • **estar a ~ de algo** to be safe from sth

mansamente ADV gently, meekly

mansarda SF (*esp LAm*) attic

mansedumbre SF **1** [*de persona*] gentleness, meekness

2 [*de animal*] tameness

mansión SF mansion

manso ADJ **1** [*persona*] meek, gentle

2 [*animal*] tame

3 (*Chile**) (= *tremendo*) huge, tremendous

SM (*Esp‡*) mattress

manta¹ SF **1** (*para taparse*) blanket • MODISMOS: • **a ~**: • **repartieron vino y comida a ~** they handed out food and wine in abundance • **llovía a ~** it was raining buckets • **la policía dio palos a ~** the police didn't hold back with their truncheons • **liarse la ~ a la cabeza** to take the plunge • **tirar de la ~** to let the cat out of the bag, give the game away ▸ **manta de viaje** travelling rug, traveling rug (*EEUU*) ▸ **manta eléctrica** electric blanket ▸ **manta**

ignífuga fire blanket
2 (*LAm*) (= *calicó*) *coarse cotton cloth*; (= *poncho*) poncho
3* (= *paliza*) hiding • **les dieron una buena ~ de palos** they gave them a good hiding *o* beating with a stick
4 (*Zool*) manta ray
manta²* ADJ bone-idle
SMF idler, slacker
SF idleness
mantadril SM (*CAm*) denim
mantarraya SF (*LAm*) manta ray
mantear ▸ CONJUG 1a VT **1** (= *lanzar*) to toss in a blanket
2 (*Caribe*) (= *maltratar*) to ill-treat, abuse
3 (*Caribe*) (= *golpear*) to beat up
manteca SF **1** (= *grasa*) fat, animal fat ▸ **manteca de cerdo** lard
2 (*esp Cono Sur*) (= *mantequilla*) butter ▸ **manteca de cacahuete** peanut butter ▸ **manteca de cacao** cocoa butter ▸ **manteca de maní** (*Arg, Uru*) peanut butter ▸ **manteca de vaca** butter ▸ **manteca vegetal** vegetable fat
3‡ (= *dinero*) dough‡, dosh‡; (= *géneros*) goods (*pl*)
4 (*LAm*‡) (= *marihuana*) pot*, grass*
5 (*And*) (= *criada*) servant girl
mantecada SF small cake, iced bun
mantecado SM *Christmas sweet made from flour, almonds and lard*
mantecón* SM milksop, mollycoddle
mantecoso ADJ (= *grasiento*) greasy; (= *cremoso*) creamy, buttery • **queso ~** soft cheese
mantel SM (*para comer*) tablecloth; (*Rel*) altar cloth • **una cena de ~ largo** (*Cono Sur**) a formal dinner • **levantar los ~es** to clear the table • **poner los ~es** to lay the table ▸ **mantel individual** place mat
mantelería SF table linen • **una ~ blanca** a set of white table linen
mantelillo SM table runner
mantelito SM doily
mantención SF (*LAm*) = **manutención**
mantenedor(a) SM/F (*Esp*) [*de certamen*] chairman/chairwoman, chairperson, president ▸ **mantenedor(a) de la familia** breadwinner
mantener ▸ CONJUG 2k VT **1** (= *sostener*) (*gen*) to hold; [+ *puente, techo*] to support • **mantén la caja un momento** hold the box a minute • **los pilares que mantienen el puente** the pillars which support the bridge
2 (= *preservar*) **a** (*en un lugar*) to store, keep • **"una vez abierto manténgase refrigerado"** "once opened keep in a refrigerator" • **"manténgase en un lugar fresco y seco"** "store in a cool dry place"
b (*en un estado o situación*) to keep • **la ilusión es lo único que lo mantiene vivo** hope is the only thing that keeps him alive *o* going • **hay que ~ actualizada la base de datos** we have to keep the database up to date • **para ~ el motor en buen estado** to keep the engine in good condition • **"mantenga limpia su ciudad"** "keep your city clean" • **"manténgase fuera del alcance de los niños"** "keep out of the reach of children" • **~ algo caliente** to keep sth hot • **~ algo en equilibrio** to balance sth, keep sth balanced • **~ algo en secreto** to keep sth a secret • **mantuvo en secreto que tenía dos hijos** she kept her two children a secret; ▹ **raya¹**
3 (= *conservar*) [+ *opinión*] to maintain, hold; [+ *costumbre, ideales*] to keep up, maintain; [+ *disciplina*] to maintain, keep; [+ *promesa*] to keep • **un alto porcentaje mantenía su opinión sobre la crisis** a high percentage maintained *o* held their opinion about the crisis • **me marcho manteniendo mi opinión** I'm leaving, but I stand by my opinion • **una civilización que lucha por ~ sus tradiciones** a civilization struggling to uphold *o* maintain its traditions • **eran partidarios de ~ el antiguo orden social** they were in favour of preserving the old social order • **~ el orden público** to keep the peace • **al conducir hay que ~ la distancia de seguridad** you have to keep (at) a safe distance when driving • **~ el equilibrio** to keep one's balance • **le cuesta ~ el equilibrio** he finds it difficult to keep his balance • **hemos conseguido ~ el equilibrio entre ingresos y gastos** we have managed to maintain a balance between income and expenditure • **~ el fuego** to keep the fire going • **~ la línea** to keep one's figure, keep in shape • **~ la paz** to keep the peace, maintain peace
• MODISMO: • **mantenella y no emendalla** (*Esp*) to stand one's ground; ▹ **calma, distancia**
4 (*económicamente*) to support, maintain • **ahora tiene una familia que ~** now he has a family to support *o* maintain • **ya no pienso ~la más** I refuse to keep *o* support *o* maintain her any longer
5 [+ *conversación, contacto*] to maintain, hold • **es incapaz de ~ una conversación coherente** he is incapable of maintaining *o* holding a coherent conversation • **en las conversaciones que hemos mantenido con el presidente** in the talks we have held with the president • **¿han mantenido ustedes relaciones sexuales?** have you had sexual relations?; ▹ **correspondencia**
6 (= *afirmar*) to maintain • **siempre he mantenido lo contrario** I've always maintained the opposite
VPR **mantenerse 1** (= *sostenerse*) to be supported • **el techo se mantiene con cuatro columnas** the roof is supported by four columns • **~se en pie** [*persona*] to stand up, stay on one's feet; [*edificio*] to be still standing • **la iglesia es lo único que se mantiene en pie** only the church is still standing
2 (*en un estado o situación*) to stay, remain • **se mantenía despierto a base de pastillas** he stayed *o* remained awake by taking pills • **el precio del petróleo se mantendrá estable** the price of oil will remain stable • **el motor se mantiene en perfectas condiciones** the engine is still in perfect condition • **"manténgase a su derecha"** (*Aut*) "keep right", "keep to the right" • **~se en contacto** to keep in touch (**con** with) • **¿os seguís manteniendo en contacto?** do you still keep in touch? • **se mantenía en contacto telefónico permanente con su familia** he maintained permanent telephone contact with his family • **~se al día en algo** to keep up to date with sth • **~se en forma** to keep fit, keep in shape • **~se en su puesto** keep *o* retain one's post • **~se en vigor** [*costumbre*] to remain in existence; [*ley*] to remain in force
• MODISMO: • **~se en su sitio** *o* **en sus trece*** to stand one's ground, stick to one's guns; ▹ **firme, flote**
3 (*económicamente*) to support o.s.
4 (= *alimentarse*) • **~se a base de algo** to live on sth • **se mantiene a base de verduras** he lives on vegetables
mantenibilidad SF ease of maintenance
mantenido/a ADJ **1** [*esfuerzo, tensión*] constant
2 [*persona*] kept
SM/F (= *amante*) kept man/kept woman
SM (*CAm, Méx**) (= *proxeneta*) pimp; (= *aprovechado*) sponger*, parasite
mantenimiento SM **1** (= *continuación*) maintenance • **el ~ de la paz** the maintenance of peace • **el ~ de las tradiciones** the upholding of traditions • **tras el ~ de las conversaciones de paz** after maintaining *o* holding peace talks
2 (= *conservación*) (*Mec, Téc*) maintenance • **el ~ de las carreteras** upkeep of the roads, road maintenance • **el coste del ~ de una familia** the upkeep of a family, the cost of running a family • **costes** *o* **gastos de ~** maintenance costs, upkeep • **servicio de ~** maintenance service
3 (*Dep*) keep-fit • **clase de ~** keep-fit class • **ejercicios** *o* **gimnasia de ~** keep-fit exercises
manteo SM [*de hombre*] long cloak; [*de mujer*] full skirt
mantequera SF **1** (*para batir*) churn
2 (*para servir*) butter dish
mantequería SF (*LAm*) (= *lechería*) dairy, creamery; (= *ultramarinos*) grocer's, grocer's shop
mantequilla SF butter • **pan con ~** bread and butter • **tostadas con ~** buttered toast • **manos de ~** butterfingers ▸ **mantequilla de cacahuete** peanut butter
mantequillera SF butter dish
mantilla SF **1** [*de mujer*] mantilla ▸ **mantilla de blonda, mantilla de encajes** lace mantilla
2 [*de bebé*] **mantillas** baby clothes
• MODISMOS: • **estar en ~s** [*persona*] to be very naive; [*proyecto, técnica*] to be in its infancy • **dejar a algn en ~s** to leave sb in the dark
mantillo SM humus, mould, mold (*EEUU*)
mantillón SM **1** (*CAm, Méx*) (= *manta*) horse-blanket
2 (*Méx**) (= *amante*) kept man/woman (*pey*); (= *parásito*) sponger
mantis SF INV ▸ **mantis religiosa** praying mantis
manto SM **1** (= *capa*) (*para abrigarse*) cloak; (*Rel, Jur*) robe, gown
2 (*Zool*) mantle
3 (*liter*) (= *velo*) • **cuando la noche tiende su ~** when the world is cloaked in darkness • **un ~ de nieve cubría la colina** a blanket of snow covered the hill
4 (*Min*) layer, stratum
5 (*tb* **manto de chimenea**) mantel
mantón SM shawl ▸ **mantón de manila** embroidered shawl
mantra SM mantra
mantudo ADJ **1** [*ave*] with drooping wings
2 (*CAm*) (= *disfrazado*) masked, in disguise
manú‡, manús‡ SM (*Esp*) bloke*
manuable ADJ handy, easy to handle
manual ADJ **1** (= *de manos*) manual • **habilidad ~** manual dexterity • **tener habilidad ~** to be clever with one's hands • **trabajo ~** manual labour, manual labor (*EEUU*)
2 = **manuable**
SM manual, guide ▸ **manual de consulta** reference book, reference manual ▸ **manual de estilo** style book, style guide ▸ **manual de funcionamiento** operating manual ▸ **manual de instrucciones** instruction manual ▸ **manual del usuario** user's manual ▸ **manual de mantenimiento** service manual, maintenance manual ▸ **manual de operación** instructions manual ▸ **manual de reparaciones** repair manual ▸ **manual sexual** sex manual
manualidades SFPL handicrafts, craftwork (*sing*) • **hacer ~** to do craftwork • **talleres de ~** craft workshops
manualmente ADV manually, by hand
manubrio SM **1** (*Mec*) (= *manivela*) handle,

crank; (= *torno*) winch
2 (*Mús*) barrel organ
3 (*LAm*) [*de bicicleta*] handlebar, handlebars (*pl*)
4 (*Para*) (*Aut*) steering wheel
manudo ADJ (*LAm*) with big hands
Manuel SM Emmanuel
manuelita SF (*Caribe*) rolled pancake
manufactura SF **1** (= *fabricación*) manufacture
2 (= *producto*) product
3 (= *fábrica*) factory
manufacturado ADJ manufactured
manufacturar ▷ CONJUG 1a VT to manufacture
manufacturero/a ADJ manufacturing
SM/F (*esp LAm*) manufacturer, manufacturing company
manumitir ▷ CONJUG 3a VT to manumit
manús SM ▸ **manú**
manuscrito ADJ handwritten
SM manuscript ▸ **manuscritos del mar Muerto** Dead Sea scrolls
manutención SF **1** [*de una familia*] maintenance, upkeep • **le pasa la ~ para sus hijos** he pays for their children's maintenance *o* upkeep • **gastos de ~** maintenance costs, upkeep
2 (*Mec, Téc*) maintenance
manyar‡ ▷ CONJUG 1a VT, VI (*Caribe, Cono Sur*) to eat
manzana SF **1** (= *fruta*) apple • **~ ácida** cooking apple • **~ de mesa** eating apple • **~ de sidra** cider apple • **~ silvestre** wild apple, crabapple • **tarta de ~** apple tart • MODISMO: • **~ de la discordia** bone of contention
2 ▸ **manzana de Adán** (*esp LAm*) (*Anat*) Adam's apple
3 [*de casas*] block (of houses)
4 (= *medida*) (*CAm*) *land measure (= 1.75 acres)*; (*Cono Sur*) *land measure (= 2.5 acres)*
manzanal SM **1** (= *huerto*) apple orchard
2 (= *manzano*) apple tree
manzanar SM apple orchard
manzanilla SF **1** (*Bot*) (= *flor*) camomile; (= *infusión*) camomile tea
2 (= *jerez*) manzanilla sherry
3 (= *aceituna*) *a variety of small olive*
manzano SM apple tree
maña SF **1** (= *habilidad*) skill • **tiene mucha ~ para hacer arreglos caseros** he's a dab hand at mending things around the house
2 (= *ardid*) trick • **con ~** craftily, slyly • **malas ~s** (*gen*) bad habits; [*de niño*] naughty ways
mañana ADV tomorrow • **~ por la mañana** tomorrow morning • **~ por la noche** tomorrow night • **¡hasta ~!** see you tomorrow! • **pasado ~** the day after tomorrow • **~ temprano** early tomorrow • **~ será otro día** tomorrow's another day
SM future • **el ~ es incierto** the future is uncertain, tomorrow is uncertain • **el día de ~** in the future
SF morning • **la ~ siguiente** the following morning • **a las siete de la ~** at seven o'clock in the morning, at seven a.m. • **de** *o* **por la ~** in the morning • **muy de ~** very early in the morning • **en la ~ de ayer** yesterday morning • **en la ~ de hoy** this morning • **de la noche a la ~** overnight
mañanero/a ADJ **1** (= *madrugador*) • **ser ~** to be an early riser
2 (= *matutino*) morning (*antes de s*)
SM/F early riser
mañanita SF **1** (= *mañana*) early morning • **de ~** very early in the morning, at the crack of dawn
2 (= *chal*) bed jacket
3 mañanitas (*Méx*) (= *canción*) serenade (*sing*)
mañear ▷ CONJUG 1a VT to manage cleverly, contrive skilfully
VI **1** (*con ingenio*) to act shrewdly, go about things cunningly
2 (*con picardía*) to get up to one's tricks
mañero ADJ **1** = **mañoso**
2 (*Cono Sur*) [*animal*] (= *fiero*) vicious; (= *obstinado*) obstinate; (= *asustadizo*) nervous, skittish
maño/a ADJ, SM/F Aragonese
mañosamente ADV **1** (= *ingeniosamente*) cleverly, ingeniously, skilfully, skillfully (*EEUU*)
2 (= *con picardía*) craftily, cunningly
mañosear ▷ CONJUG 1a VI (*And, Cono Sur*) [*niño*] to be difficult (*esp about food*)
mañoso/a ADJ **1** [*persona*] (= *hábil*) clever, ingenious; (= *astuto*) crafty, cunning
2 (*And*) (= *perezoso*) lazy
3 (*LAm*) [*animal*] (= *violento*) vicious; (= *terco*) obstinate; (= *tímido*) shy, nervous; (*And, Cono Sur, Méx*) difficult (*esp about food*)
SM/F (*CAm*) (= *ladrón*) thief
maoísmo SM Maoism
maoísta ADJ, SMF Maoist
maorí ADJ, SMF Maori
Mao Zedong SM Mao Tse-tung
MAPA SM ABR (= **Ministerio de Agricultura, Pesca y Alimentación**) ≈ MAFF, ≈ USDA (*EEUU*)
mapa SM map • **el ~ político** (= *escena*) the political scene; (= *abanico*) the political spectrum • MODISMO: • **desaparecer del ~** to vanish off the face of the earth ▸ **mapa de carreteras** road map ▸ **mapa del sitio** (*Internet*) site map ▸ **mapa del tiempo** weather map ▸ **mapa en relieve** relief map ▸ **mapa geológico** geological map ▸ **mapa hipsométrico** contour map ▸ **mapa meteorológico** weather map ▸ **mapa mural** wall map
mapache SM racoon, raccoon
mapamundi SM **1** (= *mapa*) world map
2* (= *trasero*) bottom
mapeado SM mapping
mapeango ADJ (*Caribe, Méx*), **mapiango** ADJ (*Caribe, Méx*) useless, incompetent
mapear ▷ CONJUG 1a VT to map
mapucha SF (*esp Chile*) = **mapuche**
mapuche ADJ Mapuche, Araucanian
SMF Mapuche (Indian), Araucanian (Indian); ▷ ARAUCANO
SM (*Ling*) Mapuche, Araucanian
mapurite SM (*CAm, Caribe*), **mapurito** SM (*CAm, Caribe*) skunk
maque SM lacquer
maquear ▷ CONJUG 1a VT to lacquer
VPR **maquearse‡** to get ready (to go out), get dressed up • **ir (bien) maqueado** to be all dressed up
maqueta SF **1** (= *modelo*) model, scale model, mock-up
2 (= *libro*) dummy
3 (*Mús*) demo, demo tape
maquetación SF layout, design
maquetar ▷ CONJUG 1a VT, **maquetear** ▷ CONJUG 1a VT to lay out, design
maquetista SMF (*Arquit*) model maker; (*Tip*) typesetter
maqueto SM (*pey*) immigrant worker (*in the Basque Country*)
maquiavélico ADJ Machiavellian
Maquiavelo SM Machiavelli
maquiladora SF (*Méx*) (*Com*) bonded assembly plant
maquilar ▷ CONJUG 1a VT (*Méx*) to assemble
maquillado ADJ made up • **muy ~** wearing a lot of make-up
maquillador(a) SM/F (*Teat*) make-up artist
maquillaje SM **1** (= *pintura*) make-up; (= *acto*) making up ▸ **maquillaje base, maquillaje de fondo** foundation
2* [*de cuentas*] massaging*
maquillar ▷ CONJUG 1a VT **1** (= *persona*) to make up
2* [+ *cifras, cuentas*] to massage*
VPR **maquillarse** to make o.s. up
máquina SF **1** (= *aparato*) (*gen*) machine • **a toda ~** at full speed • **coser algo a ~** to machine-sew sth • **entrar en ~** to go to press • **escribir a ~** to type • **escrito a ~** typed, typewritten • **hecho a ~** machine-made • **pasar algo a ~** to type sth (up) • MODISMO: • **forzar la ~** (= *ir deprisa*) to go full steam ahead; (= *abusar de las posibilidades*) to pull out all the stops ▸ **máquina copiadora** copier, copying machine ▸ **máquina cosechadora** combine harvester, combine ▸ **máquina de afeitar** razor, safety razor ▸ **máquina de afeitar eléctrica** electric razor, shaver ▸ **máquina de azar** fruit machine ▸ **máquina de bolas*** pinball machine ▸ **máquina de calcular** calculator ▸ **máquina de contabilidad** adding machine ▸ **máquina de coser** sewing machine ▸ **máquina de discos** jukebox ▸ **máquina de escribir** typewriter ▸ **máquina de franquear** franking machine ▸ **máquina de hacer punto** knitting machine ▸ **máquina de lavar** washing machine ▸ **máquina de sumar** adding machine ▸ **máquina de tabaco*** cigarette machine ▸ **máquina de tejer, máquina de tricotar** knitting machine ▸ **máquina de vapor** steam engine ▸ **máquina excavadora** mechanical digger, steam shovel (*EEUU*) ▸ **máquina expendedora** vending machine ▸ **máquina fotográfica** camera ▸ **máquina franqueadora** franking machine ▸ **máquina herramienta** machine tool ▸ **máquina ordeñadora** milking machine ▸ **máquina picadora** mincer ▸ **máquina quitanieves** snowplough, snowplow (*EEUU*) ▸ **máquina registradora** (*LAm*) cash register ▸ **máquina tejedora** knitting machine ▸ **máquina tragaperras** fruit machine, one-armed bandit; (*Com*) vending machine
2 (*Transportes*) [*de tren*] engine, locomotive; (= *moto**) motorbike; (*CAm, Cuba*) (= *coche*) car; (= *taxi*) taxi
3 (*Fot*) camera
4 (*Pol*) machine ▸ **máquina electoral** electoral machine
5 (= *maquinaria*) machinery, workings (*pl*); (= *plan*) scheme of things
maquinación SF machination, plot
maquinador(a) SM/F schemer, plotter
maquinal ADJ mechanical
maquinalmente ADV mechanically
maquinar ▷ CONJUG 1a VT, VI to plot
maquinaria SF **1** (= *conjunto de máquinas*) machinery ▸ **maquinaria agrícola** agricultural machinery, farm implements (*pl*) ▸ **maquinaria pesada** heavy plant
2 (= *mecanismo*) mechanism • **la ~ de un reloj** the mechanism of a watch
3 (*Pol*) machine • **la ~ electoral** the campaign machine • **la ~ propagandística** the propaganda machine
maquinilla SF (= *máquina*) small machine; (= *torno*) winch; (*para el pelo*) clippers (*pl*) • **~ para liar cigarrillos** cigarette(-rolling) machine ▸ **maquinilla de afeitar** razor, safety razor ▸ **maquinilla eléctrica** electric razor, shaver
maquinista SMF **1** (*Ferro*) engine driver, engineer (*EEUU*); (*Náut*) engineer
2 (*Téc*) operator, machinist
3 (*Teat*) scene-shifter; (*Cine*) cameraman's

assistant

maquis SM INV (= *movimiento*) resistance movement, maquis; (= *persona*) member of the resistance, maquis

mar¹ SM, (*a veces*) SF **1** (*Geog*) sea • **el fondo del mar** the bottom of the sea, the seabed • **una casa al lado del mar** a house by the sea *o* on the coast • **el avión cayó en el mar** the plane came down in the sea • **el** *o* **la mar estaba en calma** the sea was calm • **iban navegando en mar abierto** they were sailing on the open sea • **mar adentro** [*ir, llevar*] out to sea; [*estar*] out at sea • **en alta mar** on the high seas • **un buque de alta mar** an ocean-going vessel • **pesca de alta mar** deep-sea fishing • **mar arbolada** heavy sea • **caer(se) al mar** (*desde tierra*) to fall into the sea; (*desde un barco*) to fall overboard • **echarse a la mar** to set sail • **mar de fondo** (*lit*) groundswell; (*fig*) underlying tension • **mar gruesa** heavy sea • **hacerse a la mar** (*liter*) [*barco*] to set sail, put to sea (*frm*); [*marinero*] to set sail • **mar picada** choppy sea • **por mar** by sea, by boat • **toda la mercancía llegará por mar** all the goods will arrive by sea *o* by boat • **mar rizada** rough sea • **los siete mares** the seven seas • **MODISMOS**: • **arar en el mar** to labour in vain • **eso es hablar de la mar** that's just wishful thinking, that's just pie in the sky* • **me cago en la mar (salada)** (*Esp‡*) shit!‡ • **mecachis en la mar** (*Esp*) (*euf*) sugar! • **REFRÁN**: • **quien no se arriesga no pasa la mar** nothing ventured, nothing gained ▸ **mar Adriático** Adriatic Sea ▸ **mar Báltico** Baltic Sea ▸ **mar Cantábrico** Bay of Biscay, Cantabrian Sea ▸ **mar Caribe** Caribbean Sea ▸ **mar Caspio** Caspian Sea ▸ **mar de arena** (*poét*) sand dunes (*pl*), desert wastes (*pl*) (*poét*) ▸ **mar de las Antillas** Caribbean Sea ▸ **mar del Norte** North Sea ▸ **mar Egeo** Aegean Sea ▸ **mar interior** inland sea ▸ **mar Jónico** Ionian Sea ▸ **mar Mediterráneo** Mediterranean Sea ▸ **mar Muerto** Dead Sea ▸ **mar Negro** Black Sea ▸ **mar Rojo** Red Sea ▸ **mar Tirreno** Tyrrhenian Sea; ▹ **brazo, golpe**
2 (= *marea*) tide • **hay demasiada mar para salir de pesca** the tide is too high to go fishing ▸ **mar llena** high tide
3 (= *abundancia*) **a** • **un mar de diferencia** a world of difference • **hay un mar de diferencia entre las dos expresiones** there is a world of difference between the two expressions • **existe un mar de diferencia entre nosotros** we're poles apart • **estar hecho un mar de dudas** to be full of doubt, be beset with doubts (*frm*) • **estar hecho un mar de lágrimas** to be in floods of tears • **se fue hecha un mar de lágrimas** she left in floods of tears
b • **a mares**: • **estaba llorando a mares** she was crying her eyes out • **estaba sudando a mares** he was sweating buckets* • **estuvo lloviendo a mares todo el camino** it was raining cats and dogs *o* it was pouring (down) the whole way • **el vino corría a mares en la fiesta** wine flowed like water at the party
c • **MODISMO**: • **la mar de***: • **tengo la mar de cosas que hacer** I've got no end of things to do • **hace la mar de tiempo que no la veo** I haven't seen her for ages • **es la mar de guapa** she's ever so pretty • **estoy la mar de contento** I'm ever so happy, I'm over the moon* • **lo hemos pasado la mar de bien** we had a whale of a time* *o* a great time • **en Lisboa vivimos la mar de bien** we live ever so well in Lisbon, we love living in Lisbon • **ese traje te queda la mar de bien** that suit looks wonderful on you

mar² SF *eufemismo de* **madre** *in obscene expressions*

mar³ EXCL (*Mil*) march!

mar. ABR **1** (= **marzo**) Mar
2 (= **martes**) Tues.

mara* SF crowd, gang*

marabunta SF **1** [*de hormigas*] plague
2 (= *multitud*) crowd
3 (= *daños*) havoc, ravages (*pl*)

maraca SF **1** (*Mús*) maraca
2 (*Cono Sur*) (= *prostituta*) whore
3 (*And, Caribe*) (= *inútil*) dead loss*

maraco* SM (*Caribe*) youngest child, baby of the family

maracucho/a ADJ of/from Maracaibo
SM/F native/inhabitant of Maracaibo • **los ~s** the people of Maracaibo

maracuyá SM passion fruit

marajá SM = **maharajá**

maraña SF **1** (= *maleza*) thicket, tangle of plants
2 [*de hilos*] tangle
3 (= *enredo*) mess, tangle • **una ~ de pasillos** a maze *o* labyrinth of passages • **una ~ de burocracia** a bureaucratic maze *o* labyrinth • **una ~ de mentiras** a web of lies
4* (= *truco*) trick, ruse
5 (*And*) small tip

marañero/a ADJ scheming
SM/F schemer

marañón SM (*Bot*) cashew

maraquear ▹ CONJUG 1a VT (*LAm*) to shake, rattle

maraquero SM (*And, Caribe*) maraca player

marar‡ ▹ CONJUG 1a VT **1** (= *matar*) to do in*
2 (= *pegar*) to bash*, beat up*

marasmo SM **1** (*Med*) wasting, atrophy
2 (= *estancamiento*) paralysis, stagnation • **hay que sacar al país del ~ económico en que está sumido** we have to pull the country out of its economic stagnation

maratón SM, (*a veces*) SF marathon ▸ **maratón radiofónico** radiothon

maratoniano/a ADJ marathon (*antes de s*)
SM/F marathon runner

maratonista ADJ, SMF = **maratoniano**

maravedí SM (PL: **maravedís** *o* **maravedises**) *old Spanish coin*

maravilla SF **1** (= *prodigio*) wonder • **las ~s de la tecnología** the wonders of technology • **¡qué ~ de tiempo tenemos!** what wonderful weather we're having! • **el concierto fue una ~** the concert was wonderful, it was a wonderful concert • **pinta que es una ~** she paints in the most wonderful way • **contar** *o* **hablar ~s de algn/algo** to rave about sb/sth • **hacer ~s** to work wonders • **una dieta que hace ~s con tu silueta** a diet that works wonders for your figure • **hace ~s con la flauta** she plays the flute like a dream • **las siete ~s del mundo** the seven wonders of the world • **MODISMOS**: • **a ~** (*Esp*) • **a las mil ~s** • **de ~** wonderfully, wonderfully well, marvellously • **el horno funciona a las mil ~s** the oven works wonderfully (well) *o* beautifully *o* marvellously • **representa a ~ ese tipo de poesía** he is a wonderful *o* marvellous exponent of that type of poetry • **siempre nos hemos llevado de ~** we've always got on like a house on fire* *o* wonderfully (well) *o* marvellously • **—¿cómo te va con el coche nuevo? —¡de ~!** "how are you getting on with the new car?" — "really well!" *o* "great!*" • **este dinero me viene de ~** this money couldn't have come at a better time
2 (= *asombro*) amazement • **para ~ de todos se puso a cantar** to the amazement of us all she burst into song
3 (*Bot*) (= *caléndula*) marigold; (= *enredadera*) morning glory; (*Chile*) (= *girasol*) sunflower

maravillado ADJ astonished, amazed

maravillar ▹ CONJUG 1a VT to astonish, amaze • **su actuación maravilló a todo el mundo** his performance astonished *o* amazed everybody, everybody was astonished *o* amazed at his performance
VPR **maravillarse** • **~se con** *o* **de algo** to be astonished *o* amazed at *o* by sth • **nos maravillamos con su increíble paciencia** we were astonished *o* amazed at *o* by his incredible patience, we marvelled at his incredible patience

maravillosamente ADV wonderfully, marvellously, marvelously (*EEUU*) • **una figura ~ tallada** a wonderfully *o* marvellously carved figure • **ese vestido te sienta ~** you look wonderful *o* marvellous in that dress

maravilloso ADJ **1** (= *magnífico*) wonderful, marvellous, marvelous (*EEUU*) • **tengo dos hijos ~s** I have two wonderful *o* marvellous children • **he tenido una maravillosa idea** I've had a wonderful *o* marvellous idea
2 (= *mágico*) magic • **la lámpara maravillosa de Aladino** Aladdin's magic lamp

marbellí ADJ of/from Marbella
SMF native/inhabitant of Marbella • **los ~es** the people of Marbella

marbete SM **1** (= *etiqueta*) label, tag ▸ **marbete engomado** sticker
2 (*Cos*) edge, border

marca SF **1** (= *señal*) mark • **dejó una ~ al principio del libro** he left a mark at the beginning of the book • **se te nota la ~ del bañador** I can see your tan line*, I can see the mark where your swimming costume was • **haz una ~ en la casilla correcta** tick the appropriate box • **la película lleva la ~ inconfundible de su director** the film bears all the hallmarks of its director • **sello de ~** hallmark ▸ **marca de agua** watermark ▸ **marca de la casa** • **un vino ~ de la casa** a house wine • **la mala educación parece ser la ~ de la casa** bad manners seem to be the norm here ▸ **marca de ley** hallmark ▸ **marca de nacimiento** birthmark ▸ **marca transparente** watermark
2 (= *huella*) [*de pie*] footprint, footmark; [*de dedos*] fingerprint • **seguí las ~s que habían dejado sobre la arena** I followed the tracks they had left in the sand, I followed their footprints *o* footmarks in the sand
3 (*Com*) [*de comida, jabón, tabaco*] brand; [*de electrodoméstico, coche*] make; [*de ropa*] label • **¿qué ~ de tabaco fumas?** what brand do you smoke? • **¿de qué ~ es tu televisor?** what make is your television? • **venden productos de su propia ~** they sell own-brand goods • **siempre va vestido de ~** he always wears fashion labels • **ropa de ~** designer-label clothes, designer-label clothing • **MODISMO**: • **de ~ mayor*** [*susto, borrachera*] incredible • **es un imbécil de ~ mayor** he's a total idiot* ▸ **marca de calidad** quality mark ▸ **marca de fábrica** trademark ▸ **marca registrada** registered trademark; ▹ **imagen**
4 (*Dep*) [*de especialidad*] record; [*de deportista*] best time • **su mejor ~ personal** his personal best (time) • **batir una ~** to break a record • **establecer una ~** to set a record • **acaba de establecer la mejor ~ de la temporada** he's just set the best time of the season • **mejorar** *o* **superar una ~** to break a record
5 (*Náut*) (*en tierra*) seamark; (*en el mar*) marker, buoy
6 (*Naipes*) bid
7 (*en el ganado*) (= *señal*) brand; (= *acción*)

branding
8 (= *herramienta*) brand, iron
9 (*Hist*) march, frontier area • **la Marca Hispánica** the Spanish March (*Catalonia*)
marcable ADJ (*Naipes*) biddable
marcación SF 1 (*Náut*) bearing
2 (*Telec*) dialling, dialing (EEUU)
▸ **marcación automática** autodial, automatic dial
marcadamente ADV markedly
marcado ADJ marked • **con ~ acento argentino** with a marked Argentinian accent • **ese vestido le hacía las caderas muy marcadas** that dress accentuated her hips *o* made her hips stand out • **su visita tiene un ~ significado político** his visit has a strong political significance
SM 1 [*de pelo*] set
2 [*de ganado*] branding
marcador(a) SM 1 (*Dep*) scoreboard • **el ~ va dos a uno** the score is 2-1 • **dieron la vuelta al ~** they turned the match round • **abrir** *o* **inaugurar el ~** to open the scoring ▸ **marcador electrónico** electronic scoreboard; ▹ **igualar**
2 (= *indicador*) (*gen*) marker; [*de libro*] bookmark ▸ **marcador de caminos** road sign
3 (*LAm*) (= *rotulador*) marker
4 (*Billar*) marker
5 (*Telec*) dial
SM/F (*Esp*) scorer
marcaje SM 1 (*Dep*) marking; (= *entrada*) tackle, tackling ▸ **marcaje al hombre, marcaje personal** man-marking, one-to-one marking ▸ **marcaje por zonas, marcaje zonal** zonal *o* defence marking
2 [*de criminal*] shadowing, following • **hacer ~ a algn** to shadow sb, tail sb
marcapasos SM INV pacemaker
marcar ▹ CONJUG 1g VT 1 (= *señalar*) **a** [+ *objeto, ropa*] to mark; [+ *ganado*] to brand • **ha marcado las toallas con mis iniciales** she has put my initials on the towels, she has marked the towels with my initials • **el accidente lo dejó marcado para siempre** the accident marked him for life • **seguimos el procedimiento marcado por la ley** we followed the procedures required *o* laid down by law • **¿qué precio marca la etiqueta?** (*Com*) what's the price (marked) on the label? • **están marcando las camisas** (*Com*) they are putting prices on the shirts, they are pricing the shirts
b [+ *límites*] to mark • **el Mediterráneo marca los límites por el este** the Mediterranean marks the eastern limit
c (*Inform*) [+ *bloque, texto*] to flag
d (*Mús*) [+ *partitura*] to mark up
2 [*experiencia, suceso*] to mark • **ese encuentro la ~ía para siempre** that meeting would mark her for life • **una vida marcada por el sufrimiento** a life marked by suffering
3 [*termómetro*] to read • **mi reloj marca las dos** it's two o'clock by my watch, my watch says two o'clock • **este reloj marca la hora exacta** this watch keeps the right time
4 (= *designar*) [+ *tarea*] to assign; [+ *política, estrategia*] to lay down; [+ *directrices, pautas*] to lay down, give; [+ *comienzo, período*] to mark • **la empresa nos ha marcado algunas pautas a seguir** the company has given us *o* has issued some guidelines to follow • **la paz marcó el comienzo de una nueva era** peace marked the beginning of a new era • **esta obra marca el paso de la música medieval a la renacentista** this work marks the transition from medieval to renaissance music • **como marca la ley** as specified by law; ▹ **hito, pauta**
5 (= *hacer resaltar*) to accentuate • **ese vestido te marca mucho las caderas** that dress really accentuates your hips *o* makes your hips stand out; ▹ **paquete**
6 (= *seguir*) [+ *sospechoso*] to shadow, tail
7 (*Dep*) **a** [+ *gol*] to score
b [+ *tiempo*] to record, clock • **ha marcado un tiempo de 9,46** he recorded *o* clocked a time of 9.46
c [+ *jugador, contrario*] to mark, shadow; (*Méx*) to tackle
8 (*Mús*) • **~ el compás** to keep time, beat time; ▹ **paso²**
9 (*Telec*) to dial
10 (*Naipes*) to bid
11 (*Peluquería*) to set • **he ido a que me marquen el pelo** I went to get my hair set
VI 1 (*Dep*) to score
2 (*Telec*) to dial
3 (*Peluquería*) to set • **"lavar y marcar"** "shampoo and set"
VPR **marcarse** 1 [*figura, formas*] to stand out • **se le marcan mucho las venas de las manos** the veins on his hands really stand out • **~se con relieve** to stand out in relief
2 (*Esp**) • **¿nos marcamos un baile?** do you fancy a dance? • **se marcó un detalle bien majo conmigo** that was a really nice touch of hers; ▹ **farol**
3 (*Peluquería*) • **~se el pelo** to have one's hair set, have one's hair styled
4 (*Náut*) to take one's bearings
marcha SF 1 [*de soldados, manifestantes*] march • **una ~ de protesta** a protest march • **el batallón salió de ~ hacia el campamento** the battalion marched towards the camp • **¡en ~!** let's go!, let's get going; (*Mil*) forward march! • **abrir la ~** to head the march • **cerrar la ~** to bring up the rear • **encabezar la ~** to head the march • **ponerse en ~** [*persona*] (*lit*) to set off; (*fig*) to set about; [*máquina, motor*] to start • **antes de ponerse en ~, se recomienda que revisen sus vehículos** before setting off, we recommend that you check your vehicles • **ya se han puesto en ~ para preparar la querella** they have already set a lawsuit in motion, they have already set about bringing a lawsuit ▸ **marcha a pie** [*de caminantes*] (= *excursión*) hike; (= *actividad*) hiking; [*de manifestantes*] march ▸ **marcha forzada** forced march • **hemos trabajado a ~s forzadas** we've been working against the clock • **intenta recuperar a ~s forzadas su imagen pública** he is trying to rebuild his public image as quickly as possible ▸ **marcha triunfal** [*de ejército*] triumphal march; (*hacia la meta*) winning run
2 (= *partida*) departure • **su ~ fue muy precipitada** her departure was very sudden • **tras tu ~** after you left • **¿a qué hora tenéis la ~?** (*Esp**) what time do you set off?
3 (= *velocidad*) speed • **¡vaya ~ que llevas!** (*Esp*) what a speed you go at! • **he tardado en coger la ~ pero ya estoy al día** it took me a while to get into it *o* to get the hang of it but I'm on top of it now* • **"marcha moderada"** (*Aut*) "slow" • **acelerar la ~** to speed up, go faster • **deberíamos acelerar un poco la ~** we should speed up a little *o* go a little faster • **moderar la ~** to slow down • **a toda ~** at top speed • **un coche venía a toda ~ cuesta abajo** a car was coming down the hill at full *o* top speed • **han elaborado el informe a toda ~** the report has been prepared at top speed
4 (*Mús*) march ▸ **marcha fúnebre** funeral march ▸ **marcha militar** military march ▸ **marcha nupcial** wedding march ▸ **la Marcha Real** *Spanish national anthem*
5 (*Aut*) gear • **meter la cuarta ~** to change into fourth gear • **cambiar de ~** to change gear • **~ corta/directa** low/top gear • **~ larga** high gear • **primera ~** first gear ▸ **marcha atrás** (*en vehículo*) reverse, reverse gear; (*en negociaciones*) withdrawal; (*en el acto sexual**) withdrawal • **fue ~ atrás unos cuantos metros** he reversed a few metres • **dar ~ atrás** (*con un vehículo*) to reverse, put the car/van *etc* into reverse; (*en negociaciones, en el acto sexual*) to withdraw • **a última hora han dado ~ atrás** they pulled out *o* withdrew at the last minute • **si pudiese dar ~ atrás en el tiempo ...** if I could go back in time ...
6 • **en ~** (= *en funcionamiento*) [*máquina, sistema*] in operation; [*motor*] running; [*electrodoméstico, ordenador*] on; [*proyecto*] under way, in progress, on the go • **un país en ~** a country on the move *o* that is going places • **la televisión ha estado en ~ todo el día** the television has been on all day • **nos apeamos del autobús en ~** we got off the bus while it was moving • **tiene varios proyectos en ~** he has various projects under way *o* in progress *o* on the go • **poner en ~** [+ *máquina, motor*] to start; [+ *electrodoméstico, ordenador*] to turn on; [+ *proyecto, actividad*] to set in motion; [+ *ley, resolución*] to implement
7 (*Dep*) (= *carrera*) walk; (= *excursión*) walk, hike • **ganó los 20kms ~** he won the 20km walk ▸ **marcha atlética, marcha de competición** walk
8 (= *desarrollo*) [*de enfermedad*] course; [*de huracán*] progress • **la ~ de los acontecimientos** the course of events • **la larga ~ de las conversaciones** the long drawn-out process *o* course of the talks
• MODISMO: • **sobre la ~** (= *en el momento*) there and then; (= *durante una actividad*) as I/you *etc* go along • **le hicieron los análisis sobre la ~** he had his tests done there and then • **los cambios los haremos sobre la ~** we'll make the changes as we go along
9 (*Esp‡*) (= *animación*) • **no tengo ganas de ~** I don't feel like going out • **un sitio con mucha ~** a very lively place, a place with a lot of action‡ • **yo necesito un novio que me dé ~** I need a boyfriend with a bit of life • **en Granada hay mucha ~ por la noche** Granada has a great nightlife • **¿dónde está la ~ de Vigo?** where's the nightlife in Vigo?, where are the good bars in Vigo? • **me va la ~ tecno** I'm really into techno‡ • **les pegan y no se quejan, parece que les va la ~** they get hit but never complain, it seems they like a bit of suffering • **estar/ir o salir de ~** (*a bares*) to be out/go out (on the town)*; (*a discotecas*) to be out/go (out) clubbing* • **estuvimos de ~ hasta las cinco** we were out (on the town) *o* out clubbing until five in the morning* • **¿estuviste de ~ hasta muy tarde?** were you out very late last night? • **hace siglos que no vamos de ~** we haven't had a night out *o* been out for ages, we haven't been out on the town *o* (out) clubbing for ages* • **tener ~*** [*persona, música*] to be lively; [*ciudad*] to be full of action, be buzzing* • **mi abuela tiene mucha ~** my grandma is really lively • **hoy no tengo ninguna ~** I'm not in a very lively mood tonight
10 (*Méx*) (*Aut*) self-starter, self-starter motor
11 (*Caribe*) [*de caballo*] slow trot
marchador(a) SM/F walker
marchamo SM (= *etiqueta*) label, tag; [*de aduana*] customs mark; (*fig*) stamp
marchand SMF art dealer
marchantaje SM (*LAm*) clients (*pl*), clientele
marchante/a SM/F 1 (= *comerciante*)

dealer, merchant ▸ **marchante de arte** art dealer
2 (*LAm**) (= *cliente*) client, customer; (= *vendedor*) (*ambulante*) pedlar, peddler (EEUU); (*en mercado*) stall holder
3 (*Caribe*) (= *embaucador*) trickster
marchantía* (SF) (*CAm, Caribe*) clients (*pl*), clientele
marchar ▸ CONJUG 1a (VI) **1** (= *ir*) to go; (= *andar*) to walk • **~on a pie** they went on foot • **~on hacia el pueblo** they walked towards the village
2 (*Mil*) to march
3 • **¡marchando, que llegamos tarde!** get a move on, we'll be late! • **—¡un café! —¡marchando!** "a coffee, please" — "right away, sir!"
4 [*mecanismo*] to work • **mi reloj no marcha** my watch isn't working • **el motor no marcha** the engine isn't working, the engine won't work • **el motor marcha mal** the engine isn't running properly • **~ en vacío** to idle
5 (= *desarrollarse*) to go • **todo marcha bien** everything is going well • **el proyecto marcha** the plan is working (out) • **el negocio no marcha** the business is getting nowhere • **¿cómo marcha eso** *o* **marchan las cosas?** (*esp LAm*) how's it going?, how are things?
6 (*Caribe, Cono Sur*) [*caballo*] to trot
7 (*Méx**) to do military service
(VPR) **marcharse** to go (away), leave • **¿os marcháis?** are you leaving? • **con permiso, me marcho** if you don't mind I must go • **es tarde, me marcho a casa** it's late, I'm going home • **me marché de casa a los veinte años** I left home when I was twenty • **¿cuándo te marchas de vacaciones?** when are you going on holiday? • **se marchó de la capital** he left the capital • **~se a otro sitio** to go somewhere else
marchista (SMF) **1** (= *manifestante*) marcher, protest marcher
2 (*LAm*) (*Dep*) walker
marchitado (ADJ) wilted, wilting
marchitar ▸ CONJUG 1a (VT) to wither, dry up
(VPR) **marchitarse 1** [*flores*] to wither, fade
2 [*belleza, juventud*] to fade
3 [*esperanzas*] to fade; [*ideales*] to fade away
4 [*persona*] to languish, fade away
marchitez (SF) withered state, faded condition
marchito (ADJ) [*flores*] withered; [*belleza, juventud, esperanzas*] faded
marchoso/a* (ADJ) (= *animado*) lively • **he conocido a gente muy marchosa** I've met some really lively people • **es un tío muy ~** he's really into going out, he's really lively
(SM/F) • **es un ~ profesional** (*hum*) he's really into the action‡ • **un sitio para los más ~s** a place for those who can really take the pace*
Marcial (SM) Martial
marcial (ADJ) [*ley*] martial; [*porte, disciplina*] military
marcianitos (SMPL) (= *juego*) space-invaders
marciano/a (ADJ), (SM/F) Martian
marco (SM) **1** (*Arquit, Arte*) frame • **~ para cuadro** picture frame • **poner ~ a un cuadro** to frame a picture ▸ **marco de la chimenea** mantelpiece ▸ **marco de la puerta** doorframe ▸ **marco de ventana** window frame
2 (*Dep*) goal posts (*pl*), goal
3 (= *escenario*) setting • **un ~ incomparable** a perfect setting • **el paisaje ofreció un bello ~ para la fiesta** the countryside made a splendid setting for the festivity
4 (= *contexto*) framework ▸ **marco de referencia** frame of reference ▸ **marco institucional** institutional framework ▸ **marco jurídico** judicial framework ▸ **marco legal** legal framework
5 (*Econ*) mark
6 [*de pesos*] standard
(ADJ INV) • **acuerdo ~** framework agreement • **ley ~** framework law • **plan ~** draft *o* framework plan • **programa ~** framework programme
márcola (SF) pruning hook
Marcos (SM) Mark
marduga* (SMF) (*CAm*) tramp
marea (SF) **1** (*Geog*) tide ▸ **marea alta** high tide, high water ▸ **marea baja** low tide, low water ▸ **marea creciente** rising tide ▸ **marea menguante** ebb tide ▸ **marea muerta** neap tide ▸ **marea negra** oil slick ▸ **marea viva** spring tide
2 (= *flujo*) tide • **la ~ de la rebelión** the tide of revolt • **una auténtica ~ humana** a real flood of people
3 (= *brisa*) light sea breeze
4 (= *llovizna*) drizzle; (*Cono Sur*) sea mist
mareado (ADJ) **1** • **estar ~** (= *con náuseas*) to be *o* feel sick; (*en coche*) to be *o* feel carsick; (*en barco*) to be *o* feel seasick; (*en avión*) to be *o* feel airsick; (= *aturdido*) to feel dizzy
2 (= *achispado*) tipsy
mareaje (SM) **1** (= *marinería*) navigation, seamanship
2 (= *rumbo*) ship's course
mareante (ADJ) • **el perfume es tan intenso que llega a ser ~** the perfume is so strong that it makes you feel light-headed • **cantidades ~s de dinero** mind-boggling sums *o* amounts of money
marear ▸ CONJUG 1a (VT) **1** (*Med*) • **~ a algn** to make sb feel sick • **el olor a alquitrán me marea** the smell of tar makes me feel sick • **el fuerte oleaje me marea** the swell is making me feel seasick
2 (= *aturdir*) • **~ a algn** to make sb (feel) dizzy • **las alturas me marean** heights make me (feel) dizzy
3 (= *emborrachar*) • **~ a algn** to make sb feel drunk *o* light-headed
4 (= *confundir*) • **no grites tanto, que me mareas** don't shout so much, I can't hear myself think • **¡decídete y no me marees más!** make up your mind and stop going on at me!
5 (*Caribe, Méx*) (= *engañar*) to cheat
(VI) †† (*Náut*) to sail, navigate
(VPR) **marearse 1** (*Med*) to feel sick; (*en coche*) to get carsick, get travel-sick; (*en barco*) to get seasick • **se mareó con el calor** he felt sick because of the heat, the heat made him feel sick • **¿te mareas cuando vas en barco?** do you get seasick when you travel by boat? • **siempre me mareo en el coche** I always get carsick
2 (= *aturdirse*) to feel dizzy • **te ~ás si das tantas vueltas** you'll get dizzy going round like that
3 (= *emborracharse*) to get drunk *o* light-headed
4 (= *confundirse*) to get confused
5 (= *preocuparse*) • **no te marees con esto** don't bother your head about this
6 (*Caribe, Cono Sur*) [*paño*] to fade
marejada (SF) **1** (*Náut*) swell, heavy sea
2 (= *oleada*) [*de descontento, protesta*] wave, upsurge
marejadilla (SF) slight swell
maremagno (SM), **maremágnum** (SM)
1 (= *cantidad*) ocean, sea
2 (= *confusión*) confusion
maremoto (SM) (= *movimiento sísmico*) seaquake; (= *ola*) tidal wave
marengo (ADJ INV) • **gris ~** dark grey
mareo (SM) **1** (*Med*) sickness; (*en coche*) carsickness, travel sickness; (*en mar*) seasickness; (*en avión*) airsickness
2 (= *aturdimiento*) dizziness, giddiness • **le dio un ~ a causa del calor** the heat made her feel dizzy
3 (= *confusión*) • **¡qué ~ de cifras!** all these numbers are making me dizzy
4 (= *pesadez*) pain*, nuisance • **es un ~ tener que ...** it is a pain *o* nuisance having to ... • **¡qué ~ de hombre!** what a pest that man is!
mareomotriz (ADJ) [*energía*] wave (*antes de s*), tidal (*antes de s*) • **central ~** tidal power station
marfil (SM) **1** (= *material*) ivory • **(de) color ~** ivory, ivory-coloured *o* (*EEUU*) ivory-colored
2 (*LAm*) (= *peine*) fine-toothed comb
marfileño (ADJ) ivory
marga (SF) marl, loam
margal (SM) (= *terreno*) marly patch; (= *hoyo*) marl pit
margarina (SF) margarine
Margarita (SF) Margaret
margarita (SF) **1** (*Bot*) daisy • **deshojar la ~** (= *juego*) to play "she loves me, she loves me not"; (= *dudar*) to waver • MODISMOS: • **criar ~s*** to be pushing up the daisies* • **ir a coger ~s‡** to (go and) spend a penny*
2 (= *perla*) pearl • MODISMO: • **echar ~s a los cerdos** to cast pearls before swine
3 (*Zool*) winkle
4 (*Tip*) daisywheel
5 (= *cóctel*) margarita (*cocktail of tequila and lime or lemon juice*)
margen (SM) **1** [*de página*] margin • **una nota al ~** a marginal note, a note in the margin • **un comentario al ~** an aside
2 (= *espacio*) • **ganaron las elecciones por un escaso ~** they won the election by a narrow margin • **existe un amplio ~ para el fraude** there is plenty of scope for fraud • **la victoria no daba ~ para pensar que ...** the victory did not give any reason to think that ... • **en un escaso ~ de tiempo** in a short space of time • **dejen un ~ de una semana para la entrega** allow a week for delivery ▸ **margen de acción, margen de actuación** scope for action, room for manoeuvre, room for maneuver (*EEUU*) ▸ **margen de confianza, margen de credibilidad** credibility gap ▸ **margen de error** margin of error ▸ **margen de maniobra** = **margen de acción** ▸ **margen de seguridad** safety margin
3 • **al ~ de** [+ *opinión, resultado*] regardless of, despite • **al ~ de lo que tú digas** regardless of *o* despite what you say • **una vida al ~ del sistema** a life on the fringes of society • **al ~ de la ley** outside the law • **al ~ de que las acusaciones sean o no fundadas** whether the accusations are true or not • **dejar algo al ~** to leave sth aside, set sth aside • **dejando al ~ nuestras creencias, la idea es muy buena** leaving *o* setting aside our beliefs, it's a very good idea • **lo dejaron** *o* **mantuvieron al ~ de las negociaciones** they excluded him from the negotiations, they left him out of the negotiations • **mantenerse** *o* **quedarse al ~ de** [+ *negociaciones, situación, escándalo*] to keep out of, stay out of; [+ *sociedad, vida pública*] to remain on the sidelines of, remain on the fringes of
4 (*Econ*) (= *beneficio*) margin • **la competencia ha reducido nuestros márgenes** our margins have been squeezed by the competition ▸ **margen bruto** gross margin ▸ **margen comercial** mark-up ▸ **margen de beneficio** profit margin ▸ **margen de explotación** trading profit ▸ **margen de**

fluctuación rate of fluctuation ▸ **margen de ganancia(s)** profit margin ▸ **margen neto** net margin
SF *[de río]* bank • **la ~ derecha del Tajo** the right bank of the Tagus

marginación SF **1** (= *aislamiento*) *[de persona]* alienation; *[de grupo]* alienation, marginalization • **tiene miedo a la ~** she's scared of being alienated • **la ~ que sienten los inmigrantes** the alienation *o* marginalization felt by immigrants ▸ **marginación social** (= *discriminación*) social alienation; (= *pobreza*) social deprivation
2 (= *discriminación*) discrimination • **la ~ laboral de la mujer** discrimination against women in the workplace
3 (= *población marginada*) marginalization • **países con un alto índice de ~** countries with a high rate of marginalization

marginado/a ADJ **1** (= *aislado*) marginalized • **un poeta ~ a lo largo de su vida** a poet marginalized during his lifetime • **estar** *o* **quedar ~ de algo** (= *aislado*) to be alienated from sth; (= *excluido*) to be excluded from sth • **siguen estando ~s de la sociedad** they remain alienated from society • **estos países han quedado ~s del comercio internacional** these countries have been excluded from international trading • **sentirse ~** to feel discriminated against • **los agricultores se sienten ~s por la nueva ley** farmers feel discriminated against as a result of the new law
2 (= *pobre*) deprived • **una de las zonas más marginadas de Madrid** one of the most deprived areas in *o* of Madrid
SM/F *(por elección)* outsider, drop-out*; *(por discriminación)* underprivileged person, deprived person • **los ~s de nuestra sociedad** the underprivileged in our society

m

marginal ADJ **1** (= *al margen*) *[corrección, nota]* marginal, in the margin • **una nota ~** a marginal note, a note in the margin • **una observación ~** an aside
2 (= *pobre*) deprived • **un barrio ~** a deprived neighbourhood
3 (= *alternativo*) *[teatro]* fringe *(antes de s)*; *[publicación]* underground *(antes de s)*; *[artista]* alternative
4 (= *poco importante*) *[asunto]* marginal; *[papel, personaje]* minor • **la literatura ocupa una situación ~ en nuestra sociedad** literature holds a marginal position in our society
5 *(Econ)* *[coste, tipo]* marginal

marginalidad SF **1** *[de persona]* state of alienation
2 *[de grupo]* marginalization • **zonas de ~** marginalized areas

marginalización SF marginalization, exclusion

marginalizar ▷ CONJUG 1f VT to marginalize, exclude

marginar ▷ CONJUG 1a VT **1** (= *aislar*) *[+ persona]* to alienate; *[+ grupo]* to marginalize • **la marginaban en la escuela** she was alienated at school • **la sociedad margina a los toxicómanos** society marginalizes drug addicts • **la televisión margina los programas culturales** cultural programmes are marginalized on television
2 (= *discriminar*) • **no se ~á a nadie por su ideología** nobody will be discriminated against because of their ideology
3 (= *excluir*) to push out (**de** of), exclude (**de** from) • **acabaron marginándola del grupo** they ended up pushing her out of the group *o* excluding her from the group
4 *(Tip)* *[+ texto]* to write notes in the margin of; *[+ página]* to leave margins on
VPR **marginarse** to alienate oneself (**de** from)

margoso ADJ marly, loamy

margullo SM *(Caribe)* *(Bot)* shoot, runner

Mari SF *forma familiar de* **María**

María SF Mary • **Santa ~, madre de Dios** Holy Mary, mother of God ▸ **María Antonieta** Marie Antoinette ▸ **María Estuardo** Mary Stuart ▸ **María Magdalena** Mary Magdalene ▸ **María Santísima** the Virgin Mary

maría[1]* SF *(Esp)* (= *marihuana*) grass*, pot*

maría[2]* SF *(hum, pey)* (= *ama de casa*) housewife

maría[3]* SF *(Escol)* unimportant subject • MODISMO: • **las tres ~s** *(Hist)* *religious instruction, civics and PE*

maría[4]* SF *(Méx)* *female Indian immigrant from the country to Mexico City*

maría[5]‡ SF (= *caja de caudales*) peter*, safe

mariachi ADJ *(Méx)* mariachi
SM (= *música*) mariachi music; (= *conjunto*) mariachi band
SMF (= *persona*) mariachi musician

> **CONJUNTO MARIACHI**
> The **conjuntos mariachis**, bands of itinerant Mexican musicians, are mostly to be seen in the Plaza Garibaldi in Mexico City, wearing their traditional **charro** costumes: sequin-studded cowboy-style suits and wide-brimmed Mexican hats. Besides being a major tourist attraction, they provide music in the form of love songs for weddings, birthdays and **quinceañeras** (special parties for Mexican girls who have reached their 15th birthday). The term **mariachi** is said to derive from the French word for wedding.

marial ADJ, **mariano** ADJ Marian

marianismo SM Marianism

maribén‡ SF *(Esp)* death

marica SF (= *urraca*) magpie
SM **1*** (= *cobarde*) sissy
2‡ = **maricón**

Maricastaña SF • **en los días** *o* **en tiempos de ~** way back, in the good old days • **son ideas trasnochadas del año de ~** those ideas are out of the Ark • **va vestida como en tiempos de ~** her clothes are so old-fashioned

maricón** SM **1** (= *homosexual*) queer‡, fag (EEUU‡), poof‡ • **¡~ el último!** the last one's a sissy!*
2 (= *sinvergüenza*) bastard** • **¡~ de mierda!** you bastard!**

mariconada‡ SF **1** (= *mala pasada*) dirty trick
2 (= *tontería*) • **¡déjate ya de ~s!** stop pissing about!‡, stop behaving like a prat *o* (EEUU) jerk!*

mariconear* ▷ CONJUG 1a VI to camp it up *(pey)*

mariconeo* SM homosexual activities *(pl)*

mariconera* SF (man's) handbag

maridaje SM **1** (= *unión*) marriage, combination • **un ~ de tradiciones orientales y españolas** a marriage *o* combination of oriental and Spanish traditions • **un perfecto ~ gastronómico** a perfect gastronomic combination
2 (= *conexión*) close association; *(Pol)* *(pey)* unholy alliance
3 (= *matrimonio*) (= *vida*) conjugal life; (= *unión*) marriage ties *(pl)*

maridar ▷ CONJUG 1a VT **1** (= *combinar*) to combine, marry
2 (= *casar*) to marry

marido SM husband

marielito* SM *(Caribe)* Cuban exile

marihuana SF, **mariguana** SF, **marijuana** SF marijuana

marihuanero/a, mariguanero/a, marijuanero/a ADJ marijuana *(antes de s)*
SM/F (= *cultivador*) marijuana grower; (= *fumador*) marijuana smoker

marimacha* SF *(And)* = **marimacho**

marimacho* ADJ butch*, mannish
SM mannish woman, butch woman* *(pey)*

marimandón/ona* ADJ overbearing, bossy
SM/F bossyboots*

marimba SF **1** *(Mús)* (= *xilófono*) marimba; (= *tambor*) *kind of drum*; *(Caribe, Cono Sur)* *out-of-tune instrument*
2 *(Cono Sur)* (= *paliza*) beating
3 *(And)* *(Med)* large goitre
ADJ *(CAm, Caribe)* cowardly

marimoña SF buttercup

marimorena SF fuss, row • **armar la ~** to kick up a fuss *o* a row

marina SF **1** (= *organización*) navy; (= *barcos*) fleet • **la ~ española** the Spanish navy, the Spanish fleet • **servir en la ~** to serve in the navy ▸ **marina de guerra** navy ▸ **marina mercante** merchant navy, merchant marine (EEUU)
2 (= *marinería*) seamanship; (= *navegación*) navigation • **término de ~** nautical term
3 *(Geog)* coast, coastal area
4 *(Arte)* seascape

marinar ▷ CONJUG 1a VT to marinate, marinade

marinera SF **1** (= *blusa*) matelot top
2 *(Perú)* (= *baile*) *Peruvian folk dance*; ▷ **marinero**

marinería SF **1** (= *arte*) seamanship
2 (= *tripulación*) ship's crew; (= *marineros*) seamen *(pl)*, sailors *(pl)*

marinero ADJ **1** = **marino**
2 *[gente]* seafaring
3 *[barco]* seaworthy
4 • **a la marinera** sailor-fashion • **mejillones a la marinera** *(Culin)* moules marinières
SM *(gen)* sailor, mariner *(liter)*; (= *hombre de mar*) seafarer, seaman • **gorra de ~** sailor's cap • **traje de ~** sailor suit • **niños vestidos de ~** children in sailor suits ▸ **marinero de agua dulce** fair-weather sailor, landlubber ▸ **marinero de cubierta** deckhand ▸ **marinero de primera** able seaman; ▷ **marinera**

marinesco ADJ seamanly • **a la marinesca** in a seamanlike way, sailor-fashion

marino ADJ sea *(antes de s)*, marine • **pez ~** sea fish • **fauna marina** marine life, sea creatures *(pl)*
SM (= *marinero*) sailor, seaman; (= *oficial*) naval officer ▸ **marino mercante** merchant seaman

mariolatría SF Mariolatry

marioneta SF puppet, marionette • **es una ~ en manos del ejército** he is the army's puppet • **régimen ~** puppet régime

marionetista SMF puppeteer

mariposa SF **1** *(Entomología)* butterfly ▸ **mariposa cabeza de muerte, mariposa de calavera** death's head moth ▸ **mariposa de la col** cabbage white butterfly ▸ **mariposa nocturna** moth
2 *(Natación)* butterfly • **100 metros ~** 100 metres butterfly • **nadaba en el estilo ~** she was swimming butterfly
3 (= *tuerca*) wing nut, butterfly nut
4 ▸ **mariposa cervical** orthopaedic pillow, butterfly pillow
5 *(And, CAm)* (= *juguete*) toy windmill
6 *(And)* (= *juego*) blind-man's buff
7** (= *homosexual*) poof‡, fag (EEUU‡), fairy*

mariposear ▷ CONJUG 1a VI **1** (= *revolotear*) to flutter about, flit to and fro

2 (= *ser inconstante*) to be fickle; (= *coquetear*) to flit from one girl/man to the next • ~ **alrededor de algn** to dance attendance on sb, be constantly fluttering round sb
mariposilla SF small moth; [*de ropa*] clothes-moth
mariposo‡* SM poof‡, fag (*EEUU*‡), fairy*
mariposón SM **1*** (= *flirteador*) flirt, Romeo*
2‡* (= *homosexual*) poof‡*, fag (EEUU‡), fairy*
Mariquita SF *forma familiar de* **María**
mariquita SF **1** (= *insecto*) ladybird, ladybug (*EEUU*)
2 (*Orn*) parakeet
3 (*Méx*‡) pot*, grass*
SM * (= *homosexual*) poof‡, fag (*EEUU*‡), fairy*
marisabidilla SF know-all
mariscada SF seafood platter
mariscador(a) SM/F gatherer of shellfish
mariscal SM **1** (*Mil*) marshal ▸ **mariscal de campo** field marshal
2 (*Hist*) blacksmith, farrier
3 (*Chile*) (= *guiso*) seafood stew
mariscala SF (= *esposa*) marshal's wife
mariscar ▹ CONJUG 1g VI (= *pescar*) to gather shellfish (= *robar*) to nick*, swipe*
marisco SM shellfish, seafood • **no me gusta el ~** • **no me gustan los ~s** I don't like shellfish *o* seafood
marisma SF (= *pantano*) salt marsh; (= *tierras de arena*) mud flats (*pl*) • **las ~s del Guadalquivir** the Guadalquivir marshes
marisqueo SM shellfishing
marisquería SF (= *restaurante*) shellfish bar, seafood restaurant; (= *tienda*) seafood shop
marisquero ADJ shellfish (*antes de s*), seafood (*antes de s*) • **barco ~** shellfishing boat
marital ADJ marital • **convivencia ~** living together as husband and wife • **hacer vida ~** to live together as husband and wife • **obligaciones ~es** marital duties • **problemas ~es** marital problems
maritatas SFPL (*esp LAm*), **maritates** SMPL (*CAm, Méx*) gear (*sing*), tackle (*sing*), tools; (*pey*) things, junk* (*sing*)
marítimo ADJ (*de barcos, costeño*) maritime; (*de navegación*) shipping (*antes de s*); (*del mar*) marine, sea (*antes de s*) • **ciudad marítima** coastal town • **ruta marítima** sea route, seaway • **seguro ~** marine insurance; ▹ **estación, paseo**
maritornes* SF INV (= *criada*) slovenly maidservant
marjal SM marsh, fen
márketing ['marketin] SM marketing ▸ **márketing directo** direct marketing
marmaja‡ SF (*Méx*) dough*, money
marmellas‡ SFPL (*Esp*) tits‡, breasts
marmita SF **1** (*Culin*) pot; (*Mil*) mess tin
2 (*Geol*) (*tb* **marmita de gigante**) pothole
marmitón SM kitchen boy, scullion
mármol SM marble; [*de cocina*] (= *encimera*) worktop; (*para picar*) chopping-block
marmolejo SM small marble column
marmolería SF marble mason's (workshop) ▸ **marmolería funeraria** monumental masonry
marmolista SMF monumental mason
marmóreo ADJ marble (*antes de s*), marmoreal (*frm*)
marmosete SM (*Tip*) vignette
marmota SF **1** (*Zool*) marmot • MODISMO: • **dormir como una ~** to sleep like a log ▸ **marmota de Alemania** hamster ▸ **marmota de América** woodchuck, whistler (EEUU)
2 (= *dormilón*) sleepyhead*
3* (= *criada*) maid, servant

maroma SF **1** (= *cuerda*) rope
2 (*LAm*) (= *cuerda floja*) tightrope
3 maromas (*LAm*) acrobatics (*pl*), acrobatic stunts • **hacer ~s** = **maromear**
maromear ▹ CONJUG 1a VI (*LAm*) **1** (*en cuerda floja*) to walk the tightrope; (= *hacer volatines*) to do acrobatics, do acrobatic stunts
2 (*Pol*) (= *ser diplomático*) to do a balancing act; (= *ser chaquetero*) to change one's political allegiance
maromero/a SM/F (*LAm*) **1** (= *funámbulo*) tightrope walker; (= *acróbata*) acrobat
2 (= *político*) opportunist (politician)
maromo* SM (*esp Esp*) bloke*, guy*
marona* SF • **tiene 60 años y ~** (*Caribe*) he's well over sixty
marqués/esa SM marquis/marchioness
marquesina SF (= *cobertizo*) glass canopy, porch; (= *techo*) glass roof, cantilever roof; [*de parada*] bus shelter; [*de tienda de campaña*] fly sheet; (*Ferro*) roof, cab (*of locomotive*)
marquetería SF marquetry
márquetin SM marketing
marquezote SM (*CAm*) sweet bread
marquito SM slide mounting
marrajo ADJ [*toro*] vicious, dangerous; [*persona*] sly
SM **1** (= *tiburón*) shark
2 (*Méx*) (= *tacaño*) skinflint
3 (= *candado*) padlock
marramizar ▹ CONJUG 1f VI [*gato*] to howl, caterwaul
marrana SF **1** (*Zool*) sow
2‡* (= *mujer*) slut‡; ▹ **marrano**
marranada* SF, **marranería*** SF
1 (= *inmundicia*) filthiness
2 (= *acto*) filthy act • **decir ~s** to talk filth
3 (= *mala pasada*) dirty trick
marrano/a ADJ* filthy, dirty
SM (*Zool*) pig, hog (*EEUU*)
SM/F **1*** (= *persona*) (*despreciable*) swine*; (*sucio*) dirty pig*
2 (*Hist*) converted Jew; ▹ **marrana**
Marraquech SM, **Marraqués** SM Marrakech, Marrakesh
marrar ▹ CONJUG 1a VT • ~ **el tiro/golpe** to miss
VI **1** [*disparo*] to miss
2 [*comentario*] to miss the mark; [*plan*] to fail, go wrong • **no me marra una** everything's going well for me
marras ADV **1** • **de ~: es el problema de ~** it's the same old problem • **el individuo de ~** you-know-who • **volver a lo de ~** to go back over the same old stuff
2 (*And**) • **hace ~ que no lo veo** it's ages since I saw him
marrazo SM (*Méx*) (= *bayoneta*) bayonet; (= *pico*) mattock; (= *cuchillo*) short machete
marrocata‡ SF Moroccan hashish
marrón ADJ brown
SM **1** (= *color*) brown
2 (*Culin*) ▸ **marrón glacé** marron glacé
3‡ (= *acusación*) charge; (= *condena*) sentence; (= *situación comprometida*) mess • **le dieron cinco años de ~** they gave him five years' bird* • **le pillaron de** *o* **en un ~** they caught him red-handed • MODISMO: • **comerse un ~** to own up
4‡ (= *policía*) pig‡, cop*
5 (*LAm*) (*Hist*) maroon
6 (*And*) (= *papillote*) curlpaper
7 (*Caribe*) (= *café con leche*) coffee with milk
marroncito SM (*Caribe*) coffee with milk
marroquí ADJ, SMF Moroccan
SM (= *piel*) morocco, morocco leather
marroquinería SF **1** (= *artículos*) (fine) leather goods (*pl*); (= *tienda*) leather goods shop
2 (= *arte*) (fine) leatherwork

marrubio SM (*Bot*) horehound
marrueco/a ADJ, SM/F = **marroquí**
Marruecos SM Morocco • **el ~ Español** (*Hist*) Spanish Morocco
marrullería SF **1** (= *cualidad*) smoothness, glibness
2 (= *excusa*) plausible excuse
3 marrullerías (= *engatusamiento*) cajolery (*sing*), wheedling (*sing*); (*Dep*) dirty play (*sing*)
marrullero/a ADJ (= *lenguaraz*) smooth, glib; (= *engatusador*) cajoling, wheedling; [*equipo, jugador*] dirty
SM/F smooth type, smoothie*
Marsella SF Marseilles
Marsellesa SF Marseillaise
marsopa SF porpoise
marsupial ADJ, SM marsupial
mart. ABR (= **martes**) Tues.
marta SF (= *animal*) (pine) marten; (= *piel*) sable ▸ **marta cebellina, marta cibelina** sable
martajar ▹ CONJUG 1a VT (*CAm, Méx*)
1 [+ *maíz*] to pound, grind
2 • ~ **el español** to speak broken Spanish
Marte SM Mars
martellina SF sledgehammer
martes SM INV Tuesday • ~ **y trece** ≈ Friday 13th ▸ **martes de carnaval, martes de carnestolendas** Shrove Tuesday; ▹ **sábado, CARNAVAL**

> **MARTES Y TRECE**
> According to Spanish superstition Tuesday is an unlucky day, even more so if it falls on the 13th of the month. As the proverb goes, "**En martes, ni te cases ni te embarques**". In many Latin American countries it is Friday 13th that is considered unlucky.

martiano/a (*Cuba*) (*Pol*) ADJ supporting the ideas of José Martí
SM/F supporter of José Martí
martillada SF hammer blow, blow with a hammer
martillar ▹ CONJUG 1a VT, VI = **martillear**
martillazo SM (heavy) blow with a hammer • **recibió un ~ en la cabeza** he was hit on the head with a hammer, he received a hammer blow to the head • **me di un ~ en el dedo** I hit my finger with the hammer • **a ~s: destrozar algo a ~s** to smash sth to pieces with a hammer • **dar forma a algo a ~s** to hammer sth out, hammer sth into shape
martilleante ADJ insistent, repetitious
martillear ▹ CONJUG 1a VT **1** (= *golpear*) [+ *puerta*] to hammer on, pound on; [+ *piano*] to pound away at; (= *machacar*) to pound
2 (= *atormentar*) to worry, torment
VI [*motor*] to knock
martilleo SM hammering; (= *machaqueo*) pounding
martillero/a SM/F (*And, Caribe*) auctioneer
martillo SM **1** (*tb Dep*) hammer; [*de presidente de asamblea*] gavel ▸ **martillo de hielo** ice-pick ▸ **martillo de madera** mallet ▸ **martillo de orejas** claw-hammer ▸ **martillo mecánico** power hammer ▸ **martillo neumático, martillo picador** pneumatic drill, jackhammer (*EEUU*) ▸ **martillo pilón** steam hammer ▸ **martillo sacaclavos** claw hammer
2 (*Com*) auction room
3 (*Arquit*) house that sticks out from the row; (*LAm*) wing (*of a building*)
4 (= *persona*) hammer, scourge
Martín SM Martin • **San ~** (= *santo*) St Martin; (= *fiesta*) Martinmas; (*Agr*) *season for slaughtering pigs* • REFRÁN: • **a cada cerdo** *o*

puerco le llega su San ~ everyone comes to his day of reckoning; ▹ **veranillo**

martín SM ▸ **martín pescador** kingfisher

martinete SM **1** [*de construcción*] drop hammer, pile driver

2 (*Mús*) hammer

3 (*Zool*) heron

martingala SF (= *truco*) trick, ruse; (*LAm*) (*pey*) trick, fiddle*

Martinica SF Martinique

mártir SMF martyr

martirio SM **1** (*Rel*) martyrdom

2 (= *tormento*) torment, torture; (= *persona*) pain* ▸ **martirio chino** Chinese torture

martirizador ADJ agonizing, excruciating

martirizante ADJ agonizing, excruciating

martirizar ▹ CONJUG 1f VT **1** (*Rel*) to martyr

2 (= *atormentar*) to torture, torment

martirologio SM martyrology

Marucha SF *forma familiar de* **María**

marucha SF (*And*) rump steak

Maruja SF *forma familiar de* **María**

maruja* SF traditional housewife • **soy una ~** I'm only a housewife

marujeo* SM chitchat, gossip

marula SF (*Méx*) teat, nipple (*EEUU*)

marullero ADJ = **marrullero**

marusa SF (*Caribe*) shoulder bag

maruto SM (*Caribe*) **1** (*Anat*) navel

2 (*Med*) (= *verruga*) wart; (= *moradura*) bruise, welt

marxismo SM Marxism

marxista ADJ, SMF Marxist

marzal ADJ March (*antes de s*), of March

marzo SM March; ▹ **septiembre**

mas CONJ but

m

más

ADVERBIO
ADJETIVO
SUSTANTIVO MASCULINO

Para expresiones como ***más aún, más de la cuenta, a más tardar, las más de las veces,*** *ver la otra entrada.*

ADVERBIO

1 *comparativo* **a** (*con adjetivo, adverbio*) more • **más cómodo** more comfortable • **más inteligente** more intelligent

La mayoría de los adjetivos y adverbios de una sílaba o de dos sílabas terminados en "-y" forman el comparativo añadiendo la terminación "-er". A veces se produce un cambio ortográfico.

• **más barato** cheaper • **más grande** bigger • **más joven** younger • **más largo** longer • **más feliz** happier • **más lejos** further • **más deprisa** faster, more quickly • **vete más lejos de la cámara** move further away from the camera • **échate más hacia la derecha** move more *o* further to the right

b (*con verbo*) • **¿quieres más?** would you like some more? • **ahora salgo más** I go out more these days • **últimamente nos vemos más** we've been seeing more of each other lately • **correr más** to run faster • **durar más** to last longer • **me gusta más sin chocolate** I like it better *o* I prefer it without chocolate • **trabajar más** to work harder

c (*con numerales, sustantivos*) • **quisiera dos libros más** I'd like another two books, I'd like two more books • **un kilómetro más y llegaremos** one more kilometre and we'll be there • **ahora pesa veinte kilos más** he's twenty kilos heavier now, he weighs twenty kilos more now • **solo se lo repetiré una vez más** I will only repeat it once more *o* one more time • **¡no aguanto aquí ni un minuto más!** I can't stand it here a minute longer!

d • **más de** more than • **no tiene más de dieciséis años** he isn't more than sixteen • **se estima en más de mil** it is reckoned at more than a thousand • **en la clase somos más de diez** there are over ten *o* more than ten of us in the class • **son más de las diez** it's past *o* gone *o* after ten o'clock • **más de lo que yo creía** more than I thought • **lo hizo con más destreza de la que esperaba** he did it more skilfully than he had expected

e • **más que** more than • **el alemán es más difícil que el inglés** German is more difficult *o* harder than English • **tiene más dinero que yo** he has more money than I do *o* than me • **él ha viajado más que yo** he has travelled more (widely) than I have *o* than me • **se trata de voluntad más que de fuerza** it's a question of willpower rather than of strength, it's more a question of willpower than of strength; ▹ **cada**

2 *superlativo* **a** (*con adjetivos, sustantivos*) most • **su película más innovadora** his most innovative film • **él es el más inteligente** he is the most intelligent (one)

La mayoría de los adjetivos y adverbios de una sílaba o de dos sílabas terminados en "-y" forman el superlativo añadiendo la terminación "-est". A veces se produce un cambio ortográfico.

• **el bolígrafo más barato** the cheapest pen • **el niño más joven** the youngest child • **el coche más grande** the biggest car • **el punto más lejano** the furthest point • **la persona más feliz** the happiest person • **siempre está donde haya más diversión** he's always to be found where the most fun is going on

b (*con verbos*) • **salió cuando más llovía** he left when it was raining the heaviest *o* the hardest, he left when the rain was at its heaviest • **el/la que más:** • **él es el que sabe más** he's the one who knows (the) most • **es el que más viene a verme** he's the one who comes to see me (the) most (often) • **el que más me gusta es el de flores** the one I like (the) best *o* most is the flowery one • **fue el que más trabajó** he was the one who worked (the) hardest • **trabaja tanto como el que más** he works as hard as anyone

c • **más ... de:** • **el más alto de la clase** the tallest in the class • **ella es la más guapa de todas** she is the prettiest of them all • **el tren más rápido del mundo** the fastest train in the world

d • **lo más posible** as much as possible • **lo más temprano** the earliest • **lo más que puede** as much as he can • **a lo más** at (the) most • **un libro de lo más divertido** a most *o* highly amusing book • **es un hombre de lo más honrado** he's entirely honest • **todo lo más** at (the) most; ▹ **quien**

3 • **algo más:** • **quisiera decirle algo más** there's something else I wanted to say to you • **¿desea algo más?** would you like anything else? • **no dijo nada más** he didn't say anything else, he said nothing else • **no lo sabe nadie más** no one else knows, nobody else knows • **¿qué más?** what else? • **¿quién más?** anybody else?; ▹ **nada, nadie**

4 *al sumar* and, plus • **14 más 20 menos 12 es igual a 22** 14 plus 20 minus 12 equals 22 • **dos más tres (son) cinco** two and *o* plus three is five • **seremos nosotros más los niños** it will be us plus the kids • **estos, más los que ya teníamos, hacen 200** these together with *o* plus the ones we had before, make 200 • **España más Portugal** Spain together with Portugal

5 *en frases negativas* **a** (*con sentido restrictivo*) • **no veo más solución que ...** I see no other solution than *o* but to ... • **no hay más que mirar alrededor para darse cuenta** you only have to look around you to see • **al final no fue más que un susto** it gave us a fright, but that's all • **no hace más de tres semanas** only *o* just three weeks ago, no more than three weeks ago

b (= *otra vez*) • **no vengas más por aquí** don't come round here any more • **nunca más le ofreceré mi ayuda** I'll never offer to help her again

6 *con valor intensivo* • **qué ... más:** • **¡qué perro más feo!** what an ugly dog! • **¡es más bueno!** he's (ever) so kind!

7 de más • **tenemos uno de más** we have one too many • **trae una manta de más** bring an extra blanket • **estar de más** to be unnecessary, be superfluous • **aquí yo estoy de más** I'm not needed here, I'm in the way here • **unas copas no estarían de más** a few drinks wouldn't do any harm • **no estará (por) de más preguntar** there's no harm in asking

8 no más (*LAm*) just, only • **así no más** just like that • **ayer no más** just *o* only yesterday • **dos días no más** just *o* only two days • **¡espera no más!** just you wait! • **pruébelo no más** just try it • **siga no más** just carry on • **habían llegado no más** they had just arrived • **no más llegué me echaron** no sooner had I arrived than they threw me out • **vengo no más a verlo** I've come just to see it • **¡pase no más!** (= *entre*) please *o* do go in; (= *venga*) please *o* do come in • **siéntese no más** please *o* do sit down • **sírvase no más** please *o* do help yourself • **hasta no más** to the utmost, to the limit

9 *otras locuciones* • **es más** what's more, furthermore, moreover • **creo que eso es así, es más, podría asegurártelo** I believe that it is the case, and what's more *o* furthermore *o* moreover I could prove it to you • **dos más, dos menos** give or take two • **ni más ni menos:** • **él es uno más de entre nosotros, ni más ni menos** he's just one of the group, that's all • **desciende ni más ni menos que de Carlomagno** he is descended from none other than Charlemagne, he is descended from Charlemagne no less • **más o menos:** • **me dijo más o menos lo mismo de ayer** he said more or less the same thing to me yesterday • **me levanté a las siete más o menos** I got up at around *o* about seven o'clock • **por más que:** • **por más que se esfuerce** however much *o* hard he tries, no matter how (hard) he tries • **por más veces que se lo he dicho** no matter how many times I've told him • **por más que quisiera ayudar** much as I should like to help • **sin más (ni más)** without further ado

• MODISMOS: • **a más no poder:** • **está lloviendo a más no poder** it really is pouring down • **esa noche bebimos a más no poder** that night we drank until we could drink no more, we really had a lot to drink that night • **corrimos a más no poder** we ran as fast as we could • **a más y mejor:** • **está nevando a más y mejor** it really is snowing, it's snowing and then some • **ir a más:** • **discutieron, pero la cosa no fue a más** they argued, but things didn't get out of hand • **el problema de la droga va a más** the drugs problem is getting out of hand *o* out of control; ▹ **allá, bien, dar, nunca, valer**

ADJETIVO*

• esta es más casa que la otra this is a better house than the last one • es más hombre he's more of a man

SUSTANTIVO MASCULINO

1 (Mat) plus, plus sign

2 • MODISMO: • tiene sus más y sus menos it has its good and its bad points, there are things to be said on both sides

masa¹ (SF) 1 [*de pan*] dough
2 (*Cono Sur*) (= *pastelillo*) small bun, teacake; (*And, Cono Sur*) (= *hojaldre*) puff pastry ▸ **masa quebrada** short pastry, shortcrust pastry
3 (= *argamasa*) mortar

masa² (SF) 1 (= *conjunto*) mass • **una ~ de gente** a mass of people • **una ~ de aire** a mass of air • **una ~ de nubes** a bank of clouds ▸ **masa coral** choir
2 (= *volumen*) mass • MODISMO: • **llevar algo en la ~ de la sangre** to have sth in one's blood, have a natural inclination towards sth ▸ **masa atómica** atomic mass ▸ **masa crítica** (*Fís*) critical mass; (*fig*) (= *mínimo*) requisite number ▸ **masa encefálica** brain matter ▸ **masa molecular** molecular mass ▸ **masa polar** polar icecap
3 (*Sociol*) • **las ~s** the masses • **los medios de comunicación de ~s** the mass media
4 • **en ~** (= *en multitud*) en masse • **fueron en ~ a recibir al equipo** they went en masse to greet the team • **protestaron en ~** they held a mass protest • **producir algo en ~** to mass-produce sth • **despidos en ~** mass redundancies
5 (*Econ*) ▸ **masa de acreedores** body of creditors ▸ **masa monetaria** money supply ▸ **masa salarial** total wage bill
6 (*Elec*) earth, ground (*EEUU*) • **conectar un aparato con ~** to earth *o* (*EEUU*) ground an appliance

masacrar ▹ CONJUG 1a (VT) to massacre

masacre (SF) massacre

masacrear‡ ▹ CONJUG 1a (VT) (*Caribe*) to touch up*

masada (SF) farm

masadero/a (SM/F) farmer

masaje (SM) massage • **dar (un) ~ a algn** to give sb a massage • **salón de ~** massage parlour ▸ **masaje cardíaco** cardiac massage

masajear ▹ CONJUG 1a (VT) to massage

masajista (SMF) masseur/masseuse; (*Dep*) physio* ▸ **masajista terapéutico/a** physiotherapist

masar* ▹ CONJUG 1a (VT) to massage

masato (SM) (*And, CAm*) (= *bebida*) *drink made from fermented maize, bananas, yucca etc*; (*And*) (= *dulce de coco*) *coconut sweet*; (*And*) [*de plátanos*] *banana custard*

mascada (SF) 1 (*LAm*) (= *tabaco*) plug of chewing tobacco
2 (*CAm*) (= *ahorros*) nest egg; (*Cono Sur*) (= *ganancias*) illicit gains (*pl*); (= *tajada*) rake-off*, cut
3 (*And, CAm*) (= *tesoro*) buried treasure
4 (*CAm**) (= *reprimenda*) rebuke
5 (*Méx*) (= *pañuelo*) silk handkerchief *o* scarf

mascado* (ADJ) (*CAm*) creased, rumpled

mascadura (SF) chewing

mascar ▹ CONJUG 1g (VT) 1 (= *masticar*) to chew
2* [+ *palabras*] to mumble, mutter
• MODISMOS: • **~ un asunto** • **dar mascado un asunto** to explain sth in very simple terms
(VI) (= *masticar*) to chew; (*esp LAm*) (= *mascar tabaco*) to chew tobacco; (*And*) (= *mascar coca*) to chew coca
(VPR) **mascarse** to sense • **en la plaza de toros se mascaba la tragedia** you could sense tragedy in the bullring

máscara (SF) 1 (= *careta*) mask • **baile de ~s** masked ball • **~ para esgrima** fencing mask ▸ **máscara antigás** gas mask ▸ **máscara de oxígeno** oxygen mask ▸ **máscara facial** face mask *o* pack
2 **máscaras** (= *mascarada*) masque (*sing*), masquerade (*sing*)
3 (= *apariencia*) mask; (= *disfraz*) disguise • **bajo su ~ de cinismo** beneath his mask of cynicism • **quitar la ~ a algn** to unmask sb • **quitarse la ~** to reveal o.s.
4 (= *rímel*) (*tb* **máscara de pestañas**) mascara
(SMF) masked person

mascarada (SF) 1 (= *fiesta*) masque, masquerade
2 (= *farsa*) charade, masquerade

mascarilla (SF) (= *máscara*) (*tb Med*) mask; (*en cosmética*) face mask *o* pack ▸ **mascarilla capilar** (= *sustancia*) hair oil; (= *tratamiento*) hair-conditioning treatment ▸ **mascarilla de arcilla** mudpack ▸ **mascarilla facial** face mask, face pack ▸ **mascarilla de oxígeno** oxygen mask ▸ **mascarilla mortuoria** death mask

mascarón (SM) large mask ▸ **mascarón de proa** figurehead

mascota (SF) 1 [*de club, acontecimiento*] mascot
2 (= *animal doméstico*) pet

masculinidad (SF) masculinity, manliness

masculinizador (ADJ), **masculinizante** (ADJ) masculinizing

masculinizar ▹ CONJUG 1f (VT) to make more masculine; (*Bio*) to masculinize

masculino (ADJ) 1 (*Bio*) male; [*apariencia*] masculine, manly • **ropa masculina** men's clothing, menswear
2 (*Ling*) masculine
(SM) (*Ling*) masculine

> **MASCULINO**
>
> **Masculino** *se traduce al inglés por* **male** *y* **masculine**.
>
> ▹ **Masculino** *se traduce por* **male** *cuando nos referimos a la condición masculina de los seres vivos (en oposición al sexo femenino):*
> **Un veinticinco por ciento de la población masculina sobrepasa ya el metro ochenta de estatura**
> Twenty-five per cent of the male population is now six foot or over
>
> ▹ *Se traduce por* **masculine** *para referirse a las cualidades y características que tradicionalmente se han relacionado con los hombres:*
> **Una mujer tosca de rasgos más bien masculinos**
> A rough woman with rather masculine features
>
> ▹ *También se utiliza en el ámbito gramatical:*
> **Escribe cinco palabras españolas del género masculino que terminen en -e**
> Write five masculine words in Spanish ending in -e
>
> *Para otros usos y ejemplos ver la entrada.*

mascullar ▹ CONJUG 1a (VT) to mumble, mutter

masectomía (SF) mastectomy

masera (SF) kneading trough

masía (SF) (*Aragón, Cataluña*) farm

masificación (SF) (= *abarrotamiento*) overcrowding; (= *propagación*) growth, spread • **la ~ de la universidad** overcrowding in universities • **la ~ de la producción de alimentos** mass production of food • **la ~ de la cultura** the bringing of culture to the masses

masificado (ADJ) (= *abarrotado*) overcrowded; (= *de masas*) mass (*antes de s*) • **una sociedad masificada** a mass society • **el esquí es ahora un deporte ~** skiing is a sport practised by everyone these days

masificarse ▹ CONJUG 1g (VPR) (= *abarrotarse*) to get overcrowded; (= *crecer demasiado*) to get too big

masilla (SF) (*para ventanas*) putty; (*para agujeros*) filler

masillo (SM) (*Caribe*) plaster

masita (SF) (*LAm*) small cake, pastry

masitero (SM) (*And, Caribe, Cono Sur*) pastry cook, confectioner

masivamente (ADV) en masse • **votaron ~ al partido socialista** they voted en masse for the socialist party • **la huelga fue apoyada ~** there was overwhelming support for the strike

masivo (ADJ) [*ataque, dosis etc*] massive; [*evacuación, ejecución*] mass (*antes de s*) • **se espera una asistencia masiva** a huge turnout is expected • **reunión masiva** mass meeting

masmediático (ADJ) mass-media (*antes de s*) • **mucha atención masmediática** a lot of attention from the mass media

masoca* (ADJ) masochistic
(SMF) masochist

masocotudo (ADJ) (*And, Cono Sur*) = **amazacotado**

masón (SM) (free)mason

masonería (SF) (free)masonry

masónico (ADJ) masonic

masoquismo (SM) masochism

masoquista (ADJ) masochistic
(SMF) masochist

masoterapia (SF) massage (therapy)

mastate (SM) (*CAm, Méx*) (*Hist*) loincloth

mastectomía (SF) mastectomy

mastelero (SM) topmast

master, máster (ADJ) [*copia*] master
(SM) (PL: **masters**) 1 (*Univ*) master's degree (en in) ▸ **Master de Administración de Empresas** Master of Business Administration, MBA
2 (*Cine, Mús*) master copy
3 (*Dep*) masters' (competition) • **el Master de Augusta** the Augusta Masters

masticación (SF) chewing, mastication (*frm*)

masticar ▹ CONJUG 1g (VT) to chew, masticate (*frm*)

mástil (SM) 1 (= *palo*) pole; (= *sostén*) support; (*para bandera*) flagpole; (*Náut*) mast; (*Arquit*) upright ▸ **mástil de tienda** tent pole
2 [*de guitarra*] neck
3 [*de pluma*] shaft

mastín (SM) mastiff ▸ **mastín danés** Great Dane ▸ **mastín del Pirineo** Pyrenean mountain dog, Great Pyrenees (*EEUU*)

mastique (SM) (= *escayola*) plaster; (= *cemento*) cement; (= *masilla*) putty

mastitis (SF INV) mastitis

masto (SM) (*Agr, Hort*) stock (*for grafting*)

mastodonte (SM) 1 (= *animal*) mastodon
2* (= *persona*) (great) hulk*; (= *organización*) behemoth; (= *máquina*) huge great thing*

mastodóntico (ADJ) colossal, huge

mastoides (ADJ), (SF INV) mastoid

mastuerzo (SM) 1 (*Bot*) cress; (*tb* **mastuerzo de agua**) watercress
2* (= *persona*) clodhopper*

masturbación (SF) masturbation

masturbar ▹ CONJUG 1a (VT) to masturbate
(VPR) **masturbarse** to masturbate

masturbatorio (ADJ) masturbatory

m

Mat. ABR = **Matemáticas**

mata SF **1** (= *arbusto*) bush, shrub; (*esp LAm*) (= *planta*) plant; (*en tiesto*) potted plant ▸ **mata de coco** (*Caribe*) coconut palm ▸ **mata de plátano** (*Caribe*) banana tree ▸ **mata rubia** kermes oak
2 (= *ramita*) sprig; (= *manojo*) tuft; (= *raíz*) clump; (= *ramo*) bunch
3 matas (= *matorral*) thicket (*sing*), scrub (*sing*), bushes
4 (*Agr*) (= *terreno*) field, plot; (*And*) (= *huerto*) orchard
5 (*LAm*) (= *arboleda*) clump, grove; (*LAm*) (= *bosque*) forest ▸ **mata de bananos** banana plantation
6 ▸ **mata de pelo** mop of hair

mataburros SM INV (*Caribe, Cono Sur*) (*hum*) dictionary

matacaballo • MODISMO: • **a ~** ADV at breakneck speed

matacán SM **1** (*And, Caribe*) (= *cervato*) fawn, young deer
2 (*CAm*) (= *ternero*) calf

matachín SM bully

matadero SM **1** [*de ganado*] slaughterhouse, abattoir (*frm*) • **son como las ovejas que van al ~** they go like lambs to the slaughter
2* (= *trabajo*) killer*, exhausting task
3 (*Méx, Cono Sur**) (= *prostíbulo*) brothel

matador(a) ADJ **1** (= *que mata*) killing
2* (= *horrible*) horrible; (= *ridículo*) ridiculous; (= *absurdo*) absurd • **el vestido te está ~** that dress looks terrible on you
SM/F **1** (= *asesino*) killer
2 (*Taur*) matador, bullfighter

matadura SF sore

matafuego SM fire extinguisher

matagigantes SM INV giant-killer

matalahúga SF, **matalahúva** SF aniseed

matalobos SM INV aconite, wolf's-bane

matalón ADJ [*caballo*] old, worn-out
SM nag

matalotaje SM **1** (*Náut*) ship's stores
2* (= *revoltijo*) jumble, mess

matambre SM (*Cono Sur*) stuffed rolled beef

matamoros SM INV swashbuckler, braggart

matamoscas SM INV (= *paleta*) fly swat; (= *papel*) flypaper; (= *aerosol*) fly spray

matanza SF **1** (*en batalla*) slaughter, killing; (*Agr*) slaughtering; (= *temporada*) slaughtering season; (*fig*) slaughter, massacre
2 (*Caribe*) (= *matadero*) slaughterhouse; (*And*) (= *tienda*) butcher's, butcher's shop; (*CAm*) (= *mercado*) meat market

mataperrada* SF (*And, Cono Sur*) (= *broma*) prank; (= *granujada*) dirty trick

mataperrear* ▹ CONJUG 1a VI (*And, Cono Sur*) to wander the streets

mataperros* SM INV (= *niño*) urchin; (= *adolescente*) hooligan

matapolillas SM INV mothballs (*pl*)

matar ▹ CONJUG 1a VT **1** [+ *persona*] to kill; [+ *reses, ganado*] to kill, slaughter • **la mató en un ataque de celos** he killed her in a fit of jealousy • **el jefe me va a ~** the boss will kill me • **~ a algn a golpes** to beat sb to death • **~ a algn a disgustos** to make sb's life a misery • **así me maten** for the life of me • **que me maten si …** I'll be damned if …
• MODISMOS: • **~las callando** to go about things slyly • **entre todos la ~on (y ella sola se murió)** they are all to blame
2 [+ *tiempo, pelota*] to kill; [+ *sed*] to quench; [+ *sello*] to postmark, cancel; [+ *pieza*] (*en ajedrez*) to take; [+ *cal*] to slake; [+ *ángulo, borde*] to file down; [+ *color*] to dull • **cómete una manzana para ~ el hambre** have an apple to keep you going
3* (= *molestar*) • **los zapatos me están matando** these shoes are killing me* • **me mata tener que trabajar en sábado** it's a pain having to work on a Saturday*
4* (= *sorprender*) • **¿se van a casar? ¡me has matado!** they're getting married? you're kidding!*
VI to kill • **no ~ás** (*Rel*) thou shalt not kill • **entrar a ~** (*Taur*) to go in for the kill • MODISMO: • **estar o llevarse a ~ con algn** to be at daggers drawn with sb
VPR **matarse 1** (= *suicidarse*) to kill o.s. • **se mató de un tiro** he shot himself
2 (= *morir*) to be killed, get killed • **se ~on en un accidente de aviación** they were killed in a plane crash
3 (= *esforzarse*) to kill o.s. • **convendría revisar estas facturas, pero no te mates** these invoices need checking but don't kill yourself • **~se trabajando** *o* **a trabajar** to kill o.s. with work • **se mata para mantener a su familia** he has to work like crazy to keep his family • **se mata por sacar buenas notas** he goes all out to get good marks

matarife SM **1** [*de animales*] slaughterman, butcher ▸ **matarife de caballos** knacker
2 (= *matón*) thug

matarratas SM INV **1** (= *veneno*) rat poison
2* (= *alcohol*) rotgut, bad liquor

matasanos* SM INV quack (doctor)

matasellado SM postmark, franking

matasellar ▹ CONJUG 1a VT to postmark, frank

matasellos SM INV (= *marca*) postmark; (= *instrumento*) franking machine • **la carta tenía ~ de Madrid** the letter was postmarked Madrid ▸ **matasellos de puño** hand stamp

matasiete SM braggart, bully

matasuegras SM INV party blower

matasuelo SM • MODISMO: • **darse un ~** (*And**) to come a cropper*, take a flat beating (*EEUU*)

matate SM (*CAm*) canvas bag

matazón SF (*And, CAm, Caribe*) = **matanza**

match [matʃ] SM (PL: **matchs** [matʃ]) match, game (*EEUU*)

mate[1] ADJ (= *sin brillo*) matt; [*sonido*] dull

mate[2] SM (*Ajedrez*) mate • **dar ~ a** to mate, checkmate

mate[3] SM (*LAm*) **1** (= *bebida*) maté ▸ **mate cocido** maté infusion ▸ **mate de coca** coca leaf tea ▸ **mate de menta** mint tea
2 (= *vasija*) gourd, maté pot • MODISMOS: • **pegar ~** (*CAm*) to go crazy • **tener mucho ~** (*CAm*) to be sharp
3 (*Cono Sur‡*) (= *cabeza*) head, nut*, noggin (*EEUU**)

mate[4] SM (*Tenis*) smash

matear[1] ▹ CONJUG 1a VT (*Agr*) to plant at regular intervals, sow in groups
VI **1** (*Bot*) to sprout (thickly)
2 [*perro*] to hunt among the bushes

matear[2] ▹ CONJUG 1a VI (*LAm*) to drink maté

matear[3] ▹ CONJUG 1a VT (*Cono Sur*) **1** (*Ajedrez*) to checkmate
2 (= *mezclar*) to mix

matemáticamente ADV **1** (*Mat*) mathematically
2 (= *exactamente*) exactly • **siempre llegan ~ a la misma hora** they always arrive at exactly the same time • **las dos versiones coinciden casi ~** the two versions tally in almost every detail
3 (*Dep*) • **nuestro equipo se sitúa ~ en Primera División** mathematically, our team is guaranteed a place in the First Division

matemáticas SFPL, **matemática** SF mathematics (*sing*) ▸ **matemáticas aplicadas** applied mathematics ▸ **matemáticas puras** pure mathematics

matemático/a ADJ **1** (*Mat*) mathematical; [*cálculo*] precise
2 (= *exacto*) exact • **con puntualidad matemática** dead on time
3 (*Dep*) • **con esa victoria aseguró el ascenso ~** with that win they made sure of promotion
4 • **es ~** (= *no falla*): • **¡es ~!, ¡cada vez que me siento, suena el teléfono!** it's like clockwork!, every time I sit down the phone rings!
SM/F mathematician, math specialist (*EEUU*)

Mateo SM Matthew • **el evangelio según San ~** the Gospel according to St Matthew • **la Pasión según San ~** the St Matthew Passion

materia SF **1** (*Fís*) matter; (= *material*) material, substance • **~ inorgánica** inorganic matter • **~ vegetal** vegetable matter • **una ~ esponjosa y blanda** a soft spongy material *o* substance • **hay ~ para escribir varios libros** there is enough material to write several books • **hay mucha ~ para investigar** there is a lot of material to research • **ya tenéis ~ para pensar** that should give you something to think about *o* food for thought ▸ **materia colorante** dyestuff ▸ **materia fecal** faeces (*pl*), feces (*pl*) (*EEUU*) ▸ **materia grasa** fat ▸ **materia gris** grey *o* (*EEUU*) gray matter ▸ **materia prima** raw material
2 (= *tema*) subject matter; (*Escol*) subject • **índice de ~s** table of contents • **en ~ de** as regards • **entrar en ~** to get down to business, get to the point • **son expertos en la ~** they are experts on the subject • **será ~ de muchas discusiones** it will be the subject of a lot of debate ▸ **materia optativa** (*Escol*) option, optional subject

material ADJ **1** [*ayuda, valor etc*] material • **bienestar ~** material well-being
2 (= *físico*) physical • **la presencia ~ de algn** sb's physical *o* bodily presence • **dolor ~** physical pain • **daños ~es** physical damage, damage to property
3 (= *real*) • **la imposibilidad ~ de …** the physical impossibility of … • **el autor ~ del hecho** the actual perpetrator of the deed • **no tengo tiempo ~ para ir** I literally don't have time to go
SM **1** (= *materia*) material • **hecho de mal ~** made of poor-quality material(s) • **tengo ya ~ para una novela** I've got enough material now for a novel ▸ **material de construcción** building materials (*pl*) ▸ **material de desecho** waste material ▸ **materiales de derribo** rubble (*sing*) ▸ **materiales plásticos** plastics ▸ **material impreso** printed matter ▸ **material reciclado** recycled material
2 (= *equipo*) equipment ▸ **material bélico, material de guerra** war material, military equipment ▸ **material de envasado** packaging materials (*pl*) ▸ **material de limpieza** cleaning materials (*pl*) ▸ **material de oficina** office supplies (*pl*), stationery ▸ **material deportivo** sports equipment ▸ **material escolar** school equipment ▸ **materiales didácticos** teaching materials ▸ **material fotográfico** photographic equipment ▸ **material informático** hardware ▸ **material móvil, material rodante** rolling stock
3 (*Tip*) copy
4* (= *cuero*) leather
5 • **de ~** (*LAm*) made of bricks, brick-built

materialidad SF (= *naturaleza*) (material) nature; (= *apariencia*) outward appearance • **percibe solamente la ~ del asunto** he sees only the superficial aspects of the question • **es menos la ~ del insulto que ...** it's not so much the insult itself as ...

materialismo SM materialism ▸ **materialismo dialéctico** dialectical materialism

materialista ADJ materialist(ic)
SMF materialist
SM 1 (*Méx*) (= *camionero*) lorry driver, truckdriver (*EEUU*)
2 (*Méx*) (= *contratista*) building contractor

materializable ADJ realizable, attainable

materialización SF materialization

materializar ▹ CONJUG 1f VT to materialize
VPR **materializarse** to materialize

materialmente ADV 1 (= *de manera material*) materially • **no ha beneficiado ~ a este pueblo** it has brought no material benefit to this town
2 (= *físicamente*) physically • **~ posible** physically possible • **se vio ~ asaltada por los fans** she was physically assaulted by the fans
3 (= *absolutamente*) absolutely • **nos es ~ imposible** it is quite *o* absolutely impossible for us • **estaba ~ mojado** he was absolutely soaked

maternal ADJ [*instinto*] maternal; [*amor*] motherly, maternal; [*leche*] mother's; [*faja, sujetador*] maternity (*antes de s*) • **baja ~** maternity leave
SM (*Caribe*) (= *guardería*) nursery

maternidad SF 1 (= *estado*) motherhood, maternity
2 (= *hospital*) (*tb* **casa de maternidad**) maternity hospital

materno ADJ [*lengua*] mother (*antes de s*); [*amor, tono*] motherly, maternal; [*casa*] mother's • **el hogar ~** one's childhood home • **el útero ~** the mother's womb • **abuelo ~** maternal grandfather, grandfather on one's mother's side • **leche materna** mother's milk • **hospital ~-infantil** maternity hospital

matero ADJ (*Cono Sur*) 1 (= *de mate*) of maté, relating to maté
2 [*persona*] fond of drinking maté

mates* SFPL maths* (*sing*), math (*sing*) (*EEUU*)

matete* SM (*Cono Sur*) 1 (= *revoltijo*) mess, hash*
2 (= *riña*) quarrel, brawl
3 (= *confusión*) confusion

Matilde SF Mat(h)ilda

matinal ADJ morning (*antes de s*)
SF matinée

matinée SM 1 (*Teat*) matinée
2 (*And*) (= *fiesta infantil*) children's party

matiz SM 1 [*de color*] shade
2 [*de sentido*] shade, nuance; (= *ironía*) touch

matización SF 1 (*Arte*) blending
2 (= *teñido*) tinging, tinting
3 (= *aclaración*) qualification • **conviene hacer algunas matizaciones al respecto** some clarifications are required • **esta opinión, con ciertas matizaciones, es compartida por todos** this opinion, with certain qualifications, is shared by everyone • **quiero hacer una ~** I'd like to qualify *o* clarify that

matizado ADJ • **~ de** *o* **en** tinged with, touched with (*tb fig*) • **una explicación más matizada** a more thorough *o* exhaustive explanation

matizar ▹ CONJUG 1f VT 1 (*Arte*) to blend; [+ *tono*] to vary, introduce some variety into; [+ *contraste, intensidad de colores*] to tone down
2 (= *teñir*) to tinge, tint (**de** with)
3 (= *aclarar*) to qualify • **creo que deberías ~ lo que acabas de decir** I think what you just said needs qualifying • **~ que ...** to explain that ..., point out that ... • **el ministro defendió su postura, aunque matizó que ...** the minister defended his position, although he explained *o* pointed out that ...

matojal SM (*Caribe*), **matojo** SM (*And, Caribe, Méx*) = **matorral**

matón SM (= *bravucón*) thug; (*en el colegio*) bully, thug ▸ **matón de barrio** local thug, local bully-boy*

matonismo SM (= *bravuconería*) thuggery; (*en el colegio*) bullying

matorral SM (= *conjunto de matas*) thicket, bushes (*pl*); (= *terreno*) scrubland

matorro SM (*And*) = **matorral**

matra SF (*Cono Sur*) horse blanket

matraca SF 1 (= *carraca*) rattle
2* (= *lata*) nuisance, pain*; (= *burla*) teasing, banter • **dar la ~ a algn** (= *molestar*) to pester sb; (= *burlarse de*) to tease sb
3 (*And‡*) (= *marihuana*) hash*, pot*
4 **matracas** (*Escol‡*) maths* (*sing*), math (*sing*) (*EEUU*)
5 (*Méx**) (= *metralleta*) machine gun
SMF* (= *persona*) nuisance, pain*

matraquear ▹ CONJUG 1a VT 1 (= *hacer sonar*) to rattle
2* (= *molestar*) to pester; (= *burlarse de*) to tease

matraz SM flask

matreraje SM (*Cono Sur*) banditry

matrero (*LAm*) ADJ 1 (= *astuto*) cunning, sly
2 (= *desconfiado*) suspicious, distrustful
SM (= *bandido*) bandit, brigand; (= *fugitivo*) fugitive from justice; (= *tramposo*) trickster

matriarca SF matriarch

matriarcado SM matriarchy

matriarcal ADJ matriarchal

matricería SF die-stamping

matricida SMF matricide

matricidio SM matricide

matrícula SF 1 (= *inscripción*) registration, enrolment, enrollment (*EEUU*) • **el plazo de ~ finaliza el día 15** the last day for registration *o* enrolment is the 15th • **fui a la universidad a hacer la ~** I went to University to matriculate • **tasas de ~** registration fees
2 (= *nota*) ▸ **matrícula de honor** *top marks in a subject at university with the right to free registration the following year*
3 (= *alumnado*) roll
4 (*Aut*) (= *número*) registration number, license number (*EEUU*); (= *placa*) number plate, license plate (*EEUU*) • **un coche con ~ de Toledo** a car with a Toledo number plate ▸ **matrícula de encargo** personalized number plate
5 (*Náut*) registration • **un buque de ~ extranjera** a ship with foreign registration, a foreign-registered ship • **un barco con ~ de Bilbao** a Bilbao-registered boat
6 (= *registro*) register

matriculación SF 1 (= *inscripción*) registration, enrolment, enrollment (*EEUU*)
2 [*de barco, vehículo*] registration

matricular ▹ CONJUG 1a VT 1 (= *inscribir*) to register, enrol, enroll (*EEUU*)
2 [+ *barco, vehículo*] to register
VPR **matricularse** to register, enrol • **~se en el curso de ...** to sign on *o* enrol *o* (*EEUU*) enroll for the course in ...

matrilineal ADJ matrilineal

matrilinealidad SF matrilineal descent

matrimonial ADJ matrimonial • **agencia ~** marriage bureau • **enlace ~** wedding • **vida ~** married life, conjugal life (*frm*) • **capitulaciones ~es** marriage settlement (*sing*)

matrimonialista ADJ • **abogado ~** lawyer specializing in matrimonial cases

matrimoniar ▹ CONJUG 1b VI to marry, get married

matrimonio SM 1 (= *institución*) marriage, matrimony (*frm*) • **contraer ~ (con algn)** to marry (sb) • **tras 26 años de ~** after 26 years of marriage • **hacer vida de ~** to live together as man and wife • **hacer uso del ~** (*hum*) to make love ▸ **matrimonio abierto** open marriage ▸ **matrimonio canónico** canonical marriage ▸ **matrimonio civil** civil marriage ▸ **matrimonio clandestino** secret marriage ▸ **matrimonio consensual** common-law marriage ▸ **matrimonio de conveniencia, matrimonio de interés** marriage of convenience ▸ **matrimonio homosexual** homosexual marriage, gay marriage ▸ **matrimonio religioso** church wedding
2 (= *pareja*) (married) couple • **el ~ García** the Garcías, Mr and Mrs García • **cama de ~** double bed

matritense ADJ, SMF = **madrileño**

matriz SF 1 (*Anat*) womb, uterus
2 (*Téc*) mould, mold (*EEUU*), die; (*Tip*) matrix
3 [*de talonario*] stub, counterfoil
4 (*Jur*) original, master copy
5 (*Mat*) matrix; (*Inform*) array
ADJ • **casa ~** (*Com*) (= *sede*) head office; (= *compañía*) parent company; (= *convento*) parent house

matrona SF 1 (= *mujer*) matron
2 (= *comadrona*) midwife

matronal ADJ matronly

matungo‡ (*Caribe, Cono Sur*) ADJ old, worn-out
SM (= *caballo*) old horse, nag; (= *persona*) beanpole*, string bean (*EEUU**)

maturrango ADJ (*Cono Sur*) (= *torpe*) clumsy, awkward; (*And, Cono Sur*) [*jinete*] poor, incompetent
SM (*And, Cono Sur*) poor rider, incompetent horseman

Matusalén SM Methuselah

matute SM 1 (= *acto*) smuggling, contraband • **de ~** (= *de contrabando*) smuggled, contraband (*antes de s*); (= *en secreto*) secretly, on the sly • **se colaron de ~** they sneakily jumped the queue • **introducir una idea de ~** to surreptitiously slip an idea in
2 (= *géneros*) smuggled goods (*pl*), contraband
3 (= *casa de juego*) gambling den

matuteo SM smuggling, contraband

matutero SM smuggler

matutino ADJ morning (*antes de s*)
SM morning newspaper

maula ADJ [*animal*] useless, lazy; [*persona*] good-for-nothing, unreliable
SMF 1 (= *vago*) idler, slacker
2 (= *tramposo*) cheat, trickster; (= *moroso*) bad payer
SF 1 (= *retal*) remnant; (= *trasto*) piece of junk, useless object; (= *persona*) dead loss*
2 (= *truco*) dirty trick

maulería SF cunning, trickiness

maulero SM 1 (= *tramposo*) cheat, trickster; (= *engañador*) swindler
2 (= *ilusionista*) conjurer

maullar ▹ CONJUG 1a VI to mew, miaow

maullido SM mew, miaow

Mauricio[1] SM Maurice

Mauricio[2] SM (*Geog*) Mauritius ▸ **isla Mauricio** Mauritius

Mauritania SF Mauritania

mauritano/a ADJ, SM/F Mauritanian

maurofilia SF (*Hist*) *admiration for the Moors and Moorish culture*

maurofobia SF (*Hist*) *hatred of the Moors and*

Moorish culture
mausoleo SM mausoleum
máx. ABR (= **máximo**) max
maxi... PREF maxi...
maxiabrigo SM maxi-coat
maxifalda SF maxiskirt
maxilar ADJ maxillary
SM jaw, jawbone • **recibió un puñetazo en el ~** he received a punch in the jaw
maxilofacial ADJ maxillofacial
máxima¹ SF (= *frase*) maxim
máxima² SF (*Meteo*) maximum (temperature), high • **~s de 44 grados en Sevilla y Córdoba** top temperatures *o* highs of 44 degrees in Seville and Córdoba
maximalismo SM maximalism
maximalista ADJ, SMF maximalist
máxime ADV (= *sobre todo*) especially; (= *principalmente*) principally • **y ~ cuando ...** and all the more so when ...
maximización SF maximization
maximizar ▹ CONJUG 1f VT to maximize
máximo ADJ [*altura, temperatura, velocidad, carga*] maximum • **el ~ dirigente** the leader • **~ jefe** *o* **líder** (*esp LAm*) President, leader • **llegar al punto ~** to reach the highest point • **lo ~ en ordenadores** the last word in computers • **acortaron el viaje lo ~ posible** they shortened their journey as much as they could
SM maximum • **un ~ de 100 euros** a maximum of 100 euros • **el ~ de tiempo que se te permite** the maximum time you're allowed • **al ~** to the maximum • **debemos aprovechar al ~ nuestros recursos** we must exploit our resources to the maximum, we must make the best of the resources we have • **sube la calefacción al ~** put the heating up as high as it'll go • **como ~** (= *como mucho*) at the most, at the outside; (= *como muy tarde*) at the latest • **te costará 5.000 como ~** it'll cost you 5,000 at the most • **llegaré a las nueve como ~** I'll be there by nine o'clock at the latest ▸ **máximo histórico** all-time high
máximum SM maximum
maxisencillo SM, **maxisingle** SM twelve-inch (record)
maxtate SM (*Méx*) straw basket
may. ABR (= **mayúscula(s)**) cap, caps
maya¹ SF **1** (*Bot*) daisy
2 (= *muchacha*) May Queen
maya² (*Hist*) ADJ Mayan
SMF Maya, Mayan • **los ~** the Maya(s)
mayal SM flail
mayestático ADJ majestic, royal • **el plural ~** the royal "we"
mayo SM **1** (= *mes*) May • **el primero de ~** May Day • **el ~ francés** May 68; ▹ **septiembre**
2 (= *palo*) maypole
mayólica SF (*And*) wall tile
mayonesa SF mayonnaise
mayor ADJ **1** (*comparativo*) **a** (= *más grande*) • **necesitamos una habitación ~** we need a bigger *o* larger room • **un ~ número de visitantes** a larger *o* greater number of visitors, more visitors • **son temas de ~ importancia** they are more important issues, they are issues of greater importance • **sin ~es complicaciones** without further ado • **la ~ parte de los ciudadanos** most citizens • **ser ~ que algo**: • **mi casa es ~ que la suya** my house is bigger *o* larger than his • **el índice de paro es ~ que hace un año** unemployment is higher than (it was) a year ago • MODISMO: • **llegar a ~es** [*situación*] to get out of hand, get out of control
b (= *de más edad*) older • **es mi hermana ~** she's my older *o* elder sister • **Emilio es el ~ de los dos** Emilio is the older of the two • **~ que algn** older than sb • **Paco es ~ que Nacho** Paco is older than Nacho • **es tres años ~ que yo** he is three years older than me • **vivió con un hombre muchos años ~ que ella** she lived with a man many years her senior, she lived with a man who was several years older than her
2 (*superlativo*) **a** (= *más grande*) • **esta es la ~ iglesia del mundo** this is the biggest *o* largest church in the world • **su ~ problema** his biggest *o* greatest problem • **su ~ enemigo** his biggest *o* greatest enemy • **viven en la ~ miseria** they live in the greatest *o* utmost poverty • **hacer algo con el ~ cuidado** to do sth with the greatest *o* utmost care
b (= *de más edad*) oldest • **Juan es el ~** Juan is the oldest • **mi hijo (el) ~** my oldest *o* eldest son
3 (= *principal*) [*plaza, mástil*] main; [*altar, misa*] high • **calle ~** high street, main street (EEUU); ▹ **colegio, libro**
4 (= *adulto*) grown-up, adult • **nuestros hijos ya son ~es** our children are grown-up now • **las personas ~es** grown-ups, adults • **ya eres muy ~ para hacer esas tonterías** you're too old now to do silly things like that • **ser ~ de edad** to be of age • **hacerse ~** to grow up
5 (= *de edad avanzada*) old, elderly • **mis padres son muy ~es** my parents are very old
6 (= *jefe*) head (*antes de s*) • **el cocinero ~** the head chef • **montero ~** head huntsman
7 (*Mús*) major
SMF **1** (= *adulto*) grown-up, adult • **los ~es se fueron a una fiesta** the grown-ups *o* adults went to a party • **los ~es no hacen cosas así** grown-ups don't do things like that ▸ **mayor de edad** adult, *person who is legally of age*
2 (= *anciano*) • **los ~es** elderly people • **¡más respeto con los ~es!** be more respectful to your elders (and betters)!
3 (*LAm*) (*Mil*) major
SM • **al por ~** wholesale • **vender al por ~** to sell wholesale • **repartir golpes al por ~** to throw punches left, right and centre
mayoral SM **1** (= *capataz*) foreman, overseer
2 [*de finca*] farm manager, steward; [*de ovejas*] head shepherd
3 (*Hist*) (= *cochero*) coachman
mayorazgo SM **1** (= *institución*) primogeniture
2 (= *tierras*) entailed estate
3 (= *hijo*) eldest son, first-born
mayorcito ADJ • **eres ~ ya** you're a big boy now • **ya es ~ para saber lo que hace** he's old enough to know what he's doing • **ya eres un poco ~ para hacer eso** you're too old now to be doing that
mayordomo SM [*de casa*] butler; [*de hacienda*] steward; (*Cono Sur*) (= *capataz*) foreman; (*And*) (= *criado*) servant; (*LAm*) (*Rel*) patron (saint)
mayorear* ▹ CONJUG 1a VI (*CAm*) to be in charge, be the boss
mayoreo SM (*LAm*) wholesale (trade)
mayorete SF majorette
mayoría SF **1** (= *mayor parte*) majority • **la ~ de los españoles** the majority of Spaniards, most Spaniards • **la ~ de las veces** usually, on most occasions • **en la ~ de los casos** in most cases • **en su ~** mostly • **islas inhabitadas en su ~** islands, most of which are *o* which are mostly uninhabited • **una ~ del 20 por ciento** a 20 per cent majority • **una ~ de las cuatro quintas partes** a four-fifths majority • **la abrumadora ~** the overwhelming majority • **por una ~ arrolladora** by an overwhelming majority • **gobierno de la ~** majority rule • **la inmensa ~** the vast majority ▸ **mayoría absoluta** absolute majority ▸ **mayoría minoritaria** simple majority, relative majority ▸ **mayoría relativa** simple majority, relative majority ▸ **mayoría silenciosa** silent majority ▸ **mayoría simple** simple majority
2 ▸ **mayoría de edad** adulthood, majority ▸ **mayoría de edad penal** age of majority • **cumplir** *o* **llegar a la ~ de edad** to come of age
mayorista ADJ wholesale
SMF wholesaler
mayoritariamente ADV **1** (= *principalmente*) mainly, mostly • **gente ~ joven** mainly *o* mostly young people, young people for the most part
2 (*al votar*) by a majority • **el Parlamento votó ~ en contra de la reforma** a majority of the Parliament voted against the reform
mayoritario ADJ majority (*antes de s*) • **gobierno/accionista ~** majority government/shareholder
mayormente ADV (= *principalmente*) chiefly, mainly; (= *especialmente*) especially; (= *tanto más*) all the more so • **no me interesa ~** I'm not especially *o* particularly interested, I'm not all that interested
mayúscula SF capital (letter); (*Tip*) upper case letter • **se escribe con ~** it's written with a capital (letter) • **con el título en ~s** with the title in capitals *o* capital letters • **la Literatura, con ~s** literature with a capital L, heavyweight literature • **un intelectual con ~s** an intellectual with a capital I, a heavyweight intellectual
mayúsculo ADJ **1** [*letra*] capital
2 (= *enorme*) tremendous • **un susto ~** a tremendous fright *o* scare • **un error ~** a tremendous mistake
maza SF **1** (= *arma*) mace; (*Dep*) bat; (*Polo*) stick, mallet; (*Mús*) drumstick; [*de taco de billar*] handle; (*Téc*) flail; [*de cáñamo, lino*] brake • **la declaración del Gobierno cayó como una ~ sobre la oposición** the government statement was a bombshell for the opposition ▸ **maza de fraga** drop hammer ▸ **maza de gimnasia** Indian club
2* (= *persona*) bore
3 (*LAm*) [*de rueda*] hub
4 (*And, Caribe*) [*de ingenio*] drum (of a sugar mill)
mazacote SM **1** (*Culin*) • **el arroz se ha hecho un ~** the rice is just one sticky mass
2 (= *hormigón*) concrete
3 (*Arte*) (= *mezcla*) mess, hotchpotch, hodgepodge (EEUU); (= *monstruosidad*) eyesore, monstrosity
4 (*CAm, Méx*) (= *dulce*) sweet mixture
5* (= *lata*) bore
6 (*Caribe***) (= *culo*) arse**, ass (EEUU**)
mazacotudo ADJ = **amazacotado**
mazada SF **1** (= *golpe*) bash*, blow (with a club)
2 (*fig*) blow • **fue una ~ para él** it came as a blow to him • **dar ~ a algn** to hurt sb, injure sb
mazamorra (*LAm*) SF **1** [*de maíz*] maize mush, maize porridge; (*pey*) mush
2 (= *ampolla*) blister
mazamorrero/a* (*And*) ADJ of/from Lima
SM/F native/inhabitant of Lima • **los ~s** the people of Lima
mazapán SM marzipan
mazazo SM heavy blow • **fue un ~ para él** it came as a real blow to him • **la noticia cayó como un ~** the news was a bombshell • **el Gobierno asestó ayer un auténtico ~ a la oposición** the government dealt a real blow to the opposition yesterday

mazmorra SF dungeon
mazo SM **1** (= *martillo*) mallet; [*de mortero*] pestle; (= *porra*) club; [*de croquet*] mallet; [*de campana*] clapper; (*Agr*) flail • REFRÁN: • **a Dios rogando y con el ~ dando** God helps those who help themselves
2 (= *manojo*) bunch, handful; (= *fardo*) bundle, packet, package (*EEUU*); [*de papeles*] sheaf, bundle; [*de naipes*] pack; [*de billetes*] wad, roll
3* (= *persona*) bore
mazorca SF **1** [*de maíz*] cob, ear ▸ **mazorca de maíz** corncob
2 (*Téc*) spindle
3 (*Cono Sur*) (= *gobierno*) despotic government; (= *banda*) political gang
mazota SF (*And, Méx*) = **mazorca**
mazote SM (*And, Méx*) handful • **de a ~** free
Mb ABR (= **megabyte**) Mb
mb ABR (= **milibar(es)**) mb
Mbytes ABR (= **megabytes**) Mbytes
MCAC SM ABR = **Mercado Común de la América Central**
MCCA SM ABR (= **Mercado Común Centroamericano**) CACM
MCD SM ABR (= **Máximo Común Divisor**) HCF
MCM SM ABR (= **Mínimo Común Múltiplo**) LCM
MDF SM ABR (= **medium-density fibreboard**) MDF
MDP SM ABR (*Chile*) = **Movimiento Democrático Popular**
me PRON PERS **1** (*como complemento directo*) me • **me llamó por teléfono** he telephoned *o* rang me • **ya no me quiere** he doesn't love me any more
2 (*como complemento indirecto*) (to) me • **¡dámelo!** give it to me! • **me lo compró** (*de mí*) he bought it from me; (*para mí*) he bought it for me • **me lo presentó mi primo** my cousin introduced him to me • **¿por qué me lo preguntas?** why do you ask? • **me lo dijeron ayer** they told me yesterday
3 (*con partes del cuerpo, ropa*) • **me rompí el brazo** I broke my arm • **me lavé la cara** I washed my face • **me quité el abrigo** I took my coat off • **se me está cayendo el pelo** my hair is falling out
4 (*uso enfático*) • **me lo comí todo** I ate it all up • **se me ha caído el bolígrafo** I've dropped my pen • **me preparé un café** I made myself a coffee
5 (*uso reflexivo o pronominal*) • **me lavé** I washed (myself) • **me miré al espejo** I looked at myself in the mirror • **me voy a enfadar** I'm going to get cross • **me marcho** I am going
meada‡ SF **1** (= *orina*) piss** • **echar una ~** to have a piss *o* a slash**
2 (= *mancha*) urine mark, urine stain
meadero‡ SM bog‡, loo*, john (*EEUU*‡)
meado‡ ADJ **1** • **esto está ~** it's a cinch*, it's dead easy*
2 (*Cono Sur*) • **estar ~** to be pissed**
meados‡ SMPL piss** (*sing*)
meaja SF crumb
meandro SM meander
meapilas‡ ADJ sanctimonious, holier-than-thou
SMF INV (= *santito*) goody-goody*
mear‡ ▸ CONJUG 1a VT **1** (= *orinar*) to piss on**
2 (= *humillar, ganar*) to piss on**
VI to piss**, have *o* (*EEUU*) take a piss** • MODISMO: • **~ fuera del tiesto** to miss the point completely
VPR **mearse** to wet o.s. • **~se de risa** to piss o.s. laughing**
MEC SM ABR (*Esp*) = **Ministerio de Educación y Ciencia**
Meca SF • **La ~** Mecca

meca[1] SF • **la ~ del cine** the Mecca of the film world
meca[2]** EXCL (*Chile*) shit!**
meca[3]* SF (*And*) prostitute
mecachis* EXCL (*Esp*) (*eufemismo de ¡me cagó!*) sugar!*, shoot!* • **~ en la mar** sugar!*, shoot!*
mecánica SF **1** (= *técnica*) mechanics (*sing*) ▸ **mecánica cuántica** quantum mechanics (*sing*) ▸ **mecánica de precisión** precision engineering
2 (= *mecanismo*) mechanism, works
3 (= *funcionamiento*) mechanics (*pl*) • **la ~ del concurso es sencilla** the mechanics of the competition are simple • **la ~ parlamentaria** parliamentary procedure • **la ~ electoral** electoral procedure
mecánicamente ADV mechanically
mecanicista ADJ mechanistic
mecánico/a ADJ **1** (*gen*) mechanical; (*con motor*) power (*antes de s*); (= *de máquinas*) machine (*antes de s*)
2 [*gesto, trabajo*] mechanical
SM/F [*de coches*] mechanic, grease monkey (*EEUU**); (= *operario*) machinist; (= *ajustador*) fitter, repair man/woman; (*Aer*) rigger, fitter; (= *conductor*) driver, chauffeur ▸ **mecánico/a de vuelo** flight engineer
mecanismo SM **1** [*de reloj, cerradura, fusil*] mechanism ▸ **mecanismo de dirección** steering gear ▸ **mecanismo de seguridad** safety mechanism
2 (= *procedimiento*) mechanism • **el ~ electoral** the electoral procedure ▸ **mecanismo de defensa** defence mechanism
mecanización SF mechanization
mecanizado ADJ mechanized
mecanizar ▸ CONJUG 1f VT to mechanize
mecano® SM Meccano®
mecanografía SF typing ▸ **mecanografía al tacto** touch-typing
mecanografiado ADJ typewritten
SM (= *texto*) typescript; (= *acción*) typing
mecanografiar ▸ CONJUG 1c VT to type
mecanógrafo/a SM/F typist
mecapal SM (*CAm, Méx*) leather strap (*for carrying*)
mecapalero SM (*CAm, Méx*) porter
mecatazo SM (*CAm*) **1** (= *golpe*) lash
2* (= *trago*) swig*
mecate SM **1** (*CAm, Méx*) (= *cuerda*) rope, twine; (= *fibra*) strip of pita fibre • **¡es todo ~!** (*Méx**) it's terrific! • MODISMO: • **jalear el ~ a algn*** to suck up to sb*
2 (*Méx**) (= *persona*) boor, oaf
mecateada SF (*CAm, Méx*) lashing, beating
mecatear[1] ▸ CONJUG 1a VT **1** (*CAm, Méx*) (= *atar*) to tie up; (= *azotar*) to lash, whip
2 (*LAm**) (= *dar coba a*) to suck up to*
VPR **mecatearse** (*Méx*‡) • **~se** • **mecateárselas** to beat it*, leg it*
mecatear[2] ▸ CONJUG 1a VI (*And*) to eat cakes
mecatero‡ SM (*LAm*) creep*, toady
mecato SM (*And*) cakes (*pl*), pastries (*pl*)
mecedor ADJ rocking
SM **1** (= *columpio*) swing
2 (*CAm, Caribe, Méx*) (= *silla*) rocking chair
3 (*Caribe*) (= *cuchara*) stirrer
mecedora SF rocking chair
Mecenas SM Maecenas
mecenas SMF INV patron • **~ de las artes** patron of the arts
mecenazgo SM patronage
mecer ▸ CONJUG 2b VT **1** [+ *cuna, niño*] to rock; (*en columpio*) to swing; [+ *rama*] to cause to sway, move to and fro; [*olas*] [+ *barco*] to rock
2 [+ *líquido*] to stir; [+ *recipiente*] to shake
VPR **mecerse** (*en mecedora*) to rock (to and fro); (*en columpio*) to swing; [*rama*] to sway, move to and fro

mecha SF **1** [*de vela, lámpara*] wick; [*de explosivo*] fuse • **encender la ~** (*lit, fig*) to light the fuse • MODISMOS: • **aguantar ~** to grin and bear it • **tener mucha ~ para algo** to be very good at sth, have a knack for sth • **a toda ~*** at full speed ▸ **mecha lenta** slow fuse ▸ **mecha tardía** time fuse
2 [*de pelo*] = **mechón**[1]
3 mechas (*en el pelo*) highlights
4 [*de tocino*] rasher
5 (*And, Cono Sur*) (*Téc*) bit (*of brace*)
6 (*And, Caribe**) (= *broma*) joke
7 (*LAm*) (= *miedo*) fear
8* (= *ratería*) shoplifting
9 (*And*) (= *baratija*) trinket
mechado ADJ • **carne mechada** larded meat • **~ de anglicismos** full of Anglicisms
mechar ▸ CONJUG 1a VT (*Culin*) (= *poner tocino*) to lard; (= *rellenar*) to stuff
mechero[1] SM **1** (= *encendedor*) cigarette lighter; (= *estufa*) burner; (*And, Cono Sur*) (= *candil*) oil lamp ▸ **mechero Bunsen** Bunsen burner ▸ **mechero de gas** gas burner ▸ **mechero encendedor, mechero piloto** pilot light
2 (*CAm, Méx*) [*de pelo*] mop of hair
3** (= *pene*) prick**
mechero[2]**/a*** SM/F **1** (= *ladrón*) shoplifter
2 (*Caribe*) (= *bromista*) joker
mechificar* ▸ CONJUG 1g VT (*And, Caribe*) (= *engañar*) to trick, deceive; (= *mofarse de*) to mock
mecho SM (*And, CAm*) (= *vela*) candle; (= *cabo*) candle end; (= *candelero*) candlestick
mechón[1] SM [*de pelo*] lock; (= *hilos*) bundle
mechón[2]**/ona*** SM/F (*Chile*) fresher, freshman
mechudo ADJ (*LAm*) tousled, unkempt
meción SM (*CAm, Caribe*) jerk, jolt
meco* ADJ (*CAm, Méx*) (= *ordinario*) coarse, vulgar; (= *bruto*) thick*; (= *salvaje*) uncivilized, wild; (*Hist*) wild (Indian)
medalla SF (*Dep, Mil*) medal; (= *joya*) medallion • **una ~ de la Virgen** a medallion with the Virgin Mary on it • **ser ~ de bronce/plata/oro** to be a bronze/silver/gold medallist *o* (*EEUU*) medalist, get a bronze/silver/gold (medal) ▸ **medalla al valor** medal for bravery
medallero SM medal table
medallista SMF **1** (*Dep*) medallist, medalist (*EEUU*) ▸ **medallista de bronce** bronze medallist ▸ **medallista de oro** gold medallist ▸ **medallista de plata** silver medallist
2 (= *diseñador*) medal designer
medallón SM **1** (= *medalla*) medallion
2 (= *relicario*) locket
3 (*Culin*) medallion, médaillon ▸ **medallón de pescado** fish cake
médano SM, **medaño** SM (*en tierra*) sand dune; (*en el mar*) sandbank
media SF **1 medias** (= *hasta la cintura*) tights, pantyhose (*sing*) (*EEUU*); (*hasta el muslo*) stockings ▸ **medias de compresión** support tights ▸ **medias de malla** (*hasta el muslo*) fishnet stockings; (*hasta la cintura*) fishnet tights ▸ **medias de red, medias de rejilla** = **medias de malla** ▸ **medias pantalón** (*Col*) tights (*pl*); ▸ PANTALONES, ZAPATOS, GAFAS
2 (*LAm*) (= *calcetín*) sock
3 • **de ~** [*aguja*] knitting (*antes de s*); [*punto*] plain • **hacer ~** to knit
4 (*Dep*) midfield
5 (= *promedio*) average • **100 de ~ al día** an average of 100 a day • **dan una ~ de cinco conciertos al mes** they give an average of five concerts a month ▸ **media aritmética** arithmetic mean ▸ **media ponderada**

weighted average
6 ▸ **media de cerveza** 1/4 litre bottle of beer
mediación SF mediation, intercession • **por ~ de** through
mediado ADJ **1** [*local*] half-full, half-empty; [*trabajo*] half-completed • **el local estaba ~** the place was half-full *o* half-empty • **mediada la tarde** halfway through the afternoon • **llevo ~ el trabajo** I am halfway through the job, I have completed half the work
2 • **a ~s de marzo** in the middle of March, halfway through March • **a ~s del siglo pasado** around the middle of the last century
mediador(a) SM/F mediator
mediagua SF (*Cono Sur*) hut, shack
medial ADJ medial
medialuna SF (*LAm*) croissant
mediana SF **1** (*Aut*) central reservation, median (*EEUU*)
2 (*Mat*) median
medianamente ADV **1** (= *bastante*) fairly • **una calle ~ concurrida** a fairly busy street • **me gusta comer ~ bien** I like to eat at least fairly well • **cualquier persona ~ sensata** any half-sensible person
2 (= *regular*) moderately • **un trabajo ~ bueno** a moderately good piece of work • **quedó ~ en los exámenes** he did moderately well in the exams
medianera SF (*And, Cono Sur*) party wall, dividing wall
medianería SF **1** (= *pared*) party wall
2 (*Caribe, Méx*) (*Com*) partnership; (*Agr*) sharecropping
medianero ADJ **1** [*pared*] party (*antes de s*), dividing; [*valla*] boundary (*antes de s*)
2 [*vecino*] adjacent, next
SM **1** [*de casa*] owner of the adjoining house/property *etc*
2 (*Caribe, Méx*) (= *socio*) partner; (*Agr*) sharecropper
medianía SF **1** (= *promedio*) average; (= *punto medio*) halfway point; (*Econ*) moderate means (*pl*), modest circumstances (*pl*); (*en sociedad*) undistinguished social position
2 (= *mediocridad*) mediocrity • **no pasa de ser una ~** he's no better than average, he's little more than mediocre
3 (*Com*) middleman
mediano ADJ **1** (= *regular*) average; (*en tamaño*) medium-sized; [*empresa*] medium-sized • **una bomba de mediana potencia** a medium-sized bomb • **una cebolla mediana** a medium onion • **camisetas de talla mediana** medium T-shirts • **es ~ de estatura** he is of average *o* medium height • **de mediana edad** middle-aged
2 (= *del medio*) middle • **es el hermano ~** he is the middle brother
3 (= *indiferente*) mediocre, average
medianoche SF midnight • **a ~** at midnight
mediante PREP **1** (= *por medio de*) by means of • **izan las cajas ~ una polea** the crates are lifted by means of a pulley • **se comunicaban ~ mensajes en clave** they communicated by means of coded messages • **se comunican ~ gestos** they communicate through signs • **lograron abrir la puerta ~ una palanca** they managed to open the door with a metal bar • **vigilaban el edificio ~ cámaras ocultas** hidden cameras were used to keep a watch on the building • **un diseño ~ ordenador** a computer-generated design
2 • **Dios ~** God willing • **volveré, Dios ~, el lunes** I'll be back on Monday, God willing
mediar ▹ CONJUG 1b VI **1** (= *estar en medio*) to be halfway through; (= *llegar a la mitad*) to get to the middle, get halfway; [*tiempo*] to elapse, pass • **entre A y B median 30kms** it is 30kms from A to B • **media un abismo entre los dos gobiernos** the two governments are poles apart • **entre los dos sucesos ~on varios años** the two events were separated by several years, several years elapsed between the two events • **mediaba el otoño** autumn was half over, it was halfway through autumn • **mediaba el mes de julio** it was halfway through July
2 (= *ocurrir*) to come up, happen; (= *intervenir*) to intervene; (= *existir*) to exist • **pero medió la muerte de su madre** but his mother's death intervened • **media el hecho de que ...** we must take into account the fact that ... • **median relaciones cordiales entre los dos** cordial relations exist between the two • **sin ~ palabra se abalanzó sobre ellos** he fell upon them without a word
3 (= *interceder*) to mediate (**en** in, **entre** between), intervene • **~ en favor de algn** • **~ por algn** to intercede *o* intervene on sb's behalf • **~ con algn** to intercede with sb
mediático ADJ media (*antes de s*)
mediatizar ▹ CONJUG 1f VT **1** (= *estorbar*) to interfere with, obstruct; (= *influir*) to influence
2 (*Pol*) to annexe, take control of
medible ADJ (= *mensurable*) measurable; (= *observable*) detectable, appreciable
medicación SF (= *medicinas*) medication; (= *tratamiento*) medication, treatment
medicalizar ▹ CONJUG 1f VT to medicalize
médicamente ADV medically
medicamento SM medicine
▸ **medicamento de patente** patent medicine
medicamentoso ADJ • **incompatibilidad medicamentosa** incompatibility between drugs • **el tratamiento ~ será diferente** the drugs prescribed will vary
medicar ▹ CONJUG 1g VT to give medicine to • **estar medicado** to be on medication • **jabón medicado** medicated soap
VPR **medicarse** to take medicine
medicastro SM (*pey*) quack (doctor)
medicina SF **1** (= *ciencia*) medicine • **estudia ~ en la universidad** he's studying medicine at university • **un estudiante de ~** a medical student ▸ **medicina de empresa** industrial medicine ▸ **medicina forense** forensic medicine ▸ **medicina general** general medicine, general practice ▸ **medicina homeopática** homeopathic medicine ▸ **medicina interna** internal medicine ▸ **medicina legal** forensic medicine, legal medicine ▸ **medicina natural** natural medicine ▸ **medicina preventiva** preventive medicine
2 (= *medicamento*) medicine • **¿te has tomado ya la ~?** have you taken your medicine yet?
medicinal ADJ medicinal
medicinar ▹ CONJUG 1a VT to give medicine to
VPR **medicinarse** to take medicine • **~se con algo** to dose o.s. with sth
medición SF **1** [*de presión, distancia*] (= *acción*) measuring; (= *resultado*) measurement • **pronto comenzarán los trabajos de ~** measuring *o* measurement works will begin soon • **un nuevo método de ~** a new measuring system • **¿cómo se realiza la ~ de la temperatura?** how is the temperature measured? • **un método de ~ de audiencias** an audience tracking system • **aparatos de ~** measuring instruments • **hacer mediciones** to take measurements • **instrumentos de ~** measuring instruments
2 (*Literat*) [*de versos*] measuring, scansion
médico/a ADJ medical • **asistencia médica** medical attention • **receta médica** prescription
SM/F doctor ▸ **médico/a de cabecera** family doctor, GP ▸ **médico/a (de medicina) general** general practitioner ▸ **médico/a dentista** dental surgeon ▸ **médico/a deportivo/a** sports doctor ▸ **médico/a forense** forensic surgeon, expert in forensic medicine; (*Jur*) coroner ▸ **médico/a interno/a** houseman, intern (*EEUU*) ▸ **médico/a naturista** naturopath ▸ **médico/a partero/a** obstetrician ▸ **médico/a pediatra, médico/a puericultor(a)** paediatrician ▸ **médico/a residente** houseman, intern (*EEUU*) ▸ **médico/a rural** country doctor
medida SF **1** (= *unidad de medida*) measure • **una ~ de harina y dos de azúcar** one measure of flour and two of sugar • **puedes usar un vaso como ~** you can use a glass as a measure • **la libra es una ~ de peso** the pound is a measure of weight • MODISMO: • **esto colma la ~** this is the last straw ▸ **medida agraria** land measure ▸ **medida de capacidad** cubic measure ▸ **medida de superficie** square measure ▸ **medida de volumen** cubic measure ▸ **medida para áridos** dry measure ▸ **medida para líquidos** liquid measure
2 (= *medición*) measuring, measurement • **la ~ del tiempo se realizará con unos cronómetros especiales** time will be measured using some special chronometers
3 medidas (= *dimensiones*) measurements • **¿qué ~s tiene la mesa?** what are the measurements of the table? • **¿cuáles son tus ~s?** what are your measurements? • **tomar las ~s a algn/algo** (*lit*) to measure sb/sth, take sb's/sth's measurements; (*fig*) to size sb/sth up* • **tómale bien las ~s antes de proponerle nada** make sure you've got him well sized up before you propose anything
4 (= *proporción*) • **no sé en qué ~ nos afectará la nueva ley** I don't know to what extent the new law will affect us • **en cierta ~** to a certain extent • **en gran ~** to a great extent • **en menor ~** to a lesser extent • **en la ~ de lo posible** as far as possible, insofar as it is possible • **a ~ que** as • **a ~ que vaya bajando el nivel** as the level goes down • **a ~ que van pasando los días** as the days go by • **en la ~ en que** (+ *indic*) in that; (+ *subjun*) if • **el relato era bueno en la ~ en que reflejaba el ambiente de la época** the story was good in that it reflected the atmosphere of the time • **solo cambiarán el tratamiento en la ~ en que los resultados sean negativos** the treatment will only be altered if the results are negative
5 (*Cos*) • **a (la) ~** [*ropa, zapatos*] made to measure; [*trabajo, vacaciones*] tailor-made • **un traje (hecho) a la ~** a made-to-measure suit • **no tenemos un sombrero a su ~** we don't have a hat in your size *o* to fit you • **un papel hecho a su ~** a tailor-made role • **le respondió a la ~ de las circunstancias** she replied as the circumstances required • **lo hice a la ~ de tus deseos** I did it according to your wishes • **un hotel a la ~ de tus necesidades** a hotel that suits all your needs • **de *o* sobre ~** (*Chile*) [*ropa, zapatos*] made-to-measure • **venir a (la) ~** (*lit*) to be the right size; (*fig*) to be tailor-made • **este pantalón me viene a ~** these trousers are just the right size • **este trabajo me viene a**

la ~ this job is tailor-made for me
6 (*LAm*) (= *talla*) size • **¿cuál es su ~?** what size do you take? • **¿qué ~ de cuello tiene usted?** what collar size are you?, what is your collar measurement? • **ropa a sobre ~** (*Méx*) outsize clothing
7 (= *disposición*) measure • **~s destinadas a reducir el desempleo** measures aimed at reducing unemployment • **adoptar** *o* **tomar ~s** to take measures, take steps • **una de las ~s urgentes adoptadas** one of the emergency measures *o* steps taken
▸ **medida cautelar, medida de precaución** precautionary measure ▸ **medida de presión** form of pressure ▸ **medida preventiva** preventive measure ▸ **medida represiva** form of repression ▸ **medidas de seguridad** (*contra ataques, robos*) security measures; (*contra incendios*) safety measures
▸ **medidas represivas** repressive measures; ▹ **paquete**
8 (= *moderación*) • **con ~** in moderation • **sin ~** to excess • **bebía sin ~** he drank to excess • **gastos sin ~** excessive spending
9 [*de versos*] (= *medición*) measuring, scansion; (= *longitud*) measure

medidor(a) ADJ measuring
SM/F (= *persona*) measurer
SM (*esp LAm*) (= *aparato*) meter ▸ **medidor de agua** water meter ▸ **medidor de lluvia** rain gauge ▸ **medidor de presión** pressure gauge ▸ **medidor Geiger** Geiger counter

mediero/a SM/F (*LAm*) share-cropper

medieval ADJ medieval

medievalismo SM medievalism

medievalista SMF medievalist

medievo SM Middle Ages (*pl*)

medio ADJ **1** (= *la mitad de*) half • **nos queda media botella** we've half a bottle left • **~ limón** half a lemon • **~ litro** half a litre • **acudió media ciudad** half the town turned up • **~ luto** half-mourning • **media pensión** (*en hotel*) half-board • **media hora** half an hour • **estuve esperando media hora** I was waiting for half an hour • **el enfermo ha empeorado en la última media hora** the patient has got worse in the last half hour • **una hora y media** an hour and a half • **tardamos tres horas y media en llegar** we took three and a half hours to get there • **son las ocho y media** it's half past eight • **media luna** (*Astron*) half-moon • **en forma de media luna** crescent-shaped • **la Media Luna** (*en el Islam*) the Crescent; ▹ **asta, luz, mundo, naranja, palabra, voz, vuelta**
2 (= *intermedio*) • **la clase media** the middle class • **café de media mañana** mid-morning coffee • **a media tarde** halfway through the afternoon • **a ~ camino**: • **estamos a ~ camino** we're halfway there • **a ~ camino entre Madrid y Barcelona** halfway between Madrid and Barcelona; ▹ **plazo**
3 (= *promedio*) average • **la temperatura media** the average temperature; ▹ **término**
4 (= *normal*) average • **el francés ~** the average Frenchman • **el hombre ~** the man in the street
5 • **a medias**: • **lo dejó hecho a medias** he left it half-done • **está escrito a medias** it's half-written • **estoy satisfecho solo a medias** I am only partly satisfied • **una verdad a medias** a half truth • **ir a medias** to go fifty-fifty • **lo pagamos a medias** we share *o* split the cost
ADV **1** (*con adjetivo*) half • **está ~ borracha** she's half drunk • **~ dormido** half asleep • **es ~ tonto** he's not very bright, he's a bit on the slow side
2 (*con verbo, adverbio*) • **está a ~ escribir/terminar** it is half-written/finished • **~ se sonrió** she gave a half-smile • **lo dijo ~ en broma** he was only half-joking • **Ana ~ se enamoró de Gonzalo** Ana kind of fell in love with Gonzalo • **eso no está ni ~ bien** that isn't even close to being right
3 (*LAm*) (= *bastante*) rather, quite, pretty* • **fue ~ difícil** it was pretty hard
SM **1** (= *centro*) middle, centre, center (*EEUU*) • **justo en el ~ de la plaza hay una fuente** there's a fountain right in the middle *o* centre of the square • **coger algo por el ~** to take sth round the middle • **el justo ~** a happy medium • **de en ~**: • **la casa de en ~** the middle house • **quitar algo de en ~** to get sth out of the way • **quitarse de en ~** to get out of the way • **de por ~**: • **hay droga de por ~** drugs are involved • **hay dificultades de por ~** there are difficulties in the way • **meterse de por ~** to intervene • **día (de) por ~** (*LAm*) every other day • **en ~**: • **iba a besarla, pero él se puso en ~** I was going to kiss her, but he got between us • **no dejes las cosas por en ~** don't leave your things in the middle of the floor • **en ~ de la plaza** in the middle of the square • **en ~ de tanta confusión** in the midst of such confusion • **en ~ de todos ellos** among all of them • **por ~ de**: • **pasar por ~ de** to go through (the middle of) • MODISMO: • **de ~ a ~**: • **equivocarse de ~ a ~** to be completely wrong
2 (*Dep*) midfielder ▸ **medio apertura** (*Rugby*) fly-half ▸ **medio centro** centre-half ▸ **medio (de) melé** (*Rugby*) scrum-half
3 (= *método*) means (*pl*), way • **lo intentaré por todos los ~s (posibles)** I'll try everything possible • **no hay ~ de conseguirlo** there is no way of getting it, it's impossible to get • **poner todos los ~s para hacer algo** • **no regatear ~s para hacer algo** to spare no effort to do sth • **por ~ de**: • **se mueve por ~ de poleas** it moves by means of *o* using a pulley system • **me avisó por ~ de mi vecino** she let me know through my neighbour • **respira por ~ de las agallas** it breathes through *o* using *o* by means of its gills • **lo consiguió por ~ de chantajes** he obtained it by *o* through blackmail ▸ **medio de transporte** means of transport
4 **los medios** (*tb* **los medios de comunicación** *o* **difusión**) the media • **los ~s de comunicación de masas** the mass media • **los ~s informativos** the news media
5 **medios** (= *recursos*) means, resources • **es un hombre de (muchos) ~s** he's a man of means • **no tienen ~s económicos suficientes** they do not have sufficient financial resources
6 (*Bio*) (*tb* **medio ambiente**) environment
7 (= *círculo*) circle • **en los ~s financieros** in financial circles • **encontrarse en su ~** to be in one's element *o* milieu

medioambiental ADJ environmental

medioambientalista SMF environmentalist

medioambiente SM environment

mediocampista SMF midfield player

mediocampo SM midfield

mediocre ADJ average; (*pey*) mediocre

mediocridad SF (*pey*) mediocrity • **es una ~** he's a nonentity

mediodía SM **1** (= *las doce*) midday, noon; (= *hora de comer*) ≈ lunchtime • **a ~** (= *a las doce*) at midday *o* noon; (= *a la hora de comer*) ≈ at lunchtime
2 (*Geog*) south • **el ~ de Francia** the French Midi

medioevo SM Middle Ages (*pl*)

mediofondista SMF middle-distance runner

mediofondo SM (*Caribe*) petticoat

mediogrande ADJ medium large

mediometraje SM medium-length film

medioeste SM Midwest

mediooriental ADJ Middle Eastern

Medio Oriente SM Middle East

mediopensionista SMF day pupil, day student

mediopequeño ADJ medium small

mediquillo SM (*pey*) quack (doctor)

medir ▹ CONJUG 3k VT **1** (= *tomar la medida de*) [+ *habitación, ángulo*] to measure; [+ *distancia, temperatura*] to measure, gauge, gage (*EEUU*); [+ *tierra*] to survey, plot • **~ algo por millas** to measure sth in miles • MODISMOS: • **~ a algn (con la vista)** to size sb up* • **~ las calles** (*Méx**) to hang around on the streets*
2 (= *calcular*) to weigh up • **deberías ~ las consecuencias de lo que dices** you should consider *o* weigh up the consequences of what you say • **deberíamos ~ los pros y los contras de esta decisión** we should weigh up the pros and cons of this decision
3 (= *enfrentar*) • **los dos púgiles ~án sus fuerzas** the two boxers will be pitted against each other *o* will take each other on; ▹ **rasero**
4 (= *moderar*) [+ *comentarios*] to choose carefully • **mide tus palabras** (*aconsejando*) choose your words carefully; (*regañando*) mind your language
5 (*Literat*) to scan • **¿cómo se mide este verso?** how does this line scan?
VI to measure, be • **el tablero mide 80 por 20** the board measures *o* is 80 by 20 • **¿cuánto mides?** how tall are you? • **mido 1,80m** I am 1.80m • **la caja mide 20cm de ancho** the box is 20cm wide • **mide 88cm de pecho** her bust measurement is 88cms
VPR **medirse 1** (= *tomarse la medida*) (*uno mismo*) to measure o.s.; [+ *cintura, pecho*] to measure
2 (= *enfrentarse*) • **~se con algn** to take on sb • **una final en la que se ~án los dos equipos** a final in which the two teams will be pitted against each other *o* will take each other on
3 (= *moderarse*) to restrain o.s. • **deberías ~te un poco en tus actos** you should act with a bit more restraint *o* restrain yourself a bit
4 (*Méx**) (= *no perder la calma*) to keep one's head
5 (*Col, Méx*) [+ *sombrero, zapatos*] to try on

meditabundo ADJ pensive, thoughtful

meditación SF meditation; **meditaciones** meditations (**sobre** on) ▸ **meditación trascendental** transcendental meditation

meditar ▹ CONJUG 1a VT (= *pensar*) to ponder, meditate (on); [+ *plan*] to think out
VI to meditate, ponder

mediterraneidad SF Mediterranean feel *o* spirit • **un concepto de ~ muy interesante** a very interesting notion of what being Mediterranean is

Mediterráneo SM • **el ~** the Mediterranean • MODISMO: • **descubrir el ~*** to reinvent the wheel

mediterráneo ADJ **1** (*Geog*) Mediterranean
2 (= *sin salida al mar*) land-locked

médium SMF (PL: **médiums**) (= *persona*) medium

mediúmnico ADJ • **sesión mediúmnica** session with a medium • **revelaciones mediúmnicas** revelations from a medium

medo SM • **los ~s y los persas** the Medes and the Persians

medra SF (= *aumento*) increase, growth; (= *mejora*) improvement; (*Econ*) prosperity

medrar ▹ CONJUG 1a VI (= *aumentar*) to increase, grow; (= *mejorar*) to improve, do well; (= *prosperar*) to prosper, thrive; [*animal,*

planta etc] to grow, thrive • **¡medrados estamos!** (*iró*) we're in a real pickle now!
medro SM = **medra**
medroso ADJ fearful, timid
médula SF, **medula** SF **1** (*Anat*) marrow, medulla (*frm*) ▸ **médula espinal** spinal cord ▸ **médula ósea** bone marrow • **hasta la ~** (*fig*) to the core • **es irlandés hasta la ~** he is Irish through and through • **estoy convencido hasta la ~** I am totally *o* absolutely convinced • **estoy mojado hasta la ~** I am soaked to the skin
2 (*Bot*) pith
3 (= *esencia*) essence
medular ADJ **1** (*Anat*) bone-marrow (*antes de s*) • **trasplante ~** bone-marrow transplant
2 (= *fundamental*) central, fundamental, essential
medusa SF jellyfish
Mefistófeles SM Mephistopheles
mefistofélico ADJ diabolic, Mephistophelian
mefítico ADJ mephitic(al)
mefitismo SM mephitis
mega SM (*Inform*) meg, mega
mega... PREF mega...
megabyte ['megabait] SM megabyte
megaciclo SM megacycle
megafonía SF (= *sistema*) public address system; (*en la calle*) loudspeakers (*pl*)
megáfono SM megaphone
megahercio SM, **megaherzio** SM megahertz
megalítico ADJ megalithic
megalito SM megalith
megalomanía SF megalomania
megalómano/a SM/F megalomaniac
megalópolis SF INV megalopolis, super-city
megaocteto SM megabyte
megapíxel (**megapixels** *o* **megapíxeles**) SM megapixel
megatón SM megaton
megavatio SM megawatt
megavoltio SM megavolt
meiga SF (*Galicia*) wise woman, witch
mejicanada SF typically Mexican thing
mejicanismo SM Mexicanism, *word or phrase etc peculiar to Mexico*
mejicano/a ADJ, SM/F Mexican
Méjico SM Mexico
mejido ADJ [*huevo*] beaten
mejilla SF cheek
mejillón SM mussel
mejillonera SF mussel-bed
mejillonero ADJ mussel (*antes de s*) • **industria mejillonera** mussel industry
mejor ADJ **1** (*comparativo*) **a** (= *más bueno*) [*resultado, producto*] better; [*calidad, oferta*] better, higher • **a falta de otra cosa ~ que hacer** for lack of anything better to do • **nunca he visto nada ~** I've never seen anything better • **es ~ de lo que creía** it's better than I thought • **y lo que es ~** and even better, and better still • **~ que algo** better than sth • **este es ~ que aquel** this one is better than that one • **no hay nada ~ que una buena comida** there's nothing better than a good meal
b (= *preferible*) • **ser ~** to be better • **sería ~ callarse** it'd be better to keep quiet • **hubiera sido ~ no decir nada** it would have been better to say nothing • **será ~ que te vayas** you'd better go
2 (*superlativo*) **a** (*de dos*) better • **de estos dos refrescos, ¿cuál es el ~?** which is the better (out) of these two drinks?
b (*de varios*) [*persona, producto*] best; [*calidad*] top, highest; [*oferta*] highest, best • **¿quién es tu ~ amigo?** who is your best friend? • **está entre las diez ~es** she is among the ten best • **ser el ~ de la clase** to be the best in the class, be top of the class • **es el ~ de todos** he's the best of all • **vive el ~ momento de su carrera deportiva** he is at the peak of his sporting career • **un jamón de la ~ calidad** a top quality ham, a ham of the highest quality • MODISMO: • **llevarse la ~ parte** to take the lion's share
c • **lo ~** the best • **os deseo (todo) lo ~** I wish you all the best, my best wishes (to you) • **lo ~ de España es el clima** the best thing about Spain is the climate • **lo ~ del caso es que ...** the good thing is that ..., the best part of it is that ... • **os deseo lo ~ del mundo** I wish you all the best • **tengo unos abuelos que son lo ~ del mundo** my grandparents are the best in the world • **tenéis que hacerlo lo ~ posible** you have to do the best you can, you have to do your best • **lo hice lo ~ que pude** I did it the best I could, I did it as well as I could • **lo ~ que podemos hacer es callarnos** the best thing we can do is keep quiet • **estar en lo ~ de la vida** to be in the prime of life; ▹ **partir**
ADV **1** (*comparativo de bien*) better • **ahora lo entiendo todo un poco ~** I understand everything a bit better now • **yo canto ~ que tú** I can sing better than you • **lo hace cada vez ~** he's getting better and better • **¿te sientes algo ~?** do you feel any better? • **ahora estoy un poco ~ de dinero** I'm a bit better off now • **así está mucho ~** it's much better like that • **¡pues si no quieres venir con nosotros, ~!** well, if you don't want to come with us, so much the better! • **~ dicho** or rather, or I should say • **lleva tres años en Inglaterra, o ~ dicho, en el Reino Unido** she's been in England, or rather *o* or I should say the United Kingdom, for three years • **mucho ~** much better, a lot better* • **~ o peor**: • **~ o peor, ya saldremos adelante** for better or (for) worse, we'll come through this • **~ que ~** • **tanto ~** so much the better, all the better; ▹ **nunca**
2 (*superlativo de bien*) best • **¿quién es el que lo hace ~?** who does it best? • **este es el texto ~ redactado de todos** this text is the best written of all
3 (= *preferiblemente*) • **~ quedamos otro día** why don't we meet another day?, it'd be better if we met another day • **~ vámonos** we'd better go • **tú, ~ te callas*** you'd better keep quiet* • **~ me voy*** I'd better go; ▹ **cuanto**
4 • **a lo ~** maybe • **a lo ~ viene mañana** he might come tomorrow, maybe he'll come tomorrow • **a lo ~ hasta nos toca la lotería** we might even win the lottery • —**¿crees que lloverá hoy?** —**a lo ~** "do you think it will rain today?" — "maybe" *o* "it might"
mejora SF **1** (= *progreso*) improvement
2 (= *aumento*) increase • **~s de productividad** increases in productivity
3 mejoras (= *obras*) improvements, alterations
4 (*en subasta*) higher bid
5 (*Méx*) (*Agr*) weeding
mejorable ADJ improvable
mejoramiento SM improvement
mejorana SF marjoram
mejorar ▹ CONJUG 1a VT **1** [+ *servicio, resultados*] to improve; [+ *enfermo*] to make better; (= *realzar*) to enhance; [+ *oferta*] to raise, improve; [+ *récord*] to break; (*Inform*) to upgrade • MODISMO: • **mejorando lo presente** present company excepted
2 • **~ a algn** (= *ser mejor que*) to be better than sb
VI **1** [*situación*] to improve, get better; (*Meteo*) to improve, clear up; (*Econ*) to improve, pick up; [*enfermo*] to get better • **han mejorado de actitud/imagen** their attitude/image has improved • **los negocios mejoran** business is picking up • **está mejorado de sus dolores** the pain has gone away
2 (*en subasta*) to raise one's bid
VPR **mejorarse** to get better, improve • **¡que se mejore!** get well soon!
mejorcito ADJ • **lo ~ del programa** the best thing in the programme • **lo ~ de la clientela** the top customers • **este queso es de lo ~ que hay*** this cheese is the best you can get
mejoría SF improvement • **¡que siga la ~!** I hope the improvement continues
mejunje SM **1** (= *mezcla*) (*gen*) concoction; (= *bebida*) brew
2* (= *fraude*) fraud
3 (*LAm‡*) (= *lío*) mess, mix-up
melado ADJ [*color*] honey-coloured *o* (*EEUU*) -colored
SM treacle, syrup; (*LAm*) [*de caña*] cane syrup
meladura SF (*Caribe, Méx*) cane syrup
melancolía SF melancholy, sadness; (*Med*) melancholia
melancólicamente ADV (= *con tristeza*) sadly, in a melancholy way; (= *soñando*) wistfully
melancólico ADJ (= *triste*) melancholy, sad; (= *soñador*) wistful
melanésico ADJ Melanesian
melanesio/a ADJ, SM/F Melanesian
melanina SF melanin
melanismo SM melanism
melanoma SM melanoma ▸ **melanoma maligno** malignant melanoma
melarchía SF (*CAm*) = **melancolía**
melaza SF treacle, molasses (*pl*) (*EEUU*)
melcocha SF (= *melaza*) treacle, molasses (*pl*) (*EEUU*); (= *azúcar de cande*) candy, molasses toffee
melcochado ADJ [*fruta*] candied; (*de color*) golden, honey-coloured *o* (*EEUU*) -colored
melcocharse ▹ CONJUG 1a VPR to thicken (*in boiling*)
mele* SM bash*, punch
melé SF, **mêlée** [me'le] SF (*Rugby*) scrum; (= *follón*) melee, confusion
melena SF **1** [*de persona*] long hair • **lleva una ~ rubia** she has long blond hair • MODISMOS: • **andar a la ~** to be at daggers drawn • **soltarse la ~** to let one's hair down
2 [*de león*] mane
3 melenas (*pey*) (= *greñas*) mop of hair (*sing*)
melenas* SM INV = **melenudo**
melenudo/a* ADJ long-haired
SM long-haired guy
melga SF (*Cono Sur, Méx*) *plot of land prepared for sowing*
melifluo ADJ sickly-sweet
Melilla SF Melilla
melillense ADJ of/from Melilla
SMF native/inhabitant of Melilla • **los ~s** the people of Melilla
melindre SM **1** (= *bollo*) sweet cake, iced bun; (= *buñuelo*) honey fritter
2 melindres (= *afectación*) affected ways; (= *aprensión*) squeamishness (*sing*); (= *mojigatería*) prudery (*sing*), prudishness (*sing*) • **déjate de ~s y cómelo** don't be so finicky, just eat it • **no me vengas con ~s y elige el que más te guste** stop humming and hawing and choose the one you like best • **gastar ~s** = **melindrear**
melindrear ▹ CONJUG 1a VI (= *ser afectado*) to be affected; (= *ser aprensivo*) to be squeamish; (= *ser mojigato*) to be prudish; (= *ser quisquilloso*) to be finicky, be terribly fussy
melindroso ADJ (= *afectado*) affected;

(= *aprensivo*) squeamish; (= *mojigato*) prudish; (= *quisquilloso*) finicky, fussy
meliorativo (ADJ) ameliorative
melisca (SF) (*Cono Sur*) gleaning
mella (SF) **1** (= *rotura*) nick, notch; (*en dientes*) gap
2 • **MODISMO**: • **hacer ~ en algo/algn** (= *impresión*) to make an impression on sth/sb • **la crisis ha hecho ~ en los bolsillos de los europeos** Europeans are feeling the pinch because of the crisis • **la compra de unos terrenos parece haber hecho ~ en su imagen** the purchase of some land seems to have damaged his image • **la fatiga habrá hecho ~ en los reflejos de muchos corredores** fatigue will have affected the reflexes of many runners
mellado (ADJ) **1** [*filo*] jagged, nicked
2 [*persona*] gap-toothed; (*Cono Sur*) (= *con labio leporino*) hare-lipped
mellar ▹ CONJUG 1a (VT) **1** [+ *cuchillo, filo*] to nick, notch; [+ *diente*] to chip; [+ *madera*] to take a chip out of
2 (= *dañar*) to damage, harm; [+ *afán*] to hold back; [+ *entusiasmo*] to dampen
mellizo/a (ADJ), (SM/F) twin
melo* (SM) = **melodrama**
melocotón (SM) (= *fruto*) peach; (= *árbol*) peach tree
melocotonero (SM) peach tree
melodía (SF) **1** (= *música*) melody, tune; [*de móvil*] ringtone • **una ~ conocida** a familiar tune
2 (= *cualidad*) melodiousness
melódico (ADJ) melodic
melodiosamente (ADV) melodiously, tunefully
melodiosidad (SF) melodiousness
melodioso (ADJ) melodious, tuneful
melodrama (SM) melodrama
melodramáticamente (ADV) melodramatically
melodramático (ADJ) melodramatic
melómano/a (SM/F) music lover
melón¹ (SM) **1** (*Bot*) melon • **REFRÁN**: • **los melones, a cata** the proof of the pudding is in the eating
2* (= *cabeza*) head, nut*, noggin (*EEUU**)
• **estrujarse el ~** to rack one's brains
3* (= *tonto*) twit*, lemon*
4 melones‡ (= *pechos*) melons‡, tits**
melón² (SM) (*Zool*) = **meloncillo**
melonada* (SF) silly thing, stupid remark
melonar (SM) bed of melons, melon plot
meloncillo (SM) (*Zool*) ichneumon, *kind of mongoose*
melopea* (SF) • **coger** *o* **agarrar** *o* **pillar una ~** to get sloshed *o* plastered*
melosidad (SF) **1** (= *dulzura*) sweetness
2 (= *empalago*) [*de persona, voz*] sickly-sweetness; [*de canción, música*] schmaltziness, sickly-sweetness
meloso (ADJ) **1** (= *dulce*) sweet
2 (= *empalagoso*) [*persona, voz*] sickly-sweet; [*canción, música*] schmaltzy, sickly-sweet
membrana (SF) **1** (= *capa*) membrane; (*Orn*) membrane, web ▸ **membrana mucosa** mucous membrane ▸ **membrana virginal** hymen
2 (*Cono Sur*) (*Med*) diphtheria
membranoso (ADJ) membranous
membresía (SF) (*Méx*) membership
membretado (ADJ) • **papel ~** headed notepaper
membrete (SM) letterhead, heading
• **papel con ~** headed notepaper
membrillero (SM) quince tree
membrillo (SM) **1** (= *fruta*) quince • **(carne de) ~** quince jelly
2* (= *tonto*) fool, idiot
3* (= *cobarde*) softie*, coward
4* (= *chivato*) nark*, grass*
membrudo (ADJ) burly, brawny, tough
meme* (SM) meme
memela (SF) (*CAm, Méx*) (= *tortilla*) maize tortilla; (*rellena*) *fried tortilla filled with beans*
memez* (SF) stupid thing • **eso es una ~** that's stupid • **decir memeces** to talk rubbish
memo¹/a* (ADJ) silly, stupid
(SM/F) idiot
memo²* (SM) memo*, memorandum
memorabilia (SF) memorabilia
memorable (ADJ) memorable
memorablemente (ADV) memorably
memorando (SM), **memorándum** (SM) (PL: **memorándums**) **1** (= *nota*) memorandum
2 (= *libreta*) notebook
memoria (SF) **1** (= *facultad*) memory • **lo había olvidado ¡qué ~ la mía!** I'd forgotten, what a terrible memory I have! • **el accidente se le había borrado** *o* **ido de la ~** he had forgotten about the accident, he had erased the accident from his memory • **de ~** [*aprender, saber*] by heart; [*hablar, recitar, tocar*] from memory • **si no me falla la ~** if my memory serves me right, if I remember right(ly) *o* correctly • **falta de ~** (*permanente*) poor memory, forgetfulness; (*repentina*) lapse of memory • **hacer ~** to try to remember • **hacer ~ de algo** to recall sth • **perder la ~** to lose one's memory • **pérdida de ~** loss of memory • **refrescar la ~ a algn** to refresh sb's memory, jog sb's memory • **tener buena/mala/poca ~** to have a good/bad/poor memory • **traer algo a la ~** to bring sth back • **una canción que trae momentos pasados a la ~** a song that brings back the past *o* reminds you of the past • **venir a la ~**: • **¡en este sitio me vienen tantos recuerdos a la ~!** this place brings back so many memories! • **no me viene su número a la ~** her number's slipped my mind, I can't remember her number
• **MODISMO**: • **tener (una) ~ de elefante** to have the memory of an elephant
▸ **memoria asociativa** associative memory
▸ **memoria fotográfica** photographic memory
2 (= *recuerdo*) memory • **ha sido fiel a la ~ de su esposa** he has been faithful to his wife's memory • **fue un discurso digno de ~** it was a speech worth remembering *o* a highly memorable speech • **a la** *o* **en ~ de algn** [*acto, monumento*] in memory of sb • **un homenaje a la ~ de las víctimas de la guerra** a tribute to the memory of *o* in memory of war victims • **hemos guardado un minuto de silencio en su ~** we observed a minute's silence in his memory • **haber** *o* **quedar ~ de algo**: • **la peor tormenta de la que hay ~** the worst storm in living memory • **el único suceso del que me queda ~** the only event I remember *o* of which I have any memory
▸ **memoria colectiva** collective memory
▸ **memoria histórica** historical memory
3 (= *informe*) (*gen*) report; (*Educ*) paper
• **tenemos que presentar una ~ de todas nuestras actividades** we have to present a report on all our activities ▸ **memoria anual** annual report ▸ **memoria de licenciatura** dissertation
4 (= *relación*) record • **una ~ de todos los libros adquiridos** a record of all the books acquired
5 (*Inform*) memory ▸ **memoria auxiliar** backing storage ▸ **memoria burbuja** bubble memory ▸ **memoria central** main memory
▸ **memoria de acceso aleatorio** random access memory, RAM ▸ **memoria del teclado** keyboard memory ▸ **memoria de núcleos** core memory ▸ **memoria de solo lectura** read-only memory, ROM ▸ **memoria externa** external storage ▸ **memoria intermedia** buffer ▸ **memoria interna** internal storage, main memory ▸ **memoria muerta** read-only memory, ROM
▸ **memoria principal** main memory
▸ **memoria programable** programmable read-only memory ▸ **memoria RAM** RAM
▸ **memoria ROM** ROM ▸ **memoria virtual** virtual memory
6 memorias: **a** (*Literat*) (= *autobiografía*) memoirs, records
b† • **dar ~s a algn** to send *o* give one's regards to sb
memorial (SM) (= *escrito*) memorial; (*Jur*) brief
memorialista (SMF) amanuensis
memorión* (ADJ) • **es muy ~** he has an amazing memory
(SM) amazing memory
memorioso (ADJ) • **es muy ~** he has a very good memory
memorista (ADJ) (*esp LAm*) • **es ~** he just memorizes things
memorístico (ADJ) [*concurso*] memory (*antes de s*); [*aprendizaje, educación*] rote (*antes de s*)
• **una prueba memorística** a memory test
• **enseñanza memorística** rote learning, learning by rote
memorización (SF) memorizing
memorizar ▹ CONJUG 1f (VT) to memorize
mena (SF) ore
menaje (SM) **1** (= *muebles*) furniture, furnishings (*pl*)
2 (= *utensilios*) (*tb* **artículos de menaje**) household items (*pl*) • **sección de ~** (*en tienda*) hardware and kitchen department
3 (= *tareas*) housework; (= *economía doméstica*) housekeeping
4 (= *familia*) family, household • **vida de ~** (*LAm*) family life, domestic life ▸ **menaje de tres** ménage à trois
menarquía (SF) menarche
menchevique (ADJ), (SMF) Menshevik
Menchu (SF) *forma familiar de* **Carmen**
mención (SF) mention ▸ **mención honorífica** honourable *o* (*EEUU*) honorable mention • **hacer ~ de algo** to mention sth
mencionado (ADJ) aforementioned
mencionar ▹ CONJUG 1a (VT) to mention • **sin ~** ... not to mention ..., let alone ... • **dejar de ~** to fail to mention
menda* (PRON) (*tb* **mendas**) (= *yo*) yours truly • **lo tuvo que hacer este ~ (lerenda)** yours truly had to do it*, muggins here had to do it* • **el ~ no está de acuerdo** I, for one, don't agree
(SMF) (= *persona*) • **un ~** a bloke*, a guy*
mendacidad (SF) **1** (= *cualidad*) untruthfulness, mendacity (*frm*)
2 (= *mentira*) untruth
mendaz (ADJ) untruthful, mendacious (*frm*)
mendeliano (ADJ) Mendelian
mendelismo (SM) Mendelism, Mendelianism
mendicante (ADJ) **1** (*Rel*) mendicant • **las órdenes ~s** the mendicant orders
2 [*actitud*] begging
(SMF) **1** (*Rel*) mendicant
2 (= *mendigo*) beggar
mendicidad (SF) begging, mendicity (*frm*)
mendigar ▹ CONJUG 1h (VT) to beg for
(VI) to beg
mendigo/a (SM/F) beggar
(ADJ) (*Méx**) (= *cobarde*) yellow*, yellow-bellied*
mendrugo (SM) **1** (= *trozo*) (*tb* **mendrugo de pan**) crust of bread
2* (= *tonto*) dimwit*

m

meneado (ADJ) (*Caribe*) drunk
meneallo • **más vale no ~*** let sleeping dogs lie, the less said the better
menear ▸ CONJUG 1a (VT) **1** [+ *cola*] to wag; [+ *cabeza*] to shake; [+ *líquido*] to stir; [+ *pelo*] to toss; [+ *caderas*] to swing • **sin ~ un dedo** without lifting a finger • **peor es ~lo** it's best not to stir things up • **MODISMO:** • **¡me la menean!**** I don't give a shit!**
2 [+ *asunto*] to get on with, get moving on; [+ *negocio*] to handle, conduct
3 • **~ cálamo** to wield a pen
(VPR) **menearse 1** (*gen*) to shake; [*cola*] to wag; (= *contonearse*) to swing, sway • **yo de aquí no me meneo** I'm staying right here, I'm staying put • **MODISMOS:** • **de no te menees***: • **un vapuleo de no te menees** a good hiding • **una multa de las que no te menees** a hefty fine • **~se** *o* **meneársela**** to wank**
2 (= *apresurarse*) to get a move on • **¡~se!** get going!, jump to it!
Menelao (SM) Menelaus
meneo (SM) **1** [*de cola*] wag; [*de cabeza*] shake, toss; [*de líquido*] stir, stirring; [*de caderas*] swing(ing), sway(ing); (= *sacudida*) jerk, jolt • **dar un ~ a algo** to jerk sth
2* (= *paliza*) hiding*; (= *bronca*) dressing-down*
3 (= *actividad*) = **movida**
menequear ▸ CONJUG 1a (VT) (*Cono Sur, Méx*), **menequetear** ▸ CONJUG 1a (VT) (*Cono Sur, Méx*) to shake, wag
menequeo (SM) (*Cono Sur, Méx*), **menequeteo** (SM) (*Cono Sur, Méx*) shaking, wagging
menester (SM) **1** • **ser ~** (*frm*) (= *ser necesario*): **es ~ hacer algo** we must do something, it is necessary to do something • **cuando sea ~** when necessary • **todo es ~** everything is welcome
2 (= *trabajo*) job; (= *recado*) errand • **salir para un ~** to go out on an errand
3 menesteres (= *deberes*) duties, business (*sing*); (= *ocupación*) occupation (*sing*); (= *función*) function (*sing*) • **no estamos capacitados para esos ~es** we are not trained to do that • **venden un aparatito para esos ~es** you can buy a little machine to do those jobs • **MODISMO:** • **hacer sus ~es** (*euf*) to do one's business
4 menesteres (*Téc*) gear (*sing*), tools
menesteroso/a (ADJ) needy
(SM/F) • **los ~s** the needy
menestra (SF) (*tb* **menestra de verduras**) vegetable stew
menestral (SMF), **menestrala** (SF) skilled worker, artisan
menestrón (SM) (*And*) ≈ minestrone soup
mengano/a (SM/F) Mr/Mrs/Miss so-and-so; ▸ **fulano**
mengua (SF) **1** (= *disminución*) decrease, reduction; (= *decadencia*) decay, decline • **ir en ~ de algo** to be to the detriment of sth • **en ~ de la unidad del partido** to the detriment of party unity • **sin ~** (= *íntegro*) complete, whole; (= *intacto*) intact, untouched • **sin ~ de la relación de compañerismo** without affecting one's relationship as colleagues
2 (= *falta*) lack; (= *pérdida*) loss
3 (= *pobreza*) poverty
4 [*de persona*] (= *debilidad*) spinelessness, weakness of character
5 (= *descrédito*) discredit • **ir en ~ de algn** to be to sb's discredit
menguadamente (ADV)
1 (= *desgraciadamente*) wretchedly; (= *cobardemente*) cravenly (*liter*); (= *sin fuerza*) weakly, spinelessly
2 (= *con tacañería*) meanly
3 (= *estúpidamente*) foolishly
menguado (ADJ) **1** (= *disminuido*) [*ejército, tropas*] depleted; [*esfuerzos*] diminished; [*fuerzas, presupuesto*] reduced • **un hombre de menguada estatura** a diminutive man
2 (= *desgraciado*) wretched, miserable; (= *cobarde*) cowardly, craven (*liter*); (= *débil*) weak, spineless
3 (= *tacaño*) mean
4 (= *tonto*) foolish
5 (= *aciago*) unlucky • **en hora menguada** at an unlucky moment
6 • **medias menguadas** fully-fashioned stockings
(SM) (*en labor de punto*) decrease
menguante (ADJ) (= *que disminuye*) decreasing, diminishing; (= *decadente*) decaying; [*luna*] waning; [*marea*] ebb (*antes de s*)
(SF) **1** (*Náut*) ebb tide
2 [*de luna*] waning; ▸ **cuarto**
3 (= *decadencia*) decay, decline • **estar en ~** to be in decline
menguar ▸ CONJUG 1i (VT) **1** (= *disminuir*) to lessen, reduce; [+ *labor de punto*] to decrease
2 (= *desacreditar*) to discredit
(VI) **1** (= *disminuir*) to decrease, dwindle; [*número, nivel del agua*] to go down; [*marea*] to go out, ebb; [*luna*] to wane
2 (= *decaer*) to wane, decay, decline
mengue* (SM) the devil • **¡malos ~s te lleven!** go to hell!*
menhir (SM) menhir
meninges* (SFPL) • **MODISMO:** • **estrujarse las ~** to rack one's brains
meningitis (SF INV) meningitis
menisco (SM) meniscus
menjunje (SM), **menjurje** (SM) = **mejunje**
menopausia (SF) menopause
menopáusico (ADJ) menopausal
menor (ADJ) **1** (*comparativo*) **a** (*de tamaño*) smaller • **una caja de ~ tamaño** a smaller box • **los libros están ordenados de ~ a mayor** the books are arranged by size, from small to large
b (*de cantidad*) fewer, less • **necesito una cantidad ~ de botellas** I need fewer bottles • **echa sal en ~ cantidad** add less salt • **~ que algo** less than sth • **su aportación es diez veces ~ que la nuestra** his contribution is ten times less than ours • **tres es ~ que siete** three is less than seven
c (*de importancia, tiempo*) • **heridas de ~ importancia** minor injuries • **existe un ~ control en las aduanas** customs controls are not as strict *o* tight as they were • **el crecimiento de la economía es cada vez ~** the economy is growing at an ever slower rate • **viene con ~ frecuencia que antes** she doesn't come as often now • **en ~ grado** to a lesser extent
d (*de edad*) younger • **mis dos hermanos ~es** my two younger brothers • **si eres ~ de 18 años no puedes entrar** if you are under 18 you can't go in • **~ que algn** younger than sb • **soy tres años ~ que mi marido** I am three years younger than my husband • **ser ~ de edad** to be under age; (*Jur*) to be a minor • **dos jóvenes ~es de edad se han escapado de su casa** two under-age youngsters have run away from home
e (*Mús*) minor • **concierto en Mi ~** concerto in E minor
f (*Rel*) [*orden*] minor
2 (*superlativo*) **a** [*de tamaño*] smallest • **es el país de ~ tamaño de Europa** it is the smallest country in Europe • **este es el ~ de todos** this is the smallest of all
b [*de cantidad*] lowest, smallest • **el partido de ~ asistencia de la liga** the match with the lowest *o* smallest attendance in the league • **realizó la vuelta en el ~ número de golpes** he finished the round in the lowest number of shots • **hagan el ~ ruido posible** make as little noise as possible • **se despierta con el ~ ruido** he wakes up at the slightest noise
c [*de importancia, tiempo*] least • **no le doy la ~ importancia** I don't attach the slightest *o* least importance to it • **no tiene la ~ importancia** it is not in the least important • **en el ~ tiempo posible** in the shortest possible time; ▸ **idea**
d [*de edad*] youngest • **este es Miguel, mi hijo ~** this is Miguel, my youngest son
(SMF) (= *niño*) child, minor (*frm*) • **un programa educativo para ~es** an educational programme for children • **los ~es deben ir acompañados** children who are under age *o* minors (*frm*) must be accompanied • **lo detuvieron por vender drogas a ~es** he was arrested for selling drugs to minors • **un ~ de 15 años** a boy of 15 • **un campeonato para ~es de 16 años** a championship for under-16s • **apto/no apto para ~es** suitable/not suitable for (young) children • **"apto para menores acompañados"** (*Cine*) ≈ "certificate PG"
▸ **menor de edad** (*Jur*) minor • **los ~es de edad** those who are under age, minors • **delitos cometidos por ~es de edad** crimes committed by minors; ▸ **tribunal**
(SM) **1** (*Com*) • **(al) por ~** retail (*antes de s*) • **venta (al) por ~** retail sales • **un establecimiento de venta al por ~** a retail establishment
2 (*Esp*) • **contar algo al por ~** to recount sth in detail
Menorca (SF) Minorca
menoría (SF) **1** (*Jur*) minority
2 (= *inferioridad*) inferiority; (= *subordinación*) subordination
menorista (*LAm*) (ADJ) retail (*antes de s*)
(SMF) retailer
menorquín/ina (ADJ), (SM/F) Minorcan
menos (ADV) **1** (*comparativo*) less • **ahora salgo ~** I go out less these days • **últimamente nos vemos ~** we've been seeing less of each other recently • **me gusta cada vez ~** I like it less and less • **una película ~ conocida** a less well-known film • **Juan está ~ deprimido** Juan is less depressed • **es ~ difícil de lo que parece** it's less difficult than it seems • **~ aún** even less • **este me gusta ~ aún** I like this one even less • **~ de** (*con sustantivos incontables, medidas, dinero, tiempo*) less than; (*con sustantivos contables*) fewer than • **está a ~ de tres horas en tren** it's less than three hours away by train • **llegamos en ~ de diez minutos** we got there in less than *o* in under ten minutes • **~ de lo que piensas** less than you think • **tiene ~ de dieciocho años** he's under eighteen • **~ de 50 cajas** fewer than 50 boxes • **en ~ de nada** in no time at all • **por ~ de nada** for no reason at all • **~ que** less than • **me gusta ~ que el otro** I like it less than the other one • **trabaja ~ que yo** he doesn't work as hard as I do • **este es ~ caro que aquel** this one is less expensive than that one • **lo hizo ~ cuidadosamente que ayer** he did it less carefully than yesterday
2 (*superlativo*) least • **su película ~ innovadora** his least innovative film • **es el ~ inteligente de los cuatro** he is the least intelligent of the four • **el chico ~ desobediente de la clase** the least disobedient boy in the class • **es el que habla ~** he's the one who talks (the) least • **fue el que trabajó ~** he was the one who did the least work

m

3 • al ~ at least • **hay al ~ cien personas** there are at least a hundred people • **si al ~ lloviera** if only it would rain • **de ~**: • **hay siete de ~** we're seven short, there are seven missing • **me dieron un paquete con medio kilo de ~** they gave me a packet which was half a kilo short *o* under weight • **me han pagado dos libras de ~** they have underpaid me by two pounds • **darse de ~** to underestimate o.s. • **hacer a algn de ~** to put sb down • **echar de ~ a algn** to miss sb • **ir a ~** to come down in the world • **lo ~ diez** at least ten • **lo ~ posible** as little as possible • **es lo ~ que se puede esperar** it's the least one can expect • **eso es lo de ~** that's the least of it • **¡~ mal!** thank goodness! • **¡~ mal que habéis venido!** thank goodness you've come! • **era nada ~ que un rey** he was a king, no less • **no es para ~** quite right too • **por lo ~** at least • **¡qué ~!**: • **—le di un euro de propina —¡qué ~!** "I tipped her a euro" —"that was the least you could do!" • **¿qué ~ que darle las gracias?** the least we can do is say thanks! • **quedarse en ~**: • **no se quedó en ~** he was not to be outdone • **tener a ~ hacer algo** to consider it beneath o.s. to do sth • **venir a ~** to come down in the world • **y ~**: • **no quiero verle y ~ visitarle** I don't want to see him, let alone visit him • **¡ya será ~!** come off it!; ▸ **cuando, poder**

(ADJ) **1** (*comparativo*) (*con sustantivos incontables, medidas, dinero, tiempo*) less; (*con sustantivos contables*) fewer • **~ harina** less flour • **~ gatos** fewer cats • **aquí hay ~ gente** there are fewer people here • **~ ... que**: • **A tiene ~ ventajas que B** A has fewer advantages than B • **Ana tiene ~ años que Carlos** Ana is younger than Carlos • **no soy ~ hombre que él*** I'm as much of a man as he is • **este es ~ coche que el anterior*** this is not as good a car as the last one • **ser ~ que**: • **ganaremos porque son ~ que nosotros** we'll win because there are fewer of them than there are of us • **para no ser ~ que los vecinos** to keep up with the neighbours

2 (*superlativo*) (*con sustantivos incontables, medidas, dinero, tiempo*) least; (*con sustantivos contables*) fewest • **el método que lleva ~ tiempo** the method which takes (the) least time • **es el que ~ culpa tiene** he is the least to blame • **el examen con ~ errores** the exam paper with the fewest mistakes

(PREP) **1** (= *excepto*) except • **todos ~ él** everybody except him • **¡todo ~ eso!** anything but that!

2 (*Mat*) (*para restar*) minus, less • **cinco ~ dos** five minus *o* less two • **siete ~ dos (son) cinco** seven minus two is five • **son las siete ~ veinte** it's twenty to seven

(CONJ) • **a ~ que** unless • **no iré a ~ que me acompañes** I won't go unless you come with me

(SM) **1** (*Mat*) minus sign

2 • los ~ the minority

3 ▸ **más**

menoscabar ▸ CONJUG 1a (VT) **1** (= *disminuir*) to lessen, reduce; (= *dañar*) to damage

2 (= *desacreditar*) to discredit

menoscabo (SM) (= *disminución*) lessening, reduction; (= *daño*) damage • **con** *o* **en ~ de** to the detriment of • **reducción de jornada sin ~ salarial** reduction in the working day with no loss of salary • **debe haber cierta reserva, sin ~ de la amistad** certain things must remain in confidence, without being detrimental to one's friendship • **sufrir ~** to be damaged

menospreciable (ADJ) contemptible

menospreciador (ADJ) scornful, contemptuous

menospreciar ▸ CONJUG 1b (VT)

1 (= *despreciar*) to scorn, despise

2 (= *ofender*) to slight

3 (= *subestimar*) to underrate, underestimate

menospreciativo (ADJ) (= *despreciativo*) scornful, contemptuous; (= *ofensivo*) slighting

menosprecio (SM) **1** (= *desdén*) scorn, contempt

2 (= *subestimación*) underrating, underestimation

3 (= *falta de respeto*) disrespect • **con ~ del sexo de la víctima** without regard for the sex of the victim

mensáfono (SM) bleeper, pager

mensaje (SM) (*gen*) message; (*por móvil**) text (message) • **un ~ de apoyo** a message of support ▸ **mensaje de buenos augurios** goodwill message ▸ **mensaje de error** (*Inform*) error message ▸ **mensaje de la corona** (*Parl*) Queen's/King's speech ▸ **mensaje de texto** text message • **envío de ~s de texto** text messaging • **enviar ~s de texto/un ~ de texto a algn** to text sb ▸ **mensaje instantáneo** instant message ▸ **mensaje subliminal** subliminal message

mensajería (SF) **1** [*de paquetes*] (= *servicio*) courier service; (= *empresa*) courier firm

2 [*de avisos*] messaging service ▸ **mensajería electrónica** electronic messaging, electronic message handling

mensajero/a (SM/F) **1** (*para empresa de mensajería*) courier

2 (= *recadero*) messenger

menso* (ADJ) (*Chile, Méx*) silly, stupid

menstruación (SF) menstruation

menstrual (ADJ) menstrual • **dolores ~es** period pains

menstruar ▸ CONJUG 1e (VI) to menstruate

menstruo (SM) **1** (= *menstruación*) menstruation

2 (= *sangre*) menses (*pl*)

mensual (ADJ) monthly • **50 dólares ~es** 50 dollars a month

mensualidad (SF) (= *salario*) monthly salary; (= *plazo*) monthly instalment *o* (*EEUU*) installment, monthly payment • **se puede pagar en diez ~es** payment can be made in ten monthly instalments

mensualmente (ADV) monthly

mensuario (SM) (*LAm*) monthly (magazine)

ménsula (SF) (= *repisa*) bracket; (*Arquit*) corbel

mensura (SF) measurement

mensurable (ADJ) measurable

mensuración (SF) mensuration

menta¹ (SF) mint • **un caramelo de ~** a mint sweet ▸ **menta romana, menta verde** spearmint

menta² (SF) **1** (*Arg**) (= *fama*) reputation

2 mentas (*Chile**) (= *chismes*) rumours, rumors (*EEUU*), gossip (*sing*)

mentada (SF) (*Méx*) serious insult • **hacerle a algn una ~** to seriously insult sb

mentado (ADJ) **1** (= *mencionado*) aforementioned

2 (= *famoso*) well-known, famous

mental (ADJ) [*esfuerzo, salud*] mental; [*capacidad, trabajo*] intellectual

mentalidad (SF) mentality • **tiene ~ de criminal** he has a criminal mentality • **tienes (una) ~ de un niño de tres años** you've got the mentality of a three-year old • **tiene una ~ muy abierta** he is very open-minded, he's got a very open outlook

mentalización (SF) **1** (= *preparación*) mental preparation • **la importancia de la ~ de los jugadores en la victoria** the importance of players' mental preparation to achieving victory

2 (= *concienciación*) • **la ~ de la opinión pública respecto al problema del paro** the raising of public awareness about the problem of unemployment • **campañas de ~ contra la bebida** campaigns to raise awareness of the risks of drinking

3 (= *persuasión*) persuasion; (*pey*) brainwashing

mentalizado (ADJ) • **están ~s para imponerse a cualquier dificultad** they are mentally prepared to overcome any problem • **el equipo salió ~ para el triunfo** the team went out with their minds set on victory

mentalizar ▸ CONJUG 1f (VT) **1** (= *preparar*) to prepare mentally

2 (= *concienciar*) to make aware

3 (= *persuadir*) to persuade, convince; (*pey*) to brainwash

(VPR) **mentalizarse 1** (= *prepararse*) to prepare o.s. mentally • **me había mentalizado para lo peor** I had prepared myself for the worst

2 (= *concienciarse*) to become aware (**de** of)

mentalmente (ADV) mentally

mentar ▸ CONJUG 1j (VT) to mention • **~ la madre a algn** (*esp Méx*) to insult sb seriously

mentas* (SFPL) (*And, Cono Sur*) **1** (= *reputación*) good name (*sing*), reputation (*sing*) • **una persona de buenas ~** a highly-regarded *o* well-respected person

2 (= *chismes*) rumours, rumors (*EEUU*), gossip (*sing*)

mente (SF) **1** (= *pensamiento*) mind • **tiene una ~ analítica** he's got an analytical mind • **irse algo de la ~**: • **se le fue completa~ de la ~** it completely slipped his mind • **quitarse algo de la ~**: • **no me lo puedo quitar de la ~** I can't get it out of my mind • **tener en ~ hacer algo** to be thinking of doing sth • **tiene en ~ cambiar de empleo** he's thinking of changing jobs • **traer a la ~** to call to mind • **venir a la ~** to come to mind ▸ **mente consciente** conscious mind ▸ **mente subconsciente** subconscious mind

2 (= *mentalidad*) • **tiene una ~ muy abierta** she's very open-minded, she's got a very open outlook

3 (= *intelectual*) mind • **una de las grandes ~s de nuestro tiempo** one of the great minds of our time

mentecatería (SF), **mentecatez** (SF) stupidity, foolishness

mentecato/a (ADJ) silly, stupid

(SM/F) idiot, fool

mentidero (SM) gossip shop*

mentir ▸ CONJUG 3i (VI) to lie • **nos mintió** he lied to us • **miente quien diga que hubo un acuerdo** whoever says there was an agreement is lying • **~ no está bien** it's wrong to tell lies • **no he mentido en mi vida** I've never told a lie in all my life • **¡miento!** sorry!, I'm wrong!, my mistake! • **¡esta carta no me dejará ~!** this letter will bear me out *o* confirm what I say

mentira (SF) **1** (= *embuste*) lie • **¡mentira!** it's a lie! • **no digas ~s** don't tell lies • **sus ~s le causaron problemas** his lying got him into trouble • **coger a algn en una ~** to catch sb in a lie • **de ~**: • **una pistola de ~** a toy pistol • **parecer ~**: • **aunque parezca ~** however incredible it seems, strange though it may seem • **¡parece ~!** it's unbelievable!, I can't *o* don't believe it! • **parece ~ que no te acuerdes** I can't believe that you don't remember • MODISMOS: • **una ~ como una casa** *o* **como una catedral** *o* **un templo** a whopping great lie* • **la ~ tiene las patas cortas** • **no hay ~ que no salga** truth will out

m

▸ **mentira caritativa, mentira oficiosa** (*Cono Sur*), **mentira piadosa, mentira reverenda** (*Cono Sur*) white lie
2 (*en uñas*) white mark (*on fingernail*)
3 (= *errata*) erratum
mentirijillas* SFPL • **es** *o* **va de ~** it's only a joke; (*a niño*) it's only pretend *o* make-believe • **lloraba de ~** she was pretending to cry • **jugar de ~** to play for fun (*ie not for money*)
mentirilla SF fib*, white lie
mentirosillo/a SM/F fibber*
mentiroso/a ADJ **1** (= *que miente*) lying • **¡es tan ~!** he's such a liar! • **¡mentiroso!** you liar!
2 [*texto*] full of errors, full of misprints
SM/F (= *que miente*) liar • **~ profesional** compulsive liar
mentís SM INV denial • **dar el ~ a algo** to refute sth, deny sth
mentol SM menthol
mentolado ADJ mentholated
mentolatum* SM • **ser un ~** (*Cono Sur*) to be a jack of all trades
mentón SM chin ▸ **doble mentón** double chin
mentor SM mentor
menú SM **1** [*de comida*] menu ▸ **menú de la casa** main menu, standard menu ▸ **menú del día** (*Esp*) set meal
2 (*Inform*) menu • **guiado por ~** (*Inform*) menu-driven ▸ **menú desplegable** pull-down menu, drop-down menu
menudear ▹ CONJUG 1a VI **1** (= *ser frecuente*) to be frequent, happen frequently; [*misiles, insultos*] to come thick and fast • **en la campaña menudean las acusaciones** accusations are flying thick and fast in the campaign • **un texto en el que menudean las erratas** a text full of mistakes
2 (*al explicarse*) to go into great detail
3 (*Cono Sur, Méx*) (= *abundar*) to abound; (= *proliferar*) to increase, grow in number
VT **1** (= *repetir*) to repeat frequently, do repeatedly • **menudea sus visitas** he often comes to visit
2 (*LAm*) (= *vender*) to sell retail
menudencia SF **1** (= *bagatela*) trifle, small thing • **~s** odds and ends
2 (= *minuciosidad*) minuteness; (= *exactitud*) exactness; (= *meticulosidad*) meticulousness
3 menudencias (*Culin*) [*de cerdo*] offal (*sing*); (= *menudillos*) [*de ave*] giblets
menudeo SM (*Com*) retail trade • **vender al ~** to sell retail
menudez SF smallness, minuteness
menudillos SMPL giblets
menudo ADJ **1** (= *pequeño*) small, minute; [*persona*] diminutive, slight; (*fig*) slight, insignificant • **moneda menuda** small change • **la gente menuda** the little ones, kids* • MODISMOS: • **a la menuda** • **por la menuda** (*Com*) retail • **contar algo por ~** to tell sth in detail
2 (*uso admirativo*) • **¡~ lío!** what a mess! • **¡menuda plancha!** what a boob!* • **¡menuda vidorra nos vamos a dar!** we won't half live it up!* • **¡menuda me la han hecho!** they've really gone and pulled a fast one on me!* • **¡~ viento hizo anoche!** it wasn't half windy last night!*
3 (= *minucioso*) exact, meticulous
ADV • **a ~** often
SM **1** (= *dinero*) small change
2 menudos (*Culin*) offal (*sing*); [*de ave*] giblets; (*Méx*) (= *guisado*) tripe stew (*sing*)
meñique SM (*tb* **dedo meñique**) little finger
meódromo‡ SM bog‡, loo*, john (*EEUU‡*)
meollo SM **1** (*Anat*) marrow
2 [*de asunto*] heart, crux • **el ~ de la cuestión** the heart *o* crux of the matter
3 [*de persona*] brains (*pl*) • **estrujarse el ~** to rack one's brains
4 [*de pan*] crumb, soft part
meón/ona* ADJ • **es muy ~** [*niño*] he's always wetting himself; [*adulto*] he's got a weak bladder
SM/F **1** • **este niño es un ~** this boy's always wetting himself
2 (= *bebé*) baby, baby boy/baby girl
meos‡ SMPL piss** (*sing*)
meque* SM (*Caribe*) rap
mequetrefe SMF (= *inútil*) good-for-nothing; (= *curiosón*) busybody
meramente ADV merely, only
merca SF (*Méx*) (= *compra*) shopping, purchases (*pl*); (*Cono Sur*) (= *contrabando*) contraband goods (*pl*)
mercachifle SM **1** (*pey*) (= *comerciante*) small-time trader; (= *vendedor ambulante*) hawker, huckster
2 (= *avaricioso*) money grabber
mercadear ▹ CONJUG 1a VT (= *vender*) to market; (= *regatear*) to haggle over
VI to deal, trade
mercadeo SM marketing
mercader SM (*esp Hist*) merchant
mercadería SF merchandise • **~s** goods, merchandise (*sing*)
mercadillo SM street market; (*benéfico*) (charity) bazaar
mercado SM market • **inundar el ~ de algo** to flood the market with sth • **salir al ~** to come on to the market ▸ **mercado bursátil** stock market ▸ **mercado cambiario** foreign exchange market ▸ **mercado cautivo** captive market ▸ **Mercado Común** Common Market ▸ **mercado de compradores** buyer's market ▸ **mercado de demanda** seller's market ▸ **mercado de dinero** money market ▸ **mercado de divisas** currency market, foreign exchange market ▸ **mercado de futuros** futures market ▸ **mercado de la vivienda** housing market ▸ **mercado de oferta** buyer's market ▸ **mercado de productos básicos** commodity market ▸ **mercado de signo favorable al comprador** buyer's market ▸ **mercado de signo favorable al vendedor** seller's market ▸ **mercado de trabajo** labour (*EEUU*) labor market ▸ **mercado de valores** stock market ▸ **mercado de vendedores** seller's market ▸ **mercado de viejo** flea market ▸ **mercado en alza** bull market ▸ **mercado en baja** bear market ▸ **mercado exterior** foreign market, overseas market ▸ **mercado inmobiliario** property market ▸ **mercado interior** domestic market ▸ **mercado laboral** labour *o* (*EEUU*) labor market ▸ **mercado libre** free market (**de** in) ▸ **mercado mundial** world market ▸ **mercado nacional** domestic market ▸ **mercado negro** black market ▸ **mercado objetivo** target market ▸ **mercado persa** (*Cono Sur*) cut-price store ▸ **mercado único** single market
mercadológico ADJ market (*antes de s*), marketing (*antes de s*)
mercadotecnia SF marketing • **estudios de ~** market research
mercadotécnico ADJ marketing (*antes de s*)
mercancía SF merchandise • **~s** goods, merchandise (*sing*) ▸ **mercancías en depósito** bonded goods ▸ **mercancías de general** (*Náut*) general cargo (*sing*) ▸ **mercancías perecederas** perishable goods
SM INV **mercancías** goods train (*sing*), freight train (*sing*) (*EEUU*)
mercante ADJ merchant (*antes de s*); ▹ **buque, marina**
SM merchantman, merchant ship
mercantil ADJ (*gen*) mercantile, commercial; [*derecho*] commercial; ▹ **registro, sociedad**
mercantilismo SM mercantilism
mercantilización SF commercialization • **la ~ de la cultura** the commercialization of culture
mercantilizar ▹ CONJUG 1f VT to commercialize
mercar†† ▹ CONJUG 1g VT to buy
VPR **mercarse** • **~se algo** to get sth
merced SF **1†** (= *favor*) favour, favor (*EEUU*) • **hacer a algn la ~ de hacer algo** to do sb the favour of doing sth • **tenga la ~ de hacerlo** please be so good as to do it
2 • **merced a** thanks to
3 • **estar a la ~ de algo/algn** to be at the mercy of sth/sb • **el barco quedó a la ~ de los vientos** the boat was left to the mercy of the winds
4 (*antaño*) • **vuestra ~** your worship, sir
mercedario/a ADJ, SM/F Mercedarian
mercenario ADJ mercenary
SM (*Mil*) mercenary; (*Agr*) day labourer; (*pey*) (= *asalariado*) hireling
mercería SF **1** (= *artículos*) haberdashery, notions (*pl*) (*EEUU*)
2 (= *tienda*) haberdasher's (shop), notions store (*EEUU*); (*Caribe, Méx*) (= *lencería*) draper's (shop), dry-goods store (*EEUU*); (*Cono Sur*) (= *ferretería*) ironmonger's, hardware store
mercero/a SM/F haberdasher, notions dealer (*EEUU*); (*And, Caribe, Méx*) draper
Merche SF *forma familiar de* **Mercedes**
merchero/a* SM/F petty criminal, delinquent
Mercosur SM ABR (= **Mercado Común del Cono Sur**) *Argentina, Brazil, Paraguay and Uruguay*
mercromina® SF Mercurochrome®
mercurial ADJ mercurial
Mercurio SM Mercury
mercurio SM mercury
mercurocromo SM Mercurochrome®
merdoso‡ ADJ filthy
merecedor ADJ deserving, worthy (**de** of) • **es ~ de aplauso** it is to be applauded • **~ de confianza** trustworthy • **~ de crédito** solvent • **hacerse ~ de algo** to earn sth • **ser ~ de algo** to deserve sth, be deserving of sth
merecer ▹ CONJUG 2d VT **1** [+ *recompensa, castigo*] to deserve • **~ hacer algo** to deserve to do sth • **merece (que se le dé) el premio** he deserves (to receive) the prize • **no merece sino elogios** she deserves nothing but praise • **el trato que él nos merece** the treatment he deserves from us • **merece la pena** it's worth it • **no merece la pena discutir** it's not worth arguing
2 (*And*) (= *atrapar*) to catch; (= *robar*) to snatch, pinch*; (= *encontrar*) to find
VI to be deserving, be worthy • **~ mucho** to be very deserving
VPR **merecerse** • **~se algo** to deserve sth • **te mereces el premio** you deserve the prize • **tienes unos hijos que no te los mereces** you don't deserve your children • **te mereces eso y más** you deserve that and more • **se lo mereció** he deserved it, he got what he deserved • **se lo merece por tonto** (it) serves him right for being so stupid
merecidamente ADV deservedly
merecido ADJ [*premio, descanso*] well-deserved • **bien ~ lo tiene** it serves him right
SM just deserts (*pl*) • **llevarse su ~** to get one's just deserts
merecimiento SM **1** (= *lo merecido*) just deserts (*pl*)

2 (= *mérito*) merit, worthiness • **perdimos con todo ~** we deserved to lose • **lo logró sin ningún ~** she didn't deserve to achieve it • **otra persona de mayor ~** another more deserving person

merendar* ▷ CONJUG 1j VI to have an afternoon snack, have tea; (*en el campo*) to have a picnic
VT **1** (= *comer*) to have as an afternoon snack, have for tea
2 (= *mirar*) • **~ lo que escribe otro** to look at what somebody else is writing • **~ las cartas de otro** to peep at sb else's cards
VPR **merendarse 1** • **~se a algn** [+ *adversario*] to thrash sb*, walk all over sb*; (*LAm*) (= *matar*) to bump sb off*; (*And*) (= *pegar*) to beat sb up*; (*Cono Sur*) (= *estafar*) to fleece sb*
2 (= *acabar con*) [+ *libro*] to devour; [+ *país, territorio*] to take over
3 • **~se una fortuna** to squander a fortune

merendero SM (= *café*) open-air café, snack bar; (*en el campo*) picnic area; (*Méx*) (= *restaurán*) café, lunch counter

merendola* SF (= *fiesta*) tea party; (*campestre*) picnic

merengar‡ ▷ CONJUG 1h VT to upset, annoy

merengue ADJ* of/relating to Real Madrid F.C.
SM **1** (*Culin*) meringue
2 (= *persona*) (= *blandengue*) wimp*, weed*; (*LAm*) (= *enfermizo*) sickly person
3 (*And, Caribe*) (= *baile*) merengue
4 (*Cono Sur**) (= *alboroto*) row, fuss
5 • **los ~s*** Real Madrid F.C.

meretriz SF prostitute

mergo SM cormorant

meridiana SF **1** (= *diván*) divan, couch; (= *cama*) day bed
2 • **a la ~** at noon

meridianamente ADV clearly, with complete clarity • **eso queda ~ claro** that is crystal clear

meridiano ADJ **1** [*calor*] midday (*antes de s*) • **la hora meridiana** noon
2 [*luz*] very bright
3 [*hecho*] clear as day, crystal-clear • **lo veo con claridad meridiana** I can see it perfectly clearly • **sus razones eran claras y meridianas** her reasons were crystal-clear
SM (*Astron, Geog*) meridian

meridional ADJ southern
SMF southerner

merienda SF tea, afternoon snack; [*de viaje*] packed meal; (*en el campo*) picnic; (*And*) supper • **ir de ~** to go for a picnic • MODISMO: • **juntar ~s** to join forces, pool one's resources ▸ **merienda cena** high tea, early evening meal ▸ **merienda de negros*** (= *confusión*) bedlam, free-for-all; (= *chanchullo*) crooked deal

merino/a ADJ merino
SM/F (= *oveja*) merino (sheep)
SM (= *lana*) merino wool

mérito SM **1** (= *valor*) merit, worth • **de ~** of merit, worthy • **una obra de gran ~ artístico** a work of great artistic merit • **restar ~ de algo** to detract from sth • **tener ~: eso tiene mucho ~** that's very commendable • **el chico tiene mucho ~** he's a worthy lad • **la han ascendido por ~s** she was promoted on merit • **alega los siguientes ~s** he quotes the following facts in support • **"serán ~s los idiomas"** (*en anuncio*) "languages an advantage" • MODISMO: • **hacer ~s** to strive for recognition • **hizo ~s suficientes para merecer el honor** he had done enough to deserve the honour ▸ **méritos de guerra** mention in dispatches (*sing*)
2 (= *mención*) • **hacer ~ de algo** to mention sth

meritocracia SF meritocracy

meritócrata SMF meritocrat

meritoriaje SM actor's apprenticeship

meritorio/a ADJ (= *de mérito*) meritorious (*frm*), worthy; (= *merecedor*) deserving • **~ de alabanza** praiseworthy • **hizo una meritoria labor en beneficio de la infancia** her work in aid of children was commendable • **su meritoria actuación del domingo** his commendable performance on Sunday • **consiguió una meritoria sexta posición** he came a well-deserved sixth
SM/F unpaid trainee

merla SF = mirlo

merlan SM whiting

merlango SM haddock

Merlín SM Merlin • MODISMO: • **saber más que ~** to know all there is to know

merlo¹ SM (= *pez*) black wrasse

merlo²* SM (*LAm*) (= *persona*) idiot

merlucera SF *type of fishing boat, used especially for fishing hake*

merluza SF **1** (= *pez*) hake
2* (= *borrachera*) • **coger una ~** to get sozzled* • **estar con la ~*** to be sozzled*

merluzo/a* ADJ silly, stupid
SM/F idiot

merma SF (= *disminución*) [*de interés, ganancia*] decrease; (*al secarse*) shrinkage; (= *pérdida*) loss • **sin ~ de calidad** without loss of quality, without compromising on quality • **para que su honor no sufra ~** so that his honour is not diminished

mermar ▷ CONJUG 1a VT (= *disminuir*) [+ *crecimiento, capacidad*] to reduce; [+ *autoridad, prestigio*] to undermine; [+ *reservas*] to deplete; [+ *pago, raciones*] to cut
VI, VPR **mermarse** (= *disminuir*) to decrease, dwindle; [*reservas*] to become depleted; [*líquido*] to go down; [*carne*] to shrink

mermelada SF jam ▸ **mermelada de albaricoques** apricot jam ▸ **mermelada de naranja** marmalade

mero¹ ADJ **1** (= *simple*) mere, simple • **el ~ hecho de ...** the mere *o* simple fact of ... • **les detuvieron por el ~ hecho de protestar** they were arrested merely *o* simply for protesting • **soy un ~ espectador** I'm only *o* just a spectator • **es algo más que un ~ producto de consumo** it is more than just a consumer product, it is more than a mere consumer product • **fue una mera casualidad** it was pure coincidence
2 (*Méx*) (= *exacto*) precise, exact • **a la mera hora** (*lit*) right on time; (*fig**) when it comes down to it*
3 (*Méx*) (= *justo*) right • **en el momento ~** at the right moment
4 (*Méx*) (= *mismo*) • **el ~ centro** the very centre • **la mera verdad** the plain truth • **el ~ Pedro** Pedro himself • **en la mera calle** right there on the street • **en la mera esquina** right on the corner • **tu ~ papá** your own father
ADV **1** (*CAm, Méx*) (= *justo*) right, just • **aquí ~** (= *exacto*) right here, just here; (= *cerca*) near here • **¡eso ~!** right!, you've got it!
2 (*CAm, Méx*) • **ahora ~** (= *ahora mismo*) right now; (= *pronto*) in a minute • **¡ya ~!*** just coming! • **ya ~ llega** he'll be here any minute now • **él va ~ adelante** he's just ahead
3 (*CAm*) (= *de verdad*) really, truly
4 (*Méx*) (= *muy*) very
5 (*Méx*) (= *hace poco*) just • **ahora ~ llegó** he's just got here
6 (*And*) (= *solo*) only
SM • **el ~ ~** (*Méx**) the boss*

mero² SM (*Pesca*) grouper

merodeador(a) ADJ prowling; [*pandilla, tropas*] marauding
SM/F prowler

merodear ▷ CONJUG 1a VI **1** (= *rondar*) to prowl (about); [*pandillas, tropas*] to maraud • **vio a un hombre merodeando entre los coches** she saw a man prowling around among the cars
2 (*Méx*) to make money by illicit means

merodeo SM (= *acecho*) prowling; [*de pandillas, tropas*] marauding

merolico* SM (*Méx*) (= *curandero*) quack*; (= *vendedor*) street salesman

merovingio/a ADJ, SM/F Merovingian

mersa* (*Arg*), **merza*** (*Arg*) ADJ INV (= *de mal gusto*) common, naff*; (= *ostentoso*) flashy
SMF INV common person
SF (= *hampa*) mob, gang

mes SM **1** month • **al mes llegó él** he came a month later • **50 dólares al mes** 50 dollars a month • **el mes corriente** this month • **el mes que viene** • **el mes próximo** next month ▸ **mes lunar** lunar month
2 (= *sueldo*) month's pay; (= *renta*) month's rent; (= *pago*) monthly payment • **facilidades de pago 36 meses** 36 months credit available
3 (*Med**) • **estar con** *o* **tener el mes** to have one's period

mesa SF **1** table; [*de despacho*] desk • **¡a la ~!** dinner's ready! • **bendecir la ~** to say grace • **de ~:** • **vino de ~** table wine • **poner la ~** to lay the table • **recoger la ~** • **quitar la ~** to clear the table • **sentarse a la ~** to sit down to table • **servir la ~** to wait at table • MODISMO: • **estar sobre la ~** [*asunto*] to be on the table, be under consideration *o* discussion ▸ **mesa auxiliar** side table, occasional table ▸ **mesa de alas abatibles** gate-leg(ged) table ▸ **mesa de billar** billiard table ▸ **mesa de café, mesa de centro** coffee table ▸ **mesa de comedor** dining table ▸ **mesa de despacho** office desk ▸ **mesa de juntas** conference table ▸ **mesa de mezclas** mixer, mixing desk ▸ **mesa de negociación** negotiating table ▸ **mesa de noche** bedside table, night stand *o* table (EEUU) ▸ **mesa de operaciones** operating table ▸ **mesa de tijera** folding table ▸ **mesa de trabajo** desk ▸ **mesa(s) nido** nest of tables ▸ **mesa operatoria** operating table ▸ **mesa ratona** (*Cono Sur*) coffee table ▸ **mesa redonda** (*Pol*) (= *discusión*) round table; (= *conferencia*) round-table conference; (*Hist*) Round Table
2 (= *personas*) (= *comité*) committee; [*de empresa*] board; (*en mitin*) platform ▸ **Mesa de la Cámara, Mesa del Parlamento** parliamentary assembly ▸ **mesa electoral** *officials in charge of a polling station* ▸ **Mesa Nacional** National Committee
3 (= *pensión*) board • **~ y cama** bed and board • **tener a algn a ~ y mantel** to give sb free board
4 (*Geog*) (= *meseta*) tableland, plateau
5 (*Arquit*) landing
6 [*de herramienta*] side, flat

mesada SF **1** (= *dinero*) monthly payment
2 (*Arg*) worktop

mesana SF mizzen

mesarse ▷ CONJUG 1a VPR • **~ el pelo** *o* **los cabellos** to tear one's hair (out) • **~ la barba** to pull one's beard

mescalina SF mescaline

mescolanza SF = mezcolanza

mesenterio SM mesentery

mesero/a SM/F (*Méx*) waiter/waitress

meseta SF **1** (*Geog*) tableland, plateau
2 (*Arquit*) landing

mesetario ADJ (*Esp*) (= *de la meseta*) of/from the Castilian meseta; (= *castellano*) Castilian

mesiánico ADJ messianic

Mesías SM INV Messiah

mesilla SF **1** *(pequeña)* small table; *(auxiliar)* side table, occasional table ▸ **mesilla de noche** bedside table, night stand *o* *(EEUU)* table ▸ **mesilla de ruedas** trolley, cart *(EEUU)* ▸ **mesilla plegable** folding table
2 *(Caribe)* market stall
mesmeriano ADJ mesmeric
mesmerismo SM mesmerism
mesmerizante ADJ mesmerizing
mesmerizar ▹ CONJUG 1f VT to mesmerize
mesnada SF **1** *(Hist)* armed retinue
2 mesnadas (= *partidarios*) followers, supporters • **las ~s del orden** the forces of order
Mesoamérica SF Middle America *(Mexico, Central America and the West Indies)*
mesoamericano/a ADJ, SM/F Middle American
mesolítico ADJ Mesolithic
SM • **el ~** the Mesolithic
mesolito SM mesolith
mesomorfo SM mesomorph
mesón¹ SM **1** *(Hist)* inn; *(moderno) restaurant and bar with period décor*, olde worlde inn
2 *(CAm)* (= *pensión*) lodging house, rooming house *(EEUU)*
3 *(Chile, Ven)* (= *mostrador*) counter
4 *(Cono Sur)* (= *mesa grande*) large table
mesón² SM *(Fís)* meson
mesonero/a SM/F **1**†† innkeeper
2 *(en bar)* landlord/landlady
3 *(Caribe)* waiter/waitress
mesozoico ADJ Mesozoic
SM • **el ~** the Mesozoic, the Mesozoic era
mesteño *(Méx)* ADJ *[caballo]* wild, untamed
SM mustang
mestizaje SM **1** (= *cruce*) crossbreeding, miscegenation *(frm)*
2 (= *grupo de mestizos*) mestizos *(pl)*, half-castes *(pey) (pl)*
mestizar ▹ CONJUG 1f VT *[+ raza]* to crossbreed; *[+ razas]* to mix *(by crossbreeding)*
mestizo/a ADJ *[persona]* mixed-race; *[sociedad]* racially mixed; *[raza]* mixed; *[animal]* crossbred, mongrel *(pey)*; *[planta]* hybrid
SM/F (= *persona*) mestizo, half-caste *(pey)*; (= *animal*) crossbreed, mongrel *(pey)*; (= *planta*) hybrid
mesura SF **1** (= *moderación*) moderation, restraint • **con ~** in moderation • **gastan dinero sin ~** they spend money like water
2 (= *calma*) calm
mesurado ADJ **1** (= *moderado*) moderate, restrained • **estilo ~** restrained style • **precios ~s** reasonable prices
2 (= *tranquilo*) calm
mesurar ▹ CONJUG 1a VT **1** (= *contener*) to restrain
2 *(Ecu)* (= *medir*) to measure
VPR **mesurarse** to restrain o.s., act with restraint
meta SF **1** *(Ftbl)* goal; *(en hípica)* winning post; *(Atletismo)* finishing line • **chutar a ~** to shoot at goal • **entrar en** *o* **pasar por ~** to cross the finishing line ▸ **meta volante** *(en ciclismo)* bonus sprint
2 (= *objetivo*) goal, aim • **¿cuál es tu ~ en la vida?** what is your goal *o* aim in life? • **fijarse una ~** to set o.s. a goal
SMF (= *portero*) (goal)keeper
meta... PREF meta...
metabólico ADJ metabolic
metabolismo SM metabolism
metabolizador ADJ metabolizing
metabolizar ▹ CONJUG 1f VT to metabolize
metacarpiano SM metacarpal
metacrilato SM methacrylate
metadona SF methadone
metafísica SF metaphysics *(sing)*
metafísico/a ADJ metaphysical
SM/F metaphysician
metáfora SF metaphor
metafóricamente ADV metaphorically
metafórico ADJ metaphoric(al)
metal SM **1** (= *material*) metal; *(Mús)* brass • **el vil ~** filthy lucre ▸ **metal en láminas, metal laminado** sheet metal ▸ **metal noble** precious metal ▸ **metal pesado** heavy metal
2 *[de voz]* timbre
metalenguaje SM metalanguage
metalero ADJ *(And, Cono Sur)* metal *(antes de s)*
metálico ADJ *[objeto]* metal *(antes de s)*; *[color, sonido, brillo]* metallic • **un Cadillac azul ~** a metallic blue Cadillac
SM (= *dinero*) cash; (= *moneda*) coin; *(en barras)* specie, bullion • **pagar en ~** to pay (in) cash • **premio en ~** cash prize
metalingüístico ADJ metalinguistic
metalista SMF metalworker
metalistería SF metalwork
metaliteratura SF metaliterature
metalizado ADJ **1** *[pintura]* metallic
2 (= *materialista*) mercenary, only interested in making money • **el mundo actual está ~** the modern world revolves around money
metalizar ▹ CONJUG 1f VT *[+ material]* to metallize
VPR **metalizarse 1** *[persona]* to become mercenary
2 *[material]* to become metallized
metalmecánico ADJ • **industria metalmecánica** *(Cono Sur)* metallurgical industry
metalurgia SF metallurgy
metalúrgico/a ADJ metallurgic(al) • **industria metalúrgica** engineering industry
SM/F (= *trabajador*) metalworker; (= *científico*) metallurgist
metamórfico ADJ metamorphic
metamorfosear ▹ CONJUG 1a VT to metamorphose *(frm)*, transform (**en** into)
VPR **metamorfosearse** to be metamorphosed *(frm)*, be transformed
metamorfosis SF INV metamorphosis *(frm)*, transformation
metanfetamina SF methylamphetamine
metano SM methane
metástasis SF INV metastasis
metastatizar ▹ CONJUG 1f VI, **metastizar** ▹ CONJUG 1f VI to metastasize
metatarsiano SM metatarsal
metate SM *(CAm, Méx)* flat stone for grinding
metátesis SF INV metathesis
metedor¹ SM *[de bebé]* nappy liner
metedor²(a)†† SM/F (= *contrabandista*) smuggler
metedura SF ▸ **metedura de pata*** blunder, clanger*
meteduría SF smuggling
metegol SM *(Arg)* table football, table soccer *(EEUU)*
metejón* SM **1** *(Cono Sur)* violent love
2 *(And)* (= *enredo*) mess
metelón ADJ *(Méx)* meddling
metempsicosis SF INV metempsychosis
meteórico ADJ meteoric
meteorito SM meteorite
meteoro SM meteor
meteoroide SM meteoroid
meteorología SF meteorology
meteorológico ADJ meteorological, weather *(antes de s)* • **boletín** *o* **parte ~** weather report
meteorologista SMF meteorologist
meteorólogo/a SM/F meteorologist
metepatas* SMF INV • **eres un ~** you're always putting your foot in it
meter ▹ CONJUG 2a VT **1** (= *poner, introducir*) to put • **¿dónde has metido las llaves?** where have you put the keys? • **metió el palo por el aro** she stuck *o* put the stick through the ring • **mete las hamacas que está lloviendo** bring the hammocks in, it's raining • **~ algo en algo** to put sth in(to) sth • **metió la mano en el bolsillo** she put her hand in(to) her pocket • **metió el dedo en la sopa** he dipped *o* put his finger in the soup • **tienes que ~ la pieza en su sitio** you have to fit *o* put the part in the correct place • **consiguió ~ toda la ropa en la maleta** she managed to get *o* fit all the clothes in(to) the suitcase • **~ dinero en el banco** to put money in the bank • **¿quién le metió esas ideas en la cabeza?** who gave him those ideas? • MODISMO: • **a todo ~*** (= *rápido*) as fast as possible • **está lloviendo a todo ~** it's pelting with rain, it's pelting down • **le están dando antibióticos a todo ~** he's being stuffed with antibiotics*
2 *(Dep)* to score • **~ un gol** to score a goal
3 *(Cos)* *(para estrechar)* to take in; *(para acortar)* to take up • **métele la falda que le queda larga** take her skirt up a bit, it's too long
4 *(Aut)* *[+ marcha]* to go into • **mete primera** go into first gear • **¡mete el acelerador!** put your foot down!
5 (= *internar*) • **~ a algn en la cárcel** to put sb in prison • **lo metieron en un colegio privado** they put him in *o* sent him to a private school
6 *(en una profesión)* • **lo metieron a trabajar en el banco** they got him a job in a bank • **metieron a su hija (a) monja** they sent their daughter to a convent • **lo metieron a** *o* **de fontanero** they apprenticed him to a plumber
7 (= *implicar*) • **~ a algn en algo** to get sb involved in sth • **él me metió en el negocio** he got me involved in the business • **tú me metiste en este lío** you got me into this mess • **no metas a mi madre en esto** don't drag *o* bring my mother into this • **Luis metió a Fernando en muchos disgustos** Luis let Fernando in for a lot of trouble
8 (= *ocasionar*) • **~ miedo a algn** to scare *o* frighten sb • **~ prisa a algn** to hurry sb, make sb get a move on • **tenemos que ~le prisa a Adela** we need to hurry Adela, we need to make Adela get a move on • **¡no me metas prisa!** don't rush me! • **~ ruido** to make a noise • **~ un susto a algn** to give sb a fright
9* (= *dar*) • **le metieron un golpe en la cabeza** they hit him on the head • **le metió una torta delante de todos** she hit him in front of everyone
10* (= *endosar*) • **me han metido dos billetes falsos** they gave me two false banknotes • **me metieron una multa por no llevar puesto el cinturón** I was fined for not wearing a seat belt • **nos metió un rollo inacabable** he went on and on for ages • **le metieron cinco años de cárcel** they gave him five years in prison • **nos van a ~ más trabajo** they're going to lumber us with more work
11* (= *aplicar*) • **me metió la maquinilla y me peló al cero** he took the clippers to me and shaved all my hair off • **le quedaba largo el traje y le metió las tijeras** her dress was too long, so she took the scissors to it
12* (= *hacer entender*) • **no hay quien le meta que aquello era mentira** nobody seems able to make him understand that it was a lie, nobody is able to get it into his head that it was a lie
13 • **~las** *(And‡)* to beat it*
VPR **meterse 1** (= *introducirse*) • **métete por la primera calle a la derecha** take the first street on the right • **¿dónde se habrá metido**

m

el lápiz? where can the pencil have got to? • **no sabía dónde ~se de pura vergüenza** she was so ashamed, she didn't know where to hide • **~se en algo**: • **después de comer siempre se mete en el despacho** after lunch she always goes into her study *o* shuts herself away in her study • **se metió en la tienda** she went into the shop • **se metió en la cama** she got into bed • **se metió en un agujero** he got into a hole • **se metieron en el agua nada más llegar** they got straight into the water as soon as they arrived • **se me metió una avispa en el coche** a wasp got into my car • **el río se mete en el mar** the river flows into the sea • **un trozo de tierra que se mete en el mar** a finger of land that sticks out into the sea
2 (= *introducir*) • **métete la camisa** tuck your shirt in • **~se una buena cena*** to have a good dinner • **~se un pico**‡ to give o.s. a fix‡
• MODISMO: • **¡métetelo donde te quepa!**** you can stuff it!‡
3 (= *involucrarse*) • **~se en algo**: • **se metió en un negocio turbio** he got involved in a shady affair • **~se en política** to go into politics • **~se en líos** to get into trouble • **se metió en peligro** he got into danger • **no te metas en explicaciones** don't bother giving any explanations • **me metí mucho en la película** I really got into *o* got involved in the film
4 (= *entrometerse*) • **~se en algo** to interfere in sth, meddle in sth • **¿por qué te metes (en esto)?** why are you interfering (in this matter)? • **¡no te metas en lo que no te importa!** • **¡no te metas donde no te llaman!** mind your own business!
5 (*de profesión*) • **~se a algo**: • **~se a monja** to become a nun • **~se a escritor** to become a writer • **~se de algo**: • **~se de aprendiz en un oficio** to go into trade as an apprentice
6 • **~se a hacer algo** (= *emprender*) to start doing sth, start to do sth • **se metió a pintar todas las paredes de la casa** he started painting *o* to paint the whole house
7 • **~se con algn*** (= *provocar*) to pick on sb*; (= *burlarse de*) to tease sb

meterete/a* (*Arg*), **metete/a*** (*Chile, Méx*)
ADJ interfering
SM/F busybody, meddler

metiche* ADJ (*CAm, Chile, Méx*) interfering, meddling

meticón/ona* ADJ interfering, meddling
SM/F busybody, meddler

meticulosamente ADV meticulously, scrupulously

meticulosidad SF meticulousness, scrupulousness

meticuloso ADJ meticulous

metida* SF = **metedura**

metido* ADJ **1** • **estar muy ~ en algo** to be deeply involved in sth • **anda ~ en un lío** he's in a bit of trouble
2 • **~ en años** elderly, advanced in years • **está algo metidita en años** she's getting on a bit now • **~ en carnes** plump
3 • **~ en sí mismo** introspective
4 • **estar muy ~ con algn** to be well in with sb
5 (*LAm*) (= *entrometido*) interfering, meddling
6 (*Caribe, Cono Sur**) (= *bebido*) half cut*
SM **1** (= *reprimenda*) ticking-off • **dar** *o* **pegar un ~ a algn** to give sb a ticking-off
2‡ (= *sablazo*) • **pegar un ~ a algn** to touch sb for money*
3* (= *golpe*) bash*; (= *empujón*) shove • **le pegó un buen ~ a la tarta** she took a good chunk out of the cake

metijón/ona* SM/F busybody, meddler

metílico ADJ, **metilado** ADJ • **alcohol ~** methylated spirit

metilo SM methyl

metimiento SM **1** (= *inserción*) insertion
2* (= *influencia*) influence, pull*

metódicamente ADV methodically

metódico ADJ methodical

metodismo SM Methodism

metodista ADJ, SMF Methodist

método SM **1** (= *procedimiento*) method • **sus ~s de enseñanza son un poco anticuados** his teaching methods are a bit old-fashioned • **el mejor ~ para acabar con los gérmenes** the best way of killing off germs ▸ **método anticonceptivo** method of contraception ▸ **método audiovisual** audiovisual method ▸ **método del ritmo** rhythm method
2 (= *organización*) • **no obtienen resultados porque les falta ~** they don't get any results because they are not methodical (enough) • **trabajar con ~** to work methodically
3 (= *manual*) manual

metodología SF methodology

metodológicamente ADV methodologically

metodológico ADJ methodological

metomentodo* ADJ INV interfering, meddling
SMF busybody, meddler

metonimia SF metonymy

metraje SM **1** (*Cine*) length • **cinta de largo ~** feature(-length) film; ▹ **cortometraje, mediometraje, largometraje**
2 (= *distancia*) distance

metralla SF **1** (*Mil*) shrapnel
2* (= *calderilla*) coppers (*pl*), small change

metralleta SF submachine gun, tommy gun

métrica SF metrics (*sing*)

métrico ADJ metric(al) • **cinta métrica** tape measure

metro¹ SM **1** (= *medida*) metre, meter (*EEUU*) • **~s por segundo** metres per second • **mide tres ~s de largo** it's three metres long • **vender algo por ~s** to sell sth by the metre ▸ **metro cuadrado** square metre ▸ **metro cúbico** cubic metre; ▹ KILOS, METROS, AÑOS
2 (= *regla*) rule, ruler; (= *cinta métrica*) tape measure
3 (*Literat*) metre, meter (*EEUU*)

metro² SM underground, tube, subway (*EEUU*)

metrobús SM combined bus and underground railway ticket

metrónomo SM metronome

metrópoli SF (= *ciudad*) metropolis; [*de imperio*] mother country

metropolitano ADJ metropolitan • **área metropolitana de Madrid** Greater Madrid
SM **1** (*Rel*) metropolitan
2 (= *tren*) = **metro²**

metrosexual ADJ, SM metrosexual

mexicano/a ADJ, SM/F Mexican

México SM Mexico

mezanine SM mezzanine

mezcal SM (*Méx*) mescal

mezcla SF **1** (= *acción*) [*de ingredientes, colores*] mixing; [*de razas, culturas*] mixing; [*de sonidos*] mixing; [*de cafés, tabacos, whiskies*] blending • **la ~ de lo dulce y lo amargo** mixing sweet and sour flavours; ▹ **mesa**
2 (= *resultado*) [*de ingredientes, colores*] mixture; [*de razas, culturas*] mix; [*de cafés, tabacos, whiskies*] blend • **añade más agua a la ~** add some more water to the mixture • **sin ~** [*sustancia*] pure; [*gasolina*] unadulterated • **costumbres transmitidas sin ~ de influencias externas** customs passed on without any external influence ▸ **mezcla explosiva** (*lit*) explosive mixture; (*fig*) lethal combination • **los dos hermanos formaban una ~ explosiva** the two brothers formed a lethal combination
3 (*Mús*) mix
4 (*Constr*) mortar
5 (*Cos*) blend, mix

mezclado SM mixing • **el proceso de ~** the mixing process

mezclador(a) ADJ [*vaso, mesa*] mixing
SM/F (*Radio, TV*) (= *persona*) mixer ▸ **mezclador(a) de imágenes** vision mixer ▸ **mezclador(a) de sonido** sound mixer, dubbing mixer
SM **1** (*Radio, TV*) (= *aparato*) (*tb* **mezclador de sonido**) mixer, mixing desk ▸ **mezclador de vídeo, mezclador de video** (*LAm*) video mixer
2 (*Culin*) (*tb* **vaso mezclador**) mixing bowl

mezcladora SF mixer; (*tb* **mezcladora de sonido**) mixer, mixing desk ▸ **mezcladora de hormigón** concrete mixer

mezclar ▹ CONJUG 1a VT **1** (= *combinar*) [+ *ingredientes, colores*] to mix, mix together; [+ *estilos*] to mix, combine; [+ *personas*] to mix • **los materiales deben ~se muy despacio** the materials should be mixed (together) very slowly • **no mezcles los colores en la paleta** don't mix the colours on the palette • **un artista que mezcla estilos diferentes en su obra** an artist who mixes *o* combines different styles in his work • **han mezclado a niños de distintos niveles en la misma clase** they have mixed children of different abilities in the same class • **~ algo con algo** to mix sth with sth • **he mezclado el agua caliente con la fría** I've mixed the hot and cold water together, I've mixed the hot water with the cold • **no se debe ~ la religión con la política** one shouldn't mix religion with politics • **la banda sonora mezcla la música tradicional con el rock** the soundtrack is a mixture of traditional and rock music • **la harina y el azúcar se mezclan por partes iguales** equal quantities of flour and sugar are mixed (together) • **la comida china mezcla sabores salados y dulces** Chinese food combines *o* mixes savoury and sweet flavours
2 (= *confundir, desordenar*) [+ *fotos, papeles*] to mix up, mess up; [+ *idiomas*] to mix up, muddle up; [+ *naipes*] to shuffle • **¿quién me ha mezclado todos los papeles?** who's mixed *o* messed up all my papers? • **cuando habla mezcla los dos idiomas** when he talks he mixes *o* muddles up the two languages
3 [+ *café, tabaco, whisky*] to blend
4 (*Mús*) [+ *sonido*] to mix
5 (= *implicar*) • **~ a algn en algo** to involve sb in sth, get sb involved in sth • **no quiero que me mezcles en ese asunto** I don't want you to involve me *o* get me involved in that business
VI* (*con bebidas alcohólicas*) to mix (one's) drinks • **no me gusta ~** I don't like mixing (my) drinks
VPR **mezclarse 1** (= *combinarse*) [*ingredientes, colores*] to mix; [*culturas, elementos*] to mix, combine • **el aceite y el agua no se mezclan** oil and water don't mix • **en la película se mezclan la realidad y la ficción** the film mixes *o* combines reality and fiction • **lo que sentía era amor mezclado con odio** what she felt was a mixture of love and hate
2 (= *confundirse*) [*papeles, intereses*] to get mixed up • **se me han mezclado todos los documentos** all my documents have got mixed up • **los problemas políticos se mezclan con los amorosos** political issues get mixed up with romantic ones • **la vi ~se entre la multitud** I saw her merge into the

crowd • **los muertos se mezclaban con los supervivientes** the dead lay amongst the survivors
3 (= *involucrarse*) • **~se en algo** to get involved in sth • **procura no ~te en eso** try not to get involved *o* get mixed up in that
4 (= *relacionarse*) • **~se con algn** to mix with sb, get involved with sb • **no quiero que te mezcles con esa gente** I don't want you mixing with *o* getting involved with those people

mezclillo SM (*Cono Sur*) denim

mezcolanza SF hotchpotch, hodgepodge (*EEUU*), jumble

mezquinamente ADV meanly

mezquinar ▸ CONJUG 1a (*LAm*) VT **1** • **~ algo** to be stingy with sth, skimp on sth
2 (*Cono Sur*) • **~ el cuerpo** to dodge, swerve
3 (*And*) • **~ a algn** to defend sb • **~ a un niño** to let a child off a punishment
VI to be mean, be stingy

mezquindad SF **1** (= *tacañería*) meanness, stinginess
2 (= *insignificancia*) paltriness, wretchedness • **esa cantidad es una ~** that amount's a pittance
3 (= *acto vil*) mean thing (to do)

mezquino/a ADJ **1** (= *tacaño*) mean, stingy
2 (= *insignificante*) [*pago*] miserable, paltry
SM/F **1** (= *tacaño*) mean person, miser
2 (*LAm*) (= *verruga*) wart

mezquita SF mosque

mezquite SM (*Méx*) mesquite (tree *o* shrub)

mezzanine [metsa'nine] SM mezzanine; (*And*) (*Teat*) circle

mezzosoprano ['metso-so'prano] SF mezzo-soprano

M.F. ABR (= **modulación de frecuencia**) FM

mg ABR (= **miligramo(s)**) mg

MHz ABR (= **megahertzio(s)**, **megahercio(s)**) MHz

mi[1] ADJ POSES my

mi[2] SM (*Mús*) E ▸ **mi mayor** E major

mí PRON (*después de prep*) me, myself • **unos para ti y otros para mí** some for you and some for me • **tengo confianza en mí mismo** I have confidence in myself • **¡a mí con esas!** come off it!*, tell me another! • **¿y a mí qué?** so what?, what has that got to do with me? • **¡a mí!** (= *socorro*) help! • **para mí no hay duda** as far as I'm concerned there's no doubt • **por mí puede ir** as far as I'm concerned she can go • **por mí mismo** by myself

miaja SF **1** (= *migaja*) crumb
2 (= *poquito*) tiny bit • **ni (una) ~** not the least little bit
3 (*como adv*) a bit • **me quiere una ~** she likes me a bit

mialgia SF myalgia

miasma SM miasma

miasmático ADJ miasmic

miau SM mew, miaow • MODISMO: • **hizo ~ como el gato** you couldn't see him for dust

Mibor SM ABR = **Madrid inter-bank offered rate**

mica[1] SF **1** (*Min*) mica
2 (*Caribe*) (*Aut*) sidelight

mica[2] SF (*And*) (= *orinal*) chamber pot

mica[3]* SF (*CAm*) (= *borrachera*) • **ponerse una ~** to get drunk

micada SF (*CAm, Méx*) flourish

micción SF (*Med*) (*frm*) urination

miccionar ▸ CONJUG 1a VI (*Med*) (*frm*) to urinate

miche SM **1** (*Méx*) (= *gato*) cat
2 (*Caribe*) (= *licor*) liquor, spirits (*pl*)
3 (*Cono Sur*) (= *juego*) game of marbles
4 (*CAm*) (= *pelea*) fight, brawl

michelín* SM spare tyre*, spare tire (*EEUU**), roll of fat • **yo no tengo michelines como otras** I haven't got a spare tyre like some people*

michi SM (*And*) noughts and crosses, tick-tack-toe (*EEUU*)

michino/a SM/F, **micho/a*** SM/F puss, pussycat

micifuz* SM puss, pussycat

mico SM **1** (*Zool*) long-tailed monkey; (*como término genérico*) monkey • **¡cállate, ~!*** (*a niño*) shut up, you little monkey! • MODISMO: • **volverse ~**: • **se volvió ~ buscándolo** he was getting into a real state looking for it
2* • **ser un ~** (= *feo*) to be an ugly devil
3 (*CAm***) (= *vagina*) fanny**, twat**

micoleón SM (*CAm*) kinkajou

micología SF mycology

micra SF micron

micrero/a SM/F (*And, Cono Sur*) minibus driver; (*Cono Sur*) bus driver

micro[1] SM (*Radio*) mike*

micro[2] SM (= *microbús*) (*And, Cono Sur*) (*de corta distancia*) minibus; (*Cono Sur*) (*de larga distancia*) bus

micro[3] SM (*Inform*) micro, microcomputer

micro... PREF micro...

microalgas SFPL micro-algae

microbiano ADJ microbial

microbicida ADJ germicidal

microbio SM microbe (*frm*), germ

microbiología SF microbiology

microbiológico ADJ microbiological

microbiólogo/a SM/F microbiologist

microbús SM minibus

microcámara SF microcamera

microcasete SM o SF, **micro-cassette** SM o SF micro-cassette player, mini-cassette player

microchip SM (PL: **microchips**) microchip

microcircuitería SF microcircuitry

microcircuito SM microcircuit

microcirugía SF microsurgery

microclima SM microclimate

microcomputador SM, **microcomputadora** SF micro, microcomputer

microcosmos SM INV microcosm

microcrédito SM microcredit

microeconomía SF microeconomics (*sing*)

microeconómico ADJ microeconomic

microelectrónica SF microelectronics (*sing*)

microelectrónico ADJ microelectronic

microemisor ADJ microtransmitter (*antes de s*)

microespaciado SM microspacing

microestructural ADJ microstructural

microfalda SF micro-skirt

microficha SF microfiche

microfilm SM (PL: **microfilms** *o* **microfilmes**) microfilm

microfilmar ▸ CONJUG 1a VT to microfilm

micrófono SM **1** (*Radio, TV*) microphone • **hablar por el ~** to speak over the microphone ▸ **micrófono espía** hidden microphone, bug ▸ **micrófono inalámbrico**, **micrófono sin hilos** cordless microphone
2 [*de ordenador*] mouthpiece

microforma SF microform

microfotografiar ▸ CONJUG 1c VT to microphotograph

microfundio SM smallholding, small farm

micrograbador SM micro-cassette recorder, mini-cassette recorder

microinformática SF microcomputing

microinyectar ▸ CONJUG 1a VT to microinject

microlentillas SFPL contact lenses

micromecenazgo SM crowdfunding

micrómetro SM micrometer

microonda SF microwave

microondas SM INV (*tb* **horno microondas**) microwave (oven) • **apto para ~** microwavable, suitable for microwaving

microordenador SM microcomputer

microorganismo SM microorganism

micropastilla SF (*Inform*) chip, wafer

microplaqueta SF, **microplaquita** SF ▸ **microplaqueta de silicio** silicon chip

microprocesador SM microprocessor

microprograma SM (*Inform*) microprogram

micropunto SM microdot

microquirúrgico ADJ microsurgical

microscopía SF microscopy

microscópico ADJ microscopic • **se controló por observación microscópica** it was monitored through *o* with a microscope • **vistos a través del examen ~** seen through a microscope

microscopio SM microscope ▸ **microscopio electrónico** electron microscope

microsegundo SM microsecond

microsurco SM microgroove

microtaxi SM minicab

microtecnia SF, **microtecnología** SF microtechnology

microtécnica SF, **microtecnología** SF microtechnology

microtenis SM INV (*LAm*) table-tennis

microtransmisor SM micro-transmitter

Midas SM Midas • **ser un rey ~** to have the Midas touch

midi SM, **midifalda** SF midiskirt

MIE SM ABR (*Esp*) = **Ministerio de Industria y Energía**

miéchica EXCL (*LAm*) (*euf*) sugar!*, shoot!*

miedica* SMF chicken*, coward

mieditis* SF INV (= *nervios*) jitters* • **me da ~** it gives me the jitters • **tengo ~** I'm scared *o* petrified

miedo SM **1** fear • **~ a las represalias** fear of reprisals • **¡qué ~!** how scary! • **coger ~ a algo** to become afraid of sth • **dar ~** to scare • **me da ~ subir al tejado** I'm scared to go up on the roof • **le daba ~ hacerlo** he was afraid *o* scared to do it • **me da ~ dejar solo al niño** I'm frightened to leave the child alone • **de ~**: • **una película de ~** a horror film • **entrar ~ a algn**: • **me entró un ~ terrible** I suddenly felt terribly scared • **meter ~ a algn** to scare *o* frighten sb • **pasar ~**: • **pasé mucho ~ viendo la película** I was very scared watching the film • **perder el ~ a algo** to lose one's fear of sth • **por ~ a** *o* **de algo** for fear of sth • **por ~ a** *o* **de quedar en ridículo** for fear of looking ridiculous • **por ~ de que ...** for fear that ... • **tener ~** to be scared *o* frightened • **no tengas ~** don't be scared *o* frightened • **tener ~ a** *o* **de algn/algo** to be afraid of sb/sth • **tengo ~ a morir** I'm afraid of dying • **tenemos ~ a** *o* **de que nos ataquen** we're afraid that they may attack us • **tengo ~ de que le ocurra algo** I'm scared something will happen to him • **tener ~ de** *o* **a hacer algo** to be afraid to do sth, be afraid of doing sth • MODISMO: • **meterle el ~ en el cuerpo a algn** to scare the wits out of sb, scare the pants off sb* ▸ **miedo al público** (*Teat*) stage fright ▸ **miedo cerval** great fear ▸ **miedo escénico** stage fright
2 • MODISMO: • **de ~***: • **es un coche de ~** it's a fantastic car • **lo pasamos de ~** we had a fantastic time • **hace un frío de ~** it's freezing • **mi madre cocina de ~** my mum's a fantastic cook

miedoso/a ADJ (= *cobarde*) scared • **¿por qué eres tan ~?** why are you always so scared of everything • **no seas ~, que no te**

hace nada don't be scared, it's not going to hurt you

(SM/F) coward

miel (SF) [*de abejas*] honey; (= *melaza*) (*tb* **miel de caña, miel negra**) molasses • **las ~es del triunfo** the sweet taste of success

• MODISMOS: • **~ sobre hojuelas**: • **me gusta el trabajo, y si está bien pagado, pues es ~ sobre hojuelas** I enjoy the work, and if it's also well-paid, so much the better • **dejar a algn con la ~ en los labios** to leave sb feeling cheated • **quedarse con la ~ en los labios** to be left feeling cheated • REFRANES: • **hazte de ~ y te comerán las moscas** if you are too nice people will take advantage of you • **no hay ~ sin hiel** there's no rose without a thorn

mielero (SM) honeypot

mielga (SF) alfalfa

miembro (SM) **1** (*Anat*) limb, member ▸ **miembro viril** male member, penis

2 (*Ling, Mat*) member

(SMF) [*de club*] member; [*de institución, academia*] fellow, associate • **no ~** non-member • **hacerse ~ de** to become a member of, join

(ADJ) member (*antes de s*) • **los países ~s** the member states

mientes (SFPL) • **¡ni por ~!** never!, not on your life! • **parar ~ en algo** to reflect on sth • **traer a las ~** to recall • **se le vino a las ~** it occurred to him

mientras (CONJ) **1** (= *durante*) while • **sonreía ~ hablaba** he smiled as he spoke • **~ él estaba fuera** while he was out • **fue bonito ~ duró** it was nice while it lasted • **~ duró la guerra** while *o* when the war was on

2 (*expresando condición*) as long as • **seguiré ~ pueda caminar** I'll carry on (for) as long as I can still walk • **no podemos comenzar ~ no venga** we can't start until he comes

3 (= *en tanto que*) while, whereas • **tú trabajas ~ que yo estoy en el paro** you're working while *o* whereas I'm unemployed

4 (*esp LAm*) (= *cuanto*) • **~ más lo repetía, menos lo creía** the more he repeated it the less I believed him • **~ más tienen más quieren** the more they have the more they want

(ADV) (*tb* **mientras tanto**) (= *entre tanto*) meanwhile, in the meantime • **llegaré en seguida, ~ (tanto), prepáralo todo** I'll be right there, meanwhile *o* in the meantime, you get it all ready

miér. (ABR), **miérc.** (ABR) (= **miércoles**) Wed.

miércoles (SM INV) Wednesday ▸ **miércoles de ceniza** Ash Wednesday; ▹ **sábado**

mierda** (SF) **1** (= *excremento*) shit**, crap** • **una ~ de perro** some dog shit** • **estar hecho una ~** (= *sucio*) to be filthy; (= *cansado*) to be knackered* • **irse a la ~**: • **nuestros planes se han ido a la ~** our plans have gone down the pan* • **¡vete a la ~!** go to hell!‡, piss off!** • **mandar a algn a la ~** to tell sb to piss off**

2 (= *suciedad*) crap** • **había mucha ~ debajo de la alfombra** there was a lot of crap under the carpet** • **tienes la casa llena de ~** your house is filthy, your house is a pigsty

3 (= *cosa sin valor*) crap** • **el libro es una ~** the book is crap** • **es una ~ de coche** it's a crappy car** • **—¿cuánto te han pagado? —una ~** "how much did they pay you?" — "a pittance" • **de ~** crappy** • **una película de ~** a crappy film** • **esos políticos de ~** those crappy politicians**

4 (= *borrachera*) • **coger** *o* **pillar una ~** to get pissed‡, get sloshed‡

5 (= *suerte*) • **marcó un gol de pura ~** he scored a goal by an almighty fluke

6 (*uso enfático*) • **¿qué ~ quieres?** what the hell do you want?‡

7 (= *hachís*) shit**

(SMF) (= *persona*) • **tu hermana es una ~** your sister is a shit** • **es un (don) ~** he's a little shit**, he's a nobody

(EXCL) shit!** • **¡mierda! ya me he equivocado** shit, I've made a mistake** • **—¡ven aquí! —¡una ~!** "come here!" — "piss off!"**

mierdoso‡ (ADJ) filthy

mies (SF) **1** (= *cereal*) (ripe) corn, (ripe) grain

2 (= *temporada*) harvest time

3 mieses cornfields

miga (SF) **1** [*de pan*] • **la ~** the inside part of the bread, the crumb • **se separa la corteza de la ~** remove the crust from the bread

2 migas (*Culin*) fried breadcrumbs

• MODISMO: • **hacer buenas ~s con algn** to get on well with sb

3 (= *sustancia*) substance • **esto tiene su ~** there's more to this than meets the eye

4 (= *pedazo*) bit • **hacer algo ~s** to break *o* smash sth to pieces • **hacer ~s a algn** to shatter sb • **tener los pies hechos ~s** to be footsore

migajas (SFPL) **1** [*de pan*] crumbs

2 (= *trocitos*) bits; (= *sobras*) scraps • **tuvieron que contentarse con las ~ del reparto** they had to be content with the scraps when it was shared out

migar ▹ CONJUG 1h (VT) to crumble

migra* (SF) (*LAm*) immigration police *o* authorities

migración (SF) migration

migrante (SMF) migrant

migraña (SF) migraine

migrañoso/a (SM/F) migraine sufferer

migrar ▹ CONJUG 1a (VI) to migrate

migratorio (ADJ) migratory

Miguel (SM) Michael • **~ Ángel** (= *artista*) Michelangelo

mijo (SM) millet

mil (ADJ INV), (PRON), (SM) a *o* one thousand • **tres mil coches** three thousand cars • **mil doscientos dólares** one thousand two hundred dollars • **mil veces** a thousand times, thousands of times • **miles y miles** thousands and thousands • MODISMO: • **a las mil*** at some ungodly hour*; ▹ **seis**

miladi (SF) milady

milagrero/a* (ADJ) **1** (= *que cree en milagros*) • **personas milagreras** people who believe in miracles

2 [*curación*] miracle (*antes de s*), miraculous; [*poder*] miraculous; [*persona*] with miraculous powers

(SM/F) **1** (= *que cree en milagros*) believer in miracles

2 (= *que hace milagros*) miracle-worker

milagro (SM) (*Rel*) miracle; (*fig*) miracle, wonder • **es un ~ que ...** it is a miracle *o* wonder that ... • **~ (sería) que ...** it would be a miracle if ... • **de ~**: • **se salvaron de ~** they had a miraculous escape, it was a miracle they escaped • **vivir de ~** to somehow manage to keep body and soul together • **ese CD aquí no se consigue ni de ~** you can't get that CD here for love nor money • **hacer ~s**: • **un buen maquillaje puede hacer ~s** decent make-up can work wonders • **no podemos hacer ~s** we can't work miracles ▸ **milagro económico** economic miracle

(ADJ INV) miracle (*antes de s*), miraculous • **cura ~** miracle cure • **entrenador ~** super-coach, wonder-coach

milagrosa* (SF) (*Rel*) *image of the Virgin Mary believed to perform miracles*; ▹ **milagroso**

milagrosamente (ADV) miraculously

milagroso (ADJ) miraculous; ▹ **milagrosa**

Milán (SM) Milan

milanesa (SF) (*esp LAm*) (*Culin*) escalope, schnitzel

milano (SM) (*Orn*) kite ▸ **milano real** red kite

mildeu (SM), **mildiu** (SM), **mildiú** (SM) mildew

mildo (ADJ) (*Cono Sur*) timid, shy

milenariamente (ADV) • **un pueblo ~ libre** a people which has been free since time immemorial

milenario (ADJ) (= *de mil años*) thousand-year-old (*antes de s*); (= *antiquísimo*) ancient, age-old

(SM) millennium

milenio (SM) millennium

milenrama (SF) yarrow

milésima (SF) thousandth • **ganó con 91 ~s de ventaja** she won by 91 thousandths of a second • **una ~ de segundo** a thousandth of a second; (*fig*) a split second

milésimo/a (ADJ) thousandth

(SM) thousandth • **hasta el ~** to three decimal places; ▹ **sexto**

mileurista (ADJ) of (around) a thousand euros • **un sueldo ~** a salary of (around) a thousand euros a month

(SMF) *person earning around a thousand euros* • **un ~ no puede comprar ese piso** no one on a salary of a thousand euros could afford that flat

milhojas (SM o SF INV) (= *pastel*) millefeuille, *cake made with puff pastry, filled with meringue*

mili* (SF) military service • **un amigo que está en la ~** a friend who is doing his military service • **hacer la ~** to do one's military service

miliar (ADJ) • **piedra ~** milestone

milibar (SM) millibar

milicia (SF) **1** (= *arte*) art of war; (= *profesión*) military profession

2 (= *tropa*) militia • **~s armadas** armed militias

3 (= *militares*) military

4 (= *servicio militar*) military service

miliciano/a (SM/F) militiaman/militiawoman; (*And, Cono Sur*) (= *conscripto*) conscript, draftee (*EEUU*)

milico* (SM) **1** (*And, Cono Sur*) (*pey*) (= *soldado*) soldier; (= *soldado raso*) squaddie* • **los ~s** the military

2 (*And*) = **miliciano**

miligramo (SM) milligramme, milligram (*EEUU*)

mililitro (SM) millilitre, milliliter (*EEUU*)

milimetrado (ADJ) (*fig*) minutely calculated • **papel ~** graph paper

milimétricamente (ADV) precisely, minutely, down to the last detail • **analizan las cuentas ~** they go through the accounts down to the last detail • **todo está ~ preparado** every last detail is prepared • **las previsiones se han cumplido ~** things have turned out exactly as foreseen

milimétrico (ADJ) (= *preciso*) precise, minute • **con precisión milimétrica** with pinpoint accuracy

milímetro (SM) millimetre, millimeter (*EEUU*) • **no hemos avanzado ni un ~** we have got absolutely nowhere • **no ceder ni un ~** not to give an inch • **sin salirse un ~ del programa** keeping strictly to the programme • **lo calculó al** *o* **hasta el ~** he calculated it very precisely • **coinciden casi al ~** they tally in almost every detail • **cumplen las instrucciones al ~** they carry out their orders to the letter

milisegundo (SM) millisecond

militancia (SF) **1** (*en partido*) membership • **está prohibida su ~ en los partidos políticos** they are not permitted to be a member of *o*

m

join a political party • **dejó el partido tras casi 20 años de ~** she left the party after almost 20 years as a member ▸ **militancia de base** rank-and-file members (*pl*)
2 (= *afiliación*) • **¿cuál es su ~ política?** what is his political affiliation?

militante ADJ (= *radical*) militant • **una feminista ~** a militant feminist
SMF [*de partido*] member ▸ **militante de base** rank and file member

militantismo SM militancy

militar ADJ military • **ciencia ~** art of war
SM (= *soldado*) soldier, military man; (*en la mili*) serviceman • **los ~es** the military
VI ▸ CONJUG 1a **1** (*Mil*) to serve (*in the army*)
2 (*Pol*) • **~ en un partido** to be a member of a party

militarada SF military rising, putsch

militarismo SM militarism

militarista ADJ militaristic
SMF militarist

militarización SF militarization

militarizar ▸ CONJUG 1f VT to militarize

militarmente ADV militarily

militarote SM (*LAm*) (*pey*) rough soldier

milla SF mile ▸ **milla marina** nautical mile; ▸ **KILOS, METROS, AÑOS**

millar SM thousand • **a ~es** by the thousand • **los había a ~es** there were thousands of them

millarada SF (about a) thousand

millardo SM thousand million, billion

millas-pasajero SFPL passenger miles

millo SM, **millón¹** SM (*esp LAm*) (variety of) millet

millón² SM million • **un ~ a** *o* one million • **un ~ y medio de visitantes** a million and a half visitors, one-and-a-half million visitors • **un ~ de sellos** a *o* one million stamps • **tres ~es de niños** three million children • **millones de años** millions of years • **¡un ~ de gracias!** thanks a million!, thanks ever so much!

millonada* SF • **costó una ~** it cost a fortune • **lo vendió por una ~** he sold it for a fortune

millonario/a SM/F millionaire/ millionairess

millonésima SF millionth

millonésimo/a ADJ, SM/F millionth

milonga (*Cono Sur*) SF **1*** (= *mentirilla*) fib*, tale
2 (= *baile*) *type of dance and music from the River Plate Region*
3 (= *fiesta*) party
4 (= *cotilleo*) gossip

milonguero/a SM/F **1** (*Mús*) singer of milongas
2 (*Cono Sur*) (= *fiestero*) partylover

milor SM, **milord** [mi'lor] SM milord • **vive como un ~** he lives like a lord

milpa SF (*CAm, Méx*) (= *plantación*) maize field, cornfield (*EEUU*); (= *planta*) maize, corn (*EEUU*)

milpear ▸ CONJUG 1a (*CAm, Méx*) VT to prepare for the sowing of maize, prepare for the sowing of corn (*EEUU*)
VI **1** (= *plantar*) to sow a field with maize, sow a field with corn (*EEUU*)
2 [*maíz*] (= *brotar*) to sprout

milpero/a SM/F (*CAm, Méx*) maize grower, corn grower (*EEUU*)

milpiés SM INV millipede

milrayas ADJ INV • **pantalón ~** fine pinstripe trousers

miltomate SM (*CAm, Méx*) *small green or white tomato*

mimado ADJ spoiled, pampered

mimar ▸ CONJUG 1a VT to spoil, pamper

mimbre SM o SF **1** (*Bot*) osier, willow
2 (= *material*) wicker • **de ~** wicker (*antes de s*), wickerwork (*antes de s*) • **MODISMO:** • **con este ~ hay que hacer el cesto** one has to make the best of what one has

mimbrearse ▸ CONJUG 1a VPR to sway

mimbrera SF osier

mimbreral SM osier bed

mimeografiar ▸ CONJUG 1c VT to mimeograph

mimeógrafo SM mimeograph

miméticamente ADV mimetically, by way of imitation

mimético ADJ mimetic, imitation (*antes de s*)

mimetismo SM mimicry

mimetizar ▸ CONJUG 1f (*esp LAm*) VT (= *imitar*) to imitate
VPR **mimetizarse 1** (*Zool*) to change colour, change color (*EEUU*)
2 (*Mil*) to camouflage o.s.

mímica SF **1** (= *arte*) mime; (= *lenguaje*) sign language; (= *gestos*) gesticulation
2 (= *imitación*) imitation, mimicry

mímico ADJ mimic • **intérprete ~** sign language interpreter • **lenguaje ~** sign language

mimo/a SM/F (*Teat*) mime
SM **1** (*Teat*) mime
2 (= *copia*) • **hacer ~ de algo** to mime sth
3 (= *caricia*) cuddle • **una casa diseñada con ~** a house designed with loving care • **manejó el balón con ~** he caressed the ball • **escribe con ~** she's very careful in the way she writes • **dar ~s a algn** (= *consentir*) to spoil *o* pamper sb

mimosa SF mimosa

mimoso ADJ **1** (= *cariñoso*) affectionate • **es muy mimosa con su novio** she's very affectionate towards her boyfriend • **¡no te pongas tan ~!** don't be so clingy!
2 (= *mimado*) spoilt, pampered

Min. ABR (= **Ministerio**) Min • **~ de AA.EE.** FO, ≈ FCO • **~ de D.** MOD

min. ABR **1** (= **minuto(s)**) m, min
2 (= **minúscula(s)**) lc, l.c.

mín. ABR (= **mínimo**) min

mina¹ SF **1** (*Min*) mine ▸ **mina a cielo abierto** opencast mine, open cut mine (*EEUU*) ▸ **mina de carbón, mina hullera** coal mine
2 (= *galería*) gallery; (= *pozo*) shaft
3 (*Mil, Náut*) mine ▸ **mina antipersonal** anti-personnel mine ▸ **mina terrestre** land mine
4 [*de lápiz*] lead
5 (= *ganga*) (*tb* **mina de oro**) gold mine • **este negocio es una ~ (de oro)** this business is a gold mine ▸ **mina de información** mine of information

mina²‡ SF (*Cono Sur*) (= *mujer*) bird*, chick (*EEUU‡*)

minada SF (*Mil*) mining

minador(a) SM **1** (*Mil*) sapper
2 (*Náut*) (*tb* **buque minador**) minelayer
SM/F (*Min*) mining engineer

minar ▸ CONJUG 1a VT **1** (*Min, Mil, Náut*) to mine
2 (= *debilitar*) to undermine

minarete SM minaret

mineral ADJ mineral
SM **1** (*Geol*) mineral
2 (*Min*) ore ▸ **mineral de hierro** iron ore
3 (*Chile*) (= *mina*) mine

mineralero SM ore-carrier

mineralizar ▸ CONJUG 1f VT to mineralize

mineralogía SF mineralogy

mineralogista SMF mineralogist

minería SF mining

minero/a ADJ mining
SM/F miner ▸ **minero/a de carbón** coalminer ▸ **minero/a de interior** face worker

Minerva SF Minerva

minestrone SF minestrone

minga¹‡ SF prick‡

minga² SF (*LAm*) **1** (= *trabajo*) voluntary communal labour *o* (*EEUU*) labor, cooperative work
2 (= *equipo*) crew *o* gang of cooperative workers

mingaco SM (*And, Cono Sur*) = **minga²**

mingar ▸ CONJUG 1h VI (*LAm*) (= *trabajar*) to work communally, work cooperatively
VT **1** (*And, Cono Sur*) [+ *trabajadores*] to call together for a communal task
2 (*And*) (= *atacar*) to set (up)on, attack

mingitorio SM, **mingitorios** SMPL (*hum*) urinal

Mingo SM *forma familiar de* **Domingo**

mini SM **1** (*Aut*) Mini
2 (*Inform*) minicomputer
SF (= *falda*) mini, miniskirt

mini... PREF mini... • **minicoche** minicar

miniacería SF small steelworks

miniar ▸ CONJUG 1b VT [+ *manuscrito*] to illuminate

miniatura ADJ miniature • **golf ~** crazy golf
SF miniature • **en ~** in miniature • **una réplica exacta de la casa en ~** an exact replica of the house in miniature • **relojes en ~** miniature clocks • **un barco en ~** a model ship

miniaturista SMF miniaturist

miniaturización SF miniaturization

miniaturizar ▸ CONJUG 1f VT to miniaturize

minibar SM minibar

minibikini SM mini bikini

minicadena SF mini hi-fi, mini stereo system

minicalculadora SF pocket calculator

minicámara SF minicam

minicasino SM small gambling club

minicines SMPL *cinema with several small screens*

minicomputador SM minicomputer

MiniDisc®, minidisc SM (= *disco*) MiniDisc®, minidisc; (= *aparato*) MiniDisc® (player), minidisc (player)

minidisco SM diskette

miniestadio SM small sports arena

minifalda SF miniskirt

minifaldero/a ADJ miniskirted • **una chica minifaldera** a girl in a miniskirt
SF • **una atrevida minifaldera** a daring girl in a miniskirt • **las minifalderas** girls in miniskirts

minifundio SM smallholding, small farm

minifundismo SM **1** (*Agr*) *small-scale farming*
2 (*fig*) (= *fragmentación*) tendency to fragment, fragmentation • **~ sindical** parochial trade unionism (*pey*)

minifundista SMF smallholder

minigira SF short tour

minigolf SM crazy golf

minihorno SM small oven

mínima SF (*Meteo*) low, lowest temperature; ▸ **mínimo**

minimal ADJ minimalist

minimalismo SM minimalism

minimalista ADJ, SMF minimalist

minimalizar ▸ CONJUG 1f VT to minimize

mínimamente ADV • **la población se verá afectada ~** the population will be minimally affected • **si fueras ~ inteligente** if you had a modicum of intelligence • **la situación no es ni ~ aceptable** the situation is not acceptable in the slightest

minimizar ▸ CONJUG 1f VT **1** (= *reducir al*

mínimo) [*+ gastos, efectos*] to minimize • **han minimizado el empleo de insecticidas** they have minimized the use of insecticides
2 (*= quitar importancia a*) [*+ problema, suceso*] to make light of, minimize, play down • **el ministro minimizó las pérdidas económicas** the minister made light of *o* played down *o* minimized the economic losses

mínimo ADJ **1** (*= inferior*) [*nivel, cantidad*] minimum • **no llegaron a alcanzar el nivel ~ exigido** they did not manage to reach the minimum level required • **la temperatura mínima fue de 15 grados** the minimum temperature was 15 degrees • **quería conseguirlo todo con el ~ esfuerzo** he wanted to achieve everything with a *o* the minimum of effort • **"tarifa mínima: 2 euros"** "minimum fare: 2 euros" • **el tamaño ~ del dibujo deberá ser de 20 x 30 centímetros** the drawing should not be less than 20 x 30 centimetres • **lo ~**: • **es lo ~ que podemos hacer** it's the least we can do • **intente hablar lo ~ posible** try and talk as little as possible • **lo más ~** the least *o* the slightest • **el dinero no me interesa lo más ~** I'm not the least *o* the slightest bit interested in money • **los sueldos no se verán afectados en lo más ~** salaries will not be affected in the least *o* in the slightest • **precio ~** minimum price • **en un tiempo ~** in no time at all • **el microondas calienta la comida en un tiempo ~** the microwave heats up food in next to no time *o* in no time at all • **~ común denominador** lowest common denominator; ▷ **múltiplo, salario, servicio**
2 (*= muy pequeño*) [*habitación, letra*] tiny, minute; [*detalle*] minute; [*gasto, beneficio*] minimal • **escribía con una letra mínima** his writing was tiny *o* minute • **una habitación de tamaño ~** a tiny room • **esto es solo una mínima parte de lo que hemos gastado** this is just a tiny fraction of what we have spent • **este teléfono ocupa un espacio ~** this telephone takes up hardly any space • **me contó hasta el más ~ detalle** he told me everything in minute detail • **un vehículo de consumo ~** a vehicle with minimal fuel consumption
3 [*plazo*] • **no existe un plazo ~ para entregar el trabajo** there's no set date for the work to be handed in
SM **1** (*= cantidad mínima*) minimum • **¿cuál es el ~?** what is the minimum? • **bajo ~s** (*Esp*) [*credibilidad, moral*] at rock bottom; [*consumo, presupuesto*] very low • **el equipo salió al campo con la moral bajo ~s** the team took to the field with their morale at rock bottom • **su credibilidad se halla bajo ~s** his credibility is at an all-time low • **con el presupuesto bajo ~s** with the budget cut back to a minimum, with a very low budget • **como ~** at least • **eso costará, como ~, 40 euros** that will cost at least 40 euros • **como ~ te he llamado cinco veces** I've phoned you at least five times • **un ~ de algo** a minimum of sth • **necesitas hacer un ~ de esfuerzo** you need to make a minimum of effort • **necesitamos un ~ de dos millones** we need a minimum of two million • **si tuviera un ~ de vergüenza no vendría más por aquí** if he had any shame at all he wouldn't come back here • **necesito un ~ de intimidad** I need a modicum of privacy • **reducir algo al ~** to keep *o* reduce sth to a minimum • **han intentado reducir los gastos al ~** they have tried to keep *o* reduce expenditure to a minimum
2 (*Econ*) record low, lowest point • **hoy se ha llegado en la bolsa al ~ anual** today the stock exchange reached this year's record low *o* lowest point ▸ **mínimo histórico** all-time low
3 (*Mat*) [*de una función*] minimum
4 (*Meteo*) ▸ **mínimo de presión** low-pressure area, trough; ▷ **mínima**
5 (*Caribe*) (*Aut*) choke

mínimum SM minimum

minina‡ SF (*Esp*) (*= pene*) willy*, peter (*EEUU***)

minino/a SM/F (*= gato*) puss, pussycat

minio SM red lead, minium

miniordenador SM minicomputer

minipíldora SF minipill

Minipimer® SM electric mixer

miniserie SF miniseries

ministerial ADJ (*de ministro, ministerio*) ministerial • **reunión ~** cabinet meeting

ministerio SM **1** (*Pol*) ministry, department (*esp EEUU*) ▸ **Ministerio de Asuntos Exteriores** Foreign Office, State Department (*EEUU*) ▸ **Ministerio de Comercio e Industria** Department of Trade and Industry ▸ **Ministerio de (la) Gobernación** *o* **del Interior** ≈ Home Office, Department of the Interior (*EEUU*) ▸ **Ministerio de Hacienda** Treasury, Treasury Department (*EEUU*) ▸ **Ministerio Fiscal** Attorney General's office
2 (*Jur*) • **el ~ público** the Prosecution, the State Prosecutor (*EEUU*)

ministrable SMF (*= candidato*) candidate for minister

ministro/a SM/F (*en gobierno*) minister, secretary (*esp EEUU*) • **primer ~** prime minister • **consejo de ~s** (*= grupo*) cabinet; (*= reunión*) cabinet meeting ▸ **ministro/a de Asuntos Exteriores** Foreign Secretary, Secretary of State (*EEUU*) ▸ **ministro/a de Hacienda** Chancellor of the Exchequer, Secretary of the Treasury (*EEUU*) ▸ **ministro/a de (la) Gobernación, ministro/a del Interior** Home Secretary, Secretary of the Interior (*EEUU*) ▸ **ministro/a en la sombra** shadow minister ▸ **ministro/a en visita** (*Chile*) examining magistrate ▸ **ministro/a portavoz** government spokesperson ▸ **ministro/a sin cartera** minister without portfolio

minivacaciones SFPL minibreak (*sing*)

minoración SF reduction, diminution

minorar ▷ CONJUG 1a VT to reduce, diminish

minoría SF minority • **estar en ~** to be in a *o* the minority • **gobernar en ~** to govern without an overall majority ▸ **minoría de edad** minority ▸ **minoría étnica** ethnic minority

minoridad SF minority (*of age*)

minorista ADJ retail (*antes de s*)
SMF retailer

minoritario ADJ minority (*antes de s*) • **gobierno ~** minority government

Minotauro SM Minotaur

minucia SF **1** (*= detalle insignificante*) trifle, insignificant detail • **describir algo con ~** to describe sth in detail; **minucias** petty details, minutiae
2 (*= bagatela*) mere nothing

minuciosamente ADV [*limpiar*] thoroughly, meticulously; [*examinar, inspeccionar*] minutely • **analizó ~ las diferencias** he analysed the differences in minute detail • **marfiles tallados ~** delicately carved pieces of ivory

minuciosidad SF • **lo limpió con ~** she cleaned it thoroughly *o* meticulously • **debes inspeccionarlo con ~** you should inspect it thoroughly • **describió la situación con ~** she described the situation in minute detail

minucioso ADJ **1** (*= meticuloso*) thorough, meticulous
2 (*= detallado*) very detailed

minué SM minuet

minuetto SM minuet

minúscula SF small letter; (*Tip*) lower case letter • **se escribe con ~** [*la primera letra*] it is written with a small letter; [*toda una frase*] it is written in small letters *o* lower case letters • **la verdad con ~** truth with a small T

minúsculo ADJ **1** (*= muy pequeño*) tiny, minuscule
2 (*Tip*) • **letra minúscula** lower-case letter • **en letra minúscula** in lower-case letters

minusvalía SF **1** (*Med*) disability, handicap • **personas con ~** disabled people ▸ **minusvalía física** physical disability *o* handicap ▸ **minusvalía psíquica** mental disability *o* handicap
2 (*Com*) depreciation, capital loss

minusvalidez SF disablement, disability

minusválido/a ADJ (*físico*) physically handicapped, physically disabled; (*psíquico*) mentally handicapped, mentally disabled
SM/F disabled person, handicapped person • **los ~s** the disabled ▸ **minusválido/a físico/a** physically handicapped person, physically disabled person ▸ **minusválido/a psíquico/a** mentally handicapped person, mentally disabled person

minusvalorar ▷ CONJUG 1a VT to undervalue, underestimate
VPR **minusvalorarse** to hold o.s. in low esteem, have a low opinion of o.s.

minusvalorizar ▷ CONJUG 1f VT to undervalue

minuta SF **1** [*de abogado*] lawyer's bill
2 (*= menú*) menu
3 (*= borrador*) rough draft, first draft
4 (*= lista*) list, roll
5 (*Arg*) quick meal
6 (*Caribe, Cono Sur*) • **a la ~** rolled in breadcrumbs
7 (*Cono Sur*) (*= basura*) junk, trash; (*= tienda*) junk shop
8 (*CAm*) (*= bebida*) flavoured ice drink

minutado SM, **minutaje** SM timing, running time

minutar ▷ CONJUG 1a VT **1** [*+ contrato*] to draft
2 [*+ cliente*] to bill

minutario SM minute book

minutero SM (*= manecilla*) minute hand; (*= reloj*) timer

minutisa SF sweet william

minuto SM minute • **llegó al ~** she arrived one minute later • **volverá dentro de un ~** she'll be back in a minute • **a medida que pasaban los ~s** as the minutes ticked by • **guardar un ~ de silencio** to observe a minute's silence • MODISMO: • **tengo los ~s contados** I have no time to spare

miñango* SM (*And, Cono Sur*) bit, small piece • **hecho ~s** smashed to pieces, in smithereens

Miño SM • **el (río) ~** the Miño

miñoco SM (*And*) grimace

miñón ADJ (*LAm*) sweet, cute

mío ADJ POSES mine • **es mío** it's mine • **no es amigo mío** he's no friend of mine • **¡Dios mío!** my God!, good heavens! • **¡hijo mío!** my dear boy!
PRON POSES **1** • **el mío/la mía** mine • **este es el mío** this one's mine • **la mía está en el armario** mine's in the cupboard • **lo mío: lo mío es tuyo** what is mine is yours, what belongs to me belongs to you • **he puesto lo mío en esta caja** I've put my stuff *o* things in this box • **lo mío con Ana acabó hace tiempo** Ana and I finished a while ago • **lo**

m

mío son los deportes I'm a sports person myself • **el tenis no es lo mío** tennis is not for me, tennis is not my cup of tea *o* my thing
2 • **los míos** (= *mis familiares*) my folks, my family • **echo de menos a los míos** I miss my folks
3 • **la mía** (= *mi oportunidad*): • **¡esta es la mía, entraré ahora que no me ven!** now's my chance, I'll slip in now while they aren't watching!
miocardio (SM) myocardium (*frm*); ▹ **infarto**
mioceno (ADJ) Miocene
(SM) • **el ~** the Miocene, the Miocene period
miope (ADJ) short-sighted, near-sighted (*EEUU*), myopic (*frm*)
(SMF) short-sighted person, near-sighted person (*EEUU*), myopic person (*frm*)
miopía (SF) short-sightedness, near-sightedness (*EEUU*), myopia (*frm*)
miosis (SF INV) miosis, myosis
miosotis (SF INV) myosotis, myosote, forget-me-not
MIPS (SMPL ABR) (= **millones de instrucciones por segundo**) MIPS
MIR (SM ABR) 1 (*Esp*) (*Med*) = **Médico interno residente**
2 (*Bol*) = **Movimiento de Izquierda Revolucionaria**
mira (SF) 1 (*Mil, Téc*) sight • **MODISMO**: • **estar con** *o* **tener la ~ puesta en algo** to have one's sights set on sth ▸ **mira de bombardeo** bombsight ▸ **mira telescópica** telescopic sight
2 (= *intención*) aim, intention • **con la ~ de hacer algo** with the aim of doing sth • **con ~s a** with a view to • **llevar una ~ interesada** to have (only) one's own interests at heart • **tener ~s sobre algo/algn** to have designs on sth/sb
3 **miras** (= *actitud*) • **corto de ~s** narrow-minded • **amplio** *o* **ancho de ~s** (= *tolerante*) broad-minded • **de ~s estrechas** narrow-minded
4 • **estar a la ~** to be on the lookout (**de** for)
5 (= *torre*) watchtower; (= *puesto*) lookout post
mirada (SF) 1 (= *forma de mirar*) look • **tiene una ~ melancólica** he has a sad look about him • **con una ~ triste** with a sad look in his eyes • **tenía la ~ penetrante** she had a penetrating gaze • **no podía resistir su ~** I couldn't resist those eyes • **con la ~ fija en el infinito** staring into space • **MODISMO**: • **hay ~s que matan** if looks could kill
2 (= *acto*) (*rápida*) glance; (*detenida*) gaze • **le dirigió una ~ de sospecha** he gave her a suspicious look *o* glance, he looked *o* glanced at her suspiciously • **le echó una ~ por encima del hombro** she gave him a condescending look, she looked at him condescendingly • **era capaz de aguantarle** *o* **resistirle la ~ a cualquiera** he could outstare anybody, he could stare anybody out • **nos dirigimos una ~ de complicidad** we glanced at each other knowingly • **tuvo que aguantar las ~s compasivas de toda la familia** he had to suffer the pitying looks of the whole family • **echar una ~ de reojo** *o* **de soslayo a algo/algn** to look out of the corner of one's eye at sth/sb, cast a sidelong glance at sth/sb ▸ **mirada perdida** • **tenía la ~ perdida en el horizonte** she was gazing into the distance • **tenían la ~ perdida de quienes están próximos a la locura** they had the empty look of people on the verge of madness
3 (= *vista*) • **recorrió la habitación con la ~** he looked around the room • **apartar la ~ (de algn/algo)** to look away (from sb/sth) • **sin apartar la ~ de ella** without looking away from her • **bajar la ~** to look down • **clavar la ~ en algo/algn** to fix one's eyes on sth/sb • **desviar la ~ (de algn/algo)** (*lit*) to look away (from sb/sth), avert one's eyes (from sb/sth); (*fig*) to turn one's back (on sb/sth) • **es solo una excusa para desviar su ~ de los verdaderos problemas** it's just an excuse to turn their backs on the real problems • **dirigir la ~ a** *o* **hacia algn/algo** (*lit*) to look at sb/sth; (*fig*) to turn one's attention to sb/sth • **dirigió la ~ a Rosa** he looked at Rosa • **ahora están dirigiendo su ~ hacia los más necesitados** they are now turning their attention to those most in need • **echar una ~ a algn/algo** (*varias veces*) to keep an eye on sb/sth, check on sb/sth; (*una sola vez*) to have a look at sb/sth • **échale una miradita al arroz de vez en cuando** keep an eye *o* check on the rice every now and then • **echa una ~ a ver si te has dejado la luz encendida** have a look to see if you've left the light on • **antes de irse a dormir les echó una ~ a los niños** before going to bed he had a look in on the children *o* he had a quick look at the children • **le echó una última ~ a la casa antes de irse** she had a *o* one last look at the house before leaving • **le deberíais echar una última ~ al examen** you should give your exam paper a final read through • **levantar la ~** to look up, raise one's eyes • **al vernos entrar levantó la ~** on seeing us enter, he looked up *o* raised his eyes • **no levantó la ~ del libro** he didn't take his eyes off the book • **tener la ~ puesta en algo** (*lit*) to have one's gaze fixed on sth; (*fig*) to be looking towards sth, have one's sights set on sth • **seguir algo/a algn con la ~** to follow sth/sb with one's eyes • **volver la ~** to look back • **salió de la casa sin volver la ~** she left the house without looking back • **si volvemos la ~ hacia atrás, nos daremos cuenta de nuestros errores** if we look back we will realize our mistakes • **volvió su ~ a Amelia** she looked round at Amelia *o* turned her eyes towards Amelia • **volvió la ~ a su izquierda** he looked round to his left, he turned his eyes to the left; ▹ **devorar**
4 **miradas** (= *atención*) • **todas las ~s estarán puestas en el jugador brasileño** all eyes will be on the Brazilian player • **me fui, huyendo de las ~s de todo el pueblo** I left, fleeing from the prying eyes of the whole village
miradero (SM) 1 (= *lugar*) vantage point, lookout
2 (= *atracción*) centre of attention, center of attention (*EEUU*)
mirado (ADJ) 1 (= *estimado*) • **bien ~** well *o* highly thought of, highly regarded • **no estaba bien ~ que llevaran falda corta** wearing short skirts was frowned upon • **mal ~** ▹ **malmirado**
2 (= *sensato*) sensible; (= *cauto*) cautious, careful; (= *considerado*) considerate, thoughtful; (= *educado*) well-behaved • **ser ~ en los gastos** to watch what one spends, be a careful spender
3 (*pey*) finicky*, fussy
4 • **bien ~ ...** all things considered ..., when you think about it ...
mirador (SM) 1 (= *lugar de observación*) viewpoint, vantage point
2 (= *ventana*) bay window; (= *balcón*) (enclosed) balcony
3 (*Náut*) ▸ **mirador de popa** stern gallery
miraguano (SM) (*LAm*) (type of) kapok tree, kapok
miramiento (SM) 1 (= *consideración*) considerateness; (= *cortesía*) courtesy • **sin ~** without consideration
2 (= *circunspección*) care, caution; (*pey*) (= *timidez*) timidity, excessive caution
3 **miramientos** (= *respeto*) respect (*sing*); (= *cortesías*) courtesies, attentions • **andar con ~s** to tread carefully • **sin ~s** unceremoniously
miranda†* (SF) • **estar de ~** (= *gandulear*) to be loafing *o* lazing around; (= *no participar*) to be an onlooker
mirar ▹ CONJUG 1a (VT) 1 (= *ver*) to look at • **estaba mirando la foto** she was looking at the photo • **me miró con tristeza** she looked at me sadly • **miraban boquiabiertos el nuevo aparato** they stared open-mouthed at the new machine • **~ a algn de arriba abajo** to look sb up and down • **~ algo/a algn de reojo** *o* **de través** to look at sth/sb out of the corner of one's eye • **~ fijamente algo/a algn** to gaze *o* stare at sth/sb • **~ algo por encima** to glance over sth • **MODISMOS**: • **~ bien** *o* **con buenos ojos a algn** to approve of sb • **~ mal** *o* **con malos ojos a algn** to disapprove of sb • **de mírame y no me toques** delicate, fragile; ▹ **hombro**
2 (= *observar*) to watch • **se quedó mirando cómo jugaban los niños** she stood watching the children play • **miraba los barcos** she was watching the boats • **estuvo mirando la tele todo el día** he spent all day watching TV
3 (= *comprobar*) • **le ~on la maleta en la aduana** they searched his suitcase at customs • **mira que no hierva el agua** make sure the water doesn't boil • **mira a ver lo que hace el niño** go and see *o* check what the boy's up to • **mira a ver si ha venido el taxi** (look and) see if the taxi has come • **míralo en el diccionario** look it up in the dictionary
4 (= *pensar en*) • **no mira las dificultades** he doesn't think of the difficulties • **lo hago mirando el porvenir** I'm doing it with the future in mind • **¡no gastes más, mira que no tenemos dinero!** don't spend any more, remember we've no money! • **mirándolo bien**: • **bien mirado** *o* **si bien se mira** *o* **mirándolo bien, la situación no es tan grave** all in all, the situation isn't that bad, if you really think about it, the situation isn't all that bad • **bien mirado** *o* **mirándolo bien, creo que lo haré más tarde** on second thoughts, I think I'll do it later
5 (= *ser cuidadoso con*) • **mira mucho el dinero** he's very careful with money • **deberías ~ lo que gastas** you should watch what you spend • **mira mucho todos los detalles** she pays great attention to detail
6 (*uso exclamativo*) **a** (*en imperativo*) • **¡mira qué cuadro tan bonito!** look, what a pretty painting! • **¡mira cómo me has puesto de agua!** look, you've covered me in water! • **¡mira lo que has hecho!** (just) look what you've done! • **¡mira quién fue a hablar!** look who's talking! • **¡mira (bien) lo que haces!** watch what you do! • **¡mira con quién hablas!** just remember who you're talking to!
b (*indicando sorpresa, disgusto*) • **mira que**: • **¡mira que es tonto!** he's so stupid! • **¡mira que te avisé!** didn't I warn you? • **¡mira que ponerse a llover ahora!** it would have to start raining right now!
c (*indicando esperanza, temor*) • **mira que si**: • **¡mira que si ganas!** imagine if you win! • **¡mira que si no viene!** just suppose he doesn't come! • **¡mira que si es mentira!** just suppose it isn't true!, what if it isn't true?
7 (*LAm*) (= *ver*) to see • **¿lo miras?** can you see it?
(VI) 1 (*con la vista*) to look • **me vio pero miró**

hacia otro lado she saw me, but she looked the other way • **estaba mirando por la ventana** he was looking out of the window • **miré por el agujero** I looked through the hole • **miró alrededor para ver si veía a alguien** she looked around to see if she could see anyone • **~ de reojo** *o* **de través** to look out of the corner of one's eye
2 (= *comprobar*) to look • **¿has mirado en el cajón?** have you looked in the drawer?
3 (= *estar orientado hacia*) to face • **la casa mira al sur** the house faces south • **el balcón mira al jardín** the balcony looks out onto the garden
4 (= *cuidar*) • **~ por algn** to look after sb, take care of sb • **debes de ~ por tus hermanos** you should look after *o* take care of your brothers • **mira mucho por su ropa** she takes great care of her clothes • **solo mira por sus intereses** he only looks after his own interests • **tienes que ~ por ti mismo** you have to look out for yourself
5 (*uso exclamativo*) **a** (*en imperativo*) • **¡mira! un ratón** look, a mouse! • **mira, yo creo que ...** look, I think that ... • **mira, déjame en paz ahora** look, just leave me alone now • **mire usted, yo no tengo por qué aguantar esto** look here, I don't have to put up with this
b (*indicando sorpresa, admiración*) • **mira si**: • **¡mira si estaría buena la sopa que todos repitieron!** the soup was so good that everyone had seconds! • **¡mira si es listo el niño!** what a clever boy he is! • MODISMO: • **¡(pues) mira por dónde ...!** you'll never believe it!
6 • **~ a** (= *proponerse*) to aim at • **este proyecto mira a mejorar la calidad del agua** this project is aimed at improving water quality
7 (*frm*) • **por lo que mira a** as for, as regards
VPR **mirarse 1** (*reflexivo*) to look at o.s. • **~se al o en el espejo** to look at o.s. in the mirror
2 (*recíproco*) to look at each other *o* one another • **Juan y María se ~on asombrados** Juan and María looked at each other *o* one another in amazement • **los amantes se ~on a los ojos** the lovers looked into each other's eyes
3 • **se mire por donde se mire** whichever way you look at it
4 • **~se mucho** *o* **muy bien de hacer algo** to think carefully before doing sth

mirasol SM sunflower
miríada SF myriad • **~(s) de moscas** myriads of flies, a myriad of flies
mirilla SF (*en puerta*) peephole, spyhole; (*Fot*) viewfinder
miriñaque SM **1** (*Hist*) crinoline, hoop skirt
2 (*Cono Sur*) (*Ferro*) cowcatcher
3 (*Caribe, Méx*) (= *tela*) thin cotton cloth
miriópodo SM myriapod
miristiquívoro ADJ myristicivorous
mirlarse ▷ CONJUG 1a VPR to put on airs, act important
mirlo SM **1** (*Orn*) blackbird ▸ **mirlo blanco** (*fig*) rare bird
2 (= *presuntuosidad*) self-importance, pompousness
3‡ (= *lengua*) tongue • MODISMO: • **achantar el ~** to shut one's trap*
mirobrigense ADJ of/from Ciudad Rodrigo
SMF native/inhabitant of Ciudad Rodrigo • **los ~s** the people of Ciudad Rodrigo
mirón/ona* ADJ nosey*, curious
SM/F (= *espectador*) onlooker; (= *mirón*) nosey-parker*; (= *voyer*) voyeur, peeping Tom • **estar de ~** to stand around watching, stand around doing nothing • **ir de ~** to go along just to watch • MODISMO: • **los mirones son de piedra** those watching the game are not allowed to speak

mironismo* SM voyeurism
mirra SF **1** (= *resina*) myrrh
2 (*Caribe*) (*trocito*) small piece
mirtilo SM bilberry, whortleberry
mirto SM myrtle
mis SF = miss
misa SF mass • **vamos a ~ todos los domingos** we go to mass every Sunday • **dijeron/celebraron ~ en la catedral** they said/celebrated mass in the cathedral • MODISMOS: • **como en ~**: • **los niños estaban como en ~** the children were really quiet • **decir ~**: • **¡por mí, que digan ~!** let them say what they like! • **estar en ~ y repicando** to have one's cake and eat it • **ir a ~**: • **lo que yo diga va a ~** what I say goes • **no saber de la ~ la media** *o* **la mitad** not to know anything about it, not to have a clue • **ser como ~ de pobre** to last all too short a time ▸ **misa cantada** sung mass ▸ **misa de campaña** open-air mass ▸ **misa de corpore insepulto, misa de cuerpo presente** funeral mass ▸ **misa de difuntos** requiem mass ▸ **misa del alba** early morning mass ▸ **misa del domingo** Sunday mass ▸ **misa del gallo** midnight mass (*on Christmas Eve*) ▸ **misa mayor** high mass ▸ **misa negra** black mass ▸ **misa rezada** low mass ▸ **misa solemne** high mass
misacantano SM (= *sacerdote*) ordained priest; (*en primera misa*) *priest saying his first mass*
misal SM missal
misantropía SF misanthropy
misantrópico ADJ misanthropic
misántropo/a SM/F misanthrope, misanthropist
misario SM acolyte (*frm*), altar boy
miscelánea SF **1** (*frm*) (= *mezcla*) miscellany
2 (*Méx*) (= *tienda*) corner shop
misceláneo ADJ miscellaneous
misera SF lobster
miserable ADJ **1** (= *tacaño*) mean, stingy; (= *avaro*) miserly
2 [*sueldo*] miserable, paltry
3 (= *vil*) vile, despicable
4 [*lugar, habitación*] squalid, wretched
5 (= *desdichado*) wretched
SMF **1** (= *desgraciado*) wretch
2 (= *canalla*) swine, wretch • **¡miserable!** you miserable wretch!
miserablemente ADV miserably
miseramente ADV wretchedly, in poverty
miserando ADJ (*esp LAm*) pitiful
miseria SF **1** (= *pobreza*) poverty, destitution • **caer en la ~** to fall into poverty • **vivir en la ~** to live in poverty
2 (= *insignificancia*) • **una ~** a pittance
3 (= *tacañería*) meanness, stinginess
4† (= *parásitos*) fleas (*pl*), lice (*pl*) • **estar lleno de ~** to be covered with vermin
misericordia SF compassion, mercy • **Señor, ten ~ de nosotros** (*Rel*) Lord, have mercy upon us
misericordioso ADJ merciful • **Alá es ~** Allah is merciful • **mentira misericordiosa** white lie • **obras misericordiosas** charitable works
misero* ADJ churchy, fond of going to church
mísero ADJ **1** (= *tacaño*) mean, stingy; (= *avaro*) miserly
2 [*sueldo*] miserable, paltry
3 (= *vil*) vile, despicable
4 [*lugar, habitación*] squalid, wretched
5 (= *desdichado*) wretched
misérrimo ADJ *superl de* **mísero**
Misiá* SF (*Cono Sur*), **Misia*** SF (*Cono Sur*) (*tratamiento*) Missis*, Missus* • **~ Eugenia** Miss Eugenia

misil SM missile ▸ **misil antiaéreo** anti-aircraft missile ▸ **misil antimisil** anti-missile missile ▸ **misil autodirigido** guided missile ▸ **misil balístico** ballistic missile ▸ **misil buscador del calor** heat-seeking missile ▸ **misil de alcance medio** medium-range missile ▸ **misil (de) crucero** cruise missile ▸ **misil tierra-aire** ground-to-air missile
misilístico ADJ missile (*antes de s*)
misión SF **1** (= *cometido*) mission; (= *tarea*) task; (*Pol*) assignment ▸ **misión de buena voluntad** goodwill mission ▸ **misión humanitaria** humanitarian mission ▸ **misión investigadora** fact-finding mission
2 (= *delegación*) mission ▸ **misión comercial** trade mission ▸ **misión diplomática** diplomatic mission
3 misiones (*Rel*) overseas missions, missionary work (*sing*)
misional ADJ missionary
misionero/a SM/F missionary • **postura** *o* **posición del ~** missionary position
Misisipí SM Mississippi
misiva SF missive
miskito SM Miskito
mismamente* ADV (= *solo*) only, just; (= *textualmente*) literally; (= *incluso*) even; (= *en realidad*) really, actually • **~ anoche estuve allí** I was there only *o* just last night • **~ cerca de mi casa hay uno** there's actually one right near my house
mismísimo ADJ (*superl*) very (same) • **con mis ~s ojos** with my own eyes • **es usted el ~ diablo** you're the devil incarnate • **este niño es el ~ demonio** this child is a real little devil • **estuvo el ~ obispo** the bishop himself was there • **es el ~ que yo perdí** it's the very (same) one I lost
SMPL • **los ~s**: **estoy hasta los ~s*** I'm up to here with it*
mismo ADJ **1** (= *igual*) same • **el ~ coche** the same car • **estos dos vestidos son de la misma talla** these two dresses are the same size • **respondieron al ~ tiempo** they answered together, they answered at the same time • **el ~ ... que** the same ... as • **lleva la misma falda que ayer** she's wearing the same skirt as yesterday • **tengo el ~ dinero que tú** I've got the same amount of money as you • **tiene el ~ pelo que su padre** his hair's the same as his father's
2 (*reflexivo*) • **hablaba consigo ~** he was talking to himself • **lo hizo por sí ~** he did it by himself • **perjudicarse a sí ~** to harm oneself; ▷ **valer**
3 (*enfático*) **a** (*relativo a personas*) • **yo ~ lo vi** I saw it myself, I saw it with my own eyes • **estuvo el ~ ministro** the minister himself was there • **ni ella misma lo sabe** she doesn't even know herself • **ella misma se hace los vestidos** she makes her own dresses • **—¿quién responde? —a ver, tú ~** "who's going to answer?" — "well, why don't you answer yourself!"
b (*relativo a cosas*) • **—¿cuál quieres? —ese ~** "which one do you want?" — "that one there" • **—¡es un canalla! —eso ~ pienso yo** "he's a swine!" — "my thoughts exactly" • **viven en el ~ centro de Córdoba** they live right in the centre of Córdoba • **en todos los países europeos, España misma incluida** in all European countries, including Spain itself • **Ana es la generosidad misma** Ana is generosity itself, Ana is the epitome of generosity • **en ese ~ momento** at that very moment • **por eso ~**: • **era pobre y por eso ~ su ascenso tiene más mérito** he was poor and for that very reason his promotion is

m

all the more commendable
4 (*como pronombre*) • **es el ~ que nos alquilaron el año pasado** it's the same one they rented us last year • **—¿y qué edad tienes tú? —la misma que él** "and how old are you?" — "I'm the same age as him" • **no es la misma desde su divorcio** she hasn't been the same since her divorce • **—¿es usted la señorita Sánchez? —¡la misma!** "are you Miss Sánchez?" — "I am indeed!" • **leyó el texto pero no reveló el origen del ~** he read the text without revealing its source
• MODISMO: • **estamos en las mismas** we're no better off than before, we're no further forward
5 • **lo mismo a** (= *la misma cosa*) the same (thing) • **los políticos siempre dicen lo ~** politicians always say the same (thing) • **hizo lo ~ que ayer** he did the same as yesterday • **¡hombre, no es lo ~!** it's not the same (thing) at all! • **—son unos canallas —lo ~ digo yo** "they're swine" — "that's (exactly) what I say" • **—¡enhorabuena! —lo ~ digo** "congratulations!" — "likewise" *o* "the same to you" • **—eres un sinvergüenza —lo ~ te digo** "you're completely shameless" — "you too" *o* "so are you" • **nos contó lo ~ de siempre** she told us the usual story • **—¿qué desea de beber? —lo ~ (de antes), por favor** "what would you like to drink?" — "(the) same again, please" • **cuando le interese a él, o lo que es lo ~, nunca** when it suits him, in other words never • **por lo ~**: • **no es inteligente y por lo ~ tiene que estudiar el doble** he's not clever, which is exactly why he has to study twice as hard • **lo ~ que**: • **le dijo lo ~ que yo** she told him the same thing *o* the same as she told me • **le multaron por lo ~ que a mí** she got fined for the same thing as me • **no es lo ~ hablar en público que en privado** it's not the same thing to talk in public as to talk in private
b • **dar lo ~**: • **da lo ~** it's all the same, it makes no difference • **me da lo ~** • **lo ~ me da** I don't mind, it's all the same to me • **da lo ~ que vengas hoy o mañana** it doesn't matter whether you come today or tomorrow
c* (= *a lo mejor*) • **lo ~ no vienen** maybe they won't come • **no lo sé todavía, pero lo ~ voy** I don't know yet, but I may well come • **pídeselo, lo ~ te lo presta** ask him for it; you never know, he may lend it to you
d • **lo ~ que** (= *al igual que*): • **en Europa, lo ~ que en América** in Europe, (just) as in America • **lo ~ que usted es médico yo soy ingeniero** just as you are a doctor, so I am an engineer • **suspendí el examen, lo ~ que Íñigo** I failed the exam, just like Íñigo • **yo, lo ~ que mi padre, odio el baloncesto** I hate basketball, just like my father • **nos divertimos lo ~ que si hubiéramos ido al baile** we had just as good a time as if we had gone to the dance
e • **lo ~ … que** (= *tanto … como*): • **lo ~ te puede criticar que alabar** she's just as likely to criticize you as to praise you • **lo ~ puede durar una hora que dos** it could last anywhere between one and two hours • **aquí lo ~ te venden una vajilla que una bicicleta** they'll sell you anything here, from a dinner service to a bicycle • **lo ~ si viene que si no viene** whether he comes or not
(ADV) (*enfático*) • **delante ~ de la casa** right in front of the house • **en la capital ~ hay barrios de chabolas** even in the capital there are shanty towns • **ahora ~** (= *inmediatamente*) right away *o* now; (= *hace un momento*) just now • **hazlo ahora ~** do it right away *o* now • **ahora ~ acabo de hablar con él** I've just been talking to him, I was talking to him only a moment ago • **aquí ~**: • **—¿dónde lo pongo? —aquí ~** "where shall I put it?" — "right here" • **aquí ~ acampamos el año pasado** this is the exact spot where we camped last year • **así ~**: • **—¿cómo quieres el filete? —así ~ está bien** "how would you like your steak?" — "it's fine as it is" • **ayer ~** only yesterday • **hoy ~**: • **he llegado hoy ~** I just arrived today • **me dijo que me contestarían hoy ~** he told me they'd give me an answer today • **mañana ~**: • **llegará mañana ~** he's arriving tomorrow, no less • **me contestarán mañana ~** they'll give me an answer tomorrow

misogamia (SF) misogamy
misógamo/a (SM/F) misogamist
misoginia (SF) misogyny
misógino (SM) misogynist
miss [mis] (SF) beauty queen • **concurso de ~es** beauty contest ▸ **Miss España 1997** Miss Spain 1997
míster (SM) **1** (*Dep*) trainer, coach
2† (*hum*) (= *británico*) (any) Briton
misterio (SM) **1** (= *incógnita*) mystery • **no hay ~** there's no mystery about it • **ahora conozco mejor los ~s del país** now I know more of the country's secrets • **una novela de ~** a mystery (story)
2 (= *secreto*) secrecy • **¿a qué viene tanto ~?** why all this secrecy?, why are you being so mysterious? • **obrar con ~** to act in secret
3 (*Teat*) mystery play
misteriosamente (ADV) mysteriously
misterioso (ADJ) mysterious
mística (SF), **misticismo** (SM) mysticism
místico/a (ADJ) mystic(al)
(SM/F) mystic
mistificación (SF) mystification
mistificar ▸ CONJUG 1g (VT) to mystify
mistongo* (ADJ) (*Cono Sur*) wretched, miserable
Misuri (SM) Missouri
mita (*And, Cono Sur*) (*Hist*) (SF) (= *dinero*) *tax paid by Indians*; (= *trabajo*) *common service to landlord*
mitad (SF) **1** half • **basta tomar la ~ de un comprimido** half a tablet is enough • **me queda la ~** I have half left • **a ~ de precio** half-price • **reducir en una ~** to cut by half, halve; (*Culin*) to reduce by half • **doblado por la ~** folded in half • **~ (y) ~** half-and-half • **paguemos ~ y ~** let's go halves • **es ~ blanco y ~ rojo** it's half white and half red
• MODISMO: • **mi otra ~** my other half, my better half
2 (*Dep*) half • **la primera ~** the first half
3 (= *centro*) middle • **a ~ de la comida** in the middle of the meal, halfway through the meal • **está a ~ de camino entre Madrid y Barcelona** it's halfway between Madrid and Barcelona • **en ~ de la calle** in the middle of the street • **el depósito está a la ~** the tank is half empty • **ya estamos a la ~** we're halfway there • **hacia la ~ de la película** about halfway through the film • **atravesar de ~ a ~** to pierce right through • **cortar por la ~** to cut in half • **corta las uvas por la ~** cut the grapes in half • MODISMO: • **me parte por la ~** it upsets my plans
mítico (ADJ) mythical
mitificar ▸ CONJUG 1g (VT) to mythologize, convert into a myth
mitigación (SF) mitigation (*frm*); (= *de dolor*) relief; [*de sed*] quenching
mitigar ▸ CONJUG 1h (VT) (*gen*) to mitigate (*frm*); [+ *dolor*] to relieve, ease; [+ *sed*] to quench; [+ *ira*] to calm, appease; [+ *temores*] to allay; [+ *calor*] to reduce; [+ *soledad*] to alleviate, relieve
mitin (SM) **1** (*Pol*) rally
2 (= *discurso*) political speech • **dar un ~** to make a speech
mitinear ▸ CONJUG 1a (VI) to make a (political) speech; (*pey*) to make a rabble-rousing speech
mitinero/a (ADJ) demagogic, rabble-rousing
(SM/F) demagogue, rabble-rouser
mitinesco (ADJ) rabble-rousing
mito (SM) myth • **este hombre es un ~ del cine** this man is a film legend
mitocondrial (ADJ) mitochondrial
mitología (SF) mythology
mitológico (ADJ) mythological
mitómano/a (SM/F) **1** (= *idólatra*) mythomaniac
2 (*Psic*) person who exaggerates
mitón (SM) mitten
mitote (SM) (*Méx*) **1** (*Hist*) Aztec ritual/dance
2 (= *pelea*) brawl
3* (= *jaleo*) uproar
4* (= *charla*) chat • **estar en el ~** to have a chat
Mitra (SM) Mithras
mitra (SF) **1** (= *gorro*) mitre, miter (*EEUU*)
2 (= *obispado*) bishopric; (= *arzobispado*) archbishopric
mitrado (SM) bishop, prelate
mitraico (ADJ) Mithraic
mitraísmo (SM) Mithraism
mítulo (SM) mussel
mixomatosis (SF INV) myxomatosis
Mixteca (SF) (*Méx*) southern Mexico
mixteco (SM) • **el ~** (*Méx*) (*Hist*) (= *pueblo*) the Mixtecs; (= *civilización*) Mixtec civilization
mixtificar ▸ CONJUG 1g (VT) = **mistificar**
mixtión (SF) (*frm*) mixture
mixto (ADJ) (= *mezclado*) mixed; [*comité*] joint; [*empresa*] joint
(SM) **1** (= *sandwich*) *(toasted) cheese and ham sandwich*
2 (= *fósforo*) match
3 (*Mil*) explosive compound
4 (*Ferro*) passenger and goods train
mixtolobo (SM) Alsatian (dog)
mixtura (SF) (*frm*) mixture
mixturar ▸ CONJUG 1a (VT) (*frm*) to mix
Mk (ABR) (= **Marco**) Mk
ml (ABR) (= **mililitro(s)**) ml
MLN (SM ABR) (*LAm*) = **Movimiento de Liberación Nacional**
mm (ABR) (= **milímetro(s)**) mm
MMS (SM ABR) (= **multimedia message service**) MMS
M.N. (ABR), **m/n** (ABR) (*LAm*) = **moneda nacional**
mnemotécnica (SF), **mnemónica** (SF) mnemonics (*sing*)
mnemotécnico (ADJ) mnemonic • **un recurso ~** a mnemonic
Mnez. (ABR) = **Martínez**
MNR (SM ABR) (*Bol*) = **Movimiento Nacionalista Revolucionario**
M.º (ABR) **1** (*Pol*) (= **Ministerio**) Min
2 (*Escol*) = **Maestro**
m/o (ABR) (*Com*) = **mi orden**
moai (SM) (PL: **moais**) (*Chile*) Easter Island statue
moaré (SM) moiré
mobbing (SM) (*en el trabajo, en una vivienda*) harassment, bullying • **le están haciendo ~ para que se vaya de la empresa** they're trying to bully him into leaving the company
mobiliario (SM) (= *muebles*) furniture • ▸ **mobiliario auxiliar** small pieces of furniture (*pl*) ▸ **mobiliario de cocina** (= *armarios*) kitchen units (*pl*) ▸ **mobiliario de cuarto de baño** bathroom fittings (*pl*)

▸ **mobiliario de oficina** office furniture ▸ **mobiliario sanitario** sanitary ware, bathroom fittings (*pl*) ▸ **mobiliario urbano** street furniture
moblaje (SM) = **mobiliario**
MOC (SM ABR) (*Esp*) = **Movimiento de Objeción de Conciencia**
moca[1] (SM) (*Culin*) mocha
moca[2] (SF) (*Méx*) coffee-flavoured cake/biscuit
moca[3] (SF) (= *barrizal*) quagmire, muddy place
mocarro* (SM) snot*
mocasín (SM) moccasin
mocear† ▹ CONJUG 1a (VI) to play around, live a bit wildly, sow one's wild oats
mocedad† (SF) **1** (= *juventud*) youth • **en mis ~es** in my youth, in my young days
2 mocedades (= *travesuras*) youthful pranks; (= *vida licenciosa*) wild living (*sing*) • **pasar las ~es** to sow one's wild oats
moceril† (ADJ) youthful
mocerío† (SM) young people (*pl*), lads and lasses (*pl*)
mocero† (ADJ) (= *libertino*) rakish, loose-living; (= *mujeriego*) fond of the girls
mocetón/ona† (SM/F) strapping youth/girl
mocha‡ (SF) (*Esp*) nut*, noggin (*EEUU**)
mochales* (ADJ) (*Esp*) • **estar ~** to be nuts *o* crazy* • **estar ~ por algn** to be nuts *o* crazy about sb*
mochar ▹ CONJUG 1a (VT) **1** (*LAm*) (= *cortar*) to chop off (clumsily), hack off
2 (*And**) (= *despedir*) to fire*, sack*
3 (*Cono Sur*) (= *robar*) to pinch*, nick*
4 = **desmochar**
(VPR) **mocharse** (*Méx*) • **~se con** [+ *cantidad de dinero*] to contribute • **~se con algn** to go halves with sb
moche (SM) = **troche**
mochila (SF) **1** rucksack, knapsack, backpack; (*Mil*) pack • **turistas de ~** backpackers • **viajar en plan de ~** to backpack • MODISMO: • **tener algo casi en la ~*** to have sth almost in the bag* ▸ **mochila portabebés** baby-carrier, baby-sling
2 [*de bicicleta*] pannier
3 (*Cono Sur*) (= *cartera*) satchel
mochilear ▹ CONJUG 1a (VI) to backpack, go backpacking
mochilero/a (SM/F) backpacker
mocho/a (ADJ) **1** (= *desafilado*) blunt, short
2 [*árbol*] lopped, pollarded; [*vaca*] hornless, polled; [*torre*] flat-topped; [*muñón*] stubby
3 (= *mutilado*) mutilated; (*Caribe*) (= *manco*) one-armed
4 (*And*) (= *grande*) big, huge
5 (*Méx*) (= *reaccionario*) reactionary; (= *beato*) sanctimonious
(SM/F) **1** (*CAm**) (= *huérfano*) orphan
2 (*Méx*) (= *reaccionario*) reactionary; (= *beato*) sanctimonious person
(SM) **1** [*de utensilio*] blunt end, thick end; [*de cigarrillo*] butt
2* (= *carga*) = **mochuelo**
3 (*And, Caribe**) (= *caballo*) nag
mochuelo (SM) **1** (*Orn*) (*tb* **mochuelo común**) little owl • MODISMO: • **cada ~ a su olivo** let's all go back to our own homes
2 • MODISMOS: • **cargar con el ~** to get landed with it • **colgar** *o* **echar el ~ a algn** to lumber sb with the job*; (= *culpa*) to make sb carry the can*; (= *crimen*) to frame sb
moción (SF) **1** (*Parl*) motion • **hacer** *o* **presentar una ~** to propose *o* table a motion ▸ **moción compuesta** composite motion ▸ **moción de censura** motion of censure, censure motion ▸ **moción de confianza** vote of confidence
2 (= *movimiento*) motion
mocionante (SMF) (*CAm, Méx*) proposer (of a motion)
mocionar ▹ CONJUG 1a (VT) (*CAm, Méx*) to move, propose
mocito/a† (ADJ) very young
(SM/F) youngster • **mocitas casaderas** girls of marriageable age • **está hecha una mocita** she's a very grown-up young lady
moco (SM) **1** mucus, snot* • **limpiarse los ~s** to blow one's nose • **sorberse los ~s** to sniff • **tener ~s** to have a runny nose • MODISMOS: • **llorar a ~ tendido** to cry one's eyes out • **soltar el ~** to burst into tears • **tirarse el ~*** (= *mentir*) to lie; (= *exagerar*) to exaggerate, shoot a line*; (= *jactarse*) to brag
2 (*Orn*) crest • MODISMO: • **no es ~ de pavo** (= *es importante*) it's no trifle, it's not to be sneezed at; (= *es grave*) you can't laugh this one off
3 (= *mecha*) snuff, burnt wick; (= *cera derretida*) candle drippings (*pl*) • **a ~ de candil** by candlelight
4 (*Téc*) slag
mocoso/a* (SM/F) brat • **ese ~ no tiene derecho a opinar** that little brat has no right to give his opinion • **no puedes salir solo porque eres un ~** you can't go out on your own because you're just a kid • **un ~ de 19 años** a snotty-nosed youth of 19*
moda (SF) fashion • **la ~ de primavera** spring fashion • **el rap es la última ~** rap is the latest craze *o* fashion • **en los noventa llegó la ~ del acid-jazz** in the nineties acid-jazz became fashionable *o* trendy* • **la ~ esa de salir tarde por la noche** that habit of going out late at night • **ha vuelto la ~ de la minifalda** mini-skirts are back in (fashion) again • **es solo una ~ pasajera** it's just a passing fad • **a la ~** fashionable • **un sombrero a la ~** a fashionable hat • **un vestido a la ~ de París** a dress in the Paris fashion *o* style • **tienes que ponerte** *o* **vestirte un poco más a la ~** you should try and dress a bit more fashionably • **siempre va vestida a la última ~** she always dresses in the latest fashion • **estar de ~** to be in fashion, be fashionable, be in*, be all the rage*, be trendy* • **los vaqueros ajustados están muy de ~** tight jeans are really fashionable *o* in fashion, tight jeans are all the rage *o* really trendy *o* really in* • **esa teoría está muy de ~ ahora** that theory is very trendy* *o* fashionable at the moment • **pasado de ~** out of fashion, old-fashioned, outdated, out* • **pasarse de ~** to go out of fashion • **ponerse de ~** to become fashionable, get trendy* • **esta zona se está poniendo muy de ~** this area is becoming very fashionable, this area is getting very trendy*; ▹ **imponer**
modal (ADJ) modal
modales (SMPL) manners • **te lo daré si lo pides con buenos ~** I'll give it to you if you ask nicely *o* politely
modalidad (SF) **1** (= *tipo*) form, type • **una nueva ~ de contrato** a new form *o* type of contract ▸ **modalidad de pago** (*Com*) method of payment
2 (*Dep*) category • **es campeón de Europa en la ~ de cross-country** he's the European champion in the cross-country category • **ha ganado una medalla en la ~ de salto de altura** he won a medal in the high-jump
3 (*Ling, Fil*) modality
4 (*Inform*) mode ▸ **modalidad de texto** text mode
modding* (SM) modding*
modelado (SM) modelling
modelador(a) (SM/F) modeller
modelaje (SM) modelling
modelar ▹ CONJUG 1a (VT) (= *dar forma a*) to shape, form; [*escultor*] to sculpt; [*alfarero*] to model • **la vida nos modela** life moulds *o* (*EEUU*) molds us • **~ el futuro** to shape the future
(VPR) **modelarse** • **~se sobre algn** to model o.s. on sb
modélicamente (ADV) in a model *o* an exemplary fashion
modélico (ADJ) model, exemplary
modelismo (SM) modelling, model-making
modelista (SMF) model-maker, modeller
modelización (SF) modelling, creation of models ▸ **modelización cognoscitiva** cognitive modelling ▸ **modelización informática** computer modelling ▸ **modelización matemática** mathematical modelling
modelizar ▹ CONJUG 1f (VT) to model, make a model of
modelo (SM) **1** (= *tipo*) model • **se fabrica en varios ~s** it comes in several models • **un coche último ~** the latest-model car
2 (= *ejemplo*) • **presentar algo como ~** to hold sth up as a model • **servir de ~** to serve as a model • **tomar por ~** to take as a model • **~ de maridos** model husband • **~ de vida** lifestyle, way of life ▸ **modelo a escala** scale model ▸ **modelo estándar** standard model
3 (= *patrón*); (*para hacer punto*) pattern
4 (= *prenda*) model, design • **un ~ de Valentino** a Valentino model *o* design
(SMF) (*Arte, Fot, Moda*) model • **desfile de ~s** fashion show • **servir de ~ a un pintor** to sit *o* pose for a painter ▸ **modelo de alta costura** fashion model, haute couture model ▸ **modelo de portada** cover girl
(ADJ INV) (= *ejemplar*) model, exemplary • **cárcel ~** model prison • **niño ~** model child
módem (SM) (PL: **módems**) modem
moderación (SF) **1** (= *mesura*) moderation • **le recomiendo ~ en la comida** I recommend you (to) eat in moderation • **con ~** [*actuar*] with restraint; [*beber, comer*] in moderation; [*crecer*] moderately • **fume con ~** smoke in moderation • **deberías hablar con ~** you should speak in a moderate tone
2 (*Econ*) • **ha sido necesaria una ~ del gasto** we have had to cut *o* reduce expenses ▸ **moderación salarial** wage restraint
3 [*de debate, coloquio*] • **la ~ del debate correrá a cargo de ...** the debate will be chaired by ...
moderadamente (ADV) moderately
moderado (ADJ) moderate • **un candidato de izquierda moderada** a moderate left-wing candidate • **es muy ~ en la expresión** he is very moderate in tone • **vientos de ~s a fuertes** moderate to strong winds
moderador(a) (ADJ) [*papel, poder*] moderating
(SM/F) **1** (*en un debate, coloquio*) moderator, chairperson; (*TV*) presenter
2 (*Pol*) moderator • **el ministro actuó de ~ en las conversaciones** the minister acted as a moderator in the talks
(SM) (*Fís*) moderator
moderar ▹ CONJUG 1a (VT) **1** (= *controlar*) **a** [+ *impulsos, emociones*] to restrain, control; [+ *violencia, deseo*] to curb, control; [+ *ambición, opiniones, actitud*] to moderate • **lo convencieron para que ~a su postura** they persuaded him to moderate his position • **he tenido que ~ mis aspiraciones** I've had to lower my sights
b [+ *palabras, lenguaje, tono*] to tone down, mind • **ambos líderes han ido moderando su lenguaje** both leaders have gradually toned

m

down their language • **por favor, caballero, modere sus palabras** please, sir, mind your language • **moderen su lenguaje en este tribunal** I will not have such language in court

2 (= *reducir*) [+ *gastos, consumo*] to cut, reduce; [+ *velocidad*] to reduce; [+ *tensión*] to ease • **medidas para ~ la inflación** measures to curb *o* cut *o* reduce inflation • **modere su velocidad** reduce your speed, slow down; ▹ **marcha**

3 [+ *debate, coloquio*] to chair, moderate • **la mesa redonda fue moderada por Jesús Sánchez** the round table was chaired by Jesús Sánchez

VPR **moderarse 1** [*persona*] to restrain o.s., control o.s. • **prometo ~me más la próxima vez** I promise to restrain *o* control myself a bit more next time • **iba a decir una grosería, pero me ~é** I was going to say a rude word but I won't • **tuvo que ~se en sus palabras** he had to tone down his language • **hemos tenido que ~nos un poco en los gastos** we've had to cut down our spending a little

2 [*inflación, precio*] • **se están moderando los precios** prices are being kept in check *o* being held back • **la inflación se moderó relativamente** inflation slowed slightly

modernamente ADV (= *actualmente*) nowadays, in modern times; (= *recientemente*) recently

modernez* SF modernity

modernidad SF modernity

modernismo SM modernism

modernista ADJ modernist(ic)
SMF modernist

modernización SF modernization

modernizador/a ADJ modernizing
SM/F modernizer

modernizar ▹ CONJUG 1f VT to modernize
VPR **modernizarse** to modernize, move with the times

moderno/a ADJ **1** (= *actual*) modern • **una revista dirigida a la mujer moderna** a magazine aimed at the modern woman, a magazine for the woman of today • **siempre va vestida muy moderna** she always wears very trendy clothes*, she always dresses very trendily* • **tiene un equipo de música muy ~** he's got a very up-to-date hi-fi • **le gusta todo lo ~** he likes all things modern • **tienes unos abuelos muy ~s** your grandparents are very with it* • **a la moderna**† in the modern way

2 (*Hist*) modern • **la edad moderna** the modern period
SM/F trendy*

modestamente ADV **1** (= *humildemente*) modestly • —**no estoy de acuerdo —dijo ~** "I don't agree," he said modestly • **yo creo, ~, que están equivocados** in my humble opinion, they are wrong • **contribuyeron ~ a la causa** they contributed to the cause in a modest way

2 (= *sin lujo*) modestly • **~ vestido** modestly dressed • **vivía ~** he lived modestly

modestia SF **1** (= *humildad*) modesty • **~ aparte, no soy mal cocinero** though I say so myself *o* (*frm*) modesty aside, I'm not a bad cook • **con ~** modestly • **vive con ~** he lives modestly • **le respondió con ~** she answered modestly • **falsa ~** false modesty

2 (= *escasez*) • **con ~ de medios** with quite limited resources • **pese a la ~ de sus recursos económicos** despite her limited means

3 (= *falta de lujo*) modesty • **me sorprendió la ~ de su casa** I was surprised by how humble *o* modest his house was

4† (= *recato*) modesty

modesto ADJ **1** (= *humilde*) modest • **no seas tan ~** don't be so modest • **era hijo de un ~ contable** he was the son of a modest accountant • **en mi modesta opinión** in my humble opinion

2 (= *de poca importancia*) modest • **vivía de un sueldo ~** he lived on a modest salary • **nuestra modesta aportación a la causa** our modest *o* humble contribution to the cause • **un ~ paso hacia la paz** a modest step towards peace

3 (= *sin lujo*) modest • **se alojaron en una modesta pensión** they stayed in a modest guesthouse • **visten de forma muy modesta** they dress very modestly

4† (= *recatado*) [*mujer*] modest

modex SM (*Caribe*) press-on sanitary towel

modicidad SF (*frm*) reasonableness, moderateness

módico ADJ [*precio*] reasonable, modest; [*suma*] modest

modificable ADJ modifiable, that can be modified • **los precios son ~s** prices are subject to change

modificación SF (*en producto, vehículo*) modification; (*en texto*) change, alteration; (*en precio*) change ▸ **modificación de (la) conducta** behaviour modification • **técnicas de ~ de conducta** behaviour modification techniques

modificador SM (*Ling*) modifier

modificar ▹ CONJUG 1g VT [+ *producto, vehículo*] to modify; [+ *texto*] to change, alter; [+ *vida*] to change

modismo SM idiom

modistilla SF seamstress

modisto/a SM/F (= *sastre*) dressmaker; [*de alta costura*] fashion designer, couturier ▸ **modisto/a de sombreros** milliner

modo SM **1** (= *manera*) way, manner (*frm*) • **los han distribuido del siguiente ~** they have been distributed in the following way *o* (*frm*) manner • **¿no hay otro ~ de hacerlo?** isn't there another way of doing it? • **no me gusta su ~ de actuar** I don't like the way he does things • **de un ~ u otro** one way or another • **a mi ~ de pensar** *o* **ver** in my view, the way I see it ▸ **modo de empleo** instructions for use ▸ **modo de gobierno** form of government ▸ **modo de producción** mode of production ▸ **modo de vida** way of life; ▹ MANERA, FORMA, MODO

2 (*locuciones*) • **a mi/tu ~** (in) my/your (own) way • **cada uno lo interpreta a su ~** everyone interprets it in his or her own way • **a ~ de** as • **utilizó una bolsa a ~ de maleta** she used a bag as a suitcase • **a ~ de ejemplo/respuesta** by way of example/reply • **en cierto ~** in a way, to a certain extent • **de cualquier ~** (*antes de verbo*) anyway, in any case; (= *después de verbo*) anyhow • **de cualquier ~, ahora tenemos que irnos** we have to go now anyway *o* in any case • **hazlo de cualquier ~** do it anyway you like, do it anyhow, do it any old how* • **de ~** (+ *adj*): • **tenemos que actuar de ~ coherente** we must act consistently • **eso nos afectará de ~ directo** this will have a direct effect on us, this will affect us directly • **el accidente influyó de ~ negativo en el niño** the accident had a negative effect on the child • **de ese ~** (*antes de verbo*) (in) this way; (*después de verbo*) like that • **de ese ~ no habrá problemas** this way there won't be any problems • **no hables de ese ~** don't talk like that • **grosso ~** broadly speaking • **esa fue, grosso ~, la contestación que nos dio** broadly speaking, that was the answer he gave us • **de mal ~** rudely • **me lo pidió muy mal ~** he asked me for it very rudely • **del mismo** *o* **de igual ~** in the same way • **todos van vestidos del mismo** *o* **de igual ~** they are all dressed the same *o* in the same way • **del mismo** *o* **deigual ~ sucedió con los agricultores** the same thing happened with the farmers • **del mismo ~ que** in the same way as *o* that, just as • **de ningún ~** *o* **en ~ alguno**: • **no quiero de ningún ~** *o* **en ~ alguno implicarla en esto** I don't want to involve her in this in any way • **no puedo permitir eso de ningún ~** there's no way I can allow that • **no se parece de ningún ~ a lo que habíamos imaginado** it's nothing like we had imagined • **¡de ningún ~!** certainly not!, no way!* • **de todos ~s** anyway, all the same, in any case • **aunque no me dejes, me iré de todos ~s** even if you don't let me, I'll go anyway *o* all the same *o* in any case • **aunque lo esperaba, de todos ~s me sorprendió** even though I was expecting it, I was still surprised

3 • **de ~ que** (*antes de verbo*) so; (*después de verbo*) so that • **¡de ~ que eras tú el que llamaba!** so it was you that was calling! • **apílalos de ~ que no se caigan** stack them up so (that) they won't fall over

4 (*Esp*) (*frm*) (= *moderación*) moderation • **bebe con ~** drink in moderation

5 (*LAm*) • **¡ni ~!** (= *de ninguna manera*) no way*, not a chance*; (= *no hay otra alternativa*) what else can I/you *etc* do? • **ni ~ que lo va a hacer** no way she's going to do it • **si no me quieres, ni ~** if you don't love me, what else can I do?

6 modos (= *modales*) manners • **buenos ~s** good manners • **con buenos ~s** politely • **malos ~s** bad manners • **me contestó con muy malos ~s** he answered me very rudely

7 (*Ling*) [*del verbo*] mood • **de ~** manner (*antes de s*) • **adverbio de ~** manner adverb ▸ **modo adverbial** adverbial phrase ▸ **modo conjuntivo** conjunctional phrase ▸ **modo imperativo** imperative mood ▸ **modo indicativo** indicative mood ▸ **modo subjuntivo** subjunctive mood

8 (*Inform*) mode

9 (*Mús*) mode • **~ mayor/menor** major/minor mode

modorra SF **1** (= *sueño*) drowsiness • **me entró la ~** I began to feel drowsy • **sacudirse la ~** to rouse o.s.

2 (*Vet*) staggers

modorro ADJ **1** (= *soñoliento*) drowsy

2* (= *tonto*) dull, stupid

3 [*fruta*] soft, squashy

modosito ADJ, **modoso** ADJ (= *educado*) well-mannered; (= *recatado*) demure

modulación SF modulation ▸ **modulación de frecuencia** (*Radio*) frequency modulation

modulado ADJ modulated

modulador SM modulator

modulador-demodulador SM (*Inform*) modem

modular ▹ CONJUG 1a ADJ modular
VT to modulate
SM (*Cono Sur*) shelf unit

modularidad SF modularity

módulo SM **1** (*Educ*) module

2 [*de mobiliario*] unit • **estantería por ~s** modular *o* combination shelving units (*pl*)

3 (*And*) platform

4 (*Espacio*) ▸ **módulo de mando** command module ▸ **módulo lunar** lunar module

moer SM moiré

mofa SF (= *burla*) mockery, ridicule • **hacer ~ de algo/algn** to scoff at sth/sb, make fun of sth/sb • **exponer a algn a la ~ pública** to hold sb up to public ridicule • **es una ~ de nuestras creencias** it makes a mockery of our beliefs

mofador(a) ADJ mocking, scoffing, sneering
SM/F mocker, derider

mofar ▷ CONJUG 1a VI to mock, scoff, sneer
VPR **mofarse** • **~se de algo/algn** to mock sth/sb, scoff at sth/sb, sneer at sth/sb

mofeta SF **1** (*Zool*) skunk
2 (*Min*) firedamp
3‡ (= *pedo*) fart‡

mofinco‡ SM (*Caribe*) firewater*, gut-rot*

mofle SM (*LAm*) (*Aut*) silencer, muffler (*EEUU*)

moflete SM (= *mejilla*) chubby cheek

mofletudo ADJ chubby-cheeked

mogol SM **1** = **mongol**
2 (*Hist*) • **el Gran Mogol** the Great Mogul

Mogolia SF = **Mongolia**

mogólico/a ADJ, SM/F = **mongólico**

mogolla SF (*And, Cono Sur*) bargain

mogollón* SM **1** (= *gran cantidad*) loads (*pl*), masses (*pl*) • **(un) ~ de gente** • **gente a ~** loads *o* masses of people • **tengo (un) ~ de discos** I've got loads *o* masses of records
2 (= *confusión*) commotion, upheaval; (= *lío*) fuss, row • **hay mucho ~ aquí** it's a bit wild here
3 • **de ~** (= *gratis*) • **colarse de ~ en un sitio** to get into a place without paying • **comer de ~** to scrounge a meal* • **lograr un puesto de ~** to wangle a job*
ADV (= *mucho*) • **me gusta ~** I think it's great *o* fantastic*

mogollónico* ADJ huge, massive

mogote SM (= *otero*) flat-topped hillock; (= *montón*) heap, pile; [*de gavillas*] stack

mohair [mo'xair, mo'air] SM mohair

mohín SM (= *pucheros*) pout • **hacer un ~** to make a face • **con un leve ~ de extrañeza** with a faintly surprised expression

mohína SF **1** (= *enfado*) annoyance, displeasure
2 (= *mal humor*) the sulks
3 (= *tristeza*) depression • **ser fácil a las ~s** to be easily depressed

mohíno ADJ **1** (= *enfadado*) annoyed
2 (= *malhumorado*) sulky, sullen
3 (= *triste*) sad, depressed • **se fue ~ y cabizbajo** he went off, sad and downcast

moho SM **1** (*en metal*) rust
2 (*en alimentos*) mould, mold (*EEUU*), mildew • **cubierto de ~** mouldy, moldy (*EEUU*) • **olor a ~** musty smell • MODISMOS: • **no cría ~** he's always on the go, he doesn't let the grass grow under his feet • **no dejar criar ~ a algn** to keep sb on the go

mohoso ADJ **1** [*metal*] rusty
2 [*alimento*] mouldy, moldy (*EEUU*); [*olor, sabor*] musty
3 [*chiste*] stale

Moisés SM Moses

moisés SM INV (= *cuna*) Moses basket, cradle; (*portátil*) carrycot

moja‡ SF (= *puñalada*) stab, thrust; (= *herida*) stab wound

mojada SF **1** (*con agua*) wetting, soaking
2 (= *herida*) stab (wound)

mojado ADJ (= *húmedo*) damp, wet; (= *empapado*) soaked, drenched • **le pasé por la frente un trapo ~** I mopped her brow with a damp cloth • **por la mañana la hierba estaba mojada** the grass was wet in the morning • **llegamos a casa completamente ~s** we were completely soaked *o* drenched when we got home; ▷ **llover**
SM (*Méx*) wetback (*EEUU*), illegal immigrant

mojama SF salted tuna • MODISMOS: • **está más seco que una ~** he's as wrinkled as a prune • **estar más tieso que la ~** to be practically in the grave • **~ tiesa**: • **todo escritor que no sea una ~ tiesa** any writer worth his salt

mojar ▷ CONJUG 1a VT **1** (*involuntariamente*) to get wet; (*voluntariamente*) to wet; (= *humedecer*) to damp(en), moisten; (= *empapar*) to drench, soak • **¡no mojes la alfombra!** don't get the carpet wet! • **~ la cabeza al niño** to wet the baby's head • **el niño ha mojado la cama** the baby's wet the bed • **moja un poco el trapo** dampen the cloth • **la lluvia nos mojó a todos** we all got soaked in the rain • **moje ligeramente el sello** moisten the stamp a little • **~ la ropa en agua** to soak *o* steep the washing in water
2 (= *meter*) to dip • **~ el pan en el café** to dip *o* dunk one's bread in one's coffee • **~ la pluma en la tinta** to dip one's pen into the ink
3* [+ *triunfo*] to celebrate with a drink
4 • MODISMOS: • **~la** • **~ el churro**** to dip one's wick**
5 (*Ling*) to palatalize
6 (= *apuñalar*) to stab
7 (*Caribe*) [+ *camarero*] to tip; (= *sobornar**) to bribe
VI • **~ en** (= *hacer pinitos*) to dabble in; (= *entrometerse*) to meddle *o* get involved in
VPR **mojarse 1** (= *humedecerse*) **a** (*reflexivo*) to get wet • **~se hasta los huesos** to get soaked to the skin
b • **~se el pelo** (*involuntariamente*) to get one's hair wet; (*voluntariamente*) to wet one's hair • **me he mojado las mangas** I got my sleeves wet
2* (= *comprometerse*) to get one's feet wet • **no se mojó** he kept out of it, he didn't get involved
3 • MODISMO: • **~se las orejas** (*Cono Sur*) to give way, back down

mojarra SF **1‡** (= *lengua*) tongue
2 (*LAm*) (= *cuchillo*) short broad knife
3 (= *pez*) *type of bream*

mojera SF whitebeam

mojicón SM **1** (= *bizcocho*) sponge cake; (= *bollo*) bun
2* (= *bofetada*) punch in the face, slap

mojiganga SF **1** (= *farsa*) farce, piece of clowning
2 (*Hist*) masquerade, mummery

mojigatería SF (= *beatería*) sanctimoniousness; (= *puritanismo*) prudery, prudishness

mojigato/a ADJ (= *santurrón*) sanctimonious; (= *puritano*) prudish, strait-laced
SM/F (= *santurrón*) sanctimonious person; (= *puritano*) prude

mojinete SM [*de techo*] ridge; [*de muro*] tiling, coping; (*Cono Sur*) (= *aguilón*) gable

mojito SM (*Cuba*) *long drink with a base of rum*

mojo SM (*esp Méx*) garlic sauce

mojón[1] SM **1** (= *piedra*) boundary stone; (*tb* **mojón kilométrico**) milestone
2 (= *montón*) heap, pile
3 (*And***) (= *mierda*) shit**, crap**

mojón[2]/ona SM/F (*Caribe‡*) (= *bruto*) idiot, thickhead*; (= *chaparro*) shortie*

mol. ABR (*Fís*) (= **molécula**) mol

mola SF rounded mountain

molar[1] SM molar

molar[2]‡ ▷ CONJUG 1a VI (*Esp*) **1** (= *gustar*) • **lo que más me mola es ...** what I'm really into is ...* • **tía, me molas mucho** I'm crazy about you, baby* • **¡cómo mola esa moto!** that bike is really cool!‡ • **¿te mola un pitillo?** do you fancy a smoke?* • **no me mola** I don't go for that*, I don't fancy that
2 (= *estar de moda*) to be in* • **eso mola mucho ahora** that's very in right now*, that's all the rage now
3 (= *dar tono*) to be classy*, be real posh*
4 (= *valer*) to be OK* • **por partes iguales, ¿mola?** equal shares then, OK?*
5 (= *marchar*) • **la cosa no mola** it's not going well at all

molcajete SM (*esp Méx*) mortar

Moldavia SF Moldavia

moldavo/a ADJ, SM/F Moldavian, Moldovan

molde SM **1** (*Culin, Téc*) mould, mold (*EEUU*); (= *vaciado*) cast; (*Tip*) form
• MODISMO: • **romper ~s** to break the mould ▸ **molde de corona** ring mould *o* (*EEUU*) mold
2 (*Cos*) (= *patrón*) pattern; (= *aguja*) knitting needle
3 (= *modelo*) model
4 • MODISMO: • **de ~** (= *perfecto*) perfect, just right • **el vestido le está de ~** the dress is just right for her • **esto me viene de ~** this is just what I want *o* need, this is just the job*; ▷ **letra, pan**

moldeable ADJ [*material*] malleable; [*carácter, persona*] easily influenced, impressionable

moldeado SM **1** (= *modelado*) moulding, molding (*EEUU*); (*en yeso*) casting
2 [*del pelo*] soft perm

moldear ▷ CONJUG 1a VT **1** (= *modelar*) to mould, mold (*EEUU*); (*en yeso*) to cast
2 [+ *pelo*] to give a soft perm
3 [+ *persona*] to mould, mold (*EEUU*), shape

moldeo SM moulding, molding (*EEUU*)

moldura SF **1** (= *marco*) frame ▸ **moldura lateral** (*Aut*) side stripe
2 (*Arquit*) moulding, molding (*EEUU*)

mole[1] SF (= *masa*) mass, bulk; (= *edificio*) pile • **la enorme ~ del buque** the vast bulk of the ship • **ese edificio/hombre es una ~** that building/man is massive • **se sentó con toda su ~** he sat down with his full bulk *o* weight

mole[2] (*Méx*) SM (= *salsa*) thick chilli sauce; (= *plato*) meat in chilli sauce • MODISMO: • **ser el ~ de algn*** to be sb's favourite thing ▸ **mole de olla** meat stew ▸ **mole poblano** *meat dish from Puebla*

molécula SF molecule

molecular ADJ molecular

moledor ADJ grinding, crushing
SM grinder, crusher

moledora SF (*Téc*) grinder, crusher

moledura SF **1** (= *acción*) [*de café*] grinding; [*de trigo*] milling
2* (= *agotamiento*) • **¡qué ~ traigo!** I'm shattered*

moler ▷ CONJUG 2h VT **1** [+ *café*] to grind; [+ *trigo*] to mill; (= *machacar*) to crush; (= *pulverizar*) to pound • MODISMO: • **~ a algn a palos** to give sb a beating
2 (= *fastidiar*) to annoy; (= *aburrir*) to bore

molestar ▷ CONJUG 1a VT **1** (= *importunar*) to bother, annoy • **¿no la estarán molestando, verdad?** they're not bothering *o* annoying you, are they? • **no la molestes más con tus tonterías** stop pestering *o* bothering *o* annoying her with your silly games
2 (= *interrumpir*) to disturb • **que no me moleste nadie** I don't want to be disturbed by anyone • **siento ~te, pero necesito que me ayudes** I'm sorry to disturb *o* trouble *o* bother you, but I need your help
3 (= *ofender*) to upset • **espero no haberte molestado** I hope I didn't upset you
VI **1** (= *importunar*) to be a nuisance • **quita de en medio, que siempre estás molestando** get out of the way, you're always being a nuisance • **no quisiera ~, pero necesito**

m

hablar contigo I don't want to bother you *o* be a nuisance, but I need to talk to you • "no molestar" "(please) do not disturb" • me molesta mucho que me hablen así it really annoys *o* irritates me when they talk to me like that • ese ruido me molesta that noise is bothering *o* annoying *o* irritating me • me molesta el jarrón, ¿puedes apartarlo? the vase is in the way, can you move it? • me molesta tener que repetirlo it annoys me to have to repeat it
2 (= *incomodar*) to feel uncomfortable, bother • ¿te molesta el humo? does the smoke bother you? • me está empezando a ~ la herida the injury is starting to play up* *o* bother me • me molesta al tragar it hurts when I swallow • la radio no me molesta para estudiar the radio doesn't bother me when I'm studying • si le sigue molestando, acuda a su médico if it goes on giving you trouble, see your doctor
3 (= *ofender*) to upset • me molestó mucho lo que dijiste what you said really upset me • le molestó que no lo invitárais a la fiesta he was hurt that you didn't invite him to the party
4 (= *importar*) (*en preguntas*) • ¿le molesta la radio? does the radio bother you?, do you mind the radio being on? • ¿te ~ía prestarme un paraguas? would you mind lending me an umbrella? • ¿le molesta que abra la ventana *o* si abro la ventana? do you mind if I open the window?
VPR **molestarse** 1 (= *tomarse la molestia*) to bother o.s. • no se moleste, prefiero estar de pie don't trouble *o* bother yourself, I prefer to stand • —¿quiere que abra la ventana? —por mí no se moleste "shall I open the window?" — "don't mind me" • no te molestes por él, sabe arreglárselas solo don't put yourself out for him, he can manage on his own • ~se en hacer algo to take the trouble to do sth • se molestó en llevarnos al aeropuerto she took the trouble to drive us to the airport, she went to the trouble of driving us to the airport • no te molestes en venir a por mí don't bother to come and pick me up, you needn't take the trouble to come and pick me up • ni siquiera te has molestado en responder a mis cartas you didn't even bother to answer my letters
2 (= *disgustarse*) (*con enfado*) to get annoyed, get upset; (*con ofensa*) to take offence, take offense (*EEUU*) • no deberías ~te, lo hizo sin mala intención you shouldn't get annoyed *o* upset/take offence, he didn't mean any harm • ~se con algn to get annoyed *o* cross with sb • ~se por algo to get annoyed at sth, get upset about sth • se molesta por nada he gets annoyed at *o* upset about the slightest thing • ¿te has molestado por ese comentario? did that comment upset *o* offend you?

molestia SF 1 (= *trastorno*) bother, trouble • el retraso nos causó muchas ~s the delay caused us a lot of bother *o* trouble • ¿me podrías llevar a casa, si no es mucha ~? could you take me home, if it's not too much bother *o* trouble? • andar con muletas es una gran ~ walking with crutches is a real nuisance *o* bother • perdone la ~, pero ... sorry to bother you, but ... • ¡no es ninguna ~, estaré encantado de ayudarte! it's no trouble at all, I'll be happy to help! • "perdonen las ~s" "we apologize for any inconvenience" • ahorrarse la ~ de hacer algo to save o.s. the bother *o* trouble of doing sth • tomarse la ~ de hacer algo to take the trouble to do sth • se tomaron la ~ de visitarlos en persona they took the trouble to visit them in person • no tenías que haberte tomado la ~ you shouldn't have bothered *o* taken the trouble, you shouldn't have put yourself out
2 (*Med*) discomfort • al andar noto una pequeña ~ I feel a slight discomfort when I walk • si persisten las ~s, consulte a un especialista if the discomfort *o* trouble persists, consult a specialist • tengo una pequeña ~ en la garganta I have a bit of a sore throat • tengo ~s en el estómago I have an upset stomach

molesto ADJ 1 (= *que causa molestia*) [*tos, picor, ruido, persona*] irritating, annoying; [*olor, síntoma*] unpleasant • es una persona muy molesta he's a very irritating *o* annoying person • es sumamente ~ que ... it's extremely irritating *o* annoying that ... • una sensación bastante molesta quite an uncomfortable *o* unpleasant feeling • lo único ~ es el viaje the only nuisance is the journey, the only annoying thing is the journey • si no es ~ para usted if it's no trouble to you *o* no bother for you
2 (= *que incomoda*) [*asiento, ropa*] uncomfortable; [*tarea*] annoying; [*situación*] awkward, embarrassing • las faldas ajustadas son muy molestas tight skirts are very uncomfortable
3 (= *incómodo*) [*persona*] uncomfortable • me sentía ~ en la fiesta I felt uneasy *o* uncomfortable at the party • me siento ~ cada vez que me hace un regalo I feel awkward *o* embarrassed whenever she gives me a present • estaba ~ por la inyección he was in some discomfort *o* pain after the injection
4 (= *enfadado*) [*persona*] annoyed • estaba muy molesta con su actitud she was very annoyed at their attitude • ¿estás ~ conmigo por lo que dije? are you annoyed at me for what I said?
5 (= *disgustado*) [*persona*] upset • ¿estás molesta por algo que haya pasado? are you upset about something that's happened?

molestoso ADJ (*LAm*) annoying

molibdeno SM molybdenum

molicie SF 1 (= *blandura*) softness
2 (= *comodidad*) • reblandecido por la ~ de la vida moderna made complacent by the comforts *o* ease of modern life • una vida sin concesiones de ~ a life with no concessions to luxury *o* comfort
3 (= *afeminamiento*) effeminacy

molido ADJ 1 [*café, especias*] ground
2 • estar ~* (= *cansado*) to be shattered* • estoy ~ de tanto viajar I'm shattered with all this travelling* • tengo todo el cuerpo ~ I'm aching all over • tengo los riñones ~s my back is killing me*

molienda SF 1 (= *acto*) [*de café*] grinding; [*de trigo*] milling
2 (= *cantidad*) *quantity of grain to be ground*
3* (= *cansancio*) weariness
4* (= *molestia*) nuisance

moliente ADJ ▸ corriente

molinero/a SM/F miller

molinete SM (toy) windmill

molinillo SM 1 (*para moler*) hand mill ▸ molinillo de aceite olive press ▸ molinillo de café coffee mill *o* grinder ▸ molinillo de carne mincer
2 (= *juguete*) (toy) windmill, pinwheel (*EEUU*)

molino SM 1 (*gen*) mill; (= *trituradora*) grinder ▸ molino de agua water mill ▸ molino de cubo waterwheel ▸ molino de viento windmill
2* (= *persona*) fidget

molla SF [*de persona*] fleshy part; [*de carne*] lean part; [*de fruta*] flesh; [*de pan*] doughy part

mollar ADJ 1 [*fruta*] (= *blanda*) soft; (= *fácil de pelar*) easy to peel; [*almendra*] easily shelled
2 [*carne*] boned, boneless
3* [*trabajo*] cushy*, easy
4* (= *crédulo*) gullible

mollate SM plonk*

molledo SM 1 [*del brazo*] fleshy part
2 [*de pan*] doughy part

molleja SF 1 [*de ave*] gizzard
2 mollejas [*de res, cordero*] sweetbreads

mollejón* SM softie*; (*pey*) fat slob*

mollera SF 1* (= *seso*) brains (*pl*), sense • tener buena ~ to have brains, be brainy • MODISMOS: • cerrado *o* duro de ~ (= *estúpido*) dense*, dim*; (= *terco*) pig-headed • no les cabe en la ~ they just can't get their heads round it* • secar la ~ a algn to drive sb crazy
2 (= *coronilla*) crown of the head

mollete SM 1 (*Culin*) muffin
2 [*del brazo*] fleshy part
3 (= *mejilla*) fat cheek

molo SM (*Cono Sur*) breakwater, mole

molón‡ ADJ 1 (*Esp*) (= *bueno*) fantastic*, brilliant*
2 (*Esp*) (= *elegante*) posh*, classy*
3 (*CAm, Méx*) (= *pesado*) tiresome

molondra‡ SF bonce*

molote SM 1 (*Méx*) (= *ovillo*) ball of wool
2 (*Méx*) (*Culin*) fried maize pancake
3 (*And, Méx*) (= *jugarreta*) dirty trick
4 (*CAm, Caribe, Méx*) (= *alboroto*) riot, commotion

molotov ADJ INV • cóctel ~ Molotov cocktail, petrol bomb

molturar ▸ CONJUG 1a VT to grind, mill

Molucas SFPL • las (islas) ~ the Moluccas, the Molucca Islands

molusco SM mollusc, mollusk (*EEUU*)

momentáneamente ADV momentarily

momentáneo ADJ momentary

momento SM 1 (= *instante*) moment • la miró un ~ he looked at her for a moment • espera un ~ hold on a minute *o* moment • —¡Juan, ven aquí! —¡un ~! "come here, Juan" — "just a minute *o* moment!" • llegará dentro de un ~ she'll be here in a minute *o* moment • está protestando desde el ~ en que llegó he's been complaining from the moment he arrived • hace un ~ just a moment ago • en ese preciso ~ se paró el coche at that very moment *o* right then, the car stopped • este es un ~ histórico this is a historic moment • no paró de hablar ni un solo ~ he never stopped talking for a single second • no creí ni por un ~ que llegaría a divorciarse I never thought for a moment that she'd get divorced • llegará en breves ~s she'll be here shortly • en este ~ at the moment, right now • en este ~ el doctor no puede atenderle the doctor can't see you at the moment *o* right now • no dejó de apoyarme en ningún ~ she never stopped supporting me for a moment • en un primer ~ at first • en un primer ~ creí que era un resfriado at first I thought it was a cold • estuvo a mi lado en todo ~ he was at my side the whole time • en un ~ in next to no time • limpió el cuarto en un ~ he cleaned the room in next to no time
2 (= *rato*) • los mejores ~s del partido the highlights of the match • pasamos ~s inolvidables en Madrid we had an unforgettable time in Madrid
3 (= *época*) time • en el ~ actual at the present time • deben usarse las técnicas disponibles en el ~ the currently available techniques should be used • del ~: • la música más representativa del ~ the music which is

most representative of current trends • **el grupo favorito del ~** the most popular group at the moment
4 (= *coyuntura*) • **nuestra empresa pasa por un ~ magnífico** our company is doing splendidly at the moment • **atravesamos un ~ difícil** we are going through a difficult time *o* patch • **el actor estaba en su mejor ~** the actor was in his prime • **llegué en buen ~** I arrived at a good time • **ha llegado el ~ de hacer algo** the time has come to do sth • **en el ~ oportuno** at the right time • **ser buen/mal ~ para hacer algo** to be a good/bad time to do sth • **es el mejor ~ para invertir en bolsa** it's the ideal time to invest in the stock market • **todo se hará en su ~** we'll do everything in good time o when the time comes • **ya te avisarán en su ~** they'll let you know in due course
5 (*otras locuciones*) • **al ~** at once • **a cada ~ se despertaba y pedía agua** she kept waking up and asking for water, she was constantly waking up and asking for water • **en cualquier ~** any time now • **puede llegar en cualquier ~** she could arrive at any moment • **en un ~ dado**: • **en un ~ dado, conseguí sujetarlo del brazo** at one stage I managed to grab hold of his arm • **en un ~ dado, yo mismo puedo echarte una mano** I could give you a hand some time, if necessary • **de ~** for the moment • **de ~ continúa en el trabajo** he's staying in the job for the time being *o* for the moment • **de ~ déjalo y piénsatelo mejor** leave it for the moment and think it over • **de ~ no lo reconocí, pero luego recordé su cara** at first I didn't recognize him, but then I remembered his face • **desde el ~ en que**: • **los impuestos, desde el ~ en que son obligatorios, son una extorsión** since taxes are compulsory, they amount to extortion • **en el ~** straight away • **la llamé y acudió en el ~** I called her and she came over straight away • **de un ~ a otro** any minute now • **en el ~ menos pensado** when least expected • **esas cosas pasan en el ~ menos pensado** those things happen when you least expect them • **por ~s** by the minute • **está cambiando por ~s** it is changing by the minute • **por el ~** for the time being, for now
6 (*Mec*) momentum, moment

momería SF mummery, clowning
momia SF mummy • **parece una ~** she looks like a zombie • **no te quedes ahí como una ~** don't stand there like a dummy
momificación SF mummification
momificar ▹ CONJUG 1g VT to mummify
VPR **momificarse** to mummify, become mummified
momio[1] SM (= *ganga*) bargain; (= *extra*) extra; (= *sinecura*) cushy job*; (= *trato*) profitable deal • **de ~** free
ADJ [*carne*] lean
momio[2]/a* (*Chile*) ADJ reactionary, right-wing (*antes de s*)
SM/F **1** (= *carroza*) square*, fuddy-duddy*
2 (*Pol*) reactionary, right winger
momo SM **1** (= *cara*) funny face
2 (= *payasadas*) clowning, buffoonery
mona SF **1** (*Zool*) (= *hembra*) female monkey; (= *especie*) Barbary ape • MODISMO: • **mandar a algn a freír ~s*** to tell sb where to go*, tell sb to get lost* • REFRÁN: • **aunque la ~ se vista de seda (~ se queda)** you can't make a silk purse out of a sow's ear
2* (= *copión*) copycat*
3* (= *borrachera*) • **coger** *o* **pillar una ~** to get sloshed *o* plastered* • **dormir la ~** to sleep it off
4 ▸ **mona de Pascua** Easter cake
5 (*LAm**) (= *droga*) *Colombian golden marijuana*
6 • MODISMO: • **andar** *o* **estar como la ~** (*Cono Sur*) (= *sin dinero*) to be broke*; (= *desgraciado*) to feel terrible; ▹ **mono[3]**
monacal ADJ monastic
monacato SM monasticism, monastic life ▸ **monacato femenino** convent life, life as a nun
monacillo SM acolyte, altar boy
Mónaco SM Monaco
monada SF **1** (= *cosa*) • **la casa es una ~** the house is gorgeous *o* lovely • **¡qué ~!** isn't it gorgeous *o* lovely? • **¡qué ~ de perrito!** what a cute *o* lovely little dog!
2 (= *chica*) pretty girl • **¡hola, ~!** hello gorgeous *o* beautiful!*
3 (= *tontería*) • **deja de hacer ~s** stop clowning around
4 [*de niño*] charming habit, sweet little way
5* **monadas** (= *zalamería*) flattery (*sing*)
6 (= *cualidad*) silliness, childishness
mónada SF monad
monaguillo SM, **monago** SM altar boy, acolyte
monarca SMF monarch
monarquía SF monarchy
monárquico/a ADJ monarchic(al); (*Pol*) royalist, monarchist
SM/F royalist, monarchist
monarquismo SM monarchism
monarquista SM monarchist
monasterio SM [*de hombres*] monastery; [*de mujeres*] convent
monástico ADJ monastic
Moncho SM *forma familiar de* **Ramón**
Moncloa SF • **la ~** *official residence of the Spanish prime minister (Madrid)*
monclovita ADJ of the Moncloa palace, of the prime minister, prime ministerial
monda[1] SF **1** (= *peladura*) [*de naranja*] peel; [*de patata*] peelings (*pl*); [*de plátano*] skin
2 (= *acción*) peeling
3 (= *poda*) pruning; (= *temporada*) pruning season
4 (*LAm**) (= *paliza*) beating
monda[2]* SF • **¡es la ~!** (= *fantástico*) it's great!*, it's fantastic!*; (= *el colmo*) (*refiriéndose a algo*) it's the limit!; (*refiriéndose a algn*) he's the limit *o* end!*; [*algo divertido*] it's a scream*; [*persona divertida*] he's a scream* • **este nuevo baile es la ~** (= *fantástico*) this new dance is great *o* fantastic*; (*pey*) this new dance is the pits*
mondadientes SM INV toothpick
mondador SM (*Méx*) shredder
mondadura SF = **monda[1]**
mondante* ADJ • **es un chaval ~** he's a scream* • **nos pasó una cosa ~** something hilarious *o* really funny happened to us
mondar ▹ CONJUG 1a VT **1** [+ *fruta, patata*] to peel; [+ *nueces, guisantes*] to shell; [+ *palo*] to pare, remove the bark from
2* [+ *persona*] (= *cortar el pelo*) to scalp*; (= *desplumar*) to fleece*, clean out*
3 (= *podar*) to prune
4 (= *limpiar*) (*gen*) to clean, cleanse; [+ *canal*] to clean out
5 (*LAm**) (= *pegar*) to beat (up), thrash; (*Caribe*) • **~ a algn** to wipe the floor with sb*
VPR **mondarse 1** (*tb* **mondarse de risa***) to die laughing*
2 • **~se los dientes** to pick one's teeth
mondo ADJ **1** [*cabeza*] completely shorn
2 (= *sin añadidura*) plain • **el asunto ~ es esto** the plain fact of the matter is this • **tiene su sueldo ~ y nada más** he has just what he earns, nothing more • MODISMO: • **~ y lirondo*** pure and simple
3* (= *sin dinero*) • **me he quedado ~** I'm cleaned out*, I haven't a cent
mondongo SM (= *entrañas*) guts (*pl*), insides (*pl*); (= *callos*) tripe
mondongudo ADJ (*esp Cono Sur*) paunchy, pot-bellied
monear ▹ CONJUG 1a VI **1** (= *comportarse*) to monkey around, clown around; (= *hacer muecas*) to make faces
2 (*Cono Sur, Méx**) (= *jactarse*) to boast, swank*
moneda SF **1** (= *pieza*) coin • **una ~ falsa** a counterfeit coin • **una ~ de cinco dólares** a five-dollar piece • **la máquina funciona con ~s** the machine is coin-operated • **tirar una ~ al aire** to toss a coin ▸ **moneda menuda, moneda suelta** small change
2 [*de un país*] currency • **en ~ española** in Spanish money • **la casa de la ~** the mint • MODISMO: • **pagar a algn con** *o* **en la misma ~** to pay sb back in his own coin *o* in kind ▸ **moneda blanda** soft currency ▸ **moneda convertible** convertible currency ▸ **moneda corriente** currency • MODISMO: • **es ~ corriente** it's a common occurrence ▸ **moneda débil** soft currency ▸ **moneda decimal** decimal currency ▸ **moneda de curso legal** legal tender ▸ **moneda dura** hard currency ▸ **moneda fraccionaria** money in small denominations ▸ **moneda fuerte** hard currency ▸ **moneda nacional** national currency • **el precio es 1.000 pesos, ~ nacional** (*LAm*) the price is 1,000 pesos ▸ **moneda única** single currency
monedar ▹ CONJUG 1a VT, **monedear** ▹ CONJUG 1a VT to mint, coin
monedero SM **1** (*para monedas*) purse, coin purse (*EEUU*) ▸ **monedero electrónico** electronic purse
2 ▸ **monedero falso** counterfeiter
monegasco/a ADJ of/from Monaco, Monegasque • **el principado ~** the Principality of Monaco
SM/F native/inhabitant of Monaco, Monegasque • **los ~s** the people of Monaco
monería SF **1** (= *mueca*) funny face, monkey face; (= *imitación*) mimicry
2 (= *payasada*) antic, prank • **hacer ~s** to monkey around, clown around
3 (= *banalidad*) trifle, triviality
monetario ADJ monetary
monetarismo SM monetarism
monetarista ADJ, SMF monetarist
mongol(a) ADJ, SM/F Mongol, Mongolian
SM (*Ling*) Mongolian
Mongolia SF Mongolia
mongólico/a ADJ **1** (*Med*†) mongoloid† • **niños ~s** children with Down's syndrome
2 (*pey*) (= *estúpido*) moronic • **ideas mongólicas** moronic ideas
3 (= *mongol*) Mongolian
SM/F **1** (*Med*†) Down's syndrome sufferer
2 (*pey*) (= *estúpido*) moron*
3 (= *mongol*) Mongolian
mongolismo† SM Down's syndrome, mongolism†
mongoloide ADJ (*Med*†) mongoloid†
moni* SF (*LAm*) money
monicaco/a* SM/F twit*
monicongo SM (*LAm*) cartoon film
monigote SM **1** (= *muñeco*) rag doll; [*de papel*] paper doll • MODISMO: • **hacer el ~** to fool around, clown around ▸ **monigote de nieve** snowman ▸ **monigote de paja** straw man ▸ **monigote de tebeo** cartoon character; ▹ DÍA DE LOS (SANTOS) INOCENTES
2 (= *niño*) little monkey
3 (*sin personalidad*) weak character
4 (= *garabato*) doodle
monises‡ SMPL brass* (*sing*), dough* (*sing*)
monitor(a) SM/F (= *persona*) (*Dep*) instructor, coach; [*de gira*] group leader

▸ **monitor(a) de campamento** camp leader ▸ **monitor(a) de esquí** ski instructor ▸ **monitor(a) de fitness** fitness trainer ▸ **monitor(a) de natación** swimming instructor ▸ **monitor(a) deportivo/a** *(gen)* sports coach; *(en escuela)* games coach
SM *(tb Inform, Téc)* monitor
monitoreado SM monitoring
monitorear ▹ CONJUG 1a VT to monitor
monitorio ADJ admonitory
monitorización SF monitoring
monitorizar ▹ CONJUG 1f VT to monitor
monitos SMPL *(And, Méx)* cartoon *(sing)*
monja SF nun ▸ **monja de clausura** cloistered nun, nun in a closed order
monje SM **1** *(Rel)* monk
2 *(Caribe)* (= *dinero*) five-peso note
monjil ADJ *(lit)* nun's; *(fig)* *(pey)* excessively demure
SM *(hábito)* nun's habit
mono[1] SM **1** *(Zool)* monkey • **¡mono!** *(a niño)* you little monkey! ▸ **mono araña** spider monkey ▸ **mono aullador** howler monkey
2‡ *[de drogadicto]* withdrawal symptoms *(pl)*, cold turkey* • **estar con el ~** to be suffering withdrawal symptoms, have gone cold turkey* • **tener ~ de fama** to crave fame
3 (= *traje de faena*) overalls *(pl)*, boiler suit; *[de calle]* jumpsuit; *(con peto)* dungarees *(pl)* ▸ **mono de aviador** flying suit ▸ **mono de esquí** ski suit ▸ **mono de vuelo** flying suit
4* (= *hombre feo*) ugly devil
5 (= *figura*) *cartoon or caricature figure*; **monos** *(Cono Sur)* doodles ▸ **monos animados** *(Cono Sur)* cartoons
6 *(Naipes)* joker
7‡ *(policía)* cop*
8* (= *seña*) sign *(between lovers)* • **hacerse ~s** to make eyes at each other
9 *(Caribe*)* (= *deuda*) debt
10 • MODISMOS: • **tener ~s en la cara**: • **no me mirarían más ni que tuviera ~s en la cara** they couldn't have stared at me more if I had come from the moon • **estar de ~s** to be at daggers drawn • **meter los ~s a algn** *(LAm)* to put the wind up sb* • **ser un ~ de repetición** to repeat things like a parrot • **ser el último ~** to be a nobody ▸ **mono de imitación** copycat*
mono[2] ADJ **1** (= *bonito*) pretty, lovely; (= *simpático*) nice, cute • **una chica muy mona** a lovely *o* very pretty girl • **¡qué sombrero más ~!** what a nice *o* cute little hat!
2 *(Mús)* mono
mono[3]**/a** ADJ *(LAm)* (= *amarillo*) yellow; (= *rubio*) blond; (= *rojizo*) reddish blond
SM/F *(Col)* (= *rubio*) blond(e) (person); ▹ **mona**
mono... PREF mono...
monoaural ADJ monophonic, mono
monocarril SM monorail
monocasco SM monohull
monocigótico ADJ, **monocigoto** ADJ monozygotic
monocolor ADJ one-colour, of a single colour • **gobierno ~** one-party government
monocorde ADJ **1** *(Mús)* single-stringed
2 (= *monótono*) monotonous, unvaried
monocromo ADJ monochrome; *(TV)* black-and-white
SM monochrome
monóculo SM monocle
monocultivo SM single crop farming, monoculture • **el ~ es un peligro para muchos países** in many countries dependence upon a single crop is risky
monofónico ADJ monophonic
monogamia SF monogamy
monógamo ADJ monogamous
monografía SF monograph
monográfico ADJ monographic • **estudio ~** monograph • **número ~** *[de revista]* issue devoted to a single subject • **programa ~** programme devoted to a single subject
SM monograph, special edition
monograma SM monogram
monokini SM topless swimsuit
monolingüe ADJ monolingual
SMF monoglot
monolingüismo SM monolingualism
monolítico ADJ monolithic
monolitismo SM (= *naturaleza*) monolithic nature; (= *sistema*) monolithic system
monolito SM monolith
monologar ▹ CONJUG 1h VI to soliloquize; *(Teat)* to give a monologue
monólogo SM monologue, monolog *(EEUU)* ▸ **monólogo interior** stream of consciousness
monomando SM mixer tap, mixing faucet *(EEUU)*
monomanía SF *(gen)* mania, obsession; *(Psic)* monomania
monomaniaco/a ADJ, SM/F, **monomaníaco/a** ADJ, SM/F monomaniac
monomio SM monomial
monomotor ADJ single-engined
monono* ADJ *(Cono Sur)* (= *atractivo*) lovely, pretty; (= *acicalado*) dressed up
mononucleado ADJ mononuclear
mononucleosis SF INV ▸ **mononucleosis infecciosa** glandular fever
monoparental ADJ • **familia ~** single-parent family, one-parent family
monoparentalidad SF single parenthood
monopartidismo SM single-party system
monopatín SM skateboard
monopatinaje SM skateboarding
monoplano SM monoplane
monoplaza SM single-seater
monopolio SM monopoly ▸ **monopolio total** absolute monopoly
monopolista ADJ, SMF monopolist
monopolístico ADJ monopolistic
monopolización SF monopolization
monopolizador ADJ **1** *(Econ)* monopolistic • **una empresa ~a del mercado** a company with a monopoly in the market
2 *[persona]* • **un niño ~ del cariño materno** a child who monopolizes his mother's attention
monopolizar ▹ CONJUG 1f VT to monopolize
monopsonio SM monopsony
monoquini SM = **monokini**
monorrail SM monorail
monorrimo ADJ *[estrofa]* having the same rhyme throughout
monosabio SM **1** *(Zool)* trained monkey
2 *(Taur)* picador's assistant *(employee who leads the horse team dragging the dead bull)*
monosilábico ADJ monosyllabic
monosílabo ADJ monosyllabic
SM monosyllable • **responder con ~s** to answer in monosyllables
monoteísmo SM monotheism
monoteísta ADJ monotheistic
SMF monotheist
monotema SM • **ese fue el ~ de la entrevista** that was the only issue discussed in the interview • **su ~ de siempre** his old hobbyhorse
monotemático ADJ on a single subject
monoterapia SF monotherapy, single-drug therapy
monotipia SF Monotype®
monótonamente ADV monotonously
monotonía SF **1** (= *uniformidad*) *(gen)* monotony; *[de voz, sonido]* monotone
2 (= *aburrimiento*) monotony • **la ~ (de la existencia) cotidiana** the daily grind
monótono ADJ **1** (= *uniforme*) *[voz, sonido]* monotonous
2 (= *aburrido*) *[trabajo, discurso]* tedious, monotonous; *[vida]* dreary, humdrum
monousuario ADJ *(Inform)* single-user
monovalente ADJ monovalent, univalent
monovía ADJ INV monorail *(antes de s)*
monovolumen ADJ • **vehículo ~** people carrier, minivan *(EEUU)*
SM people carrier, minivan *(EEUU)*
monóxido SM monoxide ▸ **monóxido de carbono** carbon monoxide ▸ **monóxido de cloro** chlorine monoxide
Mons. ABR (= **Monseñor**) Mgr, Mons, Msgr
monseñor SM monsignor
monserga SF (= *pesadez*) boring spiel*; (= *tontería*) drivel* • **dar la ~** (= *fastidiar*) to be irritating; (= *aburrir*) be a bore • **¡no me vengas con ~s!** (= *no molestes*) give it a rest!; (= *no te enrolles*) don't talk drivel!*
monstruo SM **1** *(Mit)* monster • **el ~ del lago Ness** the Loch Ness monster
2 (= *engendro*) freak*, monster • **~ de circo** circus freak
3 (= *persona malvada*) monster • **su jefe es un ~** her boss is a monster • **ese niño es un monstruito** that child is a little monster
4 (= *prodigio*) giant • **es un ~ del ajedrez** he's a fantastic chess player • **es un ~ jugando al fútbol** he's a sensational footballer • **Borges, ~ sagrado de la literatura sudamericana** Borges, the revered figure of South American literature
5 (= *cosa enorme*) monster • **¡mira, vaya ~ de camión!** look at that lorry, what a monster!
ADJ INV* **1** (= *maravilloso*) fantastic, brilliant • **idea ~** fantastic *o* brilliant idea
2 (= *grande*) huge • **mitin ~** huge meeting • **dos proyectos ~** two huge projects
monstruosidad SF **1** (= *cosa fea*) monstrosity • **¡qué ~ de casa!** what a monstrosity of a house!
2 (= *crueldad*) atrocity
3 (= *deformidad*) • **la ~ de sus facciones** his monstrous features
monstruoso ADJ **1** (= *terrible*) monstrous • **es ~ que ...** it is monstrous that ...
2 (= *horrible*) monstrous, hideous; (= *deforme*) freak *(antes de s)*
3 (= *enorme*) monstrous, huge
monta SF **1** (= *suma*) total, sum
2 *(en equitación)* (= *caballo*) mount; (= *acción*) mounting
3 (= *apareamiento*) mating; (= *temporada de apareamiento*) mating season
4 • MODISMO: • **de poca ~** third-rate *(antes de s)* • **un cantante/hotel de poca ~** a third-rate singer/hotel • **un ladrón de poca ~** a small-time thief
montacargas SM INV service lift, freight elevator *(EEUU)*
montada SF • **la ~** *(CAm)* the mounted rural police
montadito SM *(Esp)* small sandwich
montado ADJ **1** *[persona]* • **iba ~ a caballo** he was riding a horse, he was on horseback • **estaba montada en la bicicleta** she was riding her bicycle • **artillería montada** horse artillery • **guardia montada** horse guards *(pl)* • **policía montada** mounted police
2 *[caballo]* saddled
3 *(Esp)* *(Culin)* *[nata]* whipped; *[clara]* whisked
4 *(Esp*)* • MODISMO: • **estar ~ (en el dólar)** to be rolling in it*, be loaded*
SM *(Esp)* small sandwich ▸ **montado de lomo** *hot sandwich made with pork loin*
montador(a) SM/F **1** *(Téc)* *[de máquinas,*

aparatos] fitter; [*de joyas*] setter
2 (*Cine, TV*) film editor ▸ **montador(a) de escena** set designer
(SM) (= *poyo*) (*para montar*) mounting block
montadura (SF) **1** (= *acto*) mounting
2 = **montura**
montaje (SM) **1** (*Téc*) [*de estantería, aparato*] assembly; [*de ordenador*] set up; [*de joyas*] setting • **instrucciones para el ~** assembly instructions • **el telescopio se encuentra en fase de ~** the telescope is being assembled • **para el ~ de la estantería basta con un destornillador** to put up *o* assemble the shelves all you need is a screwdriver; ▹ **cadena**
2 [*de exposición*] mounting, setting up; [*de obra de teatro*] staging • **el ~ de la exposición durará tres semanas** mounting *o* setting up the exhibition will take three weeks • **un nuevo ~ de una obra de Jean Genet** a new staging of one of Jean Genet's plays
3* (= *engaño*) set-up* • **el accidente fue solo un ~** the accident was just a set-up* • **todo era un ~ policial** the whole thing was set up by the police *o* was a police set-up* ▸ **montaje publicitario** advertising stunt, publicity stunt
4 (*Cine, Fot*) montage ▸ **montaje fotográfico** photomontage
5 (*Radio*) hookup
montante (SM) **1** (= *suma*) total ▸ **montante compensatorio monetario** amount of financial compensation
2 (= *poste*) upright, post; (= *soporte*) stanchion; (*Arquit*) [*de puerta*] transom; [*de ventana*] mullion
3 (= *ventana*) fanlight, transom (*EEUU*)
montaña (SF) **1** (= *monte*) mountain • **una ~ de papeles** a mountain of papers • **~ de mantequilla** butter mountain • **MODISMO**: • **hacer una ~ de un granito de arena** to make a mountain out of a molehill ▸ **montaña rusa** roller coaster, big dipper ▸ **Montañas Rocosas** Rocky Mountains
2 (= *zona*) (= *sierra*) mountains (*pl*) • **pasamos un mes en la ~** we spent a month in the mountains
3 (*LAm*) (= *bosque*) forest
(SMF) ▸ **montaña del Pirineo** Pyrenean mountain dog, Great Pyrenees (*EEUU*)
montañero/a (SM/F) mountaineer, climber
(ADJ) mountain (*antes de s*)
montañés/esa (ADJ) **1** (= *de montaña*) mountain (*antes de s*); (= *de tierras altas*) highland (*antes de s*)
2 (= *de Santander*) of/from the Santander region
(SM/F) **1** (*gen*) highlander
2 [*de Santander*] native/inhabitant of the Santander region
montañismo (SM) mountaineering, mountain climbing
montañoso (ADJ) mountainous
montaplatos (SM INV) dumb waiter
montar ▹ CONJUG 1a (VT) **1** (= *cabalgar*) to ride • **montaba una yegua blanca** she was riding a white mare
2 (= *subir*) • **~ a algn en *o* sobre algo** to lift sb onto sth, sit sb on sth • **se lo montó sobre las rodillas** she lifted him onto her knees, she sat him on her knees
3 (*Téc*) [+ *estantería, ventana*] to assemble, put together; [+ *coche*] to assemble; [+ *tienda de campaña*] to put up, pitch
4 (= *instalar*) [+ *consulta, oficina*] to set up, open; [+ *galería de arte, tienda*] to open; [+ *campamento, espectáculo*] to set up; [+ *exposición*] to set up, mount • **han montado una tienda de animales** they've opened a pet shop • **~ una casa** to set up house *o* home • **~ un negocio** to set up *o* start up a business
5 (= *engarzar*) [+ *joya*] to set; [+ *pistola*] to cock; [+ *reloj, resorte*] to wind, wind up • **una perla montada sobre un anillo de oro** a pearl set in a gold ring
6 (*Fot*) [+ *foto, diapositiva*] to mount
7 (= *organizar*) [+ *operación*] to mount; [+ *sistema de control*] to put into operation • **toda la operación se montó en una semana** the whole operation was mounted in a week • **la policía montó un fuerte dispositivo de seguridad** the police put strict security measures into operation • **~ guardia** to stand guard
8 (*Esp**) (= *crear*) • **~ una bronca *o* un escándalo** to kick up a fuss/scandal* • **¡menudo escándalo se montó con lo de la boda!** what a fuss they kicked up about that wedding!* • **~ un número *o* un show** to make a scene • **nos montó un show sin motivo ninguno** he made a big scene for no reason at all
9 (= *solapar*) • **~ algo sobre algo** to overlap sth with sth • **han montado unos colores sobre otros** they have overlapped some colours with others
10 (*Cine*) [+ *película*] to edit
11 (*Teat*) [+ *decorado*] to put up; [+ *obra*] to stage, put on • **~on la obra con muy bajo presupuesto** they staged *o* put on the play on a small budget
12 (*Esp*) (*Culin*) [+ *nata*] to whip; [+ *clara*] to whisk, beat • **~ la clara a punto de nieve** to whisk *o* beat the egg white until stiff
13 (= *aparear*) (*Zool*) [+ *yegua, vaca*] to mount; [+ *persona***] to mount**
14 (*Cos*) [+ *puntos*] to cast on
(VI) **1** (= *ir a caballo*) to ride • **antes montaba a diario** I used to go riding every day • **monta para una cuadra de carreras** he rides for a racing stable • **¿tú montas bien a caballo?** do you ride well?
2 (= *subirse*) **a** (*a un caballo*) to get on, mount • **ayúdame a ~** help me up, help me to get on *o* to mount
b (*en un vehículo*) • **~ en avión** to fly, travel by air *o* by plane • **~ en barco** to travel by boat • **~ en bicicleta** to ride a bicycle, cycle • **aprendí a ~ en bici a los seis años** I learned to ride a bike *o* to cycle when I was six; ▹ **cólera**
3 (*Econ*) (= *sumar*) [*factura, gastos*] to amount to, come to • **el total monta (a) 2.500 euros** the total amounts *o* comes to 2,500 euros • **REFRÁN**: • **tanto monta (monta tanto, Isabel como Fernando)** (*Esp*) it makes no difference, it's all the same • **tanto monta que vengas o no** it makes no difference *o* it's all the same whether you come or not
4 (= *solapar*) • **~ sobre algo** to overlap sth, cover part of sth • **el mapa monta sobre el texto** the map overlaps the text, the map covers part of the text • **el texto está montado sobre la foto** the text covers part of the photo
(VPR) **montarse 1** (= *subirse*) • **~se en** [+ *coche*] to get in(to); [+ *autobús, tren*] to get on(to); [+ *caballo, bicicleta*] to get on(to), mount; [+ *atracción de feria*] to go on • **¿te has montado alguna vez en avión?** have you ever been on a plane?, have you ever flown? • **~se en barco** to get on a boat, travel by boat
2 • **MODISMOS**: • **montárselo** (*Esp**) (= *organizarse*): • **montátelo como puedas** you'll have to manage the best you can • **¡tú sí que te lo has montado bien!** • **¡tú sí que lo tienes bien montado!** you're on to a good thing there!*, you've got it made!* • **se lo montó fatal con lo del regalo** he messed things up with the present* • **se lo ha montado muy mal contigo** he's behaved very badly towards you • **~se en el dólar** to make big money*
montaraz (ADJ) (= *salvaje*) wild, untamed; (= *tosco*) rough, coarse; (= *huraño*) unsociable
montarrón (SM) (*And*) forest
monte (SM) **1** (= *montaña*) mountain; (= *cerro*) hill • **el ~ de los Olivos** the Mount of Olives • **el ~ Sinaí** Mount Sinai • **los ~s Pirineos** the Pyrenees • **los ~s Urales** the Urals • **los ~s Apalaches** the Appalachian Mountains • **los ~s Cárpatos** the Carpathian Mountains • **MODISMO**: • **echarse al ~** to take to the hills
2 (= *campo*) countryside, country; (= *bosque*) woodland • **los domingos salimos al ~ a pasear** on Sundays we go walking in the countryside • **un conejo de ~** a wild rabbit • **batir el ~** to beat for game, go hunting • **MODISMOS**: • **hacérsele un ~ a algn**: • **todo se le hace un ~** he makes mountains out of molehills • **no todo el ~ es orégano** it's not all plain sailing ▸ **monte alto** forest ▸ **monte bajo** scrub
3 ▸ **monte de piedad** pawnshop
4 (*Naipes*) (= *baraja*) pile; (= *banca*) bank
5 ▸ **monte de Venus** mons veneris
6 (*CAm, Caribe*) (= *alrededores*) outskirts (*pl*), surrounding country; (*Méx*) (= *hierba*) grass, pasture
7 (*LAm**) (= *hachís*) hash*, pot*
montear ▹ CONJUG 1a (VT) to hunt
montecillo (SM) mound, hump
montenegrino/a (ADJ) Montenegrin
(SM/F) Montenegrin
Montenegro (SM) Montenegro
montepío (SM) **1** (= *sociedad*) friendly society; (= *fondo*) charitable fund for dependents
2 (*And, Cono Sur*) (= *viudedad*) widow's pension
3 (= *monte de piedad*) pawnshop
montera (SF) **1** (= *sombrero*) cloth cap; [*de torero*] bullfighter's hat • **MODISMO**: • **ponerse algo por ~** to laugh at sth; ▹ **mundo**
2 (*Téc*) rise
3 (*Arquit*) skylight; ▹ **montero**
montería (SF) **1** (= *arte*) hunting; (= *caza*) hunt, chase
2 (= *animales*) game
3 (= *personas*) hunting party
4 (= *lugar*) hunting ground
5 (*Arte*) hunting scene
6 (*And*) (= *canoa*) canoe
7 (*CAm*) (= *concesión*) concession
8 (*CAm, Méx*) (= *madedería*) logging camp
montero/a (SM/F) (= *cazador*) hunter; (= *ojeador*) beater; ▹ **montera**
montés (ADJ) wild
montevideano/a (ADJ), (SM/F) Montevidean
Montevideo (SM) Montevideo
montgomery [mon'gomeri] (SM) (*Cono Sur*) duffle coat
montículo (SM) mound, hump
monto (SM) amount • **un cheque por un ~ aproximado de nueve millones** a cheque for approximately nine million
montón (SM) **1** (*gen*) heap, pile; [*de nieve*] pile • **MODISMOS**: • **del ~** ordinary, average • **un hombre del ~** just an ordinary *o* average chap • **salirse del ~** to stand out from the crowd • **en ~** all jumbled together
2* (= *mucho*) • **sabe un ~** he knows loads* • **tenemos montones** we've got loads *o* masses* • **un ~ de** loads of*, masses of* • **un ~ de gente** loads of people*, masses of people* • **tardaron un ~ de tiempo** they took ages • **tengo un ~ de cosas que decirte** I've got

m

loads to tell you* • **a montones: ejemplos hay a montones** there is no shortage of examples • **tenía baches a montones** it was full of potholes

montonera (SF) (*LAm*) **1** (= *montón*) pile, heap; (*And*) (= *almiar*) haystack
2 (= *guerrilla*) band of guerrilla fighters
3 (*Cono Sur*) (*Hist*) troop of mounted rebels

montonero/a (ADJ) **1** (*Cono Sur*) urban guerrilla (*antes de s*)
2 (*LAm*) (= *autoritario*) overbearing
(SM/F) urban guerrilla • **los Montoneros** *armed wing of the Peronist movement in Argentina*

Montreal (SM) Montreal

montuno (ADJ) **1** (= *de montaña*) mountain (*antes de s*); (= *de bosque*) forest (*antes de s*)
2 (*LAm*) (= *salvaje*) wild, untamed; (= *rústico*) rustic

montuosidad (SF) hilliness, mountainous nature

montuoso (ADJ) hilly, mountainous

montura (SF) **1** [*de gafas*] frame; [*de joya*] mount, setting
2 (= *animal*) mount
3 (= *silla*) saddle; (= *arreos*) harness, trappings (*pl*) • **cabalgar sin ~** to ride bareback

monumental (ADJ) **1** (= *de monumentos*) • **conjunto ~** collection of historical monuments • **la riqueza ~ del país** the country's wealth of monuments • **un catálogo ~ de España** a catalogue of the (historical) monuments of Spain
2 (= *enorme*) [*esfuerzo, error, éxito*] monumental; [*atasco*] enormous; [*bronca, paliza*] tremendous
3* (= *excelente*) tremendous*, terrific*

monumentalidad (SF) monumental character

monumentalismo (SM) *tendency to construct vast buildings or monuments*

monumento (SM) **1** (= *construcción*) monument • **el ~ a la paz** the monument to peace, the peace monument • **visitar los ~s de una ciudad** to visit a city's historical buildings ▸ **monumento a los caídos** war memorial ▸ **monumento al soldado desconocido** tomb of the unknown soldier ▸ **monumento histórico-artístico** (= *edificio*) listed building; (= *zona*) ≈ conservation area ▸ **monumentos prehistóricos** prehistoric remains
2* (= *mujer*) beauty
3 monumentos (= *documentos*) documents, source material (*sing*)

monzón (SM) monsoon

monzónico (ADJ) monsoon (*antes de s*) • **lluvias monzónicas** monsoon rains

moña (SF) **1** (= *lazo*) bow; (= *cinta*) ribbon
2* (= *muñeca*) doll
3* (= *borrachera*) • **cogerse una ~** to get sloshed* • **estar con la ~** to be sloshed*

moñita (SF) (*Uru*) bow tie

moño (SM) **1** [*de pelo*] bun, chignon; (*en lo alto de la cabeza*) topknot; [*de caballo*] forelock • **se peina con un ~ alto** she piles her hair on top of her head • **hacerse (un) ~** to put one's hair up (in a bun) • **agarrarse del ~** to pull each other's hair out • MODISMOS: • **estar hasta el ~*** to be fed up to the back teeth* • **estar con el ~ torcido** (*Caribe, Méx*) to have got out of the wrong side of the bed • **ponerse ~s*** to give o.s. airs
2 (*Orn*) crest
3 (= *lazo*) bow
4 moños (= *adornos*) fripperies, buttons and bows
5 (*LAm*) (= *altivez*) pride, haughtiness • MODISMOS: • **bajar el ~ a algn** to take sb down a peg • **agachar el ~** (*Cono Sur**) to give in
6 (*Cono Sur*) bar

mopa (SF) mop

MOPTMA (SM ABR) (*Esp*) = **Ministerio de Obras Públicas, Transportes y Medio Ambiente**

moquear ▹ CONJUG 1a (VI) to have a runny nose

moquera (SF), **moqueo** (SM) • **tener ~** to have a runny nose

moquero* (SM) hankie*

moqueta (SF) fitted carpet

moquete (SM) punch on the nose

moquillo (SM) [*de perro, gato*] distemper; [*de ave*] pip

mor • **por mor de** (PREP) because of, on account of • **por mor de la amistad** for friendship's sake

mora¹ (SF) **1** (*Bot*) (= *zarzamora*) blackberry; [*del moral*] mulberry
2 (*And*) (= *bala*) bullet
3 (*Méx**) (= *droga*) pot*, grass*

mora² (SF) (*Econ, Jur*) delay • **ponerse en ~** to default

mora³ (SF) (*Cono Sur*) (= *morcilla*) black pudding, blood sausage (*EEUU*)

morada (SF) **1** (= *casa*) dwelling (*liter*), abode (*liter*), dwelling place • **bienvenido a mi humilde ~** welcome to my humble abode • **no tener ~ fija** to be of no fixed abode ▸ **última morada** final resting place; ▹ **allanamiento**
2 (= *estadía*) stay, period of residence

morado (ADJ) purple • **terciopelo ~** purple velvet • **ojo ~** black eye • MODISMOS: • **pasarlas moradas** to have a tough time of it • **ponerse ~ (de algo)*** to stuff one's face (with sth)*
(SM) **1** (= *color*) purple
2 (= *cardenal*) bruise

morador(a) (SM/F) inhabitant

moradura (SF) bruise

moral¹ (SM) (*Bot*) mulberry tree

moral² (ADJ) **1** (= *ético*) moral • **toda persona necesita una formación ~** everyone needs a moral education • **tenemos la obligación ~ de ayudarle** we are morally obliged to help him, we have a moral obligation to help him
2 (= *espiritual*) moral • **demostró una gran fortaleza ~** he showed great moral strength • **le daremos todo el apoyo ~ que necesite** we will give her all the moral support she needs • **ideas que quedan dentro del plano ~** ideas which fall within the sphere of morality
(SF) **1** (= *ética, moralidad*) morality, morals (*pl*) • **la ~ cristiana** Christian morality, Christian morals • **una película de dudosa ~** a film of dubious morality *o* morals • **no existe una ~ absoluta** there isn't an absolute morality • **doble ~** double standards (*pl*) • **faltar a la ~** to behave immorally
2 (= *estado de ánimo*) morale • **intentó subirle la ~ al equipo** he tried to boost the team's morale • **la victoria nos dio mucha ~** the victory boosted our morale • **tener baja la ~** • **estar bajo de ~** to feel a bit low • **ando muy bajo de ~ últimamente** I've been feeling a bit low lately • **levantar la ~ a algn** to raise sb's spirits *o* morale • **la ~ de las tropas estaba por los suelos** the morale of the troops was at rock bottom • **la ~ se me cayó por los suelos cuando la vi con otro hombre** my heart sank when I saw her with another man • MODISMO: • **tener más ~ que el alcoyano** (*Esp**) to keep going against all the odds, have real fighting spirit
3 (= *valor*) moral courage • **yo no habría tenido ~ para hablarles así** I wouldn't have had the moral courage to speak to them like that

moraleja (SF) moral

moralidad (SF) **1** (= *moral*) [*de persona, acto*] morality, morals (*pl*) • **una obra de ~ dudosa** a play of dubious morality *o* morals • **su falta de ~** his immorality • **faltar a la ~** to behave immorally
2 (= *moraleja*) moral

moralina (SF) moral

moralista (ADJ) moralistic
(SMF) moralist

moralizador(a) (ADJ) moralizing, moralistic • **la literatura ~a de la época** the moralizing *o* moralistic literature of the period • **su actitud era ~a** his attitude was moralistic, he had a moralistic attitude
(SM/F) moralizer

moralizante (ADJ) moralizing, moralistic • **sus novelas tienen un tono ~** his novels have a moralizing *o* moralistic tone • **el relato era bastante ~** the story was quite moralistic

moralizar ▹ CONJUG 1f (VT) to raise the moral standards of • **quiso ~ el país** he wanted to raise the country's moral standards
(VI) to moralize • **en su afán de ~** in their eagerness to moralize

moralmente (ADV) morally • **me sentía ~ obligado** I felt morally obliged • **~ no está bien** morally speaking, it's no good

morapio* (SM) cheap red wine

morar ▹ CONJUG 1a (VI) (= *vivir*) dwell (*liter*), to live; (= *alojarse*) to stay

moratón (SM) bruise

moratoria (SF) moratorium

morbidez (SF) softness, delicacy

morbididad (SF) = **morbilidad**

mórbido (ADJ) **1** (= *enfermo*) morbid
2 (= *suave*) soft, delicate

morbilidad (SF) morbidity, sickness rate

morbo (SM) **1*** (= *curiosidad*) morbid curiosity • **la prensa amarilla alimenta el ~ de la gente** the gutter press feeds people's morbid curiosity
2* (= *atractivo sexual*) • **no es guapa pero tiene ~** she's not pretty but she's sexy
3 (*Med*) (= *enfermedad*) disease, illness

morbosamente (ADV) morbidly

morbosidad (SF) **1** (= *curiosidad*) morbid curiosity, morbid interest
2 (= *enfermedad*) morbidity, sickness
3 (= *estadística*) morbidity, sick rate

morboso (ADJ) **1** (= *malsano*) [*persona, mente*] morbid; [*espectáculo*] gruesome • **curiosidad morbosa** morbid curiosity
2 (= *atractivo*) sexually attractive
3 (= *enfermo*) morbid, sickly; [*clima, zona*] unhealthy

morcilla (SF) **1** (*Culin*) blood sausage, black pudding; (*Méx*) (= *callos*) tripe • MODISMO: • **¡que te den ~!‡** get stuffed!‡
2 (*Teat*) ad lib
3** (= *pene*) prick**
4 (*Caribe*) (= *mentira*) lie

morcillo (ADJ) [*caballo*] black with reddish hairs
(SM) (= *carne*) shank (*of beef*)

morcón (SM) **1** (*Culin*) large blood sausage
2* (= *rechoncho*) stocky person
3* (= *descuidado*) sloppy individual, slob*

mordacidad (SF) sharpness, bite • **no posee ni la gracia ni la ~ de Wilder** he has neither the humour nor the acid wit of Wilder • **con ~** sharply

mordaga‡ (SF), **mordaguera‡** (SF) • **coger** *o* **pillar una ~** to get plastered*

mordaz (ADJ) [*crítica, persona*] sharp, scathing; [*estilo*] incisive; [*humor*] caustic

mordaza (SF) **1** (*en la boca*) gag

m

2 (*Téc*) clamp

mordazmente ADV bitingly, scathingly

mordedura SF bite • **una ~ de serpiente** a snake bite

mordelón ADJ **1** (*LAm*) [*perro*] prone to biting
2 (*CAm, Méx**) (= *sobornable*) given to taking bribes
SM (*Méx‡*) traffic cop*

morder ▹ CONJUG 2h VT **1** (*con los dientes*) to bite
2 (= *corroer*) (*Quím*) to corrode, eat away; [+ *recursos*] to eat into
3 (*Mec*) [+ *embrague*] to catch
4 (*CAm, Méx*) (= *exigir soborno*) to take a bribe from
5 (*Méx*) (= *estafar*) to cheat
6* (= *denigrar*) to gossip about, run down
7‡ (= *reconocer*) to recognize
VI to bite • MODISMO: • **está que muerde** he's hopping mad
VPR **morderse** to bite • **~se las uñas** to bite one's nails • MODISMO: • **~se la lengua** to bite one's tongue

mordicar ▹ CONJUG 1g VI to smart, sting

mordida SF **1** (= *mordisco*) bite
2 (*CAm, Méx*) (= *soborno*) bribe; (= *tajada*) rake-off*, cut*; (= *acción*) bribery

mordiscar ▹ CONJUG 1g = **mordisquear**

mordisco SM **1** (= *bocado*) bite • **el perro me dio un ~** the dog bit me • **le arrancó la oreja de un ~** he took his ear off in one bite • **deshacer algo a ~s** to bite sth to pieces
2 (= *trozo*) bite
3‡ (= *beso*) love bite, hickey (EEUU)

mordisquear ▹ CONJUG 1a VT (*gen*) to nibble (at); [*caballo*] to champ
VI (*gen*) to nibble; [*caballo*] to champ

morena¹ SF (*Geol*) moraine

morena² SF (= *pez*) moray

morenal SM (*CAm*) shanty town

morenear ▹ CONJUG 1a VT to tan
VPR **morenearse** to tan

morenez SF suntan, brownness

moreno/a ADJ **1** [*persona*] (= *de pelo moreno*) dark-haired; (= *de tez morena*) dark(-skinned), swarthy; (= *bronceado*) brown, tanned; (*euf*) coloured, colored (EEUU); (*And, Caribe*) mulatto • **ponerse ~** to tan, go brown
2 [*pelo*] (dark) brown; [*azúcar, pan*] brown
SM/F [*de pelo*] dark-haired man/woman; [*de tez*] dark(-skinned) man/woman • **una morena** a brunette
SM tan

morera SF mulberry tree

morería SF (*Hist*) (= *territorio*) Moorish lands (*pl*), Moorish territory; (= *barrio*) Moorish quarter

moretón SM bruise

morfa‡ SF = **morfina**

morfar‡ ▹ CONJUG 1a (*Cono Sur*) VT to eat, scoff*
VI to eat, nosh*, chow down (EEUU*) • **ni siquiera les alcanza para ~** they don't even have enough money to pay for grub‡

morfema SM morpheme

morfémico ADJ morphemic

morfi‡ SM (*Cono Sur*) grub*, nosh*, chow (EEUU*)

morfina SF morphine

morfinomanía SF morphine addiction

morfinómano/a ADJ addicted to morphine
SM/F morphine addict

morfofonología SF morphophonology

morfología SF morphology

morfológicamente ADV morphologically

morfológico ADJ morphological

morfón‡ ADJ (*Cono Sur*) piggish, greedy

morfosintaxis SF INV morphosyntax

morganático ADJ morganatic

morgue SF (*esp LAm*) morgue

moribundo/a ADJ **1** [*persona*] dying • **estaba ~** he was dying, he was at death's door
2 [*proceso, negocio*] moribund • **el régimen está ~** the regime is moribund *o* on the way out
SM/F dying person • **los ~s** the dying

moricho SM (*Caribe*) hammock

morigeración SF restraint, moderation

morigerado ADJ well-behaved, law-abiding

morigerar ▹ CONJUG 1a VT to restrain, moderate

morillo SM firedog

morir ▹ CONJUG 3j (PP: **muerto**) VI **1** [*persona, animal, planta*] to die • **ha muerto de repente** she died suddenly • **murió a consecuencia de un infarto** he died as a result of a heart attack • **lo asfixió hasta ~** she suffocated him to death • **¡muera el tirano!** down with the tyrant!, death to the tyrant! • **~ ahogado** to drown • **~ ahorcado** (*por un verdugo*) to be hanged; (*suicidándose*) to be found hanged • **murió ahorcado en su celda** he was found hanged in his cell • **~ asesinado** [*persona*] to be murdered; [*personaje público*] to be assassinated • **~ de algo** to die of sth • **murió de cáncer/del corazón** he died of cancer/of a heart attack • **~ de frío** to die of cold, freeze to death • **~ de hambre** to die of hunger, starve to death • **~ de muerte natural** to die a natural death, die of natural causes • **~ de vejez** *o* **de viejo** to die of old age • **~ por algo** to die for sth • **no merece la pena ~ por amor** it is not worth dying for love • MODISMO: • **~ al pie del cañón** to die with one's boots on; ▹ **bota**
2 (= *extinguirse*) [*civilización*] to die, die out, come to an end; [*amor*] to die; [*fuego*] to die down; [*luz*] to fade • **con él moría toda una generación** with him died an entire generation • **moría el día** (*liter*) the day was drawing to a close (*liter*) • **las olas iban a ~ a la playa** (*liter*) the waves ran out on the beach • **ese camino muere en la ermita** that path comes to an end at the chapel • MODISMO: • **y allí muere** (*LAm*) and that's all there is to it
VPR **morirse 1** [*persona, animal, planta*] to die • **se murió tras una larga enfermedad** he died after a long illness • **se acaba de ~ su abuelo** her grandfather has just died • **se le ha muerto el gato** her cat has died • **¡ojalá** *o* **así se muera!** I hope he drops dead! • **~se de algo** to die of sth • **se murió de una pulmonía** she died of pneumonia
2* (*para exagerar*) to die • **por poco me muero cuando me lo contaron** I nearly died when they told me* • **si me descubren me muero** I'll die if they find me out* • **¡muérete! primero se casa con una millonaria y luego se divorcia** you'll never guess what! first he marries a millionairess, then he gets divorced* • **¡no se va a ~ por llamar por teléfono alguna vez!** it wouldn't kill him to ring me some time!* • **¡que me muera si miento!** cross my heart and hope to die!*, may God strike me dead if I'm lying!* • **~se de algo**: • **en esta casa me muero de frío** I'm freezing in this house • **¡me muero de hambre!** I'm starving! • **¡me muero de sed!** I'm dying of thirst!* • **me moría de pena de verla llorar** it broke my heart to see her cry • **se moría de envidia** he was green with envy • **por poco me muero de vergüenza** I nearly died of embarrassment* • **me moría de miedo** I was scared stiff* • **se van a ~ de risa** they'll kill themselves laughing* • **la película era para ~se de risa** the film was hilarious *o* incredibly funny • **~se de ganas de hacer algo** to be dying to do sth* • **me moría de ganas de verte** I was dying to see you* • **~se por algo** (*de deseo*) to be dying for sth*; (*de afición*) to be crazy *o* mad about sth* • **¡me muero por una cerveza fresquita!** I'm dying for *o* I could murder a nice cold beer!* • **se muere por el fútbol** he's crazy *o* mad about football* • **~se por algn** to be crazy *o* mad about sb* • **~se por hacer algo** to be dying to do sth* • **me muero por tener una moto** I'm dying to have a motorbike* • MODISMO: • **de** *o* **para ~se**: • **ese jamón estaba de** *o* **para ~se** that ham was just amazing!* • **el Caribe es como para ~se** the Caribbean is just amazing!* • **las fotos del terremoto eran para ~se** the pictures of the earthquake were just horrific*
3 (= *entumecerse*) [*brazo, pierna*] to go to sleep, go numb

morisco/a ADJ Moorish; (*Arquit*) Moorish
SM/F **1** (*Hist*) Moslem convert to Christianity, subject Moslem (*of 15th and 16th centuries*)
2 (*Méx*) (= *cuarterón*) quadroon

morisma SF Moors (*pl*)

morisqueta SF fraud, dirty trick

mormón/ona SM/F Mormon

mormónico ADJ Mormon

mormonismo SM Mormonism

moro/a ADJ **1** (*Hist*) Moorish
2 (*Esp**) (*pey*) (= *del norte de África*) North African
3 (*Esp**) (= *machista*) macho*
4 [*caballo*] dappled, piebald
SM/F **1** (*Hist*) Moor • MODISMOS: • **¡hay ~s en la costa!** watch out! • **no hay ~s en la costa** the coast is clear • **dar a ~ muerto gran lanzada** to kick a man when he's down
2 (*Esp**) (*pey*) (= *del norte de África*) North African
3 (*LAm*) (= *caballo*) piebald (horse)
SM **1*** (= *marido*) domineering husband
2 • **~s y cristianos** (*Caribe**) (*Culin*) rice with black beans
3 (*Esp**) (= *Marruecos*) Morocco • **bajar al ~** to go to Morocco
4 (*Mús**) wrong note

morocha SF (*Caribe*) double-barrelled gun

morocho (*LAm*) ADJ **1** [*pelo*] dark; [*persona*] dark, swarthy; [*chica*] brunette • **de piel morocha** dark-skinned
2 (= *fuerte*) strong, tough; (= *apuesto*) well-built; (= *bien conservado*) well-preserved
3 (*Caribe*) (= *gemelo*) twin
SM **1** (= *maíz*) hard maize, corn (EEUU)
2 (= *persona*) tough guy*
3 morochos (*Ven*) (= *gemelos*) twins

morón SM hillock

morondanga SF hotchpotch, hodgepodge (EEUU)

morondo ADJ **1** (= *calvo*) bald; (= *sin hojas*) leafless, bare
2 (= *mondo*) bare, plain

moronga SF (*CAm, Méx*) black pudding, blood sausage (EEUU)

morosidad SF **1** (*Econ*) slowness in paying; (= *atrasos*) arrears (*pl*)
2 (= *lentitud*) slowness; (= *apatía*) apathy

moroso/a ADJ **1** (*Econ*) slow to pay • **deudor ~** slow payer, defaulter
2 (= *lento*) slow • **una película de acción morosa** a slow-moving film • **delectación morosa** lingering enjoyment
SM/F (*Econ*) bad debtor, defaulter • **cartera de ~s** bad debts (*pl*)

morra SF top of the head • MODISMO: • **andar a la ~** to exchange blows

morrada* SF **1** (= *cabezazo*) (*contra objeto*) bang on the head; (*contra otra persona, animal*) butt • **darse una ~** to fall flat on one's face
2 (= *bofetada*) bash*, punch
morral SM **1** (= *mochila*) haversack, knapsack; [*de caza*] pouch, game bag; [*de caballo*] nosebag
2* (= *matón*) lout, rough type
morralla SF **1** (= *peces*) small fry, little fish
2 (= *cosas*) junk*; (= *basura*) rubbish, garbage (EEUU)
3 (= *personas*) rabble, riff-raff
4 (*Méx*) (= *calderilla*) small change
morrazo* SM (= *golpe*) thump
morrear* ▷ CONJUG 1a VT, VI to snog*, neck
morrena SF moraine
morreo* SM snogging*, necking
morrera‡ SF (= *labios*) lips (*pl*); (= *boca*) kisser*
morrillo SM (*Zool*) fleshy part of the neck; (= *cuello**) neck, back of the neck
morriña SF (*Esp*) homesickness • **tener ~** to be homesick
morriñoso ADJ homesick
morrión SM helmet, morion
morrito* SM • **hacer ~s** to pout
morro SM **1** (*Zool*) snout, nose
2 (*Esp**) (= *labio*) (thick) lip • **beber a ~** to drink from the bottle • **¡cierra los ~s!** shut your trap!‡ • **dar a algn en los ~s** (*lit*) to bash sb*; (*fig*) to get one's own back on sb • **partir los ~s a algn** to bash sb's face in*
• MODISMOS: • **estar de ~(s)** to be in a bad mood • **estar de ~(s) con algn** to be cross with sb • **poner ~** • **torcer el ~** (= *ofenderse*) to look cross; (= *hacer una mueca*) to turn up one's nose • **poner morritos** to look sullen
3‡ (= *descaro*) cheek*, nerve* • **tener ~** to have a cheek*, have a nerve* • **¡qué ~ tienes!** you've got a nerve!* • **echarle mucho ~** to have a real nerve* • MODISMOS: • **tiene un ~ que se lo pisa*** he's got a real brass neck* • **por el ~**: • **me lo quedé por el ~** I just held on to it and to hell with them!*
4 (*Aer, Aut etc*) nose • **caer de ~** to nose-dive
5 (*Geog*) (= *promontorio*) headland, promontory; (= *cerro*) small rounded hill
6 (= *guijarro*) pebble
morrocotudo* ADJ **1** (= *fantástico*) smashing*, terrific*
2 (= *grande*) [*riña, golpe*] tremendous; [*susto*] terrible
3 (*And*) (= *rico*) rich
4 (*Cono Sur*) (= *torpe*) clumsy, awkward
morrocoy SM (*CAm*) turtle
morrón ADJ • **pimiento ~** sweet red pepper
SM **1** (= *pimiento*) sweet red pepper
2 (*Esp**) (= *golpe*) blow • **se dio un ~ con la puerta** he banged into the door and hurt his face
morrongo/a SM/F cat
morronguero* ADJ (*Caribe*) **1** (= *tacaño*) stingy
2 (= *cobarde*) yellow*
morroñoso ADJ **1** (*CAm*) (= *áspero*) rough
2 (*And*) (= *pequeño*) small; (= *endeble*) feeble; (= *miserable*) wretched, poverty-stricken
morrudo ADJ **1** (= *de labios gruesos*) thick-lipped
2 (*Cono Sur*) (= *musculoso*) tough, brawny
morsa SF walrus
morse SM Morse code
mortadela SF mortadella
mortaja SF **1** [*de muerto*] shroud
2 (*Téc*) mortise
3 (*LAm**) (= *papel*) cigarette paper
mortal ADJ **1** [*ser*] mortal
2 [*herida, golpe*] fatal, deadly; [*disparo, accidente*] fatal; [*veneno, virus, sustancia, dosis*] deadly, lethal; [*peligro*] mortal • **la película es un aburrimiento ~** the film is a real bore • **salto ~** somersault
3 [*pecado*] mortal; [*odio*] deadly
4 • **quedarse ~†** to be thunderstruck
5 • MODISMO: • **las señas son ~es†** there's no escaping the evidence
SMF (= *ser*) mortal • **como cualquier ~** just like anybody else
SM (= *salto*) somersault • **doble ~** double somersault
mortalidad SF **1** (= *condición de mortal*) mortality
2 (*en demografía*) mortality; (*en accidente*) death toll ▸ **mortalidad infantil** infant mortality
mortalmente ADV fatally • **le disparó ~ en el abdomen** he shot him fatally in the stomach • **resultó ~ herido** he was mortally wounded • **pecar ~** to commit a mortal sin
mortandad SF **1** (= *víctimas*) (*humanas*) loss of life; (*animales*) death
2 (= *matanza*) slaughter, carnage
mortecino ADJ **1** [*luz*] dim, faint; [*color*] dull; [*fuego, llamas*] dying
2 (= *débil*) weak, failing • **hacer la mortecina** to pretend to be dead
morterada* SF • **gana una ~** he earns a small fortune, he earns a tidy bit*
mortero SM mortar
mortífero ADJ deadly, lethal
mortificación SF **1** (= *sufrimiento*) torture • **era una ~ para él** it was torture *o* hell for him
2 (= *humillación*) humiliation
3 (*Rel*) mortification
mortificante ADJ mortifying
mortificar ▷ CONJUG 1g VT **1** (= *atormentar*) to torment, plague • **sus compañeros les mortifican con crueldad** their workmates treat them cruelly • **me han mortificado toda la noche los mosquitos** I was tormented all night by the mosquitos • **estos zapatos me mortifican** these shoes are killing me
2 (= *humillar*) to humiliate
3 (*Rel*) • **~ la carne** to mortify the flesh
4 (*Med*) to damage seriously
VPR **mortificarse 1** (= *atormentarse*) to torment o.s., distress o.s.
2 (*Rel*) to mortify the flesh
3 (*CAm, Méx*) (= *avergonzarse*) to feel ashamed, be mortified
mortuorio ADJ mortuary • **casa mortuoria** home of the deceased • **coche ~** hearse • **esquela mortuoria** death notice
morueco SM ram
moruno ADJ (*pey*) Moorish; ▷ **pincho**
morza SF (*Cono Sur*) carpenter's vice
Mosa SM • **el (río) ~** the Meuse
mosaico¹ ADJ Mosaic, of Moses
mosaico² SM **1** (*Arte*) (*gen*) mosaic; (= *pavimento*) tessellated pavement • **un ~ romano** a Roman mosaic • **un suelo de ~** a mosaic floor ▸ **mosaico de madera** marquetry
2 (= *conjunto*) • **un ~ de grupos étnicos** a whole spectrum of ethnic groups
mosca SF **1** (= *insecto*) fly • **pescar a la ~** to fish with a fly, fly-fish • MODISMOS: • **asarse las ~s**: • **se asaban las ~s** it was baking hot • **caer como ~s** to drop like flies • **cazar ~s** to daydream • **mandar a algn a capar ~s*** to tell sb to go to blazes* • **papar ~s** to daydream • **por si las ~s*** just in case • **me llevaré el impermeable por si las ~s** I'll take my raincoat just in case • **¿qué ~ te/le ha picado?*** what's got into you/him? • **tener la ~ en** *o* **detrás de la oreja*** to smell a rat*
▸ **mosca artificial** (*en pesca*) fly ▸ **mosca azul**, **mosca blanca** whitefly ▸ **mosca de burro** horsefly ▸ **mosca de España** Spanish fly, cantharides ▸ **mosca de la carne** meat fly ▸ **mosca de la fruta** fruit fly ▸ **mosca doméstica** house fly ▸ **mosca drosofila** drosophila, fruit fly ▸ **mosca muerta** = **mosquita** ▸ **mosca tsetsé** tsetse fly
2* (= *pesado*) pest
3† (= *dinero*) dough* • MODISMO: • **aflojar** *o* **soltar la ~** to fork out*, stump up
4† (= *barba*) small goatee beard
5 moscas (= *centellas*) sparks ▸ **moscas volantes** spots before the eyes, floaters
6 (*Méx**) (= *parásito*) sponger*
ADJ INV (*Esp**) • MODISMOS: • **estar ~** (= *suspicaz*) to be suspicious, smell a rat*; (= *preocupado*) to be worried • **estar ~ con algn** (= *enfadado*) to be cross *o* annoyed with sb
moscada ADJ • **nuez ~** nutmeg
moscarda SF bluebottle, blowfly
moscardón SM **1** (= *moscarda*) bluebottle, blowfly; (= *abejón*) hornet
2* (= *persona molesta*) pest, nuisance
moscatel¹ ADJ, SM muscatel
moscatel² SM **1** (= *pesado*) bore, pest
2 (= *mocetón*) big lad, overgrown lad
moscón SM **1** (= *insecto*) bluebottle, blowfly
2 (*Bot*) maple
3* (= *pesado*) pest, nuisance
moscoso* SM day off (*for personal matters, not deducted from annual leave*)
moscovita ADJ, SMF Muscovite
Moscú SM Moscow
Mosela SM Moselle
mosqueado ADJ **1*** (= *enfadado*) cross, angry
2* (= *desconfiado*) suspicious • **ya andaba yo ~** I already had my suspicions
3 (= *moteado*) spotted
mosqueador SM (*para moscas*) (= *instrumento*) fly-whisk; (= *cola*) tail
mosqueante* ADJ **1** (= *molesto*) annoying, irritating
2 (= *sospechoso*) suspicious, fishy*
mosquear* ▷ CONJUG 1a VT **1** (= *hacer enfadar*) to annoy • **sus tonterías acabaron por mosquearme** his nonsense annoyed me in the end
2 (= *hacer sospechar*) to puzzle • **hay algo en este caso que me mosquea** there's something about this case that puzzles me
VPR **mosquearse 1** (= *enfadarse*) to get cross, get annoyed; (= *ofenderse*) to get offended
2 (= *desconfiar*) to smell a rat*
3 (= *preocuparse*) to worry • **me mosqueé porque a las once no había llamado** I got worried because he hadn't called by eleven
mosqueo* SM • **coger** *o* **pillar** *o* **llevarse un ~** (= *enfadarse*) to get cross, get annoyed; (= *ofenderse*) to get offended; (= *desconfiar*) to smell a rat*; (= *preocuparse*) to worry
mosquete SM musket
mosquetero SM (*Hist, Mil*) musketeer; (*Teat*) groundling
mosquita SF • **~ muerta** hypocrite • **hacerse la ~ muerta** to look as if butter wouldn't melt in one's mouth
mosquitero SM mosquito net
mosquito SM (*gen*) mosquito; (*pequeño*) gnat
mosso SM • **Mossos d'esquadra** *Catalan autonomous police*
mostacera SF, **mostacero** SM mustard pot
mostacho SM moustache, mustache (EEUU)
mostachón SM macaroon
mostacilla SF (*And*) bead necklace
mostaza SF **1** (*Culin*) mustard • **~ de Dijon** (French) Dijon mustard • **~ inglesa** English mustard • **un vestido ~** a mustard-yellow dress
2 (*And, Méx‡*) pot*, hash*
mostela SF sheaf

mosto (SM) [*de uva*] grape juice; (*en la elaboración de vino*) must
mostrador (SM) 1 [*de tienda*] counter; [*de café, bar*] bar; [*de oficina, biblioteca*] desk ▸ **mostrador de caja** cash desk ▸ **mostrador de facturación** check-in desk ▸ **mostrador de tránsito** transit desk
2 [*de reloj*] face, dial
3‡ (= *pecho*) tits** (*pl*)
mostrar ▹ CONJUG 1l (VT) (= *señalar, explicar*) to show; (= *exponer*) to display, exhibit • **nos mostró el camino** he showed us the way • **~ en pantalla** (*Inform*) to display
(VPR) **mostrarse** (+ *adj*) • **se mostró interesado en la oferta** he was interested *o* showed interest in the offer • **se mostró partidario de aceptar la propuesta** he was in favour of accepting the proposal
mostrenco/a (ADJ) 1* [*persona*] (= *bruto*) oafish; (= *poco inteligente*) dense, slow; (= *gordo*) fat
2* [*objeto*] crude, roughly made
3†† (= *sin dueño*) ownerless, unclaimed; (= *sin hogar*) homeless, rootless
(SM/F)* oaf
mostro* (ADJ) (*And*) great*, superb
mota (SF) 1 (= *partícula*) speck, tiny bit • **~ de polvo** speck of dust • **~ de carbonilla** smut, speck of coal dust • REFRÁN: • **ver la ~ en el ojo ajeno** to see the mote in sb else's eye
2 (= *dibujo*) dot • **una mariposa blanca con ~s azules** a white butterfly speckled with blue • **a ~s** [*dibujo*] dotted
3 (*en tela*) (= *nudillo*) burl; (= *jaspeado*) fleck
4 (= *defecto*) fault, blemish
5 • **no hace (ni) ~ de aire** there isn't a breath of air
6 (*Geog*) hillock
7 (= *mojón*) boundary mark; (= *césped*) turf, clod (*used to block off irrigation channel*)
8 (*LAm*) (= *pelo*) lock of wavy hair
9 (*And, Caribe, Méx*) (= *borla*) powder puff
10 (*LAm*) (= *lana*) tuft (*of wool*)
11 (*LAm*) (= *planta*) marijuana plant; (= *droga*) grass*, pot‡; ▹ **moto²**
mote¹ (SM) 1 (= *apodo*) nickname • **le pusieron el ~ de "el abuelo"** they nicknamed him *o* they gave him the nickname "Grandad"
2 (*Hist*) motto, device
mote² (SM) 1 (*And, Cono Sur*) (= *trigo*) boiled wheat; (= *maíz*) boiled maize, boiled corn (*EEUU*) ▸ **mote con huesillos** (*Chile*) maize and peach drink
2 (*Cono Sur*) • MODISMOS: • **pelar ~** to gossip • **como ~** in large numbers
moteado (ADJ) 1 [*piel*] (= *con manchas pequeñas*) speckled; (= *con manchas grandes*) dappled, mottled • **un caballo gris ~** a dapple-grey horse
2 [*tela*] (*de forma irregular*) flecked; (= *con lunares*) dotted
motear ▹ CONJUG 1a (VT) to speck (**de** with)
motejar ▹ CONJUG 1a (VT) to nickname • **~ a algn de algo** to brand sb sth, accuse sb of being sth
motel (SM) motel
motero/a* (SM/F) biker*
motete (SM) motet
motín (SM) [*de presos*] riot; (*en barco, de tropas*) mutiny ▸ **motín carcelario** prison riot
motivación (SF) 1 (= *estimulación*) motivation
2 (= *motivo*) motive
motivacional (ADJ) motivational
motivar ▹ CONJUG 1a (VT) 1 (= *estimular*) to motivate • **los estudios ya no la motivan** she is no longer motivated by her studies
2 (= *causar*) to cause • **un retraso motivado por circunstancias ajenas a su voluntad** a delay caused by circumstances beyond his control
3 (= *explicar*) to justify, explain • **motivó su decisión con razonamientos muy válidos** she had some very sound reasons to justify her decision
motivo (SM) 1 (= *causa*) reason • **dejó el trabajo por ~s personales** he left the job for personal reasons • **por cuyo ~** for which reason • **fue ~ de descalificación del atleta** it was the reason for the athlete's disqualification • **con este** *o* **tal ~** for this reason • **con ~ de** (= *debido a*) because of, owing to; (= *en ocasión de*) on the occasion of • **se informatizará el sistema con ~ de las elecciones** the system will be computerized because of *o* owing to the elections • **con ~ de nuestra boda le invitamos a ...** on the occasion of our wedding we invite you to ... • **~ de**: • **me dio ~ de preocupación** it gave me cause for concern • **la decisión fue ~ de críticas** the decision became the object of criticism • **sin ~** for no reason, without good reason • **dejó de hablarme sin ~** he stopped talking to me for no reason • **ser ~ sobrado** *o* **suficiente**: • **es ~ suficiente** *o* **sobrado para seguir votándolo** that's reason enough to continue voting for him, that's all the more reason to continue voting for him • **hay suficientes** *o* **sobrados ~s para odiarlo** there are more than enough reasons for hating him ▸ **motivos de divorcio** grounds for divorce ▸ **motivos ocultos** ulterior motives
2 (= *móvil*) motive • **¿cuál fue el ~ del crimen?** what was the motive for the crime?
3 (*Arte, Mús*) motif • **decorado con ~s orientales** decorated with oriental motifs ▸ **motivo conductor** leitmotif ▸ **motivo decorativo** decorative motif ▸ **motivo ornamental** ornamental motif
(ADJ) motive
moto¹ (SF) (motor)bike • **voy al trabajo en ~** I travel to work by (motor)bike • MODISMOS: • **ir como una ~‡** to be in a rush • **ponerse como una ~‡** (*sexualmente*) to get really turned on‡, get horny‡; (*con droga*) to get high*; (= *cabrearse*) to go off one's head* ▸ **moto acuática, moto de agua** jet ski
moto²/a (ADJ) 1 (*CAm*) orphaned, abandoned
2 (*And*) tailless
(SM/F) (*CAm*) orphan; ▹ **mota**
motobomba (SF) motor pump, fire engine
motocarro (SM) *light delivery van with three wheels*
motocicleta (SF) motorcycle, motorbike • **~ con sidecar** motorbike *o* motorcycle with a sidecar
motociclismo (SM) motorcycling
motociclista (SMF) motorcyclist ▸ **motociclista de escolta** outrider
moto-cross (SM INV) motocross
motocultor (SM) cultivator
motón (SM) pulley
motonauta (SMF) jet skier
motonáutica (SF) motorboat racing, speedboat racing
motonave (SF) motor ship, motor vessel
motoneta (SF) (*LAm*) (motor) scooter
motoneurona (SF) motor neurone
motonieve (SF) snowmobile
motoniveladora (SF) bulldozer
motor (ADJ) 1 (*Téc*) motive, motor (*EEUU*) • **potencia ~a** motive power
2 (*Anat*) motor
(SM) motor, engine • **~ eléctrico** electric motor *o* engine • **un ~ de seis cilindros** a six-cylinder engine • **con seis ~es** six-engined • **con ~** power-driven • **aviación con ~** powered flight ▸ **motor a chorro, motor a reacción** jet engine ▸ **motor de arranque** starter, starter motor ▸ **motor de aviación** aircraft engine ▸ **motor de búsqueda** (*Internet*) search engine ▸ **motor de combustión interna, motor de explosión** internal combustion engine ▸ **motor de inyección** fuel-injected engine ▸ **motor delantero** front-mounted engine ▸ **motor de puesta en marcha** starter, starter motor ▸ **motor diesel** diesel engine ▸ **motor fuera (de) borda** outboard motor ▸ **motor refrigerado por aire** air-cooled engine ▸ **motor trasero** rear-mounted engine
motora (SF), **motorbote** (SM) motorboat, speedboat
motorismo (SM) motorcycling
motorista (SMF) 1 (= *motociclista*) motorcyclist
2 (*esp LAm*) (= *automovilista*) motorist, driver
motorístico (ADJ) motor-racing (*antes de s*)
motorización (SF) 1 (= *acto*) motorization; (= *mecanización*) mechanization
2 (= *capacidad*) engine size
motorizado (ADJ) motorized; [*tropas*] mechanized, motorized • **trineo ~** motor sleigh • **un largo convoy ~** a long convoy of vehicles • **en autobús u otro medio ~** by bus or some other means of transport • **patrulla motorizada** motorized patrol, mobile unit • **personas no motorizadas** people who do not own a car, people who do not have their own transport • **estar ~*** to have wheels*, have a car
motorizar ▹ CONJUG 1f (VT) (*Mil, Téc*) to motorize
(VPR) **motorizarse** (*hum**) to get o.s. some wheels*
motosegadora (SF) motor mower, motorized lawn mower
motosierra (SF) power saw
motoso (ADJ) (*LAm*) [*pelo*] kinky
motricidad (SF) 1 (= *capacidad*) mobility
2 (*Fisiol*) motor functions (*pl*)
motriz (ADJ) 1 (*Téc*) motive, motor (*EEUU*) • **potencia ~** motive power • **fuerza ~** driving force
2 (*Anat*) motor • **la actividad ~** motor functions
motu • **de ~ propio** (ADV) of one's own accord
motudo (ADJ) (*Cono Sur*) [*pelo*] kinky
mousse [mu:s] (SF), (*a veces*) (SM) 1 (*Culin*) mousse ▸ **mousse de chocolate** chocolate mousse
2 [*de pelo*] (styling) mousse; [*de afeitar*] shaving foam
movedizo (ADJ) 1 (= *no fijo*) [*terreno, suelo*] moving, shifting; [*objeto*] movable; [*persona, animal*] restless; ▹ **arena**
2 (= *cambiante*) [*persona*] fickle; [*situación*] unsettled, changeable
mover ▹ CONJUG 2h (VT) 1 (= *cambiar de posición*) **a** [+ *objeto, mano, pierna*] to move • **no muevas la mesa** don't move the table • **~ a algn de algún sitio** to move sb from somewhere • **de aquí no nos mueve nadie** we're staying right here, we're not moving from here • **"no nos ~án"** "we shall not be moved"
b (*en juegos*) [+ *ficha, pieza*] to move
2 (= *agitar*) to stir • **muévelo para que no se pegue** stir it *o* give it a stir so that it doesn't stick • **el perro se acercó moviendo la cola** the dog came up to us wagging its tail • **el viento movía sus cabellos** the wind blew her hair • **~ la cabeza** (*para negar*) to shake one's head; (*para asentir*) to nod, nod one's head • **movió la cabeza negando la pregunta** she shook her head in answer to the question • **movió la cabeza afirmativamente** she nodded (her head)
3 (*Mec*) (= *accionar*) [+ *máquina*] to work, power • **el agua movía el molino** the water turned *o*

m

drove the wheel • **el vapor mueve el émbolo** the steam drives *o* works the piston
4 (= *incitar*) • **el interés propio nos mueve a todos** self-interest motivates all of us • **lo hice movida por la curiosidad** it was curiosity that prompted *o* moved me to do it • **actuaba movido por sus instintos** he acted on his instincts • **su mensaje movía a las masas** his message roused the masses • **~ a algn a algo** to move sb to sth • **su pobreza te mueve a la compasión** their poverty moves you to pity • **~ a algn a las lágrimas** to move sb to tears • **~ a algn a la risa** to make sb laugh • **~ a algn a hacer algo** to prompt sb to do sth, move sb to do sth • **¿qué fue lo que te movió a actuar de ese modo?** what prompted *o* moved you to act in that way?
5 (= *agilizar*) [+ *asunto, tema*] to push; [+ *trámite*] to handle • **ella le movió todo el papeleo** she handled all the paperwork for him • **~ una guerra contra algn** to wage war on sb • **~ un pleito contra algn** to start proceedings against sb
6 [+ *dinero*] to move, handle • **esta empresa mueve miles de millones anualmente** this company moves *o* handles thousands of millions each year • **el tráfico de armas mueve mucho dinero** arms trading involves *o* moves a lot of money
7* [+ *droga*] to push
(VI) **1** (*en juegos*) to move • **¿con qué ficha has movido?** what piece have you moved? • **¿a quién le toca ~?** whose move is it?
2 (= *incitar*) • **~ a algo:** • **esta situación mueve a la risa** this situation makes you (want to) laugh
3 (*Bot*) to bud, sprout
(VPR) **moverse 1** (= *cambiar de posición o lugar*) to move • **se mueve con dificultad** he has difficulty moving, he finds it difficult to move • **no te muevas, que te voy a hacer una foto** keep still *o* don't move, I'm going to take your photo • **se mueve mucho en la cama** she fidgets *o* moves around a lot in bed • **muévete un poco para allá** move up a bit • **no te muevas de ahí hasta que yo vuelva** stay right there *o* don't move until I come back • **lleva horas sin ~se de ese sofá** he hasn't moved *o* stirred from that sofa in hours • **no hay quien la haga ~se** no one can get her to move • **la máquina se movía sola** the machine moved on its own
2 (= *agitarse*) [*mar*] to be rough; [*barco*] to roll; [*cortina, hojas*] to move • **las cortinas se movían con el viento** the curtains stirred *o* moved in the wind • **¿se ha movido mucho el barco?** was the sea rough?
3 (= *ponerse en marcha*) to move o.s., get a move on* • **¡venga, muévete, que tenemos prisa!** come on, move yourself *o* get a move on, we're in a hurry!*
4 (= *ser activo*) [*persona*] to be on the move*, be on the go*; [*ciudad*] to be lively • **esta moviéndose continuamente** she's always on the move *o* go* • **tuvo que ~se mucho para conseguir ese trabajo** he had to pull out all the stops to get that job • **Londres es una ciudad que se mueve** London is a really lively city
5 (= *relacionarse*) (*en un ambiente*) to move; (*entre cierta gente*) to mix • **siempre me he movido en ambientes financieros** I have always moved in financial circles • **se mueve mucho entre aristócratas** he mixes a lot with the aristocracy

movible (ADJ) **1** (= *no fijo*) [*objeto*] movable; ▸ **fiesta**
2 (= *voluble*) [*carácter, persona*] fickle

movida (SF) **1*** (= *animación*) scene* • **un bar en el centro de la ~** a bar at the heart of the club scene* • **la ~ cultural** the cultural scene* • **la ~ madrileña** the Madrid scene* • **la ~ está en la costa** the coast is where it's at‡
2‡ (= *asunto*) thing, stuff‡ • **a mí no me va esa ~** I'm not into that scene* *o* stuff‡ • **la ~ es que ...** the thing is that ... • **¡qué ~! ¡ahora tengo que ponerme a trabajar!** what a pain! I've got to get down to work now!* • **ese tío anda en ~s raras** that guy is into really weird stuff‡
3 (*Esp**) (= *pelea*) trouble • **cuando vuelva a casa me espera una buena ~** there's going to be real trouble when I get home*
4 (*Ajedrez*) move ▸ **movida clave** key-move
5 (*Pol*) movement
6 (*Chile‡*) bash*, do*

MOVIDA MADRILEÑA
The **Movida Madrileña** was a cultural movement that sprang up in Madrid towards the end of the **Transición a la Democracia** (Transition to Democracy - 1975-82). In post-Franco Spain many were glad to shake off Catholic social and sexual mores and to experiment. This was the period that saw the emergence of exciting and innovative film directors like Pedro Almodóvar and bands like Radio Futura and Alaska y los Pegamoides. At the same time the media, music and fashion industries sought to distance themselves from the mass-produced popular culture of the US and UK and to establish their own Spanish identity.

movido (ADJ) **1** (*Fot*) blurred • **la foto ha salido un poco movida** the photo has come out a bit blurred
2 [*persona*] (= *activo*) on the move*, on the go*; (= *inquieto*) restless • **es una persona muy movida** he's always on the move *o* go*
3 (= *agitado*) **a** [*mar*] rough, choppy; [*viaje*] (*en barco*) rough; (*en avión*) bumpy
b [*día, semana*] hectic, busy; [*reunión, sesión*] stormy • **he tenido una mañana muy movida** I had a very hectic *o* busy morning • **sabíamos que la reunión sería bastante movidita** we knew that the meeting would be quite stormy
4 (*And, CAm*) [*huevo*] soft-shelled
5 (*CAm*) (= *débil*) weak, feeble; (= *lento*) slow, sluggish; (= *indeciso*) irresolute

movidón* (SM) rave-up*, wild party, hot party (*EEUU*)

móvil (SM) **1** (= *motivo*) motive • **un crimen sin ~ aparente** a crime with no apparent motive • **el ~ del asesinato** the motive for the murder • **este es el verdadero ~ de su política** this is the real reason behind his policies
2 (= *teléfono*) mobile (phone) (*Brit*), cellphone (*EEUU*) ▸ **móvil con cámara** camera phone
3 (*Arte*) mobile
(ADJ) [*teléfono, unidad*] mobile

movilidad (SF) mobility ▸ **movilidad ascendente** upward mobility ▸ **movilidad social** social mobility

movilización (SF) **1** (*Mil*) mobilization
2 (*Pol*) (= *manifestación*) • **habrá varias jornadas de ~** there will be several days of industrial action • **una llamada a la ~ de los trabajadores** a call for the mobilization of the workforce
3 (*Econ*) ▸ **movilización de capital** raising of capital ▸ **movilización de recursos** mobilization of resources

movilizar ▹ CONJUG 1f (VT) **1** (= *organizar*) to mobilize
2 (*Cono Sur*) to unblock, free
3 (*Chile*) to transport
(VPR) **movilizarse** to mobilize

movimiento (SM) **1** (*Mec, Fís*) movement • **el ~ ascendente del aire** the upward movement of the air • **~ hacia abajo/arriba** downward/upward movement • REFRÁN: • **el ~ se demuestra andando** actions speak louder than words ▸ **movimiento acelerado** acceleration ▸ **movimiento continuo** continuous movement, continuous motion ▸ **movimiento de pinza** pincer movement ▸ **movimiento de rotación** rotatory movement ▸ **movimiento de traslación** orbital movement *o* motion ▸ **movimiento ondulatorio** wave movement, wave motion ▸ **movimiento perpetuo** perpetual motion ▸ **movimiento retardado** deceleration ▸ **movimiento sísmico** seismic tremor
2 (= *desplazamiento*) [*de persona, animal*] movement • **todos nuestros ~s fueron filmados** all our movements were filmed • **esta máquina puede detectar el menor ~** this machine can detect the slightest movement • **he hecho un mal ~ con el hombro** I moved my shoulder awkwardly • **no hagas ningún ~** don't move a muscle, don't make a move • **~ de cabeza** (*para negar*) shake; (*para asentir*) nod ▸ **movimiento en falso** false move • **¡un ~ en falso y disparo!** one false move and I'll shoot! • **hizo un ~ en falso y tropezó** he missed his step and tripped over ▸ **movimiento migratorio** migratory movement
3 • **en ~** [*figura, persona*] moving; [*vehículo*] in motion • **una célula en ~** a moving cell *o* a cell in motion • **a lo lejos vi una figura en ~** I saw a moving figure in the distance • **está siempre en ~** (*fig*) she's always on the move *o* go* • **mantener algo en ~** to keep sth moving *o* in motion • **poner en ~** [+ *máquina, motor*] to set in motion; [+ *vehículo*] to get going; [+ *actividad, negocio*] to start, start up • **nos pusimos en ~ demasiado tarde** we got going too late
4 (*Econ, Com*) [*de cuenta*] transaction; [*de dinero*] movement • **¿puedo consultar los ~s de mi cuenta?** can I have a statement of my account? • **"últimos ~s"** "latest transactions" • **hubo mucho ~ de dinero en el mercado** there was a lot of movement in the money market • **el ~ de los precios** changes in prices • **el ~ ascensional de los precios de las acciones** the upward movement of share prices ▸ **movimiento de caja** cash flow ▸ **movimiento de efectivo** cash flow ▸ **movimiento de mercancías** turnover, volume of business ▸ **movimientos de existencias** stock movements
5 (= *actividad*) (*en oficina, tribunal*) activity; (*en aeropuerto, carretera*) traffic • **hoy ha habido mucho ~ en la Bolsa** there was a lot of activity on the Stock Market today • **un día de poco ~ en la Bolsa** a light trading day on the Stock Market • **el ~ de pasajeros ha sido intenso estos días** passenger traffic has been very heavy in recent days • **un día de poco ~ en las carreteras** a day with little traffic on the roads ▸ **movimiento máximo** (*Aut*) peak traffic
6 (= *tendencia*) movement • **el ~ de liberación de la mujer** the women's liberation movement • **el Movimiento (Nacional)** (*Esp*) (*Hist*) *the Falangist Movement* ▸ **movimiento obrero** workers' movement ▸ **movimiento pacifista** pacifist movement ▸ **movimiento sindical** trade union movement
7 (*Mús*) [*de compás*] tempo; [*de sinfonía*] movement
8 (*Inform*) ▸ **movimiento de bloques** block move

9 (= *jugada*) move
moviola® SF **1** (*Cine*) Moviola®
2 (= *repetición*) action replay
mozalbete SM lad
Mozambique SM Mozambique
mozambiqueño/a ADJ, SM/F Mozambican
mozárabe ADJ Mozarabic
SMF Mozarab; ▹ **RECONQUISTA**
SM (*Ling*) Mozarabic
mozarrón SM big lad, strapping young fellow
mozo/a ADJ **1** (= *joven*) young • **en sus años ~s** in his youth, in his young days
2 (= *soltero*) single, unmarried
SM/F **1** (= *joven*) lad/girl • **buena moza** good-looking girl
2 (= *criado*) servant ▸ **moza de taberna** (*Esp*†) barmaid
SM (= *camarero*) waiter; (*Ferro etc*) porter ▸ **mozo de almacén** warehouse assistant ▸ **mozo de caballos** groom ▸ **mozo de café** waiter ▸ **mozo de cámara** cabin boy ▸ **mozo de cuadra** stable boy ▸ **mozo de cuerda, mozo de equipajes, mozo de estación** porter ▸ **mozo de hotel** bellboy, bellhop (*EEUU*) ▸ **mozo de laboratorio** laboratory assistant ▸ **mozo de panadería** baker's boy
mozuelo/a SM/F lad/girl
MP3 SM MP3 • **reproductor de MP3** MP3 player
MPAIAC SM ABR (*Esp*) = **Movimiento para la Autodeterminación y la Independencia del Archipiélago Canario**
MPEG SM ABR (= **Moving Picture Experts Group**) (*Inform*) MPEG
MRTA SM ABR (*Perú*) = **Movimiento Revolucionario Túpac Amaru**
ms. ABR, **mss.** ABR (= **manuscrito**) MS., ms.
Mtro. ABR = **Maestro**
mu‡ SM • **MODISMO**: • **no decir ni mu** not to say a word
SF • **¡achanta la mu!** (*Méx*) shut your face!‡
muaré SM moiré
mucamo/a SM/F (*And, Cono Sur*) houseboy/maid, servant
muceta SF cape
muchá SMF (*LAm*) = **muchacho**
muchachada SF **1** (= *travesura*) childish prank
2 (*LAm*) (= *grupo de jóvenes*) group of young people, bunch of kids*
muchacha-guía SF (PL: **muchachas-guías**) girl guide, girl scout (*EEUU*)
muchachería SF **1** (= *travesura*) childish prank
2 (= *muchachos*) boys and girls (*pl*), kids* (*pl*); (= *pandilla*) group of young people, bunch of kids*
muchachil ADJ boyish/girlish
muchacho/a SM/F **1** (= *joven*) boy/girl
2 (*tb* **muchacho de servicio**) (= *hombre*) servant; (= *mujer*) maid, servant
SM (*Chile*) (= *cuña*) wedge; (*LAm*) (= *abrazadera*) clamp; (*Cono Sur*) [*de zapato*] shoehorn; (*And*) (= *lámpara*) miner's lamp; (= *sostén*) prop
muchedumbre SF **1** [*de personas*] crowd, throng; (*pey*) mob, herd • **una ~ de admiradores** a crowd of admirers
2 [*de pájaros*] flock
muchísimo ADJ a lot of, lots of • **había muchísima gente** there were a lot of people, there were lots of people • **había muchísima comida** there was a lot of food, there was lots of food • **hace ~ tiempo** a very long time ago, ages ago
ADV very much, a lot • **me quiere ~** he loves me very much *o* a lot, he really loves me
• **llovía ~** it was raining really *o* very hard, it was pouring down
mucho ADJ **1** (*en singular*) (*en oraciones afirmativas*) a lot of, lots of; (*en oraciones interrogativas y negativas*) a lot of, much • **tengo ~ dinero** I have a lot of *o* lots of money • **había mucha gente** there were a lot of *o* lots of people there • **¿tienes ~ trabajo?** do you have a lot of *o* much work? • **no tengo ~ dinero** I don't have a lot of *o* much money • **hace ~ calor** it's very hot • **tengo ~ frío** I'm very cold • **tengo mucha hambre** I'm very hungry • **tengo mucha sed** I'm very thirsty • **tuve mucha suerte** I was very lucky • **no hace ~ tiempo** not long ago • **llevo aquí ~ tiempo** I've been here a long time
2 (*en plural*) (*en oraciones afirmativas*) a lot of, lots of; (*en oraciones interrogativas y negativas*) a lot of, many • **tiene muchas plantas** he has got a lot of *o* lots of plants • **muchas personas creen que no** a lot of *o* lots of people don't think so • **se lo he dicho muchas veces** I've told him many *o* lots of times • **¿había ~s niños en el parque?** were there a lot of *o* many children in the park? • **no había ~s patos en el lago** there weren't a lot of *o* many ducks on the lake
3* (*con singular colectivo*) • **había ~ borracho** there were a lot of *o* lots of drunks there • **hay ~ tonto suelto** there are a lot of *o* lots of idiots around • **~ beso, pero luego me critica por la espalda** she's all kisses, but then she criticizes me behind my back
4 (= *demasiado*) • **es ~ dinero para un niño** it's too much money for a child • **es mucha mujer para ti*** that woman is too much for you • **esta es mucha casa para nosotros*** this house is too big for us
PRON **1** (*en singular*) **a** (*en frases afirmativas*) a lot, lots; (*en frases interrogativas y negativas*) a lot, much • **tengo ~ que hacer** I have a lot *o* lots to do • **tiene la culpa de ~ de lo que pasa** he's to blame for a lot of *o* much of what has happened • **el plan tiene ~ de positivo** there's a lot about the plan that is positive • **su discurso tiene ~ de fascista** his rhetoric contains a lot of fascist elements • **¿has aprendido ~ en este trabajo?** have you learnt a lot *o* much from this job? • **no tengo ~ que hacer** I haven't got a lot *o* much to do • **—¿cuánto vino queda? —mucho** "how much wine is left?" — "a lot" *o* "lots"
b (*referido a tiempo*) long • **¿te vas a quedar ~?** are you staying long? • **no tardes ~** don't be long • **¿falta ~ para llegar?** will it be long till we arrive? • **—¿cuánto nos queda para acabar? —mucho** "how long till we finish?" — "ages" • **hace ~ que no salgo a bailar** it's a long time *o* ages since I went out dancing
2 (*en plural*) (*en frases afirmativas*) a lot, lots; (*en frases interrogativas y negativas*) a lot, many • **somos ~s** there are a lot of *o* lots of us • **son ~s los que no quieren** there are a lot *o* lots who don't want to • **~s dicen que ...** a lot of *o* lots of *o* many people say that ... • **~s de los ausentes** many of *o* a lot of those absent • **—¿hay manzanas? —sí, pero no muchas** "are there any apples?" — "yes, but not many *o* not a lot" • **¿vinieron ~s?** did many *o* a lot of people come? • **—¿cuántos había? —muchos** "how many were there?" — "a lot" *o* "lots"
ADV **1** (= *en gran cantidad*) a lot • **come ~** she eats a lot • **te quiero ~** I love you very much *o* a lot • **viene ~** he comes often *o* a lot • **me gusta ~ el jazz** I really like jazz, I like jazz a lot • **sí señor, me gusta y ~** I do indeed like it and I like it a lot • **—son 75 euros —es mucho** "that will be 75 euros" — "that's a lot" • **alegrarse ~** to be very glad • **correr ~** to run fast • **lo siento ~** I'm very *o* really sorry • **¡~ lo sientes tú!*** a fat lot you care!* • **trabajar ~** to work hard • **~ antes** long before • **~ más** much *o* a lot more • **~ menos** much *o* a lot less • **muy ~**: • **se guardará muy ~ de hacerlo*** he'll jolly well be careful not to do it* • **si no es ~ pedir** if that's not asking too much • **eso es ~ pedir** it's a lot to ask • **pensárselo ~**: • **se lo pensó ~ antes de contestar** he thought long and hard about it before replying • **~ peor** much *o* a lot worse
2 (*en respuestas*) • **—¿estás cansado? —¡mucho!** "are you tired?" — "I certainly am!" • **—¿te gusta? —no mucho** "do you like it?" — "not really"
3 (*otras locuciones*) • **como ~** at (the) most • **como ~ leo un libro al mes** at (the) most I read one book a month • **con ~** by far, far and away • **fue, con ~, el mejor** he was by far the best, he was far and away the best • **no se puede comparar, ni con ~, a ninguna de nuestras ideas** it bears no comparison at all *o* you can't begin to compare it with any of our ideas • **cuando ~** (*frm*) at (the) most • **tener a algn en ~** to think highly of sb • **ni ~ menos**: • **Juan no es ni ~ menos el que era** Juan is nothing like the man he was • **mi intención no era insultarte, ni ~ menos** I in no way intended to insult you, I didn't intend to insult you, far from it • **por ~ que**: • **por ~ que estudies** however hard you study • **por ~ que lo quieras no debes mimarlo** no matter how much you love him, you shouldn't spoil him
mucilaginoso ADJ mucilaginous
mucílago SM mucilage
mucosa SF (= *membrana*) mucous membrane; (= *secreción*) mucus
mucosidad SF mucus
mucoso ADJ mucous
múcura SF (*And, Caribe*) earthenware jug
muda SF **1** [*de ropa*] change of underwear
2 (*Zool*) [*de piel*] slough; [*de pelo, plumaje*] moult, molt (*EEUU*)
3 [*de la voz*] breaking
mudable ADJ, **mudadizo** ADJ
1 (= *variable*) changeable, variable
2 [*persona*] fickle
mudanza SF **1** (= *cambio*) change • **sufrir ~** to undergo a change
2 [*de casa*] move • **estar de ~** to be moving; **mudanzas** removals • **camión de ~s** removal van, moving van (*EEUU*) • **empresa de ~s** removals company, moving company (*EEUU*)
3 (*Baile*) figure
4 mudanzas (= *inconstancia*) fickleness (*sing*), moodiness (*sing*)
mudar ▹ CONJUG 1a VT **1** (= *cambiar*) to change; (= *transformar*) to change, turn (**en** into) • **esto mudó la tristeza en alegría** this changed *o* turned the sadness into joy • **le mudan las sábanas todos los días** they change his sheets every day • **le han mudado a otra oficina** they've moved him to another office
2 (*Zool*) [+ *piel*] to shed; [+ *pelo, plumaje*] to moult, molt (*EEUU*)
VI **1** (= *cambiar*) • **~ de** to change • **he mudado de parecer** I've changed my mind • **~ de color** to change colour • **su cara mudó de color** his face changed colour; ▹ **mandar**
2 (*Zool*) • **~ de** [+ *piel*] to shed; [+ *pelo, plumaje*] to moult, molt (*EEUU*)
VPR **mudarse 1** (*tb* **mudarse de ropa**) to change one's clothes
2 (*tb* **mudarse de casa**) to move, move house
3 [*voz*] to break

m

mudéjar ADJ Mudejar
SMF (*Hist*) Mudejar (*Moslem permitted to live under Christian rule*); ▹ RECONQUISTA
mudejarismo SM *Mudejar character or style*
mudenco ADJ (*CAm*) (= *tartamudo*) stuttering; (= *tonto*) stupid
mudengo ADJ (*And*) silly
mudez SF dumbness
mudo ADJ **1** (*Med*) dumb, mute (*frm*) • **es ~ de nacimiento** he was born dumb *o* (*frm*) mute
2 (= *callado*) silent, mute • **sufrió con resignación muda** he suffered with silent *o* mute resignation • **no podemos permanecer ~s ante lo que está ocurriendo** we cannot remain silent in the face of what is happening • **ser testigo ~ de algo** to stand in mute witness *o* testimony to sth
• **quedarse ~ (de)** to be struck dumb (with)
• **quedarse ~ de asombro** to be left speechless, be dumbfounded • **se quedó ~ durante tres horas** he did not speak for three hours • **quedarse ~ de envidia** (*Esp*) to be green with envy
3 (*Ling*) [*letra*] mute, silent; [*consonante*] voiceless
4 [*película*] silent
5 • **papel ~** (*Teat*) walk-on part
6 (*And, CAm*) (= *tonto*) foolish, silly
mueblaje SM = **mobiliario**
mueble ADJ movable • **bienes ~s** movable *o* personal property (*sing*)
SM **1** (= *objeto*) piece of furniture
• **~s** furniture (*sing*) • **con ~s** furnished • **sin ~s** unfurnished • **~s y enseres** furniture and fittings • MODISMO: • **salvar los ~s** to save face ▸ **mueble de elementos adicionables** unit, piece of unit furniture ▸ **mueble librería** bookcase ▸ **muebles de cocina** kitchen units ▸ **muebles de época** period furniture (*sing*) ▸ **muebles de oficina** office furniture (*sing*)
2 (*Méx**) (= *coche*) car

MUEBLE

▹ *Para traducir la palabra* **mueble** *al inglés, hay que recordar que el sustantivo* **furniture** *es incontable y lleva el verbo en singular:*
Los muebles del comedor son muy antiguos
The dining-room furniture is very old
▹ *Si queremos traducir expresiones en las que se habla de un solo mueble, o en las que se precisa el número de muebles, utilizamos la construcción* **piece/pieces of furniture**:
Este es un mueble muy valioso
This is a very valuable piece of furniture
He comprado un par de muebles antiguos
I bought one or two pieces of antique furniture
Para otros usos y ejemplos ver la entrada.

mueblé* SM brothel
mueble-bar SM cocktail cabinet, drinks cabinet
mueblería SF (= *fábrica*) furniture factory; (= *tienda*) furniture shop
mueca SF (wry) face, grimace • **hacer ~s** to make faces, pull faces (**a** at) • **una ~ de asco/estupor/desesperación** a disgusted/astonished/despairing expression
muela SF **1** (*Anat*) (*gen*) tooth; (*para especificar*) back tooth, molar • **dolor de ~s** toothache • MODISMOS: • **está que echa las ~s** he's hopping mad • **hacer la ~** (*Caribe‡*) to skive‡ ▸ **muela del juicio** wisdom tooth
2 (*Téc*) [*de molino*] millstone; [*de afilar*] grindstone
3 (*Geog*) (= *cerro*) mound, hillock
4 (*And*) gluttony
5 (*Caribe*) trickery
muellaje SM wharfage
muelle¹ SM (= *resorte*) spring • **colchón de ~s** interior sprung mattress ▸ **muelle helicoidal** coil spring ▸ **muelle real** mainspring
ADJ **1** (= *blando*) soft; (= *delicado*) delicate; (= *elástico*) springy, bouncy
2 [*vida*] soft, easy
muelle² SM **1** (*Náut*) (= *puerto*) wharf, quay; (= *malecón*) pier • **cargador de ~s** docker ▸ **muelle de atraque** (*Náut*) mooring quay; (*Aer*) docking bay
2 (*Ferro*) (*tb* **muelle de carga**) loading bay
muenda SF (*And*) thrashing
muera *etc* ▹ **morir**
muérdago SM mistletoe
muerdo* SM bite
muérgano/a SM/F (*And*) (= *desharrapado*) shabby person; (*And*) (= *maleducado*) ill-bred person, lout
SM **1** (*And, Caribe*) (= *cacharro*) useless object, piece of junk
2 (*And*) (= *caballo*) vicious horse
muermo/a* (*Esp*) ADJ (= *pesado*) boring; (= *aburrido*) wet*
SM/F (= *pesado*) crashing bore*; (= *aburrido*) drip*, wet fish*
SM **1** (= *aburrimiento*) boredom; (= *depresión*) the blues* (*pl*)
2 (= *asunto*) bore
3 [*de droga*] bad trip*
muerte SF **1** (= *por enfermedad, accidente*) death • **tuvo una buena ~** he had a good death, he died a good death • **hasta que la ~ nos separe** till death us do part • **murió de ~ natural** he died a natural death *o* of natural causes • **se debatía entre la vida y la ~** he was fighting for his life • **una lucha a ~** a fight to the death • **defenderé mis derechos a ~** I will defend my rights to the death • **mantuvo una guerra a ~ con la enfermedad** he fought his illness to the bitter end • **luchar a ~** to fight to the death • **odiar algo/a algn a ~** to detest sth/sb, loathe sth/sb • **causar la ~ a algn** to kill sb, cause the death of sb • **las heridas que le causaron la ~** the injuries that killed him *o* caused his death • **encontrar la ~** to die, meet one's death • **herido de ~** fatally injured • **el ciervo escapó herido de ~** the deer escaped fatally injured • **la democracia estaba herida de ~** democracy was on its last legs • **pena de ~** death sentence • **estar a las puertas de la ~** to be at death's door • **un susto de ~** a terrible fright • **me diste un susto de ~** you scared me to death, you gave me a terrible fright • MODISMOS: • **estar de ~** (*Esp**) to be out-of-this-world*; (*Chile**) to be extremely upset • **la comida estaba de ~** the meal was out of this world* • **de mala ~*** [*trabajo, película*] crappy**, crap** (*antes de s*); [*casa, pueblo*] grotty‡ • **nos detuvimos en un pueblucho de mala ~** we stopped in a grotty little town‡ • **era un hotel de mala ~** the hotel was a real dump‡, the hotel was really grotty‡ • **cada ~ de obispo** (*LAm**) once in a blue moon • **ser la ~*** (= *ser horrible*) to be hell*; (= *ser estupendo*) to be amazing* • **este trabajo es la ~** this job is really hell* • **este calor es la ~** this heat is killing me* • **esa noria es la ~** that big wheel is amazing*
▸ **muerte cerebral** brain death ▸ **muerte civil** loss of civil rights ▸ **muerte clínica** • **en situación de ~ clínica** clinically dead
▸ **muerte súbita** (*Med*) sudden death; (*Tenis*) tie-break; (*Golf*) sudden death play-off; (*Ftbl*) sudden death ▸ **muerte prematura** premature death ▸ **muerte repentina** sudden death ▸ **muerte violenta** violent death; ▹ **vida**
2 (= *asesinato*) murder • **fue declarado culpable de varias ~s** he was found guilty of various murders • **dar ~ a algn** to kill sb ▸ **muerte a mano airada** violent death
3 (= *desaparición*) [*de imperio, civilización*] death, demise (*frm*) • **la ~ de las civilizaciones indígenas** the death *o* demise of native civilizations
muerto/a PP *de* **morir**
ADJ **1** [*persona, animal*] dead • **mis abuelos están ~s** my grandparents are dead • **el golpe lo dejó medio ~** the blow left him half-dead • **resultó ~ en el acto** he died instantly • **~ en acción** *o* **campaña** killed in action • **dar por ~ a algn** to give sb up for dead • **ser ~ a tiros** to be shot, be shot dead • **vivo o ~** dead or alive • MODISMOS: • **estar más ~ que vivo** to be more dead than alive • **estar ~ y enterrado*** • **estar más ~ que una piedra*** • **estar más que ~*** to be as dead as a doornail*, be as dead as a dodo*, be stone dead* • **no tener donde caerse ~** not to have a penny to one's name; ▹ **ángulo, cal, lengua, marea, naturaleza, punto, tiempo, vía**
2* (*para exagerar*) **a** (= *cansado*) dead tired*, ready to drop* • **después del viaje estábamos ~s** we were dead tired *o* ready to drop after the journey* • **caí muerta en la cama** I dropped flat out on the bed
b (= *sin animación*) dead • **en invierno este pueblo está ~** this town is dead in winter
c • **estar ~ de algo**: • **estaba ~ de la envidia** I was green with envy • **me voy a la cama, que estoy muerta de sueño** I'm going to bed, I'm dead tired* • **estaba ~ de miedo** I was scared to death • **estaba ~ del aburrimiento** he was dead bored • **estoy muerta de cansancio** I'm dead tired *o* dog tired*, I'm ready to drop* • **comes como si estuvieras ~ de hambre** you're eating as if you were starving hungry • **estar ~ de risa** [*persona*] to laugh one's head off, kill o.s. laughing; [*casa*] to be going to rack and ruin; (*Esp*) [*ropa*] to be gathering dust • **estaba ~ de risa con sus chistes** I laughed my head off at his jokes, I killed myself laughing at his jokes • **compró una casa para tenerla muerta de risa** he bought a house and let it go to rack and ruin* • **el piano sigue ahí ~ de risa** the piano is still there gathering dust • **el solar sigue todavía ~ de risa** nothing has been done yet with that plot of land
3 (= *relajado*) [*brazo, mano*] limp • **se me quedó la mano muerta** my hand went limp • **deja el brazo ~** let your arm go limp
4 (= *apagado*) [*color*] dull
SM/F **1** (= *persona muerta*) (*en accidente, guerra*) • **¿ha habido ~s en el accidente?** was anyone killed in the accident? • **el conflicto ha causado 45.000 ~s** the conflict has caused 45,000 deaths *o* the deaths of 45,000 people • **el número de ~s va en aumento** the death toll *o* the number of deaths is rising • **doblar a ~** to toll the death knell • **los ~s** the dead • **resucitó de entre los ~s** he rose from the dead • **los ~s vivientes** the living dead • **tocar a ~** to toll the death knell
• MODISMOS: • **¡me cago en los ~s!** (*Esp***) fucking hell!** • **¡te lo juro por mis ~s!*** I swear on my mother's grave!* • **un ~ de hambre** a nobody • **ni ~***: • **no me pondría ese traje ni ~** I wouldn't be seen dead in that suit* • **resucitar a un ~**: • **esta sopa resucita a un ~** (*hum*) this soup really hits the spot*

2* (= *cadáver*) body • **han encontrado un ~ en el río** they have found a (dead) body in the river • **el ~ fue trasladado en avión** the body was taken by plane • **hacer el ~** to float • **¿sabes hacer el ~ boca arriba?** can you float on your back? • **hacerse el ~** to pretend to be dead • **MODISMO**: • **callarse como un ~** to keep dead quiet • **REFRANES**: • **los ~s no hablan** dead men tell no tales • **el ~ al hoyo y el vivo al bollo** dead men have no friends
SM **1*** (= *tarea pesada*) drag* • **¡vaya ~ que nos ha caído encima!** (*Esp*) what a drag!* • **lo siento, pero te ha tocado a ti el ~ de decírselo al jefe** I'm sorry, but you've drawn the short straw - you've got to tell the boss • **MODISMOS**: • **cargar con el ~** to carry the can*, take the rap* • **ese ~ yo no me lo cargo, yo soy inocente** I'm not taking the blame *o* rap*, I'm innocent • **cargar con el ~ de hacer algo** to be lumbered with doing sth* • **siempre me cargan con el ~ de cuidar a los niños** I always get lumbered with looking after the children • **cargar** *o* **echar el ~ a algn** to pin the blame on sb • **a mí no me cargas tú ese ~, yo no tengo nada que ver en este asunto** don't try and pin the blame on me, I've got nothing to do with this
2 (*Naipes*) dummy

DÍA DE LOS MUERTOS

2 November, All Souls' Day, called the **Día de los Muertos** elsewhere in the Spanish-speaking world and **Día de los Difuntos** in Spain, is the day when Christians throughout the Spanish-speaking world traditionally honour their dead. In Mexico the festivities are particularly spectacular with a week-long festival, starting on 1 November, in which Christian and ancient pagan customs are married. 1 November itself is for children who have died, while 2 November is set aside for adults. Families meet to take food, flowers and sweets in the shape of skeletons, coffins and crosses to the graves of their loved ones. In Spain people celebrate the **Día de los Difuntos** by taking flowers to the cemetery.

muesca SF **1** (= *hendidura*) notch, nick; (*para encajar*) groove, slot
2 (= *marca*) mark
muesli SM muesli
muestra SF **1** (= *señal*) sign, indication • **no ir es ~ de desprecio** not going is a sign of contempt • **es (una) ~ de cariño** it is a token of affection • **dar ~s de algo** to show signs of sth • **MODISMO**: • **para ~ (basta) un botón** by way of example • **¿que si es listo? para ~ un botón, ha sacado un diez en el examen** is he clever? by way of example he got full marks in the exam
2 (= *prueba*) proof • **eso es (la) ~ de que estaba mintiendo** this is proof that he was lying
3 (*Com*) sample ▸ **muestra gratuita** free sample
4 (*Med*) sample, specimen
5 (= *exposición*) trade fair
6 (= *en estadística*) sample ▸ **muestra aleatoria, muestra al azar** random sample ▸ **muestra representativa** representative sample
7 (*Cos*) pattern
8 (= *esfera de reloj*) face
9† [*de tienda*] sign, signboard
muestral ADJ sample (*antes de s*)
muestrario SM **1** (= *muestras*) collection of samples; (= *libro*) pattern book
2 [*de personajes, objetos*] collection
muestrear ▹ CONJUG 1a VT to sample
muestreo SM (= *acto*) sampling; (= *muestra*) sample • **hacer un ~ de la población** to select a sample of the population
mueva *etc* ▹ **mover**
mufa* SF (*Cono Sur*) (= *mala suerte*) bad luck, misfortune; (= *mal humor*) bad mood; (= *aburrimiento*) boredom, tedium
mufado* ADJ (*Cono Sur*) • **estar ~** to be in a bad mood
mugido SM **1** [*de vaca*] moo; [*de toro*] bellow
2 [*de dolor*] roar, howl
mugir ▹ CONJUG 3c VI **1** [*vaca*] to moo; [*toro*] to bellow
2 (*con dolor*) to roar, howl
mugre SF (= *suciedad*) dirt; (= *inmundicia*) filth; (= *grasa*) grime, grease • **MODISMO**: • **sacarse la ~** (*Cono Sur**) (= *trabajar*) to work like a dog*; (= *sufrir un percance*) to have a nasty accident
mugriento ADJ (= *sucio*) dirty, filthy; (= *grasiento*) grimy, greasy
mugrón SM (= *vástago*) shoot, sprout; [*de vid*] sucker, layer
mugroso ADJ (*LAm*) dirty, mucky*
muguete SM lily of the valley
mui‡ SF = **muy**
muina* SF (*Méx*) • **me da la ~** it gets on my nerves
mujahedín SM, **mujahidín** SM, **mujaidín** SM mujaheddin
mujer SF **1** woman • **ser muy ~ • ser toda una ~** to be a real woman • **ser muy ~ de su casa** to be very house-proud • **nombre de ~** woman's name • **ropa de ~** women's clothes *o* clothing • **hacerse ~** to become a woman ▸ **mujer bandera†** striking woman ▸ **mujer de la limpieza** cleaning lady, cleaning woman, cleaner ▸ **mujer de la vida** (*euf*), **mujer de mala vida** prostitute ▸ **mujer de negocios** businesswoman ▸ **mujer de vida alegre** loose woman ▸ **mujer empresaria** businesswoman ▸ **mujer fatal** femme fatale ▸ **mujer objeto** sex object ▸ **mujer piloto** (woman) pilot ▸ **mujer policía** policewoman ▸ **mujer pública** (*euf*) prostitute ▸ **mujer sacerdote** woman priest
2 (= *esposa*) wife • **mi ~** my wife • **mi futura ~** my wife-to-be • **tomar ~** to take a wife ▸ **mujer maltratada** battered wife
3 (*uso apelativo*) (*en oración directa no se traduce*) • **¡déjalo, mujer, no te preocupes!** forget about it, don't worry! • **¡mujer, no digas esas cosas!** please! don't say such things!
mujeraza* SF shrew
mujercita SF little woman, little lady
mujerengo ADJ (*CAm, Cono Sur*)
1 (= *afeminado*) effeminate
2 (= *mujeriego*) • **es muy ~** he's a real womanizer
mujerero ADJ (*LAm*) • **es muy ~** he's a real womanizer
mujeriego ADJ **1** [*hombre*] • **es muy ~** he's a real womanizer
2 • **cabalgar a mujeriegas** to ride sidesaddle
SM womanizer
mujeril ADJ womanly
mujerío* SM (*Esp*) • **ir de ~** (= *de putas*) to go whoring; (= *de ligue*) to go looking for a woman
mujer-objeto SF (PL: **mujeres-objeto**) (female) sex object
mujerona SF big woman
mujer-rana SF diver
mujerzuela‡ SF tart‡, slut‡
mújol SM grey mullet
mula SF **1** (= *animal*) mule • **MODISMO**: • **más terco que una ~** as stubborn as a mule
2 (*Méx*) (= *bravucón*) tough guy
3 (*Méx*) (= *trastos*) junk, trash (*EEUU*)
4 (*CAm*) (= *vergüenza*) shame
5 (*And*) (= *pipa*) pipe
6 (*And*) (= *idiota*) idiot
7 (*Cono Sur**) (= *mentira*) lie; (= *engaño*) trick • **MODISMOS**: • **meter la ~** to tell lies • **meter la ~ a algn** to trick sb
mulada SF drove of mules
muladar SM **1** (= *estercolero*) dungheap
2 (= *casa*) pigsty, pigpen (*EEUU*)
mulato/a ADJ, SM/F mulatto
mulé‡ SM • **dar ~ a algn** to bump sb off*
mulero/a SM/F **1** (= *mozo*) muleteer
2 (*Cono Sur**) (= *mentiroso*) liar
muleta SF **1** (*para andar*) crutch
2 (*Taur*) *matador's stick with red cloth attached*
3 (= *apoyo*) prop, support
muletazo SM *movement of the "muleta" in bullfighting*
muletilla SF **1** (= *frase*) pet word, tag
2 (= *bastón*) cross-handled cane; (*Téc*) (= *botón*) wooden toggle, wooden button
3 (*Taur*) = **muleta**
muletón SM flannelette
mulillas SFPL *team of mules which drag the dead bull from the bullring*
mulita SF (*Arg, Uru*) armadillo
mullido ADJ **1** [*cama, sofá, alfombra, hierba*] soft, springy; [*almohada, terreno*] soft; [*pelo, tela*] fluffy
2 • **dejar a algn ~*** to wear sb out
SM (= *relleno*) stuffing, filling
mullir ▹ CONJUG 3a VT **1** (= *ablandar*) to soften; [+ *almohada*] to fluff up; [+ *cama*] to shake up; [+ *tierra*] to hoe, fork over
2 [+ *plantas*] to hoe round, loosen the earth round
mullo SM (red) mullet
mulo SM mule • **MODISMO**: • **trabaja como un ~** he works like a dog
mulón ADJ (*And, Cono Sur*) (= *tartamudo*) stammering; [*niño*] slow in learning to talk, backward
multa SF fine • **echar** *o* **poner una ~ a algn** to fine sb ▸ **multa de tráfico** traffic fine ▸ **multa por aparcamiento indebido** parking ticket
multar ▹ CONJUG 1a VT to fine • **~ a algn con 100 dólares** to fine sb 100 dollars
multi... PREF multi...
multiacceso ADJ (*Inform*) multi-access
multicampeón/ona SM/F several times champion
multicanal ADJ (*TV*) multichannel
multicapa ADJ INV multilayer(ed)
multicelular ADJ multicellular
multicine SM multiscreen cinema, multiplex
multicolor ADJ [*camisa, bandera, pájaro*] multicoloured, multicolored (*EEUU*); [*espectáculo*] colourful, colorful (*EEUU*); [*planta, diseño*] variegated
multiconferencia SF three-way call
multiconfesional ADJ multidenominational
multicopiar ▹ CONJUG 1b VT to duplicate
multicopista SF duplicator • **a ~** duplicated, mimeographed
multicultural ADJ multicultural
multiculturalidad SF multiculturalism
multiculturalismo SM multiculturalism
multidimensional ADJ multidimensional
multidireccional ADJ multidirectional
multidisciplinar ADJ, **multidisciplinario** ADJ multidisciplinary • **estudio ~** multidisciplinary study, cross-disciplinary study
multifacético ADJ many-sided, multifaceted • **un hombre ~** a man of many talents
multifamiliar ADJ • **edificio ~** block of flats, apartment block (*EEUU*)
multifásico ADJ polyphase
multiforme ADJ multiform, multifarious

multifuncional (ADJ) multifunctional
multigrado (ADJ) multigrade
multilaminar (ADJ) • **madera ~** plywood
multilateral (ADJ), **multilátero** (ADJ) multilateral
multilingüe (ADJ) multilingual
multimedia (ADJ INV) multimedia (*antes de s*)
multimillonario/a (SM/F) multimillionaire/multimillionairess
(ADJ) **1** (= *persona*) • **ser ~** to be a multimillionaire/multimillionairess
2 • **un contrato ~** (*de euros*) a multi-million euro contract; (*de dólares*) a multi-million dollar contract
multimotor (ADJ) multi-engined
(SM) multi-engined aircraft
multinacional (ADJ) multinational
(SF) multinational, multinational company
multiorgánico (ADJ) • **donante ~** multiple organ donor
multipartidismo (SM) multi-party system
multipartidista (ADJ) multi-party (*antes de s*)
múltiple (ADJ) **1** [*colisión, embarazo, fractura*] multiple • **enchufe ~** multiple socket • **misiles de cabeza ~** multiple-warhead missiles • **preguntas de elección ~** multiple choice questions • **orgasmo ~** multiple orgasm
2 múltiples (= *muchos*) [*aplicaciones, problemas, ocasiones*] many, numerous • **esta mesa tiene ~s usos** this table has many *o* numerous uses, this is a multipurpose table
3 (*Inform*) • **de tarea ~** multi-task • **de usuario ~** multi-user
multiplexor (SM) multiplexor
multiplicación (SF) **1** (*Mat, Bio*) multiplication
2 (= *aumento*) increase • **gracias a la ~ de los satélites de comunicación** thanks to the rapid increase in the number of communications satellites • **la ~ de los panes y los peces** (*Rel*) the feeding of the five thousand, the miracle of the loaves and the fishes
multiplicado (SM) multiplicand
multiplicador (ADJ) • **efecto ~** multiplier effect
(SM) multiplier
multiplicar ▷ CONJUG 1g (VT) (*Mat*) to multiply (**por** by); (= *aumentar*) to increase, multiply
(VPR) **multiplicarse 1** (*Mat, Bio*) to multiply; (= *aumentar*) to increase, multiply
2 [*persona*] to be everywhere at once • **no puedo ~me** I can't be in half a dozen places at once, I've only got one pair of hands
multiplicidad (SF) multiplicity, great variety
múltiplo (ADJ) multiple
(SM) multiple ▸ **mínimo común múltiplo** lowest common multiple
multiprocesador (SM) multiprocessor
multiprocesamiento (SM), **multiproceso** (SM) multiprocessing
multipropiedad (SF) time-share • **el sistema de ~** time-sharing
multirracial (ADJ) multiracial
multirregional (ADJ) multi-regional
multirregulable (ADJ) adjustable (to a variety of positions)
multirreincidencia (SF) persistent offending
multirreincidente (SMF) persistent offender
multirriesgo (ADJ INV) • **póliza ~** fully comprehensive policy, all-risks policy
multisecular (ADJ) age-old, centuries-old
multitarea (ADJ INV) multitasking (*antes de s*)
(SF) multitasking
multitud (SF) **1** (= *gentío*) crowd • **una ~ de curiosos y periodistas** a crowd of curious onlookers and journalists • **la ~** the crowd, the masses (*pl*)
2 • **~ de: tengo ~ de cosas que hacer** I've got a mountain of things to do • **existen ~ de posibilidades** there are any number of possibilities
multitudinario (ADJ) [*manifestación*] mass (*antes de s*); [*reunión*] large; [*recepción*] tumultuous • **asamblea multitudinaria** mass meeting
multiuso (ADJ INV) multipurpose
multiusuario (ADJ INV) multiuser
multiviaje (ADJ INV) • **billete ~** multiple-journey ticket
Mumbai (SF) Mumbai
mun. (ABR) = **municipio**
mundanal (ADJ) worldly • **lejos del ~ ruido** far from the madding crowd (*liter*) • **alejarse del ~ ruido** to get away from it all
mundanalidad (SF) (*liter*) worldliness
mundanería (SF) worldliness
mundano/a (ADJ) **1** (= *del mundo*) worldly
2 (= *de alta sociedad*) society (*antes de s*); (= *de moda*) fashionable • **son gente muy mundana** they're great society people • **una reunión mundana** a fashionable gathering, a gathering of society people
(SM/F) society person, socialite
mundial (ADJ) [*acontecimiento, esfuerzo, organismo*] worldwide; [*economía, figura, población*] world (*antes de s*) • **una crisis a escala ~** a crisis on a worldwide scale, a global crisis • **las comunicaciones ~es** worldwide communications • **la primera guerra ~** the First World War, World War I • **la segunda guerra ~** the Second World War, World War II
(SM) world championship • **el Mundial** *o* **los Mundiales (de Fútbol)** the World Cup • **el Mundial** *o* **los Mundiales de Atletismo** the Athletics World Cup *o* Championship
mundialización (SF) globalization
mundialmente (ADV) worldwide, universally • **~ famoso** world-famous • **hacer algo ~ popular** to make sth universally popular • **una palabra ~ utilizada** a word used throughout *o* all over the world • **un especialista ~ conocido** a world-famous specialist, a specialist of world renown
mundillo (SM) world, circle • **en el ~ teatral** in the theatre world, in theatrical circles
mundo (SM) **1** (= *lo creado*) world • **la Copa del Mundo** the World Cup • **no hay nada mejor en el ~** there's nothing better in the whole (wide) world • **artistas de todo el ~ exponen sus obras** artists from all over the world are exhibiting their work • **la prensa de todo el ~ dio la noticia** the world press reported the news • **es conocido en todo el ~** he is known throughout the world *o* the world over • **es lo que más desea en el ~** it's what she wants most in (all) the world • **el ~ antiguo** ancient world • **el Nuevo Mundo** the New World • **el otro ~** the next world, the hereafter • **irse al otro ~** to pass away • **el Tercer Mundo** the Third World • **el Viejo Mundo** the Old World; ▷ **hombre**
2 (= *humanidad*) • **medio ~** almost everybody • **conoce a medio ~** he knows almost everybody • **estaba medio ~** there were loads of people there • **todo el ~** everyone, everybody
3 (= *ámbito*) world • **el ~ de la moda** the fashion world • **el ~ hispánico** the Hispanic world • **en el ~ de las ideas** in the world *o* realm of ideas • **en el ~ científico** in scientific circles • **el ~ del espectáculo** show business • **incorporarse al ~ del trabajo** to get a job • **no piensa volver al ~ de la política** she doesn't intend to return to politics
4 (= *vida mundana*) world • **decidió volver la espalda al ~** he decided to abandon worldly things • **los placeres del ~** worldly pleasures • **las tentaciones del ~** the temptations of the flesh
5 • MODISMOS: • **así va el ~** no wonder things are as they are • **correr ~** to see the world • **ha corrido mucho ~** he's been around a bit • **echar a algn al ~** to bring sb into the world • **echarse al ~** (*euf*) to go on the streets • **desde que el ~ es ~** since time began • **se le cayó el ~ encima** his world fell apart • **por esos ~s (de Dios)** all over, here there and everywhere • **no es el fin del ~** it's not the end of the world • **aunque se hunda el ~** come what may • **no por eso se hundirá el ~** it won't be the end of the world • **por nada del** *o* **en el ~** not for all the world • **no lo cambiaría por nada del ~** I wouldn't change it for anything in the world *o* for all the world • **no es nada del otro ~** it's nothing special *o* to write home about • **hacer algo del otro ~** to do something quite extraordinary • **ponerse el ~ por montera**: • **se cansó de trabajar en una oficina, se puso el ~ por montera y se hizo artista** he grew tired of working in an office, so he threw caution to the wind and became an artist • **se puso el ~ por montera y se fue a vivir al campo** he decided to go and live in the country and damn the consequences • **el ~ es un pañuelo** it's a small world • **tener mucho ~** to be very experienced, know one's way around • **tener poco ~** to be wet behind the ears, be inexperienced • **traer a algn al ~** to bring sb into the world • **como Dios lo trajo al ~** stark naked, as naked as the day he was born • **venir al ~** to come into the world, be born • **tal como vino al ~** stark naked • **ver ~** to see the world • **ha visto mucho ~** he's been around a bit; ▷ **comer**
6 • **un ~** (= *mucho*): • **había todo un ~ de posibilidades** there was a whole world of possibilities • **hay un ~ de distancia entre las dos ideologías** the two ideologies are worlds apart • **no debemos hacer un ~ de sus comentarios** there's no need to blow her comments out of proportion, we shouldn't read too much into her comments
mundología (SF) worldly wisdom, experience of the world, savoir-faire
mundonuevo (SM) peep show
Munich (SM) Munich
munición (SF) **1** (*tb* **municiones**) (= *balas*) ammunition, munitions (*pl*); (= *pertrechos*) stores (*pl*), supplies (*pl*) • **fábrica de municiones** munitions factory
▸ **municiones de boca** provisions, rations
2 (*Mil*) • **de ~** army (*antes de s*), service (*antes de s*) • **botas de ~** army boots
3 (*CAm*) uniform
municionera (SF) (*Caribe*) ammunition pouch
municipal (ADJ) [*elección*] municipal; [*concejo*] town (*antes de s*), local; [*empleado, oficina*] council (*antes de s*); [*impuesto*] local, council (*antes de s*); [*piscina*] public • **la empresa ~ de transportes** the municipal transport company
(SMF) (= *guardia*) local policeman/policewoman
municipalidad (SF) **1** (= *distrito*) municipality

2 (= *ayuntamiento*) town council, local council
3 (= *edificio*) town hall
municipio SM 1 (= *distrito*) municipality; (= *población*) town
2 (= *ayuntamiento*) town council, local council
3 (= *edificio*) town hall
munido ADJ (*Arg, Uru*) (*frm*) • ~ **de** [+ *aparato, objeto*] armed with, bearing
munificencia SF munificence
munífico ADJ munificent
muniqués/esa ADJ of/from Munich
SM/F native/inhabitant of Munich • **los muniqueses** the people of Munich
muñeca SF 1 (*Anat*) wrist
2 (= *juguete*) doll ▸ **muñeca de trapo** rag doll ▸ **muñeca rusa** Russian doll
3‡ (= *chica*) doll‡, chick (EEUU‡)
4 (= *trapo*) polishing rag
5 (*And, Cono Sur*) (= *mutualidad*) friendly society, benefit society (EEUU)
6 (*Cono Sur**) (= *influencia*) pull, influence
muñeco SM 1 (= *juguete*) (*con forma humana*) doll; (= *con forma animal*) toy ▸ **muñeco de peluche** soft toy
2 [*de ventrílocuo*] dummy; [*de marionetas*] puppet; (= *efigie*) [*de político, famoso*] effigy; (= *dibujo*) figure; (= *espantapájaros*) scarecrow ▸ **muñeco de guante** glove puppet ▸ **muñeco de nieve** snowman
3 (= *pelele*) puppet, pawn
4* (= *niño*) sweetie*, little angel
5* (*lío*) row, shindy*
6 **muñecos** (*And*) • **me entraron los ~s** I had butterflies in my stomach
muñeira SF *a popular Galician dance*
muñequado* ADJ (*And*) jumpy, nervous
muñequera SF wristband
muñequero/a SM/F puppeteer
muñir ▹ CONJUG 3h VT 1 (= *convocar*) to summon, call, convoke
2 (*pey*) (= *amañar*) to rig, fix
muñón SM 1 (*Anat*) stump
2 (*Mec*) pivot, journal; [*de cañón*] trunnion
mural ADJ mural, wall (*antes de s*) • **mapa ~** wall map • **periódico ~** wall newspaper
SM mural
muralismo SM muralism
muralista ADJ, SMF muralist
muralla SF 1 [*de ciudad*] (= *muro*) (city) wall, walls (*pl*); (= *terraplén*) rampart ▸ **la Gran Muralla china** the Great Wall of China
2 (*LAm*) (= *pared*) wall
murar ▹ CONJUG 1a VT to wall
Murcia SF Murcia
murciano/a ADJ of/from Murcia, Murcian
SM/F native/inhabitant of Murcia, Murcian
murciélago SM bat
murga SF 1* (= *lata*) nuisance, bind* • **dar la ~** to be a pain*, be a pest
2 (= *banda*) band of street musicians
murguista SM 1 (= *músico*) street musician; (*hum**) bad musician
2* (= *pesado*) bore
múrido SM rodent
murmullo SM 1 (= *susurro*) murmur(ing), whisper(ing); (= *queja*) muttering
2 [*de hojas, viento*] rustle, rustling; [*de agua*] murmur; (= *ruido confuso*) hum(ming)
murmuración SF gossip
murmurador(a) ADJ (= *chismoso*) gossiping; (= *criticón*) backbiting
SM/F (= *chismoso*) gossip; (= *criticón*) backbiter
murmurar ▹ CONJUG 1a VT (= *susurrar*) to murmur, whisper; (= *quejarse*) to mutter • **murmuró unas palabras de agradecimiento** she murmured a few words of thanks • **la tranquilizaba murmurando palabras en su oído** he calmed her by whispering in her ear
VI 1 (= *cotillear*) to gossip (**de** about); (= *quejarse*) to grumble, mutter (**de** about) • **siempre están murmurando del jefe** they're always grumbling *o* muttering about the boss
2 [*hojas*] to rustle; [*viento*] to whisper; [*agua*] to murmur
muro SM wall • **enfrentarse con un ~ de silencio** to come up against a wall of silence ▸ **muro de Berlín** Berlin Wall ▸ **muro de contención** retaining wall ▸ **Muro de las Lamentaciones** Wailing Wall
murria SF depression, the blues (*pl*) • **tener ~** to be down in the dumps*, feel blue
murrio ADJ depressed
murruco* ADJ (*CAm*) curly-haired
mus[1] SM *a card game*
mus[2]* SM • MODISMO: • **sin decir ni mus** without saying a word; ▹ **tus**[2]
musa SF Muse • **las ~s** the Muses
musaraña SF 1 (*Zool*) shrew
2 (= *mota*) speck floating in the eye
• MODISMOS: • **mirar a las ~s** to stare vacantly *o* into space • **pensar en las ~s** to daydream
musculación SF muscle-building
muscular ADJ muscular
musculatura SF muscles (*pl*), musculature (*frm*) • **la ~ abdominal** the abdominal muscles • **combinar ~ con inteligencia** to have brains as well as brawn
músculo SM muscle
musculoso ADJ (= *de muchos músculos*) muscular; (= *fortachón*) muscly*
museística SF museum studies
museístico ADJ museum (*antes de s*)
muselina SF muslin
museo SM (*gen*) museum; [*de pintura, escultura*] museum, gallery ▸ **museo de arte moderno** modern art gallery ▸ **museo de cera** wax museum, waxworks ▸ **museo de historia natural** natural history museum ▸ **museo de pintura** art gallery
museografía SF museography
musgaño SM shrew
musgo SM moss ▸ **musgo irlandés** carrageen moss
musgoso ADJ mossy, moss-covered
música SF 1 music • **poner ~ a algo** to set sth to music • MODISMOS: • **irse con la ~ a otra parte** to clear off* • **¡vete con la ~ a otra parte!** clear off!* • **me suena a ~ de caballitos** it sounds all too familiar ▸ **música ambiental, música ambiente** background music ▸ **música antigua** early music ▸ **música celestial** heavenly music • **sus ideas me suenan a ~ celestial** (*iró*) his ideas sound like hot air to me ▸ **música clásica** classical music ▸ **música concreta** concrete music ▸ **música coreada** choral music ▸ **música culta** classical music ▸ **música de cámara** chamber music ▸ **música de fondo** background music ▸ **música de las esferas, música de los planetas** music of the spheres ▸ **música disco** disco music ▸ **música enlatada** canned music, piped music ▸ **música étnica** world music ▸ **música folk** folk music ▸ **música ligera** light music ▸ **música militar** military music ▸ **música pop** pop music ▸ **música rock** rock music ▸ **música sacra, música sagrada** sacred music
2 (= *banda*) band
3 **músicas*** (= *tonterías*) drivel (*sing*) • **no estoy para ~s** I'm not in the mood to listen to such drivel
4 (*Esp†*) (= *cartera*) wallet, billfold (EEUU); (= *dinero*) bread‡, money; ▹ **músico**
musical ADJ, SM musical
musicalidad SF musicality, musical quality
musicalizar ▹ CONJUG 1f VT to set to music
musicar ▹ CONJUG 1g VT to set to music
músico/a ADJ musical
SM/F 1 (= *instrumentista*) musician • **~s de jazz** jazz musicians ▸ **músico/a callejero/a** street musician, busker ▸ **músico/a mayor** bandmaster
2 (= *compositor*) musician; ▹ **música**
musicología SF musicology
musicólogo/a SM/F musicologist
musiqueo SM monotonous sound
musiquilla SF (= *melodía*) tune ▸ **musiquilla de fondo** background music
musitar ▹ CONJUG 1a VT, VI to mumble, mutter
muslada‡ SF, **muslamen‡** SM thighs (*pl*)
muslera SF Tubigrip®, thigh strap
muslime ADJ, SMF Moslem
muslímico ADJ Moslem
muslo SM thigh
mustango SM mustang
mustela SF weasel
mustiarse ▹ CONJUG 1b VPR to wither, wilt
mustio ADJ 1 [*planta*] withered; [*lechuga*] limp
2 [*tela, bandera*] faded
3 [*persona*] depressed, gloomy
4 (*Méx**) (= *hipócrita*) hypocritical
musulmán/ana ADJ, SM/F Moslem
mutabilidad SF mutability (*frm*), changeableness
mutable ADJ (= *que puede mutar*) mutable; (= *variable*) mutable (*frm*), changeable
mutación SF 1 (= *cambio*) change
2 (*Bio*) mutation
3 (*Ling*) mutation
4 (*Teat*) scene change
mutagene SM mutagen
mutágeno ADJ mutagenic
SM mutagen
mutante ADJ, SMF mutant
mutar ▹ CONJUG 1a VI to mutate
VT 1 (*Bio*) to mutate
2 (= *cambiar*) to transform, alter
VPR **mutarse** to mutate (**en** into)
mutil SM (*Hist*) Carlist soldier
mutilación SF mutilation
mutilado/a ADJ 1 [*persona*] crippled, disabled; [*cadáver*] mutilated
2 [*escultura, monumento*] vandalized, defaced
SM/F cripple, disabled person ▸ **mutilado/a de guerra** disabled veteran
mutilar ▹ CONJUG 1a VT 1 (*gen*) to mutilate; (= *lisiar*) to cripple, disable
2 [+ *escultura, monumento*] to vandalize, deface; [+ *texto*] to butcher, hack about
mutis SM INV (*Teat*) exit • **¡mutis!** sh! • **tú ~** you keep quiet • **hacer ~** (*Teat*) (= *retirarse*) to exit; (*fig*) to say nothing, keep quiet
• MODISMO: • **hacer ~ por el foro** to make o.s. scarce*
mutismo SM (= *silencio*) silence • **guardar un ~ absoluto** to remain tight-lipped
mutua SF friendly society, benefit society (EEUU)
mutual SF (*And, Cono Sur*) friendly society, benefit society (EEUU)
mutualidad SF 1 (= *asociación*) friendly society, benefit society (EEUU)
2 (= *reciprocidad*) reciprocity, reciprocal nature
3 (= *ayuda*) mutual aid, reciprocal aid
mutualista ADJ mutualist
SMF *member or associate of a friendly society or benefit society*

SF (*Cono Sur*) friendly society, benefit society (EEUU)

mutuamente ADV mutually, reciprocally

mutuo ADJ (= *recíproco*) mutual; (= *conjunto*) joint

muy ADJ **1** (= *mucho*) very • **muy bueno** very good • **eso es muy español** that's very Spanish • **fue una reacción muy suya** it was a very typical reaction of his • **somos muy amigos** we're great friends • **es muy hombre** he's very manly • **es muy mujer** she's a real woman • **muy bien/tarde/mucho** very well/late/much • **muy bien, que venga** all right, he can come (along) • **Muy Señor mío** Dear Sir • **muy pero que muy guapo** really, really handsome • **muy de:** • **muy de noche** very late at night • **muy de mañana** very early in the morning • **eso es muy de él** that's just like him • **yo soy muy de la siesta** I'm very fond of a siesta • **su apoyo es muy de agradecer** his support is very much appreciated • **es muy de sentir** (*frm*) it is much to be regretted • **el/la muy:** • **el muy tonto de Pedro** that great idiot Pedro • **las muy presumidas se gastaron todo en ropa** they're so self-obsessed they spent all their money on clothes • **¡el muy bandido!** the rascal! • **por muy:** • **por muy cansado que estés** however tired you are, no matter how tired you are

2 (= *demasiado*) too • **ya es muy tarde para cenar** it's too late to have dinner now • **es muy joven para salir contigo** she's too young to be going out with you

3 (*con participio*) greatly, highly • **muy buscado** highly sought-after • **fue un tema muy comentado** the topic was very much discussed

SF † (= *lengua*) tongue; (= *boca*) trap‡, mouth • MODISMOS: • **achantar la muy** to shut one's trap‡ • **irse de la muy** to spill the beans* • **largar por la muy** to natter*

m

Nn

N¹, n ['ene] SF (= *letra*) N, n
N² SF ABR (*Aut*) = **nacional**
ABR **1** (= **Norte**) N
2 (= **noviembre**) Nov • **20-N** *20 November, day of Franco's death*
3 (*LAm*) = **Moneda Nacional** • **le entregaron solo N$2.000** they only gave him 2,000 new pesos

> **20-N**
> **20-N** is commonly used as shorthand to refer to the anniversary of General Franco's death on 20 November 1975. Every year supporters of the far right hold a commemorative rally in Madrid's Plaza de Oriente, the scene of many of Franco's speeches to the people.

n. ABR **1** = **nuestro/nuestra**
2 (= **nacido**) b
3 (= **número**) no., No.
na* PRON, **ná** PRON = **nada**
naba SF (*Bot*) swede, rutabaga (*EEUU*)
nabab SM nabob
nabina SF rapeseed
nabiza SF (*Esp*) turnip greens (*pl*)
nabo SM **1** (*Bot*) turnip; (= *raíz gruesa*) root vegetable ▸ **nabo gallego** rape ▸ **nabo sueco** swede, rutabaga (EEUU)
2 (*Anat*) root of the tail
3 (*Arquit*) newel, stair post
4 (*Náut*) mast
5** (= *pene*) prick**
Nabucodonosor SM Nebuchadnezzar
nácar SM mother-of-pearl, nacre (*frm*)
nacarado ADJ, **nacarino** ADJ mother-of-pearl (*antes de s*), pearly
nacatamal SM (*CAm, Méx*) *maize, meat and rice wrapped in banana leaf*
nacatete SM (*Méx*), **nacatón/ona** SM/F (*CAm, Méx*) unfledged chick
nacedera SF (*CAm*) (*tb* **cerca nacedera**) hedge
nacencia SF (*LAm*) = **nacimiento**
nacer ▸ CONJUG 2d VI **1** [*persona, animal*] to be born; [*ave, insecto, reptil*] to hatch • **nací en Cuba** I was born in Cuba • **cuando nazca el niño** when the baby is born • **nació para poeta** he was born to be a poet • **no nació para sufrir** she was not born to suffer • **al ~** at birth • **~ en el seno de una familia adinerada** to be born into a wealthy family • **~ muerto** to be stillborn • **~ antes de tiempo** to be born prematurely • MODISMOS: • **¡oye, que no nací ayer!** I wasn't born yesterday, you know! • **~ con estrella** to be born under a lucky star • **~ de pie** to be born lucky • **nadie nace enseñado** we all have to learn • **~ parado** (*And**) to be born with a silver spoon in one's mouth • **volver a ~** to have a lucky escape • REFRÁN: • **unos nacen con estrella y otros estrellados** fortune smiles on some but not on others
2 [*planta*] (*gen*) to sprout, bud; (= *aparecer*) to come up; [*pelo, plumas*] to grow, sprout • **le nacieron alas** it sprouted wings
3 [*estrella, sol*] to rise; [*día*] to dawn
4 [*agua*] to spring up, appear, begin to flow; [*camino*] to begin, start (**de** from, **en** in)
5 [*revolución, miedo*] to spring (**de** from); [*idea*] to come (**de** from), originate, have its origin (**de, en** in) • **el error nace del hecho de que ...** the error springs *o* stems from the fact that ... • **entre ellos ha nacido una fuerte simpatía** a strong friendship has sprung up between them • **nació una sospecha en su mente** a suspicion formed in her mind • **¿de dónde nace la idea?** where does the idea come from?
6 • **~ a: con esa exposición nació a la vida artística** that exhibition saw the beginning of his artistic career • **~ al amor** to awaken to love
VPR **nacerse 1** (*Bot*) to bud, sprout
2 (*Cos*) to split
Nacho SM *forma familiar de* **Ignacio**
nacido ADJ born • **~ de padres ricos** born of wealthy parents • **~ a la libertad** born free • **~ para el amor** born to love • **recién ~** newborn • **ser bien ~** (= *de noble linaje*) to be of noble birth; (= *educado*) to be well-bred • **ser mal ~** (= *mala persona*) to be mean, be wicked; (= *maleducado*) to be ill-mannered, be ill-bred; ▹ **malnacido**
SM • **los ~s a finales de siglo** those born *o* people born at the end of the century
• MODISMOS: • **ningún ~** nobody • **todos los ~s** everybody, all mankind
naciente ADJ (= *que nace*) nascent (*frm*); (= *nuevo*) new, recent; (= *creciente*) growing; [*sol*] rising • **el ~ interés por ...** the new-found *o* growing interest in ...
SM **1** (= *este*) east
2 nacientes (*Cono Sur*) (= *manantial*) spring (*sing*), source (*sing*)
nacimiento SM **1** (*gen*) birth; (*Orn etc*) hatching • **de ~: ciego de ~** blind from birth, born blind • **un tonto de ~** a born fool • **este defecto lo tiene de ~** he has had this defect since birth, he was born with this defect ▸ **nacimiento sin violencia** painless childbirth
2 (= *estirpe*) birth, family • **de ~ noble** of noble birth, of noble family
3 (= *manantial*) spring, source
4 [*del pelo*] roots (*pl*)
5 (= *origen*) [*de nación*] birth; [*de amistad*] beginning, start • **el partido tuvo su ~ en ...** the party had its origins in ... • **dar ~ a** to give rise to
6 (*Arte, Rel*) nativity (scene)
nación SF (= *país*) nation; (= *pueblo*) people • **de ~ española** of Spanish nationality • **trato de ~ más favorecida** most favoured nation treatment ▸ **Naciones Unidas** United Nations
SMF (*Cono Sur*) (= *extranjero*) foreigner
nacional ADJ (= *de la nación*) national; (*Econ, Com*) domestic, home (*antes de s*) • **la deuda ~** national debt • **los periódicos ~es** national newspapers • **la economía ~** the domestic economy • **solo consumen productos ~es** they buy only home-produced goods *o* British/Spanish *etc* goods • **lloverá en todo el territorio ~** there will be rain throughout the country • **páginas de ~** (*Prensa*) home news pages • **"vuelos nacionales"** "domestic flights"; ▹ **carretera, fiesta, moneda**
SMF **1** (*LAm*) (= *ciudadano*) national
2 • **los ~es** (*en la guerra civil española*) the Franco forces
nacionalcatolicismo SM *Spanish Catholicism considered as an ally of Franco*
nacionalidad SF **1** (*gen*) nationality • **ser de ~ argentina** to be of Argentinian nationality, have Argentinian citizenship • **tener doble ~** to have dual nationality
2 (*Esp*) (*Pol*) (= *región autonómica*) autonomous region
nacionalismo SM nationalism
nacionalista ADJ nationalist, nationalistic
SMF nationalist
nacionalización SF **1** [*de persona*] naturalization
2 [*de industria*] nationalization
nacionalizado ADJ [*persona*] naturalized; [*industria*] nationalized • **un chileno ~ español** a Chilean who has become a naturalized Spaniard
nacionalizar ▹ CONJUG 1f VT [+ *persona*] to naturalize; [+ *industria*] to nationalize
VPR **nacionalizarse** [*persona*] to become naturalized; [*industria*] to be nationalized • **~se español** to become a Spanish citizen, become a naturalized Spaniard
nacionalmente ADJ nationally
nacionalsocialismo SM national socialism
naco* ADJ (*Méx*) (= *bobo*) stupid; (= *cobarde*) yellow*
SM **1** (*CAm*) (= *cobarde*) coward; (= *endeble*) weakling, milksop
2 (*And, Cono Sur*) (= *tabaco*) plug of tobacco
3 (*And*) (= *maíz*) *maize kernels cooked with salt*; (= *puré de patatas*) mashed potatoes
4 (*Cono Sur*) (= *susto*) fright, scare
nada PRON **1** (= *ninguna cosa*) (*con el verbo inglés en forma afirmativa*) nothing; (*con el verbo inglés en forma negativa*) anything • **no dijo ~ en toda la tarde** he said nothing all afternoon, he didn't say anything all afternoon • **no encontrarás ~ que te guste** you won't find anything you like • **no hay ~ como un café después de comer** there's nothing like a coffee after your meal, nothing beats a coffee after your meal • **—¿qué has comprado? —nada** "what have you bought?" — "nothing" • **no entiende ~** he doesn't understand a thing *o* anything • **~ de: • no sabe ~ de español** he knows no Spanish at all, he doesn't know any Spanish at all • **no tiene ~ de particular**

there's nothing special about it • **—¿qué te cuentas? —~ de particular** "what's new?" — "nothing much" *o* "not a lot" • **no creo que ~ de eso te convenga** I don't think that's what you want at all • **¡~ de eso!** not a bit of it! • **¡~ de marcharse!** forget about leaving! • **~ de ~** absolutely nothing, nothing at all • MODISMOS: • **¡de eso ~, monada!*** no way, José!* • **esto y ~, es lo mismo** it all boils down to nothing; ▷ **ahí**

2 (*en locuciones*) **a** (*con verbo*) • **estuvo en ~ que lo perdiesen** they very nearly lost it • **no me falta de ~** I've got everything I need • **a la cocina no le falta de ~** the kitchen has everything • **hace ~** just a moment ago • **no se parecen en ~** they're not at all alike • **quedar(se) en ~** to come to nothing • **no reparar en ~** to stop at nothing • **no servir para ~** to be utterly useless • **no sirves para ~** you're utterly useless • **no sirve de ~ que os quejéis** there's no point in you complaining • **no ha sido ~** it's nothing, it doesn't matter

b (*con preposición, adverbio*) • **antes de ~**: • **antes de ~ tengo que telefonear** before I do anything else I must make a phone call • **se fue antes de ~** she left almost at once • **a cada ~** (*LAm**) constantly • **casi ~**: • **no costó casi ~** it cost next to nothing • **¡había unas cien mil personas! ¡casi ~!** there were no fewer than a hundred thousand people there! • **como si ~**: • **se lo advertí, pero como si ~** I warned him but it was as if I hadn't spoken • **le dijo que estaba despedido y se quedó como si ~** she told him he was fired and he didn't even bat an eyelid • **de ~**: • **—¡gracias! —de ~** "thanks!" — "don't mention it" *o* "you're welcome" • **fue una mentira de ~** it was only a little lie • **¡tanto revuelo por un premio de ~!** all that fuss over such a silly little prize! • **dentro de ~** very soon • **~ más**: • **—¿desea algo más? —~ más, gracias** "can I get you anything else?" — "no, that's all thank you" • **no dijo ~ más** he didn't say anything else, he said nothing else • **son las siete ~ más** it's only seven o'clock • **quiero uno ~ más** I only want one • **encendió la tele ~ más llegar** he turned on the TV as soon as he got in • **ocurrió ~ más iniciado el partido** it happened just after the beginning of the game • **estas flores aparecen ~ más terminado el invierno** these flowers come out just after the winter *o* as soon as the winter is over • **~ más que estoy muy cansado** (*And, Méx*) it's just that I'm very tired • **(~ más y) ~ menos que …** (no more and) no less than … • **han ganado ~ menos que un coche** they've won a car, no less • **entró ~ menos que el rey** who should come in but the king! • **ni ~** or anything • **es raro que no haya llamado ni ~** it's odd that she hasn't called or anything • **no quiere comer ni ~** he won't even eat • **pues no es feo ni ~** (*iró*) he's not ugly … much! • **para ~** at all • **no los mencionó para ~** he never mentioned them at all • **—¿te gusta? —para ~** "do you like it?" — "not at all" • **por ~**: • **por ~ se echa a llorar** she's always crying over nothing *o* for no reason at all • **no me subiría a un avión por ~ del mundo** I wouldn't get on a plane for anything in the world • **no por ~ le llaman "apestoso"** he's not called "smelly" for nothing • **no por ~ decidimos comprar** we had good reason to buy • **por ~ y menos puedes hacerte un vestido** you can make your own dress for next to nothing • **¡por ~!** (*Cono Sur*) not at all!, don't mention it! • **por menos de ~** for two pins

3 (*como coletilla*) • **pues ~, me voy** well, I'm off then • **—¿qué pasó? —pues ~, que estuve esperando y no llegó** "what happened?" — "well, I was there waiting and he didn't arrive" • **y ~, al final nos fuimos** anyway, in the end we left

4 (*Tenis*) love • **treinta-nada** thirty-love

ADV not at all, by no means • **no es ~ fácil** it's not at all easy, it's by no means easy • **esto no me gusta ~** I don't like this at all • **no está ~ triste** he isn't sad at all • **pues no eres tú ~ ambicioso** (*iró*) well you're not very ambitious, are you? … much!

SF • **la ~** the void • **el avión pareció salir de la ~** the aircraft seemed to come from nowhere

nadaderas SFPL water wings

nadador(a) SM/F swimmer

nadar ▷ CONJUG 1a VI **1** (*gen*) to swim; (= *flotar*) to float; (*And*) (= *bañarse*) to take a bath • **¿no sabes ~?** can't you swim? • **~ a braza** to do (the) breaststroke, swim breaststroke • **~ a crol** to do the crawl, swim crawl • **~ a espalda** to do backstroke, swim backstroke • **~ a mariposa** to do (the) butterfly, swim butterfly • MODISMOS: • **~ contra corriente** to go against the tide • **~ en la abundancia** to be rolling in it*, be rolling in money* • **querer ~ y guardar la ropa** to want to have it both ways, want to have one's cake and eat it; ▷ **agua**

2 (*en prenda, zapatos*) • **en estos pantalones va nadando** these trousers are much too big for him, he's lost inside these trousers

nadería SF • **discutir por ~s** to argue over nothing *o* over stupid things • **me regaló una ~** she gave me a little nothing, she gave me a small trifle

nadie PRON **1** (= *ninguna persona*) (*verbo inglés en afirmativo*) nobody, no one; (*verbo inglés en negativo*) anybody, anyone • **~ lo tiene** • **no lo tiene ~** nobody has it • **no he visto a ~** I haven't seen anybody • **casi ~** hardly anybody • **lo hace como ~** she does it really well • **~ más** nobody else, no one else • **vino mi familia y ~ más** just my family came and nobody *o* no one else • **no vi a ~ más que a Juan** I didn't see anybody apart from *o* except Juan • **no lo sabe ~ más que tú** nobody else knows, apart from you, nobody but you knows

2 (= *persona insignificante*) • **no es ~** he's nobody (that matters) • MODISMO: • **es un don ~** he's a nobody, he's a nonentity

nadir SM nadir

nadita* (*esp LAm*) = **nada**

nado SM • **cruzar** *o* **pasar a ~** to swim across ▸ **nado sincronizado** (*LAm*) synchronized swimming

nafta SF (= *hidrocarburo*) naphtha; (*Arg*) (= *gasolina*) petrol, gasoline (*EEUU*)

naftaleno SM naphthalene, naphthaline

naftalina SF **1** (*Quím*) naphthalene, naphthaline

2 (*para la ropa*) mothballs (*pl*)

nagual SM **1** (*CAm, Méx*) (= *brujo*) sorcerer, wizard

2 (*Méx**) (= *mentira*) lie

3 (*CAm*) (= *mascota*) inseparable companion

nagualear‡ ▷ CONJUG 1a VI (*Méx*) **1** (= *mentir*) to lie

2 (= *robar*) to nick things*

3 (= *jaranear*) to paint the town red

naguas SFPL (*LAm*) petticoat (*sing*)

nagüeta SF (*CAm*) overskirt

nahual SM (*CAm, Méx*) (*Mit*) spirit, phantom; (= *doble*) double; (= *ladrón**) cat burglar

náhuatl ADJ INV Nahuatl

SMF INV Nahuatl Indian

SM (*Ling*) Nahuatl language

NÁHUATL

Náhuatl is the indigenous Mexican language that was once spoken by the Aztecs and which has given us such words as "tomato", "avocado", "chocolate" and "chilli". The first book to be printed on the American continent was a catechism in **náhuatl**, edited by a Franciscan monk in 1539. Today **náhuatl** is spoken in the central plateau of Mexico by a million bilingual and monolingual speakers.

naide* PRON (*hum*) = **nadie**

naif ADJ (PL: **naifs** *o* **naif**) (*Arte*) naive, primitivist

SM naive art

nailon SM nylon

naipe SM (= *carta*) playing card; **naipes** cards • **una baraja de ~s** a pack *o* deck of cards ▸ **naipe de figura** court card, picture card

naipeador ADJ (*Cono Sur*) fond of cards

naipear ▷ CONJUG 1a VI (*Cono Sur*) to play cards

naja‡ SF • MODISMOS: • **de ~(s)** at full speed, like the clappers* • **darse** *o* **salir de ~s*** to get out, beat it*

najarse‡ ▷ CONJUG 1a VPR to beat it*

najencia‡ EXCL scram!*

nal. ABR (= **nacional**) nat

nalga SF buttock; **nalgas** buttocks, backside (*sing*) • **darse de ~s** to fall on one's backside

nalgada SF **1** (*Culin*) ham

2 (= *azote*) smack on the bottom; **nalgadas** spanking (*sing*)

nalgudo ADJ, **nalgón** ADJ (*And*), **nalguiento** ADJ (*And*) big-bottomed (*antes de s*), broad in the beam*

Namibia SF Namibia

namibio/a ADJ Namibian

SM/F Namibian • **los ~s** the Namibians, the people of Namibia

nana¹ SF **1** (*Mús*) lullaby, cradlesong

2 (*CAm, Méx*) (= *nodriza*) wet nurse; (= *niñera*) nursemaid

3 (= *pelele*) Babygro®, rompers (*pl*); ▷ **nano**

nana² SF **1** (= *abuela*) grandma*, granny*; ▷ **año**

2 (*CAm*) (= *mamá*) mum*, mom (*EEUU**), mummy*, mommy (*EEUU**); ▷ **nano**

nana³* SF (*Cono Sur*) (= *dolor*) pain; ▷ **nano**

nanai* EXCL, **nanay*** EXCL (*tb* **nanai de la China**) no way!* • **me hizo ver que ~ (de la China)** he made me see there was nothing doing, he showed me it just wasn't on*

nandrolona SF nandrolone

nano/a‡ SM/F kid*; ▷ **nana**

nanopartícula SF nanoparticle

nanotecnología SF nanotechnology

nanotubo SM nanotube

nao SF (*Hist*) ship

napa SF imitation leather

napalm SM napalm

napia* SF, **napias*** SFPL snout*, hooter*

napo‡ SM (*Hist*) 1000-peseta note

Napoleón SM Napoleon

napoleón SM (*Chile*) (= *alicates*) pliers (*pl*), pair of pliers

napoleónico ADJ Napoleonic

Nápoles SM Naples

napolitano/a ADJ of/from Naples, Neapolitan

SM/F Neapolitan • **los ~s** the Neapolitans, the people of Naples

narajái‡ SM (*Esp*) priest

naranja SF **1** (= *fruta*) orange ▸ **naranja amarga, naranja cajel** Seville orange

▸ **naranja navel** navel orange ▸ **naranja sanguina** blood orange ▸ **naranja zajarí** Seville orange
2* • MODISMOS: • **¡naranjas!** • **¡~s de la China!** no way!*, nothing doing!* • **encontrar su media ~** to meet one's match • **esperar la media ~** to wait for Mr Right/one's ideal woman • **mi media ~** my better half
3 (*Caribe*) bitter orange
ADJ INV [*color*] orange
SM (= *color*) orange

naranjada SF orangeade, orange squash

naranjado ADJ orange, orange-coloured

naranjal SM orange grove

naranjero/a ADJ [*país, comarca, región*] orange-growing
SM/F (= *agricultor*) orange grower; (= *vendedor*) orange seller
SM (= *árbol*) orange tree

naranjo SM orange tree

Narbona SF Narbonne

narcisismo SM narcissism

narcisista ADJ narcissistic
SMF narcissist

Narciso SM Narcissus

narciso SM **1** (*Bot*) narcissus ▸ **narciso atrompetado, narciso trompón** daffodil
2 (= *presumido*) narcissist

narco* SMF = **narcotraficante**
SM = **narcotráfico**

narco... PREF narco..., drug(s) (*antes de s*)

narcocorrupción SF drugs-related corruption

narcodependencia SF drug dependency, drug dependence

narcodólar SM drug dollar • **~es** drug money (*sing*)

narcoguerrilla SF drug terrorists (*pl*)

narcosala SF needle exchange and drop-in centre *o* (*EEUU*) center

narcosis SF INV narcosis

narcoterrorismo SM drug-related terrorism, narco-terrorism

narcótico ADJ narcotic
SM **1** (*gen*) narcotic; (= *somnífero*) sleeping pill, sleeping tablet
2 narcóticos (= *estupefacientes*) narcotics

narcotismo SM narcosis, narcotism

narcotizante ADJ, SM narcotic

narcotizar ▸ CONJUG 1f VT to drug, narcotize (*frm*)

narcotraficante SMF drug(s) trafficker, drug dealer

narcotráfico SM drug trafficking *o* dealing

nardo SM nard, spikenard

narguile SM hookah

naricear* ▸ CONJUG 1a VT (*And*) **1** (= *olfatear*) to smell (out)
2 (= *curiosear*) to poke one's nose into

narigada SF (*LAm*) snuff

narigón ADJ big-nosed
SM (*Méx*) nose ring

narigudo ADJ big-nosed

narigueta ADJ (*Cono Sur*) big-nosed

nariz SF **1** (*Anat*) nose • **tengo un grano en la ~** I have a spot on my nose • **tengo la ~ tapada** I have a blocked nose, my nose is blocked • **no te metas el dedo en la ~** don't pick your nose • **tiene las narices muy grandes** he has a very big nose • **hablar con *o* por la ~** to talk through one's nose ▸ **nariz aguileña** aquiline nose ▸ **nariz chata** snub nose ▸ **nariz de boxeador** boxer's nose ▸ **nariz griega** Greek profile ▸ **nariz respingona** turned-up nose; ▹ **sangre**, **sonarse**
2 • MODISMOS: • **darle en la ~ a algn***: • **me da en la ~ que no está diciendo la verdad** I get the feeling *o* something tells me that she is not telling the truth • **darse de narices con algo/algn*** to bump into sth/sb* • **darse de narices con la puerta** to bump into the door* • **darse de narices contra el suelo** to fall flat on one's face • **de las narices** (*Esp**) damn*, bloody‡ • **ya estamos otra vez con el ruidito ese de las narices** there's that damn* *o* bloody‡ noise again • **de narices** (*Esp**): • **me echó una bronca de narices** he gave me a hell of a telling off* • **hace un frío de narices** it's absolutely freezing* • **era guapa de narices** she was a real stunner* • **he dormido de narices** I slept really well • **me encuentro de narices** I feel fantastic *o* great • **delante de *o* en las narices de algn***: • **le robaron el coche en sus propias narices** they stole his car right under his nose* • **estar hasta las narices (de algo/algn)*** to be fed up to the back teeth (with sth/sb)* • **hinchar las narices a algn** (*Esp**) to get up sb's nose* • **ese tío me hincha las narices** that guy really gets up my nose* • **hinchársele las narices a algn** (*Esp**): • **se le hincharon las narices** he blew his top*, he hit the roof • **meter las narices en algo*** to poke one's nose into sth • **pasarse algo por las narices***: • **eso me lo paso por las narices*** I couldn't care less* *o* I don't give two hoots* about that • **por narices** (*Esp**): • **dijo que su hija no iba y por narices tuvo que ser así** she said that her daughter was not going and that was that • **con una alineación así tienen que ganar por narices** with a lineup like this they'd better win • **esto tiene que estar listo para el lunes por narices** this has to be ready by Monday no matter what • **pasar *o* restregar por las narices***: • **le gustaba pasar a su novia por las narices de su ex** he liked to show off his girlfriend in front of his ex • **siempre nos están restregando por las narices que tienen mucho dinero** they're always rubbing our noses in the fact that they have a lot of money • **romper las narices a algn*** to smash sb's face in* • **hazlo o te rompo las narices** do it or I'll smash your face in* • **tener narices** (*Esp**): • **¡tiene narices la cosa!** it's outrageous! • **tocar las narices a algn** (*Esp**): • **ya me está tocando las narices con sus comentarios** his comments really get up my nose • **me toca las narices lo que diga ella** I don't give a damn what she says* • **tocarse las narices*** to sit around twiddling one's thumbs • **en esa oficina se están todo el día tocando las narices** they sit around all day twiddling their thumbs in that office • **no ven más allá de sus narices*** they can't see beyond the end of their nose; ▹ **palmo**
3 (*Esp**) (*frases de sentido exclamativo*) • **¡narices!** rubbish!, nonsense! • **¿dónde narices están mis calcetines?** where on earth are my socks?* • **¿qué días de fiesta ni que narices? ¡aquí todo el mundo trabaja!** holidays! what are you talking about? here everybody has to work!
4 (= *olfato*) nose, sense of smell • **perros de presa con muy buena ~** gun dogs with a good nose *o* keen sense of smell
5 [*del vino*] nose

narizota* SF big nose

narizotas* SMF INV (*Esp*) • **ser un ~** to have a really big nose

narizudo ADJ (*CAm, Méx*) big-nosed

narpias* SFPL = **napia**

narración SF (= *relato, versión*) account; (*Literat*) narration

narrador(a) SM/F narrator

narrar ▸ CONJUG 1a VT [+ *historia*] to tell; [+ *suceso, aventuras, experiencia*] to recount

narrativa SF **1** (= *narración*) narrative, story
2 (= *arte*) narrative skill, skill in storytelling
3 (= *género*) fiction

narrativo ADJ narrative

narval SM narwhal

NASA SF ABR (= **National Aeronautics and Space Administration**) NASA

nasa SF **1** [*de pan*] bread bin
2 (*Pesca*) basket, creel; (= *trampa*) fish trap

nasal ADJ, SF nasal

nasalidad SF nasality

nasalización SF nasalization

nasalizar ▸ CONJUG 1f VT to nasalize

nasalmente ADV nasally

naso* SM (*Cono Sur*) nose, conk*, schnozzle (*esp EEUU*‡), hooter*

N.ª S.ra ABR = **Nuestra Señora**

nasti‡ EXCL (*tb* **nasti de plasti**) no way!* • **¡de eso ~ (, monasti)!** no way!*

nata SF **1** (*Esp*) (*gen*) cream; (*en leche cocida*) skin ▸ **nata batida** whipped cream ▸ **nata líquida** cream ▸ **nata montada** whipped cream ▸ **nata para montar** whipping cream
2 (*fig*) cream • **la flor y ~ de la sociedad** the cream of society

natación SF **1** (*gen*) swimming
2 (= *estilo*) style (of swimming), stroke ▸ **natación a braza** breast-stroke ▸ **natación de costado** sidestroke ▸ **natación de espalda** backstroke ▸ **natación de pecho** breast-stroke ▸ **natación en cuchillo** sidestroke ▸ **natación sincronizada** synchronized swimming ▸ **natación submarina** (*gen*) underwater swimming; (*con aparato respiratorio*) skin diving

natal ADJ [*país*] native; [*pueblo*] home (*antes de s*)

natalicio ADJ birthday (*antes de s*)
SM birthday

natalidad SF birth rate

natalista ADJ • **una política ~** a policy aimed at raising the birth rate

natatorio ADJ • **técnica natatoria** swimming technique • **vejiga natatoria** air bladder
SM (*Arg*) swimming pool

natillas SFPL (*Esp*) custard (*sing*) ▸ **natillas de huevo** egg custard (*sing*)

natividad SF nativity

nativo/a ADJ **1** [*persona, país*] native • **lengua nativa** mother tongue
2 (= *innato*) natural, innate
3 (*Min*) native
SM/F native ▸ **nativo/a digital** digital native

nato ADJ **1** (*gen*) born • **un actor ~** a born actor • **un criminal ~** a natural-born criminal • **es un pintor ~** he's a natural painter
2 (*por derecho*) ex officio • **el secretario es miembro ~ de ...** the secretary is ex officio a member of ...

natura†† SF **1** (= *naturaleza*) nature • **contra ~**: **un pecado contra ~** a sin against nature • **inclinaciones contra ~** unnatural leanings
2 (= *genitales*) genitals (*pl*)

naturaca‡ EXCL naturally!, natch!*

natural ADJ **1** (= *no artificial*) [*calor*] natural; [*luz, frontera*] natural; [*seda*] pure; [*flor*] real • **los fenómenos ~es** natural phenomena • **es rubia ~** she's a natural blonde
2 (= *fresco*) fresh • **fruta ~** fresh fruit
3 (= *sin aditivos*) natural • **yogur ~** natural yoghurt • **con ingredientes ~es** with natural ingredients
4 (= *a temperatura ambiente*) • **este vino se sirve ~** this wine should be served at room temperature
5 (= *innato*) natural • **tiene un talento ~ para la música** she has a natural talent for music • **la bondad es ~ en él** kindness is in his nature, it's in his nature to be kind

6 (= *normal*) natural • **es ~ que estés cansado** it's natural that you should be tired • **es lo más ~ del mundo** it's perfectly natural, it's the most natural thing in the world
7 (= *no afectado*) natural • **has salido muy ~ en la foto** you look very natural in the photo
8 (= *ilegítimo*) illegitimate • **hijo ~** illegitimate child
9 (= *nativo*) • **es ~ de Córdoba** he is a native of Cordoba • **¿de dónde es usted ~?** where are you from?, where were you born?
10 • **de tamaño ~** life-size(d)
11 (*Mús*) natural
SMF native • **un ~ de Badajoz** a native of Badajoz
SM **1** (= *carácter*) nature • **un ~ optimista** an optimistic nature • **es de ~ reservado** he's reserved by nature
2 • **al ~: fruta al ~** (= *sin aditamentos*) fruit in its own juice • **está muy guapa al ~** she is very pretty just as she is (without make-up) • **se sirve al ~** (= *a temperatura ambiente*) it is served at room temperature
3 (*Arte*) • **del ~: pintar del ~** to paint from life • **clase de dibujo del ~** life class
4 (*Taur*) *type of pass*

naturaleza SF **1** (= *universo físico*) nature • **las leyes de la ~** the laws of nature • **las ciencias de la ~** the natural science(s)
2 (= *campo*) nature • **viven en plena ~** they live surrounded by nature
3 (= *carácter*) nature • **son de ~ tímida** they're shy by nature • **es despistado por ~** he's naturally absent-minded • **la ~ humana** human nature
4 (= *constitución*) constitution • **es de ~ fuerte** he has a strong constitution
5 (= *especie*) nature • **situaciones de ~ poco común** situations of an unusual nature
6 (*Arte*) ▸ **naturaleza muerta** still life
7† (*Pol*) nationality • **el joven es suizo de ~** the young man is Swiss by nationality

naturalidad SF naturalness • **con la mayor ~ (del mundo)** as if it were the most natural thing in the world • **se levantó y siguió caminando con la mayor ~ del mundo** she picked herself up and carried on walking as if nothing had happened • **lo dijo con la mayor ~** he said it in a perfectly ordinary voice • **hacer algo con ~** to do sth in a natural way

naturalismo SM **1** (*Arte*) naturalism; (= *realismo*) realism
2 (= *nudismo*) naturism

naturalista ADJ (*Arte*) naturalistic; (= *realista*) realistic
SMF **1** (*Arte*) naturalist
2 (= *nudista*) naturist

naturalización SF naturalization

naturalizar ▷ CONJUG 1f VT to naturalize
VPR **naturalizarse** to become naturalized

naturalmente ADV **1** (= *de modo natural*) in a natural way
2 (= *por supuesto*) • **¡naturalmente!** naturally!, of course!

naturismo SM **1** (= *nudismo*) naturism
2 (= *naturopatía*) naturopathy

naturista SMF **1** (= *nudista*) naturist
2 (= *naturópata*) naturopath

naturópata SMF naturopath

naturopatía SF naturopathy

naufragar ▷ CONJUG 1h VI **1** [*barco*] to be wrecked, sink; [*gente*] to be shipwrecked
2 [*película, obra, asunto*] to fail; [*negocio*] to go under, fail

naufragio SM **1** (*Náut*) shipwreck
2 (*fig*) failure, ruin

náufrago/a ADJ shipwrecked
SM/F shipwrecked person, castaway

náusea SF (= *malestar físico*) nausea, sick feeling; (= *repulsión*) disgust, repulsion • **dar ~s a** to nauseate, sicken, disgust • **tener ~s** (*lit*) to feel nauseated, feel sick; (*fig*) to be nauseated, be sickened ▸ **náuseas del embarazo** morning sickness

nauseabundo ADJ nauseating, sickening

náutica SF navigation, seamanship

náutico ADJ nautical • **club ~** yacht club

nautilo SM nautilus

navaja SF **1** (= *cuchillo*) clasp knife, penknife ▸ **navaja automática** flick knife ▸ **navaja barbera** cutthroat razor ▸ **navaja de afeitar** razor ▸ **navaja de muelle, navaja de resorte** flick knife ▸ **navaja multiuso(s)** Swiss army knife
2 (= *molusco*) razor shell
3 (*Zool*) (= *colmillo*) tusk
4 (*Entomología*) sting
5 (*pey*) (= *lengua*) sharp tongue, evil tongue

navajada SF, **navajazo** SM knife wound, slash, gash

navajeo SM (*con navaja*) knifing, stabbing; (*fig*) infighting; (*por la espalda*) back-stabbing, stabbing in the back

navajero/a SM/F *criminal who carries a knife*

navajo ADJ Navaho, Navajo
SMF Navaho, Navajo

naval ADJ [*base*] naval; [*oficial*] navy (*antes de s*), naval; [*compañía, industria*] shipping (*antes de s*); [*constructor*] ship (*antes de s*); [*capitán*] sea (*antes de s*); [*bloqueo*] naval

Navarra SF Navarre

navarrica ADJ, SMF = **navarro**

navarro/a ADJ of/from Navarre
SM/F native/inhabitant of Navarre • **los ~s** the people of Navarre

nave SF **1** (*Náut*) ship, vessel • **MODISMOS:** • **la Nave de San Pedro** (*Rel*) the Roman Catholic Church • **quemar las ~s** to burn one's boats ▸ **nave insignia** flagship
2 (*Aer*) ▸ **nave espacial** spaceship, spacecraft
3 (*Arquit*) [*de iglesia*] nave; [*de fábrica etc*] bay ▸ **nave central** nave ▸ **nave lateral** aisle
4 (= *almacén*) warehouse ▸ **nave de laminación** rolling mill ▸ **nave industrial** factory premises (*pl*)
5 (*Méx**) (= *coche*) car

navegabilidad SF [*de río, canal*] navigability; [*de barco*] seaworthiness

navegable ADJ [*río, canal*] navigable; [*barco*] seaworthy

navegación SF (= *arte*) navigation; (= *buques*) ships (*pl*), shipping; (= *viaje*) sea voyage • **cerrado a la ~** closed to shipping ▸ **navegación aérea** (= *acción*) aerial navigation; (= *tráfico*) air traffic ▸ **navegación a vela** sailing ▸ **navegación costera** coastal traffic ▸ **navegación fluvial** river navigation ▸ **navegación por satélite** satnav*, satellite navigation

navegador(a) SM/F navigator
SM **1** (*Internet*) browser
2 [*de coche*] satnav*, satellite navigation

navegante SMF **1** (= *marinero*) seafarer • **pueblo de ~s** a seafaring nation ▸ **navegante a vela** yachtsman/yachtswoman
2 (= *que lleva el rumbo*) navigator

navegar ▷ CONJUG 1h VI **1** (*Náut*) to sail • **a 15 nudos** to sail at 15 knots, go at 15 knots • **~ a (la) vela** to sail, go sailing
2 (*Inform*) • **~ por Internet** to surf the net
VT **1** [*barco*] to sail • **~ los mares** to sail the seas
2 [*avión*] to fly
3 (= *llevar el rumbo*) to navigate

Navidad SF Christmas • **(día de) ~** Christmas Day • **¡feliz ~!** happy Christmas!; **Navidades** Christmas (time) • **por ~es** at Christmas (time)

navideño ADJ Christmas (*antes de s*)

naviera SF shipping company

naviero/a ADJ shipping (*antes de s*)
SM/F shipowner

navío SM ship ▸ **navío de alto bordo, navío de línea** (*Hist*) ship of the line

náyade SF naiad

naylón SM nylon

nazarenas SFPL (*And, Cono Sur*) large gaucho spurs

nazareno/a ADJ (*Hist*) Nazarene
SM/F **1** (*Hist*) Nazarene
2 (*Rel*) penitent in a Holy Week procession; ▷ SEMANA SANTA
SM* **1** (= *fraude*) con trick*
2 (= *persona*) con man*

Nazaret SM Nazareth

nazi ADJ, SMF Nazi

nazismo SM Nazism

nazista ADJ Nazi

NB ABR (= **nota bene**) NB

N. de la R. ABR = **nota de la redacción**

N. de la T ABR = **Nota de la Traductora**

N. del T ABR = **Nota del Traductor**

NE ABR (= **nordeste**) NE

neanderthal ADJ Neanderthal
SM Neanderthal

neblina SF **1** (*Meteo*) mist, mistiness
2 (*fig*) fog

neblinoso ADJ misty

nebulizador SM nebulizer

nebulosa SF nebula

nebulosidad SF **1** (*Astron*) nebulosity; [*del cielo*] cloudiness; [*del aire*] mistiness; (= *penumbra*) gloominess
2 (= *imprecisión*) vagueness; (= *oscuridad*) obscurity

nebuloso ADJ **1** (*Astron*) nebular, nebulous; [*cielo*] cloudy; [*aire*] misty; (= *tétrico*) dark, gloomy
2 (= *impreciso*) nebulous, vague; (= *oscuro*) obscure

necedad SF **1** (= *cualidad*) crassness, foolishness, silliness
2 (= *cosa tonta*) • **una ~** a silly thing • **~es** nonsense (*sing*)

necesariamente ADV necessarily • **el escalador más rápido no es ~ el mejor** the quickest climber is not necessarily the best • **no tenemos que estar allí ~** we don't necessarily need to be there

necesario ADJ **1** (*tras sustantivo*) necessary • **los empleados carecen de la formación necesaria** the employees lack the necessary training • **no quiero estar aquí más del tiempo ~** I don't want to be here any longer than necessary • **no disponen del dinero ~ para acabar las obras** they do not have the money they need *o* the money necessary to finish the work • **haremos todo lo ~ para avanzar en las conversaciones de paz** we will do everything (that is) necessary to advance the peace talks • **esta es una condición necesaria para que una democracia funcione** this is a necessary condition for a democracy to work • **no gastes más de lo estrictamente ~** don't spend more than is strictly necessary
2 • **hacer ~: estos graves incidentes hicieron necesaria la intervención de la policía** these serious incidents made it necessary for the police to intervene, these serious incidents made police intervention necessary • **hacerse ~: se hace necesaria una completa renovación antes de la próxima temporada** a complete overhaul is now necessary *o* required before next season • **se hizo necesaria la intervención del estado en la economía** state intervention in the economy became necessary *o* was required

3 • ser ~ to be needed, be necessary • **no será necesaria la intervención del ejército** no military intervention will be needed *o* necessary • **para hacerse monja son ~s dos años en el noviciado** it takes two years as a novice to become a nun • **fueron necesarias varias reuniones para llegar a un acuerdo** a number of meetings were needed to reach an agreement • **haremos huelga si es ~** if necessary we will go on strike, we will go on strike if need be • **si fuera ~** if necessary, if need be, if it should be necessary • **de ser ~** if necessary, if need be
4 • es ~ hacer algo: • **es muy ~ tener una infraestructura sólida** it is essential *o* vital to have a solid infrastructure • **para ir a Francia no es ~ tener pasaporte** you don't need a passport *o* it is not necessary to have a passport to go to France • **es ~ que** (*+ subjun*): • **era ~ que continuara con el tratamiento** he needed to continue *o* it was necessary for him to continue with the treatment • **no es ~ que le pidas disculpas** there is no need for you to apologize to him

neceser SM toilet bag ▸ **neceser de belleza** vanity case ▸ **neceser de costura** workbox ▸ **neceser de fin de semana** overnight bag, weekend bag

necesidad SF **1** (= *urgencia*) **a • la ~ de algo** the need for sth • **la ~ de que la OTAN cumpla su promesa** the need for NATO to carry out its promise • **hay ~ de discreción en este momento** there is a need for discretion at this moment • **la ~ de hacer algo** the need to do sth • **se habló de la ~ de encontrar una nueva vía de diálogo** the need to find a new approach to the talks was discussed • **no hay ~ de hacerlo** there is no need to do it • **tener ~ de algo** to need sth • **tienen ~ urgente de ayuda alimenticia** they urgently need food aid, they are in urgent need of food aid • **con la nueva tarjeta bancaria no tendrá ~ de llevar dinero** with the new bank card you won't need to carry money with you • **y ¿qué ~ tienes de irte a un hotel habiendo camas en casa?** why would you need to go to a hotel when there are spare beds at home? • MODISMO: • **hacer de la ~ virtud** to make a virtue of necessity • REFRÁN: • **la ~ aguza el ingenio** necessity is the mother of invention
b • de ~: • **en caso de ~** in an emergency • **una situación de ~** an emergency • **una herida mortal de ~** a fatal wound • **artículos** *o* **productos de primera ~** basic essentials, staple items
c • por ~: • **tuve que aprenderlo por ~** I had to learn it out of necessity • **el que se llame John no significa que tenga que ser inglés por ~** the fact that he is called John does not necessarily mean that he is English
d • sin ~: • **no corra riesgos sin ~** don't take unnecessary risks • **sin ~ de algo** without the need for sth • **podemos llegar a un acuerdo sin ~ de que intervenga el director** we can come to an agreement without any need for the director to intervene • **ahora podemos ir de compras sin ~ de movernos de casa** now we can go shopping without needing to leave the house
e (= *cosa necesaria*) (*personal*) need; (*objetiva*) necessity • **satisfacer las ~es de algn** to satisfy sb's needs • **para un representante un coche no es un lujo, es una ~** for a sales rep, a car is not a luxury, it's a necessity
2 (= *pobreza*) need • **están en la mayor ~** they are in great need
3 (= *apuro*) tight spot • **encontrarse en una ~** to be in a tight spot
4 necesidades: a (= *privaciones*) hardships • **pasar ~es** to suffer hardship *o* hardships
b • MODISMO: • **hacer sus ~es** (*euf*) to relieve o.s.

necesitado ADJ **1** (= *falto*) • **andar** *o* **estar** *o* **verse ~ de algo** to need sth • **estamos ~s de mano de obra** we need workers, we are in need of labour • **anda ~ de afecto** he's in need of affection, he needs affection
2 (= *pobre*) in need • **ayuda a familias necesitadas** help for needy families, help for families in need • **las naciones más necesitadas** the nations in greatest need
SMPL • **los ~s** the needy

necesitar ▸ CONJUG 1a VT to need • **necesitamos dos más** we need two more • **para comprarse un barco así se necesita mucho dinero** you need a lot of money to buy a boat like that • **póngase en contacto con nosotros si necesita más información** get in touch with us if you need *o* (*frm*) require more information • **"se necesita coche"** "car wanted" • **~ hacer algo** to need to do sth • **no necesitas hacerlo** you don't need to do it, you needn't do it • **necesito verte ahora mismo** I need to see you right now • **se necesita ser caradura para presentarse sin avisar** you'd have to be cheeky to turn up without warning • **~ que** (*+ subjun*): • **necesito que me lo mandes urgentemente** I need you to send it to me urgently • **no necesito que nadie me lo recuerde** I don't need to be reminded, I don't need anyone to remind me
VI • **~ de algo** to need sth • **el ser humano necesita del oxígeno para vivir** human beings need oxygen to survive

neciamente ADV foolishly, stupidly

necio/a ADJ **1** (= *tonto*) foolish, stupid
2 (*Méx*) (= *terco*) stubborn, pig-headed
3 (*And*) (= *displicente*) peevish
4 (*And, Caribe, Cono Sur*) (= *quisquilloso*) touchy, hypersensitive
5 (*CAm*) [*enfermedad*] hard to shake off
SM/F fool

nécora SF small crab

necrófago SM ghoul

necrofilia SF necrophilia

necrófilo/a ADJ, SM/F necrophiliac

necrología SF, **necrológica** SF (= *lista*) obituary column; (= *noticia*) obituary

necrológico ADJ obituary (*antes de s*)

necromancia SF, **necromancía** SF necromancy

necrópolis SF INV necropolis

necropsia SF autopsy

necrosar ▸ CONJUG 1a VT, VI to necrotize
VPR **necrosarse** to necrotize

necrosis SF INV necrosis

necrotizar ▸ CONJUG 1f VT, VI to necrotize
VPR **necrotizarse** to necrotize

néctar SM (*lit, fig*) nectar • **~ de melocotón** peach nectar

nectarina SF nectarine

neerlandés/esa ADJ Dutch
SM/F Dutchman/Dutchwoman • **los neerlandeses** the Dutch
SM (*Ling*) Dutch

nefando ADJ (*liter*) unspeakable, abominable

nefario ADJ (*liter*) nefarious

nefasto ADJ **1** (= *funesto*) [*viaje*] ill-fated; [*año*] unlucky; [*resultado*] unfortunate; [*influencia*] pernicious; [*corrupción*] harmful, damaging; [*alcohol, ácido*] harmful
2 (*LAm*) (= *atroz*) dreadful, terrible

nefato* ADJ (*Caribe*) stupid, dim*

nefrítico ADJ nephritic

nefritis SF INV nephritis

negación SF **1** (*gen*) negation; (= *negativa*) denial
2 (*Ling*) negative

negado/a ADJ hopeless, useless • **ser ~ para algo** to be hopeless *o* useless at sth
SM/F • **es un ~** he's hopeless *o* useless, he's a dead loss*

negar ▸ CONJUG 1h, 1j VT **1** (= *desmentir*) to deny • **niega haber robado los documentos** he denies having stolen the documents • **el ministro ha negado todas las acusaciones** the minister has denied all the accusations • **no me ~ás que ha valido la pena** you can't deny it's been worth it • **negó que lo hubieran despedido** he denied that they had sacked him, he denied having been sacked
2 (= *rehusar*) to refuse, deny (a to) • **le ~on el paso por la frontera** they refused to let him cross the border • **nos ~on la entrada al edificio** we were refused *o* denied entry to the building • **~ el saludo a algn** to blank sb*, snub sb* • **~ la mano a algn** to refuse to shake hands with sb
3 (*frm*) [*+ persona*] to disown • **negó a su hija** he disowned his daughter
VI • **~ con la cabeza** to shake one's head
VPR **negarse 1 • ~se a hacer algo** to refuse to do sth • **se negó a pagar la multa** he refused to pay the fine
2 • ~se a la evidencia to deny the obvious

negativa SF refusal • **me sorprendió su ~ a cooperar** I was surprised at his refusal to cooperate ▸ **negativa rotunda** flat refusal

negativamente ADV negatively • **contestar ~** to answer in the negative • **valorar algo ~** to take a negative view of sth

negatividad SF, **negativismo** SM negative attitude

negativizar ▸ CONJUG 1f VT to neutralize

negativo ADJ **1** (*gen*) negative • **voto ~** vote against, no vote
2 (*Mat*) minus
3 (*Fot*) negative
SM (*Fot*) negative

negligencia SF negligence

negligente ADJ negligent
SMF careless person

negligentemente ADV negligently

negociabilidad SF negotiability

negociable ADJ negotiable

negociación SF (*gen*) negotiation; (= *transacción*) deal, transaction; [*de cheque*] clearance • **entrar en negociaciones con** to enter into negotiations with ▸ **negociación colectiva de salarios** collective bargaining

negociadamente ADV • **resolver un problema ~** to settle a problem by negotiation

negociado SM **1** (= *sección*) department, section
2 (*And, Cono Sur*) (= *negocio turbio*) shady deal
3 (*Cono Sur*) (= *establecimiento*) shop, store (*EEUU*)

negociador(a) ADJ negotiating • **comisión ~a** negotiating committee
SM/F negotiator

negociante SMF businessman/businesswoman

negociar ▸ CONJUG 1b VT to negotiate
VI **1** (*Pol etc*) to negotiate
2 (*Com*) • **~ en** *o* **con** to deal in, trade in

negocio SM **1** (*Com, Econ*) (= *empresa*) business; (= *tienda*) shop, store (*EEUU*) • **el ~ del espectáculo** show business • **el ~ del libro** the book trade • **montar un ~** to set up *o* start a business • **traspasar un ~** to transfer a business, sell a business
2 (= *transacción*) deal, transaction • **el ~ es el ~** business is business • **hacer un buen ~** to pull off a good deal • **¡hiciste un buen ~!** (*iró*)

that was a fine deal you did! • **un ~ redondo** a real bargain, a really good deal • **MODISMO**: • **cuidar de su propio ~** to look after one's own interests, look after number one ▸ **negocio sucio, negocio turbio** shady deal

3 negocios (*Com, Econ*) business (*sing*), trade (*sing*) • **el mundo de los ~s** the business world • **estar en viaje de ~s** to be (away) on business • **hablar de ~s** to talk business • **hombre/mujer de ~s** businessman/ businesswoman • **retirarse de los ~s** to retire from business • **REFRÁN**: • **a malos ~s sombrero de copa** one must make the best of a bad job

4 (= *asunto*) affair • **eso es ~ tuyo** that's your affair • **mal ~** bad business • **¡mal ~!** it looks bad!

5 (*And, Cono Sur*) (= *firma*) firm, company; (= *casa*) place of business

6 (*And, Caribe**) • **el ~** the fact, the truth • **pero el ~ es que ...** but the fact is that ...

7 (*And*) (= *cuento*) tale, piece of gossip

negocioso ADJ (= *diligente*) industrious; (*en las maneras*) businesslike

negra SF **1** (*Mús*) crotchet, quarter note (*EEUU*)

2 (= *mala suerte*) bad luck • **ese me trae la ~** he brings me bad luck • **le tocó la ~** he had bad luck • **tener la ~** to be out of luck, be having a run of bad luck; ▸ **negro**

3 (*Ajedrez*) black piece

4 (*CAm*) black mark

negrada SF (*LAm*) **1** (*Hist*) (= *grupo*) group of Negroes†, Negroes† (*pl*)

2 (= *fraude*) cheat, fraud

negrear ▸ CONJUG 1a VI **1** (= *ponerse negro*) to go black, turn black; (= *parecer negro*) to appear black

2 (= *tirar a negro*) to be blackish

negrería SF (*LAm*), **negrerío** SM (*LAm*) = negrada

negrero SM (*Hist*) slave trader; (= *explotador*) exploiter of labour *o* (*EEUU*) labor, slave driver*

negriazul ADJ black and blue • **la nueva estrella ~** (*Dep*) the new star to wear the black and blue strip

negrilla SF **1** (*Tip*) = **negrita**

2 (*Bot*) elm

negrita SF **1** (*Tip*) boldface • **en ~** in bold (type), in boldface

2 (*CAm*) black mark

negrito[1] SM golliwog

negrito[2] SM (*Caribe*) black coffee

negritud SF negritude

negro/a ADJ **1** [*color, pelo*] black; [*ojos, tabaco*] dark; [*raza*] black, Negro†

• **MODISMOS**: • **más ~ que el azabache** jet-black • **~ como boca de lobo** • **~ como un pozo** pitch-black, pitch-dark

2 (= *moreno*) [*piel*] dark, swarthy; (*por el sol*) tanned, brown • **ponerse ~** to go brown, tan

3 (= *sucio*) filthy, black

4 [*estado de ánimo, humor*] black, gloomy; [*suerte*] terrible, atrocious • **la cosa se pone negra** it's not going well, it looks bad • **lo ve todo ~** he always sees the negative side of things, he's terribly pessimistic about everything • **ve muy ~ el porvenir** he's very gloomy about the future • **MODISMOS**: • **pasarlas negras** to have a tough time of it • **verse ~** to be in a jam* • **verse ~ para hacer algo** to have one's work cut out to do sth • **nos vimos ~s para salir del apuro** we had a tough time getting out of it • **vérselas negras** to find o.s. in trouble

5* (= *enfadado*) cross, peeved* • **estoy ~ con esto** I'm getting desperate about it • **poner ~ a algn** to make sb cross, upset sb • **ponerse ~** to get cross, cut up rough

6 (= *ilegal*) black • **dinero ~** hot money • **economía negra** black economy • **mercado ~** black market

7 (*Pol*) fascist • **terrorismo ~** fascist terrorism

SM **1** (= *color*) black • **en ~** (*Fot*) in black and white ▸ **negro de humo** lampblack

2 (*Caribe*) (= *café*) black coffee

SM/F **1** (= *persona*) black, coloured person†, Negro† • **¡no somos ~s!** we won't stand for it!, you can't do that to us! • **MODISMO**: • **trabajar como un ~** to work like a dog, slave away*

2* (= *escritor*) ghostwriter

3 • **mi ~** (*And, Cono Sur**) (= *cariño*) darling, honey; ▸ **negra**

negroide ADJ negroid

negrura SF blackness

negruzco ADJ blackish

nel‡ EXCL (*Méx*) yep*

neli‡ ADV = **nada**

nema SF (*Méx*) (*Admin*) seal

neme SM (*And*) asphalt

nemotécnica SF mnemonics (*sing*)

nemotécnico ADJ mnemonic • **un recurso ~** a mnemonic

nene/a SM/F **1** (= *niño pequeño*) baby, small child

2 (*uso apelativo*) • **¡sí, nena!** (*a mujer*) yes dear!, yes darling! • **¿vamos al cine, ~?** (*a hombre*) shall we go to the cinema, darling?

nenúfar SM water lily

neo SM neon

neo... PREF neo...

neoaristotelismo SM neo-Aristotelianism

neocapitalista ADJ, SMF neo-capitalist

neocelandés/esa ADJ of/from New Zealand

SM/F New Zealander • **los neocelandeses** the New Zealanders

neoclasicismo SM neoclassicism

neoclásico ADJ neoclassical

neocolonialismo SM neocolonialism

neoconservador(a) ADJ neo-conservative, neocon (*EEUU**)

SM/F neo-conservative, neocon (*EEUU**)

neofascismo SM neofascism

neofascista ADJ, SMF neofascist

neófito/a SM/F neophyte

neogótico ADJ neogothic, neo-Gothic

neoimpresionismo SM neo-impressionism

neolatino ADJ • **lenguas neolatinas** Romance languages

neolengua SF newspeak

neolítico ADJ neolithic

neologismo SM neologism

neón SM (= *gas, luz*) neon

neonatal ADJ [*asistencia*] neonatal

neonato/a SM/F newborn baby

neonatólogo/a SM/F neonatologist

neonazi ADJ, SMF neonazi

neonazista ADJ neonazi

neoplatónico ADJ neoplatonic

neoplatonismo SM neoplatonism

neoplatonista SMF neoplatonist

neopreno® SM neoprene • **traje de ~** wetsuit

neoyorquino/a ADJ of/from New York

SM/F New Yorker • **los ~s** the New Yorkers

neozelandés/esa ADJ of/from New Zealand

SM/F New Zealander • **los neozelandeses** the New Zealanders

Nepal SM Nepal

nepalés/esa, nepalí ADJ Nepalese

SM/F Nepalese • **los nepaleses** the Nepalese

nepalí ADJ, SMF = **nepalés**

nepotismo SM nepotism

Neptuno SM Neptune

nereida SF nereid

Nerón SM Nero

nervadura SF (*Arquit*) ribs (*pl*); (*Bot, Entomología*) nervure (*frm*), vein

nervio SM **1** (*Anat*) nerve; (*en carne*) sinew • **este filete tiene mucho ~** this steak is very sinewy *o* gristly ▸ **nervio ciático** sciatic nerve ▸ **nervio dental** nerve of the tooth ▸ **nervio óptico** optic nerve

2 nervios (= *ansiedad*) nerves • **MODISMOS**: • **crispar los ~s a algn** to get *o* grate on sb's nerves • **de los ~s***: • **estoy de los ~s** my nerves are on edge • **poner de los ~s a algn** to get on sb's nerves, put sb's nerves on edge • **ponerse de los ~s** to get wound up* • **tener ~s de acero** to have nerves of steel • **tener los ~s como las cuerdas de un violín** to be as jumpy as a cat • **tener los ~s destrozados** • **estar destrozado de los ~s** to be a nervous wreck • **tener los ~s a flor de piel** to be ready to explode • **poner los ~s de punta a algn** to get *o* grate on sb's nerves

3 (*Arquit, Tip, Bot*) rib; [*de insectos*] vein; (*Mús*) string; [*de libro*] rib

4 (= *vigor*) vigour, vigor (*EEUU*), strength • **tener ~** to have character • **un hombre sin ~** a spineless man, a weak man • **MODISMO**: • **ser puro ~** to live on one's nerves

5 [*de persona, sociedad*] (= *eje*) leading light, guiding spirit • **él es el ~ de la sociedad** he is the guiding spirit of the club

6 [*de cuestión, problema*] (= *fondo*) crux, heart

nerviosamente ADV nervously

nerviosera SF attack of nerves

nerviosismo SF, **nerviosidad** SM nervousness, nerves (*pl*); (= *agitación*) agitation, restlessness

nervioso ADJ **1** (*Anat*) nerve (*antes de s*), nervous • **centro ~** nerve centre • **crisis nerviosa** nervous breakdown • **depresión nerviosa** nervous depression • **sistema ~** nervous system • **ataque ~** (attack of) hysterics

2 (= *excitable*) • **ser ~** to be highly strung, be nervous • **es un niño muy ~** he's a very highly strung *o* nervous child • **los foxterriers son muy ~s** fox terriers are very highly strung

3 (= *intranquilo*) • **estar ~** to be nervous • **está nerviosa porque tiene un examen** she's nervous because she has an exam • **está muy ~ porque aún no han llegado** he's very anxious because they haven't arrived yet • **esperaban ~s los resultados** they waited nervously to hear the results • **los caballos estaban ~s antes de la tormenta** the horses were restless before the storm • **poner ~ a algn** to make sb nervous • **ponerse ~** to get nervous • **me pongo muy nerviosa en las entrevistas** I get very nervous in interviews • **¡no te pongas ~!** keep cool!*

nervoso ADJ **1** [*persona*] = **nervioso**

2 [*carne*] sinewy, tough

nervudo ADJ **1** (= *robusto*) tough

2 [*mano, brazo*] sinewy

nesga SF (*Cos*) flare, gore

nesgado ADJ (*Cos*) flared

nesgar ▸ CONJUG 1h VT (*Cos*) to flare, gore

netamente ADV (= *claramente*) clearly; (= *puramente*) purely; (= *genuinamente*) genuinely • **una construcción ~ española** a purely Spanish construction, a genuinely Spanish construction

netiqueta SF netiquette

neto ADJ **1** (*Com, Econ*) net • **peso ~** net weight • **sueldo ~** net salary, salary after deductions

2 (= *claro*) clear • **un perfil ~** a clear outline

neumático ADJ [*martillo, bomba*] pneumatic; [*freno*] air (*antes de s*), pneumatic

SM [*de rueda*] tyre, tire (*EEUU*) ▸ **neumático balón** balloon tyre ▸ **neumático de**

recambio, neumático de repuesto spare tyre ▸ **neumático radial** radial tyre ▸ **neumático sin cámara** tubeless tyre
neumoconiosis (SF INV) pneumoconiosis
neumonía (SF) pneumonia ▸ **neumonía asiática** SARS
neura* (SF) **1** (= *manía*) obsession • **¡menuda ~ te ha cogido con lo de adelgazar!** you've got a real obsession with losing weight! • **tiene la ~ de lavarse continuamente las manos** he's obsessed with washing his hands all the time
2 (= *depresión*) • **estar con la ~: está con la ~ desde que la despidieron** she's been very down since she lost her job
neural (ADJ) neural
neuralgia (SF) neuralgia
neurálgico (ADJ) **1** (*Med*) neuralgic, nerve (*antes de s*)
2 (*fig*) [*centro*] nerve (*antes de s*); [*punto*] crucial, key (*antes de s*)
neuras* (SMF INV) • **es un ~** he's neurotic
neurastenia (SF) **1** (*Med*) neurasthenia (*frm*), nervous exhaustion
2 (*fig*) nerviness, excitability
neurasténico (ADJ) **1** (*Med*) neurasthenic
2 (*fig*) neurotic, nervy, excitable
neuritis (SF INV) neuritis
neuro... (PREF) neuro...
neuroanatomía (SF) neuroanatomy
neurobiología (SF) neurobiology
neurociencia (SF) neuroscience
neurocirugía (SF) neurosurgery
neurocirujano/a (SM/F) neurosurgeon
neurofisiología (SF) neurophysiology
neurofisiológico (ADJ) neurophysiological
neuroléptico (SM) (*Farm*) neuroleptic
neurología (SF) neurology
neurológico (ADJ) neurological
neurólogo/a (SM/F) neurologist
neurona (SF) neuron, nerve cell
neurópata (SMF) neuropath
neuropatía (SF) neuropathy
neuropático (ADJ) neuropathic
neuropatológico (ADJ) neuropathological
neuropsicología (SF) neuropsychology
neuropsicólogo/a (SM/F) neuropsychologist
neuropsiquiatra (SMF) neuropsychiatrist
neuropsiquiatría (SF) neuropsychiatry
neuropsiquiátrico (ADJ) neuropsychiatric
neuroquirúrgico (ADJ) neurosurgical
neurosiquiatra (SMF) neuropsychiatrist
neurosiquiatría (SF) neuropsychiatry
neurosis (SF INV) neurosis ▸ **neurosis de guerra** shell shock
neurótico/a (ADJ), (SM/F) neurotic
neurotizar ▸ CONJUG 1f (VT) to make neurotic
(VPR) **neurotizarse** to become neurotic
neurotransmisor (SM) neurotransmitter
neurovascular (ADJ) neurovascular
neutral (ADJ), (SMF) neutral
neutralidad (SF) neutrality
neutralismo (SM) neutralism
neutralista (ADJ), (SMF) neutralist
neutralización (SF) neutralization
neutralizar ▸ CONJUG 1f (VT) (*gen*) to neutralize; [+ *tendencia, influencia*] to counteract
(VPR) **neutralizarse** (*gen*) to neutralize each other; [*influencias*] to cancel (each other) out
neutro (ADJ) **1** (*gen*) neutral
2 (*Bio*) neuter, sexless • **abeja neutra** worker bee
3 (*Ling*) neuter • **género ~** neuter • **verbo ~** intransitive verb
(SM) (*Ling*) neuter
neutrón (SM) neutron
nevada (SF) snowfall
nevado (ADJ) **1** (= *cubierto de nieve*) snow-covered; [*montaña*] snow-capped
2 (*fig*) snowy, snow-white
(SM) (*LAm*) snow-capped mountain
nevar ▸ CONJUG 1j (VI) to snow
(VT) to whiten
nevasca (SF) snowstorm
nevazón (SF) (*And, Cono Sur*) snowstorm
nevera (SF) **1** (= *frigorífico*) refrigerator, fridge*, icebox (*EEUU*)
2 (= *casa, habitación*) icebox
nevera-congelador (SF) fridge-freezer
nevería (SF) (*Méx*) ice-cream parlour, ice-cream parlor (*EEUU*)
nevero (SM) snowfield, ice field, place of perpetual snow
nevisca (SF) light snowfall, flurry of snow
neviscar ▸ CONJUG 1g (VI) to snow lightly
nevoso (ADJ) snowy
newtoniano (ADJ) Newtonian
newtonio (SM) newton
nexo (SM) link, connection, nexus (*frm*)
n/f. (ABR) = **nuestro favor**
n/g. (ABR) = **nuestro giro**
ni (CONJ) **1** (= *y no*) (*con verbo negativo en inglés*) or; (*con verbo afirmativo en inglés*) nor • **no le gustan las plantas ni los animales** he doesn't like plants or animals • **no bebe ni fuma** he doesn't smoke or drink • **un edificio sin puertas ni ventanas** a building without doors or windows • **—a mí no me gusta —ni a mí** "I don't like it" — "nor do I" *o* "neither do I" • **ni... ni ...: no tenía ni amigos ni familiares** he had no friends and no family (either), he had no friends or family, he had neither friends nor family • **no es ni blanco ni negro** it's not black and it's not white (either), it's neither black nor white • **no vinieron ni Juan ni Pedro** Juan didn't come and neither did Pedro, neither Juan nor Pedro came • **ni vino ni llamó por teléfono** he didn't come and he didn't phone (either), he neither came nor phoned • **ni lo sé ni me importa** I don't know and I don't care • **ni que lo hagas bien ni que lo hagas mal te dirán nada** whether you do it well or badly, they won't say anything
2 (*para dar más énfasis*) even • **no sabe ni dónde está Moscú** he doesn't even know where Moscow is • **ni a ti te lo dirá** he won't tell even YOU • **no lo compraría ni aunque tuviera dinero** I wouldn't buy it even if I had the money • **no tengo ni idea** I have no idea • **no ha llamado ni nada** he hasn't phoned or anything • **ni se sabe** God knows, who knows? • **ni siquiera** not even • **ni siquiera nos ha visto** he didn't even see us • **ni siquiera me llamó** he didn't even phone me • **ni uno**: • **—¿cuántos tienes? —ni uno** "how many have you got?" — "not a single one" *o* "none" • **no hemos comprado ni un regalo** we haven't bought a single present • **no me ha dicho ni una palabra desde que llegó** she hasn't said a single word to me since she got here • **ni uno de sus parientes lo ha felicitado** not (a single) one of his relatives has congratulated him • **no tengo ni un duro** I haven't got a penny
3 (*exclamaciones*) • **¡ni hablar!** no way!, not on your life! • **¿yo? ¿votar a esos? ¡ni hablar!** me vote for them? no way! *o* not on your life! • **¡ni por esas!**: • **he intentado convencerla prometiéndole un regalo, pero ni por esas** I tried to persuade her with a present but even that didn't work • **ni que**: • **siempre cuidando de él, ¡ni que fueras su madre!** you're always taking care of him, anyone would think you were his mother! • **vaya unos humos que tiene, ¡ni que fuese un dios!** he's so arrogant, he must think he's God! • **¡pero tú qué te has creído!, ¡ni que yo fuese tonto!** you must think I'm stupid or something! • **¡qué curso ni qué curso! ¡yo he aprendido por mi cuenta!** what are you talking about, taking a course? I've studied by myself!
4 • **ni bien** (*Arg, Uru*) as soon as • **ni bien me fui, sonó el teléfono** as soon as I left, the phone rang
Niágara (SM) Niagara
niara (SF) (*Agr*) stack, rick
nica (ADJ), (SMF) (*CAm*) (*pey*) Nicaraguan
nicabar‡ ▸ CONJUG 1a (VT) to rip off*, nick*
Nicaragua (SF) Nicaragua
nicaragüense (ADJ) Nicaraguan
(SMF) Nicaraguan • **los ~s** the Nicaraguans
nicaragüismo (SM) *word/phrase peculiar to Nicaragua*
nicho (SM) (*gen*) niche; (= *receso*) recess ▸ **nicho ecológico** ecological niche
nick (SM) (*Internet*) nickname, user name, nick
Nico (SM) *forma familiar de* **Nicolás**
Nicolás (SM) Nicholas
nicotiana (SF) nicotiana, tobacco plant
nicotina (SF) nicotine
nicotínico (ADJ) nicotinic, nicotine (*antes de s*)
nidada (SF) [*de huevos*] clutch; [*de pajarillos*] brood
nidal (SM) **1** (*Orn*) nest; (= *nido artificial*) nesting box
2 [*de dinero*] nest egg
3* (= *guarida*) haunt, hang-out*; (= *escondite*) hiding place
nidificación (SF) nesting, nest-building
nidificante (ADJ) • **ave ~** nesting bird
nidificar ▸ CONJUG 1g (VI) to nest
nido (SM) **1** (*gen*) nest • MODISMOS: • **caer del ~** to come down to earth with a bump • **parece que se ha caído de un ~** he's a bit wet behind the ears* • **manchar el propio ~** to foul one's own nest ▸ **nido de abeja** (*en tela*) honeycomb pattern ▸ **nido de amor** love-nest ▸ **nido de víboras** nest of vipers
2 (= *escondrijo*) hiding place • **un ~ de ladrones** a den of thieves
3 [*de conflictos*] hotbed; [*de discusiones*] focus • **el reparto de premios fue un ~ de polémicas** the prize giving gave rise to heated arguments
4 (*en hospital*) baby unit
5 [*de bebé*] (= *camita*) cot; (= *corralito*) play-pen
6 (= *emplazamiento*) ▸ **nido de ametralladoras** machine-gun nest
niebla (SF) **1** (= *bruma*) fog • **un día de ~** a foggy day • **hay ~** it is foggy ▸ **niebla artificial** smoke screen ▸ **niebla de humo** smog
2 (*en asunto, negocio*) confusion
3 (*Bot*) mildew
niego, niegue *etc* ▸ **negar**
nietísimo/a (SM/F) (*hum*) extra-special grandchild
nieto/a (SM/F) **1** (*lit*) grandson/granddaughter • **~s** grandchildren
2 (*fig*) descendant
nieva *etc* ▸ **nevar**
nieve (SF) **1** (*Meteo*) snow • **~ abundante** *o* **copiosa** heavy snow • **copo de ~** snowflake • **las primeras ~s** the first snows, the first snowfall ▸ **nieve artificial** artificial snow ▸ **nieve en polvo** powdery snow ▸ **nieves perpetuas** perpetual snow
2 (*Culin*) • **a punto de ~** stiff, beaten stiff • **batir a punto de ~** to beat until stiff
3 (*LAm*) (= *polo*) ice lolly; (= *sorbete*) sorbet, water-ice
4‡ (= *cocaína*) snow*, coke*
5 (*TV*) (= *interferencia*) snow

NIF SM ABR (= **número de identificación fiscal**) *ID number used for tax purposes*
Nigeria SF Nigeria
nigeriano/a ADJ Nigerian
SM/F Nigerian • **los ~s** the Nigerians
night* [naɪt] SM nightclub
nigromancia SF necromancy
nigromante SM necromancer
nigua SF (*Caribe, CAm*) (= *pulga*) chigoe, chigger
nihilismo SM nihilism
nihilista ADJ nihilistic
SMF nihilist
niki SM (*Esp*) T-shirt
Nilo SM Nile
nilón [ni'lon] SM nylon
nimbo SM **1** (*Arte, Astron, Rel*) halo
2 (*Meteo*) nimbus
nimbostrato SM nimbostratus
nimiamente ADV trivially
nimiedad SF **1** (= *cualidad*) insignificance, triviality
2 • **una ~** a trifle, a tiny detail • **riñeron por una ~** they quarrelled over nothing
3 (= *minuciosidad*) meticulousness; (*pey*) fussiness; (= *prolijidad*) long-windedness
4 (= *exceso*) excess
nimiez SF trifle, bagatelle
nimio ADJ **1** (= *insignificante*) insignificant, trivial • **un sinfín de detalles ~s** endless trivial details
2 [*persona*] (= *minucioso*) meticulous; (*pey*) fussy (about details); (= *prolijo*) long-winded
3 (= *excesivo*) excessive (**en** in)
ninfa SF **1** (*Mit*) nymph
2 (*Esp‡*) (= *chica*) bird*, chick (*EEUU‡*)
ninfeta SF, **ninfilla** SF, **ninfita** SF nymphet
ninfómana SF nymphomaniac
ninfomanía SF nymphomania
ninfómano ADJ nymphomaniac
nínfula SF nymphet
ningún ADJ ▸ **ninguno**
ningunear* ▸ CONJUG 1a VT (*esp CAm, Méx*) • **~ a algn** (= *hacer el vacío a*) to pretend that sb doesn't exist, ignore sb; (= *despreciar*) to look down one's nose at sb; (= *empequeñecer*) to make sb feel small; (= *tratar mal*) to treat sb like dirt*
ninguneo* SM (*esp CAm, Méx*) • **le condenaron al ~** they completely ostracized him
ninguno ADJ (*con verbo negativo en inglés*) any; (*con verbo afirmativo en inglés*) no • **no practica ningún deporte** he doesn't do any sport, he does no sport • **no hay ningún riesgo de contagio** there is no risk of infection • **no voy a ninguna parte** I'm not going anywhere • **no es ningún tonto** he's no fool • **no es molestia ninguna** it's no trouble at all
PRON **1** (*entre más de dos*) (*con verbo negativo en inglés*) any; (*con verbo afirmativo en inglés*) none • **hizo cuatro exámenes pero no aprobó ~** he took four exams but didn't pass any (of them) • —**¿cuál te gusta?** —**ninguno** "which one do you like?"—"none of them" • **~ de: no me creo ninguna de sus historias** I don't believe any of his stories • **no me interesa ~ de ellos** I'm not interested in any of them • **no lo sabe ~ de sus amigos** none of his friends know
2 (*entre dos*) (*con verbo negativo en inglés*) either; (*con verbo afirmativo en inglés*) neither • **no me gusta ~ (de los dos)** I don't like either (of them) • **no os quiero ver a ~ de los dos por aquí** I don't want to see either of you round here • **no nos ha escrito ~ de los dos** neither of them has written to us • **~ de los dos equipos pasará a la final** neither of the teams *o* neither team will get through to the final
3 (= *nadie*) nobody, no-one • **lo hace como ~** he does it like nobody *o* no-one else • **los invité a los dos pero no vino ~** I invited both but neither of them came

NINGUNO

Adjetivo

▷ *Se traduce por* **any** *si el verbo va en forma negativa y por* **no** *si el verbo va en forma afirmativa. En general es más frecuente usar* **not + any** *(salvo como sujeto, posición en la que se debe emplear* **no***), ya que* **no** *se utiliza normalmente con carácter más enfático:*
No tengo ninguna pregunta
I haven't got any questions
No se ha cometido ningún delito
No crime has been committed
No fui a ningún sitio
I didn't go anywhere
No hay ningún peligro
There is no danger, There isn't any danger

Hay que tener en cuenta que el sustantivo que sigue a **any** *va en plural si es contable, como en el primer ejemplo.*

▷ *Con palabras que poseen un sentido negativo tales como* **hardly, without** *y* **never** *hay que utilizar* **any**:
Conseguí hacerlo sin ninguna ayuda
I managed to do it without any help

Pronombre

▷ *El uso de los pronombres* **any** *y* **none** *sigue las mismas pautas que los adjetivos* **any** *y* **no**, *ya que se emplea preferiblemente la forma* **any** *con verbos en forma negativa y* **none** *si la forma es afirmativa, e igualmente se prefiere la forma* **none** *para la posición de sujeto:*
No quiero ninguno de estos
I don't want any of these
No me gusta ninguno de ellos
I don't like any of them
No queda ninguno
There are none left
No va a venir ninguno de sus amigos
None of her friends is *o* are coming

Si el verbo va detrás de **none** *puede ir tanto en singular como en plural.*

▷ *En lugar de* **none** *y* **any**, *si* **ninguno** *se refiere a dos personas o cosas se emplea* **neither** *y* **either**, *siguiendo las mismas reglas anotadas anteriormente:*
Ninguno de los dos equipos está jugando bien
Neither of the teams *o* Neither team is playing well
No conozco a ninguno de los dos
I don't know either of them

El verbo va en singular si sigue a **neither**.
▸ **ALGUNO, ALGO**

Para otros usos y ejemplos ver la entrada.

nini* ADJ of *o* relating to young people who are not studying or working, ≈ NEET* (*antes de s*) • **la generación ~** the NEET generation
SMF young person who is not studying or working, ≈ NEET*
niña SF **1** ▸ **niña bonita*** (*en lotería*) (= 15) number fifteen • **ser la ~ bonita de algn** to be the apple of sb's eye
2 [*de los ojos*] pupil • **ser la ~ de los ojos de algn** to be the apple of sb's eye; ▸ **niño**
niñada SF = **niñería**
niñato* ADJ • **no seas tan ~** don't be so childish, don't be such a baby
SM (*pey*) (= *niño*) kid*
niñear ▸ CONJUG 1a VI to act childishly
niñera SF nanny, child's nurse (*EEUU*), nursemaid†
niñería SF **1** (= *cualidad*) childishness
2 (= *acto*) childish thing; (= *trivialidad*) silly thing, triviality • **llora por cualquier ~** she cries at the slightest thing
niñero ADJ fond of children
niñez SF [*de persona*] childhood; [*de proyecto, teoría*] infancy
niño/a ADJ **1** (= *joven*) young; (*pey*) childish • **es muy ~ todavía** he's still very young • **¡no seas ~!** don't be so childish!
2 (*And*) [*fruta*] green, unripe
SM/F **1** (= *crío*) child, (little) boy/(little) girl • **los ~s** the children • **de ~** as a child • **desde ~** since childhood, since I *etc* was a child
• MODISMOS: • **ser el ~ mimado de algn** to be sb's pet • **¡qué coche ni qué ~ muerto!*** all this nonsense about a car!, car my foot!* • **como ~ con zapatos nuevos** (*por regalo, compra*) like a child with a new toy, as pleased as punch; (*por noticia, sorpresa*) as pleased as punch ▸ **niño/a bien, niño/a bonito/a** Hooray Henry* • **el ~ bonito del toreo** the golden boy of bullfighting ▸ **niño/a de la calle** street kid ▸ **niño/a expósito/a** foundling ▸ **niño/a pera, niño/a pijo/a*** pampered child, daddy's boy/girl ▸ **niño/a prodigio/a** child prodigy ▸ **niño/a terrible** enfant terrible
2 (= *bebé*) baby • **va a tener un ~** she's going to have a baby • **hacer un ~ a una** to get a girl in the family way • **cuando nazca el ~** when the baby is born, when the child is born ▸ **niño/a azul** blue baby ▸ **el Niño de la bola** (*lit*) the infant Jesus; (*fig*) fortune's favourite ▸ **niño/a de pecho** babe-in-arms ▸ **el Niño Jesús** the Christ-child; (*con menos formalidad*) the Baby Jesus ▸ **niño/a probeta** test-tube baby
3* (*uso apelativo*) • **¡~, que te vas a caer!** watch out, lad, you're going to fall! • **¡niña, no seas tan tonta!** don't be such a silly girl!
4 (*LAm*) (*esp Hist*) (= *título*) master/mistress, sir/miss • **el ~ Francisco** (young) master Francisco
5 (*Cono Sur*) undesirable; ▸ **niña**
nipón/ona ADJ Japanese
SM/F Japanese • **los nipones** the Japanese
nipos‡ SMPL dough* (*sing*), cash* (*sing*)
níquel SM **1** (*gen*) nickel; (*Téc*) nickel-plating
2 (*LAm*) (= *moneda*) small coin, nickel (*EEUU*) • **~es** (*Cono Sur, Méx*) dough* (*sing*)
niquelado ADJ nickel-plated
SM nickel plating
niquelar ▸ CONJUG 1a VT to nickel-plate
VI (*Esp‡*) to shoot a line*
niquelera SF (*And*) purse, coin purse (*EEUU*)
niqui SM T-shirt
nirvana SM Nirvana
níspero SM medlar ▸ **níspero del Japón** loquat
níspola SF medlar
nítidamente ADV clearly, sharply
nitidez SF **1** [*de imagen, fotografía*] sharpness, clarity; [*de aire, agua*] clarity
2 [*de explicación, orden*] clarity; [*de conducta*] irreproachability
nítido ADJ **1** [*imagen, fotografía*] sharp, clear; [*aire, agua*] clear
2 [*explicación, orden*] clear; [*conducta*] irreproachable
nitral SM nitrate deposit, saltpetre bed,

n

saltpeter bed (*EEUU*)
nitrato SM nitrate ▸ **nitrato de cloro** chlorine nitrate ▸ **nitrato potásico** potassium nitrate
nitrera SF (*Cono Sur*) nitrate deposit
nítrico ADJ nitric
nitro SM nitre, niter (*EEUU*), saltpetre, saltpeter (*EEUU*)
nitrobenceno SM nitrobenzene
nitrogenado ADJ nitrogenous
nitrógeno SM nitrogen
nitroglicerina SF nitroglycerin(e)
nitroso ADJ nitrous
nivel SM **1** (= *altura*) level, height • **a 900m sobre el ~ del mar** at 900m above sea level • **la nieve alcanzó un ~ de 1,5m** the snow reached a depth of 1.5m • **a ~** (*gen*) level, flush; (= *horizontal*) horizontal • **al ~ de** on a level with, at the same height as, on the same level as • **paso a ~** level crossing, grade crossing (*EEUU*) ▸ **nivel de(l) aceite** (*Aut etc*) oil level ▸ **nivel de crucero** cruising altitude ▸ **nivel del agua** water level ▸ **nivel del mar** sea level ▸ **nivel freático** water table
2 (*escolar, cultural*) level, standard • **el ~ cultural del país** the cultural standard of the country • **alto ~ de empleo** high level of employment • **conferencia al más alto ~** • **conferencia de alto ~** high-level conference, top-level conference • **de primer ~** top-level • **a ~ internacional** at an international level • **estar al ~ de** to be equal to, be on a level with • **estar al ~ de las circunstancias** to rise to the occasion • **no está al ~ de los demás** he is not up to the standard of the others • MODISMO: • **dar el ~** to come up to scratch ▸ **nivel de vida** standard of living ▸ **niveles de audiencia** ratings, audience rating (*sing*); (*TV*) viewing figures
3 (= *instrumento*) (*tb* **nivel de aire, nivel de burbuja**) spirit level
4 • **a ~ de** (= *en cuanto a*) as for, as regards; (= *como*) as; (= *a tono con*) in keeping with • **a ~ de ministro es un desastre** as a minister he's a disaster • **a ~ de viajes** so far as travel is concerned, regarding travel
nivelación SF **1** [*de superficie*] levelling (out), leveling (out) (*EEUU*)
2 [*de presupuesto*] balancing
nivelado ADJ **1** [*superficie*] level, flat; (*Téc*) flush
2 [*presupuesto*] balanced
SM levelling, leveling (*EEUU*)
niveladora SF bulldozer
nivelar ▸ CONJUG 1a VT **1** [+ *superficie*] to level (out); (*Ferro*) to grade
2 [+ *diferencias, deficiencias*] to even (out), even (up)
3 [+ *presupuesto*] to balance (**con** against), adjust (**con** to); [+ *déficit*] to cover
níveo ADJ (*liter*) snowy, snow-white
nivosidad SF snowfall, (depth of) snow
nixtamal SM (*CAm, Méx*) (= *maíz cocido*) boiled maize, boiled corn (*EEUU*)
Niza SF Nice
n/l. ABR = **nuestra letra**
NN ABR (= **ningún nombre**) no name (*mark on grave of unknown person*)
NNE ABR (= **nornordeste**) NNE
NNO ABR (= **nornoroeste**) NNW
NN.UU. SFPL ABR (= **Naciones Unidas**) UN
N.º ABR, **n.º** ABR (= **número**) No., no.
NO ABR (= **noroeste**) NW
no ADV **1** (= *para negar*) **a** (*en respuestas independientes*) no; (*con adverbios*) not • **—¿quieres un café? —no, gracias** "would you like a coffee?" —"no, thanks" • **—¿quieres venir? —no** "do you want to come?" — "no" *o* "no, I don't" • **—¿te gusta? —no mucho** "do you like it?" — "not really" • **todavía no** not yet • **¡no a la bajada de sueldos!** no to wage cuts! • **¡yo no!** not me!, not I!†
b (*para formar la negación de los verbos*) • **no sé** I don't know • **María no habla inglés** María doesn't speak English • **no puedo ir esta noche** I can't come tonight • **no tengo tiempo** I haven't got time • **no debes preocuparte** you mustn't worry • **no hace frío** it isn't cold
c • **que no** • **decir que no** to say no • **creo que no** I don't think so • **me rogó que no lo hiciera** he asked me not to do it • **—¿eras tú el que llamaba? —¡que no, que no era yo!** "was it you who was calling?" — "no, I've already told you it wasn't!" • **¡a que no eres capaz!** I bet you can't! • **¡a que no lo sabes!** I bet you don't know!
d (*con doble negación*) • **no conozco a nadie** I don't know anyone • **no quiero nada** I don't want anything, I want nothing; ▹ **de, bien, más, si¹**
2 (*para confirmar*) • **esto es tuyo, ¿no?** this is yours, isn't it? • **fueron al cine, ¿no?** they went to the cinema, didn't they? • **puedo salir esta noche, ¿no?** I can go out tonight, can't I?
3 (*para enfatizar*) • **es mejor que lo diga que no que se calle** it's better that he should speak up rather than saying nothing • **hasta que no pagues no te lo darán** they won't give it to you until you pay • **¿pues no va y le da el dinero a ella?** so what does he do? he goes and gives the money to her!
4 (*modificando a adjetivos y sustantivos*) non- • **pacto de no agresión** non-aggression pact • **los países no alineados** the non-aligned nations • **no beligerancia** non-belligerence • **el no conformismo** non-conformism • **los no fumadores** non-smokers • **la política de no intervención** the policy of non-intervention, the non-intervention policy • **no renovable** non-renewable • **la no necesidad del latín en partes de la misa** the fact that Latin is not obligatory in parts of the mass • MODISMO: • **el no va más** the ultimate • **lo que en los sesenta era el no va más** what was the ultimate in the sixties • **ese barco es el no va más del lujo** that boat is the ultimate in luxury
SM • **un no contundente** a resounding no • **le dieron un no por respuesta** they answered him no • **no hubo ni un solo no en la votación** not a single person voted no
n/o. ABR = **nuestra orden**
Nobel SM **1** (*tb* **Premio Nobel**) Nobel Prize
2 (= *persona*) Nobel prizewinner
nobiliario ADJ **1** • **título ~** title
2 [*libro*] genealogical
nobilizar ▸ CONJUG 1f VT to enhance, dignify, ennoble
noble ADJ **1** (= *aristocrático*) noble
2 (= *honrado*) noble
3 [*madera*] fine
SMF nobleman/noblewoman • **los ~s** the nobility (*sing*), the nobles
noblemente ADV nobly
nobleza SF **1** (= *cualidad*) nobility • **~ obliga** noblesse oblige
2 (= *aristocracia*) nobility
nobuk SM nubuck
nocaut SM (*LAm*), **nocáut** SM (*LAm*) knockout
nocautear ▸ CONJUG 1a VT (*LAm*) to knock out, K.O.*
nocdáun SM (*LAm*) knockdown
noche SF **1** (= *parte del día*) night • **a las once de la ~** at eleven o'clock at night • **la alarma no dejó de sonar en toda la ~** the alarm didn't stop ringing all night • **"Las mil y una ~s"** "The Arabian Nights" • **ayer ~** last night • **¡buenas ~s!** (= *al atardecer*) good evening!; (= *al despedirse o al acostarse*) good night! • **de ~** (*como adv*) at night; (*como adj*) night (*antes de s*) • **tiene miedo a salir de ~ a la calle** she is afraid to go out after dark *o* at night • **viajaban de ~ y dormían durante el día** they travelled by night and slept during the day • **crema de ~** night cream • **turno de ~** night shift • **traje de ~** evening dress • **en la ~ de ayer** last night • **en la ~ de hoy** tonight • **en la ~ del martes** on Tuesday night • **hasta muy entrada la ~** till late into the night, into the small hours • **esta ~** (= *hoy por la noche*) tonight; (= *anoche*) last night • **¿qué hay en la tele esta ~?** what's on TV tonight? • **no he podido dormir esta ~** I couldn't sleep last night • **hacer ~ en un sitio** to spend the night somewhere • **media ~** midnight • **por** *o* (*LAm*) **en** *o* (*Arg, Uru*) **a la ~** at night • **cuando se echa una siesta luego por la ~ no duerme** when he has a siesta, he doesn't sleep at night • **mañana por la ~** tomorrow night • **el lunes por la ~** on Monday night • MODISMOS: • **de la ~ a la mañana** overnight • **pasar la ~ en blanco** *o* **(de claro) en claro** *o* **en vela** to have a sleepless night • **perderse en la ~ de los tiempos** to be lost in the mists of time ▸ **noche de amor** night of passion ▸ **noche de bodas** wedding-night ▸ **noche de estreno** (*Teat*) first night, opening night ▸ **noche de los cuchillos largos** night of the long knives ▸ **noche toledana** sleepless night ▸ **Noche Vieja** New Year's Eve; ▹ **función, gato**
2 (= *oscuridad*) • **al caer la ~** at nightfall • **ya es ~ cerrada** it's completely dark now • **es de ~** it is dark • **ahora es de ~ y no se ve nada** it's dark now and you can't see a thing • **cuando sea de ~, volveremos al refugio** when night falls *o* when it's dark, we'll return to the shelter • **hacerse de ~** to get dark
3 • **la ~** (= *vida nocturna*) nightlife • **aquí se vive intensamente la ~** the nightlife is very lively here • **es el local de moda de la ~ neoyorquina** it is the trendiest nightspot on the New York scene
Nochebuena SF Christmas Eve

> **NOCHEBUENA**
> Traditional Christmas celebrations in Spanish-speaking countries mainly take place on the night of **Nochebuena**, Christmas Eve. These include a large Christmas meal, going to Midnight Mass, **Misa del Gallo**, if you are a Catholic, and, in Spain, watching the seasonal message from the King on TV. Presents are traditionally given at the Epiphany by **los Reyes Magos**, the Three Kings, but due to ever-increasing Anglo-Saxon influence many people also give presents on Christmas Day.
> ▹ **DÍA DE REYES**

nochecita SF (*LAm*) dusk, nightfall
nocherniego ADJ nocturnal, given to wandering about at night
SM night owl
nochero/a ADJ (*LAm*) nocturnal
SM/F (*Guat*) night worker
SM **1** (*Chile, Col*) (= *vigilante*) night watchman
2 (*Col*) (= *mesilla*) bedside table, night stand (*EEUU*)

Nochevieja SF, **nochevieja** SF New Year's Eve

> **NOCHEVIEJA**
> **Nochevieja**, or New Year's Eve, is one of the most important seasonal celebrations in Spanish-speaking countries. Whereas **Nochebuena** is traditionally spent at home with the family, **Nochevieja** is an occasion for going out. In Spain, the highlight of the evening is **las campanadas**, the chimes of the clock at midnight. Until quite recently the **Puerta del Sol** clock in Madrid was the most viewed image in live broadcasts ushering in the New Year, but nowadays different TV stations choose different cities when it comes to broadcasting the chimes. As the bells strike it is traditional to eat twelve grapes, one for each chime, a custom known as **las uvas de la suerte** or **las doce uvas**.

nochote SM (*Méx*) cactus beer

noción SF **1** (= *idea*) notion, idea • **no tener la menor ~ de algo** not to have the faintest idea about sth
2 nociones (= *conocimientos*) [*de electrónica, música*] basics, rudiments; [*de lenguas*] smattering (*sing*) • **tiene algunas nociones de árabe** he has a smattering of Arabic

nocional ADJ notional

nocivamente ADV harmfully

nocividad SF harmfulness

nocivo ADJ harmful, injurious (*frm*) (**para** to)

noctambulear ▸ CONJUG 1a VI to wander about at night

noctambulismo SM sleepwalking, somnambulism (*frm*)

noctámbulo/a ADJ active at night
SM/F (= *sonámbulo*) sleepwalker; (= *jaranero*) night owl

noctiluca SF (*Entomología*) glow-worm

noctívago/a ADJ, SM/F = **noctámbulo**

nocturnidad SF evening hours (*pl*), night hours (*pl*) • **con la agravante de la ~** made more serious by the fact that it was done at night • **obrar con ~** to operate under cover of darkness

nocturno ADJ **1** [*servicio, tarifa, ceguera*] night (*antes de s*) • **un vuelo ~** a night flight • **locales ~s** nightspots • **vigilante ~** night watchman • **el barrio no tiene mucho ambiente ~** there's not much nightlife in the area • **clases nocturnas** evening classes, night school (*EEUU*) • **su primera salida nocturna de las vacaciones** her first night out during the holidays
2 (*Zool, Bot*) nocturnal
SM **1** (*Mús*) nocturne
2 (*Escol*) evening classes (*pl*), night school (*EEUU*)

nodo¹ SM node

nodo² SM, **No-do** SM (*Cine, Hist*) newsreel

nodriza SF wet nurse • **barco ~** supply ship

nodular ADJ nodular

nódulo SM nodule

Noé SM Noah

nogal SM (= *madera*) walnut; (= *árbol*) walnut tree

noguera SF walnut tree

noluntad SF unwillingness, reluctance

nómada ADJ nomadic
SMF nomad

nomadear ▸ CONJUG 1a VI to wander

nomadeo SM wanderings (*pl*)

nomadismo SM nomadism

nomás ADV (*LAm*) (*gen*) just; (= *tan solo*) only; ▸ **más**

nombradía SF fame, renown

nombrado ADJ **1** (= *susodicho*) aforementioned
2 (= *famoso*) famous, renowned

nombramiento SM **1** (*gen*) naming; (= *designación*) designation
2 (*para un puesto etc*) nomination, appointment; (*Mil*) commission
3 (= *mención*) mention

nombrar ▸ CONJUG 1a VT **1** (*gen*) to name; (= *designar*) to designate
2 (*para puesto, cargo*) to nominate, appoint; (*Mil*) to commission • **~ a algn embajador** to appoint sb ambassador
3 (= *mencionar*) to mention

nombre SM **1** [*de persona, cosa*] name • **~ y apellidos** name in full, full name • **de rey no tenía más que el ~** he was king in name only • **a ~ de:** • **un sobre a ~ de …** an envelope addressed to … • **no hay nadie a ~ de María** there's no one by the name of María • **bajo el ~ de** under the name of • **de ~** by name • **de ~ García** García by name • **conocer a algn de ~** to know sb by name • **no existe sino de ~** it exists in name only • **era rey tan solo de ~** he was king in name only • **en ~ de** in the name of, on behalf of • **en ~ de la libertad** in the name of liberty • **¡abran en ~ de la ley!** open up in the name of the law! • **poner ~ a** to call, name • **¿qué ~ le van a poner?** what are they going to call him? • **por ~** by the name of, called • **sin ~** nameless • MODISMOS: • **llamar a las cosas por su ~** to call a spade a spade • **no tener ~**: • **su conducta no tiene ~** his conduct is utterly despicable ▸ **nombre artístico** [*de escritor*] pen-name, nom de plume; [*de actor*] stage name ▸ **nombre comercial** trade name ▸ **nombre de bautismo** christian name, given name (*EEUU*) ▸ **nombre de familia** family name ▸ **nombre de fichero** (*Inform*) file name ▸ **nombre de lugar** place name ▸ **nombre de pila** first name, Christian name, given name (*EEUU*) ▸ **nombre de religión** name in religion ▸ **nombre de soltera** maiden name ▸ **nombre gentilicio** family name ▸ **nombre social** corporate name
2 (*Ling*) noun ▸ **nombre abstracto** abstract noun ▸ **nombre colectivo** collective noun ▸ **nombre común** common noun ▸ **nombre concreto** concrete noun ▸ **nombre propio** proper name
3 (= *reputación*) name, reputation • **se ha hecho un ~ en el mundo editorial** she's made a name for herself in the world of publishing • **tiene ~ en el mundo entero** it has a world-wide reputation • **un médico de ~** a famous *o* renowned doctor

nomenclátor SM, **nomenclador** SM catalogue of names

nomenclatura SF nomenclature

nomeolvides SF INV **1** (*Bot*) forget-me-not
2 (= *pulsera*) bracelet (*with lover's name etc*)

nómina SF **1** (= *lista de empleados*) payroll • **tiene una ~ de 500 personas** he has 500 on his payroll • **entrar en ~** to be put on the payroll • **estar en ~** to be on the staff
2 (= *sueldo*) salary; (= *hoja de pago*) payslip • **cobrar la ~** to get paid, get one's pay-packet

nominación SF (*esp LAm*) nomination

nominal ADJ **1** [*cargo*] nominal; [*jefe, rey*] in name only
2 [*valor*] face (*antes de s*), nominal; [*sueldo etc*] nominal
3 (*Ling*) noun (*antes de s*)

nominalismo SM nominalism

nominalización SF nominalization

nominalizar ▸ CONJUG 1f VT to nominalize

nominalmente ADV nominally, in name • **al menos ~** at least in name

nominado/a SM/F nominee, candidate

nominar ▸ CONJUG 1a VT to nominate

nominativo ADJ **1** (*Ling*) nominative
2 (*Com, Econ*) • **el cheque será ~ a favor de García** the cheque should be made out *o* made payable to García
SM (*Ling*) nominative

non ADJ [*número*] odd
SM (= *impar*) odd number • **los nones** the odd ones • **pares y nones** odds and evens • **estar de non** (= *persona*) to be odd man out; (*fig*) to be useless • **queda uno de non** there's an odd one, there's one left over • **un zapato de non** an odd shoe • MODISMO: • **andar de nones** to have nothing to do, be at a loose end

nonada SF trifle, mere nothing

nonagenario/a ADJ nonagenarian, ninety-year-old
SM/F nonagenarian

nonagésimo ADJ ninetieth; ▸ **sexto**

nonato ADJ (= *no nacido*) unborn; (*mediante cesárea*) not born naturally, born by Caesarean section

noneco ADJ (*CAm*), **nonejo** ADJ (*CAm*) thick*

nones* ADV no • **decir que ~** to say no, flatly refuse • **¡nones!** no way!*

noningentésimo ADJ nine-hundredth

nono¹ ADJ ninth

nono²/a* SM/F (*Cono Sur*) granddad*, grandma*

nopal SM prickly pear

nopalera SF patch of prickly pears

noqueada SF (*esp LAm*) (= *acto*) knockout; (= *golpe*) knockout blow

noqueado* ADJ (*LAm*) shattered*, knackered*, pooped (*EEUU**)

noquear ▸ CONJUG 1a VT (*esp LAm*) to knock out, K.O*

noqueo SM (*esp LAm*) knockout

noratlántico ADJ north-Atlantic

noray SM bollard

norcoreano/a ADJ North Korean
SM/F North Korean • **los ~s** the North Koreans

nordeste ADJ [*región, parte*] north-east, north-eastern; [*dirección*] north-easterly; [*viento*] north-east, north-easterly
SM **1** (= *región*) northeast
2 (= *viento*) north-east wind

nordestino ADJ north-eastern

nórdico/a ADJ **1** (*gen*) northern, northerly • **es la ciudad más nórdica de Europa** it is the most northerly city in Europe
2 (*Hist*) Nordic, Norse
SM/F **1** (*gen*) northerner
2 (*Hist*) Norseman
SM (*Ling*) Norse

noreste ADJ, SM = **nordeste**

noria SF **1** (*Agr*) waterwheel
2 [*de feria*] big wheel, Ferris wheel (*EEUU*)

norirlandés/esa ADJ Northern Irish
SM/F native/inhabitant of Northern Ireland • **los norirlandeses** the people of Northern Ireland

norma SF **1** (= *regla*) (*tb Educ*) rule; (*oficial*) regulation • **los centros educativos tienen autonomía para elaborar sus propias ~s** schools and colleges have the power to make their own rules • **la primera ~ de autodefensa** the first rule of self-defence • **el comercio internacional está sujeto a ciertas ~s** international trade is subject to certain regulations • **una nueva ~ europea sobre emisiones acústicas** a new European regulation on sound emissions • **como** *o* **por ~ general** as a general rule, as a rule of thumb • **tener por ~ hacer algo** to make it a rule to do sth • **tengo por ~ no hablar nunca de estos temas** I make it a rule never to talk

about such matters ▸ **norma de comprobación** (*Fís*) control ▸ **normas de conducta** (*sociales*) rules of behaviour; [*de periódico, empresa*] policy (*sing*) ▸ **norma de vida** principle ▸ **normas de seguridad** safety regulations
2 (= *situación, costumbre*) norm • **un país donde la pobreza es la ~** a country where poverty is the norm • **es ~ ofrecer una copa de bienvenida** it is standard practice *o* it is the norm to offer a complimentary drink • **como es ~ en estos casos** as is standard practice *o* as is the norm in these cases
3 • **la ~** (*Ling*) the standard form • **la ~ andaluza** standard Andalusian Spanish
4 (*Arquit, Téc*) square

normal ADJ **1** (= *usual*) normal • **una persona ~** a normal person • **es perfectamente ~** it's perfectly normal • **es ~ que quiera divertirse** it's only normal that he wants to enjoy himself • **no es ~ que no quiera venir** it's unusual for him not to want to come • **lleva una vida muy ~** he leads a very ordinary life • **~ y corriente** ordinary • **—¿es guapo? —no, ~ y corriente** "is he handsome?" — "no, just ordinary" • **como alumno es ~ y corriente** he's an average pupil
2 [*gasolina*] three-star, regular (*EEUU*)
3 (*Téc*) standard; (*Mat, Quím*) normal
4 • **Escuela Normal** (*esp LAm*) teacher training college

normalidad SF normality, normalcy (*EEUU*) • **la situación ha vuelto a la ~** the situation has returned to normality *o* normal • **se comportaba con total ~** he was behaving perfectly normally • **el acto discurrió con toda ~** the ceremony passed off without incident

normalillo ADJ, **normalito** ADJ quite ordinary, run-of-the-mill

normalista (*LAm*) ADJ INV [*de estudiante*] student teacher (*antes de s*); [*de maestro*] schoolteacher (*antes de s*)
SMF (= *estudiante*) student teacher; (= *maestro*) schoolteacher

normalización SF **1** [*de relaciones, servicio, situación*] normalization • **la ~ del uso del catalán en las escuelas** the standardization of Catalan in the schools ▸ **normalización lingüística** *policy of making the local language official within an autonomous region*
2 (*Com, Téc*) standardization

normalizado ADJ (*Com, Téc*) standard, standardized

normalizar ▸ CONJUG 1f VT **1** [+ *relaciones, servicio, situación*] to restore to normal, normalize
2 (*Com, Téc*) to standardize
VPR **normalizarse** to return to normal, normalize • **el servicio se normalizó a mediodía** the service returned to normal at midday

normalmente ADV (*gen*) normally; (= *usualmente*) usually

Normandía SF Normandy

normando/a ADJ **1** (*gen*) of/from Normandy; (*Hist*) Norman • **las islas Normandas** the Channel Islands
2 (= *vikingo*) Norse
SM/F **1** (*gen*) native/inhabitant of Normandy; (*Hist*) Norman • **los ~s** the people of Normandy; (*Hist*) the Normans
2 (= *vikingo*) Norseman

normar ▸ CONJUG 1a VT (*LAm*) to lay down rules for, establish norms for

normativa SF rules (*pl*), regulations (*pl*), guidelines (*pl*) • **según la ~ vigente** according to current rules *o* regulations *o* guidelines

normativo ADJ **1** (= *preceptivo*) [*aspecto, carácter*] normative; [*gramática*] prescriptive • **es ~ en todos los coches nuevos** it is mandatory in all new cars
2 (= *legal*) • **el marco ~ vigente** the existing regulatory framework • **el actual vacío ~** the present lack of regulation

noroccidental ADJ north-western

noroeste ADJ [*región*] north-west, north-western; [*dirección*] north-westerly; [*viento*] north-west, north-westerly
SM **1** (= *región*) north-west
2 (= *viento*) north-west wind

nororiental ADJ north-eastern

norovirus SM norovirus

norsa SF (*LAm*) (= *enfermera*) nurse; (= *institutriz*) governess; (= *niñera*) nursemaid

nortada SF (steady) northerly wind

norte ADJ [*región*] northern; [*dirección*] northerly; [*viento*] north • **el hemisferio ~** the northern hemisphere • **la zona ~ de la ciudad** the northern part of the city, the north of the city • **en la costa ~** on the north coast
SM **1** (= *punto cardinal*) north ▸ **norte magnético** magnetic north
2 [*de región, país*] north • **el ~ del país** the north of the country • **al ~ de Huelva** to the north of Huelva • **eso cae más hacia el ~** that lies further (to the) north • **viajábamos hacia el ~** we were travelling north • **en la parte del ~** in the northern part • **vientos del ~** northerly winds
3 (= *viento*) north wind
4 (= *meta*) aim, objective • **aún no ha encontrado su ~ en la vida** she still hasn't found her aim in life • **pregunta sin ~** aimless question • **perder el ~** to lose one's way, go astray
5 (*Caribe*) (= *Estados Unidos*) ≈ United States
6 (*Caribe*) (= *llovizna*) drizzle

norteafricano/a ADJ North African
SM/F North African man/woman • **los ~s** the people of North Africa

Norteamérica SF North America

norteamericano/a ADJ North American; (*de Estados Unidos*) American
SM/F North American; (*de Estados Unidos*) American • **los ~s** the North Americans, the people of North America; (*de Estados Unidos*) the Americans

nortear ▸ CONJUG 1a VI (*And, CAm, Caribe*) • **nortea** the north wind is blowing

norteño/a ADJ northern
SM/F northerner

nortino/a (*And, Cono Sur*) ADJ northern
SM/F northerner

Noruega SF Norway

noruego/a ADJ Norwegian
SM/F Norwegian • **los ~s** the Norwegians
SM (*Ling*) Norwegian

norvietnamés/esa (*LAm*) ADJ North Vietnamese
SM/F North Vietnamese man/North Vietnamese woman • **los norvietnameses** the North Vietnamese, the people of North Vietnam

norvietnamita ADJ North Vietnamese
SMF North Vietnamese man/North Vietnamese woman • **los ~s** the North Vietnamese, the people of North Vietnam

nos PRON PERS PL **1** (*directo*) us • **nos quiere mucho** she loves us dearly • **nos vinieron a ver** they came to see us
2 (*indirecto*) us • **nos dio un consejo** he gave us some advice • **nos lo compró** (*de nosotros*) he bought it from us; (*para nosotros*) he bought it for us • **nos tienen que arreglar el ordenador** they have to fix the computer for us • **nos dolían los pies** our feet were hurting
3 (*reflexivo*) ourselves • **tenemos que defendernos** we must defend ourselves • **nos lavamos** we washed • **nos levantamos a las siete** we get up at seven • **nos pusimos los abrigos** we put our coats on
4 (*mutuo*) each other • **nos dimos un beso** we gave each other a kiss • **no nos hablamos** we don't speak to each other • **nos hemos enamorado** we fell in love

nosocomio SM (*esp LAm*) hospital

nosotros/as PRON PERS PL **1** (*sujeto*) we • **~ no somos italianos** we are not Italian • **se lo podemos llevar ~ mismos** we can deliver it to you ourselves
2 (*tras prep y conj*) us • **tu hermano vino con ~** your brother came with us • **no irán sin ~** they won't go without us • **no pedimos nada para ~** we ask nothing for ourselves • **han jugado peor que nosotras** they played worse than us

nostalgia SF [*del pasado*] nostalgia; [*de casa, patria, amigos*] homesickness

nostálgico ADJ [*del pasado*] nostalgic; (*de casa, patria, amigos*) homesick

nostalgioso ADJ (*Cono Sur*) = **nostálgico**

nota SF **1** (= *mensaje corto*) note; (*Admin*) memo • **te he dejado una ~ encima de la mesa** I've left you a note on the table ▸ **nota de aviso** advice note ▸ **nota de entrega** delivery note ▸ **nota de inhabilitación** (*Aut*) endorsement (*on licence*) ▸ **nota de quita y pon** Post-it®
2 (= *apunte*) note • **tomar ~s** to take notes • **tomar (buena) ~ (de algo)** (*fijarse*) to take (good) note (of sth)
3 (= *comentario*) note • **texto con ~s de ...** text edited with notes by ..., text annotated by ... ▸ **nota a pie de página** footnote ▸ **notas al margen** marginal notes
4 (*Escol*) mark, grade (*EEUU*) • **sacar buenas ~s** to get good marks • **ir para** *o* **a por ~*** to go *o* aim for a high mark • **¿ya te han dado las ~s?** have you had your report yet?
5 (*Mús*) note • **entonar la ~** to pitch a note • **dar la ~** (*lit*) to give the keynote; (*fig*) to get oneself noticed, act up ▸ **nota discordante** (*lit*) discordant note, discord • **sus críticas fueron la única ~ discordante** his criticisms struck the only discordant note • **Juan siempre tiene que dar la ~ discordante** Juan always has to disagree ▸ **nota dominante** (*lit*) dominant note; (*fig*) dominant feature *o* element
6 (= *adorno, detalle*) • **una ~ de color** a colourful note • **una ~ de buen gusto** a tasteful note
7 (*Prensa*) note ▸ **nota de la redacción** editor's note ▸ **nota de prensa** press release ▸ **nota de sociedad** gossip column ▸ **nota informativa** press release
8 • **digno de ~** (= *notable*) notable, worthy of note
9 (*Com*) (= *recibo*) receipt; (= *vale*) IOU; (*Méx*) (= *cuenta*) bill ▸ **nota de cargo, nota de débito** debit note ▸ **nota de crédito** credit note ▸ **nota de gastos** expense account
10† (= *reputación*) reputation • **de ~** of note, famous • **de mala ~** notorious • **tiene ~ de tacaño** he has a reputation for meanness
11 (*LAm*‡) effects (*pl*) of drugs
SM **notas**‡ (= *tío*) bloke‡, dude (*EEUU*‡)

notabilidad SF **1** (= *cualidad*) noteworthiness, notability
2 (= *persona notable*) notable person

notable ADJ **1** (= *destacado*) notable • **una actuación verdaderamente ~** an outstanding performance, a truly notable performance • **un poema ~ por su belleza lírica** a poem notable for its lyrical beauty • **la exposición reúne a pintores tan ~s como**

... the exhibition brings together such notable *o* distinguished painters as ...
2 (= *considerable*) [*aumento, mejoría, diferencia*] significant, considerable • **el enfermo ha experimentado una ~ mejoría** the patient has experienced a significant *o* considerable improvement • **la disminución de la contaminación ha sido ~** there has been a significant *o* considerable reduction in pollution • **la obra fue un fracaso ~** the play was a signal failure
SM (*Esp*) (= *calificación*) *mark or grade between 7 and 8 out of 10* • **he sacado un ~** ≈ I got a B
SMPL • **los ~s** the notables

notablemente ADV [*mejorar, disminuir, aumentar*] significantly, considerably • **nuestro déficit es ~ superior a la media** our deficit is significantly *o* considerably above average • **apareció ~ cansado** he appeared visibly tired

notación SF notation ▸ **notación binaria** binary notation ▸ **notación hexadecimal** hexadecimal notation ▸ **notación musical** musical notation

notar ▹ CONJUG 1a VT **1** (= *darse cuenta de*) to notice • **no lo había notado** I hadn't noticed • **los usuarios apenas han notado los efectos de la huelga** customers have hardly noticed the effects of the strike • **noté que la gente la miraba** I noticed people looking at her, I noticed that people were looking at her • **un niño nota cuando hay tensión en casa** a child can tell when there is tension at home • **dejarse ~**: • **la subida de los precios se dejará ~ sobre todo en los alimentos** the rise in prices will be most noticeable in the case of food • **su ausencia en el equipo se dejó ~ ayer** his absence from the team was noticeable yesterday • **hacer ~ algo** to point sth out • **le hice ~ que había sido él, no yo, quien dio la orden** I pointed out to him that it had been him and not me who had given the order • **hacerse ~**: • **los resultados se hicieron ~ sin tardanza** the consequences soon became apparent • **solo se comportan así para hacerse ~** they only behave like that to get noticed *o* get attention • **la esposa del presidente apenas se ha hecho ~ en todo este tiempo** the president's wife has been almost invisible all this time
2 (= *sentir*) [+ *dolor, pinchazo, frío*] to feel • **no noto frío alguno** I don't feel at all cold • **empiezo a ~ el cansancio** I'm beginning to feel tired
3 (+ *adj*) • **te noto muy cambiado** you seem very different • **lo noté preocupado** he seemed worried (to me) • **he notado la casa más silenciosa últimamente** the house has seemed quieter recently • **te noto raro** you're acting strangely
4 (= *anotar*) to note down
5 (= *marcar*) to mark, indicate
6 [+ *persona*] (= *criticar*) to criticize; (= *desacreditar*) to discredit • **~ a algn de algo** to brand sb as sth, criticize sb for being sth
VPR **notarse 1** (*uso impersonal*) **a** (= *ser obvio*) to be noticeable • **en la reunión se notó mucho la ausencia de la antigua directora** the absence of the former director was very noticeable at the meeting • **notársele algo a algn: —estás disgustada, ¿verdad? —sí, ¿se me nota mucho?** "you're upset, aren't you?" — "yes, is it (that) obvious?" • **no se le nota que es extranjero** you can't tell he's a foreigner, you wouldn't know he's a foreigner • **se le notaba muy agitado** he was obviously very agitated • **~se que**: • **se notaba que no se sentía muy seguro de sí mismo** you could tell he didn't feel very confident, he obviously didn't feel very confident • **¡se nota que acabas de cobrar!** you can tell you've just been paid!, you've obviously just been paid! • **no se notaba que acabaran de limpiar la escalera** you wouldn't know they had just cleaned the stairs
b (= *sentirse*) to be felt • **el impacto de la subida de los precios se ~á en febrero** the impact of the price increases will be felt in February • **la inflación se ha notado en el bolsillo de los españoles** the Spanish have felt the effect of inflation on their pocket • **fue un terremoto tan pequeño que no se notó** it was such a small earthquake that it went unnoticed *o* that no-one felt it
c (= *verse*) [*mancha, defecto*] to show • **no se nota nada la mancha** the stain doesn't show at all • **notársele algo a algn: —tienes una carrera en la media —¿se me nota mucho?** "you've got a ladder in your tights" — "does it show much?" • **solo se le nota la edad en la cara** his age only shows in his face
2 (*uso reflexivo*) to feel • **me noto más relajado** I feel more relaxed • **me noto con menos energía estos días** I've been feeling less energetic recently

notaría SF **1** (= *profesión*) profession of notary • **gastos de ~** legal fees, lawyer's fees
2 (= *despacho*) notary's office

notariado SM **1** (= *profesión*) profession of notary
2 (= *notarios*) notaries (*pl*)

notarial ADJ (*gen*) notarial; [*estilo*] legal, lawyer's

notarialmente ADV by legal process • **recurrir ~ a algn** to bring a legal action against sb • **tiene que certificarse ~** it must be legally certified, it must be certified before a commissioner for oaths

notario/a SM/F notary, notary public, attorney-at-law (*EEUU*)

notebook ['notbuk] SM notebook, notebook computer

noticia SF **1** (= *información*) news • **¿hay alguna ~?** any news? • **eso no es ~** that's not news • **tengo una buena ~ que darte** I've got some good news for you • **fue una ~ excelente para la economía** it was an excellent piece of news for the economy • **la última ~ fue sobre las inundaciones** the last news item was about the flooding • **vi las ~s de las nueve** I watched the nine o'clock news • **según nuestras ~s** according to our information • **estar atrasado de ~s** to be behind the times, lack up-to-date information • **¡~s frescas!** (*iró*) tell me a new one! ▸ **noticia bomba*** bombshell* ▸ **noticia de portada** front-page news, headline news
2 (= *conocimiento*) • **tener ~s de algn** to have news of sb • **hace tiempo que no tenemos ~s suyas** we haven't heard from her for a long time • **no tener ~ de algo** to know nothing about a matter • **no tenemos ~ de su paradero** we have no idea of his whereabouts

> **NOTICIA**
>
> ▹ *Para traducir la palabra* **noticia** *al inglés, hay que tener en cuenta que el sustantivo* **news** *es incontable y lleva el verbo en singular:*
>
> **Las noticias de hoy no son nada buenas**
> Today's news isn't very good
> **Cuando recibió la noticia se puso a llorar**
> When she received the news she burst into tears
>
> ▹ *Cuando queremos precisar que se trata de una noticia en particular o de un número determinado de noticias utilizamos la expresión* **piece/pieces of news**:
>
> **Había dos noticias que nos parecieron preocupantes**
> There were two pieces of news that we found worrying
>
> *Para otros usos y ejemplos ver la entrada.*

noticiable ADJ newsworthy

noticiar ▹ CONJUG 1b VT to notify

noticiario SM (*TV, Radio*) news bulletin; (*Cine*) newsreel

noticiero ADJ **1** (*TV, Radio*) news (*antes de s*)
2 (= *portador de noticias*) news-bearing, news-giving
SM **1** (= *periódico*) newspaper, gazette
2 (*LAm*) (*TV*) news bulletin; (*Caribe*) (*Cine*) newsreel

notición* SM bombshell

noticioso ADJ **1** (*esp LAm*) [*reportaje*] news (*antes de s*); [*fuente etc*] well-informed; [*suceso*] newsworthy • **agencia noticiosa** news agency • **texto ~** news report
2† • **~ de que usted quería verme ...** hearing that you wished to see me ...
SM (*LAm*) (*TV, Radio*) news bulletin

notificación SF notification

notificar ▹ CONJUG 1g VT to notify, inform

notoriamente ADV (= *obviamente*) obviously; (= *evidentemente*) glaringly, blatantly, flagrantly • **una sentencia ~ injusta** a glaringly unjust sentence

notoriedad SF (= *fama*) fame, renown; (= *dominio público*) wide knowledge • **hechos de amplia ~** widely-known facts

notorio ADJ **1** (= *conocido*) well-known, publicly known; (= *famoso*) famous • **es ~ que ...** it is well-known that ... • **un hecho ~** a well-known fact
2 (= *obvio*) obvious; [*error*] glaring, blatant, flagrant

nov. ABR (= **noviembre**) Nov

novador(a) ADJ innovative, revolutionary
SM/F innovator

noval ADJ [*tierra*] newly-broken

novamás* SM INV • **es el ~** (= *lo mejor*) it's the ultimate; (= *lo último*) it's the latest thing

novatada SF **1** (= *burla*) rag, ragging, hazing (*EEUU*)
2 (= *error*) beginner's mistake, elementary blunder • MODISMO: • **pagar la ~** to learn the hard way

novato/a ADJ raw, green
SM/F beginner, tyro

novecientos/as ADJ, PRON (*gen*) nine hundred; (*ordinal*) nine hundredth • **línea** *o* **número ~** freefone number
SM nine hundred • **en el ~** in the twentieth century; ▹ **seiscientos**

novedad SF **1** (= *cualidad*) novelty, newness • **la ~ del método sorprendió a todos** the novelty *o* newness of the method surprised everyone
2 (= *cosa nueva*) novelty • **hace tiempo que la reflexología ha dejado de ser (una) ~** reflexology ceased to be a novelty a long time ago • **las ~es discográficas** new releases • **las últimas ~es en moda infantil** the latest in children's fashions • **¿llegó tarde? ¡vaya ~!** (*iró*) so he was late? surprise, surprise!

3 (= *cambio*) • **llegar sin ~** to arrive safely • **la jornada ha transcurrido sin ~** it has been a quiet day, it has been a normal day • **el enfermo sigue sin ~** the patient's condition is unchanged • **sin ~ en el frente** (*Mil*) (*hum*) all quiet on the Western front
4 novedades (= *noticias*) news • **cuéntame todas las ~es** tell me all the news

novedoso ADJ **1** [*idea, método*] novel, new, original
2 (*Cono Sur, Méx*) = **novelesco**

novel ADJ (= *nuevo*) new; (= *inexperto*) inexperienced • **una escritora ~** a new writer
SMF (= *principiante*) beginner, novice

novela SF novel • **la ~ española en el siglo XX** the 20th century Spanish novel ▸ **novela de amor** love story, romance ▸ **novela de aprendizaje** Bildungsroman, *novel concerned with a person's formative years* ▸ **novela de ciencia ficción** science fiction novel ▸ **novela de misterio** mystery (story) ▸ **novela epistolar** epistolary novel ▸ **novela gótica** Gothic novel ▸ **novela histórica** historical novel ▸ **novela iniciática** Bildungsroman, *novel concerned with a person's formative years* ▸ **novela negra** thriller ▸ **novela policíaca** detective story, whodunit* ▸ **novela por entregas** serial ▸ **novela radiofónica** radio serial ▸ **novela río** saga ▸ **novela rosa** romantic novel

novelación SF fictionalization

novelado ADJ fictionalized

novelar ▹ CONJUG 1a VT to make a novel out of, fictionalize
VI to write novels

novelero/a ADJ **1** (= *imaginativo*) highly imaginative
2 (= *romántico*) dreamy, romantic
3 (= *aficionado*) (*a novedades*) fond of novelty; (*a novelas*) fond of novels; (*a habladurías*) gossipy, fond of gossiping
4 [*cuento, historia*] romantic, novelettish
SM/F novel reader

novelesco ADJ **1** (*Literat*) fictional • **el género ~** fiction, the novel
2 (= *romántico*) romantic, fantastic, novelettish; [*aventura etc*] storybook (*antes de s*)

novelista SMF novelist

novelística SF • **la ~** fiction, the novel

novelón* SM big novel, epic (novel); (*pey*) pulp novel

novelucha SF (*pey*) cheap novel, pulp novel

novena SF (*Rel*) novena

noveno ADJ ninth; ▹ **sexto**

noventa ADJ INV, PRON, SM (*gen*) ninety; (*ordinal*) ninetieth • **los (años) ~** the nineties • **los escritores del ~ y ocho** the writers of the 1898 Generation; ▹ **seis**

noventayochista ADJ • **un escritor ~** a writer of the 1898 Generation

noventón/ona ADJ ninety-year-old, ninetyish
SM/F person of about ninety

novia‡ SF (*Mil*) rifle, gun, rod (*EEUU*); ▹ **novio**

noviar ▹ CONJUG 1b VI • **~ con** (*Cono Sur*) to go out with, date, court (*frm*)

noviazgo SM engagement

noviciado SM (*gen*) apprenticeship, training; (*Rel*) novitiate

novicio/a SM/F (*gen*) beginner, novice; (= *aprendiz*) apprentice; (*Rel*) novice

noviembre SM November; ▹ **septiembre**

noviero* ADJ • **es muy ~** (*gen*) he has had lots of girlfriends; (= *enamoradizo*) he's always falling in love

novilla SF heifer

novillada SF (*Taur*) training fight (*bullfight with young bulls and novice bullfighters*)

novillero/a SM/F **1** (*Taur*) apprentice bullfighter, novice
2 (*Escol**) truant

novillo SM **1** (*Zool*) young bull, bullock, steer (*EEUU*)
2 novillos (*Taur*) = **novillada**
3 • MODISMO: • **hacer ~s** (*gen*) to stay away, not turn up, skive off*; (*Escol*) to play truant, play hooky (*EEUU**), skive off*

novilunio SM (*Astron*) new moon

novio/a SM/F (= *amigo*) boyfriend/ girlfriend, sweetheart†; (= *prometido*) fiancé/ fiancée; (*en boda*) (bride)groom/bride; (= *recién casado*) newly-married man/woman • **los ~s** (= *prometidos*) the engaged couple; (*en boda*) the bride and groom; (= *recién casados*) the newly-weds • **ser ~s formales** to be formally engaged • **viaje de ~s** honeymoon

novísimo ADJ (*gen*) newest, latest, most recent; (*Com*) brand-new

ns ABR (= **no sabe(n)**) *don't know(s)*

N.S. ABR = **Nuestro Señor**

ns/nc ABR (= **no sabe(n)/no contesta(n)**) *don't know(s)*

N.T. ABR **1** (*Rel*) (= **Nuevo Testamento**) NT
2 (*Téc*) = **nuevas tecnologías**

ntra. ABR = **nuestra**

ntro. ABR = **nuestro**

NU SFPL ABR (= **Naciones Unidas**) UN

nubada SF, **nubarrada** SF **1** (= *chaparrón*) downpour, sudden heavy shower
2 (*fig*) abundance

nubarrón SM storm cloud

nube SF **1** (*gen*) cloud ▸ **nube de lluvia** rain-cloud ▸ **nube de tormenta** storm cloud ▸ **nube de verano** (*lit*) summer shower; (*fig*) brief burst of annoyance
2 [*de humo, insectos, polvo*] cloud; [*de gente*] crowd, multitude • **una ~ de periodistas** a crowd *o* pack of journalists • **una ~ de críticas** a storm of criticism • **una ~ de pordioseros** a swarm of beggars
3 (*Med*) (*en el ojo*) cloud, film
4 • MODISMOS: • **andar por las ~s** • **estar en las ~s** to have one's head in the clouds • **estar en una ~** to be on cloud nine • **los precios están por las ~s** prices are sky high • **poner a algn en** *o* **por** *o* **sobre las ~s** to praise sb to the skies • **ponerse por las ~s** [*persona*] to go up the wall*; [*precio*] to rocket, soar
5 (*Internet*) **la ~** the cloud • **computación en la ~** cloud computing
6 (= *golosina*) candy-floss, cotton candy (*EEUU*)

núbil ADJ nubile

nublado ADJ [*cielo*] cloudy, overcast
SM **1** (= *nube*) storm cloud, black cloud
2 (= *amenaza*) threat; (= *peligro*) impending danger
3 (= *enfado*) anger, black mood • MODISMO: • **pasó el ~** the trouble's over
4 (= *multitud*) swarm, crowd, multitude

nublar ▹ CONJUG 1a VT **1** (*gen*) to darken, obscure
2 [+ *vista, mente*] to cloud; [+ *razón*] to affect, cloud; [+ *felicidad*] to cloud, mar
VPR **nublarse** to become cloudy, cloud over

nublazón SM (*LAm*) = **nublado**

nublo ADJ (*LAm*) cloudy

nubloso ADJ **1** [*cielo*] cloudy
2 (= *desafortunado*) unlucky, unfortunate; (= *triste*) gloomy

nubosidad SF cloudiness, clouds (*pl*) • **habrá ~ de desarrollo** *o* **evolución** it will become increasingly cloudy

nuboso ADJ cloudy

nubuck SM nubuck

nuca SF nape (of the neck), back of the neck

nuclear ADJ (*gen*) nuclear • **central ~** nuclear power station
SF (= *central nuclear*) nuclear power station
VT ▹ CONJUG 1a **1** (= *reunir*) to bring together; (= *combinar*) to combine; (= *concentrar*) to concentrate; [+ *miembros etc*] to provide a focus for, act as a forum for
2 (= *liderar*) to lead

nuclearización SF (= *proceso*) introduction of nuclear energy (**de** to); [*de un país*] conversion to nuclear energy

nuclearizado ADJ • **países ~s** countries possessing nuclear weapons

nuclearizarse ▹ CONJUG 1f VPR **1** (*Elec*) to build nuclear power stations, go nuclear
2 (*Mil*) to make *o* acquire nuclear weapons

nucleizar ▹ CONJUG 1f VT = **nuclear**

núcleo SM (*Bio, Fís, Quím*) nucleus; (*Elec*) core; (*Bot*) kernel, stone; (*fig*) core, essence ▸ **núcleo de población** population centre, population center (*EEUU*) ▸ **núcleo duro** hard core ▸ **núcleo rural** (new) village, village settlement ▸ **núcleo tormentoso** thunderstorm ▸ **núcleo urbano** city centre, city center (*EEUU*)

nudillo SM knuckle

nudismo SM nudism

nudista SMF nudist

nudo¹ ADJ • **nuda propiedad** bare ownership, bare title to property

nudo² SM **1** (*en hilo, cuerda*) knot • **el ~ de la corbata** the tie knot • **no sabe hacerse el ~ de la corbata** he doesn't know how to tie his tie • **atar con un ~** to tie in a knot • MODISMO: • **un ~ en la garganta** a lump in one's throat • **se me hizo un ~ en la garganta** I got a lump in my throat ▸ **nudo corredizo** slipknot ▸ **nudo de rizos** reef knot ▸ **nudo gordiano** Gordian knot ▸ **nudo llano, nudo marinero** reef knot
2 [*de carreteras, ferrocarriles*] junction
3 (= *vínculo*) bond, tie
4 [*de problema, cuestión*] core, crux; [*de obra, narración*] crisis, point of greatest complexity
5 (*en tallo*) node; (*en madera*) knot

nudoso ADJ [*madera*] knotty, full of knots; [*tronco*] gnarled; [*bastón*] knobbly, knobby (*EEUU*)

nueces SFPL *de* **nuez**

nuégado SM nougat

nuera SF daughter-in-law

nuestro/a ADJ POSES our; (*tras sustantivo*) of ours • **~ perro** our dog • **~s hijos** our children • **un barco ~** a boat of ours, one of our boats • **un amigo ~** a friend of ours
PRON POSES ours • **—¿de quién es esto? —es ~** "whose is this?" — "it's ours" • **esta casa es la nuestra** this house is ours • **es el ~** it is ours • **el tenis no nos gusta, lo ~ es el fútbol** we don't like tennis, we're more into football • **no servimos para pintar, lo ~ es la fotografía** we're no use at painting, we're better at photography • **los ~s** (= *nuestra familia*) our people, our family; (*Dep*) (= *nuestro equipo*) our men, our side • **es de los ~s** he's one of ours, he's one of us

nueva SF (= *noticia*) piece of news • **~s** news • MODISMOS: • **coger a algn de ~s** to take sb by surprise • **me cogió de ~s** it took me by surprise, it was news to me • **hacerse de ~s** to pretend to be surprised

Nueva Caledonia SF New Caledonia

Nueva Delhi SF New Delhi

Nueva Escocia SF Nova Scotia

Nueva Gales SF (*tb* **Nueva Gales del Sur**) New South Wales

Nueva Guinea SF New Guinea

Nueva Inglaterra SF New England

nuevamente ADV again

nuevaolero ADJ new-wave (*antes de s*)

n

Nueva Orleáns SF New Orleans
Nueva York SF New York
Nueva Zelanda SF, **Nueva Zelandia** SF (*LAm*) New Zealand
nueve ADJ INV, PRON (*gen*) nine; (*ordinal, en la fecha*) ninth • **las ~** nine o'clock • **le escribí el día ~** I wrote to him on the ninth
SM (= *número*) nine; (= *fecha*) ninth; ▹ **seis**
nuevecito ADJ brand-new
nuevo ADJ **1** (= *no usado*) new • **ha presentado su nueva película** he launched his new film • **la casa es nueva** the house is new • **la casa está nueva** the house is as good as new • **como ~: estos pantalones están como ~s** these trousers are just like new • **con una mano de pintura quedará como ~** it'll look like new after a coat of paint • **después de una buena siesta quedarás como ~** you'll feel like new after a good nap • MODISMO: • **no hay nada ~ bajo el sol** there's nothing new under the sun
2 (= *recién llegado*) new • **es ~ en el oficio** he's new to the trade • **es ~ en la ciudad** he's new to the town • **soy ~ en el colegio** I'm new at the school
3 • **de ~** (= *otra vez*) again • **tuve que leer el libro de ~** I had to read the book again
nuevomexicano/a ADJ New Mexican
SM/F New Mexican • **los ~s** the New Mexicans, the people of New Mexico
Nuevo México SM New Mexico
nuez SF **1** (= *fruto*) (*gen*) nut; [*del nogal*] walnut; (*Méx*) pecan nut ▸ **nuez de Brasil** Brazil nut ▸ **nuez de Castilla** (*Méx*) walnut ▸ **nuez de la India** (*Méx*) cashew nut ▸ **nuez de Pará** Brazil nut ▸ **nuez moscada** nutmeg ▸ **nuez nogal** (*Méx*) walnut
2 (*Anat*) (*tb* **nuez de Adán**) Adam's apple
nulidad SF **1** (*Jur*) nullity
2 (= *incapacidad*) incompetence, incapacity
3 (= *persona*) nonentity • **es una ~** he's a dead loss*, he's useless
nulo ADJ **1** (*Jur*) void, null, null and void • **~ y sin efecto** null and void • **el matrimonio fue declarado ~** the marriage was annulled
2 [*persona*] useless*, hopeless* • **es ~ para la música** he's useless at music*
3 (*en boxeo*) • **combate ~** draw
SMPL **nulos** (*Naipes*) misère (*sing*) • **bridge con ~s** bridge with the misère variation
núm. ABR (= **número**) No., no.
Numancia SF **1** (*Hist*) Numantia
2 (*fig*) *symbol of heroic or last-ditch resistance*
numantino/a ADJ **1** (*Hist*) of/from Numantia
2 [*resistencia*] heroic, last-ditch; (*pey*) diehard, stubborn
SM/F native/inhabitant of Numantia • **los ~s** the people of Numantia
numen SM **1** (*Literat*) (= *inspiración*) inspiration ▸ **numen poético** poetic inspiration
2 (= *deidad*) numen
numeración SF **1** (= *acto*) numeration, numbering
2 (= *números*) numbers (*pl*), numerals (*pl*) ▸ **numeración arábiga** Arabic numerals (*pl*) ▸ **numeración de línea** (*Inform*) line numbering ▸ **numeración romana** Roman numerals (*pl*)
numerador SM numerator
numeral ADJ numeral, number (*antes de s*)
SM numeral
numerar ▹ CONJUG 1a VT (*gen*) to number • **páginas sin ~** unnumbered pages
VPR **numerarse** (*Mil etc*) to number off
numerario ADJ **1** (*del número*) numerary
2 [*socio, miembro*] full; [*catedrático*] tenured • **profesor ~** permanent member of teaching staff • **no ~** non-established
SM (*Econ*) cash, hard cash
numerero* ADJ over-the-top, outrageous
numéricamente ADV numerically
numérico ADJ (*gen*) numerical; (*Inform*) numeric
numerito SM (*Teat*) short act; [*de relleno*] fill-in act • MODISMO: • **montar el** *o* **un ~*** to make a scene, kick up a fuss
número SM **1** (*Mat*) number • **en ~s redondos** in round numbers • **estar en ~s rojos** to be in the red • **volver a ~s negros** to get back into the black, return to profitability • **de ~**: • **miembro de ~** full member • **profesor de ~** tenured teacher, teacher with a permanent post • **echar** *o* **hacer ~s*** to do one's sums, number-crunch • **sin ~**: • **calle Aribau, sin ~** Aribau street, no number • **problemas sin ~** countless problems ▸ **número arábigo** Arabic numeral ▸ **número binario** (*Inform*) binary number ▸ **número cardinal** cardinal number ▸ **número de identificación fiscal** *ID number used for tax purposes* ▸ **número de lote** batch number, batch code ▸ **número de matrícula** (*Aut*) registration number ▸ **número de referencia** reference number ▸ **número de serie** serial number ▸ **número de teléfono** telephone number, phone number ▸ **número dos** (*lit*) number two • **el ~ dos del partido** the second in command of the party, the party's number two ▸ **número entero** whole number ▸ **número fraccionario** fraction ▸ **número impar** odd number ▸ **número negativo** negative number ▸ **número ordinal** ordinal number ▸ **número par** even number ▸ **número perfecto** perfect number ▸ **número personal de identificación** (= *clave*) personal identification number ▸ **número primo** prime number ▸ **número quebrado** fraction ▸ **número romano** Roman numeral ▸ **número uno** number one • **para mí, Sinatra será siempre el ~ uno** for me Sinatra will always be number one • **el jugador ~ uno de su país** the number one player in his country, the top player in his country
2 [*de zapatos*] size
3 [*de periódico, revista*] number, issue ▸ **número atrasado** back number ▸ **número cero** dummy number, dummy run ▸ **número extraordinario** special edition, special issue ▸ **número suelto** single issue
4 (= *billete de lotería*) ticket
5 (*Teat*) act, number • MODISMO: • **montar el** *o* **un ~*** to make a scene, kick up a fuss
6 (*Gram*) number
7 (*Mil*) man; (= *soldado raso*) private; (= *policía*) policeman • **un sargento y cuatro ~s** a sergeant and four men
numerología SF numerology
numerológico ADJ numerological
numeroso ADJ numerous • **familia numerosa** large family
numerus clausus SM *system of restricted entry (to university etc)*, quota system
numísmata SMF numismatist
numismática SF numismatics (*sing*)
numismático/a ADJ numismatic
SM/F numismatist
núms. ABR (= **números**) Nos, nos
nunca ADV never • **no viene ~** he never comes • **~ volveré a confiar en ella** I'll never trust her again • **ninguno de nosotros había esquiado ~** neither of us had ever skied before • **¿has visto ~ cosa igual?** have you ever seen anything like this? • **casi ~ me escribe** he hardly ever writes to me • **¡hasta ~!** I don't care if I never see you again! • **~ jamás** never ever • **no lo he visto ~ jamás** I've never ever seen it • **no lo haré ~ jamás** I'll never ever do it again • **~ más**: • **no lo hizo ~ más** he never did it again • **no lo veré ~ más** I'll never see him again • **más que ~** more than ever • **~ mejor dicho**: • **el primer paso hacia el coche popular lo dio - ~ mejor dicho - el Volkswagen** the first step towards a popular car was the appropriately-named Volkswagen • REFRÁN: • **~ es tarde si la dicha es buena** better late than never
nunciatura SF nunciature
nuncio SM **1** (*Rel*) nuncio • MODISMOS: • **¡cuéntaselo al ~!** tell that to the marines! • **¡que lo haga el ~!** get somebody else to do it! ▸ **nuncio apostólico, nuncio pontificio** papal nuncio
2 (= *mensajero*) messenger; (*liter*) herald, harbinger ▸ **nuncio de la primavera** harbinger of spring
nunquita ADV (*LAm*) = **nunca**
nupcial ADJ wedding (*antes de s*), nuptial (*frm*)
nupcialidad SF rate of marriage, marriage statistics
nupcias SFPL wedding (*sing*), nuptials (*frm*) • **casarse en segundas ~** to marry again, get married for the second time, remarry • **Jesús, que se casó en segundas ~ con Rosa** Jesús, who got married for the second time to Rosa
nurse ['nurse] SF **1** (*LAm*) (= *enfermera*) nurse
2 (= *institutriz*) governess; (= *niñera*) nursemaid
nutria SF otter
nutrición SF nutrition
nutricional ADJ nutritional
nutricionista SMF nutritionist
nutrido ADJ **1** (= *alimentado*) • **bien ~** well-nourished • **mal ~** undernourished, malnourished
2 (= *grande*) large, considerable; (= *numeroso*) numerous; (= *abundante*) abundant • **una nutrida concurrencia** a large crowd, a large attendance • **~ de** full of, abounding in (*frm*) • **fuego ~** (*Mil*) heavy fire • **~s aplausos** enthusiastic applause
nutriente SM nutrient
nutrimento SM nutriment, nourishment
nutrir ▹ CONJUG 3a VT **1** (= *alimentar*) to feed, nourish
2 (= *fortalecer*) [+ *confianza, relaciones*] to strengthen
3 (= *proveer*) (*de agua, ayuda*) to provide
4 (= *llenar*) to fill
VPR **nutrirse 1** (= *alimentarse*) to receive nourishment
2 (= *fortalecerse*) to feed (**de** on)
3 (= *abastecerse*) • **el acuífero del que se venía nutriendo el río** the aquifer which fed the river • **las multinacionales que se nutren de las ayudas públicas** the multinationals which have been benefitting from State aid
nutritivo ADJ nutritious, nourishing • **valor ~** nutritional value, food value
nylon ['nailon] SM nylon

Ññ

Ñ, ñ ['eɲe] SF (= *letra*) Ñ, ñ
ña* SF (*LAm*) = **doña**
ñaca* EXCL (*para dar envidia*) so there!
ñaca-ñaca‡ SM rumpy-pumpy‡
ñácara SF (*CAm*) ulcer, sore
ñaco SM (*Méx*) popcorn
ñafiar ▷ CONJUG 1b VT (*Caribe*) to pilfer
ñam* EXCL • **¡ñam ñam!** yum yum!*
ñame SM yam
ñandú SM (*Cono Sur*) South American ostrich, rhea
ñandutí SM (*Cono Sur*) Paraguayan lace
ñanga SF **1** (*CAm*) (= *pantano*) marsh, swampy ground
2 (*And*) (= *trozo*) bit, small portion
ñangada SF (*CAm*) **1** (= *mordedura*) nip, bite
2* (= *tontería*) • **¡qué ~ hiciste!*** that was a stupid thing to do!
ñangado ADJ (*Caribe*) (= *patizambo*) knock-kneed; (= *estevado*) bow-legged
ñangara SMF (*Caribe*) (*Pol*) guerrilla
ñango* ADJ (*LAm*) awkward, clumsy
ñangotarse* ▷ CONJUG 1a VPR (*And, Caribe*)
1 (= *agacharse*) to squat, crouch down
2 (= *desanimarse*) to lose heart
ñangué SM • **en los tiempos de ~** (*And**) way back, in the dim and distant past
ñaña* SF (*LAm*) (= *nodriza*) nursemaid, wet nurse
ñaño/a* (*LAm*) ADJ [*amigo*] close; (= *consentido*) spoiled
SM/F (= *amigo*) friend; (= *hermano mayor*) elder brother/sister
ñapa SF (*LAm*) (= *prima*) extra, bonus; (= *propina*) tip • **de ~** as an extra
ñapango SM (*Col*) mulatto, mestizo
ñaque SM junk
ñata¹ SF (*And*) (= *muerte*) death
ñata²* SF (*LAm*), **ñatas*** SFPL (*LAm*) nose, conk*
ñato ADJ (*LAm*) flat-nosed, snub-nosed
ñau EXCL (*LAm*) mew, miaow • **hacer ñau ñau** (*lit*) to miaow, mew; (= *arañar*) to scratch
ñauar ▷ CONJUG 1a VI (*LAm*) to miaow, mew
ñeque* SM (*And, Cono Sur*) (= *fuerza*) strength
ñique* SM (*CAm, Cono Sur*) (= *cabezazo*) butt with the head; (*CAm*) (= *puñetazo*) punch
ñiquiñaque SM **1** (= *trastos*) trash, junk
2 (= *persona*) worthless individual
ñisca SF **1** (*And, CAm, Cono Sur*) (= *pedazo*) bit, small piece
2 (*And, CAm‡*) (= *excremento*) crap**
ño* SM (*LAm*) = **don²**
ñoca SF (*And*) crack, fissure
ñoco ADJ (*LAm*) (= *sin un dedo*) lacking a finger; (= *manco*) one-handed
ñola SF **1** (*And, CAm‡*) (= *excremento*) crap**
2 (*CAm**) (= *úlcera*) ulcer, sore
ñongarse ▷ CONJUG 1h VPR (*And*)
1 (= *agacharse*) to squat, crouch down
2 • **~ el pie** to twist one's foot
ñongo ADJ **1** (*Caribe, Cono Sur, Méx**) (= *estúpido*) stupid; (*Cono Sur*) (= *lento*) slow, lazy; (= *perdido*) good-for-nothing; (= *humilde*) creepy
2 (*And, Caribe*) (= *lisiado*) crippled
3 (*Caribe*) (= *tramposo*) tricky, deceitful; (= *feo*) unsightly; (= *infausto*) of ill omen; (= *quisquilloso*) touchy
ñoña** SF (*Chile, Ecu*) shit**; ▷ **ñoño**
ñoñería SF, **ñoñez** SF **1** (= *sosería*) insipidness
2 (= *falta de carácter*) spinelessness; (= *melindres*) fussiness
ñoño/a ADJ **1** (= *soso*) characterless, insipid
2 [*persona*] (= *débil*) spineless; (= *melindroso*) fussy, finicky
SM/F spineless person, drip*; ▷ **ñoña**
ñoqui SM **1 ñoquis** (*Culin*) gnocchi
2 (*Cono Sur**) (= *golpe*) thump
ñorba SF (*And*), **ñorbo** SM (*And*) passionflower
ñorda** SF turd**, shit** • **¡una ~!** get away!* • **ser una ~** to be a shit**
ñu SM gnu
ñuco ADJ (*And*) [*animal*] dehorned; [*persona*] limbless
ñudo • **al ~** ADV (*LAm*) in vain
ñudoso ADJ = **nudoso**
ñufla* ADJ worthless
SF (*Cono Sur*) piece of junk
ñuño* SF (*And*) wet-nurse
ñusca‡ SF (*And*) crap**
ñusta SF (*And*) (*Hist*) princess of royal blood
ñutir ▷ CONJUG 3a VI (*And*) to grunt
ñuto* ADJ (*And*) crushed, ground

Oo

O[1], o[1] [o] SF (= *letra*) O, o
O[2] ABR **1** (*Geog*) (= **oeste**) W
2 (= **octubre**) Oct
o[2] CONJ or • **o … o** either … or; ▹ **ser**
o[3] ABR (*Com*) (= **orden**) o
ó CONJ or • **5 ó 6** 5 or 6
OACI SF ABR (= **Organización de la Aviación Civil Internacional**) ICAO
oasis SM INV oasis
ob. ABR, **obpo.** ABR (= **obispo**) Bp
obcecación SF (= *ofuscación*) blindness; (= *terquedad*) blind obstinacy • **en un momento de ~** in a moment of blind rage
obcecadamente ADV (= *con ofuscación*) blindly; (= *con terquedad*) obstinately, stubbornly, obdurately (*frm*)
obcecado ADJ (= *ofuscado*) blind, mentally blinded; (= *terco*) obstinate, stubborn, obdurate (*frm*); (= *trastornado*) disturbed
obcecamiento SM = **obcecación**
obcecar ▹ CONJUG 1g VT (= *ofuscar*) to blind (mentally); (= *trastornar*) to disturb the mind of • **el amor lo ha obcecado** love has blinded him (to all else)
VPR **obcecarse** to become obsessed • **~se con una idea** to become obsessed with an idea
ob. cit. ABR (= **obra citada**) op. cit.
obducción SF obduction
obedecer ▹ CONJUG 2d VT, VI **1** [+ *persona, norma*] to obey • **~ a algn** to obey sb, do as sb says
2 (= *deberse*) • **~ a algo** to be due to sth • **los síntomas obedecen a una reacción alérgica** the symptoms are due to an allergic reaction • **su viaje obedece a dos motivos** there are two reasons for his journey, his journey is due to two reasons • **~ al hecho de que …** to be due to …, arise from …
3 [*mecanismo*] to respond • **el volante no me obedecía** the steering wheel did not respond
obediencia SF obedience
obediente ADJ obedient
obelisco SM **1** (= *monumento*) obelisk
2 (*Tip*) dagger
obenques SMPL (*Náut*) shrouds
obertura SF overture
obesidad SF obesity
obeso ADJ obese
óbice SM obstacle, impediment • **eso no es ~ para que lo haga** that should not prevent him (from) *o* stop him doing it
obispado SM bishopric
obispo SM bishop
óbito SM (*liter*) death
obituario SM **1** (= *esquela*) obituary; (= *sección de periódico*) obituary section
2 (*Rel*) (= *registro*) register of deaths and burials
objeción SF objection • **poner objeciones** to object to, make *o* raise objections • **no ponen ninguna ~** they don't object, they make *o* raise no objection ▸ **objeción de conciencia** conscientious objection
objetable ADJ (= *criticable*) open to objection; (= *inaceptable*) objectionable
objetante SMF (*gen*) objector; (*en mitin*) heckler
objetar ▹ CONJUG 1a VT (*gen*) to object; [+ *argumento, plan*] to put forward, present • **¿algo que ~?** any objections? • **le objeté que no había dinero suficiente** I pointed out to him that there was not enough money
VI (*Mil*) to be a conscientious objector
objetivamente ADV objectively
objetivar ▹ CONJUG 1a VT to objectify, put in objective terms
objetividad SF objectivity
objetivo ADJ objective
SM **1** (= *propósito*) objective, aim
2 (*Mil*) objective, target
3 (*Fot*) lens ▸ **objetivo zoom** zoom lens
objeto SM **1** (= *cosa*) object • **"objetos perdidos"** "lost property" ▸ **objeto contundente** blunt instrument ▸ **objeto de arte** objet d'art ▸ **objetos de escritorio** writing materials ▸ **objetos de regalo** giftware (*sing*), gifts ▸ **objetos de tocador** toilet articles ▸ **objetos de valor** valuables ▸ **objeto sexual** sex object ▸ **objeto volante no identificado** unidentified flying object
2 (= *propósito*) object, aim • **desconocían el ~ de su visita** they did not know the object *o* aim of his visit • **al** *o* **con ~ de hacer algo** with the object *o* aim of doing sth • **estas medidas tienen por ~ reducir la inflación** the aim of these measures is to reduce inflation • **no tiene ~ que sigas preguntándome** there's no point in you continuing to ask me, it's no use you continuing to ask me
3 (= *blanco*) object • **me hizo ~ de sus obsesiones** I became the object of his obsessions • **fue ~ de sus burlas** she was the butt of their jokes • **fue ~ de un asalto** he was the target of an attack, he suffered an attack
4 (*Ling*) object ▸ **objeto directo** direct object ▸ **objeto indirecto** indirect object
objetor(a) SM/F objector ▸ **objetor(a) de conciencia** conscientious objector
oblación SF oblation, offering
oblar ▹ CONJUG 1a VT (*Cono Sur*) [+ *deuda*] to pay in cash
oblata SF oblation, offering
oblea SF **1** (= *galleta*) (*Culin*) wafer-thin slice; (*Rel*) wafer • MODISMO: • **quedar como una ~** to be as thin as a rake
2 (*Inform*) chip, wafer
3 (*Cono Sur*) (*Correos*) stamp
oblicua SF (*Mat*) oblique line
oblicuamente ADV obliquely
oblicuar ▹ CONJUG 1d VT to slant, place obliquely, cant, tilt
VI to deviate from the perpendicular
oblicuidad SF obliquity, oblique angle, oblique position
oblicuo ADJ [*línea*] oblique; [*ojos*] slanting; [*mirada*] sidelong
obligación SF **1** (= *responsabilidad*) obligation, duty • **cumplir con una ~** to fulfil an obligation • **faltar a sus obligaciones** to fail in one's obligations *o* duty, neglect one's obligations *o* duty • **tener ~ de hacer algo** to have a duty to do sth, be under an obligation to do sth • REFRÁN: • **primero es la ~ que la devoción** business before pleasure
2 (*Com, Econ*) bond, security ▸ **obligación convertible** convertible bond, convertible debenture ▸ **obligación de banco** bank bill ▸ **obligaciones del Estado** government bonds, government securities ▸ **obligación tributaria** (*Méx*) tax liability
obligacional ADJ compulsory, binding
obligacionista SMF bondholder
obligado ADJ **1** (= *forzado*) forced • **no estás ~ a dar dinero** you're not being forced to give money • **se vieron ~s a vender su casa** they were forced to sell their house • **no te sientas obligada a venir** don't feel obliged to come
2 (= *obligatorio*) • **normas de ~ cumplimiento** regulations that must be complied with
3 (= *inexcusable*) • **es ~ hacerle una visita** you're expected to pay her a visit • **este museo es visita obligada para el amante del arte** this museum is a must for the art lover
4 (*frm*) (= *agradecido*) • **estar** *o* **quedar ~ a algn** to be obliged to sb, be in sb's debt
SM (*Mús*) obbligato
obligar ▹ CONJUG 1h VT **1** (= *forzar*) to force • **~ a algn a hacer algo** to force sb to do sth • **me han obligado a venir** they forced me to come • **la obligan a estudiar francés** they make her study French
2 [*ley, norma*] • **la disposición obliga a todos los contribuyentes** all taxpayers are bound to observe this requirement, this requirement is binding on all taxpayers
3 (= *empujar*) to force • **solo se puede cerrar el cajón obligándolo** you can't get the drawer shut except by forcing it
VPR **obligarse** • **tengo que ~me a ir al gimnasio cada día** I have to force myself to go to the gym every day • **me obligo a cumplir los términos del contrato** (*frm*) I undertake to fulfil the terms of the contract
obligatoriamente ADV **1** (= *preceptivamente*) compulsorily
2 (= *forzosamente*) of necessity
obligatoriedad SF obligatory nature • **de ~ jurídica** legally binding
obligatorio ADJ (= *preceptivo*) (*gen*) obligatory, compulsory; [*promesa, acuerdo*] binding • **es ~ hacerlo** it is obligatory to do it • **escolaridad obligatoria** compulsory schooling
obliteración SF (*Med*) obliteration
obliterar ▹ CONJUG 1a VT **1** (*Med*) (*gen*) to obliterate; [+ *herida*] to staunch

2 (= *inutilizar*) to obliterate, destroy
oblongo ADJ oblong
obnubilación SF = **ofuscación**
obnubilar ▷ CONJUG 1a VT = **ofuscar**
oboe SM (= *instrumento*) oboe
SMF (= *músico*) oboist, oboe player
oboísta SMF oboist
óbolo SM mite, small contribution • **~ de San Pedro** Peter's pence
obra SF **1** (= *acción*) deed • **hoy he hecho una buena ~** I did a good deed today • **pecar de ~** to sin by deed • **buenas ~s** good works, good deeds • **ser ~ de algn** to be sb's doing • **esto no puede ser ~ de mi hijo** this can't be my son's doing • **la policía cree que podría ser ~ de la Mafia** the police think this could be the work of the Mafia • **poner por ~ un plan** to set a plan in motion • **por ~ (y gracia) de** thanks to • **un país destrozado por ~ del turismo** a country totally spoilt by tourism • **una gimnasta convertida en ídolo mundial por ~ y gracia de su entrenador** a gymnast who became a world famous idol thanks to her coach • **por ~ y gracia del Espíritu Santo** (*Rel*) through the working of the Holy Spirit, by the power of the Holy Spirit • **cree que el trabajo va a estar terminado mañana por ~ y gracia del Espíritu Santo** (*iró*) he thinks that the work will miraculously get done tomorrow • MODISMO: • **ser ~ de romanos** to be a huge task, be a herculean task • REFRÁN: • **~s son amores y no buenas razones** actions speak louder than words ▸ **obra benéfica** (= *acción*) charitable deed; (= *organización*) charitable organization, charity • **el dinero se destinará a ~s benéficas** the money will go to charity ▸ **obra de caridad** charitable deed, act of charity ▸ **obra de misericordia** (*Rel*) work of mercy ▸ **obra pía** religious foundation ▸ **obra piadosa** charitable deed ▸ **obra social** (= *organización*) *benevolent fund for arts, sports etc*; (= *labor*) charitable work
2 [*de creación artística*] **a** (= *producción total*) (*Arte, Literat, Teat, Mús*) work • **la vida y la ~ de San Juan de la Cruz** the life and work of Saint John of the Cross • **el tema de la muerte en la ~ de Lorca** the subject of death in Lorca *o* in Lorca's work
b (= *pieza*) (*Arte, Mús*) work; (*Teat*) play; (*Literat*) book, work • **una ~ de Goya** a work *o* painting by Goya • **una ~ de Lope de Vega** a play by Lope de Vega • **las ~s de Cervantes** the works of Cervantes • **~s completas** complete works, collected works ▸ **obra de arte** work of art ▸ **obra de consulta** reference book ▸ **obra de divulgación** *non-fiction book aimed at a popular audience* ▸ **obra de teatro, obra dramática** play ▸ **obra maestra** masterpiece ▸ **obra teatral** play
3 (*Constr*) **a** (= *edificio en construcción*) building site, construction site • **hemos estado visitando la ~** we've been visiting the building *o* construction site • **¿cuándo acaban la ~?** when do they finish the building work? • MODISMO: • **ser** *o* **parecer la ~ del Escorial** to be a never-ending job
b • **de ~** [*chimenea*] brick (*antes de s*); [*estantería, armario*] built-in
c obras (*en edificio*) building work (*sing*), construction work (*sing*); (*en carretera*) roadworks • **las ~s de construcción del hospital** building *o* construction work on the hospital • **las ~s de remodelación del estadio** redevelopment work at the stadium • **las ~s de ampliación del aeropuerto** work on expanding the airport • **los vecinos están de ~s** they're having building work done next door, they have the builders in next door* • **"obras"** (*en edificio*) "building under construction"; (*en carretera*) "roadworks" • **"cerrado por obras"** "closed for refurbishment" • **"página en obras"** (*Internet*) "site under construction" • **la autopista está en ~s** there are roadworks on the motorway • **estamos haciendo ~s en la cocina** we're having some building work done in the kitchen ▸ **obras públicas** public works • **Ministerio de Obras Públicas** Ministry of Public Works ▸ **obras viales, obras viarias** roadworks
4 (= *ejecución*) workmanship • **la ~ es buena pero los materiales son de mala calidad** the workmanship is good but the materials are of a poor quality • MODISMO: • **poner manos a la ~** to get down to work; ▷ **mano**
5 (*Chile*) brickwork
6 • **~ de** about • **en ~ de ocho semanas** in about eight weeks
7 • **la Obra** (*Esp*) (*Rel*) Opus Dei; ▷ OPUS DEI
obradera* SF (*And, CAm*) (*euf*) diarrhoea, diarrhea (*EEUU*)
obrador SM [*de artesano*] workshop, workroom; [*de pastelería*] bakery
obraje SM **1** (*Cono Sur*) (= *aserradero*) sawmill, timberyard
2 (*Méx*) (= *carnicería*) pork butcher's, pork butcher's shop
3 (*And*) (= *fábrica textil*) textile plant
obrajero SM **1** (*Cono Sur*) (= *maderero*) timber merchant
2 (*Bol*) (= *artesano*) craftsman, skilled worker
3 (*Méx*) (= *carnicero*) pork butcher
obrar ▷ CONJUG 1a VI **1** (= *actuar*) to act • **~on correctamente en todo momento** they acted correctly at all times • **debemos ~ de acuerdo con nuestra conciencia** we must act in accordance with our consciences • **~ con precaución** to act cautiously
2 (= *tener efecto*) [*medicinas*] to work, have an effect
3 (*frm*) (= *estar*) • **~ en manos** *o* **en poder de algn** to be in sb's possession • **los dos documentos obran ya en poder del abogado** both documents are now in the possession of the lawyer
4 (= *hacer obras*) to have building work done, do building work
5 (*euf*) (= *defecar*) to go*, go to the toilet *o* (*EEUU*) bathroom, pass a stool (*euf*)
VT **1** (*frm*) [+ *mejoría*] to make; [+ *milagro*] to work • **el medicamento no obró ningún efecto en el enfermo** the medicine had no effect on *o* did not work on the patient
2 (= *trabajar*) [+ *madera*] to work
3 (*Cono Sur*) (= *construir*) to build
obrerado SM work force
obrerismo SM labour movement, labor movement (*EEUU*)
obrero/a ADJ [*clase*] working; [*movimiento*] labour (*antes de s*), labor (*antes de s*) (*EEUU*) • **condiciones obreras** working conditions
SM/F (= *empleado*) worker; (= *peón*) labourer, laborer (*EEUU*) ▸ **obrero/a autónomo/a** self-employed worker ▸ **obrero/a cualificado/a** skilled worker ▸ **obrero/a escenógrafo/a** stagehand ▸ **obrero/a especializado/a** skilled worker ▸ **obrero/a portuario/a** dock worker
obscenamente ADV obscenely
obscenidad SF obscenity
obsceno ADJ obscene
obscu… ▷ **oscu…**
obsecuente ADJ humble, obsequious
obseder ▷ CONJUG 2a VT (*LAm*) to obsess
obsequiar ▷ CONJUG 1b VT **1** (= *regalar*) • **le ~on un reloj** they presented him with a watch, they gave him a watch
2 (*Esp*) (= *agasajar*) • **lo van a ~ con un banquete** they are going to hold a dinner in his honour *o* (*EEUU*) honor
obsequio SM **1** (= *regalo*) (*gen*) gift, present; (*para jubilado*) presentation; (*Com*) free gift • **ejemplar de ~** complimentary copy
2 (*frm*) (= *agasajo*) courtesy, kindness • **en ~ de** in honour *o* (*EEUU*) honor of • **hágame el ~ de** (+ *infin*) do me the kindness of (+ *ger*)
obsequiosamente ADV **1** (= *servicialmente*) deferentially, obligingly
2 (= *aduladoramente*) obsequiously
obsequiosidad SF **1** (= *amabilidad*) deference, complaisance
2 (= *adulación*) obsequiousness
obsequioso ADJ **1** (= *servicial*) deferential, obliging
2 (= *adulador*) obsequious
3 (*Méx*) (= *dadivoso*) fond of giving presents
observable ADJ observable
observación SF **1** (= *acto*) (*gen*) observation; (*Jur*) observance • **estar en ~** to be under observation ▸ **observación de aves** birdwatching ▸ **observación postal** interception of mail
2 (= *comentario*) remark, comment, observation • **hacer una ~** to make a remark *o* comment *o* observation, comment
3 (= *objeción*) objection • **hacer una ~ a** to raise an objection to
observador(a) ADJ observant
SM/F observer ▸ **observador(a) extranjero/a** foreign observer
observancia SF observance
observar ▷ CONJUG 1a VT **1** (= *mirar*) to observe, watch; (*Astron*) to observe
2 (= *notar*) to see, notice • **se observa una mejoría** you can see *o* detect an improvement • **~ que** to observe that, notice that
3 (*LAm*) • **~ algo a algn** to point sth out to sb, draw sb's attention to sth
4 [+ *leyes*] to observe; [+ *reglas*] to abide by, adhere to • **~ buena conducta** (*Perú*) to behave o.s.
5 (= *mostrar*) to show, give signs of
observatorio SM observatory ▸ **observatorio del tiempo, observatorio meteorológico** weather station
obsesión SF obsession
obsesionado ADJ obsessed • **estar ~ con** *o* **por algo** to be obsessed with *o* by sth
obsesionante ADJ [*recuerdo*] haunting; [*manía, afición*] obsessive
obsesionar ▷ CONJUG 1a VT [*recuerdo*] to haunt; [*manía, afición*] to obsess
VPR **obsesionarse** to become *o* get obsessed • **~se con** *o* **por algo** to become *o* get obsessed with *o* by sth
obsesivo ADJ obsessive
obseso ADJ obsessed
obsidiana SF obsidian
obsolescencia SF obsolescence ▸ **obsolescencia incorporada** (*Com*) built-in obsolescence
obsoleto ADJ obsolete
obstaculización SF hindering, hampering
obstaculizar ▷ CONJUG 1f VT [+ *negociaciones, progreso*] to hinder, hamper; [+ *tráfico*] to hold up
obstáculo SM **1** (*físico*) obstacle; ▷ **carrera**
2 (= *dificultad*) obstacle, hindrance • **no es ~ para que yo lo haga** that does not prevent me (from) *o* stop me doing it • **poner ~s a algo/algn** to hinder sth/sb
obstante • **no ~** ADV **1** (= *sin embargo*) nevertheless, however
2 (= *de todos modos*) all the same
PREP (= *a pesar de*) in spite of
obstar ▷ CONJUG 1a VI • **~ a** *o* **para** to hinder, prevent • **eso no obsta para que lo haga** that

does not prevent him (from) *o* stop him doing it

obstetra SMF obstetrician

obstetricia SF obstetrics (*sing*)

obstétrico/a ADJ obstetric(al)
SM/F obstetrician

obstinación SF obstinacy, stubbornness

obstinadamente ADV obstinately, stubbornly

obstinado ADJ obstinate, stubborn

obstinarse ▹ CONJUG 1a VPR to be obstinate • **~ en hacer algo** to persist in doing sth, insist on doing sth

obstrucción SF obstruction

obstruccionar ▹ CONJUG 1a VT (*esp LAm*) to obstruct

obstruccionismo SM (*gen*) obstructionism; (*Pol*) filibustering

obstruccionista ADJ (*gen*) obstructionist, obstructive; (*Pol*) filibustering
SMF (*gen*) obstructionist; (*Pol*) filibusterer

obstructivismo SM obstructiveness

obstructivo ADJ, **obstructor** ADJ obstructive

obstruir ▹ CONJUG 3g VT **1** (= *bloquear*) [+ *carretera, vena*] to obstruct; [*desagüe, tubería*] to block, clog; (*Dep*) to block
2 [+ *desarrollo, proceso*] to hinder, hamper, hold up

obtención SF • **el único requisito que se exige para la ~ del permiso** the only requirement for obtaining the permit • **esta medida facilitará la ~ de préstamos** this measure will make it easier to obtain a loan • **las ventas de acciones orientadas a la ~ rápida de beneficios** the sale of shares with a view to receiving a quick return

obtener ▹ CONJUG 2k VT [+ *resultado, información, permiso*] to get, obtain; [+ *mayoría, votos*] to win, obtain; [+ *premio, medalla, victoria*] to win; [+ *apoyo*] to gain, get, obtain; [+ *beneficios*] to make • **esperamos ~ mejores resultados este año** we are hoping to get *o* obtain *o* achieve better results this year • **los socialistas obtuvieron la mayoría absoluta** the socialists won *o* obtained an absolute majority • **ambos obtuvieron el premio Nobel en 1993** they both won the Nobel prize in 1993 • **el equipo español confía en ~ la victoria** the Spanish team is confident of victory • **la empresa está obteniendo grandes beneficios** the company is making large profits • **con la venta de los derechos la editorial obtuvo varios millones de dólares** the publishers got several million dollars from the sale of the copyright • **nunca obtuvo respuesta** he never got *o* received a reply • **el acusado obtuvo la libertad provisional** the accused was granted bail

obtenible ADV [*información, resultado*] obtainable; [*meta*] achievable

obturación SF (*gen*) plugging, sealing, stopping; [*de diente*] filling • **velocidad de ~** (*Fot*) shutter speed

obturador SM (*gen*) plug, seal; (*Aut*) choke; (*Fot*) shutter

obturar ▹ CONJUG 1a VT (*gen*) to plug, seal, stop (up); [+ *diente*] to fill

obtuso ADJ **1** (= *sin punta*) blunt
2 (*Mat*) obtuse
3 (*de mente, entendimiento*) obtuse

obús SM **1** (*Mil*) (= *cañón*) howitzer; (= *proyectil*) shell
2 (*Aut*) tyre valve, tire valve (EEUU)

obvención SF bonus, perquisite

obvencional ADJ **1** (= *adicional*) bonus, extra
2 (= *incidental*) incidental

obviamente ADV obviously

obviar ▹ CONJUG 1c VT **1** (= *evitar*) (*gen*) to obviate, get round, avoid • **~ un problema** to get round a problem
2 (= *no mencionar*) to leave out • **obvió los detalles más peliagudos** he left out the more awkward details
VI (= *estorbar*) to stand in the way

obviedad SF **1** (= *cualidad*) obvious nature, obviousness
2 • **una ~** an obvious remark • **la respuesta parece ser una ~** the answer seems to be obvious

obvio ADJ obvious

OC ABR (= **onda corta**) SW

oca SF **1** (= *ganso*) goose • MODISMO: • **¡es la oca!*** it's the tops!*
2 • **la Oca** (= *juego*) *board game similar to snakes and ladders*
3 (*And*) (= *planta*) oca (*root vegetable*)

ocarina SF ocarina

ocasión SF **1** (= *vez*) occasion • **en aquella ~** on that occasion • **en algunas ocasiones** sometimes • **venir en una mala ~** to come at a bad time • **con ~ de** on the occasion of
2 (= *oportunidad*) chance, opportunity • **el delantero perdió una magnífica ~ de gol** the forward missed a great goal scoring opportunity *o* a great chance of scoring • **aprovechar la ~** to take one's chance, seize one's opportunity • **dar a algn la ~ de hacer algo** to give sb the chance *o* opportunity of doing sth • MODISMO: • **la ~ la pintan calva** it's an offer one can't refuse
3 (= *motivo*) cause • **no hay ~ para quejarse** there is no cause for complaint
4 • **de ~** (*Com*) secondhand, used • **librería de ~** secondhand bookshop
5 (*LAm*) (= *ganga*) bargain • **precio de ~** bargain price, reduced price

ocasional ADJ **1** (= *accidental*) chance, accidental
2 (= *eventual*) [*trabajo*] casual, temporary; [*lluvia, visita, fumador*] occasional • **solo consigue trabajo ~** he can only find casual *o* temporary work

ocasionalmente ADV **1** (= *accidentalmente*) by chance, accidentally
2 (= *de vez en cuando*) occasionally

ocasionar ▹ CONJUG 1a VT to cause • **lamento ~le tantas molestias** I'm sorry to cause you *o* to be so much trouble • **la espesa niebla ocasionó el accidente** the accident was caused by thick fog

ocaso SM **1** (*Astron*) [*del sol*] sunset, sundown (EEUU); [*de astro*] setting
2 [*de civilización*] decline • **en el ~ de su vida** in his declining years, in the twilight of his life (*liter*)
3 (*Geog*) west

occidental ADJ western
SMF westerner

occidentalidad SF (*Pol*) allegiance to the western bloc, pro-Western stance

occidentalista ADJ (*Pol*) pro-Western

occidentalizado ADJ westernized

occidentalizar ▹ CONJUG 1f VT to westernize
VPR **occidentalizarse** to become westernized

Occidente SM (*Pol*) the West, the Western world

occidente SM west

occipital (*Anat*) ADJ occipital
SM occipital, occipital bone

occipucio SM occiput

occiso/a SM/F (*Jur*) • **el ~** (*gen*) the deceased; [*de asesinato*] the victim

Occitania SF Occitania

OCDE SF ABR (= **Organización para la Cooperación y el Desarrollo Económico**) OECD

oceanario SM oceanarium

Oceanía SF Oceania

oceánico ADJ oceanic

océano SM ocean ▸ **océano Atlántico** Atlantic Ocean ▸ **océano Glacial Ártico** Arctic Ocean ▸ **océano Índico** Indian Ocean ▸ **océano Pacífico** Pacific Ocean

oceanografía SF oceanography

oceanográfico ADJ oceanographic

oceanógrafo/a SM/F oceanographer

ocelote SM ocelot

ochar* ▹ CONJUG 1a (*Cono Sur*) VT **1** [+ *perro*] to urge on, provoke to attack
2 (= *espiar*) to spy on
VI (= *ladrar*) to bark

ochavado ADJ octagonal

ochavo SM ochavo • MODISMO: • **no tener ni un ~*** to be broke*

ochenta ADJ INV, PRON, SM eighty; (*ordinal*) eightieth • **los (años) ~** the eighties; ▹ **seis**

ochentón/ona ADJ eighty-year-old (*antes de s*), eightyish
SM/F person of about eighty

ocho ADJ INV, PRON (*gen*) eight; (*ordinal, en la fecha*) eighth • **las ~** eight o'clock • **le escribí el día ~** I wrote to him on the eighth • **dentro de ~ días** within a week
SM **1** (= *número*) eight; (= *fecha*) eighth
2 ochos (*Cos*) cable stitch (*sing*); ▹ **seis**

ochocentista ADJ nineteenth-century (*antes de s*)

ochocientos/as ADJ, PRON, SM (*gen*) eight hundred; (*ordinal*) eight hundredth; ▹ **seiscientos**

ochote SM choir of eight voices

OCI SF ABR (*Ven, Perú*) (*Pol*) = **Oficina Central de Información**

ocio SM **1** (= *tiempo libre*) leisure • **ratos de ~** leisure time, spare time, free time • **cultura del ~** leisure culture • **guía del ~** what's on
2 (= *inactividad*) idleness
3 ocios (= *actividades*) leisure pursuits

ociosamente ADV idly

ociosear* ▹ CONJUG 1a VI (*Cono Sur*) (*gen*) to be at leisure; (*pey*) to laze around, loaf about

ociosidad SF idleness • REFRÁN: • **la ~ es la madre de todos los vicios** the devil finds work for idle hands

ocioso ADJ **1** [*persona*] idle
2 (= *inútil*) [*acto*] useless, pointless; [*promesa*] idle, empty • **dinero ~** money lying idle • **es ~ especular** there is no point in speculating

ocluir ▹ CONJUG 3g (*Med*) VT to occlude
VPR **ocluirse** to become occluded

oclusión SF **1** (*Ling*) occlusion ▸ **oclusión glotal** glottal stop
2 (*Meteo*) occluded front

oclusiva SF (*Ling*) occlusive, plosive

oclusivo ADJ (*Ling*) occlusive, plosive

ocote SM (*CAm, Méx*) **1** (*Bot*) ocote pine
2 (= *tea*) torch • MODISMO: • **echar ~** to make trouble

ocozoal SM (*Méx*) rattlesnake, rattler (EEUU*)

-ocracia ▹ **Aspects of Word Formation in Spanish 2**

ocre SM ochre ▸ **ocre amarillo** yellow ochre ▸ **ocre rojo** red ochre

OCSHA SF ABR (*Rel*) = **Obra de la Cooperación Sacerdotal Hispanoamericana**

oct. ABR (= **octubre**) Oct

octaedro SM octahedron

octagonal ADJ octagonal

octágono SM octagon

octanaje SM (*Téc*) octane number • **de alto ~** high-octane (*antes de s*)

octano SM octane

octava SF (*Mús, Literat*) octave

octavilla (SF) pamphlet, leaflet
octavín (SM) piccolo
Octavio (SM) Octavian
octavo (ADJ) eighth
(SM) **1** (= *número*) eighth; ▹ **sexto**
2 (*Tip*) • **libro en ~** octavo book
3 (*Dep*) ▸ **octavos de final** quarterfinals
4 [*de droga*] small dose, small shot*
octeto (SM) (*Mús*) octet; (*Inform*) byte
octogenario/a (ADJ), (SM/F) octogenarian, eighty-year-old
octogésimo (ADJ) eightieth; ▹ **sexto**
octosílabo (ADJ) octosyllabic
(SM) octosyllable
octubre (SM) October; ▹ **septiembre**
OCU (SF ABR) (*Esp*) = **Organización de Consumidores y Usuarios**
ocular (ADJ) ocular (*frm*), eye (*antes de s*) • **mediante examen ~** by visual inspection, with the eye • **testigo ~** eyewitness
(SM) eyepiece
oculista (SMF) oculist, eye doctor (*EEUU*)
ocultación (SF), **ocultamiento** (SM) hiding, concealment
ocultamente (ADV) (= *secretamente*) secretly; (= *misteriosamente*) mysteriously; (= *furtivamente*) stealthily
ocultar ▹ CONJUG 1a (VT) **1** [+ *objeto, mancha*] to hide (**a, de** from), conceal (**a, de** from)
2 [+ *sentimientos, intenciones*] to hide, conceal
(VPR) **ocultarse** to hide (o.s.) • **~se con o tras algo** to hide behind sth • **~se a la vista** to keep out of sight • **no se me oculta que …** I am fully aware that… • **se me oculta la razón** I cannot see the reason, the reason is a mystery to me
ocultismo (SM) occultism
ocultista (SMF) occultist
oculto (ADJ) **1** (= *escondido*) hidden, concealed • **permanecer ~** to stay hidden
2 (= *misterioso*) (*gen*) mysterious; [*pensamiento*] inner, secret; [*motivo*] ulterior
3 [*poderes*] occult; ▹ **ciencia**
ocupa‡ (SMF) squatter
ocupable (ADJ) [*persona*] employable; [*puesto, posición*] available • **plaza ~** job available, position available
ocupación (SF) **1** (= *empleo*) (*en general*) employment; (*en concreto*) occupation • **ha bajado el nivel de ~ entre los jóvenes** the level of employment among young people has dropped • **desea volver a su ~ habitual, la enseñanza** he wishes to return to his usual occupation, teaching
2 (= *actividad*) activity • **lee mucho cuando sus ocupaciones políticas se lo permiten** he reads a lot when his political activities allow it • **abandonaron sus ocupaciones para unirse a la manifestación** they stopped what they were doing to join the march
3 [*de viviendas*] (= *acción*) occupation; (= *nivel de ocupación*) occupancy • **para fomentar la ~ de viviendas rurales** to encourage the occupation of rural dwellings • **la ~ hotelera ha aumentado este año** hotel occupancy has increased this year • **"se alquila piso, ~ inmediata"** "apartment available for immediate rent"
4 (*Mil, Pol*) occupation • **durante la ~ de la embajada por los guerrilleros** during the occupation of the embassy by the guerrillas • **las fuerzas de ~** the occupying forces
ocupacional (ADJ) [*actividad, taller, terapia, salud*] occupational • **formación ~** job training
ocupado/a (ADJ) **1** [*sitio*] [*asiento, plaza*] taken; [*habitación*] taken, occupied; [*retrete*] engaged • **¿está ocupada esta silla?** is this seat taken? • **todas las habitaciones del hotel están ocupadas** all the rooms in the hotel are taken *o* occupied • **el vuelo está todo ~** the flight is completely full • **¿está ~ el baño?** is the toilet occupied *o* engaged? • **"ocupado"** "engaged"
2 (*Telec*) engaged, busy (*EEUU*) • **la línea está ocupada** the line is engaged *o* busy • **señal de ~** engaged tone, busy signal (*EEUU*) • **da señal de ~** the line is engaged *o* busy
3 (*Pol, Mil*) [*territorio, país*] occupied
4 [*persona*] **a** (= *atareado*) busy (**con** with) • **estoy muy ~** I'm very busy • **estaba ocupada lavando el coche** she was busy washing the car • **no podía abrir la puerta porque tenía las dos manos ocupadas** I couldn't open the door because my hands were full *o* I had my hands full
b (= *empleado*) in work, working • **la población ocupada** the working population
5 (*Esp††*) (= *embarazada*) pregnant
(SM/F) • **el porcentaje de ~s** the percentage of people in work
ocupante (ADJ) (*Pol, Mil*) [*tropas, país*] occupying
(SMF) **1** [*de vehículo*] occupant; [*de vivienda*] occupant, occupier • **ningún ~ del vehículo resultó herido** none of the occupants of the vehicle were injured • **~s ilegales de viviendas** squatters
2 (*Pol, Mil*) [*de país*] occupier • **el ~ ruso** the occupying Russians, the Russian occupiers
ocupar ▹ CONJUG 1a (VT) **1** [+ *espacio*] to take up • **la noticia ocupaba dos páginas del periódico** the story took up two pages in the newspaper • **el armario ocupa toda la pared** the wardrobe takes up *o* covers the length of the wall • **el nuevo museo se construirá en el espacio que ocupaba el antiguo** the new museum is to be built on the site of the old one
2 [+ *posición*] • **el equipo español ocupa el puesto número diez en la clasificación** the Spanish team are tenth *o* are in tenth place in the league table • **la posición que ocupa nuestra empresa en el mercado europeo** our company's position in the European market, the position that our company occupies *o* has *o* holds in the European market • **vuelvan a ~ sus asientos** go back to your seats
3 (*Com*) [+ *puesto, cargo*] to hold; [+ *vacante*] to fill • **la persona que ocupaba el cargo antes que ella** her predecessor in the post, the person who held the post before her • **desde 1990 ocupa un escaño en el parlamento** he has held a seat in parliament since 1990 • **~á su escaño el próximo mes** he will take his seat next month • **él ocupó el puesto que quedó vacante cuando me jubilé** he filled the position left vacant when I retired
4 (*Mil, Pol*) [+ *ciudad, país*] to occupy • **los obreros ~on la fábrica** the workers occupied the factory
5 (= *habitar*) [+ *vivienda*] to live in, occupy; [+ *local*] to occupy • **la vivienda que ocupan desde hace dos años** the house they have been living in *o* have occupied for the last two years • **los jóvenes que ~on la vivienda abandonada** the youths that squatted *o* occupied the empty building • **la agencia ocupa el último piso del edificio** the agency has *o* occupies the top floor of the building • **la fundación ocupa un piso en el centro de Barcelona** the foundation is based in *o* occupies a flat in the centre of Barcelona • **la celda que ocupa ahora** the cell he currently occupies
6 [+ *tiempo*] [*labor, acción*] take up; [*persona*] to spend • **los niños y las labores de la casa me ocupan mucho tiempo** the children and the housework take up a lot of my time • **escribir el artículo me ocupó toda la mañana** my whole morning was taken up with writing the article • **ocupa sus ratos libres pintando** he spends his spare time painting • **no sabe en qué ~ su tiempo libre** he doesn't know how to fill *o* spend his spare time
7 (= *dar trabajo a*) to employ • **la agricultura ocupa a un 10% de la población activa** 10% of the working population is employed in agriculture, agriculture employs 10% of the working population
8 (= *concernir*) • **pero, volviendo al tema que nos ocupa …** however, returning to the subject under discussion …, however, returning to the subject we are concerned with *o* that concerns us … • **en el caso que nos ocupa** in this particular case, in the case under discussion
9 (= *confiscar*) to confiscate • **les ~on todo el contrabando** all their smuggled goods were seized *o* confiscated • **la policía le ocupó la navaja** the police confiscated his knife
10 (*Méx*) (= *usar*) to use • **¿está ocupando la pluma?** are you using the pen?
(VPR) **ocuparse 1** • **~se de a** (*como profesión, obligación*) to deal with • **este organismo se ocupa de conceder las licencias** this organization deals with the issuing of licences • **me ~é de ello mañana a primera hora** I will deal with it first thing tomorrow • **los servicios de seguridad no se ocupan de cuestiones económicas** the security services do not deal with economic matters • **no tiene tiempo para ~se de esos asuntos** she doesn't have time to deal with those matters • **no es esta la primera vez que nos hemos ocupado de su obra** this is not the first time that we have discussed *o* looked at his work • **ella es quien se ocupó de los detalles de la boda** it was her that took care of *o* saw to the details of the wedding
b (*por interés*) to take an interest in • **los críticos no se ~on del libro** the book was ignored by the critics, the critics took no interest in the book • **me ocupo muy poco de las tareas domésticas** I don't bother much with *o* about the housework, I take very little interest in the housework • **¡tú ocúpate de lo tuyo!** mind your own business!
c (= *cuidar de*) [+ *enfermo, niños*] to take care of, look after; [+ *enemigo*] to take care of
d [*libro, conferencia, programa*] • **el libro se ocupa de los aspectos económicos del problema** the book deals with the economic aspects of the problem • **el programa de esta noche se ~á de las elecciones en Francia** tonight's programme will take a look at the French elections • **nos ocupamos ahora de la información deportiva** (*Radio, TV*) and now a look at today's sports
2 • **~se en:** • **varias empresas se ocupan en proyectos de este tipo** a number of companies are involved in projects of this kind • **tras jubilarse solo se ocupaba en cuidar el jardín** after her retirement she spent all her time doing the garden
ocurrencia (SF) **1** (= *idea*) idea • **tuvo una ~ genial** he had a brilliant idea • **¡vaya ~!** (*iró*) what a bright idea! • **tuvo la ~ de lavarse los zapatos en la lavadora** (*iró*) he had the bright idea of washing his shoes in the washing machine
2 (= *dicho gracioso*) funny remark • **este niño tiene unas ~s divertidísimas** this child comes out with the funniest remarks
3 (*frm*) (= *acontecimiento*) occurrence
ocurrente (ADJ) **1** (= *chistoso*) witty
2 (= *listo*) bright, clever

o

3 (= *gracioso*) entertaining, amusing
ocurrido ADJ **1** (= *sucedido*) • **lo ~** what has/had happened
2 (*And*) (= *gracioso*) witty, funny
ocurrir ▷ CONJUG 3a VI to happen • **ha ocurrido algo horrible** something terrible has happened • **lo que ocurrió podría haberse evitado** what happened could have been avoided • **por lo que pudiera ~** because of what might happen • **ocurre que ...** it (so) happens that ... • **¿qué ocurre?** what's going on? • **¿qué te ocurre?** what's the matter? • **lo que ocurre es que ...** the thing is ...
VPR **ocurrirse** • **se nos ocurrió una idea buenísima** we had a brilliant idea • **¿se te ocurre algo?** can you think of anything? • **se le ocurrió hacerlo** he thought of doing it • **¡ni se te ocurra (hacerlo)!** don't even think about (doing) it! • **¡se te ocurren unas cosas!** you've got some right ideas! • **si se le ocurre huir** if he takes it into his head to escape • **¿cómo no se te ocurrió pensar que ...?** didn't it cross your mind that ...? • **se me ocurre que ...** it occurs to me that ... • **nunca se me había ocurrido** it had never crossed my mind • **¿a quién se le ocurre presentarse a medianoche?** who in their right mind would turn up in the middle of the night?
oda SF ode
odalisca SF odalisque
ODECA SF ABR (= **Organización de los Estados Centroamericanos**) OCAS
ODEPA SF ABR = **Organización Deportiva Panamericana**
odiar ▷ CONJUG 1b VT **1** (= *sentir odio por*) to hate
2 (*Chile*) (= *molestar*) to pester, annoy; (= *aburrir*) to bore
odio SM **1** (*gen*) hatred • **almacenar ~** to store up hatred • **tener ~ a algn** to hate sb ▸ **odio de clase** class hatred ▸ **odio de sangre** feud, vendetta ▸ **odio mortal** mortal hatred
2 (*Chile*) (= *molestia*) nuisance, bother
odiosear* ▷ CONJUG 1a VT (*Chile*) to pester, annoy
odiosidad SF **1** (*gen*) odiousness, hatefulness; (= *repelencia*) nastiness
2 (*Arg, Chile, Perú*) (= *molestia*) nuisance, annoyance
odioso ADJ **1** (= *detestable*) odious, hateful, detestable
2 (= *repelente*) nasty, unpleasant • **hacerse ~ a algn** to become a nuisance to sb
3 (*Arg, Chile, Perú*) (= *molesto*) annoying
Odisea SF Odyssey
odisea SF odyssey, epic journey • **fue toda una ~** it was a real odyssey
Odiseo SM Odysseus
odómetro SM milometer, odometer (*EEUU*)
odonto- PREF odonto-
odontología SF dentistry, odontology
odontólogo/a SM/F dentist, dental surgeon, odontologist
odorífero ADJ, **odorífico** ADJ sweet-smelling, odoriferous (*frm*)
odre SM **1** (= *recipiente*) wineskin
2* (= *borracho*) drunk, drunkard, old soak*
OEA SF ABR (= **Organización de Estados Americanos**) OAS
OECE SF ABR (= **Organización Europea de Cooperación Económica**) OEEC
OELA SF ABR = **Organización de Estados Latinoamericanos**
oeste ADJ [*región*] western; [*dirección*] westerly; [*viento*] west, westerly • **la zona ~ de la ciudad** the western part of the city, the west of the city • **en la costa ~** on the west coast
SM **1** (= *punto cardinal*) west
2 [*de región, país*] west • **el ~ del país** the west of the country • **al ~ de Girona** to the west of Girona • **eso cae más hacia el ~** that lies further (to the) west • **viajábamos hacia el ~** we were travelling west • **en la parte del ~** in the western part • **vientos del ~** westerly winds • **una película del Oeste** a Western
3 (= *viento*) west wind
Ofelia SF Ophelia
ofender ▷ CONJUG 2a VT **1** (= *agraviar*) to offend • **por temor a ~lo** for fear of offending him • **perdona si te he ofendido** I'm sorry if I've offended you • **(dicho) sin ánimo de ~, no es que tu marido sea un santo** no offence meant, but your husband's no saint • **no ofendas la memoria de tu madre** don't insult your mother's memory
2 [+ *sentido*] to offend, be offensive to • **~ a la vista** to offend the eye
3 (*Méx*‡) [+ *mujer*] to touch up‡, feel‡
VPR **ofenderse** to take offence *o* (*EEUU*) offense • **se ofendió porque no lo invitaron** he took offence at not being invited • **no te ofendas por lo que te voy a decir** don't be offended by what I'm going to tell you
ofendido ADJ offended • **darse por ~** to take offence *o* (*EEUU*) offense
ofensa SF **1** (= *insulto*) offence, offense (*EEUU*)
2 (= *desprecio*) slight
ofensiva SF offensive • **pasar a la ~** to go on the offensive • **tomar la ~** to take the offensive ▸ **ofensiva de paz** peace offensive
ofensivamente ADV (*Dep*) in attack
ofensivo ADJ **1** (= *de ataque*) (*tb Mil*) offensive
2 [*conducta, palabra*] offensive, rude, insulting
ofensor(a) ADJ offending
SM/F offender
oferta SF **1** (= *ofrecimiento*) offer
2 (*Com*) (*gen*) offer; (*para contrato, concurso*) tender; (*en subasta*) bid; (*Econ*) supply; (= *ganga*) special offer • **estar de *o* en ~** to be on offer • **la ley de la ~ y la demanda** the law of supply and demand • **la ~ es superior a la demanda** supply exceeds demand ▸ **oferta cerrada** sealed bid ▸ **oferta condicional** conditional offer ▸ **oferta excedentaria** excess supply ▸ **oferta monetaria** money supply ▸ **oferta promocional** promotional offer ▸ **oferta pública de adquisición (de acciones)** takeover bid ▸ **oferta pública de venta (de acciones)** share offer ▸ **ofertas de trabajo** (*en periódico*) situations vacant (column), job openings (*EEUU*)
3 (= *regalo*) gift, present
ofertante SMF (*Com*) bidder
ofertar ▷ CONJUG 1a VT **1** (*esp LAm*) (= *ofrecer*) [+ *suma de dinero, producto*] to offer
2 (*Com*) (*en concurso*) to tender; (*en subasta*) to bid
3 (= *ofrecer barato*) to sell on special offer
ofertorio SM offertory
off [of] SM • **en off** (*Cine*) off-screen; (*Teat*) offstage • **pasa algo en off** (*Cine*) something happens off-screen • **hay una discusión en off** there is an argument offstage • **poner un aparato en off** to switch a machine off • **ruido en off** background noise; ▷ **voz**
office ['ofis] SM **1** (*Esp*) (*Arquit*) (= *comedor pequeño*) breakfast room; (= *trascocina*) scullery; (= *despensa*) pantry; (= *lavadero*) utility room
2 (*Aer*) galley
off-line ADJ, ADV (*Inform*) offline
offset ['ofset] SM (*Tip*) offset
off-shore ADJ (*Econ*) offshore
offside [of'sai] SM (*Dep*) offside • **¡offside!** offside! • **estar en ~** (*Dep*) to be offside
oficial ADJ [*viaje, documento, comunicado*] official
SMF **1** (*Mil*) officer • **primer ~** (*Náut*) first mate ▸ **oficial de enlace** liaison officer ▸ **oficial de guardia** (*Náut*) officer of the watch ▸ **oficial del día** orderly officer ▸ **oficial de marina** naval officer ▸ **oficial ejecutivo** executive officer ▸ **oficial médico** medical officer ▸ **oficial pagador** paymaster
2 (= *obrero*) (*en fábrica*) skilled worker; (*en taller artesano*) craftsman/craftswoman; (*por cuenta ajena*) journeyman; (*en oficina*) clerk ▸ **oficial mayor** chief clerk
oficiala SF = **oficial**
oficialada SF (*Cono Sur, Méx*) = **oficialidad**
oficialidad SF (*Mil*) officers (*pl*)
oficialismo SM **1** (= *tendencia*) [*de un partido*] party-liners (*pl*); (= *del gobierno*) pro-government political forces (*pl*)
2 (*LAm*) (= *autoridades*) • **el ~** government authorities, the ruling *o* governing party
oficialista ADJ (*LAm*) (*del gobierno*) (pro-)government (*antes de s*), of the party in power • **el candidato ~** the ruling *o* governing party's candidate
SMF **1** [*del partido*] party-liner
2 (*LAm*) [*del gobierno*] government supporter
oficializar ▷ CONJUG 1f VT to make official, give official status to
oficialmente ADV officially
oficiante SM (*Rel*) celebrant, officiant
oficiar ▷ CONJUG 1b VT **1** (*Rel*) [+ *misa*] to celebrate; [+ *funeral, boda*] to conduct, officiate at
2 (= *informar*) to inform officially
VI **1** (*Rel*) to officiate
2 • **~ de** to officiate as, act as
oficina SF **1** (= *despacho*) (*gen*) office; (*Mil*) orderly room; (*Farm*) laboratory; (*Téc*) workshop • **horas de ~** office hours ▸ **oficina de colocación, oficina de empleo** job centre ▸ **oficina de información** information bureau ▸ **oficina de objetos perdidos** lost property office, lost-and-found department (*EEUU*) ▸ **oficina de prensa** press office ▸ **oficina meteorológica** weather bureau ▸ **oficina paisaje** open-plan office
2 (*Chile*) (*Min*) nitrate works
oficinesco ADJ **1** [*ambiente, mobiliario*] office (*antes de s*); [*versión*] clerical
2 (*pey*) bureaucratic
oficinista SMF office worker, clerk • **los ~s** office workers
oficio SM **1** (= *profesión*) trade • **aprender un ~** to learn a trade • **sabe su ~** he knows his job • **los deberes del ~** the duties of the post • **mi ~ es enseñar** my job is to teach • **un profesional con mucho ~** a seasoned professional • **tiene mucho ~** he is very experienced • **MODISMOS:** • **sin ~ ni beneficio**: • **un pobre temporero sin ~ ni beneficio** just a poor seasonal worker without a penny to his name • **se encontró sin ~ ni beneficio al salir del colegio** he found himself with no means of earning a living when he left school • **es un vago sin ~ ni beneficio** he's a good-for-nothing layabout • **ser del ~** (= *ser experto*) to be an old hand; (= *prostituirse*) to be on the game*
2 (= *función*) function • **el ~ de esta pieza es de ...** what this part does is ...
3 • **de ~: miembro de ~** ex officio member • **matones de ~** professional thugs • **fue enterrado de ~** he was buried at the State's expense • **le informaremos de ~** we will inform you officially; ▷ **abogado**
4 (= *comunicado*) official letter
5 (*Rel*) service, mass ▸ **oficio de difuntos** funeral service, mass for the dead, office for

the dead ▸ **oficio divino** divine office
6 · Santo Oficio (*Hist*) Holy Office, Inquisition
7 · buenos ~s good offices **· ofrecer sus buenos ~s** to offer one's good offices
8 (= *trascocina*) scullery
oficiosamente ADV **1** (= *extraoficialmente*) unofficially
2 (= *con entrometimiento*) officiously
3 (= *solícitamente*) helpfully, obligingly
oficiosidad SF **1** (= *entrometimiento*) officiousness
2 (= *solicitud*) helpfulness, obligingness
oficioso ADJ **1** (= *extraoficial*) unofficial, informal **· de fuente oficiosa** from an unofficial source
2 (= *entrometido*) officious
3 (= *solícito*) helpful, obliging **· mentira oficiosa** white lie
ofimática SF office automation, office computerization
ofimático ADJ **· sistema ~** office computer system **· gestión ofimática integrada** integrated computer system for office management
Ofines SF ABR = **Oficina Internacional de Información y Observación del Español**
ofrecer ▹ CONJUG 2d VT **1** (= *presentar voluntariamente*) **a** [+ *servicios, ayuda, trabajo, dinero*] to offer **· nos ofreció un té** he offered us tea **· me ofrecieron la posibilidad de trabajar para ellos** they offered me the chance to work for them **· ¿cuánto te ofrecieron por el coche?** how much did they offer you for the car? **· ~ hacer algo** to offer to do sth **· el club le ha ofrecido prorrogar su contrato** the club has offered to extend his contract **· me ofrecieron participar en la coproducción** they asked me if I would like to take part in the co-production
b [+ *espectáculo, programa*] (*en TV*) to show **· varias cadenas ofrecen el partido en directo** several channels are showing the match live **· los principales espectáculos que ofrece el festival** the main events featured in the festival **· la Filarmónica ~á un concierto el día de Navidad** the Philharmonic are giving a concert on Christmas Day
c (*frm*) [+ *respetos*] to pay (*frm*) **· ~ la bienvenida a algn** to welcome sb
2 (= *tener*) **a** [+ *ventaja*] to offer; [+ *oportunidad, garantías*] to offer, give; [+ *solución*] to offer, provide **· el formato electrónico ofrece algunas ventajas** the electronic format offers some advantages **· la sanidad pública ofrece más posibilidades de investigación** public health care offers *o* provides more scope for research **· no ofrece las suficientes garantías** it's not sufficiently reliable **· no ~ duda**: **· la gravedad del caso no ofrece duda** there is no doubt about the seriousness of the case **· el resultado no ofrecía dudas** the result left no room for doubt
b [+ *dificultad*] to present **· el caso no ofrece dificultad alguna** the case presents no difficulty **· el ladrón no ofreció resistencia** the burglar did not put up a struggle, the burglar offered no resistance (*frm*)
c [+ *imagen*] to present **· el partido necesita ~ una imagen de estabilidad** the party needs to present an image of stability **· el palacio abandonado ofrecía un aspecto desolador** the deserted palace looked depressingly bleak **· la zona ofrece un deprimente espectáculo a sus visitantes** the area is a depressing sight for visitors
3 (= *celebrar*) [+ *acto, fiesta, cena*] to hold, give **· un portavoz del Ministerio ofreció una rueda de prensa** a Ministry spokesman gave *o* held a press conference **· los compañeros le ofrecieron una comida de despedida** her colleagues held a farewell lunch for her
4 [+ *sacrificio, víctima*] to offer up **· ofrecieron un cordero en sacrificio a los dioses** they offered up a lamb to the gods **· ofrecieron su vida por la causa** they gave their lives for the cause
5 (*Rel*) to make a vow **· ha ofrecido que va a dejar de fumar** he made a vow to stop smoking
VPR **ofrecerse 1** [*persona*] **· un joven se ofreció como guía** a young man offered to act as a guide **· la vecina se ha ofrecido para cualquier cosa que necesitemos** the woman next door offered to help us in any way she could **· ~se a *o* para hacer algo** to offer to do sth **· me ofrecí a acompañarla hasta la puerta** I offered to see her to the door **· "profesor de inglés se ofrece para dar clases particulares"** "English teacher offers private tuition" **· ~se (como) voluntario** to volunteer (a for)
2 · ofrecérsele a algn [*oportunidad*] to offer itself (to sb), present itself (to sb); [*obstáculo, dificultad*] to present itself (to sb) **· se le ofreció una maravillosa oportunidad** a wonderful opportunity offered *o* presented itself (to him) **· se le ofrece ahora la oportunidad de demostrar su valía** he has now been given *o* he now has the opportunity to prove himself **· los obstáculos que se le ofrecieron** the obstacles that she was now faced with, the obstacles that had presented themselves **· un hermoso espectáculo se ofrecía ante sus ojos** (*liter*) a beautiful sight presented itself to her eyes (*liter*)
3 (*frm*) (= *desear*) **· buenos días, ¿qué se le ofrece?** good morning, what can I do for you? *o* what would you like? **· ¿se le ofrece algo?** is there anything I can do for you?
4 (= *ocurrir*) to occur **· se me ofrece una duda** I have a doubt, a problem has occurred to me **· ¿qué se ofrece?** what's going on?, what's happening?
ofrecimiento SM offer
ofrenda SF **1** (= *tributo*) tribute; (*Rel*) offering ▸ **ofrenda floral** floral tribute
2 (= *regalo*) gift
ofrendar ▹ CONJUG 1a VT **1** (= *ofrecer*) to give, contribute
2 (*Rel*) to offer up
oftalmía SF ophthalmia
oftálmico ADJ ophthalmic
oftalmología SF ophthalmology
oftalmólogo/a SM/F ophthalmologist
ofuscación SF, **ofuscamiento** SM **1** [*de la vista*] blurring
2 (*al pensar*) bewilderment, confusion; (*al actuar*) blindness
ofuscar ▹ CONJUG 1g VT **1** [*luz*] to dazzle
2 [+ *persona*] (= *confundir*) to bewilder, confuse; (= *cegar*) to blind **· estar ofuscado por la cólera** to be blinded by rage
VPR **ofuscarse · ~se por algo** to be blinded by sth
Ogino SM, **ogino** SM **· método ~** rhythm method (*of birth control*)
ogro SM ogre
oh EXCL oh!
ohmio SM ohm
oíble ADJ audible
OIC SF ABR **1** (= **Organización Internacional del Comercio**) ITO
2 = **Organización Interamericana del Café**
OICE SF ABR = **Organización Interamericana de Cooperación Económica**
OICI SF ABR (= **Organización Interamericana de Cooperación Intermunicipal**) IAMO
OID SF ABR = **Oficina de Información Diplomática**
oída SF hearing **· de *o* por ~s** by *o* from hearsay
-oide ▹ **Aspects of Word Formation in Spanish 2**
oído SM **1** (*Anat*) ear **· le estarán zumbando los ~s** his ears must be burning **· decir algo al ~ de algn** to whisper sth to sb, whisper sth in sb's ear **· MODISMOS: · aguzar los ~s** to prick up one's ears **· aplicar el ~** to listen carefully **· ¡~ a la caja!** pay attention! **· dar ~s a algo** (= *escuchar*) to listen to sth; (= *creer*) to believe sth **· entra por un ~ y sale por otro** it goes in one ear and out (of) the other **· hacer ~s a algo** to pay attention to sth, take heed of sth **· hacer ~s sordos a algo** to turn a deaf ear to sth **· llegar a ~s de algn** to come to sb's attention **· ¡~ al parche!** pay attention! **· prestar ~(s) a algo** to give ear to sth **· regalarle a algn el ~ *o* los ~s** to flatter sb, sweet-talk sb **· ser todo ~s** to be all ears; ▹ **crédito** ▸ **oído externo** external ear ▸ **oído interno** inner ear ▸ **oído medio** middle ear
2 (= *sentido*) (sense of) hearing **· duro de ~** hard of hearing **· es una canción que se pega al ~** it's a catchy song **· tiene un ~ muy fino** he has a very keen sense of hearing
3 (*Mús*) ear **· de ~** by ear **· siempre toca de ~** she always plays by ear **· tener (buen) ~** to have a good ear
oidor SM (*Hist*) judge
OIEA SM o SF ABR (= **Organismo** *u* **Organización Internacional de la Energía Atómica**) IAEA
oigo *etc* ▹ **oír**
OIN SF ABR (= **Organización Internacional de Normalización**) ISO
OIP SF ABR (*Aer*) = **Organización Iberoamericana de Pilotos**
OIR SF ABR (= **Organización Internacional para los Refugiados**) IRO
oír ▹ CONJUG 3p VT **1** (= *percibir sonidos*) to hear **· he oído un ruido** I heard a noise **· ¿me oyes bien desde tu habitación?** can you hear me all right from your room? **· le oí abrir la puerta** I heard him open the door, I heard him opening the door **· —la han despedido —¡no me digas! —como lo oyes** "she's been sacked" — "no, really!" — "she has, I'm telling you" **· oír hablar de algn** to hear about *o* of sb **· he oído decir que ...** I've heard it said that ..., rumour *o* (EEUU) rumor has it that ... **· MODISMOS: · lo oyó como quien oye llover** she paid no attention, she turned a deaf ear to it **· ¡me van a oír!** they'll be having a few words from me!
2 (= *escuchar*) to listen to **· oír la radio** to listen to the radio **· óyeme bien, no vuelvas a hacerlo** now listen to what I'm telling you, don't do it again **· no han querido oír nuestras quejas** they didn't want to listen to our complaints **· fui a oír un concierto** I went to a concert, I attended a concert
3 [+ *misa*] to attend, hear
4 [+ *confesión*] to hear
5 [+ *ruego*] to heed, answer **· ¡Dios te oiga!** I just hope you're right!
VI **1** (= *percibir sonidos*) **· oír mal** (= *ser medio sordo*) to be hard of hearing; (*al teléfono*) to be unable to hear (properly)
2 · oír de algn (*LAm*) to hear from sb
3 (*en exclamaciones*) **· ¡oye, que te dejas el cambio!** hey, you've forgotten your change! **· oiga, ¿es usted el encargado?** excuse me, are you in charge? **· ¡oye, que yo no he dicho eso!** hold on *o* just a minute, that's not what I said! **· ¡oiga!** (*Telec*) hello?

OIT SF ABR (= **Oficina** *u* **Organización Internacional del Trabajo**) ILO
ojada SF (*And*) skylight
ojal SM buttonhole, boutonniere (*EEUU*)
ojalá EXCL • **—mañana puede que haga sol —¡ojalá!** "it might be sunny tomorrow" — "I hope so!" *o* "I hope it will be!" • **—¿te darán el trabajo? —¡ojalá!** "will you get the job?" — "let's hope so!"
CONJ **1** • **¡~ venga pronto!** I wish he'd come!, I hope he comes soon! • **¡~ que gane la carrera!** let's hope she wins the race! • **—¿vendrás con nosotros? —¡~ pudiera!** "will you come with us?" — "I wish I could!" • **¡~ pudiera andar de nuevo!** if only he could walk again!
2 (*LAm*) (= *aunque*) even though • **no lo haré, ~ me maten** I won't do it even if they kill me
ojazos SMPL (= *ojos grandes*) big eyes, wide eyes; (= *ojos bonitos*) lovely big eyes • **echar los ~ a algn** to make eyes at sb
OJD SF ABR (= **Oficina de Justificación de la Difusión**) *office which keeps statistics of newspaper circulations*
OJE SF ABR = **Organización Juvenil Española**
ojeada SF glance • **echar una ~ a algo** to glance at sth, take a quick look at sth
ojeador(a) SM/F (*Caza*) beater; (*Dep*) talent scout, talent spotter
ojear[1] ▸ CONJUG 1a VT (*gen*) to eye; (*fijamente*) to stare at • **voy a ~ cómo va el trabajo** I'm going to see how the work is getting on
ojear[2] ▸ CONJUG 1a VT **1** (= *ahuyentar*) to drive away, shoo away
2 (*Caza*) to beat, put up
3 (*Cono Sur*) (= *hechizar*) to put the evil eye on
ojén SM anisette
ojeo SM (*Caza*) beating
ojeras SFPL bags under the eyes • **tener ~** to have bags under the eyes
ojeriza SF spite, ill will • **tener ~ a algn** to have a grudge against sb, have it in for sb*
ojeroso ADJ haggard • **estar ~** to have bags under the eyes
ojete SM **1** (*Cos*) eyelet
2** (= *ano*) arsehole**, asshole (*EEUU***)
ojiabierto ADJ wide-eyed
ojillos SMPL (*brillantes*) bright eyes; (*bonitos*) lovely eyes; (*pícaros*) roguish eyes • **¡tiene unos ~!** you should see the eyes she's got!
ojímetro SM • **a ~*** roughly, at a rough guess
ojinegro ADJ black-eyed
ojito SM **1** • MODISMOS: • **hacer ~s a algn*** to make eyes at sb, give sb the eye • **poner ~s a algn** to look longingly at sb • **ser el ~ derecho de algn** to be the apple of sb's eye
2 (= *cuidado*) • **¡ojito!** careful!, look out!
ojituerto ADJ cross-eyed
ojiva SF **1** (*Arquit*) pointed arch, ogive
2 (*Mil*) warhead
ojival ADJ ogival, pointed
ojo SM **1** (*Anat*) eye • MODISMOS: • **a ojo (de buen cubero)**: • **calculé a ojo (de buen cubero) cuántas personas había** I roughly calculated *o* made a rough guess at how many people were there • **no hace falta medir la harina, échala a ojo** there's no need to weigh out the flour, just add roughly the right amount • **abrir los ojos (a algo)** to open one's eyes (to sth) • **abrirle los ojos a algn** to open sb's eyes • **en un abrir y cerrar de ojos** in the twinkling of an eye • **avivar el ojo** to be on the alert • **mirar** *o* **ver algo con buenos ojos** to look kindly on sth, approve of sth • **con los ojos cerrados** • **a ojos cerrados** without a second thought • **lo aceptaría con los ojos cerrados** I'd accept it without a second thought • **cerrar los ojos a** *o* **ante algo** to shut one's eyes to sth • **tener ojo clínico** to have good intuition • **costar un ojo de la cara*** to cost an arm and a leg* • **dar en los ojos** to be conspicuous • **ser el ojo derecho de algn** to be the apple of sb's eye • **echar un ojo a algo/algn** to keep an eye on sth/sb • **tener el ojo echado a algn/algo** to have one's eye on sb/sth • **le tiene echado el ojo a Elisa desde que llegó** he's had his eye on Elisa ever since he arrived • **le tengo echado el ojo a ese vestido** I've got my eye on that dress • **tener a algn entre ojos** to have it in for sb • **hacer del ojo**† to wink • **mirar** *o* **ver algo con malos ojos** to disapprove of sth • **veían con malos ojos que se hubiese nacionalizado español** they disapproved of him adopting Spanish nationality • **¡no es nada lo del ojo!** (*iró*) it's no big deal! • **no pegué ojo en toda la noche** I didn't get a wink of sleep all night • **se le salieron los ojos de las órbitas** his eyes popped out of his head • **se le pusieron los ojos como platos** she was wide-eyed with amazement • **poner ojos a algn** to look longingly at sb • **en mis propios ojos** before my very eyes • **no quitar ojo a algo/algn** not to take one's eyes off sth/sb • **salir de ojo** to be obvious • **tener (buen) ojo para algo** to have a good eye for sth, be a good judge of sth • **ser todo ojos** to be all eyes • **a ojos vistas** visibly • REFRANES: • **ojo por ojo (, diente por diente)** an eye for an eye (, a tooth for a tooth) • **ojos que no ven, corazón que no siente** out of sight, out of mind ▸ **ojo a la funerala***, **ojo a la virulé***, **ojo a la pava*** shiner* ▸ **ojo amoratado** black eye ▸ **ojo de cristal** glass eye ▸ **ojo de pez** (*Fot*) fish-eye lens ▸ **ojo en compota** (*Cono Sur**) shiner* ▸ **ojo mágico** magic eye ▸ **ojos almendrados** almond eyes; ▹ **avizor**, **dichoso**, **niña**
2 ojos (= *vista*) • **pasar los ojos por algo** to look sth over • **paseó los ojos por la sala** he looked round the hall • **torcer los ojos** to squint • MODISMOS: • **a los ojos de algn** in sb's eyes • **clavar los ojos en algo/algn** to fix one's gaze on sth/sb, stare at sth/sb • **comerse** *o* **devorar a algn con los ojos** (*con deseo*) to devour sb with one's eyes; (*con ira*) to look daggers at sb • **entrar por los ojos**: • **esa comida no me termina de entrar por los ojos** that meal is not exactly mouth-watering • **los anuncios bien hechos nos entran por los ojos** well-made adverts captivate us • **irse los ojos tras algo/algn**: • **se le fueron los ojos tras la chica** he couldn't keep his eyes off the girl • **tener los ojos puestos en algo** (= *prestar atención a*) to centre one's attention on sth; (= *desear*) to have one's heart set on sth • **España tiene los ojos puestos en los novios reales** all eyes in Spain are on the royal couple • **recrear los ojos en algo/algn** to feast one's eyes on sth/sb • **saltar a los ojos** to be blindingly obvious
3 (= *cuidado*) • **¡ojo!** careful!, look out! • **¡ojo! es muy mentiroso** be careful! he's an awful liar • **ojo con el escalón** mind the step • **hay que tener mucho ojo con los carteristas** one must be very careful of *o* beware pickpockets • **ir con ojo** to keep one's eyes open for trouble
4 (= *orificio*) [*de aguja*] eye; [*de queso*] hole; [*de puente*] span • **el ojo de la cerradura** *o* (*LAm*) **llave** the keyhole • **un puente de cuatro ojos** a bridge with four arches *o* spans ▸ **ojo de buey** (*Náut*) porthole ▸ **ojo del culo**‡ hole‡, arsehole**, asshole (*EEUU***) ▸ **ojo del huracán** eye of the hurricane • **el presidente vuelve a estar en el ojo del huracán** the president is once again at the centre of a controversy
5 (*LAm*) (= *depósito natural*) ▸ **ojo de agua** pool, natural pool
ojón ADJ (*LAm*) big-eyed, with big eyes
ojota SF **1** (*LAm*) (= *sandalia*) rough sandal
2 (*And, Cono Sur*) (= *piel de llama*) *tanned llama leather*
ojotes* SMPL (*And, CAm*) (*pey*) bulging eyes, goggle eyes; (*bonitos*) lovely big eyes
ojuelos SMPL = **ojillos**
okapi SM okapi
okey EXCL (*esp LAm*) okay!*, OK!*
okupa‡ SMF squatter
OL ABR (= **onda larga**) LW
ola SF **1** [*de mar*] wave • **la ola** (*en un estadio*) the Mexican wave • MODISMOS: • **la nueva ola** [*de moda*] the new wave • **batir las olas** to ply the seas • **estar en la cresta de la ola** to be on the crest of a wave • **hacer olas** to make waves, rock the boat; [*de personas*] the new generation; (*Mús, Cine*) the new wave ▸ **ola de marea** tidal wave ▸ **ola sísmica** tidal wave
2 (= *abundancia*) [*de indignación, prosperidad*] wave; [*de atentados, huelgas*] spate; [*de gripe*] (sudden) outbreak ▸ **ola de calor** heat wave ▸ **ola de frío** cold spell, cold snap ▸ **ola delictiva** crime wave
OLADE SF ABR = **Organización Latinoamericana de Energía**
olán SM (*Méx*) frill
OLAVU SF ABR = **Organización Latinoamericana del Vino y de la Uva**
olé EXCL bravo!
oleada SF **1** (*Náut*) big wave
2 (= *gran cantidad*) [*de jóvenes, artistas*] wave; [*de atentados, huelgas*] spate; [*de inflación*] surge • **una gran ~ de gente** a great surge of people • **la primera ~ del ataque** the first wave of the attack
oleaginosa SF oil product
oleaginoso ADJ oily, oleaginous (*frm*)
oleaje SM swell, surge
olear[1] ▸ CONJUG 1a VI to wave, flutter
olear[2] ▸ CONJUG 1a VT to shout "olé" to, cheer, encourage
oleícola ADJ oil (*antes de s*), olive-oil (*antes de s*)
oleicultor(a) SM/F olive-grower
oleicultura SF olive-growing
óleo SM **1** (*gen*) oil • **santo(s) ~(s)** (*Rel*) holy oil(s)
2 (*Arte*) oil painting • **pintar al ~** to paint in oils
3 (*LAm*) (= *bautismo*) baptism
oleo... PREF oleo...
oleoducto SM pipeline, oil pipeline
oleoso ADJ oily
oler ▸ CONJUG 2i VT **1** (= *percibir por la nariz*) to smell • **me gusta ~ las flores** I like smelling the flowers
2* (= *sospechar*) to suspect • **ha olido lo que estás tramando** he suspects what you're up to, he's smelt a rat*
3* (= *curiosear*) to poke one's nose into* • **siempre anda oliendo lo que hacen los demás** he's always poking his nose into other people's affairs
VI **1** (= *despedir olor*) to smell (**a** of, like) • **huele muy bien** [*comida*] it smells very good; [*flor, perfume*] it smells very nice • **huele fatal** it smells foul • **huele que apesta** it stinks • **¡qué mal huelen estos zapatos!** these shoes smell awful! • **huele a humedad** it smells of damp • **huele a tabaco** it smells of cigarette smoke • **aquí huele a quemado** there's a smell of burning in here • **le huele el aliento** his breath smells • **te huelen los pies** your feet smell • **huele que alimenta*** (= *muy bien*) it smells heavenly; (= *muy mal*) it

smells foul, it stinks to high heaven*
2 (*indicando desconfianza*) • **sus excusas me huelen a camelo*** his excuses sound a bit fishy to me* • MODISMO: • **~ a chamusquina: todo esto me huele a chamusquina** the whole thing sounds fishy to me
(VPR) **olerse*** (= *sospechar*) to suspect • **nadie se había olido nada** nobody had suspected anything • **se olía que no iban a venir** he had the feeling *o* suspicion that they weren't going to come
oletear ▹ CONJUG 1a (VT) (*And*) to pry into
oletón (ADJ) (*And*) prying
olfa* (SMF) (*Cono Sur*) (= *lameculos*) creep*, bootlicker*, brown-nose (*EEUU*‡); (= *admirador*) admirer, follower
olfacción (SF) smelling, act of smelling, olfaction (*frm*)
olfatear ▹ CONJUG 1a (VT) **1** [+ *comida*] to smell, sniff; [+ *presa*] to scent, smell out
2 (= *curiosear*) to pry into, poke one's nose into
olfativo (ADJ) olfactory
olfato (SM) **1** (= *sentido*) smell, sense of smell
2 (= *instinto*) instinct, intuition
olfatorio (ADJ) olfactory
oliente (ADJ) • **bien ~** sweet-smelling • **mal ~** foul-smelling
oligarca (SMF) oligarch
oligarquía (SF) oligarchy
oligárquico (ADJ) oligarchic, oligarchical
oligo... (PREF) oligo...
oligoceno (ADJ) Oligocene
(SM) • **el ~** the Oligocene
oligoelemento (SM) trace element
oligofrénico/a (ADJ) mentally handicapped
(SM/F) mentally handicapped person
oligopolio (SM) oligopoly
oligopolístico (ADJ) oligopolistic
oligopsonio (SM) oligopsony
olimpiada (SF), **olimpíada** (SF) Olympiad • **las Olimpiadas** the Olympics • **Olimpiada de Invierno** Winter Olympics
olímpicamente* (ADV) • **pasó de nosotros ~*** he completely snubbed us
olímpico/a (ADJ) **1** [*deporte, título*] Olympic; (*Hist*) Olympian
2* (= *enorme*) • **nos despreció de forma olímpica** he was utterly contemptuous of us • **fue una sesión de trabajo olímpica** it was a marathon work session
3 (= *despectivo*) dismissive
(SM/F) Olympic athlete
olimpismo (SM) (= *movimiento*) Olympic movement; (= *juegos*) Olympic Games (*pl*)
Olimpo (SM) Olympus
oliscar ▹ CONJUG 1g (VT) **1** (= *olfatear*) to smell, sniff (gently)
2 (= *curiosear*) to investigate, look into
(VI) (= *apestar*) to start to smell (bad)
olisco (ADJ) (*Cono Sur*), **oliscón** (ADJ) (*And*), **oliscoso** (ADJ) (*LAm*) [*carne*] high*
olisquear ▹ CONJUG 1a (VT), (VI) = **oliscar**
oliva (SF) **1** (= *aceituna*) olive • **(color) verde ~** olive green
2 (= *árbol*) olive tree
3 (*Orn*) = **lechuza**
(ADJ INV) olive
oliváceo (ADJ) olive, olive-green
olivar (SM) olive grove
olivarero/a (ADJ) olive (*antes de s*)
(SM/F) olive-producer, olive-oil producer
Oliverio (SM) Oliver
olivero (ADJ) olive (*antes de s*), olive-growing (*antes de s*) • **región olivera** olive-growing region
olivicultor(a) (SM/F) olive grower
olivicultura (SF) olive growing
olivo (SM) olive tree • MODISMO: • **tomar el ~‡** to beat it*
olla (SF) **1** (= *cacharro*) pot, pan • MODISMO: • **se me va la ~*** (*por volverse loco*) I'm losing my head; (*hablando sin parar*) I'm going over the top; (*por borrachera*) I'm out of my head*; (*al perder el hilo*) I'm losing the thread, I'm getting lost ▸ **olla a presión, olla de presión** pressure cooker ▸ **olla exprés** pressure cooker
2 (*Culin*) stew ▸ **olla podrida** hotpot
3 (*en río*) eddy, whirlpool
4 (*Alpinismo*) chimney
5 ▸ **olla común, olla popular** (*Cono Sur*) soup kitchen
ollar (SM) [*de caballo*] nostril
ollero/a (SM/F) (= *artesano*) *maker of pots and pans*; (= *vendedor*) *dealer in pots and pans*
olmeca (ADJ) Olmec
(SMF) Olmec • **los ~s** the Olmecs
olmeda (SF), **olmedo** (SM) elm grove
olmo (SM) elm, elm tree ▸ **olmo campestre** common elm ▸ **olmo de montaña** wych elm
ológrafo (ADJ), (SM) holograph
olor (SM) **1** (*gen*) smell (**a** of) • **buen ~** nice smell • **mal ~** bad smell, nasty smell • **tiene mal ~** it smells horrible ▸ **olor a quemado** smell of burning ▸ **olor a sudor** smell of sweat, body odour *o* (*EEUU*) odor, B.O.* ▸ **olor corporal** body odour *o* (*EEUU*) odor, B.O.*
2 (= *atracción*) smell • **acudir al ~ del dinero** to be attracted by the smell of money
3 (= *fama*) ▸ **olor de santidad** odour of sanctity
4 olores (*Cono Sur, Méx*) (*Culin*) spices
olorcillo (SM) (*ligero*) faint smell; (*delicado*) delicate aroma; (*pey*) whiff (**a** of)
oloroso (ADJ) sweet-smelling, fragrant, scented
(SM) (= *jerez*) oloroso, oloroso sherry
olote (SM) (*CAm, Méx*) **1** (*Agr*) (= *mazorca*) corncob; (= *tallo*) maize stalk
2 • **un ~** a nobody, a nonentity
olotear ▹ CONJUG 1a (VI) (*CAm, Méx*) to gather maize *o* (*EEUU*) corn, harvest maize *o* (*EEUU*) corn
olotera (SF) (*CAm, Méx*) **1** (= *montón*) heap of corncobs
2 (= *máquina*) maize thresher
OLP (SF ABR) (= **Organización para la Liberación de Palestina**) PLO
olvidadizo (ADJ) **1** (= *desmemoriado*) forgetful
2 (= *ingrato*) ungrateful
olvidado (ADJ) **1** (= *abandonado*) forgotten • **~ de Dios** godforsaken
2 = **olvidadizo**
olvidar ▹ CONJUG 1a (VT) **1** (= *no acordarse de*) to forget • **he olvidado su nombre** I've forgotten his name • **~ hacer algo** to forget to do sth • **no olvides comprar el pan** don't forget to buy the bread • **¡olvídame!*** get lost!*
2 (= *dejar olvidado*) to forget, leave behind, leave • **no olvides los guantes** don't forget your gloves, don't leave your gloves behind • **olvidé las llaves encima de la mesa** I left the keys on the table • **olvidé el paraguas en la tienda** I left my umbrella in the shop
3 (= *omitir*) to leave out, omit
(VPR) **olvidarse 1** (= *no acordarse*) to forget • **se me olvidó por completo** I forgot all about it • **se me olvida la fecha** I forget the date, I can't think of the date • **~se de hacer algo** to forget to do sth • **me olvidé de decírtelo** I forgot to tell you
2 (= *dejarse olvidado*) to forget, leave behind, leave • **se me olvidó el paraguas** I forgot my umbrella, I left my umbrella behind • **me he olvidado el maletín en casa** I have left my briefcase at home
3 (*fig*) (*pey*) to forget o.s.

> **OLVIDAR**
>
> *Si se* **nos olvida un objeto** *en algún lugar,* **olvidar** *se puede traducir por* **forget, leave** *o* **leave behind**:
>
> ▹ *Por regla general, si no mencionamos el lugar donde se nos ha olvidado,* **olvidar** *se traduce por* **forget** *o* **leave behind**:
> **He olvidado la cartera**
> I have forgotten my wallet, I have left my wallet behind
> **No olvides el pasaporte**
> Don't forget your passport, Don't leave your passport behind
>
> ▹ *Si mencionamos el lugar donde se nos ha olvidado,* **olvidar** *se suele traducir por* **leave**:
> **He olvidado la cartera en el restaurante**
> I have left my wallet in the restaurant
>
> *Para otros usos y ejemplos ver la entrada.*

olvido (SM) **1** (*absoluto*) oblivion • **caer en el ~** to fall into oblivion • **echar al ~** to forget • **enterrar** *o* **hundir en el ~** to cast into oblivion (*liter*) • **rescatar del ~** to rescue from oblivion
2 (= *estado*) forgetfulness
3 (= *descuido*) slip, oversight • **ha sido por ~** it was an oversight
olvidón (ADJ) (*And*) forgetful
OM (ABR) **1** (*Pol*) = **Orden Ministerial**
2 (*Radio*) (= **onda media**) MW
Omán (SM) Oman
omaní (ADJ) Omani
(SMF) Omani
ombligo (SM) navel, belly button* • MODISMOS: • **se le arrugó** *o* **encogió el ~** he got cold feet* • **meter a algn el ~ para dentro*** to put the wind up sb* • **mirarse el ~** to contemplate one's navel
ombliguera (SF) (*And*) striptease artiste
ombú (SM) (*Arg*) ombú, ombú tree
ombudsman (SM) ombudsman
OMC (SF ABR) (= **Organización Mundial del Comercio**) WTO
omega (SF) omega
OMG (SM ABR) (= **Organismo Modificado Genéticamente**) GMO
OMI (SF ABR) (= **Organización Marítima Internacional**) IMO
OMIC (SF ABR) (*Esp*) = **Oficina Municipal de Información al Consumidor**
ominoso (ADJ) **1** (= *de mal agüero*) ominous
2 (= *pasmoso*) awful, dreadful
omisión (SF) **1** (*gen*) omission, oversight • **su ~ de hacer algo** his failure to do sth ▸ **omisión de auxilio** (*Jur*) failure to give assistance, failure to go to somebody's aid
2 (= *descuido*) slip, oversight
omiso (ADJ) • **hacer caso ~ de algo** to ignore sth
omitir ▹ CONJUG 3a (VT) **1** (= *no decir*) to leave out, miss out, omit
2 • **~ hacer algo** to omit to do sth, fail to do sth
OMM (SF ABR) (= **Organización Meteorológica Mundial**) WMO
omni... (PREF) omni...
ómnibus (ADJ) • **tren ~** slow train
(SM) **1** (*Aut, Hist*) omnibus
2 (*LAm*) bus
omnibús (SM) (*Cono Sur*) bus
omnicomprensivo (ADJ) all-inclusive
omnidireccional (ADJ) omnidirectional
omnímodo (ADJ) (*gen*) all-embracing; [*poder*] absolute

omnipotencia (SF) omnipotence
omnipotente (ADJ) omnipotent, all-powerful
omnipresencia (SF) omnipresence
omnipresente (ADJ) omnipresent
omnisapiente (ADJ) omniscient, all-knowing
omnisciencia (SF) omniscience
omnisciente (ADJ), **omniscio** (ADJ) omniscient, all-knowing
omnívoro (ADJ) omnivorous
omoplato (SM), **omóplato** (SM) shoulder blade
OMS (SF ABR) (= **Organización Mundial de la Salud**) WHO
OMT (SF ABR) (*Esp*) = **Oficina Municipal de Transportes**
-ón, -ona ▸ **Aspects of Word Formation in Spanish 2**
onagra (SF) evening primrose
onanismo (SM) onanism
onanista (ADJ) onanistic
(SMF) onanist
ONCE (SF ABR) (*Esp*) = **Organización Nacional de Ciegos Españoles**

> **ONCE**
> The **Organización Nacional de Ciegos Españoles** began life as a charity for the blind and is now one of the wealthiest and most successful organizations in Spain, with a wide-ranging sphere of activities, including assisting other disabled groups as well as the blind. The popular lottery which it set up to provide employment for its members is its main source of income, generating plentiful capital for investment.

once (ADJ INV), (PRON) (*gen*) eleven; (*ordinal, en la fecha*) eleventh • **las ~** eleven o'clock • **le escribí el día ~** I wrote to him on the eleventh • **MODISMOS:** • **tomar las ~*** to have elevenses* • **tomar ~** *o* **la(s) ~** *o* *a veces* **~s** (*Chile*) to have afternoon tea, have an afternoon snack
(SM) (*gen*) eleven; (= *fecha*) eleventh; (*Ftbl*) team • **el ~ titular** the first team; ▸ **seis**
oncear ▸ CONJUG 1a (VI) (*And*) to have an afternoon snack
onceavo/a (ADJ), (SM/F), **onceno/a** (ADJ), (SM/F) eleventh; ▸ **sexto**
oncogén (SM) oncogene
oncología (SF) oncology ▸ **oncología clínica** clinical oncology
oncólogo/a (SM/F) oncologist
onda (SF) **1** (*gen*) wave • **tratamiento de ~ ultravioleta** ultra-violet treatment ▸ **onda corta** short wave • **de ~ corta** shortwave (*antes de s*) ▸ **onda de choque** shock wave ▸ **onda de radio** radio wave ▸ **onda expansiva** shock wave ▸ **onda explosiva** blast, shock wave ▸ **onda extracorta** ultra-short wave ▸ **onda larga** long wave ▸ **onda luminosa** light wave ▸ **onda media** medium wave ▸ **ondas cerebrales** brain waves ▸ **onda sísmica** shock wave ▸ **onda sonora** sound wave
2* (= *ambiente*) wavelength • **estamos en la misma ~** we're on the same wavelength • **¡qué buena ~!*** that's great!* • **MODISMOS:** • **agarrar** *o* **coger la ~** (= *entender*) to get it*, get the point*; (= *coger el tino*) to get the hang of it • **estar en la ~*** (= *de moda*) to be in*; (= *al tanto*) to be on the ball*, be up to date; [*persona*] (= *a la moda*) to be hip* • **estar en ~‡** (= *drogado*) to be high‡ (*on drugs*) • **estar en ~ gay** to be into the gay thing* • **se merece un regalo en su ~*** he deserves a present he'll really like • **estar fuera de ~** to be out of touch • **perder la ~*** to lose one's touch • **¿qué ~?** (*LAm**) what's up?*
3 (*Cos*) scallop
ondeante (ADJ) = **ondulante**
ondear ▸ CONJUG 1a (VT) **1** [+ *bandera*] to wave
2 (*Cos*) to pink, scallop
(VI) **1** (= *moverse*) [*agua*] to ripple; [*bandera*] to fly, flutter; [*pelo*] to flow • **la bandera ondea en lo alto del edificio** the flag flies from the top of the building • **la bandera ondea a media asta** the flag is flying at half mast
2 (= *flotar al viento*) to stream
(VPR) **ondearse** to swing, sway
ondia* (EXCL) (*euf*) = **hostia**
ondímetro (SM) wave meter
ondina (SF) undine, water nymph
ondulación (SF) **1** [*de movimiento*] undulation, wavy motion; (*en agua*) wave, ripple; (*en pelo*) wave ▸ **ondulación permanente†** permanent wave
2 ondulaciones (*en paisaje*) undulations, ups and downs; (*en terreno*) unevenness (*sing*)
ondulado (ADJ) [*carretera*] uneven, rough; [*paisaje, terreno*] undulating, rolling; [*superficie*] undulating, uneven; [*cartón, hierro*] corrugated; [*pelo*] wavy
(SM) (*en pelo*) wave
ondulante (ADJ) **1** [*movimiento*] (*gen*) undulating; (= *de lado a lado*) from side to side, (gently) swaying
2 [*sonido*] rising and falling
3 = **ondulado**
ondular ▸ CONJUG 1a (VT) [+ *pelo*] to wave; [+ *cuerpo*] to wiggle • **hacerse ~ el pelo** to have one's hair waved
(VI), (VPR) **ondularse** (*gen*) to undulate; (= *balancearse*) to sway
ondulatorio (ADJ) undulatory, wavy
oneroso (ADJ) **1** (= *pesado*) onerous, burdensome
2 (*Jur*) onerous
ONG (SF ABR) (= **Organización No Gubernamental**) NGO
ónice (SM) onyx
onírico (ADJ) oneiric, dream (*antes de s*)
ónix (SM) onyx
ONL (SF ABR) (= **Organización No Lucrativa**) non-profit-making organization
on-line [on'lain] (*Inform*) (ADV), (ADJ) online
ONO (ABR) (= **oesnoroeste**) WNW
onomástica (SF) **1** [*del nombre*] saint's day; ▸ **SANTO**
2 (= *ciencia*) onomastics (*sing*), study of personal names
onomástico (ADJ) onomastic, name (*antes de s*), of names • **fiesta onomástica** saint's day • **índice ~** index of names • **lista onomástica** list of names
(SM) saint's day, name day
onomatopeya (SF) onomatopoeia
onomatopéyico (ADJ) onomatopoeic
ontología (SF) ontology
ontológico (ADJ) ontological
ONU (SF ABR) = **Organización de las Naciones Unidas** • **la ONU** the UN
onubense (ADJ) of/from Huelva
(SMF) native/inhabitant of Huelva • **los ~s** the people of Huelva
ONUDI (SF ABR) (= **Organización de las Naciones Unidas para el Desarrollo Industrial**) UNIDO
onusiano (ADJ) United Nations (*antes de s*)
onza¹ (SF) ounce
onza² (SF) (*LAm*) (*Zool*) snow leopard, ounce
onzavo/a (ADJ), (SM/F) eleventh; ▸ **sexto**
oolítico (ADJ) oolitic
oolito (SM) oolite
O.P. (ABR) **1** = **Obras Públicas**
2 (*Rel*) (= **Orden de Predicadores**) O.S.D.
op. (ABR) (= **opus**) op
OPA (SF ABR) (= **oferta pública de adquisición**) *takeover bid* ▸ **OPA hostil** hostile takeover bid
opa¹ (ADJ) (*And, Arg*) **1** (= *sordomudo*) deaf and dumb
2* (= *tonto*) stupid; (= *retrasado*) mentally retarded
(SMF)* (= *tonto*) idiot
opa² (EXCL) (*Arg*) stop it!
opacar ▸ CONJUG 1g (*LAm*) (VT) **1** (= *hacer opaco*) to make opaque; (= *oscurecer*) to darken; (= *empañar*) to mist up; (= *deslustrar*) to dull, tarnish
2 [+ *persona*] to outshine, overshadow
(VPR) **opacarse 1** (*LAm*) (= *hacerse opaco*) to become opaque; (= *oscurecerse*) to darken, get dark; (= *empañarse*) to mist up; (= *deslustrarse*) to lose its shine, become tarnished
2 (*And, CAm*) [*cielo*] to cloud over
opacidad (SF) **1** (= *falta de transparencia*) opacity, opaqueness
2 (= *falta de brillo*) dullness, lifelessness
3 (= *tristeza*) gloominess, sadness
opaco (ADJ) **1** (= *no transparente*) opaque • **una pantalla opaca a los rayos X** a screen which does not let X-rays through, a screen opaque to X-rays
2 (= *sin brillo*) dull, lifeless
3 (= *triste*) gloomy, sad
opado (ADJ) (*And, Caribe*) pale
OPAEP (SF ABR) (= **Organización de Países Árabes Exportadores de Petróleo**) OAPEC
opalescencia (SF) opalescence
opalescente (ADJ) opalescent
ópalo (SM) opal
opaparado (ADJ) (*And*) bewildered
opar ▸ CONJUG 1a (VT), (VI) to put in a takeover bid (for); ▸ **OPA**
opción (SF) **1** (= *elección*) option • **opciones por defecto** default options • **no hay ~** there is no other option, there is no alternative *o* choice
2 (= *derecho*) right, option • **tiene ~ a viajar gratis** he has the right *o* option to travel free
3 (*Com*) option (**a on**) • **con ~ a** *o* **para ocho más** with an option on eight more • **este dispositivo es de ~** this gadget is optional • **suscribir una ~ para la compra de algo** to take out an option on sth ▸ **opción a compra, opción de adquisición, opción de compra** (*gen*) option to buy, option to purchase; (*en Bolsa*) call option ▸ **opción de venta** (*en Bolsa*) put option ▸ **opciones sobre acciones** stock options, share options
opcional (ADJ) optional
opcionalmente (ADV) optionally
op. cit. (ABR) (= **opere citato**) op. cit.
Op.D. (ABR) (*Rel*) = **Opus Dei**
opear* ▸ CONJUG 1a (VI) (*And, Cono Sur*) to act the fool, fool about
open ['open] (SM INV) (*Golf*) open
OPEP (SF ABR) (= **Organización de Países Exportadores del Petróleo**) OPEC
ópera (SF) (*Teat*) (= *género*) opera; (= *edificio*) opera, opera house • **gran ~** grand opera ▸ **ópera bufa** comic opera ▸ **ópera prima** debut, first work
operable (ADJ) [*cataratas, tumor*] operable; [*regulaciones*] workable; [*medidas*] workable, feasible
operación (SF) **1** (= *acción*) operation ▸ **operaciones de rescate, operaciones de salvamento** rescue operations ▸ **operación retorno** (*Esp*) *effort to control traffic returning to a big city after a major holiday*
2 (*Med*) operation • **una ~ de estómago** a stomach operation, an operation on the stomach ▸ **operación a corazón abierto** open-heart surgery ▸ **operación cesárea** Caesarean, Caesarean operation

▸ **operación quirúrgica** surgical operation
3 (*Mil*) operation ▸ **operaciones conjuntas** joint operations ▸ **operación de ablandamiento** softening-up operation ▸ **operación de limpia**, **operación de limpieza** mopping up operation
4 (*Com*) transaction, deal ▸ **operación a plazo** forward transaction ▸ **operaciones bursátiles**, **operaciones de bolsa** stock-exchange transactions ▸ **operación "llave en mano"** turnkey operation ▸ **operación mercantil** business deal
5 (*Mat*) operation
6 (*LAm*) (*Min*) operation, working, exploitation; (*Com*) management
7 ▸ **operaciones accesorias** (*Inform*) housekeeping (*sing*)

operacional ADJ operational

operador(a) SM/F (*gen*) operator; (*Med*) surgeon; (*Cine*) [*de rodaje*] cameraman/camerawoman; [*de proyección*] projectionist ▸ **operador(a) de cabina** projectionist, operator ▸ **operador(a) de grúa** crane operator, winchman ▸ **operador(a) del telégrafo** (*LAm*) telegraph operator ▸ **operador(a) de sistemas** systems operator ▸ **operador(a) de télex** telex operator ▸ **operador(a) turístico/a** tour operator
SM = **operadora**

operadora SF (= *compañía*) provider, operator

operante ADJ 1 (= *en funcionamiento*) operating
2 (= *influente*) powerful, influential • **los medios más ~s del país** the most influential circles in the country

operar ▸ CONJUG 1a VT 1 (= *producir*) [+ *cambio*] to produce, bring about; [+ *cura*] to effect; [+ *milagro*] to work
2 (*Med*) [+ *paciente*] to operate on • **~ a algn de apendicitis** to operate on sb for appendicitis
3 [+ *máquina*] to operate, use
4 (= *dirigir*) [+ *negocio*] to manage, run; [+ *mina*] to work, exploit
VI 1 (*tb Mat*) to operate
2 (*Com*) to deal, do business • **hoy no se ha operado en la bolsa** there has been no dealing *o* trading on the stock exchange today
VPR **operarse** 1 (= *producirse*) to occur, come about • **se han operado grandes cambios** great changes have been made *o* have come about, there have been great changes
2 (*Med*) to have an operation (**de** for)

operario/a SM/F (*gen*) operative; (*esp LAm*) (= *obrero*) worker ▸ **operario/a de máquina** machinist

ópera-rock SF (PL: **óperas-rock**) rock opera

operatividad SF 1 [*de proyecto*] operating capacity
2 (= *eficacia*) effectiveness, efficiency

operativizar ▸ CONJUG 1f VT to put into operation, make operative

operativo ADJ operative
SM (*Cono Sur*) (*esp militar, policial*) operation

operatorio ADJ (*Med*) operating (*antes de s*)

opereta SF operetta, light opera

operia SF (*And, Cono Sur*) stupidity

operista SMF opera singer

operístico ADJ operatic, opera (*antes de s*)

operófilo/a SM/F opera-lover

operoso* ADJ (*Caribe*) irritable

opiáceo SM opiate

opiante* ADJ (*Arg, Uru*) boring • **sus clases son ~s** his lessons are a real drag*, his lessons are really boring

opiarse* ▸ CONJUG 1b VPR (*Cono Sur*) to get bored, get fed up*

opiata SF opiate

opimo ADJ plentiful, abundant, rich

opinable ADJ debatable, open to a variety of opinions

opinar ▸ CONJUG 1a VT to think • **~ que ...** to think that ..., be of the opinion that ...
VI 1 (= *pensar*) to think
2 • **~ bien de algo/algn** to think well of sth/sb, have a good *o* high opinion of sth/sb
3 (= *dar su opinión*) to give one's opinion • **fueron opinando uno tras otro** they gave their opinions in turn • **hubo un 7% que no quiso ~** (*en sondeo*) there were 7% "don't knows"

opinión SF opinion, view • **en mi ~** in my opinion *o* view • **ser de la ~ (de) que ...** to be of the opinion that ..., take the view that ... • **cambiar de ~** to change one's mind • **compartir la ~ de algn** to share sb's opinion *o* view • **formarse una ~** to form an opinion • **mudar de ~** to have a change of mind *o* opinion ▸ **opinión pública** public opinion

opio SM 1 (= *sustancia*) opium • MODISMO: • **dar el ~ a algn*** to enchant sb, captivate sb • **ella le dio el ~** she swept him off his feet
2 (*Cono Sur**) (= *tostón*) drag* • **la película es un ~** the film is a drag*

opiómano/a SM/F opium addict

opíparo ADJ [*banquete*] sumptuous

oponente ADJ opposing, contrary
SMF opponent

oponer ▸ CONJUG 2q (PP: **opuesto**) VT
1 [+ *resistencia*] to put up
2 [+ *argumentos*] to set out • **estaba en desacuerdo y opuso sus razones** he set out the reasons for his disagreement
3 (= *poner contra*) • **opusieron un dique contra el mar** they built a dyke as a defence against the sea
VPR **oponerse** to be opposed; (*mutuamente*) to oppose each other • **yo no me opongo** I don't object • **~se a algo** to oppose sth • **se opone rotundamente a ello** he is flatly opposed to it

Oporto SM Oporto

oporto SM port

oportunamente ADV 1 (*en el tiempo*) opportunely
2 (= *pertinentemente*) appropriately

oportunidad SF 1 (= *ocasión*) chance, opportunity • **darle una/otra ~ a algn** to give sb a/another chance • **tener la ~ de hacer algo** to have a chance to do sth, have the chance of doing sth • **no tuvo la ~ de ir** he didn't have a chance to go • **a** *o* **en la primera ~** at the first opportunity
2 (= *vez*) occasion, time • **en dos ~es** on two occasions
3 (*Jur*) • **igualdad de ~es** equality of opportunity
4 • **"oportunidades"** (= *rebajas*) "bargains"
5 (= *cualidad*) opportuneness, timeliness

oportunismo SM opportunism

oportunista ADJ opportunist, opportunistic
SMF opportunist

oportuno ADJ 1 [*ocasión*] opportune • **en el momento ~** at an opportune moment, at the right moment • **su llamada no pudo ser más oportuna** his call could not have come at a better moment, his call could not have been better timed
2 (= *pertinente*) appropriate • **no me ha parecido ~ decírselo** I didn't think it appropriate to tell him • **una respuesta oportuna** an apt reply • **sería ~ hacerlo en seguida** it would be best to do it at once
3 [*persona*] • **¡ella siempre tan oportuna!** (*iró*) you can always rely on her!

oposición SF 1 (*gen*) opposition ▸ **oposición frontal** direct opposition, total opposition
2 (*Esp*) (*tb* **oposiciones**) *Civil Service examination* • **hay varias plazas de libre ~** *o* **de ~ libre** there are several places that will be filled on the basis of a competitive examination • **sacar unas oposiciones** to be successful in a public competition • **hacer oposiciones a ...** • **presentarse a unas oposiciones a ...** to sit an examination for ... • **hacer oposiciones para una cátedra** to compete for a chair

> **OPOSICIONES**
> Being a civil servant in Spain means having a job for life, but applicants for public-sector jobs must pass competitive exams called **oposiciones**. The candidates (**opositores**) must sit a series of written exams and/or attend interviews. Some applicants spend years studying for and resitting exams, so preparing candidates for **oposiciones** is a major source of work for many **academias**. All public-sector appointments that are open to competition are published in the **BOE**, an official government publication.
> ▸ ACADEMIA, BOE

oposicional ADJ opposition (*antes de s*)

oposicionista ADJ opposition (*antes de s*)
SMF member of the opposition

opositar ▸ CONJUG 1a VI (*Esp*) to go in for a public competition (*for a post*), sit for a public entrance/promotion examination

opositor(a) ADJ (= *contrario*) opposing; (*Pol*) opposition (*antes de s*), of the opposition • **el líder ~** the leader of the opposition
SM/F 1 (*Univ*) competitor, candidate (**a** for)
2 (*Pol*) opponent

opresión SF 1 (= *sensación*) oppression; [*de situación, lugar*] oppressiveness
2 (*Med*) difficulty in breathing, tightness of the chest • **sentir ~** to find it difficult to breathe

opresivo ADJ oppressive

opresor(a) ADJ oppressive
SM/F oppressor

oprimente ADJ oppressive

oprimido/a ADJ oppressed
SM/F • **los ~s** the oppressed

oprimir ▸ CONJUG 3a VT 1 (= *apretar*) [+ *objeto*] to squeeze, press, exert pressure on; [+ *gas*] to compress • **la blusa me estaba oprimiendo el cuello** the blouse was too tight round my neck
2 [+ *botón, tecla*] to press
3 [+ *pueblo, nación*] (= *tiranizar*) to oppress; (= *cargar*) to burden, weigh down; (= *aplastar*) to crush

oprobio SM (*frm*) opprobrium (*frm*), ignominy

oprobioso ADJ (*frm*) opprobrious (*frm*), ignominious

optar ▸ CONJUG 1a VI 1 (*gen*) to choose, decide • **~ entre** to choose *o* decide between • **~ por** to choose, decide on, opt for • **~ por hacer algo** to choose to do sth, opt to do sth
2 • **~ a** to compete for • **~ a un premio** to compete for a prize • **(poder) ~ a** to (have the right to) apply for *o* go in for • **ellos no pueden ~ a las becas** they are not entitled to apply for the scholarships

optativa SF (*Educ*) option, elective (*EEUU*)

optativamente ADV optionally

optativo ADJ 1 (= *opcional*) optional
2 (*Ling*) optative
SM (*Ling*) optative

óptica SF 1 (= *ciencia*) optics (*sing*)
2 (= *tienda*) optician's
3 (= *punto de vista*) viewpoint, point of view • **desde esta ~** from this point of view

óptico/a ADJ [*instrumentos, fibra*] optical; [*nervio*] optic • **fue solo una ilusión óptica** it was just an optical illusion

SM/F optician
óptico-cinético SM light show
optimación SF optimization
óptimamente ADV ideally
optimar ▷ CONJUG 1a VT to optimize
optimismo SM optimism ▸ **optimismo cauto, optimismo matizado** cautious optimism
optimista ADJ optimistic, hopeful
SMF optimist
optimización SF optimization
optimizar ▷ CONJUG 1f VT to optimize
óptimo ADJ ideal, optimum (*antes de s*)
• **condiciones óptimas para la navegación a vela** ideal *o* optimum conditions for sailing • **hemos obtenido ~s resultados con este producto** we've had top *o* the best results with this product
SM ▸ **óptimo de población** (*Econ*) optimum population
optometrista SMF optometrist
opuesto PP de **oponer**
ADJ **1** [*ángulo, lado*] opposite • **están en el extremo ~ de la ciudad** they are on the opposite side of town • **chocó con un coche que venía en dirección opuesta** he crashed into a car coming in the opposite direction
2 (*Dep*) [*equipo*] opposing
3 [*intereses, versiones*] conflicting • **tenemos gustos ~s** we have very different tastes
4 • **ser ~ a algo** to be opposed to sth
opugnar ▷ CONJUG 1a VT to attack
opulencia SF **1** (= *lujo*) luxury; (= *riqueza*) opulence, affluence • **vivir en la ~** to live in luxury • **sociedad de la ~** affluent society
2 (= *abundancia*) • **la ~ de sus cabellos** the luxuriance of her hair • **la ~ de sus carnes** her abundant *o* ample flesh (*liter o hum*)
opulento ADJ **1** (= *lujoso*) luxurious; (= *rico*) opulent, affluent
2 (= *abundante*) abundant
opuncia SF (*Méx*) prickly pear
opus SM (*Mús*) opus
opúsculo SM tract, brief treatise

OPUS DEI
The **Opus Dei**, also referred to as **la Obra**, is an influential but very controversial Catholic association formed in 1928 with the aim of spreading Christian principles in society. It has a direct link to the Vatican by virtue of a special "Personal Prelature" granted by John Paul II in 1982, which in practice means that it enjoys complete independence from local diocesan authorities. During the Franco era members of the **Opus** formed the intellectual backbone of the régime. Members of the **Opus** are particularly well-represented in educational circles: the universities of Pamplona in Spain and Piura in Peru are run by it. In 2002 the priest who founded **Opus Dei**, Josemaría Escrivá de Balaguer, was canonized by Pope John Paul II.

opusdeísta SMF member of Opus Dei
opusino ADJ (*pey*) sanctimonious
OPV SF ABR (= **Oferta Pública de Venta (de acciones)**) *share offer*
oquedad SF **1** (= *cavidad*) hollow, cavity
2 [*de escrito, habla*] emptiness, hollowness
3 (= *vacío*) void
oquedal SM wood of grown timber, plantation
ORA SF ABR = **Operación de Regulación de Aparcamientos**
ora ADV (*frm*) • **ora A, ora B** (*uso temporal*) now A, now B; (= *a veces*) sometimes A, sometimes B
oración SF **1** (*Rel*) prayer • **oraciones por la paz** prayers for peace • **estar en ~** to be at prayer
2 (*Ling*) sentence • **partes de la ~** parts of speech ▸ **oración compuesta** complex sentence ▸ **oración directa** direct speech ▸ **oración indirecta** indirect speech, reported speech ▸ **oración subordinada** subordinate clause
3 (= *discurso*) oration (*frm*), speech • **pronunciar una ~** to make a speech ▸ **oración fúnebre** funeral oration
4 (*LAm*) (= *invocación*) pagan invocation, magic charm
oracional ADJ sentence (*antes de s*)
oráculo SM oracle
orador(a) SM/F speaker, orator (*frm*)
oral ADJ oral • **por vía ~** (*Med*) orally
órale* EXCL (*Méx*) (= *¡venga!*) come on!; (= *¡oiga!*) hey!
oralmente ADV orally
orangután SM orangutan
orante ADJ • **actitud ~** kneeling position, attitude of prayer
SMF (= *persona*) worshipper, person at prayer
orar ▷ CONJUG 1a VI **1** (*Rel*) to pray (**a** to, **por** for)
2 (= *disertar*) to speak, make a speech
orate SMF lunatic
orático ADJ (*CAm*) crazy, lunatic
oratoria SF oratory • **concurso de ~** public speaking competition
oratorio ADJ oratorical
SM (*Mús*) oratorio; (*Rel*) oratory, chapel
orbe SM **1** (= *globo*) orb, sphere
2 (= *mundo*) world • **en todo el ~** all over the world *o* globe
órbita SF **1** (*gen*) orbit • **entrar en ~ alrededor de la luna** to go into orbit round the moon • **estar en ~** to be in orbit • **poner en ~** to put in orbit • **está fuera de su ~ de acción** it's outside his field
2 (*Anat*) (*ocular*) socket, eye-socket
orbital ADJ orbital
orbitar ▷ CONJUG 1a VT to orbit
orca SF killer whale
Órcadas SFPL Orkneys, Orkney Islands
órdago • **de ~*** ADJ (*gen*) fantastic; (*pey*) awful, tremendous* • **tienen un yate de ~** they've got a fantastic yacht • **se cogieron una borrachera de ~** they got well and truly drunk
ordalías SFPL (*Hist*) ordeal (*sing*), trial (*sing*) by ordeal
orden SM **1** (*en colocación, sucesión*) **a** (*con objetos, personas*) order • **fueron archivados por ~ alfabético** they were filed alphabetically *o* in alphabetical order • **se fueron sentando por ~ de llegada** they sat down in order of arrival • **por ~ de antigüedad** in order of seniority • **por ~ cronológico** in chronological order • **por ~ de importancia** in order of importance • **poner ~ en algo** to sort sth out • **el ministro supo poner ~ en el departamento** the minister managed to sort out *o* put some order into the department • **los policías trataban de poner ~ en aquel caos de tráfico** the police attempted to sort out the traffic chaos • **voy a poner ~ en mi mesa** I'm going to tidy up my desk
b • **en ~** in order • **todo en ~, mi capitán** everything is in order, captain • **en ~ de combate** in battle order • **poner en ~** [+ *papeles, documentos*] to sort out • **en unas cuantas horas consiguieron poner todas sus cosas en ~** in a few hours they managed to sort everything out • **poner en ~ las ideas** to sort out one's ideas • MODISMOS: • **poner la casa en ~** to put one's house in order • **sin ~ ni concierto** without rhyme or reason ▸ **orden del día** agenda ▸ **orden natural** natural order ▸ **orden sucesorio** order of succession
2 (*tb* **orden social**) order • **el ~ establecido** the established order • **las fuerzas del ~** the forces of law and order • **llamar al ~** to call to order • **mantener el ~** to keep order • **restablecer el ~** to restore *o* reestablish order ▸ **orden público** public order, law and order • **fueron detenidos por alterar el ~ público** they were arrested for breach of the peace *o* for disturbing the peace
3 (= *tipo*) nature • **motivos de ~ moral** moral reasons • **en otro ~ de cosas ...** at the same time ..., meanwhile ... • **de primer ~** [*figura*] leading; [*factor*] of prime importance, prime • **una figura política de primer ~** a leading political figure • **un pensador de primer ~** a first-rate thinker • **un problema de primer ~** a major problem • **en todos los órdenes** on all fronts
4 • **del ~ de** in the order of, in the region of • **el coste sería del ~ de diez millones de dólares** the cost would be in the order *o* region of ten million dollars • **necesitamos del ~ de 1.500 euros para comprarlo** we need approximately 1,500 euros to buy it
5 • **en ~ a** (= *con miras a*) with a view to; (= *en cuanto a*) with regard to • **en ~ a hacer algo** in order to do sth
6 (*Arquit*) order ▸ **orden corintio** Corinthian order ▸ **orden dórico** Doric order ▸ **orden jónico** Ionic order
7 (*Bio*) order
8 (*Rel*) (*tb* **orden sacerdotal**) ordination
SF **1** (= *mandato*) order • **¡es una ~!** (and) that's an order! • **tenemos órdenes de no dejar pasar a nadie** we are under orders not to let anybody through • **dar una ~ a algn** to give sb an order, order sb • **dar (la) ~ de hacer algo** to give the order to do sth • **hasta nueva ~** until further notice • **por ~ de** by order of • **fue encarcelado por ~ del juez** he was imprisoned by order of the judge
• MODISMO: • **estar a la ~ del día**: • **los robos están a la ~ del día en esta zona** robberies have become the norm in this area • **en los setenta llevar coleta estaba a la ~ del día** in the seventies ponytails were the in thing ▸ **orden de allanamiento** (*LAm*) search warrant ▸ **orden de arresto, orden de búsqueda y captura** arrest warrant ▸ **orden de citación** (*Méx*), **orden de comparación** (*Méx*) summons, subpoena (*EEUU*) ▸ **orden de desalojo** eviction order ▸ **orden de detención** arrest warrant ▸ **orden del día** (*Mil*) order of the day ▸ **orden de registro** search warrant ▸ **orden judicial** court order ▸ **orden ministerial** ministerial order, ministerial decree
2 • **a la ~ a** (*Mil*) yes, sir!
b (*LAm*) (*en tienda*) what can I get you?; (= *no hay de qué*) you're welcome, don't mention it! • **estoy a la ~ para lo que necesites** if there is anything you need, just ask
c • **a las órdenes de algn** (*Mil*) at sb's command; (*en la policía*) under sb's instructions *o* orders; (*en otros trabajos*) under sb • **el personal que estará a las órdenes del nuevo director** the staff who will be working under the new director • **¡a sus órdenes!** (*Mil*) yes sir; (*esp LAm*) at your service
3 (*Mil, Hist, Rel*) (= *institución*) order • **la Orden de Calatrava** the Order of Calatrava • **la Orden de San Benito** the Benedictine Order ▸ **orden de caballería** order of knighthood ▸ **orden militar** military order ▸ **orden monástica** monastic order ▸ **orden religiosa** religious order

4 **órdenes** (*Rel*) orders ▸ **órdenes mayores** major orders ▸ **órdenes menores** minor orders ▸ **órdenes sagradas** holy orders
5 (*Com, Econ*) order; (*Méx*) (= *pedido*) order • **cheques a la ~ de Suárez** cheques (to be made) payable to Suárez ▸ **orden bancaria** banker's order ▸ **orden de compra** purchase order ▸ **orden de pago** money order
6 (*Méx*) (= *ración*) dish

ordenación (SF) **1** (= *colocación*) (*estado*) order, arrangement; (*acción*) ordering, arranging ▸ **ordenación del territorio, ordenación territorial** town and country planning ▸ **ordenación del tráfico** traffic planning ▸ **ordenación urbana** town planning
2 (*Rel*) ordination

ordenada (SF) ordinate

ordenadamente (ADV) [*entrar, salir*] in an orderly fashion; [*trabajar*] in an organized *o* ordered manner • **evacuaron ~ a los heridos** they evacuated the wounded in an orderly fashion • **~ colocados** neatly arranged

ordenado (ADJ) **1** (= *en orden*) [*habitación, escritorio*] tidy; [*oficina*] well-organized, ordered • **tiene toda la casa muy limpia y ordenada** she keeps the house very clean and tidy • **llevan una vida normal y ordenada** they lead a normal, ordered *o* orderly life • **los niños entraron de forma ordenada en el museo** the children entered the museum in an orderly fashion
2 [*persona*] (*al colocar algo*) tidy; (*en el trabajo*) organized
3 (*Rel*) ordained, in holy orders

ordenador (SM) computer • **pasar a ~** to type up on computer ▸ **ordenador analógico** analogue computer, analog computer (*EEUU*) ▸ **ordenador central** mainframe computer ▸ **ordenador de bolsillo** palmtop (computer) ▸ **ordenador de gestión** business computer ▸ **ordenador de (sobre)mesa** desktop computer ▸ **ordenador doméstico** home computer ▸ **ordenador personal** personal computer ▸ **ordenador portátil** (*gen*) portable computer; (*pequeño*) laptop computer ▸ **ordenador torre** tower unit ▸ **ordenador transportable** portable computer

ordenamiento (SM) **1** (*Jur*) (= *leyes*) legislation • **el nuevo ~ eléctrico** the new legislation on electricity ▸ **ordenamiento constitucional** constitution ▸ **ordenamiento jurídico** legal system
2 (*al colocar algo*) ordering, arranging

ordenancista (SMF) disciplinarian, martinet

ordenando (SM) (*Rel*) ordinand

ordenanza (SF) (= *decreto*) ordinance, decree • **honores de ~** official honours • **ser de ~** to be the rule ▸ **ordenanzas municipales** bylaws
(SMF) **1** (*en oficina*) messenger
2 (= *bedel*) porter
3 (*Mil*) orderly

ordenar ▹ CONJUG 1a (VT) **1** (= *poner en orden*) (*siguiendo un sistema*) to arrange; (*colocando en su sitio*) to tidy; (*Inform*) to sort • **hay que ~ los recibos por fechas** we have to put the receipts in order of date, we have to arrange the receipts by date • **voy a ~ mis libros** I'm going to sort out *o* organize my books • **ordenó los relatos cronológicamente** he arranged the stories chronologically *o* in chronological order • **nunca ordena sus papeles** he never tidies his paperwork • **~ sus asuntos** to put one's affairs in order • **~ su vida** to put *o* get one's life in order
2 (= *mandar*) to order • **la juez ordenó su detención** the judge ordered his arrest • **les habían ordenado que siguieran al vehículo** they had been ordered to follow the vehicle • **un tono de ordeno y mando** a dictatorial tone
3 (*Rel*) to ordain • **fue ordenado sacerdote en octubre** he was ordained as a priest in October
(VPR) **ordenarse** (*Rel*) to be ordained

ordeña (SF) (*LAm*) milking

ordeñadero (SM) milking pail

ordeñadora (SF) milking machine

ordeñar ▹ CONJUG 1a (VT) [+ *vaca, oveja*] to milk; [+ *aceitunas*] to harvest

ordeño (SM), **ordeñe** (SM) (*Caribe*) [*de leche*] milking; [*de aceitunas*] harvest

órdiga‡ (SF) • **¡la ~!** (*Esp*) bloody hell!‡

ordinal (ADJ), (SM) ordinal

ordinariamente (ADV) ordinarily, usually

ordinariez (SF) **1** (= *cualidad*) coarseness, vulgarity, commonness
2 • **una ~** a coarse remark

ordinario (ADJ) **1** (= *normal*) ordinary • **de ~** usually • **de ~ coge el autobús para ir a trabajar** he usually takes the bus to work
2 (= *vulgar*) [*persona*] common; [*comportamiento, modales*] coarse • **son gente muy ordinaria** they're very common people • **solo cuenta chistes ~s** he only tells crude jokes
(SM) **1** (*Rel*) ordinary ▸ **ordinario de la misa** Ordinary of the mass
2† (= *gastos*) daily household expenses (*pl*)
3† (= *recadero*) carrier, delivery man

ordinograma (SM) (*gen*) organization chart; [*de flujo*] flowchart

orear ▹ CONJUG 1a (VT) [+ *casa, habitación*] to air
(VPR) **orearse 1** [*ropa*] to air
2 [*persona*] to get some fresh air, take a breather

orégano (SM) **1** (= *hierba*) oregano
2 (*Méx*‡) (= *marihuana*) grass‡

oreja (SF) **1** (*Anat*) ear • MODISMOS: • **aguzar las ~s** to prick up one's ears • **calentar las ~s a algn** (= *pegar*) to box sb's ears; (= *irritar*) to get on sb's nerves; (= *despachar*) to send sb away with a flea in his ear* • **chafar la ~** to have a kip* • **descubrir** *o* **enseñar la ~** (= *traicionarse*) to give o.s. away, show one's true colours; (= *aparecer*) to show up • **con las ~s gachas** with one's tail between one's legs, crestfallen • **estar hasta las ~s de algo** to be up to one's ears *o* eyes in sth* • **hacer ~s** to listen to sense, see sense • **hacer ~s de mercader** to turn a deaf ear • **pegar la ~ (en algo)** to eavesdrop (on sth), listen in (on *o* to sth) • **planchar ~**‡ to have a kip* • **ponerle a algn las ~s coloradas** to embarrass sb • **sonreír de ~ a ~** (*con alegría*) to beam; (*con autosatisfacción*) to grin from ear to ear • **verle las ~s al lobo** to get a sudden fright • **vérsele la ~ a algn***: • **se le ve la ~** you can see his little game*; ▹ **tirón**[1]
2 (= *pieza*) [*de sillón*] wing; [*de zapato*] tab; [*de jarra*] handle; [*de envase de zumo, leche*] flap; (*de martillo*) claw; [*de libro*] flap; (*de tambor*) lug
3 (*LAm*) (= *curiosidad*) curiosity; (= *escucha*) eavesdropping; (= *prudencia*) caution
(SMF)‡ (= *soplón*) grass*, fink (*EEUU**), informer

orejano/a (ADJ) **1** (*And, Cono Sur*) [*ganado*] unbranded, ownerless
2 (*LAm*) (= *tímido*) shy, easily scared; (= *huraño*) unsociable
3 (*Caribe*) (= *cauteloso*) cautious
(SM/F) (*CAm, Caribe*) peasant, countryman/countrywoman

orejear ▹ CONJUG 1a (VI) **1** (*LAm*) (= *escuchar*) to eavesdrop
2 (*Cono Sur**) (*Naipes*) to show one's cards one by one
3 (*And, Caribe, Cono Sur*) (= *sospechar*) to be suspicious, be distrustful

orejera (SF) **1** (*para el frío*) earflap
2 (*Agr*) mouldboard, moldboard (*EEUU*)

orejero (ADJ)* **1** (*LAm*) (= *receloso*) suspicious; (= *prudente*) cautious
2 (*Cono Sur*) (= *chismoso*) telltale, tattletale (*EEUU*)
3 (*And*) (= *rencoroso*) malicious
(SM) **1** [*de sillón*] wing chair
2 (*Cono Sur**) (= *hombre de confianza*) boss's right-hand man

orejeta (SF) (*Téc*) lug

orejón (ADJ) **1** (*esp LAm*) = **orejudo**
2 (*CAm, Méx*) (= *tosco*) rough, coarse
3 (*And*) (= *distraído*) absent-minded
(SM) **1** (= *tirón*) pull on the ear
2 [*de fruta*] *strip of dried peach/apricot*
3 (*And*) (*Hist*) *Inca officer*
4 (*And*) (*Med*) goitre, goiter (*EEUU*)
5 (*And*) (= *vaquero*) herdsman; (= *llanero*) plainsman
6 (*Méx*‡) (= *marido*) cuckold

orejonas (SFPL) (*And, Caribe*) big spurs

orejudo (ADJ) big-eared, with big ears

orensano/a (ADJ) of/from Orense
(SM/F) native/inhabitant of Orense • **los ~s** the people of Orense

Orense (SM) Orense

orfanato (SM), **orfanatorio** (SM) (*LAm*) orphanage

orfandad (SF) **1** (= *estado*) orphanage (*frm*)
2 (= *desamparo*) helplessness, destitution

orfebre (SMF) silversmith, goldsmith

orfebrería (SF) **1** (= *oficio*) silversmithing, goldsmithing, craftsmanship in precious metals
2 (= *objetos*) [*de oro*] gold articles (*pl*); [*de plata*] silverware

orfelinato (SM) orphanage

Orfeo (SM) Orpheus

orfeón (SM) choral society

organdí (SM) organdie

orgánicamente (ADV) organically

orgánico (ADJ) organic; ▹ **ley**

organigrama (SM) [*de entidad, empresa*] organization chart; (*Inform*) flow chart

organillero (SM) organ grinder

organillo (SM) barrel organ, hurdy-gurdy

organismo (SM) **1** (*Bio*) organism
2 (*Pol*) (*gen*) organization; (= *institución*) body, institution; (= *agencia*) agency ▸ **organismo de sondaje** polling organization ▸ **Organismo Internacional de Energía Atómica** International Atomic Energy Agency ▸ **organismo rector** governing body, Board of Trustees (*EEUU*) ▸ **organismos de gobierno** organs of government, government bodies

organista (SMF) organist

organito (SM) (*Cono Sur*) = **organillo**

organización (SF) organization ▸ **Organización de Estados Americanos** Organization of American States ▸ **Organización de las Naciones Unidas** United Nations Organization ▸ **organización no gubernamental** non-governmental organization; ▹ **OPEP**

organizadamente (ADV) in an organized way

organizado (ADJ) [*persona*] organized

organizador(a) (ADJ) organizing • **el comité ~** the organizing committee
(SM/F) organizer

organizar ▹ CONJUG 1f (VT) **1** [+ *fiesta, espectáculo*] to organize
2* [+ *jaleo, pelea*] • **los marineros ~on un auténtico alboroto** the sailors created *o* made a real commotion • **¡menuda has organizado!** you've really stirred things up,

haven't you!
VPR **organizarse 1** [*persona*] to organize o.s., get o.s. organized • **te tienes que ~ mejor** you need to organize yourself better, you need to get yourself better organized
2* [*jaleo, pelea*] • **se organizó una pelea tremenda** there was a terrific punch-up*
organizativo ADJ organizational
órgano SM **1** (*Anat, Mec*) organ ▸ **órgano del habla** speech organ ▸ **órgano sexual** sexual organ, sex organ
2 (*Mús*) organ ▸ **órgano eléctrico** electric organ
3 (= *medio*) means, medium ▸ **órgano de enlace** means of communication
organofosfato SM organophosphate
orgásmico ADJ orgasmic
orgasmo SM orgasm
orgía SF orgy
orgiástico ADJ orgiastic
orgullo SM **1** (= *satisfacción*) pride • **eres el ~ de la familia** you're the pride of the family • **me llena de ~ ver crecer a mis hijos** it makes me really proud to see my children growing up
2 (= *altanería*) pride • **su ~ le costará caro** his pride will cost him dear • **su ~ le impedía disculparse** he was too proud to say sorry
orgullosamente ADV proudly
orgulloso ADJ **1** (= *satisfecho*) proud • **estar ~ de algo/algn** to be proud of sth/sb • **estar ~ de hacer algo** to be proud to do sth
2 (= *altanero*) proud • **es muy orgullosa y nunca saluda** she's very proud, she never says hello
oricio SM sea-urchin
orientable ADJ adjustable
orientación SF **1** [*de casa*] aspect; [*de habitación*] position, orientation; (= *dirección*) direction • **una casa con ~ sur** a house facing south • **la ~ actual del partido** the party's present course *o* position ▸ **orientación sexual** sexual orientation
2 (= *guía*) guidance, orientation • **me ayudó en la ~ bibliográfica** he helped me with bibliographical information • **lo hizo para mi ~** he did it for my guidance ▸ **orientación profesional** careers guidance ▸ **orientación vocacional** vocational guidance
3 (*Dep*) orienteering
orientador(a) SM/F careers adviser, (school) counselor (*EEUU*)
oriental ADJ **1** [*persona*] oriental; [*región, zona*] eastern
2 (*Cono Sur*) (= *uruguayo*) Uruguayan • **la Banda Oriental** Uruguay
3 (*Cuba*) of/from Oriente province
SMF **1** (= *persona de Oriente*) oriental
2 (*Cono Sur*) (= *uruguayo*) Uruguayan
3 (*Cuba*) native/inhabitant of Oriente province • **los ~es** the people of Oriente province
orientalismo SM orientalism
orientalista ADJ, SMF orientalist
orientar ▸ CONJUG 1a VT **1** (= *situar*) • **~ algo hacia** *o* **a algo** to position sth to face sth • **~on la parabólica hacia el norte** they positioned the satellite dish to face north, they put the satellite dish facing north • **la casa está orientada hacia el suroeste** the house faces south-west, the house looks south-west
2 (= *enfocar*) to direct • **tenemos que ~ nuestros esfuerzos hacia un aumento de la productividad** we must direct our efforts towards improving productivity • **hay que ~ las investigaciones en otro sentido** we shall have to follow a different path of enquiry • **cómics orientados a un público adulto** comics oriented *o* targeted at adult readers
3 (= *guiar*) to guide • **me ha orientado en la materia** he has guided me through the subject, he has given me guidance about the subject
4 (*Náut*) [+ *vela*] to trim
VPR **orientarse 1** (= *encontrar el camino*) to get one's bearings • **es difícil ~se en esta ciudad** it's hard to get one's bearings in this city, it's hard to find one's way around in this city
2 (= *tender*) • **su estilo se orienta hacia lo abstracto** his style tends towards the abstract
orientativamente ADV by way of guidance
orientativo ADJ guiding, illustrative • **los pesos reseñados son puramente ~s** the weights shown are for guidance only
oriente SM **1** (= *este*) east
2 • **el Oriente** the Orient, the East • **el Cercano** *o* **Próximo Oriente** the Near East • **el Extremo** *o* **Lejano Oriente** the Far East • **el Oriente Medio** the Middle East
3 (= *viento*) east wind
4 [*de masones*] masonic lodge
orificación SF gold filling
orificar ▸ CONJUG 1g VT [+ *muela*] to fill with gold
orificio SM (= *agujero*) orifice (*frm*), hole; (*para aire, gas*) vent ▸ **orificio de bala** bullet hole ▸ **orificio de entrada** (*en herida*) entry wound ▸ **orificio de salida** (*en herida*) exit wound
origen SM **1** (= *causa, principio*) origin • **el ~ del hombre** the origin of man • **un trabajo de investigación sobre los orígenes del flamenco** a piece of research on the origins of flamenco • **la policía está investigando el ~ de las llamadas telefónicas** the police are investigating the source of the phone calls • **dar ~ a** [+ *rumores, movimiento, organización*] to give rise to • **esta situación ha dado ~ a múltiples procesos judiciales** this situation has given rise to numerous lawsuits • **el Big Bang, la gran explosión que dio ~ al Universo** the Big Bang, the great explosion that created the Universe • **de ~:** • **proteínas de ~ animal/vegetal** animal/vegetable proteins • **problemas de ~ psicológico** psychological problems, problems of psychological origin • **un deporte de ~ inglés** a sport of English origin, a sport originally from England • **desde sus orígenes** [*de movimiento, corriente*] from its origins; [*de ciudad, país*] from the very beginning, right from the start • **una historia de la medicina desde sus orígenes hasta nuestros días** a history of medicine from its origins up to the present day • **en su ~** originally • **la obra fue escrita en su ~ para cuatro voces** the work was originally written for four voices • **en su ~ la organización no tenía más de veinte miembros** at the outset *o* at the start *o* originally the organization had no more than twenty members • **tener su ~ en** [+ *lugar*] to originate in; [+ *inicio*] to originate from; [+ *fecha*] to date back to • **la paella tuvo su ~ en Valencia** paella had its origin *o* originated in Valencia • **el vals tiene su ~ en las danzas austriacas "Ländler"** the waltz originates *o* comes from Austrian "Ländler" dances • **el fuego tuvo su ~ en un cortocircuito** the fire was caused by a short circuit • **tiene su ~ en el siglo XV** it dates back to the 15th century
2 [*de persona*] background, origins (*pl*) • **son gente de ~ humilde** they are from a humble background, they are of humble origins • **sabemos poco de sus orígenes** we know little about his background • **de ~ argentino/árabe** of Argentinian/Arab origin *o* (*más frm*) extraction • **país de ~** country of origin, native country
3 • **en ~** (*Com, Econ*) at source • **el reciclado de residuos en ~** the recycling of waste at source • **este impuesto se retiene en ~** this tax is deducted at source
original ADJ **1** (= *inicial*) [*idea, documento, idioma*] original; [*edición*] first • **van a intentar devolver la zona a su estado ~** they are going to try to return the area to its original state; ▸ **pecado**
2 (= *novedoso*) original • **el guión tiene poco de ~** the script is not very original
3 (= *raro*) unusual, original; (= *extravagante*) eccentric • **él siempre tiene que ser tan ~** (*iró*) he always has to be so different
4 (= *creativo*) original • **es un escritor muy ~** he's a very original writer
5 (= *procedente*) • **ser ~ de** [*planta, animal*] to be native to
SM **1** (= *modelo*) original • **no se parece en nada al ~** it doesn't look anything like the original
2 (*Tip*) (*tb* **original de imprenta**) manuscript, original, copy
originalidad SF **1** (= *novedad*) originality
2 (= *excentricidad*) eccentricity
originalmente ADV originally
originar ▸ CONJUG 1a VT to cause • **el terremoto originó la estampida de los elefantes** the earthquake caused the elephants to stampede • **la lucha de clases originó el conflicto** the class struggle led to *o* gave rise to the conflict • **están buscando las causas que ~on el fuego** they're looking for the cause of the fire
VPR **originarse** [*enfermedad, crisis, conflicto, incendio*] to start, originate; [*universo*] to begin • **la saeta se origina en la antigua música religiosa cristiana** "saeta" originates in ancient Christian religious music • **casi un 30% de la deuda externa del Tercer Mundo se origina por la compra de armas** nearly 30% of foreign debt in the Third World results from arms purchases
originariamente ADV originally
originario ADJ **1** (= *inicial*) original • **el sentido ~ del término** the original sense of the term • **en su forma originaria** in its original form • **país ~** country of origin, native country
2 • **~ de** [*animal, planta*] native to; [*persona*] from • **el lichi es ~ de China** lychees originated in China, the lychee is native to China • **un joven ~ de Cabo Verde** a young man from Cape Verde • **los escoceses son ~s de Irlanda** the Scots originally came from Ireland
orilla SF **1** (= *borde*) [*de río*] bank; [*de lago*] shore, edge; [*de mesa*] edge; [*de taza*] rim, lip • **la ~ del mar** the seashore • **a ~s de** on the banks of • **vive ~ de mi casa*** he lives next door to me
2 (*Cos*) (= *orillo*) selvage; (= *dobladillo*) hem
3 (*LAm*) (= *acera*) pavement, sidewalk (*EEUU*)
4 • MODISMO: • **de ~** (*Caribe*) (= *sin importancia*) trivial, of no account; (= *sin valor*) worthless
5 orillas (*LAm*) (= *arrabales*) outlying districts; (*pey*) poor quarter (*sing*); (*Méx*) shanty town (*sing*)
orillar ▸ CONJUG 1a VT **1** [+ *lago, bosque*] to skirt, go round
2 (= *esquivar*) [+ *dificultad*] to avoid, get round; [+ *tema*] to touch briefly on
3 (= *arreglar*) [+ *negocio*] to put in order, tidy up; [+ *obstáculo*] to overcome
4 (= *concluir*) to wind up
5 (*Cos*) to edge (**de with**), trim (**de with**)
6 • **~ a algn a hacer algo** (*Méx*) to lead sb

to do sth
VPR **orillarse** (*Méx*) (*Aut*) to pull over
orillero/a (*LAm*) ADJ (*gen*) lower-class, working-class; (= *arrabalero*) common, vulgar
SM/F (*gen*) lower-class person, working-class person; (= *arrabalero*) common person, vulgar person
orillo SM selvage
orín¹ SM rust • **tomarse de ~** to get rusty
orín² SM, **orina** SF urine
orinacamas SM INV dandelion
orinal SM **1** (= *bacín*) chamber pot; [*de niños*] potty ▸ **orinal de cama** bedpan
2 (*Mil**) tin hat*, helmet
orinar ▹ CONJUG 1a VI (*gen*) to urinate
VT • **~ sangre** to pass blood (*in the urine*)
VPR **orinarse** to wet o.s. • **~se en la cama** to wet one's bed • **~se encima** to wet o.s.
orines SMPL urine (*sing*)
Orinoco SM • **el río ~** the Orinoco River
orita* (*LAm*) = **ahorita**
oriundo/a ADJ • **~ de** [*planta, animal*] indigenous to, native to • **el melocotón, aunque ~ de China, se propagó rápidamente por el Oriente Medio** the peach, although indigenous *o* native to China, rapidly spread through the Middle East • **Pepa es oriunda de Granada** Pepa comes from *o* (*hum*) hails from Granada
SM/F (= *nativo*) native, inhabitant
orla SF, **orladura** SF **1** (= *borde*) [*de vestido, cuadro*] border; [*de flecos*] fringe ▸ **orla litoral** coastal strip
2 (= *ribete*) trimming
3 (*Educ*) (= *fotografía*) class graduation photograph
orlar ▹ CONJUG 1a VT to edge, trim (**con, de** with)
ornamentación SF ornamentation, adornment
ornamental ADJ ornamental
ornamentar ▹ CONJUG 1a VT to adorn (**de** with)
ornamento SM **1** (= *adorno*) ornament, adornment
2 ornamentos (*Rel*) vestments; (= *cualidades*) good qualities
ornar ▹ CONJUG 1a VT to adorn (**de** with)
ornato SM adornment, decoration
ornitofauna SF birds (*pl*), bird population
ornitología SF ornithology
ornitológico ADJ ornithological
ornitólogo/a SM/F ornithologist
ornitorrinco SM platypus
oro SM **1** (= *metal*) gold • **de oro** gold (*antes de s*), golden (*frec liter*) • **regla de oro** golden rule • **tiene una voz de oro** she has a wonderful voice • MODISMOS: • **apalear oro** to be rolling in money • **de oro y azul** very smart and elegant, all dressed up • **como un oro** like new • **es de oro** he's a treasure • **guardar algo como oro en paño** to treasure sth • **hacerse de oro** to make a fortune • **prometer el oro y el moro** to promise the earth *o* moon • REFRÁN: • **no es oro todo lo que reluce** all that glitters is not gold ▸ **oro amarillo** yellow gold ▸ **oro batido** gold leaf ▸ **oro en barras** gold bars (*pl*), bullion ▸ **oro en polvo** gold dust ▸ **oro laminado** rolled gold ▸ **oro molido** ormolu ▸ **oro negro** black gold, oil ▸ **oro viejo** old gold
2 oros (*Esp*) (*Naipes*) *one of the suits in the Spanish card deck, represented by gold coins*; ▹ BARAJA ESPAÑOLA
orografía SF orography
orográfico ADJ orographical
orondo ADJ **1** (= *grueso*) [*persona*] potbellied, big-bellied; [*vasija*] rounded, potbellied
2 (= *satisfecho*) smug, self-satisfied; (= *pomposo*) pompous
3 (*LAm*) (= *sereno*) calm, serene
oropel SM tinsel • **de ~** flashy, gaudy
• MODISMO: • **gastar mucho ~** to make a pretence of being wealthy
oropéndola SF golden oriole
oroya SF (*And*) **1** (= *cesta*) *basket of a rope bridge*
2 (*Ferro*) funicular railway
orozuz SM liquorice
orquesta SF orchestra ▸ **orquesta de baile** dance band ▸ **orquesta de cámara** chamber orchestra ▸ **orquesta de cuerdas** string orchestra ▸ **orquesta de jazz** jazz band ▸ **orquesta sinfónica** symphony orchestra
orquestación SF orchestration (*tb fig*)
orquestal ADJ orchestral
orquestar ▹ CONJUG 1a VT to orchestrate (*tb fig*)
orquestina SF band
orquídea SF orchid
orsay SM = **offside**
ortiga SF nettle, stinging nettle
orto¹ SM sunrise
orto²** SM (*Cono Sur*) (= *culo*) arse**, ass (*EEUU***); (= *ano*) arsehole**, asshole**
orto... PREF ortho...
ortodoncia SF orthodontics (*sing*), dental orthopedics (*sing*) (*EEUU*)
ortodoncista SMF orthodontist
ortodoxia SF orthodoxy
ortodoxo ADJ orthodox
ortofonista SMF speech therapist
ortografía SF spelling, orthography (*frm*)
ortográfico ADJ spelling (*antes de s*), orthographic(al) (*frm*) • **reforma ortográfica** spelling reform
ortopeda SMF orthopaedist, orthopedist (*EEUU*)
ortopedia SF orthopaedics (*sing*), orthopedics (*sing*) (*EEUU*)
ortopédico ADJ orthopaedic, orthopedic (*EEUU*)
ortopedista SMF orthopaedist, orthopedist (*EEUU*)
oruga SF **1** (= *gusano*) caterpillar
2 (*Bot*) rocket
3 (= *vehículo*) (*Téc*) caterpillar, caterpillar track; (*Mil*) tracked personnel carrier
• **tractor de ~** caterpillar tractor
orujo SM **1** (= *bebida*) *liquor distilled from grape remains*
2 (= *restos*) marc
orza¹ SF (= *jarra*) glazed earthenware jar
orza² SF (*Náut*) luff, luffing • MODISMO: • **ir de ~** to be on the wrong track
orzar ▹ CONJUG 1f VI (*Náut*) to luff
orzuelo SM (*Med*) stye
os¹ PRON PERS PL **1** (*directo*) you • **os quiero mucho** I love you very much • **no os oigo** I can't hear you
2 (*indirecto*) you • **os lo di** I gave it to you • **os lo compré** (= *de vosotros*) I bought it from you; (= *para vosotros*) I bought it for you • **¿os han arreglado ya el ordenador?** have they fixed the computer for you yet?
3 (*reflexivo*) yourselves • **¿os habéis hecho daño?** did you hurt yourselves? • **lavaos las manos** wash your hands • **cuando os marchéis** when you leave • **no hace falta que os quitéis el abrigo** you don't need to take your coats off
4 (*mutuo*) each other • **quiero que os pidáis perdón** I want you to say sorry to each other • **¿os conocéis?** have you met?, do you know each other?
os² EXCL shoo!
osa SF **1** (= *animal*) she-bear • MODISMOS: • **¡anda la osa!*** what a carry-on!* • **¡la osa!*** gosh!*
2 (*Astron*) ▸ **Osa Mayor** Ursa Major, Great Bear ▸ **Osa Menor** Ursa Minor, Little Bear
osadamente ADV daringly, boldly
osadía SF **1** (= *audacia*) daring, boldness
2 (= *descaro*) impudence, audacity, temerity
osado ADJ **1** (= *audaz*) daring, bold
2 (= *descarado*) impudent, audacious
osamenta SF **1** (= *esqueleto*) skeleton
2 (= *huesos*) bones (*pl*)
osar ▹ CONJUG 1a VI to dare • **~ hacer algo** to dare to do sth
osario SM ossuary, charnel house
Oscar SM, **óscar** SM Oscar
oscarizado/a ADJ Oscar-winning
SM/F Oscar winner
OSCE SF ABR (= **Organización para la Seguridad y Cooperación en Europa**) OSCE
oscense ADJ of/from Huesca
SMF native/inhabitant of Huesca • **los ~s** the people of Huesca
oscilación SF **1** [*de péndulo*] swinging, swaying, oscillation
2 [*de luz*] winking, blinking; [*de llama*] flickering
3 [*de precios, peso, temperatura*] fluctuation
4 [*de parecer, pensar*] hesitation, wavering
oscilador ADJ oscillating
SM oscillator
oscilante ADJ oscillating (*frm*)
oscilar ▹ CONJUG 1a VI **1** [*péndulo*] to swing, oscillate
2 [*luz*] to wink, blink; [*llama*] to flicker
3 [*precio, peso, temperatura*] to fluctuate (**entre** between); [*calidad, diseño*] to vary (**entre** between); [*distancia, intensidad*] to range (**entre** between) • **la distancia oscila entre los 100 y 500m** the distance ranges between 100 and 500m *o* from 100 to 500m • **los precios oscilan mucho** prices are fluctuating a lot
4 (= *dudar*) to hesitate (**entre** between), waver (**entre** between) • **oscila entre la alegría y el pesimismo** his mood swings from cheerfulness to pessimism
oscilatorio ADJ oscillatory
osciloscopio SM oscilloscope
oscular ▹ CONJUG 1a VT (*liter*) to osculate (*frm, hum*), kiss
ósculo SM (*liter*) osculation (*frm, hum*), kiss
oscuramente ADV obscurely
oscurana SF **1** (*CAm*) [*de polvo*] cloud of volcanic dust
2 (*And**) (= *oscuridad*) darkness
oscurantismo SM obscurantism
oscurantista ADJ, SMF obscurantist
oscuras • **a ~** ADV in the dark, in darkness; ▹ **oscuro**
oscurear ▹ CONJUG 1a VT, VI (*Méx*) = **oscurecer**
oscurecer ▹ CONJUG 2d VT **1** [+ *color, espacio*] to darken
2 (= *quitar importancia a*) [+ *cuestión*] to confuse, cloud; [+ *rival*] to overshadow, put in the shade; [+ *fama*] to tarnish
3 (*Arte*) to shade
VI, VPR **oscurecerse** to grow dark, get dark
oscurecimiento SM **1** [*de color, piel*] darkening
2 [*de memoria*] failing
oscuridad SF **1** (= *ausencia de luz*) • **tiene pánico a la ~** he's terrified of the dark • **la ~ envolvía el pueblo** the village was wrapped in darkness • **pasaba horas sentado en la ~** he would sit for hours in the dark *o* in darkness
2 [*de texto, explicación*] obscurity • **la ~ de su prosa** the obscurity of his prose
3 (= *anonimato*) obscurity • **salir de la ~** to emerge from obscurity
oscuro ADJ **1** (= *sin luz*) dark • **¡qué casa tan**

oscura! what a dark house!
2 [*color, cielo, día*] dark • **un hermoso azul ~** a beautiful dark blue • **tiene el pelo castaño ~** she has dark brown hair
3 [*texto, explicación*] obscure
4 (= *sospechoso*) • **oscuras intenciones** dubious intentions, sinister intentions • **un asunto ~** a shady business
5 (= *incierto*) [*porvenir, futuro*] uncertain • **de origen ~** of obscure origin(s)
6 (= *poco conocido*) obscure • **un ~ escritor** an obscure writer
óseo ADJ **1** (*gen*) bony
2 (*Med*) osseous, bone (*antes de s*)
osezno SM bear cub
osificación SF ossification
osificar ▹ CONJUG 1g VT to ossify
VPR **osificarse** to ossify, become ossified
-osis ▹ **Aspects of Word Formation in Spanish 2**
osito SM **1** (= *juguete*) teddy, teddy bear ▸ **osito de felpa, osito de peluche** teddy, teddy bear ▸ **osito panda** panda
2 (*Cono Sur*) [*de bebé*] Babygro®
Oslo SM Oslo
osmosis SF INV, **ósmosis** SF INV osmosis
osmótico ADJ osmotic
OSO ABR (= **oessudoeste**) WSW
oso SM bear • **MODISMOS**: • **hacer el oso** to play the fool • **ser un oso** to be a prickly sort ▸ **oso blanco** polar bear ▸ **oso colmenero** (*LAm*) anteater ▸ **oso de las cavernas** cave bear ▸ **oso de peluche** teddy bear ▸ **oso gris** grizzly, grizzly bear ▸ **oso hormiguero** anteater ▸ **oso marsupial** koala bear ▸ **oso panda** panda ▸ **oso pardo** brown bear ▸ **oso perezoso** sloth
Ostende SM Ostend
ostensible ADJ obvious, evident • **hacer algo ~** to make sth quite clear; (*LAm*) to express sth, register sth • **procurar no hacerse ~** to keep out of the way, lie low
ostensiblemente ADV **1** (= *evidentemente*) obviously, evidently
2 (= *visiblemente*) visibly, openly • **se mostró ~ conmovido** he was visibly moved
ostensivo ADJ evident
ostensorio SM monstrance
ostenta SF (*And, Cono Sur*) = **ostentación**
ostentación SF **1** (= *exhibición*) ostentation
2 (= *acto*) show, display • **hacer ~ de** to flaunt, parade, show off
ostentar ▹ CONJUG 1a VT **1** (= *exhibir*) to show; (= *hacer gala de*) to flaunt, parade, show off
2 (= *tener*) [+ *poderes legales*] to have, possess; [+ *cargo, título*] to have, hold • **~ el título mundial en patinaje sobre hielo** to hold the world title in ice-skating • **ostenta todavía las cicatrices** he still has *o* carries the scars
ostentativo ADJ ostentatious
ostentosamente ADV ostentatiously
ostentoso ADJ ostentatious
osteo... PREF osteo...
osteoartritis SF INV osteoarthritis
osteópata SMF osteopath
osteopatía SF osteopathy
osteoporosis SF INV osteoporosis
osti‡ EXCL = **hostia**
ostión SM (*esp LAm*) large oyster
ostionería SF (*LAm*) (= *tienda*) sea food shop; (= *restaurante*) sea food restaurant; (= *bar*) oyster bar
ostra SF **1** (*Zool*) oyster ▸ **ostra perlera** pearl oyster; ▹ **aburrir**
2 (= *persona*) (*pesado*) bore; (*huraño*) shrinking violet; (= *cliente fijo*) regular • **es una ~** he's a fixture here
EXCL **ostras*** (*euf*) (*denota sorpresa*) crikey!*; (*denota enfado o desagrado*) sugar!*, shoot! (EEUU*)
ostracismo SM ostracism
ostracista ADJ discriminatory
ostral SM oyster bed
ostrería SF oyster bar
ostrero SM **1** (= *lugar*) oyster bed
2 (*Orn*) oystercatcher
ostricultura SF oyster farming
osuno ADJ bear-like
OTAN SF ABR (= **Organización del Tratado del Atlántico Norte**) NATO
otánico ADJ NATO (*antes de s*)
otanista SMF supporter of NATO
otario/a* (*Cono Sur*) ADJ gullible
SM/F sucker*
OTASE SF ABR (= **Organización del Tratado del Sudeste Asiático**) SEATO
otate SM (*Méx*) (= *caña*) cane, stick; (= *junco*) reed, rush
-ote, -ota ▹ **Aspects of Word Formation in Spanish 2**
oteadero SM look-out post
otear ▹ CONJUG 1a VT **1** [+ *horizonte*] to scan
2 [+ *objeto lejano*] (*desde arriba*) to look down on, look down over; (*de forma poco clara*) to make out, glimpse
3 (= *espiar*) to watch (from above), spy on
4 (= *examinar*) to examine, look into
Otelo SM Othello
otero SM low hill, hillock, knoll
OTI SF ABR (*TV*) = **Organización de la Televisión Iberoamericana**
otitis SF INV inflammation of the ear, otitis (*frm*) ▸ **otitis media** inflammation of the middle ear, otitis media (*frm*)
otomano/a (*Hist*) ADJ Ottoman
SM/F Ottoman • **los ~s** the Ottomans
otomía SF (*Méx*) atrocity • **hacer ~s*** to get up to no good, misbehave
Otón SM Otto
otoñada SF autumn, autumn time, fall (EEUU)
otoñal ADJ autumnal, autumn (*antes de s*), fall (*antes de s*) (EEUU)
otoño SM (= *estación*) autumn, fall (EEUU) • **en el ~ de la vida** in the autumn of one's life
otorgamiento SM **1** (= *concesión*) [*de privilegio, ayuda, permiso, independencia*] granting; [*de premio*] awarding
2 (*Jur*) (= *acción*) execution; (= *documento*) legal document, deed • **~ de una escritura** execution of a deed
otorgar ▹ CONJUG 1h VT **1** (= *conceder*) [+ *privilegio, ayuda, independencia, permiso*] to grant (**a** to); [+ *premio*] to award (**a** to); [+ *poderes, título*] to confer (**a** on); [+ *esfuerzo, tiempo*] to devote (**a** to)
2 (*Jur*) (= *ejecutar*) to execute; [+ *testamento*] to make
3 (= *consentir en*) to consent to, agree to
otoronco SM (*And*) (*Zool*) mountain bear
otorrino SMF ear, nose and throat specialist, ENT specialist
otorrinolaringología SF otolaryngology (*frm*), otorhinolaryngology (*frm*)
otorrinolaringólogo SMF ear, nose and throat specialist, otolaryngologist (*frm*)
otramente ADV †† in a different way, differently
otredad SF (*liter*) otherness
otro ADJ **1** (= *diferente*) (*en singular*) another; (*en plural*) other • **dame otra revista** give me another magazine • **necesito ~ destornillador más grande** I need a bigger screwdriver • **tengo ~s planes** I have other plans • **no puedo venir ningún ~ día** I can't come any other day • **¿tiene algún ~ modelo?** do you have any other models? • **¿hay alguna otra manera de hacerlo?** is there any other way of doing it? • **son ~s tiempos** times have changed • **de ~ modo** otherwise • **le pago, de ~ modo no lo haría** I'm paying her, otherwise she wouldn't do it • **está en otra parte** it's somewhere else • **por otra parte** on the other hand • **por otra parte, he de admitir que me gusta** on the other hand, I have to admit I like it • **~ tanto**: • **Juan me insultó y Antonio hizo ~ tanto** Juan insulted me and so did Antonio • **ayer subió tres puntos y hoy aumentará ~ tanto** it went up by three points yesterday and will rise by the same amount today; ▹ **mundo**
2 (= *uno más*) (*en singular, con cifras*) another; (*en plural*) other • **¿quieres otra taza de café?** would you like another cup of coffee? • **tropezamos con otra nueva dificultad** we came up against yet another difficulty • **va a ser ~ Hitler** he's going to be a second *o* another Hitler • **luego me enseñó ~s trajes** then he showed me some other dresses • **después volvió con ~s ocho libros** then he came back with another eight books *o* with eight more books • **otra cosa**: • **me gustaría preguntarle otra cosa** I'd like to ask you something else • **¿desea alguna otra cosa?** would you like anything else? • **otra vez** again
3 (*en una secuencia temporal*) **a** (*en el futuro*) next • **yo me bajé aquí y él en la otra parada** I got off here and he got off at the next stop • **se fue y a la otra semana me escribió*** he left and wrote to me the next week
b (*en el pasado*) other • **me encontré con él el ~ día** I met him the other day
PRON **1** (= *diferente*) (*en singular*) another, another one; (*en plural*) others • **—he perdido mi lápiz —no importa, tengo ~** "I have lost my pencil" — "it doesn't matter, I've got another (one)" • **tengo ~s en el almacén** I've got some others in the warehouse • **todos los países europeos y alguno que ~ de África** all the countries in Europe and some from Africa • **es más eficaz que ningún ~** it's more efficient than any other one • **el ~** the other one • **lo ~ no importa** the rest doesn't matter
2 (= *uno más*) (*en singular*) another, another one; (*en plural*) others • **¿quieres ~?** do you want another (one)? • **¿me puede enseñar ~s?** could you show me some others *o* more? • **se me perdieron y me dieron ~s** I lost them, but they gave me some more • **¡otra!** (*en concierto*) encore!; (*en bar*) (the) same again, please
3 (*en una secuencia temporal*) • **un día sí y ~ no** every other day • **el jueves que viene no, el ~** a week on Thursday
4 (*referido a personas*) (*en singular*) somebody else; (*en plural*) others • **que lo haga ~** let somebody else do it • **tomé el sombrero de ~** I took somebody else's hat • **parece otra desde que se casó** she's a different person since she got married • **como dijo el ~** as somebody *o* someone said • **no fue ~ que el obispo** it was none other than the bishop • **unos creen que ganará, ~s que perderá** some think he'll win, others that he'll lose • **no sabe adaptarse a las costumbres de los ~s** he doesn't know how to fit in with other people • **uno y ~** both, both of them • **unos y ~s coinciden en que ...** both sides *o* groups agree that ..., they all agree that ... • **están enamorados el uno del ~** they're in love with each other
• **MODISMO**: • **¡~ que tal (baila)!** here we go again!
otrora (*liter*) ADV (= *antiguamente*) formerly, in olden times
ADJ INV one-time, former • **el ~ señor del país** the one-time ruler of the country
otrosí ADV †† (*frm*) furthermore

O

OUA (SF ABR) (= **Organización de la Unidad Africana**) OAU
OUAA (SF ABR) (= **Organización de la Unidad Afro-americana**) OAAU
ouija (SF), **oui-ja®** (SF) Ouija® board
ourensano/a (ADJ), (SM/F) = **orensano**
output ['autpu] (SM) (PL: **outputs** ['autpu]) *(Inform)* printout
ovación (SF) ovation
ovacionar ▸ CONJUG 1a (VT) to cheer, applaud, give an ovation to
oval (ADJ), **ovalado** (ADJ) oval
óvalo (SM) **1** (= *figura*) oval
2 *(Méx) (Med)* pessary
ovárico (ADJ) *[tejido, hormonas, quiste]* ovarian
ovario (SM) ovary
ovas (SFPL) fish eggs, roe *(sing)*
oveja (SF) **1** (= *animal*) *(sin distinción de sexo)* sheep; (= *hembra*) ewe • **MODISMOS**: • **apartar las ~s de los cabritos** to separate the sheep from the goats • **cargar con la ~ muerta** to be left holding the baby • **ser la ~ negra de la familia** to be the black sheep of the family • **REFRÁN**: • **cada ~ con su pareja** birds of a feather flock together
2 *(Cono Sur)* (= *prostituta*) whore
ovejera (SF) *(Méx)* sheepfold
ovejería (SF) *(Chile)* (= *ovejas*) sheep *(pl)*; (= *actividad*) sheep farming; (= *hacienda*) sheep farm
ovejero (SM) sheepdog ▸ **ovejero alemán** German shepherd, German shepherd dog, Alsatian
ovejita* (SF) *(Arg)* whore
ovejo (SM) *(LAm)*, **ovejón** (SM) *(LAm)* ram
ovejuno (ADJ) **1** *(Agr)* sheep *(antes de s)* • **ganado ~** sheep
2 (= *parecido a la oveja*) sheeplike

overbooking [oβer'βukin] (SM) overbooking
overear ▸ CONJUG 1a (VT) *(And, Cono Sur) (Culin)* to cook to a golden colour, brown
overol (SM) *(LAm)* overalls *(pl)*
ovetense (ADJ) of/from Oviedo
(SMF) native/inhabitant of Oviedo • **los ~s** the people of Oviedo
Ovidio (SM) Ovid
oviducto (SM) oviduct
Oviedo (SM) Oviedo
oviforme (ADJ) egg-shaped, oviform *(frm)*
ovillar ▸ CONJUG 1a (VT) to wind, wind into a ball
(VPR) **ovillarse** to curl up into a ball
ovillo (SM) **1** *[de lana, cuerda]* ball • **hacerse un ~** *(gen)* to curl up into a ball; *[de miedo]* to cower; *(en el habla)* to get tied up in knots
2 (= *enredo*) tangle
ovino (ADJ) ovine *(frm)*, sheep *(antes de s)* • **ganado ~** sheep
(SM) (= *animales*) sheep *(pl)* • **carne de ~** *[de oveja añeja]* mutton; *[de cordero]* lamb
ovíparo (ADJ) oviparous
OVNI (SM ABR) (= **objeto volante** *o* **volador no identificado**) UFO
ovoide (ADJ) ovoid *(frm)*, egg-shaped
(SM) **1** (= *figura*) ovoid
2 *(LAm) (Dep)* rugby ball
ovolactovegetariano/a (ADJ), (SM/F) lacto-ovo-vegetarian
ovovegetariano/a (ADJ), (SM/F) ovo-vegetarian
ovulación (SF) ovulation
ovular ▸ CONJUG 1a (VI) to ovulate
óvulo (SM) ovule, ovum
ox [os] (EXCL) shoo!
oxálico (ADJ) oxalic
oxear ▸ CONJUG 1a (VT) to shoo away

oxiacanta (SF) hawthorn
oxiacetilénico (ADJ) oxyacetylene *(antes de s)* • **soplete ~** oxyacetylene torch
oxidación (SF) **1** *[de metal]* rusting
2 *(Quím)* oxidation
oxidado (ADJ) **1** *[metal]* rusty
2 *(Quím)* oxidized
oxidar ▸ CONJUG 1a (VT) **1** *[+ metal]* to rust
2 *(Quím)* to oxidize
(VPR) **oxidarse 1** *[metal]* to rust, go rusty
2 *(Quím)* to oxidize
óxido (SM) **1** *(en metal)* rust
2 *(Quím)* oxide ▸ **óxido de hierro** iron oxide ▸ **óxido nítrico** nitric oxide ▸ **óxido nitroso** nitrous oxide
oxigenación (SF) oxygenation
oxigenado (ADJ) **1** *(Quím)* oxygenated
2 *[pelo]* bleached • **una rubia oxigenada** a peroxide blonde
(SM) peroxide *(for hair)*
oxigenar ▸ CONJUG 1a (VT) to oxygenate
(VPR) **oxigenarse 1** *(gen)* to become oxygenated
2 *[persona]* to get some fresh air
oxígeno (SM) oxygen
oxímoron (SM) oxymoron
oxte (EXCL) † *(a animal)* shoo!; *(a persona)* get out!, hop it!* • **MODISMO**: • **sin decir ~ ni moxte** without a word
oye, oyendo *etc* ▸ **oír**
oyente (SMF) **1** *(Radio)* listener • **queridos ~s** dear listeners
2 *(Univ)* unregistered student, occasional student, auditor (EEUU) • **voy de ~ a las clases de Derecho Romano** I attend the classes on Roman Law as an unregistered student
ozono (SM) ozone
ozonosfera (SF) ozonosphere

O

Pp

P, p [pe] SF (= *letra*) P, p
P. ABR **1** (*Rel*) (= **Padre**) F., Fr.
2 = **Papa**
3 (= **presidente**) P
4 (= **Príncipe**) P
p. ABR **1** (*Tip*) (= **página**) p
2 (*Cos*) = **punto**
p.ª ABR = **para**
pa* PREP *informal or humorous pronunciation of "para"*
p.a. ABR **1** = **por autorización**
2 = **por ausencia**
PAAU SFPL ABR = **Pruebas para el Acceso a la Universidad**
pabellón SM **1** (*Arquit*) [*de muestras, exposiciones*] pavilion; [*de jardín*] summerhouse; [*de hospital*] (= *ala*) wing; (= *anexo*) block, section ▸ **pabellón de aduanas** customs house ▸ **pabellón de caza** shooting box ▸ **pabellón de conciertos** bandstand ▸ **pabellón de hidroterapia** pumproom ▸ **pabellón de música** bandstand ▸ **pabellón deportivo, pabellón polideportivo** sports hall
2 (= *carpa*) bell tent
3 (*Med*) ▸ **pabellón de la oreja** outer ear
4 [*de cama*] canopy
5 (*Mús*) [*de trompeta*] mouth
6 (*Mil*) stack
7 (*Náut etc*) (= *bandera*) flag • **un buque de ~ panameño** a ship flying the Panamanian flag ▸ **pabellón de conveniencia** flag of convenience ▸ **pabellón nacional** national flag
pabilo SM, **pábilo** SM wick
Pablo SM Paul
pábulo SM **1** (= *motivo*) food, fuel; (= *estímulo*) encouragement • **dar ~ a** to feed, encourage • **dar ~ a las llamas** to add fuel to the flames • **dar ~ a los rumores** to fuel rumours
2 (*liter*) (= *alimento*) food
PAC SF ABR (= **Política Agraria Común**) CAP
Paca SF *forma familiar de* **Francisca**
paca[1] SF (*Agr*) bale
paca[2] SF (*LAm*) (*Zool*) paca, spotted cavy
pacapaca SF (*And*) owl • MODISMO: • **le vino la ~*** it all went wrong for him
pacatería SF (*pey*) **1** (= *timidez*) timidity
2 (= *modestia*) excessive modesty, prudishness
pacato ADJ (*pey*) **1** (= *tímido*) timid
2 (= *modesto*) excessively modest, prudish
pacense ADJ of/from Badajoz
SMF native/inhabitant of Badajoz • **los ~s** the people of Badajoz
paceño/a ADJ of/from La Paz
SM/F native/inhabitant of La Paz • **los ~s** the people of La Paz
pacer ▹ CONJUG 2d VT **1** [+ *hierba*] to eat, graze
2 [+ *ganado*] to graze, pasture
VI to graze
pacha SF (*CAm*) baby's bottle
pachá SM pasha • MODISMO: • **vivir como un ~** to live like a king
pachacho* ADJ (*Cono Sur*) (= *rechoncho*) chubby; (= *achaparrado*) squat
pachaco* ADJ (*CAm*) weak, feeble
pachamama SF (*And, Cono Sur*) Mother Earth, the earth mother
pachamanca SF (*Perú*) barbecue
pachanga* SF **1** (= *fiesta*) lively party; (= *juerga*) binge*, booze-up‡
2 (*Caribe*) (= *lío*) mix-up
3 (*Mús*) Cuban dance
pachanguear* ▹ CONJUG 1a VI to go on a spree
pachanguero* ADJ **1** (= *bullicioso*) noisy, rowdy
2 [*música*] catchy
pacharán SM sloe brandy
pacho* ADJ **1** (*CAm, Cono Sur**) [*persona*] (= *rechoncho*) chubby; (= *achaparrado*) squat
2 (*CAm*) [*objeto*] flat, flattened; [*sombrero*] flat-brimmed
3 (*Caribe*) (= *calmoso*) phlegmatic
pachocha* SF (*LAm*) = **pachorra**
pachol SM (*Méx*) mat of hair
pachón ADJ **1*** [*persona*] lackadaisical
2 (*CAm, Cono Sur**) (= *peludo*) shaggy, hairy; (*CAm, Méx**) (= *lanudo*) woolly, wooly (EEUU)
3 (*And**) (= *gordito*) plump
4 (*And**) (= *lerdo*) dim*, dense*
SM **1** (= *perro*) basset hound
2* (= *persona*) dull person, slow sort
pachorra* SF (= *indolencia*) slowness, sluggishness; (= *tranquilidad*) calmness • **Juan, con su santa ~ ...** Juan, as slow as ever ...
pachorrada* SF (*Caribe, Cono Sur*) blunder, gaffe
pachorrear* ▹ CONJUG 1a VI (*CAm*) to be slow, be sluggish
pachorriento* ADJ (*And, Cono Sur*),
pachorro* ADJ (*And, Caribe*),
pachorrudo* ADJ **1** (= *indolente*) slow, sluggish
2 (= *tranquilo*) calm
pachotada* SF (*And, Méx*) = **patochada**
pachucho* ADJ [*fruta*] overripe; [*persona*] off-colour, off-color (EEUU), poorly
pachuco/a* (*Méx*) ADJ (= *llamativo*) flashy, flashily dressed
SM/F **1** (*pey*) (= *chicano*) Chicano, Mexican-American
2 (= *bien vestido*) sharp dresser, snappy dresser
pachulí SM **1** (= *planta, perfume*) patchouli
2 (*Esp‡*) (= *tío*) bloke‡, guy*
paciencia SF patience • **¡paciencia!** (*gen*) be patient!; (*Cono Sur*) that's just too bad! • **acabársele** *o* **agotársele la ~ a algn: se me acaba** *o* **agota la ~** my patience is running out *o* wearing thin • **armarse** *o* **cargarse** *o* **revestirse de ~** to resolve to be patient • **perder la ~** to lose patience • **tener ~** to be patient • **no tengo más ~** my patience is at an end • MODISMO: • **¡~ y barajar!** keep trying!, don't give up!
paciencioso ADJ (*And, Cono Sur*) long-suffering
paciente ADJ, SMF patient
pacientemente ADV patiently
pacienzudo* ADJ very patient, long-suffering
pacificación SF pacification
pacificador(a) ADJ pacifying, peace-making • **operación ~a** peace-keeping operation
SM/F peacemaker
pacíficamente ADV pacifically, peaceably
pacificar ▹ CONJUG 1g VT **1** (*Mil*) to pacify
2 (= *calmar*) to calm; (= *apaciguar*) to appease
3 (= *reconciliar*) to bring together, reconcile
VPR **pacificarse** to calm down
Pacífico SM (*tb* **océano Pacífico**) Pacific (Ocean)
pacífico ADJ [*lugar, proceso, arreglo*] peaceful; [*carácter*] peaceable; [*ciudadano*] peace-loving
pacifismo SM pacifism
pacifista ADJ, SMF pacifist
pack SM [*de yogures, latas*] pack; [*de vacaciones*] package
Paco SM (*forma familiar de* **Francisco**) • MODISMO: • **ya vendrá el tío ~ con la rebaja** they *etc* will soon come down to earth with a bump
paco[1] SM (*Mil Hist*) sniper, sharpshooter
paco[2]‡ SM (*LAm*) cop‡, policeman
paco[3] ADJ (*And, Cono Sur*) (= *rojizo*) reddish
SM (*And, Cono Sur*) (= *mamífero*) alpaca
pacota* SF (*Méx*) **1** (= *género*) = **pacotilla**
2 (= *persona*) layabout*
pacotada* SF (*And*) blunder, gaffe
pacotilla SF **1** (= *género*) trash, junk, inferior stuff • **de ~** trashy, shoddy • **hacer su ~** to be doing nicely, make a nice profit
2 (*And, CAm, Cono Sur*) rabble, crowd, mob
pacotillero ADJ (*And*) (= *rústico*) rude, uncouth
SM (*And, Caribe, Cono Sur*) (= *vendedor ambulante*) pedlar, peddler (EEUU), hawker
pactable ADJ negotiable
pactar ▹ CONJUG 1a VT **1** (= *acordar*) to agree to • **~ una tregua** to agree to a truce
2 (= *estipular*) to stipulate
VI **1** (= *llegar a un acuerdo*) to come to an agreement, make a pact
2 (= *transigir*) to compromise
pacto SM agreement, pact • **hacer un ~** to make an agreement, make a pact • **romper un ~** to break an agreement • MODISMO: • **hacer un ~ con el diablo** to make a pact with the devil ▸ **Pacto Andino** Andean Pact ▸ **pacto de caballeros** gentlemen's agreement ▸ **pacto de no agresión** non-aggression pact ▸ **pacto de recompra** repurchase agreement ▸ **Pacto de Varsovia** Warsaw Pact ▸ **pacto entre caballeros** gentlemen's agreement ▸ **pacto social** (*gen*) social contract; [*de salarios*] wages settlement

PACTOS DE LA MONCLOA

In the unstable political environment in Spain that followed Franco's death and the narrow victory of Adolfo Suárez's **UCD** party in the 1977 general election, it became obvious that a great deal of cross-party cooperation would be needed if progress was to be made. The result was the **Pactos de la Moncloa**, named after the prime minister's official residence, where the pacts were signed in October 1977. They were designed to bring together all political groups in a spirit of consensus in order to push through vital legislation, specifically the Constitution, but also budgets and regional policies.

▷ LA CONSTITUCIÓN ESPAÑOLA

padecer ▷ CONJUG 2d VI to suffer • **ha padecido mucho** she has suffered a lot • **~ de** to suffer from • **padece del corazón** he has heart trouble • **ella padece por todos** she suffers on everybody's account • **padece en su amor propio** his self-respect suffers • **se embala bien para que no padezca en el viaje** it is well packed so that it will not get damaged on the journey
VT **1** (= *sufrir*) to suffer • **eso hace ~ el metal de los goznes** that puts a strain on the metal of the hinges
2 (= *aguantar*) [+ *malos tratos, adversidades*] to endure, put up with • **~ un error** to labour under a misapprehension

padecimiento SM (*gen*) suffering; (*Med*) ailment

pádel SM paddle tennis

padrastro SM **1** (= *pariente*) stepfather
2 (*en dedo*) hangnail
3† (= *mal padre*) harsh father, cruel parent
4† (= *dificultad*) obstacle, difficulty

padrazo SM indulgent father

padre SM **1** (= *progenitor*) father; (*Zool*) father, sire • **lo quiero como a un ~** I love him as you would a father • **su señor ~** your father • **Gutiérrez ~** Gutiérrez senior, the elder Gutiérrez • MODISMOS: • **de ~ y muy señor mío**: • **una paliza de ~ y muy señor mío** an almighty thrashing, the father and mother of a thrashing • **no tiene ~ ni madre, ni perrito que le ladre** he is (all) alone in the world ▸ **padre de familia** family man; (*Jur*) head of a household ▸ **padre político** father-in-law ▸ **padre soltero** single father
2 padres (= *padre y madre*) parents
3 (*Rel*) father • **el Padre Las Casas** Father Las Casas ▸ **padre espiritual** confessor ▸ **Padre Nuestro** Lord's Prayer, Our Father ▸ **Padre Santo** Holy Father ▸ **padres de la Iglesia** Church Fathers
4 [*de disciplina*] father • **es el ~ de la lingüística moderna** he is the father of modern linguistics
5* • **¡mi ~!** you don't say!* • **¡tu ~!** up yours!‡ • **¡eres mi ~!** you're a marvel!
ADJ* (= *enorme*) huge • **un éxito ~** a huge success • **se armó un lío ~** there was an almighty row • **darse una vida ~** to live the life of Riley*

padrejón SM (*Arg*) stallion

padrenuestro SM Lord's Prayer • MODISMO: • **en menos que se reza un ~** in no time at all

padrillo SM (*And, Cono Sur*) stallion

padrinazgo SM **1** (*Rel*) godfathership
2 (= *patrocinio*) sponsorship, patronage; (= *protección*) protection

padrino SM **1** (*en bautizo*) godfather; **padrinos** godparents
2 (*en boda*) ≈ best man
3 (*en duelo*) second
4 [*de mafia*] godfather
5 (= *patrocinador*) sponsor, patron
6†‡ (= *víctima*) sucker‡, victim

padrísimo* ADJ (*Méx*) = **padre**

padrón SM **1** (= *censo*) census; (*Pol*) electoral register, electoral roll; [*de miembros*] register
2 (*Téc*) pattern
3 (= *columna*) commemorative column, inscribed column
4 (= *infamia*) stain, blot • **será un ~ (de ignominia) para todos nosotros** it will be a disgrace for all of us
5 (*LAm*) (*Agr*) stud; (= *caballo*) stallion; (*And*) (= *toro padre*) breeding bull
6 (*Chile*) (*Aut*) car registration documents (*pl*)
7* (= *padrazo*) indulgent father

padrote SM **1** (*CAm, Méx**) (= *chulo*) pimp
2 (*LAm*) (= *caballo*) stallion; (= *toro*) breeding bull

paella SF **1** (*Culin*) paella
2 (= *recipiente*) paella dish

paellada SF paella party

paellera SF **1** (*Culin*) (= *recipiente*) paella dish; (= *cocinera*) paella cook
2 (*hum*) dish aerial, dish antenna (EEUU), TV satellite dish

paellero/a ADJ [*arroz, ingredientes*] paella (*antes de s*)
SM/F

paf EXCL wham!, zap!

pág. ABR (= **página**) p

paga SF **1** (= *sueldo*) (*semanal*) wages (*pl*); (*mensual*) salary; [*de jubilado, viuda*] pension; [*de niño*] pocket money • **14 ~s al año** 14 yearly payments • **día de ~** payday ▸ **paga de Navidad** Christmas bonus (*equivalent to a month's salary*) ▸ **paga extra, paga extraordinaria** salary bonus (*usually paid in July and December*)
2 (*Com*) (= *pago*) payment • **entrega contra ~** cash on delivery

PAGA EXTRAORDINARIA

Most long-term and permanent employment contracts in Spain stipulate that annual salary will be paid in 14 instalments. This means that most Spanish workers receive twice the normal monthly wage in June and December. These extra payments are generally known as **paga extraordinaria** or **paga extra**.

pagadero ADJ payable • **una hipoteca pagadera en diez años** a mortgage payable over ten years • **~ a plazos** payable in instalments • **~ al portador** payable to bearer • **~ a la entrega** payable on delivery

pagado ADJ **1** (= *ya abonado*) [*impuesto, factura, vacaciones*] paid • **con todos los gastos ~s** with all expenses paid • **"no pagado"** "unpaid" • **~ por adelantado** paid in advance, prepaid; ▷ **porte**
2 (= *con sueldo*) [*asesino, mercenario*] hired • **el futbolista mejor ~ de la historia** the most highly paid *o* the best paid footballer in history
3 (= *satisfecho*) [*persona*] • **~ de uno mismo** self-satisfied, smug

pagador(a) ADJ • **la entidad ~a** the payer
SM/F **1** (= *persona*) payer • **ser buen/mal ~** to be a good/bad payer
2 (*Mil*) (*tb* **oficial pagador**) paymaster

pagaduría SF (*gen*) pay office, cashier's office; (*Mil*) paymaster's office

paganini* SMF • **ser el ~** to be the one who pays

paganismo SM paganism, heathenism

pagano/a ADJ (*Rel*) pagan, heathen
SM/F **1** (*Rel*) pagan, heathen
2* = **paganini**
3 (= *chivo expiatorio*) scapegoat, dupe, victim

pagar ▷ CONJUG 1h VT **1** (= *abonar*) [+ *factura, rescate, sueldo*] to pay; [+ *compra*] to pay for; [+ *intereses, hipoteca*] to pay off, repay • **paga 200 dólares de alquiler** he pays 200 dollars in rent • **los menores de tres años no pagan entrada** children under three get in free • **ya han pagado las bebidas** the drinks have been paid for • **su tío le paga los estudios** his uncle is paying for his education • **estamos pagando la hipoteca del piso** we're paying off *o* repaying the mortgage on the flat • **cantidad a ~** amount payable • **"a pagar en destino"** (*Correos*) "postage due" • **~ algo con tarjeta de crédito** to pay for sth by credit card • **¿lo puede ~ con dólares?** can I pay in dollars? • **~ algo al contado** *o* **en efectivo** *o* **en metálico** to pay cash for sth, pay for sth in cash • **~ algo a plazos** to pay for sth in instalments *o* (EEUU) installments • **~ algo por** to pay sth for • **¿cuánto pagasteis por el coche?** how much did you pay for the car? • **hemos pagado un precio muy alto por haberlo traicionado** betraying him cost us dear, we paid a high price for betraying him • MODISMOS: • **ni aunque me paguen** not if you paid me • **~ a algn con la misma moneda** to give sb a taste of their own medicine; ▷ **pato, plato, vidrio**
2 (= *costar*) to cost • **el pavo se está pagando a 23 euros el kilo** turkey costs 23 euros a kilo at the moment • **sus cuadros se pagan a peso de oro** his paintings fetch a very high price
3 (= *corresponder*) [+ *ayuda, favor*] to repay; [+ *visita*] to return • **¿cómo puedo ~te lo que has hecho por mis hijos?** how can I repay you for what you've done for my children?
4 (= *sufrir las consecuencias de*) • **lo pagó con su vida** he paid for it with his life • **pagó su error con diez años de cárcel** his mistake cost him ten years in jail • MODISMOS: • **~ algo caro** to pay dearly for sth • **¡lo ~ás caro!** you'll pay dearly for this! • **~las**: • **¡las vas a ~!** you've got it coming to you!*, you'll pay for this! • **¡me las ~ás todas juntas!** I'll get you for this! • **¡que Dios se lo pague!** God bless you! • REFRÁN: • **el que la hace la paga** you have to face the consequences for what you do
VI **1** (= *satisfacer un pago*) to pay • **hoy pago yo** I'm paying today, it's my turn to pay today • **en este trabajo pagan bien** this job pays well
2 (*Col, Méx*) (= *compensar*) to pay • **el negocio no paga** the business doesn't pay
VPR **pagarse 1** [+ *estudios, gastos*] to pay for • **yo me lo pago todo** I support myself, I pay for everything myself • **él mismo está pagándose sus estudios** he's paying for his own education
2 (= *vanagloriarse*) • **~se de algo** to be pleased with sth • **se paga mucho de su pelo** she's terribly vain about her hair • **~se de uno mismo** to be conceited, be full of o.s.*

pagaré SM promissory note, IOU ▸ **pagaré del Tesoro** Treasury bill, Treasury bond

página SF page • **anuncio a toda ~** • **anuncio a ~ entera** full-page advertisement • **primera ~** front page • MODISMO: • **currarse la ~**‡ to try it on* ▸ **página de inicio** (*Internet*) home page ▸ **página personal** (*Internet*) personal web page ▸ **páginas amarillas, páginas doradas** (*Arg*) Yellow Pages® ▸ **página web** web page

paginación SF pagination

paginar ▷ CONJUG 1a VT to paginate, number the pages of • **con seis hojas sin ~** with six unnumbered pages

pago[1] SM **1** (*Econ*) payment • **el primer ~ fue de 150 euros** the first payment was 150

euros • tras el ~ de la primera letra after paying the first instalment • atrasarse en los ~s to be in arrears • huésped de ~ paying guest • día de ~ payday • suspender ~s to stop payments ▸ pago a cuenta payment on account ▸ pago adelantado advance payment ▸ pago a la entrega cash on delivery ▸ pago a la orden direct debit ▸ pago a la presentación de factura payment on invoice ▸ pago al contado cash payment ▸ pago anticipado advance payment ▸ pago a plazos payment by instalments *o* (*EEUU*) installments ▸ pago a título gracioso ex gratia payment ▸ pago contra reembolso cash on delivery ▸ pago domiciliado direct debit ▸ pago en especie payment in kind ▸ pago fraccionado payment in instalments *o* (*EEUU*) installments, part-payment ▸ pago inicial down payment, deposit ▸ pago íntegro gross payment ▸ pago por resultados payment by results ▸ pago por visión pay per view ▸ pago simbólico token payment; ▹ balanza, colegio, condición, suspensión
2 (= *recompensa*) return, reward • este es el ~ que me dais por mis esfuerzos this is what you give me in return for *o* as a reward for my efforts • en ~ de *o* por algo in return for sth, as a reward for sth
ADJ paid • estar ~ (*lit*) to be paid; (*fig*) to be even, be quits

pago² SM (= *zona*) district; (= *finca*) estate (*esp planted with vines or olives*); (*Cono Sur*) region, area; (= *tierra natal*) home turf • por estos ~s round here, in this neck of the woods*

pago³ (*Arg*) PP *de* pagar

pagoda SF pagoda

pagote* SM scapegoat

págs. ABR (= páginas) pp

pagua SF 1 (*Cono Sur*) (= *hernia*) hernia; (= *hinchazón*) large swelling
2 (*Méx*) large avocado pear

paguacha SF (*Cono Sur*) 1 = pagua
2 (= *melón*) large melon
3‡ (= *cabeza*) nut*, noggin (*EEUU**), bonce*

paguala SF (*Caribe*) swordfish

paguro SM edible crab

pai SM (*LAm*) pie

paiche SM (*And*) dried salted fish

paila SF 1 (*esp Chile*) (= *sartén*) frying pan; (= *cacerola*) large pan
2 (*Cono Sur*) (= *comida*) meal of fried food

pailero/a SM/F 1 (*And, Méx**) (= *italiano*) immigrant Italian, Wop**
2 (*CAm, Caribe, Méx*) (= *cobrero*) coppersmith; (= *calderero*) tinker

pailón SM 1 (*And, Caribe*) (= *cazo*) pot, pan
2 (*And, CAm*) (*Geog*) (= *cuenca*) bowl
3 (*Caribe*) (= *remolino*) whirlpool

paíño SM petrel

paipai SM *oriental-style fan*

pairo SM • estar al ~ (*Náut*) to lie to • MODISMO: • quedarse al ~ to sit back and do nothing

país SM 1 (= *nación*) country • los ~es miembros *o* participantes the member countries ▸ país de las maravillas wonderland ▸ país de nunca jamás never-never land ▸ país deudor debtor nation ▸ país en desarrollo, país en vías de desarrollo developing nation ▸ país natal native land ▸ país satélite satellite country *o* state
2 (= *tierra*) land, region • vino del ~ local wine
3 (*Arte*) (= *paisaje*) landscape

paisa* SMF (*LAm*) = paisano

paisaje SM 1 (= *terreno*) landscape • el ~ montañoso del Tirol the mountainous landscape of Tyrol ▸ paisaje interior state of mind
2 (= *vista panorámica*) • estaba contemplando el ~ I was looking at the scenery • desde aquí se divisa un ~ magnífico you get a magnificent view from here
3 (*Arte*) landscape

paisajismo SM (*Arte*) landscape painting; [*de jardines*] landscaping, landscape gardening

paisajista SMF (= *pintor*) landscape painter; (= *jardinero*) landscape gardener

paisajístico ADJ landscape (*antes de s*), scenic

paisanada SF (*Cono Sur*) (*gen*) group of peasants; (*colectivamente*) peasants (*pl*)

paisanaje SM 1 (= *población civil*) civil population
2 (*Arg*) (*gen*) group of peasants; (*colectivamente*) peasants (*pl*)

paisano/a ADJ (= *del mismo país*) from the same country; (= *de la misma región*) from the same region; (= *del mismo pueblo*) from the same town
SM/F 1 (= *civil*) civilian • traje de ~ plain clothes (*pl*) • vestir de ~ [*soldado*] to be wearing civilian clothes, be in civvies*; [*policía*] to be in plain clothes
2 (= *del mismo país*) compatriot, fellow countryman/countrywoman • es ~ mío he's a fellow countryman (of mine); (= *del mismo pueblo*) person from the same town; (= *de la misma región*) person from the same region
3 (*esp Arg*) (= *campesino*) peasant
4 (*Cono Sur*) (= *extranjero*) foreigner; (*Cono Sur*) (= *árabe*) Arab; (*Méx*) (= *español*) Spaniard; (*And, Cono Sur*) (= *chino*) Chinaman/Chinese woman

Países Bajos SMPL • los ~ (= *Holanda*) the Netherlands; (*Hist*) the Low countries

paisito* SM (*Uru*) homeland

País Vasco SM • el ~ the Basque Country

paja SF 1 (*Agr*) straw; (*de beber*) straw; (*LAm*) (= *leña*) dried brushwood • sombrero de ~ straw hat • techo de ~ thatched roof • hombre de ~* front man* • MODISMOS: • lo hizo en un quitarme las ~s* she did it in a jiffy* • riñeron por un quítame allá esas ~s they quarrelled *o* (*EEUU*) quarreled over nothing • REFRÁN: • ver la ~ en el ojo ajeno y no la viga en el propio to see the mote in sb else's eye and not the beam in one's own
2 (*fig*) trash, rubbish, garbage (*EEUU*); (*en libro, ensayo*) padding, waffle* • hinchar un libro con mucha ~ to pad a book out • meter ~ to waffle
3** (= *masturbación*) • hacerse una ~ • volarse la ~ (*CAm*) to wank**, jerk off**
4 (*And, Chile*) ▸ paja brava tall altiplano grass
5 (*And, CAm*) (*tb* paja de agua) (= *grifo*) tap, faucet (*EEUU*); (= *canal*) canal
6 (*Cono Sur*‡) (= *droga*) dope‡
7 (*CAm*‡) (= *mentira*) lie, fib*

pajar SM straw loft

pájara SF 1 (*Orn*) hen, hen bird; (= *perdiz hembra*) hen partridge
2* (= *mujer taimada*) sneaky bitch*; (= *ladrona*) thieving woman
3 (*Dep*) (= *desfallecimiento*) collapse
4 (= *pájaro de papel*) paper bird; (= *cometa*) kite
5 ▸ pájara pinta (game of) forfeits
6 • MODISMO: • dar ~ a algn (*And, CAm*) to swindle sb

pajarada SF (*And*) flock of birds

pajarear ▹ CONJUG 1a VT 1 (*LAm*) [+ *pájaros*] to scare, keep off
2 (*And*) (= *observar*) to watch intently
3 (*And*) (= *matar*) to murder
VI 1* (= *holgazanear*) to loaf; (= *vagar*) to loiter
2 (*LAm*) [*caballo*] to shy
3 (*Cono Sur**) (= *estar distraído*) to have one's head in the clouds
4 (*Méx**) (= *escuchar*) to keep an ear open

pajarera SF aviary; ▹ pajarero

pajarería SF 1 (= *tienda*) pet shop
2 (= *bandada de pájaros*) large flock of birds
3 (*Caribe**) (= *vanidad*) vanity

pajarero/a ADJ 1 (*Orn*) bird (*antes de s*)
2 [*persona*] (= *alegre*) merry, fun-loving; (= *chistoso*) facetious, waggish
3 [*ropa*] flashy, loud
4 (*LAm*) [*caballo*] nervous
5 (*Caribe**) (= *entrometido*) meddlesome
SM/F (*Com*) bird dealer; (= *cazador*) bird catcher; (= *criador*) bird breeder, bird fancier; (*And, CAm*) (= *ahuyentador*) bird-scarer; ▹ pajarera

pajarilla SF paper kite • MODISMO: • se le alegraron las ~s* he laughed himself silly*

pajarita SF 1 (= *corbata*) bow tie
2 (= *pájaro de papel*) paper bird; (= *cometa*) paper kite
3 (*Orn*) ▸ pajarita de las nieves white wagtail

pajarito SM 1 (*Orn*) (= *cría*) baby bird, fledgling; (*hum*) birdie
2 (= *persona*) very small person • MODISMOS: • me lo dijo un ~ a little bird told me • quedarse como un ~ to die peacefully
3 (*Caribe*) (= *bichito*) bug, insect

pájaro SM 1 (*Orn*) bird • MODISMOS: • matar dos ~s de un tiro to kill two birds with one stone • quedarse como un ~ to die peacefully • tener la cabeza a ~s • tener la cabeza llena de ~s • tener ~s en la cabeza to be featherbrained • REFRÁN: • más vale ~ en mano que ciento volando a bird in the hand is worth two in the bush ▸ pájaro azul bluebird ▸ pájaro bobo penguin ▸ pájaro cantarín, pájaro cantor songbird ▸ pájaro carpintero woodpecker ▸ pájaro de mal agüero bird of ill omen ▸ pájaro mosca (*Esp*) hummingbird
2* (= *astuto*) clever fellow, sharp sort ▸ pájaro bravo (*Ven**) smart Alec* ▸ pájaro de cuenta (= *importante*) big shot*, big noise*; (= *de cuidado*) nasty piece of work; (= *taimado*) wily bird
3** (= *pene*) prick**
4 (*Caribe*‡) (= *homosexual*) queer‡, poof‡, fag (*EEUU*‡)
ADJ 1 (*Cono Sur*) (= *atolondrado*) scatty, featherbrained
2 (*Cono Sur*) (= *sospechoso*) shady, dubious
3 (*Cono Sur*) (= *chillón*) loud, flashy
4 (*Caribe*‡) (= *afeminado*) poofy‡, queer‡
5 (*Cono Sur*) (= *distraído*) vague, distracted

pajarón/ona* (*Cono Sur*) ADJ vague, ineffectual, stupid
SM/F 1 (= *poco fiable*) untrustworthy sort; (= *ineficaz*) unbusinesslike person
2 (= *charro*) flashily dressed person

pajarota* SF (*Esp*) false rumour, canard

pajarraca* SF to-do*, fuss

pajarraco SM 1 (*Orn*) big ugly bird
2* (= *pillo*) slyboots*

paje SM (*gen*) page; (*Náut*) cabin boy

pajel SM sea-bream

pajera SF straw loft

pajero/a SM/F 1** (*en sentido sexual*) tosser**, wanker**
2 (*CAm**) (= *mentiroso*) liar
3 (*CAm*) (= *fontanero*) plumber
ADJ (*CAm**) (= *mentiroso*) fibbing*

pajilla SF 1 (*CAm, Caribe, Méx*) (= *sombrero*) straw hat
2 (*LAm*) (= *cigarrillo*) *type of cigarette made from rolled maize*

pajillero** SM tosser**, wanker**

pajita SF (drinking) straw • MODISMO:

• **quedarse mascando ~** (*Caribe**) to be left feeling foolish

pajizo ADJ **1** (= *de paja*) straw, made of straw; [*techo*] thatched
2 [*color*] straw-coloured, straw-colored (EEUU)

pajolero‡ ADJ (*Esp*) **1** (= *condenado*) bloody‡, damn(ed)* • **no tener ni pajolera idea** not to have a clue*
2 (= *tonto*) stupid
3 (= *travieso*) naughty, mischievous
4 (= *molesto*) irritating

pajón* ADJ (*Méx*) [*pelo*] (= *lacio*) lank; (= *crespo*) curly

pajonal SM (*LAm*) scrubland

pajoso ADJ **1** [*grano*] full of chaff
2 [*color*] straw-coloured; (= *como paja*) like straw

pajuela SF (= *tira*) spill; (*And*) (= *fósforo*) match; (*And, Cono Sur, Méx*) (= *de dientes*) toothpick; (*Caribe*) (*Mús*) plectrum
• **MODISMO:** • **el tiempo de la ~** olden days, bygone times

pajúo* ADJ (*Caribe*) daft, stupid

Pakistán SM Pakistan

pakistaní ADJ Pakistani
SMF Pakistani • **los ~es** the Pakistanis

pala SF **1** (*para cavar*) spade; (*para nieve, carbón, tierra*) shovel ▸ **pala cargadora** mechanical loader ▸ **pala de patatas** potato fork ▸ **pala excavadora** digger ▸ **pala mecánica** power shovel ▸ **pala quitanieves** snowplough, snowplow (EEUU) ▸ **pala topadora** (*Arg*) bulldozer
2 (*Culin*) slice ▸ **pala para el pescado** fish slice
3 (*Dep, Béisbol*) bat; (*en ping-pong*) bat, paddle (EEUU); (*en tenis*) racket • **jugar a ~** to play beach-tennis
4 [*de hélice, remo*] blade
5 ▸ **pala matamoscas** fly swat
6 [*de zapato*] vamp
7‡ (= *mano*) mitt‡ • **¡choca la ~!** shake on it!*
8† (= *astucia*) cunning, wiliness

palabra SF **1** (= *vocablo*) word • **un título de dos ~s** a two-word title • **lo tradujo ~ por ~** he translated it word for word • **me lo resumió en dos ~s** he summarized it for me in a couple of words • **¿me permiten decir unas ~s?** could I say a few words? • **eso no son más que ~s** those are just (empty) words • **no tengo ~s** *o* **me faltan ~s para expresar lo que siento** I haven't got the *o* there aren't words to express how I feel, words fail to express how I feel • **tuvo ~s de elogio para el ministro** he had words of praise for the minister • **sin decir** *o* **chistar* ~** without a word • **no dijo ni media ~** he didn't give us the slightest hint • **no entiendo ~** I can't understand a word • **es ~ de Dios** it is the word of God • **con buenas ~s:** • **me lo dijo con muy buenas ~s** he told me as cool as you like* • **nos entretenía con buenas ~s, pero nunca nos daba el dinero** he palmed us off with smooth talk, but he never gave us the money • **medias ~s** hints • **lo dijo todo con medias ~s** he said everything indirectly • **en una ~** in a word • **¡ni una ~ más!** not another word!
• **MODISMOS:** • **coger a algn la ~** (= *creer*) to take sb at his word; (= *obligar*) to keep sb to his word • **comerse las ~s** to mumble • **no cruzar (una) ~ con algn** not to say a word to sb • **decir la última ~** to have the last word • **dejar a algn con la ~ en la boca** to cut sb off in mid-sentence • **me dejó con la ~ en la boca y se fue de la habitación** he walked out of the room while I was in mid-sentence • **gastar ~s** to waste one's breath • **medir las ~s** to choose one's words carefully • **negar la ~ de Dios a algn** to concede absolutely nothing to sb • **quitar la ~ de la boca a algn** to take the words right out of sb's mouth • **tener unas ~s con algn** to have words with sb • **trabarse de ~s** to wrangle, squabble • **tener la última ~** to have the final say
• **REFRANES:** • **a ~s necias, oídos sordos** it's best not to listen to the silly things people say • **las ~s se las lleva el viento** words count for nothing ▸ **palabra clave** keyword ▸ **palabras cruzadas** (*LAm*) (= *crucigrama*) crossword (*sing*) • **un juego de ~s cruzadas** a word puzzle ▸ **palabras gruesas** crude language (*sing*) ▸ **palabras mayores†** offensive language (*sing*) • **MODISMO:** • **ser ~s mayores** (= *ser importante*): • **¿te han hecho directora? ¡eso ya son ~s mayores!** so you've been appointed director, that's really something!; ▹ **juego²**
2 (= *facultad de hablar*) • **la ~** speech • **perdió el uso de la ~** he lost the power of speech • **tiene el don de la ~** • **es de ~ fácil** he has a way with words, he has the gift of the gab* • **de ~:** • **he pecado solo de ~** I've sinned in word only • **nos acusó de ~** he accused us verbally • **dirigir la ~ a algn:** • **hace tiempo que no me dirige la ~** he hasn't spoken to me for a long time
3 (*frm*) (= *turno para hablar*) floor • **ceder la ~ a algn** • **conceder la ~ a algn** to give sb the floor, invite sb to speak • **pedir la ~** to ask for the floor, ask to be allowed to speak • **tener la ~** to have the floor • **tiene la ~ el señor presidente** the president has the floor • **yo no tengo la ~** it's not for me to say • **tomar la ~** to take the floor, speak • **hacer uso de la ~** to take the floor, speak
4 (= *promesa*) word • **es hombre de ~** he is a man of his word • **cumplió su ~** he kept his word, he was true to his word • **~ que yo no tengo nada que ver*** I've got nothing to do with it, (I) promise! • —**¿de verdad que no sabías nada?** —**¡palabra!** *o* (*hum*) **¡palabrita del Niño Jesús!** "you really didn't know anything?" — "cross my heart and hope to die!" • **bajo ~** (*Mil*) on parole • **dar** *o* **empeñar su ~** to give one's word • **faltar a su ~** to go back on *o* break one's word ▸ **palabra de casamiento** • **dar ~ de casamiento** to promise to marry ▸ **palabra de honor** word of honour, word of honor (EEUU) • **¿me das tu ~ de honor de que no dirás nada?** do you give me your word of honour you won't say anything? • **¡~ de honor!** word of honour!

palabrear ▹ CONJUG 1a VT **1** (*And, Cono Sur*) (= *acordar*) to agree verbally to • **~ a algn** to promise to marry sb
2 (*Cono Sur*) (= *insultar*) to abuse

palabreja SF (*gen*) strange word; (= *palabrota*) swearword

palabrería SF, **palabrerío** SM verbiage, hot air

palabrero/a ADJ wordy, long-winded
SM/F windbag‡

palabro* SM (= *palabrota*) swearword; (= *palabra rara*) odd word; (= *palabra petulante*) pretentious term; (= *barbarismo*) barbarism

palabrota SF swearword

palabrudo* ADJ (*Cono Sur*) foulmouthed

palacete SM small palace

palacial ADJ (*LAm*) palatial

palaciego ADJ palace (*antes de s*), court (*antes de s*)
SM (= *persona*) courtier

palacio SM (*gen*) palace; (= *mansión*) mansion • **el ~ del marqués de Mudéjar** the house of the Marquis of Mudéjar • **ir a ~** to go to court • **tener un puesto en ~** to have a post at court ▸ **palacio de congresos** conference centre, conference hall ▸ **palacio de deportes** sports centre ▸ **palacio de justicia** courthouse ▸ **Palacio de las Comunicaciones** (*en Madrid*) General Post Office ▸ **palacio de los deportes** sports centre ▸ **palacio episcopal** bishop's palace ▸ **palacio municipal** city hall ▸ **Palacio Nacional** (*p.ej. en Guatemala*) Parliament Building ▸ **palacio real** royal palace

palada SF **1** (*con pala*) shovelful, spadeful
2 (*con remo*) stroke

paladar SM **1** (*Anat*) (hard) palate, roof of the mouth
2 (= *gusto*) palate • **tener un ~ delicado** to have a delicate palate

paladear ▹ CONJUG 1a VT (*gen*) to taste; (= *degustar*) to savour, savor (EEUU) • **beber algo paladeándolo** to have a sip of sth (to see what it tastes like)

paladeo SM (*gen*) tasting; (= *degustación*) [*de comida*] savouring, savoring (EEUU); [*de bebida*] sipping

paladín SM **1** (*Hist*) paladin
2 [*de la libertad, justicia*] champion

paladinamente (*liter*) ADV (= *públicamente*) openly, publicly; (= *claramente*) clearly

paladino (*liter*) ADJ (= *público*) open, public; (= *claro*) clear • **más ~ no puede ser** it couldn't be clearer

palafrén SM palfrey

palafrenero SM groom

palana SF (*And*) **1** (= *pala*) shovel, spade
2 (= *azadón*) hoe

palanca SF **1** (= *barra*) lever ▸ **palanca de arranque** kick-starter ▸ **palanca de cambio** gear lever, gearshift (EEUU) ▸ **palanca de freno** brake lever ▸ **palanca de mando** joystick
2* (= *influencia*) pull, influence • **mover ~s** to pull strings • **tener ~** to have pull, know people in the right places ▸ **palancas del poder** levers of power
3 (*And, Méx*) [*de barca*] punting pole

palangana SF **1** (= *jofaina*) washbasin, washbowl (EEUU)
2 (*And, CAm*) (= *fuente*) platter, serving dish
SMF **1** (*Cono Sur**) (= *intruso*) intruder
2 (*LAm*) (= *frívolo*) shallow person
3 (*LAm*) (= *charlatán*) charlatan
4 (*LAm*) (= *jactancioso*) braggart

palanganear* ▹ CONJUG 1a VI (*LAm*) to brag, show off*

palanganero SM washstand

palangre SM fishing line (*with multiple hooks*)

palanquear ▹ CONJUG 1a VT **1** (*And, CAm*) (= *apalancar*) to lever (along), move with a lever
2 (*And, Caribe, Méx*) [+ *barca*] to punt, pole along
3 (*Cono Sur**) (= *ayudar*) • **¿quién te palanqueó?** who got you fixed up?
VI (*And, Caribe, Cono Sur**) to pull strings

palanquera SF stockade

palanquero SM **1** (*And, Cono Sur*) (*Ferro*) brakeman
2 (*And*) (= *leñador*) lumberman
3 (*Cono Sur**) (= *ladrón*) burglar, housebreaker

palanqueta SF **1** (*gen*) small lever; [*de forzar puertas*] jemmy, crowbar
2 (*Cono Sur, Méx*) (= *peso*) weight

palanquetazo* SM break-in, burglary

palanquista* SM burglar

p'alante‡ ADV = **para adelante**, ▹ **adelante**

palapa SF (*Méx*) **1** (= *palmera*) palm tree
2 (*como tejado*) palm roof

palatal ADJ, SF palatal

palatalización SF palatalization

palatalizar ▹ CONJUG 1f VT to palatalize
VPR **palatalizarse** to palatalize

palatinado SM palatinate

P

palatino ADJ **1** (*Pol*) palace (*antes de s*), court (*antes de s*); (*del palatinado*) palatine
2 (*Anat*) palatal

palatosquisis SF INV cleft palate

palca SF (*And*) crossroads (*sing*)

palco SM (*Teat*) box; (*Ftbl*) director's box ▸ **palco de autoridades, palco de honor** royal box, box for distinguished persons ▸ **palco de la presidencia** (*Taur*) president's box ▸ **palco de proscenio** stage box ▸ **palco presidencial** (*Taur*) president's box

palde SM (*Cono Sur*) (= *herramienta*) pointed digging tool; (= *puñal*) dagger

palé SM board game similar to Monopoly

palear ▸ CONJUG 1a VT **1** (*LAm*) [+ *barca*] to punt, pole
2 (*LAm*) [+ *tierra*] to shovel; [+ *zanja*] to dig
3 (*Cono Sur*) [+ *granos*] to thresh
VI [*piragüista*] to paddle

palenque SM **1** (= *estacada*) stockade, palisade
2 (= *recinto*) arena, ring; [*de gallos*] pit
3 (*Cono Sur*) [*de caballos*] tethering post
4 (*Cono Sur**) (= *alboroto*) din, racket

palenquear ▸ CONJUG 1a VT (*Cono Sur*) to tether

palentino/a ADJ of/from Palencia
SM/F native/inhabitant of Palencia • **los ~s** the people of Palencia

paleo... PREF paleo...

paleografía SF paleography

paleógrafo/a SM/F paleographer

paleolítico ADJ paleolithic

paleontología SF paleontology

paleontólogo/a SM/F paleontologist

paleozoico ADJ Palaeozoic, Paleozoic (*EEUU*)
SM • **el ~** the Palaeozoic, the Paleozoic (*EEUU*)

palero* ADJ (*And*) big-headed*
SM (*Méx*) front man*

Palestina SF Palestine

palestino/a ADJ Palestinian
SM/F Palestinian • **los ~s** the Palestinians

palestra SF (*Hist*) arena; (= *liza*) lists (*pl*) • **salir** *o* **saltar a la ~** (= *participar*) to take the floor; (= *darse a conocer*) to come to the fore

paleta SF **1** (*para cavar*) small shovel, small spade; [*de albañil*] trowel; (*Culin*) (*con ranuras*) fish slice; (= *plana*) spatula; (*para el fuego*) fire shovel
2 (*Arte*) palette
3 (*Téc*) [*de turbina*] blade; [*de noria*] paddle, bucket; (= *plataforma*) pallet
4 (*Anat*) shoulder blade
5 (*LAm*) (= *polo*) ice lolly, popsicle (*EEUU*)
6 (*LAm*) (= *pala*) wooden paddle for beating clothes
7 (*LAm*) (*Culin*) topside of beef
SM* (= *albañil*) building worker, brickie*; ▸ **paleto**

paletada SF shovelful, spadeful

paletear ▸ CONJUG 1a VT (*Cono Sur*) [+ *caballo*] to pat; (*fig*) to flatter
VI (*Cono Sur*) to be out of work

paletería[1] SF (*Culin*) palate, sense of taste

paletería[2]* SF collection of yokels, shower‡

paletero SM (*And*) tuberculosis

paletilla SF shoulder blade

paletización SF (*Com*) palletization

paleto/a ADJ* boorish, stupid
SM/F* yokel, country bumpkin, hick (*EEUU*); ▸ **paleta**
SM (*Zool*) fallow deer

palia SF altar cloth, pall

paliacate SM (*Méx*) kerchief, scarf

paliar ▸ CONJUG 1b VT **1** (= *mitigar*) [+ *dolor*] to relieve, alleviate, palliate (*frm*); [+ *efectos*] to lessen, mitigate, palliate (*frm*); [+ *importancia*] to diminish
2 (= *disimular*) [+ *defecto*] to conceal, gloss over; [+ *ofensa*] to mitigate, excuse

paliativo ADJ palliative, mitigating
SM palliative • **sin ~s** [*desastre, fracaso*] unmitigated; [*rechazo*] unreserved; [*vulgaridad*] utter • **un edificio feo sin ~s** an ugly building with no redeeming features • **condenar sin ~s** to condemn unreservedly

palidecer ▸ CONJUG 2d VI to turn pale

palidez SF paleness, pallor

pálido ADJ pale, pallid

palidoso ADJ (*And*) = **pálido**

paliducho/a* ADJ pale

palier SM **1** (*Mec*) bearing
2 (= *plataforma*) pallet
3 (*Arg*) (= *descanso*) landing

palillero SM (*para palillos*) toothpick holder; (*para plumillas*) penholder

palillo SM **1** (= *mondadientes*) (*tb* **palillo de dientes**) toothpick • **unas piernas como ~s de dientes** legs like matchsticks
2 (*Mús*) [*de tambor, batería*] drumstick; **palillos** (= *instrumento*) castanets
3 (*para comida oriental*) chopstick
4* (*hum*) very thin person • MODISMO: • **estar hecho un ~** to be as thin as a rake
5 (*Taur**) banderilla
6 (*Cono Sur*) (= *aguja de tejer*) knitting needle
7 (*CAm, Méx*) (= *portalápices*) penholder

palimpsesto SM palimpsest

palíndromo SM palindrome

palinodia† SF recantation • **cantar la ~** to recant

palio SM **1** (= *dosel*) canopy
2 (*Rel*) pallium • MODISMO: • **recibir bajo ~ a algn** to roll out the red carpet for sb
3†† (= *manto*) cloak

palique* SM chat, chitchat • **darle al ~** • **estar de ~** to chat, natter

palista SMF (*Dep*) canoeist

palito SM (*Arg*) ice lolly, Popsicle (*EEUU*)

palitroque SM **1*** (= *palo*) stick
2 (*Taur**) banderilla
3 (*Cono Sur*) (= *juego*) skittles (*pl*), bowling (*EEUU*); (= *local*) skittle alley, bowling alley (*EEUU*)

paliza SF **1** (= *tunda*) beating, thrashing • **dar** *o* **propinar una ~ a algn** to give sb a beating, beat sb up* • **los críticos le dieron una ~ a la novela** the critics panned *o* slated the novel*
2* (= *pesadez*) bore • **el viaje fue una ~** the journey was a real bore *o* drag* • **dar la ~** to be a pain • MODISMO: • **darse la ~** (*al estudiar, trabajar*) to slog away; (*al tocarse, besarse*) to be all over each other
3* (*Dep etc*) drubbing, thrashing • **el Betis le dio una ~ al Barcelona** Betis gave Barcelona a real thrashing, Betis thrashed Barcelona
SMF INV* (= *pesado*) bore, pain*

palizada SF **1** (= *valla*) fence, palisade
2 (= *cercado*) fenced enclosure

palizas* SMF INV bore, pain*

palizón SM = **paliza**

palla SF (*And*) (*Hist*) Inca princess

pallador SM (*LAm*) = **payador**

pallar[1] ▸ CONJUG 1a VT (*Min*) to extract; (*Agr*) to glean

pallar[2] SM (*And, Cono Sur*) Lima bean

pallasa SF mattress

pallasca SF (*And, Cono Sur*), **pallaso** SM (*And, Cono Sur*) mattress

Palma SF ▸ **Palma de Mallorca** Palma

palma SF **1** (*Anat*) palm • **leerle la ~ de la mano a algn** to read sb's palm • MODISMOS: • **conocer algo como la ~ de la mano** to know sth like the back of one's hand • **ser liso** *o* **llano como la ~ de la mano** to be as flat as a pancake • **llevar a algn en ~s** *o* **palmitas** to wait on sb hand and foot
2 palmas (= *aplausos*) clapping (*sing*), applause (*sing*) • **batir** *o* **dar** *o* **hacer ~s** to clap (one's hands), applaud • **tocar las ~s** to clap in time ▸ **palmas de tango** slow hand-clap
3 (*Bot*) palm (tree); (= *hoja*) palm leaf • MODISMO: • **llevarse la ~**: • **las tres son muy antipáticas, pero Ana se lleva la ~** the three of them are very unfriendly, but Ana wins hands down

palmada SF **1** [*de amistad*] slap, pat • **darse una ~ en la frente** to clap one's hand to one's brow
2 palmadas (= *aplausos*) clapping (*sing*), applause (*sing*) • **dar ~s** to clap (one's hands), applaud

palmadita SF pat, light tap

palmado‡ ADJ (*CAm*) skint‡, flat broke*

palmar[1] SM (*Bot*) palm grove, cluster of palms

palmar[2]‡ ▸ CONJUG 1a VI **1** (= *morir*) to kick the bucket*, peg out‡
2 (*en juego*) to lose
VT • MODISMO: • **~la** to kick the bucket*, to peg out‡

palmar[3] ADJ, **palmario** ADJ obvious, self-evident

palmarés SM **1** (*Dep*) [*de ganadores*] list of winners
2 (= *historial*) record

palmariamente ADV [*demostrar*] clearly • **estar plamariamente claro** to be abundantly clear

palmarote‡ SM (*Caribe*) yokel, hick (*EEUU**)

palmatoria SF **1** [*de vela*] candlestick
2 [*de castigo*] cane

palmazón* SM • MODISMO: • **estar en el ~** (*CAm*) to be broke*

palmeado ADJ [*pata*] webbed

palmear ▸ CONJUG 1a VT (*LAm*) [+ *perro etc*] to pat
VI to clap

palmense ADJ of/from Las Palmas
SMF native/inhabitant of Las Palmas • **los ~s** the people of Las Palmas

palmera SF, **palmero[1]** SM (*And, Cono Sur, Méx*) palm (tree) • MODISMO: • **estar en la ~*** to be broke* ▸ **palmera datilera** date palm

palmero[2]/a ADJ of/from La Palma
SM/F native/inhabitant of La Palma • **los ~s** the people of La Palma

palmeta SF (= *vara*) cane; (= *acto*) caning, swish with a cane

palmetazo SM **1** (= *acto*) caning, swish with a cane
2 (= *desaire*) slap in the face

palmetón SM slap

palmípedo ADJ web-footed

palmista SMF (*LAm*) palmist

palmiste SM (= *grano*) palm kernel; (= *aceite*) palm oil

palmitas SFPL • MODISMO: • **tener** *o* **llevar** *o* **traer a algn en ~** (= *mimar*) to spoil sb; (= *tratar con cuidado*) to handle sb with kid gloves

palmito SM **1** (*LAm*) palm heart
2 (*Esp**) (= *buen cuerpo*) body, beautiful body • MODISMO: • **lucir ~** to show off one's figure

palmo SM **1** (= *medida*) span; (*fig*) few inches (*pl*), small amount • MODISMOS: • **~ a ~** inch by inch • **avanzar ~ a ~** to inch forward • **conocer el terreno ~ a ~** *o* **a ~s** to know every inch of the ground • **tener medido el terreno a ~s** to know every inch of the ground • **con un ~ de lengua fuera** with his tongue hanging out • **crecer a ~s** to shoot up • **dejar a algn con un ~ de narices** to disappoint sb, let sb down • **no hay un ~ de A a B** there's hardly any distance *o* difference between A and B • **no levantaba un ~ del**

suelo cuando ... he was knee-high to a grasshopper when ...
2 (*CAm***) (= *coño*) cunt**
palmotear ▹ CONJUG 1a (VI) to clap, applaud
palmoteo (SM) clapping, applause
palo (SM) **1** (= *vara*) (*de poco grosor*) stick; (*fijo en el suelo*) post; [*de telégrafos, tienda de campaña*] pole; [*de herramienta*] handle, shaft • **le pegó con un ~** he hit him with a stick • **las gallinas estaban subidas en el ~** the hens were sitting on the perch • **el ~ de la fregona** the mop handle • **política de ~ y zanahoria** carrot and stick policy • MODISMOS: • **estar hecho un ~** to be as thin *o* skinny as a rake • **meter ~s en las ruedas** to throw a spanner in the works • **más tieso que un ~**: • **andaba más tieso que un ~** he walked bolt upright • **te voy a poner más tieso que un ~** I'm going to give you a good hiding • REFRÁN: • **de tal ~ tal astilla** like father like son ▸ **palo de amasar** (*Arg, Uru*) rolling pin ▸ **palo de escoba** broomstick ▸ **palo ensebado** greasy pole
2 (= *madera*) • **cuchara de ~** wooden spoon • **pata de ~** wooden leg, peg leg
3 (= *golpe*) blow • **un par de ~s es lo que tú necesitas** what you need is a good hiding • **dar** *o* **pegar un ~ a algn** (= *golpear*) to hit sb with a stick;* (= *timar*) to rip sb off* • **los críticos le dieron un ~ a la obra** the critics slated the play* • **vaya ~ me pegaron en ese restaurante** they really ripped me off in that restaurant* • **dar de ~s a algn** to give sb a beating • MODISMOS: • **andar a ~s*** to be always squabbling *o* fighting • **dar ~s de ciego** (*peleando*) to lash out wildly; (*buscando una solución*) to take a stab in the dark • **no dar** *o* **pegar (ni) ~ al agua*** to not lift a finger • **moler a algn a ~s** to give sb a beating • **ni a ~s***: • **ni a ~s va a aprender la lección** there's no way he's going to learn the lesson* • **ni a ~s me voy yo de aquí dejándote sola** wild horses wouldn't make me go off and leave you on your own, there's no way I would go off and leave you on your own*
4* (= *disgusto*) bummer‡, nightmare* • **es un ~ que te bajen el sueldo** it's a real bummer‡ *o* nightmare* that they're cutting your salary • **¡qué ~ si suspendo!** it'll be a real bummer‡ *o* nightmare* if I fail! • **dar ~**: • **me daría ~ que se enterase** I would hate it if he found out • **llevarse un ~**: • **nos llevamos un ~ muy gordo cuando descubrimos la verdad** it was a real blow when we found out the truth • **Manuel se ha llevado un gran ~ con Luisa** Manuel has been badly let down by Luisa
5 (*Náut*) mast • MODISMO: • **a ~ seco** [*navegar*] under bare poles; [*comer, beber*] • **nos tomamos el vino a ~ seco** we had the wine on its own • **nos comimos el jamón a ~ seco** we had the ham on its own, we had the ham with nothing to wash it down • **no pasa un día a ~ seco** (*Ven*) he never goes a single day without a drink • **vermut a ~ seco** straight vermouth • REFRÁN: • **que cada ~ aguante su vela** everyone should face up to their responsibilities ▸ **palo de mesana** mizzenmast ▸ **palo de trinquete** foremast ▸ **palo mayor** mainmast
6 (*Dep*) **a** [*de portería*] post • **el balón se coló entre los ~s** the ball went between the posts
b (*para golpear*) (*en hockey*) stick; (*en golf*) club ▸ **palo de golf** golf club
7 (= *de uva*) stalk
8 (*Tip*) (*de b, d*) upstroke; (*de p, q*) downstroke • **hace los ~s muy largos** he makes long strokes
9 (*Naipes*) suit • **cambiar de ~** to change suit • **seguir el ~** to follow suit ▸ **palo del triunfo** trump suit, trumps (*pl*)
10 (*Mús*) (*en flamenco*) style
11 (*esp LAm*) (*Bot*) tree ▸ **palo de hule** (*CAm*) rubber tree ▸ **palo de mango** mango tree ▸ **palo dulce** liquorice root ▸ **palo (de) rosa** rosewood ▸ **palo santo** lignum vitae
12 (*Ven**) [*de licor*] swig*, slug* • **pegarse unos ~s** to have a few drinks • MODISMOS: • **darse al ~** to take to drink • **a medio ~** half-drunk
13 (*Chile**) • MODISMO: • **tirar el ~*** to brag ▸ **palo blanco** man of straw ▸ **palo grueso** big shot*
14 (*Méx***) (= *acto sexual*) screw** • **echar un ~** to have a screw**
15 (*Col, Ven*) • **un ~ de: un ~ de casa** a marvellous house • **es un ~ de hombre** he's a great guy • **cayó un ~ de agua** the rain came pouring down, there was a huge downpour*
paloma (SF) **1** (*Orn*) dove, pigeon • MODISMO: • **¡palomita!** darling! ▸ **paloma buscadora de blancos** homing pigeon ▸ **paloma de la paz** dove of peace ▸ **paloma mensajera** carrier pigeon, homing pigeon ▸ **paloma torcaz** wood pigeon, ringdove
2 (= *persona*) meek and mild person; (*Pol*) dove ▸ **paloma sin hiel** pet, lamb
3 (= *ejercicio*) handstand
4 (*CAm, Caribe, Méx*) (= *cometa*) kite
5 palomas (*Náut*) white horses, whitecaps (EEUU)
palomar (SM) dovecot(e)
palomear ▹ CONJUG 1a (VT) **1** (*Caribe*) (= *engañar*) to swindle
2 (*And*) [+ *enemigos*] to hunt down one by one; (= *tirar a matar*) to shoot to kill, shoot dead; (= *matar a traición*) to shoot down in cold blood
palometa (SF) harvestfish, pompano, derbio
palomilla (SF) **1** (*Entomología*) moth; (*esp*) grain moth; (= *crisálida*) nymph, chrysalis
2 (*Téc*) (= *tuerca*) wing nut
3 (= *soporte*) wall bracket, angle iron
4 [*de caballo*] back, backbone
5* (*And, Cono Sur*) (= *niño vagabundo*) urchin, ragamuffin; (*CAm, Cono Sur, Méx*) [*de niños*] mob of kids; (= *pandilla*) crowd of layabouts, band of hooligans
palomino (ADJ) (*And, Cono Sur, Méx*) [*caballo*] palomino (*antes de s*); (= *blanco*) white
(SM) **1** (*Orn*) young pigeon
2 (*And, Cono Sur, Méx*) (= *caballo palomino*) palomino (horse); (= *caballo blanco*) white horse
3* (*en ropa interior*) skidmark*
palomita (SF) **1** (*Méx*) (= *aprobación*) tick
2 (*Dep*) full-length dive
3 palomitas (*tb* **palomitas de maíz**) popcorn (*sing*)
palomo (ADJ) (*And, Cono Sur, Méx*) = **palomino**
(SM) (cock) pigeon ▸ **palomo de arcilla** clay pigeon
palotada† (SF) • MODISMO: • **no dar ~** (= *no trabajar*) not to do a stroke of work; (= *no hacer nada*) to do nothing; (= *hacerlo mal*) to get nothing right
palote (SM) **1** (*en escritura*) (*gen*) downstroke; (*en forma de "S"*) pothook
2 (*Mús*) drumstick
3 (*Caribe, Cono Sur*) (*Culin*) [*de amasar*] rolling pin
4 (*Cono Sur**) (= *persona*) beanpole*, stringbean (EEUU*)
palotear ▹ CONJUG 1a (VI) to bicker, wrangle
paloteo (SM) bickering, wrangling
palpable (ADJ) **1** (*con las manos*) palpable, tangible
2 (= *claro, evidente*) palpable, obvious, palpable
palpablemente (ADV) clearly
palpamiento (SM) (*LAm*) frisking, body-search
palpar ▹ CONJUG 1a (VT) **1** (= *tocar*) to touch, feel; (= *tantear*) to feel one's way along; (*amorosamente*) to caress, fondle; (*esp LAm*) [+ *sospechoso*] to frisk
2 (= *notar*) to appreciate, understand • **ahora palpa las consecuencias** now he's really feeling the consequences • **ya ~ás lo que es esto** one day you'll really understand all this
(VPR) **palparse** [*miedo, ansiedad*] to be felt • **se palpaba el descontento** you could feel the restlessness • **hay una enemistad que se palpa** you can feel the hostility, the hostility is tangible
palpitación (SF) (*gen*) palpitation; (*nerviosa*) quiver, quivering; (*con fuerza*) flutter, fluttering
palpitante (ADJ) **1** (*gen*) palpitating; [*corazón*] throbbing
2 [*interés, cuestión*] burning
palpitar ▹ CONJUG 1a (VI) **1** (*gen*) to palpitate; [*corazón*] to throb, beat; (*nerviosamente*) to quiver; (*con fuerza*) to flutter
2 (*fig*) to throb • **en la poesía palpita la emoción** the poem throbs with emotion
3 (*Cono Sur*) • MODISMOS: • **me palpita** I have a hunch • **ya me palpitaba el fracaso** I had a hunch it would be a failure
pálpito (SM), **palpite** (SM) hunch • **tener un ~** to have a hunch
palquista‡ (SM) cat burglar
palta (SF) (*And, Cono Sur*) avocado (pear)
palto (SM) (*And, Cono Sur*) avocado (pear) tree
paltó (SM) (*esp LAm*) topcoat, overcoat
palúdico (ADJ) **1** [*pantano, terreno*] marshy
2 (*Med*) malarial
paludismo (SM) malaria
palurdo/a* (ADJ) coarse, uncouth
(SM/F) (= *paleto*) yokel, hick (EEUU*); (*pey*) lout
palustre¹ (SM) (*Téc*) trowel
palustre² (ADJ) marsh (*antes de s*)
pamela (SF) sun hat, picture hat
pamema (SF) **1** (= *bagatela*) trivial thing, trifle
2 pamemas (= *aspavientos*) fuss (*sing*) • **¡déjate de ~s!** stop your fussing! • **deja de decir ~s** stop talking nonsense
3 pamemas (= *halagos*) flattery (*sing*); (= *persuasión*) coaxing (*sing*), wheedling (*sing*)
pampa¹ (SF) **1** (*LAm*) (*Geog*) pampa(s), prairie • **la Pampa** the Pampas; ▹ GAUCHO
2 (*Cono Sur*) (*Min*) *region of nitrate deposits*; (= *descampado*) *open area on the outskirts of a town*
3 (*And*) (*en la sierra*) *high grassy plateau*
4 • MODISMOS: • **a** *o* **en la ~** (*LAm**) in the open • **en ~** (*LAm**) in the nude • **estar en ~ y la vía** (*Cono Sur**) to be flat broke* • **quedarse en ~** (*Cono Sur**) to come to nothing, fall through
pampa² (ADJ) **1** (*And, Cono Sur**) [*negocio*] shady, dishonest
2 (*And*) (= *endeble*) weak, feeble
(SMF) (*Arg*) (pampean) Indian
(SM) (*Ling*) *language of the pampean Indians*
pámpana (SF) vine leaf • MODISMO: • **zurrar la ~ a algn** (*Esp*†*) to give sb a hiding*
pámpano (SM) vine shoot, vine tendril
pampeano/a (*LAm*) (ADJ) of/from the pampas
(SM/F) native/inhabitant of the pampas • **los ~s** the people of the pampas
pampear¹ ▹ CONJUG 1a (VI) (*Cono Sur*) to travel over the pampas
pampear² ▹ CONJUG 1a (VT) (*And*) **1** (= *tocar*) to tap, pat (on the shoulder)
2 [+ *masa*] to roll out

P

pampero/a (*LAm*) ADJ of/from the pampas
SM/F native/inhabitant of the pampas • **los ~s** the people of the pampas
SM (*Meteo*) strong westerly wind (*blowing over the pampas from the Andes*)

pampinflar‡ ▸ CONJUG 1a VT • **¡me la pampinflas!** you stupid git!‡

pampino/a ADJ (*LAm*) of/from the Chilean pampas
SM/F (*Cono Sur*) native/inhabitant of the Chilean pampas • **los ~s** the people of the Chilean pampas

pamplina SF **1*** (= *tontería*) silly remark • **¡pamplinas!** rubbish!, nonsense! • **eso son ~s** that's a load of rubbish • **sin más ~s** without any more beating about the bush
2* (= *aspaviento*) fuss
3* (= *zalamería*) soft soap* • **no me vengas con ~s** don't come to me with that soft soap*
4 (*Bot*) chickweed

pamplinero* ADJ **1** (= *tonto*) silly, nonsensical
2 (= *aspaventero*) given to making a great fuss
3 (= *zalamero*) sweet-talking

pamplonada SF (*LAm*) (= *trivialidad*) triviality; (= *tontería*) silly thing, piece of nonsense

pamplonés/esa ADJ, SM/F = **pamplonica**

pamplonica ADJ of/from Pamplona
SMF native/inhabitant of Pamplona • **los ~s** the people of Pamplona

pampon SM (*And*) open space, open ground

pamporcino SM cyclamen

pan SM **1** (*Culin*) bread; (= *hogaza*) loaf • **les gusta mucho el pan con mantequilla** they love bread and butter • **compré dos panes** I bought two loaves • **estar a pan y agua** to be on bread and water ▸ **pan blanco, pan candeal** white bread ▸ **pan casero** home-made bread ▸ **pan cenceño** unleavened bread ▸ **pan de centeno** rye bread ▸ **pan de flor** white bread ▸ **pan de molde** tin loaf ▸ **pan dulce** (*Méx*) pastry ▸ **pan duro** stale bread ▸ **pan francés** (*Arg*) baguette ▸ **pan integral** wholemeal bread ▸ **pan lactal** (*Arg*) sandwich loaf ▸ **pan molido** (*Méx*) breadcrumbs (*pl*) ▸ **pan moreno** brown bread ▸ **pan rallado** breadcrumbs (*pl*) ▸ **pan tostado** toast
2 (= *bloque*) ▸ **pan de azúcar** sugar loaf ▸ **pan de hierba** turf, sod ▸ **pan de higos** block of dried figs ▸ **pan de jabón** bar *o* cake of soap
3 (*Agr*) wheat • **un año de mucho pan** a year of a heavy wheat crop
4 (*Téc*) gold *o* silver leaf
5 • MODISMOS: • **con su pan se lo coma** that's his look-out • **contigo pan y cebolla** (with you I'd gladly have) love in a cottage • **echar panes** (*And, Cono Sur*) to boast, brag • **ganarse el pan** to earn one's living • **hacer un pan como unas hostias** to make a real mistake *o* gaffe • **llamar al pan pan y al vino vino** to call a spade a spade • **más bueno que el pan***: • **estar más bueno que el pan** [*persona*] to be gorgeous, be dishy* • **ser más bueno que el pan** to be as good as gold • **ser pan comido**: • **eso es pan comido** it's a piece of cake, it's a cinch • **ser el pan nuestro de cada día**: • **aquí los atracos son el pan nuestro de cada día** muggings happen all the time around here • **venderse como pan bendito** to sell like hot cakes

pan... PREF pan... • *p.ej.* **panasiático** pan-Asiatic

pana¹ SF (= *paño*) corduroy

pana² SF (*Chile*) (*Aut*) breakdown • **quedar en ~** to break down

pana³ SF (*Chile*) **1** (= *hígado*) liver
2* (= *valor*) guts* (*pl*), courage • MODISMO: • **se le heló la ~** (*Cono Sur*) he lost his nerve
3 • MODISMO: • **tirar ~s** (*And**) to put on airs

pana⁴ SMF (*Caribe*) (= *compañero*) pal*, buddy (*EEUU*)

panacea SF panacea

panaché SM mixed salad

panadería SF **1** (= *tienda*) baker's (shop), bakery
2 (= *oficio*) breadmaking

panadero/a SM/F baker

panadizo SM (*Med*) whitlow

panafricano ADJ Pan-African

panal SM honeycomb

Panamá SM Panama

panamá SM Panama hat

panameñismo SM *word/phrase peculiar to Panama*

panameño/a ADJ Panamanian
SM/F Panamanian • **los ~s** the Panamanians

panamericanismo SM Pan-Americanism

panamericano ADJ Pan-American
SF • **la Panamericana** the Pan-American highway

panamitos SMPL (*And*), **panamos** SMPL (*And*) **1** (= *judías*) beans
2 (*fig*) food (*sing*), daily bread (*sing*)

panárabe ADJ Pan-Arab

panca SF (*And*) dry leaf of maize

pancarta SF placard, banner

panceta SF (*Arg*) streaky bacon

pancha* SF = **panza**

panchanguero* ADJ **1** (= *ruidoso*) noisy, rowdy
2 (*Méx*) (= *alegre*) merry; (= *chistoso*) witty
3 (*Méx*) (= *campechano*) expansive

pancho¹ ADJ (= *tranquilo*) calm, unruffled • **estar tan ~** (*Cono Sur, Esp*) to remain perfectly calm, not turn a hair

pancho² ADJ **1** (*Cono Sur*) (= *marrón*) brown, tan
2 (*And, Caribe*) (= *aplastado*) broad and flat; (= *achaparrado*) squat • MODISMO: • **ni tan ~ ni tan ancho** (*Caribe‡*) neither one thing nor the other
SM (*Arg*) (*Culin*) hot dog

pancho³ SM (= *pez*) young sea-bream

Pancho SM *forma familiar de* **Francisco**

pancista ADJ, SMF opportunist

pancita SF (*Méx*) (*Culin*) tripe

pancito SM (*LAm*) (bread) roll

páncreas SM INV pancreas

pancreático ADJ pancreatic

pancromático ADJ panchromatic

panda¹ SMF (*Zool*) panda

panda² SF = **pandilla**

panda³ SF (*Caribe*) = **pandeo**

pandear ▸ CONJUG 1a VI, VPR **pandearse** [*madera*] to bend, warp; [*pared*] to sag, bulge

pandemia SF pandemic

pandémico ADJ pandemic

pandemonio SM, **pandemónium** SM pandemonium • **fue el ~*** all hell broke loose, there was pandemonium

pandeo SM [*de madera*] bend; [*de pared, tejado*] sag(ging), bulge, bulging

pandereta SF tambourine • MODISMOS: • **la España de ~*** tourist Spain • **zumbar la ~ a algn** (*Esp**) to tan sb's hide*

panderetear ▸ CONJUG 1a VI to play the tambourine

pandero SM **1** (*Mús*) tambourine
2* (= *culo*) backside, butt (*EEUU‡*)
3† (= *cometa*) kite
4†* (= *tonto*) idiot

pandibó‡ SM slammer‡, can (*EEUU**), prison

pandilla SF **1** [*de amigos*] group of friends • **ayer salí con la ~ de mi hermano** I went out with my brother's friends yesterday
2 [*de criminales*] gang; [*de gamberros*] bunch, load

pandillero/a SM/F (*esp LAm*) member of a gang

pando ADJ **1** [*pared*] bulging; [*madera*] warped; [*viga*] sagging
2 [*río, persona*] slow
3 [*plato*] shallow; [*terreno*] flat
4 (*CAm*) (= *oprimido*) oppressed
5 (*CAm**) (= *saciado*) full (up)
6 (*CAm, Méx*) (*de hombros*) round-shouldered

Pandora SF • MODISMO: • **la caja de ~** Pandora's box

pandorga SF **1*** (= *jamona*) fat woman
2 (= *cometa*) kite
3 (*And**) (= *molestia*) bother, nuisance
4 (*And*) (= *mentira*) lie
5 (*Méx**) (= *broma*) (*gen*) practical joke; (*estudiantil*) student prank

pandorgo ADJ **1** (*Méx*) (= *lerdo*) dim, stupid
2 (*Caribe*) (= *gordinflón*) fat and slow-moving

pane SM (*And*) (*Aut*) breakdown

panear ▸ CONJUG 1a VI (*And, Cono Sur*) to boast, show off

panecillo SM (bread) roll

panegírico SM panegyric

panel SM **1** [*de pared, puerta*] panel • **~es** (*Arquit*) panelling (*sing*), paneling (*EEUU*) ▸ **panel de información de vuelos** flight information board ▸ **panel de instrumentos** (*Aut*) dashboard ▸ **panel de mandos** (*Aer etc*) control panel, controls (*pl*) ▸ **panel explicativo** display panel ▸ **panel solar** solar panel
2 (= *jurado*) panel ▸ **panel de audiencia** TV viewers' panel

panela SF **1** (*LAm*) (*Culin*) brown sugar loaf
2 (*Méx*) (= *sombrero*) straw hat
3 (*And, Méx**) (= *pesado*) bore, drag; (= *zalamero*) creep‡

panelería SF panelling, paneling (*EEUU*)

panelista SMF panellist, panelist (*EEUU*)

panera SF bread basket

panero ADJ **1** [*industria, producción*] bread (*antes de s*)
2 • **ser muy ~*** to love bread

paneuropeo ADJ Pan-European

pánfilo ADJ **1** (= *crédulo*) simple, gullible; (= *tonto*) stupid; (= *lento*) sluggish, lethargic
2 (*And*) (= *pálido*) pale, discoloured, discolored (*EEUU*)

panfletario ADJ [*estilo*] highly-coloured, highly-colored (*EEUU*); [*propaganda*] cheap, demagogic

panfletista SMF (*gen*) pamphleteer; (*esp LAm*) satirist, lampoonist

panfleto SM (*gen*) pamphlet; (*esp LAm*) lampoon

panga SF (*CAm, Méx*) (= *lancha*) barge, lighter; (= *transbordador*) ferry(boat)

pangolín SM scaly anteater

paniaguado SM **1** (= *criado*) servant
2 (= *protegido*) protégé

paniaguarse ▸ CONJUG 1i VPR (*Méx*) to become friends, pal up*

pánico ADJ panic (*antes de s*)
SM **1** (= *miedo*) panic • **el ~ comprador** panic buying • **yo le tengo un ~ tremendo** I'm scared stiff of him
2 • MODISMO: • **de ~*** excellent, brilliant

paniego ADJ (*Agr*) • **tierra paniega** wheatland

panificable ADJ • **granos ~s** bread grains

panificación SF breadmaking

panificadora SF bakery

panil SM (*Cono Sur*) celery

panizo SM **1** (*Bot*) (= *mijo*) millet; (= *maíz*) maize
2 (*Chile*) [*de mineral*] mineral deposit

3 (*Chile*) (= *tesoro*) treasure; (= *negocio*) gold mine
panocha (SF), **panoja** (SF) **1** (*Bot*) [*de maíz*] corncob; [*de trigo*] ear of wheat
2 (*Méx*) (= *azúcar*) unrefined brown sugar; (= *dulce*) brown sugar candy
3 (*And, CAm, Cono Sur*) (= *torta*) *large pancake of maize and cheese*
4* (= *dinero*) brass*, dough*
5 (*Méx*‡) (= *vulva*) cunt‡
panocho/a (ADJ) of/from Murcia (SM/F) native/inhabitant of Murcia • **los ~s** the Murcians, the people of Murcia (SM) (*Ling*) Murcian dialect
panoli* (SMF), **panolis*** (SMF INV) chump*, idiot
panoplia (SF) **1** (= *armadura*) panoply
2 (= *colección de armas*) collection of arms
panorama (SM) **1** (*gen*) panorama (*tb fig*); (= *vista*) view; (= *perspectiva*) outlook • **el ~ actual político** the present political scene
2 (*Arte, Fot*) view
panorámica (SF) general view, survey
panorámico (ADJ) panoramic • **punto ~** viewpoint, vantage point
panoramizar ▸ CONJUG 1f (VT), (VI) (*Cine*) to pan
panqué (SM) (*CAm, Caribe*), **panqueque** (SM) (*LAm*) pancake
panquequera (SF) (*LAm*) pancake iron
panquequería (SF) (*LAm*) pancake house
pantagruélico (ADJ) lavish
pantaleta (SF) (*LAm*), **pantaletas** (SFPL) (*LAm*) (= *bombachos*) bloomers, drawers; (= *bragas*) panties
pantalla (SF) **1** [*de lámpara*] shade, lampshade
2 (*Cine*) screen • **los personajes de la ~** screen personalities • **la pequeña ~** the small screen, the TV • **llevar una historia a la ~** to film a story ▸ **pantalla acústica** baffle ▸ **pantalla de plasma** plasma screen ▸ **pantalla de televisión** television screen ▸ **pantalla de vídeo** video screen ▸ **pantalla grande** big screen ▸ **pantalla panorámica** wide screen ▸ **pantalla plana** flat screen
3 (*Inform*) screen, display ▸ **pantalla de ayuda** help screen ▸ **pantalla de cristal líquido** liquid crystal display ▸ **pantalla de radar** radar screen ▸ **pantalla de rayos** (*en aeropuerto*) X-ray security apparatus ▸ **pantalla táctil** touch screen
4 (*CAm*) (= *abanico*) fan
5 (*fig*) front; (= *señuelo*) decoy • **servir de ~ a algo** to be a front for sth • **MODISMO**: • **hacer la ~** (*Dep*) to protect the goalkeeper
6 [*de chimenea*] fireguard
7 (= *biombo*) screen
8 (*LAm*) (= *esbirro*) henchman
9 (*CAm*) (= *espejo*) large mirror
pantallazo (SM) (*Inform*) screenshot, screen dump
pantalón (SM), **pantalones** (SMPL) **1** trousers, pants (*EEUU*) • **un ~** • **unos pantalones** • **un par de pantalones** a pair of trousers *o* (*EEUU*) pants • **bajarse los pantalones** (*lit*) to take *o* pull one's trousers down; (*Esp**) (*fig*) to swallow one's pride • **MODISMOS**: • **es ella la que lleva los pantalones*** she's the one who wears the trousers • **llevar los pantalones bien puestos** (*Caribe**) to have guts ▸ **pantalones cortos** shorts ▸ **pantalones de corsario** pirate trousers ▸ **pantalones de esquí** ski pants ▸ **pantalón de montar** riding breeches (*pl*) ▸ **pantalón pitillo** drainpipe trousers (*pl*) ▸ **pantalones tejanos, pantalones vaqueros** jeans
2 (*And*) (= *hombre*) man, male
3 (*Caribe*) (= *coraje*) guts, courage

> **PANTALONES, ZAPATOS, GAFAS**
>
> **Uso de "pair"**
>
> ▸ *Para especificar el número de objetos que constan de dos piezas que forman parte de un juego de dos, se debe usar en inglés el partitivo* **pair of** *+ SUSTANTIVO:*
>
> **Tengo dos pares de zapatos**
> I've got two pairs of shoes
>
> ▸ *La misma regla se aplica cuando se trata de objetos compuestos por dos piezas simétricas:*
>
> **¿Cuántos pantalones meto en la maleta?**
> How many pairs of trousers shall I pack?
>
> *NOTA: Si no queremos especificar el número de objetos, no es necesario utilizar* **pair**:
>
> **¿Puede arreglarme las gafas?**
> I wondered if you could mend my glasses?
>
> *Para otros usos y ejemplos ver* **gafa, pantalón, zapato**

pantanal (SM) marshland
pantano (SM) **1** (= *embalse*) reservoir
2 (= *ciénaga*) bog, marsh
3† (= *atolladero*) fix*, mess* • **salir de un ~** to get out of a jam*
pantanoso (ADJ) **1** [*terreno, región*] boggy, marshy
2 [*situación*] difficult, tricky*
panteísmo (SM) pantheism
panteísta (ADJ) pantheistic (SMF) pantheist
panteón (SM) **1** (= *monumento*) pantheon • **el ~ de los reyes** the burial place of the royal family ▸ **panteón familiar** family vault
2 (*LAm*) (= *cementerio*) cemetery
3 (*Cono Sur*) (= *mineral*) ore, mineral
panteonero (SM) (*LAm*) gravedigger
pantera (SF) **1** (*Zool*) (*gen*) panther; (*Caribe*) (= *jaguar*) jaguar
2 (*Méx*) (= *matón*) heavy*; (= *atrevido*) risk-taker
pantimedias (SFPL) (*Méx*) tights, pantyhose (*EEUU*)
pantis (SMPL) tights, pantyhose (*EEUU*)
pantógrafo (SM) pantograph
pantomima (SF) mime
pantoque (SM) (*Náut*) bilge • **agua de ~** bilge water
pantorra* (SF) (fat) calf
pantorrilla (SF) **1** (*Anat*) calf
2 (*And*) (= *vanidad*) vanity
pantorrilludo (ADJ) **1** (= *de piernas gordas*) thick-calved
2 (*And**) (= *vanidoso*) vain
pants (SMPL) (*LAm*) tracksuit (*sing*), sweat suit (*sing*) (*EEUU*)
pantufla (SF), **pantuflo** (SM) (carpet) slipper
panty (SM), **pantys** (SMPL) tights, pantyhose (*EEUU*)
panucho (SM) (*Méx*) stuffed tortilla
panudo/a* (*And*) (ADJ) boastful, bragging (SM/F) loudmouth*
panul (SM) (*Cono Sur*) celery
panza* (SF) belly, paunch • **estrellarse de ~** to do a belly flop, make a pancake landing ▸ **panza de burro** (*Alpinismo*) overhang ▸ **panza mojada** (*Méx**) wetback (*EEUU*)
panzada* (SF) **1** (= *hartazgo*) • **darse una ~ de algo: nos dimos una ~ de cordero** we stuffed ourselves with lamb • **me he dado una buena ~ de dormir** I had a really good sleep
2 (= *golpe*) (*en el agua*) belly flop • **aterrizaje de ~** belly landing
panzazo (SM) **1** (*And, Cono Sur*) (= *golpe*) belly flop
2 (*Méx*) = **panzada**
3 • **MODISMO**: • **pasar de ~** (*LAm*‡) to get through by the skin of one's teeth
panzón (ADJ), **panzudo** (ADJ) paunchy, potbellied
pañal (SM) **1** [*de bebé*] nappy, diaper (*EEUU*) • **MODISMOS**: • **estar todavía en ~es** [*persona*] to be still wet behind the ears; [*ciencia, técnica*] to be still in its infancy • **yo de informática estoy todavía en ~es** when it comes to computing, I'm still a little wet behind the ears • **esto ha dejado en ~es a los rivales** this has left the competition way behind ▸ **pañal desechable** disposable nappy
2 [*de camisa*] shirt-tail
3 pañales (= *canastilla*) baby clothes • **MODISMOS**: • **criarse en buenos ~es** to be born with a silver spoon in one's mouth • **de humildes ~es** of humble origins
pañería (SF) (= *géneros*) drapery; (= *tienda*) draper's (shop), dry-goods store (*EEUU*)
pañero/a (SM/F) draper, dry-goods dealer (*EEUU*), clothier
pañete (SM) **1** (= *tela*) light cloth
2 pañetes (= *calzones*) shorts, trunks
3 (*And*) (= *enlucido*) coat of fine plaster
4 (*Cono Sur*) [*del caballo*] horse blanket
pañí¹ (SM) (*Cono Sur*) sun trap
pañí²‡ (SF) • **MODISMO**: • **dar la ~** to give a tip-off, tip the wink*
pañito (SM) (*Esp*) [*de mesa*] table-runner; [*de bandeja*] traycloth
paño (SM) **1** (= *tela*) cloth • **MODISMOS**: • **conocerse el ~** to know the score* • **le conozco el ~** I know his sort • **REFRÁN**: • **el buen ~ en el arca se vende** good wine needs no bush
2 (= *pieza*) cloth; (= *trapo*) duster • **MODISMO**: • **jugar a dos ~s** to play a double game ▸ **paño de altar** altar cloth ▸ **paño de cocina** dishcloth ▸ **paño de lágrimas** • **soy su ~ de lágrimas** I'm a shoulder for him to cry on ▸ **paño de los platos** tea towel ▸ **paño de manos** hand towel ▸ **paño de secar** tea towel ▸ **paño higiénico** (*Esp*†) sanitary towel, sanitary napkin (*EEUU*) ▸ **paño mortuorio** pall ▸ **paños calientes** half measures • **no andarse con ~s calientes** (*para solucionar algo*) not to go in for half-measures; (*al criticar algo*) to pull no punches • **poner ~s calientes** to make a half-hearted attempt ▸ **paños tibios** (*fig*) half-measures
3 (*Cos*) (= *ancho*) piece of cloth, width
4 paños (= *ropa*) clothes; (*Arte*) drapes ▸ **paños menores** underwear (*sing*)
5 • **al ~** (*Teat*) offstage
6 (*Arquit*) wall section
7 (*en cristal*) cloud of mist; [*de diamante*] flaw
8 (*Caribe*) (= *red*) fishing net
9 (*And*) (= *tierra*) plot of land
pañol (SM) (*Náut*) store, storeroom ▸ **pañol del agua** water store ▸ **pañol del carbón** coal bunker
pañolada (SF) (*Taur, Ftbl*) *waving of handkerchiefs by spectators at a bullfight, football match etc to convey approval or disapproval*
pañoleta (SF) **1** [*de mujer*] (*sobre los hombros*) shawl; (*sobre la cabeza*) headscarf
2 [*de torero*] tie
pañolón (SM) shawl
pañuelo (SM) (*para limpiarse*) handkerchief; (*para la cabeza*) scarf, headscarf; (*para el cuello*) scarf; [*de hombre*] cravat ▸ **pañuelo de papel** paper handkerchief
papa¹ (SM) (*Rel*) pope ▸ **papa negro** black pope (*General of the Jesuits*)
papa² (SF) **1** (*esp LAm*) (= *patata*) potato

P

• MODISMOS: • **cuando las ~s queman** (*Cono Sur*) when things hot up • **echar las ~s** (*Esp**) to throw up* • **ni ~***: • **no entiendo ni ~** I don't understand a word • **no oyó ni ~** he didn't hear a thing • **no sabe ni ~** he hasn't got a clue ▸ **papa dulce** sweet potato ▸ **papas colchas** (*CAm*) crisps, potato chips (*EEUU*) ▸ **papas fritas** chips, French fries (*EEUU*)
2 (*Méx**) (= *mentira*) fib*
3 (*Cono Sur**) (= *golpe*) bash*
4 (*Caribe**) (= *trabajo fácil*) soft job*
5 (*Méx*) (= *sopa*) porridge, gruel; (*Cono Sur*) (= *de bebé*) baby food

papa[3] ADJ INV (*Cono Sur**) jolly good*, first-rate

papá* SM dad*, daddy*, pop (*EEUU**) • **mis ~s** my mum and dad*, my mom and pop (*EEUU*) ▸ **papá grande** (*Méx*) grandfather, grandpa* ▸ **Papá Noel** Father Christmas; ▹ **hijo**

papachar* ▹ CONJUG 1a (*Méx*) VT
1 (= *acariciar*) to caress, stroke
2 (= *mimar*) to pamper, spoil

papachos* SMPL (*Méx*) (= *caricias*) caresses; (= *abrazos*) cuddles

papacote (*CAm*) SM (= *cometa*) kite
SMF (= *persona influyente*) bigwig, big shot*

papada SF [*de persona*] double chin; [*de animal*] dewlap

papadeno/a‡ SM/F (*Caribe*) Jehovah's Witness

papadilla SF dewlap

papado SM papacy

papagayo SM 1 (= *pájaro*) parrot
2 (= *charlatán*) chatterbox • **como un ~** parrot-fashion • **deja de repetir todo lo que digo como un ~** don't just repeat what I say parrot-fashion
3 (*Caribe, Méx*) (= *cometa*) large kite
4 (*And*) (= *bacinilla*) bedpan

papaíto* SM dad*, daddy*, pop (*EEUU**)

papal[1] ADJ (*Rel*) papal

papal[2] SM (*LAm*) potato field

papalina SF 1 (= *gorro*) (*con orejeras*) cap with earflaps; (*de esquiar*) ski-cap; (*para atar al cuello*) bonnet; (= *toca*) mobcap
2* (= *juerga*) binge* • **coger una ~** to get plastered*
3 **papalinas** (*CAm*) (= *patatas fritas*) (*Culin*) crisps, potato chips (*EEUU*)

papalón* SM (*Méx*) rat*, swine*

papalote SM (*CAm, Méx*) 1 (= *cometa*) kite
2 (= *molino*) [*de niño*] windmill

papalotear* ▹ CONJUG 1a VI 1 (*CAm, Méx*) (= *vagabundear*) to wander about
2 (*Méx*) (= *agonizar*) to give one's last gasp

papamoscas SM INV 1 (*Orn*) flycatcher
2 = **papanatas**

papamóvil SM popemobile

papanatas* SM INV sucker*, simpleton

papanatería SF, **papanatismo** SM gullibility, simple-mindedness

papandujo* ADJ (*Esp*) soft, overripe

papanicolau SM (*LAm*) cervical smear, smear test, Pap test

papapa SF (*CAm*) stupidity

papar* ▹ CONJUG 1a VT (= *tragar*) to swallow, gulp (down)
VPR **paparse 1** (= *comer*) to scoff* • **se lo papó todo** he scoffed the lot* • MODISMO: • **¡pápate esa!** (*Esp*) put that in your pipe and smoke it!*
2 (= *recibir un golpe*) to get a sudden knock, be hit real hard*

paparazzo [papa'ratso] SM (PL: **paparazzi**) paparazzo • **los paparazzi** the paparazzi

paparrucha* SF, **paparruchada*** SF
1 (= *disparate*) silly thing • **~s** rubbish (*sing*), nonsense (*sing*)
2† (= *chapuza*) worthless object
3† (= *infundio*) hoax

paparruta SMF (*Cono Sur*) humbug

paparulo* SM (*Cono Sur*) sucker‡

papas* SFPL (= *gachas*) pap (*sing*), mushy food (*sing*); (= *comida*) grub‡ (*sing*), chow (*sing*) (*EEUU*‡)

papaya SF 1 (= *fruta*) papaya, pawpaw
2 (*Caribe***) (= *vulva*) fanny**, beaver (*esp EEUU***)

papayo SM papaya tree, pawpaw tree

papear‡ ▹ CONJUG 1a VI to eat, scoff*

papel SM 1 (= *material*) paper • **una bolsa de ~** a paper bag • **un ~** (*pequeño*) a piece of paper; (= *hoja, folio*) a sheet of paper • **lo escribí en un ~** I wrote it on a piece of paper • MODISMO: • **sobre el ~** on paper ▸ **papel absorbente** kitchen roll ▸ **papel atrapamoscas** flypaper ▸ **papel biblia** India paper ▸ **papel carbón** carbon paper ▸ **papel cel(l)o** adhesive tape ▸ **papel charol** shiny wrapping paper ▸ **papel confort** (*Chile*) toilet paper ▸ **papel continuo** continuous feed paper ▸ **papel craft** (*CAm, Méx*) waxed paper ▸ **papel cuadriculado** squared paper, graph paper ▸ **papel de aluminio** tinfoil, aluminium *o* (*EEUU*) aluminum foil ▸ **papel de arroz** rice paper ▸ **papel de calcar, papel de calco** tracing paper ▸ **papel de cartas** notepaper ▸ **papel de celofán** Cellophane® ▸ **papel de China** India paper ▸ **papel de desecho** waste paper ▸ **papel de embalaje, papel de embalar** wrapping paper ▸ **papel de empapelar** wallpaper ▸ **papel de envolver** wrapping paper ▸ **papel de estaño** tinfoil, aluminium *o* (*EEUU*) aluminum foil ▸ **papel de estraza** (grey) wrapping paper ▸ **papel de excusado**† toilet paper ▸ **papel de filtro** filter paper ▸ **papel de fumar** cigarette paper • **entre ellos no cabía un ~ de fumar** (*Esp*) you couldn't have got a razor's edge between them ▸ **papel de grasa** greaseproof paper ▸ **papel de lija** sandpaper ▸ **papel de mano** handmade paper ▸ **papel de oficio** (*LAm*) official foolscap paper ▸ **papel de paja de arroz** rice paper ▸ **papel de paredes** wallpaper ▸ **papel de plata** silver paper ▸ **papel de regalo** gift wrap, wrapping paper ▸ **papel (de) seda** tissue paper ▸ **papel de tina** handmade paper ▸ **papel de tornasol** litmus paper ▸ **papel encerado** wax(ed) paper ▸ **papel engomado** gummed paper ▸ **papel estucado** art paper ▸ **papel fiduciario** fiduciary issue, fiat currency ▸ **papel higiénico** toilet paper ▸ **papel indicador** litmus paper ▸ **papel madera** (*Cono Sur*) brown wrapping paper ▸ **papel mojado** scrap of paper, worthless bit of paper • **el documento no es más que ~ mojado** the document isn't worth the paper it's written on ▸ **papel ondulado** corrugated paper ▸ **papel para máquina de escribir** typing paper ▸ **papel pautado** ruled paper ▸ **papel pergamino** parchment paper ▸ **papel pintado** wallpaper ▸ **papel prensa** newsprint ▸ **papel reciclado** recycled paper ▸ **papel sanitario** (*Méx*) toilet paper ▸ **papel secante** blotting paper ▸ **papel sellado** stamped paper ▸ **papel timbrado** stamp, stamp paper ▸ **papel transparente** tracing paper ▸ **papel usado, papeles usados** wastepaper (*sing*) ▸ **papel vegetal** film ▸ **papel vitela** vellum paper
2 **papeles** (= *documentos*) papers, documents; (= *carnet*) identification papers • **los ~es, por favor** your papers, please • **tiene los ~es en regla** his papers are in order • **los sin ~es** illegal immigrants • MODISMO: • **perder los ~es** to lose it
3 (= *actuación*) (*Cine, Teat*) part, role; (*fig*) role • **hizo el ~ de Cleopatra** she played the part of Cleopatra • **el ~ del gobierno en este asunto** the government's role in this matter • **tuvo que desempeñar un ~ secundario** he had to play second fiddle, he had to take a minor role • **jugó un ~ muy importante en las negociaciones** he played a very important part in the negotiations • **hacer buen/mal ~** to make a good/bad impression • **el equipo hizo un buen ~ en el torneo** the team did well in the tournament ▸ **papel estelar** star part
4 (= *billetes*) • **mil dólares en ~** a thousand dollars in notes ▸ **papel moneda** paper money, banknotes (*pl*)
5 (*Econ*) (= *bonos*) stocks and shares (*pl*) ▸ **papel del Estado** government bonds (*pl*)
6 (*Esp*‡) 1,000-peseta note; (*And*) one-peso note
7 (*LAm*) (= *bolsa*) bag

PAPEL

El sustantivo **papel** *se puede traducir en inglés por* **paper** *o por* **piece of paper**.

▹ *Lo traducimos por* **paper** *cuando nos referimos al* **papel** *como material:*
¿Todo el mundo tiene lápiz y papel?
Has everybody got a pencil and paper?

▹ *Si* **papel** *se refiere a una hoja de papel no lo traducimos por* **paper**, *sino por* **a piece of paper** *si nos referimos a un trozo de papel pequeño y por* **a sheet of paper** *si nos referimos a una hoja de papel o a un folio:*
¿Has visto el papel en el que estaba apuntando mis notas?
Have you seen that sheet of paper I was making notes on?
Apúntalo en este papel
Write it down on this piece of paper

▹ *Si nos referimos a varias hojas o trozos de papel en blanco utilizamos* **sheets** *o* **pieces**:
Necesitamos varios papeles
We need several pieces of paper

▹ *Si nos referimos a* **papeles** *que ya están escritos, se pueden traducir por* **papers**:
Tengo que ordenar todos estos papeles
I must sort out all these papers

Para otros usos y ejemplos ver la entrada.

papela‡ SF (*Esp*) 1 (= *documento*) (*gen*) paper, document; (= *carné*) identity card, ID
2 (= *droga*) = **papelina**

papelada SF (*Col*) pretence

papelear ▹ CONJUG 1a VI 1 (= *revolver papeles*) to rummage through papers
2 (= *atraer la atención*) to make a splash, draw attention to o.s.

papeleo SM (= *trámites*) paperwork; (*pey*) red tape

papelera SF 1 (= *recipiente*) (*en la oficina, en casa*) wastepaper bin, wastepaper basket; (*en la calle*) litter bin, trash can (*EEUU*); (*Inform*) (*tb* **papelera de reciclaje**) wastebasket
2 (= *fábrica*) paper mill
3 (= *escritorio*) writing desk

papelería SF 1 (= *tienda*) stationer's (shop)
2 (= *artículos de escribir*) stationery
3 (= *montón*) mass of papers, heap of papers; (= *lío*) sheaf of papers

papelerío SM (*LAm*) = **papelería**

papelero/a ADJ 1 (*Com*) paper (*antes de s*)
2 (= *farolero*) pretentious
SM/F 1 (= *fabricante*) paper manufacturer

2 (= *vendedor*) [*de artículos de escribir*] stationer; (*Méx*) [*de periódicos*] newspaper seller
3 (*Cono Sur*) (= *hazmerreír*) ridiculous person

papeleta SF **1** (*gen*) slip of paper; (= *ficha*) index card, file card; [*de rifa*] ticket; (*Univ*) (*tb* **papeleta de examen**) *exam results slip*; (*CAm*) [*de visita*] visiting card, calling card (*EEUU*) • **MODISMO**: • **¡vaya ~!** this is a tough one! ▸ **papeleta de empeño** pawn ticket ▸ **papeleta de examen** (*Univ*) *exam results slip*
2 (*Pol*) ballot paper, voting paper ▸ **papeleta en blanco** blank ballot paper ▸ **papeleta nula** spoiled ballot paper
3 (*LAm*) (= *bolsa*) bag
4 (*And**) (= *multa*) fine

papelillo SM **1** (= *papel*) cigarette paper
2 (= *cigarro*) cigarette
3 (*Med*) sachet

papelina* SF paper, sheet (*containing drug*)

papelista SMF (*Caribe, Cono Sur*) = **picapleitos**

papelito SM **1** (= *trozo de papel*) slip of paper, bit of paper
2 (*Teat, Cine*) minor role, bit part

papelón/ona SM/F (= *impostor*) impostor; (= *engreído*) show-off*
SM **1** (*Teat, Cine*) leading role, big part • **MODISMO**: • **hacer un ~** to show o.s. up, make o.s. a laughing stock
2 (= *papel usado*) (piece of) wastepaper; (= *cartulina*) pasteboard
3 (*And, Caribe*) (= *pan de azúcar*) sugar loaf

papelonero ADJ (*Cono Sur*) ridiculous

papelote SM (*pey*), **papelucho** SM (*pey*) (*gen*) useless bit of paper; (*sin valor*) worthless document; (*Literat*) trashy piece of writing

papeo‡ SM **1** (= *comida*) grub‡, chow (*EEUU*‡), food
2 (= *el comer*) eating

papera SF **1** (= *bocio*) goitre, goiter (*EEUU*)
2 paperas (= *enfermedad*) mumps (*sing*)

papero/a ADJ **1** (*LAm*) [*exportación, producción*] potato (*antes de s*)
2 (*Méx*) (= *embustero*) lying, deceitful
SM/F (*Agr*) potato grower; (*Com*) potato dealer

papi* SM dad*, daddy*, pop (*EEUU**)

papiamento SM (*Ling*) Papiamento

papila SF papilla ▸ **papila gustativa** taste bud

papilla SF **1** [*de bebé*] baby food • **MODISMO**: • **estar hecho ~*** (= *cansado*) to be shattered*; (= *roto*) to be smashed to pieces
2† (= *astucia*) guile, deceit

papillote SM buttered paper, greased paper • **en ~** (*Culin*) en papillote

papiloma SM wart, papilloma (*frm*) ▸ **papiloma genital** genital wart

papilomavirus SM INV papillomavirus

papira‡ SF letter

papiro SM papyrus

pápiro‡ SM (*Esp*) (= *billete*) 1,000-peseta note • **~s** (= *dinero*) brass* (*sing*), cash (*sing*) • **tener afán de ~s** to be greedy for money

papiroflexia SF origami

papirotazo SM, **papirote** SM flick

papismo SM (*pey*) papism

papista ADJ (*pey*) papist • **MODISMO**: • **es más ~ que el papa** he's more Catholic than the Pope
SMF papist

papo SM **1** (= *papada*) double chin, jowl; [*de ave*] crop; [*de animal*] dewlap • **MODISMOS**: • **estar de ~ de mona** (*Esp**) to be first-rate • **pasarlo de ~ de mona** (*Esp**) to have a super time*
2 (= *bocio*) goitre, goiter (*EEUU*)
3** (= *vulva*) pussy**

paprika SF paprika

papú ADJ Papuan
SMF Papuan

papudo ADJ [*persona*] double-chinned, with a heavy jowl; (*Zool*) dewlapped

papujado ADJ swollen, puffed up

papujo ADJ **1** (*Méx*) (= *hinchado*) swollen, puffed up; (*And*) (*de mejillas*) chubby-cheeked
2 (*Méx*) (= *anémico*) anaemic, anemic (*EEUU*); (= *macilento*) wan; (= *enfermizo*) sickly

paquebote SM packet boat

paquero SM (*Méx*) swindler, crook

paquete SM **1** [*de correos*] (*grande*) parcel; (*pequeño*) package • **me mandaron un ~ por correo** I got a parcel in the post • **MODISMO**: • **ir** *o* **viajar de ~*** (*en moto*) to ride pillion ▸ **paquete bomba** parcel bomb ▸ **paquetes postales** (*como servicio*) parcel post (*sing*)
2 [*de cigarrillos, galletas*] packet, pack (*EEUU*); [*de harina, azúcar*] bag
3 (*Econ, Inform*) (= *conjunto*) package ▸ **paquete accionarial, paquete de acciones** parcel of shares ▸ **paquete de aplicaciones** software package ▸ **paquete de beneficios** benefits package ▸ **paquete de medidas** package of measures ▸ **paquete estadístico** statistical package ▸ **paquete integrado** integrated package
4* (= *persona torpe*) • **ser un ~** to be useless, be a dead loss* • **es un auténtico ~ para las matemáticas** he's completely useless at maths
5* (= *castigo*) • **el sargento le metió un ~ por abandonar su puesto** the sergeant threw the book at him for leaving his post • **nos van a pegar un ~ si nos saltamos las clases** we'll get a rocket if we skip classes*
6* (= *bebé*) • **dejar a una con el ~** to put a woman in the family way • **soltar el ~** to give birth
7‡ (= *genitales masculinos*) bulge, lunchbox‡ • **MODISMO**: • **marcar ~** to wear very tight trousers
8* (= *pañal*) (*limpio*) nappy; (*sucio*) dirty nappy • **aún lleva ~ por las noches** she still wears a nappy at night
9 (*Náut*) packet (boat)
10†* (= *majo*) dandy • **estar hecho un ~** to be all dressed up, be dressed in style
11 (*Med*‡) dose (of VD)‡
12 (*LAm*) (= *cosa pesada*) nuisance, bore • **¡menudo ~!** • **¡vaya ~!** what a bore!
13 • **MODISMO**: • **darse ~** (*esp CAm, Méx*) to give o.s. airs
14 (*Méx*) (= *asunto*) tough job, hard one
15 (*Cono Sur*‡) queer‡, poof‡, fag (*EEUU*‡)
16 (*LAm*) (= *vacaciones*) package holiday
ADJ INV (*And, Arg**) elegant, chic

paquetear ▸ CONJUG 1a VI (*LAm*) to be very smart

paquete-bomba SM (PL: **paquetes-bomba**) parcel bomb

paquetería SF **1** (= *paquetes*) parcels (*pl*) • **servicio de ~** parcel service
2 (*Cono Sur**) • **¡qué ~!** how elegant! • **se puso toda su ~** she put on her Sunday best • **¡vaya ~ que lleva!** she's wearing everything but the kitchen sink!*

paquetero/a* SM/F card sharper

paquetudo* ADJ (*LAm*) **1** = **paquete**
2 (= *orgulloso*) stuck-up*

paquidermo SM pachyderm

paquistaní = **pakistaní**

Paquita SF *forma familiar de* **Francisca**

Paquito SM *forma familiar de* **Francisco**

PAR SM ABR (*Esp*) = **Partido Aragonés Regionalista**

par ADJ **1** [*número*] even
2 (= *igual*) equal • **son pares en altura** they're of equal height
SM **1** (= *pareja*) pair; (= *número indeterminado*) couple • **un par de guantes** a pair of gloves • **a pares** in pairs, in twos • **por un par de dólares** for a couple of dollars • **un par de veces** a couple of times • **le dio un par de bofetadas** he slapped him a couple of times • **MODISMO**: • **de tres pares de narices***: • **se cogió un cabreo de tres pares de narices** he went totally off his head* • **te piden un currículum de tres pares de narices** they are asking for an amazing CV ▸ **par de fuerzas** (*Mec*) couple ▸ **par de torsión** (*Mec*) torque
2 (= *igual*) equal • **está al par de los mejores** it is on a par with the best • **caminar al par de algn** to walk abreast of sb • **sin par** unparalleled, peerless (*frm*) • **no tener par** to be unparalleled *o* peerless (*frm*)
3 (*Mat*) even number • **pares o nones** odds or evens
4 (*Golf*) par • **dos bajo par** two under par • **lo hizo con cuatro por debajo del par** he did it in four under par • **bajar del par** to finish under par
5 • **MODISMO**: • **de par en par** wide open
6 (*Pol*) peer • **los doce pares** the twelve peers
SF **1** (*esp Com, Econ*) par • **estar por encima de la par** to be above *o* over par • **estar por debajo de la par** to be under *o* below par • **a la par** (= *al mismo nivel*) on a par; (= *a la vez*) at the same time • **las acciones de las hidroeléctricas están a la par** shares in the hydroelectric companies are at par • **caminaban a la par** they were walking alongside each other, they were walking side by side
2 • **a la par que**: **es útil a la par que divertido** it is both useful and amusing, it is useful as well as being amusing

> **PAR**
>
> *A la hora de traducir* **par (de)** *seguido de un sustantivo, hay que tener en cuenta la diferencia entre* **pair (of)** *y* **couple (of)**.
>
> ▹ *Se traduce por* **pair (of)** *cuando nos referimos a objetos que normalmente se usan por* **pares**:
>
> **... tres pares de guantes ...**
> ... three pairs of gloves ...
> **Voy a necesitar dos pares más de calcetines**
> I'll need two more pairs of socks
>
> ▹ *Lo traducimos por* **couple (of)** *en los demás casos, en los que* **un par de** *se puede emplear además en el sentido más vago de "dos o más de dos"*:
>
> **Me he comprado un par de camisas**
> I've bought a couple of shirts
> **Regresaré en un par de minutos**
> I'll be back in a couple of minutes
>
> ▹ **PANTALONES, ZAPATOS, GAFAS**
> *Para otros usos y ejemplos ver la entrada.*

para[1] PREP **1** (*indicando finalidad, uso*) for • **un regalo ~ ti** a present for you • **psicológicamente no estoy pre~do ~ eso** I'm not psychologically ready for that • **es demasiado cara ~ nosotros** it's too dear for us, it's beyond our means • **no tengo ~ el viaje** I haven't got enough money for the trip • **léelo ~ ti** read it to yourself • **nació ~ poeta** he was born to be a poet • **ya no estoy ~ estos trotes** I'm not up to this sort of thing anymore • **yo no valgo ~ esto** I'm no good at this • **una taza ~ café** a coffee cup • **laca ~ el pelo** hairspray • **~ esto, podíamos habernos quedado en casa** if this is it, we might as well have stayed at home
2 • **~ que a** (+ *subjun*) • **lo traje ~ que lo vieras** I

P

brought it so (that) you could see it • **es ~ que lo leas** it's for you to read • **un regalo ~ que te acuerdes de mí** a present for you to remember me by • **~ que eso fuera posible tendrías que trabajar mucho** you would have to work hard for that to be possible
b (*en preguntas*) • **¿~ qué lo quieres?** why do you want it?, what do you want it for? • **¿~ qué sirve?** what's it for? • **—¿por qué no se lo dices? —¿~ qué?** "why don't you tell her?" — "what's the point *o* use?" • **tú ya has pasado por eso, ¿~ qué te voy a contar?** you've already been through that, so there's no point *o* use me telling you
• **MODISMO:** • **que ~ qué*:** • **tengo un hambre que ~ qué** (*uso enfático*) I'm absolutely starving* • **hay un embotellamiento que ~ qué** there's a huge traffic jam
3 (*+ infin*) **a** (*indicando finalidad*) to • **lo hizo ~ salvarse** he did it (in order) to save himself • **~ comprarlo necesitas cinco dólares más** to buy it you need another five dollars • **estoy ahorrando ~ comprarme una moto** I'm saving up to buy a motorbike, I'm saving up for a motorbike • **entré despacito ~ no despertarla** I went in slowly so as not to wake her • **no es ~ comer** it's not for eating, it's not to be eaten • **tengo bastante ~ vivir** I have enough to live on • **es muy tarde ~ salir** it's too late to go out
b (*indicando secuencia temporal*) • **se casaron ~ se~rse en seguida** they married only to separate soon after • **el rey visitará Argentina ~ volar después a Chile** the king will visit Argentina and then fly on to Chile
4 (*con expresiones de tiempo*) • **con esto tengo ~ rato** this will take me a while • **lo dejamos ~ mañana** let's leave it till tomorrow • **tengo muchos deberes ~ mañana** I have a lot of homework to do for tomorrow • **lo recordaré ~ siempre** I'll remember it forever • **ahora ~ las vacaciones de agosto hará un año** it'll be a year ago this *o* come the August holiday • **va ~ un año desde la última vez** it's getting on for a year since the last time • **lo tendré listo ~ fin de mes** I'll have it ready by *o* for the end of the month • **~ entonces ya era tarde** it was already too late by then • **~ las dos estaba lloviendo** by two o'clock it was raining • **un cuarto ~ las diez** (*LAm*) a quarter to ten • **son cinco ~ las ocho** (*LAm*) it's five to eight
5 (*indicando dirección*) • **~ atrás** back, backwards • **~ la derecha** to the right • **el autobús ~ Marbella** the bus for Marbella, the Marbella bus • **iba ~ el metro** I was going towards the underground • **ir ~ casa** to go home, head for home • **salir ~ Panamá** to leave for Panama
6 (*indicando opiniones*) • **~ mí que miente** in my opinion *o* if you ask me he's lying • **no hay niño feo ~ una madre** all mothers think their baby is beautiful
7 (*en comparaciones*) • **es mucho ~ lo que suele dar** this is a lot in comparison with what he usually gives • **¿quién es usted ~ gritarme así?** who are you to shout at me like that? • **~ profesor habla muy mal** he doesn't speak very clearly for a teacher • **~ ser un niño lo hace muy bien** he does it very well for a child • **~ patatas, las de mi pueblo** if it's potatoes you want, look no further than my home town • **~ ruidosos, los españoles** there's nobody like the Spaniards for being noisy
8 (*indicando trato*) • **~ con** to, towards • **tan amable ~ con todos** so kind to *o* towards everybody; ▸ **estar, ir**
para²* (SM) paratrooper, para*
para... (PREF) para...
parabellum® (SM INV) (automatic) pistol • **balas del calibre 9mm Parabellum** 9mm Parabellum bullets
parabién (SM) congratulations (*pl*) • **dar el ~ a algn** to congratulate sb (**por** on)
parábola (SF) **1** (*Mat*) parabola
2 (*Literat*) parable
parabólica (SF) satellite dish
parabólico (ADJ) parabolic
parabrisas (SM INV) windscreen, windshield (*EEUU*)
paraca¹* (SM) paratrooper, para*
paraca² (SF) (*And*) *strong wind from the sea*
paracaídas (SM INV) parachute • **lanzar algo en ~** to send sth down by parachute • **aterrizar en ~ en un lugar** to parachute into a place • **lanzarse** *o* **saltar** *o* **tirarse en ~** (*gen*) to parachute; (*en emergencia*) to parachute, bale out; (*una sola vez*) to do a parachute jump
paracaidismo (SM) **1** (*Dep, Mil*) parachuting ▸ **paracaidismo acrobático** skydiving
2 (*Méx**) (*= ocupación*) squatting
paracaidista (SMF) **1** (*gen*) parachutist; (*Mil*) paratrooper; (*acrobático*) skydiver • **los ~s** (*Mil*) the paratroops
2 (*Méx**) (*= ocupante*) squatter
3 (*Méx**) (*= colado*) gatecrasher
paracetamol (SM) paracetamol
parachispas (SM INV) fireguard, fire screen
parachoques (SM INV) (*Aut*) bumper, fender (*EEUU*); (*Ferro*) buffer; (*Mec*) shock absorber
parada (SF) **1** (*= acción*) stop • **hicimos varias ~s en el camino** we made several stops on the way • **un tren sin ~s** a direct train • **el autobús hace ~ en Valencia** the bus stops at Valencia • **correr en ~** to run on the spot, run in place (*EEUU*) • **hacer una ~ a algn** (*Chile**) to stop sb ▸ **parada biológica** (*en pesca*) temporary fishing ban (*to allow stocks to recover*) ▸ **parada cardíaca** cardiac arrest ▸ **parada de manos** (*Chile*) handstand ▸ **parada en firme** (*Equitación*) dead stop, dead halt ▸ **parada en seco** sudden stop
2 (*= lugar*) stop • **la próxima ~ es la nuestra** the next stop is ours ▸ **parada de autobús** bus stop ▸ **parada de taxis** taxi rank ▸ **parada discrecional** request stop ▸ **parada y fonda** food and shelter • **hicimos ~ y fonda en un monasterio** they gave us food and shelter in a monastery
3 [*de caballos*] relay, team
4 (*= desfile*) (*Mil*) parade • **formar en ~** to parade • **MODISMO:** • **ir a todas las ~s** (*Chile*) to be up for anything* ▸ **parada nupcial** (*Orn*) courtship display
5 (*Dep*) save, stop
6 (*Mús*) pause
7 (*Esgrima*) parry
8 (*en el juego*) bet, stake
9 (*= presa*) dam
10 (*Agr*) stud farm
11 (*Cono Sur*) (*= vanidad*) snobbery, pretension; (*= jactancia*) boastfulness • **MODISMO:** • **hacer la ~*:** • **hizo la ~ como que estudiaba** he put on a show of studying* • **no me dio asiento, solo hizo la ~** he made as if to give me his seat, but didn't
12 (*Chile**) (*= traje*) outfit
13 (*Perú*) open market, farmer's market (*EEUU*)
paradear* ▸ CONJUG 1a (VI) (*Cono Sur*) to brag, show off • **~ con algo** to brag about sth, show sth off
paradero (SM) **1** (*gen*) whereabouts (*pl*) • **averiguar el ~ de algn** to ascertain sb's whereabouts • **García se halla en ~ desconocido** García's whereabouts are unknown • **no sabemos su ~** we do not know his whereabouts
2 (*= fin*) end • **seguramente tendrá mal ~** he'll surely come to a bad end
3 (*And, Cono Sur*) [*de autobús*] bus stop
4 (*LAm*) (*= apeadero*) wayside halt
paradigma (SM) paradigm
paradigmático (ADJ) paradigmatic
paradisiaco (ADJ), **paradisíaco** (ADJ) heavenly
parado/a (ADJ) **1** (*= detenido*) • **me quedé ~ para que no me oyese** I stood still so that he couldn't hear me • **estuve un momento ~ delante de su puerta** I stopped for a moment in front of his door • **¿por qué no nos echas una mano en vez de estar ahí ~?** can't you give us a hand instead of just standing there *o* around? • **no le gusta estar ~, siempre encuentra algo que hacer** he doesn't like to be idle *o* doing nothing, he always finds himself something to do • **¿qué hace ese coche ahí ~?** what's that car doing standing there? • **la producción estuvo parada durante unos meses** production was at a standstill *o* stopped for a few months • **salida parada** (*Dep*) standing start
2 (*Esp*) (*= sin trabajo*) unemployed • **llevo dos años parada** I've been out of work *o* unemployed for two years • **se ha quedado ~ hace poco tiempo** he was made redundant a short time ago
3 (*= desconcertado*) • **me quedé ~ sin saber qué hacer después** I was taken aback and did not know what to do next • **me dejó ~ con lo que me dijo** what he said really took me aback, I was really taken aback by what he said
4 (*LAm*) (*= de pie*) standing (up) • **estuve ~ durante dos horas** I was standing for two hours • **MODISMO:** • **caer ~ (como los gatos)** to land on one's feet
5 (*Esp**) • **ser ~** (*= ser tímido*) to be tongue-tied; (*= tener poca iniciativa*) to be a wimp*
6 (*Caribe, Cono Sur*) (*= engreído*) vain
7 • **bien/mal ~:** **en este libro la mujer queda muy bien parada** women are shown in a good light in this book, women come out well in this book • **la crítica ha dejado mal parada a la película** the film got a battering from the critics • **salir bien/mal ~:** **salió mejor ~ de lo que cabía esperar** he came out of it better than could be expected • **salió muy mal ~ del accidente** he was in a bad way after the accident • **la imagen del partido ha salido muy mal parada de todo este escándalo** the party's image has suffered because of this scandal
8 (*And, Caribe*) (*= afortunado*) • **estar bien ~** to be lucky • **estar mal ~** to be unlucky
9 (*Méx, Col*) • **estar bien ~ con algn** to be well in with sb*
10 (*LAm*) (*= hacia arriba*) [*pelo*] stiff; [*poste*] upright; [*orejas*] pricked-up • **con la cola parada** with its tail held high
11 (*Méx, Ven*) (*= levantado*) up, out of bed
12 (*Chile*) (*= en huelga*) (out) on strike
(SM/F) (*Esp*) unemployed person • **Miguel López, un ~ de 27 años ...** Miguel López, an unemployed, 27-year-old man ... • **el número de ~s** the number of people out of work *o* the number of unemployed • **los ~s de larga duración** the long-term unemployed
(SM) **1** (*Ven*) • **dar un ~ a algn** to stop sb
2 (*Méx*) (*= parecido*) air, look, resemblance • **tener ~ de algn** to look like sb
paradoja (SF) paradox
paradójicamente (ADV) paradoxically
paradójico (ADJ) paradoxical
paradón* (SM) (*Dep*) great save, fantastic stop*

parador SM (*Esp*) (*tb* **parador nacional de turismo**) (state-run) tourist hotel; (*Hist*) inn

> **PARADOR NACIONAL**
> In the early days of the Spanish tourist industry in the 1950s, the government set up a network of high-class tourist hotels known as **paradores**. They are sited in rural beauty spots and places of historical interest, often in converted castles and monasteries.

paraestatal ADJ [*organismo*] public; [*actividad*] semi-official
parafarmacia SF chemist's shop (*not selling prescription medicines*) (*Brit*), drugstore (*EEUU*)
parafernalia SF paraphernalia
parafina SF (*sólida*) paraffin wax; (*Cono Sur*) (= *combustible*) paraffin ▸ **parafina líquida** liquid paraffin
parafinado ADJ waxed, waterproofed
parafrasear ▹ CONJUG 1a VT to paraphrase
paráfrasis SF INV paraphrase
paragolpes SM INV (*Cono Sur*) (*Aut*) bumper, fender (*EEUU*)
parágrafo SM (*Caribe*) paragraph
paraguas SM INV **1** (*para la lluvia*) umbrella ▸ **paraguas nuclear** nuclear umbrella ▸ **paraguas protector** protective umbrella
2* (= *condón*) rubber*, French letter‡
3 (*And, Caribe, Méx*) (= *seta comestible*) mushroom; (= *hongo venenoso*) toadstool; (= *moho*) fungus
Paraguay SM Paraguay
paraguayismo SM *word or phrase peculiar to Paraguay*
paraguayo/a ADJ of/from Paraguay
SM/F native/inhabitant of Paraguay • **los ~s** the people of Paraguay
SM **1** (*And*) (= *látigo*) whip
2 (*Caribe*) (= *machete*) long straight knife
paragüero/a ADJ (*hum*) of/from Orense
SM/F (*hum*) native/inhabitant of Orense • **los ~s** the people of Orense
SM umbrella stand
paraíso SM **1** (*Rel*) paradise, heaven ▸ **paraíso fiscal** tax haven ▸ **paraíso terrenal** Garden of Eden
2 (*Teat*) upper gallery, gods (*pl*)
paraje SM place, spot
paral SM (*Méx*) (= *madero*) post; (= *puntal*) shore, prop
paralela SF **1** (= *línea*) parallel (line)
2 paralelas parallel bars ▸ **paralelas asimétricas** (*Dep*) asymmetric bars
paralelamente ADV **1** (= *en la misma dirección*) • **la carretera avanza ~ a la vía del tren** the road runs parallel to the rail track
2 (= *al mismo tiempo*) • **los ministros de finanzas se reunieron ~ en Washington** the Finance Ministers held a parallel meeting in Washington • **~ a esta expansión económica tuvieron lugar importantes cambios sociales** significant social changes occurred in parallel with the economic expansion • **~, los rebeldes prosiguen su campaña de terror** similarly, the rebels are continuing with their campaign of terror
paralelismo SM parallelism, parallel
paralelo ADJ **1** [*líneas*] parallel (**a** to); [*vidas, caracteres*] parallel
2 (= *no oficial*) unofficial, irregular; (*pey*) illegal • **importaciones paralelas** unauthorized imports, illegal imports • **medicina paralela** alternative medicine
SM parallel • **en ~** (*Elec*) in parallel • **en ~ con** in parallel with • **rodar en ~** [*ciclistas*] to cycle two abreast • **un éxito sin ~** an unparalleled success
paralelogramo SM parallelogram
paralimpiada SF = paraolimpiada
paralímpico/a ADJ, SM/F = paraolímpico
parálisis SF INV paralysis ▸ **parálisis cerebral** cerebral palsy ▸ **parálisis infantil** infantile paralysis ▸ **parálisis progresiva** creeping paralysis
paralítico/a ADJ, SM/F paralytic
paralización SF (*gen*) stoppage; (*Med*) paralysation, paralyzation; (*fig*) blocking; (*Com*) stagnation • **la ~ fue total** everything came to a complete standstill
paralizador ADJ, **paralizante** ADJ [*miedo, gas*] paralysing, paralyzing
paralizar ▹ CONJUG 1f VT (*gen*) to stop; (*Med*) to paralyse, paralyze; [+ *tráfico*] to bring to a standstill • **estar paralizado de un brazo** to be paralysed in one arm • **estar paralizado de miedo** to be paralysed with fright
VPR **paralizarse 1** [*pierna, brazo*] to become paralysed
2 [*demanda, inversiones, obra*] to grind to a halt
paramar[1] SM (*And, Caribe*) *season of wind and snow*
paramar[2] ▹ CONJUG 1a VI (*And, Caribe*), **paramear** ▹ CONJUG 1a VI (*And, Caribe*) to drizzle
paramédico ADJ paramedic, paramedical
paramento SM **1** (= *adorno*) ornamental cover; [*de caballo*] trappings (*pl*); (= *colgadura*) hangings (*pl*) ▸ **paramentos sacerdotales** liturgical vestments
2 [*de pared, piedra*] face
paramera SF **1** (*Geog*) high moorland
2 (*Caribe*) (= *malestar*) mountain sickness
paramero/a ADJ (*And, Caribe*) (*Geog*) upland, highland
SM/F (= *persona*) highlander
parámetro SM parameter
paramilitar ADJ, SMF paramilitary
páramo SM **1** (= *brezal*) bleak plateau, high moor
2 (= *descampado*) waste land
3 (*And*) (= *llovizna*) drizzle; (= *tormenta*) blizzard
4 (*Caribe*) (= *cumbres*) mountain heights (*pl*)
paramoso ADJ (*And*) drizzly
paramotor SM paramotor
paramuno ADJ (*And*) upland, highland
paranera SF (*LAm*) grassland
parangón SM comparison • **no tiene ~ en otro país** there is nothing comparable in any other country • **sin ~** incomparable, matchless
parangonable ADJ comparable (**con** to)
parangonar ▹ CONJUG 1a VT to compare (**con** to)
paraninfo SM (*Univ*) (= *salón de actos*) assembly hall; (= *auditorio*) auditorium
paranoia SF paranoia
paranoico/a ADJ, SM/F paranoid
paranoide ADJ paranoid
paranormal ADJ paranormal
paranza SF (*Caza*) hide, blind (*EEUU*)
paraolimpiada SF, **paraolimpiadas** SFPL Paralympics, Paralympic Games
paraolímpico/a ADJ Paralympic • **Juegos Paraolímpicos** Paralympics, Paralympic Games
SM/F Paralympic athlete
parapente SM (= *deporte*) paragliding; (= *aparato*) paraglider
parapetarse ▹ CONJUG 1a VPR
1 (= *protegerse*) to protect o.s., shelter (**tras** behind)
2 (*fig*) • **~ tras media docena de excusas** to take refuge in half a dozen excuses
parapeto SM **1** (*como defensa*) (*gen*) defence, defense (*EEUU*), barricade; (*Mil*) parapet
2 [*de puente, escalera*] parapet
paraplejia SF, **paraplejía** SF paraplegia
parapléjico/a ADJ, SM/F paraplegic
parapsicología SF parapsychology
parapsicológico ADJ parapsychological
parar ▹ CONJUG 1a VT **1** [+ *persona, coche, respiración*] to stop • **me paró a punta de pistola** he stopped me at gunpoint • **nos paró la policía** we were stopped by the police • **~on el tráfico en el centro** they stopped the traffic in the centre • **no hay quien pare el avance tecnológico** there is no stopping technological progress
2 [+ *tiro, penalti, gol*] to save, stop; [+ *pase*] to intercept, cut off; [+ *golpe*] to ward off; (*Esgrima*) to parry
3 [+ *atención*] to fix (**en** on); ▹ **mientes**
4 (*Naipes*) to bet, stake
5† (= *conducir*) to lead • **ahí le paró esa manera de vida** that's where that way of life led him
6† (= *arreglar*) to prepare, arrange
7 (*LAm*) (= *levantar*) to raise; (= *poner de pie*) to stand upright
8 • **~la con algn** (*And**) to take it out on sb
VI **1** (= *detenerse, terminar*) to stop • **¡pare!** stop! • **el autobús para enfrente** the bus stops opposite • **paramos a echar gasolina** we stopped to get some petrol • **¡no para! siempre está haciendo algo** he never stops! he's always doing something • **¡y no para!** [*hablante*] he just goes on and on! • **no ~á hasta conseguirlo** he won't stop *o* give up until he gets it • **~ en seco** to stop dead • **sin ~:** • **los teléfonos sonaban sin ~** the phones never stopped ringing • **lloraba sin ~** he didn't stop crying • **fumaba sin ~** she smoked non-stop, she chain-smoked • **hablar sin ~** to talk non-stop • **estuvo una semana lloviendo sin ~** it rained uninterruptedly *o* without a break for a week • MODISMO: • **¡dónde va a ~!***: • **es mucho mejor este ¡dónde va a ~!** this one's much better, there's no comparison!
2 • **~ de hacer algo** to stop doing sth • **ha parado de llover** it has stopped raining • **no para de quejarse** he never stops complaining, he complains all the time • MODISMO: • **y para de contar*** and that's that
3 • **ir a ~** to end up • **la empresa podría ir a ~ a manos extranjeras** the firm could end up in foreign hands • **nos equivocamos de tren y fuimos a ~ a Manchester** we got on the wrong train and ended up in Manchester • **fueron a ~ a la comisaría** they ended up at the police station • **la herencia fue a ~ a manos de su primo** the inheritance went to his cousin • **no sabemos en qué va a ir a ~ todo esto** we don't know where all this is going to end • **¿dónde habrá ido a ~ todo aquel dinero?** what can have become of *o* happened to all that money? • **¿dónde vamos a ir a ~?** where's it all going to end?, what is the world coming to?
4 (= *hospedarse*) to stay (**en** at) • **siempre paro en este hotel** I always stay at this hotel
5 (= *hacer huelga*) to go on strike
6 • **~ con algn** (*And**) to hang about with sb
7 [*perro*] to point
VPR **pararse 1** [*persona*] to stop; [*coche*] to stop, pull up; [*proceso*] to stop, come to a halt; [*trabajo*] to stop, come to a standstill • **se paró en la puerta** he stopped at the door • **no se paran ante nada** they will let nothing stop them • **el reloj se ha parado** the clock has stopped • **~se a hacer algo** to stop to do sth, pause to do sth
2 • **~se en algo** (= *prestar atención*) to pay attention to sth
3 (*LAm*) (= *ponerse de pie*) to stand (up); (*de la cama*) to get up; [*pelo*] to stand on end

4 (*Tip*) to set
5 (*LAm**) (= *enriquecerse*) to make one's pile*, get rich
pararrayos SM INV lightning conductor, lightning rod (*EEUU*)
parasitar ▹ CONJUG 1a VT to parasitize
VI • **~ en** to parasitize
parasitario ADJ, **parasítico** ADJ parasitic(al)
parasitismo SM parasitism
parásito ADJ parasitic (**de** on)
SM **1** (*Bio*) parasite (*tb fig*)
2 parásitos (*Radio*) atmospherics (*pl*), statics (*sing*)
3 (*CAm*) squatter
parasitología SF parasitology
parasitólogo/a SM/F parasitologist
parasitosis SF INV parasitism
parasol SM parasol, sunshade
parateatral ADJ theatre-related, quasi-dramatic
paratifoidea SF paratyphoid
paratopes SM INV (*Ferro*) buffer
parcamente ADV (= *frugalmente*) frugally, sparingly; (= *moderadamente*) moderately
Parcas SFPL • **las ~** the Parcae, the Fates
parcela SF **1** (= *solar*) plot, piece of ground; (*Agr*) smallholding
2 [*de conocimientos, autonomía*] (= *parte*) part, portion; (= *área*) area ▸ **parcela de poder** (*político*) power base; (*de influencia*) sphere of influence
parcelar ▹ CONJUG 1a VT (*gen*) to divide into plots; [+ *finca*] to break up, parcel out
parcelario ADJ • **tierra parcelaria** land divided into plots
parcelero/a SM/F, **parcelista** SMF owner of a plot, smallholder
parchar ▹ CONJUG 1a VT (*esp LAm*) to patch, put a patch on
parche SM **1** (= *pieza*) patch; (*para un ojo*) eye patch • MODISMO: • **pegar un ~ a algn*** to put one over on sb* ▸ **parche de nicotina** nicotine patch
2 (*provisional*) temporary remedy, stopgap solution • **poner ~s** to paper over the cracks
3 (*Med*) (= *cataplasma*) poultice; (*Chile*) (= *tirita*) sticking plaster, Band-Aid® (*EEUU*)
4 (*Mús*) (= *piel de tambor*) drumhead; (= *tambor*) drum • MODISMO: • **dar el ~** to busk
parchear¹ ▹ CONJUG 1a VT to patch (up)
parchear²‡ ▹ CONJUG 1a VT to feel‡, touch up‡
parcheo SM temporary remedies (*pl*), stopgap solutions (*pl*)
parchís SM *board game similar to ludo*, Parcheesi® (*EEUU*)
parchita SF (*Caribe*) passion fruit
parcho SM (*Caribe*) = **parche**
parcial ADJ **1** (= *incompleto*) partial • **eclipse ~** partial eclipse • **examen ~** mid-term exam • **a tiempo ~** part-time
2 (= *no ecuánime*) biased, partial; (*Pol*) partisan
SM (= *examen*) mid-term exam
parcialidad SF **1** (= *falta de ecuanimidad*) partiality, bias; (*Pol*) partisanship
2 (= *grupo*) (*gen*) faction, group; (*de rebeldes*) rebel group
parcialmente ADV partially, partly
parcidad SF = **parquedad**
parco ADJ (*gen*) frugal, sparing; (= *moderado*) moderate, temperate; (*en el gasto*) parsimonious • **muy ~ en comer** very frugal in one's eating habits • **~ en elogios** sparing in one's praises
parcómetro SM parking meter
pardal SM **1** (*Orn*) (= *gorrión*) sparrow; (= *pardillo*) linnet
2 (*Bot*) aconite
3†* (= *pillo*) sly fellow, rogue • **¡pardal!** (*a niño*) you rascal!
pardear ▹ CONJUG 1a VI to look brown(ish)
pardiez†† EXCL good heavens!, by gad!††
pardillo/a SM/F **1*** (= *ingenuo*) simpleton
2* (= *rústico*) yokel, hick (*EEUU**)
SM **1** (*tb* **pardillo común**) linnet
2 (= *paño*) brown cloth
pardo/a ADJ **1** [*color*] grey-brown, brownish-grey
2 [*cielo*] overcast
3 [*voz*] flat, dull
SM/F (*Caribe, Cono Sur*) (*pey*) (= *mulato*) mulatto, half-breed; (*Méx‡*) (= *persona humilde*) poor devil
pardusco ADJ = **pardo**
pareado ADJ **1** [*verso*] rhyming
2 [*chalet*] semi-detached
SM couplet
parear ▹ CONJUG 1a VT **1** (= *emparejar*) to pair up
2 (*Bio*) to mate, pair
VI (*Caribe‡*) to skive‡
VPR **parearse** to pair off
parecer SM **1** (= *opinión*) opinion, view • **a mi ~** in my opinion *o* view • **somos del mismo ~** we are of the same opinion *o* view • **cambiar** *o* **mudar de ~** to change one's mind
2† (= *aspecto*) • **de buen ~** good-looking, handsome • **de mal ~** unattractive
VI ▹ CONJUG 2d **1** (*uso copulativo*) **a** (*por el aspecto*) (+ *adj*) to look; (+ *sustantivo*) to look like • **esos zapatos no parecen muy cómodos** those shoes don't look very comfortable • **pareces más joven** you look younger • **parece una modelo** she looks like a model • **¡pareces una reina!** you look like a queen! • **una casa que parece un palacio** a house that looks like a palace • **parece una foca*** she's huge *o* enormous* • **estos guantes parecen de seda** these gloves feel like silk
b (= *por el carácter, el comportamiento*) to seem • **parece muy afectado por la noticia** he seems very upset by the news • **parecía una persona muy amable** she seemed very nice • **desde que se divorció no parece la misma** since she got divorced she seems a different person
2 (*uso impersonal*) (= *dar la impresión de*) to seem • **todo parecía indicar que estaba interesado** everything seemed to point towards him being interested • **aunque no lo parezca** surprising though it may seem *o* (*más frm*) appear • **así parece** so it seems *o* (*más frm*) appears • **al ~** • **a lo que parece** apparently, seemingly • **parece como si** (+ *subjun*): • **parece como si quisiera ocultar algo** it's as if he were trying to hide something • **en mi sueño parecía como si volara** in my dream it was as if I was flying • **parece que** (+ *indic*): • **parece que va a llover** it looks as though *o* as if it's going to rain, it looks like rain • **parece que fue ayer** it seems only yesterday • **parece que huele a gas** I think I can smell gas • **según parece** apparently, seemingly • **parece ser que** (+ *indic*): • **parece ser que van a aumentar las temperaturas** it seems *o* (*más frm*) appears (that) it's going to get warmer • **parece ser que ha habido algún problema** it seems *o* (*más frm*) appears (that) there has been a problem
3 (*indicando opinión*) • **~le a algn: ¿qué os pareció la película?** what did you think of the film? • **¿no te parece extraño que no haya llamado?** don't you think it's strange that she hasn't called? • **me parece bien que vayas** I think it's a good idea for you to go • **te llamaré luego, si te parece bien** I'll phone you later, if that's all right with *o* by you • **¡me parece muy mal!** I think it's shocking! • **si a usted no le parece mal** if you don't mind • **me parece mentira que haya pasado tanto tiempo** I can't believe it has been so long • **podríamos ir al cine si te parece** we could go to the cinema if you like • **vamos a la piscina, ¿te parece?** what do you say we go to the swimming pool?, what about going to the swimming pool? • **como te parezca** as you wish • **~ que:** • **me parece que se está haciendo tarde** it's getting rather late, I think • **me parece que sí** I think so • **me parece que no** I don't think so • **¿te parece que está bien no acudir a una cita?** do you think it's acceptable not to turn up for an appointment?
4† (= *aparecer*) to appear; [*objeto perdido*] to turn up • **pareció el sol entre las nubes** the sun appeared through the clouds • **ya parecieron los guantes** the gloves have turned up • **¡ya pareció aquello!** so that was it!
VPR **parecerse 1** (= *asemejarse*) • **~se a algn** (*en el aspecto*) to look like sb, be like sb; (*en el carácter*) to be like sb • **en esta foto se parece mucho a su abuelo** in this photo he looks *o* is a lot like his grandfather • **el retrato no se le parece** the portrait isn't a bit like him • **es muy sensible, se parece a su madre** she's very sensitive, she's like her mother • **~se a algo** to look like sth, be like sth • **su jersey se parece al mío** his jumper looks *o* is like mine • **ni cosa que se parezca** nor anything of the sort
2 (*uso recíproco*) (*en el aspecto*) to look alike, be alike; (*en el carácter*) to be alike • **son hermanas pero no se parecen mucho** they're sisters but they don't look *o* they aren't very much alike • **¿en qué se parecen estos dos objetos?** what's the similarity between these two objects?, in what way are these two objects alike?
parecidamente ADV similarly, equally
parecido ADJ **1** (= *similar*) similar • **tienen apellidos ~s** they have similar surnames • **las casas son todas parecidas** the houses are all similar *o* alike • **nunca he visto cosa parecida** I've never seen anything like it • **ser ~ a algo** to be similar to sth, be like sth • **mi reloj es muy ~ al tuyo** my watch is very similar to yours, my watch is very like yours • **ser ~ a algn** (*de aspecto*) to look like sb; (*de carácter*) to be like sb
2 • **bien ~** good-looking, nice-looking, handsome • **no es mal parecida** she's not bad-looking
SM resemblance, likeness • **yo no te veo el ~ con tu hermano** I can't see the resemblance *o* likeness between you and your brother • **hay un gran ~ entre las dos historias** there is a great resemblance *o* likeness between the two stories, the two stories are very alike • **tiene un cierto ~ con Marlon Brando** he bears a slight resemblance to Marlon Brando
parecimiento SM **1** (*Cono Sur, Méx*) = **parecido**
2 (*Cono Sur*) (= *comparecencia*) appearance; (= *aparición*) apparition
pared SF **1** [*de edificio, habitación*] wall • **estar ~ con ~ con algo** to be right next door to sth • **estar cara a la ~** (*Escol*) to be stood in the corner • MODISMOS: • **entre cuatro ~es:** • **se pasa la vida entre cuatro ~es** he spends his life cooped up at home • **hablar a la ~:** • **es como hablarle a la ~** it's like talking to a brick wall • **las ~es oyen** the walls have ears • **ponerse (blanco) como la ~** to go as white as a sheet • **subirse por las ~es*** to go up the wall* ▸ **pared de carga** load-bearing wall

P

▸ **pared divisoria** dividing wall ▸ **pared maestra** main wall ▸ **pared medianera** party wall
2 (*Anat*) wall ▸ **pared arterial** arterial wall ▸ **pared abdominal** abdominal wall ▸ **pared celular** cell wall
3 (*Alpinismo*) face wall
4 (*Ftbl*) • **hacer la ~** to make *o* do a one-two*
paredeño (ADJ) adjoining, next-door (**con** to)
paredón (SM) **1** (*Arquit*) (= *muro*) thick wall; [*de ruinas*] standing wall
2 [*de roca*] wall of rock, rock face
3 (*Mil*) • **¡al ~!** put him up against the wall and shoot him! • **llevar a algn al ~** to put sb up against the wall, shoot sb
pareja (SF) **1** (= *par*) pair • **en este juego hay que formar ~s** for this game you have to get into pairs
2 [*de esposos, compañeros sentimentales*] couple • **había varias ~s bailando** there were several couples dancing • **vivir en ~** to live as a couple • **nuestra vida como ~** our life together • **llevamos una relación de ~** we are an item ▸ **pareja abierta** open marriage ▸ **pareja de hecho** unmarried couple ▸ **pareja reproductora** (*Orn*) breeding pair
3 (= *compañero*) partner; (= *cónyuge*) spouse • **vino con su ~** he came with his partner ▸ **pareja de baile** dancing partner ▸ **pareja estable** regular partner
4 [*de calcetín, guante, zapato*] • **no encuentro la ~ de este zapato** I can't find the shoe that goes with this one *o* my other shoe
5 [*de hijos*] • **ya tenemos la parejita** now we've got one of each
6 [*de guardias civiles*] *pair of Civil Guard officers on patrol*
7 (*LAm*) (= *caballos*) pair (*of horses*); [*de tiro*] team (*of draught animals*); [*de bueyes*] yoke (*of oxen*)

PAREJA

Para traducir el sustantivo **pareja** *referido a dos personas, hay que tener en cuenta la diferencia entre los sustantivos* **pair** *y* **couple**:

▸ *Se traduce por* **couple** *cuando se trata de un matrimonio o de dos personas que parecen tener una relación íntima, o cuando se refiere a una pareja de baile:*
En Salford conocí a una pareja de Ecuador
In Salford I met a couple from Ecuador
Algunas parejas prefieren no tener hijos
Some couples prefer not to have children
Había muchas parejas mayores bailando
There were a lot of older couples dancing

▸ *En un contexto de trabajo o de competiciones deportivas o cuando a la* **pareja** *no se le asocia ningún vínculo afectivo, se traduce por* **pair**:
Ahora vamos a trabajar por parejas
Now we're going to work in pairs
Detuvieron a la pareja al cruzar la frontera
The pair were arrested when they were crossing the border

▸ *La expresión* **pareja de** *se puede traducir tanto por* **couple of** *como por* **pair of** *cuando tiene el sentido de* **par de**:
Una pareja de pillos me robaron el reloj
A couple *o* A pair of thugs stole my watch

▸ PAR

Para otros usos y ejemplos ver la entrada.

parejamente (ADV) equally
parejería* (SF) (*Caribe*) vanity, conceit
parejero (ADJ) (*Caribe**) (= *demasiado confiado*) cheeky, sassy (*EEUU**); (= *presumido*) cocky, over-confident
(SM) **1** (*LAm*) (= *caballo*) racehorse
2 (*Caribe**) (= *persona*) hanger-on
parejo (ADJ) **1** (= *igual*) similar, alike • **seis todos ~s** six all the same • **ir ~s** to be neck and neck • **ir ~ con** to be on a par with • **por ~** on a par
2 (*LAm*) (= *nivelado*) (*Téc*) even, flush; [*terreno*] flat, level
(ADV) (*LAm*) (= *al mismo tiempo*) at the same time, together
(SM) (*CAm, Caribe*) [*de baile*] dancing partner
paremiología (SF) study of proverbs
parentela (SF) relations (*pl*), family
parenteral (ADJ) parenteral • **inyección ~** intravenous injection
parentesco (SM) relationship, kinship
paréntesis (SM INV) **1** (*Tip*) parenthesis, bracket ▸ **paréntesis cuadrados** square brackets
2 (*Ling*) (= *pausa*) parenthesis; (= *digresión*) digression; (= *aparte*) aside • **hacer un ~** (*en discurso, escrito*) to digress • **entre ~** (*como adj*) parenthetical, incidental; (*como adv*) parenthetically, incidentally • **y, entre ~ ...** and, by the way ..., and I may add in passing ...
3 (= *intervalo*) interval, break; (= *hueco*) gap; (= *descanso*) lull • **el ~ vacacional** the break for the holidays • **hacer un ~** to take a break
pareo¹ (SM) (*tradicional*) pareo; [*de playa*] beach wrap; (= *chal*) rectangular shawl
pareo² (SM) (*gen*) matching; (= *unión*) pairing off; (*Zool*) mating
paria (SMF) pariah
parián (SM) (*Méx*) market
parida (SF) **1‡** (= *dicho*) silly thing, stupid remark • **salir con una ~** to come out with a silly remark • **~s** nonsense (*sing*) ▸ **parida mental** dumb idea*
2 (= *mujer*) *woman who has recently given birth*
paridad (SF) **1** (= *igualdad*) parity, equality; (= *semejanza*) similarity
2 (= *comparación*) comparison
parido* (ADJ) • **bien ~** good-looking
paridora (ADJ FEM) fertile, productive
parienta (SF) • **la ~*** the wife*, the missus*
pariente/a (SM/F) (= *familiar*) relative, relation • **un medio ~** a distant relative *o* relation • **un ~ pobre** a poor relation • **es un ~ político** he's related to me by marriage • **los ~s políticos** the in-laws
(SM) • **el ~*** the old man*, my hubby*
parietal (ADJ) parietal
(SM) parietal bone
parihuela (SF), **parihuelas** (SFPL) stretcher
paripé* (SM) • **hacer** *o* **montar el ~** to put on a show
parir ▸ CONJUG 3a (VI) [*mujer*] to give birth, have a baby; [*yegua*] to foal; [*vaca*] to calve; [*cerda*] to farrow; [*perra*] to pup • MODISMOS: • **éramos pocos y parió la abuela*** that's the limit* • **poner a ~ a algn*** to slag sb off*
(VT) **1** (= *dar a luz*) [*mujer*] to give birth to, have, bear (*frm*); [*animal*] to have • **¡la madre que te parió!**** you bastard!**
2 (= *producir*) to produce • **ha parido una magnífica novela** he has produced a brilliant novel
3 • **~la‡** to drop a clanger‡
París (SM) Paris
parisién (ADJ) Parisian
parisiense (ADJ), (SMF), **parisino/a** (ADJ), (SM/F) Parisian

paritario (ADJ) peer (*antes de s*) • **grupo ~** peer group
paritorio (SM) delivery room
parka (SF) parka
parking ['parkin] (SM) (PL: **parkings**), **párking** ['parkin] (SM) (PL: **párkings**) car park, parking lot (*EEUU*)
párkinson (SM), **Parkinson** (SM) Parkinson's (disease)
parkour (SM) free running, parkour
parla (SF) chatter, gossip
parlador (ADJ) talkative
parlamentar ▸ CONJUG 1a (VI) (*gen*) to converse, talk; (*Mil*) to parley
parlamentario/a (ADJ) parliamentary
(SM/F) (= *diputado*) M.P., member of parliament; (*más veterano*) parliamentarian ▸ **parlamentario/a autónomo/a** member of a regional parliament
parlamento (SM) **1** (*Pol*) parliament ▸ **parlamento autónomo** regional parliament ▸ **Parlamento Europeo** European Parliament
2 (= *discurso*) speech
3 (*Mil*) parley
parlana (SF) (*CAm*) turtle
parlanchín/ina* (ADJ) talkative
(SM/F) chatterbox*
parlante (ADJ) talking
(SM) (*LAm*) loudspeaker
...parlante (SUF) • **castellanoparlante** (*adj*) Castilian-speaking; (*smf*) Castilian speaker
parlar ▸ CONJUG 1a (VI) **1*** [*persona*] to chatter (away), talk (a lot)
2 [*pájaro*] to chatter
parlero (ADJ) **1** (= *hablador*) talkative, garrulous; (= *chismoso*) gossipy
2 [*pájaro*] talking; (= *cantor*) singing, song (*antes de s*)
3 [*arroyo*] musical; [*ojos*] expressive
parleta* (SF) chat, small talk
parlotear* ▸ CONJUG 1a (VI) to chatter, prattle
parloteo* (SM) chatter, prattle
PARM (SM ABR) (*Méx*) = **Partido Auténtico de la Revolución Mexicana**
parmesano (ADJ) Parmesan • **queso ~** Parmesan cheese
(SM) Parmesan
Parnaso (SM) Parnassus
parné‡ (SM) dough‡, cash*
paro¹ (SM) (*Orn*) tit
paro² (SM) **1** (= *desempleo*) unemployment • **índice de ~** level of unemployment • **estar en ~** to be unemployed • **lo han enviado al ~** they have put him out of a job, they have made him unemployed ▸ **paro cíclico** cyclical unemployment ▸ **paro encubierto** underemployment ▸ **paro estacional** seasonal unemployment ▸ **paro obrero** unemployment
2 (= *subsidio*) unemployment benefit, unemployment insurance (*EEUU*) • **cobrar el ~** to be on the dole*, receive unemployment benefit (*frm*)
3 (= *interrupción*) stoppage • **se produjo un ~ en la cadena de montaje** there was a stoppage on the assembly line ▸ **paro biológico** (*Pesca*) temporary fishing ban ▸ **paro cardíaco** cardiac arrest ▸ **paro del sistema** (*Inform*) system shutdown ▸ **paro forzoso** enforced stoppage ▸ **paro técnico** technical breakdown
4 (= *huelga*) strike • **un ~ de tres días** a three-day strike • **hay ~ en la industria** work in the industry is at a standstill
5 (*And, Caribe*) (*Dados*) throw
6 • **en ~** (*And*) (= *de una vez*) all at once, in one go
parodia (SF) **1** (= *imitación*) parody, takeoff*

P

2 [*de la justicia, investigación*] travesty
parodiar ▹ CONJUG 1b (VT) to parody, take off*
paródico (ADJ) parodic
parodista (SMF) parodist, writer of parodies
parola (SF) **1** (*cualidad*) (= *soltura*) fluency; (= *verborrea*) verbosity; (= *labia*) gift of the gab*
2 (= *charla*) (*gen*) chitchat; (*cansina*) tiresome talk • **son ~s** (*Cono Sur**) it's all hot air*
parolimpiada (SF) = **paraolimpiada**
parolímpico/a (ADJ), (SM/F) = **paraolímpico**
parón (SM) • **la obras sufrieron un ~ ayer** building work came to a halt yesterday • **tras un ~ por la lluvia, continuó el partido** after rain had halted play, the matched restarted • **parones en una de las líneas del metro** stoppages on one of the underground lines
paroxismo (SM) paroxysm ▸ **paroxismo de risa** convulsions (*pl*) of laughter ▸ **paroxismo histérico** hysterics (*pl*)
parpadeante (ADJ) flickering
parpadear ▹ CONJUG 1a (VI) [*ojos*] to blink; [*luz*] to flicker; [*estrella*] to twinkle
parpadeo (SM) [*de ojos*] blinking; [*de luz*] flickering; [*de estrella*] twinkling
párpado (SM) eyelid • **restregarse los ~s** to rub one's eyes
parpichuela** (SF) • **hacerse una ~** to wank**
parque (SM) **1** (= *terreno, recinto*) park ▸ **parque acuático** water park ▸ **parque central** (*Méx*) town square ▸ **parque de atracciones** amusement park ▸ **parque de chatarra** scrap yard ▸ **parque de diversiones** (*Arg, Uru*) amusement park ▸ **parque de estacionamiento** car park, parking lot (*EEUU*) ▸ **parque eólico** wind farm ▸ **parque infantil** children's playground ▸ **parque nacional** national park ▸ **parque natural** nature reserve ▸ **parque tecnológico** technology park ▸ **parque temático** theme park ▸ **parque zoológico** zoo
2 [*de material*] depot ▸ **parque de artillería** artillery depot, artillery stores (*pl*) ▸ **parque de bomberos** fire station, fire *o* station house (*EEUU*)
3 [*de vehículos*] fleet • **el ~ nacional de automóviles** the total number of cars in the country • **el ~ provincial de tractores** the number of tractors in use in the province ▸ **parque automotor** (*LAm*), **parque automovilístico** car fleet ▸ **parque cerrado** parc fermé ▸ **parque móvil** fleet of official cars
4 (*para niños*) playpen
5 (*Méx*) (= *munición*) ammunition, ammo*; (= *depósito*) ammunition dump
6 (*LAm*) (= *equipo*) equipment
parqué (SM), **parquet** [par'ke] (SM) (PL: **parquets** [par'kes]) **1** (= *entarimado*) parquet
2 (*Econ*) • **el ~** the Floor (*of the stock exchange*); (*fig*) the stock market
parqueadero (SM) (*LAm*) car park, parking lot (*EEUU*)
parquear ▹ CONJUG 1a (VT), (VI) (*LAm*) to park
parquedad (SF) (= *frugalidad*) frugality, sparingness; (= *moderación*) moderation
parqueo (SM) (*LAm*) **1** (= *acto*) parking
2 (= *aparcamiento*) car-park, parking lot (*EEUU*)
parquímetro (SM) parking meter
párr. (ABR) (= **párrafo**) par, para
parra (SF) (*Bot*) grapevine; (= *trepadora*) climbing vine • MODISMO: • **subirse a la ~*** (= *engreírse*) to get all high and mighty; (= *enfadarse*) to blow one's top*
parrafada* (SF) **1** (= *charla*) chat, talk • **echar la ~** to have a chat
2 (= *discurso*) spiel*, talk • **soltar** *o* **tirarse una ~** to give a lengthy spiel*
párrafo (SM) paragraph • **hacer ~ aparte** (*lit*) to start a new paragraph; (*fig*) to change the subject • MODISMO: • **echar un ~ (con algn)*** to have a chat (with sb)
parral (SM) vine arbour, vine arbor (*EEUU*)
parrampán* (SM) (*Pan*) pretentious person
parranda (SF) **1*** (= *juerga*) spree • **andar** *o* **ir de ~** to go out on the town*
2 (*And, Cono Sur, Méx*) [*de cosas*] lot, heap; [*de personas*] group • **una ~ de** a lot of
parrandear* ▹ CONJUG 1a (VI) to go on a binge*
parricida (SMF) parricide
parricidio (SM) parricide
parrilla (SF) **1** (*Culin*) grill • **carne a la ~** grilled meat
2 (*Dep*) (*tb* **parrilla de salida**) [*de coches*] starting grid; [*de caballos*] starting stalls
3 (*Aut*) [*de radiador*] radiator grille; (*LAm*) (= *baca*) roof rack
4 [*de bicicleta*] carrier
5 (= *restaurante*) grillroom, steak restaurant
6 ▸ **parrilla televisiva** TV schedule, television schedule
parrillada (SF) **1** (= *plato*) (mixed) grill; (*en barbacoa*) barbecue
2 (*Cono Sur*) (= *restaurante*) grillroom, steak restaurant
párroco (SM) parish priest
parroquia (SF) **1** (*Rel*) (= *zona*) parish; (= *iglesia*) parish church; (= *feligreses*) parishioners (*pl*)
2 (= *clientes*) customers (*pl*), clientele • **hoy hay poca ~** there aren't many customers today • **una tienda con mucha ~** a shop with a large clientele, a well-patronized shop
parroquial (ADJ) parochial, parish (*antes de s*)
parroquiano/a (SM/F) **1** (*Rel*) parishioner
2 (*Com*) patron, customer • **ser ~ de** to shop regularly at, patronize
parsi (SMF) Parsee
parsimonia (SF) **1** (= *calma*) calmness; (= *flema*) phlegmatic nature • **con ~** calmly, unhurriedly
2 (= *frugalidad*) sparingness; (*con el dinero*) carefulness
parsimonioso (ADJ) **1** (= *tranquilo*) calm, unhurried; (= *flemático*) phlegmatic
2 (= *frugal*) sparing; (*con el dinero*) careful
parte[1] (SM) **1** (= *informe*) report • **dar ~ a algn** to report to sb • **han dado ~ del robo a la policía** they have reported the break-in to the police ▸ **parte de alta** certificate of starting employment ▸ **parte de baja (laboral)** (*por enfermedad*) doctor's note; (*por cese*) certificate of leaving employment, ≈ P45 ▸ **parte de defunción** death certificate ▸ **parte facultativo, parte médico** medical report, medical bulletin ▸ **parte meteorológico** weather forecast, weather report
2 (*Mil*) dispatch, communiqué ▸ **parte de guerra** military communiqué, war report
3 (*Radio†*) news bulletin • **el ~ de las tres** the three o'clock news (bulletin)
4 (*Cono Sur*) [*de boda*] wedding invitation; (*Aut*) speeding ticket
parte[2] (SF) **1** (= *sección*) part • **el examen consta de dos ~s** the exam consists of two parts • **¿en qué ~ del libro te has quedado?** where are you in the book?, which bit of the book are you on at the moment? • **~ de lo que pasa es culpa mía** I'm partly to blame for the situation • **la ~ de abajo** the bottom • **la ~ de arriba** the top • **la ~ de atrás** the back • **la cuarta ~** a quarter • **han perdido la cuarta ~ de las ganancias** they've lost a quarter of the profits • **la ~ delantera** the front • **ser ~ esencial de algo** to be an essential part of sth • **la mayor ~ de algo**: • **pasé la mayor ~ del tiempo leyendo** I spent most of the time reading • **la mayor ~ de los españoles** most Spanish people • —**¿os queda dinero? —sí, aunque ya hemos gastado la mayor ~** "do you have any money left?" — "yes, though we've spent most of it" • **la tercera ~** a third • **reducir algo en una tercera ~** to reduce sth by a third ▸ **parte de la oración** part of speech
2 (*en locuciones*) • **de ~ de**: • **llamo de ~ de Juan** I'm calling on behalf of Juan • **de ~ de todos nosotros** on behalf of us all • **salúdalo de mi ~** give him my regards • **dale esto de mi ~** give her this from me • **¿de ~ de quién?** (*al teléfono*) who's calling? • **en ~** partly, in part • **se debe en ~ a su falta de experiencia** it's partly due to his lack of experience, it's due in part to his lack of experience • **tienes razón solo en ~** you're only partly right • **formar ~ de algo**: • **¿cuándo entró a formar ~ de la organización?** when did she join the organization? • **no formaba ~ del equipo** he was not in the team • **forma ~ de sus obligaciones** it is part of his duties • **en gran ~** to a large extent • **por otra ~** on the other hand • **por una ~ ... por otra (parte)** on the one hand, ... on the other • **por ~ de** on the part of • **exige un gran esfuerzo por ~ de los alumnos** it requires a great effort on the part of *o* from the pupils • **yo por mi ~, no estoy de acuerdo** I, for my part, disagree • **¡vayamos por ~s!** let's take it one step at a time!
3 (= *participación*) share • **mi ~ de la herencia** my share of the inheritance • **como ~ del pago** in part exchange • **a ~s iguales** in equal shares • **ir a la ~** to go shares • **tener ~ en algo** to share in sth • **tomar ~ (en algo)** to take part (in sth) • **¿cuántos corredores tomarán ~ en la prueba?** how many runners will take part in the race? • **yo no tomé ~ en ese asunto** I had no part in it • MODISMOS: • **llevarse la mejor ~** to come off best, get the best of it • **poner de su ~** to do one's bit *o* share • **tienes que poner de tu ~** you have to do your bit *o* share • **quedarse con la ~ del león** to take the lion's share; ▹ **partir**
4 (= *lugar*) part • **¿de qué ~ de Inglaterra eres?** what part of England are you from? • **¿en qué ~ de la ciudad vives?** where *o* whereabouts in the city do you live? • **en alguna ~** somewhere • **en alguna ~ de Europa** somewhere in Europe • **en cualquier ~** anywhere • **en ninguna ~** nowhere • **en ninguna ~ del país** nowhere in the country • **por ahí no se va a ninguna ~** (*lit*) that way doesn't lead anywhere; (*fig*) that will get us nowhere • **ir a otra ~** to go somewhere else • **debe de estar en otra ~** it must be somewhere else • **en** *o* **por todas ~s** everywhere • **en todas ~s de España** all over Spain • MODISMOS: • **en las cinco ~s del mundo** (*Esp*) in the four corners of the earth • **de una ~ a otra** back and forth, to and fro • **tomar algo en buena ~†** to take sth in good part • **echar algo a mala ~†** to look on sth with disapproval • **de algún** *o* **un tiempo a esta ~** for some time now • **en salva sea la ~** (*Esp*) (*euf*) (= *trasero*): • **le dio una patada en salva sea la ~** she gave him a kick up the behind; ▹ **haba**
5 (= *bando*) side • **estar de ~ de algn** to be on sb's side • **estoy de tu ~** I'm on your side • **¿de ~ de quién estás tú?** whose side are you on? • **todo está de su ~** everything is in his favour • **ponerse de ~ de algn** to side with

sb, take sb's side
6 (*indicando parentesco*) side • **es primo por ~ de madre** he's a cousin on my mother's side
7 (*Dep*) (*en partido*) half • **primera ~** first half • **segunda ~** second half
8 (*Teat*) part
9 (*Jur*) (*en contrato*) party • **las ~s contratantes** the parties to the contract • **el documento debe ser firmado por ambas ~s** the document should be signed by both parties • **sin la intervención de terceras ~s** without the involvement of third parties • MODISMO: • **ser juez y ~** to be judge and jury (*in one's own case*) ▸ **parte actora** plaintiff ▸ **parte acusadora** prosecution ▸ **parte contraria** opposing party
10 partes (*euf*) (= *genitales*) private parts (*euf*), privates (*euf*) • **recibió un golpe en sus ~s** he was hit in the privates (*euf*) ▸ **partes íntimas, partes pudendas** private parts
11 partes† (= *cualidades*) parts, qualities, talents • **buenas ~s** good parts
12 (*Méx*) spare part

parteaguas SM INV (*LAm*) (*gen*) divide, ridge; (= *línea divisoria*) watershed ▸ **parteaguas continental** continental divide

partear ▹ CONJUG 1a VT to deliver

parteluz SM mullion

partenaire [parte'ner] SMF partner

partenogénesis SF INV parthenogenesis

Partenón SM Parthenon

partenueces SM INV nutcracker

partero/a SM/F **1** (= *comadrona*) midwife/male midwife
2 (*Méx*) (= *obstetra*) obstetrician; (= *ginecólogo*) gynaecologist, gynecologist (*EEUU*)

parterre SM **1** [*de flores*] flower bed
2 (*Teat*) stalls (*pl*)

partición SF (= *reparto*) division, sharing-out; (*Pol*) partition; (*Mat*) division

participación SF **1** (= *acto*) • **negó su ~ en el atentado** he denied taking part *o* any involvement in the attack • **queremos fomentar la ~ de los ciudadanos en la política** we want to encourage public participation *o* involvement in politics • **habló de ello durante su ~ en el programa** he spoke about it when he was on the programme ▸ **participación electoral** turnout
2 (*Econ*) (= *parte*) share; (= *inversión*) holding, interest • **la ~ de la empresa Ceresa en Rodex** Ceresa's holding in Rodex ▸ **participación accionarial** holding, shareholding ▸ **participación en el mercado** market share ▸ **participación en los beneficios** profit-sharing ▸ **participación minoritaria** minority interest
3 (= *número de participantes*) entry • **hubo una nutrida ~** there was a big entry, there were a lot of entries
4 (= *parte*) share; [*de lotería*] (share in a) lottery ticket; ▹ LOTERÍA
5 (= *aviso*) notice, notification • **dar ~ de algo** to give notice of sth ▸ **participación de boda** notice of a forthcoming wedding

participante ADJ participating • **los países ~s** the participating countries
SMF (*gen*) participant; (*Dep*) entrant

participar ▹ CONJUG 1a VI **1** (= *tomar parte*) to take part, participate (*frm*) • **~ en un concurso** to take part *o* participate in a competition • **20 países ~án en la cumbre** 20 countries will take part in the summit • **~ en una carrera** to take part in a race
2 (*Econ*) • **~ en una empresa** to own shares in a company • **~ de los beneficios** to share in the profits • **~ de** *o* **en una herencia** to share in an estate
3 (= *compartir*) • **~ de una cualidad/opinión** to share a quality/an opinion
VT (*frm*) (= *informar*) to inform • **~ algo a algn** to inform sb of sth

participativo ADJ [*sociedad, público*] participative; [*deporte, juego*] participative, participatory; [*democracia*] participatory

partícipe SMF (*gen*) participant; (*Com*) interested party • **hacer ~ a algn de algo** (= *informar*) to inform sb of sth; (= *compartir*) to share sth with sb; (= *implicar*) to make sb party to sth

participial ADJ participial

participio SM (*Ling*) participle ▸ **participio activo** present participle ▸ **participio de pasado** past participle ▸ **participio (de) presente** present participle ▸ **participio de pretérito, participio pasivo** past participle

partícula SF particle ▸ **partícula alfa** alpha particle ▸ **partícula atómica** atomic particle ▸ **partícula elemental** elementary particle

particular ADJ **1** (= *especial*) special • **nada de ~** nothing special • **el vestido no tiene nada de ~** the dress is nothing special • **lo que tiene de ~ es que ...** what's remarkable about it is that ...
2 (= *específico*) • **en este caso ~** in this particular case • **tiene un sabor ~** it has a flavour of its own • **en ~** in particular • **me gustan todas, pero esta en ~** I like all of them, but this one in particular
3 (= *privado*) [*secretario, coche*] private • **clase ~** private lesson • **casa ~** private home
SM (= *asunto*) matter • **no dijo mucho sobre este ~** he didn't say much about this matter • **sin otro ~, se despide atentamente ...** (*en correspondencia*) yours faithfully, sincerely yours (*EEUU*)
SMF (= *persona*) (private) individual • **no comerciamos con ~es** we don't do business with individuals

particularidad SF **1** (= *propiedad*) particularity, peculiarity; (= *rasgo distintivo*) special feature, characteristic • **tiene la ~ de que ...** one of its special features is (that) ..., it has the characteristic that ...
2 (= *amistad*) friendship, intimacy

particularizar ▹ CONJUG 1f VT **1** (= *distinguir*) to distinguish, characterize
2 (= *especificar*) to specify
3 (= *singularizar*) to single out
4 (= *preferir*) to prefer
5 (= *pormenorizar*) to particularize, give details about
VPR **particularizarse 1** (= *distinguirse*) [*cosa*] to distinguish itself, stand out; [*persona*] to make one's mark
2 • **~se con algn** to single sb out (*for special treatment etc*)

particularmente ADV **1** (= *especialmente*) particularly, specially
2 (= *personalmente*) privately, personally

partida SF **1** (= *documento*) certificate ▸ **partida bautismal, partida de bautismo** baptismal certificate ▸ **partida de defunción** death certificate ▸ **partida de matrimonio** marriage certificate ▸ **partida de nacimiento** birth certificate
2 (*Econ*) [*de cuenta*] entry, item; [*de presupuesto*] item, heading ▸ **partida doble** double entry • **por ~ doble** on two accounts ▸ **partida simple** single entry
3 (*Com*) (= *envío*) consignment • **han enviado una ~ de 10.000 euros** they have sent a consignment worth 10,000 euros
4 (*Naipes, Ajedrez*) game • **echar una ~** to have a game • MODISMO: • **jugarle una mala ~ a algn** to play a dirty trick on sb
5 (= *salida*) departure
6 (= *grupo*) party; (*Mil*) band, group ▸ **partida de campo** picnic (party) ▸ **partida de caza** hunting party

partidario/a ADJ • **ser ~ de algo** to be in favour *o* (*EEUU*) favor of sth • **ser ~ de hacer algo** to be in favour of doing sth
SM/F **1** (= *defensor*) [*de persona*] supporter, follower; [*de idea, movimiento*] supporter • **el candidato a la presidencia tiene muchos ~s** the presidential candidate has many supporters *o* followers • **los ~s del aborto** supporters *o* those in favour of abortion, those who support abortion
2 (*And, Caribe*) (= *aparcero*) sharecropper

partidillo SM (*Dep*) practice game

partidismo SM partisanship

partidista ADJ partisan, party (*antes de s*)
SMF partisan

partido SM **1** (*Pol*) party • **sistema de ~ único** one-party system • **tomar ~** to take sides • **tomar ~ por algo/algn** to side with sth/sb ▸ **partido de la oposición** opposition party ▸ **partido político** political party ▸ **Partido Verde** Green Party
2 (*Dep*) game, match ▸ **partido amistoso** friendly (game *o* match) ▸ **partido de casa** home game *o* match ▸ **partido de desempate** replay ▸ **partido de dobles** (*Tenis*) doubles match, game of doubles ▸ **partido de exhibición** exhibition game *o* match ▸ **partido de fútbol** football game *o* match ▸ **partido (de) homenaje** benefit game *o* match ▸ **partido de ida** away game *o* match, first leg ▸ **partido de vuelta** return game *o* match, second leg ▸ **partido internacional** international (match)
3 (= *provecho*) • **sacar ~ de algo** to make the most of sth
4 • **ser un buen ~** [*persona*] to be a good match
5 (= *distrito*) district, administrative area ▸ **partido judicial** *district under the jurisdiction of a local court*
6 (*frm*) (= *apoyo*) support • **tiene ~ entre todas las clases sociales** he has support among all social classes
7 (*frm*) • **darse a ~** • **venir(se) a ~** to give way
8 (*Cono Sur*) (*Naipes*) hand
9 (*And, Caribe*) (= *aparcería*) crop share

partija SF **1** (= *partición*) partition, division
2 (*pey*) = **parte²**

partiota SF (*Caribe*) dollar bill

partir ▹ CONJUG 3a VT **1** (= *dividir*) [+ *tarta, sandía, baraja*] to cut; [+ *tableta de chocolate*] to break; [+ *tronco*] to split • **parte la barra de pan por la mitad** (*con cuchillo*) cut the baguette in half; (*con las manos*) break the baguette in half • **¿te parto un trozo de queso?** shall I cut you (off) a piece of cheese?
2 (= *romper*) [+ *hueso, diente*] to break; [+ *rama*] to break off; [+ *nuez, almendra*] to crack • **se sentó en la mesa y la partió** he sat on the table and broke it in two • **partió el plato en varios trozos** he broke the plate into several pieces • **la piedra no llegó a ~ el cristal** the stone didn't break the window • **le partió el labio de un puñetazo** he gave him a punch and split his lip • **¡te voy a ~ la cara!*** I'm going to smash your face in!* • **~ la cabeza a algn** to split sb's head open • MODISMO: • **~ el corazón a algn** to break sb's heart
3 (= *distribuir*) to share out; (= *compartir*) to share • **~ algo con otros** to share sth with others • REFRÁN: • **quien parte y reparte se queda con la mejor parte** the person in charge of sharing out always keeps the biggest bit for himself
4* (= *fastidiar*) to mess up* • **no soporto estas reuniones a las 11, me parten toda la mañana** I hate these 11 o'clock meetings,

P

they mess up the whole morning* • **salir a comprar ya me ha partido la tarde** going shopping has wasted my whole afternoon

(VI) **1** (= *ponerse en camino*) [*persona, expedición*] to set off; [*tren, avión*] to depart (**de** from, **para** for, **hacia** in the direction of) • **~emos a primera hora de la mañana** we'll set off first thing in the morning • **la expedición ~á mañana de París** the expedition will set out *o* depart from Paris tomorrow • **partieron del puerto de Palos con destino a América** they set sail for America from the port of Palos

2 • **~ de algo** to start from sth • **hemos partido de un supuesto falso** we have started from a false assumption • **partiendo de la base de que …** working on the principle that …, assuming that … • **¿de quién partió la idea?** whose idea was it?

3 • **a ~ de** from • **a ~ de hoy** from today • **a ~ de mañana** from tomorrow • **a ~ del lunes** from Monday, starting on Monday • **a ~ de ahora** from now on • **la tercera casa a ~ de la esquina** the third house from the corner • **a ~ del puente la carretera se estrecha** the road gets narrower after the bridge • **¿qué podemos deducir a ~ de estos datos?** what can we deduce from these data?

(VPR) **partirse 1** (= *romperse*) to break • **el remo se partió en dos** the oar broke in two • **me he partido un brazo** I've broken my arm • **se le partió el labio del golpe** the blow split his lip • MODISMO: • **~se de risa** to split one's sides laughing

2† (= *irse*) to leave; (= *ponerse en camino*) to set off

partisano/a (ADJ), (SM/F) partisan

partitivo (ADJ) partitive

partitura (SF) (*Mús*) score

parto (SM) **1** (*Med*) (*gen*) birth, delivery; (= *contracciones*) labour, labor (EEUU); (*Zool*) parturition • **asistir en un ~** to deliver a baby • **estar de ~** to be in labour • **tuvo un ~ difícil** it was a difficult birth • **mal ~** miscarriage • **murió de ~** she died in childbirth • MODISMO: • **costar un ~** to be a real effort ▸ **parto múltiple** multiple birth ▸ **parto natural** natural childbirth ▸ **parto prematuro** premature birth ▸ **parto provocado** induced labour ▸ **parto sin dolor** painless childbirth

2 (= *creación*) product, creation • **el ensayo ha sido un ~ difícil** I sweated blood over the essay ▸ **parto del ingenio** brainchild ▸ **parto de los montes** anticlimax, bathos

parturición (SF) parturition

parturienta (SF) (*antes del parto*) woman in labour, woman in labor (EEUU); (*después del parto*) woman who has just given birth

party (PL: **partys**) (SM) (*gen*) party; (= *cóctel*) cocktail party, reception

parva (SF) **1** [*de trigo, cebada, centeno*] unthreshed grain

2 (= *montón*) heap, pile

parvada (SF) (*LAm*) flock

parvedad (SF) (*con nombres incontables*) small amount; (*con nombres contables*) small number • **una ~** a tiny bit • **~ de recursos** limited resources (*pl*), scant resources (*pl*)

parvulario (SM) nursery school, kindergarten

parvulista (SMF) nursery teacher

párvulo/a (SM/F) (*gen*) infant, child; (*Escol*) infant • **colegio de ~s** nursery school

pasa (SF) raisin • MODISMO: • **está hecho una ~*** he's as shrivelled as a prune ▸ **pasa de Corinto** currant ▸ **pasa de Esmirna** sultana

pasable (ADJ) **1** (= *tolerable*) passable, tolerable

2 (*LAm*) [*arroyo etc*] fordable

3 (*Cono Sur*) (= *vendible*) saleable

pasablemente (ADV) passably, tolerably (well)

pasabocas (SMPL) (*Col*) tasty snacks

pasacalle (SM) passacaglia

pasacintas (SM INV) suspender-belt, garter belt (EEUU)

pasada (SF) **1** [*de pintura, barniz*] coat; (*con un trapo*) wipe • **dale dos ~s de jabón a la ropa** soap the clothes twice • **le di una ~ con la plancha a la camisa** I ran the iron over the shirt

2 (*Cos*) (= *puntada*) • **dale una ~ al pantalón** give it a quick sew

3 • **de ~** in passing • **me comentó de ~ que no vendría mañana** she mentioned in passing that she wouldn't be coming tomorrow • **ya que vas al estanco de ~ cómprame unos sellos** (*LAm*) if you are going to the tobacconist's could you buy me some stamps while you're there *o* while you're at it • **solo estoy aquí de ~** (*LAm*) I'm only just passing by *o* through

4* (= *barbaridad*) • **¡este coche es una ~!** this car is amazing! • **¿has visto cómo ha saltado? ¡qué ~!** did you see him jump? amazing! • **¡qué ~! me han cobrado 75 euros** what a rip-off! they charged me 75 euros* • **una ~ de …*** (= *un montón de*) lots of …, tons of …* • **había una ~ de gente** there were lots *o* tons* of people

5 (= *jugarreta*) • **hacerle** *o* **jugarle una mala ~ a algn** to play a dirty trick on sb

6 (*CAm, Cono Sur**) (= *reprimenda*) telling-off*

7 (*Col*) (= *vergüenza*) shame, embarrassment

pasadera (SF) stepping stone

pasadero (ADJ) (= *tolerable*) passable, tolerable; (*Aut etc*) passable, open

(SM) (= *piedra*) stepping stone

pasadizo (SM) (*interior*) passage; (*entre calles*) passageway, alley

pasado (ADJ) **1** [*tiempo*] • **el jueves ~** last Thursday • **el mes ~** last month • **~ mañana** the day after tomorrow • **~s dos días** after two days • **ya eran pasadas las seis** it was already after six • **lo ~** the past • MODISMO: • **lo ~, ~ (está)** let bygones be bygones

2 (*Culin*) (= *en mal estado*) [*pan*] stale; [*fruta*] overripe • **esta leche está pasada** this milk is off

3 (*Culin*) (= *muy hecho*) [*carne*] overdone; [*arroz, pasta*] overcooked • **me gustan los filetes muy ~s** I like my steaks very well done • **la carne estaba demasiado pasada** the meat was overdone • **huevo ~ por agua** soft-boiled egg

4 (= *no actual*) [*ropa, zapatos*] old-fashioned; [*noticia*] stale; [*idea*] [*costumbre*] antiquated, out-of-date

5 (= *muy usado*) worn • **esta tela está muy pasada y se rompe con facilidad** this material is very worn and it tears easily • **estar ~ de vueltas** *o* **de rosca** [*grifo, tuerca*] to be worn; [*persona*] to have seen it all before

6 [*belleza*] faded

7‡ (= *borracho, drogado*) • **estar ~** to be out of one's box‡

(SM) **1** • **el ~** the past • MODISMO: • **el ~, ~ (está)** let bygones be bygones

2 [*de persona*] past • **tiene un ~ muy turbio** he has a very murky past

3 (*Ling*) past (tense)

pasador(a) (SM/F) (= *contrabandista*) smuggler; (*LAm*) (= *correo*) drug courier

(SM) **1** (*Culin*) (*gen*) colander; [*de té*] strainer

2 (*Téc*) (= *filtro*) filter; (= *pestillo*) bolt, fastener; [*de bisagra*] pin

3 [*de corbata*] tie pin; [*de camisa*] collar stud

4 [*de pelo*] hairpin

5 pasadores (= *gemelos*) cufflinks; (*LAm*) (= *cordones*) shoelaces

pasaje (SM) **1** (= *acción*) passage, passing; (*Náut*) voyage, crossing

2 (*esp LAm*) (= *boleto*) ticket ▸ **pasaje electrónico** e-ticket

3 (= *tarifa*) fare • **cobrar el ~** to collect fares

4 (= *viajeros*) passengers (*pl*)

5 (= *callejón*) passageway, alleyway; (*con tiendas*) arcade; (*Caribe, Cono Sur, Méx*) cul-de-sac

6 (*Literat, Mús*) passage

7 (*And, Caribe*) (= *cuento*) story, anecdote

8 (*And*) (= *pisos*) tenement building

pasajeramente (ADV) fleetingly

pasajero/a (ADJ) **1** [*momento*] fleeting, passing • **ave ~** bird of passage, migratory bird

2 [*sitio*] busy

(SM/F) passenger

(SM) (*Méx*) ferryman

pasamanos (SM INV), **pasamano** (SM)

1 (*Arquit*) (*gen*) handrail, rail; [*de escalera*] banister

2 (*Cono Sur*) (*Ferro etc*) strap (*for standing passenger*)

3 (*Cos*) braid

4 (*Cono Sur*) (= *propina*) tip

pasamontañas (SM) Balaclava (helmet), ski mask

pasandito* (ADV) (*CAm, Méx*) on tiptoe

pasante (SMF) **1** (*gen*) assistant; (*Jur*) articled clerk

2 (*Escol*) assistant teacher; (= *tutor*†) tutor

pasapalos (SMPL) (*Méx, Ven*) tasty snacks

pasapasa (SM) sleight of hand

pasaportar‡ ▹ CONJUG 1a (VT) to bump off‡

pasaporte (SM) passport • MODISMO: • **dar el ~ a algn*** (= *despedir*) to boot sb out*; (= *matar*) to bump sb off‡ ▸ **pasaporte biométrico** biometric passport

pasapurés (SM INV), **pasapuré** (SM) manual food mill

pasar

VERBO INTRANSITIVO
VERBO TRANSITIVO
VERBO PRONOMINAL
SUSTANTIVO MASCULINO

▹ CONJUG 1a

Para las expresiones ***pasar lista, pasar de moda, pasar desapercibido, pasarse de rosca*** *etc, ver la otra entrada*

VERBO INTRANSITIVO

1 (= *ocurrir*) **a** [*suceso*] to happen • **¿qué pasó?** what happened? • **¿pasa algo?** is anything up?, is anything wrong?, is anything the matter? • **como si no hubiese pasado nada** as if nothing had happened • **aquí pasa algo misterioso** there's something odd going on here • **siempre pasa igual** *o* **lo mismo** it's always the same • **¿qué pasa?** what's happening?, what's going on?, what's up?; (*como saludo*) how's things?* • **¿qué pasa que no entra?** why doesn't she come in? • **¿qué pasa contigo?** what's up with you?; (*como saludo**) how's it going?* • **¿qué ha pasado con ella?** what's become of her? • **lo que pasa es que …** well, you see…, the thing is that … • **pase lo que pase** whatever happens, come what may

b • **~le a algn: nunca me pasa nada** nothing ever happens to me • **no me ha pasado otra (igual) en la vida** nothing like this has ever happened to me before • **siempre me pasa lo mismo, lo pierdo todo** it's always the same, I keep losing things • **tuvo un accidente, pero por suerte no le pasó nada** he had an accident, but fortunately he wasn't hurt • **esto te pasa por no hacerme caso** this is what comes of not listening to me, this wouldn't have happened (to you) if you'd listened to me • **¿qué te pasa?** what's the matter? • **¿qué le pasa a ese?** what's the matter with him?

2 (*= cambiar de lugar*) **a** [*objeto*] • **la cuerda pasa de un lado a otro de la calle** the rope goes from one side of the street to the other • **cuando muera la empresa ~á al hijo** when he dies the company will go to his son • **la foto fue pasando de mano en mano** the photo was passed around • **pasó de mis manos a las suyas** it passed from my hands into his
b [*persona*] to go • **~ a un cuarto contiguo** to go into an adjoining room • **~ de Inglaterra al Canadá** to go from England to Canada

3 (*= entrar*) • **¡pase!** come in!; (*cediendo el paso*) after you! • **no se puede ~** you can't go through, you can't go in • **pasamos directamente a ver al jefe** we went straight in to see the boss • **los moros ~on a España** the Moors crossed over into Spain • **hacer ~ a algn** to show sb in

4 (*= transitar*) • **pasó una bicicleta** a bicycle went past • **¿a qué hora pasa el cartero?** what time does the postman come? • **ya ha pasado el tren de las cinco** (= *sin hacer parada*) the five o'clock train has already gone by; (= *haciendo parada*) the five o'clock train has already been and gone • **¿ha pasado ya el camión de la basura?** have the dustmen been? • **~ de largo** to go *o* pass by • **~ por:** • **el autobús pasa por delante de nuestra casa** the bus goes past our house • **ese autobús no pasa por aquí** that bus doesn't come this way

5 (*= acercarse a*) • **tengo que ~ por el banco** I've got to go to the bank • **~é por la tienda mañana** I'll go *o* pop into the shop tomorrow • **tendrá que ~ por mi despacho** he'll have to come to my office • **pase por caja** please pay at the cash desk • **~é por tu casa** I'll drop in
pasar a (+ *infin*) • **te ~é a buscar a las ocho** I'll pick you up at eight • **pasa a verme cuando quieras** come round whenever you like

6 (*= cambiar de situación*) to go • **el equipo ha pasado a primera división** the team has gone up to the first division • **y luego ~on a otra cosa** and then they went on to something else • **ha pasado de ser tímida a no tenerle miedo a nada** she has gone from being shy to fearing nothing • **~ de teniente a general** to go from lieutenant to general • **~ a ser** to become • **en muy poco tiempo ha pasado a ser un gran profesional** he has become a real professional in a very short space of time

7 (*= transcurrir*) [*tiempo*] to pass, go by • **han pasado cuatro años** four years have passed *o* gone by • **el tiempo pasa deprisa** time passes *o* goes so quickly • **¡cómo pasa el tiempo!** how time flies! • **ya ha pasado una hora** it's been an hour already

8 (*= acabar*) [*problema, situación*] to be over; [*efectos*] to wear off • **ha pasado la crisis** the crisis is over • **ya pasó aquello** that's all over (and done with) now

9 (*= aceptarse*) • **puede ~** it's passable, it's OK • **por esta vez pase** I'll let it go this time • **que me llames carroza, pase, pero fascista, no** you can call me an old fuddy-duddy if you like, but not a fascist

10 pasar por a (= *atravesar, caber*) to go through • **el hilo pasa por el agujero** the thread goes through the hole • **pasamos por un túnel muy largo** we went through a very long tunnel • **no pasamos por el pueblo** we didn't go through the village • **el río pasa por la ciudad** the river flows *o* goes through the city • **~ por la aduana** to go through customs • **está pasando por un mal momento** he's going through a bad patch • **no creo que el sofá pase por esa puerta** I don't think the settee will go through the door
b (= *depender de*) to depend on • **el futuro de la empresa pasa por este acuerdo** the company's future depends on *o* hangs on this agreement
c (= *ser considerado*) to pass as • **podrían perfectamente ~ por gemelos** they could easily pass as twins • **Juan pasa por francés** most people think Juan is French • **hacerse ~ por** to pass o.s. off as • **se hace ~ por médico** he passes himself off as a doctor

11 (*otras formas preposicionales*) **pasar a** (+ *infin*) (= *empezar*) • **paso ahora a explicar mi postura** I will now go on to explain my position • **~ a decir algo** to go on to say sth • **ya va siendo hora de ~ a la acción** it is time for action
pasar de (= *exceder*) • **pasa ya de los 70** he's over 70 • **esto pasa de ser una broma** this is beyond a joke • **no pasa de ser un jugador mediocre** he's no more than an average player • **no pasan de 60 los que lo tienen** those who have it do not number more than 60, fewer than 60 people have it • **yo de ahí no paso** that's as far as I'm prepared to go • **de ésta no pasa** this is the very last time • **de hoy no pasa que le escriba** I'll write to him this very day
pasar sin • **tendrá que ~ sin coche** he'll have to get by *o* manage without a car • **no puede ~ sin ella** he can't manage without her

12 (*Naipes*) to pass • **yo paso** pass

13 (*esp Esp*)* (= *mostrarse indiferente*) • **yo paso** count me out • **~ de algo/algn:** • **yo paso de política** I'm not into politics • **paso de todo** I couldn't care less • **pasa olímpicamente de todo lo que le dicen** he doesn't take the blindest bit of notice of anything they say to him • **paso de ti, chaval** I couldn't care less about you, pal

VERBO TRANSITIVO

1 (*= dar, entregar*) (*gen*) to pass; (*en una serie*) to pass on • **¿me pasas la sal, por favor?** could you pass (me) the salt, please? • **le pasó el sobre** he handed *o* passed her the envelope • **pásale una nota con disimulo** slip him a note • **cuando termines pásasela a Isabel** when you've finished pass it on to Isabel

2 (*= traspasar*) [+ *río, frontera*] to cross; [+ *límite*] to go beyond • **el túnel pasa la montaña** the tunnel goes right through the mountain • **esto pasa los límites de lo razonable** this goes beyond the realm of what is reasonable

3 (*= llevar*) • **nos ~on a ver al director** they took us to see the manager • **nos ~on a otra habitación** they moved us into another room • **he pasado mi despacho al dormitorio** I've moved my office into the bedroom

4 (*= hacer atravesar*) • **pasa el alambre por este agujero** put the wire through this hole • **pasó el hilo por el ojo de la aguja** she threaded the thread through the eye of the needle

5 (*= colar*) to strain • **~ el café por el colador** to strain the coffee

6 (*= introducir*) [+ *moneda falsa*] to pass (off); [+ *contrabando*] to smuggle • **han pasado billetes falsos** they've passed (off) forged notes • **han pasado un alijo de cocaína por la frontera** a consignment of cocaine has been smuggled across the border

7 (*= hacer deslizar*) • **voy a ~le un trapo** I'm going to wipe it down • **~ la mano por algo** to run one's hand over sth • **~ el cepillo por el pelo** to run a brush through one's hair • **~ la aspiradora por la alfombra** to vacuum the carpet, run the vacuum cleaner over the carpet • **~ la aspiradora** to do the vacuuming

8 (*= deslizar*) to slip • **le pasó el brazo por los hombros/la cintura** she slipped *o* put her arm around his shoulders/waist

9 (*= contagiar*) to give • **me has pasado tu catarro** you've given me your cold

10 (*= volver*) [+ *página*] to turn • **MODISMO:** • **~ página** to make a fresh start

11 (*= escribir*) • **~ algo a limpio** to make a neat *o* fair *o* clean copy of sth • **~ algo a máquina** to type sth up

12 (*= tragar*) (*lit*) to swallow; (*fig*) to bear, stand • **no puedo ~ esta pastilla** I can't swallow this pill, I can't get this pill down • **no puedo ~ a ese hombre** I can't bear *o* stand that man

13 (*= tolerar*) • **se lo pasan todo** they let him get away with anything • **no te voy a ~ más** I'm not going to indulge you any more

14 (*= aprobar*) [+ *examen*] to pass

15 (*= proyectar*) [+ *película, programa*] to show, screen

16 (*= poner en contacto*) • **te paso con Pedro** (*al mismo teléfono*) I'll put you on to Pedro; (*a distinto teléfono*) I'll put you through to Pedro

17 (*= realizar*) • **pasa consulta** *o* **visita a unas 700 personas diarias** he sees 700 patients a day; ▷ **revista**

18 (*= superar*) • **los pasa a todos en inteligencia** she's more intelligent than any of them • **para ganar debes ~ a muchos contrincantes** to win you have to beat a lot of opponents • **me pasa ya 3cm** he's already 3cm taller than I am

19 (*Aut*) to pass, overtake

20 (*= omitir*) • **~ algo por alto** to overlook sth • **~ por alto un detalle** to overlook a detail

21 (*+ tiempo*) to spend • **~ las vacaciones** to spend one's holidays • **voy a ~ el fin de semana con ella** I'm going to spend the weekend with her • **fuimos a ~ el día en la playa** we went to the seaside for the day • **lo ~emos tan ricamente** we'll have such a good time
pasarlo (+ *adv*) • **~lo bien** to have a good time • **¡que lo pases bien!** have a good time!, enjoy yourself! • **~lo mal** to have a bad time • **lo pasamos muy mal** we had an awful time

22 (*= dejar atrás*) • **hemos pasado el aniversario** the anniversary has passed, the anniversary is behind us • **ya hemos pasado lo peor** we're over the worst now, the worst is behind us now

23 (*= sufrir*) • **ha pasado una mala racha** she's been through a bad patch • **ha pasado muchas enfermedades** he's had a lot of illnesses • **~ frío** to be cold • **~ hambre** to be hungry

24 (*Cono Sur*)* (= *engañar*) to cheat, swindle

VERBO PRONOMINAL pasarse

1 (*= cesar*) • **¿se te ha pasado el mareo?** have you stopped feeling dizzy? • **ya se te ~á** [*enfado, disgusto*] you'll get over it; [*dolor*] it'll stop

2 (*= perder*) to miss • **se me pasó el turno** I missed my turn • **que no se te pase la oportunidad** don't miss this chance

3 (*= trasladarse*) to go over • **~se al enemigo** to go over to the enemy

4 (*= estropearse*) [*flor etc*] to fade; [*carne, pescado*] to go bad *o* off; [*fruta*] to go bad *o* soft; [*ropa*] to show signs of wear, get threadbare • **no se ~á si se tapa la botella** it will keep if you put the cap back on the bottle

5 (= *recocerse*) • **se ha pasado el arroz** the rice is overcooked
6 (*tornillo, tuerca*) to get overscrewed
7* (= *excederse*) • **está bien hacer ejercicio pero no hay que ~se** it's good to exercise but there's no point in overdoing it • **¡no te pases, o nos echarán del bar!** steady on *o* cool it or they'll throw us out of the bar!* • **¡no te pases, que te voy a dar una torta!** just watch it or I'll smack you in the face! • **¡te has pasado, tío!** (*censurando*) you've really gone and done it now!; (*felicitando*) well done, man!*, nice one!* • **se pasa en mostrar agradecimiento** he overdoes the gratitude • **te has pasado mucho con ella, gritándole así** you went much too far shouting at her like that • **~se de:** • **se pasa de bueno/generoso** he's too good/generous • **~se de listo** to be too clever by half • **~se de la raya** to go too far, overstep the mark
8 (+ *tiempo*) to spend • **se ha pasado todo el día leyendo** he has spent the whole day reading
9 (= *olvidarse de*) • **se le pasó la fecha del examen** he forgot the date of the exam • **se me pasó llamarle** I forgot to ring him
10 • **no se le pasa nada** nothing escapes him, he doesn't miss a thing
11 (*seguido de preposición*) **pasarse por** [+ *lugar*] • **pásate por casa si tienes tiempo** come round if you've got time • **ya que tienes que ~te por el banco ingrésame este talón** seeing as you have to go to the bank anyway, you can pay this cheque in for me • **se me pasó por la cabeza** *o* **imaginación** it crossed my mind
pasarse sin algo to do without sth
SUSTANTIVO MASCULINO†
• **un modesto ~** a modest competence
• **tener un buen ~** to be well off

PASAR

En expresiones temporales

▹ *Se traduce por* **spend** *cuando* **pasar** *tiene un uso transitivo y queremos indicar un período de tiempo concreto, seguido de la actividad que en ese tiempo se desarrolla, o del lugar:*

Me pasé la tarde escribiendo cartas
I spent the evening writing letters
Ha pasado toda su vida en el campo
He has spent his whole life in the country

▹ *En cambio, cuando se describe la forma en que se pasa el tiempo mediante un adjetivo, se debe emplear en inglés la construcción* **have + (a) +** *adjetivo + sustantivo:*

Pasamos una tarde entretenida
We had a lovely afternoon
Pasamos un rato estupendo jugando al squash
We had a fantastic time playing squash

la expresión **pasar el rato** *se traduce por* **pass the time**:

No sé qué hacer para pasar el rato
I don't know what to do to pass the time

▹ *Cuando el uso es intransitivo,* **pasar** *se traduce por* **pass** *o* **go by**.

A medida que pasaba el tiempo se deprimía cada vez más
As time passed *o* went by, he became more and more depressed

Para otros usos y ejemplos ver la entrada.

pasarela SF (= *puente*) footbridge; (*Teat*) catwalk, walkway; [*de modelos*] catwalk; (*Náut*) gangway, gangplank ▸ **pasarela telescópica** airport walkway, jetty walkway
pasarrato SM (*Caribe, Méx*) = **pasatiempo**
pasatiempo SM **1** (= *entretenimiento*) pastime; (= *afición*) hobby
2 pasatiempos (*en periódicos, revistas*) puzzles
pascana SF **1** (*And, Cono Sur*) (= *fonda*) wayside inn
2 (*And, Cono Sur*) (= *etapa*) stage, part (of a journey)
3 (*And*) *part of a journey done without stopping*
pascícola ADJ grazing (*antes de s*), pasture (*antes de s*)
Pascua SF **1** (= *Navidad*) Christmas time, Christmas period; (= *Epifanía*) Epiphany • **¡felices ~s!** merry Christmas! ▸ **Pascua(s) de Navidad** Christmas
2 (*en Semana Santa*) Easter ▸ **Pascua de Pentecostés** Pentecost, Whitsun, Whitsuntide ▸ **Pascua de Resurrección, Pascua florida** Easter
3 ▸ **Pascua de los hebreos, Pascua de los judíos** Passover
4 • MODISMOS: • **de ~s a Ramos** once in a blue moon • **estar como unas ~s** to be as happy as a lark • **hacer la ~ a algn*** (= *molestar*) to annoy sb, bug sb*; (= *perjudicar*) to do the dirty on sb • **¡que se hagan la ~!** (*Esp**) they can lump it! • **y santas ~s** and that's that, and that's the lot
pascual ADJ Paschal • **cordero ~** (older) lamb
pascualina SF (*Arg, Uru*) *spinach and cheese quiche*
pase SM **1** (= *documento*) pass ▸ **pase de embarque** (*Aer*) boarding pass ▸ **pase de favor** (*Pol*) safe conduct; (= *invitación*) complimentary ticket ▸ **pase de prensa** press pass ▸ **pase de temporada** (*Teat, Mús*) season ticket ▸ **pase pernocta** (*Mil*) overnight pass
2 (*Cine*) showing ▸ **pase de modas, pase de modelos** fashion show
3 (*Com*) permit
4 (*Jur*) licence, license (*EEUU*)
5 (*Dep*) pass ▸ **pase adelante** forward pass ▸ **pase (hacia) atrás** back pass
6 ▸ **pase de lista** (*Mil*) roll call
7 (*Taur*) ▸ **pase de pecho** chest-level pass
8‡ (= *contrabando*) drug smuggling; (*LAm‡*) (= *dosis*) fix‡
paseandero ADJ (*Cono Sur*) fond of strolling
paseante SMF **1** (*gen*) walker, stroller; (= *transeúnte*) passer-by; (*tb* **paseante en corte**) (*pey*) loafer, idler
2† (= *pretendiente*) suitor
pasear ▹ CONJUG 1a VT **1** [+ *perro, niño*] to take for a walk, walk
2 (= *exhibir*) [+ *ropa, coche*] to parade, show off
3 • **~ la calle a una muchacha** (*Esp†*) to walk up and down the street where a girl lives
4 (*CAm*) [+ *dinero*] to squander
5 (*Esp*) (*Hist**) to execute summarily
VI, VPR **pasearse 1** (*gen*) to go for a walk, go for a stroll; (= *de un lado a otro*) to walk about, walk up and down • **~ en bicicleta** to go for a ride, go cycling • **~ en coche** to go for a drive, go for a run in the car • **~ a caballo** to ride, go riding • **~ en bote** to go sailing
2 (*Esp*) (= *estar ocioso*) to idle, loaf about
3 • **~se por un tema** (*Esp*) to deal superficially with a subject
4 • **~se** (*Méx*) to take a day off
paseíllo SM (*Taur*) *ceremonial entry of bullfighters*
paseíto SM little walk, gentle stroll
paseo SM **1** (*gen*) walk, stroll; (= *excursión*) outing • **dar un ~** (*andando*) to go for a walk *o* stroll, take a walk *o* stroll; (*en coche*) to go for a ride • **estar de ~** to be out for a walk • **llevar** *o* **sacar a un niño de ~** to take a child out for a walk • MODISMOS: • **dar el ~ a algn*** to take sb for a ride* • **enviar** *o* **mandar a ~*** [+ *estudios, trabajo*] to jack in* • **enviar** *o* **mandar a algn a ~*** to tell sb to go to blazes*, send sb packing, chuck sb out • **no va a ser un ~** (*Esp*) it's not going to be easy • **¡vete a ~!‡** get lost!‡ ▸ **paseo a caballo** ride (on horseback) ▸ **paseo de vigilancia** round, tour of inspection ▸ **paseo en barco** boat trip ▸ **paseo en bicicleta** (bike) ride ▸ **paseo en coche** drive, ride ▸ **paseo espacial** space walk ▸ **paseo por la naturaleza** nature trail
2 (= *avenida*) parade, avenue ▸ **paseo marítimo** promenade, esplanade
3 (= *distancia*) short walk • **entre las dos casas no hay más que un ~** it's only a short walk between the two houses
4 ▸ **paseo cívico** (*Méx*) procession, fiesta procession
5 (*Esp**) (*Hist*) *(journey leading to the) summary execution of a political opponent* • **dar el ~ a algn** (*Hist*) to execute sb summarily; (*moderno*) to bump sb off‡
pasero SM (*And*) ferryman
pashá SM = **pachá**
pashmina SF pashmina
pasible ADJ (*liter*) able to endure, long-suffering
pasillear ▹ CONJUG 1a VI (*Parl*) to engage in lobby discussions, lobby
pasilleo SM lobby discussions (*pl*), lobbying
pasillo SM **1** (= *corredor*) (*en casa, oficina*) corridor; (*en avión, teatro*) aisle ▸ **pasillo aéreo** air corridor, air lane ▸ **pasillo móvil, pasillo rodante** travelator
2 (*Pol*) lobby • **hacer ~s** to engage in lobby discussions, lobby
3 (*Teat*) (= *pieza corta*) short piece, sketch
pasión SF **1** (= *amor intenso*) passion • **noches de ~** nights of passion • **la quería con ~** he loved her passionately • **tener ~ por algn** to love sb passionately
2 (= *gran afición*) passion • **le gusta el cine con ~** he's passionate about films, he's mad about films • **tener ~ por algo** to have a passion for sth • **tiene ~ por los animales** he has a passion for animals, he loves animals
3 (= *exaltación*) passion • **lo mató cegada por la ~** she killed him in a blind fit of passion • **defendía su postura con ~** she argued her case with passion *o* passionately
4 (*Rel*) • **la Pasión** the Passion
pasional ADJ passionate • **crimen ~** crime of passion
pasionaria SF passionflower
pasito ADV (*Col*) gently, softly
pasiva SF (*Ling*) passive (voice)
pasivamente ADV passively
pasividad SF passiveness, passivity
pasivo ADJ **1** [+ *persona, comportamiento*] passive • **es un niño muy ~ y nunca toma la iniciativa** he is a very passive child, he never takes the initiative
2 (*Ling*) passive • **la voz pasiva** the passive voice
SM (*Com, Econ*) liabilities (*pl*); [*de cuenta*] debit side ▸ **pasivo circulante, pasivo corriente** current liabilities (*pl*) ▸ **pasivo diferido** deferred liabilities (*pl*)
pasma‡ (*Esp*) SMF cop*
SF • **la ~** the fuzz‡, the cops* (*pl*)
pasmado ADJ **1** (= *asombrado*) astonished, amazed • **dejar ~ a algn** to astonish *o* amaze sb • **estar** *o* **quedar ~ de** to be amazed at, be astonished at • **mirar con cara de ~** to look in astonishment at

2 (= *atontado*) stunned, dumbfounded • **se quedó ahí ~** he just stood there gaping • **¡oye, ~!*** hey, you dope!
3 (= *frío*) frozen stiff; (*Bot*) frostbitten
4 (*LAm*) [*herida*] infected; [*persona*] unhealthy-looking, ill-looking
5 (*CAm, Méx*) (= *estúpido*) stupid; (= *torpe*) clumsy
6 (*LAm*) [*fruta*] overripe

pasmar ▷ CONJUG 1a (VT) **1** (= *asombrar*) to amaze, astonish
2 (= *atontar*) to stun, dumbfound
3 (= *enfriar*) to chill to the bone; (*Bot*) to nip, cut
(VPR) **pasmarse 1** (= *asombrarse*) to be amazed, be astonished (**de** at); (= *maravillarse*) to marvel, wonder (**de** at)
2 (= *estar helado*) to be chilled to the bone; (= *resfriarse*) to catch a chill
3 (*LAm*) (*Med*) (= *infectarse*) to become infected; (= *enfermar*) to fall ill; (*con trismo*) to get lockjaw; (*con fiebre*) to catch a fever
4 [*colores*] to fade
5 (*Caribe, Méx*) [*fruta*] to wither

pasmarota (SF), **pasmarotada** (SF) display of shocked surprise, exaggerated reaction

pasmarote* (SMF) idiot, halfwit • **¡no te quedes ahí como un ~!** don't just stand there like an idiot!

pasmazón (SM) (*CAm, Caribe, Méx*) = **pasmo**

pasmo (SM) **1** (= *asombro*) amazement, astonishment; (= *admiración*) wonder • **es el ~ de cuantos lo ven** it is a marvel *o* a source of wonder to all who see it
2 (= *enfriamiento*) chill • **le dio un ~*** he was frozen stiff
3 (*Med*) (= *trismo*) lockjaw, tetanus
4 (*LAm*) (= *fiebre*) fever

pasmosamente (ADV) (= *asombrosamente*) amazingly, astonishingly; (= *admirablemente*) wonderfully

pasmoso (ADJ) (= *asombroso*) amazing, astonishing; (= *admirable*) wonderful

paso¹ (ADJ) dried • **higo ~** dried fig • **ciruela pasa** prune • **uva pasa** raisin

paso² (SM) **1** (= *acción de pasar*) • **contemplaban el ~ de la procesión desde un balcón** they watched the procession go by from a balcony • **para evitar el ~ del aire** to prevent the air getting through • **por estas fechas tiene lugar el ~ de las cigüeñas por nuestra región** this is the time of year when the storks fly over our region • **los detuvieron en el ~ del estrecho** they were arrested while crossing the channel • **el presidente, a su ~ por nuestra ciudad ...** the president, during his visit to our city ... • **el huracán arrasó con todo lo que encontró a su ~** the hurricane flattened everything in its path • **con el ~ del tiempo** with (the passing of) time • **"prohibido el paso"** "no entry" • **ceder el ~** to give way, yield (*EEUU*) • **"ceda el ~"** "give way", "yield" (*EEUU*) • **dar ~ a algo**: • **el invierno dio ~ a la primavera** winter gave way to spring • **ahora vamos a dar ~ a nuestro corresponsal en Lisboa** we now go over to our correspondent in Lisbon • **las protestas dieron ~ a una huelga** the protests led to *o* were followed by a strike • **de ~**: • **mencionaron el tema solo de ~** they only mentioned the matter in passing • **¿puedes ir al supermercado, de ~ que vas a la farmacia?** could you go to the supermarket on your way to the chemist's? • **de ~ recuérdale que tiene un libro nuestro** remind him that he's got a book of ours while you're at it • **el banco me pilla de ~** the bank is on my way • **dicho sea de ~** incidentally • **entrar de ~** to drop in • **estar de ~** to be passing through • **están solo de ~ por Barcelona** they're just passing through Barcelona ▸ **paso del Ecuador** *party or trip organized by university students to celebrate the halfway stage in their degree course* ▸ **paso franco, paso libre** free passage; ▷ **ave**
2 (= *camino*) way; (*Arquit*) passage; (*Geog*) pass; (*Náut*) strait • **estás en mitad del ~** you're blocking the way • **¡paso!** make way! • **la policía le abría ~** the police cleared a path for him • **abrirse ~** to make one's way • **se abrió ~ entre la multitud** he made his way through the crowd • **se abrió ~ a tiros** he shot his way through • **se abrieron ~ luchando** they fought their way through • **cerrar el ~** to block the way • **dejar el ~ libre** to leave the way open • **dejar ~ a algn** to let sb past • **impedir el ~** to block the way • MODISMOS: • **salir al ~ a algn** to collar sb • **salir al ~ de algo** to be quick to deny sth • **han salido al ~ de la acusación** they've been quick to deny the accusation • **salir del ~** to get out of trouble ▸ **paso a desnivel, paso a distinto nivel** (*Aut*) flyover, overpass (*EEUU*) ▸ **paso a nivel** level crossing, grade crossing (*EEUU*) ▸ **paso a nivel sin barrera** unguarded level crossing ▸ **paso (de) cebra** (*Esp*) zebra crossing, crosswalk (*EEUU*) ▸ **paso de peatones** pedestrian crossing, crosswalk (*EEUU*) ▸ **paso elevado** (*Aut*) flyover, overpass (*EEUU*) ▸ **paso fronterizo** border crossing ▸ **paso inferior** underpass, subway ▸ **paso salmonero** salmon ladder ▸ **paso subterráneo** underpass, subway ▸ **paso superior** (*Aut*) flyover, overpass (*EEUU*)
3 (*al andar*) (= *acción*) step; (= *ruido*) footstep; (= *huella*) footprint • **he oído ~s** I heard footsteps • **coger el ~** to fall into step • **dar un ~** to take a step • **¿ha dado ya sus primeros ~s?** has she taken her first steps yet? • **no da ni un ~ sin ella** he never goes anywhere without her • **dirigir sus ~s hacia** to head towards • **dar un ~ en falso** (= *tropezar*) to miss one's footing; (= *equivocarse*) to make a false move • **hacer ~s** (*Baloncesto*) to travel (with the ball) • **volvió sobre sus ~s** she retraced her steps • MODISMOS: • **a cada ~** at every step, at every turn • **a ~s agigantados** by leaps and bounds • **el proyecto avanza a ~s agigantados** the project is advancing by leaps and bounds • **la demanda aumenta a ~s agigantados** demand is increasing at a rate of knots *o* extremely quickly • **andar en malos ~s** to be mixed up in shady affairs • **dar un mal ~** make a false move • **~ a ~** step by step • **por sus ~s contados** step by step, systematically • **seguir los ~s a algn** to tail sb • **seguir los ~s de algn** to follow in sb's footsteps ▸ **paso adelante** (*lit, fig*) step forward ▸ **paso a dos** pas de deux ▸ **paso atrás** (*lit, fig*) step backwards • **dio un ~ atrás** he took a step backwards
4 (= *modo de andar*) [*de persona*] walk, gait; [*de caballo*] gait • **caminaba con ~ decidido** he was walking purposefully • **acelerar el ~** to go faster, speed up • **aflojar el ~** to slow down • **apretar** *o* **avivar el ~** to go faster, speed up • **a buen ~** at a good pace • **iba andando a buen ~** I was walking at a good pace • **las conversaciones marchan a buen ~** the talks are proceeding at a good pace *o* rate • **establecer el ~** to make the pace, set the pace • **a ~ lento** at a slow pace, slowly • **a ~ ligero** (*gen*) at a swift pace; (*Mil*) at the double • **llevar el ~** to keep in step, keep time • **marcar el ~** (*gen*) to keep time; (*Mil*) to mark time • **a ~ redoblado** (*LAm*) (*Mil*) at the double • **romper el ~** to break step • MODISMO: • **a ~ de tortuga** at a snail's pace ▸ **paso de ambladura, paso de andadura** (*Equitación*) amble ▸ **paso de ganso** (*LAm*), **paso de (la) oca** goose step ▸ **paso de vals** waltz step
5 (= *ritmo*) rate, pace • **a este ~** at this rate • **a este ~ no terminarán nunca** at this rate they'll never finish • **al ~ que vamos no acabaremos nunca** at the rate we're going we'll never finish
6 (= *distancia*) • **vive a un ~ de aquí** he lives round the corner from here • **estaba a unos diez ~s** it was about ten paces away • **de eso al terrorismo no hay más que un ~** it's a small step from there to terrorism
7 (= *avance*) step • **es un ~ hacia nuestro objetivo** it's a step towards our objective • **el matrimonio es un ~ muy importante en la vida** marriage is an important step in life • MODISMOS: • **dar el primer ~** • **dar los primeros ~s** to make the first move
8 (*Téc*) [*de tornillo*] pitch; [*de contador, teléfono*] unit
9 (*Teat, Hist*) sketch, interlude
10 (*Rel*) (*en procesión*) *float in Holy Week procession, with statues representing part of Easter story*; ▷ SEMANA SANTA
11 ▸ **paso de armas** (*Mil, Hist*) passage of arms
12 (*LAm*) (= *vado*) ford
(ADV) softly, gently • **¡paso!** not so fast!, easy there!

pasodoble (SM) paso doble

pasón‡ (SM) = **pasada**

pasoso (ADJ) **1** (*LAm*) (= *poroso*) porous, permeable; (= *absorbente*) absorbent
2 (*Cono Sur*) (= *sudoroso*) perspiring, sweaty
3 (*And*) (*Med*) contagious

pasota* (ADJ INV) **1** (*Esp*) [*persona*] • **Jesús va de ~ por la vida** Jesús doesn't care much about anything • **filosofía ~** couldn't-care-less attitude
2 (*Méx*) (= *pasado de moda*) passé, out of fashion
(SMF) • **eres un ~** you just don't care, do you?

pasote* (SM) (*Esp*) (= *ultraje*) outrage; (= *exceso*) exaggeration

pasotismo (SM) (*Esp*) couldn't-care-less attitude

paspa (SF) (*And*), **paspadura** (SF) (*And, Cono Sur*) chapped skin, cracked skin

pasparse ▷ CONJUG 1a (VPR) (*And, Cono Sur*) [*piel*] to chap, crack

paspartú (SM) passe-partout

pasquín (SM) **1** (*Pol*) wall poster
2 (*Literat*) skit, lampoon

pássim (ADV) passim

pasta (SF) **1** (= *masa*) paste ▸ **pasta de celulosa** wood pulp ▸ **pasta de coca** cocaine paste ▸ **pasta de dientes** toothpaste ▸ **pasta de madera** wood pulp ▸ **pasta dentífrica** toothpaste ▸ **pasta de papel** paper pulp
2 [*de pan*] dough; (*en repostería*) pastry; (= *pastelillo*) biscuit, cookie (*EEUU*) ▸ **pasta quebrada** shortcrust pastry ▸ **pastas de té** biscuits, cookies (*EEUU*)
3 (= *macarrones, fideos*) pasta ▸ **pasta al huevo** egg pasta ▸ **pasta de sopa** pasta for soup
4 (*para untar*) paste ▸ **pasta de anchoas** anchovy paste ▸ **pasta de carne** meat paste
5* (= *dinero*) money, cash, dough* • **¡suelta la ~!** hand over the dough!* • **me ha costado una ~ gansa** it cost me an arm and a leg*
6 (*Tip*) boards (*pl*) • **media ~** half-binding • **libro en ~** hardback ▸ **pasta española** marbled leather binding
7 (= *talante*) • **tiene ~ de futbolista** he has the makings of a footballer • **ser de buena ~** to be a good sort

pastaje (SM) (*And, CAm, Cono Sur*), **pastal**

SM (*LAm*) (= *pastizal*) pasture, grazing land; (= *pasto*) grass, pasture

pastar ▸ CONJUG 1a VT, VI to graze

pastear ▸ CONJUG 1a VT to graze

pastejón SM solid mass, lump

pastel SM **1** (*Culin*) (= *dulce*) cake; [*de carne*] pie • **"pasteles"** "pastry (*sing*)", confectionery (*sing*) • **MODISMO:** • **repartirse el ~** to divide up the cake *o* (*EEUU*) pie ▸ **pastel de boda** wedding cake ▸ **pastel de cumpleaños** birthday cake
2 (*Arte*) pastel • **pintura al ~** pastel drawing
3* (= *chanchullo*) scam* • **se descubrió el ~** the scam came to light*
4† (= *chapuza*) botch, mess
ADJ pastel • **tono ~** pastel shade

pastelado SM (*Caribe*) choc-ice, ice-cream bar (*EEUU*)

pastelear ▸ CONJUG 1a VI **1** (= *trampear*) to go in for sharp practice; (= *maquinar*) to plot; (= *chanchullear*) to make cynical compromises
2 (= *temporizar*) to stall, spin it out to gain time
3* (= *adular*) to creep*, be a bootlicker*

pastelería SF **1** (= *arte*) pastry-making, (art of) confectionery
2 (= *pasteles*) cakes (*pl*), pastries (*pl*)
3 (= *tienda*) baker's, cake shop

pastelero/a ADJ **1** (*Culin*) • **masa pastelera** pastry • **rodillo ~** rolling-pin
2 • **MODISMO:** • **no tengo ni pastelera idea*** (*euf*) I haven't a clue*
3 (*Cono Sur*) (= *intrigante*) meddlesome, intriguing
SM/F **1** (*Culin*) pastry cook
2 (*Com*) baker
3 (*LAm*) (*Pol*) turncoat
4 (*And‡*) (= *traficante*) drug trafficker

pastelillo SM (*Culin*) tart ▸ **pastelillo de hígado de ganso** (*Esp*) pâté de foie gras ▸ **pastelillo de mantequilla** (*Esp*) pat of butter

pastelón SM (*Cono Sur*) large paving stone

pasterizar ▸ CONJUG 1f VT = **pasteurizar**

pasteurización SF pasteurization

pasteurizado ADJ pasteurized

pasteurizar ▸ CONJUG 1f VT to pasteurize

pastiche SM pastiche

pastilla SF **1** (*Med*) tablet, pill; (= *anticonceptivo*) Pill ▸ **pastilla para la tos** cough drop
2 (*de jabón*) bar; (*de chocolate*) piece, square • **MODISMO:** • **ir a toda ~** (*Esp**) to go full-belt* ▸ **pastilla de caldo** stock cube ▸ **pastilla de freno(s)** (*Aut*) brake pad *o* shoe ▸ **pastilla de fuego** firelighter
3 (*Inform*) chip ▸ **pastilla de silicio** silicon chip
ADJ INV (*Esp‡*) (= *aburrido*) deadly boring

pastillero[1]/a‡ SM/F pill popper‡

pastillero[2] SM pillbox

pastinaca SF parsnip

pastizal SM pasture

pastizara‡ SF • **una ~** a whole heap of money*

pasto SM **1** (*Agr*) (= *acción*) grazing; (= *sitio*) pasture; (= *hierba*) grass, pasture; (= *pienso*) feed, fodder; (*LAm*) (= *césped*) lawn • **derecho de ~** grazing rights • **un sitio abundante en ~s** a place with rich grazing • **echar el ganado al ~** to put the animals out to pasture ▸ **pasto seco** fodder
2 (*fig*) (= *alimento*) food, nourishment; [*del fuego*] fuel • **es ~ de la murmuración** it is a subject for gossip • **fue ~ del fuego** *o* **de las llamas** the flames devoured it • **ser ~ de la actualidad** to be newsworthy • **sirvió de ~ a los mirones** the onlookers lapped it up* ▸ **pasto espiritual** spiritual nourishment
3 • **MODISMO:** • **a todo ~*** abundantly • **beber a todo ~** to drink for all one is worth, drink to excess • **cita refranes a todo ~** he quotes vast quantities of proverbs • **correr a todo ~** to run like hell* • **había fruta a todo ~** there was fruit in unlimited quantities
4 • **vino de ~** ordinary wine
5 (*Méx‡*) (= *hierba*) grass‡, pot‡

pastón‡ SM • **un ~** a whole heap of money*

pastor(a) SM/F **1** (*Agr*) [*de ovejas*] shepherd/shepherdess; [*de cabras*] goatherd; [*de vacas*] cowherd • **el Buen Pastor** the Good Shepherd
2 (*Rel*) minister, clergyman/clergywoman
SM (*Zool*) sheepdog • **viejo ~ inglés** old English sheepdog ▸ **pastor alemán** Alsatian, German shepherd ▸ **pastor escocés** rough collie

pastorada SF Nativity procession, moving tableau of the Nativity

pastoral ADJ pastoral
SF **1** (*Literat*) pastoral
2 (*Rel*) pastoral letter

pastorear ▸ CONJUG 1a VT **1** (*Agr*) to shepherd; [+ *rebaño*] to pasture, graze; (= *cuidar*) to look after
2 (*Rel*) to guide, shepherd
3 (*LAm**) (= *acechar*) to lie in wait for
4 (*CAm*) (= *mimar*) to spoil, pamper

pastorela SF (*Literat*) pastourelle

pastoreo SM grazing

pastoril ADJ (*Literat*) pastoral

pastoso ADJ **1** [*masa*] doughy; [*pasta*] pasty
2 [*lengua*] furry; [*voz, vino*] rich, mellow
3 (*Cono Sur*) (= *con hierba*) grassy
4 (*And**) (= *vago*) lazy

pastura SF **1** (= *campo*) pasture
2 (= *comida*) food, fodder, feed

pasturaje SM common pasture

pasudo ADJ (*Méx*) [*pelo*] kinky

pat SM (PL: **pats** [pat]) putt

pat. ABR (= **patente**) pat.

pata SF **1** (*Zool*) **a** (= *pierna*) leg • **~ delantera** front leg • **~ trasera** back *o* hind leg • **pantalones de ~ de elefante** flared trousers, flares • **de ~ negra** (*Esp*) [*cerdo, jamón*] prime • **un fútbol de ~ negra** top-notch football*
b (= *pie*) [*de mamífero*] (*tb Peletería*) paw; [*de ave*] foot ▸ **pata de cabra** (*Téc*) crowbar ▸ **pata de cangrejo** crab stick ▸ **pata de gallo** (*en tela*) houndstooth check; (= *disparate†*) silly remark, piece of nonsense • **una chaqueta de ~ de gallo** a houndstooth jacket ▸ **pata hendida** cloven hoof ▸ **patas de gallo** (*en el ojo*) crow's feet
2* [*de persona*] leg • **quita la ~, que no veo** get your leg out of the way, I can't see* • **es un diccionario con dos ~s** (*hum*) he's a walking dictionary, he's a dictionary on legs (*hum*) • **a ~*** on foot, on Shanks' pony*, on Shanks' mare (*EEUU**) • **a la ~ coja** hopping • **entró saltando a la ~ coja** he came hopping in • **a cuatro ~s** on all fours ▸ **pata de palo** wooden leg, peg leg
3 [*de mueble*] leg • **~s arriba** (= *invertido*) upside down; (= *revuelto*) in a complete mess, topsy-turvy* • **después de la mudanza estaba toda la casa ~s arriba** after the move the whole house was in a complete mess *o* was topsy-turvy*
4 (*Chile*) (= *etapa*) stage, leg
5 patas (*Chile**) (= *caradura*) cheek* (*sing*) • **tener ~s** to be brash, be cheeky*
6 • **MODISMOS:** • **a la ~** (*Chile**) to the letter • **enseñar la ~** to give oneself away • **estirar la ~*** to kick the bucket* • **hacer la ~ a algn** (*Chile**) to soft-soap sb*, suck up to sb* • **hacer algo con las ~s** (*Col, Méx**) to make a pig's ear of sth* • **a la ~ la llana** (*Esp**): • **estaba escrito a la ~ la llana** it was written in plain language • **aunque se ha hecho famosa, se sigue comportando a la ~ la llana** although she has become famous, she is as down to earth as ever • **mala ~** bad luck • **trae mala ~ casarse en martes** it's bad luck to get married on a Tuesday • **¡qué mala ~ tuviste!** you were really unlucky! • **meter ~** (*Cono Sur*) (*Aut*) to step on the gas* • **meter la ~** to put one's foot in it • **a ~ pelada** (*Chile, Perú**) in bare feet* • **sacar la ~** to give oneself away • **saltar en una ~** (*Cono Sur*) to jump with joy • **ser ~** (*Arg*) to be game*, be up for it* • **es ~ para todo** he's game for anything*, he's up for anything* • **ser ~ de perro** (*Chile, Méx**) to have itchy feet; ▹ **metedura, pato**
SM (*And**) **1** (= *amigo*) pal*, mate*, buddy (*EEUU*)
2 (= *tipo*) bloke‡

pataca SF Jerusalem artichoke

patache SM **1** (= *barca*) flat-bottomed boat
2 (*And*) (= *sopa*) soup; (= *comida‡*) food, grub‡, chow (*EEUU‡*)

patacho SM **1** (*Cono Sur*) (= *lancha*) flat-bottomed boat
2 (*CAm, Méx*) (= *recua*) train of mules

patacón SM **1** (*And*) (*Culin*) slice of fried banana
2 (*Cono Sur*) (= *moretón*) bruise, welt

patada SF **1** (= *puntapié*) kick • **una ~ en la espinilla** a kick in the shin • **abrieron la puerta de una ~** they kicked the door open • **a ~s:** • **echar a algn a ~s** to kick *o* boot sb out • **tratar a algn a ~s** to treat sb very badly *o* like dirt* • **dar ~s** to kick • **ya noto como da pataditas** I can feel it kicking now • **dar** *o* **meter** *o* **pegar una ~ a algn/algo** to kick sb/sth, give sb/sth a kick • **le dio una fuerte ~ al balón** he kicked the ball hard, he gave the ball a hard kick • **¡como te meta una ~ en el culo, verás!*** if you don't watch it, I'll give you a kick up the arse!* • **cada vez que habla le mete una ~ al diccionario** (*hum*) every time he opens his mouth his words come out all wrong • **dar ~s en el suelo** to stamp (the floor)
2 • **MODISMOS:** • **a ~s*** (= *en gran cantidad*): • **ejemplos de eso los hay a ~s** there are loads of examples of that* • **había comida a ~s** there was loads *o* heaps of food* • **a las ~s** (*LAm**) really badly • **hace todo a las ~s** he makes a real mess of everything, he does everything really badly • **dar la ~ a*** [+ *empleado*] to kick out*, give the boot to*; [+ *novio, marido*] to ditch*, dump* • **darse ~s por algo:** • **la gente se daba ~s por conseguir una entrada** people would do anything to get a ticket • **dar cien ~s a algn*** to bug sb* • **me da cien ~s no poder hablar con libertad** it bugs me that I can't speak freely* • **de la ~** (*CAm, Méx**): • **me fue de la ~** it was a disaster, it all went pear-shaped on me* • **me cae de la ~** I can't stand the sight of him* • **en dos ~s*** (= *sin esfuerzo*) with no trouble at all; (= *en seguida*) in a jiffy* • **caer** *o* **sentar como una ~ en el estómago*** [*bebida, comida*] to upset one's stomach; [*acción*] to be like a kick in the teeth • **me cayó** *o* **sentó como una ~ en los cojones**‡ it really pissed me off**

patadón* SM (= *puntapié*) big kick; (*Dep*) long kick, long ball, long clearance

patagón/ona ADJ Patagonian
SM/F native/inhabitant of Patagonia • **los patagones** the people of Patagonia

Patagonia SF Patagonia • **voy a la ~** I'm going to Patagonia

patagónico ADJ Patagonian

patalear ▸ CONJUG 1a VI **1** (*en el suelo*) to

stamp (angrily)
2 [*bebé, niño*] to kick out
3 (= *protestar*) to protest; (= *montar follón*) to make a fuss • **por mí, que patalee** as far as I'm concerned he can make all the fuss he likes
pataleo (SM) **1** (*en el suelo*) stamping
2 (*en el aire*) kicking
3 (= *protesta*) protest; (= *follón*) scene, fuss • **derecho al ~** right to protest • **tener derecho al ~** to have the right to complain
pataleta* (SF) **1** (= *rabieta*) tantrum
2 (*Med*) (= *soponcio*) fit, convulsion
3 • **dar ~s** (*LAm*) [*niño*] to stamp one's feet
patán (SM) rustic, yokel, hick (*EEUU**); (*pey*) lout
pataplaf (EXCL), **pataplás** (EXCL), **pataplún** (EXCL) (*LAm*) bang!, crash!
patarata† (SF) **1** (= *afectación*) gush, affectation; (= *aspaviento*) emotional fuss, excessive show of feeling
2 (= *disparate*) silly thing; (= *bagatela*) triviality • **~s** nonsense (*sing*), tomfoolery (*sing*)
pataratero† (ADJ) **1** (= *afectado*) gushing, affected
2 (= *tonto*) silly
pataruco (ADJ) (*Caribe*) **1** (= *tosco*) coarse, rough
2 (= *cobarde*) cowardly
patasca (SF) (*And*) (*Culin*) *pork stew with corn*
• MODISMO: • **armar una ~*** to kick up a racket
patata (SF) (*Esp*) **1** (= *tubérculo*) potato • **puré de ~s** mashed potatoes (*pl*) ▸ **patata caliente** (*fig*) hot potato ▸ **patata de siembra** seed potato ▸ **patatas bravas** *fried potatoes with spicy tomato sauce* ▸ **patatas con su piel** jacket potatoes ▸ **patatas deshechas** mashed potatoes ▸ **patatas enteras** jacket potatoes ▸ **patatas fritas** (*en tiras*) chips, French fries (*EEUU*); (*de bolsa*) crisps, potato chips (*EEUU*) ▸ **patatas nuevas** new potatoes ▸ **patata temprana** early potato
2 • MODISMOS: • **ni ~*** nothing at all • **no entendió ni ~** he didn't understand a single word • **(no) me importa una ~** • **no se me da una ~** I don't care two hoots • **pasar la ~ caliente*** to pass the buck* • **ser una ~*** to be rubbish*
3** (= *vulva*) fanny**, beaver (*EEUU***)
patatal (SM), **patatar** (SM) potato field, potato patch
patatera (SF) potato plant
patatero* (ADJ) • **oficial ~** ranker; ▹ **rollo**
patatín* • MODISMOS: • **en el año ~** in such-and-such a year • **que (si) ~, que (si) patatán** this, that and the other • **y ~ patatán** and so on
patato* (ADJ) (*Caribe*), **patatuco*** (ADJ) (*Caribe*) short
patatús* (SM) (= *ataque*) fit*; (= *desmayo*) dizzy spell • **le daría un ~ si lo supiera** he'd have a fit if he knew*
paté (SM) pâté
pateada (SF) **1** (*Cono Sur*) (= *paseo largo*) long tiring walk
2 = **pateadura**
pateador (SM) (*Dep*) kicker
pateadura (SF), **pateamiento** (SM) **1** (*con los pies*) stamping, kicking
2 (*en discusión*) vehement denial; (*más agresiva*) violent interjection; (*Teat*) noisy protest, catcalls (*pl*)
patear¹ ▹ CONJUG 1a (VT) **1** (*en el suelo*) to stamp on; (= *dar patadas a*) to kick, boot; (*Dep*) [+ *pelota*] to kick
2 (*Esp**) (= *andar por*) to tramp round • **tuve que ~ toda la ciudad** I had to tramp round the whole town
3 (= *maltratar*) to treat roughly, treat inconsiderately; (*Teat*) (= *abuchear*) to boo, jeer
4 (*Caribe*) (= *insultar*) to abuse
5 • **la comida me ha pateado** (*Cono Sur**) the meal has upset my stomach
(VI) **1** (= *patalear*) to stamp one's foot; (*Teat*) to stamp
2 (*LAm*) [*arma, animal*] to kick
3* (= *ir a pata*) to walk (it); (*Cono Sur*) to go long distances on foot
4* (= *ir y venir*) to be always on the go, bustle about
(VPR) **patearse* 1** (= *recorrer a pie*) • **nos hemos pateado Madrid** we explored *o* did Madrid on foot
2 (= *malgastar*) • **~se el dinero** to blow one's money*
patear² ▹ CONJUG 1a (VI) to putt
patena (SF) paten
patentado (ADJ) patent(ed), proprietary (*frm*) • **marca patentada** registered trade mark
patentar ▹ CONJUG 1a (VT) to patent
patente (ADJ) **1** [*mentira, muestra*] clear • **es prueba ~ de su ineficacia** it's clear proof of his inefficiency • **me decepcionó su ~ desinterés** I was disappointed by his patent *o* clear lack of interest • **su enojo era ~** his annoyance was plain to see, he was plainly *o* patently *o* clearly annoyed • **la culpabilidad era ~ en su rostro** he had guilt written all over his face • **hacer algo ~** to reveal sth, show sth clearly • **aquella reacción hizo ~ su rencor** that reaction clearly showed *o* revealed his resentment • **quedar ~** to become patently clear *o* obvious • **con ese comentario su ignorancia quedó ~** with that comment his ignorance became patently clear *o* obvious
2 (*Com*) patent
3 (*Cono Sur**) (= *excelente*) superb, great
(SF) **1** [*de invento, producto*] patent • **derechos de ~** patent rights • **de ~** (*Cono Sur*) first-rate ▸ **patente de invención** patent
2 (*Jur*) (= *permiso*) licence, license (*EEUU*), authorization ▸ **patente de corso** (*Hist*) letter(s) of marque • **se cree que tiene ~ de corso** he thinks he's got a licence to do whatever he pleases ▸ **patente de navegación** ship's registration certificate ▸ **patente de privilegio** letters patent ▸ **patente de sanidad** bill of health
3 (*Cono Sur*) (*Aut*) licence plate, license plate (*EEUU*); (= *carnet*) driving licence, driver's license (*EEUU*)
(SM) (*Caribe*) patent medicine
patentizar ▹ CONJUG 1f (VT) to show, make evident
(VPR) **patentizarse** to show plainly, become obvious
pateo (SM) stamping
páter* (SM) (*Mil*) padre*
patera (SF) (*Esp*) boat, small boat (*often used for illegal immigration*)
paterfamilias (SM INV) paterfamilias
paternal (ADJ) fatherly, paternal
paternalismo (SM) paternalism; (*pey*) patronizing attitude
paternalista (ADJ) paternalistic; (*pey*) patronizing
(SMF) paternalist; (*pey*) patronizing person
paternalmente (ADV) paternally, in a fatherly fashion
paternidad (SF) **1** (= *estado, situación*) fatherhood, parenthood
2 (*Jur*) paternity • **prueba de ~** paternity test ▸ **paternidad literaria** authorship
paterno (ADJ) paternal • **abuelo ~** paternal grandfather
patero* (ADJ) **1** (*Cono Sur*) (= *adulador*) fawning
2 (*And*) (= *embustero*) slippery, wily
patéticamente (ADV) pathetically, movingly, poignantly
patético (ADJ) **1** (= *digno de lástima*) pathetic, moving
2 (*Cono Sur*) (= *evidente*) clear, evident
3 (= *andador*) • **es muy ~** (*And**) he loves walking
patetismo (SM) pathos, poignancy
patiabierto (ADJ) bow-legged
patibulario (ADJ) **1** (= *horroroso*) horrifying, harrowing
2 [*persona*] sinister
patíbulo (SM) scaffold, gallows
paticorto (ADJ) short-legged
patidifuso* (ADJ) (= *estupefacto*) astounded, taken aback; (= *perplejo*) nonplussed • **dejar a algn ~** (= *estupefacto*) to take sb aback; (= *perplejo*) to nonplus sb
patiestevado (ADJ) bandy-legged
patihendido (ADJ) cloven-hoofed
patilargo (ADJ) long-legged
patilla (SF) **1** [*de gafas*] sidepiece, temple (*EEUU*); [*de vestido*] pocket flap
2 [*de hombre*] sideburn; (= *rizo*) kiss curl
• MODISMO: • **tener ~s*** to have a brass neck*
3 (*Arg*) (= *banco*) bench
4 (*Caribe, Col*) (= *sandía*) watermelon
5 (*Inform*) pin
6 (*Cono Sur*) (*Bot*) layer
patilludo* (ADJ) (*Arg, Uru*) fed up*, sick*
patimocho (ADJ) (*LAm*) lame
patín (SM) **1** (*gen*) skate; [*de trineo*] runner; (*Aer*) skid; **patines** (*Cono Sur*) soft over-slippers ▸ **patín de cola** (*Aer*) tailskid ▸ **patín de cuchilla, patín de hielo** ice skate ▸ **patín de ruedas** roller skate ▸ **patines en línea** rollerblades
2 (= *patinete*) scooter
3 (*Náut*) ▸ **patín de pedal, patín playero** pedalo, pedal-boat
4 (*Aut**) old banger‡
pátina (SF) patina
patinadero (SM) skating rink
patinado (ADJ) shiny, glossy
patinador(a) (SM/F) skater
patinadura (SF) (*Caribe*) skid, skidding
patinaje (SM) **1** (*Dep*) skating ▸ **patinaje artístico, patinaje de figuras** figure skating ▸ **patinaje sobre hielo** ice-skating ▸ **patinaje sobre ruedas** roller-skating
2 (*Aut*) skidding
patinar ▹ CONJUG 1a (VI) **1** (*con patines*) (*sobre ruedas*) to roller-skate; (*sobre hielo*) to skate, ice-skate
2 (= *resbalar*) [*coche*] to skid; [*persona*] to slide • **el suelo estaba húmedo y patiné** the ground was wet and I slid
3* (= *equivocarse*) to make a blunder, boob*
4 (*Arg**) to fail
patinazo (SM) **1** (*Aut*) skid
2* (= *error*) boob*, blunder • **dar** *o* **pegar un ~** to blunder, make a boob*
patinete (SM), **patineta** (SF) scooter
patio (SM) **1** [*de casa*] courtyard; [*de escuela*] playground • MODISMOS: • **¡cómo está el ~!***: • **¡cómo está el ~! hoy todos están de mal humor** what an atmosphere! everybody is in a bad mood today! • **¡cómo está el ~! varios diputados se han liado a puñetazos** several MPs got involved in a punch-up — what's the world coming to? • **llevar el ~** to rule the roost ▸ **patio de armas** parade ground ▸ **patio de luces** well (*of a building*) ▸ **patio de operaciones** floor (*of the stock exchange*) ▸ **patio de recreo** playground
2 (*Teat*) pit ▸ **patio de butacas** stalls (*pl*), orchestra (*EEUU*)
3 (*Méx*) (*Ferro*) shunting yard

P

patiquín SM (*Caribe*) fop, dandy
patita SF ▸ calle
patitieso* ADJ **1** (= *paralizado*) • **me quedé patitiesa** (*de frío*) I was frozen stiff; (*de miedo*) I was scared stiff
2 (*fig*) = **patidifuso**
3 (= *presumido*) stuck-up*, conceited
patito SM duckling • MODISMO: • **los dos ~s*** all the twos*, twenty-two ▸ **patito feo** ugly duckling
patituerto ADJ bandy-legged
patizambo ADJ knock-kneed
pato SM **1** (*Orn*) duck • MODISMOS: • **pagar el ~*** to carry the can* • **ser el ~ de la boda** *o* **fiesta** (*LAm*) to be a laughing stock • **salga ~ o gallareta** (*LAm*) whatever the results ▸ **pato a la naranja** duck à l'orange ▸ **pato colorado** red-crested pochard ▸ **pato de reclamo** decoy duck ▸ **pato (macho)** drake ▸ **pato malvasía** white-headed duck ▸ **pato real, pato silvestre** mallard, wild duck
2* (= *persona aburrida*) bore • **estar hecho un ~** to be terribly dull
3 (= *torpe*) • **ser un ~** to be clumsy
4* (= *aburrimiento*) boredom; (= *período aburrido*) boring time; (= *fiesta*) bore, drag
5 (*And**) (= *gorrón*) sponger* • **viajar de ~** to stow away
6 (*And**) (= *inocentón*) sucker‡
7 (*Méx*) • MODISMO: • **hacer el ~** *o* **hacerse ~** to act the fool
8 (*Cono Sur**) • **ser un ~** *o* **estar ~** to be broke* • MODISMO: • **pasarse de ~ a ganso** to go too far
9 (*LAm*) (= *bacineta*) bedpan
patochada SF blunder, bloomer*
patógeno SM pathogen
patojo/a* ADJ (*LAm*) lame
SM/F (*And, CAm*) (= *niño*) child; (= *novio*) sweetheart, boyfriend/girlfriend; (*pey*) urchin, ragamuffin
patología SF pathology
patológicamente ADV pathologically
patológico ADJ pathological
patólogo/a SM/F pathologist
patomachera* SF (*Caribe*) slanging match*
patoso/a* ADJ **1** (= *torpe*) clumsy
2 (= *molesto*) troublesome • **ponerse ~** to make trouble
SM/F **1** (= *torpe*) clumsy oaf
2 (= *sabihondo*) clever Dick*, smart Aleck*
3 (= *agitador*) troublemaker
patota* SF **1** (*Cono Sur*) (= *pandilla*) street gang, mob of young thugs; (= *grupo*) large group
2 (*Caribe, Cono Sur*) (= *amigos*) mob, crowd (of friends)
patotear* ▸ CONJUG 1a VT (*Cono Sur*) to beat up*
patotero* SM (*Cono Sur*) rowdy, young thug
patraña SF **1** (= *embuste*) tall story
2 (= *narración confusa*) rigmarole, long involved story
patraquear ▸ CONJUG 1a VT (*Cono Sur*) [+ *objeto*] to steal; [+ *persona*] to hold up, mug*
patraquero/a SM/F (*Cono Sur*) (= *ladrón*) thief; (= *atracador*) holdup man/woman, mugger*
patria SF native land, fatherland • **madre ~** mother country • **luchar por la ~** to fight for one's country • MODISMO: • **hacer ~** to fly the flag* ▸ **patria adoptiva** adopted country ▸ **patria chica** home town, home area
patriada SF (*Cono Sur*) (*Hist*) rising, revolt
patriarca SM patriarch
patriarcado SM patriarchy
patriarcal ADJ patriarchal

Patricia SF Patricia
Patricio SM Patrick
patricio/a ADJ, SM/F patrician
patrilineal ADJ patrilineal
patrimonial ADJ hereditary
patrimonio SM **1** (= *bienes*) (*adquiridos*) assets (*pl*), wealth; (*heredados*) inheritance, patrimony (*frm*); (*dejados en herencia*) estate • **su ~ personal es de 300 millones** his personal assets are 300 million, his personal wealth is some 300 million • **el ~ heredado por mis padres** my parents' inheritance *o* (*frm*) patrimony • **dejó un ~ valorado en miles de millones** his estate was valued at thousands of millions • **gestión de ~s** asset management
2 (*artístico, cultural*) heritage ▸ **patrimonio de la humanidad** world heritage ▸ **patrimonio nacional** national heritage
3 (*Com*) net worth, capital resources (*pl*)
patrio ADJ **1** (*Pol*) native, home (*antes de s*) • **el suelo ~** one's native land, one's native soil • **amor ~** love of one's country, patriotism
2 (*Jur*) [*poder*] paternal
patriota ADJ patriotic
SMF patriot
SM (*CAm*) banana
patriotería SF, **patrioterismo** SM (= *chauvinismo*) chauvinism; (= *jingoísmo*) jingoism
patriotero/a ADJ (= *chauvinista*) chauvinistic; (= *jingoísta*) jingoistic
SM/F (= *chauvinista*) chauvinist; (= *jingoísta*) jingoist
patrióticamente ADV patriotically
patriótico ADJ patriotic
patriotismo SM patriotism
patrocinado/a SM/F (*Jur*) client
patrocinador(a) ADJ sponsoring • **empresa ~a** sponsor, sponsoring company
SM/F (*Com*) sponsor; [*de artes, causas benéficas*] patron/patroness; (= *promotor*) promoter
patrocinar ▸ CONJUG 1a VT (*Com*) to sponsor; [+ *artes, causas benéficas*] to act as patron to; (= *respaldar*) to back, support • **un movimiento patrocinado por ...** a movement under the auspices of *o* under the patronage of ...
patrocinazgo SM (*Com*) sponsorship; [*de artes, causas benéficas*] patronage
patrocinio SM (*Com*) sponsorship; [*de artes, causas benéficas*] patronage; (= *respaldo*) backing, support ▸ **patrocinio empresarial** commercial sponsorship
patrón/ona SM/F **1** (= *jefe*) boss*; (= *dueño*) employer, owner; (*Hist*) [*de esclavo*] master/mistress
2 [*de pensión*] landlord/landlady
3 (*Náut*) (*gen*) skipper; [*de barco mercante*] master/mistress
4 (*Rel*) (*tb* **santo patrón**) (= *santo*) patron saint; (= *virgen*) patron
5 (= *protector*) patron/patroness
SM **1** (*Cos*) pattern; (*Téc*) standard, norm ▸ **patrón de distribución** distribution pattern ▸ **patrón oro** gold standard ▸ **patrón picado** stencilled pattern
2 (*Bot*) stock (*for grafting*)
3 (= *puntal*) prop, shore
ADJ INV (*gen*) standard, regular; (= *muestra*) sample (*antes de s*)
patronaje SM pattern designing
patronal ADJ **1** (*Com*) employers' (*antes de s*) • **sindicato ~** employers' association • **cierre ~** (management) lockout • **organización ~** employers' organization • **la clase ~** management, the managerial class • **cerrado por acto ~** closed by the owners *o* management
2 (*Rel*) • **fiesta ~** local holiday (*on the feast day of the local patron saint*)
SF employers' organization; (= *dirección*) management
patronato SM **1** [*de artes, causas benéficas*] patronage; (*Com*) sponsorship • **bajo el ~ de** under the patronage of, under the auspices of
2 (*Com, Econ*) employers' association; (*Pol*) owners (*pl*) • **el ~ francés** French industrialists
3 (= *junta*) board of management, board of trustees • **el ~ de turismo** the tourist board
4 (= *fundación*) trust, foundation
patronear ▸ CONJUG 1a VT [+ *barco*] to skipper
patronímico ADJ, SM patronymic
patronista SMF pattern designer
patronizar ▸ CONJUG 1f VT to patronize
patrono/a SM/F **1** (*Com, Econ*) owner, employer
2 (= *mecenas*) patron; (= *patrocinador*) sponsor; (= *protector*) protector, supporter
3 (*Rel*) patron saint
patrulla SF patrol • **coche ~** patrol car ▸ **patrulla ciudadana** vigilante group
patrullaje SM patrolling • **bajo un fuerte ~ policial** under heavy police patrol
patrullar ▸ CONJUG 1a VT to patrol, police
VI to patrol
patrullera SF patrol boat
patrullero ADJ patrol (*antes de s*)
SM **1** (*Aut*) patrol car
2 (*Náut*) patrol boat
3 (*Méx*) (= *policía*) patrolman, policeman
patucho ADJ (*And*) short, squat
patucos SMPL [*de bebé*] bootees
patudo ADJ (*Cono Sur*) rough, brash
SM (*And*) • **el ~** the devil
patueco/a ADJ, SM/F (*CAm*) = **patojo**
patulea SF mob, rabble
patuleco/a ADJ, SM/F (*LAm*), **patulejo/a** ADJ, SM/F (*Cono Sur*), **patuleque** ADJ, SMF (*Caribe*) = **patojo**
patulenco* ADJ (*CAm*) clumsy, awkward
patullar ▸ CONJUG 1a VI **1** (= *pisar*) to trample about, stamp around
2 (= *trajinar*) to bustle about
3 (= *charlar*) to chat; (= *hacer ruido*) to talk noisily, make a lot of noise
paturro ADJ (*And, Cono Sur*) (= *rechoncho*) chubby, plump; (= *chaparro*) squat
paúl SM marsh
paular SM marshy ground
paulatinamente ADV gradually, slowly
paulatino ADJ gradual, slow
paulina* SF **1** (= *reprimenda*) telling-off*
2 (= *carta*) poison-pen letter
Paulo SM Paul
pauperismo SM (*frm*) pauperism
pauperización SF (*frm*) impoverishment
paupérrimo ADJ very poor, poverty-stricken
pausa SF **1** (= *en programa, reunión*) break; (*al hablar, leer*) pause; (*Mús*) rest • **con ~** slowly, deliberately ▸ **pausa publicitaria** commercial break
2 (*Téc*) (*en casette*) pause (button); (*en vídeo*) hold
pausadamente ADV slowly, deliberately
pausado ADJ slow, deliberate
pausar ▸ CONJUG 1a VT (= *retardar*) to slow down; (= *interrumpir*) to interrupt
VI to go slow
pauta SF **1** (= *modelo*) model; (= *guía*) guideline; (= *regla*) rule, guide • **marcar la ~** to set the standard • **París marca la ~ de la moda en todo el mundo** Paris sets the trend *o* the standard for fashion all over the world

P

• **servir de ~ a** to act as a model for
2 (*en papel*) lines (*pl*)
pautado ADJ • **papel ~** ruled paper
SM (*Mús*) stave
pautar ▸ CONJUG 1a VT 1 (*Tip*) [+ *papel*] to rule
2 (*esp CAm*) (= *marcar*) to mark, characterize; (= *reglar*) to establish a norm for, lay down a pattern for
pava SF 1 (*Orn*) turkey (hen) • **MODISMOS**:
• **es una ~** (*Esp**) she's a complete bore
• **echar la ~** (*Esp**) to puke up*, throw up
• **pelar la ~** (*Esp**) to whisper sweet nothings
▸ **pava real** peahen
2 (*Cono Sur*) (*para hervir*) kettle; (*para mate*) pot for making maté
3 (*Col, Ven*) (= *sombrero*) broad-brimmed straw hat
4 (*And, CAm*) (= *fleco*) fringe, bangs (*pl*) (*EEUU*)
5 (*Cono Sur, Méx*) (= *orinal*) chamber pot
6 (*And, Cono Sur*) (= *guasa*) coarse banter; (= *chiste*) tasteless joke • **MODISMO**: • **hacer la ~ a algn*** to make sb look stupid
7 (*And, CAm**) (= *colilla*) cigarette-end, fag-end‡
8‡ (= *chica*) bird‡
pavada SF 1 (*esp Arg**) (= *tontería*) silly thing • **no digas ~s** don't talk rubbish
2 (*Orn*) flock of turkeys
3 (*Cono Sur*) (= *bagatela*) trivial thing • **cuesta una ~** it costs next to nothing
4 (*Caribe*) (= *mala suerte*) bit of bad luck
pavear ▸ CONJUG 1a VT 1 (*And*) (= *asesinar*) to kill treacherously
2 (*And, Cono Sur*) (= *burlarse de*) to play a joke on
VI 1 (*Cono Sur, Perú**) (= *hacer el tonto*) to act the fool, mess about
2 (*Cono Sur**) [*enamorados*] to whisper sweet nothings
3 (*And**) (= *hacer novillos*) to play truant, play hooky (*EEUU**)
pavería SF (*Cono Sur*) silliness, stupidity
pavero/a SM/F (*And, Cono Sur*) practical joker
pavesa SF piece of ash; **pavesas** SFPL hot ash (*sing*)
pavimentación SF paving
pavimentado ADJ [*exteriores*] paved; [*interiores*] tiled
pavimentar ▸ CONJUG 1a VT [+ *exteriores*] to pave; [+ *interiores*] to floor
pavimento SM 1 (*de asfalto*) roadway, road surface
2 (*de losas*) (*gen*) paving; (*en interior*) flooring
pavipollo SM 1 (*Orn*) young turkey
2* (= *bobo*) twit*, idiot
pavisoso* ADJ dull, graceless
pavitonto* ADJ silly
pavo SM 1 (*Orn*) turkey • **MODISMOS**:
• **comer ~*** to be a wallflower (*at a dance*); (*LAm*) to be disappointed • **estar en la edad del ~** to be at an awkward age • **ir de ~** (*LAm**) to travel free, get a free ride • **tener mucho ~** to blush a lot • **tener un ~ encima**: • **esta niña tiene un ~ encima que no se aclara** it looks like she'll never grow out of being a giggling teenager • **subírsele el ~ a algn**: • **se le subió el ~** he went bright red ▸ **pavo real** peacock
2 (*Esp**) (= *tonto*) silly thing, idiot
3‡ (= *moneda*) five-peseta coin
4* (= *primo*) sucker‡
5 (*Chile**) (= *polizón*) stowaway
6 (*And*) (= *cometa*) large kite
7 (*And**) (= *espadón*) big shot*; (= *sospechoso*) evil-looking person
8 (*Caribe**) (= *reprimenda*) telling-off*
9‡ (= *hombre*) bloke‡; (*Caribe*‡) (= *joven*) youngster, kid*
10‡ (= *síndrome de abstinencia*) cold turkey*

ADJ* silly • **¡no seas ~!** don't be silly!
pavón SM 1 (*Orn*) peacock
2 (*Téc*) bluing, bronzing
pavonearse ▸ CONJUG 1a VPR (= *presumir*) (*gen*) to show off (**de** about); (*al hablar*) to brag (**de** about); (*al andar*) to swagger, strut
pavoneo SM (*gen*) showing-off; (*al hablar*) bragging; (*al andar*) swagger, strutting
pavor SM dread, terror
pavorosamente ADV terrifyingly
pavoroso ADJ terrifying
pavoso ADJ (*Caribe*) (= *desafortunado*) unlucky; (= *que trae mala suerte*) that brings bad luck
pay SM (*LAm*) pie
paya SF (*Cono Sur*) = **payada**
payacate SM (*Méx*) [*de bolsillo*] handkerchief; (= *prenda*) scarf, kerchief
payada SF (*Cono Sur*) *improvised gaucho folksong* ▸ **payada de contrapunto** *contest between two "payadores"*
payador SM (*Cono Sur*) gaucho minstrel
payar ▸ CONJUG 1a VI 1 (*Cono Sur*) (= *cantar*) *to improvise songs to a guitar accompaniment*
2* (= *contar cuentos*) to talk big*, shoot a line*
payasada SF clownish trick, stunt; (*pey*) ridiculous thing (to do); **payasadas** clowning (*sing*); (*Teat*) slapstick (*sing*), knockabout humour (*sing*), knockabout humor (*sing*) (*EEUU*)
payasear ▸ CONJUG 1a VI (*LAm*) to clown around
payaso/a SM/F clown (*tb fig*)
payés/esa SM/F (*Cataluña, Baleares*) peasant farmer
payo/a ADJ 1 (*Arg*) (= *albino*) albino
2 (*Méx*) (= *simple*) rustic, simple
3 (*Méx*) [*ropa*] loud, flashy
SM/F (*para gitanos*) non-gipsy, non-gypsy (*EEUU*)
payuelas SFPL chickenpox (*sing*)
paz SF 1 (*gen*) peace; (= *tranquilidad*) peace and quiet, tranquillity, tranquility (*EEUU*)
• **¡a la paz de Dios!** God be with you! • **en paz y en guerra** in peace and war, in peacetime and wartime • **dejar a algn en paz** to leave sb alone, leave sb in peace • **¡déjame en paz!** leave me alone! • **descansar en paz** to rest in peace • **su madre, que en paz descanse** her mother, God rest her soul • **estar en paz** (*gen*) to be at peace; (*fig*) to be even, be quits (**con** with); (*Méx*‡) to be high‡ • **¡haya paz!** stop it!, that's enough! • **mantener la paz** to keep the peace • **perturbar la paz** to disturb the peace • **MODISMOS**: • **no dar paz a la lengua** to keep on and on • **¡... y en paz!, ¡aquí paz y después gloria!** and that's that!, and Bob's your uncle!*
2 (= *tratado*) peace, peace treaty • **la paz de los Pirineos** the Peace of the Pyrenees (*1659*)
• **firmar paz** to sign a peace treaty • **hacer las paces** (*gen*) to make peace; (*fig*) to make (it) up • **poner paz** to make peace
3 (*Rel*) kiss of peace, sign of peace
pazguato ADJ 1 (= *necio*) simple, stupid
2 (= *remilgado*) prudish
pazo SM (*Galicia*) country house
PC SM ABR 1 (= **personal computer**) PC
2 = **Partido Comunista**
p.c. ABR (= **por cien**) p.c.
PCB SM ABR (= **policlorobifenilo**) PCB
PCE SM ABR = **Partido Comunista Español**
PCN SM ABR (*El Salvador*) = **Partido de Conciliación Nacional**
PCUS SM ABR (*Pol, Hist*) = **Partido Comunista de la Unión Soviética**
PCV SM ABR (*Ven*) = **Partido Comunista Venezolano**
PD ABR, **P.D.** ABR (= **posdata**) PS
PDA SF o SF ABR (= **Personal Digital Assistant**) PDA
PDC SM ABR (*LAm*) = **Partido Demócrata Cristiano**
PDF SM ABR (*Inform*) PDF • **un archivo en PDF** a PDF file
pdo. ABR (= **pasado**) ult.
Pdte. ABR (*Chile*) (*Prensa*) = **presidente**
pe SF (*name of the*) *letter* P • **MODISMO**: • **de pe a pa*** from A to Z, from beginning to end
P.^e^ ABR (= **Padre**) F., Fr.
pea* SF • **coger una pea** to get smashed*, get legless*
peaje SM toll • **autopista de ~** toll motorway, turnpike (*EEUU*) ▸ **peaje anti-congestión** (*en Londres*) congestion charge
peajista SMF collector of tolls
peal SM (*LAm*) lasso
pealar ▸ CONJUG 1a VT (*LAm*) to lasso
peana SF 1 (= *pedestal*) base, pedestal
2 (*Golf*) tee
3* (= *pie*) foot
peatón SM pedestrian • **paso de peatones** pedestrian crossing, crosswalk (*EEUU*)
peatonal ADJ pedestrian (*antes de s*) • **calle ~** pedestrian precinct
peatonalización SF pedestrianization
peatonalizar ▸ CONJUG 1f VT to pedestrianize
pebete/a SM/F (*Arg, Uru**) (= *niño*) kid*; (= *persona baja*) short person
SM 1 (= *incienso*) joss stick
2 [*de cohete*] fuse
3 (= *olor*) stink
4 (*Cono Sur*) (= *panecillo*) roll
pebre SM (*esp Chile*) (*Culin*) *mild sauce made from vinegar, garlic, parsley and pepper*
peca SF freckle
pecado SM 1 (*Rel*) sin • **por mis ~s** for my sins • **un ~ de juventud** a youthful indiscretion, a sin of youth • **estar en ~** to be in a state of sin • **MODISMO**: • **en el ~ llevas la penitencia** you've made your bed now lie in it ▸ **pecado capital** deadly sin ▸ **pecado de comisión** sin of commission ▸ **pecado nefando** sodomy ▸ **pecado original** original sin ▸ **pecado venial** venial sin
2 (= *cosa lamentable*) crime, sin • **sería un ~ no aprovecharlo** it would be a crime *o* sin not to make use of it • **¡es un ~ darle el filete al gato!** it's a crime to give steak to the cat!
pecador(a) ADJ sinful
SM/F sinner
pecaminosidad SF sinfulness
pecaminoso ADJ sinful
pecar ▸ CONJUG 1g VI 1 (*Rel*) to sin; (*fig*) to err
• **si he pecado en esto, ha sido por ...** if I have been at fault in this, it has been because ... • **si me lo pones delante, acabaré pecando** if you put temptation in front of me, I shall fall
2 • **~ de** (+ *adj*) to be too (+ *adj*) • **peca de generoso** he is too generous, he is generous to a fault • **peca por exceso de confianza** he is too confident
pécari SM (*LAm*), **pecarí** SM (*LAm*) (*Zool*) peccary
peccata minuta SF • **ser ~** to be no big deal, be unimportant
pecé* SM (*Esp*) (= *partido*) Communist Party
SMF (= *persona*) Communist
pecera SF (*redonda*) fishbowl; (*rectangular*) fish tank
pecero/a* SM/F (*Pol*) member of the Communist Party
pecha SF (*Cono Sur*) push, shove
pechada* SF 1 (= *hartazgo*) • **llevamos una ~ de andar** that's more than enough walking (for one day), it's been a real slog* • **se dieron una ~ de trabajar** they really slogged

their guts out*
2 (*LAm*) (= *empujón*) push, shove
3 (*LAm**) (= *sablazo*) scrounging*
pechador* ADJ (*Cono Sur*) demanding
pechar¹* ▷ CONJUG 1a VT 1 (*LAm*) (= *empujar*) to push, shove
2 (*Cono Sur*) (= *pedir dinero a*) to tap*, touch for
3 (*Cono Sur*) (= *atrapar*) to collar*, grab
VI • **~ con** (*gen*) to put up with; [+ *cometido*] to shoulder, take on; [+ *problema*] to face up to
pechar² ▷ CONJUG 1a VT, VI to pay (as a tax)
pechazo* SM (*LAm*) 1 (= *empujón*) push, shove
2 [*de dinero*] touch (for a loan)*
pechblenda SF pitchblende
peche‡ (*CAm*) ADJ skinny
SM child
pechera SF 1 (*Cos*) [*de camisa*] shirt front; [*de vestido*] front; (*Mil*) chest protector ▸ **pechera postiza** dicky
2 (*Anat**) (*hum*) big bosom
pechero¹/a SM/F (*Hist*) commoner, plebeian
pechero² SM (= *babero*) bib; [*de vestido*] front
pechicato ADJ (*Caribe*) = **pichicato**
pechina SF scallop
pecho¹ SM 1 (= *tórax*) chest • **le dieron una puñalada en el ~** he was stabbed in the chest • **tenía una herida en el ~** he had a chest injury • **estar de ~ sobre algo** to be leaning on sth • **estaba de ~ sobre la barandilla** he was leaning on the railing • **sacar ~** to stick one's chest out • **ponte firme y saca ~** stand up straight and stick your chest out • **el presidente ha sacado ~ ante las críticas** the president put on a brave face under the criticism • MODISMOS: • **abrir el ~ a algn** to confide in sb, open one's heart to sb • **no caberle a algn la alegría en el ~:** • **no me/le cabía la alegría en el ~** I/he was bursting with happiness • **dar el ~** to face things squarely • **a ~ descubierto** (= *sin armas*) unarmed, defenceless, defenseless (*EEUU*); (= *francamente*) openly, frankly • **echarse entre ~ y espalda** [+ *comida*] to put away*; [+ *bebida*] to knock back* • **gritar a todo ~** (*And, Caribe*) to shout at the top of one's voice • **partirse el ~*** to bust a gut* • **quedarse con algo en el ~** to keep sth back • **tomarse algo a ~** to take sth to heart
2 [*de mujer*] **a** (= *busto*) bust • **un sujetador que realza el ~** a bra which makes your bust look bigger • **de ~ plano** flat-chested • **tener mucho ~** to have a big bust • **tener poco ~** to be flat-chested
b (= *mama*) breast • **le han extirpado un ~** she had a breast removed • **dar el ~** to breast-feed • **un niño de ~** a baby at the breast
3 (= *valor*) • MODISMOS: • **¡~ al agua!** courage! • **a lo hecho, ~** we must make the best of it now
4 (*Geog*) slope, gradient
pecho² SM (*Hist*) tax, tribute
pechoño ADJ (*And, Cono Sur*) sanctimonious
pechuga SF 1 (*Culin*) breast; [*de mujer**] tits‡ (*pl*), bosom; (= *escote*) cleavage ▸ **pechuga de pollo** chicken breast
2 (*Geog*) slope, hill
3 (*LAm**) (*pey*) (= *descaro*) nerve, cheek*
4 (*And, CAm**) (= *abuso de confianza*) abuse of trust
5 (*CAm*) (= *molestia*) trouble, annoyance
pechugón/ona* ADJ 1 (= *de mucho pecho*) busty*, big-bosomed
2 (*LAm*) (= *descarado*) shameless; (= *franco*) outspoken; (= *chupón*) sponging; (= *egoísta*) selfish
3 (*Cono Sur*) (= *resuelto*) single-minded
4* (= *atractivo*) dishy*
SM/F (*LAm*) 1 (= *descarado*) shameless individual
2 (= *gorrón*) sponger*
pechuguera SF (*And, Méx*) (= *ronquera*) hoarseness; (= *resfriado*) chest cold
pecio SM wrecked ship, shipwreck; **pecios** flotsam (*sing*), wreckage (*sing*)
pecíolo SM, **peciolo** SM (leaf) stalk, petiole (*Téc*)
pécora SF (*tb* **mala pécora**)* (= *arpía*) bitch‡; (= *prostituta*) loose woman, whore
pecoso ADJ freckled
pecotra SF (*Cono Sur*) (*Anat*) bump, swelling; (*en madera*) knot
pectina SF pectin
pectoral ADJ (*Anat*) pectoral • **pastillas ~es** cough drops
SM 1 (*Rel*) pectoral cross
2 **pectorales** (*Anat*) pectorals
pecuaca SF (*And, Caribe*) = **pecueca**
pecuario ADJ livestock (*antes de s*)
pecueca SF (*And, Caribe*) (= *pezuña*) hoof; (*hum*) (= *olor*) smell of feet
peculado SM embezzlement
peculiar ADJ 1 (= *particular, característico*) particular • **su ~ manera de ver las cosas** his particular way of seeing things, his own individual way of seeing things • **un rasgo ~ de su carácter** a particular characteristic trait of his • **tiene un carácter muy ~** he's got a very individual personality • **una característica ~ del paisaje andaluz** a characteristic peculiar to the landscape of Andalusia
2 (= *raro*) peculiar, unusual • **su comportamiento es un tanto ~** his behaviour is a bit peculiar *o* unusual
peculiaridad SF peculiarity, special characteristic • **cada país tiene sus ~es** each country has its own peculiarities
peculio SM (= *dinero*) one's own money; (= *ahorros*) modest savings (*pl*) • **de su ~** out of one's own pocket
pecunia* SF (= *dinero*) brass*; (*Caribe*) (= *moneda*) coin
pecuniario ADJ pecuniary, money (*antes de s*) • **pena pecuniaria** fine
PED SM ABR (= **Procesamiento Electrónico de Datos**) EDP
pedagogía SF pedagogy
pedagógicamente ADV pedagogically
pedagógico ADJ pedagogic(al)
pedagogo/a SM/F (= *profesor*) teacher, educator; (= *teórico*) educationalist
pedal SM 1 [*de bicicleta, automóvil*] pedal ▸ **pedal de acelerador** accelerator (pedal) ▸ **pedal de(l) embrague** clutch (pedal) ▸ **pedal de freno** brake (pedal) ▸ **pedal dulce** (*Mús*) soft pedal ▸ **pedal fuerte** (*Mús*) loud pedal ▸ **pedal piano, pedal suave** (*Mús*) soft pedal
2‡ (= *borrachera*) • **coger un ~** to get canned‡
pedalear ▷ CONJUG 1a VI to pedal • **~ en agua** to tread water
pédalo SM pedal boat, pedalo
pedáneo ADJ • **alcalde ~** mayor of a small town • **juez ~** local magistrate
pedanía SF district
pedante ADJ (*gen*) pedantic; (= *pomposo*) pompous, conceited
SMF pedant
pedantería SF (*gen*) pedantry; (= *pomposidad*) pomposity, conceit
pedantescamente ADV pedantically
pedantesco ADJ pedantic
pedazo SM 1 (= *trozo*) piece • **un ~ de papel** a piece of paper • **un ~ de pan** a piece of bread • **trabaja por un ~ de pan** he works for a mere pittance • **hacer algo a ~s** to do sth in pieces, do sth piecemeal • **caerse a ~s** to fall to bits • **hacer ~s** [+ *papel*] to rip, tear (up); [+ *vidrio, cristal*] to shatter, smash; [+ *persona*] to tear to shreds • **estoy hecho ~s** I'm worn out • **hacerse ~s** [*objeto*] to fall to pieces; [*vidrio, cristal*] to shatter, smash • MODISMO: • **ser un ~ de pan** to be a really nice person, be an angel
2 (*con insultos*) • **es un ~ de alcornoque** *o* **animal** *o* **bruto*** he's a blockhead*, he's an idiot
3 (*con expresiones de cariño*) • **¡~ de mi alma** *o* **mi corazón** *o* **mis entrañas!** my darling!
pederasta SMF pederast, paedophile, pedophile (*EEUU*)
pederastia SF pederasty, paedophilia, pedophilia (*EEUU*)
pedernal SM flint • **como un ~** of flint, flinty
pederse* ▷ CONJUG 2a VPR to fart‡
pedestal SM pedestal, stand
pedestre ADJ 1 (= *a pie*) pedestrian • **carrera ~** walking race
2 [*metáfora, arte, razón*] pedestrian
pedestrismo SM walking
pediatra SMF paediatrician, pediatrician (*EEUU*)
pediatría SF paediatrics (*sing*), pediatrics (*sing*) (*EEUU*)
pediátrico ADJ paediatric, pediatric (*EEUU*)
pedicura SF chiropody, podiatry (*EEUU*)
pedicuro/a SM/F chiropodist, podiatrist (*EEUU*)
pedida SF (*Esp*) (*tb* **pedida de mano**) engagement; ▷ **anillo, pulsera**
pedidera SF (*And, CAm, Caribe*) = **petición**
pedido SM 1 (*Com*) order • **su ~ será atendido inmediatamente** your order will be dealt with immediately • **cursar** *o* **hacer un ~** to place an order • **servir un ~** (*Esp*) to deliver an order ▸ **pedido al contado** cash order ▸ **pedido atrasado** outstanding order ▸ **pedido de ensayo** trial order ▸ **pedido de repetición** repeat order ▸ **pedido pendiente** outstanding order ▸ **pedido por teléfono** telephone order; ▷ **cartera, hoja**
2 (= *petición*) request • **a ~ de algn** at the request of sb • **hacer algo bajo** *o* **sobre ~** to make sth to order
pedigrí SM, **pedigree** [pedi'gri] SM pedigree
pedigüeño ADJ cadging, mooching (*EEUU**)
pedilón ADJ (*LAm*) = **pedigüeño**
SM (*LAm*) pest, nuisance
pedimento SM (*gen*) petition; (*Jur*) claim, bill; (*Méx*) (*Com*) licence, license (*EEUU*), permit
pedir ▷ CONJUG 3k VT 1 (= *rogar, solicitar*) to ask for • **¿habéis pedido ya la cuenta?** have you asked for the bill yet? • **lo único que pido es que no llueva mañana** all I ask is that it doesn't rain tomorrow • **necesito ~te consejo** I need to ask your advice • **a ti nadie te ha pedido tu opinión** nobody asked your opinion • **estuve pidiendo auxilio durante un buen rato** I was calling for help for some time • **una manifestación pidiendo la libertad de los secuestrados** a demonstration calling for the release of the hostages • **llamé para ~ que me pusieran una canción** I phoned to request a song • **~ cuentas a algn** to demand an explanation from sb • **~ algo a Dios** to pray to God for sth • **~ disculpas** to apologize • **~ algo por favor:** • **me pidió por favor que fuera discreto** he asked me to please keep it to myself • **te lo pido por favor, quédate conmigo** please stay with me • **~ hora** to

make an appointment • ~ **limosna** to beg • ~ **la palabra** to ask for permission to speak • **pido la palabra, señoría** permission to speak, my lord • ~ **perdón** (= *disculparse*) to apologize; (*suplicando*) to beg (for) forgiveness • ~ **permiso** to ask (for) permission • **MODISMOS**: • **te lo pido por Dios** I'm begging you • **¿qué más se puede ~?** what more can you ask (for)?
2 (*Com*) (= *encargar*) to order • **he pedido unos zapatos por correo** I've ordered some shoes by post • **tengo pedidos varios libros** I've got some books on order
3 (*en un restaurante*) to order; (*en un bar*) to ask for, order • **de primero hemos pedido sopa** we've ordered soup as a starter • **hemos pedido dos cafés y un té** we've asked for *o* ordered two coffees and a tea
4 (*para casarse*) to propose to • **fue a su casa a ~la** he went to her house to propose to her • **mis dos hermanas ya están pedidas** my two sisters are already spoken for • ~ **la mano de algn** to ask for sb's hand • ~ **a algn en matrimonio** to ask for sb's hand in marriage
5 (*Jur*) [+ *condena*] to ask for • **el fiscal pidió siete años de cárcel** the prosecution asked for a seven-year sentence
6 (= *requerir*) to need • **esta planta pide mucho sol** this plant needs lots of sunlight • **ese sofá pide una cortina azul** that sofa needs a blue curtain to go with it • ~ **algo a gritos** *o* **voces** to be crying out for sth • **la casa está pidiendo a voces que la pinten** the house is crying out to be painted
7 (*tb* **pedir prestado**) to borrow • **tengo que ~te unos libros** I need to borrow some books off you • **me pidió prestado el coche** he asked if he could borrow the car, he asked to borrow the car
(VI) **1** (= *rogar*) • **este niño está todo el día pidiendo** that child is always asking for things • ~ **por algn** (*Rel*) to pray for sb • **pido a Dios por los difuntos** I pray to God for the dead • **MODISMO**: • **por ~ que no quede** there's no harm in asking
2 (= *pedir dinero*) [*mendigo*] to beg; [*voluntario*] to collect money • **iba pidiendo por los vagones** he went begging from carriage to carriage • **piden para una buena causa** they are collecting money for a good cause
3 (*en un bar, restaurante*) to order • **¿habéis pedido ya?** have you ordered yet?; ▹ **boca**
(VPR) **pedirse*** (= *elegir*) to bag* • **se pidió el mejor asiento** he bagged the best seat* • **yo me pido el de fresa** I bags the strawberry one*, bags I get the strawberry one*

pedo (ADJ) ‡ • **estar ~** (= *borracho*) to be pissed**, be sloshed‡; (= *drogado*) to be high‡ • **ponerse ~** (= *borracho*) to get pissed**, get sloshed‡; (= *drogado*) to get high‡
(SM) **1*** fart‡ • **tirarse un ~** to fart‡
2‡ [*de alcohol, drogas*] • **agarrar** *o* **coger un ~** (= *emborracharse*) to get pissed**, get sloshed‡; (= *drogarse*) to get high‡ • **estar en ~** (*Cono Sur*) to be pissed**, be sloshed‡ • **¡estás en ~!** (*al hablar*) you must be kidding! • **MODISMO**: • **al ~** (*Cono Sur*): • **no me gusta trabajar al ~** I don't like working for the sake of it
3 ▸ **pedo de lobo** (*Bot*) puffball
4 ▸ **pedo de monja** (*Culin*) very light pastry

pedofilia (SF) paedophilia, pedophilia (*EEUU*)
pedófilo/a (SM/F), **pedofílico/a** (SM/F) paedophile, pedophile (*EEUU*)
pedología (SF) pedology, study of soils
pedorrera‡ (SF) string of farts‡
pedorrero‡ (ADJ) given to farting‡, windy
pedorreta* (SF) raspberry*
pedorro/a* (ADJ) (= *tonto*) daft; (= *pelmazo*) annoying
(SM/F) (= *tonto*) twit*; (= *pelmazo*) pain*
pedrada (SF) **1** (= *acción*) throw of a stone; (= *golpe*) hit *o* blow from a stone • **matar a algn a ~s** to stone sb to death • **pegar una ~ a algn** to throw a stone at sb
2 (= *comentario molesto*) snide remark, dig*
3 • **MODISMOS**: • **sentar como una ~**: • **la cosa le sentó como una ~** he took it very ill, the affair went down very badly with him • **me sienta como una ~ tener que irme** I hate having to go • **venir como ~ en ojo de boticario** to be just what the doctor ordered
pedrea (SF) **1** (= *combate*) stone-throwing, fight with stones
2 (*Meteo*) hailstorm
3 [*de lotería*] minor prizes (*pl*)
pedregal (SM) [*de piedras*] rocky ground, stony place; (*Méx*) [*de lava*] lava field
pedregón (SM) (*LAm*) rock, boulder
pedregoso (ADJ) stony, rocky
pedregullo (SM) (*Cono Sur*) gravel
pedrejón (SM) big stone, rock, boulder
pedrera (SF) quarry
pedrería (SF) precious stones (*pl*), jewels (*pl*)
pedrero (SM) **1** (= *persona*) quarryman, stone cutter
2 (*And, CAm, Cono Sur*) = **pedregal**
pedrisco (SM) **1** (= *granizo*) hail; (= *granizada*) hailstorm
2 (= *montón*) heap of stones; (= *lluvia de piedras*) shower of stones
Pedro (SM) Peter • **MODISMO**: • **entrar como ~ por su casa** to come in as if one owned the place
pedrusco (SM) **1** (= *piedra*) rough stone; (= *trozo de piedra*) piece of stone, lump of stone
2 (*LAm*) = **pedregal**

PEDIR

¿"Ask" o "ask for"?

▷ *La expresión* **pedir algo** *se traduce por* **ask for something**:
Pidieron muchas cosas diferentes
They asked for many different things

Si el verbo **pedir** *lleva dos complementos, el complemento de persona siempre va delante*:
Pídele un lápiz a la profesora
Ask the teacher for a pencil

▷ *La estructura* **pedir a alguien que haga algo**, *se traduce al inglés por* **ask** + *objeto* + *construcción de infinitivo*:
Le pedí a mi hermana que me trajera una alfombra de Turquía
I asked my sister to bring me a rug from Turkey
Le pediremos que nos haga un descuento
We'll ask him to give us a discount

Si el contexto es más formal **pedir** *también se puede traducir por* **request**:
Ambas partes en conflicto están pidiendo ayuda al extranjero
Both sides are requesting help from abroad

Para otros usos y ejemplos ver la entrada.

peduncular (ADJ) stalk (*antes de s*), peduncular (*Téc*)
pedúnculo (SM) stem, stalk
peerse* ▹ CONJUG 2a (VPR) = **pederse**
pega (SF) **1** (= *dificultad*) snag, problem • **todo son ~s** there's nothing but problems • **poner ~s** (= *objetar a algo*) to raise objections; (= *crear problemas*) to cause trouble
2 • **de ~*** (= *falso*) false, dud*; (= *de imitación*) fake, sham, bogus • **un billete de ~** a dud banknote*
3 (= *acción*) sticking
4 (= *chasco*) practical joke; (= *truco*) hoax, trick
5 (= *paliza*) beating, beating-up*
6 (*Caribe, Cono Sur, Méx*) (= *trabajo*) work
7 (*Caribe*) (= *liga*) birdlime
8 (*Cono Sur*) [*de enfermedad*] infectious period
9 • **MODISMOS**: • **estar en la ~** (*Cono Sur*) to be at one's best • **jugar a la ~** (*And*) to play tag
(SM) • **MODISMO**: • **ser el ~*** to be the one who always sees problems
pegachento (ADJ) sticky
pegada (SF) **1*** (= *atractivo*) appeal • **un cantante con mucha ~** a singer with great appeal
2 ▸ **pegada de carteles** (*Pol*) • **dio comienzo la campaña con la tradicional ~ de carteles** the campaign began with the traditional sticking up of posters
3 (*Cono Sur*) (= *mentira*) fib, lie
4 (*Cono Sur*) (= *acierto*) • **¡qué ~!** what a piece *o* stroke of luck! • **fue una ~ y por casualidad** it was a complete fluke
5 • **tiene una excelente ~** (*Boxeo*) he packs an excellent punch; (*Ftbl**) he has a good shot on him*
pegadillo (SM) (*And*) lace
pegadizo/a (ADJ) **1** (*Esp*) [*canción, melodía*] catchy
2 [*risa, enfermedad*] contagious
3 (= *pegajoso*) sticky
4 (= *postizo*) false
5 (*Esp*) (= *gorrón*) sponging*
(SM/F) (*Esp*) sponger*
pegado (ADJ) **1** (= *adherido*) (*gen*) stuck; (*con pegamento*) glued • **me desperté con los ojos ~s** I woke up with my eyes stuck together • **¿está bien pegada la foto?** is the photo stuck on properly? • **el póster estaba ~ a la pared con chinchetas** the poster was stuck *o* fixed to the wall with drawing pins; ▹ **falda**
2 (= *junto*) • ~ **a algo**: **el estadio está ~ al río** the stadium is right beside the river • **íbamos muy ~s al coche de delante** we were right behind the car in front • **pon el piano ~ a la pared** put the piano right up *o* flush against the wall • **la lámpara estaba muy pegada al techo** the lamp was almost touching the ceiling • **los corredores iban muy ~s unos a otros** the runners were bunched together • **se tira las horas pegada al ordenador** she spends hours glued to the computer • **se pasan el día ~s a los libros** they spend all day with their noses stuck in books* • **está todo el día ~ a su madre** he's a real mother's boy
3 (= *quemado*) [*arroz, leche*] burnt, burned (*EEUU*) • **oler a ~** to smell burnt • **MODISMO**: • **quedarse ~*** to get an electric shock, get fried (*EEUU**)
4 (*Esp*) (= *asombrado*) stunned • **me has dejado ~ con esa noticia** what you've just said has really stunned me *o* taken me aback, I'm really stunned by what you've just said
5 (*Esp‡*) • **estar ~** to not have a clue* • **no me sé nada del examen, estoy ~** I haven't got a clue about the exam*
(SM) (*Med*) (= *parche*) sticking plaster,

P

Band-Aid® (EEUU)

pegadura SF (*And*) practical joke

pegajoso ADJ **1** (= *que se adhiere*) [*superficie, suelo, manos*] sticky; [*miel*] sticky, gooey* • **la mesa está muy pegajosa** the table is all sticky • **hoy hace un calor ~** it's really sticky today
2 [*persona*] clingy*
3 (*LAm*) [*canción, melodía*] catchy
4 (= *contagioso*) contagious

pegamento SM glue, adhesive ▸ **pegamento de caucho** (*Aut*) rubber solution ▸ **pegamento de contacto** contact adhesive

pegar ▹ CONJUG 1h VT **1** (= *adherir*) **a** (*gen*) to stick; (*con cola*) to glue, stick; [+ *cartel*] to stick up; [+ *dos piezas*] to fix together; (*Inform*) to paste • **tengo que ~ las fotos en el álbum** I have to stick the photos into the album • **~ un sello** to stick a stamp on • **lo puedes ~ con celo** you can stick it on with Sellotape®, you can sellotape it on
• MODISMO: • **no ~ sello*** not to lift a finger
b (= *coser*) [+ *botón*] to sew on
2 (= *golpear*) (*gen*) to hit; (= *dar una torta a*) to smack • **Andrés me ha pegado** Andrés hit me • **hazlo o te pego** do it or I'll hit you • **es un crimen ~ a los niños** it's a crime to hit *o* smack children • **dicen que pega a su mujer** they say he beats his wife
3* (= *dar*) • **me pegó un golpe** he hit me • **~ un grito** to shout, cry out • **le han pegado un puntapié** they gave him a kick, they kicked him • **~ un salto** to jump (*with fright etc*) • **~ un susto a algn** to scare sb, give sb a fright • **¡qué susto me has pegado!** what a fright you gave me! • **le ~on un tiro** they shot him; ▹ fuego
4 (= *arrimar*) • **~ una silla a una pared** to move *o* put a chair up against a wall • **~ el oído a la puerta** to put one's ear to the door
• MODISMO: • **~ el oído** *o* **la oreja** to prick up one's ears
5* (= *contagiar*) to give (**a** to) • **me has pegado la gripe** you've given me the flu • **él me pegó la costumbre** I picked up the habit off him
6 • MODISMO: • **~la** (*And, Arg**) (= *tener suerte*) to be lucky; (= *lograrlo*) to manage it; (= *caer en gracia*) to have a hit (**con** with)
7 (*Méx*) (= *atar*) to tie, fasten (down); [+ *caballo*] to hitch up
8 (*Caribe*) [+ *trabajo*] to start
VI **1** (= *adherir*) to stick; (*Inform*) to paste
2 (= *agarrar*) [*planta*] to take (root); [*remedio*] to take; [*fuego*] to catch
3 • **~ contra algo** to hit sth • **pegamos contra un muro** we hit a wall • **~ en algo** (= *dar*) to hit sth; (= *rozar*) to touch sth • **la flecha pegó en el blanco** the arrow hit the target • **la pelota pegó en el árbol** the ball hit the tree • **pegaba con un palo en la puerta** he was pounding on *o* hitting the door with a stick • **las ramas pegan en los cristales** the branches beat against the windows • **el sol pega en esta ventana** the sun beats down through this window • **el piano pega en la pared** the piano is touching the wall
4* (= *armonizar*) to go well, fit; [*dos colores*] to match, go together • **es un ingrediente que no pega** it's an ingredient which does not go well with other dishes • **este sillón no pega aquí** this armchair doesn't look right here • **la cita no pega** the quotation is out of place • **~le a algn: no le pega nada actuar así** it's not like him to act like that • **~ con algo** to match sth, go with sth • **ese sombrero no pega con el abrigo** that hat doesn't match *o* go with the coat
5* (= *ser fuerte*) to be strong • **este vino pega (mucho)** this wine is really strong *o* goes to your head • **a estas horas el sol pega fuerte** the sun is really hot at this time of day
6* (= *tener éxito*) • **ese autor está pegando** that author's a big hit • **esta canción está pegando muy fuerte** this song is rocketing up the charts • **los jóvenes vienen pegando (fuerte)** the younger generation's coming up fast
7* (= *creer*) • **me pega que ...: me pega que no vendrá** I have a hunch that he won't come
8 • **~le a algo*** to be a great one for sth* • **~le a la bebida** to be a heavy drinker
9 (*Caribe, Méx**) (= *trabajar duro*) to slog away*
VPR **pegarse 1** (= *adherirse*) to stick • **vigila o se ~á el arroz** be careful or the rice will stick
2 (= *pelearse*) to hit each other, fight
3 • **~se a algn** (= *arrimarse*) to stay close to sb; (*Dep*) to stick close to sb • **pégate al grupo y no te perderás** stay close to the group and you won't get lost • **el niño se pegó a su madre** the boy clung to his mother • **si vamos a algún sitio siempre se nos pega** if we go anywhere he always latches on to us • **~se a una reunión** to gatecrash a meeting*
• MODISMO: • **~se a algn como una lapa** (*Esp*) to stick to sb like glue *o* a limpet
4* (= *contagiarse*) (*lit*) to be catching; (*fig*) to be infectious, be catchy • **todo se pega (menos la hermosura)** everything's catching (except good looks) • **se te ha pegado el acento andaluz** you've picked up an Andalusian accent
5* (= *darse*) • **~se un tiro** to shoot o.s. • **¡es para ~se un tiro!** it's enough to make you scream! • **~se un golpe** to hit o.s. • **me pegué un golpe en la cabeza** I hit my head • **se pega una vida padre** he lives the life of Riley
• MODISMOS: • **pegársela*** (= *fracasar*) to fail, come a cropper* • **pegársela a algn** (= *traicionar*) to double-cross sb; (= *ser infiel*) to cheat on sb

Pegaso SM Pegasus

pegatina SF sticker

pegativo ADJ (*CAm, Cono Sur*) sticky

pego* SM (*Esp*) • MODISMO: • **dar el ~:** • **es una imitación barata pero da el ~** it's a cheap imitation but it looks like the real thing

pegón* ADJ **1** [*persona*] tough, hard, given to violence
2 [*vino*] strong

pegoste SM **1** (*LAm*) (= *esparadrapo*) surgical tape
2 (*Caribe**) (= *colado*) gatecrasher
3 (*CAm‡*) (= *parásito*) scrounger*

pegote* SM **1** (*Culin*) sticky mess
2 • MODISMOS: • **echarse un ~** • **tirarse ~s** to brag*, exaggerate, show off
3 (= *gorrón*) hanger-on
4 (= *chapuza*) botch; (= *parche*) patch

pegotear* ▹ CONJUG 1a VI to sponge*, cadge

pegujal SM **1** (*Econ*) wealth, money; (= *hacienda*) estate
2 (*Agr*) small plot, small private plot, smallholding

peina SF back comb, ornamental comb

peinada SF combing • **darse una ~** to comb one's hair

peinado ADJ **1** • **bien ~** [*pelo*] well-combed; [*persona*] neat, well-groomed
2 (= *relamido*) [*persona*] foppish; [*estilo, ingenio*] affected
SM **1** [*de pelo*] hairdo, hairstyle ▸ **peinado de paje** pageboy hairstyle
2* (= *investigación*) check, investigation; (= *redada*) sweep, raid; (= *casa por casa*) house-to-house search

peinador(a) SM/F (= *persona*) hairdresser
SM **1** (= *bata*) dressing gown, peignoir
2 (*LAm*) (= *tocador*) dressing table

peinadura SF **1** (= *acción*) combing
2 peinaduras (= *pelos*) combings

peinar ▹ CONJUG 1a VT **1** [+ *pelo*] (*con peine*) to comb; (*con cepillo*) to brush • **me peinan en Zoila's** I get my hair done at Zoila's
2 [+ *caballo*] to comb, curry
3 [+ *zona*] to comb
4 (*LAm*) [+ *roca*] to cut
5 (*Arg**) (= *adular*) to flatter
6 (*Dep**) [+ *balón*] to head
VPR **peinarse** to comb one's hair • **~se a la griega** to do one's hair in the Greek style

peine SM comb • MODISMO: • **¡te vas a enterar de lo que vale un ~!** (*Esp**) now you'll find out what's what! ▸ **peine de púas** fine-toothed comb, nit comb

peinecillo SM fine comb

peineta SF back comb, ornamental comb

peinilla SF (*And, Caribe*) large machete

p.ej. ABR (= **por ejemplo**) e.g.

peje ADJ (*Méx*) stupid
SM **1** (*Zool*) fish ▸ **peje araña** weever ▸ **peje sapo** monkfish
2* (= *listillo*) twister, sharpie (*EEUU**)

pejiguera* SF bother, nuisance

Pekín SM Beijing, Peking

pela SF **1** (*Culin*) peeling
2 (*Esp**) (= *peseta*) peseta • **~s** (= *dinero*) money (*sing*) • **unas buenas ~s** a good few bucks* • **mucha ~** *o* **~ larga** lots of dough‡ • **mirar la ~** to be concerned only about money
• MODISMO: • **cambiar** *o* **echar la ~‡** to throw up*, puke (up)*
3 (*LAm**) (= *zurra*) beating
4 (*Méx**) [*de trabajo*] slog, hard work; (*CAm*) (= *fatiga*) exhaustion

pelada SF **1** (*LAm*) (= *corte de pelo*) haircut
2 (*Cono Sur*) (= *calva*) bald head
3 (*And, CAm, Caribe*) (= *error*) blunder
4 • **la Pelada** (*And, Caribe, Cono Sur*) (= *muerte*) Death

peladar SM (*Cono Sur*) arid plain

peladera SF **1** (*Med*) alopecia
2 (*CAm, Méx*) (= *chismes*) gossip, backbiting
3 (*Cono Sur*) (= *erial*) arid plain

peladero SM (*LAm*) = **pelador**

peladez* SF **1** (*Méx*) (= *vulgaridad*) vulgarity; (= *palabrota*) rude word, obscenity
2 (*And*) (= *pobreza*) poverty

peladilla SF (*Esp*) sugared almond

PELADO

A stock figure in Mexican theatre and film, the **pelado** is a kind of rural anti-hero cum lovable rogue who survives by his quick wits in the foreign environment of the city. The Mexican actor and comedian Mario Moreno (1911-94) based the character **Cantinflas**, for which he is famous all over the Spanish-speaking world, on the **pelado**. The **pelado** is closely related to the literary figure of the **pícaro** and forms part of a long line of anti-heroic characters in Hispanic literature.

▹ PÍCARO, CARPA

pelado/a ADJ **1** (= *sin pelo*) • **lleva la cabeza pelada** he has his head shaved
2 (*por el sol*) • **tengo la espalda pelada del sol** my back is peeling from being in the sun
3 [*fruta, patata*] peeled; [*gamba*] shelled • **tomates ~s** peeled tomatoes • **solo han dejado los huesos ~s** they left nothing but the bones
4 [*terreno*] treeless, bare; [*paisaje*] bare; [*tronco*] bare, smooth • **una montaña pelada**

a bare mountain
5 (= *escueto*) bare • **cobra el sueldo ~** he gets just his bare salary • **he sacado un cinco ~** I just scraped a five
6* (= *sin dinero*) broke*, penniless
7 (*Méx*) (= *grosero*) coarse, rude
8* [*número*] round • **el cinco mil ~** a round five thousand
9 (*CAm, Caribe*) (= *descarado*) impudent
SM * (= *corte de pelo*) haircut
SM/F **1**† (= *pobre*) pauper
2 (*Méx**) (= *obrero*) working-class person
3 (*And, CAm**) (= *bebé*) baby

pelador SM (*Culin*) peeler

peladura SF **1** (= *acción*) peeling
2 peladuras (= *mondaduras*) peel (*sing*), peelings
3 (= *calva*) bare patch

pelafustán/ana SM/F layabout, good-for-nothing

pelagatos SM INV, **pelagallos** SM INV nobody

pelágico ADJ pelagic, deep-sea (*antes de s*)

pelaje SM **1** (*Zool*) fur, coat
2 (= *apariencia*) • **tenía muy mal ~** he looked very suspicious *o* dodgy • **no me gusta nada el ~ de esa gente** I don't like the look of them at all • **¡qué ~ llevas! pareces un pedigüeño** just look at you! you look like a right tramp! • **y otros de ese ~** and others of that ilk • **de todo ~** of every kind
3 (= *pelo**) mop of hair*

pelambre SM **1** (*Zool*) skin, fleece (*cut from animal*)
2* [*de persona*] mop of hair*
3 (*en cabeza, piel*) bare patch
4 (*Cono Sur*) (= *murmullos*) gossip, slander

pelambrera* SF mop of hair*

pelanas SM INV nobody

pelandusca* SF (*Esp*) tart‡, slut‡

pelapatatas SM INV, **pelapapas** SM INV (*LAm*) potato peeler

pelar ▸ CONJUG 1a VT **1** (= *rapar*) • **lo han pelado al cero** *o* **al rape** they've cropped his hair*, they've completely shaved his hair off
2 [+ *fruta, patata*] to peel; [+ *habas, mariscos*] to shell
3 (= *despellejar*) to skin; (= *desplumar*) to pluck
4† (= *criticar*) to flay, criticize
5† (= *quitar el dinero a*) to clean out*, fleece*
6† (= *matar*) to do in‡, bump off‡
7 (*LAm*) (= *azotar*) to beat up*
8 • **~la** (*And**) (= *morir*) to kick the bucket‡, die
VI **1** (*Cono Sur*) (= *cotillear*) to gossip
2 (*Esp**) • **que pela: hace un frío que pela** it's bitterly cold • **la sopa está que pela** this soup is piping hot
VPR **pelarse 1** (= *cortarse el pelo*) to get one's hair cut • **voy a ~me** I'm going to get my hair cut
2 [*nariz, hombros*] to peel • **se me está pelando la espalda** my back is peeling
3 • MODISMOS: • **pelársela**** (= *masturbarse*) to toss off** • **pelárselas***: • **se las peló en cuanto vio a su padre** he ran off as soon as he saw his dad • **me las pelo** I'm off* • **corre que se las pela** he runs like nobody's business*
4 (*Méx*‡) (= *morir*) to kick the bucket‡

pelazón SF (*CAm, Méx*) **1** (= *chismes*) gossip, backbiting
2 (= *pobreza*) chronic poverty

peldaño SM (*Arquit*) step, stair; [*de escalera portátil*] rung

pelea SF (*a golpes, patadas*) fight; (= *discusión, riña*) quarrel, row • **armar una ~** to start a fight • **gallo de ~** fighting cock, gamecock ▸ **pelea de gallos** cockfight

peleado ADJ • **estoy peleada con dos amigas** I've fallen out with two friends • **María está peleada con su novio** María has broken up *o* split up with her boyfriend

peleador ADJ quarrelsome

pelear ▸ CONJUG 1a VI **1** (*físicamente*) to fight • **los dos púgiles ~án por el título mañana** the two boxers will fight for the title tomorrow • **los perros peleaban por un hueso** the dogs were fighting over a bone • **siempre me toca ~ con los niños a la hora del baño** I'm always the one who has to battle with the children at bathtime
2 (= *esforzarse*) to struggle • **tuvo que ~ mucho para mantener a su familia** he had to struggle hard to support his family, it was a hard struggle for him to support his family
VPR **pelearse 1** (*físicamente*) to fight • **dos niños se estaban peleando en el patio** there were two children fighting in the playground • **estaban peleándose a puñetazos** they were punching each other *o* laying into each other with their fists • **los hermanos se peleaban a patadas** the two brothers were kicking each other • **se estaban peleando por unos caramelos** they were fighting over some sweets • **~se con algn** to fight sb
2 (= *discutir*) to argue, quarrel • **siempre nos peleamos cuando hablamos de política** we always end up arguing whenever we talk about politics
3 (= *romper una relación*) [*dos amigos*] to fall out; [*novios*] to split up, break up • **se ha peleado con todas sus amigos** he's fallen out with all his friends • **se ha peleado con su novio** she has broken up *o* split up with her boyfriend

pelechar ▸ CONJUG 1a VI **1** (*Zool, Orn*) (= *perder pelo*) to moult, molt (*EEUU*); (= *criar pelo*) to grow new hair
2 (= *recuperarse*) [*persona*] to be on the mend, regain one's strength; [*negocio*] to be turning the corner
3 (*Cono Sur*) (= *enriquecerse*) prosper

pelecho SM (*Cono Sur, Méx*) **1** (= *pelo*) moulted fur; (= *piel*) sloughed skin
2 (= *ropa*) old clothing

pelele SM **1** (= *figura*) guy, straw doll; (*fig*) tool, puppet
2 (= *bobo*) simpleton
3 [*de bebé*] Babygro®, rompers (*pl*), creepers (*pl*) (*EEUU*)

pelendengue SM = **perendengue**

peleón ADJ **1** (= *belicoso*) aggressive
2 (= *discutidor*) argumentative
3 [*vino*] cheap, rough

peleona* SF (*gen*) row, set-to*; (*más violenta*) brawl

peleonero ADJ (*LAm*) = **peleón**

pelero SM **1** (*CAm, Cono Sur*) horse blanket
2 (*Caribe*) = **pelambre**

pelés** SMPL (*Esp*) balls** • MODISMO: • **estar en ~** to be stark naked

pelete SM **1** = **pelado**
2 • **en ~** stark naked

peletería SF **1** (= *tienda*) furrier's, fur shop; (= *oficio*) furriery
2 (*Caribe*) (= *zapatería*) shoe shop

peletero/a SM/F furrier

peli* SF = **película**

peliagudo ADJ [*tema*] tricky

pelicano[1] ADJ grey-haired

pelícano SM, **pelicano**[2] SM pelican

pelicorto ADJ short-haired

película SF **1** (*Cine*) film, movie (*EEUU*) • **hoy echan** *o* **ponen una ~ de Hitchcock por la tele** there's a Hitchcock film on TV tonight • **pasar una ~** to show a film • MODISMOS: • **una cosa de ~** like something in the movies, an astonishing thing, something out of this world • **fue de ~** it was incredible • **¡allá ~s!*** it's nothing to do with me! ▸ **película de acción** action film ▸ **película de animación** cartoon ▸ **película de aventuras** adventure film ▸ **película de dibujos (animados)** cartoon ▸ **película de época** period film ▸ **película de gángsters** gangster film ▸ **película de la serie B** B film, B movie (*esp EEUU*) ▸ **película del Oeste** western ▸ **película de miedo** horror film ▸ **película de terror** horror film ▸ **película en color** colour film, color film (*EEUU*) ▸ **película muda** silent film ▸ **película S** porn film ▸ **película sonora** talkie ▸ **película (de) vídeo** video film
2 (*Fot*) film ▸ **película virgen** unexposed film
3 (*Téc*) film ▸ **película autoadherible** (*Méx*) Clingfilm®, Saran Wrap® (*EEUU*)
4* (= *narración*) story, catalogue of events; (= *cuento*) tall story, tale • **¡cuánta ~!** what a load of rubbish!*
5 (*Caribe*) (= *disparate*) silly remark; (= *lío*) row, rumpus

peliculero* ADJ **1** (= *aficionado al cine*) fond of films *o* (*EEUU*) movies, fond of the cinema
2* (= *afectado*) showy

peligrar ▸ CONJUG 1a VI to be in danger • **~ de hacer algo** to be in danger of doing sth

peligro SM (*gen*) danger, peril (*liter*); (= *riesgo*) risk • **en ~ de extinción** in danger of extinction • **no hay ~ de la vida de la madre** the mother's life is not in danger • **estos gases constituyen un ~ para la salud** these gases pose a risk to health, these gases pose a health hazard • **¡ese niño es un ~ andante!** (*hum*) that child is a walking disaster area! • **correr ~**: • **corre el ~ de que lo descubran** he runs the risk of being found out • **bajo esta roca no corremos ~** we're in no danger under this rock, we're free from danger under this rock • **estar en ~** to be in danger • **está fuera de ~** he's out of danger • **poner en ~** to endanger, put at risk, jeopardize • **"peligro de incendio"** "fire risk", "fire hazard" • **"peligro de muerte"** "danger" ▸ **peligro amarillo** yellow peril

peligrosamente ADV (*gen*) dangerously; (= *arriesgadamente*) riskily

peligrosidad SF (*gen*) danger; (= *riesgo*) riskiness

peligroso ADJ (*gen*) dangerous; (= *arriesgado*) risky; [*herida*] ugly, nasty

pelilargo ADJ long-haired

pelillo* SM trifle, trivial thing • **no se para en ~s** he is not easily deterred • MODISMOS: • **echar ~s a la mar** to bury the hatchet • **¡~s a la mar!** (*Esp*) let bygones be bygones!

pelín* SM bit, small amount • **un ~ de música** a bit of music
ADV a bit, just a bit • **es un ~ tacaño** he's just a bit mean • **te pasaste un ~** you went a bit too far

pelinegro ADJ black-haired

pelirrojo/a ADJ red-haired, red-headed
SM/F redhead • **la pequeña pelirroja** the little redhead

pelirrubio ADJ fair-haired

pella SF **1** (*gen*) ball, round mass; (*sin forma*) dollop; (*Culin*) lump of lard
2 [*de coliflor*] head
3* (= *suma de dinero*) sum of money
4 • MODISMO: • **hacer ~s** to play truant*, play hooky (*EEUU**)

pelleja SF **1** (= *piel*) skin, hide
2* (= *prostituta*) whore
3* (= *mujer delgada*) thin woman
4 (*Esp*‡) (= *cartera*) wallet, billfold (*EEUU*)

pellejería SF **1** (= *pieles*) skins (*pl*), hides (*pl*)
2 (= *curtiduría*) tannery
3 pellejerías (*Cono Sur*) (= *dificultades*)

difficulties

pellejero/a‡ SM/F pickpocket

pellejo SM **1** [*de animal*] skin, hide; [*de persona**] skin; [*de uva*] skin • **MODISMOS**: • **no caber en el ~** to be bursting with pride • **estar en el ~ de algn**: • **no quisiera estar en su ~** I wouldn't like to be in his shoes • **ponerse en el ~ de algn**: • **ponte en su ~** put yourself in her shoes • **quitarle el ~ a algn** to flay sb, criticize sb harshly • **no tener más que el ~** to be all skin and bones
2* (= *vida*) neck* • **arriesgar el ~** to risk one's neck* • **perder el ~** to snuff it* • **salvar el ~** to save one's skin *o* neck*
3 (= *odre*) wineskin
4* (= *borracho*) drunk

pellet SM (PL: **pellets**) pellet

pellingajo SM (*And, Cono Sur*) **1** (= *trapo*) dishcloth
2 (= *objeto*) piece of junk

pelliza SF (*hecha de piel*) fur jacket; (*forrada de piel*) fur-lined jacket

pellizcar ▷ CONJUG 1g VT **1** [+ *persona, mejilla*] to pinch
2 [+ *comida*] to nibble, pick at

pellizco SM **1** (*en mejilla, brazo*) pinch
2 (= *cantidad pequeña*) small bit • **un ~ de sal** a pinch of salt • **MODISMO**: • **un buen ~*** a tidy sum*
3 [*de sombrero*] pinch, dent

pellón SM (*LAm*) *sheepskin saddle blanket*

pelma SMF* bore • **¡no seas ~!** don't be such a bore!
SM lump, solid mass

pelmazamente* ADV boringly

pelmazo/a* ADJ boring
SMF bore

pelo SM **1** (= *filamento*) [*de persona, animal*] hair; [*de barba*] whisker; (*Téc*) fibre, fiber (*EEUU*), strand • **un ~ rubio** a blond hair
2 (*en conjunto*) [*de persona*] hair; (= *piel*) fur, coat; [*de fruta*] down; [*de jersey*] fluff; [*de tejido*] nap, pile • **tiene el ~ rubio** she has blond hair • **tiene el ~ rizado** he has curly hair • **tienes mucho ~** you have thick hair • **tiene poco ~** his hair is thin • **se me está cayendo el ~** I am losing my hair • **cortarse el ~** to have one's hair cut • **dos caballos del mismo ~** two horses of the same colour ▸ **pelo de camello** camel-hair, camel's hair (*EEUU*)
3 [*de reloj*] hairspring
4 [*de diamante*] flaw
5 (= *grieta*) hairline crack
6 (= *sierra*) hacksaw blade
7 • **MODISMOS**: • **a pelo***: • **cabalgar** *o* **montar a ~** to ride bareback • **cantar a ~** to sing unaccompanied • **hacerlo a ~** (*sexualmente*) to have unprotected sex • **está más guapa a ~ que con maquillaje** she's prettier just as she is, without her make-up on • **ir a ~** (= *sin sombrero*) to go bareheaded; (= *desnudo*) to be stark naked • **pasar el mono a ~** (*de drogas*) to go through cold turkey • **agarrarse a un ~** to clutch at straws • **al ~***: • **te queda al ~** it looks great on you, it fits like a glove • **este regalo me viene al ~** this present is just what I needed *o* wanted • **viene al ~ el comentario** that comment is spot on • **un tema que viene muy al ~ en esta discusión** a subject which is highly relevant to this debate • **caérsele el ~ a algn** (*esp Esp**): • **¡se te va a caer el ~!** you're (in) for it now! • **cortar un ~ en el aire** to be pretty smart • **dar a algn para el ~*** (= *pegar*) to beat the living daylights out of sb*; (*en discusión*) to wipe the floor with sb*; (= *regañar*) to give sb a rollicking* • **con estos ~s***: • **¡Juan viene a cenar y yo con estos ~s!** Juan is coming to dinner and look at the state I'm in! • **ser de dos ~s** (*Cono Sur*) to be two-faced • **echar el ~** (*Cono Sur**) to waste time, idle • **lucirle el ~ a algn***: • **así nos luce el ~** and that's the awful state we're in, that's why we're so badly off • **de medio ~** (= *de baja calidad*) second-rate; (= *de baja categoría social*) of no social standing • **de ~ en pecho** manly • **un hombre de ~ en pecho** a real man • **hacer a ~ y pluma**‡ to be AC/DC‡ • **por los ~s** by the skin of one's teeth • **pasó el examen por los ~s** he passed the exam by the skin of his teeth, he scraped through the exam • **parece traído por los ~s** it seems far-fetched • **con ~s y señales** in minute detail • **soltarse el ~*** to let one's hair down* • **tener el ~ de la dehesa** to be unable to hide one's rustic *o* humble origins • **no tener ~s en la lengua** not to mince one's words • **no tocar un ~ de la ropa a algn** not to lay a finger on sb • **tomar el ~ a algn** to pull sb's leg • **no ver el ~ a algn*** not to see hide nor hair of sb • **no se les ve el ~ desde hace mucho** there's been no sign of them for ages; ▷ **punta**
8 • **un ~*** (= *un poco*) • **no se mueve un ~ de aire** *o* **viento** there isn't a breath of wind stirring • **no me fío un ~ de ellos** I don't trust them an inch • **me temo que te pasas un ~** I am afraid you are going a bit too far • **no afloja un ~** (*Cono Sur*) he won't give an inch • **no tiene un ~ de tonto** he's no fool • **no perdí el avión por un ~** I only just caught the plane • **nos escapamos por un ~** we had a close shave

pelón ADJ **1** (= *calvo*) bald, hairless; (= *rapado*) with a crew-cut, close-cropped
2 (= *sin recursos*) broke*, penniless; (= *pobre*) poor
3 (= *tonto*) thick*, stupid
4 (*And*) (= *con mucho pelo*) hairy, long-haired
SM **1** (= *pobre diablo*) poor wretch
2 (*LAm*) (= *niño*) child, baby
3 (*Cono Sur*) (= *melocotón*) nectarine
4 (*Caribe**) (= *error*) blunder, boob*

pelona SF **1** (= *calvicie*) baldness
2 • **la Pelona*** (= *muerte*) death

peloso ADJ hairy

pelota SF **1** (*Dep*) ball • **jugar a la ~** to play ball • **MODISMOS**: • **devolver la ~ a algn** to turn the tables on sb • **hacer la ~ a algn*** to suck up to sb • **lanzar ~s fuera** to dodge the issue • **pasarse la ~** to pass the buck* • **la ~ sigue en el tejado** it's all still up in the air ▸ **pelota base** baseball ▸ **pelota de goma** (*Mil*) rubber bullet ▸ **pelota vasca** pelota
2 pelotas*‡ (= *testículos*) balls*‡ • **¿que te deje el coche? ¡las ~s!** you expect me to lend you the car? what a bloody cheek!‡ • **en ~s** (= *desnudo*) stark naked, starkers‡; (= *sin dinero*) broke* • **coger** *o* **pillar a algn en ~s** to catch sb with their trousers down* • **dejar a algn en ~s** to strip sb clean *o* naked; (*en un juego*) to clean sb out* • **MODISMOS**: • **hinchar las ~s a algn** to get on sb's tits‡, bug sb* • **tener ~s** to have balls • **tocar las ~s a algn** to get on sb's tits‡, bug sb*
3* (= *cabeza*) nut*, noggin (*EEUU**), head
4 (*LAm*‡) [*de amigos*] bunch, gang
5 (*CAm, Caribe, Méx*) (= *pasión*) passion • **tener ~ por** to have a passion for
6 (*CAm, Caribe, Méx*) (= *amante*) girlfriend
SMF* creep*

pelotari (*Esp*) SMF pelota player

pelotazo SM **1** (*Esp*‡) drink • **pegarse un ~** to have a drink
2 (*Dep*) (*fuerte*) fierce shot; (*largo*) long ball
3 (*Esp**) (= *enriquecimiento*) • **la operación fue un ~ para los directivos** the directors made a fortune out of the deal • **la cultura del ~** the get-rich-quick culture

pelote‡ SM five-peseta coin

pelotear ▷ CONJUG 1a VT **1** (*Econ*) [+ *cuenta*] to audit
2 (*And**) • **~ un asunto** to turn sth over in one's mind
3 (*LAm**) (= *captar*) to catch, pick up
VI **1** (*Dep*) to knock a ball about, kick a ball about; (*Tenis*) to knock up
2 (= *reñir*) to bicker, argue

peloteo SM **1** (*Tenis*) (*como entrenamiento*) knock-up; (= *tirada larga*) rally
2 (*Ftbl*) kick-about*; [*de entrada*] warm-up
3* (= *adulación*) flattery
4 (= *intercambio*) exchange, sending back and forth • **hubo mucho ~ diplomático** there was a lot of diplomatic to-ing and fro-ing

pelotera* SF row, set-to*

pelotero/a ADJ* = **pelotillero**
SM/F **1** (*LAm*) (= *jugador*) ball player; [*de fútbol*] footballer; [*de béisbol*] baseball player
2* (= *lameculos*) creep‡

pelotilla* SF **1** (= *adulación*) • **hacer la ~ a algn** to suck up to sb*
2 [*de nariz*] bogey‡ • **hacer ~s** to pick one's nose

pelotilleo* SM crawling*, bootlicking*, brownnosing (*EEUU*‡)

pelotillero/a* ADJ crawling*, bootlicking*, brownnosing (*EEUU*‡)
SM/F crawler*, bootlicker*, brownnose (*EEUU*‡)

pelotón SM **1** [*de gente*] crowd; [*de atletas, ciclistas*] pack ▸ **pelotón de cabeza** leading group
2 (*Mil*) detachment, squad ▸ **pelotón de abordaje** boarding party ▸ **pelotón de demolición** demolition squad ▸ **pelotón de ejecución, pelotón de fusilamiento** firing squad
3 [*de hilos*] tangle, mat

pelotudez‡ SF (*LAm*) stupidity

pelotudo/a‡ ADJ **1** (= *valiente*) tough, gutsy
2 (*LAm*) (= *imbécil*) bloody stupid‡; (= *inútil*) useless; (= *descuidado*) slack, sloppy
3 (*CAm**) [*salsa*] lumpy
SM/F (*LAm*) bloody fool‡, jerk (*EEUU**)

pelpa‡ SF (*LAm*) joint‡, reefer‡

peltre SM pewter

peluca SF **1** (*para cabeza*) wig
2* (= *rapapolvo*) dressing-down*

peluche SM felt, plush; ▷ **oso**

peluchento ADJ silky, smooth

peluco‡ SM clock, watch

pelucón/ona ADJ (*And*) long-haired
SM/F (*Cono Sur*†) (= *conservador*) conservative; (*And*) (= *de alta posición*) bigwig, big shot*

peludo ADJ **1** (= *con mucho pelo*) hairy, shaggy; (= *con pelo largo*) long-haired; [*animal*] furry, shaggy; [*barba*] bushy
2 (*CAm**) (= *difícil*) hard
SM **1** (= *felpudo*) round felt mat
2 (*Cono Sur*) (*Zool*) (species of) armadillo
3 (*Cono Sur*‡) (= *borrachera*) • **agarrarse un ~** to get sloshed‡

peluquearse ▷ CONJUG 1a VPR (*LAm*) to have a haircut

peluquería SF **1** (= *establecimiento*) [*de mujeres, hombres*] hairdresser's; [*de hombres solo*] barber's (shop)
2 (= *oficio*) hairdressing

peluquero/a SM/F [*de mujeres, hombres*] hairdresser; [*de hombres solo*] barber

peluquín SM toupée, hairpiece • **MODISMO**: • **¡ni hablar del ~!*** no way!*

pelusa SF **1** (*Bot*) down; (*Cos*) fluff; (*en cara*) down, fuzz; (*bajo muebles*) fluff, dust
2* (*entre niños*) envy, jealousy

pelusiento ADJ (*And, Caribe*) hairy, shaggy

peluso‡ SM (*Mil*) squaddie*, recruit

pélvico ADJ pelvic

pelvis SF INV pelvis

P

peme‡ SM military policeman

PEMEX SM ABR = **Petróleos Mexicanos**

PEN SM ABR **1** (*Esp*) = **Plan Energético Nacional**
2 (*Arg*) = **Poder Ejecutivo Nacional**

pena SF **1** (= *tristeza*) sorrow • **tenía mucha ~ después de la muerte de su hijo** she grieved a lot *o* was extremely upset after her son's death • **tengo una ~ muy grande porque no está con nosotros** I'm very sad that he is not here with us • **alma en ~** lost soul • **dar ~**: • **da ~ verlos sufrir así** it's sad to see them suffer like that • **me daba ~ dejar España** I was sad *o* sorry to leave Spain • **Pepe me da mucha ~** I feel very sorry for Pepe • **morir de (la) ~** to die of a broken heart • MODISMO: • **sin ~ ni gloria**: • **ese año pasó sin ~ ni gloria** it was an uneventful sort of year • **la exposición pasó sin ~ ni gloria** the exhibition went almost unnoticed
2 (= *lástima*) shame, pity • **¿no podéis venir? ¡qué ~!** you can't come? what a shame *o* a pity! • **¡es una ~ que no tengamos más tiempo!** it's a shame *o* a pity that we haven't got more time!, it's too bad we haven't got more time! (*EEUU*) • **mi habitación está que da ~ verla** my room is in a terrible state* • **de ~**: • **la economía va de ~** the economy is in a terrible state • **el vestido le quedaba de ~** the dress looked terrible on her • **estar hecho una ~** to be in a sorry state
3 penas (= *problemas*) • **cuéntame tus ~s** tell me all your troubles • **logramos superarlo con muchas ~s** we had to struggle to overcome it • MODISMOS: • **ahogar las ~s** to drown one's sorrows • **¡allá ~s!** I don't care!, that's not my problem! • **a duras ~s** with great difficulty • **a duras ~s consiguió alcanzar la orilla** he only managed to reach the shore with great difficulty • **a duras ~s llegamos a fin de mes** we can barely make ends meet
4 (= *esfuerzo*) • **ahorrarse la ~** to save o.s. the trouble, save o.s. the bother* • **merecer** *o* **valer la ~** to be worth • **no merece la ~** it's not worth it • **una película que vale la ~ ver** a film that's worth seeing • **¿merece la ~ visitar la catedral?** is the cathedral worth a visit? • **no vale la ~ que perdamos el tiempo discutiendo eso** it's not worth wasting time arguing about it
5 (*Jur*) sentence • **el juez le impuso una ~ de tres años de prisión** the judge sentenced him to three years in prison • **bajo** *o* **so ~ de** [*+ castigo, multa, prisión*] on *o* under penalty of • **bajo ~ de muerte** on pain of death, on *o* under penalty of death • **tiene prohibido hacerlo, so ~ de ser expulsado** he is forbidden to do it, on *o* under penalty of expulsion ▸ **pena capital** capital punishment ▸ **pena de muerte** death penalty ▸ **pena máxima** maximum sentence; (*Ftbl*) penalty ▸ **pena pecuniaria** fine ▸ **pena privativa de libertad** custodial sentence
6 (*Méx, And*) (= *vergüenza*) embarrassment • **me da mucha ~** I'm very embarrassed • **¡qué ~!** how embarrassing! • **sentir** *o* **tener ~** to be *o* feel embarrassed, be *o* feel ill at ease
7 (*And*) (= *fantasma*) ghost

penable ADJ punishable

penacho SM **1** (*Orn*) tuft, crest
2 [*de casco, sombrero*] plume
3 (= *orgullo*) pride, arrogance
4 [*de humo*] plume

penado/a ADJ = **penoso**
SM/F convict

penal ADJ penal
SM **1** (= *prisión*) prison, (state) penitentiary (*EEUU*)
2 (*LAm*) (*Dep*) (= *penalty*) penalty (kick)

penales* SM INV police record (*sing*)

penalidad SF **1 penalidades** (= *dificultades*) hardship (*sing*)
2 (*Jur*) penalty, punishment

penalista SMF expert in criminal law, penologist

penalización SF **1** (= *sanción*) penalty, penalization • **recorrido sin penalizaciones** (*Dep*) clear round
2 (*Jur*) criminalization

penalizar ▸ CONJUG 1f VT **1** (= *sancionar*) to penalize
2 (*Jur*) to criminalize

penalti (PL: **penaltis**) SM, **penalty** (PL: **penaltys, penalties**) SM (*Dep*) penalty (kick) • **marcar de ~** to score from a penalty • **punto de ~** penalty spot • **pitar** *o* **señalar ~** to award a penalty • **transformar un ~** to convert a penalty, score a penalty • MODISMO: • **casarse de ~*** to have a shotgun wedding ▸ **penalti córner** penalty corner

penar ▸ CONJUG 1a VT **1** (*Jur*) to punish • **la ley pena el asesinato** the law punishes murder • **un delito penado con diez años de cárcel** a crime punishable by ten years' imprisonment
2 (*And*) [*difunto*] to haunt
VI **1** (= *sufrir*) [*persona*] to suffer; [*alma*] to be in torment • **ha penado mucho con su hijo enfermo** she has suffered terribly with her sick child • **ella pena por todos** she takes everybody's sufferings upon herself • **~ de amores** (*liter*) to go through the pains of love (*liter*)
2 (= *desear*) • **~ por algo** to pine for sth, long for sth • **~ por hacer algo** to pine to do sth, long to do sth
3 (*And*) [*difunto*] • **en ese lugar penan** that place is haunted
VPR **penarse** to grieve, mourn

penca SF **1** (*Bot*) (= *hoja*) leaf; (= *nervio*) main rib; (= *chumbera*) prickly pear
2 (*Méx*) [*de cuchillo*] blade
3 • MODISMOS: • **agarrar una ~** (*LAm**) to get sloshed* • **hacerse de ~s** to have to be coaxed into doing something
4 (*And*) • **una ~ de casa** a great big house • **una ~ de hombre** a fine-looking man • **una ~ de mujer** a fine-looking woman
5 (*LAm***) (= *pene*) prick**

pencar‡ ▸ CONJUG 1g VI to slog away*, slave away*

pencazo* SM (*CAm*) (= *golpe*) smack • **cayó un ~ de agua** it pelted down*, the skies opened

penco ADJ (*CAm**) (= *trabajador*) hard-working
SM **1** (= *persona*) dimwit*, nitwit*
2 (= *caballo*) nag
3 (*And*) • **un ~ de hombre** a fine-looking man
4 (*Caribe*‡) (= *homosexual*) poof‡, queer‡, fag (*EEUU*‡)

pendango ADJ (*Caribe*) (= *afeminado*) effeminate; (= *miedoso*) cowardly

pendejada* SF (*LAm*) **1** (= *tontería*) foolish thing
2 (= *acto cobarde*) cowardly act
3 (= *molestia*) curse, nuisance
4 (= *cualidad*) [*de necio*] foolishness, stupidity; [*del cobarde*] cowardliness

pendejear* ▸ CONJUG 1a VI (*And, Méx*) to act the fool

pendejeta* SMF (*And*) idiot

pendejo/a* ADJ **1** (*LAm*) (= *imbécil*) idiotic; (= *cobarde*) cowardly, yellow*
2 (*And*) (= *listo*) smart; (= *taimado*) cunning
3 (*Caribe, Méx*) (= *torpe*) ham-fisted
SM/F **1** (*LAm*) (= *imbécil*) fool, idiot; (= *cobarde*) coward
2 (*Cono Sur*) (= *muchacho*) kid*; (= *sabelotodo*) know-all
SM [*del pubis*] pubic hair, pube‡

pendencia SF (= *riña*) quarrel; (= *pelea*) fight, brawl • **armar ~** to stir up trouble

pendenciero/a ADJ quarrelsome, argumentative
SM/F troublemaker

pender ▸ CONJUG 2a VI **1** (= *colgar*) to hang (**de**, **en** from, **sobre** over) • **la amenaza que pende sobre nosotros** the threat hanging over us
2 (*Jur*) to be pending
3 (= *depender*) to depend (**de** on)

pendiente ADJ **1** (= *a la expectativa*) • **estar ~ de algo: estaban ~s de su llegada** they were waiting for him to arrive • **estamos ~s de lo que él decida** we are waiting to see what he decides • **quedamos ~s de sus órdenes** we await your instructions
2 (= *atento*) • **estar ~ de algo/algn: está muy ~ de la salud de su madre** he always keeps an eye on his mother's health • **está demasiado ~ de su novio** she's too wrapped up in her boyfriend • **estaban muy ~s de lo que decía** they were listening to her intently
3 [*juicio, caso, pedido*] pending • **aún tenemos un par de asuntos ~s** we still have a couple of matters pending
4 [*cuenta*] outstanding, unpaid
5 [*asignatura*] • **tengo las matemáticas ~s** I have to resit maths
6 (= *colgado*) hanging
SM (= *arete*) earring
SF [*de un terreno*] slope; [*de un tejado*] pitch • **subieron por una ~ muy pronunciada** they climbed up a steep slope • **en ~** sloping • MODISMO: • **estar en la ~ vital** to be over the hill*

pendil SM (woman's) cloak • MODISMO: • **tomar el ~*** to pack up*, clear out*

péndola SF **1** (= *pluma*) pen, quill
2 [*de puente*] suspension cable

pendolear ▸ CONJUG 1a VI **1** (*LAm*) (= *escribir mucho*) to write a lot; (*Cono Sur*) (= *tener buena letra*) to write neatly
2 (*Méx*) to be good in difficult situations, know how to manage people sensibly

pendolista SMF penman, calligrapher

pendón SM **1** (= *bandera*) banner, standard; [*de forma triangular*] pennant
2* (= *vaga*) lazy woman; (= *mujer promiscua*) tart‡, slut‡
3 • MODISMO: • **ser un ~**†* to be an awkward customer*

pendona* SF = **pendón**

pendonear* ▸ CONJUG 1a VI to loaf around*, hang out*

pendoneo* SM • **irse de ~** to go out round the streets*

péndulo SM pendulum ▸ **péndulo de Foucault** Foucault's Pendulum

pene SM penis

Penélope SF Penelope

penene* SMF = PNN

peneque ADJ ‡ (= *borracho*) • **estar ~** to be pickled‡
SM (*Méx*) (*Culin*) stuffed tortilla

penetrable ADJ penetrable

penetración SF **1** (= *acción*) penetration
2 (= *agudeza*) sharpness, acuteness; (= *visión*) insight

penetrador ADJ = **penetrante**

penetrante ADJ **1** [*herida*] deep
2 [*arma*] sharp; [*frío, viento*] biting; [*sonido*] piercing; [*vista*] acute; [*aroma*] strong;

P

[*mirada*] sharp, penetrating
3 [*genio, mente*] keen, sharp; [*ironía*] biting

penetrar ▹ CONJUG 1a VI **1** (= *entrar*) • **~on a través de** *o* **por una claraboya** they entered through a skylight • **el humo penetraba a través de las rendijas** the smoke was filtering through the cracks • **el agua había penetrado a través de** *o* **por las paredes** the water had seeped into the walls • **~ en: penetramos en un túnel** we went into *o* entered a tunnel • **la luz apenas penetra en la habitación** hardly any light enters the room • **el cuchillo penetró en la carne** the knife went into *o* entered *o* penetrated the flesh • **ocho hombres armados ~on en la embajada** eight gunmen broke into the embassy • **penetramos poco en el mar** we did not go far out to sea • **su ingratitud penetró hondamente en mi corazón** her ingratitude pierced me to the bone
2 (*frm*) (= *descifrar*) to penetrate • **~ en el sentido de algo** to penetrate the meaning of sth
VT **1** (= *atravesar*) to go right through • **un frío glacial le penetró los huesos** an icy cold went right through to her bones
2 (*sexualmente*) to penetrate
3 (*frm*) (= *descubrir*) [+ *misterio*] to fathom; [+ *secreto*] to unlock; [+ *sentido*] to grasp; [+ *intención*] to see through, grasp
VPR **penetrarse** • **~se de algo** (*frm*) (= *absorber*) to become imbued with sth; (*Esp*) (= *comprender*) to understand sth fully, become fully aware of (the significance of) sth

peneuvista (*Esp*) ADJ • **política ~** policy of the PNV, PNV policy; ▹ **PNV**
SMF member of the PNV

penga SF (*And*) bunch of bananas

penicilina SF penicillin

península SF peninsula ▸ **la Península Ibérica** the Iberian Peninsula

peninsular ADJ peninsular
SMF • **los ~es** peninsular Spaniards

penique SM penny • **~s** pence • **un ~** a penny, one penny

penitencia SF **1** (= *estado*) penitence
2 (= *castigo*) penance • **en ~** as a penance • **imponer una ~ a algn** to give sb a penance • **hacer ~** to do penance (**por** for)

penitenciado/a SM/F (*LAm*) convict

penitencial ADJ penitential

penitenciar ▹ CONJUG 1b VT to impose a penance on

penitenciaría SF prison, (state) penitentiary (*EEUU*)

penitenciario ADJ penitentiary, prison (*antes de s*)
SM confessor

penitente ADJ **1** (*Rel*) penitent
2 (*And*) (= *tonto*) silly
SMF (*Rel*) penitent; ▹ **SEMANA SANTA**
SM (*Cono Sur*) **1** (= *pico*) rock pinnacle, isolated cone of rock
2 (= *figura de nieve*) snowman

penol SM yardarm

penosamente ADV arduously, laboriously, with great difficulty

penoso ADJ **1** (= *doloroso*) painful • **me veo en la penosa obligación de comunicarles que …** I regret to have to inform you that …
2 (= *difícil*) [*tarea*] arduous, laborious; [*viaje*] gruelling, grueling (*EEUU*)
3 (= *lamentable*) pitiful • **fue un espectáculo ~** it was a sorry *o* pitiful sight • **era ~ ver la casa en ese estado** the house was a sorry *o* pitiful sight, it was pitiful to see the house in such a state
4 (*And, Méx*) (= *tímido*) shy, timid
5 (*And, Méx*) (= *embarazoso*) embarrassing

penquista (*Chile*) ADJ of/from Concepción
SMF native/inhabitant of Concepción • **los ~s** the people of Concepción

pensado ADJ • **un proyecto poco ~** a badly-thought-out *o* an ill-thought-out scheme • **lo tengo bien ~** I have thought it over *o* out carefully • **tengo ~ hacerlo mañana** I mean *o* intend to do it tomorrow • **bien ~, creo que …** on reflection, I think that … • **en el momento menos ~** when you least expect it

pensador(a) SM/F thinker

pensamiento SM **1** (= *facultad*) thought • MODISMO: • **como el ~** in a flash
2 (= *mente*) mind • **acudir** *o* **venir al ~ de algn** to come to sb's mind • **no le pasó por el ~** it never occurred to him, it never entered his mind • **envenenar el ~ de algn** to poison sb's mind (**contra** against) • **ni por ~** I wouldn't dream of it
3 (= *cosa pensada*) thought • **mal ~** nasty thought • **el ~ de Quevedo** Quevedo's thought • **adivinar los ~s de algn** to read sb's thoughts, guess what sb is thinking • **nuestro ~ sobre este tema** our thinking on this subject ▸ **pensamiento único** (*Pol*) single system of values
4 (= *propósito*) idea, intention • **mi ~ es hacer algo** my idea *o* intention is to do sth
5 (*Bot*) pansy

pensante ADJ thinking

pensar ▹ CONJUG 1j VT **1** (= *opinar*) to think • **~ de**: • **¿qué piensas de ella?** what do you think of her? • **¿qué piensas del aborto?** what do you think about abortion? • **~ que** to think that • **—¿piensas que van a venir? —pienso que sí** "do you think they'll come?" — "I think so" • **dice que las mujeres no tendrían que trabajar, yo pienso que sí** he says women shouldn't work, I think they should • **yo pienso que no** I don't think so
2 (= *considerar*) to think about, think over • **lo ~é** I'll think about it, I'll think it over • **esto es para ~lo** this needs thinking about *o* careful consideration • **lo pensó mejor** she thought better of it • **me pongo triste solo con ~lo** the mere thought of it makes me sad • **pensándolo bien …** on second thoughts …, on reflection … • **piénsalo bien antes de responder** think carefully before you answer • **¡ni ~lo!** no way!*
3 (= *decidir*) • **~ que** to decide that, come to the conclusion that … • **he pensado que no vale la pena** I've decided that it's not worth it, I've come to the conclusion that it's not worth it
4 (= *tener la intención de*) • **~ hacer algo** to intend to do sth • **pienso seguir insistiendo** I intend to keep on trying • **no pensaba salir** I wasn't intending *o* planning to go out • **no pienso volver a Cuba** I have no intention of going back to Cuba • **no pienso decir nada** I won't be saying anything
5 (= *concebir*) to think up • **¿quién pensó este plan?** who thought this plan up?, whose idea was this plan?
6 (= *esperar*) • **cuando menos lo pienses** when you least expect it • **sin ~lo** unexpectedly
VI **1** (= *tener ideas*) to think • **eso me hace ~** that makes me think • **quieren imponer su forma de ~** they want to impose their way of thinking • **después de mucho ~ tuve una idea** after much thought I had an idea • **~ en algo/algn** to think about sth/sb • **¿en qué piensas?** what are you thinking about? • **estaba pensando en ir al cine esta tarde** I was thinking of going to the cinema this evening • **solo piensa en pasarlo bien** all he thinks about is having a good time • **pienso mucho en ti** I think about you a lot • **~ para sí** to think to o.s. • **dar que ~**: • **el hecho de que no llamara a la policía da que ~** the fact that she didn't call the police makes you think • **un reportaje que da que ~** a thought-provoking article • **dar que ~ a la gente** to set people thinking, arouse suspicions • **sin ~** without thinking • **~ sobre algo** to think about sth • MODISMO: • **~ con los pies**: • **estás pensando con los pies** you're not using your head
2 • **~ bien de algo/algn** to think well of sth/sb • **~ mal de algo/algn** to think ill of sth/sb • **¡no pienses mal!** don't be nasty! • **¡siempre pensando mal!** what a nasty mind you've got! • REFRÁN: • **piensa mal y acertarás** you can't trust anybody
3 (= *aspirar*) • **~ en algo** to aim at sth • **piensa en una cátedra** he's aiming at a chair
VPR **pensarse** • **piénsatelo** think it over • **tienes nueve días para pensártelo** you have nine days to think it over *o* to think about it • **sin pensárselo dos veces** without a second thought • **después de pensárselo mucho** after thinking about it long and hard, after much thought

pensativamente ADV pensively, thoughtfully

pensativo ADJ pensive, thoughtful

Pensilvania SF Pennsylvania

pensión SF **1** (*por vejez*) pension; (*por invalidez, de divorciada*) allowance • **cobrar la ~** to draw one's pension ▸ **pensión alimenticia** alimony, maintenance ▸ **pensión asistencial** state pension ▸ **pensión contributiva** contributory pension ▸ **pensión de invalidez, pensión de inválidos** disability allowance ▸ **pensión de jubilación, pensión de retiro** retirement pension ▸ **pensión de viudedad** widow's/widower's pension ▸ **pensión escalada** graduated pension ▸ **pensión vitalicia** annuity
2 (= *casa de huéspedes*) boarding house, guest house; (*Univ*) lodgings (*pl*); (*And*) (= *bar*) bar, café
3 (= *precio*) board and lodging • **media ~** half board ▸ **pensión completa** full board
4 (*Univ*) scholarship; [*de viaje*] travel grant
5 (*And, Cono Sur*) (= *preocupación*) worry, anxiety; (= *remordimiento*) regret
6† (= *molestia*) drawback, snag

pensionado/a ADJ pensioned
SM/F (= *pensionista*) pensioner
SM (= *internado*) boarding school

pensionar ▹ CONJUG 1a VT **1** [+ *jubilado*] give a pension to; [+ *estudiante*] to give a grant to
2 (*And, Cono Sur*) (= *molestar*) to bother; (= *preocupar*) to worry

pensionista SMF **1** (= *jubilado*) pensioner, old-age pensioner ▸ **pensionista por invalidez** recipient of disability allowance
2 (= *huésped*) lodger, paying guest
3 (*Escol*) boarder
4 (*LAm*) (= *subscriptor*) subscriber

pentagonal ADJ pentagonal

pentágono SM pentagon • **el Pentágono** (*en EEUU*) the Pentagon

pentagrama SM stave, staff

pentámetro SM pentameter

Pentateuco SM Pentateuch

pentatlón SM pentathlon

pentatónico ADJ pentatonic

Pentecostés SM **1** (*cristiano*) Whitsun, Whitsuntide • **domingo de ~** Whit Sunday
2 (*judío*) Pentecost

penúltima SF **1** (*Ling*) penult, penultima
2* (= *bebida*) • **vamos a tomarnos la ~** let's have one for the road*

penúltimo/a ADJ, SM/F penultimate, last but one

penumbra SF half-light, semi-darkness • sentado en la ~ seated in the shadows
penuria SF (= pobreza) poverty; (= escasez) shortage, dearth
peña SF 1 (Geog) crag
2 (= grupo) group, circle; (pey) coterie, clique; (LAm) (= club) folk club; (= fiesta) party • forma parte de la ~ he's a member of the circle • hay ~ en el café los domingos the group meets in the café on Sundays ▸ peña deportiva supporters' club ▸ peña taurina club of bullfighting enthusiasts
3* (= gente) crowd • hay mucha ~ there's loads of people*
4 (Cono Sur) (= montepío) pawnshop
peñascal SM (gen) rocky place; (= colina) rocky hill
peñasco SM 1 (= piedra) large rock, boulder
2 (= risco) rock, crag • MODISMO: • no se me pasó por el ~* it never occurred to me
peñascoso ADJ rocky, craggy
peñazo* ADJ • ¡no seas tan ~! don't be such a pain!*
SM pain (in the neck)* • dar el ~ to be a pain*, be a bore*
peñista SMF (Dep) member of a supporters' club
peñón SM 1 (= roca) wall of rock, crag
2 • el Peñón the Rock (of Gibraltar)
peños‡ SMPL ivories*, teeth
peñusco* SM (Caribe, Cono Sur) crowd
peo‡ SM • ¡vete al peo! go to hell!*
peón SM 1 (Téc) labourer, laborer (EEUU); (esp LAm) (Agr) farm labourer, farmhand; (Taur) assistant; (Méx) (= aprendiz) apprentice; (= ayudante) assistant ▸ peón caminero navvy, roadmender ▸ peón de albañil bricklayer's mate
2 (Ajedrez) pawn
3 (Mil, Hist) infantryman, foot-soldier
4 (= peonza) spinning top
5 (Mec) spindle, shaft
peonada SF 1 (Agr) day's stint, day's shift
2 (= trabajadores) gang of labourers, gang of laborers (EEUU)
peonaje SM (= trabajadores) group of labourers, group of laborers (EEUU); (Taur) assistants (pl)
peonar ▹ CONJUG 1a VI (Cono Sur) to work as a labourer
peoneta SM (Chile) (Aut) lorry driver's mate, truck driver's mate (EEUU)
peonía SF peony
peonza SF 1 (= trompo) (spinning) top
2* (= persona) busy bee* • ser una ~ to be always on the go
3 • MODISMO: • ir a ~‡ to go on foot, hoof it*
peor ADJ 1 (comparativo de malo) [producto, resultado, situación] worse; [oferta] lower; [calidad] poorer • la película era ~ de lo que yo pensaba the film was worse than I thought • su situación es ~ que la nuestra their situation is worse than ours • un vino de ~ calidad an inferior wine • ir a ~ to get worse • la situación fue a ~ the situation got worse • y lo que es ~ and what's worse • ~ es nada (LAm) it's better than nothing; ▹ tanto
2 (superlativo de malo) worst • no se lo deseo ni a mi ~ enemigo I wouldn't wish it on my worst enemy • es el ~ de la clase he is the worst in the class • en el ~ de los casos if the worst comes to the worst • lo ~: • lo ~ de todo es que no podemos hacer nada the worst thing is that there is nothing we can do • ponerse en lo ~ to imagine the worst • la ~ parte the worst part • ya hemos hecho la ~ parte del trabajo we have already done the worst part of the job • te ha tocado la ~ parte en este asunto you came off worst in this business
ADV 1 (comparativo de mal) worse • ahora veo mucho ~ my sight is much worse now • escribo cada vez ~ my handwriting is getting worse and worse • hoy hemos jugado ~ que nunca we played worse than ever today • si no le gusta, ~ para él if he doesn't like it, that's his loss o that's just too bad; ▹ mal, mejor
2 (superlativo de mal) worst • ¿quién es el que lo hace ~ de los tres? who does it worst out of the three?, which of the three does it worst? • esta es la carta ~ redactada que he leído nunca this is the most badly o the worst written letter I've ever read
peoría SF worsening, deterioration
Pepa SF (forma familiar de Josefa, María José) • MODISMO: • ¡viva la ~! (por despreocupación) and to hell with everybody else!*; (por regocijo) jolly good!*
pepa SF 1 (LAm) (= semilla) [de uva, tomate] pip; [de melocotón, dátil] stone • MODISMO: • aflojar la ~* to spill the beans*
2 (LAm) (= canica) marble
3 (And*) (= mentira) lie
4 (And) (= pillo) rogue
pepazo SM 1 (LAm) (= tiro) shot, hit; (= pedrada) throw
2 (And*) (= mentira) lie
Pepe SM (forma familiar de José) • MODISMO: • ponerse como un ~* to have a great time*
pepe SM 1 (And, Caribe*) (= petimetre) dandy
2 (CAm) (= biberón) feeding bottle
pepenado/a SM/F (CAm, Méx) (= huérfano) orphan; (= expósito) foundling
pepenador(a) SM/F (Méx) scavenger (on rubbish tip)
pepenar ▹ CONJUG 1a VT 1 (CAm, Méx) (= recoger) to pick up; (en la basura) to search through; (= escoger) to choose; (= obtener) to get, obtain
2 (Méx) (= agarrar) to grab hold of; (= registrar) to pick through, poke about in; (= robar) to steal
3 (Méx) [+ huérfano] to take in, bring up
VI (CAm, Méx) to search through rubbish tips
pepián SM (And, CAm, Méx) (= salsa) thick chilli sauce; (= guiso) meat cooked in thick chilli sauce
pepinazo* SM 1 (= explosión) bang
2 (Ftbl) screamer*, scorcher*
3 (= accidente) smash
pepinillo SM gherkin
pepino SM 1 (Bot) cucumber • MODISMOS: • me importa un ~ • no se me da un ~* I don't care two hoots*, I don't give a damn*
2‡ (= cabeza) nut*, bonce*, noggin (EEUU*)
3** (= pene) prick**
Pepita SF forma familiar de Josefa
pepita SF 1 (Vet) pip • MODISMO: • no tener ~ en la lengua to be outspoken, not to mince one's words
2 (Bot) pip
3 (Min) nugget
Pepito SM forma familiar de José
pepito SM 1 (Culin) meat sandwich
2 (And, CAm, Caribe*) (= petimetre) dandy
pepitoria SF 1 (Esp) (Culin) • pollo en ~ chicken fricassée
2 (fig) hotchpotch, hodgepodge (EEUU)
3 (CAm) (= semillas) dried pumpkin seeds (pl)
pepón‡ ADJ (And) good-looking, dishy*
pepona SF large cardboard doll
pepsina SF pepsin
péptico ADJ peptic
péptido SM peptide
peptona SF peptone
peque* SMF kid*, child
pequeñajo/a* ADJ little, tiny
SM/F little rascal, little devil
pequeñez SF 1 [de tamaño] smallness, small size; [de altura] shortness
2 [de miras] pettiness, small-mindedness
3 (= nada) trifle, trivial thing • preocuparse por pequeñeces to worry about trifles
pequeñín/ina ADJ tiny, little
SM/F little one
pequeño/a ADJ small, little; [cifra] small, low; (= bajo) short • el hermano ~ the youngest brother • un niño ~ a small child • cuando era ~ • de ~ when I was a child, when I was little • un castillo en ~ a miniature castle • un negocio en ~ a small-scale business
SM/F child • los ~s the children, the little ones • soy el ~ I'm the youngest
pequeñoburgués/esa ADJ petit bourgeois
SM/F petit bourgeois/petite bourgeoise
pequero* SM (Cono Sur) cardsharp
pequinés/esa ADJ of/from Peking
SM/F native/inhabitant of Peking • los pequineses the people of Peking
SM (= perro) Pekinese, Pekingese
pera[1] SF 1 (Bot) pear • MODISMOS: • eso es pedir ~s al olmo that's asking the impossible • es~r a ver de qué lado caen las ~s to wait and see which way the cat will jump • hacerse una ~** to wank** • partir ~s con algn to fall out with sb • poner a algn las ~s a cuarto to tell sb a few home truths • ser la ~* to be the limit • tirarse la ~ (And*) to play truant, play hooky (EEUU) • tocarse la ~‡ to sit on one's backside (doing nothing)
2 (= barba) goatee; (Chile*) (= barbilla) chin
3 [de atomizador, bocina] bulb
4 (Elec) (= bombilla) bulb; (= interruptor) switch
5‡ (= cabeza) nut*, bonce*, noggin (EEUU*)
6 peras* (= pechos) tits**
7* (= empleo) cushy job*
8 (LAm) (Dep) punchball
pera[2]* ADJ INV (= pijo) posh* • un barrio ~ a posh area • fuimos a un restaurante muy ~ we went to a really swish o posh restaurant* • niño o pollo ~ spoiled upper-class brat
pera[3]‡ SM fence*, receiver (of stolen goods)
peral SM pear tree
peraltado ADJ (Arquit) canted, sloping; [curva, carretera] banked, cambered
SM = peralte
peraltar ▹ CONJUG 1a VT [+ curva, carretera] to bank, camber
peralte SM (Arquit) cant, slope; [de curva, carretera] banking, camber
perca SF perch
percal SM, percala SF (And, Méx)
1 (= tejido) percale • MODISMO: • conocer el ~* to know what the score is*
2‡ (= dinero) dough‡, cash
percán SM (Chile) mould, mold (EEUU), mildew
percance SM 1 (gen) misfortune, mishap; (= accidente) accident; (en plan) setback, hitch • sufrir o tener un ~ to suffer a mishap
2 (Econ) perquisite, perk*
percanque SM (Cono Sur) mould, mold (EEUU), mildew
per cápita ADV per capita
percatarse ▹ CONJUG 1a VPR • ~ de (= observar) to notice; (= comprender) to realize; (= hacer caso de) to heed; (= guardarse de) to guard against
percebe SM 1 (Zool) barnacle
2* (= tonto) idiot, twit*
percentil SM percentile
percepción SF 1 (facultad) perception ▸ percepción extrasensorial extrasensory perception

2 (= *idea*) perception, idea
3 (*Com, Econ*) collection; (= *recibo*) receipt

perceptible ADJ **1** (= *visible*) perceptible, noticeable
2 (*Com, Econ*) payable, receivable

perceptiblemente ADV perceptibly, noticeably

perceptivo ADJ perceptive

perceptor(a) SM/F (*gen*) recipient; [*de impuestos*] collector, receiver ▸ **perceptor(a) de subsidio de desempleo** *person who draws unemployment benefit*

percha SF **1** (*para ropa*) (clothes) hanger; (= *colgador*) clothes rack; (*para sombreros*) hat stand • **vestido de ~** ready-made dress, off-the-peg dress
2 (*Téc*) rack ▸ **percha de herramientas** toolrack
3 (*para pájaros*) perch
4 (= *tronco*) pole
5* (= *tipo*) build, physique; [*de mujer*] figure
6 (*And*) (= *ostentación*) showiness • **tener ~** (*Cono Sur*) to be smart
7 (*And*) (= *ropa*) new clothes (*pl*), smart clothing; (*Caribe*) (= *chaqueta*) jacket; (= *traje*) suit
8 (*Cono Sur*) (= *montón*) pile
9 (*Méx**) (= *grupo*) gang

perchero SM [*de pared*] clothes rack; [*de pie*] coat stand

perchudo ADJ (*And*) smart, elegant

percibir ▹ CONJUG 3a VT **1** (= *notar*) to perceive, notice; (= *ver*) to see, observe; [+ *peligro*] to sense, scent • **~ que ...** to perceive that ..., observe that ...
2 [+ *sueldo, subsidio*] to draw, receive

percollar ▹ CONJUG 1a VT (*And*) to monopolize

percuchante SM (*And*) fool

percudir ▹ CONJUG 3a VT (= *deslustrar*) to tarnish, dull; [+ *ropa*] to dirty, mess up; [+ *cutis*] to spoil

percusión SF percussion • **instrumento de ~** percussion instrument

percusionar ▹ CONJUG 1a VT to hit, strike

percusionista SMF percussionist

percusor SM (*Téc*) hammer; [*de arma*] firing pin

percutir ▹ CONJUG 3a VT to strike, tap

percutor SM = **percusor**

perdedor(a) ADJ **1** [*baza, equipo*] losing
2 (= *olvidadizo*) forgetful, given to losing things
SM/F loser • **buen ~** good loser

perder ▹ CONJUG 2g VT **1** [+ *objeto, dinero, peso*] to lose • **he perdido el monedero** I've lost my purse • **a los seis años perdió a su padre** she lost her father when she was six • **he perdido cinco kilos** I've lost five kilos • **había perdido mucha sangre** she had lost a lot of blood • **ha perdido mucho dinero en la bolsa** she has lost a lot of money on the stock market • **no tienes nada que ~** you have nothing to lose • **~ el conocimiento** to lose consciousness • **~ la costumbre** to get out of the habit • **~ algo de vista** to lose sight of sth • **nunca pierde de vista el fin que persigue** he never loses sight of his goal • **no lo pierdas de vista** don't let him out of your sight • **conviene no ~ de vista que ...** we mustn't forget that ..., we mustn't lose sight of the fact that ...
2 [+ *tiempo*] to waste • **¡me estás haciendo ~ el tiempo!** you're wasting my time! • **sin ~ un momento** without wasting a moment
3 [+ *aire, aceite*] to leak • **el vehículo pierde aceite** the car is leaking oil, the car has an oil leak • **la pelota perdió aire** the ball went flat
4 (= *no coger*) [+ *tren, avión*] to miss; [+ *oportunidad*] to miss, lose • **no pierde detalle** he doesn't miss a thing
5 (= *destruir*) to ruin • **ese vicio le ~á** that vice will ruin him, that vice will be his ruin • **ese error le perdió** that mistake was his undoing • **lo que le pierde es ...** where he comes unstuck is ...
6 (*Jur*) to lose, forfeit
VI **1** (*en competición, disputa*) to lose • **el equipo perdió por 5-2** the team lost 5-2 • **tienen** *o* **llevan todas las de ~** they look certain to lose • **saber ~** to be a good loser • **salir perdiendo**: • **salí perdiendo en el negocio** I lost out on the deal • **salí perdiendo en la discusión** I came off worst in the argument
2 (= *empeorar*) • **era un buen cantante, pero ha perdido mucho** he was a good singer, but he's gone downhill • **era muy guapo, pero ha perdido bastante** he isn't nearly as good-looking as he used to be • **ha perdido mucho en mi estimación** he has gone down a lot in my estimation
3 [*tela*] to fade
4 • **echar a ~** [+ *comida, sorpresa*] to ruin, spoil; [+ *oportunidad*] to waste • **echarse a ~** [*comida*] to go off; [*sorpresa*] to be ruined, be spoiled
VPR **perderse 1** [*persona*] to get lost • **tenía miedo de ~me** I was afraid of getting lost *o* losing my way • **se perdieron en el bosque** they got lost in the wood • **se perdió en un mar de contradicciones** he got lost in a mass of contradictions • **¡piérdete!*** get lost!*
2 [*objeto*] • **se me han perdido las llaves** I've lost my keys • **¿qué se les ha perdido en Alemania?** what business have they in Germany?
3 [+ *programa, fiesta*] to miss • **~se algo interesante** to miss something interesting • **¡no te lo pierdas!** don't miss it! • **no se pierde ni una** she doesn't miss a thing
4 (= *desaparecer*) to disappear • **el tren se perdió en la niebla** the train disappeared into the fog • **el arroyo se pierde en la roca** the stream disappears into the rock
5 (= *desperdiciarse*) to be wasted, go to waste • **se pierde mucho tiempo** a lot of time is wasted • **se pierden muchos talentos naturales** a lot of natural talent goes to waste • **nada se pierde con intentar** there's no harm in trying
6 (= *arruinarse*) [*persona*] to lose one's way; [*cosecha*] to be ruined, get spoiled • **se perdió por el juego** gambling was his ruin *o* undoing • **con la lluvia se ha perdido la cosecha** the rain has ruined the crops
7 • **~se por algo/algn** to be mad about sth/sb • **~se por hacer algo** to be dying to do sth, long to do sth
8 (*LAm*) (= *prostituirse*) to go on the streets

perdición SF (*Rel*) perdition; (*fig*) undoing, ruin • **fue su ~** it was his undoing • **será mi ~** it will be the ruin of me

perdida SF loose woman*; ▹ **perdido**

pérdida SF (*gen*) loss; (*Téc*) leakage, wastage; (*Jur*) forfeiture, loss • **~s** (*Econ, Mil etc*) losses • **es una ~ de tiempo** it's a waste of time • **¡no tiene ~!** you can't miss it! • **vender algo con ~** to sell sth at a loss • **a ~ de vista** as far as the eye can see • **entrar en ~** (*Aer*) to stall ▸ **pérdida contable** (*Com*) book loss ▸ **pérdida de conocimiento** loss of consciousness ▸ **pérdida efectiva** actual loss; ▹ **perdido**

perdidamente ADV • **~ enamorado** hopelessly in love

perdidizo ADJ • **hacer algo ~** to hide sth away, deliberately lose sth • **hacerse el ~** (*en juego*) to lose deliberately; (= *irse*) to make o.s. scarce, slip away

perdido/a ADJ **1** (= *extraviado*) lost; [*bala*] stray • **estaban ~s y tuvieron que preguntar el camino** they were lost and had to ask the way • **paraíso ~** paradise lost • **objetos ~s** lost property (*sing*) • **dar algo por ~** to give sth up for lost • **eso es tiempo ~** that's a waste of time; ▹ **rato, bala**
2 (= *aislado*) remote, isolated • **un pueblo ~ en las montañas** a remote *o* isolated village in the mountains
3 (= *sin remedio*) • **estaba borracho ~** he was totally *o* dead* drunk • **está loco ~** he's raving mad • **es tonto ~** he's a complete idiot • **es un caso ~** he's a hopeless case • **¡estamos ~s!** we're done for! • MODISMO: • **de ~s, al río** in for a penny, in for a pound
4 (= *enamorado*) • **estar ~ por algn** to be mad *o* crazy about sb
5* (= *sucio*) • **ponerlo todo ~ de barro** to get everything covered in mud, get mud everywhere • **te has puesto ~ el pantalón** you've ruined your trousers
6 (*LAm*) (= *vago*) idle; (= *pobre*) down and out
SM/F libertine; ▹ **perdida**

perdidoso ADJ **1** (= *que pierde*) losing
2 (= *que se pierde fácilmente*) easily lost, easily mislaid

perdigar ▹ CONJUG 1h VT [+ *perdiz*] to singe

perdigón SM **1** (*Orn*) young partridge
2 (= *bala*) pellet; **perdigones** shot (*sing*), pellets ▸ **perdigón zorrero** buckshot

perdigonada SF **1** (= *disparo*) shot
2 (= *herida*) shotgun wound

perdigonazo SM **1** (= *impacto*) blast of shot
2 = **perdigonada**

perdiguero ADJ • **perro ~** gundog
SM gundog

perdis* SM INV rake

perdiz SF partridge • MODISMO: • **marear la ~** to mess about* ▸ **perdiz blanca, perdiz nival** ptarmigan

perdón SM **1** (= *acción*) **a** (*Rel*) forgiveness • **el ~ de los pecados** the forgiveness of sins
b (*Jur*) pardon • **el ~ del juez** the judge's pardon
c (*Econ*) write-off • **el ~ de la deuda externa** the write-off of the foreign debt
d (*locuciones*) • **no cabe ~** it is inexcusable • **con ~** if you don't mind me saying so • **son todos unos imbéciles, con ~** they're all idiots, if you don't mind me saying so • **con ~ de la expresión** pardon my language, if you'll pardon the expression • **pedir ~ (a algn)** (*por algo leve*) to apologize (to sb); (*por algo grave*) to ask (sb's) forgiveness • **os pido ~ por el retraso** I'm sorry *o* I apologize for the delay • **le pido mil perdones por lo que le dije** I'm terribly sorry for what I said to you • **pido ~ a Dios** I ask God to forgive me, I ask God for forgiveness • **con ~ de los presentes** (= *con permiso*) if you'll permit me; (= *excepto*) present company excepted • MODISMO: • **no tener ~**: • **no tenéis ~ por lo que hicisteis** what you did was unforgivable, there's no excuse for what you did • **hace siglos que no voy al cine, no tengo ~ de Dios** (*hum*) I haven't been to the cinema for ages, I should be ashamed of myself (*hum*)
2 (*independiente*) **a** • **¡perdón!** (*disculpándose*) sorry!; (*tras eructar, toser*) excuse me!, pardon me!; (*llamando la atención*) excuse me!, pardon me! (*EEUU*) • **~, ¿te ha dolido?** sorry, did I hurt you? • **~ ¿me puede indicar dónde está la estación?** excuse me, can you tell me where the station is?
b • **¿perdón?** (*cuando no se ha entendido algo*) sorry?, pardon?, pardon me? (*EEUU*)

perdonable ADJ [*error, pecado*] forgivable, pardonable

perdonador ADJ forgiving
perdonar ▷ CONJUG 1a VT **1** (= *disculpar*) **a** [+ *falta, pecado*] to forgive • **es algo que no puedo ~ fácilmente** it's something I can't easily forgive • **perdona nuestras ofensas** (*Rel*) forgive us our trespasses • **perdona que te interrumpa** (I'm) sorry to interrupt • **perdona que te diga** if you don't mind me saying (so)
b • **~ a algn** to forgive sb • **¿me perdonas?** do you forgive me? • **que Dios me perdone si me equivoco, pero ...** may God forgive me if I'm wrong, but ...
2 (= *excusar*) **a** [+ *curiosidad, ignorancia*] to pardon, excuse • **perdone mi ignorancia, pero ...** pardon *o* excuse my ignorance, but ... • **"perdonen las molestias"** "we apologize for any inconvenience" • **las plantas no perdonan la falta de luz** plants don't do well without light
b • **~ una obligación/una deuda a algn** to let sb off an obligation/a debt • **te perdono los 50 euros que me debes** I'll let you off the 50 euros you owe me • **le han perdonado la pena** he's been pardoned • **~ la vida a algn** to spare sb's life; (*Dep*) to let sb off the hook • **va con aires de ir perdonándole la vida a todo el mundo** he acts as if the world owes him a living
c (*Econ*) [+ *deuda*] to write off
3 (= *perder*) [+ *detalle, ocasión*] to miss • **no perdona ni una sola ocasión de lucirse** he won't miss a single chance of showing off • MODISMO: • **no perdona ni una*** he doesn't miss a trick*
VI (= *disculpar*) • **¿perdona?** • **¿perdone?** (*cuando no se ha entendido algo*) sorry?, pardon?, pardon me? (EEUU) • **¡perdona!** • **¡perdone!** (= *disculpándose*) (I'm) sorry!; (= *llamando la atención*) excuse me!, pardon me! • **¡ay, perdona, no te había visto!** oh, I'm sorry, I didn't see you there! • **perdone, ¿me podría decir el precio de este traje?** excuse me, could you tell me how much this suit is? • **perdona, pero yo iba primero** excuse me, but I was first • **los años no perdonan** time shows no mercy • **~ por algo**: • **perdona por la interrupción, pero necesito hablar contigo** I'm sorry to interrupt, but I need to talk to you • **perdona por haberte ofendido** please forgive me if I have offended you, I'm sorry to have offended you
perdonavidas SMF INV **1** (= *matón*) bully, thug
2 (= *persona suficiente*) • **es un ~** he's Mister High and Mighty
perdulario ADJ **1** (= *olvidadizo*) forgetful
2 (= *descuidado*) careless, sloppy
3 (= *vicioso*) dissolute
SM rake
perdurabilidad SF durability
perdurable ADJ (= *duradero*) lasting, abiding; (= *perpetuo*) everlasting
perdurar ▷ CONJUG 1a VI (= *durar*) to last, endure; (= *subsistir*) to remain, still exist
perecedero ADJ (*Com*) perishable; [*vida*] transitory; [*persona*] mortal • **géneros no ~s** non-perishable goods
perecer ▷ CONJUG 2d VI **1** [*persona*] to die, perish (*frm*) • **~ ahogado** (*en agua*) to drown; (*por falta de oxígeno*) to suffocate
2 [*objeto*] to shatter
VPR **perecerse**† **1** • **~se de risa** to die laughing • **~se de envidia** to be dying of jealousy
2 • **~se por algo** to long for sth, be dying for sth • **~se por una mujer** to be crazy about a woman • **se perece por los calamares** he's crazy about squid • **~se por** (+ *infin*) to long to (+ *infin*), be dying to (+ *infin*)
peregrinación SF **1** (*Rel*) pilgrimage • **ir en ~** to make a pilgrimage, go on a pilgrimage (**a** to)
2 (= *viajes*) long tour, travels (*pl*); (*hum*) peregrination
peregrinar ▷ CONJUG 1a VI **1** (*Rel*) to go on a pilgrimage, make a pilgrimage (**a** to)
2 (= *ir*) to go to and fro; (= *viajar*) to travel extensively
peregrino/a ADJ **1** (= *que viaja*) wandering, travelling, traveling (EEUU); (*Orn*) migratory
2 (= *exótico*) exotic; (= *extraño*) strange, odd; (= *singular*) rare, extraordinary • **ideas peregrinas** harebrained ideas
3 [*costumbre, planta*] alien, newly-introduced
SM/F pilgrim
perejil SM **1** (*Bot*) parsley
2 perejiles* (*Cos*) buttons and bows, trimmings; (= *títulos*) extra titles, handles (to one's name)*
3 • MODISMO: • **andar como ~** (*Cono Sur*) to be shabbily dressed
perendengue SM **1** (= *adorno*) trinket, cheap ornament
2 perendengues* (= *pegas*) snags, problems • **el problema tiene sus ~s** the question has its tricky points • **un proyecto de muchos ~s** a plan with a lot of snags
3 perendengues* (= *categoría*) (high) standing (*sing*), importance (*sing*); (= *valor*) spirit (*sing*), guts
perengano/a SM/F somebody or other, someone or other
perenne ADJ (*gen*) perennial, constant; (*Bot*) perennial • **de hoja ~** evergreen
perennemente ADV constantly
perennidad SF (*gen*) perennial nature; (= *perpetuidad*) perpetuity
perentoriamente ADV (= *urgentemente*) urgently; (= *imperiosamente*) peremptorily
perentorio ADJ (= *urgente*) urgent; (= *imperioso*) peremptory • **plazo ~** final deadline
pereque* SM (*LAm*) nuisance, bore
perestroika SF perestroika
pereza SF laziness • **me da ~ ducharme** I can't be bothered to have a shower • **tener ~** to feel lazy • **¡qué ~!*** what a drag!* • **¡qué ~, tener que limpiar la casa!** what a drag, having to clean the house!*
perezosa SF (*And, Cono Sur*) deckchair
perezosamente ADV lazily
perezoso/a ADJ lazy
SM/F (= *vago*) idler, lazybones*
SM **1** (*Zool*) sloth
2 (*Caribe, Méx*) (= *imperdible*) safety pin
perfección SF **1** (= *cualidad*) perfection • **a la ~** to perfection
2 (= *acto*) completion
perfeccionamiento SM (= *proceso*) perfection; (= *mejora*) improvement
perfeccionar ▷ CONJUG 1a VT **1** (*gen*) to perfect; (= *mejorar*) to improve
2 (= *acabar*) to complete, finish
perfeccionismo SM perfectionism
perfeccionista SMF perfectionist
perfectamente ADV perfectly • **te entiendo ~** I perfectly understand what you mean, I know exactly what you mean • —**¿cómo está tu hermano?** —**¡perfectamente!** "how's your brother?" — "he's doing just fine"
perfectibilidad SF perfectibility
perfectible ADJ perfectible
perfecto ADJ **1** (= *ideal*) perfect • **¡perfecto!** fine! • **me parece ~ que lo hagan** I think it quite right that they should do it
2 (= *completo*) complete • **un ~ imbécil** a complete idiot • **era un ~ desconocido** he was a complete *o* total stranger
SM (*Ling*) perfect, perfect tense
pérfidamente ADV perfidiously, treacherously
perfidia SF perfidy, treachery
pérfido ADJ perfidious, treacherous
perfil SM **1** (*gen*) profile (*tb fig*); (= *contorno*) silhouette, outline; (*Geol, Arquit*) section, cross section; (*Fot*) side view • **de ~** in profile, from the side • **ponerse de ~** to stand side on ▸ **perfil aerodinámico** streamlining ▸ **perfil bajo** • **neumáticos de ~ bajo** low-profile tyres *o* (EEUU) tires
2 (*profesional*) profile ▸ **perfil del cliente** (*Com*) customer profile ▸ **perfil psicológico** psychological profile
3 perfiles (= *rasgos*) features, characteristics; (= *cortesías*) social courtesies; (= *retoques*) finishing touches
perfilado ADJ **1** (*gen*) well-shaped, well-finished; [*rostro*] long; [*nariz*] well-formed, shapely
2 (*Aer*) streamlined
perfilador SM ▸ **perfilador de cejas** eyebrow pencil ▸ **perfilador de labios** lip-liner, lip pencil ▸ **perfilador de ojos** eye-liner
perfilar ▷ CONJUG 1a VT **1** (*gen*) to outline; (*fig*) to shape • **son los lectores los que perfilan los periódicos** it is the readers who shape their newspapers
2 (*Aer*) to streamline
3 (= *rematar*) to put the finishing touches to, round off
VPR **perfilarse 1** [*modelo*] to show one's profile, stand sideways on; [*edificio*] to be silhouetted; (*Taur*) to prepare for the kill (**en** against)
2 (*fig*) to take shape • **el proyecto se va perfilando** the project is taking shape
3 (*LAm*) (= *adelgazar*) to slim, get slim
4 (*Cono Sur*) (*Dep*) to dribble and shoot
perforación SF **1** (= *orificio*) (*Tip*) perforation; (*Cine, Fot*) sprocket; (*Téc*) punch-hole; (*Min*) bore hole
2 (= *proceso*) (*gen*) piercing, perforation; (*Min*) drilling, boring; (*Tip*) punching, perforating
perforado ADJ [*papel*] holed; [*labios*] pierced
SM hole-punching
perforadora SF **1** (*Tip*) punch ▸ **perforadora de tarjetas** card punch
2 (*Téc*) drill ▸ **perforadora neumática** pneumatic drill
perforar ▷ CONJUG 1a VT (*gen*) to perforate, pierce; (*Min*) to drill, bore; [+ *tarjeta*] to punch, punch a hole in; [+ *ficha*] to punch; [+ *pozo*] to sink; (= *pinchar*) to puncture (*tb Med*)
VI (*Min*) to drill, bore
VPR **perforarse** [*úlcera*] to get perforated
perforista SMF (*Inform*) card puncher
performance [perˈformans] SF performance
perfumado ADJ scented, perfumed
perfumador SM perfume spray
perfumar ▷ CONJUG 1a VT to perfume, scent
perfume SM perfume, scent
perfumería SF perfumery, perfume shop
perfumista ADJ [*empresa*] perfumery
SMF perfumer
pergamino SM parchment • **una familia de muchos ~s** a very blue-blooded family, a family of very noble lineage • **los ~s del mar Muerto** the Dead Sea scrolls
pergenio* SM (*Cono Sur*) (*hum*) bright boy, clever kid*
pergeñar ▷ CONJUG 1a VT **1** (= *tramar*) [+ *plan*] to sketch; [+ *asesinato*] to plot; [+ *texto*] to draft

2* (= *arreglar*) [+ *cita*] to fix up, arrange
3 (*Cono Sur**) [+ *persona*] to eye from head to toe
pergeño SM aspect, appearance
pérgola SF pergola
peri... PREF peri...
perica SF 1 (*And, CAm*) (= *navaja*) razor, knife; (= *machete*) machete; (= *espada*) short sword
2 (*And, CAm**) (= *borrachera*) • **agarrar una ~** to get sloshed*, get trashed (*EEUU*‡)
3‡ (= *chica*) bird‡, chick (*EEUU*‡); (= *puta*) tart‡, slut‡, whore
4‡ (= *droga*) snow‡, cocaine
pericia SF (= *habilidad*) skill; (= *experiencia*) expertise
pericial ADJ expert • **tasación ~** expert valuation • **testigo ~** expert witness
periclitar ▸ CONJUG 1a VI (*frm*) 1 (= *declinar*) to decay, decline; (= *quedar anticuado*) to become outmoded • **esos quedan ya periclitados** those are out of date now
2 (= *peligrar*) to be in danger
Perico SM (*forma familiar de* **Pedro**)
• **MODISMOS**: • **~ el de los palotes** (*Esp*) Mister So-and-So • **ser ~ entre ellas** to be a ladies' man
perico SM 1 (*Orn*) parakeet
2 (*Bot*) giant asparagus
3‡ (= *droga*) snow‡, cocaine
4 (*Col*) (= *café*) white coffee
5 (= *peluca*) wig, toupé
6* (= *orinal*) chamberpot
7‡ (= *puta*) tart*, slut‡
8 • (**huevos**) **~s** (*And, Caribe*) *scrambled eggs with fried onions*
pericote SM (*And, Cono Sur*) 1 (= *ratón*) large rat
2* (= *niño*) kid*, nipper*
periferia SF 1 (*Mat*) periphery; (*Geog*) [*de población*] outskirts (*pl*) • **los que viven en la ~ social** those who live on the fringes of society
2 (*Inform*) peripherals (*pl*)
periférico ADJ peripheral • **barrio ~** outlying district • **unidad periférica** peripheral (unit) • **carretera periférica** ring road
SM 1 **periféricos** (*Inform*) peripherals
2 (*Méx*) (*Aut*) ring road, beltway (*EEUU*)
perifollo SM 1 (*Bot*) chervil
2 **perifollos** (= *adornos*) buttons and bows, trimmings
perífrasis SF INV periphrasis
perifrástico ADJ periphrastic
perilla SF 1 (= *barba*) goatee • **MODISMO**: • **venir de ~(s)** to be more than welcome
▸ **perilla de la oreja** ear lobe
2 (= *joya*) pear-shaped ornament, drop
3 (*Elec*) switch ▸ **perilla del timbre** bellpush
4 (*Méx*) (= *manija*) handle
5 (= *tirador*) doorknob
perillán†* SM rogue, rascal • **¡perillán!** (*a un niño*) you little rascal!
perimetral ADJ perimeter (*antes de s*)
• **vallado ~** perimeter fence
perímetro SM perimeter
perimido ADJ (*Arg, Uru*) (*frm*) [*ideas, teorías*] outdated
perinatal ADJ perinatal
perinola SF teetotum
ADV • **de ~** (*Caribe*) utterly, absolutely
periódicamente ADV periodically
periodicidad SF 1 [*de acción, evento*] regularity; [*de publicación*] frequency (*of publication*) • **una revista de ~ mensual** a monthly magazine
2 (*Téc*) periodicity
periódico ADJ (*gen*) periodic(al); (*Mat*) recurrent
SM (= *diario*) newspaper, paper; (= *publicación periódica*) periodical ▸ **periódico de la tarde** evening newspaper, evening paper ▸ **periódico del domingo, periódico dominical** Sunday newspaper, Sunday paper ▸ **periódico mural** wall newspaper
periodicucho* SM (*pey*) rag*
periodismo SM journalism ▸ **periodismo amarillo** sensationalist journalism, ≈ tabloid journalism ▸ **periodismo deportivo** sports journalism ▸ **periodismo de investigación** investigative journalism
▸ **periodismo gráfico** photoreportage
periodista SMF journalist ▸ **periodista de radio** radio reporter ▸ **periodista de televisión** television reporter, TV reporter
periodístico ADJ journalistic • **estilo ~** journalistic style, journalese (*pey*) • **el mundo ~** the newspaper world • **de interés ~** newsworthy
periodización SF periodization
periodo SM, **período** SM 1 [*de tiempo*] period ▸ **periodo contable** (*Com*) accounting period ▸ **período de incubación** incubation period
2 (= *menstruación*) period
3 (*Ling*) sentence, period
periodoncia SF periodontics (*sing*), periodontology
peripatético ADJ peripatetic
peripecia SF 1 (= *incidente*) adventure, incident
2 (= *vicisitud*) vicissitude, sudden change
periplo SM (*gen*) (long) journey, tour; (*Náut*) (long) voyage; (*Hist*) periplus; (= *errabundeo*) wanderings (*pl*); (*hum*) peregrination
peripuesto* ADJ (*gen*) dressed-up, smart; (*excesivamente*) overdressed • **tan ~** all dressed-up (to the nines)
periquear* ▸ CONJUG 1a (*And*) VI to get dressed up, get dolled up*
VPR **periquearse** to get dressed up, get dolled up*
periquete SM • **en un ~*** in a tick
periquito SM 1 (*Orn*) parakeet
2‡ (= *droga*) snow‡, cocaine
periscopio SM periscope
perista* SMF fence*, receiver of stolen goods
peristilo SM peristyle
perita¹* ADJ = **pera**²
perita² SF • **MODISMO**: • **ser una ~ en dulce** to be gorgeous
peritaje SM 1 (= *informe*) specialist's report, expert's report; (= *trabajo*) expert work; (= *pericia*) expertise
2 (= *honorarios*) expert's fee
3 (= *estudios*) professional training
peritar ▸ CONJUG 1a VT to judge expertly, give an expert opinion on
perito/a ADJ (= *experto*) expert; (= *con experiencia*) experienced, seasoned • **ser ~ en** [+ *actividad*] to be expert at; [+ *materia*] to be an expert on
SM/F (*gen*) expert; (= *técnico*) technician; (= *ingeniero técnico*) technical engineer
▸ **perito/a agrónomo/a** agronomist
▸ **perito/a electricista** qualified electrician
▸ **perito/a en metales** metal expert, specialist in metals ▸ **perito/a testigo** (*Méx*) expert witness
peritoneo SM peritoneum
peritonitis SF INV peritonitis
perjudicado/a ADJ affected
SM/F • **los ~s** those affected
perjudicar ▸ CONJUG 1g VT 1 (= *dañar*) to harm • **me perjudica que digan eso** their saying that is damaging to me
2† (= *desfavorecer*) • **ese sombrero la perjudica** that hat doesn't suit her, she doesn't look good in that hat
3 (*LAm*) (= *calumniar*) to malign, slander
VPR **perjudicarse** to lose out
perjudicial ADJ damaging, harmful, detrimental (*frm*)
SM (*Méx*‡) secret policeman
perjuicio SM damage, harm • **el escándalo ha reportado graves ~s al ministro** the scandal has done the minister serious damage *o* harm • **sufrir grandes ~s** to suffer great damage • **la crisis ha causado enormes ~s económicos** the crisis has caused severe financial damage • **en ~ de algo** to the detriment of sth, at the expense of sth • **han bajado los precios en ~ de la calidad** prices have fallen to the detriment *o* at the expense of quality • **redundar en ~ de algo** to be detrimental to sth, harm sth • **sin ~ de** (*Jur*) without prejudice to • **sin ~ de que luego me pueda arrepentir** even though I might change my mind later, in spite of the fact that I might change my mind later;
▸ **daño**
perjurar ▸ CONJUG 1a VI 1 (*Jur*) to perjure o.s., commit perjury
2 (= *jurar*) to swear a lot
VPR **perjurarse** to perjure o.s., commit perjury
perjurio SM perjury
perjuro/a ADJ perjured
SM/F perjurer
perla SF pearl • **MODISMOS**: • **de ~s**: • **me parece de ~s** it's absolutely splendid • **me viene de ~s** it suits me perfectly *o* just fine
▸ **perla cultivada** cultured pearl, cultivated pearl ▸ **perla negra** black pearl ▸ **perlas de imitación** imitation pearls
perlado ADJ pearly • **cebada perlada** pearl barley
perlático ADJ paralytic, palsied
perlesía SF paralysis, palsy
perlífero ADJ pearl-bearing • **ostra perlífera** pearl oyster
perlino ADJ pearly
permagel SM permafrost
permanecer ▸ CONJUG 2d VI 1 (*en un lugar*) to stay, remain • **¿cuánto tiempo vas a ~ en Toledo?** how long are you staying in Toledo?
• **permaneció en cama durante toda la convalecencia** he stayed in bed throughout his convalescence
2 (*en un estado*) to remain • **~ en silencio** to remain silent • **permanezcan sentados** (please) remain seated
permanencia SF 1 (= *continuidad*) • **su ~ en el equipo depende de su rendimiento** his presence in the team will depend on his performance
2 (= *estancia*) stay • **escribió la novela durante su ~ en el sanatorio** he wrote the novel during his stay in the sanatorium
▸ **permanencia en filas** (period of) military service
3 **permanencias** [*de profesores*] obligatory administrative duties
permanente ADJ (*gen*) permanent; (= *constante*) constant; [*color*] fast; [*comisión*] standing
SF (*en pelo*) permanent wave, perm*
• **hacerse una ~** to have one's hair permed
permanentemente ADV (= *perennemente*) permanently; (= *constantemente*) constantly
permanganato SM permanganate
permeabilidad SF permeability
permeable ADJ permeable (**a** to)
permisible ADJ permissible
permisionario/a SM/F (*LAm*) official agent, official agency, concessionaire
permisividad SF (*gen*) permissiveness; (*Econ*) liberal policies (*pl*)

P

permisivo ADJ permissive

permiso SM **1** (= *autorización*) permission • **solicitó ~ para abandonar la reunión** he asked for permission to leave the meeting • **¡permiso!** (*para pasar*) excuse me! • **con ~** (*pidiendo ver algo*) if I may; (*queriendo entrar, pasar*) (*esp LAm*) excuse me • **con ~ de ustedes me voy** excuse me but I must go • **con su ~, ¿se puede?** excuse me, may I come in? • **dar ~** to give permission • **no me dieron ~ para salir del cuartel** they didn't give me permission to leave the barracks • **¿me da ~ para salir hoy un poco antes?** will you let me leave a little earlier today?, could I leave a little earlier today? • **tener ~ para hacer algo** to have permission to do sth
2 (= *documento*) permit, licence, license (*EEUU*) ▸ **permiso de armas** gun licence, firearms certificate ▸ **permiso de circulación** registration document ▸ **permiso de conducción** (*Esp*), **permiso de conducir** (*Esp*) driving licence, driver's license (*EEUU*) ▸ **permiso de entrada** entry permit ▸ **permiso de exportación** export licence ▸ **permiso de importación** import licence ▸ **permiso de obras** planning permission, building permit ▸ **permiso de residencia** residence permit ▸ **permiso de salida** exit permit ▸ **permiso de trabajo** work permit, green card (*EEUU*)
3 (*para no trabajar*) leave • **ha pedido unos días de ~** he has asked for a few days' leave • **estar de ~** to be on leave ▸ **permiso por maternidad** maternity leave ▸ **permiso por paternidad** paternity leave

permitir ▹ CONJUG 3a VT **1** (= *autorizar*) **a** [+ *entrada, movimiento*] to allow, permit (*más frm*) • **no permiten la entrada a menores de 18 años** under-18s are not allowed in • **—no puedo abrir la puerta —permítame** "I can't open the door" — "allow me" • **"no está permitido el uso de teléfonos móviles"** "the use of mobile phones is not permitted" • **si se me permite la expresión** *o* **la palabra** if you'll pardon the expression • **~ que**: • **no le permitas que te hable así** don't allow her to talk to you like that • **permítame que la ayude, señora** please allow me to help you, madam
b (*en preguntas*) • **¿me permite?** (*al entrar*) may I (come in)?; (*al pasar al lado de algn*) excuse me, please; (*al ayudar a algn*) may I (help you)? • **¿me permite su pasaporte, por favor?** may I see your passport please? • **¿me permite que le diga una cosa?** may I say something to you?
2 (= *hacer posible*) to allow, permit (*más frm*) • **las nuevas tecnologías ~án una mayor producción anual** the new technologies will allow *o* (*más frm*) permit a higher annual production • **este tejido permite el paso del aire** this material allows the air through • **si el tiempo lo permite** weather permitting • **~ (a algn) hacer algo** to allow (sb) to do sth • **la televisión nos permite llegar a más público** television lets us reach *o* allows us to reach a wider audience • **todos los datos permiten hablar de una epidemia** all the data points to *o* indicates an epidemic • **~ que** (+ *subjun*) to allow (+ *infin*) • **un marco legal que permita que una persona decida libremente** a legal framework to allow people to choose freely • **el buen tiempo permitió que se celebrase el concierto al aire libre** the good weather allowed us to hold the concert outdoors
VPR **permitirse 1** (= *atreverse a*) • **se permite demasiadas libertades con su secretaria** he takes too many liberties with his secretary • **me permito recordarle que está prohibido fumar** (*frm*) may I remind you that smoking is forbidden (*frm*)
2 (= *concederse*) to allow o.s. • **me permito dos cigarrillos al día** I allow myself two cigarettes a day • **poder ~se (hacer) algo** to be able to afford (to do) sth • **no me puedo ~ más gastos este mes** I can't afford any more expense this month • **no puedo ~me comer fuera todos los días** I can't afford to eat out every day • **no podemos ~nos el lujo de ser ingenuos** we can't afford to be naive

permuta SF [*de bienes, mercancías*] exchange; [*de puesto de trabajo*] interchange

permutación SF **1** (*Mat*) permutation
2 = **permuta**

permutar ▹ CONJUG 1a VT **1** (*Mat*) to permute
2 [+ *puesto de trabajo*] to exchange, swap; [+ *acciones, edificios*] to switch, exchange; [+ *intervenciones, actuaciones*] to interchange • **~ algo con algn** to exchange sth with sb • **~ destinos con algn** to exchange *o* swap jobs with sb

pernada SF **1** • **derecho de ~** (*Hist*) droit de seigneur
2 (= *coz*) kick • **dar ~s** to kick out

pernear ▹ CONJUG 1a VI **1** (= *agitar las piernas*) to kick one's legs, shake one's legs
2 (= *patear*) to stamp one's foot (with rage)
3* (= *darse prisa*) to get cracking*

pernera SF trouser leg

perneta SF • **en ~s** bare-legged, with bare legs

perniabierto ADJ bow-legged

perniche* SM blanket

perniciosamente ADV perniciously • **la crisis afectará ~ a la economía mundial** the crisis will have a pernicious effect on the world economy

pernicioso ADJ pernicious (*tb Med*); [*influencia, sustancia*] harmful; [*insecto*] injurious (**para** to); [*persona*] wicked, evil

pernicorto ADJ short-legged

pernigordo ADJ fat-legged

pernil SM **1** (*Zool*) upper leg, haunch; (*Culin*) leg; (*Caribe*) leg of pork, pork
2 (*Cos*) trouser leg

pernio SM hinge

perno SM bolt • MODISMO: • **estar hasta el ~** (*And**) to be at the end of one's tether

pernocta SF • **pase (de) ~** overnight pass

pernoctación SF overnight stay • **con tres pernoctaciones en hotel** with three nights in a hotel

pernoctar ▹ CONJUG 1a VI to spend the night, stay the night

pero[1] CONJ **1** but • **me gusta, ~ es muy caro** I like it, but it's very expensive • **yo no quería ir, ~ bueno ...** I didn't want to go, but still ...
2 (*al principio de frase*) • **~, ¿dónde está Pedro?** where on earth is Pedro? • **~ bueno, ¿vienes o no?** now look, are you coming or not? • **~ vamos a ver** well let's see • **¡~ qué guapa estás!** you look great! • **¡~ si no tiene coche!** I tell you he hasn't got a car!
3 (*uso enfático*) • **~ que muy**: **una chica guapa, ~ que muy guapa** what you call a really pretty girl, a pretty girl and no mistake • **hizo muy, ~ que muy mal** he was wrong, really, really wrong • **¡estoy ~ que muy harto!** I'm damn well fed up!* • **¡~ que muy bien!** well done!
SM **1** (= *falta, defecto*) snag • **el plan no tiene ~s** the plan hasn't any snags, there's nothing wrong with the plan
2 (= *pega*) objection • **encontrar** *o* **poner ~s a algo** to raise objections to sth, find fault with sth • **¡no hay ~ que valga!** there are no buts about it!

pero[2] SM (*And, Cono Sur*) pear tree

perogrullada SF platitude, truism

perogrullesco ADJ platitudinous

Perogrullo SM, **Pero Grullo** SM • MODISMO: • **verdad de ~** platitude, truism

perol SM **1** (= *cazuela*) (*grande*) pot; (*más pequeña*) saucepan
2 (*Caribe*) (= *utensilio*) kitchen utensil; (= *trasto*) piece of junk, worthless object

perola SF saucepan

perolero SM **1** (*Caribe*) (= *hojalatero*) tinsmith
2 (= *objetos*) pile of junk, collection of odds and ends

peronacho* SM (*Cono Sur*) (*pey*) Peronist

peroné SM fibula

peronismo SM Peronism

> **PERONISMO**
> General Juan Domingo Perón (1895-1974) came to power in Argentina in 1946, on a social justice platform known as **justicialismo**. He aimed to break Argentina's dependence on exports by developing the domestic economy through state-led industrialization. **Peronismo** stood for nationalization of industry, trade unions, paid holidays, the welfare state and the provision of affordable housing. Women were given the vote in 1947, a move championed by Perón's charismatic wife "Evita" (María Eva Duarte). Following her death in 1952, Perón's support began to crumble and he was driven into exile in 1955. His party was banned for almost a decade and did not regain power until 1973, when he was recalled from exile to become President. He died the following year. **Peronismo** as a movement has survived, and the Peronist party returned to power in 1989 under Carlos Menem.

peronista ADJ, SMF Peronist

peroración SF **1** (= *discurso*) peroration, speech; (= *perorata*) long-winded speech
2 (= *conclusión*) conclusion of a speech

perorar ▹ CONJUG 1a VI to make a speech; (*hum*) to spout

perorata SF (= *rollo*) long-winded speech; (= *soflama*) violent speech, harangue • **echar una ~** to rattle on* (**sobre** about)

peróxido SM peroxide ▸ **peróxido de hidrógeno** hydrogen peroxide

perpendicular ADJ perpendicular (**a** to) • **el camino es ~ al río** the road is at right angles to the river
SF perpendicular • **salir de la ~** to be out of the perpendicular

perpendicularmente ADV perpendicularly

perpetración SF perpetration

perpetrador(a) SM/F perpetrator

perpetrar ▹ CONJUG 1a VT to perpetrate

perpetuación SF perpetuation

perpetuamente ADV perpetually

perpetuar ▹ CONJUG 1e VT to perpetuate

perpetuidad SF perpetuity • **a ~** in perpetuity, for ever • **condena a ~** life sentence • **le condenaron a prisión a ~** he was sentenced to life

perpetuo ADJ (*gen*) perpetual; [*condena, exilio*] life (*antes de s*); (*Bot*) everlasting • **cadena perpetua** life imprisonment

Perpiñán SM Perpignan

perplejamente ADV perplexedly, in a puzzled way

perplejidad SF **1** (= *confusión*) perplexity, puzzlement
2 (= *indecisión*) hesitation
3 (= *situación perpleja*) perplexing situation

perplejo ADJ perplexed, puzzled • **me miró**

~ he gave me a perplexed *o* puzzled look • **dejar a algn ~** to perplex sb, puzzle sb • **se quedó ~ un momento** he hesitated a moment, he looked perplexed for a moment

perra SF **1** (*Zool*) bitch
2 (*Esp**) (= *moneda*) copper, penny • **ahorró unas ~s** he saved a few coppers* • **no tener una ~*** to be broke*, be skint* ▸ **perra chica** (*Hist*) 5-céntimo coin ▸ **perra gorda** (*Hist*) 10-céntimo coin
3* (= *rabieta*) tantrum • **el niño cogió una ~** the child had a tantrum
4* (= *obsesión*) obsession, crazy idea • **está con la ~ de comprárselo** he's taken it into his head to buy it • **le cogió la ~ de ir a México** he got obsessed about going to Mexico*
5 (*Cono Sur*) (= *sombrero*) old hat
6 (*Cono Sur*) (= *cantimplora*) leather water bottle

perrada SF **1** (= *perros*) pack of dogs
2* (= *acción*) dirty trick

perraje SM (*And*) **1** [*de perros*] pack of dogs
2* [*de personas*] lower orders (*pl*), lower ranks (*pl*)

perramus SM INV (*Arg*) raincoat

perrera SF **1** (*para perros callejeros*) dog pound; (*para perros con dueño*) kennels (*pl*), kennel (*EEUU*)
2 (= *furgoneta*) dogcatcher's van
3 (*Chile**) (= *rabieta*) tantrum
4 (*Caribe*) (= *pelea*) row, shindy
5 (*en el trabajo*) grind; ▷ **perrero**

perrería SF **1** (= *perros*) pack of dogs; (*fig*) gang of villains
2* (= *trampa*) dirty trick
3 (= *palabra*) harsh word, angry word • **decir ~s de algn** to say harsh things about sb

perrero/a SM/F dog catcher; ▷ **perrera**

perrilla SF (*Méx*) stye

perrillo SM **1** (*Zool*) puppy
2 (*Mil*) trigger

perrito/a SM/F puppy ▸ **perrito/a faldero/a** lapdog
SM ▸ **perrito caliente** hot dog

perro SM **1** (*Zool*) dog • **"cuidado con el perro"** "beware of the dog" ▸ **perro afgano** Afghan hound ▸ **perro antiexplosivos**, **perro buscadrogas** sniffer dog ▸ **perro callejero** stray (dog) ▸ **perro cobrador** retriever ▸ **perro dálmata** dalmatian ▸ **perro de agua** (*CAm*) coypu ▸ **perro de aguas** spaniel ▸ **perro de casta** pedigree dog ▸ **perro de caza** hunting dog ▸ **perro de ciego** guide dog ▸ **perro de lanas** poodle ▸ **perro de muestra** pointer ▸ **perro de presa** bulldog ▸ **perro de raza** pedigree dog ▸ **perro de San Bernardo** St Bernard ▸ **perro de Terranova** Newfoundland dog ▸ **perro de trineo** husky, sled dog ▸ **perro dogo** bulldog ▸ **perro esquimal** husky ▸ **perro faldero** lapdog ▸ **perro guardián** guard dog ▸ **perro guía** guide dog ▸ **perro lazarillo** guide dog ▸ **perro lebrel** whippet ▸ **perro lobo** alsatian, German shepherd ▸ **perro marino** dogfish ▸ **perro pastor** sheepdog ▸ **perro pequinés** Pekinese ▸ **perro policía** police dog ▸ **perro raposero** foxhound ▸ **perro rastreador, perro rastrero** tracker dog ▸ **perro salchicha*** sausage dog*, dachshund ▸ **perro vagabundo** stray (dog) ▸ **perro zorrero** foxhound
2 • **MODISMOS:** • **¡a otro ~ con ese hueso!** pull the other one, it has bells on it!* • **atar ~s con longaniza:** • **se cree que allí atan los ~s con longaniza** he thinks it's the land of milk and honey • **de ~s** foul • **estaba de un humor de ~s** he was in a foul *o* stinking mood • **tiempo de ~s** foul *o* dirty weather • **echarle los ~s a algn*** to come down on sb like a ton of bricks* • **echar una hora a ~s** to waste a whole hour, get absolutely nothing done in an hour • **hacer ~ muerto** (*Chile, Perú**) to avoid paying • **heder a ~ muerto** to stink to high heaven • **meter los ~s en danza** to set the cat among the pigeons • **¿qué ~ te/le mordió?** (*Caribe**) what's up with you/him?* • **llevarse como (el) ~ y (el) gato** to fight like cat and dog • **ser como el ~ del hortelano** to be a dog in the manger • **ser ~ viejo** to be an old hand • **tratar a algn como a un ~** to treat sb like dirt • **vida de ~** dog's life • **REFRANES:** • **a ~ flaco todo son pulgas** it never rains but it pours • **~ ladrador, poco mordedor** • **~ que ladra no muerde** his bark is worse than his bite
3 (*Culin*) ▸ **perro caliente** hot dog
4* (*pey*) (= *holgazán*) lazy sod**‡
5* (*pey*) (= *persona despreciable*) swine‡
6 (*And*) (= *modorra*) drowsiness
7 (*Cono Sur*) clothes peg, clothes pin (*EEUU*)
ADJ* rotten* • **¡qué perra suerte la mía!** what rotten luck I have!* • **esta perra vida** this wretched life • **¡qué perra vida!** life's a bitch!* • **he pasado una temporada perra** I've been through a rough patch*

perroflauta* SMF hippy, bum*

perro-guía SM (PL: **perros-guía**) guide dog

perrona† SF (= *moneda*) 10-céntimo coin • **de (a) ~*** cheapo*, cheap

perronero* ADJ cheapo*, cheap

perrucho SM (*pey*) hound, cur

perruna SF dog biscuit

perruno ADJ canine, dog (*antes de s*); [*afecto, devoción*] doglike

persa ADJ, SMF Persian
SM (*Ling*) Persian
SF (*Cono Sur*) (= *mercado*) market, bazaar

per saecula saeculorum ADV (*frm*), **per secula seculorum** ADV for ever and ever

persecución SF **1** (= *acoso*) pursuit • **estar en plena ~** to be in full cry ▸ **persecución individual** (*Ciclismo*) individual pursuit ▸ **persecución por equipos** team pursuit ▸ **persecución sexual** sexual harassment
2 (*Pol, Rel*) persecution

persecutorio ADJ • **manía persecutoria** persecution complex • **trato ~** cruel treatment

perseguible ADJ (*Jur*) [*delito*] indictable; [*persona*] liable to prosecution • **~ a instancia de parte** liable to private prosecution • **~ de oficio** liable to prosecution by the state

perseguidor(a) SM/F **1** (*gen*) pursuer
2 (*Rel, Pol*) persecutor

perseguimiento SM pursuit, hunt, chase • **en ~ de** in pursuit of

perseguir ▷ CONJUG 3d, 3k VT **1** [+ *presa, fugitivo*] (*gen*) to pursue, chase; (*por motivos ideológicos*) to persecute; (= *acosar*) to hunt down, hunt out
2 [+ *persona, empleo*] to chase after, go after; [+ *propósito, fin*] to pursue • **la persiguió durante dos años** he was after her for two years, he pursued her for two years • **me persiguieron hasta que dije que sí** they pestered me until I said yes • **lo persiguen los remordimientos** he is plagued by remorse • **lo persigue la mala suerte** he is dogged by ill luck

perseverancia SF perseverance, persistence

perseverante ADJ persevering, persistent

perseverantemente ADV perseveringly, persistently

perseverar ▷ CONJUG 1a VI to persevere, persist • **~ en** to persevere in, persist with

Persia SF Persia

persiana SF [*de lamas*] (Venetian) blind; [*de tablitas*] slatted shutter; (*enrollable*) roller blind • **MODISMO:** • **enrollarse como una ~*** to go on and on

persignarse ▷ CONJUG 1a VPR to cross o.s.

persistencia SF persistence

persistente ADJ persistent

persistentemente ADV persistently

persistir ▷ CONJUG 3a VI to persist (**en** in)

persoga SF (*CAm, Méx*) halter (*of plaited vegetable fibre*)

persona SF **1** (= *individuo*) person • **es una ~ encantadora** he's a charming person • **20 ~s** 20 people • **aquellas ~s que lo deseen** those who wish • **es buena ~** he's a good sort • **en la ~ de** in the person of • **en ~** in person, in the flesh • **vendrá él en ~ a recoger los papeles** he will come and collect the papers in person • **vi al príncipe en ~** I saw the prince in the flesh *o* in person • **por ~** per person • **20 kilos por ~** 20 kilos per person • **tres caramelos por ~** three sweets per person *o* each • **dos dólares por ~** two dollars per person, two dollars a head • **tercera ~** third party • **sin inmiscuir a terceras ~s** without involving third parties ▸ **persona de edad** elderly person, senior citizen ▸ **persona de historia**† dubious individual ▸ **persona mayor** adult ▸ **persona no grata, persona non grata** persona non grata ▸ **personas reales** (*frm*) royalty (*sing*), king and queen
2 (*Jur*) ▸ **persona física** natural person ▸ **persona jurídica** legal entity
3 (*Ling*) person • **la tercera ~ del singular** the third person singular
4 (*Rel*) • **las tres ~s de la Santísima Trinidad** the three persons of the Holy Trinity

PERSONA

Mientras que **persona** *en singular se traduce por* **person**, *el plural tiene dos traducciones:* **people** *y* **persons.**

▷ **People** *es la forma más utilizada, ya que* **persons** *se emplea solamente en el lenguaje formal o técnico. Las dos formas llevan el verbo en plural:*

Acaban de llegar tres personas preguntando por un tal Sr. Oliva
Three people have just arrived asking for a Mr Oliva
"Peso máximo: 8 personas"
"Weight limit: 8 persons"

Para otros usos y ejemplos ver la entrada.

personaje SM **1** (= *sujeto notable*) personage, important person; (= *famoso*) celebrity, personality • **ser un ~** to be somebody, be important
2 (*Literat, Teat*) character

personajillo SM (*gen*) insignificant person; (*Literat, Teat*) minor character; (*hum*) minor celebrity

personal ADJ personal
SM **1** (= *plantilla*) staff, personnel; (*esp Mil*) force; (*Náut*) crew, complement • **estar falto de ~** to be shorthanded *o* shortstaffed ▸ **personal de cabina** cabin staff *o* crew ▸ **personal de exterior** surface workers (*pl*) ▸ **personal de interior** underground workers (*pl*) ▸ **personal de servicios** maintenance staff ▸ **personal de tierra** (*Aer*) ground crew, ground staff
2* (= *gente*) people • **había mucho ~ en el cine** there was a big crowd in the cinema • **MODISMO:** • **quedarse con el ~*** to be a hit with people
SF (*Baloncesto*) personal foul

personalidad SF **1** (= *modo de ser*)

personality • **doble ~** dual personality ▸ **personalidad desdoblada** split personality
2 (= *personaje público*) public figure • **~es** personalities, dignitaries
3 (*Jur*) legal entity
personalísimo ADJ intensely personal, highly individualistic
personalismo SM 1 (= *parcialidad*) partiality • **obrar sin ~s** to act impartially *o* without favouritism
2 (= *alusión personal*) personal reference • **tenemos que proceder sin ~s** we must carry on without getting personal
3 (= *egoísmo*) selfishness, egoism
personalizado ADJ (= *individualizado*) [*servicio, instrucciones*] personalized; (= *hecho a medida*) [*coche, ordenador, solución*] customized
personalizar ▹ CONJUG 1f VT (*gen*) to personalize; (= *personificar*) to embody, personify
VI 1 (= *nombrar en particular*) to name names
2 (= *hacer alusiones personales*) to get personal
VPR **personalizarse** to become personal
personalmente ADV personally
personarse ▹ CONJUG 1a VPR to appear in person • **~ en** to present o.s. at, report to • **~ en forma** (*Jur*) to be officially represented • **el juez se personó en el lugar del accidente** the judge made an official visit to the scene of the accident
personería SF 1 (*Cono Sur*) (= *personalidad*) personality; (= *talento*) aptitude, talent
2 (*LAm*) (*Jur*) legal status
personero/a SM/F (*LAm*) (*Pol*) (= *representante*) (government) official; (= *portavoz*) spokesperson; (*Jur*) proxy
personificación SF 1 (= *representación*) personification, embodiment • **es la ~ de los celos** he is the embodiment of jealousy, he is jealousy personified
2 (*Literat*) personification
personificar ▹ CONJUG 1g VT 1 (= *encarnar*) to personify, embody • **es la codicia personificada** he is greed personified • **en esta mujer el autor personifica la maldad** the author makes this woman a personification of wickedness
2 (*en discurso*) to single out for special mention
perspectiva SF 1 (*Arte*) perspective • **en ~** in perspective • **le falta ~** he lacks a sense of perspective
2 (= *vista*) view, scene
3 (= *posibilidad*) prospect • **la ~ no es nada halagüeña** it's a most unwelcome prospect • **buenas ~s de mejora** good prospects for *o* of improvement • **se alegró con la ~ de pasar un día en el campo** he cheered up with the prospect of spending a day in the country • **encontrarse ante la ~ de hacer algo** to be faced with the prospect of doing sth • **tener algo en ~** to have sth in prospect • **las ~s de la cosecha son favorables** the harvest outlook is good
perspicacia SF 1 (= *agudeza mental*) perceptiveness, shrewdness
2 (= *agudeza visual*) keen-sightedness
perspicaz ADJ 1 (= *agudo, sagaz*) perceptive, shrewd
2 [*vista*] keen; [*persona*] keen-sighted
perspicazmente ADV perceptively, shrewdly
perspicuidad SF (*frm*) perspicuity (*frm*), clarity
perspicuo ADJ perspicuous (*frm*), clear
persuadir ▹ CONJUG 3a VT to persuade • **~ a algn de algo/para hacer algo** to persuade sb of sth/to do sth • **dejarse ~** to allow o.s. to be persuaded
VPR **persuadirse** to be persuaded
persuasión SF 1 (= *acción de persuadir*) persuasion
2 (= *convicción*) conviction • **tener la ~ de que …** to have the conviction that …, be convinced that …
persuasiva SF persuasiveness, power of persuasion
persuasivo ADJ [*vendedor, carácter*] persuasive; [*argumento, razones*] persuasive, convincing
pertenecer ▹ CONJUG 2d VI 1 (= *ser propiedad*) • **~ a algn** to belong to sb • **los terrenos pertenecen al ayuntamiento** the land belongs to the council, the land is council property • **este diccionario te pertenece** this dictionary belongs to you
2 (= *formar parte*) • **~ a algo** to belong to sth • **pertenecemos a un grupo pacifista** we belong to a pacifist group
3 (*frm*) (= *competer*) • **~ a algn hacer algo** to be sb's responsibility to do sth • **le pertenece a él acabar el trabajo** it's his responsibility to finish the job, it's up to him to finish the job
perteneciente ADJ 1 (= *que pertenece*) belonging (**a** to) • **los países ~s** the member countries • **las personas ~s al organismo** members of the organization
2 (= *relacionado*) • **~ a** pertaining to
pertenencia SF 1 (= *posesión*) ownership • **las cosas de su ~** his possessions, his property
2 **pertenencias** (= *objetos personales*) personal belongings; [*de finca*] appurtenances, accessories
3 (*a club, asociación*) membership (**a** of)
pértica SF *land measure* (= *2.70 metres*)
pértiga SF pole • **salto de ~** (*Dep*) pole vault ▸ **pértiga de trole** trolley pole
pertiguero SM verger
pertiguista SMF pole-vaulter
pertinacia SF 1 (= *persistencia*) persistence
2 (= *obstinación*) obstinacy
pertinaz ADJ 1 [*tos*] persistent; [*sequía*] long-lasting, prolonged
2 [*persona*] obstinate
pertinencia SF (= *relevancia*) relevance, pertinence; (= *idoneidad*) appropriateness
pertinente ADJ 1 (= *relevante*) relevant, pertinent; (= *adecuado*) appropriate • **no es ~ hacerlo ahora** this is not the appropriate time to do it
2 • **~ a** concerning • **en lo ~ a libros** as regards books, as far as books are concerned
pertinentemente ADV (= *relevantemente*) relevantly, pertinently; (= *adecuadamente*) appropriately
pertrechar ▹ CONJUG 1a VT (*gen*) to supply (**con, de** with); (= *equipar*) to equip (**con, de** with); (*Mil*) to supply with ammunition and stores, equip
VPR **pertrecharse** • **~se de algo** to provide o.s. with sth
pertrechos SMPL 1 (= *útiles*) gear (*sing*) ▸ **pertrechos de pesca** fishing tackle (*sing*)
2 (*Mil*) (*gen*) supplies and stores; (= *provisiones*) provisions; (= *munición*) munitions
perturbación SF 1 (*Meteo, Pol*) disturbance ▸ **perturbación del orden público** breach of the peace
2 (*Med*) upset, disturbance; (*mental*) mental disorder
perturbado/a ADJ mentally unbalanced
SM/F mentally unbalanced person
perturbador(a) ADJ 1 [*noticia*] disturbing, perturbing
2 [*conducta*] unruly, disorderly; [*movimiento*] subversive
SM/F disorderly element, unruly person
perturbadoramente ADV disturbingly
perturbar ▹ CONJUG 1a VT 1 (= *alterar*) [+ *orden*] to disturb; [+ *plan*] to upset; [+ *calma*] to disturb, ruffle
2 (*Med*) to disturb, mentally disturb
Perú SM Peru
peruanismo SM *word or phrase peculiar to Peru*
peruano/a ADJ Peruvian
SM/F Peruvian • **los ~s** the Peruvians
Perucho* SM (*Caribe*) • MODISMO: • **viven en plan de ~** they get on like a house on fire
peruétano* ADJ (*And, Caribe, Méx*) boring, tedious
SM (*And, Caribe, Méx*) (= *pelma*) bore; (= *necio*) dolt • **ese muchacho es un ~** (*Cono Sur*) (= *entrometido*) that lad is always sticking his nose where it doesn't belong
perversamente ADV wickedly
perversidad SF 1 (= *cualidad*) [*de depravado*] depravity; [*de malvado*] wickedness
2 (= *acto*) evil deed
perversión SF 1 (= *depravación*) perversion ▸ **perversión sexual** sexual perversion
2 (= *maldad*) wickedness
perverso ADJ (= *depravado*) depraved; (= *malvado*) wicked
pervertido/a ADJ perverted, deviant
SM/F pervert, deviant
pervertidor(a) SM/F corruptor ▸ **pervertidor(a) de menores** child corruptor, corruptor of minors (*frm*)
pervertimiento SM perversion, corruption
pervertir ▹ CONJUG 3i VT [+ *persona*] to pervert; [+ *texto*] to distort, corrupt; [+ *gusto*] to corrupt
VPR **pervertirse** to become perverted
pervinca SF (*Bot*) periwinkle
pervivencia SF survival
pervivir ▹ CONJUG 3a VI to survive
pesa SF 1 (*Dep*) weight • **hacer ~s** to do weight training, do weights* • **levantamiento de ~s** weightlifting
2 [*de balanza, reloj*] weight
3 (*And, CAm, Caribe*) butcher's shop
pesabebés SM INV baby scales (*pl*)
pesadamente ADV 1 (= *con mucho peso*) heavily • **caer ~** to fall heavily
2 (= *lentamente*) slowly, sluggishly
3 (= *de manera aburrida*) boringly, tediously
pesadez SF 1 (= *peso*) weight
2 (= *lentitud*) slowness, sluggishness
3 (*Med*) (= *malestar*) heaviness; (= *somnolencia*) drowsiness ▸ **pesadez de estómago** bloated feeling in the stomach
4 (= *aburrimiento*) tediousness, boring nature; (= *molestia*) annoyance • **es una ~ tener que …** it's a bore having to … • **¡qué ~!** what a bore!
pesadilla SF 1 (= *mal sueño*) nightmare, bad dream • **una experiencia de ~** a nightmarish experience
2 (= *tormento*) nightmare • **ha sido la ~ de todos** it has been a nightmare for everybody • **ese equipo es nuestra ~** that is our bogey team
pesado/a ADJ 1 [*paquete, comida*] heavy • **industria pesada** heavy industry
2 (= *lento*) [*persona*] slow, sluggish; [*mecanismo*] stiff
3 (*Meteo*) heavy, sultry
4 [*sueño*] deep, heavy
5 (*Med*) heavy • **tengo la cabeza pesada** my head feels heavy • **tener el estómago ~** to feel bloated, feel full up
6 [*tarea*] (= *difícil*) tough, hard; (= *aburrido*) tedious, boring; (= *molesto*) annoying; [*lectura*] heavy, stodgy • **esto se hace ~** this is becoming tedious • **la lectura del libro**

P

resultó pesada the book was heavy going • **es una persona de lo más ~** he's a terribly dull sort • **ese me cae ~** (*Caribe, Méx**) that chap gets on my nerves* • **es ~ tener que …** it's such a bore having to … • **¡no seas ~!** stop being such a pain!
SM/F **1** (= *aburrido*) bore • **es un ~** he's such a bore
2 (*Caribe**) (= *pez gordo*) big shot*
SM (= *acto*) weighing

pesador SM (*And, CAm, Caribe*) butcher

pesadumbre SF grief, sorrow

pesaje SM **1** (= *acción*) weighing
2 (*Dep*) weigh-in

pésame SM condolences (*pl*) • **dar el ~** to express one's condolences, send one's sympathy (**por** for, on) • **mi más sentido ~** my deepest sympathy, my heartfelt condolences

pesantez SF weight, heaviness; (*Fís*) gravity

pesar ▷ CONJUG 1a VI **1** [*objeto, persona*] **a** (= *tener peso*) to weigh; (*Boxeo, Hípica*) to weigh in at; (*Inform*) to be • **pesa cinco kilos** it weighs five kilos • **pesa cinco kilos** it weighs five kilos • **¿cuánto pesas?** how much *o* what do you weigh? • **el boxeador pesó 90kg** the boxer weighed in at 90kg • **esta foto pesa 50k** this photo is 50k (in size)
b (= *tener mucho peso*) to be heavy • **ese paquete no pesa** that parcel isn't heavy, that parcel hardly weighs anything • **¿pesa mucho?** is it heavy? • **¡cómo pesa esta bolsa!** this bag's really heavy! • **¡no pesa nada!** it's not heavy at all! • **~ como una losa** to weigh like a millstone round one's neck
2 (= *resultar pesado*) • **~le a algn: le pesaba la mochila** his rucksack was weighing him down • **los pies me pesan, estoy muy cansado** I'm so tired, I can hardly lift my feet up any more
3 (= *afligir*) • **me pesa mucho** I am very sorry about it *o* to hear it • **¡ya le ~á!** he'll be sorry!, he'll regret this! • **me pesa haberlo hecho** I regret having done it, I'm sorry I did it • **le pesa que no le hayan nombrado** he is hurt that he has not been appointed
4 (= *ser una carga*) • **le pesa tanta responsabilidad** all that responsibility weighs heavily on him • **me pesan los años** I feel my age • **~ sobre** [*responsabilidad, preocupación*] to weigh heavily on; [*amenaza, acusación*] to hang over • **pesa sobre mi conciencia** it is weighing heavily on my conscience • **sobre ella pesan muchas obligaciones** she is burdened with many responsibilities • **las sospechas que pesan sobre Aguirre** the suspicions surrounding Aguirre • **pesa sobre ellos una orden de busca y captura** there is a warrant out for their arrest • **la hipoteca que pesa sobre el piso** the mortgage with which the flat is burdened • **la maldición que pesa sobre nuestra familia** the curse afflicting our family
5 (= *influir*) to carry weight • **sus opiniones no pesan en el partido** her opinions do not carry any weight in the party • **sus razones no han pesado en mi decisión** his arguments did not influence my decision
6 • **pese a (que)** in spite of (the fact that), despite (the fact that) • **pese a las dificultades** in spite of *o* despite the difficulties • **lo creo, pese a que ellos lo niegan** I believe it, even though they deny it, I believe it, in spite of *o* despite the fact that they deny it • **lo haré pese a quien pese** I'll do it whether people like it or not, I'll do it, no matter who I offend; ▷ **mal**
7 (*And, CAm*) (= *vender carne*) to sell meat
VT **1** [+ *carta, fruta etc*] to weigh
2 (= *sopesar*) to weigh up • **~ las posibilidades** to weigh up one's chances • **~ los pros y los contras** to weigh up the pros and cons
VPR **pesarse** to weigh o.s.; (*Boxeo, Hípica*) to weigh in • **tengo que ~me** I must weigh myself
SM **1** (= *aflicción*) sorrow • **la noticia le causó un hondo ~** the news caused him deep sorrow • **expresó su ~ a la familia de las víctimas** he expressed his sorrow to the families of the victims
2 (= *arrepentimiento*) regret • **expresó su ~ por el accidente** he expressed his regret at the accident • **a mi ~** to my regret • **con gran ~ mío** much to my regret • **sentir** *o* **tener ~ por no haber …** to regret not having …
3 • **a pesar de** in spite of, despite • **a ~ de todo** in spite of *o* despite everything • **a ~ del mal tiempo** in spite of *o* despite the bad weather • **a ~ de que** even though • **a ~ de que no tiene dinero** even though he has no money, in spite of *o* despite the fact that he has no money • **a ~ de que la quiero** even though I love her • MODISMO: • **a ~ de los ~es*** in spite of *o* despite everything

pesario SM pessary

pesaroso ADJ (= *arrepentido*) regretful; (= *afligido*) sorrowful, sad

pesca SF **1** (= *actividad*) fishing • **allí la ~ es muy buena** the fishing is very good there • **ir de ~** to go fishing • **andar a la ~ de** (*fig*) to fish for, angle for ▸ **pesca a caña** angling ▸ **pesca a mosca** fly-fishing ▸ **pesca de altura** deep sea fishing ▸ **pesca de bajura** coastal fishing, shallow water fishing ▸ **pesca de la ballena** whaling ▸ **pesca de perlas** pearl fishing ▸ **pesca submarina** underwater fishing
2 (= *lo pescado*) catch • **la ~ ha sido mala** it's been a poor catch • MODISMO: • **… y toda la ~*** … and all the rest of it, … and whatnot*

pescada SF hake

pescadería SF (= *tienda*) fish shop, fishmonger's; (= *mercado*) fish market

pescadero/a SM/F fishmonger, fish merchant (EEUU)

pescadilla SF whiting, small hake

pescado SM **1** (*Culin*) fish • **quiero comprar ~** I want to buy some fish ▸ **pescado azul** blue fish
2 (*And, Cono Sur**) (= *policía*) secret police

pescador(a) ADJ fishing
SM/F fisherman/fisherwoman ▸ **pescador(a) a mosca** fly-fisherman/fly-fisherwoman ▸ **pescador(a) de caña** angler

pescante SM **1** [*de carruaje*] driver's seat, coachman's seat
2 (*Teat*) wire
3 (*Téc*) jib
4 (*Náut*) davit

pescar ▷ CONJUG 1g VT **1** [+ *peces, mariscos*] to catch • **pescamos varias truchas** we caught several trout • **fuimos a ~ salmón** we went salmon-fishing
2* (= *agarrar*) • **lo ha pescado la policía** he's been caught *o* nabbed* by the police • **¡si no te abrigas vas a ~ una pulmonía!** if you don't wrap up you'll catch pneumonia! • **viene a ~ un marido** she's come to get *o* bag* a husband • **me ~on fumando** I got caught smoking • **¡te pesqué!** caught you!, got you!
3* (= *entender*) to get • **¿aún no has pescado el chiste?** haven't you got the joke yet? • **en la clase de matemáticas no pesco nada** I don't understand a thing in maths
VI **1** [*pescador*] to fish • **ir a ~** to go fishing • **~ a mosca** to fish with a fly, flyfish • **~ a la rastra** • **~ al arrastre** to trawl • MODISMO: • **~ en río revuelto** to fish in troubled waters
2 (*And, Cono Sur*) (= *dormitar*) to nod, doze
VPR **pescarse** • MODISMO: • **no sabe lo que se pesca*** he hasn't a clue*, he has no idea

pescata SF catch, haul

pescocear ▷ CONJUG 1a VT (*LAm*) to grab by the scruff of the neck

pescozón SM slap on the neck

pescozudo ADJ thick-necked, fat in the neck

pescuezo SM **1** (*Zool*) neck; (*Anat*) scruff of the neck • **retorcer el ~ a una gallina** to wring a chicken's neck • **¡calla, o te retuerzo el ~!** shut up, or I'll wring your neck!
2† (= *vanidad*) vanity; (= *altanería*) haughtiness, pride

pescuezón ADJ (*LAm*) **1** = **pescozudo**
2 (= *de cuello largo*) long-necked

pese PREP • **~ a** despite, in spite of

pesebre SM **1** (*Agr*) manger
2 (*Rel*) nativity scene, crib

pesebrera SF (*Cono Sur, Méx*) = **pesebre**

pesera SF (*Méx*) = **pesero**

pesero SM **1** (*Méx*) (= *colectivo*) minibus
2 (*And, CAm, Caribe*) (= *carnicero*) butcher

peseta SF peseta • MODISMO: • **cambiar la ~*** to throw up

pesetada SF (*LAm*) joke, trick

pesetera SF (*CAm, Méx*) prostitute

pesetero ADJ **1** (= *avaro*) money-grabbing*, mercenary
2 (*Méx*) [*comerciante*] small-time
3 (*And, CAm, Caribe*) (= *gorrón*) sponging*

pésimamente ADV awfully, dreadfully

pesimismo SM pessimism

pesimista ADJ pessimistic
SMF pessimist

pésimo ADJ awful, dreadful
ADV (*Méx**) • **lo hiciste ~** you did it awfully *o* dreadfully

peso SM **1** (*Fís, Téc*) weight • **no puedo levantar mucho ~** I can't lift much weight • **¿cuál es tu ~?** how much do you weigh? • **un vehículo de mucho/poco ~** a heavy/light vehicle • **las telas se venden al ~** the fabrics are sold by weight • **coger ~** (*Esp*) (= *engordar*) to put on weight; (= *levantar peso*) to lift weight • **no dar el ~** (*al pesarse*) [*boxeador*] not to make the weight; [*recién nacido*] to be below normal weight, be underweight; (*en una categoría*) not to make the grade, not come up to scratch • **ese escultor no da el ~** that sculptor doesn't make the grade *o* come up to scratch • **sostener algo en ~** to support the full weight of sth • **falto de ~** underweight • **ganar ~** to put on weight • **~s y medidas** weights and measures • **perder ~** to lose weight • MODISMOS: • **caer por su propio ~** (= *ser obvio*) to go without saying, be obvious; (= *no tener lógica*) not to stand up (to scrutiny) • **valer su ~ en oro** to be worth one's weight in gold ▸ **peso atómico** atomic weight ▸ **peso bruto** gross weight ▸ **peso en vivo** live weight ▸ **peso escurrido** net weight ▸ **peso específico** (*lit*) specific gravity; (*fig*) influence ▸ **peso máximo autorizado** gross weight ▸ **peso molecular** (*Quím*) molecular weight ▸ **peso muerto** (*Náut*) (*tb fig*) dead weight ▸ **peso neto** net weight
2 (= *acción*) • **van a proceder al ~ de la fruta** they're going to weigh the fruit • **el ~ de la leña se hace en unas balanzas enormes** the firewood is weighed on enormous scales
3 [*de culpa, responsabilidad*] weight • **le cayó encima todo el ~ de la justicia** he felt the full weight of the law • **el delantero llevó todo el ~ del ataque** the forward carried the full weight of the attack • **el ~ de los años** the

burden of old age • **quitarse un ~ de encima** to take a load *o* weight off one's mind • **me quitarías un buen ~ de encima** it would be a weight off my mind, you would take a weight off my mind
4 (= *importancia*) weight • **su opinión era la de mayor ~ en la reunión** his opinion carried the most weight at the meeting • **España tiene poco ~ en esa organización** Spain does not carry much weight in that organization • **de ~** [*persona*] influential; [*argumento*] weighty, forceful • **un argumento de poco ~** a lightweight argument • **razones de ~** good *o* sound reasons ▸ **peso político** political influence
5 (= *balanza*) scales (*pl*) ▸ **peso de baño** bathroom scales (*pl*) ▸ **peso de cocina** kitchen scales (*pl*) ▸ **peso de muelle** spring balance
6 (*Med*) heaviness • **noto un ~ muy grande en la cabeza** I can feel a great heaviness in my head
7 (*Dep*) **a** (*Esp*) (*Atletismo*) shot • **lanzamiento de ~** shot putting • **lanzar el ~** to put the shot
b (*Halterofilia*) • **levantamiento de ~s** weightlifting
c (*Boxeo*) weight ▸ **peso completo** (*CAm, Méx, Ven*) heavyweight ▸ **peso gallo** bantamweight ▸ **peso ligero, peso liviano** (*Chile, Ven*) lightweight ▸ **peso medio** middleweight ▸ **peso medio fuerte** light heavyweight, cruiserweight ▸ **peso mosca** flyweight ▸ **peso pesado** heavyweight ▸ **peso pluma** featherweight ▸ **peso welter** welterweight
8 (*Econ*) peso • **MODISMO**: • **no valer un ~** to be no good

pesor SM (*CAm, Caribe*) weight, heaviness
pespunte SM (*Cos*) backstitch(ing)
pespuntear ▹ CONJUG 1a VT, VI to backstitch
pesquera SF 1 (= *zona*) fishing-ground, fishery
2 (= *presa*) weir
pesquería SF fishing ground, fishery
pesquero ADJ fishing (*antes de s*)
SM fishing boat
pesquis* SM (= *agudeza*) (*intelectual*) nous*; (*técnica*) know-how • **tener el ~ para hacer algo** to have the nous to do sth*
pesquisa SF (= *indagación*) investigation, inquiry; (= *búsqueda*) search
SM (*And, Cono Sur**) (= *policía*) secret police; (= *detective*) detective
pesquisador(a) SM/F (= *investigador*) investigator, inquirer; (= *detective*) detective; (*And, Cono Sur**) (= *policía*) member of the secret police
pesquisar ▹ CONJUG 1a VT to investigate, inquire into
pesquisidor(a)† SM/F investigator, inquirer
pestaña SF 1 [*de ojo*] eyelash • **MODISMOS**: • **no pegué ~*** I didn't get a wink of sleep • **quemarse las ~s** (= *excederse*) (*gen*) to burn one's fingers; (*estudiando*) to burn the midnight oil • **tener ~** to be pretty smart
2 (*Bot*) fringe
3 (= *saliente*) [*de caja*] flap; [*de neumático*] rim; (*en página web*) tab
4 (*Esp*‡) (= *policía*) • **la ~** the fuzz‡, the cops* (*pl*)
pestañear ▹ CONJUG 1a VI, **pestañar** ▹ CONJUG 1a VI (*LAm*) to blink • **sin ~** without batting an eyelid
pestañeo SM blink(ing)
pestazo* SM stink, stench
peste SF 1 (*Med*) plague • **una ~ de ratones** a plague of mice • **MODISMOS**: • **huir de algo/algn como de la ~** to avoid sth/sb like the plague • **ser la ~*** to be a nuisance, be a pain* ▸ **peste aviar** fowl pest ▸ **peste bubónica** bubonic plague ▸ **peste negra** Black Death ▸ **peste porcina** swine fever
2 (= *mal olor*) stink, foul smell • **¡qué ~ hay aquí!** there's a real stink in here!
3 • **MODISMO**: • **decir** *o* **echar ~s de algn** to slag sb off* • **siempre anda echando ~s de su jefe** she's always slagging off her boss*
4 (*Cono Sur*) (*gen*) infectious disease; (= *viruela*) smallpox
5 (*And*) (= *resfriado*) cold
pesticida SM pesticide
pestífero ADJ (= *dañino*) pestiferous; [*olor*] foul; [*influencia*] noxious, harmful
pestilencia SF 1 (= *plaga*) pestilence, plague
2 (= *mal olor*) stink, stench
pestilencial ADJ pestilential
pestilente ADJ 1 (= *dañino*) pestilent
2 (= *que huele mal*) smelly, foul
pestillo SM [*de puerta, ventana*] bolt; [*de cerradura*] latch; (*Cono Sur*) (= *picaporte*) door handle
pestiño SM (*Esp*) 1 (*Culin*) honey-coated fritter
2* (= *lata*) bore, drag • **fue un ~** it was a real drag
3* (= *chica*) plain girl
pestozos‡ SMPL socks
pesuña SF (*LAm*) = **pezuña**
peta[1]‡ SF (*Esp*) peseta
peta[2]‡ SM 1 (= *droga*) joint‡, reefer‡
2 (= *nombre*) name ▸ **peta chungo** false name
3 (= *documentación*) papers (*pl*)
petabyte SM petabyte
petaca SF 1 [*de cigarrillos*] cigarette case; [*de puros*] cigar case; [*de pipa*] tobacco pouch; [*de alcohol*] flask • **MODISMO**: • **hacerle la ~ a algn** to make an apple-pie bed for sb
2 (*LAm*) (= *cesto*) wicker basket; (= *baúl*) leather-covered chest; (*Méx*) (= *maleta*) suitcase • **MODISMO**: • **se le fueron las ~s** (*Arg**) he lost his patience
3 (*CAm, Méx*) (*Anat*) hump
4 **petacas** (*Caribe, Méx*‡) (= *nalgas*) buttocks; (= *pechos*) big breasts
SMF (*Arg**) 1 (= *rechoncho*) short squat person
2 (= *vago*) lazy person
ADJ INV* 1 (*Chile*) (= *torpe*) slow, sluggish; (= *vago*) lazy, idle
2 (*Caribe*) (= *grosero*) coarse
petacho SM patch, mend
petacón* ADJ 1 (*Méx, And, Cono Sur*) (= *rechoncho*) plump, chubby
2 (*Méx*) (= *nalgudo*) fat-bottomed, broad in the beam* • **está petacona** she's rather broad in the beam*
petacudo* ADJ 1 (*And*) (= *grueso*) stout, fat
2 (*CAm*) (= *con joroba*) hunchbacked
3 (*Méx*) (= *nalgudo*) broad in the beam*
4 (*Col*) (= *lento*) slow, ponderous, sluggish
petado* ADJ • **estar ~ (de gente)** to be packed (with people) • **estar ~ (de algo)** to be crammed (with sth)
pétalo SM petal
petanca SF pétanque
petar* ▹ CONJUG 1a VI • **no le peta trabajar en una oficina** he's not into working in an office • **ahora mismo no me peta** I don't feel like it now
petardazo SM 1 (= *fuegos artificiales*) firework display
2 (= *sonido*) crack, bang
3 (= *sorpresa*) shock result, upset
petardear ▹ CONJUG 1a VI (*Aut*) to backfire
VT* (= *estafar*) to cheat, swindle
petardista* SM/F 1 (*Méx*) (= *político*) crooked politician*
2 (*CAm*) (= *estafador*) cheat, swindler
petardo SM 1 (= *cohete*) banger, firecracker; (= *explosivo*) small explosive device; (*Mil*) petard
2* (= *lo que aburre*) bore, drag • **ser un ~** to be dead boring*
3‡ (= *mujer fea*) hag‡, old hag‡
4‡ (= *droga*) joint‡
5* (= *estafa*) fraud, swindle • **pegar un ~** pull a fast one (**a** on)
petate SM 1 (= *estera*) grass mat; (*esp LAm*) [*de palma*] mat of palm leaves; (*para dormir*) sleeping mat
2 (= *equipaje*) bundle of bedding and belongings; (*Mil*) kit bag • **liar el ~*** (*lit*) to pack; (= *irse*) to pack up and go, clear out*; (= *morir*) to kick the bucket*
3* (= *estafador*) cheat, trickster
4* (= *pobre hombre*) poor devil
5 • **MODISMO**: • **se descubrió el ~*** the fraud was uncovered
petatearse‡ ▹ CONJUG 1a VPR (*Méx*) to peg out‡, kick the bucket*
peteneras SFPL (*Esp*) • **MODISMO**: • **salir por ~** to say/do something quite inappropriate
petición SF 1 (= *solicitud*) (*gen*) request; (= *documento*) petition • **con referencia a su ~ del 20 de mayo** with reference to your request of 20 May • **vamos a oír las peticiones de los oyentes** we are going to hear the listeners' requests • **a ~ popular** by popular request • **a ~ de la familia** at the request of the family • **"consulta previa petición de cita"** "consultation by appointment" • **una ~ firmada por cinco mil personas** a petition signed by five thousand people ▸ **petición de divorcio** petition for divorce ▸ **petición de extradición** request for extradition ▸ **petición de indulto** appeal for a reprieve ▸ **petición de mano** proposal (of marriage) ▸ **petición de orden** (*Inform*) prompt
2 (*Jur*) (= *alegato*) plea; (= *reclamación*) claim • **una ~ de 12 años de condena** a recommendation to serve 12 years
peticionar ▹ CONJUG 1a VT (*LAm*) to petition
peticionario/a SM/F petitioner (*frm*), applicant
petimetre ADJ foppish
SM fop, dandy
petirrojo SM robin
petiso/a (*LAm*), **petizo/a** (*LAm*) ADJ (= *pequeño*) small, short; (= *rechoncho*) chubby
SM (= *caballo bajo*) small horse
SM/F (= *persona baja*) small person
petisú SM cream puff
petitorio ADJ • **mesa petitoria** stall (*for charity collection*)
petizón ADJ (*And, Cono Sur*) = **petiso**
peto SM [*de falda*] bodice; [*de pantalón*] bib; (*Mil*) breastplate; (*Taur*) horse's padding • **(pantalones con) ~** dungarees (*pl*), overalls (*pl*) (*EEUU*)
petral SM breast-strap (*of harness*)
Petrarca SM Petrarch
petrarquismo SM Petrarchism
petrarquista ADJ Petrarchan
petrel SM petrel
pétreo ADJ stony, rocky
petrificación SF petrifaction
petrificado ADJ petrified
petrificar ▹ CONJUG 1g VT (*lit, fig*) to petrify
VPR **petrificarse** (*lit*) to become petrified; (*fig*) to be petrified
petrodólar SM petrodollar
petroleado ADJ [*animal, ave*] oiled
petróleo SM (*Min*) oil, petroleum; (*LAm*) (= *kerosene*) paraffin ▸ **petróleo combustible** fuel oil ▸ **petróleo crudo** crude oil ▸ **petróleo de alumbrado** paraffin (oil), kerosene (*EEUU*)
petrolero ADJ oil (*antes de s*) • **flota**

P

petrolera oil tanker fleet • **industria petrolera** oil industry • **sindicato ~** oil workers' union
(SM) **1** (*Náut*) oil tanker
2 (*Com*) (*gen*) oil man; (= *obrero*) oil worker
3† (= *incendiario*) arsonist, incendiary
petrolífero (ADJ) **1** (*Min*) oil-bearing
2 (*Com*) oil (*antes de s*) • **compañía petrolífera** oil company
petrología (SF) petrology
petroquímica (SF) (= *ciencia*) petrochemistry; (*Com*) petrochemical company; (= *fábrica*) petrochemical factory
petroquímico (ADJ) petrochemical
petulancia (SF) opinionated nature
petulante (ADJ) opinionated
petunia (SF) petunia
peuquino (ADJ) (*Cono Sur*) greyish, grayish (EEUU)
peyorativamente (ADV) pejoratively
peyorativo (ADJ) pejorative
peyote (SM) (*LAm*) peyote cactus
pez[1] (SM) fish • **cogimos tres peces** we caught three fish • MODISMOS: • **estar como el pez en el agua** to feel completely at home, be in one's element • **ser un buen pez**†* to be a rogue, be a rascal • **quien quiera peces que se moje el culo*** if you want something, you have to go and get it ▸ **pez de colores** goldfish • **¡me río de los peces de colores!*** I couldn't care less! ▸ **pez espada** swordfish ▸ **pez gordo*** big shot* ▸ **pez martillo** hammerhead ▸ **pez mujer** manatee ▸ **pez sierra** sawfish ▸ **pez volador, pez volante** flying fish
(ADJ)* • MODISMO: • **estar pez en algo** to know nothing at all about sth • **están algo peces en idiomas** they're pretty clueless about languages
pez[2] (SF) (= *brea*) pitch, tar
pezón (SM) **1** [*de persona*] nipple; [*de animal*] teat
2 (*Bot*) stalk
3 (*Mec*) ▸ **pezón de engrase** lubrication point, grease nipple
pezonera (SF) (*Cono Sur*) feeding bottle
pezuña (SF) **1** (*Zool*) hoof; [*de persona**] hoof*, foot
2 (*Méx, Perú**) (= *olor*) smell of sweaty feet
PFCRN (SM ABR) (*Méx*) = **Partido del Frente Cardenista de Reconstrucción Nacional**
PGB (SM ABR) (*Chile*) (= **Producto Geográfico Bruto**) GDP
pgdo. (ABR) (= **pagado**) pd
PGP (SM ABR) (*Uru*) = **Partido por el Gobierno del Pueblo**
PGR (SF ABR) (*Méx*) = **Procuraduría General de la República**
phishing [fiʃin] (SM) (*Internet*) phishing • **ataque (de) ~** phishing attack
piada (SF) **1** (*Orn*) cheep, cheeping
2 (= *expresión copiada*) borrowed phrase
piadosamente (ADV) **1** (*Rel*) piously, devoutly
2 (= *bondadosamente*) kindly, mercifully
piadoso (ADJ) **1** (*Rel*) pious, devout
2 (= *bondadoso*) kind, merciful (**para, con** to); ▸ **mentira**
piafar ▸ CONJUG 1a (VI) [*caballo*] to paw the ground, stamp
pial (SM) lasso
pialar ▸ CONJUG 1a (VT) to lasso
Piamonte (SM) Piedmont
piamontés/esa (ADJ) of/from Piedmont
(SM/F) native/inhabitant of Piedmont • **los piamonteses** the people of Piedmont
pianista (SMF) pianist
pianístico (ADJ) piano (*antes de s*)
piano (SM) piano • **tocar el ~** (*lit*) to play the piano; (= *fregar**) to do the washing-up; (= *robar**) to rob, steal; (= *registrar huellas*‡) to have one's fingerprints taken, be fingerprinted • MODISMO: • **como un ~** (*Esp**) huge, massive ▸ **piano de cola** grand piano ▸ **piano de media cola** baby grand ▸ **piano mecánico** pianola ▸ **piano recto, piano vertical** upright piano
piantado/a‡ (*Cono Sur*) (ADJ) nuts*, crazy
(SM) nutcase*
piantarse‡ ▸ CONJUG 1a (VPR) (*Cono Sur*) to escape, get out
piante* (SMF) • **es un ~** he's a pain*
piar ▸ CONJUG 1c (VI) **1** [*ave*] to cheep
2* (= *hablar*) to talk, chatter
3* (= *quejarse*) to whine, grouse* • **~las*** to be forever whining *o* grousing*
4* (= *soplar*) to spill the beans* • **¡no la píes!** don't let on!*
piara (SF) herd
piastra (SF) piastre, piaster (EEUU)
PIB (SM ABR) (= **producto interior bruto**) GDP
pibe/a* (SM/F) (*esp Arg*) (= *niño*) kid*; (= *muchacho*) boy/girl; (= *novio*) boyfriend/ girlfriend
pibil (SM) (*Méx*) chilli sauce
pica[1] (SF) (*Orn*) magpie
pica[2] (SF) (*Mil*) pike; (*Taur*) goad; (= *pene***) prick** • MODISMO: • **poner una ~ en Flandes** to bring off a real coup, achieve a signal success
pica[3] (SF) (*And*) (*Agr*) tapping (*of rubber trees*)
pica[4] (SF) **1** (*And*) (= *resentimiento*) pique, resentment
2 (*Cono Sur*) (= *mal humor*) annoyance, irritation • **sacar ~ a algn*** to annoy sb
pica[5]* (SMF) [*de autobús*] inspector
pica[6] (SF) (*And, CAm, Caribe*) (= *camino*) forest trail, narrow path
picacera* (SF) (*And, Cono Sur*) irritation
picacho (SM) peak, summit
picada[1] (SF) **1** [*de abeja, avispa*] sting; [*de serpiente, mosquito*] bite; [*de ave*] peck
2 (*Cono Sur*) (= *mal humor*) bad temper, anger
3 • **ir en ~** (*LAm*) (*lit*) to nose-dive; (*fig*) to plummet, take a nose-dive
4 (*Culin*) (= *salsa picante*) spicy sauce; (*Cono Sur*) (= *tapas*) snacks (*pl*)
picada[2] (SF) **1** (*LAm*) (= *senda*) forest trail, narrow path
2 (*And*) (= *vado*) ford
picada[3] (SF) (*Cono Sur*) small restaurant
picadero (SM) **1** (= *escuela*) riding school
2‡ (= *apartamento*) bachelor pad*, *apartment used for sexual encounters*
3 (*LAm*‡) [*de drogas*] shooting gallery‡
4 (*And*) (= *matadero*) slaughterhouse
picadillo (SM) [*de carne*] mince, ground meat (EEUU) • **~ de cebolla** finely chopped onions (*pl*) • **los hizo ~** he made mincemeat out of them • MODISMO: • **ser como el ~** (*Caribe**) to be boring
picado (ADJ) **1** (= *podrido*) [*diente*] rotten, decayed; [*fruta*] rotten; [*metal*] rusty, rusted • **tengo tres muelas picadas** I have three cavities
2 (*Culin*) [*ajo, cebolla, patata*] chopped; (*Esp, Cono Sur*) [*carne*] minced, ground (EEUU)
3 (= *triturado*) [*tabaco*] cut; [*hielo*] crushed
4 [*vino*] pricked, sour
5 [*mar*] choppy
6 • **~ de viruelas** pockmarked
7* (= *enfadado*) • **estar ~** to be in a huff*
• **están ~s desde hace muchos años** they fell out years ago
8* (= *interesado*) • **estar ~ con *o* por algo** to go for sth in a big way* • **está muy ~ con la lotería** he's really been bitten by the lottery bug*, he's gone for the lottery in a big way*
9 (= *borracho*) tipsy
10 (*Mús*) [*nota*] staccato
(SM) **1** (= *acción*) **a** (*Culin*) [*de ajo, cebolla, patata*] chopping; (*Esp, Cono Sur*) [*de carne*] mincing, grinding (EEUU)
b [*de billete, boleto*] punching
c (= *triturado*) [*de tabaco, de piedra*] cutting; [*de hielo*] crushing
2 (*Aer, Orn*) dive • **caer en ~** (*Esp*) (*Aer*) to plummet, nose-dive; [*precios, popularidad, producción*] to plummet, fall sharply
3 (*Mús*) staccato
picador (SM) **1** [*de caballos*] (*gen*) horse-trainer, horse-breaker; (*Taur*) picador
2 (*Min*) faceworker
picadora (SF) (*tb* **picadora de carne**) mincer, mincing machine
picadura (SF) **1** (*gen*) prick; (= *pinchazo*) puncture; [*de abeja, avispa*] sting; [*de serpiente, mosquito*] bite
2 (= *tabaco picado*) cut tobacco
picaflor (SM) (*LAm*) **1** (*Orn*) hummingbird
2* (= *tenorio*) ladykiller*, Don Juan; (= *mariposón*) flirt; (= *amante*) lover, boyfriend
picafuego (SM) poker
picahielos (SM INV) ice axe, ice ax (EEUU)
picajón* (ADJ), **picajoso*** (ADJ) touchy
picamaderos (SM INV) woodpecker
picana (SF) (*LAm*) cattle prod, goad ▸ **picana eléctrica** electric prod (*esp for torture*)
picanear ▸ CONJUG 1a (*LAm*) (VT) (*gen*) to spur on, goad on; [+ *persona*] to torture with electric shocks
picante (ADJ) **1** (= *que pica*) [*comida, sabor*] hot, spicy; [*vino*] tart, sour
2 (= *malicioso*) [*comentario*] sharp, cutting; [*chiste*] dirty; [*comedia, película*] naughty, spicy; [*persona*] naughty
(SM) **1** (*Culin*) **a** (= *especia*) chilli • **esta salsa tiene mucho ~** this sauce is very hot *o* spicy
b (*And, Cono Sur*) (= *guisado*) *meat stew with chilli sauce*
2 (= *picardía*) (*en persona*) zip, zest; (*en chiste, situación*) piquancy
3 picantes (*Esp*‡) (= *calcetines*) socks
picantería (SF) (*And, Cono Sur*) (cheap) restaurant (*specializing in spicy dishes*)
picantón (SM) spicy sauce
picapedrero (SM) stonecutter
picapica (SF) **1** (*And*) (= *serpentina*) streamer
2 • **polvos de ~** itching powder
picapleitos (SMF INV) (*pey*) (= *pleitista*) litigious person; (= *abogado*) shark lawyer
picaporte (SM) (= *manija*) door handle; (= *pestillo*) latch; (= *aldaba*) doorknocker; (= *llave*) latchkey
picar ▸ CONJUG 1g (VT) **1** (*con el pico, la boca*) [*abeja, avispa*] to sting; [*mosquito, serpiente, pez*] to bite; [*ave*] to peck (at) • **me ha picado un bicho en el cuello** an insect has bitten me on the neck • **los pájaros han picado toda la fruta** the birds have pecked holes in *o* pecked (at) all the fruit • **~ el anzuelo** (*lit*) to take *o* swallow the bait; (*fig*) to rise to the bait, fall for it* • MODISMO: • **¿qué mosca le habrá picado?** what's got into her?, what's eating her? (EEUU)
2 (= *comer*) [*persona*] to nibble at • **he estado picando unos cacahuetes** I've been nibbling at some peanuts • **he picado algo antes de comer** I had a little nibble before lunch
3 (= *agujerear*) [+ *hoja, página*] to punch a hole/some holes in; [+ *billete, entrada*] to punch
4 (= *trocear*) **a** (*Culin*) [+ *ajo, cebolla, patata*] to chop; (*Esp, Cono Sur*) [+ *carne*] to mince, grind (EEUU) • **pica la cebolla muy picadita** chop the onion very finely
b [+ *tabaco*] to cut; [+ *hielo*] to crush
c [+ *tierra*] to dig over, break up; [+ *piedra*] (*en trozos pequeños*) to chip at; (*en trozos grandes*) to break up • **acabó sus días picando piedra**

P

en una cantera he ended his days breaking up stone in a quarry
5 (= *provocar*) [+ *persona*] to needle, goad; [+ *caballo*] to spur on • **estaba siempre picándome** he was always needling *o* goading me • **eso me picó la curiosidad** that aroused my curiosity • **lo que dijiste lo picó en su amor propio** what you said wounded *o* hurt his pride
6 (= *corroer*) [+ *diente, muela, madera*] to rot; [+ *hierro, metal*] to rust; [+ *cable*] to corrode; [+ *goma, neumático*] to perish • **las polillas han picado la lana** the moths have made holes in the wool
7 (*Inform*) [+ *texto*] to key in
8 (*Mús*) [+ *nota*] to play staccato
9 (*Taur*) [+ *toro*] to stick, prick (*with the goad*)
10 (*Mil*) [+ *enemigo*] to harass
11 (*Ven**) (= *sablear*) to scrounge*
12 (*Ven**) • **~ el ojo a algn** to wink at sb
VI 1 (*con el pico, la boca*) [*abeja, avispa*] to sting; [*mosquito, serpiente*] to bite; [*ave*] to peck
2 (= *comer*) [*persona*] to nibble, snack • **llevo todo el día picando** I've been nibbling *o* snacking all day
3 (= *morder el cebo*) [*pez*] to bite; [*persona**] to fall for it* • **hoy parece que no pican** it seems they aren't biting today • **ha picado mucha gente** a lot of people have fallen for it* • MODISMO: • **~ muy alto** to aim too high, be over-ambitious
4 (= *ser picante*) [*comida*] to be hot, be spicy • **esta salsa sí que pica** this sauce is really hot *o* spicy
5 (= *causar picor*) [*herida, espalda*] to itch • **me pica la espalda** my back itches • **me pica por todo el cuerpo** I'm itching all over • **me pica la barba** I've got an itchy beard • **un jersey que pica** an itchy jumper • **¿le pica la garganta?** do you have a tickle in your throat?, do you have a tickly throat? • **me pican los ojos** my eyes are stinging *o* smarting • **el alcohol te va a ~ un poco** the alcohol is going to sting you a little • **¿qué te pica?** (*lit*) where does it itch?; (*fig*) what's got into you?, what's eating you? (EEUU) • REFRÁN: • **a quien le pique que se rasque** if you don't like it, you can lump it
6 [*sol*] to burn • **hoy sí que pica el sol** the sun is really burning today
7 (= *probar*) • **~ en algo** to dabble in sth • **ha picado en todos los géneros literarios** he has dabbled in all the literary genres
8 (*Esp**) (= *llamar a la puerta*) to knock
9 (*Cono Sur‡*) (= *largarse*) to split‡
10 (*Esp*) (*Aut*) to pink
11 • **~le** (*Méx**) (= *darse prisa*) to hurry up
12 (*LAm*) [*pelota*] to bounce
VPR **picarse 1** (= *corroerse*) [*diente, muela*] to rot, decay; [*hierro, metal*] to rust; [*goma, neumático*] to perish; [*cable*] to corrode; [*ropa*] to get moth-eaten • **se ha picado la chapa del coche** the bodywork has rusted
2 (*Culin*) [*fruta*] to go rotten; [*vino*] to go sour, turn sour
3* **a** (= *enfadarse*) to get into a huff* • **¿no te habrás picado por lo que te he dicho?** you're not in a huff about what I said, are you? • REFRÁN: • **el que se pica ajos come** if the cap fits, wear it
b (= *sentirse provocado*) • **se picó y pisó el acelerador** he rose to the challenge and stepped on the accelerator • **~se con algn** to compete with sb • **siempre se están picando a ver quién es el primero** they're always competing to be the first
c (= *aficionarse*) • **~se con algo** to get hooked on sth* • **se ha picado con los videojuegos** he's got into video games in a big way*, he's got hooked on video games*
4 [*mar*] to get choppy
5 (*Caribe*) • **~se de pecho** to become consumptive
6‡ (= *inyectarse droga*) to shoot up* • **ese tío se pica** that guy shoots up* • **~se heroína** to shoot heroin*

picarazado ADJ (*Caribe*) pockmarked
picardear ▸ CONJUG 1a VT • **~ a algn** to get sb into bad habits, lead sb into evil ways
VI (= *jugar*) to play about; (= *dar guerra*) to play up, be mischievous
VPR **picardearse** to get into evil ways, go to the bad
Picardía SF Picardy
picardía SF 1 (= *cualidad*) (*del taimado*) slyness, craftiness; (*del travieso*) naughtiness
2 (= *acción*) prank, naughty thing (to do)
3 (= *grosería*) naughty thing (to say); (= *insulto*) insult • **le gusta decir ~s a la gente** he likes saying naughty things to people
picardías SM INV baby-doll pyjamas (*pl*)
picaresca SF 1 (*Literat*) (genre of the) picaresque novel
2 (= *astucia*) guile, chicanery (*liter*), subterfuge • **la ~ española** Spanish guile, Spanish wiliness
3 (= *hampa*) (criminal) underworld
picaresco ADJ 1 (= *travieso*) roguish, rascally
2 (*Literat*) picaresque
pícaro/a ADJ 1 (= *taimado*) sly, crafty; (= *travieso*) [*niño*] naughty, mischievous
2 (= *deshonesto*) crooked; (= *pillo*) roguish, knavish
3 (*hum*) naughty, wicked • **¡este ~ siglo!** what naughty times we live in! • **tiene inclinación a los ~s celos** she is prone to wicked jealousy
4 (= *precoz*) [*niño*] precocious, knowing (*esp sexually aware before the proper age*)
SM/F 1 (= *granuja*) rogue, scoundrel; (= *ladino*) sly sort; (= *niño*) rascal, scamp • **¡pícaro!** you rascal!
2 (*Literat*) rogue

PÍCARO
In Spanish literature, especially of the Golden Age, the **pícaro** is a roguish character whose travels and adventures are used as a vehicle for social satire. The anonymous **Lazarillo de Tormes** (1554), which relates the life and adventures of one such character, is thought to be the first of the genre known as the picaresque novel, or **novela picaresca**. Other well-known picaresque novels were written by Cervantes (**Rinconete y Cortadillo**) and Francisco de Quevedo (**El Buscón**).

picarón ADJ* naughty, roguish
SM (*LAm*) (*Culin*) fritter
picaruelo* ADJ roguish, naughty, sly • **me dio una mirada picaruela** she gave me a roguish look
picas SFPL (*Naipes*) spades
picatoste SM fried bread
picaza SF magpie
picazo SM (= *picotazo*) peck; (= *golpe*) jab, poke
picazón SF 1 (*Med*) (= *picor*) itch; (= *ardor*) sting, stinging feeling
2 (= *desazón*) uneasiness
píccolo SM piccolo
pícea SF spruce
picha¹ SF (*Méx*) 1 (= *manta*) blanket
2 (*hum*) (= *querida*) mistress
picha²** SF prick**
pichado ADJ (*Cono Sur*) easily embarrassed
pichana SF (*And, Cono Sur*) broom
pichanga SF 1 (*And*) (= *escoba*) broom
2 (*Cono Sur*) (*Dep*) friendly soccer match
3 (*Cono Sur*) (*Culin*) tray of cocktail snacks
pichango SM (*Cono Sur*) dog
piche SM 1 (*CAm*) (= *avaro*) miser, skinflint*
2 (*And, Cono Sur*) (*Zool*) *kind of armadillo*
3 (*Caribe, Cono Sur*) (= *miedo*) fright
4 (*And*) (= *empujón*) shove
5 (*And*) (= *suero*) whey
6 (*And*) (= *rojo*) red
pichel SM (= *vaso*) tankard, mug; (*Méx*) water jug
pichi¹‡ ADJ (= *elegante*) smart, elegant
SM 1 (= *chulapo*) *Madrid man in traditional dress*
2 (*en oración directa*) mate*, man*, buddy (EEUU*)
pichi²* SM • **hacer ~** (*And, Cono Sur*) to have a pee*
pichi³ SM (= *prenda*) pinafore dress
pichicata* SF (*LAm*) 1 (= *droga*) cocaine powder
2 (= *inyección*) shot*
pichicatero/a* SM/F (*LAm*) (= *adicto*) druggie*; (= *comerciante*) drug peddler
pichicato* ADJ (*LAm*) stingy
pichichi SM top goal-scorer
pichicote ADJ (*And*) mean, miserly
pichilingo SM (*Méx*) lad, kid*
pichincha* SF (*And, Cono Sur*) (= *ganga*) bargain; (= *precio*) bargain price; (= *trato*) good deal; (= *suerte*) lucky break
pichingo SM (*CAm*) jar, vessel; (*pey*) piece of junk
pichintún SM (*Cono Sur*) dash, smidgen*
pichirre* ADJ (*And, Caribe*) mean, stingy
picholear* ▸ CONJUG 1a VI 1 (*CAm, Cono Sur*) (= *jaranear*) to have a good time
2 (*CAm, Méx*) (= *apostar*) to have a flutter*
pichón SM 1 (= *paloma*) young pigeon; (*Culin*) pigeon ▸ **pichón de barro** clay pigeon
2 (*LAm*) (= *pollo*) chick
3 (*LAm**) (= *novato*) novice, greenhorn; (*Dep*) rookie
4 (*Cono Sur*) • **un ~ de hombre** a well-bred man
5 (= *apelativo*) darling, dearest • **sí, ~** yes, darling *o* dearest
pichonear* ▸ CONJUG 1a VT 1 (*Méx*) (= *engañar*) to swindle, con*
2 (*And, CAm*) (= *pillar*) to catch out; (= *matar*) to kill, murder
3 (*Cono Sur*) = **pinchar**
4 (*And, CAm*) (= *tener prestado*) to borrow
VI (*And, Cono Sur, Méx*) to win an easy victory
pichoso ADJ (*Caribe*) dirty
pichula** SF (*And*) cock**, prick**
pichuleador* SM (*Cono Sur*) money-grubber
pichulear* ▸ CONJUG 1a VI 1 (*Cono Sur*) (= *negociar*) to be a smalltime businessman; (= *ser mercenario*) to be mercenary, be greedy for money
2 (*CAm, Méx*) (= *gastar poco*) to be careful with one's money
pichuleo* SM 1 (*Cono Sur*) (= *mezquindad*) meanness, stinginess*
2 (*CAm, Méx*) (= *negocio*) small business, retail business
pichulín‡ SM (*Arg, Uru*) willy*, peter (EEUU‡)
pichulina‡ SF willy*, peter (EEUU‡)
picia* SF prank
pickles ['pikels] SMPL (*Cono Sur*) pickles
pick-up [pi'kap, pi'ku] SM 1† (= *tocadiscos*) pickup
2 (*LAm*) (= *camioneta*) pickup (truck)
picnic SM 1 (= *excursión*) picnic
2 (= *cesta*) picnic basket, picnic set
pico SM 1 [*de ave*] beak, bill; [*de insecto*] beak
2 (= *punta*) corner, sharp point • **dobló el ~ de la página** he folded back the corner of the

P

page • el ~ de la plancha the sharp point of the iron • se sentó en el ~ de la cama he sat on the edge *o* corner of the bed • cuello de ~ V-neck • sombrero de tres ~s cocked hat, three-cornered hat • MODISMO: • irse de ~s pardos* to go out on the town*, have a night on the town*
3 [*de jarra*] lip, spout
4 [*de montaña*] peak, summit; (*fig*) peak
5 (= *herramienta*) pick, pickaxe, pickax (*EEUU*)
6 [*de una cantidad*] • quédese con el ~ keep the change • son las tres y ~ it's just after three • tiene 50 libros y ~ he has 50-odd books *o* over 50 books • tiene cuarenta y ~ años she's forty-odd • veinte euros y ~ just over twenty euros
7* • MODISMO: • costar un ~ to cost a fortune*
8* (= *boca*) trap* • ¡cierra el ~! shut your trap!*, shut up!* • MODISMOS: • darle al ~ to gab a lot* • darse el ~ to kiss • hincar el ~ (= *morir*) to peg out*; (= *ceder*) to give up, give in • irse del ~ to gab a lot* • ser un ~ de oro • tener buen *o* mucho ~ to have the gift of the gab
9 (= *pájaro*) woodpecker
10* [*de droga*] fix*, shot*
11 (*Naipes*) spade
12 (*And, Cono Sur***) (= *pene*) prick**

picolargo* ADJ (*Cono Sur*) (= *respondón*) pert, saucy, sassy (*EEUU**); (= *murmurador*) backbiting; (= *intrigante*) intriguing, scheming

picoleto‡ SM (*Esp*) Civil Guard

picón/ona* ADJ 1 (*And, Caribe*) (= *respondón*) cheeky*, sassy (*EEUU**)
2 (*And, Caribe*) (= *quisquilloso*) touchy
3 (*Caribe*) (= *burlón*) mocking
SM/F (*And*) gossip, telltale

picor SM = picazón

picoreto ADJ (*And, CAm, Caribe*) loose-tongued, indiscreet

picoso ADJ 1 (*LAm*) (= *picante*) very hot, spicy
2 (*de viruela*) pockmarked

picota SF 1 (*Arquit*) point, top; (*Geog*) peak
2 (*Bot*) bigarreau cherry
3 (*Hist*) pillory • MODISMO: • poner a algn en la ~ to pillory sb
4‡ (= *nariz*) hooter‡, conk‡

picotada SF, **picotazo** SM [*de pájaro*] peck; [*de abeja, avispa*] sting; [*de serpiente, mosquito*] bite • MODISMO: • tener mala ~ to be bad-tempered

picotear ▷ CONJUG 1a VT to peck (at)
VI 1 (*al comer*) to nibble
2* (= *parlotear*) to gas*, gab*
VPR **picotearse** to squabble

picotero/a* ADJ chattering, gossipy, talkative
SM/F gossip, chatterer, gasbag*

picotón SM (*And, Cono Sur*) peck

picto/a ADJ Pictish
SM/F Pict • los ~s the Picts
SM (*Ling*) Pictish

pictograma SM pictogram

pictóricamente ADV pictorially

pictórico ADJ (*gen*) pictorial; [*paisaje*] worth painting • tiene dotes pictóricas she has a talent for painting

picú† SM record player, phonograph (*EEUU*)

picúa SF (*Caribe*) 1 (= *cometa*) small kite
2 (= *comerciante*) sharp businessman
3 (= *prostituta*) prostitute

picuda SF 1 (*Orn*) woodcock
2 (*Caribe*) (= *pez*) barracuda

picudo ADJ 1 (= *puntiagudo*) pointed; [*jarra*] with a spout; [*persona*] pointy-nosed
2 (*Méx**) (= *astuto*) crafty, clever
3* = picotero
4 (*Caribe*) = cursi

piculina‡ SF (*Esp*) tart‡, slut‡, whore

picup SM (*LAm*) pickup (truck)

picure SM 1 (*And*) (= *fugitivo*) fugitive; (= *gandul*) slacker
2 (*Caribe*) (= *salsa picante*) spicy sauce

picurearse* ▷ CONJUG 1a VPR (*And, Caribe*) to scarper‡

PID SM ABR (= **proceso integrado de datos**) IDP

pida, pido ▷ pedir

pídola SF leapfrog

pie SM 1 (*Anat*) foot • levanta el pie izquierdo lift your left foot • las plantas de los pies the soles of the feet • no arrastres los pies al andar don't drag your feet while you walk • con los pies descalzos barefoot • se le fueron los pies he slipped • poner el pie en el acelerador (*lit*) to step on the gas*; (*fig*) to speed things up, step up the pace • volverse pies atrás to retrace one's steps ▸ pie de atleta athlete's foot ▸ pie de cabra crowbar ▸ pie de rey slide gauge ▸ pies de barro feet of clay ▸ pies de cerdo (*Culin*) (pig's) trotters ▸ pies de gato climbing boots ▸ pies planos flat feet
2 (*locuciones*) • a pie on foot • ir a pie to go on foot, walk • estar de pie to be standing (up) • estaba de pie junto a mi cama he was standing next to my bed • permanecieron mucho tiempo de pie they were standing for a long time, they were on their feet a long time • en pie: • llevo en pie desde las cuatro I've been up since four • mantenerse en pie [*persona*] to stay standing *o* on one's feet; [*objeto*] to remain upright • la oferta sigue en pie the offer still stands • ganado en pie (*LAm*) cattle on the hoof • a pie enjuto† (*lit*) dry-shod; (*fig*) without danger, without any risk • a pie firme†: • permanecer a pie firme to remain steadfast • ponerse de *o* en pie to stand up • MODISMOS: • de a pie common, ordinary • gente de a pie common *o* ordinary folk • el hombre de a pie the man in the street • el español de a pie the average Spaniard • soldado de a pie (*Hist*) foot-soldier • andar con pies de plomo to tread carefully *o* warily • de pies a cabeza from head to foot • se mojó de pies a cabeza she got soaked from head to foot • es un caballero de pies a cabeza he's a gentleman through and through • caer de pie to fall on one's feet • cojear del mismo pie to suffer from the same problem • hacer algo con los pies*: • han redactado este contrato con los pies they've made a mess of drawing up this contract • estás pensando con los pies you're not using your head • con los pies por delante feet first • se lo llevaron con los pies por delante he left feet first, he left in a (wooden) box • no dar pie con bola* to get everything wrong • hoy no doy pie con bola I can't seem to get anything right today • dale el pie y se tomará la mano give him an inch and he'll take a mile • entrar con buen pie *o* con el pie derecho to get off to a good start • estar con un pie en el hoyo to have one foot in the grave • hacer pie (*en el agua*) to touch the bottom • no hacer pie to be out of one's depth • a pies juntillas blindly • se lo creyeron a pies juntillas they blindly believed it • levantarse con el pie izquierdo to get out of the wrong side of the bed • nacer de pie to be born lucky • parar los pies a algn take sb down a peg or two • perder el pie to lose one's footing, slip • poner el pie *o* los pies en to set foot in • desde el pasado sábado, mi padre no ha puesto los pies en casa my father hasn't set foot in the house since last Saturday • poner los pies en el suelo to put your feet firmly on the ground • poner (los) pies en polvorosa to take to one's heels • sacar los pies del plato *o* tiesto to kick over the traces • salir por pies* to take to one's heels, leg it* • sin pies ni cabeza: • un argumento sin pies ni cabeza an absurd argument • el mensaje no tenía ni pies ni cabeza the message didn't make any sense at all, I couldn't make head or tail of the message • el plan no tiene ni pies ni cabeza the plan is totally unworkable; ▷ buscar
3 (= *base*) [*de columna, estatua, lámpara*] base; [*de cama*] foot; [*de colina, escalera*] foot, bottom; [*de copa*] stem; [*de calcetín*] foot • a los pies de la cama at the foot of the bed • al pie del monte at the foot *o* bottom of the mountain • al pie de ese edificio next to that building, right beside that building • al pie de fábrica ex-works • al pie de la obra (*Com*) including delivery charges • MODISMO: • al pie del cañón: • este fin de semana estará al pie del cañón he'll be hard at work this weekend • ha cumplido 30 años al pie del cañon he spent 30 years on the job • morir al pie del cañón to die in harness
4 [*de página*] foot, bottom; [*de foto*] caption • notas a pie de página footnotes • MODISMO: • al pie de la letra [*citar*] literally, verbatim; [*copiar*] word for word; [*cumplir*] to the letter, down to the last detail ▸ pie de imprenta imprint
5 (*Bot*) [*de árbol*] trunk; [*de planta*] stem; [*de rosa*] stock
6 (= *unidad de medida*) foot • tiene cuatro pies de largo it is four feet long ▸ pie cuadrado square foot
7 (*Teat*) cue
8 [*de vino*] sediment
9 (= *causa*) • dar pie a to give cause for • dar pie para que algn haga algo to give sb cause to do sth
10 (= *posición*) • estar en pie de igualdad to be on an equal footing (con with) • estar en pie de guerra (*lit*) to be on a war footing, be ready to go to war; (*fig*) to be on the warpath • poner a algn en pie de guerra to get sb up in arms
11 (*Literat*) foot
12 (*Cono Sur**) (= *pago*) deposit, down payment
13 ▸ pie de vía (*CAm*) (*Aut*) indicator, turn signal (*EEUU*)

piecería SF, **piecerío** SM (*Mec*) parts (*pl*)

piecero/a SM/F tailor's cutter, garment worker

piedad SF 1 (= *compasión, pena*) pity • tuvo ~ del mendigo he took pity on the beggar • ten un poco de ~ con el pobrecillo show some pity *o* sympathy for the poor boy • ¡por ~! for pity's sake! • mover a algn a ~ (*frm*) to move sb to pity, arouse compassion in sb
2 (= *clemencia*) mercy • el rey tuvo ~ de sus súbditos the king showed mercy to his subjects • ¡Dios, ten ~ de mi! God, have mercy on me!
3 (*Rel*) piety
4† (= *respeto*) respect ▸ piedad filial filial respect
5 (*Arte*) • la Piedad the Pietà

piedra SF 1 (= *material*) stone; (= *trozo*) stone, rock (*EEUU*) • la ~ de la torre está gastada the stone in the tower is ruined • un puente de ~ a stone bridge • nos tiraban ~s they were throwing stones at us • primera ~ foundation stone • colocar la primera ~ to lay the foundation stone • ¿quién se atreve a lanzar la primera ~? which of you shall cast the first stone? • MODISMOS: • no dejar

~ por mover to leave no stone unturned • no dejar ~ sobre ~ to raze to the ground • hablar ~s (And‡) to talk through the back of one's head* • menos da una ~ it's better than nothing • pasarse a algn por la ~‡ to lay sb* • no ser de ~: • no soy de ~ I'm not made of stone, I do have feelings • tener el corazón de ~ to be hard-hearted • tirar la ~ y esconder la mano to be a grass snake • tirar ~s a o contra su propio tejado to shoot o.s. in the foot ▸ piedra angular cornerstone ▸ piedra arenisca sandstone ▸ piedra caliza limestone ▸ piedra de afilar, piedra de amolar grindstone ▸ piedra de cal limestone ▸ piedra de escándalo source of scandal ▸ piedra de molino millstone ▸ piedra de toque touchstone ▸ piedra filosofal philosopher's stone ▸ piedra fundamental (lit) foundation stone; (fig) basis, cornerstone ▸ piedra imán lodestone ▸ piedra poma (Méx), piedra pómez pumice (stone) ▸ piedra preciosa precious stone; ▹ tiro
2 [de mechero] flint
3 (Med) stone
4 (Meteo) hailstone
5 • en ~ (Cono Sur) (Culin) with hot sauce
SMF (Caribe) (= pesado) bore

piel SF 1 [de persona] skin • tiene la ~ grasa/seca she has oily/dry skin • estirarse la ~* to have a facelift • MODISMOS: • dejarse la ~ to give one's all • ponerse en la ~ de algn to put o.s. in sb else's shoes • se me/le puso la ~ de gallina I/he came out in goose pimples o goose flesh • ser de la ~ de Barrabás o del diablo* to be a little devil o monster ▸ piel de naranja (por celulitis) orange-peel skin
2 [de animal] (gen) skin; [de vaca, búfalo, elefante] hide; [de foca, zorro, visón] fur; (= cuero) leather • abrigo de ~es fur coat • artículos de ~ leather goods • una maleta de ~ a leather suitcase • MODISMO: • la ~ de toro Iberia ▸ piel de ante suede ▸ piel de becerro calf, calfskin ▸ piel de cabra goatskin ▸ piel de cerdo pigskin ▸ piel de ternera calfskin
3 [de frutas] (gen) skin; [de naranja, limón] peel; [de manzana] skin, peel
SMF ▸ piel roja redskin • los ~es rojas the redskins

piélago SM (liter) 1 (= océano) ocean
2 (fig) • un ~ de dificultades a sea of difficulties

pienso¹ SM 1 (Agr) feed, fodder • ~s feeding stuffs
2‡ (= comida) grub‡, chow (EEUU‡)

pienso²†† SM thought • MODISMO: • ¡ni por ~! never!, the very idea!

piercing ['pirsin] SM piercing • lleva tres ~s en la oreja he's got three piercings in his ear • me voy a hacer un ~ en el ombligo I'm going to have my navel pierced

pierna SF 1 (Anat) leg • en ~s bare-legged • estirar las ~s to stretch one's legs • mañana iremos hasta el pueblo para hacer ~s we'll walk into the village tomorrow to get some exercise o for the exercise • MODISMOS: • dormir a ~ suelta o tendida to sleep like a log* • salir por ~s* to take one's heels, leg it*
2 (= muslo de animal) leg • ~ de cordero leg of lamb
3 [de letra] stroke; (con pluma) downstroke
4 (Cono Sur) player

piernas* SM INV twit*, idiot

piernicorto ADJ short-legged

pierrot [pie'ro] SM pierrot

pietista ADJ pietistic

pieza SF 1 (= componente) a [de rompecabezas, colección] piece • una vajilla de 60 ~s a 60-piece dinner service • un traje de baño de dos ~s a two-piece swimsuit • poco a poco fueron encajando todas las ~s del misterio little by little all the pieces of the mystery fell into place
b [de una exposición] exhibit • la colección expuesta consta de 30 ~s the collection on display includes 30 exhibits • una exposición de ~s de cerámica/orfebrería an exhibition of ceramics/silverware
c [de mecanismo, motor] part, component • las ~s del motor the engine parts o components
d • de una ~: el capó estaba construido de una ~ the bonnet was made in one piece • un bañador de una ~ a one-piece swimsuit • un caballero de una ~ an upright gentleman • me dejas de una ~ con lo que me acabas de contar I'm astonished at what you've just told me • me quedé de una ~ I was totally dumbstruck o gobsmacked* • MODISMO: • ser de una (sola) ~ (LAm) to be as straight as a die ▸ pieza arqueológica artefact ▸ pieza clave (lit) essential part; (fig) key element ▸ pieza de convicción (Jur) piece of evidence ▸ pieza de museo museum piece ▸ pieza de oro (= moneda) gold coin, gold piece; (= objeto) gold object ▸ pieza de recambio, pieza de repuesto spare (part), extra (EEUU)
2 (= ejemplar) a [de carne, fruta] piece • dos ~s de fruta two pieces of fruit • vender algo por ~s to sell sth by the piece • solo vendemos la carne por ~s enteras we only sell meat in whole cuts • "vendemos el queso por piezas" "we sell individual cheeses"
b (Arte) example • una ~ única del Románico a unique example of the Romanesque
c (tb pieza de caza) specimen • se cobró dos buenas ~s he shot two fine specimens
3 (Ajedrez) piece
4 (Cos) (= remiendo) patch; (= rollo de tela) roll
5 (esp LAm) (= habitación) room ▸ pieza amueblada furnished room ▸ pieza de recibo reception room
6 (= obra) (Mús) piece, composition; (Literat) work; (Teat) play ▸ pieza corta (Mús) short piece; (Teat) playlet ▸ pieza literaria literary work ▸ pieza musical piece of music, musical piece ▸ pieza oratoria speech
7 (Mil) ▸ pieza de artillería artillery piece
8 (Odontología) tooth ▸ pieza bucal, pieza dental, pieza dentaria tooth
9* (= persona) • ¡buena ~ estás tú hecho! you're a fine one! • MODISMOS: • ser una ~ para algo (Méx*) to be very good at sth • ser mucha ~ para algn (Méx*) to be in a different league from sb
SMF ‡ (= camello) pusher*

pífano SM fife

pifia SF 1 (Billar) miscue
2* (= error) blunder, bloomer*
3 (And, Cono Sur) (= burla) mockery; (= chiste) joke • hacer ~ de (= burlarse) to mock, poke fun at; (= bromear) to make a joke of, joke about
4 (And, Cono Sur) (= rechifla) hiss

pifiador ADJ (And, Cono Sur) joking, mocking

pifiar ▹ CONJUG 1b VT 1 (And, Arg) (= burlarse de) to joke about, mock; (= engañar) to play a trick on
2 (And, Cono Sur) (= arruinar) to mess up, botch
3 (And, Cono Sur) (= chiflar) to boo, hiss at
4 (Méx‡) (= robar) to nick‡, lift*
5* • ~la (= meter la pata) to blunder, make a bloomer*
VI 1 (Cono Sur) (= fracasar) to fail, come a cropper*; (en el juego) to mess up one's game
2 (And, CAm) (= llevarse un chasco) to be disappointed, suffer a setback

pigmentación SF pigmentation

pigmentado/a ADJ (gen) pigmented; (euf) [persona] coloured, colored (EEUU)
SM/F (euf) coloured person, colored person (EEUU)

pigmento SM pigment

pigmeo/a ADJ, SM/F pigmy

pignorable ADJ • objeto fácilmente ~ a thing which it is easy to pawn

pignorar ▹ CONJUG 1a VT to pawn

pigricia SF 1 (And) (= bagatela) trifle, bagatelle; (= pizca) small bit, pinch
2 (= pereza) laziness

pija✱✱ SF prick✱✱; ▹ pijo

pijada* SF 1 (= cosa absurda) • eso es una ~ that's utter nonsense o rubbish
2 (= cosa sin importancia) trifle
3 (= capricho) expensive toy

pijama SM pyjamas (pl), pajama (EEUU) ▸ pijama de playa beach pyjamas (pl)

pijar✱✱ ▹ CONJUG 1a VT to fuck✱✱

pije SM (Chile) toff*, snob*

pijo/a ADJ * 1 [persona, ropa, discoteca] posh
2 (= tonto) stupid
SM/F * 1 (= niño bien) spoilt brat, spoilt rich kid
2 (= tonto) berk*, twit*, jerk (EEUU*)
SM 1 (Esp✱✱) (= pene) prick✱✱
2‡ • MODISMOS: • no te oyen ni ~ they can't hear you at all • ¡qué ~s! hell's bells!* • ¿qué ~s haces aquí? what in hell's name are you doing here?*; ▹ pija

pijolero/a* ADJ, SM/F = pijotero

pijoprogre* (pey) SMF trendy, middle-class left winger

pijotada* SF 1 = pijada
2 (Méx) (= dinero) insignificant sum

pijotear* ▹ CONJUG 1a VI (And, Cono Sur, Méx) to haggle

pijotería* SF 1 (= esnobismo) snobbery, snobbishness
2 (= molestia) nuisance, annoying thing; (= petición) trifling request, silly demand
3 (LAm) (= pequeña cantidad) insignificant sum, tiny amount; (= bagatela) trifle, small thing
4 (LAm) (= tacañería) stinginess*

pijotero* a ADJ 1 (= molesto) tedious, annoying; (= condenado) bloody‡, bleeding‡
2 (LAm) (= tacaño) mean, stingy*
3 (Cono Sur) (= no fiable) untrustworthy
SM/F 1 (= persona molesta) pain* • ¡no seas ~! don't be such a pain!*
2 (= tonto) berk‡, twit*

pijudo* ADJ 1 = pijotero
2 (CAm) (= muy bueno) great*, terrific*

pila¹ SF 1 [de libros, juguetes] pile, stack
2* [de deberes, trabajo] heap • una ~ de heaps of, piles of • tengo una ~ de cosas que hacer I have heaps o piles of things to do • una ~ de años ages • una ~ de ladrones a bunch of thieves
3 (Arquit) pile

pila² SF 1 (= fregadero) sink; (= artesa) trough; (= abrevadero) drinking trough; [de fuente] basin; (LAm) (public) fountain ▸ pila de cocina kitchen sink
2 (Rel) (tb pila bautismal) font • nombre de ~ Christian name, first name • MODISMO: • sacar de ~ a algn to act as godparent to sb ▸ pila de agua bendita holy water stoup
3 (Elec) battery • aparato a ~s battery-run apparatus, battery-operated apparatus • MODISMO: • cargar las ~s to recharge one's batteries ▸ pila alcalina alkaline battery, alkaline cell ▸ pila atómica atomic pile ▸ pila (de) botón watch battery, calculator battery ▸ pila seca dry cell ▸ pila solar solar battery
4 • MODISMO: • ponerse las ~s* to get one's act together, put one's skates on
5 (Caribe) (= grifo) tap, faucet (EEUU)

pilado‡ ADJ • MODISMO: • está ~ (And)

(*= seguro*) it's a cert*; (*= fácil*) it's a cinch‡
pilar¹ SM **1** (*= poste*) post, pillar; (*= mojón*) milestone; [*de puente*] pier
2 (*fig*) pillar, mainstay • **un ~ de la monarquía** a mainstay of the monarchy
pilar² SM [*de fuente*] basin, bowl
pilastra SF (*gen*) pilaster; (*Cono Sur*) [*de puerta*] frame
Pilates SM Pilates
Pilatos SM Pilate
pilatuna* SF (*LAm*) dirty trick
pilatuno ADJ (*And*) manifestly unjust
pilcha* SF (*Cono Sur*) **1** (*= prenda*) [*de persona*] garment, article of clothing; [*de caballo*] harness
2 pilchas (*= ropa vieja*) old clothes; (*= ropa elegante*) fine clothes
3 (*= querida*) mistress
pilche SM (*LAm*) (coconut) gourd, calabash
píldora SF pill • **la ~ (anticonceptiva)** the (contraceptive) pill • MODISMOS: • **dorar la ~** to sugar *o* sweeten the pill • **tragarse la ~** to be taken in ▸ **píldora abortiva** morning-after pill ▸ **píldora antibaby** contraceptive pill ▸ **píldora anticalvicie** anti-baldness pill ▸ **píldora anticonceptiva** contraceptive pill ▸ **píldora antifatiga** anti-fatigue pill, pep pill* ▸ **píldora del día después, píldora del día siguiente** morning-after pill
pildorazo* SM (*Mil*) burst of gunfire, salvo; (*Dep*) fierce shot
pildorita SF (*Cono Sur*) small cocktail sausage
pileta SF **1** (*gen*) basin, bowl; [*de cocina*] sink; (*= artesa*) trough
2 (*LAm*) [*de baño*] wash basin ▸ **pileta de natación** swimming pool
pilgua SF (*Cono Sur*) wicker basket
pilier SM prop forward
piligüe ADJ (*CAm*) [*fruta*] shrivelled, empty
SMF (*CAm, Méx*) poor devil
pilila* SF willy*, peter (*EEUU*‡)
pililo SM (*Cono Sur*) tramp, hobo (*EEUU*)
pilintruca SF (*Cono Sur*) slut
pillada SF **1** (*= trampa*) dirty trick
2 (*Cono Sur*) (*= sorpresa*) surprise revelation; (*= encuentro*) surprise encounter
pillaje SM pillage, plunder
pillar ▸ CONJUG 1a VT **1** (*= atrapar*) to catch • **nunca lo pillo en casa** I can never catch him at home • **lo pilló la policía** the police caught *o* nabbed* him • **el perro le pilló el pantalón** the dog caught his trouser leg • **me pilló el dedo con la puerta** he got my finger caught in the door • **¡como te pille ...!** if I get hold of you ...!
2* (*= tomar, coger*) to catch, get • **~ el autobús** to catch *o* get the bus • **píllame un asiento al lado tuyo** grab me a seat beside you*
3 (*= sorprender*) to catch • **lo pillé fumando** I caught him smoking • **¡te he pillado!** caught *o* got you!
4 (*= alcanzar*) to catch up with • **salí corriendo y la pillé a medio camino** I ran out and caught up with her on the way
5 (*= atropellar*) to hit, run over • **la pilló una moto** she was hit by a motorbike
6 [*+ resfriado, pulmonía*] to catch, get • **~ una borrachera** to get drunk
7* [*+ puesto*] to get, land
8 [*+ broma, significado*] to get, catch on to
VI (*Esp**) • **me pilla lejos** it's too far for me • **me pilla muy cerca** it's handy *o* near for me • **me pilla de camino** it's on my way
VPR **pillarse** to catch • **se pilló el dedo con la puerta** he caught his finger in the door
pillastre* SMF scoundrel
pillería SF **1** (*= acción*) dirty trick
2 [*de niños*] naughtiness; [*de adultos*] craftiness
3 (*= pandilla*) gang of scoundrels
pillete SM rascal, scamp
pillín/ina SM/F rascal, scamp
pillo/a ADJ [*adulto*] sly, crafty; [*niño*] naughty
SM/F (*= adulto*) rogue, scoundrel; (*= niño*) rascal, scamp
pilluelo SM rascal, scamp
pilmama SF (*Méx*) (*= nodriza*) wet-nurse; (*= niñera*) nursemaid
pilme ADJ (*Cono Sur*) very thin
pilón¹ SM **1** (*gen*) pillar, post; (*Elec*) pylon
2 (*Téc*) drop hammer
3 [*de romana*] weight
4 [*de azúcar*] sugar loaf
5 (*Caribe*) (*Agr*) dump, store
pilón² SM **1** (*= abrevadero*) drinking trough; [*de fuente*] basin; (*Méx*) drinking fountain
2 (*= mortero*) mortar
3 (*Méx**) extra, bonus; (*= propina*) tip
4 (*Cono Sur*) (*= capacho*) pannier
piloncillo SM (*Méx*) powdered brown sugar
pilongo ADJ **1** (*= flaco*) thin, emaciated
2 [*castaña*] dried
pilosidad SF hairiness
piloso ADJ hairy
pilotaje SM (*Náut, Aer*) piloting • **fallo de ~** navigational error
pilotar ▸ CONJUG 1a VT [*+ avión*] to pilot; [*+ coche*] to drive; [*+ barco*] to steer, navigate
pilote SM **1** (*Arquit*) pile
2 (*CAm**) (*= fiesta*) party
pilotear ▸ CONJUG 1a VT **1** = **pilotar**
2 (*LAm*) (*= dirigir*) [*+ persona*] to guide, direct; [*+ negocio*] to run, manage
3 (*Cono Sur*) [*+ persona*] to exploit
piloto SMF **1** (*Aer*) pilot • **segundo ~** co-pilot ▸ **piloto de caza** fighter pilot ▸ **piloto de pruebas** test pilot
2 [*de coche*] driver, racing driver; [*de moto*] rider ▸ **piloto de pruebas** (*Aut*) test driver
3 (*Náut*) navigator, navigation officer ▸ **piloto de puerto** harbour pilot
4 (*= guía*) guide; (*en exploración*) pathfinder
SM **1** (*= aparato*) ▸ **piloto automático** automatic pilot ▸ **piloto de combate** fighter pilot
2 (*= luz*) pilot, pilot light; (*Aut*) tail light, rear light ▸ **piloto de alarma** flashing light ▸ **piloto de niebla** fog light, fog lamp
ADJ INV pilot (*antes de s*) • **estudio ~** pilot study • **planta ~** pilot plant • **programa ~** pilot programme *o* (*EEUU*) program • **piso ~** show flat
pilpinto SM (*And, Cono Sur*) butterfly
pilsen SF, **pílsener** SF (*Chile*) beer
piltra‡ SF kip*
piltrafa SF **1** [*de carne*] poor quality meat • **~s** scraps
2 (*fig*) (*= cosa*) worthless object; (*= persona*) wretch
3 piltrafas (*LAm*) [*de ropa*] rags, old clothes
4 (*And, Cono Sur*) (*= ganga*) bargain; (*= suerte*) piece of luck; (*= ganancia*) profit
piltrafiento ADJ **1** (*Cono Sur, Méx*) (*= harapiento*) ragged
2 (*Cono Sur*) (*= marchito*) withered
piltrafoso ADJ (*And*) ragged
piltrafudo ADJ (*And*) weak, languid
piltre ADJ **1** (*And, Caribe*) (*= petimetre*) foppish
2 (*Chile*) [*fruta*] (*= madura*) over-ripe; (*= seca*) shrivelled, dried up
SMF (*And**) snappy dresser*
pilucho (*Cono Sur*) ADJ* naked
SM [*de bebé*] cotton vest, dress
pimentero SM **1** (*Bot*) pepper plant
2 (*Culin*) pepperpot, pepper shaker (*EEUU*)
pimentón SM **1** (*= especia*) (*tb* **pimentón dulce**) paprika ▸ **pimentón picante** hot paprika, cayenne pepper
2 (*LAm*) (*= fruto*) sweet pepper, capsicum
pimienta SF pepper ▸ **pimienta de cayena** cayenne pepper ▸ **pimienta inglesa** allspice ▸ **pimienta negra** black pepper
pimiento SM **1** (*= fruto*) pepper • MODISMO: • **(no) me importa un ~** I don't care two hoots* ▸ **pimiento del piquillo, pimiento morrón, pimiento rojo** red pepper ▸ **pimiento verde** green pepper
2 (*Bot*) pepper plant
pimpampúm* SM **1** [*de ferias*] shooting gallery
2 (*= ruido*) crash, bang, wallop
pimpante* ADJ **1** (*= acicalado*) smart, spruce
2 (*tb* **tan pimpante**) (*= ufano*) smug, self-satisfied
pimpinela SF pimpernel
pimplar* ▸ CONJUG 1a VI to booze*
VPR **pimplarse** • **~se una botella** to down a bottle*, quaff a bottle*
pimpollo SM **1** (*Bot*) (*= serpollo*) sucker, shoot; (*= brote*) sapling; (*= capullo*) bud
2* (*= niño*) bonny child; (*= mujer*) attractive woman • **hecho un ~** (*= elegante*) very smart; (*= joven*) very young for one's age
pimpón SM ping-pong
pimponista SMF ping-pong player
PIN SM PIN
pin SM (PL: **pins**) **1** (*= insignia*) badge
2 (*Elec*) pin
pinabete SM fir, fir tree
pinacate SM (*Méx*) black beetle
pinacoteca SF art gallery
pináculo SM pinnacle
pinar SM pine grove
pinaza SF pinnace
pincel SM **1** (*para pintar*) paintbrush; [*de cocina*] brush • MODISMO: • **estar hecho un ~** to be very smartly dressed
2 (*= pintor*) painter
pincelada SF brushstroke • **última ~** (*fig*) finishing touch
pincha¹* SF (*Caribe*) job, spot of work
pincha² SF (*Cono Sur*) hair-grip
pinchadiscos* SMF INV (*Esp*), **pincha³*** SMF INV (*Esp*) disc jockey, D.J.
pinchado ADJ [*rueda*] flat
pinchante ADJ [*grito*] piercing
pinchar ▸ CONJUG 1a VT **1** (*= reventar*) [*+ globo, pelota*] to burst; [*+ neumático, rueda*] to puncture • **me han pinchado las ruedas** my tyres have been slashed
2 (*= picar*) **a** (*con algo punzante*) to prick • **le pinchó en el brazo con un alfiler** she pricked his arm with a pin
b (*Culin*) to test • **pincha la carne con el tenedor** test the meat with your fork, stick the fork in the meat • MODISMO: • **ni ~ ni cortar*** to count for nothing
3 (*= comer*) to nibble (at) • **hemos pinchado unos taquitos de queso** we nibbled (at) a few cubes of cheese
4* (*= poner una inyección a*) to give a jab to*, give a shot to* • **tuvimos que ~lo para que se le calmase el dolor** we had to give him a jab *o* shot to ease the pain* • **me han pinchado un antibiótico** I got an antibiotic jab *o* a shot of antibiotics*
5* (*= apuñalar*) to knife • **amenazó con ~lo si no le daba el dinero** he threatened to knife him if he didn't give him the money
6* (*= presionar*) (*gen*) to prod; (*pey*) to pester • **hay que ~lo para que se mueva** he needs prodding to get him going • **no dejan de ~me para que me case** they keep getting on at me *o* pestering me to get married
7* (*= provocar*) to wind sb up* • **siempre me está pinchando** he's always winding me up*
8* [*+ línea, teléfono*] to tap, bug

9 (*Esp**) (*Mús*) • **~ discos** to deejay*, be a disc jockey
VI **1** (= *hincarse*) [*espina*] to prick; [*clavo*] to stick • **ten cuidado con el rosal, que pincha** careful of the rosebush, it's prickly *o* it will prick you • **te pincha la barba** your beard is bristly *o* prickly
2 (= *tener un pinchazo*) to get a puncture • **pinchamos al salir de la curva** we got a puncture coming out of the bend
3 (*Esp**) (= *fracasar*) to come a cropper* • **hemos pinchado con este proyecto** we have come a cropper with this project* • **el Real Madrid ha pinchado en casa** Real Madrid have come a cropper at home*
4 (= *hacer clic*) to click (**en** on)
5 (*Chile**) (= *ligar*) • **cuando era joven pinchaba harto** when he was young he had a lot of girlfriends • **~ con algn** to get off with sb*
VPR **pincharse 1** (= *clavarse*) (*en dedo, brazo*) to prick o.s. • **me he pinchado con una aguja** I've pricked myself with a needle • **¿te has pinchado en el pie?** did you get something stuck in your foot?
2 (= *reventarse*) [*globo, pelota*] to burst; [*neumático, rueda*] to puncture • **se nos pinchó la rueda** we got a puncture • **tener un neumático pinchado** to have a puncture, have a flat tyre
3 (*Med*) [+ *antibiótico, insulina*] to inject o.s. with • **tengo que ~me insulina a diario** I have to inject myself with insulin every day • **hoy no tengo que ir a ~me** I don't have to go for an injection today
4‡ (= *drogarse*) to shoot up* • **había un hombre pinchándose en el callejón** there was a man shooting up in the alley* • **se pincha heroína** he shoots heroin*

pinchazo SM **1** (*con objeto punzante*) prick • **me he metido un ~ cosiendo** I've pricked my finger *o* myself sewing
2 (*en neumático*) puncture • **tuvimos un ~** we got a puncture
3* (= *inyección*) [*de antibiótico, insulina*] jab*, shot; [*de cocaína, heroína*] shot, fix‡ • **le encontraron varios ~s en el brazo** they found a number of needle marks on his arm
4 [*de dolor*] shooting pain, sharp pain
5 (*Telec**) tap*, bug*
6 (*Esp*) (= *fracaso*) fiasco • **las elecciones supusieron un gran ~ para el gobierno** the elections proved to be a disaster *o* fiasco for the government

pinche ADJ **1** (*Méx‡*) (= *maldito*) bloody‡, lousy‡ • **todo por unos ~s centavos** all for a few measly cents
2 (*CAm, Méx*) (= *miserable*) wretched
3 (*CAm**) (= *tacaño*) stingy, tight-fisted
SMF **1** [*de cocina*] kitchen hand, kitchen-boy
2 (*Cono Sur*) (= *oficinista*) minor office clerk; (= *criminal*) small-time criminal
3 (*Caribe, Méx*) (= *granuja*) rascal
SM **1** (*And*) (= *jamelgo*) nag
2 (*Cono Sur*) (= *horquilla*) hairpin, bobby pin (EEUU)

pinchito SM (*Esp*) tapa

pincho SM **1** (= *punta*) point; (= *varilla*) pointed stick, spike
2 [*de zarza, flor*] thorn, prickle; [*de cactus, animal*] spike, prickle
3‡ (= *navaja*) knife
4 (*Culin*) tapa • **un ~ de tortilla** a small portion of omelette ▸ **pincho moruno** kebab
5** (= *pene*) prick**

pinchota‡ SMF *user of drugs by injection*

pinciano/a (*Esp*) ADJ of/from Valladolid
SM/F native/inhabitant of Valladolid • **los ~s** the people of Valladolid

pindárico ADJ Pindaric

Píndaro SM Pindar

pindonga* SF gadabout

pindonguear* ▸ CONJUG 1a VI to gad about

pindongueo* SM • **ir de ~** to wander round, roam the streets

pinga SF **1** (*LAm***) (= *pene*) prick**
2 (*Caribe*) • MODISMO: • **de ~*** amazing, terrific*

pingajo SM rag, shred • **ir hecho un ~** to look a right mess*

pinganilla* SM **1** (*LAm*) (= *pretencioso*) sharp dresser
2 (*Méx*) • **en ~s** (= *de puntillas*) on tiptoe; (= *en cuclillas*) squatting; (= *poco firme*) wobbly

pinganillo ADJ (*And*) chubby

pinganitos†* SMPL • **estar en ~** to be well up, be well-placed socially • **poner a algn en ~** to give sb a leg up (socially)

pingo ADJ INV* (*pey*) loose*, promiscuous
SM **1** (= *harapo*) rag; (= *prenda*) old garment • **~s*** cheap women's clothes • **no tengo ni un ~ que ponerme*** I haven't a single thing I can wear • MODISMOS: • **andar** *o* **ir de ~** to gad about • **poner a algn como un ~** to slag sb off*
2* (= *callejeador*) gadabout; (*pey*) (= *mujer*) slut‡
3* (= *caballo*) (*Arg, Uru*) (*bueno*) good horse; (*Chile, Perú*) (*malo*) nag
4 (*Méx*) (= *niño*) scamp • **el ~** the devil
5 (*Cono Sur*) (= *niño*) lively child

pingonear* ▸ CONJUG 1a VI to gad about

pingorotear ▸ CONJUG 1a VI (*LAm*), **pingotear** ▸ CONJUG 1a VI (*LAm*) to skip about, jump

ping-pong ['pimpon] SM ping-pong

pinguchita* SF (*Cono Sur*) beanpole*, string bean (*EEUU**)

pingucho (*Cono Sur*) ADJ poor, wretched
SM urchin, ragamuffin

pingüe ADJ **1** (*gen*) abundant, copious; [*ganancias*] rich, fat; [*cosecha*] bumper; [*negocio*] lucrative
2 (= *grasiento*) greasy

pingui* SM swank

pingüinera SF penguin colony

pingüino SM penguin ▸ **pingüino de Humboldt** Humboldt's penguin

pinitos SMPL, **pininos** SMPL (*esp LAm*) • **hacer sus ~** [*niño*] to toddle, take his/her first steps; [*novato*] to take his/her first steps; [*enfermo*] to start to get about again, get back on one's feet again • **hago mis ~ como pintor** I play *o* dabble at painting

pinja** SF (*And*) prick**

pino¹ SM **1** (*Bot*) pine, pine tree • MODISMOS: • **ponerle ~** (*Cono Sur**) to make a great effort • **vivir en el quinto ~** to live at the back of beyond • **eso está en el quinto ~** that's miles away ▸ **pino albar** Scots pine ▸ **pino araucano** monkey-puzzle (tree) ▸ **pino bravo** cluster pine ▸ **pino de tea** pitch pine ▸ **pino marítimo, pino rodeno** cluster pine ▸ **pino silvestre** Scots pine
2 (*en gimnasia*) • **hacer el ~** to do a handstand
3 pinos = **pinitos**

pino² ADJ steep • **en ~** (= *vertical*) upright, vertical; (= *de pie*) standing

pinocha SF pine needle

Pinocho SM Pinocchio

pinol SM (*CAm, Méx*), **pinole** SM (*CAm, Méx*) *drink made of roasted maize flour or* (EEUU) *roasted cornflour*

pinolero/a* (*CAm*) ADJ Nicaraguan
SM/F Nicaraguan • **los ~s** the Nicaraguans

pinrel* SM hoof*, foot

pinsapo SM (*Esp*) Spanish fir

pinta¹ SF **1** (= *lunar*) (*gen*) spot, dot; (*Zool*) spot, mark • **una tela a ~s azules** a cloth with blue spots
2 [*de líquidos*] drop, spot; [*de lluvia*] drop; (= *bebida**) drop to drink • **una ~ de grasa** a grease spot
3* (= *aspecto*) appearance • **por la ~** by the look of it • **tener buena ~** [*persona*] to look good, look well; [*comida*] to look good • **tener ~ de listo** to look clever • **tiene ~ de criminal** he looks like a criminal • **tiene ~ de español** he looks Spanish, he looks like a Spaniard • **¿qué ~ tiene?** what does he look like? • **con esa(s) ~(s) no puedes ir** you can't go looking like that • MODISMOS: • **¡a la ~!** (*Cono Sur*) perfect!, that's fine! • **estar a la ~** (*Cono Sur*) • **tener ~** (*Cono Sur*) (= *atractivo*) to be attractive; (= *elegante*) to be smart, be well-dressed • **no se le vio ni ~** (*LAm**) there wasn't a sign *o* trace of him • **tirar ~*** to impress
4 (*LAm*) (*Zool*) (= *colorido*) colouring, coloring (EEUU), coloration; (= *característica*) family characteristic, distinguishing mark
5 (*CAm, Méx*) (= *pintada*) piece of graffiti
6 (*Naipes*) spot (*indicating suit*) • **¿a qué ~?** what's trumps?, what suit are we in?
7 (*And, Cono Sur*) (= *juego*) draughts (*pl*); (= *dados*) dice
8 (*Cono Sur*) (*Min*) high-grade ore
9 • MODISMOS: • **hacer ~** (*Méx*) • **irse de ~** (*CAm*) to play truant • **ser de la ~** (*Caribe*) (*euf*) to be coloured

pinta² SF (= *medida inglesa*) pint

pinta³* SM rogue

pintada¹ SF (*Orn*) guinea-fowl

pintada² SF piece of graffiti • **~s** graffiti

pintado ADJ **1** (*Zool*) (= *moteado*) spotted; (= *pinto*) mottled, dappled
2* (= *igual*) • **~ a algn** exactly like sb, identical to sb • **el niño salió ~ al padre** the boy turned out exactly like his father *o* identical to his father
3 • MODISMOS: • **el más ~*** anybody • **eso podría pasarle al más ~** that could happen to anybody • **lo hace como el más ~** he does it as well as anybody • **sentar/venir que ni ~ a algn*** to suit sb down to the ground*
SM **1** (= *acción*) (*gen*) painting; (*Téc*) coating ▸ **pintado de campo** marking-out of the pitch
2 (*Esp*) *wine and vermouth cocktail*

pintalabios SM INV lipstick

pintamonas* SMF INV (*pey*) **1** (= *pintor*) dauber*
2 (= *don nadie*) • **un ~** a nobody

pintar ▸ CONJUG 1a VT **1** (*Arte*) (*con óleo, acuarela*) to paint; (*con lápices, rotuladores*) (= *dibujar*) to draw; (= *colorear*) to colour, color (EEUU) • **el primer cuadro que pintó** the first picture he painted • **~ algo al óleo/temple** to paint sth in oils/tempera • **píntame una casa** paint *o* draw me a house
2 (= *dar una capa de pintura a*) [+ *pared, habitación*] to paint • **hace falta ~ esta habitación** this room needs painting *o* decorating • **"recién pintado"** "wet paint" • **tengo que ~ el coche** the car needs a coat of paint *o* a respray • **~ algo de** *o* **en blanco/azul** to paint sth white/blue • **~ algo con pistola** to spray-paint sth
3 (= *describir*) to paint • **lo pinta todo muy negro** he paints it all very black • **tal como lo pintas, no parece que haya una solución fácil** the way you describe it *o* paint things, it seems there is no easy solution; ▸ **fiero, ocasión**
4* (= *tener importancia*) • **¿acaso tú pintas algo en esta cuestión?** what's this got to do with you?, what business is this of yours? • **¿pero qué pintamos aquí?** what on earth are we doing here? • **yo en esa fiesta no pinto nada**

I'd be out of place at that party • **no pinta nada en la empresa** he's nobody important in the company • **antes me consultaban, pero ya no pinto nada** before I was consulted but my opinion counts for nothing now

VI **1** (*Arte*) to paint • **no pinto desde hace años** I haven't painted for years
2 (*para decorar*) to decorate • **cuando terminen la obra ~emos** when they finish the building work we'll decorate *o* do the decorating
3 (= *manchar*) (*de pintura, tinta*) • **ten cuidado con ese banco, que pinta** be careful, that bench has wet paint on it • **"¡ojo, pinta!"** "wet paint"
4* (= *escribir*) to write • **este boli ya no pinta** this biro doesn't work *o* write • **no pintéis en las mesas** don't write on the desks
5 (*Bot*) (= *madurar*) to ripen • **en agosto pintan las uvas** the grapes ripen in August
6 (*Naipes*) to be trumps • **¿qué pinta?** what's trumps? • **pintan corazones** hearts are trumps
7 (*LAm**) (= *mostrarse*) to look • **la situación pinta mejor** things are looking up • **no me gusta cómo pinta esto** I don't like the look of this

VPR **pintarse 1** (= *maquillarse*) (*una vez*) to put one's make-up on, make o.s. up; (*con frecuencia*) to use make-up • **tardó una hora en ~se** she took an hour to put her make-up on *o* to make herself up • **no me gusta nada ir pintada** I don't like using make-up • **se ~on la cara para la fiesta de disfraces** they painted their faces for the fancy-dress party • **~se los labios** to put lipstick on • **~se los ojos**: • **¿te has pintado los ojos?** have you got any eye make-up on?, did you put on your eye make-up? • **¿con qué te pintas los ojos?** what eye make-up do you use? • **~se las uñas** to paint one's nails • MODISMO: • **pintárselas solo para algo*** to be an expert *o* a dab hand at sth • **se las pinta solo para conseguir lo que quiere** he's an expert *o* a dab hand at getting what he wants • **a la hora de meter la pata se las pinta solo** he's a specialist *o* an expert at putting his foot in it
2 (= *mancharse*) [+ *manos, ropa*] • **te has pintado las manos de tinta** you've got ink on your hands
3 (= *notarse*) to show • **el cansancio se pintaba en su rostro** you could see the tiredness in her face, the tiredness showed on her face
4 (*Méx‡*) (= *largarse*) to beat it‡

pintarrajeado ADJ daubed-on, scrawled-on

pintarrajear* ▸ CONJUG 1a VT, VI to daub

pintarrajo* SM daub

pintarroja SF dogfish

pintas* SMF INV scruff*, scruffily dressed person

pintear ▸ CONJUG 1a VI to drizzle, spot with rain

pintiparado ADJ **1** (= *idéntico*) identical (a to)
2 • MODISMO: • **me viene (que ni) ~** it suits me a treat

pintiparar ▸ CONJUG 1a VT to compare

Pinto SM • MODISMO: • **estar entre ~ y Valdemoro** (*Esp**) (= *indeciso*) to be in two minds; (= *borracho*) to be tipsy • **el examen está entre ~ y Valdemoro** the exam's a borderline case

pinto ADJ **1** (*LAm*) (= *con manchas*) spotted, dappled; (= *marcado*) marked (*esp in black and white*); (= *abigarrado*) motley, colourful, colorful (*EEUU*)
2 [*tez*] blotchy
3 (*Cuba*) (= *listo*) clever; (*pey*) sharp, shrewd
4 (*Caribe*) (= *borracho*) drunk

pintor(a) SM/F **1** painter ▸ **pintor(a) de brocha gorda** (*de paredes*) painter and decorator; (*de cuadros*) (*pey*) bad painter, dauber ▸ **pintor(a) decorador(a)** painter and decorator ▸ **pintor(a) de suelo** pavement artist
2 (*Cono Sur**) (= *fachendoso*) swank*

pintoresco ADJ picturesque

pintoresquismo SM picturesqueness

pintura SF **1** (= *forma artística, cuadro*) painting • MODISMO: • **no lo podía ver ni en ~** she couldn't stand the sight of him ▸ **pintura a la acuarela, pintura a la aguada** watercolour, watercolor (*EEUU*) ▸ **pintura al óleo** oil painting ▸ **pintura al pastel** pastel drawing ▸ **pintura rupestre** cave painting
2 (= *descripción*) depiction
3 (= *material*) paint ▸ **pintura a la cola, pintura al temple** (*para paredes*) distemper; (*para cuadros*) tempera ▸ **pintura emulsionada** emulsion, emulsion paint
4 (= *lápiz de color*) crayon ▸ **pintura de cera** wax crayon

pinturero/a* ADJ swanky*
SM/F show-off*, swank*

pinza SF **1** [*de ropa*] clothes peg, clothespin (*EEUU*) ▸ **pinza de pelo** hairgrip
2 pinzas (*de depilar*) tweezers; (*para hielo, azúcar*) tongs; (*Med*) forceps • MODISMOS: • **había que cogerlo con ~s** I had to take it very carefully • **no se lo sacan ni con ~s** wild horses won't drag it out of him
3 (*Cos*) pleat • **pantalones de ~s** trousers with waist pleats, pleated trousers
4 [*de cangrejo, langosta*] pincer, claw

pinzamiento SM ▸ **pinzamiento discal** slipped disc, slipped disk (*EEUU*)

pinzón SM (*Orn*) finch ▸ **pinzón real** bullfinch ▸ **pinzón vulgar** chaffinch

piña SF **1** [*de pino*] pine cone
2 (= *fruta*) pineapple ▸ **piña de América, piña de las Indias** pineapple
3 [*de personas*] (= *grupo*) group; (= *conjunto*) cluster, knot; (= *corrillo*) clique, closed circle • MODISMO: • **como una ~** • **estaban unidos como una ~** they were a very close-knit group
4 (*Caribe, Méx*) [*de rueda*] hub
5* (= *golpe*) punch, bash* • **darse una ~** to have a crash • **darse ~s** to fight, exchange blows
6 (*Méx*) [*de revólver*] chamber
7 (*And**) • **¡qué ~!** bad luck! • **estar ~** to be unlucky
SM (*CAm‡*) poof‡, faggot (*EEUU‡*)

piñal SM (*LAm*) pineapple plantation

piñar* SM (*Méx*) lie

piñata¹ SF (*en fiestas*) *container hung up at parties to be beaten with sticks until sweets or presents fall out*

piñata²‡ SF (= *dientes*) ivories* (*pl*), teeth (*pl*)

piñata³ SF (*Cono Sur*) brawl, scrap*

piñatería SF (*Cono Sur*) armed hold-up

piño¹* SM (= *diente*) ivory*, tooth

piño²* SM (*Chile*) (= *reunión*) crowd, lot

piñón¹ SM (*Bot*) pine kernel • MODISMO: • **estar** *o* **llevarse a partir un ~** to be the best of buddies, be bosom pals* (**con** with)

piñón² SM (*Orn, Téc*) pinion • MODISMOS: • **seguir a ~ fijo*** (= *sin moverse*) to be rooted to the spot; (= *sin cambiar de idea*) to go on in the same old way, be stuck in one's old ways • **quedarse a ~ fijo*** to have a mental block

piñonate SM candied pine-nut

piñonear ▸ CONJUG 1a VI to click

piñoneo SM click

piñoso* ADJ (*And*) unlucky

Pío SM Pius

pío¹ ADJ [*caballo*] piebald, dappled

pío² ADJ **1** (*Rel*) pious, devout; (*pey*) sanctimonious
2 (= *compasivo*) merciful

pío³ SM **1** (*Orn*) cheep, chirp • MODISMO: • **no decir ni pío** not to breathe a word • **¡de esto no digas ni pío!** don't you breathe a word! • **irse sin decir ni pío** to go off without a word
2 • MODISMO: • **tener el pío de algo*** to long for sth

piocha SF **1** (*LAm*) (= *piqueta*) pickaxe, pickax (*EEUU*)
2 (*Chile*) (= *distintivo*) badge
3† (= *joya*) jewel (worn on the head)
4 (*Méx*) (= *barba*) goatee
ADJ (*Méx*) nice

piojería SF **1** (= *lugar*) lousy place, verminous place
2 (= *pobreza*) poverty
3* (= *miseria*) tiny amount, very small portion

piojo SM **1** (*Zool*) louse • MODISMOS: • **dar el ~** (*Méx**) to show one's nasty side • **estar como ~s en costura** to be packed in like sardines ▸ **piojo resucitado*** jumped-up fellow, vulgar parvenu
2 (*And*) gambling den

piojoso ADJ **1** (= *con piojos*) lousy
2 (= *sucio*) filthy
3 (= *mezquino*) mean

piojuelo SM louse

piola SF **1** (*LAm*) (= *soga*) rope, tether
2 (*And, Caribe*) (= *cuerda*) cord, string; (= *maguey*) agave
3 (*Cono Sur‡*) (= *pene*) cock‡
ADJ INV (*Arg**) (= *astuto*) smart, clever; (= *listo*) bright; (= *taimado*) sly; (= *servicial*) helpful; (= *bueno*) great*, terrific*; (= *elegante*) classy*

piolet [pio'le] SM (PL: **piolets** [pio'les]) ice axe, ice ax (*EEUU*)

piolín SM (*LAm*) cord, twine

pionco ADJ **1** (*Cono Sur*) naked from the waist down
2 (*Méx*) (= *en cuclillas*) squatting
3 (*Méx*) [*caballo*] short-tailed

pionero/a ADJ pioneering
SM/F pioneer

pioneta SM (*Chile*) (*Aut*) lorry driver's mate, truck driver's mate (*EEUU*)

piorrea SF pyorrhoea

PIP SM ABR (*Puerto Rico*) = **Partido Independentista Puertorriqueño**

pipa¹ SF **1** (*de fumar*) pipe • **fumar en ~** • **fumar una ~** to smoke a pipe
2 [*de vino*] (= *barril*) cask, barrel; (= *medida*) pipe
3 (*Bot*) (= *semilla*) pip, seed; [*de girasol*] (edible) sunflower seed • MODISMO: • **no tener ni para ~s** to be broke, be skint*
4 (*Mús*) reed
5 (*LAm**) (= *barriga*) belly* • **tener ~** to be potbellied
6‡ (= *pistola*) rod‡, pistol; (= *ametralladora*) machine-gun
7 • MODISMO: • **pasarlo ~*** to have a great time*
8 (*And, CAm*) (*Bot*) green coconut

pipa²* SM **1** (*Mús*) assistant
2 (= *mozo de carga*) porter
3 (= *utillero*) boy, mate

pipear‡ ▸ CONJUG 1a VT to look at
VI to look

pipero¹/a SM/F **1** (= *vendedor ambulante*) street vendor
2 (= *fumador*) pipe smoker

pipero² SM (= *estante*) pipe rack

pipeta SF pipette

pipi‡ SM **1** (*Mil*) squaddie*, recruit

2 (= *novato*) new boy
pipí* SM (= *orín*) pee*; (*entre niños*) wee-wee* • **hacer ~** (*gen*) to do a wee-wee*, have a pee* • **hacerse ~** to need a wee-wee; (*involuntariamente*) to wet oneself
pipián SM (*CAm, Méx*) (= *salsa*) thick chilli sauce; (= *guiso*) *meat cooked in thick chilli sauce*
pipiar ▸ CONJUG 1c VI to cheep, chirp
pipiciego ADJ (*And*) short-sighted, near-sighted (EEUU)
pipil* SM (*CAm*) (*hum*) Mexican
pipiolero* SM (*Méx*) crowd of kids*
pipiolo/a* SM/F **1** (= *joven*) youngster; (*LAm*) (= *chico*) little boy/little girl; (= *novato*) novice, greenhorn
2 (*Caribe, Cono Sur*) (= *tonto*) fool
3 **pipiolos** (*CAm*) (= *dinero*) money (*sing*)
pipirigallo SM sainfoin
pipiripao SM **1**†* (= *convite*) slap-up do*, beanfeast*
2 • MODISMO: • **de ~** (*LAm*) worthless
pipo ADJ (*And, Caribe*) potbellied • **estar ~** (*Caribe*) to be bloated
SM **1** (*Caribe*) (= *niño*) child
2 (*And, Caribe*) (= *empleado*) crooked employee*
3 (*And*) (= *golpe*) punch, bash*
4 (*And*) (= *licor*) contraband liquor
pipón* ADJ (*And, Caribe, Cono Sur*) (= *barrigón*) potbellied; (= *lleno de comida*) bloated
piporro SM **1** (= *instrumento*) bassoon
2 (= *persona*) bassoonist
pipote SM **1** (= *barril*) keg, cask
2 (*Ven*) (= *cubo de basura*) dustbin, trash can (EEUU)
pipudo‡ ADJ great*, super*
pique[1] SM **1** (= *resentimiento*) resentment, pique; (= *inquina*) grudge; (= *rivalidad*) rivalry, competition • **tener un ~ con algn** to have a grudge against sb • **tienen (un) ~ sobre sus coches** they're always trying to outdo one another with their cars • **estar de ~** to be at loggerheads
2 • **echar a ~** [+ *barco*] to sink; [+ *futuro, carrera*] to wreck, ruin • **irse a ~** [*barco*] to sink; [*esperanza, familia*] to be ruined
3 • **estar a ~ de hacer algo** (= *a punto de*) to be on the point of doing sth; (= *en peligro de*) to be in danger of doing sth
4 (*LAm*) (*Min*) (= *galería*) mine shaft; (*Méx*) (= *pozo*) drill, well
5 (*LAm*) (= *rebote*) bounce, rebound
6 (*CAm, Cono Sur*) (= *sendero*) trail, narrow path
7 (*And*) (= *insecto*) jigger flea
pique[2] SM (*Naipes*) spades
pique[3]‡ SM [*de droga*] fix‡, shot*
piquera SF **1** [*de tonel, colmena*] hole, vent
2 (*CAm, Méx**) (= *taberna*) dive*
3 (*Caribe*) [*de taxis*] taxi rank
piquero SM **1** (*Hist*) pikeman
2 (*And, Cono Sur*) (= *minero*) miner
3‡ (= *ratero*) pickpocket
piqueta SF (= *herramienta*) pick, pickaxe, pickax (EEUU); [*de tienda de campaña*] peg
piquetazo SM (*LAm*) **1** (= *tijeretazo*) snip, small cut
2 [*de pájaro*] peck
piquete SM **1** [*de personas*] (*Mil*) squad, party; (*en huelga*) picket ▸ **piquete de ejecución** firing squad ▸ **piquete informativo** picket ▸ **piquete móvil** flying picket ▸ **piquete secundario** secondary picket ▸ **piquete volante** flying picket
2 (*Arg*) (= *corral*) yard, small corral
3 (= *pinchazo*) prick, jab
4 (= *agujero*) small hole (*in clothing*)
5 (*And*) (= *merienda*) picnic
6 (*Caribe*) (*Mús*) street band
piquin SM **1** (*And*) (= *galán*) boyfriend
2 (*Cono Sur**) (= *pizca*) pinch, dash

3 (*Cono Sur*) (= *persona*) irritable sort
piquiña SF **1** (*And, Caribe*) = **picazón**
2 (*Caribe*) (= *envidia*) envy
pira[1] SF (= *hoguera*) pyre
pira[2]‡ SF • MODISMOS: • **hacer ~** • **irse de ~** (= *largarse*) to clear off*; (*Escol*) to cut class*, play truant
pirado/a‡ ADJ (= *loco*) round the bend*, crazy; (= *drogado*) high‡, out of one's head‡
SM/F (= *majareta*) nutcase*; (= *drogado*) druggy‡
piragua SF canoe
piragüismo SM canoeing
piragüista SMF canoeist
piramidal ADJ **1** [*forma*] pyramidal
2 (*And**) terrific*, tremendous*
pirámide SF pyramid ▸ **pirámide de edad(es)** age pyramid
Píramo SM Pyramus
piraña SF piranha
pirarse* ▸ CONJUG 1a VPR (*tb* **pirárselas**) (= *largarse*) to beat it*, clear out*; (*And*) to escape from prison; (*Méx*) to peg out‡ • **~ las clases** to cut class*
pirata SMF **1** (= *corsario*) pirate ▸ **pirata aéreo** hijacker
2 (*Inform*) ▸ **pirata informático/a** hacker
3 (*Literat**) plagiarist
4* (= *granuja*) rogue, scoundrel
5 (*Com*) cowboy, shark
6†* (= *persona cruel*) hard-hearted person
ADJ • **barco ~** pirate ship • **disco ~** bootleg record • **edición ~** pirated edition • **emisora ~** pirate radio station
pirateado ADJ [*CD, DVD, software*] pirated
piratear ▸ CONJUG 1a VT (*Aer*) to hijack; [+ *CD, DVD, software*] to pirate; (*Inform*) to hack into; [+ *libro*] to plagiarize
VI **1** [*barcos*] to buccaneer, practise piracy, practice piracy (EEUU)
2 (= *robar*) to steal
piratería SF, **pirateo** SM **1** [*de buque*] piracy ▸ **piratería aérea** highjacking
2 [*de disco, concierto, grabación*] bootlegging • **~ de vídeo** video piracy ▸ **piratería digital** digital piracy ▸ **piratería informática** (= *acceso prohibido*) hacking; (= *copia pirata*) software piracy
3 (= *robo*) theft, stealing
4 **piraterías** (= *estragos*) depredations
pirático ADJ piratical
piraya SF (*LAm*) piranha
pirca SF (*And, Chile*) dry-stone wall
pire‡ SM (= *drogas*) trip‡
pirenaico ADJ Pyrenean
pirético ADJ pyretic
piretro SM pyrethrum
pirgua SF (*And, Cono Sur*) shed, small barn
piri‡ SM grub‡, nosh‡, chow (EEUU‡)
piridina SF pyridine
pirineísta SMF mountaineer (*who climbs in the Pyrenees*)
Pirineo SM, **Pirineos** SMPL Pyrenees • **el ~ catalán** the Catalan (part of the) Pyrenees
pirineo ADJ Pyrenean
pirinola* SF (*Méx*) kid*, child
piripez†* SF • **coger una ~** to get sozzled
piripi* ADJ • **estar ~** to be sozzled*
pirita, piritas SF pyrite, pyrites
pirlán SM (*And*) doorstep
piro‡ SM • **darse el ~ de** to escape from • **darse el ~** to beat it*
piro... PREF pyro...
pirófago/a SM/F fire-eater
piromanía SF pyromania
pirómano/a SM/F pyromaniac
piropear ▸ CONJUG 1a VT to compliment, pay an amorous compliment to, make a flirtatious remark to
piropo SM **1** (= *cumplido*) flirtatious remark; (= *lisonja*) flattery • **echar ~s a** to make a flirtatious remark to
2 (= *granate*) garnet; (= *rubí*) ruby
3 (*And**) ticking-off*

piroso* ADJ lewd, dirty
pirotecnia SF (*gen*) pyrotechnics (*pl*), fireworks (*pl*); (= *fuegos artificiales*) firework display
pirotécnico ADJ pyrotechnic, firework (*antes de s*)
piroxidina SF pyridoxine
pirquén SM • **mina al ~** (*Chile*) rented mine
pirrar* ▸ CONJUG 1a, **pirriar** ▸ CONJUG 1b VT • **le pirraba el cine** he was really into the cinema*
VPR **pirr(i)arse** • **~se por** to be crazy about
pírrico ADJ • **victoria pírrica** Pyrrhic victory
Pirro SM Pyrrhus
pirucho SM (*CAm*) (ice-cream) cone *o* cornet
pirueta SF (= *movimiento ágil*) pirouette; (= *cabriola*) caper • MODISMO: • **hacer ~s** to perform a balancing act
piruetear ▸ CONJUG 1a VI (*gen*) to pirouette; (= *saltar*) to caper
piruja* SF (*Col, Méx*) prostitute, hooker*
pirula‡ SF **1** • MODISMO: • **hacer la ~ a*** (= *molestar*) to upset, annoy; (= *jugarla*) to play a dirty trick on; (= *embaucar*) to cheat
2 (*Anat*) willy*, peter (EEUU**); ▸ **pirulo**
piruleta SF lollipop
pirulí SM **1** (= *piruleta*) lollipop • MODISMO: • **durar lo que un ~ a la puerta de un colegio** not to last five minutes
2** (= *pene*) prick**
3 • **el Pirulí*** Madrid television tower
pirulo[1] (*Cono Sur‡*) SM • **tiene 40 ~s** he's the big four O, he's forty
pirulo[2]/a SM/F (= *niño*) slim child; ▸ **pirula**
pis* SM pee* • **hacer pis** to have a pee*, do a wee* • **hacerse pis en la cama** to wet the *o* one's bed
Pisa SF Pisa
pisa SF **1** [*de uvas*] treading
2* (= *zurra*) beating
pisacorbatas SF INV (*Col*) tiepin
pisada SF (= *paso*) footstep; (= *huella*) footprint
pisadera SF (*And*) carpet
pisadero SM (*Méx*) brothel
pisado SM treading (of grapes)
pisano/a ADJ Pisan
SM/F native/inhabitant of Pisa • **los ~s** the people of Pisa
pisapapeles SM INV paperweight
pisar ▸ CONJUG 1a VT **1** (= *andar sobre*) to walk on • **¿se puede ~ el suelo de la cocina?** can I walk on the kitchen floor?
2 (= *poner el pie encima de*) to tread on, step on • **perdona, te he pisado** sorry, I trod *o* stepped on your foot • **vio una cucaracha y la pisó** she saw a cockroach and trod *o* stood on it • **~ el acelerador a fondo** to step on the accelerator, put one's foot down*
• **"prohibido pisar el césped"** "keep off the grass" • MODISMOS: • **ir pisando huevos** to tread carefully • **tiene un morro que se lo pisa*** he's a cheeky devil*
3 (= *ir a*) to set foot in • **no volvimos a ~ ese sitio** we never set foot in that place again • **hace años que no pisa un bar** he hasn't been in a pub for years
4 [+ *uvas*] to tread; [+ *tierra*] to tread down
5 (= *avasallar*) to trample on, walk all over • **no se deja ~ por nadie** he doesn't let anybody trample on *o* walk all over him
6 (*Mús*) [+ *tecla*] to strike, press; [+ *cuerda*] to hold down
7 (*And*) [+ *hembra*] to cover; (*CAm**) to fuck**, screw**

8* (= *adelantarse a*) • **otro le pisó el puesto** somebody got in first and collared the job • **el periódico le pisó la noticia** the newspaper got in first with the news • **~ una baza a algn** to trump sb's trick; ▹ **talón**
VI (= *andar*) to tread • **hay que ~ con cuidado** you have to tread carefully
• MODISMO: • **~ fuerte*** to make great strides • **entrar pisando fuerte** to burst onto the scene*
VPR **pisarse** (*Col**) to push off*

pisaverde† SMF toff*

pisca SF **1** (*Méx*) (= *cosecha*) maize harvest, corn harvest (EEUU)
2 (*And*) (= *prostituta*) prostitute
3 (= *parte*) = **pizca**

piscador SM (*Méx*) harvester

piscar ▹ CONJUG 1g (*Méx*) VT to pinch, nip
VI to harvest maize, harvest corn (EEUU)

piscicultor(a) SM/F fish farmer

piscicultura SF fish farming

piscifactoría SF fish farm

piscigranja SF (*LAm*) fish farm

piscina SF **1** (*Dep*) swimming pool ▸ **piscina climatizada** heated swimming pool ▸ **piscina cubierta** indoor swimming pool ▸ **piscina de saltos** diving pool ▸ **piscina olímpica** Olympic pool
2 (= *estanque*) fishpond

Piscis SM (*Astron, Astrol*) Pisces • **es de ~** (*LAm*) she's (a) Pisces, she's a Piscean

piscis (*Astrol*) SMF INV Pisces (*inv*), Piscean • **los ~ son así** that's what Pisces *o* Pisceans are like
ADJ INV Pisces, Piscean • **soy ~** I'm (a) Pisces, I'm a Piscean

pisco[1] SM (*And*) **1** (= *pavo*) turkey
2 (= *persona*) fellow, guy*

pisco[2] SM (*And, Chile*) strong grape liquor ▸ **pisco sauer** (*And*) pisco cocktail

piscoiro* SM, **piscoira** SF (*Cono Sur**) bright child

piscola SF (*Chile*) pisco and coca cola (drink)

piscolabis SM INV **1** (= *tentempié*) snack
2 (*CAm, Méx*) money

pisicorre SM (*Caribe*) small bus

piso SM **1** (*esp LAm*) (= *suelo*) floor; (= *materiales para suelo*) flooring
2 [*de edificio*] floor, storey, story (EEUU); [*de autobús, barco*] deck; [*de cohete*] stage; [*de pastel*] layer, tier • **primer ~** first floor, second floor (EEUU) • **viven en el quinto ~** they live on the fifth floor • **un edificio de ocho ~s** an eight-storey building • **autobús de dos ~s** double-decker bus • **ir en el ~ de arriba** to travel on the top deck, travel upstairs ▸ **piso alto** top floor ▸ **piso bajo** ground floor, first floor (EEUU)
3 (= *apartamento*) flat, apartment (EEUU) • **poner un ~ a una** (*Esp*) to set a woman up in a flat ▸ **piso de seguridad, piso franco** (*Esp*) safe house ▸ **piso piloto** show flat
4 (*Aut*) [*de neumático*] tread
5 [*de zapato*] sole • **poner ~ a un zapato** to sole a shoe
6 (*LAm*) (= *tapete*) table runner; (= *estera*) mat; (*And, Cono Sur*) (= *alfombra*) long narrow rug ▸ **piso de baño** bathmat
7 (*Min*) set of workings; (*Geol*) layer, stratum
8 (*Cono Sur*) (= *taburete*) stool; (= *banco*) bench

pisón SM **1** (*para aplastar tierra*) ram, rammer
2 (*LAm*) = **pisotón**
3 (*Cono Sur*) (= *mortero*) mortar

pisotear ▹ CONJUG 1a VT **1** (*gen*) to tread down, trample (underfoot); (= *hollar*) to stamp on
2 (= *humillar*) to trample on; [+ *ley*] to abuse, disregard

pisoteo SM (*gen*) treading, trampling; (= *holladura*) stamping

pisotón SM **1** (*con el pie*) stamp • **me ha dado un ~** he trod on my foot
2 (*Periodismo**) scoop

pispar* ▹ CONJUG 1a VI (*Cono Sur*) (= *acechar*) to spy, keep watch
VT ‡ (= *robar*) to nick‡

pis-pas* SM, **pispás*** SM • **en un pis-pas** in a flash, in no time at all

pisporra SF (*CAm*) wart

pista SF **1** (= *rastro*) track, trail; (*Inform*) track • **estar sobre la ~** to be on the scent • **estar sobre la ~ de algn** to be on sb's trail *o* track, be after sb • **seguir la ~ de algn** (*gen*) to be on sb's trail *o* track; [*de cerca*] to shadow sb
2 (= *indicio*) clue • **dame una ~** give me a clue • **la policía tiene una ~** ya the police already have a lead ▸ **pista falsa** (*gen*) false trail; (= *ardid*) red herring
3 (*Dep*) [*de atletismo*] track; (= *cancha*) court; [*de circo*] ring; (*Aut*) carriageway; (*CAm*) (= *avenida*) avenue • **reunión de ~ cubierta** indoor athletics meeting • **atletismo en ~** track athletics ▸ **pista de aprendizaje** nursery slope ▸ **pista de aterrizaje** (*en aeropuerto*) runway; (*para aviones militares, privados*) landing strip ▸ **pista de atletismo** athletics track ▸ **pista de baile** dance floor ▸ **pista de bolos** bowling alley ▸ **pista de carreras** racetrack ▸ **pista de ceniza** dirt track ▸ **pista de esquí** piste, ski run ▸ **pista de hielo** ice rink ▸ **pista de hierba** grass court ▸ **pista de patinaje** skating rink ▸ **pista de squash** squash court ▸ **pista de tenis** tennis court ▸ **pista de tierra batida** clay court ▸ **pista dura** hard court ▸ **pista forestal** forest trail
4 [*de cinta*] track

pistacho SM pistachio

pistero ADJ (*CAm*) mercenary, fond of money

pistilo SM (*Bot*) pistil

pisto SM **1** (*Esp*) (*Culin*) fried vegetable hash, ratatouille
2 • MODISMO: • **darse ~*** to show off, swank*
3 (= *revoltijo*) hotchpotch, hodgepodge (EEUU)
4 (*LAm*‡) (= *dinero*) dough*
5 (*And*) [*de revólver*] barrel
6 (*Méx*‡) (= *trago*) shot of liquor*
7† (= *caldo de pollo*) chicken broth
8† • MODISMO: • **a ~s** (= *poco a poco*) little by little; (= *con escasez*) sparingly

pistola SF **1** (= *arma*) pistol, gun; (*Téc*) (*para pintar*) spray gun ▸ **pistola ametralladora** submachine-gun, tommy-gun ▸ **pistola de agua** water pistol ▸ **pistola de engrase** grease gun ▸ **pistola de juguete** toy pistol ▸ **pistola de pintar** spray gun ▸ **pistola engrasadora** grease gun ▸ **pistola rociadora de pintura** spray gun
2 (*Esp*) [*de pan*] French stick, baguette
3**‡ (= *pene*) prick**‡

pistolera SF **1** (*para pistola*) holster
• MODISMO: • **salir de ~s** to get out of a tight spot
2 pistoleras (*Anat**) flabby thighs

pistolerismo SM gun law, rule by terror

pistolero SM gunman ▸ **pistolero a sueldo** hired gunman

pistoleta SF (*And, Cono Sur*) small pistol

pistoletazo SM (= *disparo*) pistol shot; (*Dep*) (*tb* **pistoletazo de salida**) starting signal

pistolete SM pocket pistol

pistolo‡ SM soldier

pistón SM **1** (*Mec*) piston
2 (*Mús*) key; (*Col*) (= *corneta*) bugle, cornet
3 (*CAm, Méx*) (= *tortilla*) corn tortilla
4 • MODISMO: • **de ~*** smashing*, terrific*

pistonudo* ADJ smashing*, terrific*

pistudo* ADJ (*CAm*) filthy rich*

pita SF **1** (= *planta*) agave, pita; (= *fibra*) pita fibre, pita thread; (*Chile, Perú*) (= *hilo*) string
• MODISMO: • **enredar la ~** (*LAm**) to stir things up
2 pitas (*CAm*) (= *mentiras*) lies

pitada SF **1** (= *silbido*) whistle; (= *rechifla*) hiss
2 (*LAm**) [*de cigarrillo*] puff, drag*
3* (= *salida inoportuna*) silly remark

pitador/a* SM/F (*LAm*) smoker

Pitágoras SM Pythagoras

pitagorín* SM brainbox*

pitandero/a* SM/F (*Cono Sur*) smoker

pitanza SF **1** (= *ración*) daily ration
2‡ (= *alimento*) grub‡, chow (EEUU‡)
3* (= *precio*) price
4 (*Cono Sur*) (= *ganga*) bargain; (= *ventaja*) profit

pitar ▹ CONJUG 1a VI **1** (= *sonar*) (*con silbato*) to blow one's whistle; (*con claxon*) to hoot, blow one's horn • **el policía nos pitó** the policeman blew his whistle at us • **el camionero me pitó** the lorry driver hooted at us, the lorry driver blew his horn at us
2 (= *abuchear*) to whistle
3 • MODISMO: • **ir** *o* **salir pitando***: • **cuando la vio venir salió pitando** as soon as he saw her coming he was off like a shot* • **adiós, me tengo que ir pitando** bye, I must dash* • **vámonos pitando, que no llegamos** let's get a move on or we won't get there in time*
4 (*LAm**) (= *fumar*) to smoke
5† (= *funcionar*) to work • **el negocio no pita** the business isn't going well
VT **1** (*Dep*) • **el árbitro pitó falta** the referee whistled *o* blew for a foul • **¿quién pita el partido?** who's refereeing the match?
2 (*LAm**) (= *fumar*) to smoke

pitarra‡ SF grub‡, chow (EEUU‡), food

pitay SM (*And, Cono Sur*) rash

pitazo SM (*LAm*) whistle, hoot • MODISMO: • **dar el ~ a algn** (*Caribe**) to tip sb the wink*

pítcher [pitʃer] SMF (*Béisbol*) pitcher

pitear ▹ CONJUG 1a VI (*LAm*) = **pitar**

pitido SM (= *silbido*) whistle; (= *sonido agudo*) beep; (= *sonido corto*) pip

pitilla SF (*Cono Sur*) string

pitillera SF cigarette case

pitillo SM **1*** (= *cigarrillo*) cigarette • **echarse un ~** to have a smoke
2 (*And, Caribe*) (= *pajita*) drinking straw

pítima SF **1** (*Med*) poultice
2 (= *borrachera**) • **coger una ~** to get plastered*

pitiminí SM • MODISMO: • **de ~** trifling, trivial

pitinsa* SF (*CAm*) overalls

pitiusa ADJ of/from Ibiza *o* Formentera (*as opposed to the other Balearic islands*)
SF • **las Pitiusas** Ibiza and Formentera

pitiyanqui‡ SMF, **pitiyanki**‡ SMF (*Caribe*) Yankee-lover

pito SM **1** [*de coche, camión*] horn, hooter; [*de tren*] whistle, hooter • **el camionero tocó el ~** the lorry driver blew the horn *o* hooted
2 (= *silbato*) whistle • **el arbitro tocó el ~** the referee blew his whistle • **tener voz de ~** to have a squeaky voice • MODISMOS: • **cuando ~s, flautas*** it's always the same, one way or another it always happens • **cuando no es por ~s es por flautas*** if it isn't one thing it's another • **entre ~s y flautas*** what with one thing and another • **(no) importar un ~***: • **no me importa un ~** I don't care two hoots* • **no tocar un ~ en algo***: • **en este asunto no toca ~** he's got nothing to do with this matter • **tomar a algn por el ~ de un sereno**:

• **me tomaron por el ~ de un sereno** (*Esp**) they thought I was something the cat dragged in • **no vale un ~*** it's not worth tuppence
3* (= *cigarrillo*) fag*, ciggy*; (*LAm*) (= *pipa*) pipe
4* (= *pene*) willy*, peter (*EEUU**‡*) • MODISMO: • **tocarse el ~‡** to do damn-all‡, be bone-idle
5 (*LAm*) ▸ **pito de ternera** steak sandwich
6 (*Orn*) ▸ **pito real** green woodpecker • MODISMO: • **~ ~ colorito** ≈ eeny meeny miny mo

pitón¹ SM (*Zool*) python

pitón² SM (= *cuerno*) horn; [*de jarra*] spout; (*LAm*) [*de manguera*] nozzle; (*Bot*) sprig, young shoot; (= *bulto*) bump, lump; **pitones‡** (= *senos*) tits‡ ▸ **pitón de roca** sharp point of rock

pitonisa SF (= *adivinadora*) fortune teller; (= *hechicera*) witch, sorceress

pitopausia‡ SF male menopause

pitorrearse* ▷ CONJUG 1a VPR • **~ de** to scoff at, make fun of

pitorreo* SM teasing, joking • **estar de ~** to be in a joking mood

pitorro SM spout

pitote* SM fuss, row

pitra SF (*Cono Sur*) rash

pituco* a (*And, Cono Sur*) ADJ posh* SM/F toff*, posh person*

pitufa‡ SF bird‡, chick (*EEUU**)

pitufo‡ SM 1 (*Pol*) career politician
2 (*Méx*) (= *policía*) cop*, policeman

pituitario ADJ pituitary • **glándula pituitaria** pituitary (gland)

pituto* SM (*Cono Sur*) 1 (= *enchufe*) useful contact, connection
2 (= *chapuza*) odd job

piuco ADJ (*Cono Sur*) timid, scared

piular ▷ CONJUG 1a VI to cheep, chirp

pívot SMF (*Dep*) pivot

pivotar ▷ CONJUG 1a VI 1 (*Dep*) to pivot
2 (= *oscilar*) • **~ alrededor de** to revolve around • **~ en política** to switch allegiances in politics

pivote SMF (*Dep*) pivot
SM pivot

píxel SM (*Inform*) pixel

pixelar ▷ CONJUG 1a VT pixelate

píxide SF pyx

pixtón SM (*CAm*) thick tortilla

piyama SM (*LAm*) pyjamas (*pl*), pajama (*EEUU*)

pizarra SF 1 (= *piedra*) slate; (= *esquisto*) shale
2 (*Escol*) board, blackboard ▸ **pizarra blanca** whiteboard ▸ **pizarra interactiva** interactive whiteboard
3 (*Cono Sur*) (= *tablero*) notice board, bulletin board (*EEUU*)
4 (*LAm*) (= *marcador*) scoreboard

pizarral SM 1 (= *cantera*) slate quarry
2 ▷ **pizarra**

pizarrín SM slate pencil

pizarrón SM (*LAm*) (*Escol*) blackboard; (*Dep*) scoreboard

pizarroso ADJ slaty

pizca SF 1 (= *partícula*) tiny bit; (= *migaja*) crumb • **una ~ de sal** a pinch of salt
2 (= *rastro*) • **ni ~** not a bit • **no tiene ni ~ de gracia** it's not funny at all • **no tiene ni ~ de verdad** there's not a shred of truth in it
3 (*Méx*) (*Agr*) maize harvest

pizcar ▷ CONJUG 1g VT to pinch, nip

pizco SM pinch, nip

pizcucha SF (*CAm*) kite (*toy*)

pizote SM (*CAm*) coati(-mundi)

pizpireta* SF spirited girl, lively girl

pizpireto* ADJ flirty

pizza SF (*Culin*) pizza

pizzería [pitse'ria] SF pizzeria

PJ SM ABR (*Arg*) (= **Partido Justicialista**) *Peronist party*

p.j. SM ABR = **partido judicial**

PJF SF ABR (*Méx*) = **Policía Judicial Federal**

placa SF 1 (*gen*) plate; (= *lámina*) sheet; [*de cocina*] plate; (= *radiador*) radiator ▸ **placa conmemorativa** commemorative plaque ▸ **placa de hielo** icy patch ▸ **placa del nombre** nameplate ▸ **placa de matrícula** number plate, license plate (*EEUU*), registration plate ▸ **placa dental** (dental) plaque ▸ **placa de silicio** silicon chip ▸ **placa giratoria** (*Ferro*) turntable ▸ **placa madre** (*Inform*) motherboard ▸ **placa solar** (*en techo*) solar panel; (*en pared*) radiator; ▷ **vitrocerámica**
2 (*Fot*) (*tb* **placa fotográfica**) plate ▸ **placa esmerilada** focusing screen
3 (*LAm*) (*Mús*) gramophone record, phonograph record (*EEUU*)
4 (= *distintivo*) badge, insignia
5 (*LAm*) (= *erupción*) blotch, skin blemish

placaje SM (*Rugby*) tackle

placaminero SM persimmon

placar ▷ CONJUG 1g VT to tackle

placard SM (*Cono Sur*) built-in cupboard, (clothes) closet (*EEUU*)

placebo SM placebo • **efecto ~** placebo effect

pláceme SM (= *felicitación*) congratulations (*pl*), message of congratulations • **dar el ~ a algn** to congratulate sb

placenta SF placenta, afterbirth

placentero ADJ pleasant, agreeable

placentino/a (*Esp*) ADJ of/from Plasencia SM/F native/inhabitant of Plasencia • **los ~s** the people of Plasencia

placer¹ SM 1 (*gen*) pleasure • **es un ~ hacerlo** it is a pleasure to do it • **con mucho *o* sumo ~** with great pleasure • **tengo el ~ de presentarle a ...** it's my pleasure to introduce ... • **viaje de ~** pleasure trip • **a ~** as much as one wants ▸ **placer de dioses** heavenly delight
2 (= *deleite*) pleasure • **los ~es del ocio** the pleasures of idleness • **darse a los ~es** to give o.s. over to pleasure
VT ▷ CONJUG 2w (= *agradar*) to please • **me place poder hacerlo** I am glad to be able to do it

placer² SM 1 (*Geol, Min*) placer
2 (*Náut*) sandbank
3 (*Col*) (= *solar*) plot, patch; (*Agr*) ground prepared for sowing
4 (*Caribe*) field

placero/a SM/F 1 (= *vendedor*) stallholder, market trader
2 (*ocioso*) gossip

plácet SM blessing • **tiene el ~ de la dirección del partido** he has the blessing of the party leadership • **dar el ~ a algn** to give one's blessing to sb

placeta SF (*Cono Sur*) plateau

plácidamente ADV placidly

placidez SF placidity

plácido ADJ placid

pladur® SM plasterboard

plaf EXCL bang!, crash!

plafón SM 1 (*en el techo*) (= *rosetón*) ceiling rosette; (= *lámpara*) flush-fitting ceiling light
2 (*Arquit*) (= *panel*) soffit
3 (*LAm*) (*Constr*) ceiling

plaga SF 1 (*Agr, Zool*) pest; [*de langostas*] plague; (*Bot*) blight ▸ **plaga de la vid** grape vine blight ▸ **plaga del jardín** garden pest ▸ **plagas forestales** forest pests
2 (= *azote*) scourge • **aquí la sequía es una ~** drought is a scourge here • **una ~ de turistas** a plague of tourists
3 (= *exceso*) glut, abundance • **ha habido una ~ de lechugas** there has been a glut of lettuces
4 (= *aflicción*) affliction, grave illness

plagar ▷ CONJUG 1h VT (= *infestar*) to infest, plague • **han plagado la ciudad de carteles** they have covered *o* plastered the town with posters • **un texto plagado de errores** a text riddled with errors • **esta sección está plagada de minas** this part has mines everywhere
VPR **plagarse** • **~se de** to become infested with

plagiar ▷ CONJUG 1b VT 1 (= *copiar*) to plagiarize; [+ *producto*] to pirate, copy illegally
2 (*Méx*) (= *secuestrar*) to kidnap

plagiario/a SM/F 1 (= *imitador*) plagiarist
2 (*Méx*) (= *secuestrador*) kidnapper

plagio SM 1 (= *copia*) plagiarism; [*de producto*] piracy, illegal copying
2 (*Méx*) (= *secuestro*) kidnap(ping)

plaguicida SM pest-control substance, insecticide

plan SM 1 (= *proyecto*) plan; (= *intención*) idea, intention • **¿qué ~es tienes para este verano?** what are your plans for the summer? • **no tengo ~es para el futuro** I have no plans for the future • **realizar su ~** to put one's plan into effect • **mi ~ era comprar otro nuevo** my idea *o* intention was to buy a new one • **tengo un ~ estupendo para mañana** I've got a splendid idea about what to do tomorrow ▸ **plan de choque** action plan, plan of action ▸ **plan de desarrollo** development plan ▸ **plan de incentivos** incentive scheme ▸ **plan de jubilación** retirement plan ▸ **plan de pensiones** pension plan ▸ **plan de vuelo** flight plan ▸ **plan quinquenal** five-year plan
2 [*de curso*] programme, program (*EEUU*) ▸ **plan de estudios** curriculum, syllabus
3* (= *manera, actitud*) • **este niño está en un ~ imposible** this child is really playing up • **si te pones en ese ~** if that's your attitude • **como sigas en ese ~** if you go on like that • **lo hizo en ~ bruto** he did it in a brutal way • **viajar en ~ económico** to travel cheap • **el negocio es en ~ timo** the deal is really a swindle • **chaparrones en ~ disperso** scattered showers • **viven en ~ pasota** they live like hippies • **en ~ de: lo dije en ~ de broma** I said it as a joke *o* for a laugh • **vamos en ~ de turismo** we're going as tourists • **salieron en ~ de divertirse** they went out looking for a good time • **está en ~ de rehusar** he's in a mood to refuse, he's likely to refuse at the moment
4* • MODISMOS: • **eso no es ~** • **tampoco es ~** that's not on* • **a todo ~†** sparing no expense • **no me hace ~†** (+ *infin*) it doesn't suit me to (+ *infin*)
5†* (= *aventura*) date; (*pey*) fling* • **¿tienes ~ para esta noche?** have you got a date for tonight? • **buscar ~** to try to pick somebody up* • **tiene un ~ con la mujer del alcalde** he's having a fling with the mayor's wife*
6 (*Med*) course of treatment • **estar a ~** to be on a course of treatment
7 (*Topografía*) (= *nivel*) level; (= *altura*) height
8 (*Cono Sur, Méx*) [*de barco etc*] flat bottom
9 (*LAm*) (= *llano*) level ground; (*Cono Sur*) (= *falda de cerro*) foothills (*pl*)
10 (*And, CAm, Caribe*) [*de espada etc*] flat

plana SF 1 [*de hoja*] side, page; (*Tip*) page; (*Escol*) writing exercise, copywriting • **noticias de primera ~** front-page news • **en primera ~** on the front page • **escribir una ~ de castigo** to write lines as a punishment • MODISMO: • **corregir *o* enmendar la ~ a algn** to put sb right; (*pey*) to find fault with sb, improve upon sb's efforts ▸ **plana de**

P

anuncios advertisement page
2 ▸ plana mayor (*Mil*) staff; (*fig*) top brass*
3 (*Téc*) trowel; [*de tonelero*] cooper's plane

planazo SM **1** (*LAm**) • **se dio un ~** he fell flat on his face
2 (*Caribe*) (= *trago*) shot of liquor

plancha SF **1** (= *lámina*) plate, sheet; (= *losa*) slab; (*Tip*) plate; (*Náut*) gangway; (*Med*) dental plate • **hacer la ~** [*bañista*] to float
2 (= *utensilio*) iron; (= *acción*) ironing; [*de traje*] pressing; (= *ropa para planchar*) ironing
▸ plancha a *o* **de vapor** steam iron
▸ plancha eléctrica electric iron
3 (*Culin*) grill; (*Cono Sur*) griddle pan • **a la ~** grilled • **pescado a la ~** grilled fish
4 (= *ejercicio*) press-up
5* (= *error*) bloomer* • **hacer** *o* **tirarse una ~** to drop a clanger‡, put one's foot in it
• **MODISMO:** • **pasar ~** (*Cono Sur*) to be embarrassed
6 (*Dep*) dive • **entrada en ~** sliding tackle
• **lanzarse en ~** to dive (for the ball)
• **cabecear en ~** to do a diving header

planchada SF **1** (*para barcas*) landing stage
2 (*LAm*) = **plancha**

planchado ADJ **1** [+ *ropa*] ironed; [+ *traje*] pressed
2 (*CAm, Cono Sur*) (= *elegante*) very smart, dolled up*
3 (*LAm**) (= *sin dinero*) broke*
4 (*Culin*) pressed • **jamón ~** pressed ham
5 (*Méx*) (= *listo*) clever; (= *valiente*) brave
SM **1** (*a la ropa*) ironing; (*a un traje*) pressing
• **una prenda que no necesita ~** a non-iron garment • **dar un ~ a** [+ *ropa*] to iron; [+ *traje*] to press
2 (*And, Cono Sur*) (*Aut*) panel beating

planchador(a) SM/F *person who does the ironing*

planchadora SF (= *máquina*) press, trouser press

planchar ▸ CONJUG 1a VT **1** [+ *ropa*] to iron; [+ *traje*] to press • **prenda de no ~** non-iron garment
2 (*LAm**) (= *adular*) to suck up to*
3 (*Méx**) (= *dejar plantado*) to stand up*
VI **1** (= *desarrugar*) to iron, do the ironing
2 (*LAm**) (= *no bailar*) to be a wallflower
3 (*Chile**) (= *meter la pata*) to drop a clanger‡; (= *parecer absurdo*) to look ridiculous

planchazo* SM = **plancha**

planchear ▸ CONJUG 1a VT to plate

plancheta SF **1** (*Agrimensura*) plane table
2 • **MODISMO:** • **echárselas de ~*** to show off, swank*

planchón SM (*Cono Sur*) (*en campo*) ice field; (*en montaña*) snowcap

plancton SM plankton

planeación SF (*Méx*) planning

planeador SM glider

planeadora SF **1** (= *niveladora*) leveller, bulldozer
2 (*Náut*) speedboat, powerboat

planear ▸ CONJUG 1a VT (= *proyectar*) to plan
• **~ hacer algo** to plan to do sth
VI (*Aer*) to glide; (*fig*) to hang, hover (**sobre** over)

planeo SM (*gen*) gliding • **un ~** glide

planeta SM planet • **el ~ rojo** the red planet, Mars

planetario ADJ planetary
SM planetarium

planicie SF (= *llanura*) plain; (= *llano*) flat area, level ground; (= *superficie plana*) flat surface

planificación SF (*gen*) planning; (*Inform*) scheduling **▸ planificación corporativa** corporate planning **▸ planificación familiar** family planning **▸ planificación urbana** town planning

planificador(a) ADJ planning (*antes de s*)
SM/F planner

planificar ▸ CONJUG 1g VT to plan

planilla SF (*LAm*) **1** (= *lista*) list; (= *tabla*) table; (= *nómina*) payroll; (= *sujetapapeles*) clipboard; (= *papelito*) slip of paper
2 (*Ferro*) ticket
3 (*And, Cono Sur*) (= *formulario*) application form; (*Econ*) (= *cuenta*) account; [*de gastos*] expense account
4 (*And, Cono Sur*) (*para votar*) ballot paper, voting slip; (= *nómina de electores*) electoral roll *o* register; (= *candidatos*) ticket

planimetría SF surveying, planimetry

planing, planning ['planin] SM (PL: **plan(n)ings** ['planin]) schedule, agenda

plano ADJ (= *llano*) flat, level • **tiene los pies ~s** he has flat feet • **es muy plana de pecho** she is very flat-chested
SM **1** (*Mat, Mec*) plane **▸ plano focal** focal plane **▸ plano inclinado** inclined plane
2 (= *posición, nivel*) plane • **están en un ~ distinto** they're on a different plane • **de distinto ~ social** of a different social plane *o* position
3 (*Cine, Fot*) shot • **unos preciosos ~s de elefantes** some beautiful elephant shots
• **un primer ~** a close-up • **en primer ~** (*Cine, Fot*) in close-up; (*Arte*) in the foreground
• **estar en (un) segundo ~** (*fig*) to be in the background **▸ plano aéreo** aerial shot
▸ plano corto close-up **▸ plano general** general view **▸ plano largo** long shot
4 (*Aer*) **▸ plano de cola** tailplane
5 (*Arquit, Mec*) plan; (*Geog*) map; [*de ciudad*] map, street plan • **levantar el ~ de** [+ *país*] to survey, make a map of; [+ *edificio*] to draw up the designs for **▸ plano acotado** contour map
6 • **de ~:** **caer de ~** to fall flat • **confesar de ~** to make a full confession • **le daba el sol de ~** the sun shone directly on it • **rechazar algo de ~** to turn sth down flat
7 [*de espada*] flat

planta¹ SF (*Bot*) plant **▸ planta carnívora** carnivorous plant **▸ planta de interior** indoor plant, houseplant **▸ planta de Navidad** poinsettia

planta² SF **1** (= *piso*) floor • **vivo en la tercera ~** I live on the third floor • **un edificio de tres ~s** a three-storey building **▸ planta baja** ground *o* (EEUU) first floor **▸ planta noble** function suite
2 (*Arquit*) (= *plano*) ground plan • **construir un edificio de (nueva) ~** to build a completely new building
3 (*tb* **planta del pie**) the sole of the foot
• **asentar sus ~s en** (*iró*) to install o.s. in
4 (= *aspecto*) • **de buena ~** fine-looking
5 (= *fábrica*) plant **▸ planta de embotellado** bottling plant **▸ planta de enlatado** canning factory **▸ planta de ensamblaje** assembly plant **▸ planta depuradora** water purification plant **▸ planta de tratamiento térmico** (waste) incineration plant **▸ planta piloto** pilot plant **▸ planta potabilizadora** waterworks (*sing*), water treatment plant
6 (*Baile, Esgrima*) position (of the feet)
7 (= *plan*) plan, programme, program (EEUU), scheme

plantación SF **1** (= *acción*) planting • **ha comenzado la ~ de pinos** they have started to plant pine trees
2 (= *terreno cultivado*) plantation • **una ~ de tabaco** a tobacco plantation

plantado ADJ **1** (*Bot*) planted (**de** with) • **un campo ~ de viñedos** a field planted with vines
2 • **dejar ~ a algn*** (*en una cita*) to stand sb up*; (*en una relación sentimental*) to dump sb*, ditch sb*; (*en una situación difícil*) to leave sb in the lurch*, leave sb high and dry; (*mientras se habla*) to leave sb in mid-sentence • **me dejó plantada el día de la boda** he stood me up *o* left me in the lurch on my wedding day* • **lo dejó todo ~ y se fue del país** he packed *o* chucked everything in and left the country*; (*con prisa*) he dumped everything and left the country*
3* (= *de pie*) standing • **sigue ahí ~** he's still standing there
4 • **bien ~*** (= *persona*) well-groomed • **un equipo muy bien ~ en el terreno de juego** a very well organized team on the pitch

plantador(a) SM/F (= *persona*) planter
SM (= *utensilio*) dibber, dibble

plantadora SF (*Agr*) (= *máquina*) planter, planting machine

plantaje* SM (*And, Caribe*) looks (*pl*)

plantar ▸ CONJUG 1a VT **1** (*Bot*) [+ *árbol, bulbo, jardín*] to plant; [+ *semilla*] to plant, sow
• **plantó todo el jardín de flores** she planted the whole garden with flowers
2 (= *colocar*) [+ *estaca, poste*] to put, stick
• **plantó el piano al lado de la ventana** he stuck the piano by the window • **le plantó sus cosas en mitad de la calle*** she dumped his things in the middle of the street*
• **MODISMO:** • **~ el pie en algo** to set foot in sth • **no vuelvas a ~ el pie en mi casa** don't you ever set foot in my house again
3* (= *dar*) [+ *beso*] to plant; [+ *insulto*] to hurl
• **me plantó un beso en los labios** he planted a kiss on my lips • **~ una bofetada a algn** to slap sb* • **MODISMOS:** • **~ cara a** [+ *persona, críticas*] to stand up to; [+ *problema*] to face up to, confront • **no se atreven a ~le cara al jefe** they don't dare stand up to the boss
• **durante seis años le estuvo plantando cara a la muerte** he held out against death for six years • **~ cuatro verdades a algn** to give sb a piece of one's mind*
4* (= *abandonar*) (*en una cita*) to stand up*; [+ *novio*] to dump*, ditch*; [+ *actividad, estudios*] to pack in*, chuck in* • **plantó sus estudios y se marchó a Francia** he packed *o* chucked in his studies and went to France*
5* (= *dar un corte*) • **¿por qué no lo plantas de una vez?** why don't you tell him where to go once and for all? • **la planté para que no te insultara más** I cut her short before she insulted you any more
VPR **plantarse 1** (= *colocarse*) to plant o.s., plonk o.s.* • **se nos plantó delante y no nos dejaba ver** he planted *o* plonked* himself in front of us so we couldn't see • **se plantó aquí con todas sus maletas** he planted *o* plonked* himself here with all his suitcases
2 (= *llegar*) • **~se en** to get to, make it to • **en tres horas se plantó en Sevilla** he got to *o* made it to Seville in three hours • **se plantó sin esfuerzo en la final** he made it to the final easily
3 (= *mantenerse firme*) • **~se en** to stick to • **se plantó en su decisión** she stuck to her decision • **debes ~te ahí y no dejarte influenciar** you should stick to that and not be swayed
4 (= *detenerse*) [*caballo*] to stop dead, pull up short
5 (*Naipes*) to stick • **me planto** I stick
6 (*And, CAm**) (= *arreglarse*) to doll o.s. up*

plante SM **1** (= *huelga*) stoppage, protest strike
2 (= *postura*) stand, agreed basis for resistance; (= *programa*) common programme of demands

planteamiento SM **1** (= *exposición*) [*de novela, película*] first part, exposition (*frm*) • **el**

~ **de la sinfonía** the way the symphony is structured • **el ~ del problema** (*Mat*) the way the problem is set out
2 (= *punto de vista*) approach • **el entrenador ha propuesto un ~ distinto del ataque** the coach has suggested a different approach in attack • **un ~ nuevo de la cuestión** a new way of looking at *o* approaching the issue • **sus ~s estéticos** his aesthetics
3 (= *idea*) plan • **yo me había hecho otro ~ de este fin de semana** I had made other plans for this weekend
4 (*Arquit*) (*tb* **planteamiento urbanístico**) town planning

plantear ▹ CONJUG 1a VT **1** (= *exponer*) **a** [+ *situación, problema*] to bring up, raise • **no me atrevo a ~les el tema a mis padres** I don't dare bring up *o* raise the issue with my parents • **planteáselo todo tal como es** explain *o* put the situation to him exactly as it is • **planteado el problema en estos términos ...** with the problem expressed *o* put in these terms ...
b (*Mat*) [+ *ecuación, problema*] to set out
2 (= *proponer*) [+ *cambio, posibilidad*] to suggest • **he planteado la necesidad de un cambio** I have suggested that a change is necessary • **el futuro plantea un reto al que habrá que hacer frente** the future presents a challenge that will have to be met
3 (= *causar*) [+ *problema*] to pose, create • **esta decisión nos plantea un problema moral** this decision poses *o* creates a moral problem • **esta novela ~á problemas para adaptarla al cine** adapting this novel for the cinema will pose *o* create various problems
VPR **plantearse 1** (= *cuestionarse*) to think about, consider • **ya es hora de que te plantees qué vas a hacer con tu vida** it's time you started thinking about *o* it's time you considered what you're going to do with your life • **yo no me planteo ese tipo de cosas** I don't think about that sort of thing • **me estoy planteando si merece la pena el esfuerzo** I'm thinking about *o* considering whether it is worth the effort
2 (= *considerar*) to see • **yo me planteo la vida como una lucha por sobrevivir** I see life as a struggle for survival • **en tu lugar, yo me lo ~ía de otro modo** if I were you, I would see things differently • **~se hacer algo** to think of doing sth, consider doing sth • **me estoy planteando seriamente dejar de fumar** I'm seriously thinking of *o* considering giving up smoking
3 (= *presentarse*) [*cuestión, problema*] to arise, come up • **esa cuestión volverá a ~se en el futuro** this question will arise *o* come up again in the future • **ahora se plantea el problema de la inflación** this raises the question of inflation, there arises the question of inflation (*frm*) • **en el futuro se nos ~á el mismo dilema** we will be faced with the same dilemma in the future • **ahora se nos plantea la duda de qué hacer con todo este dinero** now we have the problem of what to do with all this money

plantel SM **1** (= *grupo*) • **un ~ de jóvenes pintoras** a group of young painters • **un excelente ~ de actores** an excellent pool of actors • **un ~ de jugadores prometedores** an promising squad of players
2 (= *centro educativo*) training establishment
3 (*Bot*) nursery
4 (*LAm*) (= *escuela*) school

plantificar ▹ CONJUG 1g VT* (= *colocar*) to plonk down, dump down*
VPR **plantificarse 1** (*Caribe, Cono Sur, Méx**) (= *plantarse*) to plant o.s.; (= *no ceder*) to stand firm, stand one's ground • **se plantificó en la puerta** he planted himself in the doorway, he stood there in the doorway
2 (*Méx*) (= *ataviarse*) to get dolled up*

plantilla SF **1** [*de zapato*] inner sole, insole; [*de media etc*] sole
2 (*Téc*) pattern, template; (= *patrón*) stencil
3 (= *personas*) staff, personnel; (*Dep*) playing staff; (= *lista*) list, roster • **estar de ~** to be on the payroll ▸ **plantilla de personal** staff

plantillada* SF (*And*) bragging

plantío SM **1** (= *acto*) planting
2 (= *terreno*) bed, patch

plantista SMF braggart

plantón SM **1*** (= *espera*) long wait • **dar (un) ~ a algn** to stand sb up* • **estar de ~** (*gen*) to be stuck, have to wait around; (*Mil*) to be on sentry duty • **tener a algn de ~** to keep sb waiting
2 (*Bot*) (= *plántula*) seedling; (= *esqueje*) cutting

plántula SF seedling

plañidera SF (paid) mourner

plañidero ADJ mournful, plaintive

plañir ▹ CONJUG 3h VT to mourn, grieve over

plaqueta SF platelet

plas¹ EXCL = **plaf**

plas²(a)‡ SM/F brother/sister

plasma SM plasma ▸ **plasma sanguíneo** blood plasma

plasmación SF shape, form

plasmar ▹ CONJUG 1a VT **1** (= *dar forma a*) to embody • **sus ideas quedaron plasmadas en un manifiesto** his ideas were embodied in a manifesto
2 (= *reflejar*) to capture, reflect • **la novela plasma perfectamente la angustia del autor** the novel captures *o* reflects the author's anguish perfectly
VPR **plasmarse** • **~se en algo** to manifest itself in sth • **la indignación ciudadana se plasmó en revueltas callejeras** the anger among the population manifested itself in street riots

plasta SF **1** (*gen*) soft mass, lump; (= *cosa aplastada*) flattened mass
2* (= *desastre*) botch, mess • **es una ~ de edificio** it's a mess of a building • **el plan es una ~** the plan is one big mess, the plan is a complete botch
SMF* (= *pelmazo*) bore
ADJ INV boring

plástica SF plastic art, (art of) sculpture and modelling *o* (*EEUU*) modeling

plasticar ▹ CONJUG 1g VT (*LAm*) [+ *documento*] to cover with plastic, seal in plastic, laminate

plasticidad SF **1** [*de material*] plasticity
2 (= *expresividad*) expressiveness; [*de descripción*] richness

plasticina® SF (*Cono Sur*) Plasticine®

plástico ADJ **1** (*gen*) plastic • **artes plásticas** plastic arts
2 [*imagen*] expressive; [*descripción*] rich, evocative
3 (*CAm**) • **chico ~** young trendy
SM **1** (*gen*) plastic • **es de ~*** it's fake, it's not real*
2* (= *disco*) record, disc • **pinchar un ~** spin a disc*
3 (*Mil*) plastic explosive

plasticoso ADJ plastic, plasticky*

plastificación SF treatment with plastic, lamination

plastificado ADJ treated with plastic, laminated

plastificar ▹ CONJUG 1g VT **1** [+ *documento*] to cover with (laminated) plastic, laminate
2 (*Mús*) to record, make a record of

plastilina® SF Plasticine®

plastrón SM (*LAm*) floppy tie, cravat

plata SF **1** (= *metal*) silver; (= *vajilla*) silverware; (*Econ*) silver • **MODISMOS:** • **como una ~** bright as a pin • **hablar en ~** to speak bluntly, speak frankly
2 (*esp LAm*) (= *dinero*) money; (= *riqueza*) wealth • **podrido en ~*** stinking rich*, rolling in it*
3 • **La Plata** (= *río*) the (River) Plate

platacho SM (*Cono Sur*) *dish of raw seafood*

platada SF (*LAm*) dish, plateful

plataforma SF **1** (*gen*) platform; (= *tablado*) stage • **zapatos de ~** platforms, platform shoes ▸ **plataforma continental** continental shelf ▸ **plataforma de carga** loading platform ▸ **plataforma de lanzamiento** launch pad, launching pad ▸ **plataforma de perforación** drilling rig, oil rig ▸ **plataforma digital** (*TV*) digital platform ▸ **plataforma espacial** space station ▸ **plataforma giratoria** turntable ▸ **plataforma petrolera, plataforma petrolífera** oil rig
2 (*Pol*) (*tb* **plataforma electoral**) platform; (= *programa*) programme; [*de negociación*] package, set of proposals ▸ **plataforma reivindicativa** set of demands
3 (*fig*) (*para lograr algo*) springboard

platal* SM (*LAm*) fortune

platanal SM, **platanar** SM (*Col*), **platanera** SF (*LAm*) banana plantation

platanero/a ADJ banana (*antes de s*)
SM/F (*LAm*) (= *cultivador*) banana grower; (*Com*) dealer in bananas

plátano SM **1** (= *fruta*) banana; (*para cocinar*) plantain; (= *árbol*) banana tree
2 (= *árbol ornamental*) plane (tree)
3‡ banana‡, prick**

platea SF (*Cine, Teat*) stalls (*pl*), orchestra (section) (*EEUU*)

plateado ADJ **1** (= *de plata*) [*color*] [*objeto*] silver; [*cabello*] silver, silvery; [*brillo*] silvery; (*Téc*) silver-plated
2 (*Méx*) wealthy
SM silver-plating

platear ▹ CONJUG 1a VT **1** (*Téc*) to silver-plate, silver
2 (*CAm, Méx*) to sell, turn into money
VI to turn silver

platense (*Arg*) ADJ **1** = **rioplatense**
2 (*de la ciudad de La Plata*) of/from La Plata
SMF **1** = **rioplatense**
2 native/inhabitant of La Plata • **los ~s** the people of La Plata

plateresco ADJ plateresque

platería SF **1** (= *arte*) silversmith's craft
2 (= *tienda*) silversmith's
3 (= *objetos*) silverware, silver

platero/a SM/F silversmith

plática SF (*esp Méx*) (= *charla*) talk, chat; (*Rel*) sermon • **estar de ~** to be chatting, be having a talk

platicador* ADJ (*Méx*) chatty, talkative

platicar ▹ CONJUG 1g VI (= *charlar*) to talk, chat
VT (*Méx*) (= *decir*) to tell

platija SF plaice, flounder

platilla SF (*Caribe*) water melon

platillo SM **1** (= *plato*) (*gen*) small plate; (*para taza*) saucer; [*de limosnas*] collecting bowl; (*de balanza*) pan • **pasar el ~** to pass the hat round ▸ **platillo volante, platillo volador** flying saucer
2 platillos (*Mús*) cymbals
3 (*CAm, Méx*) dish • **el tercer ~ de la comida** the third course of the meal

platina SF **1** [*de microscopio*] slide
2 (*Mús*) [*de tocadiscos*] deck; [*de casete*] tape (deck) • **doble ~** twin deck
3 (*Tip*) platen

platino SM **1** (= *metal*) platinum **2 platinos** (*Aut*) contact points ADJ • **rubia ~** platinum blonde

plato SM **1** (= *recipiente*) (*para comer*) plate; (*de balanza*) pan • **fregar los ~s** to wash *o* do the dishes, wash up • MODISMOS: • **pagar los ~s rotos** to carry the can* • **estar en el ~ y en la tajada** • **estar al ~ y a las tajadas** to have one's cake and eat it • REFRÁN: • **del ~ a la boca se pierde la sopa** there's many a slip 'twixt cup and lip ▸ **plato de postre** dessert plate ▸ **plato frutero** fruit dish ▸ **plato hondo** soup dish, soup plate ▸ **plato llano** dinner plate ▸ **plato sopero** soup dish, soup plate
2 (= *contenido del plato*) plate, plateful • **un ~ de arroz** a plate *o* plateful of rice • MODISMO: • **vender algo por un ~ de lentejas** to sell sth for a mess of pottage
3 (*Culin*) (*en menú*) course; (= *guiso*) dish • **un menú de tres ~s** a three-course meal • **es un ~ típico español** it's a typical Spanish dish • **es mi ~ favorito** it's my favourite dish • MODISMOS: • **no es ~ de mi gusto** it's not my cup of tea • **comen del mismo ~** they're great pals • **ser ~ de segunda mesa*** [*cosa*] to be second-best; [*persona*] play second fiddle ▸ **plato central** (*Ven*) main course ▸ **plato combinado** set main course, *meat or fish etc served with vegetable accompaniment as one dish* ▸ **plato de fondo** main course ▸ **plato dulce** sweet course ▸ **plato fuerte** (= *comida principal*) main course; (= *abundante*) big meal; (= *tema principal*) main topic, central theme; (= *punto fuerte*) strong point ▸ **plato precocinado** pre-cooked meal ▸ **plato preparado** ready-to-serve meal ▸ **plato principal** main course
4 [*de tocadiscos*] turntable ▸ **plato giradiscos, plato giratorio** turntable
5 ▸ **plato de (la) ducha** shower tray
6 (*Téc*) plate
7 (*Dep*) • **tiro al ~** clay pigeon shooting
8 (*Cono Sur**) • **es un ~** (= *guapo*) he's a dish*, he's very dishy* • **¡qué ~!** (= *divertido*) what a laugh!

plató SM set

Platón SM Plato

platón SM (*LAm*) **1** (*Culin*) (= *plato grande*) large dish; (*de servir*) serving dish **2** (= *palangana*) washbasin, washbowl (EEUU)

platónicamente ADV platonically

platónico ADJ platonic

platonismo SM Platonism

platonista SMF Platonist

platudo* ADJ (*LAm*) rich, well-heeled*

plausible ADJ **1** [*argumento, motivo*] acceptable, admissible **2** [*comportamiento, intento, esfuerzo*] commendable, praiseworthy

plausiblemente ADV **1** [*alegar*] reasonably, believably **2** [*comportarse*] commendably, laudably

playa SF **1** (= *orilla del mar*) beach • **una ~ de arenas doradas** a beach with golden sands • **pasar el día en la ~** to spend the day at *o* on the beach • **pescar desde la ~** to fish from the beach *o* shore ▸ **Playa Girón** (*Caribe*) Bay of Pigs
2 (= *costa*) seaside • **ir a veranear a la ~** to spend the summer at the seaside, go to the seaside for one's summer holidays
3 (*LAm*) (= *llano*) flat open space ▸ **playa de carga y descarga** (*Ferro*) goods yard ▸ **playa de estacionamiento** car park, parking lot (EEUU) ▸ **playa de juegos** playground
4 • MODISMO: • **una ~ de algo** (*Caribe**) loads of sth*

playera SF **1** (*CAm, Méx*) (= *camiseta*) T-shirt **2** (= *zapatilla*) canvas shoe; [*de tenis*] tennis shoe

playero ADJ beach (*antes de s*) • **es muy ~** he loves going down the beach

playo ADJ (*Arg, Méx*) flat

play-off ['pleiof] SM (PL: **play-offs**) (*Dep*) play-off

plaza SF **1** (*entre calles*) square • **la Plaza Roja** Red Square • MODISMOS: • **abrir ~** (*Taur*) to open a bullfight • **regar la ~** (*Esp**) to have a beer (as a starter) ▸ **plaza de armas** parade ground ▸ **plaza de toros** bullring ▸ **plaza mayor** main square
2 (= *mercado*) market, market place • **hacer la ~** to do the daily shopping
3 (= *espacio*) (*gen*) room, space; [*de vehículo*] seat • **un vehículo de dos ~s** a two-seater vehicle • **el avión tiene 90 ~s** the plane carries 90 passengers • **reservar una ~** to book a seat • **"no hay plazas"** "no vacancies" • **abrir ~** to make way • **¡plaza!** make way! ▸ **plaza de atraque** berth, mooring ▸ **plaza de garaje** parking space (*in garage*) ▸ **plaza hotelera** hotel bed
4 (= *puesto de trabajo*) (*gen*) post; (= *vacante*) vacancy • **cubrir una ~** to fill a vacancy *o* post *o* job • **sentar ~** (*Mil*) to enlist, sign on (**de** as)
5† (= *ciudad*) town, city
6 (*tb* **plaza fuerte**) (*Mil*) fortress, fortified town; (*Pol*) stronghold

plazo SM **1** (= *período*) period • **dentro del ~ previsto** within the specified period • **en un ~ de diez días** within a period of ten days • **nos dan un ~ de ocho días para acabar el trabajo** they've given us eight days to finish the job • **¿cuándo vence el ~?** when is the deadline? • **a ~** (*Com*) on credit • **a ~ fijo** (*Com*) fixed-term • **a corto ~** (*adj*) short-term; (*adv*) in the short term • **a largo ~** (*adj*) long-term; (*adv*) in the long term • **es una tarea a largo ~** it's a long-term job • **veremos los resultados a largo ~** we'll see the results in the long term • **a medio ~** (*adj*) medium-term; (*adv*) in the medium term ▸ **plazo de entrega** delivery time, delivery date ▸ **plazo de prescripción** (*Jur*) time limit
2 (= *pago*) instalment, installment (EEUU), payment • **no pagó el ~ de marzo** he didn't pay the March instalment • **a ~s** in instalments • **pagar algo a ~s** pay for sth in instalments

plazoleta SF, **plazuela** SF small square

pleamar SF high tide

plebe SF • **la ~** (*gen*) the common people (*pl*), the masses (*pl*); (*pey*) the mob, the rabble, the plebs* (*pl*) (*pey*)

plebeyez SF plebeian nature; (*fig*) coarseness, commonness

plebeyo/a ADJ **1** (= *de la plebe*) plebeian **2** (= *ordinario*) coarse, common SM/F plebeian, commoner

plebiscito SM plebiscite

pleca SF (*Inform*) backslash

plectro SM plectrum

plegable ADJ [*mesa, cama*] folding, collapsible

plegadera SF paperknife

plegadizo ADJ = **plegable**

plegado SM **1** (= *acto*) [*de papel*] folding, creasing; [*de algo duro*] bending; [*de tela*] pleating **2** (= *pliegue*) fold

plegamiento SM **1** (*Geol*) fold **2** [*de camión*] jack-knifing

plegar ▸ CONJUG 1h, 1j VT **1** (= *doblar*) [+ *papel*] to fold; [+ *algo duro*] to bend **2** (*Cos*) to pleat
VI to fold up
VPR **plegarse 1** (= *someterse*) to yield, submit (**a** to) **2** (= *doblarse*) [*algo duro*] to bend; [*mesa, cama*] to fold away, be collapsible

plegaria SF prayer

pleitear ▸ CONJUG 1a VI **1** (*Jur*) (= *litigar*) to go to court • **~ con** *o* **contra algn** to take sb to court **2** (*esp LAm**) (= *reñir*) to argue

pleitesía SF • **rendir ~ a algn** (= *respeto*) to show respect for sb, show sb courtesy; (= *homenaje*) to pay tribute to sb

pleitista ADJ **1** (*Jur*) litigious **2** (= *reñidor*) quarrelsome, argumentative SMF **1** (*Jur*) litigious person **2** (*fig*) troublemaker **3** (*LAm*) (= *peleón*) brawler

pleitisto ADJ (*LAm*) quarrelsome, argumentative

pleito SM **1** (*Jur*) lawsuit, case; **pleitos** litigation (*sing*) • **andar en ~s** to be engaged in lawsuits *o* litigation • **entablar ~** to bring an action, bring a lawsuit • **ganar el ~** to win one's case • **poner ~** to sue, bring an action • **poner ~ a algn** to bring an action against sb, take sb to court ▸ **pleito civil** civil action ▸ **pleito de acreedores** bankruptcy proceedings (*pl*)
2 (= *litigio*) dispute
3 (*esp LAm*) (= *discusión*) quarrel, argument; (= *pelea*) fight, brawl • **estar a ~ con algn** to be at odds with sb • **no quiero meterme en ~s** I don't want to get into an argument
4 ▸ **pleito homenaje** homage

plenamente ADV [*consciente, recuperado*] fully; [*satisfecho*] completely • **me satisface ~** it gives me complete satisfaction • **acertó ~** he was absolutely right • **vivir la vida ~** to live life to the full

plenaria SF plenary, plenary session

plenario ADJ plenary, full; ▸ **indulgencia**

plenilunio SM full moon

plenipotenciario/a ADJ, SM/F plenipotentiary

plenitud SF **1** (= *apogeo*) • **en la ~ de sus poderes** at the height of his powers • **estaba en la ~ de la vida** he was in the prime of life **2** (= *totalidad*) plenitude, fullness

pleno ADJ full • **~ empleo** full employment • **~s poderes** full powers • **en ~ día** • **a plena luz del día** in broad daylight • **en ~ verano** in the middle of the summer • **vive en ~ centro de Bilbao** he lives right in the center of Bilbao • **le dio en plena cara** she hit him full in the face • **en plena vista** in full view
SM **1** (= *reunión*) plenary, plenary session **2** (*en las quinielas*) *maximum number of points* **3** • **en ~**: **el gobierno en ~ asistió al funeral** the entire Cabinet attended the funeral • **ha dimitido la junta directiva en ~** the board of directors resigned en masse

pleonasmo SM pleonasm

pleonástico ADJ pleonastic

plepa SF **1** (= *persona enfermiza*) sickly person **2*** (= *antipático*) unpleasant sort **3*** (= *pesado*) pain*, nuisance

pletina SF = **platina**

plétora SF (*frm*) (= *abundancia*) plethora (*frm*), abundance; (= *exceso*) excess, surplus

pletórico ADJ • **estar ~** [*jugador*] to be on top form • **~ de** [+ *fuerza, energía, entusiasmo*] full of, bursting with; [+ *vida, ilusiones*] full of; [+ *felicidad, salud*] bursting with • **el equipo está ~ de moral** the team's morale couldn't be higher

pleuresía SF pleurisy

plexiglás® SM Perspex®, Plexiglas® (EEUU)

plexo SM (*Anat*) ▸ **plexo solar** solar plexus

pléyade SF **1** (*Literat*) distinguished group *o* gathering **2 Pléyades** (*Mit*) Pleiades

P

plica SF (= *carta cerrada*) sealed envelope *o* document; (*en un concurso*) sealed entry; (*en concurso de obras*) sealed bid

pliego SM (= *hoja de papel*) sheet; (= *carpeta*) folder; (*Tip*) section, signature ▸ **pliego cerrado** (*Náut*) sealed orders (*pl*) ▸ **pliego de cargos** list of accusations ▸ **pliego de condiciones** specifications (*pl*) (of a tender) ▸ **pliego de descargo** evidence (for the defendant) ▸ **pliego de reivindicaciones**, **pliego petitorio** (*Cono Sur*) list of demands

pliegue SM **1** (= *doblez*) fold, crease
2 (*Cos*) (*gen*) pleat; (= *alforza*) tuck
3 (*Geol*) fold

plima SF • **flor de la ~** (*Cono Sur*) wisteria

plin EXCL • **¡a mí, ~!** I couldn't care less!

Plinio SM Pliny ▸ **Plinio el Joven** Pliny the Younger ▸ **Plinio el Viejo** Pliny the Elder

plinto SM plinth

plisado ADJ pleated
SM **1** (= *acción*) pleating
2 (= *tablas*) pleats (*pl*)

plisar ▸ CONJUG 1a VT to pleat

PLN SM ABR (*C. Rica*) = **Partido de Liberación Nacional**

plomada SF **1** (*Arquit*) plumb
2 (*Náut*) lead
3 (*Pesca*) weights (*pl*), sinkers (*pl*)

plomar ▸ CONJUG 1a VT to seal with lead

plomazo SM **1*** (= *pelmazo*) bore
2 (*CAm, Méx*) (= *tiro*) shot; (= *herida*) bullet wound

plombagina SF plumbago

plomería SF **1** (*Arquit*) lead roofing
2 (*LAm*) (= *sistema*) plumbing; (= *taller*) plumber's workshop

plomero/a SM/F (*esp LAm*) plumber

plomífero* ADJ deadly boring

plomizo ADJ (*de plomo*) grey, gray (EEUU); [*cielo*] leaden (*liter*), grey, gray (EEUU)

plomo SM **1** (= *metal*) lead • **~ derretido** molten lead • **gasolina con ~** leaded petrol • **gasolina sin ~** unleaded petrol • **soldadito de ~** tin soldier • MODISMO: • **sacar ~ a algo** to make light of sth, play sth down
2 (= *plomada*) plumb line; [*de pesca*] weight, sinker • **a ~** true, vertical(ly); (*fig*) (= *justo*) just right • **caer a ~** to fall heavily *o* flat
3 (*Elec*) fuse • **se han fundido los ~s** the fuses have blown • **se le fundieron los ~s** (*Esp**) he blew his top*
4* (= *pesadez*) bore
5 (*esp LAm*) (= *bala*) bullet
6 (*Méx*) (= *tiroteo*) gunfight
ADJ **1** (*LAm*) (= *gris*) grey, gray (EEUU), lead-coloured, lead-colored (EEUU)
2 • **ponerse ~*** (= *enfadarse*) to dig one's heels in
3* (= *pesado*) boring, dull • **no seas ~** don't be such a bore

plomoso ADJ (*CAm*) boring

plotter ['ploter] SM (PL: **plotters** ['ploter]) (*Inform*) plotter

plugo, pluguiere *etc* ▸ **placer¹**

pluma SF **1** [*de ave*] feather; (*como adorno*) plume, feather • **colchón de ~s** feather bed • MODISMOS: • **hacer a ~ y a pelo** to be versatile, be ready to undertake anything • **tener ~** (*Esp*) to be camp
2 (*para escribir*) (*de metal, plástico*) pen; (*de ave*) quill • **y otras obras de su ~** and other works from his pen • **dejar correr la ~** to write spontaneously • MODISMO: • **escribir algo a vuela ~** to scribble sth down ▸ **pluma atómica** (*Méx*) ballpoint pen ▸ **pluma electrónica** light pen ▸ **pluma esferográfica** (*LAm*) ballpoint pen ▸ **pluma estilográfica**, **pluma fuente** fountain pen
3 (= *caligrafía*) penmanship, writing
4 (*Bádminton*) (= *volante*) shuttlecock
5 (*CAm*) (= *mentira*) fib, tale; (= *truco*) hoax
6 (*Cono Sur**) (= *puta*) prostitute
7 (*And, Caribe, Cono Sur*) (= *grifo*) tap, faucet (EEUU)
8 (*Cono Sur*) (= *grúa*) crane, derrick
9 (*Esp‡*) (= *peseta*) one peseta
10 (*Esp***) (= *pene*) prick**
11 (*Esp**) (= *periodista*) hack
SM (*Dep*) featherweight

plumada SF (= *plumazo*) stroke of the pen; (= *letra adornada*) flourish

plumado ADJ feathered

plumafuente SF (*LAm*) fountain pen

plumaje SM **1** (*Orn*) plumage, feathers (*pl*)
2 (= *adorno*) plume, crest
3 (= *penacho*) bunch of feathers

plumario/a SM/F (*CAm, Méx*) (= *periodista*) hack, journalist; (= *funcionario**) penpusher, pencilpusher (EEUU)

plumazo SM **1** (= *trazo fuerte*) stroke of the pen • **de un ~** with one stroke of the pen; (*Caribe*) in a jiffy* • **es un cuento que escribió de un ~** it's a story which she dashed off
2 (= *colchón*) feather mattress; (= *almohada*) feather pillow

plumbemia SF lead poisoning

plúmbeo ADJ **1** (= *de plomo*) lead (*antes de s*), leaden (*liter*)
2 (= *que pesa mucho*) weighty, heavy
3 (= *aburrido*) boring, dull

plúmbico ADJ plumbic

plumear ▸ CONJUG 1a VT (*CAm, Méx**) to write, scribble
VI **1** [*ave*] to hatch
2 (*Méx‡*) (= *ser prostituta*) to be on the game*

plumero SM **1** (*para limpiar*) feather duster
2 (= *adorno*) plume
3 (= *penacho*) bunch of feathers • MODISMO: • **se le ve el ~*** you can see what his game is*
4 (= *portaplumas*) penholder
5 (= *estuche*) pencil case
6 (*And*) (= *fontanero*) plumber
7 (*Cono Sur*) (= *borla*) powder puff
ADJ* (= *homosexual*) camp

plumier, plumiere SM pencil case

plumífero¹ SM quilted anorak

plumífero²/a SM/F (*hum*) (= *escritor*) hack; (= *periodista*) hack

plumilla SF nib
SMF (= *periodista*) hack journalist

plumín SM nib

plumista SMF clerk, scrivener

plumón SM **1** (*Orn*) down
2 (*para abrigar*) (= *abrigo*) quilted jacket; (= *edredón*) continental quilt, duvet, comforter (EEUU); (= *saco de dormir*) quilted sleeping bag
3 (*LAm*) (= *rotulador*) felt-tip pen

plumoso ADJ feathery, downy

plural ADJ **1** (*Ling*) plural
2 (*esp LAm*) (= *muchos*) many
SM plural • **en ~** in the plural

pluralidad SF **1** (= *diversidad*) plurality • **hay una alta ~ temática** there are many different themes
2 • **una ~ de** (= *varios*) a number of • **el asunto tiene ~ de aspectos** there are a number of sides to this question • **países con una ~ de culturas** countries with several cultures • **una ~ de ideas** diverse ideas, a variety of ideas
3 ▸ **pluralidad de votos** majority of votes

pluralismo SM pluralism

pluralista ADJ **1** (= *abierto*) pluralist, pluralistic
2 (= *polifacético*) many-sided, diverse
SMF pluralist

pluralización SF pluralization

pluralizar ▸ CONJUG 1f VT **1** (*Ling*) to pluralize
2 (= *generalizar*) to generalize

pluri... PREF pluri..., many ..., multi...

plurianual ADJ (= *de varios años*) lasting for several years; (= *largo*) long-term

pluricelular ADJ multicellular

pluricultural ADJ multicultural

pluridimensional ADJ multidimensional, multifaceted, many-sided

pluridisciplinar ADJ multidisciplinary

pluriempleado/a ADJ having more than one job
SM/F person with more than one job, moonlighter*

pluriempleo SM having more than one job, moonlighting*

plurifamiliar ADJ • **vivienda ~** multi-family housing unit

pluriforme ADJ very diverse, multifaceted

plurilingüe ADJ multilingual

plurilingüismo SM multilingualism

plurinacional ADJ • **estado ~** state consisting of several nationalities

pluripartidismo SM multi-party system

pluripartidista ADJ • **sistema ~** multi-party system

plurivalencia SF (= *valores*) many-sided value; (= *versatilidad*) versatility; (= *aplicaciones*) wide applicability

plurivalente ADJ (= *polivalente*) multivalent, having numerous values; (= *versátil*) versatile; (= *aplicable*) widely applicable

plus SM bonus • **con cinco dólares de ~** with a bonus of five dollars ▸ **plus de antigüedad** seniority bonus ▸ **plus de carestía de vida** cost-of-living bonus ▸ **plus de exclusividad** *bonus in return for working exclusively for one employer* ▸ **plus de nocturnidad** extra pay for unsocial hours ▸ **plus de peligrosidad** danger money ▸ **plus de productividad** productivity bonus ▸ **plus salarial** bonus

pluscafé SM (*LAm*) liqueur

pluscuamperfecto SM (*Ling*) pluperfect, past perfect

plusmarca SF record • **batir la ~** to break the record

plusmarquista SMF (= *poseedor*) record holder; (= *que mejora*) record-breaker; (= *ganador*) top scorer

plusvalía SF (*gen*) appreciation, added value; [*de capital*] capital gain • **impuesto sobre la ~** capital gains tax

Plutarco SM Plutarch

pluto‡ ADJ (*And*) drunk, sloshed*

plutocracia SF plutocracy

plutócrata SMF plutocrat

plutocrático ADJ plutocratic

Plutón SM Pluto

plutonio SM plutonium

pluvial ADJ rain (*antes de s*)

pluviometría SF rainfall, precipitation

pluviométrico ADJ rainfall (*antes de s*) • **media pluviométrica** average rainfall

pluviómetro SM rain gauge, pluviometer

pluviosidad SF rainfall

pluvioso ADJ rainy

pluviselva SF rainforest

PM ABR (= **Policía Militar**) MP

p.m. ABR **1** (= **post meridiem**) pm
2 = **por minuto**

pm. ABR = **próximo**

PMA SM ABR **1** (= **Programa Mundial de Alimentos**) WFP
2 (*Aut*) = **peso máximo autorizado**

p/mes ABR (= **por mes**) pcm

PMM SM ABR (= **parque móvil de ministerios**) *official government cars*

PN SMF ABR (*Esp*) = **profesor numerario/profesora numeraria**

PNB SM ABR (= **producto nacional bruto**) GNP

P.N.D. SM ABR (*Educ*) (= **personal no docente**) *non-teaching staff*

PNN SMF ABR (*Educ*) = **profesor(a) no numerario/a**

SM ABR (*Econ*) (= **producto nacional neto**) NNP

PNP SM ABR (*Puerto Rico*) = **Partido Nuevo Progresista**

PNR SM ABR (*Méx*) (*Hist*) = **Partido Nacional Revolucionario**

PNUD SM ABR (= **Programa de las Naciones Unidas para el Desarrollo**) UNDP

PNV SM ABR (*Esp*) (*Pol*) = **Partido Nacionalista Vasco**

P.° ABR (= **Paseo**) Ave., Av.

p.o. ABR = **por orden**

poblacho SM, **poblachón** SM dump, one-horse town

población SF **1** (= *gente*) population ▸ **población activa** working population ▸ **población flotante** floating population ▸ **población marginada** marginalized sectors of society (*pl*) • **el aumento de la ~ marginada** the increasing marginalization of society ▸ **población ocupada** working population ▸ **población pasiva** non-working population
2 (= *lugar habitado, ciudad*) town; (= *pueblo*) village; (*Cono Sur*) (= *caserío*) small hamlet
3 (= *acción*) settlement
4 (*Chile*) (*tb* **población callampa**) (= *suburbio*) shanty town; (= *barrio pobre*) slum area, poor quarter

poblacional ADJ population (*antes de s*) • **estudio ~** population study

poblada SF (*LAm††*) (= *revuelta*) rural revolt; (= *muchedumbre*) crowd

poblado ADJ **1** (= *habitado*) inhabited • **poco ~** sparsely populated • **densamente ~** densely populated • **la ciudad más poblada del país** the city with the largest population in the country
2 • **~ de** (= *habitado*) peopled *o* populated with; (= *lleno*) full of; (= *cubierto*) covered with
3 [*barba, cejas*] bushy, thick
SM (= *pueblo*) village; (= *población*) town; (= *lugar habitado*) settlement; (*Aut*) built-up area ▸ **poblado de absorción, poblado dirigido** new town, satellite town

poblador(a) SM/F **1** (= *colonizador*) settler, colonist; (= *fundador*) founder; (= *habitante*) inhabitant • **los primeros ~es** the first settlers
2 (*Chile*) slum dweller

poblano/a ADJ (*LAm*) village (*antes de s*), town (*antes de s*); (*Méx*) of/from Puebla
SM/F **1** (*LAm*) villager
2 (*Méx*) native/inhabitant of Puebla

poblar ▸ CONJUG 1l VT **1** [*colonos, conquistadores*] to settle, populate
2 [*animales, plantas*] inhabit • **los peces que pueblan las profundidades** the fish that inhabit the depths • **las estrellas que pueblan el espacio** the stars that fill space • **~ una colmena** (*Agr*) to stock a beehive
3 • **~ de algo: han poblado el río con varias especies de peces** they have stocked the river with various species of fish • **~on el monte de abetos** they planted the trees with fir trees
VPR **poblarse 1** (= *llenarse*) to fill (**de** with) • **la región se pobló en pocos años** the area was settled *o* populated in the space of a few years • **el centro de la ciudad se pobló de gente** the city centre filled up with people
2 (*Bot*) (= *cubrirse de hojas*) to come into leaf

pobo SM white poplar

pobre ADJ **1** [*persona, familia, barrio*] poor • **aquí vive gente muy ~** the people who live here are very poor
2 (= *escaso*) poor • **sus conocimientos de inglés son muy ~s** his knowledge of English is very poor • **una dieta ~ en vitaminas** a diet poor in vitamins
3 (*indicando compasión*) poor • **¡~ hombre!** poor man!, poor fellow! • **¡~ Francisco!** poor old Francisco! • **¡~ de mí!** poor me! • **¡~ de él!** poor man!, poor fellow! • **¡~ de ti si te pillo!** you'll be sorry if I catch you! • **~ diablo** poor wretch, poor devil
SMF **1** (= *necesitado*) poor person; (= *mendigo*) beggar • **un ~** a poor man • **los ~s** the poor, poor people • **un ~ pedía dinero** a beggar *o* poor man was asking for money
2 (*indicando compasión*) poor thing • **la ~ estaba mojada** the poor thing was wet through

pobrecillo/a SM/F poor thing

pobremente ADV poorly

pobrería SF (*Cono Sur*), **pobrerío** SM (*Cono Sur*) the poor, poor people

pobrete/a SM/F poor thing, poor wretch
ADJ poor, wretched

pobretería SF **1** (= *los pobres*) the poor, poor people
2 (= *pobreza*) poverty
3 (= *tacañería*) miserliness, meanness

pobretón/ona ADJ very poor, terribly poor
SM/F poor man/woman

pobreza SF **1** (= *falta de dinero*) poverty • **vivían en la más absoluta ~** they lived in abject poverty • REFRÁN: • **~ no es vileza** poverty is not a crime
2 (= *escasez*) • **nos sorprendió la ~ de su razonamiento** we were surprised by the poverty of his arguments • **~ de vocabulario** poverty of vocabulary
3 (*Rel*) • **voto de ~** vow of poverty

poca SM (*LAm*), **pócar** SM (*Méx*) poker

pocero SM well-digger

pocerón SM (*CAm, Méx*) large pool

pocha¹ SF (*Culin*) haricot bean

pocha² SF (*Cono Sur*) (= *mentira*) lie; (= *trampa*) trick

pochar, pochear ▸ CONJUG 1a VT (*Culin*) to fry lightly

pochismo* SM (*Méx*) (*Ling*) *incorrect use of language caused by interference from American English*

pocho/a ADJ **1** (= *estropeado*) [*flor*] withered; [*persona*] peaky*, off-colour*, off-color (*EEUU**); [*fruta*] soft, overripe
2 [*color*] faded
3 (= *deprimido*) depressed, gloomy
4 (*Cono Sur*) (= *gordito*) chubby; (= *bajo*) squat
SM/F (*Méx*) *United States national of Mexican origin*, Mexican-American

pochoclo SM (*Arg*) popcorn

pocholada* SF nice thing, pretty thing • **es una ~** it's lovely • **una ~ de niño** a sweet *o* cute little baby

pocholez* SF gem, treasure • **el vestido es una ~** it's a gorgeous dress

pocholo/a* ADJ nice, cute
SM/F pretty boy/pretty girl; (*en oración directa*) my little angel, my poppet

pocilga SF **1** (= *porqueriza*) pigsty, pigpen (*EEUU*)
2 (= *lugar asqueroso*) pigsty, pigpen (*EEUU*)

pocillo SM **1** (= *tazón*) mug
2 (= *cuenco*) (small) bowl, (small) dish
3 (*LAm*) [*de café*] coffee cup
4 (*Méx*) (= *jarra*) [*de cerveza*] tankard

pócima SF, **poción** SF **1** (*Farm*) potion, draught, draft (*EEUU*)
2 (*Vet*) drench; (= *brebaje*) concoction

poco ADJ **1** (*en singular*) little, not much • **tenemos ~ tiempo** we have little time, we don't have much time • **hay muy ~ queso** there's very little cheese, there's hardly any cheese • **de ~ interés** of little interest • **con ~ respeto** with little respect, with scant respect • **el provecho es ~** the gain is small, there isn't much to gain • **poca cosa**: • **no te preocupes por tan poca cosa** don't worry about such a little thing • **poca cosa se podría haber hecho** there wasn't much we could have done • **comemos, jugamos a cartas, leemos y poca cosa más** we eat, play cards, read and do little else *o* and that's about it • **es poca cosa** (= *no mucho*) it's not much; (= *no importante*) it's nothing much • **somos tan poca cosa** we're so insignificant • **es muy guapa pero poca cosa** she's very pretty, but there isn't much to her • **y por si fuera ~** and as if that weren't enough, and to cap it all
2 (*en plural*) few, not many • **~s niños saben que ...** few *o* not many children know that ... • **tiene ~s amigos** he has few friends, he hasn't got many friends • **~s días después** a few days later • **compré unos ~s libros** I bought a few books • **me quedan pocas probabilidades** I don't have much chance • **todas las medidas son pocas** no measure will be enough
PRON **1** (*en singular*) **a** (= *poca cosa*) • **la reforma servirá para ~** the reform won't do much good *o* won't be much use • **una hora da para ~** you can't get much done in an hour • **con lo ~ que me quedaba** with what little I had left • **ya sabes lo ~ que me interesa** you know how little it interests me
b • **un ~** a bit, a little • **—¿tienes frío? —un ~** "are you cold?" — "a bit *o* a little" • **he bebido un ~, pero no estoy borracho** I've had a bit to drink, but I'm not drunk • **voy a dormir un ~** I am going to have a little sleep • **le conocía un ~** I knew him a bit *o* slightly • **necesito descansar un ~** I need to rest for a while • **espera un ~** wait a minute *o* moment • **estoy un ~ triste** I am rather *o* a little sad • **es un ~ lo que yo comentaba** that's more or less what I was saying • **un ~ como**: • **es un ~ como su padre** he's rather *o* a bit like his father • **lo hice un ~ como protesta** I did it partly as a protest • **un ~ de**: • **un ~ de dinero** a little money • **dame un ~ de vino** can I have some wine? • **¡un ~ de silencio!** let's have some quiet here!
c (*referido a tiempo*) not long • **tardaron ~ en hacerlo** it didn't take them long to do it, they didn't take long to do it • **lleva ~ trabajando aquí** he hasn't been working here long • **a ~ de** shortly after • **a ~ de haberlo firmado** shortly after signing it • **cada ~** every so often • **dentro de ~** shortly, soon • **~ después** shortly after • **hace ~** not long ago • **fuimos a verla hace ~** we visited her not long ago, we visited her quite recently • **tu hermana ha llamado hace ~** your sister called a short while ago • **la conozco desde hace ~** I haven't known her long, I've only known her for a short while • **hasta hace ~** until recently
2 (*en plural*) few • **~s son los que ...** there are few who ... • **ya somos ~s los que nos sentimos así** there are now very few of us who feel this way • **~s de entre ellos** few of them • MODISMO: • **como hay ~s**: • **es tonto como hay ~s** he's as stupid as they come
ADV **1** (*con verbos*) not much, little • **cuesta ~** it doesn't cost much, it costs very little • **habla ~** he doesn't say much • **ahora trabaja ~** he doesn't work much now • **vamos ~ a Madrid** we don't go to Madrid

much, we hardly ever go to Madrid • **lo estiman ~** they hardly value it at all, they value it very little
2 (*con adjetivos: se traduce a menudo por medio de un prefijo*) • **~ dispuesto a ayudar** disinclined to help • **~ amable** unkind • **~ probable** unlikely • **~ inteligente** unintelligent, not very intelligent • **sus libros son ~ conocidos aquí** his books are not very well known here
3 (*otras locuciones*) • **~ a ~** little by little • **¡~ a ~!** steady on!, easy does it! • **a ~** (*Méx**) • **¿a ~?** never!, you don't say! • **¡a ~ no!** not much!* • **¿a ~ no?** (well) isn't it? • **¿a ~ crees que ...?** do you really imagine that ...? • **de a ~** (*LAm*) gradually • **tener en ~**: • **tiene en ~ a su jefe** she doesn't think much of her boss • **tiene la vida en ~** he doesn't value his life • **~ más o menos** more or less • **por ~** almost, nearly • **por ~ me ahogo** I almost *o* nearly drowned • **a ~ que**: • **a ~ que pueda** if at all possible • **a ~ que corras, lo alcanzas** if you run now you'll catch it

poda SF **1** (= *acto*) pruning
2 (= *temporada*) pruning season

podadera SF (= *cuchillo*) pruning knife, billhook; (= *tijera*) pruning shears (*pl*); (*de tipo yunque*) secateurs (*pl*)

podadora SF (*Méx*) lawnmower

podar ▷ CONJUG 1a VT **1** [+ *árbol*] to lop, prune; [+ *rama*] to lop, trim, trim off; [+ *rosal*] to prune
2 (= *acortar*) [+ *texto*] to prune; [+ *pasaje, parte*] to cut out

podcast SM (PL: **podcasts**) podcast

podenco SM hound

poder

VERBO AUXILIAR
VERBO INTRANSITIVO
VERBO IMPERSONAL
SUSTANTIVO MASCULINO

▷ CONJUG 2S

VERBO AUXILIAR

1 (= *tener la posibilidad o capacidad de*) • **yo puedo ayudarte** I can help you • **puedo hacerlo solo** I can do it on my own *o* by myself • **¿se puede llamar por teléfono desde aquí?** can you phone from here? • **no puede venir** he can't *o* cannot come • **llevo varios días sin ~ salir** I haven't been able to go out for several days • **no ha podido venir** he couldn't come, he was unable to come • **creo que mañana no voy a ~ ir** I don't think I'll be able to come tomorrow • **este agua no se puede beber** this water isn't fit to drink

2 (= *tener permiso para*) • **puedes irte** you can *o* may go • **¿puedo usar tu teléfono?** can *o* may I use your phone? • **¿puedo abrir la ventana?** can *o* may I open the window? • **aquí no se puede fumar** you aren't allowed to smoke here, you can't smoke here

3 (*en peticiones*) • **¿puedes/puede darme un vaso de agua?** can I/may I have a glass of water please? • **¿me puede usted decir cuándo sale el autobús?** can *o* could you tell me when the bus leaves?

4 (*indicando eventualidad*) • **puede** *o* **podría estar en cualquier sitio** it could *o* might be anywhere • **¡cuidado, te puedes hacer daño!** careful, you could *o* might hurt yourself! • **podías haberte roto una pierna** you could *o* might have broken your leg • **puede haber salido** he may have gone out • **por lo que pueda pasar** just in case

5 (*indicando obligación moral*) • **¡no pueden tratarnos así!** they can't treat us like this! • **bien podrían cuidarla un poco mejor** they really ought to take better care of her • **es lo menos que podemos hacer por ellos** it's the least we can do for them • **no podíamos dejarlo solo** we couldn't leave him alone

6 (*en cálculos, aproximaciones*) • **¿qué edad puede tener?** I wonder what age he is?, how old do you reckon he is? • **puede costar unos cien euros** it could cost as much as a hundred euros

7 (*en sugerencias*) • **podríamos ir al cine** we could go to the cinema • **siempre puedes volverlo a intentar** you can always try again later

8 (*en reproches*) • **¡podías habérmelo dicho!** you could *o* might have told me! • **habría podido ser más amable** she could *o* might have been a bit nicer • **¡al menos podrías disculparte!** you could at least say sorry!

VERBO INTRANSITIVO

1 (= *tener la posibilidad o capacidad*) • **no puedo** I can't • **lo haré si puedo** I'll do it if I can • **¡no puedo más!** (= *estoy agotado*) I can't go on!; (= *estoy desesperado*) I can't cope any more!; (= *he comido mucho*) I can't eat another thing!

2 (= *tener permiso*) • **¿se puede?** may I come in? • **¿puedo?** may I?

3 (= *tener dominio, influencia*) • **los que pueden** those who can, those who are able • **el dinero puede mucho** money can do almost anything, money talks • **la curiosidad pudo más que el temor** his curiosity got the better of his fear • **él puede mucho en el partido** he has a lot of influence in the party • **~ a algn: yo le puedo** I'm a match for him; (*entre niños*) I could have him* **poder con** • **¿puedes con la maleta?** can you manage the suitcase? • **no puedo con él** (= *no puedo controlarle*) I can't handle him; (= *pesa mucho*) he's too heavy for me • **no puedo con la hipocresía** I can't stand hypocrisy

4 (*en locuciones*) • **a más no ~**: • **es tonto a más no ~** he's as stupid as they come • **su actuación fue correcta a más no ~** he behaved entirely properly • **comió a más no ~** he ate until he couldn't eat any more • **no ~ por menos que**: • **no pude por menos que decirle lo que pensaba de él** I just had to tell him what I thought of him

5 (*CAm, Méx*)* (= *molestar*) (*con irritación*) to annoy; (*con disgusto*) to upset • **su actitud me pudo** his attitude annoyed me *o* got on my nerves • **me pudo esa broma** that joke upset me

VERBO IMPERSONAL

puede (ser) (= *es posible*) maybe, it may be so, perhaps • **¡no puede ser!** that can't be!, that's impossible!
puede (ser) que (+ *subjun*) • **puede (ser) que esté en la biblioteca** he could *o* may be in the library, perhaps he's in the library • **puede (ser) que tenga uno ya** he may *o* might have one already • **puede (ser) que no venga** he may *o* might not come • **puede (ser) que tenga razón** she may *o* could be right • **puede (ser) que sí** maybe (so)

SUSTANTIVO MASCULINO

1 (= *capacidad, facultad*) power • **tiene un enorme ~ de concentración** she has tremendous powers of concentration • **afirma tener ~es mágicos** he claims to have magic powers ▸ **poder adquisitivo** purchasing power ▸ **poder de convocatoria** • **tienen un gran ~ de convocatoria** they really pull in the crowds, they're real crowd-pullers* ▸ **poder de negociación** bargaining power

2 (= *autoridad, influencia*) power • **ejercen un ~ enorme sobre la juventud** they have a lot of power *o* influence over young people • **en este país los militares tienen mucho ~** the military are very powerful in this country • **no tienen ~ para oponerse a estas medidas** they are not powerful enough to oppose these measures • **un partido jugado de ~ a ~** an evenly-matched game

3 (*Pol*) • **el ~** power • **¡el pueblo al ~!** power to the people! • **¡Herrera al ~!** Herrera for leader! • **bajo el ~ de algn**: • **estar en el ~** • **ocupar el ~** to be in power • **subir al ~** to come to power • **el ~ central** central government • **el cuarto ~** the fourth estate • **el ~ establecido** the establishment • **los ~es fácticos** the powers that be • **los ~es públicos** the authorities ▸ **poder absoluto** absolute power ▸ **poder civil** civil power ▸ **poder ejecutivo** executive power ▸ **poder judicial** judiciary ▸ **poder legislativo** legislative power

4 (= *fuerza, eficacia*) • **un detergente de gran ~ limpiador** a powerful detergent • **este medicamento no tiene ~ contra la tuberculosis** this drug is ineffective *o* isn't effective against tuberculosis

5 (= *potestad*) **poderes** powers • **les dieron amplios ~es para dirigir la empresa** they were given wide-ranging powers to run the company • **tiene plenos ~es para intervenir en el asunto** he has full authority to intervene in the matter

6 (*Jur*) • **por ~es** *o* (*LAm*) **poder** by proxy • **casarse por ~es** to get married by proxy ▸ **poder notarial** power of attorney

7 (= *posesión*) possession • **tengo en mi ~ información confidencial** I am in possession of confidential information • **estar** *u* **obrar en ~ de algn** to be in sb's hands *o* possession • **esa información está** *u* **obra en ~ de la juez** that information is in the hands of the judge, that information is in the judge's possession • **pasar a ~ de algn** to pass to sb, pass into sb's possession

8 (*Fís, Mec*) power • **el ~ del motor** the power of the engine ▸ **poder calorífico** calorific value

9 (*LAm*) (= *persona*) drug pusher

poderhabiente SMF proxy, attorney (*EEUU*)

poderío SM **1** (= *poder*) power; (= *fuerza*) might; (= *señorío*) authority, jurisdiction
2 (*Econ*) wealth

poderosamente ADV powerfully

poderoso ADJ powerful • REFRÁN: • **~ caballero es don dinero** money talks
SMPL • **los ~s** (= *dirigentes*) the people in power; (= *ricos*) the rich and powerful

podiatría SF podiatry

podio SM (= *estrado*) podium; (*Méx*) rostrum • **subir al ~** (*Dep*) to mount the winners' podium • **estar en el ~ de la actualidad** to be in the limelight

pódium SM (PL: **pódiums**) = podio

podología SF chiropody, podiatry (*EEUU*)

podólogo/a SM/F chiropodist, podiatrist (*EEUU*)

podómetro SM pedometer

podón SM billhook

podre SF pus

podredumbre SF **1** (= *cualidad*) rottenness, putrefaction; (= *parte podrida*) rot
2 (= *corrupción*) rottenness, corruption
3 (*Enología*) ▸ **podredumbre noble** noble rot
4 (= *tristeza*) secret sorrow, secret sadness
5 (*Med*) pus

podrida SF • **armar la ~** (*Cono Sur**) to start a fight

podrido ADJ **1** (*putrefacto*) rotten
2 (= *corrupto*) rotten, corrupt • **el sistema está ~ por dentro** there is corruption inside the system • **están ~s de dinero*** they're filthy rich*
3 (*Cono Sur**) (= *harto*) fed-up*

P

podrir ▸ CONJUG 3a = pudrir
poema SM poem • **MODISMO**: • **ser todo un ~** to be quite a sight, be just like a fairy tale; (*pey*) to be a complete farce
poemario SM book of poems
poemático ADJ poetic
poesía SF **1** (= *arte*) poetry • **la ~ del Siglo de Oro** Golden Age poetry
2 (= *poema*) poem
3 (= *encanto*) poetry
poeta SMF **1** (= *compositor de versos*) poet
2 (*LAm*) (= *escritor*) writer, author
poetastro SM poetaster
poética SF poetics (*sing*), art of poetry
poéticamente ADV poetically
poético ADJ poetic, poetical
poetisa SF poetess, woman poet
poetizar ▸ CONJUG 1f VT **1** [+ *texto*] to poeticize, put into poetry
2 (= *idealizar*) to idealize
VI to write poetry
pogrom SM, **pogromo** SM pogrom
póker SM poker
polaca SF (*And, Cono Sur*) (= *blusa*) smock
polaco¹/a ADJ (= *de Polonia*) Polish
SM/F Pole
SM **1** (*Ling*) Polish
2 (*CAm*) (= *policía*) cop*
polaco²/a (*pey*) ADJ, SM/F Catalan
polaina SF **1** (= *sobrecalza*) leggings (*pl*)
2 (*And, CAm, Cono Sur*) (= *molestia*) nuisance; (= *chasco*) setback
polar ADJ polar
polaridad SF polarity
polarización SF polarization
polarizado ADJ polarized
SM polarizing
polarizar ▸ CONJUG 1f VT to polarize
VPR **polarizarse** to polarize, become polarized (**en torno a** around)
polca SF **1** (*Mús*) polka
2* (= *jaleo*) fuss, to-do*
3 (*And*) (= *blusa*) blouse
4 (*And, Cono Sur*) (= *chaqueta*) long jacket
polcata* SF row, shindy*
pólder SM (PL: **pólders**) polder
pole SF pole (position)
polea SF pulley; (*Aut*) fan belt; (*Náut*) tackle, tackle block
poleada SF (*CAm*) *hot drink made of milk and flour*
polémica SF **1** (= *discusión*) controversy
2 (= *género*) polemics (*sing*)
polémico ADJ controversial, polemical (*frm*)
polemista SMF polemicist • **un brillante ~** a brilliant polemicist
polemizar ▸ CONJUG 1f VI to argue (**en torno a** about) • **se ha polemizado mucho en torno al tema** the matter has been the subject of much controversy • **no quiero ~** I have no wish to get involved in an argument • **~ con algn en la prensa** to have a debate with sb in the press
polemología SF war studies (*pl*)
polen SM pollen
polenta SF **1** (*And, Cono Sur*) (= *maicena*) cornflour, cornstarch (*EEUU*); (= *sémola de maíz*) ground maize, polenta
2 • **tener ~** (= *entusiasmo*) to be enthusiastic; (= *calidad*) to be first-rate
poleo SM pennyroyal
polera SF **1** (*Chile*) (= *camiseta*) T-shirt
2 (*Cono Sur*) (= *jersey*) polo neck
poli* SM/F cop*
SF • **la ~** the cops* (*pl*)
poli... PREF poly-
poliamida SM polyamide
poliandria SF polyandry
poliándrico ADJ polyandrous
polibán SM hip-bath
Polichinela SM Punch
policía SMF policeman/policewoman, police officer ▸ **policía de paisano** plain-clothes policeman ▸ **policía de tránsito** (*LAm*) traffic police ▸ **policía informático/a** *police officer specializing in computer crime* ▸ **policía local, policía municipal** local policeman/policewoman
SM ▸ **policía acostado** (*Ven*) (*Aut**) speed bump, sleeping policeman
SF (= *organización*) police • **¡llama a la ~!** call the police! • **Cuerpo Nacional de Policía** (*Esp*) ≈ the Police Force ▸ **policía antidisturbios** riot police ▸ **policía autonómica** *police force of a regional autonomy* ▸ **policía de barrio** community police ▸ **Policía de Tráfico** traffic police ▸ **Policía Local** Local Police ▸ **Policía Militar** military police ▸ **Policía Montada** mounted police ▸ **Policía Municipal** local police ▸ **Policía Nacional** national police ▸ **Policía Secreta** secret police

> **POLICÍA**
> In Spain the **policía nacional** is the force in charge of national security and general public order while the **policía municipal** deals with regulating traffic and policing the local community. The Basque Country and Catalonia also have their own police forces, the **Ertzaintza** and the **Mossos d'Esquadra** respectively. In rural areas it is the **Guardia Civil** that is responsible for policing duties.
> ▸ **GUARDIA CIVIL, ERTZAINTZA**

policiaco ADJ, **policíaco** ADJ police (*antes de s*) • **novela policíaca** detective story
policial ADJ police (*antes de s*)
SM (*CAm*) policeman
policivo ADJ (*Col*) police (*antes de s*)
policlínica SF, **policlínico** SM (*tb* **hospital policlínico**) general hospital
policromado ADJ polychrome
SM polychrome painting
policromo ADJ, **polícromo** ADJ polychromatic, polychrome
polideportivo SM sports centre, sports center (*EEUU*)
poliducto SM (*Perú, Ven*) oil pipeline
poliedro SM polyhedron
poliéster SM polyester
poliestireno SM polystyrene
polietileno SM polythene, polyethylene (*EEUU*)
polifacético ADJ multi-faceted, versatile
polifacetismo SM many-sidedness, versatility
Polifemo SM Polyphemus
polifonía SF polyphony
polifónico ADJ polyphonic
polifuncional ADJ multi-purpose, multi-functional
poligamia SF polygamy
polígamo ADJ polygamous
SM polygamist
poligénesis SF INV polygenesis
políglota ADJ, SMF, **poliglota** ADJ, SMF polyglot
polígloto/a ADJ, SM/F, **poligloto/a** ADJ, SM/F polyglot
poligonal ADJ polygonal
polígono SM **1** (*Mat*) polygon
2 (= *terreno*) building lot ▸ **polígono de descongestión** overspill area ▸ **polígono de ensayos** test site, testing ground ▸ **polígono de tiro** shooting range; (*Mil*) firing range, artillery range ▸ **polígono industrial** industrial estate ▸ **polígono residencial** housing estate
polígrafo/a SM/F writer on a wide variety of subjects
poliinsaturado ADJ polyunsaturated
SM polyunsaturate
polilla SF (= *mariposa*) moth; (= *oruga*) grub; [*de la ropa*] clothes moth; [*de la madera*] woodworm; [*de libros*] bookworm
polímata SMF polymath
polimerización SF polymerization
polímero SM polymer
poli-mili SMF (*Esp*) (*Hist*) *member of the political-military wing of ETA*
polimorfismo SM polymorphism
polimorfo ADJ polymorphic
Polinesia SF Polynesia
polinesio/a ADJ, SM/F Polynesian
polínico ADJ pollen (*antes de s*)
polinización SF pollination ▸ **polinización cruzada** cross-pollination
polinizar ▸ CONJUG 1f VT to pollinate
polinomio SM (*Mat*) polynomial
polinosis SF INV hay fever
polio SF polio
poliomielitis SF INV poliomyelitis
polipiel® SF imitation leather
pólipo SM polyp, polypus
polipropileno SM polypropylene
Polisario SM ABR (*tb* **El Frente Polisario**) = **Frente Popular de Liberación del Sáhara y Río de Oro**
polisemia SF polysemy
polisémico ADJ polysemic
polisílabo ADJ polysyllabic
SM polysyllable
polisón SM **1** (= *armazón*) bustle
2* (= *trasero*) bottom
polista SMF polo player
politécnica SF ≈ technical college
politécnico ADJ polytechnic • **universidad politécnica** polytechnic
politeísmo SM polytheism
politeísta ADJ polytheistic
politene SM, **politeno** SM polythene, polyethylene (*EEUU*)
política SF **1** (*Pol*) politics (*sing*) • **meterse en (la) ~** to get involved in politics • **la ~ en la posguerra** postwar politics ▸ **política de pasillo(s)** lobbying
2 (= *programa*) policy ▸ **política agraria** agricultural policy ▸ **política de cañonera** gunboat diplomacy ▸ **política de ingresos y precios, política de jornales y precios** prices and incomes policy ▸ **política de mano dura** strong-arm policy, tough policy ▸ **política de silla vacía** empty-chair policy, refusal to take one's seat (in parliament) ▸ **política de tierra quemada** scorched earth policy ▸ **política económica** economic policy ▸ **política exterior** foreign policy ▸ **política interior** [*de país*] domestic policy; [*de organización*] internal politics ▸ **política presupuestaria** budget policy ▸ **política salarial** incomes policy
3 (= *tacto*) tact, skill; (= *cortesía*) politeness, courtesy; (= *educación*) good manners (*pl*)
políticamente ADV politically • **~ correcto** politically correct
politicastro/a SM/F (*pey*) politico* (*pey*)
político/a ADJ **1** (*Pol*) political
2 [*persona*] (= *diplomático*) tactful; (= *hábil*) skilful, skillful (*EEUU*); (= *cortés*) polite, well-mannered; (= *reservado*) stiff, reserved
3 [*pariente*] • **padre ~** father-in-law • **es tío ~ mío** he's an uncle of mine by marriage • **familia política** in-laws (*pl*)
SM/F politician ▸ **político/a de café** armchair politician
politicón* ADJ **1** (*Pol*) strongly political, keenly interested in politics
2 (= *ceremonioso*) very ceremonious, obsequious
politiquear ▸ CONJUG 1a VI (= *actuar*) to play

at politics, dabble in politics; (= *hablar*) to talk politics

politiqueo SM, **politiquería** SF (*pey*) political manoeuvring *o* (*EEUU*) maneuvering

politiquero/a SM/F (*pey*) political intriguer

politiqués SM political jargon

politiquillo/a SM/F minor politician

politización SF politicization

politizado ADJ politicized • **tiene un trabajo muy ~** he has a politically sensitive job

politizar ▷ CONJUG 1f VT to politicize

politología SF political science, study of politics

politólogo/a SM/F political scientist, political expert

politono SM (*Telec*) polyphonic ringtone, polytone

politoxicomanía SF multiple drug-addiction

politraumatismo SM multiple injuries (*pl*)

poliuretano SM polyurethane

polivalente ADJ **1** (*Quím, Med*) polyvalent
2 (= *versátil*) (*gen*) multi-purpose; [*avión*] multi-role
3 (= *con varios aspectos*) multi-faceted, many-sided

polivinilo SM polyvinyl

póliza SF **1** (*Com*) (= *certificado*) certificate, voucher; (= *giro*) draft • **pagar una ~** to pay out on an insurance policy ▸ **póliza de seguro(s)** insurance policy ▸ **póliza dotal** endowment policy
2 (= *impuesto*) tax stamp, fiscal stamp

polizón SM **1** (*Aer, Náut*) stowaway • **viajar de ~** to stow away (**en** on)
2 (= *vago*) tramp, vagrant, bum (*EEUU*)

polizonte‡ SM cop*

polla SF **1** (*Orn*) pullet; (= *polluelo*) chick ▸ **polla de agua** moorhen
2** (= *pene*) prick** • **MODISMOS:** • **¡una ~!** get away!* • **¡ni qué ~s!** no way!* • **¿qué ~s quieres?** what the hell do you want?* • **¡qué duquesa ni que ~s en vinagre!** duchess my arse!** • **dejarse de ~s** to stop farting about‡
3 (*LAm*) (*Naipes*) stakes (*pl*), pool
4 (*Cono Sur*) (= *lotería*) lottery

pollaboba‡ SM berk*, wimp*

pollada SF brood

pollastre* SM = pollo

pollastro* SM, **pollastrón*** SM sly fellow

pollera SF **1** (*para pollos*) (= *criadero*) hencoop, chicken run; (= *cesto*) basket for chickens
2 (*LAm*) (= *falda*) skirt, overskirt
3 (*Cono Sur*) (*Rel*) soutane
4 (= *aparato*) walker; ▷ **pollero**

pollería SF poulterer's (shop)

pollero/a SM/F **1** (= *criador*) chicken farmer; (= *vendedor*) poulterer
2 (*LAm*) (= *jugador*) gambler
3 (*Méx**) (= *guía*) *guide for illegal immigrants to USA*; ▷ **pollera**

pollerudo ADJ (*Cono Sur*) **1** (= *cobarde*) cowardly
2 (= *chismoso*) backbiting, gossipy
3 (= *santurrón*) self-righteous, sanctimonious

pollino/a SM/F **1** (= *burro*) donkey
2* (= *persona*) ass*, idiot

pollita* SF **1** (= *gallina*) young pullet
2 (= *chica*) bird*, chick (*EEUU**) • **ya está hecha una ~*** she's turned into quite a good-looking chick‡
3 • **MODISMO:** • **echar ~s** to tell lies

pollito SM **1** (*Orn*) chick ▸ **pollito de un día** day-old chick
2* = **pollo**

pollo SM **1** (*Orn*) (= *adulto*) chicken; (= *cría*) chick; (*Culin*) chicken • **~ asado** *o* (*LAm*) **rostizado** roast chicken • **MODISMOS:** • **echarse el ~** (*Cono Sur*) to pack up and go • **¡qué duquesa ni qué ~s en vinagre!*** duchess my foot!* • **¡ni eso ni ~s en vinagre!*** no way!* • **montar un ~** to make a fuss, make a scene ▸ **pollo de corral** free-range chicken ▸ **pollo de granja** broiler chicken
2 (*Pol*) *torture where the victim is suspended from a pole or spit*
3* (= *joven*) young lad • **¿quién es ese ~?** who's that young lad?* • **es un ~ nada más** he's only a kid* ▸ **pollo pera*** (= *pijo*) rich kid; (= *chanchullero*) spiv*, flash Harry*
4 (*Esp*‡) (= *esputo*) gob* • **soltar un ~** to gob*
5 (*Méx**) (= *emigrante*) *would-be immigrant to USA from Mexico*

polluelo SM chick

polo¹ SM **1** (*Geog*) pole • **de ~ a ~** from pole to pole ▸ **polo magnético** magnetic pole ▸ **Polo Norte** North Pole ▸ **Polo Sur** South Pole
2 (*Elec*) [*de imán*] pole; [*de enchufe*] pin • **una clavija de cuatro ~s** a four-pin plug ▸ **polo negativo** negative pole ▸ **polo positivo** positive pole
3 (= *centro*) centre, center (*EEUU*), focus ▸ **polo de atracción** centre *o* (*EEUU*) center of attraction ▸ **polo de desarrollo, polo de promoción** (*Com*) development area
4 (= *extremo*) • **los dos generales son ~s opuestos** the two generals are poles apart • **esto es el ~ opuesto de lo que dijo antes** this is the exact opposite of what he said before ▸ **polo de referencia** point of reference
5 (*para comer*) ice lolly, Popsicle® (*EEUU*)

polo² SM (*Dep*) polo ▸ **polo acuático** water polo

polo³ SM (= *jersey*) polo-neck; (= *camisa*) polo shirt

polola SF (*Cono Sur*) (= *coqueta*) flirt; (= *amiga*) girlfriend; ▷ **pololo**

pololear ▷ CONJUG 1a (*Chile**) VI **1** (= *salir*) to go out • **~ con algn** to be going out with sb, be dating sb*
2 (= *coquetear*) to flirt (**con** with)
VT **1** (= *pretender*) to court
2 (= *coquetear con*) to flirt with

pololeo* SM (*Chile*) **1** [*de novios*] dating*
2 [*de pretendiente*] courting
3 (= *coqueteo*) flirting

pololito* SM (*Chile*) odd job, casual job

pololo/a (*Chile*) SM/F* boyfriend/girlfriend; ▷ **polola**
SM **1** (= *insecto*) moth
2 (= *pesado*) bore
3 (= *coqueto*) flirt
4 (= *pretendiente*) (persistent) suitor
5 (= *chulo*) pimp

polonesa SF polonaise

Polonia SF Poland

poltergeist SM INV poltergeist

poltrón ADJ idle, lazy

poltrona SF **1** (= *butaca*) easy chair
2 (*pey*) (= *cargo*) • **abandonar la ~ ministerial** to resign one's post as minister • **pasó demasiado tiempo en la ~** he spent too long in power *o* office

poltronear ▷ CONJUG 1a VI (*Cono Sur, Méx*) to laze around, loaf around

polución SF **1** (= *contaminación*) pollution ▸ **polución ambiental** environmental pollution ▸ **polución de la atmósfera** air pollution
2 [*de semen*] ▸ **polución nocturna** nocturnal emission (*frm*), wet dream

polucionante ADJ polluting

polucionar ▷ CONJUG 1a VT to pollute

polvareda SF **1** (= *polvo*) cloud of dust
2 (= *jaleo*) fuss, rumpus* • **levantar una ~** to create a storm, cause a rumpus*, kick up a fuss*

polvera SF **1** (= *estuche*) powder compact
2 (*Méx*) cloud of dust

polvero SM **1** (*LAm*) cloud of dust
2 (*CAm*) (= *pañuelo*) handkerchief

polvete** SM = polvo

polvillo SM **1** (*LAm*) (*Agr*) blight
2 (*And, Cono Sur*) [*de tabaco*] *tobacco refuse*
3 (*CAm*) (= *cuero*) *leather for shoemaking*
4 (*And*) [*de arroz*] rice bran

polvo SM **1** (*en el aire*) dust • **lleno de ~** dusty • **limpiar** *o* **quitar el ~** to dust • **MODISMOS:** • **hacer algo ~*** to ruin sth • **hacer ~ a algn*** (= *agotar*) to wear sb out; (= *deprimir*) to depress sb; (*en discusión*) to wipe the floor with sb* • **hecho ~*:** • **estoy hecho ~** (= *cansado*) I'm shattered*, I'm knackered‡; (= *deprimido*) I feel really down • **el coche está hecho ~** the car is a wreck • **el libro está hecho ~** the book is falling to pieces • **limpio de ~ y paja:** • **ganó 50 millones, limpios de ~ y paja** he won 50 million in his hand • **matar el ~** to lay the dust • **hacer morder el ~ a algn** to humiliate sb • **sacudir el ~ a algn** to thrash sb, beat sb up* • **REFRÁN:** • **aquellos ~s traen estos lodos** such are the consequences ▸ **polvo espacial** space dust
2 (*Quím, Culin, Med*) powder; [*de tocador*] face powder • **ponerse ~s** to powder one's face • **en ~** [*leche, canela, cocaína*] powdered • **solo se encuentra en ~** it's only available in powdered form ▸ **polvos de arroz** rice powder (*sing*) ▸ **polvos de blanqueo** bleaching powder (*sing*) ▸ **polvos de chile** chilli powder (*sing*) ▸ **polvo(s) de hornear, polvo(s) de levadura** baking powder (*sing*) ▸ **polvo dentífrico** tooth powder (*sing*) ▸ **polvos de picapica** itching powder (*sing*) ▸ **polvos de talco** talcum powder (*sing*) ▸ **polvos para dientes** tooth powder (*sing*)
3‡ (= *droga*) snow‡, coke*
4 (= *porción*) pinch • **un ~ de rapé** a pinch of snuff
5** screw**, shag** • **echar un ~** to have a screw *o* shag** • **está para un buen ~** she's hot stuff‡

pólvora SF **1** (= *explosivo*) gunpowder • **MODISMOS:** • **no ha descubierto** *o* **inventado la ~** it's not as if he's done anything amazingly original • **gastar la ~ en salvas** (= *desperdiciar*) to waste time and energy; (= *hacer gestos inútiles*) to make empty gestures; (= *hacer aspavientos*) to make a great song and dance • **levantar ~** to create *o* make a stir • **oler a ~** to smell fishy* • **propagarse como la ~** to spread like wildfire ▸ **pólvora de algodón** guncotton
2 (= *fuegos artificiales*) fireworks (*pl*)
3 (= *mal genio*) bad temper, crossness
4 (= *viveza*) life, liveliness

polvorear ▷ CONJUG 1a VT to powder, sprinkle (**de** with)

polvoriento ADJ **1** [*superficie*] dusty
2 [*sustancia*] powdery

polvorilla* SMF • **ser un(a) ~** (= *de genio vivo*) to be really touchy*; (= *inquieto*) to be a live wire

polvorín SM **1** (*Mil*) (= *almacén*) arsenal; (= *pólvora*) fine powder
2 (= *situación peligrosa*) powder keg
3 (*Cono Sur*) (= *insecto*) gnat
4 (*Cono Sur, Méx*) = **polvorilla**
5 (*And, Caribe*) (= *polvareda*) cloud of dust

polvorón SM *type of light, crumbly shortbread*

polvorosa SF • **MODISMO:** • **poner pies en ~*** to beat it*, scarper*

polvoroso ADJ dusty

P

polvoso ADJ (*LAm*) dusty
pom SM (*CAm*) incense
poma SF **1** (= *manzana*) apple
2 (= *frasco*) scent bottle; (*Cono Sur*) small flask; (*And*) carafe
3 (*Méx*) (= *piedra*) pumice, pumice stone
pomada SF **1** (= *crema*) cream, ointment
• MODISMOS: • **estar en la ~*** (= *metido*) to be mixed up in it, be involved; (= *al tanto*) to be in the know • **hacer algo ~** (*Cono Sur**) to break sth to bits, ruin sth
2 (= *gente*) • **la ~‡** the cream, the top people
pomar SM apple orchard
pomelo SM grapefruit, pomelo (EEUU)
pómez SF • **piedra ~** pumice (stone)
pomo SM **1** [*de puerta*] knob, handle; [*de espada*] pommel
2 (= *frasco*) scent bottle
3 (*Bot*) pome
4 (*And*) (= *borla*) powder puff
pompa SF **1** (= *burbuja*) bubble ▸ **pompa de jabón** soap bubble
2 (*Náut*) pump
3 (= *fasto*) pomp, splendour, splendor (EEUU); (= *ostentación*) show, display; (= *boato*) pageant, pageantry ▸ **pompas fúnebres** (= *ceremonia*) funeral (*sing*); (= *cortejo*) funeral procession (*sing*)
▸ **"Pompas fúnebres"** (= *funeraria*) "Undertaker's" (*sing*), "Funeral parlour" (*sing*), "Funeral parlor" (EEUU) (*sing*)
Pompeya SF Pompeii
Pompeyo SM Pompey
pompis* SM INV bottom, behind*, butt (EEUU‡)
pompo ADJ (*And*) blunt
pompón SM pompom
pomposamente ADV (= *con esplendor*) splendidly, magnificently; (= *con majestuosidad*) majestically; (= *con ostentación*) pompously
pomposidad SF (= *esplendor*) splendour, splendor (EEUU), magnificence; (= *majestuosidad*) majesty; (*pey*) (= *ostentación*) pomposity, pompousness
pomposo ADJ (= *espléndido*) splendid, magnificent; (= *majestuoso*) majestic; (= *ostentoso*) pompous
pómulo SM (= *hueso*) cheekbone; (= *mejilla*) cheek
p.º n.º SM ABR (= **peso neto**) nt. wt.
ponchada[1] SF (*LAm*) **1** [*de poncho*] ponchoful
2 (= *mucho*) large quantity, large amount
• **costó una ~** it cost a bomb*
ponchada[2] SF [*de ponche*] bowlful of punch
ponchada[3] SF (*Méx*), **ponchadura** SF (*Méx*) (*Aut*) puncture, flat (EEUU)
ponchar ▸ CONJUG 1a VT (*Méx*) **1** [+ *neumático*] to puncture
2 [+ *billete*] to punch
VI (*LAm**) (= *resistir*) to champ at the bit
VPR **poncharse** (*Méx*) • **se ponchó el balón** the ball got punctured • **se le ponchó una llanta** he had a flat tyre *o* (EEUU) tire, he had a puncture
ponchazos* SMPL (*Arg*) • **a los ~** with great difficulty
ponche SM punch
ponchera SF **1** (*para ponche*) punch bowl
2 (*And, Caribe, Méx*) (= *palangana*) washbasin, washbowl (EEUU); (*And*) (= *bañera*) bath
3 (*Cono Sur**) (= *barriga*) paunch, beer belly*, beer gut*
poncho[1] ADJ **1** (= *perezoso*) lazy, idle
2 (= *tranquilo*) quiet, peaceable
3 (*And*) (= *gordito*) chubby
poncho[2] SM (= *ropa*) poncho, cape; (= *manta*) blanket • **los de a ~** (*And**) the poor
• MODISMOS: • **estar a ~** (*And**) to be in the dark • **arrastrar el ~** (*LAm**) to be looking *o* spoiling for a fight • **donde el diablo perdió el ~** (*Cono Sur**) at the back of beyond*
• **pisarle el ~ a algn** (*And*) to humiliate sb
• **pisarse el ~** (*Cono Sur**) to be mistaken
ponchura SF (*Ven*) wash basin
Poncio Pilato SM Pontius Pilate
ponderable ADJ (= *considerable*) considerable
ponderación SF **1** (*al decir algo*) (= *contrapeso*) weighing, consideration; (= *cuidado*) deliberation
2 (= *alabanza*) high praise • **está sobre toda ~** I can't praise it highly enough
3 [*de índice*] weighting
4 (= *equilibrio*) balance
ponderado ADJ **1** (= *alabado*) praised • **mi querido y nunca bien ~ amigo** my dear and unappreciated friend
2 (= *equilibrado*) balanced
3 (*Estadística*) weighted • **media ponderada** weighted average • **voto ~** proportional voting
ponderar ▸ CONJUG 1a VT **1** (= *alabar*) to praise highly, speak highly of • **~ algo a algn** to speak warmly of sth to sb, tell sb how good sth is • **le ponderan de inteligente** they speak highly of his intelligence
2 (= *considerar*) to weigh up, consider
3 (*Estadística*) to weight
pondré *etc* ▸ **poner**
ponedero SM nest, nesting box
ponedora ADJ • **gallina ~** laying hen • **ser buena ~** to be a good layer
ponencia SF **1** (= *exposición*) paper, learned paper, communication; (= *informe*) report
2 (= *comisión*) committee, board
ponente SMF speaker (*at a conference*)

poner

VERBO TRANSITIVO
VERBO INTRANSITIVO
VERBO PRONOMINAL

▸ CONJUG 2q

Para las expresiones ***poner cuidado, poner en duda, poner por las nubes, poner a parir, poner como un trapo, poner verde, poner de vuelta y media, poner por testigo, ponerse por delante,*** *ver la otra entrada.*

VERBO TRANSITIVO

1 (= *colocar, situar*) to put • **¿dónde pongo mis cosas?** where shall I put my things? • **pon los libros en la estantería** put the books on the shelf • **le puso la mano en el hombro** she put a hand on his shoulder • **me han puesto en la habitación de arriba** they've put me in the upstairs bedroom • **han puesto un anuncio en el periódico** they've put an advertisement in the paper • **voy a ~ las patatas** I'm going to put the potatoes on
• **ponle un poco de mantequilla y verás qué bueno** put some butter in it and you'll see how good it is
• **~ algo aparte** to put sth aside, put sth to one side • **ponlo en su sitio** put it back
2 (+ *ropa, calzado*) to put on • **le pusieron un vestido nuevo** they dressed her in a new dress • **ponle los zapatos** can you put his shoes on?
3 (= *añadir*) to add • **ponle más sal** add some salt, put some more salt in it • **pongo 20 más para llegar a 100** I'll add 20 more to make it 100
4 (= *aplicar, administrar*) to put • **le pusieron una tirita en la herida** they put a plaster on her wound • **ponle talco al cambiarle el pañal** put some talcum powder on him when you change his nappy • **le han puesto muchas inyecciones** she's been given a lot of injections
5 (= *disponer, preparar*) • **pon cubiertos para 12 personas** set the table for 12 people • **~ la mesa** to lay *o* set the table
6 (= *instalar*) **a** [+ *teléfono, calefacción*] to put in
• **queremos ~ moqueta** we want to have a carpet fitted
b [+ *tienda*] to open; [+ *casa*] to furnish • **han puesto una tienda de muebles** they've opened a furniture shop • **han puesto la casa con todo lujo** they have furnished the house luxuriously
7 (= *exponer*) • **ponlo al sol** leave *o* put it out in the sun • **~ algo a secar** to put sth out to dry
8 (= *hacer funcionar*) [+ *radio, televisión, calefacción*] to put on, turn on; [+ *disco*] to put on, play
• **pon el radiador** put the radiator on
• **¿pongo música?** shall I put some music on?
9 (= *ajustar*) [+ *despertador*] to set • **puse el despertador para las siete** I set the alarm for seven o'clock • **pon el horno al máximo** put the oven on maximum • **~ el reloj en hora** to put one's watch right • **ponlo más alto** turn it up
10 (= *adoptar*) • **¿por qué pones esa voz tan tonta?** why are you speaking in that silly voice? • **puso acento francés al decirlo** she put on a French accent when she said it
• **¡no pongas esa cara!** don't look at me like that! • **puso muy mala cara cuando se lo dije** he looked very annoyed when I told him
• **puso cara de asombro** he looked surprised
11 (= *volver*) (+ *adj, adv*) to make • **me pone furiosa** he makes me mad • **para no ~le de mal humor** so as not to make him cross, so as not to put him in a bad mood • **la has puesto colorada** you've made her blush • **la medicina lo puso bueno** the medicine made him better • **¡cómo te han puesto!** (= *te han manchado*) look what a mess you are!; (= *te han pegado*) they've given you a right thumping!
12 (= *servir*) • **¿qué te pongo?** what can I get you?, what would you like? • **¿me pones más patatas?** could I have some more potatoes?
13 (= *conectar por teléfono*) to put through
• **póngame con el conserje** put me through to the porter • **¿me pone con el Sr. García, por favor?** could you put me through to Mr García, please? • **le pongo en seguida** I'll put you through
14 (= *exhibir*) • **¿qué ponen en el cine?** what's on at the cinema? • **¿ponen alguna película esta noche?** is there a film on tonight?
15 (= *enviar*) to send • **le puso un telegrama** he sent her a telegram
16 (= *escribir*) to put • **¿qué pongo en la carta?** what shall I put in the letter? • **¿te has acordado de ~ el remite?** did you remember to put the return address on it?
17 (= *decir, estar escrito*) to say • **¿qué pone aquí?** what does it say here?
18 (= *imponer*) [+ *examen, trabajo*] to give, set
• **nos pone mucho trabajo** he gives *o* sets us a lot of work • **el ayuntamiento pone muchos impuestos** council taxes are very high • **me han puesto una multa** I've been fined, I've been given a fine
19 (= *oponer*) [+ *inconvenientes*] to raise • **nos han puesto muchos problemas** they've put a lot of obstacles in our way • **le pone peros a todo** he's always finding fault with everything
20 (= *aportar, contribuir*) [+ *dinero*] • **he puesto 50 euros de mi bolsillo** I put in 50 euros out of my own pocket • **todos pusimos diez euros**

para el regalo we all put in ten euros towards the present • **yo pongo el dinero pero ella escoge** I do the paying, but she does the choosing • **yo pongo la bebida y vosotros el postre** I'll get the drink and you can get the dessert
21 (= *invertir*) to put in • **hemos puesto más de cinco millones** we have put in over five million • **puso todos sus ahorros en aquel negocio** he put all his savings into that business
22 (= *apostar*) • **pon tres fichas al rojo** put three chips on red • **pongo cinco euros a que mañana llueve** I bet five euros that it will rain tomorrow
23 (= *llamar*) to call • **¿qué nombre** *o* **cómo le van a ~?** what are they going to call him?, what name are they giving him? • **al niño le pusieron Luis** they called the child Luis
24 (= *criticar, alabar*) • **te puso muy bien ante el jefe** she was very nice about you to the boss • **me han puesto muy bien esa película** I've heard that film is very good • **¡cómo te han puesto!** (= *te han criticado*) they had a real go at you!; (= *te han alabado*) they were really nice about you! • **tu cuñada te ha puesto muy mal** your sister-in-law was very nasty about you
25 (= *tildar*) • **~ a algn de:** • **la han puesto de idiota para arriba** they called her an idiot and worse
26 (= *suponer*) • **pongamos 120** let's say 120 • **pongamos que ganas la lotería** suppose *o* supposing you win the lottery • **poniendo que …** supposing that …
27 • **~ a algn a** (+ *infin*): • **nada más llegar nos pusieron a barrer** no sooner had we arrived than we were set to sweeping the floor • **puso a sus hijos a trabajar** she sent her children out to work
28 • **~ a Juan bien con Pedro** to make things up between Juan and Pedro • **~ a Juan mal con Pedro** to make Juan fall out with Pedro, cause a rift between Juan and Pedro
29 (*en trabajo*) • **~ a algn de:** • **puso a su hija de sirvienta** she got her daughter a job as a servant • **lo han puesto de dependiente en una tienda** they got him a job as a shop assistant
30 • MODISMO: • **¡no pongo ni una!** (*Caribe**) I just can't get anything right!
31 (*gallina*) [+ *huevos*] to lay
VERBO INTRANSITIVO
1 (*aves*) to lay (eggs)
2 (= *apostar*) • **no pongo a la lotería** I don't play the lottery
VERBO PRONOMINAL **ponerse**
1 (= *colocarse, situarse*) (*de pie*) to stand; (*sentado*) to sit; (*echado*) to lie • **se puso delante de la ventana** he stood in front of the window • **se ponía a mi lado en clase** he used to sit next to me in class • **póngase de lado** lie on your side • **~se cómodo** to make o.s. comfortable • **ponte en mi lugar** put yourself in my place • **todos se pusieron de** *o* **en pie** everyone stood up • **se puso de rodillas** she knelt down
2 (+ *ropa, calzado, joyas*) to put on • **~se un traje** to put a suit on • **ponte las zapatillas** put your slippers on • **no sé qué ~me** I don't know what to wear
3 (= *aplicarse, administrarse*) • **ponte más perfume** put some more perfume on • **te pones demasiado maquillaje** you wear too much make-up • **se puso un supositorio** he used a suppository
4 (*sol*) to set
5 (= *volverse*) (+ *adj, adv*) • **~se enfermo/gordo** to get ill/fat • **se puso hecho una furia** he got absolutely furious • **cuando se lo dije se puso muy triste** he was very sad when I told him • **¡no te pongas así!** don't be like that! • **¡qué guapa te has puesto!** you look lovely! • **en el agua se pone verde** it turns green in water
6 (*al teléfono*) • **dile que se ponga** tell him to come to *o* on the phone • **no se quiere ~** she doesn't want to come on (the phone) • **¿se puede ~ María, por favor?** could I speak to María, please?
7 (= *empezar*) • **~se a hacer algo** to start *o* begin to do sth, start *o* begin doing sth • **se pusieron a gritar** they started *o* began shouting, they started *o* began to shout • **se va a ~ a llover** it's going to start raining • **si me pongo a pensar en lo que me espera …** if I start thinking *o* to think about what awaits me … • **~se con algo:** • **ahora me pongo con los deberes** I'm going to start on my homework now
8 (= *llenarse*) • **~se de algo:** • **¡cómo te has puesto de barro!** you're all covered in mud! • **se puso perdida de alquitrán** she got covered in tar • **nos hemos puesto bien de comida** we ate our fill
9 (= *llegar*) • **~se en** to get to, reach • **se puso en Madrid en dos horas** he got to *o* reached Madrid in two hours
10 (= *emplearse*) • **me puse a servir** I went into service • **~se de conserje** to take a job as a porter
11 • **~se a bien con algn** to get on good terms with sb; (*pey*) to get in with sb • **~se a mal con algn** to get on the wrong side of sb
12‡ (= *drogarse*) to get high‡
13 (= *parecerle*) • **se me pone que …** (*LAm*) (= *me parece*) it seems to me that …
14 • MODISMO: • **ponérselos a algn**‡ to cheat on sb

poney ['poni] SM (PL: **poneys**) pony
ponga *etc* ▸ **poner**
pongaje SM (*And, Cono Sur*) = **pongueaje**
pongo¹ ▸ **poner**
pongo² SM orang-utan
pongo³ SM (*And*) **1** (= *criado*) (*unpaid*) *Indian servant*; (= *inquilino*) *Indian tenant*
2 (*Geog*) ravine
pongueaje SM (*And, Cono Sur*) (*esp Hist*) *domestic service which Indian tenants are obliged to give free*
poni SM pony
ponible ADJ wearable
poniente ADJ west, western
SM **1** (= *oeste*) west
2 (= *viento*) west wind
ponja‡ ADJ, SMF (*And*) Jap**
ponqué SM (*Col, Méx*) cake
pontaje SM, **pontazgo** SM toll
pontevedrés/esa (*Esp*) ADJ of/from Pontevedra
SM/F native/inhabitant of Pontevedra • **los pontevedreses** the people of Pontevedra
pontificado SM papacy, pontificate
pontifical ADJ papal, pontifical
pontificar ▸ CONJUG 1g VI to pontificate
pontífice SM pope, pontiff • **el Sumo Pontífice** the Supreme Pontiff
pontificio ADJ papal, pontifical
pontón SM **1** (= *barco*) pontoon • **puente de pontones** pontoon bridge
2 (= *puente*) bridge of planks
3 (*Aer*) [*de hidroavión*] float
4 (= *buque viejo*) hulk
pony ['poni] SM (PL: **ponys**) pony
ponzoña SF (= *tóxico*) poison, venom; (= *ideas*) poison
ponzoñoso ADJ [*ataque*] venomous, poisonous; [*propaganda*] poisonous; [*costumbre, idea*] pernicious
pool [pul] SM (PL: **pools** [pul]) (*Econ*) consortium
pop ADJ pop
SM (*Mús*) pop, pop music
EXCL bingo!*
popa SF **1** (*Náut*) stern • **a ~** astern, abaft • **de proa a ~** fore and aft, from stem to stern; ▸ **viento**
2 (= *culo*) rear*, backside, bottom
popar ▸ CONJUG 1a VT **1** (= *mimar*) to spoil, make a fuss of; (= *halagar*) flatter
2 (= *mofarse de*) to scorn, jeer at
pope SM **1** (*Rel*) priest of the Orthodox Church
2* (= *líder*) guru, spiritual leader; (= *ídolo*) idol
popelín SM, **popelina** SF poplin
popería* SF pop fans (*pl*)
popero/a* ADJ • **música popera** pop music
SM/F pop fan
popi* ADJ pop
SMF pop fan
popó‡ SM poo-poo‡ • **hacer ~** to do a poo-poo‡
popof* ADJ INV, **popoff*** ADJ INV (*Méx*) posh*, society (*antes de s*)
poporo SM **1** (*And, Caribe*) (= *bulto*) bump, swelling
2 (*Caribe*) (= *porra*) truncheon, nightstick (EEUU)
popote SM (*Méx*) (= *pajita*) drinking straw; (= *tallo*) long thin stem; (= *hierba*) *tough grass used for making brooms*
populachería SF cheap popularity, playing to the gallery
populachero ADJ **1** (= *plebeyo*) common, vulgar; (= *chabacano*) cheap
2 [*discurso, política*] rabble-rousing; [*político*] demagogic (*frm*), who plays to the gallery
populacho SM (= *capa social*) plebs* (*pl*) (*pey*); (= *multitud*) mob
popular ADJ **1** (= *del pueblo*) [*cultura, levantamiento*] popular; [*música*] popular, folk (*antes de s*); [*tradiciones*] popular, folk (*antes de s*); [*lenguaje*] popular, colloquial • **el tribunal ~** the people's court
2 (= *de clase obrera*) • **un barrio ~** a working-class neighbourhood *o* (EEUU) neighborhood
3 (= *muy conocido*) popular • **es un actor muy ~** he is a very popular actor • **es la más ~ de su clase** she's the most popular child in her class
popularidad SF popularity
popularismo SM popularism
popularización SF popularization
popularizar ▸ CONJUG 1f VT to popularize
VPR **popularizarse** to become popular
populismo SM populism; (= *política*) populist policies (*pl*)
populista ADJ, SMF populist
populoso ADJ populous
popurrí SM potpourri
poquedad SF **1** (= *timidez*) timidity, pusillanimity (*frm*)
2 (= *escasez*) scantiness; (= *pequeñez*) smallness
3 • **una ~** (= *algo pequeño*) a small thing; (= *nimiedad*) a trifle
póquer SM poker
poquísimo ADJ **1** (*con nombres incontables*) (*gen*) very little; (= *casi nada*) hardly any, almost no • **con ~ dinero** with very little money
2 poquísimos very few
poquitín SM • **un ~** a little bit
poquito SM **1** • **un ~** a little bit (**de** of); (*como adv*) a little, a bit
2 • **a ~s** bit by bit, little by little • **¡~ a poco!**

P

gently!, easy there! • **se añade la leche ~ a poco** the milk is added a little at a time *o* gradually

por

PREPOSICIÓN

1 (causa) **a** (+ *sustantivo*) because of • **tuvo que suspenderse por el mal tiempo** it had to be cancelled because of the weather • **no se realizó por escasez de fondos** it didn't go ahead because of a shortage of funding • **nos encontramos por casualidad** we met by chance • **lo hago por gusto** I do it because I like to • **fue por necesidad** it was out of necessity • **por temor a** for fear of • **no se lo dijo por temor a ofenderla** he didn't tell her for fear of offending her

b (+ *infin*) • **no aprobó por no haber estudiado** he didn't pass because he hadn't studied • **por venir tarde se perdió la mitad** because he arrived late he missed half of it • **me castigaron por mentir** I was punished for lying

c (+ *adj*) • **le expulsaron por revoltoso** they expelled him for being a troublemaker • **lo dejó por imposible** he gave it up as (being) impossible • **esto te pasa por tonto** this is what you get for being stupid

2 (objetivo) **a** (+ *sustantivo*) for • **trabajar por dinero** to work for money • **daría lo que fuera por un poco de tranquilidad** I'd give anything for a bit of peace and quiet • **brindemos por nuestro futuro** let's drink to our future

b (+ *infin*) • **lo hizo por complacerle** he did it to please her • **por no llegar tarde** so as not to arrive late, in order not to be late • **hablar por hablar** to talk for the sake of talking

3 (= *en favor, defensa de*) for • **lo hice por mis padres** I did it for my parents • **hazlo por mí** do it for me, do it for my sake • **luchar por la patria** to fight for one's country

4 (elección) • **su amor por la pintura** his love of painting • **está loca por ti** she's crazy about you • **no sabía por cuál decidirme** I couldn't decide which to choose

5 (evidencia) judging by, judging from • **por lo que dicen** judging by *o* from what they say • **por la cara que pone no debe de gustarle** judging by *o* from his face I don't think he likes it • **por las señas no piensa hacerlo** apparently he's not intending to do it, it doesn't seem like he's intending to do it

6 (medio) • **por su propia mano** by his own hand • **lo obtuve por un amigo** I got it through a friend • **la conozco por mi hermano** I know her through my brother • **por correo** by post • **por mar** by sea • **hablar por señas** to use sign language

7 (agente) by • **hecho por él** done by him • **"dirigido por"** "directed by" • **fueron apresados por la policía** they were captured by the police

8 (modo) by • **me agarró por el brazo** he grabbed me by the arm • **punto por punto** point by point • **buscaron casa por casa** they searched house by house • **están dispuestos por tamaños** they are arranged according to size *o* by size • **por orden alfabético** in alphabetical order

9 (lugar) • **se va por ahí** it's that way • **¿por dónde?** which way? • **ir a Bilbao por Santander** to go to Bilbao via Santander • **cruzar la frontera por Canfranc** to cross the border at Canfranc • **pasar por Madrid** to go through Madrid • **se asomaron por la ventana** they leaned out of the window • **iban cantando por la calle** they were walking along the street singing • **paseábamos por la playa** we were walking along the beach • **por todas partes** everywhere • **por todo el país** throughout the country • **viajar por el mundo** to travel (around) the world

10 (aproximación) • **busca por ahí** look over there • **viven por esta zona** they live around here • **por aquí cerca** near *o* around here • **aquello ocurrió por abril** it happened around April • **por la feria** round about *o* around carnival time • **está por el norte** it's somewhere up north

11 (tiempo) • **se levanta por la mañana temprano** she gets up early in the morning • **por la mañana siempre tengo mucho trabajo** I always have a lot of work in *o* during the morning • **no sale por la noche** he doesn't go out at night

12 (duración) for • **será por poco tiempo** it won't be for long • **se quedarán por 15 días** they will stay for a fortnight

13 (sustitución, intercambio) (= *a cambio de*) for; (= *en lugar de*) instead of • **te doy este por aquel** I'll swap you this one for that one • **le dieron uno nuevo por el viejo** they gave him a new one (in exchange) for the old one • **lo vendí por 15 dólares** I sold it for 15 dollars • **me dieron 13 francos por una libra** I got 13 francs to the pound • **hoy doy yo la clase por él** today I'm giving the class for him *o* in his place • **ha puesto B por V** he has put B instead of V

14 (representación) • **hablo por todos** I speak on behalf of *o* for everyone • **interceder por algn** to intercede on sb's behalf, intercede for sb • **diputado por Madrid** a member of parliament for Madrid • **vino por su jefe** he came instead of *o* in place of his boss

15 (distribución) • **10 dólares por hora** 10 dollars an hour • **80km por hora** 80km per *o* an hour • **revoluciones por minuto** revolutions per minute • **tres dólares por persona** three dollars each, three dollars per person

16 (en multiplicaciones) • **cinco por tres, quince** five times three is fifteen, five threes are fifteen • **mide 6 metros de alto por 4 de ancho** it is 6 metres high by 4 wide

17 (= *en cuanto a*) • **por mí no hay inconveniente** that's fine as *o* so far as I'm concerned • **por mí, que se vaya** as *o* so far as I'm concerned he can go, for all I care he can go • **por mí, como si quieres pasar una semana sin comer** I don't care if you want to go for a week without eating • **si por mí fuera, tú estarías trabajando** if it were *o* was down to me, you'd be working

18 (= *como*) • **tomar a algn por esposo/esposa** to take sb to be one's husband/wife • **le dan por muerto** they have given him up for dead • **le tienen por tonto** they think he's stupid

19 (concesión) (+ *subjun*) • **por (muy) difícil que sea** however hard it is *o* may be • **por mucho que lo quisieran** however much they would like to, much as they would like to • **por más que lo intente** no matter how *o* however hard I try, try as I might

20 (acción inacabada) (+ *infin*) • **quedan platos por lavar** there are still some dishes to do • **aún me quedan tres páginas por traducir** I still have three pages left to translate

21 **ir (a) por algo/algn** (= *en busca de*) to go and get sth/sb • **ha ido (a) por vino** she's gone to get some wine • **voy por el médico** I'll go and fetch *o* get the doctor • **voy a por él** (*a buscarle*) I'll go and get him; (*a atacarle*) I'm going to get him • **solo van a por las pelas*** they're only in it for the money • **¡a por ellos!** get them! • MODISMO: • **ir a por todas** to really go for it

22 (en preguntas) **por qué** why • **¿por qué no vienes conmigo?** why don't you come with me? • **no tengo por qué ir** there's no reason why I should go **¿por?*** why (do you ask)?

porcachón* ADJ = **porcallón**
porcada* SF = **porquería**
porcallón* ADJ filthy, dirty
porcelana SF (= *material*) porcelain; (= *loza*) china, chinaware, porcelain • **tienda de ~** china shop • **estantes llenos de ~s** shelves full of china *o* chinaware *o* porcelain
porcentaje SM percentage • **un elevado ~ de algo** a high percentage *o* proportion of sth • **el ~ de defunciones** the death rate • **trabajar a ~** to work on a percentage basis ▸ **porcentaje de accesos** (*Inform*) hit rate
porcentual ADJ percentage (*antes de s*)
porcentualmente ADV (= *en porcentaje*) in percentage terms, percentage-wise; (= *proporcionalmente*) proportionately
porche SM 1 [*de casa*] porch
2 (= *soportal*) arcade
Porcia SF Portia
porcino ADJ pig (*antes de s*), porcine (*frm*) • **ganado ~** pigs (*pl*); ▸ **fiebre, peste**
SM 1 (= *animal*) pig, hog (*esp EEUU*); (= *lechón*) young pig • **carne de ~** pork
2 (*Med*) bump, swelling
porción SF 1 (= *parte*) (*gen*) portion; (*en un reparto*) share; (*en recetas*) quantity, amount; (*de chocolate, pastel*) piece • **una ~ de patatas fritas** a portion *o* helping of chips • **quesitos en porciones** cheese portions • **grandes porciones del presupuesto** large chunks of *o* a large proportion of the budget
2 (= *montón*) • **una ~ de** a number of • **tengo una ~ de cosas que hacer** I have a number of things to do • **tuvimos una ~ de problemas** we had quite a few problems *o* a number of problems
porcuno ADJ pig (*antes de s*)
pordiosear ▸ CONJUG 1a VI to beg
pordiosero/a SM/F beggar
porende†† ADV hence, therefore
porfa* EXCL please
porfía SF 1 (= *cualidad*) (= *terquedad*) stubbornness, obstinacy; (= *persistencia*) persistence
2 (= *disputa*) dispute; (= *contienda*) continuous struggle, continuous competition
3 • **a ~** in competition
porfiadamente ADV (= *tercamente*) stubbornly, obstinately; (= *con insistencia*) persistently
porfiado ADJ (= *terco*) stubborn, obstinate; (= *insistente*) persistent
SM (*LAm*) (= *muñeco*) roly-poly doll, tumbler, tumbler toy
porfiar ▸ CONJUG 1c VI 1 (= *persistir*) to persist, insist • **~ en algo** to persist in sth • **porfía en que es así** he insists that it is so, he will have it that it is so • **~ por hacer algo** to struggle obstinately to do sth • **porfían por escapar** they are bent on escaping
2 (= *disputar*) to argue stubbornly • **~ con algn** to argue with sb
pórfido SM porphyry
porfión ADJ dogged, stubborn
porfirismo SM porphyria
porfirista SMF (*Méx*) supporter of Porfirio Díaz
pormenor SM detail, particular
pormenorización SF • **sin entrar en la ~** without going into detail
pormenorizadamente ADV in detail

P

pormenorizado ADJ detailed
pormenorizar ▹ CONJUG 1f VT **1** (= *describir*) to describe in detail
2 (= *detallar*) to detail, set out in detail
VI to go into detail
porno* ADJ INV porn*, porno*
SM porn* ▸ **porno blando** soft porn*
▸ **porno duro** hard porn*
pornografía SF pornography
▸ **pornografía dura** hard porn ▸ **pornografía infantil** child pornography
pornográfico ADJ pornographic
pornografista SMF pornographer
poro¹ SM (*Anat*) pore
poro² SM (*LAm*) (= *puerro*) leek
poronga‡ SF (*Cono Sur*) prick‡, cock‡
porongo SM (*LAm*) **1** (= *planta*) gourd, calabash, squash (EEUU)
2 (= *persona*) nobody
pororó SM (*Cono Sur*) popcorn
porosidad SF porousness, porosity
poroso ADJ porous
porotal SM (*LAm*) **1** (= *terreno*) beanfield, bean patch
2 • **un ~ de*** a whole lot of, a whole heap of
poroto SM **1** (*And, Cono Sur*) (= *judía*) bean; **porotos*** grub* (*sing*), chow (*sing*) (EEUU‡), food (*sing*) • MODISMOS: • **ganarse los ~s** to earn one's daily bread • **no valer un ~*** to be worthless ▸ **poroto verde** green bean, runner bean
2 (*Cono Sur*) (*Dep*) (*tb fig*) point • **anotarse un ~*** to score a point • **¡te anotaste un ~!** you made it!
3 (*Cono Sur**) (= *niño*) kid*; (= *alfeñique*) weakling
porpuesto SM (*Caribe*) minibus, taxi
porque CONJ **1** (= *por causa de que*) (+ *indic*) because • **no pudo ir ~ estaba enferma** she couldn't go because she was ill • **¿por qué no contestas? —~ no me da la gana** "why don't you answer?" — "because I don't feel like it" • **—¿por qué te vas? —porque sí** "why are you going?" — "just because" • **—¿por qué no puedo ir? —porque no** "why can't I go?" — "just because"
2 (= *para que*) (+ *subjun*) so that, in order that • **elevó la voz ~ todos pudieran oírlo** he raised his voice so that everyone could hear him *o* in order that everyone might hear him • **recemos ~ vuelvan** let us pray that they may return
porqué SM **1** (= *motivo*) reason (**de** for) • **me gustaría saber el ~ de su actitud** I'd like to know the reason for her attitude • **no me interesan los ~s** I'm not interested in the whys and wherefores • **el ~ de la revolución** the causes of the revolution
2† (= *cantidad*) amount • **tiene mucho ~** he's got plenty of the ready*
porquería SF **1** (= *suciedad*) dirt, muck* • **¿qué es toda esta ~ que hay el suelo?** what's all this dirt *o* muck on the floor? • **estar hecho una ~** to be covered in dirt *o* muck*
2 (= *guarrada*) • **no hagas ~s con la comida** don't make such a mess with your food
3 (= *indecencia*) • **estas ~s no deberían salir por la tele** that filth *o* smut shouldn't be shown on TV • **decir ~s** to say filthy things
4 (= *cosa de poca calidad*) junk*, rubbish*, garbage (EEUU*) • **si comes tantas ~s, luego no vas a cenar** if you eat all that junk *o* rubbish now you won't want your dinner* • **en esta tienda solo venden ~s** this shop only sells cheap rubbish* • **la novela es una ~** the novel is just rubbish*
5 (= *poco dinero*) pittance • **me han pagado una ~** they paid me a pittance • **lo vendieron por una ~** they sold it for next to nothing
6 (= *mala pasada*) • **¡vaya ~ te han hecho despidiéndote así!** what a lousy thing they did to you, sacking you like that!*
7 • **de ~** (*LAm**) (= *condenado*) lousy*
porqueriza SF pigsty, pigpen (EEUU)
porquerizo SM, **porquero** SM swineherd
porra SF **1** [*de policía*] truncheon, billyclub (EEUU)
2 (*Téc*) large hammer
3 (*Culin*) *large club-shaped fritter*
4* (= *nariz*) conk*, hooter*, schnozzle (*esp* EEUU‡)
5 (= *juego*) sweep, sweepstake
6* (*exclamaciones*) • **¡porras!** (= *¡maldición!*) damn!‡; (= *¡mentira!*) rubbish! • **¡una ~!** no way!* • **¡a la ~!** get out! • **¡a la ~ el ministro!** the minister can go to hell!* • **mandar a algn a la ~** to tell sb to go to hell*, send sb packing • **¡vete a la ~!** go to hell!* • **¡qué coche ni que ~s!** car my foot!
7 (*Méx*) (*Dep*) fans (*pl*); (*Teat*) claque
8 (*And, Cono Sur*) (= *mechón*) curl
9 (*CAm, Méx*) (*Pol*) political gang
10 (*CAm*) (= *olla*) metal cooking pot
11‡ (= *pene*) prick‡
12* (= *pesado*) bore
13* (= *jactancia*) • **gasta mucha ~** he's always boasting, he's always shooting his mouth off*
porracear* ▹ CONJUG 1a VT (*Caribe, Méx*) to beat up
porrada SF **1*** (= *montón*) • **una ~ de** loads of* • **hace una ~ de tiempo** ages ago
2 (= *porrazo*) thump, blow
porrata‡ SMF dope smoker*
porrazo SM **1** (= *golpe*) thump, blow; (= *caída*) bump • **le di un ~ con la silla** I whacked him with the chair • **me di un ~ contra la puerta** I banged myself on the door
2 • MODISMOS: • **de ~** (*LAm*) in one go • **de golpe y ~** suddenly
porrear ▹ CONJUG 1a VI **1** (= *insistir*) to go on and on
2 (= *drogarse*) to smoke dope*
porrería* SF **1** (= *petición*) annoying request
2 (= *necedad*) stupidity
porrero/a‡ SM/F dope smoker*
porreta SF (*Bot*) green leaf • MODISMO: • **en ~(s)*** stark naked, starkers*
porretada SF = **porrada**
porrillo* • **a ~** ADV loads of*, galore • **tiene ropa a ~** he's got loads of clothes* • **gana dinero a ~** he earns loads of money*
porrista (*Col, Méx*) SMF (= *seguidor*) fan
SF (= *animadora*) cheerleader
porro* SM **1** (*Esp*) (*de droga*) joint*
2 (= *idiota*) idiot, oaf
3 (*And, Caribe*) (= *baile*) *folk dance*
ADJ stupid, oafish
porrón¹ SM **1** (= *recipiente*) *jar with a long spout for drinking from*
2 • **un ~ de*** loads of* • **la película me gustó un ~*** the film is the business* • **esa tía me gusta un ~*** I fancy the pants off her*
3 (*Arg*) [*de cerveza*] bottle of beer
porrón² ADJ (= *lerdo*) slow, stupid; (= *soso*) dull; (= *torpe*) sluggish
porrón³ SM (*Orn*) pochard ▸ **porrón moñudo** tufted duck
porrudo ADJ **1** (= *abultado*) big, bulging
2 (*Arg*) (= *melenudo*) long-haired
3 (*Cono Sur*) (= *engreído*) big-headed, swollen-headed
porsiacaso SM (*Arg, Ven*) knapsack
port. ABR = **portugués**
porta SF port, porthole
portaaeronaves SM INV aircraft carrier
portaaviones SM INV aircraft carrier
portabebés SM INV baby carrier
portabiberón SM bottle holder
portabilidad SF portability
portable ADJ portable
SM portable computer
portabotellas SM INV (= *botellero*) wine rack; (= *carrito*) bottle carrier • **carro ~** bottle carrier
portabultos SM INV carrier
portabusto, portabustos SM (*Méx*) brassiere (*frm*), bra
portacargas SM INV (= *caja*) crate; [*de bicicleta*] carrier
portacheques SM INV chequebook, checkbook (EEUU)
portación SF • **~ de armas** carrying (of) a weapon
portacoches SM INV car transporter
portacontenedor SM, **portacontenedores** SM INV container ship
portacubiertos SM INV cutlery tray
portada SF **1** (= *primera plana*) [*de libro*] title page, frontispiece (*frm*); [*de periódico*] front page
2 (= *cubierta*) [*de revista, libro*] cover; [*de disco*] sleeve, jacket (EEUU)
3 (*Arquit*) (= *fachada*) façade; (= *pórtico*) porch, doorway; (= *portal*) carriage door, gateway
portadiscos SM INV record rack
portado ADJ • **bien ~** (= *elegante*) well-dressed; (= *cortés*) well-behaved; (= *respetable*) respectable
portadocumentos SM INV document holder
ADJ INV • **agenda ~** Filofax® • **cartera ~** briefcase
portador(a) SM/F **1** [*de cheque, carta*] bearer • **el ~ de esta carta** the bearer of this letter • **páguese al ~** pay the bearer
2 (*Med*) [*de germen, virus*] carrier
portaequipajes SM INV **1** (*en un coche*) (= *maletero*) boot, trunk (EEUU); (= *baca*) roof-rack
2 (*en tren, autocar*) luggage rack
3 [*de bicicleta*] carrier
portaesquíes SM INV, **portaesquís** SM INV ski rack
portaestandarte SMF standard bearer
portafolio SM, **portafolios** SM INV briefcase, attaché case
portafotos SM INV locket
portafusil SM rifle sling
portahachón SM torchbearer
portal SM **1** [*de edificio*] (= *vestíbulo*) hallway; (= *puerta*) front door • **la llave del ~** the front door key • **un vecino de su ~** a neighbour who lives in the same block
2 [*de casa*] hall, vestibule (*frm*)
3 (*Rel*) ▸ **portal de Belén** (= *representación navideña*) Nativity scene • **el ~ de Belén** (*Biblia*) the stable at Bethlehem
4 (*Dep*) goal
5 [*de muralla*] gate
6 (*Internet*) portal
7 portales (= *soportales*) arcade (*sing*)
portalada SF = **portalón**
portalámparas SM INV (light)bulb socket
portalápices SM INV (= *estuche*) (*para llevar*) pencil case; (*para escritorio*) pencil holder, pen holder
portalibros SM INV book strap
portaligas SM INV suspender belt, garter belt (EEUU)
portalón SM **1** (*Arquit*) large gate, imposing entrance
2 (*Náut*) gangway
portamaletas SM INV **1** (*Aut*) (= *baca*) roof rack; (*Chile*) (= *maletero*) boot, trunk (EEUU)
2 (*en tren, autobús*) luggage rack

portamanteo SM (*Esp*) travelling bag
portaminas SM INV propelling pencil
portamisiles SM INV missile carrier
portamonedas SM INV purse, coin purse (EEUU)
portante SM • MODISMO: • **tomar el ~*** to clear off*
portañuela SF fly (*of trousers*)
portaobjeto SM, **portaobjetos** SM INV slide, microscope slide
portapapeles SM INV **1** (= *maletín*) briefcase
2 (*Inform*) clipboard
portaplacas SM INV plate holder
portaplatos SM INV plate rack
portapliegos SM INV (*And*) office boy
portaplumas SM INV pen holder
portar ▸ CONJUG 1a VT [+ *bolsa, documentación*] to carry; [+ *arma*] to carry, bear (*frm*); [+ *gafas, ropa*] to wear
VPR **portarse 1** (= *comportarse*) to behave, conduct o.s. (*frm*) • **~se bien** to behave well • **~se mal** to misbehave, behave badly • **se portó muy bien conmigo** he treated me very well, he was very decent to me • **se ha portado como un cerdo** he has behaved like a swine
2 (= *distinguirse*) to show up well, come through creditably
3 (*LAm*) (= *comportarse bien*) to behave well
portarretratos SM INV photo frame, picture frame
portarrevistas SM INV magazine rack
portarrollos SM INV [*de en baño*] toilet-roll holder; [*de en cocina*] kitchen-roll holder
portasenos SM INV (*LAm*) brassiere (*frm*), bra
portátil ADJ portable
SM portable, portable computer
portatostadas SM INV toast rack
portatrajes SM INV suit bag
portavelas SM INV candle holder
portaviandas SM INV lunch box, dinner pail (EEUU)
portaviones SM INV aircraft carrier
portavocía SF office of spokesperson
portavoz SMF spokesman/spokeswoman, spokesperson
SM **1** (*pey*) (= *periódico, emisora*) mouthpiece
2 (= *altavoz*) megaphone, loudhailer
portazgo SM toll
portazo SM slam • **cerrar la puerta de un ~** to slam the door (shut) • **dar** *o* **pegar un ~** to slam the door
porte SM **1** (*Com*) (= *acto*) carriage, transport; (= *costos*) carriage; (*Correos*) postage ▸ **franco de porte** (*Com*) carriage paid; (*Correos*) post free ▸ **porte debido** (*Com*) freight C.O.D. ▸ **porte pagado** (*Com*) carriage paid; (*Correos*) post paid ▸ **porte por cobrar** freight forward
2 (*esp Náut*) (= *tonelaje*) capacity
3 (= *presencia*) bearing, demeanour, demeanor (EEUU) • **de ~ distinguido** with a distinguished bearing *o* air
4 (= *conducta*) behaviour, behavior (EEUU), conduct (*frm*)
porteador(a) SM/F (*en expedición*) porter; (*en la caza*) bearer; (*Com*) carrier
portear[1] ▸ CONJUG 1a VT to carry, transport
portear[2] ▸ CONJUG 1a VI **1** [*puerta*] to slam, bang
2 (*Cono Sur*) to get out in a hurry
portento SM (= *prodigio*) marvel, wonder; (= *genio*) genius, wizard • **es un ~ de belleza** she is stunningly beautiful • **¡qué ~ de memoria!** what a prodigious memory!, what an amazing memory!
portentosamente ADV marvellously, marvelously (EEUU), extraordinarily
portentoso ADJ marvellous, marvelous (EEUU), extraordinary
porteño/a ADJ (*Arg*) of/from Buenos Aires; (*Chile*) of/from Valparaíso
SM/F (*Arg*) native/inhabitant of Buenos Aires; (*Chile*) native/inhabitant of Valparaíso • **los ~s** the people of Buenos Aires/Valparaíso
porteo SM carriage, conveyance
portería SF **1** (= *conserjería*) caretaker's office, concierge's office; (= *vivienda*) caretaker's flat, concierge's flat
2 (*Dep*) (= *meta*) goal
portero/a SM/F **1** [*de edificio*] caretaker, concierge, (apartment house) manager (EEUU)
2 (*en hotel, hospital*) porter
3 (*Dep*) goalkeeper
SM ▸ **portero automático, portero eléctrico, portero electrónico** entry phone
portezuela SF **1** (= *puerta*) door ▸ **portezuela de la gasolina** fuel-filler flap
2 (*Cos*) pocket flap
portezuelo SM (*Cono Sur*) pass
pórtico SM **1** [*de iglesia, monumento*] portico
2 [*de tiendas*] arcade
3 (= *entrada*) gateway ▸ **pórtico de entrada** gateway
portilla SF porthole
portillo SM **1** (*en la pared*) (= *abertura*) gap, opening; (= *brecha*) breach; (= *puerta falsa*) side entrance
2 (= *postigo*) wicket, wicket gate
3 (*Geog*) narrow pass
4 (*en objeto frágil*) (= *abolladura*) dent; (= *desportilladura*) chip
5 (*para lograr algo*) (= *punto débil*) weak spot, vulnerable point; (*para solución*) opening
pórtland® SM (*LAm*) cement
portón SM **1** (= *puerta grande*) large door
2 (= *puerta principal*) main door; (*LAm*) [*de casa*] front door
3 (*en cerca*) gate
4 (*Cono Sur*) (= *puerta trasera*) back door
5 (*Aut*) (*tb* **portón trasero**) hatch, hatchback, tailgate (EEUU)
portorriqueño/a ADJ, SM/F Puerto Rican
portuario ADJ (= *del puerto*) port (*antes de s*), harbour (*antes de s*), harbor (*antes de s*) (EEUU); (= *del muelle*) dock (*antes de s*) • **trabajador ~** docker
Portugal SM Portugal
portugués/esa ADJ, SM/F Portuguese
SM (*Ling*) Portuguese
portuguesismo SM portuguesism, *word/phrase etc borrowed from Portuguese*
porvenir SM future • **en el ~** in the future • **labrarse un ~** to carve out a future for o.s. • **un hombre sin ~** a man with no prospects *o* future • **le espera un brillante ~** he has a brilliant future ahead of him • **leer el ~ a algn** to tell sb's fortune
pos[1] SM • **en pos de** (*liter*) after, in pursuit of • **ir en pos de algo/algn** to chase (after) sth/sb, pursue sth/sb • **va en pos de triunfo** she's after success
pos[2]* CONJ (*esp LAm*) = **pues**
posada SF **1** (= *hospedaje*) shelter, lodging • **dar ~ a algn** to give shelter to sb, take sb in
2 (= *lugar*) (*para comer*) inn; (*para dormir*) boarding house
3 (= *morada*) house, dwelling
4 (*CAm, Méx*) (= *fiesta*) Christmas party
posaderas* SFPL backside* (*sing*), butt (*sing*) (EEUU‡), buttocks
posadero/a SM/F innkeeper
posar ▸ CONJUG 1a VT [+ *carga*] to lay down, put down; [+ *mano*] to place, lay • **posó la mirada en el horizonte** his gaze rested on the horizon, his eyes came to rest on the horizon
VI (*Arte*) to sit, pose
VPR **posarse 1** (= *pararse en tierra*) [*pájaro*] to perch, sit, alight; [*insecto*] to alight; [*avión*] to land • **el avión se encontraba posado** the aircraft was on the ground
2 [*líquido, polvo*] to settle
posas* SFPL backside* (*sing*), butt (*sing*) (EEUU‡), buttocks
posavasos SM INV (*de corcho, madera*) coaster; (*de cartón*) beer mat
posbélico ADJ postwar (*antes de s*)
poscolonial ADJ post-colonial
poscombustión SF • **dispositivo de ~** afterburner
posconciliar ADJ post-conciliar
posconcilio SM • **los 20 años de ~** the 20 years following Vatican II
posdata SF postscript
posdoctoral ADJ post-doctoral
pose SF **1** (*para foto, cuadro*) pose; (*Fot*) exposure, time exposure
2 (= *actitud*) attitude
3 (*pey*) (= *afectación*) affectation, pose; (= *postura afectada*) affected pose
4 (= *elegancia*) poise
poseedor(a) SM/F **1** (= *dueño*) owner, possessor (*frm*)
2 [*de puesto, récord*] holder
poseer ▸ CONJUG 2e VT **1** (= *ser dueño de*) [+ *bienes*] to own; [+ *fortuna*] to own, have; [+ *talento, cultura*] to have • **poseía una inteligencia excepcional** he had an exceptional mind, he was exceptionally intelligent • **posee conocimientos de inglés** she has some knowledge of English • **lo poseyó un temblor convulso** he was overcome by *o* with a compulsive fit
2 [+ *ventaja*] to have, enjoy; [+ *puesto, récord*] to hold
3 (*sexualmente*) to possess, have
poseído/a ADJ **1** (= *poseso*) possessed (**por** by); (= *enloquecido*) maddened, crazed
2 (= *engreído*) • **estar muy ~ de algo** to be very vain about sth, have an excessively high opinion of sth
SM/F • **gritar como un ~** to scream like one possessed
Poseidón SM Poseidon
poselectoral ADJ post-electoral
posesión SF **1** (= *propiedad*) possession; [*de un puesto*] tenure, occupation; [*de lengua, tema*] complete knowledge, perfect mastery • **dar ~ a algn** to hand over to sb • **él está en ~ de las cartas** he is in possession of the letters • **está en ~ del récord** he holds the record • **tomar ~** to take over • **tomar ~ de algo** to take possession of sth, take sth over • **tomar ~ de un cargo** to take up a post
2 (= *cosa poseída*) possession; (= *finca*) piece of property, estate • **huyen con sus escasas posesiones** they flee carrying their few possessions
3 (*Chile*) (*Agr*) tenant's house and land
4 (*Caribe*) ranch, estate
posesionar ▸ CONJUG 1a VT • **~ a algn de algo** to hand sth over to sb
VPR **posesionarse** • **~se de algo** to take possession of sth, take sth over
posesividad SF possessiveness
posesivo ADJ, SM possessive
poseso/a ADJ = **poseído**
SM/F = **poseído**
posestructuralismo SM post-structuralism
posestructuralista ADJ, SMF post-structuralist
posfechar ▸ CONJUG 1a VT to postdate
posfeminismo SM post-feminism
posfeminista ADJ post-feminist

(SMF) post-feminist
posfranquismo (SM) *period after the death of Franco*
posfranquista (ADJ) • **cultura ~** post-Franco culture, culture since Franco
posglacial (ADJ) post-glacial
posgrado (SM) • **curso de ~** postgraduate course
posgraduado/a (ADJ) postgraduate
(SM/F) (= *persona*) graduate student, postgraduate
(SM) (= *título*) postgraduate degree
posgradual (ADJ) postgraduate
posguerra (SF) postwar period • **en la ~** in the postwar period, after the war • **los años de la ~** the postwar years
posibilidad (SF) **1** (= *oportunidad*) chance, possibility • **no existe ~ de que venga** there's no chance *o* possibility that he'll come • **no tenemos ninguna ~** we don't have the slightest chance, we don't stand a chance • **este chico tiene ~es** this boy has got potential • **la ~ de hacer algo** the chance of doing sth • **¿tienes ~ de aprobar el examen?** do you have any chance of passing the exam? • **tiene pocas ~es de ganar** he hasn't got much chance of winning • **me han dado la ~ de elegir** they have given me the choice *o* the chance to choose
2 (= *alternativa*) possibility • **hemos descartado la ~ de una huelga** we've ruled out the possibility of a strike • **hay dos ~es: operación o radioterapia** there are two alternatives *o* possibilities: an operation or radiotherapy
3 posibilidades (= *recursos*) means • **un deportivo no está dentro de mis ~es** a sports car is beyond my means *o* out of my price range • **vive por encima de sus ~es** he lives above his means
posibilista (ADJ) optimistic, positive
(SMF) optimist, positive thinker
posibilitar ▷ CONJUG 1a (VT) (= *hacer posible*) [+ *acuerdo, acceso*] to make possible; [+ *idea, plan*] to make feasible • **los satélites posibilitan las operaciones a gran distancia** satellites make long distance operations possible • **esto posibilita la realización del proyecto** this makes the project feasible • **~ que algn haga algo** to allow sb to do sth, make it possible for sb to do sth
posible (ADJ) **1** [*opción, solución*] possible • **un ~ comprador** a possible *o* potential buyer • **hemos hecho todas las concesiones ~s** we have made all possible concessions *o* all the concessions we can • **hay una ~ infección** there is a suspected *o* possible infection • **hacer algo ~** to make sth possible • **su colaboración hizo ~ el acuerdo** her contribution made the agreement possible • **entra dentro de lo ~** it is within the bounds of possibility • **en la medida de lo ~** as far as possible, insofar as possible (*frm*) • **haremos todo lo ~ por evitarlo** we shall do everything possible *o* all we can to avoid it
2 • **es ~** (= *probable, permitido*) it is possible; (= *realizable*) it is feasible • **—¿crees que vendrá? —es ~** "do you think he'll come?" — "possibly *o* he might *o* it's possible" • **¡eso no es ~!** it can't be!, that's not possible! • **esa propuesta es bastante ~** that proposal is quite feasible • **es ~ hacer algo** it is possible to do sth • **¿sería ~ comprar todavía las entradas?** would it still be possible to buy tickets? • **no me fue ~ llegar a tiempo** I was unable to get there in time • **es ~ que** (+ *subjun*): • **es ~ que no pueda ir** I might *o* may not be able to go • **es muy ~ que vuelva tarde** it's quite possible that I'll be back late, I may well be back late • **a o de ser ~** if possible • **si es ~** if possible • **si es ~, me gustaría verlo** I'd like to see him if possible • **le ruego que, si le es ~, acuda a la reunión** please come to the meeting if you possibly can • **si me fuera ~, te lo diría** if I could *o* if it were possible, I would tell you • MODISMO: • **¿será ~?*** I can't believe it! • **¡pues sí que eres descarado! ¿será ~?** I can't believe you are so cheeky! • **¿será ~ que no haya venido?** I can't believe he hasn't come!
(ADV) • **lo más ... ~** as ... as possible • **lo más pronto ~** as soon as possible; ▷ **mejor**
(SMPL) **posibles** (*Esp*) means • **una señora de ~s** a woman of means • **vive dentro de sus ~s** she lives within her means • **una familia de ~s** a well-to-do family
posiblemente (ADV) possibly • **~ el mejor vino del mundo** possibly the best wine in the world • **—¿crees que vendrá? —posiblemente** "do you think she'll come?" — "possibly *o* she might" • **~ tengamos que mudarnos** we might have to move, it's possible that we'll have to move
posición (SF) **1** (= *postura*) position • **mantener el frasco en ~ vertical** keep the bottle in an upright position • **estar en ~ de firme** (*Mil*) to be at attention • **estar en ~ de guardia** to be on guard ▸ **posición del misionero** missionary position
2 (= *lugar*) position • **la ~ de los jugadores en el terreno de juego** the position of the players on the pitch
3 (= *categoría*) position, standing • **disfrutan de una elevada ~ social** they enjoy a high social position
4 (= *punto de vista*) position, stance • **¿cuál es su ~ en este conflicto?** what's your position *o* stance on this dispute?
5 (*en competición, liga*) place, position • **ganó Alemania con Italia en segunda ~** Germany won, with Italy in second place *o* position • **terminó en primera ~** he finished first *o* in first place • **posiciones de honor** first three places, medal positions • **perder posiciones** (*en lucha, enfrentamiento*) to lose ground
6 (*LAm*) (= *puesto de trabajo*) position, post
posicionado (SM) positioning
posicionamiento (SM) (= *acción*) positioning; (= *postura*) stance, attitude
posicionar ▷ CONJUG 1a (VT) to position
(VPR) **posicionarse** (= *tomar posición*) to adopt an attitude, take up a stance; (= *declarar su posición*) to define one's position, declare oneself
posimperial (ADJ) post-imperial
posimpresionismo (SM) post-impressionism
posimpresionista (ADJ), (SMF) post-impressionist
posindustrial (ADJ) post-industrial
positiva (SF) (*Fot*) positive, print
positivado (SM) (*Fot*) printing
positivamente (ADV) positively
positivar ▷ CONJUG 1a (VT) (*Fot*) (= *imprimir*) to print; (= *revelar*) to develop
positivismo (SM) positivism
positivista (ADJ), (SMF) positivist
positivo (ADJ) **1** (= *afirmativo, beneficioso*) positive • **la prueba de embarazo dio ~** the pregnancy test was positive • **el atleta dio ~** the athlete tested positive • **el conductor dio ~** the driver tested positive
2 (*Mat*) positive, plus
3 [*idea*] constructive • **es ~ que ...** it is good that ..., it is encouraging that ...
(SM) **1** (*Ling*) positive
2 (*Fot*) positive, print
3 (*Dep*) point
pósito (SM) **1** (= *granero*) granary, public granary
2 (= *cooperativa*) cooperative • **~ de pescadores** fishing cooperative
positrón (SM) positron
posmeridiano (ADJ) postmeridian, afternoon (*antes de s*)
posmodernidad (SF) post-modernity
posmodernismo (SM) postmodernism
posmoderno/a (ADJ) postmodern
(SM/F) postmodernist
posnatal (ADJ) postnatal
poso (SM) **1** (= *sedimento*) [*de mineral*] sediment, deposit; [*de vino*] sediment, dregs (*pl*), lees (*pl*); [*de café*] dregs (*pl*), grounds (*pl*) ▸ **posos de té** tea leaves
2 (= *huella*) trace
posol (SM) (*CAm*) *maize drink*
posología (SF) dosage
posoperativo (ADJ) post-operative
posoperatorio (ADJ) post-operative
(SM) post-operative period, period of recovery after an operation
pososo (ADJ) (*CAm*) (= *poroso*) porous, permeable; (= *absorbente*) absorbent
posparto (ADJ) postnatal
(SM) postnatal period, postpartum (*frm*)
posponer ▷ CONJUG 2q (VT) **1** (= *aplazar*) to postpone
2 (= *subordinar*) • **~ la salud al trabajo** to put one's career before one's health • **~ el amor propio al interés general** to subordinate one's pride to the general interest • **~ a algn** to downgrade sb
posposición (SF) **1** (= *aplazamiento*) postponement
2 (*Ling*) postposition
3 (= *subordinación*) subordination
pospositivo (ADJ) postpositive
posproducción (SF) post-production
posquemador (SM) afterburner
post... (PREF) post...
posta (SF) **1**† (= *caballos*) relay, team; (= *tramo*) stage; (= *parada*) staging post • **por la ~** post-haste, as quickly as possible
2 • MODISMO: • **a ~** on purpose, deliberately
3 (*Caza*) (= *munición*) slug, pellet
4 (*Chile*) (*Med*) first-aid post, first-aid station
5 (*Naipes*) stake
6 (*Culin*) slice ▸ **posta de pierna** (*CAm*) leg of pork
(SM) courier
postal (ADJ) postal • **giro ~** postal order; ▷ **caja, código**
(SF) postcard ▸ **postal ilustrada** picture postcard
postcolonial (ADJ) post-colonial
postdata (SF) postscript
postdoctoral (ADJ) post-doctoral
poste (SM) (= *palo*) post, pole; (= *columna*) pillar; [*de ejecución*] stake; (*Dep*) post, upright • **el balón pasó entre los ~s** the ball went in between the posts • MODISMOS: • **dar ~ a algn*** to keep sb hanging about • **mover los ~s** to move the goalposts • **oler el ~** (= *peligro*) to scent danger, see trouble ahead; (= *algo sospechoso*) to smell a rat* ▸ **poste de cerca** fence post ▸ **poste de llegada** winning post ▸ **poste del tendido eléctrico** electricity pylon ▸ **poste de portería** goalpost ▸ **poste de salida** starting post ▸ **poste indicador** signpost ▸ **poste restante** (*LAm*) poste restante (*esp Brit*), general delivery (*EEUU*) ▸ **poste telegráfico** telegraph pole
postear ▷ CONJUG 1a (VT) (*en blog, redes sociales*) to post
postelectoral (ADJ) post-electoral
postema (SF) **1** (*Med*) (= *absceso*) abscess
2 (*Méx*) (= *divieso*) boil; (= *pus*) pus
3* (= *pelmazo*) bore, dull person
postemilla (SF) (*LAm*) gumboil
póster (SM) (PL: **pósteres** *o* **pósters**) poster
postergación (SF) **1** [*de acto*] postponement

P

2 (= *relegación*) disregard, neglect • **ha sufrido una ~ en el trabajo** she has been passed over for promotion at work
postergar ▸ CONJUG 1h VT 1 (= *aplazar*) to defer, postpone; (= *retrasar*) to delay
2 (= *relegar*) (*en el trato*) to disregard, neglect; (*en ascenso*) to pass over, ignore
posteridad SF 1 (= *futuro*) posterity
2 (*Esp**) (= *culo*) bottom, backside*
posterior ADJ 1 (= *trasero*) [*lugar*] back, rear; [*máquina, motor*] rear-mounted • **en la parte ~ del jardín** at the back of the garden
2 (*en tiempo*) later, subsequent • **ser ~ a algo** to be later than sth
3 (*en orden*) later, following
posteriori ▸ **a posteriori**
posterioridad SF • **con ~** subsequently, later • **con ~ a algo** subsequent to sth, after sth
posteriormente ADV later, subsequently, afterwards
postgrado SM = **posgrado**
postgraduado/a ADJ, SM/F = **posgraduado**
postguerra SF = **posguerra**
postigo SM 1 (= *contraventana*) shutter
2† (= *puerta chica en otra mayor*) wicket, wicket gate; (= *portillo*) postern; (= *puerta falsa*) side door, side gate
postillón SM postillion
postín* SM 1 (= *lujo*) elegance • **de ~** posh*
2 (= *jactancia*) • **darse ~** to show off • **se da mucho ~ de que su padre es ministro** he boasts about his father being a minister
postinear* ▸ CONJUG 1a VI to show off
postinero* ADJ 1 [*persona*] vain, conceited (**de** about)
2 [*traje*] posh*
postizas SFPL (*Esp*) *small castanets*
postizo ADJ [*dientes, sonrisa, bigote*] false; [*cuello de camisa*] detachable
SM [*de pelo*] hairpiece, switch
postnatal ADJ postnatal
postoperatorio ADJ, SM = **posoperatorio**
postor SM bidder • **al mejor ~** to the highest bidder
postparto ADJ, SM = **posparto**
postproducción SF post-production
postración SF prostration
postrado ADJ prostrate • **~ por el dolor** prostrate with grief
postrar ▸ CONJUG 1a VT 1 (*Med*) (= *debilitar*) to weaken, prostrate
2 (= *derribar*) to cast down, overthrow
VPR **postrarse** to prostrate o.s.
postre SM dessert, pudding • **¿qué hay de ~?** what's for dessert? • **de ~ tomé un helado** I had ice cream for dessert • MODISMOS: • **para ~** to cap it all, on top of everything • **y, para ~, vamos y nos perdemos** and to cap it all *o* on top of everything, we went and got lost • **llegar para los ~s** to come very late
SF • MODISMO: • **a la ~** when all is said and done, at the end of the day • **a la ~, todos defendemos los mismos intereses** when all is said and done *o* at the end of the day, we all have the same interests
postremo ADJ = **postrero**
postrer ADJ = **postrero**
postrero ADJ (= *último*) last; (= *rezagado*) rear, hindmost • **palabras postreras** dying words
postrimerías SFPL 1 (= *final*) final stages, closing stages • **en las ~ del siglo** in the last few years of the century, at the end *o* close of the century
2 (= *agonía*) dying moments
3 (*Teología*) four last things
postulación SF 1 (= *proposición*) proposition, postulation
2 (*Rel*) postulancy
3 (= *colecta*) collection
4 (*LAm*) [*de candidato*] nomination, candidature
postulado SM (= *supuesto*) assumption, postulate (*frm*); (= *proposición*) proposition
postulador SM postulator
postulante SMF 1 (*Rel*) postulant, candidate
2 (*en colecta*) collector
3 (*LAm*) [*de trabajo*] candidate
postular ▸ CONJUG 1a VT 1 (= *defender*) [+ *teoría*] to postulate
2 (= *pedir*) to demand, seek • **en el artículo postula la reforma de …** in the article he sets out demands for the reform of …
3 (*en colecta*) to collect (for charity)
4 (*LAm*) (= *proponer*) [+ *candidato*] to nominate
VI 1 (*en colecta*) to collect (for charity)
2 (*LAm*) to apply (**para** for)
VPR **postularse** (*LAm*) (*Pol*) to stand
póstumamente ADV posthumously
póstumo ADJ posthumous
postura SF 1 [*del cuerpo*] position • **no sé cómo puedes estar en una ~ tan incómoda** I don't know how you can stand being in such an uncomfortable position ▸ **postura del loto** lotus position
2 (= *actitud*) stance, position • **adoptó una ~ poco razonable** he adopted an unreasonable stance *o* position • **tomar ~** to take a stand
3 (*en una subasta*) bid • **hacer ~** to make a bid
4 (*en juego de azar*) bet, stake
5 [*de ave*] (= *acción*) egg-laying; (= *conjunto de huevos*) eggs (*pl*), eggs laid (*pl*)
6‡ (= *droga*) *1000-pesetas' worth of hashish*
postural ADJ postural
posturear* ▸ CONJUG 1a VI to pose
postureo* SM posing
postvacacional ADJ post-vacation (*antes de s*) • **depresión ~** post-vacation depression
post-venta ADJ INV, **posventa** ADJ INV after-sales (*antes de s*) • **servicio** *o* **asistencia post-venta** after-sales service
pota SF 1 (= *calamar*) cuttlefish
2 • **echar la(s) ~(s)‡** to puke‡, throw up*
potabilización SF purification
potabilizadora SF water-treatment plant, waterworks
potabilizar ▸ CONJUG 1f VT • **~ el agua** to make the water drinkable
potable ADJ 1 drinkable • **agua ~** drinking water
2* (= *aceptable*) good enough, passable
potaje SM 1 (*Culin*) *vegetable and pulse stew*
2 (= *revoltijo*) jumble
potar‡ ▸ CONJUG 1a VI to puke‡, throw up*
potasa SF potash
potasio SM potassium
pote SM 1 (= *tarro*) jar; (= *jarra*) jug; (= *vaso*) glass; (= *olla*) pot; (= *maceta*) flowerpot, pot; (*Ven*) (= *bote*) tin, can; (*Méx*) (= *vasija*) mug; (*And, Caribe*) (= *termo*) flask • MODISMOS: • **a ~** in plenty • **darse ~*** to show off
2 (*Culin*) stew ▸ **pote gallego** Galician stew
3* (= *gesto*) pout, sulky look
4* (= *trago*) drink • **tomar unos ~s** to have a few drinks
potear* ▸ CONJUG 1a VI to have a few drinks
potencia SF 1 (= *capacidad*) power ▸ **potencia de fuego** firepower ▸ **potencia electoral** voting power, power in terms of votes ▸ **potencia hidráulica** hydraulic power ▸ **potencia muscular** muscular power, muscular strength ▸ **potencia nuclear** nuclear power
2 (*Mec*) power ▸ **potencia (en caballos)** horsepower ▸ **potencia al freno** brake horsepower ▸ **potencia real** effective power
3 (*Pol*) power • **las grandes ~s** the great powers • **éramos una ~ naval** we used to be a naval power ▸ **potencia colonial** colonial power ▸ **potencia mundial** world power
4 (*Mat*) power • **elevado a la quinta ~** raised to the power of five
5 (*Rel*) (*tb* **potencia del alma**) faculty
6 • **en ~** potential, in the making • **es una guerra civil en ~** it is a civil war in the making
potenciación SF = **potenciamiento**
potenciador ADJ • **ser ~ de algo** to stimulate sth
SM ▸ **potenciador del sabor** flavour enhancer
potencial ADJ potential
SM 1 (= *capacidad*) potential ▸ **potencial comercial** market potential ▸ **potencial de ventas** sales potential ▸ **potencial ganador** (*Econ*) earning potential; (*Dep*) potential to win
2 (*Ling*) conditional
potencialidad SF potentiality
potencialización SF = **potenciamiento**
potencializar ▸ CONJUG 1f VT = **potenciar**
potencialmente ADV potentially
potenciamiento SM 1 [*de turismo, artes, nuevo producto*] promotion
2 [*de economía, producción, cooperación*] boosting, strengthening
potenciar ▸ CONJUG 1b VT 1 [+ *turismo, artes, nuevo producto*] to favour, favor (EEUU), foster, promote; (= *desarrollar*) to develop; (= *mejorar*) to improve
2 (= *fortalecer*) to boost, strengthen
3 (*Inform*) to upgrade
potentado/a SM/F 1 (*en la industria*) tycoon, magnate • **un ~ de la construcción** a construction tycoon *o* magnate • **los ~s que veranean en Marbella** the idle rich who spend the summer in Marbella
2 (= *poderoso*) big shot*
potente ADJ 1 (= *poderoso*) powerful
2* (= *grande*) mighty, big • **un grito ~** a great yell, an almighty shout*
3 (= *viril*) virile
4 (*Chile*) [*salsa*] hot
poteo* SM drinking • **ir de ~*** to go for a few drinks
potestad SF authority, jurisdiction • **patria ~** paternal authority • **~ marital** husband's (legal) authority
potestativo ADJ (*Jur*) (= *optativo*) optional, facultative
potingue* SM 1 (= *brebaje*) concoction, brew
2 (= *crema*) face cream
potito SM 1 (*Esp*) (= *tarro*) jar of baby food
2 (*LAm**) (= *culo*) backside, bum‡, butt (EEUU‡)
poto* SM (*And, Cono Sur*) 1 (= *culo*) backside, bum‡, butt (EEUU‡)
2 (= *fondo*) lower end
3 (*Bot*) calabash
4 (= *vasija*) earthenware jug
potoco* ADJ (*And, Cono Sur*) squat
potón (*Cono Sur*) ADJ coarse
SM rustic, peasant
potosí SM fortune • **cuesta un ~** it costs the earth, it costs a fortune • **vale un ~** it's worth a fortune • **ella vale un ~** she's a treasure, she's worth her weight in gold • **en ese negocio tienen un ~** they've got a gold mine in that business
potra SF 1 (*Zool*) filly
2* (= *suerte*) luck, jam* • **de ~** luckily, by luck • **tener ~** to be jammy*
3 (*Med*) (= *hernia*) rupture, hernia
potranca SF filly, young mare
potranco/a SM/F colt/filly, young horse/mare
potrear ▸ CONJUG 1a VT 1 (*And, CAm*) (= *zurrar*) to beat

P

2 (*Caribe, Méx*) [+ *caballo*] to break, tame
VI (*CAm, Cono Sur*) to caper about, chase around

potrero SM (*LAm*) **1** (= *pasto*) pasture; (= *cercado*) paddock
2 (= *finca*) [*de ganado*] cattle ranch; [*de cría*] stud farm
3 (*Cono Sur*) (= *parque*) playground
4 (*Méx*) (= *llanura*) open grassland
ADJ ‡ (= *afortunado*) lucky, jammy*

potrillo SM **1** (= *caballo*) colt
2 (*Chile*) (= *copa*) tall glass
3 (*And*) (= *canoa*) small canoe

potro SM **1** (*Zool*) colt
2 (*Dep*) (vaulting) horse
3 [*de tortura*] rack
4 [*de herrar*] shoeing frame
5 (*LAm*) (*Med*) hernia

potroso‡ ADJ jammy*, lucky

POUM SM ABR (*Esp*) (*Hist*) = **Partido Obrero de Unificación Marxista**

poyo SM (*para sentarse*) stone bench; (*en cocina*) stone kitchen top; (*de ventana*) stone ledge

poza SF **1** (= *charca*) (*gen*) puddle, pool; [*de río*] backwater, pool
2 (*LAm‡*) (= *escupitajo*) gob* of spit

pozanco SM puddle, pool

pozo SM **1** [*de agua*] well • MODISMOS: • **es un ~ de maldad** he is wicked through and through, he is rotten to the core • **ser un ~ de sabiduría** to be a fount of wisdom • **ser un ~ sin fondo** to be a bottomless pit • **caer en el ~** to fall into oblivion ▸ **pozo artesiano** artesian well ▸ **pozo ciego** cesspool ▸ **pozo de petróleo** oil well ▸ **pozo de riego** well used for irrigation ▸ **pozo negro** cesspool ▸ **pozo petrolífero** oil well ▸ **pozo séptico** septic tank
2 [*de río*] deep part
3 (*Min*) (= *hueco*) shaft; (= *mina*) pit, mine ▸ **pozo de aire** air shaft ▸ **pozo de registro, pozo de visita** manhole ▸ **pozo de ventilación** ventilation shaft
4 (*Náut*) hold
5 (*LAm*) (*Astron*) black hole

pozol SM (*LAm*) = **posol**

pozole SM (*Méx*) (*Culin*) maize stew

PP SM ABR (*Esp*) (*Pol*) = **Partido Popular**

PP. ABR (= **Padres**) Frs

pp. ABR (= **porte pagado**) CP, c/p

p.p. ABR (*Jur*) (= **por poder**) pp, per pro

p.p.m. ABR **1** (= **palabras por minuto**) wpm
2 (= **partes por millón**) ppm

p.p.p. ABR (= **puntos por pulgada**) d.p.i.

PR SM ABR = **Puerto Rico**

práctica SF **1** [*de actividad*] practice • **aprender con la ~** to learn by practice • **la ~ hace al maestro** practice makes perfect • **llevar algo a la ~** • **poner algo en ~** to put sth into practice • **en la ~** in practice ▸ **práctica de riesgo** high-risk practice ▸ **práctica establecida** standard practice ▸ **prácticas restrictivas (de la competencia)** restrictive practices
2 prácticas (= *aprendizaje*) (*gen*) practice (*sing*), training (*sing*); [*de profesor*] teaching practice (*sing*); [*de laboratorio*] experiments • **hacer ~s** to do one's training • **hacer ~s de clínica** to do one's hospital training • **contrato en ~s** work experience placement • **estudiantes en ~s** students doing work experience • **período de ~s** (practical) training period ▸ **prácticas de tiro** target practice ▸ **prácticas en empresa** work experience ▸ **prácticas profesionales** professional training, practical training (*for a profession*)

practicable ADJ **1** (= *factible*) practicable, workable, feasible
2 [*camino*] passable, usable
3 (*Teat*) [*puerta*] that opens, that is meant to open

prácticamente ADV practically • **está ~ terminado** it's practically finished, it's almost finished

practicante ADJ (*Rel*) practising, practicing (EEUU)
SMF (*Med*) (= *ayudante*) medical assistant, nurse (*specializing in giving injections, taking blood pressure etc*); (*Méx*) (= *estudiante*) final year medical student

practicar ▸ CONJUG 1g VT **1** [+ *habilidad, virtud*] to practise, practice (EEUU), exercise
2 (= *hacer prácticas de*) [+ *actividad, profesión*] to practise, practice (EEUU); [+ *deporte*] to play • **le conviene ~ algún deporte** it would be good for him to play a sport *o* do some sport • **practica el francés con su profesor** she practises French with her teacher
3 (= *ejecutar*) [+ *operación quirúrgica*] to carry out, do, perform (*frm*); [+ *detención*] to make; [+ *incisión*] to make
4 [+ *hoyo*] to cut, make
VI (*en deporte, juego*) to practise, practice (EEUU); (*en profesión*) to do one's training *o* practice

practicidad SF (= *viabilidad*) practicality; (= *resultado*) effectiveness

practicismo SM down-to-earth attitude, sense of realism

práctico ADJ **1** (= *útil*) (*gen*) practical; [*herramienta*] handy; [*ropa*] sensible, practical • **no resultó ser muy ~** it turned out to be not very practical • **resulta ~ vivir tan cerca de la fábrica** it's convenient *o* handy to live so close to the factory
2 (= *no teórico*) [*estudio, formación*] practical • **conocimientos ~s de informática** practical experience of computers
3 (= *pragmático*) • **sé ~ y búscate un trabajo que dé dinero** be practical *o* sensible and find a job with money
4 (*frm*) (= *experto*) • **ser muy ~ en algo** to be very skilled at sth, be an expert at sth
SM **1** (*Náut*) pilot (*in a port*)
2 (*Med*) practitioner

pradera SF (= *prado*) meadow, meadowland; (*de Canadá, EEUU*) prairie • **unas extensas ~s** extensive grasslands

pradería SF meadowlands (*pl*), grasslands (*pl*)

prado SM (= *campo*) meadow, field; (= *parque*) green grassy area; (= *pastizal*) pasture; (*LAm*) (= *césped*) grass, lawn

Praga SF Prague

pragmática SF **1** (*Ling*) pragmatics (*sing*)
2 (*Hist*) decree, proclamation

pragmático ADJ pragmatic

pragmatismo SM pragmatism

pragmatista SMF pragmatist

prángana* ADJ INV (*Méx*) poor

PRD SM ABR **1** (*Méx*) = **Partido de la Revolución Democrática**
2 (*República Dominicana*) = **Partido Revolucionario Dominicano**

pre... PREF pre...

preacordar ▸ CONJUG 1l VT to reach a preliminary agreement on, make a draft agreement on

preacuerdo SM preliminary agreement, outline *o* draft agreement

preadolescente ADJ pre-adolescent, pre-pubescent (*pey*)
SMF pre-adolescent boy/girl

prealarma SF early warning

prealerta SF standby, yellow alert • **en estado de ~** on standby, on yellow alert

preámbulo SM **1** (= *introducción*) [*de libro, discurso*] introduction; [*de ley, constitución*] preamble
2 (= *rodeo*) • **andarse con ~s** • **gastar ~s** to beat about the bush, avoid the issue • **sin más ~s** without further ado, without preamble
3 (= *preliminar*) prelude • **la visita del rey es el ~ de las conversaciones** the royal visit is a prelude to the negotiations

preasignación SF (*Telec*) carrier pre-selection

preautonómico ADJ (*Esp*) (*Pol*) *before the creation of the autonomous regional governments*

preaviso SM forewarning, early warning

prebélico ADJ prewar

prebenda SF **1** (*Rel*) (= *renta*) prebend
2 (= *gaje*) perk* • **las ~s del cargo** the perks of the job* ▸ **prebendas corporativas** business perks*

prebendado SM prebendary

preboste SM **1** (*Hist*) provost
2 (*Pol*) chief, leader

precalentamiento SM (*Dep*) warm-up; (*Aut*) warming up

precalentar ▸ CONJUG 1j VT to preheat; (*Dep*) to warm up
VPR **precalentarse** (*Dep*) to warm up

precampaña SF (*tb* **precampaña electoral**) run-up to the election campaign

precanceroso ADJ precancerous, pre-cancer

precandidato/a SM/F (*esp Méx*) (*Pol*) *official shortlisted Presidential candidate*

precariamente ADV precariously

precariedad SF **1** [*de empleo, salud, situación*] precariousness
2 [*de recursos, medios*] scarcity

precario ADJ [*salud*] precarious; [*situación*] precarious, difficult; [*economía, democracia*] unstable; [*vivienda*] poor, inferior; [*medios*] unpredictable, reduced
SM precarious state • **dejar a algn en ~** to leave sb in a difficult situation • **estamos en ~** we are in a difficult situation • **vivir en ~** to live from hand to mouth, scrape a living

precarización SF • **los sindicatos han denunciado la constante ~ del empleo** the unions have condemned the trend towards poorer working conditions and greater job insecurity

precarizar ▸ CONJUG 1f VT • **esas medidas van a conseguir ~ el empleo en la región** these measures will lead to poorer working conditions and greater job insecurity in the area

precaución SF **1** (*al hacer algo*) (= *cuidado*) precaution; (= *medida*) preventive measure • **tomar precauciones** to take precautions • **extremar las precauciones** to be extra careful • **lo hicimos por ~** we did it to be on the safe side, we did it as a precautionary measure *o* as a precaution
2 (= *previsión*) foresight; (= *cautela*) caution • **ir con ~** to proceed with caution

precautorio ADJ precautionary

precaver ▸ CONJUG 2a VT (= *prevenir*) to try to prevent, guard against; (= *anticipar*) to forestall; (= *evitar*) to stave off
VPR **precaverse** to be on one's guard, take precautions (**contra** against) • **~se de algo** to be on one's guard against sth, beware of sth

precavidamente ADV cautiously

precavido ADJ **1** (= *cauteloso*) cautious • REFRÁN: • **hombre ~ vale por dos** forewarned is forearmed
2 (= *preparado*) prepared • **vengo ~** I came prepared

precedencia SF **1** (= *prioridad*) precedence, priority
2 (= *preeminencia*) greater importance, superiority

precedente ADJ preceding, previous,

foregoing (*frm*) • **cada uno mejor que el ~** each one better than the one before
SM precedent • **de acuerdo con el ~** according to precedent • **establecer** *o* **sentar un ~** to set a precedent • **sin ~(s)** (= *sin antecedentes*) unprecedented, without precedent; (= *sin igual*) unparalleled • **sin que sirva de ~** just this once • **por primera vez y sin que sirva de ~, voy a seguir tu consejo** just this once, I'll follow your advice

precedentemente ADV earlier, at an earlier stage, previously

preceder ▸ CONJUG 2a VT **1** (= *anteceder*) • **~ a algo/algn** to precede sth/sb • **le precedía un coche** he was preceded by a car • **los años que precedieron a la Guerra Civil** the years leading up to the Civil War, the years preceding the Civil War • **el título precede al nombre** the title goes before the name
2 (= *tener prioridad*) • **~ a algo/algn** to have priority over sth/sb, take precedence over sth/sb
VI to precede • **todo lo que precede** all the preceding (part), all that which comes before

preceptista SMF theorist

preceptiva SF precepts (*pl*)

preceptivo ADJ compulsory, obligatory, mandatory • **es ~ utilizar el formulario** the application form must be used

precepto SM (= *regla*) precept; (= *mandato*) order, rule • **día** *o* **fiesta de ~** (*Rel*) holy day of obligation

preceptor/a SM/F (*en colegio*) teacher; (*particular*) (private) tutor

preceptorado SM tutorship

preceptoral ADJ tutorial

preceptuar ▸ CONJUG 1e VT to lay down, establish

preces SFPL prayers, supplications

preciado ADJ **1** (= *estimado*) [*posesión*] prized; [*amigo*] valued, esteemed
2 (= *presuntuoso*) presumptuous

preciarse ▸ CONJUG 1b VPR • **~ de algo** to pride o.s. on sth • **~ de hacer algo** to pride o.s. on doing sth

precintado ADJ [*de paquete*] sealed, presealed; [*calle, zona*] sealed off
SM [*de paquete*] sealing; [*de calle, zona*] sealing off

precintar ▸ CONJUG 1a VT [+ *paquete*] to seal, preseal; [+ *calle, zona*] to seal off

precinto SM **1** (*Com*) seal
2 (= *acción*) [*de paquete*] sealing; [*de calle, zona*] sealing off

precio SM **1** (= *importe*) [*de producto*] price; [*de viaje*] fare; (*en hotel*) rate, charge • **han subido los ~s** prices have gone up • **¿qué ~ tiene?** how much is it? • **a ~ de saldo** at a knockdown price • **a** *o* **por un ~ simbólico** for a nominal *o* token sum • **"no importa precio"** "cost no object" • **"precio a discutir"** "offers" • **último ~** closing price • MODISMOS: • **poner** *o* **señalar ~ a la cabeza de algn** to put a price on sb's head • **no tener ~** to be priceless • **este cuadro no tiene ~** this painting is priceless • **su lealtad no tiene ~** his loyalty is of enormous value ▸ **precio al contado** cash ▸ **precio al detalle, precio al por menor** retail price ▸ **precio de compra** purchase price ▸ **precio de coste, precio de costo** cost-price • **a ~ de coste** at cost price ▸ **precio de fábrica** ex works price • **a ~ de fábrica** at factory prices ▸ **precio de intervención** intervention price ▸ **precio de mercado** market price ▸ **precio de ocasión** bargain price ▸ **precio de oferta** offer price ▸ **precio de referencia** suggested price ▸ **precio de salida** starting price ▸ **precio de situación** (*LAm*) bargain price ▸ **precio de venta** sale price, selling price ▸ **precio de venta al público** retail price ▸ **precio de venta recomendado** recommended retail price ▸ **precio neto** net price ▸ **precio obsequio** giveaway price ▸ **precio orientativo** manufacturer's recommended price ▸ **precios al consumo** retail prices ▸ **precio tope** top price, ceiling price ▸ **precio unitario** unit price
2 (= *coste, sacrificio*) • **pagó un ~ muy alto por su libertad** he paid a very high price for his freedom • **lo hará a cualquier ~** he'll do it whatever the cost *o* at any price • **evítelo a cualquier ~** avoid it at all costs • **al ~ de** (*frm*) at the cost of • **ganó las elecciones, pero al ~ de su integridad** he won the election but at the cost *o* expense of his integrity
3 (*frm*) (= *valor*) worth, value • **un hombre de gran ~** a man of great worth • **tengo en gran ~ su amistad** I value his friendship very highly

preciosamente ADV (= *maravillosamente*) beautifully; (= *con encanto*) charmingly

preciosidad SF **1*** (= *objeto*) (*bello*) beautiful thing; (*apreciado*) precious object • **es una ~** he's adorable • **¡oye, ~!** hey, beautiful!
2 (*como cualidad*) (= *excelencia*) preciousness; (= *valor*) value, worth
3 (*pey*) (= *afectación*) preciousness, preciosity

preciosismo SM preciosity

preciosista ADJ precious, affected
SMF affected writer, precious writer

precioso ADJ **1** (= *valioso*) precious, valuable; ▸ **piedra**
2 (= *hermoso*) (*gen*) lovely, beautiful; (= *primoroso*) charming • **un vestido ~** a beautiful dress • **tienen un niño ~** they have a lovely child • **¿verdad que es ~?** isn't it lovely *o* beautiful?

preciosura SF = **preciosidad**

precipicio SM **1** (*en monte, peñasco*) cliff, precipice
2 (= *situación arriesgada*) abyss • **un país al borde del ~** a country on the edge of the abyss, a country on the brink of disaster *o* ruin

precipitación SF **1** (*al hacer algo*) (= *prisa*) haste; (= *imprudencia*) rashness • **con ~** hastily, precipitately (*frm*)
2 (*Meteo*) rainfall, precipitation (*frm*) • **precipitaciones abundantes** heavy rainfall • **precipitaciones débiles** light rain • **abundantes precipitaciones de nieve** heavy snow
3 (*Quím*) precipitation

precipitadamente ADV [*huir, lanzarse*] headlong; [*irse*] very suddenly; [*actuar*] rashly, precipitately (*frm*) • **escribí una nota ~** I dashed off a note • **tuvieron que casarse ~** they had to get married in a hurry • **ha abandonado ~ el país** he left the country very suddenly

precipitado ADJ [*huida*] headlong; [*partida*] hasty, sudden; [*conducta*] hasty, rash
SM (*Quím*) precipitate

precipitador SM precipitant

precipitar ▸ CONJUG 1a VT **1** (= *arrojar*) to hurl down, throw (**desde** from)
2 (= *apresurar*) to hasten, precipitate (*frm*) • **aquello precipitó su salida** that affair hastened *o* (*frm*) precipitated his departure • **la dimisión precipitó la crisis** her resignation brought on *o* (*frm*) precipitated the crisis • **no precipitemos los acontecimientos** let's not rush things
3 (*Quím*) to precipitate
VPR **precipitarse 1** (= *arrojarse*) to throw o.s., hurl o.s. (**desde** from) • **~se sobre algo** [*pájaro*] to swoop down on sth; [*animal*] to pounce on sth • **~se sobre algn** to throw *o* hurl o.s. on sb
2 (= *correr*) to rush, dash • **~se a hacer algo** to rush to do sth • **~se hacia la salida** to rush towards the exit
3 (= *actuar sin reflexión*) to act hastily • **se ha precipitado rehusándolo** he acted hastily in rejecting it, it was rash of him to refuse it • **no te precipites** don't rush into things

precipitoso ADJ **1** [*lugar*] precipitous, very steep
2 [*huida etc*] = **precipitado**

precisa SF **1** (*CAm*) (= *urgencia*) urgency
2 • **tener la ~** (*Cono Sur**) to be on the ball

precisado ADJ • **verse ~ a hacer algo** to be forced *o* obliged to do sth

precisamente ADV **1** (= *con precisión*) precisely
2 (= *exactamente*) precisely, exactly • **¡precisamente!** exactly!, precisely! • **~ por eso** for that very reason, precisely because of that • **~ fue él quien lo dijo** as a matter of fact it was he who said it • **~ estamos hablando de eso** we're just talking about that • **llegó ~ cuando nos íbamos** he arrived just as we were leaving • **yo no soy un experto ~** I'm not exactly an expert • **no es eso ~** it's not quite that

precisar ▸ CONJUG 1a VT **1** (= *necesitar*) to need, require • **no precisa lavado** it needs no washing, it doesn't require washing • **el jefe precisa tu ayuda** the boss needs your help • **no precisamos que el candidato tenga experiencia** we do not require that the candidate should be experienced • **"se precisan mensajeros"** "messengers required", "messengers wanted"
2 (= *especificar*) to specify • **no precisó a qué hora llegaría** he didn't specify when he would arrive • **aún no han precisado los detalles del contrato** they have not specified the details of the contract yet • **¿puedes ~ un poco más?** can you be a little more specific? • **precisó que no se trataba de un virus** he said specifically that it was not a virus
VI • **~ de algo** to need *o* require sth • **no precisamos de sus servicios** we do not need *o* require your services

precisión SF **1** (= *exactitud*) precision, accuracy, preciseness • **instrumento de ~** precision instrument
2 • **hacer precisiones** to clarify matters
3 (= *necesidad*) need, necessity • **tener ~ de algo** to need sth, be in need of sth • **verse en la ~ de hacer algo** to be forced *o* obliged to do sth
4 (*Méx*) (= *urgencia*) urgency

preciso ADJ **1** (= *exacto*) precise • **una descripción precisa** a precise description • **hemos recibido instrucciones precisas** we have received precise instructions • **un reloj muy ~** a very precise *o* accurate watch
2 (= *justo*) • **en aquel ~ momento** at that precise *o* very moment • **tengo el tiempo ~ para comer y ducharme** I have just enough time to eat and shower
3 (= *necesario*) necessary • **las cualidades precisas** the necessary qualities • **cuando sea ~** when it becomes necessary • **si es ~ iré yo mismo** I'll go by myself if necessary • **es ~ tener coche** it is essential to have a car • **es ~ que lo hagas** you must do it • **no es ~ que vengas** there's no need for you to come • MODISMO: • **ser un Don Preciso** (*Cono Sur*) to believe o.s. to be indispensable
4 [*estilo, lenguaje*] concise
5 (*Caribe*) [*persona*] conceited

precitado ADJ above-mentioned

preclaro ADJ illustrious

precocidad SF **1** (= *cualidad*)

P

precociousness, precocity
2 (*Bot*) earliness

precocinado ADJ pre-cooked • **platos ~s** ready meals, pre-cooked meals

precocinar ▸ CONJUG 1a VT to precook

precognición SF foreknowledge, precognition (*frm*)

precolombino ADJ pre-Columbian • **la América precolombina** America before Columbus

preconcebido ADJ preconceived • **idea preconcebida** preconceived idea, preconception

preconcepción SF preconception

preconciliar ADJ preconciliar, before Vatican II

precondición SF precondition

preconización SF 1 (= *recomendación*) recommendation
2 (= *apoyo*) advocacy

preconizar ▸ CONJUG 1f VT 1 (= *elogiar*) to praise
2 (= *recomendar*) to recommend, advise
3 (= *apoyar*) to advocate

precontrato SM pre-contract

precordillera SF (*LAm*) Andean foothills (*pl*)

precoz ADJ 1 (= *prematuro*) [*envejecimiento, calvicie, eyaculación*] premature; [*diagnóstico, pronóstico*] early; [*niño*] precocious
2 (*Bot*) early

precozmente ADV 1 (= *prematuramente*) [*envejecer, eyacular*] prematurely; [*diagnosticar, detectar*] early • **inició su actividad sexual ~** he became sexually active at an early age
2 (*Bot*) early

precristiano ADJ pre-Christian

precursor(a) SM/F precursor, forerunner

predación SF (*Bio*) predation; (*fig*) depredation, plundering

predador SM, **predator** SM predator

predecesor(a) SM/F predecessor

predecible ADJ predictable • **la ~ subida de los tipo de interés preocupa a muchos** many people are worried about the predicted rise in interest rates • **el resultado no es fácilmente ~** the result isn't easy to predict

predecir ▸ CONJUG 3o VT to predict, forecast

predemocrático ADJ prior to the establishment of democracy

predestinación SF predestination

predestinado ADJ predestined • **estar ~ a hacer algo** to be predestined to do sth

predestinar ▸ CONJUG 1a VT to predestine

predeterminación SF predetermination

predeterminado ADJ predetermined

predeterminar ▸ CONJUG 1a VT to predetermine

prédica SF (= *sermón*) sermon; (= *arenga*) harangue • **~s** preaching

predicación SF preaching

predicado SM predicate

predicador/a SM/F preacher

predicamento SM 1 (= *prestigio*) standing, prestige • **no goza ahora de tanto ~** it has less prestige now, it is not so well thought of now
2 (*LAm*) (= *situación difícil*) predicament

predicar ▸ CONJUG 1g VT, VI to preach • **~ con el ejemplo** to practise what one preaches

predicativo ADJ predicative

predicción SF [*de catástrofe, hecho futuro*] prediction; [*del tiempo*] forecast ▸ **predicción del tiempo** weather forecasting

predicho ADJ aforementioned

predictivo ADJ [*texto*] predictive

predigerido ADJ predigested

predilección SF predilection • **tener ~ por algo** to have a predilection for sth • **predilecciones y aversiones** likes and dislikes

predilecto ADJ favourite, favorite (*EEUU*) • **fue nombrado hijo ~ de Madrid** he was named one of Madrid's honorary citizens

predio SM (= *finca*) property, estate; (*LAm*) (= *local*) premises (*pl*) • **~s** land (*sing*) ▸ **predio rústico** rural property, country estate ▸ **predio urbano** town property

predisponente ADJ [*factor, efecto*] underlying • **factores ~s de algo** the underlying factors of sth

predisponer ▸ CONJUG 2q VT to predispose; (*con prejuicios*) to prejudice, bias (**contra** against)

predisposición SF (= *tendencia*) predisposition; (= *prejuicio*) prejudice, bias (**contra** against); (*Med*) tendency, predisposition (**a** to)

predispuesto ADJ predisposed • **ser ~ a los catarros** to have a tendency to get colds • **es ~ al abatimiento** he tends to get depressed • **estar ~ contra algn** to be prejudiced against sb

predocumento SM draft, preliminary paper

predominante ADJ 1 (= *preponderante*) [*papel, poder*] predominant; [*opinión, ideología, viento*] prevailing
2 (*Com*) [*interés*] controlling

predominantemente ADV predominantly

predominar ▸ CONJUG 1a VI [*papel, poder*] to predominate, dominate; [*opinión, ideología, viento*] to prevail
VT to dominate, predominate over

predominio SM predominance

preelectoral ADJ pre-election (*antes de s*) • **sondeo ~** pre-election survey

preeminencia SF pre-eminence

preeminente ADJ pre-eminent

preeminentemente ADV pre-eminently

preempción SF pre-emption

preenfriar ▸ CONJUG 1c VT to precool

preescoger ▸ CONJUG 2c VT [+ *jugadores*] to seed

preescolar ADJ preschool • **educación ~** preschool education, nursery education
SM (= *escuela*) nursery school, nursery
SMF (= *niño*) child of nursery school age

preestablecido ADJ pre-established

preestrenar ▸ CONJUG 1a VT to preview, give a preview of

preestreno SM preview, press view

preexistencia SF pre-existence

preexistente ADJ pre-existing, pre-existent

preexistir ▸ CONJUG 3a VI to pre-exist, exist before

prefabricado ADJ prefabricated
SM prefabricated building, prefab*

prefabricar ▸ CONJUG 1g VT to prefabricate

prefacio SM preface, foreword

prefecto SM prefect

prefectura SF prefecture

preferencia SF 1 (= *prioridad*) preference • **tendrán ~ los que no lleguen al salario mínimo** preference will be given to those earning less than the minimum wage • **tienen ~ los vehículos que circulan por la derecha** vehicles coming from the right have priority • **localidad de ~** reserved seat • **tratamiento de ~** preferential treatment
2 (= *predilección*) preference • **no tengo ninguna ~** I have no preference • **tiene una clara ~ por la hija mayor** he has a clear preference for his eldest daughter, his eldest daughter is his clear favourite

preferencial ADJ preferential

preferente ADJ 1 [*trato*] (= *especial*) preferential; (= *prioritario*) priority (*antes de s*); [*lugar*] prominent; [*derecho*] prior; (*Econ*) [*acción*] preference (*antes de s*)
2 • **clase ~** (*Aer*) club class

preferentemente ADV preferably

preferible ADJ preferable (**a** to)

preferiblemente ADV preferably

preferido/a ADJ favourite, favorite (*EEUU*) • **es mi cantante ~** he's my favourite singer
SM/F favourite, favorite (*EEUU*) • **yo era la preferida de mi madre** I was my mother's favourite

preferir ▸ CONJUG 3i VT to prefer • **~ el té al café** to prefer tea to coffee • **¿cuál prefieres?** which do you prefer? • **¿qué prefieres (tomar)?** what will you have? • **prefiero ir a pie** I prefer to walk, I'd rather walk

PREFERIR

Más verbo

▸ *Cuando se habla de generalizaciones,* **preferir** *+ infinitivo se traduce por* **prefer** *+* **-ing**:

Prefiero nadar a correr
I prefer swimming to running
Juan siempre prefería leer a trabajar
Juan always preferred reading to working

▸ *Cuando se habla de lo que se quiere hacer en una ocasión determinada,* **prefiero/preferiría** *se traducen por* **would rather** *+ infinitivo sin* **to** *o, en un contexto más formal, por* **would prefer** *+ infinitivo con* **to**:

—¿Vamos al cine? —Preferiría quedarme en casa
"Shall we go to the cinema?" — "I'd rather stay *o* I'd prefer to stay at home"
Prefiero quedarme en un hotel a alquilar un apartamento
I'd rather stay in a hotel than rent an apartment, I'd prefer to stay in a hotel rather than rent an apartment

Como se puede ver en el ejemplo anterior, **would prefer to** *se usa en correlación con* **rather than** *+ infinitivo sin* **to** *y nunca con* **than** *solo.*

▸ *Cuando se trata de traducir estructuras como* **preferiría que** *+ oración subordinada, en inglés se emplea la siguiente estructura: sujeto de la oración principal +* **would rather** *+ sujeto + verbo en pasado:*

Preferiría que él me llamara
I'd rather he phoned me
—¿Te importa que hable con ella?
—Preferiría que no lo hicieras
"Do you mind if I talk to her?" — "I'd rather you didn't"

Otra posibilidad de expresar esta construcción en inglés sería: **would prefer it if** *+ resto de la oración o* **would prefer** *+ objeto + construcción de infinitivo:*

Preferiría que él me llamara
I'd prefer it if he phoned me *o* I'd prefer him to phone me

Para otros usos y ejemplos ver la entrada.

prefiguración SF foreshadowing, prefiguration

prefigurar ▸ CONJUG 1a VT to foreshadow, prefigure

prefijar ▸ CONJUG 1a VT 1 (= *predeterminar*) to fix beforehand, prearrange
2 (*Ling*) to prefix (**a** to)

prefijo SM 1 (*Ling*) prefix
2 (*Telec*) (dialling) code, STD code, area code (*EEUU*)

preformateado ADJ preformatted

pregón SM (= *proclama*) proclamation, announcement (*by town crier*); (*Com*) street cry, vendor's cry ▸ **pregón de las fiestas** local festival opening speech

pregonar ▹ CONJUG 1a VT [+ *inocencia propia, interés*] to proclaim, announce; [+ *secreto*] to disclose, reveal; [+ *mercancía*] to hawk; [+ *méritos*] to proclaim (for all to hear) • **no estaría bien que lo fueras pregonando por ahí** you shouldn't go spreading it around

pregonero/a SM/F **1** (*municipal*) town crier
2 [*de fiestas*] person who makes the opening speech
3 (*Méx*) (= *subastador*) auctioneer

pregrabado ADJ pre-recorded

pregrabar ▹ CONJUG 1a VT to pre-record

preguerra SF prewar period • **el nivel de la ~** the prewar level • **en la ~** in the prewar period, before the war

pregunta SF question • **contestar a una ~** to answer a question • **hacer una ~** to ask *o* put a question • **acosar a algn a ~s** to bombard sb with questions • **lo negó, a ~s de los periodistas** questioned by the press he denied it • **presentar una ~** (*Pol*) to put down a question, table a question • **"preguntas frecuentes"** "FAQs", "frequently asked questions" • MODISMO: • **andar** *o* **estar a la cuarta ~** (*Esp**) to be broke* ▸ **pregunta capciosa** trick question ▸ **pregunta de elección múltiple** multiple-choice question ▸ **pregunta indiscreta** indiscreet question, tactless question ▸ **pregunta retórica** rhetorical question ▸ **pregunta sugestiva** (*Jur*) leading question ▸ **pregunta tipo test** multiple-choice question

preguntar ▹ CONJUG 1a VT to ask • **~ algo a algn** to ask sb sth • **siempre me preguntas lo mismo** you're always asking me the same question • **le pregunté la hora** I asked him the time • **pregúntale cómo se llama** ask her what her name is • **pregúntale si quiere venir** ask him if he wants to come, ask him whether he wants to come or not • **le fue preguntada su edad** (*frm*) he was asked his age
VI to ask, inquire • **~ por algn: si te preguntan por mí di que no he llegado** if they ask about me, tell them I haven't arrived • **cuando la vi ayer me preguntó por ti** she asked after you when I saw her yesterday • **hay alguien al teléfono que pregunta por el jefe** there's someone on the phone asking for the boss • **~ por la salud de algn** to ask after sb's health
VPR **preguntarse** to wonder • **me pregunto si vale la pena** I wonder if it's worthwhile

preguntón* ADJ inquisitive

prehispánico ADJ pre-Hispanic

prehistoria SF prehistory

prehistórico ADJ prehistoric

preignición SF pre-ignition

preimpositivo ADJ • **beneficios ~s** pre-tax profits, profits before tax

preinforme SM preliminary report

preinscripción SF (*para cursar estudios*) pre-enrolment, pre-enrollment (EEUU); (*para congreso, cursillo*) provisional booking

preinstalación SF • **~ de radio** radio fitted as standard • **~ de aire acondicionado** air conditioning pre-installed

preinstalado ADJ [*software*] pre-installed

prejubilación SF early retirement

prejubilado/a SM/F person who takes early retirement

prejubilar ▹ CONJUG 1a VT to force to take early retirement

prejuiciado ADJ (*LAm*) prejudiced (**contra** against)

prejuicio SM **1** (= *parcialidad*) prejudice, bias (**contra** against) • **no tienen ~s contra los españoles** they are not prejudiced against Spaniards
2 (= *idea preconcebida*) preconception
3 (= *acto*) prejudgement

prejuzgar ▹ CONJUG 1h VT to prejudge

prelación SF precedence, priority • **tener ~ sobre algo** to have precedence *o* priority over sth

prelado SM prelate

prelatura SF prelature ▸ **prelatura personal** personal prelature

prelavado SM prewash

preliminar ADJ [*estudio, resultado*] preliminary; (*Dep*) • **fase ~** qualifying round(s)
SM **1** (*gen*) preliminary
2 preliminares (*en el sexo*) foreplay (*sing*)

preludiar ▹ CONJUG 1b VT to herald • **el calor que preludia la primavera** the warmth that heralds the coming of spring
VI (*Mús*) [*cantante*] to warm up; [*pianista*] to play a few scales; [*orquesta*] to tune up

preludio SM **1** (*Mús*) (= *comienzo*) prelude (**de** to); (= *ensayo*) warm-up
2 (= *comienzo*) prelude

premamá ADJ • **vestido (de) ~** maternity dress

premarital ADJ premarital

prematrimonial ADJ premarital, before marriage; ▹ **relación**

prematuramente ADV prematurely

prematuro/a ADJ premature • **es ~ hablar de detalles** it's too early to talk about details, it would be rather premature to talk about details
SM/F premature baby

premedicación SF premedication

premeditación SF premeditation • **con ~** with premeditation, deliberately

premeditadamente ADV with premeditation, deliberately

premeditado ADJ [*acto, crimen, tiro*] premeditated; [*ironía*] deliberate; [*negligencia*] wilful; [*insulto*] calculated

premeditar ▹ CONJUG 1a VT (= *pensar*) to premeditate, think out (in advance); (= *planear*) [+ *crimen*] to premeditate, plan

premenstrual ADJ premenstrual; ▹ **síndrome**

premiación SF (*LAm*) **1** (= *acción*) • **no estoy de acuerdo con su ~** I don't think the award should go/should have gone to him
2 (= *ceremonia*) awards ceremony; (*Escol*) prize-giving

premiado/a ADJ [*novela*] prizewinning; [*número, boleto*] winning • **tu billete resultó** *o* **salió ~ con 60 millones** your ticket won 60 million
SM/F prizewinner

premiar ▹ CONJUG 1b VT **1** (= *dar un premio a*) to award a prize to • **el jurado ha premiado la película italiana** the jury awarded a prize to the Italian film • **fue premiado el director italiano** the Italian director received an award • **han premiado el documental** the documentary won an award
2 (= *recompensar*) to reward (**con** with) • **han premiado su esfuerzo con un aumento de sueldo** they rewarded his efforts with a pay rise

premier [pre'mjer] SMF prime minister, premier

premiere [pre'mjer] SF premiere

premio SM **1** (*en competición*) prize • **Gran Premio de Fórmula Uno** Formula One Grand Prix • **llevarse un ~** to get a prize ▸ **premio de consolación** consolation prize ▸ **premio de fin de carrera** final-year prize ▸ **premio en metálico** cash prize ▸ **premio extraordinario** (*Univ*) award with special distinction ▸ **premio gordo** jackpot
2 (= *recompensa*) reward • **como ~ a sus servicios** as a reward for her services
3 (*Com, Econ*) (= *prima*) premium • **a ~** at a premium
SMF (= *persona galardonada*) • **una entrevista con la ~ Nobel de la Paz** an interview with the winner of the Nobel Peace Prize • **intervendrá en el debate el actual ~ Cervantes** the current Cervantes Prize winner will take place in the debate

premioso ADJ **1** (= *apremiante*) pressing, urgent
2 [*orden*] strict
3 [*persona*] (*al hablar*) reticent, shy of speaking; (*al escribir*) slow (in writing); (*al moverse*) slow, awkward
4 [*estilo*] laboured, labored (EEUU)
5 [*vestido*] tight

premisa SF premise

premonición SF premonition

premonitoriamente ADV as a warning

premonitorio ADJ premonitory (*frm*), warning (*antes de s*)

premunirse ▹ CONJUG 3a VPR (*LAm*) = **precaver**

premura SF **1** (= *prisa*) haste, urgency
2 (= *aprieto*) pressure • **con ~ de tiempo** under pressure of time, with very little time • **debido a ~ de espacio** because of pressure on space

prenatal ADJ antenatal, prenatal

prenavideño ADJ before Christmas, pre-Christmas (*antes de s*)

prenda SF **1** (*tb* **prenda de vestir**) garment, article of clothing ▸ **prenda interior** undergarment, piece of underwear • **~s interiores** underwear (*sing*) ▸ **prendas de cama** bedclothes ▸ **prendas deportivas** sportswear (*sing*) ▸ **prendas de mesa** table linen (*sing*) ▸ **prendas de punto** knitwear (*sing*) ▸ **prendas de trabajo** work clothes
2 (= *garantía*) pledge • **dejar algo en ~** (*por dinero*) to pawn sth; (*como garantía*) to leave sth as security • **en** *o* **como ~ de algo** as a token of sth • MODISMOS: • **no soltar ~** to give nothing away • **no dolerle ~s a algn**: • **a mí no me duelen ~s** I don't mind saying nice things about others, it doesn't worry me that I'm not as good as others • REFRÁN: • **al buen pagador no le duelen ~s** a good payer is not afraid of giving guarantees
3 prendas (= *cualidades*) talents, gifts • **buenas ~s** good qualities • **de todas ~s** first class, excellent
4 (= *juego*) forfeit • **pagar ~** to pay a forfeit
5* (*en oración directa*) darling • **¡oye, ~!** hi, gorgeous!*
6 • **la ~** (*Cono Sur*) one's sweetheart, one's lover

prendar ▹ CONJUG 1a VT **1** [+ *persona*] (= *cautivar*) to captivate, enchant; (= *ganar la voluntad de*) to win over • **volvió prendado de la ciudad** by the time he came back he had fallen in love with the town
2 (*Méx*) (= *empeñar*) to pawn
VPR **prendarse** • **~se de algo** to be captivated by sth, be enchanted with sth • **~se de algn** to fall in love with sb

prendedera SF (*And*) waitress

prendedor SM, **prendedero** SM clasp, brooch, broach (EEUU)

prender ▹ CONJUG 2a VT **1** [+ *persona*] (= *capturar*) to catch, capture; (= *detener*) to arrest
2 (*Cos*) (= *sujetar*) to fasten; (*con alfiler*) to pin,

attach (**en to**) • **~ el pelo con horquillas** to pin one's hair with grips
3 (= *atar*) to tie, do up
4 (*esp LAm*) [+ *fuego, horno, vela, cigarrillo*] to light; [+ *cerilla*] to strike; [+ *luz, TV*] to switch on; [+ *cuarto*] to light up
VI 1 [*fuego*] to catch • **sus ideas prendieron fácilmente en la juventud** his ideas soon caught on with the young
2 (= *engancharse*) to catch, stick • **el ancla prendió en el fondo** the anchor buried itself in the seabed
3 [*planta*] to take, take root
4 [*vacuna*] to take
VPR **prenderse 1** (= *encenderse*) to catch fire
2 [*mujer*] to dress up
3 (*Caribe*) (= *emborracharse*) to get drunk
prendería† SF [*de cosas usadas*] secondhand (clothes) shop; [*de baratijas*] junkshop; [*de empeños*] pawnbroker's (shop)
prendero/a† SM/F 1 [*de cosas usadas*] secondhand (clothes) dealer, junk dealer
2 (= *prestamista*) pawnbroker
prendido ADJ 1 • **quedar ~** (= *enganchado*) to be caught (fast), be stuck; (= *cautivado*) to be captivated
2 (*Cono Sur*) (*Med*) constipated
3 (*Méx*) (= *vestido*) dressed up
SM (= *adorno*) clip, brooch
prendimiento SM 1 (= *captura*) (*gen*) capture; [*de droga, contrabando*] seizure
2 (= *detención*) arrest
3 (*Cono Sur*) (*Med*) constipation
prensa SF 1 (= *publicaciones*) • **la ~** the press, the (news)papers • **leer la ~** to read the (news)papers • **salir en la ~** to appear in the press *o* (news)papers • **tener mala ~** to have *o* get a bad press ▸ **la prensa amarilla** the gutter press ▸ **prensa del corazón** celebrity and gossip magazines (*pl*) ▸ **prensa roja** (*Cono Sur*) *sensationalist press specializing in crime stories* ▸ **prensa rosa** celebrity and gossip magazines (*pl*)
2 (= *máquina*) (*Mec, Dep*) press; (*Tip*) printing press; [*de raqueta*] press • **aprobar un libro para la ~** to pass a book for the printers • **dar algo a la ~** to send sth to the printers • **entrar en ~** to go to press • **estar en ~** to be at the printers • **"libros en prensa"** "forthcoming titles"

PRENSA DEL CORAZÓN

The **prensa del corazón** is the generic term given in Spain to weekly or fortnightly magazines specializing in society gossip and the social lives of the rich and famous. The pioneer was **¡Hola!**, which first appeared in 1944 - **Hello!** magazine is the English-language version - while other popular titles include **Pronto**, **Lecturas**, **Semana** and **Diez Minutos**. In recent years TV stations have followed their lead with seemingly more and more celebrity and gossip programmes (**programas del corazón**) appearing all the time.

prensaajos SM INV garlic press
prensado ADJ compressed
SM 1 (= *acto*) pressing
2 (= *lustre*) sheen, shine, gloss
prensador SM press, pressing machine ▸ **prensador de paja** straw baler
prensaestopas SM INV (*Náut*) stuffing box
prensaje SM (*Mús*) recording
prensalimones SM INV lemon-squeezer
prensar ▹ CONJUG 1a VT to press
prensil ADJ prehensile
prenupcial ADJ prenuptial
preñado ADJ 1 [*mujer, animal*] pregnant • **está preñada de seis meses** she's six months pregnant
2 • **~ de algo** pregnant with sth, full of sth • **una situación preñada de peligros** a situation fraught with danger • **ojos ~s de lágrimas** eyes brimming with tears
3 [*muro*] bulging, sagging
SM (= *embarazo*) pregnancy
preñar ▹ CONJUG 1a VT 1 (= *dejar embarazada*) to get pregnant; (*Zool*) to impregnate, fertilize
2 (= *llenar*) to fill
preñez SF pregnancy
preocupación SF 1 (= *inquietud*) worry, concern; (= *miedo*) fear • **tiene la ~ de que su mujer le es infiel** he is worried that his wife is unfaithful to him
2 (*LAm*) (= *preferencia*) special consideration, priority, preference
preocupado ADJ worried, concerned (**por** about)
preocupante ADJ worrying
preocupar ▹ CONJUG 1a VT (= *inquietar*) to worry; (= *molestar*) to bother • **esto me preocupa muchísimo** I'm extremely worried about this, this worries me very much • **me preocupa cómo decírselo** I'm worried about how to tell him • **no le preocupa el qué dirán** he's not bothered about what people may say
VPR **preocuparse 1** (= *inquietarse*) to worry (**de, por** about) • **¡no se preocupe!** (*para calmar a algn*) don't worry!; (*para que algn no haga algo*) don't bother! • **no te preocupes por eso** don't worry about that • **no se preocupa en lo más mínimo** he doesn't care in the least
2 (= *ocuparse*) to concern o.s. (**de** about) • **tú preocúpate de que todo esté listo** you see to it that everything is ready
3 (= *dar prioridad*) • **~se de algo** to give special attention to sth, give sth priority
preolímpico/a ADJ • **torneo ~** Olympic qualifying tournament
SM (= *competición*) Olympic qualifying tournament *o* round
SM/F (= *clasificado*) Olympic qualifier; (= *participante*) *athlete etc taking part in an Olympic qualifying tournament*
preoperatorio ADJ pre-operative, pre-op*
SM pre-operative period
preorgásmico ADJ pre-orgasmic
prepagado ADJ [*sobre*] pre-paid
prepago SM prepayment • **tarjeta de ~** prepayment card
preparación SF 1 (= *realización*) preparation • **tiempo de ~: 30 minutos** preparation time: 30 minutes • **un plato de fácil ~** an easy dish to make • **estar en ~** to be in preparation • **tengo varios libros en ~** I have several books in preparation
2 (*antes de hacer algo*) • **¿cuánto tiempo dedicas a la ~ de un examen?** how long do you spend studying for *o* preparing an exam? • **la ~ de las vacaciones me llevó varias semanas** it took me weeks to prepare for the holidays • **clases de ~ al parto** ante-natal classes ▸ **preparación de datos** data preparation
3 (= *formación*) (*de estudios*) education; (*profesional*) training • **salió de la universidad con una buena ~** he left university with a good education • **buscamos a alguien con una buena ~ informática** we're looking for someone with good computer training *o* with a good training in computers ▸ **preparación física** (= *entrenamiento*) training; (= *estado*) physical condition
4 (*tb* **estado de preparación**) preparedness, readiness • **~ militar** military preparedness
5 (*Farm*) preparation
preparado ADJ 1 (= *dispuesto*) [*persona*] prepared, ready • **—¿te vas a presentar al examen? —no, todavía no estoy ~** "are you going to take the exam?" — "no, I'm not prepared *o* ready yet" • **¡~s, listos, ya!** (*gen*) ready, steady, go!; (*Dep*) on your marks, get set, go! • **no estoy ~ mentalmente para la entrevista** I am not mentally prepared for the interview
2 (*Culin*) (= *listo para servir*) ready to serve; (= *precocinado*) ready cooked; ▹ **comida**
3 (*Educ*) (*con estudios*) educated; (*como salida profesional*) trained; (*con título*) qualified • **está muy bien ~ para este trabajo** he's very well trained for this job • **un candidato muy ~** a highly-qualified candidate
4 (= *informado*) well-informed
SM (*Farm*) preparation
preparador(a) SM/F 1 (= *instructor*) [*de deportista*] trainer, coach; [*de opositor*] private tutor ▸ **preparador(a) físico/a** fitness trainer
2 [*de caballo*] trainer
3 (*en laboratorio*) assistant
preparar ▹ CONJUG 1a VT 1 (= *dejar listo*) [+ *comida*] to make, prepare; [+ *habitación, casa*] to prepare, get ready; [+ *compuesto, derivado*] (*Quím*) to prepare, make up • **estoy preparando la cena** I'm making *o* preparing dinner, I'm getting dinner ready • **¿te preparo un café?** shall I make you a coffee? • **¿me puedes ~ la cuenta, por favor?** can you make my bill up, please?; ▹ **terreno**
2 (= *organizar*) [+ *acción, viaje*] to prepare; [+ *ejemplar, revista*] to prepare, work on • **tardaron semanas en ~ el atraco** it took them weeks to set up *o* prepare the robbery • **tengo una sorpresa preparada para ti** I've got a surprise for you • **estamos preparando el siguiente número de la revista** we're working on *o* preparing the next issue of the magazine
3 (= *instruir*) (*para un partido*) to train, coach; (*para examen, oposición*) to coach, tutor • **lleva meses preparando al equipo** he has been training *o* coaching the team for months • **la están preparando en una academia** they are preparing *o* coaching her in a private school, she is being tutored in a private school • **~ a algn en algo** to coach sb in sth • **busco a alguien que me prepare en inglés** I'm looking for someone to coach me in English
4 [+ *examen, prueba*] to study for, prepare for • **llevo semanas preparando este examen** I have been studying *o* preparing for this exam for weeks
VPR **prepararse 1** (= *disponerse*) to get ready • **venga, prepárate, que nos vamos** come on, get ready, we're going • **~se a hacer algo** to get ready to do sth • **se preparaba a salir de casa cuando sonó el teléfono** he was just about *o* getting ready to leave the house when the telephone rang • **prepárate a oír esto** get ready for this • **~se para** to get ready for, prepare for • **nos estamos preparando para las vacaciones** we are getting ready *o* preparing for the holidays
2 (= *estudiar*) [+ *discurso*] to prepare; [+ *examen*] to prepare for, study for • **lleva todo el día preparándose el discurso** she has been preparing her speech all day • **no me había preparado bien el examen** I hadn't done enough preparation for the exam, I hadn't prepared *o* studied properly for the exam
3 (= *formarse*) to prepare • **se están preparando para la prueba de acceso a la universidad** they are preparing for the university entrance exam • **me estoy preparando para el campeonato nacional**

P

I'm preparing for the national championship
4 (= *aproximarse*) [*problemas, tormenta*] to loom • **vimos como se preparaba la tormenta** we saw how the storm was brewing *o* looming • **se prepara una reestructuración ministerial** a cabinet reshuffle is imminent *o* afoot *o* looming

preparativo ADJ preparatory, preliminary
SMPL **preparativos** preparations • **los ~s para la conferencia** the preparations for the conference • **hacer sus ~s** to make one's preparations, prepare

preparatoria SF (*CAm, Méx*) (= *colegio*) secondary school, high school (EEUU)

preparatorio ADJ [*curso, trabajo, material*] preparatory; [*diseño, dibujo, boceto*] preliminary • **ejercicios ~s** preliminary exercises, warm-up exercises

pre-Pirineo SM Pyrenean foothills

preponderancia SF (= *predominio*) preponderance; (= *superioridad*) superiority • **sus propuestas tienen ~ sobre las mías** his proposals carry more weight than mine

preponderante ADJ **1** (= *predominante*) predominant, preponderant (*frm*)
2 (= *superior*) superior

preponderantemente ADV predominantly

preponderar ▸ CONJUG 1a VI **1** (= *predominar*) to predominate, preponderate (*frm*)
2 (= *prevalecer*) to dominate, prevail

preponente ADJ (*And*) arrogant, self-important, conceited

preponer ▸ CONJUG 2q VT to place before

preposición SF preposition

preposicional ADJ prepositional

prepósito SM superior

prepotencia SF **1** (= *arrogancia*) high-handedness • **el incidente fue un ejemplo más de su ~** the incident was yet another example of his high-handedness • **nunca me habían tratado con tanta ~** I had never been treated in such a high-handed manner *o* with such arrogance
2 (= *poder*) power • **su ~ en el Congreso es absoluta** he has absolute power in Congress

prepotente ADJ **1** (= *arrogante*) high-handed • **actitud ~** high-handed attitude • **un ministro fatuo y ~** a conceited and arrogant minister
2 (= *poderoso*) powerful

preproducción SF pre-production

preprogramado ADJ pre-programmed

preprogramar ▸ CONJUG 1a VT to pre-programme, pre-program (EEUU)

prepucio SM foreskin, prepuce (*frm*)

prerrequisito SM prerequisite

prerrogativa SF prerogative

prerrománico ADJ pre-romanesque

presa SF **1** (= *animal apresado*) (*por cazador*) catch; (*por otro animal*) prey • **ave de ~** bird of prey • **huyó ~ del pánico** he fled in panic • **hacer ~ en algo: la desesperación hizo ~ en los soldados** the soldiers were seized with despair • **ser ~ de algo** to be a prey to sth • **los ancianos son ~ fácil de los vendedores sin escrúpulos** old people are easy prey for unscrupulous salesmen
2 (*en un río*) (= *dique*) dam; (= *represa*) weir, barrage
3 (*Mil*) (= *botín*) spoils (*pl*), booty; (*Náut*) prize
4 (*Agr*) ditch, channel
5 (= *colmillo*) tusk, fang; (*Orn*) claw
6 (*esp LAm*) [*de carne*] piece (of meat)

presagiador ADJ ominous

presagiar ▸ CONJUG 1b VT to betoken, forebode, presage

presagio SM omen, portent

presbicia SF long-sightedness

presbiopía SF presbyopia

présbita ADJ, **présbite** ADJ long-sighted

presbiteriano/a ADJ, SM/F Presbyterian

presbiterio SM presbytery, chancel

presbítero/a SM/F priest

presciencia SF prescience, foreknowledge

presciente ADJ prescient

prescindencia SF (*LAm*) (= *privación*) doing without, going without; (= *abstención*) non-participation, abstention

prescindente ADJ (*LAm*) non-participating

prescindible ADJ dispensable • **y cosas fácilmente ~s** and things we can easily do without

prescindir ▸ CONJUG 3a VI • **~ de**
1 (= *renunciar a*) to do without, go without • **no puede ~ de su secretaria** he can't do without his secretary • **han prescindido del coche** they've given up their car
2 (= *ignorar*) to disregard • **no deberían ~ de su opinión** they shouldn't disregard *o* ignore her opinion
3 (= *omitir*) to dispense with • **prescindamos de los detalles inútiles** let's dispense with *o* skip the unnecessary details

prescribir ▸ CONJUG 3a (PP: **prescrito**) VT to prescribe
VI [*plazo*] to expire, run out

prescripción SF **1** (*Med*) prescription ▸ **prescripción facultativa, prescripción médica** medical prescription • **por ~ facultativa** on the doctor's orders
2 (*Méx*) (*Jur*) legal principle

prescriptivo ADJ prescriptive

prescripto ADJ (*Arg*) prescribed

prescrito ADJ prescribed

presea SF **1** (*liter*) (= *joya*) jewel, gem; (= *cosa preciada*) treasure, precious thing
2 (*LAm*) (= *premio*) prize

preselección SF **1** (*Dep*) (= *acción*) seeding; (= *equipo*) squad, team
2 [*de candidatos, participantes*] shortlist, shortlisting • **hacer una ~** to draw up a shortlist

preseleccionado/a SM/F (*Dep*) squad member, member of the squad; (*en candidatura*) short-listed candidate; (*en concurso*) short-listed entry

preseleccionar ▸ CONJUG 1a VT
1 [+ *candidatos*] to shortlist
2 (*Dep*) to seed

presencia SF **1** (*al estar*) presence • **en ~ de algn** in the presence of sb, in sb's presence • **estamos en ~ de un gran escritor** we have here a great writer
2 (= *aspecto*) appearance • **buena ~** smart appearance • **tener buena ~** to look smart ▸ **presencia de ánimo** presence of mind

presencial ADJ **1** • **testigo ~** eyewitness
2 (*Educ*) • **un curso ~ en el campus** a campus-based course • **formación ~** on-campus learning, classroom learning

presenciar ▸ CONJUG 1b VT (= *asistir a*) to be present at, attend; (= *ver*) to witness, see

presentable ADJ presentable

presentación SF **1** (*entre personas*) introduction • **tras las oportunas presentaciones** after the appropriate introductions; ▸ **carta, tarjeta**
2 (= *introducción*) [*de personaje, proyecto*] presentation; [*de producto*] launch, presentation; [*de campaña*] launch • **el cantante llevó a cabo la ~ del acto** the singer presented *o* hosted the event • **texto de ~** introduction ▸ **presentación de modelos** fashion parade, fashion show ▸ **presentación editorial** (*dentro del libro*) publisher's foreword; (*en contraportada*) publisher's blurb ▸ **presentación en público** first public appearance, debut ▸ **presentación en sociedad** coming out, debut
3 (= *concurrencia*) • **tras su ~ al concurso** after entering the competition • **¿cuáles son los motivos de su ~ a las elecciones?** what are your reasons for standing in these elections?
4 (= *llegada*) turning up • **su ~ en mitad de la reunión** her turning up in the middle of the meeting • **no entendemos el por qué de su ~ sin avisar** we don't understand why he turned up unannounced
5 (= *entrega*) submission • **la fecha de ~ del escrito** the date the document was submitted, the submission date of the document • **la ~ del trabajo tendrá que hacerse antes del día 31** the work must be submitted before the 31st • **el plazo de ~ de solicitudes está ya cerrado** applications are no longer being accepted, the closing date for applications is now past
6 (= *muestra*) presentation • **previa ~ de su carné de socio** on presentation of your membership card • **se requiere la ~ de la invitación** invitations must be presented *o* shown on request
7 (= *aspecto*) [*de persona*] appearance; [*de comida, producto, trabajo*] presentation • **se requiere buena ~ a los candidatos** candidates must be of good appearance
8 (*Chile*) (= *solicitud*) petition

presentador(a) SM/F **1** [*de acto*] host/hostess, presenter
2 (*TV, Radio*) [*de debate, documental, informativo*] presenter; [*de programa de variedades, concurso*] host/hostess, presenter

presentar ▸ CONJUG 1a VT **1** (= *enseñar, exponer*) (*gen*) to present; [+ *moción, candidato*] to propose, put forward; [+ *pruebas, informe*] to submit; [+ *documento, pasaporte*] to show • **~ una propuesta** to make *o* present a proposal • **~ algo al cobro** *o* **al pago** (*Com*) to present sth for payment
2 (= *entregar*) to hand in • **mañana tengo que ~ un trabajo** I have to hand in an essay tomorrow • **presentó la dimisión** he handed in his resignation, he resigned
3 (= *mostrar*) [+ *señal, síntoma*] to show • **presenta señales de deterioro** it is showing signs of wear
4 (= *exponer al público*) [+ *producto, disco, libro*] to launch • **presentó su obra en la Galería Mons** she showed her work at the Galería Mons
5 (*en espectáculo*) [+ *obra*] to perform; [+ *actor, actriz*] to present, feature • **el grupo presentó una obra en un solo acto** the group performed a one-act play
6 (= *ser presentador de*) [+ *programa televisivo*] to present, host • **J. Pérez presenta el programa** the programme is presented *o* hosted by J. Pérez • **¿quién presenta ahora las noticias de las nueve?** who presents *o* reads the nine o'clock news now?
7 (= *tener*) to have • **este año el examen presenta novedades** this year the exam has some new features • **el ferrocarril presenta ventajas evidentes** the train offers *o* has obvious advantages • **el cadáver presentaba varios impactos de bala** the body had several bullet wounds • **el coche presenta ciertas modificaciones** the car has had certain changes made to it
8 [+ *persona*] to introduce • **me presentó a sus padres** he introduced me to his parents • **permítanme ~les a don Narciso Gómez** allow me to introduce Mr Narciso Gómez (to you) • **te presento a Carlos** this is Carlos • **a ver si te presento a mi amiga Jacinta** you must meet my friend Jacinta, I must introduce you to my friend Jacinta • **ser presentada en sociedad** to come out, make one's début

9 (= *ofrecer*) [+ *disculpa*] to offer, make • **presentó sus respetos** she paid her respects • **le presento mis consideraciones** (*en carta*) yours faithfully
10 (*Mil*) • **~ armas** to present arms • **~ batalla** (*lit*) to draw up in battle array; (*fig*) to offer resistance
VPR **presentarse 1** (= *aparecer*) to turn up • **se ~on sin avisar** they turned up unexpectedly • **se presentó en un estado lamentable** he turned up in a dreadful state
2 (= *comparecer*) • **el atracador se presentó a la policía** the robber gave himself up to the police • **tengo que ~me ante el juez** I have to appear before the judge • **tendrá que ~se ante el juez cada semana** he'll have to report to the judge once a week • **hay que ~se el lunes por la mañana en la oficina del paro** we have to go to the Job Centre on Monday morning • **~se voluntario** to volunteer
3 (= *hacerse conocer*) to introduce o.s. (**a** to) • **antes de nada, me voy a ~** first of all, let me introduce myself
4 [*candidato*] to run, stand • **~se a** [+ *puesto*] to apply for; [+ *examen*] to sit, enter for; [+ *concurso*] to enter • **he decidido no ~me a las elecciones** I've decided not to stand *o* run in the elections
5 (= *surgir*) [*problema*] to arise, come up; [*oportunidad*] to present itself, arise • **se presentó un caso singular** a strange case came up • **el futuro no se presenta optimista** the future isn't looking too good • **el día se presenta muy hermoso** it looks like it's going to be a lovely day

presente ADJ **1** (*en el espacio*) • **el objeto del ~ trabajo** the purpose of this essay • **los firmantes del ~ escrito** we the undersigned • **el público ~** those present in the audience • **según uno de los testigos ~s** according to one of the witnesses • —**¡Miguel García!** —**¡presente!** "Miguel García!" — "here!" • **un problema siempre ~** an ever-present problem • **estar ~** to be present • **¿estabas tú ~ en esa reunión?** were you present at that meeting? • **la mezcla de estilos está siempre ~ en sus películas** the mixing of styles is a permanent feature in his films • **esa posibilidad está siempre ~** there is always that possibility, that possibility always exists • **hacerse ~** to manifest o.s. • **su espíritu se hizo ~ a través de la médium** his spirit manifested itself through the medium • **tener algo ~** to bear sth in mind • **hay que tener ~ esa posibilidad** we have to bear that possibility in mind • **te tendré ~ si me entero de algún trabajo** I will bear you in mind if I hear of any jobs • **siempre os tendré ~s en mis pensamientos** you will always be in my thoughts, I will never forget you • MODISMO: • **mejorando lo ~** as you are yourself, just like you • **es muy buena actriz, mejorando lo ~** she's a very good actress, as you are yourself *o* just like you; ▷ **cuerpo**
2 (*en el tiempo*) [*año, mes, temporada*] current; [*momento*] present • **los acontecimientos ~s** current events • **en el ~ ejercicio fiscal** in the current tax year • **hasta el momento ~** up to the present time • **el día 28 del ~ mes** the 28th of this month
3 (*LAm*) (*en sobre*) • **"presente"** "by hand"
SMF • **los/las ~s** those present • **todos los allí ~s** all those present
SM **1** (*tb* **momento presente**) present • **hay que vivir el ~** you have to live in the present • **hasta el ~** up to the present
2 (*Ling*) present, present tense ▸ **presente de indicativo** present indicative ▸ **presente de subjuntivo** present subjunctive; ▷ **participio**
3 (= *regalo*) present, gift
SF (*frm*) • **le comunico por la ~ que ...** I hereby inform you that ... (*frm*)

presentimiento SM premonition, presentiment • **tener un mal ~** to have a sense of foreboding

presentir ▷ CONJUG 3i VT to feel, be aware of • **presiento que ...** I have a feeling that ..., I feel that ...

preservación SF preservation, protection

preservante SM preservative

preservar ▷ CONJUG 1a VT **1** (= *proteger*) to protect, preserve (**contra** against, **de** from)
2 (*LAm*) (= *conservar*) to maintain, preserve

preservativo SM condom, contraceptive sheath (*frm*)

presi* SMF = **presidente**

presidencia SF **1** (= *gobierno*) [*de nación*] presidency; [*de comité*] chairmanship • **ocupar la ~ de** [+ *empresa*] to be the president of; [+ *comité*] to be the chairman of • **ocupar la ~ del gobierno** to be president • **España ocupa actualmente la ~ de la UE** Spain currently holds the presidency of the EU
2 • **Presidencia** (= *oficina*) Prime Minister's office

presidenciable ADJ • **ministro ~** minister who has the makings of a president
SMF possible candidate *o* contender for the presidency

presidencial ADJ presidential • **las (elecciones) ~es** the presidential elections

presidencialismo SM presidential rule

presidente/a SM/F (SF A VECES: **presidente**) **1** (*Pol, Com*) [*de país, asociación*] president; [*de comité, reunión*] chair, chairperson, chairman/chairwoman; (*Esp*) (*Pol*) (*tb* **Presidente del Gobierno**) prime minister; [*de la cámara*] speaker • **candidato a ~** (*Pol*) presidential candidate • **es candidato a ~ de Cruz Roja/del Real Madrid** he is a candidate for the presidency of the Red Cross/he is a candidate to be chairman of the board of Real Madrid ▸ **presidente/a de honor** honorary president ▸ **presidente/a vitalicio/a** president for life
2 (*Jur*) (= *magistrado*) presiding magistrate; (= *juez*) presiding judge
3 (*LAm*) (= *alcalde*) mayor

PRESIDENTE DEL GOBIERNO
The head of the Spanish government, or **Presidente del Gobierno**, is elected not just by the winning party but by the entire **Congreso de los Diputados** following a general election. The **Presidente** is appointed for a four-year term and called upon by the King to form a cabinet. As in Britain, he has the power to call an early election, and can be forced to do so by a censure motion in the **Congreso**.

presidiario/a SM/F convict

presidio SM **1** (= *cárcel*) prison, penitentiary (*EEUU*) • **meter a algn en ~** to put sb in prison
2 (= *trabajos forzados*) hard labour, penal servitude
3 (*Pol*) praesidium, presidium
4 (*Mil*) (= *plaza fuerte*) garrison; (= *fortaleza*) fortress

presidir ▷ CONJUG 3a VT **1** (= *estar al frente de*) [+ *gobierno*] to preside over, be president of; [+ *reunión*] to chair, be chairman of
2 (= *dominar*) to dominate • **los temores presidieron la jornada de ayer** fear dominated *o* held sway the whole day yesterday • **la inoperancia y el recurso a medidas de emergencia presidieron su política** the predominant features of his policy were ineffectiveness and recourse to emergency measures
VI (*en gobierno*) to hold the presidency; (*en ceremonia*) to preside; (*en reunión*) to be the chair

presilla SF **1** (*para botón, corchete*) [*de hilo, tela*] loop; [*de metal*] eye
2 (= *cierre*) fastener, clip
3 (*LAm*) (*Mil*) shoulder badge, flash; (*Méx*) epaulette

presintonía SF presetting, preprogram(m)ing

presión SF **1** (*Meteo, Fís, Téc*) pressure; (*con la mano*) press, squeeze • **olla a ~** pressure cooker • **reactor de agua a ~** pressurized water reactor • **indicador/medidor de ~** pressure gauge • **tres atmósferas de ~** three atmospheres of pressure • **hacer ~ sobre algo** to press (on) sth ▸ **presión arterial** blood pressure ▸ **presión atmosférica** atmospheric pressure, air pressure ▸ **presión sanguínea** blood pressure
2 (= *influencia*) pressure • **ejercer** *o* **hacer ~ para que se haga algo** to press for sth to be done; (*Pol*) to lobby for sth to be done • **hay ~ dentro del partido** there are pressures within the party • **hacer algo bajo ~** to do sth under pressure ▸ **presión fiscal, presión impositiva** tax burden

presionar ▷ CONJUG 1a VT **1** [+ *botón, tecla*] to press
2 [+ *persona*] to pressure, pressurize, put pressure on • **~ a algn para que haga algo** to pressure *o* pressurize sb into doing sth, put pressure on sb to do sth • **el ministro, presionado por los fabricantes, accedió** the minister, under pressure from the manufacturers, agreed
VI to press • **~ para algo** to press for sth • **~ para que sea permitido algo** to press for sth to be allowed

preso/a ADJ • **llevar ~ a algn** to take sb prisoner • **estuvo ~ durante tres años** he was in prison for three years • **la cárcel donde estuvo ~** the prison where he served his sentence • **estar ~ del pánico** to be panic-stricken • MODISMO: • **~ por mil, ~ por mil quinientos** (*Esp*) in for a penny, in for a pound
SM/F (= *prisionero*) prisoner ▸ **preso/a común** ordinary prisoner ▸ **preso/a de conciencia** prisoner of conscience ▸ **preso/a de confianza** trusty ▸ **preso/a político/a** political prisoner ▸ **preso/a preventivo/a** remand prisoner

pressing ['presin] SM **1** (*Dep*) pressure
2 = **presión**

prestación SF **1** (= *subsidio*) benefit; (*Méx*) fringe benefit, perk* ▸ **prestación asistencial** social security benefit, welfare benefit (*EEUU*) ▸ **prestación por desempleo** unemployment benefit, unemployment compensation (*EEUU*) ▸ **prestación por jubilación** retirement benefit ▸ **prestaciones sociales** (= *dinero*) social security benefits; (= *servicios*) social services
2 (= *acción*) • **se limitaron a la ~ de ayuda técnica** they limited themselves to giving technical aid • **le agradecemos la ~ de sus servicios** we are grateful for the services rendered ▸ **prestación de juramento** oath-taking, swearing in ▸ **prestación personal** obligatory service ▸ **prestaciones sanitarias** health services ▸ **prestación social sustitutoria** community service (*alternative to national service*)
3 (*Econ*) (= *préstamo*) lending, loan
4 prestaciones (*Téc, Inform*) features,

P

facilities; (*Aut*) (= *equipamiento*) features; (= *rendimiento*) performance (*sing*)

prestado ADJ (*gen*) borrowed; (*en biblioteca*) on loan • **llevaba un traje ~** he was wearing a borrowed suit • **de ~**: • **fue a la boda de ~** he went to the wedding in borrowed clothes • **tuvo que vivir un tiempo de ~** he had to live at other people's expense for a while • **dejar algo ~** to lend sth • **pedir algo ~** (= *tomar prestado*) to borrow sth; (= *preguntar*) to ask to borrow sth • **tomar algo ~** to borrow sth

prestador(a) SM/F lender

prestamista SMF [*de dinero*] moneylender; [*de empeños*] pawnbroker

préstamo SM **1** (= *acción*) (*de prestar*) lending; (*de pedir prestado*) borrowing • **servicio de ~ de libros** book lending service • **buscamos una alternativa al ~ bancario** we are looking for an alternative to bank borrowing • **en ~** on loan ▸ **préstamo a domicilio** home lending ▸ **préstamo interbibliotecario** interlibrary loan
2 (= *dinero prestado*) loan • **necesitamos un ~ de cinco millones** we need a loan of five million • **conceder un ~** to grant a loan • **hacer un ~ a algn** to give sb a loan • **pedir un ~** to ask for a loan ▸ **préstamo bancario** bank loan ▸ **préstamo cobrable a la vista** call loan ▸ **préstamo colateral** collateral loan ▸ **préstamo con garantía** secured loan ▸ **préstamo hipotecario** mortgage (loan), real-estate loan (*EEUU*) ▸ **préstamo para la vivienda** home loan ▸ **préstamo personal** personal loan ▸ **préstamo pignoraticio** collateral loan ▸ **préstamo puente** bridging loan; ▹ **casa**
3 (*Ling*) loanword

prestancia SF (= *elegancia*) elegance, poise; (= *excelencia*) excellence, distinction

prestar ▹ CONJUG 1a VT **1** (= *dejar prestado*) to lend • **¿me puedes ~ el coche?** can I borrow your car?, can you lend me your car? • **prestó su imagen para un anuncio** he allowed his image to be used in an advertisement
2 (*LAm*) (= *pedir prestado*) to borrow (**a** from)
3 (= *dedicar*) [+ *esfuerzo*] to devote; [+ *apoyo, auxilio, ayuda*] to give • **le agradecemos los servicios prestados** we thank you for the services rendered • **la embajada también prestó su colaboración** the embassy also cooperated • **~ atención a algn/algo** to pay attention to sb/sth • **~ crédito a algo** to believe sth • **no podía ~ crédito a mis oídos** I couldn't believe my ears • **~ declaración** (*ante la policía*) to make a statement; (*en un juicio*) to give evidence, testify • **~ juramento** (*gen*) to take the oath, be sworn in • **prestó juramento sobre la Biblia** he swore on the Bible • **~ oídos a algo** to take notice of sth
4 (*frm*) (= *aportar*) • **los jóvenes prestaban alegría a la fiesta** the young people brought good cheer to *o* brightened up the party • **el color azul le prestaba un encanto especial a la habitación** the blue colour gave *o* lent a special charm to the room
5 (*Ven*) • **~ a algn** to do good to sb • **no le prestó el viaje** the trip didn't do him any good
VI **1** (= *dar de sí*) [*zapatos*] to give; [*cuerda*] to stretch
2 (= *servir*) • **~ para algo** to be big enough for sth
VPR **prestarse 1** • **~se a** [*persona*] **a** (= *aceptar*) to accept • **yo nunca me ~ía a esa petición** I would never agree to that request • **no se ~á a participar en ese tipo de juego** he will never agree to be involved in that kind of game
b (= *ofrecerse*) to volunteer to • **se prestó a echarnos una mano si hacía falta** he volunteered to give us a hand if we needed it
2 (= *dar lugar a*) • **~se a algo**: • **sus palabras se ~on a confusión** his words were misinterpreted • **la situación actual se presta a varias interpretaciones** the present situation could be interpreted in several ways • **ese argumento se presta a discusión** that argument is open to debate
3 (= *servir*) • **~se para algo** to be suitable for sth • **se presta para cualquier uso** it is suitable for any purpose • **esta sala se presta muy bien para este tipo de concierto** this hall is perfectly suited to this type of concert
4 • **~se de algo** (*Caribe*) to borrow sth

prestatario/a SM/F borrower

preste SM (*hum*) priest

presteza SF promptness, alacrity (*frm*) • **con ~** speedily, promptly, with alacrity (*frm*)

prestidigitación SF (= *ilusionismo*) conjuring, sleight of hand, prestidigitation (*frm*); (= *malabarismo*) juggling

prestidigitador(a) SM/F (= *ilusionista*) conjurer, prestidigitator (*frm*); (= *malabarista*) juggler

prestigiado ADJ (*LAm*) (= *respetable*) worthy, estimable; (= *prestigioso*) prestigious

prestigiar ▹ CONJUG 1b VT (= *dar prestigio*) to give prestige to; (= *dar fama*) to make famous; (= *honrar*) to honour, honor (*EEUU*) (**con** with); (= *realzar*) to enhance

prestigio SM **1** (= *fama*) prestige • **de ~** prestigious
2 (= *ensalmo*) spell, magic spell
3 (= *truco*) trick

prestigioso ADJ prestigious, famous

presto ADJ **1** (= *rápido*) quick, prompt, swift
2 (= *listo*) ready (**para** for, **a** to)
3 (*Mús*) presto
ADV (= *rápidamente*) quickly, swiftly; (= *en seguida*) right away, at once

presumible ADJ presumable, probable • **es ~ que la cifra sea mucho más alta** we can assume that the figure is much higher, the figure is likely to be much higher, the figure is probably much higher • **es ~ la existencia de restos más antiguos** we can assume the existence of older remains, we can assume that older remains exist

presumiblemente ADV presumably

presumido ADJ (= *creído*) conceited; (= *coqueto*) vain

presumir ▹ CONJUG 3a VI (= *alardear*) to give o.s. airs, show off; (= *envanecerse*) to be conceited • **lo hizo para ~ ante sus amistades** he did it to show off in front of his friends • **no presumas tanto** don't be so conceited • **~ de listo** to think o.s. very smart • **presume de experto** he likes to think he's an expert, he considers himself an expert • **~ demasiado de sus fuerzas** to overestimate one's strength
VT **1** (= *suponer*) to presume • **presumo que quedarán campeones de la liga** I presume that they will end up as league champions • **según cabe ~** as may be presumed, presumably • **es de ~ que** presumably, supposedly
2 (*Arg, Bol*) (= *pretender*) to court; (= *coquetear con*) to flirt with

presunción SF **1** [*de un conocimiento*] (= *conjetura*) supposition, presumption; (= *sospecha*) suspicion • **el principio de ~ de inocencia** the principle that one is presumed innocent until proven guilty
2 (= *vanidad*) conceit, presumptuousness

presuntamente ADV supposedly, allegedly • **un hombre ~ rico** a supposedly *o* an allegedly rich man • **~ causó la muerte de su hermano** he is alleged to have caused the death of his brother

presunto ADJ **1** (= *supuesto*) (*gen*) supposed, presumed; [*criminal*] suspected, alleged • **el ~ asesino** the alleged murderer • **Gómez, ~ implicado en ...** Gómez, allegedly involved in ...
2 [*heredero*] presumptive
3 (= *llamado*) so-called • **estos ~s expertos** these so-called experts

presuntuosamente ADV (= *con vanidad*) conceitedly, presumptuously; (= *con pretensión*) pretentiously

presuntuoso ADJ (= *vanidoso*) conceited, presumptuous; (= *pretencioso*) pretentious

presuponer ▹ CONJUG 2q VT to presuppose, assume

presuposición SF presupposition, assumption

presupuestal ADJ (*Méx*) = **presupuestario**

presupuestar ▹ CONJUG 1a VT [+ *gastos*] to budget for • **costó mucho más de lo presupuestado inicialmente** it cost much more than was initially budgeted for • **su costo está presupuestado en 16 millones** its cost is estimated at 16 million

presupuestario ADJ budget (*antes de s*), budgetary

presupuestívoro/a SM/F (*LAm*) (*hum*) public employee

presupuesto SM **1** (*Econ*) budget • **~ de ventas** sales budget ▸ **los Presupuestos Generales (del Estado)** the national budget ▸ **presupuesto operante** operating budget
2 (*para obra, encargo etc*) estimate • **pedir ~** to ask for an estimate • **"presupuesto sin compromiso"** "free estimates — no obligation"
3 (= *supuesto*) premise, assumption

presurizado ADJ pressurized

presurizar ▹ CONJUG 1f VT to pressurize

presurosamente ADV (= *con rapidez*) quickly, promptly; (= *con prisa*) hastily

presuroso ADJ (= *rápido*) quick, speedy; (= *precipitado*) hasty; [*paso*] quick, brisk • **entró ~** he rushed in • **acudieron ~s a ayudarnos** they rushed to our aid

pretal SM (*esp LAm*) strap, girth

prêt-à-porter ADJ INV off-the-peg, ready-to-wear, off-the-rack (*EEUU*)

pretecnología SF (*Escol*) practical subjects (*pl*)

pretemporada SF (*Dep*) pre-season

pretenciosidad SF **1** (= *pretensiones*) pretentiousness; (= *fanfarronería*) showiness
2 (*LAm*) vanity, boastfulness

pretencioso ADJ **1** (= *vanidoso*) pretentious, presumptuous; (= *fanfarrón*) showy
2 (*LAm*) (= *presumido*) vain, stuck-up*

pretender ▹ CONJUG 2a VT **1** (= *aspirar a*) • **¿qué pretende usted?** what are you after?, what do you hope to achieve? • **~ el trono** to pretend to the throne • **~ hacer algo**: • **pretendió convencerme** he tried to convince me • **pretendo sacar algo de provecho** I intend to get something out of it • **¿qué pretende usted decir con eso?** what do you mean by that? • **no pretendo ser rico** I've no aspirations to be rich • **pretende llegar a ser médico** she hopes to become a doctor • **~ que** (+ *subjun*) to expect that ... • **¡no ~ás que te pague la comida!** you're not expecting me to pay for your meal, are you?
2 (*frm*) (= *afirmar*) to claim • **pretende que el coche le atropelló adrede** he claims that the car deliberately knocked him down
3† (= *cortejar*) to woo, court

pretendidamente ADV supposedly, allegedly

pretendido ADJ supposed, alleged

pretendiente/a SM/F (= *aspirante*) (*a cargo*) candidate, applicant (**a** for); (*al trono*) pretender (**a** to)
SM † [*de una mujer*] suitor

pretensado ADJ prestressed

pretensión SF **1** (= *intención*) aim; (= *aspiración*) aspiration • **un libro sin más ~ que divertir** a book which only aims to entertain • **tiene la ~ de que yo lo acompañe** he expects me to go with him
2 pretensiones (= *aspiraciones*) • **tiene pretensiones de artista** she is an aspiring artist • **tiene pretensiones intelectuales** he likes to think of himself as an intellectual • **tiene pocas pretensiones** he doesn't aspire to much • **enviar historial profesional indicando pretensiones económicas** send curriculum vitae indicating desired salary • **una simple chaqueta sin pretensiones** a simple jacket, nothing fancy
3 (*LAm*) (= *vanidad*) vanity; (= *presunción*) presumption, arrogance

pretensioso ADJ (*LAm*) = **pretencioso**

pretensor SM • **cinturón con ~** inertia-reel seatbelt

preterir ▷ CONJUG 3a VT to leave out, omit, pass over

pretérito ADJ **1** (*Ling*) past
2 (= *pasado*) past, former • **las glorias pretéritas del país** the country's former glories
SM (*Ling*) (*tb* **pretérito indefinido**) preterite, past historic ▸ **pretérito imperfecto** imperfect ▸ **pretérito perfecto** present perfect

preternatural ADJ preternatural

pretextar ▷ CONJUG 1a VT to use as an excuse • **~ que ...** to claim that ..., use as an excuse the fact that ...

pretexto SM pretext • **vino con el ~ de ver al abuelo** he came on the pretext of visiting Granddad • **con el ~ de que ...** on the pretext that ... • **era solo un ~ para no venir** it was only an excuse not to come • **bajo ningún ~** under no circumstances • **so ~ de** (*frm*) under pretext of • **tomar a ~** (*frm*) to use as an excuse

pretil SM **1** (*Constr*) (= *muro*) parapet; (= *barandilla*) handrail, railing
2 (*And*) [*de garaje, hotel*] forecourt
3 (*Caribe, Méx*) (= *banco*) bench
4 (*Méx*) (= *encintado*) kerb

pretina SF **1** (= *cinturilla*) waistband; (= *cinturón*) belt, girdle (*liter*)†
2 (*And, Cono Sur*) (= *correa*) leather strap
3 (*Caribe*) (= *bragueta*) flies (*pl*), fly

pretor SM **1** (*Méx*) (= *juez*) lower-court judge, magistrate
2 (*Hist*) praetor

pretoriano ADJ • **guardia pretoriana** praetorian guard

preu†* SM one-year pre-university course

preuniversitario/a† ADJ pre-university • **curso ~** one-year pre-university course
SM/F *student on a pre-university course*

prevalecer ▷ CONJUG 2d VI **1** (= *imponerse*) to prevail (**sobre** against, over)
2 (= *triunfar*) to triumph, win through
3 (*Bot*) (= *arraigar*) to take root and grow; (= *prosperar*) to thrive

prevaleciente ADJ prevailing, dominant

prevalerse ▷ CONJUG 2p VPR • **~ de algo** (= *valerse*) to avail o.s. of sth; (= *aprovecharse*) to take advantage of sth

prevaricación SF, **prevaricato** SM (*Jur*) perversion of the course of justice, corrupt practice

prevaricar ▷ CONJUG 1g VI to pervert the course of justice, be guilty of corrupt practice

preve* SF = **prevención**

prevención SF **1** [*de accidente, enfermedad*] prevention • **en ~ de algo** in order to prevent sth • **medidas de ~** emergency measures, contingency plans
2 (= *medida*) precautionary measure, precaution • **hemos tomado ciertas prevenciones** we have taken certain precautionary measures *o* precautions
3 (= *previsión*) foresight, forethought • **obrar con ~** to act with foresight
4 (= *prejuicio*) prejudice • **tener ~ contra algn** to be prejudiced against sb
5 (= *comisaría*) police-station
6 (*Mil*) guardroom, guardhouse

prevenido ADJ **1** • **ser ~** (= *cuidadoso*) to be cautious; (= *previsor*) to be far-sighted
2 • **estar ~** (= *preparado*) to be ready, be prepared; (= *advertido*) to be forewarned, be on one's guard (**contra** against) • REFRÁN: • **hombre ~ vale por dos** forewarned is forearmed

prevenir ▷ CONJUG 3r VT **1** (= *evitar*) to prevent; (= *prever*) to foresee, anticipate • **hay accidentes que no se pueden ~** some accidents cannot be prevented • REFRÁN: • **más vale ~ que curar** prevention is better than cure, better safe than sorry
2 (= *advertir*) to warn • **~ a algn** to warn sb, put sb on his guard (**contra, de** against, about) • **pudieron ~le a tiempo** they were able to warn him in time
3 (= *predisponer*) to prejudice, bias (**a favor de** in favour of, **en contra de** against)
4 (= *preparar*) to prepare, get ready (**para** for)
5 (= *proveer*) • **~ a algn de algo** to provide sb with sth
VPR **prevenirse 1** (= *prepararse*) to get ready, prepare • **~se para un viaje** to get ready for a trip • **~se contra algo** to take precautions against sth, prepare for sth
2 (= *proveerse*) • **~se de ropa adecuada** to provide o.s. with suitable clothing
3 • **~se en contra de algn** to set o.s. against sb

preventiva SF (*Méx*) amber light

preventivo ADJ [*medida*] preventive, precautionary; (*Med*) preventive; ▷ **prisión**

prever ▷ CONJUG 2u VT **1** (= *adivinar*) to foresee; (= *predecir*) to predict, forecast • **~ que ...** to anticipate that ..., expect that ... • **ya lo preveía** I expected as much • **se prevé un descenso de precios** a drop in prices is predicted *o* forecast • **si ganan como se prevé** if they win as expected *o* predicted
2 (= *proyectar*) to plan • **la elección está prevista para ...** the election is scheduled *o* planned for ... • **tenemos previsto atravesar el desierto** we are planning to cross the desert • **un embarazo no previsto** an unplanned pregnancy • **no teníamos previsto nada para eso** we had not made any allowance for that
3 (= *establecer*) to provide for, establish • **la ley prevé que ...** the law provides *o* stipulates that ...

previamente ADV previously

previo ADJ **1** (= *anterior*) [*experiencia, programa, conocimiento*] previous; [*examen*] preliminary; [*compromiso*] prior • **sin ~ aviso** without prior warning • **autorización previa** prior authorization, prior permission
2 • **~ a** before, prior to
3 [*idea*] preconceived, received
PREP (= *tras*) • **~ acuerdo de todas las partes afectadas** subject to the agreement of all interested parties • **~ pago de los derechos** on payment of the fees • **"previa cita"** "by appointment only", "appointment required"

SM (*Cine*) playback

previsible ADJ foreseeable, predictable

previsiblemente ADV predictably

previsión SF **1** (*como cualidad*) (= *clarividencia*) foresight, far-sightedness; (= *prudencia*) caution
2 (= *acto*) precaution, precautionary measure • **en ~ de algo** (= *como precaución*) as a precaution against sth; (= *esperando*) in anticipation of sth
3 (= *pronóstico*) forecast • **previsiones económicas** economic forecast (*sing*) • **~ de ventas** sales forecast • **las previsiones del plan quinquenal** the forecasts of the five-year plan ▸ **previsión del tiempo, previsión meteorológica** weather forecast, weather forecasting
4 ▸ **previsión social** social security; (*Chile*) ≈ pension fund

previsional ADJ (*Cono Sur*) social security (*antes de s*)

previsivo ADJ (*Méx*) = **previsor**

previsor ADJ (= *precavido*) far-sighted; (= *prudente*) thoughtful, prudent

previsoramente ADV **1** (*previendo*) far-sightedly; (= *con prudencia*) prudently
2 (= *por si acaso*) just in case

previsto ADJ [*resultados*] predicted, anticipated • **la reunión prevista para el día 20** the meeting planned for the 20th • **empezó a la hora prevista** it started on time • **todo salió según lo ~** everything went as planned *o* (according) to plan

prez† SM honour, honor (*EEUU*), glory

PRI SM ABR (*Méx*) (*Pol*) = **Partido Revolucionario Institucional**

pribar* ▷ CONJUG 1a VT, VI = **privar²**

prieta SF (*Cono Sur*) black pudding

prieto ADJ **1** (= *apretado*) tight • **no hagas el nudo tan ~** don't tie the knot so tight • **de carnes prietas** firm-bodied • **un siglo ~ de historia** a century packed full of history, a century rich in history
2 (= *oscuro*) blackish, dark; (*esp Méx*) dark, swarthy
SM (*LAm*) (= *dado*) loaded dice

prietuzco ADJ (*CAm, Caribe, Méx*) blackish

priísta (*Méx*) (*Pol*) ADJ *of or pertaining to the PRI party*
SMF supporter of the PRI party

prima SF **1** [*de seguro*] premium
2 (= *gratificación*) bonus ▸ **prima a la producción, prima de incentivo** incentive bonus ▸ **prima de peligrosidad** danger money ▸ **prima de productividad** productivity bonus ▸ **prima por coste de la vida** cost of living bonus
3 (*Rel*) prime
4 (*Cono Sur*) • **bajar la ~** to moderate one's language • **subir la ~** to use strong language; ▷ **primo**

primacía SF **1** (*como cualidad*) (= *superioridad*) primacy, first place; (= *supremacía*) supremacy; (= *prioridad*) priority • **tener la ~ sobre algo** to be superior to sth ▸ **primacía de paso** (*Aut*) priority, right of way
2 (*Rel*) primacy

primada* SF (= *estupidez*) piece of stupidity; (= *error*) silly mistake

primado SM (*Rel*) primate

primadona SF, **primadonna** SF prima donna

primal(a) ADJ yearling
SM/F yearling

primar ▷ CONJUG 1a VI (= *predominar*) • **una zona en la que prima la actividad comercial** an area in which commercial activity predominates • **en el acuerdo bilateral prima la cooperación militar** military

cooperation is key to the bilateral agreement • **en sus diseños prima la elegancia** elegance is the keynote in his designs • **~ sobre algo** to take precedence over sth, have priority over sth • **el materialismo prima sobre la espiritualidad** materialism takes precedence over spirituality
VT (*Dep*) to give a bonus to

primaria SF **1** (*Educ*) primary education
2 (*Pol*) (*tb* **primarias**) primary election(s)

primariamente ADV primarily

primariedad SF primacy

primario ADJ [*color, sector*] primary; [*instinto, necesidad*] basic • **escuela primaria** primary school

primate SM **1** (*Zool*) primate
2 (= *prócer*) outstanding figure, important person
ADJ most important

primavera SF **1** (= *estación*) spring • **en ~** in spring, in springtime • REFRÁN: • **la ~ la sangre altera** spring is in the air
2 (*liter*) (= *esplendor*) • **está en la ~ de la vida** he is in the prime of life
3 primaveras (*liter*) (= *años*) summers (*liter*) • **tenía quince ~s** she was a girl of fifteen summers (*liter*)
4 (*Orn*) blue tit
5 (*Bot*) primrose
SM • **ser un ~** (*Esp**) to be a simple soul

primaveral ADJ spring (*antes de s*), springlike

prime* ADJ = **primero**

primer ADJ ▹ **primero**

primera SF **1** (*Aut*) first gear, bottom gear • **meter (la) ~** to change into first gear; ▹ **bueno**
2 (*en viajes*) first class • **ir en ~** to go first class • **viajar en ~** to travel first class
3 • **a la ~** (= *primera ocasión*) [*acertar*] first time • **las cosas no salen siempre a la ~** you don't always get it right first time • **saqué el carnet de conducir a la ~** I got my driving licence at the first attempt • **dijo sí a la ~** he said yes straight away
4 • MODISMO: • **de ~*** (= *excelente*) excellent, brilliant* • **el partido fue de ~** the match was excellent *o* brilliant* • **aquí vendemos un jamón de ~** here we sell the finest quality ham • **aquí se come de ~** you eat really well here, the food is excellent *o* brilliant* here • **hoy me encuentro de ~** I feel great today* • **esta cerveza me ha sentado de ~** this beer has gone down a treat* • **ese dinero me viene de ~** that money suits me down to the ground*; ▹ **clase**
5 (*Com*) ▸ **primera de cambio** first of exchange • MODISMO: • **a la(s) ~(s) de cambio** (= *sin avisar*) without warning; (= *tras la primera dificultad*) at the first sign of trouble; ▹ **primero**

primeramente ADV (= *en primer lugar*) first, firstly; (= *principalmente*) chiefly

primerear ▹ CONJUG 1a VI (*Cono Sur*) to land the first blow, get in first

primerizo/a ADJ **1** (= *novato*) green, inexperienced
2 (= *primero*) first • **novela primeriza** first novel
SM/F (= *principiante*) beginner
SF (*Med*) first time mother

primero/a ADJ (ANTES DE SM SING: **primer**) **1** (*en el espacio*) [*página, planta*] first; [*fila*] front, first • **vivo en el primer piso** I live on the first *o* (EEUU) second floor • **una foto en primera página** a front-page photo, a photo on the front page • **las primeras páginas del libro** the first few pages of the book • **un apartamento en primera línea de playa** an apartment right on the sea front • **estar ~** (*en una cola*) to be first; (*en importancia*) to come first • **perdone, pero yo estaba ~** excuse me, but I was first • **para mí ~ están mis estudios** my studies take priority *o* come first • **~ está la obligación y después la diversión** business before pleasure; ▹ **plana, plano**
2 (*en el tiempo*) [*día, semana, fase*] first; [*época, poemas*] early; [*síntoma*] first, early • **la primera parte del partido** the first half of the match • **una novela escrita en primera persona** a novel written in the first person • **no es la primera vez** it is not the first time • **Juan Carlos Primero** Juan Carlos the First • **los ~s días estaba contento** I was happy for the first few days • **sus dos primeras novelas** his first two novels • **la primera época de Picasso** Picasso's early period • **en los ~s años del siglo** in the early years of the century • **a primera hora (de la mañana)** first thing in the morning • **mañana a primera hora** first thing tomorrow (morning) • **a primeras horas de la tarde de ayer** early yesterday afternoon • **en primer lugar** (*dentro de un orden*) first of all; (*para dar énfasis*) in the first place • **en primer lugar vamos a visitar el Partenón** first of all we are going to visit the Parthenon • **en primer lugar, tú no deberías haber dicho nada** in the first place, you shouldn't have said anything; ▹ **hora, guerra**
3 (= *principal*) [*deber, objetivo*] main, primary • **lo ~ es que te pongas bueno** the main thing is that you get well • **productos de primera calidad** top quality products • **artículos de primera necesidad** basic essentials, staple items • **primer actor** leading man • **primera actriz** leading lady • **~s auxilios** first aid • **el botiquín de ~s auxilios** the first-aid box • **de primera categoría** first-class • **un puerto de primera categoría** (*Ciclismo*) a first-category climb • **primer espada** (*Taur*) principal bullfighter • **primer violín** (= *concertino*) leader; (*de sección*) first violin • MODISMO: • **lo ~ es lo ~** first things first; ▹ **bailarín, dama, mandatario, ministro, piedra**
SM/F first • **soy el ~ de la lista** I'm top of the list, I'm first on the list • **quedó entre los diez ~s** he was in *o* among the first ten • **es la primera de la clase** she is the best in the class, she is top of the class • **fui la primera en darme cuenta del fallo** I was the first to realize the mistake • **llegar el ~** to be the first to arrive; ▹ **bueno, vista, primera**
SM **1** • **a ~s (de mes)** at the beginning of the month • **a ~s de junio** at the beginning of June
2 (*tb* **primer plato**) starter, first course • **¿qué van a tomar de ~?** what will you have as a starter *o* for the first course?
ADV **1** (= *en primer lugar*) first • **~ iremos a comprar y luego al cine** first, we'll do the shopping and then go to the cinema
2 (*indicando preferencia*) sooner, rather • **~ se queda en casa que pedir dinero** she'd sooner *o* rather stay at home than ask for money • **¡~ morir!** I'd rather die!

primicia SF **1** (= *novedad*) novelty; (= *estreno*) first appearance ▸ **primicia informativa** scoop
2 primicias (= *primeros frutos*) first fruits

primigenio ADJ primitive, original

primípara SF first-time mother, primipara (*frm*)

primitiva SF • **la ~*** = **lotería primitiva** ▹ **lotería**

primitivamente ADV **1** (= *al principio*) at first
2 (= *de un modo primitivo*) primitively, in a primitive way

primitivo ADJ **1** [*arte, pueblo*] primitive; (= *salvaje*) uncivilized • **en condiciones primitivas** in primitive conditions • **el hombre ~** primitive man
2 (= *original*) first, original • **el texto ~** the original text • **quedan 200 de los ~s 850** there remain 200 from the original 850 • **devolver algo a su estado ~** to restore sth to its original state • **es una obra primitiva** it is an early work
3 [*color*] primary
4 (*Econ*) [*acción*] ordinary

primo/a ADJ **1** [*número*] prime
2 [*materia*] raw
SM/F **1** (= *pariente*) cousin • MODISMOS: • **le vino el ~ de América†*** she started her period • **ser ~s hermanos** (*referido a cosas*) to be extraordinarily alike ▸ **primo/a carnal, primo/a hermano/a** first cousin
2* (= *incauto*) dupe, sucker* • MODISMOS: • **hacer el ~** to be taken for a sucker*, be taken for a ride* • **tomar a algn por ~** to do sb down*, take sb in*; ▹ **prima**

primogénito/a ADJ, SM/F first-born

primogenitura SF **1** (*al nacer*) primogeniture
2 (= *patrimonio*) birthright

primor SM **1** (= *delicadeza*) delicacy
2 (= *maestría*) care, skill • **hecho con ~** done most skilfully, delicately made • **cose que es un ~** she sews beautifully
3 (= *objeto primoroso*) fine thing, lovely thing • **hace ~es con la aguja** she makes lovely things with her needlework • **hijos que son un ~** delightful children, charming children

primordial ADJ fundamental, essential • **esto es ~** this is top priority • **es de interés ~** it is of fundamental concern • **es ~ saberlo** it is essential to know it • **ha desempeñado un papel de ~ importancia** it has played a crucial role

primordialidad SF (= *importancia*) overriding importance; (= *supremacía*) supremacy

primordialmente ADV basically, fundamentally

primorosamente ADV (= *con delicadeza*) exquisitely, delicately, elegantly; (= *con esmero*) neatly, skilfully, skillfully (EEUU)

primoroso ADJ (= *delicado*) exquisite, fine; (= *esmerado*) neat, skilful, skillful (EEUU)

prímula SF primrose

princesa SF princess ▸ **princesa real** ≈ Princess Royal

principado SM principality • **el Principado de Asturias** (the principality of) Asturias

principal ADJ **1** (= *más importante*) (*gen*) principal, main; [*crítico, adversario*] foremost; [*piso*] first, second (EEUU) • **interpreta el papel ~** she plays the leading role • **lo ~ es que el problema se ha solucionado** the main thing is the problem has been solved
2 [*persona, autoridad*] illustrious
SM **1** (= *persona*) head, chief, principal
2 (*Econ*) principal, capital
3 (*Teat*) dress circle
4 (= *piso*) first floor, second floor (EEUU)

principalmente ADV principally, chiefly, mainly

príncipe SM prince • **el ~ de Asturias** the heir to the Spanish throne ▸ **príncipe azul** Prince Charming, knight in shining armour ▸ **príncipe consorte** prince consort ▸ **príncipe de Gales** Prince of Wales ▸ **príncipe heredero** crown prince
ADJ INV • **edición ~** first edition

principesco ADJ princely

principiante/a ADJ [*actor, fotógrafo, jugador*] inexperienced • **conductor ~** learner driver
SM/F (= *novato*) beginner, novice; (= *aprendiz*) learner • **cometen errores de ~** they make basic mistakes

principiar ▸ CONJUG 1b VT to begin
VI to begin • **~ a hacer algo** to begin to do sth, begin doing sth • **~ con algo** to begin with sth

principio SM **1** (= *comienzo*) beginning • **al ~** at first, in the beginning • **a ~s del verano** at the beginning of the summer, early in the summer • **desde el ~** from the first, from the outset • **desde el ~ hasta el fin** from start to finish, from beginning to end • **en un ~** at first, to start with • **dar ~ a algo** to start sth off • **tener ~ en algo** to start from sth, be based on sth
2 principios (= *nociones*) rudiments, first notions • **"Principios de física"** "Introduction to Physics", "Outline of Physics"
3 (= *norma*) principle • **persona de ~s** man of principles • **en ~** in principle • **por ~** on principle • **es inmoral por ~** it is immoral in principle • **sin ~s** unprincipled • **el ~ de la legalidad** the force of law, the rule of law
4 (*Fil*) principle
5 (*Quím*) element, constituent ▸ **principio activo** active ingredient
6 (*Culin*) entrée

principote* SM (= *jactancioso*) show-off*, swank*; (= *arribista*) parvenu, social climber

pringada SF *bread dipped in gravy etc*

pringado/a* SM/F **1** (= *víctima*) (innocent) victim; (= *sin suerte*) unlucky person; (= *infeliz*) poor devil, wretch • **el ~ del grupo** the odd man out, the loser
2 (= *tonto*) fool, idiot • **¡no seas ~!** don't be an idiot!
3 (= *gafe*) bringer of bad luck

pringao* SM = **pringado**

pringar ▸ CONJUG 1h VT **1** (*Culin*) [+ *pan*] to dip, dunk; [+ *asado*] to baste • **~ el pan en la sopa** to dip one's bread in the soup
2 (= *ensuciar*) to dirty, soil (with grease); (*esp LAm*) to splash
3* (= *implicar*) • **~ a algn en un asunto** to involve sb in a matter • **están pringadas en esto unas altas personalidades** some top people are mixed up in this
4* (= *herir*) • **~ a algn** to wound sb, make sb bleed
5* (= *denigrar*) to blacken, run down*
6 (*Cono Sur*) [+ *enfermedad*] to give
7 (*Cono Sur**) [+ *mujer*] to put in the family way
8 • **~la‡** (= *meter la pata*) to drop a brick*, make a boob*; (*Med*) to get a dose of the clap‡ • **~la(s)‡** (= *morir*) to kick the bucket*, snuff it*
VI **1*** (= *perder*) to come a cropper*, take a beating • **hemos pringado** we're done for
2 (= *trabajar*) to sweat one's guts out*, slog away*
3 • **~ en algo** (*superficialmente*) to dabble in sth; (*implicándose*) to take a hand in sth, get mixed up in sth
4* (= *morir*) to kick the bucket*, snuff it*
5 (*CAm, Caribe, Méx*) (= *lloviznar*) to drizzle
VPR **pringarse 1** (= *ensuciarse*) to get covered (**con, de** with, in)
2* (= *involucrarse*) to get mixed up (**en** in)
3* (= *comprometerse*) to get one's fingers burnt • **o nos pringamos todos, o ninguno** either we all carry the can or none of us does*
4* (= *ganar por medios dudosos*) to make money on the side; (= *sacar tajada*) to get a rake-off*; (= *enriquecerse*) to make a packet*

pringo SM (*LAm*) (= *gota*) drop; (= *pizca*) bit, pinch • **con un ~ de leche** with a drop of milk

pringón ADJ (= *sucio*) dirty, greasy
SM **1** (= *mancha*) grease stain, grease spot
2‡ (= *tajada*) rake-off*; (= *ganancias*) packet*

pringoso ADJ (= *grasiento*) greasy; (= *pegajoso*) sticky

pringue SM o SF **1** (= *grasa*) grease, dripping
2 (= *mancha*) grease stain, grease spot; (= *suciedad*) dirt
3* (= *molestia*) nuisance • **es un ~ tener que ...** it's a bind having to ...*
4 (*CAm, Méx*) (= *salpicadura*) splash (*of mud etc*)
5 (*And*) (= *quemadura*) burn
6‡ (= *dinero*) dosh‡, money
7‡ (= *policía*) Crime Squad

prior(a) SM/F prior/prioress

priorato SM (*Rel*) priory

priori ▸ **a priori**

prioridad SF (= *precedencia*) priority; (= *antigüedad*) seniority, greater age; (*Aut*) right of way, priority • **tener ~** to have *o* take priority (**sobre** over); (*Aut*) to have the right of way ▸ **prioridad de paso** (*Aut*) right of way

prioritariamente ADV (= *en primer lugar*) as a priority, first; (= *mayormente*) mainly, principally

prioritario ADJ (= *primero*) priority (*antes de s*); (= *principal*) main, principal; (*Inform*) foreground (*antes de s*) • **un proyecto de carácter ~** a plan with top priority, a (top) priority plan • **lo ~ es ...** the first thing (to do) is ...

priorizar ▸ CONJUG 1f VT to give priority to, treat as a priority, prioritize
VI to determine priorities

prisa SF (= *prontitud*) hurry, haste; (= *premura*) urgency • **con las ~s me olvidé el paraguas** in the rush I forgot my umbrella • **voy con mucha ~** I'm in a great hurry • **a ~** quickly, hurriedly • **a toda ~** as quickly as possible • **correr ~** (*Esp*) to be urgent • **no corre ~** it's not urgent • **¿corren ~ estas cartas?** are these letters urgent?, is there any hurry for these letters? • **¿te corre ~?** are you in a hurry? • **darse ~** to hurry, hurry up • **¡date ~!** hurry (up)!, come along! • **de ~** quickly, hurriedly • **meter ~ a algn** to make sb get a move on, make sb hurry up • **tener ~** to be in a hurry • MODISMO: • **sin ~ pero sin pausa** slow but steady

prisco ADJ (*LAm**) simple
SM (*esp Cono Sur*) (= *albaricoque*) apricot

prisión SF **1** (= *cárcel*) prison • **~ de alta** *o* **máxima seguridad** top-security prison
2 (= *encarcelamiento*) imprisonment • **cinco años de ~** five years' imprisonment, prison sentence of five years ▸ **prisión domiciliaria** house-arrest ▸ **prisión mayor** *sentence of more than six years and a day* ▸ **prisión menor** *sentence of less than six years and a day* ▸ **prisión perpetua** life imprisonment ▸ **prisión preventiva** preventive detention • **el juez ha decretado la ~ preventiva** the judge remanded him in custody
3 prisiones (= *grillos*) shackles, fetters

prisionero/a SM/F prisoner • **hacer ~ a algn** to take sb prisoner ▸ **prisionero/a de conciencia** prisoner of conscience ▸ **prisionero/a de guerra** prisoner of war ▸ **prisionero/a político/a** political prisoner

prisma SM **1** (*Fís, Ópt*) prism
2 (= *punto de vista*) point of view, angle • **bajo** *o* **desde el ~ de** from the point of view of

prismático ADJ prismatic
SMPL **prismáticos** binoculars, field glasses

pristinidad SF pristine nature, original quality

prístino ADJ pristine, original

priva* SF (*Esp*) • **la ~** the booze*, the drink

privacidad SF (= *intimidad*) privacy; (= *secreto*) secrecy

privación SF **1** (= *acto*) deprivation, deprival • **sufrir ~ de libertad** to suffer loss of liberty
2 privaciones (= *miserias*) hardship (*sing*), privations • **durante la guerra sufrimos muchas privaciones** we suffered a lot of hardship during the war

privada SF (*Méx*) private road

privadamente ADV privately

privado ADJ **1** [*club, colegio, avión*] private • **"privado y confidencial"** "private and confidential"
2 (*LAm*) (= *alocado*) mad, senseless
3 (*Caribe*) (= *débil*) weak, faint
SM **1** • **en ~** privately, in private
2 (*Pol*) (= *favorito*) favourite, favorite (EEUU), protégé; (*Hist*) royal favourite, chief minister

privanza SF favour • **durante la ~ de Lerma** when Lerma was royal favourite, when Lerma was chief minister

privar¹ ▸ CONJUG 1a VT **1** (= *despojar*) • **~ a algn de algo** to deprive sb of sth, take sth away from sb • **~ a algn del conocimiento** to render sb unconscious • **lo ~on del carnet de conducir** they suspended his driving licence, they took away his driving licence • **quedaron privados de electricidad** they were without electricity • **nos vimos privados de su compañía** we found ourselves deprived of her company
2 (= *prohibir*) • **~ a algn de hacer algo** to forbid sb to do sth, prevent sb from doing sth • **no me prives de verte** don't forbid me to come to see you, don't tell me not to come again
3 (= *impedir*) to prevent • **lo cual me privó de verlos** which prevented me from seeing them
4 (= *extasiar*) to delight, overwhelm
VI **1*** (= *gustar mucho*) • **las motos me privan** I'm mad about motorbikes*
2* (= *estar de moda*) to be in fashion, be the thing, be all the rage* • **en ese periodo privaba la minifalda** at that time miniskirts were in *o* were all the rage* • **la cualidad que más priva entre ellos** the quality which is most strongly present in them • **priva en algunos públicos** it's popular with some audiences
VPR **privarse** • **~se de algo** (= *abstenerse*) to deprive o.s. of sth; (= *renunciar*) to give sth up, forgo sth • **no se privan de nada** they don't want for anything, they lack nothing

privar²* ▸ CONJUG 1a VT, VI (= *beber*) to booze*

privata‡ SF = **priva**

privativo ADJ **1** (= *exclusivo*) exclusive • **esa función es privativa del presidente** that function is the president's alone • **el hecho no es ~ de España** it's not only *o* exclusively a Spanish phenomenon • **la planta es privativa del Brasil** the plant is peculiar *o* restricted to Brazil
2 (*Jur*) • **una pena privativa de libertad** a prison sentence

privatización SF privatization

privatizador ADJ [*proceso, política*] privatisation (*antes de s*), of privatisation • **organismo ~** privatisation body

privatizar ▸ CONJUG 1f VT to privatize

prive‡ SM = **priva**

privilegiado/a ADJ [*vida, posición, persona*] privileged; [*clima, inteligencia, memoria*] exceptional
SM/F privileged person • **los ~s** the privileged

privilegiar ▸ CONJUG 1b VT (= *favorecer*) to

P

favour, favor (*EEUU*); (*= dar privilegio*) to grant a privilege to

privilegio SM privilege • **los ~s de la aristocracia** the privileges of the aristocracy • **tuve el ~ de conocerla en persona** I had the privilege of meeting her in person • **disfrutar** *o* **gozar de un ~** to enjoy a privilege • **conceder un ~** to grant a privilege ▸ **privilegio de invención** patent ▸ **privilegio fiscal** tax concession

privota‡ SMF piss artist‡, boozer‡

pro SM **1** (*= provecho*) profit, advantage • **en pro de** (*= en nombre de*) on behalf of; (*= en favor de*) in favour of • **los pros y los contras** the pros and cons, for and against • MODISMO: • **buena pro le haga** and much good may it do him

2 • **de pro** (*= bueno*) worthy; (*= verdadero*) real, true • **hombre de pro** worthy man, honest man • **para los cinéfilos de pro** for real film buffs

PREP (*= en favor de*) for, on behalf of • **asociación pro ciegos** association for (aid to) the blind • **campaña pro paz** peace campaign

pro- PREF pro- • **pro-norteamericano** pro-American • **gestoras pro-amnistía** pro-amnesty lobby

pro... PREF pro-... • *p.ej.* **proárabe** pro-Arab

proa SF (*Náut*) bow, prow; (*Aer*) nose • **de ~** bow (*antes de s*), fore • **de ~ a popa** from stem to stern • **en la ~** in the bows • **poner la ~ a** (*Náut*) to head for, set a course for • MODISMO: • **poner la ~ a algn** to take a stand against sb, set o.s. against sb

proabortista ADJ pro-abortion

proactivo ADJ proactive

proamnistía ADJ INV pro-amnesty • **gestora ~** (*Esp*) *organization calling for an amnesty for ETA prisoners*

probabilidad SF **1** (*= capacidad de suceder*) likelihood, probability • **según toda ~** in all probability • **nubes y claros con pocas ~es de lluvia** cloud and sunny periods with little likelihood of rain

2 (*= oportunidad*) chance, prospect • **hay pocas ~es de que venga** there is little prospect of his coming • **tenemos grandes ~es de ganar** we've got a good chance of winning • **apenas tiene ~es** he hasn't much chance ▸ **probabilidades de vida** expectation of life, life expectancy

probabilístico ADJ probabilistic

probable ADJ **1** (*= posible*) probable, likely • **es ~ que ...** it is probable that ..., it is likely that ... • **es ~ que no venga** he probably won't come

2 (*= demostrable*) provable

probablemente ADV probably

probadamente ADV • **un método ~ ineficaz** a method of proven inefficiency

probado ADJ **1** (*= demostrado*) proven • **un sistema de probada eficacia** a system of proven efficiency • **es un hecho ~ que ...** it has been proved that ...

2 (*= analizado*) tested • **es un método ~ y eficaz** it is a tested, effective method • **productos de probada calidad** tried and tested products

probador SM **1** (*para cambiarse*) changing room, fitting room

2 [*de perfume*] tester

3 (*tb* **piloto probador**) test pilot

probanza SF proof, evidence

probar ▸ CONJUG 1l VT **1** (*= demostrar*) [*+ eficacia, inocencia, teoría*] to prove • **eso ~ía la existencia de vida en Marte** that would prove the existence of life on Mars • **~ que** to prove that • **¿cómo puedes ~ que no estabas allí?** how can you prove that you weren't there? • **el juez consideró probado que era culpable** the judge considered that he had been proved guilty

2 (*= poner a prueba*) [*+ sustancia, vacuna, persona*] to test; [*+ método*] to try; [*+ aparato, arma*] to test, try out; [*+ actor, músico*] to audition • **hemos dejado dinero en el suelo para ~lo** we've left some money lying on the floor to test him • **prueben su puntería, señoras y señores** try your aim, ladies and gentlemen • **te dan diez días para ~ el vídeo** they give you a ten-day trial period for the video, they give you ten days to try out the video • **~on a muchos actores para el papel** they auditioned a lot of actors for the part; ▹ **fortuna, suerte**

3 (*= catar*) to try, taste • **prueba un poco de este pescado** try *o* taste a bit of this fish • **el médico me ha prohibido que pruebe el marisco** the doctor says I'm not allowed (to eat) seafood • **yo el vino no lo pruebo** I never touch *o* drink wine • **llevamos horas sin ~ bocado** it's hours since we've had a bite to eat • REFRÁN: • **al ~ se ve el mosto** the proof of the pudding is in the eating

4 [*+ ropa*] (*hecha a medida*) to fit; (*de confección*) to try on • **¿puede venir mañana a que le pruebe el traje?** can you come tomorrow to have your suit fitted? • **tengo que ir a la modista a que me pruebe** I have to go to the dressmaker for a fitting • **te voy a ~ este abrigo a ver como te queda** I'm going to try this coat on you to see what it looks like

VI **1** (*= intentar*) to try, have a go • **déjame que pruebe yo** let me try, let me have a go • **¿has probado con este bolígrafo?** have you tried this pen? • **~ a hacer algo** to try doing sth • **he probado a hacerlo yo sola, pero no he podido** I tried doing it on my own but I couldn't • MODISMO: • **con** *o* **por ~ nada se pierde** there's no harm in trying, nothing ventured, nothing gained

2 (*= sentar*) [*actividad, ropa*] to suit; [*comida*] to agree with • **le probó mal ese oficio** that trade didn't suit him • **no me prueba bien el café** coffee doesn't agree with me

3 • **~ de algo** ▹ VT

VPR **probarse** [*+ ropa, zapatos*] to try on • **¿me puedo ~ esta camisa?** can I try this shirt on? • **pruébate una talla más** try (on) a larger size

probatorio ADJ (*Jur*) [*dato, documento*] • **un hecho de limitado valor ~** a fact of limited evidential value • **documentos ~s de su culpabilidad** documents in proof of his guilt, documents proving his guilt

probeta SF test tube

ADJ INV test-tube (*antes de s*) • **bebé ~** test-tube baby

probidad SF integrity, honesty

probiótico ADJ probiotic

problema SM **1** (*= dificultad*) problem • **el ~ del paro** the problem of unemployment • **el ~ es que no tengo tiempo** the problem is I don't have time • **si hay algún ~ dímelo** let me know if there is any problem • **¿tienes ~s de dinero?** do you have any money worries *o* financial problems? • **este coche nunca me ha dado ~s** this car has never given me any trouble • **no quiero ~s** I don't want any trouble

2 (*Mat*) problem

3 (*Méx*) (*= accidente*) accident, mishap

ADJ INV (*= problemático*) problem (*antes de s*) • **niño ~** problem child

problemática SF problems (*pl*), questions (*pl*)

problemático ADJ problematic

problematizar ▸ CONJUG 1f VT [*+ asunto*] to make problematic; [*+ persona*] to burden with problems

probo ADJ honest, upright

probóscide SF proboscis

procacidad SF **1** [*de persona*] (*= desvergüenza*) insolence, impudence; (*= descaro*) brazenness

2 [*de comentario, chiste*] indecency, obscenity

procaz ADJ **1** [*persona*] (*= atrevido*) insolent, impudent; (*= descarado*) brazen

2 [*comentario, chiste*] indecent, obscene

procedencia SF **1** (*= origen*) source, origin

2 (*= lugar de salida*) [*de tren, avión*] point of departure; [*de barco*] port of origin

3 (*Jur*) propriety, legitimacy

4 (*= conveniencia*) properness

procedente ADJ **1** • **~ de** from • **un queso ~ de Noruega** a Norwegian cheese, a cheese from Norway • **llegó a Madrid ~ de Colombia** he arrived in Madrid from Colombia • **el tren ~ de Sevilla** the train from Seville

2 (*= conveniente*) proper, fitting

3 (*Jur*) proper • **procedimiento ~** proper procedure

procedentemente ADV properly, in a right and proper fashion

proceder ▹ CONJUG 2a VI **1** (*= provenir*) • **~ de** to come from, originate in • **procede de una familia rica** she comes from *o* belongs to a wealthy family • **todo esto procede de su negativa** all this springs from his refusal • **de donde procede que ...** (from) whence it happens that ... (*frm*)

2 (*al actuar*) (*= obrar*) to act; (*= conducirse*) to proceed, behave • **ha procedido precipitadamente** he has acted hastily • **conviene ~ con cuidado** it is best to go carefully, it would be best to proceed with caution • **~ contra algn** (*Jur*) to take proceedings against sb

3 (*= pasar*) to proceed • **~ a una elección** to proceed to an election • **procedieron a la detención de los sospechosos** they proceeded to arrest the suspects • **procedieron a despejar la carretera** they proceeded to clear the road

4 (*= ser correcto*) to be right (and proper), be fitting • **no procede obrar así** it is not right to act like that • **si el caso procede** if the case warrants it • **luego, si procede, ...** then, if appropriate, ... • **táchese lo que no proceda** cross out what does not apply

5* (*= estar de moda*) to be in*, be in fashion

SM (*= conducta*) behaviour, behavior (*EEUU*); (*= línea de acción*) course of action

procedimental ADJ procedural; (*Jur*) legal

procedimiento SM (*= sistema*) process; (*= método*) means, method; (*= trámites*) procedure; (*Jur*) proceedings • **un ~ para abaratar el producto** a method of making the product cheaper • **por un ~ deductivo** by a deductive process • **los ~s establecidos en el Tratado** the procedures established by the Treaty

proceloso ADJ (*liter*) stormy, tempestuous

prócer SM **1** (*= persona eminente*) worthy, notable; (*= magnate*) important person; (*esp LAm*) (*Pol*) famous son, famous citizen • **~ de las letras** literary figure, eminent writer

2 (*= líder*) great man, leader; (*LAm*) leader of the independence movement

procesado[1] ADJ [*alimento*] processed

SM (*Téc*) processing ▸ **procesado de aguas** water treatment ▸ **procesado de imágenes** image processing

procesado[2]**/a** ADJ, SM/F accused

procesador SM processor ▸ **procesador de datos** data processor ▸ **procesador de textos** word processor

procesadora SF (*LAm*) (*tb* **procesadora de alimentos**) food processor

procesal ADJ [*derecho, obligación*] procedural; [*gasto*] legal • **defecto ~** procedural technicality • **costas ~es** legal costs

procesamiento SM **1** (*Jur*) (*gen*) prosecution; (= *juicio*) trial; ▹ **auto²**
2 (*Inform*) processing ▸ **procesamiento concurrente** concurrent processing ▸ **procesamiento de datos** data processing ▸ **procesamiento de textos** word processing ▸ **procesamiento interactivo** interactive processing ▸ **procesamiento por lotes** batch processing ▸ **procesamiento simultáneo** simultaneous processing
3 (*Téc*) processing

procesar ▹ CONJUG 1a VT **1** (= *juzgar*) [*juez*] to try, put on trial; [*estado, acusación*] to prosecute, put on trial
2 (= *demandar*) to sue, bring an action against
3 (*Téc, Inform*) to process

procesión SF **1** (*Rel*) procession
2 (= *hilera*) stream • **una ~ de mendigos/hormigas** a never-ending stream of beggars/ants • **una ~ de quejas** a never-ending series of complaints • MODISMO: • **la ~ va por dentro** he keeps his troubles *o* problems to himself

procesional ADJ processional

procesionaria SF (= *mariposa*) processionary moth; (= *oruga*) processionary caterpillar

proceso SM **1** (= *desarrollo*) (*tb Anat, Quím*) process • **el ~ de una enfermedad** the course *o* progress of a disease ▸ **proceso de paz** peace process ▸ **proceso de selección** selection process ▸ **proceso mental** mental process
2 (*Med*) • **un ~ gastroenterítico** an attack of gastroenteritis • **un ~ gripal** a bout of flu ▸ **proceso infeccioso** infection ▸ **proceso pulmonar** lung disease
3 (= *transcurso*) lapse of time • **en el ~ de un mes** in the course of a month
4 (*Jur*) (= *juicio*) trial; (= *pleito*) lawsuit, proceedings (*pl*) • **abrir** *o* **entablar ~** to bring a suit (**a** against) ▸ **proceso verbal** (= *escrito*) record; (= *audiencia*) hearing
5 (*Inform*) processing ▸ **proceso de imágenes** image processing ▸ **proceso de textos** word processing ▸ **proceso electrónico de datos** electronic data processing ▸ **proceso no prioritario** background processing ▸ **proceso por lotes** batch processing ▸ **proceso prioritario** foreground processing

procesual ADJ **1** (*Jur*) procedural
2 (= *en progreso*) evolving

proclama SF **1** (*Pol*) (= *bando*) proclamation; (= *discurso*) address; (= *manifiesto*) manifesto
2 proclamas (= *amonestaciones*) banns

proclamación SF proclamation

proclamar ▹ CONJUG 1a VT to proclaim • **~ a algn algo** to proclaim sb sth • MODISMO: • **~ algo a los cuatro vientos** to shout sth from the rooftops
VPR **proclamarse** • **~se campeón** to become champion, win the championship • **~se rey** to proclaim o.s. king

proclive ADJ inclined, prone (**a** to)

proclividad SF proclivity (*frm*), inclination

procónsul SM proconsul

procrastinación SF procrastination

procrastinar VI to procrastinate

procreación SF procreation (*frm*), breeding

procrear ▹ CONJUG 1a VT, VI to procreate (*frm*), breed

procura SF (*esp LAm*) obtaining, getting • **en ~ de** in search of • **andar en ~ de algo** to be trying to get sth

procuración SF (*Jur*) power of attorney, proxy

procurador(a) SM/F **1** (*Jur*) (= *abogado*) attorney, solicitor ▸ **procurador(a) general** attorney general
2 (= *apoderado*) proxy
3 (*tb* **procurador en Cortes**) (*Pol, Hist*) deputy, *member of Spanish parliament under Franco; (actualmente) member of a regional parliament*

procuraduría SF **1** (= *despacho*) lawyer's office
2 (*tb* **procuraduría general**) (*Méx*) attorney general's office
3 (= *costas*) legal costs (*pl*), lawyers' fees (*pl*)

procurar ▹ CONJUG 1a VT **1** (= *intentar*) • **~ hacer algo** to try to do sth, endeavour *o* (*EEUU*) endeavor to do sth • **procura conservar la calma** do try to keep calm • **procura que no te vean** don't let them see you, take care not to let them see you
2 (= *conseguir*) to get, obtain • **~ un puesto a algn** to get sb a job, find a job for sb • **esto nos ~á grandes beneficios** this will bring us great benefits
3 (= *lograr*) • **~ hacer algo** to manage to do sth, succeed in doing sth • **por fin procuró dominarse** eventually he managed to control himself
VPR **procurarse** • **~se algo** to secure sth

procurón* ADJ (*Méx*) interfering, nosey*

Procustes SM, **Procusto** SM Procrustes • **lecho de ~** Procrustes' bed

prodigalidad SF **1** (= *abundancia*) bounty, richness
2 (= *liberalidad*) lavishness, generosity
3 (= *despilfarro*) wastefulness, extravagance

pródigamente ADV **1** (= *abundantemente*) bountifully
2 (= *generosamente*) lavishly
3 (= *con prodigalidad*) prodigally
4 (= *con despilfarro*) wastefully

prodigar ▹ CONJUG 1h VT (= *dar mucho*) to lavish, give lavishly; (= *despilfarrar*) to squander • **prodiga las alabanzas** he is lavish in his praise • **nos prodigó sus atenciones** he was very generous in his kindnesses to us • **~ algo a algn** to lavish sb with sth, lavish sth on sb
VPR **prodigarse 1** (= *ser generoso*) to be generous (*with what one has*) • **se ~on en alabanzas** they were lavish with *o* in their praise
2 (= *dejarse ver*) to show o.s. • **no te prodigas mucho que digamos** we don't see much of you to say the least

prodigio SM **1** (= *cosa*) wonder • **los ~s de la tecnología moderna** the wonders of modern technology • **este nuevo chip es un ~ electrónico** this new chip is an electronic wonder *o* marvel
2 (= *persona*) prodigy • **este niño es un auténtico ~** this child is a real prodigy
3 (*Rel*) miracle
ADJ INV • **niño ~** child prodigy

prodigiosamente ADV prodigiously, marvellously, marvelously (*EEUU*)

prodigioso ADJ prodigious, marvellous, marvelous (*EEUU*)

pródigo/a ADJ **1** (= *exuberante*) bountiful • **un discurso ~ en citas bíblicas** a discourse rich in biblical quotations • **fui tan ~ en los pormenores que ...** I was so lavish in *o* with details that ... • **la pródiga naturaleza** bountiful nature
2 (= *generoso*) lavish, generous (**de** with) • **ser ~ de sus talentos** to be generous in offering one's talents
3 (= *derrochador*) prodigal, wasteful • **hijo ~** prodigal son
SM/F (= *derrochador*) spendthrift, prodigal

producción SF **1** (*Com*) (= *acción*) production; (= *cantidad*) output • **en fase de ~** in the production phase • **la ~ maderera de Brasil** Brazil's timber output ▸ **producción bruta** gross production ▸ **producción en cadena** production-line assembly ▸ **producción en serie** mass production
2 (*Literat, Mús*) output • **la ~ poética de Lorca** Lorca's poetic output • **su abundante ~ operística** his prolific operatic work
3 (*Cine, Teat*) production • **departamento de ~** production department • **una ~ italiana** an Italian production ▸ **producción propia** (*TV*) in-house production • **programas de ~ propia** in-house programmes

producir ▹ CONJUG 3n VT **1** [+ *cereales, fruta, petróleo*] to produce • **se producen miles de toneladas de aceitunas al año** thousands of tons of olives are produced each year • **este país produce buenos deportistas** this country produces good sportsmen
2 (= *fabricar*) [+ *aceite, coche*] to produce, make; [+ *electricidad, energía*] to produce, generate • **esta factoría ha producido cinco mil vehículos en un mes** this factory has turned out *o* produced *o* made five thousand vehicles in a month • **~ algo en serie** to mass-produce sth
3 [+ *cambio, efecto, herida, daños*] to cause • **el virus que produce la neumonía** the virus which causes pneumonia • **un fallo en los frenos produjo el accidente** the accident was caused by brake failure • **tanto ruido me produce dolor de cabeza** all this noise is giving me a headache • **el polvo me produce alergia** I'm allergic to dust • **¿qué impresión te produjo?** what impression did it make on you? • **~ alegría a algn** to make sb happy • **~ tristeza a algn** to make sb sad
4 (*Econ*) [+ *interés*] to yield; [+ *beneficio*] to yield, generate • **mis ahorros me producen un interés anual del 5%** my savings yield an annual interest of 5%
5 (= *crear*) [+ *novela, cuadro*] to produce • **llevo tiempo sin ~ nada** I haven't produced anything for some time
6 (*Cine, TV*) to produce
VPR **producirse 1** (= *ocurrir*) [*cambio, efecto*] to take place; [*accidente, explosión, terremoto*] to occur; [*guerra, incendio, revolución*] to break out • **a no ser que se produzca un cambio** unless there is a change, unless a change takes place • **el accidente se produjo al salir de la autopista** the accident occurred as they left the motorway • **se produjo un aumento sensible de la demanda de viviendas** there was a significant increase in the demand for houses • **se desconoce a qué hora se produjo la muerte** the time of death is unknown • **se ha producido una disminución de la inversión** investment has fallen
2 (= *provocarse*) [+ *herida, fractura*] • **se produjo varias heridas con una cuchilla** he inflicted wounds on himself with a razor blade • **al caerse se produjo una fractura en el pie** she fractured a bone in her foot when she fell • **él mismo se produjo la muerte** he caused his own death

productividad SF productivity

productivo ADJ [*tierra, fábrica, encuentro*] productive; [*negocio*] profitable • **~ de interés** [*bono*] interest-bearing

producto SM **1** (= *artículo*) product • **nuestra gama de ~s cosméticos** our range of cosmetic products • **~s de primera necesidad** staple items, staple products, basic necessities • **"consuma ~s españoles"** "buy Spanish goods" • **los ~s del campo** country produce ▸ **productos agrícolas** agricultural produce (*sing*), farm produce

(*sing*) ▸ **productos alimenticios** foodstuffs ▸ **productos de belleza** beauty products ▸ **productos de consumo** consumer goods ▸ **productos de desecho** waste products ▸ **productos de limpieza** cleaning products ▸ **producto derivado** by-product • **~s derivados de la leche** dairy products, dairy produce (*sing*) • **~s derivados del petróleo** oil products ▸ **producto químico** chemical product, chemical ▸ **productos de marca** branded goods, brand name goods ▸ **producto secundario** by-product ▸ **productos estancados** goods sold by state monopoly ▸ **productos lácteos** dairy products, dairy produce (*sing*) ▸ **productos perecederos** perishable goods
2 (= *producción*) production • **ha aumentado el ~ de este año** production has increased this year
3 (= *resultado*) result, product • **la clonación es ~ de años de investigación** cloning is the result *o* product of years of research • **eso es ~ de tu imaginación** that is a figment of your imagination
4 (*Econ*) (= *beneficio*) yield, profit ▸ **producto interior bruto** gross domestic product ▸ **producto interno bruto** (*Arg*) gross domestic product ▸ **producto nacional bruto** gross national product
5 (*Mat*) product

productor(a) ADJ **1** (*Com, Agr*) producing • **países ~es de petróleo** oil producing countries • **las naciones ~as** producer nations
2 (*Cine, TV, Mús*) production (*antes de s*) • **la compañía ~a** the production company
SM/F **1** (*Com*) producer; (*Agr*) producer, grower • **el principal ~ de refrescos del mundo** the largest producer of soft drinks in the world • **los ~es de aceite de oliva** olive oil producers • **los ~es de vino** wine producers *o* growers
2 (*Cine, TV*) producer ▸ **productor(a) asociado/a** associate producer ▸ **productor(a) ejecutivo/a** executive producer
3 (= *obrero*) labourer

productora SF (= *empresa*) (*Com*) producer; (*Cine, TV*) production company; (*Mús*) record company

produje, produzco *etc* ▹ **producir**

proemio SM preface, introduction

proeza SF **1** (= *hazaña*) exploit, feat, heroic deed
2 (*LAm*) (= *alarde*) boast

Prof. ABR, **prof.** ABR (= **profesor**) Prof

Profa. ABR, **profa.** ABR (= **profesora**) Prof

profanación SF desecration

profanar ▹ CONJUG 1a VT [+ *tumba, templo*] to desecrate, defile • **~ la memoria de algn** to blacken the memory of sb

profano/a ADJ **1** (= *laico*) profane, secular
2 (= *irrespetuoso*) irreverent
3 (= *no experto*) lay, uninitiated; (= *ignorante*) ignorant • **soy ~ en la materia** I don't know anything about the subject • **soy ~ en música** I don't know anything about music, I'm a layman when it comes to music
4 (= *deshonesto*) indecent, immodest
SM/F (= *inexperto*) layman/laywoman; (= *ajeno*) outsider

profe* SMF = **profesor(a)**

profecía SF prophecy

proferir ▹ CONJUG 3i VT [+ *palabra, sonido, maldición*] to utter; [+ *insinuación*] to drop, throw out; [+ *insulto*] to hurl, let fly (**contra** at); [+ *suspiro*] to fetch, heave

profesar ▹ CONJUG 1a VT **1** (*Rel*) [+ *religión*] to profess; [+ *admiración, creencia*] to profess, declare
2 [+ *profesión*] to practise, practice (*EEUU*)
3 [+ *materia*] to teach; (*Univ*) to hold a chair in
VI (*Rel*) to take vows

profesión SF **1** (= *ocupación*) profession; (*en formulario*) occupation; (= *vocación*) calling, vocation • **abogado de ~** • **de ~ abogado** a lawyer by profession ▸ **profesión liberal** liberal profession
2 (*Rel*) [*de fe*] profession, declaration; (*en orden religiosa*) taking of vows

profesional ADJ professional • **no ~** non-professional
SMF professional • **un ~ del diseño** a professional designer • **esta gran ~ del cine** this great professional of the cinema ▸ **profesional del amor** prostitute ▸ **profesional del sexo** sex worker

profesionalidad SF **1** [*de asunto*] professional nature
2 (= *actitud*) professionalism, professional attitude

profesionalismo SM professionalism

profesionalización SF • **la ~ del ejército** the professionalization of the army • **ingresar en la ~** to become a professional

profesionalizar ▹ CONJUG 1f VT to professionalize, make more professional
VPR **profesionalizarse** to become professional, turn professional

profesionalmente ADV professionally

profesionista SMF (*Méx*) professional

profeso ADJ (*Rel*) professed

profesor(a) SM/F **1** (= *enseñante*) (*gen*) teacher; (= *instructor*) instructor ▸ **profesor(a) de autoescuela** driving instructor ▸ **profesor(a) de canto** singing teacher, singing tutor ▸ **profesor(a) de educación física** P.E. teacher ▸ **profesor(a) de equitación** riding teacher ▸ **profesor(a) de esgrima** fencing master/mistress ▸ **profesor(a) de esquí** ski instructor, skiing instructor ▸ **profesor(a) de gimnasia** gym instructor ▸ **profesor(a) de natación** swimming instructor ▸ **profesor(a) de piano** piano teacher ▸ **profesor(a) particular** private tutor ▸ **profesor(a) robot** teaching machine
2 (*Escol*) teacher ▸ **profesor(a) de biología** biology teacher, biology master/mistress ▸ **profesor(a) de instituto** secondary teacher
3 (*Univ*) (= *titular*) lecturer, professor (*EEUU*); (= *catedrático*) professor • **es ~ de griego** he is a lecturer in Greek, he lectures in Greek • **nuestros ~es de la universidad** our university teachers *o* lecturers • **se reunieron los ~es** the staff met, the faculty met (*esp EEUU*) ▸ **profesor(a) adjunto/a** assistant lecturer, assistant professor (*EEUU*) ▸ **profesor(a) agregado/a** assistant lecturer, assistant professor (*EEUU*)

profesorado SM **1** (= *profesores*) teaching staff, faculty (*EEUU*)
2 (= *profesión*) teaching profession; (= *enseñanza*) teaching, lecturing
3 (= *cargo*) professorship

profesoral ADJ [*actitud, tono*] professorial; [*plantilla, materiales*] teaching (*antes de s*)

profesoril ADJ donnish

profeta SM prophet • MODISMO: • **no ser ~ en su tierra** not to be a prophet in one's own land

proféticamente ADV prophetically

profético ADJ prophetic

profetisa SF prophetess

profetizar ▹ CONJUG 1f VT (= *predecir*) to prophesy; (= *adivinar*) to guess, conjecture

profiláctico ADJ prophylactic
SM (= *condón*) condom, sheath (*frm*), prophylactic (*frm*)

profilaxis SF INV prophylaxis

prófugo SM (= *fugitivo*) fugitive; (= *desertor*) deserter • **continúa ~** he is still at large *o* on the run ▸ **prófugo de la justicia** fugitive from justice

profundamente ADV **1** (*con verbos*) [*creer, meditar, desconfiar*] deeply, profoundly; [*dormir*] deeply, soundly
2 (*con adjetivos*) [*religioso, afectado*] deeply, profoundly; [*dividido*] deeply; [*conservador*] extremely

profundidad SF **1** (= *hondura*) depth; (*Mat*) depth, height • **tener una ~ de 30cm** to be 30cm deep • **¿qué ~ tiene?** how deep is it? • **la poca ~ del río** the shallowness of the river • **la ~ de la crisis** the severity of the crisis ▸ **profundidad de campo** (*Fot*) depth of field; ▹ **carga**
2 • **las ~es del océano** the depths of the ocean
3 (= *meticulosidad*) depth, profundity • **investigación en ~** in-depth investigation • **reforma en ~** radical *o* far-reaching reform • **limpieza de cutis en ~** deep skin cleansing

profundímetro SM depth gauge

profundización SF [*de conocimientos, crisis*] deepening • **es necesaria una ~ de los conocimientos históricos** we need to deepen our awareness of historical knowledge • **hemos de avanzar en la ~ de la democracia** we must consolidate democracy

profundizar ▹ CONJUG 1f VI • **~ en algo** to go more deeply into sth • **no voy a ~ en este tema** I'm not going to go any more deeply into this topic • **un libro que ayuda a ~ en el conocimiento de las culturas americanas** a book which helps us to understand American cultures more deeply
VT **1** [+ *hoyo, pozo*] to deepen, make deeper
2 (= *investigar*) [+ *asunto*] to study in depth, go deeply into; [+ *misterio*] to fathom, get to the bottom of

profundo ADJ **1** (= *hondo*) deep • **tener 20cm de ~** to be 20cm deep, be 20cm in depth • **¿cuánto tiene de ~?** how deep is it? • **poco ~** shallow
2 (= *intenso*) [*suspiro, voz, respiración*] deep; [*nota*] low, deep; [*sueño*] deep, sound; [*misterio, pensador*] profound • **siento un ~ respeto hacia él** I have great *o* a deep respect for him • **las imágenes le produjeron una profunda impresión** the pictures made a profound impression on him • **conocedor ~ del arte** expert in the art • **en lo ~ del alma** in the depths of one's soul • **estaban inmersos en una profunda oscuridad** (*liter*) they were enveloped by a profound darkness (*liter*)
3 • **en la Francia profunda** in the French heartland • **en el Sussex ~** in deepest Sussex, deep in Sussex

profusamente ADV (= *con abundancia*) profusely; (= *con extravagancia*) lavishly, extravagantly

profusión SF **1** (= *abundancia*) profusion
2 (= *prodigalidad*) wealth • **con ~ de detalles** with a wealth of detail

profuso ADJ (= *abundante*) profuse; (= *pródigo*) lavish, extravagant

progenie SF **1** (= *hijos*) progeny (*frm*), offspring, brood (*pey*)
2 (= *ascendencia*) family, lineage

progenitor(a) SM/F (= *antepasado*) ancestor; (= *padre*) father/mother; **progenitores** (*hum*) parents

progenitura SF offspring

progesterona SF progesterone

programa SM **1** (*de curso, actividades, TV, Radio*) programme, program (*EEUU*) • **~ de**

actividades programme of activities • **~ de gimnasia** exercise plan *o* regime
▸ **programa coloquio** chat show
▸ **programa concurso** game show
▸ **programa debate** TV debate ▸ **programa de consumo** consumer affairs programme
▸ **programa de estudios** curriculum, syllabus ▸ **programa de fomento de empleo** job creation scheme ▸ **programa electoral** electoral programme, electoral program (EEUU), election manifesto ▸ **programa nuclear** nuclear programme, nuclear program (EEUU) ▸ **programa piloto** pilot scheme
2 (*Cine*) ▸ **programa continuo** continuous showing ▸ **programa doble** double bill
3 (*Inform*) program ▸ **programa de aplicación** application program ▸ **programa fuente** source program ▸ **programa objeto** object program ▸ **programa verificador de ortografía** spellchecker
4 (*Cono Sur**) (= *amorío*) love affair

programable ADJ that can be programmed, programmable

programación SF 1 (*Inform*) programming, programing (EEUU) ▸ **programación de ordenadores** computer programming *o* (EEUU) programing
2 (*Radio, TV*) programme planning, program planning (EEUU); (*en periódico*) programme guide, viewing guide • **ha habido ciertos cambios en la ~** there have been a few changes to the schedule ▸ **programación abierta** uncoded programmes (*pl*), non-scrambled programmes (*pl*)
▸ **programación codificada** scrambled programmes (*pl*)
3 (*Ferro*) scheduling, timetabling

programado ADJ planned, scheduled

programador(a) SM/F programmer; (*Inform*) (computer) programmer
▸ **programador(a) de aplicaciones** applications programmer
▸ **programador(a) de sistemas** systems programmer

programar ▸ CONJUG 1a VT 1 [+ *actividades, vacaciones*] (= *planear*) to plan; (*detalladamente*) to draw up a programme *o* (EEUU) program for
2 (*Inform*) [+ *ordenador*] to program; [+ *vídeo*] to programme, program (EEUU)
3 (*TV, Radio*) to show
4 (*Ferro*) to schedule, timetable
5 [+ *futuro*] to shape, mould, mold (EEUU), determine

programático ADJ programmatical

programería SF (*Inform*) ▸ **programería fija** firmware

progre* ADJ (= *moderno*) (*gen*) trendy; (*en política*) leftish, liberal; (*en lo sexual*) liberal, permissive (*in outlook*)
SMF (= *moderno*) (*gen*) trendy; (*en política*) lefty*, liberal; (*en lo sexual*) sexual liberal

progresar ▸ CONJUG 1a VI to progress, make progress

progresía SF 1 • **la ~** (= *personas*) [*de moda*] the trendies; (*en política*) the lefties*, the liberals; (*en lo sexual*) the sexual liberals
2 (= *actitud*) (*gen*) trendiness; (*Pol*) leftish outlook

progresión SF progression ▸ **progresión aritmética** arithmetic progression
▸ **progresión geométrica** geometric progression

progresista ADJ, SMF progressive

progresivamente ADV progressively

progresividad SF progressiveness, progressive nature

progresivo ADJ (= *que avanza*) progressive; (= *paulatino*) gradual; (= *continuo*) continuous; (*Ling*) continuous

progreso SM (= *mejora*) progress; (= *avance*) advance; **progresos** progress (*sing*) • **hacer ~s** to progress, make progress, advance

progubernamental ADJ pro-government

prohibición SF 1 (= *veto*) ban (**de** on), prohibition (**de of**) • **la ~ total de las pruebas nucleares** the total ban on *o* the total prohibition of nuclear testing • **la ~ de exportar cereales** the banning *o* prohibition of cereal exports, the ban on cereal exports • **levantar la ~ de algo** to remove *o* lift the ban on sth
2 [*de exportaciones, venta*] embargo (**de** on)

prohibicionismo SM prohibitionism

prohibicionista ADJ, SMF prohibitionist

prohibido ADJ [*libro*] banned; [*droga*] prohibited; [*fruta*] forbidden

prohibir ▸ CONJUG 3a VT 1 (= *vedar*) [+ *venta, consumo, publicidad, prueba nuclear*] to ban, prohibit • **han prohibido la venta ambulante** street selling has been banned *o* prohibited • **la ley lo prohíbe** it is banned by law • **han prohibido la circulación de camiones este fin de semana** lorries have been banned from the roads this weekend • **quieren ~ la caza de ballenas** they want to put a ban on whaling, they want to ban whaling • **está totalmente prohibido hacer publicidad del tabaco** there is a total ban on tobacco advertising, tobacco advertising is completely banned *o* forbidden • **queda terminantemente prohibido** it is strictly forbidden
2 (= *no permitir*) • **~ algo a algn: prohibieron el acceso a la prensa** the press were banned • **el médico me ha prohibido los dulces** the doctor says I'm not allowed (to eat) sweet things, the doctor has banned me from eating sweet things • **~ a algn hacer algo**: • **me prohibió entrar en su casa** he banned me from his house, he forbade me to enter his house • **la dirección nos prohibía usar maquillaje** the management prohibited us from wearing make-up, the management forbade us to wear make-up • **~ a algn que haga algo** to forbid sb to do sth • **te prohíbo que me hables así** I forbid you to talk to me like that • **tener algo prohibido**: • **tengo prohibido el tabaco** I'm not allowed to smoke • **le tenían prohibido salir de casa** he was not allowed out • **me tienen prohibida la entrada** I'm banned, they have banned me • **me tienen prohibido hablar de política mientras comemos** I'm banned from talking politics at the dinner-table, I'm not allowed to talk politics at the dinner-table
3 (*en letreros*) • **"prohibida la caza"** "no hunting" • **"prohibida la entrada a menores de 18 años"** "no (admission to) under-18s" • **"prohibido el paso a toda persona ajena a la obra"** "no unauthorized entry", "authorized personnel only" • **"queda prohibido el consumo de alcohol en este local"** "no alcohol may be consumed on these premises" • **"prohibido fumar"** "no smoking" • **"prohibido jugar a la pelota"** "no ball games" • **"prohibido fijar carteles"** "stick no bills"

prohibitivo ADJ 1 [*coste, precio*] prohibitive • **los precios del marisco son ~s** seafood is prohibitively expensive, the price of seafood is prohibitive
2 [*ley, señal*] prohibitive

prohibitorio ADJ prohibitory

prohijar ▸ CONJUG 1a VT to adopt

prohombre SM (= *eminencia*) outstanding man, great man; (= *líder*) leader

prójima* SF 1 (= *fulana*) loose woman, woman of dubious character
2 • **la ~*** (= *esposa*) my old woman*, the wife*

projimidad SF (*And, Caribe, Cono Sur*) (= *compasión*) fellow feeling, compassion (for one's fellows); (= *solidaridad*) solidarity

prójimo SM 1 (= *semejante*) fellow man, fellow creature; (= *vecino*) neighbour, neighbor (EEUU) • **el dinero del ~** other people's money • **meterse en los asuntos del ~** to meddle in other people's affairs • **amar al ~** to love one's neighbour
2* (= *tío*) so-and-so*, creature

prolapso SM prolapse

prole SF (= *descendencia*) offspring; (*pey, hum*) brood (*pey, hum*), spawn (*pey*) • **padre de numerosa ~** father of a large family

prolegómeno SM preface, introduction • **los ~s del partido** (= *comienzo*) the early stages of the match; (= *ceremonias*) the pre-match ceremonies

proletariado SM proletariat

proletario/a ADJ proletarian
SM/F proletarian (*frm*), worker • **se negaron a disparar sobre sus hermanos ~s** they refused to shoot their fellow workers

proletarismo SM proletarianism

proletarizar ▸ CONJUG 1f VT to proletarianize

proliferación SF proliferation • **tratado de no ~ (de armas nucleares)** non-proliferation treaty (for nuclear weapons)

proliferar ▸ CONJUG 1a VI to proliferate

prolífico ADJ prolific (**en** of)

prolijamente ADV (= *interminablemente*) long-windedly; (= *con pesadez*) tediously; (= *con minuciosidad*) with an excess of detail

prolijidad SF (= *extensión*) long-windedness, prolixity (*frm*); (= *minuciosidad*) excess of detail

prolijo ADJ 1 (= *extenso*) prolix (*frm*); (= *largo*) long-winded; (= *pesado*) tedious; (= *muy minucioso*) excessively meticulous
2 (*Arg*) (= *pulcro*) smart, neat
3 (*Cono Sur*) (= *incansable*) untiring

prologar ▸ CONJUG 1h VT to preface, write an introduction to • **un libro prologado por Ortega** a book with a preface by Ortega

prólogo SM 1 [*de libro*] prologue, prolog (EEUU) (**de** to) • **un texto con ~ y notas de García Márquez** a text edited by García Márquez
2 (= *principio*) prelude (**de** to)
ADJ INV • **etapa ~** preliminary stage, preparatory stage

prologuista SMF prologue *o* (EEUU) prolog writer

prolongación SF 1 (= *acto*) prolongation, extension
2 [*de carretera*] extension • **por la ~ de la Castellana** along the new part of the Castellana, along the extension of the Castellana
3 (*Elec*) extension, flex

prolongado ADJ [*reunión, viaje*] lengthy • **no se recomienda su uso ~** not suitable for prolonged use

prolongar ▸ CONJUG 1h VT 1 (= *alargar*) (*gen*) to prolong, extend; [+ *tubo*] to make longer, extend; [+ *reunión*] to prolong
2 (*Mat*) [+ *línea*] to produce
VPR **prolongarse** (= *alargarse*) to extend, go on • **la carretera se prolonga más allá del bosque** the road goes on beyond the wood • **la sesión se prolongó bastante** the meeting went on quite a long time, it was a pretty long meeting • **la fiesta se prolongó hasta la madrugada** the party went on until the early hours

prom. ABR (= **promedio**) av

promedial ADJ average

promedialmente ADV on the average, as an average

promediar ▸ CONJUG 1b VT **1** (*Mat*) to work out the average of, average (out)
2 (= *tener un promedio de*) to average • **la producción promedia 100 barriles diarios** production averages 100 barrels a day
VI **1** (= *mediar*) to mediate (**entre** between)
2 • **promediaba el mes** it was halfway through the month • **antes de ~ el mes** before the month is halfway through

promedio SM **1** (= *término medio*) average • **el ~ es de 35%** the average is 35% • **el ~ de asistencia diaria** the average daily attendance • **para aprobar hace falta sacar un cinco de ~** you need an average of five to pass
2 [*de distancia*] middle, mid-point

promesa SF **1** (= *ofrecimiento*) (*gen*) promise; (*con compromiso formal*) pledge • **absolver a algn de su ~** to release sb from his promise • **cumplir una ~** to keep a promise • **faltar a una ~** to break a promise, go back on one's word ▸ **promesa de matrimonio** promise of marriage
2 (= *persona*) • **la joven ~ del deporte español** the bright hope of Spanish sport
ADJ INV • **jugador ~** promising player

promesante SMF (*Cono Sur*), **promesero/a** SM/F (*And, Cono Sur*) pilgrim

prometedor ADJ, **prometente** ADJ promising

prometedoramente ADV promisingly

Prometeo SM Prometheus

prometer ▸ CONJUG 2a VT **1** (= *dar palabra*) to promise • **le han prometido unas vacaciones** they've promised her a holiday • **¡te lo prometo!** I promise! • **prometió llevarnos al cine** he promised to take us to the cinema
2* (= *asegurar*) to assure • **te prometo que se acordará de mí** I can assure you he will remember me • **no me verás más, te lo prometo** you won't see me again, (that) I can assure you
3 (= *augurar*) to promise • **esto promete ser interesante** this promises to be interesting • **esto no nos promete nada bueno** this does not look at all hopeful for us, this promises to be pretty bad for us
4 (*Rel*) • **~ hacer algo** to take a vow to do sth
VI (= *tener porvenir*) to have promise, show promise • **este jugador promete** this player has *o* shows promise
VPR **prometerse 1** • **~se algo** to expect sth, promise o.s. sth • **nos habíamos prometido algo mejor** we had expected sth better
• MODISMO: • **prometérselas muy felices** to have high hopes
2 [*novios*] to get engaged • **se prometió con él en abril** she got engaged to him in April

prometido/a ADJ **1** [*ayuda, favor*] promised
• REFRÁN: • **lo ~ es deuda** a promise is a promise, you can't break a promise • **la Tierra Prometida** the Promised Land
2 [*persona*] engaged • **estar ~ con algn** to be engaged to sb
SM/F (= *novio*) fiancé/fiancée
SM (= *promesa*) promise

prominencia SF **1** (= *abultamiento*) bump, protuberance (*tb Med*); (= *hinchazón*) swelling; [*del terreno*] rise
2 (*esp LAm*) (= *importancia*) prominence

prominente ADJ **1** [*mentón, tripa*] prominent
2 (= *importante*) prominent

promiscuidad SF **1** (*sexual*) promiscuity
2 (= *heterogeneidad*) mixture, confusion
3 (= *ambigüedad*) ambiguity

promiscuo ADJ **1** (*sexualmente*) promiscuous
2 (= *heterogéneo*) (*con intención*) mixed; (*por casualidad*) motley
3 [*sentido*] ambiguous

promisión SF • **tierra de ~** land of promise, promised land

promisorio ADJ **1** [*futuro, artista*] promising
2 (*Jur*) promissory

promoción SF **1** (= *ascenso*) (*gen*) promotion, advancement; (*profesional*) promotion
2 [*de producto, oferta*] promotion ▸ **promoción de ventas** sales promotion ▸ **promoción por correspondencia directa** direct mail advertising
3 ▸ **promoción inmobiliaria** property development
4 (= *año*) class, year • **la ~ de 1975** the 1975 class • **estaba en mi ~** he was from my class *o* year, he was the same class *o* year as me
5 (= *ganga*) special offer • **está en ~** it's on (special) offer

promocional ADJ promotional

promocionar ▸ CONJUG 1a VT **1** [+ *producto, artista*] to promote
2 [+ *empleado*] to promote
VPR **promocionarse** to improve o.s., better o.s.

promontorio SM (= *altura*) promontory; (*en la costa*) promontory, headland

promotor(a) SM/F (*gen*) promoter; [*de disturbios*] instigator, prime mover; [*de ley*] sponsor • **el ~ de los disturbios** the instigator of the rioting ▸ **promotor(a) de ventas** sales promoter ▸ **promotor(a) inmobiliario/a** property developer

promotora SF property development company

promovedor(a) SM/F (*gen*) promoter; [*de disturbios etc*] instigator

promover ▸ CONJUG 2h VT **1** (= *impulsar*) [+ *proceso, plan, intereses, desarrollo*] to promote; [+ *ley*] to sponsor; [+ *debate, conflicto*] to provoke • **normas destinadas a ~ el libre comercio** regulations aimed at promoting free trade • **~ un pleito** to bring an action, file a suit
2 (= *provocar*) to cause • **su discurso promovió un enorme alboroto en la sala** his speech caused a tremendous uproar in the hall
3 (= *ascender*) [+ *persona, equipo*] to promote (a to)

promulgación SF **1** (= *anuncio solemne*) announcement
2 [*de ley*] enactment

promulgar ▸ CONJUG 1h VT **1** (= *anunciar solemnemente*) to announce
2 [+ *ley*] to enact, pass

pronombre SM pronoun ▸ **pronombre personal** personal pronoun ▸ **pronombre posesivo** possessive pronoun ▸ **pronombre reflexivo** reflexive pronoun

pronominal ADJ pronominal

pronominalización SF pronominalization

pronosticación SF prediction, forecasting, prognostication (*frm*)

pronosticador(a) SM/F (*gen*) forecaster; (*Carreras*) tipster

pronosticar ▸ CONJUG 1g VT to forecast • **han pronosticado nevadas** they are forecasting snow • **pronosticó un aumento de la inflación** he forecast *o* predicted an increase in inflation

pronóstico SM **1** (= *predicción*) (*gen*) prediction, forecast; (*en carreras*) tip • **~s para el año nuevo** predictions for the new year ▸ **pronóstico del tiempo** weather forecast
2 (*Med*) prognosis • **de ~ leve** slight, not serious • **su ~ es reservado** (*por falta de datos*) his condition is uncertain; (*por posibilidad de agravamiento*) his condition is unstable

prontamente ADV promptly

prontico* ADV, **prontito** ADV **1** (= *rápido*) double-quick; (= *enseguida*) right away
2 (= *temprano*) very early, nice and early

prontitud SF **1** (= *rapidez*) quickness, promptness • **respondió con ~** he replied promptly
2 (= *viveza*) quickness, sharpness

pronto ADV **1** (= *dentro de poco*) soon • **el tren estará ~ aquí** the train will be here soon • **~ hará diez años que nos casamos** it will soon be ten years since we got married • **todavía es ~ para salir** it's too soon *o* early to leave • **cuanto más ~ mejor** the sooner the better • **¡hasta ~!** see you soon! • **lo más ~ posible** as soon as possible
2 (*Esp*) (= *temprano*) early • **hoy he comido un poco ~** I ate a bit early today • **acostarse ~** to go to bed early • **levantarse ~** to get up early
3 (= *rápidamente*) quickly • **se hizo famoso muy ~** he became famous very quickly • **¡venid aquí, ~!** come here, right now *o* quickly! • MODISMO: • **se dice (muy) ~*** (*algo difícil*) it's easier said than done; (*algo sorprendente*) it's quite a thought
4 (*otras locuciones*) • **al ~** at first • **de ~** (= *repentinamente*) suddenly; (= *inesperadamente*) unexpectedly; (*Col, Cono Sur*) (= *a lo mejor*) maybe, perhaps • **de ~ se cayó el cuadro de la pared** the picture suddenly fell off the wall • **se presentó de ~ en la casa** he turned up at the house unexpectedly • **de ~ no sabe** maybe *o* perhaps he doesn't know • **por de *o* lo ~** (= *por ahora*) for now, for the moment; (= *en primer lugar*) for a start, for one thing • **por lo ~ toma setenta euros, mañana te daré el resto** take seventy euros for now *o* for the moment, and I'll give you the rest tomorrow • **—¿por qué no viniste? —bueno, por lo ~ estaba demasiado cansado** "why didn't you come?" — "well, for a start *o* for one thing I was too tired" • **tan ~ se ríe, tan ~ llora** one minute he's laughing, the next he's crying • **tan ~ es amigo tuyo, como de repente ya no lo es** one minute he's your friend, the next he doesn't want to know • **tan ~ como** (+ *subjun*) as soon as • **te llamaré tan ~ como sepa algo** I'll call you as soon as I hear anything
ADJ **1** (*frm*) (= *rápido*) [*regreso, solución, mejoría*] swift; [*respuesta*] prompt; [*servicio, persona*] quick • **le deseo una pronta recuperación** I wish you a swift recovery • **quedo a la espera de su pronta respuesta** I look forward to your prompt reply • **es ~ en las decisiones** he is quick about making decisions • **estuvo muy ~ para irse** he was very quick to leave
2 (*Cono Sur*) (= *preparado*) ready • **la comida está pronta** lunch is ready • **estar ~ para algo** to be ready for sth • **los republicanos estamos ~s para este desafío** we republicans are ready for this challenge • **estar ~ para hacer algo** to be ready to do sth
SM (*Esp**) (= *arrebato*) • **le dio un ~ y se largó** he left on a sudden impulse • **tiene unos ~s muy malos** he gets ratty all of a sudden* • **le dio un ~ de enojo y me golpeó** she flew into a sudden rage and hit me

prontuario SM **1** (= *libro*) handbook, manual, compendium
2 (*Arg*) (*Jur*) criminal record

pronuncia SF (*Méx*) = **pronunciamiento**

pronunciable ADJ pronounceable

pronunciación SF pronunciation

pronunciado ADJ [*acento*] pronounced, strong; [*curva*] sharp; [*facciones*] marked, noticeable; [*pendiente*] steep; [*tendencia*] marked, noticeable

pronunciamiento SM military revolt, military uprising

pronunciar ▸ CONJUG 1b (VT) **1** (*Ling*) [+ *palabra, idioma*] to pronounce; [+ *sonido*] to make, utter
2 (= *decir*) [+ *discurso*] to make, deliver; [+ *brindis*] to propose • **~ unas palabras de elogio** to say a few words of tribute • **pronunció unas palabras en las que ...** she said that ...
3 (*Jur*) [+ *sentencia*] to pass, pronounce
(VPR) **pronunciarse 1** to be pronounced • **no sé cómo se pronuncia esta palabra** I don't know how to pronounce this word
2 (= *expresarse*) to declare o.s., state one's opinion • **~se a favor de algo** to pronounce in favour of sth, declare o.s. in favour of sth • **~se sobre algo** to pronounce on sth, make a pronouncement about sth • **un 20% no se pronunció** 20% expressed no opinion
3 (*Pol, Mil*) (= *rebelarse*) to revolt, rise
4 (= *acentuarse*) to become (more) pronounced
5* (= *apoquinar*) to cough up*, fork out*

pronuncio (SM) (*And*) = **pronunciamiento**

propagación (SF) **1** (= *extensión*) [*de enfermedad, infección, fuego*] spreading; [*de ruido*] spreading, diffusion (*frm*); [*de ideas*] spreading, dissemination (*frm*)
2 (*Bio*) propagation

propaganda (SF) **1** (*Pol*) propaganda ▸ **propaganda electoral** electoral propaganda
2 (*Com*) (= *publicidad*) advertising • **las revistas están llenas de ~** magazines are full of advertising • **hacer ~ de algo** to advertise sth • **han hecho mucha ~ del concierto** the concert has been well-advertised
3 (= *panfletos, octavillas*) advertising leaflets (*pl*) • **repartía ~ por la calle** he was handing out advertising leaflets in the street • **me han llenado el buzón de ~** I've been inundated with junk mail

propagandista (SMF) propagandist

propagandístico (ADJ) **1** (*Pol*) propaganda (*antes de s*)
2 (*Com*) advertising (*antes de s*)

propagar ▸ CONJUG 1h (VT) **1** (= *extender*) [+ *ideas*] to spread, disseminate; [+ *rumor, enfermedad, fuego*] spread
2 (*Bio*) to propagate
(VPR) **propagarse 1** [*ideas, rumores, enfermedad, incendio*] to spread
2 (*Bio*) to propagate

propalación (SF) (= *divulgación*) disclosure; (= *diseminación*) dissemination

propalar ▸ CONJUG 1a (VT) (= *divulgar*) to divulge, disclose; (= *diseminar*) to disseminate; (= *publicar*) to publish an account of

propano (SM) propane

propasarse ▸ CONJUG 1a (VPR) (= *excederse*) to go too far, overstep the bounds; (*sexualmente*) to take liberties, overstep the bounds of propriety

propela (SF) (*Caribe, Méx*) (= *hélice*) propeller; (= *fuerabordo*) outboard motor

propelente (SM) propellent

propender ▸ CONJUG 2a (VI) • **~ a algo** to tend towards sth, incline to sth • **~ a hacer algo** to tend to do sth, have a tendency to do sth

propensión (SF) inclination, tendency (a to); (*Med*) tendency

propenso (ADJ) **1** • **~ a** (= *predispuesto*) prone to, subject to; (*Med*) prone to • **es muy ~ a enfadarse** he has a tendency to get angry, he's prone to getting angry • **soy propensa a los resfriados** I am very prone to colds, I catch colds easily
2 (= *dispuesto*) inclined to • **ser ~ a hacer algo** to be *o* feel inclined to do sth

propi* (SF) = **propina**

propiamente (ADV) **1** (*tb* **propiamente dicho, propiamente hablando**) strictly speaking • **este es, ~, el centro del pueblo** this is, strictly speaking, the town centre • **~ hablando, esto no es un vaso, sino una taza** strictly speaking, that is a cup not a glass • **la ceremonia religiosa ~ dicha comenzará a las doce** the religious ceremony itself will begin at twelve
2 (= *auténticamente*) really, exactly • **la novela no es ~ autobiográfica** the novel is not really *o* exactly autobiographical

propiciación (SF) propitiation

propiciador(a) (SM/F) (*LAm*) sponsor

propiciar ▸ CONJUG 1b (VT) **1** [+ *cambio, revolución*] (= *favorecer*) to favour, favor (EEUU); (= *crear condiciones*) to create a favourable atmosphere for; (= *provocar*) to cause, give rise to • **tal secreto propicia muchas conjeturas** such secrecy gives rise to *o* causes a lot of speculation • **un hecho que propició que el fuego se extendiera** a fact which helped the fire to spread
2 (= *atraer*) to propitiate (*frm*), win over
3 (*LAm*) to sponsor

propiciatorio (ADJ) propitiatory • **víctima propiciatoria** scapegoat

propicio (ADJ) [*momento, condiciones*] favourable, favorable (EEUU); [*persona*] kind, well-disposed

propiedad (SF) **1** (= *pertenencia*) possession, ownership • **ser de la ~ de algn** to be the property of sb, belong to sb • **es ~ del municipio** it is the property of the town, it belongs to the council, it's council property • **una finca de la ~ del marqués** an estate belonging to the marquis • **en ~**: • **tener un puesto de trabajo en ~** to have tenure • **tener un piso/una parcela en el cementerio en ~** to own a flat/a plot of land in the cemetery • **adquirir una vivienda/un terreno en ~** to purchase a home/a piece of land (*land or property*) • **ceder algo a algn en ~** to transfer to sb the full rights (of ownership) over sth, transfer sth completely to sb ▸ **propiedad privada** private ownership • **"no pasar — propiedad privada"** "no entry — private property" ▸ **propiedad pública** public ownership
2 (= *objeto poseído*) property • **una ~** a property, a piece of property • **este diamante es una de sus ~es más preciadas** this diamond is one of her most treasured possessions ▸ **propiedad particular** private property
3 (*Quím, Med*) property
4 (= *característica*) property, attribute
5 (= *adecuación*) propriety • **discutir la ~ de una palabra** to discuss the appropriateness of a word • **hablar con ~** to speak properly *o* correctly • **hablar español con ~** (= *expresarse bien*) to have a good command of Spanish; (= *hablar correctamente*) to speak Spanish correctly, speak correct Spanish
6 (= *exactitud*) accuracy • **lo reproduce con toda ~** he reproduces it faithfully
7 (*Com*) (= *derechos*) right, rights (*pl*) • **"es propiedad"** "copyright" ▸ **propiedad industrial** patent rights (*pl*) ▸ **propiedad intelectual, propiedad literaria** copyright

propietario/a (ADJ) • **la inmobiliaria propietaria del piso** the property company which owns the flat
(SM/F) **1** (= *poseedor*) (*gen*) owner, proprietor/proprietress; [*de tierras*] landowner • **es ~ de una cadena de restaurantes** he owns a chain of restaurants
2 (= *casero*) landlord/landlady

propina (SF) **1** (= *dinero extra*) (*en restaurante, bar*) tip, gratuity (*frm*); [*de los niños*] pocket money • **dar algo de ~** to give sth extra • **me dieron diez euros de ~** they gave me a ten-euro tip • **si compras seis te dan uno de ~** if you buy six you get one free
2 (*Mús*) encore

propinar ▸ CONJUG 1a (VT) **1** (= *dar*) [+ *golpe*] to strike, deal; [+ *azotes*] to give • **le propinó una buena paliza** he gave him a good thrashing • **le propinó una serie de consejos** he gave him a lot of advice, he made him listen to several bits of advice
2 (= *invitar*) • **~ a algn** to buy sb a drink
(VPR) **propinarse** • **~se algo** to treat o.s. to sth

propincuidad (SF) propinquity, nearness, proximity

propincuo (ADJ) near

propio (ADJ) **1** (*uso enfático*) **a** (*con posesivos*) own • **salió del hospital por su ~ pie** he left the hospital on his own two feet • **lo vi con mis ~s ojos** I saw it with my own eyes • **MODISMO**: • **en mis propias narices** under my very nose
b (= *mismo*) • **me lo ha dicho el ~ ministro** the minister himself told me so • **la solicitud debe ser firmada por el ~ interesado** the application must be signed by the applicant himself • **hacer lo ~** to do the same, follow suit • **se marchó sin decir nada y pretendía que nosotros hiciéramos lo ~** he left without a word and wanted us to do the same *o* follow suit • **yo haría lo ~ que tú** I'd do the same as you • **al ~ tiempo** at the same time • **están subiendo los impuestos al ~ tiempo que baja la inflación** they are raising taxes at the same time as inflation is going down • **la novela es al ~ tiempo romántica y dinámica** the novel is both romantic and fast-moving at the same time
c • **al ~** (*CAm*) on purpose • **de ~** especially
2 (*indicando posesión*) own • **¿tiene coche ~?** do you have your own car? • **esos rizos parecen ~s** those curls look as if they are your own • **lo hizo en defensa propia** he did it in self-defence • **hablo en nombre ~ y en el de mis compañeros** I speak for myself and my colleagues
3 (= *característico*) • **~ de algo/algn** typical of sth/sb • **una bebida propia del país** a drink typical of the country • **este sol es más ~ de un país mediterráneo** this sunshine is more typical of a Mediterranean country • **ese gesto era muy ~ de él** that gesture was very like him *o* very typical of him • **fruta propia del tiempo** seasonal fruit • **preguntas propias de un niño** questions that a child would ask
4 (= *inconfundible*) all (of) its own • **este perfume tiene un olor muy ~** this perfume has a scent all (of) its own
5 (= *adecuado*) suitable • **recibieron al rey con los honores que le son ~s** they received the king with the honours which are his due *o* with all suitable honours • **~ para algo** suitable for sth • **esa corbata no es muy propia para la ocasión** that tie is not very suitable for the occasion • **no es lugar ~ para este tipo de comportamiento** this is not the place for that sort of behaviour
6 (= *correcto*) strict, true • **utiliza las palabras en sentido ~** he uses the words in their strict *o* true sense
7 (*Esp**) (= *parecido*) • **las manzanas están tan propias que dan ganas de comérselas** the apples look so real that you want to eat them • **has salido muy ~ en ese retrato** that portrait of you is a good likeness, that portrait looks really like you
8 (*esp Méx, CAm*) • **—con su permiso —propio**

P

"excuse me" — "certainly"
SM **1** (= *mensajero*) messenger
2 • ~s y extraños all and sundry • **su triunfo sorprendió a ~s y extraños** her victory surprised all and sundry

proponente SMF proposer

proponer ▹ CONJUG 2q (PP: **propuesto**) VT
1 (= *sugerir*) [+ *idea, proyecto*] to suggest, propose; [+ *candidato*] to propose, put forward; [+ *brindis, moción de censura*] to propose; [+ *teoría*] to put forward, propound (*frm*) • **hemos propuesto la creación de un centro de acogida** we have suggested *o* proposed the setting up of a reception centre • **el plan propuesto por el sindicato** the plan put forward *o* suggested *o* proposed by the union • **no creo que la solución sea esa, como parece que algunos proponéis** I do not believe that is the solution, as some of you seem to suggest • **la cifra de ventas propuesta asciende a un millón de libras** the sales target comes to one million pounds • **te voy a ~ un trato** I'll make you a deal *o* a proposition • **~ a algn hacer algo** to suggest to sb that they should do sth • **fue ella quien me propuso hacer ese papel** it was her who suggested (to me) that I should play this part • **~ que** to suggest *o* propose that • **propongo que la reunión se aplace hasta mañana** I suggest *o* propose that the meeting be postponed till tomorrow, I suggest we put the meeting off till tomorrow • **yo propongo que lo paguemos a medias** I suggest we go halves on it • **le propuse que se casara conmigo** I proposed to her
2 (= *recomendar*) • **~ a algn para** [+ *cargo*] to nominate sb for, propose sb as; [+ *premio*] to nominate sb for • **lo han propuesto para el cargo de secretario** they have nominated him for secretary, they have proposed him as secretary • **he sido propuesta para la beca de investigación** I've been nominated *o* proposed for the research scholarship • **la película ha sido propuesta como candidata para los Oscars** the film has been nominated for an Oscar
3 (= *plantear*) [+ *problema*] (*gen*) to pose; (*Mat*) to set
VPR **proponerse** • **~se algo** to put one's mind to sth • **cuando me propongo algo seriamente, lo consigo** when I really set out to do something *o* put my mind to something, I get it done • **~se hacer algo** (*con intención*) to mean to do sth, intend to do sth; (*con empeño*) to be determined to do sth, be intent on doing sth • **me he propuesto dejar de fumar este año** I mean *o* intend to give up smoking this year • **no me había propuesto hacerte daño** I didn't mean *o* intend to hurt you • **me he propuesto terminar el libro hoy** I am determined to finish the book today, I am intent on finishing the book today • **~se que:** • **¿es que te has propuesto que lleguemos tarde?** you're determined to make us late, aren't you?, you're intent on making us late, aren't you? • **sin proponérselo** unintentionally • **y así, sin proponérmelo, me convertí en empresario** so, without exactly meaning to, I became a businessman, so I became a businessman unintentionally

proporción SF **1** (*gen*) proportion; (*Mat*) ratio; (= *relación*) relationship; (= *razón, porcentaje*) rate • **la ~ entre azules y verdes** the proportion of blues to greens • **está en ~ con los gastos** it is in proportion to the expenses • **ganaron la votación por una ~ de cinco a uno** they won the vote by a ratio of five to one • **esto no guarda ~ con lo otro** this is out of proportion to the rest
2 proporciones [*de objeto*] proportions; [*de plan, escándalo*] scope • **una máquina de proporciones gigantescas** a machine of huge size *o* proportions • **se desconocen las proporciones del desastre** the size *o* extent *o* scope of the disaster is unknown • **guarda bien las proporciones** it remains in proportion • **de proporciones** (*LAm*) (= *enorme*) huge, vast
3 (= *oportunidad*) chance, opportunity, right moment
4 proporciones (*Méx*) (= *riqueza*) wealth (*sing*) • **de proporciones** wealthy

proporcionadamente ADV proportionately, in proportion

proporcionado ADJ **1 • bien ~** [*persona, cara*] well-proportioned; [*talle*] shapely
2 (= *en proporción*) proportionate (**a** to)
3 (= *adecuado*) appropriate (**a** to) • **de tamaño ~** of the appropriate size

proporcional ADJ proportional (**a** to)

proporcionalmente ADV proportionally

proporcionar ▹ CONJUG 1a VT **1** (= *dar*) to supply, provide • **~ dinero a algn** to supply sb with money • **esto le proporciona una renta anual de ...** this brings him in a yearly income of ... • **esto proporciona mucho encanto a la narración** this lends *o* gives great charm to the story • **su tío le proporcionó el puesto** his uncle found him the job, his uncle helped him into *o* helped him get the job
2 (= *adaptar*) to adjust, adapt (**a** to)

proposición SF **1** (= *sugerencia, oferta*) proposal • **aceptó nuestra ~ de vender la casa** he accepted our proposal to sell the house • **¿cuál es tu ~?** what do you propose?, what is your proposal *o* proposition?
▸ **proposición de ley** bill ▸ **proposición de matrimonio** marriage proposal, proposal of marriage ▸ **proposiciones deshonestas** indecent proposals, indecent suggestions
▸ **proposición no de ley** motion
2 (*Ling*) clause
3 (*Fil, Mat*) proposition

propósito SM **1** (= *intención*) purpose • **¿cuál es el ~ de su visita?** what is the purpose of his visit? • **para lograr este ~ se han desplazado a Madrid** with this in mind *o* for this purpose, they have gone to Madrid • **buenos ~s** (*para el futuro*) good intentions; (*para el año nuevo*) resolutions • **de ~** on purpose, deliberately • **fuera de ~** off the point • **hacer(se) (el) ~ de hacer algo** to resolve to do sth, decide to do sth • **los tres hicieron firme ~ de no atacar** the three of them resolved *o* decided not to attack • **nunca nos hemos hecho el ~ de gastar más dinero** it has never been our intention to spend more money • **sin ~** [*caminar, moverse*] aimlessly; [*actuar*] unintentionally • **tener (el) ~ de hacer algo** to intend *o* mean to do sth, be one's intention to do sth • **no tenía ~ ninguno de pelearme** I didn't intend *o* mean to get into a fight, it was not my intention to get into a fight • **tengo el firme ~ de irme de casa** I am determined to leave home, I am intent on leaving home ▸ **propósito de enmienda** • **no veo ~ de enmienda en su comportamiento** I don't see him mending his ways *o* turning over a new leaf
2 • a ~ a (*como adjetivo*) suitable, right (**para** for) • **era la persona a ~ para el trabajo** he was very suitable for the job, he was the right person for the job • **hizo varios comentarios a ~** he made various comments on the matter
b (*como adverbio*) on purpose, deliberately • **lo siento, no lo hice a ~** I'm sorry, I didn't do it on purpose *o* deliberately • **me he comprado un traje a ~ para la boda** I've bought a dress especially for the wedding • **venir a ~** (= *venir expresamente*) to come especially; (= *ser adecuado*) [*comentario, observación*] to be well-timed; [*dinero*] to come in handy • **he venido a ~ para verte** I have come especially to see you • **esa observación vino muy a ~** that was a timely remark, that remark was very well-timed • **el dinero que me diste me vino muy a ~** the money you gave me was just what I needed *o* came in very handy
c (= *por cierto*) by the way • **a ~, ¿qué vais a hacer en Semana Santa?** by the way, what are you doing at Easter?
d • a ~ de (*después de verbo*) about; (*uso independiente*) talking of, à propos of • **estuvieron discutiendo a ~ de las elecciones** they were having a discussion about the election • **a ~ de Picasso, ¿has visto alguna vez el Guernica?** talking of *o* à propos of Picasso, have you ever seen Guernica? • **a ~ de dinero, ¿cuándo me vas a pagar?** now you mention it *o* talking of money, when are you going to pay me? • **¿a ~ de qué me dices eso ahora?** why do you say that now?

propuesta SF **1** (= *sugerencia*) proposal • **me hizo varias ~s de trabajo** he made me several work proposals • **a ~ de algn** at the proposal *o* suggestion of sb • **aprobar una ~** to approve a proposal • **desestimar una ~** to turn down *o* reject a proposal • **rechazar una ~** to reject a proposal, turn down a proposal
▸ **propuesta de ley** bill
2 (= *recomendación*) (*para un cargo*) candidature; (*para un premio*) nomination • **todos apoyaron su ~ como candidato** everyone supported his candidature • **la ~ de Elena como presidenta fue la más votada** Elena received most votes in the election for president
3 (= *proyecto*) design • **concurso de ~s** design competition

propuesto PP de **proponer**

propugnación SF advocacy

propugnar ▹ CONJUG 1a VT (= *proponer*) to advocate, propose, suggest; (= *apoyar*) to defend, support

propulsado ADJ • **un avión ~ por tres motores** a plane driven by four engines • **el coche está ~ por un motor de ocho cilindros** the car has an eight-cylinder engine, the car runs on eight cylinders • **~ a chorro** jet-propelled

propulsante SM fuel, propellent

propulsar ▹ CONJUG 1a VT **1** (*Mec*) [+ *vehículo*] to drive, propel; [+ *avión, cohete*] to propel
2 [+ *actividad, cambio*] to promote, encourage

propulsión SF propulsion ▸ **propulsión a chorro** jet propulsion • **con ~ a chorro** jet-propelled ▸ **propulsión a cohete** rocket propulsion ▸ **propulsión por reacción** jet propulsion

propulsor(a) ADJ **1** [*motor*] jet (*antes de s*)
2 [*medidas*] driving
SM (*Téc*) (= *combustible*) propellent, fuel; (= *motor*) motor, engine
SM/F (= *persona*) promoter

propuse *etc* ▹ **proponer**

prorrata SF share, quota, prorate (*EEUU*)
• **a ~** proportionately, pro rata

prorratear ▹ CONJUG 1a VT to share out, distribute proportionately, prorate (*EEUU*)
• **~emos el dinero** we will share out the money pro rata • **los daños se ~án entre las cuatro aseguradoras** damages will be shared by the four insurers

prorrateo SM sharing (in proportion),

apportionment • **a ~ pro rata**, proportionately
prórroga SF (= *plazo extra*) extension; (*Dep*) extra time; (*Mil*) deferment; (*Jur*) stay (of execution), respite
prorrogable ADJ which can be extended
prorrogación SF deferment, prorogation (*frm*)
prorrogar ▸ CONJUG 1h VT [+ *período*] to extend; [+ *decisión*] to defer, postpone; [+ *sesión*] to prorogue, adjourn; (*Mil*) to defer; (*Jur*) to grant a stay of execution to • **prorrogamos una semana las vacaciones** we extended our holiday by a week • **no les ~on el contrato** their contract was not extended
prorrumpir ▸ CONJUG 3a VI to burst forth, break out • **la multitud prorrumpió en aplausos** the crowd burst (out) into applause • **~ en gritos** to start shouting • **~ en lágrimas** to burst into tears
prosa SF **1** (*Literat*) prose • **poema en ~** prose poem ▸ **prosa poética** prose poetry
2 (= *prosaísmo*) prosaic nature, ordinariness • **la ~ de la vida** the ordinariness of life
3* (= *verborrea*) verbiage
4 (*Cono Sur*) (= *vanidad*) vanity, haughtiness
5 (*And, CAm*) (= *afectación*) pomposity, affectation
prosador(a) SM/F **1** (= *escritor*) prose writer
2* (= *hablador*) chatterbox*, great talker
prosaicamente ADV prosaically
prosaico ADJ [*tono, lenguaje*] prosaic; [*explicación*] mundane, prosaic; [*ambición, objetivo*] mundane • **la realidad es mucho más prosaica** the truth is much more mundane
prosaísmo SM [*de lo cotidiano*] prosaic nature; (*Literat*) prosaicism
prosapia SF (= *alcurnia*) lineage, ancestry • **una familia de (mucha) ~** a (very) illustrious family • **es un liberal de ~** he comes from a long line of liberals
proscenio SM proscenium
proscribir ▸ CONJUG 3a VT **1** (= *prohibir*) (*gen*) to prohibit, ban; [+ *partido*] to proscribe, outlaw; [+ *criminal*] to outlaw; [+ *asunto*] to ban • **~ un tema de su conversación** to banish a topic from one's conversation
2 (= *desterrar*) to banish, exile
proscripción SF **1** (= *prohibición*) (*gen*) prohibition (*frm*) (**de** of), ban (**de** on); [*de partido*] proscription, outlawing
2 (= *destierro*) banishment
proscripto ADJ (*Arg*) = **proscrito**
proscrito/a PP *de* **proscribir**
ADJ **1** (= *prohibido*) (*gen*) banned, prohibited; [*actividad*] outlawed, proscribed • **un libro ~** a banned book
2 (= *desterrado*) exiled
SM/F (= *exiliado*) exile; (= *bandido*) outlaw
prosecución SF **1** (= *continuación*) continuation
2 [*de objetivo*] pursuit; [*de demanda*] pressing
3 (= *caza*) pursuit
proseguir ▸ CONJUG 3d, 3k VT (= *seguir*) [+ *charla, reunión*] to continue, carry on; [+ *demanda*] to go on with, press; [+ *investigación, estudio*] to pursue
VI **1** • **~ en** *o* **con una actitud** to continue in one's attitude, maintain one's attitude
2 [*condición*] to continue, go on • **prosiguió con el cuento** he went on with the story • **¡por favor, prosiga!** please go on! *o* continue! • **prosigue el mal tiempo** the bad weather continues
proselitismo SM proselytism
proselitista ADJ proselytizing
prosélito/a SM/F convert, proselyte (*frm*) • **hacer ~s** to win over converts
prosificación SF **1** (= *texto*) prose version
2 (= *acción*) rewriting as prose, turning into prose
prosificar ▸ CONJUG 1g VT to write a prose version of, rewrite as *o* in prose
prosista SMF prose writer
prosodia SF prosody
prosopopeya SF **1** (= *personificación*) personification, prosopopoeia (*frm*)
2 (= *pomposidad*) pomposity, affectation
prospección SF **1** (= *exploración*) exploration (**de** for) ▸ **prospección de mercados** market research
2 (*Min*) prospecting (**de** for) ▸ **prospección de petróleo** prospecting for oil, drilling for oil
3 (*Mil*) prospecting
prospeccionar ▸ CONJUG 1a VT to look to, examine
prospectar ▸ CONJUG 1a VT to survey
prospectiva SF futurology
prospectivo ADJ [*estudio, informe*] pilot • **análisis ~** forecast
prospecto SM **1** (= *folleto*) leaflet
2 (= *instrucciones*) (*gen*) sheet of instructions; [*de medicamento*] directions for use; [*de empresa, universidad*] prospectus
prospector(a) SM/F prospector • **~(a) de mercados** market researcher
prósperamente ADV (= *con mejoras*) prosperously; (= *con éxito*) successfully
prosperar ▸ CONJUG 1a VI [*industria*] to prosper, thrive; [*idea, proyecto*] to prosper; (= *tener éxito*) to be successful • **la moción de censura no prosperó** the censure motion was unsuccessful *o* was defeated
prosperidad SF (= *bienestar*) prosperity; (= *éxito*) success • **en época de ~** in a period of prosperity, in good times • **desear a algn muchas ~es** to wish sb all success
próspero ADJ (= *floreciente*) prosperous, thriving; (= *venturoso*) successful • **feliz Navidad y ~ Año Nuevo** Happy Christmas and a prosperous new year • **con próspera fortuna** with good luck, favoured by fortune
próstata SF prostate
prosternarse ▸ CONJUG 1a VPR (= *postrarse*) to prostrate o.s.; (= *humillarse*) to bow low, bow humbly
prostético ADJ prosthetic
prostibulario ADJ brothel (*antes de s*)
prostíbulo SM brothel
prostitución SF prostitution • **casa de ~** brothel ▸ **prostitución infantil** child prostitution
prostituir ▸ CONJUG 3g VT [+ *persona*] to prostitute; [+ *ideales*] to prostitute
VPR **prostituirse 1** (*en sentido sexual*) (*por primera vez*) to become a prostitute; (*como profesión*) to work as a prostitute
2 (= *corromperse*) to prostitute o.s.
prostituto/a SM/F male prostitute/ prostitute
prosudo ADJ (*And, Cono Sur*) affected, pompous
protagónico ADJ leading, major
protagonismo SM **1** (= *papel*) leading role; (= *liderazgo*) leadership • **conceder el ~ al pueblo** to grant power to the people
2 (= *importancia*) prominence; (*en sociedad*) taking an active part, being socially active • **afán de ~** urge to be in the limelight • **tuvo poco ~** he made little showing • **el tema adquiere gran ~ en este texto** the theme takes on major importance in this text • **le gusta hacer las cosas sin ~s** he likes to do things without making a fuss
3 (= *defensa*) defence, defense (*EEUU*)
4 (= *apoyo*) support
protagonista ADJ central, leading • **tuvo un papel ~ en las negociaciones** she played a central *o* leading role in the negotiations
SMF **1** (*en hecho real*) main figure • **los ~s del conflicto** the main figures in the dispute
2 (= *personaje*) [*de obra literaria*] main character, protagonist (*frm*); [*de película, serie*] main character, lead • **el ~ no muere en la película** the main character *o* lead doesn't die in the film
3 (= *actor, actriz*) star • **la ~ de la película es Bette Davies** the star of the film is Bette Davies
protagonístico ADJ leading • **papel ~** leading role
protagonizar ▸ CONJUG 1f VT **1** (*Cine, Teat*) to play the lead in • **una película protagonizada por Greta Garbo** a film starring Greta Garbo
2 (= *formar parte de*) [+ *proceso, rebelión*] to lead; [+ *manifestación, protesta, accidente*] to be involved in; [+ *escándalo*] to be caught up in, be involved in; [+ *derrota, victoria*] to figure in, be involved in • **el mes ha estado protagonizado por ...** the month has been notable for ... • **un encuentro protagonizado por los dos actores principales** a meeting between the two main protagonists
proteaginosa SF protein product
protección SF protection ▸ **protección civil** civil defence *o* (*EEUU*) defense ▸ **protección de datos** data protection ▸ **protección policial** police protection
proteccionismo SM protectionism
proteccionista ADJ [*medida*] protectionist; [*arancel*] protective
SMF protectionist
protector(a) ADJ **1** (= *defensivo*) protecting, protective • **cubierta ~a** protective cover • **medidas ~as de la industria** measures to protect industry, protective measures towards industry • **crema ~a** barrier cream
2 [*tono*] patronizing
SM/F (= *defensor*) (*gen*) protector; [*de artista*] patron; [*de la tradición*] guardian • **El Protector** (*LAm*) (*Hist Pol*) the Protector
SM **1** (*Inform*) ▸ **protector de pantalla** screen saver
2 ▸ **protector solar** sun protection
3 (*Boxeo*) ▸ **protector bucal** gum shield
protectorado SM protectorate
proteger ▸ CONJUG 2c VT **1** (= *resguardar*) to protect (**contra, de** against, from) • **esta bufanda te ~á del frío** this scarf will protect you from the cold • **la policía protegió al árbitro de las iras del público** the police protected *o* shielded the referee from the wrath of the public • **sus padres la protegen demasiado** her parents are overprotective towards her • **protegemos los derechos de los trabajadores** we defend the rights of the workers • **~ contra grabación** *o* **escritura** (*Inform*) to write-protect
2 [+ *artista*] to act as patron to
VPR **protegerse** • **~se de** *o* **contra algo** to protect o.s. from *o* against sth • **nos protegimos de** *o* **contra la lluvia en la cabaña** we sheltered from the rain in the hut • **se protegió del** *o* **contra el sol con una gorra** he wore a cap for protection against the sun • **~se de las miradas indiscretas** to shield o.s. from prying eyes
protegido/a ADJ **1** (= *resguardado*) protected • **especie protegida** protected species
2 [*vivienda*] subsidised
SM/F protégé, protégée
proteico ADJ **1** (= *cambiante*) protean
2 [*alimento, contenido*] protein (*antes de s*)
proteína SF protein
proteínico ADJ protein (*antes de s*) • **contenido ~** protein content
protervidad SF wickedness, perversity

P

protervo ADJ wicked, perverse
protésico/a ADJ prosthetic
SM/F prosthetist, limb-fitter ▸ **protésico/a dental** dental technician
prótesis SF INV (*Med*) (*gen*) prosthesis; (= *brazo, pierna*) artificial limb ▸ **prótesis de cadera** artificial hip ▸ **prótesis de mama** breast implant ▸ **prótesis dental** dental prosthesis ▸ **prótesis de silicona** silicone implant ▸ **prótesis de uñas** nail extensions
protesta SF **1** (= *queja*) protest • **el ministro desoyó las ~s ciudadanas** the minister ignored the people's protests • **una manifestación de ~ contra la nueva ley** a protest demonstration against the new law • **los gritos de ~ fueron silenciados con aplausos** shouts of protest were drowned by the applause • **canción (de) ~** protest song • **déjate de ~s porque no pienso dejarte ir** you can stop protesting because I'm not going to let you go • **en señal de ~ contra** *o* **por algo** in protest against sth
2 (*frm*) (= *declaración*) protestation • **hacer ~s de lealtad** to protest one's loyalty
protestación SF protestation
▸ **protestación de fe** profession of faith
▸ **protestación de lealtad** protestation of loyalty, declaration of loyalty
protestante ADJ, SMF Protestant
protestantismo SM Protestantism
protestar ▸ CONJUG 1a VI **1** (= *quejarse*) to complain • **~on contra la subida de la gasolina** they complained *o* (*frm*) protested against the rise in the price of petrol • **protestó por lo mal que la habían tratado** she complained *o* (*frm*) protested about how badly she had been treated • **no protestes tanto y acábate la cena** stop complaining and finish your dinner
2 (*Jur*) • **¡protesto, Su Señoría!** objection, Your Honour! • **¡protesto contra esa observación!** I resent that!, I object to that remark!
VT **1** [+ *letra, pagaré*] to protest, note • **un cheque protestado por falta de fondos** a cheque referred to drawer
2 (*frm*) (= *declarar*) to protest
protesto SM **1** [*de letra*] protest
2 (*LAm*) protest
protestón/ona* ADJ whingeing (*pey**), perpetually moaning
SM/F perpetual moaner, whinger (*pey**)
proto... PREF proto...
protocolario ADJ **1** (= *ceremonial*) required by protocol, established by protocol
2 (= *formulario*) ceremonial, formal
protocolo SM **1** (*Pol, Inform*) protocol
2 (= *reglas ceremoniales*) protocol, convention
3 (= *formalismo*) • **sin ~s** informal(ly), without formalities
4 (*Med*) medical record
protón SM proton
protoplasma SM protoplasm
prototípico ADJ archetypal, typical
prototipo SM (= *arquetipo*) prototype; (= *modelo*) model
protuberancia SF **1** (= *bulto*) protuberance
2 (*en estadística*) bulge
protuberante ADJ protuberant
prov. ABR = **provincia**
provecho SM (= *ventaja*) advantage; (= *beneficio*) benefit; (*Econ*) (= *ganancia*) profit • **de ~** [*negocio*] profitable; [*actividad*] useful; [*persona*] worthy, honest • **¡buen ~!** enjoy your meal! • **¡buen ~ le haga!** and much good may it do him! • **en ~ de** to the benefit of • **un pueblo que lucha consigo mismo, en ~ de otros** a people who fight amongst themselves, to the benefit *o* advantage of others • **en ~ del prójimo** for the benefit of others • **en ~ propio** for one's own benefit, to one's own advantage • **sacar ~ de algo** to benefit from sth, profit by *o* from sth
provechosamente ADV advantageously, beneficially, profitably
provechoso ADJ (= *ventajoso*) advantageous; (= *beneficioso*) beneficial, useful; (= *rentable*) profitable
provecto ADJ aged, elderly • **de edad provecta** aged, elderly
proveedor(a) SM/F (= *abastecedor*) supplier, purveyor; (= *distribuidor*) dealer • **consulte a su ~ habitual** consult your usual dealer • **"Proveedores de la Casa Real"** "By appointment to His/Her Majesty"
▸ **proveedor de servicios de Internet** internet service provider, ISP
proveeduría SF (*Cono Sur*) grocer's, grocery
proveer ▸ CONJUG 2e (PP: **provisto y proveído**) VT **1** (= *suministrar*) to supply, furnish (**de** with)
2 (= *preparar*) to provide, get ready • **~ todo lo necesario** to provide all that is necessary (**para** for)
3 [+ *vacante*] to fill
4 [+ *negocio*] to transact, dispatch
5 (*Jur*) to decree
VI • **~ a** to provide for • **~ a las necesidades de algn** to provide for sb's needs • **~ a un vicio de algn** to pander to sb's vice
VPR **proveerse** • **~se de algo** to provide o.s. with sth
proveniente ADJ • **~ de** from • **gente ~ de diferentes países** people from different countries • **inversiones ~s de Japón** Japanese investment, investment from Japan
provenir ▸ CONJUG 3r VI • **~ de** to come from • **la palabra "ruleta" proviene del francés** the word "roulette" comes from (the) French • **esto proviene de no haberlo curado antes** this stems from *o* comes from *o* is a result of not having treated it earlier
Provenza SF Provence
provenzal ADJ Provençal
SMF Provençal
SM (*Ling*) Provençal
proverbial ADJ proverbial
proverbialmente ADV proverbially
proverbio SM proverb
provida ADJ INV, **pro-vida** ADJ INV pro-life
próvidamente ADV providently
providencia SF **1** (*Rel*) • **la (Divina) Providencia** (Divine) Providence
2 providencias (= *precauciones*) measures, steps • **tomar las ~s necesarias para evitar accidentes** to take the steps necessary to avoid accidents
3 (*Jur*) ruling, decision
providencial ADJ providential
providencialmente ADV providentially
providente ADJ, **próvido** ADJ provident
provincia SF **1** (= *distrito*) province; (*Esp*) (*Admin*) ≈ county • **la capital de la ~** the provincial capital • **las Provincias Vascongadas** (*Hist*) the Basque Provinces, the Basque Country
2 • **de ~s: un pueblo de ~s** a country town, a provincial town • **lleva una vida de ~s** she lives a provincial life • **una gira por ~s** a tour of the provinces

> **PROVINCIA**
> Spain is divided into 55 administrative **provincias**, including the islands and Ceuta and Melilla in North Africa. Each one has a **capital de provincia**, which generally has the same name as the province itself. **Provincias** are grouped by geography, history and culture into **comunidades autónomas**.
> ▸ **COMUNIDAD AUTÓNOMA**

provincial[1] ADJ provincial, ≈ county (*antes de s*)
provincial[2]**(a)** SM/F (*Rel*) provincial
provincialismo SM **1** (= *cualidad*) provincialism
2 (*Ling*) *dialect word, phrase etc*
provincianismo SM provincialism • **~ de cortas luces** • **~ de vía estrecha** narrow provincialism, deadening provincialism
provinciano/a ADJ **1** (= *rural*) country (*antes de s*)
2 (= *paleto*) provincial
3† (= *vasco*) Basque, of the Basque Provinces
SM/F **1** (= *de provincias*) provincial country dweller
2† (= *vasco*) Basque
proviniente ADJ = **proveniente**
provisión SF **1** (= *acto*) provision • **concurso para la ~ de 84 plazas de profesorado** competition to fill 84 teaching jobs
2 (= *abastecimiento*) provision, supply
3 provisiones (= *alimentos*) provisions, supplies
4 (*Econ*) • **cheque sin ~** bad cheque, bad check (*EEUU*) ▸ **provisión de fondos** financial cover
5 (= *medida*) precautionary measure, step
provisional ADJ provisional
provisionalidad SF provisional nature, temporary character
provisionalmente ADV provisionally
provisionar ▸ CONJUG 1a VT to cover, make bad-debt provision for
provisorio ADJ (*esp LAm*) provisional
provista SF (*Cono Sur*) provisions (*pl*), supplies (*pl*)
provisto VB (*pp de* **proveer**) • **~ de algo** [*persona*] provided with sth, supplied with sth; [*automóvil, máquina*] equipped with sth • **no iban ~s de suficiente comida** they didn't have enough food with them • **el televisor viene ~ de mando a distancia** the television comes with remote control included *o* complete with remote control
provocación SF provocation
provocador(a) ADJ provocative • **agente ~** agent provocateur
SM/F trouble-maker
provocadoramente ADV provocatively
provocar ▸ CONJUG 1g VT **1** (= *causar*) [+ *protesta, explosión*] to cause, spark off; [+ *fuego*] to cause, start (deliberately); [+ *cambio*] to bring about, lead to; [+ *proceso*] to promote • **~ risa a algn** to make sb laugh • **incendio provocado** arson
2 [+ *parto*] to induce, bring on
3 [+ *persona*] (*gen*) to provoke; (= *incitar*) to rouse, stir up (to anger); (= *tentar*) to tempt, invite • **¡no me provoques!** don't start me! • **~ a algn a cólera** *o* **indignación** to rouse sb to fury • **~ a algn a lástima** to move sb to pity • **el mar provoca a bañarse** the sea invites one to go for a swim
4 (*sexualmente*) to rouse
VI **1** (*LAm*) (= *gustar, apetecer*) • **me provoca comer** I feel like eating • **¿te provoca un café?** would you like a coffee?, do you fancy a coffee? • **¿qué le provoca?** what would you like?, what do you fancy? • **no me provoca la idea** the idea doesn't appeal to me, I don't fancy the idea • **—¿por qué no vas? —no me provoca** "why aren't you going?" — "I don't feel like it" • **no me provoca estudiar hoy** I'm not in the mood for studying today, I don't feel like studying today
2* (= *vomitar*) to be sick, throw up*
provocativo ADJ **1** (= *incitante*) provocative
2 (*sexualmente*) [*mirada, vestido*] provocative; [*risa, gesto*] inviting, provocative
proxeneta SMF pimp, procurer/procuress

proxenetismo SM procuring

próximamente ADV shortly, soon

proximidad SF nearness, closeness • **en las ~es de Madrid** in the vicinity of Madrid

próximo ADJ **1** (= *cercano*) near, close; [*pariente*] close • **un lugar ~ a la costa** a place near the coast • **vivimos muy ~s** we live very close by • **en fecha próxima** soon, at an early date • **estar ~ a algo** to be close to sth, be near sth • **estar ~ a hacer algo** to be on the point of doing sth, be about to do sth
2 (= *siguiente*) next • **el mes ~** next month • **el ~ 5 de junio** on 5th June next • **se bajarán en la próxima parada** they will get off at the next stop

proyección SF **1** (= *acto*) [*de imagen*] projection; [*de luz*] casting, throwing
2 (*Cine*) screening • **el tiempo de ~ es de 35 minutos** the film runs for 35 minutes, the screening lasts 35 minutes
3 (= *diapositiva*) slide, transparency
4 (= *alcance*) hold, influence • **la ~ de los periódicos sobre la sociedad** the hold of newspapers over society • **un intelectual con gran ~ social** a very influential intellectual • **un artista de una gran ~ internacional** an internationally renowned artist

proyeccionista SMF projectionist

proyectable ADJ • **asiento ~** (*Aer*) ejector seat

proyectar ▸ CONJUG 1a VT **1** (= *planear*) • **~ hacer algo** to plan to do sth • **tenía proyectado hablar con él** I was planning to speak to him
2 (*Arquit*) to plan; (*Mec*) to design • **está proyectado para ...** it is designed to ...
3 (*Cine, Fot*) to project, screen
4 [+ *luz*] to cast, project; [+ *sombra*] to cast
5 (= *dirigir*) [+ *objeto*] to hurl, throw; [+ *chorro, líquido*] to shoot out
6 (*Mat*) to project
VPR **proyectarse** [*sombra*] to be cast

proyectil SM **1** (= *arma*) projectile, missile ▸ **proyectil balístico intercontinental** intercontinental ballistic missile ▸ **proyectil de iluminación** flare, rocket ▸ **proyectil (tele)dirigido** guided missile
2 (*Mil*) (*de cañón*) shell; (*con cohete*) missile

proyectista SMF **1** (*Aer, Aut, Téc*) (= *diseñador*) designer; (= *delineante*) draughtsman, draftsman (EEUU)
2 (*Cine*) projectionist

proyecto SM **1** (= *intención*) plan • **cambiar de ~** to change one's plans • **está en ~ la publicación de los catálogos para el año que viene** the publication of the catalogues is planned for next year • **tener algo en ~** to be planning sth • **tener ~s para algo** to have plans for sth • **tener ~s sobre algo** to have designs on sth ▸ **proyecto piloto** pilot scheme
2 (*Téc*) plan, design; (= *idea*) project
3 (*Econ*) detailed estimate
4 (*Pol*) ▸ **proyecto de declaración** draft declaration ▸ **proyecto de ley** bill
5 (*Univ*) ▸ **proyecto de fin de carrera, proyecto final de carrera** (*práctico*) final-year project; (*teórico*) final-year dissertation

proyector SM **1** (*Cine*) projector ▸ **proyector de diapositivas** slide projector
2 (= *foco de luz*) (*Teat*) spotlight; (*para monumentos*) floodlight; (*Mil*) (= *reflector*) searchlight ▸ **proyector antiniebla** fog lamp

prudencia SF (= *cuidado*) care, caution; (= *cordura*) wisdom, prudence; (= *sensatez*) sound judgment, soundness • **actuar con ~** to be careful *o* cautious • **el problema debe ser analizado con ~** the problem must be carefully studied • **extremar la ~** to proceed with extreme caution

prudencial ADJ **1** (= *adecuado*) prudential; (= *sensato*) sensible • **tras un intervalo ~** after a decent interval, after a reasonable time
2 [*cantidad, distancia*] roughly correct

prudenciarse ▸ CONJUG 1b VPR (*And, CAm, Méx*) (= *ser cauteloso*) to be cautious; (= *contenerse*) to hold back, control o.s.

prudente ADJ sensible, prudent • **lo más ~ sería ir ahora mismo al médico** the most sensible *o* prudent thing to do would be to go straight to the doctor • **es una conductora muy ~** she's a very careful driver • **manténgase a una distancia ~ del vehículo delantero** keep a safe distance from the car in front

prudentemente ADV (= *con sensatez*) sensibly, wisely, prudently; [*decidir*] judiciously, soundly; [*conducir*] carefully

prueba SF **1** (= *demostración*) proof • **esta es una ~ palpable de su incompetencia** this is clear proof of his incompetence • **¿tiene usted ~ de ello?** can you prove it?, do you have proof? • **eso es la ~ de que él lo hizo** this proves that he did it, this is the proof that he did it • **es ~ de que tiene buena salud** that proves *o* shows he's in good health • **sin dar la menor ~ de ello** without giving the faintest sign of it • **ser buena ~ de algo** to be clear proof of sth • **el resultado es buena ~ de su profesionalidad** the result is clear proof of her professionalism • **Alonso dio buena ~ de su calidad como orador** Alonso clearly demonstrated his quality as a speaker, Alonso gave clear proof of his quality as a speaker • **como *o* en ~ de** in proof of • **como *o* en ~ de lo cual** in proof of which • **me lo dio como *o* en ~ de amistad** he gave it to me as a token of friendship • **como *o* en ~ de que no es así te lo ofrezco gratis** to prove that that isn't the case, I'll give it to you for free • **a las ~s me remito** (I'll let) the facts speak for themselves
2 (*Jur*) piece of evidence • **~s** evidence (*sing*) • **el fiscal presentó nuevas ~s** the prosecutor presented new evidence • **se encuentran en libertad por falta de ~s** they were released for lack of evidence ▸ **pruebas documentales** documentary evidence (*sing*) ▸ **pruebas indiciarias** circumstantial evidence (*sing*)
3 (= *examen*) (*Escol, Univ, Med*) test; [*de actor*] (*Cine*) screen test; (*Teat*) audition • **la maestra nos hizo una ~ de vocabulario** our teacher gave us a vocabulary test • **el médico me hizo más ~s** the doctor did some more tests on me • **se tendrán que hacer la ~ del SIDA** they'll have to be tested for AIDS • MODISMO: • **ser la ~ de fuego de algo** to be an acid test of sth ▸ **prueba de acceso** entrance test, entrance examination ▸ **prueba de alcoholemia** Breathalyzer® test ▸ **prueba de aptitud** aptitude test ▸ **prueba de capacitación** proficiency test ▸ **prueba de(l) embarazo** pregnancy test ▸ **prueba de inteligencia** intelligence test ▸ **prueba de nivel** placement test ▸ **prueba de paternidad** paternity test ▸ **prueba de selectividad** (*Univ*) entrance examination ▸ **prueba de tornasol** litmus test ▸ **prueba nuclear** nuclear test ▸ **prueba práctica** practical, practical test
4 (= *ensayo*) **a** (*gen*) • **haz la ~** try it • **período de ~** [*de persona*] probationary period; [*de producto*] trial period • **piloto de ~s** test pilot • **vuelo de ~s** test flight • **estar en (fase de) ~s** to be on trial • **emitir en ~s** (*TV*) to broadcast test transmissions
b • **a prueba** (*Téc*) on trial; (*Com*) on approval, on trial • **el nuevo secretario está a ~ durante un mes** the new secretary is on trial for a month • **ingresar con un nombramiento a ~** to take up a post for a probationary period • **matrimonio a ~** trial marriage • **poner *o* someter a ~** to put to the test • **poner a ~ la paciencia de algn** to try sb's patience • **poner a ~ los nervios de algn** to test sb's nerves
c • **a ~ de**: • **a ~ de agua** waterproof • **a ~ de bala(s)** bulletproof • **a ~ de bomba(s)** (*lit*) bombproof, shellproof • **un método a ~ de bombas** a surefire method • **es de una honestidad a ~ de bomba** he's completely honest • **a ~ de choques** shockproof • **a ~ de ladrones** burglarproof • **a ~ de ruidos** soundproof ▸ **prueba clínica** clinical trial ▸ **prueba de campo** field trial ▸ **prueba en carretera** (*Aut*) test drive
5 (*Dep*) (= *disciplina*) event; (= *carrera*) race • **la ~ de los cien metros lisos** the hundred metres • **la ~ de descenso** the downhill • **la ~ individual** (*Tenis*) the singles ▸ **prueba campo a través** (*Atletismo*) cross-country race; (*Hípica*) cross-country trial ▸ **prueba clasificatoria** heat ▸ **prueba contrarreloj** time trial ▸ **prueba de carretera** (*Ciclismo*) road race ▸ **prueba de obstáculos** obstacle race ▸ **prueba de relevos** relay, relay race ▸ **prueba de resistencia** endurance test ▸ **prueba de vallas** hurdles, hurdles race ▸ **prueba eliminatoria** heat ▸ **prueba en ruta** (*Ciclismo*) road race ▸ **prueba por equipos** (*Ciclismo*) team trial
6 (*Cos*) fitting • **sala de ~s** fitting room
7 (*Fot*) print ▸ **prueba negativa** negative ▸ **prueba positiva** print
8 [*de comida*] (= *acto*) testing, sampling; (= *cantidad*) taste, sample
9 (*LAm*) (*en el circo*) (= *número*) circus act; (*And*) (= *función*) circus show, performance
10 pruebas (*Tip*) proofs • **primeras ~s** first proofs, galleys • **~s de planas** page proofs • **corrector de ~s** proofreader

pruebista SMF **1** (*LAm*) (= *acróbata*) acrobat; (= *funámbulo*) tightrope walker; (= *prestidigitador*) conjurer; (= *malabarista*) juggler; (= *contorsionista*) contortionist
2 (*Cono Sur*) [*de libros*] proofreader

prurito SM **1** (*Med*) (= *picor*) itching, pruritus (*frm*)
2 (= *anhelo*) itch, urge • **tener el ~ de hacer algo** to have the urge to do sth • **por un ~ de exactitud** out of an excessive desire for accuracy, because of his eagerness to get everything just right

Prusia SF Prussia

prusiano/a ADJ, SM/F Prussian

PS SM ABR (*Pol*) = **Partido Socialista**

pse... PREF, **psi...** PREF psy... (*all forms are pronounced with silent "p"*)

PSE-EE SM ABR (*Esp*) = **Partido Socialista de Euskadi-Euskadiko Eskerra**

psefología SF psephology

psefólogo/a SM/F psephologist

pseudocientífico ADJ pseudo-scientific

psic... PREF psych...

psicoactivo ADJ psychoactive

psicoafectivo ADJ mental, psychological

psicoanálisis SM INV psychoanalysis

psicoanalista SMF psychoanalyst

psicoanalítico ADJ psychoanalytic, psychoanalytical • **diván ~** psychiatrist's couch

psicoanalizar ▸ CONJUG 1f VT to psychoanalyse

psicocirugía SF psychosurgery

psicodélico ADJ psychedelic

psicodepresor SM depressant

psicodinámica SF psychodynamics (*sing*)

psicodrama SM psychodrama

P

psicoestimulante SM (mental) stimulant

psicofármaco SM psychotropic drug, mood-altering drug

psicolingüística SF psycholinguistics (*sing*)

psicolingüístico ADJ psycholinguistic

psicología SF psychology ▸ **psicología conductista** behavioural psychology, behavioral psychology (*EEUU*) ▸ **psicología de masas** mass psychology ▸ **psicología educativa** educational psychology ▸ **psicología femenina** feminine psychology, female psychology ▸ **psicología masculina** male psychology ▸ **psicología médica** medical psychology

psicológicamente ADV psychologically

psicológico ADJ psychological

psicólogo/a SM/F psychologist

psicomotor ADJ psychomotor

psicomotricidad SF psychomotor activity

psiconeurosis SF INV psychoneurosis

psicópata SMF psychopath

psicopático ADJ psychopathic

psicopatología SF psychopathology

psicopedagogo/a SM/F educational psychologist

psicoquinesis SF INV psychokinesis

psicoquinético ADJ psychokinetic

psicosis SF INV psychosis

psicosocial ADJ psychosocial

psicosomático ADJ psychosomatic

psicotécnico ADJ • **test ~ • prueba psicotécnica** response test

psicoterapeuta SMF psychotherapist

psicoterapia SF psychotherapy

psicótico/a ADJ psychotic
SM/F psychotic

psicotrópico ADJ psychotropic, psychoactive

psiqu... PREF psych...

Psique SF Psyche

psique SF psyche

psiquiatra SMF psychiatrist

psiquiatría SF psychiatry

psiquiátrico ADJ psychiatric
SM mental hospital ▸ **psiquiátrico penitenciario** psychiatric prison

psíquico ADJ psychic, psychical • **enfermedades psíquicas** mental illnesses, psychological illnesses

psitacosis SF INV psittacosis

PSOE [pe'soe] SM ABR (*Esp*) = **Partido Socialista Obrero Español**

psoriasis SF INV psoriasis

PSS SF ABR = **prestación social sustitutoria**

PSUM SM ABR (*Méx*) = **Partido Socialista Unificado de México**

pta ABR **1** (*Econ*) = **peseta**
2 = **presidenta**

Pta. ABR (*Geog*) (= **Punta**) Pt

ptas ABR = **pesetas**

PTB SM ABR (*And*) (= **Producto Territorial Bruto**) GDP

pte. ABR = **presidente**

pterodáctilo [tero'daktilo] SM pterodactyl

ptmo. ABR (*Com*) = **préstamo**

ptomaína [toma'ina] SF ptomaine

ptomaínico [toma'iniko] ADJ • **envenenamiento ~** ptomaine poisoning

pts ABR = **pesetas**

púa SF **1** (= *pincho*) (*gen*) sharp point; (*Bot, Zool*) prickle, spine; [*de erizo*] quill; [*de peine*] tooth; [*de tenedor*] prong, tine; [*de alambre*] barb; (*LAm*) [*de gallo de pelea*] spur
2 (*Mús*) [*de guitarrista*] plectrum, pick; [*de tocadiscos*] gramophone needle, phonograph needle (*EEUU*)
3 (*Bot*) graft, cutting
4‡ one peseta

puaf* EXCL yuck!*

puazo* SM (*Arg*) slash

pub [pub, paβ] SM (PL: **pubs** [pub, paβ]) *bar where music is played*

púber ADJ adolescent
SMF adolescent

pubertad SF puberty

pubescencia SF pubescence

pubescente ADJ pubescent

púbico ADJ pubic

pubis SM INV pubis

publicación SF publication

públicamente ADV publicly, in public • **lo admitió ~** he admitted it publicly *o* in public

publicar ▷ CONJUG 1g VT **1** (*Com*) [+ *libro, artículo*] to publish; [+ *disco, grabación*] to issue
2 (= *difundir*) (*gen*) to publicize; [+ *secreto*] to make public, divulge

publicidad SF **1** (*Com*) advertising • **hacer ~ de** to advertise • **se ha prohibido la ~ del tabaco** cigarette advertising has been banned ▸ **publicidad de lanzamiento** advertising campaign to launch a product, advance publicity ▸ **publicidad directa** direct advertising ▸ **publicidad en el punto de venta** point-of-sale advertising ▸ **publicidad estática** (advertising on) hoardings ▸ **publicidad gráfica** display advertising
2 (= *divulgación*) publicity • **dar ~ a algo** to give publicity to sth

publicista SMF publicist

publicitar ▷ CONJUG 1a VT **1** (*Com*) to advertise
2 (= *divulgar*) to publicize
VPR **publicitarse** to advertise

publicitario/a ADJ advertising (*antes de s*), publicity (*antes de s*) • **campaña publicitaria** advertising campaign
SM/F advertising agent, advertising executive

público ADJ **1** (= *de los ciudadanos, del Estado*) [*transporte, teléfono, organismo, gasto*] public • **la gravedad de la situación es de dominio ~** the seriousness of the situation is public knowledge • **colegio ~** state school • **dinero ~** public money, government funds (*pl*) • **es un peligro ~ en la carretera** he is a danger to the public, he's a public menace on the roads* • **la vía pública** the street, the public highway (*frm*); ▷ **administración, deuda, opinión, sector**
2 (= *no íntimo*) [*acto, escándalo*] public • **los acusaron de escándalo ~** they were accused of public indecency • **se retiró de la vida pública** he retired from public life • **hacer algo ~** to make sth public • **en un comunicado de prensa hecho ~ ayer** in a press release issued yesterday • **su incompetencia fue pública y notoria** his incompetence was blatantly obvious *o* was plain for all to see; ▷ **relación**
SM **1** (= *audiencia*) (*Mús, Teat*) audience; (*Dep, Taur*) spectators (*pl*), crowd; (*TV*) (*en el plató*) audience; (*en casa*) viewers (*pl*), audience • **había poco ~ en la sala** there weren't many people in the audience • **"apta para todos los publicos"** "certificate U", "G movie" (*EEUU*) • **el estadio estaba lleno de ~** the stadium was full of spectators, there was a big crowd in the stadium • **el ~ presente en el plató** the studio audience • **un programa con gran audiencia de ~** a programme with a large number of viewers *o* a large audience • **"aviso al público"** "public notice" • **en ~** [*actuar, hablar*] in public; [*actuación, presentación, aparición*] public • **el gran ~** (*gen*) the general public • **escribe para el gran ~** she writes for the average reader ▸ **público adulto** adult audience ▸ **público infantil** children's audience • **un programa de televisión dirigido al ~ infantil** a television programme for children *o* aimed at a children's audience ▸ **público objetivo** (*Com*) target customers (*pl*); (*TV*) target audience
2 (= *seguidores*) **a** [*de periódico, escritor*] readers (*pl*), readership • **no es lo que quiere nuestro ~** it's not what our readers want *o* our readership wants • **un diario para un ~ muy especializado** a newspaper for a very specialized readership
b [*de cantante*] fans (*pl*) • **su ~ le sigue siendo fiel** her fans are still loyal to her
3 [*de oficina, banco, museo*] • **nuestros precios están expuestos al ~** our prices are displayed publicly • **a las dos cerramos al ~** we close (to the public) at two o'clock • **"horario de atención al público"** (*en bancos*) "hours of business"; (*en tiendas*) "opening hours"

publirreportaje SM advertising feature

pucará SF **1** (*Arg, And*) (*Hist*) (= *fortaleza*) Indian fortress
2 (*LAm*) (*Arqueología*) (= *fuerte*) pre-Columbian fort; (= *tumba*) Indian burial mound

pucelano/a* ADJ of/from Valladolid
SM/F native/inhabitant of Valladolid • **los ~s** the people of Valladolid

pucha¹ SF **1** (*Cuba*) (= *ramo*) bouquet
2 (*Méx*) (= *pan*) ring-shaped loaf

pucha²* SF **1** (*LAm*) (*euf*) = **puta**
2 • **¡(la) ~!** (*con sorpresa*) well I'm damned!; (*con irritación*) drat!

puchana SF (*Cono Sur*) broom

puchar‡ ▷ CONJUG 1a VT to speak, say

puchera SF stew

pucherazo* SM electoral fiddle* • **dar ~** to rig an election, fiddle the votes*

puchero SM **1** (= *olla*) cooking pot
2 (= *guiso*) stew
3 (= *sustento*) daily bread • **ganar(se) el ~*** to earn one's crust • **apenas gana para el ~** he hardly earns enough to live on
4* (= *mueca*) pout • **hacer ~s** to pout, screw up one's face

puches SMPL porridge (*sing*), gruel (*sing*)

puchica‡ EXCL (*And*) blast!*, damn!

puchito/a* SM/F (*Cono Sur*) youngest child

pucho SM **1** (*Cono Sur*) (= *colilla*) [*de cigarrillo*] fag end‡, dog end‡; [*de puro*] cigar stub
2 (*LAm*) (= *cigarrillo*) fag‡
3 (*LAm*) (= *resto*) (*gen*) scrap, left-over(s) (*pl*); [*de bebida*] dregs (*pl*); [*de tela*] remnant; (*Econ*) coppers (*pl*), small change
4 (*LAm*) (= *nimiedad*) trifle, mere nothing • **a ~s** in dribs and drabs
5 (*And, Cono Sur*) (= *hijo*) youngest child

puco SM (*And, Cono Sur*) earthenware bowl

pude *etc* ▷ **poder**

pudendo ADJ • **partes pudendas** private parts, pudenda (*frm*)
SM (= *pene*) penis

pudibundez SF (= *afectación*) false modesty; (= *remilgos*) excess of modesty

pudibundo ADJ (= *mojigato*) prudish; (= *vergonzoso*) bashful, modest; (= *tímido*) over-shy

pudicicia SF (= *pudor*) modesty; (= *castidad*) chastity

púdico ADJ (= *recatado*) modest; (= *casto*) chaste

pudiendo ▷ **poder**

pudiente ADJ (= *rico*) wealthy, well-to-do; (= *poderoso*) powerful, influential • **las gentes menos ~s** the less well-off • **las clases ~s** the upper classes

pudín SM pudding

pudinga SF puddingstone

pudo *etc* ▹ poder

pudor SM **1** (= *recato*) modesty; (= *timidez*) shyness; (= *vergüenza*) (sense of) shame, (sense of) decency • **con ~** modestly, discreetly • **tenía ~ de confesarlo** he was ashamed to confess it • **alardea sin ~ de su riqueza** she boasts unashamedly *o* openly about her wealth • **lo dijo sin ningún ~** she said it without embarrassment
2 (= *castidad*) chastity, virtue • **atentado al ~** indecent assault

pudorosamente ADV (= *recatadamente*) modestly; (= *con timidez*) shyly; (= *castamente*) chastely, virtuously

pudoroso ADJ (= *recatado*) modest; (= *tímido*) shy; (= *casto*) chaste, virtuous

pudrición SF **1** (= *proceso*) rotting
2 (= *lo podrido*) rot ▸ **pudrición seca** dry rot

pudridero SM rubbish heap

pudrimiento SM **1** (= *proceso*) rotting
2 (= *lo podrido*) rot

pudrir ▹ CONJUG 3a VT **1** (= *descomponer*) to rot, decay
2* (= *molestar*) to upset, vex
VI (*fig*) (= *haber muerto*) to rot, be dead and buried
VPR **pudrirse 1** (= *corromperse*) [*comida*] to rot, decay; [*valores*] to deteriorate
2 [*persona*] to rot, languish • **mientras se pudría en la cárcel** while he was languishing in jail • **te vas a ~ de aburrimiento** you'll die of boredom • **¡que se pudra!*** let him rot! • **¡ahí *o* así te pudras!*** get away!*, not on your nelly!‡

pueblada* SF **1** (*LAm*) (= *motín*) riot; (= *revuelta*) revolt, uprising
2 (*Cono Sur*) (= *multitud*) (*gen*) mob; [*de obreros*] gathering of workers

pueblerino/a ADJ [*carácter, ambiente*] small-town (*antes de s*), countrified; [*persona*] rustic, provincial
SM/F (= *aldeano*) rustic, country person; (*pey*) country bumpkin*, hick (*EEUU**)

pueblero/a (*LAm*) ADJ town (*antes de s*), city (*antes de s*)
SM/F townsman/townswoman, city dweller; (*pey*) city slicker

pueblito SM (*LAm*) little town; (*más pequeño*) little village

pueblo SM **1** (*Pol*) people, nation • **el ~ español** the Spanish people • **la voluntad del ~** the people's will • **hacer un llamamiento al ~** to call on the people ▸ **pueblo elegido** chosen people
2 (= *plebe*) common people (*pl*), lower orders (*pl*) • **el ~ llano** the common people
3 (= *localidad pequeña*) (*gen*) small town; (*en el campo*) country town; (*de pocos habitantes*) village • **ser de ~** (*gen*) to be a country person, be from the countryside; (*pey*) to be a country bumpkin*, be a country hick (*EEUU**) ▸ **pueblo fantasma** ghost town ▸ **pueblo joven** (*Perú*) shanty town

puedo *etc* ▹ poder

puente SM **1** (*Arquit*) bridge • **sirven de ~ entre los refugiados y la Administración** they act as intermediaries *o* as a link between the refugees and the Government • MODISMOS: • **tender un ~** • **tender ~s** to offer a compromise, go part-way to meet sb's wishes • **tender ~s de plata a algn** to make it as easy as possible for sb ▸ **puente aéreo** (*de servicio frecuente*) shuttle service; (*en crisis*) airlift ▸ **puente atirantado** suspension bridge ▸ **puente colgante** suspension bridge ▸ **puente de barcas** pontoon bridge ▸ **puente de peaje** toll bridge ▸ **puente de pontones** pontoon bridge ▸ **puente giratorio** swing bridge ▸ **puente grúa** bridge crane ▸ **puente levadizo** drawbridge ▸ **puente peatonal** footbridge ▸ **puente voladizo** cantilever bridge
2 [*de gafas, entre dientes*] bridge
3 (*Elec*) • **hacer un ~ a un coche** to hot-wire a car
4 (*Náut*) (*tb* **puente de mando**) bridge; (= *cubierta*) deck ▸ **puente del timón** wheelhouse
5 (*entre fiestas*) long weekend • **hacer ~** to take a long weekend
6 (= *brecha*) gap • **habrá que salvar el ~ de una cosecha a otra** something will have to be done to fill *o* bridge the gap between one harvest and the next
7 (*And*) (= *clavícula*) collarbone
ADJ INV (= *temporal*) temporary; (= *de transición*) provisional, transitional • **crédito ~** bridging loan • **curso ~** intermediate course (*between two degrees*) • **gabinete ~** caretaker government • **hombre ~** linkman, intermediary • **préstamo ~** bridging loan • **solución ~** temporary solution

> **HACER PUENTE**
> When a public holiday falls on a Tuesday or Thursday it is common practice for employers to make the Monday or Friday a holiday as well and to give everyone a four-day weekend. This is known as **hacer puente**. When a named public holiday such as the **Día de la Constitución** in Spain falls on a Tuesday or a Thursday, people refer to the whole holiday period as e.g. the **puente de la Constitución**.

puentear* ▹ CONJUG 1a VT **1** [+ *autoridad*] to bypass, pass over • **le ~on con el ascenso** they passed him over for the promotion
2 (*Econ*) to take out a bridging loan on sth
VI to jump a grade (in the hierarchy), go up to the grade next but one

puenting ['pwentin] SM bungee jumping (*from a bridge*)

puerca SF **1**** (= *puta*) slut‡
2 (= *cochinilla*) woodlouse; ▹ **puerco**

puercada SF (*And, CAm, Caribe*) (= *acto*) dirty trick; (= *dicho*) obscene remark

puerco/a SM/F **1**** (= *cerdo*) pig/sow, hog/sow (*EEUU*) ▸ **puerco de mar** porpoise ▸ **puerco espín** porcupine ▸ **puerco jabalí** wild boar, wild pig ▸ **puerco marino** dolphin ▸ **puerco montés, puerco salvaje** wild boar, wild pig; ▹ **Martín**
2* (= *sinvergüenza*) pig*; (= *canalla*) swine*, rotter*
ADJ **1** (= *asqueroso*) dirty, filthy
2 (= *repugnante*) nasty, disgusting
3 (= *grosero*) coarse
4 (= *mezquino*) rotten*, mean; ▹ **puerca**

puericia SF boyhood

puericultor(a) SM/F • **médico ~** paediatrician, pediatrician (*EEUU*)

puericultura SF paediatrics (*sing*), pediatrics (*sing*) (*EEUU*)

pueril ADJ **1** (*gen*) childish, child (*antes de s*) • **edad ~** childhood
2 (*pey*) puerile (*frm*), childish

puerilidad SF puerility (*frm*), childishness

puerperal ADJ puerperal • **fiebre ~** puerperal fever

puerqueza SF (*Cono Sur*) **1** (= *objeto*) dirty thing, filthy object
2 (= *trampa*) dirty trick
3 (*Zool*) bug, creepy-crawly*

puerro SM leek

puerta SF **1** (*para bloquear el paso*) [*de casa, vehículo, armario*] door; [*de jardín, ciudad*] gate • **llaman a la ~** there's somebody at the door • **espero no haberme equivocado de ~** I hope this is the right door • **un coche de dos ~s** a two-door car • **nos encontramos en la ~ del Ministerio** we met at the entrance to the Ministry • **le esperé a la ~ de la escuela** I waited for him outside the entrance to the school • **Susana me acompañó a la ~** Susana saw me out ▸ **puerta accesoria** side door ▸ **puerta acristalada** glass door ▸ **puerta corredera** sliding door ▸ **puerta cortafuegos** fire door ▸ **puerta de artistas** stage door ▸ **puerta de servicio** tradesman's entrance ▸ **puerta excusada** side door ▸ **puerta giratoria** revolving door ▸ **puerta oscilante** swing door ▸ **puerta principal** [*de una casa*] front door; [*de edificio público*] main entrance ▸ **puerta trasera** back door ▸ **puerta ventana, puerta vidriera** French window
2 (= *abertura en la pared*) doorway
3 (*locuciones*) • **~ a ~**: • **servicio ~ a ~** door-to-door service • **tardo tres horas de ~ a ~** it takes me three hours door-to-door • **hacer el ~ a ~** (*Pol*) to doorstep • **de ~s abiertas**: • **jornada de ~s abiertas** open day • **política de ~s abiertas** open-door policy • **a ~ cerrada** (*gen*) behind closed doors; (*Jur*) in camera • **de ~ en ~** from door to door • **iban de ~ en ~ pidiendo firmas** they went from door to door collecting signatures • **vendedor de ~ en ~** door-to-door salesman • MODISMOS: • **a las ~s de**: • **a las ~s de la muerte** at death's door • **ahora, a las ~s de la vejez, lo comprendo** now that I am approaching old age, I understand • **en septiembre, ya a las ~s del otoño** in September, with autumn just around the corner • **dejar la ~ abierta a algo** to leave the way open to sth • **dejar una ~ abierta a otras opciones** to leave the way open for other options • **abrir la ~ a algo** to open the door to sth • **de ~s adentro** behind closed doors, in private • **política de ~s adentro** domestic *o* home policy • **un sirviente de ~s adentro** (*LAm*) a live-in servant • **de ~s afuera**: • **lo que pasa de ~s afuera** (= *fuera de casa*) what happens outside of this home; (= *en el extranjero*) what happens abroad • **de ~s afuera se dice que ...** publicly it is being said that ... • **la gente empieza a vivir menos de ~s afuera** people are starting to be less concerned about appearances • **cerrarle todas las ~s a algn** to close off all avenues to sb • **por la ~ chica**: • **entrar por la ~ chica** to get in by the back door • **coger la ~*** to leave • **dar con la ~ en las narices a algn** to slam the door in sb's face • **dar ~ a algn*** to chuck sb out • **estar en ~s**: • **el invierno está en ~s** winter is just around the corner • **estar en ~s de hacer algo** to be about to do sth • **enseñar la ~ a algn** to show sb the door • **equivocarse de ~**: • **te has equivocado de ~** you've come to the wrong person • **franquear las ~s a algn** to welcome sb in • **por la ~ grande**: • **entrar por la ~ grande** to make a grand entrance • **salir por la ~ grande** [*torero*] to make a triumphant exit • **si me voy, lo haré por la ~ grande** if I leave, I'll leave with my head held high • **quedarse a la ~** to fall at the last hurdle • **querer poner ~s al campo** to try to stem the tide • **salir por la ~ de los carros** (= *apurado*) to leave in a hurry; (= *destituido*) to leave in disgrace
4 (*Aer*) gate ▸ **puerta de embarque** boarding gate
5 (*Dep*) goal • **un disparo *o* remate a ~** a shot at goal • **sacar de ~** to take a goal kick
6 (*Inform*) port

puertaventana SF (= *puerta*) French window; (= *contraventana*) shutter

puertear ▹ CONJUG 1a VI (*Cono Sur*) to make

a dash for the exit
puerto SM **1** (*para embarcaciones*) port, harbour, harbor (*EEUU*) • **entrar a** *o* **tomar ~** to enter (into) port • MODISMO: • **llegar a buen ~** to get over a difficulty, come through safely ▸ **puerto comercial** trading port ▸ **puerto de contenedores** container port ▸ **puerto de entrada** port of entry ▸ **puerto de escala** port of call ▸ **puerto de gran calado** deep-water port ▸ **puerto de mar** seaport ▸ **puerto de origen** home port ▸ **puerto deportivo** marina, yachting harbour ▸ **puerto franco, puerto libre** free port ▸ **puerto naval** naval port, naval harbour ▸ **puerto pesquero** fishing port
2 (*tb* **puerto de montaña**) pass
3 (*Inform*) port ▸ **puerto de expansión** expansion port ▸ **puerto de serie** serial port ▸ **puerto (de transmisión en) paralelo** parallel port ▸ **puerto (de transmisión en) serie, puerto en serie** serial port ▸ **puerto USB** USB port
Puerto Rico SM Puerto Rico
puertorriqueñismo SM word *o* phrase peculiar to Puerto Rico
puertorriqueño/a ADJ, SM/F Puerto Rican
pues CONJ **1** (*con valor consecutivo*) then • **—tengo sueño —¡~ vete a la cama!** "I'm tired" — "then go to bed!" • **llegó, ~, con dos horas de retraso** so he arrived two hours late • **¿no vas con ella, ~?** aren't you going with her after all?
2 (*con valor enfático*) well • **~ no voy** well I'm not going • **~, como te iba contando ...** well, as I was saying ... • **¡~ no lo sabía!** well, I didn't know! • **¡~ claro!** yes, of course! • **~ sí** well, yes; (= *naturalmente*) certainly • **~ no** well, no; (= *de ningún modo*) not at all • **¡~ qué!** come now!, what else did you expect!
3 (*indicando duda*) • **~, no sé** well, I don't know
4 (*frm*) (*con valor causal*) since, for • **cómpralo, ~ lo necesitas** buy it, since you need it
puesta SF **1** (= *acto*) ▸ **puesta a cero** (*Inform*) reset ▸ **puesta al día** updating ▸ **puesta a punto** fine tuning ▸ **puesta de largo** coming-out (in society) ▸ **puesta en antena** (*TV*) showing, screening ▸ **puesta en común** idea-sharing session ▸ **puesta en escena** staging ▸ **puesta en libertad** freeing, release ▸ **puesta en marcha** (= *acto*) starting; (= *dispositivo*) self-starter ▸ **puesta en práctica** putting into effect, implementation
2 (*Astron*) setting ▸ **puesta del sol** sunset
3 [*de huevos*] egg-laying • **una ~ anual de 300 huevos** an annual lay *o* output of 300 eggs
4 (*Naipes*) stake, bet
5 (*Cono Sur*) • **¡puesta!** it's a tie!, it's a draw!; (*en carrera*) it's a dead heat!
puestero/a SM/F **1** (*esp LAm*) (*en mercado*) stallholder, market vendor
2 (*Cono Sur*) (*Agr*) (= *mayoral*) farm overseer, ranch caretaker; (= *agricultor*) small farmer, tenant farmer; (= *trabajador*) ranch hand
puesto PP *de* **poner**
ADJ **1** • **con el sombrero ~** with one's hat on, wearing a hat • **una mesa puesta para nueve** a table laid for nine • **salieron del país con lo ~** they left the country with nothing but the clothes they were wearing
• MODISMO: • **tenerlos bien ~s** (*Esp‡*) to be a real man
2 [*persona*] • **bien ~** • **muy ~** well dressed, smartly turned out
3 • **ir ~*** (= *estar drogado*) to be high*; (= *estar borracho*) to be steaming*, be soused (*EEUU**)
4 • **no está muy ~ en este tema** he's not very well up on this subject
SM **1** (= *lugar*) place; (= *posición*) position • **ocupa el tercer ~ en la liga** it is in third place in the league • **ceder el ~ a algn** to give up one's place to sb • **guardar** *o* **mantener su ~** to keep the proper distance • **sabe estar en su ~** he knows his place ▸ **puesto de amarre** berth, mooring ▸ **puesto de honor** leading position
2 (= *empleo*) post, position, job • **tiene un ~ de conserje** he works as a porter ▸ **puesto de decisión** position of power ▸ **puesto de trabajo** post, position, job • **se crearán 200 ~s de trabajo** 200 new jobs will be created
3 [*de vigilancia*] post ▸ **puesto de control** checkpoint ▸ **puesto de escucha** listening-post ▸ **puesto de observación** observation post ▸ **puesto de policía** police post ▸ **puesto de socorro** first-aid post ▸ **puesto de vigilancia** (= *garita*) guard post; (= *torre*) watchtower ▸ **puesto fronterizo** border post
4 (*Caza*) stand, place
5 (*Com*) (*en mercado*) stall; (*en feria de muestras*) stand, booth ▸ **puesto callejero** street stall ▸ **puesto de mercado** market stall ▸ **puesto de periódicos** newspaper stand
6 (*Cono Sur*) *land and house held by ranch caretaker*
• **~ que** (*conj*) since, as
puf¹ EXCL ugh!
puf² SM (PL: **pufs**) pouffe
pufo* SM **1** (= *trampa*) trick, swindle • **dar el ~ a algn** to swindle sb
2 (= *deuda*) debt
3 (= *persona*) con man*
púgil SM boxer
pugilato SM (= *boxeo*) boxing; (= *disputa*) conflict
pugilismo SM boxing
pugilista SM boxer
pugilístico ADJ boxing (*antes de s*)
pugío SM (*And, Cono Sur*) spring
pugna SF struggle, conflict • **entrar en ~ con algn** to clash with sb, come into conflict with sb • **estar en ~ con algn** to clash with sb, conflict with sb
pugnacidad SF pugnacity, aggressiveness
pugnar ▸ CONJUG 1a VI **1** (= *luchar*) to fight (por for) • **~ en defensa de algo** to fight in defence of sth
2 (= *esforzarse*) to struggle, strive • **~ por hacer algo** to struggle *o* strive to do sth • **~ por no reírse** to struggle not to laugh
3 • **~ con** [+ *opinión, idea*] to clash with, conflict with; [+ *persona*] to battle it out with
pugnaz ADJ pugnacious, aggressive
puja SF **1** (= *lucha*) struggle • **la ~ por el control de la empresa** the struggle for control of the firm
2 (*en una subasta*) bidding ▸ **puja de salida** opening bid
3 • **sacar de la ~ a algn** (= *adelantarse*) to get ahead of sb; (= *sacar de apuro*) to get sb out of a jam*
4 (*And**) ticking-off*
pujante ADJ (= *fuerte*) strong, vigorous; (= *potente*) powerful; (= *enérgico*) forceful; (= *poderoso económicamente*) booming
pujanza SF [*de grupo, país*] power, strength; [*de idioma, industria, economía*] strength; [*de carácter*] forcefulness, drive
pujar ▸ CONJUG 1a VI **1** (*en subasta*) to bid, bid up; (*Naipes*) to bid • **~ en** *o* **sobre el precio** to bid the price up
2 (= *esforzarse*) to struggle, strain • **~ por hacer algo** to struggle to do sth
3 • **~ para adentro** (*Méx**) to grin and bear it
4 (= *vacilar*) to falter, dither, hesitate
5 (= *no encontrar palabras*) to struggle for words, be at a loss for words
6 (= *hacer pucheros*) to be on the verge of tears
7 (*CAm‡*) (= *quejarse*) to moan, whinge*
puje* SM (*And*) ticking-off*
pujo SM **1** (*Med*) difficulty in relieving o.s., tenesmus (*frm*)
2 (= *ansia*) longing, strong urge • **sentir ~ de llorar** to be on the verge of tears • **sentir ~ de reírse** to have an uncontrollable urge to laugh
3 (= *intento*) attempt, try, shot • **tiene ~s de caballero** he has pretensions to being a gentleman
pulcramente ADV (= *con orden*) neatly, tidily, smartly; (= *con delicadeza*) exquisitely, delicately
pulcritud SF (= *orden*) neatness, tidiness; (= *delicadeza*) exquisiteness, delicacy
pulcro ADJ (= *ordenado*) neat, tidy; (= *elegante*) smartly dressed; (= *exquisito*) exquisite; (= *delicado*) dainty, delicate
pulga SF **1** (= *insecto*) flea • MODISMOS: • **buscar las ~s a algn*** to tease sb, needle sb* • **no aguantar ~s*** to stand no nonsense • **tener malas ~s*** to be short-tempered, be bad-tempered • **un tío con muy malas ~s** a bad-tempered chap • **hacer de una ~ un elefante** *o* **un camello** (= *dar importancia*) to make a mountain out of a molehill; (= *buscar defectos*) to nit-pick
2 [*de juego*] tiddlywink • **juego de ~s** tiddlywinks
3 (*Inform*) bug
pulgada SF inch
pulgar SM thumb
pulgarada SF **1** (= *capirotazo*) flick, flip
2 [*de rapé*] pinch
Pulgarcito SM Tom Thumb
pulgón SM plant louse
pulgoso ADJ (*And*) flea-ridden, verminous
pulguero‡ SM **1** (*Esp*) (= *cama*) kip‡, bed
2 (*CAm, Caribe*) (= *cárcel*) jail
pulguiento ADJ (*And*) flea-ridden, verminous
pulidamente ADV **1** (= *con pulcritud*) neatly, tidily; (= *con esmero*) carefully; (= *refinadamente*) in a polished way; (*pey*) affectedly
2 (= *con cortesía*) courteously
pulido ADJ **1** [*madera, metal*] polished
2 [*estilo, lenguaje*] refined, polished
SM polish, polishing
pulidor(a) SM/F polisher
pulidora SF polishing machine
pulimentado SM polishing
pulimentar ▸ CONJUG 1a VT (= *pulir*) to polish; (= *dar lustre a algo*) to put a gloss on sth, put a shine on sth; (= *alisar*) to smooth
pulimento SM **1** (= *acto*) polishing
2 (= *brillo*) gloss
3 (= *sustancia*) polish
pulique SM (*CAm*) *dish of chillies and maize*
pulir ▸ CONJUG 3a VT **1** [+ *cristal, metal, suelo*] to polish
2 (= *perfeccionar*) to polish • **hace falta ~ esta traducción** this translation still needs polishing
3 [+ *persona*] • **nadie ha logrado ~lo** nobody has managed to polish his manners • **en este colegio ~án su educación** they will finish off *o* round off her education at this school
4‡ (= *birlar*) to pinch* • **ya me han pulido el bolígrafo** they've gone and pinched my pen*
VPR **pulirse 1** (= *refinarse*) to acquire polish
2 (= *acicalarse*) to spruce o.s. up
3* (= *gastar*) to go through, get through
pull [pul] SM pullover
pulla SF **1** (= *insulto*) cutting remark, wounding remark; (= *mofa*) taunt; (= *indirecta*) dig
2 (= *obscenidad*) obscene remark, rude word

pullman ['pulman] SM **1** (*And, Cono Sur*) (*Ferro*) sleeping car
2 (*Chile*) (= *autobús*) long-distance coach

pullover [pu'loβer] SM pullover, jumper

pulmón SM (*Anat*) lung • **a pleno ~** [*respirar*] deeply; [*gritar*] at the top of one's lungs ▸ **pulmón de acero** iron lung

pulmonar ADJ pulmonary (*frm*), lung (*antes de s*)

pulmonía SF pneumonia ▸ **pulmonía doble** double pneumonia

pulmotor SM iron lung

pulóver SM pullover

pulpa SF **1** (*como resultado de machacar*) (*gen*) pulp; [*de fruta, planta*] flesh ▸ **pulpa de madera** wood pulp ▸ **pulpa dental, pulpa dentaria** pulp ▸ **pulpa de papel** paper pulp
2 (= *pasta blanda*) soft mass
3 (*Anat*) soft flesh
4 (*LAm*) (= *carne*) meat off the bone, fillet

pulpejo SM fleshy part, soft part

pulpería SF (*LAm*) (= *tienda*) general store, food store; (= *taberna*) bar, tavern

pulpero/a SM/F (*LAm*) (= *comerciante*) storekeeper, grocer; (= *tabernero*) tavern keeper

púlpito SM pulpit

pulpo SM **1** (*Zool*) octopus • MODISMOS: • **estar más perdido que un ~ en un garaje*** not to have a clue • **ser como un ~** to be all arms
2 (*Aut*) elastic strap

pulposo ADJ fleshy

pulque SM (*Méx*) pulque

> **PULQUE**
> **Pulque** is a traditional alcoholic drink from Mexico. Thick, slightly sweet and milky, it is brewed from the juice of the agave plant, or **maguey**, and is roughly equivalent in strength to beer. It was the sacred drink of the Aztecs, who used it in offerings to the gods and also for medicinal purposes. In modern-day Mexico it is often given to children since it is rich in vitamins, and in the cities it is sold in special bars called **pulquerías**.

pulquear ▸ CONJUG 1a (*Méx*) VI to drink pulque
VPR **pulquearse** to get drunk on pulque

pulquería SF (*Méx*) bar

pulquérrimo ADJ *superl de* **pulcro**

pulsación SF **1** (= *latido*) beat
2 [*de tecla*] (*Tip, Inform*) keystroke • **hace 200 pulsaciones por minuto** she does 200 keystrokes a minute ▸ **pulsación doble** (*Inform*) strikeover
3 [*de pianista, mecanógrafo*] touch

pulsador SM (= *botón*) button, push-button; (= *interruptor*) switch

pulsar¹ ▸ CONJUG 1a VT **1** [+ *botón*] to press; [+ *tecla*] to strike, touch, tap; (*Mús*) to play
2 [+ *opinión*] to sound out
3 • **~ a algn** (*Med*) to take sb's pulse, feel sb's pulse
VI to beat

pulsar² SM (= *estrella*) pulsar; (= *agujero negro*) black hole

pulsátil ADJ pulsating

pulseada SF (*Cono Sur*) arm-wrestling; (*fig*) intense competition • **hacer una ~** to arm-wrestle

pulsear ▸ CONJUG 1a VI (*Cono Sur*) **1** (= *echar un pulso*) to arm-wrestle
2 (= *apuntar*) to take aim

pulsera SF bracelet, wristlet • **~ para reloj** watch strap • **reloj de ~** wristwatch ▸ **pulsera de pedida** (*Esp*) engagement bracelet

pulsión SF urge, drive, impulse

pulso SM **1** (*Anat*) pulse • **tomar el ~ a algn** to take sb's pulse, feel sb's pulse • MODISMOS: • **perder el ~ de algo**: • **la Iglesia ha perdido el ~ de la sociedad** the church has lost touch with society • **tomar el ~ a algo**: • **tomar el ~ a la opinión pública** to sound out public opinion • **tomar el ~ al mercado** to gauge the mood of the market
2 (= *seguridad en la mano*) • **tener buen ~** to have a steady hand • **tener mal ~** to have an unsteady hand • **tener ~** (*Cono Sur*) to have a good aim • **con ~ firme** with a firm hand • **le tiembla el ~** his hand is shaking
3 • **a ~**: **levantar algo a ~** to lift sth with one hand • **levantar una silla a ~** to lift a chair with one hand • **tomar un mueble a ~** to lift a piece of furniture clean off the ground • **dibujo (hecho) a ~** freehand drawing • MODISMOS: • **ganar(se) algo a ~** (= *con esfuerzo*) to get sth through one's own hard work; (= *con dificultad*) to get sth the hard way • **hacer algo a ~** (= *sin ayuda*) to do sth without help from anyone
4 (= *pelea*) • **echar un ~** to arm-wrestle
5 (= *contienda*) trial of strength, showdown • **el ~ entre el gobierno y la oposición** the confrontation *o* showdown between the government and the opposition • **echar un ~ a algn** (= *contender*) to have a trial of strength with sb; (= *desafiar*) to challenge sb
6 (= *tacto*) tact • **con mucho ~** with great tact
7 (*Col*) (= *pulsera*) bracelet; (= *reloj*) wristwatch

pulular ▸ CONJUG 1a VI **1** (= *bullir*) to swarm (**por** around) • **los turistas pululan por el vestíbulo del hotel** the tourists are swarming around the hotel lobby, the hotel lobby is throbbing *o* swarming with tourists
2 (= *abundar*) to swarm (**de** with) • **aquí pululan los mosquitos** this place is teeming *o* swarming with mosquitoes
VT (*LAm*) to infest, overrun

pululo* ADJ (*CAm*) short and fat

pulverización SF **1** [*de sólidos*] pulverization
2 [*de perfume, insecticida*] spraying

pulverizador SM [*de colonia, ambientador*] spray; [*de pintura*] spray gun ▸ **pulverizador nasal** nasal inhaler

pulverizar ▸ CONJUG 1f VT **1** [+ *sólido*] (*gen*) to pulverize; (= *reducir a polvo*) to powder, convert into powder
2 [+ *líquido*] to spray
3 (= *aniquilar*) [+ *enemigo, ciudad*] to pulverize, smash; [+ *rival, oponente*] to hammer, thrash • **pulverizó el récord** she smashed the record

pulverulento ADJ **1** [*sustancia*] powdered, powdery
2 [*superficie*] dusty

pum EXCL (*en disparo*) bang!; (*en golpe*) thud! • MODISMO: • **ni pum** not a thing • **no entendí ni pum** I didn't understand a thing

puma SM puma

pumba EXCL (*imitando un golpe*) bang!, crash!; (*imitando una explosión*) boom!, bang!

puna SF (*And*) **1** (*Geog*) (= *altiplano*) puna; (= *páramo*) bleak upland
2 (= *soroche*) mountain sickness
3 (= *viento*) cold mountain wind

punch SM (*LAm*) **1** (= *puñetazo*) punch
2 (*al hacer algo*) (= *empuje*) strength, punch; (= *agilidad*) agility
3 punches (*CAm*) popcorn (*sing*)

punchar ▸ CONJUG 1a VT (*LAm*) to punch

punching ['punʃin] SM punchball

punching-ball ['punʃinbal] SM (*Boxeo*) punchball, whipping-boy

punción SF puncture ▸ **punción en la médula** lumbar puncture

pundonor SM (= *dignidad*) self-respect, amour propre; (= *honra*) honour, honor (*EEUU*); (= *desfachatez*) nerve, cheek*

pundonoroso ADJ (= *digno*) honourable, honorable (*EEUU*); (= *puntilloso*) punctilious, scrupulous

punga‡ SF (*Cono Sur*) thieving, nicking‡
SMF (*Cono Sur*) pickpocket, thief

pungir ▸ CONJUG 3c VT **1** (= *punzar*) to prick, puncture; (= *picar*) to sting
2 (= *hacer sufrir*) to cause suffering to

punguista‡ SMF (*And, Cono Sur*) (= *carterista*) pickpocket; (= *ladrón*) thief

punible ADJ punishable

punición SF punishment

púnico ADJ, SM (*Ling*) Punic

punitivo ADJ, **punitorio** ADJ punitive

punki, punkie ['punki] ADJ, SMF punk

punta SF **1** (= *extremo*) [*de dedo, lengua, pincel*] tip; [*de ciudad*] side; [*de mesa*] end; [*de pañuelo*] corner • **la ~ de los dedos** the fingertips, the tips of one's fingers • **colocad la ~ del pie hacia arriba** point your toes upwards • **vivimos en la otra ~ de Barcelona** we live on the other side of Barcelona • **se sentó en la otra ~ de la mesa** she sat at the other end of the table • **de ~ a cabo** *o* **de ~ a punta** from one end to the other • **nos recorrimos la ciudad de ~ a ~** we went from one end of the city to the other • **me leí el periódico de ~ a cabo** I read the paper from cover to cover • MODISMOS: • **la ~ del iceberg** the tip of the iceberg • **tener algo en la ~ de la lengua** to have sth on the tip of one's tongue
2 (= *extremo puntiagudo*) [*de cuchillo, tijeras, lápiz*] point; [*de flecha*] tip • **un rotulador de ~ fina** a felt-tip pen with a fine point • **un cuchillo con ~** a pointed knife • **una estrella de cinco ~s** a five-pointed star • **de ~**: • **tenía todo el pelo de ~** her hair was all on end • **las tijeras le cayeron de ~ en el pie** the scissors fell point down *o* point first on his foot • **unos zapatos de ~** a pair of pointed shoes • **acabado en ~** pointed • **a ~ de navaja** at knife point • **a ~ de pistola** at gunpoint • **sacar ~ a** [+ *lápiz*] to sharpen; (*Esp*) [+ *comentario, opinión*] to twist • **le saca ~ a todo lo que digo** she twists everything I say • MODISMOS: • **a ~ de** (*LAm**): • **salió adelante a ~ de esfuerzo** he got ahead by sheer effort *o* by dint of hard work • **va a entender a ~ de patadas** he has to have sense beaten into him • **vive a ~ de remedios** he lives on medicines • **estar de ~** [*persona*] to be irritable • **estar de ~ con algn** to be annoyed with sb • **ponerse de ~ con algn** to fall out with sb • **ir de ~ en blanco** to be all dressed up, be dressed up to the nines • **ponerse de ~ en blanco** to get all dressed up • **poner a algn los pelos** *o* **el vello de ~** to make sb's hair stand on end • **se me ponen los pelos de ~ de pensar en el miedo que pasamos** my hair stands on end when I think of how scared we were • **esas imágenes me pusieron el vello de ~** those images were really spine-chilling, those images made my hair stand on end • **estar hasta la ~ de los pelos con** *o* **de algn*** to be fed up to the back teeth with sb* • **a ~ (de) pala** (*Esp**): • **había gente a ~ pala** there were loads of people* • **tienen dinero a ~ pala** they're loaded*, they've got loads of money* ▸ **punta de diamante** (= *cortador*) diamond glass cutter; (= *diseño*) diamond point • **cristal tallado a ~ de diamante** diamond-cut glass ▸ **punta de lanza** spearhead • **son la ~ de lanza de nuestra ofensiva comercial** they are spearheading our marketing campaign; ▸ **nervio**
3 (= *cantidad pequeña*) (*lit*) bit; (*fig*) touch • **una**

P

puntita de sal a pinch of salt • **tiene sus ~s de filósofo** there's a touch of the philosopher about him • **tiene una ~ de loco** he has a streak of madness
4 (= *clavo*) tack
5 (*Geog*) (= *cabo*) point; (= *promontorio*) headland
6 (= *asta*) [*de toro*] horn; [*de ciervo*] point, tine
7 (*Ftbl*) • **juega en la ~** he plays up front
8 (= *colilla*) stub, butt
9 (*Cos*) (= *encaje*) dentelle
10 puntas: **a** [*del pelo*] ends • **tengo las ~s abiertas** I have split ends • **quiero cortarme las ~s** I'd like a trim, I'd like to have my hair trimmed
b (*Ballet*) points, ballet shoes
c (*Culin*) ▸ **puntas de espárrago** asparagus tips ▸ **puntas de solomillo** *finest cuts of pork*
11 (*Cono Sur, Méx*) • **una ~ de algo** a lot of sth • **pagó una ~ de pesos por eso** he paid a lot of money for that • **son todos una ~ de ladrones** they are all a bunch of thieves
12 (*Cuba*) [*de tabaco*] *leaf of best tobacco*
13 (*Bol*) *eight-hour shift of work*
14 (*Caribe*) (= *mofa*) taunt, snide remark
(ADJ INV) peak • **horas ~** [*de electricidad, teléfono*] peak times • **la hora ~** [*del tráfico*] the rush hour • **el tráfico en la hora ~** rush-hour traffic • **tecnología ~** latest technology, leading edge technology • **velocidad ~** maximum speed, top speed
(SMF) (*Dep*) striker, forward • **media ~** midfield player

puntada (SF) **1** (*Cos*) stitch • **se ven las ~s** you can see the stitching • **dale unas puntaditas más a la manga** put a few more stitches in the sleeves • MODISMO: • **no dar ~**: • **hoy no ha dado ~** he hasn't done a stroke all day • **no ha dado ~ en el asunto** he's done nothing at all about it ▸ **puntada cruzada** cross-stitch ▸ **puntada invisible** invisible mending
2* (= *insinuación*) hint • **pegar** *o* **soltar una ~** to drop a hint
3 (= *dolor*) stitch, sharp pain
4 (*Méx*) witty remark, witticism

puntaje (SM) (*LAm*) score

puntal (SM) **1** (= *soporte*) (*Arquit*) prop, support; (*Agr*) prop; (*Téc*) strut
2 (= *persona*) (*que sirve de apoyo*) chief supporter; (*que ayuda a resistir*) cornerstone; (*que está al frente*) leading light
3 (*LAm*) snack

puntapié (SM) kick • **echar a algn a ~s** to kick sb out • **pegar un ~ a algn** to give sb a kick ▸ **puntapié colocado** place kick ▸ **puntapié de bote pronto** drop kick ▸ **puntapié de saque** drop-out

puntazo (SM) **1** (*Taur*) jab (*with a horn*)
2 (*LAm*) (= *pinchazo*) jab, poke; (= *puñalada*) stab; (= *herida*) stab wound, knife wound
3* • **fue un ~** it went down really well* • **¡qué ~ de fiesta!** the party was just perfect!

punteado (ADJ) (= *moteado*) (*gen*) dotted, covered with dots; [*pintura*] stippled; [*diseño*] of dots; [*plumaje*] flecked
(SM) **1** (= *moteado*) (*en diseño*) series of dots, stippling; (*en plumaje*) flecking
2 (*Mús*) picking

puntear ▷ CONJUG 1a (VT) **1** (*con puntos*) (= *motear*) to dot, cover *o* mark with dots; (= *pintar*) to stipple; (= *jaspear*) to fleck
2 (= *comprobar*) [+ *artículos*] to tick, put a mark against, check (*EEUU*); (*LAm*) [+ *lista*] to check off
3 (*Cos*) to stitch, stitch up
4 (*Mús*) [+ *guitarra*] to pluck; [+ *violín*] to play pizzicato
5 (*Cono Sur*) [+ *tierra*] to fork over
6 (*LAm*) [+ *desfile*] to head, lead
(VI) (*Náut*) to luff

punteo (SM) plucking

puntera (SF) **1** [*de zapato*] (= *punta*) toe; (= *refuerzo*) toecap
2 [*de lapicero*] pencil tip
3* (= *puntapié*) kick

punterazo (SM) powerful shot, drive

puntería (SF) **1** (*al apuntar*) aim, aiming • **enmendar** *o* **rectificar la ~** to correct one's aim • **hacer la ~ de un cañón** to aim a gun, sight a gun
2 (= *destreza*) marksmanship • **tener buena ~** to be a good shot • **tener mala ~** to be a bad shot

puntero (ADJ) (= *primero*) top, leading; (= *moderno*) up-to-date • **más ~** (= *sobresaliente*) outstanding, furthest ahead; (= *último*) latest • **empresa puntera** leading company • **equipo ~** top club • **tecnología puntera** the latest technology, state-of-the-art technology
(SM) **1** (*para señalar*) pointer ▸ **puntero luminoso** light pen
2 (= *cincel*) stonecutter's chisel
3 (= *persona que destaca*) outstanding individual; (= *líder*) leader, top man
4 (*LAm*) (= *equipo*) leading team; [*de rebaño*] leading animal; [*de desfile*] leader
5 (*LAm*) [*de reloj*] hand

puntiagudo (ADJ) sharp, sharp-pointed

puntilla (SF) **1** (*Cos*) lace edging
2 (*Taur*) *short dagger for giving the coup de grâce* • MODISMOS: • **dar la ~** to finish off the bull, give the coup de grâce • **dar la ~ a algo/algn** to finish sth/sb off • **aquello fue la ~** that was the last straw
3 • **de ~s** on tiptoe • **andar de ~s** to walk on tiptoe
4 (*Téc*) tack
5 [*de pluma*] point, nib

puntillazo (SM) **1** (*Taur*) *the decisive, mortal blow in a bullfight*
2 • **dar el ~ a algo** to put an end to sth

puntillismo (SM) pointillism

puntillo (SM) **1** (*pey*) (= *amor propio*) exaggerated sense of honour *o* (*EEUU*) honor, excessive amour propre, punctilio (*frm*)
2‡ • **coger** *o* **ligar un ~** (*con bebida*) to get merry*; (*con drogas*) to get high* • **tener un ~** (*con bebida*) to be merry*; (*con drogas*) to be high*

puntilloso (ADJ) (= *detallista*) punctilious; (= *susceptible*) touchy, sensitive

punto (SM) **1** (= *topo*) (*en un diseño*) dot, spot; (*en plumaje*) spot, speckle; (*en carta, dominó*) spot, pip • **aparecen en la piel unos ~s rojos** red spots appear on the skin • **línea de ~s** dotted line ▸ **punto de luz** light ▸ **punto negro** (= *espinilla*) blackhead
2 (= *signo*) (*en la i*) dot; (*de puntuación*) full stop, period (*EEUU*) • **dos ~s** colon • MODISMOS: • **con ~s y comas** down to the last detail • **les contó con ~s y comas lo que había pasado** she told them what had happened down to the last detail • **poner los ~s sobre las íes** to dot the i's and cross the t's • **le puso los ~s sobre las íes** she corrected him, she drew attention to his inaccuracies • **sin faltar ~ ni coma** down to the last detail • **y ~**: • **¡lo digo yo y ~!** I'm telling you so and that's that! ▸ **punto acápite** (*LAm*) (*en dictado*) full stop, new paragraph, period, new paragraph (*EEUU*) ▸ **punto final** full stop, period (*EEUU*); (*fig*) end • **poner ~ final a la discusión** to put an end to the argument, draw a line under the argument ▸ **puntos suspensivos** (*gen*) suspension points; (*en dictado*) dot, dot, dot ▸ **punto y aparte** (*en dictado*) full stop, new paragraph, period, new paragraph (*EEUU*) • **esto marca un ~ y aparte en la historia del teatro** this marks a break with tradition *o* the past in the theatre • **este es un vino ~ y aparte** this is an uncommonly good *o* exceptional wine ▸ **punto y coma** semicolon ▸ **punto y seguido** (*en dictado*) full stop (no new paragraph), period (no new paragraph) (*EEUU*)
3 (*Dep*) point • **con ocho ~s a favor y tres en contra** with eight points for and three against • **los dos están empatados a ~s** the two of them are level on points • **ganar** *o* **vencer por ~s** to win on points • **perdieron por tres ~s** they lost by three points • **completó la ronda con cero ~s** she had a clear round • MODISMO: • **perder (muchos) ~s** to lose (a lot of) prestige • **¡qué ~ te has marcado con lo que has dicho!*** what you said was spot-on*
4 (= *tema*) (*gen*) point; (*en programa de actividades*) item • **no quiero extenderme sobre ese ~** I don't wish to elaborate on that point • **los ~s en el orden del día son ...** the items on the agenda are ... • **contestar ~ por ~** to answer point by point ▸ **punto capital** crucial point ▸ **puntos a tratar** matters to be discussed ▸ **puntos de consulta** terms of reference
5 (= *labor*) knitting; (= *tejido*) knitted fabric, knit • **prendas de ~** knitwear (*sing*) • **falda de ~** knitted skirt • **chaqueta de ~** cardigan • **hacer ~** to knit ▸ **punto del derecho** plain knitting ▸ **punto del revés** purl ▸ **punto de media** plain knitting
6 (*Cos, Med*) (= *puntada*) stitch; [*de media*] loose stitch • **me tuvieron que dar cinco ~s** I had to have five stitches • **me van a quitar los ~s** I am having my stitches out • MODISMO: • **¡~ en boca!** mum's the word! ▸ **punto de costado** (= *dolor*) stitch • **tengo un ~ de costado** I've got a stitch, I've got a pain in my side ▸ **punto de cruz** cross stitch ▸ **punto de sutura** stitch
7 (= *lugar*) (*gen*) spot, place; (*Geog, Mat*) point; [*de proceso*] point, stage; (*en el tiempo*) point, moment • **al llegar a este ~** at this point *o* stage ▸ **punto cardinal** cardinal point • **los cuatro ~s cardinales** the four points of the compass ▸ **punto ciego** (*Anat*) blind spot ▸ **punto clave** key point • **el ~ clave de su razonamiento** the key point of her argument ▸ **punto crítico** critical point ▸ **punto culminante** high point • **llegar a su ~ culminante** to reach its climax ▸ **punto de asistencia** (*Aut*) checkpoint ▸ **punto débil** weak point *o* spot ▸ **punto de calor** heat source ▸ **punto de congelación** freezing point ▸ **punto de contacto** point of contact ▸ **punto de control** checkpoint ▸ **punto de ebullición** boiling-point ▸ **punto de encuentro** meeting point ▸ **punto de equilibrio** (*Com*) break-even point ▸ **punto de fuga** vanishing point ▸ **punto de fusión** melting-point ▸ **punto de inflamación** flashpoint ▸ **punto de información** information centre ▸ **punto de mira** [*de rifle*] sight; (= *objetivo*) aim, objective; (= *punto de vista*) point of view • MODISMO: • **estar en el ~ de mira de algn**: • **su comportamiento está en el ~ de mira de la prensa** his behaviour has come under scrutiny in the press • **el fraude fiscal está en el ~ de mira de Hacienda** the Treasury has targeted tax evasion • **Tokio está en el ~ de mira de sus misiles** their missiles are pointing towards Tokyo ▸ **punto de inflexión** turning point ▸ **punto de no retorno** point of no return ▸ **punto de partida** starting point ▸ **punto de penalti** penalty spot ▸ **punto de referencia** point of reference ▸ **punto de**

P

taxis taxi stand, cab rank ▸ **punto de venta** point of sale • **terminales ~ de venta** point of sale terminals • **está presente en 3.000 ~s de venta** it's available at 3,000 outlets ▸ **punto de vista** point of view, viewpoint • **él lo mira desde otro ~ de vista** he sees it differently, he looks at it from another point of view ▸ **punto flaco** weak point, weak spot ▸ **punto muerto** (*Mec*) dead centre; (*Aut*) neutral (gear); (= *estancamiento*) deadlock, stalemate • **las negociaciones están en un ~ muerto** the negotiations are deadlocked, the talks have reached a stalemate ▸ **punto negro** (*Aut*) (accident) black spot; (*fig*) blemish ▸ **punto neurálgico** (*Anat*) nerve centre *o* (*EEUU*) center; (*fig*) key point ▸ **punto neutro** (*Mec*) dead centre; (*Aut*) neutral (gear)
8 (*otras locuciones*) • **a punto** ready • **está a ~** it's ready • **con sus cámaras a ~ para disparar** with their cameras at the ready • **llegar a ~** to come just at the right moment • **poner un motor a ~** to tune an engine • **al ~** at once, immediately • **estar al ~** (*LAm**) to be high‡ • **bajar de ~** to decline, fall off, fall away • **a ~ de**: • **a ~ de caramelo** caramelized • **poner el azúcar a ~ de caramelo** to caramelize the sugar • **batir las claras a ~ de nieve** beat the egg whites until stiff *o* until they form stiff peaks • **estar a ~ de hacer algo** to be on the point of doing sth, be about to do sth • **estábamos a ~ de salir cuando llamaste** we were about to go out when you phoned • **estuve a ~ de llamarte** I almost called you • **estaba a ~ de llorar** he was on the verge of tears • **estuve a ~ de perder el tren** I very nearly missed the train • **en ~**: • **a las siete en ~** at seven o'clock sharp *o* on the dot • **llegó en ~** he arrived right on time • **en su ~** [*carne*] done to a turn; [*fruta*] just ripe • **el arroz está en su ~** the rice is just right • **pongamos las cosas en su ~** let's be absolutely clear about this • **hasta cierto ~** up to a point, to some extent • **hasta tal ~ que …** to such an extent that … • **la tensión había llegado hasta tal ~ que …** the tension had reached such a pitch that … • **subir de ~** (= *aumentar*) to grow, increase; (= *empeorar*) to get worse • MODISMOS: • **coger** *o* **ligar** *o* **pillar un buen ~**‡ (*con alcohol*) to get merry*; (*con drogas*) to get high* • **cogerle** *o* **pillarle el ~ a algn**‡ to work sb out • **darle el ~ a algn**‡: • **si me da el ~, voy** if I feel like it, I'll go • **si le da el ~ es capaz de cualquier cosa** if he gets it into his head he can do anything • **saber algo a ~ fijo** to know sth for sure • **de todo ~** completely, absolutely
9 (*Esp**) (= *hombre*) guy*; (*pey*) rogue • **¡vaya un ~!** • **¡está hecho un ~ filipino!** he's a right rogue!*
10 (= *agujero*) hole • **darse dos ~s en el cinturón** to let one's belt out a couple of holes
11 (*Inform*) pixel ▸ **punto de parada** break-point ▸ **punto de referencia** benchmark

puntocom SF INV, ADJ INV dotcom, dot. com

puntuable ADJ • **una prueba ~ para el campeonato** a race which counts towards *o* scores in the championship

puntuación SF **1** (*Ling, Tip*) punctuation
2 (= *puntos*) mark, marks (*pl*); (= *grado*) class, grade; (*Dep*) score
3 (= *acto*) (*Escol*) marking, grading (*EEUU*); (*Dep*) scoring • **sistema de ~** system of scoring

puntual ADJ **1** [*persona, llegada*] punctual
2 (= *detallado*) [*informe*] detailed; [*cálculo*] exact, accurate
3 (= *aislado*) • **se trata de casos muy ~es** they are very isolated cases • **ha tenido unos cuantos éxitos ~es en su carrera** he's had the odd success in his career, he's had a few successes at odd times during his career
ADV (= *a tiempo*) • **nunca llega ~** he's never on time

puntualidad SF **1** [*de llegada*] punctuality • **pagar con ~** to pay promptly
2 (= *exactitud*) exactness, accuracy
3 (= *fiabilidad*) reliability, conscientiousness

puntualización SF specification, detailed statement *o* explanation

puntualizador ADJ specific, detailed

puntualizar ▸ CONJUG 1f VT **1** [+ *detalles*] to specify
2 (= *recordar*) to fix in one's mind, fix in one's memory

puntualmente ADV **1** (= *con puntualidad*) [*llegar*] punctually; [*pagar*] promptly
2 (= *con exactitud*) precisely, exactly, accurately
3 (= *con fiabilidad*) reliably, conscientiously

puntuar ▸ CONJUG 1e VT **1** (*Ling, Tip*) to punctuate
2 (= *evaluar*) [+ *clase, estilo*] to evaluate, assess; [+ *examen*] to mark, grade (*EEUU*)
VI **1** (= *valer*) to count • **eso no puntúa** that doesn't count
2 (*Dep*) (= *marcar*) to score

puntudo ADJ (*LAm*) sharp

puntura SF puncture, prick

punzada SF **1** (= *puntura*) prick, jab
2 (*Med*) (= *punto*) stitch; (= *dolor*) twinge (of pain), shooting pain; (= *espasmo*) spasm
3 [*de pena, remordimiento*] pang, twinge
4 (*Caribe**) (= *insolencia*) cheek*, nerve

punzante ADJ **1** [*dolor*] shooting, stabbing
2 [*instrumento*] sharp
3 [*comentario*] biting, caustic

punzar ▸ CONJUG 1f VT **1** (= *pinchar*) (*gen*) to puncture, prick, pierce; (*Téc*) to punch; (= *perforar*) to perforate
2 (= *doler*) to hurt, grieve • **las sienes le punzaban** her temples were throbbing • **le punzan los remordimientos** he feels pangs of regret, his conscience pricks him

punzó ADJ (*And, Cono Sur*) bright red

punzón SM (*Téc*) punch; (*Tip*) bodkin

puñada SF punch, clout • **dar de ~s en** to punch, pound, beat on

puñado SM handful • **a ~s** by handfuls, in plenty • **me mola un ~*** I like it a lot, I love it

puñal SM dagger • MODISMO: • **poner un ~ al pecho a algn** to put sb on the spot

puñalada SF **1** (= *herida*) stab, wound, knife wound • MODISMO: • **coser a ~s** to stab repeatedly, carve up*
2 (= *traición*) terrible blow ▸ **puñalada trapera** stab in the back

puñeta** SF **1** (*indicando enojo*) • **¡no me vengas con ~s!** give me peace!, stop your whining! • **¡qué coche ni que ~s!** car my arse!** • **tengo un catarro de la ~** I've got a hellish *o* a stinking cold*, I've got a bloody awful cold‡ • MODISMO: • **irse a hacer ~s** to go to hell* • **¡vete a hacer ~s!** go to hell!*
2 • **hacer la ~ a algn** to screw sb around**
EXCL • **¡~s!** • **¡qué ~s!** (*indicando enojo*) shit!**, hell!*; (*indicando asombro*) bugger me!**, well I'm damned!

puñetazo SM punch • **a ~s** with one's fists • **dar a algn de ~s** to punch sb

puñetería‡ SF bore, drag

puñetero‡ ADJ (= *maldito*) damned*; (= *despreciable*) rotten

puño SM **1** (*Anat*) fist • **con el** *o* **a ~ cerrado** with one's clenched fist • **apretar los ~s** (*lit*) to clench one's fists; (*fig*) to struggle hard • MODISMOS: • **comerse los ~s** to be starving • **como un ~**: • **su piso es como un ~** his flat is tiny *o* a matchbox • **es una verdad como un ~** it's as plain as a pikestaff • **mentiras como ~s** whopping great lies* • **de mi/tu/su ~**: • **de ~ y letra del poeta** in the poet's own handwriting • **ganar algo con los ~s** to get sth by sheer hard work • **tener a algn (metido) en un ~** to have sb under one's thumb ▸ **puño de hierro** knuckle-duster; ▸ **virgen**
2 [*de camisa, chaqueta*] cuff
3 [*de espada*] hilt; [*de herramienta*] handle, haft, grip; [*de velero, vasija, puerta*] handle
4 (= *puñado*) handful, fistful

pupa SF **1** (*Med**) (= *ampolla*) blister; (*en los labios*) cold sore; (= *úlcera*) ulcer
2* (*en lenguaje infantil*) pain • **hacer ~ a algn** to hurt sb • **hacerse ~** to get hurt
3* (= *error*) gaffe, blunder
4 (*Entomología*) pupa
SMF INV **pupas*** unpredictable person; (= *gruñón*) moaner*

pupila SF **1** (*Anat*) pupil
2 (= *perspicacia*) sharpness, intelligence
3 (*Arg**) (= *prostituta*) prostitute, whore, hooker (*EEUU**)

pupilo/a SM/F **1** (*en pensión*) boarder; (*en un orfelinato*) inmate
2 (*Jur*) ward
3 (*Dep**) player

pupitre SM desk

pupo SM (*And, Cono Sur*) navel

pupón ADJ **1** (*Cono Sur, Méx**) (= *lleno*) stuffed, full, full up
2 (*Cono Sur*‡) (= *barrigón*) pot-bellied, paunchy

pupurrí SM pot-pourri

pupusa SF (*CAm*) (*Culin*) stuffed tortilla

pupusería SF (*CAm*) *shop selling stuffed tortillas*

puque ADJ (*Méx*) (= *podrido*) rotten, bad; (= *débil*) weak, sickly; (= *estéril*) sterile

puquío SM (*LAm*) spring, fountain

pura SF • MODISMO: • **por las ~s** (*Cono Sur**) just for the hell of it

puramente ADV purely, simply

purasangre SMF (PL: **purasangres**) thoroughbred

puré SM (*Culin*) purée, (thick) soup • **~ de guisantes** (*lit*) pea soup; (*fig*) peasouper*, thick fog • **~ de patatas** mashed potatoes (*pl*) • **~ de tomate** tomato purée, tomato paste • **~ de verduras** thick vegetable soup • MODISMO: • **estar hecho ~*** to be knackered*

purear ▸ CONJUG 1a VI (*And*) to drink one's liquor neat

pureta* ADJ old, elderly
SMF **1** (= *viejo*) old crock
2 (= *carca*) old square*

pureza SF purity

purga SF **1** (*Med*) purge, purgative
2 (*Pol*) purge
3 (= *drenaje*) venting, draining • **válvula de ~** vent

purgación SF **1** (= *acción*) purging; (= *medicina*) purgative
2 [*de mujer*] menstruation
3 • **tener purgaciones*** to have the clap*

purgante SM, ADJ purgative

purgar ▸ CONJUG 1h VT **1** (*Med*) to purge, administer a purgative to
2 (*Pol*) (= *depurar*) to expel • **~ a los fascistas del partido** to purge the party of fascists, expel fascists from the party
3 (= *limpiar de*) [+ *pecado*] to purge, expiate; [+ *delito*] to pay for; [+ *pasiones*] to purge • **~ la religión de supersticiones** to purge *o* cleanse religion of superstition
4 (*Mec*) (= *drenar*) [+ *depósito, tubería*] to drain;

[+ *radiador*] to bleed, drain; [+ *frenos*] to bleed
5 (= *purificar*) to purify, refine
VPR **purgarse 1** (*Med*) to take a purge
2 (*fig*) • **~se de algo** to purge o.s. of sth
purgativo ADJ purgative
purgatorio SM purgatory • **¡fue un ~!** it was purgatory!
puridad SF • **en ~** (= *claramente*) plainly, directly; (= *estrictamente*) strictly speaking; (= *secretamente*) in secret
purificación SF purification ▸ **purificación étnica** ethnic cleansing
purificador ADJ purifying
SM ▸ **purificador de agua** water filter ▸ **purificador de aire** air purifier, air filter
purificante ADJ cleansing
purificar ▹ CONJUG 1g VT [+ *agua, raza*] to purify; [+ *metales*] to refine, purify; [+ *pulmones*] to cleanse
purili‡ SMF old geezer‡
Purísima ADJ • **la ~** the Virgin
purismo SM purism
purista SMF purist
puritanismo SM puritanism
puritano/a ADJ **1** (*Rel*) Puritan
2 [*actitud, tradición*] puritanical, puritan
SM/F **1** (*Rel*) Puritan
2 (*fig*) puritan
puro ADJ **1** (= *sin mezcla*) [*color, lenguaje*] pure; [*aire*] clean; [*oro*] solid ▸ **pura sangre** (= *caballo*) thoroughbred
2 (*con valor enfático*) pure, simple • **de ~ aburrimiento** out of sheer boredom • **por pura casualidad** by sheer chance • MODISMO: • **~ y duro***: • **fue un timo ~ y duro** it was a straightforward *o* downright swindle • **es un reaccionario ~ y duro** he's an out-and-out reactionary
3 (= *casto*) pure, chaste
4 (*LAm*) (= *uno solo*) only, just • **me queda una pura porción** I have just one portion left
5 (*esp And, Caribe, Méx*) (= *idéntico*) identical • **el hijo es ~ el padre** the son is exactly like his father
ADV • **de ~ bobo** out of sheer stupidity • **de ~ cansado** out of sheer tiredness • **no se le ve el color de ~ sucio** it's so dirty you can't tell what colour it is • **cosas que se olvidan de ~ sabidas** things which are so well known that they get overlooked
SM **1** (*tb* **cigarro puro**) cigar ▸ **puro habano** Havana cigar
2 • MODISMO: • **meter un ~ a algn*** (*gen*) to throw the book at sb*; (*Mil*) to put sb on a charge
3 • **a ~ de**† by dint of, thanks only to
púrpura SF **1** (= *color*) purple
2 (= *cargo*) ▸ **púrpura cardenalicia** cardinal purple ▸ **la púrpura imperial** the mantel of emperor
purpurado SM (= *persona*) cardinal; (= *cargo*) purple
purpurar ▹ CONJUG 1a VT to dye purple
purpúreo ADJ purple
purpurina SF **1** (= *pintura*) (*gen*) metallic paint; (*para decoración, maquillaje*) glitter
2 (= *oropel*) glitz, tinsel
purpurino ADJ purple
purrela SF **1** (= *vino*) bad wine, cheap wine, plonk*
2 • **una ~** a mere trifle, chicken feed (*pey*)
purrete* SM (*Cono Sur*) kid*, child
purulento ADJ purulent
pus SM pus
puse *etc* ▹ **poner**
pusilánime ADJ fainthearted, pusillanimous
pusilanimidad SF faintheartedness, pusillanimity
pústula SF pustule
put [pʊt] SM (PL: **puts** [pʊt]) (*Golf*) putt
puta** SF **1** (= *prostituta*) whore, prostitute • **casa de ~s** brothel • **¡la muy ~!** the slut!, the bitch!‡ • **ir(se) de ~s** to go whoring ▸ **puta callejera** streetwalker
2 (*expresando fastidio*) • **¡puta!** bloody hell!‡ • **¡la ~!** (*expresando sorpresa*) well I'm damned!
3 (*Naipes*) jack, knave
4 • **pasarlas ~s** to have a shitty time*, have a rotten time*; ▹ **puto**
putada** SF (= *mala pasada*) dirty trick • **¡es una ~!** it's a real bugger!‡
putañear* ▹ CONJUG 1a VI to go whoring
putañero* ADJ **1** (= *que va de putas*) whoring
2 (= *cachondo*) randy, oversexed
SM whoremonger
putativo ADJ putative (*frm*), supposed
puteada* SF (*LAm*) (= *insultos*) shower of gross insults; (= *palabrota*) swearword
puteado** ADJ **1** (= *fastidiado*) • **nos tienen ~s** they're really screwing us around‡ • **el ~ pueblo español** the long-suffering *o* hard done-by Spanish people
2 (= *harto*) fed up to the back teeth*, browned off* • **estar ~** to be fed up to the back teeth*, be browned off
3 (= *maleado*) corrupted, perverted
putear ▹ CONJUG 1a VT **1**** (= *fastidiar*) to bugger about‡, muck around
2** (= *enfadar*) to upset, send up the wall*
3 (*LAm**) (= *insultar*) to swear at, curse
VI* **1** (= *ir de putas*) to go whoring
2 (= *ser prostituta*) to be on the game*
3 (*Cono Sur*) (= *jurar*) to swear, curse, eff and blind*
puteo* SM • **ir de ~** (*Esp*) to go whoring
putería* SF **1** (*de putas*) (= *prostitución*) prostitution, whoring; (= *vida*) life of the prostitute
2 (= *prostitutas*) gathering of prostitutes
3 (= *prostíbulo*) brothel
4 (= *artimañas*) womanly wile(s)
5 (= *zalamería*) soft soap*
puterío* SM whoring, prostitution
putero SM whoremonger
puticlub* [putɪ'klu] SM (*hum*) pick up joint‡
putilla* SF scrubber‡
putiza‡ SF (*Méx*) brawl, set-to*
puto** ADJ bloody*, bloody awful* • **no me hizo ni ~ caso** she completely bloody ignored me‡ • **no tengo ni un ~ duro** I'm absolutely skint* • **¡ni puta idea!** I've no bloody idea!* • **por toda la puta calle** all along the bloody street‡ • **¡qué puta suerte!** (= *mala*) what bloody awful luck!*; (= *buena*) what incredible luck!* • MODISMO: • **de puta madre** (= *bueno*) terrific*, smashing*; (= *malo*) bloody awful‡; (*uso adverbial*) marvellously • **cocina de puta madre** she's a bloody marvellous cook‡; ▹ **puta**
SM **1** (= *prostituto*) male prostitute
2 (= *insulto*) sod**
putrefacción SF rotting, putrefaction • **basura en ~** rotting rubbish • **alimentos sujetos a ~** perishable foods • **el cadáver estaba en avanzado estado de ~** the body was in an advanced estate of decomposition ▸ **putrefacción fungoide** dry rot ▸ **putrefacción política** political corruption
putrefacto ADJ (= *podrido*) rotten, putrid; (= *descompuesto*) decayed
putrescente ADJ rotting, putrefying
pútrido ADJ putrid, rotten
putt [pʊt] SM (PL: **putts** [pʊt]) putt
putter ['puter] SM (PL: **putters** ['puter]) putter
puya SF **1** (= *vara*) (*gen*) goad, pointed stick; (*Taur*) point of the picador's lance
2 (= *sarcasmo*) gibe, barbed comment
3 (*Caribe*) one cent
puyar ▹ CONJUG 1a VT **1** (*LAm*) to jab, prick
2 (*Col**) (= *molestar*) to upset, needle*
VI (*Caribe*) [*planta*] to shoot, sprout
puyazo SM **1** (*Taur*) jab with the lance
2 (= *palabras*) gibe, barbed comment
puyero SM (*Caribe*) pile of money • **divertirse un ~*** to have a great time*, have a whale of a time*
puyo SM (*Cono Sur*) coarse woollen poncho
puyón SM **1** (*And, Cono Sur*) (= *espolón*) cock's spur
2 (*Méx*) (= *puya*) sharp point; (= *espina*) thorn, prickle
3 (*And, CAm, Caribe*) (= *pinchazo*) jab, prick
4 (*And, CAm, Méx*) (= *brote*) shoot, bud
puzcua SF (*Méx*) puffed maize
puzle, puzzle ['puθle] SM puzzle (*tb fig*)
PVC SM ABR (= **polyvinyl-chloride**) PVC
PVP SM ABR (= **precio de venta al público**) RRP
PYME SF ABR, **pyme** SF ABR = **Pequeña y Mediana Empresa**
PYRESA SF ABR = **Prensa y Radio Española, Sociedad Anónima**

Qq

Q, q [ku] SF (= *letra*) Q, q
Qatar SM Qatar
q.b.s.m. ABR (= **que besa su mano**) *courtesy formula*
q.b.s.p. ABR (= **que besa sus pies**) *courtesy formula*
q.D.g. ABR, **Q.D.G** ABR (= **que Dios guarde**) *courtesy formula*
QED ABR (= **quod erat demonstrandum**) QED
q.e.g.e. ABR (= **que en gloria esté**) ≈ RIP
q.e.p.d. ABR (= **que en paz descanse**) RIP
q.e.s.m. ABR (= **que estrecha su mano**) *courtesy formula*
QH SF ABR (= **quiniela hípica**) *horse-racing totalizator*
qm ABR = **quintal(es) métrico(s)**
qts. ABR (= **quilates**) c
quad SM quad, quad bike
Quáker® SM (*LAm*) porridge
quantum ['kwantum] SM (PL: **quanta** ['kwanta]) (*Fís*) quantum
quark SM (PL: **quarks**) quark
quásar SM quasar
quattrocentista ADJ quattrocento (*antes de s*)
que[1] PRON REL **1** (*refiriéndose a personas*) **a** (*como sujeto*) who, that • **el hombre que vino ayer** the man who *o* that came yesterday • **hable con alguien que entienda de esto** talk to someone who knows about this
b (*como complemento: a menudo se omite*) that • **el hombre que vi en la calle** the man (that) I saw in the street • **la chica que conoció durante las vacaciones** the girl (that) he met on holiday
2 (*refiriéndose a cosas*) **a** (*como sujeto*) that, which • **la película que ganó el premio** the film that *o* which won the award
b (*como complemento: a menudo se omite*) that, which • **el coche que compré** the car (that *o* which) I bought • **el libro del que te hablé** the book (that *o* which) I spoke to you about • **el día que ella nació** the day (when *o* that) she was born • **la cama en que pasé la noche** the bed in which I spent the night, the bed I spent the night in
3 • **el/la/los/las que** ▹ **el**
4 • **lo que** ▹ **lo**[1]
que[2] CONJ **1** (*en subordinada sustantiva: a menudo se omite*) **a** (+ *indic*) that • **creo que va a venir** I think (that) he will come • **dijo que vendría** he said (that) he'd come • **dile a Rosa que me llame** tell Rosa to call me • **estoy seguro de que lloverá** I am sure (that) it will rain • **aceptan la idea de que el diálogo es útil** they accept the idea that a dialogue is useful • **eso de que no lo sabía es un cuento** all that about him not knowing is pure fiction
b (+ *subjun*) that • **no sabía que tuviera coche** I didn't know (that) he had a car • **me alegro de que hayan ganado** I am glad (that) they have won • **es una pena que no tengamos más tiempo** it's a pity (that) we haven't got more time • **no digo que sea un traidor** I'm not saying (that) he's a traitor • **espero que os sea útil** I hope you'll find it useful • **no creo que te sea difícil encontrarlo** I don't think you'll have any difficulty finding it • **quieren que les esperes** they want you to wait for them
c • **decir que sí** to say yes; ▹ **claro**
2 (*en comparaciones*) • **eres igual que mi padre** you're just like my father • **más que** more than • **ganas más que yo** you earn more than me • **es más alto que tú** he's taller than you • **más que nada** more than anything • **menos que** less than • **prefiero estar aquí que en mi casa** I'd rather be here than at home • **prefiero las películas serias que las comedias** I prefer serious films to comedies • **yo que tú** if I were you • **yo que tú, iría** I'd go, if I were you
3 (*expresando resultado*) **a** (*a menudo se omite*) that • **tan ... que**: • **es tan grande que no lo puedo levantar** it's so big (that) I can't lift it • **soplaba tan fuerte que no podíamos salir** it was blowing so hard (that) we couldn't go out • **tanto ... que**: • **las manos le temblaban tanto que apenas podía escribir** her hands were shaking so much (that) she could hardly write
b • **tengo una sed que me muero** I'm dying of thirst • **huele que es un asco** it smells disgusting; ▹ **bendición, primor**
4 (*expresando causa*) • **llévate un paraguas, que está lloviendo** take an umbrella, it's raining • **no lo derroches, que es muy caro** don't waste it, it's very expensive • **¡vamos, que cierro!** come on now, I'm closing! • **¡cuidado, que te caes!** careful or you'll fall!, mind you don't fall! • **¡suéltame, que voy a gritar!** let go or I'll scream!
5 (*expresando reiteración o insistencia*) • **siguió toca que toca** he kept on playing • **estuvieron habla que habla toda la noche** they talked and talked all night • **¡que sí!**: • **—es verde —¡que no! —¡que sí!** "it's green" — "no it isn't!" — "yes it is!" • **—no funciona —que sí, es que lo haces mal** "it doesn't work" — "yes it does, you're just doing it wrong"
6 (*sin antecedente expreso*) **a** (*expresando mandato*) • **¡que lo haga él!** let him do it!, he can do it himself! • **¡que entre!** send him in!, let him come in!
b (*expresando deseo*) • **¡que venga pronto!** let's hope he comes soon! • **¡que te mejores!** get well soon! • **¡que os guste la película!** enjoy the film!
c (*expresando sorpresa*) • **¿que no estabas allí?** (are you telling me) you weren't there?
7 • **el que** (+ *subjun*) (= *el hecho de que*) the fact that • **el que viva en Vitoria no es ningún problema** the fact that he lives in Vitoria isn't a problem • **el que quiera estar con su madre es natural** it is natural (that) he should want to be with his mother

qué PRON **1** (*interrogativo*) • **¿qué?** what? • **¿qué has dicho?** what did you say? • **¿a qué has venido?** why have you come?, what have you come for? • **¿con qué lo vas a pagar?** how are you going to pay for it?, what are you going to pay with? • **¿de qué lo conoces?** how do you know him?, where do you know him from? • **¿en qué lo notas?** how can you tell? • **no sé qué quiere decir** I don't know what it means • **¿qué tan grande es?** (*LAm*) how big is it? • **¿qué más?** (*gen*) what else?; (*en tienda*) anything else? • **¿para qué?**: • **¿para qué lo quiere?** why does he want it?, what does he want it for? • **¿para qué, si nunca me hace caso?** what's the point? he never listens to me anyway • **¿por qué?** why? • **¿por qué no se lo dices?** why don't you tell him? • **¿qué tal?** how are things? • **¿qué tal estás?** how are you? • **¿qué tal el trabajo?** how's work? • **¿qué tanto?** (*LAm*) (= *¿cuánto?*) how much? • **¿qué tanto lo quiere?** how much do you love him? • **¿y qué?** so what? • **no lo he hecho, ¿y qué?** so what if I haven't done it? • **¿y a mí qué?** so what?, what has that got to do with me? • MODISMOS: • **ahí estaba el qué** that was the reason • **sin qué ni para qué** without rhyme or reason
2 (*exclamativo*) • **¡qué de gente había!** what a lot of people there were! • **¡qué de cosas te diría!** what a lot I'd have to say to you! • **¡qué va!**: • **¡qué va!, no me parece caro** no, I don't think it's expensive at all! • **—es muy fea —¡qué va! a mí me parece monísima** "she's very ugly" — "you're joking, I think she's really pretty!" • **¿aquí, en España, corrupción? ¡qué va!** corruption, here in Spain? come off it!
ADJ **1** (*interrogativo*) • **¿qué día del mes es hoy?** what's today's date?, what's the date today? • **¿qué camisa le regalarías?** which shirt would you give him? • **dime qué libro buscas** tell me which book you are looking for • **—¿has encontrado mi lápiz? —¿qué lápiz?** "have you found my pencil?" — "what pencil?" • **¿qué edad tiene?** how old is he?, what age is he? • **¿a qué velocidad?** how fast?, at what speed? • **¿de qué tamaño es?** how big is it?, what size is it?
2 (*exclamativo*) • **¡qué día más espléndido!** what a glorious day! • **¡qué casualidad!** what a coincidence! • **¡qué susto!** what a fright! • **¡qué asco!** how revolting! • **¡qué maravilla!** how wonderful! • **¡qué maravilla de casa!** what a wonderful house!
ADV • **¡qué bonito!** isn't it pretty!, how pretty it is! • **¡qué boba eres!** you're so silly! • **¡qué mala eres!** you're awful! • **¡qué mala suerte!** what rotten luck! • **¡qué bien!** (= *estupendo*) great!, excellent!; (= *bravo*) well done! • **¡qué bien se vive solo!** it's great living on your own! • **¡qué bien canta!** she sings so well!, she's such a good singer! • **¡qué bien se oye!** you can hear so clearly!

quebracho (SM) **1** (= *árbol*) quebracho, quebracho tree; (= *madera*) break axe, break ax (EEUU)
2 (*Téc*) *extract used in leather-tanning*
quebrada (SF) **1** (= *hondonada*) ravine, gorge; (= *puerto*) gap, pass
2 (*LAm*) (= *arroyo*) brook, mountain stream
quebradero (SM) ▸ **quebradero de cabeza** headache, worry
quebradizo (ADJ) **1** (= *frágil*) (*gen*) fragile, brittle; [*hojaldre*] short; [*galleta*] crumbly; [*voz*] weak, faltering
2 (= *enfermizo*) sickly, frail
3 (= *muy sensible*) emotionally fragile, sensitive, easily upset
4 (*moralmente*) weak, easily tempted
quebrado (ADJ) **1** (= *roto*) (*gen*) broken; [*terreno*] rough, uneven; [*línea*] irregular, zigzag
2 • **~ de color** [*rostro*] pale; [*tez*] pallid
3 (*Med*) ruptured
4 (*Econ*) bankrupt
(SM) **1** (*Mat*) fraction
2 (*Econ*) bankrupt ▸ **quebrado no rehabilitado** undischarged bankrupt ▸ **quebrado rehabilitado** discharged bankrupt
quebradora (SF) (*CAm*) (*Med*) dengue fever
quebradura (SF) **1** (= *grieta*) fissure, crack
2 (*Geog*) = **quebrada**
3 (*Med*) rupture
quebraja (SF) fissure, slit, crack
quebrantadura (SF), **quebrantamiento** (SM) **1** (= *rotura*) (*gen*) breaking; (*al formarse una grieta*) cracking; [*de resistencia*] weakening; [*de cerradura*] forcing; [*de ley*] violation ▸ **quebrantadura de forma** (*Jur*) breach of normal procedure
2 (= *estado*) exhaustion, exhausted state
3 (= *mala salud*) broken health
quebrantahuesos (SM INV) bearded vulture
quebrantar ▹ CONJUG 1a (VT) **1** (= *romper*) (*gen*) to break; (*haciendo grietas*) to crack; (*haciendo añicos*) to shatter
2 (= *debilitar*) [+ *resistencia*] to weaken, break; [+ *salud, posición*] to destroy, undermine; [+ *persona*] to break; [+ *cimientos, furia, moral*] to weaken
3 (= *abrir*) [+ *cerradura*] to force; [+ *caja fuerte, sello*] to break open; [+ *cárcel*] to break out of; [+ *recinto sagrado*] to break into, violate; [+ *terreno vedado*] to trespass on
4 [+ *ley, promesa*] to break
5 [+ *color*] to tone down
6 (*LAm*) [+ *caballo*] to break in
(VPR) **quebrantarse** [*persona*] to be broken (in health *etc*)
quebranto (SM) **1** (= *perjuicio*) damage, harm
2 [*de persona*] (= *agotamiento*) exhaustion; (= *depresión*) depression; (= *mala salud*) broken health
3 (= *aflicción*) sorrow, affliction
quebrar ▹ CONJUG 1j (VT) **1** (= *romper*) to break, smash
2 (= *doblar*) (*gen*) to bend; [+ *cuerpo*] to bend (at the waist)
3 (= *torcer*) to twist
4 [+ *proceso*] (= *interrumpir*) to interrupt; (= *modificar*) to alter the course of, seriously interfere with
5 [+ *color*] to tone down
6 (*Méx**) (= *matar*) to bump off*, waste*
7 = **quebrantar**
(VI) **1** (*Econ*) to fail, go bankrupt
2 (= *debilitarse*) to weaken
3 • **~ con algn** to break with sb
(VPR) **quebrarse 1** to break, get broken, smash
2 (*Med*) to rupture
quebraza (SF) **1** (= *grieta*) crack
2 (*Med*) crack (*on the skin*), chap
quebrazón (SF) **1** (*LAm*) [*de vidrio*] smashing, shattering
2 (*Cono Sur*) (= *contienda*) quarrel
quebroso (ADJ) (*And*) brittle, fragile
queche (SM) smack, ketch
quechua (ADJ) Quechua, Quechuan
(SMF) Quechua(n) Indian
(SM) (*Ling*) Quechua

> **QUECHUA**
> **Quechua**, the language spoken by the Incas, is the most widely spoken indigenous language in South America, with some 13 million speakers in the Andean region. The first Quechua grammar was compiled by a Spanish missionary in 1560, as part of a linguistic policy intended to aid the process of evangelization. In 1975 Peru made Quechua an official state language. From Quechua come words such as "llama", "condor" and "puma".

queda (SF) • **toque de ~** curfew
quedada[1]†† (SF) (*CAm, Caribe, Méx*) spinster, old maid (*pey*)
quedada[2]* (SF) (= *broma*) joke, tease; (= *engaño*) hoax
quedado (ADJ) (*Cono Sur, Méx*) lazy

quedar

VERBO INTRANSITIVO
VERBO PRONOMINAL

▹ CONJUG 1a

Para expresiones como ***quedarse tan ancho, quedarse con las ganas, quedársele grabado algn, quedarse helado, quedarse parado****, ver la otra entrada.*

VERBO INTRANSITIVO

1 (*indicando lugar*) to be • **eso queda muy lejos** that's a long way away • **queda un poco más al oeste** it is a little further west • **queda a 6 km de aquí** it's 6 km from here • **queda hacia la derecha** it's over to the right • **¿por dónde queda Correos?** where's the post office? • **queda por aquí** it's around here somewhere • **esa cuestión queda fuera de nuestra responsabilidad** that matter lies outside our responsibility
2 (*indicando posición*) • **quedó el penúltimo** he was second last • **~ atrás**: • **no quieren ~ atrás en la carrera espacial** they don't want to be left behind *o* fall behind in the space race • **la crisis ha quedado atrás** the crisis is behind us
3 (*indicando resultado*) **a** (*con adjetivos, adverbios, locuciones preposicionales, participios*) • **el autocar quedó destrozado** the coach was wrecked • **te ha quedado muy bonita la cocina** you've made a great job of the kitchen • **quedó paralítico tras el accidente** the accident left him paralysed • **la cara le ha quedado desfigurada** her face has been disfigured • **al final quedamos como amigos** we were still friends afterwards • **aún no han quedado definidos los criterios** the criteria still haven't been established • **la junta ha quedado constituida** the board has been elected • **~ ciego** to go blind • **~ huérfano** to be orphaned • **quedó huérfano de padre a los seis años** he lost his father when he was six years old • **~ viuda/viudo** to be widowed, lose one's husband/wife • MODISMO: • **ahí quedó la cosa** that's how we left it
b • **~ en algo**: • **¿en qué quedó la conversación?** how did the conversation end? • **todas sus promesas ~on en nada** all her promises came to nothing • **al final todo quedó en un susto** it gave us a scare but it turned out all right in the end
c • **~ sin**: • **miles de personas han quedado sin hogar** thousands of people have been left homeless • **el proyecto quedó sin realizar** the project was never carried out • **la reconstrucción del puente ha quedado sin hacer por falta de presupuesto** the rebuilding of the bridge has been abandoned because of a shortage of funds
4 (*en el trato, al hablar*) • **ha quedado como un canalla** he has shown himself to be a rotter • **~ bien**: • **regalando flores siempre queda uno bien** taking flowers always makes a good impression • **solo lo ha hecho por ~ bien** he only did it to make himself look good • **~ bien con algn** to make a good impression on sb • **~ mal**: • **nos hiciste ~ mal haciendo esas preguntas** you made us look bad by asking those questions • **no quiero ~ mal con ellos** I don't want to get on the wrong side of them • **por no ~ mal** so as not to cause any offence • **~ por algo** to be left looking like sth • **quedé por idiota** I was left looking like an idiot • **aunque fue idea de todos, yo quedé por el culpable** although everyone was to blame, it ended up looking as if it was my fault • **~ en ridículo**: • **ha quedado en ridículo** he ended up looking a fool • **quería que su marido ~a en ridículo** she wanted to make her husband look a fool, she wanted to show her husband up
5 (= *permanecer*) to stay • **~on allí una semana** they stayed there a week • **quedo a la espera de sus noticias** (*en carta*) I look forward to hearing from you
6 (= *haber todavía*) to be left • **no queda ninguno** there are none left • **¿queda algo de la cena?** is there any dinner left? • **no quedan más que escombros** there is nothing left but rubble • **no quedaba nadie en el autobús** there was nobody left on the bus • **de la ciudad solo queda el castillo** all that remains *o* is left of the city is the castle • **no quedó ni un solo edificio en pie** not a single building was left standing • **se me cayó un poco de vino, pero no ha quedado ninguna mancha** I spilt some wine, but it didn't leave a stain • **si a 8 le quito 2, quedan 6** if I take 2 from 8, I'm left with *o* it leaves 6 • **~le a algn**: • **¿le quedan entradas para esta noche?** do you have any tickets left for tonight? • **me quedan cinco euros** I've got five euros left • **no nos queda mucho dinero** we don't have much money left • **~ a deber algo** to owe sth • **no tenía suficiente y tuve que ~le a deber** I didn't have enough money on me, so I had to owe him • **me quedó a deber 25 euros** he was left owing me 25 euros • **quedan pocos días para la fiesta** the party is only a few days away • **nos quedan 12 km para llegar a Badalona** we've still got 12 km to go to Badalona • **~ por hacer**: • **nos queda por pagar la luz** we still have to pay the electricity bill • **queda por limpiar la cocina** the kitchen still needs cleaning • **eso queda todavía por estudiar** that remains to be studied • **no me queda más remedio** I have no alternative (left) • MODISMO: • **que no quede**: • **por mí que no quede, yo he ayudado en lo que he podido** it won't be for want of trying on my part, I helped as much as I could • **por probar que no quede** there's no harm in trying • **tú por ser amable que no quede** nobody could accuse

q

you of not being nice
7 Educ [*asignatura*] • **me han quedado las matemáticas** I failed mathematics
8 *ropa* (= *ser la talla*) to fit; (= *sentar*) to suit • **¿qué tal (de grande) te queda el vestido?** does the dress fit you? • **me queda pequeño** it's too small for me • **no te queda bien ese vestido** that dress doesn't suit you • **te queda bien** it suits you • **no queda bien así/aquí** it doesn't look right like that/here
9 • **~ en** (= *acordar*): • **¿quedamos en eso, entonces?** we'll do that, then, all right? • **~ en** *o* (*LAm*) **de hacer algo** to agree to do sth • **~on en esperar unos días antes de tomar una decisión definitiva** they agreed to wait a few days before taking a final decision • **quedamos en vernos mañana** we arranged to meet tomorrow • **~ en que** to agree that • **quedamos en que cada uno traería una botella** we agreed that everyone would bring a bottle • **¿en qué quedamos? ¿lo compras o no?** so what's it to be then? are you going to buy it or not?
10 *= citarse* to arrange to meet • **hemos quedado en la puerta del cine** we've arranged to meet outside the cinema • **habíamos quedado, pero no se presentó** we had arranged to meet, but he didn't turn up • **¿quedamos a las cuatro?** shall we meet at four? • **¿cómo quedamos?** where shall we meet and what time? • **~ con algn** to arrange to meet sb • **¿quedamos con ella en la parada?** shall we meet her at the bus stop?

VERBO PRONOMINAL **quedarse**
1 *= permanecer, estar* **a** (*gen*) to stay • **ve tú, yo me quedo** you go, I'll stay • **se quedó toda la mañana en la cama** she stayed in bed all morning • **me quedé en casa** I stayed at home • **mis compañeros salieron de trabajar a las cinco, pero yo me quedé hasta las ocho** my colleagues all left work at five, but I stayed behind until eight • **sus preguntas se ~on sin respuesta** his questions remained *o* were left unanswered • **~se con unos amigos** to stay with some friends • **~se atrás** (= *atrasarse*) to fall behind, be left behind; (= *en posición retrasada*) to stay behind • **generalmente se queda atrás hasta la última vuelta** (*Dep*) he usually stays behind until the last lap
b (+ *gerundio*) • **me quedé estudiando hasta que cerraron la biblioteca** I carried on *o* stayed working in the library until it closed • **id vosotros, yo me quedo un rato más viendo el museo** you go, I want to stay and look round the museum a bit more • **me quedé viendo la tele hasta muy tarde** I stayed up late watching TV • **se nos quedó mirando asombrado** he stared at us in amazement
2 *indicando resultado* **a** (*con adjetivos, locuciones preposicionales*) • **me estoy quedando sordo** I'm going deaf • **se ha quedado viudo** he has been widowed, he has lost his wife • **~se en nada** to come to nothing • **se me ha quedado pequeña esta camisa** I've outgrown this shirt
b • **~se sin**: • **nos hemos quedado sin café** we've run out of coffee • **~se sin empleo** to lose one's job • **al final nos quedamos sin ver el concierto** we didn't get to see the concert in the end
3 *= conservar* (*gen*) to keep; (= *comprar*) to take • **quédatela como recuerdo** keep it as a memento • **me la quedo** I'll take it • **~se con** (= *retener*) to keep; (= *comprar*) to take; (= *preferir*) to go for, take • **quédese con la vuelta** keep the change • **se quedó con mi pluma** he kept my pen • **me quedo con este paraguas** I'll take this umbrella • **el vencedor se queda con todo** winner takes all • **entre A y B, me quedo con B** given a choice between A and B, I'd go for *o* take B • **así que me quedé con el más tonto de los tres** so I got (left with) the stupidest of the three • **~se con hambre** to be still hungry
4 *= retener en la memoria* • **está muy mayor, no se le quedan las cosas** he's really old now, he can't remember things • **lo siento, no me quedé con su nombre** sorry, I can't quite remember your name • **tiene mucha facilidad para ~se con los números** she's very good at remembering numbers
5 Esp • **~se con algn*** (= *engañar*) to con sb*; (= *tomar el pelo a*) to take the mickey out of sb*, pull sb's leg* • **¿te estás quedando conmigo?** are you trying to kid me?*
6 *= calmarse* [*viento*] to drop; [*mar*] to calm down

quedito ADV very softly, very gently
quedo ADJ **1** (= *inmóvil*) still
2 (= *tranquilo*) [*voz*] quiet, gentle; [*paso*] soft
ADV softly, gently • **¡quedo!** (= *con cuidado*) careful now!; (= *suave*) gently now!
quedón‡ ADJ (*Esp*) **1** (= *guasón*) jokey, waggish
2 (= *ligón*) flirtatious, fond of the men/the ladies
quehacer SM job, task • **~es domésticos** housework (*sing*), household chores • **agobiado de ~** overburdened with work • **atender a sus ~es** to go about one's business • **tener mucho ~** to have a lot to do
queimada SF *traditional Galician hot drink made with flamed "orujo", sugar and lemon*
queja SF **1** (= *reclamación*) (*gen*) complaint; (*refunfuñando*) grumble, grouse*; (*con rencor*) grudge, resentment • **una ~ infundada** an unjustified complaint • **presentar una ~** to make *o* lodge a complaint • **tener ~ de algn** to have a complaint to make about sb • **tener motivo de ~** to have cause for complaint • **estoy harto de tus ~s** I'm tired of your complaining
2 (= *gemido*) moan, groan ▸ **queja de dolor** groan of pain
3 (*Jur*) protest
quejadera SF (*And, Méx*), **quejambre** SF (*And, Méx*) moaning
quejarse ▹ CONJUG 1a VPR **1** (= *reclamar*) (*gen*) to complain (**de** about, of); (*refunfuñando*) to grumble (**de** about, at); (*protestando*) to protest (**de** about, at) • **~ a la dirección** to complain to the management • **~ de que** to complain (about the fact) that • **se quejó de que nadie lo escuchaba** he complained that nobody listened to him • **~ de vicio*** to be always complaining
2 (= *gemir*) (*gen*) to moan, groan; (*lloriqueando*) to whine
quejica ADJ moaning
SMF moaner, grumbler
quejido SM (= *gemido*) moan, groan; (= *lloriqueo*) whine • **dar ~s** (= *gemir*) to moan, groan; (= *lloriquear*) to whine
quejigal SM, **quejigar** SM gall-oak grove
quejigo SM gall-oak
quejón/ona* ADJ moaning, grumbling
SM/F moaner, grumbler
quejoso ADJ [*persona*] complaining; [*tono*] plaintive • **está ~ de mí** he is annoyed with me
quejumbre SF moan, groan
quejumbroso ADJ = **quejoso**
queli¹‡ SM, **quel‡** SF, **quela‡** SF house • **irse a la ~** to go home
queli²‡ SM mate*, pal*, buddy (*EEUU**)
quelite SM (*CAm, Méx*) (= *verduras*) any green vegetable; (= *brote*) shoot, tip, green part • MODISMO: • **poner a algn como un ~** (*Méx**) to make mincemeat of sb
quelonia SF (*Caribe*) turtle
quelonio SM chelonian
quelpo SM kelp
quema SF **1** (= *incendio*) fire; (= *combustión*) burning; (*LAm*) (*Agr*) burning-off (of scrub) • MODISMO: • **salvarse de la ~**: • **fue el único atleta que se salvó de la ~** he was the only athlete to escape the carnage
2 (*Arg*) (= *vertedero*) rubbish dump
3 • **hacer ~** (= *acertar*) to hit the target
4 (*Méx*) (= *peligro*) danger
quemable ADJ inflammable
quemado ADJ **1** (*por fuego, sol*) burned, burnt • **llegó muy ~ de la playa** he got back really burned *o* burnt from the beach • **esto sabe a ~** this tastes burned *o* burnt • **aquí huele a ~** there's a smell of burning in here
2 (= *desprestigiado*) • **se le considera un político ya ~** he's regarded as a political has-been • **ya está ~ como futbolista** he's had it as a footballer* • **un artista ~ por salir demasiado en televisión** an artist who has become overexposed through being on television too much
3* (= *harto*) sick and tired* • **la vecina me tiene ~** I've had it up to here with the woman next door*, I'm sick and tired of the woman next door* • **estar ~ con algo** to be sick and tired of sth*
4 (*LAm*) (= *bronceado*) tanned
5 (*Chile**) (= *falto de suerte*) unlucky • **nací ~** I was born unlucky • **es tan ~ el pobre** he's such an unlucky guy*
SM **1** (= *acto*) burning; (*Med*) cauterization
2 (*LAm*) burnt field
3 quemados (= *heridos*) burn victims • **los ~s evolucionan favorablemente** the burn victims are making good progress; ▹ **unidad**
quemador SM burner ▸ **quemador de gas** gas burner
quemadura SF **1** (= *herida*) (*por fuego, sol*) burn; (*por líquido hirviendo*) scald • **una ~ de cigarro** a cigarette burn • **~ de primer/segundo grado** first-/second-degree burn ▸ **quemaduras de sol, quemaduras solares** sunburn (*sing*)
2 [*de fusible*] blow-out
3 (*Bot*) (*por helada*) cold blight; (= *tizón*) smut
quemar ▹ CONJUG 1a VT **1** (= *hacer arder*) **a** [*fuego, sol*] [+ *papeles, mueble, arroz, patatas*] to burn; [+ *edificio*] to burn down; [+ *coche*] to set fire to • **lo ~on vivo** he was burned alive • **las ~on en la hoguera** they were burned at the stake • **tenía el rostro quemado por el sol** he had a sunburned face • **el incendio ha quemado varias hectáreas de bosque** the fire has destroyed *o* burned down several hectares of woodland • **he quemado la camisa con la plancha** I scorched *o* burned my shirt with the iron • **los guerrilleros ~on varias aldeas** the guerrillas set fire to *o* burned several villages; ▹ **nave**
b [*líquido hirviendo*] to scald; [*ácido, frío, helada*] to burn • **la pomada parece que te quema el brazo** the cream makes your arm burn
2 (= *dar sensación de calor*) [*radiador, especia picante*] to burn • **el radiador me está quemando la espalda** the radiator is burning my back • **esta bebida te quema la garganta** this drink burns your throat
3 [+ *fusible*] to blow
4 (= *gastar*) **a** [+ *calorías*] to burn, burn up; [+ *energías*] to burn off
b [+ *fortuna*] to squander; [+ *dinero*] to blow*,

squander; [+ *recursos*] to use up • **quemó su dinero en la lotería** he blew his money on the lottery* • **MODISMO**: • **~ etapas** to rush ahead with things
5* (= *fastidiar*) to bug*, get* • **lo que más me quemó fue que me tratara como a un estúpido** what bugged* me *o* got* me most was the way he treated me as if I was stupid
6 (= *desgastar*) [+ *político, gobierno*] to destroy, be the ruin of • **un escándalo sexual puede ~ a cualquier político** a sex scandal can destroy *o* can be the ruin of any politician • **tanto aparecer en televisión va a ~ su carrera** all these TV appearances will damage his career
7 (*Com*) [+ *precios*] to slash, cut; [+ *géneros*] to sell off cheap
8 (*Cuba*) (= *estafar*) to swindle
9 (*CAm*) (= *denunciar*) to denounce, inform on
10 (*Ven**) (*con arma de fuego*) to shoot
11 (*Arg, Uru*) • **~ a algn** to make a fool of sb
VI 1 (= *arder*) [*comida, líquido, metal*] to be boiling (hot); [*mejillas*] to be burning • **la sopa está quemando** the soup is boiling (hot) • **ya no quema** it's not too hot now • **le quemaban las mejillas** her cheeks were burning • **¡cómo quema el sol!** the sun's really scorching (hot)! • **este sol no quema nada** (*LAm*) you won't get tanned in this sun
2 (= *picar*) [*especia, picante*] to burn • **es una especia que quema en la lengua** this spice burns your tongue
VPR **quemarse** 1 [*persona*] (*con fuego*) to burn o.s.; (*con el sol*) to get burned • **se quemó con aceite hirviendo** he burned himself on hot oil • **me quemé la lengua con la sopa** I burned my tongue on the soup • **para no ~se con el sol** to avoid getting sunburnt • **~se a lo bonzo** to set fire to o.s.; ▹ **ceja**
2 (= *arder*) [*cuadros, papeles*] to get burned; [*edificio*] to burn down; [*comida*] to burn • **se está quemando la cortina** the curtain is getting burned • **se me ha quemado la cena** I've burned the dinner, the dinner has burned • **se han quemado 100 hectáreas de pinares en el incendio** 100 hectares of pinewood have been destroyed in the fire • **no te acerques a la chimenea que se te va a ~ la ropa** don't go too close to the fire or you'll scorch *o* burn your clothes • **por el olor parece que algo se está quemando** it smells like something is burning
3 (= *desprestigiarse*) • **tantos años trabajando en esto y aún no se ha quemado** so many years working on this and he's still going strong • **quiere hacer menos en televisión para no ~se en poco tiempo** he wants to do less television to avoid overexposure *o* becoming overexposed • **te quemás si salís con él** (*Arg, Uru*) you'll look really bad if you go out with him
4 (*en juego, adivinanzas*) • **caliente, caliente ... ¡que te quemas!** (you're getting) warm, warmer ... you're really hot *o* you're boiling!
5 (*Caribe*) (= *deprimirse*) to get depressed

quemarropa • **a ~** ADV point-blank

quemazón SF 1 (= *acción*) burning, combustion; (*CAm, Caribe, Méx*) fire
2 (= *calor intenso*) intense heat
3 (= *picazón*) (*Med*) burning sensation; (*fig*) itch
4 (= *comentario*) cutting remark
5 (= *resentimiento*) pique, resentment
6 (*Com*) (= *saldo*) bargain sale, cut-price sale
7 (*Cono Sur*) (= *espejismo*) mirage (*on the pampas*)

quemón¹* SM (*Méx*) (= *chasco*) disappointment, let-down

quemón²/ona‡ SM/F (*Méx*) dope smoker*

quena SF (*And, Cono Sur*) Indian flute

queo¹‡ SM (*Esp*) house

queo²* SM • **dar el ~** to shout a warning

quepis SM INV (*esp LAm*) (*Mil*) kepi, round military cap

quepo *etc* ▹ **caber**

queque SM (*LAm*) cake (*of various kinds*)

queratina SF keratin

queratinizarse ▹ CONJUG 1f VPR to keratinize

querella SF 1 (*Jur*) (= *acusación*) charge, accusation; (= *proceso*) suit, case • **interponer** *o* **presentar una ~ contra algn** to bring a lawsuit *o* an action against sb ▸ **querella por difamación** action for libel *o* defamation ▸ **querella privada** action for damages
2 (= *disputa*) dispute • **han olvidado sus viejas ~s** they have set aside their old disputes • **antiguas ~s familiares** old family feuds
3† (= *queja*) complaint

querellado/a SM/F defendant

querellante SMF (*Jur*) plaintiff • **la parte ~** the plaintiff

querellarse ▹ CONJUG 1a VPR 1 (= *quejarse*) to complain
2 (*Jur*) to file a complaint, bring an action (**ante** before, **contra, de** against)

querencia SF 1 (*Zool*) (= *instinto*) homing instinct
2 (*Zool*) (= *guarida*) lair, haunt
3 (*Taur*) (bull's) favourite spot
4 (= *terruño*) favourite haunt, home ground • **buscar la ~** to head for home
5 (= *morriña*) homesickness, longing for home

querendón/ona* (*LAm*) ADJ affectionate, loving
SM/F (= *cariñoso*) loving *o* affectionate person; (= *favorito*) favourite, favorite (*EEUU*), pet; (= *amante*) lover

querer

VERBO TRANSITIVO
VERBO INTRANSITIVO
VERBO PRONOMINAL
SUSTANTIVO MASCULINO

▹ CONJUG 2t

Para la expresión **querer decir**, *ver la otra entrada.*

VERBO TRANSITIVO

1 *a una persona* (= *amar*) to love; (= *apreciar*) to like • **¡te quiero!** I love you! • **quiero mucho a mis abuelos** I love my grandparents very much • **no estoy enamorado, pero la quiero mucho** I'm not in love with her, but I'm very fond of her • **la quiero con locura** I'm madly in love with her • **me quiere ... no me quiere** (*deshojando una margarita*) she loves me ... she loves me not • **en la oficina lo quieren mucho** he is well liked at the office • **~ bien a algn** to want the best for sb • **hacerse ~ por algn** to endear o.s. to sb • **~ mal a algn** to wish sb ill • **MODISMOS**: • **¡por lo que más quieras!** (*rogando*) by all that's sacred!; (*regañando*) for Heaven's sake! • **~ a algn como a la niña de sus ojos** to dote on sb • **la quiere como a la niña de sus ojos** she's the apple of his eye, he dotes on her

2 = *desear* a [+ *objeto*] to want • **¿cuál quieres?** which one do you want? • **¿qué más quieres?** (*lit*) what else do you want?; (*iró*) what more do you want? • **hace lo que quiere** she does what she wants *o* as she pleases • **se lo di, pero no lo quiso** I gave it to him, but he didn't want (to take) it • **¡lo que quieras!** as you wish!, have it your own way! • **¿quieres un café?** would you like some coffee? • **~ pelea** to be looking for trouble • **todo lo que tú quieras**: • **será muy feo y todo lo que tú quieras, pero es muy buena persona** he may be ugly and all that, but he's a very nice person
b (+ *infin*) to want • **~ hacer algo** to want to do sth • **quiere ser ingeniero** he wants to be an engineer • **lleva días que no quiere comer** she's been off her food for several days • **¿qué quieres comer hoy?** what would you like for dinner today? • **no quiso pagar** he refused to pay, he wouldn't pay • **ha querido quedarse en casa** he preferred to stay at home
c • **~ que algn haga algo** to want sb to do sth • **no quiero que vayas** I don't want you to go • **el destino quiso que volvieran a verse** fate decreed that they should see each other again • **la tradición quiere que ...** tradition has it that ... • **este quiere que le rompan la cabeza*** this guy is asking to get his head kicked in* • **¿quieres que me crea que tú solo te has bebido todo el whisky?** are you asking me to believe that you drank all the whisky by yourself? • **¿qué quieres que te diga?** what can I say? • **¿qué quieres que le haga?**: • **si se va por ahí sin hacer caso, ¿qué quieres que le haga?** if he goes off without taking any notice, what am I supposed to do *o* what can I do about it? • **si estudio y no apruebo, ¿qué quieres que le haga?** if I study and still don't pass, what can I do? • **¡qué más quisiera yo!** if only I could! • **¿qué más quisiera yo que ver juntos a mis hijos?** what more could I wish for *o* want than to see my children together?

3 = *tener intención de* (+ *infin*) • **no quería hacerte daño** I didn't mean to hurt you • **al ~ abrir la botella, saltó el tapón** the cork exploded while she was trying to open the bottle • **quiso hacerlo pero no pudo** he tried to do it but he couldn't

4 *pidiendo algo* • **quería dos kilos de patatas, por favor** I'd like two kilos of potatoes, please, could I have two kilos of potatoes, please? • **¿quieres darme tu nueva dirección?** would *o* could you give me your new address? • **¿querría participar en nuestra oferta?** would you like to take advantage of our offer? • **¿cuánto quieren por el coche?** what are they asking for the car?, how much do they want for the car?

5 = *requerir* • **¿para qué me querrá?** I wonder what he wants me for?, what can he want me for? • **el traje quiere un sombrero ancho** that dress needs a big hat to go with it

6 *uso impersonal* • **quería amanecer** dawn was about to break • **quiere llover** it looks like rain

VERBO INTRANSITIVO

1 = *desear* • **¿quieres?** (*ofreciendo algo*) do you want some?, would you like some? • **lo hago porque quiero** I do it because I want to • **—¿quieres casarte conmigo? —sí, quiero** "will you marry me?" — "yes, I will" • **—¿puedes enviar tú el correo? —como usted quiera** "could you take the post?" — "as you wish" • **mientras el jefe no quiera, no hay nada que hacer** as long as the boss is opposed, there's nothing to be done *o* nothing we can do about it • **ven cuando quieras** come whenever you like
• **MODISMOS**: • **como quiere**: • **¡está como quiere!** (*Esp‡*) she's a bit of all right!‡ • **tiene tanto dinero que vive como quiere** he's so rich he can live as he pleases • **quiera o no** • **quiera que no** whether he *etc* likes it or not

• **quieras o no, eso cambiará nuestras vidas** whether you like it or not, that's going to change our lives • **con el cambio de trabajo, quieras que no, se ha animado un poco** you may agree or disagree, but the fact is he's perked up a bit since he changed jobs
• REFRÁN: • **~ es poder** where there's a will there's a way
2 (= *tener intención*) • **lo hizo queriendo** he did it deliberately *o* on purpose • **lo hizo sin ~** he didn't mean to do it, he did it inadvertently
3 • **como quiera que** = **comoquiera** • **donde quiera que** = **dondequiera**
VERBO PRONOMINAL **quererse**
(*recíproco*) • **nosotros nos queremos** we love each other • **se quieren como hermanos** they love each other like brothers
SUSTANTIVO MASCULINO
• **cosas del ~** affairs of the heart • **dimitieron por culpa de algún ~** they resigned because of love affairs • **tener ~ a** to be fond of

---

querida SF mistress
querido/a ADJ **1** (= *amado*) dear • **~s amigos, nos hemos reunido para ...** dear friends, we are assembled here to ... • **nuestra querida patria** our beloved country • **sus seres ~s** his loved ones • **~s hermanos** (*Rel*) dearly beloved • **un alcalde ~ por todos** a mayor who is well-liked in the community, a popular mayor
2 (*en cartas*) dear • **Queridos padres:** Dear parents,
3 (*And*) nice
SM/F **1** (*uso apelativo*) darling • **¡sí, ~!** yes, darling!
2 (= *amante*) lover
querindongo/a SM/F lover
quermes SF, **quermés** SF kermes
querosén SM, **querosene** SM (*LAm*), **queroseno** SM kerosene, paraffin
querúbico ADJ cherubic
querubín SM cherub
quesadilla SF **1** (= *pastel*) cheesecake
2 (*LAm*) pasty, folded tortilla
quesera SF cheese dish; ▷ **quesero**
quesería SF **1** (= *tienda*) cheese shop, dairy
2 (= *fábrica*) cheese factory
3 (= *quesos*) cheeses (*pl*)
4 (= *productos lácteos*) dairy products (*pl*)
quesero/a ADJ • **la industria quesera** the cheese industry
SM/F cheesemaker; ▷ **quesera**
quesillo SM (*CAm*) *tortilla with cream cheese filling*
quesito SM cheese triangle
queso SM **1** (= *alimento*) cheese • **le huelen los pies a ~** he's got cheesy feet*
• MODISMOS: • **dársela a algn con ~*** to take sb in* • **estar como un ~*** to be tasty *o* dishy*
▸ **queso azul** blue cheese ▸ **queso crema** (*LAm*) cream cheese ▸ **queso de bola** Edam ▸ **queso de nata** cream cheese ▸ **queso de oveja** sheep's cheese ▸ **queso de puerco** (*Méx*) jellied pork ▸ **queso de untar** cheese spread ▸ **queso fundido** processed cheese, process cheese (*EEUU*) ▸ **queso helado**† ice-cream brick ▸ **queso manchego** *sheep's milk cheese made in La Mancha* ▸ **queso parmesano** Parmesan cheese ▸ **queso rallado** grated cheese
2 quesos‡ (= *pies*) plates*, feet
quetzal SM **1** (= *moneda*) *monetary unit of Guatemala*
2 (= *ave*) quetzal
quevedos SMPL pince-nez
quey SM (*And*) cake
quiá† EXCL never!, not on your life!
quíbole* EXCL (*Méx*) how's things?
quiche SM quiche
quichua ADJ Quechua, Quechuan
SMF Quechua(n) Indian
SM (*Ling*) Quechua
quichuismo SM Quechuan word *o* expression
quichuista SMF **1** (*LAm*) (= *especialista*) Quechua specialist
2 (*And, Cono Sur*) (= *hablante*) Quechua speaker
quicio SM doorjamb • MODISMOS: • **estar fuera de ~** to be out of joint • **sacar a algn de ~** to drive sb up the wall*, get on sb's nerves • **estas cosas me sacan de ~** these things make me see red *o* drive me mad
quico SM • MODISMO: • **ponerse como el ~** (*Esp*)* (= *comer mucho*) to stuff o.s.*; (= *engordar*) to get as fat as a pig
quid SM gist, crux • **dar en el ~** to hit the nail on the head • **he aquí el ~ de la cuestión** this is the crux of the matter
quídam SM **1** (= *alguien*) somebody (or other)
2 (= *don nadie*) nobody
quiebra SF **1** (*Econ*) bankruptcy • **ir a la ~** to go bankrupt ▸ **quiebra bancaria** bank failure ▸ **quiebra fraudulenta** fraudulent bankruptcy ▸ **quiebra voluntaria** voluntary bankruptcy
2 (= *deterioro*) breakdown • **la ~ de los valores tradicionales** the breakdown of traditional values
3† (= *grieta*) crack, fissure
4† (= *fracaso*) failure • **es algo que no tiene ~** it just can't go wrong
quiebre SM breaking, rupture
quiebro SM **1** (*Taur*) dodge, swerve
• MODISMO: • **dar el ~ a algn** to dodge sb
2 (*Mús*) grace note(s), trill
quien PRON REL **1** (*con antecedente*) **a** (*como sujeto*) who • **hablé con mi abogado, ~ me dio la razón** I spoke to my solicitor, who said I was right • **él es ~ se ocupa de estos asuntos** he is the one who deals with these things • **el Ayuntamiento será ~ se haga cargo de eso** it'll be the Council that take care of that
b (*como complemento*) who, whom (*frm*) • **su profesor, a ~ está dedicado el libro, siempre lo apoyó** his teacher, who the book is dedicated to, always supported him, his teacher, to whom the book is dedicated, always supported him (*frm*) • **el pintor a ~ describe en su libro** the painter he describes in his book, the painter whom he describes in his book (*frm*) • **la señorita con ~ hablaba** the young lady I was talking to, the young lady to whom I was talking (*frm*)
2 (*como indefinido*) **a** (+ *subjun*) • **un libro muy interesante para ~ sepa poco del tema** a very interesting book for anyone who knows little about the subject • **~es no estén de acuerdo que se vayan** anyone who doesn't agree can leave • **pregúntale a ~ quieras** ask anyone *o* whoever you like • **"a ~ corresponda"** "to whom it may concern"
b (+ *indic*) • **~ más se quejaba era él** the person who complained most was him, he was the one that *o* who complained the most • **yo hablo con ~ quiero** I'll speak to who I like • **la tierra es para ~ la trabaja** the land belongs to he who works it • **lo dijo como ~ anuncia una gran noticia** he said it like someone announcing some really important news • **hay ~ no piensa lo mismo** there are some *o* those who do not think the same • **no hay ~ lo aguante** no one can stand him • **¡no hay ~ te entienda!** there's no understanding you!
C • MODISMOS: • **~ más, ~ menos**: • **~ más, ~ menos tiene un amigo que ha estudiado en el extranjero** most of us have a friend who has studied abroad • **~ más, ~ menos, todos hemos tenido miedo a la oscuridad de pequeños** all of us, to some extent, have been afraid of the dark as children • **como ~ dice** so to speak • **nací en Navarra, a un paso, como ~ dice, de Francia** I was born in Navarre, just a stone's throw from France, so to speak • **como ~ no quiere la cosa**: • **se acercó, como ~ no quiere la cosa, a enterarse de lo que decíamos** he casually moved closer to us to find out what we were saying • **era capaz de beberse una botella de vino, como ~ no quiere la cosa** he was quite capable of drinking a whole bottle of wine, just like that *o* as if it were nothing • **como ~ oye llover**: • **estuve una hora intentando convencerlo, y él, como ~ oye llover** I spent an hour trying to persuade him but it was like water off a duck's back • **no ser ~**: • **él no es quién para decirme lo que tengo que hacer** it's not for him to tell me what to do • **tú no eres ~ para decirme si tengo que llegar a casa antes de las diez** it's not for you to tell me whether I should come home before ten
quién PRON **1** (*interrogativo*) (*como sujeto*) who; (*como complemento*) whom • **no sé ~ lo dijo primero** I don't know who said it first • **¿~ es esa chica?** who's that girl? • **—te han llamado —¿~ era?** "somebody phoned you" — "who was it?" • **¿a ~ se lo diste?** who did you give it to? • **¿a ~ le toca?** whose turn is it? • **¿con ~ estabas anoche?** who were you with last night? • **¿de ~ es la bufanda esa?** whose scarf is that? • **¿~ de ustedes lo reconoce?** which of you recognizes it?
2 (*exclamativo*) • **¡~ sabe!** who knows!
• **¡~ pudiese!** if only I could! • **¡~ lo hubiera dicho!** who would have thought it!
quienquiera PRON INDEF (PL: **quienesquiera**) whoever • **le cazaremos ~ que sea** we'll catch him whoever he is
• **~ que sea el responsable lo pagará** whoever is responsible will pay • **~ que críe un niño** whoever brings up a child, anybody who brings up a child • **dondequiera que estén y con ~ que estén** wherever and whoever they may be
quiera *etc* ▷ **querer**
quietismo SM quietism
quietista SMF quietist
quieto ADJ **1** [*animal, persona*] (= *parado*) still; (= *inmóvil*) motionless • **¡quieto!** (*al perro*) down boy!; (*a un niño*) keep still!, stop fidgeting!; (= *sé bueno*) behave yourself!
• **dejar algo ~** to leave sth alone • **¡estáte ~!** keep still! • **estar ~ como un poste** *o* **una estatua** to stand stock-still, be as still as a statue
2 [*carácter*] calm, placid
quietud SF [*de persona, noche*] stillness, quietude (*frm*); [*de situación*] calm
quif SM hashish
quihubo‡ EXCL (*Méx*) how's it going?
quijada SF jaw, jawbone
quijotada SF quixotic act
quijote SM quixotic person, dreamer, do-gooder*; (*pey*) well-meaning busybody
• **Don Quijote** Don Quixote
quijotería SF **1** = **quijotismo**
2 = **quijotada**
quijotescamente ADV quixotically
quijotesco ADJ quixotic
quijotismo SM quixotism
quil. ABR (= **quilates**) c
quilar** ▷ CONJUG 1a VT (*Esp*) to screw**
quilatar ▷ CONJUG 1a VT = **aquilatar**
quilate SM carat • **oro de 18 ~s** 18 carat gold
• MODISMO: • **de muchos ~s** high class, quality

quilco SM (*Chile*) large basket
quiligua SF (*Méx*) large basket
quilla[1] SF (*Náut*) keel • **colocar la ~ de un buque** to lay down a ship • **dar de ~** to keel over • MODISMO: • **pasar a algn por la ~** to keelhaul sb
quilla[2] SF (*LAm*) (= *cojín*) cushion
quillango SM (*Cono Sur*) blanket of furs, fur blanket
quilo[1] SM kilogramme, kilogram (EEUU)
quilo[2] SM (*Anat*) chyle • MODISMO: • **sudar el ~*** (= *sufrir*) to have a tough time; (= *trabajar*) to slave *o* slog away
quilo... PREF = **kilo...**
quilombear‡ ▷ CONJUG 1a VI (*Cono Sur*) to go whoring
quilombera‡ SF (*Cono Sur*) tart‡, slut‡, whore
quilombero‡ ADJ (*Cono Sur*) rowdy
quilombo SM (*And, Cono Sur*) **1** (= *burdel*) brothel
2 (= *choza*) rustic hut, shack
3* (= *lío*) mess
quiltrear* ▷ CONJUG 1a VT (*Cono Sur*) to annoy
quiltro* SM (*Cono Sur*) **1** (= *perrito*) (*gen*) lapdog; (*callejero*) stray dog, mongrel
2* (= *tipo pesado*) pest, nuisance
quimba SF **1** (*And, Caribe*) (= *calzado*) sandal
2 (*And*) (= *mueca*) grimace
3 quimbas (*And*) (= *dificultades*) difficulties; (= *deudas*) debts
quimbo SM (*Caribe*) knife, machete
quimera SF **1** (*Mit*) (= *monstruo imaginario*) chimera
2 (= *alucinación*) hallucination; (= *ilusión*) illusion, chimera; (= *noción*) fancy, fantastic idea; (= *sueño*) pipe dream
3 (= *sospecha*) unfounded suspicion • **tener la ~ de que ...** to suspect quite wrongly that ...
4 (= *riña*) quarrel
quimérico ADJ [*plan, proyecto, idea*] fanciful; [*esperanza*] impossible
quimerista ADJ **1** (= *soñador*) dreamy
2 (= *pendenciero*) quarrelsome; (= *ruidoso*) rowdy
SMF **1** (= *soñador*) dreamer, visionary
2 (= *pendenciero*) quarrelsome person; (= *ruidoso*) rowdy, brawler
quimerizar ▷ CONJUG 1f VI to indulge in fantasy *o* pipe dreams
química SF chemistry ▸ **química física** physical chemistry ▸ **química inorgánica** inorganic chemistry ▸ **química orgánica** organic chemistry
químicamente ADV chemically
químico/a ADJ chemical
SM/F chemist
quimio* SF (= *quimioterapia*) chemo*
quimioterapia SF chemotherapy
quimono SM kimono
quimoterapia SF chemotherapy
quina SF **1** (*Bot*) quinine, Peruvian bark • MODISMOS: • **ser más malo que la ~*** to be a little horror • **tragar ~*** to have to put up with it
2 (= *vino*) tonic wine
quinaquina SF (*Med*) quinine, cinchona bark
quincalla SF **1** (= *ferretería*) hardware, ironmongery
2 (= *baratija*) trinket
quincallería SF ironmonger's (shop), hardware store (EEUU)
quincallero/a SM/F ironmonger, hardware dealer (EEUU)
quince ADJ INV, PRON (*gen*) fifteen; (*ordinal, en la fecha*) fifteenth • **le escribí el día ~ I** wrote to him on the fifteenth • **~ días** a fortnight • MODISMO: • **dar ~ y raya a algn** to be able to beat sb with one hand tied behind one's back; ▷ **seis**
SM (= *número*) fifteen; (= *fecha*) fifteenth • **los Quince** the 15 member nations (*of the EU*)
quinceañera SF (*Méx*) *coming-out ball for girls who have reached their 15th birthday*
quinceañero/a ADJ fifteen-year-old; (*en general*) teenage
SM/F fifteen-year-old; (*en general*) teenager
quinceavo ADJ, SM fifteenth
quincena SF **1** (= *quince días*) fortnight, two weeks • **la segunda ~ de enero** the second half of January, the last two weeks in January
2 (= *condena*) fortnight's imprisonment
3 (= *pago*) fortnightly pay
quincenal ADJ fortnightly, bimonthly (EEUU)
quincenalmente ADV fortnightly, once a fortnight, semimonthly (EEUU)
quinceno ADJ fifteenth
quincha SF (*LAm*) *wall or roof etc made of rushes and mud*
quinchar ▷ CONJUG 1a VI (*LAm*) to build walls *etc* of "quincha"
quincho SM (*Cono Sur*) (= *choza*) mud hut; (*And, Cono Sur*) (= *cerco*) mud wall; (*Cono Sur*) (= *restaurán*) steak restaurant
quincuagenario/a ADJ, SM/F fifty-year-old
Quincuagésima SF Quinquagesima Sunday
quincuagésimo ADJ fiftieth; ▷ **sexto**
quindécimo ADJ fifteenth
quinfa SF (*And*) sandal
quingentésimo ADJ five-hundredth; ▷ **sexto**
quingo SM **1** (*And*) twist, turn
2 quingos zigzag (*sing*)
quinguear ▷ CONJUG 1a VI (*And*) (= *girar*) to twist, turn; (= *zigzaguear*) to zigzag
quiniela SF **1** (= *boleto*) pools coupon • **echar la ~** to hand in one's coupon
2 (= *juego*) football pool(s) • **jugar a la ~** *o* **a las ~s** to do the (football) pools ▸ **quiniela hípica** horse-racing totalizator

QUINIELA
The **quiniela** is the Spanish equivalent of the football pools and coupons are available from **estancos**. Players can predict a home win (1), a draw (X) or an away win (2) for most premier and first division matches. 15 correct forecasts gets the biggest prize but 10 or more correct forecasts also wins some money. The sums won vary from week to week depending on the takings or **recaudación**. There is also a version for horse racing known as the **quiniela hípica**.
▷ ESTANCO

quinielista SMF pools punter, participant in a football pool
quinielístico ADJ pools (*antes de s*) • **boleto ~** pools coupon • **peña quinielística** pools syndicate
quinientos/as ADJ, PRON, SMPL/SFPL (*gen*) five hundred; (*ordinal*) five hundredth • **en el ~** in the sixteenth century • MODISMO: • **volvió a las (mil) quinientas*** he got back at some ungodly hour; ▷ **seiscientos**
quinina SF quinine
quino SM (*LAm*) cinchona, cinchona tree
quinqué SM **1** (*para iluminar*) oil lamp
2* (= *astucia*) know-how, shrewdness • **tener mucho ~** to know what's what, know what the score is*
quinquenal ADJ quinquennial • **plan ~** five-year plan
quinquenalmente ADV every five years
quinquenio SM quinquennium, five-year period
quinqui* SM (= *delincuente*) small-time delinquent; (= *vendedor*) small-time dealer
quinta SF **1** (= *casa de campo*) villa, country house; (*LAm*) (= *chalet*) house; (= *finca*) *small estate on the outskirts of a town*
2 (*Mil*) draft, call-up • **ser de la (misma) ~ de algn** to be the same age as sb • **la ~ de 1998** the 1998 call-up, the class called up in 1998 • **entrar en ~s** (= *tener edad*) to reach the call-up age; (= *ser llamado*) to be called up
3 (*Mús*) fifth
quintacolumnista SMF fifth columnist
quintada* SF joke, trick
quintaescencia SF, **quintaesencia** SF quintessence
quintaesencial ADJ quintessential
quintal SM **1** (= *medida*) 100lbs • **esto pesa un ~*** (*fig*) this weighs a ton* ▸ **quintal métrico** ≈ 100kg
2 (*Castilla*) (= *peso*) ≈ 46kg
quintar ▷ CONJUG 1a VT (*Mil*) to call up, conscript, draft (EEUU)
quintería SF farmhouse
quintero SM (= *agricultor*) farmer; (= *bracero*) farmhand, labourer, laborer (EEUU)
quinteto SM quintet
quintilla SF (*Literat, Hist*) *five-line stanza*
quintillizo/a SM/F quintuplet
Quintín SM • MODISMOS: • **se armó la de San ~*** all hell broke loose* • **se va a armar la de San ~** there will be an almighty row* • **costó la de San ~*** it cost a bomb*
quinto ADJ fifth • **quinta columna** fifth column; ▷ **sexto**
SM **1** (*Mat*) fifth
2 (*Mil*) conscript, draftee (EEUU), national serviceman
3* (= *juego*) bingo
4 (*Méx*) (= *moneda*) nickel
5 (= *botellín*) small bottle of beer
quíntral SM (*And, Cono Sur*) **1** (*Zool*) armadillo
2 (*Mús*) ten-stringed guitar
quíntuple SMF (*Chile, Ven*) quintuplet
quintuplicar ▷ CONJUG 1g VT to quintuple
VPR **quintuplicarse** to quintuple • **el número de casos se ha quintuplicado** the number of cases has increased fivefold, there has been a fivefold increase in the number of cases
quíntuplo ADJ quintuple, fivefold
SM quintuple • **25 es el ~ de 5** 25 is five times more than 5
quinzavo ADJ, SM = **quinceavo**
quiña SF (*And*), **quiñadura** SF (*And*) scratch
quiñar* ▷ CONJUG 1a VT (*And*) to scratch
quiñazo SM (*LAm*) smash, collision
quiño SM (*LAm*) (= *puñetazo*) punch
quiñón SM piece of land, plot of land
quiñonero SM part owner (of a piece of land)
quiosco SM [*de venta*] kiosk, stand, stall; (= *pabellón*) summerhouse, pavilion ▸ **quiosco de música** bandstand ▸ **quiosco de necesidad** public lavatory ▸ **quiosco de periódicos** news stand
quiosquero/a SM/F owner of a news-stand, newspaper seller
quipe SM (*And*) knapsack, rucksack, backpack (EEUU)
quipo SM, **quipos** SMPL (*And*) (*Hist*) quipu, *Inca system of recording information using knotted strings*
quipu SM = **quipo**

quique (SM) (*Chile*) grison
quiqui** (SM) screw** • **echar un ~** to have a screw**, play hide the sausage*
quiquiriquí (SM) cock-a-doodle-doo
quirico (SM) (*Caribe*) (= *criado*) servant; (= *mensajero*) messenger; (= *ladrón*) petty thief
quirófano (SM) operating theatre, operating room (*EEUU*) • **pasar por la mesa del ~** to go under the knife*
quirógrafo (SM) (*Méx*) IOU
quirología (SF) palmistry, chiromancy
quiromancia (SF) palmistry
quiromántico/a (SM/F) palmist
quiromasaje (SM) massage
quiropedia (SF), **quiropodia** (SF) chiropody, podiatry (*EEUU*)
quiropodista (SMF) chiropodist, podiatrist (*EEUU*)
quiropráctica (SF) osteopathy
quiropráctico/a (SM/F) chiropractor
quiroterapeuta (SMF) chiropractor
quirquincho (SM) (*Cono Sur*) *species of armadillo*
quirúrgicamente (ADV) surgically • **intervenir ~ a algn** to operate on sb
quirúrgico (ADJ) surgical • **se puede tratar sin intervención quirúrgica** it can be treated without surgery
quise *etc* ▷ **querer**
quisicosa* (SF) puzzle, conundrum
quisling ['kizlin] (SM) (PL: **quislings** ['kizlin]) quisling
quisque* (SM), **quisqui*** (SM) • **cada** *o* **todo ~** (absolutely) everyone, every man-Jack • **como cada ~** like everyone else • **ni ~** not a living soul • **ser un ~** (*gen*) to be a fusspot*; (= *detallista*) to have a mania for details
quisquilla (SF) **1** (*Zool*) shrimp
2 (= *nimiedad*) trifle, triviality
3 (= *pega*) slight snag, minor problem
4 quisquillas (= *sofisterías*) quibbles, quibbling, hair-splitting • **¡déjate de ~s!** (= *no seas quisquilloso*) stop fussing!; (= *no protestes*) stop quibbling! • **pararse en ~s** (= *reñir*) to bicker; (= *protestar*) to quibble
quisquilloso (ADJ) **1** (= *susceptible*) touchy, oversensitive; (= *irritable*) irritable; (= *perfeccionista*) pernickety*, persnickety (*EEUU**), choosy, fussy
2 (= *preocupado por nimiedades*) too bothered about petty details
quiste (SM) cyst ▸ **quiste ovárico** ovarian cyst ▸ **quiste sebáceo** sebaceous cyst
quístico (ADJ) cystic • **fibrosis quística** cystic fibrosis
quisto (ADJ) • **bien ~** = **bienquisto** • **mal ~** = **malquisto**
quita (SF) **1** [*de deuda*] release
2 (*LAm*) (= *descuento*) rebate
3 • **de ~ y pon: un cuello de ~ y pon** a detachable collar • **una moda de ~ y pon** a passing fashion • **la actitud que adopta es de ~ y pon** he's just adopting that attitude because it's expedient
quitacutículas (SM INV) cuticle cream, cuticle conditioner
quitaesmalte (SM), **quitaesmaltes** (SM INV) nail-polish *o* nail-varnish remover
quitagusto (SM) (*And*) intruder, gatecrasher
quitahielo (SM) windscreen scraper
quitaipón • **de ~** (= *de quita y pon*) ▷ **quita**
quitalodos (SM INV) boot scraper
quitamanchas (SM INV) **1** (= *producto*) stain remover
2† (= *oficio*) dry cleaner; (= *tienda*) dry-cleaner's (shop)
quitamiedos (SM INV) (*Esp*) handrail
quitamotas* (SM INV) bootlicker*, toady
quitanieves (SM INV) snowplough, snowplow (*EEUU*)
quitapelillos* (SM INV) bootlicker*, toady
quitapenas (SM INV) **1‡** (= *pistola*) pistol, rod (*EEUU‡*); (= *navaja*) knife, chiv‡
2 (= *consuelo*) comforter, solace
3 (= *licor*) stiff drink
quitapesares (SM INV) comfort, distraction
quitapiedras (SM INV) (*Ferro*) cowcatcher
quitapintura (SF) paint remover, paint stripper
quitapón = **quitaipón** ▷ **quita**
quitar ▷ CONJUG 1a (VT) **1** (= *sacar*) (*gen*) to remove; [+ *ropa, zapatos*] to take off; [+ *póster, estantes*] to take down • **le ~on las vendas** they took her bandages off, they removed her bandages • **tardaron dos días en ~ los escombros** it took two days to clear *o* remove the rubble • **~on las banderas de los balcones** they took the flags down from the balconies, they removed the flags from the balconies • **quita eso de allí** get that away from there • **querían ~le de su puesto** they wanted to remove him from his post • **~ la mesa** to clear the table • MODISMOS: • **~ de en medio a algn** to get rid of sb • **no ~le ojo a algn** not to take one's eyes off sb
2 (= *arrebatar*) (*gen*) to take away; (*para robar*) to take, steal; [+ *vida*] to take • **su hermana le quitó la pelota** his sister took the ball away from him • **me ~on la licencia** I had my licence taken away • **le ~on la cartera en el tren** someone took his wallet on the train, he had his wallet stolen on the train • **me quitó la novia** he stole my girlfriend • **~ el sitio a algn** to steal sb's place
3 (= *eliminar*) [+ *mancha*] to remove, get rid of; [+ *dolor*] to relieve, stop; [+ *felicidad, ilusión, ganas*] to take away; [+ *preocupaciones, temores*] to allay • **me quitó las ganas de comer** it took my appetite away • **trataba de ~me esa idea de la cabeza** she tried to make me change my mind • **~ el hambre**: • **un par de rodajas deben ~ el hambre** a couple of slices should stop you feeling hungry • **no alimenta mucho, pero quita el hambre** it's not very nutritious, but it's filling • **~ la sed** to quench one's thirst • **el vino no quita la sed** wine doesn't quench your thirst, wine isn't thirst-quenching • **~ el sueño**: • **el café me quita el sueño** coffee stops me sleeping • **ese asunto no me quita el sueño** I'm not losing any sleep over that matter
4 (= *restar*) • **no quita nada de su valor** it does not detract at all from its value • **no le quiero ~ méritos** I don't want to detract from him • **eso le quita la razón** that shows he's wrong, that proves him wrong • **quiero ~ unos cuantos centímetros a mi cintura** I want to lose a few centimetres from around the waist • **me quita mucho tiempo** it takes up a lot of my time • **~ extensión a un campo** to reduce the size of a field • **~ importancia a algo** to play sth down • **quitando el postre comimos bien** apart *o* aside from the dessert we had a good meal • **quitando tres o cuatro, van a ir todos** except for three or four (people), everybody is going
5 (= *impedir*) • **~ a algn de hacer algo** to stop *o* prevent sb (from) doing sth
6 (*Mat*) to take away, subtract
7 [+ *golpe*] to ward off; (*Esgrima*) to parry
8‡ [+ *dinero*] to make
(VI) • **¡quita!, ¡quita de ahí!** (= *¡aparta!*) get out of the way!; (= *¡qué va!*) get away!, come off it! • MODISMOS: • **eso no quita**: • **eso no quita para que me ayudes** that doesn't stop *o* prevent you helping me, that doesn't mean you can't help me • **eso no quita que eche de menos a mi mujer** that doesn't mean I don't miss my wife • **ni quito ni pongo** I'm neutral, I'm not saying one thing or the other; ▷ **quita**
(VPR) **quitarse 1** (= *apartarse*) • **¡quítate de ahí!** • **¡quítate de en medio!** get out of the way! • **¡quítate de mi vista!** get out of my sight! • **me quito** (*And**) I'm off, I must be going
2 (= *desaparecer*) [*dolor*] to go, go away; [*mancha*] to come out • **esa mancha de vino no se quita** that wine stain won't come out
3 (= *acabarse*) • **se me quitan las ganas de ir** I don't feel like going now • **se me ~on las ganas de viajar** I no longer felt like travelling
4 (= *sacarse*) **a** [+ *ropa, zapatos*] to take off; [+ *barba*] to shave; [+ *lentillas*] to take out • **~se años: te has quitado diez años (de encima)** you look ten years younger • **no te quites años** don't lie about your age • **~se la preocupación** to stop worrying • **~se una muela** to have a tooth out
b • **~se algo/a algn de encima** to get rid of sth/sb • **¡ya me he quitado de encima el coche viejo!** at last I've got rid of the old car! • **¡no me la puedo ~ de encima!** I can't get rid of her! • **¡qué peso nos hemos quitado de encima!** what a relief!, that's a real weight off our minds!
5 • **~se de** (= *dejar*): • **~se de un vicio** to give up a bad habit • **~se del tabaco** to give up smoking • **quitémonos de tonterías** let's stop being silly
quitasol (SM) sunshade, parasol
quitasueño (SM) worry, problem
quite (SM) **1** (= *acción*) removal
2 (= *movimiento*) (*gen*) dodge, sidestep; (*Esgrima*) parry; (*Taur*) distracting manoeuvre *o* (*EEUU*) maneuver • **estar al ~** to be always ready to help *o* be at hand • **hacer el ~ a algn** (*Cono Sur*) to avoid sb • **esto no tiene ~** there's no help for it
3 (*LAm*) (*Dep*) tackle
quiteño/a (ADJ) of *o* from Quito (SM/F) native *o* inhabitant of Quito • **los ~s** the people of Quito
Quito (SM) Quito
quitrín (SM) (*CAm, Caribe, Cono Sur*) (= *vehículo*) trap
quiubo* (EXCL) (*Chile, Méx*) hi!, how's it going?*
quizá (ADV), **quizás** (ADV) perhaps, maybe • —**¿vienes o no?** —**quizá** "are you coming?" — "perhaps" • **~ llegue mañana, si tenemos suerte** if we're lucky it may arrive tomorrow *o* perhaps it will arrive tomorrow • **~ no** maybe not
quórum ['kworum] (SM) (PL: **quórums** ['kworum]) quorum • **constituir ~** to make up a quorum • **la reunión no pudo celebrarse por falta de ~** the meeting could not be held because there wasn't a quorum *o* (*frm*) because it was inquorate

Rr

R, r ['ere] SF (= *letra*) R, r

R. ABR **1** (*Rel*) (= **Reverendo**) Rev, Revd
2 (= **Real**) R
3 = **Rey, Reina**
4 = **remite, remitente**
5 (= **río**) R

rabada SF hindquarter, rump

rabadán SM head shepherd

rabadilla SF **1** (*Anat*) coccyx
2 (*Culin*) [*de pollo*] parson's nose*, pope's nose (*EEUU*)

rabanillo SM wild radish

rábano SM radish • MODISMOS: • **¡un ~!*** get away! • **me importa un ~*** I don't care *o* give two hoots* • **tomar el ~ por las hojas** to get the wrong end of the stick* ▸ **rábano picante** horseradish

rabear ▹ CONJUG 1a VI to wag its tail

rabelasiano ADJ Rabelaisian

rabí SM (PL: **rabíes**) rabbi

rabia SF **1** (*Med*) rabies
2 (= *ira*) fury, anger • **me da ~** it makes me mad *o* infuriates me • **¡qué ~!** (= *ira*) isn't it infuriating!; (= *pena*) what a pity! • MODISMO: • **con ~**: • **llueve con ~** it's raining with a vengeance • **es fea con ~** she's as ugly as sin*
3 (= *antipatía*) • **tener ~ a algn** to have a grudge against sb, have it in for sb* • **el maestro le tiene ~** the teacher has it in for him*, the teacher doesn't like him • **tomar ~ a algn/algo** to take a dislike to sb/sth

rabiadero SM (*And*) fit of rage

rabiar ▹ CONJUG 1b VI **1** (*Med*) to have rabies, be rabid
2* (= *sufrir*) (*de dolor*) to be in great pain • **estaba rabiando de dolor de muelas** she had a raging toothache
3* (= *encolerizarse*) • **hacer ~ a algn** to infuriate sb, make sb see red • **las cosas así le hacen ~** things like that infuriate him *o* make him see red • **¡para que rabies!** so there! • MODISMOS: • **a ~***: • **me gusta a ~** (= *muchísimo*) I just love it • **que rabia**: • **está que rabia** (= *furioso*) he's hopping mad*, he's furious • **esta sopa quema que rabia** this soup is hot enough to burn the roof of your mouth off* • **este cóctel está que rabia** (= *buenísimo*) this cocktail has a real kick to it*
4* (= *anhelar*) • **~ por algo** to long for sth, be dying for sth • **~ por hacer algo** to be dying to do sth

rabiasca SF (*Caribe*) fit of temper

rabicorto ADJ short-tailed

rabieta SF tantrum • **coger(se) una ~** to throw a tantrum, fly into a rage

rabietas* SMF INV touchy sort, bad-tempered person

rabilargo ADJ long-tailed

rabillo SM **1** (*Bot*) leaf stalk
2 (*Anat*) small tail
3 (= *punta*) tip; (= *parte delgada*) thin part; (= *tira*) thin strip of material • **mirar por el ~ del ojo** to look out of the corner of one's eye

rabimocho ADJ (*And, Caribe, Méx*) short-tailed

rabínico ADJ rabbinical

rabino SM rabbi • **gran ~** chief rabbi

rabión SM (*tb* **rabiones**) rapids (*pl*)

rabiosamente ADV **1** (= *furiosamente*) furiously, in a rage
2 [*doler*] terribly
3 (= *fanáticamente*) rabidly

rabioso ADJ **1** (*Med*) rabid • **perro ~** (*lit*) rabid dog; (*fig*) mad dog
2 (= *furioso*) [*persona*] furious; [*aficionado*] rabid, fervent • **poner ~ a algn** to enrage sb, make sb livid • **de rabiosa actualidad** highly topical
3 [*dolor*] terrible

rabo SM **1** (*Zool*) tail • MODISMOS: • **con el ~ entre las piernas** with one's tail between one's legs • **queda el ~ por desollar** the hardest part is still to come ▸ **rabo cortado** docked tail ▸ **rabo de buey** oxtail; ▹ **cabo**
2** (= *pene*) cock**, dick** ▸ **rabo verde** (*CAm*) dirty old man*

rabón ADJ **1** [*animal*] (= *de rabo pequeño*) short-tailed; (= *sin rabo*) tailless
2 (*LAm*) (= *pequeño*) short, small
3 (*Cono Sur*) (= *desnudo*) stark naked
4 (*Caribe, Cono Sur*) [*cuchillo*] damaged
5 (*Méx*) (= *desgraciado*) down on one's luck

rabona SF **1** • **hacer (la) ~** (*Escol*) to play truant, skip school, play hookey (*EEUU**)
2 (*LAm*) (= *prostituta*) camp follower

rabonear ▹ CONJUG 1a VI (*Cono Sur*) to play truant, skip school, play hookey (*EEUU**)

rabosear ▹ CONJUG 1a VT to mess up, rumple, crumple

rabotada SF rude remark

rabudo ADJ long-tailed

raca[1]* SF (*CAm*) (= *mamá*) mummy*

raca[2] (**†) SM (*Aut*) banger*

racanear* ▹ CONJUG 1a VI **1** (*con el dinero*) to be stingy*
2 (*en el trabajo*) to slack

racaneo* SM, **racanismo*** SM **1** (*con el dinero*) stinginess
2 (*en el trabajo*) slackness, idleness

rácano/a* ADJ **1** (= *tacaño*) stingy*, mean
2 (= *vago*) bone idle
3 (= *artero*) sly, cunning
SM/F **1** (= *tacaño*) mean devil, scrooge*
2 (= *vago*) slacker, idler • **hacer el ~** to slack

RACE SM ABR (= **Real Automóvil Club de España**) ≈ RAC, ≈ AA, ≈ AAA (*EEUU*)

racha SF **1** (*Meteo*) gust of wind
2 (= *periodo*) string, series • **buena ~** run of good luck • **mala ~** run of bad luck • MODISMOS: • **a ~s** by fits and starts • **estar de ~** (= *de suerte*) to be in luck; (*Dep*) (= *en forma*) to be in form

rache SM (*Caribe*) zip, zipper (*EEUU*)

racheado ADJ gusty, squally

rachi‡ SM night

rachir ▹ CONJUG 3h VT (*Cono Sur*) to scratch

rachoso ADJ (*Cono Sur*) ragged

racial ADJ racial, race (*antes de s*) • **odio ~** racial hatred, race hatred • **disturbios ~es** race riots

racialmente ADV racially

racimo SM **1** [*de uvas*] bunch, cluster
2 [*de flores*] (= *ramo*) bunch; (*Bot*) raceme

raciocinación SF ratiocination

raciocinar ▹ CONJUG 1a VI to reason

raciocinio SM **1** (= *facultad*) reason
2 (= *razonamiento*) reasoning

ración SF **1** (*Mat*) ratio
2 (= *porción*) portion, helping; (*Mil*) ration • **una ~ de jamón** a portion of ham • **una ~ de albóndigas** a portion *o* plate of meatballs • **darse una ~ de vista†** to have a good look ▸ **ración de campaña** field rations (*pl*) ▸ **ración de hambre** starvation wage
3 (*Rel*) prebend

racional ADJ **1** (*Mat, Fil*) rational
2 (= *razonable*) reasonable, sensible

racionalidad SF rationality

racionalismo SM rationalism

racionalista ADJ, SMF rationalist

racionalización SF **1** (*Psic, Fil*) rationalization
2 (*Com*) streamlining, rationalization

racionalizador ADJ **1** (*Psic, Fil*) rationalizing
2 (*Com*) streamlining, rationalizing

racionalizar ▹ CONJUG 1f VT **1** (*Psic, Fil*) to rationalize
2 (*Com*) to streamline, rationalize (*euf*)

racionalmente ADV rationally, reasonably, sensibly

racionamiento SM rationing

racionar ▹ CONJUG 1a VT **1** (= *limitar*) to ration • **estar racionado** to be rationed
2 (= *distribuir*) to ration out, share out

racionero SM (*Rel*) prebendary

racionista SMF **1** (= *que percibe pensión*) person living on an allowance
2 (= *actor*) (*de papeles pequeños*) player of bit parts; (*de ínfima clase*) ham*, third-rate actor/actress

racismo SM racism, racialism

racista ADJ, SMF racist, racialist

raco* SM (*CAm*) (= *papá*) daddy*

rada SF (*Náut*) roads (*pl*), roadstead

radar SM (= *sistema*) radar; (= *estación*) radar station

radárico ADJ radar (*antes de s*)

radiación SF **1** (*Fís*) radiation ▸ **radiación solar** solar radiation ▸ **radiación ultravioleta** ultraviolet radiation
2 (*Radio*) broadcasting

radiactividad SF radioactivity • **detector de ~** Geiger counter

radiactivo ADJ radioactive

radiado ADJ **1** (*Radio*) radio (*antes de s*) • **en una entrevista radiada** in a radio interview
2 (*Bot*) radiate

radiador SM radiator

radial ADJ **1** (*Mec*) radial
2 (*LAm*) (*Radio*) radio (*antes de s*) • **comedia ~** radio play

3 (*Aut*) • **carretera ~** radial trunk road, *trunk road leading from periphery of a country to its centre*
radiante ADJ **1** (*Fís*) radiant
2 [*persona*] radiant • **estaba ~** she was radiant (**de** with)
radiar[1] ▸ CONJUG 1b VT **1** (*Fís*) to radiate
2 (*Radio*) to broadcast
3 (*Med*) to treat with radiation
radiar[2] ▸ CONJUG 1b VT **1** (*LAm*) (= *borrar*) to delete, cross off; (= *suprimir*) to remove
2 (= *expulsar*) to expel
radicado ADJ • **~ en** based in
radical ADJ, SMF radical
SM **1** (*Ling*) root
2 (*Mat*) square-root sign
3 (*Quím*) radical
radicalidad SF (= *cualidad*) radical nature; (*Pol*) radicalism
radicalismo SM radicalism
radicalización SF [*de pensamiento*] increasing radicalism, radicalization (*frm*); [*de posturas, política*] toughening, radicalization (*frm*); [*de conflicto*] intensification
radicalizar ▸ CONJUG 1f VT to radicalize
VPR **radicalizarse 1** (*Pol*) to become more radical, radicalize
2 [*conflicto*] to intensify
radicalmente ADV radically
radicar ▸ CONJUG 1g VI **1** [*dificultad, problema*] • **~ en** to lie in • **el problema no radicaba en la situación política** the (root) cause of the problem was not the political situation
2 (*frm*) (= *localizarse*) to be, be situated, lie • **la sede principal radica en Barcelona** the headquarters are in Barcelona • **el centro de acogida radica dentro de la reserva natural** the reception centre is inside the nature reserve
3 (*Bot*) to take root
VPR **radicarse** to establish o.s. (**en** in)
radicha* SMF (*Cono Sur*) radical
radicheta* SF (*Cono Sur*) (*hum*) radical
radícula SF radicle
radiestesia SF water divining, dowsing
radio[1] SM **1** (*Mat*) radius • **en un ~ de 10km** within a radius of 10km • **de corto ~** short-range (*antes de s*) • **de largo ~** long-range (*antes de s*) ▸ **radio de acción** [*de autoridad*] jurisdiction, extent of one's authority; (*Aer*) range • **un avión de largo ~ de acción** a long-range aircraft ▸ **radio de giro** turning circle
2 [*de rueda*] spoke
3 (*Quím*) radium
4 (*Anat*) radius
5 (= *mensaje*) wireless message
6 (*LAm*) = **radio**[2]
radio[2] SF radio • **por ~** by radio, on the radio, over the radio • **hablar por ~** to talk on the radio ▸ **radio digital** digital radio ▸ **radio libre** pirate radio ▸ **radio macuto*** • **enterarse de algo por ~ macuto** to hear sth on the grapevine ▸ **radio pirata** (= *sistema*) pirate radio; (= *emisora*) pirate radio station
radio... PREF radio...
radioactividad SF = **radiactividad**
radioactivo ADJ = **radiactivo**
radioaficionado/a SM/F radio ham*, amateur radio enthusiast
radioantena SF (*Radio*) antenna; (*Astron*) radio telescope
radioastronomía SF radio astronomy
radiobaliza SF radio beacon
radiobiología SF radiobiology
radiobúsqueda SF radiopaging
radiocaptar ▸ CONJUG 1a VT to listen in to, pick up
radiocarbono SM radiocarbon
radiocasete SM radio cassette, radio-cassette player
radiocomunicación SF radio contact, contact by radio
radiodespertador SM clock radio, radio alarm
radiodiagnóstico SM X-ray diagnosis
radiodifundir ▸ CONJUG 3a VT to broadcast
radiodifusión SF broadcasting
radiodifusora SF (*LAm*) radio station
radioemisora SF radio station
radioenlace SM radio link
radioescucha SMF listener
radioestesia SF water divining, dowsing
radiofaro SM radio beacon
radiofonía SF radiotelephony
radiofónico ADJ radio (*antes de s*)
radiogoniómetro SM direction finder
radiografía SF **1** (= *técnica*) radiography, X-ray photography
2 • **una ~** an X-ray, a radiograph (*frm*)
radiografiar ▸ CONJUG 1c VT **1** (*Med*) to X-ray
2 (*Radio*) to radio, send by radio
radiográfico ADJ X-ray (*antes de s*), radiographic (*frm*)
radiógrafo/a SM/F radiographer
radiograma SM radio message, radiogram
radiogramola† SF (*Esp*) radiogram
radioisótopo SM radioisotope
radiola SF (*Perú*) jukebox
radiólisis SF INV radiolysis
radiolocalización SF radiolocation
radiología SF radiology
radiológico ADJ **1** [*examen, diagnóstico*] X-ray (*antes de s*)
2 [*material, arma, ataque*] radiological
radiólogo/a SM/F radiologist
radiomensajería SF radiopaging
radionavegación SF radio navigation
radionovela SF radio serial
radiooperador(a) SM/F radio operator
radiopatrulla SM patrol car
radiorreceptor SM radio receiver, radio set ▸ **radiorreceptor de contrastación** monitor set
radioscopia SF radioscopy
radioso ADJ (*LAm*) radiant
radiotaxi SM radio cab, radio taxi
radiotécnica SF radio engineering
radiotécnico/a SM/F radio engineer
radiotelefonía SF radiotelephony
radiotelefonista SMF radiotelephonist
radioteléfono SM radiotelephone
radiotelegrafía SF radiotelegraphy
radiotelegrafiar ▸ CONJUG 1c VT to radiotelegraph
radiotelegrafista SMF radio operator
radiotelescopio SM radiotelescope
radioterapeuta SMF radiotherapist
radioterapia SF radiotherapy
radiotransmisión SF (= *acto*) transmission, broadcasting; (= *programa*) transmission, broadcast
radiotransmisor SM radio transmitter
radioyente SMF listener
radón SM radon
RAE SF ABR (*Esp*) = **Real Academia Española**

> **RAE**
> The **Real Academia Española de la Lengua** was created in 1713 to protect the purity of the Spanish language. There are 46 members appointed for life from among Spain's most prestigious writers and linguists. It works in collaboration with the 21 other Spanish language academies, which represent all the countries where Spanish is a native language. Its first dictionary, the six-volume **Diccionario de Autoridades**, was published between 1726 and 1739.

raedera SF scraper
raedura SF **1** (= *acto*) scrape, scraping
2 raeduras scrapings, filings
3 (*Med*) abrasion, graze
raer ▸ CONJUG 2y VT **1** (= *rascar*) to scrape; (= *quitar*) to scrape off
2 (*Med*) to graze, abrade (*frm*)
3 [+ *contenido*] to level off, level with the brim
VPR **raerse** (= *excoriarse*) to chafe; [*paño*] to fray
raf SM rough
Rafael SM Raphael
ráfaga SF **1** (*Meteo*) gust
2 [*de tiros*] burst
3 [*de intuición, luz*] flash
4 (*And, Cono Sur*) (= *racha*) run of luck • **estar de** o **en (mala) ~** to have a spell o run of bad luck, be going through a bad patch
rafaguear ▸ CONJUG 1a VT *to direct a burst of machine gun fire at*
VI *to fire a burst with a machine gun*
rafañoso* ADJ (*Cono Sur*) (= *sucio*) dirty; (= *ordinario*) coarse, common
rafia SF raffia
rafting ['raftin] SM white-water rafting
raglán ADJ INV • **manga ~** raglan sleeve
RAH SF ABR (*Esp*) = **Real Academia de la Historia**
rai ADJ, SM rai
raicear ▸ CONJUG 1a VI (*LAm*) to take root
raicero SM (*LAm*) root system, roots (*pl*)
raid [raid] SM (PL: **raids** [raid]) **1** (= *incursión*) [*de soldados*] raid; [*de policías*] police raid
2 (= *plaga*) attack, infestation
3 (*Aer*) long-distance flight; (*Aut*) rally drive
4 (= *esfuerzo*) attempt, endeavour, endeavor (*EEUU*); (= *empresa*) enterprise; (= *hazaña*) heroic undertaking; (*Dep*) endurance test
5 (*esp Méx*) (*Aut*) lift, ride (*EEUU*) • **pedir ~** to hitch a lift
raído ADJ **1** [*paño*] frayed, threadbare; [*ropa, persona*] shabby
2 (= *desvergonzado*) shameless
raigambre SF, (*a veces*) SM **1** (*Bot*) root system, roots (*pl*)
2 (= *tradición*) tradition; (= *antecedentes*) antecedents (*pl*), history • **tienen ~ liberal** they have a liberal tradition • **una familia de fuerte ~ local** a family with deep roots in the area
raigón SM **1** (*Bot*) thick root, stump
2 [*de diente*] root
rail SM, **raíl** SM rail ▸ **rail electrizado** electrified rail, live rail
Raimundo SM Raymond
raíz SF **1** [*de planta*] root • MODISMOS: • **de ~**: • **arrancar algo de ~** to root sth out completely • **cortar un problema de ~** to nip a problem in the bud • **echar raíces** [*planta*] to take root; [*persona*] to put down roots
2 [*de diente, pelo*] root
3 (*Mat*) ▸ **raíz cuadrada** square root ▸ **raíz cúbica** cube root
4 (= *origen*) root • **ha vuelto a sus raíces** he has gone back to his roots • **hay que llegar a la ~ del problema** we have to get to the root of the problem • **la bebida fue la ~ de todos sus males** drink was the root cause o was at the root of all his troubles
5 • **a ~ de** as a result of • **a ~ de su depresión dejó el trabajo** as a result of his depression he gave up his job
6 (*Ling*) root
7 (*Inform*) root
raja SF **1** (= *hendidura*) (*en la piel*) gash; (*en muro*) chink; (*en porcelana, cristal, madera*) crack
2 [*de melón, sandía*] slice
3** (= *vagina*) cunt**
4 • **sacar ~*** (= *sacar tajada*) to get a rake-off*,

get one's cut*
5 (Caribe) (= sangre negra) • tener ~ to have some black blood, be of African descent
6 (And) • MODISMO: • estar en la ~* (= sin dinero) to be broke*
7 rajas (Méx) (Culin) pickled green pepper
rajá (SM) rajah
rajada* (SF) 1 (Cono Sur) (= huida) flight, hasty exit
2 (Méx) (= cobardía) cowardly act
rajado/a* (SM/F) 1 (= canalla) swine*
2 (= cobarde) coward, chicken*
rajador (ADJ) (Cono Sur) fast
rajadura (SF) = raja
rajamacana* (SM) (Caribe) 1 (= trabajo duro) tough job
2 (= persona) (duro) tough character; (terco) stubborn person
3 (= experto) expert
4 • a ~ = a rajatabla ▸ rajatabla
rajante* (ADJ) (Cono Sur) (= perentorio) peremptory, sharp; (= inmediato) immediate
rajar ▸ CONJUG 1a (VT) 1 [+ papel, tejido] to tear, rip; [+ neumático, rueda] to slash; [+ vidrio, cerámica] to crack; [+ leña] to chop up
2* (= acuchillar) to cut up*
3 (LAm) (= calumniar) to slander, run down
4 (LAm‡) [+ examen] to flunk*, fail
5 (And, Caribe) (= aplastar) to crush, defeat; (= arruinar) to ruin; (= fastidiar) to annoy
6 (Cono Sur*) [+ trabajador] to fire*
(VI) 1* (= hablar mucho) to natter* • ~ de algn* (= criticar) to slag sb off*
2* (= jactarse) to brag
(VPR) **rajarse 1** [papel, tejido] to tear, rip; [vidrio, cerámica] to crack; [neumático] to get ripped
2* (= echarse atrás) to back out* • **no te irás a ~ ahora que tenemos las entradas** you are not going to back out now we've got the tickets • **¡me rajé!** (LAm) that's enough for me!, I'm quitting!
3 (LAm) (= huir) to run away
rajatabla • a ~ (ADV) 1 (= estrictamente) strictly, rigorously; (= exactamente) exactly • **debéis seguir estas instrucciones a ~** you should follow these instructions exactly *o* to the letter • **cumplir las órdenes a ~** to carry out one's orders to the letter
2 (LAm) • **pagar a ~** to pay on the dot, pay promptly
rajatablas* (SM INV) (And, Caribe) ticking-off*, telling-off*
raje* (SM) (Cono Sur) 1 (= despido) firing*, sacking* • **dar el ~ a algn** (= despedir) to fire sb*, sack sb*
2 (= prisa) • **al ~** in a hurry • **tomar(se) el ~** to beat it*
rajita (SF) slice, thin slice
rajo (SM) (LAm) tear, rip
rajón/ona (ADJ) 1 (LAm) (= liberal) generous, lavish, free-spending
2 (CAm, Méx) (= cobarde) cowardly
3 (CAm, Méx) (= pesimista) readily disheartened
4 (Méx) (= de poca confianza) unreliable
(SM) (Andalucía, LAm) (= raja) tear, rip
(SM/F) 1 (CAm, Méx) (= remolón) quitter
2 (CAm, Méx) (= matón) bully; (= jactancioso) braggart
3 (And, Méx) (= chismoso) gossip, telltale, tattletale (EEUU)
rajonada (SF) (CAm) 1 (= baladronada) boast, brag; (= jactancia) bragging
2 (= ostentación) ostentation
rajuñar* ▸ CONJUG 1a (VT) (Arg) = **rasguñar**
rala (SF) (And) birdlime
rale (SM) (Cono Sur) wooden bowl, wooden dish
ralea (SF) (pey) kind, sort • **de esa ~** of that sort *o* (liter) ilk • **gente de baja ~** riffraff, common people
ralear ▸ CONJUG 1a (VI) to become thin, become sparse
ralentí (SM) 1 (Cine) slow motion • **al ~** in slow motion
2 (Aut) • **estar al ~** • **funcionar al ~** to be ticking over
ralentización (SF), **ralentizamiento** (SM) (= desaceleración) slowing down, deceleration; (Econ) slowing down
ralentizar ▸ CONJUG 1f (VT), (VI) to slow down
(VPR) **ralentizarse** to slow down
rallado (ADJ) grated; ▸ **pan**
rallador (SM) grater
ralladura (SF) • ~ **de limón** grated lemon rind • **~s de patata/queso** grated potato/cheese (sing)
rallar ▸ CONJUG 1a (VT) 1 (Culin) to grate
2‡ (= fastidiar) to grate on • **me ralla esa actitud** that attitude grates on me
3 (Caribe) (= provocar) to goad
rallo (SM) (Culin) grater; (Téc) file
rallón (ADJ) (And) bothersome, irritating
rally ['rrali] (PL: **rallys**) (SM) 1 (Aut) rally ▸ **rally de coches de época** vintage car rally
2 (Econ) rally
rallye ['rrali] (SM) = **rally**
ralo (ADJ) 1 (= claro) [pelo] thin, sparse; [bosque] sparse; [tela] loosely woven; [aire] thin
2 (Cono Sur) (= insustancial) insubstantial
(ADV) • **ralo-ralo** (Cono Sur) sometimes
RAM (SF ABR) (= **Random Access Memory**) RAM
rama (SF) 1 [de árbol] branch • **en ~: algodón en ~** raw cotton • **canela en ~** cinnamon sticks (pl) • MODISMOS: • **andarse** *o* **irse por las ~s** to beat about the bush • **poner algo en la última ~** to leave sth till last ▸ **rama de olivo** (lit, fig) olive branch ▸ **rama de perejil** sprig of parsley
2 [de ciencia, familia, organización] branch • **Yolanda pertenece a la ~ materna de su familia** Yolanda is on his mother's side of the family
3 (Tip) • **en ~** unbound
4 (LAm*) (= hachís) pot*, hash*
ramada (SF) 1 (= ramaje) branches (pl)
2 (LAm) (= cobertizo) shelter or covering made of branches
ramadán (SM), **Ramadán** (SM) Ramadan
ramaje (SM) branches (pl)
ramal (SM) 1 (= cabo) strand; (para el caballo) halter
2 (= desvío) (Aut) branch; (Ferro) branch line
3 (= derivación) offshoot
ramalazo (SM) 1 (= azote) lash
2 [de depresión, locura] fit • **me dio un ~ de dolor** I felt a sudden stab of pain • MODISMO: • **tener ~** to be effeminate
3 (= ráfaga) [de viento] gust; [de lluvia] blast
ramazón (SF) (CAm, Cono Sur, Méx) antler, horns (pl)
rambla (SF) 1 (= avenida) boulevard, avenue
2 (= arroyo) watercourse
3 (LAm) (= paseo marítimo) esplanade, promenade; (= muelle) quayside
ramera (SF) whore, prostitute
ramificación (SF) ramification
ramificarse ▸ CONJUG 1g (VPR) to branch, branch out, ramify (frm)
ramiforme (ADJ) ramiform
ramillete (SM) 1 [de flores] bouquet, bunch; (de adorno) corsage; (Bot) (= inflorescencia) cluster
2 (= conjunto selecto) choice bunch, select group
ramita (SF) [de árbol, planta] twig, sprig; (ramo) spray
ramo (SM) 1 [de flores] bouquet, bunch ▸ **ramo de novia** bride's bouquet
2 [de árbol] branch
3 (Com) (= sector) field, section, department • **es del ~ de la alimentación** he's in the food business • **el ministro del ~** the appropriate minister, the minister concerned with this • **es del ~*** (= homosexual) he's one of them*, he's a poof‡, he's a fag (EEUU‡)
4* (= ramalazo) (tb **ramos**) • **tiene ~s de loco** he has a streak of madness in him, he has a mad streak in him
ramojo (SM) brushwood
Ramón (SM) Raymond
ramonear ▸ CONJUG 1a (VT) 1 [+ árboles] to lop, lop the twigs of
2 [ovejas] to browse on
rampa (SF) ramp ▸ **rampa de acceso** entrance ramp ▸ **rampa de desperdicios, rampa de la basura** refuse chute ▸ **rampa de lanzamiento** launch(ing) ramp ▸ **rampa de misiles** missile launcher ▸ **rampa móvil** mobile launch pad, mobile launching pad
rampante (ADJ) rampant
rampla (SF) (Chile) (truck) trailer
ramplón (ADJ) common, coarse
ramplonería (SF) commonness, coarseness
rana (SF) 1 (Zool) frog • MODISMOS: • **cuando las ~s críen pelo** when pigs fly, when pigs learn to fly • **¡hasta que las ~s críen pelo!** if I never see you again it'll be too soon! • **pero salió ~*** but he turned out badly, but he was a big disappointment ▸ **rana toro** bullfrog
2 (= juego) game of throwing coins into the mouth of an iron frog
ranchada (SF) 1 (CAm) (= canoa) canoe
2 (LAm) (= cobertizo) shed, improvised hut
ranchar ▸ CONJUG 1a (VI) 1 (Cono Sur, Méx) (= vagar) to wander from farm to farm
2 (And, Caribe, Méx) (= pernoctar) to spend the night; (= establecerse) to settle
3 (Caribe) (= obstinarse) to persist
ranchear ▸ CONJUG 1a (VT) (Caribe, Méx) (= saquear) to loot, pillage; (= robar) to rob
(VI) 1 (LAm) (= formar rancho) to build a camp
2 (And, Cono Sur) (= comer) to have a meal
ranchera (SF) 1 (Méx) (Mús) Mexican folk song
2 (= coche) station wagon; ▸ **ranchero**
ranchería (SF) 1 (LAm) (para trabajadores) labourers' quarters, laborers' quarters (EEUU)
2 (LAm) = **ranchería**
3 (Caribe) (= taberna) poor country inn
4 (Caribe) (= chabolas) shantytown
ranchería (SM) (LAm) settlement
ranchero/a (ADJ) (Méx) 1 (= rudo) uncouth; (= ridículo) ridiculous, silly
2 (= conocedor del campo) • **es muy ~** he's a real countryman *o* country person
3 (Culin) • **huevos ~s** fried eggs in a hot chilli and tomato sauce
4 (Mús) • **música ranchera** ≈ country and western music
(SM/F) 1 (LAm) (= jefe de rancho) rancher
2 (= cocinero) mess cook
3 (Méx) peasant, country person; ▸ **ranchera**
ranchitos (SMPL) (Ven) shantytown (sing)
rancho (SM) 1 (Méx) (= granja) ranch, small farm
2 (LAm) (= choza) hut, thatched hut; (LAm) (= casa de campo) country house, villa
3 (Caribe) (= chabola) shanty, shack • **~s** (And, Caribe) shanty town
4 (Náut) crew's quarters (pl)
5 (= campamento) camp, settlement
6 (Mil) mess, communal meal; (pey) (= comida) bad food, grub* • **asentar el ~** (= preparar la comida) to prepare a meal; (fig) (= organizarse) to settle in, get things

organized • **hacer el ~** to have a meal • MODISMO: • **hacer ~ aparte** to set up on one's own, go one's own way
7 (*Cono Sur*) (= *sombrero*) straw hat
rancidez SF, **ranciedad** SF **1** [*de vino*] age, mellowness; [*de mantequilla, tocino*] staleness
2 (= *antigüedad*) great age, antiquity; (*pey*) antiquatedness
rancio ADJ **1** [*vino*] old, mellow; [*mantequilla, tocino*] rancid
2 [*linaje*] ancient; [*tradición*] very ancient, time-honoured, time-honored (*EEUU*); (*pey*) antiquated, old-fashioned • **esas dos son muy rancias** those two are a couple of old fogeys*
SM = **rancidez**
rancontán ADV (*And, CAm, Caribe*) in cash
rand [ran] SM (PL: **rands** [ran]) rand
randa¹ SF (*Cos*) lace, lace trimming
randa²* SM (= *ladrón*) pickpocket, petty thief; (= *sospechoso*) suspicious character, prowler
randar‡ ▷ CONJUG 1a VT to nick‡, rip off‡
randevú SM (*Cono Sur*) rendezvous
randevuses SMPL (*Cono Sur*) courtesies
ranfaña* SM (*And, Cono Sur*) scruff*
ranfañoso* (*And, Cono Sur*) ADJ shabby, scruffy
SM scruff*
ranfla SF (*LAm*) ramp
ranga SF (*And*) nag, old horse
ranglán ADJ INV = **raglán**
rango¹ SM **1** (= *categoría*) rank; (= *prestigio*) standing, status • **de ~** of high standing, of some status • **de alto ~** of high standing, of some status
2 (*LAm*) (= *lujo*) luxury; (= *pompa*) pomp, splendour, splendor (*EEUU*)
rango² SM (*And*) = **ranga**
rangosidad* SF (*Cono Sur*) generosity
rangoso* ADJ (*Cono Sur*) generous
Rangún SM Rangoon
ranita SM Baby-gro®, rompers (*pl*), romper suit
ránking ['raŋkin] SM (PL: **ránkings** ['raŋkin]) **1** (= *clasificación*) ranking
2 (*And*) (*Mús*) top twenty, hit parade
rantifuso ADJ (*Cono Sur*) **1** (= *sucio*) dirty, grubby; (= *ordinario*) common
2 (= *sospechoso*) suspicious
ranúnculo SM (*Bot*) ranunculus; (*esp Esp*) buttercup
ranura SF (= *hendedura*) groove; (*para monedas*) slot ▸ **ranura de expansión** (*Inform*) expansion slot
rap SM rap, rap music • **hacer rap** to rap
rapacidad SF rapacity
rapado/a ADJ [*pelo*] close-cropped
SM/F (= *persona*) skinhead
SM (= *corte de pelo*) • **tiene un buen ~** he has his hair close shaven
rapadura SF (*LAm*) (= *azúcar*) brown sugar; (= *caramelo*) *sweet made of milk and syrup*
rapapolvo SM telling-off*, ticking-off* • **echar un ~ a algn** to give sb a telling-off *o* ticking-off*
rapar ▷ CONJUG 1a VT **1** [+ *pelo*] to crop; [+ *barba*] to shave
2* (= *arrebatar*) to snatch*, pinch*
VPR **raparse** • **~se la cabeza** to shave one's head
rapaz¹ ADJ **1** (*Zool*) predatory; (*Orn*) of prey
2 (= *avaricioso*) rapacious, greedy; (= *inclinado al robo*) thieving
SF (*Zool*) predatory animal; (*Orn*) bird of prey
rapaz²(a)†† SM/F (*Esp*) (*hum*) boy/girl, lad/lass
rape¹ SM **1** [*de barba*] quick shave; [*de pelo*] rough haircut • **al ~** cut close
2* (= *bronca*) ticking-off*, telling-off*
rape² SM (*Zool*) angler fish
rapé SM snuff
rapel SM, **rápel** SM = **rappel**
raper SMF (PL: **rapers**) = **rapper**
rapero/a* ADJ rap (*antes de s*)
SM/F rapper
rápida SF (*Méx*) chute
rápidamente ADV fast, quickly
rapidez SF speed • **me sorprendió la ~ con que acabó el trabajo** the speed with which he finished the job surprised me, it surprised me how quickly he finished the job • **con ~** quickly • **se vistió con ~** she got dressed quickly
rápido ADJ **1** (= *veloz*) fast, quick; [*tren*] fast, express
2 (*And, Caribe, Cono Sur*) [*campo, paisaje*] fallow
3 (*Caribe*) [*tiempo*] clear
ADV quickly • **¡y ~, eh!** and make it snappy!*
SM **1** (*Ferro*) express
2 (*And, Caribe, Cono Sur*) (= *campo*) open country
3 • **rápidos** (= *rabiones*) rapids
rapiña SF robbery, robbery with violence; ▸ **ave**
rapiñar ▷ CONJUG 1a VT to steal
raposa SF **1** (*Zool*) (= *zorro*) fox; (= *zorra*) vixen
2 (*Caribe*) (= *bolsa*) carrier bag; ▸ **raposo**
raposera SF foxhole
raposero ADJ • **perro ~** foxhound
raposo SM **1** (= *zorro*) fox
2 (*And, Caribe*) (= *mocoso*) kid*; ▸ **raposa**
rappel SM abseiling • **a ~** by abseiling • **hacer ~** to abseil, abseil down
rappelar ▷ CONJUG 1a VI to abseil, abseil down
rapper SMF (PL: **rappers**) rapper, rap artist
rapsodia SF rhapsody
rapsódico ADJ rhapsodic
raptar ▷ CONJUG 1a VT to kidnap, abduct
rapto SM **1** (= *secuestro*) kidnapping, kidnaping (*EEUU*), abduction
2 (= *impulso*) sudden impulse • **en un ~ de celos** in a sudden fit of jealousy
3 (= *éxtasis*) ecstasy, rapture
raptor(a) SM/F kidnapper
raque¹ SM beachcombing • **andar al ~** to beachcomb, go beachcombing
raque² SM (*Caribe*) bargain
raquear¹ ▷ CONJUG 1a VI to go beachcombing
raquear² ▷ CONJUG 1a VT (*Caribe*) to rob, hold up
Raquel SF Rachel
raquero/a SM/F beachcomber
raqueta SF [*de tenis, bádminton*] racket; [*de ping pong*] bat ▸ **raqueta de nieve** snowshoe
raquetazo SM shot, hit, stroke
raquítico ADJ **1** (*Med*) rachitic
2 [*cantidad, sueldo*] paltry, miserly
3 [*árbol*] stunted
raquitis SF INV, **raquitismo** SM rickets (*pl*)
raramente ADV rarely, seldom
rarefacción SF rarefaction
rareza SF **1** (= *calidad*) rarity
2 (= *objeto*) rarity
3 (= *rasgo singular*) oddity, peculiarity • **tiene sus ~s** he has his peculiarities, he has his little ways • **tiene alguna ~** there's something odd about him
raridad SF rarity
rarificado ADJ rarefied
rarificar ▷ CONJUG 1g VT to rarefy
rarífico ADJ (*Cono Sur*) = **raro**
raro ADJ **1** (= *extraño*) strange, odd • **es un hombre muy ~** he's a very strange *o* odd man • **es ~ que no haya llamado** it's strange *o* odd that he hasn't called • **¡qué ~!** • **¡qué cosa más rara!** how (very) strange!, how (very) odd!
2 (= *poco común*) rare • **una especie muy rara** a very rare species • **con alguna rara excepción** with few *o* rare exceptions • **de rara perfección** of rare perfection, of remarkable perfection • **rara vez nos visita** • **rara es la vez que nos visita** he rarely visits us
3 (*Fís*) rare, rarefied
ras SM levelness, evenness • **a ras de** level with, flush with • **volar a ras de tierra** to fly (almost) at ground level • **ras con ras** level, on a level
rasado ADJ level • **cucharada rasada** level teaspoonful
rasante ADJ low • **tiro ~** low shot • **vuelo ~** low-level flight
SM slope • **cambio de ~** (*Aut*) brow of a hill
rasar ▷ CONJUG 1a VT **1** [+ *contenido*] to level, level with the brim
2 (= *rozar*) to skim, graze • **la bala pasó rasando su sombrero** the bullet grazed his hat
3 = **arrasar**
VPR **rasarse** [*cielo*] to clear
rasca¹‡ SF **1** (*Esp*) (= *frío*) cold • **¿cómo se te ocurre salir con esta ~?** what do you think you're doing going out in this cold? • **¡menuda ~ hace!** it's freezing!
2 (*And, CAm, Caribe*) (= *borrachera*) drunkenness
rasca²* ADJ (*Cono Sur*) (= *vulgar*) tacky*; (= *de mala calidad*) inferior
rascacielos SM INV skyscraper
rascacio SM scorpion fish
rascadera SF **1** (= *utensilio*) scraper
2 (= *almohaza*) currycomb
rascado* ADJ **1** (*LAm*) (= *borracho*) drunk
2 (*CAm*) (= *casquivano*) feather-brained
rascador SM **1** (= *utensilio*) scraper
2 [*de pelo*] ornamental hairclasp
rascaespalda SM backscratcher
rascamoño SM **1** = **rascador**
2 (*Bot*) zinnia
rascapies SM INV (*And*) firecracker
rascar ▷ CONJUG 1g VT **1** (*con uñas*) to scratch
2 [+ *puerta, pared*] to scrape; [+ *pintura*] to scrape off
3 (*hum*) [+ *instrumento*] to scrape, scratch *o* saw away at
VI (*LAm*) (= *picar*) to itch
VPR **rascarse 1** (*con uñas*) to scratch, scratch o.s. • MODISMOS: • **~se la barriga** • **~se la panza** to take it easy
2 (*LAm*) (= *emborracharse*) to get drunk
3 • **~se juntos** (*CAm, Cono Sur*) to band together • MODISMO: • **no ~se con algn** (*And*) not to hit it off with sb
rasca-rasca SM scratch-card game ▸ **tarjetas rasca-rasca** scratch cards
rascatripas* SMF INV fiddler, third-rate violinist
rasco* ADJ (*Chile*) common, ordinary
rascón¹ ADJ **1** (= *amargo*) sharp, sour (to taste)
2 (*Méx*) (= *pendenciero*) quarrelsome
rascón² SM (*Orn*) water rail
rascuache ADJ (*CAm, Méx*) **1** (= *pobre*) poor, penniless
2 (= *desgraciado*) wretched
3 (= *ridículo*) ridiculous, in bad taste
4 (= *grosero*) coarse, vulgar
5 (= *tacaño*) mean, tightfisted
rascucho ADJ (*Cono Sur*) drunk
RASD SF ABR = **República Árabe Saharaui Democrática**
raseado ADJ level • **cucharada raseada** level spoonful

rasear ▸ CONJUG 1a VT **1** (= *rozar*) to skim, graze
2 (= *nivelar*) to level, level off
3 [+ *balón*] to play low, play along the ground

rasera SF fish slice

rasero SM strickle • **doble ~** double standards (*pl*) • MODISMO: • **medir dos cosas con el mismo ~** to treat two things alike

rasete SM satinet, satinette

rasgado ADJ **1** [*ojos*] almond-shaped; [*boca*] wide, big
2 [*ventana*] wide
3 (*LAm*) (= *franco*) outspoken
4 (*And*) (= *generoso*) generous

rasgadura SF tear, rip

rasgar ▸ CONJUG 1h VT **1** [+ *tejido, piel*] to tear, rip; [+ *papel*] to tear up, tear to pieces
2 = **rasguear**
VPR **rasgarse** to tear

rasgo SM **1** (*Anat*) feature • **tiene unos ~s muy marcados** she has very pronounced (facial) features • **de ~s enérgicos** of energetic appearance
2 (= *peculiaridad*) characteristic, feature
▸ **rasgos característicos** typical features
▸ **rasgos distintivos** distinctive features
3 (*con pluma*) stroke, flourish
• **~s** characteristics (*of one's handwriting*)
• MODISMO: • **a grandes ~s** broadly speaking
4 (= *acto*) ▸ **rasgo de generosidad** act of generosity; (= *acción noble*) noble gesture
▸ **rasgo de ingenio** flash of wit, stroke of genius
5 (*LAm*) (= *acequia*) irrigation channel; (= *terreno*) plot, plot of land

rasgón SM tear, rip, rent (*liter*)

rasguear ▸ CONJUG 1a VT **1** (*Mús*) to strum
2 (= *al escribir*) to write with a flourish; (*fig*) (= *escribir*) to write

rasguñadura SF (*LAm*) scratch

rasguñar ▸ CONJUG 1a VT **1** (= *rascar*) to scratch
2 (*Arte*) to sketch, draw in outline

rasguño SM **1** (= *arañazo*) scratch • **salir sin un ~** to come out of it without a scratch
2 (*Arte*) sketch, outline drawing

rasmillón SM (*Cono Sur*) scratch

raso ADJ **1** [*campo, terreno*] (= *llano*) flat, level; (= *sin árboles*) clear, open; (= *liso*) smooth
2 [*asiento*] backless
3 [*cielo*] clear • **está ~** the sky is clear
4 [*contenido*] level, level with the brim • **una cucharada rasa** a level spoonful
5 [*pelota, vuelo*] very low, almost at ground level • **marcó el gol por ~** he scored with a low shot
6 (= *simple*) • **soldado ~** private • **aprobado ~** bare pass, bare pass mark
ADV • **tirar ~** (*Dep*) to shoot low
SM **1** (*Cos*) satin
2 (= *campo llano*) flat country; (= *campo abierto*) open country • **dormir al ~** to sleep out in the open

raspa SF **1** (*Bot*) [*de cebada*] beard; [*de uva*] stalk
2 [*de pez*] (= *espina*) fishbone; (= *espinazo*) backbone
3* (= *persona irritable*) grouch*
4* (= *persona delgada*) beanpole*, string bean (*EEUU**)
5 (*LAm**) (= *reprimenda*) scolding, telling-off*, ticking-off*
6 (*Caribe, Méx*) (= *azúcar*) brown sugar
7 (*Cono Sur*) (= *herramienta*) rasp
8 • **ni de ~** (*And*) (= *de ninguna manera*) under no circumstances, no way*
9 (*CAm, Méx*) (= *burla*) joke
10 (*LAm*) (= *chusma*) riffraff

raspada* SF (*Caribe, Méx*) scolding, telling-off*, ticking-off*

raspado ADJ **1** (*CAm, Caribe*) shameless
2 • **un aprobado ~** a bare pass • **lo aprobé ~** I just scraped through
SM **1** (*Med*) D and C, dilation and curettage
2 (*LAm*) (= *bebida*) water ice, sherbet (*EEUU*)

raspador SM **1** (= *herramienta*) scraper, rasp
2 (*Méx*) (*Culin*) grater

raspadura SF **1** (= *acto*) scrape, scraping, rasping
2 raspaduras [*de papel*] scrapings; [*de hierro*] filings
3 (= *raya*) scratch, mark
4 (= *borradura*) erasure
5 (*LAm*) (= *azúcar*) brown sugar, brown sugar scrapings

raspante ADJ sharp, rough

raspar ▸ CONJUG 1a VT **1** [+ *pintura*] to scrape off • **raspó la pintura de la pared** he scraped the paint off the wall • **has raspado la pared con la bicicleta** you've scraped the wall with your bike • **tienes que ~ la puerta para quitarle el barniz** you have to sand the door to get the varnish off
2 [+ *piel*] to scratch • **este jersey me raspa el cuello** this jumper scratches my neck • **los socialistas quedaron raspando la mayoría absoluta** the Socialists were a whisker *o* an inch away from achieving an absolute majority, the Socialists were within a whisker *o* an inch of achieving an absolute majority
3 [*vino, licor*] to be rough on • **este vino raspa la garganta** this wine is rough on your throat
4* (= *hurtar*) to pinch*, swipe*
5 (*Caribe**) (= *matar*) to kill
6 (*LAm**) (= *regañar*) to tick off*, tell off*, scold
7 (*Méx*) (= *injuriar*) to say unkind things to, make wounding remarks to
8 (*en un escrito*) to scratch out • **han raspado la firma** they have scratched out the signature
VI **1** [*manos, tejido, licor*] to be rough • **esta toalla raspa** this towel is rough
2 (*LAm**) (= *irse*) to leg it*; (= *morir*) to kick the bucket*

raspear* ▸ CONJUG 1a VT (*LAm*) to tick off*, tell off*, scold
VI [*pluma*] to scratch

raspón SM **1** (= *rasguño*) scratch, graze; (*LAm*) (= *abrasión*) abrasion; (= *cardenal*) bruise
2 (*LAm**) (= *regaño*) scolding, telling-off*, ticking-off*, scolding
3 (*Col*) (= *sombrero*) straw hat
4 (*Méx**) (= *comentario hiriente*) cutting remark

rasponear* ▸ CONJUG 1a VT (*And*) to scold, tick off*, tell off*

rasposo ADJ **1** [*sabor*] sharp, rough
2 (*LAm**) (= *tacaño*) stingy*
3 (*Cono Sur*) (= *raído*) scruffy, threadbare; (= *miserable*) wretched

rasqueta SF **1** (= *herramienta*) scraper, rasp
2 (*Cono Sur*) (= *almohaza*) horse brush, currycomb

rasquetear ▸ CONJUG 1a VT (*Cono Sur*) to brush down

rasquiña SF (*LAm*) itch

rasta ADJ, SMF Rasta

rastacuerismo* SM (*LAm*) (= *ambición social*) social climbing; (= *tren de vida*) rich living; (= *ostentación*) ostentation, display

rastacuero/a* ADJ, SM/F (*LAm*) nouveau riche

rastafario/a ADJ, SM/F Rastafarian

rasterizar ▸ CONJUG 1f VT to rasterize

rastra SF **1** (*Agr*) (= *rastrillo*) rake; (= *grada*) harrow
2 • **a ~s**: **tuvo que sacar al niño a ~s de la juguetería** she had to drag the child out of the toyshop • **llevaba la bolsa a ~s** she was dragging the bag along behind her • **el herido fue a ~s hasta la puerta** the injured man crawled to the door • **no voy al fútbol ni a ~s** wild horses wouldn't get me to a football match* • **desde hace años lleva este problema a ~s** she's been dogged by this problem for years • **con un sueldo tan bajo siempre vamos a ~s** with such a low salary we're always struggling (along)
3 (*Pesca*) trawl • **pescar a la ~** to trawl
4 (*para transportar*) trolley (*for moving heavy objects*), cart (*EEUU*)
5 (= *ristra*) string
6 (= *huella*) trail, track
7 (*Cono Sur*) (= *cinturón*) *metal ornament on gaucho's belt*
8† (= *consecuencia*) unpleasant consequence, disagreeable result; (= *castigo*) punishment

rastreabilidad SF traceability

rastreable ADJ traceable

rastreador(a) SM/F (= *persona*) tracker
SM (*Náut*) (*tb* **barco rastreador**) trawler
▸ **rastreador de minas** minesweeper

rastrear ▸ CONJUG 1a VT **1** (= *buscar*) to track, trail; [+ *satélite*] to track; [+ *río*] to drag • **~ el monte** to comb the woods • **~ los archivos** to trawl through the files
2 [+ *minas*] to sweep
3 (*Pesca*) to trawl
VI **1** (*Agr*) to rake, harrow
2 (*Pesca*) to trawl
3 (*Aer*) to skim the ground, fly very low

rastreo SM **1** (*en agua*) dredging, dragging; (*Pesca*) trawling
2 [*de satélite*] tracking

rastrerismo* SM (*LAm*) toadying, bootlicking*, brown-nosing (*EEUU‡*)

rastrero ADJ **1** (*Zool*) creeping, crawling; (*Bot*) creeping
2 [*vestido*] trailing
3 [*vuelo*] very low
4 (*fig*) [*conducta*] mean, despicable; [*persona*] cringing; [*método*] low; [*disculpa*] abject, humble

rastrillada SF (*Cono Sur*) track, trail

rastrillar ▸ CONJUG 1a VT **1** (*Agr*) to rake; (= *recoger*) to rake up; (= *alisar*) to rake smooth
2 (*LAm*) [+ *fusil*] to fire; [+ *fósforo*] to strike
3 (*CAm, Méx*) [+ *pies*] to drag
VI **1** (*And, Caribe, Cono Sur*) (= *errar el tiro*) to miss; (*Caribe, Cono Sur*) (= *disparar*) to fire, shoot
2 (*Cono Sur**) (= *robar*) to shoplift

rastrillazo SM (*CAm*) **1** (= *sueñecito*) light sleep
2 (= *piscolabis*) light meal, snack

rastrillero/a* SM/F (*Cono Sur*) shoplifter

rastrillo SM **1** (*Agr*) rake
2 (*Mil*) portcullis; (*Arquit*) spiked gate
3 (*Téc*) hackle, flax comb
4 [*de cerradura, llave*] ward
5 (*Ferro*) ▸ **rastrillo delantero** cowcatcher
6 (*Com*) (= *mercadillo*) jumble sale
7 (*Méx*) (= *cuchilla*) razor, safety razor

rastro SM **1** (= *pista*) trail; (= *olor*) scent • **la policía ha seguido el ~ a** *o* **de los atracadores** the police have followed the robbers' trail • **los perros le perdieron el ~** the dogs lost his scent
2 (= *señal*) trace • **quedaban ~s de sangre en el suelo** there were traces of blood on the floor • **desaparecer sin dejar ~** to vanish without trace • **ni ~**: **no ha quedado ni ~ del jamón** there isn't a scrap of ham left
3 (*Agr*) (= *rastrillo*) rake; (= *grada*) harrow
4 (= *mercadillo*) fleamarket • **el Rastro** *fleamarket in Madrid*
5† (= *matadero*) slaughterhouse

rastrojear ▸ CONJUG 1a VI (*LAm*) (= *espigar*)

to glean; [animales] to feed in the stubble
rastrojera (SF) stubble field
rastrojero (SM) 1 (Cono Sur) (= campo) stubble field
2 (Cono Sur) (Aut) jeep
3 (Méx) (= maíz) maize o (EEUU) corn stalks (used as fodder)
rastrojo (SM) 1 (Agr) (= residuo) [de campo] stubble • **campo de ~** stubble field
2 (Cono Sur) (= terreno cultivado) ploughed field, plowed field (EEUU)
3 **rastrojos** (LAm) (= sobras) waste (sing), remains, leftovers
rasura (SF) 1 (= llanura) flatness, levelness; (= lisura) smoothness
2 (= afeitado) shave, shaving; (Téc) scrape, scraping
3 **rasuras** (= raspaduras) [de papel] scrapings; [de hierro] filings
rasurado (SM) shave
rasurador (SM), **rasuradora** (SF) (Méx) electric shaver, electric razor
rasurar ▹ CONJUG 1a (VT) 1 (= afeitar) to shave
2 (Téc) to scrape
(VPR) **rasurarse** to shave
rata (SF) rat • MODISMO: • **ser una ~ de biblioteca** to be a bookworm ▸ **rata común** house rat ▸ **rata gris** brown rat ▸ **rata negra** black rat, house rat
(SMF)* 1 (= tacaño) miser, mean devil, stingy devil*
2 (= ladrón) sneak thief
rataplán (SM) drumbeat, rub-a-dub
ratear ▹ CONJUG 1a (VT) 1 (= hurtar) to steal, pilfer
2 (= repartir) to share out
3 (= reducir) to reduce proportionately
(VI) (= arrastrarse) to crawl, creep
ratera (SF) (Méx) rat trap
ratería (SF) 1 (= robo) petty thieving • **una ~** a theft
2 (= cualidad) crookedness, dishonesty
raterismo (SM) (LAm) thieving
ratero/a (ADJ) 1 (= que roba) thieving, light-fingered
2 (= despreciable) despicable
(SM/F) (= ladrón) thief, petty thief; (= carterista) pickpocket; (Méx) [de casas] burglar
raticida (SM) rat poison
ratificación (SF) ratification
ratificar ▹ CONJUG 1g (VT) [+ tratado] to ratify; [+ noticia] to confirm; [+ opinión] to support • **~ que ...** to confirm that ...
rating ['ratin] (SM) (PL: **ratings** ['ratin])
1 (Náut) class
2 (TV etc) popularity rating
ratio (SM), (a veces) (SF) ratio
Ratisbona (SF) Regensburg, Ratisbon
rato (SM) 1 (= espacio de tiempo) **a** (uso incontable) • **lleva bastante ~ hablando** he's been talking for quite a while o for quite some time • **hace ~** a while ago, some time ago • **hace ~ que se fue** he left a while ago, he left some time ago • **largo ~** a long time • **hablamos largo ~** we talked a long time • **más ~** (Chile) later • **déjalo para más ~** leave it for later • **nos vemos más ~** see you later • **mucho ~** a long time • **¿vas a tardar mucho ~?** will you be long? • MODISMO: • **para ~**: • **tenemos carretera para ~** we still have quite a way to go • **tenemos para ~ con este trabajo** we still have quite a lot to do to get this work finished, we're still a long way from finishing this work • **aún queda presidente para ~** the president will still be around for some time to come; ▹ **cuerda**
b (uso contable) • **durante el ~ que estuve esperando** during the short time I was waiting • **estoy encantada de haber tenido este ~ para charlar contigo** I'm delighted to have had this time to chat to you • **en esos ~s me olvido de todo** at such moments I forget about everything • **otro ~**: • **ya lo llamaré otro ~** I'll call him back another time • **dile que se ponga otro ~ al teléfono** can you call her back to the phone for a minute? • **¡hasta otro ~!** so long!, I'll see you! • **todo el ~** the whole time, all the time
c • **un ~** a (short) while • **al cabo de un ~ dijo ...** after a (short) while he said ... • **dentro de un ~** in a (short) while • **solo estuvo allí un ~** he was only there a (short) while • **todavía tardará un ~ en salir** it'll still be a while before he comes out • **me quedaré un ~ más** I'll stay a bit longer • **me tuvo esperando un buen ~** she kept me waiting a good while o quite some time • **escríbeme cuando tengas un ~** write to me when you have a spare moment • **no regresó hasta pasado un buen ~** he didn't come back for a while • **dar un mal ~ a algn** to give sb a hard time • **estos hijos no dan más que malos ~s** these children give you nothing but grief • **mujer, no te des mal ~** don't let yourself be upset • **pasar un buen/mal ~** to have a good/bad time • **me hizo pasar un mal ~** I had a terrible time because of him • **pasar el ~** to pass the time • **tener sus ~s** to have one's moments ▸ **ratos de ocio** leisure time ▸ **ratos libres** spare time, free time
2 (otras expresiones temporales) • **al ~** shortly afterwards, shortly after, a short while later • **al poco ~ sonó el teléfono** shortly afterwards o shortly after o a short while later the phone rang • **llamaron al poco ~ de irte** they called a short while after o shortly after you left • **al ~ viene** (Méx*) he'll be here soon o in a (short) while • **voy a comer al ~** (Méx*) I'm going to eat soon o in a moment • **a cada ~** every other minute • **caminaba despacio, parándose a cada ~** she walked slowly, stopping all the time o every other minute • **de ~ en ~** every so often
3 • **~s: a ~s** at times • **a ~s, me parece sincero y a otros no** at times he seems sincere and at other times not • **el enfermo solo se levanta a ~s** the patient only gets up from time to time o now and again • **de a ~s** (Arg, Uru) from time to time, now and again • **a ~s perdidos** in one's spare moments • **trabajo en el jardín a ~s perdidos** I work in the garden in my spare moments
4* • **un ~** (Esp) (uso adverbial) (= bastante): • **es un ~ difícil** it's pretty tricky* • **es un ~ listo** he's pretty smart* • **pesan un ~** they weigh quite a bit, they're pretty heavy* • **sabe un ~ largo de matemáticas** she knows quite a bit of maths*
ratón (SM) 1 (Zool) mouse • MODISMO: • **mandar a algn a capar ratones‡** to tell sb to go to blazes* ▸ **ratón almizclero** muskrat ▸ **ratón de archivo, ratón de biblioteca** bookworm
2 (Inform) mouse ▸ **ratón inalámbrico** cordless mouse, wireless mouse ▸ **ratón óptico** optical mouse
3 (Caribe) (= petardo) squib, cracker
4 (Caribe*) (= resaca) hangover
5* (= pelusa) ball of fluff
ratonar ▹ CONJUG 1a (VT) to gnaw, nibble
ratonera (SF) 1 (= trampa) mousetrap
2 (= agujero) mousehole
3 (fig) (= trampa) trap • **caer en la ~** to fall into the trap
4 (And, Cono Sur*) (= barrio bajo) hovel, slum
5 (Caribe) (= tienda) ranch store
ratonero (SM) (tb **ratonero común**) buzzard
RAU (SF ABR) (= **República Árabe Unida**) UAR
raudal (SM) 1 (= torrente) torrent, flood
2 (= abundancia) plenty, abundance • **a ~es** in abundance, in great numbers • **entrar a ~es** to pour in, come flooding in
raudo (ADJ) (frm) (= rápido) swift
ravioles (SMPL) ravioli
raya[1] (SF) 1 (= línea) line; (en mano) line; (en tela, diseño) stripe • **a ~s** striped • MODISMOS: • **hacer ~** to mark off • **mantener a ~ a algn** to keep sb at bay • **pasarse de la ~** to overstep the mark, go too far • **poner a ~** to check, hold back • **tener a ~** (= impedir el avance) to keep off, keep at bay; (= controlar) to keep in check, keep under control ▸ **raya diplomática** (en tejido) pinstripe ▸ **raya en negro** black line ▸ **raya magnética** magnetic stripe
2 (= marca) (en una superficie) scratch, mark
3 (en el pelo) parting, part (EEUU) • **hacerse la ~** to part one's hair
4 (en el pantalón) crease
5 (Tip) line, dash; (Telec) dash
6‡ (= droga) fix*, dose
7 (Méx††) (= sueldo) pay, wages (pl)
raya[2] (SF) (= pez) ray, skate ▸ **raya manta** butterfly ray, California butterfly ray
rayadillo (SM) (Cos) [de rayas] striped material; [de rayas azules y blancas] blue-and-white striped material
rayado (ADJ) 1 [papel] ruled, lined; [tela, diseño] striped
2 [disco, mueble] scratched
3 [cheque] crossed
4* (= loco) cracked*, crazy
5 (Cono Sur) (= fanático) extreme, fanatical
(SM) 1 (en papel) ruling, ruled lines (pl); (en tela, diseño) stripes (pl), striped pattern
2 (Caribe) (Aut) no parking area
rayador (SM) 1 (Méx††) (= contador) paymaster, accountant
2 (Cono Sur) (= árbitro) umpire
3 (Cono Sur) = **rallador**
rayadura (SF) scratch
rayajo* (SM) scrawl
rayano (ADJ) 1 (= lindante) adjacent, contiguous (frm); (= fronterizo) bordering
2 • **~ en** bordering on
rayar ▹ CONJUG 1a (VT) 1 [+ papel] to rule, draw lines on
2 [+ disco, mueble] to scratch
3 [+ cheque] to cross
4 (= garabatear) to scribble on
5 [+ caballo] to spur on
6 (Méx) (= pagar) to pay, pay his wages to
7 (Cono Sur) = **rallar**
(VI) 1 • **~ con** (= lindar) to be next to, be adjacent to
2 • **~ en** (= asemejarse) to border on, verge on • **esto raya en lo increíble** this verges on the incredible • **raya en los cincuenta** he's pushing fifty*
3 (= arañar) to scratch • **este producto no raya al fregar** this product cleans without scratching
4 • **al ~ el alba** at break of day, at first light
5 (Méx) (= cobrar) to draw one's wages
(VPR) **rayarse** 1 [objeto] to get scratched
2 (And) (= ver realizados sus deseos) to see one's dreams come true
3 (Méx) (= enriquecerse) to get rich
4 (And, Cono Sur*) (= enojarse) to lose one's temper
5 (Cono Sur) (= enloquecer) to go crazy
rayero/a (SM/F) (Cono Sur) linesman, assistant referee
rayo[1] (SM) 1 [de luz] ray, beam ▸ **rayo de luna** moonbeam ▸ **rayo de la muerte** death ray ▸ **rayo de partículas** particle beam ▸ **rayo de sol** sunbeam, ray of sunlight ▸ **rayo láser** laser beam ▸ **rayos catódicos** cathode rays ▸ **rayos cósmicos** cosmic rays ▸ **rayos**

r

gamma gamma rays ▸ **rayos infrarrojos** infrared rays ▸ **rayos luminosos** light rays ▸ **rayo solar** sunbeam, ray of sunlight ▸ **rayos ultravioleta** ultraviolet rays ▸ **rayos X** X-rays
2 [*de rueda*] spoke
3 (*Meteo*) lightning, flash of lightning • **cayó un ~ en la torre** the tower was struck by lightning • MODISMOS: • **a ~s**: • **huele a ~s*** it smells awful • **sabe a ~s*** it tastes awful • **como un ~** like lightning, like a shot • **la noticia le sentó como un ~** the news hit him like a bombshell • **entrar como un ~** to dash in • **salir como un ~** to dash out • **pasar como un ~** to rush past, flash past • **echar ~s y centellas** to rage, fume • **¡que le parta un ~!*** damn him!* • **¡que me parta un ~ si lo sé!** I'm damned if I know!* • **¡a los demás que les parta un ~!** and the rest of them can go to hell!* • **ser un ~** to be as sharp as they come
4 (*como exclamativo*) • **¡~s!*** dammit!* • **¿qué ~s es eso?*** what in hell's name is that?*

rayo[2] ▸ **raer**

rayón SM rayon

rayuela SF (= *juego de adultos*) pitch-and-toss; (*Arg*) (= *juego de niños*) hopscotch

raza[1] SF 1 (= *grupo étnico*) race; [*de animal*] breed • **de ~** • **de pura ~** [*caballo*] thoroughbred; [*perro*] pedigree ▸ **raza blanca** white race ▸ **raza humana** human race ▸ **raza negra** black race
2 (= *estirpe*) stock

raza[2] SF 1 (= *grieta*) crack, slit, fissure; (*en tela*) run
2 (= *rayo*) ray of light
3 (*Perú**) (= *descaro*) cheek* • **¡qué tal ~!** some cheek!*, what a cheek!*

razano ADJ (*And*) thoroughbred

razia SF raid

raziar ▸ CONJUG 1b VI to raid

razón SF 1 (= *facultad*) reason • **entrar en ~** to see sense, listen to reason • **hacer que algn entre en ~** to make sb see sense • **perder la ~** to go out of one's mind • **tener uso de ~**: **escribo desde que tengo uso de ~** I've been writing for as long as I can remember • **apenas tenían uso de ~ cuando ...** they were mere babes in arms when ...
2 (= *verdad*) • **asistir la ~**: • **le asiste la ~** he has right on his side • **cargarse de ~** to have right fully on one's side • **quiero cargarme de ~ antes de ...** I want to be sure of my case before ... • **con ~ o sin ella** rightly or wrongly • **dar la ~ a algn** (= *estar de acuerdo*) to agree that sb is right; (= *apoyar*) to side with sb • **al final me dio la ~** in the end he agreed that I was right • **quitar la ~ a algn** to say sb is wrong • **tratar de quitar a algn la ~** to try to put sb in the wrong • **~ le sobra** she's only too right • **tener ~** to be right • **no tener ~** to be wrong • **tener parte de ~** to be partly right • **tienen toda la ~ (del mundo)** they're absolutely right
3 (= *motivo*) reason • **¿cuál era la ~ de su visita?** what was the reason for his visit? • **la ~ por la que lo hizo** the reason why he did it, the reason for his doing it • **sus razones tendrá** he must have his reasons • **con ~** with good reason • **están hartos con toda la ~ (del mundo)** they're fed up and they have good reason to be, they're fed up and rightly so • **¡con ~!** naturally! • **~ de más**: • **~ de más para ayudarlas** all the more reason to help them • **en ~ a** *o* **de** (= *debido a*) owing to; (= *de acuerdo con*) according to • **no atender a razones**: • **no atiende a razones** he won't listen to reason ▸ **razón de ser** raison d'être ▸ **razones de Estado** reasons of State
4 (= *información*) • **"razón: Princesa 4"** "inquiries to 4 Princesa Street", "for further details apply to 4 Princesa Street" • **dar ~ de algo/algn** to give information about sth/sb • **nadie me daba ~ de ella** nobody could tell me anything about her *o* give me any information about her • **nadie supo dar ~ de su paradero** no one knew *o* could tell us his whereabouts • **mandar a algn ~ de que haga algo**† to send word (to sb) to do sth
5 (*Mat*) ratio • **en ~ directa con** in direct ratio to • **a ~ de**: • **a ~ de cinco a siete** in the ratio of five to seven • **lo devolverán a ~ de mil dólares mensuales** they will pay it back at a rate of a thousand dollars a month • **abandonan el país a ~ de 800 cada año** they are leaving the country at the rate of 800 a year
6 (*Com*) ▸ **razón social** trade name, firm's name

razonabilidad SF reasonableness

razonable ADJ reasonable

razonablemente ADV reasonably

razonado ADJ 1 (= *fundado en razones*) reasoned
2 [*cuenta*] itemized, detailed

razonamiento SM reasoning

razonar ▸ CONJUG 1a VT 1 (= *argumentar*) to reason, argue
2 [+ *problema*] to reason out
3 [+ *cuenta*] to itemize
VI 1 (= *argumentar*) to reason, argue
2 (= *hablar*) to talk, talk together

razzia ['raθia] SF = **razia**

razziar ▸ CONJUG 1b VI = **raziar**

rbdo. ABR (*Com*) (= **recibido**) recd, rec'd

RCE SF ABR (*Esp*) = **Radio Cadena Española**

RCN SF ABR (*Méx, Col*) = **Radio Cadena Nacional**

RD ABR (*Esp*) = **Real Decreto**

RDA SF ABR (*Hist*) (= **República Democrática Alemana**) GDR

Rdo. ABR (= **Reverendo**) Rev, Revd

RDSI SF ABR (= **Red Digital de Servicios Integrados**) ISDN

re SM (*Mús*) D ▸ **re mayor** D major

re... PREF 1 (*esp LAm*) (*repetición*) re...
2 (*intensivo*) very • **refrío** very cold • **reguapa** really pretty • **¡rebomba!** (*Esp*†) that's amazing! • **¡rediez!** (*Esp*†) well I'm damned!*

reabastecer ▸ CONJUG 2d VT [*de combustible, de gasolina*] to refuel
VPR **reabastecerse** to refuel

reabastecimiento SM refuelling, refueling (EEUU)

reabrir ▸ CONJUG 3a (PP: **reabierto**) VT to reopen • MODISMO: • **~ las heridas** to open old wounds
VPR **reabrirse** to reopen

reabsorber ▸ CONJUG 2a VT to reabsorb

reacción SF 1 (*Fís, Quím*) reaction (**a, ante** to) ▸ **reacción nuclear** nuclear reaction
2 (= *respuesta*) response (**a** to) • **la ~ blanca** the white backlash ▸ **reacción en cadena** chain reaction
3 (*Téc*) • **avión a** *o* **de ~** jet plane • **propulsión por ~** jet propulsion

reaccionar ▸ CONJUG 1a VI 1 (= *responder*) (*tb Fís, Quím*) to react (**a, ante** to, **contra** against, **sobre** on), respond (**a** to) • **¿cómo reaccionó?** how did she react?
2 (= *sobreponerse*) to pull o.s. together

reaccionario/a ADJ, SM/F reactionary

reacio ADJ reluctant • **ser ~ a** to resist, resist the idea of • **ser ~ a hacer algo** to be reluctant *o* unwilling to do sth

reacondicionamiento SM [*de motor*] reconditioning; [*de empresa, organización*] reorganization, restructuring

reacondicionar ▸ CONJUG 1a VT [+ *motor*] to recondition; [+ *empresa, organización*] to reorganize, restructure

reactivación SF reactivating • **~ de la economía** economic recovery, economic upturn

reactivar ▸ CONJUG 1a VT to reactivate
VPR **reactivarse** [*precios, actividad económica*] to recover

reactividad SF reactivity

reactivo SM reagent

reactor SM 1 (*Fís*) reactor ▸ **reactor de agua a presión** pressurized water reactor ▸ **reactor enfriado por gas** gas-cooled reactor ▸ **reactor generador** breeder reactor ▸ **reactor nuclear** nuclear reactor ▸ **reactor reproductor** breeder reactor
2 (*Aer*) (= *motor*) jet engine; (= *avión*) jet plane ▸ **reactor ejecutivo** executive jet

readaptación SF readjustment ▸ **readaptación profesional** retraining ▸ **readaptación social** social rehabilitation

readaptar ▸ CONJUG 1a VT 1 [+ *datos*] to readjust, adapt
2 [+ *persona*] (*profesionalmente*) to retrain; (*socialmente*) to rehabilitate

readmisión SF readmission

readmitir ▸ CONJUG 3a VT to readmit

readquirir ▸ CONJUG 3i VT to recover

reafirmación SF reaffirmation

reafirmar ▸ CONJUG 1a VT to reaffirm, reassert

reagrupación SF regrouping

reagrupar ▸ CONJUG 1a VT to regroup
VPR **reagruparse** to regroup

reagudizarse ▸ CONJUG 1f VPR [*problema*] to get worse again; [*enfermedad*] to get worse again, recrudesce

reaje‡ SM (*Cono Sur*) mob, rabble

reajustar ▸ CONJUG 1a VT 1 (= *volver a ajustar*) to readjust
2 (*Pol*) to reshuffle
3 (= *subir*) [+ *precios*] to increase, put up
VPR **reajustarse** to readjust

reajuste SM 1 (= *acción*) readjustment • **un doloroso ~ de sus ideas** an agonizing reappraisal of his ideas
2 (*Pol*) reshuffle ▸ **reajuste ministerial** cabinet reshuffle
3 (*Econ*) ▸ **reajuste de precios** (= *subida*) price rise, price increase ▸ **reajuste salarial** (= *recorte*) wage cut

real[1] ADJ (= *verdadero*) real • **esta vez el dolor era ~** this time the pain was real • **en la vida ~** in real life • **la película está basada en hechos ~es** the film is based on real *o* actual events

real[2] ADJ 1 (= *de la realeza*) royal • **la familia ~** the royal family • **porque no me da la ~ gana*** because I don't damn well feel like it*
2† (= *espléndido*) grand, splendid • **una ~ hembra** (*hum*) a fine figure of a woman
SM 1 (*tb* **real de la feria**) fairground
2 (*Hist*) army camp • MODISMO: • **asentar** *o* **sentar los ~es** (*Mil*) to set up camp; [*persona*] to install o.s. • **ha asentado sus ~es en mi casa y de aquí no lo sacas** he's installed himself in my house and you won't get him out of here
3 (*Hist, Econ*) *old Spanish coin of 25 céntimos, one quarter of a peseta* • **no tiene un ~*** he hasn't a bean*

reala SF (*CAm, Méx*) rope

realada SF (*Méx*) roundup, rodeo

realar ▸ CONJUG 1a VT (*Méx*) to round up

realce SM 1 (*Téc*) embossing
2 (*Arte*) highlight
3 (= *esplendor*) lustre, luster (EEUU), splendour, splendor (EEUU); (= *importancia*) importance, significance • **dar ~ a** (= *añadir*

esplendor) to add lustre to, enhance; (= *destacar*) to highlight • **poner de ~** to emphasize

realengo ADJ **1** *(LAm)* *[animal]* ownerless
2 *(Méx, Caribe)* (= *ocioso*) idle; (= *libre*) free, unattached

realeza SF royalty

realidad SF reality • **la ~ de la política** the realities of politics • **la ~ siempre supera a la ficción** truth is stranger than fiction • **atengámonos a la ~** let's stick to the facts • **la dura ~** the harsh reality • **en ~** in fact, actually • **la ~ es que ...** the fact (of the matter) is that ... ▸ **realidad virtual** virtual reality

realimentación SF *(Radio, Inform)* feedback; *(Aer)* refuelling, refueling *(EEUU)*

realineamiento SM realignment

realinear ▷ CONJUG 1a VT to realign

realismo SM realism ▸ **realismo mágico** magical realism ▸ **realismo social** social realism ▸ **realismo sucio** dirty realism

REALISMO MÁGICO

Realismo mágico, which derives from a term coined by the Cuban writer Alejo Carpentier in 1949, **lo real maravilloso**, refers to a primarily Latin American literary genre in which the writer combines elements of the fantastic and realistic in a conscious effort to reconcile tradition with modernity and American-Indian and Black oral culture with European literary writing. The most celebrated magical realist writer is Colombian Nobel prize winner Gabriel García Márquez.

realista ADJ realistic
SMF realist

reality SM (PL: **realities**) reality show

reality show [re'alitiʃow] SM (PL: **reality shows**) reality show

realizable ADJ **1** *[propósito]* attainable; *[proyecto]* practical, feasible
2 *(Econ)* *[activo]* realizable

realización SF **1** *[de proyecto]* carrying out
2 *[de promesa]* fulfilment, fulfillment *(EEUU)*
3 *[de propósito]* achievement, realization
4 *[de viaje, vuelo, visita, compra]* making • **tras la ~ de su primer vuelo** after making his first flight
5 *(Econ)* realization; (= *venta*) sale, selling-up; (= *liquidación*) clearance sale ▸ **realización de beneficios, realización de plusvalías** profit taking
6 *(Cine, TV)* production; *(Radio)* broadcast
7 *(Ling)* performance

realizado ADJ • **sentirse ~** to feel fulfilled

realizador(a) SM/F *(Cine, TV)* producer

realizar ▷ CONJUG 1f VT **1** *[+ propósito]* to achieve, realize; *[+ promesa]* to fulfil, fulfill *(EEUU)*, carry out; *[+ proyecto]* to carry out, put into effect
2 *[+ viaje, vuelo, visita, compra]* to make; *[+ expedición]* to carry out, go on
3 *(Econ)* *[+ activo]* to realize; *[+ existencias]* to sell off, sell up; *[+ ganancias]* to take
VPR **realizarse 1** *[sueño]* to come true; *[esperanzas]* to materialize; *[proyecto]* to be carried out
2 *[persona]* to fulfil o.s., fulfill o.s. *(EEUU)* • **~se como persona** to achieve personal fulfilment *o* *(EEUU)* fulfillment, fulfil *o* *(EEUU)* fulfill o.s. as a person

realmente[1] ADV **1** (= *verdaderamente*) really • **fue una época ~ difícil** it was a really difficult period
2 (= *de hecho*) really, actually • **lo prometió, aunque ~ no pensaba hacerlo** she promised to do it although she didn't actually *o* really intend to • **nunca me creí que fuera él ~ el autor** I never really *o* actually believed that he was the author

realmente[2] ADV *(referente a la realeza)* royally

realojar ▷ CONJUG 1a VT to rehouse

realojo SM rehousing

realquilado/a ADJ sublet
SM/F sublessee

realquilar ▷ CONJUG 1a VT (= *subarrendar*) to sublet; (= *alquilar de nuevo*) to relet

realzar ▷ CONJUG 1f VT **1** (= *dar más importancia*) to enhance, heighten, add to
2 *(Téc)* to emboss, raise
3 *(Arte)* to highlight

reanimación SF (= *restablecimiento*) *(tb fig)* revival; *[de un enfermo, accidentado]* resuscitation

reanimar ▷ CONJUG 1a VT **1** (= *dar fuerzas*) to revive • **un té bien caliente te ~á** a nice hot cup of tea will revive you
2 *[+ enfermo, accidentado]* to revive
3 (= *dar ánimo*) to cheer up • **sus palabras de consuelo lograron ~la** his words of comfort cheered her up
VPR **reanimarse** to revive

reanudación SF renewal, resumption

reanudar ▷ CONJUG 1a VT *[+ diálogo, viaje]* to resume • **~on su amistad tras una larga separación** they resumed their friendship after a long separation, they took up their friendship again after a long separation • **han reanudado las negociaciones** they have resumed the talks
VPR **reanudarse** to resume • **las clases se ~án el lunes** classes will resume on Monday

reaparecer ▷ CONJUG 2d VI (= *volver a aparecer*) to reappear; *[síntomas]* to recur

reaparición SF (= *nueva aparición*) reappearance; *[de síntomas]* recurrence

reapertura SF reopening

reaplicar ▷ CONJUG 1g VT to reapply

reaprovisionamiento SM replenishment, restocking

reaprovisionar ▷ CONJUG 1a VT to replenish, restock

rearmar ▷ CONJUG 1a VT to rearm
VPR **rearmarse** to rearm

rearme SM rearmament

reasegurar ▷ CONJUG 1a VT to reinsure

reaseguro SM reinsurance

reasentar ▷ CONJUG 1j VT to resettle

reasfaltado SM resurfacing

reasfaltar ▷ CONJUG 1a VT to resurface

reasumir ▷ CONJUG 3a VT to resume, reassume

reata SF **1** (= *cuerda*) rope *(joining string of pack animals)*; *(LAm)* (= *lazo*) rope, lasso; *(LAm)* (= *correa*) strap; *(And)* (= *tira de algodón*) strip of cotton cloth
2 (= *caballos*) string, string of horses, pack train • **de ~** (= *en hilera*) in single file, one after the other; (= *sumisamente*) submissively
3 *(And, Caribe, Méx)* *[de flores]* flowerbed, border
4 *(Méx)* (= *enrejado*) bamboo screen
5 *(Méx**)* (= *pene*) prick**, cock** • **echar ~** to fuck**

reavivar ▷ CONJUG 1a VT to revive

rebaja SF **1** (= *descuento*) reduction, discount • **me hicieron una ~ de seis euros** they gave me a six-euro reduction *o* discount • **¿me puede hacer alguna ~?** could you give me a discount? • **no hacemos devolución en los artículos de ~** sales goods cannot be returned
2 (= *reducción*) *[de impuestos, tarifas, condena]* reduction • **la empresa propone una ~ de los salarios de un 8%** the company is proposing an 8% wage cut *o* an 8% reduction in wages
3 rebajas *(en comercios)* sales • **las ~s de marzo** the spring sales • **"rebajas"** "sale" • **"grandes rebajas"** "big reductions", "sale" • **están de ~s en Harrods** Harrods have a sale, Harrods are having a sale

rebajado ADJ **1** *[precio]* reduced
2 *[producto]* cut-price
3 *[acera]* dropped

rebajamiento SM **1** (= *humillación*) • **nunca creí que llegara a tal ~** I never thought that he would lower himself *o* he would stoop so far • **~ de sí mismo** self-abasement
2 (= *rebaje*) *[de puerta, salario, condena, nivel del agua]* lowering
3 (= *reducción*) = **rebaja**

rebajar ▷ CONJUG 1a VT **1** (= *reducir*) **a** *(en dinero)* *[+ impuesto, coste, precio]* to reduce, cut, lower • **algunos bancos ~on ayer sus tipos de interés** some banks reduced *o* cut *o* lowered their interest rates yesterday • **le ~on el precio en un cinco por ciento** they reduced *o* cut the price by five per cent, they took five per cent off • **¿nos han rebajado algo?** have they taken something off?, have they given us a reduction *o* discount? • **hemos rebajado todos nuestros artículos** we have reduced all our stock
b *(en tiempo)* *[+ condena, castigo]* to reduce; *[+ edad, límite]* to lower • **le ~on la condena por buen comportamiento** his sentence was reduced for good behaviour • **han rebajado la edad penal a los 16 años** they have lowered the age of criminal responsibility to 16 • **propusieron ~ la jornada de trabajo** they proposed shortening the working day • **rebajó la plusmarca mundial en 1,2 segundos** he took 1.2 seconds off the world record
c *(en cantidad)* *[+ nivel, temperatura]* to reduce, lower; *[+ luz, tensión, intensidad]* to reduce; *[+ peso]* to lose; *[+ dolor]* to ease, alleviate • **la OMS aconseja ~ el consumo de azúcar en la dieta** the WHO recommends reducing *o* lowering the sugar intake in one's diet • **quiere ~ cinco kilos** he wants to take off *o* lose five kilos • **el hotel rebajó su categoría de cinco a cuatro estrellas** the hotel reduced its rating from five-star to four-star
2 (= *diluir*) *[+ líquido]* to dilute; *[+ pintura]* to thin; *[+ color]* to tone down; *[+ droga]* to cut, adulterate • **siempre rebaja el vino con gaseosa** he always dilutes his wine with soda water • **echa un poco más de agua al caldo para ~lo de sal** put a bit more water in the soup to make it less salty
3 (= *bajar la altura de*) *[+ terreno]* to lower, lower the level of; *[+ tejado]* to lower; *[+ puerta]* to rabbet
4 (= *humillar*) to humiliate, put down • **rebajó a su mujer delante de sus amigos** he put his wife down *o* humiliated his wife in front of their friends • **piensa que ese trabajo lo rebaja** he thinks that job is beneath him *o* is humiliating • **ese tipo de comportamiento te rebaja** that sort of behaviour does you no credit
5 *(Mil)* (= *eximir*) to exempt (**de** from)
VI • **~ de peso** *(Arg, Uru)* to slim, lose weight • **una dieta para ~ de peso** a diet to lose weight, a slimming diet
VPR **rebajarse 1** • **~se a hacer algo** to lower o.s. to do sth, stoop to do sth • **yo no me ~ía a hablar con él** I wouldn't lower myself *o* I wouldn't stoop to talk to him • **~se ante algn** to humble o.s. before sb • **es demasiado orgulloso para ~se ante ti** he's too proud to humble himself before you
2 *(Arg, Uru)* • **me rebajé el pelo** I had my hair cut in layers

rebaje SM **1** *[de terreno, nivel]* lowering

2 (*Téc*) (*en madera*) rabbet
3 (*Econ*) cut
rebajo SM (*Téc*) rabbet
rebalsa SF pool, puddle
rebalsar ▷ CONJUG 1a VT 1 [+ *agua*] to dam, dam up, block
2 (*LAm*) [+ *orillas*] to burst, overflow
VPR **rebalsarse** to form a pool, form a lake, become dammed up
rebanada SF 1 (*Culin*) slice
2 (*Méx*) (= *pestillo*) latch
rebanar ▷ CONJUG 1a VT [+ *pan*] to slice; [+ *árbol*] to slice through, slice down; [+ *pierna**] to slice off
rebañar ▷ CONJUG 1a VT [+ *restos*] to scrape up • **rebañó la salsa (del plato) con pan** he wiped *o* mopped the sauce up (from the plate) with bread • **rebañó el plato de arroz** she mopped up the rice from the plate • **logró ~ ciertos fondos** he managed to scrape some money together
rebaño SM 1 [*de ovejas*] flock; [*de cabras*] herd
2 [*de personas*] (*tb Rel*) flock
rebasar ▷ CONJUG 1a VT 1 [+ *límite*] to pass; [+ *punto*] to pass, go beyond; [+ *límite de tiempo*] to exceed; (*en cualidad, cantidad*) to exceed, surpass; (*en carrera, progreso*) to overtake, leave behind • **han rebasado ya los límites razonables** they have already gone beyond all reasonable limits • **el inglés lo rebasó en la última vuelta** the Englishman overtook *o* passed him on the last lap • **nuestro sistema educativo ya ha rebasado al europeo** our education system has now overtaken the European one
2 (*esp Méx*) (*Aut*) to overtake, pass (*EEUU*); (*Náut*) to sail past
rebatible ADJ 1 [*argumento*] easily refuted
2 [*silla*] tip-up
rebatinga SF (*CAm, Méx*) = **rebatiña**
rebatiña SF (*LAm*) scramble, rush • **les echó caramelos a la ~** he threw sweets so that they could scramble for them • **andar a la ~ de algo** (= *pelear por algo*) to scramble for sth, fight over sth; (= *discutir por algo*) to argue fiercely over sth
rebatir ▷ CONJUG 3a VT 1 [+ *ataque*] to repel; [+ *golpe*] to parry, ward off
2 [+ *argumento*] to reject, refute; [+ *sugerencia*] to reject; [+ *tentación*] to resist
3 [+ *suma*] to reduce; [+ *descuento*] to deduct, knock off
rebato SM (= *alarma*) alarm; (*Mil*) surprise attack • **llamar** *o* (*frm*) **tañer** *o* **tocar a ~** to sound the alarm
rebautizar ▷ CONJUG 1f VT to rechristen
Rebeca SF Rebecca
rebeca SF cardigan
rebeco SM chamois, ibex
rebelarse ▷ CONJUG 1a VPR to rebel • **~ contra** to rebel against
rebelde ADJ 1 (= *que se rebela*) rebellious • **el gobierno ~** the rebel government • **ser ~ a algo** to rebel against sth
2 [*niño*] unruly; [*resfriado*] persistent; [*mancha*] stubborn; [*pelo*] wild; [*problema*] difficult; [*sustancia*] difficult to work with
3 (*Jur*) defaulting
SMF 1 (*Mil, Pol*) rebel
2 (*Jur*) defaulter
rebeldía SF 1 (= *cualidad*) rebelliousness; (= *desafío*) defiance, disobedience • **estar en plena ~** to be in open revolt
2 (*Jur*) default • **caer en ~** to be in default • **fue juzgado en ~** he was judged by *o* in default
rebelión SF rebellion
rebelón ADJ hard-mouthed
rebencudo ADJ (*Caribe*) stubborn
rebenque SM (*LAm*) whip, riding crop
rebenqueada* SF (*LAm*) whipping, lashing
rebenquear* ▷ CONJUG 1a VT (*LAm*) to whip, lash
reblandecer ▷ CONJUG 2d VT to soften
VPR **reblandecerse** to go soft
reblandecido* ADJ (*And*) (= *loco*) soft in the head; (= *senil*) senile
reblandecimiento SM softening • **~ cerebral** softening of the brain
reble‡ SM bum‡, ass (*EEUU**‡), bottom
rebobinado SM rewinding
rebobinar ▷ CONJUG 1a VT to rewind
rebojo SM crust, piece of bread
rebolichada SF (*Méx*) opportunity
rebolludo ADJ thickset, chunky*
reborde SM (= *saliente*) ledge; (*Téc*) flange, rim
rebosadero SM overflow
rebosante ADJ • **~ de** (*lit, fig*) brimming with, overflowing with
rebosar ▷ CONJUG 1a VI 1 [*líquido, recipiente*] to overflow • **el café rebosa de la taza** the coffee cup is running over, the coffee is running *o* spilling over the edge of the cup • **la alegría le rebosa** he bubbles over with happiness • **les rebosa el dinero** they have pots of money • **el grupo llenó la sala a ~** the group filled the room to overflowing
2 • **~ de algo** to overflow with sth, be brimming with sth • **~ de salud** to be radiant with health
3 (= *abundar*) to abound, be plentiful
VT to abound in • **su rostro rebosaba salud** he was the picture of health
reboso SM (*Caribe, Cono Sur*) driftwood
rebotado* SM (= *sacerdote*) ex-priest; (= *monje*) former monk
rebotar ▷ CONJUG 1a VT 1 [+ *pelota*] to bounce; [+ *ataque*] to repel, beat back; [+ *rayos*] to bounce back, cause to bounce off
2 [+ *clavo*] to clinch
3* [+ *persona*] to annoy
4 (*And, Méx*) [+ *agua*] to muddy, stir up
VI [*pelota*] to bounce; [*bala*] to ricochet, glance (**de** off)
VPR **rebotarse*** to get cheesed off* • **~se con algn** to have a dig at sb*, have a go at sb*
rebote SM bounce, rebound • **de ~** (= *en el segundo bote*) on the rebound; (*fig*) (= *de rechazo*) indirectly
reboteador(a) SM/F rebounder
rebotear ▷ CONJUG 1a VI to get rebounds
rebotica SF back room
rebozado ADJ (*Culin*) fried in batter, fried in breadcrumbs
rebozar ▷ CONJUG 1f VT 1 (*Culin*) to roll in batter, roll in breadcrumbs
2 (*frm*) [+ *rostro*] to muffle up, cover
VPR **rebozarse** to muffle (o.s.) up
rebozo SM 1 (= *mantilla*) muffler, wrap; (*LAm*) (= *chal*) shawl
2 (*frm*) (= *ocultación*) dissimulation • **de ~** secretly • **sin ~** openly, frankly
rebrotar ▷ CONJUG 1a VI to break out again, reappear
rebrote SM new outbreak, reappearance
rebufar ▷ CONJUG 1a VI to snort loudly
rebufo SM loud snort
rebujo SM (= *maraña*) mass, knot, tangle; (= *paquete*) badly-wrapped parcel
rebullicio SM (= *bullicio*) hubbub, uproar; (= *agitación*) agitation
rebullir ▷ CONJUG 3a VT (*Méx*) to stir up
VPR **rebullirse** to stir, begin to move
rebultado ADJ bulky
rebumbio* SM (*Méx*) racket, din, hubbub
rebusca SF 1 (= *busca*) search
2 (*Agr*) gleaning
3 (= *restos*) leftovers (*pl*), remains (*pl*)
4 (*And, Cono Sur*) (= *negocio*) small business; (= *negocio ilegal**) shady dealing, illicit trading; (= *ganancia*) profit on the side
rebuscado ADJ 1 [*estilo*] affected; [*palabra*] recherché
2 (*LAm*) (= *afectado*) affected, stuck-up*
rebuscar ▷ CONJUG 1g VT 1 [+ *objeto*] to search carefully for; (*Agr*) to glean
2 [+ *lugar*] to search carefully; [+ *montón*] to search through, rummage in
VI (= *buscar minuciosamente*) to search carefully; (*Agr*) to glean • **estuve rebuscando en los armarios y no lo encontré** I was looking in the cupboards and I couldn't find it
VPR **rebuscarse*** 1 (*And, Cono Sur*) (= *buscar trabajo*) to look for work
2 (*And*) (= *ingeniárselas*) to get by
rebuznar ▷ CONJUG 1a VI to bray
rebuzno SM bray, braying
recabar ▷ CONJUG 1a VT 1 (= *obtener*) to manage to get (**de** from) • **~ fondos** to raise funds
2 (= *reclamar*) to claim as of right, assert one's claim to
3 (= *solicitar*) to ask for, apply for; (= *exigir*) to demand, insist on
recadero/a SM/F (= *mensajero*) messenger; (= *repartidor*) errand boy/girl
recado SM 1 (= *mensaje*) message • **chico de los ~s** messenger, errand boy • **coger** *o* **tomar un ~** (*por teléfono*) to take a message • **dejar ~** to leave a message • **enviar a algn a un ~** to send sb on an errand • **mandar ~** to send word • **salir a un ~** • **salir a hacer un ~** to go out on an errand
2 (= *provisión*) provisions (*pl*), daily shopping
3 (= *equipo*) equipment, materials (*pl*)
▸ **recado de escribir** writing case, set of writing materials
4 (*LAm*) (= *montura*) saddle and trappings
5 (*Caribe*) (= *saludos*) greetings (*pl*) • **déle ~s a su familia** give my regards to his family
6†† (= *regalo*) gift, small present
recaer ▷ CONJUG 2n VI 1 (*Med*) to suffer a relapse, relapse
2 [*criminal etc*] to fall back, relapse (**en** into)
3 • **~ en** *o* **sobre** [*elección*] to fall on, fall to; [*premio*] to go to; [*legado*] to pass to; [*deber*] to devolve upon • **las sospechas recayeron sobre el conserje** suspicion fell on the porter • **esta carga ~á más sobre los pobres** the poor will be the hardest hit by this burden • **la acusación recayó sobre él mismo** the charge came back on him
4 (*Arquit*) • **~ a** to look out on, look over
recaída SF relapse (**en** into)
recalar ▷ CONJUG 1a VT to saturate, soak
VI 1 (*Náut*) to sight land, reach port
2* (= *terminar en*) to end up (**en** at)
3 • **~ a algn** (*LAm*) (= *recurrir*) to go to sb for help
recalcar ▷ CONJUG 1g VT 1 (= *subrayar*) to stress, emphasize • **~ algo a algn** to stress the importance of sth to sb • **~ a algn que ...** to tell sb emphatically that ... • **~ cada sílaba** to stress every syllable
2 [+ *contenido*] to press down, squeeze in; [+ *recipiente*] to cram, stuff (**de** with)
VI 1 (*Náut*) to list, heel
2 (*esp LAm*) (= *terminar en*) to end up (**en** at, in)
VPR **recalcarse** • **~se un hueso** (*LAm*) to dislocate a bone
recalcitrante ADJ recalcitrant
recalcitrar ▷ CONJUG 1a VI 1 (= *echarse atrás*) to take a step back
2 (= *resistir*) to resist, be stubborn, refuse to take heed
recalentado ADJ warmed-up

recalentamiento SM **1** (= *calentamiento*) overheating ▸ **recalentamiento del planeta** global warming
2 (*Culin*) warming-up, reheating
recalentar ▸ CONJUG 1j VT **1** (*demasiado*) to overheat
2 [+ *comida*] to warm up, reheat
VPR **recalentarse** to get too hot
recalificación SF reassessment
recalificar ▸ CONJUG 1g VT to reassess
recalmón SM lull
recamado SM embroidery
recamar ▸ CONJUG 1a VT to embroider
recámara SF **1** (= *cuarto*) side room; (= *vestidor*) dressing room; (*esp Méx*) (= *dormitorio*) bedroom
2 [*de fusil*] breech, chamber
3 (= *cautela*) caution, wariness • **tener mucha ~** to be on the careful side, be naturally cautious
recamarera SF (*esp Méx*) chambermaid, maid
recambiar ▸ CONJUG 1b VT to change over
recambio SM (*Mec*) spare; [*de pluma*] refill • **neumático de ~** spare tyre, spare tire (EEUU) • **piezas de ~** spares, spare parts
recañí‡ SF window
recapacitar ▸ CONJUG 1a VT to think over, reflect (up)on
VI to think things over, reflect
recapitulación SF recapitulation, summing-up
recapitular ▸ CONJUG 1a VT, VI to recapitulate, sum up
recargable ADJ rechargeable
recargado ADJ (= *sobrecargado*) overloaded; [*estilo, diseño*] overelaborate
recargar ▸ CONJUG 1h VT **1** [+ *encendedor, bolígrafo*] to refill; [+ *batería, pila*] to recharge; [+ *arma*] to reload; [+ *tarjeta de móvil*] to top up
2 (= *cargar demasiado*) to clutter • **han recargado la habitación con muebles** they have cluttered the room with furniture
3 (*Econ*) • **nos han recargado un 20%** we have to pay a 20% surcharge
4 (*Jur*†) [+ *sentencia*] to increase
recargo SM **1** (*Econ*) extra charge, surcharge; (= *aumento*) increase
2 (*Jur*) new charge, further charge
3 (*Med*) rise in temperature
4 (= *carga nueva*) new burden; (= *aumento de carga*) extra load, additional load
recatadamente ADV modestly
recatado ADJ **1** (= *modesto*) modest, shy, demure
2 (= *prudente*) cautious, circumspect
recatar ▸ CONJUG 1a VT to hide
VPR **recatarse 1** (= *ser discreto*) to act discreetly • **sin ~se** openly
2 (= *ser prudente*) to be cautious; (= *vacilar*) to hesitate • **~se de algo** to fight shy of sth • **no se recata ante nada** nothing daunts her
3 (= *ocultarse*) to hide o.s. away (**de** from)
recato SM **1** (= *modestia*) modesty, shyness
2 (= *cautela*) caution, circumspection; (= *reserva*) reserve, restraint • **sin ~** openly, unreservedly
recatón SM (*And*) miner's pick
recauchado SM, **recauchaje** SM (*Chile*) retreading, remoulding, remolding (EEUU)
recauchar ▸ CONJUG 1a VT to retread, remould, remold (EEUU)
recauchutado SM **1** [*de neumático*] retread
2 (= *proceso*) retreading, remoulding, remolding (EEUU)
recauchutar ▸ CONJUG 1a VT [+ *neumático*] to retread, remould, remold (EEUU)
recaudación SF **1** (= *acción*) collection ▸ **recaudación de fondos** fundraising
2 (= *cantidad*) takings (*pl*); (*Dep*) gate, gate money; ▸ QUINIELA
3† (= *oficina*) tax office
recaudador(a) SM/F ▸ **recaudador(a) de impuestos** tax collector
recaudadora SF (*And*) tax office, Internal Revenue Service (EEUU)
recaudar ▸ CONJUG 1a VT [+ *impuestos*] to collect; [+ *dinero*] to raise; (*Com*) to take; [+ *fondos*] to raise; [+ *deuda*] to recover
recaudería SF (*Méx*) greengrocer's shop
recaudo SM **1** (*Econ*) collection
2 (= *cuidado*) care, protection; (= *precaución*) precaution • **estar a buen ~** to be in a safe place • **poner algo a buen ~** to put sth in a safe place
3 (*Jur*) surety, security
4 (*CAm, Cono Sur, Méx*) (= *especias*) spices, condiments
5 (*CAm, Cono Sur, Méx*) (= *legumbres*) *daily supply of fresh vegetables*
recebo SM gravel
recechar ▸ CONJUG 1a VT to stalk
rececho SM stalking • **cazar a** *o* **en ~** to stalk
recechor(a) SM/F stalker
recelar ▸ CONJUG 1a VT • **~ que ...** to suspect that ..., fear that ...
VI • **~ de** to be suspicious of • **~ de hacer algo** to be wary of doing sth
recelo SM (= *suspicacia*) suspicion; (= *temor*) misgiving, apprehension; (= *desconfianza*) distrust, mistrust
receloso ADJ (= *suspicaz*) suspicious; (= *desconfiado*) distrustful; (= *temeroso*) apprehensive
recensión SF review
recepción SF **1** (= *acto*) reception
2 (*Radio*) reception
3 (= *ceremonia*) reception
4 (= *cuarto*) drawing room; [*de hotel*] reception, reception desk
recepcionar ▸ CONJUG 1a VT (*esp LAm*) to receive, accept
recepcionista SMF receptionist, hotel receptionist
receptación SF receiving, crime of receiving
receptáculo SM receptacle
receptar ▸ CONJUG 1a VT to receive
receptividad SF receptivity
receptivo ADJ receptive
receptor(a) SM (*Elec, Radio, TV*) receiver ▸ **receptor de televisión** television set
SM/F **1** (*Med*) recipient ▸ **receptor(a) universal** universal recipient
2 (*Béisbol*) catcher; (*en fútbol americano*) receiver
3 (*Ling*) recipient
recesar ▸ CONJUG 1a VI (*LAm*) (*Pol*) to recess, go into recess
recesión SF (*Com, Econ*) recession; [*de precios*] slide, fall
recesivo ADJ **1** (*Bio*) recessive
2 (*Econ*) recession (*antes de s*), recessionary
receso SM **1** (*LAm*) (*Parl*) recess
2 (*Econ*) ▸ **receso económico** downturn in the economy
receta SF **1** (*Culin*) recipe (**de** for)
2 (*Med*) prescription • **"con receta médica"** "available on prescription only"
recetar ▸ CONJUG 1a VT **1** (*Med*) to prescribe
2 (*CAm, Méx*) [+ *golpe*] to deal
recetario SM collection of recipes, recipe book
rechace SM **1** (= *rechazo*) rejection
2 (*Dep*) rebound
rechazamiento SM **1** [*de ataque, enemigo*] repelling, repulsion
2 [*de acusación, idea*] rejection; [*de oferta*] refusal; [*de tentación*] resistance, rejection
3 [*de luz*] reflection
4 (*Med*) [*de órgano*] rejection
rechazar ▸ CONJUG 1f VT **1** [+ *persona*] to push away; [+ *ataque*] to repel, beat off; [+ *enemigo*] to drive back
2 [+ *acusación, idea*] to reject; [+ *oferta*] to turn down, refuse; [+ *tentación*] to resist
3 [+ *luz*] to reflect; [+ *agua*] to throw off
4 (*Med*) [+ *órgano*] to reject
rechazo SM **1** (= *negativa*) refusal • **~ frontal** [*de propuesta*] outright rejection; [*de oferta*] flat refusal
2 (*Med*) rejection
3 (= *rebote*) bounce, rebound • **de ~** on the rebound
4 (= *desaire*) rebuff
5 [*de fusil*] recoil
rechifla SF **1** (= *silbido*) whistling; (= *abucheo*) booing; (*Teat*) catcall
2 (= *burla*) mockery
rechiflar ▸ CONJUG 1a VT (= *silbar*) to whistle at; (= *abuchear*) to boo
VI (= *silbar*) to whistle; (= *abuchear*) boo
VPR **rechiflarse 1** • **~se de algn** to make a fool of sb
2 (*Cono Sur*) (= *enojarse*) to get cross, lose one's temper
rechín SM (*And*) piece of burnt food • **huele a ~** I can smell food burning
rechinamiento SM [*de madera, puerta*] creak, creaking; [*de máquina*] clank, clanking; [*de metal seco*] grating; [*de motor*] grinding, whirr, whirring; [*de dientes*] grinding
rechinar ▸ CONJUG 1a VI **1** (= *chirriar*) [*madera, puerta*] to creak; [*máquina*] to clank; [*metal seco*] to grate; [*motor*] to grind, whirr; [*dientes*] to grind, gnash • **hacer ~ los dientes** to grind one's teeth
2 (*And, Cono Sur, Méx**) (= *rabiar*) to rage, fume
3 (*Caribe*) (= *quejarse*) to grumble; (= *contestar*) to answer back
VT (*CAm, Méx*) (*Culin*) to burn, overcook
VPR **rechinarse 1** (*CAm, Méx*) (= *quemarse*) to burn, overcook
2 (*Cono Sur**) (= *enojarse*) to get cross, lose one's temper
rechinido SM, **rechino** SM = **rechinamiento**
rechistar ▸ CONJUG 1a VI to complain • **se fue a la cama sin ~** he went to bed without complaint, he went to bed without a word of complaint • **nadie se atrevió a ~** nobody dared complain
rechonchez SF stockiness
rechoncho ADJ thickset, stocky
rechupete • **de ~*** ADJ (= *estupendo*) splendid, jolly good*; [*comida*] delicious, scrumptious*
ADV splendidly, jolly well* • **pasarlo de ~** to have a fantastic time* • **el examen me ha salido de ~** the exam went like a dream for me
recial SM rapids (*pl*)
reciamente ADV (= *fuertemente*) strongly; (= *con intensidad*) intensely
recibí SM "received with thanks" • **poner el ~ en algo** to sign for sth
recibidero ADJ receivable
recibido ADJ (*LAm*) qualified
recibidor[1] SM [*de casa*] hall
recibidor[2]**(a)** SM/F (= *persona*) recipient, receiver
recibimiento SM **1** (= *acogida*) welcome, reception • **dispensar a algn un ~ apoteósico** to give sb a tremendous *o* (*frm*) rapturous welcome *o* reception
2† (= *antesala*) anteroom, vestibule; (= *sala*) reception room; (= *vestíbulo*) hall

recibir ▷ CONJUG 3a (VT) **1** (= *ser beneficiario de*) **a** [+ *dinero, apoyo, llamada, noticias*] to receive, get; [+ *ayuda, homenaje*] to receive • **~án una compensación económica** they'll get compensation, they will receive financial compensation (*más frm*) • **he recibido del Sr Gómez la cantidad de ...** (*en recibo*) received from Sr Gómez the sum of ... • **¿recibiste mi carta?** did you get my letter? • **estamos a la espera de ~ más mercancía** we're waiting for some new stock to arrive • **recibió el premio a la mejor película extranjera** it won the prize for best foreign film • **recibió la orden de vender las acciones** he was instructed to sell the shares • **no reciben bien el Canal 8** the reception is not very good on Channel 8 • **"mensaje recibido"** (*Radio*) "message received" • **~ asistencia médica** to receive medical assistance, be given medical assistance • **~ el calificativo de** to be labelled (as) • **~ el nombre de** (*frm*) (= *llamarse*) to be called; (*al nacer*) to be named
b [*lago, río, mar*] • **el río recibe las aguas de numerosos afluentes** a great many tributaries flow into the river
2 (= *sufrir*) [+ *susto*] to get • **recibió un susto tremendo** she got a terrible shock • **~ un disparo** to be shot • **~ un golpe** to be hit, be struck
3 [+ *persona*] **a** (= *acoger*) to welcome • **estaba en la puerta para ~ a los invitados** she was at the door to welcome the guests • **los recibieron muy mal** they were given a very poor welcome • **nos recibieron con gran alegría** they gave us a very warm welcome • **recibía a sus invitados en el salón** she entertained her guests in the drawing room • **ir a ~ a algn** to meet sb • **fueron a ~los a la estación** they went to meet them at the station • **salieron a ~los al jardín** they received them in the garden • MODISMO: • **~ a algn con los brazos abiertos** to welcome sb with open arms
b (*para reunión, entrevista*) (*gen*) to see; (*formalmente*) to receive • **el doctor lo ~á enseguida** the doctor will see you in a moment • **el rey se negó a ~los** the king refused to receive them • **hoy no puede ~ visitas** she can't receive visitors today • **no se les permite ~ visitas de sus familiares** they are not allowed family visits
c (*en el matrimonio*) to take • **la recibió por esposa** he took her as *o* for his wife
4 (*Taur*) • **~ al toro** to meet the bull's charge
5 (= *aceptar*) [+ *propuesta, sugerencia*] to receive • **la oferta fue mal recibida** the offer was badly received
6 (*en correspondencia*) • **recibe un fuerte abrazo de tus padres** lots of love from Mum and Dad • **reciba un saludo de ...** yours sincerely ... • **recibe mi más sincera felicitación** my sincerest congratulations
7 (= *sostener*) [+ *peso*] to bear • **estas paredes reciben el peso de la casa** these are load-bearing walls
(VI) **1** (*frm*) (*en casa*) (= *tener invitados*) to entertain; (= *tener visitas*) to receive visitors • **reciben mucho en casa** they entertain a lot • **la baronesa solo puede ~ los lunes** the baroness is only at home on Mondays, the baroness can only receive visitors on Mondays
2 [*médico*] to see patients • **el dentista no recibe los viernes** the dentist doesn't see patients on Fridays
(VPR) **recibirse** (*LAm*) (*Univ*) to graduate • **aún no se ha recibido** he hasn't graduated yet • **me faltan dos años para ~me** I've got two years to go before I graduate • **~se de** to qualify as • **~se de abogado** to qualify as a lawyer • **~se de doctor** to get *o* (*frm*) take one's doctorate, receive one's doctor's degree

recibo (SM) **1** (= *factura*) bill, account • **~ de la luz** electricity bill
2 [*de dinero*] receipt • **acusar ~ (de algo)** to acknowledge receipt (of sth)
3 • MODISMO: • **ser de ~**: • **no es de ~ que...** it is unacceptable that ...
4 (*frm*) • **estar de ~** [*persona*] to be at home, be at home to callers; [*traje, objeto*] to be ready for collection

reciclable (ADJ) recyclable
reciclado (ADJ) recycled
(SM) (*Téc*) recycling; [*de persona*] retraining
reciclador (ADJ) recycling
recicladora (SF) (= *planta*) recycling plant; (= *empresa*) recycling firm
reciclaje (SM), **reciclamiento** (SM) [*de papel, vidrio*] recycling; [*de profesional*] retraining; [*de plan*] modification, adjustment
reciclar ▷ CONJUG 1a (VT) (*Téc*) to recycle; [+ *profesional*] to retrain; [+ *plan*] to modify, adjust
(VPR) **reciclarse** [*profesional*] to retrain
recidiva (SF) relapse
reciedumbre (SF) (= *fuerza*) strength; (= *vigor*) vigour, vigor (EEUU)
recién (ADV) **1** (*antepuesto a participio*) newly • **~ casado** newly married • **los ~ casados** the newlyweds • **~ hecho** newly-made • **~ llegado** newly arrived • **los ~ llegados** (*a un lugar*) the newcomers; (*a una reunión*) the latecomers • **el ~ nacido** the newborn • **un ~ nacido** a newborn child
2 (*LAm*) (= *apenas*) just, recently • **~ llegó** he has only just arrived, he arrived only recently • **~ se acordó** he has just remembered it • **~ me lo acaban de decir** they've only just told me • **~ ahora** right now, this very moment • **~ aquí** right here, just here
reciente (ADJ) recent • **un descubrimiento muy ~** a very recent discovery • **su muerte está aún muy ~ en nuestra memoria** her death is still very fresh in our memory
recientemente (ADV) recently
Recife (SM) Recife
recinto (SM) (= *cercado*) enclosure; (= *área*) area, place; (= *zona delimitada*) precincts (*pl*) • **dentro del ~ universitario** on the university campus ▸ **recinto amurallado** walled enclosure ▸ **recinto ferial** exhibition site ▸ **recinto fortificado** fortified place ▸ **recinto penitenciario** prison grounds (*pl*)
recio (ADJ) **1** (= *fuerte*) [*persona*] strong, tough; [*cuerda*] thick, strong; [*prueba*] tough, demanding, severe; [*tierra*] solid
2 [*voz*] loud
3 [*tiempo*] harsh, severe
4 (= *intenso*) • **en lo más ~ del combate** in the thick of the fight • **en lo más ~ del invierno** in the depths of winter
(ADV) [*soplar, golpear*] hard; [*cantar, gritar*] loudly
recipiendario/a (SM/F) (*frm*) newly-elected member
recipiente (SMF) (= *persona*) recipient
(SM) (= *vaso*) container
reciprocación (SF) reciprocation
recíprocamente (ADV) reciprocally, mutually
reciprocar ▷ CONJUG 1g (VT) to reciprocate
reciprocidad (SF) reciprocity • **usar de ~** to reciprocate
recíproco (ADJ) (= *mutuo*) reciprocal; (= *inverso*) inverse • **a la recíproca** vice versa • **estar a la recíproca** to be ready to respond

recitación (SF) recitation
recitado (SM) (= *recitación*) recitation; (*Mús*) recitative
recital (SM) [*de música*] recital; [*de literatura*] reading • **dio todo un ~ del arte de torear** he gave a virtuoso demonstration of the bullfighter's art ▸ **recital de poesía** poetry reading
recitar ▷ CONJUG 1a (VT) to recite
recitativo (SM) recitative
reclamable (ADJ) reclaimable
reclamación (SF) **1** (= *queja*) complaint • **formular** *o* **presentar una ~** to make *o* lodge a complaint
2 (= *reivindicación*) claim ▸ **reclamación salarial** wage claim
reclamar ▷ CONJUG 1a (VT) **1** [+ *herencia, tierras*] to claim; [+ *derechos*] to demand • **reclama su parte de los beneficios** he is claiming his share of the profits • **~ daños y perjuicios** to claim damages • **reclaman mejores condiciones de trabajo** they're demanding better working conditions • **~ una deuda** to demand payment of a debt • **~on su presencia ante el tribunal** they demanded him to appear before the court
2 [+ *atención, solución*] to demand • **esto reclama toda nuestra atención** this demands our full attention
3 [+ *aves*] to call to
(VI) (= *quejarse*) to complain • **fui a ~ al director** I went and complained to the manager • **~ contra algo** to complain about sth • **~ contra una sentencia** (*Jur*) to appeal against a sentence
(VPR) **reclamarse** [*aves*] to call to one another
reclame (SM o SF) (*LAm*) advertisement • **mercadería de ~** loss leader
reclamo (SM) **1** (*Orn*) call; (*Caza*) decoy, lure
2 (= *llamada*) call • **acudir al ~** to answer the call
3 (= *anuncio*) advertisement; (= *slogan*) advertising slogan; (= *aliciente*) lure, attraction; (*Tip*) catchword ▸ **reclamo publicitario** advertising ploy
4 (*Jur*) claim
5 (= *afirmación*) claim, statement
6 (*LAm*) (= *protesta*) complaint
reclasificar ▷ CONJUG 1g (VT) to reclassify
reclinable (ADJ) • **asiento ~** reclining seat
reclinar ▷ CONJUG 1a (VT) to lean, recline, rest (**contra** against, **sobre** on)
(VPR) **reclinarse** to lean back
reclinatorio (SM) prie-dieu
recluir ▷ CONJUG 3g (VT) (= *encerrar*) to shut away; (*Jur*) (= *encarcelar*) to imprison
(VPR) **recluirse** to shut o.s. away
reclusión (SF) **1** (= *encarcelamiento*) imprisonment, confinement ▸ **reclusión mayor** imprisonment in conditions of maximum security ▸ **reclusión perpetua** life imprisonment
2 (= *cárcel*) prison
3 (= *encierro voluntario*) seclusion
recluso/a (ADJ) imprisoned • **población reclusa** prison population
(SM/F) **1** (*Jur*) inmate, prisoner ▸ **recluso/a de confianza** trusty ▸ **recluso/a preventivo/a** prisoner on remand, remand prisoner
2 (= *ermitaño*) recluse
reclusorio (SM) (*esp Méx*) prison
recluta (SMF) (= *persona*) recruit
(SF) (= *reclutamiento*) recruitment
reclutamiento (SM) recruitment
reclutar ▷ CONJUG 1a (VT) **1** [+ *soldados*] to recruit; [+ *trabajadores*] to contract, take on
2 (*Arg*) [+ *ganado*] to round up
recobrar ▷ CONJUG 1a (VT) [+ *salud*] to

r

recover, get back; [+ *ciudad, fugitivo*] to recapture; [+ *amistad*] to win back • **~ las fuerzas** to get one's strength back • **~ el conocimiento** to regain consciousness, come to • **solo ha recobrado parte del dinero que le robaron** he has recovered only part of the money stolen from him • **el país ha recobrado la calma** the country is calm again, calm has returned to the country
(VPR) **recobrarse 1** (*Med*) (= *recuperarse*) to recover • **aún no se ha recobrado del accidente** he still hasn't recovered from the accident
2 (*frm*) (= *volver en sí*) to regain consciousness, come to
3 (*frm*) (= *serenarse*) to collect o.s.

recobro (SM) [*de salud*] recovery; [*de ciudad, fugitivo*] recapture; [*de dinero*] recovery, retrieval

recocer ▸ CONJUG 2b, 2h (VT) **1** (= *calentar*) to warm up, heat up; (= *cocer demasiado*) to overcook
2 (*Metal*) to anneal
3 (*Cono Sur*) (= *cocer*) to cook
(VPR) **recocerse*** (= *reconcomerse*) to be eaten up inside

recochinearse* ▸ CONJUG 1a (VPR) • **~ de algn** (*Esp*) to take the mickey out of sb*

recochineo* (SM) mickey-taking*

recocido (ADJ) **1** (= *demasiado cocido*) overcooked
2 (= *vuelto a cocinar*) warmed up, heated up

recocina (SF) scullery

recodar ▸ CONJUG 1a (VI) to form a bend

recodo (SM) bend, turn

recogecables (SM INV) automatic cable retractor

recogedor (SM) (= *recipiente*) dustpan; (= *herramienta*) rake, scraper

recogepelotas (SMF INV) ball boy/ball girl

recoger ▸ CONJUG 2c (VT) **1** (= *levantar*) [+ *objeto caído*] to pick up; [+ *objetos dispersos*] to gather (up), gather together • **se agachó para ~ la cuchara** he bent down to pick up the spoon • **recogí el papel del suelo** I picked the paper up off the floor • **recogió la ropa del suelo** she gathered the clothes up off the floor • **si tiras agua en el suelo recógela con la fregona** if you spill water on the floor mop it up
2 (= *recolectar*) [+ *datos, información*] to gather, collect; [+ *dinero, firmas*] to collect; [+ *correo, basura*] to collect, pick up • **¿a qué hora recogen el correo?** what time is the mail *o* post collected?, what time do they collect the mail *o* post? • **a las diez recogen la basura** the rubbish gets collected at ten o'clock
3 (= *ordenar*) [+ *objetos*] to clear up, clear away; [+ *casa, habitación*] to tidy up, straighten up • **recógelo todo antes de marcharte** clear up everything before you leave • **recogí los platos y los puse en el fregadero** I cleared away the plates and put them in the sink • **~ la mesa** to clear the table • **recoge tus cosas** get your things together, gather up your things
4 (= *guardar*) [+ *ropa lavada*] to take in, get in; [+ *herramientas*] to put away
5 (*Agr*) to harvest, gather in, take in; [+ *fruta, guisantes*] to pick; [+ *flores*] to pick, gather
6 (= *reducir, ajustar*) [+ *cuerda, vela*] to take in; [+ *alas*] to fold; [+ *cuernos*] to draw in; [+ *falda*] to gather up, lift up; [+ *mangas*] to roll up; (*Cos*) to take in, reduce, shorten
7 (= *almacenar*) [+ *polvo*] to gather; [+ *líquido*] to absorb, take up; (*en recipiente*) to collect
8 (= *ir a buscar*) [+ *persona*] to pick up, fetch, collect; [+ *billetes, paquete*] to collect, pick up • **te vendremos a ~ a las ocho** we'll come and pick you up *o* fetch you *o* collect you at eight o'clock, we'll come for you at eight o'clock
9 (= *mostrar*) to show • **la imagen recoge uno de los momentos más dramáticos** the picture shows *o* captures one of the most dramatic moments • **el informe recoge la situación** the situation is described in the report
10 (= *incluir*) to include • **el informe recoge diversas sugerencias** various suggestions are included in the report, the report includes various suggestions • **vocablos que no están recogidos en el diccionario** words not included in the dictionary
11 [+ *demandas, reivindicaciones*] to take into account • **el acuerdo recoge las demandas de los indígenas** the agreement takes into account the demands of the native people
12 (= *recibir*) • **ahora empieza a ~ los frutos de su esfuerzo** she's beginning to reap the reward(s) of her efforts • **no recogió más que censuras** he received nothing but condemnation • **de todo esto van a ~ muy poco** they won't get much back out of all this, they will get very little return from all this
13 (= *retirar*) [+ *periódico, libro*] to seize; [+ *moneda*] to call in • **las autoridades recogieron todos los ejemplares** the authorities seized all the copies • **van a ~ las monedas antiguas** they are going to call in the old coins
14 (= *dar asilo*) to take in, shelter
(VI) (= *ordenar*) to tidy up, straighten up; (*al cerrar, terminar*) to clear up
(VPR) **recogerse 1** (= *retirarse*) to withdraw, retire; (*a casa*) to go home; (= *acostarse*) to go to bed
2 (= *refugiarse*) to take shelter
3 [+ *falda*] to gather up, lift up; [+ *mangas, pantalones*] to roll up • **~se el pelo** to put one's hair up • **se recogió el pelo en un moño** she put her hair up in a bun • **se recogió el pelo en una coleta** he tied his hair back in a ponytail

recogida (SF) **1** [*de basura, correo*] collection • **hay seis ~s diarias** there are six collections a day ▸ **recogida de basuras** refuse collection, garbage collection (EEUU) ▸ **recogida de datos** (*Inform*) data capture ▸ **recogida de equipajes** (*Aer*) baggage reclaim
2 (*Agr*) harvest
3 (= *retiro*) withdrawal, retirement
4 (*Méx*) (*Agr*) round-up; (*Cono Sur*) [*de policía*] sweep, raid

recogido (ADJ) **1** [*vida*] quiet; [*lugar*] secluded; [*persona*] reserved, retiring • **ella vive muy recogida** she lives very quietly
2 (= *apretado*) bunched up, tight
(SM) tuck, gathering

recogimiento (SM) **1** (= *estado*) absorption • **vivir con ~** to live in seclusion, live in peace and quiet
2 (*Rel*) recollection
3 (= *retirada*) withdrawal

recolección (SF) **1** [*de dinero*] collection ▸ **recolección de basura** (*esp LAm*) refuse collection, garbage collection (EEUU)
2 (*Agr*) (= *acto*) harvesting; (= *época*) harvest time
3 (= *recopilación*) compilation; (= *resumen*) summary
4 (*Rel*) retreat

recolectar ▸ CONJUG 1a (VT) = recoger

recolector(a) (SM/F) (*Agr*) picker

recoleto (ADJ) **1** [*persona*] quiet, retiring
2 [*calle*] quiet

recolocación (SF) relocation

recolocar ▸ CONJUG 1g (VT) to relocate

recomendable (ADJ) recommendable • **poco ~** inadvisable • **es una persona muy poco ~** he's someone I wouldn't recommend

recomendación (SF) **1** (= *consejo*) recommendation
2 (*para un trabajo*) to recommend • **carta de ~** letter of introduction *o* recommendation (**para to**) • **tiene buenas recomendaciones** he is strongly recommended
3 (*Rel*) ▸ **recomendación del alma** prayers for the dying (*pl*)

recomendado (ADJ) (*LAm*) registered

recomendar ▸ CONJUG 1j (VT) **1** (= *aconsejar*) to recommend • **~ a algn que haga algo** to recommend *o* advise sb to do sth • **le recomiendo esta novela** I recommend this novel to you
2 (*para un trabajo*) • **lo ~on para el puesto** he was recommended for the job
3 (*LAm*) (*Correos*) to register

recomendatorio (ADJ) recommendatory • **carta recomendatoria** letter of introduction (**para to**)

recomenzar ▸ CONJUG 1f, 1j (VT), (VI) to begin again, recommence

recomerse ▸ CONJUG 2a (VPR) to bear a secret grudge, harbour *o* (EEUU) harbor resentment

recompensa (SF) **1** (*por un servicio*) reward, recompense • **como** *o* **en ~ por los servicios prestados** (in return) for services rendered
2 (*por daño, perjuicio*) (= *compensación*) compensation (**de for**)

recompensar ▸ CONJUG 1a (VT) **1** [+ *servicio*] to reward, recompense • **"se recompensará"** "reward offered"
2 [+ *daño, perjuicio*] to compensate

recomponer ▸ CONJUG 2q (VT) **1** (= *arreglar*) to mend, repair
2 (*Tip*) to reset

recompra (SF) repurchase, buying back

recomprar ▸ CONJUG 1a (VT) to repurchase, buy back

reconcentrar ▸ CONJUG 1a (VT)
1 (= *concentrar*) [+ *atención*] to concentrate, devote (**en to**)
2 (= *juntar*) to bring together
3 [+ *solución*] to make more concentrated
4 (= *disimular*) to hide
(VPR) **reconcentrarse** (= *concentrarse*) to concentrate hard, become totally absorbed

reconciliable (ADJ) reconcilable

reconciliación (SF) reconciliation

reconciliar ▸ CONJUG 1b (VT) to reconcile
(VPR) **reconciliarse** to become reconciled, be reconciled

reconcomerse ▸ CONJUG 2a (VPR) to bear a secret grudge, harbour *o* (EEUU) harbor resentment

reconcomio (SM) **1** (= *rencor*) grudge, resentment
2 (= *deseo*) urge, longing, itch
3 (= *sospecha*) suspicion

recóndito (ADJ) recondite • **en lo más ~ de** in the depths of • **en lo más ~ del corazón** in one's heart of hearts • **en lo más ~ de mi ser** deep down inside

reconducir ▸ CONJUG 3n (VT) **1** [+ *persona*] to take back, bring back (**a to**)
2 (*Jur*) to renew, extend

reconexión (SF) reconnection • **si el sistema se cae, se produce la ~ automática** you are automatically reconnected if the system goes down

reconfirmar ▸ CONJUG 1a (VT) to reconfirm

reconfortante (ADJ) (= *que conforta*) comforting; (= *que anima*) cheering
(SM) (*LAm*) tonic

reconfortar ▸ CONJUG 1a (VT) **1** (= *confortar*) to comfort; (= *animar*) to cheer, encourage

r

2 (*Med*) to strengthen
VPR **reconfortarse** • **~se con** to fortify o.s. with

reconocer ▹ CONJUG 2d VT **1** (= *conocer*) to recognize • **no te he reconocido con ese sombrero** I didn't recognize you in that hat • **le reconocí por la voz** I knew *o* recognized him by his voice
2 (= *identificar*) to identify • **tuvo que ~ el cadáver de su hermano** he had to identify his brother's body
3 (= *considerar*) [+ *gobierno, hijo*] to recognize • **no le reconocieron como jefe** they did not recognize him as their leader
4 (= *admitir*) to admit • **reconócelo, ha sido culpa tuya** admit it, it was your fault • **hay que ~ que no es normal** you have to admit (that) it isn't normal • **reconozco que no existen pruebas** I admit that there is no evidence • **el acusado reconoció los hechos** the accused admitted what he had done • **me reconoció el mérito de haberlo hecho** he gave me the credit for doing it
5 (= *agradecer*) [+ *servicio*] to be grateful for
6 (*Med*) [+ *paciente*] to examine
7 [+ *terreno*] to survey; (*Mil*) to reconnoitre, spy out
8 (= *registrar*) to search
VPR **reconocerse** • **se ha reconocido culpable** he has admitted his guilt

reconocible ADJ recognizable

reconocido ADJ **1** [*jefe*] recognized, accepted
2 (*frm*) (= *agradecido*) • **estar** *o* **quedar ~** to be grateful

reconocimiento SM **1** (= *aprobación*) recognition • **en ~ a** • **como ~ por** in recognition of
2 (= *registro*) search, searching; (= *inspección*) inspection, examination ▸ **reconocimiento de firma** (*Méx*) authentication of a signature
3 (*Mil*) reconnaissance • **vuelo de ~** reconnaissance flight
4 (*Med*) examination, checkup ▸ **reconocimiento físico** physical examination ▸ **reconocimiento médico** medical (examination)
5 (*Inform*) ▸ **reconocimiento de la voz** speech recognition ▸ **reconocimiento óptico de caracteres** optical character recognition

reconquista SF reconquest, recapture • **la Reconquista** the Reconquest (*of Spain*)

RECONQUISTA
The term **Reconquista** refers to the eight centuries during which the Christian kings of the Spanish kingdoms gradually reclaimed their country from the Moors, who had invaded the Iberian Peninsula in 711. It is generally accepted that the reconquest began in 718 with the Christian victory at Covadonga in Asturias, and ended in 1492, when Ferdinand and Isabella, the **Reyes Católicos**, retook Granada, the last Muslim stronghold. In the intervening centuries there had been a great deal of contact and overlap between the two cultures. Christians living under Arab rule were called **mozárabes**, while **mudéjares** were practising Muslims living under Christian rule. In contrast with the pluralistic society that had existed under the Arabs, the final years of the **Reconquista** were a time of great intolerance, with Arabs and Jews being forcibly converted to Christianity, after which they were known as **conversos**. Those refusing to be converted were expelled in 1492.

reconquistar ▹ CONJUG 1a VT **1** (*Mil*) [+ *terreno*] to regain, reconquer; [+ *ciudad*] to recapture (**a** from)
2 (*fig*) [+ *estima*] to recover, win back

reconsideración SF reconsideration

reconsiderar ▹ CONJUG 1a VT to reconsider

reconstitución SF (= *acto*) reconstitution, reforming; [*de crimen, escena*] reconstruction

reconstituir ▹ CONJUG 3g VT (= *rehacer*) to reconstitute; [+ *crimen, escena*] to reconstruct

reconstituyente SM tonic

reconstrucción SF reconstruction

reconstruir ▹ CONJUG 3g VT to reconstruct

recontar ▹ CONJUG 1l VT **1** [+ *cantidad*] to recount, count again
2 [+ *cuento*] to retell, tell again

recontra* PREF (*LAm*) extremely, terribly • **~caro** terribly dear • **~bueno** really good • **estoy ~cansado** I'm terribly tired
EXCL well I'm ...!*

reconvención SF **1** (*frm*) (= *reprensión*) reprimand
2 (*Jur*) counterclaim

reconvenir ▹ CONJUG 3r VT **1** (= *reprender*) to reprimand
2 (*Jur*) to counterclaim

reconversión SF (= *reestructuración*) restructuring, reorganization
▸ **reconversión industrial** industrial rationalization ▸ **reconversión profesional** retraining

reconvertir ▹ CONJUG 3i VT **1** (= *transformar*) to reconvert (**en** to)
2 (= *reestructurar*) to restructure, reorganize; [+ *industria*] to rationalize
• **~ profesionalmente** to retrain
VPR **reconvertirse 1** [*profesional*] to retrain
2 [*empresa*] to restructure • **~se en** to be converted into

recopa SF cup-winners' cup

recopilación SF **1** (= *recolección*) compilation; (= *resumen*) summary
▸ **recopilación de datos** (*Inform*) data collection
2 (*Jur*) code • **la Recopilación** *Spanish law code of 1567* • **la Nueva Recopilación** *Spanish law code of 1775*

recopilador(a) SM/F compiler

recopilar ▹ CONJUG 1a VT **1** (= *reunir*) to compile; (= *resumir*) to summarize
2 [+ *leyes*] to codify

recopilatorio ADJ compilation (*antes de s*)
SM compilation

récord, record ['rekor] ADJ INV record • **cifras ~** record numbers • **en un tiempo ~** in a record time
SM (PL: **récords, records** ['rekor]) record • **batir el ~** to break the record

recordable ADJ memorable

recordación SF recollection • **digno de ~** memorable

recordar[1] ▹ CONJUG 1l VT **1** (= *acordarse de*) to remember • **prefieren no ~ aquellos tiempos** they prefer not to remember those times • **1999 será recordado como un año estupendo para todos** 1999 will be remembered as a great year for everybody • **recuerdo que un día se me acercó y me dijo ...** I remember that one day she came over to me and said ... • **no lo recuerdo** I can't remember, I don't remember • **creo ~ que ...** I seem to remember *o* recall that ... • **~ haber hecho algo** to remember doing *o* having done sth • **recuerda haberlo dicho** he remembers saying *o* having said it • **no recuerdo haberte dado permiso para salir** I don't remember *o* recall giving *o* having given you permission to go out • **~ que** to remember that • **recuerdo que no llegó hasta por la noche** I remember that he didn't arrive until nighttime
2 (= *traer a la memoria*) to remind • **estas botas me recuerdan a las que llevábamos de pequeños** these boots remind me of the ones we used to wear as children • **¿a qué te recuerda esa foto?** what does that photo remind you of? • **el poema recuerda a García Lorca** the poem is reminiscent of García Lorca • **~ algo a algn** to remind sb of sth • **recuérdale que me debe 50 dólares** remind him that he owes me 50 dollars • **te recuerdo que son las tres** let me remind you that it's three o'clock • **me permito ~le que aún no hemos recibido el pago** I would remind you *o* may I remind you that we have not yet received payment • **~ a algn que haga algo** to remind sb to do sth • **recuérdame que ponga la lavadora** remind me to put the washing (machine) on
3 (*Méx**) (= *despertar*) to wake up
VI to remember • **no recuerdo** I can't *o* don't remember • **si mal no recuerdo** if my memory serves me right *o* correctly, if I remember rightly *o* correctly • **que yo recuerde** as far as I can remember, as I recall (*frm*)
VPR **recordarse 1** (*Cono Sur, Méx**) (= *despertar*) to wake up
2 (*And, Caribe*) (= *volver en sí*) to come to, come round
3 (*Chile*) (= *acordarse*) • **ahora que me estoy recordando, la conocí en Madrid** now that I remember, I met her in Madrid • **apenas me recuerdo de mi antigua casa** I (can) hardly remember my old house

recordar[2] ▹ CONJUG 1l VT (*CAm, Caribe, Méx*) [+ *voz*] to record

recordativo ADJ reminiscent • **carta recordativa** reminder

recordatorio SM **1** (= *tarjeta*) [*de fallecimiento*] in memoriam card; [*de primera comunión*] First Communion card
2 (= *aviso*) reminder • **esto te servirá de ~** let this be a reminder to you

recordman SM, **récordman** SM (PL: **recordmans** *o* **récordmans**) record holder

recorrer ▹ CONJUG 2a VT **1** [+ *ciudad, país*] to travel around • **recorrimos Francia en moto** we travelled around France on a motorbike • **~ una ciudad a pie** to walk round a city, do a city on foot
2 [+ *trayecto*] to cover, do • **ese día recorrimos 100 kilómetros** we covered *o* did 100 kilometres that day • **aún nos quedan diez kilómetros por ~** we still have ten kilometres to go
3 (= *inspeccionar*) to go round • **he recorrido todas las librerías buscando esa novela** I've been round all the bookshops looking for that novel
4 (*Tip*) [+ *letras*] to take over
5† (= *leer por encima*) • **~ un escrito** to run one's eye over *o* look through a document
6† (= *reparar*) to repair, mend

recorrido SM **1** (= *viaje*) run, journey • **hicimos un ~ por los pueblos de Andalucía** we travelled round the villages of Andalusia • **el ~ del primer día fue de 450km** we covered 450kms on the first day
2 (= *distancia*) • **de corto ~** (*Aer*) short-haul • **de largo ~** (*Aer*) long-haul • **tren de largo ~** intercity train ▸ **recorrido de aterrizaje** (*Aer*) landing run
3 (= *ruta*) route • **este es el ~ más largo** this is the longest route *o* way
4 [*de émbolo*] stroke
5 (*Golf*) round • **un ~ en cinco bajo par** a round of five under par
6 (*Hípica*) • **un ~ sin penalizaciones** a clear round

7 (*Mec*) repair
recortable SM cut-out
recortada SF sawn-off shotgun
recortado ADJ **1** [*borde*] uneven, irregular
2 (*CAm, Caribe*) (= *achaparrado*) short and stocky
3 (*CAm, Caribe**) (= *necesitado*) broke*
SM (*And, Caribe, Cono Sur*) sawn-off shotgun, pistol
recortar ▸ CONJUG 1a VT **1** [+ *pelo*] to trim; [+ *exceso, sobras*] to cut away, cut off
2 [+ *figura, diseño*] to cut out
3 [+ *escopeta*] to saw off
4 [+ *presupuesto*] to cut, reduce; [+ *plantilla*] to cut, cut back; [+ *víveres*] to cut down
5 (= *perfilar*) to draw in outline
VPR **recortarse** to stand out, be silhouetted (**en, sobre** against)
recorte SM **1** (= *acción*) cutting, trimming
2 [*del pelo*] trim
3 (*para economizar*) cut • **han anunciado un ~ de** *o* **en los gastos** they have announced a cut *o* cutback in spending ▸ **recorte presupuestario** spending cut ▸ **recorte salarial** wage cut ▸ **recortes de personal, recortes de plantilla** staff cutbacks
4 [*de periódico, revista*] cutting, clipping • **~s de periódico** newspaper cuttings *o* clippings • **el libro está hecho de ~s** the book is a scissors-and-paste job • **álbum de ~s** scrapbook
5 (*CAm**) (= *comentario*) nasty remark
recoser ▸ CONJUG 2a VT to patch up, darn
recosido SM patch, darn
recostable ADJ • **asiento ~** reclining seat
recostado ADJ reclining • **estar ~** to be lying down
recostar ▸ CONJUG 1l VT to lean (**en** on)
VPR **recostarse** (= *reclinarse*) to lie back, recline (*frm*); (= *tumbarse*) to lie down
recotín* ADJ (*Cono Sur*) restless
recova SF **1** [*de aves*] (= *negocio*) poultry business, dealing in poultry; (= *mercado*) poultry market
2 (*And, Cono Sur*) (= *mercado*) food market; (*And*) (= *carnicería*) butcher's, butcher's shop
3 (*Cono Sur*) (*Arquit*) arcade, covered corridor (*along the front of a house*)
recoveco SM **1** [*de calle etc*] turn, bend
2 (*en casa*) nook, odd corner
3 recovecos (= *complejidades*) ins and outs • **el asunto tiene muchos ~s** it's a very complicated matter • **hablar sin ~s** to speak plainly *o* frankly
recovero/a SM/F poultry dealer
recreación SF (= *esparcimiento*) recreation; (= *diversión*) amusement
recrear ▸ CONJUG 1a VT **1** (= *crear de nuevo*) to recreate
2 (= *divertir*) to amuse, entertain
VPR **recrearse** to enjoy o.s. • **se recrea viendo los infortunios de otros** he takes pleasure in *o* gloats over others' misfortunes
recreativo ADJ recreational • **instalaciones recreativas** recreational facilities
SM games arcade
recrecer ▸ CONJUG 2d VT to increase
VI **1** (= *crecer*) to increase, grow
2 (= *volver a ocurrir*) to happen again
VPR **recrecerse** to cheer up, recover one's spirits
recreo SM **1** (= *esparcimiento*) recreation; (= *diversión*) amusement
2 (*Escol*) break, playtime, recess (*EEUU*)
recriminación SF **1** (= *reproches*) recrimination ▸ **recriminación mutua** mutual recrimination
2 (*Jur*) countercharge
recriminar ▸ CONJUG 1a VT **1** (= *reprochar*) to reproach
2 (*Jur*) to countercharge
VI to recriminate
VPR **recriminarse** to reproach each other
recrudecer ▸ CONJUG 2d VT to worsen
VI ▸ VPR
VPR **recrudecerse** (= *intensificarse*) to intensify; (= *empeorar*) to intensify, worsen; (= *aumentar*) to recrudesce, break out again
recrudecimiento SM, **recrudescencia** SF new outbreak, flare-up
recrudescente ADJ recrudescent
recta SF **1** (= *línea*) straight line
2 (*Dep*) straight ▸ **recta de llegada, recta final** home straight
3 (= *última fase*) closing stages (*pl*), final stage
rectal ADJ rectal
rectamente ADV **1** (= *correctamente*) [*comportarse, entender*] properly, correctly
2 (= *directamente*) straight • **mirar a algn ~ a los ojos** to look sb straight in the eyes
rectangular ADJ rectangular
rectángulo ADJ [*forma*] rectangular; [*triángulo*] right-angled
SM rectangle, oblong
rectificable ADJ rectifiable • **fácilmente ~** easily rectified
rectificación SF correction • **publicar una ~** to publish a correction
rectificador(a) SM/F rectifier
rectificar ▸ CONJUG 1g VT **1** (= *corregir*) to rectify, correct; [+ *cálculo*] to correct; [+ *conducta*] to change, reform
2 (= *enderezar*) to straighten, straighten out
3 (*Mec*) to rectify; [+ *cilindro*] to rectify, rebore
4 (*Culin*) to add • **~ de sal si hace falta** add salt to taste
VI to correct o.s. • **—no, eran cuatro, —rectificó** "no," he said, correcting himself, "there were four" • **rectifique, por favor** please see that this is put right
rectilíneo ADJ straight, rectilinear
rectitud SF **1** (= *calidad de justo*) rectitude, honesty
2 [*de una línea*] straightness
recto ADJ **1** (= *derecho*) straight; (= *vertical*) upright
2 • ángulo ~ right angle
3 [*persona*] (= *honrado*) honest, upright; (= *estricto*) strict; [*juez*] fair, impartial; [*juicio*] fair; [*intención*] honest
4 (= *literal*) [*sentido*] proper • **en el sentido ~ de la palabra** in the proper sense of the word
5 (*Ling*) [*caso*] nominative
ADV • **siga todo ~** go straight on • **la flecha fue recta al blanco** the arrow went straight to the target
SM (*Anat*) rectum
rector(a) ADJ [*entidad*] governing; [*idea, principio*] guiding, governing • **una figura ~a** an outstanding *o* leading figure • **los principios ~es del régimen** the régime's guiding principles
SM/F **1** (*Univ*) ≈ vice-chancellor, rector (*EEUU*), president (*EEUU*)
2 [*de colegio*] principal
rectorado SM **1** (= *cargo*) ≈ vice-chancellorship, principalship, presidency (*EEUU*)
2 (= *oficina*) ≈ vice-chancellor's office, president's office (*EEUU*)
rectorar ▸ CONJUG 1a VT (*CAm*) to rule, govern, direct
rectoría SF **1** = **rectorado**
2 (*Rel*) rectory
recua SF mule train, train of pack animals • **una ~ de chiquillos** a bunch of kids
recuadro SM box
recubrir ▸ CONJUG 3a (PP: **recubierto**) VT (= *cubrir*) to cover (**con, de** with); (= *pintar*) to coat (**con, de** with)
recuento SM (= *acto*) recount; (= *inventario*) inventory • **hacer el ~ de** to count up, reckon up ▸ **recuento de espermas** sperm count ▸ **recuento polínico** pollen count
recuerdo ADJ (*And**) awake
SM **1** (= *memoria*) memory • **guardar un feliz ~ de algn** to have happy memories of sb • **contar los ~s** to reminisce • **"Recuerdos de la vida de hace 80 años"** "Reminiscences of life 80 years ago" • **entrar en el ~** • **pasar al ~** (*euf*) to pass away
2 (= *regalo*) souvenir, memento • **"~ de Mallorca"** "present from Majorca" • **toma esto como ~** take this as a keepsake ▸ **recuerdo de familia** family heirloom
3 recuerdos (= *saludos*) regards • **¡~s a tu madre!** give my regards to your mother! • **os manda muchos ~s para todos** he sends you all his warmest regards
recuero SM muleteer
recuesto SM slope
reculada SF **1** (*con el cuerpo, vehículo*) backward movement
2 (*del fusil*) recoil
3 (*Méx*) (*Mil*) retreat
recular ▸ CONJUG 1a VI **1** (= *ir hacia atrás*) [*animal, vehículo*] to move backwards, go back; [*fusil*] to recoil
2 (= *ceder*) to back down
3 [*ejército*] to fall back, retreat
reculativa SF (*Méx*) = **reculada**
reculón SM **1** (*LAm*) = **reculada**
2 • andar a reculones to go backwards
recuperable ADJ [*dinero, pérdidas*] recoverable; [*envases*] returnable
recuperación SF **1** (= *vuelta a la normalidad*) [*de economía, divisa*] recovery; [*de enfermo, paciente*] recovery, recuperation (*más frm*) • **la lenta ~ del consumo privado** the slow recovery of consumer spending • **la pierna necesita un periodo de ~** your leg needs some time to recuperate
2 (= *reutilización*) **a** [*de edificio*] restoration; [*de tierras*] reclamation; [*de chatarra, vidrio*] salvage • **un plan de ~ de edificios históricos de la ciudad** a restoration plan for historic buildings in the city
b [*de algo perdido, olvidado*] revival • **el movimiento de ~ de la música tradicional italiana** the movement for the revival of traditional Italian music
3 [*de dinero, joyas*] recovery; (*Com*) [*de costes, pérdidas*] recovery, recoupment (*frm*)
4 (*Esp*) (*Educ*) (= *examen*) resit • **examen de ~** resit • **tendrá que ir a clases de ~** he will have to do classes for the resits
5 (*Inform*) retrieval
recuperar ▸ CONJUG 1a VT **1** (= *recobrar*) **a** [+ *bienes*] to recover; [+ *costes, pérdidas, inversión*] to recoup, recover • **no recuperamos el dinero robado** we didn't get the stolen money back, we didn't recover the stolen money (*más frm*) • **nunca ~ás lo que te gastas en lotería** you'll never get back what you spend on the lottery
b [+ *credibilidad, poder, libertad, control*] to regain; [+ *fuerzas*] to get back, regain • **ella ha hecho que recupere la confianza en la gente** she has made me regain my trust in people • **el jugador ha recuperado la forma física** the player has regained fitness • **el país comienza a ~ la normalidad** the country is beginning to return to normality • **al verte recuperó la sonrisa** the smile came back *o* returned to her face when she saw you • **el dólar recupera posiciones** the dollar is recovering • **nunca recuperó la memoria** she never got her memory back, she never regained *o* recovered her memory

r

c [+ *clase, día*] to make up • **ayer trabajaron el doble para ~ el tiempo perdido** they worked double time yesterday to make up the time lost • **esta clase tendremos que ~la** we'll have to make up this class
d (*Inform*) to retrieve
2 (= *reutilizar*) **a** [+ *edificio*] to restore; [+ *tierras*] to reclaim; [+ *chatarra, vidrio*] to salvage
b (*del olvido*) [+ *artista, obra*] to revive; [+ *tradiciones*] to restore, revive • **esta exposición recupera a un gran pintor olvidado** this exhibition has revived a great but forgotten painter
3 (*Educ*) to retake, resit • **tengo que ~ una asignatura** I have to retake *o* resit one subject
VPR **recuperarse 1** [*enfermo*] to recover (**de** from) • **la ciudad se recupera poco a poco tras la intensa nevada** the city is gradually recovering from the heavy blizzard • **~se de** [+ *operación, enfermedad, crisis, viaje*] to recover from
2 (*Com*) [*economía, mercado, divisa*] to recover • **los mercados financieros parecen ~se** the money markets seem to be recovering

recuperativo ADJ recuperative

recurrencia SF **1** (= *repetición*) recurrence
2 (= *apelación*) recourse, appeal

recurrente ADJ (= *repetitivo*) recurrent
SMF (*Jur*) appellant

recurrir ▹ CONJUG 3a VT (*Jur*) to appeal against
VI **1** • **~ a** [+ *medio, violencia*] to resort to; [+ *persona*] to turn to
2 (*Jur*) to appeal (**a** to, **contra** against)

recursivo ADJ recursive

recurso SM **1** (= *medio*) • **es una mujer de ~s** she's a resourceful woman • **tiene infinidad de ~s** he's infinitely resourceful • **como último ~** as a last resort
2 (*Jur*) appeal • **interponer ~ contra algn** to lodge an appeal against sb ▸ **recurso de apelación** appeal to the Supreme Court
3 recursos (= *bienes*) resources • **la familia está sin ~s** the family has nothing to fall back on ▸ **recursos ajenos** borrowed capital ▸ **recursos económicos** economic resources ▸ **recursos energéticos** energy resources ▸ **recursos financieros** financial resources ▸ **recursos humanos** human resources ▸ **recursos naturales** natural resources ▸ **recursos no renovables** non-renewable resources

recusable ADJ objectionable

recusación SF **1** (= *rechazo*) rejection
2 (*Jur*) challenge

recusante ADJ, SMF recusant

recusar ▹ CONJUG 1a VT **1** (= *rechazar*) to reject, refuse
2 (*Jur*) to challenge, challenge the authority of

red SF **1** (*para pescar*) net; [*de portería*] net; [*del pelo*] hairnet; (= *malla*) mesh; (= *para equipajes*) (luggage) rack; (= *cerca*) fence; (= *enrejado*) grille ▸ **red barredera** trawl ▸ **red de alambre** wire mesh, wire netting ▸ **red de seguridad** safety net ▸ **red metálica** metal screen
2 [*de cosas relacionadas*] network; [*de agua, suministro eléctrico*] mains, main (*EEUU*), supply system; [*de tiendas*] chain • **la Red** (*Internet*) the Net • **con agua de la red** with mains water, with water from the mains ▸ **red de área extendida** wide area network ▸ **red de área local** local network, local area network ▸ **red de comunicaciones** communications network ▸ **red de conmutación de circuito** circuit switching network ▸ **red de distribución** distribution network ▸ **red de emisoras** radio network ▸ **red de espionaje** spy network ▸ **red de rastreo** tracking network ▸ **red de transmisión de datos** data network ▸ **Red Digital de Servicios Integrados** Integrated Services Digital Network ▸ **red ferroviaria** railway network, railway system ▸ **red informática** network ▸ **red local** (*Inform*) local network, local area network ▸ **red rastreadora** tracking network ▸ **red social** social network • **las redes sociales** social media ▸ **red terrorista** terrorist network ▸ **red vascular** vascular system ▸ **red viaria** road network
3 (= *trampa*) snare, trap • **aprisionar a algn en sus redes** to have sb firmly in one's clutches, to have sb well and truly snared • **caer en la red** to fall into the trap • **tender una red para algn** to set a trap for sb

redacción SF **1** (= *acción*) writing • **la ~ del texto me llevó dos horas** it took me two hours to write the text
2 (= *expresión*) wording • **dices cosas interesantes, pero tendrías que cuidar la ~** what you say is interesting, but you need to pay more attention to how you word it
3 (*Escol*) essay, composition
4 (= *oficina*) newspaper office; (= *personas*) editorial staff

redactar ▹ CONJUG 1a VT **1** [+ *carta, noticia, artículo*] to write; [+ *acuerdo, contrato*] to draw up • **un ensayo mal redactado** a badly written essay
2 (*Prensa*) [+ *periódico*] to edit
VI to write • **redacta muy mal** he writes very badly

redactor(a) SM/F **1** (*en periódico*) editor
2 (= *escritor*) writer, drafter

redada SF **1** [*de policía*] raid
2 (*Pesca*) (= *acción*) cast, throw; (= *captura*) catch, haul

redaje SM (*And*) (= *red*) net; (= *maraña*) mess, tangle

redaño SM **1** (*Anat*) mesentery
2 redaños* (= *valor*) guts*

redargüir ▹ CONJUG 3g VT **1** (*Jur*) to impugn, hold to be invalid
2 (*frm*) • **~ que …** to argue on the other hand that …
VI (*frm*) to turn an argument against its proposer

redecilla SF hairnet

redecorar ▹ CONJUG 1a VT to redecorate

rededor • **al ~** • **en ~** = **alrededor**

redefinición SF redefinition

redefinir ▹ CONJUG 3a VT to redefine

redemocratización SF return to democracy, reestablishment of democracy

redención SF (*Rel*) redemption; (*Econ*) repayment, redemption (*frm*); (*Jur*) reduction in sentence

redentor(a) ADJ redeeming
SM/F redeemer • **MODISMO**: • **meterse a ~** (*pey*) to stick one's oar in
SM • **Redentor** Redeemer, Saviour, Savior (*EEUU*)

redescubrir ▹ CONJUG 3a (PP: **redescubierto**) VT to rediscover

redesignar ▹ CONJUG 1a VT (*Inform*) to rename

redespachar ▹ CONJUG 1a VT (*Cono Sur*) (*Com*) to send on, forward, forward directly

redicho* ADJ affected

redil SM sheepfold

redimensionamiento SM (= *reestructuración*) remodelling, remodeling (*EEUU*); (*euf*) (= *racionalización*) rationalization

redimensionar ▹ CONJUG 1a VT (*Econ*) (= *reestructurar*) to remodel; (*euf*) (= *racionalizar*) to rationalize, streamline, cut back

redimible ADJ redeemable

redimir ▹ CONJUG 3a VT **1** (*Rel*) to redeem
2 (*Econ*) to redeem (*frm*), repay
3 (= *liberar*) [+ *cautivo*] to ransom, redeem (*frm*); [+ *esclavo*] to redeem (*frm*), purchase the freedom of
VPR **redimirse** • **~se de algo** to redeem o.s. after sth

rediós* EXCL good God!

rediseñar ▹ CONJUG 1a VT to redesign

redistribución SF redistribution

redistribuir ▹ CONJUG 3g VT to redistribute

redistributivo ADJ redistributive • **programa ~** programme for the redistribution of wealth

rédito SM return, interest

redituable ADJ (*Cono Sur*) profitable

redituar ▹ CONJUG 1e VT to yield, produce, bear

redivivo ADJ revived, resuscitated

redoba SF (*Méx*) *wooden board hung round neck and used as a percussion instrument*

redoblado ADJ **1** (*Mec*) reinforced
2 [*persona*] stocky, thickset
3 [*paso*] double-quick
4 [*fuerzas*] renewed • **volvió al ataque con fuerzas redobladas** he went back on the attack with renewed strength

redoblante SM side drum, long-framed side drum

redoblar ▹ CONJUG 1a VT **1** (= *aumentar*) to redouble
2 (= *plegar*) [+ *papel etc*] to bend back; [+ *clavo*] to clinch
VI (*Mús*) to play a roll on the drum; [*trueno*] to roll, rumble

redoble SM [*de tambor*] drumroll; [*de trueno*] roll, rumble

redoma SF **1** (= *frasco*) flask, phial
2 (*Cono Sur*) [*de pez*] fishbowl
3 (*Caribe*) (*Aut*) roundabout, traffic circle (*EEUU*)

redomado ADJ **1** [*mentiroso, estafador*] inveterate
2 (= *taimado*) sly, artful

redomón ADJ **1** (*LAm*) [*caballo*] (= *no domado por completo*) half-trained, not fully broken-in
2 (*Méx*) [*caballo*] (= *salvaje*) wild, unbroken
3 [*persona*] (= *inexperto*) untrained, unskilled; (= *torpe*) slow, dense
4 (= *ordinario*) crude, rough

redonda SF **1** (*Mús*) semibreve, whole note (*EEUU*)
2 (*Tip*) roman
3 • **a la ~**: **en muchas millas a la ~** for many miles around • **se olía a un kilómetro a la ~** you could smell it a mile off

redondeado ADJ rounded

redondear ▹ CONJUG 1a VT **1** (= *curvar*) to round off
2 (= *completar*) to round off • **~ un negocio** to close a deal
3 [+ *cifra*] (*tomando un valor superior*) to round up; (*tomando un valor inferior*) to round down
4 (= *complementar*) to supplement, top up
VPR **redondearse 1** (= *enriquecerse*) to become wealthy
2 (= *librarse de deudas*) to get clear of debts

redondel SM **1** (= *círculo*) ring, circle ▸ **redondel de humo** smoke ring
2 (*Taur*) bullring, arena
3 (*Aut*) roundabout, traffic circle (*EEUU*)

redondez SF roundness • **en toda la ~ de la tierra** in the whole wide world

redondilla SF quatrain

redondo ADJ **1** [*forma*] round • **tiene la cara redonda** he has a round face • **tres metros en ~** three metres (a)round • **MODISMO**: • **caer ~**: **le dispararon y cayó ~** he was shot

and collapsed in a heap • **cayó ~ en la cama** he went out like a light as soon as he got into bed
2 [*cantidad, cifra*] round • **en números ~s** in round numbers, in round figures
3* (= *completo*) complete, finished • **todo le ha salido ~** it all went well for him • **será un negocio ~** it will be a really good deal • **el negocio era ~** the business was really profitable • **triunfo ~** complete *o* resounding success
4 (= *definitivo*) • **dijo un no ~** he flatly refused
5 (*Méx*) [*viaje*] round
6 (*Méx**) (= *lerdo*) dense*, thick*; (= *débil*) weak
SM 1 • **en ~: girar en ~** to turn right round • **negarse en ~** to refuse flatly
2 (*Mús**) disc, record
3 (*Culin*) rump steak

redopelo SM (*frm*) 1* (= *riña*) scrap*, rough-and-tumble
2 • **a ~:** • **una lógica a ~** logic stood on its head, logic in reverse • **traer al ~ a algn** to treat sb very badly, ride roughshod over sb

redor SM • **en ~** = **alrededor**

redro ADV behind

redrojo SM 1 (*Bot*) late fruit, withered fruit
2 (*Cono Sur*) (= *exceso*) rest, remainder
3 (*Méx**) (= *harapos*) rags (*pl*)

redropelo SM = **redopelo**

reducción SF 1 (= *disminución*) **a** [*de cantidad, precios, consumo, tamaño*] reduction • **una ~ del número de atentados** a reduction in the number of terrorist attacks • **una ~ del gasto público** a cut *o* reduction in public spending • **una ~ en el tamaño de los envases** a reduction in the size of containers • **estudian nuevas reducciones de personal** they are considering new staff cuts *o* reductions in staff
b [*de tiempo*] reduction • **la ~ a cinco años del mandato presidencial** the reduction of the presidential term to five years • **los sindicatos piden la ~ de la jornada laboral** they unions are calling for a shorter working day ▸ **reducción de jornada** reduction of working hours ▸ **reducción del activo** divestment ▸ **reducciones presupuestarias** budget cuts ▸ **reducciones salariales** wage cuts
2 (*Mat*) (= *conversión*) [*de unidades, medidas*] conversion; [*de ecuaciones*] reduction
3 [*de rebeldes*] defeat
4 (*Med*) setting, reduction (*frm*)
5 (*Chile*) [*de indígenas*] reservation (*of natives*)
6 (*LAm*) (*Hist*) *settlement of Christianized Indians*

reduccionismo SM reductionism

reduccionista ADJ reductionist

reducible ADJ reducible

reducido ADJ [*grupo, número*] small; [*ingresos, recursos*] limited; [*tarifa, precio*] reduced; [*espacio*] confined • **una sala de dimensiones reducidas** a small-sized room • **personas con capacidad auditiva reducida** people with a hearing impairment • **a precios ~s** at reduced prices • **quedar ~ a** to be reduced to • **la plantilla quedó reducida a 70 personas** the staff was reduced to 70 people • **todo quedó ~ a un malentendido** everything boiled down to a misunderstanding

reducidor(a) SM/F (*LAm*) fence*, receiver (of stolen goods)

reducir ▸ CONJUG 3n VT 1 (= *disminuir*) **a** (*en cantidad*) [+ *gastos, inflación, precio*] to reduce, bring down, cut; [+ *tensión, ansiedad*] to reduce; [+ *riesgo*] to reduce, lessen • **medidas encaminadas a ~ el número de parados** measures designed to reduce *o* bring down *o* cut the number of unemployed • **han reducido las listas de espera en los hospitales** they have reduced *o* cut hospital waiting lists • **el autobús redujo su velocidad** the bus reduced speed, the bus slowed down • **conviene ~ el consumo de grasas** it is advisable to cut down on fatty foods • **el banco redujo su beneficio un 12%** the bank saw its profits fall by 12% • **un tratamiento para ~ la celulitis** a treatment to reduce cellulite • **~ algo en algo** to reduce sth by sth, cut sth by sth • **tenemos que ~ la producción en un 20%** we have to reduce *o* cut production by 20% • **~ a la mínima expresión** to reduce to the bare minimum • **~ algo al mínimo** to reduce *o* cut sth to the minimum • **~ algo a la mitad** to cut sth by half
b (*en tiempo*) [+ *jornada laboral*] to reduce, shorten; [+ *sentencia*] to reduce • **han reducido la mili a nueve meses** they have reduced *o* cut military service to nine months • **sus abogados consiguieron ~ la sentencia a dos meses** his lawyers managed to get his sentence reduced to two months
c (*en tamaño*) [+ *copia*] to reduce; [+ *discurso, artículo*] to cut down, shorten
2 • **~ algo a algo a** (= *limitar*) to limit sth to sth; (= *simplificar*) to reduce sth to sth • **redujo su intervención a criticar al gobierno** her participation was limited to criticizing the government • **todo lo reduce a cosas materiales** he reduces everything to material terms
b (= *convertir*) [+ *cantidad, medida*] to convert sth into sth; [+ *fracción, ecuación*] to reduce sth into sth • **~ un kilómetro a metros** to convert a kilometre into metres • **el techo fue reducido a cenizas por el fuego** the roof was reduced to ashes by the fire • MODISMO: • **~ algo al absurdo** to expose the absurdity of sth
3 (= *someter*) [+ *ladrón, fugitivo, loco*] to overpower; [+ *alborotadores*] to subdue; [+ *fortaleza*] to subdue, reduce (*frm*) • **entre los tres lograron ~ al atracador** the three of them managed to overpower the robber • **~ a algn a la obediencia** to bring sb to heel • **~ a algn al silencio** (*por la fuerza, por miedo*) to silence sb; (*por vergüenza, humillación*) to reduce sb to silence
4 (*Med*) [+ *hueso, hernia*] to set, reduce (*frm*)
5 (*Quím*) to reduce
6 (*LAm*) (*en el mercado negro*) to get rid of*
VI (*Aut*) to change down • **reduce a segunda** change down to second gear
VPR **reducirse 1** (= *disminuir*) [*inflación, población, beneficios*] to fall; [*calor*] to become less intense, decrease; [*salsa*] to reduce • **el número de accidentes se ha reducido en un 16,5%** the number of accidents has fallen by 16.5% • **sus gastos se redujeron a la mitad** their expenses were cut *o* reduced by half
2 (= *limitarse*) • **~se a a** (*en cantidad*) • **el mobiliario se reduce a unas pocas mesas y sillas** the furniture amounts to no more than *o* is simply a few tables and chairs • **sus ingresos se reducen a una pensión por invalidez de 500 euros** his income is limited to *o* consists only of a disability pension of 500 euros
b (*en extensión*) • **el consumo de heroína se ha ido reduciendo a la población más joven** heroin consumption has gradually been reduced to just the younger population • **el problema se reduce a una pura cuestión económica** the problem comes down to *o* boils down to simple economics, the problem is simply a question of economics • **la entrevista se redujo a un cuarto de hora escaso** the interview lasted barely a quarter of an hour • **el pensamiento del autor se puede ~ a lo siguiente** the author's thinking can be simplified *o* summarized as follows
c [*persona*] to limit o.s. to • **en este ensayo nos ~emos a la situación en el siglo XVIII** in this essay we will limit ourselves to considering the situation in the 18th century • **se vieron reducidos a pedir limosna** they were reduced to begging for alms

reductible ADJ reducible

reductivo ADJ 1 (= *simplificador*) [*noción, enfoque*] reductive
2 [*régimen*] weight-losing • **mamoplastia reductiva** breast reduction

reducto SM [*de ideología, rebeldes*] stronghold, redoubt • **el último ~ del águila imperial** the last stronghold *o* redoubt of the imperial eagle • **el último ~ de los árabes en el reino de Castilla** the last Arab stronghold in the kingdom of Castile

reductor ADJ 1 (*Aut*) [*marcha*] reduction (*antes de s*)
2 (= *adelgazante*) [*crema*] slimming, reducing
3 (= *simplificador*) reductive

reductora SF (*Aut*) reduction gear

reduje *etc* ▹ **reducir**

redundancia SF redundancy • **valga la ~** forgive the repetition

redundante ADJ redundant, superfluous

redundar ▹ CONJUG 1a VI • **~ en** to redound to (*frm*) • **~ en beneficio de algn** to benefit sb, be to sb's advantage

reduplicación SF 1 (= *duplicación*) reduplication
2 [*de esfuerzos*] redoubling
3 (*Ling*) reduplication

reduplicar ▹ CONJUG 1g VT 1 (= *duplicar*) to reduplicate
2 [+ *esfuerzo*] to redouble

reedición SF reissue, reprint, reprinting

reedificación SF rebuilding

reedificar ▹ CONJUG 1g VT to rebuild

reeditar ▹ CONJUG 1a VT to reissue, republish, reprint

reeducación SF re-education
▸ **reeducación profesional** retraining

reeducar ▹ CONJUG 1g VT to re-educate • **~ profesionalmente** to give industrial retraining to

reelaborar ▹ CONJUG 1a VT to rework

reelección SF re-election

reelecto ADJ (*LAm*) re-elected

reelectoral ADJ (*LAm*) re-electoral

reelegible ADJ eligible for re-election

reelegir ▹ CONJUG 3c, 3k VT to re-elect

reembalar ▹ CONJUG 1a VT to repack

reembolsable ADJ 1 [*gastos*] refundable, repayable
2 (*Com*) redeemable, refundable • **no ~** [*valores*] irredeemable; [*depósito*] non-returnable, non-refundable

reembolsar ▹ CONJUG 1a VT [+ *persona*] to reimburse; [+ *dinero*] to repay, pay back; [+ *depósito*] to refund, return
VPR **reembolsarse** to reimburse o.s. • **~se una cantidad** to recover a sum

reembolso SM [*de gastos*] reimbursement; [*de depósito*] refund • **enviar algo contra ~** to send sth cash on delivery ▸ **reembolso fiscal** tax rebate

reemisor SM booster station

reemplazable ADJ replaceable

reemplazante SMF (*esp LAm*) replacement, substitute

reemplazar ▹ CONJUG 1f VT 1 [+ *modelo, pieza*] to replace • **tenemos que encontrar la forma de ~ este sistema** we have to find a way of replacing this system • **~ a algo/algn** to replace sth/sb • **este motor ~á a los**

r

actuales de 11 litros this engine will replace current 11 litre engines • **el nilón nunca podrá ~ al algodón** nylon will never be able to replace cotton • **~ algo con** *o* **por algo** to replace sth with sth • **van a ~ los discos duros por tarjetas de memoria RAM** hard disks will be replaced by RAM memory boards
2 [*+ persona*] **a** (*= ocupar el lugar de*) (*gen*) to replace; (*brevemente*) to stand in for • **durante la baja por maternidad mi ayudante me ~á** my assistant will take my place *o* will replace me while I am on maternity leave • **el subdirector lo reemplazó en la reunión** the assistant director stood in for him at the meeting • **tras el descanso, Pérez reemplazó a Carlos** Pérez came on for Carlos after half-time, Carlos was substituted by Pérez after half-time
b (*= poner en lugar de*) to replace • **el entrenador no pretende ~ a ningún jugador** the coach does not intend to replace any player • **~ a algn con** *o* **por algn** to replace sb with sb • **los ~án por obreros extranjeros** they are going to be replaced by foreign workers, they will replace them with foreign workers

reemplazo (SMF) (*= persona sustituta*) replacement
(SM) **1** (*= sustitución*) replacement • **el coste del ~ de los productos sanguíneos sospechosos** the cost of replacing suspect blood products • **el entrenador decidió el ~ del portero** the coach decided to substitute the goalkeeper • **vino en ~ del profesor de física** he came to replace the physics teacher, he came as the replacement for the physics teacher
2 (*Esp*) (*Mil*) *intake of conscripts* • **los soldados pertenecientes al último ~ de 1994** soldiers recruited in the last call-up *o* draft of 1994 • **soldados de ~** conscripts, draftees (*EEUU*)

reemprender ▸ CONJUG 2a (VT) to resume

reencarnación (SF) reincarnation

reencarnar ▸ CONJUG 1a (VT) to reincarnate
(VPR) **reencarnarse** to be reincarnated • **~se en algn/algo** to be reincarnated as sb/sth

reencauchado (SM) (*LAm*) retread, remould

reencauchar ▸ CONJUG 1a (VT) (*LAm*) to retread, remould

reencender ▸ CONJUG 2g (VT) to light again, rekindle

reencontrarse ▸ CONJUG 1l (VPR) to meet again

reencuadernar ▸ CONJUG 1a (VT) to rebind

reencuentro (SM) reunion

reengancharse ▸ CONJUG 1a (VPR) to re-enlist

reenganche (SM) (*Mil*) re-enlistment

reentrada (SF) re-entry

reenvasar ▸ CONJUG 1a (VT) to repack, rewrap

reenviar ▸ CONJUG 1c (VT) (*a nuevo domicilio*) to forward; (*a diferente dirección*) to redirect; (*al remitente*) to return

reenvío (SM) cross-reference

reequilibrar ▸ CONJUG 1a (VT) **1** (*Pol*) to restabilize
2 [*+ peso, carga*] to rebalance

reescribible (ADJ) rewritable

reescribir ▸ CONJUG 3a (VT) to rewrite

reestatificación (SF) renationalization

reestatificar ▸ CONJUG 1g (VT) to renationalize

reestrenar ▸ CONJUG 1a (VT) (*Teat*) to revive, put on again; (*Cine*) to re-release

reestreno (SM) (*Teat*) revival; (*Cine*) re-release

reestructuración (SF) restructuring, reorganizing

reestructurar ▸ CONJUG 1a (VT) to restructure, reorganize

reevaluación (SF) reappraisal

reevaluar ▸ CONJUG 1e (VT) to reappraise

reexaminación (SF) re-examination

reexaminar ▸ CONJUG 1a (VT) to re-examine

reexpedir ▸ CONJUG 3k (VT) (*a nuevo domicilio*) to forward; (*a diferente dirección*) to redirect; (*al remitente*) to return

reexportación (SF) re-export

reexportar ▸ CONJUG 1a (VT) to re-export

REF (SM ABR) (*Esp*) (*Econ*) = **Régimen Económico Fiscal**

Ref.ª (ABR) (= **referencia**) ref

refacción (SF) **1** (*frm*) (*= colación*) light refreshment, collation (*frm*)
2 (*LAm*) (*Mec*) repair; (*Arquit*) refurbishment, repair
3 (*LAm*) (*Agr*) (*= gastos*) running costs (*pl*)
4 (*Caribe, Méx*) (*= préstamo*) short-term loan; (*= subvención*) financial assistance
5 refacciones (*Méx*) (*= repuestos*) spares, spare parts

refaccionar ▸ CONJUG 1a (*LAm*) (VT) **1** (*Mec*) to repair; (*Arquit*) to refurbish, repair
2 (*= subvencionar*) to finance, subsidize

refaccionaria (SF) (*LAm*) repair shop

refajo† (SM) (*= enagua*) flannel underskirt; (*= combinación*) slip

refalar* ▸ CONJUG 1a (*Cono Sur*) (VT) **1** • **~ algo a algn** (*= quitar*) to take sth from sb, take sth off sb
2 (*= hurtar*) to steal
(VPR) **refalarse*** **1** (*= quitarse*) • **~se los zapatos** to kick off one's shoes
2 (*= huir*) to make off, beat it*
3 (*= resbalar*) to slip

refalón* (SM) (*Cono Sur*) slip, fall

refaloso* (ADJ) (*Cono Sur*) **1** (*= resbaladizo*) slippery
2 (*= tímido*) shy, timid

refanfinflar* ▸ CONJUG 1a (VT) • **me la refanfinfla** I couldn't give a damn*

refectorio (SM) refectory

referencia (SF) **1** (*= mención*) reference • **con ~ a** with reference to • **hacer ~ a** to refer to, allude to ▸ **referencia comercial** trade reference ▸ **referencia cruzada** cross reference ▸ **referencia múltiple** general cross reference
2 (*= informe*) account, report • **una ~ completa del suceso** a complete account of what took place • **me han dado buenas ~s de ella** I have had good reports of her ▸ **referencia bancaria** banker's reference

referenciar ▸ CONJUG 1b (VT) to index

referendo (SM) referendum

referéndum (SM) (PL: **referéndums**) referendum

referente (ADJ) • **~ a** relating to, about, concerning

referí (SMF) (*LAm*) referee, umpire

referible (ADJ) • **~ a** referable to

referido (ADJ) **1** (*= antedicho*) above-mentioned
2 (*Ling*) • **discurso ~** reported speech

referir ▸ CONJUG 3i (VT) **1** (*= contar*) to tell, recount • **~ que ...** to say that ..., tell how ...
2 (*= dirigir*) • **~ al lector a un apéndice** to refer the reader to an appendix
3 (*= relacionar*) to refer, relate • **todo lo refiere a su teoría favorita** he refers *o* relates everything to his favourite theory • **han referido el cuadro al siglo XVII** they have dated the picture as 17th-century
4 • **~ a** (*Econ*) to convert into
5 (*CAm*) (*= insultar*) to abuse, insult
6 • **~ algo a algn en cara** (*Méx*) to throw sth in sb's face
(VPR) **referirse** • **~se a** to refer to • **me refiero a lo de anoche** I refer to what happened last night • **¿a qué te refieres?** what exactly do you mean? • **por lo que se refiere a eso** as for that, as regards that, as far as that is concerned

refilón • **de ~** (ADV) obliquely, on the slant • **el sol da de ~** the sun falls on the slant, the sun comes slanting in • **mirar a algn de ~** to look out of the corner of one's eye at sb

refinación (SF) refining

refinado (ADJ) refined
(SM) refining

refinador(a) (SM/F) refiner

refinadura (SF) refining

refinamiento (SM) refinement • **con todos los ~s modernos** with all the modern refinements ▸ **refinamiento por pasos** (*Inform*) stepwise refinement

refinanciación (SF) refinancing

refinanciar ▸ CONJUG 1b (VT) to refinance

refinar ▸ CONJUG 1a (VT) **1** (*Téc*) to refine
2 (*= perfeccionar*) [*+ sistema*] to refine, perfect; [*+ estilo*] to polish

refinería (SF) refinery ▸ **refinería de petróleo** oil refinery

refino (ADJ) extra fine, pure, refined
(SM) refining

refirmar ▸ CONJUG 1a (VT) (*LAm*) to reaffirm

refistolería (SF) **1** (*CAm*) (*= intriga*) scheming nature
2 (*Méx*) (*= presunción*) vanity
3 (*Caribe**) (*= zalamería*) boot-licking*

refistolero (ADJ) **1** (*CAm*) (*= intrigante*) intriguing, scheming
2 (*Méx*) (*= presuntuoso*) vane
3 (*Caribe*) (*= zalamero*) greasy, oily

reflación (SF) reflation

reflacionar ▸ CONJUG 1a (VT) to reflate

reflectante (ADJ) reflective

reflector (SM) **1** (*= cuerpo que refleja*) reflector ▸ **reflector posterior** (*Aut*) rear reflector
2 (*Elec*) spotlight; (*Aer, Mil*) searchlight

reflejar ▸ CONJUG 1a (VT) **1** [*+ imagen, luz*] to reflect
2 (*= manifestar*) to reflect • **la novela refleja la problemática social de la época** the novel reflects the social problems of the time • **su expresión reflejaba inquietud** you could see the worry in her face, she wore a worried expression (on her face)
(VPR) **reflejarse 1** [*imagen, luz*] to be reflected
2 (*= manifestarse*) • **el temor se reflejaba en su rostro** fear was written on his face

reflejo (ADJ) **1** [*luz*] reflected
2 [*movimiento*] reflex
3 [*verbo*] reflexive
(SM) **1** (*= imagen*) reflection • **miraba su ~ en el agua** he was looking at his reflection in the water
2 (*= índice*) reflection • **este es un ~ de la inquietud del pueblo** this reflects *o* is a reflection of people's unease
3 (*Anat*) reflex; (*= acción*) reflex action • **tener buenos ~s** to have good reflexes • **perder ~s** (*fig*) to lose one's touch
4 reflejos (*= brillo*) gleam (*sing*), glint (*sing*) • **tiene ~s metálicos** it has a metallic glint
5 reflejos (*en el pelo*) highlights • **tiene el pelo castaño con ~s rubios** she has chestnut hair with blond highlights
6 (*= tinte para el pelo*) rinse • **darse un ~ azul** to have a blue rinse

reflejoterapia (SF) reflexology

reflex, réflex (ADJ INV) SLR, reflex
(SF) SLR camera

reflexión (SF) **1** (*Fís*) reflection
2 (*= consideración*) reflection, thought • **con ~** on reflection • **sin ~** without thinking • **mis reflexiones sobre el problema** my

reflections on the problem • **hacer reflexiones** to reflect

reflexionar ▸ CONJUG 1a VT to reflect on, think about, think over
VI (= *considerar*) to reflect (**sobre** on); (*antes de actuar*) to think, pause • **¡reflexione!** you think about it!, think for a moment!

reflexivamente ADV 1 (*Ling*) reflexively
2 [*obrar*] thoughtfully, reflectively

reflexividad SF (*Ling*) reflexiveness

reflexivo ADJ 1 [*verbo*] reflexive
2 [*persona*] thoughtful, reflective
3 [*acto*] considered

reflexología SF reflexology

reflexólogo/a SM/F reflexologist

reflexoterapia SF reflex therapy

reflotar ▸ CONJUG 1a VT [+ *barco*] to refloat; [+ *empresa, negocio*] to relaunch, re-establish

refluir ▸ CONJUG 3g VI to flow back

reflujo SM ebb, ebb tide

refocilación SF, **refocilamiento** SM (= *placer*) huge enjoyment, great pleasure; (*pey*) (= *regodeo*) unhealthy pleasure, cruel pleasure

refocilar ▸ CONJUG 1a (*frm*) VT (= *encantar*) to delight; (= *divertir*) to amuse hugely; (= *alegrar*) to cheer up
VI (*And, Cono Sur*) [*rayo*] to flash
VPR **refocilarse** 1 (= *divertirse*) • **~se con algo** to enjoy sth hugely, take great delight in sth • **se refocila viendo lo que sufre otro** he delights in *o* gloats over sb else's sufferings
2 (= *alegrarse*) to cheer up no end

refocilo SM 1 = **refocilación**
2 (*And*) (= *relámpago*) lightning

reforestación SF reforestation

reforestar ▸ CONJUG 1a VT to reforest

reforma SF 1 (= *modificación*) reform • **~s políticas** political reforms • **la Reforma** (*Rel*) the Reformation; (*Méx*) (*Pol*) 19th century reform movement ▸ **reforma agraria** land reform ▸ **reforma educativa** education reform
2 **reformas** (*en edificio, local*) alterations • **cerrado por ~s** closed for refurbishment, closed for alterations
3 (*Cos*) alteration

reformación SF reform, reformation

reformado ADJ reformed

reformador(a) SM/F reformer

reformar ▸ CONJUG 1a VT 1 [+ *edificio*] to renovate • **van a ~ todas las casas del casco antiguo** they are going to renovate all the houses in the old quarter
2 [+ *ley, sistema*] to reform • **han reformado los estatutos del partido** they have reformed the party statutes
3 [+ *persona*] to reform • **su novia ha conseguido ~le y ya no bebe** his girlfriend has managed to reform him and he doesn't drink any more
4 (*Cos*) to alter
5 (*frm*) (= *formar de otro modo*) to re-form
VPR **reformarse** [*persona*] to reform, mend one's ways

reformatear ▸ CONJUG 1a VT (*Inform*) to reformat

reformatorio SM reformatory ▸ **reformatorio de menores** remand home, reform school (EEUU)

reformismo SM reforming policy, reforming attitude

reformista ADJ reforming
SMF reformist, reformer

reformular ▸ CONJUG 1a VT 1 [+ *sistema, estructura*] to reformulate
2 [+ *pregunta*] to rephrase

reforzado ADJ reinforced

reforzador SM (*Elec*) booster; (*Fot*) intensifier

reforzamiento SM reinforcement, strengthening

reforzar ▸ CONJUG 1f, 1l VT 1 (*Arquit, Carpintería*) to reinforce
2 (= *fortalecer*) to reinforce, strengthen • **debemos ~ nuestra estrategia de ventas** we must reinforce *o* strengthen our sales strategy
3 (*Mil*) to reinforce
4 [+ *dosis*] to increase
5 (*Fot*) to intensify

refracción SF refraction

refractante ADJ refractive

refractar ▸ CONJUG 1a VT to refract

refractario ADJ 1 (*Téc*) fireproof, heat-resistant; (*Culin*) ovenproof
2 • **ser ~ a la reforma** to be resistant *o* opposed to reform • **ser ~ a las lenguas** to have no aptitude for languages, be hopeless where languages are concerned

refractivo ADJ refractive

refractor SM refractor

refrán SM proverb, saying • **como dice el ~** as the saying goes

refranero SM collection of proverbs

refraniento ADJ (*Cono Sur*) much given to quoting proverbs

refregar ▸ CONJUG 1h, 1j VT 1 (= *frotar*) to rub, rub hard; (= *limpiar*) to scrub
2 (*fig*) (= *restregar*) • **~ algo a algn** *o* **en las narices de algn** to rub sth in to sb, harp on about sth to sb

refregón SM 1 (= *frotamiento*) (*sin darse cuenta*) rub, rubbing; (*limpiando*) scrub, scrubbing
2 (= *señal*) rub mark

refrenar ▸ CONJUG 1a VT 1 [+ *caballo*] to rein back
2 [+ *pasiones, ánimos*] to restrain, hold in check
VPR **refrenarse** to restrain o.s.

refrendar ▸ CONJUG 1a VT 1 (= *dar validez a*) [+ *documento*] to countersign; [+ *decisión, nominación*] to endorse
2 [+ *pasaporte*] to stamp
3* (= *repetir*) to do again, repeat; [+ *comida*] to order more of, have a second helping of

refrendo SM 1 (= *acto*) [*de decisión*] endorsement; [*de documento*] countersigning
2 (= *firma*) countersignature

refrescante ADJ refreshing, cooling

refrescar ▸ CONJUG 1g VT 1 (= *enfriar*) to cool, cool down
2 [+ *conocimiento*] to brush up, polish up • **~ la memoria** to refresh one's memory
3 [+ *acto*] to repeat; [+ *enemistad, interés*] to renew
VI 1 (*Meteo*) to get cooler, cool down • **en septiembre ya refresca** it starts to get cooler in September
2 [*bebida*] to be refreshing
3 (*Méx*) (*Med*) to get better
VPR **refrescarse** 1 (= *tomar el aire*) to go out for a breath of fresh air
2 (= *lavarse*) to freshen up
3 (= *beber*) to have a drink; (*And, esp Col*) (= *tomar té*) to have tea

refresco SM soft drink • **nos tomamos unos ~s** we had some soft drinks *o* refreshments • **después del concierto nos ofrecieron un ~** they laid on some refreshments for us after the concert ▸ **refresco de cola** cola

refresquería SF (*LAm*) refreshment stall

refri* SM (*Méx*) fridge*

refriega SF (*de poca importancia*) scuffle; (*violenta*) brawl

refrigeración SF [*de comida*] refrigeration; (*Mec*) cooling; [*de casa*] air conditioning ▸ **refrigeración por agua** water cooling ▸ **refrigeración por aire** air cooling

refrigerado ADJ [*comida*] chilled; [*sala*] air-conditioned • **~ por agua** water-cooled • **~ por aire** air-cooled

refrigerador ADJ cooling, refrigerating
SM 1 (= *frigorífico*) refrigerator, fridge
2 (*para el aire acondicionado*) cooling unit, cooling system

refrigeradora SF (*LAm*) refrigerator, fridge

refrigerante ADJ cooling, refrigerating
SM (*Quím*) refrigerant, coolant

refrigerar ▸ CONJUG 1a VT (= *enfriar*) to chill, refrigerate; (*Téc*) to refrigerate; (*Mec*) to cool; [+ *sala*] to air-condition

refrigerio SM 1 (= *piscolabis*) snack; (= *bebida*) cooling drink
2 (= *alivio*) relief

refrior SM chill, chill in the air

refrito ADJ 1 (*Culin*) refried
2 [*obra*] revised, rehashed
SM rehash, revised version

refucilar ▸ CONJUG 1a VI (*And, Cono Sur*) = **refocilar**

refucilo SM (*And, Cono Sur*) lightning

refuerzo SM 1 (= *reforzamiento*) reinforcement
2 (*Téc*) support
3 **refuerzos** (*Mil*) reinforcements
4 (= *ayuda*) aid

refugiado/a ADJ, SM/F refugee

refugiarse ▸ CONJUG 1b VPR (= *acogerse a un refugio*) to take refuge; (= *cobijarse*) to shelter (**en** in) • **se refugió en un país vecino** he fled to a neighbouring country

refugio SM 1 (= *sitio*) refuge, shelter • **acogerse a un ~** to take refuge, (take) shelter (**en** in) ▸ **refugio alpino** mountain hut ▸ **refugio antiaéreo** air-raid shelter ▸ **refugio antiatómico, refugio antinuclear, refugio atómico** fallout shelter ▸ **refugio de caza** hunting lodge ▸ **refugio de montaña** mountain hut ▸ **refugio fiscal** tax shelter ▸ **refugio nuclear** fallout shelter ▸ **refugio subterráneo** (*Mil*) underground shelter, dugout
2 (*Esp*) (*Aut*) street island

refulgencia SF (*frm*) brilliance, refulgence (*frm o liter*)

refulgente ADJ (*frm*) brilliant, refulgent (*frm o liter*)

refulgir ▸ CONJUG 3c VI (*frm*) to shine, shine brightly

refundar ▸ CONJUG 1a VT to relaunch

refundición SF 1 (*Téc*) recasting
2 [*de obra*] new version, adaptation

refundidor(a) SM/F reviser, adapter

refundir ▸ CONJUG 3a VT 1 (*Téc*) to recast
2 [+ *obra*] to adapt, rewrite
3 (*And, CAm, Méx*) (= *perder*) to lose, mislay
4 (*Cono Sur*) (= *arruinar*) to ruin, crush; [+ *candidato*‡] to plough‡, plow (EEUU)
5 (*CAm*) (= *guardar*) to keep carefully
VPR **refundirse** (*And, CAm, Méx*) to get lost, be mislaid

refunfuñar ▸ CONJUG 1a VI (= *gruñir*) to growl; (= *quejarse*) to grumble

refunfuño SM (= *gruñido*) growl, grunt; (= *queja*) grumble

refunfuñón/ona* ADJ grumpy
SM/F grouch*

refusilo SM (*And, Chile*) lightning

refutable ADJ refutable • **fácilmente ~** easily refuted

refutación SF refutation

refutar ▸ CONJUG 1a VT to refute

regada SF watering

regadera SF 1 (*Hort*) watering can • MODISMO: • **estar como una ~** (*Esp**) to be crazy
2 (*Méx*) shower

r

regadío SM • **de ~** irrigated • **tierra de ~** irrigated land • **cultivo de ~** crop that grows on irrigated land

regadizo ADJ irrigable

regador SM (*Cono Sur*) watering can

regadura SF (*en jardín*) sprinkling, watering; (*Agr*) irrigation

regala SF gunwale

regaladamente ADV [*vivir*] in luxury • **comer ~** to eat extremely well

regalado ADJ **1** (= *cómodo*) comfortable, pleasant; (*pey*) (= *fácil*) soft • **MODISMO:** • **hace su regalada gana** (*LAm**) she does exactly what she likes *o* goes her own sweet way
2 (= *delicado*) dainty, delicate
3 (= *gratis*) free, given away • **me lo dio medio ~** he gave it to me for a song • **no lo quiero ni ~** I wouldn't have it at any price

regalar ▸ CONJUG 1a VT **1** (= *dar como regalo*) to give, give as a present • **~ algo a algn** to give sb sth, make sb a present of sth • **en su jubilación le ~on este reloj** they gave him this clock on his retirement, they presented him with this clock on his retirement • **están regalando plumas** they're giving pens away • **regaló el balón** (*Dep*) he gave the ball away
2 (*frm*) (= *agasajar*) • **~ a algn con un banquete** to hold a dinner in sb's honour *o* (*EEUU*) honor • **le ~on con toda clase de atenciones** they lavished attention on him
VPR **regalarse** (= *darse gusto*) to indulge o.s., pamper o.s.

regalía SF **1** (= *privilegio*) privilege, prerogative
2 regalías [*del rey*] royal prerogatives; (*Com*) (= *bonificación*) bonus (*sing*), perquisite (*sing*); (= *derechos*) royalties (*pl*); (= *adelanto*) advance payment (*sing*)
3 (*esp LAm*) (= *regalo*) gift, present
4 (*Caribe*) (= *excelencia*) excellence, goodness

regaliz SM, **regaliza** SF liquorice, licorice ▸ **regaliz de palo** stick of liquorice

regalo SM **1** (= *obsequio*) present, gift • **dar** *o* **hacer a algn un ~** to give sb a present *o* gift • **de ~: dan estos libros de ~** they're giving these books away • **entrada de ~** complimentary ticket • **estuche de ~** presentation case • **un libro de ~** a free book ▸ **regalo de boda** wedding present ▸ **regalo de cumpleaños** birthday present ▸ **regalo de Navidad, regalo de Reyes** Christmas present
2 (= *deleite, placer*) pleasure; [*de comida*] treat, delicacy • **es un ~ para el oído** it's a treat to listen to • **un ~ del cielo** a godsend
3†† (= *comodidad*) luxury, comfort

regalón ADJ **1** (= *comodón*) comfort-loving
2 [*vida*] (= *de lujo*) of luxury; (*pey*) (= *fácil*) soft, easy
3 (*LAm*) (= *predilecto*) • **es el ~ de su padre** he's the apple of his father's eye, he's his daddy's pet
4 (*And*) (= *obsequioso*) fond of giving presents

regalonear ▸ CONJUG 1a (*Cono Sur*) VT (= *mimar*) to spoil, pamper
VI (= *dejarse mimar*) to allow o.s. to be pampered

regañada* SF (*CAm, Méx*) = **regaño**

regañadientes • **a ~** ADV unwillingly, reluctantly

regañado ADJ • **estar ~ con algn** to be at odds with sb

regañar ▸ CONJUG 1a VT to scold, tell off*
VI **1** [*persona*] to grumble, grouse*
2 [*dos personas*] to fall out, quarrel
3†† [*perro*] to snarl, growl

regañina SF = **regaño**

regaño SM **1** (= *reprimenda*) scolding, telling-off* • **merecerse un ~** to get a telling off*
2 (= *gruñido*) snarl, growl; (= *mueca*) scowl; (= *queja*) grumble, grouse*

regañón ADJ (= *gruñón*) grumbling; [*mujer*] nagging

regar ▸ CONJUG 1h, 1j VT **1** [+ *planta, parterre*] to water; [+ *campo, terreno*] to irrigate; [+ *calle*] to hose down • **regó la carta con lágrimas** (*liter*) she cried all over the letter
2 (*Culin*) • **~on la cena con Rioja** they washed the meal down with some Rioja • **durante la cocción se riega la carne con su jugo** whilst it is cooking, baste the meat in its own juice
3 (*Geog*) [*río*] to water; [*mar*] to wash • **una costa regada por un mar tranquilo** a coast washed by a calm sea
4 [+ *herida*] to wash, bathe (**con, de** with)
5 (= *esparcir*) to sprinkle, scatter • **iba regando monedas** he was dropping money all over the place
6 (*And, CAm**) (= *derramar*) to spill; (= *derribar*) to knock over, knock down
7 (*Caribe*) (= *pegar*) to hit
VI **1** (*Caribe**) (= *bromear*) to joke • **está regando** she's having us on*
2 (*Caribe*) (= *actuar sin pensar*) to act rashly
3 • **~la** (*Méx‡*) (= *fracasar*) to screw it up‡, make a mess of it
VPR **regarse 1** (*CAm, Méx*) (= *dispersarse*) to scatter, scatter in all directions
2 (*Caribe**) (= *enfadarse*) to get cross
3 (*LAm*) (= *ducharse*) to shower, take a shower

regata[1] SF (*Agr*) irrigation channel

regata[2] SF (*Náut*) (= *una carrera*) race, boat race; (= *varias carreras*) regatta

regate SM **1** (= *movimiento*) swerve, dodge; (*Dep*) dribble
2 (= *treta*) dodge, ruse

regatear[1] ▸ CONJUG 1a VI (*Náut*) to race

regatear[2] ▸ CONJUG 1a VT **1** (*Com*) [+ *objeto, precio*] to haggle over, bargain over
2 (= *economizar*) to be mean with, economize on • **aquí regatean el vino** they are mean with their wine here • **su padre no le regatea dinero** her father does not keep her short of money • **no hemos regateado esfuerzos para terminarlo** we have spared no effort to finish it
3 (*frm*) (= *negar*) to deny, refuse to allow • **no le regateo buenas cualidades** I don't deny his good qualities
VI **1** (*Com*) to haggle, bargain
2 (= *esquivar*) to swerve, dodge; (*Dep*) to dribble
VPR **regatearse** • **~se algo** (*LAm*) to haggle over sth

regateo SM **1** (*Com*) haggling, bargaining
2 (*Dep*) dribbling

regatista SMF (= *participante*) competitor (*in yacht race*); (= *aficionado*) yachtsman/yachtswoman

regato SM pool

regatón[1] SM [*de bastón*] tip, ferrule

regatón[2] ADJ (*Com*) haggling
SM (*Caribe**) (= *restos*) dregs (*pl*)
SMF (*Méx**) (= *comerciante*) small-time dealer

regazo SM lap

regencia SF regency

regeneración SF regeneration

regenerado ADJ regenerate

regenerador ADJ regenerative

regeneramiento SM regeneration

regenerar ▸ CONJUG 1a VT to regenerate

regenta SF wife of the regent

regentar ▸ CONJUG 1a VT **1** (= *dirigir*) [+ *hotel, negocio*] to run, manage; [+ *destinos*] to guide, preside over
2 (= *ocupar*) [+ *puesto permanente*] to occupy, hold; [+ *puesto temporal*] to hold temporarily

regente ADJ **1** [*príncipe*] regent
2 [*director*] managing
SMF **1** (*Pol*) regent
2 [*de fábrica*] manager; (*Esp*) (*Farm*) chief pharmacist
SM (*Méx*) (= *alcalde*) mayor

reggae ['reɣe] SM reggae

reggaetón SM (*Mús*) = **reguetón**

regiamente ADV regally

regicida SMF regicide

regicidio SM regicide

regidor(a) ADJ [*principio*] governing, ruling
SM/F **1** (*Teat*) stage manager
2 (*TV*) floor manager
SM (*Hist*) alderman

regiego ADJ, SM = **rejego**

régimen SM (PL: **regímenes**) **1** (*Pol*) régime • **antiguo ~** ancien régime • **bajo el ~ del dictador** under the dictator's régime *o* rule ▸ **régimen del terror** reign of terror
2 (*Med*) (*tb* **régimen alimenticio**) diet • **estar a ~** to be on a diet • **poner a algn a ~** to put sb on a diet • **ponerse a ~** to go on a diet • **hacer ~** to be on a diet ▸ **régimen de adelgazamiento** diet, slimming diet ▸ **régimen lácteo** milk diet
3 (= *reglas*) rules (*pl*), set of rules • **en ~ de franquicia** under franchise • **prisión de ~ abierto** open prison • **he cambiado de ~ de vida** I have changed my whole way of life • **alojamiento en ~ de pensión completa** full board • **viviendas en ~ de alquiler** homes for rent ▸ **régimen tributario** tax system

regimentación SF regimentation

regimiento SM **1** (*Mil*) regiment
2* (= *multitud*) crowd

Reginaldo SM Reginald

regio ADJ **1** (= *real*) royal, regal
2 (= *suntuoso*) splendid, majestic
3 (*And, Cono Sur**) (= *genial*) great*, terrific*
EXCL (*And, Cono Sur**) great!*, fine!

regiomontano/a ADJ of/from Monterrey
SM/F native/inhabitant of Monterrey • **los ~s** the people of Monterrey

región SF **1** (*Geog, Pol*) region; (= *área*) area, part
2 (*Anat*) region

regional ADJ regional

regionalismo SM regionalism

regionalista ADJ, SMF regionalist

regionalización SF regionalization

regir ▸ CONJUG 3c, 3k VT **1** [+ *país*] to rule, govern; [+ *colegio*] to run; [+ *empresa*] to manage, run
2 (*Econ, Jur*) to govern • **según el reglamento que rige estos casos** according to the statute which governs these cases • **los factores que rigen los cambios del mercado** the factors which govern *o* control changes in the market
3 (*Ling*) to take • **ese verbo rige el dativo** that verb takes the dative
VI **1** (= *estar en vigor*) [*ley, precio*] to be in force; [*condición*] to prevail, obtain • **esa ley ya no rige** that law is no longer in force • **cuando estas condiciones ya no rijan** when these conditions no longer obtain
2 (*con mes, año*) • **el mes que rige** the present month, the current month
3 (= *funcionar*) to work, go • **el timbre no rige** the bell doesn't work
4* (= *estar cuerdo*) • **no ~** to have a screw loose*, not be all there*
VPR **regirse** • **~se por** to be ruled by, be guided by, go by

regista SMF producer

registrado ADJ **1** (= *anotado*) registered
2 (*Méx*) (*Correos*) (= *certificado*) registered

registrador(a) SM/F **1** (*Admin*) (= *persona*) recorder, registrar

2 ▸ **registrador(a) de sonido** (*TV*) sound recordist
SM ▸ **registrador de vuelo** flight recorder

registradora SF (*Com*) cash register

registrar ▹ CONJUG 1a VT **1** [*+ equipaje, lugar, persona*] to search • **lo hemos registrado todo de arriba abajo** we have searched the whole place from top to bottom • MODISMO: • **¡a mí que me registren!*** search me!*
2 (= *anotar*) to register, record • **han registrado el nacimiento de su hijo** they have registered the birth of their son
3 [*+ temperatura, terremoto*] to record, register; [*+ terremoto, temblor*] to register • **el termómetro registró una mínima de diez grados** the thermometer recorded *o* registered a minimum temperature of ten degrees
4 (*Mús*) to record • **~ la voz en una cinta** to record one's voice on tape
5 (*Méx*) [*+ correo*] to register
6 • **~ un libro**† to mark one's place in a book
VPR **registrarse 1** (= *apuntarse*) to register • **tienes que ~te en el consulado** you have to register at the consulate • **me registré en el hotel** I checked into the hotel
2 (= *ocurrir*) • **hoy se han registrado las temperaturas más altas del año** the highest temperatures this year were recorded today • **se han registrado lluvias en toda la región** there was rain throughout the whole region • **se han registrado algunos casos de tifus** a few cases of typhus have been reported • **el cambio que se ha registrado en su actitud** the change which has occurred in his attitude

registro SM **1** (= *acción*) registration, recording
2 (= *libro*) register; (*Inform*) record • **firmar el ~** to sign the register • **capacidad de ~** storage facility, recording capacity ▸ **registro catastral** land registry ▸ **registro de casamientos** register of marriages ▸ **registro de defunciones** register of deaths ▸ **registro de la propiedad inmobiliaria** land registry ▸ **registro de nacimientos** register of births ▸ **registro electoral** electoral register, electoral roll ▸ **registro lógico** logical record ▸ **registro mercantil** business register ▸ **registro parroquial** parish register
3 (= *lista*) list, record; (= *apunte*) note ▸ **registro de erratas** list of errata
4 (= *entrada*) entry
5 (= *oficina*) registry, record office ▸ **registro civil** ≈ registry office, ≈ county clerk's office (EEUU) ▸ **registro de la propiedad** (= *oficina*) land registry, land registry office ▸ **registro de patentes y marcas** patent office
6 (= *búsqueda*) search; (= *inspección*) inspection • **practicar un ~** to make a search (en of) • **orden de ~** search warrant ▸ **registro domiciliario** house search ▸ **registro policíaco** police search
7 (*Mús*) (= *grabación*) recording • **es un buen ~ de la sinfonía** it is a good recording of the symphony
8 (*Mús*) (= *timbre*) [*de la voz*] register; [*del órgano*] stop; [*del piano*] pedal • MODISMOS: • **adoptar un ~ muy raro** • **salir por un ~ muy raro** to adopt a very odd tone • **mira por qué ~ nos sale ahora** look what he's coming out with now • **tocar todos los ~s** to pull out all the stops
9 (*Téc*) manhole
10 (*Ling*) register
11 (*Dep*) (= *marca*) personal best; (= *récord*) record
12 [*de reloj*] regulator
13 (*Tip*) register • **estar en ~** to be in register
14 (*And, Cono Sur*) (= *tienda*) wholesale textiles store

regla SF **1** (= *instrumento*) ruler ▸ **regla de cálculo** slide rule ▸ **regla de un pie** 12-inch rule ▸ **regla en T, regla T** T-square
2 (= *norma*) rule • **las ~s del ajedrez** the rules of chess • **~s para utilizar una máquina** instructions for the use of a machine • **no hay ~ sin excepción** every rule has its exception • **las cuatro ~s** *addition, subtraction, multiplication and division* • **en ~** in order • **no tenía los papeles en ~** his papers were not in order • **todo está en ~** everything is in order • **poner algo en ~** to put sth straight • **por ~ general** generally, as a rule • **salir de ~** to overstep the mark • **en toda ~**: • **hacer algo en toda ~** to do sth properly • **es un español en toda ~** he's a real Spaniard, he's a Spaniard through and through ▸ **reglas del juego** rules of the game ▸ **regla de tres** rule of three • **¿por qué ~ de tres ...?** (*Esp**) why on earth ...? ▸ **reglas de oro** golden rules
3 (= *menstruación*) period
4 (= *moderación*) moderation, restraint • **comer con ~** to eat in moderation
5 (*Rel*) rule, order • **viven según la ~ benedictina** they live according to the Benedictine rule

reglable ADJ adjustable

reglaje SM **1** (*Mec*) adjustment ▸ **reglaje de neumáticos** wheel alignment
2 (*Mil*) correction, correction of aim

reglamentación SF **1** (= *acción*) regulation
2 (= *reglas*) regulations (*pl*), rules (*pl*)

reglamentar ▹ CONJUG 1a VT to regulate

reglamentariamente ADV in due form, according to the rules

reglamentario ADJ [*uniforme*] regulation (*antes de s*) • **pistola reglamentaria** standard issue pistol • **en el traje ~** in the regulation dress • **en la forma reglamentaria** in the properly established way • **es ~** (*+ infin*) the regulations stipulate that

reglamento SM (= *reglas*) rules (*pl*), regulations (*pl*); [*de reunión, sociedad*] standing order, standing orders (*pl*); (*municipal*) by-law; [*de profesión*] code of conduct • **pistola de ~** standard issue pistol ▸ **reglamento de aduana** customs regulations (*pl*) ▸ **reglamento del tráfico** highway code

reglar ▹ CONJUG 1a VT **1** [*+ papel*] to rule
2 [*+ acciones*] to regulate
3 (*Mec*) to check, overhaul
4 (*Mil*) [*+ puntería*] to correct
VPR **reglarse** • **~se a** to abide by, conform to • **~se por** to be guided by

regleta SF space

regletear ▹ CONJUG 1a VT to space out

regocijadamente ADV merrily, joyfully

regocijado ADJ **1** [*carácter*] jolly, cheerful
2 [*estado, humor*] merry, joyful

regocijar ▹ CONJUG 1a VT to gladden, delight • **la noticia regocijó a la familia** the news delighted the family, the news filled the family with joy • **un chiste que regocijó a todos** a joke which made everyone laugh • **creó un personaje para ~ a los niños** she created a character to amuse children
VPR **regocijarse 1** (= *alegrarse*) to rejoice, be glad (**de, por** about, at) • **se regocija de la mala suerte de otros** he delights in other people's misfortunes
2 (= *reírse*) to laugh • **~se con un chiste** to laugh at a joke
3 (= *pasarlo bien*) to have a good time

regocijo SM **1** (= *alegría*) joy, happiness; (= *júbilo*) delight, elation
2†† (= *regodeo*) gloating (**por** over)
3 regocijos†† (= *fiestas*) festivities, celebrations ▸ **regocijos navideños** Christmas festivities ▸ **regocijos públicos** public rejoicing

regodearse ▹ CONJUG 1a VPR **1** • **~ con** *o* **en algo** to gloat over sth
2 (*LAm**) (= *ser exigente*) to be fussy, be hard to please

regodeo SM **1** (= *broma*) joking
2 (= *deleite*) delight; (*pey*) (= *refocilo*) perverse pleasure *o* delight

regodeón (*LAm*) ADJ **1** (= *exigente*) fussy, hard to please
2 (= *egoísta*) self-indulgent

regodiente ADJ (*And*) fussy, hard to please

regojo SM **1** (= *pan*) piece of left-over bread
2* (= *persona*) tich*, titch*

regoldar* ▹ CONJUG 1l VI to belch

regordete ADJ [*persona*] chubby, plump; [*manos*] fat

regosto SM longing, craving (**de** for)

regrabadora SF rewriter ▸ **regrabadora de DVDs** DVD rewriter

regresar ▹ CONJUG 1a VI (= *venir*) to return, come back; (= *irse*) to return, go back
VT (*LAm*) to give back, return
VPR **regresarse** (*LAm*) ▹ VI

regresión SF **1** (= *acción*) (*tb Psic*) regression
2 (= *retroceso*) [*de productividad*] fall, decrease; [*de actividad cultural*] decline ▸ **regresión demográfica** population decline, fall in population

regresivo ADJ regressive, backward

regreso SM return • **viaje de ~** return trip • **emprender el ~ a** to return to, come/go back to • **estar de ~** to be back • **de ~** on the way back, on my/his/our *etc* way back • **de ~ a casa tuvimos una avería** the car broke down on the way home • **nos enteraremos al ~** we'll find out once we get back

regro ADJ (*Caribe*) great*, fabulous*

regto. ABR (= **regimiento**) Regt., Rgt

regüeldo SM (*frm*) belch, belching

reguera SF **1** (*Agr*) irrigation channel
2 (*Náut*) cable, mooring rope, anchor chain

reguero SM **1** (= *señal*) track; [*de sangre*] trickle; [*de humo, pólvora*] trail • MODISMO: • **propagarse como un ~ de pólvora** to spread like wildfire
2 (*Agr*) irrigation ditch

reguetón SM (*Mús*) reggaeton

reguío SM (*And*) = **riego**

regulable ADJ adjustable

regulación SF **1** (*con reglas*) regulation; (*Mec*) adjustment; (= *control*) control ▸ **regulación de la natalidad** birth control ▸ **regulación del tráfico** traffic control ▸ **regulación del volumen sonoro** (*Radio*) volume control
2 (*euf*) (= *reducción*) reduction ▸ **regulación de empleo** redundancy ▸ **regulación de jornada** cut in working hours ▸ **regulación de plantilla** staff cut

regulador ADJ regulating, regulatory
SM (*Mec*) regulator, throttle; (*Radio*) control, button ▸ **regulador de intensidad (de luz)** dimmer, dimmer switch ▸ **regulador del volumen (sonoro)** volume control

regular[1] ADJ **1** (= *normal*) normal, usual
2 (= *común*) ordinary • **por lo ~** as a rule, generally
3 (= *uniforme*) regular • **a intervalos ~es** at regular intervals • **tiene un latido ~** it has a regular beat
4 (= *mediano*) medium, average • **de tamaño ~** medium-sized, average-sized
5 (= *no muy bueno*) so-so, not too bad • **es una novela ~** it's an average sort of novel • **—¿qué tal la fiesta? —regular** "what was the party like?" — "it was O.K. *o* all right *o* not too bad" • **—¿qué tal estás? —regular**

r

"how are you?" — "so-so *o* all right *o* can't complain"
6 (*Rel, Mil*) regular
regular² ▹ CONJUG 1a (VT) **1** (= *ajustar*) to regulate, control; [*ley*] to govern; [+ *tráfico, precio*] to control
2 (*Mec*) to adjust, regulate; [+ *reloj*] to put right; [+ *despertador*] to set
3 (*Méx*) (= *calcular*) to calculate
regularcillo* (ADJ) = regular¹
regularidad (SF) regularity • **con ~** regularly
regularización (SF) (= *legalización*) regularization; (= *acomodación*) standardization
regularizar ▹ CONJUG 1f (VT) (= *ajustar, legalizar*) to regularize; (= *acomodar*) to standardize, bring into line
regularmente (ADV) regularly
régulo (SM) (*frm*) kinglet, petty king
regurgitación (SF) regurgitation
regurgitar ▹ CONJUG 1a (VT) to regurgitate
regustado (ADJ) (*Caribe*) well-satisfied
regustar ▹ CONJUG 1a (VT) (*Caribe, Méx*) to taste, relish, savour, savor (*EEUU*)
regusto (SM) aftertaste • **queda siempre el ~** it leaves a bad taste in the mouth
rehabilitación (SF) **1** [*de enfermo, delincuente*] rehabilitation
2 (*en cargo*) reinstatement
3 [*de edificio*] restoration
4 [*de una máquina*] overhaul
rehabilitar ▹ CONJUG 1a (VT) **1** [+ *persona*] to rehabilitate; (*en cargo*) to reinstate
2 (*Arquit*) to restore, renovate; (*Mec*) to overhaul
rehacer ▹ CONJUG 2r (VT) **1** (= *hacer de nuevo*) to do again, redo • **tengo que ~ toda la carta** I have to do the whole letter again, I have to redo the whole letter again
2 (= *recomponer*) • **no ha podido ~ su vida** he hasn't been able to piece his life together again *o* rebuild his life
(VPR) **rehacerse 1** (= *reponerse*) to recover • **~se de algo** to get over sth, recover from sth
2 (*Mil*) to re-form
rehecho (ADJ) **1** (= *robusto*) thickset, chunky
2 (= *descansado*) rested
rehén (SMF) hostage
rehenchir ▹ CONJUG 3l (VT) to fill, stuff, pack (de with)
rehilar ▹ CONJUG 1a (VI) **1** (= *temblar*) to quiver, shake
2 [*flecha*] to hum
rehilete (SM) **1** (= *flecha*) dart; (*Taur*) banderilla
2 (*Dep*) (= *volante*) shuttlecock
3 (= *comentario*) taunt
rehogado (ADJ) sautéed, tossed in oil
rehogar ▹ CONJUG 1h (VT) to sauté, toss in oil
rehostia** (EXCL) damn it!
(SF) • **esto es la ~** this is the absolute limit • **se cree que es la ~** he thinks he's the best thing since sliced bread*
rehuir ▹ CONJUG 3g (VT) to avoid • **Juan me rehúye** Juan is avoiding me • **rehúye de las situaciones difíciles** she avoids *o* runs away from difficult situations
rehusar ▹ CONJUG 1a (VT) to refuse • **~ hacer algo** to refuse to do sth
(VI) to refuse
reidero* (ADJ) amusing, funny
reidor (ADJ) (*frm*) merry, laughing
reiki (SM) reiki
reilón (ADJ) (*Caribe*) (= *que se ríe*) given to laughing a lot, giggly; (= *alegre*) merry
reimplantar ▹ CONJUG 1a (VT) to re-establish, reintroduce
reimponer ▹ CONJUG 2q (VT) to reimpose
reimpresión (SF) reprint, reprinting
reimprimir ▹ CONJUG 3a (VT) to reprint
reina (SF) **1** (= *monarca*) queen ▸ **reina de (la) belleza** beauty queen ▸ **reina de la fiesta** carnival queen ▸ **reina madre** queen mother ▸ **reina mora** (= *juego*) hopscotch ▸ **reina viuda** dowager queen
2 (*Ajedrez*) queen
3 (*Entomología*) queen
4 (*Bot*) ▸ **reina claudia** greengage
5* (= *droga*) pure heroin
(ADJ INV) • **la prueba ~** the main event
reinado (SM) reign • **bajo el ~ de** in the reign of
Reinaldo (SM) Reginald
reinante (ADJ) **1** (= *soberano*) reigning
2 (*fig*) (= *que prevalece*) prevailing
reinar ▹ CONJUG 1a (VI) **1** [*rey, reina*] to reign, rule
2 [*caos, confusión, paz*] to reign • **reina una confusión total** total confusion reigns, there is total confusion • **entre la población reinaba el descontento** there was widespread discontent among the population • **reinan las bajas temperaturas** there are low temperatures everywhere, low temperatures prevail everywhere
reinauguración (SF) reinauguration
reinaugurar ▹ CONJUG 1a (VT) to reinaugurate
reincidencia (SF) **1** (= *acto*) relapse (en into)
2 (= *tendencia*) recidivism
reincidente (SMF) recidivist, persistent offender
reincidir ▹ CONJUG 3a (VI) (= *recaer*) to relapse (en into); [*criminal*] to reoffend; [*pecador*] to backslide
reincorporación (SF) **1** [*de trabajador*] (*tras descanso, vacaciones*) return; (*tras despido*) reinstatement
2 [*de colonia, territorio*] reincorporation
reincorporar ▹ CONJUG 1a (VT) **1** [+ *colonia, territorio*] to reincorporate
2 [+ *trabajador*] to reinstate
(VPR) **reincorporarse** • **~se a algo** to rejoin sth • **~se al trabajo** (*tras vacaciones, descanso*) to return to work; (*tras despido*) to be reinstated
reindustrialización (SF) restructuring of industry
reineta (ADJ) • **manzana ~** pippin
(SF) pippin
reingresar ▹ CONJUG 1a (VI) • **~ en** to re-enter
reingreso (SM) re-entry (en into)
reinicializar ▹ CONJUG 1f (VT) (*Inform*) to reset, reboot
reiniciar ▹ CONJUG 1b (VT) to begin again
reinicio (SM) new beginning
reino (SM) kingdom ▸ **reino animal** animal kingdom ▸ **reino vegetal** plant kingdom ▸ **el Reino Unido** the United Kingdom
reinona‡ (SF) (= *mariquita*) fairy‡, fag (*EEUU‡*)
reinoso/a (SM/F) **1** (*And*) [*del interior*] inlander, inhabitant of the interior (*esp of the cold eastern upland*)
2 (*Caribe*) Colombian
reinserción (SF) ▸ **reinserción en la sociedad, reinserción social** social rehabilitation, assimilation into society
reinsertado/a (SM/F) (= *ex-terrorista*) reformed terrorist
reinsertar ▹ CONJUG 1a (VT) to rehabilitate, assimilate into society
(VPR) **reinsertarse** • **~se en la sociedad** to resume an ordinary social life
reinstalar ▹ CONJUG 1a (VT) **1** [+ *aparato*] to reinstall
2 (*en un puesto*) to reinstate
reinstauración (SF) restoration
reinstaurar ▹ CONJUG 1a (VT) to restore
reintegrable (ADJ) returnable, refundable
reintegración (SF) **1** (*a cargo*) reinstatement (a in)
2 (*Econ*) refund, repayment
3 (= *vuelta*) return (a to)
reintegrar ▹ CONJUG 1a (VT) **1** (= *restituir, reconstituir*) to reintegrate
2 [+ *persona*] to reinstate (a in)
3 (*Econ*) [+ *dinero*] to pay back • **~ a algn una cantidad** to refund *o* pay back a sum to sb • **le han reintegrado todos sus gastos** he has been reimbursed for all his expenses
4 [+ *documento*] to attach a fiscal stamp to
(VPR) **reintegrarse** • **~se a** to return to
reintegro (SM) **1** (*Econ*) refund, reimbursement; (*en banco*) withdrawal
2 [*de lotería*] return of one's stake
3 (= *sello*) fiscal stamp, cost of a fiscal stamp
reintroducción (SF) reintroduction
reintroducir ▹ CONJUG 3n (VT) to reintroduce
reinvención (SF) reinvention • **su capacidad de ~** his ability to reinvent himself
reinventar ▹ CONJUG 1a (VT) to reinvent
reinversión (SF) reinvestment
reinvertir ▹ CONJUG 3i (VT) to reinvest
reír ▹ CONJUG 3l (VI) **1** [*persona*] to laugh • **no me hagas ~** don't make me laugh • **echarse a ~** to burst out laughing • MODISMO: • **~ como un loco** to laugh one's head off • REFRÁN: • **el que ríe el último, ríe mejor** *o* **más fuerte** he who laughs last laughs longest
2 (*liter*) [*ojos*] to laugh (*liter*), sparkle; [*campo, mañana, naturaleza*] to sparkle, glow
(VT) to laugh at • **todos le ríen los chistes** everybody laughs at his jokes
(VPR) **reírse 1** to laugh • **~se con algo/algn**: • **todos se ríen con sus chistes** everybody laughs at his jokes • **siempre nos reímos con él** we always have a good laugh with him • **~se de algn/algo** to laugh at sb/sth • **se está riendo de mí** he's laughing at me • **¿de qué te ríes?** what are you laughing at? • MODISMO: • **¡déjame que me ría!** that's a good one!
2* (= *estar roto*) • **estos zapatos se ríen** these shoes are split wide open at the toes • **la chaqueta se me ríe por los codos** my jacket has worn through at the elbows
reiteración (SF) reiteration (*frm*), repetition • **llamada de ~** (*Com*) follow-up call • **visita de ~** (*Com*) follow-up visit
reiteradamente (ADV) repeatedly
reiterado (ADJ) repeated
reiterar ▹ CONJUG 1a (VT) to reiterate (*frm*), repeat
reiterativo (ADJ) reiterative
reivindicable (ADJ) recoverable, recoverable at law
reivindicación (SF) **1** (= *reclamación*) demand • **el gobierno ha rechazado las reivindicaciones de los sindicatos** the government have rejected the union's demands ▸ **reivindicación salarial** pay claim, wage claim
2 [*de asesinato, crimen*] • **se produjo la ~ del atentado** responsibility for the attack has been claimed
3 (= *desagravio*) • **una lucha por la ~ de la memoria de Galileo** a fight to vindicate Galileo's memory • **era la justa ~ de los políticos de la República** it was a fair reappraisal of the politicians of the Republic
4 (*Jur*) recovery
reivindicar ▹ CONJUG 1g (VT) **1** (= *reclamar*) [+ *derechos, condiciones, independencia*] to demand; [+ *herencia*] to claim • **reivindican subidas salariales** they are demanding pay

increases
2 [+ *asesinato, crimen*] to claim responsibility for • **han reivindicado la autoría del atentado** they have claimed responsibility for the attack
3 (= *desagraviar*) [+ *reputación*] to vindicate • **reivindican la memoria de los poetas asesinados** they're demanding a reappraisal of the murdered poets
4 (*Jur*) to recover
5 (*LAm**) (= *exigir*) to demand
VPR **reivindicarse** (*LAm*) to vindicate o.s.

reivindicativo ADJ, **reivindicatorio** ADJ [*movimiento, acto, plataforma*] protest (*antes de s*) • **adoptar una postura más reivindicativa** to be more aggressive in one's demands

reja SF **1** [*de ventana*] bars (*pl*), grille; [*de cercado*] railing • MODISMO: • **entre ~s**: • **estar entre ~s** to be behind bars • **meter a algn entre ~s** to put sb behind bars
2 (*Rel*) screen
3 (*Agr*) ▸ **reja del arado** ploughshare, plowshare (EEUU)
4 (*LAm**) (= *cárcel*) prison, nick‡
5 (*Méx*) (*Cos*) darn, darning
6 (*Cono Sur*) (*Agr*) cattle truck

rejado SM grille, grating

rejeada SF (*And, CAm*) thrashing

rejear ▸ CONJUG 1a VT (*CAm*) to jail, put in jail

rejego* ADJ (*Méx*) **1** (= *rebelde*) wild, rebellious
2 (= *lento*) slow, sluggish
SM (*CAm*) stud bull

rejiego ADJ (*Caribe, Méx*) = **rejego**

rejilla SF **1** [*de caño, alcantarilla*] grating, grille; [*de equipaje*] luggage rack; [*de horno*] shelf; [*de ventilador*] vent ▸ **rejilla de ventilación** ventilation grille
2 (= *muebles*) wickerwork • **silla de ~** wicker chair
3 (= *braserillo*) small stove, footwarmer
4 (*Cono Sur*) (= *fresquera*) meat safe, cooler (EEUU)

rejo SM **1** (= *punta*) spike, sharp point
2 [*de insecto*] sting
3 (*Bot*) radicle
4 (*fig*) (= *vigor*) strength, vigour, vigor (EEUU), toughness
5 (*LAm*) (= *látigo*) whip; (= *soga*) cattle rope
6 (*Caribe*) (= *tira*) strip of raw leather; (= *porra*) stick, club ▸ **rejo tieso** brave person
7 (*And*) (= *ordeño*) milking; (= *vacas*) herd of cows

rejón SM (= *barra de hierro*) pointed iron bar, spike; (*Taur*) lance

rejoneador(a) SM/F (*Taur*) *mounted bullfighter who uses the lance*

rejonear ▸ CONJUG 1a (*Taur*) VT [+ *toro*] to wound with the lance
VI to fight the bull on horseback with the lance

rejoya SF (*CAm*) (*Geog*) deep valley

rejudo ADJ (*And, Caribe*) (= *pegajoso*) sticky, viscous; (*Caribe*) [*líquido*] runny

rejugado ADJ **1** (*And, Caribe*) (= *astuto*) cunning, sharp
2 (*CAm*) (= *tímido*) shy

rejunta SF (*Cono Sur, Méx*) round-up, rodeo

rejuntar ▸ CONJUG 1a VT **1** (*esp Cono Sur*) (= *recoger*) to collect, gather in
2 (*Méx*) [+ *ganado*] to round up
3 (*Cono Sur*) [+ *suma*] to add up

rejuvenecedor ADJ rejuvenating

rejuvenecer ▸ CONJUG 2d VT to rejuvenate
VPR **rejuvenecerse** to be rejuvenated, become young again

rejuvenecimiento SM rejuvenation

relación SF **1** (= *vínculo*) connection • **no existe ninguna ~ entre los dos accidentes** there is no connection between the two accidents • **existe una ~ entre el tabaco y el cáncer** there is a connection *o* relation *o* relationship between cigarettes and cancer • **guardar** *o* **tener ~ con algo** [*suceso*] to be connected with sth, be related to sth; [*persona*] to be connected with sth • **no guardar ~ (alguna) con algo** (= *no parecerse*) to bear no relation (whatsoever) to sth; (= *no estar relacionado*) to have no connection *o* relation (at all) with sth ▸ **relación calidad/precio** value for money • **tener buena ~ calidad/precio** to be good value for money ▸ **relación causa-efecto** cause and effect relationship ▸ **relación real de intercambio** terms of trade (*pl*)
2 • **con ~ a** • **en ~ a** *o* **con** (= *comparado con*) compared to, compared with; (= *en lo referente a*) with regard to, in connection with • **un aumento del 3% con ~ al año anterior** an increase of 3% over *o* compared to *o* compared with the previous year • **con ~ a la encuesta publicada por este periódico** with regard to *o* in connection with the survey published by this newspaper • **fue interrogado en ~ con el secuestro** he was questioned in connection with the kidnapping
3 (= *entre personas*) **a** (*en el momento presente*) relations (*pl*) • **¿cómo es su ~** *o* **son sus relaciones con su jefe?** how are relations between you and your boss? • **estar en** *o* **mantener buenas relaciones con** [+ *persona*] to be on good terms with; [+ *organización*] to have good relations with • **romper las relaciones con** [+ *país, organización*] to break off relations with; [+ *familiar, amigo*] to break off all contact with
b (*de larga duración*) relationship • **¿cómo eran las relaciones con su padre?** what was your relationship with your father like? • **tenía una ~ de amistad con algunos de sus alumnos** he had a friendly relationship with some of his students • **¿sigues manteniendo las relaciones con tus antiguos compañeros de universidad?** do you still keep in touch with people from your university days? ▸ **relaciones humanas** human relations
4 (*con empresa, organización*) connection • **¿tiene alguna ~ con esa empresa?** do you have any connection with that company? • **ha sido detenido por sus relaciones con la Mafia** he has been arrested because of his connections with the Mafia ▸ **relaciones comerciales** trade relations ▸ **relaciones diplomáticas** diplomatic relations ▸ **relaciones empresariales** business relations ▸ **relaciones laborales** labour relations, labor relations (EEUU) ▸ **relaciones públicas** (= *actividad*) public relations, PR; (= *profesional*) public relations officer, PR officer
5 (*tb* **relación amorosa**) relationship • **nuestra ~ duró hasta 1997** our relationship lasted until 1997 • **no veían con buenos ojos sus relaciones con una extranjera** they did not view his relationship with a foreign woman favourably • **tu ~ de pareja** your relationship with your partner • **llevan varios meses de relaciones** they've been seeing each other for some months • **tienen una ~ formal desde hace un año** they've been formally going out for a year ▸ **relación sentimental** relationship
6 (*tb* **relación sexual**) (= *acto*) sex; (= *trato*) sexual relationship • **mantener** *o* **tener relaciones sexuales con algn** (*de forma esporádica*) to have sex with sb; (*de forma continuada*) to be in a sexual relationship with sb ▸ **relaciones carnales** carnal relations ▸ **relaciones extramatrimoniales** extra-marital relationships ▸ **relaciones ilícitas** illicit sexual relations ▸ **relaciones prematrimoniales** premarital sex, sex before marriage
7 (= *referencia*) • **hacer ~ a algo** to refer to sth • **no hizo ~ a ese tema** she did not refer to that subject
8 relaciones (= *personas conocidas*) acquaintances; (= *enchufes*) contacts, connections • **tener (buenas) relaciones** to be well connected, have good contacts *o* connections
9 (*Mat*) (= *proporción*) ratio • **los superan numéricamente en una ~ 46-36%** they outnumber them by a ratio of 46-36% ▸ **relación de compresión** compression ratio
10 (*frm*) (= *narración*) account • **hacer una ~ de algo** to give an account of sth • **hizo una ~ detallada de lo que vio** she gave a detailed account of what she saw
11 (= *lista*) list • **la ~ de aprobados se publicará en marzo** the list of those who have passed will be issued in March • **el usuario dispone, junto a la factura telefónica, de una ~ de sus llamadas** the customer receives, together with the telephone bill, a breakdown of calls made
12 (*Jur*) (= *informe*) record, (official) return

relacionado ADJ **1** [*acontecimiento, tema, problema*] related • **las dos cuestiones están íntimamente relacionadas** the two matters are closely related • **~ con algo** related to sth • **delitos ~s con el narcotráfico** crimes related to drug trafficking • **actividades relacionadas con el teatro** theatre-related activities • **me interesa todo lo ~ con el tema** I'm interested in everything to do with *o* connected with *o* related to the subject
2 [*persona*] • **una persona bien relacionada** a well-connected person • **~ con algn/algo** connected with sb/sth, linked to sb/sth • **J.S. podría estar ~ con el atentado** J.S. could be connected with *o* linked to the bomb attack • **empresas relacionadas con la industria automovilística** companies connected with *o* linked to the car industry • **se le considera muy bien ~ con los servicios secretos** he is thought to have very close connections with the secret service

relacional ADJ **1** (*Inform, Mat*) relational
2 (*Sociol*) • **estudio ~** study of (human) relationships

relacionar ▸ CONJUG 1a VT **1** (= *asociar*) to connect (**con** with) • **ya hay tres documentos que lo relacionan con el caso** there are now three documents connecting him with *o* linking him to the case
2 (= *enumerar*) to list • **los ejemplos que se relacionan a continuación** the examples listed below
VPR **relacionarse 1** [*persona*] • **un hombre que sabe ~se** a man who mixes with the right people • **~se con algn** to mix with sb • **en el colegio no se relacionaba con nadie** he didn't mix with anybody at school • **se relacionaba poco con los vecinos** she had little contact with her neighbours
2 [*sucesos, temas*] to be connected, be related • **los dos hechos no se relacionan** the two events are not connected *o* related • **~se con algo** to be related to sth • **palabras que se relacionan con el mar** words related to the sea
3 (*frm*) (= *referirse*) • **en lo que se relaciona a** as for, with regard to

relai [re'le] SM, **relais** [re'le] SM relay

r

relajación SF **1** (= *sosiego*) relaxation
2 (= *suavización*) slackening, loosening
3 (*moral*) laxity
4 (*Med*) hernia, rupture

relajado ADJ **1** (= *sosegado*) relaxed
2 (= *inmoral*) dissolute, loose
3 (*Med*) ruptured

relajadura SF (*Méx*) hernia, rupture

relajamiento ADV **1** [*de músculo*] relaxation
2 [*de sanciones, actitud*] relaxation, loosening

relajante ADJ **1** [*ejercicio, actividad*] relaxing
2 (*Med*) sedative
3 (*Cono Sur*) [*comida*] sickly, sweet and sticky
4 (= *repugnante*) revolting, disgusting
SM sedative

relajar ▸ CONJUG 1a VT **1** (= *sosegar*) to relax
2 (= *suavizar*) to slacken, loosen
3 (*moralmente*) to weaken, corrupt
4 (*LAm*) [*comida*] to cloy, sicken, disgust
5 (*Caribe*) (= *hacer mofa de*) to mock, deride; (= *escarnecer*) to poke fun at
VPR **relajarse 1** (= *sosegarse*) to relax
2 (= *aflojarse*) to slacken off, loosen
3 (*moralmente*) [*persona*] to go off the straight and narrow, go to the bad; [*moralidad*] to become lax
4 (*Med*) • **~se un tobillo** to sprain one's ankle • **~se un órgano** to rupture an organ

relajo SM (*LAm*) **1** (= *libertinaje*) laxity, dissipation, depravity; (= *indecencia*) lewdness
2 (= *acción inmoral*) immoral act; (= *acto indecente*) indecent act
3 (= *ruido*) row, din; (= *fiesta*) lewd party; (= *desorden*) commotion, disorder; (= *lío*) fuss, row • **¡qué ~!** what a row/mess!
4 (= *burla*) rude joke; (= *trastada*) practical joke; (= *escarnio*) derision • **echar algo a ~** to make fun of sth • **cuento de ~** blue joke
5* (= *relajación*) relaxation; (= *descanso*) rest, break
6 (*Méx*) (= *opción fácil*) easy ride, soft option

relajón ADJ **1** (*Caribe*) (= *mofador*) mocking; (= *obsceno**) dirty
2 (*Méx*) (= *depravado*) depraved, perverse

relamer ▸ CONJUG 2a VT to lick repeatedly
VPR **relamerse 1** [*animal*] to lick its chops; [*persona*] (*tb* **relamerse los labios**) to lick one's lips
2 (*fig*) • **~se con algo** to relish the prospect of sth; (*pey*) to gloat over the prospect of sth
3 (= *gloriarse*) to brag
4†† (= *maquillarse*) to paint one's face

relamido ADJ **1** (= *afectado*) affected
2 (= *acicalado*) overdressed
3 (= *remilgado*) prim and proper
4 (*CAm, Caribe**) (= *descarado*) shameless, cheeky*

relámpago SM (= *rayo*) flash of lightning • **vi un ~ en el horizonte** I saw a flash of lightning on the horizon • **ayer hubo ~s** there was lightning yesterday • **MODISMO**: • **como un ~** as quick as lightning, in a flash
▸ **relámpago difuso** sheet lightning
ADJ INV • **guerra ~** blitzkrieg • **visita ~** lightning visit • **viaje ~** lightning trip

relampagucear ▸ CONJUG 1a VI (*Caribe, Méx*) (= *parpadear*) to twinkle, flicker; (= *brillar*) to gleam

relampaguceo SM (*Caribe, Méx*) (= *parpadeo*) twinkle, flicker; (= *brillo*) gleam

relampagueante ADJ flashing

relampaguear ▸ CONJUG 1a VI **1** (*Met*) • **relampagueó toda la noche** there was lightning all night
2 (= *arrojar luz*) to flash
3 (*Caribe*) (= *parpadear*) to twinkle, flicker; (= *brillar*) to gleam, shine

relampagueo SM **1** [*de luz*] flashing
2 (*Caribe*) (= *parpadeo*) twinkle, flicker; (= *brillo*) gleam, shine

relampuso ADJ (*Caribe*) shameless, brazen

relance SM (*Cono Sur*) **1** = **piropo**
2 • **de ~** (= *al contado*) in cash

relanzamiento SM relaunch, relaunching

relanzar ▸ CONJUG 1f VT **1** [+ *plan*] to relaunch
2 [+ *ataque*] to repel, repulse

relatar ▸ CONJUG 1a VT to relate, tell

relativamente ADV relatively

relatividad SF relativity

relativismo SM relativism

relativista ADJ relativistic
SMF relativist

relativizar ▸ CONJUG 1f VT to play down, diminish the importance of

relativo ADJ **1** (= *no absoluto*) relative • **una humedad relativa del 60%** a relative humidity of 60% • **todo es ~** everything is relative • **un problema de una importancia muy relativa** a relatively unimportant problem • **fueron momentos de relativa riqueza** it was a time of relative prosperity • **sus conocimientos son muy ~s** his knowledge is very limited
2 (= *referente*) • **~ a algo** relating to sth • **cuestiones relativas a la economía** matters relating to the economy • **en lo ~ a la educación ...** as regards education ..., with regard to education ...
3 (*Ling*) relative
SM relative

relato SM (= *narración*) story, tale; (= *informe*) account, report

relator(a) SM/F [*de cuentos*] teller, narrator; (*Jur*) court reporter

relatoría SF (*Jur*) post of court reporter

relauchar* ▸ CONJUG 1a VI (*Cono Sur*) to skive off‡

relax [re'las] SM (*Esp*) **1** (= *sosiego*) relaxation, state of relaxation • **hacer ~** to relax • **vamos a hacer un poco de ~** let's take a break
2 • **"relax"** (*euf*) (*anuncio*) "massage"

relé SM relay

releer ▸ CONJUG 2e VT to reread

relegación SF **1** (= *acción*) relegation
2 (*Hist*) (= *destierro*) exile, banishment

relegar ▸ CONJUG 1h VT **1** (= *apartar*) to relegate • **~ algo al olvido** to consign sth to oblivion
2 (*Hist*) (= *desterrar*) to exile, banish

relente SM night dew

releso ADJ (*Cono Sur*) stupid, thick*

relevación SF **1** (= *sustitución*) relief (*tb Mil*)
2 (*Jur*) [*de obligación*] exoneration; [*de contrato*] release

relevante ADJ **1** (= *destacado*) outstanding
2 (= *pertinente*) relevant

relevar ▸ CONJUG 1a VT **1** (*Mil*) [+ *guardia*] to relieve; [+ *colega*] to replace, substitute for • **~ la guardia** to relieve the guard
2 (= *destituir*) • **~ a algn de un cargo** to remove sb from office • **ser relevado de su mando** to be relieved of one's command
3 (= *dispensar*) • **~ a algn de una obligación** to relieve sb of a duty, free sb from an obligation • **~ a algn de hacer algo** to free sb from the obligation to do sth • **~ a algn de la culpa** to exonerate sb, free sb from blame
4 (*Téc*) to emboss

relevista SMF (= *corredor*) relay runner; (= *nadador*) relay swimmer

relevo SM **1** (= *acto*) relief, change; (= *personas*) relief • **tomar el ~** to take over • **~ de la guardia** changing of the guard • **~ de los tiros** change of horses
2 relevos (*Dep*) relay (*sing*), relay race (*sing*) • **100 metros ~s** 100 metre relay ▸ **relevos femeninos** women's relay (*sing*) ▸ **relevos masculinos** men's relay (*sing*)

reliar ▸ CONJUG 1c VT to roll

relicario SM **1** (*Rel*) shrine, reliquary
2 (= *medallón*) locket

relieve SM **1** (*Arte, Téc*) relief • **alto ~** high relief • **bajo ~** bas-relief • **en ~** in relief • **estampar** *o* **grabar en ~** to emboss
2 (*Geog*) • **un país de ~ montañoso** a mountainous country
3 (= *importancia*) importance • **un personaje de ~** an important *o* prominent figure • **dar ~ a algo** to lend importance to sth • **la asistencia del ministro dio ~ a la celebración** the minister's presence lent an added importance to the event • **poner algo de ~** to highlight sth • **el colapso circulatorio puso de ~ la falta de planificación** the traffic chaos highlighted the lack of planning
4 relieves†† (= *restos*) leftovers

religión SF (*Rel*) religion • **entrar en ~** to take vows, enter a religious order

religiosamente ADV religiously

religiosidad SF **1** (= *devoción*) piety, religiousness, religiosity
2 (= *puntualidad*) religiousness

religioso/a ADJ religious
SM/F monk/nun, member of a religious order

relimpio* ADJ absolutely clean

relinchada SF (*Méx*) = **relincho**

relinchar ▸ CONJUG 1a VI to neigh, snort

relincho SM neigh, neighing, snort, snorting

reliquia SF **1** (*Rel*) relic
2 reliquias (= *restos*) relics, remains; (= *vestigios*) traces, vestiges ▸ **reliquia de familia** family heirloom
3 (*Med*) • **reliquias** after effects
4 (*Méx*) (= *exvoto*) offering, votive offering

rellano SM landing

rellena SF (*Col, Méx*) (= *morcilla*) black pudding, blood sausage (*EEUU*)

rellenable ADJ refillable, reusable

rellenado SM (= *llenado*) refill, replenishment; (*Aut*) refuelling, refueling (*EEUU*)

rellenar ▸ CONJUG 1a VT **1** (= *volver a llenar*) to refill, replenish; (*Aer*) to refuel
2 (= *llenar hasta arriba*) to fill up
3 [+ *formulario*] to fill in, fill out; [+ *espacios*] to fill in
4 (*Culin*) to stuff (**de** with)
5 (*Cos*) to pad
VPR **rellenarse** to stuff o.s. (**de** with)

rellenito ADJ plump

relleno ADJ **1** (= *lleno hasta arriba*) full up (**de** of)
2 (*Culin*) stuffed (**de** with)
3 (= *gordito*) [*persona*] plump; [*cara*] full
SM **1** (*Culin*) (*para dulces*) filling; (*para carnes*) stuffing
2 [*de caramelo*] centre, center (*EEUU*) ▸ **relleno blando** soft centre ▸ **relleno duro** hard centre
3 (*en un escrito*) • **frases de ~** padding
4 (*Arquit*) plaster filling
5 (*Cos*) padding
6 (*Mec*) packing
7 (*And*) (= *vertedero*) tip, dump

reloj [re'lo] SM (*grande*) clock; [*de pulsera*] watch • **contra (el) ~** against the clock • **MODISMO**: • **como un ~** like clockwork • **marchar como un ~** to go like clockwork ▸ **reloj automático** timer, timing mechanism ▸ **reloj biológico** biological clock ▸ **reloj de arena** hourglass, sandglass ▸ **reloj de bolsillo** pocket watch ▸ **reloj de caja** grandfather clock ▸ **reloj de carillón** chiming clock ▸ **reloj de cuco** cuckoo clock

▸ **reloj de estacionamiento** parking meter ▸ **reloj de fichar** time clock ▸ **reloj de la muerte** (*Entomología*) deathwatch beetle ▸ **reloj de pie** grandfather clock ▸ **reloj de pulsera** wristwatch ▸ **reloj de sol** sundial ▸ **reloj despertador** alarm clock ▸ **reloj digital** digital watch ▸ **reloj eléctrico** electric clock ▸ **reloj fichador** time clock ▸ **reloj parlante** talking clock ▸ **reloj registrador** time clock

relojear ▸ CONJUG 1a VT (*Cono Sur*)
1 [*+ carrera*] to time
2* (= *vigilar*) to spy on, keep tabs on; (= *controlar*) to check, keep a check on

relojería SF **1** (= *tienda*) watchmaker's, watchmaker's shop
2 (= *arte*) watchmaking, clockmaking • **aparato de ~** clockwork • **bomba de ~** time bomb • **mecanismo de ~** timing device

relojero/a SM/F (= *fabricante*) (*de relojes de pulsera*) watchmaker; (*de relojes de pared*) clockmaker

reluciente ADJ **1** (= *brillante*) shining, brilliant; [*joyas*] glittering, sparkling
2 [*persona*] (= *de buen aspecto*) healthy-looking; (= *gordo*) well-fed

relucir ▸ CONJUG 3f VI (= *brillar*) to shine; [*joyas*] to glitter, sparkle • MODISMO: • **sacar algo a ~** [*+ tema*] to bring sth up, mention sth • **siempre saca a ~ sus éxitos** he's always going on about how successful he is

relujar ▸ CONJUG 1a VT (*CAm, Méx*) to shine

relumbrante ADJ (= *brillante*) brilliant, dazzling; (= *deslumbrante*) glaring

relumbrar ▸ CONJUG 1a VI (= *brillar*) to dazzle; (= *deslumbrar*) to glare

relumbrón SM **1** [*de luz*] flash
2 (= *ostentación*) flashiness, ostentation • **vestirse de ~** to dress ostentatiously • **joyas de ~** flashy jewellery *o* (*EEUU*) jewelry

remachado ADJ (*And*) quiet, reserved

remachador(a) SM/F (= *persona*) riveter
SF (= *máquina*) riveting machine, riveter

remachar ▸ CONJUG 1a VT **1** (*Téc*) [*+ metales*] to rivet; [*+ clavo*] to clinch
2 [*+ aspecto, asunto, punto*] • **quisiera ~ este punto que considero de extrema importancia** I would like to stress this point, which I think is extremely important • **el político remachó ese punto recordándoles qué había pasado** the politician really hammered home the point by reminding them what had happened
3 (= *finalizar*) to finish off
VPR **remacharse** (*And**) to remain stubbornly silent

remache SM **1** (*Téc*) rivet
2 (= *acción*) [*de metal*] riveting; [*de clavo*] clinching
3 (*And*) (= *terquedad*) stubbornness, obstinacy

remada SF stroke

remador(a) SM/F rower

remaduro ADJ (*LAm*) overripe

remake [ri'meik] SM remake

remalladora SF mender, darner

remallar ▸ CONJUG 1a VT to mend, darn

remalo* ADJ (*LAm*) really bad

remandingo SM (*Caribe*) row, uproar

remanente ADJ **1** (= *que queda*) remaining
2 (*Com*) [*de producto*] surplus
3 (*Fís*) remanent
SM (= *lo que queda*) remainder; (*Com*) [*de producto*] surplus

remangar ▸ CONJUG 1h VT = **arremangar**

remango* ADJ lively, energetic, vigorous

remangue* SM liveliness, energy, vigour, vigor (*EEUU*) • **hacer algo con ~** to do sth energetically, tackle sth vigorously

remansarse ▸ CONJUG 1a VPR to form a pool

remanso SM **1** (*en río*) pool
2 (= *lugar*) quiet place • **un ~ de paz** an oasis of peace

remaque SM remake

remar ▸ CONJUG 1a VI **1** (*Náut*) to row • **~ en seco** to go on a rowing machine
2†† (= *pasar penurias*) to toil, struggle

remarcable ADJ (*esp LAm*) remarkable

remarcación SF mark-up

remarcar ▸ CONJUG 1g (*esp LAm*) VT
1 (= *observar*) to notice, observe
2 (= *señalar*) to point out
3 (= *subrayar*) to emphasize, underline
4 [*+ precio*] to mark up

remasterizar ▸ CONJUG 1f VT to remaster

rematadamente ADV terribly, hopelessly • **~ mal** terribly *o* hopelessly bad • **es ~ tonto** he's utterly stupid

rematado ADJ **1** (= *total*) hopeless, complete • **es un loco ~** he's a raving lunatic • **es un tonto ~** he's an utter fool *o* a complete idiot
2 (*Esp*†) [*niño*] very naughty

rematador(a) SM/F **1** (*Dep*) goal scorer
2 (*And, Cono Sur*) auctioneer

rematadora SF auction house, auctioneer's

rematante SMF highest bidder

rematar ▸ CONJUG 1a VT **1** (= *matar*) to finish off
2 (= *terminar*) [*+ discurso, actuación*] to round off, conclude; [*+ trabajo*] to finish off; [*+ bebida, comida*] to finish up, finish off • **remató el concierto cantando su último éxito** she rounded off the concert by singing her latest hit
3 (*Tenis*) to smash; (*Ftbl*) (*con el pie*) to shoot; (*con la cabeza*) to head • **remató el centro (de cabeza)** he met the cross (with a header) • **remató la jugada** he finished off the move
4 (*Cos*) to cast off
5 (*Arquit*) to top, crown
6 (*LAm*) (*Com*) (= *subastar*) to auction; (= *liquidar*) to sell off cheap
7 (*Cono Sur*) [*+ caballo*] to pull up
VI **1** (= *terminar*) to end, finish off • **remató con un par de chistes** he ended *o* finished off with a couple of jokes
2 • **~ en** to end in • **es del tipo que remata en punta** it's the sort which ends in a point • **fue una broma que remató en tragedia** it was a prank which ended in tragedy
3 (*Tenis*) to smash; (*Ftbl*) (*con el pie*) to shoot; (*con la cabeza*) to head • **~ de cabeza** to head the ball towards goal

remate SM **1** (= *cabo*) end; (= *punta*) tip, point; [*de edificio, mueble*] ornamental top
2 (= *toque final*) • **como ~ al concierto hizo un bis** to round off the concert he played an encore • **poner ~ a algo** to cap sth • **de ~***: • **está loco de ~** he's stark raving mad* • **para ~*** to crown it all, to top it all • **para ~ va y me insulta** to crown *o* top it all he went and insulted me
3 (*Ftbl*) (*con el pie*) shot; (*con la cabeza*) header • **un ~ de cabeza** a header • **un equipo sin ~** a team with no finishing power
4 (*LAm*) (*Com*) (= *liquidación*) bargain sale; (= *subasta*) auction
5 (*Bridge*) bidding

rematista SMF (*And, Caribe*) auctioneer

rembolsar *etc* ▸ CONJUG 1a VT = **reembolsar**

remecer ▸ CONJUG 2d VT (*LAm*) (*de lado a lado*) to shake; (= *agitar*) to wave
VPR **remecerse** to rock, swing, swing to and fro

remedar ▸ CONJUG 1a VT (= *imitar*) to imitate, copy; (*para burlarse*) to ape, mimic

remediable ADJ that can be remedied *o* put right • **fácilmente ~** easily remedied *o* put right

remediar ▸ CONJUG 1b VT **1** (= *solucionar*) to remedy • **no podemos ~ este problema** we cannot remedy this problem • **si el gobierno no lo remedia se perderán muchos puestos de trabajo** if the government does not remedy the situation a lot of jobs will be lost • **llorando no remedias nada** you're not going to solve anything by crying, crying won't solve anything
2 (= *evitar*) • **no pudo ~ echarse a reír** she couldn't prevent herself from laughing • **es un mujeriego pero le quiero, no puedo ~lo** he's a womanizer but I love him, I can't help it
3 [*+ necesidades*] to meet, help with

remedio SM **1** (= *alternativa*) choice, alternative • **no tengo más ~ que ir** I've got no alternative *o* choice but to go • **—¿tienes que trabajar este sábado? —¡qué ~!** "are you working this Saturday?" — "I've got no choice!" • **¿qué ~ me queda?** what else can I do?, what choice have I got? • **no hay más ~ que operarle** there is nothing for it but to operate on him • **¡si no hay más ~, iré!** well, if I have to, I'll go!
2 (= *solución*) • **Juan no tiene ~** Juan's a hopeless case, Juan's beyond redemption • **como último ~** as a last resort • **sin ~**: **tenemos que hacerlo hoy sin ~** we have to do it today without fail • **es un tonto sin ~** he's hopelessly stupid, he's so stupid he's beyond redemption • **poner ~ a algo** to remedy sth, correct sth
3 (*Med*) cure, remedy • **un buen ~ contra** *o* **para el resfriado** a good cure *o* remedy for colds • **un ~ contra** *o* **para la tos** a cough remedy • MODISMOS: • **es peor el ~ que la enfermedad** the solution is worse than the problem • **¡ni por un ~!** not on your life! • **ni para un ~**: • **no se le podía encontrar ni para un ~** it couldn't be had for love nor money • **no ha dejado leche ni para un ~** she hasn't left a single drop of milk ▸ **remedio casero** home remedy ▸ **remedio heroico** drastic action
4 (*frm*) (= *alivio*) relief, help • **es un ~ en su aflicción** it's a relief in her distress
5 (*Jur*) remedy, recourse

remedo SM (= *imitación*) imitation, copy; (*pey*) parody

rememorar ▸ CONJUG 1a VT to recall

remendar ▸ CONJUG 1j VT **1** [*+ ropa*] to darn, mend; (*con parche*) to patch
2 (*fig*) (= *corregir*) to correct

remendón/ona ADJ • **zapatero ~** cobbler
SM/F cobbler

remera SF (*Arg*) (= *camiseta*) T-shirt

remero/a SM/F oarsman/oarswoman, rower
SM (= *máquina*) rowing machine

remesa SF [*de dinero*] remittance; [*de bienes*] shipment ▸ **remesa de fondos** (*Méx*) (*Com*) settlement, financial settlement

remesar ▸ CONJUG 1a VT [*+ dinero*] to remit, send; [*+ bienes*] to send, ship

remeter ▸ CONJUG 2a VPR (= *volver a meter*) to put back; [*+ camisa*] to tuck in

remezcla SF remix

remezón SM (*LAm*) earth tremor, slight earthquake

remiendo SM **1** [*de ropa*] mending; (*con parche*) patching
2 (= *arreglo*) mend, darn; (= *parche*) patch • **a ~s** piecemeal • **echar un ~ a algo** (= *coser*) to darn sth; (= *poner un parche*) to patch sth, put a patch on sth
3 (= *corrección*) correction
4 (*Med*) improvement
5 (*Zool*) spot, patch

r

remilgado ADJ **1** (= *melindroso*) finicky, fussy, particular
2 (= *mojigato*) prudish, prim
3 (= *afectado*) affected
remilgo SM **1** (= *melindre*) fussiness • **él no hace ~s a ninguna clase de trabajo** he won't turn up his nose at any kind of work
2 (= *mojigatería*) prudery, primness
3 (= *afectación*) affectation
remilgoso ADJ (*LAm*) = **remilgado**
reminiscencia SF reminiscence
remirado ADJ **1** (= *prudente*) cautious, circumspect, careful; (*pey*) overcautious
2 (*pey*) (= *gazmoño*) prudish; (= *afectado*) affected, over-nice; (= *melindroso*) fussy, pernickety*, persnickety (EEUU*)
remirar ▹ CONJUG 1a VT to look at again • **lo miraba y lo remiraba y aún no se lo creía** she stared and stared at it, but she still couldn't believe it
VPR **remirarse** to be extra careful (**en** about), take great pains (**en** over)
remise SM • **auto de ~** (*Arg*) hire car
remisión SF **1** (= *envío*) sending; (*esp LAm*) (*Com*) shipment, consignment
2 (*al lector*) reference (**a** to)
3 (= *aplazamiento*) postponement
4 (= *disminución*) (*tb Med*) remission
5 (*Rel*) forgiveness, remission
remiso ADJ **1** [*persona*] • **estar** *o* **mostrarse ~ a hacer algo** to be reluctant to do sth, be unwilling to do sth
2 [*movimiento*] slow, sluggish
remisor(a) SM/F (*LAm*) sender
remite SM sender
remitente SMF sender
remitido SM **1** (*en periódico*) paid insert
2 (*Méx*) (= *consignación*) shipment, consignment
remitir ▹ CONJUG 3a VT **1** (= *enviar*) to send; [+ *dinero*] to remit, send; (*Com*) to ship, send
2 [+ *lector*] to refer (**a** to)
3 (= *aplazar*) to postpone
4 • **~ una decisión a algn** to refer a decision to sb
5 (*Rel*) to forgive, pardon
VI (= *disminuir*) to slacken, let up
VPR **remitirse** • **a las pruebas me remito** the proof of the pudding is in the eating
remix SM remix
remo SM **1** (*Náut*) oar • **cruzar un río a ~** to row across a river • **pasaron los cañones a ~** they rowed the guns across • MODISMO: • **a ~ y vela** speedily
2 (*Dep*) rowing • **practicar el ~** to row
3 (*Anat**) limb; [*de pájaro*] wing
4†† (= *penuria*) toils (*pl*) • **andar al ~** to be hard at it
remoción SF (*esp LAm*) (= *acción de remover*) removal; (= *cese*) dismissal
remodelación SF **1** (*Arquit*) remodelling, remodeling (EEUU)
2 (*Aut*) restyling
3 [*de organización*] restructuring; (*Pol*) reshuffle ▸ **remodelación de gobierno** government reshuffle ▸ **remodelación ministerial** cabinet reshuffle
remodelar ▹ CONJUG 1a VT (*Arquit*) to remodel; (*Aut*) to restyle; (*Pol*) to reshuffle; [+ *organización*] to restructure
remojar ▹ CONJUG 1a VT **1** [+ *legumbres*, *prenda*] to soak, steep (**en** in); [+ *galleta*] to dip (**en** in, into)
2* (= *celebrar bebiendo*) • **¡este triunfo habrá que ~lo!** this victory calls for a drink!
3 (*Méx**) (= *sobornar*) to bribe
VPR **remojarse** (*en playa, piscina*) to have a dip • **ir a ~se** to go for a dip
remojo SM **1** • **poner algo a** *o* **en ~** to leave sth to soak
2 (*LAm*) (= *regalo*) gift, present; (= *propina*) tip
remojón SM **1** (*en piscina, playa*) • **darse un ~*** to go in for a dip
2 (*Culin*) piece of bread soaked in milk *etc*
remolacha SF beetroot, beet (EEUU) ▸ **remolacha azucarera** sugar beet ▸ **remolacha de mesa, remolacha roja** beetroot, beet (EEUU)
remolachero/a ADJ beet (*antes de s*)
SM/F beet farmer
remolcable ADJ that can be towed, towable
remolcador SM **1** (*Náut*) tug
2 (*Aut*) breakdown lorry, tow truck (EEUU)
remolcar ▹ CONJUG 1g VT **1** (*Náut*) to tug
2 (*Aut*) to tow
remoledor* ADJ (*And, Cono Sur*) roistering, party-going
remoler ▹ CONJUG 2h VT **1** (= *moler*) to grind up small
2 (*LAm**) (= *fastidiar*) to annoy, bug*
VI (*Cono Sur, And**) to live it up*
remolienda* SF (*And, Cono Sur*) party, wild time*
remolinar ▹ CONJUG 1a VI, **remolinear** ▹ CONJUG 1a VI = **arremolinarse**
remolino SM **1** [*de agua*] (*pequeño*) swirl, eddy; (*grande*) whirlpool
2 [*de aire*] (*pequeño*) eddy; (= *grande*) whirlwind; [*de humo, polvo*] whirl, cloud
3 [*de pelo*] cowlick
4 [*de gente*] crowd, throng
5 (= *conmoción*) commotion
remolón/ona* ADJ (= *vago*) lazy
SM/F **1** (= *vago*) slacker, shirker
2 (= *ignorante*) • **hacerse el ~: le tocaba pagar pero se hizo el ~** it was his turn to pay, but he made as if it wasn't
remolonear ▹ CONJUG 1a VI (= *vaguear*) to slack, shirk
VPR **remolonearse** • **cuando llegó la hora de pagar empezó a ~se** when it came to paying, he started making as if it had nothing to do with him
remolque SM **1** (= *vehículo*) trailer; (= *caravana*) trailer, semitrailer (EEUU), caravan; (*Náut*) ship on tow
2 (= *acción*) towing • **a ~** on tow • **ir a ~** to be on tow • **llevar un coche a ~** to tow a car • **dar ~ a un coche** to tow a car • **ir a ~ de algn** to go along with sb (*in what they say or do*)
3 (= *cuerda*) towrope
remonda†* SF • **¡es la ~!** this is the end!
remonta SF **1** (*Cos*) mending, repair
2 (*Mil*) remount, supply of cavalry horses
remontada SF recovery
remontar ▹ CONJUG 1a VT **1** [+ *río*] to go up; [+ *obstáculo*] to negotiate, get over; ▹ **vuelo²**
2 [+ *zapato*] to mend, repair; [+ *media*] to mend, mend a ladder in
3 (*Mil*) [+ *caballo*] to remount
4 [+ *reloj*] to wind
5 (*Caza*) [+ *animales*] to frighten away
VPR **remontarse 1** [*avión, pájaro*] to rise, soar; [*edificio*] to soar, tower • **~se en alas de la imaginación** (*liter*) to take flight on the wings of fantasy
2 (*Econ*) • **~se a** to amount to
3 (*en tiempo*) • **~se a** to go back to • **este texto se remonta al siglo XI** this text dates from *o* dates back to the 11th century • **sus recuerdos se remontan a la Guerra Civil** her memories go back to the Civil War
• **tenemos que ~nos a los mismos orígenes** we must go back to the roots of this
remonte SM ski lift
remoquete SM **1** (= *apodo*) nickname
• **poner ~ a algn** to give sb a nickname
2 (= *puñetazo*) punch
3 (= *comentario*) cutting remark, dig*
4* (= *coqueteo*) flirting, spooning*; (= *pretendiente*) suitor
rémora SF **1** (*Zool*) remora
2 (= *obstáculo*) hindrance
remorder ▹ CONJUG 2h VI (= *reconcomer*) • **me remuerde el haberle tratado así** I have a guilty conscience about treating him like that • **no me remuerde la conciencia** I don't have any qualms about it
VPR **remorderse** to feel/show remorse
remordimiento SM (*tb* **remordimientos**) remorse, regret • **tener ~s** to feel remorse, suffer pangs of conscience
remotamente ADV **1** [*parecerse, recordar*] vaguely
2 [*pensar*] vaguely, tentatively
remotidad* SF (*CAm*) remote spot, distant place
remoto ADJ **1** (*en el tiempo*) far-off, distant • **en épocas remotas** in far-off *o* distant times
2 (*en el espacio*) faraway, distant • **en un país ~** in a faraway *o* distant country
3 (= *poco probable*) remote • **existe la remota posibilidad de que venga** there is a remote possibility *o* a very slight chance he may come • **no tengo ni la más remota idea** I haven't the faintest *o* remotest idea • **no se me ocurriría insultarle ni por lo más ~** it would never enter my head to insult him • —**¿te enfrentarías a él?** —**¡ni por lo más ~!** "would you stand up to him?" — "no way *o* not on your life!"
remover ▹ CONJUG 2h VT **1** [+ *tierra*] to turn over, dig up; [+ *objetos*] to move round; [+ *fuego, brasas*] to poke, stir; [+ *sopa*] to stir; [+ *ensalada*] to toss; [+ *cóctel*] to shake • **~ el pasado** to stir up the past • **~ un asunto** to go into a matter • **~ un proyecto** to revive a scheme • MODISMOS: • **~ cielo y tierra** • **~ Roma con Santiago** to move heaven and earth
2 (= *quitar*) to remove; (*Med*) to remove
3 (*esp LAm*) (= *cesar*) to dismiss
removimiento SM removal
remozado SM [*de persona*] rejuvenation; [*de edificio, fachada*] renovation
remozamiento SM [*de persona*] rejuvenation; [*de edificio, fachada*] renovation
remozar ▹ CONJUG 1f VT [+ *persona*] to rejuvenate; [+ *aspecto*] to brighten up; [+ *organización*] to give a new look to, give a face-lift to; [+ *edificio, fachada*] to renovate
VPR **remozarse** to be rejuvenated • **la encuentro muy remozada** she looks so much younger
remplazar ▹ CONJUG 1f VT = **reemplazar**
rempujar* ▹ CONJUG 1a VT to shove, push
rempujón* SM shove, push
remuda SF (= *cambio*) change, alteration; (= *reemplazo*) replacement; (*tb* **remuda (de ropa)**) change of clothes, spare clothes (*pl*) ▸ **remuda de caballos** change of horses
remudar ▹ CONJUG 1a VT (= *cambiar*) to change, alter; (= *reemplazar*) to replace
remunerable ADJ remunerable
remuneración SF remuneration
remunerado ADJ • **trabajo mal ~** badly-paid job
remunerador ADJ **1** (= *retribuido*) remunerative • **poco ~** unremunerative
2 (= *gratificante*) rewarding, worthwhile
remunerar ▹ CONJUG 1a VT (= *retribuir*) to remunerate; (= *premiar*) to reward
remunerativo ADJ remunerative
renacentista ADJ Renaissance (*antes de s*)
renacer ▹ CONJUG 2d VI **1** (= *volver a nacer*) to be reborn; (*Bot*) to reappear, come up again
2 (= *reavivar*) to revive • **hacer ~** to revive • **hoy me siento ~** today I feel like a new person *o*

as if I've come to life again • **sentían ~ la esperanza** they felt new hope
renaciente ADJ renascent
renacimiento SM rebirth, revival • **el Renacimiento** the Renaissance
renacionalizar ▹ CONJUG 1f VT to renationalize
renacuajo SM **1** (*Zool*) tadpole
2* (= *niño*) shrimp
3 (*pey*) (= *pequeñajo*) runt, little squirt*
renal ADJ renal, kidney (*antes de s*)
Renania SF Rhineland
renano ADJ Rhenish, Rhine (*antes de s*)
rencilla SF **1** (= *disputa*) quarrel • **~s** arguments, bickering (*sing*)
2 (= *rencor*) bad blood • **me tiene ~** he's got it in for me*, he bears me a grudge
rencilloso ADJ quarrelsome
renco ADJ lame
rencor SM (= *amargura*) rancour, rancor (*EEUU*), bitterness; (= *resentimiento*) ill feeling, resentment; (= *malicia*) spitefulness • **guardar ~** to bear malice, harbour *o* (*EEUU*) harbor a grudge (**a** against) • **no le guardo ~** I bear him no malice
rencorosamente ADV **1** (= *con resentimiento*) resentfully; (= *con amargura*) bitterly
2 (= *con malicia*) spitefully, maliciously
rencoroso ADJ **1** [*ser*] spiteful, nasty
2 [*estar*] (= *resentido*) resentful; (= *amargado*) bitter
rendición SF **1** (*Mil*) surrender ▸ **rendición incondicional** unconditional surrender
2 (*Econ*) yield, profit, profits (*pl*)
3 (*Cono Sur*) (*Com, Econ*) trading balance; (*tb* **rendición de cuentas**) balance
rendidamente ADV (= *sumisamente*) submissively; (= *servilmente*) obsequiously; (= *con devoción*) devotedly
rendido ADJ **1** (= *cansado*) exhausted, worn-out
2 (= *sumiso*) submissive; (= *servil*) obsequious; (= *enamorado*) devoted
rendidor ADJ (*LAm*) highly productive, highly profitable
rendija SF **1** (= *hendedura*) crack, cleft; (= *abertura*) aperture
2 (*en la ley*) loophole
rendimiento SM **1** [*de una máquina*] output; (= *capacidad*) capacity; (= *producción*) output • **aumentar el ~ de una máquina** to increase the output of a machine • **el ~ del motor** the performance of the engine • **funcionar a pleno ~** to work all-out, work at full throttle
2 [*de persona*] performance, achievement • **tiene muy bajo ~ escolar** he's not doing very well *o* achieving much academically • **Centro de Alto Rendimiento** *specialized sports training centre* ▸ **rendimiento académico** academic achievement ▸ **rendimiento laboral** performance at work
3 (*Econ*) yield, profit, profits (*pl*) • **ley del ~ decreciente** law of diminishing returns ▸ **rendimiento del capital** return on capital
4 (= *sumisión*) submissiveness; (= *servilismo*) obsequiousness; (= *devoción*) devotion • **su ~ total a la voluntad de ella** his complete submission to her will
5 (= *agotamiento*) exhaustion
6 (= *parte útil*) usable part, proportion of usable material
rendir ▹ CONJUG 3k VT **1** (= *producir*) to produce; [+ *beneficios etc*] to yield; [+ *producto, total etc*] to produce; [+ *interés*] to bear
2 (= *cansar*) to exhaust, tire out • **le rindió el sueño** he was overcome by sleep
3 • **~ homenaje a** to pay tribute to • **~ culto a** to worship • **~ las gracias** (*frm*) to give thanks
4 (*Mil*) [+ *ciudad*] to surrender; [+ *fortaleza*] to take, capture • **~ la guardia** to hand over the guard
5 (*Mil*) [+ *bandera*] to dip; [+ *armas*] to lower, reverse
6 (*Esp*) (= *vomitar*) to vomit, bring up
7 (*Com*) [+ *factura*] to send
8 • **~ examen** (*Cono Sur*) to sit *o* take an exam
9 (*frm*) (= *vencer*) [+ *país*] to conquer, subdue
10 (*frm*) (= *dominar*) to dominate • **logró ~ el albedrío de la joven** he came to dominate the young woman's will completely • **había que ~ su entereza** he had to overcome his moral objections
11 (*frm*) (= *devolver*) to give back, return; (= *entregar*) to hand over
VI **1** (= *producir*) to yield, produce; (= *dar resultados*) to give good results • **el negocio no rinde** the business is not profitable *o* doesn't pay • **la finca rinde para mantener a ocho familias** the estate produces enough to keep eight families • **este año ha rendido poco** it has done poorly this year • **trabajo, pero no rindo** I work hard but without much to show for it
2 [*arroz*] to swell up
3 (*LAm*) (= *durar*) to last longer, keep going
VPR **rendirse 1** (= *ceder*) to yield (**a** to); (*Mil*) to surrender; (= *entregarse*) to give o.s. up • **~se a la razón** to yield to reason • **~se a la evidencia** to bow before the evidence • **~se a la fuerza** to yield to violence • **¡me rindo!** I give in!
2 (= *cansarse*) to wear o.s. out
renditivo ADJ (*Cono Sur*) productive
renegado/a ADJ **1** (= *traidor*) renegade; (*Rel*) apostate (*antes de s*); (*Pol*) rebel (*antes de s*)
2* (= *brusco*) gruff*; (= *malhumorado*) cantankerous, bad-tempered
SM/F (= *traidor*) renegade; (*Rel*) apostate; (*Pol*) rebel
renegar ▹ CONJUG 1h, 1j VI **1** • **~ de: renegó de su fe** he renounced his faith • **ha renegado de su familia** she has disowned her own family
2 (= *maldecir*) to curse, swear; (= *blasfemar*) to blaspheme
3 (= *refunfuñar*) to complain (**de** about) • **se pasa el día renegando de todo** she spends her time complaining about everything
4 (*And, Méx*) (= *enojarse*) to get angry, get upset
5 (*And, Méx*) (= *gritar*) to shout, rage
VT • **negar y ~ algo** to deny sth vigorously • **niega y reniega haber provocado el incendio** he vigorously denies having started the fire
renegociación SF renegotiation
renegociar ▹ CONJUG 1b VT to renegotiate
renegón* ADJ grumbling, cantankerous, grouchy*
renegrido ADJ very black, very dark
RENFE SF ABR, **Renfe** SF ABR (*Ferro*) = **Red Nacional de los Ferrocarriles Españoles**
renglón SM **1** (= *línea*) line, line of writing • **escribir unos renglones** to write a few lines *o* words • **estos pobres renglones** (*liter*) these humble jottings • MODISMOS: • **a ~ seguido** immediately after • **leer entre renglones** to read between the lines
2 (*Com*) item of expenditure
3 (*LAm*) (*Com*) (= *género*) line of goods; (= *departamento*) department, area
rengo ADJ (*LAm*) lame, crippled
rengue‡ SM train
renguear ▹ CONJUG 1a VI **1** (*LAm*) (= *cojear*) to limp, hobble
2 (*Cono Sur*) (= *perseguir*) to pursue a woman
renguera SF (*LAm*) limp, limping
reniego SM **1** (= *juramento*) curse, oath; (*Rel*) blasphemy
2 (= *queja*) grumble, complaint
reno SM reindeer
renombrado ADJ renowned, famous
renombrar ▹ CONJUG 1a VT to rename
renombre SM (= *fama*) renown, fame • **de ~** renowned, famous
renovable ADJ renewable
renovación SF **1** [*de contrato, pasaporte, suscripción*] renewal
2 [*de edificio*] renovation • **han invertido 100 millones en la ~ del museo** they have invested 100 million in the renovation of the museum • **subvenciones para la ~ de los sistemas informáticos** subsidies for updating *o* upgrading computer systems
3 [*de partido, asamblea*] clearout • **el comité necesita una completa ~** the committee needs a complete clearout
4 (= *reanudación*) renewal • **la ~ de las hostilidades acabó con las esperanzas de paz** the renewal of hostilities scuppered hopes of peace
5 (*Rel*) ▸ **renovación espiritual** spiritual renewal
renovado ADJ renewed, redoubled • **con renovada energía** with renewed energy
renovador(a) (*Pol*) ADJ reformist
SM/F restorer • **~ de muebles** furniture restorer
renoval SM (*Cono Sur, Méx*) area of young trees
renovar ▹ CONJUG 1l VT **1** [+ *contrato, pasaporte, suscripción*] to renew
2 [+ *edificio*] to renovate; [+ *sistema informático*] to update, upgrade
3 [+ *muebles*] to change • **han renovado el mobiliario de la casa** they've changed the furniture in the house
4 [+ *partido, asamblea*] to clear out
5 (= *reanudar*) [+ *ataques*] to renew; [+ *conversaciones*] to resume
VPR **renovarse 1** (= *reanudarse*) • **se han renovado los ataques** there have been renewed attacks, the attacks have resumed
2 [*persona*] • **~se o morir** adapt or perish
renqueante ADV **1** (= *con cojera*) limping
2 (= *irregular*) shaky
renquear ▹ CONJUG 1a VI **1** (= *cojear*) to limp, hobble
2* (= *ir tirando*) to get by, just about manage
3 [*motor*] to splutter
4 (= *vacilar*) to dither
renqueo SM limp
renta SF **1** (= *ingresos*) income; (= *ganancia*) interest, return • **tiene ~s particulares** she has a private income • **vivir de (las) ~s** to live on one's private income • **política de ~s** incomes *o* (*EEUU*) income policy • **título de ~ fija** fixed-interest bond • **valores de ~ fija** fixed-yield securities ▸ **renta bruta nacional** gross national income ▸ **renta del trabajo** earned income ▸ **renta devengada** earned income ▸ **renta disponible** disposable income ▸ **renta gravable** taxable income ▸ **renta imponible** taxable income ▸ **renta nacional** national income ▸ **renta no salarial** unearned income ▸ **renta sobre el terreno** ground rent ▸ **rentas públicas** revenue (*sing*) ▸ **renta vitalicia** annuity
2 (= *deuda*) public debt, national debt
3 (*esp LAm*) (= *alquiler*) rent • **"casa de renta"** "house to let"
rentabilidad SF profitability
rentabilizar ▹ CONJUG 1f VT (= *hacer rentable*) to make profitable, make more profitable; (= *sacar provecho de*) to exploit to the full; (*pey*) to cash in on
rentable ADJ profitable • **no ~** unprofitable • **la línea ya no es ~** the line is no longer economic (to run)

r

rentado ADJ (*Cono Sur*) paid

rentar ▹ CONJUG 1a VT **1** (= *producir*) to produce, yield
2 (*LAm*) [+ *casa*] to let, rent out • **"rento casa"** "house to let"
VPR **rentarse** • **"se renta"** (*Méx*) "to let"

rentero/a SM/F tenant farmer

rentista SMF **1** (= *accionista*) stockholder; (*que vive de sus rentas*) rentier
2 (= *especialista*) financial expert

rentístico ADJ financial

renuencia SF **1** [*de persona*] reluctance, unwillingness
2 [*de materia*] awkwardness

renuente ADJ **1** [*persona*] reluctant, unwilling
2 [*materia*] awkward, difficult

renuevo SM **1** (= *acto*) renewal
2 (*Bot*) shoot, sprout

renuncia SF **1** (*a derecho, trono*) renunciation • **la paz depende de una ~ total a la violencia** peace is dependent on a total renunciation of violence • **está considerando una posible ~ a sus derechos al trono** he is thinking of renouncing his rights to the throne • **han hecho pública la ~ a sus exigencias/planes** they announced that they have abandoned *o* dropped their claims/plans • **confirmó su ~ a participar en el proyecto** he confirmed his refusal to take part in the project
2 [*de empleado*] resignation • **presentó su ~** he tendered his resignation, he resigned
3 (= *abnegación*) renunciation • **una vida de ~ y sacrificio** a life of renunciation and sacrifice

renunciar ▹ CONJUG 1b VI **1** • **~ a** [+ *derecho, trono*] to renounce; [+ *exigencia, plan*] to abandon, drop • **han renunciado a la violencia** they have renounced violence • **ha renunciado a su puesto de jefe de prensa** he has resigned his post as press officer • **tras su enfermedad renunció al tabaco** after his illness he gave up smoking • **¿renuncias a Satanás?** do you renounce Satan?
2 (= *dimitir*) to resign • **el ministro no ~á** the minister will not resign
3 (*Naipes*) to revoke

renuncio SM **1** (*Naipes*) revoke
2 (= *mentira*) • **coger a algn en un ~** to catch sb in a fib, catch sb out

reñidamente ADV bitterly, hard, stubbornly

reñidero SM ▸ **reñidero de gallos** cockpit

reñido ADJ **1** [*batalla, concurso*] hard-fought, close • **un partido ~** a hard-fought *o* close game • **en lo más ~ de la batalla** in the thick of the fight
2 (= *enfadado*) • **estar ~ con algn** to have fallen out with sb, be on bad terms with sb • **está ~ con su familia** he has fallen out with his family, he is on bad terms with his family
3 (= *en contradicción*) • **estar ~ con algo: está ~ con el principio de igualdad** it goes against *o* is contrary to the principle of equality

reñidor ADJ quarrelsome

reñir ▹ CONJUG 3h, 3k VT **1** (= *regañar*) to scold; (= *reprender*) to tell off*, reprimand (**por** for)
2 [+ *batalla*] to fight, wage
VI (= *pelear*) to quarrel, fall out (**con** with) • **ha reñido con su novio** she's fallen out *o* had a fight with her boyfriend • **se pasan la vida riñendo** they spend their whole time quarrelling • **riñeron por cuestión de dinero** they quarrelled about money, they quarrelled over money

reo[1] SMF **1** (= *delincuente*) culprit, offender; (*Jur*) accused, defendant ▸ **reo de Estado** person accused of a crime against the state ▸ **reo de muerte** person under sentence of death
2 (*Cono Sur*) (= *vagabundo*) tramp, bum (*EEUU**)

reo[2] SM (= *pez*) sea trout

reoca* SF • **es la ~** (*Esp*) (= *bueno*) it's the tops*; (= *malo*) it's the pits*

reojo • **de ~** ADV • **mirar a algn de ~** (= *disimuladamente*) to look at sb out of the corner of one's eye; (= *con recelo*) to look askance at sb

reorganización SF reorganization

reorganizar ▹ CONJUG 1f VT to reorganize
VPR **reorganizarse** to reorganize

reorientación SF [*de negocio, economía*] reorientation; [*de recursos*] redeployment

reorientar ▹ CONJUG 1a VT [+ *economía*] to reorientate; [+ *dirección, costumbre*] to change; [+ *recursos*] to redeploy

reóstato SM rheostat

Rep. ABR (= **República**) Rep

repanchigarse* ▹ CONJUG 1h VPR,

repantigarse* ▹ CONJUG 1h VPR to lounge, sprawl, loll (back) • **estar repanchigado en un sillón** to be sprawled *o* lolling (back) in a chair

repanocha* SF • **¡eres la ~!** you're unbelievable! • **¡aquello fue la ~!** it was unbelievable!

reparable ADJ repairable

reparación SF **1** (= *acción*) repairing, mending
2 (*Téc*) repair • **efectuar reparaciones en** to carry out repairs to *o* on • **"reparaciones en el acto"** "repairs while you wait"
3 (= *desagravio*) reparation
4 (*Jur*) redress

reparador(a) ADJ **1** [*sueño*] refreshing; [*comida*] fortifying, restorative
2 (*frm*) [*persona*] critical, faultfinding
SM/F (= *criticón*) critic, faultfinder
SM (*Téc*) repairer

reparadora SF ▸ **reparadora de calzados** (*Méx*) shoe repairer's

reparar ▹ CONJUG 1a VT **1** (= *arreglar*) to repair, mend, fix
2 [+ *energías*] to restore; [+ *fortunas*] to retrieve
3 [+ *ofensa*] to make amends for; [+ *suerte*] to retrieve; [+ *daño, pérdida*] to make good; [+ *consecuencia*] to undo
4 [+ *golpe*] to parry
5 (= *observar*) to observe, notice
6 (*Cono Sur*) (= *imitar*) to mimic, imitate
VI **1** • **~ en** (= *darse cuenta de*) to observe, notice • **no reparó en la diferencia** he didn't notice the difference • **sin ~ en que ya no funcionaba** without noticing it didn't work any more
2 • **~ en** (= *poner atención en*) to pay attention to, take heed of; (= *considerar*) to consider • **no ~ en las dificultades** not to consider the problems • **repara en lo que vas a hacer** consider what you are going to do, reflect on what you are going to do • **sin ~ en los gastos** regardless of the cost • **no ~ en nada** to stop at nothing
3 (*LAm*) [*caballo*] to rear, buck
VPR **repararse 1** (= *controlarse*) to restrain o.s.
2 (*CAm, Méx*) [*caballo*] to rear, buck

reparista ADJ (*And, CAm, Caribe*), **reparisto** ADJ (*CAm*) (= **reparón**)

reparo SM **1** (= *escrúpulo*) scruple, qualm • **no tuvo ~ en hacerlo** he had no qualms about doing it, he did not hesitate to do it
2 (= *objeción*) objection; (= *crítica*) criticism; (= *duda*) doubt • **poner ~s** (= *oponerse*) to raise objections (**a** to); (= *criticar*) to criticize, express one's doubts
3 (*frm*) (= *reparación*) repair; (*Arquit*) restoration
4 (*Esgrima*) parry
5 (= *protección*) defence, defense (*EEUU*), protection
6 (*Med*) remedy
7 (*CAm, Méx*) [*de caballo*] bucking, rearing • **tirar un ~** to rear, buck

reparón/ona ADJ critical, faultfinding
SM/F critic, faultfinder

repartición SF **1** (= *distribución*) distribution; (= *división*) sharing out, division
2 (*Cono Sur*) (*Admin*) government department
3 (*LAm*) (*Pol*) [*de tierras*] redistribution

repartida SF (*LAm*) = **repartición**

repartidor(a) SM/F (= *distribuidor*) distributor; (*Com*) deliveryman/deliverywoman ▸ **repartidor(a) de leche** milkman/milkwoman ▸ **repartidor(a) de periódicos** paperboy/papergirl ▸ **repartidor(a) de pizzas** pizza delivery boy/girl

repartija SF (*LAm*) (*pey*) share-out, carve-up*

repartimiento SM (= *distribución*) distribution; (= *división*) division

repartir ▹ CONJUG 3a VT **1** (= *dividir entre varios*) to divide (up), share (out) • **tendremos que ~ el pastel** we'll have to share (out) *o* divide (up) the cake • **~ dividendos** to share the profits • **los estudiantes están repartidos en cuatro grupos** the students are divided into four groups • **el premio está muy repartido** the prize is shared among many
2 (= *distribuir, dar*) [+ *correo, periódicos*] to deliver; [+ *folletos, premios*] to give out, hand out; [+ *naipes*] to deal • **repartieron golpes a todo el que se les acercaba** they lashed out at anyone who came near them
3 (= *esparcir*) • **hay guarniciones repartidas por todo el país** there are garrisons dotted about *o* spread about *o* distributed all over the country
VPR **repartirse 1** (= *dividirse entre varios*) • **se repartieron el botín** they divided (up) *o* shared (out) the spoils among themselves
2 (= *distribuir*) • **"se reparte a domicilio"** "home delivery (service)"

reparto SM **1** (= *partición*) sharing out • **el ~ de la herencia originó conflictos** the sharing out of the inheritance gave rise to disputes • **no existe un equilibrado ~ de la riqueza** there is not an even distribution of wealth, wealth is not evenly distributed ▸ **reparto de beneficios** profit sharing ▸ **reparto de dividendos** distribution of dividends
2 (= *entrega*) [*de correo, periódicos*] delivery • **"reparto a domicilio"** "home delivery (service)" • **vamos a efectuar el ~ de premios** we are going to give out the prizes
3 (*Cine, Teat*) cast • **un ~ estelar** a star cast
4 (*LAm*) (= *solar*) building site; (= *barrio*) suburb

repasador SM (*Cono Sur*) dishcloth

repasar ▹ CONJUG 1a VT **1** [+ *cuenta*] to check; [+ *texto, lección*] to revise; [+ *apuntes*] to go over (again); [+ *publicación etc*] to put the finishing touches to, polish up
2 (*Mec*) (= *arreglar*) to check, overhaul
3 • **~ la plancha por una prenda** to iron a garment again, give a garment another iron
4 (*Cos*) (= *coser*) to sew, sew up
5 (*Cono Sur*) [+ *platos*] to wipe; [+ *mueble*] to dust, polish; [+ *ropa*] to brush, brush down
6 [+ *lugar*] to pass again, pass by again • **pasar y ~ una calle** to go up and down a street

repaso SM **1** (= *revisión*) revision • **ejercicios de ~** revision exercises • **dale un ~ a esta**

lección revise this lesson • **los técnicos daban el último ~ a la nave** the technicians were giving the ship a final check • **le di un último ~ a la carta antes de enviarla** I read through the letter again quickly before sending it • **un ~ de los temas tratados más importantes** a quick run-through *o* review of the main points I've dealt with
• MODISMO: • **dar** *o* **pegar un buen ~ a algn*** (= *regañar*) to give sb a proper ticking-off*; (= *ganar*) to thrash sb
2 (*Cos*) (= *arreglo*) • **tengo que darles un ~ a estos pantalones** I have to mend these trousers • **ropa de ~** mending, darning

repatear* ▸ CONJUG 1a VT • **ese tío me repatea** that guy gets on my wick‡ *o* turns me right off*

repatingarse* ▸ CONJUG 1h VPR to lounge, sprawl, loll (back)

repatriación SF repatriation

repatriado/a ADJ repatriated
SM/F repatriate, repatriated person

repatriar ▸ CONJUG 1b VT to repatriate; [+ *criminal*] to deport • **van a ~ el famoso monumento** they are going to send the famous monument back to its country of origin
VPR **repatriarse** to return home, go back to one's own country

repe[1]* ADJ repeated, duplicated • **este sello lo tengo ~** I've got this stamp twice
SF (*TV*) repeat

repe[2] SM (*And*) mashed bananas with milk

repechar ▸ CONJUG 1a VI • **~ contra** (*Méx*) to lean against, lean one's chest against

repecho SM **1** (= *vertiente*) sharp gradient, steep slope • **a ~** uphill
2 (*Caribe, Méx*) (= *parapeto*) parapet
3 (*Méx*) (= *refugio*) shelter, refuge

repela SF (*And, CAm*) gleaning, gleaning of coffee crop

repelar ▸ CONJUG 1a VT **1** (= *pelar*) [+ *cabeza*] to leave completely bare, shear; [+ *persona*] to leave completely shaven, shear; [+ *hierba*] to nibble, crop; [+ *uñas*] to clip
2 (= *arrancar pelo*) • **~ a algn** to pull sb's hair
3 (*Méx*) (= *criticar*) to raise objections to, call into question
4 (*Méx*) (= *reprender*) to scold, tell off*
VPR **repelarse** (*Cono Sur*) to feel remorse

repelencia SF (*esp LAm*) revulsion, disgust

repelente ADJ **1** (= *repulsivo*) repellent, repulsive
2* (= *sabelotodo*) • **es ~** he's a know-all
SM repellent, insect repellent

repeler ▸ CONJUG 2a VT **1** [+ *enemigo*] to repel, repulse, drive back
2 (= *rechazar*) • **el material repele el agua** the material is water-resistant • **la pared repele la pelota** the wall sends the ball back, the ball bounces off the wall
3 [+ *idea, oferta*] to reject
4 (= *repugnar*) to repel, disgust
VPR **repelerse** • **los dos se repelen** the two are incompatible, the two are mutually incompatible

repellar ▸ CONJUG 1a VT **1** [+ *pared, muro*] to plaster, stucco
2 (*LAm*) (= *enjalbegar*) to whitewash
3 (*Caribe*) (= *menear*) to wriggle, wiggle

repello SM **1** (*en pared, muro*) • **la pared tenía ~s** the cracks on the wall had been filled in with plaster
2 (*LAm*) (= *jalbegue*) whitewash, whitewashing
3 (*Caribe*) (*en baile*) wiggle, grind

repelo SM **1** (= *pelo*) hair out of place, hair that sticks up
2 (*en madera*) snag, knot
3 (*en la piel*) hangnail
4* (= *riña*) tiff, slight argument
5 (= *aversión*) aversion
6 (*And, Méx*) (= *baratijas*) junk, bric-a-brac
7 (*And, Méx*) (= *trapo*) rag, tatter

repelón ADJ (*Méx*) grumbling, grumpy
SM **1** (= *tirón*) tug, tug at one's hair
2 (*Cos*) ruck, snag
3 (= *pedacito*) small bit, tag, pinch
4 [*de caballo*] dash, short run
5 (*Méx*) (= *reprimenda*) telling-off*, scolding

repelús* SM • **me da ~** it gives me the willies* *o* shivers

repeluz SM • **en un ~** (*Cono Sur*) in a flash, in an instant

repeluzno* SM nervous shiver, slight start of fear

repensar ▸ CONJUG 1j VT to rethink, reconsider

repente SM **1** (= *movimiento*) sudden movement, start; (*fig*) (= *impulso*) sudden impulse ▸ **repente de ira** fit of anger
2 • **de ~** (= *de pronto*) suddenly; (= *inesperadamente*) unexpectedly
3 (*Méx*) (*Med*) (= *acceso*) fit; (= *desmayo*) fainting fit

repentinamente ADV • **torcer ~** to turn sharply, make a sharp turn; ▸ **repente**

repentino ADJ **1** (= *súbito*) sudden; (= *imprevisto*) unexpected; [*curva, vuelta*] sharp
2 • **tener repentina compasión** (*frm*) to be quick to pity

repentización SF (*Mús*) sight-reading; (= *improvisación*) ad-lib, improvisation

repentizar ▸ CONJUG 1f VI (*Mús*) to sight-read; (= *improvisar*) to ad-lib, improvise

repentón* SM violent start

repera* SF • **es la ~** it's the tops*

repercusión SF **1** (= *consecuencia*) repercussion • **repercusiones** repercussions • **las repercusiones de esta decisión** the repercussions of this decision • **de amplia** *o* **de ancha ~** far-reaching, with profound effects • **tener ~** *o* **repercusiones en** to have repercussions on
2 [*de sonido*] repercussion; (= *reverberación*) reverberation, echo

repercutir ▸ CONJUG 3a VI **1** (= *influenciar*) • **~ en** to have repercussions on, affect
2 (= *reverberar*) [*sonido*] to echo, reverberate
3 (= *rebotar*) to rebound, bounce off
4 (*Méx*) (= *oler mal*) to smell bad, stink
VT (*And*) to contradict
VPR **repercutirse** to reverberate

reperiquete SM (*Méx*) **1** (= *baratija*) cheap jewellery, cheap jewelry (*EEUU*)
2 (= *baladronada*) brag, boast

repertoriar ▸ CONJUG 1b VT to catalogue, catalog (*EEUU*), list

repertorio SM **1** (= *lista*) list, index; (= *catálogo*) catalogue, catalog (*EEUU*)
2 (*Teat*) repertoire
3 (*Inform*) repertoire

repesca SF **1** (*Escol*) repeat, repeat exam
2 (*Dep*) play-off, play-off for third place

repescar ▸ CONJUG 1g VT to give a second chance to

repeso SM (*And*) bonus, extra

repetición SF **1** (= *acción*) repetition; (= *reaparición*) recurrence
2 (*Teat*) encore
3 • **fusil de ~** repeating rifle

repetidamente ADV repeatedly

repetido ADJ **1** (= *reiterado*) repeated • **el tan ~ aviso** the oft-repeated warning
2 (= *numeroso*) numerous • **en repetidas ocasiones** on numerous occasions • **repetidas veces** repeatedly, over and over again
3 [*sello*] duplicate

repetidor SM (*Radio, TV*) booster, booster station

repetidora SF repeater rifle

repetir ▸ CONJUG 3k VT (= *reiterar*) to repeat; (= *rehacer*) to do again • **le repito que es imposible** I repeat that it is impossible • **los niños repiten lo que hacen las personas mayores** children imitate adults • **~ el postre** to have a second helping *o* seconds* of dessert • **~ un curso** to repeat a year
VI **1** (= *servirse de nuevo*) to have a second helping • **se comió un buen plato y repitió** she ate a large plateful and then had a second helping
2 [*ajo, pepino, chorizo*] • **el pepino repite mucho** cucumber keeps repeating on you • **las cebollas me repiten** onions repeat on me
VPR **repetirse 1** [*persona*] to repeat o.s.
2 [*suceso*] to recur • **¡ojalá no se repita esto!** I hope this won't happen again!
3 [*comida*] • **el ajo se me repite mucho** garlic repeats on me

repetitivo ADJ repetitive

repicado SM copying of tapes, copying of video tapes, video piracy

repicar ▸ CONJUG 1g VT **1** [+ *campanas*] to ring • MODISMO: • **~ gordo un acontecimiento** to celebrate an event in style
2 [+ *carne*] to chop up finely
3 [+ *cinta*] to copy, pirate
VPR **repicarse‡** to boast (**de** about, of)

repintar ▸ CONJUG 1a VT (= *volver a pintar*) to repaint; (= *pintar de prisa*) to paint hastily
VPR **repintarse** to pile the make-up on

repipi* ADJ (= *afectado*) affected; (= *esnob*) la-di-dah*; (= *engreído*) stuck-up* • **es una niña ~** she's a little madam

repique SM **1** [*de tambor*] beating
2 [*de campanas*] ringing, pealing
3* (= *riña*) tiff, squabble

repiquete SM **1** [*de tambor*] beating; [*de campana*] pealing, ringing
2 (*Mil*) clash
3 (*Cono Sur*) (*Orn*) trill, song
4 (*And*) (= *resentimiento*) pique, resentment

repiquetear ▸ CONJUG 1a VT **1** [+ *campanas*] to ring
2 [+ *tambor*] to tap, beat rapidly
VI **1** (*Mús*) to peal, ring out
2 [*máquina*] to clatter
VPR **repiquetearse*** to squabble

repiqueteo SM **1** [*de tambor*] beating; [*de campana*] pealing, ringing
2 (*en mesa*) tapping
3 [*de máquina*] clatter

repisa SF (= *estante*) shelf • **la ~ de la chimenea** the mantelpiece • **la ~ de la ventana** the windowsill

replana SF (*And*) underworld slang

replantar ▸ CONJUG 1a VT to replant

replanteamiento SM rethink, reconsideration

replantear ▸ CONJUG 1a VT [+ *cuestión*] to raise again, reopen
VPR **replantearse** • **~se algo** to rethink *o* reconsider sth, think again about sth • **me lo estoy replanteando** I'm thinking it over again

replantigarse* ▸ CONJUG 1h VPR (*LAm*) = **repanchigarse**

repleción SF repletion

replegable ADJ **1** (= *que se pliega*) folding, that folds, that folds up
2 (*Aer*) [*tren de aterrizaje*] retractable

replegar ▸ CONJUG 1h, 1j VT **1** (= *plegar*) to fold over; (*de nuevo*) to fold again, refold
2 [+ *tren de aterrizaje*] to retract, draw up
VPR **replegarse** (*Mil*) to withdraw, fall back

repletar ▹ CONJUG 1a (*frm*) VT to fill completely, stuff full, pack tight
VPR **repletarse** to stuff o.s., eat to repletion (*frm*)

repleto ADJ **1** (= *lleno*) full up • **~ de** full of, crammed with • **el cuarto estaba ~ de gente** the room was crammed with people • **una colección repleta de rarezas** a collection containing many rare pieces
2 • **estar ~** [*persona*] to be full up (*with food*)
3 [*aspecto*] well-fed

réplica SF **1** (= *respuesta*) answer; (*Jur*) replication • **derecho de ~** right of reply • **~s** backchat (*sing*) • **dejar a algn sin ~s** to leave sb speechless
2 (*Arte*) replica, copy

replicar ▹ CONJUG 1g VI **1** (= *contestar*) to answer, retort
2 (= *objetar*) to argue, answer back • **¡no repliques!** don't answer back!

replicón* ADJ argumentative

repliegue SM **1** (= *pliegue*) fold, crease
2 (*Mil*) withdrawal, retreat ▸ **repliegue táctico** tactical withdrawal, tactical retreat

repoblación SF [*de personas*] repopulation; [*de peces*] restocking; [*de árboles*] reafforestation ▸ **repoblación forestal** reafforestation

repoblar ▹ CONJUG 1l VT [+ *país*] to repopulate; [+ *río*] to restock; (*con árboles*) to plant trees on

repollita SF (*Col*), **repollito** SM ▸ **repollita de Bruselas** (*Col*), **repollito de Bruselas** (*Cono Sur*) Brussels sprout

repollo SM cabbage

repollonco* ADJ (*Cono Sur*), **repolludo*** ADJ tubby*, chunky*

reponer ▹ CONJUG 2q (PP: **repuesto**) VT
1 [+ *productos, surtido*] to replenish
2 (= *devolver*) [+ *objeto dañado*] to replace, pay for, pay for the replacement of • **~ el dinero robado** to pay back the stolen money
3 (*en un cargo*) to reinstate
4 (= *recuperar*) • **~ fuerzas** to get one's strength back
5 (*Teat*) to revive, put on again; (*TV*) to repeat
6 (*frm*) (= *replicar*) to reply (**que** that)
VPR **reponerse** (= *recuperarse*) to recover • **~se de** to recover from, get over

repóquer SM (*tb* **repóquer de ases**) *four aces plus a wild card*

reportaje SM report, article ▸ **reportaje gráfico** illustrated report

reportar ▹ CONJUG 1a (*frm*) VT **1** (= *traer*) to bring, carry; (= *producir*) to give, bring • **esto le habrá reportado algún beneficio** this will have brought him some benefit • **la cosa no le reportó sino disgustos** the affair brought him nothing but trouble • **esto le habrá reportado dos millones** it must have landed him two million
2 (*LAm*) (= *informar*) to report; (= *denunciar*) to denounce, accuse; (= *notificar*) to notify, inform
VI (*LAm*) (*a cita*) to turn up (*for an appointment*)
VPR **reportarse 1** (= *contenerse*) to control o.s.; (= *calmarse*) to calm down
2 (*Méx*) (= *presentarse*) to turn up

reporte SM (*esp CAm, Méx*) report, piece of news

reportear ▹ CONJUG 1a VT (*LAm*)
1 (= *fotografiar*) to photograph (*for the press*)
2 [+ *suceso*] to report, report on

repórter SMF = **reportero**

reportero/a SM/F reporter ▸ **reportero/a gráfico/a** news photographer, press photographer

reposabrazos SM INV armrest

reposacabezas SM INV headrest

reposacodos SM INV elbow rest

reposadamente ADV (= *con tranquilidad*) quietly; (= *descansadamente*) gently, restfully; (= *sin prisa*) unhurriedly, calmly

reposadera SF (*CAm*) drain, sewer

reposado ADJ (= *tranquilo*) quiet; (= *descansado*) gentle, restful; (= *lento*) unhurried, calm

reposamuñecas SM INV wrist rest

reposapiés SM INV footrest

reposaplatos SM INV table mat, hot pad (EEUU)

reposar ▹ CONJUG 1a VI **1** (= *descansar*) to rest
2 (= *dormir*) to sleep
3 (= *apoyarse*) to lie, rest • **su mano reposaba sobre mi hombro** her hand lay *o* rested on my shoulder • **la columna reposa sobre una base circular** the column is resting *o* sitting on a circular base
4 [*restos mortales*] to lie, rest
5 (*Culin*) • **dejar ~ algo** to let sth stand
VT **1** (= *apoyar*) to lay, rest • **reposó la cabeza sobre la almohada** she lay *o* rested her head on the pillow
2 • **~ la comida** to let one's food settle *o* go down
VPR **reposarse** [*líquido*] to settle

reposera SF (*Cono Sur*) canvas chair, deck chair

reposición SF **1** (= *recambio*) replacement
2 (*Econ*) reinvestment
3 (*Teat*) revival; (*TV*) repeat
4 (*Med*) (*tb fig*) recovery

reposicionar ▹ CONJUG 1a VT to reposition

repositorio SM repository

reposo SM rest, repose (*frm o liter*) • **estar en ~** to be resting • **guardar ~** (*Med*) to rest, stay in bed ▸ **reposo absoluto** (*Med*) complete rest

repostada SF (*LAm*) rude reply, sharp answer

repostadero SM refuelling stop, refueling stop (EEUU)

repostaje SM refuelling, refueling (EEUU), filling up

repostar ▹ CONJUG 1a VT [+ *surtido*] to replenish • **~ combustible** *o* **gasolina** (*Aer*) to refuel; (*Aut*) to fill up, fill up with petrol
VI to refuel
VPR **repostarse** to replenish stocks, take on supplies • **~se de combustible** to refuel

repostería SF **1** (= *tienda*) confectioner's, confectioner's shop, cake shop
2 (= *arte*) confectionery
3 (= *despensa*) larder, pantry

repostero/a SM/F confectioner, pastry cook
SM (*And, Chile*) (= *despensa*) pantry, larder; (= *estantería*) kitchen shelf unit

repostón* ADJ (*CAm, Méx*) rude, surly

repregunta SF (*Jur*) cross-examination, cross-questioning

repreguntar ▹ CONJUG 1a VT (*Jur*) to cross-examine, cross-question

reprender ▹ CONJUG 2a VT (= *amonestar*) to reprimand, tell off*; [+ *niño*] to scold • **~ algo a algn** to criticize sb for sth

reprensible ADJ reprehensible

reprensión SF (= *amonestación*) (*a un adulto*) reprimand, telling-off*; (*a un niño*) scolding

represa SF **1** (= *presa*) dam; (= *lago artificial*) lake, pool; (= *vertedero*) weir ▸ **represa de molino** millpond
2 (= *parada*) check, stoppage
3 (= *represión*) repression
4 (= *captura*) recapture

represalia SF reprisal • **como ~ por** in reprisal for • **tomar ~s** to retaliate, take reprisals (**contra** against)

represaliado/a SM/F victim of a reprisal

represaliar ▹ CONJUG 1b VT to take reprisals against

represar ▹ CONJUG 1a VT **1** (*Náut*) to recapture
2 (= *detener*) to check, put a stop to
3 (*Pol*) (= *reprimir*) to repress
4 [+ *agua*] to dam, dam up; (*fig*) to stem

representable ADJ **1** (= *ilustrable*) • **es ~ en un gráfico** it can be represented in a graph
2 (*Teat*) • **la obra no es ~** the play cannot be staged *o* performed

representación SF **1** [*de concepto, idea, imagen*] representation • **la ~ gráfica** the graphic representation • **en este cuadro el buitre es una ~ de la muerte** in this painting the vulture represents death
2 [*de país, pueblo, organización*] (= *acto*) representation; (= *delegación*) delegation • **partidos políticos con ~ parlamentaria** political parties represented in parliament • **en el congreso había una nutrida ~ de empresarios** there was a large representation of businessmen at the conference • **la ~ española en la feria** the Spanish delegation at the fair • **en ~ de**: **el abogado que actúa en ~ del banco** the lawyer representing the bank • **me invitaron a ir en ~ de la empresa** they invited me to go as a representative of the company, they invited me to go to represent the company • **habló en ~ de todos** she spoke on behalf of everyone
▸ **representación diplomática** (= *actividad*) diplomatic representation; (= *oficina*) embassy ▸ **representación legal** (= *acto*) legal representation; (= *abogado*) lawyer(s) • **la ~ legal del acusado** (= *acto*) the defendant's legal representation; (= *abogado*) the lawyers representing the defendant, the defendant's lawyers
▸ **representación proporcional** proportional representation
3 (*Teat*) (= *función*) performance; (= *montaje*) production • **durante una ~ teatral** during a theatre performance • **una ~ financiada por el Patronato de Turismo** a production financed by the Tourist Board
4 (*Com*) representation • **ha conseguido la ~ de varias firmas farmacéuticas** he has managed to become an agent for various pharmaceutical companies, he has managed to obtain the representation of various pharmaceutical companies • **tener la ~ exclusiva de un producto** to be sole agent for a product, have sole agency of a product (*frm*)
5† (= *súplica*) • **hacer representaciones a algn** to make representations to sb (*frm*)
6†† (= *importancia*) standing • **un hombre de ~** a man of some standing

representado/a SM/F client

representante SMF **1** [*de organización, país, en parlamento*] representative • **la única ~ española en esta prueba** Spain's only representative in this event • **uno de los máximos ~s del surrealismo** one of the greatest exponents *o* representatives of surrealism ▸ **representante legal** legal representative ▸ **representante sindical** union representative
2 (*Com*) representative
3 [*de artista, deportista*] agent
4† (= *actor*) performer, actor/actress

representar ▹ CONJUG 1a VT **1** (= *actuar en nombre de*) [+ *país, votantes*] to represent; [+ *cliente, acusado*] to act for, represent • **la cantante que ~á a España en el festival** the singer who will represent Spain at the festival • **el príncipe representó al rey en la ceremonia** the prince attended the

ceremony on behalf of the king *o* representing the king
2 (= *simbolizar*) to symbolize, represent • **Don Quijote representa el idealismo** Don Quixote symbolizes *o* represents idealism • **cuando éramos pequeños nuestros padres representaban el modelo a seguir** when we were small our parents were our role models
3 (= *reproducir*) to depict • **este grabado representa a la amada del pintor** this engraving depicts the painter's lover • **nuevas formas de ~ el mundo** new ways of representing *o* portraying *o* depicting the world • **esta columna del gráfico representa los síes** this column of the graph shows *o* represents those in favour
4 (= *equivaler a*) [+ *porcentaje, mejora, peligro*] to represent; [+ *amenaza*] to pose, represent • **obtuvieron unos beneficios de 1,7 billones, lo que representa un incremento del 28% sobre el año pasado** they made profits of 1.7 billion, which represents an increase of 28% on last year • **los kurdos representan el 9% de los habitantes de Siria** the Kurds account for *o* represent 9% of the inhabitants of Syria • **la ofensiva de ayer representa una violación de la tregua** yesterday's offensive constitutes a violation of the truce • **no sabes lo mucho que representa este trabajo para él** you don't know how much this job means to him
5 (= *requerir*) [+ *trabajo, esfuerzo, sacrificio*] to involve • **representa mucho esfuerzo** it involves a great deal of effort
6 (*Teat*) [+ *obra*] to perform; [+ *papel*] to play • **el teatro donde se representa la obra** the theatre where the play is being performed • **en esta película represento el papel de un abogado** in this film I play the part of a lawyer • **¿quién va a ~ el papel que tenía antes la URSS?** who's going to play the part *o* role previously played by the USSR?
7 (= *aparentar*) [+ *edad*] to look • **no representa los años que tiene** she doesn't look her age • **representa unos 55 años** he looks about 55
8 (= *hacer imaginar*) to point out • **nos representó las dificultades con que nos podíamos encontrar** she pointed out the difficulties we might come up against
VPR **representarse** (= *imaginarse*) to imagine • **no puedo representármelo siendo fiel** I can't imagine him being faithful

representatividad SF • **el sindicato con mayor ~ en la enseñanza** the union with the greatest representation in the teaching profession • **carece de la suficiente ~ para poder hablar en nombre del grupo** he is not representative enough of the group to speak on its behalf

representativo ADJ **1** (= *simbólico, característico*) representative • **estas cifras no son muy representativas** these figures are not very representative • **uno de los artistas más ~s de la época** one of the most representative artists of the age
2 (*Pol*) [*democracia, institución, organización*] representative • **organizaciones representativas de los indígenas** organizations representing the indigenous people

represión SF **1** [*de deseos, impulsos*] repression
2 (*Pol*) [*de rebelión*] suppression • **la brutal ~ de la rebelión por las tropas del gobierno** the brutal suppression of the rebellion by government troops • **la ~ es una realidad en China** repression is a fact of life in China

represivo ADJ, **represor** ADJ repressive

reprimenda SF reprimand, rebuke

reprimido/a ADJ repressed
SM/F repressed person

reprimir ▷ CONJUG 3a VT **1** [+ *deseos, impulsos*] to repress
2 [+ *rebelión*] to suppress
3 [+ *bostezo*] to suppress; [+ *risa*] to hold in, hold back
VPR **reprimirse** • **~se de hacer algo** to stop o.s. (from) doing sth

reprisar ▷ CONJUG 1a VT (*CAm, Cono Sur, Méx*) to revive, put on again

reprise[1] SF (*esp LAm*) (*Teat*) revival

reprise[2] [re'pris] SM, (*a veces*) SF (*Aut*) acceleration

repristinación SF (*frm*) restoration to its original state

repristinar ▷ CONJUG 1a VT (*frm*) to restore to its original state

reprivatización SF privatization, reprivatization

reprivatizar ▷ CONJUG 1f VT to privatize, reprivatize

reprobable ADJ reprehensible

reprobación SF (= *desaprobación*) reproval, reprobation • **escrito en ~ de ...** written in condemnation of ...

reprobador ADJ reproving, disapproving

reprobar ▷ CONJUG 1l VT **1** (= *desaprobar*) to reprove, condemn
2 (*LAm*) (*Escol*) (= *suspender*) to fail

reprobatorio ADJ = **reprobador**

réprobo ADJ damned

reprocesado SM, **reprocesamiento** SM reprocessing

reprocesar ▷ CONJUG 1a VT to reprocess

reprochable ADJ blameworthy, culpable

reprochar ▷ CONJUG 1a VT (= *reconvenir*) to reproach • **~ algo a algn** to reproach sb for sth • **le reprochan su descuido** they reproach him for his negligence
VPR **reprocharse** to reproach o.s. • **no tienes nada que ~te** you have nothing to reproach yourself for

reproche SM reproach (**a** for) • **nos miró con ~** he looked at us reproachfully

reproducción SF reproduction
▸ **reproducción asexual** asexual reproduction ▸ **reproducción asistida** assisted reproduction

reproducir ▷ CONJUG 3n VT **1** (= *volver a producir*) to reproduce
2 (*Bio*) to reproduce, breed
3 (= *copiar*) to reproduce
VPR **reproducirse 1** (*Bio*) to reproduce, breed
2 [*condiciones*] to be reproduced; [*suceso*] to happen again, recur • **se le han reproducido los síntomas** the symptoms have reappeared *o* recurred • **si se reproducen los desórdenes** if the disturbances happen again

reproductor ADJ [*yegua*] brood (*antes de s*); [*órgano, sistema*] reproductive
SM ▸ **reproductor de CD** CD player ▸ **reproductor de compact disc, reproductor de discos compactos** compact disc player ▸ **reproductor de DVD** DVD player ▸ **reproductor MP3/MP4** MP3/MP4 player

reprografía SF reprography

reprogramar ▷ CONJUG 1a VT [+ *película*] to reprogramme, reprogram (*EEUU*); [+ *deuda*] to reschedule

reps SM INV rep

reptar ▷ CONJUG 1a VI to creep, crawl

reptil ADJ reptilian
SM reptile

reptilario SM reptile house

república SF republic ▸ **república bananera** banana republic ▸ **República Dominicana** Dominican Republic ▸ **República Árabe Unida** United Arab Republic

republicanismo SM republicanism

republicano/a ADJ, SM/F republican

repudiación SF repudiation

repudiar ▷ CONJUG 1b VT **1** [+ *violencia*] to repudiate
2 (= *no reconocer*) to disown
3 (= *renunciar a*) to renounce

repudio SM repudiation

repudrir ▷ CONJUG 3a VT **1** (= *pudrir*) to rot
2 (*fig*) (= *consumir*) to gnaw at, eat up
VPR **repudrirse** to eat one's heart out, pine away

repuesto PP *de reponer*
SM **1** [*de pluma*] refill
2 (*Aut, Mec*) spare, spare part • **rueda de ~** spare wheel • **y llevamos otro de ~** and we have another as a spare *o* in reserve
3 (*Esp*) (= *mueble*) sideboard, buffet
4 (= *provisión*) stock, store; (= *abastecimiento*) supply

repugnancia SF **1** (= *asco*) disgust, repugnance; (= *aversión*) aversion (**hacia, por** to)
2 (= *desgana*) reluctance • **lo hizo con ~** he was loathe to do it
3 (*moral*) repugnance
4 (*Fil*) opposition, incompatibility

repugnante ADJ disgusting, revolting

repugnar ▷ CONJUG 1a VT **1** (= *causar asco*) to disgust, revolt • **ese olor me repugna** that smell is disgusting • **me repugna mirarlo** it disgusts *o* sickens me to watch it
2 (= *odiar*) to hate, loathe • **siempre ha repugnado el engaño** he's always hated deceit
3 (*Fil*) (= *contradecir*) to contradict
VI **1** [*ser repugnante*] to be disgusting, be revolting
2 ▷ VPR
VPR **repugnarse** (*Fil*) (= *ser opuestos*) to conflict, be in opposition; (= *contradecirse*) to contradict each other • **las dos teorías se repugnan** the two theories contradict each other

repujado ADJ embossed

repujar ▷ CONJUG 1a VT to emboss, work in relief

repulgado ADJ (*frm*) affected

repulgar ▷ CONJUG 1h VT **1** (*Cos*) to hem, edge
2 (*Culin*) to crimp

repulgo SM **1** (*Cos*) (= *dobladillo*) hem; (= *punto*) hemstitch
2 (*Culin*) crimping, fancy edging, decorated border ▸ **repulgos de empanada*** silly scruples

repulido ADJ **1** [*objeto*] polished
2 [*persona*] dressed up, dolled up*

repulir ▷ CONJUG 3a VT **1** [+ *objeto*] to polish up
2 [+ *persona*] to dress up
VPR **repulirse** (= *arreglarse*) to dress up, get dolled up*

repulsa SF **1** [*de oferta, persona*] rejection; [*de violencia*] • **sufrir una ~** to meet with a rebuff
2 (*Mil*) check

repulsar ▷ CONJUG 1a VT (*frm*) **1** (= *rechazar*) [+ *solicitud*] to reject, refuse; [+ *oferta, persona*] to rebuff; [+ *violencia*] to condemn
2 (*Mil*) to repulse

repulsión SF **1** = **repulsa**
2 (= *aversión*) repulsion, disgust
3 (*Fís*) repulsion

repulsivo ADJ disgusting, revolting

repunta SF **1** (*Geog*) point, headland
2 (= *indicio*) sign, indication, hint
3 (= *resentimiento*) pique
4 (= *disgusto*) slight upset, tiff
5 (*LAm*) (*Agr*) round-up

6 *(And)* (= *riada*) sudden rise (*of a river*), flash flood
repuntar ▷ CONJUG 1a VT *(LAm)* [+ *ganado*] to round up
VI 1 [*marea*] to turn
2 *(LAm)* (= *manifestarse*) to begin to show; [*persona*] to turn up unexpectedly
3 *(LAm)* [*río*] to rise suddenly
VPR **repuntarse 1** [*vino*] to begin to sour, turn
2 [*persona*] to get cross, get annoyed
3 [*dos personas*] to fall out, have a tiff
repunte SM 1 [*de mar*] turn of the tide; [*de río*] level
2 (= *mejora*) upturn, recovery • **ha habido un ~ económico** there has been an economic upturn *o* recovery
3 *(And)* *(Econ)* rise in share prices
4 *(LAm)* *(Agr)* round-up
reputación SF reputation
reputado ADJ *(frm)* • **muy ~** highly reputed, reputable • **una colección reputada en mucho** a highly regarded collection
reputar ▷ CONJUG 1a VT *(frm)* (= *considerar*) to deem, consider • **~ a algn de** *o* **por inteligente** to consider sb intelligent • **le reputan no apto para el cargo** they consider him unsuitable for the post • **una colección reputada en mucho** a highly regarded collection
requebrar ▷ CONJUG 1j VT *(liter)* (= *halagar*) to flatter, compliment; (= *flirtear*) to flirt with
requemado ADJ [*objeto, terreno, planta*] scorched; [*comida*] overdone, overcooked
requemar ▷ CONJUG 1a VT (= *quemar*) to scorch; *(Culin)* to burn • MODISMO: • **~le la sangre a algn:** • **todo esto me requema la sangre** the whole thing makes my blood boil
VPR **requemarse 1** (= *quemarse*) to get scorched; (= *secarse*) to get parched, dry up; [*comida*] to burn • MODISMO: • **~se la lengua** to burn one's tongue
2 (= *guardar rencor*) to harbour a grudge, harbor a grudge (EEUU)
requenete ADJ *(Caribe)*, **requeneto** ADJ *(And, Caribe)* = **rechoncho**
requerimiento SM 1 (= *petición*) request • **se personó en el juzgado a ~ del juez** she appeared in court after being summonsed by the judge
2 (= *notificación*) notification
requerir ▷ CONJUG 3i VT 1 (= *necesitar*) to need, require • **esto requiere cierto cuidado** this requires some care • **"se requiere dominio del inglés"** "fluent English required", "good command of English required"
2 (= *solicitar*) to request, ask • **~ a algn que haga algo** to request *o* ask sb to do sth • **el ministro requirió los documentos** the minister sent for his papers
3 (= *llamar*) to send for, summon *(frm)* • **el juez le requirió para que lo explicara** the judge summonsed him to explain it
4†† (= *requebrar*) (*tb* **requerir de amores**) to court, woo
VI • **~ de** (*esp LAm*) to need, require
requesón SM cottage cheese
requeté SM 1 *(Hist)* Carlist militiaman
2† (= *machote*) he-man*, tough guy*
requete...* PREF extremely ... • **una chica requeteguapa** a really attractive girl • **me parece requetebién** it seems absolutely splendid to me • **lo tendré muy requetepensado** I'll think it over very thoroughly
requiebro SM *(liter)* compliment, flirtatious remark
réquiem SM (PL: **réquiems**) requiem
requilorios SMPL† 1 (= *trámites*) tedious formalities, red tape (*sing*)
2 (= *adornos*) silly adornments, unnecessary frills
3 (= *preliminares*) time-wasting preliminaries; (= *rodeos*) roundabout way of saying something
4 (= *elementos dispersos*) bits and pieces
requintar ▷ CONJUG 1a VT 1 *(LAm)* (= *apretar*) to tighten
2 • **~ a algn** *(And, Méx)* to impose one's will on sb, push sb around
3 *(And)* (= *insultar*) to abuse, swear at
VI *(Caribe)* (= *parecerse*) to resemble each other
requisa SF 1 (= *inspección*) survey, inspection
2 *(Mil)* requisition
3 *(esp LAm)* (= *confiscación*) seizure, confiscation
requisar ▷ CONJUG 1a VT 1 (= *confiscar*) to seize, confiscate
2 *(Mil)* to requisition
3 *(esp LAm)* (= *registrar*) to search
requisición SF 1 (= *confiscación*) seizure, confiscation
2 *(Mil)* requisition
3 *(esp LAm)* (= *inspección*) search
requisito SM requirement, requisite • **cumplir los ~s** to fulfil *o* (EEUU) fulfill the requirements • **cumplir los ~s para un cargo** to have the essential qualifications for a post ▸ **requisito previo** prerequisite
requisitoria SF 1 *(Jur)* (= *citación*) summons; (= *orden*) writ
2 *(LAm)* (= *interrogatorio*) examination, interrogation
res SF 1 (= *animal*) beast, animal • **100 reses** 100 animals, 100 head of cattle ▸ **res lanar** sheep ▸ **res vacuna** (= *vaca*) cow; (= *toro*) bull; (= *buey*) ox
2 *(Méx)* (= *carne*) steak
resabiado ADJ [*persona*] knowing, crafty; [*caballo*] vicious
resabiarse ▷ CONJUG 1b VPR to acquire bad habits, get into bad habits
resabido ADJ 1 [*dato*] well known • **lo tengo sabido y ~** I know all that perfectly well
2 [*persona*] pretentious, pedantic
resabio SM 1 (= *gusto malo*) unpleasant aftertaste • **tener ~s de** *(fig)* to smack of
2 (= *mala costumbre*) [*de persona*] bad habit
resabioso ADJ *(And, Caribe)* = **resabiado**
resaca SF 1 [*de mar*] undertow, undercurrent
2 [*de borrachera*] hangover
3 (= *reacción*) reaction, backlash • **la ~ blanca** the white backlash
4 *(LAm*)* (= *aguardiente*) high-quality liquor
5 *(Cono Sur)* (*en playa*) line of driftwood and rubbish (*left by the tide*)
6 *(Cono Sur*)* (= *personas*) dregs (*pl*) of society
7 *(Caribe)* (= *paliza*) beating
resacado* ADJ *(Méx)* (= *tacaño*) mean, stingy; (= *débil*) weak; (= *estúpido*) stupid • **es lo ~** it's the worst of its kind
SM *(And)* liquor, contraband liquor
resacar ▷ CONJUG 1g VT *(LAm)* to distil
resacoso* ADJ hungover
resalado* ADJ (= *vivo*) lively
resaltable ADJ notable, noteworthy
resaltante ADJ *(LAm)* outstanding
resaltar ▷ CONJUG 1a VI 1 (= *destacarse*) to stand out • **lo escribí en mayúsculas para que ~a** I wrote it in capitals to make it stand out • **entre sus cualidades resalta su elegancia** her most striking quality is her elegance • **hacer ~ algo** to set sth off; *(fig)* to highlight sth • **este maquillaje hace ~ sus delicadas facciones** this makeup sets off her delicate features • **la encuesta hace ~ el descontento con el sistema educativo** the survey highlights the dissatisfaction with the education system
2 (= *sobresalir*) to jut out, project
VT (= *destacar*) to highlight • **el conferenciante resaltó el problema del paro** the speaker highlighted the problem of unemployment • **quiero ~ la dedicación de nuestros empleados** I would like to draw particular attention to the dedication of our staff
resalte SM, **resalto** SM 1 (= *saliente*) projection
2 (= *rebote*) bounce, rebound
resanar ▷ CONJUG 1a VT to restore, repair, make good
resaquero ADJ *(LAm)* = **remolón**
resarcimiento SM (= *pago*) repayment; (= *compensación*) compensation
resarcir ▷ CONJUG 3b VT (= *pagar*) to repay; (= *compensar*) to indemnify, compensate • **~ a algn de una cantidad** to repay sb a sum • **~ a algn de una pérdida** to compensate sb for a loss
VPR **resarcirse** • **~se de** to make up for
resbalada SF *(LAm)* slip
resbaladero SM 1 (= *lugar*) slippery place
2 (= *tobogán*) slide, chute
resbaladilla SF *(Méx)* slide, chute
resbaladizo ADJ slippery
resbalar ▷ CONJUG 1a VI 1 (*al andar*) to slip (**en, sobre** on); *(Aut)* to skid • **había llovido y resbaló** it had been raining and she slipped • **el coche resbaló y se dio contra el árbol** the car skidded into the tree • **le resbalaban las lágrimas por las mejillas** tears were trickling down her cheeks
2 (= *equivocarse*) to slip up, make a slip
3* (= *ser indiferente*) • **me resbala** it leaves me cold • **las críticas le resbalan** criticism runs off him like water off a duck's back
VPR **resbalarse** to slip • **se resbaló bajando la calle** she slipped walking down the street
resbalón SM 1 (= *acción*) slip; *(Aut)* skid
2 (= *equivocación*) slip, error • **dar** *o* **pegar un ~** to slip up
resbalosa SF *Peruvian dance*
resbaloso ADJ 1 *(LAm)* (= *resbaladizo*) slippery
2 *(Méx*)* (= *coqueto*) flirtatious
rescatar ▷ CONJUG 1a VT 1 (= *salvar*) to save, rescue
2 [+ *cautivo*] to rescue, free; [+ *pueblo*] to recapture, recover
3 [+ *objeto empeñado*] to redeem
4 [+ *póliza*] to surrender
5 [+ *posesiones*] to get back, recover
6 [+ *tiempo perdido*] to make up
7 [+ *delitos*] to atone for, expiate *(frm)*
8 [+ *terreno*] to reclaim
9 *(LAm)* (= *revender*) to resell
VI *(And)* to peddle goods from village to village
rescate SM 1 (*en incendio, naufragio*) rescue • **operaciones de ~** rescue operations • **acudir al ~ de algn** to go to sb's rescue
2 [*de cautivo*] rescue, freeing; [*de pueblo*] recapture, recovery
3 [*de algo empeñado*] redemption
4 (*en secuestro*) (= *dinero*) ransom
5 [*de posesiones*] recovery
6 [*de delitos*] atonement, expiation *(frm)*
7 ▸ **rescate de terrenos** land reclamation
rescindible ADJ • **contrato ~ por ambas partes** contract that can be cancelled by either side
rescindir ▷ CONJUG 3a VT 1 [+ *contrato*] to cancel, rescind
2 [+ *privilegio*] to withdraw
rescisión SF 1 [*de contrato*] cancellation
2 [*de privilegio*] withdrawal
rescoldo SM 1 (= *brasa*) embers (*pl*), hot ashes (*pl*)

2 (= *recelo*) doubt, scruple • MODISMO: • **avivar el ~** to stir up the dying embers
rescontrar ▸ CONJUG 1l (VT) (*Com, Econ*) to offset, balance
resecación (SF), **resecamiento** (SM) drying
resecar¹ ▸ CONJUG 1g (VT) (= *secar*) to dry off, dry thoroughly
(VPR) **resecarse** to dry up
resecar² ▸ CONJUG 1g (VT) (*Med*) (= *quitar*) to cut out, remove; (= *amputar*) to amputate
resección (SF) resection
reseco (ADJ) **1** (= *muy seco*) very dry, too dry
2 (= *flaco*) skinny, lean
reseda (SF) (*LAm*), **resedá** (SF) (*LAm*) mignonette
resellarse†* ▸ CONJUG 1a (VPR) to switch parties, change one's views
resembrado (SM) re-sowing, re-seeding
resembrar ▸ CONJUG 1j (VT) to re-sow, re-seed
resentido/a (ADJ) **1** (= *disgustado*) resentful • **aún está ~ porque no le felicitaste** he still feels resentful that you didn't congratulate him, he still resents the fact that you didn't congratulate him
2 (= *dolorido*) painful • **aún tiene la mano resentida por el golpe** his hand is still painful *o* hurting from the knock
(SM/F) • **es un ~** he has a chip on his shoulder, he is resentful
resentimiento (SM) (= *rencor*) resentment; (= *amargura*) bitterness
resentirse ▸ CONJUG 3i (VPR) **1** (= *estar resentido*) • **~ con** *o* **por algo** to resent sth, feel bitter about sth
2 (= *debilitarse*) to be weakened, suffer • **con los años se resintió su salud** his health suffered *o* was affected over the years • **los cimientos se resintieron con el terremoto** the foundations were weakened by the earthquake • **sin que se resienta el dólar** without the dollar being affected
3 (= *sentir*) • **~ de** [+ *defecto*] to suffer from • **~ de las consecuencias de** to feel the effects of • **me resiento todavía del golpe** I can still feel the effects of the injury
reseña (SF) **1** (= *resumen*) outline, summary; [*de libro*] review
2 (= *descripción*) brief description
3 (*Mil*) review
4 (*Cono Sur, esp Chile*) (= *procesión*) procession held on Passion Sunday
reseñable (ADJ) **1** (= *destacado*) noteworthy, notable; (= *digno de mencionar*) worth mentioning
2 [*ofensa*] bookable
reseñante (SMF) reviewer
reseñar ▸ CONJUG 1a (VT) **1** (= *resumir*) to write up, write a summary of
2 [+ *libro*] to review
3 [+ *delincuente*] to book
reseñista (SMF) reviewer
resero/a (*LAm*) (SM) (= *vaquero*) cowboy, herdsman
(SM/F) (= *comerciante*) cattle dealer
reserva (SF) **1** (= *provisiones*) [*de minerales, petróleo, armamentos, vitaminas*] reserve; [*de agua*] supply; [*de productos ya almacenados*] stock • **las ~s de agua están al mínimo** water supplies are at a minimum • **acumularon grandes ~s de carbón para el invierno** they built up large stocks of coal for the winter • **pasta, arroz, legumbres, tienen ~s de todo** pasta, rice, pulses, they have stocks of everything • **~s de víveres** food supplies • **estos chicos tienen grandes ~s de energía** these kids have endless amounts *o* reserves of energy • **de ~** [*precio, jugador, fondo*] reserve (*antes de s*); [*zapatos, muda*] spare • **el equipo de ~** the reserve team
2 (*Econ*) reserve • **las ~s de divisas** currency reserves ▸ **reserva de caja** cash reserves (*pl*) ▸ **reserva en efectivo, reserva en metálico** cash reserves (*pl*) ▸ **reserva para amortización, reserva para depreciaciones** depreciation allowance ▸ **reservas de oro** gold reserves ▸ **reservas monetarias** [*de un país*] currency reserves ▸ **reservas ocultas** hidden reserves, secret reserves
3 (= *solicitud*) (*en hotel, avión*) reservation; (*en teatro, restaurante*) reservation, booking • **no se cobra por la ~ de asientos** there is no booking *o* reservation charge • **se pueden hacer ~s por teléfono** you can book by phone, you can make a telephone booking *o* reservation • **ya he hecho la ~ de plaza en la academia de baile** I've reserved *o* booked my place at the dance school
4 (= *territorio*) reserve ▸ **reserva biológica** wildlife sanctuary, wildlife reserve ▸ **reserva de caza** game reserve ▸ **reserva de indios** Indian reservation ▸ **reserva de pesca** protected fishing area, fishing preserve ▸ **reserva nacional** national park ▸ **reserva natural** nature reserve
5 (*Mil*) • **nuestro ejército tiene una importante ~ de soldados** our army has significant reserves of soldiers • **pasar a la ~** to join the reserve ▸ **reserva activa** active reserve
6 (*Dep*) • **estar en la ~** to be a reserve
7 (*Aut*) [*de gasolina*] reserve tank • **con la ~ tenemos para diez kilómetros** with the reserve tank we have enough to go ten kilometres
8 (= *recelo*) reservation • **el pacto será aprobado, aunque con algunas ~s** the agreement will be sanctioned, but with certain reservations • **contestó con ciertas ~s** she answered with some reservation • **nos apoyaron sin ~s** they gave us their unreserved support
9 [*de carácter*] (= *inhibición*) reserve; (= *discreción*) discretion • **confiamos en tu ~ al manejar este asunto** we are counting on your discretion in this matter
10 (= *secreto*) confidence • **se ruega absoluta ~** your strictest confidence is requested • **han mantenido la más absoluta ~ sobre este incidente** they have maintained the utmost confidence over this incident • **sus nombres se mantienen en ~ por razones de seguridad** their names have not been revealed for security reasons
11 • **a ~ de** subject to • **a ~ de un estudio más detallado** subject to more detailed study • **a ~ de consultar antes con mis superiores** subject to prior consultation with my superiors • **a ~ de que ...** unless ...
(SMF) (*Dep*) reserve • **el banquillo de los ~s** the reserves' bench
(SM) (= *vino*) vintage wine (*that has been aged for a minimum of three years*)

RESERVA
Quality Spanish wine is often graded **Crianza**, **Reserva** or **Gran Reserva** according to the length of bottle-ageing and barrel-ageing it has undergone. Red **Reserva** wines are at least three years old, having spent a minimum of one year in cask, and white **Reserva** wines are at least two years old with at least six months spent in cask. A **Gran Reserva** wine is a top-quality wine. A red must be aged for at least two years in an oak cask and three years in the bottle. White wine must be aged for four years, with at least six months in cask.
▸ CRIANZA

reservación (SF) (*LAm*) reservation
reservadamente (ADV) in confidence
reservado (ADJ) **1** [*actitud, persona*] (= *poco comunicativo*) reserved; (= *discreto*) discreet
2 (= *confidencial*) [*asunto, documento*] confidential • **estos documentos son materia reservada** these documents are confidential, these documents contain confidential material
(SM) **1** (= *habitación aparte*) (*en restaurante*) private room; (*en tren*) reserved compartment
2 (*Cono Sur*) (= *vino*) vintage wine
reservar ▸ CONJUG 1a (VT) **1** [+ *asiento, habitación, mesa*] to reserve, book; [+ *billete, entrada*] to book • **~ en exceso** to overbook
2 (= *guardar*) to keep, keep in reserve, set aside • **lo reserva para el final** he's keeping it till last • **ha reservado lo mejor para sí** he has kept the best part for himself
(VPR) **reservarse 1** (*para luego*) to save o.s. (**para** for) • **no bebo porque me reservo para más tarde** I'm not drinking because I'm saving myself for later on
2 (= *encubrir*) to conceal; (= *callar*) to keep to o.s. • **prefiero ~me los detalles** I prefer not to reveal the details
reservista (SMF) reservist
reservón* (ADJ) excessively reserved
reservorio (SM) (*Med*) reservoir
resfriado (ADJ) **1** (= *acatarrado*) • **estar ~** to have a cold
2 (*Arg**) (= *indiscreto*) indiscreet
(SM) cold • **coger un ~** to catch a cold
resfriar ▸ CONJUG 1c (VT) **1** (*Med*) • **~ a algn** to give sb a cold
2 (= *enfriar*) to cool, chill
3 [+ *ardor*] to cool
(VI) (*Meteo*) to turn cold
(VPR) **resfriarse 1** (*Med*) to catch a cold
2 [*relaciones*] to cool off
resfrío (SM) (*LAm*) cold
resguardar ▸ CONJUG 1a (VT) to protect, shield (**de** from)
(VPR) **resguardarse 1** (= *protegerse*) to defend o.s., protect o.s.
2 (= *obrar con cautela*) to proceed with caution
resguardo (SM) **1** [*de compra*] slip, receipt; [*de cheque*] stub ▸ **resguardo de consigna** cloakroom ticket, cloakroom check (*EEUU*)
2 (= *protección*) defence, defense (*EEUU*), protection • **servir de ~ a algn** to protect sb
3 (*Náut*) sea room
residencia (SF) **1** (= *casa*) residence • **la reunión tuvo lugar en la ~ del primer ministro** the meeting took place at the prime minister's residence • **segunda ~** second home ▸ **residencia canina** dogs' home, kennels (*pl*), kennel (*EEUU*) ▸ **residencia de estudiantes** hall of residence ▸ **residencia oficial** official residence ▸ **residencia para ancianos, residencia para jubilados** residential home, old people's home ▸ **residencia sanitaria** hospital ▸ **residencia universitaria** hall of residence
2 (= *domicilio*) residence • **fijó su ~ en Barcelona** he took up residence in Barcelona • **con ~ en Bogotá** resident in Bogotá
3 (= *hotel*) guest house, boarding house
4 (= *estancia*) residence • **la conoció durante su ~ en Madrid** (*frm*) he got to know her during his residence *o* while he was living in Madrid • **permiso de ~** residence permit
5 (*Jur*) (= *investigación*) investigation, inquiry
6 (*And*) (*Jur*) ▸ **residencia vigilada** house arrest
residencial (ADJ) residential
(SF) (*And, Cono Sur*) boarding house, small hotel

r

residenciar ▹ CONJUG 1b VT (*Jur*) to investigate
VPR **residenciarse** (*frm*) to take up residence, establish o.s., settle

residente ADJ, SMF resident • **no ~** non-resident

residir ▹ CONJUG 3a VI **1** (= *vivir*) to reside, live
2 • **~ en** (= *radicar en*) to reside in, lie in; (= *consistir en*) to consist in • **la dificultad reside en que ...** the difficulty resides in *o* lies in the fact that ... • **la autoridad reside en el gobernador** authority rests with the governor

residual ADJ residual, residuary • **aguas ~es** sewage (*sing*)

residuo SM **1** (= *parte que queda*) residue; (*Mat*) remainder; (*Quím*) residuum
2 residuos (= *restos*) remains; (= *basura*) refuse (*sing*), waste (*sing*); (*Téc*) waste products • **~s tóxicos** toxic waste (*sing*)
▸ **residuos atmosféricos** fallout (*sing*)
▸ **residuos nucleares** nuclear waste (*sing*)
▸ **residuos radiactivos** radioactive waste (*sing*) ▸ **residuos sólidos** solid waste (*sing*)

resignación SF resignation

resignadamente ADV resignedly, with resignation

resignado ADJ resigned

resignar ▹ CONJUG 1a VT (*frm*) [+ *puesto*] to resign; [+ *mando*] to hand over (**en** to)
VPR **resignarse** to resign o.s. (**a, con** to) • **~se a hacer algo** to resign o.s. to doing sth

resina SF resin

resinoso ADJ resinous

resistencia SF **1** (= *oposición*) resistance • **la Resistencia** (*Hist*) the Resistance • **los acusaron de ~ a la autoridad** they were charged with resisting arrest • **ofrecer** *o* **oponer ~** to offer resistance, resist
▸ **resistencia pasiva** passive resistance
2 (= *aguante*) stamina • **los alpinistas necesitan mucha ~** mountaineers need lots of stamina • **el maratón es una carrera de ~** the marathon is an endurance race • **escribir una tesis es una prueba de ~** doing a thesis is a test of endurance • **carrera de ~** long-distance race
3 (*a la enfermedad, al frío*) resistance
4 [*de materiales*] strength • **este plástico es valorado por su ~** this plastic is valued for its strength
5 (*Elec*) (= *cualidad*) resistance; (= *componente de circuito*) resistor; [*de plancha, secador*] element

resistente ADJ (= *que ofrece resistencia*) resistant (**a** to); [*tela*] hard-wearing, tough; [*ropa*] strong; (*Bot*) hardy • **~ al calor** resistant to heat, heat-resistant • **~ al fuego** fireproof • **hacerse ~** (*Med*) to build up a resistance (**a** to)
SMF resistance fighter

resistible ADJ resistible

resistir ▹ CONJUG 3a VT **1** [+ *peso*] to bear, take, support; [+ *presión*] to take, withstand
2 [+ *ataque, tentación*] to resist; [+ *propuesta*] to resist, oppose, make a stand against • **resisto todo menos la tentación** I can resist anything but temptation
3 (= *tolerar*) to put up with, endure • **no puedo ~ este frío** I can't bear *o* stand this cold • **no lo resisto un momento más** I'm not putting up with this a moment longer
4 • **~le la mirada a algn** to stare sb out
VI **1** (= *oponer resistencia*) to resist
2 (= *durar*) to last (out), hold out • **el equipo no puede ~ mucho tiempo más** the team can't last *o* hold out much longer • **el coche resiste todavía** the car is still holding out *o* going
3 (= *soportar peso*) • **¿~á la silla?** will the chair take it?
VPR **resistirse 1** (= *oponer resistencia*) to resist
2 (= *no estar dispuesto*) • **~se a hacer algo** to be reluctant to do sth, resist doing sth • **no me resisto a citar algunos versos** I can't resist quoting a few lines • **me resisto a creerlo** I find it hard to believe
3 (= *encontrar difícil*) • **se me resiste la química** I'm not very good at chemistry

resituar ▹ CONJUG 1e VT [+ *país*] to put back on track; [+ *debate, concepto*] to redefine

resma SF ream

resobado ADJ hackneyed, trite, well-worn

resobar ▹ CONJUG 1a VT **1** (= *manosear*) to finger, paw
2 [+ *tema*] to work to death

resobrino/a SM/F first cousin once removed

resol SM glare of the sun

resolana SF (*LAm*) (= *resol*) glare of the sun; (= *sitio*) sunspot, suntrap

resolano SM sunspot, suntrap

resollar ▹ CONJUG 1l VI **1** (= *respirar*) to breathe noisily; (= *jadear*) to puff and pant
2 (*fig*) • **escuchar sin ~** to listen without saying a word in reply • **hace tiempo que no resuella** it's a long time since we heard from him

resoltarse ▹ CONJUG 1l VPR (*And*) to overstep the mark

resolución SF **1** (= *decisión*) decision • **tomar una ~** to take a decision ▸ **resolución fatal** decision to take one's own life
2 [*de problema*] (= *acción*) solving; (= *respuesta*) solution • **el problema no tiene ~** there is no solution to the problem
3 [*de conflicto*] resolution
4 (*Jur*) ▸ **resolución judicial** legal ruling
5 (= *determinación*) resolve, determination • **obrar con ~** to act with determination
6 (*frm*) (= *resumen*) • **en ~** in a word, in short, to sum up
7 (*Inform*) • **alta ~** high resolution • **baja ~** low resolution
8 (*Cono Sur*) (= *terminación*) finishing, completion

resolutivo ADJ decisive

resoluto ADJ = **resuelto**

resolver ▹ CONJUG 2h (PP: **resuelto**) VT **1** [+ *problema*] to solve; [+ *duda*] to settle; [+ *asunto*] to decide, settle; [+ *crimen*] to solve • **crimen sin ~** unsolved crime
2 (*Quím*) to dissolve
3 [+ *cuerpo de materiales*] to analyse, divide up, resolve (**en** into)
VI **1** (= *juzgar*) to rule, decide • **~ a favor de algn** to rule *o* decide in sb's favour
2 (= *decidirse por*) • **~ hacer algo** to resolve to do sth
VPR **resolverse 1** [*problema*] to resolve itself, work out
2 (= *decidir*) to decide, make up one's mind • **~se a hacer algo** to resolve to do sth • **~se por algo** to decide on sth • **hay que ~se por el uno o el otro** you'll have to make up your mind one way or the other
3 (*frm*) • **~se en** to be transformed into • **todo se resolvió en una riña más** it all came down to one more quarrel

resonador SM resonator

resonancia SF **1** (= *reverberación*) resonance; (= *eco*) echo
2 (*Med*) (*tb* **resonancia magnética**) magnetic resonance scanning
3 (= *consecuencia*) wide impact, wide effect • **tener ~** to have repercussions, have a far-reaching effect

resonante ADJ **1** (= *que resuena*) resonant; (= *sonoro*) ringing, resounding
2 [*éxito*] tremendous, resounding

resonar ▹ CONJUG 1l VI to resound, ring (**de** with)

resondrar* ▹ CONJUG 1a VT (*And, Cono Sur*) to tell off, tick off*

resongar ▹ CONJUG 1a VT (*LAm*) = **rezongar**

resoplar ▹ CONJUG 1a VI **1** (*con ira*) to snort
2 (*por cansancio*) to puff

resoplido SM **1** (*de cansancio*) puff, puffing; (*de ira*) snort
2 (= *respiración fuerte*) • **dar ~s** [*persona*] to breathe heavily, puff; [*motor*] to chug, puff
3 (= *exabrupto*) sharp answer

resorber ▹ CONJUG 2a VT to reabsorb

resorción SF resorption, reabsorption

resorte SM **1** (= *muelle*) spring
2 (= *medio*) means, expedient; (= *enchufe*) contact; (= *influencia*) influence • **tocar ~s** to pull strings • **tocar todos los ~s** to use all one's influence, pull all the strings one can
3 (*LAm**) (= *incumbencia*) concern; (= *competencia*) province • **no es de mi ~** it's not my concern *o* province

resortera SF (*Méx*) catapult (*Brit*), slingshot (*EEUU*)

respaldar ▹ CONJUG 1a VT **1** [+ *documento*] to endorse
2 (= *apoyar*) to back, support
3 (*Inform*) to support
4 (= *garantizar*) to guarantee
VPR **respaldarse 1** (= *apoyarse*) • **~se con** *o* **en** to base one's arguments on
2 (= *reclinarse*) to lean back (**contra** against, **en** on)

respaldo SM **1** [*de silla*] back; [*de cama*] head
2 [*de documento*] (= *dorso*) back; (= *cosa escrita*) endorsement • **firmar al** *o* **en el ~** to sign on the back
3 (= *apoyo*) support, backing; (*LAm*) (= *ayuda*) help; (= *garantía*) guarantee • **operación de ~** back-up operation, support operation
4 (*Hort*) wall

respectar ▹ CONJUG 1a VT • **por lo que respecta a** as for, with regard to

respectivamente ADV respectively

respectivo ADJ **1** (= *correspondiente*) respective
2 • **en lo ~ a** as regards, with regard to

respecto SM • **al ~** on this matter • **a ese ~** in that respect • **no sé nada al ~** I know nothing about it • **bajo ese ~** in that respect • **(con) ~ a** • **~ de** with regard to, in relation to • **(con) ~ a mí** as for me

respetabilidad SF respectability

respetable ADJ respectable
SM • **el ~** (*Teat*) the audience; (*hum*) the public

respetablemente ADV respectably

respetado ADJ well-respected

respetar ▹ CONJUG 1a VT **1** [+ *persona, derecho*] to respect • **respeto tu decisión** I respect your decision • **nunca ha respetado a sus padres** she has never respected *o* had any respect for her parents • **hacerse ~** to win respect, earn respect • **"respetad las plantas"** "be careful of the plants"
2 (= *obedecer*) to observe • **respeten las normas de seguridad** observe the safety regulations • **no respetan los semáforos** they ignore the traffic lights, they do not observe the traffic lights
3 (= *conservar*) to conserve • **al remodelar la zona ~on las murallas romanas** when they redeveloped the area they conserved the Roman walls
VPR **respetarse** (*reflexivo*) to have self-respect, respect o.s.; (*mutuo*) to respect each other • **no se respeta a sí misma** she has no self-respect • **un periodista que se**

respete no revela sus fuentes no self-respecting journalist would reveal his sources

respeto (SM) 1 (= *consideración*) respect • ~ a la opinión ajena respect for other people's opinion • ~ a las personas mayores respect for one's elders • con todos mis ~s, creo que se equivoca with all due respect, I think you're wrong • ~ a *o* de sí mismo self-respect • ¡un ~! show some respect! • faltar al ~ a algn to be disrespectful to sb, be rude to sb • guardar ~ a algn to respect sb • perder el ~ a algn to lose one's respect for sb • por ~ a algn out of consideration for sb • presentar sus ~s a algn to pay one's respects to sb • tener ~ a algn to respect sb • MODISMO: • campar por sus ~s to do as one pleases
2* (= *miedo*) • volar me impone mucho ~ I'm very wary of flying • le tengo mucho ~ a las tormentas I'm fearful of thunderstorms
3† • de ~ best, reserve (*antes de s*) • cuarto de ~ best room • estar de ~ to be dressed up

respetuosamente (ADV) respectfully

respetuosidad (SF) respectfulness

respetuoso (ADJ) respectful

réspice (SM) (*frm*) 1 (= *respuesta*) sharp answer, curt reply
2 (= *reprensión*) severe reprimand

respingado (ADJ) snub, turned-up

respingar ▷ CONJUG 1h (VI) 1 [*vestido*] to ride up
2 [*caballo*] to shy, balk
3 (= *mostrarse reticente*) to show o.s. unwilling, dig one's heels in

respingo (SM) 1 (= *sobresalto*) start, jump • dar un ~ to start, jump
2 (*Cos*) • la chaqueta me hace un ~ aquí the jacket rides up here
3 = réspice

respingón (ADJ) turned-up

respingona (SF) *traditional Castilian dance*

respirable (ADJ) breathable

respiración (SF) 1 [*de persona, animal*] breathing • ejercicios de ~ breathing *o* (*más frm*) respiration exercises • llegué sin ~ I arrived breathless *o* out of breath • sus arriesgados saltos cortaban la ~ her dangerous leaps took your breath away • contener la ~ to hold one's breath • dejar a algn sin ~ to leave sb breathless, take sb's breath away • quedarse sin ~ to be out of breath • se quedó sin ~ después de correr tras el autobús after running for the bus he was out of breath • al ver aquello se quedó sin ~ the sight of it left him breathless *o* took his breath away ▸ respiración artificial artificial respiration ▸ respiración asistida artificial respiration (*by machine*) • está con ~ asistida she is on a ventilator *o* respirator ▸ respiración boca a boca mouth-to-mouth resuscitation • se le hizo la ~ boca a boca he was given mouth-to-mouth resuscitation, he was given the kiss of life ▸ respiración mecánica = respiración asistida
2 [*de lugar cerrado*] ventilation

respiradero (SM) 1 (*Téc*) vent, valve
2 (*fig*) (= *respiro*) respite, breathing space

respirador (SM) (*tb* respirador artificial) ventilator, (artificial) respirator

respirar ▷ CONJUG 1a (VI) 1 (= *tomar aire*) to breathe • no respires por la boca don't breathe through your mouth • respire hondo take a deep breath, breathe deeply • ~ con dificultad to breathe with difficulty • salí al balcón a ~ un poco I went out to the balcony to get some air
2 (= *descansar*) • estos niños no me dejan ni tiempo para ~ these children don't give me time to breathe • tengo tanto trabajo que no puedo ni ~ I'm up to my ears *o* eyes in work • sin ~ without a break, without respite
3 (= *sentir alivio*) to breathe again • ¡respiro! I can breathe again!, what a relief! • ~ aliviado to breathe a sigh of relief • ~ tranquilo to breathe easily *o* freely (again)
4 (= *hablar*) • no respiró en toda la reunión he didn't utter a word in the whole meeting • los niños lo miraban sin poder ~ the children watched him with bated breath
5 (= *ventilarse*) a [*fruta, vino*] to breathe
b (*Aut*) • levanta el capó para que respire el motor put the bonnet up to ventilate the engine
(VT) 1 [+ *aire, oxígeno*] to breathe • necesito ~ un poco de aire fresco I need to get some fresh air • se podía ~ el aroma de las flores you could breathe in the smell of the flowers • se respiraba un aire cargado de humo the air was thick with smoke
2 (= *mostrar*) [+ *optimismo, felicidad*] to exude, radiate • respira confianza she exudes *o* radiates confidence
3 (= *notar*) • se respiraba un ambiente festivo en la manifestación there was an air of festivity at the demonstration • se respiraba ya un ambiente prebélico there was a sense of war in the air • ¿cuál es el clima que se respira en el país tras el atentado? what is the feeling in the country following the bomb attack?

respiratorio (ADJ) [*insuficiencia, sistema, vías*] respiratory; [*problemas, dificultades*] breathing (*antes de s*), respiratory

respiro (SM) 1 (= *respiración*) breath • dio un ~ hondo he took a deep breath • lanzó un ~ de alivio she breathed a sigh of relief
2 (= *descanso*) [*de trabajo, esfuerzo*] break, rest; [*de ataque, preocupación*] respite • llevas toda la semana trabajando, necesitas un ~ you've been working all week, you need a break *o* a rest • los clientes no nos dan un momento de ~ the customers don't give us a moment's peace • su rival no le concedió ningún ~ his rival gave him no respite • trabajaba sin ~ she worked without respite • tomarse un ~ to take a break, take a breather*
3 (= *alivio*) [*de enfermedad, preocupación*] relief • las pastillas le dan algún que otro ~ del dolor the pills ease the pain for a while, the pills give her some relief from the pain • es un ~ saber que han encontrado trabajo it's a relief to know that they have found work • poder escaparse unos días a la playa es un ~ getting away to the beach for a few days is like a breath of fresh air
4 (= *prórroga*) extension • los acreedores acordaron conceder un ~ de seis meses en el pago de la deuda the creditors agreed to an extension of six months *o* agreed to grant six months' grace on the debt payment • el gobierno necesita un ~ antes de las elecciones the government needs a breathing space before the elections

respis (SM) = réspice

resplandecer ▷ CONJUG 2d (VI) 1 (= *relucir*) to shine; [*joyas*] to sparkle, glitter
2 (*de alegría*) to shine • ~ de felicidad to be radiant *o* shine with happiness

resplandeciente (ADJ) 1 (= *brillante*) shining; [*joyas*] sparkling, glittering
2 (*de alegría*) radiant (de with)

resplandor (SM) 1 (= *brillantez*) brilliance, brightness; [*de joyas*] sparkle, glitter
2 (*Méx*) (= *luz del sol*) sunlight; (= *calor del sol*) warmth of the sun; (= *brillo*) glare

responder ▷ CONJUG 2a (VI) 1 (= *contestar*) (*a pregunta, llamada*) to answer; (*en diálogo, carta*) to reply • la mayor parte de los encuestados respondió afirmativamente the majority of people surveyed said yes *o* (*frm*) answered positively • aunque llamen al timbre varias veces no respondas even if they ring the bell a number of times don't answer • respóndame lo antes posible please reply as soon as possible • respondió de forma contundente he gave a forceful reply • ~ a [+ *pregunta*] to answer; [+ *carta*] to reply to, answer; [+ *críticas, peticiones*] to respond to, answer • la primera ministra eludió ~ a las acusaciones de la oposición the prime minister avoided answering the opposition's accusations • ~ al nombre de [*persona*] to go by the name of; [*animal*] to answer to the name of • el detenido, cuyo nombre responde a las iniciales A. M., ... the person under arrest, whose initials are A.M., ...
2 (= *replicar*) to answer back • no me respondas don't answer me back
3 (= *reaccionar*) to respond • nunca se imaginó que la gente fuera a ~ tan bien he never imagined that people would respond so well • los frenos no respondieron the brakes didn't respond • si las abonas bien verás qué bien responden if you feed them well you'll see how well they respond • ~ a • no respondió al tratamiento he did not respond to the treatment • el pueblo respondió a su llamada the population answered his call *o* (*más frm*) responded to his call
4 (= *rendir*) [*negocio*] to do well; [*máquina*] to perform well; [*empleado*] to produce results • debes preparar un equipo de profesionales que responda you must train a team of professionals that can produce results *o* come up with the goods*
5 (= *satisfacer*) • ~ a [+ *exigencias, necesidades*] to meet; [+ *expectativas*] to come up to • este tipo de productos no responde ya a las exigencias del mercado this type of product no longer meets market demands • el equipo italiano no ha respondido a las expectativas the Italian team has not come up to expectations • la construcción de esta nueva carretera responde a una necesidad social this new road has been built in response to public need
6 (= *corresponder*) • ~ a [+ *idea, imagen, información*] to correspond to; [+ *descripción*] to answer, fit • una imagen de fragilidad que no responde a la realidad an image of fragility that does not correspond to reality • uno de los detenidos responde a la descripción del sospechoso one of those arrested answers *o* fits the description of the suspect
7 (= *responsabilizarse*) • yo ya te avisé, así que no respondo I warned you before, I'm not responsible • ~ de [+ *acto, consecuencia*] to answer for; [+ *seguridad, deuda*] to be responsible for; [+ *honestidad*] to vouch for • cada cual debe ~ de sus actos every person must answer for his or her actions • tendrá que ~ de su gestión económica ante un tribunal he will have to answer for his financial management in a court of law • yo no respondo de lo que pueda pasar I cannot answer for the consequences • la empresa no responde de la seguridad del edificio the company is not responsible for the security of the building
8 • ~ por algn to vouch for sb • yo respondo por él I can vouch for him
9 [*material*] to be workable, be easily worked
(VT) (= *contestar*) [+ *pregunta, llamada*] to answer • responde algo, aunque sea al azar give an answer *o* say something, even if it's

r

a guess • —**no quiero** —**respondió** "I don't want to," he replied • **me respondió que no sabía** she told me that she didn't know, she replied that she didn't know • **le respondí que sí** I said yes

respondida SF (*LAm*) reply

respondón* ADJ cheeky, lippy*, mouthy*

responsabilidad SF responsibility; (*Jur*) liability • **hay que exigir ~es al gobierno por los hechos** the government must be held accountable *o* responsible for what happened • **bajo mi ~** under my responsibility • **cargo de ~** position of responsibility • **de ~ limitada** limited liability (*antes de s*) ▸ **responsabilidad civil** public liability, public liability insurance ▸ **responsabilidad contractual** contractual liability ▸ **responsabilidad ilimitada** (*Com*) unlimited liability ▸ **responsabilidad objetiva** (*Jur*) strict liability ▸ **responsabilidad solidaria** joint responsibility

responsabilizar ▸ CONJUG 1f VT to blame, hold responsible • **~ a algn de algo** to hold sb responsible for sth, place the blame for sth on sb
VPR **responsabilizarse** • **no me responsabilizo de sus actos** I'm not responsible for her actions • **cada uno de nosotros debe ~se de sus actos** we must all accept responsibility for our actions • **~se de un atentado** to claim responsibility for an attack

responsable ADJ **1** (= *sensato*) responsible • **es un niño muy ~ para su edad** he is very a responsible boy for his age
2 (= *encargado*) responsible, in charge • **la persona ~ del departamento** the person in charge of the department, the person responsible for the department • **es ~ de la política municipal** she is responsible for *o* in charge of council policy
3 (= *culpable*) responsible • **el conductor ~ del accidente** the driver responsible for the accident • **cada cual es ~ de sus acciones** everybody is responsible for their own actions • **el fabricante es ~ de los daños causados** the manufacturer is liable for the damage caused • **ser ~ ante algn de algo** to be accountable *o* answerable to sb for sth • **hacer a algn ~ de algo** to hold sb responsible for sth • **hacerse ~ de algo** to take responsibility for sth • **no me hago ~ de lo que pueda pasar** I take no responsibility for what may happen
SMF **1** (= *culpable*) • **tú eres la ~ de lo ocurrido** you're responsible for what happened • **la policía busca a los ~s** the police are looking for the culprits
2 (= *encargado*) • **quiero hablar con el ~** I wish to speak to the person in charge • **Ramón es el ~ de la cocina** Ramón is in charge of the kitchen ▸ **responsable de prensa** press officer

responso SM prayer for the dead

responsorio SM response

respuesta SF **1** (= *contestación*) (*a pregunta, en examen, test*) answer; (*a carta, comentario*) reply • **preguntas y ~s** questions and answers • **demasiadas preguntas sin ~** too many unanswered questions • **su única ~ fue encogerse de hombros** his only reply was to shrug his shoulders
2 (= *reacción*) **a** (*ante un estímulo, ataque*) response • **la inflamación es una ~ defensiva del organismo** the inflammation is a defensive response of the body • **estoy satisfecho de la ~ positiva del público** I am satisfied with the positive response from the public
b (*a problema*) answer • **la falta de ~ del gobierno a los problemas medioambientales** the government's failure to answer environmental problems ▸ **respuesta inmune, respuesta inmunitaria** immune response

resquebradura SF, **resquebrajadura** SF crack, split

resquebrajar ▸ CONJUG 1a VT to crack, split
VPR **resquebrajarse** to crack, split

resquebrar ▸ CONJUG 1j VI to begin to crack

resquemar ▸ CONJUG 1a VT **1** (= *quemar*) to burn slightly; (*Culin*) to scorch, burn; [+ *lengua*] to burn, sting; [+ *planta*] to parch, dry up
2 (= *amargar*) to cause bitterness to, upset

resquemor SM **1** (= *resentimiento*) resentment, bitterness
2 (= *sospecha*) secret suspicion
3 (= *sensación*) burn, sting; (*Culin*) burnt taste

resquicio SM **1** (= *abertura*) chink, crack
2 (= *oportunidad*) opening, opportunity • **un ~ de esperanza** a glimmer of hope ▸ **resquicio legal** legal loophole
3 (*LAm*) (= *vestigio*) sign, trace
4 (*Caribe*) (= *pedacito*) little bit, small piece

resta SF (*Mat*) **1** (= *sustracción*) subtraction
2 (= *residuo*) remainder

restablecer ▸ CONJUG 2d VT [+ *relaciones*] to re-establish; [+ *orden*] to restore
VPR **restablecerse** (*Med*) to recover

restablecimiento SM **1** [*de relaciones*] re-establishment; [*de orden*] restoration
2 (*Med*) recovery

restallar ▸ CONJUG 1a VI [*látigo*] to crack; [*papel*] to crackle; [*lengua*] to click

restallido SM [*de látigo*] crack; [*de papel*] crackle; [*de lengua*] click

restante ADJ remaining • **lo ~** the rest, the remainder • **los ~s** the rest

restañar ▸ CONJUG 1a VT to stanch, stop, stop the flow of • **~ las heridas** (*fig*) to heal the wounds

restañasangre SM bloodstone

restar ▸ CONJUG 1a VT **1** (*Mat*) to take away, subtract • **réstale 10 a 24** subtract 10 from 24, take away 10 from 24 • **a esta cifra hay que ~le los gastos de comida** you have to deduct *o* subtract the meals allowance from this figure
2 [+ *autoridad, importancia*] • **~ autoridad a algn** to take away authority from sb • **le restó importancia** he did not give it much importance
3 (*Dep*) [+ *pelota*] to return
VI (*frm*) to remain, be left • **restan tres días para terminarse el plazo** there are three days left before the closing date • **ahora solo me resta hacerlo** it only remains for me now to do it, all I have to do now is do it

restauración SF **1** (= *acción*) restoration • **la Restauración** (*Esp*) *the restoration of the Spanish monarchy (1873)*
2 (= *hostelería*) • **la ~** the restaurant industry • **la ~ rápida** the fast-food industry

restaurador(a) SM/F **1** (*Arte*) restorer
2 [*de hotel*] restaurateur, restaurant owner
SM ▸ **restaurador de cabello** hair restorer

restaurante SM, **restaurán** [resto'ran] SM, **restaurant** SM restaurant

restaurar ▸ CONJUG 1a VT (*tb Inform*) to restore

restinga SF sandbar, shoal, mud bank

restiramiento SM (*Méx*) ▸ **restiramiento facial** facelift

restitución SF **1** (= *devolución*) return
2 (= *restablecimiento*) restoration

restituir ▸ CONJUG 3g VT **1** (= *devolver*) to return, give back (**a** to)
2 (= *restablecer*) to restore
3 (*Arquit*) to restore
VPR **restituirse** (*frm*) • **~se a** to return to, go back to

resto SM **1** (= *lo que queda*) rest; (*Mat*) remainder • **yo haré el ~** I'll do the rest • **no hace falta que te cuente el ~** I don't need to tell you the rest • MODISMO: • **para los ~s***: • **yo me quedo aquí para los ~s** I'm staying here for good
2 restos [*de edificio, muralla*] remains; [*de comida*] leftovers, scraps; [*de avión, naufragio*] wreckage (*sing*); (= *escombros*) debris (*sing*), rubble (*sing*) ▸ **restos de edición** remainders ▸ **restos de serie** leftovers, remainders ▸ **restos humanos** human remains ▸ **restos mortales** (mortal) remains
3 (*Dep*) (= *devolución de pelota*) return (of service); (= *jugador*) receiver • **estar al ~** to receive
4 (= *apuesta*) stake • **echar el ~*** (= *apostar*) to stake all one's money; (= *esforzarse al máximo*) to do one's utmost • **echar el ~ por hacer algo** to go all out to do sth, do one's utmost to do sth

restorán [resto'ran] SM (*LAm*) restaurant

restregar ▸ CONJUG 1h, 1j VT (*con cepillo, estropajo*) to scrub; (*con trapo*) to rub, rub hard

restricción SF (= *limitación*) restriction, limitation • **sin ~ de** without restrictions as to • **hablar sin restricciones** to talk freely ▸ **restricciones eléctricas** electricity cuts, power cuts ▸ **restricción mental** mental reservations (*pl*) ▸ **restricciones presupuestarias** budgetary constraints ▸ **restricción salarial** wage restraint

restrictivo ADJ restrictive

restrillar ▸ CONJUG 1a VT (*And, Caribe*) [+ *látigo*] to crack
VI (*Caribe*) [*madera*] to crack, creak

restringido ADJ restricted, limited

restringir ▸ CONJUG 3c VT to restrict, limit (**a** to)

resucitación SF resuscitation

resucitador SM respirator

resucitar ▸ CONJUG 1a VT **1** (*Rel*) [+ *persona*] to raise from the dead • **podía ~ a los muertos** he could bring back the dead
2 [+ *ley*] to resurrect
VI to rise from the dead • **al tercer día resucitó** (*Biblia*) on the third day He rose again

resudar ▸ CONJUG 1a VT, VI **1** (= *sudar*) to sweat a little
2 [+ *recipiente*] to leak slightly

resuello SM **1** (= *aliento*) breath; (= *respiración*) breathing • **corto de ~** short of breath • **sin ~** out of breath, out of puff* • MODISMO: • **sumir el ~ a algn** (*LAm*‡) to bump sb off*
2 (= *jadeo*) puff; (= *respiración ruidosa*) wheeze • MODISMO: • **meter a algn el ~ en el cuerpo** to put the wind up sb*
3 (*LAm*) (= *respiro*) breathing space; (= *descanso*) rest • **tomar un ~** to take a breather
4‡ (= *dinero*) bread*, money

resueltamente ADV (= *con determinación*) resolutely, with determination; (= *audazmente*) boldly; (= *firmemente*) steadfastly

resuelto PP de **resolver**
ADJ (= *determinado*) resolute, resolved, determined; (= *audaz*) bold; (= *firme*) steadfast • **estar ~ a algo** to be set on sth • **estar ~ a hacer algo** to be determined to do sth

resulta SF result • **de ~s de** as a result of • **estar a ~s de** (*esp Esp*) to keep track of, keep up-to-date with

resultado (SM) **1** (= *dato resultante*) [*de elecciones, examen, competición, investigación*] result; [*de partido*] score, result • **la publicación de los ~s económicos de la empresa** the publication of the company's economic results • **el ~ fue de empate a dos** the result was a two-two draw • **los ~s de la jornada futbolística** the football scores
2 (= *efecto*) result • **el pacto fue el ~ de meses de trabajo** the pact was the result of months of work • **dar ~** [*plan, método*] to succeed, be successful; [*tratamiento*] to produce results • **la jugada no ha dado ~** the move didn't come off* *o* wasn't successful • **la prueba no siempre da ~s fiables** the test does not always give *o* provide reliable results • **las negociaciones están dando ~s positivos** the negotiations are proving positive
3 (*Mat*) result

resultante (ADJ) resulting (*antes de s*), resultant (*frm*) (*antes de s*) • **~ de** resulting from
(SF) (*Fís*) resultant

resultar ▹ CONJUG 1a (VI) **1** (= *tener como resultado*) **a** (+ *adj, sustantivo*) to be • **varias personas ~on heridas en el atentado** several people were wounded in the attack • **el conductor resultó muerto** the driver was killed • **resultó ganador un escritor desconocido** the winner was an unknown writer • **varios corredores han resultado positivos** a number of runners have tested positive • **la operación resultó un fracaso** the operation was a failure, the operation resulted in failure (*frm*)
b (+ *infin*) • **resultó no saber nada de aquel asunto** he turned out to know nothing about that matter, it turned out that he knew nothing about that matter • **~ ser** to turn out to be • **resultó ser el padre de mi amigo** he turned out to be my friend's father • **si resulta ser verdadero** if it proves (to be) true, if it turns out to be true • **el causante del incendio resultó ser un cable de la luz** the cause of the fire turned out *o* proved to be an electric cable
c • **resulta que** it turns out that • **ahora resulta que no vamos** now it turns out *o* now it seems (that) we're not going after all • **dijeron que lo había hecho él solo, cuando resulta que tenía varios cómplices** he was said to have done it on his own, when it turns out that he had several accomplices • **al final resultó que era inocente** he proved *o* he turned out to be innocent in the end, in the end it turned out that he was innocent • **me gustaría ir, pero resulta que no tengo dinero** I'd like to go, but the thing is *o* the fact is that I haven't got any money
2 (= *salir*) to turn out, work out • **todo resultó bien** everything turned out *o* worked out well • **aquello no resultó muy bien** that didn't turn out *o* work out very well • **no resultó** it didn't work
3 (*frm*) (= *ser*) (+ *adj*) **a** (*uso impersonal*) • **resulta difícil decidir si ...** it is hard to decide whether ... • **su versión resulta difícil de creer** his story is hard to believe, it's hard to believe his story • **este trabajo está resultando un poco aburrido** this job is getting a bit boring • **resulta más barato hacerlo así** it works out cheaper to do it this way
b (*con complemento de persona*) • **me está resultando fácil** I'm finding it easy • **la casa nos resulta muy pequeña** the house is too small for us • **me resulta simpático** he seems like a nice guy to me
4 (*frm*) • **~ de** to be the result of, result from • **la mayor parte de sus problemas resultan de su falta de diplomacia** most of his problems are the result of a lack of tact • **¿quién sabe lo que ~á de todo esto?** who knows what will come of all this?, who knows what the outcome of all this will be?
5 (*frm*) • **~ en** to result in, lead to • **el latifundismo resulta en beneficios privados** large-scale landholding results in *o* leads to individual profits
6 (*Esp**) (= *agradar*) • **tu prima no es una belleza, pero resulta** your cousin is no beauty, but she's got something (about her) • **esa corbata no resulta con ese traje** that tie doesn't look right *o* go with that suit

resultón* (ADJ) attractive

resumen (SM) summary, résumé • **hizo un ~ de lo que dijo** she gave a summary *o* résumé of what he said • **en ~** (= *en conclusión*) to sum up; (= *brevemente*) in short
(ADJ INV) • **comparencia ~** brief concluding appearance • **exposición ~** summary • **programa ~** programme in summary form

resumidero (SM) (*LAm*) = **sumidero**

resumido (ADJ) condensed

resumir ▹ CONJUG 3a (VT) (= *recapitular*) to sum up; (= *condensar*) to summarize; (= *cortar*) to abridge, shorten
(VI) • **bueno, resumiendo, ...** so, to sum up, ..., so, in short, ...
(VPR) **resumirse 1** • **la situación se resume en pocas palabras** the situation can be summed up in a few words
2 [*asunto*] • **~se en** to boil *o* come down to • **todo se resumió en algunos porrazos** all it boiled *o* came down to was a few punches

resunta (SF) (*And*) summary

resurgimiento (SM) resurgence

resurgir ▹ CONJUG 3c (VI) **1** (= *reaparecer*) to reappear, revive
2 (*Med*) to recover

resurrección (SF) resurrection

retablo (SM) altarpiece

retacada (SF) foul stroke

retacado (ADJ) (*Méx*) full

retacarse ▹ CONJUG 1g (VPR) (*LAm*) to refuse to budge

retacear ▹ CONJUG 1a (VT) (*And, Cono Sur*) to give grudgingly

retachar ▹ CONJUG 1a (VT), (VI) (*LAm*) to bounce

retacitos (SMPL) (*CAm*) confetti

retaco (SM) **1*** (= *persona*) midget
2 (*Billar*) short cue

retacón* (ADJ) (*esp And, Cono Sur*) short, squat

retador(a) (ADJ) challenging, defiant
(SM/F) (*LAm*) (*Dep*) challenger

retaguardia (SF) **1** (*Mil*) rearguard • **a ~** in the rear • **tres millas a ~** three miles to the rear, three miles further back • **estar** *o* **ir a** *o* **en ~** to bring up the rear
2* (= *culo*) rear*, posterior (*hum*)

retahíla (SF) (= *serie*) string, series; [*de injurias*] stream

retajado/a (*Cono Sur*) (ADJ) (*Zool*) castrated, gelded
(SM/F) ‡ wanker**‡

retajar ▹ CONJUG 1a (VT) **1** (= *cortar*) to cut out, cut round
2 (*LAm*) (= *castrar*) to castrate, geld

retal (SM) remnant

retaliación (SF) (*LAm*) retaliation

retallones (SMPL) (*Caribe*) leftovers

retama (SF), **retamo** (SM) (*LAm*) (*Bot*) broom

retar ▹ CONJUG 1a (VT) **1** (= *desafiar*) to challenge
2 (*Arg**) (= *regañar*) to tell off, tick off*
3 (*Cono Sur**) (= *insultar*) to insult, abuse • **~ a algn algo** to throw sth in sb's face

retardación (SF) (= *enlentecimiento*) retardation, slowing down; (= *retraso*) delaying; (*Mec*) deceleration

retardado (ADJ) • **bomba de efecto ~** time bomb

retardar ▹ CONJUG 1a (VT) (= *frenar*) to slow down, slow up; [+ *marcha*] to hold up; [+ *tren*] to delay, make late

retardatriz (ADJ) delaying

retardo (SM) (*frm*) delay

retazar ▹ CONJUG 1f (VT) **1** (= *cortar*) to cut up, snip into pieces; [+ *leña*] to chop
2 (= *dividir*) to divide up

retazo (SM) **1** (*Cos*) remnant, bit, piece; **retazos** snippets, bits and pieces • **a ~s** in bits
2 (*Caribe*) bargain

RETD (SF ABR) (*Esp*) (*Telec*) = **Red Especial de Transmisión de Datos**

rete... (PREF) (*esp LAm*) very, extremely • **retebién** very well • **una persona retefina** a really refined person*

retemblar ▹ CONJUG 1j (VI) to shudder, shake (**de** at, with)

retemplar ▹ CONJUG 1a (VT) (*And, CAm, Cono Sur*) to cheer up

retén (SM) **1** (*Téc*) stop, catch; (*Aut*) oil seal
2 (= *reserva*) reserve, store • **tener algo de ~** to have sth in reserve
3 (*Mil*) reserves (*pl*), reinforcements (*pl*) • **hombre de ~** reserve • **estar de ~** to be on call
4 (*LAm*) [*de policía*] roadblock, police roadblock
5 (*Caribe*) (= *correccional*) remand home

retención (SF) **1** (= *contención*) retention ▸ **retención de tráfico** traffic delay, traffic hold-up
2 (*Econ*) deduction, stoppage ▸ **retención a cuenta** deduction at source ▸ **retención fiscal** deduction for tax purposes
3 (*Med*) retention
4 (*Telec*) hold facility

retener ▹ CONJUG 2k (VT) **1** (= *no dejar marchar*) to keep; [*la policía*] to detain, hold • **lo retiene su familia** his family is what keeps him there • **no intentes ~me porque pienso ir** don't try and keep *o* stop me because I'm going • **retuvieron a los inmigrantes en la aduana** they held *o* detained the immigrants at customs • **una llamada de última hora me retuvo en la oficina** a last-minute phone call held me up *o* kept me back at the office • **~ a algn preso** to hold *o* keep sb prisoner
2 (= *conservar*) [+ *datos, información*] to withhold; [+ *pasaporte*] to retain • **el Atlético ha conseguido ~ el título de Liga** Atlético managed to hold on to *o* keep *o* retain the league title
3 (= *memorizar*) to retain • **es incapaz de ~ los nombres de la gente** he's incapable of retaining people's names
4 (*Econ*) [+ *dinero*] to deduct
5 [+ *calor*] to retain; [+ *líquido*] to hold • **no puede ~ la orina** he can't hold his water
6 (*frm*) [+ *atención, interés*] to retain
7 (*frm*) [+ *deseo, pasión*] to restrain; [+ *aliento*] to hold
(VPR) **retenerse** to restrain o.s.

retenida (SF) guy rope

retentiva (SF) memory

retentivo (ADJ) retentive

reteñir ▹ CONJUG 3h, 3k (VT) to redye

reticencia (SF) **1** (= *renuencia*) unwillingness, reluctance
2 (= *reserva*) reticence, reserve
3 (= *ironía*) irony, sarcasm

reticente (ADJ) **1** (= *reacio*) unwilling, reluctant • **estar** *o* **ser ~ a hacer algo** to be

r

unwilling *o* reluctant to do sth • **se mostró ~ a aceptar** she was unwilling *o* reluctant to accept • **se declara ~ a meterse en política** he says he doesn't like the idea of getting involved in politics
2 (= *con reserva*) reticent, reserved
3 (= *irónico*) ironical, sarcastic
rético/a ADJ, SM/F Romansch
SM (*Ling*) Romansch
retícula SF **1** (*Ópt*) reticle
2 (*Fot*) screen
reticular ADJ reticulated
retículo SM **1** (= *red*) reticle
2 [*de medir*] grid
retina SF retina
retinol SM retinol
retintín SM **1** (= *tono sarcástico*) sarcastic tone • **decir algo con ~** to say sth sarcastically
2 (= *tilín*) tinkle, tinkling; [*de llaves*] jingle, jangle; (*en el oído*) ringing
retinto ADJ (*esp LAm*) very dark
retiñir ▷ CONJUG 3a VI (= *resonar*) to tinkle; [*llaves*] to jingle, jangle; (*en el oído*) to go on ringing, go on ringing in one's ears
retirada SF **1** (*Mil*) retreat, withdrawal • **batirse en ~** • **emprender la ~** to retreat, beat a retreat
2 [*de dinero, embajador*] withdrawal
3 [*de vehículo, objeto*] removal
4†† (= *refugio*) safe place, place of refuge
retiradamente ADV [*vivir*] quietly, in seclusion
retirado ADJ **1** [*lugar*] remote
2 [*vida*] quiet
3 (= *jubilado*) retired
4 (*Esp*††) • **la tiene retirada** he keeps her as his mistress
retirar ▷ CONJUG 1a VT **1** [+ *acusación, apoyo, subvención*] to withdraw; [+ *demanda*] to withdraw, take back • **han retirado su apoyo al Gobierno** they have withdrawn their support for the Government • **les ~on las subvenciones** they had their subsidies taken away *o* withdrawn • **retiró su candidatura a la Presidencia** he stood down from the presidential election, he withdrew his candidacy for the presidency • **la mayoría del electorado le ha retirado la confianza** he has lost the confidence *o* trust of the majority of the electorate • **~ la palabra a algn** to stop speaking to sb • **~ el saludo a algn** to stop saying hello to sb
2 [+ *moneda, sello*] to withdraw (from circulation); [+ *autobús, avión*] to withdraw (from service) • **estos aviones serán retirados de** *o* **del servicio** these planes are to be withdrawn from service • **el producto fue retirado del mercado** the product was withdrawn from the market *o* taken off the market
3 [+ *permiso, carnet, pasaporte*] to withdraw, take away • **le han retirado el permiso de conducir** he's had his driving licence taken away
4 [+ *dinero*] to withdraw • **fui a ~ dinero de la cuenta** I went to withdraw some money from my account
5 [+ *tropas*] to withdraw; [+ *embajador*] to recall, withdraw; [+ *atleta, caballo*] to withdraw, scratch
6 (= *quitar*) to take away, remove • **la camarera retiró las copas** the waitress took the glasses away • **le ~on todos los objetos afilados de la celda** all sharp objects were removed from his cell
7 [+ *cabeza, cara*] to pull back, pull away; [+ *mano*] to draw back, withdraw; [+ *tentáculo*] to draw in
8 (= *jubilar*) to retire, pension off

VPR **retirarse 1** (= *moverse*) to move back *o* away (**de** from) • **retírate de la entrada para que pueda pasar la gente** move back *o* away from the door so that people can get through • **~se ante un peligro** to shrink back from a danger
2 (= *irse*) • **puede usted ~se** you may leave • **el testigo puede ~se** the witness may stand down • **se retiró enfadado a la cocina** he withdrew to the kitchen in a huff • **~se de las negociaciones** to withdraw from the negotiations • **se ~on del torneo** (*antes de su inicio*) they withdrew from *o* pulled out of the tournament; (*después de su inicio*) they retired from *o* pulled out of the tournament • **tuvo que ~se del terreno de juego** he had to leave the pitch
3 • **~se (a su habitación)** to retire (to one's room *o* to bed) (*frm, liter*)
4 (*al teléfono*) • **¡no se retire!** hold the line!
5 (*Mil*) to withdraw, retreat
6 (= *jubilarse*) to retire (**de** from) • **mi padre se retira el año que viene** my father will be retiring next year • **cuando me retire de los negocios** when I retire from business • **se retiró anticipadamente** she took early retirement
retiro SM **1** (= *jubilación*) retirement • **un oficial en ~** a retired officer ▸ **retiro prematuro** early retirement
2 (= *pensión*) retirement pension, pension
3 (= *lugar*) quiet place, secluded spot; (*Rel*) retreat
4 [*de dinero*] withdrawal
reto SM **1** (= *desafío*) challenge
2 (*Cono Sur*) (= *reprimenda*) telling off, scolding
3 (*Cono Sur*) (= *insulto*) insult
retobado ADJ **1** (*LAm*) [*animal*] (= *salvaje*) wild
2 (*LAm*) [*persona*] (= *taimado*) sly, crafty; (= *rebelde*) rebellious; (= *terco*) obstinate; (= *hosco*) sullen; (= *caprichoso*) unpredictable, capricious
3 (*And, CAm, Méx**) (= *gruñón*) grumbling; (= *descarado*) saucy, sassy (EEUU), cheeky*
retobar ▷ CONJUG 1a VT **1** (*And, Cono Sur*) (= *forrar*) to line with leather, line with sacking, line with oilcloth; (= *cubrir*) to cover with leather
2 (*And*) [+ *pieles*] to tan
VI ▷ VPR
VPR **retobarse** (*LAm*) (= *obstinarse*) to be stubborn, dig one's heels in; (= *quejarse*) to grumble, protest
retobo SM **1** (*LAm*) (= *forro*) lining; (= *cubierta*) covering
2 (*Cono Sur*) (= *hule*) sacking, oilcloth
3 (*LAm*) (= *terquedad*) stubbornness; (= *protesta*) grumble, moan
4 (= *capricho*) whim
5 (*And, CAm*) (*Agr*) old stock, useless animals; (= *persona*) useless person; (= *objeto*) worthless object; (= *trastos*) junk, rubbish, garbage (EEUU)
6 (*LAm*) (= *resabio*) aftertaste
retobón ADJ (*Cono Sur*) = **retobado**
retocar ▷ CONJUG 1g VT **1** [+ *dibujo, foto*] to touch up
2 [+ *grabación*] to play back
VPR **retocarse** (*Esp*) to freshen one's make-up
retomar ▷ CONJUG 1a VT to take up again
retoñar ▷ CONJUG 1a VT **1** (*Bot*) to sprout, shoot
2 (= *reaparecer*) to reappear, recur
retoño SM **1** (*Bot*) sprout, shoot
2* (= *niño*) kid*
retoque SM **1** (= *acción*) touching-up; (= *último trazo*) finishing touch
2 (*Med*) symptom, sign, indication

retorcer ▷ CONJUG 2b, 2h VT **1** [+ *brazo*] to twist; [+ *manos, lavado*] to wring; [+ *hebras*] to twine, twine together • **~le el pescuezo a algn*** to wring sb's neck*
2 [+ *argumento*] to turn, twist; [+ *sentido*] to twist
VPR **retorcerse 1** [*cordel*] to get into knots, get tangled (up) *o* twisted
2 [*persona*] to writhe, squirm • **~se de dolor** to writhe in pain • **~se de risa** to double up with laughter
3 • **~ el bigote** to twirl one's moustache
retorcido ADJ **1** [*estilo*] involved
2 [*método, persona, mente*] devious
retorcijón SM (*LAm*) = **retortijón**
retorcimiento SM **1** [*de brazo*] twisting; [*de manos, ropa lavada*] wringing; [*de hebras*] entwining, twisting together
2 [*de estilo*] involved nature
3 [*de método, persona, mente*] deviousness
retórica SF **1** (*Literat*) rhetoric
2 retóricas* (= *palabrería*) hot air (*sing*), mere words
retóricamente ADV rhetorically
retórico/a ADJ rhetorical
SM/F rhetorician
retornable ADJ returnable • **envase no ~** non-returnable container/bottle
retornar ▷ CONJUG 1a VI (= *venir*) to return, come back; (= *irse*) to return, go back
VT **1** (= *devolver*) to return, give back
2 (= *reponer*) to replace, put back
3 (= *mover*) to move back
retorno SM **1** (= *vuelta*) return • **viaje de ~** return journey • **operación ~** *traffic control operation for the mass return home after holidays or public holiday*
2 (*frm*) (= *recompensa*) reward; (= *pago*) repayment; (= *cambio*) exchange, barter; [*de regalo, servicio*] return
3 (*Elec*) ▸ **retorno terrestre** earth wire, ground wire (EEUU)
4 (*Inform*) ▸ **retorno del carro** (*tb Tip*) carriage return ▸ **retorno del carro automático** (*Inform*) word wrap, word wraparound
5 (*Méx*) (*Aut*) turning place • **"retorno prohibido"** "no U turns"
retorsión SF [*de brazo*] twisting; [*de manos, ropa mojada*] wringing
retorta SF retort
retortero* SM • **andar al ~** to bustle about, have heaps of things to do • **andar al ~ por algo** to crave sth • **andar al ~ por algn** to be madly in love with sb • **llevar** *o* **traer a algn al ~** to have sb under one's thumb
retortijón SM rapid twist ▸ **retortijón de tripas** stomach cramp
retostar ▷ CONJUG 1l VT to burn, overcook
retozar ▷ CONJUG 1f VI to romp, frolic, frisk about
retozo SM (= *holgorio*) romp, frolic; (= *jugueteo*) gambol • **~s** romping (*sing*), frolics
retozón ADJ **1** (= *juguetón*) playful, frisky
2 [*risa*] bubbling
retracción SF retraction
retractable ADJ retractable
retractación SF retraction, recantation
retractar ▷ CONJUG 1a VT to retract, withdraw
VPR **retractarse** to retract, recant • **me retracto** I take that back • **me retracto de la acusación hecha** I withdraw the accusation
retráctil ADJ **1** (*Aer*) retractable
2 (*Bio*) retractile
retraer ▷ CONJUG 2o VT **1** [+ *uñas*] to draw in, retract
2 (= *volver a traer*) to bring back
3 (*frm*) (= *disuadir*) to dissuade
VPR **retraerse 1** (= *retirarse*) • **se retrajo a la**

r

aldea para su convalecencia she withdrew to the village to convalesce
2 (= intimidarse) • se retrae cuando le preguntan algo she goes into her shell when she's asked a question
retraído ADJ (= tímido) shy, reserved
retraimiento SM (= timidez) shyness, reserve
retranca SF (LAm) brake
retrancar ▷ CONJUG 1g VT (LAm) to brake
VPR **retrancarse** (LAm) (= frenar) to brake, apply the brakes
retransmisión SF (TV, Radio) • Canal Cinco realizará la ~ del partido (TV) the match will be shown o broadcast on Channel Five; (Radio) the match will be broadcast on Channel Five • durante la ~ no habrá cortes publicitarios there will be no commercial breaks during the broadcast
▸ retransmisión en diferido delayed transmission ▸ retransmisión en directo live broadcast, live transmission
retransmitir ▷ CONJUG 3a VT 1 (TV) to show, broadcast; (Radio) to broadcast
2†† [+ recado] to relay, pass on
retrasado/a ADJ 1 (en una actividad) • estar o ir ~ to be behind • va muy ~ en química he is very behind in chemistry, he has a lot to make up in chemistry • estar ~ en los pagos to be behind in o with one's payments, be in arrears • vamos ~s en la producción we are lagging behind in the production
2 (en el tiempo) [persona] late • llegó ~ a la reunión he was late for the meeting, he got to the meeting late
3 (en el desarrollo) [país, pueblo, sociedad] backward • nuestro sistema universitario va ~ respecto a otros países our university system is very backward compared with o is behind that of other countries
4 (= no actual) [ideas, estilo] outdated, outmoded
5 [reloj] slow • tengo el reloj ocho minutos ~ my watch is eight minutes slow
6 (mentalmente) mentally retarded
SM/F (tb retrasado/a mental) (pey) mentally handicapped
retrasar ▷ CONJUG 1a VT 1 (= aplazar) [+ suceso, acción] to postpone, put off; [+ fecha] to put back • retrasó en una hora su comparecencia ante la prensa he postponed o put off his appearance before the press for an hour • el sorteo ha sido retrasado una semana the draw has been postponed for a week o put back a week • han retrasado la fecha del examen they've put back the date of the exam • quieren ~ la edad de jubilación they want to raise the retirement age
2 (= retardar) to delay, hold up • varios problemas burocráticos ~on la salida del avión a number of bureaucratic problems delayed o held up the departure of the plane • la nieve está retrasando el tráfico the snow is holding up o delaying traffic
3 [+ reloj] to put back • esta noche tenemos que ~ los relojes we have to put the clocks back tonight
VI [reloj] to be slow
VPR **retrasarse** 1 (al llegar) [persona, tren] to be late • siento haberme retrasado I'm sorry I'm late • el avión se retrasó más de cuatro horas the plane was more than four hours late
2 (en una actividad) to be late • siempre se retrasaba en el cumplimiento de sus promesas she was always late in fulfilling her promises • se han retrasado en el pago de los sueldos este mes they're late in paying the wages this month • se han retrasado en el pago del alquiler they're in arrears with the rent, they've fallen behind with the rent
3 [acontecimiento, producción] to be delayed, be held up • el inicio del campeonato se retrasó por la lluvia the start of the championship was delayed o held up by rain
4 (= quedarse atrás) (en los estudios) to get behind, fall behind; (andando) to lag behind • empezó a ~se en los estudios cuando cayó enfermo he began to fall o get behind in his studies when he fell ill
5 [reloj] to be slow
retraso SM 1 (al llegar) delay • perdona el ~ sorry for the delay • el ~ en la llegada de los bomberos the delay in the arrival of the fire brigade • nuestro vuelo ha sufrido un ~ de dos horas our flight has been delayed by two hours • ir con ~ to be running late • llegar con ~ to be late, arrive late • llegó con 25 minutos de ~ he was o arrived 25 minutes late
2 (en una actividad) delay • protestaron por el ~ en el cobro de sus salarios they complained about the delay in the payment of their wages • llevo un ~ de seis semanas en mi trabajo I'm six weeks behind with my work • las obras de la catedral se iniciaron con ~ the building work at the cathedral started late • el mitin comenzó con una hora de ~ the rally began an hour late, the rally was delayed (by) an hour
3 (en país, investigación) backwardness • el ~ cultural del país con relación a los países vecinos the cultural backwardness of the country compared to its neighbours • llevamos años de ~ en la investigación espacial we are years behind in space investigation
4 ▸ retraso mental mental deficiency • padece un leve ~ mental he has mild learning difficulties, he's slightly retarded
retratar ▷ CONJUG 1a VT 1 (Arte) to paint the portrait of; (Fot) to photograph, take a picture of • hacerse ~ (en cuadro) to have one's portrait painted; (en fotografía) to have one's photograph taken
2 (= representar) to portray, depict, describe
VPR **retratarse** (en cuadro) to have one's portrait painted; (en fotografía) to have one's photograph taken
retratería SF (LAm) photographer's, photographer's studio
retratista SMF (Arte) portrait painter; (Fot) photographer
retrato SM 1 (Arte) portrait; (Fot) photograph, portrait • MODISMO: • ser el vivo ~ de algn to be the spitting image of sb ▸ retrato hablado (LAm) Identikit picture
2 (= descripción) portrayal, depiction, description
retrato-robot SM (PL: retratos-robot) Identikit picture
retrechería SF 1 (= truco) dodge*, wheeze*, crafty trick; (hum) rascally trick
2 retrecherías (= encantos) winning ways, charming ways
3 (= atractivo) charm, attractiveness
retrechero ADJ 1 (= dado a trucos) full of dodges*; (= astuto) wily, crafty; (hum) rascally
2 (= encantador) winning, charming, attractive
3 (LAm) (= tacaño) mean; (= tramposo) unreliable, deceitful; (= sospechoso) suspicious
retreparse ▷ CONJUG 1a VPR to lean back
retreta SF 1 (Mil) retreat; (= exhibición) tattoo, display
2 (LAm) (= concierto) open-air band concert
retrete SM lavatory, bathroom (EEUU)
retribución SF 1 (= pago) pay, payment; (= recompensa) reward
2 (Téc) compensation
retribuido ADJ [esfuerzos] rewarded; [puesto] salaried • un puesto mal ~ a badly-paid post
retribuir ▷ CONJUG 3g VT 1 (= pagar) to pay; (= recompensar) to reward
2 (LAm) [+ favor] to repay, return
retro* ADJ INV 1 [moda] retro
2 (Pol) reactionary
SM (Pol) reactionary
retro... PREF retro...
retroacción SF feedback
retroactivamente ADV retroactively, retrospectively
retroactividad SF [de ley] retroactivity, retrospective nature • estas leyes carecen de ~ these laws do not have retroactive effect • la ~ de los aumentos salariales no es negociable backdating the wage increases is not negotiable
retroactivo ADJ retroactive, retrospective • ley con o de efecto ~ retroactive o retrospective law • un aumento ~ desde abril a rise backdated to April • dar efecto ~ a un pago to backdate a payment
retroalimentación SF (tb Inform) feedback
retroalimentador ADJ feedback (antes de s)
retroalimentar ▷ CONJUG 1a VT to feed back
retrocarga SF • de ~ breechloading • arma de ~ breechloader
retroceder ▷ CONJUG 2a VI 1 (= moverse hacia atrás) to move back, move backwards, go back, go backwards; [ejército] to fall back, retreat; [aguas] to go down • retrocedió unos pasos he went o moved back a few steps • la policía hizo ~ a la multitud the police made the crowd move back • tienes que ~ a la primera casilla you have to go back to the first square
2 [rifle] to recoil
3 (= desistir) to give up; (= rajarse) to back down; (ante un peligro) to flinch • no ~ to stand firm
retroceso SM 1 (= movimiento) backward movement; (Mil) retreat
2 [de rifle] recoil • cañón sin ~ recoil-less gun
3 (Com) (= recesión) recession, depression; [de precio] fall, drop
4 (Med) new outbreak
5 (Tip) backspace
retrocohete SM retrorocket
retrocuenta SF countdown
retrogradación SF retrogression
retrógrado ADJ 1 (Pol) reactionary
2 (= que retrocede) retrograde, retrogressive
retrogresión SF retrogression
retroiluminación SF backlighting
retronar ▷ CONJUG 1l VI = retumbar
retropropulsión SF jet propulsion
retroproyección SF (con retroproyector) overhead projection; (Cine) (= efecto especial) back projection
retroproyector SM overhead projector
retrospección SF retrospection
retrospectiva SF 1 (Arte) retrospective, retrospective exhibition
2 • en ~ with hindsight
retrospectivamente ADV retrospectively; [considerar] in retrospect
retrospectivo ADJ retrospective • escena retrospectiva flashback • mirada retrospectiva backward glance, look back (a at)
retrotraer ▷ CONJUG 2o VT to carry back (in time), take back • retrotrajo su relato a los tiempos del abuelo he carried his tale back into his grandfather's day • ahora podemos ~ su origen al siglo XI now we can take its origin further back to the 11th century

r

• **piensa ~ el problema a su origen** he hopes to trace the problem back to its origin
retroventa SF resale • **precio de ~** resale price
retroviral ADJ retroviral
retrovírico ADJ retroviral
retrovirus SM INV retrovirus
retrovisión SF hindsight; (*Cine*) flashback, flashback technique
retrovisor SM (*tb* **espejo retrovisor**) driving mirror, rear-view mirror
retrucar ▸ CONJUG 1g VI **1** [+ *argumento*] to turn against its user
2 (*Cono Sur*) (= *replicar*) to retort • **le retruqué diciendo que …** I retorted to him that …
3 (*Billar*) to kiss
retruécano SM pun, play on words
retruque SM **1** (*And, Cono Sur*) sharp retort
2 • **de ~** (*Cono Sur, Méx*) on the rebound
retuit SM (PL: **retuits**) (*en Twitter*) retweet
retuitear ▸ CONJUG 1a VT (*en Twitter*) to retweet
retumbante ADJ **1** (= *que retumba*) booming, rumbling; (= *sonoro*) resounding
2 (= *enfático*) bombastic
retumbar ▸ CONJUG 1a VI **1** [*artillería*] to boom, thunder; [*trueno*] to roll, crash • **la cascada retumbaba a lo lejos** the waterfall roared in the distance
2 [*voz, pasos*] to echo • **la caverna retumbaba con nuestros pasos** the cave echoed with our steps • **sus palabras retumban en mi cabeza** his words are still reverberating in my mind
retumbo SM [*de artillería*] boom, thunder; [*de trueno*] roll, rolling, crash, crashing; [*de voz*] boom, booming; [*de pasos*] echo
reubicación SF [*de trabajadores, empresas*] relocation; [*de comunidad, pueblo*] resettlement
reubicar ▸ CONJUG 1g VT [+ *trabajador, empresa*] to relocate; [+ *comunidad, pueblo*] to resettle
reuma SM, **reúma** SM rheumatism
reumático ADJ rheumatic
reumatismo SM rheumatism
reumatoide ADJ rheumatoid
reunido ADJ • **está ~** (*Esp*) he's in a meeting • **el jefe está ~ con el director** the boss is in a meeting with his director
reunificación SF reunification
reunificar ▸ CONJUG 1g VT to reunify
reunión SF **1** (*de trabajo, deportiva*) meeting; (*social*) gathering • **¿irás a la ~ de padres?** are you going to the parents' meeting? • **no pudo ir a la ~ familiar** he couldn't go to the family gathering • **celebrar una ~** to hold a meeting • **convocar una ~** to call a meeting ▸ **reunión de trabajo** business meeting ▸ **reunión de ventas** sales meeting ▸ **reunión en la cumbre** summit (meeting) ▸ **reunión ilícita** unlawful assembly ▸ **reunión informativa** briefing ▸ **reunión plenaria** plenary session
2 (= *gente reunida*) meeting • **el director se dirigió a la ~** the director addressed the meeting
reunir ▸ CONJUG 3a VT **1** (= *juntar*) to join, join together
2 (= *recolectar*) [+ *cosas dispersas*] to gather, gather together, get together; [+ *datos*] to collect, gather; [+ *recursos*] to pool; [+ *colección*] to assemble, make; [+ *dinero*] to collect; [+ *fondos*] to raise • **la producción de los demás países reunidos no alcanzará al nuestro** the production of the other countries put together will not come up to ours • **los cuatro reunidos no valen lo que él** he is better than the four of them put together • **~ esfuerzos** to join forces
3 [+ *personas*] to bring together, get together • **reunió a sus amigos para discutirlo** he got his friends together to talk it over
4 [+ *cualidades*] to combine; [+ *condiciones*] to have, possess • **la casa no reúne las condiciones** the house doesn't match up to requirements • **creo ~ todos los requisitos** I think I meet all the necessary requirements
VPR **reunirse 1** (= *unirse*) to join together; (*de nuevo*) to reunite
2 [*personas*] (*en asamblea*) to meet, gather; (*en casa*) to get together • **~se para hacer algo** to get together to do sth
3 [*circunstancias*] to conspire (**para** to)
reurbanizar ▸ CONJUG 1f VT to redevelop
reutilizable ADJ reusable
reutilización SF reuse, recycling
reutilizar ▸ CONJUG 1f VT to reuse
reválida SF final examination
revalidar ▸ CONJUG 1a VT (= *ratificar*) to confirm, ratify • **~ un título** (*Dep*) to regain a title
revalorar ▸ CONJUG 1a VT = **revalorizar**
revalorización SF, **revaloración** SF [*de moneda*] revaluation; (*Econ*) reassessment
revalorizar ▸ CONJUG 1f VT [+ *moneda*] to revalue; (*Econ*) to reassess
VPR **revalorizarse** [*divisa*] to rise; [*mercancía*] to rise in value • **el euro se ha revalorizado frente a la libra** the euro has risen against the pound
revaluación SF revaluation
revaluar ▸ CONJUG 1e VT to revalue
revancha SF **1** (= *venganza*) revenge • **tomarse la ~** to get one's revenge, get one's own back
2 (*Dep*) return match; (*Boxeo*) return fight
revanchismo SM revanchism
revanchista ADJ, SMF revanchist
revejido ADJ (*And*) weak, feeble
revelación SF revelation; [*de un secreto*] disclosure • **fue una ~ para mí** it was a revelation to me
ADJ INV • **el coche ~ del año** the surprise car of the year • **el diputado ~ del año** the surprise of the year among MPs
revelado SM developing
revelador ADJ [*información, documento*] revealing; (= *incriminador*) telltale
SM (= *sustancia*) developer
revelar ▸ CONJUG 1a VT **1** (= *descubrir*) to reveal • **reveló los nombres de sus cómplices** she revealed the names of her accomplices • **no quiso ~ su identidad** he did not want to reveal *o* disclose his identity, he did not want to identify himself • **~ un secreto** to reveal *o* give away a secret
2 (*frm*) (= *evidenciar*) to reveal, show • **su expresión revelaba desprecio** his expression revealed *o* showed contempt
3 (*Fot*) to develop • **todavía no hemos revelado las fotos** we haven't had the photos developed yet
VPR **revelarse** • **~se como**: • **se ha revelado como una gran pianista** she has turned out to be *o* shown herself to be a great pianist
revendedor(a) SM/F **1** [*de entradas*] ticket tout, scalper (*EEUU**)
2 (*Com*) (*al por menor*) retailer
revender ▸ CONJUG 2a VT **1** [+ *entradas*] to tout, resell, scalp (*EEUU**)
2 (= *vender*) to retail
revendón SM (*And*) middleman
revenido ADJ stale
revenirse ▸ CONJUG 3r VPR **1** [*pan, galletas, fritos*] to go stale; [*vino*] to go sour
2 [*pintura, escayola*] to dry out
3 (= *encogerse*) to shrink
4 (= *ceder*) to give way
reventa SF **1** [*de entradas*] touting, scalping (*EEUU**)
2 (= *venta al por menor*) resale • **precio de ~** resale price
SMF (= *persona*) ticket tout, scalper (*EEUU**)
reventadero SM **1** (= *trabajo*) tough job, heavy work, grind
2 (= *terreno áspero*) rough ground; (= *terreno escarpado*) steep terrain
3 (*And, Cono Sur, Méx*) (= *hervidero*) bubbling spring
4 (*Cono Sur*) = **rompiente**
reventado* ADJ (= *cansado*) exhausted
reventador(a) SM/F **1** (*en mitín*) troublemaker, heckler
2 (= *ladrón*) safe-breaker
reventar ▸ CONJUG 1j VT **1** (*por presión*) [+ *globo, neumático, tubería, ampolla*] to burst; [+ *espinilla*] to squeeze • **tengo una cubierta reventada** I've got a puncture, I have a flat tyre • **el ruido de las discotecas me revienta los oídos** I find the racket inside clubs deafening, the noise in clubs is enough to burst your eardrums • **"reventamos los precios"** "prices slashed" • **tanto alcohol le va a ~ el hígado** all this drink is going to do his liver in*
2 (*por una explosión*) [+ *puente, vehículo*] to blow up; [+ *cristales*] to shatter, blow out • **la granada le reventó la mano** the grenade blew off his hand • **los ladrones ~on la caja fuerte** the robbers blew (open) the safe • **~on la puerta de un disparo** they shot open the door
3 (= *estropear*) to ruin • **~ás la moto conduciendo así** you'll ruin the motorbike riding it like that
4 (= *agotar*) [+ *caballo*] to ride into the ground
5* (= *golpear*) • **lo ~on a palos** they beat the living daylights out of him* • **te voy a ~ a patadas** I'm going to kick your face in* • **si me desobedece lo reviento** if he doesn't obey me, I'll kill him*
6* (= *hacer fracasar*) [+ *plan, espectáculo*] to wreck; [+ *asamblea, mitin, ceremonia*] to disrupt; [+ *huelga*] to smash, quash; [+ *manifestación*] to break up • **le encanta ~ nuestros planes** he loves wrecking our plans • **un grupo de sindicalistas intentó ~ la intervención del conferenciante** a group of trade union members heckled the delegate's speech *o* tried to shout down the delegate during his speech
7* (= *fastidiar*) • **le revienta tener que levantarse temprano** he can't stand having to get up early • **me revienta que nos traten así** being treated like that really bugs me*
VI **1** (= *explotar*) [*globo, tubería, depósito*] to burst; [*neumático*] to burst, blow out; [*granada, proyectil*] to blow up; [*cristal*] to break, shatter • **la presa reventó e inundó el valle** the dam burst, flooding the valley • **parecía que las venas del cuello le iban a ~** it looked as if the veins in his neck were about to burst • **le va a ~ el pantalón** his trousers are going to split • **hacer ~** [+ *neumático*] to burst; [+ *costuras*] to split • MODISMO: • **a todo ~** (*Chile*) at the most • **es bastante joven, a todo ~ tiene 30 años** he's pretty young, 30 years old at the most • **no llegué tan tarde anoche, a todo ~ debían ser las once** I didn't get back so late last night, it must have been eleven at the latest
2 [*persona*] **a** (*por estar lleno*) • **no puedo comer más, voy a ~** I can't eat any more, I'm full to bursting • **necesito entrar al baño, voy a ~** I need to go to the toilet, I'm bursting*
b (*por enfado*) to explode • **cuando dijeron que no querían trabajar, reventé** when they told me they didn't want to work, I just exploded • **como esto dure un día más, creo que reviento** if this carries on one more day, I think I'll explode • **sus relaciones son tan tensas que van a ~ en cualquier momento**

relations between them are so tense that things are going to blow up at any moment
3 [*lugar*] • **el teatro estaba a ~** the theatre was packed full, the theatre was full to bursting • **más de 20.000 personas llenaron la plaza de toros a ~** more than 20,000 people packed the bullring, the bullring was full to bursting with more than 20,000 people
4 • **~ de: reventaba de ganas de decirlo todo** I was dying *o* bursting to tell him all about it • **~ de cansancio** to be worn out, be shattered • **~ de indignación** to be bursting with indignation • **~ de ira** to be livid, be absolutely furious • **~ de risa** to kill o.s. laughing, split one's sides (laughing)
5 • **~ por** to be dying to, be bursting to • **reventaba por ver lo que pasaba** he was dying *o* bursting to see what was going on • **revienta por saber lo que dicen** she's dying *o* bursting to know what they're saying
6* (= *morir*) to drop dead* • **por mí como si revientas** you can drop dead for all I care*
7 [*ola*] to break
VPR **reventarse 1** (= *romperse*) **a** (*por presión*) [*tubería*] to burst; [*pantalón, vestido*] to split
b (*por explosión*) [*depósito, tanque*] to explode, blow up
2* (= *agotarse*) • **se revienta a trabajar** he's slogging *o* sweating his guts out*, he's working his butt off (EEUU‡) • **el toro se reventó corriendo** the bull ran itself into the ground
3 (*Arg, Col, Uru**) to crash • **se reventó contra un poste** it crashed into a post
4 (*Méx**) to have a great time • **nos reventamos en la boda de Rosa** we had a great time at Rosa's wedding

reventazón SF **1** (*Cono Sur*) (= *colina*) low ridge
2 (*Méx*) [*de estómago*] flatulence
3 (*Méx*) (= *fuente*) bubbling spring

reventón SM **1** (= *explosión*) [*de neumático*] blowout; [*de tubería*] burst
2 (= *esfuerzo grande*) • **le dio un ~ al caballo** he rode his horse into the ground • **darse** *o* **pegarse un ~*** to slog *o* sweat one's guts out*, work one's butt off (EEUU‡) • **se da cada ~ de trabajar** he kills himself working
3 (*Esp**) • **dar un ~** (= *morirse*) to drop dead*
4 (= *cuesta*) steep slope; (= *subida*) tough climb
5 (= *apuro*) jam*, fix
6 (*Méx**) (= *juerga*) rave-up*
7 (*Cono Sur*) (*Min*) outcrop of ore
8 (*CAm*) (= *empujón*) shove, push

rever ▷ CONJUG 2u (PP: **revisto**) VT **1** (*Jur*) [+ *sentencia*] to review; [+ *pleito*] to retry
2 (= *ver de nuevo*) to see again, look at again

reverberación SF reverberation

reverberador SM reverberator

reverberar ▷ CONJUG 1a VI **1** [*luz*] to play, be reflected; [*superficie*] to shimmer, shine; [*nieve*] to glare • **la luz reverberaba en el agua** the light played *o* danced on the water • **la luz del farol reverberaba en la calle** the lamplight was reflected on the street
2 [*sonido*] to reverberate

reverbero SM **1** [*de luz*] play, reflection; [*de superficie*] shimmer, shine; [*de nieve*] glare • **el ~ de la nieve** the glare of the snow, the dazzle of the snow
2 [*de sonido*] reverberation
3 (= *reflector*) reflector
4 (*LAm*) (= *cocinilla*) small spirit stove
5 (*Caribe*) (= *licor*) cheap liquor

reverdecer ▷ CONJUG 2d VI **1** (*Bot*) to grow green again
2 (= *renacer*) to come to life again, revive
VT (= *reavivar*) to revive, reawaken

reverencia SF **1** (= *inclinación*) bow • **hacer una ~** to bow
2 (= *respeto*) reverence
3 (*Rel*) • **Reverencia** (*tb* **Su Reverencia, Vuestra Reverencia**) Your Reverence

reverencial ADJ reverential

reverenciar ▷ CONJUG 1b VT to revere, venerate

reverenciosamente ADV reverentially

reverencioso ADJ reverent, respectful

reverendísimo ADJ Most Reverend

reverendo ADJ **1** (*Rel*) reverend • **el ~ padre Pabón** Reverend Father Pabón
2 (= *estimado*) respected, revered
3* (= *solemne*) solemn
4 (*LAm**) (= *inmenso*) big, awful • **un ~ imbécil** a complete idiot

reverente ADJ reverent

reverentemente ADV reverently

reversa SF (*LAm*) reverse

reversible ADJ reversible

reversión SF reversion

reversionario ADJ reversionary

reverso SM (= *revés*) back, other side; [*de moneda*] reverse • MODISMO: • **el ~ de la medalla** *o* **moneda** the other side of the coin

revertir ▷ CONJUG 3i VI **1** [*posesión*] to revert (a to)
2 (= *volver*) • **~ a su estado primitivo** to revert to its original state
3 (= *venir a parar*) • **~ en** to end up as • **~ en beneficio de** to benefit • **~ en perjuicio de** to be to the detriment of

revés SM **1** (= *lado contrario*) • **el ~** [*de papel, sello, mano, tela*] the back; [*de prenda*] the inside • **siempre empieza las revistas por el ~** he always reads magazines from the back, he always begins magazines at the end • MODISMO: • **el ~ de la moneda** *o* **medalla** the other side of the coin
2 • **al** *o* **del ~** (*con sustantivo*) (= *lo de arriba abajo*) upside down; (= *lo de dentro fuera*) inside out; (= *lo de delante atrás*) back to front • **tienes el libro al ~** you are holding the book the wrong way round *o* upside down • **llevas los calcetines al ~** you've got your socks on inside out • **te has puesto la gorra del ~** you've put your cap on back to front • **has puesto los cables al ~** you've put the wires on the wrong way round • **llevas los zapatos al ~** you've got your shoes on the wrong feet • **volver al** *o* **del ~** [+ *prenda, objeto*] to turn the other way; [+ *argumento, situación*] to turn on its head
3 • **al ~** (*con verbo*) the other way round; (*como nexo*) on the contrary • **ponte al ~** turn the other way round • **Luis le dejó dinero a Gerardo, ¿o fue al ~?** Luis lent Gerardo some money, or was it the other way round? • **todo nos salió al ~** everything went wrong for us, nothing went right for us • **cuando tienes prisa lo haces todo al ~** when you're in a hurry you do everything wrong • **a mí no me produce ningún complejo, al ~, es un orgullo** I'm not embarrassed by it, on the contrary, I feel very proud • **al ~ de:** • **fue al ~ de lo que dices** it was the opposite of what you say • **al ~ de lo que se cree, ...** contrary to popular belief, ... • **entender algo al ~** to get hold of the wrong end of the stick • **y al ~** and vice versa • **cuando yo quiero salir él quiere trabajar, y al ~** when I want to go out he wants to work, and vice versa
4 (= *bofetada*) slap, backhand slap • **como me vuelvas a insultar te doy un ~** you insult me again and you'll get a slap *o* you'll feel the back of my hand
5 (*Dep*) backhand • **un ~ a dos manos** a two-handed backhand • **un ~ cruzado** a cross-court backhand
6 (= *contratiempo*) setback • **los reveses de la fortuna** changes in fortune • **sufrir un ~** to suffer a setback

revesado ADJ **1** [*asunto*] complicated, involved
2 (= *rebelde*) [*niño*] unruly, uncontrollable

revesero ADJ (*And*) treacherous

revestido ADJ covered • **~ de algo** covered with sth

revestimiento SM (*Téc*) coating, covering; (= *forro*) lining; [*de carretera*] surface; (*Mil*) revetment ▸ **revestimiento antiadherente** non-stick coating

revestir ▷ CONJUG 3k VT **1** (= *recubrir*) [+ *pared, suelo*] to cover (**de, con** with); [+ *tubo*] to sheathe (**de, con** in); [+ *fachada*] to face (**de, con** with, in) • **revestimos el suelo con láminas de corcho** we covered the floor with cork tiles • **revistieron el techo con fibra de vidrio** they lined the ceiling with fibreglass • **un armazón de acero revestido de hormigón** a steel frame clad in concrete
2 (*frm*) (= *presentar, tener*) to have, possess • **el acto revestía gran solemnidad** the ceremony was very solemn • **el asunto no reviste importancia** the matter is not important • **sus heridas no revisten importancia** his injuries are not serious
3 (*frm*) (= *encubrir*) • **revistió de ingenuidad sus comentarios maliciosos** he cloaked his barbed comments with apparent innocence
4 (*frm*) [+ *lenguaje, texto*] to lard (**de** with) • **revistió su discurso de frases grandilocuentes** he larded his speech with high-flown phrases
5 [*sacerdote*] to put on, don
VPR **revestirse 1** (*frm*) (= *recubrirse*) • **~se de paciencia** to summon up all one's patience • **se revistió de valor y fue a hablarle** he summoned all his courage and went to speak to her • **está revestido de autoridad** he is invested with authority • **los árboles se revisten de hojas** the trees are coming into leaf
2 [*sacerdote*] to put on one's vestments
3 (*frm*) (= *apasionarse*) to get carried away

reviejo ADJ (= *muy viejo*) very old; [*niño*] wise beyond his years

revientapisos SMF INV burglar, housebreaker

revirado* ADJ (*Cono Sur*) **1** (= *de mal genio*) bad-tempered, irritable; (= *revoltoso*) unruly, wild
2 (= *loco*) crazy

revirar ▷ CONJUG 1a VT to turn (round), twist (round)
VPR **revirarse 1** (*Caribe, Cono Sur*) (= *rebelarse*) to rebel
2 (*Cono Sur*) (= *enloquecer*) to go crazy
3 • **~se contra algn** (*Caribe, Cono Sur*) to turn on sb

revirón ADJ (*CAm, Caribe*) disobedient, rebellious, unruly
SM (*CAm, Caribe, Méx*) rebellion, revolt

revisación SF (*Cono Sur*), **revisada** SF (*LAm*) medical examination

revisar ▷ CONJUG 1a VT **1** [+ *texto*] to revise, look over, go through; [+ *edición*] to revise
2 [+ *cuenta*] to check; (*Econ*) to audit
3 (*Jur*) to review
4 [+ *teoría*] to reexamine, review
5 (*Mil*) to review
6 (*Mec*) to check, overhaul; (*Aut*) to service

revisión SF **1** [*de cuenta*] check; [*de teoría, método*] review ▸ **revisión aduanera** customs inspection ▸ **revisión de cuentas** audit ▸ **revisión salarial** wage review
2 (*Mec*) check, overhaul; (*Aut*) service

revisionismo SM revisionism

r

revisionista ADJ, SMF revisionist
revisor(a) SM/F **1** (*Ferro*) ticket collector, inspector
2 (*Cine, TV*) ▸ **revisor(a) de guión** script editor
3 (*Econ*) ▸ **revisor(a) de cuentas** auditor
SM ▸ **revisor ortográfico** spellchecker, spelling checker
revista SF **1** [*de información general*] magazine; (*especializada*) journal, review ▸ **revista científica** scientific journal ▸ **revista comercial** trade journal ▸ **revista de destape**† erotic magazine ▸ **revista de información general** current affairs magazine ▸ **revista del corazón** *magazine featuring celebrity gossip and real-life romance stories* ▸ **revista de moda** fashion magazine ▸ **revista gráfica**† illustrated magazine ▸ **revista juvenil** teenage magazine ▸ **revista literaria** literary review ▸ **revista semanal** weekly (magazine)
2 (= *sección*) section ▸ **revista de libros** books section ▸ **revista de toros** bullfighting news
3 (= *inspección*) inspection; (*Mil, Náut*) review, inspection • **pasar ~ a la tropa** to review *o* inspect the troops • **ahora pasaremos ~ a la actualidad deportiva** now we'll review today's sporting events • **¿ya has pasado ~ a todos los invitados?*** have you given all the guests the once-over, then?*
4 (*Teat*) variety show, revue
5 (*Jur*) retrial
6 (*And*) [*del pelo*] trim
revistar ▸ CONJUG 1a VT (*Mil*) to review, inspect; (*Náut*) to review
revistero/a SM (= *mueble*) magazine rack
SM/F (*en periódico*) (= *crítico*) reviewer, critic; (= *escritor*) contributor ▸ **revistero/a deportivo/a** sports journalist ▸ **revistero/a literario/a** literary critic, book reviewer
revisto PP *de* **rever**
revitalización SF revitalization
revitalizador ADJ revitalizing
SM stimulant
revitalizante ADJ revitalizing, invigorating
revitalizar ▸ CONJUG 1f VT to revitalize
revival SM (*Mús*) revival; [*de persona*] comeback
ADJ INV • **canción ~** hit song from the past
revivificar ▸ CONJUG 1g VT to revitalize
revivir ▸ CONJUG 3a VT **1** (= *recordar*) to revive memories of
2 (= *vivir de nuevo*) to relive, live again
VI **1** (= *volver a vivir*) to revive, be revived
2 (= *renacer*) to come to life again
revocación SF (*Jur*) revocation; (= *decisión contraria*) reversal
revocar ▸ CONJUG 1g VT **1** [+ *decisión*] to revoke, reverse; [+ *orden*] to cancel; [+ *persona*] to remove from his/her post, axe, ax (EEUU)
2 [+ *humo*] to blow back
3 (*Arquit*) (= *enlucir*) to plaster; (= *encalar*) to whitewash
4 (= *disuadir*) to dissuade (**de** from)
revocatoria SF (*LAm*) revocation, repeal
revoco SM **1** (*Jur*) revocation; (= *decisión contraria*) reversal
2 = revoque
revolar ▸ CONJUG 1l VI (= *alzar el vuelo*) to take to flight again; (= *revolotear*) to flutter about, fly around
revolcadero SM mudhole, mud bath
revolcar ▸ CONJUG 1g, 1l VT **1** [+ *persona*] to knock down, knock over; (*Taur*) to knock down and trample on
2* [+ *adversario*] to wipe the floor with*
3 (= *humillar*) to bring down, deflate
VPR **revolcarse 1** [*persona*] to roll about; [*animal*] to wallow; [*amantes**] to have a romp in the hay* • **~se de dolor** to writhe in pain • MODISMOS: • **~se en el vicio** to wallow in vice • **~se en la tumba** to turn in one's grave
2 (= *obstinarse*) to dig one's heels in
revolcón* SM fall, tumble • **dar un ~ a algn** to wipe the floor with sb* • **darse un ~ con algn** to have a roll in the hay with sb*
revolear ▸ CONJUG 1a VT (*Cono Sur*) [+ *lazo*] to twirl, spin
VI to fly round
revolera SF whirl, twirl
revolica SF (*CAm*) confusion
revolotear ▸ CONJUG 1a VI [*pájaro*] to flutter, fly about; [*mariposa*] to flit (about)
revoloteo SM [*de pájaro*] fluttering; [*de mariposa*] flitting
revolqué ▸ revolcar
revoltijo SM, **revoltillo** SM (= *confusión*) jumble, confusion; (= *desorden*) mess ▸ **revoltijo de huevos** scrambled eggs (*pl*)
revoltoso/a ADJ (= *rebelde*) rebellious, unruly; [*niño*] naughty, unruly
SM/F (= *alborotador*) troublemaker, agitator
revoltura SF **1** (*LAm*) (= *confusión*) confusion, jumble
2 (*Méx*) (= *mezcla*) mixture; (*Culin*) *scrambled eggs with vegetables*; (*Arquit*) mortar, cement
revolución SF **1** (*Téc*) revolution • **revoluciones por minuto** revolutions per minute
2 (*Pol*) revolution ▸ **Revolución Cultural** Cultural Revolution ▸ **Revolución de Octubre** October Revolution ▸ **revolución de palacio** palace revolution ▸ **Revolución Industrial** Industrial Revolution ▸ **revolución islámica** Islamic revolution ▸ **Revolución Verde** Green Revolution
revolucionar ▸ CONJUG 1a VT **1** [+ *industria, moda*] to revolutionize
2 (*Pol*) to stir up, sow discontent among
3 [+ *persona*] to get excited
revolucionario/a ADJ, SM/F revolutionary
revoluta SF (*CAm*) revolution
revolvedora SF (*Cono Sur, Méx*) concrete mixer
revolver ▸ CONJUG 2h (PP: **revuelto**) VT
1 [+ *líquido*] to stir
2 [+ *papeles*] to look through
3 [+ *tierra*] to turn over, turn up, dig over
4 (= *enredar*) • **¡deja de ~!** • **¡no revuelvas!** (*a niño*) stop messing about with things!, stop fidgeting! • MODISMO: • **~la** to mess everything up
5 (= *desordenar*) to mix up, mess up • **han revuelto toda la casa** they've turned the whole house upside down
6 [+ *asunto*] to go into, investigate • **~ algo en la cabeza** to turn sth over in one's mind
7 (*Pol*) to stir up, cause unrest among; [+ *persona*] to provoke, rouse to anger
8 • **~ los ojos** to roll one's eyes • **~ el estómago** to turn one's stomach
9 (= *envolver*) to wrap up
VI • **~ en** to go through, rummage in, rummage about in • **~ en los bolsillos** to feel in one's pockets, fumble in one's pockets
VPR **revolverse 1** (= *volver*) to turn round; (*en cama*) to toss and turn • **~se de dolor** to writhe in pain • **se revolvía en su silla** he was fidgeting about on his chair • **se me revuelve el estómago solo de pensarlo** it turns my stomach just thinking about it • **~se al enemigo** to turn to face the enemy
2 (= *enfrentarse*) • **~se contra algn** to turn on *o* against sb
3 [*sedimento*] to be stirred up; [*líquido*] to become cloudy
4 (*Meteo*) to break, turn stormy
5 (*Astron*) to revolve
6 (*And**) (= *prosperar*) to get a lucky break, have a change of fortunes; (*pey*) to look after Number One
revólver SM revolver
revoque SM (*Arquit*) **1** (= *enlucimiento*) plastering; (= *encaladura*) whitewashing
2 (= *enlucido*) plaster; (= *cal*) whitewash
revuelco SM fall, tumble
revuelo SM **1** [*de aves*] flutter, fluttering
2 (= *conmoción*) stir, commotion; (= *jaleo*) row, rumpus • **de ~** incidentally, in passing • **armar** *o* **levantar un gran ~** to cause a great stir
revuelta SF **1** (*Pol*) disturbance, riot • **las ~s populares del siglo pasado** the civil disturbances of the last century • **la ~ militar acabó con la democracia** the military uprising put an end to democracy
2 (= *agitación*) commotion, disturbance
3 (= *curva*) bend, turn
4 (= *vuelta*) turn • **dar vueltas y ~s a algo** to turn sth over and over in one's mind
revuelto PP *de* **revolver**
ADJ **1** [*objetos*] mixed up, in disorder; [*huevos*] scrambled; [*agua*] cloudy, turbid; [*mar*] rough; [*tiempo*] unsettled • **todo estaba ~** everything was in disorder *o* upside down • **los tiempos están ~s** these are troubled times • **tengo el pelo ~** my hair's all untidy *o* in a mess • **tener el estómago ~** to have an upset stomach, have a stomach upset
2 (= *inquieto*) [*adulto*] restless, discontented; [*niño*] mischievous, naughty; [*población*] rebellious, mutinous • **la gente está revuelta por abusos como ese** people are up in arms about scandals like this
3 [*asunto*] complicated, involved
SM **1** (*Culin*) *scrambled eggs with vegetables* ▸ **revuelto de gambas** *scrambled eggs with prawns*
2 (*And*) (= *mosto*) must, grape juice
revulsar* ▸ CONJUG 1a VT (*Méx*) to vomit, throw up
revulsionar ▸ CONJUG 1a VT (*frm*) • **~ a algn** to turn sb's stomach
revulsivo SM **1** (*Med*) enema, revulsive
2 (= *acicate*) • **el mal resultado electoral fue un ~ para la izquierda** the bad election results were a salutary lesson for the left
rey SM **1** (= *monarca*) king • **los Reyes inauguraron la exposición** the King and Queen opened the exhibition • **los Reyes Católicos** the Catholic Monarchs (*Ferdinand and Isabella of Aragon and Castile*) • **el rey de la selva** the king of the jungle • MODISMOS: • **se cree el rey del mambo** he really fancies himself*, he thinks he's the bee's knees* • **hablando del rey de Roma (por la puerta asoma)** talk of the devil (and he'll appear) • **lo mismo me da rey que roque** it's all the same to me, it's all one to me • **ni rey ni roque** no-one at all, not a single living soul • REFRÁN: • **a rey muerto rey puesto** off with the old, on with the new ▸ **rey de armas** (*Hist*) king of arms
2 Reyes (= *fecha*) Epiphany • **los Reyes Magos** the Magi, the Three Kings, the Three Wise Men • **¿qué te han traído los Reyes?** ≈ what did Father Christmas bring you?
3 (*en ajedrez, naipes*) king
4 (*uso apelativo*) pet* • **anda, rey, cómetelo todo** come on, pet, eat it all up*
ADJ INV • **el fútbol es el deporte rey** football is the king of sports

DÍA DE REYES
In the Spanish-speaking world, **los Reyes** or **El Día de Reyes** is the day when people traditionally receive presents for the Christmas season. When they go to bed on January 5, children leave their shoes outside their bedroom doors or by their windows in the expectation that the **Reyes Magos** (Wise Men) will leave presents beside them. They may already have written letters to **SS.MM. los Reyes Magos de Oriente** with a list of what they would like. For **Reyes** it is traditional to eat **Roscón de Reyes**, a ring-shaped cake studded with frosted fruits and containing a little trinket or coin.

reyerta SF quarrel
reyezuelo SM **1** (= *monarca*) petty king, kinglet
2 (*Orn*) • **~ (sencillo)** goldcrest
Reykiavik SM Reykjavik
rezaga SF (*LAm*) = **zaga**
rezagado/a ADJ • **quedar ~** (= *quedar atrás*) to be left behind; (= *estar retrasado*) to be late, be behind; (*en pagos, progresos*) to fall behind • **carta rezagada** (*And, Méx*) (*sin reclamar*) unclaimed letter
SM/F (= *que llega tarde*) latecomer; (*Mil*) straggler
rezagamiento SM (= *atraso*) falling behind, lagging behind; (*en pagos, progresos*) backwardness
rezagar ▸ CONJUG 1h VT (= *dejar atrás*) to leave behind; (= *retrasar*) to delay, postpone
VPR **rezagarse** (= *atrasarse*) to fall behind • **nos rezagamos en la producción** we are falling behind in production
rezago SM **1** (= *material sobrante*) unused material, material which is left over
2 (*Cono Sur*) (= *mercancías*) unsold goods (*pl*), remaindered goods (*pl*); (= *ganado*) cattle rejected at the abattoir
3 (= *vacas dispersas*) group of straggling cattle
4 (*And, Méx*) (*Correos*) (= *cartas*) unclaimed letters (*pl*)
rezar ▸ CONJUG 1f VT [+ *oración*] to say
VI **1** (*Rel*) to pray (**a** to)
2 [*texto*] to read, go • **el anuncio reza así** the notice reads *o* goes as follows
3 • **~ con** (= *tener que ver con*) to concern, have to do with • **eso no reza conmigo** that has nothing to do with me
4* (= *quejarse*) to grumble
rezo SM **1** (= *oración*) prayer, prayers (*pl*) • **estar en el ~** to be at prayer
2 (= *acto*) praying
rezondrada* SF (*And*) scolding
rezondrar ▸ CONJUG 1a VT, VI (*And*) = **rezongar**
rezongador ADJ = **rezongón**
rezongar ▸ CONJUG 1h VT (*LAm*) (= *regañar*) to scold
VI (= *gruñir*) to grumble; (= *murmurar*) to mutter; (= *refunfuñar*) to growl
rezongo SM **1** (= *quejido*) grumble, moan
2 (*CAm*) (= *reprimenda*) reprimand; (= *regaño*) scolding
rezongón ADJ grumbling, grouchy*, cantankerous
rezumar ▸ CONJUG 1a VT to ooze, exude
VI **1** [*contenido*] to ooze (out), seep (out), leak (out); [*recipiente*] to ooze, leak
2 (= *transpirar*) to ooze • **le rezuma el orgullo** he oozes pride • **le rezuma el entusiasmo** he is bursting with enthusiasm
VPR **rezumarse 1** [*contenido*] to ooze (out), seep (out), leak (out); [*recipiente*] to ooze, leak
2 (= *traslucirse un hecho*) to leak out, become known

RFA SF ABR (*Hist*) (= **República Federal Alemana**) FRG
RFE SF ABR = **Revista de Filología Española**
Rh ABR (= **Rhesus**) Rh • **soy Rh positivo** I'm rhesus positive
ría¹ SF estuary ▸ **Rías Altas** northern coast of Galicia ▸ **Rías Bajas** southern coast of Galicia
ría² ▸ **reír**
riachuelo SM brook, stream
Riad SM Riyadh
riada SF flood • MODISMO: • **hasta aquí llegó la ~** that's how bad things were
ribazo SM steep slope, steep bank
ribeiro SM *young white wine from Galicia*
ribera SF **1** [*de río, lago*] bank; [*del mar*] beach, shore; (= *área*) riverside
2 (*Agr*) irrigated plain
3 (*Cono Sur, Méx*) [*de campo*] riverside community; (= *chabolas*) shanty town, slum quarter
riberano/a ADJ, SM/F (*LAm*) = **ribereño**
ribereño/a ADJ (= *de río*) riverside (*antes de s*); (= *costero*) coastal
SM/F *person who lives near a river*, riverside dweller
ribete SM **1** (*Cos*) border
2 (= *adorno*) addition, adornment
3 ribetes (= *toques*) • **tiene sus ~s de pintor** he's got a bit of the painter about him
ribetear ▸ CONJUG 1a VT to edge, border, trim (**de** with)
ribo SM (*And*) [*de río*] bank; [*de mar*] shore
riboflavina SF riboflavin
ricacho/a* SM/F, **ricachón/ona*** SM/F fabulously rich man/woman; (*pey*) well-heeled bourgeois*, dirty capitalist*
ricamente ADV **1** (= *lujosamente*) richly
2 (= *estupendamente*) • **muy ~** very well • **viven muy ~ sin él** they manage very *o* perfectly well without him • **tan ~** very well • **he dormido tan ~** I've had such a good sleep • **comeremos tan ~** we'll have a really good meal
Ricardo SM Richard
ricino SM castor-oil plant • **aceite de ~** castor oil
ricito SM ringlet, kiss curl
rico/a ADJ **1** (= *adinerado*) rich, wealthy • REFRÁN: • **llueva sobre el más ~** to him who has more shall be given
2 [*suelo*] rich • **~ de** *o* **en** rich in
3 (= *valioso*) valuable, precious; (= *lujoso*) luxurious, sumptuous, valuable; [*tela*] fine, rich, sumptuous
4 (= *sabroso*) delicious, tasty • **estos pasteles están muy ~s** these cakes are delicious
5* (= *bonito*) cute, lovely; (*en oración directa*) • **¡rico!** darling! • **¡oye, ~!** hey, watch it!* • **¡que no, ~!** (*Esp*) no way, mate!* • **¡qué ~ es el pequeño!** isn't he a lovely baby! • **está muy rica la tía** she's a bit of all right‡ • **¡qué ~!** (*iró*) (isn't that just) great!
SM/F rich person • **nuevo ~** nouveau riche
rictus SM INV [*de desprecio*] sneer; [*de burla*] grin ▸ **rictus de amargura** bitter smile ▸ **rictus de dolor** wince of pain
ricura* SF **1** (= *sabrosura*) tastiness, delicious quality • **¡qué ~ de pastel!** isn't this cake delicious?
2 (= *hermosura*) • **¡qué ~ de criatura!** what a gorgeous baby!
3 (= *chica*) • **¡oye, ~!** hey, gorgeous!
ridi* ADJ ridiculous • **¡no seas ~!** don't be ridiculous!
SM • **hacer el ~** to make a fool of o.s.
ridículamente ADV ridiculously, absurdly
ridiculez SF **1** (= *dicho absurdo*) • **¡qué ~!** how ridiculous! • **no digas más ridiculeces** don't be so ridiculous
2 (= *insignificancia*) • **¿y no os habláis por una ~ así?** (do) you mean you've stopped talking to each other because of a silly little thing like that? • **¿solo vas a comer esta ~? ¡coge un poco más!** is that all you're eating? have a bit more!
ridiculización SF mockery
ridiculizador ADJ, **ridiculizante** ADJ mocking, derisive
ridiculizar ▸ CONJUG 1f VT to ridicule, deride • **~ a sus adversarios** to make one's opponents look silly
ridículo ADJ ridiculous • **¿a que suena ~?** doesn't it sound ridiculous?
SM • **hiciste el ~** you made a fool of yourself • **puso a Ana en ~ delante de todos** he made a fool of Ana in front of everyone, he showed Ana up in front of everyone • **no te pongas en ~** don't make a fool of yourself, don't show yourself up • **no tiene sentido del ~** he isn't afraid of making a fool of himself • **exponerse al ~** (*frm*) to lay o.s. open to ridicule
riego SM **1** (= *aspersión*) watering; (= *irrigación*) irrigation • **la política de ~** irrigation policy ▸ **riego por aspersión** watering by spray, watering by sprinklers ▸ **riego por goteo** trickle irrigation
2 (*Anat*) ▸ **riego sanguíneo** blood flow, blood circulation
riel SM **1** (*Ferro*) rail • **~es** rails, track (*sing*)
2 (*Téc*) ingot
rielar ▸ CONJUG 1a VI (*poét*) to shimmer (*liter*)
rielazo* SM (*CAm*) blow, smack
rielero/a SM/F (*Méx*) railroad worker
ríen *etc* ▸ **reír**
rienda SF **1** (= *correa*) rein • MODISMOS: • **aflojar las ~s** to let up • **empuñar las ~s** to take charge • **llevar las ~s** to be in charge, be in control • **soltar las ~s** to let go • **a ~ suelta** (= *con toda libertad*) without the least restraint; (= *con celeridad*) at top speed • **dar ~ suelta a** to give free rein to • **dar ~ suelta a los deseos** to really indulge o.s. • **dar ~ suelta a la imaginación** to let one's imagination run wild • **dar ~ suelta al llanto** to weep uncontrollably • **dar ~ suelta a algn** to give sb a free hand
2 (= *moderación*) restraint, moderating influence
riendo ▸ **reír**
riente ADJ (*liter*) **1** (= *risueño*) laughing, merry
2 [*paisaje*] bright, pleasant
riesgo SM risk (**de** of) • **esta operación presenta mayores ~s** the risks are higher with this operation, this operation is riskier • **un ~ para la salud** a health hazard *o* risk • **factor de ~** risk factor • **grupos de ~** risk groups • **de alto ~** high-risk • **seguro a** *o* **contra todo ~** fully comprehensive insurance policy • **a ~ de: a ~ de que me expulsen** at the risk of being expelled • **correr ~s** to take risks • **no quiero correr ese ~** I'd rather not take that risk • **correr el ~ de hacer algo** to run the risk of doing sth • **corres el ~ de que te despidan** you run the risk of being dismissed • MODISMO: • **por su cuenta y ~**: • **los que se adentren en el bosque lo harán por su cuenta y ~** those who enter the forest do so at their own risk • **la compañía autorizó los pagos por su cuenta y ~, sin consultar** the company authorized the payments on their own behalf, without consulting ▸ **riesgo calculado** calculated risk ▸ **riesgo profesional** occupational hazard
riesgoso ADJ (*LAm*) risky, dangerous
Rif SM Rif, Riff
rifa SF **1** (= *lotería*) raffle

2†† (= *riña*) quarrel, fight

rifar ▹ CONJUG 1a (VT) to raffle • **~ algo con fines benéficos** to raffle sth for charity

(VI) †† to quarrel, fight

(VPR) **rifarse 1*** (= *contender por*) • **~se algo** to quarrel over sth, fight for sth • **~se el amor de algn** to vie for sb's love

2 (*CAm*) (= *arriesgarse*) to take a risk

rifeño/a (ADJ) [*persona*] of/from Rif, of/from Riff; [*dialecto*] Riffian

(SM/F) Rif, Riff • **los ~s** the Rifs *o* Riffs, the Rif *o* Riff

(SM) (*Ling*) Riff

rifirrafe* (SM), **rifirirafe*** (SM) shindy*, row

rifle (SM) (= *arma*) rifle; (*Dep*) sporting rifle; (*Caza*) hunting gun ▸ **rifle de repetición** repeating rifle

riflero/a (ADJ) (*Cono Sur, Méx*) [*tirador*] ace, crack

(SM/F) **1** (*Mil*) rifleman/riflewoman

2 (*Cono Sur, Méx*) (= *tirador*) marksman/ markswoman

rígidamente (ADV) **1** [*moverse*] rigidly, stiffly

2 [*comportarse*] rigidly

3 (= *estrictamente*) strictly, harshly

4 (= *sin expresividad*) woodenly

rigidez (SF) **1** [*de material*] stiffness, rigidity; [*de pierna, tendón*] stiffness ▸ **rigidez cadavérica** rigor mortis

2 (= *inflexibilidad*) [*de actitud*] inflexibility; [*de carácter*] strictness, inflexibility

3 [*de expresión*] woodenness

rígido (ADJ) **1** (= *tieso*) rigid, stiff • **quedarse ~** (*gen*) to go rigid; (*de frío*) to get stiff, get stiff with cold

2 [*actitud*] rigid, inflexible

3 (*moralmente*) strict, harsh

4 [*expresión*] wooden, expressionless

rigor (SM) **1** (= *severidad*) severity, harshness; (= *dureza*) toughness

2 (*Meteo*) harshness, severity • **el ~ del verano** the hottest part of the summer • **los ~es del clima** the rigours *o* (*EEUU*) rigors of the climate

3 (= *exactitud*) rigour, rigor (*EEUU*) • **con todo ~ científico** with scientific precision • **una edición hecha con el mayor ~ crítico** an edition produced to rigorous critical standards

4 • **ser de ~** (= *esencial*) to be de rigueur, be absolutely essential • **después de los saludos de ~** after the usual *o* customary greetings • **me dio los consejos de ~** he gave me the advice you would have expected • **en ~** strictly speaking

5 • **un ~ de cosas** (*And*) (= *muchos*) a whole lot of things

6 (*Cono Sur**) (= *paliza*) • **dar un ~ a algn** to give sb a hiding*

rigorismo (SM) strictness, severity

rigorista (ADJ) strict

(SMF) strict disciplinarian

rigue (SM) (*CAm*) tortilla

rigurosamente (ADV) **1** (= *severamente*) severely, harshly

2 (= *con exactitud*) rigorously

3 (= *completamente*) • **eso no es ~ exacto** that is not strictly accurate • **un estudio ~ científico** a thoroughly scientific study

rigurosidad (SF) rigour, rigor (*EEUU*), harshness, severity

riguroso (ADJ) **1** [*control, dieta, disciplina*] strict; [*actitud, castigo*] severe, harsh; [*medida*] tough • **es muy ~ con sus empleados** he's very strict with his employees • **iban de luto ~** they were wearing deep mourning • **exigen un cumplimiento ~ de los acuerdos** they're demanding strict compliance with the agreement • **en ~ orden alfabético** in strict alphabetical order

2 [*invierno, clima*] harsh

3 (= *concienzudo*) [*método, estudio*] rigorous • **es fruto de una investigación rigurosa** it's a product of rigorous research • **un trabajo poco ~** a sloppy piece of work

4 (*liter*) cruel • **los hados ~s** cruel fate (*sing*)

rija (SF) quarrel, fight

rijio (SM) **1** (*CAm*) = **rijo**

2 (*CAm, Méx*) (= *espíritu*) spirit, spirited temperament (*of a horse*)

rijioso (ADJ) (*CAm, Méx*) = **rijoso**

rijo (SM) lustfulness, sensuality

rijosidad (SF) **1** (= *susceptibilidad*) touchiness, susceptible nature

2 (= *disposición para reñir*) quarrelsomeness

3 (= *deseo sexual*) lustfulness, sensuality

rijoso (ADJ) **1** (= *susceptible*) sensitive, susceptible

2 (= *peleador*) quarrelsome

3 (= *sensual*) lustful, sensual

4 [*caballo*] in rut

rila (SF) **1** (*And, Méx*) [*de carne*] gristle

2 (*And*) (= *excremento*) bird droppings (*pl*)

rilarse‡ ▹ CONJUG 1a (VI) **1** (= *agotarse*) to knacker o.s.*, get shagged out‡

2 (= *rajarse*) to back out, fall down on the job

3 (= *asustarse*) to be dead scared

4 (= *temblar*) to shiver

5 (= *peerse*) to fart**

rima (SF) **1** (= *consonancia*) rhyme • **octava ~** ottava rima • **tercia ~** terza rima ▸ **rima imperfecta** assonance, half rhyme ▸ **rima interna** internal rhyme ▸ **rima perfecta** full rhyme

2 (= *composición*) **rimas** verse (*sing*), poetry (*sing*)

rimado (ADJ) rhymed, rhyming

rimador(a) (SM/F) rhymester

rimar ▹ CONJUG 1a (VT), (VI) to rhyme (**con** with)

rimbombancia (SF) **1** (= *pomposidad*) pomposity, bombast

2 (= *ostentosidad*) showiness, flashiness

3 (= *resonancia*) resonance, echo

rimbombante (ADJ) **1** (= *pomposo*) pompous, bombastic

2 (= *ostentoso*) showy, flashy

3 (= *resonante*) resounding, echoing

rimbombar ▹ CONJUG 1a (VI) to resound, echo, boom

rímel (SM), **rimmel** (SM) mascara

rimero (SM) stack, pile, heap

Rin (SM) Rhine

rin (SM) **1** (*Méx*) (*Aut*) rim, wheel rim

2 (*Perú*) (*Telec*) metal phone token

rinche (ADJ) (*And, Cono Sur*) full to the brim, brimming over

rincón (SM) **1** (= *ángulo*) corner (*inside*)

2 (= *escondrijo*) corner, nook; (= *retiro*) retreat • **en un ~ de mi mente** somewhere in the back of my mind

3 (*esp LAm*) (= *terreno*) patch of ground

rinconada (SF) corner

rinconera (SF) **1** (= *mesita*) corner table, corner unit; (= *armario*) corner cupboard, dresser

2 (*Arquit*) wall between corner and window

ring ['rrin] (SM) (*esp LAm*) ring, boxing ring

ringla (SF), **ringle** (SM), **ringlera** (SF) row, line

ringlete (*And, Cono Sur*) (ADJ) fidgety*, restless

(SMF) fidget*, restless person

ringletear ▹ CONJUG 1a (VI) (*Cono Sur*) to fidget

ringorrango (SM) **1** (*en escritura*) flourish

2 ringorrangos (= *adornos*) frills, buttons and bows, useless adornments

ringuelete (SMF) (*Cono Sur, And*) (= *inquieto*) rolling stone (*fig*)

(SM) (*And*) (= *rehilete*) dart; (= *molinillo*) toy windmill

ringueletear ▹ CONJUG 1a (VI) (*And, Cono Sur*) = **callejear**

rinitis (SF INV) ▸ **rinitis alérgica** hay fever

rinoceronte (SM) rhinoceros ▸ **rinoceronte blanco** white rhinoceros

rinoplastia (SF) rhinoplasty

rintoso‡ (SM) (*Caribe*) skiver‡, shirker

riña (SF) (= *discusión*) quarrel, argument; (= *lucha*) fight, brawl ▸ **riña de gallos** cockfight ▸ **riña de perros** dogfight, dogfighting

riñendo *etc* ▹ **reñir**

riñón (SM) **1** (*Anat*) (= *órgano*) kidney • **me duelen los riñones** my lower back hurts

• MODISMOS: • **me costó un ~*** it cost me a fortune, it cost the earth • **tener el ~ bien cubierto*** to be well off • **tener riñones*** to have guts, be tough ▸ **riñón artificial** artificial kidney

2 (= *centro*) heart, core • **en el ~ de Castilla** in the very heart of Castile

riñonada* (SF) • MODISMO: • **me costó una ~** it cost the earth, it cost me a fortune

riñonera (SF) money belt, money pouch

riñonudo* (ADJ) tough

río¹ (SM) **1** (= *corriente de agua*) river • **es un río de oro** it's a gold mine • REFRANES: • **a río revuelto, ganancia de pescadores** there is always somebody ready to take advantage of a chaotic situation • **cuando el río suena, agua lleva** • **cuando el río suena, piedras trae** there's no smoke without fire ▸ **río abajo** downstream ▸ **río arriba** upstream

2 (= *torrente*) stream, torrent • **un río de gente** a stream of people, a flood of people

(ADJ INV)† • **novela río** saga, roman fleuve • **programa río** blockbuster of a programme • **serie río** long-running series

río², **rió** *etc* ▹ **reír**

Río de Janeiro (SM) Rio de Janeiro

Río de la Plata (SM) River Plate

Rioja (SF) • **La ~** La Rioja

rioja (SM) Rioja (wine)

riojano/a (ADJ) Riojan, of/from La Rioja

(SM/F) Riojan, native/inhabitant of La Rioja • **los ~s** the Riojans, the people of La Rioja

(SM) **1** (= *vino*) Rioja

2 (*Ling*) Riojan dialect

riolada* (SF) flood, stream

rioplatense (ADJ) of/from the River Plate region

(SMF) native/inhabitant of the River Plate region • **los ~s** the people of the River Plate region

riostra (SF) brace, strut

ripiado (ADJ) **1** (*And*) (= *harapiento*) ragged

2 (*Caribe*) (= *pobre*) wretched, down-at-heel

ripiar ▹ CONJUG 1b (VT) **1** (*Arquit*) to fill with rubble

2 (*And, Caribe*) (= *cortar*) to shred, cut into shreds; (= *desmenuzar*) to crumble

3 (*And, Caribe*) (= *despilfarrar*) to squander

4 (*And*) [+ *persona*] to leave badly off; [+ *dos personas*] to mix up

5 (*Méx*) (= *espigar*) to glean

6 (*Caribe*) (= *pegar*) to hit

ripiería (SF) (*And*) mob, populace

ripio (SM) **1** (= *palabras inútiles*) padding, empty words (*pl*); (*en poesía*) trite verse

• MODISMO: • **no perder ~** not to miss a trick

2 (= *residuo*) refuse, waste

3 (= *escombro*) rubble, debris

4 (*Chile*) (= *grava*) gravel

ripioso (ADJ) (*And, Caribe*) ragged

riqueza (SF) **1** (= *bienes*) wealth • **la distribución de la ~** the distribution of

wealth • **no le importaba nada toda su ~** all her riches meant nothing to her • **vivir en la ~** to live in luxury ▸ **riqueza imponible** taxable assets (*pl*)
2 (= *abundancia*) richness • **su enorme ~ espiritual** his enormous spiritual wealth *o* richness of spirit • **tiene una gran ~ de vocabulario** she has a very extensive *o* rich vocabulary
3 (= *fertilidad*) richness • **la ~ del suelo** the richness of the soil
riquiña SF (*Caribe*) sewing basket
riquiñeque SM (*And*) quarrel
risa SF laugh • **el libro es una verdadera ~** the book is a real laugh • **hubo ~s** there was laughter • **causar ~ a algn** (*frm*) to make sb laugh • **dar ~**: • **daba ~ la manera en que lo explicaba** it was so funny the way he told it • **me dio la ~** I got (a fit of) the giggles • **de ~**: • **no es cosa de ~** it's no laughing matter • **le pagan un sueldo de ~** they pay him a pittance, what they pay him is a joke • **entrarle a algn la ~**: • **me entró la ~** I got (a fit of) the giggles • **mover** *o* **provocar a algn a ~** (*frm*) to make sb laugh • **¡qué ~!**: • **¡qué ~! ¿cómo se llama este humorista?** he's hilarious *o* so funny! what's that comedian's name again? • **¡qué ~, casi se cae de culo!** what a laugh *o* it was so funny *o* it was such a laugh, she nearly fell on her backside! • **soltar la ~** to burst out laughing • **tomarse algo a ~** to treat sth as a joke • **no te tomes a ~ todo lo que te digo** don't treat everything I tell you as a joke • **MODISMOS**: • **ahogarse de ~** to fall about laughing • **caerse de ~** to fall about laughing • **descoserse** *o* **desternillarse de (la) ~** to split one's sides laughing, laugh one's head off • **morirse de ~** to die laughing, kill o.s. laughing • **mondarse de ~** to split one's sides laughing, laugh one's head off • **muerto de ~**: • **estaba muerto de ~ con la película** he was killing himself laughing at the film • **la bicicleta está muerta de ~ en el garaje** the bike is gathering dust in the garage • **partirse** *o* **troncharse de ~** to split one's sides laughing, laugh one's head off • **REFRÁN**: • **la ~ va por barrios** every dog has his day ▸ **risa contagiosa** infectious laugh ▸ **risa de conejo** false laugh, affected laugh ▸ **risa floja, risa tonta** • **me dio** *o* **entró la ~ floja** *o* **tonta** I got (a fit of) the giggles ▸ **risas enlatadas** canned laughter (*sing*)
risco SM **1** (= *peñasco*) cliff, crag
2 riscos (= *terreno áspero*) rough parts
riscoso ADJ steep
risible ADJ ludicrous, laughable
risión SF derision, mockery • **ser un objeto de ~** to be a laughing stock
risotada SF guffaw, loud laugh
rispiar ▸ CONJUG 1b VI (*CAm*) to rush off
rispidez SF **1** (*esp LAm*) (= *mala educación*) coarseness, uncouthness
2 (= *aspereza*) roughness, sharpness
ríspido ADJ **1** (*esp LAm*) (= *maleducado*) rough, coarse
2 (= *áspero*) [*terreno*] rough, rocky
risquería SF (*Cono Sur*) craggy place
ristra SF string • **una ~ de ajos** a string of garlic
ristre SM • **en ~** at the ready, all set; ▸ **lanza**
risueñamente ADV smilingly
risueño ADJ **1** [*cara*] smiling • **muy ~** with a big smile
2 [*temperamento*] cheerful
3 (*liter*) [*paisaje*] bright, pleasant
4 (*liter*) (= *favorable*) favourable, favorable (*EEUU*)
RITD SF ABR (*Telec*) = **Red Iberoamericana de Transmisión de Datos**

rítmicamente ADV rhythmically
rítmico ADJ rhythmic, rhythmical
ritmo SM **1** (*Mús*) rhythm • **tiene mucho sentido del ~** she has a very good *o* strong sense of rhythm • **daban palmas al ~ de la música** they were clapping in time to the music • **marcar el ~**: **marcaba el ~ con el pie** he kept time with his foot • **París marca el ~ de la moda** Paris sets the fashion trends
2 (= *marcha*) pace • **el trabajo se mantiene a un ~ intenso** work is proceeding at a fast pace • **lo haré a mi ~** I'll do it at my own pace • **trabaja a ~ lento** she works slowly, she works at a slow pace • **MODISMO**: • **a todo ~** flat out ▸ **ritmo cardíaco** heart rate ▸ **ritmo de crecimiento, ritmo de expansión** growth rate ▸ **ritmo de vida** • **el tranquilo ~ de vida de los pueblos** the quiet pace of life in the villages • **sin un sueldo no puedo llevar este ~ de vida** without a salary I can't keep up with this lifestyle ▸ **ritmo respiratorio** respiratory rate
3 (*frm*) (= *periodicidad*) rhythm • **de acuerdo con el ~ de las estaciones** in keeping with the rhythm of the seasons
rito SM rite ▸ **rito de iniciación** initiation rite ▸ **rito iniciático** initiation rite ▸ **ritos de paso** rites of passage
ritual ADJ ritual
SM ritual • **de ~** ritual, customary
ritualismo SM ritualism
ritualista ADJ ritualistic, ritual
SMF ritualist
ritualizado ADJ ritualized
ritualmente ADV ritually
rival ADJ rival, competing
SMF rival, competitor • **el eterno ~** the old enemy
rivalidad SF rivalry, competition
rivalizar ▸ CONJUG 1f VI to compete, contend • **~ con** to rival, compete with • **los dos rivalizan en habilidad** they rival each other in skill
rizado ADJ [*pelo*] curly; [*superficie*] ridged; [*terreno*] undulating; [*mar*] choppy
rizador SM curling iron, hair curler
rizadura SF ripple
rizapestañas SM INV eyelash curlers (*pl*)
rizar ▸ CONJUG 1f VT [+ *pelo*] to curl; [+ *superficie*] to ridge; [+ *mar*] to ripple, ruffle
VPR **rizarse** [*agua*] to ripple • **~se el pelo** to perm one's hair, have one's hair permed
rizo[1] ADJ curly
SM **1** [*de pelo*] curl; [*de superficie*] ridge; (*en agua*) ripple
2 (*Aer*) loop • **hacer el ~** (*Aer*) to loop the loop • **MODISMO**: • **rizar el ~** (= *complicar*) to split hairs
3 (*Aer*) looping the loop
rizo[2] SM (*Náut*) reef
rizoma SM rhizome
R.M. ABR = **Reverenda Madre**
Rma. ABR (= **Reverendísima**) Rt. Rev.
Rmo. ABR (= **Reverendísimo**) Rt. Rev.
RNE SF ABR = **Radio Nacional de España**
R.O. ABR = **Real Orden**
roano ADJ roan
SM roan, roan horse
robacarros SMF INV (*LAm*) car thief
robacarteras SMF INV pickpocket
robado ADJ stolen
robagallinas* SMF INV petty thief
robalo SM, **róbalo** SM sea bass
robaperas* SMF INV petty thief
robar ▸ CONJUG 1a VT **1** [+ *objeto, dinero*] to steal; [+ *banco*] to rob • **¡nos han robado!** we've been robbed! • **~ algo a algn** to steal sth from sb • **les robaba dinero a sus compañeros de clase** he was stealing money from his classmates • **me han robado la cartera** my wallet has been stolen • **Ana le ha robado el novio** Ana has stolen her boyfriend • **el defensa le robó el balón** the defender stole the ball off him • **no quiero ~le su tiempo** I don't want to take up your time • **tuve que ~le horas al sueño para acabar el trabajo** I had to work into the night to finish the job • **~le el corazón a algn** (*liter*) to steal sb's heart
2 [+ *atención*] to steal, capture; [+ *paciencia*] to exhaust; [+ *tranquilidad*] to destroy, take away; [+ *vida*] to take, steal
3 (= *estafar*) to cheat, rob • **en ese negocio te han robado** you've been cheated *o* robbed in that deal
4 [+ *naipes*] to take, draw • **roba una carta de la baraja** take *o* draw a card from the deck
5 (*frm*) [*río, corriente*] to carry away
6†† (= *raptar*) to kidnap, abduct
VI **1** (= *sisar*) to steal • **lo cogieron robando** he was caught stealing • **no ~ás** (*Biblia*) thou shalt not steal • **entraron a ~ en mi casa** they broke into my house
2 (*Naipes*) to take a card, draw a card
Roberto SM Robert
robinsón SM castaway
roblar ▸ CONJUG 1a VT to rivet, clinch
roble SM oak, oak tree • **de ~** oak (*antes de s*) • **de ~ macizo** of solid oak, solid oak (*antes de s*)
robledal SM, **robledo** SM oakwood
roblón SM rivet
roblonar ▸ CONJUG 1a VT to rivet
robo SM **1** [*de dinero, objetos*] theft; (*en vivienda*) burglary; (*en tienda, banco*) robbery ▸ **robo a mano armada** armed robbery ▸ **robo con allanamiento** breaking and entering ▸ **robo con escalo** breaking and entering (*climbing over a wall*) ▸ **robo de identidades** identity theft
2 (= *estafa*) • **¡esto es un ~!** this is daylight robbery! • **¿cinco mil por una camiseta? ¡vaya ~!** five thousand for a T-shirt? what a rip-off!*
3 (= *cosa robada*) stolen article; (= *cosas robadas*) stolen goods (*pl*)
robot [ro'βo] SM (PL: **robots** [ro'βo]) robot
ADJ INV • **retrato ~** Identikit picture
robótica SF robotics (*sing*)
robotización SF robotization
robotizado ADJ automated, robotized (*EEUU*)
robotizar ▸ CONJUG 1f VT (= *automatizar*) to automate, robotize (*EEUU*); (*fig*) [+ *persona*] to turn into a robot
robustecer ▸ CONJUG 2d VT to strengthen
VPR **robustecerse** to grow stronger
robustecimiento SM strengthening
robustez SF strength, toughness, robustness
robusto ADJ strong, tough, robust
ROC SM ABR (= **Reconocimiento Óptico de Caracteres**) OCR
Roca SF • **la ~** the Rock, the Rock of Gibraltar
roca SF **1** (= *piedra*) rock • **en ~ viva** in(to) the living rock • **MODISMO**: • **ser firme como una ~** to be as solid as a rock
2‡ (= *droga*) crack
rocalla SF pebbles (*pl*)
rocalloso ADJ pebbly, stony
rocambolescamente ADV (= *extraordinariamente*) bizarrely, in a bizarre fashion; (= *recargadamente*) ornately, over-elaborately
rocambolesco ADJ (= *raro*) odd, bizarre; [*estilo*] ornate, over-elaborate
rocanola† SF jukebox
rocanrol SM rock'n'roll, rock and roll
rocanrolear* ▸ CONJUG 1a VI to rock and roll

r

roce SM **1** (= *acción*) rub, rubbing; (*Téc*) friction; (*Pol*) friction
2 (= *herida*) graze
3* (= *contacto*) close contact • **tener ~ con algn** to be in close contact with sb, have a lot to do with sb
4 (= *disgusto*) brush • **tuvo algún ~ con la autoridad** he had a few brushes with the law

rochabús* SM (*Perú*) water cannon truck, police water cannon truck

Rochela SF • **La ~** La Rochelle

rochela* SF (*And, Caribe*) (= *fiesta*) rowdy party; (= *alboroto*) din, racket

rochelero* ADJ (*And, Caribe*) (= *ruidoso*) unruly, rowdy; (*Caribe*) (= *travieso*) mischievous, naughty

rociada SF **1** (= *aspersión*) shower, spray; (*en bebida*) dash, splash; (*Agr*) spray
2 [*de piedras*] shower; [*de balas*] hail; [*de injurias*] hail, stream

rociadera SF watering can

rociado SM (= *aspersión*) sprinkling; (*Agr*) spraying

rociador SM (*para rociar*) spray; (*Agr*) sprinkler ▸ **rociador de moscas** fly spray

rociar ▹ CONJUG 1C VT **1** [+ *agua*] to sprinkle, spray; [+ *balas*] to spray
2 (*Culin*) (= *acompañar*) • **~ el plato con un vino de la tierra** to wash down the dish with a local wine
VI (*Meteo*) • **empieza a ~** the dew is beginning to fall • **rocía esta mañana** there is a dew this morning

rocín SM **1** (= *caballo*) [*de trabajo*] hack, nag; (*Cono Sur*) [*de montar*] riding horse
2 (*And*) (= *buey*) draught ox
3* (= *persona*) lout

rocinante SM broken-down old horse

rocío SM **1** (*Meteo*) dew
2 (= *gotas*) sprinkling

rock ADJ, SM rock

rockabilly SM rockabilly

rockero/a ADJ rock (*antes de s*) • **música rockera** rock music • **es muy ~** he's a real rock fan
SM/F (= *cantante*) rock singer; (= *músico*) rock musician; (= *aficionado*) rock fan

rococó ADJ, SM rococo

rocola SF jukebox

rocosidades SFPL rocky places

rocoso ADJ rocky

rocote SM (*LAm*), **rocoto** SM (*LAm*) large pepper, large chilli

roda SF (*Náut*) stem

rodaballo SM turbot ▸ **rodaballo menor** brill

rodada SF **1** [*de rueda*] rut, track
2 (*Cono Sur, Méx*) (= *caída*) fall (from a horse)

rodadero SM (*And*) cliff, precipice

rodado ADJ **1** [*tráfico*] vehicular
2 [*piedra*] rounded • **canto ~** boulder • **salir** *o* **venir ~** to go smoothly
3 [*caballo*] dappled
4 [*estilo*] well-rounded, fluent
5 (= *con experiencia*) experienced
SM (*Cono Sur*) vehicle, wheeled vehicle

rodadura SF **1** (*tb* **banda de rodadura**) [*de neumático*] tread
2 (= *acto*) roll, rolling
3 (= *rodada*) rut

rodaja SF **1** [*de pan, fruta*] slice • **limón en ~s** sliced lemon
2 [*de mueble*] castor
3 (= *ruedecilla*) small wheel
4 (= *disco*) small disc

rodaje SM **1** (*Téc*) wheels (*pl*), set of wheels
2 (*Cine*) shooting, filming
3 (*Aut*) running-in, breaking in (*EEUU*) • **"en rodaje"** "running in"
4 (= *inicio*) • **período de ~** initial phase • **poner en ~** to launch
5 (= *experiencia*) experience
6 (*And*) (= *impuesto*) vehicle tax, road tax

rodamiento SM **1** ▸ **rodamiento a bolas, rodamiento de bolas** ball bearing
2 (*tb* **banda de rodamiento**) [*de neumático*] tread

Ródano SM Rhône

rodante ADJ rolling • **material ~** rolling stock

rodapié SM skirting board, baseboard (*EEUU*)

rodar ▹ CONJUG 1l VI **1** (= *dar vueltas*) [*pelota*] to roll; [*rueda*] to go round, turn • **la moneda fue rodando por el caño** the coin rolled down the drain • **rodó escaleras abajo** he fell *o* rolled downstairs • **se oía el ~ de los carros** one could hear the sound of cartwheels • **~ de suelo** (*Aer*) to taxi • MODISMOS: • **echarlo todo a ~** to mess it all up • **~ por algn** to be at sb's beck and call
2* (= *deambular*) • **me han hecho ir rodando de acá para allá** they kept shunting me about from one place to another • **tienen al niño rodando de guardería en guardería** they keep moving *o* shifting the kid about from nursery to nursery
3 (*Cine*) to shoot, film • **llevamos dos meses rodando en México** we've spent two months filming in Mexico
4* (= *existir todavía*) to be still going, still exist • **ese modelo rueda todavía por el mundo** that model is still about
5 (*Méx, Arg*) [*caballo*] to stumble, fall forwards
VT **1** [+ *vehículo*] to wheel, wheel along; [+ *coche nuevo*] to run in
2 (= *hacer rodar*) [+ *objeto*] to roll, roll along
3 (*Cine*) to shoot, film
4 (*Inform*) [+ *programa*] to run
5 (*Caribe*) (= *agarrar*) to seize; (= *encarcelar*) to imprison
6 (*LAm*) • **~ (a patadas)** to knock over, kick over
7 (*LAm*) [+ *ganado*] to round up

Rodas SF Rhodes

rodear ▹ CONJUG 1a VT **1** (= *poner alrededor de*) to encircle, enclose • **~on el terreno con alambre de púas** they surrounded the field with barbed wire, they put a barbed wire fence around the field • **le rodeó el cuello con los brazos** she threw her arms round his neck
2 (= *ponerse alrededor de*) to surround • **los soldados ~on el edificio** the soldiers surrounded the building
3 (*LAm*) [+ *ganado*] to round up
VPR **rodearse 1** (= *volverse*) to turn round
2 • **~se de** to surround o.s. with • **se rodeó de gente importante** she surrounded herself with important people

rodela SF **1** (= *escudo*) buckler, round shield
2 (*Cono Sur*) (= *rosca*) padded ring (*for carrying loads on one's head*)

rodenticida SM rat poison

rodeo SM **1** (= *ruta indirecta*) long way round, roundabout way; (= *desvío*) detour • **dar un ~** to make a detour
2 (*en discurso*) circumlocution • **andarse con ~s** to beat about the bush • **no te andes con ~s** • **déjate de ~s** stop beating about the bush • **hablar sin ~s** to speak plainly
3 (*LAm*) (*Agr*) roundup
4 (*Dep*) rodeo

rodera SF rut, wheel track

Rodesia SF (*Hist*) Rhodesia

rodesiano/a ADJ, SM/F (*Hist*) Rhodesian

rodete SM **1** [*de pelo*] coil, bun; [*de grasa*] roll; (*para llevar carga*) pad
2 [*de cerradura*] ward

rodilla SF **1** (*Anat*) knee • **de ~s** kneeling • **doblar** *o* **hincar la ~** (= *arrodillarse*) to kneel down; (= *ser servil*) to bow, humble o.s. (**ante** to) • **estar de ~s** to be kneeling, be kneeling down • **hincarse de** *o* **ponerse de ~s** to kneel, kneel down, get down on one's knees • **pusieron al país de ~s** they brought the country to its knees
2 (*para llevar carga*) pad
3 (= *paño*) floor cloth, mop

rodillazo SM push with the knee • **dar un ~ a** to knee

rodillera SF **1** (= *protección*) knee guard; (= *remiendo*) knee patch
2 (= *abombamiento*) baggy part (*in knee of trousers*)
3 (*para llevar carga*) pad

rodillo SM (*Culin*) rolling pin; (*Tip*) ink roller; [*de máquina de escribir*] cylinder, roller; (*para pintura, césped*) roller; (= *exprimidor*) mangle; (*Agr*) roller ▸ **rodillo de pintura** paint roller ▸ **rodillo de vapor** steamroller ▸ **rodillo pastelero** rolling pin

rodillón/ona‡ SMF (*And*) old geezer/old bag*

rodio SM rhodium

rododendro SM rhododendron

Rodrigo SM Roderick • **~ el último godo** Roderick, the last of the Goths

rodrigón SM stake, prop, support

Rodríguez SM • **estar de ~** (*Esp*) to be left on one's own

roedor ADJ **1** (*Zool*) gnawing
2 (= *atormentador*) [*sensación, conciencia*] gnawing; [*duda, sospecha*] nagging
SM rodent

roer ▹ CONJUG 2z VT **1** [+ *comida*] to gnaw; (= *mordiscar*) to nibble at; [+ *hueso*] to gnaw, pick
2 (= *corroer*) to corrode, eat away
3 [+ *capital*] to eat into (bit by bit)
4 [*conciencia*] to prick

rogación SF **1** (= *petición*) petition
2 rogaciones (*Rel*) rogations

rogar ▹ CONJUG 1h, 1l VT (= *suplicar*) to beg • **démelo, se lo ruego** give it to me, I beg you • **ruegue a este señor que nos deje en paz** please ask this gentleman to leave us alone • **"se ruega no fumar"** "please do not smoke"
VI **1** (= *suplicar*) to beg, plead • **hacerse de ~** to play hard to get • **no se hace de ~** he doesn't have to be asked twice
2 (*Rel*) to pray

rogativa SF (*Rel*) rogation

rogatoria SF (*LAm*) request, plea

rogatorio ADJ • **comisión rogatoria** investigative commission, committee of inquiry

rojear ▹ CONJUG 1a VI **1** (= *volverse rojo*) to redden, turn red
2 (= *tirar a rojo*) to be reddish

rojeras* SMF INV red, commie*

rojete SM rouge

rojez SF (= *cualidad*) redness; (*en la piel*) blotch

rojigualdo ADJ red-and-yellow (*colours of the Spanish flag*)

rojillo/a* ADJ, SM/F (= *izquierdista*) leftie*, pinko*

rojizo ADJ reddish

rojo/a ADJ **1** (*color*) red • **~ burdeos** maroon, dark red • **~ cereza** cherry red • **~ sangre** blood-red • **~ teja** brick-red • MODISMOS: • **poner ~ a algn** to make sb blush • **ponerse ~** to turn red, blush • **ponerse ~ de ira** to go purple with rage
2 [*pelo*] red
3 (*Pol*) red; (*Esp*) (*durante la Guerra Civil y con Franco*) Republican

SM 1 (= *color*) red, red colour *o* (*EEUU*) color • **calentar al ~ vivo** to make red-hot • **la atmósfera está al ~ vivo** the atmosphere is electric • **la emoción está al ~ vivo** excitement is at fever pitch • **un semáforo en ~** a red light
2 (= *maquillaje*) ▸ **rojo de labios** lipstick
SM/F (*Pol*) (= *de izquierdas*) red; (= *republicano*) Republican
rojura SF redness
rol SM 1 (*Teat*) role, part; (*fig*) role • **juegos de rol** role-playing games • **desempeña un rol importantísimo en la política municipal** she plays a very important role in local politics
2 (*Méx*) (= *paseo*) • **dar un rol** to take a walk
3 (*Náut*) muster
rola* SF (*Caribe*) (= *comisaría*) police station
SMF (*Cono Sur*) (= *matón*) lout; (= *zonzo*) thickhead*, dope*
Rolando SM Roland
rolar ▸ CONJUG 1a VT 1 (*And, Cono Sur*) (= *mencionar*) to touch on, mention, mention in conversation • **la conversación roló la religión** the conversation touched on religion
2 (*Méx*) (= *pasar*) to pass from hand to hand
VI 1 [*viento*] to veer round
2 (*Cono Sur*) (= *ser arribista*) to be a social climber
3 (*And, Cono Sur*) (= *hablar*) to talk, converse (**con** with)
4 (*And, Cono Sur*) (= *alternar con*) to associate, be in contact (**con** with)
Roldán SM Roland
roldana SF pulley wheel
rollazo* ADJ dead boring*
SM real pain*
rollista* ADJ (*Esp*) • **es muy ~** (= *pesado*) he's such a bore; (= *mentiroso*) he's such a storyteller *o* fibber*
SMF (*Esp*) (= *pesado*) bore; (= *mentiroso*) storyteller*, fibber*
rollito SM roll ▸ **rollito de primavera** spring roll
rollizo ADJ 1 (= *rechoncho*) plump; [*niño*] chubby; [*mujer*] plump, buxom
2 (= *redondo*) round; (= *cilíndrico*) cylindrical
rollo SM 1 (= *cilindro*) [*de tela, papel, cuerda fina, cable fino*] roll; [*de cuerda gruesa, cable grueso*] coil; [*de película de cine*] reel; [*de pergamino*] scroll • **un ~ de papel higiénico** a roll of toilet paper • **regalamos un ~ color** we offer a free colour film • **papel en ~** rolled up paper • **los ~s del mar Muerto** the Dead Sea Scrolls ▸ **rollo de pelo** (*Ven*) curler, hair curler, roller
2 (*Culin*) **a** (*tb* **rollo pastelero**) (*Esp*) rolling pin
b [*de masa, relleno*] (pastry) roll ▸ **rollo de primavera** spring roll
3 (= *tronco*) log • **en ~** whole, uncut
4* (= *michelín*) roll of fat, spare tyre* (*hum*)
5 (*Esp**) (*tb* **rollo macabeo** *o* **patatero**) (= *explicación*) spiel*; (= *sermón*) lecture; (= *mentira*) yarn • **nos soltó el ~ de siempre** he gave us the usual spiel* • **¡menudo ~ nos contó tu padre!** what a lecture your dad gave us! (*iró*) • **¡menudo ~ que tiene!** he's always waffling (on) about something!* • **nos vino con un ~ de su familia que no había quien se lo creyera** he spun us a yarn about his family that no one could possibly believe • **¡vaya ~ patatero que me estás contando!** you're talking a load of old tosh!‡, you're talking a load of baloney! (*EEUU**) • **perdona por el ~ que te he soltado** sorry if I have bored you to death with my story • MODISMOS: • **cortar el ~** to cut it short*, cut the crap*** • **corta el ~ y dime exactamente lo que quieres** cut it short* *o* cut the crap*** and tell me exactly what you want • **cinco minutos más y ya corto el ~** five minutes more and then I'll shut up* • **cortar el ~ a algn**: • **mejor que le cortes el ~, que tenemos prisa** don't let him rattle on, we're in a hurry • **¡con lo bien que lo estábamos pasando! ¡nos has cortado el ~!** we were having a great time until you went and spoiled things! • **estar de ~*** (*Esp, Méx*): • **están de ~ desde hace dos horas** they've been rattling on for two hours now • **tirarse el ~** (*Esp, Méx*): • **no te tires el ~ conmigo que te conozco** don't give me that spiel*, I know what you're like • **tírate el ~ e invítame a una copa** be a pal and get me a drink*
6* (= *aburrimiento*) • **¡qué ~!** what a pain!‡ • **ser un ~** [*discurso, conferencia*] to be dead boring*; [*persona*] to be a bore*, be a pain‡ • **lo de las lentillas es un ~** contact lenses are a real pain*
7‡ (= *asunto*) thing • **está metido en muchos ~s** he's into all sorts of things • **no sabemos de qué va el ~** we don't know what it's all about *o* what's going on • **ir a su ~** to do one's own thing
8 (*Esp*‡) (= *ambiente*) scene* • **no me va el ~ de esta gente** I'm not into their scene*
9‡ (= *sensación*) • **buen/mal ~**: • **en sus fiestas siempre hay buen ~** there's always a good atmosphere at his parties • **había muy buen ~ entre nosotros** we got on really well together • **¡qué mal ~!** what a pain!* • **me da buen/mal ~** I've got a good/nasty *o* bad feeling about it • **¡qué buen ~ me da ese tío!** that guy gives me really good vibes!* • **la película me dio tan mal ~ que me deprimí** the film was a real downer* • **tener un buen/mal ~ con algn** to get on well/badly with sb
10* (= *relación sentimental*) • **tener un ~ (con algn)** to be involved (with sb)
ADJ INV (*Esp, Méx**) boring • **esa película es muy ~** that film's dead boring* • **no seas ~, Julián** don't be a bore* *o* pain‡, Julián
rolo SM (*LAm*) stick, truncheon, billy (club) (*EEUU*)
ROM SF ABR (= **Read-Only Memory**) ROM
Roma SF Rome • MODISMOS: • **revolver ~ con Santiago** to leave no stone unturned • **~ no se construyó en un día** Rome was not built in a day • **por todas partes se va a ~** • **todos los caminos llevan a ~** all roads lead to Rome
romadizo SM 1 (= *resfriado*) head cold; (= *catarro*) catarrh
2 (*Caribe*) (= *reuma*) rheumatism
romana SF steelyard • MODISMO: • **cargar la ~** (*Cono Sur**) to heap the blame on somebody else; ▸ **romano**
romance ADJ [*idioma*] Romance
SM 1 (*Ling*) Romance language; (= *castellano*) Spanish, Spanish language • **hablar en ~** (= *con claridad*) to speak plainly
2 (*Literat*) ballad
3 (= *amorío*) romance, love affair; (= *amante*) lover
romancear ▸ CONJUG 1a VT †† to translate into Spanish
VI (*Cono Sur*) 1 (= *charlar*) to waste time chatting
2 (= *galantear*) to flirt
romancero SM collection of ballads • **el Romancero** the Spanish ballads
romancístico ADJ ballad (*antes de s*)
romaní ADJ Romany
SMF Romany
SM (*Ling*) Romany
Romania SF Romance countries (*pl*), Romance-speaking regions (*pl*)
románico ADJ 1 [*idioma*] Romance
2 (*Arte, Arquit*) Romanesque; (*en Inglaterra*) Norman
romanizar ▸ CONJUG 1f VT to romanize
VPR **romanizarse** to become romanized
romano/a ADJ, SM/F Roman
SM (*Esp*†) cop*; ▸ **romana**
romanó SM (*Ling*) Romany
románticamente ADV romantically
romanticismo SM romanticism
romántico/a ADJ, SM/F romantic
romanticón* ADJ [*persona*] sentimental, soppy*; [*película, novela*] slushy*, soppy*
romaza SF dock, sorrel
rombal ADJ rhombic
rombo SM 1 (*Mat*) rhombus; (*en diseño*) diamond, diamond shape
2 (*TV*†) diamond (*warning of scenes with adult content*) • **una película de dos ~s** an over-18 film
romboidal ADJ rhomboid
romboide SM rhomboid
Romeo SM Romeo
romereante SMF (*And, Caribe*) pilgrim
romería SF 1 (*Rel*) pilgrimage • **ir en ~** to go on a pilgrimage
2 (*Aut*) queue, tailback

ROMERÍA

In Spain **romerías** are annual religious pilgrimages to chapels and shrines associated with particular saints or miracles of the Virgin. The pilgrims, called **romeros**, make their way on foot to the particular holy site, often covering long distances, and make offerings. The day's festivities often include sports fixtures, fireworks and traditional music and dancing. Some **romerías** are large-scale events, one of the best known being the **Romería de la Virgen del Rocío** at Huelva in Andalusia, which involves spectacular processions of pilgrims in traditional Andalusian dress, some on horseback and some in brilliantly decorated wagons.

romero[1]/a SM/F (= *peregrino*) pilgrim
romero[2] SM (*Bot*) rosemary
romo ADJ 1 (= *sin punta*) blunt; [*persona*] snub-nosed
2 (= *aburrido*) dull, lifeless
rompebolas*** SMF INV (*Arg*) pain in the arse*** *o* (*EEUU*) ass***
rompecabezas SM INV 1 (= *juego*) jigsaw, jigsaw puzzle
2 (= *algo complicado*) puzzle; (= *problema*) problem, headache
rompecojones*** SMF INV pain in the arse*** *o* (*EEUU*) ass***
rompecorazones SMF INV heartbreaker
rompedero SM ▸ **rompedero de cabeza** puzzle, brain teaser
ADJ (*frm*) breakable, delicate, fragile
rompedor ADJ [*obra, movimiento, ideas, artista*] ground-breaking
rompedora-cargadora SF power loader
rompehielos SM INV icebreaker
rompehuelgas SMF INV strikebreaker, blackleg
rompenueces SM INV nutcrackers (*pl*), pair of nutcrackers
rompeolas SM INV breakwater
romper ▸ CONJUG 2a (PP: **roto**) VT 1 (= *partir, destrozar*) **a** (*intencionadamente*) [+ *juguete, mueble, cuerda*] to break; [+ *rama*] to break, break off; [+ *vaso, jarrón, cristal*] to break, smash • **los ladrones entraron rompiendo la puerta a patadas** the burglars got in by kicking down the door • **la onda expansiva rompió los cristales** the shock wave broke *o* smashed the windows

r

b (*= rasgar*) [*+ tela, vestido, papel*] to tear, rip • **¡cuidado, que vas a ~ las cortinas!** careful, you'll tear *o* rip the curtains! • **se disgustó tanto con la carta que la rompió en pedazos** he was so angry about the letter that he tore *o* ripped it up

c (*por el uso*) [*+ zapatos, ropa*] to wear out

d [*+ barrera*] (*lit*) to break down, break through; (*fig*) to break down • **tratan de ~ barreras en el campo de la informática** they are trying to break down barriers in the area of computing • **~ la barrera del sonido** to break the sound barrier

e • MODISMOS: • **~ aguas**: • **todavía no ha roto aguas** her waters haven't broken yet • **~ la cara a algn*** to smash sb's face in* • **~ el hielo** to break the ice • **~ una lanza en favor de algn/algo** to stick up for sb/sth • **no haber roto un plato**: • **se comporta como si no hubiera roto un plato en su vida** he behaves as if butter wouldn't melt in his mouth • **de rompe y rasga**: • **es una mujer de rompe y rasga** she's not someone to mess with • **quien rompe paga** one must pay the consequences for one's actions; ▸ **esquema, molde**

2 (*= terminar*) [*+ equilibrio, silencio, maleficio, contrato*] to break; [*+ relaciones, amistad*] to break off • **hagamos algo distinto que rompa la rutina** let's do something different to break the routine • **la patronal ha roto el pacto con los sindicatos** employers have broken the agreement with the unions • **~ la racha de algo** to break a run of sth • **~ el servicio a algn** (*Tenis*) to break sb's service

3 (*Mil*) [*+ línea, cerco*] to break, break through • **¡rompan filas!** fall out! • **~ (el) fuego** to open fire • **~ las hostilidades** to start hostilities

4 (*Agr*) [*+ tierra*] to break, break up

5 (*Arg, Uru***) (*= molestar*) to piss off** • **deja de ~me** stop pissing me off**

VI **1** [*olas*] to break

2 (*= salir*) [*diente*] to come through; [*capullo, flor*] to come out • **~ entre algo** to break through sth, burst through sth • **los manifestantes rompieron entre el cordón de seguridad** the demonstrators broke *o* burst through the security cordon

3 [*alba, día*] to break • **al ~ el alba** at crack of dawn, at daybreak

4 (*= empezar*) • **~ a hacer algo** to (suddenly) start doing sth, (suddenly) start to do sth • **rompió a proferir insultos contra todo el mundo** he suddenly started hurling *o* to hurl insults at everyone • **al verme rompió a llorar** when he saw me he burst into tears • **~ en llanto** to break down in tears • **cuando rompa el hervor** when it comes to the boil

5 (*= separarse*) [*pareja, novios*] to split up • **hace algún tiempo que rompieron** they split up some time ago • **~ con** [*+ novio, amante*] to split up with, break up with; [*+ amigo, familia*] to fall out with; [*+ aliado*] to break off relations with; [*+ tradición, costumbre, pasado*] to break with; [*+ imagen, tópico, leyenda*] to break away from • **ha roto con su novio** she has broken *o* split up with her boyfriend • **Albania rompió con China en 1978** Albania broke off relations with China in 1978 • **han roto con una tradición de siglos** they have broken with a centuries-old tradition

VPR **romperse 1** (*= partirse, destrozarse*) **a** [*juguete, mueble, cuerda*] to break; [*plato, cristal*] to break, smash • **la rama se ha roto con el viento** the branch broke (off) in the wind • **se me rompió un dedo en el accidente** my finger got broken in the accident, I broke a finger in the accident

b (*uso enfático*) • **me he roto la muñeca jugando al tenis** I broke my wrist playing tennis • **no te vayas a ~ de tanto trabajar** (*iró, hum*) don't strain yourself working so hard (*iró*) • MODISMO: • **~se la cabeza*** (*= pensar mucho*) to rack one's brains; (*= preocuparse*) to kill o.s. worrying; ▸ **cuerno**

2 (*= rasgarse*) [*tela, papel*] to tear, rip • **tiraron del gorro de papel hasta que se rompió** they pulled the paper hat till it tore *o* ripped • **se me han roto los pantalones** I've torn *o* ripped my trousers

3 (*= estropearse*) [*coche, motor*] to break down; [*televisor*] to break • **se ha roto la lavadora** the washing machine is broken, the washing machine has broken down

4 (*= gastarse*) [*ropa, zapatos*] to wear out • **se le han roto los pantalones por las rodillas** his trousers have worn (through) at the knees

5 (*Ciclismo*) [*pelotón*] to break up

6 (*Arg, Uru**) (*= esforzarse*) • **no me rompí mucho, no valía la pena** I didn't go to a lot of trouble, it wasn't worth it • **el pobre se rompe tanto y saca malas notas** the poor guy works like crazy and gets really bad marks* • **así se lo agradecés a tu madre que se rompe todo por vos** that's how you thank your mother, who does all she can for you

rompevientos SM INV **1** (*Arg, Méx*) (*= impermeable*) anorak
2 (*Arg*) (*= sudadera*) sweatshirt
3 (*Uru*) [*de lana*] sweater

rompiente SM **1** (*= escollo*) reef, shoal
2 rompientes (*= olas*) breakers, surf (*sing*)

rompimiento SM **1** [*de ladrillo, cristal, porcelana*] breaking, smashing; [*de muro*] breaking; [*de tela, papel*] tearing • **la tromba de agua causó el ~ del muro** the downpour caused the wall to break *o* collapse ▸ **rompimiento de aguas** downpour
2 [*de negociaciones, diálogo*] breaking-off; [*de récord*] breaking • **procederemos al ~ de contrato** we will break the contract forthwith (*frm*) • **su ~ con el resto de las vanguardias europeas** his break with the rest of the European avant-garde ▸ **rompimiento de contacto** (*Mil*) disengagement
3 (*= abertura*) opening
4 (*= comienzo*) [*de hostilidades*] outbreak

romplón • **de ~** ADV (*LAm*) suddenly, unexpectedly

rompope SM (*CAm, Méx*) eggnog

Rómulo SM Romulus

ron SM rum

ronca SF **1** (*Zool*) (*= sonido*) roar (*of rutting stag*); (*= época*) rutting season
2 (*= amenaza*) threat • **echar ~s** to bully, threaten

roncadoras SFPL (*LAm*) large spurs

roncar ▸ CONJUG 1g VI **1** (*cuando se duerme*) to snore
2 [*ciervo, mar*] to roar
3 (*= amenazar*) to threaten, bully
4 (*And, Cono Sur**) (*= ser mandón*) to be bossy *o* domineering

roncear ▸ CONJUG 1a VT **1** (*= insistir*) to pester, keep on at
2 (*LAm*) (*= espiar*) to keep watch on, spy on
3 (*LAm*) = **ronzar¹**
VI **1** (*Náut*) to move slowly
2 (*= trabajar a desgana*) to work half-heartedly; (*= gandulear*) to slack, kill time

roncería SF **1** (*= desgana*) unwillingness
2 (*= lisonja*) cajolery

roncero ADJ **1** (*Náut*) slow, slow-moving, sluggish
2 (*= desganado*) unwilling; (*= gandul*) slack, slow • **estar ~** to find reasons for shirking work
3 (*= gruñón*) grumpy, grouchy*
4 (*= cobista*) smooth, smarmy*
5 (*And, CAm, Cono Sur*) (*= taimado*) sly, sharp; (*= entrometido*) nosey*, meddling

roncha SF **1** (*= hinchazón*) swelling • MODISMOS: • **hacer ~** (*Cono Sur**) to create an impression • **levantar ~** (*Caribe**) to pass a dud cheque* • **sacar ~*** to cause an upset
2 (*= cardenal*) bruise
3 (*= rodaja*) slice

ronco ADJ [*persona*] hoarse; [*voz*] husky; [*sonido*] harsh, raucous

roncón* ADJ (*And, Caribe*) boastful, bragging

ronda SF **1** [*de guardia*] beat; (*= personas*) watch, patrol, guard • **ir de ~** to do one's round ▸ **ronda nocturna** night patrol, night watch
2 (*Mús*) group of serenaders
3 [*de bebidas*] round • **pagar una ~** to pay for a round
4 [*de negociaciones, elecciones*] round
5 [*de cartas*] hand, game
6 (*en competición, concurso*) round; (*Golf*) round
7 (*Aut*) (*tb* **ronda de circunvalación**) ring road, beltway (*EEUU*), bypass
8 (*Mil*) sentry walk
9 (*Cono Sur*) (*= juego*) ring-a-ring-a-roses • **en ~** in a ring, in a circle

rondalla SF **1** (*Mús*) band of street musicians
2 (*= ficción*) fiction, invention

rondana SF (*LAm*) pulley

rondar ▸ CONJUG 1a VT **1** [*policía, soldado*] to patrol
2 [*+ cifra, edad*] • **el precio ronda los mil dólares** the price is in the region of a thousand dollars • **rondaba los 30 años** he was about 30
3 (*= perseguir*) • **la ronda a todas horas para que le preste dinero** he pesters her night and day to lend him money • **es una idea que me rondaba la cabeza desde hace tiempo** it's an idea which I've had going round in my head for quite a while • **me está rondando un catarro** I've got a cold hanging over me • **a estas horas siempre me ronda el sueño** I always start feeling sleepy around this time
4† (*= cortejar*) to court
VI **1** [*policía, soldado*] to (be on) patrol
2 (*= deambular*) to prowl • **sospechan de un hombre que rondaba por allí** they suspect a man who was prowling around the area
3 [*pensamiento, idea*] • **debes rechazar las dudas que te rondan por la cabeza** you must dispel the doubts that are besetting you
4† [*enamorado, la tuna*] to serenade

rondeño/a ADJ of/from Ronda
SM/F native/inhabitant of Ronda • **los ~s** the people of Ronda

rondín¹ SM (*And, Cono Sur*) (*= vigilante*) night watchman

rondín² SM (*And*) (*Mús*) harmonica

rondó SM (*Literat*) rondeau; (*Mús*) rondo

rondón • **de ~** ADV unexpectedly • **entrar de ~** (*= sin aviso*) to rush in; (*en fiesta*) to gatecrash

ronquear ▸ CONJUG 1a VI to be hoarse

ronquedad SF, **ronquera** SF **1** [*de persona*] hoarseness
2 [*de voz*] (*permanentemente*) huskiness; (*temporalmente*) hoarseness

ronquido SM snore, snoring

ronronear ▸ CONJUG 1a VI to purr

ronroneo SM purr

ronzal SM halter

ronzar¹ ▸ CONJUG 1f VT (*Náut*) to move with levers, lever along

r

ronzar² ▸ CONJUG 1f (VT), (VI) (*al comer*) to munch, crunch
roña (SF) **1** (= *mugre*) dirt, grime; (*en metal*) rust
2 (= *tacañería*) meanness, stinginess
3 (*Vet*) mange
4 (= *corteza*) pine bark
5 (= *estratagema*) stratagem
6 (*Caribe, Méx*) (= *envidia*) envy; (= *inquina*) grudge, ill will
7 (*And*) (*Med*) feigned illness
8 • **jugar a la ~** to play for fun, play without money stakes
(SMF)* mean person, scrooge*
roñería (SF) meanness, stinginess
roñica* (SMF) skinflint
roñoso (ADJ) **1** (= *mugriento*) dirty, filthy; [*metal*] rusty
2 (= *tacaño*) mean, stingy
3 (= *inútil*) useless
4 (*Vet*) mangy
5 (*And*) (= *tramposo*) tricky, slippery
6 (*Caribe, Méx*) (= *rencoroso*) bitter, resentful; (= *hostil*) hostile
ropa (SF) clothes (*pl*) • **¡quítate esa ~ tan sucia!** take those dirty clothes off! • **siempre lleva ~ pasada de moda** he always wears old-fashioned clothes • **voy a cambiarme de ~** I'm going to change (my clothes) • **tender la ~** to hang out the washing • MODISMOS: • **guardar la ~** to speak cautiously • **hay ~ tendida** walls have ears • **nadar y guardar la ~** to cover one's back • **no tocar la ~ a algn** not to touch a hair of sb's head, keep one's hands off sb • REFRÁN: • **la ~ sucia se lava en casa** don't wash your dirty linen in public ▸ **ropa blanca** (= *ropa interior*) underwear; (= *ropa de cama, manteles*) linen; (*para la lavadora*) whites (*pl*) ▸ **ropa de cama** bed linen ▸ **ropa de color** coloureds (*pl*), coloreds (*pl*) (EEUU) ▸ **ropa de deporte** sportswear ▸ **ropa de mesa** table linen ▸ **ropa de trabajo** work clothes (*pl*) ▸ **ropa hecha** ready-made clothes (*pl*), off-the-peg clothes (*pl*) ▸ **ropa interior** underwear ▸ **ropa íntima** (*LAm*) underwear ▸ **ropa para lavar, ropa sucia** dirty washing, dirty clothes (*pl*), laundry ▸ **ropa usada** secondhand clothes (*pl*) ▸ **ropa vieja** (*esp Méx*) (*Culin*) meat stew
ropaje (SM) **1** (= *vestiduras*) gown, robes (*pl*); **ropajes** (*Rel*) vestments (*pl*)
2 (*Literat*) (= *adornos*) embellishments (*pl*), rhetorical adornments (*pl*)
ropalócero (SM) butterfly
ropavejería (SF) old-clothes shop
ropavejero/a (SM/F) second-hand-clothes dealer
ropería (SF) **1** (= *tienda*) clothes shop
2 (= *comercio*) clothing trade, garment industry (EEUU)
ropero (ADJ) for clothes, clothes (*antes de s*) • **armario ~** wardrobe
(SM) (= *guardarropa*) wardrobe; [*de ropa blanca*] linen cupboard
ropita (SF) baby clothes (*pl*)
ropón (SM) **1** [*de ceremonia*] long robe
2 (= *bata*) loose coat, housecoat
roque¹ (SM) (*Ajedrez*) rook, castle
roque²* (ADJ) • **estar ~** to be asleep • **quedarse ~** to fall asleep
roquedal (SM) rocky place
roqueño (ADJ) **1** (= *rocoso*) rocky
2 (= *duro*) hard as rock, rock-like, flinty; (*fig*) rock-solid
roquero/a (ADJ), (SM/F) = **rockero**
rorcual (SM) rorqual, finback, finback whale
ro-ro (SM) car ferry, roll-on/roll-off ferry
rorro (SM) **1*** (= *bebé*) baby
2 (*Méx*) (= *persona*) fair blue-eyed person
3 (*Méx*) (= *muñeca*) doll
Rosa (SF) Rose
rosa (SF) **1** (*Bot*) rose • **palo ~** rosewood • MODISMO: • **como una ~**: • **estar como una ~** to feel as fresh as a daisy • **un cutis como una ~** a skin as soft as silk • **estar como las propias ~s** to feel entirely at ease • **florecer como ~ en mayo** to bloom, flourish • REFRÁN: • **no hay ~ sin espinas** there's no rose without a thorn ▸ **rosa almizcleña** musk rose ▸ **rosa laurel** rosebay, oleander
2 • **de color ~** • **color de ~** pink; (*fig*) rosy • **vestidos color de ~** pink dresses • **verlo todo del color de ~** to see everything through rose-tinted spectacles *o* (EEUU) rose-colored glasses
3 (*en la piel*) birthmark, red birthmark
4 (*Arquit*) rose window
5 ▸ **rosa de los vientos, rosa náutica** compass, compass card, compass rose
(ADJ) pink • **revista ~** magazine of sentimental stories • **Zona Rosa** (*Méx*) (= *barrio*) *elegant (tourist) quarter of Mexico City*
rosáceo (ADJ) = **rosado**
rosacruciano (ADJ) Rosicrucian
rosado (ADJ) **1** [*color*] pink
2 [*panorama*] rosy
(SM) (= *vino*) rosé
rosal (SM) **1** (= *planta*) rose bush, rose tree ▸ **rosal de China, rosal japonés** japonica ▸ **rosal silvestre** wild rose ▸ **rosal trepador** climbing rose, rambling rose
2 (*Caribe, Cono Sur*) (= *rosaleda*) rose bed, rose garden
rosaleda (SF) rose bed, rose garden
rosario (SM) **1** (*Rel*) rosary; (= *sarta*) rosary beads (*pl*), rosary • **rezar el ~** to say the rosary • REFRÁN: • **acabar como el ~ de la aurora** *o* **del alba** to end up in confusion, end with everybody falling out
2 (= *serie*) string, series • **un ~ de maldiciones** a string of curses
3 (*Agr*) chain of buckets (*of a waterwheel*)
4 (*Anat**) backbone
5 (*Arquit*) beading
rosbif (SM) roast beef
rosca (SF) **1** [*de humo*] ring, spiral • **estaba hecho una ~** he was all curled up in a ball
2 (*Culin*) ring-shaped roll, ring-shaped pastry, ≈ doughnut • MODISMOS: • **hacer la ~ a algn*** to suck *o* (EEUU) kiss up to sb* • **no comerse una ~*** (= *no ligar*) to get absolutely nowhere ▸ **rosca de Reyes** (*LAm*) ring-shaped cake (*eaten on January 6*); ▸ DÍA DE REYES
3 [*de tornillo*] thread; [*de espiral*] turn • **pasarse de ~** [*tornillo*] to have a crossed thread; [*persona*] to go too far, overdo it
4 (*Anat*) (= *hinchazón*) swelling; [*de grasa*] roll of fat
5 (*And*) (*Pol*) ruling clique, oligarchy
6 (*Cono Sur*) (*para llevar carga*) pad
7 (*Cono Sur*) (*Naipes*) circle of card players
8 (*Cono Sur*) (= *discusión*) noisy argument; (= *jaleo*) uproar, commotion • **se armó una ~** there was uproar
rosco¹ (SM) **1** (*Culin*) ring-shaped roll, ring-shaped pastry, ≈ doughnut • MODISMO: • **no comerse un ~*** (= *no ligar*) to get absolutely nowhere (**con** with)
2* (= *nota*) zero, nought
rosco² (SM) (*LAm*) (*Com*) middleman
roscón (SM) (*tb* **roscón de Reyes**) ring-shaped cake (*eaten on January 6*); ▸ DÍA DE REYES
rosedal (SM) (*Cono Sur*) = **rosaleda**
Rosellón (SM) Roussillon
róseo (ADJ) (*liter*) rosy, roseate
roseta (SF) **1** (*Bot*) small rose
2 (*Dep*) rosette
3 [*de regadera*] rose, nozzle
4 (*en la piel*) red spot
5 (*And, Cono Sur*) [*de espuela*] rowel
6 rosetas [*de maíz*] popcorn (*sing*)
rosetón (SM) **1** (*Arquit*) rose window
2 (*Dep*) rosette
3 (*Aut*) cloverleaf, cloverleaf junction
rosicler (SM) dawn pink, rosy tint of dawn
rosita (SF) **1** (*Bot*) small rose
2 (*Cono Sur*) (= *pendiente*) earring
3 • **de ~** (*Méx*) (= *sin esfuerzo*) without effort • **andar de ~** (*LAm*) (*sin trabajo*) to be out of work
4 rositas [*de maíz*] popcorn (*sing*)
rosquero* (ADJ) (*Cono Sur*) quarrelsome
rosquete‡ (SM) (*And*) queer‡, poof‡, fag (EEUU‡)
rosquetón‡ (*Perú*) (ADJ) effeminate
(SM) queer‡, fag (EEUU‡)
rosquilla (SF) **1** [*de humo*] ring
2 (*Culin*) ring-shaped pastry, doughnut • MODISMO: • **venderse como ~s** to sell like hot cakes
3 (= *larva*) small caterpillar
rosticería (SF) (*Méx, Chile*) roast chicken shop
rostizado (ADJ) roast • **pollo ~** (*Méx*) roast chicken
rostizar ▸ CONJUG 1a (VT) to spit-roast
rostro (SM) **1** (= *semblante*) countenance; (= *cara*) face • **retrato de ~ entero** full-face portrait
2* (= *descaro*) nerve*, cheek*
3 (*Náut*) beak
4 (*Zool*) rostrum
rostropálido/a (SM/F) paleface
rotación (SF) **1** (= *giro*) rotation ▸ **rotación de la tierra** rotation of the earth
2 (*Agr*) ▸ **rotación de cultivos** crop rotation
3 (*Com*) [*de producción*] turnover ▸ **rotación de existencias** turnover of stock
rotacional (ADJ) rotational
rotaje* (SM) (*Chile*) plebs* (*pl*)
rotar ▸ CONJUG 1a (VT) to rotate
rotarianismo (SM) (*esp LAm*) Rotarianism
rotariano/a (ADJ), (SM/F) (*LAm*) = **rotario**
rotario/a (ADJ), (SM/F) (*esp LAm*) Rotarian
rotativamente (ADV) by turns
rotativo (ADJ) (= *que gira*) rotary, revolving; [*prensa*] rotary
(SM) **1** (*Tip*) rotary press
2 (= *periódico*) newspaper
3 (= *luz*) revolving light
4 (*Cono Sur*) (*Cine*) continuous performance
rotatorio (ADJ) rotating • **la secretaría será rotatoria** the secretaryship will rotate
rotería (SF) **1** (*LAm*) (= *plebe*) common people (*pl*), plebs* (*pl*)
2 (*Cono Sur*) (= *truco*) dirty trick; (= *dicho*) coarse remark
rotisería (SF) (*Cono Sur*) delicatessen
roto/a (PP) *de* **romper**
(ADJ) **1** (= *partido, destrozado*) [*juguete, mueble, cristal, puerta*] broken • **tengo la pierna rota** I've broken my leg, I've got a broken leg
2 (= *rasgado*) [*tela, papel*] torn • **la bolsa está rota** the bag is torn • **tienes rota la manga del vestido** the sleeve of your dress is ripped *o* torn • **la cuerda estaba rota por los extremos** the rope was frayed at the ends
3 (= *estropeado*) [*lavadora, televisor*] broken; [*coche, motor*] broken down
4 [*zapato*] worn, worn-out
5 (= *destrozado*) [*persona*] broken; [*vida*] shattered • **estar ~ de cansancio** to be exhausted, be worn-out
6†† (= *libertino*) debauched, dissipated
7 (*Chile**) (= *de clase baja*) common, low-class; (= *maleducado*) rude
(SM/F) **1** (= *persona chilena*) **a** (*Perú, Bol**)

Chilean, Chilean person
b (*Chile*) • **el ~ chileno** the average Chilean
2 (*Chile**) **a** (= *pobre*) pleb*
b (= *persona*) guy*/woman • **es una rota con suerte** she's a lucky woman • **el rotito quería que le pagáramos el viaje** the cheeky devil wanted us to pay for his trip*
c (= *maleducado*) • **esta rota no sabe comportarse a la mesa** she's so rude *o* such a pig‡, she doesn't know how to behave at the dinner table
(SM) (= *agujero*) (*en pantalón, vestido*) hole • **te has hecho un ~ en la manga** you've got a hole in your sleeve • MODISMO: • **valer** *o* **servir lo mismo para un ~ que para un descosido** to serve a multitude of purposes • REFRÁN: • **nunca falta un ~ para un descosido** you can always find a companion in misfortune
rotograbado (SM) rotogravure
rotonda (SF) **1** (*Aut*) roundabout, traffic circle (*EEUU*)
2 (*Arquit*) rotunda, circular gallery
3 (*Ferro*) engine shed, roundhouse
rotor (SM) rotor
rotoso* (ADJ) **1** (*LAm*) (= *harapiento*) ragged, shabby
2 (*And, Cono Sur**) (= *ordinario*) low-life, common
rótula (SF) **1** (*Anat*) kneecap
2 (*Mec*) ball-and-socket joint
rotulación (SF) **1** (= *escritura*) labelling; (*en mapa etc*) lettering
2 (= *profesión*) sign painting
rotulador (SM) felt tip pen
rotular ▷ CONJUG 1a (VT) [+ *objeto*] to label, put a label on; [+ *carta, documento*] to head, entitle; [+ *mapa*] to letter, inscribe
rotulata (SF) labels (*pl*), inscriptions (*pl*) (*collectively*)
rotulista (SMF) sign painter
rótulo (SM) **1** (= *letrero*) sign, notice; (= *cartel*) placard, poster ▸ **rótulo de salida** (*TV*) credits (*pl*) ▸ **rótulo luminoso** illuminated sign
2 (= *encabezamiento*) heading, title; (*en mapa*) lettering
3 (= *etiqueta*) label, ticket
rotundamente (ADV) [*negar*] flatly, roundly; [*afirmar, expresar acuerdo*] emphatically
rotundidad (SF) **1** [*de negativa*] flatness; [*de victoria*] clearness, convincing nature
2 (= *redondez*) rotundity
rotundo (ADJ) **1** (= *terminante*) [*negativa*] flat; [*victoria*] clear, convincing • **me dio un "sí" ~** he gave me an emphatic "yes"
2 (= *redondo*) round
rotura (SF) **1** [*de objeto*] • **varios autobuses sufrieron la ~ de cristales** a number of buses had their windscreens smashed *o* broken • **el seguro del coche cubre la ~ de cristales** the car insurance covers window breakage • **la explosión causó la ~ de la presa** the explosion caused the dam to break *o* burst *o* collapse • **la casa está sin agua por una ~ en las tuberías** the house has no water because of a broken pipe • **en la fotografía puede apreciarse la ~ del muro** in the photograph you can see where the wall is broken *o* the break in the wall
2 (*Med*) • **la ~ del hueso se produjo en el momento de la caída** the bone broke at the moment of the fall • **ingresó por ~ de cadera** he was admitted for a broken hip • **ha sufrido una ~ de ligamentos** he has torn ligaments
3 (*en tela*) tear, rip
roturación (SF) breaking-up, ploughing, plowing (*EEUU*)
roturar ▷ CONJUG 1a (VT) (*Agr*) to break up, plough, plow (*EEUU*)
rough [ruf] (SM) • **el ~** (*Golf*) the rough
roulotte [ru'lot] (SF) caravan, trailer (*EEUU*)
round [raun] (SM) (PL: **rounds**) round
router (SM) (*Inform*) router
roya (SF) rust, blight
royalty (SM) (PL: **royalties**) royalty
roza (SF) **1** (*Arquit*) groove, hollow (*in a wall*)
2 (*esp Cono Sur*) (= *hierbajos*) weeds (*pl*)
3 (*Méx*) (= *matas*) brush, stubble
4 (*And*) (*Agr*) planting in newly-broken ground
5 (*CAm*) (= *tierra limpia*) cleared ground
rozado (ADJ) worn, grazed
rozador (SM) (*Caribe*) machete
rozadura (SF) (= *marca*) mark of rubbing, chafing mark; (*en la piel*) abrasion, graze
rozagante (ADJ) (*liter*) **1** [*vestido*] showy; (= *llamativo*) striking
2 (= *ufano*) proud
rozamiento (SM) **1** (= *fricción*) rubbing, chafing; (*Mec*) friction
2 • **tener un ~ con algn*** to have a slight disagreement with sb
rozar ▷ CONJUG 1f (VT) **1** (= *tocar ligeramente*) • **la rocé al pasar** I brushed past her • **estas botas me rozan los tobillos** these boots rub my ankles • **con esa falda vas rozando el suelo** your skirt is trailing on the floor • **la mesa ha rozado la pared** the table has scraped the wall • **la pelota rozó el poste** the ball shaved *o* grazed the post • **la flecha le rozó la oreja** the arrow grazed his ear • **la gaviota volaba rozando el mar** the seagull skimmed over the sea
2 (= *acercarse a*) • **debe estar rozando los 50** she must be getting on for 50 • **su estilo de juego roza la perfección** his game is close to perfection • **es una cuestión que roza lo judicial** it's almost a judicial matter
3 (*Arquit*) to make a groove *o* hollow in
4 (*Agr*) [+ *hierba*] to graze; [+ *terreno*] to clear
(VI) • **~ con algo: eso roza con la codicia** that's bordering *o* verging on greed
(VPR) **rozarse 1** (= *tocarse ligeramente*) • **se rozó conmigo al pasar** he brushed past me • **me rocé la rodilla con el muro** I grazed *o* scraped my knee on the wall
2* (= *tratarse*) • **~se con algn** to hobnob with sb*, rub shoulders with sb
3 (= *desgastarse*) [*cuello, puños*] to become frayed *o* worn
4† (= *tropezarse*) to trip over one's own feet; (*al hablar*) to get tongue-tied • **~se en un sonido** to stutter over a sound
roznar¹ ▷ CONJUG 1a (VT), (VI) = **ronzar**
roznar² ▷ CONJUG 1a (VI) [*burro*] to bray
roznido (SM) bray, braying
R.P. (ABR) = **Reverendo Padre**
r.p.m. (ABR) (= **revoluciones por minuto**) rpm
RRPP (ABR) (= **relaciones públicas**) PR
Rte. (ABR) = **remite, remitente**
RTVE (SF ABR) = **Radiotelevisión Española**
rúa (SF) street
Ruán (SM) Rouen
ruana (SF) (*And, Caribe*) poncho, ruana
Ruanda (SF) Rwanda
ruandés/esa (ADJ), (SM/F) Rwandan
ruanetas (SMF INV) (*Col*) peasant
ruano (ADJ), (SM) = **roano**
rubeola (SF), **rubéola** (SF) German measles
rubí (SM) (= *piedra preciosa*) ruby; [*de reloj*] jewel
rubia (SF) **1** (*Esp†**) (= *peseta*) peseta
2 (*Aut*) estate car, station wagon (*EEUU*); ▷ **rubio**
rubiales* (SMF INV) blond/blonde, fair-haired person
rubiato/a (ADJ) fair, blond/blonde
(SM/F) fair-haired person, blond/blonde
Rubicón (SM) Rubicon • MODISMO: • **pasar el ~** to cross the Rubicon
rubicundo (ADJ) **1** [*cara*] ruddy; [*persona*] ruddy-faced
2 (= *rojizo*) reddish
rubiez (SF) (*liter*) blondness
rubio/a (ADJ) **1** [*persona*] fair-haired, blond/blonde; [*animal*] light-coloured, light-colored (*EEUU*), golden • **~ ceniza** ash-blond • **~ platino** platinum-blonde
2 • **tabaco ~** Virginia tobacco
(SM) Virginia tobacco
(SM/F) blond/blonde, fair-haired person ▸ **rubia ceniza** ash blonde ▸ **rubia de bote** peroxide blonde ▸ **rubia miel** honey blonde ▸ **rubia oxigenada** peroxide blonde ▸ **rubia platino** platinum blonde; ▷ **rubia**
rublo (SM) rouble
rubor (SM) **1** (*en cara*) blush, flush • **causar ~ a algn** to make sb blush
2 (= *timidez*) bashfulness
3 (= *color*) bright red
ruborizado (ADJ) (= *colorado*) blushing; (= *avergonzado*) ashamed
ruborizante (ADJ) blush-making
ruborizar ▷ CONJUG 1f (VT) to cause to blush, make blush
(VPR) **ruborizarse** to blush, redden (**de** at)
ruboroso (ADJ) (*frm*) **1** • **ser ~** to blush easily
2 • **estar ~** (= *colorado*) to blush, be blushing; (= *avergonzado*) to feel bashful
rúbrica (SF) **1** (= *señal*) red mark
2 [*de la firma*] flourish
3 (= *título*) title, heading • **bajo la ~ de** under the heading of
4 • **de ~** customary, usual
rubricar ▷ CONJUG 1g (VT) **1** (= *firmar*) to sign with a flourish; [+ *documento*] to initial
2 (= *concluir*) to sign and seal
rubro (SM) **1** (*LAm*) (= *título*) heading, title
2 (*LAm*) (*Com*) ▸ **rubro social** trading name, firm's name
3 (*LAm*) [*de cuenta*] heading
ruca (SF) **1** (*Cono Sur*) (= *cabina*) hut, Indian hut, cabin
2 (*Méx*) (= *soltera*) old maid
rucho (ADJ) (*And*) [*fruta*] overripe
rucio/a (ADJ) **1** [*caballo*] grey, gray (*EEUU*); [*persona*] grey-haired, gray-haired (*EEUU*)
2 (*Chile**) (= *rubio*) fair, blond/blonde
(SM) (= *caballo*) grey, gray (*EEUU*), grey horse, gray horse (*EEUU*)
(SM/F) (*Chile**) (= *rubio*) blond/blonde, blond/blonde person
ruco (ADJ) **1** (*LAm*) (= *usado*) worn-out, useless; (= *agotado*) exhausted
2 (*And, Méx*) (= *viejo*) old
ruda (SF) rue
rudamente (ADV) **1** (= *tosco*) coarsely
2 (= *sencillamente*) simply, plainly
rudeza (SF) **1** (= *tosquedad*) coarseness ▸ **rudeza de entendimiento** stupidity
2 (= *sencillez*) simplicity
rudimental (ADJ), **rudimentario** (ADJ) rudimentary
rudimento (SM) **1** (*Anat*) rudiment
2 rudimentos (= *lo básico*) rudiments
rudo (ADJ) **1** [*madera*] rough; (= *sin pulir*) unpolished
2 (*Mec*) [*pieza*] stiff
3 [*persona*] (= *sencillo*) simple
4 (= *tosco*) coarse
5 [*golpe*] hard • **fue un ~ golpe para mí** it was a terrible blow for me
rueca (SF) distaff
rueda (SF) **1** (*Mec*) wheel; (= *neumático*) tyre, tire (*EEUU*); [*de mueble*] roller, castor • MODISMOS: • **chupar ~** (*Ciclismo*) to tuck in; (= *aprovecharse*) to ride on sb's coattails • **ir**

sobre ~s* (*en vehículo*) to go for a spin*; (= *marchar bien*) to go smoothly ▸ **rueda auxiliar** (*Arg, Uru*) spare wheel (*esp Brit*), spare tire (*EEUU*) ▸ **rueda de agua** waterwheel ▸ **rueda de alfarero** potter's wheel ▸ **rueda de atrás** rear wheel, back wheel ▸ **rueda de auxilio** (*Arg, Uru*) spare wheel (*esp Brit*), spare tire (*EEUU*) ▸ **rueda de cadena** sprocket wheel ▸ **rueda de la fortuna** wheel of fortune ▸ **rueda delantera** front wheel ▸ **rueda de molino** millwheel • **MODISMO**: • **comulga con ~s de molino** he'd swallow anything ▸ **rueda dentada** cog ▸ **rueda de paletas** paddle wheel ▸ **rueda de recambio** spare wheel (*esp Brit*), spare tire (*EEUU*) ▸ **rueda de trinquete** ratchet wheel ▸ **rueda hidráulica** waterwheel ▸ **rueda impresora** (*Inform*) print wheel ▸ **rueda libre** freewheel ▸ **rueda motriz** driving wheel ▸ **ruedas de aterrizaje** (*Aer*) landing wheels
2 (= *círculo*) circle, ring • **en ~** in a ring ▸ **rueda de identificación** identification parade ▸ **rueda de prensa** press conference ▸ **rueda de reconocimiento** identification parade ▸ **rueda informativa** press conference
3 (= *rodaja*) slice, round
4 (*en torneo*) round
5 (*Hist*) rack
6 (= *pez*) sunfish
7 [*de pavón*] spread tail • **hacer la ~** to spread its tail • **MODISMO**: • **hacer la ~ a algn** to court sb, to play up to sb, ingratiate o.s. with sb
8 • **dar ~ (en)** (*Caribe*) (*Aut*) to drive (around)

ruedecilla SF (= *rueda pequeña*) small wheel; [*de mueble*] roller, castor

ruedero SM wheelwright

ruedo SM **1** (*Taur*) bullring, arena
2 (*Pol*) ring
3 (= *contorno*) edge, border; (= *circunferencia*) circumference; [*de vestido*] hem
4 (= *esterilla*) mat, round mat
5 (*Cono Sur*) (= *suerte*) luck, gambler's luck
6 (= *rotación*) turn, rotation

ruega *etc* ▹ **rogar**

ruego SM request • **a ~ de** at the request of • **accediendo a los ~s de** in response to the requests of • **"~s y preguntas"** (*en una conferencia*) "any other business"

rufián SM **1** (= *gamberro*) hooligan; (= *canalla*) scoundrel
2 (= *chulo*) pimp

rufianería SF, **rufianismo** SM [*de chulo*] pimping, procuring; (*Jur*) living off immoral earnings

rufianesca SF criminal underworld

rufo ADJ **1** (= *pelirrojo*) red-haired; (= *rizado*) curly-haired
2* (= *satisfecho*) smug, self-satisfied; (= *engreído*) cocky*, boastful

rugbista SMF rugby player

rugby ['rugbi] SM rugby

rugido SM roar ▸ **rugido de dolor** howl *o* roar of pain ▸ **rugido de tripas** stomach rumblings (*pl*), collywobbles* (*pl*)

rugir ▹ CONJUG 3c VI **1** [*león etc*] to roar; [*toro*] to bellow; [*mar*] to roar; [*tormenta, viento*] to roar, howl, rage; [*estómago*] to rumble; [*persona*] to roar • **~ de dolor** to roar *o* howl with pain
2‡ (= *oler mal*) to pong*, stink

rugosidad SF roughness

rugoso ADJ **1** (= *áspero*) rough
2 (= *arrugado*) wrinkled, creased

ruibarbo SM rhubarb

ruido SM **1** (= *sonido*) noise • **¿has oído ese ~?** did you hear that noise? • **no hagas tanto ~** don't make so much noise • **no hagas ~, que el niño está durmiendo** don't make a sound, the baby's sleeping • **me hace ~ el estómago*** my stomach is rumbling • **lejos del mundanal ~** (*hum, liter*) far from the madding crowd (*liter*) • **sin ~** quietly • **MODISMOS**: • **mucho ~ y pocas nueces** much ado about nothing • **es más el ~ que las nueces**: • **prometieron reformas para este año, pero era más el ~ que las nueces** they promised reforms for this year, but it was all hot air • **los grandes beneficios anunciados son más el ~ que las nueces** the large profits they announced are not all what they were cracked up to be ▸ **ruido blanco** white noise ▸ **ruido de fondo** background noise ▸ **ruido de sables** • **en los cuarteles se oye ~ de sables** there's talk of rebellion in the ranks
2 (= *escándalo*) • **hacer** *o* **meter ~** to cause a stir • **quitarse de ~s** to keep out of trouble

ruidosamente ADV **1** (= *estrepitosamente*) noisily, loudly
2 (= *de manera sensacionalista*) sensationally

ruidoso ADJ **1** (= *estrepitoso*) noisy
2 [*noticia*] sensational

ruin ADJ **1** (= *vil*) [*persona*] contemptible, mean
2 [*trato*] (= *injusto*) mean, shabby; (= *cruel*) heartless, callous
3 (= *tacaño*) mean, stingy
4 (= *pequeño*) small, weak
5 [*animal*] vicious

ruina SF **1** (*Econ*) ruin • **estaba al borde de la ~** he was on the brink of (financial) ruin • **la empresa le llevó a la ~** the venture ruined him (financially) • **estar en la ~** to be ruined • **tanto gastar en viajes va a ser mi ~** spending all this money on travel is going to cost me a fortune
2 [*de edificio*] collapse • **amenazar ~** to threaten to collapse, be about to fall down
3 [*de imperio*] fall, decline; [*de persona*] ruin, downfall • **el alcohol va a ser mi ~** alcohol will be the ruin of me, alcohol will be my downfall • **esto contribuyó a su ~ política** this contributed to his political downfall
4 (= *persona ajada*) • **estar hecho una ~** to be a wreck, look a wreck
5 ruinas ruins • **han descubierto unas ~s romanas** they have discovered some Roman ruins • **el castillo está en ~s** the castle is in ruins
6 (*Jur‡*) bird‡, prison sentence

ruindad SF **1** (= *cualidad*) meanness, lowness
2 (= *acto*) low act, mean act

ruinoso ADJ **1** (*Arquit*) ruinous; (= *destartalado*) tumbledown
2 (*Econ*) ruinous, disastrous

ruiseñor SM nightingale

rula SF (*And, CAm*) hunting knife

rular‡ ▹ CONJUG 1a VT to pass round

rulemán SM (*Cono Sur*) ball-bearing, roller bearing

rulenco ADJ (*Cono Sur*), **rulengo** ADJ (*Cono Sur*) weak, underdeveloped

rulero SM (*And*) hair curler, roller

ruleta SF roulette ▸ **ruleta rusa** Russian roulette

ruletear ▹ CONJUG 1a VI (*CAm, Méx*) to drive a taxi, drive a cab

ruleteo SM (*CAm, Méx*) taxi driving, cab driving

ruletero SM (*CAm, Méx*) taxi driver, cab driver

rulo¹ SM **1** (= *rodillo*) roller; (*Culin*) rolling pin
2 [*de pelo*] curler
3 (= *pelota*) ball, round mass
4 (*And, Cono Sur*) (= *rizo*) natural curl

rulo² SM (*Cono Sur*) (= *terreno*) well-watered ground

rulota SF caravan, trailer (*EEUU*)

ruma SF (*LAm*) heap, pile

Rumanía SF, **Rumania** SF Romania

rumano/a ADJ, SM/F Rumanian, Romanian
SM (*Ling*) Rumanian, Romanian

rumba¹ SF **1** (*Mús*) rumba
2 (*LAm*) (= *fiesta*) party, celebration

rumba² SF (*Cono Sur*) = **ruma**

rumbar ▹ CONJUG 1a VT (*LAm*) to throw
VI **1** (*And*) (= *zumbar*) to buzz
2 (*And, Cono Sur*) (= *orientarse*) to get one's bearings
VPR **rumbarse** (*And*) to make off, go away

rumbeador SM (*And, Cono Sur*) pathfinder, tracker

rumbear ▹ CONJUG 1a VI **1** (*LAm*) (*Mús*) to dance the rumba
2 (*LAm*) (= *seguir*) to follow a direction; (= *orientarse*) to find one's way, get one's bearings
3 (*Cuba**) (= *ir de rumba*) to have a party
4 (*Méx*) (*en bosque*) to clear a path (through the undergrowth)

rumbero ADJ **1** (*And, Cono Sur*) (= *rumbeador*) tracking, pathfinding
2 (*Caribe*) [*juerguista*] party-going, fond of a good time
SM (*And*) (*en bosque*) pathfinder, guide; [*de río*] river pilot

rumbo¹ SM **1** (= *dirección*) (*Aer, Náut*) course • **corregir el ~** to correct one's course • **perder el ~** (*Aer, Náut*) to go off course • **poner ~ a** to set a course for • **con ~ a**: **acababa de despegar con ~ a Rumanía** it had just taken off for Romania • **zarparon con ~ sur** they set a southerly course • **sin ~ (fijo)** [*pasear*] aimlessly; [*viajar*] with no fixed destination • **una existencia sin ~** an aimless existence
2 (= *tendencia*) • **los acontecimientos han tomado un nuevo ~** events have taken a new turn • **los nuevos ~s de la estrategia occidental** the new lines of western strategy
3 (= *generosidad*) generosity, lavishness • **de mucho ~** = **rumboso** • **viajar con ~** to travel in style
4 (*LAm*) (= *fiesta*) party
5 (*Cono Sur*) (= *herida*) cut (on the head)

rumbo² SM (*And*) (*Orn*) hummingbird

rumbón* ADJ = **rumboso**

rumbosidad SF lavishness

rumboso ADJ **1** [*persona*] (= *generoso*) generous; (= *espléndido*) big, splendid
2 [*regalo*] lavish; [*boda, fiesta*] big, showy

rumia SF, **rumiación** SF rumination

rumiante ADJ, SM ruminant

rumiar ▹ CONJUG 1b VI **1** [*rumiante*] to chew the cud
2 (= *considerar*) to ruminate, ponder; (*pey*) to take too long to make up one's mind
VT **1** (= *masticar*) to chew
2 [+ *asunto*] to chew over

rumor SM **1** (= *noticia vaga*) rumour, rumor (*EEUU*) • **circula** *o* **corre el ~ de que ...** there's a rumour going round that ...
2 (= *murmullo*) murmur; [*de voces*] buzz

rumoreado ADJ rumoured, rumored (*EEUU*)

rumorearse ▹ CONJUG 1a VPR • **se rumorea que** it is rumoured *o* (*EEUU*) rumored that

rumoreo SM murmur, murmuring

rumorología SF rumours (*pl*), rumors (*pl*) (*EEUU*)

rumorólogo/a SM/F scandalmonger

rumorosidad SF noise level

rumoroso ADJ (*liter*) murmuring; [*arroyo*] babbling

runa¹ SF rune

r

runa² (SM) (*And, Cono Sur*) Indian, Indian man
runa simi (SM) (*And*) Quechua, Quechua language
runcho (ADJ) **1** (*And*) (= *ignorante*) ignorant; (= *obstinado*) stubborn
2 (*CAm*) (= *tacaño*) mean
rundir ▹ CONJUG 3a (*Méx*) (VT) (= *guardar*) to keep; (= *ocultar*) to hide, put away
(VI) to become drowsy
(VPR) **rundirse** to fall fast asleep
rundún (SM) (*Cono Sur*) hummingbird
runfla* (SF) (*LAm*), **runflada*** (SF) (*LAm*) (= *montón*) lot, heap; (= *multitud*) crowd; (= *pandilla*) gang, gang of kids*
rúnico (ADJ) runic
runrún (SM) **1** [*de voces*] murmur
2 (= *rumor*) rumour, rumor (*EEUU*), buzz*
3 [*de una máquina*] whirr
runrunearse ▹ CONJUG 1a (VPR) • **se runrunea que** ... the rumour *o* (*EEUU*) rumor is that ...
runruneo (SM) = **runrún**
ruñir ▹ CONJUG 3h (VT) (*And, Méx, Caribe*) = **roer**
rupestre (ADJ) rock (*antes de s*) • **pintura ~** cave painting • **planta ~** rock plant
rupia (SF) (= *moneda*) rupee
ruptor (SM) contact breaker
ruptura (SF) **1** [*de cable, cerco*] • **tenemos que encontrar el punto de ~ del cable** we need to find the point where the cable broke • **la ofensiva de ~ del cerco de Sarajevo** the attack to break the siege of Sarajevo
2 (= *interrupción*) [*de pacto, contrato*] breaking; [*de relaciones, negociaciones*] breaking-off • **la construcción de la autopista puede llevar a la ~ del equilibrio ecológico** the construction of the motorway could upset the ecological balance • **el incidente causó la ~ de los lazos políticos entre ambos países** the incident led to the breaking-off of diplomatic ties between the two countries
3 (= *disolución*) break-up • **la ~ de la unidad familiar** the break-up of the family unit • **los motivos de su ~ matrimonial** the reasons for the break-up of their marriage • **la ~ de la coalición electoral** the break-up of the electoral coalition
4 (= *división*) split, rupture (*frm*) • **las diferencias entre ambos líderes pueden provocar una ~ interna** the differences between the two leaders could cause an internal split *o* (*frm*) a rupture within the party
5 (*con el pasado*) break • **este cambio supone una ~ con todo lo anterior** this change means a break with everything that went before
6 (*Tenis*) break • **seis puntos de ~** six break points ▸ **ruptura de servicio** break of service, service break
rural (ADJ) rural
(SF) (*Arg*) (*Aut*) estate car, station wagon (*EEUU*)
(SM) • **los ~es** (*Méx*) (*Hist*) (= *la policía*) the rural police
Rusia (SF) Russia ▸ **Rusia Soviética** Soviet Russia
ruso/a (ADJ) Russian
(SM/F) **1** (= *de Rusia*) Russian • **los Rusos** the Russians, the people of Russia
2 (*Arg**) Jew
(SM) (*Ling*) Russian
rústica (SF) • **libro en ~** paperback (book) • **edición (en) ~** paperback edition; ▹ **rústico**
rusticidad (SF) **1** (= *calidad*) rusticity, rural character
2 (= *tosquedad*) coarseness, uncouthness; (= *grosería*) crudity; (= *descortesía*) bad manners (*pl*), unmannerliness
rústico/a (ADJ) **1** (= *del campo*) rustic, rural, country (*antes de s*)
2 (= *tosco*) coarse, uncouth; (= *grosero*) crude; (= *descortés*) unmannerly
(SM/F) peasant, yokel, hillbilly (*EEUU*); ▹ **rústica**
rustidera (SF) roasting tin
ruta (SF) **1** [*de un viaje*] route
2 (= *camino*) ▸ **ruta aérea** air route, airway ▸ **ruta de la seda** silk route, silk road ▸ **Ruta Jacobea** Way of St James (*pilgrim road to Santiago de Compostela*)
3 (*Cono Sur*) (= *carretera*) road
rutero/a (ADJ) road (*antes de s*)
(SM/F) **1** (= *camionero*) truck driver
2 (*Esp*) (*de fin de semana*) raver
rutilancia (SF) sparkle
rutilante (ADJ) (*liter*) shining, sparkling, glowing
rutilar ▹ CONJUG 1a (VI) (*liter*) to shine, sparkle
rutina (SF) routine • **por ~** from force of habit ▸ **rutina diaria** daily routine
rutinariamente (ADV) (= *de manera rutinaria*) in a routine way; (= *sin imaginación*) unimaginatively
rutinario (ADJ) **1** [*procedimiento*] routine; (= *de cada día*) ordinary, everyday
2 [*persona*] ordinary; (= *sin imaginación*) unimaginative; [*creencia*] unthinking, automatic
rutinizarse ▹ CONJUG 1f (VPR) to become routine, become normal
Rvdo. (ABR) (= **Reverendo**) Rev, Revd

r

Ss

S, s ['ese] (SF) (= *letra*) S, s
S (ABR) **1** (= **sur**) S
2 (= **septiembre**) Sept • **el 11-S** 9-11, Nine-Eleven
3 (= **sobresaliente**) v.g.
4 (*Cine*) • **película S** pornographic film
S. (ABR) (*Rel*) (= **San, Santa, Santo**) St
s. (ABR) **1** (= **siglo**) c
2 (= **siguiente**) foll.
s/ (ABR) (*Com*) (= **su, sus**) yr
S.ª (ABR) (= **Sierra**) Mts
S.A. (ABR) **1** (*Com*) (= **Sociedad Anónima**) Ltd, plc, Corp (EEUU), Inc (EEUU)
2 (= **Su Alteza**) HH
sáb. (ABR) (= **sábado**) Sat.
sábado (SM) **1** (= *día de la semana*) Saturday • **del ~ en ocho días** Saturday week, a week on Saturday, the Saturday after next • **el ~ pasado** last Saturday • **el ~ próximo** *o* **que viene** this *o* next Saturday • **el ~ por la mañana** (on) Saturday morning • **la noche del ~** (on) Saturday night • **un ~ sí y otro no** • **cada dos ~s** every other *o* second Saturday • **no va al colegio los ~s** he doesn't go to school on Saturdays • **vendrá el ~ (25 de marzo)** he will come on Saturday (25 March) ▸ **Sábado de Gloria, Sábado Santo** Easter Saturday ▸ **sábado inglés** (*Cono Sur*) *non-working Saturday*
2 (*Rel*) [*de los judíos*] Sabbath
3 • MODISMO: • **hacer ~** to do the weekly clean
sábalo (SM) shad
sabana (SF) savannah
sábana (SF) **1** [*de cama*] sheet • **la Sábana Santa de Turín** the Holy Shroud of Turin • MODISMOS: • **encontrar las ~s*** to hit the hay* • **se le pegan las ~s** he oversleeps • **ponerse en la ~** to strike it lucky ▸ **sábana de agua** sheet of rain
2 (*Rel*) altar cloth
3‡ (= *dinero*) 1000-peseta note • **media ~** 500-peseta note ▸ **sábana verde** 1000-peseta note
sabandija (SF) **1** (= *animal*) bug, creepy-crawly* • **~s** vermin (*sing*)
2* (= *persona*) louse*
3 (*Arg**) (= *diablillo*) rascal
sabanear ▸ CONJUG 1a (VT) **1** (*CAm*) (= *agarrar*) to catch
2 (*CAm*) (= *halagar*) to flatter
3 (*CAm, Caribe*) (= *perseguir*) to pursue, chase
(VI) (*LAm*) (= *recorrer la sabana*) to travel across a plain; (= *reunir el ganado*) to round up cattle on the savannah, scour the plain for cattle
sabanero/a (*LAm*) (ADJ) (= *de la sabana*) savannah (*antes de s*), of/from the savannah
(SM/F) plainsman/plainswoman
(SM) (*CAm*) (= *matón*) bully, thug
sabanilla (SF) **1** (*Rel*) altar cloth
2 (*Cono Sur*) (= *colcha*) bedspread
sabañón (SM) chilblain
sabara (SF) (*Caribe*) light mist, haze
sabatario/a (ADJ), (SM/F) sabbatarian

sabateño (SM) (*Caribe*) boundary stone
sabático (ADJ) **1** (*Rel, Univ*) sabbatical
2 (= *del sábado*) Saturday (*antes de s*)
sabatino (ADJ) Saturday (*antes de s*)
sabedor (ADJ) • **ser ~ de algo** to know about sth
sabelotodo* (SMF INV) know-all*, know-it-all (EEUU*)
saber ▸ CONJUG 2m (VT) **1** (= *tener conocimiento de*) **a** [+ *dato, información*] to know • **no sabía que era tu cumpleaños** I didn't know it was your birthday • **sé que me has mentido** I know you've lied to me • **lo sé** I know • **sin ~lo yo** without my knowledge, without me knowing • **hacer ~ algo a algn** to inform sb of sth, let sb know about sth • **quiero hacerle ~ que …** I would like to inform *o* advise you that … • **el motivo de esta carta es hacerle ~ que …** I am writing to inform *o* advise you that …
b (*locuciones*) • **a ~** namely • **dos planetas, a ~, Venus y la Tierra** two planets, namely Venus and Earth • **a ~ si realmente lo compró** I wonder whether he really did buy it • **a ~ dónde lo tiene guardado** I wonder where he has it hidden away • **¡anda a ~!** (*LAm*) God knows! • **demasiado bien sé que …** I know only too well that … • **¡no lo sabes bien!*** not half!* • **cualquiera sabe si …** it's anybody's guess whether … • **¡de haberlo sabido!** if only I'd known! • **lo dudo, pero nunca se sabe** I doubt it, but you never know • **para que lo sepas** let me tell you, for your information • **que yo sepa** as far as I know • **que sepamos** as far as we know • **un no sé qué** a certain something • **un no sé qué de afectado** a certain (element of) affectation • **¡quién sabe!** who knows! • **¿quién sabe?** who knows?, who can tell?, who's to say? • **¡si lo sabré yo!** I should know! • **tú sabrás (lo que haces)** I suppose you know (what you're doing) • **¿tú qué sabes?** what do you know about it? • **¡vete a ~!** God knows! • **¡vete a ~ de dónde ha venido!** goodness only knows where he came from! • **vete tú a ~** your guess is as good as mine • **ya lo sabía yo** I thought as much • **¡yo qué sé!, ¡qué sé yo!** how should I know!, search me!* • MODISMOS: • **cada uno sabe dónde le aprieta el zapato** everyone knows their own weaknesses • **no sabía dónde meterse** he didn't know what to do with himself • **no ~ ni papa** not to know the first thing about sth; ▸ **Briján**
2 (= *enterarse de*) to find out • **en cuanto lo supimos fuimos a ayudarle** as soon as we found out, we went to help him • **cuando lo supe** when I heard *o* found out about it • **lograron ~ el secreto** they managed to learn the secret
3 (= *tener noticias*) to hear • **desde hace seis meses no sabemos nada de él** we haven't heard from him for six months
4 (= *tener destreza en*) • **¿sabes ruso?** do you speak Russian?, can you speak Russian? • **no sé nada de cocina** I don't know anything about cookery • **~ hacer algo:** • **sabe cuidar de sí mismo** he can take care of himself, he knows how to take care of himself • **¿sabes nadar?** can you swim? • **saben tratar muy bien al forastero** they know how to look after visitors • **¿sabes ir?** do you know the way? • **todavía no sabe orientarse por la ciudad** he still doesn't know his way around town • **pocos campeones saben perder** few champions are good losers • **es una persona que sabe escuchar** she's a good listener
5 (*LAm*) • **~ hacer** to be in the habit of doing • **no sabe venir por aquí** he doesn't usually come this way, he's not in the habit of coming along here
(VI) **1** (= *tener conocimiento*) • **~ de algo** to know of sth • **sabe mucho de ordenadores** he knows a lot about computers • **sé de un sitio muy bueno** I know of a very good place • **hace mucho que no sabemos de ella** it's quite a while since we heard from her, we haven't had any news from her for quite a while
2 (= *estar enterado*) to know • **costó muy caro, ¿sabe usted?** it was very expensive, you know • **un 5% no sabe, no contesta** there were 5% "don't knows"
3 (= *tener sabor*) to taste • **no sabe demasiado bien** it doesn't taste too good • **sabe un poco amargo** it tastes rather bitter • **~ a** to taste of • **esto sabe a queso** this tastes of cheese • **esto sabe a demonio(s)** this tastes awful • MODISMO: • **~le mal a algn:** • **me supo muy mal lo que hicieron** I didn't like what they did, I wasn't pleased *o* didn't feel good about what they did • **no me sabe mal que un amigo me gaste bromas** I don't mind a friend playing jokes on me, it doesn't bother me having a friend play jokes on me
(VPR) **saberse 1** (*uso enfático*) • **eso ya me lo sabía yo** I already knew that • **se lo sabe de memoria** she knows it by heart • MODISMO: • **se las sabe todas*** he knows every trick in the book*
2 (*uso impersonal*) **a** (= *ser conocido*) • **ya se sabe que …** it is known that …, we know that … • **no se sabe** nobody knows, it's not known • **no se saben las causas** the causes are not known *o* are unknown • **¿se puede ~ si …?** can you tell me if *o* whether …? • **¿quién es usted, si se puede ~?** who are you, may I ask? • **sépase que …** let it be known that … • **nunca más se supo de ellos** they were never heard of again
b (= *ser descubierto*) • **se supo que …** it was learnt *o* discovered that … • **por fin se supo el secreto** finally the secret was revealed
3 (*de uno mismo*) • **se saben héroes** they know they are heroes
(SM) knowledge, learning • **según mi leal ~**

y entender (*frm*) to the best of my knowledge ▸ **saber hacer** (*Téc*) know-how; (*Literat*) savoir-faire ▸ **saber popular** folk wisdom

> **SABER**
>
> *Por regla general, si* **saber** *va seguido de un infinitivo, se traduce por* **can** *cuando indica una habilidad permanente y por* **know how** *cuando se trata de la capacidad de resolver un problema concreto. La construcción correspondiente habrá de ser* **can** + INFINITIVO *sin* **to** *o* **know how** + INFINITIVO *con* **to**:
>
> **Jaime sabe tocar el piano**
> Jaime can play the piano
> **¿Sabes cambiar una rueda?**
> Do you know how to change a wheel?
>
> *Hay que tener en cuenta que* **know** *(sin* **how***) nunca puede ir seguido directamente de un infinitivo en inglés.*
>
> *Para otros usos y ejemplos ver la entrada.*

sabiamente ADV **1** (= *eruditamente*) learnedly, expertly
2 (= *prudentemente*) wisely, sensibly

sabichoso* ADJ (*Caribe*) = **sabihondo**

sabidillo/a* SM/F know-all*, know-it-all (*esp EEUU**)

sabido VB (*pp de* **saber**) • **es ~ que** it is well known that • **como es ~** as we all know
ADJ **1** (= *consabido*) well-known, familiar
2 (*iró*) [*persona*] knowledgeable, learned
3 • **de ~** (= *por supuesto*) for sure, certainly
4 (*And*) (= *travieso*) mischievous, saucy

sabiduría SF (= *saber*) wisdom; (= *instrucción*) learning ▸ **sabiduría popular** folklore

sabiendas • **a ~** ADV (= *sabiendo*) knowingly; (= *a propósito*) deliberately • **a ~ de que ...** knowing full well that ...

sabihondo/a ADJ, SM/F know-all*, know-it-all (*esp EEUU**)

sabio/a ADJ **1** [*persona*] (= *docto*) learned; (= *juicioso*) [*persona*] wise, sensible
• MODISMO: • **más ~ que Salomón** wiser than Solomon
2 [*acción, decisión*] wise, sensible
3 [*animal*] trained
SM/F (= *docto*) learned man/learned woman; (= *experto*) scholar, expert • **¡hay que escuchar al ~!** (*iró*) just listen to the professor! • REFRÁN: • **de ~s es rectificar** it takes a wise man to recognize that he was wrong

sabiondo/a ADJ, SM/F = **sabihondo**

sablazo SM **1** (= *herida*) sword wound; (= *golpe*) sabre slash, saber slash (*EEUU*)
2* (= *gorronería*) sponging*, scrounging* • **dar o pegar un ~ a algn** (*en tienda, restaurante*) to rip sb off*; (*al pedir dinero*) to touch sb for a loan* • MODISMOS: • **vivir de ~s** to live by sponging *o* scrounging* • **la cuenta fue un ~*** the bill was astronomical

sable[1] SM (= *arma*) sabre, saber (*EEUU*), cutlass

sable[2] SM (*Heráldica*) sable

sablear* ▹ CONJUG 1a VT • **~ dinero a algn** to scrounge money from *o* off sb* • **~ algo a algn** to scrounge sth from *o* off sb*

sablista* SMF sponger*, scrounger*

sabor SM taste, flavour, flavor (*EEUU*) • **con ~ a queso** cheese-flavoured • **este caramelo tiene ~ a naranja** this sweet tastes of orange, this sweet's orange-flavoured • **con un ligero ~ arcaico** with a slightly archaic flavour (to it) • **sin ~** tasteless; (*fig*) insipid • MODISMO: • **le deja a uno mal/buen ~ de boca** it leaves a nasty/pleasant taste in the mouth ▸ **sabor local** local colour, local color (*EEUU*)

saborcillo SM slight taste

saborear ▹ CONJUG 1a VT **1** [+ *comida*] (*apreciando el sabor*) to savour, savor (*EEUU*); (= *probar*) to taste
2 (= *dar sabor a*) to flavour, flavor (*EEUU*)
3 (= *deleitarse con*) [+ *venganza, momento, triunfo, victoria*] to relish, savour, savor (*EEUU*); [+ *desgracia ajena*] to delight in
VPR **saborearse** to smack one's lips (in anticipation) • **~se algo** (*fig*) to relish the thought of sth

saborete SM slight taste

saborizante SM flavouring, flavoring (*EEUU*)

sabotaje SM sabotage ▸ **sabotaje industrial** industrial sabotage

saboteador(a) SM/F saboteur

sabotear ▹ CONJUG 1a VT to sabotage

Saboya SF Savoy

saboyano/a ADJ of/from Savoy
SM/F native/inhabitant of Savoy • **los ~s** the people of Savoy

sabré *etc* ▹ **saber**

sabrosear* ▹ CONJUG 1a VI (*Ven*) to have fun

sabrosera SF (*LAm*) tasty thing, titbit

sabroso ADJ **1** [*comida*] tasty, delicious
2 (= *agradable*) [*libro*] solid, meaty; [*oferta*] substantial; [*sueldo*] fat
3 [*broma, historia*] racy, daring
4 (*And, Caribe, Méx*) (= *ameno*) pleasant
5 (*And, Caribe, Méx*) (= *parlanchín*) talkative
6 (*Méx*) (= *fanfarrón*) bigheaded, stuck-up*

sabrosón* ADJ **1** (*LAm*) = **sabroso**
2 (*And*) (= *parlanchín*) talkative, chatty

sabrosura SF (*LAm*) **1** [*de comida*] tastiness
2 (= *lo agradable*) pleasantness, delightfulness, sweetness
3 (= *placer*) delight, enjoyment

sabueso SM (*Zool*) bloodhound
SMF (= *detective*) sleuth*

saburra SF fur (*on tongue*)

saburroso ADJ coated, furred

saca[1] SF **1** (= *saco*) big sack ▸ **saca de correo, saca de correos** mailbag
2 (*LAm*) [*de ganado*] herd of cattle, moving herd of cattle

saca[2] SF (= *acción*) (*gen*) taking out, withdrawal; (*Com*) export • **estar de ~** (*Com*) to be on sale; [*mujer*] to be of marriageable age ▸ **saca carcelaria** illegal removal of a prisoner from prison (for execution)

sacabocados SM INV punch (*for making holes*)

sacabotas SM INV bootjack

sacabuche SM sackbut

sacabullas* SM INV (*Méx*) bouncer*

sacaclavos SM INV nail-puller, pincers (*pl*)

sacacorchos SM INV corkscrew

sacacuartos SM INV = **sacadineros**

sacada SF (*And, Cono Sur*) = **sacadura**

sacadera SF landing-net

sacadineros* SM INV **1** (= *baratija*) cheap trinket
2 (= *diversión*) *money-wasting spectacle, worthless sideshow etc*
3 (= *persona*) cheat

sacador(a) SM/F server

sacadura SF (*And, Cono Sur*) extraction

sacafaltas SMF INV faultfinder

sacamuelas* SMF INV **1** (*hum*) (= *dentista*) tooth-puller
2 (= *parlanchín*) chatterbox*

sacaniguas SM INV (*And*) squib, Chinese cracker

sacaperras* SMF INV con artist*

sacapuntas SM INV pencil sharpener

sacar

> VERBO TRANSITIVO
> VERBO INTRANSITIVO
> VERBO PRONOMINAL

▹ CONJUG 1g

> *Para las expresiones* ***sacar adelante, sacar brillo, sacar algo en claro, sacar los colores a algn, sacar faltas a algo, sacar algo en limpio, sacar provecho, sacar a relucir****, ver la otra entrada.*

VERBO TRANSITIVO

1 (= *poner fuera*) to take out, get out • **sacó el revólver y disparó** he drew his revolver and fired, he took *o* got his revolver out and fired • **he sacado las toallas al sol** I've put the towels out to dry in the sun • **saca la basura, por favor** please put *o* take the rubbish out • **~on a los rehenes por la ventana** they got the hostages out through the window • **~ a algn a bailar** to get sb up for a dance • **~ algo/a algn de**: • **sacó toda su ropa del armario** she took all his clothes out of the wardrobe, she removed all his clothes from the wardrobe • **sacó el regalo del paquete** he removed the present from its wrapping • **voy a ~ dinero del cajero** I'm going to take *o* get some money out of the machine • **quiero ~ un libro de la biblioteca** I want to get a book out of the library • **¡sacadme de aquí!** get me out of here! • **nunca saca a su mujer de casa** he never takes his wife out • **mañana sacan a dos terroristas de cárcel** tomorrow two terrorists will be released from jail • **~ a pasear a algn** to take sb (out) for a walk • **saqué al perro a pasear** I took the dog (out) for a walk • MODISMO: • **~ a algn de sí** to drive sb mad

2 (*de una persona*) [+ *diente*] to take out • **me han sacado una muela** I've had a tooth (taken) out • **¡deja ese palo, que me vas a ~ un ojo!** stop playing with that stick, you're going to poke my eye out! • **~ sangre a algn** to take blood from sb

3 (*con partes del cuerpo*) to stick out • **saca la lengua** stick your tongue out • **~ la lengua a alguien** to stick one's tongue out at sb • **~ la barbilla** to stick one's chin out • **saca la mano si vas a aparcar** stick your hand out if you're going to park; ▹ **pecho**[1]

4 (= *obtener*) **a** [+ *notas, diputados*] to get • **siempre saca buenas notas** he always gets good marks • **han sacado 35 diputados** they have had 35 members (elected) • **¿y tú qué sacas con denunciarlo a la policía?** and what do you get out of *o* gain from reporting him to the police? • **no consiguió ~ todos los exámenes en junio** (*Esp*) she didn't manage to pass *o* get all her exams in June • **sacó un seis** (*con dados*) he threw a six
b [+ *dinero*] • **lo hago para ~ unos euros** I do it to earn *o* make a bit of money • **sacó el premio gordo** he got *o* won the jackpot • **sacamos una ganancia de ...** we made a profit of ...
c [+ *puesto*] to get • **sacó la plaza de enfermera** she got the nursing post
d [+ *información*] to get • **los datos están sacados de dos libros** the statistics are taken *o* come from two books • **¿de dónde has sacado esa idea?** where did you get that idea? • **¿de dónde has sacado esa chica tan guapa?** where did you get *o* find such a beautiful girlfriend?
e • **~ algo de** [+ *fruto, material*] to extract sth from • **sacan aceite de las almendras** they

extract oil from the almonds • **han sacado petróleo del desierto del Sáhara** they have extracted oil from the Sahara desert
f • **~ algo a algn** to get sth out of sb • **no conseguirán ~le nada** they won't get anything out of him • **le ~on millones a base de chantajes** they got millions out of him by blackmailing him • **le ~on toda la información que necesitaban** they got all the information they needed from *o* out of him
g [*+ conclusión*] to draw • **¿qué conclusión se puede ~ de todo esto?** what can be concluded from all of this?, what conclusion can be drawn from all of this? • **lo que se saca de todo esto es que ...** the conclusion to be drawn from all this is that ...
h [*+ característica*] • **ha sacado el pelo rubio de su abuela** she gets her blonde hair from her grandmother
5 *(= comprar)* [*+ entradas*] to get • **yo ~é los billetes** I'll get the tickets
6 *(= lanzar)* [*+ modelo nuevo*] to bring out; [*+ libro*] to bring out, publish; [*+ disco*] to release; [*+ moda*] to create • **han sacado sus nuevos productos al mercado** they have brought out their new product range • **ya han sacado las nuevas monedas de dos euros** the new two-euro coins are out
7 *(= hacer)* [*+ foto*] to take; [*+ copia*] to make • **te voy a ~ una foto** I'm going to take a photo of you • **esta cámara saca buenas fotos** this camera takes good photos
8 *(= resolver)* • **no conseguí ~ el problema** I couldn't solve the problem
9 *(= mostrar)* • **le han sacado en el periódico** he was in the paper • **los ~on en la tele** they were on TV • **no me sacó en la foto** he missed me out of the photo • **estamos sacando anuncios en TV** we're running some adverts on TV
10 *(= mencionar)* • **no me saques ahora eso** don't come to me with that now
11 *(esp LAm)* (= *quitar*) [*+ ropa*] to take off; [*+ mancha*] to get out *o* off, remove (*frm*) • **~ la funda a un fusil** to take the cover off a rifle
12 *(= aventajar en)* • **al terminar la carrera le sacaba 10 metros al adversario** he finished the race 10 metres ahead of his rival • **le saca 10cm a su hermano** he is 10cm taller than his brother
13 *(= salvar)* to get out • **nos sacó de esa penosa situación** she got us out of that difficult situation; ▷ **apuro**
14 *(= poner)* [*+ apodo, mote*] to give
15 *(Dep)* **a** (*Tenis*) to serve
b (*Ftbl*) • **saca el balón Kiko** (*en saque de banda*) the throw-in is taken by Kiko; (*en falta*) Kiko takes the free kick • **~ una falta** to take a free kick
16 *(Cos)* [*+ prenda de vestir*] (= *ensanchar*) to let out; (= *alargar*) to let down
17 *(Naipes)* to play
VERBO INTRANSITIVO
1 *(Tenis)* to serve
2 *(Ftbl)* (*en córner, tiro libre*) to take the kick; (*en saque de banda*) to take the throw-in • **después de marcar un gol, saca el contrario** after a goal has been scored, the opposing team kicks off
VERBO PRONOMINAL **sacarse**
1 *(= extraer)* [*+ objeto*] to take out; [*+ diente*] to have out • **se sacó la mano del bolsillo** he took his hand out of his pocket • **casi me saco un ojo con la barra de hierro** I almost poked *o* took my eye out with the iron bar • **se tiene que ~ una muela** she has got to have a tooth out
2 *(esp LAm)* (= *quitarse*) • **~se la ropa** to take one's clothes off
3 *(= conseguir)* to get • **~se unos euros** to get *o* make a few euros • **quiero ~me un doctorado** I want to get a PhD • **~se el carnet de conducir** to get one's driving licence, pass one's driving test • **~se el título de abogado** to qualify as a lawyer
4 *(Méx)* (= *irse*) to leave, go away • **¡sáquese de aquí!** get out of here!

sacarina SF saccharin, saccharine
sacarino ADJ saccharin, saccharine
sacatín SM (*And*) still
sacerdocio SM priesthood
sacerdotal ADJ priestly
sacerdote SM priest • **sumo ~** high priest ▸ **sacerdote obrero** worker priest
sacerdotisa SF priestess
sacha ADJ INV (*LAm*) **1** (= *fingido*) false, sham • **~ médico** quack
2 (= *desmañado*) bungling, unskilled • **~ carpintero** clumsy carpenter
sachadura SF weeding
sachar ▷ CONJUG 1a VT to weed
sacho SM weeding hoe
saciado ADJ • **~ de** (*lit*) sated with; (*fig*) steeped in
saciar ▷ CONJUG 1b VT **1** [*+ hambre*] to satisfy; [*+ sed*] to quench
2 [*+ deseos, curiosidad*] to satisfy; [*+ ambición*] to fulfil, fulfill (EEUU)
VPR **saciarse 1** (*de comida, bebida*) to sate *o* satiate o.s. (**con, de** with)
2 (= *satisfacerse*) to be satisfied (**con, de** with)
saciedad SF satiation, satiety • **comer hasta la ~** to eat one's fill • **repetir hasta la ~** to repeat ad nauseam
saco¹ SM **1** (= *costal*) (*referido al contenedor*) bag, sack; (*referido al contenido*) bagful; (*Mil*) kitbag; (*Dep*) punchball • MODISMOS: • **a ~s** by the ton • **por fin lo tenemos en el ~*** we've finally talked him round* • **no es *o* no parece ~ de paja** he can't be written off as unimportant • **caer en ~ roto** to fall on deaf ears • **no echar algo en ~ roto** to be careful not to forget sth • **dar a algn por ~**‡ to screw sb‡ • **mandar a algn a tomar por ~**‡ to tell sb to get stuffed‡ • **ser un ~ sin fondo** to spend money like water • **ser un ~ de huesos** to be a bag of bones ▸ **saco de arena** sandbag ▸ **saco de dormir** sleeping bag ▸ **saco postal** mailbag, postbag ▸ **saco terrero** sandbag
2 (*Anat*) sac ▸ **saco amniótico** amniotic sac
3 (= *gabán*) long coat, loose-fitting jacket; (*LAm*) (= *chaqueta*) jacket; (*And*) (= *jersey*) jumper
4‡ (= *cárcel*) nick‡, prison
saco² SM (*Mil*) sack • **entrar a ~ en** to sack
sacón/ona* ADJ **1** (*CAm*) [*soplón*] sneaky; [*cobista*] flattering, soapy*
2 (*LAm*) (= *entrometido*) nosey*, prying
SM/F* **1** (*CAm*) (= *zalamero*) flatterer, creep‡
2 (*LAm*) (= *entrometido*) nosey-parker*
SM (*Cono Sur*) woman's outdoor coat
saconear* ▷ CONJUG 1a VT (*CAm*) to soft-soap*
saconería* SF **1** (*CAm*) (= *zalamería*) flattery, soft soap*
2 (*LAm*) (= *curiosidad*) prying
SACRA SM ABR (*Arg*) = **Sindicato de Amas de Casa de la República Argentina**
sacral ADJ religious, sacral
sacralización SF consecration, canonization
sacralizar ▷ CONJUG 1f VT to consecrate
sacramental ADJ (*Rel*) [*rito*] sacramental; [*palabras*] ritual
sacramentar ▷ CONJUG 1a VT to administer the sacraments to

SACRA

Founded in 1984, **SACRA**, or the **Sindicato de Amas de Casa de la República Argentina**, was the world's first trade union for housewives. One of its main aims has been to redefine housework as employment and to obtain for its members the salaries, pensions and health benefits traditionally associated with union membership. It has developed an educational programme designed to improve women's job opportunities, organized cheap holidays for housewives and obtained free medical treatment for its members. While union membership has allowed thousands of women to take part in public affairs, critics believe that the idea that housewives should have salaries simply reaffirms the stereotypical view that women function best in the home and, in the long run, may encourage non-participation outside.

sacramento SM sacrament • **el Santísimo Sacramento** the Blessed Sacrament • **recibir los ~s** to receive the sacraments
sacrificado ADJ **1** [*profesión, vida*] demanding
2 [*persona*] self-sacrificing
sacrificar ▷ CONJUG 1g VT **1** (*Rel*) to sacrifice (a to)
2 (= *matar*) [*+ ganado*] to slaughter; [*+ animal doméstico*] to put to sleep
VPR **sacrificarse** to sacrifice o.s.
sacrificio SM **1** (*Rel*) sacrifice • **el ~ de la misa** the sacrifice of the mass
2 [*de animal*] slaughter, slaughtering
sacrilegio SM sacrilege
sacrílego ADJ sacrilegious
sacristán SM verger, sexton, sacristan
sacristía SF **1** (*Rel*) vestry, sacristy
2‡ (= *bragueta*) flies (*pl*); (= *horcajadura*) crotch
sacro ADJ [*arte, música*] sacred • **Sacro Imperio Romano** Holy Roman Empire
SM (*Anat*) sacrum
sacrosanto ADJ sacrosanct
sacuara SF (*And*) bamboo plant
sacudida SF **1** (= *agitación*) shake, shaking • **dar una ~ a una alfombra** to beat a carpet • **avanzar dando ~s** to bump *o* jolt *o* lurch along
2 (= *movimiento brusco*) [*de cuerpo, rodilla*] jerk; [*de cabeza*] toss
3 [*de terremoto*] shock; [*de explosión*] blast • **la ~ de la bomba llegó hasta aquí** the bomb blast could be felt here ▸ **sacudida eléctrica** electric shock
4 (= *alteración brusca*) [*de situación*] violent change; (*Pol*) upheaval • **hay que darle una ~** he needs a jolt
sacudido ADJ **1** (= *brusco*) ill-disposed, unpleasant
2 (= *difícil*) intractable
3 (= *resuelto*) determined
sacudidor SM (*Méx*) feather duster
sacudidura SF, **sacudimiento** SM = sacudida
sacudir ▷ CONJUG 3a VT **1** (= *agitar*) [*+ árbol, edificio, cabeza*] to shake; [*+ ala*] to flap; [*+ alfombra*] to beat; [*+ colchón*] to shake, shake the dust out of
2 (= *quitar*) [*+ tierra*] to shake off; [*+ cuerda*] to jerk, tug
3 (= *conmover*) to shake • **una tremenda emoción sacudió a la multitud** a great wave of excitement ran through the crowd • **~ a algn de su depresión** to shake sb out of his depression • **~ los nervios a algn** to

shatter sb's nerves
4* (= *pegar*) • **~ a algn** to belt sb*
5 • ~ dinero a algn* to screw money out of sb*
(VPR) **sacudirse** (*uno mismo*) to shake o.s.; [+ *brazo, pelo*] to shake • **el perro se sacudía el rabo** the dog was wagging its tail • **salió del mar sacudiéndose el agua** he came out of the sea shaking the water off himself • **sacúdete la arena del pelo** shake the sand out of your hair • **el caballo se sacudía las moscas con la cola** the horse brushed off the flies with its tail • **por fin se la han sacudido** they've finally got rid of her

sacudón (SM) (*LAm*) violent shake

S.A. de C.V. (ABR) (*Méx*) (= **Sociedad Anónima de Capital Variable**) Ltd, plc, Corp (EEUU), Inc (EEUU)

sádico/a (ADJ) sadistic
(SM/F) sadist

sadismo (SM) sadism

sadista (SMF) sadist

sado* (ADJ) = **sadomasoquista**

sadoca‡ (SMF) = **sadomasoquista**

sado-maso* (SM) S & M*

sadomasoquismo (SM) sadomasochism

sadomasoquista (ADJ) sadomasochistic
(SMF) sadomasochist

saeta (SF) **1** (*Mil*) arrow, dart
2 (= *aguja*) [*de reloj*] hand; [*de brújula*] magnetic needle
3 (*Mús*) *sacred song in flamenco style*
4 (*Rel*) ejaculatory prayer

saetera (SF) loophole

saetín (SM) **1** [*de molino*] millrace
2 (*Téc*) tack

safado* (ADJ) **1** (*LAm*) (= *loco*) mad, crazy
2 (*Arg*) (= *despejado*) cute*, alert, bright

safagina (SF), **safajina** (SF) (*And*) uproar, commotion

safari (SM) safari • **estar de ~** to be on safari • **MODISMO:** • **contar ~s*** to shoot a line*

safo‡ (SM) hankie*, handkerchief

saga (SF) **1** (*Literat*) saga
2 (= *clan*) clan, dynasty

sagacidad (SF) (= *astucia*) shrewdness, cleverness; (= *perspicacia*) sagacity

sagaz (ADJ) **1** [*persona*] (= *astuto*) shrewd, clever; (= *perspicaz*) sagacious
2 [*perro*] keen-scented

sagazmente (ADV) (= *con astucia*) shrewdly, cleverly; (= *con perspicacia*) sagaciously

Sagitario (SM) (*Astron, Astrol*) Sagittarius • **es de ~** (*LAm*) he's (a) Sagittarius, he's a Sagittarian

sagitario (*Astrol*) (SMF INV) Sagittarius, Sagittarian • **los ~ son así** that's what Sagittariuses *o* Sagittarians are like
(ADJ INV) Sagittarius, Sagittarian • **soy ~** I'm (a) Sagittarius, I'm a Sagittarian

sagrado (ADJ) [*lugar, libro*] holy, sacred; [*deber*] sacred • **Sagradas Escrituras** Holy Scriptures • **Sagrada Familia** Holy Family; ▷ **vaca**
(SM) sanctuary, asylum • **acogerse a ~** to seek sanctuary

sagrario (SM) sacrarium

sagú (SM) sago

Sahara [sa'ara] (SM), **Sáhara** ['saxara] (SM) Sahara

saharaui [saxa'raui] (ADJ) Saharan
(SMF) native/inhabitant of the Sahara • **los ~s** the people of the Sahara

sahariana (SF) safari jacket

sahariano/a (ADJ), (SM/F) = **saharaui**

Sahel (SM) Sahel

sahumadura (SF) = **sahumerio**

sahumar ▷ CONJUG 1a (VT) **1** (= *incensar*) to perfume, perfume with incense
2 (= *fumigar*) to smoke, fumigate

sahumerio (SM) **1** (= *acto*) perfuming with incense
2 (= *humo*) aromatic smoke
3 (= *sustancia*) aromatic substance

S.A.I. (ABR) (= **Su Alteza Imperial**) HIH

saibó (SM) (*LAm*), **saibor** (SM) (*And, Caribe*) sideboard

saín (SM) **1** (= *grasa*) [*de animal*] animal fat; [*de pescado*] fish oil (*used for lighting*)
2 (*en la ropa*) dirt, grease

sainete (SM) **1** (*Teat*) one-act farce, one-act comedy
2 (*Culin*) (= *salsa*) seasoning, sauce; (= *bocadito*) titbit, delicacy

> **SAINETE**
> A **sainete** is a humorous short, generally one-act, verse play sometimes performed as an interlude between the acts of a major play. **Sainetes** were developed in the 18th century by playwrights such as Ramón de la Cruz, and were largely based on satirical observations of ordinary people's lives and reflected this in the language they were written in. They were still being written by authors such as Carlos Arniches well into the 20th century.
> ▷ **ENTREMÉS**

sainetero/a (SM/F), **sainetista** (SMF) writer of *sainetes*

sajar ▷ CONJUG 1a (VT) to cut open, lance

sajín* (SM) (*CAm*), **sajino*** (SM) (*CAm*) underarm odour, smelly armpits (*pl*)

sajón/ona (ADJ), (SM/F) Saxon

Sajonia (SF) Saxony

sajornar ▷ CONJUG 1a (VT) (*Caribe*) to pester, harass

sal¹ (SF) **1** (*Culin, Quím*) salt ▸ **sal amoníaca** sal ammoniac ▸ **sal común** kitchen salt, cooking salt ▸ **sal de cocina** kitchen salt, cooking salt ▸ **sal de eno** (*CAm*) fruit salts, liver salts ▸ **sal de fruta(s)** fruit salts ▸ **sal de la Higuera** Epsom salts ▸ **sal de mesa** table salt ▸ **sal gema** rock salt ▸ **sales aromáticas** smelling salts ▸ **sales de baño** bath salts ▸ **sales minerales** mineral salts ▸ **sal gorda** kitchen salt, cooking salt ▸ **sal volátil** sal volatile
2 [*de persona*] (= *gracia*) wit; (= *encanto*) charm • **tiene mucha sal** he's very amusing
3 (*LAm*) (= *mala suerte*) misfortune, piece of bad luck

sal² ▷ **salir**

sala (SF) **1** (*en casa*) (*tb* **sala de estar**) living room, sitting room, lounge; (= *cuarto grande*) hall; [*de castillo*] hall
2 (= *local público*) (*Teat, Mús*) auditorium; (*Cine*) cinema, movie theater (EEUU); (*Jur*) court; (*Med*) ward • **deporte en ~** indoor sport • **un cine con diez ~s** a cinema with ten screens • **Titanic lo ponen en la ~ tres** Titanic is on screen three ▸ **sala capitular** chapterhouse, meeting room ▸ **sala cinematográfica** cinema, movie theater (EEUU) ▸ **sala de alumbramiento** delivery room ▸ **sala de autoridades** (*Aer*) VIP lounge ▸ **sala de banderas** guardroom ▸ **sala de cine** cinema, movie theater (*EEUU*) ▸ **sala de conciertos** concert hall ▸ **sala de conferencias** (*gen*) conference hall; (*Univ*) lecture hall, lecture theatre, lecture theater (EEUU) ▸ **sala de consejos** meeting room, conference room ▸ **sala de consulta** reading room ▸ **sala de embarque** departure lounge ▸ **sala de espera** (*Med, Ferro*) waiting room; (*Aer*) departure lounge ▸ **sala de fiestas** night club (*with cabaret*) ▸ **sala de grados** graduation hall ▸ **sala de juegos** (*en casino*) gaming room; (*en hotel, barco*) casino ▸ **sala de juntas** (*Com*) boardroom ▸ **sala de justicia** law court ▸ **sala de lectura** reading room ▸ **sala de lo civil** civil court ▸ **sala de lo criminal, sala de lo penal** criminal court ▸ **sala de máquinas** (*Náut*) engine room ▸ **sala de muestras** showroom ▸ **sala de operaciones** operating theatre, operating room (EEUU) ▸ **sala de partos** delivery room ▸ **sala de prensa** press room ▸ **sala de profesores** staffroom ▸ **sala de recibo** parlour ▸ **sala de salidas** departure lounge ▸ **sala de subastas** saleroom, auction room ▸ **sala de urgencias** accident and emergency department, casualty department ▸ **sala VIP** (*en aeropuerto*) VIP lounge ▸ **sala X** adult cinema
3 (= *muebles*) suite of living room furniture, lounge suite

salacidad (SF) salaciousness, prurience

salacot (SM) pith helmet, topee

sala-cuna (SF) (PL: **salas-cuna**) (*Cono Sur*) day-nursery

saladar (SM) salt marsh

saladería (SF) (*Cono Sur*) meat-curing plant

saladito (SM) (*Cono Sur*) nibble, snack, bar snack

salado (ADJ) **1** (*Culin*) (= *con sal*) salt (*antes de s*), salted; (= *con demasiada sal*) salty; (= *no dulce*) savoury • **agua salada** salt water • **está muy ~** it's very salty
2 (= *persona*) (= *gracioso*) amusing; (= *encantador*) charming • **¡qué ~!** (= *divertido*) how amusing!; (*iró*) very droll! • **es un tipo muy ~** he's a very amusing chap
3 [*lenguaje*] rich, racy
4 (*LAm*) (= *desgraciado*) unlucky, unfortunate
5 (*Cono Sur**) (= *caro*) [*objeto*] expensive; [*precio*] very high

> **SALADO**
>
> ▷ **Salado** *se traduce por* **salt** *al referirse al agua de mar (por oposición a agua dulce) o a un producto que ha sido curado con sal:*
> **El Caspio es un lago de agua salada**
> The Caspian Sea is a salt lake
> **El bacalao salado se emplea mucho en la cocina española**
> Salt cod is used a great deal in Spanish cooking
>
> ▷ **Salado**, *por oposición a dulce, se traduce por* **savoury**:
> **... platos dulces y salados ...**
> ... sweet and savoury dishes ...
>
> ▷ *Si algo está* **salado** *porque sabe a sal o porque contiene demasiada sal, se debe traducir por* **salty**:
> **Estas albóndigas están muy saladas**
> These meatballs are very salty
>
> **Salty** *es la única de estas tres traducciones que se puede usar en grado superlativo o comparativo:*
> **Esta carne está mucho más salada que la de ayer**
> This meat is much saltier than what we had yesterday
>
> *Si nos referimos a almendras o cacahuetes salados se debe emplear* **salted**.
>
> *Para otros usos y ejemplos ver la entrada.*

Salamanca (SF) Salamanca

salamanca (SF) (*Cono Sur*) **1** (= *cueva*) cave, grotto
2 (= *lugar oscuro*) dark place
3 (= *brujería*) witchcraft, sorcery

S

salamandra SF salamander
salamanqués/esa ADJ, SM/F = salmantino
salamanquesa SF lizard, gecko
salame SM **1** (*Culin*) salami
2 (*Cono Sur*‡) idiot, thickhead*
salami SM salami
salar¹ SM (*And, Cono Sur*) (= *yacimiento*) salt flat, salt pan; (= *mina*) salt mine
salar² ▹ CONJUG 1a VT **1** (*Culin*) (*para poner salado*) to add salt to, put salt in; (*para conservar*) to salt
2 (*LAm*) (= *arruinar*) to ruin, spoil; (= *gafar*) to bring bad luck to, jinx*; (= *maldecir*) to curse, wish bad luck on
3 (*And*) [+ *ganado*] to feed salt to
4 (*CAm, Caribe*) (= *deshonrar*) to dishonour
VPR **salarse** (*CAm, Méx**) [*sorpresa, planes*] to go wrong, fall through
salarial ADJ wage (*antes de s*) • **reclamación ~** wage claim
salario SM wage, wages (*pl*), pay, salary ▸ **salario base** basic wage ▸ **salario de hambre, salario de miseria** starvation wage ▸ **salario inicial** starting salary ▸ **salario mínimo** minimum wage ▸ **salario mínimo interprofesional** guaranteed minimum wage
salaz ADJ salacious, prurient
salazón SF **1** (= *acto*) salting
2 (*Culin*) (= *carne*) salted meat; (= *pescado*) salted fish
3 (*CAm, Caribe, Méx*) (= *mala suerte*) bad luck
salazonera SF salting plant (*for salting fish*)
salbeque SM (*CAm*) knapsack, backpack (*esp EEUU*)
salbute SM (*Méx*) stuffed tortilla
salceda SF, **salcedo** SM willow plantation
salchicha SF sausage
salchichería SF pork butcher's (shop)
salchichón SM *salami-type sausage*
salchichonería SF (*Méx*) pork butcher's (shop)
salchipapa SF (*And*) *kind of kebab*
salcochar ▹ CONJUG 1a VT to boil in salt water
saldar ▹ CONJUG 1a VT **1** (*Com*) [+ *cuenta*] to settle, pay; [+ *deuda*] to settle, pay off
2 [+ *diferencias*] to settle
3 (= *liquidar*) [+ *existencias*] to clear, sell off; [+ *libros*] to remainder
VPR **saldarse** • **~se con algo** to result in sth • **el accidente se ha saldado con cuatro muertos** the accident resulted in four deaths, four people died in the accident
saldo SM **1** [*de cuenta*] balance • **comprobé el ~ de mi cuenta** I checked my account balance ▸ **saldo acreedor** credit balance ▸ **saldo activo** active balance ▸ **saldo a favor** credit balance ▸ **saldo anterior** balance brought forward ▸ **saldo comercial** trade balance ▸ **saldo deudor** debit balance ▸ **saldo en contra** debit balance, adverse balance ▸ **saldo final** final balance ▸ **saldo negativo** debit balance, adverse balance ▸ **saldo pasivo** debit balance ▸ **saldo positivo** credit balance ▸ **saldo vencido** balance due
2 (= *liquidación*) sale • **precio de ~** sale price • **un abrigo que compré en los ~s** a coat I bought in the sales
3 (= *pago*) settlement, payment
4 [*de móvil*] credit • **no me queda ~ en el móvil** I haven't any credit left on my mobile
5 (= *resultado final*) • **la manifestación acabó con un ~ de 20 personas heridas** a total of 20 people were injured in the demonstration • **el ~ oficial es de 28 muertos** the official toll is 28 dead
6 • **ser un ~*** [*cosa muy usada*] to have had it*; [*persona inútil*] to be hopeless, be a dead loss* • **cómprate otro abrigo, el que llevas es un auténtico ~** you should get yourself another coat, the one you're wearing has had it* • **eres un auténtico ~, no sabes ni freír un huevo** you're hopeless *o* you're a dead loss, you can't even boil an egg*
saledizo ADJ projecting
SM projection, overhang • **en ~** projecting, overhanging
salera SF (*Cono Sur*) = **salina**
salero SM **1** [*de mesa*] salt cellar, salt shaker (*EEUU*)
2 (= *almacén*) salt store
3 [*de persona*] (= *ingenio*) wit; (= *encanto*) charm; (= *atractivo*) sex appeal, allure
4 (*Agr*) salt lick
5 (*Cono Sur*) = **salina**
saleroso* ADJ = **salado**
saleta SF small room
salga *etc* ▹ **salir**
salida SF **1** [*de un lugar*] • **le prohibieron la ~ del país** he was forbidden to leave the country • **exigen la ~ de las tropas extranjeras** they are demanding the withdrawal of foreign troops • **tras su ~ de la cárcel** when he came out of prison • **a la ~**: • **te esperaremos a la ~** we'll wait for you on the way out • **a la ~ del cine fuimos a tomar una copa** after the cinema we went for a drink • **sondeos realizados a la ~ de las urnas** exit polls • **hubo ~ a hombros para el primero de los diestros** the first matador was carried out of the ring shoulder-high • **dar ~ a**: • **el pasillo que da ~ a la pista de tenis** the passageway which leads out (on)to the tennis court • **necesitaba dar ~ a su creatividad** he needed to give expression to *o* find an outlet for his creativity • **dio ~ a su indignación** he gave vent to his anger • **puerta de ~** exit door; ▹ **visado**
2 (= *aparición*) • **los fans esperaban su ~ al escenario** the fans were waiting for her to come (out) onto the stage • **tras la ~ de los futbolistas al terreno de juego** after the footballers came/went out onto the pitch • **la venda detuvo la ~ de sangre** the bandage stopped the flow of blood • **precio de ~** [*de objeto subastado*] starting price; [*de acciones*] offer price ▸ **salida del sol** sunrise
3 (= *lugar*) [*de edificio*] exit, way out; [*de autopista*] exit, turn-off • **¿dónde está la ~?** where's the exit *o* the way out? • **"salida"** (*encima de la puerta*) "exit"; (*en el pasillo*) "way out", "exit" • **una cueva sin ~** a cave with no way out • **el ejército controla las ~s de la ciudad** the army controls the roads out of the city • **tener ~ a algo**: • **nuestro edificio tiene ~ a las dos calles** our building has access onto both streets • **un país que no tiene ~ al mar** a country with no access to the sea • **la sala tiene ~ al jardín** the living room opens on to the garden ▸ **salida de artistas** stage door ▸ **salida de emergencia** emergency exit ▸ **salida de incendios** fire exit; ▹ **callejón**
4 [*de avión, tren*] departure • **la hora de ~ del vuelo** the flight departure time • **"salidas internacionales"** "international departures" • **"salidas nacionales"** "domestic departures" • **el autobús efectuará su ~ desde el andén número cuatro** the bus will depart from bay number four • **después de la ~ del tren** after the train leaves, after the departure of the train
5 (= *escapada*) [*de viaje*] trip; [*de excursión*] trip, outing; (*por la noche*) night out, evening out • **en mi primera ~ al extranjero** on my first trip abroad, on my first foreign trip • **me controlaban mucho las ~s por la noche** they kept tight control of my nights out *o* my going out at night • **es su primera ~ desde que dio a luz** it's the first time she's been out since she gave birth ▸ **salida al campo** field trip
6 (= *comienzo*) [*de carrera, desfile*] start • **fuimos a ver la ~ de la procesión** we went to see the start of the procession, we went to see the procession move off • **"salida"** "start" • **los corredores estaban preparados para la ~** the runners were ready for the start (of the race) • **acudieron a los puestos de ~** they took their starting positions • **Palmer tuvo una mala ~ del tee** (*Golf*) Palmer played a poor tee shot • **dar la ~** to give the starting signal • **es el encargado de dar la ~ a la carrera** he is the one who starts the race *o* gives the starting signal for the race • **tomar la ~** (= *empezar*) to start the race; (= *participar*) to take part, compete ▸ **salida en falso, salida falsa** false start ▸ **salida lanzada** running start, flying start ▸ **salida nula** false start ▸ **salida parada** standing start; ▹ **parrilla**
7 (*Teat*) (*al entrar en escena*) appearance; (*para recibir aplausos*) curtain-call • **hago una sola ~ al principio de la obra** I only make one appearance at the beginning of the play • **hicieron tres ~s en los aplausos** they took three curtain calls
8 (= *solución*) solution • **buscan una ~ negociada al conflicto** they are seeking a negotiated solution to the conflict • **la única ~ está en la negociación** the only way out is through negotiation, the only solution is to negotiate • **buscan en la música una ~ a sus frustraciones** they try to find an outlet for their frustration in music • **no le quedaba otra ~ que la dimisión** she had no alternative *o* option but to resign
9 (*al hablar*) • **¡qué buena ~!** that was a really witty comment! • **tiene unas ~s que te mueres de risa** some of the things he comes out with are just hilarious ▸ **salida de bombero** (*Esp*) (*hum*) • **¡vaya ~s de bombero que tuvo!** he dropped some real clangers!* ▸ **salida de tono** • **fue una ~ de tono** it was inappropriate *o* uncalled-for
10 (*Com*) [*de producto*] launch • **dar ~ a**: • **dar ~ a los excedentes agrícolas** to find an outlet for surplus produce • **dimos ~ a nuestras existencias en dos meses** we sold off our stock in two months • **tener ~** to sell well • **tener una ~ difícil** to be a hard sell • **tener una ~ fácil** to have a ready market, be a soft sell
11 (*Econ*) (= *cargo*) debit entry • **entradas y ~s** income and expenditure
12 salidas (*en el trabajo*) openings, job opportunities • **esa carrera no tiene apenas ~s** there are very few openings *o* job opportunities for someone with that degree ▸ **salidas profesionales** job opportunities
13 (*Téc*) [*de aire, gas, vapor*] vent; [*de agua*] outlet • **tiene ~s de aire caliente por los laterales** it has hot air vents on the sides • **los orificios de ~ de vapor** the steam vents • **apertura de ~ del agua** water outlet
14 (*Inform*) output ▸ **salida impresa** hard copy
15 (= *prenda*) ▸ **salida de baño** (*Cono Sur*) (*en casa*) bathrobe; (*en playa, piscina*) beach robe ▸ **salida de teatro** evening wrap
16 (*Arquit*) (= *saliente*) projection
17 (*Mil*) (*para el ataque*) sortie
18 (*Naipes*) lead
salido PP *de* **salir**

ADJ 1 (= *prominente*) [*rasgos*] prominent; [*ojos*] bulging; [*dientes*] protruding
2 (*Esp**) (= *cachondo*) randy*, horny* • **estar ~** [*animal*] to be on heat; [*persona*] to be in the mood, feel randy*, feel horny*
3* (= *osado*) daring; (*pey*) rash, reckless

salidor ADJ 1 (*LAm*) (= *fiestero*) fond of going out a lot
2 (*Caribe*) (= *buscapleitos*) argumentative

saliente ADJ 1 (*Arquit*) projecting
2 [*rasgo*] prominent
3 (= *importante*) salient
4 [*sol*] rising
5 [*miembro*] outgoing, retiring
SM 1 (*Arquit*) projection
2 [*de carretera*] hard shoulder, verge, berm (*EEUU*)
3 (*Mil*) salient

salina SF 1 (= *mina*) salt mine
2 (= *depresión*) salt pan
3 **salinas** (= *fábrica*) saltworks; (= *saladar*) salt flats

salinera SF (*And, Caribe*) = **salina**

salinidad SF salinity, saltiness

salinización SF (= *acto*) salinization; (= *estado*) salinity

salinizar ▹ CONJUG 1f VT to salinize, make salty
VPR **salinizarse** to become salty

salino ADJ saline

salir

VERBO INTRANSITIVO
VERBO PRONOMINAL

▹ CONJUG 3q

Para las expresiones ***salir adelante***, ***salir ganando***, ***salir perdiendo***, ***salir de viaje***, *ver la otra entrada.*

VERBO INTRANSITIVO

1 (= *partir*) [*persona*] to leave; [*transportes*] to leave, depart (*frm*); (*Náut*) to leave, sail • **el autocar sale a las ocho** the coach leaves at eight • **sale un tren cada dos horas** there is a train every two hours • **~ de** to leave • **salimos de Madrid a las ocho** we left Madrid at eight • **saldremos del hotel temprano** we'll leave the hotel early • **quiere ~ del país** she wants to leave the country • **¿a qué hora sales de la oficina?** what time do you leave the office? • **salgo de clase a las cinco** I finish school at five • **~ para** to set off for • **después de comer salimos para Palencia** after we had eaten we set off for Palencia

2 (= *no entrar*) (= *ir fuera*) to go out; (= *venir fuera*) to come out; (*a divertirse*) to go out • **sal ahí fuera a recoger la pelota** go out there and get the ball back • **sal aquí al jardín con nosotros** come out into the garden with us • **salió a la calle a ver si venían** she went outside *o* she went out into the street to see if they were coming • **—¿está Juan? —no, ha salido** "is Juan in?" — "no, I'm afraid he's gone out" • **¿vas a ~ esta noche?** are you going out tonight? • **nunca he salido al extranjero** I've never been abroad • **la pelota salió fuera** (*Ftbl*) the ball went out (of play) • **los rehenes salieron por la ventana** the hostages got out through the window • **salió corriendo (del cuarto)** he ran out (of the room) • **~ de**: • **nos la encontramos al ~ del cine** we bumped into her when we were coming out of the cinema • **¿de dónde has salido?** where did you appear *o* spring from? • **~ de un apuro** to get out of a jam • **~ del coma** to come out of a coma • **~ de paseo** to go out for a walk • MODISMOS: • **de esta no salimos*** we'll never get out of this one* • **~ de pobre**: • **no salió nunca de pobre** he never stopped being poor

3 (*al mercado*) [*revista, libro, disco*] to come out; [*moda*] to come in • **el libro sale el mes que viene** the book comes out next month • **acaba de ~ un disco suyo** an album of his has just come out *o* been released

4 (*en medios de comunicación*) • **la noticia salió en el periódico de ayer** the news was *o* appeared in yesterday's paper • **sus padres salieron en los periódicos** her parents were in the papers • **~ por la televisión** to be *o* appear on TV

5 (= *surgir*) to come up • **en el debate no salió el tema del aborto** the subject of abortion didn't come up in the debate • **si sale un puesto apropiado** if a suitable job comes up • **cuando salga la ocasión** when the opportunity comes up *o* arises • **¡ya salió aquello!** we know all about that! • **~le algo a algn: le ha salido novio/un trabajo** she's got herself a boyfriend/a job

6 (= *aparecer*) [*agua*] to come out; [*sol*] to come out; [*mancha*] to appear • **no sale agua del grifo** there's no water coming out of the tap • **ha salido una mancha en el techo** a damp patch has appeared on the ceiling • **me sale sangre** I'm bleeding

7 (= *nacer*) [*diente*] to come through; [*planta, sol*] to come up; [*pelo*] to grow; [*pollito*] to hatch • **me está saliendo una muela del juicio** one of my wisdom teeth is coming through • **ya le ha salido un diente al niño** the baby already has one tooth • **le han salido muchas espinillas** he's got a lot of blackheads • **nos levantamos antes de que saliera el sol** we got up before sunrise

8 (= *quitarse*) [*mancha*] to come out, come off • **el anillo no le sale del dedo** the ring won't come off her finger, she can't get the ring off her finger

9 (= *costar*) • **la calefacción de gas saldría más barata** gas heating would work out cheaper • **~ a**: • **sale a ocho euros el kilo** it works out at eight euros a kilo • **salimos a 10 libras por persona** it works out at £10 each • **~ por**: • **me salió por 1.000 pesos** it cost me 1,000 pesos

10 (= *resultar*) • **¿cómo salió la representación?** how did the performance go? • **espero que todo salga como habíamos planeado** I hope everything goes to plan • **la prueba salió positiva** the test was positive • **salió triunfador de las elecciones** he was victorious in the elections • **la secretaria salió muy trabajadora** the secretary turned out to be very hard-working • **¿qué número ha salido premiado en la lotería?** what was the winning number in the lottery? • **salió alcalde por tres votos** he was elected mayor by three votes • **tenemos que aceptarlo, salga lo que salga** we have to accept it, whatever happens • **~ bien**: • **el plan salió bien** the plan worked out well • **espero que todo salga bien** I hope everything works out all right • **¿salió bien la fiesta?** did the party go well? • **ha salido muy bien de la operación** she's come through the operation very well • **¿cómo te salió el examen?** how did your exam go? • **~ mal**: • **salió muy mal del tratamiento** the treatment wasn't at all successful • **la celebración salió mal por la lluvia** the celebrations were spoiled by the rain • **les salió mal el proyecto** their plan didn't work out • **¡qué mal me ha salido el dibujo!** oh dear! my drawing hasn't come out very well!

11 • **~le algo a algn a** (= *poder resolverse*) • **he intentado resolver el problema pero no me sale** I've tried to solve the problem but I just can't do it • **este crucigrama no me sale** I can't do this crossword
b (= *resultar natural*) • **no me sale ser amable con ella** I find it difficult being nice to her
c (= *poder recordarse*) • **no me sale su apellido** I can't think of his name

12 • **~ a** [*calle*] to come out in, lead to • **esta calle sale a la plaza** this street comes out in *o* leads to the square

13 • **~ a algn** (= *parecerse*) to take after sb • **ha salido a su padre** he takes after his father

14 • **~ con algn** to go out with sb • **está saliendo con un compañero de clase** she's going out with one of her classmates • **salen juntos desde hace dos años** they've been going out (together) for two years

15 • **~ con algo** (*al hablar*) to come out with sth • **y ahora sale con esto** and now he comes out with this • **ahora me sale con que yo le debo dinero** and now he starts complaining that I owe him money

16 • **~ de** [*proceder*] to come from • **el aceite que sale de la aceituna** oil which comes from olives

17 • **~ por algn** (= *defender*) to come out in defence of sb, stick up for sb; (*económicamente*) to back sb financially • **cuando hubo problemas, salió por mí** when there were problems, she stuck up for me *o* came out in my defence

18 (*Teat*) to come on • **sale vestido de policía** he comes on dressed as a policeman • **"sale el rey"** (*acotación*) "enter the king"

19 (= *empezar*) (*Dep*) to start; (*Ajedrez*) to have first move; (*Naipes*) to lead • **~ con un as** to lead an ace • **~ de triunfo** to lead a trump

20 (*Inform*) to exit

21 (= *sobresalir*) to stick out • **el balcón sale unos dos metros** the balcony sticks out about two metres

22 (= *pagar*) • **~ a los gastos de algn** to meet *o* pay sb's expenses

VERBO PRONOMINAL **salirse**

1 (= *irse*) to leave • **se salió del partido** he left the party • MODISMO: • **~se con la suya** to get one's way

2 (= *escaparse*) to escape (**de** from), get out (**de** of) • **el tigre se salió de la jaula** the tiger escaped from the cage, the tiger got out of the cage

3 (= *filtrarse*) [*aire, líquido*] to leak (out) • **la botella estaba rota y se salía el vinagre** the bottle was cracked and the vinegar was coming out *o* leaking (out) • **se salía el aceite del motor** oil was leaking out of the engine • **el barril se sale** (*Esp*) the barrel is leaking

4 (= *rebosar*) to overflow; (*al hervir*) to boil over • **cierra el grifo antes de que se salga el agua** turn the tap off before the water overflows • **se ha salido la leche** the milk has boiled over • **el río se salió de su cauce** the river burst its banks • MODISMO: • **~se de madre** to lose one's self-control

5 (= *desviarse*) to come off • **nos salimos de la carretera** we came off the road • **~se de la vía** to jump the rails • **~se del tema** to get off the point

6 (= *desconectarse*) to come out • **se ha salido el enchufe** the plug has come out

7 (= *excederse*) • **~se de lo normal** to go beyond what is normal • **~se de los límites** to go beyond the limits

> **SALIR**
>
> **Para precisar la forma de salir**
>
> *Aunque* **salir (de)** *se suele traducir por* **come out (of)** *o por* **go out (of)** *según la dirección del movimiento, cuando se quiere especificar la forma en que se realiza ese movimiento, estos verbos se pueden reemplazar por otros como* **run out, rush out, jump out, tiptoe out, climb out** *etc:*
>
> **Se vio a tres hombres enmascarados salir del banco corriendo**
> Three masked men were seen running out of the bank
>
> **Salió del coche con un salto**
> He jumped out of the car
>
> **Salió de puntillas de la habitación**
> He tiptoed out of the room
>
> *Para otros usos y ejemplos ver la entrada.*

salita (SF) **1** (*en casa*) sitting room
2 (*Teat*) small auditorium

salitre (SM) **1** (*= sustancia salina*) saltpetre, saltpeter (*EEUU*), nitre
2 (*Chile*) (*= nitrato de Chile*) Chilean nitrate

salitrera (SF) (*= fábrica*) nitre works; (*= mina*) nitrate fields (*pl*)

saliva (SF) saliva • MODISMOS: • **gastar ~** to waste one's breath (**en** on) • **tragar ~** to swallow one's feelings

salivación (SF) salivation

salivadera (SF) spittoon, cuspidor (*EEUU*)

salival (ADJ) salivary

salivar ▷ CONJUG 1a (VI) **1** (*= segregar saliva*) to salivate
2 (*esp LAm*) (*= escupir*) to spit

salivazo (SM) gobbet of spit • **arrojar un ~** to spit

salivera (SF) (*Cono Sur*) spittoon, cuspidor (*EEUU*)

salmantino/a (ADJ) of/from Salamanca, Salamancan
(SM/F) native/inhabitant of Salamanca, Salamancan • **los ~s** the people of Salamanca, the Salamancans

salmear ▷ CONJUG 1a (VI) to sing psalms

salmo (SM) psalm

salmodia (SF) **1** (*Rel*) psalmody
2* (*= canturreo*) drone

salmodiar ▷ CONJUG 1b (VI) **1** (*Rel*) to sing psalms
2* (*= canturrear*) to drone

salmón (SM) salmon

salmonela (SF) salmonella

salmonelosis (SF INV) salmonellosis, salmonella food-poisoning

salmonero (ADJ) • **río ~** salmon river

salmonete (SM) red mullet

salmuera (SF) pickle, brine

salobre (ADJ) salt, salty • **agua ~** brackish water

saloma (SF) **1** (*Náut*) sea shanty, sea song
2 [*de trabajo*] working song

Salomé (SF) Salome

Salomón (SM) Solomon

salomónicamente (ADV) with the wisdom of Solomon

salomónico (ADJ) • **juicio ~** judgement of Solomon

salón (SM) **1** [*de casa*] living-room, lounge • **juego de ~** parlour game, parlor game (*EEUU*) ▸ **salón comedor** lounge-dining-room
2 [*de lugar público*] (*gen*) hall, assembly room; [*de colegio*] common-room; (*Com*) show, trade fair, exhibition; (*Náut*) saloon; (*Chile*) (*Ferro*) first class ▸ **salón de actos** assembly room ▸ **salón de baile** ballroom ▸ **salón de belleza** beauty parlour, beauty parlor (*EEUU*) ▸ **salón de demostraciones** showroom ▸ **salón de fiestas** dance hall ▸ **salón de fumadores** smoking room ▸ **salón de juegos** (*en casino*) gaming room; (*en hotel, barco*) casino ▸ **salón del automóvil** motor show ▸ **salón de los pasos perdidos*** waiting room ▸ **salón de masaje** massage parlour, massage parlor (*EEUU*) ▸ **salón de pintura** art gallery ▸ **salón de plenos del Ayuntamiento** Council chamber ▸ **salón de reuniones** conference room ▸ **salón de sesiones** assembly hall ▸ **salón de té** tearoom ▸ **salón náutico** boat show
3 (*= muebles*) suite of living room furniture, lounge suite

saloncillo (SM) (*Teat*) private room

salonero (SM) (*And*) waiter

salpicadera (SF) (*Méx*) mudguard, fender (*EEUU*)

salpicadero (SM) dashboard

salpicado (ADJ) **1** • **~ de** splashed *o* spattered with • **un diseño ~ de puntos rojos** a pattern with red spots in it • **una llanura salpicada de granjas** a plain with farms dotted about on it, a plain dotted with farms • **un discurso ~ de citas latinas** a speech sprinkled with Latin quotations, a speech full of Latin quotations
2 (*Cono Sur, Méx*) [*animal*] spotted, dappled
(SM) **1** (*= acto*) splashing
2 (*= diseño*) sprinkle

salpicadura (SF) **1** (*= acto*) splashing
2 (*= mancha*) splash
3 (*en conversación, discurso*) sprinkling

salpicar ▷ CONJUG 1g (VT) **1** (*= manchar*) (*de barro, pintura*) to splash (**de** with); (*de agua*) to sprinkle (**de** with); [*+ tela*] to dot, fleck (**de** with) • **~ agua sobre el suelo** to sprinkle water on the floor • **la multitud de islas que salpican el océano** the host of islands dotted about the ocean • **este asunto salpica al gobierno** this affair hasn't left the government untouched, the government has been tainted by this affair
2 [*+ conversación, discurso*] to sprinkle (**de** with)

salpicón (SM) **1** = **salpicadura**
2 (*Culin*) ▸ **salpicón de marisco(s)** seafood salad
3 (*And*) (*= jugos mixtos*) cold mixed fruit juice
4 (*And, Cono Sur*) (*= ensalada*) raw vegetable salad

salpimentar ▷ CONJUG 1a (VT) **1** (*Culin*) to season, add salt and pepper to
2 (*= amenizar*) to spice up (**de** with)

salpiquear ▷ CONJUG 1a (VT) (*And, Caribe*) = **salpicar**

salpresar ▷ CONJUG 1a (VT) to salt, salt down

salpreso (ADJ) salted, salt

salpullido (SM) (*= erupción*) rash, skin eruption; (*= picadura*) fleabite; (*= hinchazón*) swelling (from a bite)

salsa[1] (SF) **1** (*Culin*) (*gen*) sauce; [*de carne*] gravy; (*para ensalada*) dressing • MODISMOS: • **cocerse en su propia ~** to stew in one's own juice • **estar en su ~** to be in one's element • **es la ~ de la vida** it's the spice of life ▸ **salsa blanca** white sauce ▸ **salsa de ají** chilli sauce ▸ **salsa de tomate** tomato sauce, ketchup ▸ **salsa holandesa** hollandaise sauce ▸ **salsa mahonesa, salsa mayonesa** mayonnaise ▸ **salsa tártara** tartar sauce
2‡ (*= ambiente*) scene* • **la ~ madrileña** the Madrid scene*

salsa[2] (SF) (*Mús*) salsa

salsamentaría (SF) (*Col*) pork butcher's (shop)

salsera (SF) sauce boat

salsero/a (ADJ) (*Mús*) salsa-loving • **ritmo ~** salsa rhythm
(SM/F) salsa music player

salsifí (SM) salsify

saltabanco (SM) **1** (*Hist*) quack, mountebank
2 = **saltimbanqui**

saltado (ADJ) **1** [*loza*] chipped, damaged • **la corona tiene varias piedras saltadas** the crown has several stones missing
2 [*ojos*] bulging

saltador(a) (SM/F) (*Atletismo*) jumper; (*Natación*) diver ▸ **saltador(a) de altura** high-jumper ▸ **saltador(a) de longitud** long-jumper ▸ **saltador(a) de pértiga** pole-vaulter ▸ **saltador(a) de trampolín** trampolinist ▸ **saltador(a) de triple** triple jumper
(SM) (*= comba*) skipping rope

saltadura (SF) chip

saltamontes (SM INV) grasshopper

saltante (ADJ) (*And, Cono Sur*) outstanding, noteworthy

saltaperico (SM) (*Caribe*) squib, firecracker

saltar ▷ CONJUG 1a (VI) **1** [*persona, animal*] (*= dar un salto*) (*tb Atletismo*) to jump; (*más lejos*) to leap; (*a la pata coja*) to hop • **~ de alegría** to jump with *o* for joy • **~ a la comba** to skip, jump rope (*EEUU*) • **hacer ~ un caballo** to jump a horse, make a horse jump
• MODISMO: • **está a la que salta** (*= a la caza de una oportunidad*) he never misses a trick*; (*= al día*) he lives for the day
2 (*= lanzarse*) **a** (*lit*) • **~ al campo** *o* **al césped** (*Dep*) to come out on to the pitch • **~ al agua** to jump *o* dive into the water • **~ de la cama** to leap out of bed • **~ en paracaídas** to parachute • **~ por una ventana** to jump *o* leap out of a window • **~ sobre algn** to jump *o* leap *o* pounce on sb • **~ a tierra** to leap ashore
b (*fig*) • **~ al mundo de la política** to go into politics, move into the political arena • **~ del último puesto al primero** to jump from last place to first • **~ a la fama** to win fame, be shot to fame
3 (*= salir disparado*) [*chispa*] to fly, fly out; [*líquido*] to shoot out, spurt out; [*corcho*] to pop out; [*resorte*] to break, go*; [*astilla*] to fly off; [*botón*] to come off; [*pelota*] to fly • **saltan chispas** sparks are flying • **está saltando el aceite** the oil is spitting • **la pelota saltó fuera del campo** the ball flew out of the ground • **el balón saltó por encima de la portería** the ball flew over the bar • **hacer ~ una trampa** to spring a trap • **el asunto ha saltado a la prensa** the affair has reached the newspapers • MODISMOS: • **~ a la memoria** to leap to mind • **salta a la vista** it's patently obvious, it hits you in the eye
4 (*= estallar*) [*cristal*] to shatter; [*recipiente*] to crack; [*madera*] to crack, snap, break • **la bombilla saltó en pedazos** the light bulb exploded • **hacer ~ un edificio** to blow a building up • **~ por los aires**: • **el coche saltó por los aires** the car was blown up • **el acuerdo puede ~ por los aires** the agreement could be destroyed *o* go up in smoke • **hacer ~ algo por los aires** to blow sth up; ▸ **banca**
5 (*Elec*) [*alarma*] to go off; [*plomos*] to blow
6 (*al hablar*) **a** (*de forma inesperada*) to say, pipe up* • **—¡estupendo! —saltó uno de los chavales** "great!" piped up* *o* said one of the boys • **~ con una patochada** to come out with a ridiculous *o* foolish remark • **~ de una cosa a otra** to skip from one thing *o* subject to another, skip about
b (*con ira*) to explode, blow up
7 (*= irse*) • **~ de un puesto** to give up a job

S

• **hacer ~ a algn de un puesto** to boot sb out of a job*
8 [*cantidad, cifra*] to shoot up, leap, leap up • **la mayoría ha saltado a 900 votos** the majority has shot up *o* leaped (up) to 900 votes
9 • **~ atrás** (*Bio*) to revert
(VT) **1** [+ *muro, obstáculo*] (*por encima*) to jump over, jump; (*llegando más lejos*) to leap, leap over; (*apoyándose con las manos*) to vault • **el caballo saltó la valla** the horse jumped over *o* jumped the fence
2 (= *arrancar*) • **le saltó tres dientes** he knocked out three of his teeth • **me has saltado un botón** you've torn off one of my buttons
3 (*con explosivos*) to blow up
(VPR) **saltarse 1** (= *omitir*) to skip • **nos saltamos el desayuno** we skipped breakfast • **hoy me he saltado una clase** I skipped a class today • **~se un párrafo** to skip a paragraph, miss out a paragraph • **me he saltado un par de renglones** I've skipped a couple of lines
2 (= *no hacer caso de*) • **~se un semáforo** to go through a red light, jump the lights, shoot the lights* • **~se un stop** to disobey a stop sign • **~se todas las reglas** to break all the rules; ▸ **torera**
3 (= *salirse*) [*pieza*] to come off, fly off • **se me ~on las lágrimas** I burst out crying
saltarín/ina (ADJ) **1** (= *que salta*) [*cabra, cordero, niño*] frolicking; [*rana, pulga*] jumping, leaping
2 (= *inquieto*) restless
(SM/F) dancer
salteado (ADJ) **1** (= *discontinuo*) • **—¿has leído el libro? —solo unas páginas salteadas** "have you read the book?" — "I just skipped through it" • **hizo unos cuantos ejercicios ~s y dejó el resto** he skipped through a couple of exercises and left the rest
2 (*Culin*) sauté, sautéed
salteador (SM) (*tb* **salteador de caminos**) highwayman
salteamiento (SM) highway robbery, holdup
saltear ▸ CONJUG 1a (VT) **1** (*Culin*) to sauté
2 (= *atracar*) to hold up
3 (= *sorprender*) to take by surprise
(VI) (= *hacer discontinuamente*) (*al trabajar*) to do in fits and starts; (*al leer*) to skip (over) bits • **lo leyó salteando** he read bits of it here and there
(VPR) **saltearse** (*Arg, Uru*) = **saltarse**
salteña (SF) (*And*) meat pie
salterio (SM) **1** (*Rel*) (*gen*) psalter; (*en la Biblia*) Book of Psalms
2 (*Mús*) psaltery
saltimbanqui (SM) (= *malabarista*) juggler; (= *acróbata*) acrobat; (= *volatinero*) tightrope walker
salto (SM) **1** (= *acción*) (*gen*) jump; (*de mayor altura, distancia*) leap; (*al agua*) dive • **este invento es un gran ~ adelante en tecnología** this invention is a great leap forward in technology • **la novela está narrada con numerosos ~s atrás en el tiempo** the novel is told with a lot of flashbacks in time • **a ~s**: • **cruzamos el río a ~s** we jumped across the river • **había que andar a ~s para no pisar los cristales** you had to hop about so as not to tread on the glass • **el pájaro avanzaba a saltitos** the bird hopped along • **dar** *o* **pegar un ~** [*persona, animal*] to jump; [*corazón*] to leap • **dio un ~ de dos metros** he jumped two metres • **cuando me enteré di un ~ de alegría** I jumped for joy when I found out • **al verla me dio un ~ el corazón** when I saw her my heart leapt • **empezó a dar ~s para calentarse** he started jumping about to warm up • **los niños les acompañaban dando ~s** the kids went with them, jumping *o* hopping about • **me daba ~s el corazón** my heart was pounding • **el progreso da ~s imprevisibles** progress makes unpredictable leaps • **al hablar da muchos ~s de un tema a otro** when he speaks, he jumps from *o* leaps around from one subject to the next • **de un ~**: • **se puso en pie de un ~** he leapt *o* sprang to his feet • **de un ~ se encaramó a la rama de un árbol** he leapt up onto the branch of a tree • **subió/bajó de un ~** he jumped up/down • **el libro supuso su ~ a la fama** the book marked his leap to fame, the book was his springboard to fame • MODISMOS: • **a ~ de mata**: • **vivir a ~ de mata** (= *sin organización*) to lead a haphazard life; (= *sin seguridad*) to live from hand to mouth • **estoy leyendo el libro a ~ de mata** I'm reading the book in dribs and drabs • **dar el ~** to make the leap *o* jump • **le gustaría dar el ~ al teatro profesional** he would like to make the leap *o* jump into professional theatre • **pegar el ~ a algn*** to cheat on sb* • **tirarse al ~** (*Chile**) to take a chance *o* risk ▸ **salto a ciegas, salto al vacío** leap in the dark
2 (*Atletismo*) jump; (*Natación*) dive • **un ~ de ocho metros** a jump of eight metres • **los participantes en las pruebas de ~s** the participants in the jump events • **triple ~** triple jump ▸ **salto alto** (*LAm*) high jump ▸ **salto con garrocha** (*LAm*), **salto con pértiga** pole vault ▸ **salto de altura** high jump ▸ **salto de ángel** swallow dive ▸ **salto de carpa** jack-knife dive ▸ **salto de esquí** ski-jump • **la Copa del Mundo de ~s de esquí** ski-jumping World Cup ▸ **salto de longitud** long jump ▸ **salto de palanca** high dive ▸ **salto de trampolín** springboard dive ▸ **salto en paracaídas** (= *salto*) parachute jump; (= *deporte*) parachuting ▸ **salto inicial** (*Baloncesto*) jump ball ▸ **salto largo** (*LAm*) long jump ▸ **salto mortal** somersault ▸ **salto nulo** no-jump ▸ **saltos de obstáculos** hurdles
3 (= *diferencia*) gap • **entre los dos hermanos hay un ~ de nueve años** there is a gap of nine years between the two brothers • **hay un gran ~ entre su primer libro y este último** there is a big leap between his first book and this latest one
4 (= *en texto*) • **aquí hay un ~ de 50 versos** there's a gap of 50 lines here • **he dado un ~ de varias páginas** I've skipped several pages ▸ **salto de línea** (*Inform*) line break
5 (= *desnivel*) [*de agua*] waterfall; (*en el terreno*) fault ▸ **salto de agua** (*Geog*) waterfall; (*Téc*) chute
6 ▸ **salto de cama** negligee
saltón (ADJ) **1** (= *prominente*) [*ojos*] bulging; [*dientes*] protruding
2 (*LAm*) (= *poco hecho*) undercooked, half-cooked
(SM) grasshopper
saltona (SF) (*Cono Sur*) young locust
salubre (ADJ) healthy, salubrious (*frm*)
salubridad (SF) **1** (= *cualidad*) healthiness, salubriousness (*frm*)
2 (= *estadísticas*) health statistics
salud (SF) **1** (*Med*) health • **estar bien/mal de ~** to be in good/bad health • **mejorar de ~** to get better • **tener buena ~** • **gozar de buena ~** to enjoy good health • **devolver la ~ a algn** to give sb back his health, restore sb to health • **¿cómo vamos de ~?** how are we today? ▸ **salud ambiental** environmental health ▸ **salud mental** mental health, mental well-being ▸ **salud ocupacional** occupational health ▸ **salud pública** public health
2 (= *bienestar*) welfare, wellbeing • **la ~ moral de la nación** the country's moral welfare • MODISMO: • **curarse en ~** to be prepared, take precautions
3 (*en brindis*) • **¡a su ~!** • **¡~ (y pesetas)!** cheers!, good health! • **beber a la ~ de algn** to drink to the health of sb
4 (*al estornudar*) • **¡salud!** bless you!
5 (*Rel*) salvation
saludable (ADJ) **1** (*Med*) healthy
2 (= *provechoso*) good, beneficial • **un aviso ~** a salutary warning
saludador(a) (SM/F) quack doctor
saludar ▸ CONJUG 1a (VT) **1** (*al encontrarse con algn*) (*con palabras*) to say hello to, greet (*frm*); (*con gestos*) to wave at, wave to • **entré a ~la** I went in to say hello to her • **me saludó dándome un beso** he greeted me with a kiss • **nos saludó con la mano** she waved to us • **le saludé desde la otra acera** I waved to him from the other side of the street • **les saludaban desde el barco agitando pañuelos blancos** they waved white handkerchiefs at them from the ship • **la saludó con una leve inclinación de cabeza** he greeted her with a slight nod • **la compañía en pleno salió a ~ al público** the whole company came out to take a bow • **salude de mi parte a su marido** give my regards to your husband
2 (*en carta*) • **le saluda atentamente** yours faithfully
3 (*Mil*) to salute
4 [+ *noticia, suceso*] to hail, welcome
(VI) **1** (= *dirigir un saludo*) to say hello • **nunca saluda** she never says hello
2 (*Mil*) to salute
(VPR) **saludarse** • **se ~on con un beso** they greeted each other with a kiss • **hace tiempo que no se saludan** they haven't been speaking for some time
saludo (SM) **1** (*al encontrarse con algn*) (= *palabra*) greeting; (= *gesto*) wave • **no contestó a mi ~** he didn't respond to my greeting • **nos dirigió un ~ con la mano** he gave us a wave, he waved to us • **~s** *o* **un ~ a Adela** regards to Adela • MODISMO: • **negar el ~ a algn** to cut sb dead, ignore sb, blank sb*
2 (*en carta*) • **un ~ cariñoso a Gonzalo** warm regards to Gonzalo • **un ~ afectuoso** *o* **cordial** kind regards • **~s** best wishes • **¡~s a Teresa de mi parte!** give my best wishes to Teresa!, say hello to Teresa for me! • **os envía muchos ~s** he sends you warmest regards • **atentos ~s** yours sincerely, yours truly (*EEUU*) • **~s cordiales** kind regards • **~s respetuosos**† respectfully yours
3 (*Mil*) salute
Salustio (SM) Sallust
salutación (SF) greeting, salutation
salva[1] (SF) **1** [*de aplausos*] storm
2 (*Mil*) salute, salvo ▸ **salva de advertencia** warning shots (*pl*)
3 (= *saludo*) greeting
4 (= *promesa*) oath, solemn promise
salva[2] (SF) (= *bandeja*) salver, tray
salvabarros (SM INV) mudguard, fender (*EEUU*)
salvación (SF) **1** (= *rescate*) rescue (**de** from)
2 (*Rel*) salvation ▸ **salvación eterna** eternal salvation
salvada (SF) (*LAm*) = **salvación**
salvado (SM) bran
Salvador (SM) **1** • **el ~** (*Rel*) the Saviour, the Savior (*EEUU*)
2 • **El ~** (*Geog*) El Salvador
salvador(a) (SM/F) **1** (= *que rescata*) rescuer, saviour, savior (*EEUU*)
2 [*de playa*] life-saver

salvadoreñismo (SM) *word or phrase etc peculiar to El Salvador*
salvadoreño/a (ADJ), (SM/F) Salvadoran
salvaeslip (SM) (PL: **salvaeslips**) panty liner
salvaguarda (SF) safeguard
salvaguardar ▸ CONJUG 1a (VT) **1** (= *defender*) to safeguard
2 (*Inform*) to back-up, make a backup copy of
salvaguardia (SF) **1** (= *defensa*) safeguard, defence, defense (*EEUU*)
2 (= *documento*) safe-conduct
salvajada (SF) savage deed, atrocity
salvaje (ADJ) **1** [*planta, animal, tierra*] wild
2 (= *no autorizado*) [*huelga*] unofficial, wildcat; [*construcción*] unauthorized
3 [*pueblo, tribu*] savage
4 (= *brutal*) savage, brutal • **un ~ asesinato** a brutal *o* savage murder
5 (*LAm**) (= *estupendo*) terrific*, smashing*
(SMF) (*lit, fig*) savage
salvajemente (ADV) savagely, brutally
salvajería (SF) = **salvajada**
salvajez (SF) = **salvajismo**
salvajino (ADJ) **1** (= *salvaje*) wild, savage
2 • **carne salvajina** meat from a wild animal
salvajismo (SM) savagery
salvamanteles (SM INV) table mat, hot pad (EEUU)
salvamento (SM) **1** (= *acción*) (*gen*) rescue; [*de naufragio*] salvage • **de ~** rescue (*antes de s*) • **operaciones de ~** rescue operations • **bote de ~** lifeboat ▸ **salvamento y socorrismo** life-saving
2 (= *refugio*) place of safety, refuge
salvapantallas (SM INV) screensaver
salvaplatos (SM INV) table mat, hot pad (EEUU)
salvar ▸ CONJUG 1a (VT) **1** (*de un peligro*) to save • **me salvó la vida** he saved my life • **los bomberos nos ~on del fuego** the firemen saved us from the blaze • **apenas ~on nada del incendio** they hardly managed to salvage anything from the fire • **me has salvado de tener que sentarme con ese pesado** you saved me (from) having to sit next to that old bore
2 (*Rel*) to save
3 (*Inform*) to save
4 (= *evitar*) [+ *dificultad, obstáculo*] to get round, overcome; [+ *montaña, río, barrera*] to cross; [+ *rápidos*] to shoot
5 (*frm*) [+ *distancia*] to cover • **el tren salva la distancia en dos horas** the train covers *o* does the distance in two hours
6 (= *exceptuando*) • **salvando: salvando algún detalle, la traducción está muy bien** apart from a few minor details, the translation is very good; ▸ **distancia**
7 (*frm*) [+ *altura*] to rise above
8 (*Cono Sur*) [+ *examen*] to pass
(VPR) **salvarse 1** (*de un peligro*) to escape • **pocos se ~on del naufragio** few escaped from *o* survived the shipwreck • **¡sálvese quien pueda!** • **¡sálvese el que pueda!** every man for himself!
2* (= *librarse*) • **considera incompetentes a todos los ministros, no se salva nadie** in his view all the ministers are, without exception, incompetent • **todos son antipáticos, Carlos es el único que se salva** they're an unfriendly lot, Carlos is the one exception
3 (*Rel*) to be saved
salvaslip (SM) (PL: **salvaslips**) panty liner
salvataje (SM) (*Cono Sur*) rescue
salvavidas (SM INV) (= *flotador*) lifebelt, life preserver (EEUU); (= *chaleco*) life jacket
(ADJ INV) life-saving (*antes de s*) • **bote ~** lifeboat • **cinturón ~** lifebelt, life preserver (EEUU) • **chaleco ~** life jacket
salvedad (SF) reservation, qualification • **con la ~ de que ...** with the proviso that ... • **me gustaría hacer una ~** I would like to qualify what you said *o* to make a qualification
Salvi (SM) *forma familiar de* **Salvador**
salvia (SF) sage
salvilla (SF) **1** (= *bandeja*) salver, tray
2 (*Cono Sur*) (= *vinagrera*) cruet
salvo (ADJ) safe; ▸ **sano**
(PREP) except, except for, save • **~ aquellos que ya contamos** except (for) those we have already counted • **de todos los países ~ de Italia** from all countries except Italy • **~ error u omisión** (*Com*) errors and omissions excepted
(ADV) • **a ~** out of danger • **a ~ de** safe from • **nada ha quedado a ~ de sus ataques** nothing has been safe from *o* has escaped his attacks • **para dejar a ~ su reputación** in order to safeguard his reputation • **ponerse a ~** to reach safety • **en ~** out of danger, in a safe place
(CONJ) • **~ que** • **~ si** unless • **iré ~ que me avises al contrario** I'll go unless you tell me otherwise
salvoconducto (SM) safe-conduct
salvohonor (SM) (*hum*) backside
samaritano/a (SM/F) Samaritan • **buen ~** good Samaritan
samaruco (SM) (*Cono Sur*) hunter's pouch, gamebag
samba (SF) samba; ▸ **sambo**
sambenito (SM) **1** (= *deshonra*) • **le colgaron el ~ de cobarde** they branded him a coward • **le colgaron el ~ de haberlo hecho** they put the blame for it on him • **echar el ~ a otro** to pin the blame on somebody else • **quedó con el ~ toda la vida** the stigma stayed with him for the rest of his life
2 (*Hist*) sanbenito
sambo/a (SM/F) *offspring of black person and (American) Indian*
sambumbia (SF) **1** (*CAm, Caribe, Méx*) (= *bebida*) fruit drink
2 (*Méx*) [*de ananás*] pineapple drink; (= *hordiate*) barley water drink
3 (*And*) (= *trasto*) old thing, piece of junk • **volver algo ~** to smash sth to pieces
sambutir‡ ▸ CONJUG 3a (*Méx*) (VT) (= *meter a fuerza*) to stick in, stuff in*; (= *hundir*) to sink in, shove in
samotana* (SF) (*CAm*) row, uproar
samovar (SM) samovar
sampablera (SF) (*Caribe*) racket, row
sampán (SM) sampan
Samuel (SM) Samuel
samurear ▸ CONJUG 1a (VI) (*Caribe*) to walk with bowed head
San (SM) (*apócope de santo*) saint • **San Juan** Saint John • **cerca de San Martín** near St Martin's (church) • **se casarán por San Juan** (*en sentido extenso*) they'll get married sometime in midsummer; (*estrictamente*) they'll get married round about St John's Day; ▸ **santo, lunes**
sanable (ADJ) curable
sanaco (ADJ) (*Caribe*) silly
sanalotodo (SM INV) cure-all
sanamente (ADV) healthily
sananería (SF) (*Caribe*) stupid remark, silly comment
sanar ▸ CONJUG 1a (VT) [+ *herida*] to heal; [+ *persona*] to cure (**de** of)
(VI) [*herida*] to heal; [*persona*] to recover
sanativo (ADJ) healing, curative
sanatorio (SM) sanatorium, sanitarium (EEUU) ▸ **sanatorio mental** psychiatric clinic, psychiatric hospital
San Bernardo (SM) St Bernard
sancho (SM) **1** (= *cerdo*) pig, hog (EEUU)
2 (*Méx*) (= *carnero*) ram; (= *cordero*) lamb; (= *macho cabrío*) billy goat; (= *animal abandonado*) orphan animal, suckling
sanción (SF) sanction • **sanciones comerciales** trade sanctions • **sanciones económicas** economic sanctions • **imponer sanciones** to impose sanctions • **levantar sanciones a algn** to lift sanctions against sb ▸ **sanción disciplinaria** punishment, disciplinary measure
sancionable (ADJ) punishable
sancionado/a (SM/F) guilty person • **los ~s** (*Pol*) those who have been punished for a political offence, those guilty of political crimes
sancionar ▸ CONJUG 1a (VT) **1** (= *castigar*) (*gen*) to sanction; (*Jur*) to penalize
2 (= *permitir*) to sanction
sancionatorio (ADJ) (*Jur*) penal, penalty (*antes de s*)
sancochado (SM) (*And*) = **sancocho**
sancochar ▸ CONJUG 1a (VT) (*LAm*) to parboil
sancocho (SM) **1** (*Culin*) (= *comida mal guisada*) undercooked food; (= *carne*) parboiled meat
2 (*LAm*) (= *guisado*) stew (of meat, yucca *etc*)
3 (*CAm, Caribe, Méx*) (= *lío*) fuss
4 (*Caribe*) (= *bazofia*) pigswill
San Cristóbal (SM) **1** (*Rel*) St Christopher
2 (*Geog*) St Kitts
sanctasanctórum (SM) **1** (= *lugar*) inner sanctum • **su pequeño despacho es el ~ de la casa** his small office is like the inner sanctum of the house
2 (*Rel*) holy of holies
sandalia (SF) sandal
sándalo (SM) sandal, sandalwood
sandez (SF) **1** (= *cualidad*) foolishness
2 (= *acción*) stupid thing • **decir sandeces** to talk nonsense • **fue una ~ obrar así** it was a stupid thing to do
sandía (SF) watermelon; ▸ **sandío**
sandinismo (SM) Sandinista movement
sandinista (ADJ), (SMF) (*Nic*) Sandinista
sandío/a (ADJ) foolish, silly
(SM/F) fool; ▸ **sandía**
sánduche (SM) (*LAm*) sandwich
sandunga (SF) **1*** (= *encanto*) charm; (= *gracia*) wit
2 (*LAm*) (= *juerga*) binge*, celebration
sandunguero (ADJ) (= *encantador*) charming; (= *gracioso*) witty
sándwich [san'gwitʃ, sam'bitʃ] (SM) (PL: **sándwichs, sándwiches**) sandwich
sandwichera (SF) toasted sandwich maker
sandwichería (SF) (*esp LAm*) sandwich bar
saneamiento (SM) **1** (= *limpieza*) [*de río, ciudad, alcantarillado*] clean-up; [*de terreno*] drainage • **pidió un préstamo para el ~ de la casa** she applied for a loan to upgrade the house • **materiales de ~** sanitary fittings
2 [*de empresa*] restructuring • **invirtieron 100 millones en el ~ económico de la compañía** they invested 100 million in restructuring the company's finances • **el ~ de la economía** putting the economy back on a sound footing
3 (*Econ*) [*de deuda*] write-off; [*de activo*] write-down
4 (*Jur*) compensation, indemnification
sanear ▸ CONJUG 1a (VT) **1** (= *limpiar*) [+ *río, ciudad, alcantarillado*] to clean up; [+ *casa*] to upgrade
2 [+ *empresa*] to restructure • **es preciso ~ la compañía** the company needs restructuring • **~ la economía** to put the economy back on a sound footing
3 (*Econ*) [+ *deuda*] to write off; [+ *activo*] to write down

S

4 (*Jur*) (= *compensar*) to compensate, indemnify
sanfasón* SF (*LAm*), **sanfazón** SF (*LAm*) cheek* • **a la ~** unceremoniously, informally; (*pey*) carelessly
sanfermines SMPL *festivities in celebration of San Fermín (Pamplona)*

SANFERMINES
The **Sanfermines** is a week-long festival starting on 7 July in Pamplona (Navarre) to honour **San Fermín**, the town's patron saint. One of its main events involves bulls and bullfighting. The bulls are led from their enclosure to the bullring early in the morning through the city's main streets; young men, dressed in traditional Navarrese red berets, white shirts and trousers with red sashes around their waists, run through the streets leading the fast-moving bulls. This activity, known as the **encierro**, in which people risk serious injury and even death, was popularized by writers such as Ernest Hemingway and now attracts visitors from all over the world. The festivities start with the **txupinazo**, a large rocket fired from Pamplona's main square, and for a full week Pamplona becomes one large street party punctuated by the daily **encierro**.

sanforizar ▹ CONJUG 1f VT to sanforize®
sango SM (*And*) *yucca and maize pudding*
sangradera SF **1** (*Med*) lancet
2 [*de agua*] (= *acequia*) irrigation channel; (= *desagüe*) sluice, outflow
sangradura SF **1** (*Med*) (= *incisión*) cut made into a vein; (= *sangría*) bleeding, bloodletting
2 (*Anat*) inner angle of the elbow
3 (*Agr*) drainage channel
sangrante ADJ **1** [*encías, úlcera*] bleeding
2 [*batalla, guerra*] bloody
3 (= *indignante*) scandalous • **lo más ~ del caso es que la policía no hizo nada** the most scandalous aspect of the affair was that the police did nothing
sangrar ▹ CONJUG 1a VT **1** [+ *enfermo, vena*] to bleed
2 (*Agr, Téc*) [+ *terreno*] to drain; [+ *agua*] to drain off; [+ *árbol, tubería, horno*] to tap
3 [+ *texto, línea*] to indent
4 (= *explotar*) • **~ a algn** to bleed sb dry • **siempre está sangrando a sus padres** he is always bleeding his parents dry
5* (= *robar*) to filch
VI **1** [*persona, herida, encías*] to bleed • **me sangra la nariz** (*de forma espontánea*) I've got a nosebleed; (*a consecuencia de un golpe*) my nose is bleeding
2 (*frm*) (= *doler*) to rankle • **aún le sangra la humillación** the humiliation still rankles
3 (= *ser reciente*) • **estar sangrando** to be still fresh
sangre SF **1** (*Bio*) blood • **tiene ~ de tipo O negativo** he's blood type O negative, his blood type is O negative • **las enfermedades de la ~** blood diseases • **la tela es de color rojo ~** the fabric is a blood-red colour • **chupar la ~ a algn** (*lit*) to suck sb's blood; (*fig*) (= *explotar*) to bleed sb dry; (*Méx*) (= *hacer pasar mal rato*) to give sb a hard time, make sb's life a misery • **dar ~** to give blood • **donar ~** to donate blood • **echar ~** to bleed • **estuvo echando ~ por la nariz** (*de forma natural*) he had a nosebleed; (*a consecuencia de un golpe*) his nose was bleeding, he was bleeding from the nose • **hacer ~ a algn** to make sb bleed • **me pegó y me hizo ~** he hit me and I started bleeding *o* to bleed, he hit me and made me bleed • **hacerse ~**: • **¿te has hecho ~?** are you bleeding? • **me hice ~ en la rodilla** my knee started bleeding *o* to bleed • **salirle ~ a algn**: • **me está saliendo ~ de la herida** my cut is bleeding ▸ **sangre caliente** • **a ~ caliente** in the heat of the moment • **por sus venas corre ~ caliente** he is very hot-blooded • **de ~ caliente** [*animal*] warm-blooded (*antes de s*); [*persona*] hot-blooded (*antes de s*) ▸ **sangre fría** coolness, sang-froid (*frm*) • **era el que tenía más ~ fría a la hora de tomar decisiones** he was the coolest when it came to taking decisions • **la ~ fría del asesino** the murderer's cold-blooded nature • **lo asesinaron a ~ fría** they killed him in cold blood • **de ~ fría** [*animal*] cold-blooded (*antes de s*); [*persona*] cool-headed (*antes de s*) • **mantener la ~ fría** to keep calm, keep one's cool ▸ **sangre nueva** new blood • **los inmigrantes inyectaron ~ nueva en el país** the immigrants injected new blood into the country; ▹ **banco, baño, delito**
2 • MODISMOS: • **arderle la ~ a algn**: • **me arde la ~ cada vez que me habla** each time he speaks to me it makes my blood boil • **beber la ~ a algn** (*Méx*) to give sb a hard time, make sb's life a misery • **bullirle la ~ a algn**: • **me bulle la ~ ante tanto sufrimiento** seeing such suffering makes my blood boil • **son jóvenes y les bulle la ~ en las venas** they are young and bursting with energy • **hacer correr la ~** to shed blood • **no les importa hacer correr la ~ de sus compatriotas** they are unconcerned about shedding the blood of their fellow countrymen • **dar su ~ por algo** to give one's life for sth, shed one's blood for sth (*frm*) • **dieron su ~ por sus ideales** they gave their lives for their beliefs • **encender la ~ a algn** to make sb's blood boil • **a ~ y fuego** ruthlessly, by fire and sword (*liter*) • **la revuelta fue aplastada a ~ y fuego** the revolt was crushed ruthlessly *o* by fire and sword (*liter*) • **hacerse mala ~** to get annoyed • **me hago muy mala ~ cuando me faltan al respeto** I get really annoyed when people are disrespectful to me • **helar la ~ a algn** to make sb's blood run cold • **sus gritos le helaban la ~ a cualquiera** her cries would make anyone's blood run cold • **hervirle la ~ a algn**: • **me hierve la ~ cuando nos tratan así** it really makes me mad *o* it makes my blood boil when they treat us like this • **tener la ~ de horchata** *o* (*Méx*) **atole** to be cold-hearted • **ser de ~ ligera** (*Méx*) • **ser liviano de ~** (*Chile*) to be easy-going *o* good-natured • **llegar a la ~** to come to blows • **andar con ~ en el ojo** (*Cono Sur**) to bear a grudge • **es de ~ pesada** (*Méx*) • **es pesado de ~** (*Chile*) he's not a very nice person, he's not very good-natured • **quemar la ~ a algn** to make sb's blood boil • **me quema la ~ verlo sufrir** it makes my blood boil to see him suffer • **no llegar la ~ al río**: • **discutimos un poco pero no llegó la ~ al río** we argued a bit but it didn't come *o* amount to much • **sudar ~** to sweat blood • **costar ~, sudor y lágrimas** to cost blood, sweat and tears • **no tener ~ en las venas** to be a cold fish
3 (= *linaje*) blood • **lleva ~ española en las venas** he has Spanish blood (in him) • **somos hermanos de ~** we're blood brothers • **tenemos la misma ~** we are blood relations • MODISMOS: • **llevar algo en la ~** to have sth in one's blood • **lleva la política en la ~** he's got politics in his blood • **la ~ tira (mucho)** blood is thicker than water ▸ **sangre azul** blue blood • **ser de ~ azul** to belong to the aristocracy; ▹ **puro**
sangregorda* SMF bore
sangría SF **1** (*Med*) bleeding, bloodletting ▸ **sangría suelta** excessive flow of blood
2 [*de recursos*] outflow, drain
3 (*Anat*) inner angle of the elbow
4 (*Agr*) (= *acequia*) irrigation channel; (= *desagüe*) outlet, outflow; (= *zanja*) ditch; (= *drenaje*) drainage
5 [*de alto horno*] (= *acción*) tapping; (= *metal fundido*) stream of molten metal
6 (*Culin*) sangria
7 (*Tip, Inform*) indentation
sangrientamente ADV bloodily
sangriento ADJ **1** (= *con sangre*) [*herida*] bleeding; [*arma, manos*] bloody, bloodstained
2 [*batalla, guerra*] bloody
3 (= *cruel*) [*injusticia*] flagrant; [*broma*] cruel; [*insulto*] deadly
4 (*liter*) [*color*] blood-red
sangrigordo ADJ (*Caribe*) (= *aburrido*) tedious, boring; (= *insolente*) rude, insolent
sangriligero* ADJ (*LAm*), **sangriliviano** ADJ (*LAm*) pleasant, congenial
sangripesado* ADJ (*LAm**), **sangrón** ADJ (*Cuba, Méx*), **sangruno** ADJ (*Caribe*) (= *desagradable*) unpleasant, nasty; (= *aburrido*) boring, tiresome; (= *obstinado*) obstinate, pig-headed
sanguarañas* SFPL (*And*) circumlocutions, evasions
sánguche SM (*LAm*), **sanguchito** SM (*LAm*) sandwich
sangüich SM (*Esp*) sandwich
sanguijuela SF leech
sanguinario ADJ bloodthirsty, cruel
sanguíneo ADJ **1** (*Anat*) blood (*antes de s*) • **vaso ~** blood vessel
2 [*color*] blood-red
sanguinolento ADJ **1** (= *con sangre*) [*herida*] bleeding; [*flujo*] bloody; [*ojos*] bloodshot
2 (= *manchado de sangre*) bloodstained
3 [*color*] blood-red
4 (*Culin*) underdone, rare
sanidad SF **1** (= *cualidad*) health, healthiness
2 (*Admin*) health, public health • **(Ministerio de) Sanidad** Ministry of Health • **inspector de ~** health inspector ▸ **sanidad animal** animal welfare ▸ **sanidad pública** public health (department)
San Isidro SM Saint Isidore

SAN ISIDRO
San Isidro is the patron saint of Madrid, and gives his name to the week-long festivities which take place round 15 May. Originally an 18th-century trade fair, the **San Isidro** celebrations now include music, dance, a famous **romería**, theatre and bullfighting. The **isidrada** is in fact one of the most important dates in the bullfighting calendar.
▹ **ROMERÍA**

sanitaría SF (*Cono Sur*) plumber's, plumber's shop
sanitario/a ADJ [*condiciones*] sanitary; [*centro, medidas*] health (*antes de s*) • **política sanitaria** health policy • **control ~** public health inspection • **asistencia sanitaria** medical attention
SMPL **sanitarios** (= *aparatos de baño*) sanitary ware (*sing*), bathroom fittings; (*Méx*) (= *wáter*) toilet (*sing*), washroom (*sing*) (*EEUU*)
SM/F (*Med*) stretcher bearer
sanjacobo SM *escalope with cheese filling*
San José SM (*Geog*) San José
San Juan SM Saint John

> **SAN JUAN**
> The **Día de San Juan** on 24 June fuses Christian tradition with ancient summer solstice celebrations. In many areas, particularly near the sea, it is customary to light large bonfires on open ground on the night of 23 June and to burn an effigy, usually made of pieces of wood and rags, at the stake. These **hogueras de San Juan**, which are often accompanied by fireworks and music, draw crowds of people wanting to dance or simply to enjoy the summer evening, until the fire dies out in the small hours. Some legends credit this night with magical qualities and talk of ghostly apparitions.

San Lorenzo SM • **el (río) ~** the St Lawrence (River)

San Marino SM San Marino

sano ADJ **1** (= *con salud*) [*persona*] healthy; [*órgano*] sound; [*fruta*] unblemished • **MODISMO**: • **cortar por lo ~** to take extreme measures, go right to the root of the problem
2 (= *beneficioso*) [*clima, dieta*] healthy; [*comida*] wholesome
3 (= *entero*) whole, intact • **~ y salvo** safe and sound • **no quedó plato ~ en toda la casa** there wasn't a plate in the house left unbroken • **esa silla no es muy sana** that chair is not too strong
4 (= *sin vicios*) [*persona*] healthy; [*enseñanza, idea*] sound; [*deseo*] earnest, sincere; [*objetivo*] worthy

San Salvador SM (*Geog*) San Salvador

sansalvadoreño/a ADJ of/from San Salvador
SM/F native/inhabitant of San Salvador • **los ~s** the people of San Salvador

sánscrito ADJ, SM Sanskrit

sanseacabó EXCL • **y ~*** and that's the end of it

Sansón SM Samson • **MODISMO**: • **es un ~** he's tremendously strong

Santa Bárbara SF Santa Barbara

santabárbara SF (*Náut*) magazine

santamente ADV • **vivir ~** to live a saintly life

santanderino/a (*Esp*) ADJ of/from Santander
SM/F native/inhabitant of Santander • **los ~s** the people of Santander

santateresa SF praying mantis

santería SF **1** (*Cuba*) (= *tienda*) *shop selling religious images, prints, etc*; (= *brujería*) witchcraft
2* = **santidad**
3 (*Caribe*) (*Rel*) *religion of African origin*

santero/a SM/F **1** (*Caribe*) *maker or seller of religious images, prints, etc*
2 (= *devoto*) *person excessively devoted to the saints*

Santiago SM St James ▸ **Santiago (de Chile)** Santiago (de Chile) ▸ **Santiago (de Compostela)** Santiago de Compostela

santiaguero/a* SM/F (*Cono Sur*) faith healer

santiagués/esa ADJ of/from Santiago de Compostela
SM/F native/inhabitant of Santiago de Compostela • **los santiagueses** the people of Santiago

santiaguino/a ADJ of/from Santiago (de Chile)
SM/F native/inhabitant of Santiago (de Chile) • **los ~s** the people of Santiago (de Chile)

santiamén SM • **en un ~** in no time at all, in a flash

santidad SF [*de lugar*] holiness, sanctity; [*de persona*] saintliness • **su Santidad** His Holiness

santificación SF sanctification

santificar ▸ CONJUG 1g VT **1** (*Rel*) [*+ persona*] to sanctify; [*+ lugar*] to consecrate; [*+ fiesta*] to keep • **santificado sea Tu Nombre** hallowed be Thy Name
2* (= *perdonar*) to forgive

santiguada SF (= *señal*) sign of the Cross; (= *acto*) act of crossing oneself

santiguar ▸ CONJUG 1i VT **1** (= *bendecir*) to make the sign of the cross over, bless
2* (= *pegar*) to slap, hit
3 (*LAm*) (= *sanear*) to heal, heal by blessing
VPR **santiguarse 1** (= *persignarse*) to cross o.s.
2* (= *exagerar*) to make a great fuss

santísimo ADJ (*superl*) holy, most holy
SM • **el Santísimo** the Holy Sacrament
SF • **MODISMO**: • **hacer la santísima a algn*** (= *jorobar*) to drive sb up the wall*; (= *perjudicar*) to do sb down*

santo/a ADJ **1** (*Rel*) [*vida, persona*] holy; [*tierra*] consecrated; [*persona*] saintly; [*mártir*] blessed; ▸ **semana**
2 [*remedio*] wonderful, miraculous
3 (*enfático*) blessed • **~ y bueno** well and good • **hacer su santa voluntad** to do as one jolly well pleases • **todo el ~ día** the whole blessed day • **y él con su santa calma** and he as cool as a cucumber
SM/F **1** (*Rel*) saint • **Santo Tomás** St Thomas ▸ **santo/a patrón/ona, santo/a titular** patron saint
2 • **MODISMOS**: • **¿a ~ de qué?** why on earth? • **¿a qué ~?** what on earth for? • **¡por todos los ~s!** for pity's sake! • **no es ~ de mi devoción** he's not my cup of tea* • **alzarse con el ~ y la limosna*** to clear off with the whole lot* • **comerse los ~s*** to be terribly devout • **desnudar a un ~ para vestir otro** to rob Peter to pay Paul • **se le fue el ~ al cielo** he forgot what he was about to say • **¡que se te va el ~ al cielo!** you're miles away! • **llegar y besar el ~** to pull it off at the first attempt • **fue llegar y besar el ~** it was as easy as pie • **nacer con el ~ de espaldas** to be born unlucky • **poner a algn como un ~*** to give sb a telling-off* • **quedarse para vestir ~s** to be left on the shelf • **tener el ~ de cara*** to have the luck of the devil • **tener el ~ de espaldas*** to be cursed with bad luck
3 (= *persona*) saint • **es un ~** he's a saint • **estaba hecho un ~** he was terribly sweet
SM **1** (= *onomástica*) saint's day • **mañana es mi ~** tomorrow is my name day *o* saint's day
2 (*en libro*) picture
3 ▸ **santo y seña** (*Mil*) password
4 (*Cono Sur*) (*Cos*) patch, darn

> **SANTO**
> As well as celebrating their birthday, many Spaniards and Latin Americans celebrate their **santo** or **onomástica**. This is the day when the saint whose name they have is honoured in the Christian calendar. It used to be relatively common for newborn babies to be named after the saint on whose day they were born. So a boy born on 25 July (Saint James's day) stood a good chance of being christened "Santiago". The tradition may be dying out now that parents are no longer restricted to names from the Christian calendar. In Spain, as with birthdays, the person whose **santo** it is normally buys the drinks if they go out with friends.

Santo Domingo SM **1** (= *capital*) Santo Domingo
2 (= *isla*) Hispaniola

santón* SM (*hum*) big shot*, big wheel*

santoral SM calendar of saints' days

santuario SM **1** (*Rel*) (= *templo*) sanctuary, shrine; (= *lugar sagrado*) sanctuary
2 (*And, Caribe*) (= *ídolo*) native idol; (= *tesoro*) buried treasure

santulario ADJ (*Cono Sur*) = **santurrón**

santurrón/ona ADJ (= *mojigato*) sanctimonious; (= *hipócrita*) hypocritical
SM/F (= *mojigato*) sanctimonious person; (= *hipócrita*) hypocrite

saña SF **1** (= *furor*) rage; (= *crueldad*) cruelty • **con ~** viciously
2 (= *cartera*) wallet, billfold (*EEUU*)

sañero‡ SM (*Esp*) pickpocket

sañoso ADJ = **sañudo**

sañudamente ADV (= *furiosamente*) angrily, furiously; (= *con crueldad*) cruelly; (= *brutalmente*) viciously

sañudo ADJ **1** [*persona*] (= *furioso*) furious, enraged; (= *cruel*) cruel
2 [*golpe*] vicious, cruel

sapaneco ADJ (*CAm*) plump, chubby

sáparo SM (*And*) wicker basket

sapiencia SF knowledge, wisdom

sapo[1] SM **1** (*Zool*) toad • **MODISMO**: • **echar ~s y culebras** to turn the air blue
2 (= *persona*) ugly creature
3 (*LAm*) *game of throwing coins into the mouth of an iron toad*
4 (*CAm, Caribe*) (= *soplón*) informer, grass*, fink (*EEUU**)
5 (*Cono Sur‡*) (= *soldado*) soldier

sapo[2] ADJ **1** (*And, CAm, Cono Sur*) (= *astuto*) cunning, sly
2 (*Cono Sur*) (= *hipócrita*) hypocritical, two-faced
3 (*CAm, Caribe*) (= *chismoso*) gossipy

saporro ADJ (*And, CAm*) short and chubby

sapotear ▸ CONJUG 1a VT (*And*) to finger, handle

saprófago ADJ saprophagous

saprófito ADJ saprophytic
SM saprophyte

saque SM **1** (*Tenis*) service, serve; (*Rugby*) line-out; (*Ftbl*) (*para dar comienzo al partido*) kick-off ▸ **saque de banda** (*Ftbl*) throw-in ▸ **saque de castigo** penalty kick ▸ **saque de esquina** corner, corner kick ▸ **saque de falta** free kick ▸ **saque de honor** guest appearance ▸ **saque de mano** (*LAm*) throw-in ▸ **saque de portería, saque de puerta, saque de valla** (*Cono Sur*) goal kick ▸ **saque inicial** kick-off ▸ **saque lateral** throw-in ▸ **saque libre** free kick
2 (= *apetito*) • **tener buen ~** to have a hearty appetite
SMF (*Tenis*) server

saqué *etc* ▸ **sacar**

saqueador(a) SM/F looter

saquear ▸ CONJUG 1a VT **1** (*Mil*) to sack
2 (= *robar*) to loot, plunder, pillage

saqueo SM **1** (*Mil*) sacking
2 (= *robo*) looting, plundering, pillaging

saquito SM small bag ▸ **saquito de papel** paper bag

S.A.R. ABR (= **Su Alteza Real**) HRH

sarampión SM measles

sarao SM **1** (= *fiesta*) soirée, evening party
2* (= *lío*) fuss, to-do*

sarape SM (*Méx*) blanket

sarasa‡ SM pansy*, fairy*, fag (*EEUU‡*)

saraviado ADJ (*And*) [*objeto*] spotted, mottled; [*animal*] spotted; [*persona*] freckled

sarazo ADJ (*LAm*) = **zarazo**

sarazón ADJ (*Méx*) = **zarazo**

sarcasmo SM sarcasm • **es un ~ que …** it is ludicrous that …

sarcásticamente ADV sarcastically

sarcástico ADJ sarcastic

sarcófago SM sarcophagus
sarcoma SM sarcoma
sardana SF *Catalan dance and music*
sardina SF sardine • MODISMO: • **como ~s en lata** like sardines ▸ **sardina arenque** herring ▸ **sardina noruega** brisling
sardinel SM (*Col*) **1** (= *acera*) pavement (*Brit*), sidewalk (*EEUU*)
2 (= *borde*) kerb (*Brit*), curb (*EEUU*)
sardinero ADJ sardine (*antes de s*)
sardo/a ADJ, SM/F Sardinian
sardónico ADJ sardonic, sarcastic
sargazo SM gulfweed
sargentear ▹ CONJUG 1a VT **1** (*Mil*) to command
2* (= *mandonear*) to boss about
VI* to be bossy, boss people about
sargento SMF **1** (*Mil*) sergeant ▸ **sargento de primera** [*de tierra*] staff sergeant; [*de aire*] flight sergeant
2 (*pey**) (= *mandón*) bossy person
sargentona* SF tough mannish woman
sargo SM bream
sari SM sari
sarín SM sarin
sarita SF (*And*) straw hat
sarmentoso ADJ **1** [*planta*] twining, climbing
2 (*Anat*) [*manos*] gnarled; [*dedos*] long and thin
sarmiento SM vine shoot
sarna SF (*Med*) scabies; (*Vet*) mange
sarniento ADJ, **sarnoso** ADJ **1** (*Med*) scabious; (*Vet*) mangy
2 (= *raquítico*) weak
3 (*And, Cono Sur**) (= *despreciable*) lousy*, contemptible
sarong SM sarong
sarpullido SM **1** (*Med*) rash
2 [*de pulga*] fleabite
sarraceno/a ADJ, SM/F Saracen
sarracina SF **1** (= *pelea*) brawl, free fight
2 (= *matanza*) mass slaughter • **han hecho una ~** (*Educ**) they've ploughed almost everybody*
Sarre SM Saar
sarrio SM Pyrenean mountain goat
sarro SM **1** (= *depósito*) (*en los dientes*) tartar, plaque; (*en la lengua*) fur; (*en una caldera*) scale, fur
2 (*Bot*) rust
sarroso ADJ [*dientes*] covered with tartar; [*caldera, lengua*] furred, furry
sarta SF, **sartalada** SF (*Cono Sur*) (= *serie*) string; (= *fila*) line, row • **una ~ de mentiras** a pack of lies
sartén SF, (*LAm*) SF frying pan
• MODISMO: • **coger la ~ por donde quema** to act rashly • **saltar de la ~ y dar en la brasa** to jump out of the frying pan into the fire • **tener la ~ por el mango** to have the upper hand
sarteneja SF (*And, Méx*) (= *marisma seca*) dried-out pool; (*Méx*) (= *bache*) pothole; (= *tierra seca*) cracked soil, parched soil
sasafrás SM sassafras
sastra SF seamstress
sastre/a SM/F tailor; (*Teat*) costumier
• **hecho por ~** tailor-made ▸ **sastre de teatro** costumier
ADJ INV • **traje ~** tailor-made suit
sastrería SF **1** (= *oficio*) tailor's trade, tailoring
2 (= *tienda*) tailor's, tailor's shop
Satán SM, **Satanás** SM Satan
satánico ADJ (= *diabólico*) satanic; (= *malvado*) fiendish
satanismo SM Satanism, devil-worship
satanización SF demonizing
satanizar ▹ CONJUG 1f VT to demonize
satelitario ADJ satellite (*antes de s*)
satélite SM **1** (*Astron*) satellite
• **transmisión vía ~** satellite broadcasting
▸ **satélite artificial** artificial satellite
▸ **satélite de comunicaciones** communications satellite ▸ **satélite espía** spy satellite ▸ **satélite meteorológico** weather satellite
2 (= *persona*) (*gen*) satellite; (= *esbirro*) henchman; (= *compañero*) crony
ADJ INV satellite • **ciudad ~** satellite town
• **país ~** satellite country
satén SM sateen
satín SM (*LAm*) sateen, satin
satinado ADJ glossy, shiny
SM gloss, shine
satinar ▹ CONJUG 1a VT to gloss, make glossy
sátira SF satire
satíricamente ADV satirically
satírico ADJ satiric, satirical
satirizar ▹ CONJUG 1f VT to satirize
sátiro SM **1** (*Literat*) satyr
2 (= *hombre lascivo*) sex maniac
satisfacción SF **1** (= *placer*) satisfaction • **a ~ de** to the satisfaction of • **a su entera ~** to his complete satisfaction • **con ~ de todos** to everyone's satisfaction ▸ **satisfacción laboral, satisfacción profesional** job satisfaction
2 [*de ofensa*] (= *compensación*) satisfaction, redress; (= *disculpa*) apology • **pedir una ~ a algn** to demand satisfaction from sb
3 ▸ **satisfacción de sí mismo** self-satisfaction, smugness
satisfacer ▹ CONJUG 2r VT **1** [+ *persona*] to satisfy • **el resultado no me satisface** I'm not satisfied *o* happy with the result
• **~ a algn de** *o* **por una ofensa** to give sb satisfaction for an offence
2 (= *compensar*) [+ *gastos, demanda*] to meet; [+ *deuda*] to pay; [+ *éxito*] to gratify, please; [+ *necesidad, solicitud*] to meet, satisfy; (*Com*) [+ *letra de cambio*] to honour, honor (*EEUU*)
3 [+ *culpa*] to expiate; [+ *pérdida*] to make good
VPR **satisfacerse 1** (= *contentarse*) to satisfy o.s., be satisfied • **~se con muy poco** to be content with very little
2 (= *vengarse*) to take revenge
satisfactoriamente ADV satisfactorily
satisfactorio ADJ satisfactory
satisfecho ADJ **1** (= *complacido*) satisfied; (= *contento*) content, contented • **darse por ~ con algo** to declare o.s. satisfied with sth
• **dejar ~s a todos** to satisfy everybody
2 (*después de comer*) • **quedarse ~** to be full
3 (*tb* **satisfecho consigo mismo, satisfecho de sí mismo**) self-satisfied, smug • **nos miró ~** he looked at us smugly
sativa SF (*Cono Sur*) marijuana
satrústegui* EXCL well!, gee! (*EEUU*), well I'm blowed!*
satsuma SF satsuma
saturación SF saturation
saturado ADJ saturated
saturar ▹ CONJUG 1a VT (*Fís, Quím*) to saturate • **~ el mercado** to flood the market
• **estos aeropuertos son los más saturados** those airports are the most crowded *o* stretched • **¡estoy saturado de tanta televisión!** I can't take any more television!
saturnales SFPL Saturnalia
saturnino ADJ saturnine
Saturno SM Saturn
sauce SM willow ▸ **sauce de Babilonia, sauce llorón** weeping willow
saucedal SM willow plantation
saúco SM elder
saudí ADJ, SMF, **saudita** ADJ, SMF Saudi
Saúl SM Saul
sauna SF, (*Cono Sur*) SM sauna
saurio SM saurian
savia SF sap
saxífraga SF saxifrage
saxo SM sax
SMF sax player
saxofón SM (= *instrumento*) saxophone
SMF (= *músico*) saxophonist
saxofonista SMF saxophonist
saxófono SMF = **saxofón**
saya SF **1** (*para vestir*) (= *falda*) skirt; (= *enagua*) petticoat; (= *vestido*) dress
2 (*And*) (= *mujer*) woman
sayal SM sackcloth
sayo SM (= *prenda*) smock, tunic
• MODISMO: • **cortar un ~ a algn** (*Esp*) to gossip about sb, talk behind sb's back • **¿qué ~ se me corta?** what are they saying about me?
sayón SM **1** (*Jur*) executioner
2 (= *hombre peligroso*) ugly customer*
sayuela SF (*Caribe*) long shirt, smock
sazo* SM hankie*
sazón[1] SF **1** [*de fruta*] ripeness • **en ~** [*fruta*] ripe, ready (to eat); (= *oportunamente*) opportunely • **fuera de ~** [*fruta*] out of season; (= *inoportunamente*) inopportunely
2 (*liter*) • **a la ~** then, at that time
3 (= *sabor*) flavour, flavor (*EEUU*)
sazón[2] ADJ (*And, CAm, Méx*) ripe
sazonado ADJ **1** [*fruta*] ripe
2 [*plato*] seasoned
3 • **~ de** seasoned with, flavoured *o* (*EEUU*) flavored with
4 (= *ingenioso*) witty
sazonar ▹ CONJUG 1a VT **1** [+ *fruta*] to ripen
2 (*Culin*) to season (**de** with)
3 (*Caribe*) (= *endulzar*) to sweeten
VI to ripen
s/c ABR (*Com*) **1** = **su casa**
2 = **su cuenta**
scalextric® SM **1** Scalextric® (*model motor racing set*)
2 (*Aut*) *complicated traffic interchange*, spaghetti junction*
schop [ʃop] SM (*Cono Sur*) (= *vaso*) mug, tankard; (= *cerveza*) beer, draught *o* (*EEUU*) draft beer
schopería [ʃope'ria] SF (*Cono Sur*) beer bar
scooter [es'kuter] SM motor scooter
Scotch® SM (*And, Méx*) Sellotape®, Scotch tape® (*EEUU*)
script [es'kri] SF (PL: **scripts** [es'kri]) script-girl
scruchante* SM (*Arg*) burglar
Sdo. ABR (*Com*) (= **Saldo**) bal
SE ABR (= **sudeste**) SE
se PRON PERS **1** (*complemento indirecto*) **a** (*a él*) him; (*a ella*) her; (*a ellos*) them; (*a usted, ustedes*) you • **voy a dárselo** I'll give it to him *o* her *o* them *o* you • **ya se lo dije** I (already) told him *o* her *o* them *o* you • **he hablado con mis padres y se lo he explicado** I've talked to my parents and explained it to them • **aquí tiene las flores, ¿se las envuelvo, señor?** here are your flowers, shall I wrap them for you, sir? • **no lo tenemos, pero se lo puedo encargar** we haven't got it, but I can order it for you
b (*con doble complemento indirecto*) • **dáselo a Enrique** give it to Enrique • **¿se lo has preguntado a tus padres?** have you asked your parents about it?
c (*con partes del cuerpo, ropa*) • **se rompió la pierna** he broke his leg • **Pablo se lavó los dientes** Pablo cleaned his teeth • **Carmen no podía abrocharse el vestido** Carmen couldn't do up her dress • **han prometido no cortarse la barba** they have sworn not to cut

their beards • **tiene que cortarse el pelo** he must have a haircut
d (*uso enfático*) • **se comió un pastel** he ate a cake • **no se esperaba eso** he didn't expect that
2 (*uso reflexivo*) **a** (*masculino*) himself; (*femenino*) herself; (*plural*) themselves; (*de usted*) yourself; (*de ustedes*) yourselves; (*sujeto no humano*) itself • **Marcos se ha cortado con un cristal** Marcos cut himself on a piece of broken glass • **Margarita se estaba preparando para salir** Margarita was getting (herself) ready to go out • **¿se ha hecho usted daño?** have you hurt yourself? • **se tiraron al suelo** they threw themselves to the ground • **la calefacción se apaga sola** the heating turns itself off automatically • **se está afeitando** he's shaving • **¡siéntese!** sit down • **sírvase esperar un momento** please wait a moment • **vestirse** to get dressed
b (*indefinido*) oneself • **mirarse en el espejo** to look at oneself in the mirror
3 (*como parte de un verbo pronominal*) • **se durmió** he fell asleep • **se enfadó** he got annoyed • **se marchó** he left • **mi hermana nunca se queja** my sister never complains • **se retira** he withdraws
4 (*uso recíproco*) each other, one another • **se escriben a menudo** they write to each other often • **se quieren** they love each other • **hace un año que no se ven** it's a year since they last saw each other • **procuran no encontrarse** they try not to meet each other • **se miraron todos** they all looked at one another • **no se hablan** they are not on speaking terms
5 (*uso impersonal*) **a** (*con sujeto indeterminado*) • **se registraron nueve muertos** there were nine deaths, nine deaths were recorded • **se dice que es muy rico** he's said to be very rich • **no se sabe por qué** it is not known *o* people don't know why • **se compró hace tres años** it was bought three years ago • **en esa zona se habla galés** Welsh is spoken in that area, people speak Welsh in that area • **se cree que el tabaco produce cáncer** it is believed that smoking causes cancer
b (*referido al hablante*) • **no se oye bien** you can't hear very well • **es lo que pasa cuando se come tan deprisa** that's what happens when you eat so fast • **¿cómo se dice eso en inglés?** how do you say that in English? • **se está bien aquí** it's nice here • **se hace lo que se puede** we do what we can • **se admiten sugerencias** we welcome suggestions • **"véndese coche"** "car for sale" • **se avisa a los interesados que …** those concerned are informed that …
c (*en recetas, instrucciones*) • **se pelan las patatas** peel the potatoes • **"sírvase muy frío"** "serve chilled" • **"no se admiten visitas"** "no visitors" • **"se prohíbe fumar"** "no smoking"

sé ▷ **saber, ser**
S.E. (ABR) (= **Su Excelencia**) H.E.
SEA (SM ABR) (*Esp*) (*Agr*) = **Servicio de Extensión Agraria.**
sea *etc* ▷ **ser**
SEAT (SF ABR), **Seat** (SF ABR) (*Esp*) = **Sociedad Española de Automóviles de Turismo**
sebáceo (ADJ) sebaceous
sebear ▷ CONJUG 1a (VT) (*Caribe*) to inspire love in
sebo (SM) **1** (= *grasa*) (*gen*) grease, fat; (*para velas*) tallow; (*Culin*) suet
2 (= *gordura*) fat
sebón (ADJ) (*And, CAm, Cono Sur*) idle, lazy
seboso (ADJ) (= *grasiento*) greasy; (= *mugriento*) grimy

Sec. (ABR) (= **secretario, secretaria**) sec
seca (SF) **1** (*Agr*) drought
2 (*Meteo*) dry season
3 (*Náut*) sandbank
secadero (SM) **1** (= *lugar*) drying place
2 (*And*) (= *terreno*) dry plain, scrubland
secado (SM) drying ▸ **secado a mano** blow-dry
secador (SM) drier, dryer ▸ **secador centrífugo** spin drier, spin dryer ▸ **secador de manos** hand drier, hand dryer ▸ **secador de pelo** hairdrier, hairdryer
secadora (SF) tumble drier, tumble dryer ▸ **secadora centrífuga** spin drier, spin dryer ▸ **secadora de cabello** (*CAm, Méx*) hairdrier, hairdryer
secamanos (SM INV) hand drier, hand dryer
secamente (ADV) [*contestar*] curtly; [*ordenar*] sharply • **—no sé nada —afirmó ~** "I don't know anything," he said curtly • **se comportó muy ~ con nosotros** he was very short *o* curt with us • **—ahora, ¡a dormir! —dijo ~** "now, off to sleep!," he said sharply
secano (SM) **1** (*Agr*) (*tb* **tierra de secano**) (= *sin lluvia*) dry land, dry region; (= *sin riego*) unirrigated land • **cultivo de ~** dry farming
2 (*Náut*) (= *banco de arena*) sandbank; (= *islote*) small sandy island
secante¹ (ADJ) **1** • **papel ~** blotting paper
2 (*And, Cono Sur**) (= *latoso*) annoying
(SM) blotting paper, blotter
secante² (SF) (*Mat*) secant
secapelos (SM INV) hairdrier, hairdryer
secar ▷ CONJUG 1g (VT) **1** (= *quitar la humedad*) (*con paño, toalla*) to dry; (*con fregona*) to mop up; (*con papel secante*) to blot • **me sequé las lágrimas** I dried my tears • **~ los platos** to dry the plates, dry up
2 (= *resecar*) [+ *planta, terreno*] to dry up; [+ *piel*] to dry out
3 (*Uru*) (= *fastidiar*) to annoy, vex
(VI) to dry • **lo he puesto a ~ cerca del radiador** I've left it to dry near the radiator
(VPR) **secarse 1** (*uso reflexivo*) **a** [*persona*] to dry o.s., get dry • **me encanta ~me al sol** I love drying myself in the sun
b [+ *manos, pelo*] to dry; [+ *lágrimas, sudor*] to dry, wipe • **~se la frente** to mop one's brow
2 (= *quedarse sin agua*) **a** [*ropa*] to dry, dry off • **no entres hasta que no se seque el suelo** don't come in until the floor is dry *o* has dried
b [*arroz, pasta*] to go dry; [*garganta*] to get dry; [*río, pozo*] to dry up, run dry; [*hierba, terreno*] to dry up; [*planta*] to wither
3 [*herida*] to heal up
4* (= *adelgazar*) to get thin
5* (*tb* **secarse de sed**) to be parched*
secarral (SM) dry plain, arid area
secarropa (SM) clothes-horse
sección (SF) **1** (*Arquit, Mat*) section ▸ **sección cónica** conic section ▸ **sección longitudinal** longitudinal section ▸ **sección transversal** cross section ▸ **sección vertical** vertical section
2 (= *parte*) (*gen*) section; [*de almacén, oficina*] department ▸ **sección de contactos** personal column (*containing offers of marriage etc*) ▸ **sección de cuerdas** string section ▸ **sección deportiva** sports page, sports section ▸ **sección económica** financial pages (*pl*), city pages (*pl*) ▸ **sección fija** regular feature ▸ **sección oficial** Official Section
3 (*Mil*) section, platoon
seccional (ADJ) sectional
(SF) **1** (*Cono Sur*) police station
2 (*Col*) branch office
seccionar ▷ CONJUG 1a (VT) (= *dividir*) to section, divide into sections; (= *cortar*) to cut, cut off; (= *disecar*) to dissect • **~ la garganta a algn** to cut sb's throat
secesión (SF) secession
secesionista (ADJ), (SMF) secessionist
seco (ADJ) **1** (= *no húmedo*) dry • **tengo los labios ~s** my lips are dry • **las sábanas no están secas todavía** the sheets are still not dry • **es un calor ~** it's a dry heat • **en ~** (= *sin líquido*) • **no me puedo tragar esto en ~** I can't swallow this without water • **"limpiar en seco"** "dry clean only"; ▷ **dique, ley**
2 (= *desecado*) [*higo, pescado*] dried; [*hojas*] dead, dried; [*árbol*] dead • **un cuadro de flores secas** a painting of dried flowers • **estaban ~s todos los geranios** all the geraniums had dried up • **dame una cerveza, que estoy ~*** give me a beer, I'm really parched*; ▷ **ciruela, fruto**
3 (= *no graso*) [*piel, pelo*] dry
4 (= *no dulce*) [*vino, licor*] dry • **un champán muy ~** a very dry champagne
5 (= *flaco*) thin, skinny* • MODISMO: • **está ~ como un palo** he's (as) thin as a rake
6 (= *no amable*) [*persona, carácter, respuesta*] curt; [*orden*] sharp; [*estilo*] dry • **estuvo muy ~ conmigo por teléfono** he was very curt *o* short with me on the phone • **—no se puede —contestó muy ~** "can't be done," he replied curtly
7 (= *sin resonancia*) [*tos*] dry; [*ruido*] dull; [*impacto*] sharp • **oyó el golpe ~ de la puerta** he heard the dull thud of the door • **le dio un golpe ~ en la cabeza** he gave him a sharp bang on the head
8 • **en ~** (= *bruscamente*) • **frenar en ~** to brake sharply • **pararse en ~** to stop dead, stop suddenly • **parar a algn en ~** (*al hablar*) to cut sb short
9 (= *sin acompañamiento*) • **sobrevivimos a base de pan ~** we survived on bread alone • **para vivir sólo tiene el sueldo ~** he has nothing but his salary to live on; ▷ **palo**
10 • MODISMOS: • **a secas**: • **no existe la libertad a secas** there's no such thing as freedom pure and simple • **Gerardo García, Gerardo a secas para los amigos** Gerardo García, just Gerardo to his friends • **nos alimentamos de pan a secas** we survived on nothing but bread • **dejar ~ a algn*** (= *matar*) to kill sb stone dead* • **lo dejó ~ de un tiro** he blew him away* • **cuando me dijo el precio me dejó ~** I was stunned when he told me the price • **ser ~ para algo** (*Chile**) to be a great one for sth* • **tener ~ a algn** (*Col, Cono Sur*): • **me tienen ~** I've had enough of them • **tomarse algo al ~** (*Chile*) to down sth in one • **a ver todos, ¿al ~?** come on everyone, (down) in one!
(SM) (*Col*) main course
secoya (SF) redwood, sequoia
secre* (SMF) = **secretario**
secreción (SF) secretion
secreta* (SF) secret police
(SMF) secret policeman/policewoman
secretamente (ADV) secretly
secretar ▷ CONJUG 1a (VT) to secrete
secretaría (SF) **1** (= *oficina*) secretary's office
2 (= *cargo*) secretaryship
3 • **Secretaría** (*Méx*) (= *Ministerio*) Ministry
secretariado (SM) **1** (= *oficina*) secretariat
2 (= *cargo*) secretaryship
3 (= *curso*) secretarial course
4 (= *profesión*) profession of secretary
secretario/a (SM/F) **1** (= *administrativo*) secretary ▸ **secretario/a adjunto/a** assistant secretary ▸ **secretario/a de dirección** executive secretary ▸ **secretario/a de imagen** public relations officer ▸ **secretario/a de prensa** press secretary ▸ **secretario/a de rodaje** script clerk

▸ **secretario/a general** (*gen*) general secretary; (*Pol*) secretary general ▸ **secretario/a judicial** clerk of the court ▸ **secretario/a municipal** town clerk ▸ **secretario/a particular** private secretary
2 (*Méx*) (*Pol*) Minister, Minister of State, Secretary of State (*EEUU*) ▸ **secretario/a de Estado** (*Esp*) junior minister, undersecretary (*EEUU*)

secretear ▹ CONJUG 1a VI 1 (= *conversar*) to talk confidentially
2 (= *cuchichear*) to whisper (unnecessarily)

secreter SM writing desk

secretismo SM secrecy, excessive secrecy

secreto SM 1 (= *confidencia*) secret • **alto ~** top secret • **confiar** *o* **contar un ~ a algn** to tell sb a secret • **en ~** in secret, secretly • **estar en el ~** (*frm*) to be in on the secret • **guardar un ~** to keep a secret • **hacer ~ de algo** (*frm*) to be secretive about sth, keep sth secret ▸ **secreto a voces** open secret ▸ **secreto de confesión** (*Rel*) confessional secret ▸ **secreto de estado** state secret ▸ **secreto de Polichinela** (*frm*) open secret ▸ **secreto de sumario, secreto sumarial** • **debido al ~ del sumario** *o* **sumarial** because the matter is sub judice • **se ha levantado el ~ sumarial sobre el caso** reporting restrictions have been lifted; ▹ **mantener**
2 (= *clave*) secret • **el ~ está en la salsa** the secret is in the sauce • **¿cuál es el ~ de su éxito?** what is the secret of her success?
3 (= *reserva*) secrecy • **lo han hecho con mucho ~** they have done it in great secrecy
4 (= *cajón*) secret drawer
5 (= *combinación*) combination
ADJ secret • **todo es de lo más ~** it's all highly secret

secta SF sect

sectario/a ADJ sectarian • **no ~** (*Pol*) non-sectarian; (*Rel*) non-denominational
SM/F sectarian

sectarismo SM sectarianism

sector SM 1 (*Econ, Geom*) sector ▸ **sector privado** private sector ▸ **sector público** public sector ▸ **sector terciario** tertiary sector, service industries (*pl*), service sector
2 (= *sección*) [*de opinión*] section; [*de ciudad*] area, sector ▸ **sector industrial** (*Col*) industrial estate (*Brit*), industrial park (*EEUU*)

sectorial ADJ sectorial

sectorialmente ADV *in a way which relates to a particular sector o industry etc*

secuaz SMF (= *partidario*) (*gen*) follower, supporter; (*pey*) henchman

secuela SF 1 (= *consecuencia*) consequence
2 [*de novela, película*] sequel
3 (*Méx*) (*Jur*) proceedings (*pl*), prosecution

secuencia SF sequence ▸ **secuencia de arranque** (*Inform*) startup routine, startup sequence

secuenciación SF sequencing

secuenciador SM sequencer

secuencial ADJ sequential

secuencialmente ADV sequentially, in sequence

secuenciar ▹ CONJUG 1b VT to arrange in sequence

secuestración SF 1 (*Jur*) sequestration
2 = secuestro

secuestrado/a ADJ 1 [*persona*] kidnapped
2 [*barco, avión*] hijacked
SM/F hostage

secuestrador(a) SM/F 1 [*de persona*] kidnapper
2 [*de avión*] hijacker ▸ **secuestrador(a) aéreo/a** hijacker

secuestrar ▹ CONJUG 1a VT 1 [+ *persona*] to kidnap
2 [+ *avión*] to hijack
3 (*Jur*) to seize, confiscate

secuestro SM 1 [*de persona etc*] kidnapping, kidnaping (*EEUU*) ▸ **secuestro de carbón** carbon sink
2 [*de avión*] hijack, hijacking ▸ **secuestro aéreo** hijack, hijacking
3 (*Jur*) [*de cargamento, contrabando*] seizure; [*de propiedad*] sequestration

secular ADJ 1 (*Rel*) secular, lay
2 (= *que dura 100 años*) century-old; (= *antiguo*) age-old, ancient • **una tradición ~** an age-old tradition

secularización SF secularization

secularizado ADJ [*sociedad*] secularized; [*educación*] secular

secularizar ▹ CONJUG 1f VT to secularize

secundar ▹ CONJUG 1a VT 1 [+ *moción*] to second; [+ *huelga*] to take part in, join
2 [+ *persona*] (*en un proyecto*) to support; (*para la votación*) to second

secundaria SF 1 (*esp LAm*) (= *enseñanza*) secondary education, high school education (*EEUU*)
2 (*Méx*) (= *colegio*) secondary school, high school (*EEUU*)

secundario/a ADJ (= *no principal*) (*gen*) secondary; [*carretera, efectos*] side (*antes de s*); (*Inform*) background (*antes de s*) • **actor ~** supporting actor; ▹ **educación**
SM/F supporting actor

secundinas SFPL afterbirth (*sing*)

secuoia SF (*LAm*), **secuoya** SF (*LAm*) = secoya

sed SF 1 (= *ganas de beber*) thirst • **apagar** *o* **saciar la sed** to quench one's thirst • **tener (mucha) sed** to be (very) thirsty • **sed inextinguible** *o* **insaciable** unquenchable thirst
2 (*Agr*) drought, dryness
3 (= *ansia*) thirst (**de** for), craving (**de** for) • **tener sed de** to thirst *o* be thirsty for, crave

seda SF 1 (= *hilo, tela*) silk • **de ~** silk (*antes de s*) • MODISMOS: • **hacer ~**‡ to sleep, kip‡ • **como la ~** (*adj*) as smooth as silk; (*adv*) smoothly • **ir como la ~** to go like clockwork ▸ **seda artificial** artificial silk ▸ **seda de coser** sewing silk ▸ **seda dental** dental floss ▸ **seda en rama** raw silk ▸ **seda hilada** spun silk ▸ **seda lavada** washed silk
2 (*Zool*) bristle

sedación SF sedation

sedado ADJ under sedation • **el único superviviente continúa ~ en el hospital** the only survivor is still under sedation in hospital

sedal SM fishing line

sedán SM saloon, sedan (*EEUU*)

sedante ADJ 1 (*Med*) sedative
2 (= *relajante*) soothing, calming
SM sedative

sedar ▹ CONJUG 1a VT to sedate

sedativo ADJ sedative

sede SF 1 (= *lugar*) [*de gobierno*] seat; [*de organización*] headquarters (*pl*), central office; (*Dep*) venue ▸ **sede diplomática** diplomatic quarter ▸ **sede social** head office, central office
2 (*Rel*) see • **Santa Sede** Holy See

sedentario ADJ sedentary

sedentarismo SM 1 (= *cualidad*) sedentary nature
2 (= *actitud*) sedentary lifestyle

sedente ADJ seated

sedeño ADJ 1 (= *sedoso*) silky, silken (*liter*)
2 (*Zool*) bristly

sedería SF 1 (*de seda*) (= *comercio*) silk trade; (= *manufactura*) silk manufacture, sericulture; (= *tienda*) silk shop
2 (= *géneros*) silk goods (*pl*)

sedero/a ADJ silk (*antes de s*) • **industria sedera** silk industry
SM/F silk dealer

SEDIC SF ABR = **Sociedad Española de Documentación e Información Científica**

sedicente ADJ self-styled, would-be

sedición SF sedition

sedicioso/a ADJ seditious
SM/F rebel

sediente ADJ • **bienes ~s** real estate

sediento ADJ [*persona*] thirsty; [*campos*] parched • **~ de poder** power-hungry

sedimentación SF sedimentation

sedimentar ▹ CONJUG 1a VT 1 (= *depositar*) to deposit
2 (= *aquietar*) to settle, calm
VPR **sedimentarse** 1 (= *depositarse*) to settle
2 (= *aquietarse*) to calm down, settle down

sedimentario ADJ sedimentary

sedimento SM sediment, deposit

sedosidad SF silkiness

sedoso ADJ silky, silken

seducción SF 1 (= *acción*) seduction
2 (= *encanto*) seductiveness

seducir ▹ CONJUG 3n VT 1 (*en sentido sexual*) to seduce
2 (= *cautivar*) to charm, captivate • **seduce a todos con su simpatía** she captivates everyone with her charm • **la teoría ha seducido a muchos** the theory has attracted many people • **no me seduce la idea** I'm not taken with the idea
3 (*moralmente*) to lead astray
VI to be charming • **es una película que seduce** it's a captivating film

seductivo ADJ = **seductor**

seductor(a) ADJ 1 (*sexualmente*) seductive
2 (= *cautivador*) [*persona*] charming; [*idea*] tempting
SM/F seducer/seductress

Sefarad SF 1 (*Hist*) Spain
2 (= *patria*) homeland

sefardí, sefardita ADJ Sephardic
SMF Sephardic Jew/Sephardic Jewess, Sephardi • **~es** • **sefarditas** Sephardim

segable ADJ ready to cut

segadera SF sickle

segador(a) SM/F (= *persona*) harvester, reaper

segadora SF (*Mec*) harvester ▸ **segadora de césped** lawnmower

segadora-atadora SF binder

segadora-trilladora SF combine harvester

segar ▹ CONJUG 1h, 1j VT 1 (*Agr*) [+ *mies*] to reap, cut; [+ *hierba*] to mow, cut
2 (= *acabar con*) [+ *persona*] to cut off; [+ *esperanzas*] to ruin • **~ la juventud de algn** to cut sb off in his prime

seglar ADJ secular, lay
SMF layman/laywoman • **los ~es** the laity

segmentación SF segmentation

segmentar ▹ CONJUG 1a VT 1 (= *cortar*) to segment, cut into segments
2 (= *dividir*) to divide up, separate out
VPR **segmentarse** to fragment, divide up

segmento SM (*Mat, Zool*) segment; (*Com, Econ*) sector, group ▸ **segmento de émbolo** (*Aut*) piston ring

segoviano/a ADJ of/from Segovia
SM/F native/inhabitant of Segovia • **los ~s** the people of Segovia

segregación SF 1 (= *separación*) segregation ▸ **segregación racial** racial segregation
2 (*Anat*) secretion

segregacionista SMF segregationist, supporter of racial segregation

segregar ▹ CONJUG 1h VT 1 (= *separar*) to segregate
2 (*Anat*) to secrete

seguida SF 1 • **de ~** (= *sin parar*) without a

break; (= *inmediatamente*) at once, immediately • **en ~** right away • **en ~ estoy con usted** I'll be with you right away • **en ~ voy** I'll be right there • **en ~ termino** I've nearly finished, I shan't be a minute • **en ~ tomó el avión para Madrid** he immediately caught the plane to Madrid
2 • MODISMO: • **coger la ~** to get into the swing of it
seguidamente (ADV) **1** (= *sin parar*) continuously
2 (= *inmediatamente después*) immediately after, next • **~ les ofrecemos ...** (*TV*) next ..., and next ... • **dijo ~ que ...** he went on at once to say that ...
seguidilla (SF) **1** (*Mús*) seguidilla (*dance and piece of music in a fast triple rhythm*)
2 (*Literat*) seguidilla (*poem with four to seven lines used in popular songs*)
3 • **una ~ de protestas** a series of complaints
seguidista (ADJ) copycat (*antes de s*)
seguido (ADJ) **1** [*línea*] continuous, unbroken • **una fila seguida de casas** a row of terraced houses
2 • **~s: cinco días ~s** (= *ininterrumpidos*) five days running, five days in a row • **tres blancos ~s** three bull's-eyes in a row, three consecutive bull's-eyes • **llevo dos horas seguidas esperándote** I've been waiting for you for two whole *o* solid hours • **tuvo los niños muy ~s** she had all her children one after the other
3 • **~ de algo/algn** followed by sth/sb • **llegó el ministro ~ de sus colaboradores** the minister arrived, followed by his staff
(ADV) **1** (= *directo*) straight on • **vaya todo ~** just keep going straight on • **continúe por aquí ~** go straight on past here
2 (= *detrás*) • **ese coche iba primero y ~ el mío** that car was in front and mine was immediately behind it
3 (*LAm*) (= *a menudo*) often • **le gusta visitarnos ~** she likes to visit us often
seguidor(a) (SM/F) (*gen*) follower; (*Dep*) supporter, fan*
seguimiento (SM) **1** (= *persecución*) pursuit • **ir en ~ de** to chase (after) • **estación de ~** tracking station
2 (= *continuación*) (*gen*) continuation; (*TV*) report, follow-up
3 [*de proceso*] (*tb Med*) monitoring • **el secuestro ha tenido un gran ~ por todas las televisiones** the kidnapping received plenty of coverage on all channels • **el ~ de la huelga** the support for the strike
seguir ▷ CONJUG 3d, 3k (VT) **1** (= *perseguir*) [+ *persona, pista*] to follow; [+ *indicio*] to follow up; [+ *presa*] to chase, pursue • **tú ve primero que yo te sigo** you go first and I'll follow you • **ella llegó primero, seguida del embajador** she arrived first, followed by the ambassador • **nos están siguiendo** we're being followed • **seguía todos sus pasos** I followed his every step • **la seguía con la mirada** his eyes followed her • **me sigue como un perrito faldero** he's always tramping at my heels
2 (= *estar atento a*) [+ *programa de TV*] to watch, follow; [+ *programa de radio*] to listen to, follow; [+ *proceso, progreso*] to monitor, follow up; [+ *satélite*] to track • **~ los acontecimientos de cerca** to monitor events closely • **estaba ocupada y no he seguido la conversación** I was busy and didn't follow the conversation • **esta exposición permite ~ paso a paso la evolución del artista** this exhibition allows the artist's development to be traced step by step
3 (= *hacer caso de*) [+ *consejo*] to follow, take; [+ *instrucciones, doctrina, líder*] to follow • **siguió el ejemplo de su padre** he followed his father's example • **~ los pasos de algn** to follow in sb's footsteps • **sigue la tradición de la familia** he follows in the family tradition
4 [+ *rumbo, dirección*] to follow • **seguimos el curso del río** we followed the course of the river • **siga la flecha** follow the arrow • **siga esta calle y al final gire a la derecha** carry on up *o* follow this street and turn right at the end • **~ su camino** to continue on one's way • **sigue su camino de cineasta independiente** he continues in his path of independent film-maker • **el mercado sigue su camino alcista** the market is continuing on its upward trend • **~ su curso**: • **el proyecto sigue su curso** the project is still on course, the project continues on (its) course • **la enfermedad sigue su curso** the illness is taking *o* running its course • **que la justicia siga su curso** let justice take its course
5 (= *entender*) [+ *razonamiento*] to follow • **es un razonamiento muy difícil de ~** it's an argument which is rather hard to follow • **¿me sigues?** are you with me?
6 (*Educ*) [+ *curso*] to take, do
7† [+ *mujer*] to court†
(VI) **1** (= *continuar*) to go on, carry on • **¿quieres que sigamos?** shall we go on? • **¡siga!** (= *hable*) go on!, carry on; (*LAm*) (= *pase*) come in • **¡síguele!** (*Méx*) go on! • **"sigue"** (*en carta*) P.T.O.; (*en libro*) continued • **la carretera sigue hasta el pueblo** the road goes on as far as the town • **siga por la carretera hasta el cruce** follow the road up to the crossroads • **~ por este camino** to carry on along this path
2 • **~ adelante** [*persona*] to go on, carry on; [*acontecimiento*] to go ahead • **los Juegos Olímpicos siguieron (adelante) a pesar del atentado** the Olympics went ahead despite the attack; ▷ **adelante**
3 (*en estado, situación*) to be still • **sigue enfermo** he's still ill • **sigue en Caracas** she's still in Caracas • **el ascensor sigue estropeado** the lift's still not working • **sigue soltero** he's still single • **¿cómo sigue?** how is he? • **que siga usted bien** keep well, look after yourself • **~ con una idea** to go on with an idea • **seguía en su error** he continued in his error • **seguimos sin teléfono** we still haven't got a phone • **sigo sin noticias** I still haven't heard anything • **sigo sin comprender** I still don't understand • **esas preguntas siguen sin respuesta** those questions remain unanswered
4 • **~ haciendo algo** to go on doing sth, carry on doing sth • **siguió mirándola** he went on *o* carried on looking at her • **siguió hablando con nosotros** he went on speaking to us • **el ordenador seguía funcionando** the computer carried on working, the computer was still working • **sigo pensando lo mismo** I still think the same • **sigue lloviendo** it's still raining
5 (= *venir a continuación*) to follow, follow on • **como sigue** as follows • **lo que sigue es un resumen** what follows is a summary • **entre otros ejemplos destacan los que siguen** amongst other examples, the following stand out • **mencionaré varios casos en lo que sigue** I'll now move on to mention several cases • **~ a algo**: • **las horas que siguieron a la tragedia** the hours following *o* that followed the tragedy • **a la conferencia siguió un debate** the lecture was followed by a discussion
(VPR) **seguirse 1** (= *venir a continuación*) to follow • **una cosa se sigue a otra** one thing follows another • **después de aquello se siguió una época tranquila** after that there followed a quiet period
2 (= *deducirse*) to follow • **de esto se sigue que ...** it follows from this that ...
según (PREP) **1** (= *de acuerdo con*) according to • **~ el jefe** according to the boss • **~ este mapa** according to this map • **obrar ~ las instrucciones** to act in accordance with one's instructions • **~ lo que dice** from what he says, going by what he says • **~ lo que se decida** according to what is decided • **~ parece** seemingly, apparently
2 (= *depende de*) depending on • **~ tus circunstancias** depending on your circumstances • **~ el dinero que tengamos** depending on what money we have
(CONJ) **1** (= *depende de*) depending on • **~ esté el tiempo** depending on the weather • **~ (como) me encuentre** depending on how I feel • **~ (que) vengan tres o cuatro** depending on whether three or four come
2 (*indicando manera*) as • **~ me consta** as I know for a fact • **está ~ lo dejaste** it's just as you left it • **~ están las cosas, es mejor no intervenir** the way things are, it's better not to get involved • **~ se entra, a la izquierda** to the left as you go in
3 (*indicando simultaneidad*) as • **lo vi ~ salía** I saw him as I was going out • **~ íbamos entrando nos daban la información** they gave us the information as we went in
(ADV)* • **—¿lo vas a comprar? —según** "are you going to buy it?" — "it all depends" • **~ y como** • **~ y conforme** it all depends
segunda (SF) **1** (*Aut*) second gear
2 (*Ferro*) second class • **viajar en ~** to travel second class
3 (*Mús*) second
4 segundas (= *doble sentido*) double meaning • **lo dijo con ~s** he really meant something else when he said it; ▷ **segundo**
segundar ▷ CONJUG 1a (VT) **1** (= *repetir*) to do again
2 (*Cono Sur*) [+ *golpe*] to return
(VI) to come second, be in second place
segundero (SM) second hand (*of watch*)
segundo/a (ADJ) (*gen*) second; [*enseñanza*] secondary; [*intención*] double • **en ~ lugar** (*en clasificación*) in second place; (*en discurso*) secondly; ▷ **sexto**
(SM/F) **1** (*en orden*) (*gen*) second; (*Admin, Mil*) second in command • **sin ~** unrivalled
▸ **segundo/a de a bordo** (*Náut*) first mate; (*fig*) second in command
2 (*Mús*) alto
(SM) **1** (= *medida de tiempo*) second
2 (= *piso*) second floor, third floor (*EEUU*)
3 (*Astron*) ▸ **segundos de arco** seconds of arc; ▷ **segunda**
segundón/ona (SM) second son, younger son
(SM/F) second-class citizen
segur (SF) (= *hoz*) sickle; (= *hacha*) axe, ax (*EEUU*)
seguramente (ADV) • **—están llamando a la puerta —seguramente será el cartero** "there's someone at the door" — "it'll probably be the postman" *o* "I expect it'll be the postman" • **~ llegarán mañana** they'll probably arrive tomorrow, I expect they'll arrive tomorrow • **~ nos volveremos a ver** I'm sure *o* I expect we'll see each other again • **—¿lo va a comprar? —seguramente** "is he going to buy it?" — "I expect so"
seguridad (SF) **1** (= *falta de riesgo*) **a** (*ante accidente, peligro*) safety; (*ante delito, atentado*) security • **han aumentado la ~ en el circuito** they have increased safety on the circuit • **para mayor ~ recomendamos el uso de la**

S

mascarilla for safety's sake we recommend that you use a mask • **han cuestionado la ~ del experimento** they have questioned the safety of the experiment • **cierre de ~** [*de pulsera, collar, arma*] safety catch • **cinturón de ~** safety belt • **empresa de ~** security company • **medidas de ~** (*ante accidente, incendio*) safety measures; (*ante delito, atentado*) security measures
b (*económica*) security • **le preocupa la ~ de sus inversiones** he's worried about the security of his investments • **hasta que no tenga trabajo no tendrá ~ económica** until he has a job he won't have any financial security
c (*Mil, Pol*) security • **consejo de ~** security council
2 ▸ **seguridad alimentaria** food security ▸ **seguridad ciudadana** *the security of the public from crime* • **nos preocupa mucho la ~ ciudadana** we are very concerned about crime ▸ **seguridad colectiva** collective security ▸ **seguridad contra incendios** fire precautions (*pl*) ▸ **seguridad del Estado** national security, state security • **las fuerzas de ~ del Estado** state security forces ▸ **seguridad en el trabajo** health and safety at work ▸ **seguridad en la carretera** road safety ▸ **seguridad social** (= *sistema de pensiones y paro*) social security, welfare (*EEUU*); (= *contribuciones*) national insurance; (= *sistema médico*) national health service, ≈ NHS ▸ **seguridad vial** road safety
3 (= *sensación*) (*de no tener peligro*) security; (*de confianza*) confidence, assurance • **la ~ que da tener unos buenos frenos** the security that good brakes give you • **habla con mucha ~** he speaks with great confidence *o* assurance • **quiere dar la impresión de ~** he wants to give a confident impression ▸ **seguridad en uno mismo** self-confidence, self-assurance
4 (= *certeza*) certainty • **no hay ninguna ~ de que vaya a ocurrir** there's no certainty that that will happen • **no puedo darle ~** I can't say for sure *o* for certain • **con ~:** • **no lo sabemos con ~** we don't know for sure *o* for certain • **con toda ~, podemos decir que ...** with complete certainty, we can say that ... • **tener la ~ de que ...** to be sure *o* certain that ... • **tenía la ~ de que algo iba a pasar** he was sure *o* certain that something was going to happen • **tengan ustedes la ~ de que ...** (you may) rest assured that ... (*frm*)
5 (*Jur*) [*de fianza*] security, surety

seguro ADJ **1** (= *sin peligro*) **a** [*refugio, método, vehículo*] safe • **no te subas a esa escalera porque no es muy segura** don't go up that ladder, it's not very safe • **a causa de una práctica sexual poco segura** due to unsafe sex
b [*persona, objetos de valor*] safe • **está más ~ en el banco** it's safer in the bank • **el bebé se siente ~ cerca de su madre** the baby feels safe *o* secure close to its mother
2 (= *sujeto, estable*) secure • **hay que atar mejor la carga porque no parece muy segura** the load needs to be fixed a bit better because it doesn't seem to be very securely attached *o* very secure • **su trabajo no es nada ~** his job is not at all secure
3 (= *definitivo*) [*fracaso, muerte*] certain • **su dimisión no es segura** her resignation is not certain • **aún no hay fecha segura** there's no definite date yet • **eso es lo más ~** that's the most likely thing • **lo más ~ es que no pueda ir** I almost certainly *o* most likely won't be able to go • **dar algo por ~:** • **si yo fuera tú no daría la victoria por segura** if I were you I wouldn't be sure of victory • **se da por ~ que se trataba de un secuestro** there's little doubt that it was a kidnapping • **es ~ que ...:** • **es ~ que ganaremos la copa** we're bound *o* sure *o* certain to win the cup • **lo que es ~ es que el congreso se celebrará en Barcelona** the conference is definitely going to be held in Barcelona
4 (= *convencido*) sure • **¿estás ~?** are you sure? • **sí, estoy completamente segura** yes, I'm absolutely sure *o* positive • **—¿estás ~ de que era él? —sí, segurísimo** "are you sure it was him?" — "yes, positive" • **—vamos a ganar —pues yo no estaría tan ~** "we're going to win" — "I wouldn't bet on it" *o* "I wouldn't be so sure" • **~ de algo** sure of sth • **nunca he visto un hombre tan ~ de sus opiniones** I've never seen a man so sure of his opinions • **no estoy ~ de poder ir** I'm not sure I'll be able to go • **no estés tan ~ de que vas a ganar** don't be so sure that you're going to win
5 (*de uno mismo*) confident • **se muestra cada vez más ~ en el escenario** he is more and more sure of himself *o* confident on stage • **me noto más segura al andar** I feel more steady on my feet, I feel more confident walking now • **~ de sí mismo** self-confident, self-assured
6 (= *fiable*) [*fuente, cálculo, método*] reliable • **no es un método muy ~** it's not a very reliable *o* sure method • **es la forma más segura de adelgazar** it's the surest way to lose weight
7 (*LAm*) (= *honesto*) trustworthy
ADV for sure, for certain • **no lo sabemos ~** we don't know for sure *o* certain • **—¿seguro que te interesa? —sí, seguro** "are you sure that you're interested?" — "yes, I'm sure" • **—estoy dispuesto a cambiar de actitud —sí, sí, ~** (*iró*) "I'm willing to change my attitude" — "yeah, yeah, sure!" (*iró*) • **~ que algunos se alegrarán** some people will certainly be pleased, I'm sure that some people will be pleased • **~ que llueve mañana** it's sure to rain tomorrow • **a buen ~ • de ~** certainly • **a buen ~** *o* **de ~ va a dar que hablar** it will certainly give people something to talk about • MODISMO: • **ir** *o* **jugar sobre ~** to play (it) safe • **decidieron jugar sobre ~ contratando a un buen abogado** they decided to play (it) safe and hire a good lawyer
SM **1** (= *dispositivo*) **a** [*de puerta, lavadora*] lock; [*de arma de fuego*] safety catch; [*de pulsera*] clasp • **echa el ~, que van niños en el coche** lock the doors, there are children in the car
b (*CAm, Méx*) (= *imperdible*) safety pin
2 (*Com, Econ*) insurance • **¿tienes el ~ del coche?** have you got your car insurance documents with you? • **hacerse un ~** to take out insurance ▸ **seguro a todo riesgo** comprehensive insurance ▸ **seguro contra terceros** third-party insurance ▸ **seguro de accidentes** accident insurance ▸ **seguro de crédito a la exportación** export credit guarantee ▸ **seguro de daños a terceros** third-party insurance ▸ **seguro de desempleo** unemployment benefit, unemployment compensation *o* insurance (*EEUU*) ▸ **seguro de enfermedad** health insurance ▸ **seguro de incendios** fire insurance ▸ **seguro de jubilación** retirement plan, pension plan, pension scheme ▸ **seguro de paro** (*Esp*) unemployment benefit, unemployment compensation *o* insurance (*EEUU*) ▸ **seguro de viaje** travel insurance ▸ **seguro de vida** life assurance, life insurance (*esp EEUU*) ▸ **seguro marítimo** marine insurance ▸ **seguro mixto** endowment assurance, endowment insurance (*esp EEUU*) ▸ **seguro multirriesgo** multirisk insurance ▸ **seguro mutuo** mutual insurance ▸ **seguro temporal** term insurance
3* (= *sistema médico*) national health* • **los médicos de pago y los del ~** private doctors and national health *o* NHS ones ▸ **seguro social** (*LAm*) (= *sistema de pensiones y paro*) social security, welfare (*EEUU*); (= *contribuciones*) national insurance; (= *sistema médico*) national health service

seibó SM (*And, Caribe*) sideboard

seis ADJ INV, PRON (*gen*) six; (*ordinal, en la fecha*) sixth • **~ mil** six thousand • **tiene ~ años** she is six (years old) • **un niño de ~ años** a six-year-old (child), a child of six • **son las ~** it's six o'clock • **son las cinco menos ~** it's six minutes to five • **nos fuimos los ~ al cine** all six of us went to the cinema • **somos ~ para comer** there are six of us for dinner • **unos ~** about six • **le escribí el día ~** I wrote to him on the sixth • **en la página ~** on page six
SM INV (= *número*) six; (= *fecha*) sixth • **dos más cuatro son ~** two plus four are six • **hoy es ~** today is the sixth • **llega el ~ de agosto** he arrives on the sixth of August *o* on August the sixth *o* on 6 August • **vive en el ~** he lives at number six • **el ~ de corazones** the six of hearts

seiscientos/as ADJ, PRON (*gen*) six hundred; (*ordinal*) six hundredth • **~ soldados** six hundred soldiers • **seiscientas botellas** six hundred bottles • **~ treinta y dos euros** six hundred and thirty-two euros • **—¿cuántas habitaciones tiene el hotel? —seiscientas** "how many rooms does the hotel have?" — "six hundred" • **~ cuarenta** six hundred and forty • **el año ~** the year six hundred
SM **1** (= *número*) six hundred
2* (*Aut*) *small, beetle-shaped 600cc car manufactured by SEAT and highly popular in Spain during the sixties and seventies*

seísmo SM earthquake

seisporocho SM (*Caribe*) *a Venezuelan folk dance*

SEL SF ABR = **Sociedad Española de Lingüística**

selección SF **1** (= *acción*) selection ▸ **selección biológica** natural selection ▸ **selección múltiple** multiple choice ▸ **selección natural** natural selection
2 (*Dep*) ▸ **selección absoluta, selección nacional** national team, national side
3 selecciones (*Literat, Mús*) selections

seleccionable ADJ eligible

seleccionado SM team

seleccionador(a) SM/F (*Dep*) manager, coach (*EEUU*)

seleccionar ▹ CONJUG 1a VT to select, pick, choose

selectivamente ADV selectively

selectividad SF **1** (= *cualidad*) selectivity
2 (*Esp*) (*Univ*) entrance examination

selectivo ADJ selective

selecto ADJ **1** (= *exclusivo*) [*vino, producto*] select; [*club*] exclusive
2 [*obras literarias*] selected

selector SM (*Téc*) selector ▸ **selector de programas** programme selector, program selector (*EEUU*)

selenizaje SM moon landing

selenizar ▹ CONJUG 1f VI to land on the moon

selfi, selfie SF o SM selfie • **hacerse un ~** to take a selfie

self-service SM self-service restaurant

sellado ADJ [*documento oficial*] sealed; [*pasaporte, visado*] stamped
SM [*de documento oficial*] sealing; [*de pasaporte, visado*] stamping

selladora SF primer, sealant

selladura SF (= *sello*) seal
sellar ▸ CONJUG 1a VT **1** (= *poner sello en*) [+ *documento oficial*] to seal; [+ *pasaporte, visado*] to stamp
2 (= *marcar*) to brand
3 (= *cerrar*) [+ *pacto, labios*] to seal; [+ *urna, entrada*] to seal up; [+ *calle*] to seal off
sello SM **1** (*Correos*) stamp • MODISMO: • **no pega ni un ~*** he's bone-idle* ▸ **sello aéreo** airmail stamp ▸ **sello conmemorativo** commemorative stamp ▸ **sello de correos** postage stamp ▸ **sello de urgencia** express-delivery stamp
2 (= *estampación*) (*personal, de rey*) seal; (*administrativo*) stamp, official stamp; (*LAm*) (*en reverso de moneda*) tails ▸ **sello de caucho, sello de goma** rubber stamp ▸ **sello real** royal seal
3 (*Com*) brand; (*Mús*) (*tb* **sello discográfico**) record label; (*Literat*) publishing house • **lleva el ~ de esta oficina** it carries the stamp of this office ▸ **sello fiscal** revenue stamp ▸ **sellos de prima** (*Com*) trading stamps
4 (*Med*) capsule, pill
5 (= *marca*) (*tb* **sello distintivo**) hallmark, stamp • **lleva el ~ de su genialidad** it carries the hallmark of his genius
seltz [selθ, sel] SM • **agua (de) ~** seltzer (water)
selva SF **1** (= *jungla*) jungle ▸ **selva tropical** rainforest, tropical rainforest
2 (= *bosque*) forest ▸ **Selva Negra** Black Forest
selvático ADJ **1** (= *de la selva*) forest (*antes de s*)
2 (= *de la jungla*) jungle (*antes de s*)
3 (= *rústico*) rustic
4 (*Bot*) wild
selvoso ADJ wooded, well-wooded
sem. ABR (= **semana**) wk
S.Em.ª ABR (= **Su Eminencia**) H.E.
semaforazo* SM *robbery (of occupants of a car) at traffic lights*
semáforo SM **1** (*Aut*) traffic lights (*pl*) ▸ **semáforo sonoro** pelican crossing
2 (*Náut*) semaphore; (*Ferro*) signal
semana SF **1** (= *siete días*) week • **entre ~** during the week, in the week • **podemos vernos un día entre ~** we could see each other one day during the week • **vuelo de entre ~** midweek flight • **días entre ~** weekdays ▸ **semana inglesa** five-day working week, five-day workweek (*EEUU*) ▸ **semana laboral** working week, workweek (*EEUU*) ▸ **Semana Santa** Holy Week
2 (= *salario*) week's wages (*pl*)

> **SEMANA SANTA**
> In Spain celebrations for **Semana Santa** (Holy Week) are often spectacular. **Viernes Santo**, **Sábado Santo** and **Domingo de Resurrección** (Good Friday, Holy Saturday, Easter Sunday) are all national public holidays, with additional days being given as local holidays. There are long processions through the streets with **pasos** - religious floats and sculptures. Religious statues are carried along on the shoulders of the **cofrades**, members of the **cofradías** or lay brotherhoods that organize the processions. These are accompanied by **penitentes** and **nazarenos** generally wearing long hooded robes. Seville, Málaga and Valladolid are particularly well known for their spectacular Holy Week processions.

semanal ADJ weekly
semanalmente ADV weekly, each week
semanario ADJ weekly
SM weekly, weekly magazine
semanero/a SM/F (*LAm*) weekly-paid worker
semántica SF semantics (*sing*)
semánticamente ADV semantically
semántico ADJ semantic
semblante SM (*liter*) (= *cara*) countenance (*liter*), face; (= *aspecto*) look • **alterar el ~ a algn** to upset sb • **componer el ~** to put on a serious *o* straight face • **mudar de ~** to change colour *o* (*EEUU*) color • **el caso lleva otro ~ ahora** things look different now • **tener buen ~** (*de salud*) to look well; (*de humor*) to be in a good mood
semblantear ▸ CONJUG 1a VT **1** (*CAm, Cono Sur, Méx*) (= *mirar a la cara*) • **~ a algn** to look sb straight in the face, scrutinize sb's face
2 (*CAm, Méx*) (= *examinar*) to study, examine, look at
semblanza SF biographical sketch
sembradera SF seed drill
sembradío SM = **sembrío**
sembrado SM sown field
sembrador(a) SM/F sower
sembradora SF (*Mec*) seed drill
sembradura SF sowing
sembrar ▸ CONJUG 1j VT **1** (*Agr*) to sow (**de** with) • **~ un campo de nabos** to sow *o* plant a field with turnips • REFRÁN: • **el que siembra recoge** you reap what you sow
2 [+ *superficie*] to strew (**de** with)
3 (= *extender*) [+ *objetos*] to scatter, spread; [+ *noticia*] to spread; [+ *minas*] to lay • **~ minas en un estrecho** • **~ un estrecho de minas** (*Náut*) to mine a strait, lay mines in a strait • **~ la discordia** to sow discord • **~ el pánico** to spread panic, sow panic (*liter*)
4 (*Méx*) [+ *jinete*] to throw; (= *derribar*) to knock down
sembrío SM (*LAm*) sown field
semejante ADJ **1** (= *parecido*) similar • **ser ~s** to be alike *o* similar • **~ a** like • **es ~ a ella en el carácter** she is like her in character • **son muy ~s** they are very much alike *o* very similar • **dijo eso o algo ~** she said that or something similar *o* something like that
2 (*Mat*) similar
3 (*uso enfático*) such • **nunca hizo cosa ~** he never did any such thing *o* anything of the sort • **¿se ha visto frescura ~?** did you ever see such cheek?
4 (*Cono Sur, Méx*) (= *enorme*) huge, enormous
SM **1** (= *prójimo*) fellow man, fellow creature • **nuestros ~s** our fellow men
2 • **no tiene ~** (= *equivalente*) it has no equal, there is nothing to equal it
semejanza SF similarity, resemblance • **a ~ de** like, as • **tener ~ con** to look like, resemble ▸ **semejanza de familia** family likeness
semejar ▸ CONJUG 1a VI (= *parecerse a*) to look like, resemble
VPR **semejarse** to look alike, resemble each other • **~se a** to look like, resemble
semen SM semen
semental ADJ stud (*antes de s*), breeding (*antes de s*)
SM **1** (*Zool*) stallion, stud horse
2‡ (= *hombre*) stud‡
sementera SF **1** (= *acto*) sowing
2 (= *temporada*) seedtime
3 (= *tierra*) sown land
4 (= *caldo de cultivo*) hotbed (**de** of), breeding ground (**de** for)
semestral ADJ [*reunión, examen, resultados*] half-yearly, six-monthly; [*informe, revista*] biannual
semestralmente ADV [*reunirse, examinarse*] half-yearly; [*publicarse*] biannually
semestre SM **1** (= *seis meses*) (*gen*) period of six months; (*Univ*) semester
2 (*Econ*) half-yearly payment
semi... PREF semi..., half-
semiacabado ADJ half-finished
semialfabetizado ADJ semiliterate
semiamueblado ADJ semi-furnished
semiautomático ADJ semiautomatic
semibola SF small slam
semibreve SF semibreve, whole note (*EEUU*)
semicircular ADJ semicircular
semicírculo SM semicircle
semiconductor SM semiconductor
semiconsciente ADJ semi-conscious, half-conscious
semiconsonante SF semiconsonant
semicorchea SF semiquaver, sixteenth (note) (*EEUU*)
semicualificado ADJ semiskilled
semicultismo SM half-learned word
semiculto ADJ half-learned
semicupio SM (*CAm, Caribe*) hip bath
semiderruido ADJ half-ruined, half-collapsed
semidesconocido ADJ virtually unknown
semidescremado ADJ semi-skimmed
semidesértico ADJ semidesert (*antes de s*)
semidesierto ADJ half-empty
semidesnatado ADJ semi-skimmed
semidesnudo ADJ half-naked
semidiós SM demigod
semidormido ADJ half-asleep
semidúplex ADJ half duplex
semielaborado ADJ half-finished
semienterrado ADJ half-buried
semiexperto ADJ semiskilled
semifallo SM singleton (**a** in)
semifinal SF semifinal
semifinalista SMF semifinalist
semifondo SM middle-distance race
semifracaso SM partial failure, near failure
semiinconsciente ADJ semiconscious, half-conscious
semilla SF **1** (*Bot*) seed • **uvas sin ~s** seedless grapes ▸ **semilla de césped** grass seed
2 (= *origen*) seed, source • **la ~ de la discordia** the seeds of discord
3 (*Cono Sur*) (= *niño*) baby, small child • **la ~** the kids* (*collectively*)
semillero SM (= *terreno*) seedbed, nursery; (= *caja*) seed box • **un ~ de delincuencia** a hotbed of *o* a breeding ground for crime • **la decisión fue un ~ de disgustos** the decision caused a whole series of problems
semimedio SM welterweight
seminal ADJ seminal
seminario SM **1** (*Rel*) seminary
2 (*Univ*) seminar
3 (*Agr*) seedbed
seminarista SM seminarian
seminuevo ADJ (*Com*) nearly new, pre-owned (*EEUU*)
semioficial ADJ semi-official
semiología SF semiology
semiolvidado ADJ half-forgotten
semioruga SF (*tb* **camión semioruga**) half-track
semioscuridad SF half-darkness
semiótica SF semiotics (*sing*)
semiótico ADJ semiotic
semipesado ADJ light-heavyweight
semiprecioso ADJ semiprecious
semiprofesional ADJ, SMF semi-professional
semisalado ADJ brackish
semi-seco SM medium-dry
semiseparado ADJ semidetached
semisótano SM lower ground floor
semita ADJ Semitic
SMF Semite

semítico (ADJ) Semitic
semitono (SM) semitone
semivacío (ADJ) half-empty
semivocal (SF) semivowel
semivolea (SF) half-volley
sémola (SF) semolina
semoviente (ADJ) • **bienes ~s** livestock
sempiterno (ADJ) (*lit*) eternal; (*fig*) never-ending
sen(a) (SM/F) senna
Sena (SM) Seine
senado (SM) **1** (*Pol*) senate
2 (= *reunión*) assembly, gathering

SENADO
The **Senado** is the Upper Chamber of the Spanish Parliament. Approximately 80% of its 256 members acquire their seats in the general elections while the remaining 20% are nominated by each of the Autonomous Regions (**Comunidades Autónomas**). Like the **Congreso de los Diputados**, the term of office for the **Senado** is no longer than four years.
▹ CONGRESO DE LOS DIPUTADOS

senador(a) (SM/F) senator
senatorial (ADJ) senatorial
sencillamente (ADV) simply • **es ~ imposible** it's simply impossible
sencillez (SF) **1** [*de costumbre, estilo, ropa*] simplicity • **se viste con mucha ~** she dresses very simply
2 [*de tema, problema*] simplicity, straightforwardness • **no entendió nada pese a la ~ del asunto** she didn't understand a thing despite the simplicity *o* straightforwardness of the matter
3 (= *naturalidad*) naturalness • **me gustó su ~ en el trato** I liked her naturalness
4 (*LAm*) (= *necedad*) foolishness
sencillo (ADJ) **1** [*costumbre, estilo, ropa*] simple • **su forma de hablar es sencilla y directa** his manner of speaking is simple and direct
2 [*asunto, problema*] simple, straightforward • **es un plato ~ de hacer pero apetitoso** it's a simple but tasty dish, the dish is straightforward to make, but tasty
3 (= *no afectado*) natural, unaffected • **es muy rico pero muy ~ en el trato** he's very rich, but nevertheless very natural *o* unaffected
4 [*billete*] single
5 (*LAm*) (= *necio*) foolish
(SM) **1** (= *disco*) single
2 (*LAm*) (= *cambio*) small change
senda (SF) **1** (= *sendero*) path, track
2 (*para conseguir algo*) path
3 (*Cono Sur*) (*Aut*) lane
senderismo (SM) rambling, hill walking
senderista[1] (SMF) (*Dep*) rambler, hill walker
senderista[2] (*Perú*) (*Pol*) (ADJ) *of or pertaining to the Sendero Luminoso guerrilla movement*
(SMF) member of Sendero Luminoso
sendero (SM) path, track ▸ **Sendero Luminoso** (*Perú*) (*Pol*) Shining Path guerrilla movement
sendos (ADJ PL) • **les dio ~ golpes** he hit both of them, he gave each of them a beating • **recibieron ~ regalos** each one received a present • **con sendas peculiaridades** each with its own peculiarity
Séneca (SM) Seneca
senectud (SF) old age
Senegal (SM) (*tb* **El Senegal**) Senegal
senegalés/esa (ADJ), (SM/F) Senegalese
senescencia (SF) ageing
senil (ADJ) senile
senilidad (SF) senility
senior, sénior (ADJ INV) **1** (*Dep*) senior
2 (= *con experiencia*) senior
3 (*acompañando a nombre propio*) senior
(SMF) (PL: **seniors** *o* **séniors**) (*Dep*) senior
seno (SM) **1** (= *pecho*) breast • **una operación para reducir los ~s** a breast-reduction operation
2 (= *centro*) • **en el ~ de la familia** in the bosom of the family • **el ~ del movimiento** the heart *o* core of the movement ▸ **seno de Abraham** Abraham's bosom
3 (*liter*) (= *útero*) • **lleva un niño en su ~** she is with child (*liter*) ▸ **seno materno** womb
4 (*Mat*) sine
5 (*Anat*) ▸ **seno frontal** frontal sinus ▸ **seno maxilar** maxillary sinus
6 (*Náut, Meteo*) trough
7 (*Geog*) (= *ensenada*) small bay; (= *golfo*) gulf
8 (*frm*) (= *hueco*) hollow • **un fregadero de dos ~s** a double sink
SENPA (SM ABR) (*Esp*) = **Servicio Nacional de Productos Agrarios**
sensación (SF) **1** (= *percepción*) feeling, sensation • **una ~ de placer** a feeling *o* sensation of pleasure • **tengo la ~ de que …** • **me da la ~ de que …** I have a feeling that …
2 (= *conmoción*) sensation • **causar** *o* **hacer ~** to cause a sensation
sensacional (ADJ) sensational
sensacionalismo (SM) sensationalism
sensacionalista (ADJ) sensationalist • **la prensa ~** the sensationalist press, the tabloid press
(SMF) sensationalist
sensacionalizar ▹ CONJUG 1f (VT) to sensationalize
sensatamente (ADV) sensibly
sensatez (SF) good sense • **con ~** sensibly
sensato (ADJ) sensible
sensibilidad (SF) **1** (*al dolor, al frío*) feeling • **no tiene ~ en las piernas** he has no feeling in his legs
2 (= *emotividad*) sensitivity • **~ afectiva** emotional sensitivity
3 (= *disposición*) feeling, sensitivity • **muestra una gran ~ para la música** she has a great feeling *o* sensitivity for music ▸ **sensibilidad artística** artistic feeling *o* sensitivity
4 [*de aparato, máquina*] sensitivity • **una película de alta ~** a highly sensitive film
sensibilización (SF) sensitizing
sensibilizado (ADJ) **1** (= *alérgico*) sensitized
2 (*Fot*) sensitive
sensibilizar ▹ CONJUG 1f (VT) **1** (= *concienciar*) to sensitize • **~ la opinión pública** to inform public opinion
2 (*Fot*) to sensitize
sensible (ADJ) **1** (*al dolor, al frío*) sensitive • **tiene la piel muy ~** she has very sensitive skin • **~ a algo** sensitive to sth • **es muy ~ a los cambios de temperatura** it's very sensitive to changes in temperature • **los seres ~s** sentient beings
2 (= *impresionable*) sensitive (**a** to) • **es muy ~ y llora con facilidad** he is very sensitive and cries easily
3 (= *perceptivo*) • **~ a algo** sensitive to sth • **es muy ~ a los problemas de la población** he is very sensitive to people's problems • **Ana es muy ~ al arte** Ana has an artistic sensitivity
4 (= *evidente*) [*cambio, diferencia*] appreciable, noticeable; [*pérdida*] considerable • **una ~ mejoría** a noticeable improvement
5 (*Téc*) sensitive (**a** to); (*Fot*) sensitive • **un aparato muy ~** a very sensitive piece of equipment • **una placa ~ a la luz** a light-sensitive plate
6 (= *capaz*) • **~ de** capable of • **~ de mejora** capable of improvement
(SF) (*Mús*) leading note
sensiblemente (ADV) perceptibly, appreciably, noticeably • **~ más** substantially more
sensiblería (SF) sentimentality
sensiblero (ADJ) sentimental, slushy*
sensitiva (SF) (*Bot*) mimosa
sensitivo (ADJ) **1** [*órgano*] sense (*antes de s*)
2 [*animal*] sentient, capable of feeling
sensomotor (ADJ) sensorimotor
sensor (SM) sensor ▸ **sensor de calor** heat sensor
sensorial (ADJ), **sensorio** (ADJ) sensory
sensual (ADJ) sensual, sensuous
sensualidad (SF) sensuality, sensuousness
sensualismo (SM) sensualism
sensualista (SMF) sensualist
sensualmente (ADV) sensually, sensuously
sentada (SF) **1** (= *tiempo que se está sentado*) sitting • **de** *o* **en una ~** at one sitting
2 (*Pol*) sit-in, sit-down protest • **hacer una ~** to organize a sit-in
sentadera (SF) **1** (*LAm*) (*para sentarse*) seat (*of a chair etc*)
2 sentaderas (*Méx**) (= *trasero*) backside* (*sing*)
sentadero (SM) seat
sentado (ADJ) **1** • **estar ~** to be sitting, be seated • **estaba ~ a mi lado** he was sitting *o* seated next to me • **permanecer ~** to remain seated • MODISMO: • **esperar ~***: • **si crees que te lo devolverá ya puedes esperar ~** if you think he's going to give it back to you you've got another think coming* *o* you can think again
2 • **dar por ~** to take for granted • **di por ~ que estabas de acuerdo** I took it for granted that you were in agreement, I assumed you were in agreement
3 • **dejar ~: quiero dejar ~ que …** I want to make it clear that …
4 [*carácter, personalidad*] balanced
sentador (ADJ) (*Cono Sur*) smart, elegant
sentadura (SF) (*en piel*) sore; (*en fruta*) mark
sentar ▹ CONJUG 1j (VT) **1** [+ *persona*] to sit, seat
2 (= *colocar*) [+ *objeto*] to place, place firmly • **~ las costuras** to press the seams • **~ el último ladrillo** to tap the last brick into place • **~ las bases de algo** to lay the foundations for sth
3 (= *establecer*) [+ *base, principio*] to establish; [+ *precedente*] to set
4 • **~ una suma en la cuenta de algn** (*Com*) to put a sum down to sb's account
5 (*And, Caribe*) [+ *persona*] to crush, squash
6 (*And*) [+ *caballo*] to rein in sharply, pull up sharply
(VI) **1** (*en el aspecto*) to suit • **ese peinado le sienta horriblemente** that hairstyle doesn't suit her at all, that hairstyle looks awful on her
2 • **~ bien/mal a algn** [*comida*] to agree/disagree with sb • **no me sientan bien las gambas** prawns disagree with me • **unas vacaciones le ~ían bien** he could do with a holiday
3 (= *agradar*) • **~ bien/mal** to go down well/badly • **le ha sentado mal que lo hayas hecho tú** he didn't like your doing it • MODISMO: • **~ como un tiro**: • **a mí me sienta como un tiro*** it suits me like a hole in the head*
(VPR) **sentarse 1** [*persona*] to sit, sit down, seat o.s. (*frm*) • **¡siéntese!** (do) sit down, take a seat • **sentémonos aquí** let's sit (down) here • **se sentó a comer** she sat down to eat
2 [*sedimento*] to settle
3 [*tiempo*] to settle, settle down, clear up
4 (*Arquit*) [*cimientos*] to settle
sentencia (SF) **1** (*Jur*) sentence • **dictar** *o* **pronunciar ~** to pronounce sentence • **visto para ~** ready for sentencing ▸ **sentencia de muerte** death sentence

S

2 (= *decisión*) decision, ruling; (= *opinión*) opinion
3 (*Literat*) maxim, saying
4 (*Inform*) statement

sentenciar ▷ CONJUG 1b VT **1** (*Jur*) to sentence (**a** to)
2 (*Dep*) [+ *partido*] to decide
3 (*LAm*) • **~ a algn** to swear revenge on sb
VI **1** (= *dar su opinión*) to pronounce o.s., give one's opinion
2 (*Dep*) to decide the match

sentenciosamente ADV gravely, weightily

sentenciosidad SF **1** [*de refrán*] pithiness
2 [*de lenguaje*] sententiousness

sentencioso ADJ **1** [*refrán*] pithy
2 [*lenguaje*] sententious; [*carácter*] dogmatic

sentidamente ADV **1** (= *con sentimiento sincero*) sincerely, with great feeling
2 (= *con pesar*) regretfully

sentido ADJ **1** [*carta, declaración*] heartfelt • **pronunció unas sentidas palabras en su honor** he said some heartfelt words in his honour • **una pérdida muy sentida** a deeply felt loss • **mi más ~ pésame** my deepest sympathy, my heartfelt condolences
2 (= *dolido*) hurt • **estaba muy sentida con sus amigos** she was very hurt by her friends
3 [*carácter, persona*] sensitive
SM **1** (= *capacidad*) **a** (*para sentir*) sense • **ha perdido el ~ del gusto** he has lost his sense of taste • **los cinco ~s** the five senses • MODISMOS: • **costar un ~** (*Esp*†*) to cost the earth • **poner los cinco ~s** to be on one's toes • **tener un sexto ~** to have a sixth sense
b (*para percibir*) sense • **no tiene ~ del ritmo** he has no sense of rhythm • **tiene muy buen ~ del color** he has a very good sense of colour ▸ **sentido común** common sense ▸ **sentido de la orientación** sense of direction ▸ **sentido de la proporción** sense of proportion ▸ **sentido del humor** sense of humour ▸ **sentido de los negocios** business sense ▸ **sentido del ridículo** • **su ~ del ridículo le impidió hacerlo** he felt self-conscious *o* embarrassed so he didn't do it • **tiene un gran ~ del ridículo** she easily feels self-conscious *o* embarrassed ▸ **sentido práctico** • **tener ~ práctico** to be practical
2 (= *significado*) meaning • **ser madre le ha dado un nuevo ~ a su vida** being a mother has given a new meaning to her life • **¿cuál es el ~ literal de esta palabra?** what is the literal meaning of this word? • **la vida sin ti no tendría ~** without you life would have no meaning *o* would be meaningless • **doble ~** double meaning • **esa frase tenía doble ~** that sentence had a double meaning • **sin ~** [*palabras, comentario*] meaningless • **decía cosas sin ~** he was talking nonsense
3 (= *lógica*) sense • **no le veo ~ a esta discusión** I can't see any sense *o* point in this argument • **poco a poco, todo empieza a cobrar ~** everything is gradually beginning to make sense • **sin ~** [*crueldad, violencia*] senseless • **fue un debate sin ~** it was a pointless debate • **tener ~** to make sense • **solo tiene ~ quejarse si así puedes conseguir lo que quieres** it only makes sense to complain if *o* the only point in complaining is if you can then get what you want • **no tiene ~ que te disculpes ahora** it's pointless (you) apologizing now, there's no sense *o* point in (you) apologizing now
4 (= *conciencia*) consciousness • **lo encontré en el suelo sin ~** I found him unconscious on the floor • **perder el ~** to lose consciousness • **recobrar el ~** to regain consciousness • MODISMO: • **quitar el ~ a algn** to take sb's breath away
5 (= *dirección*) direction • **los dos avanzaban en el mismo ~** they were both moving forward in the same direction • **conducía en ~ contrario** he was driving in the opposite direction • **"sentido único"** "one way" • **en el ~ de las agujas del reloj** clockwise • **en ~ contrario al de las agujas del reloj** anti-clockwise, counterclockwise (*EEUU*); ▷ **calle**
6 (*otras expresiones*) • **en ~ amplio** in the broad sense • **en el buen ~ de la palabra** in the best *o* good sense of the word • **en cierto ~** in a sense • **en ese ~** (*con nombre*) to that effect; (*con verbo*) in that sense, in that respect • **ha habido rumores en ese ~** there have been rumours to that effect • **en ese ~ no sabemos qué hacer** in that sense *o* respect, we don't know what to do • **en ~ estricto** in the strict sense of the word *o* term • **no es, en ~ estricto, un pez de río** it's not a freshwater fish in the strict sense of the word *o* term, it's not strictly speaking a freshwater fish • **en ~ figurado** in the figurative sense, figuratively • **en ~ lato** in the broad sense • **tomar algo en el mal ~** to take sth the wrong way • **en tal ~** to that effect • **están dispuestos a dar testimonio en tal ~** they are prepared to testify to that effect • **un acuerdo en tal ~ sería interpretado como una privatización** such an agreement *o* an agreement to that effect would be interpreted as privatization

sentimental ADJ **1** (= *emotivo*) [*persona, objeto*] sentimental; [*mirada*] soulful • **ponerse ~** to get sentimental
2 [*asunto, vida*] love (*antes de s*) • **aventura ~** love affair

sentimentalismo SM sentimentality

sentimentalmente ADV sentimentally

sentimentaloide* ADJ sugary, oversentimental

sentimentero ADJ (*Caribe, Méx*) = **sensiblero**

sentimiento SM **1** (= *emoción*) feeling • **pone mucho ~ cuando canta** he puts a lot of feeling into his singing • **despertó el ~ nacionalista del pueblo** it aroused the nationalistic feelings *o* sentiments of the people ▸ **sentimiento de culpa** feeling of guilt, guilty feeling ▸ **sentimiento del deber** sense of duty
2 (= *pena*) sorrow • **lloraba con mucho ~** he cried with great sorrow • **le acompaño en el ~** please accept my condolences
3 sentimientos (= *forma de sentir*) feelings • **has conseguido herir sus ~s** you've managed to hurt his feelings • **no deberías jugar con sus ~s** you shouldn't play with his emotions *o* feelings • **¿le has revelado ya tus ~s?** have you told her how you feel? • **es una persona de buenos ~s** she's a good-hearted person • **es cruel y no tiene ~s** he's cruel and unfeeling

sentina SF **1** (*Náut*) bilge
2 (*en ciudad*) sewer, drain

sentir ▷ CONJUG 3i VT **1** [+ *emoción, sensación, dolor*] to feel • **de repente he sentido frío** I suddenly felt cold • **no siento la pierna** I can't feel my leg • **empezó a ~ los efectos del alcohol** he began to feel the effects of the alcohol • **sentí ganas de contárselo** I felt the urge to tell him about it • **dejarse ~** to be felt • **están empezando a dejarse ~ los efectos de la crisis** the effects of the crisis are beginning to be felt • **en octubre ya se deja ~ el frío** by October it's already starting to get cold • **~ hambre** to feel hungry • **~ pena por algn** to feel pity for sb, feel sorry for sb • **~ sed** to feel thirsty
2 (= *percibir*) to sense • **sintió la presencia de alguien en la oscuridad** he sensed a presence in the darkness • **quizá sintió que no le estaba diciendo la verdad** maybe she sensed that I wasn't telling her the truth
3 (*con otros sentidos*) **a** (= *oír*) to hear • **no la sentí entrar** I didn't hear her come in • **no se sentía el vuelo de una mosca** you could have heard a pin drop
b (*esp LAm*) [+ *olor*] to smell; [+ *sabor*] to taste • **¿sientes el olor a quemado?** can you smell burning? • **no le siento ningún gusto a esto** this doesn't taste of anything to me
4 (= *presentir*) • **siento que esto no acabará bien** I have a feeling that this isn't going to end well
5 [+ *música, poesía*] to have a feeling for
6 (= *lamentar*) to be sorry about, regret (*más frm*) • **siento mucho lo que pasó** I'm really sorry about what happened • **siento no haber podido ir** I'm sorry I wasn't able to go • **siento informarle que no ha sido seleccionado** I'm sorry to tell you that you haven't been selected, I regret to inform you that you haven't been selected (*más frm*) • **siento molestarlo, pero necesito su ayuda** I'm sorry to bother you, but I need your help • **lo siento** I'm sorry • **lo siento muchísimo** • **¡cuánto lo siento!** I'm so sorry • **lo siento en el alma** I'm terribly sorry • **~ que ...** to be sorry that ... • **siento mucho que pienses de esa forma** I'm very sorry that you feel that way
VI to feel • **ni oía ni sentía nada** he could neither hear nor feel anything • **ama y siente como cualquier ser humano** he feels love and emotion like any human being • **el tiempo se me pasaba sin ~** I didn't notice the time passing
VPR **sentirse 1** (*en estado, situación*) to feel • **¿cómo te sientes?** how do you feel? • **no me siento con ánimos para eso** I don't feel up to it • **podemos ~nos satisfechos con el resultado** we can feel satisfied with the result • **se sentía observada** she felt she was being watched • **se sintió herido en su orgullo** his pride had been wounded • **~se como en casa** to feel at home • **~se culpable** to feel guilty • **~se mal** to feel bad • **me sentí mal por lo que había dicho** I felt bad about what I had said • **me sentí mal y me fui directamente a casa** I felt ill *o* bad and went straight home
2 (*Med*) • **~se de algo**: • **desde la operación se siente mucho de la espalda** she's had a lot of back pain since the operation • **ha vuelto a ~se del reúma** she has begun to suffer from rheumatism again
3 (*LAm*) (= *ofenderse*) to take offence • **no te sientas con él, no se refería a ti** don't be annoyed with him *o* don't take offence, he wasn't talking about you
4 (*Méx*) (= *resquebrajarse*) [*pared, hueso, vasija*] to crack
SM **1** (= *opinión*) feeling, opinion • **la decisión no refleja el ~ mayoritario** the decision does not reflect the feeling *o* opinion of the majority • **el ~ popular** popular feeling, popular opinion
2 (= *sentimiento*) feelings (*pl*) • **no quiero herir tu ~** I don't want to hurt your feelings • **el resurgimiento del ~ religioso** the upsurge in religious sentiment *o* feeling

sentón SM (*CAm, Méx*) (= *caída*) heavy fall • **dar un ~** (*Méx*) (= *caerse*) to fall on one's backside • **dar un ~ a** (*And*) [+ *caballo*] to rein in suddenly

seña SF **1** (= *gesto*) sign • **hablar por ~s** (*gen*) to communicate using signs; [*sordos*] to use sign-language • **hacer una ~ a algn** to make a sign to sb, signal to sb • **le hizo una ~ para que fuera** he signalled to him to go
2 señas (= *dirección*) address (*sing*) • **dar las ~s**

de algn to give sb's address
3 señas (= *indicios*) • **dar ~s de algo** to show signs of sth • **daba ~s de cansancio** he showed signs of tiredness • **por las ~s, parece imposible conseguirlo** it seems it's impossible to get hold of it, it's apparently impossible to get hold of it • **las ~s son mortales**† the signs are unmistakable
4 señas (= *detalles*) • **con las ~s que me diste lo reconocí enseguida** I recognized him immediately thanks to your description • **por** *o* **para más ~s** to be precise • **es colombiana, de Cali para más ~s** she's Colombian, from Cali to be precise ▸ **señas de identidad** identifying marks, distinguishing marks ▸ **señas personales** (personal) description (*sing*)
5 (*Mil*) • **santo y ~** password

señá SF = **señora**

señal SF **1** [*de aviso*] (*gen*) signal; (= *letrero*) sign • **un silbido era la ~ para que se callaran** a whistle was the signal for them to keep quiet • **el avión esperaba la ~ para despegar** the plane was waiting for the signal to take off • **una ~ acordada con anterioridad** a prearranged signal • **han puesto una ~ al principio del camino** they have put up a sign at the start of the road • **dar la ~ de** *o* **para algo** to give the signal for sth • **hacer una ~ a algn** (*con un gesto cualquiera*) to gesture to sb; (*ya acordada*) to signal to sb • **me hizo una ~ para que me apartara** he gestured to me to move aside • **subieron a la azotea para hacer ~es al helicóptero** they went up to the roof to signal to the helicopter ▸ **señal de alarma** (*ante un peligro*) warning signal; (= *síntoma*) warning sign • **dieron la ~ de alarma** they gave the warning signal • **deberían interpretar esto como una ~ de alarma** they should interpret this as a warning sign • **la muerte de varias ovejas ha hecho sonar la ~ de alarma** the death of several sheep has set alarm bells ringing ▸ **señal de auxilio** distress signal ▸ **señales de humo** smoke signals ▸ **la señal de la cruz** the sign of the cross ▸ **señal de la victoria** victory sign, V-sign ▸ **señal de salida** (*Dep, Ferro*) starting signal • **dar la ~ de salida** to give the starting signal ▸ **señal de socorro** distress signal
2 (*Aut*) sign • **la ~ de stop** the stop sign ▸ **señal de circulación** traffic sign, road sign ▸ **señal de peligro** warning sign ▸ **señal de preferencia** right of way sign ▸ **señal de tráfico** traffic sign, road sign ▸ **señal horizontal** road marking ▸ **señal vertical** road sign
3 (= *indicio*) sign • **es ~ de que las cosas van mejorando** it is a sign that things are improving • **su cuerpo mostraba ~es de violencia** his body showed signs of violent treatment • **le contestó sin la menor ~ de sorpresa** she answered him without the slightest sign of surprise • **los ladrones no dejaron la más mínima ~** the robbers didn't leave the slightest trace • **es buena ~** it's a good sign • **dar ~es de algo** to show signs of sth • **no daba ~es de nerviosismo** he showed no signs of nervousness • **lleva más de un mes sin dar ~es de vida** there's been no sign of him for more than a month • **en ~ de algo** as a sign of sth • **se dieron la mano en ~ de amistad** they shook hands as a sign of friendship • **en ~ de respeto** as a mark *o* sign of respect
4 (= *marca*) mark • **un vehículo sin ninguna ~ identificativa** a vehicle with no identifying marks • **haz una ~ en los paquetes urgentes** put a mark on the express parcels, mark the express parcels • **dejó una ~ en la esquina de la página** he marked the page • **la varicela le ha dejado la cara llena de ~es** her face has been left badly scarred *o* marked by chickenpox • **dejó ~es de dedos en el cristal** he left fingerprints on the glass
5 (*Med*) (= *síntoma*) symptom
6 (*Com, Econ*) (= *depósito*) deposit • **dejar una cantidad en ~** to leave a sum as a deposit
7 (*Radio*) signal • **se ha ido la ~** the signal has gone ▸ **señal horaria** time signal
8 (*Telec*) (*al teléfono*) tone; (*en contestador*) beep, tone • **deja tu mensaje tras oír la ~** leave your message after the beep *o* tone ▸ **señal de comunicando** engaged tone, busy signal (*EEUU*) ▸ **señal de llamada** dialling tone, ringing *o* (*EEUU*) ring tone ▸ **señal de ocupado** (*LAm*) engaged tone, busy signal (*EEUU*)

señala SF (*Cono Sur*) earmark

señaladamente ADV **1** (= *claramente*) clearly, distinctly • **mantiene una actitud ~ hostil** he maintains a clearly *o* distinctly hostile attitude
2 (= *especialmente*) especially • **eso beneficiaría ~ a los que más tienen** that would especially benefit those who are better off

señalado ADJ **1** (= *especial*) [*día*] special; [*ocasión, acontecimiento*] special, momentous • **en una fecha tan señalada como hoy** on such a special *o* momentous day as today • **los rasgos más ~s de su poesía** the most notable features of his poetry
2 [*persona*] (*gen*) distinguished; (*pey*) notorious • **un político especialmente ~ por la calidad de sus discursos** a politician particularly distinguished by the quality of his speeches • **un ~ criminal** a notorious criminal

señalador SM (*tb* **señalador de libros**) bookmark

señalar ▹ CONJUG 1a VT **1** (= *indicar*) (*gen*) to show; (*con el dedo*) to point • **me señaló el camino** he showed me the way • **como señala el informe** as shown in the report • **la aguja señala el nivel del aceite** the needle shows the oil level • **el termómetro señalaba 25 grados** the thermometer read 25 degrees • **es de mala educación ~ a la gente** it's rude to point (at people) • **~ una falta** (*Dep*) to indicate a foul
2 (= *marcar*) to mark • **señala en rojo dónde están los fallos** mark the mistakes in red • **señaló las cajas con etiquetas** he labelled the boxes • **el acné le ha señalado la cara** his face has been marked *o* scarred by acne • **eso señaló el principio de la decadencia** that marked the start of the decline
3 (= *destacar*) to point out • **tenemos que ~ tres aspectos fundamentales** we have to point out three fundamental aspects • **tuve que ~le varios errores en el examen** I had to point out several mistakes in the exam to him • **~ que** to point out that
4 (= *designar*) [+ *fecha, precio*] to fix, settle; [+ *tarea*] to set • **en el momento señalado** at the given moment, at the appointed time • **todas las encuestas lo señalan como el candidato favorito** all the opinion polls point to him as the favourite candidate
5 (*Aut*) [+ *carretera, ruta*] to signpost
6 [+ *ganado*] to brand
VPR **señalarse 1** (= *destacar*) to distinguish o.s. (**como** as) • **se señaló como el mejor saltador de todos los tiempos** he established himself as the greatest jumper of all time • **se han señalado por su generosidad** they have distinguished themselves by their generosity
2 (= *llamar la atención*) to stand out • **viste sobriamente porque no le gusta ~se** she dresses plainly because she doesn't like to stand out • **se señaló por su actitud rebelde ante la prensa** she stood out for her defiant attitude towards the press

señalero SM (*Cono Sur*) signalman

señalización SF **1** (= *acto*) (*Aut*) signposting, signing (*EEUU*); (*Ferro*) signalling, signaling (*EEUU*)
2 (= *conjunto de señales*) (*en carretera*) road signs (*pl*); (*en edificio*) signposting ▸ **señalización horizontal** markings (*pl*) on the road ▸ **señalización vertical** road signs (*pl*)

señalizado ADJ signposted

señalizador SM **1** (*tb* **señalizador vertical**) road sign
2 (*tb* **señalizador de viraje**) (*Cono Sur*) indicator, turn signal (*EEUU*)

señalizar ▹ CONJUG 1f VT **1** (*Aut*) [+ *ruta, carretera*] to signpost • **el desvío no estaba bien señalizado** the turn-off was not properly signposted • **un cartel señalizaba el área de servicio** a sign indicated the service area
2 (*Ferro*) to signal
VI (*con intermitente, con la mano*) to indicate, signal

señero ADJ **1** (= *sin par*) unequalled, unequaled (*EEUU*), outstanding
2 (= *solo*) alone, solitary

seño* SF (*Esp*) = **señorita**

señor(a) ADJ **1*** (*antes de sustantivo*) (*uso enfático*) great big* • **vive en una ~a casa** he lives in a great big house* • **eso es un ~ melón** that's some melon
2 (= *libre*) free, at liberty • **eres muy ~ de hacerlo si quieres** you're quite free *o* at liberty to do so if you want
SM/F **1** (= *persona madura*) man *o* (*más frm*) gentleman/lady • **ha venido un ~ preguntando por ti** there was a man *o* (*más frm*) a gentleman here asking for you • **le espera una ~a en su despacho** there's a lady waiting to see you in your office • **es todo un ~** he's a real gentleman • **lo he comprado en la planta de ~as** I bought it in ladieswear • MODISMO: • **dárselas de ~** to put on airs ▸ **señora de compañía** companion
2 (= *dueño*) [*de tierras*] owner; [*de criado, esclavo*] master/mistress • **el ~ no vendrá hoy a comer** the master will not be here for lunch today • **¿está la ~a?** is the lady of the house in? • **el ~ de la casa** the master of the house • **no es ~ de sus pasiones** he cannot control his passions
3 (*fórmula de tratamiento*) **a** (*con apellido*) Mr/Mrs • **es para el ~ Serrano** it's for Mr Serrano • **el ~ y la ~a Durán** Mr and Mrs Durán • **los ~es Centeno y Sánchez tuvieron que irse antes** (*frm*) Messrs Centeno and Sánchez had to leave early (*frm*) • **los ~es (de) González** Mr and Mrs González
b* (*con nombre de pila*) • **buenos días, ~ Mariano** (*a Mariano Ruiz*) good morning, Mr Ruiz • **la ~a María es de mi pueblo** (*hablando de María Ruiz*) Mrs Ruiz is from my village
c (*hablando directamente*) sir/madam • **no se preocupe ~** don't worry, sir • **¿qué desea la ~a?** (*en tienda*) can I help you, madam?; (*en restaurante*) what would you like, madam? • **¡oiga, ~a!** excuse me, madam! • **¡~as y ~es!** ladies and gentlemen!
d (*con nombre de cargo o parentesco*) • **el ~ alcalde** the mayor • **el ~ cura** the priest • **~ presidente** Mr President • **~ alcalde** Mr Mayor • **sí, ~ juez** yes, my Lord • **como diría tu ~a madre** as your mother would say
e (*frm*) (*en correspondencia*) • **muy ~ mío** Dear Sir • **muy ~a mía** Dear Madam • **muy ~es**

nuestros Dear Sirs • **~ director** (*en carta a periódico*) Dear Sir
4 (*uso enfático*) • **pues sí ~, así es como pasó** yes indeed, that's how it happened • **¡no ~, ahora no te vas!** oh no, you're not going anywhere yet!; ▹ **señora**
5 (*en letrero*) • **"señores"** "gents"
SM **1** (*Hist*) lord ▸ **señor de la guerra** warlord ▸ **señor feudal** feudal lord
2 (*Rel*) • **el Señor** the Lord • **alabemos al Señor** let us praise the Lord • **Nuestro Señor** Our Lord • **Nuestro Señor Jesucristo** Our Lord Jesus Christ • **recibir al Señor** to take communion

señora SF **1** (= *esposa*) wife • **vino con su ~** he came with his wife • **la ~ de García** Mrs García • **mi ~** my wife
2 (*Rel*) • **Nuestra Señora** Our Lady
3 (*en letrero*) • **"señoras"** "ladies"

señorear ▹ CONJUG 1a VT **1** (= *gobernar*) (*gen*) to rule; (*pey*) to domineer, lord it over
2 [+ *edificio*] to dominate, tower over
3 [+ *pasiones*] to master, control
VPR **señorearse 1** (= *dominarse*) to control o.s.
2 (= *darse humos*) to adopt a lordly manner
3 • **~se de** to seize, seize control of

señoría SF **1** • **su** *o* **vuestra Señoría** your *o* his lordship/your *o* her ladyship
2 (= *dominio*) rule, sway

señorial ADJ noble, majestic, stately

señorío SM **1** (*Hist*) manor, feudal estate
2 (= *dominio*) rule, dominion (**sobre** over)
3 (= *cualidad*) majesty, stateliness
4* (= *personas adineradas*) (*gen*) distinguished people; (*pey*) toffs*, nobs‡

señorita ADJ (= *de buenos modales*) (*Cono Sur*) polite
SF **1** (= *mujer soltera*) young lady • **una ~ ha llamado por teléfono** a young lady phoned • **ya estás hecha toda una ~** you've turned into a proper young lady • **la ~ no está contenta con nada** (*iró*) it would seem nothing pleases her ladyship • **residencia de ~s** hostel for young women ▸ **señorita de compañía** (*euf*) escort girl
2 (*fórmula de tratamiento*) **a** (*con apellido*) Miss • **~ Pérez** Miss Pérez • **¿es usted señora o ~?** is it Mrs or Miss?
b (*con nombre de pila*) • **buenos días, ~ Rosa** (*a Rosa Pérez*) good morning, Miss Pérez
c (*hablando directamente*) • **¿puedo ayudarla en algo, ~?** can I help you, madam?
d (*usado por criados*) • **la ~ no está en casa** (*referido a Rosa Pérez*) Miss Pérez is not at home • **¿a qué hora desea la ~ que la despierte?** what time would you like me to wake you, Miss?
e (*en correspondencia*) • **estimada ~** (*a Rosa Pérez*) Dear Miss Pérez, Dear Ms Pérez
3* (= *maestra*) teacher • **mi ~ no nos ha mandado tarea** my teacher didn't give us any homework • **~, Luisa me ha quitado el bolígrafo** Miss, Luisa has taken my pen

señoritingo/a* SM/F spoilt brat*

señorito ADJ (*pey*) high and mighty* • **no le gusta trabajar, es muy señorita** she doesn't like working, she's too high and mighty*
SM **1** (= *hijo de señor*) young gentleman; (*en lenguaje de criados*) master, young master
2 (*pey*) rich kid*

señorón/ona* SM/F big shot*

señuelo SM **1** (*Caza*) decoy
2 (*fig*) (= *cebo*) bait, lure
3 (*And, Cono Sur*) (= *buey*) leading ox

seo SF (*Aragón*) cathedral

sep. ABR (= **septiembre**) Sept

sepa *etc* ▹ **saber**

separable ADJ **1** (= *distinguible*) separable • **el carácter no es totalmente ~ de la forma física** character is not totally separable from physical form • **la vida privada es muy difícilmente ~ de la pública** it is very difficult to keep your private life separate from your public life
2 (= *extraíble*) [*revista*] detachable; [*teclado*] removable
SM pull-out feature

separación SF **1** (= *división*) division • **la estantería sirve de ~ entre las dos zonas** the bookcase acts as a division between the two areas • **las tropas han cruzado la línea de ~** the troops have crossed the dividing line ▸ **separación de bienes** separate estates (*pl*) ▸ **separación de poderes** separation of powers ▸ **separación racial** racial segregation
2 (*entre cónyuges, amigos*) separation • **tras varios meses de ~** after several months of separation • **en el momento de la ~ de las dos compañías** at the moment when the two companies split ▸ **separación legal, separación matrimonial** legal separation
3 (= *distancia*) gap, space • **deja un poco más de ~ entre los cuadros** leave a slightly bigger gap *o* space between the pictures
4 [*de un cargo*] removal, dismissal • **tras su ~ del cargo** after his removal *o* dismissal from the post ▸ **separación del servicio** (*Mil*) discharge

separadamente ADV separately

separado/a ADJ **1** (= *independiente*) separate • **dormimos en camas separadas** we sleep in separate beds • **tiene los ojos muy ~s** his eyes are very far apart • **por ~** separately • **los trabajos se facturan por ~** each job is invoiced separately • **puede comprar los libros juntos o por ~** you can buy the books together or separately
2 [*cónyuge*] separated • **está ~ de su mujer** he is separated from his wife • **es hija de padres ~s** her parents are separated
SM/F • **los ~s con hijos** separated people with children

separador SM **1** (*en carpeta, maletín*) divider
2 (*Téc*) separator
3 (*Inform*) delimiter
4 (*Col*) (*Aut*) central reservation, median strip (*EEUU*)

separadora SF burster

separar ▹ CONJUG 1a VT **1** (= *apartar*) to separate • **la maestra nos separó para que no habláramos** the teacher split us up *o* separated us so that we wouldn't talk • **si no los llegan a ~ se matan** if no one had pulled them apart *o* separated them, they would have killed each other • **separe la última sección del formulario** detach the bottom of the form • **~ algn/algo de algn/algo** to separate sb/sth from sb/sth • **al nacer los ~on de sus padres** they were taken (away) *o* separated from their parents at birth • **los ~on del resto de los pasajeros** they were split up *o* separated from the rest of the passengers • **separa el sofá de la pared** move the sofa away from the wall • **separe la cazuela de la lumbre** take the pot off the heat • MODISMO: • **~ el grano de la paja** to separate the wheat from the chaff
2 (= *distanciar*) • **nada conseguirá ~nos** nothing can come between us • **éramos buenos amigos, pero la política nos separó** we were good friends but politics came between us • **el trabajo la mantiene separada de su familia** work keeps her away from her family • **hasta que la muerte nos separe** till death us do part
3 (= *existir entre*) • **la distancia que separa Nueva York de Roma** the distance between New York and Rome • **el abismo que separa a los ricos de los pobres** the gulf between *o* separating (the) rich and (the) poor
4 (= *deslindar*) • **los Pirineos separan España de Francia** the Pyrenees separate Spain from France • **unas barreras de protección separaban el escenario de la plaza** there were crash barriers separating the stage from the rest of the square • **la frontera que separa realidad y ficción** the dividing line between reality and fiction, the line that separates reality from *o* and fiction
5 (= *dividir*) to divide • **separa las palabras en sílabas** divide the words into syllables • **los separé en varios montones** I sorted them out into several piles
6 (= *poner aparte*) • **¿me puedes ~ un poco de tarta?** can you put aside some cake for me?
7 (= *destituir*) (*de un cargo*) to remove, dismiss • **ser separado del servicio** (*Mil*) to be discharged
VPR **separarse 1** (*en el espacio*) to part • **caminaron hasta la plaza, donde se ~on** they walked as far as the square, where they went their separate ways *o* where they parted • **al llegar a la juventud sus destinos parecen ~se** when they became teenagers they seemed to go their separate ways • **~se de algn/algo: no se separa de él ni un solo instante** she never leaves him *o* leaves his side for a moment • **no debí ~me de las maletas** I shouldn't have left the suitcases unattended • **no se separan ni un momento del televisor** they sit there glued to the television, they never take their eyes off the television • **consiguió ~se del pelotón** he managed to leave the pack behind • **no se separen del grupo hasta que estemos dentro de la catedral** stay with the group until we are in the cathedral • **no quiere ~se de sus libros** he doesn't want to part with his books • **se separó de la vida pública** she withdrew *o* retired from public life
2 (*en una relación*) [*cónyuges*] to separate, split up; [*socios, pareja*] to split up • **sus padres se han separado** his parents have separated *o* split up • **¿en qué año se ~on los Beatles?** what year did the Beatles break up *o* split up? • **~se de** [+ *cónyuge*] to separate from, split up with; [+ *socio, pareja*] to split up with • **se separó de su marido** she separated from *o* split up with her husband • **se ha separado de todos sus amigos** he has cut himself off from all his friends • **piensa ~se de la empresa** he is thinking of leaving the company
3 (= *desprenderse*) [*fragmento, trozo*] to detach itself (**de** from), come away; [*pedazos*] to come apart
4 (*Pol, Rel*) to break away • **se separó de ellos para formar su propio partido** he broke away from them to form his own party • **cuando la Iglesia anglicana se separó de Roma** when the Anglican Church broke away *o* (*frm*) seceded from Rome
5 (*Jur*) to withdraw (**de** from)

separata SF offprint

separatismo SM separatism

separatista ADJ, SMF separatist

separo SM (*Méx*) cell

sepelio SM burial, interment

sepia ADJ, SM INV (= *color*) sepia
SF **1** (= *pez*) cuttlefish
2 (*Arte*) sepia

SEPLA SM ABR (= **Sindicato Español de Pilotos de Líneas Aéreas**) ≈ BALPA

sepsis SF INV sepsis

sept. ABR (= **septiembre**) Sept

septentrión SM (*liter*) north

septentrional ADJ north, northern

septeto SM septet

S

septicemia (SF) septicaemia, septicemia (EEUU)
séptico (ADJ) septic
septiembre (SM) September • **llegará el (día) 11 de ~** he will arrive on 11 September *o* on the 11th of September *o* on September the 11th • **en ~** in September • **en ~ del año pasado/que viene** last/next September • **a mediados de ~** in mid-September • **estamos a tres de ~** it's 3 September *o* the third of September • **todos los años, en ~** every September
septillizo/a (SM/F) septuplet
séptimo (ADJ), (SM) seventh; ▸ **sexto**
septuagenario/a (ADJ) septuagenarian, seventy-year-old
(SM/F) septuagenarian, person in his/her seventies, seventy-year-old
septuagésimo (ADJ), (SM) seventieth
séptuplo (ADJ) sevenfold
sepulcral (ADJ) **1** (= *del sepulcro*) sepulchral • **la inscripción ~** the inscription on the tomb *o* grave
2 (= *sombrío*) gloomy, dismal • **silencio ~** deathly silence
sepulcro (SM) (*esp Biblia*) tomb, grave, sepulchre, sepulcher (EEUU) • **~ blanqueado** whited sepulchre
sepultación (SF) (*Cono Sur*) burial
sepultar ▸ CONJUG 1a (VT) **1** (= *enterrar*) (*gen*) to bury; (*en mina*) to trap, bury • **quedaron sepultados bajo la roca** they were buried under the rock
2 (= *ocultar*) to hide away, conceal
sepultura (SF) **1** (= *acción*) burial • **dar ~ a** to bury • **dar cristiana ~ a algn** to give sb a Christian burial • **recibir ~** to be buried
2 (= *tumba*) grave, tomb
sepulturero (SM) gravedigger
seque *etc* ▸ **secar**
sequedad (SF) **1** (= *falta de humedad*) dryness
2 (*en contestación, carácter*) curtness
sequerío (SM) dry place, dry field
sequía (SF) **1** (= *falta de lluvias*) drought
2 (= *temporada*) dry season
3 (*And*) (= *sed*) thirst
sequiar ▸ CONJUG 1c (VI) (*Cono Sur*) to inhale
séquito (SM) **1** [*de rey, presidente*] retinue, entourage
2 (*Pol*) followers (*pl*)
3 [*de sucesos*] train, string • **con todo un ~ de calamidades** with a whole catalogue of disasters
SER (SF ABR) (*Esp*) (= **Sociedad Española de Radiodifusión**) *radio network*

S

ser

VERBO INTRANSITIVO
VERBO AUXILIAR
SUSTANTIVO MASCULINO

▸ CONJUG 2V
VERBO INTRANSITIVO
1 (*con función copulativa*) **a** (+ *adj*) to be • **es difícil** it's difficult • **es muy alto** he's very tall • **soy casado/soltero/divorciado** I'm married/single/divorced • **compra uno que no sea caro** buy one that isn't too expensive • **es pesimista** he's a pessimist • **somos seis** there are six of us • **me es imposible asistir** I'm unable to attend, it's impossible for me to attend • **¡que seas feliz!** I wish you every happiness! • **—eres estúpida —no, no lo soy** "you're stupid"—"no I'm not" • **¡será posible!** I don't believe it! • **¡serás burro!** you can be so stupid!
b (+ *sustantivo, pronombre*) • **el gran pintor que fue Goya** the great painter Goya • **hable con algún abogado que no sea Pérez** speak to some lawyer other than Pérez • **soy ingeniero** I'm an engineer • **con el tiempo fue ministro** he eventually became a minister • **yo era la reina, ¿vale?** suppose I were queen, right? • **presidente que fue de Francia** (*frm*) former president of France • **—¿dígame? —¡hola, soy Pedro!** "hello?"—"hello, it's Peter" • **—¿quién es? — soy yo** "who is it?"—"it's me" • **—¿quién será a estas horas? —será tu hermano** "who can it be at this hour?" — "it must be your brother" • **—¿qué ha sido eso? —nada, la puerta ha dado un portazo** "what was that?" — "nothing, the door slammed shut" • **es él quien debiera hacerlo** he's the one who should do it
c • **ser de** (*indicando origen*) to be from • **ella es de Calatayud** she's from Calatayud • **estas naranjas son de España** these oranges are Spanish *o* from Spain • **¿de dónde es usted?** where are you from?
d • **ser de** (*indicando composición*) to be made of • **es de lana** it's made of wool, it's woollen • **es de piedra** it's made of stone
e • **ser de** (*indicando pertenencia*) to belong to • **el parque es del municipio** the park belongs to the town • **esta tapa es de otra caja** this lid belongs to another box • **¿de quién es este lápiz?** whose pencil is this?, who does this pencil belong to? • **este es suyo** this one is his • **es de Joaquín** it's Joaquín's
f (+ *infin*) • **es de creer que**: • **continuó hablando, es de creer que sin interrupción** he went on talking, presumably without being interrupted • **si, como es de creer, ustedes también lo apoyan...** if, as may be supposed, you also support him... • **no es de creer que lo encarcelen, pero sí lo multarán** they probably won't put him in prison, but they are sure to fine him • **es de desear que ...** it is to be wished that ... • **es de esperar que ...** it is to be hoped that ... • **era de ver** it was worth seeing
2 • **ser para** (*indicando dirección, finalidad*): • **las flores son para ti** the flowers are for you • **el trofeo fue para Álvarez** the trophy went to Álvarez • **el sexto hoyo fue para García** García took the sixth hole • **este cuchillo es para cortar pan** this knife is for cutting bread • **ese coche no es para correr mucho** that car isn't made for going very fast • **esas finuras no son para mí** such niceties are not for me
3 (= *existir*) to be • **ser o no ser** to be or not to be • **Dios es** God exists • **érase que se era** • **érase una vez** once upon a time
4 (= *tener lugar*) • **la fiesta va a ser en su casa** the party will be at her house • **el crimen fue en Agosto** the crime took place in August
• MODISMO: • **otra vez será**: • **—no he podido ir a visitarla —bueno, otra vez será** "I wasn't able to visit her" — "never mind, you can do it some other time" • **—no he aprobado —¡otra vez será!** "I didn't pass" — "better luck next time!"
5 (*en preguntas retóricas*) • **¿qué será de mí?** what will become of me? • **¿qué habrá sido de él?** what can have become of him?, what can have happened to him?
6 (*con horas del día, fecha, tiempo*) to be • **es la una** it's one o'clock • **son las siete** it's seven o'clock • **serán las ocho** it must be about eight (o'clock) • **serían las nueve cuando llegó** it must have been about nine (o'clock) when he arrived • **hoy es cuatro de septiembre** today is 4 September • **es verano** it's summer • **era de noche** it was night time; ▸ **hora**
7 (= *en cálculos*) to be • **tres y dos son cinco** three plus two is five • **—¿cuánto es? —son dos euros** "how much is it?" — "two euros, please"
8 (*locuciones en infinitivo*) • **a no ser**: • **habríamos fracasado a no ser por su apoyo** we would have failed had it not been for their help • **llegaremos tarde a no ser que salgamos mañana** we'll be late unless we leave tomorrow • **como ha de** *o* **tiene que ser**: • **es un hombre como tiene que ser** he's a real man • **se lo comió con cuchillo y tenedor, como ha de** *o* **tiene que ser** she ate it with a knife and fork, the way it's supposed to be eaten • **con ser** (= *a pesar de ser*): • **con ser ella su madre no le veo el parecido** she may well be his mother, but I can't see any resemblance • **de no ser**: • **de no ser esto cierto tendríamos que eliminarlo** if this weren't the case we'd have to get rid of him • **de no ser por él me habría ahogado** if it hadn't been for him I'd have drowned • **no vaya a ser que...**: • **déjales tu teléfono, no vaya a ser que se pierdan** give them your phone number in case they get lost • **anda despacio, no vaya a ser que te caigas** walk slowly so you don't fall over
9 (*locuciones en indicativo*) • **es más**: • **creo que eso es así, es más, podría asegurártelo** I think that is the case, in fact I can assure you it is • **es que**: • **—¿por qué no llamaste? —es que no pude** "why didn't you call?" — "because I couldn't" • **es que no quiero molestarle** it's just that I don't want to upset him • **¿es que no te enteras?** don't you understand, or what? • **¿cómo es que no llamaste?** how come you didn't call?
10 (*locuciones en subjuntivo*) • **¡sea!** agreed!, all right! • **—compartiremos los gastos —¡sea!** "we'll share the cost" — "agreed!" *o* "all right!" • **(ya) sea ... (ya) sea: (ya) sea de izquierdas, (ya) sea de derechas yo no la voto** whether she's right-wing or left-wing, I'm not voting for her • **(ya) sea Juan o (ya) sea Antonio, alguien tiene que hacerlo** someone has to do it, (be it) either Juan or Antonio • **sea lo que sea**: • **—¡pero si es economista! —sea lo que sea, yo no me fío de sus opiniones** "but he's an economist!"—"be that as it may *o* he may well be, but still I don't trust his opinions" • **o sea** that is • **mis compañeros, o sea, Juan y Pedro** my colleagues, that is, Juan and Pedro • **o sea, que no vienes** so you're not coming • **no sea que** in case • **llévate el móvil no sea que llamen** take your mobile phone with you in case they call • **pon aquí las llaves, no sea que las pierdas** put the keys here so you don't lose them
VERBO AUXILIAR
(*en formas pasivas*) to be • **fue construido** it was built • **será fusilado** he will be shot • **está siendo estudiado** it is being studied • **ha sido asaltada una joyería** there has been a raid on a jeweller's
SUSTANTIVO MASCULINO
1 (= *ente*) being • **sus seres queridos** her loved ones ▸ **ser humano** human being ▸ **Ser Supremo** Supreme Being ▸ **ser vivo** living creature
2 (= *esencia, alma*) being • **todo su ser se conmovió ante tanta miseria** her whole being was moved by such poverty • **en lo más íntimo de su ser** deep within himself • **la quiero con todo mi ser** I love her with all my heart • **volver a su ser** to return *o* go back to normal
3 (*existencia*) life • **la mujer que le dio su ser** the woman who gave him (his) life, the woman who brought him into the world

> **SER**
>
> *En español decimos* **somos 15, son 28** *etc. Esta estructura se traduce al inglés por* **there are were** *etc + número +* **of us you them**:
>
> **Somos 50**
> There are 50 of us
> **Eran 38 en total**
> There were 38 of them altogether
>
> *Para otros usos y ejemplos ver la entrada.*

sera SF pannier, basket
seráficamente ADV angelically, like an angel
seráfico ADJ **1** (= *angélico*) angelic, seraphic
2* (= *humilde*) poor and humble
serafín SM **1** (*Rel*) seraph; (*fig*) angel
2 (*Caribe*) (= *broche*) clip, fastener
serape SM (*Méx*) = **sarape**
serbal SM, **serbo** SM service tree, sorb
Serbia SF Serbia
serbio/a ADJ Serbian
SM/F Serb
SM (*Ling*) Serbian
serbobosnio/a ADJ, SM/F Bosnian Serb
serbocroata ADJ, SMF Serbo-Croatian
SM (*Ling*) Serbo-Croat
serenamente ADV **1** (= *con calma*) calmly, serenely
2 (= *tranquilamente*) peacefully, quietly
serenar ▹ CONJUG 1a VT (*frm*) **1** (= *calmar*) [+ *ánimo, mente*] to calm; [+ *discusión, pelea*] to calm down; [+ *problema*] to settle
2 [+ *líquido*] to clarify
VI (*And**) to drizzle
VPR **serenarse 1** [*persona*] to calm down
2 (*Meteo*) [*mar*] to grow calm; [*tiempo*] to clear up, settle (down)
3 [*líquido*] to clear, settle
serenata SF serenade
serendipia SF serendipity
serenera SF (*And, CAm, Caribe*) cape, wrap
serenero SM (*Cono Sur*) (= *pañuelo*) headscarf; (= *chal*) wrap, cape
serenidad SF **1** (= *calma*) calmness, serenity
2 (= *tranquilidad*) peacefulness, quietness
serenísimo ADJ • **su Alteza Serenísima** His/Her Serene Highness
sereno ADJ **1** (= *apacible*) [*persona*] calm, serene; [*cara, expresión*] serene
2 (*Meteo*) [*tiempo*] settled, fine; [*cielo*] cloudless, clear
3 (= *calmado*) [*ambiente*] calm, quiet; [*tarde, noche*] still, peaceful; [*aguas*] calm, still
4 (= *sobrio*) • **estar ~** to be sober
SM **1** (= *humedad*) night dew • **dormir al ~** to sleep out in the open • **le perjudica el ~** the night air is bad for her
2 (= *vigilante*) night watchman
sereta SF builder's bucket, basket
seriado ADJ mass-produced
serial SM, (*Cono Sur*) SF serial ▸ **serial radiofónico** radio serial
serialización SF serialization
serializar ▹ CONJUG 1f VT to serialize
seriamente ADV seriously
seriar ▹ CONJUG 1b VT **1** (= *poner en serie*) to arrange in series, arrange serially
2 (*TV, Radio*) to make a serial of, serialize
3 (= *producir*) to mass-produce
sericultura SF silk-raising, sericulture
serie SF **1** (= *sucesión*) (*tb Bio, Mat*) series • **ha escrito una ~ de artículos sobre la infancia** she has written a series of articles about childhood • **asesinatos en ~** serial killings • **asesino en ~** serial killer
2 (*Industria*) • **de ~**: • **tamaño de ~** standard size • **artículo de ~** mass-produced article • **equipamiento de ~** standard equipment • **modelo de ~** (*Aut*) standard model • **el aire acondicionado es de ~** air-conditioning comes as standard • **en ~**: • **fabricación en ~** mass production • **fabricar** *o* **producir en ~** to mass-produce • **fuera de ~** (= *extraordinario*) special, out of the ordinary • **un fuera de ~** an extraordinary person, one of a kind • **artículos fuera de ~** (*Com*) goods left over, remainders
3 (*Elec*) • **en ~** in series
4 (*Inform*) • **impresora en ~** serial printer • **interface en ~** serial interface • **puerto (en) ~** serial port
5 (= *conjunto*) [*de monedas, sellos*] series; [*de inyecciones*] course
6 (*TV, Radio*) (*en episodios sueltos*) series; (*en historia continua*) serial
7 (*Cine*) • **película de ~ B** B-movie
8 (*Dep*) qualifying heat
seriedad SF **1** (= *calidad personal*) seriousness • **hablar con ~** to speak seriously *o* in earnest
2 (= *responsabilidad*) responsibility, sense of responsibility • **falta de ~** lack of responsibility, irresponsibility
3 [*de enfermedad, crisis, problema*] seriousness
4 (= *fiabilidad*) reliability, trustworthiness
serigrafía SF silk-screen printing • **una ~** a silk-screen print
serigrafiado ADJ printed, screen-printed
serigrafista SMF silk-screen printer
serimiri SM drizzle
serio ADJ **1** [*expresión, tono*] serious • **¿por qué estás hoy tan ~?** why are you (looking) so serious today? • **su padre es muy ~** his father's a very serious person • **se quedó mirándome muy ~** he looked at me very seriously, he stared gravely at me • **pareces muy ~** you're looking very serious • **ponerse ~**: **se puso seria al ver la foto** she went *o* became serious when she saw the photo • **me voy a poner seria contigo si no estudias** I'm going to get cross with you if you don't do some studying
2 • **en ~** seriously • **tomar un asunto en ~** to take a matter seriously • **no hablaba en ~** I wasn't serious • **¿lo dices en ~?** are you serious?, do you really mean it?
3 [*problema, enfermedad, pérdida*] serious • **esto se pone ~** this is getting serious
4 (= *fiable*) [*persona*] reliable; [*trato*] straight, honest • **es una persona poco seria** he's not very reliable • **una empresa seria** a reliable firm • **no es ~ que ahora decidan echarse atrás** it's not very responsible of them to back out now
5 (= *severo*) • **el negro es un color demasiado ~ para una niña** black is too serious *o* severe a colour for a young girl • **lleva un traje muy ~** he's wearing a very formal suit
6 [*estudio, libro*] serious
sermón SM **1** (*Rel*) sermon • **el Sermón de la Montaña** the Sermon on the Mount
2* (= *regañina*) lecture* • **vaya ~ que nos soltó tu padre** what a lecture your dad gave us!
sermonear* ▹ CONJUG 1a VT to lecture*
VI to sermonize
sermoneo* SM lecture*
sermonero* ADJ given to sermonizing
sernambí SM (*And, Caribe*) inferior rubber
serología SF serology
serón SM **1** (= *sera*) pannier, large basket
2 [*de bebé*] cot
seronegativo ADJ seronegative
seropositivo ADJ (*gen*) seropositive; (*con VIH*) HIV-positive
seroso ADJ serous
serotonina SF serotonin
serpa SF (*Bot*) runner
serpear ▹ CONJUG 1a VI, **serpentear** ▹ CONJUG 1a VI **1** (*Zool*) to wriggle, creep
2 [*camino*] to wind, twist and turn; [*río*] to wind, meander
serpenteante ADJ [*camino*] winding, twisting; [*río*] winding, meandering
serpenteo SM **1** (*Zool*) wriggling, creeping
2 [*de camino*] winding, twisting; [*de río*] winding, meandering
serpentín SM coil
serpentina SF **1** (*Min*) serpentine
2 (= *papel*) streamer
serpentino ADJ **1** (= *como serpiente*) snaky, sinuous
2 [*de camino*] winding, meandering
serpiente SF snake, serpent • **la Serpiente** the (European monetary) Snake ▸ **serpiente boa** boa constrictor ▸ **serpiente de anteojos** cobra ▸ **serpiente de cascabel** rattlesnake, rattler (*EEUU**) ▸ **serpiente de mar** sea serpent ▸ **serpiente de verano** silly(-season) story, non-story (*used to fill papers in the slack season*) ▸ **serpiente de vidrio** slowworm ▸ **serpiente pitón** python
serpol SM wild thyme
serpollo SM sucker, shoot
serrado ADJ serrated, toothed
serraduras SFPL sawdust (*sing*)
serrallo SM harem
serrana SF = **serranilla**
serranía SF **1** (= *terreno montañoso*) mountains (*pl*), mountainous area, hilly country
2 (*Méx*) (= *bosque*) wood, forest
serraniego ADJ = **serrano**
serranilla SF *15th-century verse-form*
serrano/a ADJ **1** (*Geog*) mountain (*antes de s*), hill (*antes de s*)
2 (= *tosco*) coarse, rustic
3 • **partida serrana** (*Esp*) dirty trick
SM/F mountain-dweller, highlander; ▹ **serrana**
serrar ▹ CONJUG 1j VT **1** [+ *madera*] to saw up
2 (= *separar*) to saw off
serrería SF sawmill
serrín SM sawdust
serrote SM (*Méx*) = **serrucho**
serruchar ▹ CONJUG 1a VT (*esp LAm*) to saw (up); (= *separar*) to saw off
serrucho SM **1** (= *herramienta*) saw, handsaw
2 (*Caribe*) (= *prostituta*) whore
3 • **hacer un ~** (*And, Caribe*) to split the cost
Servia SF = **Serbia**
servible ADJ serviceable, usable
servicial ADJ helpful, obliging
SM (*And*) servant
servicialidad SF helpfulness, obliging nature
servicio SM **1** (= *ayuda, atención*) **a** (*a empresa, país*) service • **lleva veinte años de ~ en la empresa** he has twenty years' service with the company • **no cobró nada por sus ~s** he didn't charge anything for his services • **al ~ de**: • **un agente secreto al ~ de la Corona** a secret agent in the service of the Crown • **estar de ~** to be on duty • **estar de ~ de guardia** (*Mil*) to be on guard duty • **estar fuera** *o* **libre de ~** to be off duty • **un policía libre de ~** an off-duty policeman • **prestar ~** (*gen*) to work; (*Mil*) to serve • **ha prestado sus ~s en el hospital universitario** she has worked at the university hospital • **prestó sus ~s como teniente de la marina** he served as a lieutenant in the navy
b (*a cliente*) service • **el ~ no está incluido** service is not included • **una empresa de ~s informáticos** a computing services company • **a su ~** at your service • **"servicio a domicilio"** "we deliver", "home

delivery service"
c [*de tren, autobús*] service • **el ~ a la costa ha quedado interrumpido** the service to the coast has been interrupted ▸ **servicio a bordo** (*en avión*) in-flight services (*pl*); (*en barco, tren*) services on board (*pl*) ▸ **servicio comunitario** community service ▸ **servicio contra incendios** fire service ▸ **servicio de aduana** customs service ▸ **servicio de asesoramiento** advisory service ▸ **servicio de atención al cliente** customer service ▸ **servicio de bomberos** fire service ▸ **servicio de contraespionaje** secret service ▸ **servicio de entrega** delivery service ▸ **servicio de información, servicio de inteligencia** intelligence service ▸ **servicio de limpieza** cleaning services (*pl*) ▸ **servicio de megafonía** public address system ▸ **servicio de orden** (*en manifestación*) stewards (*pl*), marshals (*pl*) ▸ **servicio de préstamo a domicilio** lending facility, home lending service ▸ **servicio de recogida de basura** refuse collection service ▸ **servicio de transportes** transport service ▸ **servicio de vigilancia aduanera** coastguard patrol ▸ **servicio médico** medical service ▸ **servicio permanente** round-the-clock service ▸ **servicio posventa** after-sales service ▸ **servicios de socorro** emergency services ▸ **servicio secreto** secret service ▸ **servicios informativos** broadcasting services ▸ **servicios mínimos** minimum service (*sing*), skeleton service (*sing*) ▸ **servicio social (sustitutorio)** community service (*performed in place of military service*) ▸ **servicios postales** postal services ▸ **servicios sociales** social services; ▹ **estación**
2 (= *funcionamiento*) • **estar en ~** to be in service • **entrar en ~** to come *o* go into service • **fuera de ~** out of service • **poner en ~** to put into service • **está previsto poner en ~ una segunda pista de aterrizaje** there are plans to open a second runway, there are plans to put a second runway into operation *o* service
3 (= *beneficio*) service • **hizo un gran ~ a su país** he did his country a great service • **es un abrigo viejo, pero me hace mucho ~** it's an old coat, but I get a lot of use out of it • **hacer un flaco ~ a algn** to do sb a disservice
4 (*Mil*) (*tb* **servicio militar**) military service • **ser apto para el ~** to be fit for military service ▸ **servicio activo** active service
5 (*en un hospital*) department • **"servicio de pediatría"** "paediatric department" ▸ **servicio de urgencias** accident and emergency department, casualty department
6 servicios (*Econ*) public services • **el sector ~s** the public service sector
7 (= *retrete público*) toilet, washroom (*EEUU*), restroom (*EEUU*) • **¿dónde están los ~s?** where are the toilets?
8 (*en la mesa*) **a** (*para cada comensal*) • **un juego de café con seis ~s** a six-piece coffee set • **faltan dos ~s** we are two places *o* settings short
b (= *juego*) set ▸ **servicio de café** coffee set, coffee service ▸ **servicio de mesa** dinner service ▸ **servicio de té** tea set, tea service
9 (= *servidumbre*) (*tb* **servicio doméstico**) (= *personas*) servants (*pl*); (= *actividad*) service, domestic service • **hay dos habitaciones para el ~** there are two rooms for the servants • **han mejorado las condiciones del ~** conditions of domestic service have improved • **escalera de ~** service staircase • **puerta de ~** tradesman's entrance
10 (*Tenis*) serve, service • **romper el ~ de algn** to break sb's serve *o* service
11 (*Rel*) service • **el ~ será oficiado por Monseñor Cipriá** Monsignor Cipriá will officiate at the service
12 (*Econ*) [*de una deuda*] servicing
13 (*LAm*) [*de un automóvil*] service • **le toca el ~ a los 3.000km** it's due (for) a service after 3000km

servidor(a) (SM/F) **1** (= *criado*) servant
2 (*como expresión cortés*) • **—¿quién es la última de la cola? —~a** "who's last in the queue?" —"I am" • **—Francisco Ruiz —¡servidor!** (*frm*) "Francisco Ruiz" — "present! *o* at your service!" (*frm*) • **¡~ de usted!** at your service! • **"su seguro ~"**† (*en cartas*) "yours faithfully" (*frm*), "yours truly" (*EEUU*) (*frm*) • **un ~: al final un ~ tuvo que fregar todos los platos** (*hum*) in the end yours truly *o* muggins had to wash all the dishes* • **él y un ~ pasamos un buen rato** he and I had a good time
3 (*Cono Sur*) ▸ **servidor(a) del orden** police officer
(SM) (*Inform*) (= *empresa*) internet service provider, ISP; (= *aparato*) server ▸ **servidor de correo** mail server ▸ **servidor de red** network server

servidumbre (SF) **1** (= *conjunto de criados*) staff, servants (*pl*)
2 (= *condición*) [*de criado*] servitude; [*de esclavo*] slavery • **la ~ de los que trabajan para un jefe** the servitude of those who work for their boss • **el dinero se ha convertido en una forma de ~** money has turned into a form of slavery
3 (*Hist*) (*tb* **servidumbre de la gleba**) serfdom
4 (*Jur*) ▸ **servidumbre de aguas** water rights (*pl*) ▸ **servidumbre de paso** rights (*pl*) of way

servil (ADJ) **1** (= *poco apreciado*) [*actitud, comportamiento*] servile, obsequious; [*trabajo*] menial
2 [*imitación, estilo*] slavish

servilismo (SM) servility, obsequiousness (*frm*)

servilla (SF) slipper, pump

servilleta (SF) serviette, napkin

servilletero (SM) serviette ring, napkin ring

servilmente (ADV) obsequiously

servir ▹ CONJUG 3k (VT) **1** [+ *persona, intereses, causa*] to serve • **seguiré sirviendo al pueblo** I will continue to serve the people • **están sirviendo a su interés personal** they are furthering *o* serving their own interests • **~ a Dios** to serve God • **~ a la patria** to serve one's country • **¿en qué puedo ~le?** how can I help you? • MODISMOS: • **para ~le**† • **para ~ a usted**† at your service • REFRÁN: • **no se puede ~ a Dios y al diablo** no man can serve two masters
2 (*para comer*) **a** (*en la mesa*) [+ *comida*] to serve; [+ *bebida*] to serve, pour • **¿a qué hora sirven el desayuno?** what time is breakfast served? • **se negaron a ~nos** they refused to serve us • **¿me ayudas a ~ la mesa?** can you help me serve (the food)? • **la cena está servida** dinner's on the table, dinner is served (*frm*) • **¿te sirvo un poco más?** would you like some more?, can I give you some more? • **había cinco criados para ~ la mesa** there were five servants waiting at *o* serving at table
b (= *proporcionar*) to give, serve (*frm*) • **ese día sirven una comida especial a la tropa** the troops are given *o* (*frm*) served a special meal that day • **sirvieron unos canapés tras la inauguración** after the opening ceremony there were canapés, canapés were served after the opening ceremony (*frm*)
3 (*Com*) [+ *pedido*] to process
4 (*Tenis*) to serve
5 (*Mec*) [+ *máquina, cañón*] to man
6 (*Naipes*) [+ *cartas*] to deal
(VI) **1** (= *ser útil*) to be useful • **todavía puede ~** it might still be useful • **este mismo me ~á** this one will do • **siempre que lo he necesitado me ha servido** whenever I've needed it, it's done the job • **eso no sirve** that's no good *o* use • **este sistema ya no sirve** this system is no good *o* use any more • **ya no me sirve** it's no good *o* use to me now • **la distinción entre derechas e izquierdas ya no sirve** the distinction between right and left is no longer valid • **~ para algo:** • **puede ~ para limpiar el metal** it can be used for *o* it is suitable for cleaning metal • **¿para qué sirve?** what is it for? • **¿para qué sirve este aparato?** what's this gadget for? • **la nueva normativa solo ha servido para crear polémica** the new regulation has only served to stir up controversy (*frm*), the only thing the new rule has done is to stir up controversy • **el acuerdo no ha servido para alcanzar la paz** the agreement has not succeeded in achieving peace • **esta huelga no está sirviendo para nada** this strike is not achieving anything • **no sirves para nada** you're completely useless • **yo no ~ía para médico** I'd be no good as a doctor
2 • **~ de algo:** • **la legislación italiana puede ~nos de guía** we can use Italian law as a guide, Italian law can serve a guide • **~ de ejemplo a algn** to be an example to sb • **esa experiencia le ha servido de lección** that experience taught him a lesson • **por si sirve de algo** in case that's any use • **no sirve de nada quejarse** it's no good *o* use complaining, there's no point in complaining • **no sirve de nada que vaya él** it's no good *o* use him going*, there's no point in him going • **¿de qué sirve mentir?** what's the good *o* use of lying?, what's the point in lying?; ▹ **precedente**
3 (*en el servicio doméstico*) to work as a servant • **estuvo sirviendo en Madrid** she was a servant in Madrid • **ponerse a ~** to become a servant
4 [*camarero*] to serve • **vete a ~ en la barra** go and serve at the bar
5 (*Mil*) to serve (*frm*) • **yo serví en la Marina** I was in the Navy, I served in the Navy (*frm*) • **está sirviendo** he's doing his military service
6 (*Tenis*) to serve
7 (*Naipes*) (*tb* **servir del palo**) to follow suit
(VPR) **servirse 1** (= *ponerse*) [+ *comida*] to help o.s. to; [+ *bebida*] to pour o.s., help o.s. to • **sírvete más ensalada** have some more salad, help yourself to more salad • **yo misma me ~é el café** I'll pour myself some coffee, I'll help myself to some coffee • **¿qué se van a ~?** (*LAm*) what will you have?
2 (= *utilizar*) • **~se de** [+ *herramienta, objeto*] to use, make use of; [+ *amistad, influencia*] to use • **se han servido de su cargo para enriquecerse** they used their position to make money • **se sirvieron de la oscuridad para escapar** (*liter*) they availed themselves of the darkness to make good their escape (*liter*)
3 (*frm*) (= *hacer el favor de*) • **~se hacer algo:** • **sírvase volver por aquí mañana** (would you) please come back tomorrow • **le ruego que se sirva acompañarme** (would you) come with me, please • **si la señora se sirve pasar por aquí** if madam would care to come this way

servo (SM) servo

servo... (PREF) servo...

servoasistido (ADJ) servo-assisted

servodirección SF power steering
servofrenos SMPL power-assisted brakes
servomecanismo SM servo, servomechanism
sésamo SM sesame • **¡ábrete ~!** open sesame!
sesapil SM sex-appeal
sesear ▹ CONJUG 1a VT *to pronounce c (before e, i) and z as s (a feature of Andalusian and much LAm pronunciation)*
sesenta ADJ INV, PRON, SM sixty; (= *ordinal*) sixtieth • **los (años) ~** the sixties; ▹ **seis**
sesentañero/a SM/F man/woman of about sixty
sesentón/ona ADJ sixty-year-old, sixtyish
SM/F man/woman of about sixty, sixty-year-old
seseo SM *pronunciation of c (before e, i) and of z as s (a feature of Andalusian and much LAm pronunciation)*
sesera* SF brains (*pl*)
sesgado ADJ **1** (= *inclinado*) slanted, slanting, oblique
2 (= *ladeado*) awry, askew
3 [*pelota*] swerving, sliced
4 [*opinión, reportaje*] bias(s)ed, slanted
sesgar ▹ CONJUG 1h VT **1** (= *inclinar*) to slant, place obliquely
2 (= *ladear*) to put askew, twist to one side
3 [+ *pelota*] to slice
4 (*Cos*) to cut on the bias
5 (*Téc*) to bevel
6 [+ *opinión, reportaje*] to bias, slant
7 [+ *vida*] to cut short
sesgo SM **1** (= *inclinación*) slant • **estar al ~** to be slanting
2 (= *torcimiento*) warp, twist
3 (*Cos*) bias • **cortar algo al ~** to cut sth on the bias
4 (*Téc*) bevel
5 (= *dirección*) direction • **ha tomado otro ~** it has taken a new turn
6* (= *truco*) dodge*
sésil ADJ sessile
sesión SF **1** (*Admin*) session • **abrir/levantar la ~** to open/close *o* adjourn the session • **celebrar una ~** to hold a session ▸ **sesión de preguntas al gobierno** ≈ question time ▸ **sesión parlamentaria** parliamentary session ▸ **sesión secreta** secret session
2 (= *espacio de tiempo*) (*para retrato*) sitting; (*para tratamiento médico*) session ▸ **sesión de entrenamiento** training session ▸ **sesión de espiritismo** séance ▸ **sesión de lectura de poesías** poetry reading ▸ **sesión de prestidigitación** conjuring show ▸ **sesión fotográfica** photo session
3 (*Cine*) showing; (*Teat*) show, performance • **la segunda ~** the second showing • **hay tres sesiones diarias** there are three showings a day ▸ **sesión continua** continuous showing
4 (*Inform*) session
sesionar ▹ CONJUG 1a VI (= *estar en sesión*) to be in session; (= *celebrar sesión*) to hold a meeting
seso SM **1** (*Anat*) brain
2 (= *inteligencia*) brains (*pl*), intelligence • MODISMOS: • **calentarse** *o* **devanarse los ~s** to rack one's brains • **eso le tiene sorbido el ~** he's crazy about it • **perder el ~** to go off one's head (**por** over)
3 sesos (*Culin*) brains
sesquicentenario SM 150th anniversary, sesquicentenary
sesquipedal ADJ sesquipedalian
sestear ▹ CONJUG 1a VI to take a siesta, have a nap
sesteo SM (*LAm*) siesta, nap
sesudamente ADV sensibly, wisely
sesudo ADJ **1** (= *sensato*) sensible, wise
2 (= *inteligente*) brainy
3 (*Cono Sur*) (= *terco*) stubborn, pig-headed
set SM (PL: **set** *o* **sets**) (*Dep*) set
set. ABR (= **setiembre**) Sept
seta SF mushroom ▸ **seta venenosa** toadstool
setecientos/as ADJ, PRON, SM (*gen*) seven hundred; (*ordinal*) seven hundredth • **en el ~** in the eighteenth century; ▹ **seiscientos**
setenta ADJ INV, PRON, SM (*gen*) seventy; (*ordinal*) seventieth • **los (años) ~** the seventies; ▹ **seis**
setentañero/a SM/F man/woman of about seventy, seventy-year-old
setentón/ona ADJ seventy-year-old, seventyish
SM/F man/woman of about seventy, seventy-year-old
setero/a ADJ mushroom (*antes de s*)
SM/F mushroom gatherer
setiembre SM = **septiembre**
seto SM **1** (= *cercado*) fence ▸ **seto vivo** hedge
2 (*Caribe*) (= *pared*) dividing wall, partition
setter [se'ter] SM (PL: **setters** [se'ter]) setter
SEU SM ABR (*Hist*) = **Sindicato Español Universitario**
seudo... PREF pseudo...
seudociencia SF pseudoscience
seudohistoria SF pseudohistory
seudónimo ADJ pseudonymous
SM (= *nombre falso*) pseudonym; (= *nombre artístico*) pen name
Seúl SM Seoul
s.e.u.o. ABR (= **salvo error u omisión**) E & OE
severamente ADV **1** (= *con dureza*) severely
2 (= *con austeridad*) sternly
severidad SF **1** (*en el trato*) severity
2 (= *austeridad*) sternness
severo ADJ **1** (= *riguroso*) [*persona*] severe, harsh; [*padre, profesor, disciplina*] strict; [*castigo, crítica*] harsh; [*estipulaciones*] stringent; [*condiciones*] harsh, stringent • **ser ~ con algn** to treat sb harshly
2 (= *duro*) [*invierno*] severe, hard; [*frío*] bitter
3 (= *austero*) [*vestido, moda*] severe; [*actitud*] stern
seviche SM = **cebiche**
Sevilla SF Seville
sevillanas SFPL **1** (= *melodía*) *popular Sevillian tune*
2 (= *baile*) *typical Sevillian dance*
sevillano/a ADJ, SM/F Sevillian
sexagenario/a ADJ sexagenarian, sixty-year-old
SM/F sexagenarian, man/woman in his/her sixties, sixty-year-old
sexagésimo ADJ, SM sixtieth; ▹ **sexto**
sexar ▹ CONJUG 1a VT to sex
sexenio SM (*esp Méx*) *six-year Presidential term of office*
sexería SF sex shop
sexi = **sexy**
sexismo SM sexism
sexista ADJ, SMF sexist
sexo SM **1** (*Bio*) sex • **el bello ~** the fair sex • **el ~ débil** the weaker sex • **el ~ femenino/masculino** the female/male sex • **el ~ fuerte** the stronger sex • **el ~ opuesto** the opposite sex • **de ambos ~s** of both sexes • **sin ~** sexless • MODISMO: • **hablar del ~ de los ángeles** to indulge in pointless discussion • **sería como discutir sobre el ~ de los ángeles** it would be a totally pointless discussion ▸ **sexo en grupo** group sex ▸ **sexo oral** oral sex ▸ **sexo seguro** safe sex
2 (= *órgano sexual*) [*de hombre*] penis, sexual organs (*pl*) (*frm*); [*de mujer*] vagina, sexual organs (*pl*) (*frm*)
sexofobia SF aversion to sex
sexología SF sexology
sexólogo/a SM/F sexologist
sex shop [sek'ʃop] SF (PL: **sex shops**) sex shop
sex symbol [sek'simβol] SMF (PL: **sex symbols**) sex symbol
sexta SF (*Mús*) sixth; ▹ **sexto**
sextante SM sextant
sexteto SM sextet
sextillizo/a SM/F sextuplet
sexto ADJ sixth • **Juan ~** John the sixth • **en el ~ piso** on the sixth floor • **en ~ lugar** in sixth place, sixth • **vigésimo ~** twenty-sixth • **una sexta parte** a sixth
SM (= *parte*) sixth • **dos ~s** two sixths; ▹ **sexta**
séxtuplo ADJ sixfold
sexual ADJ sexual, sex (*antes de s*) • **vida ~** sex life
sexualidad SF **1** (= *opción sexual*) sexuality
2 (*Bio*) sex • **determinar la ~ de** to determine the sex of
sexualmente ADV sexually • **ser acosado ~** to be sexually harassed, suffer (from) sexual harassment
sexy ADJ [*persona*] sexy; [*libro, escena*] erotic, titillating
SM sexiness, sex appeal
s.f. ABR (= **sin fecha**) n.d.
s/f ABR (*Com*) = **su favor**
SGAE SF ABR = **Sociedad General de Autores de España**
SGEL SF ABR = **Sociedad Española General de Librería**
SGML SM ABR (= **Standard Generalized Markup Language**) (*Inform*) SGML
SGR SF ABR = **sociedad de garantía recíproca**
sgte. ABR (= **siguiente**) foll., f
sgtes. ABR (= **siguientes**) foll., ff
shakespeariano ADJ Shakespearian
share [ʃear] SM (*TV*) audience share
shareware ['ʃerwer] SM INV (*Inform*) shareware
shiatsu ['sjatsu] SM shiatsu
shock [ʃok] SM (PL: **shock** *o* **shocks** [ʃok]) shock
shopping ['ʃopin] SM (*Arg, Uru*) shopping centre, shopping center (*EEUU*), shopping mall (*EEUU*)
short [ʃor] SM, **shorts** [ʃor] SMPL shorts
show [tʃo, ʃou] SM **1** (*Teat*) show
2‡ (= *jaleo*) fuss, bother • **menudo ~ montó** he made a great song-and-dance about it
3 (= *farsa*) farce, masquerade
si[1] CONJ **1** (*uso condicional*) if • **si lo quieres, te lo doy** if you want it I'll give it to you • **si lo sé, no te lo digo** I wouldn't have told you, if I'd known • **si tuviera dinero, lo compraría** if I had any money I would buy it • **si me lo hubiese pedido, se lo habría** *o* **hubiera dado** if he had asked me for it I would have given it to him • **si no** (*condición negativa*) if not; (*indicando alternativa*) otherwise, or (else) • **avisadme si no podéis venir** let me know if you can't come • **si no estudias, no aprobarás** you won't pass if you don't study, you won't pass unless you study • **ponte crema porque si no, te quemarás** put some cream on, otherwise *o* or (else) you'll get sunburned • **vete, si no, vas a llegar tarde** go, or (else) you'll be late • **llevo el paraguas por si (acaso) llueve** I've got my umbrella (just) in case it rains • **¿y si llueve?** what if it rains? • **¿y si se lo preguntamos?** why don't

S

we ask her?
2 (*en interrogativas indirectas*) whether • **no sé si hacerlo o no** I don't know whether to do it or not • **no sabía si habías venido en avión o en tren** I didn't know whether *o* if you'd come by plane or train • **me pregunto si vale la pena** I wonder whether *o* if it's worth it • **no sé si será verdad** I don't know whether *o* if it's true • **¿sabes si nos han pagado ya?** do you know if we've been paid yet?
3 (*uso concesivo*) • **no sé de qué te quejas, si eres una belleza** I don't know what you're complaining about when you're so beautiful • **si bien** although • **si bien creó un amplio consenso político ...** although it is true *o* while it may be true that he created a broad political consensus ...
4 (*uso desiderativo*) • **¡si fuera verdad!** if only it were true!, I wish it were true! • **¡si viniese pronto!** I wish he'd come!, if only he'd come!
5 (*indicando protesta*) but • **¡si no sabía que estabas allí!** but I didn't know you were there! • **¡si (es que) acabo de llamarte!** but I've only just phoned you! • **¡si tienes la tira de discos!** but you have loads of records!*
6 (*uso enfático*) • **¡si serán hipócritas!** they're such hypocrites!, they're so hypocritical! • **—es un pesado —¡si lo sabré yo!** "he's a pain" — "don't I know it!" *o* "you're telling me!" • **si lo sabré yo, que soy su mujer** I ought to know, I'm his wife • **que si engorda, que si perjudica a la salud ...** they say it's fattening and bad for your health • **que si lavar los platos, que si limpiar el suelo, que si ...** what with washing up and sweeping the floor and ...
7 (*indicando sorpresa*) • **¡pero si es el cartero!** why, it's the postman! • **¡pero si eres tú! no te había reconocido** oh, it's you, I didn't recognize you!

si² (SM) (*Mús*) B ▸ **si mayor** B major
sí¹ (ADV) **1** (*como respuesta*) yes • **—¿te gusta? —sí** "do you like it?" — "yes (I do)" • **un dedo en alto es que sí** if you put one finger up it means yes • **—¿sabes que me caso? —¿ah, sí?** "do you know I'm getting married?" — "really?" • **—el piso es bonito pero no tiene mucha luz —bueno, eso sí** "it's a nice flat but it's a bit dark" — "yes, that's true" • **sí pues** (*LAm*) of course
2 (*uso enfático*) **a** (*en oposición a una negación*) • **ellos no van pero nosotros sí** they're not going but we are • **él no quiere pero yo sí** he doesn't want to but I do • **no tiene hermanos, pero sí dos hermanas** he doesn't have any brothers but he does have two sisters • **—¿a que no eres capaz? —¿a que sí?** "I bet you can't" — "do you want a bet?"* • **—yo eso no me lo creo —¡que sí, hombre!** "I can't believe that" — "I'm telling you, it's true" • **un sábado sí y otro no** every other Saturday • **MODISMOS:** • **por sí o por no** in any case, just in case • **un sí es no es** somewhat • **resulta un sí es no es artificioso** it is somewhat contrived
b (*en oraciones afirmativas*) • **vimos que sí, que era el mismo hombre** we saw that it was indeed the same man • **ahí sí me duele** it definitely hurts there, that's where it hurts • **apenas tienen para comer, pero eso sí, el tabaco no les falta** they hardly have enough money for food, but they're certainly never short of cigarettes • **ya llevamos aquí una semana, ¿a que sí, Luisa?** we've been here a week now, isn't that right, Luisa? • **ella sí vendrá** she'll certainly come • **sí que:** • **pero nosotros sí que lo oímos** but we certainly heard it • **sí que me lo dijo** (yes) he did tell me • **¡pues sí que estoy yo para bromas!** (*iró*) this is a great time for jokes! • **eso sí que no:** • **me piden que traicione a mis amigos y eso sí que no*** they're asking me to betray my friends and that's just not on* • **—¿puedo hacer unas fotos? —¡ah, no, eso sí que no!** "can I take some photos?" — "no, absolutely not!" • **eso sí que no se puede aguantar** that is just unbearable, I just can't stand that • **MODISMO:** • **porque sí:** • **no se hacen ricos porque sí, sino a base de arriesgar mucho** they don't get rich just like that, they have to take a lot of risks • **no vamos a la huelga porque sí** we're not going on strike just for the sake of it • **—¿por qué yo? —pues porque sí** "why me?" — "(just) because!"
3 (*en oraciones subordinadas*) • **creo que sí** I think so • **—¿asistirá el presidente? —puede que sí** "will the president be there?" — "he might be" • **decir que sí** to say yes • **se lo pedimos y dijo que sí** we asked her and she agreed *o* she said yes • **dijo que sí con la cabeza** he nodded in agreement
(SM) **1** (= *consentimiento*) yes • **un sí rotundo** a definite yes • **todavía no tengo el sí por su parte** she hasn't said yes yet • **la propuesta obtuvo un sí abrumador** people voted overwhelmingly in favour of the proposal • **dar el sí** (*a una propuesta*) to say yes; (*en la boda*) to say "I do" • **le costó mucho dar el sí al proyecto** he found it hard to agree to the project • **MODISMO:** • **no tener ni un sí ni un no con algn:** • **nunca hemos tenido ni un sí ni un no** we've never had a cross word *o* the slightest disagreement
2 síes (= *votos*) votes in favour • **la mayoría necesaria era de 93 síes** a majority of 93 votes (in favour) was needed • **13 síes y 12 noes** 13 in favour and 12 against, 13 ayes and 12 noes
sí² (PRON) **1** (*uso reflexivo*) **a** (*de tercera persona*) (*referido a una persona*) himself/herself; (*referido a un objeto, concepto*) itself; (*en plural*) themselves • **no lo podrá hacer por sí solo** he won't be able to do it on his own *o* by himself • **sentía tras de sí los pasos de un hombre** she could hear the steps of a man following her • **tiene un currículum que para sí quisieran muchas actrices** she has a track record that many actresses would be envious of • **el producto en sí es inofensivo** the product itself is inoffensive • **sí mismo/a** (*referido a persona*) himself/herself; (*referido a objeto, concepto*) itself; (*uso impersonal*) yourself, oneself (*más frm*) • **aquí el escritor habla de sí mismo** here the writer is talking about himself • **vivía muy encerrada en sí misma** she was very wrapped up in herself *o* wrapped up in her own world • **ha puesto lo mejor de sí mismo en ese proyecto** he has given his all to the project • **la tierra gira sobre sí misma** the earth turns on itself • **es mejor aprender las cosas por sí mismo** it's better to learn things by yourself *o* oneself (*más frm*) • **sí mismos/as** themselves • **están muy seguros de sí mismos** they are very confident, they are very sure of themselves • **los datos hablan por sí mismos** the facts speak for themselves
b (*referido a usted*) (*en singular*) yourself; (*en plural*) yourselves • **sí mismo/a** yourself • **sí mismos/as** yourselves
c • **MODISMOS:** • **de por sí:** • **el problema ya es bastante difícil de por sí** the problem is difficult enough in itself *o* as it is • **él, de por sí, ya tiene mal carácter** he's got a really bad temper at the best of times • **estar en sí** to be in one's right mind • **estar fuera de sí** to be beside o.s. • **empezó a dar gritos fuera de sí** he started shouting hysterically • **estar sobre sí** to be on one's guard; ▸ **caber, volver**

SI

La conjunción **si** *se puede traducir al inglés por* **if** *o* **whether**; **si no** *se traduce por* **if not** *o* **unless**.

Si

▷ *Por regla general,* **si** *se traduce al inglés por* **if** *en las oraciones condicionales y por* **whether** *o* **if** *en las dubitativas:*

Si me has mentido te arrepentirás
If you have lied to me you'll regret it
Si tuviera mucho dinero me compraría un caballo
If I had lots of money, I'd buy myself a horse
No sé si me dejará quedarme
I don't know whether *o* if he'll let me stay

▷ **Si** *se puede traducir solo por* **whether**, *y nunca por* **if**, *cuando se presentan dos opciones a elegir, cuando va detrás de una preposición, delante de un infinitivo o de una oración interrogativa indirecta:*

No sé si ir a Canadá o a Estados Unidos
I can't decide whether to go to Canada or the United States
Quiero que hablemos de si deberíamos mandar a los niños a un colegio interno
I want to talk to you about whether we should send the children to boarding school
Todavía no tenemos muy claro si vamos a mudarnos o no
We still haven't made up our minds about whether to move or not

Si no

▷ **Si no** *generalmente se traduce al inglés por* **if not** *aunque, cuando en español se puede reemplazar por* **a no ser que**, *se puede utilizar también* **unless** *y cuando equivale a* **de lo contrario** *se emplea preferentemente* **otherwise** *o* **or else**:

Iría al cine más a menudo si no fuera tan caro
I would go to the cinema more often if it weren't so expensive
No te puedes quedar aquí si no pagas el alquiler
You can't stay here unless you pay your rent *o* You can't stay here if you don't pay your rent
Tenemos que estar allí antes de las diez; si no, vamos a tener problemas
We must be there by ten, otherwise *o* or else we'll be in trouble

Las oraciones del tipo **si hubieras/si no hubieras hecho algo ...** *se pueden traducir, en un registro más culto, omitiendo la partícula* **if** *e invirtiendo el orden del sujeto y el verbo auxiliar:*

Si hubieras estado aquí esto no habría ocurrido
Had you been here this would not have happened
Si no hubiese robado el dinero, ahora no estaría en la cárcel
Had he not stolen the money, he wouldn't be in prison now

Para otros usos y ejemplos ver la entrada.

S

2 • **entre sí:** • **son idénticos entre sí** they are identical to each other • **se repartieron la herencia entre sí** they shared (out) the inheritance among themselves • **las dos soluciones son incompatibles entre sí** the two solutions are mutually incompatible • **las dos ciudades distan entre sí 45km** the two cities are 45km apart

Siam SM Siam
siamés/esa ADJ, SM/F Siamese
sibarita ADJ sybaritic, luxury-loving
SMF sybarite, lover of luxury
sibarítico ADJ sybaritic, luxury-loving
sibaritismo SM sybaritism, love of luxury
Siberia SF Siberia
siberiano/a ADJ, SM/F Siberian
sibil SM **1** (= *cueva*) cave
2 (= *sótano*) vault, underground store
3 [*de trigo*] corn-storage pit
Sibila SF Sibyl
sibila SF sibyl
sibilante ADJ, SF sibilant
sibilino ADJ sibylline
sic ADV sic
sic... PREF = psic...
sicalipsis SF INV (= *erotismo*) eroticism, suggestiveness; (= *pornografía*) pornography
sicalíptico ADJ (= *erótico*) erotic, suggestive; (= *pornográfico*) pornographic
sicario SM hired killer, hitman*
sicav [si'kav] (= **sociedad de inversión de capital variable**) SICAV
Sicilia SF Sicily
siciliano/a ADJ, SM/F Sicilian
SM (= *dialecto*) Sicilian
sico... PREF = psico...
sicofanta SM, **sicofante** SM sycophant
sicomoro SM, **sicómoro** SM sycamore
sicote* SM (*LAm*) foot odour
SIDA SM ABR, **sida** SM ABR (= **síndrome de inmunodeficiencia adquirida**) AIDS
• ~ **declarado** full-blown AIDS
sidatorio SM AIDS clinic
SIDE SF ABR (*Arg*) (= **Secretaría de Inteligencia del Estado**) *Peronist secret service*
sidecar SM sidecar
sideral ADJ **1** (*Astron*) (= *de los astros*) astral; (= *del espacio exterior*) space (*antes de s*)
2 [*coste, precio*] astronomic
siderometalurgia SF iron and steel industry
siderometalúrgico ADJ iron and steel (*antes de s*)
siderurgia SF iron and steel industry
siderúrgica SF iron and steel works
siderúrgico ADJ iron and steel (*antes de s*)
sídico ADJ AIDS (*antes de s*)
sidoso/a ADJ AIDS (*antes de s*)
SM/F AIDS sufferer
sidra SF cider
sidrería SF cider bar
sidrero/a ADJ cider (*antes de s*)
SM/F cider maker
sidrina SF cider
siega SF **1** (= *acción*) (= *cosechar*) reaping, harvesting; (= *segar*) mowing
2 (= *época*) harvest, harvest time
siembra SF **1** (= *acción*) sowing • **patata de ~** seed potato
2 (= *época*) sowing time
siembre SM (*Caribe*) sowing
siempre ADV **1** (*indicando frecuencia*) always • **está ~ lloviendo** it's always raining • **una persona ~ dispuesta a ayudar** someone always ready to help • **como ~** as usual • **el día había empezado como ~** the day had begun as usual • **tú tan modesto como ~** (*iró*) modest as ever • **de ~** [*lugar, hora*] usual (*antes de s*) • **por favor, lo de ~** my usual, please • **protestan los de ~** it's the same people as usual protesting • **siguen con los mismos problemas de ~** they've still got the same old problems • **vino con el mismo cuento de ~** he came out with the same old story • **desde ~** always • **lo vienen haciendo así desde ~** they've always done it this way • **¡hasta ~!** farewell! • **para ~** forever, for good* • **se ha ido para ~** she has gone forever *o* for good* • **dijeron adiós para ~ a su país** they bade farewell to their country forever • **por ~** (*liter*) for ever • **por ~ jamás** for ever and ever
2 (= *en todo caso*) always • • **~ puedes decir que no lo sabías** you can always say you didn't know
3 (*LAm**) (= *todavía*) still • **¿~ se va mañana?** are you still going tomorrow?
4 (*esp Méx*) (= *definitivamente*) certainly, definitely • • **~ no me caso este año** I'm certainly *o* definitely not getting married this year • • **~ sí** certainly, of course
5 (*Chile*) (= *de todas maneras*) still • **lo tenían completamente rodeado y ~ se escapó** they had him completely surrounded but he still escaped • • **~ sí me voy** I'm going anyway
CONJ **1** • • **~ que** (= *cada vez*) whenever; (= *a condición de*) as long as, provided (that), providing (that) • **voy ~ que puedo** I go whenever I can • • **~ que salgo llueve** every time *o* whenever I go out it rains • **riéguelas ~ que sea necesario** water them whenever necessary • • **~ que él esté de acuerdo** as long as he agrees, provided (that) *o* providing (that) he agrees
2 • • **~ y cuando** as long as, provided (that), providing (that)
siempreverde ADJ evergreen
siempreviva SF houseleek
sien SF (*Anat*) temple
siena ADJ, SM INV (= *color*) sienna
siento *etc* ▸ **sentar, sentir**
sierpe SF snake, serpent
sierra SF **1** (= *herramienta*) saw ▸ **sierra circular** circular saw ▸ **sierra de arco** hacksaw ▸ **sierra de bastidor** frame saw, span saw ▸ **sierra de cadena** chainsaw ▸ **sierra de calados, sierra de calar** fretsaw ▸ **sierra de espigar** tenon saw ▸ **sierra de marquetería** fretsaw, coping saw ▸ **sierra de vaivén** jigsaw ▸ **sierra mecánica** power saw ▸ **sierra para metales** hacksaw
2 (*Geog*) mountain range, sierra • **la ~** (= *zona*) the hills, the mountains • **van a la ~ a pasar el fin de semana** they're off to the mountains for the weekend
3 (*Méx*) (= *pez*) swordfish
Sierra Leona SF Sierra Leone
siervo/a SM/F slave ▸ **siervo de Dios** servant of the Lord ▸ **siervo de la gleba** serf
siesta SF **1** (= *sueñecito*) siesta, nap • **la hora de la ~** siesta time (*after lunch*) • **dormir la** *o* **echarse una ~** to have an afternoon nap
2 (= *hora del día*) afternoon
siestecita SF nap, doze
siete[1] ADJ INV, PRON seven; (*ordinal, en la fecha*) seventh • **las ~** seven o'clock • **le escribí el día ~** I wrote to him on the seventh
• MODISMO: • **hablar más que ~** to talk nineteen to the dozen
SM **1** (= *número*) seven; ▸ **seis**
2 (= *roto*) • **hacerse un ~ en el pantalón** to tear one's trousers (*making an L-shaped tear*)
SF (*LAm*) • **¡la gran ~!*** wow!*, hell!* • **de la gran ~*** terrible*, tremendous* • **hijo de la gran ~**** bastard**, son of a bitch (*EEUU***)
siete[2]** SM (*LAm*) arsehole**, asshole (*EEUU***)
sietecueros SM INV (*LAm*) gumboil, whitlow
sietemesino/a ADJ [*niño*] two months premature
SM/F baby born two months premature
sífilis SF INV syphilis
sifilítico/a ADJ, SM/F syphilitic
sifón SM **1** (*Téc*) trap, U-bend
2 [*de agua*] siphon, syphon • **whisky con ~** whisky and soda
3 (*Geol*) flooded underground chamber
4 (*And*) (= *cerveza*) beer, bottled beer
sifrino ADJ (*Caribe*) stuck-up*, full of airs and graces
sig. ABR (= **siguiente**) f
siga SF (*Cono Sur*) pursuit • **ir a la ~ de algo** to chase after sth
sigilo SM (= *silencio*) stealth; (= *secreto*) secrecy • **con mucho ~** [*entrar, caminar*] very stealthily; [*reunirse, negociar*] amid great secrecy, with great secrecy ▸ **sigilo sacramental** secrecy of the confessional
sigilosamente ADV (= *silenciosamente*) stealthily; (= *secretamente*) secretly
sigiloso ADJ (= *silencioso*) stealth; (= *secreto*) secret
sigla SF (= *símbolo*) symbol; **siglas** (*pronunciadas como una palabra*) acronym (*sing*); (*pronunciadas individualmente*) abbreviation (*sing*)
siglo SM **1** (= *cien años*) century • **el jugador del ~** the player of the century • **los ~s medios** the Middle Ages • **por los ~s de los ~s** world without end, for ever and ever ▸ **Siglo de las Luces** Age of Enlightenment ▸ **siglo de oro** (*Mit*) golden age ▸ **Siglo de Oro** (*Literat*) Golden Age
2 (= *largo tiempo*) • **hace un ~** *o* **hace ~s que no le veo** I haven't seen him for ages
3 (*Rel*) • **el ~** the world • **retirarse del ~** to withdraw from the world
signar ▸ CONJUG 1a VT **1** (= *sellar*) to seal
2 (= *marcar*) to put one's mark on
3 (= *firmar*) to sign
4 (*Rel*) to make the sign of the Cross over
VPR **signarse** to cross o.s.
signatario/a ADJ, SM/F signatory
signatura SF **1** (*Mús, Tip*) signature
2 [*de biblioteca*] catalogue number, catalog number (EEUU), press mark
significación SF **1** (= *importancia*) significance
2 (= *sentido*) meaning
significado ADJ well-known
SM **1** [*de palabra*] meaning • **su ~ principal es ...** its chief meaning is ... • **una palabra de ~ dudoso** a word of uncertain meaning
2 (= *importancia*) significance
significante ADJ (*esp LAm*) significant
SM (*Ling*) signifier
significar ▸ CONJUG 1g VT **1** (= *querer decir*) [*palabra*] to mean; [*suceso*] to mean, signify • **¿qué significa "freelance"?** what does "freelance" mean?
2 (= *representar*) • **50 dólares significan muy poco para él** 50 dollars doesn't mean much to him • **él no significa nada para mí** he means nothing to me • **~á la ruina de la empresa** it will mean the end for the company • **él no significa gran cosa en estos asuntos** he doesn't count for much in these matters
3 (= *expresar*) to make known, express (**a** to) • **le significó la condolencia de la familia** he expressed *o* conveyed the family's sympathy
VPR **significarse 1** (= *distinguirse*) to become known, distinguish o.s. (**como** as)
2 (= *tomar partido*) to declare o.s., take sides • **no ~se** to refuse to take sides
significativamente ADV (= *considerablemente*) significantly; (= *expresivamente*) meaningfully
significativo ADJ **1** [*cambio, detalle, desarrollo*] significant • **es ~ que ...** it is

S

significant that ... • **calcularlo a tres cifras significativas** to work it out to three significant figures
2 [*mirada*] meaningful
signo SM **1** (= *señal*) (*gen*) sign; (*Mat*) sign, symbol • **ese apetito es ~ de buena salud** such an appetite is a sign of good health ▸ **signo de admiración** exclamation mark, exclamation point (EEUU) ▸ **signo de interrogación** question mark ▸ **signo de la cruz** sign of the Cross ▸ **signo de la victoria** victory sign, V-sign ▸ **signo de sumar** plus sign ▸ **signo igual** equals sign, equal sign (EEUU) ▸ **signo lingüístico** linguistic sign ▸ **signo más** plus sign ▸ **signo menos** minus sign ▸ **signo postal** postage stamp ▸ **signos de puntuación** punctuation marks
2 (= *carácter*) • **un ~ de los tiempos** a sign of the times • **una estrategia de ~ modernizador** a modernizing strategy • **invirtieron el ~ de la tendencia** they reversed the trend
3 (*tb* **signo del zodíaco**) star sign • **¿de qué ~ es Carmen?** what (star) sign is Carmen?
sigo *etc* ▹ **seguir**
sigs. ABR (= **siguientes**) ff
siguiente ADJ next, following • **el ~ vuelo** the next flight • **¡que pase el ~, por favor!** next please! • **el** *o* **al día ~** the following *o* next day • **dijo lo ~** he said the following
sij ADJ, SMF (PL: **sijs**) Sikh
sijolaj SM (*CAm*) (*Mús*) clay whistle, type of ocarina
sílaba SF syllable
silabario SM spelling book
silabear ▹ CONJUG 1a VT (= *dividir en sílabas*) to divide into syllables; (= *pronunciar*) to pronounce syllable by syllable
silabeo SM division into syllables
silábico ADJ syllabic
silba SF hissing, catcalls (*pl*) • **armar** *o* **dar una ~ (a)** to hiss
silbar ▹ CONJUG 1a VT **1** (*Mús*) [+ *melodía*] to whistle
2 [+ *comedia, orador*] to hiss
VI **1** [*persona*] (*con los labios*) to whistle; (*al respirar*) to wheeze
2 [*viento*] to whistle; [*bala, flecha*] to whistle, whizz
3 (*Teat*) to hiss, boo
silbatina SF (*And, Cono Sur*) hissing, booing
silbato SM whistle
silbido SM, **silbo** SM **1** [*de persona*] (*con los labios*) whistle, whistling; (*al respirar*) wheezing
2 (= *zumbido*) hum ▸ **silbido de oídos** ringing in the ears
3 (= *abucheo*) hissing
silenciador SM silencer, muffler (EEUU)
silenciamiento SM [*de oposición*] silencing; [*de suceso*] hushing up
silenciar ▹ CONJUG 1b VT **1** [+ *suceso*] to hush up; [+ *hecho*] to keep silent about
2 [+ *persona*] to silence
3 (*Téc*) to silence
VPR **silenciarse** • **se silenció el asunto** the matter was hushed up • **se silenció su labor** his work was kept secret
silencio SM **1** (= *falta de ruido*) silence • **¡silencio!** silence!, quiet! • **¡~ en la sala!** silence in court! • **nos escribió tras dos años de ~** after two years' silence she wrote to us • **un poco de ~, por favor** let's have a bit of quiet, please • **¡qué ~ hay aquí!** it's so quiet here! • **había un ~ sepulcral** it was deadly silent, there was a deathly silence • **en ~** in silence • **la casa estaba en ~** the house was silent • **en el ~ más absoluto** in dead silence • **guardar ~** to keep silent, keep quiet • **guardar un minuto de ~** to observe a one-minute *o* a minute's silence • **imponer ~ a algn** (*frm*) to make sb be quiet • **mantenerse en ~** to keep quiet, remain silent • **pasar una pena en ~** to suffer in silence • **reducir al ~** (*frm*) to silence, reduce to silence • **romper el ~** (*frm*) to break the silence ▸ **silencio administrativo** administrative silence
2 (*Mús*) rest
ADJ (*And, CAm, Méx*) (= *silencioso*) silent, quiet; (= *tranquilo*) still
silenciosamente ADV silently, quietly, noiselessly
silencioso ADJ [*persona*] silent, quiet; [*máquina*] silent, noiseless
silense ADJ (*Esp*) of Silos, of Santo Domingo de Silos
silente ADJ silent, noiseless
sílex SM silex, flint
sílfide SF sylph
silfo SM sylph
silicato SM silicate
sílice SF silica
silíceo ADJ siliceous
silicio SM silicon
silicona SF silicone
silicosis SF INV silicosis
silla SF **1** (= *asiento*) seat, chair • **política de la ~ vacía** policy of the empty chair, policy of not taking one's seat (*in parliament etc*)
• MODISMO: • **calentar la ~** to stay too long, outstay one's welcome ▸ **silla alta** high chair ▸ **silla de balanza, silla de hamaca** (*LAm*) rocking chair ▸ **silla de manos** sedan chair ▸ **silla de paseo** (*para bebé*) pushchair, stroller (EEUU) ▸ **silla de ruedas** wheelchair ▸ **silla de seguridad** child (safety) seat (*for car*) ▸ **silla de tijera** folding chair ▸ **silla eléctrica** electric chair ▸ **silla giratoria** swivel chair ▸ **silla plegable** folding chair
2 (*tb* **silla de montar**) saddle
sillar SM block of stone, ashlar
sillería SF **1** (= *asientos*) chairs (*pl*), set of chairs; (*Rel*) choir stalls (*pl*); (*Teat*) seating
2 (= *taller*) chair-maker's workshop
3 (*Arquit*) masonry, ashlar work
sillero/a SM/F (= *artesano*) chair-maker
SM (*Cono Sur*) (= *caballo*) horse, mule
silleta SF **1** (= *silla pequeña*) small chair
2 (*LAm*) (= *silla*) seat, chair; (= *taburete*) low stool
3 (*Med*) bedpan
sillico SM chamber pot
sillín SM saddle
sillita SF small chair ▸ **sillita de niño** pushchair, stroller (EEUU)
sillón SM **1** (= *butaca*) armchair, easy chair; (*LAm*) (= *mecedora*) rocking chair ▸ **sillón de dentista** dentist's chair ▸ **sillón de hamaca** (*LAm*) rocking chair ▸ **sillón de lona** deck chair ▸ **sillón de orejas** wing chair ▸ **sillón de ruedas** wheelchair ▸ **sillón orejero** wing chair
2 [*de montar*] sidesaddle
silo SM **1** (*Agr*) silo
2 (*Mil*) silo, bunker
3 (= *sótano*) underground store
4 (= *depósito*) storage pit
silogismo SM syllogism
silogístico ADJ syllogistic
silueta SF **1** (= *contorno*) silhouette • **se adivinaba una ~ detrás de la cortina** you could make out a silhouette *o* figure behind the curtain • **la ~ del castillo se recortaba sobre el horizonte** the castle was silhouetted against the horizon
2 (= *tipo*) figure • **un bañador que realza la ~** a swimsuit that shows off your figure
3 (*Arte*) silhouette, outline drawing • **en ~** in silhouette
siluetear ▹ CONJUG 1a VT (*lit*) to outline; (*fig*) to shape, mould, mold (EEUU)
silvático ADJ = **selvático**
silvestre ADJ **1** (*Bot*) wild
2 (= *agreste*) rustic, rural
silvicultor(a) SM/F forestry expert
silvicultura SF forestry
SIM SM ABR (*Esp*) = **Servicio de Investigación Militar**
sima SF **1** (= *abismo*) abyss, chasm
2 (= *grieta*) deep fissure
Simbad SM Sinbad ▸ **Simbad el marino** Sinbad the sailor
simbiosis SF INV symbiosis
simbiótico ADJ symbiotic
simbólicamente ADV symbolically
simbólico ADJ [*momento, papel*] symbolic; [*cantidad, gesto, pago, huelga*] token
simbolismo SM symbolism
simbolista ADJ, SMF symbolist
simbolizar ▹ CONJUG 1f VT to symbolize
símbolo SM symbol ▸ **símbolo de la fe, símbolo de los apóstoles** Creed ▸ **símbolo de prestigio** status symbol ▸ **símbolo gráfico** (*Inform*) icon
simbología SF **1** (= *símbolos*) symbols (*pl*), system of symbols
2 (= *estudio*) study of symbols
simbombo ADJ (*Caribe*) cowardly
simetría SF **1** (= *igualdad*) symmetry
2 (= *armonía*) harmony
simétricamente ADV **1** (= *con igualdad*) symmetrically
2 (= *con armonía*) harmoniously
simétrico ADJ **1** (= *igual*) symmetrical
2 (= *armonioso*) harmonious
simetrizar ▹ CONJUG 1f VT **1** [+ *forma*] to make symmetrical
2 (= *armonizar*) to bring into line, harmonize
símico ADJ = **simiesco**
simiente SF seed
simiesco ADJ simian
símil ADJ similar
SM **1** (= *comparación*) comparison
2 (*Literat*) simile
similar ADJ similar (**a** to)
similaridad SF = **similitud**
similitud SF similarity, resemblance
similor SM pinchbeck • **de ~** pinchbeck, showy but valueless
simiñaca SF (*Caribe*) tangle, mess
simio SM ape, simian (*frm*)
Simón SM Simon
simonía SF simony
simpatía SF **1** (= *afecto*) • **son muestras de ~ hacia** *o* **por la víctima** it's a show of sympathy towards the victim • **coger ~ a algn** to take a liking to sb • **ganarse la ~ de todos** to win everybody's affection • **tener ~ a algn** • **sentir ~ hacia** *o* **por algn** to like sb • **no le tenemos ~ en absoluto** we don't like him at all • **no tiene ~s en el colegio** nobody at school likes him • **~s y antipatías** likes and dislikes
2 (= *cordialidad*) friendly nature, friendliness • **su ~ nos cautivó** we were charmed by her friendly nature *o* friendliness • **la famosa ~ andaluza** that famous Andalusian friendliness • **tener (mucha) ~** to be (very) likeable *o* nice
3 **simpatías** (*Pol*) sympathies • **sus ~s se decantan por los socialistas** his sympathies lie with the socialists
4 (*Fís, Med*) sympathy • **explosión por ~** secondary explosion
simpático ADJ **1** (= *afectuoso*) [*persona*] nice, pleasant, likeable; [*ambiente*] congenial, pleasant • **¡qué policía más ~!** what a nice policeman! • **estuvo muy simpática con todos** she was very nice to everybody • **los cubanos son muy ~s** Cubans are very nice *o*

friendly people • **no le hemos caído muy ~s** she didn't really take to us, she didn't really like us • **siempre procura hacerse el ~** he's always trying to ingratiate himself • **me cae ~** I think he's nice, I like him • **me es ~ ese muchacho** I like that lad
2 (*Anat, Med*) sympathetic

simpatiquísimo (ADJ) *superl de* **simpático**

simpatizante (SMF) sympathizer (**de** with)

simpatizar ▸ CONJUG 1f (VI) **1** [*dos personas*] to get on, get on well together • **pronto ~on** they soon became friends
2 • **~ con algn** to get on well with *o* take to sb

simplada (SF) (*And, CAm*) (= *cualidad*) simplicity, stupidity; (= *acto*) stupid thing, stupid thing to do *o* to say

simple (ADJ) **1** (= *sin adornos*) [*peinado, objeto*] simple; [*vestido, decoración*] plain
2 [*método*] simple, easy, straightforward
3 (*antes de sustantivo*) (= *mero*) mere • **por ~ descuido** through sheer carelessness • **es cosa de una ~ plumada** it's a matter of a mere stroke of the pen • **somos ~s aficionados** we're just amateurs
4 (*antes de sustantivo*) (= *corriente*) ordinary • **es un ~ abogado** he's only *o* just a solicitor • **un ~ soldado** an ordinary soldier
5 [*persona*] (= *sin complicaciones*) simple; (= *crédulo*) gullible; (*pey*) (= *de pocas luces*) simple-minded
6 (*Ling, Quím*) simple
7 (*Bot*) single
(SMF) (= *persona*) simpleton
(SMPL) **simples** (*Tenis*) singles; (*Bot*) simples

simplemente (ADV) simply, just • **~ tendrás que aceptarlo** you'll simply *o* just have to accept it • **~ pretendía ayudarte** I was only *o* just trying to help you • **~ te llamaba para confirmar la cita** I was just calling to confirm our date • **eso se arregla ~ diciéndole que no** the simple solution to that is to say no to him, that's easily solved by saying no to him

simpleza (SF) **1** [*de persona*] (= *cualidad mental*) simpleness; (= *credulidad*) gullibility; (= *necedad*) simple-mindedness
2 (= *acto*) silly thing, silly thing to do/say • **se contenta con cualquier ~** she's happy with any little thing • **se enojó por una ~** he got annoyed over nothing *o* over some silly little thing • **eso son ~s** that's nonsense

simplicidad (SF) simplicity, simpleness

simplificable (ADJ) simplifiable

simplificación (SF) simplification

simplificado (ADJ) simplified

simplificar ▸ CONJUG 1g (VT) to simplify

simplista (ADJ) simplistic

simplón/ona (ADJ) simple, gullible
(SM/F) simple soul, gullible person

simplote/a (ADJ), (SM/F) = **simplón**

simposio (SM) symposium

simulación (SF) **1** (= *representación*) simulation ▸ **simulación por ordenador** computer simulation
2 (= *fingimiento*) pretence, pretense (*EEUU*)

simulacro (SM) **1** (= *fingimiento*) sham, pretence, pretense (*EEUU*) ▸ **un simulacro de ataque** simulated attack, mock attack ▸ **un simulacro de combate** mock battle ▸ **simulacro de incendio** fire practice, fire drill ▸ **simulacro de salvamento** (*Náut*) boat drill
2 (= *apariencia*) semblance

simulado (ADJ) (= *representado*) simulated; (= *fingido*) feigned

simulador (SM) ▸ **simulador de vuelo** flight simulator

simular ▸ CONJUG 1a (VT) **1** [+ *ataque, robo*] to simulate
2 (= *fingir*) to feign, sham • **simuló ser hermano del director** he pretended to be the director's brother

simultáneamente (ADV) simultaneously

simultanear ▸ CONJUG 1a (VT) • **~ dos cosas** to do two things simultaneously • **~ A con B** to fit in A and B at the same time, combine A with B

simultaneidad (SF) simultaneousness

simultáneo (ADJ) simultaneous

simún (SM) simoom

sin (PREP) **1** (*seguido de sustantivo, pronombre*) without • **¿puedes abrirla sin llave?** can you open it without a key? • **lo hice sin la ayuda de nadie** I did it without anybody's help • **llevamos diez meses sin noticias** it's been ten months since we've had any news, we've been ten months without news • **parejas jóvenes, sin hijos** young couples with no children • **cerveza sin alcohol** alcohol-free beer, non-alcoholic beer • **un producto sin disolventes** a solvent-free product • **un vestido sin tirantes** a strapless dress • **los sin techo** the homeless • **un hombre sin escrúpulos** an unscrupulous man • **agua mineral sin gas** still mineral water • **estar sin algo**: • **estuvimos varias horas sin luz** we had no electricity for several hours • **estoy sin dinero** I've got no money • **quedarse sin algo** (= *terminarse*) to run out of sth; (= *perder*) to lose sth • **me he quedado sin cerillas** I've run out of matches • **se ha quedado sin trabajo** he's lost his job ▸ **sin papeles** (*SMF*) illegal immigrant
2 (= *no incluyendo*) not including, excluding • **ese es el precio de la bañera sin los grifos** that is the price of the bath, excluding *o* not including the taps • **cuesta 550 euros, sin IVA** it costs 550 euros, exclusive of VAT *o* not including VAT
3 (+ *infin*) **a** (*indicando acción*) • **se fueron sin despedirse** they left without saying goodbye • **murió sin haber hecho testamento** he died without having made a will • **nos despedimos, no sin antes recordarles que ...** (*TV*) before saying goodnight we'd like to remind you that ... • **no me gusta estar sin hacer nada** I don't like having nothing to do, I don't like doing nothing
b (*indicando continuidad*) • **son las doce y el cartero sin venir** it's twelve o'clock and the postman still hasn't come • **llevan mucho tiempo sin hablarse** they haven't spoken to each other for a long time • **llevamos dos meses sin cobrar** we haven't been paid for two months • **seguir sin**: • **las camas seguían sin hacer** the beds still hadn't been made • **sigo sin entender para qué sirven** I still don't understand what they are for
c (*tras sustantivo pasivo*) • **un montón de recibos sin pagar** a pile of unpaid bills
4 • **sin que** (+ *subjun*) without • **salieron sin que nadie se diera cuenta** they left without anyone realizing • **sin que él lo sepa** without him knowing, without his knowing • **no lo haré sin que me lo pidan** I won't do it unless they ask me to
(SF) (= *cerveza sin alcohol*) alcohol-free beer

sinagoga (SF) synagogue

Sinaí (SM) Sinai

sinalefa (SF) elision

sinalefar ▸ CONJUG 1a (VT) to elide

sinapismo (SM) **1** (*Med*) mustard plaster • **hay que ponerle un ~*** he needs gingering up
2 (= *persona*) (*aburrido*) bore; (*fastidioso*) nuisance, pest

sinarquismo (SM) (*Méx*) Sinarquism (*Mexican fascist movement of the 1930s*)

sinarquista (SMF) (*Méx*) Sinarquist

sinceramente (ADV) sincerely

sincerarse ▸ CONJUG 1a (VPR) (= *justificarse*) to vindicate o.s.; (= *decir la verdad*) to tell the truth, be honest • **~ a** *o* **con** to be honest with, level with • **~ ante el juez** to justify one's conduct to the judge • **~ de su conducta** to explain *o* justify one's conduct

sinceridad (SF) sincerity • **no pongo en duda su ~** I don't doubt her sincerity • **respóndeme con ~** please answer honestly • **dime con toda ~ lo que piensas de ella** tell me in all honesty what you think of her • **con toda ~, me parece un libro pésimo** to be quite honest *o* in all sincerity, I think it's a terrible book

sincero (ADJ) sincere • **es muy ~** he's very sincere • **ser ~ con algn** to be honest with sb • **si quieres que te sea ~, no estoy en absoluto de acuerdo** if you want my honest opinion, I don't agree at all • **reciba nuestro más ~ pésame** (*frm*) please accept our deepest sympathies *o* our heartfelt condolences

síncopa (SF) **1** (*Ling*) syncope
2 (*Mús*) syncopation

sincopado (ADJ) syncopated

sincopar ▸ CONJUG 1a (VT) to syncopate

síncope (SM) **1** (*Ling*) syncope
2 (*Med*) syncope (*frm*) • **casi le da un ~ cuando lo vio** she nearly fainted when she saw it

sincopizarse ▸ CONJUG 1f (VPR) to have a blackout

sincretismo (SM) syncretism

sincronía (SF) synchrony

sincrónico (ADJ) **1** (*Téc*) synchronized
2 [*sucesos*] simultaneous
3 (*Ling*) synchronic

sincronismo (SM) (= *correspondencia*) (*gen*) synchronism; [*de sucesos*] simultaneity; [*de fechas*] coincidence

sincronización (SF) synchronization

sincronizadamente (ADV) simultaneously

sincronizador (SM) timer

sincronizar ▸ CONJUG 1f (VT) to synchronize (**con** with)

síncrono (ADJ) synchronous

sincrotrón (SM) synchrotron

sindicación (SF) **1** [*de obreros*] unionization
2 (*Prensa*) syndication
3 (*LAm*) (*Jur*) charge, accusation

sindical (ADJ) union (*antes de s*), trade-union (*antes de s*)

sindicalismo (SM) trade unionism, trades unionism

sindicalista (ADJ) union (*antes de s*), trade-union (*antes de s*)
(SMF) trade unionist, trades unionist

sindicalizar ▸ CONJUG 1f (VT) to unionize
(VPR) **sindicalizarse** to form a union

sindicar ▸ CONJUG 1g (VT) **1** [+ *trabajadores*] to unionize
2 (*LAm*) to charge, accuse
(VPR) **sindicarse** [*trabajador*] to join a trade(s) union; [*trabajadores*] to form a trade(s) union

sindicato (SM) **1** [*de trabajadores*] trade union, trades union, labor union (*EEUU*) ▸ **sindicato amarillo** yellow union, *conservative union that is in the pocket of the management* • **el problema de los ~s amarillos** the problem of company unionism ▸ **sindicato charro** (*Méx*) *conservative union that is in the pocket of the management*
2 [*de negociantes*] syndicate • MODISMO: • **casarse por el ~*** to have a shotgun wedding

sindicatura (SF) syndicate

síndico (SM) [*de organización*] trustee; (*en caso de bancarrota*) receiver, official receiver

síndrome (SM) syndrome ▸ **síndrome de**

abstinencia withdrawal symptoms (*pl*) ▸ **síndrome de Down** Down's syndrome ▸ **síndrome de Estocolmo** Stockholm syndrome ▸ **síndrome de fatiga crónica** chronic fatigue syndrome, ME ▸ **síndrome de la clase turista** economy-class syndrome ▸ **síndrome de (la) falsa memoria** false memory syndrome ▸ **síndrome de Ménière** Ménière's syndrome, Ménière's disease ▸ **síndrome premenstrual** premenstrual syndrome, premenstrual tension ▸ **síndrome tóxico** poisoning

sinécdoque SF synecdoche

sinecura SF sinecure

sine die ADV sine die

sine qua non ADJ • **condición ~** sine qua non

sinergía SF synergy

sinestesia SF synaesthesia, synesthesia (EEUU)

sinfín SM = **sinnúmero**

sinfonía SF symphony

sinfónico ADJ symphonic • **orquesta sinfónica** symphony orchestra

sinfonieta SF sinfonietta

sinfonola SF (*LAm*) jukebox

Singapur SM Singapore

singar ▸ CONJUG 1h VT (*Caribe*‡) to pester, annoy
VI (*CAm, Caribe***) to fuck**, screw**

singladura SF **1** (*Náut*) (= *recorrido*) day's run; (= *día*) nautical day
2 (*Pol*) course, direction

single SM **1** (*Mús*) single
2 singles (*Tenis*) singles

singlista SMF (*LAm*) singles player

singón SM (*Caribe, Méx*) womanizer, philanderer

singuisarra* SF (*And, Caribe*) row, racket

singular ADJ **1** (*Ling*) singular
2 • **combate ~** single combat
3 (= *destacado*) outstanding, exceptional
4 (= *raro*) singular, odd
SM (*Ling*) singular • **en ~** (*lit*) in the singular; (*fig*) in particular • **se refiere a él en ~** it refers to him in particular • **que hable él en ~** let him speak for himself

singularidad SF singularity, peculiarity

singularizar ▸ CONJUG 1f VT to single out
VPR **singularizarse** (= *distinguirse*) to distinguish o.s., stand out; (= *llamar la atención*) to be conspicuous • **~se con algn** to single sb out for special treatment

singularmente ADV **1** (= *extrañamente*) singularly, peculiarly
2 (= *especialmente*) especially

sinhueso* SF tongue • MODISMO: • **soltar la ~** to shoot one's mouth off*

siniestra SF left hand • **a mi ~** on my left

siniestrado/a ADJ damaged, wrecked, crashed • **la zona siniestrada** the affected area, the disaster zone
SM/F victim

siniestralidad SF accident rate

siniestro ADJ **1** (= *malintencionado*) [*intenciones, personaje*] sinister; [*mirada*] evil
2 (= *desgraciado*) [*día, viaje*] fateful; [*coincidencia*] unfortunate
3 (*liter*) (= *izquierdo*) left
SM (= *desastre natural*) disaster; (= *accidente*) accident ▸ **siniestro marítimo** disaster at sea ▸ **siniestro nuclear** nuclear disaster ▸ **siniestro total** total write-off • **fue declarado ~ total** it was declared a total write-off

sinnúmero SM • **un ~ de** no end of, countless

sino[1] SM fate, destiny

sino[2] CONJ **1** (= *pero*) but • **no son ocho ~ nueve** there are not eight but nine • **no lo hace solo para sí ~ para todos** he's not doing it only for himself but for everybody • **no solo ..., sino ...** not only ..., but ... • **no cabe otra solución ~ que vaya él** the only answer is that he should go
2 (= *salvo*) except, save • **todos aplaudieron ~ él** everybody except him applauded • **no lo habría dicho ~ en broma** he could only have said it jokingly, he wouldn't have said it except as a joke
3 (= *únicamente*) only • **¿quién ~ él se habría atrevido?** only he would have dared! • **no te pido ~ una cosa** I ask only *o* but one thing of you

sino... PREF Chinese ..., Sino...

sínodo SM synod

sinología SF Sinology

sinólogo/a SM/F Sinologist

sinonimia SF synonymy

sinónimo ADJ synonymous (**de** with)
SM synonym

sinopsis SF INV synopsis

sinóptico ADJ synoptic, synoptical • **cuadro ~** diagram, chart

sinovial ADJ synovial

sinovitis SF INV ▸ **sinovitis del codo** tennis elbow

sinrazón SF wrong, injustice

sinsabor SM **1** (= *disgusto*) trouble, unpleasantness
2 (= *dolor*) sorrow
3 (= *preocupación*) uneasiness, worry

sinsentido SM absurdity

sinsilico* ADJ (*Méx*) stupid, thick*

sinsonte SM (*CAm, Méx*) mockingbird

sinsustancia* SMF idiot

sintáctico ADJ syntactic, syntactical

sintagma SM syntagma, syntagm

sintagmático ADJ (*Gram*) syntagmatic

Sintasol® SM vinyl floor covering

sintaxis SF INV syntax

síntesis SF INV **1** (= *resumen*) summary • **en ~** (*frm*) in short
2 (*Bio, Quím*) synthesis
3 (*Fil*) synthesis
4 (*Inform*) synthesis ▸ **síntesis del habla** voice synthesis, speech synthesis

sintéticamente ADV synthetically

sintético ADJ synthetic

sintetizado ADJ synthesized

sintetizador SM synthesizer ▸ **sintetizador de la voz humana**, **sintetizador de voz** voice synthesizer, speech synthesizer

sintetizar ▸ CONJUG 1f VT **1** (*Quím, Mús*) to synthesize
2 (= *resumir*) to summarize

sintiendo *etc* ▸ **sentir**

sintoísmo SM Shintoism

síntoma SM **1** (*Med*) symptom
2 (= *señal*) sign, indication

sintomático ADJ symptomatic

sintomatizar ▸ CONJUG 1f VT to typify, characterize, be symptomatic of

sintomatología SF symptomatology

sintonía SF **1** (*Radio*) [*del dial*] tuning
2 (*Radio*) (= *melodía*) signature tune • **estén atentos a nuestra ~** stay tuned
3 (*entre personas*) • **estar en ~ con algn** to be in tune with sb

sintonización SF tuning

sintonizado SM tuning

sintonizador SM tuner

sintonizar ▸ CONJUG 1f VT **1** (*Radio*) [+ *estación, emisión*] to tune to, tune in to
2 (*Cine*) to synchronize
3 (*Elec*) to syntonize
VI • **~ con** to be in tune with, be on the same wavelength as

sinuosidad SF **1** (= *cualidad*) sinuosity (*liter*), intricacy
2 (= *curva*) curve • **las ~es del camino** the windings of the road, the twists and turns of the road
3 [*de persona, actitud*] deviousness

sinuoso ADJ **1** (= *con curvas*) [*camino*] winding, sinuous; [*línea, raya*] wavy; [*rumbo*] devious
2 [*persona, actitud*] devious

sinusitis SF INV sinusitis

sinvergonzón‡ SM rotter*, swine‡

sinvergüencería SF **1** (= *acción*) dirty trick*
2 (= *descaro*) shamelessness

sinvergüenza ADJ (= *pillo*) rotten; (= *descarado*) brazen, shameless
SMF (= *pillo*) scoundrel, rogue; (= *canalla*) rotter*; (= *insolente*) cheeky devil
• **¡sinvergüenza!** (*hum*) you villain! • **es una ~** she's a cheeky devil

sinvergüenzada* SF (*LAm*) rotten thing*, rotten thing to do*

sinvergüenzura SF (*LAm*) shamelessness

Sión SM Zion

sionismo SM Zionism

sionista ADJ, SMF Zionist

síper SM (*CAm, Méx, Ven*) zip (*Brit*), zipper (*EEUU*)

sipo ADJ (*And*) pockmarked

sipotazo SM (*CAm*) slap

siqu... PREF ▸ **psiqu...** (*p.ej.*) • **siquiatría** ▸ **psiquiatría**

siquiera ADV **1** (= *al menos*) at least • **una vez ~** once at least, just once • **deja ~ trabajar a los demás** at least let the others work • **dame un abrazo ~** at least give me a hug • **~ come un poquito** at least eat a bit
2 (*en frases negativas*) • **ni ~ me dio las gracias** he didn't even say thank you, he didn't so much as say thank you • **ni me miró ~** • **ni ~ me miró** she didn't even look at me • **ni él ~ vino** not even he came
CONJ **1** (= *aunque*) even if, even though • **ven ~ sea por pocos días** do come even if it's only for a few days
2 • **~ venga, ~ no venga** whether he comes or not

Siracusa SF Syracuse

sirena SF **1** (*Mit*) siren, mermaid ▸ **sirena de la playa** bathing beauty
2 (= *bocina*) siren, hooter ▸ **sirena de buque** ship's siren ▸ **sirena de niebla** foghorn

sirga SF towrope

sirgar ▸ CONJUG 1h VT to tow

sirgo SM twisted silk, piece of twisted silk

Siria SF Syria

sirimba SF (*Caribe*) faint, fainting fit

sirimbo ADJ (*Caribe*) silly

sirimbombo ADJ (*Caribe*) (= *débil*) weak; (= *tímido*) timid

sirimiri SM drizzle

siringa SF **1** (*LAm*) rubber tree
2 (*And*) panpipes (*pl*)

siringal SM (*LAm*) rubber plantation

Sirio SM Sirius

sirio/a ADJ, SM/F Syrian

sirla‡ SF **1** (= *arma*) chiv‡, knife
2 (= *atraco*) holdup, stick-up‡

sirlero/a‡ SM/F mugger

siró SM (*Caribe*) syrup

siroco SM sirocco

sirope SM (*LAm*) syrup

sirsaca SF seersucker

sirte SF shoal, sandbank

sirviendo *etc* ▸ **servir**

sirviente/a SM/F servant

sisa SF **1** (= *robo*) (*gen*) petty theft; [*de criado*] dishonest profit (*made by a servant*)
• **~s** pilfering (*sing*), petty thieving (*sing*)
2 (= *tajada*) cut, percentage*
3 (*Cos*) (*gen*) dart; (*para la manga*) armhole

sisal SM sisal

sisar ▷ CONJUG 1a VT **1** (= *robar*) to thieve, pilfer
2 (= *engañar*) to cheat
3 (*Cos*) to take in

sisear ▷ CONJUG 1a VT, VI to hiss

siseo SM hiss, hissing

Sísifo SM Sisyphus

sísmico ADJ seismic

sismo SM (*esp LAm*) = **seísmo**

sismografía SF seismography

sismógrafo SM seismograph

sismología SF seismology

sismológico ADJ seismological

sismólogo/a SM/F seismologist

sisón¹/ona ADJ thieving, light-fingered
SM/F petty thief

sisón² SM (*Orn*) little bustard

sistema SM **1** (= *conjunto ordenado*) system ▸ **sistema binario** (*Inform*) binary system ▸ **sistema de alerta inmediata** early warning system ▸ **sistema de calefacción** heating, heating system ▸ **sistema de diagnosis** diagnostic system ▸ **sistema de facturación** invoicing system ▸ **sistema de fondo fijo** (*Com*) imprest system ▸ **sistema de gestión de base de datos** database management system ▸ **sistema de lógica compartida** shared logic system ▸ **sistema de seguridad** security system ▸ **sistema educativo** education system ▸ **sistema experto** expert system ▸ **sistema financiero** financial system ▸ **sistema frontal** (*Meteo*) front, frontal system ▸ **sistema impositivo** tax system ▸ **sistema inmunitario, sistema inmunológico** immune system ▸ **sistema métrico** metric system ▸ **Sistema Monetario Europeo** European Monetary System ▸ **sistema montañoso** mountain range ▸ **sistema nervioso** nervous system ▸ **sistema nervioso central** central nervous system ▸ **sistema operativo** operating system ▸ **sistema operativo en disco** disk operating system ▸ **sistema pedagógico** educational system ▸ **sistema rastreador** (*en investigaciones espaciales*) tracking system ▸ **sistema tributario** tax system
2 (= *método*) method • **trabajar con ~** to work systematically *o* methodically • **yo por ~ lo hago así** I make it a rule to do it this way, I've got into the habit of doing it this way

sistemática SF systematics (*sing*)

sistemáticamente ADV systematically

sistematicidad SF systematicity

sistemático ADJ systematic

sistematización SF systematization

sistematizar ▷ CONJUG 1f VT to systematize

sistémico ADJ systemic

sitiado ADJ besieged

sitiador(a) SM/F besieger

sitial SM seat of honour

sitiar ▷ CONJUG 1b VT **1** (= *asediar*) to besiege, lay siege to
2 (= *acorralar*) to corner, hem in

sitio SM **1** (= *lugar*) place • **un ~ tranquilo** a peaceful place *o* spot • **Real Sitio** royal country house • **cambiar algo de ~** to move sth • **cambiarse de ~ con algn** to change places with sb • **en cualquier ~** anywhere • **en ningún ~**: • **no lo encuentro en ningún ~** I can't find it anywhere • **en ningún ~ se pasa tan bien como aquí** you'll enjoy yourself nowhere better than here, you won't enjoy yourself anywhere better than here • **en todos los ~s** everywhere
• MODISMOS: • **así no vas a ningún ~** you'll get nowhere like that • **dejar a algn en el ~** to kill sb on the spot • **poner a algn en su ~** to put sb firmly in his place • **quedarse en el ~** to die instantly, die on the spot
2 (= *espacio*) room, space • **hay ~ de sobra** there's plenty of room *o* space • **¿hay ~?** is there any room? • **te he guardado un ~ a mi lado** I've saved you a place next to me • **¿has encontrado ~ para aparcar?** have you found somewhere to park *o* a parking space?
• **¿tienes ~ para nosotros en tu casa?** do you have room for us in your house? • **hacer ~ a algn** to make room for sb • **te hemos hecho ~ en el coche** we've made room for you in the car
3 (*Mil*) siege • **poner ~ a algo** to besiege sth • **levantar el ~** to raise the siege; ▷ **estado**
4 (= *sitio web*) site ▸ **sitio web** website
5 (*CAm, Cono Sur*) (= *solar*) building site, vacant lot (*EEUU*)
6 (*Caribe, Méx*) (*Agr*) small farm, smallholding
7 (*LAm*) (= *parada*) taxi rank, cab rank (*esp EEUU*) • **carro de ~** taxi, cab (*esp EEUU*)

sito ADJ situated, located (**en** at, in)

situ • **in ~** ADV on the spot, in situ

situación SF **1** (= *circunstancias*) situation • **¿qué harías en una ~ así?** what would you do in a situation like that? • **me pones en una ~ muy difícil** you're putting me in a very difficult position • **no estoy en ~ de desmentirlo** I'm not in a position to deny it ▸ **situación jurídica** legal status ▸ **situación límite** extreme situation
2 (= *emplazamiento*) situation, location • **la casa tiene una ~ inmejorable** the house is in a superb location, the house is superbly located *o* situated
3 (*en la sociedad*) position, standing • **crearse una ~** to do well for o.s. ▸ **situación económica** financial position, financial situation
4 (= *estado*) state • **la ~ del edificio es ruinosa** the building is in a state of ruin
5 • **precio de ~** (*LAm*) bargain price

situacional ADJ situational

situado ADJ **1** (= *colocado*) situated, placed • **está ~ en ...** it's situated in ... • **el piso no está muy bien ~** the flat isn't very well situated
2 (*Econ*) • **estar (bien) ~** to be financially secure

situar ▷ CONJUG 1e VT **1** (= *colocar*) to place, put; (*Mil*) to post • **esto la sitúa entre los mejores** this places *o* puts her among the best • **van a ~ la estación en el centro de la ciudad** the station is going to be located *o* sited in the city centre
2 (= *señalar*) to find, locate • **no supo ~ Grecia en el mapa** he couldn't find *o* locate Greece on the map
3† [+ *dinero*] (= *invertir*) to place, invest; (= *depositar en banco*) to bank • **~ una pensión para algn** to settle an income on sb
VPR **situarse 1** (= *colocarse*) to position o.s. • **los jugadores se ~on cerca de la portería** the players positioned themselves near the goal • **se ha situado muy bien en la empresa** he's got himself a very good position in the company • **se ha situado entre los tres países más ricos del mundo** it has become one of the three richest countries in the world
2 [*novela, película*] to be set • **la acción se sitúa en Buenos Aires** the action is set in Buenos Aires
3 (*en la sociedad*) to do well for o.s. • **se situó muy bien en la capital** she did really well for herself in the capital

siútico* ADJ (*Chile*) = **cursi**

siutiquería SF (*Cono Sur*) = **cursilería**

skay [es'kai] SM imitation leather

sketch [es'ketʃ] SM (PL: **sketches** [es'ketʃ]) sketch

skin [es'kin] ADJ, SMF (PL: **skins**), **skinhead** [es'kinxeð] ADJ, SMF (PL: **skinheads**) skinhead

S.L. ABR **1** (*Com*) (= **Sociedad Limitada**) Ltd, Corp. (*EEUU*)
2 (= **Sus Labores**) ▷ labor

slalom [ez'lalom] SM slalom ▸ **slalom gigante** giant slalom

slam [ez'lam] SM (*Bridge*) slam • **gran ~** grand slam • **pequeño ~** little slam

slip [ez'lip] SM (PL: **slips** [ez'lip]) **1** (= *calzoncillos*) underpants (*pl*), briefs (*pl*)
2 (= *bañador*) bathing trunks (*pl*)

s.l. ni f. ABR (= **sin lugar ni fecha**) n.p. or d.

slogan [ez'loɣan] SM (PL: **slogans** [ez'loɣan]) slogan

slot [ez'lot] SM ▸ **slot de expansión** (*Inform*) expansion slot

S.M. ABR (*Esp*) **1** (*Rel*) = **Sociedad Marianista**
2 (= **Su Majestad**) HM

smart phone SM smartphone

smash [ez'mas] SM smash

SME SM ABR (= **Sistema Monetario Europeo**) EMS

SMI SM ABR = **salario mínimo interprofesional**

smiley SM smiley

smog [ez'smo] SM smog

smoking [ez'mokin] SM (PL: **smokings** [ez'mokin]) dinner jacket, tuxedo (*EEUU*)

SMS SM (= *mensaje*) text (message), SMS (message)

s/n ABR = **sin número**

snack [ez'nak] SM (PL: **snacks** [ez'nak]) **1** (= *merienda*) snack
2 (= *cafetería*) snack bar

s.n.m. ABR = **sobre el nivel del mar**

snob [ez'noβ] = **esnob**

snowboard SM snowboarding • **practicar ~** to go snowboarding

snowboarder SMF snowboarder

so¹ EXCL **1** (*para parar*) whoa!
2 (*LAm*) (¡*silencio!*) quiet!, shut up!*
3 (*Caribe*) (*a animal*) shoo!

so² EXCL (*como intensificador*) • **¡so burro!** you idiot!, you great oaf! • **¡so indecente!** you swine!*

so³ PREP ▷ **pena, pretexto**

SO ABR (= **suroeste**) SW

s/o ABR (*Com*) = **su orden**

soasar ▷ CONJUG 1a VT to roast lightly

soba* SF **1** [*de tela, persona*] fingering
2 (= *paliza*) hiding; (= *bofetada*) slap, punch • **dar una ~ a algn** to wallop sb*

sobacal ADJ underarm (*antes de s*)

sobaco SM **1** (*Anat*) armpit • MODISMO: • **se lo pasó por el ~*** he dismissed it, he totally disregarded it
2 (*Cos*) armhole

sobada* SF **1** (= *manoseo*) feel, grope
2 (= *dormida*) long sleep • **me voy a pegar una ~ de órdago** I'm going to sleep like a log

sobado ADJ **1** [*ropa*] (= *usado*) worn, shabby; (= *arrugado*) crumpled
2 [*libro*] well-thumbed, dog-eared
3 (= *trillado*) [*tema*] well-worn; [*chiste*] old, corny*
4 (*Culin*) [*masa*] short, crumbly (*EEUU*)
5 (*Cono Sur*) (= *enorme*) big, huge

sobador(a) SM/F **1** (*And, Méx*) (*Med*) (= *matasanos*) quack
2 (*And, Caribe, Méx*) (= *lisonjero*) flatterer, smooth talker

sobajar ▷ CONJUG 1a VT **1** = **sobajear**
2 (*And, Méx*) (= *humillar*) to humiliate

sobajear ▷ CONJUG 1a VT **1** (= *manosear*) to handle, finger
2 (*LAm*) (= *apretar*) to squeeze, press; (= *desordenar*) to mess up

sobandero SM (*And*) (= *matasanos*) quack
sobao ADJ * • **quedarse ~** to fall asleep;
▷ **sobado**
SM *sponge cake made with cream or lard*
sobaquera SF **1** (*Cos*) armhole
2* (= *mancha*) stain
3 (= *pistolera*) shoulder holster
4 (*CAm, Caribe*) (= *olor*) underarm odour, underarm odor (EEUU)
sobaquero ADJ • **funda sobaquera** shoulder holster
sobaquina* SF underarm odour, underarm odor (EEUU)
sobar ▷ CONJUG 1a VT **1** (= *toquetear*) [+ *tela*] to finger, dirty (with one's fingers); [+ *ropa*] to rumple, mess up; [+ *masa*] to knead; [+ *músculo*] to massage, rub
2* (= *magrear*) to grope*, paw*
3* (= *pegar*) to wallop
4* (= *molestar*) to pester
5 (*LAm*) [+ *huesos*] to set
6 (*And*) (= *despellejar*) to skin, flay
7 (*And, Caribe, Méx*) (= *lisonjear*) to flatter
8 (*CAm, Méx*) (= *reprender*) to tell off*
VI * to kip*, sleep
VPR **sobarse*** [*enamorados*] to neck, make out (*EEUU*‡), have a grope
sobasquera SF (*CAm, Caribe, Méx*) = **sobaquina**
sobeo SM fondling
soberanamente ADV supremely
soberanía SF sovereignty ▸ **soberanía popular** popular sovereignty
soberano/a ADJ **1** (*Pol*) sovereign
2 (= *supremo*) supreme
3* (= *tremendo*) real, really big • **una soberana paliza** a real walloping*
SM/F sovereign • **los ~s** the king and queen, the royal couple
soberbia SF **1** [*de persona*] (= *orgullo*) pride; (= *altanería*) haughtiness, arrogance
2 (= *magnificencia*) magnificence
3 (= *ira*) anger; (= *malhumor*) irritable nature
soberbio ADJ **1** [*persona*] (= *orgulloso*) proud; (= *altanero*) haughty, arrogant
2 (= *magnífico*) magnificent, grand
• **¡soberbio!** splendid!
3 (= *enojado*) angry; (= *malhumorado*) irritable
4* = **soberano**
sobeta* ADJ INV • **estar** *o* **quedarse ~** to be having a kip
sobijo SM **1** (*And, CAm*) = **soba**
2 (*And*) (= *desolladura*) skinning, flaying
sobijón SM (*CAm*) = **sobijo**
sobón* ADJ **1** (= *que soba*) • **es muy ~** his hands are everywhere • **¡no seas ~!** get your hands off me!, stop pawing me!*
2 (= *gandul*) lazy, workshy
3 (*And*) (= *adulón*) soapy*, greasy
sobornable ADJ bribable, venal
sobornar ▷ CONJUG 1a VT **1** (= *comprar*) to bribe
2 (*hum*) (= *engatusar*) to get round
soborno SM **1** (= *pago*) bribe • **denunció un intento de ~** he reported an attempted bribe
2 (= *delito*) bribery
3 (*And, Cono Sur*) (= *sobrecarga*) extra load; (= *prima*) extra, bonus • **de ~** extra, in addition
sobra SF **1** (= *excedente*) excess, surplus
2 sobras [*de comida*] leftovers; (*Cos*) remnants
3 • **de ~** spare, extra • **aquí tengo de ~** I've more than enough here • **tenemos comida de ~** we've got more than enough food • **tengo tiempo de ~** I've got plenty of time • **tuvo motivos de ~** he was more than justified • **lo sé de ~** I know it only too well • **sabes de ~ que yo no he sido** you know full well that it wasn't me • **aquí estoy de ~** I'm not needed *o* I'm superfluous here • **es de ~ conocido** it's common knowledge
sobradamente ADV • **lo conozco ~** I know him only too well • **con eso queda ~ satisfecho** he is more than satisfied with that • **es ~ sabido que …** it is common knowledge that …
sobradero SM overflow pipe
sobradillo SM penthouse
sobrado ADJ **1** [*cantidad, tiempo*] (= *más que suficiente*) more than enough; (= *superfluo*) superfluous, excessive; (= *sobreabundante*) superabundant • **hay tiempo ~** there's plenty of time • **motivo más que ~ para hacerlo** all the more reason to do it • **tuvo razones sobradas para …** he had good reason to … • **sobradas veces** repeatedly
2 • **estar ~ de algo** to have more than enough of sth
3 (= *acaudalado*) wealthy • **no anda muy ~** he's not very well off
4 (= *atrevido*) bold, forward
5 (*Cono Sur*) (= *enorme*) colossal
6 • **darse de ~** (*And**) to be full of oneself
ADV too, exceedingly
SM **1** (= *desván*) attic, garret
2 sobrados (*Andalucía, Cono Sur*) leftovers
sobrador* ADJ (*Cono Sur*) stuck-up*, conceited
sobrancero ADJ unemployed
sobrante ADJ (= *excedente*) spare; (= *restante*) remaining
SM **1** (= *lo que sobra*) (*gen*) surplus, remainder; (*Com, Econ*) surplus; (= *saldo activo*) balance in hand
2 sobrantes odds and ends
SMF redundant worker, laid-off worker (*EEUU*), person made redundant
sobrar ▷ CONJUG 1a VT to exceed, surpass
VI (= *quedar de más*) to remain, be left, be left over; (= *ser más que suficiente*) to be more than enough; (= *ser superfluo*) to be spare • **ha sobrado mucha comida** there's a lot of food left (over) • **por este lado sobra** there's too much on this side • **sobra uno** there's one too many, there's one left • **con este dinero ~á** this money will be more than enough • **esta pieza sobra** this piece is spare • **este ejemplo sobra** this example is unnecessary • **no es que sobre talento** it's not that there's a surplus of talent • **todo lo que has dicho sobra** all that you've said is quite unnecessary • **nos sobra tiempo** we have plenty of time • **al terminar me sobraba medio metro** I had half a metre left over when I finished • **veo que aquí sobro** I see that I'm not needed *o* I'm superfluous here • REFRÁN: • **más vale que sobre que no que falte** better too much than too little
sobrasada SF Majorcan sausage
sobre¹ SM **1** (*para cartas*) envelope ▸ **sobre de paga, sobre de pago** pay packet ▸ **sobre de primer día (de circulación)** first-day cover ▸ **sobre de sellos** packet of stamps
2‡ (= *cama*) bed • **meterse en el ~** to hit the sack*, hit the hay*
3 (*LAm*) (= *cartera*) handbag
sobre² PREP **1** (= *encima de*) on • **está ~ la mesa** it's on the table • **un puente ~ el río Ebro** a bridge across *o* over the river Ebro • **prestar juramento ~ la Biblia** to swear on the Bible • **la marcha ~ Roma** the march on Rome • **llevaba una chaqueta negra ~ camisa blanca** he wore a black jacket over a white shirt • **varios policías se abalanzaron ~ él** several policemen jumped on *o* fell upon him • **los insultos llovían ~ mí de todas partes** insults rained down on me from all sides • **la responsabilidad que recae ~ sus hombros** the responsibility which rests on *o* upon his shoulders • MODISMO: • **estar ~ algn** (= *vigilar*) to keep constant watch over sb; (= *acosar*) to keep on at sb; (= *dominar*) to control sb • **tengo que estar ~ él para que lo haga** I have to stand over him to make him do it, I have to keep a constant watch over him to make sure he does it • **quiere estar ~ todos** he wants to control everyone
2 (= *por encima de*) **a** [+ *lugar*] over • **volamos ~ Cádiz** we're flying over Cadiz • **se inclinó ~ la mesa** she leant over the table
b (*con cantidades*) above • **500 metros ~ el nivel del mar** 500 metres *o* (*EEUU*) meters above sea level • **dos grados ~ cero** two degrees above cero • **diez dólares ~ lo estipulado** ten dollars over and above what was agreed
3 (*indicando superioridad*) over • **tiene muchas ventajas ~ los métodos convencionales** it has many advantages over conventional methods • **están celebrando su victoria ~ el Atlético** they're celebrating their victory over Atlético • **amaba la belleza ~ todas las cosas** he loved beauty above all things
4 (*indicando proporción*) out of, in • **tres ~ cien** three out of every hundred, three in a hundred • **cuatro personas ~ diez no votarían** four out of ten people would not vote, four in every ten people would not vote • **una puntuación de tres ~ cinco** three (marks) out of five
5 (*Econ*) on • **un préstamo ~ una propiedad** a loan on a property • **un aumento ~ el año pasado** an increase on *o* over last year • **un impuesto ~ algo** a tax on sth
6 (= *aproximadamente*) about • **~ las seis** at about six o'clock • **ocupa ~ 20 páginas** it fills about 20 pages, it occupies roughly 20 pages
7 (= *acerca de*) about, on • **un libro ~ Tirso** a book about *o* on Tirso • **información ~ vuelos** information about flights • **hablar ~ algo** to talk about sth
8 (= *además de*) in addition to, on top of • **~ todas mis obligaciones ahora tengo una nueva** on top of all my duties I now have a new one
9 • **~ todo** (= *en primer lugar*) above all; (= *especialmente*) especially • **~ todo, no perdamos la calma** above all, let's keep calm • **~ todo me gusta este** I especially like this one
sobre… PREF super…, over…
sobreabundancia SF superabundance, overabundance
sobreabundante ADJ superabundant, overabundant
sobreabundar ▷ CONJUG 1a VI to be very abundant (**en in, with**)
sobreactuación SF overacting
sobreactuar ▷ CONJUG 1e VI to overact
sobrealimentación SF overfeeding
sobrealimentado ADJ supercharged
sobrealimentador SM supercharger
sobrealimentar ▷ CONJUG 1a VT
1 [+ *persona*] to overfeed
2 (*Mec*) to supercharge
sobreañadido ADJ (= *extra*) additional; (= *superfluo*) superfluous
sobreañadir ▷ CONJUG 3a VT to give in addition, add, add as a bonus
sobrecalentamiento SM overheating
sobrecalentar ▷ CONJUG 1j VT to overheat
sobrecama SM *o* SF bedspread
sobrecaña SF splint
sobrecapacidad SF overcapacity, excess capacity
sobrecapitalización SF overcapitalization
sobrecapitalizar ▷ CONJUG 1f VT to overcapitalize

sobrecarga (SF) **1** (= *peso excesivo*) (*lit*) overload; (*fig*) extra burden
2 (*Com*) surcharge ▸ **sobrecarga de importación** import surcharge
3 (*Correos*) overprint, overprinting
4 (= *cuerda*) rope
sobrecargado (ADJ) **1** (*de peso*) overloaded
2 (*de trabajo*) overloaded, overburdened • **estar ~ de algo** to be overloaded with sth, be overburdened with sth
sobrecargar ▸ CONJUG 1h (VT) **1** (*con peso*) [+ *camión*] to overload; [+ *persona*] to weigh down, overburden (**de** with) • **~ el mercado** (*Cono Sur*) to glut the market
2 (*Com*) to surcharge
3 (*Correos*) to surcharge, overprint (**de** with)
4 (*Elec*) to overload
sobrecargo (SMF) **1** (*Náut*) purser
2 (*Aer*) senior flight attendant
sobrecejo (SM) **1** (= *ceño*) frown
2 (*Arquit*) lintel
sobreceño (SM) frown
sobrecito (SM) sachet
sobrecogedor (ADJ) **1** [*paisaje, silencio*] imposing, impressive
2 (= *horrible*) horrific • **~as escenas de guerra** horrific scenes of war
sobrecoger ▸ CONJUG 2c (VT) (= *sobresaltar*) to startle, take by surprise; (= *asustar*) to scare, frighten
(VPR) **sobrecogerse 1** (= *sobresaltarse*) to be startled, start; (= *asustarse*) to get scared, be frightened
2 (= *quedar impresionado*) to be overawed (**de** by) • **~se de emoción** to be overcome with emotion
sobrecontrata (SF) overbooking
sobrecontratar ▸ CONJUG 1a (VT), (VI) to overbook
sobrecoste (SM) extra charges (*pl*)
sobrecubierta (SF) jacket, dust jacket
sobredicho (ADJ) aforementioned
sobredimensionado (ADJ) **1** (= *muy grande*) excessively large, oversized
2 • **estar ~ de** to have a surplus *o* excess of, have too much of
sobredimensionamiento (SM) [*de personal*] excessive number; [*de tamaño*] increase in size, expansion
sobredimensionar ▸ CONJUG 1a (VT)
1 [+ *beneficios, importancia, problema*] to inflate
2 (*Téc, Aut*) to oversize
sobredorar ▸ CONJUG 1a (VT) **1** (= *dorar*) to gild
2 (= *disimular*) to gloss over
sobredosis (SF INV) overdose
sobreentender ▸ CONJUG 2g (VT) (= *entender*) to understand; (= *adivinar*) to deduce, infer
(VPR) **sobreentenderse** • **aquí se sobreentienden dos palabras** you can see that there should be two words here • **se sobreentiende que** ... it is implied that ..., it goes without saying that ...
sobreescribir ▸ CONJUG 3a (VT) to overwrite
sobreesfuerzo (SM) **1** (= *esfuerzo enorme*) superhuman effort
2 (*Med*) overstrain
sobreestimación (SF) overestimate
sobreestimar ▸ CONJUG 1a (VT) to overestimate
sobreexcitación (SF) overexcitement
sobreexcitado (ADJ) overexcited
sobreexcitar ▸ CONJUG 1a (VT) to overexcite
(VPR) **sobreexcitarse** to get overexcited
sobreexplotación (SF) [*de recursos*] overexploitation, draining; [*de trabajadores*] exploitation
sobreexplotar ▸ CONJUG 1a (VT) [+ *recursos*] to overexploit, drain; [+ *trabajadores*] to exploit
sobreexponer ▸ CONJUG 2q (VT) to overexpose
sobreexposición (SF) overexposure
sobrefunda (SF) (*CAm*) pillowslip, pillowcase
sobregirar ▸ CONJUG 1a (VT), (VI) to overdraw
sobregiro (SM) overdraft
sobrehilar ▸ CONJUG 1a (VT) to whipstitch, overcast
sobrehumano (ADJ) superhuman
sobreimpresión (SF) (*Correos*) overprint, overprinting
sobreimpresionado (ADJ) superimposed
sobreimpresionar ▸ CONJUG 1a (VT) to superimpose
sobreimpreso (ADJ) superimposed
sobreimprimir ▸ CONJUG 3a (VT) to overprint
sobrellevar ▸ CONJUG 1a (VT) [+ *peso*] to carry, help to carry; [+ *carga de otro*] to ease; [+ *desgracia, desastre, enfermedad*] to bear, endure; [+ *faltas ajenas*] to be tolerant towards
sobremanera (ADV) exceedingly • **me interesa ~** I'm most interested in it
sobremarca (SF) overbid
sobremarcha (SF) overdrive
sobremesa (SF) **1** (= *después de comer*) sitting on after a meal • **estar de ~** to sit round the table after lunch/dinner • **conversación de ~** table talk • **charla de ~** after-dinner speech • **orador de ~** after-dinner speaker • **programa de ~** (*TV*) afternoon programme • **un cigarro de ~** an after-lunch/dinner cigar • **hablaremos de eso en la ~** we'll talk about that after lunch/dinner
2 • **lámpara de ~** table lamp • **ordenador de ~** desktop computer
3 (= *mantel*) table cover, tablecloth
4 (= *postre*) dessert

SOBREMESA
After the main meal of the day, which usually takes place at around 2 or 3 p.m., the Spanish have traditionally lingered on at table drinking coffee and either chatting or watching TV before returning to work later in the afternoon. If they have more time, they may even have a liqueur or play cards. While **estar de sobremesa** is also occasionally applied to the period after the evening meal, it is more usually taken to mean after lunch, and the **sobremesa** time band used in TV programme listings applies only to between 2.00 and 5.00 p.m.

sobremodo (ADV) very much, enormously
sobrenadar ▸ CONJUG 1a (VI) to float
sobrenatural (ADJ) **1** (= *inexplicable*) supernatural • **lo ~** the supernatural • **ciencias ~es** occult sciences • **vida ~** life after death
2 (= *misterioso*) weird, unearthly
sobrenombre (SM) nickname
sobrentender ▸ CONJUG 2g (VT) = **sobreentender**
sobrepaga (SF) extra pay, bonus
sobreparto (SM) confinement (*after childbirth*) • **dolores de ~** afterpains • **morir de ~** to die in childbirth
sobrepasar ▸ CONJUG 1a (VT) [+ *límite, esperanzas*] to exceed; [+ *rival, récord*] to beat; [+ *pista de aterrizaje*] to overshoot
(VPR) **sobrepasarse** = **propasarse**
sobrepelliz (SF) surplice
sobrepelo (SM) (*Cono Sur*) saddlecloth
sobrepesca (SF) overfishing
sobrepeso (SM) [*de paquete, persona*] excess weight; [*de camión*] extra load
sobrepoblación (SF) overpopulation
sobreponer ▸ CONJUG 2q (PP: **sobrepuesto**) (VT) **1** (= *poner encima de*) to put on top (**en** of), superimpose (**en** on)
2 (= *añadir*) to add (**en** to)
3 (= *anteponer*) • **~ A a B** to give A preference over B
(VPR) **sobreponerse 1** (= *recobrar la calma*) to control o.s., pull o.s. together
2 (= *vencer dificultades*) to win through • **~se a una enfermedad** to pull through an illness • **~se a un enemigo** to overcome an enemy • **~se a un rival** to triumph over a rival • **~se a un susto** to get over a fright
sobreprecio (SM) (= *recargo*) surcharge; (= *aumento de precio*) increase in price
sobreprima (SF) extra premium
sobreproducción (SF) overproduction
sobreproducir ▸ CONJUG 3n (VT) to overproduce
sobreprotección (SF) overprotection
sobreprotector (ADJ) overprotective
sobreproteger ▸ CONJUG 2c (VT) to overprotect
sobrepuerta (SF) lintel
sobrepuesto (PP) *de* **sobreponer**
(ADJ) superimposed
sobrepujar ▸ CONJUG 1a (VT) **1** (*en subasta*) to outbid
2 (= *superar*) to outdo, surpass • **sobrepuja a todos en talento** he outdoes all the rest in talent, he has more talent than all the rest
sobrereacción (SF) overreaction
sobrereserva (SF) overbooking
sobrereservar ▸ CONJUG 1a (VT), (VI) to overbook
sobrero (ADJ) extra, spare
(SM) (*Taur*) reserve bull
sobresaliente (ADJ) **1** (*Arquit*) projecting, overhanging
2 (= *excelente*) outstanding
3 (*Educ*) first class
(SMF) (*Teat*) understudy
(SM) (*Univ*) first class, distinction
sobresalir ▸ CONJUG 3q (VI) **1** (*Arquit*) to project, overhang, jut out; (= *salirse de la línea*) to stick out
2 (= *destacarse*) to stand out, excel
sobresaltar ▸ CONJUG 1a (VT) to startle, frighten
(VPR) **sobresaltarse** to start, be startled (**con, de** at)
sobresalto (SM) (= *sorpresa*) start; (= *susto*) fright, scare; (= *conmoción*) sudden shock • **de ~** suddenly
sobresanar ▸ CONJUG 1a (VI) **1** (*Med*) to heal superficially
2 (= *ocultarse*) to conceal itself, hide its true nature
sobrescrito (SM) (= *señas*) address; (= *inscripción*) superscription
sobreseer ▸ CONJUG 2e (VT) **1** • **~ una causa** (*Jur*) to dismiss a case
2 • **~ de algo** to desist from sth, give up sth
sobreseído (ADJ) • **causa sobreseída** (*Jur*) case dismissed
sobreseimiento (SM) stay (of proceedings)
sobresello (SM) double seal
sobrestadía (SF) demurrage
sobrestante (SM) (= *capataz*) foreman, overseer; (= *gerente*) site manager
sobrestimación (SF) overestimate
sobrestimar ▸ CONJUG 1a (VT) to overestimate
sobresueldo (SM) bonus, extra pay
sobretasa (SF) surcharge
sobretensión (SF) (*Elec*) surge
sobretiempo (SM) (*LAm*) overtime
sobretiro (SM) (*Méx*) offprint
sobretítulo (SM) (*Prensa*) general title, general heading

sobretodo SM overcoat

sobrevaloración SF **1** [*de dinero, moneda*] overvaluation
2 (*en importancia*) overrating

sobrevalorado ADJ **1** [*dinero, moneda*] overvalued
2 [*persona*] overrated

sobrevalorar ▷ CONJUG 1a VT [+ *dinero, moneda*] to overvalue; [+ *persona*] to overrate

sobrevaluado ADJ = **sobrevalorado**

sobrevender ▷ CONJUG 2a VT to overbook

sobrevenir ▷ CONJUG 3r VI (= *ocurrir*) to happen, happen unexpectedly; (= *resultar*) to follow, ensue

sobreventa SF (*tb* **sobreventa de billetes**) overbooking

sobrevirar ▷ CONJUG 1a VI to oversteer

sobrevivencia SF survival

sobreviviente ADJ, SMF = **superviviente**

sobrevivir ▷ CONJUG 3a VI **1** (= *quedar vivo*) to survive • **sobrevivir a** [+ *accidente*] to survive; [+ *persona*] to survive, outlive
2 (= *durar más tiempo que*) to outlast

sobrevolar ▷ CONJUG 1l VT to fly over

sobrevuelo SM overflying • **permiso de ~** permission to overfly

sobrexcitación SF overexcitement

sobrexcitado ADJ overexcited

sobrexcitar ▷ CONJUG 1a VT to overexcite

sobrexponer ▷ CONJUG 2q VT to overexpose

sobrexposición SF overexposure

sobriamente ADV **1** [*vestirse*] soberly
2 [*decorar, amueblar*] simply

sobriedad SF **1** [*de estilo, color, decoración*] sobriety • **vestía con ~** he was soberly dressed
2 (= *moderación*) moderation • **siempre come con ~** she always eats in moderation

sobrino/a SM/F nephew/niece • **mis ~s** (= *varones*) my nephews • **mis ~s** (= *varones y hembras*) my nieces and nephews

sobrinonieto/a SMF great nephew/niece

sobrio ADJ **1** (= *no borracho*) sober
2 [*color, estilo, decoración*] sober
3 (= *moderado*) frugal • **llevan una vida muy sobria** they live a very frugal life • **ser ~ con la bebida** to drink in moderation • **es ~ de palabras** he's a man of few words
4 (= *tranquilo*) restrained

sobros SMPL (*CAm*) leftovers, scraps

soca[1] SF **1** (*And*) [*de arroz*] young shoots of rice; [*de tabaco*] top leaf of tobacco plant, high-quality tobacco leaf
2 (*CAm**) (= *embriaguez*) drunkenness

soca[2]* SM • **hacerse el ~** to act dumb*

socaire SM **1** (*Náut*) lee • **al ~** to leeward
2 • **al ~ de algo** (= *al abrigo de*) under the protection of sth; (= *so pretexto de*) using sth as an excuse • **estar** *o* **ponerse al ~** to shirk

socaliña SF (= *astucia*) craft, cunning; (= *porfía*) clever persistence
SMF* twister, swindler

socaliñar ▷ CONJUG 1a VT to get by a swindle

socaliñero ADJ (= *astuto*) crafty, cunning; (= *porfiado*) persistent

socapa SF • **a ~** surreptitiously

socapar* ▷ CONJUG 1a VT (*And, Méx*) • **~ a algn** to cover up for sb

socar ▷ CONJUG 1g (*CAm*) VT **1** (= *comprimir*) to press down, squeeze, compress
2* (= *enojar*) to annoy, upset
VI to make an effort
VPR **socarse 1** (= *emborracharse*) to get drunk
2 • **~se con algn** to fall out *o* squabble with sb

socarrar ▷ CONJUG 1a VT to scorch, singe

socarrón ADJ **1** (= *irónico*) [*persona, comentario, tono*] sarcastic, ironical; [*humor*] snide
2 (= *astuto*) crafty, cunning, sly

socarronamente ADV (*irónicamente*) sarcastically

socarronería SF **1** (= *ironía*) [*de persona, comentario, tono*] sarcasm, irony; [*de humor*] snide humour, snide humor (*EEUU*)
2 (= *astucia*) craftiness, cunning, slyness

sócate SM (*Ven*) socket, lampholder

socava SF, **socavación** SF undermining

socavar ▷ CONJUG 1a VT **1** (= *minar*) to undermine
2 (= *excavar*) [*persona*] to dig under; [*agua*] to hollow out
3 (= *debilitar*) to sap, undermine

socavón SM **1** (*Min*) (= *galería*) gallery, tunnel; (= *hueco*) hollow; (= *cueva*) cavern; (*en la calle*) hole
2 (*Arquit*) subsidence

soche SM (*And*) [*de oveja*] tanned sheepskin; [*de cabra*] tanned goatskin

socia* SF (*Esp*) whore

sociabilidad SF [*de persona*] sociability; [*de animal*] gregariousness; [*de reunión*] conviviality

sociable ADJ [*persona*] sociable, friendly; [*animal*] social, gregarious; [*reunión*] convivial

sociablemente ADV sociably

social ADJ **1** (= *de la sociedad*) social
2 (*Com, Econ*) company (*antes de s*), company's • **acuerdo ~** • **pacto ~** wages agreement • **paz ~** industrial harmony, agreement between employers and unions
SMPL **sociales** (*Escol**) social studies

socialdemocracia SF social democracy

socialdemócrata ADJ social democrat, social-democratic
SMF social democrat

socialdemocrático ADJ social democratic

socialismo SM socialism

socialista ADJ socialist, socialistic
SMF socialist

socialización SF [*de país*] collectivization; [*de empresa*] nationalization

socializador ADJ, **socializante** ADJ
1 (= *que socializa*) socializing
2 (*Pol*) [*reformas*] with Socialist leanings

socializar ▷ CONJUG 1f VT [+ *país*] to collectivize; [+ *empresa*] to nationalize

socialmente ADV socially

sociata‡ ADJ, SMF socialist

sociedad SF **1** (*Sociol*) society • **la ~ de consumo** the consumer society • **la ~ del ocio** the leisure society • **la ~ permisiva** the permissive society • **en la ~ actual** in contemporary society • **hacer ~** to join forces
2 (= *asociación*) (*gen*) society, association; (*oficial*) body ▸ **sociedad científica** learned society ▸ **Sociedad de Jesús** Society of Jesus ▸ **Sociedad de Naciones** League of Nations ▸ **sociedad de socorros mutuos** friendly society, provident society ▸ **sociedad docta** learned society ▸ **sociedad gastronómica** dining club ▸ **sociedad inmobiliaria** building society ▸ **sociedad secreta** secret society
3 (*Com, Econ*) (= *empresa*) (*gen*) company; [*de socios*] partnership ▸ **sociedad anónima** limited liability company, corporation (*EEUU*) ▸ **Sociedad Anónima** (*en nombres de empresa*) Limited, Incorporated (*EEUU*) ▸ **sociedad anónima laboral** workers' cooperative ▸ **sociedad comanditaria** limited partnership ▸ **sociedad conjunta** (*Com*) joint venture ▸ **sociedad de beneficencia** friendly society, benefit association (*EEUU*) ▸ **sociedad de cartera** holding company ▸ **sociedad de control** holding company ▸ **sociedad en comandita** limited partnership ▸ **sociedad instrumental, sociedad limitada** limited company, private limited company, corporation (*EEUU*) ▸ **sociedad mercantil** trading company ▸ **sociedad protectora de animales** society for the protection of animals
4 • **alta** *o* **buena ~** high society • **entrar en ~** • **presentarse en (la) ~** to come out, make one's debut • **notas de ~** gossip column, society news column
5 ▸ **sociedad conyugal** marriage partnership

societal ADJ societal

socio/a SM/F **1** (= *asociado*) [*de empresa*] associate; [*de club*] member; [*de sociedad docta*] fellow • **hacerse ~ de** to become a member of, join • **se ruega a los señores ~s** … members are asked to … ▸ **socio/a de honor** honorary member ▸ **socio/a de número** full member ▸ **socio/a honorario/a** honorary member ▸ **socio/a numerario/a** full member ▸ **socio/a vitalicio/a** life member
2 (*Com, Econ*) partner ▸ **socio activo** active partner ▸ **socio capitalista, socio comanditario** sleeping partner, silent partner (*EEUU*)
3* (= *amigo*) buddy, mate*

socio... PREF socio...

sociobiología SF sociobiology

sociocultural ADJ sociocultural
• **animador ~** [*de organización*] events organizer; [*de hotel*] entertainments manager

socioeconómico ADJ socioeconomic

sociolingüística SF sociolinguistics (*sing*)

sociolingüístico ADJ sociolinguistic

sociología SF sociology

sociológicamente ADV sociologically

sociológico ADJ sociological

sociólogo/a SM/F sociologist

sociopolítico ADJ sociopolitical

sociosanitario ADJ public health (*antes de s*)

soco ADJ **1** (*CAm*) (= *borracho*) drunk, tight*
2 = **zoco**[1]
SM **1** (*And*) (*Anat, Bot*) stump
2 (*And*) (= *cuchillo*) short blunt machete
3 = **zoco**[2]

socola SF (*And, CAm*) clearing of land

socolar ▷ CONJUG 1a VT **1** (*And, CAm*) [+ *tierra*] to clear, clear of scrub
2 (*And*) [+ *trabajo*] to bungle, do clumsily

socollón SM (*CAm, Caribe*) violent shaking

socollonear ▷ CONJUG 1a VT (*CAm*) to shake violently

socón‡ ADJ (*CAm*) studious, swotty*

soconusco SM **1** (= *chocolate*) fine chocolate
2 (*Caribe**) (= *trato*) shady deal, dirty business

socorrer ▷ CONJUG 2a VT [+ *ciudad sitiada*] to relieve; [+ *expedición*] to bring aid to • **~ a algn** to help sb, come to sb's aid

socorrido ADJ **1** [*tienda*] well-stocked
2 (= *útil*) handy • **un ~ primer plato** a common starter
3 [*persona*] helpful, obliging
4 [*ejemplo, método*] hackneyed, well-worn

socorrismo SM life-saving

socorrista SMF lifeguard, life-saver

socorro SM **1** (= *ayuda*) help, aid, assistance; (= *alivio*) relief • **¡socorro!** help! • **trabajos de ~** relief *o* aid work (*sing*) • **pedir ~** to ask for help • **acudió en su ~** she went to his aid ▸ **socorros mutuos** mutual aid (*sing*)
2 (*Cono Sur*) (= *pago adelantado*) advance payment, sub*

socoyote SM (*Méx*) smallest child

Sócrates SM Socrates

socrático ADJ Socratic

socrocio SM plaster

socucha SF (*Cono Sur, Méx*), **socucho** SM (*Cono Sur, Méx*) (= *cuartito*) poky little room, den; (= *casucha*) hovel, slum

soda SF **1** (*Quím*) soda
2 (= *bebida*) soda water

sódico ADJ sodium (*antes de s*)

sodio SM sodium

Sodoma SF Sodom

sodomía SF sodomy

sodomita SMF sodomite

sodomizar ▷ CONJUG 1f VT to sodomize

SOE SM ABR (*Esp*) = **Seguro Obligatorio de Enfermedad**

soez ADJ dirty, crude, coarse

sofá SM sofa, settee

sofá-cama SM (PL: **sofás-cama**), **sofá-nido** SM (PL: **sofás-nido**) sofa bed, studio couch

sofero ADJ (*And*) huge, enormous

Sofía[1] SF (= *nombre*) Sophia

Sofía[2] SF (*Geog*) Sofia

sofión SM (= *bufido*) angry snort; (= *reprimenda*) sharp rebuke; (= *réplica*) sharp retort

sofisma SM sophism

sofista SMF sophist

sofistería SF sophistry

sofisticación SF **1** [*de persona, gestos*] sophistication
2 (= *afectación*) affectation

sofisticado ADJ **1** [*persona, gesto*] sophisticated
2 (= *afectado*) (*pey*) affected

sofístico ADJ sophistic, sophistical

soflama SF **1** (= *fuego*) flicker, glow
2 (= *sonrojo*) blush
3 (= *arenga*) fiery speech, harangue
4* (= *engaño*) deceit; (= *halagos*) cajolery, blarney
5 (*Méx*) (= *chisme*) piece of trivia, bit of gossip

soflamar ▷ CONJUG 1a VT **1** (= *quemar*) (*gen*) to scorch; (*Culin*) to singe
2 (= *hacer sonrojar*) to make blush
3* (= *engañar*) to deceive; (= *halagar*) to cajole

sofocación SF **1** suffocation
2 = **sofoco**

sofocado ADJ • **estar ~** (= *sin aire*) to be out of breath; (= *ahogándose*) to feel stifled; (= *abochornado*) to be hot and bothered

sofocante ADJ stifling, suffocating

sofocar ▷ CONJUG 1g VT **1** (= *ahogar*) [*calor*] to stifle; [*fuego, humo*] to suffocate • **este tiempo tan húmedo me sofoca** I find this humid weather stifling
2 (= *apagar*) [+ *incendio*] to smother, put out; [+ *rebelión*] to crush, put down; [+ *epidemia*] to stamp out
3 (= *enojar*) to anger, upset
4 (= *avergonzar*) to embarrass
5 (= *sonrojar*) to make ... blush
VPR **sofocarse 1** (= *ahogarse*) (*por el esfuerzo*) to get out of breath; (*por el calor*) to suffocate
2 (= *sonrojarse*) to blush
3 (= *avergonzarse*) to get embarrassed
4 (= *enojarse*) to get angry, get upset • **no vale la pena que te sofoques** it's not worth upsetting yourself about it
5 (*CAm, Méx*) (= *preocuparse*) to worry, be anxious

Sófocles SM Sophocles

sofoco SM **1** (*por el calor*) stifling sensation; (*por la menopausia*) hot flush, hot flash (*EEUU*)
2 (= *azoro*) embarrassment • **pasar un ~** to have an embarrassing time
3 (= *ira*) anger, indignation

sofocón* SM • **llevarse un ~** to get upset

sofoquina* SF **1** (= *calor*) stifling heat • hace una ~ it's stifling
2 = **sofocón**

sofreír ▷ CONJUG 3l (PP: **sofrito**) VT to fry lightly

sofrenada SF **1** (*repentino*) sudden check, sudden jerk on the reins
2* (= *bronca*) ticking-off*

sofrenar ▷ CONJUG 1a VT **1** [+ *caballo*] to rein back sharply
2 (= *controlar*) to restrain
3* (= *echar una bronca a*) to tick off*

sofrito PP de **sofreír**
SM *fried onion, garlic and tomato used as a base for cooking sauces and dishes*

sofrología SF sleep therapy

software ['sofwer] SM software
▸ **software de aplicación** application software ▸ **software del sistema** system software ▸ **software del usuario** user software ▸ **software espía** spyware
▸ **software integrado** integrated software
▸ **software libre** free software, freeware

soga SF (= *cuerda*) (*gen*) rope, cord; [*de animal*] halter; [*del verdugo*] hangman's rope
• MODISMOS: • **hacer ~** to lag behind • **dar ~ a algn** to make fun of sb • **echar la ~ tras el caldero** to chuck it all up*, throw in one's hand • **estar con la ~ al cuello** to be in deep water • **hablar de la ~ en casa del ahorcado** to say the wrong thing

sogatira SM tug of war

soguear ▷ CONJUG 1a VT **1** (*And, CAm, Cono Sur*) (= *atar*) to tie with a rope
2 (*Caribe*) (= *lazar*) to lasso
3 (*Caribe*) (= *domesticar*) to tame
4 (*And**) (= *burlarse de*) to make fun of

soguero ADJ (*Caribe*) tame

sois ▷ **ser**

soja SF soya • **semilla de ~** soya bean

sojuzgar ▷ CONJUG 1h VT (= *vencer*) to conquer; (= *subyugar*) to subjugate

sol[1] SM **1** (= *astro*) sun • **al ponerse el sol** at sunset • **al salir el sol** at sunrise • **de sol a sol** from dawn to dusk • MODISMOS: • **arrimarse al sol que más calienta** to keep in with the right people • **como un sol** (= *brillante*) as bright as a new pin • **salga el sol por donde quiera** come what may • **ser un sol**: • **María es un sol, siempre tan agradable** María is a darling, she's always so pleasant • **el niño es un sol** he's a lovely child ▸ **sol naciente** rising sun ▸ **sol poniente** setting sun ▸ **sol y luna** (*Caribe**) machete, cane knife ▸ **sol y sombra** brandy and anisette
2 (= *luz solar*) sun, sunshine • **entra mucho sol en el comedor** the dining room gets a lot of sun *o* sunshine • **ayer tuvimos nueve horas de sol** we had nine hours of sunshine yesterday • **hay** *o* **hace sol** it is sunny, the sun is shining • **un día de sol** a sunny day • **estar al sol** to be in the sun • **mirar algo a contra sol** to look at sth against the light • **tomar el sol** to sunbathe • **tumbarse al sol** to lie in the sun • MODISMOS: • **hacía un sol de justicia** the sun was blazing down • **no me deja ni a sol ni a sombra** he doesn't give me a moment's peace ▸ **sol artificial** sunlamp
3 (*uso apelativo*) • **¡sol mío, ven con mamá!** come with Mummy, darling *o* pet!*
4 (*Taur*) • **localidades de sol** *the cheapest seats in a bullring with no shade*
5 (*Perú*) (*Econ*) Sol, *former monetary unit of Peru*

sol[2] SM (*Mús*) G ▸ **sol mayor** G major

solada SF sediment

solado SM tiling, tiled floor

solamente ADV = **solo**

solana SF **1** (= *lugar soleado*) sunny spot, suntrap
2 (= *solario*) sun lounge, solarium

solanas* ADJ INV alone, all on one's own

solanera SF **1** (= *sol*) scorching sunshine
2 (*Med*) (= *quemadura*) sunburn; (= *insolación*) sunstroke

solano SM east wind

solapa SF **1** [*de chaqueta*] lapel; [*de sobre, libro, bolsillo*] flap
2 (= *pretexto*) pretext

solapadamente ADV slyly, in an underhand way, sneakily

solapado ADJ (= *furtivo*) sly, underhand; (= *evasivo*) evasive; (= *secreto*) undercover

solapamiento SM overlapping

solapante ADJ overlapping

solapar ▷ CONJUG 1a VT **1** (= *cubrir parcialmente*) to overlap
2 (= *encubrir*) to cover up, keep dark
VI to overlap (**con** with)
VPR **solaparse** to overlap • **se ha solapado** it has got covered up, it has got hidden underneath

solapo SM **1** (*Cos*) lapel
2 • **a ~*** = **solapadamente**

solar[1] SM **1** (= *terreno*) (*gen*) lot, piece of land, site; (*en obras*) building site
2 (= *casa solariega*) ancestral home, family seat
3 (= *linaje*) lineage

solar[2] ▷ CONJUG 1l VT [+ *suelo*] to tile; [+ *zapatos*] to sole

solar[3] ADJ solar, sun (*antes de s*) • **rayos ~es** solar rays

solariego ADJ **1** • **casa solariega** family seat, ancestral home
2 (*Hist*) [*ascendencia*] ancient and noble; [*títulos*] manorial • **tierras solariegas** ancestral lands

solario SM, **solárium** SM solarium

solas • **a ~** ADV alone, by oneself • **finalmente se quedó a ~ en su despacho** at last she was alone *o* on her own in her office • **lo hizo a ~** he did it (all) by himself • **volar a ~** to fly solo • **vuelo a ~** solo flight

solateras* ADJ INV alone, all on one's own

solaz SM (= *descanso*) recreation, relaxation; (= *consuelo*) solace

solazar ▷ CONJUG 1f VT (= *divertir*) to amuse, provide relaxation for; (= *consolar*) to console, comfort; (= *alegrar*) to cheer
VPR **solazarse** to enjoy o.s., relax

solazo* SM scorching sun

solazoso ADJ (= *que descansa*) restful; (= *que entretiene*) recreational, relaxing

soldada SF pay; (*Mil*) service pay

soldadera SF (*Méx*) camp follower

soldadesca SF **1** (= *profesión*) military profession, military
2 (*pey*) (= *soldados*) army rabble

soldadesco ADJ soldierly

soldadito SM ▸ **soldadito de plomo** tin soldier

soldado[1] SMF soldier • **una joven ~** a young woman soldier • **la tumba del Soldado Desconocido** the tomb of the Unknown Soldier ▸ **soldado de infantería** infantryman ▸ **soldado de marina** marine ▸ **soldado de plomo** tin soldier ▸ **soldado de primera** lance corporal ▸ **soldado raso** private, private first class (*EEUU*)

soldado[2] ADJ [*junta*] welded • **totalmente ~** welded throughout

soldador(a) SM/F (= *persona*) welder
SM (*Téc*) soldering iron

soldadura SF **1** [*de materiales*] solder
2 (= *acción*) (*con estaño*) soldering; (*sin estaño*) welding ▸ **soldadura autógena** welding
3 (= *juntura*) welded seam, weld

soldar ▷ CONJUG 1l VT **1** (*Téc*) (*con estaño*) to solder; (*fundiendo*) to weld

S

2 (= *juntar*) to join, unite
3 [+ *disputa*] to patch up
VPR **soldarse** [*huesos*] to knit, knit together

soleado ADJ sunny

solear ▷ CONJUG 1a VT (= *dejar al sol*) to put *o* leave in the sun; (= *blanquear*) to bleach

solecismo SM solecism

soledad SF **1** (= *falta de compañía*) (*voluntaria*) solitude; (*involuntaria*) loneliness, lonesomeness (EEUU) • **le gusta trabajar en la ~ de su habitación** he likes working in the solitude of his room • **tengo miedo a la ~** I have a fear of loneliness • **la ~ le deprime** being alone makes him feel depressed
2 soledades (*liter*) solitary place (*sing*) • **nadie habitaba aquellas ~es** no-one lived in that solitary place

solejar SM = **solana**

solemne ADJ **1** (= *serio*) solemn
2* (= *enorme*) [*mentira*] downright; [*tontería*] utter; [*error*] complete, terrible

solemnemente ADV solemnly

solemnidad SF **1** [*de persona*] solemnity
2 [*de acontecimiento*] (= *majestuosidad*) impressiveness; (= *dignidad*) solemnity
3 (= *ceremonia*) solemn ceremony • **~es** solemnities
4 solemnidades (= *formalismos*) formalities, bureaucratic formalities
5 • **pobre de ~** miserably poor, penniless

solemnización SF solemnization, celebration

solemnizar ▷ CONJUG 1f VT to solemnize, celebrate

solenoide SM solenoid

soler ▷ CONJUG 2h; defectivo VI
1 (= *acostumbrar*) **a** (*en presente*) • **suele pasar por aquí** he usually comes this way • **—¿bebió alcohol? —pues no suele** "did he drink?" — "well, he doesn't usually" • **como se suele hacer por estas fechas** as is normal *o* customary at this time of the year
b (*en pasado*) • **solíamos ir todos los años a la playa** we used to go to the beach every year
2 (*Cono Sur*) (= *ocurrir*) to occur rarely, happen only occasionally; ▷ ACOSTUMBRAR

solera SF **1** (= *tradición*) tradition • **este es país de ~ celta** this is a country with a long-established Celtic tradition • **vino de ~** vintage wine • **es un barrio con ~** it is a typically Spanish *etc* quarter • **es de ~ de médicos** he comes from a line of doctors
2 (= *objeto*) (*de apoyo*) prop, support; (*para saltar*) plinth
3 [*de cuneta*] bottom
4 (= *piedra de molino*) lower millstone
5 (*Méx*) (= *baldosa*) flagstone
6 (*Cono Sur*) [*de acera*] kerb, curb (EEUU)

SOLERA
Sherry does not have a specific vintage since it is a mixture of the vintages from different years; the **solera** method is used to ensure uniformity of quality. In the **bodega** (cellar) the casks are arranged in horizontal rows, with the bottom row, known as the **solera**, containing the oldest wine. When part of this is bottled, the casks are replenished with wine from the row immediately above, which in turn is refilled with wine from the next row, and so on.
▷ JEREZ

solería SF flooring

soleta SF **1** (*Cos*) patch, darn
2† (= *mujer*) shameless woman
3* • **dar ~ a algn** to chuck sb out • **tomar ~** to beat it* • **dejar a algn en ~s** (*And*) to leave sb penniless
4 (*Méx*) (*Culin*) wafer, ladyfinger

solevantamiento SM **1** [*de objeto*] pushing up, raising
2 (*Pol*) rising

solevantar ▷ CONJUG 1a VT **1** [+ *objeto*] to push up, raise
2 (*Pol*) to rouse, stir up

solfa SF **1** (*Mús*) (= *solfeo*) sol-fa; (= *signos*) musical notation
2* (= *paliza*) thrashing
3* • MODISMO: • **poner a algn en ~** to make sb look ridiculous

solfear ▷ CONJUG 1a VT **1** (*Mús*) to sol-fa
2* (= *zurrar*) to thrash
3* (= *echar una bronca a*) to tick off*
4† (*Cono Sur*) (= *hurtar*) to nick‡, swipe‡

solfeo SM **1** (*Mús*) sol-fa, singing of scales, voice practice • **clase de ~** singing lesson
2* (= *paliza*) thrashing; (= *reprensión*) ticking-off*

solicitación SF [*de beca, ayuda*] requesting; [*de votos*] canvassing

solicitado ADJ • **estar muy ~** to be in great demand, be much sought after • **está muy ~ por las chicas** all the girls are after him

solicitante SMF applicant

solicitar ▷ CONJUG 1a VT **1** (= *pedir*) [+ *permiso, apoyo*] to ask for, seek; [+ *visto bueno*] to seek; [+ *empleo, puesto*] to apply for; [+ *votos, opiniones*] to canvass; [+ *datos, información*] to ask for, request (*más frm*) • **~ algo a algn** to ask sb for sth
2 [+ *atención*] (*tb Fís*) to attract
3 (= *perseguir*) [+ *persona*] to pursue, try to attract; [+ *mujer*] to court

solícito ADJ (= *diligente*) solicitous (**por** about, for); (= *atento*) attentive; (= *servicial*) obliging

solicitud SF **1** (= *petición*) (*gen*) request; (*para puesto, beca, permiso*) application • **presenté** *o* **entregué la ~ para el trabajo** I submitted the application for the job • **denegar** *o* **rechazar una ~** to reject an application • **a ~** (*frm*) on request ▸ **solicitud de extradición** request *o* application for extradition ▸ **solicitud de pago** (*Com*) demand note
2 (= *impreso*) application form • **rellene la ~ en letra mayúscula** fill in the application (form) in block capitals
3 (*frm*) (= *atención*) • **el recepcionista atendió con ~ nuestras reclamaciones** the receptionist was very solicitous in dealing with our complaints • **cuidaba con ~ a su nieto enfermo** she looked after her sick grandson with great devotion

sólidamente ADV solidly

solidariamente ADV jointly, mutually

solidaridad SF solidarity • **por ~ con** out of solidarity with

solidario ADJ **1** (= *humanitario*) caring • **Luis es muy ~** Luis is a very caring person • **vivimos en un mundo poco ~** we live in an uncaring world, we live in a world where it's every man for himself • **un acto ~** an act of solidarity • **~ con algo/algn**: • **se ha mostrado muy ~ con nuestra causa** he has been very sympathetic to our cause, he has shown a lot of solidarity with our cause • **hacerse ~ con algo/algn** to declare one's solidarity with sth/sb • **~ de algo** (*frm*): • **hacerse ~ de una opinión** to echo an opinion
2 (*Jur*) [*compromiso*] mutually binding, shared in common; [*participación*] joint, common; [*firmante, participante*] jointly liable • **responsabilidad solidaria** joint liability

solidarizarse ▷ CONJUG 1f VPR • **~ con** to declare one's support for • **me solidarizo con esa opinión** I share that view

solideo SM calotte, skullcap

solidez SF (= *firmeza*) solidity; (= *dureza*) hardness

solidificación SF solidification, hardening

solidificar ▷ CONJUG 1g VT to solidify, harden
VPR **solidificarse** to solidify, harden

sólido ADJ **1** [*objeto*] (= *compacto*) solid; (= *duro*) hard
2 (*Téc*) (= *firme*) solidly made; (= *bien construido*) well built; [*zapatos*] stout, strong; [*color*] fast
3 (= *seguro*) [*argumento*] solid, sound; [*base, principio*] sound
SM solid

soliloquiar ▷ CONJUG 1b VI to soliloquize, talk to oneself

soliloquio SM soliloquy, monologue

solimán SM **1** (*Quím*) corrosive sublimate
2 (= *veneno*) poison

solio SM throne

solipsismo SM solipsism

solista SMF soloist

solitaria SF tapeworm

solitario/a ADJ **1** [*persona, vida*] solitary, lonely, lonesome (EEUU) • **vivir ~** to live alone *o* on one's own
2 [*lugar*] lonely, desolate • **a esa hora la calle está solitaria** at that hour the street is deserted *o* empty
SM/F (= *recluso*) recluse; (= *ermitaño*) hermit
SM **1** (*Naipes*) solitaire
2 (= *diamante*) solitaire
3 • **en ~** alone, on one's own • **vuelta al mundo en ~** solo trip around the world • **tocar en ~** to play solo

solito* ADJ • **estar ~** to be all alone, be all on one's own

sólito ADJ usual, customary

soliviantado ADJ rebellious

soliviantar ▷ CONJUG 1a VT **1** (= *amotinar*) to stir up, rouse, rouse to revolt
2 (= *enojar*) to anger
3 (= *sacar de quicio*) to exasperate
4 (= *inquietar*) to worry • **le tienen soliviantado los celos** he is eaten up with jealousy
5 (= *hacer sentir ansias*) to fill with longing
6 (= *dar esperanzas a*) to buoy up with false hopes • **anda soliviantado con el proyecto** he has tremendous hopes for the scheme

soliviar ▷ CONJUG 1b VT to lift, push up
VPR **soliviarse** to half rise, partly get up

solla SF plaice

sollamar ▷ CONJUG 1a VT to scorch, singe

sollastre SM rogue, villain

sollo SM sturgeon

sollozar ▷ CONJUG 1f VI to sob

sollozo SM sob • **decir algo entre ~s** to sob sth

solo[1] ADJ **1** (= *sin compañía*) alone, on one's own • **pasa los días ~ en su cuarto** he spends the days alone *o* on his own in his room • **iré ~** I'll go alone *o* on my own • **dejar ~ a algn** to leave sb alone • **me quedé ~** I was left alone • **habla ~** he talks to himself • **se quedó ~ a los siete años** he was left an orphan *o* alone in the world at seven • MODISMOS: • **estar más ~ que la una*** to be all on one's own • **es tonto como él ~** he's as stupid as they come • **lo hace como él ~** he does it as no one else can • **se queda ~ contando mentiras** he's as good a liar as you'll find • REFRÁN: • **más vale estar ~ que mal acompañado** it's better to be on your own than in bad company
2 (= *solitario*) lonely • **me siento muy ~** I feel very lonely
3 (= *único*) • **su sola preocupación es ganar dinero** his one *o* only concern is to make

money • **con esta sola condición** on this one condition • **hay una sola dificultad** there is only *o* just one problem • **no hubo ni una sola objeción** there was not a single objection
4 (= *sin acompañamiento*) [*café, té*] black; [*whisky, vodka, ron*] straight, neat • **tendremos que comer pan ~** we shall have to eat plain bread
5 (*Mús*) solo • **cantar ~** to sing solo
SM **1** (*Mús*) solo • **un ~ de guitarra** a guitar solo • **un ~ para tenor** a tenor solo
2 (= *café*) black coffee
3 (*Naipes*) solitaire, patience
4 (*Cono Sur*) (= *lata*) tedious conversation
solo² ADV, **sólo** ADV (= *únicamente*) only; (= *exclusivamente*) solely, merely, just • **solo quiero verlo** I only *o* just want to see it • **es solo un teniente** he's only a lieutenant, he's a mere lieutenant • **no solo A sino también B** not only A but also B • **solo con apretar un botón** at the touch of a button • **me parece bien solo que no tengo tiempo** that's fine, only *o* but I don't have the time • **ven aunque solo sea para media hora** come even if it's just for half an hour • **con solo que sepas tocar algunas notas** even if you only know how to play a few notes • **solo con que estudies dos horas diarias** by studying for as little as two hours a day • **tan solo** only, just • **solo que ...** except that ... • **viajará sólo un par de días** he'll only be away for a couple of days

*In the past the standard spelling for this adverb was with an accent (**sólo**). Nowadays the **Real Academia Española** advises that the accented form is only required where there might otherwise be confusion with the adjective **solo**.*

solomillo SM sirloin steak
solón SM (*Caribe*) scorching heat, very strong sunlight
solsticio SM solstice ▸ **solsticio de invierno** winter solstice ▸ **solsticio de verano** summer solstice
soltar ▹ CONJUG 1l VT **1** (= *dejar de agarrar*) to let go of; (= *dejar caer*) to drop • **soltó mi mano** he let go of my hand • **¡suéltenme!** let go of me!, let me go! • **no sueltes la cuerda** don't let go of the rope • **el gato me soltó el ratón en los pies** the cat dropped the mouse at my feet • **dejó de escribir y soltó el bolígrafo** she stopped writing and put down her pen
2 [+ *amarras*] to cast off; [+ *nudo, cinturón*] (= *quitar*) to untie, undo; (= *aflojar*) to loosen • **ve soltando cuerda mientras bajas** pay the rope out gradually as you descend
3 (*Aut*) [+ *embrague*] to let out, release, disengage (*frm*); [+ *freno*] to release
4 (= *dejar libre*) [+ *preso, animal*] to release, set free; [+ *agua*] to let out, run off • **soltó una paloma blanca en señal de paz** he released a white dove as a token of peace
5 (= *emitir*) [+ *gas, olor*] to give off; [+ *grito*] to let out • **suelta vapores peligrosos** it gives off dangerous fumes • **solté un suspiro de alivio** I let out *o* heaved a sigh of relief • **~ una carcajada** to burst out laughing • **~ un estornudo** to sneeze • **~ un suspiro** to sigh
6 (= *asestar*) • **~ un golpe** to deal a blow • **le soltó un puñetazo** she hit him
7 (*al hablar*) [+ *noticia*] to break; [+ *indirecta*] to drop; [+ *blasfemia*] to come out with, let fly • **les volvió a ~ el mismo sermón** he gave them the lecture all over again • **¡suéltalo ya!** out with it!, spit it out!* • **soltó un par de palabrotas** he came out with a couple of rude words, he let fly a couple of obscenities • MODISMO: • **~ cuatro verdades** a algn to tell sb a few home truths
8* (= *perder*) [+ *puesto, privilegio*] to give up; [+ *dinero*] to cough up* • **no quiere ~ el puesto por nada del mundo** he won't give up the job for anything in the world
9 [*serpiente*] [+ *piel*] to shed
10 (= *resolver*) [+ *dificultad*] to solve; [+ *duda*] to resolve; [+ *objeción*] to satisfy, deal with
11 (*And*) (= *ceder*) to cede, give, hand over
VPR **soltarse 1** (= *liberarse*) • **que no se vaya a ~ el perro** don't let the dog get out *o* get loose • **logró ~se y pedir ayuda** he managed to free himself *o* get free and call for help
2 (= *desprenderse*) to come off; (= *aflojarse*) to come loose, work loose • **~se los botones** to undo one's buttons • **~se el pelo** to let one's hair down
3 (= *deshacerse*) [*cordón, nudo*] to come undone, come untied; [*costura*] to come unstitched
4 (= *desenvolverse*) (*con actividad*) to become expert; (*con idioma*) to become fluent • **~se a andar/hablar** to start walking/talking
5 (= *independizarse*) to achieve one's independence, win freedom
6 (= *desmandarse*) to lose control of o.s. • **~se a su gusto** to let off steam, let fly
7* • **~se con: ~se con una idea absurda** to come up with a silly idea • **~se con una contribución de 50 dólares** to come up with a 50-dollar contribution • **por fin se soltó con algunos peniques** he eventually parted with a few coppers
solterear ▹ CONJUG 1a VI (*Cono Sur*) to stay single
soltería SF (*gen*) single state, unmarried state; [*de hombre*] bachelorhood; [*de mujer*] spinsterhood • **está muy bien en su ~** she's perfectly happy being single
soltero/a ADJ single, unmarried • **está soltera** she's single, she's unmarried • **madre soltera** single *o* unmarried mother
SM/F single *o* unmarried man/woman, bachelor/spinster • **apellido de soltera** maiden name • **la señora de García, Rodríguez de soltera** Mrs García, née Rodríguez
solterón/ona SMF (= *hombre*) confirmed bachelor; (= *mujer*) spinster; (*pey*) old maid • **tía solterona** maiden aunt
solterona SF spinster; (*pey*) old maid • **tía ~** maiden aunt
soltura SF **1** (*al hablar*) fluency, ease • **habla árabe con ~** he speaks Arabic fluently
2 (= *flojedad*) [*de cuerda*] slackness; [*de pieza, tornillo*] looseness; [*de brazos, piernas*] agility, nimbleness
3 (*Med*) (*tb* **soltura de vientre**) looseness of the bowels, diarrhoea, diarrhea (*EEUU*)
4 (*pey*) (= *desvergüenza*) shamelessness
solubilidad SF solubility
soluble ADJ **1** (*Quím*) soluble • **~ en agua** water-soluble, soluble in water
2 [*problema*] solvable, that can be solved
solución SF **1** (*Quím*) solution
2 (= *respuesta*) [*de problema*] solution, answer (**a** to); [*de crucigrama, pregunta*] answer (**de** to) • **esto no tiene ~** there's no answer to this, there's no solution to this one ▸ **solución final** final solution ▸ **solución salomónica** compromise solution
3 (*Teat*) climax, dénouement
4 ▸ **solución de continuidad** break in continuity, interruption
solucionar ▹ CONJUG 1a VT **1** [+ *problema*] to solve • **un problema sin ~** an unsolved problem
2 (= *decidir*) to resolve, settle
solucionista SMF solver
solvencia SF **1** (*Econ*) (= *estado*) solvency; (= *acción*) settlement, payment
2 (= *fiabilidad*) reliability • **de toda ~ moral** completely trustworthy • **fuentes de toda ~** completely reliable sources ▸ **solvencia moral** good character
3 (= *reputación*) solid reputation
4 (= *aptitud*) ability, competence
solventar ▹ CONJUG 1a VT **1** [+ *deuda*] to settle, pay
2 (= *solucionar*) [+ *dificultad*] to resolve; [+ *asunto*] to settle
solvente ADJ **1** (*Econ*) solvent, free of debt
2 (= *fiable*) [*persona*] reliable, trustworthy; [*fuente*] reliable
3 (= *decente*) respectable, worthy
4 (= *hábil*) able
SM (*Quím*) solvent
solysombra* SM brandy and anisette
somalí ADJ, SMF Somali
Somalia SF Somalia
somanta SF beating, thrashing
somantar ▹ CONJUG 1a VT to beat, thrash
somatada SF (*CAm*) blow, punch
somatar ▹ CONJUG 1a (*CAm*) VT **1** [+ *persona*] (= *zurrar*) to beat, thrash; (= *pegar*) to punch
2 (= *vender*) to sell off cheap
VPR **somatarse** to fall and hurt o.s., knock o.s. about badly
somatén SM **1** (= *alarma*) alarm • **tocar a ~** to sound the alarm
2* (= *jaleo*) uproar, confusion
somático ADJ somatic
somatizar ▹ CONJUG 1f VT **1** (= *exteriorizar*) to externalize, express externally
2 (= *caracterizar*) to characterize
somatón SM (*CAm*) = **somatada**
sombra SF **1** (*proyectada por un objeto*) shadow • **solo vi una ~** I only saw a shadow • **Juan se ha convertido en tu ~** Juan follows you round like your shadow • **dar** *o* **hacer ~** to cast a shadow • **el ciprés da** *o* **hace una ~ alargada** cypress trees cast a long shadow • **un árbol que da** *o* **hace ~** a shady tree • **no quiere que otros le hagan ~** he doesn't want to be overshadowed by anybody else • MODISMO: • **no se fía ni de su ~** he doesn't trust a soul ▸ **sombra de ojos** eyeshadow ▸ **sombras chinescas** shadow play (*sing*), pantomime (*sing*)
2 (= *zona sin sol*) shade • **ven, siéntate aquí a la ~** come and sit here in the shade • **luz y ~** light and shade • **se sentó a la ~ del olivo** she sat in the shade of the olive tree • **medró a la ~ del presidente** she flourished under the protection of the president • MODISMOS: • **a la ~*** (= *en prisión*) in the clink*, inside* • **permanecer** *o* **quedarse en la ~** to stay in the background, remain on the sidelines
3 (= *rastro*) shadow • **sin ~ de duda** without a shadow of a doubt • **no es ni ~ de lo que era** he's a shadow of his former self • **sin ~ de avaricia** without a trace of greed • **no tiene ni ~ de talento** he hasn't the least bit of talent • **tiene una ~ de parecido con su tío** he has a faint resemblance to his uncle
4 (= *suerte*) luck • **¡qué mala ~!** how unlucky!, what bad luck! • **esta vez he tenido muy buena ~** I was very lucky this time
5 (= *gracia*) • **tiene muy buena ~ para contar chistes** he's got a knack *o* gift for telling jokes, he's very funny telling jokes • **tener mala ~** to have a bad sense of humour
6 (= *mancha*) (*lit*) dark patch, stain; (*fig*) stain, blot • **es una ~ en su carácter** it is a stain *o* blot on his character
7 (= *fantasma*) shade, ghost
8 (*Arte*) shade
9 (*Boxeo*) shadow-boxing • **hacer ~** to shadow-box
10 (*CAm, Cono Sur*) (= *quitasol*) parasol, sunshade

11 (*CAm, Méx*) (= *toldo*) awning; (= *pórtico*) porch
12 (*CAm, Cono Sur*) (*para escribir*) guidelines (*pl*)
13† **sombras** (= *oscuridad*) darkness (*sing*), obscurity (*sing*); (= *ignorancia*) ignorance (*sing*); (= *pesimismo*) sombreness (*sing*)
sombraje (SM), **sombrajo** (SM) shelter from the sun • **hacer ~s** to get in the light
sombreado (ADJ) shady
(SM) (*Arte*) shading
sombreador (SM) ▸ **sombreador de ojos** eyeshadow
sombrear ▹ CONJUG 1a (VT) **1** (= *dar sombra*) to shade
2 (*Arte*) to shade
3 (= *maquillar*) to put eyeshadow on
sombrerera (SF) **1** (= *caja*) hatbox
2 (*And, Caribe*) (= *perchero*) hat stand; ▹ **sombrerero**
sombrerería (SF) **1** (= *sombreros*) hats (*pl*), millinery
2 (= *tienda*) hat shop
3 (= *fábrica*) hat factory
sombrerero/a (SM/F) (= *artesano*) (*para sombreros de hombre*) hatter; (*para sombreros de mujer*) milliner; ▹ **sombrerera**
(SM) (*And, Cono Sur*) (= *perchero*) hatstand
sombrerete (SM) **1** (= *sombrero*) little hat
2 [*de seta*] cap
3 (*Téc*) [*de carburador*] bonnet; (= *cubo de rueda*) cap; [*de chimenea*] cowl
sombrero (SM) **1** (= *gorro*) hat • MODISMO: • **quitarse el ~ ante algo** to take off one's hat to sth ▸ **sombrero apuntado** cocked hat ▸ **sombrero de ala ancha** wide-brimmed hat, broad-brimmed hat ▸ **sombrero de copa** top hat ▸ **sombrero de jipijapa** Panama hat ▸ **sombrero de paja** straw hat ▸ **sombrero de pelo** (*LAm*) top hat ▸ **sombrero de tres picos** cocked hat, three-cornered hat ▸ **sombrero flexible** soft hat, trilby, fedora (*EEUU*) ▸ **sombrero gacho** slouch hat ▸ **sombrero hongo** bowler, bowler hat, derby (*EEUU*) ▸ **sombrero safari** safari hat ▸ **sombrero tejano** stetson, ten-gallon hat
2 (*Bot*) cap
sombríamente (ADV) sombrely, somberly (*EEUU*)
sombrilla (SF) parasol, sunshade • MODISMO: • **me vale ~** (*Méx**) I couldn't care less*
sombrío (ADJ) **1** (= *con sombra*) shaded
2 (= *triste*) [*lugar*] sombre, somber (*EEUU*), gloomy, dismal; [*persona, perspectiva*] gloomy
(SM) (*Méx*) shady place
someramente (ADV) superficially
somero (ADJ) **1** (= *a poca profundidad*) shallow
2 (= *poco detallado*) superficial, summary (*frm*)
someter ▹ CONJUG 2a (VT) **1** (= *dominar*) [+ *territorio, población*] to subjugate; [+ *rebeldes*] to subdue, put down; [+ *asaltante*] to overpower, overcome • **ni entre cuatro hombres lo pudieron ~** even four men were not enough to overpower *o* overcome him
2 (= *subordinar*) • **sometió sus intereses a los de su pueblo** he put the interests of the people before his own, he subordinated his interests to those of the people (*frm*) • **~ su opinión a la de otros** to put the opinion of others above one's own
3 • **~ a a** (= *exponer*) [+ *represión, tortura, interrogatorio*] to subject to • **cuando se somete a elevadas temperaturas** when it is subjected to high temperatures • **hay que ~ a examen todas las ideas establecidas** all established ideas should be subjected to scrutiny • **lo tiene sometido a su entera voluntad** he is entirely subject to her will • **~án las propuestas a un amplio debate** the proposals will be widely debated • **han sometido a referéndum su ingreso en la UE** they have held a referendum on joining the EU • **~ algo/a algn a prueba** to put sth/sb to the test • **vamos a ~ nuestra hipótesis a prueba** we are going to put our hypothesis to the test • **la princesa sometió a sus pretendientes a una prueba** the princess made her suitors undergo a test • **~ algo a votación** to put sth to the vote
b (= *entregar*) to submit sth to • **~á el acuerdo a la aprobación de los ministros** he will submit the agreement for the approval of the ministers • **~ una obra a la censura** to submit a work to the censor
(VPR) **someterse 1** (= *aceptar*) • **~se a** [+ *disciplina, autoridad*] to submit to; [+ *normas*] to comply with • **me someto a la voluntad de Dios** I submit to God's will • **tienen que ~se a las normas urbanísticas** they must comply with urban development regulations • **~se a la mayoría** to give way to the majority • **~se a la opinión de algn** to bow to sb's opinion
2 (= *exponerse*) • **~se a** [+ *desprecio, humillación*] to subject o.s. to; [+ *operación, prueba, tratamiento*] to undergo • **me niego a ~me a tal suplicio** I refuse to subject myself to such an ordeal • **deberá ~se a un intenso entrenamiento** she will have to undergo intensive training
sometico (ADJ) (*And*), **sometido** (ADJ) (*And, CAm*) = **entrometido**
sometimiento (SM) **1** (= *dominación*) [*de un pueblo*] subjugation • **tras el ~ de los celtas, los romanos …** after the subjugation of the Celts, the Romans … • **han conseguido el ~ de los rebeldes** they have managed to subdue the rebels
2 (= *sumisión*) **a** (*por la fuerza*) subjection (**a** to) • **siglos de ~ al patriarcado** centuries of subjection to *o* being subject to patriarchy
b (*voluntariamente*) (*a la autoridad*) submission (**a** to); (*a la ley*) compliance (**a** with) • **rechazan el ~ a la autoridad** they refuse to submit to *o* bow to authority
3 (= *exposición*) • **como consecuencia de su ~ a estímulos externos** as a result of being subjected to external stimuli
4 (= *entrega*) [*de propuesta*] submission (**a** to) • **tras pocos días de su ~ a la aprobación del pleno** a few days after its submission to the plenary session for approval • **tras el ~ de la propuesta a votación** after the proposal was put to the vote
somier [so'mjer] (SM) (PL: **somiers, somieres** [so'mjer]) (*sin concretar tipo*) bed base; (*con muelles*) springs (*pl*); (*con láminas de madera*) slats (*pl*)
somnambulismo (SM) sleepwalking, somnambulism (*frm*)
somnámbulo/a (SM/F) sleepwalker, somnambulist (*frm*)
somnífero (ADJ) sleep-inducing
(SM) sleeping pill
somnílocuo/a (ADJ) given to talking in one's sleep
(SM/F) person who talks in his *o* her sleep
somnolencia (SF) sleepiness, drowsiness
somnolento (ADJ), **somnoliento** (ADJ) sleepy, drowsy
somorgujar ▹ CONJUG 1a (VT) to duck
(VPR) **somorgujarse** to dive, plunge (**en** into)
somormujo (SM) grebe ▸ **somormujo menor** dabchick
somos ▹ **ser**
sompopo (SM) (*El Salvador*) yellow ant
son¹ (SM) **1** (*Mús*) (= *sonido*) sound; (= *sonido agradable*) pleasant sound • **al son de** to the sound of • **a los sones de la marcha nupcial** to the strains of the wedding march
2 (= *rumor*) rumour, rumor (*EEUU*) • **corre el son de que …** there is a rumour *o* (*EEUU*) rumor going round that …
3 (= *estilo*) manner, style • **¿a qué son?** • **¿a son de qué?** why on earth? • **en son de** as, like • **en son de broma** as *o* for a joke • **en son de paz** in peace • **en son de guerra** in a warlike fashion • **no vienen en son de protesta** they haven't come with the idea of complaining • **por este son** in this way • **sin son** for no reason at all
4 (*LAm*) *Afro-Cuban dance and tune* ▸ **son huasteco** (*Méx*) *folk song from Veracruz*; ▹ **bailar**
son² ▹ **ser**
sonado (ADJ) **1** (= *comentado*) [*éxito, noticia*] much talked-about; [*escándalo, estafa*] notorious • **ha sido un divorcio muy ~** their divorce has caused a great stir, it has been a much talked-about divorce • **el escándalo fue muy ~** the scandal was much talked about, it was a notorious scandal • **hacer una que sea sonada*** to kick up a stink*
2* (= *chiflado*) • **estar ~** to be crazy; (*Boxeo*) to be punch drunk
sonaja (SF) **1** (= *campanilla*) little bell
2 sonajas (*para niño*) rattle (*sing*)
sonajera (SF) (*Cono Sur*), **sonajero** (SM) rattle
sonambulismo (SM) sleepwalking, somnambulism (*frm*)
sonámbulo/a (SM/F) sleepwalker, somnambulist (*frm*)
sonanta‡ (SF) guitar
sonante (ADJ) ▹ **contante**
sonar¹ ▹ CONJUG 1l (VI) **1** (= *producir sonido*) **a** [*campana, teléfono, timbre*] to ring; [*aparato electrónico*] to beep, bleep • **este timbre no suena** this bell doesn't work *o* ring • **está sonando el busca** the pager is beeping *o* bleeping • **el reloj de la iglesia no sonó** the church clock did not chime • **acaban de ~ las diez** it has just struck ten • **hacer ~** [+ *alarma, sirena*] to sound; [+ *campanilla, timbre*] to ring; [+ *trompeta, flauta*] to play • **hace ~ su vieja gaita en las grandes ocasiones** he plays his old bagpipes on special occasions • **haz ~ el claxon** blow *o* beep the horn
b [*alarma, sirena*] to go off • **a las seis sonó el despertador** the alarm clock went off at six
c [*máquina, aparato*] to make a noise; [*música*] to play • **¡cómo suena este frigorífico!** what a noise this fridge makes! • **~on tres disparos** three shots were heard • **empezó a ~ el himno nacional** the national anthem started to play • **le sonaban las tripas** his stomach was rumbling • MODISMO: • **ni ~ ni tronar** not to count; ▹ **flauta, río**
2 (*Ling*) [*fonema, letra*] to be pronounced; [*frase, palabra*] to sound • **la h de "hombre" no suena** the h in "hombre" is not pronounced *o* is silent • **escríbelo tal como suena** write it as it sounds
3 (= *parecer por el sonido*) to sound • **sonaba extraño viniendo de él** it sounded strange coming from him • **cantan en inglés y suenan muy bien** they sing in English and they sound very good • **ese título suena bien** that sounds like a good title • **~ a** to sound like • **suena a metálico** it sounds like metal • **eso me suena a excusa** that sounds like an excuse to me • **sus palabras sonaban a falso** his words rang *o* sounded false • **~ a hueco** to sound hollow • MODISMOS: • **así como suena** just like that • **le dijo que se fuera, así como suena** he told him to go, just like that • **se llama Anastasio, así como suena** he's

S

called Anastasio, believe it or not • **me suena a chino** it sounds double Dutch to me
4 (= *ser conocido*) to sound familiar, ring a bell* • **¿no te suena el nombre?** isn't the name familiar?, doesn't the name sound familiar *o* ring a bell? • **a mí su cara no me suena de nada** his face isn't at all familiar to me *o* doesn't look at all familiar to me
5 (= *mencionarse*) • **su nombre suena constantemente en relación con este asunto** her name is always coming up *o* being mentioned in connection with this affair • **no quiere que suene su nombre** he doesn't want his name mentioned
6 (*And, Cono Sur**) (= *fracasar*) to come to grief* • **sonamos en la prueba de francés** we came to grief in the French test* • **ahora sí que sonamos** now we're really in trouble
7 (*Cono Sur**) (= *morirse*) to kick the bucket*, peg out*
8 (*Cono Sur**) (= *estropearse*) to pack up*
9 • **hacer ~** (*Cono Sur**) (*gen*) to wreck; [+ *dinero*] to blow*
10 • **hacer ~ a algn** (*Cono Sur**) (= *derrotar*) to thrash sb*; (= *castigar*) to do sb‡; (= *suspender*) to fail, flunk (*EEUU**) • **lo van a hacer ~ si lo pillan** he'll get done for it if they catch him‡
VT 1 (= *hacer sonar*) [+ *campanilla*] to ring; [+ *trompeta*] to play; [+ *alarma, sirena*] to sound
2 • **~ la nariz a algn** to blow sb's nose
3 (*Méx, Ven**) (= *pegar*) to clobber*
4 (*Méx, Ven**) (= *ganar*) to thrash*
VPR **sonarse** (*tb* **sonarse los mocos** *o* **la nariz**) to blow one's nose
sonar² SM, **sónar** SM sonar
sonata SF sonata
sonda SF 1 (= *acción*) sounding
2 (*Med*) probe
3 (*Náut*) lead ▸ **sonda acústica** echo sounder ▸ **sonda espacial** space probe
4 (*Téc*) bore, drill
sondaje SM (*Náut*) sounding; (*Téc*) boring, drilling • **conversaciones de ~** exploratory talks
sondar ▸ CONJUG 1a VT, **sondear** ▸ CONJUG 1a VT 1 (*Med*) to probe
2 (*Náut*) to sound, take soundings of
3 (*Téc*) to bore, bore into, drill
4 (= *investigar*) [+ *misterio*] to fathom; [+ *persona, intenciones*] to sound out • **sondear a la opinión pública** to sound out public opinion • **sondear el terreno** to spy out the land, see how the land lies
sondeo SM 1 (*Med, Náut*) sounding
2 (*Téc*) drilling
3 (*Pol*) (= *encuesta*) poll; (= *contacto*) feeler, approach • **~ realizado a la salida de las urnas** exit poll ▸ **sondeo de audiencia** audience research ▸ **sondeo de la opinión pública** public opinion poll, Gallup Poll ▸ **sondeo de opinión** opinion poll ▸ **sondeo telefónico** telephone survey
sonería SF chimes (*pl*)
soneto SM sonnet
songa SF 1 (*Caribe*) (= *sarcasmo*) sarcasm, irony
2 (*Méx*) (= *grosería*) dirty joke, vulgar remark
3 • **a la ~ (~)** (*And, CAm, Cono Sur**) slyly, underhandedly
songo ADJ (*And, Méx*) 1* (= *estúpido*) stupid, thick*
2* (= *taimado*) sly, crafty
SM (*And*) buzz, hum
sónico ADJ sonic, sound (*antes de s*)
sonidista SMF sound engineer
sonido SM sound • **~ envolvente** surround sound
soniquete SM = **sonsonete**
sonista SMF sound engineer, sound recordist
sonitono SM (*Telec*) true tone
sonoboya SF sonar buoy
sonómetro SM sound level meter
sonoridad SF sonority
sonorización SF 1 [*de película*] adding of the soundtrack
2 [*de local*] installation of a sound system
3 (*Ling*) voicing
sonorizar ▸ CONJUG 1f VT 1 [+ *película*] to add the sound track to
2 [+ *local*] to install a sound system in
3 (*Ling*) to voice
VPR **sonorizarse** (*Ling*) to voice, become voiced
sonoro ADJ 1 (= *ruidoso*) [*cavidad*] resonant; [*voz*] rich, sonorous; [*poesía*] sonorous; [*cueva*] echoing; [*beso*] loud
2 (*Ling*) voiced
3 • **banda sonora** sound track • **efectos ~s** sound effects
sonotone SM hearing aid
sonreír ▸ CONJUG 3l VI 1 [*persona*] to smile • **~ a algn** to smile at sb • **el chiste no le hizo ni ~** she didn't even smile at the joke • **~ forzadamente** to force a smile
2 (= *favorecer*) • **le sonríe la fortuna** fortune smiles (up)on him • **el porvenir le sonríe** he has a bright future ahead of him
VPR **sonreírse** to smile
sonría *etc* ▸ **sonreír**
sonriente ADJ smiling
sonrisa SF smile • **~ amarga** wry smile • **~ forzada** forced smile • **no perder la ~** to keep smiling • **una ~ de oreja a oreja** an ear-to-ear grin
sonrojado ADJ blushing
sonrojante ADJ embarrassing
sonrojar ▸ CONJUG 1a VT • **~ a algn** to make sb blush
VPR **sonrojarse** to blush (**de** at)
sonrojo SM 1 (= *rubor*) blush
2 (= *improperio*) offensive word, embarrassing remark (*that brings a blush*)
sonrosado ADJ rosy, pink
sonrosarse ▸ CONJUG 1a VPR to turn pink
sonsacar ▸ CONJUG 1g VT to wheedle, coax • **~ a algn** to pump sb for information • **~ un secreto a algn** to worm a secret out of sb
sonsear ▸ CONJUG 1a VI (*Cono Sur*) = **zoncear**
sonsera SF (*LAm*), **sonsería** SF (*LAm*) = **zoncera**
sonso/a* ADJ, SM/F (*LAm*) = **zonzo**
sonsonete SM 1 (= *sonido*) [*de golpes*] tap, tapping; [*de traqueteo*] rattle; [*de cencerro*] jangling
2 (= *voz monótona*) monotonous delivery, singsong, singsong voice
3 (= *frase rimada*) jingle, rhyming phrase
4 (= *tono mofador*) mocking undertone
sonsoniche SM (*Caribe*) = **sonsonete**
sonza SF 1 (*Caribe*) (= *astucia*) cunning, deceit
2 (*Méx*) (= *sarcasmo*) sarcasm, mockery
soñación* SF • **¡ni por ~!** not on your life!
soñado ADJ 1 (= *ideal*) dream (*antes de s*) • **¿cómo sería su casa soñada?** what would your dream home be like?
2 (= *deseado*) dreamed-of • **llegó el ~ día del armisticio** the dreamed-of armistice day dawned
3 (*Col, Cono Sur**) (= *divino*) gorgeous • **un traje de novia ~** a gorgeous wedding dress
soñador(a) ADJ [*ojos, mirada*] dreamy • **siempre he sido un poco ~a** I've always been a bit of a dreamer • **la gente es menos ~a hoy día** nowadays people are less idealistic
SM/F dreamer
soñar ▸ CONJUG 1l VT 1 (*durmiendo*) **a** [+ *ensueño*] to dream • **no recuerdo lo que soñé anoche** I can't remember what I dreamed about last night • **soñé que me había perdido en la selva** I dreamed that I had got lost in the jungle
b (*LAm*) [+ *persona*] to dream about • **te soñé anoche** I dreamed about you last night
2 (= *imaginar*) to dream • **han ganado más dinero del que jamás habían soñado** they have won more money than they ever dreamed of *o* dreamed possible • **nunca lo hubiera soñado** I'd never have dreamed it
• MODISMOS: • **¡ni ~lo!***: • **¿ir en avión? yo eso ¡ni ~lo!** me go by plane? no chance!* • **—¿me compras un abrigo de visón? —¡ni lo sueñes!** "will you buy me a mink coat?" — "in your dreams!" *o* "dream on!"* • **que ni soñado***: • **fue un montaje teatral que ni soñado** the staging of the play was out of this world* • **me va que ni soñado** it suits me a treat*
VI 1 (*durmiendo*) to dream • **~ con algo** to dream about sth • **anoche soñé contigo** I dreamed *o* I had a dream about you last night • **"que sueñes con los angelitos"** "sweet dreams" • **~ en voz alta** to talk in one's sleep
2 (= *fantasear*) to dream • **deja ya de ~ y ponte a trabajar** stop daydreaming *o* dreaming and get on with some work • **~ con algo** to dream of sth • **soñaban con la victoria** they dreamed of victory • **soñaba con una lavadora** she dreamed of (one day) having a washing machine • **~ con hacer algo** to dream of doing sth • **sueña con ser cantante** she dreams of being a singer • **no podemos ni ~ con comprarnos un coche** we can't even think of buying a car • **~ despierto** to daydream
soñarra SF, **soñera** SF 1 (= *modorra*) drowsiness, deep desire to sleep
2 (= *sueño*) deep sleep
soñolencia SF = **somnolencia**
soñolientamente ADV sleepily, drowsily
soñoliento ADJ sleepy, drowsy
sopa SF 1 (= *caldo*) soup • MODISMOS: • **hasta en la ~**: • **los encontramos hasta en la ~** they're everywhere, they're ten a penny • **andar a** *o* **vivir a** *o* **comer la ~ boba** to scrounge one's meals* • **poner a algn como ~ de Pascua*** to give sb a ticking-off* ▸ **sopa chilena** (*And*) corn and potato soup ▸ **sopa de cebolla** onion soup ▸ **sopa de cola** (*CAm*) oxtail soup ▸ **sopa de fideos** noodle soup ▸ **sopa de sobre** packet soup ▸ **sopa de verduras, sopa juliana** vegetable soup
2 (= *pan mojado*) sop • **hacer ~s** to dunk* • MODISMOS: • **estar hecho una ~** to be sopping wet, be soaked to the skin • **dar ~s con honda a algn** to be streets ahead of sb ▸ **sopas de leche** bread and milk
3 ▸ **sopa de letras** word search, word search game
4 (*Méx*) (*tb* **sopa seca**) second course
sopaipilla SF (*And, Cono Sur*) fritter
sopapear ▸ CONJUG 1a VT 1 [+ *persona*] (= *golpear*) to slap, smack; (= *sacudir*) to shake violently
2 (= *maltratar*) to maltreat; (= *insultar*) to insult
sopapié SM (*And*) kick
sopapina SF series of punches, bashing*
sopapo SM slap, smack
sopar* ▸ CONJUG 1a (*Cono Sur*) VT [+ *pan*] to dip, dunk
VI to meddle
sopear ▸ CONJUG 1a VT (*LAm*) to soak
sopera SF soup tureen
sopero ADJ 1 [*plato, cuchara*] soup (*antes de s*)
2 (*And*) (= *curioso*) nosey*, gossipy
SM soup plate
sopesar ▸ CONJUG 1a VT 1 (= *levantar*) to try

S

the weight of
2 (= *evaluar*) [+ *situación*] to weigh up; [+ *palabras*] to weigh

sopetón SM **1** (= *golpe*) punch
2 • **de ~** suddenly, unexpectedly • **entrar de ~** to pop in, drop in • **entrar de ~ en un cuarto** to burst into a room

sopimpa SF (*Caribe*) series of punches

soplacausas* SMF INV incompetent lawyer

soplado ADJ* **1** [*persona*] (= *borracho*) tight*; (= *limpio*) clean; (= *pulcro*) extra smart, overdressed; (= *afectado*) affected; (= *engreído*) stuck-up*
2 (*Cono Sur**) • **ir ~** to drive very fast
SM (*tb* **soplado de vidrio**) glass blowing

soplador(a) SM/F **1** [*de vidrio*] glass blower
2 (= *alborotador*) troublemaker
3 (*And, CAm*) (*Teat*) prompter
SM (= *ventilador*) fan, ventilator

soplagaitas* SMF INV idiot, twit*

soplamocos* SM INV **1** (= *puñetazo*) punch, slap
2 (*Méx*) (= *comentario*) put-down

soplapollas** SMF INV berk*, wanker**, prick**

soplar ▸ CONJUG 1a VT **1** (= *echar aire sobre*) [+ *polvo*] to blow away, blow off; [+ *superficie, sopa, fuego*] to blow on; [+ *vela*] to blow out; [+ *globo*] to blow up; [+ *vidrio*] to blow
2 (= *inspirar*) to inspire
3 (= *decir confidencialmente*) • **~ la respuesta a algn** to whisper the answer to sb • **~ a algn** (= *ayudar a recordar*) to prompt sb • **~ a algn algo referente a otro** to tell sb something nasty about somebody
4* (= *delatar*) to split on*
5* (= *birlar*) to pinch*
6* (= *cobrar*) to charge, sting* • **me han soplado ocho dólares** they stung me for eight dollars • **¿cuánto te ~on?** how much did they sting you for?
7* [+ *golpe*] • **le sopló un buen mamporro** she whacked *o* clouted him one*
VI **1** [*persona, viento*] to blow • **¡sopla!*** (*indicando sorpresa*) well I'm blowed!*
2* (= *delatar*) to split*, squeal*
3* [*beber*] to drink, booze
VPR **soplarse 1*** (= *devorar*) • **~se un pastel** to wolf (down) a cake • **se sopla un litro entero** he knocks back a whole litre*
2* (= *delatar*) • **~se de algn** to split on sb*, sneak on sb
3* (= *engreírse*) to get conceited

soplete SM blowlamp, blowtorch
▸ **soplete oxiacetilénico** oxyacetylene burner ▸ **soplete soldador** welding torch

soplido SM strong puff, blast

soplo SM **1** [*de aire*] (*con la boca*) blow, puff; (*por el viento*) puff, gust • MODISMO: • **en un ~**: • **la semana pasó como *o* en un ~** the week flew by, the week was over in no time
2 (*Téc*) blast
3* tip-off • **dar el ~** to squeal* • **ir con el ~ al director** to tell tales to the headmaster, go and tell the head*
4* [*de policía*] informer, grass*, fink (*EEUU**)
5 ▸ **soplo cardíaco, soplo al corazón** heart murmur

soplón/ona* SM/F **1** [*de policía*] informer, grass*, fink (*EEUU**)
2 (*Méx*) (= *policía*) (*gen*) cop*; (*And*) [*de la policía secreta*] member of the secret police
3 (*CAm*) (*Teat*) prompter

sopón ADJ (*Caribe*) interfering

soponcio* SM • **¡qué ~! me pillaron copiando en el examen** I nearly died! they caught me copying in the exam • **si no abres las ventanas nos va a dar un ~** if you don't open the windows we're all going to pass out • **al verlo con la cabeza rapada le dio un ~** she had a fit when she saw him with his head shaved

sopor SM **1** (*Med*) drowsiness
2 (= *letargo*) torpor

soporífero, soporífico ADJ **1** (*Med*) sleep-inducing
2 (= *aburrido*) soporific
SM **1** (= *pastilla*) sleeping pill
2 (= *bebida*) sleeping draught

soportable ADJ bearable

soportal SM **1** [*de casa*] porch
2 soportales (*en una calle*) arcade (*sing*), colonnade (*sing*)

soportante ADJ supportive

soportar ▸ CONJUG 1a VT **1** (= *resistir*) [+ *peso*] to support; [+ *presión*] to resist, withstand • **cuatro pilares soportan la bóveda** the vault is supported by four pillars • **las vigas soportan el peso del techo** the beams bear *o* carry the weight of the ceiling
2 (= *aguantar*) [+ *dolor, contratiempo, clima*] to bear; [+ *persona*] to put up with • **soportaba su enfermedad con resignación** she bore her illness with resignation • **soportó a su marido durante años** she put up with her husband for years • **soporta mal el dolor** she cannot stand pain • **no soporto a ese imbécil** I can't stand that idiot • **no soporta que la critiquen** she can't stand being criticized
VPR **soportarse** • **Ruth y Blanca no se soportan** Ruth and Blanca can't stand each other

soporte SM **1** (= *apoyo*) [*de puente*] support; [*de repisa*] bracket
2 (= *pedestal*) base, stand
3 [*de persona*] support • **es un buen ~ para sus padres** she's a real support to her parents • **esto es un ~ para su opinión** this supports *o* backs up her opinion
4 (*Inform*) medium ▸ **soporte de entrada** input medium ▸ **soporte de salida** output medium ▸ **soporte físico** hardware ▸ **soporte lógico** software
5 (*Heráldica*) supporter

soprano SMF soprano

soquete SM (*LAm*) sock, ankle sock, anklet (*EEUU*)

sor SF Sister • **Sor María** Sister Mary • **una sor*** a nun

sorber ▸ CONJUG 2a VT **1** (= *beber*) (*poco a poco*) to sip; (*chupando*) to suck up • **~ por una paja** to drink through a straw • **~ por las narices** (*gen*) to sniff, sniff in, sniff up; (*Med*) to inhale
2 (= *absorber*) [*esponja, papel secante*] to soak up, absorb
3 (= *tragar*) [*mar*] to suck down, swallow up; [+ *palabras*] to drink in

sorbete SM **1** (= *postre*) sorbet, sherbet (*EEUU*)
2 (*Caribe, Cono Sur*) (= *pajita*) drinking straw
3 (*Méx*) (= *sombrero*) top hat

sorbetera SF ice-cream freezer

sorbetería SF (*CAm*) ice-cream parlour, ice-cream shop

sorbetón SM gulp, mouthful

sorbito SM sip

sorbo SM (*al beber*) (= *trago pequeño*) sip; (= *trago grande*) gulp, swallow • **un ~ de té** a sip of tea • **beber a ~s** to sip • **de un ~** in one gulp • **tomar de un ~** to down in one, drink in one gulp

sorche*‡ SM, **sorchi*‡** SM soldier

sordamente ADV dully, in a muffled way

sordera SF deafness ▸ **sordera profunda** profound deafness

sordidez SF **1** (= *suciedad*) sordidness, squalor
2 (= *inmoralidad*) sordidness

sórdido ADJ **1** (= *sucio*) dirty, squalid
2 (= *inmoral*) sordid
3 [*palabra*] nasty, dirty

sordina SF **1** (*Mús*) mute
2 • **con ~** on the quiet, surreptitiously

sordo/a ADJ **1** [*persona*] deaf • **quedarse ~** to go deaf • **mostrarse ~ a** • **permanecer ~ a** to be deaf to • **se mostró ~ a sus súplicas** he was deaf to her entreaties, her entreaties fell on deaf ears • MODISMOS: • **a la sorda** • **a sordas** on the quiet, surreptitiously • **~ como una tapia** as deaf as a post
2 (= *insonoro*) [*ruido*] dull, muffled; [*dolor*] dull; [*emoción, ira*] suppressed
3 (*Ling*) voiceless
SM/F deaf person • **hacerse el ~** to pretend not to hear, turn a deaf ear

sordociego/a ADJ blind and deaf
SM/F blind and deaf person

sordomudez SF deaf-muteness

sordomudo/a ADJ deaf and dumb
SM/F deaf-mute

sorgo SM sorghum

soriano/a (*Esp*) ADJ of/from Soria
SM/F native/inhabitant of Soria • **los ~s** the people of Soria

soriasis SF INV psoriasis

Sorlinga • **islas ~** SFPL Scilly Isles

sorna SF **1** (= *malicia*) sarcasm
2 (= *tono burlón*) sarcastic tone • **con ~** sarcastically, mockingly
3 (= *lentitud*) slowness

sornar‡ ▸ CONJUG 1a VI to kip‡, sleep

sorocharse ▸ CONJUG 1a VPR **1** (*LAm*) = **asorocharse**
2 (*Cono Sur*) (= *ponerse colorado*) to blush

soroche SM **1** (*LAm*) (*Med*) mountain sickness, altitude sickness
2 (*Cono Sur*) (= *rubor*) blush, blushing
3 (*And, Cono Sur*) (*Min*) galena, natural lead sulphide

sorprendente ADJ surprising • **no es ~ que ...** it is hardly surprising that ..., it is small wonder that ...

sorprendentemente ADV surprisingly

sorprender ▸ CONJUG 2a VT **1** (= *asombrar*) to surprise • **no me ~ía que ...** I wouldn't be surprised if ...
2 (= *coger desprevenido*) to catch; (*Mil*) to surprise • **lo sorprendieron robando** they caught him stealing
3 [+ *conversación*] to overhear; [+ *secreto*] to find out, discover; [+ *escondrijo*] to find
VI to be surprising • **sorprende observar cómo lo hace** it's surprising to see how he does it • **sorprende la delicadeza de su verso** the delicacy of her poetry is surprising
VPR **sorprenderse** to be surprised • **me sorprendí de la claridad de sus ideas** I was surprised at the clarity of his ideas • **no me sorprendí de que se enfadara** I wasn't surprised he got angry • **se sorprendió mucho** he was very surprised

sorprendido ADJ surprised

sorpresa SF **1** (= *asombro*) surprise • **¡qué *o* vaya ~!** what a surprise! • **fue una ~ verte allí** it was a surprise to see you there, I was surprised to see you there • **ante *o* para mi ~** to my surprise • **con gran ~ mía** much to my surprise • **causar ~ a algn** to surprise sb • **coger a algn de *o* por ~** to take sb by surprise • **dar una ~**: • **Pablo quería darme una ~** Pablo wanted to take me by surprise *o* surprise me • **nunca ha llegado a la final, pero esta vez podría dar una *o* la ~** she has never reached the final before but this time she may cause an upset *o* she may surprise a few people • **llevarse una ~** to get a surprise • **producir ~ a algn** to surprise sb
2 (= *regalo*) surprise • **¿me has comprado alguna ~?** have you bought a surprise for me?

3 (*Mil*) surprise attack
ADJ INV surprise (*antes de s*) • **ataques ~** surprise attacks • **inspección ~** spot check • **resultado ~** surprise result • **sobres ~** lucky dip bags • **visita ~** unannounced visit, surprise visit

sorpresivamente ADV (= *asombrosamente*) surprisingly; (= *repentinamente*) suddenly, unexpectedly

sorpresivo ADJ (*esp LAm*) (= *asombroso*) surprising; (= *imprevisto*) sudden, unexpected

sorrajar ▷ CONJUG 1a VT (*Méx*) (= *golpear*) to hit; (= *herir*) to wound

sorrasear ▷ CONJUG 1a VT (*Méx*) to part-roast, grill

sorrongar ▷ CONJUG 1h VI (*And*) to grumble

sorrostrigar ▷ CONJUG 1h VT (*And*) to pester, annoy

sortario ADJ (*Caribe*) lucky, fortunate

sortear ▷ CONJUG 1a VT 1 (= *decidir al azar*) to draw lots for
2 (= *rifar*) (*gen*) to raffle; (*Dep*) to toss up for
3 (= *evitar*) [+ *obstáculo*] to dodge, avoid • **el torero sorteó al toro** the bullfighter dodged out of the bull's way • **el esquiador sorteó las banderas con habilidad** the skier swerved skilfully round the flags • **aquí hay que ~ el tráfico** you have to weave in and out of the traffic here
4 (= *librarse de*) [+ *dificultad*] to avoid, get round; [+ *pregunta*] to handle, deal with, deal with skilfully *o* (*EEUU*) skillfully
VI 1 (*en sorteo*) to draw lots
2 (*con moneda*) to toss, toss up

sorteo SM 1 (*en lotería*) draw; (= *rifa*) raffle; (*Dep*) toss • **ganar el ~** to win the toss • **el ganador se decidirá mediante ~** lots will be drawn to decide the winner ▸ **sorteo de regalos** prize draw; ▷ LOTERÍA
2 (*al evitar algo*) dodging, avoidance

sortija SF 1 (= *anillo*) ring ▸ **sortija de compromiso, sortija de pedida** engagement ring ▸ **sortija de sello** signet ring
2 (= *bucle*) curl, ringlet

sortilegio SM 1 (= *hechizo*) spell, charm
2 (= *hechicería*) sorcery
3 (= *encanto*) charm

sos (*Arg*) = sois ▷ ser

sosa SF soda ▸ **sosa cáustica** caustic soda

sosaina* ADJ dull, boring
SMF dull person, bore

sosco SM (*And*) bit, piece

sosegadamente ADV calmly, peacefully, gently

sosegado ADJ 1 [*apariencia, vida*] calm, peaceful
2 [*persona*] calm, serene

sosegar ▷ CONJUG 1h, 1j VT 1 [+ *persona*] (= *calmar*) to calm; (= *aquietar*) to quieten, quiet (*EEUU*); (= *arrullar*) to lull
2 [+ *ánimo*] to calm
3 [+ *dudas, aprensiones*] to allay
VI to rest
VPR **sosegarse** (= *calmarse*) to calm down; (= *aquietarse*) to quieten down

soseras* ADJ = soso

sosería SF 1 (= *insulsez*) insipidness
2 (= *monotonía*) dullness • **es una ~** it's boring, it's terribly dull

sosia SM double

sosiego SM 1 [*de lugar, ambiente*] (= *tranquilidad*) calm, calmness, tranquility; (= *quietud*) peacefulness
2 [*de persona*] calmness, serenity, composure • **hacer algo con ~** to do sth calmly

soslayar ▷ CONJUG 1a VT 1 (= *poner ladeado*) to put sideways, place obliquely (*frm*)
2 (= *librarse de*) [+ *dificultad*] to get round; [+ *pregunta*] to avoid, dodge, sidestep; [+ *encuentro*] to avoid

soslayo • **al** *o* **de ~** ADV obliquely, sideways • **mirada de ~** sidelong glance • **mirar de ~** (*lit*) to look out of the corner of one's eye (at); (*fig*) to look askance (at)

soso ADJ 1 (*Culin*) (= *insípido*) tasteless, insipid; (= *sin sal*) unsalted • **estas patatas están sosas** these potatoes are unsalted *o* need more salt
2 (= *aburrido, inexpresivo*) dull, uninteresting

sospecha SF suspicion

sospechar ▷ CONJUG 1a VT to suspect • **sospecho que lo hizo él** I suspect (that) he did it • **—fue él el que lo robó —ya lo sospechaba** "it was he who stole it" — "I suspected as much" • **sospecho que no tardarán en llegar** I have a feeling they won't be long
VI • **~ de algn** to suspect sb, be suspicious of sb • **la policía siempre sospechó del marido** the police always suspected the husband, the police were always suspicious of the husband

sospechosamente ADV suspiciously

sospechoso/a ADJ suspicious • **su comportamiento es muy ~** his behaviour is very suspicious • **el bar estaba lleno de tipos ~s** the bar was full of suspicious-looking types • **todos son ~s** everybody is under suspicion • **tiene amistades sospechosas** he has some dubious acquaintances • **es ~ de asesinato** he is suspected of murder
SM/F suspect

sosquín SM (*Caribe*) 1 (= *ángulo*) wide corner, obtuse angle
2 (= *golpe*) backhander, sweetener (*EEUU*), unexpected blow

sosquinar ▷ CONJUG 1a VT (*Caribe*) to hit unexpectedly, wound unexpectedly

sostén SM 1 (*Arquit*) support, prop
2 (= *prenda femenina*) bra, brassiere
3 (= *alimento*) sustenance
4 (= *apoyo*) support • **el único ~ de su familia** the sole support of his family • **el principal ~ del gobierno** the mainstay of the government

sostener ▷ CONJUG 2k VT 1 (= *sujetar*) **a** (*en las manos, los brazos*) to hold • **¡sostén esto un momentito!** hold this a minute! • **yo llevaba las cajas mientras él me sostenía la puerta** I carried the boxes while he held the door open for me
b (*en pie*) [+ *construcción, edificio, techo*] to hold up, support • **los pilares que sostienen el puente** the pillars which hold up *o* support the bridge • **las piernas apenas me sostenían** my legs could barely hold me up *o* support me • **entró borracho, sostenido por dos amigos** he came in drunk, held up *o* supported by two friends
c (= *soportar*) [+ *peso, carga*] to bear, carry, sustain (*frm*)
2 (= *proporcionar apoyo a*) **a** (*económicamente*) to support • **no gano suficiente para ~ a una familia** I don't earn enough to support a family • **algunas de las alternativas sugeridas para ~ al club** some of the alternatives suggested to keep the club going
b (= *alimentar*) to support, sustain (*frm*) • **la tierra no da para ~ a todo el mundo** the land does not provide enough to support *o* (*frm*) sustain everyone
c (*moralmente*) to support • **la élite ha dejado de ~ al régimen** the elite has stopped supporting the regime • **una mayoría capaz de ~ al Gobierno** a majority large enough to keep *o* support the government in power • **solo lo sostiene el cariño de sus hijos** the love of his children is all that keeps him going
3 (= *mantener*) **a** [+ *opinión*] to hold • **siempre he sostenido lo contrario** I've always held the opposite opinion • **sostiene un punto de vista muy diferente** he has *o* holds a very different point of view • **no tiene datos suficientes para ~ esa afirmación** she doesn't have enough information to back up *o* support that statement • **la investigación no ha terminado, como sostiene el juez** the investigation has not concluded, as the judge maintains *o* holds • **~ que** to maintain *o* hold that • **sigue sosteniendo que es inocente** she still maintains *o* holds that she is innocent
b [+ *situación*] to maintain, keep up • **no podrán ~ su puesto en la clasificación** they won't be able to maintain *o* keep up their place in the ranking • **los campesinos han sostenido desde siempre una fuerte lucha con el medio** country people have always kept up *o* carried on a hard struggle against the environment • **~ la mirada de algn** to hold sb's gaze
4 (= *tener*) [+ *conversación, enfrentamiento, polémica*] to have; [+ *reunión, audiencia*] • **sostuvo recientemente un enfrentamiento con el presidente** he recently had a clash with the president • **sostuvo un breve encuentro con sus ministros** he held a brief meeting with his ministers
5 (*Mús*) [+ *nota*] to hold, sustain
VPR **sostenerse 1** (= *sujetarse*) to stand • **la escultura se sostiene sobre cuatro columnas** the sculpture stands on four columns • **un libro grueso que se sostiene de canto** a thick book which will stand up • **no se me sostiene el peinado** my hair won't stay up • **~se en pie** [*persona*] to stand upright, stand on one's feet; [*edificio*] to stand • **apenas podía ~me en pie** I could hardly stand upright, I could hardly stand on my feet • **la iglesia es lo único que se sostiene todavía en pie** only the church is still standing
2 (= *sustentarse*) **a** (*económicamente*) [*persona*] to support o.s.; [*empresa*] to keep going • **mientras pueda ~se con sus ingresos** as long as she can support herself on her income • **la minería se sostiene gracias a las subvenciones** the mining industry is kept going by subsidies
b (*con alimentos*) • **¿cómo puedes ~te solo con un bocadillo?** how can you keep going on just a sandwich? • **~se a base de algo** to live on sth, survive on sth
3 (= *resistir*) • **el mercado se sostiene firme** the market is holding firm • **~se en el poder** to maintain o.s. in power • **se sostiene en su negativa de no dejarlos participar** he persists in his refusal to let them take part

sostenibilidad SF sustainability

sostenible ADJ [*desarrollo, crecimiento, recuperación*] sustainable • **la situación no parece ~ a largo plazo** the situation does not seem to be sustainable in the long term • **su postura resulta difícilmente ~** his position is difficult to sustain

sostenidamente ADV continuously

sostenido ADJ 1 (= *continuo*) sustained
2 (*Mús*) sharp • **do ~** C sharp
SM (*Mús*) sharp

sostenimiento SM 1 (= *sujeción*) support • **las vigas sirven de principal ~ al edificio** the girders act as the building's main support
2 (= *conservación*) • **una política de ~ de precios** a policy of maintaining price levels • **medidas que contribuyen al ~ de la democracia** measures that contribute to

S

the upholding *o* maintenance of democracy
3 (= *apoyo*) (*financiero*) maintenance; (*con alimentos*) sustenance • **para el ~ de la economía** for the maintenance of *o* to maintain the economy
sota[1] (SF) 1 (*Naipes*) jack, knave
2† (= *descarada*) hussy, brazen woman; (= *puta*) whore
sota[2] (SM) (*Cono Sur**) overseer, foreman
sotabanco (SM) 1 (= *desván*) attic, garret
2 (*Cono Sur*) (= *cuartucho*) poky little room
sotabarba (SF) double chin, jowl
sotacura (SM) (*And, Cono Sur*) curate
sotana (SF) 1 (*Rel*) cassock, soutane
2* (= *paliza*) hiding
sotanear* ▸ CONJUG 1a (VT) to tick off*
sótano (SM) 1 (*en casa*) (*habitable*) basement; (*como almacén*) cellar
2 (*en banco*) vault
Sotavento • **islas ~** (SFPL) Leeward Isles
sotavento (SM) (*Náut*) lee, leeward • **a ~** to leeward • **de ~** leeward (*antes de s*)
sotechado (SM) shed
soterradamente (ADV) in an underhand way
soterrado (ADJ) buried, hidden
soterramiento (SM) excavation • **obras de ~** excavations, underground works
soterrar ▸ CONJUG 1j (VT) 1 (= *enterrar*) to bury
2 (= *esconder*) to hide away, bury
soto (SM) 1 (*Bot*) (= *matorral*) thicket; (= *arboleda*) grove, copse
2 (*And*) (*en la piel*) rough lump, bump; (= *nudo*) knot
sotobosque (SM) undergrowth
sotreta (SF) (*And, Cono Sur*) 1 (= *caballo*) horse; (= *caballo brioso*) frisky horse; (= *caballo viejo*) useless old nag
2 (= *persona*) loafer, idler, bum (EEUU)
soturno (ADJ) taciturn, silent
soufflé [su'fle] (SM) soufflé
soul (ADJ INV), (SM) (*Mús*) soul
soutien [su'tjen] (SM) (PL: **soutiens**) (*Arg*) bra, brassiere
souvenir [suβe'nir] (SM) (PL: **souvenirs**) souvenir
soviet (SM) soviet
soviético/a (ADJ) Soviet (*antes de s*) (SM/F) • **los ~s** the Soviets, the Russians
soy ▸ **ser**
soya (SF) (*LAm*) soya, soy (EEUU)
S.P. (ABR) 1 (*Rel*) = **Santo Padre**
2 (*Esp*) (*Aut*) = **Servicio Público**
3 (*Admin*) = **Servicio Postal**
spa (SM) spa
spaghetti, spaghettis, spaguetti, spaguettis (SMPL) [espa'ɣetis] spaghetti (*sing*)
spammer [es'pamer] (SMF) (PL: **spammers**) (*Internet*) spammer
spárring [es'parin] (SM) sparring partner
speed* [es'pið] (SM) (= *droga*) speed
spi* [es'pi] (SM) spinnaker
spinning® [es'pinin] (SM) spinning® • **sesión de ~** spin® session, spinning® session
spleen [es'plin] (SM) = **esplín**
SPM (SM ABR) (= **síndrome premenstrual**) PMS
sponsor [espon'sor] (SMF) (PL: **sponsors** [espon'sor]) sponsor
sport [es'por] (SM) sport • **chaqueta (de) ~** sports jacket, sports coat (*EEUU*) • **ropa de ~** casual wear • **vestir de ~** to dress casually • **hacer algo por ~** to do sth (just) for fun
spot [es'pot] (SM) (PL: **spots**) 1 (*TV*) ▸ **spot electoral** party political broadcast ▸ **spot publicitario** (*TV*) commercial, ad*
2 (*Cono Sur*) (*Elec*) spotlight
spray [es'prai] (SM) (PL: **sprays**) spray, aerosol
sprint [es'prin] (SM) (PL: **sprints** [es'prin])
1 (*Dep*) sprint • **imponerse al ~** to win in a sprint finish • **tengo que hacer un ~** I must dash, I must get a move on
2 (*tb* **sprint final**) (= *esfuerzo máximo*) final dash, last-minute rush
sprintar [esprin'tar] ▸ CONJUG 1a (VI) to sprint
sprínter [es'printer] (SMF) sprinter
squash [es'kwas] (SM) squash
Sr. (ABR) (= **Señor**) Mr; ▸ DON/DOÑA
Sra. (ABR) (= **Señora**) Mrs; ▸ DON/DOÑA
S.R.C. (ABR) (= **se ruega contestación**) RSVP
Sres. (ABR) (= **Señores**) Messrs
Sria. (ABR) (= **secretaria**) sec
Sri Lanka (SM) Sri Lanka
Srio. (ABR) (= **secretario**) sec
Srs. (ABR) (= **Señores**) Messrs
Srta. (ABR) (= **Señorita**) Miss, Ms; ▸ DON/DOÑA
SS. (ABR) (= **Santos, Santas**) SS
ss. (ABR) 1 (= **siguientes**) following, foll.
2 (= **siglos**) cent.
S.S. (ABR) 1 (*Rel*) (= **Su Santidad**) HH
2 = **Seguridad Social**
3 = **Su Señoría**
s.s. (ABR) (= **seguro servidor**) *courtesy formula*
SSE (ABR) (= **sudsudeste**) SSE
SSI (SM ABR) (= **Servicio Social Internacional**) ISS
SS.MM. (ABR) = **Sus Majestades**
SSO (ABR) (= **sudsudoeste**) SSW
SSS (SM ABR) = **servicio social sustitutorio**
s.s.s. (ABR) (= **su seguro servidor**) *courtesy formula*
Sta. (ABR) (= **Santa**) St
staccato [esta'kato] (ADV) staccato
staff [es'taf] (SM) (PL: **staffs** [es'taf])
1 (= *equipo*) (*Mil*) staff, command; (*Pol*) ministerial team
2 (= *persona*) top executive
3 (*Cine, Mús*) credits (*pl*), cast (and credits) (*EEUU*), credit titles (*pl*)
stage [es'teiʒ] (SM) period, phase
stagflación [estagfla'θjon] (SF) stagflation
Stalin [es'talin] (SM) Stalin
stand [es'tan] (SM) (PL: **stands** [es'tan]) stand
standard (ADJ), (SM), **stándard** (ADJ), (SM) [es'tandar] = **estándar**
standing [es'tandin] (SM) standing • **de alto ~** [*oficial*] high-ranking; [*ejecutivo*] top; [*piso*] luxury • **una mujer de alto ~** a woman of high standing
stárter [es'tarter] (SM) 1 (*Aut*) (= *aire*) choke; (*LAm*) (= *arranque*) self-starter, starter motor
2 (*LAm*) (*Equitación*) (= *persona*) starter; (= *puerta*) starting gate
statu quo (SM) status quo
status [es'tatus] (SM INV) status
step [es'tep] (SM) step (aerobics)
Sto. (ABR) (= **Santo**) St
stock [es'tok] (SM) (PL: **stocks** [es'tok]) stock, supply
stop [es'top] (SM) stop sign, halt sign
store [es'tor] (SM) sunblind, awning
story board (SM) story board
stress [es'tres] (SM) stress
stretching [es'tretʃin] (SM) stretching
stripper [es'triper] (SMF) (PL: **strippers**) stripper
strip-tease [es'triptis] (SM), **striptease** [es'triptis] (SM) striptease
su (ADJ POSES) 1 (*sing*) (= *de él*) his; (= *de ella*) her; (= *de usted*) your; (= *de animal, cosa*) its; (*impersonal*) one's • **el chico perdió su juguete** the boy lost his toy • **María vino con su padre** María came with her father • **dígame su número de teléfono** give me your telephone number • **un oso y su cachorro** a bear and its cub • **uno tiene que mirar por su negocio** one has to look after one's own business
2 (*pl*) (= *de ustedes*) your; (= *de ellos, de ellas*) their • **no olviden sus paraguas** don't forget your umbrellas • **las niñas se quedaron en su cuarto** the girls stayed in their room
3 (*uso enfático*) • **tendrá sus buenos 80 años** he must be a good 80 years old • **su dinero le habrá costado** it must have cost her a pretty penny • **una casa de muñecas con sus cortinitas y todo** a doll's house with little curtains and everything
suampo (SM) (*CAm*) swamp
suato* (ADJ) (*Méx*) silly
suave (ADJ) 1 (= *liso*) [*superficie*] smooth, even; [*piel, pasta*] smooth
2 (= *no fuerte*) [*color, movimiento, brisa, reprimenda*] gentle; [*clima, sabor*] mild; [*trabajo*] easy; [*operación mecánica*] smooth, easy; [*melodía, voz*] soft, sweet; [*ruido*] low; [*olor*] slight; [*droga*] soft • MODISMO: • **~ como el terciopelo** smooth as silk, like velvet
3 [*persona, personalidad*] gentle, sweet • **estuvo muy ~ conmigo** he was very sweet to me, he behaved very nicely to me
4 (*Chile, Méx**) (= *grande*) big, huge; (= *destacado*) outstanding
5 (*Méx‡*) (= *atractivo*) good-looking, fanciable*; (= *estupendo*) great*, fabulous* • **¡suave!** great idea!*, right on! (EEUU*)
6 • **dar la ~** (*LAm*) (= *halagar*) to flatter
(ADV) 1 (*LAm*) [*sonar*] softly, quietly
2 (*Méx*) • **toca ~** she plays beautifully
suavemente (ADV) [*golpear, llover*] gently; [*entrar*] softly; [*mover, deslizar*] smoothly
suavidad (SF) 1 (= *lisura*) [*de superficie*] smoothness, evenness; [*de piel*] smoothness
2 (= *falta de intensidad*) [*de color, movimiento, brisa, reprimenda*] gentleness; [*de clima, sabor, olor*] mildness; [*de trabajo*] easiness; [*de melodía, voz*] softness, sweetness; [*de ruido*] quietness
suavización (SF) 1 (= *de superficie*) smoothing
2 (= *ablandamiento*) [*de severidad, dureza*] softening, tempering; [*de medidas*] relaxation
suavizado (ADJ) toned-down
suavizador (SM) razor strop
suavizante (SM) (*para ropa*) softener, fabric softener; (*para pelo*) conditioner
suavizar ▸ CONJUG 1f (VT) 1 (= *alisar*) to smooth out, smooth down
2 (= *ablandar*) (*gen*) to soften; [+ *carácter*] to mellow; [+ *severidad, dureza*] to temper; [+ *medida*] to relax
3 (= *quitar fuerza a*) [+ *navaja*] to strop; [+ *pendiente*] to ease, make more gentle; [+ *color*] to tone down; [+ *tono*] to soften
(VPR) **suavizarse** to soften
sub... (PREF) sub..., under... • **subempleo** underemployment • **subprivilegiado** underprivileged • **subestimar** to underestimate • **subvalorar** to undervalue • **la selección española sub-21** the Spanish under-21 team
suba (SF) (*CAm, Cono Sur*) rise, rise in prices
subacuático (ADJ) underwater
subalimentación (SF) undernourishment
subalimentado (ADJ) undernourished, underfed
subalpino (ADJ) subalpine
subalquilar ▸ CONJUG 1a (VT) to sublet
subalterno/a (ADJ) [*importancia*] secondary; [*personal*] auxiliary
(SM/F) 1 (= *subordinado*) subordinate
2 (*Taur*) assistant bullfighter
subarbustivo (ADJ) shrubby
subarrendador(a) (SM/F) subtenant
subarrendar ▸ CONJUG 1j (VT) to sublet, sublease

subarrendatario/a (SM/F) subtenant
subarriendo (SM) subtenancy, sublease
subártico (ADJ) subarctic
subasta (SF) **1** (= *venta*) auction, sale by auction • **poner en** *o* **sacar a pública ~** to put up for auction, sell at auction ▸ **subasta a la baja, subasta a la rebaja** Dutch auction
2 (= *contrato de obras*) tender, tendering
3 (*Naipes*) auction
subastador(a) (SM/F) auctioneer
subastadora (SF) (= *casa*) auction house
subastar ▹ CONJUG 1a (VT) to auction, sell at auction
subatómico (ADJ) subatomic
subcampeón/ona (SM/F) runner-up
subcampeonato (SM) runner-up position, second place
subcomisario/a (SM/F) deputy superintendent
subcomisión (SF) subcommittee
subcomité (SM) subcommittee
subconjunto (SM) **1** (*Inform*) subset
2 (*Pol*) subcommittee
3 (*Zool*) subspecies
subconsciencia (SF) subconscious
subconsciente (ADJ) subconscious
(SM) • **el ~** the subconscious • **en el ~** in one's subconscious ▸ **subconsciente colectivo** collective subconscious
subconscientemente (ADV) subconsciously
subcontinente (SM) subcontinent
subcontrata (SF) subcontract
subcontratación (SF) subcontracting
subcontratado (ADJ) subcontracted
subcontratar ▹ CONJUG 1a (VT) to subcontract
subcontratista (SMF) subcontractor
subcontrato (SM) subcontract
subcultura (SF) subculture
subcutáneo (ADJ) subcutaneous
subdesarrollado (ADJ) underdeveloped
subdesarrollo (SM) underdevelopment
subdirección (SF) section, subdepartment
subdirector(a) (SM/F) [*de organización*] deputy director; [*de empresa*] assistant manager/manageress, deputy manager/manageress; [*de colegio*] deputy head ▸ **subdirector(a) de biblioteca** sub-librarian, deputy librarian
subdirectorio (SM) subdirectory
súbdito/a (ADJ), (SM/F) subject
subdividir ▹ CONJUG 3a (VT) to subdivide
(VPR) **subdividirse** to subdivide
subdivisible (ADJ) subdivisible
subdivisión (SF) subdivision
sube (SM) (*LAm*) • **dar un ~ a algn** to give sb a hard time ▸ **sube y baja** see-saw
subempleado (ADJ) underemployed
subempleo (SM) underemployment
subespecie (SF) subspecies
subestación (SF) substation
subestimación (SF) [*de capacidad, enemigo*] underestimation; [*de objeto, propiedad*] undervaluation; [*de argumento*] understatement
subestimado (ADJ) undervalued, underrated
subestimar ▹ CONJUG 1a (VT) [+ *capacidad, enemigo*] to underestimate, underrate; [+ *objeto, propiedad*] to undervalue; [+ *argumento*] to understate; [+ *persona, artista*] to undervalue, underrate
(VPR) **subestimarse** to underrate o.s., undervalue o.s. • **no te subestimes** don't run yourself down, don't underrate *o* undervalue yourself
subexponer ▹ CONJUG 2q (VT) to underexpose
subexposición (SF) underexposure
subexpuesto (ADJ) underexposed
subfusil (SM) automatic rifle
subgénero (SM) **1** (*Literat*) minor genre
2 (*Zool*) subspecies
subgerente (SMF) assistant director
subgrupo (SM) (*gen*) subgroup; (*Pol*) splinter group
subibaja (SM) seesaw, teeter-totter (*EEUU*)
subida (SF) **1** (= *ascensión*) [*de montaña, cuesta*] ascent • **dirigió la primera ~ al Kilimanjaro** he led the first ascent on Kilimanjaro • **es una ~ difícil** it's a tough ascent *o* climb • **una ~ en globo** a balloon ascent • **a la ~ tuvimos que parar varias veces** we had to stop several times on the way up
2 (= *pendiente*) slope, hill
3 (= *aumento*) rise, increase • **una ~ de los precios** a price rise *o* increase • **se espera una ~ de las temperaturas** temperatures are expected to rise ▸ **subida salarial** pay rise, wage increase
4* [*de drogas*] high*
subido (ADJ) **1** (= *intenso*) [*color*] bright, intense; [*olor*] strong • **un chiste ~ de tono** a risqué joke
2 [*precio*] high
3* • **hoy tienes el guapo ~** you're looking great today • **está de tonto ~** he's being really silly
subienda (SF) (*And*) shoal
subilla (SF) awl
subíndice (SM) subscript
subinquilino/a (SM/F) subtenant
subir ▹ CONJUG 3a (VT) **1** (= *levantar*) [+ *pierna, brazo, objeto*] to lift, lift up, raise; [+ *calcetines, pantalones, persianas*] to pull up • **sube los brazos** lift your arms (up), raise your arms
2 (= *poner arriba*) (*llevando*) to take up; (*trayendo*) to bring up • **¿me puedes ayudar a ~ las maletas?** can you help me to take up the cases? • **voy a ~ esta caja arriba** I'll take this box upstairs • **¿puedes ~ ese cuadro de abajo?** could you bring that picture up from down there? • **lo subieron al portaequipajes** they put it up on the rack • **lo subimos a un taxi** we put him in a taxi
3 (= *ascender*) [+ *calle, cuesta, escalera, montaña*] (= *ir arriba*) to go up; (= *venir arriba*) to come up • **subió las escaleras de dos en dos** she went up the stairs two at a time • **tenía problemas para ~ las escaleras** he had difficulty getting up *o* climbing the stairs
4 (= *aumentar*) [+ *precio, salario*] to put up, raise, increase; [+ *artículo en venta*] to put up the price of • **los taxistas han subido sus tarifas** taxi drivers have put their fares up *o* have raised their fares • **van a ~ la gasolina** they are going to put up *o* increase the price of petrol
5 (= *elevar*) [+ *volumen, televisión, radio*] to turn up; [+ *voz*] to raise • **sube la radio, que no se oye** turn the radio up, I can't hear it
6 (*en escalafón*) [+ *persona*] to promote
7 (*Arquit*) to put up, build • **~ una pared** to put up *o* build a wall
8 (*Mús*) to raise the pitch of
(VI) **1** (= *ir arriba*) to go up; (= *venir arriba*) to come up; (*en un monte, en el aire*) to climb • **suba al tercer piso** go up to the third floor • **sube, que te voy a enseñar unos discos** come up, I've got some records to show you • **seguimos subiendo hasta la cima** we went on climbing till we reached the summit • **estaba mirando como la mosca subía por la ventana** I watched the fly move slowly up the window • **tuvimos que ~ andando** we had to walk up
2 (*Transportes*) (*en autobús, avión, tren, bicicleta, moto, caballo*) to get on; (*en coche, taxi*) to get in • **~ a un autobús/avión/tren** to get on(to) a bus/plane/train • **~ a un coche** to get in(to) a car • **~ a una bicicleta** to get on(to) a bike • **~ a un caballo** to mount a horse, get on(to) a horse • **~ a bordo** to go *o* get on board
3 (*en el escalafón*) to be promoted (a to) • **nuestro objetivo es ~ a primera división** our aim is to go up *o* be promoted to the First Division
4 (= *aumentar*) [*precio, valor*] to go up, rise; [*temperatura*] to rise • **la gasolina ha vuelto a ~** (the price of) petrol has gone up again • **sigue subiendo la bolsa** share prices are still rising • **le ha subido la fiebre** her temperature has gone up *o* risen; ▹ **tono**
5 (= *aumentar de nivel*) [*río, mercurio*] to rise; [*marea*] to come in
6 [*cantidad*] • **~ a** to come to, total
(VPR) **subirse 1** (*Transportes*) (*en autobús, avión, tren*) to get on; (*en coche*) to get in; (*en bicicleta*) to get on, climb on • **~se a un autobús/avión/tren** to get on(to) a bus/plane/train • **~se a un coche** to get in(to) a car • **~se a una bicicleta** to get on(to) a bike • **~se a un caballo** to mount a horse, get on(to) a horse • **~se a bordo** to go *o* get on board
2 (= *trepar*) (*a árbol, tejado*) to climb • **el niño se le subió a las rodillas** the child climbed (up) onto her knees • MODISMO: • **~se por las paredes** to hit the roof • **están que se suben por las paredes** they're hopping mad; ▹ **barba, parra**
3 (*con ropa*) • **~se los calcetines/pantalones** to pull up one's socks/trousers • **~se la cremallera (de algo)** to zip (sth) up
4 (*a la cabeza, cara*) • **el vino se me sube a la cabeza** wine goes to my head • **el vino/el dinero se le ha subido a la cabeza** the wine/money has gone to his head • **se le subieron los colores a la cara** she blushed
5 (*en comportamiento*) (= *engreírse*) to get conceited; (= *descararse*) to become bolder; (= *portarse mal*) to forget one's manners
6 (*Bot*) to run to seed

> **SUBIR**
>
> **Otros verbos de movimiento**
>
> ▹ **Subir la cuesta/la escalera** *etc, por regla general, se suele traducir por* **to come up** *o por* **to go up**, *según la dirección del movimiento (hacia o en sentido contrario al hablante), pero* **come** *y* **go** *se pueden reemplazar por otros verbos de movimiento si la oración española especifica la forma en que se sube mediante el uso de adverbios o construcciones adverbiales:*
>
> **Tim subió las escaleras a gatas**
> Tim crept up the stairs
> **El mes pasado los precios subieron vertiginosamente**
> Prices shot up last month
>
> *Para otros usos y ejemplos ver la entrada.*

súbitamente (ADV) (= *repentinamente*) suddenly; (= *de forma imprevista*) unexpectedly
súbito (ADJ) **1** [*cambio, acción*] (= *repentino*) sudden; (= *imprevisto*) unexpected; ▹ **muerte**
2 (= *precipitado*) hasty, rash
3* (= *irritable*) irritable
(ADV) (*tb* **de súbito**) suddenly, unexpectedly
subjefatura (SF) local headquarters, local police headquarters
subjetivamente (ADV) subjectively
subjetivar ▹ CONJUG 1a (VT), **subjetivizar** ▹ CONJUG 1f (VT) to subjectivize, perceive in subjective terms
subjetividad (SF) subjectivity

S

subjetivismo SM subjectivism
subjetivo ADJ subjective
subjuntivo ADJ subjunctive
SM subjunctive, subjunctive mood
sublevación SF (= *motín*) [*de rebeldes, ciudadanos*] revolt, uprising; [*de militares*] mutiny; [*de presos*] riot
sublevar ▸ CONJUG 1a VT **1** (= *amotinar*) to rouse to revolt
2 (= *indignar*) to infuriate
VPR **sublevarse** to revolt, rise, rise up
sublimación SF sublimation
sublimado SM sublimate
sublimar ▸ CONJUG 1a VT **1** [+ *persona*] to exalt
2 [+ *deseos*] to sublimate
3 (*Quím*) to sublimate
sublime ADJ **1** (= *excelso*) sublime • **lo ~** the sublime
2 (*liter*) (= *alto*) high, lofty
sublimemente ADV sublimely
sublimidad SF sublimity
subliminal ADJ subliminal
subliteratura SF third-rate literature, pulp writing
submarinismo SM (*como deporte*) scuba diving; (*para pescar*) underwater fishing
submarinista ADJ • **exploración ~** underwater exploration
SMF scuba diver
submarino ADJ underwater, submarine • **pesca submarina** underwater fishing
SM **1** (*Náut*) submarine
2 (*Arg*) (*Culin*) *hot milk with piece of chocolate*
3 (*Arg*) (= *tortura*) *repeated submersion of victim's head in water*
submundo SM underworld
subnormal ADJ **1** (*Med*) subnormal, mentally handicapped
2* (*pey*) nuts*, mental*
SMF **1** (*Med*) subnormal person, mentally handicapped person
2* (*pey*) nutcase*, blockhead*
subnormalidad SF subnormality, mental handicap
subocupación SF (*LAm*) underemployment
subocupado/a (*LAm*) ADJ underemployed
SM/F underemployed person • **los ~s** the underemployed
suboficial SMF non-commissioned officer, NCO
subordinación SF subordination
subordinado/a ADJ subordinate • **quedar ~ a algo** to be subordinate to sth
SM/F subordinate
subordinar ▸ CONJUG 1a VT to subordinate
VPR **subordinarse** • **~se a** to subordinate o.s. to
subpárrafo SM subparagraph
subproducto SM by-product
subprograma SM subprogram
subrayable ADJ worth emphasizing • **el punto más ~** the point which should particularly be noted, the most important point
subrayado ADJ **1** (*con línea*) underlined
2 (*en cursiva*) italicized, in italics
SM **1** (*con línea*) underlining
2 (*en cursiva*) italics (*pl*) • **el ~ es mío** my italics, the italics are mine
subrayar ▸ CONJUG 1a VT **1** [+ *texto, frase*] (*con línea*) to underline; (*en cursiva*) to italicize, put in italics
2 (= *recalcar*) to underline, emphasize
subrepticiamente ADV surreptitiously
subrepticio ADJ surreptitious
subrogación SF substitution, replacement
subrogante (*Chile*) ADJ acting
SMF substitute
subrogar ▸ CONJUG 1h, 1l VT to substitute, replace
subrutina SF subroutine
subsahariano ADJ sub-Saharan
subsanable ADJ (= *perdonable*) excusable; (= *reparable*) repairable • **un error fácilmente ~** an error which is easily put right *o* rectified • **un obstáculo difícilmente ~** an obstacle which is hard to overcome *o* get round
subsanar ▸ CONJUG 1a VT [+ *falta*] to overlook, excuse; [+ *perjuicio, defecto*] to repair, make good; [+ *error*] to rectify, put right; [+ *deficiencia*] to make up for; [+ *dificultad, obstáculo*] to get round, overcome
subscribir ▸ CONJUG 3a VT = **suscribir**
subsecretaría SF undersecretaryship
subsecretario/a SM/F undersecretary, assistant secretary
subsector SM subsection, subsector
subsecuente ADJ subsequent
subsede SF secondary venue
subsidiar ▸ CONJUG 1b VT to subsidize
subsidiariedad SF subordination, subsidiary nature
subsidiario ADJ subsidiary
subsidio SM **1** (*Econ*) (= *subvención*) subsidy, grant; (= *ayuda financiera*) aid ▸ **subsidio de desempleo** unemployment benefit, unemployment compensation (EEUU) ▸ **subsidio de enfermedad** sick benefit, sick pay ▸ **subsidio de exportación** export subsidy ▸ **subsidio de huelga** strike pay ▸ **subsidio de natalidad** maternity benefit ▸ **subsidio de paro** unemployment benefit, unemployment compensation (EEUU) ▸ **subsidio de vejez** old age pension ▸ **subsidio familiar** ≈ family credit, ≈ welfare (EEUU)
2 (*And*) (= *inquietud*) anxiety, worry
subsiguiente ADJ subsequent
subsistema SM subsystem
subsistencia SF (= *supervivencia*) subsistence; (= *sustento*) sustenance • **salario de ~** subsistence wage
subsistente ADJ (= *duradero*) lasting, enduring; (= *aún existente*) surviving • **una costumbre aún ~** a custom that still exists *o* survives
subsistir ▸ CONJUG 3a VI **1** (= *malvivir*) to subsist, live (**con, de** on); (= *perdurar*) to survive, endure • **todavía subsiste el edificio** the building is still standing • **es una creencia que subsiste** it is a belief which still exists • **sin ayuda económica no podrá ~ el colegio** the school will not be able to survive without financial aid
2 (*And*) (= *vivir juntos*) to live together
subsónico ADJ subsonic
subsótano SM basement
subst... PREF = **sust...**
substituir ▸ CONJUG 3g VT = **sustituir**
subsuelo SM subsoil
subsumir ▸ CONJUG 3a VT to subsume
subte* SM (*Arg*) underground, tube*, subway (EEUU)
subteniente/a SM/F sub-lieutenant, second lieutenant
subterfugio SM subterfuge
subterráneo ADJ underground, subterranean
SM **1** (= *túnel*) underground passage
2 (= *almacén bajo tierra*) underground store, cellar
3 (*Arg*) (= *metro*) underground, subway (EEUU)
subtexto SM subtext
subtitulado SM subtitling
subtitular ▸ CONJUG 1a VT to subtitle
subtítulo SM subtitle, subheading • **~s** (*Cine, TV*) subtitles
subtotal SM subtotal
subtropical ADJ subtropical
suburbano ADJ suburban
SM (= *tren*) suburban train
suburbial ADJ suburban; (*pey*) slum (*antes de s*)
suburbio SM **1** (= *afueras*) suburb, outlying area
2 (= *barrio bajo*) slum area, shantytown
subutilizado ADJ under-used, under-utilized
subvaloración SF undervaluing
subvalorar ▸ CONJUG 1a VT (= *no valorar*) to undervalue, underrate; (= *subestimar*) to underestimate
subvención SF subsidy, subvention, grant ▸ **subvenciones agrícolas** agricultural subsidies ▸ **subvención estatal** state subsidy ▸ **subvención para la inversión** (*Com*) investment grant
subvencionado ADJ subsidized
subvencionar ▸ CONJUG 1a VT to subsidize
subvenir ▸ CONJUG 3r VI • **~ a** [+ *gastos*] to meet, defray; [+ *necesidades*] to provide for • **con eso subviene a sus vicios** he uses that to pay for his vices • **así subviene a la escasez de su sueldo** that's how he supplements his (low) salary
subversión SF **1** (= *acción*) subversion • **la ~ del orden establecido** the undermining of the established order
2 (= *revolución*) revolution
subversivo ADJ subversive
subvertir ▸ CONJUG 3i VI **1** (= *alterar*) to subvert
2 (= *derrocar*) to overthrow
subyacente ADJ underlying
subyacer ▸ CONJUG 2x VT to underlie
subyugación SF subjugation
subyugado ADJ subjugated
subyugador ADJ, **subyugante** ADJ
1 (= *que domina*) dominating
2 (= *que hechiza*) captivating, enchanting
subyugar ▸ CONJUG 1h VT **1** (= *dominar*) [+ *país*] to subjugate, subdue; [+ *enemigo*] to overpower; [+ *voluntad*] to dominate, gain control over
2 (= *hechizar*) to captivate, charm
succión SF suction
succionar ▸ CONJUG 1a VT **1** (= *sorber*) to suck
2 (*Téc*) to absorb, soak up
sucedáneo ADJ substitute
SM substitute
suceder ▸ CONJUG 2a VI **1** (= *ocurrir*) to happen • **pues sucede que no vamos** well it (so) happens we're not going • **no le había sucedido eso nunca** that had never happened to him before • **suceda lo que suceda** come what may, whatever happens • **¿qué sucede?** what's going on? • **lo que sucede es que ...** the fact *o* the trouble is that ... • **llevar algo por lo que pueda ~** to take sth just in case • **lo más que puede ~ es que ...** the worst that can happen is that ... • **lo mismo sucede con este que con el otro** it's the same with this one as it is with the other
2 (= *seguir*) • **~ a algo** to follow sth • **al otoño sucede el invierno** winter follows autumn • **a este cuarto sucede otro mayor** a larger room leads off this one, a larger room lies beyond this one
VT [+ *persona*] to succeed • **~ a algn en un puesto** to succeed sb in a post • **si muere, ¿quién la ~á?** if she dies, who will succeed?
VPR **sucederse** to follow one another
sucesión SF **1** (*al trono, en un puesto*)

succession (a to) • **en la línea de ~ al trono** in line of succession to the throne ▸ **sucesión apostólica** apostolic succession
2 (= *secuencia*) sequence, series • **una ~ de acontecimientos** a succession *o* series of events • **en rápida ~** in quick succession
3 (= *herencia*) inheritance ▸ **derechos de sucesión** death duty
4 (= *hijos*) issue, offspring • **morir sin ~** to die without issue
sucesivamente (ADV) successively, in succession • **y así ~** and so on
sucesivo (ADJ) (= *subsiguiente*) successive, following; (= *consecutivo*) consecutive • **tres días ~s** three days running, three consecutive days • **en lo ~** (= *en el futuro*) henceforth (*frm o liter*), in future; (= *desde entonces*) thereafter, thenceforth (*frm o liter*)
suceso (SM) **1** (= *acontecimiento*) event; (= *incidente*) incident • **sección de ~s** (*Prensa*) (section of) accident and crime reports
2 (= *resultado*) issue, outcome • **buen ~** happy outcome
sucesor(a) (SM/F) **1** (*al trono, a un puesto*) successor
2 (= *heredero*) heir/heiress
sucesorio (ADJ) [*lucha, derechos, crisis*] succession (*antes de s*); [*impuesto*] inheritance (*antes de s*) • **tercero en la línea sucesoria** third in (the) line of succession
suche (ADJ) (*Caribe**) sharp, bitter
(SM) (*Cono Sur*) **1*** (= *grano*) pimple
2* (= *funcionario*) penpusher, pencil pusher (EEUU)
3‡ (= *coime*) pimp
súchil (SM) (*LAm*) *an aromatic flowering tree*
sucho (ADJ) (*And*) maimed, crippled
suciamente (ADV) **1** (= *con suciedad*) dirtily, filthily
2 (= *vilmente*) vilely, meanly
3 (= *obscenamente*) obscenely
suciedad (SF) **1** (= *porquería*) dirt • **un detergente que elimina la ~** a detergent that banishes dirt
2 (= *falta de limpieza*) dirtiness
sucintamente (ADV) succinctly, concisely
sucinto (ADJ) **1** [*discurso, texto*] succinct, concise
2 [*prenda*] brief, scanty, skimpy*
sucio (ADJ) **1** (= *manchado*) [*cara, ropa, suelo*] dirty • **llevas los zapatos muy ~s** your shoes are very dirty • **tienes las manos sucísimas** your hands are filthy • **hazlo primero en ~** make a rough draft first, do it in rough first
2 [*color*] dirty
3 (= *fácil de manchar*) • **los pantalones blancos son muy ~s** white trousers show the dirt, white trousers get dirty very easily
4 (= *obsceno*) dirty, filthy • **palabras sucias** dirty words, filthy words
5 (= *deshonesto*) [*jugada*] foul, dirty; [*táctica*] dirty; [*negocio*] shady
6 [*conciencia*] bad
7 [*lengua*] coated, furred
(ADV) • **jugar ~** to play dirty
(SM) (*And*) bit of dirt
suco¹ (ADJ) (*And*) muddy, swampy
suco² (ADJ) (*And*) (= *rojizo*) bright red; (= *rubio*) blond, fair; (= *anaranjado*) orange
sucre (SM) sucre (*standard monetary unit of Ecuador*)
sucrosa (SF) sucrose
sucucho (SM) (*Caribe*) = **socucha**
suculencia (SF) (= *lo sabroso*) tastiness, richness; (= *jugosidad*) succulence
suculento (ADJ) (= *sabroso*) tasty, rich; (= *jugoso*) succulent
sucumbir ▹ CONJUG 3a (VI) to succumb (a to)
sucursal (SF) (= *oficina local*) branch, branch office; (= *filial*) subsidiary

sucusumuco (ADV) • **a lo ~** (*And, Caribe*) pretending to be stupid, feigning stupidity
sud (SM) (*esp LAm*) south
sudaca* (ADJ), (SMF) (*pey*) South American
sudadera (SF) sweatshirt ▸ **sudadera con capucha** hooded sweatshirt, hoodie*
sudado (ADJ) sweaty
(SM) (*Perú*) stew
Sudáfrica (SF) South Africa
sudafricano/a (ADJ), (SM/F) South African
Sudamérica (SF) South America
sudamericano/a (ADJ), (SM/F) South American
Sudán (SM) Sudan
sudanés/esa (ADJ), (SM/F) Sudanese
sudar ▹ CONJUG 1a (VI) **1** (= *transpirar*) to sweat • **MODISMOS:** • **~ a chorros*** • **~ a mares*** to sweat buckets* • **hacer ~ a algn** to make sb sweat
2 (= *exudar*) [*recipiente*] to ooze; [*pared*] to sweat
(VT) **1** (= *transpirar*) to sweat • **MODISMO:** • **~ la gota gorda** to sweat buckets*; ▹ **sangre, tinta**
2 (= *mojar*) [+ *ropa, prenda*] to make sweaty • **MODISMOS:** • **~ la camiseta** to sweat blood • **me la suda**‡*: • **es un asunto que me la suda** it bores the pants off me*
3 (*Bot*) (= *segregar*) to ooze, give out, give off
4* (= *conseguir con esfuerzo*) • **~lo** to sweat it out • **~ un aumento de sueldo** to sweat for a rise in pay • **ha sudado el premio** he really went flat out to get that prize
5* [+ *dinero*] to cough up*, part with
sudario (SM) shroud
sudestada (SF) (*Cono Sur*) = **surestada**
sudeste (SM) = **sureste**
sudista (ADJ) southern
(SMF) Southerner
sudoeste = **suroeste**
sudoku (SM) sudoku
sudón* (ADJ) (*LAm*) sweaty
sudor (SM) **1** (= *transpiración*) sweat • **con el ~ de su frente** by the sweat of one's brow • **estar bañado en ~** to be dripping with sweat
2 (*tb* **sudores**) (= *esfuerzo*) toil (*sing*), labour (*sing*), labor (*sing*) (EEUU)
sudoración (SF) sweating
sudoroso (ADJ), **sudoriento** (ADJ), **sudoso** (ADJ) sweaty • **trabajo ~** thirsty work
Suecia (SF) Sweden
suecia (SF) suede
sueco/a (ADJ) Swedish
(SM/F) Swede • **MODISMO:** • **hacerse el ~*** to act dumb
(SM) (*Ling*) Swedish
suegro/a (SM/F) father-in-law/ mother-in-law; **suegros** parents-in-law, in-laws
suela (SF) **1** [*de zapato*] (= *base*) sole; (= *trozo de cuero*) piece of strong leather • **media ~** half sole • **MODISMOS:** • **no llegarle a algn a la ~ del zapato** • **Juan no le llega a la ~ del zapato a Pablo** Juan can't hold a candle to Pablo • **duro como la ~ de un zapato** tough as leather, tough as old boots • **de siete ~s** utter, downright • **un pícaro de siete ~s** an utter *o* a downright *o* a proper rogue
2 (*Téc*) tap washer
3 • **~s** (*Rel*) sandals
4 (= *pez*) sole
suelazo (SM) (*LAm*) (= *caída*) heavy fall, nasty bump; (= *golpe*) blow, punch
sueldo (SM) (= *paga*) (*gen*) pay; (*mensual*) salary; (*semanal*) wages (*pl*) • **asesino a ~** hired killer, contract killer • **estar a ~** to be on a salary, earn a salary • **estar a ~ de una potencia extranjera** to be in the pay of a foreign power ▸ **sueldo atrasado** back pay ▸ **sueldo base** basic salary ▸ **sueldo en especie** payment in kind ▸ **sueldo fijo** regular salary ▸ **sueldo líquido** net salary
suelear* ▹ CONJUG 1a (VT) (*Cono Sur*) to throw, chuck
suelo (SM) **1** (*en el exterior*) (= *tierra*) ground; (= *superficie*) surface • **caer al ~** to fall to the ground, fall over • **echar al ~** [+ *edificio*] to demolish; [+ *esperanzas*] to dash; [+ *plan*] to ruin • **echarse al ~** (= *tirarse al suelo*) to hurl o.s. to the ground; (= *arrodillarse*) to fall on one's knees • **MODISMOS:** • **por los ~s:** • **los precios están por los ~s** prices are at rock bottom • **esos géneros están por los ~s** those goods are dirt cheap • **tengo el ánimo por los ~s** I feel really low • **arrastrar** *o* **poner** *o* **tirar por los ~s** [+ *persona*] to slate, slag off*; [+ *novela, película*] to pan, slam, rubbish* • **medir el ~** to measure one's length (on the ground) • **tirarse por los ~s*** to roll in the aisles (with laughter)* • **venirse al ~** to fail, collapse, be ruined ▸ **suelo natal, suelo patrio** native land, native soil
2 (*en edificio*) (= *superficie*) floor; (= *solería*) flooring • **un ~ de mármol** a marble floor
3 (= *terreno*) soil, land ▸ **suelo edificable** building land ▸ **suelo empresarial** *space for office accommodation* ▸ **suelo vegetal** topsoil
4 [*de pan, vasija*] bottom
suelta (SF) • **habrá una ~ de palomas** doves will be released
suelte *etc* ▹ **soltar**
sueltista (SMF) (*LAm*) freelance journalist
suelto (ADJ) **1** (= *libre*) (*gen*) free; [*criminal*] free, out; [*animal*] loose • **el bandido anda ~** the bandit's on the loose • **el perro anda ~** the dog is loose
2 (= *desatado*) [*cordones*] undone, untied; [*cabo, hoja, tornillo*] loose • **llevas ~s los cordones** your shoelaces are undone • **el libro tiene dos hojas sueltas** the book has two pages loose • **el arroz tiene que quedar ~** rice shouldn't stick together
3 • **dinero ~** loose change
4 [*prenda de vestir*] loose, loose-fitting • **iba con el pelo ~** she had her hair down *o* loose
5 [*vientre*] loose
6 • **~ de lengua** (= *parlanchín*) talkative; (= *respondón*) cheeky; (= *soplón*) blabbing; (= *obsceno*) foul-mouthed
7 (= *separado*) [*trozo, pieza*] separate, detached; [*ejemplar, volumen*] individual, odd; [*calcetín*] odd • **no se venden ~s** they are not sold singly *o* separately • **es un trozo ~ de la novela** it's a separate extract from the novel, it's an isolated passage from the novel • **son tres poesías sueltas** these are three separate poems • **hay un calcetín ~** there is one odd sock • **una mesa con números ~s de revistas** a table with odd copies of magazines
8 (*Com*) (= *no envasado*) loose
9 [*movimiento*] (= *libre*) free, easy; (= *ágil*) quick
10 (= *fluido*) [*estilo*] fluent; [*conversación*] easy, easy-flowing • **está muy ~ en inglés** he is very good at *o* fluent in English
11 (*moralmente*) free and easy
12 (*Literat*) [*verso*] blank
(SM) **1** (= *cambio*) loose change, small change
2 (= *artículo*) item, short article, short report
suene *etc* ▹ **sonar**
sueña *etc* ▹ **soñar**
sueñera (SF) (*LAm*) drowsiness, sleepiness
sueño (SM) **1** (= *estado*) sleep • **coger** *o* **conciliar el ~** to get to sleep • **echarse un ~** *o* **un sueñecito*** to have a nap, have a kip* • **en** *o* **entre ~s:** • **me hablaste entre ~s** you talked to me but you were half asleep • **tener el ~ ligero** to be a light sleeper • **tener el ~ pesado** to be a heavy sleeper ▸ **sueño eterno**

S

eternal rest ▸ **sueño invernal** (*Zool*) winter sleep ▸ **sueño paradójico** paradoxical sleep ▸ **sueño profundo** deep sleep ▸ **sueño REM** REM sleep; ▹ **dormir**
2 (= *ganas de dormir*) • **tienes cara de ~** you look sleepy • **tengo ~ atrasado** I haven't caught up on sleep, I haven't had much sleep lately • **caerse de ~** to be asleep on one's feet • **dar ~**: • **su conversación me da ~** his conversation sends me to sleep • **la televisión me da ~** television makes me sleepy • **morirse de ~** • **estar muerto de ~** to be asleep on one's feet, be so tired one can hardly stand • **quitar el ~ a algn** to keep sb awake • **el café me quita el ~** coffee keeps me awake • **ya se me ha quitado el ~** I'm not sleepy any more • **tener ~** to be sleepy, be tired • MODISMO: • **perder el ~ por algo** to lose sleep over sth; ▹ **vencer**
3 (= *imagen soñada*) dream • **anoche tuve un ~ espantoso** I had a horrible dream last night • **¿sabes interpretar los ~s?** do you know how to interpret dreams? • **¡que tengas dulces ~s!** sweet dreams! • MODISMO: • **¡ni en ~s!*** no chance!* • **eso no te lo crees tú ni en ~s** don't give me that!* • **no pienso volver a hablarle ni en ~s** there's no way I'd ever talk to him again* ▸ **sueño húmedo** wet dream
4 (= *ilusión*) dream • **por fin consiguió la casa de sus ~s** she finally got the house of her dreams *o* her dream home • **vive en un mundo de ~s** he lives in a dream world • **estas vacaciones son como un ~** these holidays are like a dream come true • **mi ~ dorado es vivir frente al mar** my greatest dream is to live by the sea ▸ **el sueño americano** the American Dream

suero (SM) **1** (*Med*) serum ▸ **suero fisiológico** saline solution
2 [*de leche*] whey ▸ **suero de leche** buttermilk

suertaza* (SF) great stroke of luck

suerte (SF) **1** (= *fortuna*) luck • **con un poco de ~ podemos ganar** with a bit of luck we can win • **no me cupo tal ~** I had no such luck • **no nos acompañó mucho la ~** luck wasn't on our side • **¡suerte!** • **¡buena suerte!** good luck! • **dar ~** to bring good luck • **el topacio da ~** topaz brings good luck • **este número me da ~** this is my lucky number • **día de ~** lucky day • **me considero un hombre de ~** I consider myself a lucky man • **estar de ~** to be in luck • **mala ~** bad luck • **la mala ~ está acompañando su gira** his tour is being dogged by bad luck • **¡siempre tengo tan mala ~ con los hombres!** I'm always so unlucky with men!, I always have such bad luck with men! • **¡qué mala ~!** how unlucky!, what bad luck! • **por ~** luckily, fortunately • **probar ~** to try one's luck • **tener ~** to be lucky • **¡que tengas ~!** good luck!, the best of luck! • **tuvo una ~ increíble** he was incredibly lucky • **tuvo la ~ de que el autobús saliera con retraso** he was lucky that the bus left late, luckily for him his bus left late • **tentar a la ~** to try one's luck • **traer ~** to be lucky, bring good luck • **me trajo ~** it brought me good luck • **trae mala ~** it's bad luck, it's unlucky • MODISMO: • **por ~ o por desgracia** for better or for worse; ▹ **golpe**
2 (= *destino*) fate • **la ~ que les espera** the fate which awaits them • **quiso la ~ que pasara por allí un médico** as luck *o* fate would have it a doctor was passing by • **estar resignado a su ~** to be resigned to one's fate • **los abandonaron a su ~** they left them to their fate • **no estaba contento con su ~** he wasn't happy with his lot • **correr la misma ~ que algn** to suffer the same fate as sb • **mejorar la ~ de algn** to improve sb's lot • **tentar a la ~** to tempt fate
3 (= *azar*) chance • **confiar algo a la ~** to leave sth to chance • **lo echaron a ~s** (*con cerillas, papeletas*) they drew lots; (*con moneda*) they tossed (a coin) • MODISMOS: • **caerle** *o* **tocarle en ~ a algn**: • **al equipo español le tocó en ~ enfrentarse a Turquía** as chance had it, the Spanish team were drawn to play against Turkey • **¡vaya marido que me ha tocado en ~!** what a husband I ended up with! • **la ~ está echada** the die is cast
4 (= *clase*) sort, kind • **hubo toda ~ de comentarios** there were all sorts *o* kinds of remarks • **lo explicó con toda ~ de detalles** she explained it in great detail
5 (*frm*) (= *modo*) • **de esta ~** in this way • **no podemos seguir de esta ~** we cannot go on in this way • **los molinos de agua pueden clasificarse de esta ~** water wheels can be classified in the following way *o* in this way • **de ~ que** in such a way that
6 (*Taur*) *stage of the bullfight* ▸ **suerte de banderillas** *the second stage of a bullfight, in which the "banderillas" are stuck into the bull's back* ▸ **suerte de capa** *stage of a bullfight where passes are made with the cape* ▸ **suerte de varas** *opening stage of a bullfight where the bull is weakened with the picador's lance* ▸ **suerte suprema** *final stage of a bullfight*

suertero (ADJ) (*LAm*), **suertudo** (ADJ) (*esp LAm*) lucky, jammy*

suertoso (ADJ) (*And*) lucky

suestada (SF) (*Arg*) southeast wind

sueste (SM) **1** (= *sombrero*) sou'wester
2 (*LAm*) (= *viento*) southeast wind

suéter (SM) sweater

Suetonio (SM) Suetonius

Suez (SM) Suez • **Canal de ~** Suez Canal

suficiencia (SF) **1** (= *cabida*) sufficiency • **con ~** sufficiently, adequately • **una ~ de ...** enough ...
2 (= *competencia*) competence • **demostrar su ~** to prove one's competence, show one's capabilities
3 (*Escol*) proficiency
4 (*pey*) (= *engreimiento*) self-importance; (= *satisfacción de sí mismo*) smugness, self-satisfaction

suficiente (ADJ) **1** (= *bastante*) enough • **ahora no llevo ~ dinero (como) para pagarte** I don't have enough money on me at the moment to pay you
2 (= *petulante*) smug, self-satisfied
(SM) (*Escol*) ≈ C, pass mark, passing grade (EEUU)

suficientemente (ADV) sufficiently, adequately • **no era ~ grande** it wasn't big enough *o* sufficiently big • **~ bueno** good enough

sufijo (SM) suffix

suflé (SM) soufflé

sufragáneo (ADJ) suffragan

sufragar ▹ CONJUG 1h (VT) **1** (= *ayudar*) to help, aid
2 (= *pagar*) [+ *gastos*] to meet, defray; [+ *proyecto*] to pay for, defray the costs of
(VI) (*LAm*) to vote (**por** for)

sufragio (SM) **1** (= *voto*) vote • **los ~s emitidos a favor del candidato** the votes cast for the candidate
2 (= *derecho al voto*) suffrage ▸ **sufragio universal** universal suffrage
3 (= *apoyo*) help, aid
4 (*Rel*) suffrage

sufragista (ADJ), (SMF) suffragist
(SF) (*Hist*) suffragette

sufrible (ADJ) bearable

sufrido (ADJ) **1** [*persona*] (= *fuerte*) tough; (= *paciente*) long-suffering, patient
2 [*tela*] hard wearing, tough; [*color*] that does not show the dirt, that wears well
3 [*marido*] complaisant
(SM) complaisant husband

sufridor(a) (ADJ) suffering
(SM/F) (= *persona*) sufferer
(SM) (*And*) saddlecloth

sufrimiento (SM) **1** (= *padecimiento*) suffering • **una vida marcada por el ~** a life of suffering
2†† (= *paciencia*) patience • **tener ~ en las dificultades** to be patient in hard times, bear troubles patiently

sufrir ▹ CONJUG 3a (VT) **1** (= *tener*) [+ *accidente*] to have, suffer; [+ *consecuencias, revés*] to suffer; [+ *cambio*] to undergo; [+ *intervención quirúrgica*] to have, undergo; [+ *pérdida*] to suffer, sustain • **la ciudad sufrió un ataque** the city suffered *o* sustained an attack • **sufrió un ataque al corazón** he had a heart attack • **~ un colapso** to collapse
2 (= *soportar*) • **Juan no puede ~ a su jefe** Juan can't bear *o* stand his boss • **no puede ~ que la imiten** she can't bear *o* stand people imitating her
3 [+ *examen, prueba*] to undergo
4 (*frm*) (= *sostener*) to hold up, support
(VI) to suffer • **sufría en silencio** she suffered in silence • **mi madre sufre mucho si llego tarde a casa** my mother gets terribly worried if I'm late home • **hacer ~ a algn** to make sb suffer • **~ de algo** to suffer from sth • **sufre de reumatismo** she suffers from rheumatism • **sufre mucho de los pies** she suffers a lot *o* has a lot of trouble with her feet

sugerencia (SF) suggestion • **hacer una ~** to make a suggestion; ▹ **buzón**

sugerente (ADJ) **1** (= *lleno de ideas*) [*exposición, obra*] thought-provoking; [*lenguaje*] evocative
2 (= *seductor*) [*mirada, gesto, voz*] suggestive; [*ropa, iluminación*] seductive • **con el ~ título de "Pasión tropical"** with the suggestive title of "Pasión tropical"

sugerible (ADJ) = **sugestionable**

sugerimiento (SM) suggestion

sugerir ▹ CONJUG 3i (VT) **1** (= *proponer*) to suggest • **¿tú qué me sugieres?** what do you suggest? • **nos sugirió la idea de grabar esa canción** he suggested the idea of recording that song to us • **~ hacer algo** to suggest doing sth • **yo sugiero empezar más temprano** I suggest that we begin earlier, I suggest beginning earlier • **~ a algn que** (+ *subjun*): • **me ha sugerido que escriba una novela** he has suggested that I write a novel *o* that I should write a novel
2 (= *insinuar*) to hint at, suggest • **sugirió la posibilidad de que el ministro dimitiera** he hinted at the possibility of the minister resigning, he suggested the possibility that the Minister would resign
3 (= *indicar*) to suggest • **los hallazgos arqueológicos sugieren la existencia de un asentamiento anterior** the archaeological finds suggest the existence of a previous settlement • **no es una novela histórica, como el título podría ~** it is not a historical novel, as the title might suggest
4 (= *evocar*) • **la película me ha sugerido muchas cosas** the film was very thought-provoking, the film gave me much food for thought • **la idea que nos sugiere este nuevo producto** the idea conveyed by this new product, the image this new product calls to mind

sugestión (SF) **1** (= *convencimiento*) • **sus problemas no son más que pura ~** his problems are all in his mind • **lo durmió gracias a sus poderes de ~** he made him go

S

to sleep by his hypnotic powers
2 (= *insinuación*) suggestion • **nunca acepta las sugestiones de los demás** he never listens to anyone else's suggestions • **las sugestiones del demonio** the promptings of the devil
sugestionable ADJ (= *impresionable*) impressionable, suggestible; (= *influenciable*) readily influenced
sugestionar ▹ CONJUG 1a VT to influence • **es probable que se haya dejado ~ por ...** he may have allowed himself to be influenced by ... • **~ a algn para que haga algo** to influence sb to do sth
VPR **sugestionarse** to indulge in auto-suggestion • **~se con algo** to talk o.s. into sth
sugestivo ADJ **1** (= *que invita a pensar*) stimulating, thought-provoking; (= *evocador*) evocative
2 (= *atractivo*) attractive
sugiera *etc* ▸ **sugerir**
suiche SM (*esp Méx*) **1** (*Elec*) switch
2 (*Aut*) ignition, ignition switch
suicida ADJ suicidal • **comando ~** suicide squad • **conductor ~** suicidal driver • **piloto ~** suicide pilot, kamikaze pilot
SMF (= *que ha intentado suicidarse*) suicidal case; (= *muerto*) suicide victim • **es un ~ conduciendo** he's a maniac behind the wheel
suicidado/a SM/F *person who commits suicide*
suicidar ▹ CONJUG 1a VT (*iró*) to murder, assassinate (*so as to convey an impression of suicide*), fake the suicide of
VPR **suicidarse** to commit suicide, kill o.s.
suicidario ADJ, **suicidiario** ADJ suicidal
suicidio SM suicide
sui géneris ADJ INV individual, idiosyncratic
suite [swit] SF **1** (*en hotel*) suite
2 (*Mús*) suite
Suiza SF Switzerland
suiza SF **1** (*CAm, Caribe*) (= *juego*) skipping, jumping rope (*EEUU*), skipping game
2 (*And, CAm*) (= *paliza*) beating
suizo¹/a ADJ, SM/F Swiss
suizo² SM (*Culin*) sugared bun
suje* SM bra
sujeción SF **1** (= *estado*) subjection
2 (= *acción*) (*al cerrar*) fastening; (*al apoderarse de algo*) seizure
3 (= *dominación*) subjection (**a** to) • **con ~ a** subject to
sujetacorbata SM tiepin
sujetador SM **1** (= *prenda*) [*de ropa interior*] bra, brassiere (*frm*); [*del biquini*] top
2 (*para pelo*) clip, hairgrip, bobby pin (*EEUU*)
sujetalibros SM INV book-end
sujetapapeles SM INV paper clip
sujetar ▹ CONJUG 1a VT **1** (= *agarrar*) to hold • **sujeta esto un momento** hold this a moment • **dos policías lo sujetaban contra la pared** two policemen pinned *o* held him against the wall • **lo tuvieron que ~ entre tres personas para que no huyera** he had to be held back *o* restrained by three people to stop him escaping
2 (= *afianzar*) • **lo sujeté con un esparadrapo** I fixed it with some sticking-plaster • **sujeta bien la ropa, que no se la lleve el viento** peg the clothes (up) properly so the wind doesn't blow them away • **hay que ~ bien a los niños dentro del coche** children should be properly strapped in *o* properly secured when travelling by car • **~ algo a:** • **se sujeta a la pared por medio de argollas** it is fixed *o* attached *o* secured to the wall through rings • **~ algo con:** • **~ algo con clavos** to nail sth down • **~ algo con grapas** to staple sth • **~ algo con tornillos** to screw sth down • **enrolló el mapa y lo sujetó con una goma** she rolled up the map and fastened *o* secured it with a rubber band • **sujetó las facturas con un clip** she clipped the invoices together
3 (= *contener*) [+ *rebelde*] to subdue, conquer; [+ *rival, animal enfurecido*] to keep down • **es muy rebelde y sus padres no lo pueden ~** he's very rebellious - his parents can't control him • **lograron ~ las aspiraciones de los sindicatos** they succeeded in keeping the aspirations of the unions under control • **vive sin ataduras que la sujeten** she has nothing to tie her down, she has no ties to bind her • **mis deberes como político me sujetan aquí** my duties as a politician bind me here
VPR **sujetarse 1** (= *agarrarse*) **a** [+ *pelo, sombrero*] to hold • **salió sujetándose los pantalones** he came out holding his trousers up • **¿tienes una goma para ~me el pelo?** have you got an elastic band to hold my hair up? • **inclinó la cabeza y se sujetó el sombrero** he tilted his head and held his hat on
b • **~se a algo** to hold on to sth • **tuvo que ~se a la barandilla para no caerse** he had to hold on to the handrail so as not to fall over
2 (= *someterse*) • **~se a** [+ *normas, reglas*] to abide by; [+ *autoridad*] to submit to • **no quieren ~se a un horario fijo** they don't want to tie themselves down to fixed hours, they don't want to be bound by a fixed timetable
sujeto ADJ **1** (= *fijo*) fastened, secure • **¿está sujeta la cuerda?** is the rope fastened securely?, is the rope secure? • **las ruedas van sujetas por cuatro tuercas** the wheels are held on *o* secured by four nuts • **los espejos estaban ~s a la pared** the mirrors were fastened *o* fixed to the wall
2 (= *pendiente*) • **~ a algo** subject to sth • **vivimos ~s a las vicisitudes del destino** we are all subject to the vicissitudes of fate • **la programación podría estar sujeta a cambios** the programme could be subject to changes • **una suma de dinero no sujeta a impuestos** a non-taxable sum of money
SM **1*** (= *tipo*) character* • **un ~ sospechoso** a suspicious(-looking) character*
2 (*Med, Fil*) subject • **todos los ~s estudiados** all the subjects studied
3 (*Ling*) subject
4 (*Econ*) ▸ **sujeto pasivo** taxpayer
sulfamida SF sulphonamide
sulfatar ▹ CONJUG 1a VT to fertilize, fertilize with sulphate
sulfato SM sulphate, sulfate (*EEUU*)
▸ **sulfato amónico** ammonium sulphate
▸ **sulfato de cobre** copper sulphate ▸ **sulfato de hierro** iron sulphate ▸ **sulfato magnésico** magnesium sulphate ▸ **sulfato potásico** potassium sulphate
sulfurado* ADJ cross, angry
sulfurar ▹ CONJUG 1a VT **1** (*Quím*) to sulphurate, sulfurate (*EEUU*)
2* (= *sacar de quicio a*) to rile*
VPR **sulfurarse*** (= *enojarse*) to get riled*, see red, blow up*
sulfúreo ADJ sulphurous, sulfurous (*EEUU*)
sulfúrico ADJ sulphuric, sulfuric (*EEUU*)
sulfuro SM sulphide, sulfide (*EEUU*)
sulfuroso ADJ sulphurous, sulfurous (*EEUU*)
sultán/ana SM/F sultan/sultana
sultanato SM sultanate
suma SF **1** (*Mat*) (= *acción*) addition, adding, adding up; (= *cantidad*) total, sum; (= *dinero*) sum • **una ~ de dinero** a sum of money • **¿cuánto es la ~ de todos los gastos?** what are the total expenses? • **hacer ~s** to add up, do addition • **hizo la ~ de todo lo que habían gastado** he added up everything they had spent • **~ y sigue** (*Com*) "carried forward"; (*fig**) and it's still going on ▸ **suma global** lump sum
2 (= *resumen*) summary • **en ~** in short • **una ~ de perfecciones** perfection itself • **es la ~ y compendio de todas las virtudes** she is the personification of virtue
SM • **un ~ y sigue de grandes aportaciones al mundo del automóvil** a whole host of great contributions to the motoring world • **su vida es un continuo ~ y sigue de tragedias** his life is one tragedy after another
sumador SM adder
sumadora SF adding machine
sumamente ADV extremely, exceedingly, highly
sumando SM addend
sumar ▹ CONJUG 1a VT **1** (*Mat*) to add (together) • **suma estas dos cantidades** add these two amounts (together)
2 (= *totalizar*) to add up to, come to • **la cuenta suma seis dólares** the bill adds up *o* comes to six dollars • **dos y dos suman cuatro** two and two are *o* make four
3† (= *resumir*) to summarize, sum up
VI to add up • **suma y sigue** (*Contabilidad*) carried forward
VPR **sumarse** • **~se a algo** to join sth • **~se a un partido** to join a party • **~se a una protesta** to join in a protest
sumarial ADJ summary
sumariamente ADV summarily
sumario ADJ **1** (= *breve*) brief, concise
2 (*Jur*) summary • **información sumaria** summary proceedings (*pl*)
SM **1** (= *resumen*) (*gen*) summary; (*en revista*) contents (*pl*)
2 (*Jur*) indictment • **abrir** *o* **instruir un ~** to institute legal proceedings, present *o* issue an indictment (*esp EEUU*)
sumarísimo ADJ summary
Sumatra SF Sumatra
sumergible ADJ [*nave*] submersible; [*reloj*] waterproof
SM submarine
sumergido ADJ **1** (*en agua*) submerged, sunken
2 (= *ilegal*) illegal, unauthorized • **economía sumergida** black economy • **tratos ~s** black-market deals
sumergimiento SM submersion, submergence
sumergir ▹ CONJUG 3c VT (*completamente*) to immerse; (*parcialmente*) to dip (**en** in) • **~ la bolsa en agua hirviendo** put the bag into the boiling water
VPR **sumergirse 1** (= *hundirse*) [*objeto, persona*] to sink beneath the surface; [*submarino*] to dive
2 (*en un ambiente*) • **~se en** to immerse o.s. in
sumersión SF **1** (= *inmersión*) submersion
2 (= *absorción*) absorption (**en** in)
sumidero SM **1** (*en calle, azotea, patio*) drain
2 (*Téc*) sump, oilpan (*EEUU*)
3 (= *sangría*) drain • **es el gran ~ de las reservas** it is the chief drain on our reserves
4 (*And, Caribe*) (= *pozo negro*) cesspool, cesspit
5 (*Caribe*) (= *tremedal*) quagmire
sumido ADJ • **~ en su trabajo** immersed *o* buried in one's work • **~ en mis pensamientos** lost in thought
sumiller SM wine waiter
suministrador(a) SM/F supplier
suministrar ▹ CONJUG 1a VT [+ *géneros, información*] to supply, provide; [+ *persona*] to

S

supply • **me ha suministrado muchos datos** he has given me a lot of information, he has provided *o* supplied me with a lot of information
suministro (SM) **1** (= *provisión*) supply • **~s** (*Mil*) supplies ▸ **suministro de agua** water supply ▸ **suministro de gas** gas supply ▸ **suministros de combustible** fuel supply (*sing*)
2 (= *acción*) supplying, provision
sumir ▹ CONJUG 3a (VT) **1** (= *hundir*) (*gen*) to sink, plunge; [*mar, olas*] to swallow up, suck down
2 (= *abismar*) to plunge (**en** into) • **el desastre lo sumió en la tristeza** the disaster filled him with sadness
3 (*And, Cono Sur, Méx*) (= *abollar*) to dent
(VPR) **sumirse 1** (= *hundirse*) to sink
2 [*agua*] to run away
3 • **~se en el estudio** to throw o.s. into one's studies • **~se en la duda** to be seized by doubt • **~se en la tristeza** to be filled with sadness
4 [*boca, pecho*] to sink, be sunken, become hollow
5 (*LAm*) (= *encogerse*) to cower, cringe; (= *desanimarse*) to lose heart; (= *callar*) to fall silent from fear, clam up
6 • **~se el sombrero** (*LAm*) to pull one's hat down over one's eyes
sumisamente (ADV) (= *dócilmente*) submissively, obediently; (= *sin resistir*) unresistingly; (= *sin quejarse*) uncomplainingly
sumisión (SF) **1** (= *acción*) submission
2 (= *docilidad*) submissiveness
sumiso (ADJ) (= *dócil*) submissive; (= *que no se resiste*) unresisting; (= *que no se queja*) uncomplaining
súmmum (SM) height
sumo¹ (ADJ) **1** (= *supremo*) great, supreme • **con suma dificultad** with the greatest *o* utmost difficulty • **con suma indiferencia** with supreme indifference • **con suma destreza** with consummate skill
2 [*rango*] high, highest • **~ sacerdote** high priest • **la suma autoridad** the supreme authority
3 • **a lo ~** at (the) most
sumo² (SM) (*Dep*) sumo, sumo wrestling
sunco (ADJ) (*And*) = **manco**
sungo (ADJ) (*And*) **1** (= *de raza negra*) (*gen*) black; (= *de piel lisa*) with a shiny skin
2 (= *tostado*) tanned
suní (ADJ), (SMF), **sunita** (ADJ), (SMF) Sunni
suntuario (ADJ) sumptuary
suntuosamente (ADV) (= *magníficamente*) sumptuously, magnificently; (= *pródigamente*) lavishly, richly
suntuosidad (SF) (= *magnificencia*) sumptuousness, magnificence; (= *prodigalidad*) lavishness
suntuoso (ADJ) (= *magnífico*) sumptuous, magnificent; (= *lujoso*) lavish, rich
sup. (ABR) (= **superior**) sup
supe *etc* ▹ **saber**
supeditar ▹ CONJUG 1a (VT) **1** (= *subordinar*) to subordinate (**a** to) • **tendrá que ser supeditado a lo que decidan ellos** it will depend *o* be dependent on what they decide
2 (= *sojuzgar*) to subdue
3 (= *oprimir*) to oppress, crush
(VPR) **supeditarse** • **~se a** (= *subordinarse*) to be subject to; (= *ceder*) to give in to • **no voy a ~me a sus caprichos** I am not going to give in to her whims
súper* (ADJ) super*
(SM) supermarket
(SF) (*Aut*) four-star petrol
(ADV)* • **pasarlo ~** to have a great time*
super... (PREF) super..., over... • **superambicioso** overambitious • **superatraco** major hold-up • **supercaro*** dead expensive* • **superdesarrollo** overdevelopment • **superfamoso** really famous • **superreservado** excessively shy • **un texto supercomentado** a text which has so often been commented on
superable (ADJ) [*dificultad*] surmountable, that can be overcome; [*tarea*] that can be performed • **un obstáculo difícilmente ~** an obstacle not easily overcome
superabundancia (SF) superabundance, overabundance
superabundante (ADJ) superabundant
superación (SF) **1** (= *acto*) overcoming, surmounting
2 (= *mejora*) improvement; ▹ **afán**
superagente* (SMF) supercop*, super-sleuth*
superar ▹ CONJUG 1a (VT) **1** (= *aventajar*) [+ *contrincante, adversario*] to overcome; [+ *límite*] to go beyond; [+ *récord, marca*] to break • **fue incapaz de ~ al rival** he was unable to overcome his rival • **pronto superó al resto de los corredores** she soon overtook the other runners • **las ventas han superado con creces nuestras expectativas** sales have far exceeded our expectations • **las temperaturas han superado los 20 grados** temperatures have risen (to) above 20 degrees • **~ a algn en algo: superó al adversario en cuatro puntos** she beat her opponent by four points • **nos superaban en número** they outnumbered us • **nos supera a todos en inteligencia** she's cleverer than all of us
2 (= *pasar con éxito*) [+ *dificultad*] to overcome; [+ *enfermedad, crisis*] to get over • **ha tenido que ~ muchos obstáculos en su vida** she has had to overcome a lot of obstacles in her life • **aún no ha superado el divorcio de sus padres** he still hasn't got over his parents' divorce
3 [+ *etapa*] to get past • **el equipo francés no superó la primera ronda** the French team did not get past the first round • **ya hemos superado lo peor** we're over the worst now
4 [+ *prueba, examen*] to pass
(VPR) **superarse** to excel o.s. • **esta tortilla está buenísima, ¡te has superado!** this omelette is delicious, you've excelled yourself! • **un atleta que siempre intenta ~se** an athlete who is always trying to do better
superávit (SM) (PL: **superávits**) surplus
superavitario (ADJ) surplus (*antes de s*)
superbloque (SM) (*Ven*) large block of flats (*Brit*) *o* apartment building (*EEUU*)
superbombardero (SM) superbomber
supercarburante (SM) high-grade fuel
supercarretera (SF) superhighway
superchería (SF) fraud, trick, swindle
superchero (ADJ) fraudulent
superclase (SMF) (*Dep*) top-class sportsman/sportswoman
supercola (SF) superglue
superconductividad (SF) superconductivity
superconductor (ADJ) superconductive
(SM) superconductor
superconsumo (SM) overconsumption
supercopa (SF) cup-winners' cup
supercotizado (ADJ) in very great demand
supercuenta (SF) high interest account
supercuerda (SF) (*Fís*) superstring
superdirecta (SF) overdrive
superdotado/a (ADJ) extremely gifted
(SM/F) extremely gifted person
superego (SM) superego
superempleo (SM) overemployment
superentender ▹ CONJUG 2g (VT) to supervise, superintend
supererogación (SF) supererogation
superestrella (SF) superstar
superestructura (SF) superstructure
superferolítico* (ADJ) **1** (= *afectado*) affected
2 (= *muy refinado*) excessively refined
3 (= *delicado*) overnice, finicky, choosy*
superficial (ADJ) **1** [*herida*] superficial, skin (*antes de s*)
2 (= *poco perceptible*) [*interés*] superficial; [*mirada*] brief, perfunctory; [*carácter*] shallow; [*medidas*] surface (*antes de s*)
superficialidad (SF) **1** [*de herida*] superficiality
2 (= *frivolidad*) shallowness
superficialmente (ADV) superficially
superficie (SF) **1** [*de cuerpo, líquido*] surface • **la ~ terrestre** the earth's surface • **el submarino salió a la ~** the submarine surfaced, the submarine came to the surface • **ruta de ~** surface route ▸ **superficie de rodadura** (*Aut*) tread ▸ **superficie inferior** lower surface, underside
2 (*en medidas*) area • **en una extensa ~** over a wide area • **una ~ de 200 hectáreas** an area of 200 hectares ▸ **superficie útil** useful area, usable space
3 (= *aspecto externo*) surface • **es un comentario inofensivo en la ~** it's a harmless comment on the surface
4 (*Com*) • **gran ~** (= *hipermercado*) hypermarket, superstore • **~ de venta(s)** sales area
superfino (ADJ) superfine
superfluamente (ADV) superfluously
superfluidad (SF) superfluity
superfluo (ADJ) superfluous
superfosfato (SM) superphosphate
superhéroe (SM) superhero
superhombre (SM) superman
superíndice (SM) superscript
superintendencia (SF) supervision
superintendente (SMF) (= *supervisor*) supervisor, superintendent; (= *capataz*) overseer • **~ de división** sectional head
superior¹ (ADJ) **1** (= *más alto*) [*estante, línea*] top (*antes de s*); [*labio, mandíbula*] upper • **vive en el piso ~** he lives on the top floor • **en la parte ~ de la página** at the top of the page • **el cuadrante ~ izquierdo** the top left quadrant
2 (= *mejor*) superior, better • **ser ~ a algo** to be superior to sth, be better than sth • **sentirse ~ a algn** to feel superior to sb
3 (= *excelente*) • **la orquesta estuvo ~** the orchestra was top-quality *o* top-class • **una moqueta de calidad ~** a superior quality *o* top-quality carpet
4 [*cantidad*] • **cualquier número ~ a doce** any number above *o* higher than twelve • **nos son muy ~es en número** they greatly outnumber us
5 (*en categoría*) [*animal, especie*] higher • **una casta ~** a higher caste • **tiene un cargo ~ al tuyo** he has a higher-ranking post than yours
6 (*Educ*) [*curso, nivel*] advanced; [*enseñanza*] higher
(SM) (*en rango*) superior • **mis ~es** my superiors
superior²/a (*Rel*) (ADJ) superior
(SM/F) superior/mother superior
superioridad (SF) superiority • **con aire de ~** condescendingly, patronizingly
superitar ▹ CONJUG 1a (VT) (*And, Cono Sur*)
1 (= *superar*) to overcome
2 (= *aventajar*) to improve
superlativo (ADJ), (SM) superlative
superlujo (SM) • **hotel de ~** super-luxury

hotel • **tiene categoría de ~** it is in the super-luxury class
supermercado SM supermarket
superministro/a SM/F minister with an overall responsibility, senior minister, overlord
supermoda SF • **vestido de ~** high-fashion dress
supermujer SF superwoman
supernova SF supernova
supernumerario/a ADJ, SM/F supernumerary
superordenador SM supercomputer
superpetrolero SM supertanker
superpoblación SF [*de país, región*] overpopulation; [*de barrio*] overcrowding
superpoblado ADJ [*país, región*] overpopulated; [*barrio*] overcrowded, congested
superpoder SM superpower
superponer ▷ CONJUG 2q VT **1** (= *colocar encima*) to superimpose, put on top
2 • **~ una cosa a otra** (*fig*) to give preference to one thing over another, put one thing before another
3 (*Inform*) to overstrike
superposición SF superposition
superpotencia SF superpower, great power
superpredador SM top predator, superpredator
superproducción SF overproduction
superprotector ADJ overprotective
supersecreto ADJ top secret
supersensible ADJ ultrasensitive
supersimplificación SF oversimplification
supersónico ADJ supersonic
superstición SF superstition
supersticiosamente ADV superstitiously
supersticioso ADJ superstitious
supertalla SF outsize
supervalorar ▷ CONJUG 1a VT to overvalue
superventas* ADJ best-selling
SM INV best seller • **lista de ~** (*Mús*) charts (*pl*)
supervigilancia SF (*LAm*) supervision
supervisar ▷ CONJUG 1a VT to supervise
supervisión SF supervision
supervisor(a) SM/F supervisor
supervivencia SF survival
▸ **supervivencia de los más aptos, supervivencia de los mejor dotados** survival of the fittest
superviviente ADJ surviving
SMF survivor
supervivir ▷ CONJUG 3a VI to survive
superyo SM superego
supino ADJ, SM supine
súpito ADJ **1** = **súbito**
2 (*And*) (= *atónito*) dumbfounded
suplantación SF **1** (= *sustitución*) supplanting
2 (*al hacerse pasar por otro*) impersonation
3 (*And*) (= *falsificación*) forgery
suplantar ▷ CONJUG 1a VT **1** (= *sustituir*) to supplant, take the place of; (= *hacerse pasar por otro*) to impersonate
2 (*And*) (= *falsificar*) to falsify, forge
suplefaltas SMF INV **1** (= *chivo expiatorio*) scapegoat
2 (= *suplente*) substitute, stopgap, fill-in
suplemental ADJ supplementary
suplementario ADJ [*ingresos, vitaminas, información*] supplementary • **se cobra un precio ~** a supplement is charged • **empleo** *o* **negocio ~** sideline • **tren ~** extra *o* relief train • **tiempo ~** overtime
suplementero SM (*Cono Sur*) newsboy, news vendor
suplemento SM **1** (= *recargo*) (*al pagar*) supplement; (*Ferro*) excess fare
▸ **suplemento alimenticio** dietary supplement ▸ **suplemento por habitación individual** single room supplement, single supplement
2 (= *revista*) supplement ▸ **suplemento a color** colour supplement ▸ **suplemento dominical** Sunday supplement
▸ **suplemento separable** pull-out supplement
suplencia SF (= *sustitución*) substitution, replacement; (= *etapa*) *period during which one deputizes etc*
suplente ADJ (= *sustituto*) substitute, deputy; (= *disponible*) reserve • **maestro ~** supply teacher
SMF (= *sustituto*) substitute, deputy; (= *reemplazo*) replacement; (= *jugador, deportista*) reserve; (= *profesor*) supply teacher; (= *médico*) locum; (*Teat*) understudy
supletorio ADJ [*cama, sillón*] extra; [*medida*] stopgap (*antes de s*) • **con la ventaja supletoria de que ...** with the additional advantage that ... • **llevar una lámpara supletoria** to take a spare bulb
SM (*Telec*) extension
súplica SF (= *ruego*) request; (= *petición*) supplication, entreaty, plea; (*Jur*) (= *instancia*) petition • **~s** entreaties, pleading (*sing*)
• **acceder a las ~s de algn** to grant sb's request • **se publica a ~ de ...** it is published at the request of ...
suplicante ADJ [*tono de voz*] imploring, pleading
SMF petitioner, supplicant
suplicar ▷ CONJUG 1g VT **1** (= *rogar*) to beg, beg for, plead for, implore • **~ a algn no hacer algo** to beg *o* implore sb not to do sth
• **te suplico que te quedes** I beg you to stay
• **"se suplica cerrar la puerta"** "please shut the door"
2 (*Jur*) to appeal to, petition (**de** against)
suplicatorio SM **1** (*Pol*) *Supreme Court petition asking Parliament to overlook an MP's parliamentary immunity so that (s)he can be prosecuted*
2 (*Jur*) letter supplicatory
suplicio SM **1** (= *tortura*) torture; (*Hist*) (= *ejecución*) punishment, execution
2 (= *tormento*) torment, torture • **~ de Tántalo** ordeals of Tantalus • **es un ~ tener que escucharle** it's torture having to listen to him
suplir ▷ CONJUG 3a VT **1** (= *compensar*) [+ *necesidad*] to fulfil, fulfill (*EEUU*); [+ *omisión*] to make good; [+ *falta*] to make good, make up for; [+ *palabra que falta*] to supply
2 (= *sustituir*) to replace, substitute • **~ a uno con otro** to replace one with another, substitute one for another • **está supliendo al portero lesionado** he's replacing the injured goalkeeper • **suplen el aceite con grasa animal** they replace the oil with animal fat, they substitute animal fat for the oil
supo *etc* ▷ **saber**
supondré *etc* ▷ **suponer**
suponer ▷ CONJUG 2q (PP: **supuesto**) VT
1 (= *imaginar*) to imagine • **estoy muy satisfecho, como puedes ~** I'm very pleased, as you can imagine • **ya puedes ~ lo que pasó** you can guess *o* imagine what happened • **le pagaron, supongamos, diez millones** he was paid, say, ten million • **es de ~:** • **es de ~ que haya protestas** I would imagine there will be protests, presumably there will be protests • **están muy apenados, como es de ~** they are very upset, as you would expect • **como era de ~, llegaron tarde** as was to be expected, they arrived late
2 • **~ que** (*intentando adivinar*) to imagine that, suppose that, guess that*; (*como hipótesis*) to suppose that; (*dando por sentado*) to assume that, presume that • **supongo que necesitaréis unas vacaciones** I imagine *o* suppose you'll need a holiday, I guess you'll need a holiday* • **sí, supongo que tienes razón** yes, I suppose you're right, yes, I guess you're right* • **eso nos hace ~ que ha habido un cambio de actitud** this would suggest (to us) that there has been a change of attitude • **supón que tuvieras mucho dinero, ¿qué harías?** suppose *o* supposing you had a lot of money, what would you do?
• **suponiendo que todo salga según lo previsto** assuming *o* presuming everything goes according to plan • **supongo que no:**
• **—¿crees que llegará tarde? —no lo sé, supongo que no** "do you think he'll be late?" — "I don't know, I don't suppose so"
• **—no será fácil —no, supongo que no** "it won't be easy" — "no, I suppose not"
• **supongo que no habrá problemas** I don't suppose there will be any problems
• **supongo que sí** I suppose so, I imagine so, I guess so*
3 (= *atribuir*) (*con objeto indirecto de persona*) • **os suponía informados de este asunto** I assumed *o* presumed you had been informed about this matter • **le suponía mucho más inteligente** I had imagined him to be more intelligent • **le supongo unos 60 años** I would say *o* guess he's about 60 • **se le supone una gran antigüedad** it is thought *o* believed to be very old • **el equipo no mostró la calidad que se le suponía** the team did not show the talent expected of them *o* they had been credited with
4 (= *implicar*) to mean • **la mudanza no nos supondrá grandes gastos** the move won't mean *o* involve a lot of expense for us
• **nuestra amistad supone mucho para mí** our friendship means a great deal to me • **el nuevo método supuso una auténtica revolución** the new method brought about a complete revolution
VPR **suponerse** to imagine • **el viaje resultó justo como me suponía** the trip turned out just as I had imagined • **ya me lo suponía** I thought so • **~se que:** • **suponte que os pasa algo** suppose *o* supposing something happens to you • **me supongo que no irá** I suppose he won't go
SM • **un ~:** • **a ver, un ~, si tú fueras su marido, ¿qué harías?** OK, just supposing you were her husband, what would you do?
• **si te ofrecen el puesto, es un ~, ¿lo aceptarías?** supposing *o* suppose they were to offer you the job, would you accept?
• **supongamos, es solo un ~, que eso sea verdad** let us suppose, for the sake of argument, that it is true
suponga *etc* ▷ **suponer**
suposición SF **1** (= *conjetura*) assumption
2 (= *calumnia*) slander
supositorio SM suppository
supra... PREF supra...
supradicho ADJ aforementioned
supranacional ADJ supranational
supremacía SF supremacy
supremo ADJ supreme • **jefe ~** commander-in-chief, supreme commander
supresión SF **1** (= *acción*) [*de rebelión, crítica*] suppression; [*de costumbre, derecho, institución*] abolition; [*de dificultad, obstáculo*] removal, elimination; [*de restricción*] lifting; [*de detalle, pasaje*] deletion

S

2 (= *prohibición*) banning

supresivo ADJ suppressive

supresor SM (*Elec*) suppressor

suprimido ADJ suppressed, banned

suprimir ▸ CONJUG 3a VT [+ *rebelión, crítica*] to suppress; [+ *costumbre, derecho, institución*] to abolish; [+ *dificultad, obstáculo*] to remove, eliminate; [+ *restricción*] to lift; [+ *detalle, pasaje*] to delete, cut out, omit; [+ *libro*] to suppress, ban • **~ la grasa de la dieta** to cut out *o* eliminate fat from one's diet

supuestamente ADV supposedly

supuesto PP *de* **suponer**

ADJ **1** (= *falso*) [*nombre*] assumed, false • **el ~ arquitecto resultó no tener título** the supposed architect proved not to be qualified

2 (= *no demostrado*) supposed • **en el ~ informe policial** in the supposed police report

3 • **¡por ~!** of course! • **por ~ que iré** of course I'll go • **—¿puedo usar su teléfono? —¡por ~!** "can I use your phone?" — "of course (you can)!"

4 • **dar algo por ~** to take sth for granted • **dieron por ~ que estábamos interesados** they took it for granted that we were interested

5 • **~ que** (*frm*) (= *dando por sentado que*) assuming; (= *en caso de que*) in the event of • **~ que nuestra moneda no baje** (always) assuming our currency does not fall in value • **~ que las autoridades requieran una prueba** in the event of the authorities requiring proof

SM (= *hipótesis*) assumption • **partieron del ~ de que era verdad** they started from the assumption that it was true • **en el ~ de que no venga** assuming that he doesn't come ▸ **supuesto previo** prior assumption

supuración SF suppuration

supurar ▸ CONJUG 1a VI to suppurate, fester

supuse *etc* ▸ **suponer**

sur ADJ [*región*] southern; [*dirección*] southerly; [*viento*] south, southerly • **la zona sur de la ciudad** the southern part of the city, the south of the city • **en la costa sur** on the south coast

SM **1** (= *punto cardinal*) south

2 [*de región, país*] south • **el sur del país** the south of the country • **al sur de Jaén** (to the) south of Jaén • **eso cae más hacia el sur** that lies further (to the) south • **viajábamos hacia el sur** we were travelling south • **en la parte del sur** in the southern part • **las ciudades del sur** the southern cities, the cities of the south • **vientos del sur** south *o* southerly winds

3 (= *viento*) south *o* southerly wind

sura SM sura

Suráfrica SF = **Sudáfrica**

surafricano/a ADJ, SM/F = **sudafricano**

Suramérica SF = **Sudamérica**

suramericano/a ADJ, SM/F = **sudamericano**

surazo SM (*And, Cono Sur*) strong southerly wind

surcar ▸ CONJUG 1g VT [+ *tierra*] to plough, plow (*EEUU*), plough through, plow through (*EEUU*), furrow; [+ *superficie*] to score, groove • **una superficie surcada de ...** a surface lined *o* criss-crossed with ... • **los barcos que surcan los mares** (*liter*) the ships which ply the seas • **las aves que surcan los aires** (*liter*) the birds which ride the winds

surco SM **1** (*Agr*) furrow • MODISMO: • **echarse al ~** (*por pereza*) to sit down on the job; (= *terminar*) to knock off*, think one has done enough

2 (= *ranura*) (*en metal*) groove, score; (*en disco*) groove

3 (*Anat*) wrinkle

4 (*en agua*) track, wake

surcoreano/a ADJ, SM/F South Korean

sureño/a ADJ southern

SM/F southerner

surero SM (*And*) cold southerly wind

surestada SF (*Cono Sur*) wet south-easterly wind

sureste ADJ [*parte*] southeast, southeastern; [*rumbo, viento*] southeasterly

SM **1** (*Geog*) southeast

2 (= *viento*) southeast wind

surf SM surfing • **practicar el ~** to surf ▸ **surf a vela** windsurfing

surfear ▸ CONJUG 1a VI **1** (*en el mar*) to surf

2 (*en Internet*) to surf (the net)

surfero/a ADJ surfing

SM/F surfer

surfing SM • **hacer ~** to surf, go surfing

surfista SMF surfer

surgencia SF, **surgimiento** SM emergence

surgir ▸ CONJUG 3c VI **1** (= *aparecer*) (*gen*) to arise, emerge, appear; [*líquido*] to spout, spout out, spurt; [*barco*] (*en la niebla*) to loom up; [*persona*] to appear unexpectedly • **la torre surge en medio del bosque** the tower rises up out of the woods

2 [*dificultad*] to arise, come up, crop up • **han surgido varios problemas** several problems have come up *o* cropped up

3 (*Náut*) to anchor

suriano ADJ (*Méx*) southern

surinamés/esa ADJ Surinamese

SM/F Surinamese

surja *etc* ▸ **surgir**

surmenage SM, **surmenaje** SM (= *trabajo excesivo*) overwork; (= *estrés*) stress, mental fatigue; (= *crisis*) nervous breakdown

suroeste ADJ [*parte*] southwest, southwestern; [*rumbo, viento*] southwesterly

SM **1** (*Geog*) southwest

2 (= *viento*) southwest wind

surrealismo SM surrealism

surrealista ADJ surrealist, surrealistic

SMF surrealist

surtido ADJ **1** (= *variado*) mixed, assorted, varied • **pasteles ~s** assorted cakes

2 (= *provisto*) • **estar bien ~ de** to be well supplied with, have good stocks of • **estar mal ~ de** to be badly off for

SM selection, assortment, range • **gran ~** large assortment, wide range • **artículo de ~** article from stock

surtidor SM **1** (= *chorro*) jet, spout; (= *fuente*) fountain

2 ▸ **surtidor de gasolina** (= *aparato*) petrol pump, gas pump (*EEUU*); (= *lugar*) petrol station, gas station (*EEUU*)

3 (*LAm*) [*de droga*] drug pusher

surtir ▸ CONJUG 3a VT **1** (= *suministrar*) to supply, furnish, provide • **~ a algn de combustible** to supply sb with fuel • **~ el mercado** to supply the market • **~ un pedido** to fill an order

2 (= *tener*) ▸ **efecto**

VI (= *brotar*) to spout, spurt, spurt up, rise

VPR **surtirse** • **~se de** to provide o.s. with

surto ADJ anchored

suruca SF (*Caribe*) **1** (= *algazara*) din, uproar

2 (= *borrachera*) drunkenness

suruco** SM (*Cono Sur*) crap**, shit**

surumbático ADJ (*LAm*) = **zurumbático**

surumbo ADJ (*CAm*) = **zurumbo**

surumpe SM (*And*) inflammation of the eyes (*caused by snow glare*), snow blindness

surupa SF (*Caribe*) cockroach, roach (*EEUU*)

suruví SM (*Cono Sur*) catfish

survietnamita ADJ, SMF South Vietnamese

susceptibilidad SF **1** [*de persona*] susceptibility (a to)

2 susceptibilidades (= *malentendidos*) sensibilities • **ofender las ~es de algn** to offend sb's sensibilities

susceptible ADJ **1** • **~ de** capable of • **~ de mejora(r)** capable of improvement • **~ de sufrir daño** liable to suffer damage

2 [*persona*] susceptible • **~ a las críticas** sensitive to criticism

suscitar ▸ CONJUG 1a VT [+ *rebelión*] to stir up; [+ *escándalo, conflicto*] to cause, provoke; [+ *discusión*] to start; [+ *duda, problema*] to raise; [+ *interés, sospechas*] to arouse; [+ *consecuencia*] to cause, give rise to, bring with it

suscribir ▸ CONJUG 3a (PP: **suscrito**) VT **1** [+ *contrato, memoria*] to sign

2 (= *reafirmar*) [+ *promesa*] to make; [+ *opinión*] to subscribe to, endorse

3 (*Econ*) [+ *acciones*] to take out an option on; [+ *seguro*] to underwrite

4 • **~ a algn a una revista** to take out a subscription to a magazine for sb • **lo suscribió por 100 dólares** she put him down for a 100-dollar contribution

VPR **suscribirse** to subscribe (a to) • **¿te vas a ~?** are you going to subscribe? • **~se a una revista** to take out a subscription for a magazine

suscripción SF subscription • **abrir una ~** to take out a subscription • **cerrar su ~** to cancel one's subscription • **por ~ popular** by public subscription

suscripto ADJ (*Arg*) PP *de* **suscribir**

suscriptor(a) SM/F subscriber

suscrito VB (*pp de* **suscribir**) • **~ en exceso** oversubscribed

Suso SM *familiar form of Jesús*

susodicho ADJ above-mentioned

suspender ▸ CONJUG 2a VT **1** (= *colgar*) to hang, hang up, suspend (**de** from)

2 (= *interrumpir*) [+ *pago, trabajo*] to stop, suspend; [+ *reunión, sesión*] to adjourn; [+ *línea, servicio*] to discontinue; [+ *procedimiento*] to interrupt; [+ *plan, viaje*] to call off, cancel • **~ hasta más tarde** to put off till later, postpone for a time • **~ a algn de empleo y sueldo** to suspend sb (from work) without pay • **~ la emisión de un programa** to cancel the showing of a programme • **ha suspendido su visita hasta la semana que viene** he's postponed his visit until next week • **el partido se suspendió a causa de la lluvia** the game was rained off • **han suspendido la boda** they've called the wedding off, they've cancelled the wedding

3 (*Escol*) [+ *asignatura*] to fail • **he suspendido las matemáticas** I've failed maths • **lo han suspendido en química** he's failed Chemistry

VI to fail

suspense SM suspense • **novela/película ~** thriller

suspensión SF **1** (*al colgar*) hanging, hanging up, suspension

2 (*Aut, Mec*) suspension • **con ~ independiente** with independent suspension ▸ **suspensión hidráulica** hydraulic suspension

3 (= *interrupción*) [*de campeonato*] stoppage, suspension; [*de sesión*] adjournment; [*de servicios*] stoppage ▸ **suspensión de empleo y sueldo** suspension without pay ▸ **suspensión de fuego** ceasefire ▸ **suspensión de hostilidades** cessation of hostilities ▸ **suspensión de pagos** suspension of payments

4 (*Jur*) stay

suspensivo ADJ • **puntos ~s** dots, suspension points
suspenso ADJ **1** (= *colgado*) hanging, suspended, hung (**de** from)
2 (*Escol*) [*candidato*] failed
3 • **estar** *o* **quedarse ~** (= *pasmarse*) to be astonished, be amazed; (= *maravillarse*) to be filled with wonder; (= *aturdirse*) to be bewildered, be baffled
SM **1** (*Escol*) (= *asignatura*) fail, failure • **tengo un ~ en inglés** I failed English
2 • **estar en** *o* **quedar en ~: la reunión ha quedado en ~ hasta el jueves** they've adjourned the meeting until next Thursday • **el juicio está en ~ hasta que se encuentre un nuevo juez** the trial has been suspended until a new judge can be found
3 (*LAm*) (= *misterio*) suspense • **una novela/película de ~** a thriller
suspensores SMPL **1** (*LAm*) (= *tirantes*) braces, suspenders (EEUU)
2 (*Perú*) (*Dep*) athletic support (*sing*), jockstrap (*sing*)
suspensorio ADJ suspensory
SM (= *prenda*) jockstrap; (*Med*) suspensory, suspensory bandage
suspicacia SF suspicion, mistrust
suspicaz ADJ suspicious, distrustful
suspirado ADJ longed-for, yearned for
suspirar ▷ CONJUG 1a VI to sigh • **~ por** (= *anhelar*) to long for
suspiro SM **1** (*lit, fig*) sigh • **deshacerse en ~s** to sigh deeply, heave a great sigh • **exhalar el último ~** to breathe one's last ▸ **suspiro de alivio** sigh of relief
2 (*LAm*) (*Culin*) meringue
sustancia SF **1** (= *materia*) substance • **una ~ pegajosa** a sticky substance ▸ **sustancia blanca** (*Anat*) white matter ▸ **sustancia gris** (*Anat*) grey matter
2 (= *esencia*) substance • **no has captado la ~ de su discurso** you haven't grasped the substance of his speech • **en ~** in substance, in essence • **sin ~** [*teoría, discurso*] lacking in substance; [*persona*] shallow, superficial
3 (*Culin*) [*de alimento*] substance ▸ **sustancia de carne** meat stock
4 (*Fil*) substance
sustancial ADJ **1** (= *importante*) substantial, significant • **no se han producido cambios ~es** there have been no substantial *o* significant changes
2 (= *esencial*) substantial, fundamental
3 = **sustancioso**
sustancialmente ADV (= *abundantemente*) substantially; (= *esencialmente*) essentially, vitally, fundamentally
sustancioso ADJ [*discurso*] that gives food for thought; [*comida*] solid, substantial; [*ganancias*] healthy, fat (*pey*)
sustantivación SF nominalization
sustantivar ▷ CONJUG 1a VT to nominalize
sustantivo ADJ substantive; (*Ling*) substantival, noun (*antes de s*)
SM noun, substantive ▸ **sustantivo colectivo** collective noun ▸ **sustantivo contable** count noun, countable noun ▸ **sustantivo no contable** uncount noun, uncountable noun
sustentabilidad SF viability
sustentable ADJ viable, sustainable
sustentación SF **1** (= *manutención*) maintenance
2 (= *apoyo*) support
3 (*Aer*) lift
sustentar ▷ CONJUG 1a VT **1** (= *sujetar*) to hold up, support, bear the weight of
2 (= *alimentar*) to sustain, nourish
3 [+ *familia, hijos*] to support, maintain
4 [+ *esperanzas*] to sustain, keep alive
5 [+ *idea, teoría*] to maintain, uphold
6 (*Ecología*) to sustain
VPR **sustentarse** • **~se con** to sustain o.s. with, subsist on • **~se de esperanzas** to live on hopes • **~se del aire** to live on air
sustento SM **1** (= *apoyo*) support
2 (*para vivir*) (= *alimento*) sustenance; (= *manutención*) maintenance • **ganarse el ~** to earn one's living, earn a livelihood • **es el ~ principal de la institución** it is the lifeblood of the institution
sustitución SF substitution (**por** for), replacement (**por** by)
sustituible ADJ replaceable
sustituir ▷ CONJUG 3g VT **1** (= *poner en lugar de*) to replace, substitute • **~ A por B** to replace A by *o* with B, substitute B for A • **lo quieren ~** they want him replaced • **tendremos que ~ el neumático pinchado** we shall have to replace the flat tyre
2 (= *tomar el lugar de*) (*gen*) to replace; (*temporalmente*) to stand in for • **los sellos azules sustituyen a los verdes** the blue stamps are replacing the green ones • **lo sustituí como secretario de la asociación** I replaced him as club secretary • **¿me puedes ~ un par de semanas?** can you stand in for me for a couple of weeks? • **me ~á mientras estoy fuera** he'll take my place *o* deputize for me while I'm away
sustitutivo ADJ substitute • **géneros propios ~s de los importados** home-produced goods in place of *o* to replace imported ones
SM substitute (**de** for)
sustituto/a SM/F (*temporal*) substitute, stand-in; (*para siempre*) replacement • **soy el ~ del profesor de inglés** I'm standing in for the English teacher
sustitutorio ADJ substitute, replacement (*antes de s*); ▷ **servicio**
susto SM **1** (= *impresión repentina*) fright, scare • **¡qué ~!** what a fright! • **dar un ~ a algn** to give sb a fright *o* scare • **darse** *o* **pegarse un ~*** to have a fright, get scared (EEUU) • **caerse del ~** to be frightened *o* scared to death • **meter un ~ a algn*** to put the wind up sb* • MODISMOS: • **no ganar para ~s*:** • **este año no ganamos para ~s** it's been one setback after another this year • **no pasó del ~** it was less serious than was at first thought
2 (*And*) (= *crisis nerviosa*) nervous breakdown
3 • **el ~** (*hum*) (*en restaurante*) the bill
sustracción SF **1** (= *acto*) removal
2 (*Mat*) (= *resta*) subtraction, taking away; (= *descuento*) deduction
3 (= *hurto*) theft ▸ **sustracción de menores** child abduction
sustraer ▷ CONJUG 2p VT **1** (= *llevarse*) to remove, take away
2 (*Mat*) (= *restar*) to subtract, take away; (= *descontar*) to deduct
3 (= *robar*) [+ *dinero, cuadro*] to steal; [+ *persona*] to abduct
4 [+ *agua*] to extract
VPR **sustraerse** • **~se a** (= *evitar*) to avoid; (= *apartarse de*) to withdraw from, contract out of • **no pude ~me a la tentación** I could not resist the temptation
sustrato SM substratum
susurrante ADJ [*viento*] whispering; [*arroyo*] murmuring; [*follaje*] rustling
susurrar ▷ CONJUG 1a VT to whisper • **me susurró su nombre al oído** he whispered his name in my ear
VI **1** [*persona*] to whisper • **~ al oído de algn** to whisper to sb, whisper in sb's ear
2 (= *sonar*) [*viento*] to whisper; [*arroyo*] to murmur; [*hojas*] to rustle; [*insecto*] to hum
VPR **susurrarse** • **se susurra que ...** it is being whispered that ..., it is rumoured *o* (EEUU) rumored that ...
susurro SM **1** (= *cuchicheo*) whisper
2 (= *sonido*) [*de viento*] whisper; [*de arroyo*] murmur; [*de hojas*] rustle; [*de insecto*] hum, humming
sutién SM (*Arg*) bra, brassiere
sutil ADJ **1** [*diferencia*] subtle
2 (= *perspicaz*) [*inteligencia, persona*] sharp, keen; [*comentario*] subtle
3 (= *delicado*) [*hilo, hebra*] fine; [*tela*] delicate, thin, light; [*atmósfera*] thin; [*olor*] subtle, delicate; [*brisa*] gentle
sutileza SF **1** (= *delicadeza*) fineness, delicacy
2 (= *perspicacia*) subtlety, subtleness; (= *agudeza*) sharpness, keenness
3 (= *concepto sutil*) subtlety, fine distinction
4 (*pey*) (= *maña*) artifice, artful deceit
sutilizar ▷ CONJUG 1f VT **1** [+ *objeto*] (= *reducir*) to thin down, fine down; (= *pulir*) to polish, perfect; (= *limar, mejorar*) to refine
2 [+ *concepto*] (*pey*) to quibble about *o* over, split hairs about *o* over
VI (*pey*) (= *pararse en cosas nimias*) to quibble, split hairs
sutilmente ADV subtly
sutura SF suture
suturar ▷ CONJUG 1a VT to suture
suyo/a ADJ POSES **1** (= *de él*) his; (= *de ella*) her; (= *de ellos, ellas*) their • **la culpa es suya** it's his/her *etc* fault • **—permiso —es ~** (*Chile, Méx*) "excuse me" — "yes?" • **no es amigo ~** he is not a friend of his/hers *etc* • **no es culpa suya** it's not his/her *etc* fault, it's no fault of his/hers *etc* • **varios libros ~s** (= *de ellos*) several books of theirs, several of their books • **hacer algo ~:** • **hizo suyas mis palabras** he echoed my words • **eso es muy ~** that's just like him, that's typical of him • **él es un hombre muy ~** (= *reservado*) he's a man who keeps very much to himself; (= *quisquilloso*) he's a very fussy sort
2 (= *de usted, ustedes*) your • **¿es ~ esto?** is this yours?
PRON POSES (= *de él*) his; (= *de ella*) hers; (= *de usted, ustedes*) yours; (*de animal, cosa*) its; (= *de uno mismo*) one's own; (= *de ellos, ellas*) theirs • **este libro es el ~** this book is his/hers *etc* • **los ~s** (= *familia*) one's family *o* relations; (= *partidarios*) one's own people *o* supporters • **~ afectísimo** yours faithfully *o* sincerely, yours truly (EEUU) • **de ~** in itself, intrinsically • **lo ~** (what is) his; (= *su parte*) his share, what he deserves • **aguantar lo ~** (= *su parte*) to do one's share; (= *mucho*) to put up with a lot • **él pesa lo ~** he's really heavy, he's a fair weight • MODISMOS: • **hacer de las suyas** to get up to one's old tricks • **ir a la suya** • **ir a lo ~** to go one's own way; (*pey*) to go one's own sweet way, think only of o.s. • **salirse con la suya** to get one's own way; (*en una discusión*) to carry one's point • REFRÁN: • **cada cual a lo ~** it's best to mind one's own business
svástica [ez'bastika] SF swastika
swing [es'win] SM **1** (*Mús*) swing
2 (*Golf*) swing
switch [es'witʃ] SM (*esp Méx*) **1** (*Elec*) switch
2 (*Aut*) ignition, ignition switch

S

Tt

T¹, t¹ [te] SF (= *letra*) T, t
T² ABR, **t²** ABR (= **tonelada**) t, ton
t. ABR (= **tomo(s)**) vol, vols
TA SF ABR (= **traducción automática**) AT
taba SF (= *hueso*) ankle bone; (= *juego*) jacks, knucklebones, jackstones (EEUU)
• **MODISMO:** • **menear las ~s*** (= *moverse con prisa*) to bustle about; (= *apresurarse*) to get cracking*
tabacal SM (= *plantación*) tobacco plantation; (= *terreno*) tobacco field
Tabacalera SF *Spanish state tobacco monopoly*; ▷ **ESTANCO**
tabacalera SF (*Méx*) cigarette factory
tabacalero/a ADJ tobacco (*antes de s*)
SM/F (= *tendero*) tobacconist, tobacco dealer (EEUU); (= *cultivador*) tobacco grower; (= *mayorista*) tobacco merchant
tabaco SM **1** (*para fumar*) **a** (= *producto*) tobacco; (= *planta*) tobacco plant
• **MODISMOS:** • **se le acabó el ~** (*Cono Sur**) he ran out of dough* • **estar de mal ~** (*CAm**) to be in a bad mood • **estaba hecho ~*** [*persona*] he was all in; [*objeto*] it was all torn to pieces • **quitar el ~ a algn*** to do sb in*
b (= *cigarrillos*) cigarettes (*pl*) • **¿tienes ~?** have you any cigarettes?
c (*LAm*) (= *puro*) cigar ▸ **tabaco amarillo, tabaco americano** Virginia tobacco ▸ **tabaco de hebra** loose tobacco ▸ **tabaco de liar** rolling tobacco ▸ **tabaco de mascar** chewing tobacco ▸ **tabaco de pipa** pipe tobacco ▸ **tabaco en polvo** snuff ▸ **tabaco en rama** leaf tobacco ▸ **tabaco negro** dark tobacco ▸ **tabaco picado** shag, cut tobacco ▸ **tabaco rubio** Virginia tobacco ▸ **tabaco turco** Turkish tobacco
2 (*LAm*) (= *droga*) reefer*, joint*
3 (*Caribe**) (= *golpe*) slap, smack
ADJ (*esp LAm*) dusty brown
tabacón‡ SM (*Méx*) marijuana, grass‡
tabalada SF bump, heavy fall
tabalear ▷ CONJUG 1a VI (*con los dedos*) to drum, tap
VT (= *balancear*) to rock, swing
tabaleo SM **1** (*con los dedos*) drumming, tapping
2 (= *balanceo*) rocking, swinging
tabanco SM **1** (*CAm*) (= *desván*) attic
2 (*Méx*) (= *puesto*) stall
tábano SM horsefly, gadfly
tabaqueada* SF (*Méx*) (= *paliza*) beating-up*; (= *pelea*) fist-fight
tabaquear ▷ CONJUG 1a VI (*And*) to smoke
tabaquera SF **1** (= *bolsa*) tobacco pouch
2 (= *estuche*) (*para puros*) cigar case; (*para cigarrillos*) cigarette case; (*para rapé*) snuffbox
3 (= *tarro*) tobacco jar
4 [*de pipa*] bowl; ▷ **tabaquero**
tabaquería SF (*LAm*) **1** (= *tienda*) tobacconist's (shop), cigar store (EEUU)
2 (= *fábrica*) cigar factory, tobacco factory
tabaquero/a ADJ tobacco (*antes de s*)
SM/F (= *tendero*) tobacconist, tobacco dealer (EEUU); (= *mayorista*) tobacco merchant; (= *cultivador*) tobacco grower; ▷ **tabaquera**
tabaquismo SM smoking habit ▸ **tabaquismo pasivo** passive smoking
tabaquito SM (*LAm*) small cigar
tabarra* SF nuisance, bore • **dar la ~** to be a nuisance, be a pain in the neck* • **dar la ~ a algn** to pester sb
tabasco® SM Tabasco®
tabear ▷ CONJUG 1a VI (*Cono Sur*) to gossip
taberna SF **1** (= *bar*) pub, bar; (*Hist*) tavern
2 (*Caribe*) (= *tienda*) small grocery shop
3 (*Cono Sur*) [*de juego*] gambling den
tabernáculo SM tabernacle
tabernario ADJ [*lenguaje*] rude, dirty, coarse, gutter (*antes de s*)
tabernero/a SM/F (= *dueño*) landlord/landlady, publican, bar manager; (= *camarero*) barman/barmaid, bartender
tabicar ▷ CONJUG 1g VT **1** [+ *puerta, ventana*] (*con ladrillos*) to brick up; (*con madera*) to board up
2 [+ *habitación*] to partition off
3 [+ *nariz*] to block (up)
VPR **tabicarse** [*nariz*] to get blocked up
tabicón SM (*Méx*) breeze block
tabique SM **1** (= *pared*) thin wall; (*entre habitaciones*) partition, partition wall ▸ **tabique nasal** nasal septum
2 (*Méx*) (*Constr*) brick
tabla SF **1** (= *pieza*) [*de madera*] plank, board; [*de piedra*] slab; (*Arte*) panel; (= *estante*) shelf; (*Caribe*) (= *mostrador*) shop counter
• **MODISMOS:** • **estar en las ~s** (*Caribe*) to be destitute • **escaparse en una ~** to have a narrow escape, have a close shave • **hacer ~ rasa** to make a clean sweep • **hacer ~ rasa de algo** to completely disregard sth, ride roughshod over sth • **salvarse en una ~** to have a narrow escape, have a close shave ▸ **tabla a vela** surfboard, windsurfing board ▸ **tabla de cocina, tabla de cortar** chopping board ▸ **tabla de dibujo** drawing board ▸ **tabla de esmeril** emery board ▸ **tabla de lavar** washboard ▸ **tabla del suelo** floorboard ▸ **tabla de picar** chopping board ▸ **tabla de planchar** ironing board ▸ **tabla de quesos** cheeseboard ▸ **tabla de salvación** (*fig*) last resort, only hope ▸ **tabla deslizadora, tabla de surf** surfboard ▸ **tabla de windsurf** windsurfing board
2 tablas: **a** (*Taur*) barrier (*sing*)
b (*Teat*) stage (*sing*) • **pisar las ~s** to tread the boards • **salir a las ~s** to go on the stage, become an actor/actress • **MODISMOS:** • **coger ~s** (*en teatro*) to gain acting experience; (*fig*) to get the hang of it • **tener (muchas) ~s** [*actor*] to have a good stage presence; [*político*] to be an old hand
3 tablas (*Ajedrez*) draw (*sing*); (*fig*) stalemate (*sing*) • **hacer ~s** • **quedar en ~s** (*lit*) to draw; (*fig*) to reach stalemate, be deadlocked • **el partido quedó en ~s** the game was a draw, the game was drawn ▸ **tablas por ahogado** stalemate
4 [*de falda*] box pleat, broad pleat
5 (= *lista*) (*Mat*) table; (*en libro*) (= *índice*) table; (*Dep*) (*tb* **tabla clasificatoria**) table, (league) table; (*Inform*) array ▸ **tabla de abdominales** abdominal routine ▸ **tabla de consulta** (*Inform*) lookup table ▸ **tabla de ejercicios, tabla de gimnasia** exercise routine, set of exercises ▸ **tabla de logaritmos** table of logarithms ▸ **tabla de mareas** tide table ▸ **tabla de materias** table of contents ▸ **tabla de multiplicar** multiplication table ▸ **tabla de valores** set of values ▸ **tabla salarial** wage scale ▸ **tabla trazadora** plotter
6 (*Agr*) plot, patch
7 (*And*) • **MODISMOS:** • **cantarle las ~s a algn** to tell it to sb straight • **salir con las ~s** to fail
SM‡ queer‡, fairy‡, fag (EEUU‡)
tablada SF (*Cono Sur*) slaughterhouse
tablado SM **1** (= *plataforma*) stage
2 (*Hist*) scaffold
tablaje SM, **tablazón** SF planks (*pl*), planking, boards (*pl*)
tablao SM (= *espectáculo*) flamenco show; (= *escenario*) dance floor (*for flamenco dancing*); (= *local*) flamenco venue
tablear ▷ CONJUG 1a VT **1** [+ *madera*] to cut into boards *o* planks
2 [+ *terreno*] (= *dividir*) to divide up into plots; (= *nivelar*) to level off
3 (*Cos*) to pleat
4 (*Cono Sur*) [+ *masa*] to roll out
tablero SM **1** (= *panel*) (*de madera*) board; (*para anuncios*) notice board, bulletin board (EEUU); (= *pizarra*) blackboard; [*de mesa*] top; [*de mármol*] slab; (*Elec*) switchboard ▸ **tablero de dibujante, tablero de dibujo** drawing board ▸ **tablero de gráficos** (*Inform*) graph pad ▸ **tablero de instrumentos, tablero de mandos** instrument panel ▸ **tablero posterior** tailboard
2 (*para juegos*) board ▸ **tablero de ajedrez** chessboard
3 (= *garito*) gambling den
tablet SF (PL: **tablets**) (*Inform*) tablet
tableta SF **1** [*de chocolate*] bar, slab; (*Med*) tablet
2 [*de madera*] (= *bloque*) block; (= *tablero*) board
3 (*Inform*) tablet ▸ **tableta gráfica** graphics tablet
tabletear ▷ CONJUG 1a VI to rattle
tableteo SM rattle
tablilla SF **1** (= *tabla*) small board; (*Med*) splint
2 (*Méx*) [*de chocolate*] bar
tablista SMF windsurfer
tabloide SM tabloid
tablón SM **1** (= *tabla*) plank; (= *viga*) beam ▸ **tablón de anuncios** notice board, bulletin board (EEUU)
2* (= *borrachera*) • **coger** *o* **pillar un ~** to get plastered*
3 (*LAm*) (*Agr*) plot, bed

t

tablonazo SM (*Caribe*) trick, swindle
tabú ADJ INV taboo • **palabras ~** taboo words
SM (PL: **tabús, tabúes**) taboo
tabuco SM (= *chabola*) slum, shack; (= *cuarto*) tiny room, poky little room
tabulación SF tabulation
tabulador SM tab, tabulator
tabular VT ▷ CONJUG 1a to tabulate
ADJ tabular
taburete SM stool
TAC SF/SM ABR (= **tomografía axial computerizada**) CAT
tacada SF (*Billar*) stroke; (= *serie de puntos*) break • **MODISMO**: • **de una ~** all in one go
tacana SF **1** (*And, Cono Sur*) (*Agr*) cultivated hillside terrace
2 (*Cono Sur, Méx*) [*de mortero*] pestle
3 (*Cono Sur*) (= *policía*) fuzz‡, police
tacanear ▷ CONJUG 1a VT (*Cono Sur*) (= *apisonar*) to tread down; (= *machacar*) to pound, crush
tacañería SF **1** (= *mezquindad*) meanness, stinginess
2 (= *astucia*) craftiness
tacaño ADJ **1** (= *avaro*) mean, stingy
2 (= *astuto*) crafty
tacar ▷ CONJUG 1g VT (*And*) **1** (= *disparar*) to shoot at sb
2 (= *llenar*) to fill, pack tightly (**de** with)
tacatá* SM, **tacataca** SM [*de bebé*] baby walker; [*de anciano*] walking frame, Zimmer frame®
tacha[1] SF **1** (*Téc*) large tack, stud
2 (*LAm*) = **tacho**
tacha[2] SF blemish • **sin ~** [*vida, reputación*] unblemished; [*estilo, conducta*] faultless; [*lealtad*] absolute • **una persona sin ~** a person who is beyond reproach • **poner ~ a algo** to find fault with sth
tachadura SF (= *tachón*) crossing-out, erasure (*frm*); (= *corrección*) correction
tachar ▷ CONJUG 1a VT **1** (= *suprimir*) to cross out; (= *corregir*) to correct • **~ a algn de una lista** to cross *o* take sb off a list
2 • **~ a algn de** to brand sb (as) • **lo ~on de colaboracionista** he was branded (as) a collaborator • **~ a algn de incapaz** to brand sb (as) incompetent • **tachó de inoportuna la invitación** he described the invitation as untimely • **me molesta que taches de tonterías lo que digo** I don't like the way you dismiss what I say as nonsense
3 (*Jur*) [+ *testigo*] to challenge
tachero SM (*Cono Sur*) tinsmith
tachines‡ SMPL (*Esp*) (= *pies*) plates‡, feet; (= *zapatos*) shoes
tacho SM **1** (*LAm*) (= *cubo*) bucket, pail; (= *caldera*) boiler; (= *olla*) pan; (*para azúcar*) sugar pan, sugar evaporator; (= *arcón*) bin, container ▸ **tacho de la basura, tacho para la basura** (*And, Cono Sur*) dustbin, rubbish bin, trash *o* garbage can (*EEUU*) ▸ **tacho para lavar la ropa** clothes boiler
2 (*Cono Sur*) (= *lavabo*) washbasin, bathroom sink *o* washbowl (*EEUU*) • **MODISMO**: • **irse al ~*** to be ruined, fail
tachón[1] SM **1** (*Téc*) ornamental stud, boss
2 (*Cos*) trimming
tachón[2] SM (= *tachadura*) crossing-out, deletion (*frm*) • **escribe con letra clara y sin tachones** write clearly and avoid crossing things out
tachonado ADJ • **~ de estrellas** star-studded, star-spangled • **candelabros ~s de diamantes** diamond-studded candelabras
tachonar ▷ CONJUG 1a VT to stud
tachoso ADJ defective, faulty
tachuela SF **1** (= *clavo*) (tin) tack; (*en cinturón, ropa*) stud; (*LAm*) (= *chincheta*) drawing pin
2 (*Caribe*) (= *alfiler*) long pin
3 (*Aut*) speed ramp, sleeping policeman
4 (*LAm*) (= *recipiente*) metal pan; (= *cazo*) dipper; (= *taza*) metal cup
5 (*LAm**) (= *persona*) short stocky person
tacita SF small cup • **la Tacita de Plata** Cadiz (*used affectionately*) • **MODISMO**: • **como una ~ de plata** as bright as a new pin
tácitamente ADV tacitly
Tácito SM Tacitus
tácito ADJ **1** (*gen*) tacit; [*acuerdo*] unspoken, tacit; [*ley*] unwritten
2 (*Ling*) understood
taciturnidad SF (= *reserva*) taciturnity, silent nature; (= *mal humor*) sullenness, moodiness; (= *tristeza*) glumness
taciturno ADJ (= *callado*) taciturn, silent; (= *malhumorado*) sullen, moody; (= *triste*) glum
tacizo SM **1** (*And, Caribe*) (= *hacha*) narrow-bladed axe
2 (*And*) (= *celda*) small prison cell
taco SM **1** (= *pieza*) (*para tornillo*) Rawlplug®; (= *tapón*) plug, stopper; [*de bota de fútbol*] stud; (*para fusil*) wad, wadding; (= *tarugo*) wooden peg ▸ **taco de salida** (*Dep*) starting block
2 (*Billar*) cue
3 [*de papeles*] (*para escribir*) pad; [*de billetes, cupones*] book; [*de cheque*] stub; (= *calendario*) desk calendar
4 [*de jamón, queso*] cube
5 (*Esp**) (= *palabrota*) rude word, swearword • **soltar un ~** to swear • **dice muchos ~s** he swears a lot
6 (*Esp*‡) (= *lío*) mess • **armarse** *o* **hacerse un ~** to get into a mess, get mixed *o* muddled up • **dejar a algn hecho un ~** to flatten sb (in an argument)
7‡ (= *año*) year • **tener 16 ~s** to be 16 (years old) • **cumple cinco ~s** (*en la cárcel*) he's doing five years' bird‡
8 (*Mil, Hist*) ramrod
9 (*LAm*) (= *tacón*) heel
10 (*Méx*) (*Culin*) taco, filled rolled tortilla; (= *bocado**) snack, bite • **MODISMO**: • **darse ~** (*CAm, Méx**) to give o.s. airs
11 (*Chile*) (= *trago*) swig of wine*
12 (*Cono Sur, Méx*) (= *obstáculo*) obstruction, blockage; (*Chile**) (= *atasco*) traffic jam
13 (*aplicado a personas*) (*Cono Sur*) (= *chaparro*) short stocky person; (*And**) (= *personaje*) big shot*; (*CAm, Caribe, Méx*) fop, dandy
14 (*CAm, Caribe*) (= *preocupación*) worry, anxiety; (= *miedo*) fear
tacógrafo SM tachograph, tacho*
tacómetro SM tachometer
tacón SM **1** [*de zapato*] heel • **tacones altos** high heels • **tacones bajos** low heels • **nunca llevo tacones** I never wear high heels • **zapatos de ~ (alto)** high-heeled shoes ▸ **tacón (de) aguja** stiletto heel ▸ **tacón de cuña** wedge heel
2‡ (= *monedero*) purse, coin purse (*EEUU*)
taconazo SM (= *patada*) kick (*with one's heel*); (= *golpecito*) heel tap • **dar un ~** to click one's heels; **taconazos** (*Mil*) heel-clicking (*pl*)
taconear ▷ CONJUG 1a VI **1** (= *caminar*) to walk clicking *o* tapping one's heels
2 (= *dar golpecitos*) to tap with one's heels; (*Mil*) to click one's heels
3 (= *apresurarse*) to bustle about
VT (*Cono Sur*) to pack tight, fill right up
taconeo SM **1** (*al andar*) • **podíamos oír el ~ de sus zapatos** we could hear her shoe heels clicking about
2 (= *golpecitos*) tapping with one's heels; (*Mil*) heel-clicking
tacote‡ SM (*Méx*) marijuana, grass‡
táctica SF **1** (= *estrategia*) tactic • **una nueva ~** a new tactic, new tactics • **el equipo cambió de ~** the team changed tactics • **la ~ del avestruz** the head-in-the-sand approach ▸ **táctica de cerrojo** stonewalling, negative play
2 (= *jugada*) move; (*fig*) gambit
tácticamente ADV tactically
táctico/a ADJ tactical
SM/F (= *experto*) tactician; (*Dep*) coach
táctil ADJ tactile
tacto SM **1** (= *sentido*) (sense of) touch; (= *acción*) touch • **ser áspero al ~** to be rough to the touch • **conoce las monedas por el ~** she identifies coins by touch
2 (= *cualidad*) feel • **tiene un ~ viscoso** it has a sticky feel (to it)
3 (= *diplomacia*) tact • **tener ~** to be tactful
tacuache SM (*Caribe*) fib, lie
tacuacín SM (*Méx*) sloth
tacuaco ADJ (*Cono Sur*) chubby
tacuche SM (*Méx*) bundle of rags
ADJ worthless
Tadjikstán SM, **Tadjikia** SF Tadjikistan
TAE SF ABR (= **tasa anual efectiva** *o* **equivalente**) APR
taekwondista SMF taekwondist
tae kwon do SM, **tae-kwon-do** SM taekwondo, tae-kwon-do
tafetán SM **1** (= *tela*) taffeta
2 (*tb* **tafetán adhesivo, tafetán inglés**) sticking plaster, Band-Aid® (*EEUU*)
3 tafetanes (= *banderas*) flags; (= *galas*) frills, buttons and bows
tafia SF (*LAm*) rum
tafilete SM morocco leather
tagalo/a ADJ, SM/F Tagalog
SM (*Ling*) Tagalog
tagarnia* SF • **comer hasta la ~** (*And, CAm*) to stuff o.s.*
tagarnina SF **1** (= *puro*) (cheap) cigar
2 (*Méx*) (= *petaca*) leather tobacco pouch
3 (*And, CAm, Méx**) (= *borrachera*) • **agarrar una ~*** to get tight*
tagarote* SM **1** (*Zool*) sparrowhawk
2* (= *persona*) tall shabby person
3* (= *empleadillo*) lawyer's clerk, penpusher, pencil pusher (*EEUU*)
4 (*CAm*) (= *personaje*) big shot*
tagua SF (*And*) ivory palm
taguara SF (*Ven*) cheap restaurant
tahalí SM swordbelt
Tahití SM Tahiti
tahitiano/a ADJ, SM/F Tahitian
tahona SF (= *panadería*) bakery, bakehouse; (= *molino*) flour mill
tahonero/a SM/F (= *panadero*) baker; (= *molinero*) miller
tahúr SMF (= *jugador*) gambler; (*pey*) cardsharp, cheat
tai chi SM t'ai chi, tai chi
taifa* SF gang, crew
taiga SF taiga
tailandés/esa ADJ, SM/F Thai
SM (*Ling*) Thai
Tailandia SF Thailand
taima SF **1** (= *astucia*) slyness, craftiness, slickness
2 (*Cono Sur**) (= *terquedad*) obstinacy, pigheadedness
taimadamente ADV craftily, cunningly
taimado ADJ **1** (= *astuto*) sly, crafty
2 (= *hosco*) sullen
3 (*And*) (= *perezoso*) lazy
taimarse ▷ CONJUG 1a VPR **1** (= *volverse taimado*) to get sly, adopt crafty tactics
2 (= *enfadarse*) to go into a huff, sulk; (= *obstinarse*) to be obstinate, dig one's heels in
taita* SM **1** (*And, Cono Sur*) (= *papá*) father, dad*, daddy*; (= *tío*) uncle

t

2 (*Cono Sur*) (*tratamiento*) *in direct address, term of respect used before a name*
3 (*Cono Sur*) (= *matón*) tough, bully; (= *pendenciero*) troublemaker
4†† (= *chulo*) pimp
Taiwán SM Taiwan
taiwanés/esa ADJ, SM/F Taiwanese
taja SF cut
tajada SF **1** (*Culin*) slice
2* (= *beneficio*) rake-off* • **sacar ~** to get one's share, take one's cut* • **sacaron buena ~ de ello** they did well out of it
3 (= *raja*) cut, slash • **¡te haré ~s!** I'll have your guts for garters!*
4* (= *borrachera*) • **coger** *o* **pillar una ~** to get plastered*
5 (*Med*) hoarseness
tajadera SF **1** (= *hacha*) chopper; (= *cincel*) cold chisel
2 (= *tabla*) chopping block
tajadero SM chopping block
tajado ADJ sheer
tajador SM (*And*) pencil sharpener
tajalán/ana ADJ (*Caribe*) lazy
SM/F idler, layabout
tajaleo* SM (*Caribe*) **1** (= *comida*) food, grub‡, chow (*EEUU*‡)
2 (= *pelea*) row, brawl
tajaloseo* SM (*Caribe*) row
tajamar SM **1** (*Náut*) stem; [*de puente*] cutwater
2 (*CAm, Cono Sur*) (= *muelle*) mole; (*And, Cono Sur*) (= *presa*) dam, dyke
tajante ADJ **1** (= *contundente*) [*negativa*] emphatic; [*órdenes*] strict; [*crítica, distinción*] sharp; [*comentario*] incisive • **contestó con un "no" ~** he answered with an emphatic "no" • **hacer afirmaciones ~s** to make categorical statements • **fueron ~s en su condena** they were categorical in their condemnation • **una crítica ~ del gobierno** some sharp criticism of the government • **es una persona ~** he calls a spade a spade
2 [*herramienta*] sharp, cutting
tajantemente ADV [*responder*] emphatically, sharply • **me niego ~** I categorically refuse • **la propuesta fue rechazada ~** the proposal was rejected outright
tajar ▷ CONJUG 1a VT to cut, slice, chop
tajarrazo SM (*CAm, Méx*) slash, wound; (*fig*) damage, harm
tajeadura SF (*Cono Sur*) long scar
tajear* ▷ CONJUG 1a VT (*LAm*) (= *cortar*) to cut (up), chop (up); (= *rajar*) to slash
Tajo SM Tagus
tajo SM **1** (= *corte*) cut, slash • **darse un ~ en el brazo** to cut one's arm • **cortar algo de un ~** to slice sth off • **tirar ~s a algn** to slash at sb
2 (*Geog*) (= *corte*) cut, cleft; (= *escarpa*) steep cliff, sheer drop
3* (= *trabajo*) work • **todo el verano en el ~, sin vacaciones** I have to slog away all summer, without a holiday • **largarse al ~** to get off to work, get back on the job • **¡vamos al ~!** let's get on with it!
4 (*Culin*) (= *tabla*) chopping block
5 [*del verdugo*] executioner's block
6 (= *filo*) cutting edge
7 (= *taburete*) small three-legged stool
tajón SM (*Méx*) slaughterhouse
tal ADJ **1** (*en relación con algo ya mencionado*) such • **no existía tal restaurante** no such restaurant existed • **nunca he hecho tal cosa** I never did any such thing *o* anything of the sort • **en tales casos es mejor consultar con un médico** in such cases it's better to consult a doctor • **nunca he visto a tal persona** I've never seen any such person • **hace diez años, tal día como hoy** on the same day ten years ago, ten years ago today • **el tal cura resultó estar casado** this priest (we were talking about) *o* (*pey*) this priest person turned out to be married; ▷ **cosa, palo**
2 (*indicando extrañeza o exageración*) such • **con tal atrevimiento** with such a cheek, so cheekily • **eran tales sus deseos de venganza** her desire for revenge was so great • **¡había tal confusión en el aeropuerto!** it was total chaos at the airport! • **tal era su fuerza que podía levantar a dos hombres** he was so strong that he could lift two men
3 (*indicando indeterminación*) • **se aloja en tal o cual hotel** he is staying at such-and-such a hotel • **tal día, a tal hora** on such-and-such a day, at such-and-such a time • **vivía en la calle tal, en el número cual** she lived in such-and-such a street at such-and-such a number • **necesitaba un millón para tal cosa y otro millón para tal otra** he needed a million for one thing and another million for another • **un tal García** one García, a man called García or something (*pey*)
PRON **1** (= *persona indeterminada*) • **el tal** this man I mentioned • **esa es una tal** (*pey*) she's a tart* • **me dijo que yo era un tal o un cual** she called me all sorts of names • **es su padre, y como tal, es responsable de su hijo** he's his father, and as such he is responsible for his son • MODISMO: • **son tal para cual** they're two of a kind; ▷ **fulano**
2 (= *cosa indeterminada*) • **no haré tal** I won't do anything of the sort, I'll do no such thing • **y tal***: • **fuimos al cine y tal** we went to the pictures and stuff* • **había pinchos, bebidas y tal** there were snacks and drinks and things • **estábamos charlando y tal, y de pronto me dio un beso** we were just chatting and so on, when suddenly he kissed me • **tal y cual**: • **teníamos prisa, pero entre tal y cual tardamos una hora** we were in a hurry, but between one thing and another it took us an hour • **es muy simpática y tal y cual, pero no me gusta** she's very nice and all that, but I don't like her • **me dijo que si tal y que si cual, pero no pudo convencerme** he said this, that and the other, but he wasn't able to convince me
ADV **1** (*en comparaciones*) • **tal como**: • **estaba tal como lo dejé** it was just as I had left it • **tal y como están las cosas, no creo que sea buena idea** as things are *o* given the current state of affairs, I don't think it would be a good idea • **tal y como están las cosas, es mejor que nos vayamos** under the circumstances, it would be better if we left • **tal cual**: • **déjalo tal cual** leave it just as it is • **después de tantos años sigue tal cual** she hasn't changed after all these years • **se enteró de la noticia y se quedó tal cual** when he heard the news he didn't bat an eyelid • **en la foto salió tal cual es en realidad** it came out in the photo just like it is in real life • **tal la madre, cual la hija** like mother, like daughter • **tal que**:
• **tomaremos algo ligero tal que una tortilla** we'll have something light such as *o* like an omelette
2 (*en preguntas*) • **¿qué tal?** how's things?, how are you? • **¿qué tal el partido?** what was the game like?, how was the game? • **¿qué tal tu tío?** how's your uncle? • **¿qué tal estás?** how are you? • **¿qué tal estoy con este vestido?** how do I look in this dress? • **¿qué tal has dormido?** how did you sleep? • **¿qué tal es físicamente?** what does she look like? • **¿qué tal si lo compramos?** why don't we buy it?, suppose we buy it?
3 • **tal vez** perhaps, maybe • **son, tal vez, las mejores canciones del disco** they are perhaps *o* maybe *o* possibly the best songs on the album • **—¿crees que ganarán? —tal vez** "do you think they'll win?" — "perhaps *o* maybe *o* they may do" • **tal vez me pase por tu casa mañana** I may drop in at your place tomorrow
4 • **con tal de**: • **hace lo que sea con tal de llamar la atención** he'll do anything to attract attention • **no importa el frío con tal de ir bien abrigado** the cold doesn't matter as long as *o* if you're well wrapped up • **con tal de que** provided (that), as long as • **con tal de que no me engañes** provided (that) *o* as long as you don't deceive me • **con tal de que regreséis antes de las once** provided (that) *o* as long as you get back before eleven
tala SF **1** [*de árboles*] felling, cutting down; (= *destrucción*) havoc
2 (*Caribe*) (= *hacha*) axe, ax (*EEUU*)
3 (*Caribe*) (= *huerto*) vegetable garden
4 (*Cono Sur*) (= *pasto*) grazing
talabarte SM sword belt
talabartería SF **1** (= *taller*) saddlery, harness-maker's shop
2 (*LAm*) (= *tienda*) leather-goods shop
talabartero/a SM/F saddler, harness maker
talacha SF, **talache** SM (*Méx*) mattock
talado SM felling
taladradora SF pneumatic drill, jackhammer (*EEUU*)
taladrante ADJ piercing
taladrar ▷ CONJUG 1a VT **1** [+ *pared*] to drill a hole/holes in, drill; [+ *billete, documento*] to punch • **una bala le taladró el tobillo** a bullet pierced his ankle
2 [*ruido, mirada, dolor*] to pierce • **un ruido que taladra los oídos** an ear-splitting noise • **me taladró con la mirada** she fixed me with a piercing gaze • **un llanto de bebé taladra el silencio** a baby's cry pierces the silence, the silence is shattered by a baby's cry
taladro SM **1** (= *herramienta*) drill ▸ **taladro mecánico** power drill ▸ **taladro neumático** pneumatic drill
2 (= *agujero*) drill hole
talaje SM **1** (*LAm*) (= *pasto*) pasture
2 (*Cono Sur, Méx*) (= *pastoreo*) grazing, pasturage
tálamo SM marriage bed
talamoco ADJ (*And*) albino
talante SM **1** (= *carácter*) • **un hombre de ~ liberal** a liberal-minded man
2 (= *humor*) mood • **estar de buen ~** to be in a good mood • **estar de mal ~** to be in a bad mood • **responder de mal ~** to answer bad-temperedly
3 (= *disposición*) • **hacer algo de buen ~** to do sth willingly • **recibir a algn de buen ~** to give sb a warm welcome
talar ▷ CONJUG 1a VT **1** [+ *árbol*] to fell, cut down
2 (= *devastar*) to lay waste, devastate
3 (= *podar*) to prune
talasoterapia SF thalassotherapy
talco SM (*Quím*) talc; (*tb* **polvos de talco**) talcum powder
talcualillo* ADJ so-so, middling, fair
talega SF **1** (= *bolsa*) sack, bag
2 talegas: **a** (= *dinero*) money (*sing*)
b (*Méx***) (= *testículos*) balls**
talegada SF, **talegazo** SM heavy fall
talego SM **1** (= *saco*) long sack, big sack
2* (= *persona*) lump*
3‡ (= *cárcel*) nick*, jail, can (*EEUU*‡)

4‡ (= billete) 1000 pesetas • **medio ~** 500 pesetas
5‡ [de hachís] small bar of hash
taleguilla SF bullfighter's breeches (pl)
talejo SM (And) paper bag
talento SM **1** (= inteligencia) • **una mujer de enorme ~** a woman of enormous talent
2 (= aptitud) talent • **Ana tiene ~ para la música** Ana has a talent for music
3 (= prodigio) talent • **su hijo es un auténtico ~** her son is a really gifted o talented boy
4 (Biblia) talent
talentoso ADJ talented, gifted, exceptional (EEUU)
talero SM (Cono Sur) whip
Talgo SM ABR (Esp) (= **tren articulado ligero Goicoechea-Oriol**) inter-city express train
talibán/ana (a veces invariable) ADJ Taliban (antes de s)
SM/F (= persona) member of the Taliban • **los talibanes** the Taliban
talidomida SF thalidomide
talión SM • **la ley del ~** an eye for an eye
talismán SM talisman
talla¹ SF **1** [de ropa] size • **camisas de todas las ~s** shirts in all sizes • **¿de qué ~ son estos pantalones?** what size are these trousers?
2 (= altura) height • **dar la ~** (lit) to be tall enough; (fig) to measure up • **no ha dado la ~ para ingresar en el ejército** he wasn't tall enough to join the army, he didn't satisfy the minimum height requirement for joining the army • **no dio la ~ como solista** he didn't make the grade as a soloist, he didn't measure up as a soloist • **no dio la ~ en la disputa** he couldn't hold his own in the argument • **tener poca ~** to be short
3 (= categoría, nivel) stature • **hay pocos políticos de la ~ de este ministro** there are few politicians of the stature of this minister
4 (Arte) (= escultura) sculpture; [de madera] carving; (= grabado) engraving ▸ **talla en madera** woodwork, wood carving
5 (= vara) measuring rod
6 (Naipes) hand
7 (Med†) gallstones operation
8 (Jur†) reward (for capture of a criminal) • **poner a algn a ~** to offer a reward for sb's capture
talla² SF **1** (CAm) (= mentira) fib, lie
2 (Cono Sur) (= chismes) gossip, chitchat; (= piropo) compliment • **echar ~s a algn** to pay a compliment to a woman • MODISMO: • **echar ~** to put on airs
3 (And) (= paliza) beating
4 (Méx*) (= pelea) set-to*, squabble
tallado ADJ **1** [madera] carved; [piedra] sculpted; [metal] engraved
2 • **bien ~** shapely, well-formed • **mal ~** misshapen
SM (en madera) carving; (en piedra) sculpting; (= grabado) engraving ▸ **tallado en madera** woodcarving
tallador(a) SM/F **1** (= persona) [de madera] carver; [de piedra] sculptor; [de diamantes] cutter; [de metal] engraver ▸ **tallador(a) de madera** woodworker, wood carver
2 (LAm) (Naipes) dealer, banker
tallar¹ ▸ CONJUG 1a VT **1** [+ madera] to carve, work; [+ piedra] to sculpt; [+ diamante] to cut; [+ metal] to engrave
2 [+ persona] to measure (the height of)
3 (Naipes) to deal
VI (Naipes) to deal, be banker
VPR **tallarse** (Méx) (= frotarse) to rub o.s.; (para limpiarse) to scrub o.s.
tallar²* ▸ CONJUG 1a VT **1** (And) (= fastidiar) to bother, annoy
2 (And) (= azotar) to beat
VI (Cono Sur) (= chismear) to gossip; [amantes] to whisper sweet nothings
tallarín SM **1** (Culin) noodle
2 (And*) (= galón) stripe
talle SM **1** (= cintura) waist • **un vestido de ~ bajo** a dress with a low waist ▸ **talle de avispa** wasp waist
2 (= medidas) waist and chest measurements (pl); (= talla) size, fitting
3 (= tipo) [de mujer] figure; [de hombre] build, physique • **de ~ esbelto** slim • **tiene buen ~** she has a good figure
4 (= aspecto) look, appearance; (= contorno) outline
5 (CAm, Cono Sur) (= corpiño) bodice
taller SM (Téc, Educ, Teat) workshop; (= fábrica) factory, mill; (Aut) garage, repair shop; (Arte) studio; (Cos) workroom; (en lenguaje sindical) shop ▸ **taller de coches** car repair shop, garage (for repairs) ▸ **taller de máquinas** machine shop ▸ **taller de montaje** assembly shop ▸ **taller de reparaciones** repair shop ▸ **taller de teatro** theatre workshop, drama workshop ▸ **taller de trabajo** (en congreso etc) workshop ▸ **talleres gráficos** printing works ▸ **taller mecánico** garage (for repairs) ▸ **taller ocupacional** occupational therapy workshop
tallero/a SM/F (LAm) **1** (= verdulero) vegetable merchant, produce dealer (EEUU)
2 (= embustero) liar
tallista SMF wood carver
tallo SM **1** [de flor] stem, stalk; [de hierba] blade
2 (And) (= repollo) cabbage
3 tallos (LAm) (= verdura) vegetables, greens
4 (= fruta) crystallized fruit
talludito* ADJ mature, middle-aged • **el actor es ~ ya para este papel** the actor is getting on a bit now for this role • **Sofía Loren, que está ya talludita** Sofia Loren, who is no longer as young as she was
talludo ADJ **1** [planta] tall; [persona] tall, lanky; ▹ **talludito**
2 (CAm, Méx) [fruta] (= duro) tough; (= correoso) leathery; (= difícil de pelar) hard to peel
3 (CAm, Méx*) • **es un viejo ~** he's old but there's life in him yet • **es una máquina talluda** it's an old machine but it still serves its purpose
talmente* ADV exactly, literally • **la casa es ~ una pocilga** the house is a real pigsty
Talmud SM Talmud
talmúdico ADJ Talmudic
talón SM **1** [del pie] heel; [de calcetín, zapato] heel • MODISMO: • **pisar los talones a algn** to be hard on sb's heels ▸ **talón de Aquiles** Achilles heel
2 [de neumático] rim
3 (= cheque) cheque, check (EEUU); (= matriz) stub, counterfoil; (Ferro) luggage receipt ▸ **talón al portador** bearer cheque, cheque payable to the bearer ▸ **talón en blanco** blank cheque ▸ **talón nominativo** non-negotiable cheque • **un ~ nominativo a favor de Luis González** a cheque made out to o made payable to Luis González ▸ **talón sin fondos** bad cheque
talonador(a) SM/F (Rugby) hooker
talonar ▸ CONJUG 1a VT (Rugby) to heel
talonario SM [de cheques] cheque book, check book (EEUU); [de recibos] receipt book; [de billetes] book of tickets; [de recetas] prescription pad
talonear ▸ CONJUG 1a VT **1** (LAm) [+ caballo] to spur along, dig one's heels into
2 (Dep) to heel
VI **1** (= apresurarse) to walk briskly, hurry along
2 (Méx) [prostituta] to walk the streets, ply one's trade
talonera SF heel-pad; (And) heel
talquera SF talcum powder container; (con borla) compact
talquina* SF (Cono Sur) deceit, treachery
taltuza SF (CAm) raccoon
talud SM slope, bank; (Geol) talus
tamal SM (LAm) **1** (Culin) tamale
2 (= trampa) trick, fraud; (= intriga) intrigue • **hacer un ~** to set a trap
3 (Méx) pile, bundle
tamalero/a ADJ **1** fond of tamales
2 (= intrigante) scheming, fond of intrigue
SM/F (= fabricante) tamale maker; (= vendedor) tamale seller
tamango SM (Cono Sur) **1** (= zapato) sandal
2 (= vendas) bandages (pl)
tamañito ADJ • **dejar a algn ~** (= humillar) to make sb feel very small; (en debate) to crush sb, flatten sb (in an argument) • **me quedé ~** (= achicado) I felt about so high; (= confuso) I felt utterly bewildered
tamaño SM size • **son del mismo ~** • **tienen el mismo ~** they are the same size • **¿de qué ~ es?** how big is it?, what size is it? • **un ordenador del ~ de un libro** a computer the size of a book • **una foto ~ carnet** a passport-size photo • **de ~ natural** full-size, life-size • **de ~ extra** o **extraordinario** outsize, extra large ▸ **tamaño de bolsillo** pocket-size ▸ **tamaño familiar** family-size ▸ **tamaño gigante** king-size
ADJ **1** (= tan grande) so big a, such a big; (= tan pequeño) so small a, such a small • **parece absurdo que cometiera ~ error** it seems absurd that he should make such a mistake
2 (LAm) (= enorme) huge, colossal
támara SF **1** (= planta) date-palm
2 támaras (= dátiles) dates, cluster (sing) of dates
tamarindo SM **1** (Bot) tamarind
2 (Méx‡) traffic policeman, traffic cop*
tamarisco SM, **tamariz** SM tamarisk
tambache SM (Méx) [de ropa] bundle of clothes; (= bulto) big package
tambaleante ADJ **1** [persona] staggering; [paso] unsteady; [mueble] unsteady, wobbly; [vehículo] swaying
2 [economía, democracia] shaky; [régimen] tottering
tambalear ▸ CONJUG 1a VT to shake, rock
VPR **tambalearse 1** [persona] to stagger; [vehículo] to lurch, sway; [mueble] to wobble • **ir tambaleándose** to stagger along
2 [gobierno] to totter
tambaleo SM [de persona] staggering; [de vehículo] swaying; [de mueble] wobble
tambar ▸ CONJUG 1a VT (And) to swallow
tambarria* SF (And, CAm) binge*, booze-up*
tambero/a SM/F (And) (Hist) (= mesonero) innkeeper; (= granjero) dairy farmer
también ADV **1** (= además) also, too, as well • **ha estado en China y ~ en Japón** he has been in China and also in Japan, he has been in China and in Japan too o as well • **hablaron ~ de otros temas** they also discussed other matters, they discussed other matters too o as well • **Isabel ~ sabe inglés** (uso ambiguo) Isabel knows English too o as well; (también inglés) Isabel also knows English, Isabel knows English too o as well; (también Isabel) Isabel knows English too o as well • **Italia tomará ~ parte en la competición** Italy will take part in the competition too o as well • **~ los niños tienen derecho a dar su opinión** children have the right to give their opinion too o as well • **¿tú ~ tienes la gripe?** have you got the

t

flu too *o* as well? • **si él no viene, ~ podemos ir nosotros** if he doesn't come, we can always go • **—estoy cansado —yo ~** "I'm tired" — "so am I" *o* "me too" • **—me gustó —a él ~** "I liked it" — "so did he" • **ácido ascórbico, ~ conocido como vitamina C** ascorbic acid, also known as vitamin C • **—¿y es guapa? —también** "and is she pretty?" — "yes, she is"
2 (*uso enfático*) • **tuvimos mala suerte, aunque ~ es cierto que nos faltaba preparación** we were certainly unlucky but (then again) we were also underprepared *o* we were underprepared too *o* as well • **—me fui sin despedirme —¡pues anda que tú ~!** "I left without saying goodbye" — "what a thing to do!"

tambo SM **1** (*And*) (*Hist*) (= *taberna*) wayside inn, country inn
2 (*And, Cono Sur*) (= *granja*) (small) dairy (farm)
3 (*Cono Sur*) (= *corral*) milking yard
4 (*Cono Sur*) (= *burdel*) brothel

tambocha SF (*Col*) *highly poisonous red ant*

tambor SM **1** (*Mús*) (= *instrumento*) drum; (= *persona*) drummer • MODISMO: • **venir** *o* **salir a ~ batiente** to come out with flying colours ▸ **tambor mayor** drum major
2 (*Téc*) drum; [*de lavadora*] drum ▸ **tambor del freno** brake drum
3 (*Anat*) ▸ **tambor del oído** eardrum
4 [*de detergente*] drum
5 ▸ **tambor magnético** (*Inform*) magnetic drum
6 (*Arquit*) [*de columna*] tambour
7 (*Cos*) (= *bastidor*) tambour
8 (*Caribe, Méx*) (= *tela*) burlap, sackcloth

tambora SF **1** (*Mús*) (= *tambor*) bass drum; (*Méx*) (= *banda*) brass band
2 (*Caribe**) (= *mentira*) lie, fib

tamboril SM small drum

tamborilada SF, **tamborilazo** SM (= *batacazo*) bump on one's bottom; (= *sacudida*) severe jolt; (= *espaldarazo*) slap on the shoulder

tamborilear ▸ CONJUG 1a VI **1** (*Mús*) to drum
2 (*con los dedos*) to drum
3 [*lluvia*] to patter, drum
VT* to praise up, boost

tamborileo SM **1** (*con los dedos*) drumming
2 [*de lluvia*] patter, pattering

tamborilero/a SM/F drummer

tambre SM (*And*) dam

tamegua SF (*CAm, Méx*) weeding, cleaning

tameguar ▸ CONJUG 1d VT (*CAm, Méx*) to weed, clean

Tamerlán SM Tamburlaine

Támesis SM Thames

tamil ADJ, SMF Tamil

tamiz SM sieve • MODISMO: • **pasar algo por el ~** to go through sth with a fine-tooth comb, scrutinize sth

tamizado ADJ [*harina, información*] sifted; [*luz*] filtered
SM sifting

tamizar ▸ CONJUG 1f VT [+ *harina, azúcar*] to sift, sieve; [+ *datos, información*] to sift through; [+ *luz*] to filter; [+ *rayos*] to filter out

tamo SM (= *pelusa*) fluff, down; (*Agr*) dust; (= *paja*) chaff

tampa SF (*Cono Sur*) matted hair

támpax® SM INV Tampax®, tampon

tampiqueño/a ADJ of/from Tampico
SM/F native/inhabitant of Tampico • **los ~s** the people of Tampico

tampoco ADV **1** not ... either, neither, nor • **yo no lo compré ~** I didn't buy it either • **~ lo sabe él** he doesn't know either • **ni Ana ni Cristóbal ~** neither Ana nor Cristóbal • **—yo no voy —yo ~** "I'm not going" — "nor am I *o* neither am I *o* me neither" • **—yo no fui —yo ~** "I didn't go" — "nor did I *o* neither did I *o* me neither" • **—nunca he estado en París —ni yo ~** "I've never been to Paris" — "neither have I *o* me neither" • **—¿lo sabes tú? —tampoco** "do you know?" — "no, I don't either"
2 (*uso enfático*) • **~ nos vamos a enfadar ahora por eso** we're not going to fall out over that, are we? • **bueno, ~ es como para ponerse a llorar** it's not as if it's anything to cry about

tampón SM **1** (*Med*) tampon
2 (*para entintar*) ink pad
ADJ INV • **parlamento ~** rubber-stamp parliament • **sistema ~** buffer system • **zona ~** buffer zone

tamuga SF **1** (*CAm*) (= *fardo*) bundle, pack; (= *mochila*) knapsack
2 (*LAm‡*) joint‡, reefer‡

tan ADV **1** (*tras verbo*) so • **estaba tan cansado que me quedé dormido** I was so tired I fell asleep • **no te esperaba tan pronto** I wasn't expecting you so soon • **¡no es tan difícil!** it's not so difficult!
2 (*tras sustantivo*) such • **¿para qué quieres un coche tan grande?** what do you want such a big car for? • **no es una idea tan buena** it's not such a good idea
3 (*en exclamaciones*) • **¡qué idea tan rara!** what an odd notion! • **¡qué regalo tan bonito!** what a beautiful present! • **¡que cosa tan rara!** how strange!
4 (*en comparaciones*) • **es tan feo como yo** he's as ugly as me • **tan es así que** so much so that
5 • **tan solo** only • **hace tan solo unas semanas** only a few weeks ago
6 • **tan siquiera = siquiera**
7 (*Méx*) • **¿qué tan grande es?** how big is it? • **¿qué tan grave está el enfermo?** how ill is the patient? • **¿qué tan lejos?** how far?

tanaca SF (*And*) slut

tanaceto SM tansy

tanaco ADJ (*Cono Sur*) foolish, silly

tanate SM (*CAm, Méx*) **1** (= *cesta*) basket, pannier
2 tanates (= *trastos*) odds and ends, bits and pieces, gear (*sing*)

tanatorio SM funeral home (*EEUU*)

tanda SF **1** (= *grupo*) [*de cosas, personas*] batch; [*de golpes*] series; [*de huevos*] layer; [*de inyecciones*] course, series; [*de ladrillos*] course • **por ~s** in batches ▸ **tanda de penaltis** series of penalties, penalty shoot-out
2 (= *turno*) [*de trabajo*] shift, turn; [*de riego*] turn (*to use water*) ▸ **tanda de noche** night shift
3 (*Billar*) game; (*Béisbol*) innings (*pl*)
4 (*LAm*) (= *espectáculo*) show, performance; (*Cono Sur*) (= *farsa*) farce; (*Cono Sur*) (= *musical*) musical • **primera ~** early performance, first show ▸ **tanda de avisos** (*LAm*) commercial break, ad break*

tándem SM (= *bicicleta*) tandem; (*Pol*) duo, team • **en ~** (*Elec*) tandem; (*fig*) in tandem, jointly, in association

tanga SM tanga, G-string

tangada‡ SF trick, swindle

tangana SF (*Perú*) large oar

tanganear ▸ CONJUG 1a VT (*And, Caribe*) to beat

tanganillas • **en ~** ADV (*lit*) unsteadily; (*fig*) uncertainly, dubiously

tanganillo SM prop, wedge, temporary support

tangar‡ ▸ CONJUG 1h VT to swindle • **~ algo a algn** to do sb out of sth

tangencial ADJ tangential

tangencialmente ADV tangentially

tangente SF tangent • MODISMO: • **salirse por la ~** (= *hacer una digresión*) to go off at a tangent; (= *esquivar una pregunta*) to dodge the issue

Tánger SM Tangier(s)

tangerino/a ADJ of/from Tangier(s)
SM/F native/inhabitant of Tangier(s) • **los ~s** the people of Tangier(s)

tangibilidad SF tangibility

tangible ADJ (*lit*) tangible; (*fig*) tangible, concrete

tango SM tango

tanguear ▸ CONJUG 1a VI **1** (*LAm*) (= *bailar*) to tango
2 (*And*) [*borracho*] to reel drunkenly

tanguero/a SM/F, **tanguista** SMF tango dancer

tánico ADJ tannic • **ácido ~** tannic acid

tanino SM tannin

tano/a SM/F (*Cono Sur*) (*pey*) Italian, wop** (*pey*)

tanque SM **1** (= *depósito*) tank, reservoir; (*Aut*) tanker, tanker lorry ▸ **tanque de cerebros, tanque de ideas** think tank
2 (*Mil*) tank
3 (*Esp‡*) handbag, purse (*EEUU*)

tanquero SM (*Caribe*) (*Náut*) tanker; (*Aut*) tanker, tank wagon

tanqueta SF small tank, armoured *o* (*EEUU*) armored car

tanquista SMF member of a tank crew

tanta SF (*And*) maize bread

tantán SM (= *tambor*) tomtom; (= *gong*) gong

tantarán SM, **tantarantán** SM **1** [*de tambor*] beat, rat-a-tat-tat
2* (= *golpe*) hefty punch; (= *sacudida*) violent shaking

tanteada SF **1** (*LAm*) = **tanteo**
2 (*Méx*) (= *mala pasada*) dirty trick; (= *estafa*) hoax, swindle

tanteador(a) SM/F (= *persona*) scorer
SM (= *marcador*) scoreboard

tantear ▸ CONJUG 1a VT **1** (*con la mano*) to feel • **tanteó la mesilla en busca del reloj** he felt for the watch on the bedside table
2 (= *probar*) to test, try out; (= *sondear*) to probe; [+ *intenciones, persona*] to sound out • MODISMO: • **~ el terreno** to test the water, get the lie of the land
3 (= *calcular*) [+ *tela, cantidad*] to make a rough estimate of; [+ *peso*] to feel, get the feel of; [+ *situación*] to weigh up; [+ *problema*] to consider
4 (*Arte*) to sketch in, draw the outline of
5 (*Dep*) to keep the score of
6 (*CAm, Méx*) (= *acechar*) to lie in wait for
7 (*Méx*) (= *estafar*) to swindle; (= *burlarse*) to make a fool of, take for a ride*
VI **1** (*Dep*) to score, keep (the) score
2 (*LAm*) (= *ir a tientas*) to grope, feel one's way • **¡tantee usted!** what do you think?

tanteo SM **1** (= *cálculo*) rough estimate; (= *consideración*) weighing up • **a** *o* **por ~** by guesswork
2 (= *prueba*) test, testing, trial; [*de situación*] sounding out • **al ~** by trial and error • **conversaciones de ~** exploratory talks
3 (*Dep*) score • **un ~ de 9-7** a score of 9-7

tantico* SM • **un ~** (*esp LAm*) a bit, quite a bit • **es un ~ difícil** it's a bit awkward*

tantísimo ADJ so much • **~s** so many • **había tantísima gente** there was such a crowd

tantito* (*Méx*) ADJ a bit of, a little • **~ pulque** a little pulque
SM = **tantico**
ADV a bit, a little • **~ antes** a bit *o* little earlier

tanto ADJ **1** (*indicando gran cantidad*) (*en singular*) so much; (*en plural*) so many • **ahora**

no bebo tanta leche I don't drink so *o* as much milk now • **tiene ~ dinero que no sabe qué hacer con él** he has so much money he doesn't know what to do with it • **¡tuve tanta suerte!** I was so lucky! • **¡tengo tantas cosas que hacer hoy!** I have so many things to do today! • **había ~s coches que no había donde aparcar** there were so many cars that there was nowhere to park • **~ ... como** (*en singular*) as much ... as; (*en plural*) as many ... as • **tiene ~ dinero como yo** he has as much money as I do • **no recibe tantas llamadas como yo** he doesn't get as many calls as I do • **~ gusto** how do you do?, pleased to meet you
2 (*indicando cantidad indeterminada*) • **había cuarenta y ~s invitados** there were forty-odd guests • **hay otros ~s candidatos** there are as many more candidates, there's the same number of candidates again • **se dividen el trabajo en otras tantas partes** they divide up the work into a like number of parts
PRON **1** (= *gran cantidad*) (*en singular*) so much; (*en plural*) so many • **gana ~** he earns so much • **no necesitamos tantas** we don't need so many • **vinieron ~s que no cabían en la sala** so many people came that they wouldn't all fit into the room • **~ como** (*en singular*) as much as; (*en plural*) as many as • **gano ~ como tú** I earn as much as you • **coge ~s como quieras** take as many as you like • **es uno de ~s** he's nothing special
2 (= *cantidad indeterminada*) • **nació en el mil novecientos cuarenta y ~s** she was born in nineteen forty-something *o* some time in the forties • **a ~s de marzo** on such and such a day in March • **yo no sé qué ~s de libros hay** I don't know how many books there are • MODISMO: • **las tantas (de la madrugada *o* de la noche)**: • **el tren llegó a las tantas** the train arrived really late *o* in the middle of the night • **estar fuera hasta las tantas** to stay out until all hours • —**¿qué hora es?** —**deben de ser las tantas** "what's the time?" — "it must be pretty late"
3 (*otras locuciones*) • **entre ~** meanwhile • **mientras ~** meanwhile • **no es para ~** (*al quejarse*) it's not as bad as all that; (*al enfadarse*) there's no need to get like that about it • **por lo ~** so, therefore • MODISMOS: • **ni ~ así**: • **no nos desviamos ni ~ así** we didn't deviate even by this much • **no le tengo ni ~ así de lástima** I haven't a scrap of pity for him • **¡y ~!**: • —**¿necesitarás unas vacaciones?** —**¡y ~!** "do you need a holiday?" — "you bet I do!"
ADV **1** (*con verbos*) (*indicando duración, cantidad*) so much; (*indicando frecuencia*) so often • **se preocupa ~ que no puede dormir** he gets so worried that he can't sleep, he worries so much that he can't sleep • **estoy cansada de ~ andar** I'm tired after all this walking • **¡cuesta ~ comprar una casa!** buying a house is such hard work! • **no deberías trabajar ~** you shouldn't work so hard • **¡no corras ~!** don't run so fast! • **ya no vamos ~ al cine** we don't go to the cinema so *o* as much any more • **ahora no la veo ~** I don't see so *o* as much of her now, I don't see her so often now • **~ como**: • **él gasta ~ como yo** he spends as much as I do *o* as me • **~ como corre, va a perder la carrera** he may be a fast runner, but he's still going to lose the race • **~ como habla no dice más que tonterías** all his talk is just hot air • **~ tú como yo** both you and I • **~ si viene como si no** whether he comes or not • **es así que** so much so that; ▸ **montar**
2 (*con adjetivos, adverbios*) • **los dos son ya mayores, aunque su mujer no ~** the two of them are elderly, although his wife less so • **~ como**: • **es difícil, pero ~ como eso no creo** it's difficult, but not that difficult • **es un poco tacaño, pero ~ como estafador, no** he's a bit on the mean side, but I wouldn't go so far as to call him a swindler • **es ~ más difícil** it is all the more difficult • **es ~ más loable cuanto que ...** it is all the more praiseworthy because ... • **~ mejor** so much the better • **~ mejor para ti** so much the better for you • **~ peor** so much the worse • **~ peor para ti** it's your loss *o* that's just too bad • MODISMO: • **¡ni ~ ni tan calvo!** there's no need to exaggerate!
3 (*en locuciones conjuntivas*) • **en ~** as (being) • **estoy en contra de la leyes en ~ sistema represivo** I am against laws as (being) a repressive system • **en ~ que** (= *mientras que*) while; (= *como*) as • **no puede haber democracia en ~ que siga habiendo torturas** for as long as there is torture, there can never be democracy, there cannot be democracy while there is torture • **la Iglesia en ~ que institución** the Church as an institution
SM **1** (= *cantidad*) • **me paga un ~ fijo cada semana** he pays me a fixed amount each week • **cobra un ~ por página** he gets so much per page • **¿qué ~ será?** (*LAm*) how much (is it)? • **otro ~**: • **las máquinas costaron otro ~** the machines cost as much again *o* the same again ▸ **tanto alzado** fixed price • **por un ~ alzado** for a fixed rate ▸ **tanto por ciento** percentage
2 (= *punto*) (*Ftbl, Hockey*) goal; (*Baloncesto, Tenis*) point • **Juárez marcó el segundo ~** Juárez scored the second goal • **marcó dos ~s** he scored twice • **apuntar los ~s** to keep score ▸ **tanto a favor** goal for, point for ▸ **tanto del honor** consolation goal ▸ **tanto en contra** goal against, point against; ▹ **apuntar**
3 • **estar al ~** to be up to date • **estar al ~ de los acontecimientos** to be fully abreast of events • **mantener a algn al ~ de algo** to keep sb informed about sth • **poner a algn al ~ de algo** to put sb in the picture about sth
4 • **un ~** (*como adv*) rather • **estoy un ~ cansado** I'm rather tired

Tanzania SF Tanzania

tanzano/a ADJ, SM/F Tanzanian

tañar‡ ▹ CONJUG 1a VT to grasp, understand • **~ a algn** to twig what sb is saying*

tañedor(a) SM/F [*de instrumentos de cuerda*] player; [*de campanas*] bell-ringer

tañer ▹ CONJUG 2f VT [+ *instrumento de cuerda*] to play; [+ *campana*] to ring

tañido SM (*Mús*) sound; [*de campana*] ringing

TAO SF ABR (= **traducción asistida por ordenador**) CAT

taoísmo SM Taoism

taoísta ADJ, SMF Taoist

tapa SF **1** [*de caja, olla, piano*] lid; [*de frasco*] top; [*de depósito de gasolina*] cap • MODISMO: • **levantarse la ~ de los sesos** to blow one's brains out ▸ **tapa de registro** manhole cover, inspection cover
2 [*de libro*] cover • **libro de ~s duras** hardback
3 [*de zapato*] heelplate
4 [*de canal*] sluicegate
5 (= *ración de comida*) snack (*taken at the bar counter with drinks*) • **ir de ~s** ▹ **tapeo**
6 (= *pieza de carne*) flank
7 (*And*) (= *bistec*) rump steak
8 (*Méx*) (*Aut*) hubcap
9 (*Caribe*) (= *comisión*) commission

tapaagujeros* SM INV, **tapagujeros*** SM INV **1** (*Arquit*) jerry-builder
2 (= *sustituto*) stand-in, substitute

tapabarro SM (*Cono Sur*) mudguard, fender (*EEUU*)

tapaboca SF, **tapabocas** SM INV
1 (= *prenda*) muffler
2 (= *manotada*) slap

tapaboquetes SM INV stopgap

tapacubos SM INV hubcap

tapada SF **1** • **un gay de ~*** a closet gay*
2 (= *mentira*) lie

tapadera SF **1** [*de olla*] lid; [*de tarro de plástico*] top, cap ▸ **tapadera deslizante** sliding cover
2 [*de organización*] cover, front, front organization (**de** for); [*de espía*] cover • **el restaurante es una ~ de la mafia** the restaurant is a cover *o* front for the mafia

tapadero SM stopper

tapadillo • **de ~** ADV secretly, stealthily

tapado/a ADJ **1** (*Chile*) [*animal*] *all one colour*
2 (*And*) (= *vago*) lazy, slack; (= *ignorante*) ignorant
3 (*Ven*) • **ser ~ para algo** to be useless at sth
SM/F (*Méx*) (*Pol*) *potential PRI Presidential election candidate*
SM **1** (*Uru, Chile*) (= *abrigo*) coat
2 (*Méx*) (= *chal*) shawl; (= *pañuelo*) headscarf
3 (*Bol*) (= *tesoro*) buried treasure
4 (*And, CAm*) (*Culin*) *dish of plantain and barbecued meat*

tapagrietas SM INV filler

tapalcate SM (*CAm, Méx*) (= *objeto*) piece of junk, useless object; (= *persona*) useless person

tapalodo SM (*And, Caribe*) mudguard

tapanca SF **1** (*LAm*) (= *gualdrapa*) saddle blanket; (*And, Cono Sur*) [*de caballo*] horse trappings (*pl*)
2 (*Cono Sur*) (= *culo*) backside

tapaojo SM (*LAm*) (= *venda*) blindfold, bandage (over the eyes); (= *parche*) patch

tapaporos SM INV primer

tapar ▹ CONJUG 1a VT **1** (= *cubrir*) (*gen*) to cover; (*más deliberada o completamente*) to cover up • **un velo le tapaba parte de la cara** part of her face was covered by a veil • **le tapó la boca con la mano** she covered his mouth with her hand • **le ~on los ojos y se lo llevaron** he was blindfolded and taken away • **mandaron ~ los desnudos de la Capilla Sixtina** they ordered the nudes of the Sistine Chapel to be covered up
2 (= *cerrar*) (*con tapadera*) [+ *olla, tarro*] to put the lid on; [+ *botella*] (*gen*) to put the top on; (*con corcho*) to put the cork in
3 [+ *tubo, túnel, agujero, ranura*] (= *obstruir*) block up; (= *rellenar*) to fill, fill in
4 (= *abrigar*) (*con ropa*) to wrap up; (*en la cama*) to cover up • **tapa bien al niño, que no se enfríe** wrap the child (up) well so that he doesn't catch cold
5 (= *ocultar*) [+ *objeto*] to hide; [+ *vista*] to block; [+ *hecho, escándalo*] to cover up • **los arbustos tapaban el sendero** the bushes hid the path • **las nubes siguen tapando el sol** the clouds are still blocking the sun • **la madre le tapa las travesuras** when he does something naughty, his mother always covers up for him
6 (*Chile, Méx, And*) [+ *diente*] to fill
7 (*LAm*) [+ *cañería, excusado*] to block
8 (*And*) (= *aplastar*) to crush, flatten; (= *chafar*) to crumple, rumple
9 (*And*) (= *insultar*) to abuse, insult
VPR **taparse 1** (= *cubrirse*) (*gen*) to cover o.s.; (= *envolverse*) to wrap (o.s.) up • **me tapé con la manta** I covered myself with the blanket • **tápate bien al salir** wrap yourself up well before going out
2 • **~se los oídos/ojos** to cover one's

ears/eyes • **la peste le hizo ~se la nariz** the stench was so bad that he had to cover *o* hold his nose
3 (= *atascarse*) [*oídos, nariz*] to get blocked, get blocked up; [*cañería, excusado*] (*LAm*) to get blocked • **al aterrizar se me ~on los oídos** my ears got blocked (up) when we landed • **tengo la nariz tapada** my nose is blocked (up), I have a blocked (up) nose
tapara (SF) (*Caribe*) calabash, gourd, squash (*EEUU*)
táparo (SM) (*And*) **1** (= *yescas*) tinderbox
2 (= *tuerto*) one-eyed person; (*fig*) dolt
taparrabo (SM), **taparrabos** (SM INV) loincloth
tapatío/a (*Méx*) (ADJ) of/from Guadalajara (SM/F) native/inhabitant of Guadalajara • **los ~s** the people of Guadalajara
tapayagua (SF) (*CAm, Méx*), **tapayagüe** (SM) (*Méx*) (= *nubarrón*) storm cloud; (= *llovizna*) drizzle
tape* (SM) (*Caribe*) cover
tapear ▸ CONJUG 1a (VI) (*esp Esp*) ▸ **tapeo**
tapeo (SM) (*esp Esp*) • **ir de ~** to go round the bars (*drinking and eating snacks*) • **bar de ~** tapas bar
tapeque (SM) (*And*) equipment for a journey
tapera (SF) (*LAm*) **1** (= *casa*) ruined house
2 (= *pueblo*) abandoned village
tapería (SF) tapas bar
taperujarse* ▸ CONJUG 1a (VPR) to cover up one's face
tapesco (SM) (*CAm, Méx*) (= *armazón*) bedframe; (= *cama*) camp bed
tapete (SM) (= *mantel*) tablecloth (*usually lace or embroidered*); (= *paño*) runner; (= *alfombrita*) rug; (*tb* **tapete verde**) (*Naipes*) card table • MODISMOS: • **estar sobre el ~** to be under discussion • **poner un asunto sobre el ~** to put a matter up for discussion
tapetusa (SF) (*And*) contraband liquor
tapia (SF) **1** (= *muro*) (*gen*) wall; [*de jardín*] garden wall; [*de adobe*] mud wall, adobe wall • **saltar la ~** to climb over the wall; ▸ **sordo**
2‡ (= *compañero*) partner
tapial (SM) = **tapia**
tapialera (SF) (*And*) = **tapia**
tapiar ▸ CONJUG 1b (VT) **1** [+ *jardín, terreno*] to wall in
2 [+ *puerta, ventana*] (*con ladrillos*) to brick up; (*con tablas*) to board up
tapicería (SF) **1** [*de coche, muebles*] upholstery • **tela de ~** upholstery fabric
2 (= *tapiz*) tapestry
3 (= *arte*) tapestry making
tapicero/a (SM/F) [*de muebles*] upholsterer
tapiñar‡ ▸ CONJUG 1a (VT) to scoff*, eat
tapioca (SF) tapioca
tapir (SM) tapir
tapisca (SF) (*CAm, Méx*) maize harvest, corn harvest (*EEUU*)
tapiscar ▸ CONJUG 1g (VT) (*CAm, Méx*) to harvest
tapita* (ADJ) • **estar ~** (*Caribe*) to be as deaf as a post
tapiz (SM) [*de pared*] tapestry; [*de suelo*] carpet ▸ **tapiz de empapelar** (*Méx*) wallpaper ▸ **tapiz volador** magic carpet
tapizado (SM) [*de coche, mueble*] upholstery; [*de suelo*] carpeting; [*de pared*] tapestries (*pl*)
tapizar ▸ CONJUG 1f (VT) **1** [+ *muebles*] to upholster, cover; [+ *coche*] to upholster; [+ *suelo*] to carpet, cover; [+ *pared*] to hang with tapestries
2 (*fig*) to carpet (**con, de** with)
tapón (SM) **1** [*de botella*] (*gen*) cap, top; [*de corcho*] cork; [*de vidrio*] stopper ▸ **tapón de corona, tapón de rosca** screw top
2 (*en los oídos*) (*para el ruido*) earplug; [*de cera*] plug
3 [*de lavabo*] plug
4 (*Med*) tampon
5 (*Baloncesto*) block
6 (*Aut*) (= *atasco*) traffic jam
7* (= *persona*) chubby person
8 (*Méx*) (*Elec*) fuse
9 (= *estorbo*) obstacle, hindrance; (*Aut**) slowcoach*
(ADJ) (*CAm, Cono Sur*) tailless
taponado (ADJ) [*desagüe, tubería*] blocked • **tengo los oídos ~s** my ears are blocked up
taponar ▸ CONJUG 1a (VT) [+ *tubería, puerta, carretera*] to block; [+ *agujero*] to plug, block; (*Dep*) to block, stop; (*Med*) to tampon
(VPR) **taponarse** [*nariz, oídos*] to get blocked up
taponazo (SM) pop
tapujar* ▸ CONJUG 1a (VT) to cheat, con*
(VPR) **tapujarse** to muffle o.s. up
tapujo* (SM) **1** (= *engaño*) deceit, dodge; (= *secreto*) secrecy; (= *subterfugio*) subterfuge, dodge* • **andar con ~s** to be involved in some shady business* • **llevan no sé qué ~ entre manos** they're up to something • **sin ~s** (= *claramente*) honestly, openly; (= *sin rodeos*) without beating about the bush
2 (= *embozo*) muffler
taquear ▸ CONJUG 1a (VT) (*LAm*) **1** (= *llenar*) to fill right up, pack tight (**de** with)
2 [+ *arma*] (= *cargar*) to tamp, ram; (= *disparar*) to fire
(VI) **1** (*LAm*) to play billiards *o* (*EEUU*) pool
2 (*Méx*) (= *comer tacos*) to have a snack of tacos
3 (*Caribe*) (= *vestirse*) to dress in style
(VPR) **taquearse** (*And*) to get rich
taquería (SF) **1** (*Méx*) taco stall, taco bar
2 (*Caribe*) (= *descaro*) cheek
taquete (SM) (*Méx*) plug, bung
taquicardia (SF) abnormally rapid heartbeat, tachycardia
taquigrafía (SF) shorthand, stenography (*EEUU*)
taquigráficamente (ADV) in shorthand • **tomar un discurso ~** to take down a speech in shorthand
taquigráfico (ADJ) shorthand (*antes de s*)
taquígrafo/a (SM/F) shorthand writer, stenographer (*EEUU*) • MODISMO: • **con luz y ~s** openly
taquilla (SF) **1** (*para billetes, entradas*) (= *sala*) booking office, ticket office; (= *ventanilla*) ticket window; [*de teatro, cine*] box office • **éxito de ~** box-office success, box-office hit
2 (= *recaudación*) (*Teat*) takings (*pl*), take (*EEUU*); (*Dep*) gate money, proceeds (*pl*) • **la ~ fue escasa** attendance was poor
3 (= *armario*) locker; (= *archivador*) filing cabinet; (= *carpeta*) file
4 (*CAm*) (= *bar*) bar; (= *tienda*) liquor store
5 (*And, CAm, Cono Sur*) (= *clavo*) tack
taquillaje (SM) (*Teat etc*) takings (*pl*), box-office receipts (*pl*); (*Dep*) gate-money, gate
taquillero/a (ADJ) popular, successful (at the box office) • **ser ~** to be good (for the) box office, be a draw, be popular • **función taquillera** box-office success, big draw • **el actor más ~ del año** the actor who has been the biggest box-office draw of the year
(SM/F) clerk, ticket clerk
taquimeca* (SM/F) shorthand typist, stenographer (*EEUU*)
taquimecanografía (SF) shorthand typing
taquimecanógrafo/a (SM/F) shorthand typist, stenographer (*EEUU*)
taquímetro (SM) tachymeter
taquito (SM) [*de jamón*] small cube
tara[1] (SF) **1** (= *peso*) tare
2 (= *defecto*) defect, blemish
tara[2] (SF) tally stick
tarabilla (SF) **1** [*de ventana*] latch, catch
2* (= *charla*) chatter
(SMF)* **1** (= *hablador*) chatterbox*
2 (= *casquivano*) featherbrained person; (= *inútil*) useless individual, dead loss*
tarabita (SF) **1** [*de cinturón*] tongue
2 (*And*) (*en puente*) cable of a rope bridge (*with hanging basket for carrying passengers across ravines*)
taracea (SF) inlay, marquetry
taracear ▸ CONJUG 1a (VT) to inlay
tarado/a (ADJ) **1** (*Com*) defective, imperfect
2 [*persona*] crippled
3* (= *idiota*) stupid; (= *loco*) crazy, nuts*
(SM/F)* (= *idiota*) cretin*, moron*
tarambana (SMF), **tarambanas** (SMF INV)
1 (= *casquivano*) harebrained person; (= *estrafalario*) crackpot*; (= *no fiable*) fly-by-night
2 (= *parlanchín*) chatterbox*
taranta (SF) **1** (*LAm*) (= *locura*) mental disturbance, madness; (*CAm*) (= *confusión*) bewilderment
2 (*Méx*) (= *embriaguez*) drunkenness
3 (*And, Cono Sur*) (*Zool*) tarantula
tarantear ▸ CONJUG 1a (VI) (*Cono Sur*) (= *hacer algo imprevisto*) to do sth unexpected; (= *cambiar*) to chop and change a lot; (= *hacer cosas raras*) to behave strangely, be eccentric
tarantela (SF) tarantella
tarantín (SM) **1** (*CAm, Caribe*) (*Culin*) kitchen utensil
2 (*Caribe*) (= *patíbulo*) scaffold
3 (*Caribe*) (= *puesto*) stall
4 tarantines (*Caribe**) odds and ends
taranto (ADJ) (*And*) dazed, bewildered
tarántula (SF) tarantula
tarar ▸ CONJUG 1a (VT) (*Com*) to tare
tarareable (ADJ) • **melodía ~** catchy tune, tune that you can hum
tararear ▸ CONJUG 1a (VT), (VI) to hum
tararí* (ADJ) (*Esp*) crazy
(EXCL) no way!*, you must be joking!
tarasca (SF) **1** (= *monstruo*) carnival dragon, monster
2 (= *comilón*) glutton; (= *sangría de recursos*) *person who is a drain on one's resources*
3* (= *mujer*) old hag, old bag*
4 (*And, CAm, Cono Sur*) (= *boca*) big mouth
tarascada (SF) **1** (= *mordisco*) bite
2* (= *contestación*) tart reply, snappy answer
tarascar ▸ CONJUG 1g (VT) to bite
tarasco (SM) (*And*), **tarascón** (SM) (*LAm*) bite, nip
tarasquear ▸ CONJUG 1a (VT) (*CAm, Cono Sur, Méx*) (= *morder*) to bite; (= *cortar*) to bite off
tardado (ADJ) (*Méx*) slow, time-consuming
tardanza (SF) **1** (= *demora*) delay
2 (= *lentitud*) slowness
tardar ▸ CONJUG 1a (VT) • **he tardado un poco debido a la lluvia** I'm a bit late because of the rain • **tardamos tres horas de Granada a Córdoba** it took us *o* we took three hours to get from Granada to Córdoba • **¿cuánto se tarda?** how long does it take? • **aquí tardan mucho en servirte** the service is very slow here, they take a long time to serve you here • **tardó tres horas en encontrarlo** it took him three hours to find it, he spent three hours looking for it • **tardó mucho en repararlo** he took a long time to repair it
(VI) • **vete a buscarlo, pero no tardes** go and fetch it, but don't be long • **te espero a las ocho, no tardes** I expect you at eight, don't be late • **~ en hacer algo**: • **tardó en llegar** it was late in arriving • **tarda en hacer efecto** it takes a while to take effect, it doesn't take effect immediately • **no tarde usted en informarme** please tell me as soon as you know • **el público no tardó en reaccionar** the spectators were not slow *o* were quick to react • **a más ~** at the latest • **a las ocho a**

más ~ at eight o'clock at the latest • **sin ~** without delay • **a todo ~** at the latest
VPR **tardarse** (*Méx**) to be long, take a long time • **no me tardo** I won't be long, I won't take long

tarde ADV (*gen*) late; (= *demasiado tarde*) too late • **llegar ~** to be late, arrive late • **ya es ~ para quejarse** it's too late to complain now • **se hace ~** it's getting late • **se te hará ~ si no aligeras** you'll be late if you don't hurry up • **de ~ en ~** from time to time • **más ~** later • **un poco más ~** a bit later • **~ o temprano** sooner or later
SF (= *primeras horas*) afternoon; (= *últimas horas*) evening • **a las siete de la ~** at seven in the evening • **¡buenas ~s!** good afternoon!/ good evening! • **tenlo listo a la ~** have it ready by the afternoon/evening • **en la ~ de hoy** this afternoon/evening • **en la ~ del lunes** on Monday afternoon/evening • **por la ~** in the afternoon/evening • **el domingo por la ~** on Sunday afternoon/evening
• MODISMO: • **de la ~ a la mañana** overnight

tardecer ▸ CONJUG 2d VI = **atardecer**

tardecito ADV (*LAm*) rather late

tardíamente ADV (= *tarde*) late, belatedly; (= *demasiado tarde*) too late

tardío ADJ [*periodo, producto*] late • **el Renacimiento ~** the late Renaissance • **la medicina ha sido una vocación tardía** she came to medicine late in life • **tener un hijo ~** to have a child late in life • **el interés de los historiadores ha sido relativamente ~** historians have only relatively recently *o* lately taken an interest

tardo ADJ **1** (= *lento*) slow, sluggish
2 (= *torpe*) dull, dense • **~ de oído** hard of hearing • **~ de reflejos** slow (to react)

tardo... PREF late • **tardorromano** late Roman • **el tardofranquismo** the last years of the Franco régime

tardón* ADJ **1** (= *lento*) slow
2 (= *lerdo*) dim

tarea SF **1** (= *trabajo*) task, job • **una de sus ~s es repartir la correspondencia** one of his tasks *o* jobs is to hand out the mail • **es una ~ poco grata** it's a thankless task • **todavía me queda mucha ~** I've still got a lot left to do ▸ **tareas domésticas** housework (*sing*), household chores
2 [*de colegial*] • **las ~s** homework (*sing*)
3 (*Inform*) task

tareco SM (*And*) old thing, piece of junk

tarifa SF **1** (= *precio fijado*) [*de suministros*] rate; [*de transportes*] fare ▸ **tarifa apex** apex fare ▸ **tarifa bancaria** bank rate ▸ **tarifa de suscripción** subscription rate ▸ **tarifa nocturna** (*Telec*) cheap rate ▸ **tarifa plana** (*para Internet*) flat rate, unmetered access; (*para móviles*) flat rate ▸ **tarifa postal** postal rate ▸ **tarifa reducida** (*Transportes*) reduced fare ▸ **tarifa turística** tourist rates
2 (= *lista de precios*) price list
3 (= *arancel*) tariff ▸ **tarifa aduanera** customs tariff

tarifar ▸ CONJUG 1a VT to price
VI to fall out, quarrel

tarifario ADJ • **política tarifaria** pricing policy • **revisión tarifaria** revision of prices, revision of pricing • **la tendencia tarifaria será la de reducir precios** the tendency will be to reduce prices

tarificación SF metering

tarificar ▸ CONJUG 1g VT to meter

tarima SF **1** (= *plataforma*) platform; (= *estrado*) dais; (= *soporte*) stand
2 (= *suelo*) flooring

tarimaco SM (*Caribe*) = **tareco**

tarja¹ SF (= *palo*) tally (stick)

tarja²* SF (= *golpe*) swipe, bash*

tarjar ▸ CONJUG 1a VT **1** (= *señalar*) to keep a tally of, notch up
2 (*And, Cono Sur*) (= *tachar*) to cross out

tarjeta SF card • **dejar ~** to leave one's card • **pagar con ~** to pay by (credit) card • **pasar ~** to send in one's card ▸ **tarjeta amarilla** (*Dep*) yellow card ▸ **tarjeta bancaria** banker's card, bank card ▸ **tarjeta comercial** business card ▸ **tarjeta de banda magnética** swipe card ▸ **tarjeta de circuitos** (*Inform*) circuit board ▸ **tarjeta de crédito** credit card ▸ **tarjeta de embarque** boarding pass ▸ **tarjeta de expansión** expansion card ▸ **tarjeta de felicitación** greetings card, greeting card (*EEUU*) ▸ **tarjeta de fidelidad** loyalty card ▸ **tarjeta de gráficos** graphics card ▸ **tarjeta de identidad** identity card ▸ **tarjeta de lector** reader's ticket ▸ **tarjeta de memoria** memory card ▸ **tarjeta de multifunción** multifunction card ▸ **tarjeta de Navidad** Christmas card ▸ **tarjeta de periodista** press card ▸ **tarjeta de prepago** (*de móvil*) prepaid card ▸ **tarjeta de presentación** business card ▸ **tarjeta de respuesta** reply card ▸ **tarjeta de respuesta pagada** reply-paid postcard ▸ **tarjeta de saludo** greetings card, greeting card (*EEUU*) ▸ **tarjeta de sonido** sound card ▸ **tarjeta de vídeo** (*Esp*), **tarjeta de video** (*LAm*) video card ▸ **tarjeta de visita** business card, visiting card ▸ **tarjeta dinero** cash card ▸ **tarjeta gráfica** (*Inform*) graphics card ▸ **tarjeta inteligente** smart card ▸ **tarjeta monedero** electronic purse *o* wallet ▸ **tarjeta navideña** Christmas card ▸ **tarjeta perforada** punched card ▸ **tarjeta postal** postcard ▸ **tarjeta (de) prepago** top-up card ▸ **tarjeta roja** (*Dep*) red card ▸ **tarjeta sanitaria europea** European Health Insurance card ▸ **tarjeta SIM** SIM card ▸ **tarjeta telefónica** phonecard ▸ **tarjeta verde** (*Méx*) (= *visado*) Green Card (*EEUU*)

tarjetear ▸ CONJUG 1a VT • **~ a un jugador** to show a card to a player

tarjetero ADJ • **el árbitro se mostró muy ~** (*Ftbl*) the referee was constantly reaching for his pocket, the referee booked a lot of players
SM (= *cartera*) credit card holder, credit card wallet

tarot SM tarot

tarpón SM tarpon

tarquín SM mud, slime, ooze

tarra‡ SMF old geezer‡

tarraconense ADJ of/from Tarragona
SMF native/inhabitant of Tarragona • **los ~s** the people of Tarragona

Tarragona SF Tarragona

tarrajazo SM **1** (*And, Caribe*) (= *suceso*) unpleasant event
2 (*CAm*) (= *golpe*) blow; (= *herida*) wound

tarramenta SF (*Caribe, Méx*) horns (*pl*)

tarrayazo SM **1** (*And, Caribe, Méx*) [*de red*] cast (of a net)
2 (*Caribe*) (= *golpe*) violent blow

tarrear ▸ CONJUG 1a VT (*Caribe*) to cuckold

tarrina SF [*de helado, margarina*] tub

tarro SM **1** (= *recipiente*) [*de vidrio*] jar; [*de porcelana*] pot
2 (*Esp**) (= *cabeza*) nut*, noggin (*EEUU**)
• MODISMOS: • **comer el ~ a algn** (= *engañar*) to put one over on sb*; (= *lavar el cerebro*) to brainwash sb • **comerse el ~** to rack one's brains, think hard
3 (*esp LAm*) (= *lata*) tin, can; (= *bidón*) drum
• MODISMO: • **arrancarse con los ~s*** to run off with the loot*
4 (*And††*) (= *chistera*) top hat
5 (*Cono Sur*) (= *chiripa*) stroke of luck, fluke
6 (*Caribe, Cono Sur*) (= *cuerno*) horn
7 (*Caribe*) [*del marido*] cuckolding
8 (*Caribe*) (= *asunto*) thorny question, complicated affair

tarsana SF (*LAm*) soapbark

tarso SM tarsus

tarta SF **1** (= *pastel*) cake; (*con base de hojaldre*) tart • MODISMO: • **repartir la ~** to divide up the cake ▸ **tarta de bodas** wedding cake ▸ **tarta de cumpleaños** birthday cake ▸ **tarta de frutas** fruitcake ▸ **tarta de manzana** apple tart ▸ **tarta de queso** cheesecake ▸ **tarta nupcial** wedding cake
2 (= *gráfico*) pie chart

tártago SM **1** (*Bot*) spurge
2* (= *desgracia*) mishap, misfortune
3* (= *trastada*) practical joke

tartaja* ADJ INV stammering, tongue-tied
SMF INV stammerer

tartajear ▸ CONJUG 1a VT to stammer

tartajeo SM stammer(ing)

tartajoso/a ADJ, SM/F = **tartaja**

tartalear ▸ CONJUG 1a VI **1** (*al andar*) (*aturdido*) to walk in a daze; (*tambaleándose*) to stagger, reel
2 (*al hablar*) to stammer, be stuck for words

tartamudeante ADJ stuttering, stammering

tartamudear ▸ CONJUG 1a VI to stutter, stammer

tartamudeo SM stutter(ing), stammer(ing)

tartamudez SF stutter, stammer

tartamudo/a ADJ stuttering, stammering
SM/F stutterer, stammerer

tartán SM tartan

tartana SF **1** (= *carruaje*) trap, light carriage
2* (= *auto*) banger*, clunker (*EEUU**)

tartancho ADJ (*And, Cono Sur*) = **tartamudo**

Tartaria SF Tartary

tartárico ADJ tartaric • **ácido ~** tartaric acid

tártaro¹ SM (*Quím*) tartar • **salsa tártara** tartar sauce

tártaro²/a ADJ, SM/F Tartar

tartera SF (= *fiambrera*) lunch box; (*para horno*) cake tin

Tarteso SM Tartessus; (*Biblia*) Tarshish

tarugo ADJ **1*** (= *zoquete*) stupid
2 (*Caribe*) (= *adulador*) fawning
SM **1** (= *pedazo de madera*) lump, chunk; (= *clavija*) wooden peg; (= *tapón*) plug, stopper; (= *adoquín*) wooden paving block
2 (= *pan*) chunk of stale bread
3* (= *imbécil*) chump*, blockhead*
4 (*Caribe**) (= *susto*) fright, scare
5 (*Méx*) (= *miedo*) fear, anxiety
6‡ (= *soborno*) backhander*

tarumba* ADJ • **volver ~ a algn** (= *confundir*) to confuse sb, get sb all mixed up; (= *marear*) to make sb dizzy • **volverse ~** to get all mixed up, get completely confused • **esa chica me tiene ~** I'm crazy about that girl

Tarzán SM Tarzan

tasa SF **1** (= *precio*) rate • **de cero ~** zero-rated ▸ **tasa básica** (*Com*) basic rate ▸ **tasa de aeropuerto** airport tax ▸ **tasa de basuras** refuse *o* (*EEUU*) garbage collection charge ▸ **tasa de cambio** exchange rate ▸ **tasa de descuento bancario** bank rate ▸ **tasa de instrucción** tuition fee ▸ **tasa de interés** interest rate ▸ **tasas académicas** tuition fees ▸ **tasas judiciales** legal fees ▸ **tasas locales, tasas municipales** local taxes
2 (= *índice*) rate ▸ **tasa de crecimiento, tasa de desarrollo** growth rate ▸ **tasa de desempleo** level of unemployment, unemployment rate ▸ **tasa de mortalidad** death rate, mortality rate ▸ **tasa de nacimiento, tasa de natalidad** birth rate

t

▸ **tasa de paro** level of unemployment, unemployment rate ▸ **tasa de rendimiento** (*Com*) rate of return
3 (= *tasación*) valuation, appraisal (*EEUU*)
4 (= *medida, regla*) measure • **sin ~** boundless, limitless • **gastar sin ~** to spend like there's no tomorrow
tasable (ADJ) ratable
tasación (SF) valuation, appraisal (*EEUU*) • **~ de un edificio** valuation of a building ▸ **tasación pericial** expert valuation
tasadamente (ADV) sparingly
tasador(a) (SM/F) valuer, appraiser (*EEUU*) ▸ **tasador(a) de averías** average adjuster ▸ **tasador(a) de impuestos** tax appraiser
tasajear ▸ CONJUG 1a (VT) (*LAm*) 1 (= *cortar*) to cut, slash
2 [+ *carne*] to jerk
tasajo (SM) 1 (= *cecina*) dried beef, jerked beef
2 (*And*) (= *persona*) tall thin person
tasajudo (ADJ) (*LAm*) tall and thin
tasar ▸ CONJUG 1a (VT) 1 (= *valorar*) to value
2 [+ *trabajo*] to rate (**en** at)
3 (= *restringir*) to limit, put a limit on, restrict; (= *racionar*) to ration; (= *escatimar*) to be sparing with; (*pey*) to be mean with, stint • **les tasa a los niños hasta la leche** she even rations her children's milk
tasca (SF) pub, bar • **ir de ~s** to go on a pub crawl*
tascar ▸ CONJUG 1g (VT) 1 [+ *lino*] to swingle, beat
2 [+ *hierba*] to munch, champ; [+ *freno*] to champ at sth
3 (*And*) (= *masticar*) to chew, crunch
Tasmania (SF) Tasmania
tasquear* ▸ CONJUG 1a (VI) (*Esp*) to go drinking, go round the bars
tasqueo* (SM) • **ir de ~** (*Esp*) = **tasquear**
tata* (SM) (*LAm*) (= *padre*) dad*, daddy* (SF) (= *niñera*) nanny; (= *chacha*) maid; ▸ **tato**
tatarabuelo/a (SM/F) great-great-grandfather/-mother • **mis ~s** my great-great-grandparents
tataranieto/a (SM/F) great-great-grandson/-daughter • **sus ~s** his great-great-grandchildren
tatas • **a ~** (ADV) • **andar a ~** (= *hacer pinitos*) to toddle; (= *ir a gatas*) to crawl, get down on all fours
tate[1] (EXCL) (*sorpresa*) gosh!*, crumbs!*; (*al darse cuenta*) so that's it!, oh I see!; (*aviso*) look out!; (*admiración*) bravo!; (*ira*) come now!
tate[2]‡ (SM) (= *marihuana*) hash*, pot‡
ta-te-ti (SM) (*Arg, Uru*) noughts and crosses (*sing*) (*Brit*), tic tac toe (*EEUU*)
tato/a* (SM/F) (= *hermano*) brother/sister (SM) (*LAm**) (= *padre*) dad(dy)*, pop (*EEUU**); ▸ **tata**
tatole* (SM) (*Méx*) plot
tatuaje (SM) 1 (= *dibujo*) tattoo
2 (= *acto*) tattooing
tatuar ▸ CONJUG 1d (VT) to tattoo
tauca (SF) (*And*) 1 (= *objetos*) heap of things
2 (= *bolsa*) large bag
taumaturgia (SF) miracle working, thaumaturgy
taumaturgo (SM) miracle worker
taurinamente (ADV) in bullfighting terms
taurino (ADJ) bullfighting (*antes de s*) • **el mundo ~** the bullfighting business • **una revista taurina** a bullfighting magazine
Tauro (SM) (*Astron, Astrol*) Taurus • **es de ~** (*LAm*) he's (a) Taurus, he's a Taurean
tauro (*Astrol*) (SMF INV) Taurus, Taurean • **los ~ son así** that's what Tauruses *o* Taureans are like
(ADJ INV) Taurus, Taurean • **soy ~** I'm (a) Taurus, I'm a Taurean
taurofobia (SF) dislike of bullfighting
taurófobo/a (SM/F) opponent of bullfighting
taurómaco/a (ADJ) bullfighting (*antes de s*) (SM/F) bullfighting expert
tauromaquia (SF) (art of) bullfighting, tauromachy (*frm*)
tauromáquico (ADJ) bullfighting (*antes de s*)
tautología (SF) tautology
tautológico (ADJ) tautological
TAV (SM ABR) (= **tren de alta velocidad**) HVT
taxativamente (ADV) 1 (= *específicamente*) specifically, in a restricted sense
2 (= *tajantemente*) sharply, emphatically
taxativo (ADJ) 1 (= *restringido*) limited, restricted; [*sentido*] specific
2 (= *tajante*) sharp, emphatic
taxi (SM) taxi, cab • **fuimos en ~** we went by taxi ▸ **taxi colectivo** (*Col*) minibus
taxidermia (SF) taxidermy
taxidermista (SMF) taxidermist
taximetrero/a (SM/F) (*Arg*), **taximetrista** (SMF) (*Arg*) taxi driver, cab driver
taxímetro (SM) 1 (= *aparato*) taximeter, clock
2 (*Arg*) (= *vehículo*) taxi
taxista (SMF) taxi driver, cabby*, cab driver (*EEUU*)
taxonomía (SF) taxonomy
taxonomista (SMF) taxonomist
Tayikistán (SM) Tadzhikistan
taza (SF) 1 (= *recipiente*) cup; (= *contenido*) cupful ▸ **taza de café** (= *café*) cup of coffee; (= *recipiente*) coffee cup
2 [*de fuente*] basin, bowl; [*de lavabo*] bowl; [*de retrete*] pan, bowl ▸ **taza del wáter** toilet bowl
3 (*Cono Sur*) (= *palangana*) washbasin, bathroom sink (*EEUU*) ▸ **taza de noche** (*Cono Sur*) (*euf*) chamber pot
tazado (ADJ) [*ropa*] frayed, worn; [*persona*] shabby
tazar ▸ CONJUG 1f (VT) 1 (= *cortar*) to cut; (= *dividir*) to cut up, divide
2 (= *desgastar*) to fray
(VPR) **tazarse** to fray
tazón (SM) (= *cuenco*) bowl; (= *taza*) large cup; (= *jarra*) mug
TBC (SM ABR) = **tren de bandas en caliente**
TC (SM ABR) = **Tribunal Constitucional**
TCI (SF ABR) (= **Tarjeta de Circuito Impreso**) PCB
TDT (SF ABR) (= **televisión digital terrestre**) DTT, DTTV
TDV (SF ABR) (= **tabla deslizadora a vela**) windsurfing board
te[1] (SF) *name of the letter T*
te[2] (PRON PERS) 1 (*como complemento directo*) you • **te quiero mucho** I love you very much • **ayer te vi en el centro** I saw you in the city centre yesterday
2 (*como complemento indirecto*) you • **te voy a dar un consejo** I'm going to give you some advice • **te he traído esto** I've brought you this, I've brought this for you • **me gustaría comprártelo para navidad** I'd like to buy it for you *o* buy you it for Christmas • **no te lo compro porque lo vendes muy caro** I'm not going to buy from you because you're charging too much for it • **¿te han arreglado el ordenador?** have they fixed your computer (for you)?
3 (*con partes del cuerpo, ropa*) • **¿te duelen los pies?** do your feet hurt? • **¿te has puesto el abrigo?** have you put your coat on?
4 (*uso enfático*) • **te lo comiste todo** you ate it all up • **se te ha caído el bolígrafo** you've dropped your pen • **se te ha parado el reloj** your watch has stopped
5 (*uso reflexivo o pronominal*) • **¿te has lavado?** have you washed? • **¡cálmate!** calm down! • **¿te levantas temprano?** do you get up early? • **tienes que defenderte** you have to defend yourself • **te vas a caer** you'll fall • **te equivocas** you're wrong • **¿te has hecho daño?** have you hurt yourself?
6 (*uso impersonal*) • **aquí siempre te intentan timar** they always try to cheat you here
té (SM) 1 (= *planta, bebida*) tea
2 (= *reunión*) tea party • **dar un té** to give a tea party • MODISMO: • **dar el té a algn*** to bore sb to tears ▸ **té canasta** (*LAm*) *tea party, often in aid of charity, where canasta is played*
tea (SF) 1 (= *antorcha*) torch; (= *astilla*) firelighter • MODISMOS: • **arder como una tea** • **convertirse en una tea** to go up like a torch
2‡ (= *cuchillo*) knife
teatral (ADJ) 1 [*grupo, temporada*] theatre (*antes de s*), theater (*antes de s*) (*EEUU*); [*asociación, formación*] dramatic • **obra ~** play
2 (= *aparatoso*) (= *persona*) theatrical; [*gesto, palabras*] dramatic, theatrical; (*pey*) histrionic, stagey
teatralidad (SF) 1 (= *aparato*) theatricality; (= *drama*) drama; (*pey*) histrionics (*pl*), staginess
2 (= *sentido del teatro*) sense of theatre, stage sense; (*pey*) showmanship
teatralizar ▸ CONJUG 1f (VT) [+ *obra*] to stage; [+ *situación*] to dramatize
teatralmente (ADV) theatrically
teatrero/a* (ADJ) 1 (= *exagerado*) theatrical
2 (= *aficionado*) • **ser muy ~** to be a great theatre-goer
(SM/F) 1 (= *aficionado*) theatre-goer
2 (= *profesional*) theatre-worker
teatro (SM) 1 (*gen*) theatre, theater (*EEUU*); (= *escenario*) stage • **escribir para el ~** to write for the stage • **en el ~ es una persona muy distinta** she's a very different person on the stage • **hacer que se venga abajo el ~** to bring the house down ▸ **teatro amateur, teatro de aficionados** amateur theatre, amateur dramatics ▸ **teatro de calle** street theatre ▸ **teatro del absurdo** theatre of the absurd ▸ **teatro de la ópera** opera house ▸ **teatro de repertorio** repertory theatre ▸ **teatro de títeres** puppet theatre ▸ **teatro de variedades** variety theatre, music hall, vaudeville theater (*EEUU*)
2 (*Literat*) (= *género*) drama; (= *obras de teatro*) plays (*pl*) • **el ~ del siglo XVIII** 18th century theatre *o* drama • **el ~ de Cervantes** Cervantes's plays
3 [*de suceso*] scene; (*Mil*) theatre, theater (*EEUU*) ▸ **teatro de guerra** theatre of war ▸ **teatro de operaciones** theatre of operations
4 (= *exageración*) • **hacer ~** (= *alborotar*) to make a fuss; (= *exagerar*) to exaggerate • **tiene mucho ~** he's always so melodramatic
5 (*LAm*) (= *cine*) cinema, movies (*pl*)
Tebas (SF) Thebes
tebeo (SM) (children's) comic, comic book (*EEUU*) • MODISMO: • **está más visto que el ~** that's old hat ▸ **tebeo de terror** horror comic
tebeoteca (SF) collection of comics
teca (SF) teak
techado (SM) (= *tejado*) roof; (= *cubierta*) covering • **bajo ~** under cover, indoors
techar ▸ CONJUG 1a (VT) to roof (in *o* over)
techo (SM) 1 (*interior*) ceiling; (*exterior*) (*Aut*) roof • **el ~ de mi cuarto está pintado de blanco** the ceiling in my room is painted white • **los ~s de las casas son de pizarra** the houses have slate roofs • **bajo ~** indoors • **tenis bajo ~** indoor tennis • **bajo el mismo ~** under the same roof • **un sin ~** a homeless person • **los sin ~** the homeless ▸ **techo**

corredizo, techo solar (*Aut*) sunroof
2 (= *límite, tope*) ceiling, limit; (*Econ*) ceiling • **ha tocado ~** it has reached its upper limit, it has peaked ▸ **techo de cristal** glass ceiling
3 (*Aer*) ceiling
techumbre SF roof
tecito SM (*esp LAm*) cup of tea
tecla SF (*Inform, Mús, Tip*) key • MODISMOS: • **dar en la ~*** (= *acertar*) to get it right; (= *aprender*) to get the hang of it • **dar en la ~ de hacer algo*** to fall into the habit of doing sth • **tocar ~s**: • **no le queda ninguna otra ~ por tocar** there's nothing else left for him to try ▸ **tecla con flecha** arrow key ▸ **tecla de anulación** cancel key ▸ **tecla de borrado** delete key ▸ **tecla de cambio** shift key ▸ **tecla de control** control key ▸ **tecla de desplazamiento** scroll key ▸ **tecla de edición** edit key ▸ **tecla de función** function key ▸ **tecla de iniciación** booting-up switch ▸ **tecla del cursor** cursor key ▸ **tecla de retorno** return key ▸ **tecla de tabulación** tab key ▸ **tecla programable** user-defined key ▸ **teclas de control direccional del cursor** cursor control keys
teclado SM (*tb Inform*) keyboard, keys (*pl*); [*de órgano*] keyboard, manual • **Gimbel a los ~s** Gimbel on keyboards • **marcación por ~** push-button dialling ▸ **teclado inalámbrico** wireless keyboard, cordless keyboard ▸ **teclado numérico** (*Inform*) numeric keypad
tecle ADJ (*Cono Sur*) weak, sickly
tecleado SM typing
teclear ▹ CONJUG 1a VT 1 (*gen*) to key in, type in; (*en cajero automático*) to enter
2* [+ *problema*] to approach from various angles
3 (*LAm*) [+ *instrumento*] to play clumsily, mess about on; [+ *máquina de escribir*] to mess about on
VI 1 (*en máquina de escribir, ordenador*) to type; (*en el piano*) to play
2* (= *tamborilear*) to drum, tap
3 (*Cono Sur**) [*negocio*] to be going very badly; [*persona*] to be doing very badly • **ando tecleando** I'm doing very badly
tecleo SM 1 (= *tecleado*) typing, keying
2 (*Mús*) playing
3* (= *tamborileo*) drumming, tapping
tecleteo SM = tecleo
teclista SMF (*Inform*) keyboard operator, keyboarder; (*Mús*) keyboard player
teclo/a ADJ (*And*) old
SM/F old man/woman
técnica SF 1 (= *método*) technique
2 (= *tecnología*) technology • **los avances de la ~** advances in technology
3 (= *destreza*) skill; ▹ **técnico**
técnicamente ADV technically
tecnicidad SF technicality, technical nature
tecnicismo SM 1 (= *carácter técnico*) technical nature
2 (*Ling*) technical term, technicality
técnico/a ADJ technical
SM/F 1 (*en fábrica, laboratorio*) technician ▸ **técnico/a de laboratorio** laboratory technician, lab technician* ▸ **técnico/a de mantenimiento** maintenance engineer ▸ **técnico/a de sonido** sound engineer, sound technician ▸ **técnico/a de televisión** television engineer, television repairman ▸ **técnico/a informático/a** computer programmer
2 (= *experto*) expert, specialist • **es un ~ en la materia** he's an expert on the subject
3 (*Dep*) trainer, coach; ▹ **técnica**
tecnicolor® SM Technicolor® • **en ~** in Technicolor
tecnificar ▹ CONJUG 1g VT to make more technical
VPR **tecnificarse** to become more technical
tecno ADJ [*música*] techno
SM (*Mús*) techno
tecno... PREF techno...
tecnocracia SF technocracy
tecnócrata SMF technocrat
tecnocrático ADJ technocratic
tecnofóbico ADJ technophobic
tecnología SF technology • **alta ~** high technology • **nuevas ~s** new technologies ▸ **tecnología Bluetooth**® Bluetooth® technology ▸ **tecnología de alimentos** food technology ▸ **tecnología de estado sólido** solid-state technology ▸ **tecnología de la información** information technology ▸ **tecnología inalámbrica** wireless technology ▸ **tecnología punta** leading-edge technology
tecnológicamente ADV technologically
tecnológico ADJ technological
tecnólogo/a SM/F technologist
teco* ADJ (*CAm, Méx*) drunk
tecolote SM 1 (*CAm, Méx*) (= *búho*) owl
2 (*Méx**) (= *policía*) policeman, cop*
ADJ 1 (*CAm*) [*color*] reddish-brown
2 (*CAm, Méx*) (= *borracho*) drunk
tecomate SM (*CAm, Méx*) 1 (= *calabaza*) gourd, calabash
2 (= *recipiente*) earthenware bowl
tecorral SM (*Méx*) dry-stone wall
tectónica SF tectonics (*sing*)
tectónico ADJ tectonic
tecuán ADJ (*CAm, Méx*) greedy, voracious
SM monster
tedio SM (= *aburrimiento*) boredom, tedium; (= *vaciedad*) sense of emptiness • **me produce ~** it just depresses me
tedioso ADJ tedious
tefe SM 1 (*And*) (= *cuero*) strip of leather; (= *tela*) strip of cloth
2 (*And*) (= *cicatriz*) scar on the face
tegumento SM tegument
Teherán SM Teheran
tehuacán SM (*Méx*) mineral water
Teide SM • **el (pico de) ~** Mount Teide, Mount Teyde
teína SF theine
teísmo SM theism
teísta ADJ theistic
SMF theist
teja[1] SF (roof) tile • **de color ~** brick red • MODISMOS: • **pagar a toca ~*** to pay on the nail • **de ~s abajo** in this world, in the natural way of things • **de ~s arriba** in the next world • **por fin le cayó la ~** (*Cono Sur*) finally the penny dropped ▸ **tejas de pizarra** slates
teja[2] SF (*Bot*) lime (tree)
tejadillo SM top, cover
tejado SM (tiled) roof • MODISMO: • **tiene el ~ de vidrio** people who live in glass houses shouldn't throw stones, it's the pot calling the kettle black
tejamaní SM (*LAm*), **tejamanil** SM (*LAm*) roofing board, shingle
tejano/a ADJ, SM/F Texan
SMPL **tejanos** (= *vaqueros*) jeans, denims
tejar[1] ▹ CONJUG 1a VT to tile, roof with tiles • **~ un techo** to tile a roof
tejar[2] SM tile factory
Tejas SM Texas
tejaván SM (*LAm*) (= *cobertizo*) shed; (= *galería*) gallery; (= *choza*) rustic dwelling
tejavana SF (= *cobertizo*) shed; (= *tejado*) shed roof, plain tile roof
tejedor(a) SM/F 1 (= *artesano*) weaver
2 (*And, Cono Sur*) (= *intrigante*) schemer, meddler
tejedora SF (= *máquina*) (*de hacer punto*) knitting machine; (*de tejer*) loom
tejedura SF 1 (= *acto*) weaving
2 (= *textura*) weave, texture
tejeduría SF 1 (= *arte*) (art of) weaving
2 (= *fábrica*) textile mill
tejemaneje* SM 1 (= *intriga*) intrigue; (= *chanchullo*) shady deal* • **los políticos y sus ~s** politicians and their shady deals*
2 (= *actividad*) bustle; (= *bulla*) fuss • **se trae un tremendo ~** he's making a tremendous fuss
tejer ▹ CONJUG 2a VT 1 [+ *tela*] to weave; [+ *tela de araña*] to spin, make; [+ *capullo*] to spin • **tejido a mano** hand-woven
2 (= *hacer punto*) to knit; (= *hacer ganchillo*) to crochet; (= *coser*) to sew • **tejido a mano** hand-knitted
3 [+ *complot*] to hatch; [+ *plan*] to devise; [+ *mentira*] to fabricate; [+ *cambio etc*] to bring about little by little
VI 1 (*en telar*) to weave • MODISMO: • **~ y destejer** to chop and change, do and undo (*EEUU*)
2 (= *hacer punto*) to knit; (= *hacer ganchillo*) to crochet; (= *coser*) to sew
tejerazo* SM (*Esp*) (*Hist*) • **el ~** *the coup attempted by Col Tejero on 23 February 1981*
tejeringo SM fritter
tejido SM 1 (= *tela*) fabric, material • **el ~ social** the social fabric ▸ **tejido de punto** knitting, knitted fabric
2 (= *trama*) weave; (= *textura*) texture • **un ~ de intrigas** a web of intrigue
3 (*Anat*) tissue ▸ **tejido conjuntivo** connective tissue
tejo[1] SM 1 (= *aro*) ring, quoit • MODISMO: • **echar** *o* **tirar los ~s a algn*** to make a play for sb
2 (= *juego*) hopscotch
3 (*Esp*†*) *5-peseta piece*
tejo[2] SM (*Bot*) yew (tree)
tejoleta SF shard
tejón SM badger
tejudo SM label (*on spine of book*)
tel. ABR (= **teléfono**) tel
tela SF 1 (= *tejido*) cloth, fabric; (= *trozo*) piece of cloth • **esta ~ es muy resistente** this cloth *o* fabric is very strong • **usó una ~ para hacer el remiendo** she used a piece of cloth as a patch • **un libro en ~** a clothbound book • MODISMO: • **poner en ~ de juicio** to (call into) question, cast doubt on ▸ **tela asfáltica** roofing felt ▸ **tela cruzada** twill ▸ **tela de araña** spider's web ▸ **tela de saco** sackcloth ▸ **tela metálica** wire netting ▸ **tela mosquitera** mosquito net
2 (*Arte*) (= *lienzo*) canvas, painting
3 (*en líquido*) skin
4 (*Anat*) membrane • MODISMO: • **llegarle a algn a las ~s del corazón** to touch sb's heart
5 (*Bot*) skin ▸ **tela de cebolla** onion skin
6‡ (= *dinero*) dough*, cash* • **sacudir** *o* **soltar la ~** to cough up*, fork out*
7 (*And*) (= *tortilla*) thin maize pancake
8* (*tb* **tela marinera**) • **el asunto tiene (mucha) ~** *o* **tiene ~ (marinera)** it's a complicated matter, there's a lot to it • **—ya va por el quinto marido —¡tiene ~ (marinera)!** "she's already on her fifth husband" — "that takes some beating!"* • **hay ~ para rato** there's lots to talk about
9‡ (*enfático*) • **~ de: es ~ de guapa** she's dead *o* really gorgeous*
telabrejos SMPL (*LAm*) things, gear, odds and ends
telanda* SF brass*, money
telar SM 1 (= *máquina*) loom; **telares** (= *fábrica*) textile mill (*sing*)
2 (*Teat*) gridiron
telaraña SF cobweb, spider's web

t

Tel Aviv SM Tel Aviv

tele* SF telly*, TV • **mirar** *o* **ver la ~** to watch telly • **salir en** *o* **por la ~** to be on telly*, be on the box*

tele... PREF tele...

teleadicto/a* SM/F telly addict*

telealarma SF alarm (system)

telebaby SM (PL: **telebabys**) cable car

telebanco SM cash dispenser

telebasura* SF trash TV

telebrejos SMPL (*Méx*) = **telabrejos**

telecabina SF cable-car

telecámara SF television camera

telecargar ▹ CONJUG 1h VT (*Inform*) to download

teleco* SMF (= *ingeniero*) telecoms engineer
SF **1** (= *empresa*) telecoms company
2 (= *ingeniería*) telecoms, telecommunications engineering

telecomando SM remote control

telecomedia SF TV comedy show

telecompra SF TV shopping

telecomunicación SF telecommunication

teleconferencia SF (= *reunión*) teleconference; (= *sistema*) teleconferencing

telecontrol SM remote control

telecopia SF (= *sistema*) fax (system); (= *mensaje*) fax (message)

telecopiadora SF telecopier

telediario SM television news bulletin

teledifusión SF telecast

teledirigido ADJ remote-controlled, radio-controlled

telef. ABR (= **teléfono**) tel

telefacsímil SM, **telefax** SM (= *sistema*) fax (system); (= *mensaje*) fax (message)

teleférico SM cable railway, cableway, aerial tramway (*EEUU*); (*para esquiadores*) ski lift

telefilm SM, **telefilme** SM TV film

telefonazo* SM telephone call • **te daré un ~** I'll give you a ring *o* call

telefonear ▹ CONJUG 1a VT, VI to telephone, phone (up)

telefonema SM telephone message

telefonía SF telephony • **red de ~ móvil** mobile phone (*Brit*) *o* cellphone (*EEUU*) network • **servicios de ~ móvil** mobile phone (*Brit*) *o* cellphone (*EEUU*) services ▸ **telefonía celular** mobile phone (*Brit*) *o* cellphone (*EEUU*) system ▸ **telefonía fija** landline phones (*pl*)

Telefónica SF • **la ~** *former Spanish national telephone company*

telefónicamente ADV by telephone • **fue amenazado ~** he received threatening phone calls

telefónico ADJ telephone (*antes de s*), telephonic • **llamada telefónica** telephone call • **listín ~** telephone book • **marketing ~** telemarketing, telesales (*pl*)

telefonillo SM entry phone

telefonista SMF (telephone) operator, telephonist

teléfono SM **1** (= *aparato*) telephone, phone; (= *número*) telephone number, phone number • **todas las habitaciones tienen ~** there are telephones in all the rooms • **¿tienes ~?** do you have a phone?, are you on the phone? • **apunta mi ~** write down my phone number • **coger el ~** • **contestar al ~** to answer the phone • **está hablando por ~** he's on the phone • **llamar a algn por ~** to phone sb (up), ring sb up • **te llaman por** *o* **al ~** there's someone on the phone for you ▸ **teléfono celular** mobile phone (*Brit*), cellphone (*EEUU*) ▸ **teléfono con cámara** camera phone ▸ **teléfono de la esperanza** ≈ Samaritans (*pl*) ▸ **teléfono de tarjeta** card phone ▸ **teléfono erótico** sex line ▸ **teléfono fijo** landline (phone) ▸ **teléfono gratuito** Freefone® ▸ **teléfono inalámbrico** cordless (tele)phone ▸ **teléfono inteligente** smartphone ▸ **teléfono IP** IP phone ▸ **teléfono móvil** mobile (phone) (*Brit*), cellphone (*EEUU*) ▸ **teléfono móvil de coche** car phone ▸ **teléfono particular** home telephone number ▸ **teléfono rojo** (*Pol*) hotline ▸ **teléfono sin hilos** cordless (tele) phone ▸ **teléfono wap** WAP(-enabled) phone; ▹ **colgar**
2 [*de ducha*] shower head

telefotografía SF, **telefoto** SF telephoto

telefotográfico ADJ telephoto (*antes de s*)

telegenia SF telegenic quality

telegénico ADJ telegenic

telegrafía SF telegraphy

telegrafiar ▹ CONJUG 1c VT, VI to telegraph

telegráficamente ADJ briefly

telegráfico ADJ telegraphic, telegraph (*antes de s*)

telegrafista SMF telegraphist

telégrafo SM telegraph ▸ **telégrafo óptico** semaphore

telegrama SM telegram, wire (*EEUU*) • **poner un ~ a algn** to send sb a telegram

teleimpresor SM, **teleimpresora** SF teleprinter

teleindicador SM TV monitor

teleinformático ADJ telematic

telele* SM fit, queer turn • **le dio un ~** it gave him quite a turn

telemandado ADJ remote-controlled

telemando SM remote control

telemanía SF TV addiction

telemaratón SM telethon

telemarketing SM, **telemárketing** SM telesales (*pl*)

telemática SF data transmission, telematics (*sing*)

telemático ADJ telematic

telemedida SF telemetry

telemedir ▹ CONJUG 3k VT to telemeter

telémetro SM rangefinder

telengues SMPL (*CAm*) things, gear, odds and ends

telenoticias SFPL television news (*sing*), TV news (*sing*)

telenovela SF soap (opera), TV serial

telenque ADJ (*Cono Sur*) weak, feeble

teleobjetivo SM telephoto lens, zoom lens

teleología SF teleology

teleoperador(a) SM/F telemarketing phone operator

telépata SMF telepathist, telepath

telepate SM (*CAm*) bedbug

telepatía SF telepathy

telepáticamente ADV telepathically

telepático ADJ telepathic

telepredicador(a) SMF televangelist

teleproceso SM teleprocessing

telequinesia SF telekinesis

telerrealidad SF reality TV

telerregulación SF adjustment by remote control

telescopar ▹ CONJUG 1a VT to telescope
VPR **telescoparse** to telescope

telescópico ADJ telescopic

telescopio SM telescope

teleserie SF TV series

telesilla SM o SF chair lift, ski lift

telespectador(a) SM/F viewer

telesquí SM ski lift

teletaquilla SF pay-per-view television • **partidos de fútbol en ~** pay-per-view football matches

teletaxi SM radio cab, radio taxi

teletex SM, **teletexto** SM teletext

teletienda SF home shopping

teletipista SMF teletypist, teleprinter operator

teletipo SM teletype, teleprinter

teletrabajador(a) SM/F teleworker

teletrabajar ▹ CONJUG 1a VI to telework

teletrabajo SM teleworking

teletransportar ▹ CONJUG 1a VT to teleport

teletransporte SM teleportation

teletratamiento SM teleprocessing

teletubo SM cathode-ray tube, television tube

televendedor(a) SM/F telesales person

televenta SF, **televentas** SFPL telesales

televidente SMF viewer

televisar ▹ CONJUG 1a VT to televise

televisión SF television, TV • **hacer ~** to work in television *o* TV • **salir en** *o* **por la ~** to be on television *o* TV • **ver la ~** to watch television *o* TV ▸ **televisión a la carta** TV on demand ▸ **televisión comercial** commercial television, commercial TV ▸ **televisión de alta definición** high-definition television, high-definition TV ▸ **televisión de circuito cerrado** closed-circuit television, closed-circuit TV ▸ **televisión digital** digital television, digital TV ▸ **televisión digital terrestre** digital terrestrial television, digital terrestrial TV ▸ **televisión en color** colour *o* (*EEUU*) color television, colour *o* (*EEUU*) color TV ▸ **televisión interactiva** interactive television, interactive TV ▸ **televisión matinal** breakfast television, breakfast TV ▸ **televisión pagada** pay television, pay TV ▸ **televisión por cable** cable television, cable TV ▸ **televisión por satélite** satellite television, satellite TV

televisivo/a ADJ **1** television (*antes de s*) • **serie televisiva** television series
2 (= *de interés televisivo*) televisual; [*persona*] telegenic
SM/F television personality

televisor SM television set, TV ▸ **televisor de plasma** plasma TV

televisual ADJ television (*antes de s*)

télex SM INV telex

telón SM (*Teat*) curtain ▸ **telón de acero** (*Pol*) Iron Curtain ▸ **telón de boca** front curtain ▸ **telón de fondo, telón de foro** backcloth, backdrop ▸ **telón de seguridad** safety curtain ▸ **telón metálico** fire curtain

telonero/a ADJ (*Mús*) [*grupo*] support (*antes de s*)
SM/F (*Mús*) support band, support act; (*Teat*) first turn, curtain-raiser

telúrico ADJ **1** (= *de la Tierra*) • **movimiento ~** earthquake
2 [*fuerzas, corrientes*] telluric

tema SM **1** (= *asunto*) subject • **luego hablaremos de ese ~** we'll talk about that subject later • **el ~ de su discurso** the subject *o* theme of his speech • **es un ~ muy manoseado** it's a hackneyed *o* well-worn theme • **es un ~ recurrente en su obra** it is a recurring theme in his work • **tienen ~ para rato** they have plenty to talk about • **cambiar de ~** to change the subject • **pasar del ~***: • **—¿qué piensas de las elecciones? —paso del ~** "what do you think about the elections?" — "I couldn't care less about them"* ▸ **tema de actualidad** topical issue ▸ **tema de conversación** talking point ▸ **temas de actualidad** current affairs
2 (*Ling*) [*de palabra*] stem; [*de oración*] theme
3 (*Mús*) theme

temar ▹ CONJUG 1a VI (*Cono Sur*) **1** (= *tener idea fija*) to have a mania, be obsessed
2 (= *tener inquina*) to bear ill will • **~ con algn** to have a grudge against sb

temario SM **1** (*Univ*) (= *temas*) list of topics; (= *programa*) programme, program (*EEUU*);

(= *asignaturas*) syllabus
2 [*de oposiciones*] set of topics
3 [*de conferencia, reunión*] agenda
temascal SM (*CAm, Méx*) bathroom; (*fig*) hot place, oven
temática SF **1** (= *conjunto de temas*) subjects (*pl*)
2 (= *tema*) [*de obra, película*] subject matter
temático ADJ **1** [*acuerdo, trato*] thematic • **las preguntas deben ordenarse por bloques ~s** questions must be grouped by *o* according to topic • **parque ~** theme park
2 (*Ling*) stem (*antes de s*)
3 (*And*) (= *poco prudente*) injudicious, tasteless
tembladera* SF **1** (= *tembleque*) violent shaking, trembling fit
2 (*LAm*) quagmire
tembladeral SM (*Cono Sur, Méx*) quagmire
temblar ▸ CONJUG 1j VI **1** [*persona*] **a** (*por miedo*) to tremble, shake; (*por frío*) to shiver • **me temblaba la mano** my hand was trembling *o* shaking • **~ de miedo** to tremble *o* shake with fright • **~ de frío** to shiver with cold • MODISMO: • **~ como un azogado** to shake like a leaf, tremble all over
b (= *sentir miedo*) • **echarse a ~** to get frightened • **tiemblo de pensar en lo que pueda ocurrir** I shudder to think what may happen • **~ ante la escena** to shudder at the sight • **~ por su vida** to fear for one's life
2 [*edificio*] to shake, shudder; [*tierra*] to shake • MODISMO: • **dejar una botella temblando*** to use most of a bottle
tembleque* SM **1** (= *temblor*) violent shaking, shaking fit • **le entró un ~** he got the shakes, he began to shake violently
2 (*LAm*) (= *persona*) weakling
temblequeante* ADJ [*andar*] doddery, wobbly, tottering; [*voz*] quivering, tremulous
temblequear* ▸ CONJUG 1a VI (= *temblar*) to shake violently, be all of a quiver; (= *tambalearse*) to wobble
temblequera* SF **1** (= *temblor*) shaking; (= *tambaleo*) wobbling
2 (*And, Caribe*) (= *miedo*) fear; (= *temblor*) trembling
temblón ADJ trembling, shaking • **álamo ~** aspen
SM aspen
temblor SM **1** [*de miedo*] trembling, shaking; [*de frío, fiebre*] shivering • **uno de los síntomas es un ligero ~ en las manos** one of the symptoms is a slight trembling *o* shaking of the hands • **cuando la vio le dio un ~** he trembled when he saw her • **le entró un ~ violento** he began to shake violently • **los ~es son síntomas de fiebre** shivering is a symptom of fever
2 (*tb* **temblor de tierra**) earthquake, (earth) tremor
temblorosamente ADV **1** [*hablar*] tremulously
2 [*moverse*] tremblingly
tembloroso ADJ **1** [*persona*] (*por miedo*) shaking, trembling; (*por frío*) shivering • **con voz temblorosa** in a tremulous *o* shaky voice
2 [*llama*] flickering
tembo ADJ (*And*) featherbrained, stupid
temer ▸ CONJUG 2a VT [+ *persona, castigo, consecuencias*] to be afraid of, fear • **teme al profesor** he's afraid *o* frightened of the teacher • **~ a Dios** to fear God • **~ hacer algo** to be afraid of doing sth • **temo ofenderles** I'm afraid of offending them • **~ que** to be afraid (that), fear (that) • **teme que no vaya a volver** she's afraid *o* she fears (that) he might not come back
VI to be afraid • **no temas** don't be afraid • **~ por algo** to fear for sth • **~ por la seguridad de algn** to fear for sb's safety • **el equipo de rescate temía por nuestras vidas** the rescue team feared for our lives
VPR **temerse** • **~se algo: ya me lo temía, es el carburador** it's the carburettor, I thought as much *o* I was afraid it might be • **—ha empezado a llover —me lo temía** "it has started raining" — "I was afraid it would" • **—no podré venir —me lo estaba temiendo** "I won't be able to come" — "I was afraid you wouldn't" • **se temen lo peor** they fear the worst • **~se que** to be afraid (that) • **mucho me temo que ya no lo encontrarás** I'm very much afraid (that) you won't find it now, I very much suspect (that) you won't find it now • **me temo que no** I'm afraid not
temerariamente ADV (= *sin prudencia*) rashly, recklessly; (= *sin reflexión*) hastily; (= *con audacia*) boldly
temerario ADJ **1** [*persona, acto*] (= *imprudente*) rash, reckless; (= *audaz*) bold
2 [*juicio*] hasty, rash
temeridad SF **1** (= *imprudencia*) rashness; (= *audacia*) boldness; (= *prisa*) hastiness
2 (= *acto*) rash act, folly
temerón ADJ bullying, ranting, loud-mouthed
SM bully, ranter
temerosamente ADV fearfully
temeroso ADJ **1** (= *con temor*) fearful, frightened
2 • **~ de Dios** God-fearing, full of the fear of God
3 (= *espantoso*) fearsome
temible ADJ fearsome, frightful; [*adversario*] fearsome, redoubtable
temor SM (= *miedo*) fear • **~ a** fear of • **por ~ from fear** • **por ~ a** for fear of • **por ~ a equivocarme** for fear of making a mistake • **sin ~ a** without fear of ▸ **temor de Dios** fear of God
témpano SM **1** (*tb* **témpano de hielo**) ice floe • MODISMO: • **como un ~** as cold as ice, ice-cold • **quedarse como un ~*** to be chilled to the bone
2 (= *tamboril*) small drum, kettledrum
3 (= *parche*) drumhead
4 (*Arquit*) tympan
5 ▸ **témpano de tocino** (*Culin*) flitch of bacon
témpera SM tempera
temperadero SM (*LAm*) summer resort
temperado ADJ (*And*) = **templado**
temperamental ADJ temperamental
temperamento SM **1** (= *manera de ser*) temperament, nature • **tiene un ~ muy equilibrado** he has a very balanced temperament • **es una mujer de ~ emprendedor** she is a woman with an enterprising nature
2 (= *genio*) temperament • **tener ~** to be temperamental
temperancia SF temperance
temperante (*LAm*) ADJ teetotal
SMF teetotaller, abstainer
temperar ▸ CONJUG 1a VT (= *moderar*) to temper; (= *calmar*) to calm; (= *aliviar*) to relieve
VI (*LAm*) (= *veranear*) to spend the summer, summer; (= *cambiar de aires*) to have a change of air, have a change of climate
temperatura SF temperature • **a ~ ambiente** at room temperature • **descenso/aumento de las ~s** fall/rise in temperature • **tomar la ~ a algn** to take sb's temperature
temperie SF (state of the) weather
tempestad SF storm • **levantar una ~ de protestas** to raise a storm of protest • **el libro ha cosechado una ~ de críticas** the book has provoked a storm of criticism • **"La Tempestad" de Shakespeare** Shakespeare's "Tempest" ▸ **tempestad de arena** sandstorm ▸ **tempestad de nieve** snowstorm ▸ **tempestad de polvo** dust storm
tempestivo ADJ timely
tempestuoso ADJ stormy
templado ADJ **1** [*líquido, comida*] lukewarm; [*clima*] mild, temperate; (*Geog*) [*zona*] temperate
2 (= *moderado*) moderate, restrained; (*en comer*) frugal; (*en beber*) of sober habits, abstemious • **nervios ~s** nerves of steel
3 (*Mús*) well-tuned
4 (= *valiente*) brave, courageous; (= *franco*) bold, forthright
5* (= *listo*) bright, lively; (*CAm, Méx*) (= *hábil*) able, competent
6 (*And*) (= *severo*) severe
7 (*And, Caribe*) (= *borracho*) tipsy
8 • MODISMO: • **estar ~** (*And, Cono Sur*) to be in love
SM (*Téc*) tempering, hardening
templanza SF **1** (= *virtud*) temperance
2 (*Meteo*) mildness
templar ▸ CONJUG 1a VT **1** [+ *comida*] (= *calentar*) to warm up; (= *enfriar*) to cool down
2 [+ *clima*] to make mild; [+ *calor*] to reduce
3 (= *moderar*) to moderate; [+ *ánimos*] to calm; [+ *cólera*] to restrain, control
4 (*Quím*) [+ *solución*] to dilute
5 [+ *acero*] to temper, harden
6 (*Mús*) to tune (up)
7 (*Mec*) to adjust; [+ *tornillo*] to tighten up; [+ *resorte*] to set properly
8 (*Arte*) [+ *colores*] to blend
9 (*And*) (= *derribar*) to knock down; (*CAm*) (= *golpear*) to hit, beat up; (*And*) (= *matar*) to kill, bump off*
10 (*Caribe***) to screw**, fuck**
VI **1** (*Meteo*) (= *refrescar*) to get cooler; (= *hacer más calor*) to get warmer, get milder
2 (*Caribe*) (= *huir*) to flee
VPR **templarse 1** [*agua, ambiente*] (= *calentarse*) to warm up, get warm; (= *enfriarse*) to cool down
2 [*persona*] to be moderate, act with restraint • **~se en la comida** to eat frugally
3 (*And, CAm*) (= *morir*) to die, kick the bucket*
4 (*Caribe, Méx*) (= *huir*) to flee
5 (*And, Caribe*) (= *emborracharse*) to get tipsy
6 (*Cono Sur*) (= *enamorarse*) to fall in love
7 (*Cono Sur*) (= *excederse*) to go too far, overstep the mark
8 • **templárselas** (*And*) to stand firm
templario SM Templar
temple SM **1** (*Téc*) (= *proceso*) tempering; (= *efecto*) temper
2 (*Mús*) tuning
3 (= *humor*) mood • **estar de mal ~** to be in a bad mood
4 (= *coraje*) courage, boldness; (= *espíritu*) mettle, spirit
5 (= *pintura*) distemper; (*Arte*) tempera • **pintar al ~** to distemper; (*Arte*) to paint in tempera
6 (*Meteo*) state of the weather, temperature
7 (*LAm*) (= *enamoramiento*) infatuation
templete SM **1** (*en parque*) pavilion, kiosk ▸ **templete de música** bandstand
2 (= *templo*) small temple; (= *santuario*) shrine; (= *nicho*) niche
templo SM **1** (= *edificio de culto*) temple • **el ~ de Apolo** the Temple of Apollo • MODISMOS: • **como un ~*** (= *enorme*) huge, enormous; (= *excelente*) first-rate, excellent • **una verdad como un ~** a glaring truth
2 (= *iglesia*) church ▸ **templo metodista** Methodist church *o* chapel ▸ **templo**

protestante Protestant church

templón* SM (*Ven*) pull, tug

tempo SM tempo

temporada SF **1** (= *periodo determinado*) season • **los mejores goles de la ~** the best goals of the season • **en plena ~** at the height of the season • **estar fuera de ~** to be out of season ▸ **temporada alta** high season ▸ **temporada baja** low season ▸ **temporada de caza** open season ▸ **temporada de esquí** ski season ▸ **temporada de exámenes** examination period ▸ **temporada de fútbol** football season ▸ **temporada de ópera** opera season ▸ **temporada media** mid-season
2 (= *periodo indeterminado*) period • **pasa muchas ~s en el extranjero** she spends long periods abroad • **llevan una ~ de peleas continuas** they've been going through a phase *o* period of constant squabbling • **nos vamos a pasar una temporadita al campo** we're going to spend some time in the country • **a** *o* **por ~s** on and off • **—¿tienes mucho trabajo? —va a** *o* **por ~s** "have you got a lot of work?" — "it's a bit on and off *o* it goes in phases"*

temporadista SMF (*Caribe*) holiday-maker, vacationer (EEUU)

temporal ADJ **1** (= *provisional*) temporary; [*trabajo*] temporary, casual; (*en turismo, agricultura*) seasonal • **empresa de trabajo ~** temp recruitment agency
2 (*Rel*) temporal • **poder ~** temporal power
3 (*Anat*) temporal
SM **1** (= *tormenta*) storm; (= *mal tiempo*) spell of rough weather • MODISMO: • **capear el ~** to weather the storm, ride out the storm ▸ **temporal de agua, temporal de lluvia** (= *tormenta*) rainstorm; (= *período lluvioso*) rainy weather, prolonged rain ▸ **temporal de nieve** (= *tormenta*) snowstorm; (= *período de nevadas*) snowy weather
2 (*Anat*) temporal bone
3 (*Caribe*) (= *persona*) shady character

temporalero/a SM/F (*Méx*) *wet-season agricultural worker*

temporalidad SF temporariness, temporary nature

temporalmente ADV temporarily

temporáneo ADJ temporary

temporario ADJ (*LAm*) temporary

témporas SFPL ember days; ▹ **culo**

temporero/a ADJ [*obrero*] (= *eventual*) temporary, casual; (= *de temporada*) seasonal
SM/F (= *eventual*) casual worker; (= *de temporada*) seasonal worker

temporizador ADJ • **mecanismo ~** timing device
SM timer, timing device

temporizar ▹ CONJUG 1f VI to temporize

tempozonte ADJ (*Méx*) hunchbacked

tempranal ADJ early

tempranear ▹ CONJUG 1a VI **1** (*LAm*) to get up early
2 (*Cono Sur*) (*Agr*) to sow early

tempranero ADJ **1** [*fruta*] early
2 [*persona*] • **ser ~** to be an early riser

temprano ADJ early • **a una edad temprana** at an early age
ADV early • **saldremos por la mañana ~** we shall be leaving early in the morning • **ayer me acosté ~** I went to bed early yesterday • **aún es ~ para conocer los resultados** it's too soon to know the results yet

ten ▹ **tener**

tenacidad SF **1** (= *perseverancia*) tenacity
2 (= *persistencia*) [*de dolor*] persistence; [*de mancha*] stubbornness; [*de creencia*] strength, stubbornness (*pey*); [*de resistencia*] tenacity
3 [*de material*] toughness, resilience

tenacillas SFPL (*para azúcar*) sugar tongs; (*para cabello*) curling tongs, curling iron (*sing*) (EEUU); (*Med*) tweezers, forceps; (*para velas*) snuffers

tenamaste ADJ (*CAm, Méx*) stubborn
SM **1** (*CAm, Méx*) (= *piedra*) cooking stone
2 (*CAm*) = **cachivache**

tenaz ADJ **1** [*persona*] (= *perseverante*) tenacious, persistent
2 (= *persistente*) [*dolor*] persistent; [*mancha*] stubborn; [*creencia*] firm, stubborn (*pey*); [*resistencia*] tenacious
3 [*material*] tough, durable, resistant

tenaza SF **1** (*Bridge*) squeeze (**a** in)
2 tenazas (*Téc*) pliers, pincers; [*de cocina, para el fuego*] tongs; (*Med*) forceps

tenazmente ADV (= *con perseverancia*) tenaciously; (= *con tozudez*) stubbornly

tenazón • **a** *o* **de ~** ADV (= *de pronto*) suddenly; [*disparar*] without taking aim

tenca¹ SF (= *pez*) tench

tenca² SF (*Cono Sur*) (= *engaño*) lie, swindle

tencal SM (*Méx*) wicker box, wicker poultry cage

tencel® SM Tencel®

tencha* SF (*CAm*) prison

tendajo SM = **tendejón**

tendal* SM **1** (*LAm*) (= *montón*) load*, heap* • **un ~ de** a load of*, a whole heap of*
2 (= *toldo*) awning
3 (*Agr*) (*para aceitunas*) *sheet spread to catch olives when shaken from the tree*
4 (*Cono Sur*) (*Agr*) (*para esquilar*) shearing shed; (*And, CAm*) (*para secar café*) *sunny place for drying coffee*
5 (*And*) (= *campo*) flat open field
6 (*And, Caribe*) (= *fábrica*) brickworks, tileworks

tendalada* SF (*LAm*) *a lot of scattered objects or people* • **una ~ de** a lot of, loads of*

tendear ▹ CONJUG 1a VI (*Méx*) to go window-shopping

tendedera SF **1** (*CAm, Caribe, Méx*) (= *cuerda*) clothesline
2 (*And*) = **tendal**

tendedero SM (= *lugar*) drying place; (= *cuerda*) clothesline, washing line; (= *armazón*) clothes horse

tendejón SM (= *tienda*) small shop; (= *cobertizo*) stall, booth

tendencia SF tendency, trend • **la ~ hacia el socialismo** the tendency *o* trend towards socialism • **una palabra con ~ a quedarse arcaica** a word which is tending to become archaic • **tener ~ a hacer algo** to have a tendency *o* to tend to do sth • **tengo ~ a engordar** I have a tendency *o* I tend to put on weight • MODISMO: • **marcar ~** to set a trend ▸ **tendencia a la baja** downward trend ▸ **tendencia al alza, tendencia alcista** upward trend ▸ **tendencia bajista** downward trend ▸ **tendencia imperante** dominant trend, prevailing tendency ▸ **tendencias del mercado** market trends

tendenciosidad SF tendentiousness

tendencioso ADJ tendentious

tendente ADJ • **una actitud ~ al minimalismo** an attitude tending towards minimalism • **una medida ~ a mejorar los servicios** a measure designed to improve services

tender ▹ CONJUG 2g VT **1** (= *extender*) [+ *herido, paciente*] to lay; [+ *mantel*] to spread • **lo tendieron en la cama** they laid him on the bed • **tendieron el cadáver sobre el suelo** they laid the corpse out on the floor • **tendí la toalla sobre la arena** I spread the towel (out) on the sand
2 (= *colgar*) [+ *ropa*] to hang out; [+ *cuerda*] to stretch
3 (= *alargar*) [+ *lápiz, libro*] to hold out • **me tendió la mano** he stretched *o* held out his hand to me
4 [+ *trampa*] to set, lay • **le tendieron una trampa** they set *o* laid a trap for him • **nos han tendido una emboscada** we've been ambushed
5 (= *construir*) [+ *puente, ferrocarril*] to build; [+ *cable, vía*] to lay
6 (*LAm*) • **~ la cama** to make the bed • **~ la mesa** to lay the table, set the table
7 [+ *arco*] to draw
VI **1** • **~ a hacer algo** to tend to do sth • **en octubre las temperaturas tienden a bajar** temperatures tend to fall in October • **las prendas de lana tienden a encoger** woollen clothes tend to shrink
2 • **~ a algo** to tend to *o* towards sth • **tiende al egocentrismo** she tends to self-centredness • **la inflación tiende al alza** the trend is for inflation to go up • **el color tiende a verde** the colour is verging on *o* has a tendency towards green • **las plantas tienden a la luz** plants grow *o* turn towards the light
VPR **tenderse 1** (= *acostarse*) to lie down, stretch (o.s.) out
2 [*caballo*] to run at full gallop
3 (*Naipes*) to lay down
4† (= *despreocuparse*) to give up, let things go

ténder SM (*Ferro*) tender

tenderete SM **1** (*en mercado*) (= *puesto*) (market) stall; (= *carretón*) barrow • **montar un ~** to set up a stall
2 (= *géneros*) display of goods for sale
3 (*para ropa lavada*) = **tendedero**

tendero/a SM/F (*gen*) shopkeeper, storekeeper (EEUU); [*de comestibles*] grocer

tendida SF (*Cono Sur*) shy, start

tendido ADJ **1** [*persona*] lying, lying down • **estaba tendida en el suelo** she was lying on the ground
2 [*galope*] fast
SM **1** (= *ropa lavada*) (*tb* **tendidos**) washing, clothes (*pl*) (*hung out to dry*)
2 (*Taur*) front rows of seats
3 [*de cable, vía*] (*por tierra*) laying; (*por el aire*) hanging
4 (= *cables*) wires (*pl*) ▸ **tendido de alta tensión** high voltage power line ▸ **tendido eléctrico** power line, overhead cables (*pl*), overhead lines (*pl*)
5 (*Culin*) batch of loaves
6 (*Arquit*) coat of plaster
7 (*And, Méx*) (= *ropa de cama*) bedclothes (*pl*)
8 (*CAm, Caribe*) (= *cuerda*) long tether, rope
9 (*And, Méx*) (= *puesto de mercado*) (market) stall

tendinitis SF INV tendinitis, tendonitis

tendinoso ADJ sinewy

tendón SM tendon, sinew ▸ **tendón de Aquiles** Achilles tendon

tendonitis SF INV tendinitis, tendonitis

tendré *etc* ▹ **tener**

tenducho* SM poky little shop

tenebrosidad SF **1** (*poét*) (= *oscuridad*) darkness, gloom(iness)
2 [*de perspectiva*] gloominess, blackness
3 [*de asunto, complot*] sinister nature
4 [*de estilo*] obscurity

tenebroso ADJ **1** (= *oscuro*) dark, gloomy
2 [*perspectiva*] gloomy, black
3 (*pey*) [*complot, pasado*] sinister
4 [*estilo*] obscure

tenedor(a) SM/F (*Com, Econ*) holder, bearer ▸ **tenedor(a) de acciones** shareholder ▸ **tenedor(a) de libros** book-keeper ▸ **tenedor(a) de obligaciones** bondholder ▸ **tenedor(a) de póliza** policyholder
SM [*de mesa*] fork • **restaurante de cinco ~es** ≈ five-star restaurant

teneduría SF ▸ **teneduría de libros** book-keeping

tenencia SF **1** (= *posesión*) [*de vivienda*] tenancy, occupancy; [*de propiedad*] possession • **~ de drogas** possession of drugs • **~ ilícita de armas** illegal possession of weapons
2 [*de cargo*] tenure ▸ **tenencia asegurada** security of tenure
3 (= *puesto*) • **~ de alcaldía** post of deputy mayor
4 (*Mil*) lieutenancy

tener

VERBO TRANSITIVO
VERBO AUXILIAR
VERBO PRONOMINAL

▹ CONJUG 2k

Para las expresiones como **tener cuidado, tener ganas, tener suerte, tener de particular, tener en cuenta**, *ver la otra entrada.*

VERBO TRANSITIVO

El uso de **got** *con el verbo* **have** *es más frecuente en inglés británico, pero solo se usa en el presente.*

1 (= *poseer, disponer de*) to have, have got • **¿tienes dinero?** do you have *o* have you got any money? • **¿tienes un bolígrafo?** do you have *o* have you got a pen? • **¿tiene usted permiso para esto?** do you have *o* have you got permission for this? • **tiene un tío en Venezuela** he has an uncle in Venezuela, he's got an uncle in Venezuela • **ahora no tengo tiempo** I don't have *o* I haven't got time now
2 (*referido a aspecto, carácter*) to have, have got • **tiene el pelo rubio** he has blond hair, he's got blond hair • **tenía una sonrisa preciosa** she had a lovely smile • **tiene la nariz aguileña** she has an aquiline nose, she's got an aquiline nose • **tenía el pelo mojado** his hair was wet
3 (*referido a edad*) to be • **tiene siete años** he's seven (years old) • **¿cuántos años tienes?** how old are you? • **al menos debe de ~ 55 años** she must be at least 55
4 (*referido a ocupaciones*) to have, have got • **tenemos clase de inglés a las 11** we have an English class at 11, we've got an English class at 11 • **el lunes tenemos una reunión** we're having a meeting on Monday, we've got a meeting on Monday • **mañana tengo una fiesta** I'm going to a party tomorrow
5 (= *parir*) to have • **va a ~ un niño** she's going to have a baby
6 (= *medir*) to be • **~ 5cm de ancho** to be 5cm wide
7 (= *sentir*) (+ *sustantivo*) to be (+ *adj*) • **~ hambre/sed/calor/frío** to be hungry/thirsty/hot/cold • **no tengas tantos celos** don't be so jealous • **hemos tenido mucho miedo** we have been very frightened • **le tengo mucho cariño** I'm very fond of him • **he tenido un presentimiento** I've had a premonition
8 (= *padecer, sufrir*) to have • **han tenido un accidente** they have had an accident • **hemos tenido muchas dificultades** we have had a lot of difficulties • **Luis tiene la gripe** Luis has *o* has got flu • **tengo fiebre** I have *o* I've got a (high) temperature • **¿qué tienes?** what's the matter with you?, what's wrong with you?
9 (= *sostener*) to hold • **tenía el pasaporte en la mano** he had his passport in his hand, he was holding his passport in his hand • **tenme el vaso un momento, por favor** hold my glass for me for a moment, please • **¡ten!** • **¡aquí tienes!** here you are!
10 (= *recibir*) to have • **aún no he tenido carta** I haven't had a letter yet • **¿has tenido noticias suyas?** have you heard from her?
11 (= *pensar, considerar*) • **~ a bien hacer algo** to see fit to do sth • **~ a algn en algo**: • **te tendrán en más estima** they will hold you in higher esteem • **~ a algn por** (+ *adj*) to consider sb (to be) (+ *adj*) • **le tengo por poco honrado** I consider him (to be) rather dishonest • **ten por seguro que ...** rest assured that ...
12 **tener algo que** (+ *infin*) • **tengo trabajo que hacer** I have *o* I've got work to do • **no tengo nada que hacer** I have *o* I've got nothing to do • **eso no tiene nada que ver** that has *o* that's got nothing to do with it
13 (*locuciones*) • **ya saben dónde me tienen** you always know where you can find me • **¡ahí lo tienes!** there you are!, there you have it! • **~ algo de** (+ *adj*): • **de bueno no tiene nada** there's nothing good about it • **no tiene nada de particular** it's nothing special • **¿qué tiene de malo?** what's wrong with that? • **~lo difícil** to find it difficult • **~lo fácil** to have it easy • MODISMOS: • **¿(conque) esas tenemos?** so that's the game, is it?, so it's like that, is it? • **no ~las todas consigo** (= *dudar*) to be dubious *o* unsure; (= *desconfiar*) to be uneasy, be wary • **no las tengo todas conmigo de que lo haga** I'm none too sure that he'll do it, I'm not entirely sure that he'll do it • **~ todas las de ganar** to hold all the winning cards, look like a winner • **~ todas las de perder** to be fighting a losing battle, look like losing • REFRÁN: • **quien tuvo retuvo** some things stay with you to the grave

VERBO AUXILIAR

1 **tener que** (+ *infin*) **a** (*indicando obligación*) • **tengo que comprarlo** I have to *o* I've got to buy it, I must buy it • **tenemos que marcharnos** we have to *o* we've got to go, we must be going • **tienen que aumentarte el sueldo** they have to *o* they've got to give you a rise • **tuvo que devolver todo el dinero** he had to pay all the money back • **tiene que ser así** it has to be this way
b (*indicando suposición, probabilidad*) • **¡tienes que estar cansadísima!** you must be really tired! • **tiene que dolerte mucho ¿no?** it must hurt a lot, doesn't it? • **tiene que estar en tu despacho** it must be in your office • **tiene que haberte dolido mucho** it must have hurt a lot
c (*en reproches*) • **¡tendrías que haberlo dicho antes!** you should have said so before! • **¡tendría que darte vergüenza!** you should be ashamed of yourself! • **¡tú tenías que ser!** it would be you!, it had to be you!
d (*en sugerencias, recomendaciones*) • **tendrías que comer más** you should eat more • **tendríamos que pedirle perdón** we should apologize to him
2 (+ *participio*) • **tenía puesto el sombrero** he had his hat on • **nos tenían preparada una sorpresa** they had prepared a surprise for us • **tenía pensado llamarte** I had been thinking of phoning you • **te lo tengo dicho muchas veces** I've told you hundreds of times • **yo no le tengo visto** I've never set eyes on him
3 (+ *adj*) • **procura ~ contentos a todos** he tries to keep everybody happy • **me tiene perplejo la falta de noticias** the lack of news is puzzling, I am puzzled by the lack of news
4 (*esp Méx*) (= *llevar*) • **tienen tres meses de no cobrar** they haven't been paid for three months, it's three months since they've been paid • **tengo cuatro años aquí** I've been here for four years

VERBO PRONOMINAL **tenerse**

1 (= *sostenerse*) • **~se firme** (*lit*) to stand upright; (*fig*) to stand firm • **~se de** *o* **en pie** to stand up • **la muñeca se tiene de pie** the doll stands up • **no se puede ~ de pie** • **no se tiene de pie** he can hardly stand • **estoy que no me tengo de sueño** I'm falling asleep on my feet, I'm about ready to drop
2 (= *considerarse*) • **~se en mucho** to have a high opinion of o.s. • **~se por**: • **se tiene por muy listo** he thinks himself very clever, he thinks he's very clever

teneraje SM (*LAm*) calves (*pl*)

tenería SF tannery

Tenerife SM Tenerife

tenga, tengo *etc* ▹ **tener**

tenguerengue‡ SM (*Caribe*) hovel

tenia SF tapeworm

tenida SF **1** (*Cono Sur*) (= *traje*) suit, outfit; (= *uniforme*) uniform ▸ **tenida de gala** evening dress ▸ **tenida de luto** mourning ▸ **tenida de noche** evening dress
2 (*LAm*) (= *reunión*) meeting, session; [*de masones*] meeting (*of a masonic lodge*)

tenienta SF (*Mil*) **1** = **teniente**
2† (= *esposa*) lieutenant's wife

teniente SMF **1** (*Mil*) lieutenant, first lieutenant (*EEUU*) ▸ **teniente coronel** lieutenant colonel ▸ **teniente de navío** lieutenant ▸ **teniente general** lieutenant general
2 (= *ayudante*) deputy, assistant ▸ **teniente de alcalde** deputy mayor ▸ **teniente fiscal** assistant prosecutor
ADJ • **estar ~‡** to be deaf

tenis SM INV **1** (= *deporte*) tennis ▸ **tenis de mesa** table tennis
2 (= *zapato*) tennis shoe, plimsoll • MODISMO: • **colgar los ~‡** to kick the bucket‡
3 (= *pistas*) tennis courts (*pl*); (= *club*) tennis club

tenista SMF tennis player

tenístico ADJ tennis (*antes de s*)

tenor¹ SM (*Mús*) tenor

tenor² SM (= *sentido*) meaning, sense • **el ~ de esta declaración** the tenor of this statement • **a este ~** in this fashion, like this • **del siguiente ~** as follows • **a ~ de** (= *según*) according to; (*Jur*) in accordance with

tenorio* SM ladykiller, Don Juan

tensado SM [*de cable, cuerda*] tensioning, tightening; [*de arco*] drawing

tensamente ADV tensely

tensar ▹ CONJUG 1a VT [+ *cable, cuerda*] to tighten, tauten; [+ *músculo*] to tense; [+ *arco*] to draw; [+ *relaciones*] to strain
VPR **tensarse** [*relaciones*] to become strained

tensión SF **1** [*de cable, cuerda*] tension, tautness
2 [*de músculos*] tension • **con los músculos en ~** with one's muscles all tensed up
3 (*Med*) blood pressure • **tener la ~ alta** to have high blood pressure • **tomarse la ~** to have one's blood pressure taken ▸ **tensión arterial** blood pressure
4 (*Elec*) (= *voltaje*) tension, voltage • **alta ~** high tension • **cable de alta ~** high-tension cable
5 [*de gas*] pressure
6 (= *estrés*) strain, stress • **estar en ~** to be

tense ▸ **tensión excesiva** (over)strain ▸ **tensión nerviosa** nervous strain, nervous tension ▸ **tensión premenstrual** premenstrual tension, PMT
7 (*en situación*) tension, tenseness • **hubo momentos de gran ~** there were some very tense moments • **la ~ de la situación política** the tenseness of the political situation ▸ **tensión racial** racial tension

tensionado ADJ tense, in a state of tension

tensional ADJ tense, full of tension

tensionar ▹ CONJUG 1a VT **1** [+ *músculo*] to tense
2 [+ *adversario*] to put pressure on; [+ *relaciones*] to put a strain on

tenso ADJ **1** (= *tirante*) tense, taut
2 [*persona, situación*] tense; [*relaciones*] strained • **es una situación muy tensa** it is a very tense situation • **las relaciones entre los dos están muy tensas** relations between the two are very strained

tensor SM (*Téc*) guy, strut; (*Anat*) tensor; [*de cuello*] stiffener; (*Dep*) chest expander
ADJ tensile

tentación SF **1** (= *impulso*) temptation • **resistir (a) la ~** to resist temptation • **no pude resistir la ~ de comprarlo** I couldn't resist the temptation to buy it • **vencer la ~** to overcome temptation
2* (= *cosa tentadora*) • **las gambas son mi ~** I can't resist prawns • **¡eres mi ~!** you'll be the ruin of me!

tentacular ADJ tentacular • **la envergadura ~** the width of the tentacles

tentáculo SM tentacle • **la mafia va extendiendo sus ~s** the Mafia is gradually spreading its tentacles

tentado ADJ • **estuve ~ de decírselo** I was tempted to tell him

tentador(a) ADJ tempting
SM/F tempter/temptress

tentar ▹ CONJUG 1j VT **1** (= *seducir*) to tempt • **me tentó con una copita de anís** she tempted me with a glass of anisette • **no me tienta nada la idea** I can't say I fancy the idea* • **~ a algn a hacer algo** to tempt sb to do sth
2 (= *palpar*) to feel; (*Med*) to probe • **ir tentando el camino** to feel one's way
3 (= *probar*) to test, try (out)
VPR **tentarse*** (*Cono Sur*) to give in (to temptation)

tentativa SF (= *intento*) attempt; (*Jur*) criminal attempt ▸ **tentativa de asesinato** attempted murder ▸ **tentativa de robo** attempted robbery ▸ **tentativa de suicidio** suicide attempt

tentativo ADJ tentative

tentebonete* SM (= *empleo*) cushy job‡, plum; (= *gaje*) perk*

tentempié* SM snack, bite

tenue ADJ **1** [*tela, velo*] thin, fine
2 [*olor, sonido, línea*] faint; [*neblina, lluvia*] light; [*aire*] thin
3 [*razón*] tenuous, insubstantial; [*relación*] tenuous
4 [*estilo*] simple, plain

tenuidad SF **1** [*de tela*] thinness, fineness
2 [*de sonido*] faintness; [*de neblina, lluvia*] lightness; [*del aire*] thinness
3 [*de razón, relación*] tenuousness
4 [*de estilo*] simplicity

teñido SM dyeing

teñir ▹ CONJUG 3h, 3k VT **1** [+ *pelo, ropa*] to dye • **~ una prenda de azul** to dye a garment blue • **el jersey ha teñido los pañuelos** the colour of the jersey has come out on the handkerchiefs
2 (= *manchar*) to stain • **teñido de sangre** stained with blood
3 (= *matizar*) to tinge (**de** with) • **un poema teñido de añoranza** a poem tinged with longing
4 (*Arte*) [+ *color*] to darken
VPR **teñirse 1** • **~se el pelo** to dye one's hair
2 • **el mar se tiñó de negro** the sea darkened

teocali SM (*Méx*), **teocalli** SM (*Méx*) (*Hist*) Aztec temple

teocracia SF theocracy

teocrático ADJ theocratic

teodolito SM theodolite

teogonía SF theogony

teologal ADJ • **las virtudes ~es** the three Christian virtues (*faith, hope and charity*)

teología SF theology

teológico ADJ theological

teólogo/a SM/F theologian, theologist

teorema SM theorem

teorético ADJ (*LAm*) theoretic(al)

teoría SF theory • **en ~** in theory, theoretically ▸ **teoría atómica** atomic theory ▸ **teoría cuántica** quantum theory ▸ **teoría de conjuntos** set theory ▸ **teoría de la información** information theory ▸ **teoría de la relatividad** theory of relativity ▸ **teoría del caos** chaos theory

teóricamente ADV theoretically, in theory

teoricidad SF theoretical nature

teórico/a ADJ theoretic(al) • **examen ~** theory (exam)
SM/F theoretician, theorist

teorización SF theorizing

teorizante SMF theoretician, theorist; (*pey*) theorizer

teorizar ▹ CONJUG 1f VI to theorize

teosofía SF theosophy

teosófico ADJ theosophical

teósofo/a SM/F theosophist

tepalcate SM (*CAm, Méx*) **1** (= *vasija*) earthenware jar; (= *fragmento*) fragment of pottery, shard
2 (= *trasto*) piece of junk

tepalcatero/a SM/F (*Méx*) potter

tepe SM sod, turf, clod

tepetate SM (*CAm, Méx*) **1** (= *residuo*) slag
2 (= *caliza*) limestone

tepocate SM (*CAm, Méx*) **1** (= *guijarro*) stone, pebble
2* (= *niño*) kid*

teporocho* ADJ (*Méx*) tight*, drunk

tequesquite SM (*Méx*) *salt made by evaporation from salt lakes*

tequi‡ SM car

tequila SM tequila

tequilero* ADJ (*Méx*) tight*, drunk

tequío SM (*CAm, Méx*) (= *molestia*) trouble; (= *fardo*) burden; (= *daño*) harm, damage

tequioso ADJ (*CAm, Méx*) (= *molesto*) annoying; (= *gravoso*) burdensome; (= *dañino*) harmful

terabyte SM terabyte

terapeuta SMF therapist

terapéutica SF therapeutics (*sing*)

terapéutico ADJ therapeutic(al)

terapia SF therapy ▸ **terapia aversiva** aversion therapy ▸ **terapia cognitivo-conductual** cognitive behavioural therapy ▸ **terapia de choque** shock therapy ▸ **terapia de conducta** behavioural therapy, behavioral therapy (*EEUU*) ▸ **terapia de electrochoque** electroshock therapy ▸ **terapia de grupo** group therapy ▸ **terapia electroconvulsiva** electroconvulsive therapy ▸ **terapia génica** gene therapy ▸ **terapia intensiva** (*Méx, Arg, Uru*) intensive care ▸ **terapia laboral** occupational therapy ▸ **terapia lingüística** speech therapy ▸ **terapia ocupacional** occupational therapy ▸ **terapia por aversión** aversion therapy ▸ **terapia táctil** touch therapy

teratogénico ADJ teratogenic

tercamente ADV stubbornly, obstinately

tercena SF **1** (*Méx*) (= *almacén*) government warehouse
2 (*And*) (= *carnicería*) butcher's (shop)

tercenista SMF (*And*) butcher

tercer ADJ ▹ **tercero**

tercera SF **1** (*Mús*) third
2 (*Aut*) third (gear)
3 (= *clase*) third class • **un hotel de ~** a third-rate hotel; ▹ **tercero**

tercería SF **1** (= *arbitración*) mediation, arbitration
2 (*pey*) [*de alcahuete*] procuring

tercermundismo SM **1** (= *atraso*) backwardness, under-development
2 (= *actitudes*) *attitudes or policies akin to those of a third-world country*

tercermundista ADJ third-world (*antes de s*); (*pey*) (*fig*) backward
SM third-world country

tercero/a ADJ (ANTES DE SM SING: **tercer**) third • **la tercera vez** the third time • **terceras personas** third parties • **tercer grado (penitenciario)** *lowest category within the prison system which allows day release privileges* • **Tercer Mundo** Third World • **MODISMO**: • **a la tercera va la vencida** third time lucky; ▹ **edad, sexto**
SM/F **1** (= *árbitro*) mediator, arbitrator; (*Jur*) third party ▸ **tercero en discordia** third party
2 (*pey*) (= *alcahuete*) procurer/procuress, go-between
SM (= *piso*) third floor; ▹ **tercera**

tercerola SF (*Caribe*) shotgun

terceto SM **1** (*Mús*) trio
2 (*Literat*) tercet, triplet

terciada SF (*LAm*) plywood

terciado ADJ **1** (*en tamaño*) • **una merluza terciada** a medium-sized hake
2 (= *usado*) • **está ~ ya** [*botella etc*] it's a third finished
3 • **azúcar terciada** brown sugar
4 • **llevar algo ~** [+ *bolso, arma*] to wear sth crosswise *o* across one's chest *etc* • **con el sombrero ~** with his hat at a rakish angle

terciana SF tertian (fever)

terciar ▹ CONJUG 1b VT **1** (*Mat*) (= *dividir en tres*) to divide into three
2 (= *inclinar*) to slant, slope; [+ *arma*] to wear (diagonally) across one's chest; [+ *sombrero*] to tilt, wear on the slant
3 (*Agr*) to plough a third time
4 (*And, Cono Sur, Méx*) (*al hombro*) to hoist on to *o* carry on one's shoulder
5 (*LAm*) [+ *vino*] to water down; (*Méx*) (= *mezclar*) to mix, blend
VI **1** (= *mediar*) to mediate • **~ entre dos rivales** to mediate between two rivals • **yo ~é con el jefe** I'll have a word with the boss
2 (= *participar*) • **~ en algo** to take part in sth, join in sth
3 (= *completar el número*) to fill in, make up the numbers
VPR **terciarse** • **si se tercia, él también sabe hacerlo** if it comes to that, he knows how to do it too • **si se tercia una buena oportunidad** if a good chance presents itself *o* comes up • **si se tercia alguna vez que yo pase por allí** if I should happen to go that way

terciario ADJ tertiary

tercio SM **1** (= *tercera parte*) third • **dos ~s** two thirds
2 (*Taur*) stage, part (of the bullfight) • **cambiar de ~** (*Taur*) to enter the next stage of the bullfight; (= *cambiar de tema*) to

change the subject
3 (*Mil, Hist*) regiment, corps ▸ **tercio de la guardia civil** division of the civil guard ▸ **tercio extranjero** foreign legion
4 • **hacer buen ~ a algn** (= *hacer favor*) to do sb a service; (= *ser útil*) to serve sb well, be useful to sb • **hacer mal ~ a algn** to do sb a bad turn • MODISMO: • **estar mejorado en ~ y quinto** to come out of it very well
5 (*LAm*) (= *fardo*) pack, bale
6 (*Caribe*) (= *hombre*) fellow, guy*

terciopelo (SM) velvet

terco (ADJ) **1** (= *obstinado*) stubborn, obstinate • MODISMO: • **~ como una mula** as stubborn as a mule
2 (*And*) (= *severo*) harsh, unfeeling; (= *indiferente*) indifferent
3 [*material*] hard, tough, hard to work

Tere (SF) *forma familiar de* **Teresa**

tere (ADJ) (*And*) [*niño*] weepy, tearful

terebrante (ADJ) [*dolor*] sharp, piercing

tereco (SM) (*And*) = **tereque**

Terencio (SM) Terence

tereque (SM) (*And, Caribe*) **1** = **cachivache**
2 tereques things, gear* (*sing*), odds and ends

Teresa (SF) T(h)eresa

teresiano (ADJ) • **las obras teresianas** the works of Saint Teresa (of Ávila)

tergal® (SM) Terylene®, Dacron® (*EEUU*)

tergiversación (SF) distortion

tergiversar ▹ CONJUG 1a (VT) to distort, twist (the sense of)

terliz (SM) ticking

termal (ADJ) thermal

termalismo (SM) hydrotherapy, bathing at a spa

termalista (ADJ) spa (*antes de s*)
(SMF) *person who visits a spa*

termas (SFPL) (= *baños*) thermal baths; (= *manantiales*) thermal springs, hot springs

termes (SM INV) termite

termia (SF) (gas) therm

térmica[1] (SF) (= *corriente*) thermal, hot-air current

térmica[2] (SF) (*tb* **central térmica**) power station

térmico (ADJ) thermic, heat (*antes de s*); [*cristal*] heated • **baja térmica en el norte** a drop in temperature in the North

terminacho (SM) (= *palabra malsonante*) nasty word, rude word; (= *palabra fea*) ugly word; (= *palabra incorrecta*) incorrect word, malapropism, linguistic monstrosity

terminación (SF) **1** (= *finalización*) ending, termination • **la fecha prevista para la ~ de las obras** the date work was due to be finished
2 (*Ling*) ending, termination
3 (*Cono Sur*) (*Téc*) (= *acabado*) finish, finishing
4 ▸ **terminaciones nerviosas** nerve endings

terminado (SM) (*Téc*) finish, finishing
(ADJ) (= *acabado*) finished • **bien ~** well finished

terminajo (SM) = **terminacho**

terminal (ADJ) **1** (= *final*) [*enfermedad, estación*] terminal • **un cáncer en fase ~** a terminal cancer • **un enfermo en fase ~** a terminal patient • **los enfermos ~es** the terminally ill • **el edificio ~ del aeropuerto** the airport terminal
2 (*Bot*) [*hoja, rama*] terminal
(SM), (*a veces*) (SF) (*Elec, Inform*) terminal ▸ **terminal de computadora** computer terminal ▸ **terminal de pago, terminal de punto de venta** point-of-sale terminal ▸ **terminal de vídeo** video terminal ▸ **terminal informático** computer terminal ▸ **terminal interactivo** interactive unit
(SF), (*a veces*) (SM) (*Aer, Náut*) terminal; [*de autobuses, trenes*] terminus ▸ **terminal de carga** freight terminal ▸ **terminal de contenedores** container terminal ▸ **terminal de pasajeros, terminal de viajeros** passenger terminal

terminante (ADJ) [*respuesta*] categorical, conclusive; [*negativa*] flat, outright; [*prohibición*] strict; [*decisión*] final

terminantemente (ADV) [*responder*] categorically, conclusively; [*negar*] flatly; [*prohibir*] strictly • **queda ~ prohibido fumar en clase** smoking during lectures is strictly forbidden

terminar ▹ CONJUG 1a (VT) to finish • **he terminado el libro** I've finished the book • **no me ha dado tiempo a ~ el vestido** I haven't had time to finish the dress • **quiso ~ sus días en Marbella** she wanted to end her days in Marbella
(VI) **1** [*persona*] **a** (*en una acción, un trabajo*) to finish • **¿todavía no has terminado?** haven't you finished yet? • **¿quieres dejar que termine?** would you mind letting me finish? • **~ de hacer algo** to finish doing sth, stop doing sth • **cuando termine de hablar** when he finishes *o* stops speaking • **terminó de llenar el vaso con helado** he topped *o* filled the glass up with ice-cream • **terminaba de salir del baño** she had just got out of the bath • **no termino de entender por qué lo hizo** I just can't understand why she did it • **no me cae mal, pero no termina de convencerme** I don't dislike him, but I'm not too sure about him
b (*de una forma determinada*) to end up • **terminé rendido** I ended up exhausted • **~on peleándose** they ended up fighting • **terminó mal** he ended up badly • **terminó diciendo que ...** he ended by saying that ...
c • **~ con**: • **han terminado con todas las provisiones** they've finished off all the supplies • **hace falta algo que termine con el problema del paro** we need something to put an end to the problem of unemployment • **un cáncer terminó con su vida** cancer killed him • **he terminado con Andrés** I've broken up with *o* finished with Andrés • **¡estos niños van a ~ conmigo!** these children will be the death of me!
d • **~ por hacer algo** to end up doing sth • **seguro que ~á por dimitir** I bet he ends up resigning
2 [*obra, acto*] to end • **¿cómo termina la película?** how does the film end? • **la ceremonia terminó con un baile** the ceremony ended with a dance • **esto va a ~ en tragedia** this will end in tragedy • **estoy deseando que termine este año** I can't wait for this year to be over *o* to end • **¿a qué hora termina la clase?** what time does the class finish *o* end?
3 [*objeto, palabra*] • **~ en algo** to end in sth • **termina en punta** it ends in a point • **termina en vocal** it ends in *o* with a vowel
4 (*Inform*) to quit
(VPR) **terminarse 1** [*obra, acto*] to end • **antes de que se termine el curso** before the year ends *o* finishes, before the year is over
2 [*comida, gasolina, carrete*] to run out • **se nos ha terminado el café** we've run out of coffee
3 [*persona*] to finish • **me terminé el libro en dos días** I finished the book in two days • **¡termínate toda la sopa!** finish (up) your soup! • **termínate la copa y vámonos** finish your drink and let's go, drink up and let's go

terminista (SMF) (*Cono Sur*) pedant

término (SM) **1** (= *fin*) end, conclusion (*frm*) • **al ~ del partido/del debate** at the end *o* (*frm*) conclusion of the match/of the debate • **dar ~ a** [+ *situación*] to end; [+ *labor*] to complete • **dio ~ a la obra que su antecesor dejó sin concluir** he completed the work that his predecessor had left unfinished • **llegar a ~** [*negociación, proyecto*] to be completed, come to a conclusion; [*embarazo*] to go to (full) term • **las negociaciones llegaron a buen ~** the negotiations came to a successful conclusion • **llevar algo a ~** to bring sth to a conclusion • **llevar algo a buen** *o* **feliz ~** to bring sth to a successful conclusion • **llevar a ~ un embarazo** to go to (full) term, carry a pregnancy to full term • **poner ~ a algo** to put an end to sth • **tenemos que poner ~ a tales atrocidades** we must put an end to such atrocities
2 (= *lugar*) • **primer ~** [*de imagen*] foreground • **en primer ~ podemos contemplar la torre** in the foreground, we can see the tower • **de ahí se deduce, en primer ~, que ...** thus we may deduce, firstly, that ... • **segundo ~** middle distance • **con la recesión el problema pasó a un segundo ~** with the recession the problem took second place • **en segundo ~** secondly • **en último ~** (= *en último lugar*) ultimately; (= *si no hay otro remedio*) as a last resort • **la decisión, en último ~, es suya** ultimately, the decision is his • **la causa fue, en último ~, la crisis económica de los 70** the cause was, in the final *o* last analysis, the economic crisis of the 70s • **en último ~ puedes dormir en el sofá** if the worst comes to the worst, you can always sleep on the sofa ▸ **término medio** (= *punto medio*) happy medium; (= *solución intermedia*) compromise, middle way • **ni mucho ni poco, queremos un ~ medio** neither too much nor too little, we want a happy medium • **tendrán que buscar un ~ medio** they will have to look for a compromise *o* middle way • **como** *o* **por ~ medio** on average
3 (*Ling*) (= *palabra, expresión*) term • **una lista de ~s médicos** a list of medical terms • **era una revolucionaria, en el buen sentido del ~** she was a revolutionary in the good sense of the word
4 **términos**: **a** (= *palabras*) terms • **se expresó en ~s conciliatorios** he expressed himself in conciliatory terms • **han perdido unos 10.000 millones de dólares en ~s de productividad** they have lost some 10,000 million dollars in terms of productivity • **en ~s generales** in general terms, generally speaking • **(dicho) en otros ~s, ...** in other words ... • **en ~s reales** in real terms
b (= *condiciones*) [*de contrato, acuerdo, tregua*] terms • **según los ~s del contrato** according to the terms of the contract • **los ~s del intercambio** the terms of trade • **estar en buenos ~s con algn** to be on good terms with sb
5 (*Mat, Fil*) [*de fracción, ecuación*] term • MODISMO: • **invertir los ~s** to reverse the roles
6 (= *límite*) [*de terreno*] boundary, limit; (= *en carretera*) boundary stone ▸ **término municipal** municipal district, municipal area
7 (= *plazo*) period, term (*frm*) • **en el ~ de diez días** within a period *o* (*frm*) term of ten days
8 (*Col, Méx*) (*en restaurante*) • **—¿qué ~ quiere la carne? —término medio, por favor** "how would you like the meat?" — "medium, please"
9 (*Ferro*) terminus

terminología (SF) terminology

terminológico (ADJ) terminological

terminólogo/a (SM/F) terminologist

termita (SF), **termite** (SF) termite

termitero (SM) (= *montículo*) termite

t

mound; (= *nido*) termite nest, termitarium (*frm*)
termo SM **1** (= *frasco*) Thermos flask®
2 (= *calentador*) water heater
termo... PREF thermo...
termoaislante ADJ heat-insulating
termodinámica SF thermodynamics (*sing*)
termodinámico ADJ thermodynamic
termoeléctrico ADJ thermoelectric
termoimpresora SF thermal printer
termoiónico ADJ thermionic
termómetro SM thermometer
▸ **termómetro clínico** clinical thermometer
termonuclear ADJ thermonuclear
termopar SM thermocouple
termopila SF thermopile
Termópilas SFPL • **Las ~** Thermopylae
termorresistente ADV heat-resistant
termosfera SF thermosphere
termostático ADJ thermostatic
termostato SM thermostat
termotanque SM (*Cono Sur*) immersion heater
terna SF short list (*of three candidates*)
ternario ADJ ternary
terne ADJ **1** (= *fuerte*) tough, strong, husky; (*pey*) bullying
2 (= *terco*) stubborn • **~ que ~** out of sheer stubbornness
SM **1** bully, tough*
2 (*Cono Sur*) rogue
ternejo ADJ (*And*) spirited, vigorous
ternera SF **1** (*Agr*) (heifer) calf
2 (*Culin*) veal
ternero SM (*Agr*) calf
ternerón ADJ **1*** (= *compasivo*) soft-hearted
2 (*Cono Sur, Méx*) [*mozo*] overgrown, big
terneza SF **1** (= *ternura*) tenderness
2 ternezas* (= *palabras tiernas*) sweet nothings, tender words
ternilla SF cartilage
ternilloso ADJ gristly, cartilaginous
terno SM **1** (= *grupo de tres*) set of three, group of three; (= *trío*) trio
2 (= *traje*) three-piece suit; (*LAm*) suit
3 (*Caribe*) (= *joyas*) necklace set
4* (= *palabrota*) curse, swearword • **echar** *o* **soltar ~s** to curse, swear
ternura SF **1** (= *sentimiento*) tenderness; (= *cariño*) affection, fondness • **miró a los niños con ~** she looked fondly *o* tenderly at the children
2* (= *palabra*) endearment
ternurismo SM sentimentality
ternurista ADJ sentimental, schmaltzy*
Terpsícore SF Terpsichore
terquedad SF **1** (= *obstinación*) stubbornness, obstinacy
2 (= *dureza*) hardness, toughness
3 (*And*) (= *severidad*) harshness, lack of feeling; (= *indiferencia*) indifference
terracota SF terracotta
terrado SM **1** (= *tejado*) flat roof; (= *terraza*) terrace
2* (= *cabeza*) nut*, noggin (*EEUU**), bonce*
terraja SF diestock
terral SM (*LAm*) (= *polvareda*) cloud of dust
ADJ • **viento ~** land breeze *o* wind
Terranova SF Newfoundland
terranova SM (= *perro*) Newfoundland dog
terraplén SM **1** (*en carretera, ferrocarril*) embankment
2 (*Agr*) terrace
3 (*Mil*) rampart, bank
4 (= *cuesta*) slope, gradient
terraplenar ▷ CONJUG 1a VT [+ *terreno*] (= *nivelar*) to (fill and) level (off); (= *elevar*) to bank up, raise; (*Agr*) to terrace; [+ *hoyo*] to fill in

terráqueo/a ADJ earth (*antes de s*), terrestrial (*frm*) • **globo ~** globe
SM/F earthling
terrario SM terrarium
terrateniente SMF landowner
terraza SF **1** (*Arquit*) (= *balcón*) balcony; (= *azotea*) flat roof, terrace
2 (= *café*) pavement café • **nos sentamos en la ~ de un café** we sat outside a cafe
3 (*Agr*) terrace
4 (*en jardín*) flowerbed, border
5 (*Culin*) (= *jarro*) two-handled glazed jar
6* (= *cabeza*) nut*, noggin (*EEUU**), bonce*
terrazo SM terrazzo
terregal SM **1** (*LAm*) (= *terrón*) clod, hard lump of earth
2 (*Méx*) (= *tierra*) loose earth, dusty soil; (= *polvareda*) cloud of dust
terremoto SM earthquake
terrenal ADJ worldly • **la vida ~** worldly life, earthly life; ▷ **paraíso**
terreno ADJ **1** (*Rel*) [*bienes*] earthly • **esta vida terrena** this earthly life (*liter*)
2 (*Bio, Geol*) terrestrial
SM **1** (= *extensión de tierra*) (*gen*) land; (= *parcela*) piece of land, plot of land • **30 hectáreas de ~** 30 hectares of land • **es ~ municipal** it is council land • **los ~s pertenecientes al museo** the land belonging to the museum • **vender unos ~s** to sell some land • **nos hemos comprado un ~ en las afueras** we've bought a piece of land *o* plot of land *o* some land on the outskirts of the city • **el ~ que antes ocupaba la fábrica** the site the factory used to be on
2 (*explicando sus características*) (= *relieve*) ground, terrain; (= *composición*) soil, land • **los accidentes del ~** the unevenness of the ground *o* terrain • **un ~ pedregoso** stony ground *o* terrain • **estamos sobre un ~ arenoso** we're on sandy soil *o* land • **vehículos todo ~** all-terrain vehicles
3 a (= *campo*) **a** [*de estudio*] field • **en el ~ de la química** in the field of chemistry • **ese no es mi ~** that's not my field
b [*de actividad*] sphere, field • **el gobierno debe tomar medidas urgentes en el ~ económico** the government must take urgent measures in the economic sphere *o* field • **la competencia de las empresas extranjeras en todos los ~s** competition from foreign companies in all areas • **en cuanto a las pensiones, se ha avanzado poco en este ~** as for pensions, little progress has been made in this area • **este caso entra en el ~ militar** this case is a military matter
4 • MODISMOS: • **ceder ~** to give ground (**a**, **ante** to) • **pisar ~ firme** to be on safe *o* firm *o* solid ground • **ganar ~** to gain ground • **perder ~** to lose ground • **saber** *o* **conocer el ~ que se pisa** to be on familiar ground • **preparar el ~** to pave the way • **vencer a algn en su propio ~** to defeat sb on his home *o* own ground • **recuperar ~** to recover lost ground • **sobre el ~** on the ground • **analizarán la situación sobre el ~** they will analyse the situation on the ground • **resolveremos el problema sobre el ~** we will solve the problem as we go along • **~ abonado**: • **es ~ abonado para el vicio** it is a breeding ground for vice • **dichas tendencias han encontrado el ~ abonado entre la juventud** these trends have found a fertile breeding ground amongst the young • **este país es ~ abonado para las inversiones extranjeras** this country provides rich pickings for foreign investment • **llamar a algn a ~** to tell sb off, pull sb up* ▸ **terreno de pruebas** testing-ground
5 (*Dep*) • **empataron en su ~** they drew at home • **perdieron en su propio ~** they lost on their home ground • **el equipo tuvo una nueva derrota fuera de su ~** the team suffered a fresh defeat away (from home)
▸ **terreno de juego** pitch, field
térreo ADJ (= *de tierra*) earthen; [*color*] earthy
terrero ADJ **1** (= *de la tierra*) earthy; ▷ **saco**[1]
2 [*vuelo*] low, skimming
3 (= *humilde*) humble
SM pile, heap; (*Min*) dump
terrestre ADJ **1** (= *de la Tierra*) • **la atmósfera ~** the earth's atmosphere • **la superficie ~** the surface of the earth, the earth's surface • **un observatorio que girará en órbita ~** an observatory that will orbit the earth; ▷ **corteza**
2 (= *ni de aire ni de agua*) [*fuerzas, tropas*] ground (*antes de s*), land (*antes de s*); [*minas, frontera*] land (*antes de s*); [*transporte*] land (*antes de s*), terrestrial (*frm*); [*ofensiva*] (= *no aérea*) ground (*antes de s*); (= *no por mar*) land (*antes de s*) • **la distribución de alimentos por vía ~** distribution of food overland *o* by land
3 (*Téc, TV*) terrestrial
4 [*animal, vegetación*] land (*antes de s*), terrestrial (*frm*)
5 (*Rel*) earthly
terrible ADJ terrible, awful
terriblemente ADV terribly, awfully
terrícola SMF earthling
terrier SM terrier
terrífico ADJ terrifying
terrina SF terrine
territorial ADJ (= *de territorio*) territorial; (= *de región*) regional
territorialidad SF territoriality
territorio SM territory • **en todo el ~ nacional** in the whole country ▸ **territorio bajo mandato** mandated territory
terrón SM **1** [*de tierra*] clod, lump
2 [*de azúcar*] lump • **azúcar en terrones** lump sugar
3 (= *terreno*) field, patch (of land) • **destripar terrones** to work the land
terronera SF (*And*) terror, fright
terror SM terror • **película de ~** horror film • **me da ~ pensar que tengo que hablar con él** the thought of having to speak to him terrifies me, it terrifies me to think I have to speak to him ▸ **terrores nocturnos** nightmares
terrorífico ADJ terrifying, frightening
terrorismo SM terrorism ▸ **terrorismo de Estado** state terrorism ▸ **terrorismo islamista** Islamic terrorism
terrorista ADJ terrorist
SMF terrorist ▸ **terrorista islamista** Islamic terrorist
terroso ADJ earthy
terruño SM **1** (= *parcela de tierra*) plot, piece of ground; (= *tierra nativa*) native soil, home (ground) • **apego al ~** attachment to one's native soil
2 (= *terrón*) lump, clod
terso ADJ **1** (= *liso*) smooth; (= *brillante*) shiny, glossy • **piel tersa** smooth skin, soft skin
2 [*estilo*] polished, smooth
tersura SF **1** (= *suavidad*) smoothness; (= *brillo*) shine, glossiness
2 [*de estilo, lenguaje*] smoothness, flow
tertulia SF **1** (= *reunión*) social gathering, regular informal gathering • **la ~ del Café Gijón** the Cafe Gijón circle, the in-crowd at the Cafe Gijón • **estar de ~** to talk, sit around talking • **hacer ~** to get together, meet informally and talk • **hoy no hay ~** there's no meeting today, the group is not meeting

today ▸ **tertulia literaria** literary circle, literary gathering ▸ **tertulia radiofónica** radio talk show ▸ **tertulia televisiva** talk show
2 (= *sala*) clubroom, games room
3 (*Cono Sur*) (= *galería*) gallery; (*Caribe*) (= *palcos*) boxes

TERTULIA
The term **tertulia** is used for groups of people who meet informally on a regular basis to chat about current affairs, the Arts etc, and is also used to refer to the gathering itself. In early 20th Century Spain, **tertulias literarias** were much in vogue, and critics and writers would meet to discuss the literary issues of the day in places such as the famous Café Gijón. In more recent times, the term has been used to refer to the highly organized PR platforms in which writers of the moment engage in round-table discussions to promote their latest works.

Tertuliano SM Tertullian
tertuliano/a SM/F 1 (= *contertulio*) member of a social gathering
2 (*Radio, TV*) talk show guest
tertuliar ▸ CONJUG 1b VI (*LAm*) (= *ir a una reunión*) to attend a social gathering; (= *reunirse*) to get together, meet informally and talk
Teruel SM Teruel
terylene® SM Terylene®, Dacron® (*EEUU*)
Tesalia SF Thessaly
tesar ▸ CONJUG 1j VT to tauten, tighten up
tesauro SM thesaurus
tescal SM (*Méx*) stony ground
tesela SF tessera
Teseo SM Theseus
tesina SF dissertation, minor thesis
tesis SF INV 1 (*Univ*) thesis ▸ **tesis doctoral** doctoral thesis, doctoral dissertation (*EEUU*), PhD thesis
2 (*Fil*) thesis
3 (= *teoría*) • **su ~ es insostenible** his theory is untenable • **no podemos refutar las ~ de la defensa** we cannot refute the defence's arguments • **no comparto su ~** I don't share your opinion
tesitura SF 1 (= *mental*) attitude, frame of mind
2 (*Mús*) tessitura
teso ADJ (= *tenso*) tense
SM crest
tesón SM (= *tenacidad*) tenacity, persistence; (= *insistencia*) insistence • **resistir con ~** to resist tenaciously
tesonero ADJ (*LAm*) tenacious, persistent
tesorería SF 1 (= *cargo*) treasurership, office of treasurer
2 (= *oficina*) treasury
3 (= *activo disponible*) liquid assets (*pl*)
tesorero/a SM/F treasurer
tesoro SM 1 (*de mucho valor*) treasure • **valer un ~** to be worth a fortune • **tenemos una cocinera que es todo un ~** we have a cook who is a real treasure, we have a real gem of a cook • **el libro es un ~ de datos** the book is a mine of information • **es un ~ de recuerdos** it is a treasure-house of memories ▸ **tesoro escondido** buried treasure
2 (*en oración directa*) darling • **¡sí, ~!** yes, my darling!
3 (*Econ, Pol*) treasury ▸ **Tesoro público** Exchequer, Treasury
4 (= *pagaré*) treasury bond
5 (= *diccionario*) thesaurus
Tespis SM Thespis
test [tes] SM (PL: **tests** [tes]) test • **examen tipo ~** multiple-choice exam ▸ **test de comprensión** comprehension test ▸ **test de embarazo** pregnancy test
testa SF 1 (= *cabeza*) head ▸ **testa coronada** crowned head
2* (= *inteligencia*) brains (*pl*); (= *sentido común*) gumption*
testador(a) SM/F testator/testatrix
testaduro ADJ (*Caribe*) = **testarudo**
testaferro SM front man
testamentaría SF 1 (= *acto*) execution of a will
2 (= *bienes*) estate
testamentario/a ADJ testamentary
SM/F executor/executrix
testamento SM 1 will, testament • **hacer ~** to make one's will
2 (*Biblia*) • **Antiguo Testamento** Old Testament • **Nuevo Testamento** New Testament
3* (= *escrito largo*) screed
testar¹ ▸ CONJUG 1a VI (= *hacer testamento*) to make a will
testar² ▸ CONJUG 1a VT (*And*) (= *subrayar*) to underline
testar³ ▸ CONJUG 1a VT [+ *coche, producto*] to test
testarada* SF, **testarazo*** SM bump on the head • **darse una ~** to bump *o* bang one's head
testarudez SF stubbornness, pigheadedness
testarudo ADJ stubborn, pigheaded
testear ▸ CONJUG 1a (*LAm*) VT to test
VI to do a test, undergo a test
testera SF front, face; (*Zool*) forehead
testero SM 1 = **testera**
2 [*de cama*] bedhead
3 (*Arquit*) wall
testes SMPL testes
testiculamen‡ SM equipment*, balls**
(*pl*)
testículo SM testicle
testificación SF 1 testification
2 = **testimonio**
testificar ▸ CONJUG 1g VT (= *atestiguar*) to attest; (*en juicio*) to testify to, give evidence of
VI (*en juicio*) to testify, give evidence • **~ de** (= *atestiguar*) to attest; (= *dar testimonio*) to testify to, give evidence of
testigo SMF 1 (*Jur*) witness; [*de boda, contrato*] witness • **citar a algn como ~** to call sb as a witness ▸ **testigo de cargo** witness for the prosecution ▸ **testigo de descargo** witness for the defence ▸ **testigo ocular** eyewitness ▸ **testigo pericial** expert witness ▸ **testigo presencial** eyewitness
2 (= *espectador*) witness • **declaró un ~ del accidente** a person who had witnessed the accident gave evidence • **tú eres ~ de que nunca le he pegado** you can testify to *o* vouch for the fact that I have never hit him • **estas paredes han sido ~ de nuestro amor** these walls have witnessed *o* are the witness of our love • **pongo al cielo por ~** as God is my witness
3 (*Rel*) ▸ **testigo de Jehová** Jehovah's witness
SM 1 (*Dep*) (*en relevos*) baton
2 (*Aut*) • **~ luminoso** warning light
3 (*en experimento*) control
4 (*Geol*) sample core
ADJ INV • **grupo ~** control group
testimonial ADJ token, nominal
testimonialmente ADV (= *como símbolo*) as a token gesture; (= *nominalmente*) nominally; (= *sin entusiasmo*) half-heartedly
testimoniar ▸ CONJUG 1b VT (= *testificar*) to testify to, bear witness to; (= *mostrar*) to show, demonstrate
VI to testify, bear witness
testimonio SM 1 (*Jur*) (= *declaración*) testimony, evidence; (= *afidávit*) affidavit • **dar ~** to testify (**de** to), give evidence (**de** of) • **falso ~** perjury, false testimony
2 (= *prueba*) proof; (= *indicación*) evidence • **~ de compra** proof of purchase • **los fósiles son ~ de ello** fossils are evidence of this • **las calles nos dan ~ de su pasado árabe** the streets bear witness to its Arab past • **como ~ de mi afecto** as a token *o* mark of my affection
testosterona SF testosterone
testuz SM [*de caballo*] forehead; [*de buey, toro*] nape (*of the neck*)
teta SF 1* (= *mama*) breast, tit**, boob‡ • **dar (la) ~ a** to suckle, breast-feed • **quitar la ~ a** to wean • **niño de ~** baby at the breast • MODISMO: • **mejor que ~ de monja‡** really great*
2 [*de biberón*] teat, nipple (*EEUU*)
ADJ INV • **estar ~** (*Esp‡*) to be really great*
tetamen‡ SM big bust
tétano SM, **tétanos** SM INV tetanus
tete* SM (*Cono Sur*) mess, trouble
tetelque ADJ (*CAm, Méx*) sharp, bitter
tetera¹ SF (*para té*) teapot; (= *recipiente grande*) tea urn ▸ **tetera eléctrica** electric kettle
tetera² SF (*Méx*) (= *biberón*) feeding bottle; (= *vasija*) *vessel with a spout*
tetero SM (*And, Caribe*) feeding bottle
tetilla SF 1 [*de hombre*] nipple
2 [*de biberón*] teat, nipple (*EEUU*)
tetina SF teat, nipple (*EEUU*)
Tetis SF Thetis
tetón¹ SM (*en neumático*) bubble, swelling
tetón²‡ ADJ (*Cono Sur*) stupid, thick*
tetona* ADJ busty*
tetrabrik® SM INV, **tetra brik®** SM INV Tetra-Pak® (carton)
tetracilíndrico ADJ • **motor ~** four-cylinder engine
tetracloruro SM tetrachloride ▸ **tetracloruro de carbono** carbon tetrachloride
tetraedro SM tetrahedron
tetrágono SM tetragon
tetrámetro SM tetrameter
tetramotor ADJ four-engined
tetrapak® SM INV, **tetra pak®** SM INV Tetra-Pak® (carton)
tetraplejia SF, **tetraplejía** SF quadriplegia
tetrapléjico/a ADJ, SM/F quadriplegic
tetrarreactor SM four-engined jet plane
tetratlón SM tetrathlon
tétrico ADJ [*ambiente, habitación, lugar*] gloomy, dismal; [*humor, pensamiento, cuento, relato*] gloomy, pessimistic; [*luz*] dim, wan
tetuda* ADJ busty*
tetunte SM (*CAm*) bundle
teutón/ona ADJ Teutonic
SM/F Teuton
teutónico ADJ Teutonic
teveo SM = **tebeo**
textear ▸ CONJUG 1a (*esp LAm*) VT, VI to text
textil ADJ 1 [*industria*] textile
2 [*playa*] non-nudist
SMPL **textiles** (= *tejidos*) textiles
SF textile company
texto SM text • **libro de ~** textbook • **grabado fuera de ~** full-page illustration
textual ADJ 1 (= *de un texto*) textual • **cita ~** quotation
2 (= *exacto*) exact; (= *literal*) literal • **son sus palabras ~es** those are his exact words
textualmente ADV 1 (*Literat*) textually
2 (= *exactamente*) exactly; (= *literalmente*) literally, word for word • **dice ~ que ...** he says, and I quote, that ...

t

textura (SF) texture
texturizado (ADJ) textured
tez (SF) (= *piel*) complexion, skin; (= *color*) colouring, coloring (*EEUU*) • **de tez morena** dark(-skinned), dusky (*liter*) • **de tez pálida** fair(-skinned)
tezontle (SM) (*Méx*) volcanic rock (*for building*)
Tfno. (ABR), **tfno.** (ABR) (= **teléfono**) Tel, tel
TFT (SM ABR) TFT
TGV (SM ABR) (= **tren de gran velocidad**) ≈ APT
thriller (SM) (PL: **thrillers**) thriller
ti (PRON PERS) you • **es para ti** it's for you • **ahora todo depende de ti** it all depends on you now • **esto no se refiere a ti** this doesn't refer to you • **¿a ti te gusta el jazz?** do you like jazz? • **¿a ti te han dicho algo?** have they said anything to you? • **solo piensas en ti (mismo)** you only think of yourself • **no sabes defenderte por ti misma** you don't know how to stand up for yourself
tiamina (SF) thiamine
tiangue (SM) (*CAm*) (= *mercado*) small market; (= *puesto*) booth, stall
tianguis (SM INV) (*CAm, Méx*) (open-air) market
TIAR (SM ABR) = **Tratado Interamericano de Asistencia Recíproca**
tiara (SF) tiara
tiarrón/ona* (SM/F) big guy*/big girl
tibante (ADJ) (*And*) haughty
tibe (SM) (*And, Caribe*) whetstone
Tíber (SM) Tiber
Tiberio (SM) Tiberius
tiberio* (ADJ) (*CAm, Méx*) sloshed*
(SM) **1** (= *jaleo*) uproar, row; (= *pelea*) set-to*
2 (*CAm, Méx*) binge*
Tíbet (SM) • **El ~** Tibet
tibetano/a (ADJ), (SM/F) Tibetan
(SM) (*Ling*) Tibetan
tibia (SF) tibia
tibiarse ▷ CONJUG 1b (VPR) (*CAm, Caribe*) to get cross
tibieza (SF) **1** [*de líquidos*] lukewarmness, tepidness
2 [*de creencias*] half-heartedness; [*de persona*] lukewarmness, lack of enthusiasm
tibio (ADJ) **1** [*comida, líquido*] lukewarm, tepid
2 [*creencia*] half-hearted; [*persona*] lukewarm; [*recibimiento*] cool, unenthusiastic • **estar ~ con algn** to be cool to sb, behave distantly towards sb • MODISMO: • **poner ~ a algn*** (= *insultar*) to hurl abuse at sb, give sb a verbal battering; (*por detrás*) to say dreadful things about sb
3 (*CAm, Caribe*) (= *enfadado*) cross, angry
tibor (SM) (= *jarro*) large earthenware jar; (*Caribe*) (= *orinal*) chamber pot; (*Méx*) (= *calabaza*) gourd, squash (*EEUU*)
tiburón (SM) **1** (*Zool*) shark ▸ **tiburón de río** pike
2* (= *persona sin escrúpulos*) shark*
3 (*Bolsa*) raider
4 (*Cono Sur*) wolf*, Don Juan
tiburoneo (SM) (*Bolsa*) share raiding
tic (SM) (PL: **tics**) **1** (= *sonido*) click; [*de reloj*] tick
2 (*Med*) tic ▸ **tic facial** facial tic ▸ **tic nervioso** nervous tic
3 (= *costumbre*) habit
Ticiano (SM) Titian
tícket ['tike] (SM) (PL: **tickets** ['tike]) (= *billete*) ticket; [*de compra*] receipt
tico/a* (ADJ), (SM/F) (*CAm*) Costa Rican
tictac (SM) [*de reloj*] tick, ticking; [*de corazón*] beat • **hacer ~** [*reloj*] to tick; [*corazón*] to beat
tiempecito (SM) (spell of) very bad weather
tiemple (SM) **1** (*Cono Sur*) (= *galanteo*) love-making, courting
2 (*Cono Sur*) (= *amante*) lover
3 (*LAm*) (= *enamoramiento*) infatuation
tiempo (SM) **1** (*indicando duración*) time • **no tengo ~** I haven't got time • **tenemos todo el ~ del mundo** we have all the time in the world • **el ~ pasa y no nos damos ni cuenta** time goes by *o* passes and we don't even realize it • **tómate el ~ que quieras** take as long as you want • **me llevó bastante ~** it took me quite a long time • **hace bastante ~ que lo compré** I bought it quite a while ago • **¿cuánto ~ se va a quedar?** how long is he staying for? • **¿cuánto ~ hace de eso?** how long ago was that? • **¿cuánto ~ hace que vives aquí?** how long have you been living here? • **¡cuánto ~ sin verte!** I haven't seen you for ages! • **más ~**: • **necesito más ~ para pensármelo** I need more time *o* longer to think about it • **no puede quedarse más ~** he can't stay any longer • **mucho ~**: • **una costumbre que viene de mucho ~ atrás** a long-standing custom • **has tardado mucho ~** you took a long time • **ocurrió hace mucho ~** it happened a long time ago • **hace mucho ~ que no la veo** I haven't seen her for a long time • **al poco ~ de** soon after • **al poco ~ de su muerte** soon after his death • **se acostumbró a la idea en muy poco ~** she soon got used to the idea, it didn't take her long to get used to the idea ▸ **tiempo de exposición** (*Fot*) exposure time ▸ **tiempo libre** spare time, free time
2 (*otras locuciones*) • **a tiempo** in time • **llegamos a ~ de ver la película** we got there in time to see the film • **todavía estáis a ~ de cambiar de idea** it's still not too late for you to change your minds • **el avión llegó a ~** the plane arrived on time • **cada cierto ~** every so often • **a ~ completo** full-time • **trabajar a ~ completo** to work full-time • **con ~**: • **llegamos con ~ de darnos un paseo** we arrived in time to have a walk • **si me lo dices con ~** if you tell me beforehand • **con el ~** eventually • **con el ~ lo conseguiremos** we'll manage it eventually • **dar ~**: • **no da ~ a terminarlo** there isn't enough time to finish it • **¿crees que te dará ~?** do you think you'll have (enough) time? • **dale ~** give him time • **fuera de ~** at the wrong time • **ganar ~** to save time • **hacer ~** to while away the time • **matar el ~** to kill time • **a ~ parcial** part-time • **trabajo a ~ parcial** part-time work • **trabajador a ~ parcial** part-timer • **de un *o* algún ~ a esta parte** for some time (past) • **pasar el ~** to pass time • **no es más que una forma de pasar el ~** it just a way of passing time • **perder el ~** to waste time • **estás perdiendo el ~** you're wasting your time • **me estás haciendo perder el ~** you're wasting my time • **sería simplemente perder el ~** it would just be a waste of time • **¡rápido, no perdamos (el) ~!** quick, there's no time to lose! • **sin perder ~** without delay • **sacar ~ para hacer algo** to find the time to do sth • **tener ~ para algo** to have time for sth • MODISMOS: • **andando el ~** in due course, in time • **el ~ apremia** time presses • **dar ~ al ~** to let matters take their course • **de ~ en ~** from time to time • REFRANES: • **con el ~ y una caña (hasta las verdes caen)** all good things come to those who wait • **el ~ es oro** time is precious • **el ~ dirá** time will tell • **el ~ todo lo borra** • **el ~ lo cura todo** time is a great healer
3 (= *momento*) time • **al mismo ~** • **a un ~** at the same time • **al (mismo) ~ que** at the (same) time as • **cada cosa a su ~** everything in good time • **llegamos antes de ~** we arrived early • **ha nacido antes de ~** he was born prematurely, he was premature • **a su debido ~** in due course
4 (= *época*) time • **durante un ~ vivimos en Valencia** we lived in Valencia for a time *o* while • **en ~ de los griegos** in the days of the Greeks • **en mis ~s** in my day • **en ~s de mi abuelo** in my grandfather's day • **en los buenos ~s** in the good old days • **en estos ~s que corren** these days • **en otros ~s** formerly • **en los últimos ~s** recently, lately, in recent times • **a través de los ~s** through the ages • **los ~s están revueltos** these are troubled times • **hay que ir con los ~s** you have to move with the times • MODISMO: • **en ~s de Maricastaña**: • **va vestida como en ~s de Maricastaña** her clothes went out with the ark, her clothes are really old-fashioned • **una receta del ~ de Maricastaña** an ancient *o* age-old recipe ▸ **tiempos modernos** modern times
5 (= *edad*) age • **Ricardo y yo somos del mismo ~** Ricardo and I are the same age • **¿cuánto *o* qué ~ tiene el niño?** how old is the baby?
6 (*Dep*) half • **primer ~** first half • **segundo ~** second half ▸ **tiempo muerto** (*lit*) time-out; (*fig*) breather
7 (*Mús*) [*de compás*] tempo, time; [*de sinfonía*] movement
8 (*Ling*) tense • **en ~ presente** in the present tense ▸ **tiempo compuesto** compound tense ▸ **tiempo simple** simple tense
9 (*Meteo*) weather • **hace buen ~** the weather is good • **hace mal ~** the weather is bad • **¿qué ~ hace ahí?** what's the weather like there? • **si dura el mal ~** if the bad weather continues • **del ~**: • **¿quiere el agua fría o del ~?** would you like the water chilled or at room temperature? • **prefiero la fruta del ~** I prefer fruit that's in season • REFRÁN: • **a mal ~, buena cara** one must try to put a brave face on it; ▷ **mapa, hombre**
10 (*Inform*) time ▸ **tiempo compartido** time-sharing ▸ **tiempo de ejecución** run time ▸ **tiempo real** real time • **conversación en ~ real** real-time conversation • **cada jugador está conectado en ~ real** all the players are playing in real time
11 (*Industria*) time ▸ **tiempo de paro, tiempo inactivo** downtime ▸ **tiempo preferencial** prime time
12 (*Náut*) stormy weather
13 (*Mec*) cycle • **motor de dos ~s** two-stroke engine
tienda (SF) **1** (*Com*) shop, store • **lo compré en esta ~** I bought it in this shop • **ir de ~s** to go shopping ▸ **tienda de abarrotes** (*CAm, And, Méx*) grocer's (shop) (*esp Brit*), grocery (*EEUU*) ▸ **tienda de comestibles** grocer's (shop), grocery (*EEUU*) ▸ **tienda de deportes** sports shop, sporting goods store (*EEUU*) ▸ **tienda de regalos** gift shop ▸ **tienda de ultramarinos** grocer's (shop), grocery (*EEUU*) ▸ **tienda electrónica** e-shop, (*esp Brit*) e-store (*esp EEUU*) ▸ **tienda libre de impuestos** duty-free shop ▸ **tienda por departamento** (*Caribe*) department store
2 (*tb* **tienda de campaña**) tent • **montar la ~** to pitch the tent • **desmontar la ~** to take down the tent
3 (*Náut*) awning
4 (*Med*) ▸ **tienda de oxígeno** oxygen tent
tienta (SF) **1** • **a ~s** gropingly, blindly • **andar a ~s** to grope one's way along, feel one's way; (*fig*) to feel one's way • **buscar algo a ~s** to grope around for sth • **decir algo a ~s** to throw out a remark at random, say sth to see what effect it has
2 (*Taur*) trial, test
3 (*Med*) probe
tiento (SM) **1** (= *diplomacia*) tact; (= *prudencia*)

care; (= *cautela*) wariness, circumspection • **ir con ~** to go carefully
2 (= *toque*) feel(ing), touch • **a ~** (= *por el tacto*) by touch; (= *con inseguridad*) uncertainly • **perder el ~** to lose one's touch • **a 40 dólares nadie le echó un ~** at 40 dollars nobody was biting, at 40 dollars he didn't get a tickle*
3* (= *propuesta*) pass* • **echar un ~ a una chica** to make a pass at a girl, try it on with a girl*
4 (= *buen pulso*) steadiness of hand, steady hand
5* (= *trago*) swig* • **dar un ~** to take a swig (a from)
6 (*Zool*) feeler, tentacle
7 (= *palo*) (*Circo*) balancing pole; [*de ciego*] blind man's stick
8* (= *puñetazo*) blow, punch • **dar ~s a algn** to hit sb
9 (*Cono Sur*) (= *tira*) thong of raw leather, rawhide strap

tiernamente (ADV) tenderly

tierno (ADJ) **1** (= *blando*) [*carne*] tender; [*pan*] fresh
2 [*brote*] tender
3 (= *afectuoso*) [*persona*] tender, affectionate; [*mirada, sonrisa*] tender
4 (= *joven*) tender • **a la tierna edad de cinco años** at the tender age of five • **en su más tierna infancia** in his tenderest youth

tierra (SF) **1** • **la Tierra** the earth, the Earth
2 (= *superficie*) **a** (*fuera del agua*) land • **¡~ a la vista!** land ahoy! • **permanecer en ~** to remain on land • **la industria pesquera genera unos 400.000 empleos en ~** the fishing industry provides 400,000 jobs on land • **saltar a ~** to leap ashore • **~ adentro** inland • **el desierto avanza ~ adentro** the desert is advancing inland • **soy de ~ adentro** I'm from inland • **por ~** overland, by land • **atravesar un país por ~** to go overland *o* by land across a country • **por ~ y por mar** by land and by sea • **tomar ~** to reach port, get in
b (= *no aire*) (*desde el aire*) ground; (*desde el espacio*) earth • **la explosión ocurrió cuando el avión cayó a ~** the explosion occurred when the aeroplane hit the ground • **un ataque por ~ y aire** a ground and air attack • **tocar ~** to touch down • **tomar ~** to land ▸ **tierra firme** (= *no aire*) solid ground; (= *no agua*) land
3 (= *suelo*) ground • **estaba tirado en la ~** he was lying on the ground • **caer a ~** to fall down • **caer por ~** [*persona*] to fall to the ground; [*argumento, teoría*] to fall apart • **dar con algo en ~** to knock sth over • **echar a ~** [+ *construcción, rival*] to knock down • **echarse a ~** to throw o.s. on *o* to the ground • **MODISMOS:** • **besar la ~** to fall flat on one's face • **echar** *o* **tirar por ~** [+ *trabajo, organización*] to ruin, destroy; [+ *expectativas, sueños*] to shatter; [+ *teoría, tesis*] to demolish • **perder ~** (*antes de caerse*) to lose one's footing; (*en el agua*) to get out of one's depth • **poner ~ de por medio** to get away as quickly as possible • **venirse a** *o* **por ~** to collapse • **¡~, trágame!** let me die! (*iró*)
4 (= *material*) (*gen*) earth; (= *polvo*) dust; (= *barro*) mud; (*para jardinería, cultivo*) soil • **olía a ~ mojada** it smelled of wet earth • **se levantó mucha ~** a dust cloud blew up • **con los zapatos llenos de ~** (= *polvo*) with his shoes covered in dust; (= *barro*) with his shoes covered in mud • **viviendas con suelo de ~** houses with earth *o* dirt floors • **el avión aterrizó en una pequeña pista de ~** the aeroplane landed on a small dirt runway • **un camino de ~** a dirt road • **es muy buena ~ para las plantas** it's good soil for plants • **un saco de ~** a bag of soil • **jugarán en pistas de ~** they'll play on clay courts • **sacudir la ~** (*Cono Sur, Méx*) to dust • **MODISMOS:** • **estar bajo ~** to be dead and buried • **echar ~ a** *o* **sobre algo** (= *ocultar*) to hush sth up; (= *olvidar*) to put sth behind one • **acordaron echar ~ al incidente y seguir siendo amigos** they agreed to put the incident behind them and continue to be friends • **echar ~ a algn** (*Méx, Chile*) to sling *o* throw mud at sb; (*Col**) to make sb look bad • **le vienes a echar ~ a mi carro con tu descapotable** your convertible makes my car look ridiculous *o* really bad • **echarse ~ encima** to foul one's own nest ▸ **tierra caliente** (*LAm*) *land below 1000m approximately* ▸ **tierra de batán** fuller's earth ▸ **tierra de brezo** peat ▸ **tierra fría** (*LAm*) *land above 2000m approximately* ▸ **tierra quemada** (*Pol*) scorched earth ▸ **tierra templada** (*LAm*) *land between 1000m and 2000m approximately* ▸ **tierra vegetal** topsoil; ▹ **pista, política**
5 (*Agr*) land • **trabajar la ~** to work the land • **las ~s de cereales** grain-growing land • **heredó unas ~s cerca del río** he inherited some land near the river • **MODISMO:** • **en cualquier ~ de garbanzos** all over ▸ **tierra baldía** wasteland ▸ **tierra de cultivo** arable land ▸ **tierra de labor** agricultural land ▸ **tierra de pan llevar** grain-growing land ▸ **tierra de regadío** irrigated land ▸ **tierra de secano** dry land, unirrigated land
6 (= *división territorial*) **a** (= *lugar de origen*) • **en mi ~ no se usa esa expresión** we don't use that expression where I come from • **vamos a nuestra ~ a pasar las Navidades** we're going home for Christmas • **todo refugiado siente nostalgia de su ~** every refugee feels homesick for or misses his native land *o* homeland • **de la ~** [*vino, queso*] local, locally produced; [*fruta, verduras*] locally grown • **productos de la ~** local produce
b (*en plural*) • **la expropiación de ~s palestinas** the expropriation of Palestinian land *o* lands • **su largo exilio en ~s australianas** her lengthy exile in Australia • **no es de estas ~s** he's not from these parts, he's not from this part of the world • **MODISMO:** • **ver ~s†** to see the world ▸ **Tierra del Fuego** Tierra del Fuego ▸ **tierra de nadie** no-man's-land ▸ **tierra de promisión** promised land ▸ **tierra natal** native land ▸ **tierra prometida** promised land ▸ **Tierra Santa** Holy Land
7 (*Elec*) earth, ground (*EEUU*) • **conectar un aparato a ~** to earth *o* (*EEUU*) ground an appliance; ▹ **toma**

tierra-aire (ADJ INV) • **misil tierra-aire** surface-to-air missile, ground-to-air missile

tierrafría (SMF) (*And*) highlander

tierral (SM) (*LAm*), **tierrazo** (SM) (*LAm*) = **terral**

tierra-tierra (ADJ INV) • **misil tierra-tierra** surface-to-surface missile

tierrero (SM) (*LAm*) cloud of dust

tierruca (SF) native land, native heath

tieso (ADJ) **1** (= *duro*) stiff; (= *rígido*) rigid; (= *erguido*) erect; (= *derecho*) straight; (= *tenso*) taut • **ponte tiesa** stand up straight • **con las orejas tiesas** with its ears pricked • **MODISMOS:** • **dejar ~ a algn*** (= *matar*) to do sb in*; (= *sorprender*) to amaze sb, leave sb speechless • **quedarse ~*** (*de frío*) to be frozen stiff; (= *sorprenderse*) to be left speechless; (= *morirse*) to snuff it*, peg out*
2 (= *sano*) fit; (= *vivo*) sprightly; (= *alegre*) chirpy* • **le encontré muy ~ a pesar de su enfermedad** I found him very chirpy in spite of his illness
3 (= *poco amable*) (*en conducta*) stiff; (*en actitud*) rigid • **me recibió muy ~** he received me very coldly • **MODISMO:** • **~ como un ajo** as stiff as a poker
4 (= *orgulloso*) proud; (= *presumido*) conceited, stuck-up*; (= *pagado de sí mismo*) smug • **iba tan ~ con la novia al brazo** he was walking so proudly with his girl on his arm
5 (= *terco*) stubborn; (= *firme*) firm, confident • **ponerse ~ con algn** to stand one's ground, insist on one's rights; (*pey*) to be stubborn with sb • **tenerlas tiesas con algn** to put up a firm resistance to sb, stand up for o.s.
6* (= *sin dinero*) (flat) broke*
(ADV) strongly, energetically, hard

tiesto (SM) **1** (= *maceta*) flowerpot
2 (= *cascote*) shard, piece of pottery
3 (*Cono Sur*) (= *vasija*) pot, vessel; (= *orinal*) chamber pot

tiesura (SF) **1** (= *rigidez*) stiffness
2 (= *presunción*) conceit
3 (= *terquedad*) stubbornness

tifiar‡ ▹ CONJUG 1b (VT) (*Caribe*) to nick‡, lift*

tifitifi* (SM) (*Caribe*) theft

tifo (SM) typhus ▸ **tifo asiático** cholera ▸ **tifo de América** yellow fever ▸ **tifo de Oriente** bubonic plague

tifoidea (SF) typhoid

tifoideo (ADJ) • **fiebre tifoidea** typhoid (fever)

tifón (SM) **1** (= *huracán*) typhoon
2 (= *tromba*) waterspout
3 (*Méx*) (*Min*) outcrop of ore

tifus (SM INV) **1** (*Med*) typhus ▸ **tifus exantemático** spotted fever ▸ **tifus icteroides** yellow fever
2 (*Teat**) claque • **entrar de ~** to get in free

tigra (SF) (*LAm*) (*Zool*) female tiger; (= *jaguar*) female jaguar • **MODISMO:** • **ponerse como una ~ parida** (*And, Cono Sur**) to fly off the handle*

tigre (SM) **1** (*Zool*) tiger; (*LAm*) jaguar ▸ **tigre de Bengala** Bengal tiger ▸ **tigre de colmillo de sable** sabre-toothed tiger ▸ **tigre de papel** paper tiger
2 (*And*) (= *café*) *black coffee with a dash of milk*; (*And*) (= *combinado*) cocktail
3‡ (= *wáter*) bog‡, loo*, john (*EEUU‡*) • **esto huele a ~** this stinks, this smells foul

tigrero (ADJ) (*Cono Sur*) brave
(SM) (*LAm*) jaguar hunter

tigresa (SF) **1** (= *animal*) tigress
2 (= *mujer cruel*) shrew; (= *mujer fatal*) vamp*

tigridia (SF) tiger lily

tigrillo (SM) (*LAm*) *member of the cat tribe, eg ocelot, lynx*

Tigris (SM) Tigris

tigrón* (SM) (*Caribe*) bully, braggart

tigüila (SF) (*Méx*) trick, swindle

tija (SF) (*Aut*) shank

tijera (SF) **1** (*tb* **tijeras**) scissors (*pl*); (*para jardín*) shears (*pl*), clippers (*pl*) • **unas ~s** a pair of scissors • **meter la ~ en algo** to cut into sth • **es un trabajo de ~** it's a scissors-and-paste job ▸ **tijeras de coser** sewing scissors ▸ **tijeras de podar** secateurs ▸ **tijeras para las uñas** nail scissors ▸ **tijeras podadoras** secateurs
2 [*de bicicleta*] fork
3 • **de ~** folding • **silla de ~** (= *con respaldo*) folding chair; (= *banqueta*) folding stool, camp stool • **escalera de ~** steps, step-ladder
4 (*LAm*) (*Zool*) claw, pincer
5* (= *persona*) gossip • **ser una buena ~** • **tener buena ~** (= *chismoso*) to be a great gossip; (= *mordaz*) to have a sharp tongue; (= *criticón*) be a scandalmonger

tijeral (SM) (*Cono Sur*) stork

tijereta (SF) **1** (= *insecto*) earwig
2 (*Bot*) vine tendril

3 (*Dep*) scissor(s) kick, overhead kick

tijeretazo SM **1** (*con tijeras*) snip, snick
2 (*económico*) cutback

tijeretear ▷ CONJUG 1a VT to snip, snick
VI **1** (= *entrometerse*) to meddle
2 (*CAm, Cono Sur, Méx*) (= *chismear*) to gossip, backbite

tijereteo SM **1** (*con tijeras*) snipping, snicking
2 (= *entrometimiento*) meddling
3 (*CAm, Cono Sur, Méx*) (= *chismes*) gossiping, backbiting

tila SF **1** (= *planta*) lime tree
2 (= *infusión*) lime flower tea • MODISMO: • **¡que te den ~!*** give me a break!*
3‡ (= *droga*) hash*, pot*

tildar ▷ CONJUG 1a VT **1** (= *acusar*) • **~ a algn de racista** to brand sb (as) a racist • **le ~on de vago** they dismissed him as lazy, they called him lazy
2 (*Tip*) (*gen*) to put an accent on; (*sobre la n*) to put a tilde over

tilde SF **1** (*ortográfica*) (= *acento*) (*gen*) accent; (*sobre la n*) tilde
2 (= *mancha*) blemish; (= *defecto*) defect, flaw
3 (= *bagatela*) triviality; (= *pizca*) jot, bit • MODISMO: • **en una ~*** in a jiffy*

tilichera SF (*CAm, Méx*) hawker's box, glass-covered box

tilichero/a SM/F (*CAm, Méx*) hawker, pedlar, peddler (*EEUU*)

tiliches* SMPL (*CAm, Méx*) (= *pertenencias*) belongings; (= *baratijas*) trinkets; (= *trastos*) junk (*sing*)

tilín SM [*de campanilla*] tinkle, ting-a-ling • MODISMOS: • **hacer ~ a algn***: • **me hace ~** [*persona*] I fancy him*; [*cosa*] I like it, I go for it* • **no me hace ~** [*cosa*] it doesn't do anything for me • **en un ~** (*And, Caribe, Cono Sur**) in a flash • **tener algo al ~** (*Caribe*) to have sth at one's fingertips

tilinches* SMPL (*Méx*) rags

tilingada* SF (*Cono Sur, Méx*) silly thing (to do *etc*)

tilingo/a* (*And, Cono Sur, Méx*) ADJ silly, stupid
SM/F fool

tilinguear* ▷ CONJUG 1a VI (*And, Cono Sur, Méx*) to act the fool

tilinguería* SF (*And, Cono Sur, Méx*)
1 (= *estupidez*) silliness, stupidity
2 tilinguerías nonsense (*sing*)

tilintar ▷ CONJUG 1a VT (*CAm*) to stretch, tauten

tilinte ADJ (*CAm*) **1** (= *tenso*) tight, taut
2 (= *elegante*) elegant
3 (= *repleto*) replete

tilma SF (*Méx*) blanket, cape

tilo SM **1** (= *planta*) lime tree
2 (*LAm*) (= *infusión*) lime flower tea

tiloso* ADJ (*CAm*) dirty, filthy

timador(a) SM/F swindler, trickster

timar ▷ CONJUG 1a VT to swindle, con* • **¡me han timado!** I've been conned!* • **le ~on la herencia** they swindled him out of his inheritance
VPR **timarse*** [*pareja*] to make eyes at each other • **~se con algn** (= *engatusar*) to play sb along, lead sb on; (*amorosamente*) to make eyes at sb, ogle sb

timba SF **1** (*en juego de azar*) hand
2 (= *garito*) gambling den
3 (*CAm, Caribe, Méx*) (= *tripa*) pot-belly
4 • MODISMO: • **tener ~** (*Caribe*): • **esto tiene ~** it's a sticky business

timbal SM **1** (*Mús*) small drum, kettledrum • **~es** timpani
2 (*Culin*) meat pie
3 timbales** (= *testículos*) balls**

timbembe* ADJ (*Cono Sur*) weak, trembling

timbero/a* (*Cono Sur*) ADJ given to gambling
SM/F gambler

timbiriche SM (*Caribe, Méx*) small shop

timbrado ADJ • **voz bien timbrada** well-toned voice

timbrar ▷ CONJUG 1a VT **1** [+ *documento*] to stamp
2 [+ *carta*] to postmark, frank

timbrazo SM ring • **dar un ~** to ring the bell

timbre SM **1** (*Elec*) bell • **tocar el ~** to ring the bell ▸ **timbre de alarma** alarm bell
2 (*Mús*) timbre ▸ **timbre nasal** nasal timbre, twang
3 (*Com, Econ*) (= *sello*) fiscal stamp, revenue stamp; (= *renta*) stamp duty, revenue stamp (*EEUU*)
4 (*Méx*) [*de correos*] (postage) stamp
5 (*LAm*) (= *descripción*) [*de persona*] personal description; [*de géneros*] description of goods (*etc*)
6 ▸ **timbre de gloria** (= *señal*) mark of honour; (= *acto*) *action etc which is to one's credit*

timbrear ▷ CONJUG 1a VI to ring (the bell)

timbusca SF (*And*) (= *sopa*) thick soup; (= *plato rústico*) *spicy local dish*

tímidamente ADV shyly, timidly

timidez SF shyness, timidity

tímido ADJ shy, timid

timo SM swindle, con trick* • **dar un ~ a algn** to swindle sb, con sb* • **¡es un ~!** it's a rip-off!*

timón SM **1** (*Aer, Náut*) rudder; (= *mando, control*) helm • **poner el ~ a babor** to turn to port, port the helm • MODISMO: • **coger** *o* **empuñar el ~** to take the helm, take charge ▸ **timón de deriva, timón de dirección** rudder ▸ **timón de profundidad** (*Aer*) elevator
2 [*de carruaje*] pole; [*de arado*] beam
3 (*And*) (*Aut*) steering wheel

timonear ▷ CONJUG 1a VT (*LAm*) (= *dirigir*) to direct, manage; (= *guiar*) to guide
VI to steer; (*And*) (*Aut*) to drive

timonel SMF (*Náut*) steersman/steerswoman, helmsman/helmswoman; (*en barca de remo*) cox

timonera SF wheelhouse

timonería SF (*Náut*) rudders (*pl*), steering mechanisms (*pl*); (*Ferro*) linkage

timonero SM = **timonel**

Timor SM Timor • **~ Oriental** East Timor

timorato ADJ **1** (= *tímido*) lily-livered, spineless
2 (= *mojigato*) sanctimonious, prudish
3 (= *que teme a Dios*) God-fearing

timorés/esa ADJ Timorese • **~ oriental** East Timorese
SM/F Timorese, Timorese man/woman • **los timoreses** the Timorese • **los timoreses orientales** the East Timorese

Timoteo SM Timothy

tímpano SM **1** (*Anat*) tympanum, eardrum
2 (*Arquit*) tympanum
3 (*Mús*) small drum, kettledrum; **tímpanos** (*en orquesta*) timpani

tina SF (= *recipiente*) tub, vat; (*para bañarse*) bath(tub) ▸ **tina de lavar** washtub

tinaco SM (*Méx*) (= *cisterna*) water tank; (*And, Méx*) (= *vasija*) tall earthenware jar

tinaja SF large earthenware jar

tinajero SM stone water filter

tinca SF **1** (*Cono Sur*) (= *capirotazo*) flip, flick
2 (*And*) bowls (*pl*)
3 (*Cono Sur*) (= *pálpito*) hunch

tincada SF (*Cono Sur*) hunch

tincanque SM (*Cono Sur*) = **tinca**

tincar* ▷ CONJUG 1g VI (*Chile*) **1** (= *presentir*) to have a hunch about • **me tinca que …** it seems to me that …, I have a feeling that…
2 (= *apetecer*) to like, fancy* • **me tinca** I like it • **no me tinca** I don't fancy the idea
3 (= *dar un capirotazo a*) to flip, flick

tincazo SM (*Cono Sur*) = **tinca**

tinctura SF tincture

tinerfeño/a ADJ of/from Tenerife
SM/F native/inhabitant of Tenerife • **los ~s** the people of Tenerife

tinga* SF (*Méx*) row, uproar

tingar ▷ CONJUG 1h VT (*And*) to flip, flick

tinglado SM **1** (= *tablado*) platform; (= *cobertizo*) shed
2* (= *sistema*) set-up • **está metida en el ~ del espiritismo** she's into the spiritualism thing • **conocer el ~** to know the score* • **montar el ~** to get going, set up in business • **montar su ~** to do one's own thing*
3 (= *intriga*) plot, intrigue; (= *truco*) trick • **armar un ~** to hatch a plot
4 (= *follón*) mess

tingo SM (*And*), **tingue** SM (*And*) = **tinca**

tinieblas SFPL **1** (= *oscuridad*) dark(ness) (*sing*); (= *sombras*) shadows; (= *tenebrosidad*) gloom (*sing*)
2 (= *confusión*) confusion (*sing*); (= *ignorancia*) ignorance (*sing*) • **estamos en ~ sobre sus proyectos** we are in the dark about his plans

tino¹ SM **1** (= *habilidad*) skill, knack, feel; (= *seguridad*) (sureness of) touch; (= *conjeturas*) (good) guesswork; (*Mil*) (= *puntería*) (accurate) aim • **coger el ~** to get the feel *o* hang of it • **a ~** gropingly • **a buen ~** by guesswork
2 (= *tacto*) tact; (= *perspicacia*) insight, acumen; (= *juicio*) good judgement • **sin ~** foolishly • **obrar con mucho ~** to act very wisely • **perder el ~** to act foolishly, go off the rails • MODISMO: • **sacar de ~ a algn** (= *enfadar*) to exasperate sb, infuriate sb; (= *confundir*) to confuse sb
3 (= *moderación*) moderation • **sin ~** immoderately • **comer sin ~** to eat to excess • **gastar sin ~** to spend recklessly

tino² SM **1** (= *tina*) vat; [*de piedra*] stone tank
2 (= *lagar*) winepress; [*de aceite*] olive press

tinoso ADJ (*And*) (= *hábil*) skilful, skillful (*EEUU*), clever; (= *juicioso*) sensible; (= *moderado*) moderate; (= *diplomático*) tactful

tinque SM (*Cono Sur*) = **tinca**

tinta SF **1** (*para escribir*) ink • **con ~** in ink • MODISMOS: • **saber algo de buena ~** to know sth on good authority • **sudar ~*** to slog, slave one's guts out* ▸ **tinta china** Indian ink, India ink (*EEUU*) ▸ **tinta de imprenta** printing ink, printer's ink ▸ **tinta de marcar** marking ink ▸ **tinta indeleble** indelible ink ▸ **tinta invisible, tinta simpática** invisible ink
2 [*de pulpo, calamar*] ink • **calamares en su ~** squid in their own ink
3 (*Arte*) (= *color*) colour, color (*EEUU*); **tintas** (*liter*) shades, hues • **media ~** half-tone, tint • MODISMOS: • **cargar las ~s** to exaggerate • **medias ~s** (= *medidas*) half measures; (= *ideas*) half-baked ideas; (= *respuestas*) inadequate answers
4 (= *tinte*) dye

tintar ▷ CONJUG 1a VT to dye

tinte SM **1** (= *acto*) dyeing
2 (= *producto*) dye, dyestuff; (*para madera*) stain
3 (= *tintorería*) dry cleaner's; (= *taller*) dyer's (shop)
4 (= *tendencia*) hint • **sin el menor ~ político** without the slightest hint of politics, with no political overtones whatsoever
5 (= *barniz*) veneer, gloss • **tiene cierto ~ de hombre de mundo** he has a slight touch of the man of the world about him

tinterillo SM **1** (= *empleado*) penpusher, pencil pusher (EEUU), small-time clerk
2 (*LAm*) (= *abogado*) shyster lawyer*
tintero SM **1** (= *recipiente*) inkpot, ink bottle (EEUU), inkwell • **MODISMO**: • **dejarse algo en el ~** (= *olvidar*) to forget about sth; (= *no mencionar*) to leave sth unsaid • **no se deja nada en el ~** she leaves nothing unsaid
2 (*LAm*) (= *plumas*) desk set, writing set
tintillo SM (*Cono Sur*) red wine
tintín SM [*de campanilla*] tinkle, tinkling; [*de cadena, llaves*] jingle; [*de copas, tazas*] clink, chink
tintineante ADJ **1** [*llaves*] jingling
2 [*campanilla*] tinkling
tintinear ▷ CONJUG 1a VI [*campanilla*] to tinkle; [*cadena, llaves*] to jingle; [*copas, tazas*] to clink, chink
tintineo SM = **tintín**
tinto ADJ **1** [*vino*] red
2 (= *teñido*) dyed; (= *manchado*) stained • **~ en sangre** stained with blood, bloodstained
SM **1** (= *vino*) red wine • **un ~** a (glass of) red wine
2 (*Col*) (= *café*) black coffee
tintorera SF (= *pez*) shark; (*And, CAm, Méx*) female shark; ▷ **tintorero**
tintorería SF **1** (= *tienda*) dry cleaner's
2 (= *actividad*) dyeing; (= *fábrica*) dyeworks; (= *establecimiento*) dyer's, dyer's shop
tintorero/a SM/F (= *que tiñe*) dyer; (= *que limpia en seco*) dry cleaner; ▷ **tintorera**
tintorro* SM plonk*, cheap red wine
tintura SF **1** (= *acto*) dyeing
2 (*Quím*) dye, dyestuff; (*Téc*) stain
3 (*Farm*) tincture ▸ **tintura de tornasol** litmus ▸ **tintura de yodo** (tincture of) iodine
4 (= *poquito*) smattering; (= *barniz*) thin veneer
tinturar ▷ CONJUG 1a VT **1** (= *teñir*) to dye
2 (= *instruir*) • **~ a algn** to give sb a rudimentary knowledge, teach sb superficially
tiña SF **1** (*Med*) ringworm
2 (= *pobreza*) poverty
3 (= *tacañería*) meanness
tiñoso ADJ **1** (*Med*) scabby, mangy
2 (= *miserable*) poor, wretched
3 (= *tacaño*) mean
tío/a SM/F **1** (= *pariente*) uncle/aunt • **mi tío Ignacio** my uncle Ignacio • **mis tíos** (= *solo hombres*) my uncles; (= *hombres y mujeres*) my uncle(s) and aunt(s) • **el tío Sam** Uncle Sam • **MODISMOS**: • **¡no hay tu tía!*** nothing doing! • **¡cuéntaselo a tu tía!*** pull the other one!* ▸ **tío/a abuelo/a** great-uncle/great-aunt ▸ **tío/a carnal** blood uncle/aunt
2* (= *hombre*) guy*, bloke*; (= *mujer*) woman; (= *chica*) girl • **¿quién es ese tío?** who's that guy *o* bloke?* • **los tíos** guys*, blokes* • **las tías** women • **¡qué tío! ¡no ha perdido un solo partido!** the guy's incredible, he hasn't lost a single match!* • **¡qué tío! ¡nunca me deja en paz!** the guy's a real pain, he won't leave me alone!* • **MODISMOS**: • **es un tío grande** • **es un tío con toda la barba** he's a great guy *o* bloke* ▸ **tío/a bueno/a** hunk*/stunner* • **¡tía buena!** hello gorgeous!*
3†† *title given to older people in traditional rural communities* • **ha muerto el tío Francisco** old Francisco has died
tiovivo SM roundabout, carousel (EEUU), merry-go-round
tipa SF (*And, Cono Sur*) large wicker basket; ▷ **tipo**
tipazo* SM **1** (= *tipo*) [*de hombre*] build; [*de mujer*] figure • **¡qué ~ tiene Raquel!** what a figure Raquel's got!
2 (= *hombre*) (*grande*) tall chap*, big guy*; (*arrogante*) arrogant fellow; (*And*) (= *importante*) bigwig*
tipear ▷ CONJUG 1a VT, VI (*LAm*) to type
tipejo/a* SM/F (*raro*) oddball*, queer fish*; (*despreciable*) nasty character
tiperrita SF (*Caribe*) typist
tipiadora† SF **1** (= *máquina*) typewriter
2 (= *persona*) typist
típicamente ADV typically
tipicidad SF genuineness, authenticity
típico ADJ **1** (= *característico*) typical • **es muy ~ de él** it's typical of him • **¡lo ~!** typical!
2 (= *pintoresco*) full of local colour *o* (EEUU) color; (= *tradicional*) traditional; (= *regional*) regional; [*costumbre*] typical • **es la taberna más típica de la ciudad** it's the most picturesque pub in town • **no hay que perderse tan típica fiesta** you shouldn't miss a festivity so full of local colour *o* tradition • **es un traje ~** it is a traditional costume • **baile ~** regional dance, national dance
tipificación SF classification
tipificar ▷ CONJUG 1g VT **1** (= *clasificar*) to class, consider (**como** as)
2 (= *ser típico de*) to typify, characterize
tipismo SM (= *color*) local colour, local color (EEUU); (= *interés folklórico*) picturesqueness; (= *tradicionalismo*) traditionalism; (= *regionalismo*) regional character
tiple SM **1** (*Mús*) (= *persona*) treble, boy soprano
2 (= *voz*) soprano
SF (*cantante*) soprano
tipo/a SM/F* (= *individuo*) (= *hombre*) guy*, bloke*; (= *mujer*) chick*, bird*, dame (EEUU*) • **¿quién es ese ~?** who's that guy *o* bloke?* • **dos ~s sospechosos** two suspicious characters*; ▷ **tipa**
SM **1** (= *clase*) type, kind, sort • **un coche de otro ~ pero del mismo precio** a different type *o* kind *o* sort of car but for the same price • **un nuevo ~ de bicicleta** a new type of bicycle • **no me gusta este ~ de fiestas** I don't like this kind of party • **todo ~ de ...** all sorts *o* kinds of ... • **tuvimos todo ~ de problemas** we had all sorts *o* kinds of problems
2 (*Bot, Literat, Zool*) type
3 (*Com, Econ*) rate ▸ **tipo a término** forward rate ▸ **tipo bancario, tipo base** base rate ▸ **tipo de cambio** exchange rate ▸ **tipo de descuento** discount rate ▸ **tipo de interés** interest rate ▸ **tipo impositivo** tax rate
4 (= *figura, cuerpo*) [*de hombre*] build; [*de mujer*] figure • **tiene el ~ de su padre** he has his father's build • **tener buen ~** [*hombre*] to be well built; [*mujer*] to have a good figure • **Nuria tiene un ~ horrible** Nuria has a terrible figure • **MODISMOS**: • **aguantar** *o* **mantener el ~** to keep one's composure • **jugarse el ~** to risk one's neck
5 (*Tip*) type ▸ **tipo de letra** typeface ▸ **tipo gótico** Gothic type ▸ **tipo menudo** small type
ADJ INV **1** (= *similar a*) • **un sombrero ~ Bogart** a Bogart-style hat • **una joven ~ Marilyn** a girl in the Marilyn mould • **una foto ~ carné** a passport-size photo • **un vehículo ~ jeep** a jeep-type vehicle
2 (= *típico*) average, typical • **dos conductores ~** two average *o* typical drivers • **lengua ~** standard language
tipografía SF **1** (= *arte*) typography
2 (= *taller*) printing works, printing press
tipográfico ADJ typographical, printing (*antes de s*)
tipógrafo/a SM/F printer
tipología SF typology
tiposo ADJ (*And*) ridiculous, eccentric
típula SF cranefly, daddy-long-legs
tique SM = **tíquet**
tiquear ▷ CONJUG 1a VT (*Cono Sur*) to punch
tíquet ['tike] SM (PL: **tíquets** ['tike]) (= *billete*) ticket; (= *recibo de compra*) receipt; (*And*) (= *etiqueta*) label
tiquismiquis* SMF INV (= *persona*) fusspot*, fussbudget (EEUU*)
SMPL **1** (= *escrúpulos*) silly scruples; (= *detalles*) fussy details; (= *quejas*) silly *o* trivial objections
2 (= *cortesías*) affected courtesies, bowing and scraping
3 (= *riñas*) bickering (*sing*), squabbles
4 (= *molestias*) minor irritations, pinpricks
tiquitique* SM • **estar en el ~** to be gossiping
tira[1] SF **1** [*de tela*] strip; [*de zapato*] strap • **cortar algo en ~s** to cut sth into strips ▸ **tira cómica** comic strip ▸ **tira de películas** film strip ▸ **tira publicitaria** flysheet, advertising leaflet
2* • **MODISMO**: • **la ~***: • **me gusta la ~** I love it • **ganan la ~** they earn a packet* • **de eso hace la ~** that was ages ago • **la ~ de** loads of*, masses of • **estoy desde hace la ~ de tiempo** I've been here for absolutely ages
SM ▸ **tira y afloja** (= *negociaciones*) hard bargaining; (= *concesiones*) give and take, mutual concessions (*pl*)
tira[2] SF (*CAm, Méx**) police, cops* (*pl*)
SM (*Cono Sur**) (plainclothes) cop*, detective
tirabeque SM mangetout
tirabuzón SM **1** (= *rizo*) curl, ringlet
2 (= *sacacorchos*) corkscrew • **MODISMO**: • **sacar algo a algn con ~** to drag sth out of sb
3 (*Natación*) twist, corkscrew
tirachinas SM INV catapult, slingshot (EEUU)
tirada SF **1** [*de dados, dardos*] throw • **en la primera ~ hizo diez puntos** he scored ten points in the first throw • **de una ~** in one go • **leyó la novela de una ~** he read the novel straight through in one go
2 (= *distancia*) distance • **de aquí a Almería hay una ~ de 18kms** the distance from here to Almería is 18km • **aún nos queda una buena ~** we've still got a long way to go
3 (*Tip*) (= *acto*) printing; (= *ejemplares impresos*) print run; (= *ejemplares vendidos*) circulation • **han hecho una ~ de 5.000 ejemplares** they have done a print run of 5,000 copies • **la revista tiene una ~ semanal de 200.000 ejemplares** the magazine has a weekly circulation of 200,000 copies ▸ **tirada aparte** offprint
4 (= *retahíla*) string
5 (*Cos*) length
6 (*LAm*) (= *discurso*) boring speech
7 (*Cono Sur*) (= *indirecta*) hint
8 (*Caribe*) (= *mala pasada*) dirty trick
tiradera SF **1** (*CAm, Caribe, Cono Sur*) (= *faja*) sash; (= *correa*) belt, strap; (*Caribe*) [*de caballo*] harness strap, trace
2 (*And, CAm**) (= *mofa*) taunt
tiradero SM (*Méx*) (= *vertedero*) tip, rubbish-dump; (= *suciedad, desorden*) mess • **esta casa es un ~** this house is a tip*
tirado/a ADJ **1** (= *tumbado*) • **estar ~** to be lying • **siempre está ~ en el sofá** he's always lying on the sofa • **los juguetes estaban ~s por toda la habitación** the toys were lying *o* strewn all over the room
2* (= *barato*) • **estar ~** to be dirt-cheap*
3* (= *fácil*) • **estar ~** to be dead easy *o* a cinch* • **esa asignatura está tirada** that subject is dead easy*, that subject is a cinch*
4* • **dejar ~ a algn** to leave sb in the lurch • **quedarse ~** to be left in the lurch

t

5 (= *embarcación*) rakish
SM/F * (= *colgado*) no-hoper*

tirador(a) SM/F (= *persona*) marksman/ markswoman, shooter; (*CAm, Méx*) (= *cazador*) hunter • **es un buen ~** he's a good shot ▸ **tirador(a) apostado/a** sniper ▸ **tirador(a) certero/a** sharpshooter
SM 1 [*de cajón*] handle; [*de puerta*] knob
2 [*de campanilla*] bell pull
3 (= *tirachinas*) catapult, slingshot (*EEUU*)
4 (*Arte, Téc*) (= *pluma*) drawing pen
5 (*And, Cono Sur*) (= *cinturón*) wide gaucho belt
6 **tiradores** (*Cono Sur*) (= *tirantes*) braces, suspenders (*EEUU*)

tiragomas SM INV catapult, slingshot (*EEUU*)

tiraje SM 1 (*Tip*) (= *impresión*) printing; (= *cantidad*) print run
2 (*CAm, Cono Sur, Méx*) [*de chimenea*] chimney flue

tiralevitas SMF INV bootlicker*

tiralíneas SM INV drawing pen, ruling pen

tiranía SF tyranny

tiránicamente ADV tyrannically

tiranicida SMF tyrannicide (*person*)

tiranicidio SM tyrannicide (*act*)

tiránico ADJ (*gen*) tyrannical; [*amor*] possessive, domineering; [*atracción*] irresistible, all-powerful

tiranizar ▸ CONJUG 1f VT (= *oprimir*) to tyrannize; (= *gobernar*) to rule despotically; (= *dominar*) to domineer

tirano/a ADJ (= *tiránico*) tyrannical, despotic; (= *dominante*) domineering
SM/F tyrant, despot
SM (*Méx**) (= *policía*) cop*

tirantas SFPL (*And, Méx*) braces, suspenders (*EEUU*)

tirante ADJ 1 [+ *soga*] tight, taut; (= *tensado*) tensed, drawn tight
2 [*relaciones, situación*] (= *tenso*) tense, strained • **estamos algo ~s** things are rather strained between us
3 (*Econ*) tight
SM 1 [*de vestido*] shoulder strap; **tirantes** [*de pantalones*] braces, suspenders (*EEUU*) • **vestido sin ~s** strapless dress
2 (*Arquit*) crosspiece, brace; (*Mec*) strut, brace; [*de arreos*] trace

tirantear ▸ CONJUG 1a VT (*CAm, Cono Sur*) to stretch

tirantez SF 1 (*Téc etc*) tightness, tension
2 (*fig*) (= *tensión*) tension, strain • **la ~ de las relaciones con Eslobodia** the strained relations with Slobodia, the tense state of relations with Slobodia • **ha disminuido la ~** the tension has lessened
3 (*Econ*) tightness

tirar

VERBO TRANSITIVO
VERBO INTRANSITIVO
VERBO PRONOMINAL

▸ CONJUG 1a

Para las expresiones como **tirar de la lengua, tirar de la manta, tirar por la borda, tirar por tierra,** *ver la otra entrada.*

VERBO TRANSITIVO

1 (= *lanzar*) to throw • **tiró un papel por la ventanilla** he threw a piece of paper out of the window • **~ algo a algn** (*para que lo coja*) to throw sth to sb; (*para hacer daño*) to throw sth at sb • **tírame la pelota** throw me the ball • **les tiraban piedras a los soldados** they were throwing stones at the soldiers • **me tiró un beso** she blew me a kiss

2 (= *derribar*) [+ *edificio*] to pull down; [+ *jarrón, silla, estatua*] to knock over; [+ *pared, verja*] to knock down • **van a ~ la casa** they are going to demolish *o* pull down the house • **la moto la tiró al suelo** the motorbike knocked her over • **el viento ha tirado la valla** the wind has knocked the fence down • **¡abre, o tiro la puerta abajo!** open up, or I'll break the door down!

3 (= *dejar caer*) to drop • **tropezó y tiró la bandeja** she tripped and dropped the tray • **han tirado muchas bombas en la capital** many bombs have been dropped on the capital

4 (= *desechar*) to throw away • **no tires las sobras, que se las voy a dar al perro** don't throw away the leftovers, I'll give them to the dog • **tira las sobras a la basura** throw the leftovers in the bin • **no tires el aceite por el sumidero** don't tip *o* pour the oil down the drain • **estos pantalones están para ~los** these trousers have had it, these trousers are about ready for the dustbin • **no hay que ~ la comida** you shouldn't waste food

5 (= *malgastar*) [+ *dinero*] to waste; [+ *fortuna*] to squander • **has tirado el dinero comprando eso** it was a waste of money buying that, you wasted your money buying that

6 (= *disparar*) [+ *tiro*] to fire; [+ *flecha*] to shoot; [+ *cohete*] to launch, fire • **el aparato tira el proyectil a 2.000m** the machine throws the projectile 2,000m

7 (+ *foto*) to take

8 (= *dar, pegar*) • **deja ya de ~ patadas** stop kicking • **la mula le tiró una coz** the mule kicked him *o* gave him a kick • **¡mamá, Carlos me ha tirado un mordisco!** Carlos has bitten me, Mum!

9 (*Tip*) (= *imprimir*) to print, run off

10 (= *trazar*) [+ *línea*] to draw, trace

11* (= *suspender*) • **ya me han vuelto a ~ en química** I've failed chemistry again, I've flunked chemistry again (*esp EEUU**)

12 (*And*) (= *usar*) to use • **~ brazo** to swim

13 (*And, Caribe, Cono Sur*) (= *acarrear*) to cart, haul, transport

14 • **~la de**† (= *dárselas de*) to fancy oneself as, pose as

VERBO INTRANSITIVO

1 (*haciendo fuerza*) **a** (= *traer hacia sí*) to pull • **¡tira un poco más fuerte!** pull a bit harder! • **~ de** [+ *soga, cuerda*] to pull • **tire de ese cabo** pull that end • **¡no le tires de la trenza a tu hermana!** don't pull your sister's pigtail! • **~ de la cadena (del wáter)** to flush the toilet, pull the chain • **~ de la manga a algn** to tug at sb's sleeve • **"tirar"** (*Esp*) (*en puerta etc*) "pull" • **"tire"** (*LAm*) (*en puerta etc*) "pull"
b (= *llevar tras sí*) • **~ de** to pull • **un burro tiraba de la carreta** a donkey was pulling the cart along, the cart was drawn by a donkey • **los niños tiraban del trineo** the children were pulling the sledge along

2* (= *atraer*) • **no le tira el estudio** studying does not appeal to him, studying holds no attraction for him • **la patria tira siempre** one's native land always exerts a powerful pull

3 (= *estar tirante*) [*ropa*] to be tight • **este vestido tira un poco de aquí** this dress is a bit tight here • **me tira de sisa** it's tight round my armpits

4 (= *usar*) • **~ de** [+ *espada, navaja*] to draw • **~on de cuchillos** they drew their knives • **tiramos de diccionario y lo traducimos en un minuto*** if we use a dictionary it will just take a minute to translate

5 (= *disparar*) to shoot • **¡no tires!** don't shoot! • **~ con bala** to use live ammunition • **~ al blanco** to aim • **~ a matar** to shoot to kill • **los guardas tiraban a matar** the guards were shooting to kill • **mi jefa es de las que tiran a matar** my boss is the sort of person who goes for the kill

6 (*Dep*) (*con balón*) to shoot; (*con fichas, cartas etc*) to go, play • **¡tira!** shoot! • **tiró fuera de la portería** he shot wide of the goal • **tira tú ahora** it's your go now • **~ a puerta** (*Esp*) to shoot at goal

7* (= *arreglárselas*) to get by • **podemos ~ con menos dinero** we can get by on less money • **ir tirando** to get by, manage • **—¿qué tal esa salud? —vamos tirando** "how's your health?" — "we're getting by"

8 (= *funcionar*) [*motor*] to pull; [*chimenea, puro*] to draw, pull • **el motor no tira** the engine isn't pulling • **esta moto no tira** there's no life in this motorbike

9 (= *ir*) to go • **tire usted adelante** go straight on • **¡tira de una vez!** get on with it!, go on, then! • **~ a la derecha** to turn right • **~ por una calle** to turn down a street, go off along a street

10* (= *durar*) to last • **esos zapatos ~án todavía otro invierno** those shoes will last another winter yet

11 (*seguido de preposición*) **tirar a** (= *tender*) • **tiene el pelo rubio tirando a rojizo** he has reddish blond hair • **es mediocre tirando a malo** it's middling to bad, it's mediocre verging on bad • **tira más bien a cuidadoso** he's on the careful side • **tira a su padre** he takes after his father
tirar para (= *aspirar a ser*) • **la pequeña tira para actriz** the little girl has ambitions of becoming an actress • **tira para médico** he's attracted towards a career in medicine

12 • MODISMO: • **a todo ~** at the most • **nos queda gasolina para 20km a todo ~** we have only enough petrol for 20kms at the most *o* at the outside • **llegará el martes a todo ~** he'll arrive on Tuesday at the latest

13 (*LAm*)** (*sexualmente*) to screw**

VERBO PRONOMINAL **tirarse**

1 (= *lanzarse*) to throw o.s. • **~se al suelo** to throw o.s. to the ground • **~se por una ventana** to jump from *o* out of a window, throw o.s. out of a window • **~se por un precipicio** to throw o.s. over a cliff • **~se al agua** (*gen*) to plunge into the water; (*de cabeza*) to dive *o* plunge into the water • **~se en la cama** to lie down in bed • **~se en paracaídas** to parachute (down); (*en emergencia*) to bale out • **~se sobre algn** to rush at sb, spring on sb

2* (= *pasar*) to spend • **se tiró dos horas arreglándolo** he spent two hours fixing it • **me tiré mucho tiempo haciéndolo** I spent a lot of time doing it, it took me a long time to do it

3 (= *expeler*) • **~se un eructo*** to burp*, belch, break wind • **~se un pedo‡** to fart‡

4 • **~se a algn**** (*sexualmente*) to screw sb**, lay sb‡

5* (= *irse*) • **~se a otra parte** to clear off somewhere else*

tirilla SF 1 (= *tira*) band, strip; (*Cos*) neckband
2 (*Cono Sur*) (= *ropa*) shabby dress, ragged garment

tirillas* SMF INV 1 (= *mequetrefe*) unimportant person, nobody • **¡vete, ~!** get along, little man!
2 (= *enclenque*) undersized individual, runt

tirillento ADJ (*LAm*) ragged, shabby

tirita SF 1 (*Med*) (sticking) plaster, bandaid® (*EEUU*)

2 (*Cos*) tag, tape (*for name on clothing*)
tiritaña* SF mere trifle
tiritar ▷ CONJUG 1a VI **1** (*de frío, miedo*) to shiver (**de** with)
2* • **MODISMO**: • **dejaron el pastel tiritando** they almost finished the cake off • **esta botella ha quedado tiritando** there isn't much left of this bottle
tiritón SM shiver
tiritona SF shivering (fit)
Tiro SM Tyre
tiro SM **1** (= *disparo*) shot • **oímos un ~** we heard a shot • **resultó herido con un ~ de bala en la pierna** he received a gunshot wound to the leg • **lo mataron de un ~** they shot him dead • **se oyeron varios ~s a lo lejos** gunfire was heard *o* shots were heard in the distance • **a tiros**: • **liarse a ~s con algn** (*lit*) to have a gunfight with sb; (*fig*) to get involved in a slanging match with sb • **tendrán que decidirlo a ~s** they'll have to shoot it out • **matar a algn a ~s** to shoot sb (dead) • **pegar un ~ a algn** to shoot sb • **le pegó un ~ a su amante** she shot her lover • **¡que le peguen cuatro ~s!** he ought to be shot! • **se pegó un ~** he shot himself • **MODISMOS**: • **a ~ de piedra** a stone's throw away • **a ~ fijo*** for sure • **lo sé a ~ fijo** I know for sure • **esperar a ver por dónde van los ~s** to wait and see which way the wind is blowing • **creían que era un problema de trabajo, pero por ahí no iban los ~s** they thought the problem was work-related, but they were wide of the mark • **ir de ~s largos** to be all dressed up, wear one's Sunday best • **ni a ~s***: • **no lo haría ni a ~s** I wouldn't do it for love or money • **salir el ~ por la culata**: • **le salió el ~ por la culata** it backfired on him • **sentar como un ~***: • **me sienta como un ~** [*obligación*] it's a real pain*; [*ropa, peinado*] it looks really awful *o* terrible on me*; [*comida*] it really doesn't agree with me • **me sentó como un ~ que no viniera a la cita** I was really miffed that she didn't turn up* ▸ **tiro al blanco** target practice ▸ **tiro al pichón** clay pigeon shooting ▸ **tiro al plato** trap shooting, clay pigeon shooting ▸ **tiro con arco** archery ▸ **tiro de escopeta** gunshot ▸ **tiro de gracia** coup de grâce ▸ **tiro de pichón** clay pigeon shooting ▸ **tiro olímpico** Olympic shooting; ▷ **campo, galería**
2 (= *alcance*) range • **estar a ~** to be within range • **cuando el jabalí estuvo a ~** once the boar was within range • **tenía varios ejemplares a ~** she had several copies to hand • **si se pone a ~, lo mato** if he comes near me, I'll kill him • **le pide dinero al primero que se le pone a ~** she's always asking the first person who comes along for money • **tener algo a ~** to be within one's reach, have within one's reach • **a ~ de fusil** within shooting distance
3 (*Dep*) (= *lanzamiento*) shot • **parar un ~** to stop a shot ▸ **tiro a gol** shot at goal ▸ **tiro de aproximación** (*Golf*) approach shot ▸ **tiro de castigo** (*Méx*) penalty kick ▸ **tiro de esquina** (*Col*) corner (kick) ▸ **tiro de revés** backhand (shot) ▸ **tiro libre** (*en fútbol*) free kick; (*en baloncesto*) free throw
4 [*de animales*] team • **animal de ~** draught animal • **caballo de ~** carthorse
5 [*de pantalón*] *distance between crotch and waist* • **el pantalón me va corto de ~** the trousers are too tight around my crotch
6 (*Arquit*) (*en escalera*) flight of stairs; [*de chimenea*] draught, draft (EEUU)
7 (*Min*) (= *pozo*) shaft ▸ **tiro de mina** mineshaft
8 (*para tirar*) (= *cuerda*) rope, cord; (= *cadena*) chain; [*de timbre*] bellpull; [*de arreos*] brace, strap
9 tiros (*Mil*) swordbelt (*pl*); (*Cono Sur*) braces, suspenders (EEUU)
10 (*Méx**) (= *éxito*) hit*, success
11 (*LAm*) (*otras locuciones*) • **a ~ de hacer algo** about to do sth, on the point of doing sth • **MODISMOS**: • **al ~** (*esp Chile**) at once, right away • **de a ~** completely • **del ~** consequently • **hacer algo de un ~** to do sth in one go
12 (*And, Cono Sur, Méx*) (= *canica*) marble
13 (*Cono Sur*) (*en carreras*) distance, course
14 (*Méx*) (= *ejemplar*) issue; (= *edición*) edition
15 (*Cono Sur*) (= *indirecta*) hint
16 (*Caribe*) (= *astucia*) craftiness, cunning
tiroideo ADJ thyroid
tiroides ADJ INV thyroid
SM INV, (*a veces*) SF thyroid (gland)
Tirol SM • **El ~** the Tyrol
tirolés/esa ADJ, SM/F Tyrolean
tirolina SF zip line, flying fox
tirón¹ SM **1** (= *acción*) pull, tug • **dar un ~ a algo** to give sth a pull *o* tug, pull *o* tug at sth • **me dio un ~ del jersey** she pulled *o* tugged at my jumper • **le dio un ~ de pelo** she pulled his hair • **dar un ~ de orejas a algn** (*lit*) to pull *o* tug sb's ear; (*fig*) to tell sb off • **me lo arrancó de un ~** she suddenly jerked it away from me • **MODISMO**: • **aguantar el ~** to ride out *o* weather the storm
2 (*en músculo, tendón*) • **sufrió un ~ en la pantorrilla** he pulled a calf muscle ▸ **tirón muscular** pulled muscle
3 (= *robo*) bag-snatching • **el ~ es el delito más común** bag-snatching is the most common crime • **intentó darle el ~** he tried to snatch her bag
4 (*de un coche, motor*) sudden jerk, sudden jolt
5 • **MODISMO**: • **de un ~**: • **leyó la novela de un ~** he read the novel straight through in one go • **se lo bebió de un ~** he drank it down in one go • **trabajan diez horas de un ~** they work ten hours at a stretch • **he dormido toda la noche de un ~** I slept right through the night
tirón² SM (= *persona*) tyro, novice
tironear ▷ CONJUG 1a VT (*esp LAm*) = **tirar**
tironero SM/F, **tironista** SMF bag-snatcher
tirotear ▷ CONJUG 1a VT (= *disparar*) to shoot at, fire on; (= *matar*) to shoot, shoot down
VPR **tirotearse** to exchange shots
tiroteo SM (= *tiros*) shooting, exchange of shots; (= *escaramuza*) skirmish; (= *batalla*) gunfight; (*con policía*) shoot-out ▸ **tiroteo cruzado** crossfire
Tirreno ADJ • **mar ~** Tyrrhenian Sea
tirria* SF dislike • **tener ~ a algn** to dislike sb, have a grudge against sb
tisaje SM weaving
tisana SF tisane, herbal tea
tísico/a ADJ consumptive, tubercular
SM/F consumptive
tisiquento ADJ (*Cono Sur*), **tisiquiento** ADJ (*Cono Sur*) (*Med*) consumptive; (*de aspecto*) pale and thin
tisis SF INV consumption, tuberculosis
tisú SM (PL: **tisús**) (= *tela*) lamé; (= *pañuelo*) tissue
tisular ADJ tissue (*antes de s*)
tít. ABR = **título**
Titán SM Titan
titán SM titan, giant • **una tarea de titanes** a titanic task • **un combate de titanes** a titanic struggle
titánico ADJ titanic
titanio SM titanium
titeador* ADJ (*And, Cono Sur*) mocking, derisive
titear* ▷ CONJUG 1a VT (*And, Cono Sur*) to mock, scoff at, to make fun of
titeo* SM (*And, Cono Sur*) mockery, scoffing • **tomar a algn para el ~** to scoff at sb, make fun of sb
títere SM **1** (= *marioneta*) puppet • **MODISMO**: • **no dejar ~ con cabeza** (= *cambiar*) to turn everything upside down; (= *romper*) to break up everything in sight; (= *criticar*) to spare no one
2 títeres (= *espectáculo*) puppet show (*sing*); (= *arte*) puppetry (*sing*)
3 (= *persona*) puppet, tool
ADJ INV • **gobierno ~** puppet government
titi‡ SF bird*, chick*
tití SM (*LAm*) capuchin (monkey)
titilante ADJ twinkling
titilar ▷ CONJUG 1a VI [*luz, estrella*] to twinkle; [*párpado*] to flutter, tremble
titipuchal* SM (*Méx*) (noisy) crowd
titiritaña SF (*Méx*) **1** (= *espectáculo*) puppet show
2 (= *cosa insignificante*) piece of trivia • **de ~** sickly
titiritero/a SM/F **1** (= *que maneja marionetas*) puppeteer
2 (= *acróbata*) acrobat; (= *malabarista*) juggler; (= *artista de circo*) circus artist
tito/a* SM/F uncle/ auntie*
Tito Livio SM Livy
titubeante ADJ **1** (= *que duda*) hesitant
2 (= *que balbucea*) stuttering
3 [*discurso, voz*] halting
titubear ▷ CONJUG 1a VI **1** (= *vacilar*) to hesitate, vacillate • **no ~ en hacer algo** not to hesitate to do sth • **respondió sin ~** he answered without hesitation
2 (= *balbucear*) to stutter
titubeo SM **1** (= *vacilación*) hesitation, vacillation • **proceder sin ~s** to act without hesitation, act resolutely
2 (= *balbuceo*) stuttering
titulación SF (*Univ*) degrees and diplomas (*pl*) • **"se necesita ~ universitaria"** "university degree required"
titulado/a ADJ **1** [*libro*] entitled • **una obra titulada "Sotileza"** a book entitled "Sotileza"
2 [*persona*] with a degree, qualified • **~ en ingeniería** with a degree in engineering
SM/F graduate
titular ADJ • **jugador ~** regular first-team player • **juez ~** *judge assigned to a particular court* • **médico ~** *doctor assigned to a particular post in the public health care system* • **profesor ~** *teacher assigned to a particular post in the state education system*
SMF **1** [*de puesto*] holder, incumbent; (*Rel*) incumbent
2 [*de cuenta, pasaporte*] holder; [*de coche, vivienda*] owner
3 (*Dep*) regular first-team player; (*LAm*) captain
SM (*Prensa*) headline • **los ~es** (*Radio, TV*) the (news) headlines
VT ▷ CONJUG 1a [+ *libro, película*] to title, entitle • **tituló la obra "Fiesta"** he (en)titled the play "Fiesta" • **¿cómo vas a ~ el trabajo?** what title are you going to give the essay?
VPR **titularse 1** [*novela, poema*] • **¿cómo se titula la película?** what's the title of the film?, what's the film called? • **la película se titula "Texas"** the film is called "Texas", the title of the film is "Texas"
2 (*Univ*) to graduate • **~se en algo** to graduate in sth
titularidad SF **1** (= *propiedad*) ownership • **empresa de ~ pública** publicly-owned company
2 (*de un cargo*) tenure • **durante la ~ de Bush** during Bush's period of office
3 (*Dep*) first place, first-team place, top spot

titulillo SM (*Tip*) running title, page heading; (*Prensa*) subhead, section heading • MODISMO: • **andar en ~s*** to watch out for every little thing

titulitis SF INV (*hum*) (*en una empresa etc*) *mania for employing graduate personnel*; (*en un estudiante*) *obsession with acquiring an academic degree*

titulización SF (*Econ*) securitization

titulizar ▹ CONJUG 1f VT (*Econ*) to securitize

título SM **1** [*de libro, película*] title; (*en periódico*) headline; (*Jur*) heading
2 [*de campeón*] title
3 (*Educ*) (= *diploma*) certificate; (= *licenciatura*) degree; (= *calificación*) qualification; (*Caribe*) (*Aut*) driving licence, driver's license (*EEUU*) • **maestro sin ~** unqualified teacher; **títulos** qualifications • **tener los ~s para un puesto** to have the qualifications for a job ▸ **título universitario** university degree
4 (= *dignidad*) title; (= *persona*) titled person • **casarse con un ~** to marry into the nobility, marry a titled person ▸ **título de nobleza** title of nobility
5 (= *cualidad*) quality • **no es precisamente un ~ de gloria para él** it is not exactly a quality on which he can pride himself • **tiene varios ~s honrosos** he has several noble qualities, he has a number of worthy attributes
6 (*en presupuesto*) item
7 • **a ~ de** (= *a modo de*) by way of; (= *en calidad de*) in the capacity of • **a ~ de ejemplo, ...** by way of example, ..., for example, ... • **el dinero fue a ~ de préstamo** the money was by way of (being) a loan • **a ~ de curiosidad** as a matter of interest • **ya ha comenzado a funcionar a ~ experimental** it is already being used on an experimental basis • **a ~ particular** *o* **personal** in a personal capacity, in an unofficial capacity • **a ~ póstumo** posthumously
8 [*de bienes*] title ▸ **título de propiedad** title deed
9 (*Econ*) (= *bono*) bond ▸ **título al portador** bearer bond ▸ **título de renta fija** fixed interest security ▸ **título de renta variable** variable yield security
10 (= *derecho*) right • **con justo ~** rightly • **tener ~ de hacer algo** to be entitled to do sth

tiza SF (*para escribir, de billar*) chalk • **una ~** a piece of chalk

tizar ▹ CONJUG 1f VT **1** (*Cono Sur*) (= *planear*) to plan; (= *diseñar*) to design, model
2 (*And*) [+ *traje*] to mark out for cutting

tizate SM (*CAm, Méx*) chalk

Tiziano SM Titian

tizna SF black, grime

tiznado/a** SM/F (*CAm, Méx*) bastard**, son of a bitch (*EEUU**)

tiznajo* SM = **tiznón**

tiznar ▹ CONJUG 1a VT **1** (= *ennegrecer*) to blacken, black; (= *manchar*) to smudge, stain (**de** with)
2 [+ *reputación*] to stain, tarnish; [+ *nombre, carácter*] to defame, blacken
VPR **tiznarse 1** • **~se la cara con hollín** to blacken one's face with soot
2 (= *mancharse*) to get smudged, get soiled
3 (*CAm, Cono Sur, Méx**) (= *emborracharse*) to get drunk

tizne SM (= *hollín*) soot; (= *mancha*) smut

tiznón SM [*de hollín*] speck of soot, smut; (= *mancha*) smudge

tizo SM firebrand

tizón SM **1** (= *madera*) firebrand • MODISMO: • **negro como un ~** as black as coal
2 (*Bot*) smut
3 (= *deshonra*) stain, blemish

tizonazos SMPL pains of hell

tizonear ▹ CONJUG 1a VT [+ *fuego*] to poke, stir

tizos* SMPL dabs*, fingers

tlacanear* ▹ CONJUG 1a VT (*Méx*) to feel up*

tlachique SM (*Méx*) unfermented pulque

tlacote SM (*Méx*) growth, tumour, tumor (*EEUU*)

tlacual* SM (*Méx*) **1** (= *alimentos*) food; (= *comida, cena*) meal
2 (= *olla*) cooking pot

tlapalería SF (*Méx*) (= *ferretería*) ironmonger's (shop), hardware store; (= *papelería*) stationer's

tlapiloya* SF (*Méx*) clink*, jail

tlapisquera SF (*Méx*) shed, barn, granary

tlascal SM (*Méx*) tortilla

TLC SM ABR (= **Tratado de Libre Comercio**) NAFTA

tlecuil SM (*Méx*) brazier

Tm ABR, **tm** ABR (= **tonelada(s) métrica(s)**) tonne

TNT SM ABR (= **trinitrotolueno**) TNT

toa SF (*LAm*) hawser, rope, towrope

toalla SF towel • MODISMO: • **arrojar** *o* **tirar la ~** to throw in the towel ▸ **toalla de baño** bath towel ▸ **toalla de mano** hand towel ▸ **toalla de playa** beach towel ▸ **toalla de rodillo** roller towel ▸ **toalla playera** beach towel

toallero SM towel rail

toallita SF (*tb* **toallita húmeda**) wet wipe

toba* SF **1** (= *colilla*) dog-end*
2 (= *puñetazo*) punch, bash*

tobar ▹ CONJUG 1a VT (*And*) to tow

tobera SF nozzle

tobillera SF **1** (*para tobillo*) ankle support
2* (= *chica*) teenager, bobbysoxer (*EEUU**)

tobillero ADJ [*falda*] ankle-length
SM (= *calcetín*) ankle-sock; (*Dep*) ankle-guard

tobillo SM ankle

tobo SM (*Caribe*) bucket

tobogán SM **1** (*en parque*) slide; (*en piscina*) chute, slide ▸ **tobogán acuático** water slide
2 (*para nieve*) toboggan, sledge, sled (*EEUU*)
3 [*de feria*] switchback ▸ **tobogán gigante** roller coaster

toc ADV • **¡toc, toc!** (*en puerta*) rat-a-tat!, knock, knock!

toca[1] SF **1** [*de monja*] cornet, wimple
2 (*Hist*) (= *tocado*) headdress; (= *sombrero sin ala*) toque; (= *gorrito*) bonnet ▸ **tocas de viuda** widow's weeds

toca[2] SMF (*LAm*) = **tocayo**

tocadiscos SM INV record player, phonograph (*EEUU*)

tocado[1] ADJ **1** [*fruta*] bad, rotten; [*carne etc*] tainted, bad • **estar ~** (*Dep*) to be injured • MODISMO: • **estar ~ de la cabeza** to be weak in the head
2 • **una creencia tocada de heterodoxia** a somewhat unorthodox belief

tocado[2] ADJ • **~ con un sombrero** wearing a hat
SM **1** (= *prenda*) headdress
2 (= *peinado*) coiffure, hairdo
3 (= *arreglo*) toilet, washroom (*EEUU*)

tocador[1] SM **1** (= *mueble*) dressing table • **jabón de ~** toilet soap • **juego de ~** toilet set
2 (= *cuarto*) boudoir, dressing room ▸ **tocador de señoras** ladies' room
3 (= *neceser*) toilet bag

tocador[2]**(a)** SM/F (*Mús*) player

tocadorista SMF dresser

tocamientos SMPL (sexual) molestation (*sing*)

tocante ADJ • **~ a** regarding, with regard to, about • **en lo ~ a** so far as ... is concerned, as regards

tocar[1] ▹ CONJUG 1g VT **1** (*gen*) to touch; (*para examinar*) to feel • **si lo tocas te vas a quemar** if you touch it you'll burn yourself • **¡no me toques!** don't touch me! • **que nadie toque mis papeles** don't let anyone touch my papers • **no toques el dinero como no sea para una emergencia** don't touch the money unless it's an emergency • **tócalo, verás qué suave** feel it and see how soft it is • **tócale la frente, la tiene muy caliente** feel his forehead, it's very hot • **no toques la mercancía sin guantes** don't handle the goods without gloves • **el delantero tocó la pelota con la mano** the forward handled (the ball) • MODISMO: • **~ madera** to touch wood, knock on wood (*EEUU*)
2 (= *estar en contacto con*) to touch • **la mesa está tocando la pared** the table is touching the wall • **ponte ahí, tocando la pared** stand up against the wall over there • **~ tierra** to touch down, land
3 (= *hacer sonar*) [+ *piano, violín, trompeta*] to play; [+ *campana, timbre*] to ring; [+ *tambor*] to beat; [+ *silbato*] to blow; [+ *disco*] to play • **el reloj de la iglesia ha tocado las diez** the church clock has just struck ten • **~ la bocina** *o* **el claxon** to hoot *o* sound one's horn • **~ la generala** (*Mil*) to sound the call to arms • **~ la retirada** to sound the retreat
4 [+ *tema*] to refer to, touch on • **no tocó para nada esa cuestión** he didn't refer to *o* touch on that matter at all • **prefiero no ~ lo relacionado con el trabajo** I'd prefer not to talk about work
5 (= *afectar*) to concern • **esa cuestión me toca de cerca** that issue closely concerns me • **por lo que a mí me toca** so far as I am concerned
6 (= *estar emparentado con*) to be related to • **a mí Juan no me toca nada** Juan is not related to me in any way
7 (= *conmover*) to touch • **las imágenes me ~on en lo más profundo** the pictures moved *o* touched me deeply • **el poema nos tocó el corazón** the poem touched our hearts • **me has tocado el amor propio** you've wounded my pride
8 (*Dep*) to hit • **el balón tocó el palo** the ball hit the post
9 (*Náut*) • **hacía varios días que no tocábamos puerto** it was several days since we had called at *o* put in at a port • **en este crucero ~emos el puerto de Génova** on this cruise we will call *o* stop at Genoa
10 (*Caza*) to hit
11 (*Arte*) to touch up
VI **1** (*Mús*) to play • **toca en un grupo de rock** he's in *o* he plays in a rock group
2 (= *sonar*) • **en cuanto toque el timbre** when the bell rings • **tocan a misa** they are ringing the bell for mass • **~ a muerto** to toll the death knell
3 (= *llamar*) • **~ a una puerta** to knock on *o* at a door
4 (= *corresponder*) • **no toca hacerlo hasta el mes que viene** it's not due to be done until next month • **ahora toca torcer a la derecha** now you have to turn right • **~ a algn: les tocó un dólar a cada uno** they got a dollar each • **¿les ~á algo de herencia?** will they get anything under the will? • **me ha tocado el peor asiento** I ended up with *o* got the worst seat • **le tocó la lotería** he won the lottery • **¿a quién le toca?** whose turn is it? • **~ a algn hacer algo:** • **te toca jugar** it's your turn (to play), it's your go • **nos toca pagar a nosotros** it's our turn to pay • **siempre me toca fregar a mí** I'm always the one who has to do the dishes • **a usted le toca reprenderle si lo cree conveniente** it is up to

you to reprimand him if you see fit • MODISMO: • **¡a pagar tocan!** it's time to pay up!
5 (= *rayar*) • **~ en algo** to border on sth, verge on sth • **esto toca en lo absurdo** this borders *o* verges on the ridiculous • **su conducta toca en locura** his behaviour borders *o* verges on madness
6 (= *chocar*) • **~ con algo** to touch sth
7 • **~ a su fin** to be drawing to a close • **el verano tocaba a su fin** summer was drawing to a close
VPR **tocarse 1** (*uso reflexivo*) • **no te toques los granos** don't pick your spots • **está todo el día tocándose la barba** he's always playing with his beard • **tocársela** (*Esp***) (= *masturbarse*) to jerk off**; (*fig*) to do bugger-all** • **está todo el día tocándosela** he does bugger-all all day** • MODISMO: • **tocárselas*** to beat it*
2 (*uso recíproco*) to touch • **los cables no deben ~se** the wires should not be touching
3 (*LAm‡*) (= *drogarse*) to be a junkie*
tocar[2] ▹ CONJUG 1g VT [+ *pelo*] to do, arrange, set
VPR **tocarse** to cover one's head, put on one's hat
tocata[1]* SM record player, phonograph (*EEUU*)
tocata[2] SF (*Mús*) toccata
tocateja • **a ~*** ADV on the nail*
tocayo/a SM/F **1** namesake • **es mi ~** he's my namesake • **somos ~s** we have the same name
2 (= *amigo*) friend
toche SM (*Méx*) hare
tochimbo SM (*And*) smelting furnace
tocho* SM big fat book, tome
tocineta SF (*Col*) bacon
tocinillo SM ▸ **tocinillo de cielo** *pudding made with egg yolk and syrup*
tocino SM **1** (= *grasa*) salted fresh lard; (*con vetas de carne*) salt pork; [*de panceta*] bacon ▸ **tocino entreverado, tocino veteado** streaky bacon
2 ▸ **tocino de cielo** = tocinillo de cielo
toco[1]/a SM/F (*CAm*) = tocayo
toco[2] SM (*Caribe*) = tocón[1]
toco[3]‡ SM • **costó un ~** (*Cono Sur*) it cost a hell of a lot*
tocoginecología SF obstetrics (*sing*)
tocoginecólogo/a SM/F obstetrician
tocología SF obstetrics (*sing*)
tocólogo/a SM/F obstetrician
tocolotear ▹ CONJUG 1a VI (*Caribe*) to shuffle (the cards)
tocomocho* SM • **el timo del ~** *confidence trick involving the sale of a worthless lottery ticket*
tocón[1] SM (*Bot*) stump
tocón[2]/ona* SM/F groper* • **es un ~** he's got wandering hands*
tocón[3] ADJ (*And*) (= *sin rabo*) tailless; (*Caribe*) (= *sin cuernos*) hornless
tocuyo SM (*And, Cono Sur*) coarse cotton cloth
todavía ADV **1** (*temporal*) (*en oraciones afirmativas*) still; (*en oraciones negativas*) yet, still • **está nevando ~** it is still snowing • **—¿has acabado? —todavía no** "have you finished" — "not yet" • **~ no se ha ido** she hasn't gone yet, she still hasn't gone • **~ en 1970** as late as 1970
2 (= *incluso, aun así*) even • **es ~ más inteligente que su hermano** he's even more intelligent than his brother, he's more intelligent still than his brother
3* (= *encima*) • **has aprobado sin estudiar y ~ te quejas** you passed without doing any work and (yet) you're still complaining

TODAVÍA

Todavía *se traduce principalmente al inglés por* **still** *o* **yet**.

▹ *Se traduce por* **still** *cuando nos referimos a una situación o acción que comenzó en el pasado y que todavía continúa. Generalmente* **still** *se coloca detrás de los verbos auxiliares o modales y delante de los demás verbos:*

Todavía tienen hambre
They are still hungry
Todavía toco el piano
I still play the piano
¿Puedes verlos todavía?
Can you still see them?

▹ *También se puede traducir* **todavía** *por* **still** *para expresar insatisfacción o sorpresa en oraciones negativas. En este caso,* **still** *se coloca detrás del sujeto:*

Todavía no sé cómo ayudarle
I still don't know how to help him
Después de veinte años todavía no puede olvidarlo
After twenty years she still can't forget him

▹ *Se traduce generalmente por* **yet** *en frases negativas e interrogativas cuando nos referimos a una situación o acción que no ha tenido lugar todavía y que esperamos que ocurra.* **Yet** *va al final de la frase, aunque a veces puede ponerse delante del verbo principal en frases negativas:*

El doctor no ha llegado todavía
The doctor hasn't arrived yet *o* hasn't yet arrived
¿Todavía no han llamado?
Haven't they phoned yet?

En lenguaje formal, se puede traducir **todavía** *por* **yet** *en frases afirmativas para expresar que algo no se ha realizado. Para ello utilizamos la estructura* **to have yet** *+ infinitivo con* **to**:

Todavía tienen que comunicarnos los resultados
They have yet to tell us the results

▹ *En oraciones comparativas* **todavía** *se traduce por* **even**:

Su prima es todavía más alta que ella
Her cousin is even taller than she is

El adverbio **aún** *sigue las mismas pautas que* **todavía**:

Aún no sé cómo decírselo
I still don't know how to tell him
¿Aún no has hablado con ella?
Haven't you talked to her yet?
Aún está trabajando para esa compañía de seguros
She's still working for that insurance company
Este pastel está aún mejor que el de la semana pasada
This cake is even better than last week's

Para otros usos y ejemplos ver la entrada.

todero/a* SM/F (*Col, Ven*) jack of all trades
toditito* ADJ (*LAm*), **todito** ADJ (absolutely) all
todo ADJ **1** (*en singular*) (= *en su totalidad*) all • **no han llamado en ~ el día** they haven't phoned all day • **no he dormido en toda la noche** I haven't slept all night • **lo golpeó con toda su fuerza** he hit him with all his might • **ha viajado por ~ el mundo** he has travelled throughout *o* all over the world • **lo sabe ~ Madrid** all Madrid knows it • **en toda España no hay más que cinco** there are only five in the whole of Spain • **recorrimos ~ el bosque** we searched the whole forest • **vino ~ el equipo** the whole team came • **el universo ~** the whole universe • **he limpiado toda la casa** I've cleaned the whole house • **puso una alfombra a ~ lo ancho de la habitación** she put a rug down right across the room • **en toda España no lo encuentras** you won't find it anywhere in Spain • **~ lo que usted necesite** everything *o* whatever you need • **con ~ lo listo que es, no es capaz de resolver esto** clever as he is *o* for all his intelligence, he can't solve this problem • **~ lo demás** all the rest • **a** *o* **con toda prisa** in all haste, with all speed • **a toda velocidad** at full speed • MODISMOS: • **a ~ esto** (= *entretanto*) meanwhile; (= *a propósito*) by the way • **a ~ esto, la orquesta siguió tocando** meanwhile, the band kept on playing • **a ~ esto, ¿os apetece ir al cine?** by the way, would you like to go to the cinema? • **a ~ esto, no nos olvidemos de llamarla** while we're on the subject, we mustn't forget to phone her • **¡toda la vida!** (*LAm**) yes, indeed!; ▹ **cuanto, mundo**
2 (*en plural*) **a** (*en un conjunto*) all • **~s los libros** all the books • **~s vosotros** all of you
b (= *cada*) every • **~s los días** every day • **nos vemos todas las semanas** we see each other every week • **pararon a ~s los coches que pasaban** they stopped every car that went by • **habrá un turno para ~s y cada uno de los participantes** each and every one of the participants will have their turn; ▹ **forma**
3 (*con valor enfático*) • **es ~ un hombre** he's every inch a man, he's a real man • **es ~ un héroe** he's a real hero • **ese hombre es ~ ambición** that man is all ambition • **tiene toda la nariz de su abuela** her nose is exactly like her grandmother's • **el niño era ~ ojos** the child was all eyes • **soy ~ oídos** I'm all ears • **puede ser ~ lo sencillo que usted quiera** it can be as simple as you wish • **dio un portazo por toda respuesta** his only response was to slam the door • **~ lo contrario** quite the opposite; ▹ **más**
4 (= *del todo*) • **lleva una falda toda rota** she's wearing a skirt that's all torn • **estaba ~ rendido** he was completely worn out • **vaya ~ seguido** go straight on *o* ahead
PRON **1** (*en singular*) • **se lo comió ~** he ate it all • **cree que lo sabe ~** she thinks she knows it all • **lo han vendido ~** they've sold the lot, they've sold it all • **se enfada por ~** she gets angry about everything • **lo sabemos ~** we know everything • **~ cabe en él** he is capable of anything • **~ o nada** all or nothing • **~ son reveses** it's one setback after another • **y luego ~ son sonrisas** and then it's all smiles • **~ el que quiera …** everyone *o* anyone who wants to … ▸ **todo a cien** ≈ pound store, ≈ dollar store (*EEUU*), *shop selling everyday items at low prices*
2 (*en plural*) (= *cosas*) all (of them); (= *personas*) everybody, everyone • **~s son caros** they're all expensive • **el más bonito de ~s** the prettiest of all • **~s estaban de acuerdo** everybody *o* everyone agreed • **~s los que quieran venir** all those who want to come, anyone who wants to come
3 (*locuciones con preposición*) • **ir a ~** to be prepared to do or die • **ante ~** first of all, in the first place • **con ~**: • **con ~ y** in spite of • **el coche, con ~ y ser nuevo …** the car, in spite of being new …, despite the fact that the car was new … • **con ~ (y con eso)** still, nevertheless • **con ~ y con eso llegamos una hora tarde** we still arrived an hour late,

nevertheless we arrived an hour late • **de ~**: • **lo llamaron de ~** they called him every name under the sun • **nos pasó de ~** everything possible happened to us, you name it, it happened to us • **del ~** wholly, entirely • **no es del ~ malo** it is not wholly *o* all bad • **no es del ~ verdad** it is not entirely true • **después de ~** after all • **MODISMOS**: • **estar en ~** to be on the ball* • **de todas todas**: • **¡te digo que sí de todas todas!** I tell you it jolly well is! • **es verdad de todas todas** it's absolutely true • **ir a por todas** to give it one's all; ▹ **botica, pesar, sobre²**
SM • **el ~** the whole • **como** *o* **en un ~** as a whole • **MODISMO**: • **ser el ~*** to run the show; ▹ **jugar**

TODO

▹ *Para traducir el adjetivo* **todo** *con el sentido de* **en su totalidad** *se usa* **all**, *seguido del sustantivo en singular y sin determinante:*

Se pasó toda la tarde viendo la tele
He spent all afternoon watching TV

▹ *Con el mismo sentido anterior, también se puede traducir por* **whole** *o* **entire**, *este último es más enfático. En este caso, el indefinido tiene que ir acompañado de un sustantivo contable en singular y precedido por un determinante:*

Se pasó toda la tarde viendo la tele
He spent the whole *o* the entire afternoon watching TV

▹ **Todos** *se traduce por* **every** *cuando se hace hincapié en todos y cada uno de los individuos de un grupo de personas o cosas y también cuando se habla de acciones repetidas:*

Todos los niños deben llevar el uniforme del colegio
Every child must wear school uniform
Salimos a cenar todos los viernes
We go out for dinner every Friday

El sustantivo que sigue a **every** *va en singular y nunca lleva determinante. El verbo va también en singular.*

▹ *Cuando* **todos** *se emplea para generalizar, se traduce por* **all**. *En este caso el sustantivo que sigue a* **all** *no lleva determinante:*

Todos los alemanes saben hablar inglés
All Germans can speak English

▹ **Todos** *también se traduce por* **all** *para referirse al conjunto de individuos de un grupo pero, a diferencia de* **every**, *sin dar importancia a los elementos. En este caso el sustantivo lleva determinante y va en plural, como el verbo:*

Todos los libros de la biblioteca eran antiguos
All the books in the library were old

Para otros usos y ejemplos ver la entrada.

todopoderoso ADJ almighty, all-powerful • **Dios Todopoderoso** Almighty God
SM • **el Todopoderoso** the Almighty

todoterreno SM INV (*tb* **coche todoterreno, vehículo todoterreno**) four-wheel drive vehicle, all-terrain vehicle, SUV (*esp EEUU*)
ADJ INV **1** [*objeto, máquina*] (= *versátil*) multi-purpose; (= *adaptable*) adaptable
2 [*persona*] versatile

tofo SM (*Cono Sur*) white clay

toga SF (*Hist*) toga; (*Jur*) robe, gown; (*Univ*) gown • **tomar la ~** to qualify as a lawyer

togado/a SM/F lawyer, attorney(-at-law) (*EEUU*)

Togo SM Togo

Togolandia SF Togoland

togolés/esa ADJ, SM/F Togolese

toilette [tua'le] SF (*Cono Sur*) toilet, lavatory, washroom (*EEUU*)

toisón SM (*tb* **toisón de oro**) Golden Fleece

tojo¹ SM (*Bot*) gorse, furze

tojo² ADJ (*And*) (= *gemelo*) twin

Tokio SM Tokyo

tol SM (*CAm*) gourd, squash (*EEUU*)

tolda SF **1** (*LAm*) (= *tela*) canvas
2 (*LAm*) (= *tienda de campaña*) tent; (= *refugio*) shelter; [*de barco*] awning
3 (*Caribe*) (= *bolsa grande*) large sack
4 (*Caribe*) (= *cielo nublado*) overcast sky
5 (*Caribe*) (*Pol*) • **es de la ~ Acción Democrática** he belongs to Acción Democrática

toldería SF (*And, Cono Sur*) Indian village, camp of Indian huts

toldillo SM (*And, Caribe*) mosquito net

toldo SM **1** (*en tienda, balcón*) awning; (*en la playa*) sunshade; (*para fiesta*) marquee, garden tent (*EEUU*); (*para tapar*) tarpaulin
2 (*Méx*) (*Aut*) hood, top (*EEUU*)
3 (*And, Cono Sur*) (= *choza*) Indian hut; (*Méx*) (= *tienda*) tent
4 (*And, Caribe*) (= *mosquitera*) mosquito net

tole¹* SM **1** (= *disturbio*) commotion, uproar; (= *protesta*) outcry • **levantar el ~** to kick up a fuss • **venir a algn con el ~** to pester *o* badger sb about sth, go on at sb about sth
2 (= *chismes*) gossip, rumours (*pl*)
3 • **MODISMO**: • **coger** *o* **tomar el ~** (= *irse*) to get out, pack up and go

tole² SM (*And*) track, trail

toledano/a ADJ Toledan, of/from Toledo; ▹ **noche**
SM/F Toledan, native/inhabitant of Toledo • **los ~s** the people of Toledo, the Toledans

tolempo SM (*And*) = **lempo**

tolerable ADJ tolerable

tolerado ADJ tolerated • **película tolerada (para menores)** a film suitable for children

tolerancia SF **1** (= *respeto*) tolerance; [*de ideas*] toleration ▸ **tolerancia cero** zero tolerance
2 (*Med, Téc*) tolerance

tolerante ADJ tolerant

tolerantismo SM religious toleration

tolerar ▹ CONJUG 1a VT **1** (= *consentir*) to tolerate • **no se puede ~ esto** this cannot be tolerated • **no tolera que digan eso** he won't allow them to say that • **su madre le tolera demasiado** his mother lets him get away with too much
2 (= *aguantar*) to bear, put up with • **su estómago no tolera los huevos** eggs don't agree with him • **el cosmonauta toleró muy bien esta situación difícil** the cosmonaut stood up very well to this awkward situation • **el puente no tolera el peso de los tanques** the bridge will not support the weight of the tanks
3 (*Med, Téc*) to tolerate

tolete SM **1** (*Náut*) tholepin
2 (*LAm*) (= *palo*) short club, stick, cudgel
3 (*And, Caribe*) (= *pedazo*) piece, bit
4 (*And*) (= *balsa*) raft

toletole SM **1** (*And, Cono Sur*) (= *alboroto*) row, uproar
2 (*And*) (= *terquedad*) obstinacy
3 (*Caribe**) (= *vida alegre*) high life; (= *vagabundeo*) roving life
4 (= *chismes*) gossip, rumours (*pl*)

tolla SF **1** (= *pantano*) marsh, quagmire
2 (*Caribe, Méx*) (= *abrevadero*) drinking trough

tollina* SF hiding*

Tolomeo SM Ptolemy

Tolón SM Toulon

toloncho SM (*And*) piece of wood

tolondro ADJ scatterbrained
SM (*Med*) (= *chichón*) bump, swelling

tolondrón ADJ, SM = **tolondro**

tolosarra ADJ of/from Tolosa
SMF native/inhabitant of Tolosa • **los ~s** the people of Tolosa

tolteca ADJ, SMF Toltec

tolva SF **1** (= *recipiente*) hopper; (= *vertedor*) chute
2 (*Cono Sur, Méx*) (*Ferro*) hopper wagon, hopper car (*EEUU*)
3 (*Méx*) (*Min*) shed for storing ore

tolvanera SF dustcloud

toma SF **1** (*Téc*) [*de agua, gas*] (= *entrada*) inlet; (= *salida*) outlet ▸ **toma de aire** air inlet, air intake ▸ **toma de antena** (*Radio, TV*) aerial socket ▸ **toma de corriente** power point ▸ **toma de tierra** earth (wire), ground (wire) (*EEUU*)
2 (*Cine, TV*) shot • **la película empieza con una ~ aérea** the film begins with an aerial shot • **¡escena primera, tercera ~!** scene one, take three! ▸ **toma directa** live shot
3 [*de jarabe, medicina*] dose; [*de bebé*] feed • **~ de rapé** pinch of snuff
4 (*Mil*) (= *captura*) taking, capture • **la ~ de Granada** the taking *o* capture of Granada • **la ~ de la Bastilla** the storming of the Bastille
5 (*LAm*) (= *acequia*) irrigation channel; (*CAm*) (= *arroyo*) brook
6 ▸ **toma de conciencia** realization ▸ **toma de contacto** initial contact ▸ **toma de decisiones** decision-making, decision-taking ▸ **toma de declaración** taking of evidence ▸ **toma de hábito** (*Rel*) taking of vows ▸ **toma de posesión** • **mañana tendrá lugar la ~ de posesión del nuevo presidente** the new president will take office tomorrow ▸ **toma de tierra** (*Aer*) landing, touchdown
SM ▸ **toma y daca** give and take

tomada SF (*LAm*) plug

tomadero SM **1** (= *asidero*) handle
2 (= *entrada*) inlet, intake; (= *grifo*) tap, faucet (*EEUU*)

tomado ADJ **1** [*voz*] hoarse
2 • **estar ~** (*LAm**) (= *borracho*) to be drunk
3 (*tb* **tomado de orín**) rusty

tomador(a) ADJ (*LAm**) (= *borracho*) drunken
SM/F **1** (*Com*) [*de bono, cheque*] drawee; [*de seguro*] policy holder
2 (*LAm**) (= *borracho*) drunkard
3†* (= *ladrón*) thief

tomadura SF ▸ **tomadura de pelo** (= *guasa*) leg-pull*; (= *mofa*) mockery; (= *timo*) con*, rip-off*

tomaína SF ptomaine

tomante‡ SM queer‡, fag (*EEUU*‡)

tomar

VERBO TRANSITIVO
VERBO INTRANSITIVO
VERBO PRONOMINAL

▹ CONJUG 1a

Para las expresiones **tomar las aguas, tomar las armas, tomar la delantera, tomar impulso, tomar tierra**, *ver la otra entrada.*

VERBO TRANSITIVO

1 (= *coger*) to take • **si no tienes bolígrafo toma**

este take this pen if you haven't got one • **la tomó de la mano** he took her by the hand • **lo toma o lo deja** take it or leave it • **¡toma!** here (you are)! • **vayan tomando asiento** please sit down, please be seated (*frm*) • **~ la pluma** to pick up one's pen • MODISMO: • **~ las de Villadiego** to shift it*

2 (*= ingerir, consumir*) [+ *comida*] to eat, have; [+ *bebida*] to drink, have; [+ *medicina*] to take • **si tienes hambre podemos ~ algo** if you're hungry we can get something to eat • **tomas demasiado café** you drink too much coffee • **tomamos unas cervezas** we had a few beers • **¿qué quieres ~?** what would you like?, what will you have? • **tome una cucharada de jarabe cada ocho horas** take a spoonful of syrup every eight hours • **~ el pecho** to feed at the breast, breastfeed

3 (*= viajar en*) [+ *tren, avión, taxi*] to take • **vamos a ~ el autobús** let's take *o* get the bus • **cada día toma el tren de las nueve** he catches *o* takes the nine o'clock train every day

4 (*Cine, Fot, TV*) to take • **~ una foto de algn** to take a photo of sb, take sb's photo

5 (*= apuntar*) [+ *notas, apuntes*] to take; [+ *discurso*] to take down • **nunca toma apuntes en clase** he never takes notes in class • **tomo nota de todo lo que me has dicho** I have taken note of everything you have told me • **nos ~on declaración en comisaría** they took (down) our statements *o* they took statements from us at the police station • **~ por escrito** to write down

6 (*= medir*) [+ *temperatura, pulso*] to take • **tengo que ir a que me tomen la tensión** I have to go and have my blood pressure taken • **ven, que te tomo las medidas** let me take your measurements

7 (*= adoptar*) [+ *decisión, precauciones*] to take • **~emos medidas para que no vuelva a suceder** we will take steps to ensure that it does not happen again

8 (*= adquirir*) • **la situación está tomando mal cariz** the situation is beginning to look ugly • **el proyecto ya está tomando forma** the project is taking shape; ▹ **color, conciencia**

9 (*= empezar a sentir*) • **le han tomado mucho cariño** they have become very fond of him • **les tomé asco a los caracoles** I took a dislike to snails • MODISMO: • **~la o tenerla tomada con algn*** to have (got) it in for sb* • **la jefa la ha tomado o la tiene tomada conmigo** the boss has (got) it in for me

10 (*= disfrutar de*) [+ *baño, ducha*] to have, take • **~ el aire o el fresco** to get some fresh air • **~ el sol** to sunbathe

11 (*Mil*) (*= capturar*) to take, capture; (*= ocupar*) to occupy • **la policía tomó la fábrica** the police occupied the factory

12 (*= contratar*) [+ *empleado*] to take on, engage

13 (*= ocupar*) to take • **traducirlo me ha tomado tres horas** it took me three hours to translate it

14 (*= entender, interpretar*) to take • **tomó muy a mal que la suspendieran** she took it very badly when she failed • **lo tomó como una ofensa** he took offence at it, he was offended by it • **lo han tomado a broma** they haven't taken it seriously, they are treating it as a joke • **no lo tomes en serio** don't take it seriously

15 **tomar a algn por** (*= confundir*) • **~ a algn por policía** to take sb for a policeman, think that sb is a policeman • **~ a algn por loco** to think sb mad • **¿por quién me toma?** what do you take me for?, who do you think I am?

16 (*sexualmente*) to have

17 (*And*) (*= molestar*) to upset, annoy

VERBO INTRANSITIVO

1 (*Bot*) [*planta*] to take (root); [*injerto*] to take

2 (*LAm*) (*= ir*) • **~ a la derecha** to turn right

3 (*LAm*) (*= beber*) to drink • **estaba tomando en varios bares** he was drinking in a number of bars

4 (*exclamaciones*) • **¡toma!*** • **¡toma! menuda suerte has tenido ...** well, of all the luck!, can you believe it? what luck! • **¡toma! pues yo también lo sé hacer** hey! I know how to do that too • MODISMO: • **¡toma ya!** • **¡toma ya, vaya tío tan bueno!** wow, what an amazing guy!* • **¡toma ya, vaya golazo!** look at that, what a fantastic goal!

5 (*esp LAm*)* • **tomó y se fue** off he went, he upped and went • **tomó y lo rompió** he went and broke it

VERBO PRONOMINAL **tomarse**

1 (*= cogerse*) [+ *vacaciones*] to take • **me he tomado la libertad de leer tu informe** I have taken the liberty of reading your report • **no se ~on la molestia de informarnos** they didn't bother *o* take the trouble to let us know

2 (*= ingerir*) [+ *bebida*] to drink, have; [+ *comida*] to eat, have; [+ *medicina*] to take • **se tomó 13 cervezas** he drank *o* had 13 beers • **me tomé un bocadillo** I ate *o* had a sandwich • **tómate el yogur, verás qué bueno** eat up your yogurt, you'll like it

3 (*= medirse*) [+ *pulso, temperatura*] to take

4 (*= entender, interpretar*) to take • **no te lo tomes así** don't take it that way • **no te lo tomes tan a mal** don't take it so badly, don't take it so much to heart • **se lo sabe ~ bien** he knows how to take it, he can take it in his stride • **se lo toma todo muy en serio** he takes it all very seriously

5 **tomarse por** (*= creerse*) to think o.s. • **¿por quién se toma ese ministro?** who does that minister think he is?

6 (*= tomarse de orín*) to get rusty

Tomás SM Thomas

tomatal SM **1** (*= terreno*) tomato bed, tomato field
2 (*LAm*) (*= planta*) tomato plant

tomatazo SM • **recibió una lluvia de ~s** he was pelted with tomatoes • **lo echaron del escenario a ~s** they saw him offstage, throwing tomatoes

tomate SM **1** tomato • **salsa de ~** tomato sauce • MODISMO: • **ponerse como un ~** to turn as red as a beetroot
2* (*en calcetín, media*) hole
3* (*= jaleo*) fuss, row; (*= pelea*) set-to* • **al final de la noche hubo ~** there was a fight at the end of the evening • **¡qué ~!** what a mess! • **esto tiene ~** this is tough, this is a tough one

tomatera SF **1** (*= planta*) tomato plant
2 (*Cono Sur**) (*= juerga*) drunken spree; (*= fiesta*) rowdy party

tomatero/a SM/F (*= cultivador*) tomato grower; (*= comerciante*) tomato dealer

tomavistas SM INV cine camera, movie camera (*EEUU*)

tombo‡ SM (*And*) fuzz‡, police

tómbola SF tombola

tomillo SM thyme ▸ **tomillo salsero** savory, garden thyme

tominero ADJ (*Méx*) mean

tomismo SM Thomism

tomista ADJ, SMF Thomist

tomiza SF esparto rope

tomo¹ SM volume • **en tres ~s** in three volumes

tomo² SM (*= bulto*) bulk, size • MODISMO: • **de ~ y lomo*** utter, out-and-out • **un canalla de ~ y lomo** a real swine*

tomografía SF tomography

tomo-homenaje SM (PL: **tomos-homenaje**) homage volume, Festschrift

tomón ADJ (*And*) teasing, jokey

tompiate SM (*Méx*) (*= canasta*) basket (*of woven palm leaves*); (*= bolsa*) pouch (*of woven palm leaves*)

ton SM • MODISMO: • **sin ton ni son** (*= sin motivo*) for no particular reason; (*= sin lógica*) without rhyme or reason

tonada SF **1** (*= melodía*) tune; (*= canción*) song, air
2 (*LAm*) (*= acento*) accent
3 (*Caribe*) (*= embuste*) fib; (*= juego de palabras*) pun

tonadilla SF little tune, ditty

tonal ADJ tonal

tonalidad SF **1** (*Mús*) tonality; (*Radio*) tone • **control de ~** tone control ▸ **tonalidad mayor** major key ▸ **tonalidad menor** minor key
2 (*Arte*) (*= tono*) shade; (*= colores*) colour scheme, color scheme (*EEUU*) • **una bella ~ de verde** a beautiful shade of green • **cambiar la ~ de un cuarto** to change the colour scheme of a room

tonel SM **1** (*= barril*) barrel, cask
2* (*= persona*) fat lump*

tonelada SF **1** (*= unidad*) ton ▸ **tonelada americana, tonelada corta** short ton ▸ **tonelada inglesa, tonelada larga** long ton, gross ton ▸ **tonelada métrica** metric ton, tonne
2 (*Náut*) ▸ **tonelada de registro** register ton • **un buque de 30.000 ~s de registro bruto** a ship of 30,000 gross register tons

tonelaje SM tonnage

tonelería SF cooperage, barrel-making

tonelero/a SM/F cooper

tonelete SM **1** (*= tonel*) cask, keg
2 (*= falda*) short skirt

Tonete SM *forma familiar de* **Antonio**

tonga SF **1** (*= capa*) layer, stratum; [*de ladrillos*] course
2 (*Caribe, Méx*) (*= montón*) pile
3 (*And, Aragón, Cono Sur*) (*= tarea*) job, task; (*= tanda*) spell of work
4 (*And*) (*= siesta*) nap

tongada SF (*= capa*) layer; (*= revestimiento*) coat, covering

tongo¹ SM (*Dep*) (*= trampa*) fixing • **¡hay ~!** it's been fixed!, it's been rigged! • **hubo ~ en las elecciones** the elections were rigged

tongo² SM (*And, Chile*) **1** (*= bombín*) Indian woman's hat, bowler hat
2 (*= bebida*) rum punch

tongonearse ▹ CONJUG 1a VPR (*LAm*) = **contonearse**

tongoneo SM (*LAm*) = **contoneo**

tongorí SM (*And, Cono Sur*) (*= hígado*) liver; (*= menudillos*) offal; (*= bofe*) lights (*pl*)

tongoy SM (*LAm*) bowler hat

Toni SM *forma familiar de* **Antonio**

tónica SF **1** (*= bebida*) tonic, tonic water
2 (*= tendencia*) tone, trend, tendency • **es una de las ~s del estilo moderno** it is one of the keynotes of the modern style
3 (*Mús*) tonic

tonicidad SF tonicity

tónico ADJ **1** (*Mús*) [+ *nota*] tonic; (*Ling*) [+ *sílaba*] tonic (*antes de s*), stressed
2 (*Med*) (*= estimulante*) tonic, stimulating
SM tonic

tonificador ADJ, **tonificante** ADJ invigorating, stimulating

tonificar ▹ CONJUG 1g VT [+ *músculos, piel*] to tone up; [+ *ánimo*] to invigorate

tonillo SM **1** (*especial*) (sarcastic) tone of voice
2 (*monótono*) monotonous tone of voice, monotonous drone

3 (*regional*) accent

tono SM **1** [*de sonido*] tone • **en ~ bajo** in low tones, in a low tone • **baja/sube un poco el ~ del televisor** turn down/up the television a little ▸ **tono de discado** (*Cono Sur*), **tono de marcar** (*Telec*) dialling tone, dial tone (*EEUU*) ▸ **tono de llamada** (*Telec*) ringtone ▸ **tono de voz** tone of voice • **lo noté por el ~ de su voz** I could tell from his tone of voice • **—ya me he dado cuenta —dijo, alzando el ~ de voz** "I can see that," he said, raising his voice

2 [*de palabras, discusión, escrito*] tone • **le molestó el ~ de mi carta** she was upset by the tone of my letter • **¡cómo hablas en ese ~ a tu padre!** how dare you speak to your father in that tone (of voice)! • **esa expresión tiene un ~ despectivo** that expression sounds insulting • **contestó con ~ de enfado** she replied angrily • **intenté tratar la cuestión en ~ de broma** I tried to treat the whole matter lightheartedly • **nos habló con un ~ distante** her voice was rather distant as she spoke to us • **un disco de ~ más intimista** a record with a more intimate feel (to it) • **bajar el ~** to soften one's tone • **bajar el ~ de algo** to soften the tone of sth, tone sth down • **cambiar de ~** to change one's tone • **cuando le dije eso se serenó y cambió de ~** when I told him that he calmed down and changed his tone *o* his tone changed • **fue él quien cambió el ~ de la conversación** it was him that changed the tone of the conversation • **la reunión cambió de ~ pasadas las nueve de la noche** the tone of the meeting changed after nine o'clock • **a este ~** in the same vein • **fuera de ~** [*respuesta, comentario, actitud*] uncalled for • **subir de ~** [*discusión, conversación*] to grow *o* become heated; [*conflicto*] to intensify; [*quejas*] to grow louder • **las voces empezaron a subir de ~** they began to raise their voices • **la oposición está subiendo el ~ de sus ataques al gobierno** the opposition is stepping up *o* intensifying its attacks on the government • **chistes subidos de ~** racy jokes

3 • **a ~** matching • **ropa náutica y accesorios a ~** sailing gear and matching accessories • **estar a ~ con algo** [*color*] to match sth; [*diseño, comentarios*] to be in keeping with sth • **una escena final divertida, muy a ~ con el resto de la película** an amusing final scene, very much in keeping with the rest of the film • **una ideología más a ~ con los tiempos** an ideology more in tune with the times • **ponerse a ~** (= *prepararse físicamente*) to get (o.s.) into shape; (= *animarse*) to perk o.s. up* • **voy a tomarme un whisky doble, a ver si me pongo a ~** I'm going to have a double whisky to perk myself up*

4 (= *clase, distinción*) • **una familia de ~** a good family • **eso no es de ~** that's just not done • **ser de buen/mal ~: ir a los balnearios era entonces una actividad de buen ~** visiting spas was quite the done thing then • **una fiesta de buen ~** a fashionable party • **es de mal ~ hablar de esos temas** it is bad form to talk about such matters, it's (simply) not done to talk about such things • MODISMO: • **darse ~** to put on airs

5 [*de color*] shade, tone • **en ~s grises y azules** in shades of grey and blue, in grey and blue tones • **~s pastel** pastel shades, pastel tones

6 (*Anat, Med*) tone ▸ **tono muscular** muscle tone

7 (*Mús*) (= *intervalo*) tone; (= *tonalidad*) key; (= *altura*) pitch ▸ **tono mayor** major key ▸ **tono menor** minor key

8 (*Mús*) (= *diapasón*) tuning fork; (= *corredera*) slide

tonsura SF tonsure

tonsurado ADJ tonsured

tonsurar ▸ CONJUG 1a VT **1** (*Rel*) to tonsure

2 [+ *lana*] to clip, shear

tontada SF = tontería

tontaina* SMF idiot, dimwit*

tontamente ADV stupidly • **sonreía ~ ante las cámaras** he grinned stupidly at the cameras • **se me olvidó llamar por teléfono ~** I stupidly forgot to phone • **tropezó ~** he tripped clumsily

tontear* ▸ CONJUG 1a VI **1** (= *hacer el tonto*) to fool about, act the fool

2 (= *decir tonterías*) to talk nonsense

3 (*amorosamente*) to flirt

tontera SF (*LAm*) = tontería

tontería SF **1** (= *dicho*) • **eso son ~s** • **es una ~** that's nonsense *o* rubbish *o* (*esp EEUU*) garbage • **decir ~s** to talk nonsense *o* rubbish *o* (*esp EEUU*) garbage • **¡qué ~ acabas de decir!** that was a silly thing to say! • **lo que has dicho no es ninguna ~** what you've just said isn't such a bad idea • **¡déjate de ~s!** don't be silly!, don't talk nonsense! • **dejémonos de ~s** let's be serious

2 (= *acto*) • **ha sido una ~ el negarte a verle** it was silly of you to refuse to see him • **hacer una ~** to do a silly thing *o* something silly • **no hace nada más que ~s** he's always doing silly things *o* being silly • **deja de hacer ~s** stop being silly

3 (= *insignificancia*) silly little thing • **cualquier ~ le afecta** he gets upset over any silly little thing *o* the slightest thing • **lo vendió por una ~** he sold it for next to nothing

4 (= *remilgo*) • **Juanito tiene mucha ~ a la hora de comer** Juanito is so picky about his food

5 (= *cualidad*) silliness, foolishness

tonto/a ADJ **1** [*persona*] **a** (= *bobo*) (*dicho con afecto*) silly; (*dicho con enfado*) stupid • **venga, vente con nosotros, ¡no seas ~!** come on, come with us, don't be silly! • **¡qué ~ soy!** how silly *o* stupid of me! • **fui tan ~ que me dejé engañar por ellos** I was silly enough to be taken in by them • **¿tú te has creído que yo soy ~?** • **¿me tomas por ~?** do you think I'm stupid? • MODISMO: • **es ~ del bote** *o* **de capirote** *o* **de remate** he's a total *o* complete idiot*

b (*poco inteligente*) stupid • **¡y parecía ~!** and we thought he was stupid! • MODISMOS: • **a lo ~:** • **¿para qué esforzarse a lo ~?** why go to all that trouble for nothing? • **y a lo ~, a lo ~, se le pasó la mitad del día** and before he knew it, half the day had slipped by • **es más ~ que Abundio** (*Esp**) he's as thick as two short planks* • **hacer ~ a algn** (*Chile**) to trick sb • **a tontas y a locas:** • **piénsalo bien, no quiero que actúes/hables a tontas y a locas** think carefully, don't just do/say the first thing that comes into your head • **esos jóvenes sin seso que solo hablan a tontas y a locas** these silly youngsters who chatter away without even thinking what they're saying

c (= *insolente*) silly • **¡si te pones ~ no te vuelvo a traer al cine!** if you start being silly I won't take you to the cinema again!

d (= *torpe*) • **me quedé como ~ después del golpe** I felt dazed after the knock • **hoy se me olvida todo, estoy como ~** I keep forgetting things today, I'm out of it* • **dejar a algn ~** (*Esp*) to leave sb speechless

e (= *presumido*) stuck-up* • **pasaba muy ~ por delante de ella** he walked past her showing off • **está muy ~ desde que es médico** he's such a show-off since he became a doctor*

f (*Med*) imbecile; ▸ **pelo**

2 [*risa, frase, accidente*] silly • **¡qué fallo más ~!** it was a really silly mistake! • **fue una respuesta tonta** that was a stupid answer • **me entró la risa tonta** I started giggling • **me pilló en una hora tonta y le presté el dinero** I wasn't thinking at that moment and I lent him the money; ▸ **caja**

SM/F **1** idiot • **soy un ~, ¡nunca debí haberla escuchado!** I'm such an idiot, I should never have listened to her! • **allí estaba, riéndome como una tonta** there I was, laughing like an idiot • **el ~ del pueblo** the village idiot • MODISMOS: • **hacer el ~** (*a propósito*) to act the fool, play the fool; (*sin querer*) to be a fool • **has hecho el ~ no siguiendo sus consejos** you were a fool not to take her advice • **hacerse el ~** to act dumb ▸ **tonto útil** willing stooge

2 (*Med*) imbecile

SM **1** (*Circo, Teat*) clown, funny man

2 (*And, CAm*) (= *palanca*) jemmy

tontón[1]/ona* SM/F = tonto

tontón[2]* SM (= *vestido*) smock, maternity dress

tontorrón/ona* SM/F dimwit*

tontura SF = tontería

tontureco ADJ (*CAm*) = tonto

tonudo* ADJ (*Cono Sur*) classy*

tony ['toni] SM (*LAm**) clown

toña‡ SF **1** (= *golpe*) (*con el puño*) bash*, punch; (*con el pie*) kick

2 (= *borrachera*) • **pillarse una ~** (*Esp*) to get plastered‡

toñeco/a* ADJ (*Ven*) spoilt

SM/F spoilt brat*

top* ADJ (= *mejor*) top, best; [*empresa, marca*] leading

SM INV **1** (= *prenda*) top

2 (= *persona*) top person, leading personality • **el top del top** la crème de la crème • **el top de la gama** the best in its range; ▸ **top manta**

topacio SM topaz

topadora SF (*Cono Sur, Méx*) bulldozer

topar ▸ CONJUG 1a VI **1** (= *encontrar*) • **~ con** [+ *persona*] to run into, come across, bump into; [+ *objeto*] to find, come across

2 (= *chocar*) • **~ contra** to run into, hit • **~ con un obstáculo** to run into an obstacle, hit an obstacle

3 (= *consistir*) • **la dificultad topa en eso** that's where the trouble lies, there's the rub

4 (*Méx*) (= *reñir*) to quarrel

VT **1** (*Zool*) to butt, horn

2 [+ *persona*] to run into, come across, bump into; [+ *objeto*] to find, come across • **le topé por casualidad en el museo** I happened to bump into him in the museum

3 (*And, Cono Sur, Méx*) (= *apostar*) to bet, stake

VPR **toparse** • **~se con** [+ *persona*] to run into, come across, bump into; [+ *objeto*] to find, come across • **me topé con él hoy en el bar** I bumped into him in the bar today

tope[1] ADJ INV (= *máximo*) maximum, top • **la edad ~ para el puesto** the maximum age for the job • **fecha ~** closing date, deadline • **precio ~** top price • **sueldo ~** maximum salary

SM **1** (= *límite*) limit • MODISMOS: • **estar a ~** *o* **hasta el ~** *o* **hasta los ~s*:** • **el teatro estaba (lleno) a ~** the theatre was packed out* • **el contenedor está hasta los ~s** the container is overloaded • **voy a estar a ~ de trabajo** I'm going to be up to my eyes *o* neck in work* • **ir a ~*** to go flat out* • **trabajar a ~*** to work flat out* • **vivir a ~*** to live life to the full ▸ **tope salarial** wage ceiling

2 (*Náut*) [*del mastelero*] masthead; (= *vigía*) lookout

3 (*And, Cono Sur*) (= *cumbre*) peak, summit

ADV (*Esp*‡) (= *muy*) • **es ~ enrollada** she's mega-cool* • **es ~ guay** it's well cool*

tope² SM **1** (= *golpe*) (*gen*) bump, knock; (*con la cabeza*) butt
2 (= *riña*) quarrel; (= *pelea*) scuffle
3 (= *objeto*) stop, check; [*de tren*] buffer; [*de coche*] bumper, fender (EEUU); [*de puerta*] doorstop, wedge; [*de revólver*] catch; (*Méx*) (*en una carretera*) speed bump *o* hump ▸ **tope de tabulación** tab stop
4 (= *dificultad*) snag, problem • **ahí está el ~** that's the problem, that's just the trouble
5‡ (= *robo*) burglary

topera SF **1** (*Zool*) molehill
2‡ (= *metro*) tube*, subway (EEUU)

topero/a‡ SM/F burglar

toperol SM (*Cono Sur, Méx*) brass tack

topetada SF bump, bang

topetar ▹ CONJUG 1a VT **1** (= *golpear*) to butt, bump
2 (= *encontrarse*) to bump into

topetazo SM bump, bang

topetear ▹ CONJUG 1a VT (*And*) = **topetar**

topetón SM = **topetazo**

tópicamente ADV externally

topicazo* ADJ corny, clichéd
SM cliché

tópico ADJ **1** (*Med*) local • **de uso ~** for external use
2 (= *trillado*) commonplace, trite
SM **1** (= *lugar común*) commonplace, cliché
2 (*LAm*) (= *tema*) topic, subject

topillo¹ SM (*Méx*) (= *timo*) trick, swindle

topillo² SM (*Zool*) vole

topista‡ SMF burglar

top-less SM, **topless** SM (*en playa, piscina*) topless bathing; (*en club*) topless entertainment • **ir en** *o* **hacer top-less** to go topless

top manta SM *practice of selling pirated DVDs, CDs, etc, using a blanket as a display area*

top-model SMF (PL: **top-models**) supermodel

topo¹ SM **1** (*Zool*) mole
2 (= *torpe*) clumsy person, blunderer
3 (= *espía*) mole
4 (*Esp*) (= *lunar*) polka dot
5 (*Mec*) mole, tunnelling machine

topo² SM **1** (*LAm*) (= *alfiler*) large pin
2 (*And*) (= *distancia*) *measurement of distance of 1.5 leagues*

topocho¹ ADJ (*Caribe*) (= *gordito*) plump, chubby

topocho² SM (*Caribe*) (*Bot*) plantain

topografía SF topography

topográfico ADJ topographic(al)

topógrafo/a SM/F topographer

topolino SM **1** (= *zapato*) wedge-heeled shoe
2 (= *coche*) small car (*Fiat 500 cc*)
SF (= *persona*) teenager, bobbysoxer (EEUU)

topón SM (*LAm*) = **topetada**

toponimia SF **1** (= *nombres*) toponymy (*frm*), place names (*pl*)
2 (= *estudio*) study of place names

toponímico ADJ toponymic

topónimo SM place name

toposo ADJ (*Caribe*) meddlesome

top-secret [top'sikret] ADJ, SM INV top secret

toque SM **1** (= *golpecito*) tap • **le dio un ~ en el hombro** he gave her a tap on the shoulder • **unos toquecitos con la varita y saldrá el conejo** a few taps of the magic wand and the rabbit will come out • MODISMOS: • **dar un ~ de atención a algn** • **dar un ~ a algn***: • **el jefe tuvo que darle un ~ de atención por llegar tarde** the boss had to pull him up for being late • **te van a dar un ~ si sigues portándote mal** you'll get a telling-off if you keep behaving badly
2 (= *sonido*) [*de campana*] chime, ring; [*de reloj*] stroke; [*de timbre*] ring; [*de tambor*] beat • **al ~ de las doce** on the stroke of twelve • **dar un ~ a algn** (*por teléfono*) to give sb a bell* ▸ **toque de diana** reveille ▸ **toque de difuntos** death knell ▸ **toque de oración** call to prayer ▸ **toque de queda** curfew ▸ **toque de retreta** retreat ▸ **toque de silencio** lights out
3 (= *detalle*) touch • **el ~ personal** the personal touch • **faltan algunos ~s para completarlo** it still needs a few touches to finish it off • **dar el último ~** *o* **los últimos ~s a algo** to put the finishing touch *o* touches to sth
4 (*Arte*) [*de color, brillo*] touch ▸ **toque de luz** highlight
5 (*Quím*) test
6† (= *quid*) crux, essence • **ahí está el ~** that's the crux of the matter
7 (*And*) (= *vuelta*) turn

toquetear* ▹ CONJUG 1a VT **1** (= *manosear*) to handle, finger
2 (*Mús*) to play idly, mess about on
3 (= *acariciar*) to fondle, feel up*, touch up*

toqueteo* SM **1** (= *manoseo*) handling, fingering
2 (= *caricias*) fondling, touching up*

toquido SM (*CAm, Méx*) = **toque**

toquilla SF **1** (= *chal*) knitted shawl; (*para la cabeza*) headscarf
2 (= *gorro*) woollen bonnet; (*And*) (= *sombrero*) straw hat

torácico ADJ thoracic

torada SF herd of bulls

tórax SM thorax • **radiografía de ~** chest X-ray

torbellino SM **1** [*de viento*] whirlwind; [*de polvo*] dust cloud
2 [*de cosas*] whirl
3 (= *persona*) whirlwind

torcaz ADJ • **paloma ~** wood pigeon, ring dove

torcecuello SM (*Orn*) wryneck

torcedor SM **1** (*Téc*) spindle
2 (= *angustia*) torment, torture

torcedura SF **1** (*gen*) twist(ing); (*Med*) sprain, strain
2 (= *vino*) weak wine

torcer ▹ CONJUG 2b, 2h VT **1** (= *retorcer*) [+ *dedo, muñeca, tronco*] to twist; [+ *tobillo*] to twist, sprain; [+ *madera*] to warp; [+ *soga*] to plait; (= *doblar*) to bend • **¡me torció el brazo!** he twisted my arm! • **le ha torcido el cuello** he's twisted his neck • **torció la cabeza para mirarla** he turned (his head) to look at her
2 • **~ el gesto** to scowl • **~ los ojos** *o* **la vista** to squint
3 [+ *ropa*] to wring
4 (= *cambiar*) [+ *rumbo*] to change; [+ *voluntad*] to bend; [+ *pensamientos*] to turn; [+ *significado*] to distort, twist • **el conflicto ha torcido el curso de los acontecimientos** the conflict has changed the course of events
5 (= *pervertir*) [+ *persona*] to lead astray
VI (= *girar*) [*camino, vehículo, viajero*] to turn • **el coche torció a la izquierda** the car turned left • **al llegar allí tuerza usted a la derecha** when you get there turn right
VPR **torcerse 1** (= *retorcerse*) to twist; (= *doblarse*) to bend • **me torcí el tobillo** I twisted *o* sprained my ankle
2 (= *ladearse*) • **gira el volante que te estás torciendo** turn the steering wheel, you're not driving straight • **usa papel rayado para no ~se escribiendo** use ruled paper so you write straight
3 (= *ir por mal camino*) [*persona*] to go astray, go off the rails
4 (= *ir mal*) [*proyecto*] to go off the rails; [*proceso, acontecimientos*] to take a strange turn
5 (= *agriarse*) [*leche*] to turn, go off; [*vino*] to go sour

torcida SF wick

torcidamente ADV **1** (*lit*) in a twisted way, crookedly
2 (*fig*) deviously, in a crooked way

torcido ADJ **1** (= *no derecho*) [*nariz, línea*] crooked; (= *doblado*) [*palo, alambre*] bent • **el cuadro está ~** the picture is not straight, the picture is crooked • **llevaba el sombrero algo ~** he had his hat on not quite straight
2 (= *taimado*) devious, crooked
3 (*And, CAm, Caribe*) (= *desgraciado*) unlucky
SM (= *acto*) [*de seda*] twist

torcijón SM **1** sudden twist
2 = **retortijón**

torcimiento SM = **torcedura**

tordillo ADJ dappled, dapple-grey
SM dapple

tordo ADJ dappled, dapple-grey
SM (*Orn*) thrush

torear ▹ CONJUG 1a VT **1** [+ *toro*] to fight, play
2 (= *evitar*) to dodge, avoid
3 (= *acosar*) to plague; (= *burlarse*) to tease, draw on; (= *confundir*) to confuse • MODISMO: • **¡a mí no me torea nadie!** nobody messes me around!*
4 (= *mantener a raya*) to keep at bay; (= *dar largas a*) to put off, keep guessing
5 (*CAm, Cono Sur*) [+ *animal*] to provoke, enrage; (*Cono Sur, Méx*) [+ *persona*] to infuriate
6 (*And, Cono Sur*) [*perro*] to bark furiously at
VI **1** (*Taur*) to fight (bulls) • **toreó bien Suárez** Suárez fought well • **no volverá a ~** he will never fight again • **el muchacho quiere ~** the boy wants to be a bullfighter
2* (= *dar largas*) to spin it out, procrastinate
3 (*And, Cono Sur*) (= *ladrar*) to bark furiously

toreo SM (art of) bullfighting

torera SF (= *chaqueta*) short tight jacket • MODISMOS: • **saltarse un deber a la ~** to neglect one's duty • **saltarse una ley a la ~** to flout a law; ▹ **torero**

torería SF **1** (= *toreros*) bullfighters (*pl*); (= *mundo del toreo*) bullfighting world
2 (*Caribe, CAm*) (= *broma*) prank

torero/a SM/F bullfighter • MODISMO: • **hacer una de ~*** to say sth completely off the point; ▹ **torera**

torete SM **1** (= *toro*) (*pequeño*) small bull; (*joven*) young bull
2 (= *niño*) (*fuerte*) strong child, robust child; (*travieso*) mischievous child; (*de mal genio*) bad-tempered child

toril SM bullpen

torio SM thorium

torito* SM (*And*) (*Entomología*) bluebottle

tormenta SF **1** (*Meteo*) storm • MODISMO: • **una ~ en un vaso de agua** a storm in a teacup, a tempest in a teapot (EEUU) ▸ **tormenta de arena** sandstorm ▸ **tormenta de nieve** snowstorm ▸ **tormenta de polvo** dust storm
2 (= *discusión etc*) storm; (= *trastorno*) upheaval, turmoil • **desencadenó una ~ de pasiones** it unleashed a storm of passions • **sufrió una ~ de celos** she was eaten up with jealousy ▸ **tormenta de cerebros** brainstorm, brainstorming

tormento SM (= *tortura*) torture; (*fig*) torture, torment; (= *angustia*) anguish, agony • **dar ~ a** to torment; (*fig*) to torment, plague • **darse ~** to torment o.s. • **estos zapatos son un ~** these shoes are agony • **sus dos hijos son un ~ perpetuo** her two sons are a constant trial *o* torment to her

tormentoso ADJ stormy

tormo SM lump, mass
torna SF (= *vuelta*) return • MODISMOS: • **cambiar las ~s** to turn the tables • **volver las ~s a algn** to turn the tables on sb • **se han vuelto las ~s** now the boot's on the other foot, it's a different story now
tornada SF return
tornadera SF pitchfork, winnowing fork
tornadizo/a ADJ (= *cambiadizo*) changeable; (= *caprichoso*) fickle
SM/F (*Hist*) renegade
tornado SM tornado
tornar ▸ CONJUG 1a VT **1** (= *devolver*) to give back, return
2 (= *cambiar*) to change (**en** into), alter
VI **1** (= *volver*) to return, go back
2 • **~ a hacer algo** to do sth again • **tornó a llover** it began to rain again • **tornó a estudiar el problema** he studied the problem again
3 • **~ en sí** to regain consciousness, come to
VPR **tornarse 1** (= *regresar*) to return
2 (= *volverse*) to become, turn
tornasol SM **1** (*Bot*) sunflower
2 (*Quím*) litmus • **papel de ~** litmus paper
3 (*fig*) sheen, iridescence
tornasolado ADJ (*gen*) iridescent, sheeny; [*seda*] shot
tornasolar ▸ CONJUG 1a VT to make iridescent, put a sheen on
VPR **tornasolarse** to be *o* become iridescent, show different lights
tornavía SF turntable
tornavoz SF [*de instrumento musical*] sounding board; [*de púlpito*] sounding board, canopy • **hacer ~** to cup one's hands to one's mouth
torneado ADJ **1** (*Téc*) turned (*on a lathe*)
2 [*brazo*] shapely, delicately curved; [*figura*] pleasingly rounded
SM turning
tornear ▸ CONJUG 1a VT to turn (*on a lathe*)
torneo SM **1** (*Dep*) tournament, competition ▸ **torneo de tenis** tennis tournament ▸ **torneo olímpico** Olympic tournament ▸ **torneo por equipos** team tournament
2 (*Hist*) (= *justa*) joust
tornero/a SM/F machinist, turner
tornillería SF (= *tornillos*) screws (*pl*); (*sin especificar*) nuts and bolts (*pl*)
tornillo SM **1** (*en punta*) screw; (*para tuerca*) bolt • MODISMOS: • **apretar los ~s a algn** to apply pressure on sb, put the screws on sb* • **le falta un ~*** he has a screw loose* • **hacer ~** (*Mil*) to desert ▸ **tornillo de banco** vice, vise (*EEUU*), clamp ▸ **tornillo sin fin** worm gear
2 (*Cono Sur**) (= *frío*) bitter cold
torniquete SM **1** (= *barra giratoria*) turnstile
2 (*Med*) tourniquet
torniscón SM **1** (= *apretón*) pinch, squeeze
2 (= *manotazo*) (*en la cara*) slap on the face; (*en la cabeza*) smack on the head, cuff
torno SM **1** (*para levantar pesos*) winch, windlass; (*para tensar*) winding drum
2 (*para tornear*) lathe • **labrar a ~** to turn on the lathe ▸ **torno de alfarero** potter's wheel ▸ **torno de asador** spit ▸ **torno de banco** vice, vise (*EEUU*), clamp ▸ **torno de hilar** spinning wheel ▸ **torno de tornero** turning lathe
3 [*de río*] (= *recodo*) bend; (= *rabiones*) race, rapids (*pl*)
4 • **en ~ a: se reunieron en ~ a él** they gathered round him • **la conversación giraba en ~ a las elecciones** the conversation revolved *o* centred around the election • **polemizar en ~ a un texto** to argue about a text • **todo estaba inundado en muchos kilómetros en ~** everything was flooded for miles around
toro SM **1** (*Zool*) bull • MODISMOS: • **coger el ~ por los cuernos** • **irse a la cabeza del ~** to take the bull by the horns • **echar el ~ a algn*** to give sb a severe dressing-down* • **hacer un ~*** (*Teat*) to stand in for somebody • **a ~ pasado** with hindsight, in retrospect • **soltar el ~ a algn*** to give sb a severe dressing-down* ▸ **toro bravo, toro de lidia** fighting bull
2 (= *hombre*) strong man, he-man*, tough guy* • MODISMO: • **ser ~ corrido** to be an old hand at it, be an old fox
3 • **los ~s** (= *corrida*) bullfight (*sing*); (= *toreo*) bullfighting • **ir a los ~s** to go to the bullfight • **este año no habrá ~s** there will be no bullfight this year • **no me gustan los ~s** I don't like bullfighting • MODISMOS: • **ciertos son los ~s** it turns out that it's true • **ver los ~s desde la barrera** to stand on the sidelines, remain uncommitted
4 • MODISMO: • **hacer ~s*** to play truant, cut class
5 • **Toro** (*Astrol*) Taurus
torombolo* ADJ (*Caribe*) (= *gordito*) plump; (= *barrigón*) pot-bellied
toronja SF grapefruit, pomelo (*EEUU*)
toronjil SM lemon balm
toronjo SM grapefruit tree
torpe ADJ **1** (= *poco ágil*) [*persona*] clumsy; [*movimiento*] ungainly • **¡qué ~ eres, ya me has vuelto a pisar!** you're so clumsy, you've trodden on my foot again! • **un hombre de ~s andares** a man with an ungainly walk
2 (= *necio*) dim, slow • **soy muy ~ para la informática** I'm very dim *o* slow when it comes to computers • **es bastante ~ y nunca entiende las lecciones** he's a bit dim *o* slow, he never understands the lessons
3 (= *sin tacto*) clumsy • **¡qué ~ soy! me temo que la he ofendido** how clumsy *o* stupid of me! I'm afraid I've offended her
torpear ▸ CONJUG 1a VI (*Cono Sur*) to be dishonest, behave dishonourably
torpedear ▸ CONJUG 1a VT (*Mil*) to torpedo; [+ *proyecto*] to torpedo • **~ a algn con preguntas** to bombard sb with questions
torpedeo SM bombardment
torpedero SM torpedo boat
torpedo SM torpedo
torpemente ADV **1** (= *sin destreza*) clumsily, awkwardly
2 (= *neciamente*) slow-wittedly
torpeza SF **1** (= *falta de agilidad*) [*de persona*] clumsiness; [*de movimientos*] ungainliness
2 (= *falta de inteligencia*) dimness, slowness
3 (= *falta de tacto*) • **¡menuda ~ la tuya! has ofendido a toda la familia** that was really tactless *o* clumsy of you, you've offended the whole family! • **fue una ~ por mi parte decírselo** it was stupid *o* clumsy of me to tell him
4 (= *tontería*) • **cometer una ~** to do sth stupid
torpón ADJ (*Cono Sur*) = torpe
torpor SM torpor
torrado SM **1**‡ (= *cabeza*) bonce‡, head
2 torrados (*Culin*) toasted chickpeas
torrar ▸ CONJUG 1a VT **1** (*Culin*) to toast, roast
2‡ (= *robar*) to pinch*, nick*
VPR **torrarse 1** (= *asarse*) to roast
2* (= *dormirse*) to go off to sleep
torre SF **1** (*Arquit*) tower; [*de oficinas, viviendas*] tower block; (*Radio*) mast, tower; [*de electricidad*] pylon; [*de pozo de petróleo*] derrick ▸ **torre de alta tensión, torre de conducción eléctrica** electricity pylon ▸ **Torre de Babel** Tower of Babel ▸ **torre de marfil** ivory tower ▸ **torre de música** hi-fi
2 (*Ajedrez*) rook, castle
3 (*Aer, Mil, Náut*) turret; (*Mil*) watchtower ▸ **torre de control** (*Aer*) control tower ▸ **torre de lanzamiento** launch tower ▸ **torre del homenaje** keep ▸ **torre de mando** [*de submarino*] conning tower ▸ **torre de observación** observation tower, watchtower ▸ **torre de perforación** drilling rig ▸ **torre de refrigeración** cooling tower ▸ **torre (de) vigía** (*Náut*) crow's nest; [*de submarino*] conning tower ▸ **torre de vigilancia** watchtower
4 (*Caribe, Méx*) (= *chimenea*) factory chimney
5 • MODISMO: • **dar en la ~** (*Méx*) to hit where it hurts most
torrefacción SF toasting, roasting
torrefacto ADJ high roast
torreja SF **1** (*LAm*) (*fried*) *slices of fruit and vegetables*
2 (*Cono Sur*) slice of fruit
torrencial ADJ torrential
torrencialidad SF torrential nature
torrencialmente ADV torrentially
torrente SM **1** (= *río*) torrent • **llover a ~s** to rain cats and dogs, rain in torrents ▸ **torrente de sangre, torrente sanguíneo** bloodstream
2 [*de palabras*] torrent, rush; [*de insultos*] stream, torrent; [*de lágrimas*] flood; [*de gente*] stream ▸ **torrente de voz** powerful voice
torrentera SF gully, watercourse
torrentoso ADJ (*LAm*) [*río*] torrential, rushing; [*lluvia*] torrential
torreón SM [*de castillo*] tower; [*de casa*] turret
torrero SM lighthouse keeper
torreta SF **1** (*Aer, Mil, Náut*) turret; [*de submarino*] conning tower ▸ **torreta de observación, torreta de vigilancia** watchtower
2 (*Elec*) pylon, mast
torrezno SM rasher, slice of bacon
tórrido ADJ torrid
torrificar ▸ CONJUG 1g VT (*Méx*) [+ *café*] to toast, roast
torrija SF *bread soaked in milk and fried in batter with honey or sugar and wine, eaten especially at Easter*
torsión SF **1** (= *torcedura*) twist, twisting
2 (*Mec*) torsion, torque
torsional ADJ torsional
torso SM (*Anat*) torso; (*Arte*) head and shoulders
torta SF **1*** (= *bofetada*) thump; (= *puñetazo*) punch, sock*; (= *caída*) fall; (= *choque*) crash • **liarse a ~s** to get involved in a punch-up
2 (= *pastel*) cake; (*con base de masa quebrada*) tart, flan; (= *crepe*) pancake; (*Méx*) sandwich • MODISMOS: • **la ~ costó un pan** it worked out dearer than expected, it was more trouble than it was worth • **eso es ~s y pan pintado** it's child's play, it's a cinch‡ • **¡ni ~!*** I haven't a clue!, not the foggiest! • **no entendió ni ~** he didn't understand a word of it • **nos queda la ~** there's a lot left over
3 (*CAm, Méx*) (= *tortilla*) ▸ **torta de huevos** omelet(te)
4 (*Esp*‡) (= *borrachera*) • **agarrar una ~** to get plastered*
5 (*Tip*) font
tortazo* SM (= *bofetada*) slap, sock*; (= *golpe*) thump • **pegarse un ~** to get a knock
tortear ▸ CONJUG 1a VT (*Cono Sur*) [+ *masa*] to flatten, roll; (*CAm, Méx*) [+ *tortilla*] to shape (*with the palms of one's hands*)
VI (*Méx*) (= *aplaudir*) to clap, applaud
tortero ADJ (*And*) round and flat, disc-shaped
tortícolis SF INV stiff neck • **me levanté con ~** I got up with a stiff neck *o* a crick in my neck
tortilla SF **1** [*de huevo*] omelette • MODISMOS:

• **hacer algo una ~** to smash sth up • **van a hacer el negocio una ~** they're sure to mess the deal up • **hacer a algn una ~*** to beat sb up* • **dar la vuelta a la ~** to turn the tables • **volverse la ~**: • **se ha vuelto la ~** now the boot is on the other foot, it's a different story now • **se le volvió la ~** it came out all wrong for him, it all blew up in his face ▸ **tortilla de patatas, tortilla española** Spanish potato omelette ▸ **tortilla francesa** plain omelette
2 (*CAm, Méx*) [*de maíz*] flat maize pancake, tortilla
3‡ (= *lesbianismo*) lesbian sex
tortillera SF 1 (*CAm, Méx*) (= *vendedora*) seller of maize pancakes
2‡* (= *lesbiana*) dyke‡*, lesbian
tortita SF pancake
tórtola SF turtledove
tortoleo SM (*Méx*) billing and cooing
tórtolo SM 1 (= *ave*) (male) turtledove
2* (= *amante*) lovebird, loverboy; **tórtolos** pair of lovers, lovebirds
tortuga SF [*de tierra*] tortoise; (*tb* **tortuga marina**) turtle • MODISMO: • **a paso de ~** at a snail's pace
tortuguismo SM (*Méx*) go-slow, slowdown (*EEUU*)
tortuoso ADJ 1 [*camino*] winding, full of twists and turns
2 [*conducta*] devious
tortura SF torture
torturado/a SM/F torture victim
torturador(a) SM/F torturer
torturar ▹ CONJUG 1a VT to torture
toruno SM 1 (*CAm*) (= *semental*) stud bull; (*Cono Sur*) (= *toro viejo*) old bull; (*Cono Sur*) (= *buey*) ox
2 (*Cono Sur*) (= *hombre*) fit old man
torvisca SF, **torvisco** SM spurge flax
torvo ADJ grim, fierce • **una mirada torva** a fierce look
torzal SM 1 (= *hilo*) cord, twist
2 (*Cono Sur*) (= *lazo*) plaited rope, lasso
tos SF cough • **acceso de tos** coughing fit • **tiene tos** he's got a cough ▸ **tos convulsa, tos ferina** whooping cough
toscamente ADV roughly, crudely
Toscana SF • **La ~** Tuscany
toscano/a ADJ, SM/F Tuscan
SM 1 (*Ling*) Tuscan; (*Hist*) Italian
2 (= *puro*) (a kind of) cigar
tosco ADJ coarse, rough, crude
tosedera SF (*LAm*) nagging cough
toser ▹ CONJUG 2a VI to cough
VT • MODISMO: • **no hay quien le tosa** he's in a class by himself • **no hay quien le tosa a la hora de cocinar** he's in a class by himself when it comes to cooking • **cuando se pone así no hay quien le tosa** no one gets in his way when he's in that mood
tosido SM (*CAm, Cono Sur, Méx*) cough
tósigo SM poison
tosquedad SF coarseness, roughness, crudeness
tostada SF 1 [*de pan*] piece of toast • **~s** toast (*sing*) • MODISMO: • **olerse la ~** to smell a rat
2 • **una ~ de*** a load of*, masses of • **hace una ~ de años** ages ago
3 (*Méx*) (= *tortilla*) fried tortilla; (*CAm*) (= *plátano*) toasted slice of banana
4 (*Cono Sur*) (= *conversación*) long boring conversation
tostado ADJ 1 (*Culin*) toasted
2 [*color*] dark brown, ochre; [*persona*] tanned
SM 1 (= *acción*) [*de pan*] toasting; [*de café*] roasting
2 (= *bronceado*) tan
tostador SM [*de pan*] toaster; [*de café*] roaster ▸ **tostador de pan** electric toaster
tostadora SF toaster
tostadura SF [*de café*] roasting
tostar ▹ CONJUG 1l VT 1 [+ *pan*] to toast; [+ *café*] to roast; [+ *carne*] to brown
2 (= *broncear*) to tan
3 (*Caribe, Cono Sur**) (= *pegar*) • **~ a algn** to tan sb's hide*
4 (*Méx*) (= *ofender*) to offend; (= *perjudicar*) to harm, hurt; (= *matar*) to kill
5 (*Caribe, Cono Sur*) (= *proseguir*) to push on with
VPR **tostarse** (*tb* **tostarse al sol**) to tan, get brown
tostelería SF (*CAm*) cake shop
tostón SM 1* (= *lata*) bore, nuisance; (= *discurso*) long boring speech; (= *cuento*) tedious tale • **dar el ~** (= *aburrir*) to be a bore; (= *fastidiar*) to be a nuisance
2 (*Culin*) (= *cubito*) crouton; (= *tostada*) piece of toast dipped in oil; (= *tostada quemada*) *piece of bread toasted too much*; (= *garbanzo*) toasted chickpea
3 (= *lechón*) roast sucking pig
4 (*Caribe*) (= *banana*) slice of fried green banana
5 (*Méx**) (= *moneda*) 50-cent piece
tostonear* ▹ CONJUG 1a VT, VI (*Méx*) to sell at bargain prices
total ADJ 1 (= *absoluto*) [*éxito, fracaso*] total • **una revisión ~ de su teoría** a complete revision of his theory • **una calamidad ~** a total disaster
2 (= *global*) [*importe, suma*] total
3* (= *excelente*) smashing, brilliant • **es un libro ~** it's a brilliant book
ADV 1 (= *resumiendo*) in short, all in all; (= *así que*) so • **~ que** to cut a long story short, the upshot of it all was that ... • **~, que no fuimos** so we didn't go after all • **~, que vas a hacer lo que quieras** basically then you're going to do as you please
2 (= *al fin y al cabo*) at the end of the day • **~, ¿qué más te da?** at the end of the day, what do you care? • **~, usted manda** well, you're the boss after all
SM (= *suma total*) total; (= *totalidad*) whole • **el ~ son 50 pesos** the total is 50 pesos • **el ~ de la población** the whole (of the) population • **en ~** in all • **en ~ éramos catorce** there were fourteen of us altogether ▸ **total debe** debit total ▸ **total de comprobación** hash total ▸ **total haber** assets total
totalidad SF whole • **la ~ de la población** the whole (of the) population • **la práctica ~ de los votantes** nearly all the voters • **quieren publicar el informe en su ~** they want to publish the report in its entirety • **la aseguradora cubrirá los gastos en su ~** the insurer will cover all expenses
totalitario ADJ totalitarian
totalitarismo SM totalitarianism
totalizador ADJ all-embracing, all-encompassing
SM totalizator
totalizar ▹ CONJUG 1f VT to totalize, add up
VI to add up to, total
totalmente ADV totally, completely • **Mario es ~ distinto a Luis** Mario is totally *o* completely different from Luis • **estoy ~ de acuerdo** I totally *o* completely agree • **—¿estás seguro? —totalmente** "are you sure?" — "absolutely"
totazo SM 1 (*And*) (= *explosión*) bursting, explosion
2 (*And, Caribe*) (= *golpe*) bang on the head
totear ▹ CONJUG 1a (*And, Caribe*) VI to burst, explode
VPR **totearse** (= *reventar*) to burst; (= *agrietarse*) to crack, split
tótem SM (PL: **tótems**) totem, totem pole
totémico ADJ totemic
totemismo SM totemism
totogol SM (*Col*) football pools (*pl*) (*Brit*), sports lottery (*EEUU*)
totopo SM (*CAm, Méx*), **totoposte** SM (*CAm, Méx*) crisp tortilla
totora SF (*And*) large reed
totoral SM (*LAm*) reed bed
totoreco* ADJ (*CAm*) thick*, stupid
totovía SF woodlark
totuma SF 1 (*And, Caribe*) (*Bot*) gourd, squash (*EEUU*), calabash
2 (*Cono Sur*) (= *cardenal*) bruise; (= *chichón*) bump, lump
3 (*And, Caribe, Cono Sur*) (= *cabeza*) nut‡, head • **cortarse ~** (*Caribe*) to get one's hair cut
totumo SM 1 (*LAm*) (= *árbol*) calabash tree
2 (*Cono Sur*) (= *chichón*) bump on the head
touroperador(a) SM/F tour operator
toxicidad SF toxicity
tóxico ADJ toxic, poisonous
SM poison, toxin
toxicodependencia SF drug-addiction
toxicodependiente SMF drug-addict
toxicología SF toxicology
toxicológico ADJ toxicological
toxicólogo/a SM/F toxicologist
toxicomanía SF drug-addiction
toxicómano/a ADJ addicted to drugs
SM/F drug addict
toximia SF toxaemia, toxemia (*EEUU*)
toxina SF toxin
toxinfección SF poisoning ▸ **toxinfección alimentaria** food poisoning
tozudez SF stubbornness, obstinacy
tozudo ADJ stubborn, obstinate
traba SF 1 (= *unión*) bond, tie; (*Mec*) clasp, clamp; [*de caballo*] hobble; (*Cono Sur*) hair slide
2 **trabas** [*de prisionero*] shackles
3 (= *estorbo*) obstacle, hindrance • **sin ~s** unrestrained, free • **poner ~s a** to restrain, obstruct • **ponerse ~s** to make difficulties for o.s.
4 (*Caribe, Méx*) [*de gallos*] (= *pelea*) cockfight; (= *lugar*) cockpit
trabacuenta SM mistake, miscalculation • **andar con ~s** to be engaged in endless controversies
trabado ADJ 1 (= *unido*) joined; [*discurso*] coherent, well constructed
2 (= *fuerte*) tough, strong
3 (*LAm*) (*al hablar*) stammering
4 (*And*) (= *bizco*) cross-eyed
trabajado ADJ 1 (= *elaborado*) carefully worked • **bien ~** well made, elaborately fashioned
2 (*pey*) forced, strained, artificial
3 [*persona*] (= *cansado*) worn out, weary from overwork
trabajador(a) ADJ hard-working, industrious
SM/F worker, labourer, laborer (*EEUU*); (*Pol*) worker ▸ **trabajador(a) autónomo/a** self-employed person ▸ **trabajador(a) eventual** casual worker ▸ **trabajador(a) por cuenta ajena** employee, employed person ▸ **trabajador(a) por cuenta propia** self-employed person ▸ **trabajador(a) portuario/a** docker ▸ **trabajador(a) social** social worker
trabajar ▹ CONJUG 1a VI 1 [*persona*] to work • **trabaja en las afueras** she works on the outskirts of town • **no trabajes tanto** don't work so hard • **ahora trabajo más que antes** I work harder now than I used to • **se mata trabajando para alimentar a su familia** he works himself to death to feed his family • **llevo una semana sin ~** I haven't done any

t

work for a week • **ese actor trabaja muy bien** that actor's very good • **~ de algo** to work as sth • **trabajo de camarero** I work as a waiter • **~ en algo**: • **¿en qué trabajas?** what's your job? • **¿ha trabajado antes en diseño gráfico?** do you have any previous work experience in graphic design? • **trabajan en una compañía aérea** they work for an airline • **~ por horas** to work by the hour • **~ jornada completa** to work full-time • **~ media jornada** to work half-days • **~ por hacer algo**: • **estamos trabajando por conseguir nuestros derechos** we are working towards getting our rights • **~ a tiempo parcial** to work part-time • MODISMOS: • **~ como un buey** *o* **como una mula** to work like a Trojan • **~ como un condenado** *o* **un negro** to work like a slave
2 (= *funcionar*) [*fábrica*] to work; [*máquina*] to run, work • **la fábrica trabaja día y noche** the factory works day and night • **para que el cerebro trabaje** for the brain to work (properly) • **el sistema inmunitario trabaja para vencer las infecciones** the immune system works to overcome infections • **el tiempo trabaja a nuestro favor** time is on our side • **hacer ~**: • **si quiere hacer ~ su dinero llámenos** if you want to make your money work for you, give us a call
3 [*tierra, árbol*] to bear, yield
(VT) **1** [+ *tierra, cuero, madera*] to work; [+ *masa*] to knead; [+ *ingredientes*] to mix in
2 [+ *detalle, proyecto*] to work on; [+ *mente*] to exercise • **hay que ~ un poco más los números musicales** we need to do a bit more work on the musical numbers • **el pintor ha trabajado muy bien los árboles** the painter has put a lot of work into the trees
3 (*Com*) (= *vender*) to sell • **es mi colega quien trabaja ese género** it is my colleague who sells *o* handles that line • **nosotros no trabajamos esa marca** we don't sell *o* stock that brand
4 [+ *caballo*] to train
(VPR) **trabajarse 1** [+ *persona*] to work on • **se está trabajando a su tía para sacarle los ahorros** he's working on his aunt in order to get hold of her savings
2 [+ *asunto*] to work on • **tienes que ~te el ascenso un poco más** you need to work a bit harder on getting that promotion • **tienes que ~te un poco más el alemán** you've got to work on your German a bit • **quien no se lo trabaja no consigue nada** you won't get anything if you don't work for it

trabajo (SM) **1** (= *labor*) work • **tengo mucho ~** I have a lot of work • **me queda ~ para una hora** I have an hour's work left • **¡buen ~!** good work! • **en reconocimiento a su ~ como actor** in recognition of his work as an actor • **tiene una enorme capacidad de ~** she's a very willing worker • **planchar la ropa es el ~ que menos me gusta** the ironing is the job I like least • **a veces le sale algún que otro trabajillo** he gets odd jobs now and then • **el ~ de la casa** the housework • **ropa de ~** work clothes • **estar sin ~** to be unemployed • **los que están sin ~** the unemployed • **quedarse sin ~** to find o.s. out of work, lose one's job • MODISMO: • **¡esto es un ~ de chinos!** this is really painstaking work! ▸ **trabajo a destajo** piecework ▸ **trabajo de campo**, **trabajo en el terreno** fieldwork ▸ **trabajo en equipo** teamwork ▸ **trabajo intelectual** brainwork ▸ **trabajo manual** manual labour, manual labor (EEUU) ▸ **trabajo nocturno** night work ▸ **trabajo por turnos** shiftwork ▸ **trabajos forzados** hard labour (*sing*), hard labor (EEUU) (*sing*) ▸ **trabajos manuales** (*Escol*) handicrafts ▸ **trabajo social** social work ▸ **trabajo sucio** dirty work
2 (*tb* **puesto de trabajo**) job • **le han ofrecido un ~ en el banco** he's been offered a job at the bank • **tengo un ~ de media jornada** I have a job working half-days • **no encuentro ~** I can't find work *o* a job ▸ **trabajo eventual** temporary job ▸ **trabajo fijo** permanent job
3 (*tb* **lugar de trabajo**) work • **vivo cerca de mi ~** I live near work *o* near my workplace • **está en el ~** she's at work • **me puedes llamar al ~** you can call me at work • **ir al ~** to go to work
4 (= *esfuerzo*) • **lo hizo con mucho ~** it cost him a lot of effort to do it • **han sido muchos años de ~ para ganar el pleito** it has taken many years' hard work to win the lawsuit • **ahorrarse el ~** to save o.s. the trouble • **costar ~**: • **le cuesta ~ hacerlo** he finds it hard to do • **me cuesta ~ decir que no** I find it hard to say no • **dar ~**: • **reparar la casa nos ha dado mucho ~** it was hard work *o* a real job repairing the house • **los niños pequeños dan mucho ~** small children are a lot of work • **tomarse el ~ de hacer algo** to take the trouble to do sth • REFRÁN: • **~ te doy, ~ te mando** it's no easy task, it's a tough job
5 (= *obra*) (*Arte, Literat*) work; (*Educ*) essay; [*de investigación*] study • **uno de los mejores ~s del arquitecto** one of the architect's greatest works • **tengo que entregar dos ~s mañana** I have to hand in two essays tomorrow
6 (*Econ*) **a** (= *mano de obra*) labour, labor (EEUU)
b (*tb* **Ministerio de Trabajo**) ≈ Department of Employment, ≈ Department of Labor (EEUU)

trabajoadicto/a (SM/F) workaholic

trabajosamente (ADV) (= *con trabajo*) laboriously; (= *dolorosamente*) painfully

trabajoso (ADJ) **1** (= *difícil*) hard, laborious; (= *doloroso*) painful
2 (*Med*) pale, sickly
3 (*Cono Sur*) (= *exigente*) exacting, demanding; (= *astuto*) wily
4 (*And*) (= *poco amable*) unhelpful; (= *malhumorado*) bad-tempered, tetchy
5 (*Cono Sur*) (= *molesto*) annoying

trabalenguas (SM INV) tongue twister

trabar ▸ CONJUG 1a (VT) **1** [+ *puerta, ventana*] (*para que quede cerrada*) to wedge shut; (*para que quede abierta*) to wedge open • **trabó la puerta con una silla para que no entrara** he wedged the door shut with a chair to stop her getting in • **trabó la pata de la mesa con una madera** she wedged a piece of wood under the table leg
2 [+ *salsa, líquido*] to thicken
3 (*Carpintería*) to join; (*Constr*) to point
4 (= *comenzar*) [+ *conversación, debate*] to start (up), strike up; [+ *batalla*] to join • **~ amistad** to strike up a friendship
5 (= *enlazar*) • **una serie de razonamientos muy bien trabados** a tightly woven *o* very well constructed argument
6 (= *obstaculizar*) to hold back • **la falta de recursos ha trabado el desarrollo de la investigación** research has been held back by the lack of funds
7 [+ *caballo*] to hobble
8 [+ *sierra*] to set
9 (*CAm, Caribe*) (= *engañar*) to deceive
(VI) **1** [*planta*] to take
2 [*ancla, garfio*] to grip
(VPR) **trabarse 1** (= *enredarse*) to get tangled up • **me trabé en un matorral y no podía salir** I got tangled up in a thicket and couldn't get free • **se le traba la lengua** he gets tongue-tied; (*Caribe*) he loses the thread (of what he is saying)
2 (= *atascarse*) [*cajón, puerta, mecanismo*] to jam, get jammed
3 (= *involucrarse*) • **~se en una discusión** to get involved in an argument

trabazón (SF) **1** (*Téc*) joining, assembly
2 [*de líquido*] consistency
3 (= *coherencia*) coherence

trabilla (SF) (= *tira*) small strap; (= *broche*) clasp; [*de cinturón*] belt loop; (= *puntada*) dropped stitch

trabucar ▸ CONJUG 1g (VT) (= *confundir*) to confuse; (= *desordenar*) to mix up, mess up; [+ *palabras, sonidos*] to mix up, confuse
(VPR) **trabucarse** to get all mixed up

trabuco (SM) **1** (*tb* **trabuco naranjero**) blunderbuss; (= *juguete*) popgun
2** (= *pene*) prick**

traca (SF) **1** [*de fuegos artificiales*] string of fireworks; (= *ruido fuerte*) row, racket
2 • **es de ~*** it's killingly funny

trácala (SF) **1** (*And*) (= *gentío*) crowd, mob
2 (*Caribe, Méx*) (= *trampa*) trick, ruse
3 (*Méx*) (= *tramposo*) trickster

tracalada* (SF) **1** (*LAm*) (= *gentío*) crowd • **una ~ de** a load of* • **a ~s** by the hundred
2 (*Méx*) (= *trampa*) trick, ruse

tracalero/a* (*Méx, Caribe*) (ADJ) (= *astuto*) crafty; (*tramposo*) sly, deceitful
(SM/F) cheat, trickster

tracamundana* (SF) **1** (= *jaleo*) row, rumpus
2 (= *cambio*) swap, exchange

tracatrá* (EXCL) no way!*, get away!*

tracción (SF) traction, drive ▸ **tracción a las cuatro ruedas** four-wheel drive ▸ **tracción delantera** front-wheel drive ▸ **tracción integral, tracción total** four-wheel drive ▸ **tracción trasera** rear-wheel drive

tracería (SF) tracery

tracoma (SM) trachoma

tractivo (ADJ) tractive

tractor (SM) tractor ▸ **tractor agrícola** agricultural tractor, farm tractor ▸ **tractor de oruga** caterpillar tractor
(ADJ) • **rueda ~a** drive wheel

tractorada (SF) *demonstration where farmers block the streets with their tractors*

tractorista (SMF) tractor driver

trad. (ABR) (= **traducido**) trans

tradición (SF) tradition

tradicional (ADJ) traditional

tradicionalidad (SF) traditionality, traditional character

tradicionalismo (SM) traditionalism

tradicionalista (ADJ), (SMF) traditionalist

tradicionalmente (ADV) traditionally

tráding ['tradin] (ADJ) • **empresa ~** trading company
(SF) trading company

traducción (SF) translation (**a** into, **de** from) ▸ **traducción asistida por ordenador** computer-assisted translation ▸ **traducción automática, traducción automatizada** automatic translation, machine translation ▸ **traducción directa** *translation into one's own language* ▸ **traducción simultánea** simultaneous translation

traducible (ADJ) translatable

traducir ▸ CONJUG 3n (VT) to translate (**a** into, **de** from)
(VPR) **traducirse** • **~se en** (= *significar*) to mean in practice; (= *suponer*) to entail, result in

traductor(a) (SM/F) translator ▸ **traductor(a) jurado/a, traductor(a) público/a** (*Arg, Uru*) official translator

traer ▸ CONJUG 2o (VT) **1** (= *transportar*) to

bring • **¿has traído el dinero?** have you brought the money? • **¿me traes un vaso de agua?** can you bring *o* fetch *o* get me a glass of water? • **el muchacho que trae los periódicos** the lad who delivers *o* brings the newspapers • **¿nos trae la cuenta, por favor?** can we have the bill, please? • **trae, ya lo arreglo yo** give it to me, I'll fix it • **¿me puedes ~ mañana a la oficina?** can you bring me to work *o* give me a lift to work tomorrow? • **¿qué la trae por aquí?** what brings you here? • **~ un hijo al mundo** to bring a child into the world • **~ buenas/malas notas** to get good/bad marks *o* grades (EEUU) • MODISMO: • **como su madre *o* como Dios lo trajo al mundo** as naked as the day he was born, in his birthday suit; ▷ **memoria**
2 (= *llevar encima*) [+ *ropa*] to wear; [+ *objeto*] to carry • **traía unos zapatos muy bonitos** she was wearing some very nice shoes • **¿qué traes en esa bolsa?** what have you got in that bag?, what are you carrying in that bag?
3 [*periódico, revista*] • **el periódico no trae nada sobre eso** there's nothing about it in the newspaper • **¿trae alguna noticia interesante?** is there any interesting news?
4 (= *causar*) [+ *suerte, paz, beneficios*] to bring; [+ *recuerdos*] to bring back; [+ *consecuencias*] to have • **te ~á buena suerte** it'll bring you good luck • **el embargo trajo como consecuencia la ruina económica** the embargo brought about *o* resulted in the economic ruin • **~ consigo** to bring about • **la recesión trajo consigo un aumento del paro** the recession brought with it *o* brought about an increase in unemployment; ▷ **colación, cuento¹**
5 (= *tener*) (+ *adj*) • **la ausencia de noticias me trae muy inquieto** the lack of news is making me very anxious • **el juego lo trae perdido** gambling is his ruin; ▷ **loco**
6 • MODISMOS: • **me trae sin cuidado** • **me trae al fresco*** I couldn't care less* • **me la trae floja‡** I couldn't give a damn‡ • **~ de cabeza a algn**: • **el caso trae de cabeza a la policía local** this case is proving to be a headache for local police • **el horario comercial trae de cabeza a los consumidores** shopping hours are a headache for consumers • **~la con algn** (*Méx*) to have it in for sb* • **llevar *o* ~ a mal ~ a algn** [*persona*] to give sb nothing but trouble; [*problema*] to be the bane of sb's life • **¡este hijo mío me trae a mal ~!** this son of mine is really giving me a hard time!, this son of mine is (giving me) nothing but trouble! • **~ y llevar a algn** (= *molestar*) to pester sb; (= *chismorrear*) to gossip about sb; ▷ **traído**
7 (= *atraer*) [+ *imán*] to draw, attract
VPR **traerse 1** (= *tramar*) to be up to • **estoy seguro de que esos dos se traen algún manejo sucio** I'm sure the two of them are up to something shady; ▷ **mano**
2 (*uso enfático*) to bring • **me he traído la cámara** I've brought the camera, I've brought the camera with me • **no se trajo al novio** she didn't bring her boyfriend
3* • MODISMO: • **se las trae**: • **es un problema que se las trae** it's a real nightmare of a problem • **tiene un padre que se las trae** her father is impossible, her father is a real nightmare
4 (*Esp††*) • **~se bien** (= *vestirse*) to dress well; (= *comportarse*) to behave properly • **~se mal** (= *vestirse*) to dress shabbily; (= *comportarse*) to behave badly
trafagar ▷ CONJUG 1h VI to bustle about
tráfago SM **1** (= *ajetreo*) bustle, hustle
2 (*Com*) traffic, trade
3 (= *trabajo*) (*pesado*) drudgery, toil; (*rutinario*) routine job
trafaguear ▷ CONJUG 1a VI (*Méx*) to bustle about, keep on the go
traficante SMF dealer (**en** in) ▸ **traficante de armas** arms dealer ▸ **traficante de drogas** drug dealer ▸ **traficante de esclavos** slave trader
traficar ▷ CONJUG 1g VI **1** (= *negociar*) to deal (con with, **en** in); (*pey*) to traffic (**en** in)
2† (= *moverse*) to keep on the go, be on the move; (= *viajar*) to travel a lot
tráfico SM **1** (*Aut, Ferro*) traffic • **accidente de ~** road accident, traffic accident • **cortar el ~** to interrupt traffic ▸ **tráfico de carga** (*LAm*), **tráfico de mercancías** goods traffic ▸ **tráfico por ferrocarril** rail traffic ▸ **tráfico rodado** road traffic, vehicular traffic
2 (*tb* **Dirección General de Tráfico**) *public department in charge of controlling traffic*
3 (= *negocio*) trade; (*pey*) traffic (**en** in) ▸ **tráfico de drogas, tráfico de estupefacientes** drug traffic ▸ **tráfico de influencias** peddling of political favours *o* (EEUU) favors
4 (*LAm*) (= *tránsito*) transit, passage
tragabalas SM INV (*Méx*) bully, braggart
tragadera‡ SF (*LAm*) slap-up do*, blow-out‡, chow-down (EEUU‡)
tragaderas SFPL **1** (= *garganta*) throat (*sing*), gullet (*sing*)
2 (= *credulidad*) gullibility (*sing*); (= *tolerancia*) tolerance (*sing*) • **tener buenas ~** (= *ser crédulo*) to be gullible; (= *ser permisivo*) to be very easy-going, be prepared to put up with a lot
tragadero SM throat, gullet • **la comida fue un ~** (*Méx**) we stuffed ourselves*
tragador(a) SM/F glutton
tragafuegos SMF INV fire eater
trágala* SMF (= *glotón*) glutton
SM • MODISMOS: • **cantar el ~ a algn** to laugh in sb's face • **es el país del ~** it's the country where you accept something whether you like it or not
tragaldabas* SMF INV glutton, pig*, hog (EEUU)
tragaleguas* SMF INV great walker
tragalibros SMF INV (= *lector*) bookworm; (= *empollón*) swot*, grind (EEUU)
tragallón ADJ (*Cono Sur*) greedy
tragaluz SM skylight
tragamonedas SM INV = **tragaperras**
traganíqueles* SM INV (*CAm*) = **tragaperras**
tragantada* SF swig*, mouthful
tragantón* ADJ greedy
tragantona* SF **1*** (= *comilona*) slap-up meal, blow-out*, chow-down (EEUU‡)
2 (= *trago*) gulp
3 (= *acto*) (act of) swallowing hard
tragaperras SF INV (*gen*) slot machine; (*en bar*) fruit-machine, one-armed bandit; ▷ **máquina**
tragar ▷ CONJUG 1h VT **1** [+ *comida, bebida*] to swallow • **un poco de agua te ayudará a ~ la pastilla** the tablet will be easier to swallow with a little water • **nunca he visto a nadie ~ tanta comida*** I've never seen anyone put away so much food* • **le molesta la garganta al ~ saliva** her throat bothers her when she swallows hard • **me insultó, pero tragué saliva por respeto a su padre** he insulted me, but I bit my tongue out of respect for his father
2 (= *absorber*) to soak up • **esta tierra traga el agua rápidamente** this ground soaks the water up very quickly
3* (= *gastar*) to use • **este coche traga mucha gasolina** this car uses a lot of petrol *o* guzzles* petrol
4* (= *aguantar*) [+ *insultos, reprimenda*] to put up with • **le ha hecho ~ mucho a su mujer** his wife has had to put up with a lot • **no puedo ~ a tu hermano** I can't stand your brother
5* (= *creer*) to swallow*, fall for* • **nadie se va a ~ esa historia** nobody is going to swallow *o* fall for that story*
VI **1*** (= *engullir*) • **tu hijo traga que da gusto** your son really enjoys *o* loves his food
2* (= *creer*) to swallow*, fall for* • **—¿han tragado? —no, no se han creído nada** "did they swallow it *o* fall for it?" — "no, they didn't believe a word"*
VPR **tragarse 1** [+ *comida, bebida*] to swallow • **se lo tragó entero** he swallowed it whole • **el perro se ha tragado un hueso** the dog has swallowed a bone • **eso me lo trago en dos minutos*** I could put that away in no time*
2 (= *absorber*) [*arena, tierra*] to soak up; [*mar, abismo*] to swallow up, engulf
3 [*teléfono, máquina*] to swallow • **la máquina del café se me ha tragado todas las monedas** the coffee machine has swallowed all my change
4 (= *aguantar*) [+ *insultos, reprimenda*] to put up with • **tuvo que ~se las amenazas de su jefe** he had to put up with his boss's threats • **siempre tengo que ~me los problemas de los demás** I always have to sit and listen to other people's problems • **pone la tele y se traga todo lo que le echen** he puts the TV on and watches anything that's on
5* (= *creer*) to swallow*, fall for* • **se ~á todo lo que se le diga** he'll swallow *o* fall for whatever he's told*
6 (= *reprimir*) • **~se las lágrimas** to hold back one's tears • **~se el orgullo** to swallow one's pride
tragasables SMF INV sword-swallower
tragasantos SMF INV excessively pious person
tragavenado SM (*And, Caribe*) boa constrictor
tragedia SF tragedy • **monta una ~ de cualquier tontería** he makes a drama out of every little thing
trágicamente ADV tragically
trágico ADJ tragic(al) • **lo ~ es que ...** the tragedy of it is that ..., the tragic thing about it is that ...
SM tragedian
tragicomedia SF tragicomedy
tragicómico ADJ tragicomic
trago SM **1** (*de un líquido*) drink • **un traguito de agua** a sip of water • **no vendría mal un ~ de vino** a drop of wine would not come amiss • **echar un ~** to have a drink, have a swig* • **beber algo de un ~** to drink sth in one gulp • MODISMOS: • **el ~ del estribo** one for the road • **brindar el ~ a algn** (*LAm*) to stand sb a drink
2 (= *bebida alcohólica*) drink; (*LAm*) (= *licor*) hard liquor • **¡échame un ~!** give me a drink! • **ser demasiado aficionado al ~** to be too fond of the drink
3 (= *experiencia*) • **mal ~** • **~ amargo** (= *momento difícil*) hard time, rough time; (= *golpe*) blow; (= *desgracia*) misfortune, calamity • **fue un ~ amargo** it was a cruel blow • **nos quedaba todavía el ~ más amargo** the worst of it was still to come
4 • **a ~s: hacer algo a ~s** to do sth bit by bit
tragón/ona ADJ greedy
SM/F glutton • **es un ~** he is very greedy, he's a greedy pig*
traguear* ▷ CONJUG 1a VT, VI (*CAm*)

t

(= *beber*) to drink; (*Caribe*) (= *emborracharse*) to get sloshed*
VPR **traguearse** (*And, CAm, Méx*) to get sloshed*
trai SM (*Cono Sur*) (*Rugby*) try
traición SF **1** (= *deslealtad*) betrayal; (= *alevosía*) treachery • **una ~** a betrayal • **cometer una ~ contra algn** to betray sb • **matar a algn a ~** to kill sb treacherously
2 (*Jur*) treason • **alta ~** high treason
traicionar ▸ CONJUG 1a VT to betray
traicionero ADJ treacherous
traída SF carrying, bringing ▸ **traída de aguas** water supply
traído ADJ† worn, threadbare • MODISMO: • **~ y llevado**: • **el tan ~ y llevado tema del papel de la familia hoy día** the overworked *o* time-worn subject of the role of the family today • **el tan ~ y llevado oro de Moscú** the much talked-about Moscow gold
SMPL **traídos** (*Col*) presents, gifts
traidor(a) ADJ [*persona*] treacherous; [*acto*] treasonable
SM/F traitor/traitress; (*Teat*) villain
traidoramente ADV treacherously, traitorously
traiga *etc* ▸ **traer**
trailer SM (PL: **trailers**), **tráiler** SM (PL: **tráilers**) **1** (*Cine*) trailer
2 (= *caravana*) caravan, trailer (*EEUU*); [*de camión*] trailer, trailer unit
traílla SF **1** (*Téc*) scraper, leveller; (*Agr*) harrow
2 [*de perro*] lead, leash
3 (= *conjunto de perros*) team of dogs
traillar ▸ CONJUG 1a VT (= *rascar*) to scrape; (= *allanar*) to level; (*Agr*) to harrow
traína SF sardine-fishing net, dragnet
trainera SF [*de pesca*] small fishing boat (*used for trawling*); [*de remo*] *rowing boat used for racing*
training ['treinin] SM (PL: **trainings**)
1 (= *entrenamiento*) training
2 (= *curso*) training course
traiña SF = **traína**
Trajano SM Trajan
traje[1] ▸ **traer**
traje[2] SM (*de dos piezas*) suit; (= *vestido*) dress; (*típico*) dress, costume; (*fig*) garb, guise • **~ hecho** off-the-peg suit • **~ hecho a la medida** made-to-measure suit • **un policía en ~ de calle** a plain-clothes policeman • MODISMOS: • **cortar un ~ a algn** to gossip about sb • **en ~ de Eva** in her birthday suit ▸ **traje de agua** wet suit ▸ **traje de baño** bathing costume, swimsuit, swimming costume ▸ **traje de campaña** battledress ▸ **traje de ceremonia** full dress ▸ **traje de chaqueta** suit ▸ **traje de cóctel** cocktail dress ▸ **traje de cuartel** (*Mil*) undress ▸ **traje de época** period costume ▸ **traje de etiqueta** dress suit, dinner dress ▸ **traje de luces** bullfighter's costume ▸ **traje de noche** evening dress ▸ **traje de novia** wedding dress, bridal gown ▸ **traje de oficina** business suit ▸ **traje de paisano** (*Esp*) civilian clothes; (*de policía*) plain clothes ▸ **traje de playa** sunsuit ▸ **traje espacial** spacesuit ▸ **traje isotérmico** wet suit ▸ **traje largo** evening gown ▸ **traje pantalón** trouser suit ▸ **traje regional** regional costume, regional dress ▸ **traje serio** business suit
trajeado ADJ • **ir bien ~** to be well dressed, be well turned out • **estar ~ de** to be dressed in; (*hum*) to be got up in, be rigged out in • **estar bien ~ para la temporada** to have the right clothes for the weather *o* season
trajear ▸ CONJUG 1a VT (= *vestir*) to clothe, dress (**de** in); (*hum*) to get up, rig out (**de** in)
VPR **trajearse** (= *vestirse*) to dress up; (= *adquirir*) to provide o.s. with clothes
trajelarse‡ ▸ CONJUG 1a VPR • **~ una botella** to knock a bottle back*
traje-pantalón SM (PL: **trajes-pantalón**) trouser suit
trajera *etc* ▸ **traer**
traje-sastre SM (PL: **trajes-sastre**) suit, tailor-made suit
trajín SM **1*** (= *ajetreo*) coming and going, bustle, commotion; (= *jaleo*) fuss
2 (= *transporte*) haulage, transport
3 trajines* (= *actividades*) affairs, goings-on • **trajines de la casa** household chores
trajinado ADJ [*tema*] well-worked, overworked, trite
trajinar ▸ CONJUG 1a VI (= *ajetrearse*) to bustle about; (= *viajar*) to travel around a lot; (= *moverse mucho*) to be on the go, keep on the move
VT **1** (= *transportar*) to carry, transport
2 (*Cono Sur*) (= *estafar*) to swindle, deceive
3 (*Cono Sur*) (= *registrar*) to search
4** (*sexualmente*) to lay‡
trajinería SF carriage, haulage
trajinista SMF (*Caribe, Cono Sur*) busybody, snooper
tralla SF (= *cuerda*) whipcord, whiplash; (= *látigo*) lash, whip
trallazo SM **1** [*de látigo*] (= *ruido*) crack of a whip; (= *golpe*) lash
2* (= *bronca*) telling-off*
3 (*Dep*) fierce shot, hard shot
trama SF **1** [*de un tejido*] weft, woof
2 [*de historia*] plot
3 (= *conjura*) plot, scheme, intrigue
4 (= *vínculo*) connection, link; (= *correlación*) correlation
5 (*Tip*) shaded area
tramador ADJ (*Col*) exciting
tramar ▸ CONJUG 1a VT **1** (= *tejer*) to weave
2 [+ *engaño, enredo*] to plan, plot; [+ *complot*] to lay, hatch • **están tramando algo** they're up to sth • **¿qué estarán tramando?** I wonder what they're up to?
VPR **tramarse** • **algo se está tramando** there's something going on, there's something afoot
trambucar ▸ CONJUG 1g VI **1** (*And, Caribe*) (= *naufragar*) to be shipwrecked
2 (*Caribe*) (= *enloquecer*) to go out of one's mind, lose one's marbles‡
trambuque SM (*And*) shipwreck
trámil ADJ (*Cono Sur*) awkward, clumsy
tramitación SF • **~ de divorcio** divorce proceedings (*pl*) • **~ de visado** visa application • **~ de subvención** grant application procedure
tramitar ▸ CONJUG 1a VT (= *gestionar*) [+ *pasaporte, permiso*] to process; [+ *crédito*] to negotiate • **el consulado le está tramitando el pasaporte** the consulate is processing his passport application • **vamos a empezar a ~ el permiso de obras** we're going to apply for planning permission • **estoy tramitando un préstamo con el banco** I'm negotiating a loan with the bank • **ya están tramitando su divorcio** they have started divorce proceedings
trámite SM **1** (= *fase*) step, stage • **obtener un visado implica toda una serie de ~s** there are a number of steps *o* stages involved in obtaining a visa • **tuvimos que hacer muchos ~s antes de abrir el negocio** we had a lot of paperwork to do before we could start the business • **estoy harto de tantos ~s** I'm fed up with all this red tape *o* form-filling
2 (= *formalidad*) formality • **este examen es puro ~, ya tienes el puesto asegurado** this exam is purely a formality, you've already got the job
3 (= *proceso*) procedure • **para acortar los ~s lo hacemos así** to make the procedure shorter we do it this way • **de ~: el gobierno se limita a resolver asuntos de ~** the government is dealing only with routine business matters • **en ~** in hand • **lo tenemos en ~** we have the matter in hand, we are pursuing the matter • **el proyecto de ley está en ~ parlamentario** the bill is going through parliament • **"patente en trámite"** "patent pending", "patent applied for" ▸ **trámites judiciales** court proceedings
tramo SM **1** [*de carretera*] section, stretch; [*de puente*] span; [*de escalera*] flight ▸ **tramo cronometrado** time trial
2 [*de tiempo*] period • **el ~ final de las rebajas** the last few days of the sale
3 (= *terreno*) plot
4 (*Econ*) [*de préstamo*] tranche; [*de impuestos*] band
tramontana SF **1** (= *viento*) north wind; (= *dirección*) north • MODISMO: • **perder la ~*** to lose one's head
2 (= *soberbia*) pride, conceit; (= *lujo*) luxury
tramontar ▸ CONJUG 1a VI [*sol*] to sink behind the mountains
VPR **tramontarse** to escape over the mountains
tramoya SF **1** (*Teat*) piece of stage machinery
2 (= *enredo*) plot, scheme; (= *estafa*) trick, swindle; (= *parte oculta*) secret part (of a deal)
tramoyar ▸ CONJUG 1a VT (*And, Caribe*) to swindle
tramoyero ADJ (*CAm, Caribe*) tricky, sharp
tramoyista SMF **1** (*Teat*) stagehand, scene shifter
2 (= *estafador*) swindler, trickster; (= *farsante*) humbug; (= *impostor*) impostor; (= *intrigante*) schemer
trampa SF **1** (*para cazar*) trap; (= *lazo*) snare ▸ **trampa explosiva** (*Mil*) booby trap ▸ **trampa mortal** death trap ▸ **trampa para ratas** rat trap
2 (= *engaño*) trap • **no vayas, es una ~** don't go, it's a trap • **esto tiene ~** • **aquí hay ~** there's a catch here • **caer en la ~** to fall into the trap • **coger a algn en la ~** to catch sb lying • **tender una ~ a algn** to set *o* lay a trap for sb • MODISMO: • **ni ~ ni cartón**: • **este contrato no tiene ni ~ ni cartón** there's no hidden catch in this contract
3 (*en el juego*) • **¡eso es ~!** that's cheating! • **hacer ~(s)** to cheat
4 (= *puerta*) trapdoor; [*de mostrador*] hatch
5 (*Golf*) bunker, sand trap (*EEUU*)
6 (*Com*) bad debt
7† (= *bragueta*) fly
trampantojo* SM (= *juego de manos*) sleight of hand, trick; (= *chanchullo*) fiddle*, cheat; (= *método poco limpio*) underhand method
trampear ▸ CONJUG 1a VT (*en el juego*) to cheat
VI **1** (= *hacer trampa*) to cheat; (= *conseguir dinero*) to get money by false pretences
2 (= *ir tirando*) to manage, get by
3 [*vestido, zapatos etc*] to last out
trampería SF = **tramposería**
trampero ADJ (*CAm, Cono Sur, Méx*) = **tramposo**
SM **1** (= *cazador*) trapper
2 (*Cono Sur*) (= *trampa*) trap for birds
trampilla SF **1** (= *escotilla*) trap, hatchway ▸ **trampilla de carburante** filler cap, fuel (tank) cap
2 (= *mirilla*) peephole

3 (= *bragueta*) fly
trampista (SMF) = **tramposo**
trampolín (SM) **1** (*Dep*) (*en piscina*) springboard, diving board; (*en gimnasia*) trampoline; [*de esquí*] ski-jump
2 (*para conseguir algo*) springboard
trampón* (ADJ) crooked*
tramposería (SF) crookedness
tramposo/a (ADJ) crooked, tricky • **ser ~** to be a cheat
(SM/F) **1** (*en el juego*) cheat; (= *estafador*) crook*, shyster (*EEUU*), swindler; (= *tahúr*) cardsharp
2 (*Econ*) bad payer
tranca (SF) **1** [*de puerta, ventana*] bar • MODISMO: • **a ~s y barrancas** with great difficulty, overcoming many obstacles
2 (= *garrote*) cudgel, club
3 (*esp LAm**) (= *borrachera*) • **tener una ~** to be drunk
4 trancas (*Méx**) (= *piernas*) legs • MODISMO: • **saltar las ~s** (*Méx*) (= *rebelarse*) to rebel; (= *perder la paciencia*) to lose one's patience
5 (*Cono Sur*) [*de escopeta*] safety catch
6 (*Caribe*) dollar, peso
7 (*Caribe*) (*Aut*) traffic jam
8 (*Cono Sur**) (= *complejo*) complex, neurosis
trancada (SF) (= *paso*) stride • **en dos ~s** (*lit*) in a couple of strides; (*fig*) in a couple of ticks
trancantrulla (SF) (*Cono Sur*) trick, fraud
trancaperros (SM INV) (*Caribe*) row, scrap
trancar ▹ CONJUG 1g (VT) **1** [+ *puerta, ventana*] to bar
2 (*Caribe*) (*Aut*) to box in, block in, shut in
(VI) (*al caminar*) to stride along
(VPR) **trancarse 1** (*LAm*) (= *estar estreñido*) to be constipated
2 (*Caribe**) to get drunk
trancazo (SM) **1** (= *golpe*) blow, bang (with a stick)
2* (= *gripe*) flu
trance (SM) **1** (= *momento difícil*) • **estamos pasando por un mal ~** we're going through a difficult period *o* patch • **aún no ha logrado superar el ~** he still hasn't managed to get over what he's been through • **puesto en tal ~** placed in such a predicament • **estar en ~ de muerte** to be at death's door • **estar en ~ de hacer algo** to be on the point of doing sth • **último ~** last *o* dying moments • **a todo ~** at all costs ▸ **trance mortal** last *o* dying moments (*pl*)
2 [*de médium*] trance; (*Rel*) trance, ecstasy • **entrar en ~** to fall *o* go into a trance • **estar en ~** to be in a trance
tranco (SM) **1** (= *paso*) stride, big step • **andar a ~s** to walk with long strides, take big steps • **en dos ~s** (*lit*) in a couple of strides; (*fig*) in a couple of ticks
2 (*Arquit*) threshold
trancón (SM) (*Col*) (*Aut*) traffic jam
tranque (SM) (*Cono Sur*) (= *presa*) dam; (= *embalse*) reservoir
tranquera (SF) **1** (= *cercado*) palisade, fence
2 (*LAm*) (*para ganado*) cattle gate
tranquero (SM) (*And, Caribe, Cono Sur*) cattle gate
tranqui* (EXCL) cool it!*, calm down!
(ADJ) = **tranquilo**
tranquilamente (ADV) **1** (= *plácidamente*) peacefully • **el bebé dormía ~ en su cuna** the baby was sleeping peacefully in its cot
2 (= *sin prisa*) • **fuimos paseando ~ hasta el pueblo** we took a leisurely stroll into the village • **piénsalo ~ antes de responder** take your time and think about it before you answer
3 (= *con aplomo*) calmly • **háblale ~** speak to him calmly
4 (= *sin preocupación*) • **le puedo contar todos mis secretos ~** I can tell her all my secrets with no worries
5 (= *con descaro*) • **y se fue ~ sin pagar** and he went off, cool as you please *o* like, without paying
6 (= *fácilmente*) • **se puede ver ~ tres películas seguidas** he's quite capable of watching three films in a row
tranquilidad (SF) **1** (= *placidez*) peace • **¡qué ~ se respira en el campo!** the countryside is so peaceful! • **si no hay ~ no puedo estudiar** I can't study without peace and quiet • **con tres hijos no tengo ni un momento de ~** with three children I never get a moment's peace
2 (= *falta de prisa*) • **llévatelo a casa y léelo con ~** take it home and read it at your leisure
3 (= *aplomo*) calm • **respondió con ~** he answered calmly
4 (= *falta de preocupación*) • **para mayor ~ llama a tus padres** call your parents, to put your mind at rest • **¡qué ~! ya se han acabado los exámenes** what a relief, the exams are over at last! • **puedes decírmelo con total ~, no se lo contaré a nadie** you're quite safe telling me, I won't tell anyone • **perder la ~** to lose patience
5 (= *descaro*) • **dijo con toda ~ que no pensaba pagar** she said quite calmly *o* as cool as you please *o* like that she didn't intend to pay
tranquilino/a (SM/F) (*LAm*) drunkard
tranquilizador (ADJ) [*música*] soothing; [*hecho*] reassuring
tranquilizadoramente (ADV) (*calmando*) soothingly; (*quitando ansiedad*) reassuringly
tranquilizante (ADJ) = **tranquilizador**
(SM) (*Med*) tranquillizer, tranquilizer (*EEUU*)
tranquilizar ▹ CONJUG 1f (VT) to calm down • **un brandy te ~á** a brandy will calm you down • **el árbitro intentó ~ a los jugadores** the referee tried to calm the players down • **las palabras del médico me ~on** the doctor's words reassured me • **¿por qué no llamas a tu madre para ~la?** why don't you call your mother to put her mind at rest?
(VPR) **tranquilizarse** to calm down • **¡tranquilícese!** calm down! • **se tranquilizó al saber que habían llegado bien** she stopped worrying when she found out that they had arrived safely
tranquilla (SF) **1** (= *pasador*) latch, pin
2 (*en conversación*) trap, catch
3 (*And*) (= *obstáculo*) hindrance, obstacle
tranquillo* (SM) knack • **coger el ~ a algo** to get the hang of sth, get the knack of sth
tranquilo/a (ADJ) **1** (= *plácido*) [*sitio, momento*] quiet, peaceful; [*mar*] calm • **se fueron a vivir a un pueblecito ~** they went to live in a quiet *o* peaceful little village • **una tarde tranquila** a quiet *o* peaceful afternoon
2 (= *sosegado*) calm • **es una persona muy tranquila** she's a very calm person • **el día del examen estaba bastante ~** the day of the exam I was quite calm • **contestó muy ~ a todas las preguntas** he answered all the questions calmly
3 (= *sin preocupación*) • **estad ~s que yo me encargo de todo** don't worry, I'll look after everything • **tú estáte ~ hasta que yo vuelva** you stay put till I come back • **¡deja ya ~ al pobre chico!** leave the poor boy alone! • **¡~, no merece la pena enfadarse!** calm down! there's no point getting annoyed • **¡eh, ~, sin empujar!** hey, easy does it! no pushing! • **tener la conciencia tranquila** to have a clear conscience
4 (= *descarado*) • **¡mira que es tranquila! todos esperando y ella como si nada** nothing seems to bother her! everyone's waiting and she couldn't care less • **se quedó tan ~** he didn't bat an eyelid • **lo ha suspendido todo y él tan ~** he's failed the lot, but it doesn't seem to worry him
(SM/F) • **¡es una tranquila de cuidado! aún no ha acabado los deberes** she's not bothered about anything, that one, she still hasn't finished her homework!
tranquis* (ADJ) • **hacer algo en plan ~** to take one's time to do sth
tranquiza (SF) (*And, Méx*) beating
Trans. (ABR) (*Com*) = **transferencia**
trans... (PREF) trans...; ▹ **tras...**
transacción (SF) **1** (*Com*) transaction; (= *acuerdo*) deal, bargain ▸ **transacción comercial** business deal
2 (*Jur*) (*para evitar un pleito*) compromise, compromise settlement • **llegar a una ~** to reach a compromise
transalpino (ADJ) transalpine
transandino (ADJ) trans-Andean
transar¹ ▹ CONJUG 1a (VT) (*Cono Sur*) (= *comerciar*) to trade
(VI) (*LAm*) = **transigir**
transar² ▹ CONJUG 1a (VT) (*Méx*) (= *defraudar*) to cheat, swindle, defraud
transatlántico (ADJ) transatlantic; [*travesía*] Atlantic • **los países ~s** the countries on the other side of the Atlantic
(SM) (= *barco*) (ocean) liner
transbordador (SM) (*Náut*) ferry; (*Aer*) shuttle ▸ **transbordador espacial** space shuttle ▸ **transbordador funicular** cable railway ▸ **transbordador para coches** car ferry
(ADJ) • **puente ~** transporter bridge
transbordar ▹ CONJUG 1a (VT) (*gen*) to transfer; (*Náut*) to transship
(VI) (*Ferro*) to change
transbordo (SM) **1** (*Ferro*) [*de pasajeros*] change • **hacer ~** to change (**en** at)
2 [*de equipajes*] transfer
transcendental (ADJ) = **trascendental**
transcendente (ADJ) = **trascendental**
transcender ▹ CONJUG 2g (VT) = **trascender**
transceptor (SM) transceiver
transcontinental (ADJ) transcontinental
transcribir ▹ CONJUG 3a (PP: **transcrito**) (VT) (= *copiar*) to transcribe; (*de alfabeto distinto*) to transliterate
transcripción (SF) (= *copia*) transcription; [*de alfabeto distinto*] transliteration
transcrito (PP) *de* **transcribir**
transcultural (ADJ) cross-cultural
transculturización (SF) transculturation
transcurrir ▹ CONJUG 3a (VI) **1** [*tiempo*] to pass, elapse • **han transcurrido siete años** seven years have passed
2 [*acto, celebración*] to pass, go • **la manifestación transcurrió sin incidentes** the demonstration passed without incident • **todo transcurrió normalmente** everything went normally
transcurso (SM) passing, lapse, course • **~ del tiempo** course of time, passing of time • **en el ~ de ocho días** in the course *o* space of a week • **en el ~ de los años** over the years
transecto (SM) transect
transepto (SM) transept
transeúnte (ADJ) (= *no residente*) transient, transitory; [*miembro*] temporary
(SMF) **1** (*en la calle*) passer-by • **~s** passers-by
2 (= *no residente*) non-resident; (*euf*) (= *mendigo*) vagrant
transexual (ADJ), (SMF) transsexual
transexualidad (SF) transsexuality
transexualismo (SM) transsexualism

t

transferencia (SF) **1** (*Jur, Dep*) transfer ▸ **transferencia bancaria** banker's order, bank transfer ▸ **transferencia cablegráfica** cable transfer ▸ **transferencia de crédito** credit transfer ▸ **transferencia electrónica de fondos** electronic funds transfer ▸ **transferencia por cable** cable transfer
2 (*Psic*) transference

transferible (ADJ) transferable

transferir ▹ CONJUG 3i (VT) to transfer

transfiguración (SF) transfiguration

transfigurar ▹ CONJUG 1a (VT) to transfigure (en into)

transformable (ADJ) transformable; (*Aut*) convertible

transformación (SF) **1** (= *cambio*) transformation, change (en into)
2 (*Culin*) processing
3 (*Rugby*) conversion

transformacional (ADJ) transformational

transformador (SM) (*Elec*) transformer

transformar ▹ CONJUG 1a (VT) **1** (= *convertir*) • ~ **algo en algo** to turn sth into sth • **han transformado el palacio en museo** they have turned *o* converted the palace into a museum • **pretendía ~ el plomo en oro** he aimed to turn lead into gold
2 (= *cambiar*) to transform • **su novia lo ha transformado** his girlfriend has transformed him • **las nuevas tecnologías han transformado el mundo de la comunicación** new technology has transformed the world of communications
3 (*Rugby*) to convert
(VPR) **transformarse 1** (= *convertirse*) • **~se en algo** to turn into sth • **al hervir, el agua se transforma en vapor** water turns *o* is converted into steam when it boils • **la rana se transformó en príncipe** the frog turned into a prince
2 (= *cambiar*) • **cuando sonríe se le transforma la cara** her face is transformed when she smiles • **desde que dejó de beber se ha transformado** since he stopped drinking he's a changed man

transformismo (SM) **1** (*Bio*) evolution, transmutation
2 (*sexual*) transvestism

transformista (SMF) **1** (*Teat*) quick-change artist(e)
2 (*sexual*) transvestite

transfronterizo (ADJ) cross-border (*antes de s*) • **seguridad transfronteriza** cross-border security

tránsfuga (SMF) (*Pol*) [*de partido*] turncoat; [*de nación*] defector

transfuguismo (SM) tendency to defect

transfundir ▹ CONJUG 3a (VT) **1** [+ *líquidos*] to transfuse
2 [+ *noticias*] to tell, spread

transfusión (SF) transfusion ▸ **transfusión de sangre, transfusión sanguínea** blood transfusion • **hacer una ~ de sangre a algn** to give sb a blood transfusion

transgénero (ADJ INV) transgender
(SMF INV) transgender person, transgendered person

transgenia (SF) genetic modification

transgénico (ADJ) genetically modified, GM (*antes de s*)

transgredir ▹ CONJUG 3a (VT), (VI) to transgress

transgresión (SF) transgression

transgresor(a) (SM/F) transgressor

transiberiano (ADJ) trans-Siberian

transición (SF) transition (a to, de from) • **período de ~** transitional period • **la ~** (*Esp*) (*Pol*) the transition (*to democracy after Franco's death*)

LA TRANSICIÓN

The death of General Franco on 20 November 1975 ushered in a period of transition to democracy in Spain which was to end with the democratic transfer of power to the **PSOE** (Spanish Socialist Party) on 28 November 28 1982.

On 22 November 1975 Juan Carlos I was proclaimed king. Though initially handicapped by a constitutional system devised by Franco, the King was able to appoint the **aperturista** Adolfo Suárez as Prime Minister in July 1976.

Within three months Suárez rushed through a political reform bill introducing universal suffrage and a two-chamber parliament which was put to a referendum and endorsed by 94.2% of the electorate. Political parties were legalized and elections were held on 15 June 1977. Suárez and his party, the newly-formed **UCD (Unión de Centro Democrático)**, won without gaining an overall majority. Through accords with the other parties - the **Pactos de la Moncloa** - they were able to manage the transitional process, which included the drafting and endorsement of the 1978 Constitution.

transicional (ADJ) transitional

transido (ADJ) • **~ de angustia** beset with anxiety • **~ de dolor** racked with pain • **~ de frío** frozen to the marrow • **~ de hambre** fainting with hunger

transigencia (SF) **1** (= *avenencia*) compromise; (*cediendo*) yielding
2 (= *actitud*) spirit of compromise, accommodating attitude

transigente (ADJ) **1** (= *que cede*) accommodating
2 (= *tolerante*) tolerant

transigir ▹ CONJUG 3c (VI) **1** (= *ceder*) to give way, make concessions • **hemos transigido con la demanda popular** we have bowed to popular demand
2 (= *tolerar*) • **~ con algo** to tolerate sth • **yo no transijo con tales abusos** I cannot tolerate this sort of outrage
(VT) • **~ un pleito** (*Jur*) to settle (a suit) out of court

Transilvania (SF) Transylvania

transistor (SM) transistor

transistorizado (ADJ) transistorized

transitable (ADJ) passable

transitar ▹ CONJUG 1a (VI) [*vehículo*] to travel; [*peatón*] to go, walk • **calle transitada** busy street • **~ por** to go along, pass along

transitivamente (ADV) transitively

transitivo (ADJ) transitive

tránsito (SM) **1** (= *paso*) transit, passage, movement • **"se prohíbe el ~"** "no thoroughfare" • **el ~ de este camino presenta dificultades** the going on this road is not easy • **estar de ~** to be in transit, be passing through • **en ~** in transit
2 (= *tráfico*) movement, traffic • **calle de mucho ~** busy street • **horas de máximo ~** rush hour (*sing*), peak (traffic) hours ▸ **tránsito rodado** vehicular traffic
3 [*de puesto*] transfer, move
4 (= *muerte*) passing, death
5 (= *parada*) [*de transporte público*] stop; [*de turismos*] stopping place • **hacer ~** to make a stop
6 (= *pasillo*) passageway

transitoriedad (SF) transience

transitorio (ADJ) **1** (= *provisional*) [*medida*] provisional, temporary; [*período*] transitional, of transition
2 (= *pasajero*) transitory

transliteración (SF) transliteration

transliterar ▹ CONJUG 1a (VT) to transliterate

translucidez (SF) translucence

translúcido (ADJ) translucent

transmarino (ADJ) overseas

transmigración (SF) migration, transmigration

transmigrar ▹ CONJUG 1a (VI) to migrate, transmigrate

transmisibilidad (SF) (*Med*) contagiousness, ability to be transmitted

transmisible (ADJ) transmissible; (*Med*) contagious

transmisión (SF) **1** (= *acto*) transmission; (*Jur*) transfer ▸ **transmisión de dominio** transfer of ownership
2 (*Mec*) transmission
3 (*Elec*) transmission; (*Radio, TV*) transmission, broadcast(ing) ▸ **transmisión en circuito** hookup ▸ **transmisión en diferido** recorded programme *o* (*EEUU*) program, repeat broadcast ▸ **transmisión en directo** live broadcast ▸ **transmisión exterior** outside broadcast ▸ **transmisión por satélite** satellite broadcasting
4 transmisiones (*Mil*) signals (corps)
5 (*Inform*) • **media ~ bidireccional** half duplex • **plena ~ bidireccional** full duplex ▸ **transmisión de datos** data transmission ▸ **transmisión de datos en paralelo** parallel data transmission ▸ **transmisión de datos en serie** serial data transmission

transmisor (ADJ) transmitting • **aparato ~** • **estación ~a** transmitter
(SM) transmitter

transmisora (SF) transmitter, radio relay station

transmisor-receptor (SM) transceiver; (*portátil*) walkie-talkie

transmitir ▹ CONJUG 3a (VT) **1** (*Radio, TV*) [+ *señal, sonido*] to transmit; [+ *programa*] to broadcast
2 [+ *bienes, saludos, recados*] to pass on
3 [+ *enfermedad, gérmenes*] to give, pass on
4 (*Jur*) to transfer (a to)
(VI) (*Radio, TV*) to broadcast
(VPR) **transmitirse** [*enfermedad, gérmenes*] to be transmitted, be passed on

transmutable (ADJ) transmutable

transmutación (SF) transmutation

transmutar ▹ CONJUG 1a (VT) to transmute (en into)

transnacional (ADJ) transnational, international
(SF) transnational (company), multinational (company)

transoceánico (ADJ) transoceanic

transparencia (SF) **1** [*de cristal, agua*] transparency
2 (= *claridad*) openness, transparency • **el nuevo Ejecutivo se caracteriza por su ~** the new Government is characterized by its policy of openness • **todos los partidos prometen ~ en su financiación** all the parties are promising to be open about their sources of finance, all the parties are promising financial transparency ▸ **transparencia fiscal** fiscal *o* tax transparency ▸ **transparencia informativa** information transparency *o* disclosure
3 (*Fot*) slide, transparency

transparentar ▹ CONJUG 1a (VT) (= *dejar ver*) to reveal, allow to be seen; [+ *emoción*] to reveal, betray
(VI) [*ser transparente*] to be transparent; (= *dejarse ver*) to show through
(VPR) **transparentarse 1** [*vidrio, agua*] to be transparent, be clear; [*objeto, ropa*] to show

t

through • **se te transparenta el sujetador** your bra is showing through, you can see your bra through that
2* [*ropa gastada*] to become threadbare; [*persona*] to be dreadfully thin
3 (= *insinuarse*) to show clearly, become perceptible • **se transparentaba su verdadera intención** his real intention became clear

transparente ADJ **1** [*agua, cristal*] transparent, clear; [*aire*] clear; [*vestido*] see-through
2 [*persona*] transparent; [*intenciones, motivos*] clear, transparent
3 [*gestión, contabilidad*] open, transparent • **el Presidente ha prometido una gestión ~** the President has promised open *o* transparent government
SM (= *pantalla*) blind, shade

transpiración SF **1** (= *sudor*) perspiration
2 (*Bot*) transpiration

transpirar ▷ CONJUG 1a VI **1** (= *sudar*) to perspire
2 [*líquido*] to seep through, ooze out; (*Bot*) to transpire
3 (= *revelarse*) to transpire, become known

transpirenaico ADJ [*ruta*] trans-Pyrenean; [*tráfico*] passing through *o* over the Pyrenees

transplantar ▷ CONJUG 1a VT = **trasplantar**

transpondedor SM transponder

transponer ▷ CONJUG 2q (PP: **transpuesto**) VT **1** (*gen*) to transpose; (= *cambiar de sitio*) to switch over, move about
2 (= *trasplantar*) to transplant
3 • **~ la esquina** to disappear round the corner
VI (= *desaparecer*) to disappear from view; (= *ir más allá*) to go beyond, get past; [*sol*] to go down
VPR **transponerse 1** (= *cambiarse*) to change places
2 (= *esconderse*) to hide (behind); [*sol*] to go down
3 (= *dormirse*) to doze (off)

transportable ADJ transportable • **fácilmente ~** easily carried, easily transported

transportación SF transportation

transportador SM **1** (*Mec*) conveyor, transporter ▸ **transportador de banda, transportador de correa** conveyor belt
2 (*Mat*) protractor

transportar ▷ CONJUG 1a VT **1** [+ *tropas, mercancías*] (*gen*) to transport; (*en barco*) to ship • **transportan el ganado por ferrocarril** the livestock is transported by rail • **el camión transportaba medicamentos** the lorry was carrying medicines • **el avión podrá ~ 100 pasajeros** the plane will be able to carry 100 passengers • **aquella música la transportaba a su adolescencia** that music took her back *o* transported her to when she was a teenager
2 (*Elec*) [+ *corriente*] to transmit
3 (*Mús*) to transpose
VPR **transportarse** (= *extasiarse*) to be transported, be enraptured

transporte SM **1** [*de pasajeros, tropas*] transport, transportation (EEUU); [*de mercancías*] transport, transportation (EEUU), carriage • **se me va el sueldo en ~** all my wages go on transport • **¿cuál es su medio de ~ habitual?** what is your usual means of transport? • **Ministerio de Transportes** Ministry of Transport, Department of Transportation (EEUU) ▸ **transporte colectivo** public transport, public transportation (EEUU) ▸ **transporte de mercancías** goods transport ▸ **transporte escolar** school buses (*pl*) ▸ **transporte por carretera** road transport, haulage ▸ **transporte público** public transport, public transportation (EEUU)
2 (*Náut*) transport, troopship
3 (= *éxtasis*) transport
4 (*Méx**) vehicle

transportista SMF (*Aut*) haulier, haulage contractor
SM (*Aer*) carrier

transposición SF transposition

transpuesto ADJ • **quedarse ~** to doze off

transustanciación SF transubstantiation

transustanciar ▷ CONJUG 1b VT to transubstantiate

transvasar ▷ CONJUG 1a VT = **trasvasar**

transversal ADJ transverse, cross; (= *oblicuo*) oblique • **calle ~** cross street • **otra calle ~ de la calle mayor** another street which crosses the high street
SF • **una ~ de la Gran Vía** a street crossing *o* which cuts across the Gran Vía

transversalmente ADV (= *cruzando*) transversely, across; (= *oblicuamente*) obliquely

transverso ADJ = **transversal**

transvestido/a ADJ, SM/F transvestite

transvestismo SM transvestism

tranvía SM (= *coche*) tram(car), streetcar (EEUU); (= *sistema*) tramway; (*Ferro*) local train

tranza* (*Méx*) SMF con man*
ADJ [*comerciante*] crooked, dodgy*; [*policía, juez*] crooked, bent*
SF fiddle*

tranzar ▷ CONJUG 1f VT (*Méx*) (= *defraudar*) to cheat, swindle, defraud

trapacear* ▷ CONJUG 1a VI (= *trampear*) to cheat, be on the fiddle*; (= *causar líos*) to make mischief

trapacería* SF **1** (= *trampa*) racket, fiddle*
2 (= *chisme*) piece of gossip, malicious rumour *o* (EEUU) rumor

trapacero/a* ADJ (= *tramposo*) dishonest, swindling
SM/F **1** (= *tramposo*) cheat, swindler
2 (= *chismoso*) gossip, mischief-maker

trapacista SMF = **trapacero**

trapajoso ADJ **1** (= *andrajoso*) shabby, ragged
2 [*pronunciación*] defective, incorrect; [*persona*] (*que habla mal*) who talks incorrectly; (*con defecto*) who has a speech defect

trápala SF **1** [*de caballo*] clatter, clip-clop
2* (= *jaleo*) row, uproar, shindy*; (= *parloteo*) talkativeness
3 (= *trampa*) swindle, trick
SMF **1*** (= *hablador*) chatterbox*
2* (= *tramposo*) swindler, cheat

trapalear ▷ CONJUG 1a VI **1** [*caballo*] to clatter, beat its hooves, clip-clop; [*persona*] to clatter, go clattering along
2* (= *parlotear*) to chatter, jabber
3 (= *mentir*) to fib, lie; (= *trampear*) to be on the fiddle*

trapalero* ADJ (*Caribe*) = **trapalón**

trapalón* ADJ (= *mentiroso*) lying; (= *tramposo*) dishonest, swindling

trapalonear ▷ CONJUG 1a VI (*Cono Sur*) = **trapalear**

trapatiesta* SF (= *jaleo*) commotion, uproar, shindy*; (= *pelea*) fight, brawl

trapaza SF = **trapacería**

trapeador SM (*LAm*) floor mop

trapear ▷ CONJUG 1a VT **1** (*LAm*) [+ *suelo*] to mop
2 (*CAm**) (= *pegar*) to beat, tan*; (= *insultar*) to insult; (= *regañar*) to tick off*

trapecio SM **1** (*en gimnasia, circo*) trapeze
2 (*Mat*) trapezium, trapezoid (EEUU)

trapecista SMF trapeze artist(e)

trapería SF **1** (= *trapos*) rags (*pl*); (= *ropa vieja*) old clothes (*pl*)
2 (= *tienda*) [*de ropa*] second-hand clothes shop; [*de cacharros*] junk shop

trapero/a ADJ ▷ **puñalada**
SM/F ragman/ragwoman

trapezoide SM trapezoid

trapicar ▷ CONJUG 1g VI (*Cono Sur*) [*comida*] to taste very hot; [*herida*] to sting, smart

trapichar ▷ CONJUG 1a VT (*And, Méx*) to smuggle (in); (*Caribe*) to deal in

trapiche SM **1** (*para aceite de oliva*) olive-oil press; (*para azúcar*) sugar mill
2 (*And, Cono Sur*) (*Min*) ore crusher

trapichear* ▷ CONJUG 1a VI **1** (= *hacer trampa*) to be on the fiddle*; (= *tramar*) to plot, scheme; (= *andar en malos pasos*) to be mixed up in something shady*
2 (*Cono Sur*) (= *comerciar*) to scrape a living by buying and selling
VT to deal in, trade in

trapicheo* SM fiddle*, shady deal*; **trapicheos** (= *trampas*) fiddles*, shady dealing* (*sing*); (= *intrigas*) plots, schemes, tricks

trapichero/a* SM/F **1** (= *negociante*) small-time dealer
2 (*And, Caribe*) (= *entrometido*) busybody

trapiento ADJ ragged, tattered

trapillo SM • **estar** *o* **ir de ~** to be dressed in ordinary clothes, be informally dressed

trapío* SM **1** (= *encanto*) charm; (= *garbo*) elegance, graceful way of moving • **tener buen ~** to have a fine presence, carry o.s. elegantly, move well *o* gracefully; (*fig*) to have real class
2 [*de toro*] fine appearance

trapisonda SF **1** (= *pelea*) row, brawl; (= *jaleo*) row, commotion, shindy*
2* (= *trampa*) swindle, fiddle*; (= *asunto sucio*) monkey business*, shady affair*, fiddle*; (= *intriga*) intrigue

trapisondear ▷ CONJUG 1a VI (= *intrigar*) to scheme, plot, intrigue; (= *hacer trampa*) to fiddle*, wangle*

trapisondeo* SM, **trapisondería*** SF (= *intriga*) scheming, plotting, intrigues; (= *trampa*) fiddling*, wangling*

trapisondista* SMF (= *conspirador*) schemer, intriguer; (= *tramposo*) fiddler*, wangler*

trapito* SM • **cada día se pone un ~ distinto** she puts on some different garb *o* something different every day, she wears a different outfit every day • **siempre se está comprando ~s** she's always buying clothes • **MODISMO:** • **sacar los ~s al sol** (*LAm*) to rake up the past ▸ **trapitos de cristianar**†* Sunday best, glad rags*

trapo SM **1** (= *paño para limpiar*) (*gen*) cloth; (*usado, raído*) rag • **un ~ húmedo** a damp cloth • **pasar un ~ por** [+ *suelo*] to give a wipe over *o* down; [+ *muebles*] to dust ▸ **trapo de cocina** (*para secar los platos*) tea towel, dish towel (EEUU); (*para limpiar*) dish cloth ▸ **trapo del polvo** duster, dust cloth (EEUU)
2 (= *trozo de tela*) (*gen*) piece of material; (*usado, raído*) rag, piece of rag • **un dragón de cartón y ~** a dragon made of cardboard and rags • **MODISMO:** • **tener manos de ~** to have butterfingers; ▷ **muñeca**
3 **trapos*** (= *ropa*) clothes • **gasta una barbaridad en ~s** she spends a fortune on clothes
4 (*Náut*) (= *vela*) canvas, sails (*pl*) • **a todo ~** under full sail
5 (*Taur**) cape
6 • **MODISMOS:** • **como** *o* **hecho un ~***: • **dejar a algn como un ~*** to tear sb to shreds* • **estar como un ~*** to be like a limp rag*

• **poner a algn como un ~*** to lay into sb*, slag sb off‡ • **entrar a** *o* **al ~** to go on the attack • **no pudo aguantar más críticas y entró al ~** he couldn't stand being criticized any longer and went on the attack • **soltar el ~** (*al llorar*) to burst into tears; (*al reír*) to burst out laughing • **a todo ~*** (= *muy rápido*) at full speed, flat out*; (= *a toda potencia*) full blast, at full blast; (*LAm*) (= *a todo lujo*) in style • **iban a todo ~** they were going at full speed *o* flat out* • **tenían la música puesta a todo ~** they had the music on (at) full blast • **celebraron la boda a todo ~** they celebrated the wedding in style • **llorar a todo ~** to cry one's eyes out
▸ **trapos sucios** • **no quieren que salgan a la luz los ~s sucios** they don't want the skeletons in the cupboard to come out • **lavar los ~s sucios en casa** not to wash one's dirty linen in public • **en la cena sacaron los ~s sucios (a relucir** *o* (*Esp*) **a la luz)** everyone at the dinner party washed their dirty linen in public • **le sacaron los ~s sucios a relucir** they were raking up his past

traposiento ADJ (*And*) ragged

traposo ADJ **1** (*And, Caribe, Cono Sur*) (= *harapiento*) ragged
2 (*Cono Sur*) = **trapajoso**
3 (*Cono Sur*) [*carne*] tough, stringy

trapujear ▸ CONJUG 1a VI (*CAm*) to smuggle

trapujero SM (*CAm*) smuggler

traque SM **1** (= *ruido*) crack, bang
2‡ (= *pedo*) noisy fart‡

tráquea SF trachea, windpipe

traquear ▸ CONJUG 1a VT **1** (*CAm, Cono Sur, Méx*) (= *dejar huella*) to make deep tracks on
2 (*Caribe*) [+ *persona*] to take about from place to place; (*Cono Sur*) [+ *ganado*] to move from place to place
3 (*Caribe*) (= *probar*) to test, try out; (= *entrenar*) to train
VI **1** (*con ruido*) = **traquetear**
2 (*Cono Sur*) (= *frecuentar*) to frequent a place
3 (*Caribe*) (= *beber*) to drink
VPR **traquearse** (*Caribe*) to go out of one's mind

traqueo SM = **traqueteo**

traqueotomía SF tracheotomy, tracheostomy

traqueteado ADJ hectic, busy

traquetear ▸ CONJUG 1a VT [+ *recipiente*] to shake; [+ *sillas etc*] to rattle, bang about, make a lot of noise with, muck about with
VI **1** (*con ruido*) [*vehículo*] to rattle, jolt; [*cohete*] to crackle, bang; [*ametralladora*] to rattle, clatter
2 (*Cono Sur, Méx*) (= *apresurarse*) to bustle about, go to and fro a lot; (*Cono Sur*) (= *cansarse*) to tire o.s. out at work

traqueteo SM **1** (= *acción*) [*de vehículo*] rattle, rattling, jolting; [*de cohete*] crackle, bang; [*de ametralladora*] rattle
2 (*And, Caribe, Méx*) (= *ruido*) row, din; (= *movimiento*) hustle and bustle, coming and going

traquidazo SM (*Méx*) = **traquido**

traquido SM [*de látigo*] crack; [*de disparo*] crack, bang, report

traquinar ▸ CONJUG 1a VI (*Caribe*) = **trajinar**

tras[1] PREP **1** (= *después de*) after • **~ unos días de vacaciones volvió a su trabajo** after a few days' holiday she went back to work • **~ perder las elecciones se retiró de la política** after losing the election he retired from politics • **día ~ día** day after day • **uno ~ otro** one after another *o* the other
2 (= *por detrás de*) behind • **estaba oculto ~ las cortinas** he was hidden behind the curtains • **¿qué escondes ~ esa mirada inocente?** what are you hiding behind that innocent face? • **andar** *o* **estar ~ algo** to be after sth • **anda ~ un puesto en la administración pública** he's after a job in the civil service • **correr** *o* **ir ~ algn** to chase (after) sb
3 • **~ (de): ~ (de) abollarme el coche va y se enfada** he dents my car and on top of that *o* then he gets angry
SM †* (= *trasero*) behind, rump

tras[2] EXCL • **¡tras, tras!** tap, tap!; (*llamando*) knock, knock!

tras... PREF ▸ **trans...**

trasalcoba SF dressing room

trasaltar SM retrochoir

trasbocar* ▸ CONJUG 1g VT, VI (*And, Cono Sur*) to vomit, throw up

trasbucar ▸ CONJUG 1g VT (*Caribe, Cono Sur*) to upset, overturn

trasbuscar ▸ CONJUG 1g VT (*Cono Sur*) to search carefully

trascendencia SF **1** (= *importancia*) importance, significance; (= *consecuencias*) implications (*pl*), consequences (*pl*) • **una discusión sin ~** a discussion of no particular significance • **un encuentro sin ~** an inconsequential meeting • **la matanza no ha tenido ~ informativa** the killing did not make the headlines
2 (*Fil*) transcendence

trascendental ADJ **1** (= *importante*) significant, important; (= *esencial*) vital
2 (*Fil*) transcendental

trascendente ADJ = **trascendental**

trascender ▸ CONJUG 2g VI **1** (= *conocerse*) to leak out, get out • **por fin ha trascendido la noticia** the news has leaked *o* got out at last • **no queremos que sus comentarios trasciendan** we do not want her remarks to leak out *o* to get out
2 (= *propagarse*) • **~ a algo** to extend to sth • **su influencia trasciende a los países más remotos** his influence extends to the most remote countries
3 (= *ir más allá*) • **~ de algo** to transcend sth, go beyond sth • **una cuestión que trasciende de los intereses nacionales** a matter that transcends *o* goes beyond national interests • **el debate ha trascendido de los círculos académicos** the debate has gone beyond academic circles
4 (*Fil*) to transcend
5† (= *oler*) to smell (**a** of); (= *heder*) to reek (**a** of)
VT to transcend, go beyond • **esto trasciende los confines de la razón** it transcends *o* goes beyond the boundaries of reason

trascendido SM (*Cono Sur*) leak

trascocina SF scullery

trascolar ▸ CONJUG 1l VT to strain

trasconejarse* ▸ CONJUG 1a VPR to get lost, be misplaced

trascordarse ▸ CONJUG 1l VPR • **~ algo** to forget sth, lose all memory of sth • **estar trascordado** to be completely forgotten

trascoro SM retrochoir

trascorral SM **1** (= *corral*) inner yard
2* (= *culo*) bottom

trascuarto SM back room

trasegar ▸ CONJUG 1h, 1j VT **1** (= *cambiar de sitio*) to move about, switch round; [+ *puestos*] to reshuffle
2 [+ *vino*] (*para la mesa*) to decant; (*en bodega*) to rack, pour into another container *o* bottle
3* [+ *bebida*] to knock back*
4 (= *trastornar*) to upset
VI * to drink, booze*

trasera SF back, rear

trasero ADJ [*puerta*] back; [*asiento*] back, rear • **la parte trasera del edificio** the back *o* rear of the building • **motor ~** rear-mounted engine • **rueda trasera** back wheel, rear wheel
SM **1** (*euf*) (= *culo*) bottom, behind
• MODISMO: • **quedar(se) con el ~ al aire*** to be caught with one's pants down*
2 (*Zool*) hindquarters (*pl*)
3†† **traseros** (= *antepasados*) ancestors

trasfondo SM (*gen*) background; [*de crítica*] undertone, undercurrent

trasgo SM **1** (= *duende*) goblin, imp
2 (= *niño*) imp

trasgredir ▸ CONJUG 3a VT = **transgredir**

trashojar ▸ CONJUG 1a VT to leaf through, glance through

trashumancia SF, **trashumación** SF seasonal migration, transhumance (*frm*)

trashumante ADJ migrating, on the move to new pastures

trashumar ▸ CONJUG 1a VI to make the seasonal migration, move to new pastures

trasiego SM **1** (= *cambio de sitio*) move, switch; [*de puestos*] reshuffle; [*de vino*] (*para la mesa*) decanting; (*en bodega*) racking
2 (= *trastorno*) upset
3 (= *ir y venir*) coming and going

trasigar ▸ CONJUG 1h VT (*And*) to upset, turn upside down

trasijado ADJ skinny

traslación SF **1** (*Astron*) movement, passage
2 (= *copia*) copy; (= *acción*) copy(ing)
3 (= *metáfora*) metaphor; (= *uso figurado*) figurative use

trasladar ▸ CONJUG 1a VT **1** [+ *empleado, preso*] to transfer, move; [+ *muebles, tienda, oficina*] to move • **la han trasladado de sección** she has been transferred *o* moved to another department • **ayúdame a ~ estos archivadores al otro despacho** help me move these filing cabinets into the other office • **han trasladado la oficina a otra ciudad** they have moved the office to another city, they have relocated to another city
2 (= *copiar*) [+ *carta, informe*] to copy
3 (= *aplazar*) [+ *evento*] to postpone (**a** until); [+ *reunión*] to adjourn (**a** until)
4 (= *traducir*) to translate (**a** into) • **trasladó su pensamiento al papel** she transferred her thoughts onto paper • **~ una novela a la pantalla** to transfer a novel to the screen
VPR **trasladarse 1** (= *desplazarse*) to travel • **los que se trasladan al trabajo en coche** those who travel to work by car • **después de la ceremonia nos trasladamos al hotel** after the ceremony we moved on *o* went to the hotel
2 (= *mudarse*) to move (a to) • **nos hemos trasladado a un local más céntrico** we've moved to more central premises • **~se a otro puesto** to move to a new job

traslado SM **1** [*de muebles*] removal; [*de oficina, residencia*] move • **mi cuñado nos ayudó con el ~** my brother-in-law helped us with the move
2 [*de empleado, preso*] transfer • **le han denegado el ~ a Madrid** they refused him his transfer to Madrid • **el preso se fugó durante su ~ a otro centro penitenciario** the prisoner escaped while he was being transferred *o* moved to another prison
3 ▸ **traslado de bloque** (*Inform*) cut-and-paste operation
4 (= *copia*) copy
5 (*Jur*) notification • **dar ~ a algn de una orden** to give sb a copy of an order

traslapar ▸ CONJUG 1a VT to overlap
VPR **traslaparse** to overlap

traslapo SM overlap, overlay

traslaticiamente ADV figuratively

traslaticio (ADJ) figurative

traslucir ▹ CONJUG 3f (VT) (= *mostrar*) to show; (= *revelar*) to reveal, betray
(VI) • **dejar ~ algo** to suggest sth
(VPR) **traslucirse 1** (= *ser transparente*) to be translucent, be transparent
2 (= *ser visible*) to show through
3 (= *inferirse*) to reveal itself, be revealed; (= *ser obvio*) to be plain to see • **en su cara se traslucía cierto pesimismo** his expression revealed *o* showed a certain pessimism
4 (= *saberse*) to leak out, come to light

traslumbrar ▹ CONJUG 1a (VT) to dazzle
(VPR) **traslumbrarse 1** (= *ser deslumbrado*) to be dazzled
2 (= *ir y venir*) to appear and disappear suddenly, come and go unexpectedly; (= *pasar rápidamente*) to flash across

trasluz (SM) **1** • **al ~: mirar algo al ~** to look at sth against the light
2 (= *luz difusa*) diffused light; (= *luz reflejada*) reflected light, gleam
3 (*Caribe*) (= *semblanza*) resemblance

trasmano (SM) **1** • **a ~** (= *apartado*) out of the way • **me pilla a ~** it's out of my way, it's not on my way
2 (*And*) • **por ~** (= *secretamente*) secretly, in an underhand way

trasminante (ADJ) (*Cono Sur*) [*frío*] bitter, piercing

trasminarse ▹ CONJUG 1a (VPR) to filter through, pass through

trasmundo (SM) hidden world, secret world

trasnochada (SF) **1** (= *vigilia*) vigil, watch; (= *noche sin dormir*) sleepless night
2 (*Mil*) night attack
3 (= *noche anterior*) last night, the night before

trasnochado (ADJ) **1** (= *obsoleto*) outmoded
2 (= *ojeroso*) haggard, run-down

trasnochador(a) (ADJ) • **son muy ~es** they go to bed very late, they keep very late hours
(SM/F) night bird, night owl

trasnochar ▹ CONJUG 1a (VI) **1** (= *acostarse tarde*) to stay up late, go to bed late; (= *no acostarse*) to stay up all night; (= *ir de juerga*) to have a night out, have a night on the tiles
2 • **~ en un sitio** to spend the night in a place
(VT) [+ *problema*] to sleep on
(VPR) **trasnocharse** (*Méx**) ▹ VI

trasoír ▹ CONJUG 3p (VT), (VI) to mishear

trasojado (ADJ) haggard, hollow-eyed

traspaís (SM) interior, hinterland

traspalar ▹ CONJUG 1a (VT) to shovel about, move with a shovel

traspapelar ▹ CONJUG 1a (VT) to lose, mislay
(VPR) **traspapelarse** to get mislaid

traspapeleo (SM) misplacement

traspar ▹ CONJUG 1a (VI) (*Méx*) to move house

traspasar ▹ CONJUG 1a (VT) **1** (= *penetrar*) to pierce, go through, penetrate; [*líquido*] to go/come through, soak through • **la bala le traspasó el pulmón** the bullet pierced his lung • **~ a algn con una espada** to run sb through with a sword
2 [*dolor*] to pierce, go right through • **un ruido que traspasa el oído** an ear-splitting noise • **el grito me traspasó** the yell went right through me • **la escena me traspasó el corazón** the scene pierced me to the core
3 [+ *calle*] to cross over
4 [+ *límites*] to go beyond, overstep • **esto traspasa los límites de lo aceptable** this goes beyond what is acceptable • **~ la barrera del sonido** to break the sound barrier
5 [+ *ley, norma*] to break, infringe
6 [+ *propiedad*] (= *transferir*) to transfer; (= *vender*) to sell, make over; (*Jur*) to convey • **"se traspasa negocio"** "business for sale"
7 (*Dep*) [+ *jugador*] to transfer
8 (*Pol*) [+ *poderes, competencias*] to devolve
(VPR) **traspasarse** to go too far, overstep the mark

traspaso (SM) **1** (= *venta*) transfer, sale; (*Jur*) conveyance
2 (= *propiedad*) property transferred; (*Jur*) property being conveyed
3 (*Dep*) (= *acción*) transfer; (= *pago*) transfer fee
4 (*Esp*) (*Pol*) ▸ **traspaso de competencias** transfer of powers
5 [*de ley*] infringement
6 (= *pena*) anguish, pain, grief

traspatio (SM) (*LAm*) backyard

traspié (SM) **1** (= *tropezón*) trip, stumble • **dar un ~** to trip, stumble
2 (= *error*) blunder, slip

traspintarse ▹ CONJUG 1a (VPR) **1** (*en papel*) to come through, show through
2* (= *acabar mal*) to backfire, turn out all wrong

trasplantado/a (SM/F) transplant patient

trasplantar ▹ CONJUG 1a (VT) to transplant
(VPR) **trasplantarse** to emigrate, uproot o.s.

trasplante (SM) **1** (*Med*) transplant, transplantation ▸ **trasplante de corazón** heart transplant ▸ **trasplante de órganos** organ transplant ▸ **trasplante hepático** liver transplant
2 (*Bot*) transplanting

trasponer ▹ CONJUG 2q (VT) = **transponer**

traspontín (SM) = **traspuntín**

traspuesta (SF) **1** (= *transposición*) transposition; (= *cambio*) switching, changing over
2 (*Geog*) rise
3 (= *huida*) flight, escape; (= *acto de esconderse*) hiding
4 (= *patio*) backyard; (= *dependencias*) outbuildings (*pl*)

traspuesto (ADJ) • **quedarse ~** to doze off

traspunte (SMF) prompt, prompter

traspuntín (SM) **1** (= *asiento*) tip-up seat, folding seat
2* (= *culo*) backside*, bottom

trasque (CONJ) (*LAm*) in addition to the fact that ..., besides being ...

trasquiladura (SF) shearing

trasquilar ▹ CONJUG 1a (VT) **1** [+ *oveja*] to shear; [+ *pelo, persona*] to crop • MODISMO: • **ir por lana y volver trasquilado** to get more than you bargained for
2* (= *cortar*) to cut (down)

trasquilón (SM) • **¡menudo ~ que le han dado!** what a mess they've made of his hair! • **cortado a trasquilones** unevenly cut

trastabillar ▹ CONJUG 1a (VI) (*esp LAm*) to stagger, stumble

trastabillón (SM) (*LAm*) stumble, trip

trastada* (SF) **1** (= *travesura*) prank, mischief
2 (= *mala pasada*) dirty trick • **hacer una ~ a algn** to play a dirty trick on sb

trastajo* (SM) piece of junk

trastazo* (SM) bump, bang, thump • **darse** *o* **pegarse un ~** (*lit*) to get a knock; (*fig*) to come a cropper*

traste[1] (SM) **1** (*Mús*) [*de guitarra*] fret
2 • MODISMOS: • **dar al ~ con algo** to spoil sth, mess sth up • **dar al ~ con una fortuna** to squander a fortune • **dar al ~ con los planes** to ruin one's plans • **esto ha dado al ~ con mi paciencia** this has exhausted my patience • **irse al ~** to fall through, be ruined

traste[2] (SM) **1** (*LAm*) = **trasto**
2 (*Cono Sur**) bottom, backside*

trastear ▹ CONJUG 1a (VT) **1** (*Mús*) (= *tocar*) to play (well)
2 [+ *objetos*] (= *mover*) to move around; (= *revolver*) to disarrange, mess up
3 (*Taur*) to play with the cape
4 [+ *persona*] (= *manipular*) to twist around one's little finger, lead by the nose; (= *hacer esperar*) to keep waiting, keep hanging on
5 (*Méx*‡) (= *acariciar*) to feel up*, touch up*
(VI) **1** (= *mover objetos*) to move things around • **~ con** *o* **en** (= *buscar*) to rummage among; (= *manosear*) to fiddle with; (= *desordenar*) to mess up, disarrange
2 (*And, CAm*) (= *mudarse*) to move house
(VPR) **trastearse** (*And, Cono Sur*) to move house

trastera (SF) **1** (= *cuarto*) lumber room
2 (*Méx*) (= *armario*) cupboard
3 (*Caribe*) (= *trastos*) heap of junk

trastería (SF) **1** (= *trastos*) lumber, junk
2 (= *tienda*) junkshop
3 = **trastada**

trastero (SM) **1** (= *cuarto*) lumber room
2 (*Méx*) (= *armario*) cupboard, closet (EEUU)
3 (*Méx*‡) (= *culo*) backside*
4 (*CAm, Méx*) (*para platos*) dishrack

trastienda (SF) **1** [*de tienda*] back room • MODISMO: • **obtener algo por la ~** to get sth under the counter
2* (= *astucia*) cunning • **tiene mucha ~** he's a sly one
3 (*Cono Sur, Méx**) (= *culo*) backside*

trasto (SM) **1** (= *cosa inútil*) piece of junk • MODISMO: • **tirarse los ~s a la cabeza** to have a blazing row ▸ **trastos viejos** junk (*sing*), rubbish (*sing*), garbage (*sing*) (EEUU)
2 trastos* gear (*sing*), tackle (*sing*) • **liar los ~s** to pack up and go ▸ **trastos de matar** weapons ▸ **trastos de pescar** fishing tackle (*sing*)
3 trastos (*Teat*) (= *decorado*) scenery (*sing*); (= *accesorios*) stage furniture (*sing*), properties
4* (= *persona inútil*) good-for-nothing, dead loss*
5* (= *niño*) little rascal

trastocamiento (SM) disruption

trastocar ▹ CONJUG 1g, 1l (VT) = **trastrocar**

trastornado (ADJ) [*persona*] disturbed; [*mente*] disturbed, unhinged

trastornar ▹ CONJUG 1a (VT) **1** (= *perturbar*) [+ *mente*] to disturb, unhinge; [+ *persona*] to drive crazy, mentally disturb • **esa chica le ha trastornado** that girl is driving him crazy, he's lost his head over that girl
2* (= *encantar*) to delight • **le trastornan las joyas** she's crazy about jewels, she just lives for jewels
3 (= *alterar*) [+ *persona*] to upset, trouble, disturb; [+ *ideas*] to confuse, upset; [+ *proyecto*] to upset; [+ *vida*] to mess up; [+ *sentidos*] to daze, mess up; [+ *nervios*] to shatter; [+ *orden público*] to disturb; [+ *objetos*] to mix up, turn upside down
(VPR) **trastornarse 1** [*persona*] to go out of one's mind, become deranged *o* disturbed
2 [*proyectos*] to fall through, be ruined

trastorno (SM) **1** (= *molestia*) inconvenience, trouble • **tener que esperar es un ~** it's a real nuisance having to wait
2 (*Pol*) disturbance, upheaval • **los ~s políticos** the political disturbances
3 (*Med*) upset, disorder ▸ **trastorno de personalidad** personality disorder ▸ **trastorno digestivo, trastorno estomacal** stomach upset ▸ **trastorno dismórfico corporal** body dysmorphic disorder ▸ **trastorno mental** mental disorder

trastrabillar ▹ CONJUG 1a (VI) **1** (= *tropezar*) to trip, stumble

2 (= *tambalearse*) to totter, reel, stagger
3 (= *tartamudear*) to stammer, stutter
trastrocar ▸ CONJUG 1g, 1l (VT) **1** [+ *objetos*] to switch over, change round; [+ *orden*] to reverse, invert
2 [+ *palabras*] to change, transform
trastrueco (SM), **trastrueque** (SM)
1 (= *cambio*) [*de objetos*] switch, changeover; [*de orden*] reversal, switch
2 (= *transformación*) change, transformation
trastumbar ▸ CONJUG 1a (VT) • **~ la esquina** (*Méx*) to disappear round the corner, turn the corner
trasudar ▸ CONJUG 1a (VI) [*atleta*] to sweat lightly; [*cosa*] to seep
trasudor (SM) slight sweat
trasuntar ▸ CONJUG 1a (VT) **1** (= *copiar*) to copy, transcribe
2 (= *resumir*) to summarize
3 (= *mostrar*) to show, exude • **su cara trasuntaba serenidad** his face exuded calm
trasunto (SM) **1** (= *copia*) copy, transcription
2 (= *semejanza*) image, likeness; (= *copia exacta*) carbon copy • **fiel ~** exact likeness • **esto es un ~ en menor escala de lo que ocurrió** this is a repetition on a smaller scale of what happened
trasvasable (ADJ) transferable
trasvasar ▸ CONJUG 1a (VT) **1** [+ *líquido*] to pour into another container, transfer; [+ *vino*] to decant
2 [+ *río*] to divert
trasvase (SM) **1** (= *paso*) [*de vino*] pouring, decanting; [*de río*] diversion
2 (= *fuga*) drain
trasvasijar ▸ CONJUG 1a (VT) (*Cono Sur*) = trasvasar
trasvolar ▸ CONJUG 1l (VT) to fly over, cross in an aeroplane
trata (SF) ▸ **trata de blancas** white slave trade ▸ **trata de esclavos** slave trade
tratable (ADJ) **1** (= *amable*) friendly, sociable
2 [*enfermedad*] treatable
3 (*Cono Sur*) passable
tratadista (SMF) writer (of a treatise)
tratado (SM) **1** (*Com*) agreement; (*Pol*) treaty, pact ▸ **Tratado de Adhesión** Treaty of Accession (*to EU*) ▸ **tratado de paz** peace treaty ▸ **Tratado de Roma** Treaty of Rome ▸ **Tratado de Utrecht** Treaty of Utrecht
2 (= *libro*) treatise • **un ~ de física** a treatise on physics
tratamiento (SM) **1** [*de objeto, material, tema*] treatment; [*de problema*] handling, treatment
2 (*Med*) treatment ▸ **tratamiento ambulatorio** out-patient treatment ▸ **tratamiento con rayos X** X-ray treatment ▸ **tratamiento de choque** shock treatment ▸ **tratamiento médico** medical treatment
3 (*Inform*) processing ▸ **tratamiento de datos** data processing ▸ **tratamiento de gráficos** graphics processing ▸ **tratamiento de la información** information processing ▸ **tratamiento de márgenes** margin settings ▸ **tratamiento de textos** word processing ▸ **tratamiento por lotes** batch processing
4 [*de persona*] treatment • **el ~ que recibí** the way I was treated, the treatment I received
5 (= *título*) title, style (*of address*) • **dar ~ a algn** to give sb his full title • MODISMO: • **apear el ~ a algn** to drop sb's title, address sb without formality
tratante (SMF) dealer, trader (**en** in)
tratar ▸ CONJUG 1a (VT) **1** [+ *persona, animal, objeto*] to treat • **su novio la trata muy mal** her boyfriend treats her very badly • **hay que ~ a los animales con cariño** animals should be given plenty of affection, animals should be treated lovingly • **te dejo la cámara, pero trátala bien** I'll let you have the camera, but be careful with it *o* treat it carefully • **la vida la ha tratado muy bien** life has been very kind to her, life has treated her very well • **este asunto debe ser tratado con cuidado** this matter should be handled carefully • **~ a algn de loco** to treat sb like a madman • MODISMO: • **~ a algn a patadas** to treat sb like dirt
2 (= *llamar*) • **¿cómo le tenemos que ~ cuando nos hable?** how should we address him when he speaks to us? • **~ a algn de algo** to call sb sth • **~ a algn de vago** to call sb a layabout • **~ a algn de tú/usted** to address sb as "tú"/"usted"
3 (= *relacionarse con*) • **~ a algn: ya no lo trato** I no longer have any dealings with him • **lo trato solo desde hace seis meses** I have only known him for six months • **me cae bien, pero no la he tratado mucho** I like her, but I haven't had a lot to do with her
4 (*Med*) [+ *paciente, enfermedad*] to treat • **me están tratando con un nuevo fármaco** I'm being treated with a new drug • **le ~on la neumonía con antibióticos** they treated the pneumonia with antibiotics • **¿qué médico te está tratando?** which doctor is giving you treatment?
5 [+ *tejido, madera, residuos*] to treat • **el agua se ha tratado con cloro** the water has been treated with chlorine
6 (= *discutir*) [+ *tema*] to deal with; [+ *acuerdo, paz*] to negotiate • **~emos este tema en la reunión** we'll deal with this subject in the meeting • **este asunto tiene que ~lo directamente con el director** you'll have to speak directly with the manager about this matter
7 (*Inform*) to process
(VI) **1** • **~ de** [*libro*] to be about, deal with; [*personas*] to talk about, discuss • **la película trata de un adolescente en Nueva York** the film is about a teenager in New York • **ahora van a ~ del programa** they're going to talk about *o* discuss the programme now
2 (= *intentar*) • **~ de hacer algo** to try to do sth • **~é de llegar pronto** I'll try to arrive early • **trata de no ser demasiado estricto con él** try not to be too strict with him • **~ de que:** • **~é de que esta sea la última vez** I'll try to make sure that this is the last time • **trata por todos los medios de que el trabajo esté acabado para mañana** try and do whatever you can to make sure that the job is done by tomorrow
3 (= *relacionarse*) • **~ con algn:** • **trato con todo tipo de gente** I deal with all sorts of people • **no tratamos con traidores** we don't have dealings with traitors • **no había tratado con personas de esa clase** I had not previously come into contact with people like that • **para ~ con animales hay que tener mucha paciencia** you have to be very patient when dealing with animals • **es muy difícil ~ con el enemigo** it is not at all easy to have dealings with the enemy
4 (*Com*) • **~ con** *o* **en algo** to deal in sth • **trataban con** *o* **en pieles** they dealt in furs, they were involved in the fur trade
(VPR) **tratarse 1** (= *cuidarse*) to look after o.s. • **ahora se trata con mucho cuidado** he looks after himself very carefully now • **no se trata nada mal el chico** (*iró*) he certainly looks after himself all right
2 (= *relacionarse*) • **~se con algn** to have dealings with sb • **hace tiempo que no me trato con ellos** it is a while since I've had any dealings *o* had anything to do with them • **se trató con gente rica** she mixed with wealthy people
3 (= *hablarse*) to address each other • **¿cómo nos tenemos que ~?** how should we address each other? • **no se tratan desde hace tiempo** they haven't been speaking (to each other) for some time • **~se de:** • **se tratan de usted** they address each other as "usted" • **¿aquí nos tratamos de tú o de usted?** are we on "tú" or "usted" terms here?
4 • **~se de algo a** (= *ser acerca de*) to be about sth • **se trata de la nueva piscina** it's about the new pool • **¿de qué se trata?** what's it about?
b (= *ser cuestión de*) • **se trata de aplazarlo un mes** it's a question of putting it off for a month • **se trata sencillamente de que rellenéis este formulario** all you have to do is fill in this form
c (= *ser*) • **ahora bien, tratándose de ti ...** now, seeing as it's you ... • **si no se trata más que de eso** if there's no more to it than that, if that's all it is • **se ~á de su primera visita a Colombia** it will be her first visit to Colombia
tratativas (SFPL) (*Cono Sur*) (= *negociaciones*) negotiations; (= *medidas*) steps, measures
trato (SM) **1** (= *acuerdo*) deal • **¡~ hecho!** it's a deal! • **cerrar un ~** to close *o* clinch a deal • **hacer un ~** to do a deal • **hacer buenos ~s a algn†** to offer sb advantageous terms ▸ **trato comercial** business deal
2 (= *relación*) • **ya no tengo ~ con ella** I don't have anything to do with her any more • **no quiero ~ con él** I want nothing to do with him • **romper el ~ con algn** to break off relations with sb ▸ **trato carnal, trato sexual** • **tener ~ carnal** *o* **sexual con algn** to have sexual relations with sb
3 **tratos** (= *negociaciones*) negotiations • **entrar en ~s con algn** to enter into negotiations *o* discussions with sb • **estar en ~s con algn** to be in negotiations with sb, be negotiating with sb
4 (= *tratamiento*) treatment • **daba muy mal ~ a sus empleados** he treated his employees very badly • **malos ~s** physical abuse (*sing*) • **malos ~s a menores** child abuse (*sing*) ▸ **trato de favor, trato preferente** preferential treatment
5 (= *manera de ser*) manner • **es una persona de ~ agradable** he has a pleasant manner • **de fácil ~** easy to get on with
6 (*forma de cortesía*) • **no sé qué ~ darle, si de tú o de usted** I don't know whether to address him as "tú" or as "usted" • **dar a algn el ~ debido** to give sb his proper title
7 (*Méx*) (= *puesto*) market stall; (= *negocio*) small business
trauma (SM) **1** (= *shock*) trauma
2 (= *lesión*) injury
3 (*Med*) = **traumatología**
traumar ▸ CONJUG 1a (VT) to traumatize
traumático (ADJ) traumatic
traumatismo (SM) traumatism
traumatizado (ADJ) traumatized
traumatizante (ADJ) traumatic
traumatizar ▸ CONJUG 1f (VT) (*Med, Psic*) to traumatize; (*fig*) to shock, affect profoundly
traumatología (SF) orthopedic surgery
traumatólogo/a (SM/F) traumatologist
trauque (SM) (*Cono Sur*) friend
travelling ['traβelin] (SM) (PL: **travelling(s)** ['traβelin]), **travelín** (SM) (*Cine*) (= *aparato*) dolly, travelling platform; (= *movimiento*) tracking shot
través (SM) **1** (*Arquit*) (= *viga*) crossbeam
2 (*Mil*) traverse; (= *muro*) protective wall
3 (= *curva*) bend, turn; (= *inclinación*) slant; (= *sesgo*) bias; (= *deformación*) warp
4 (= *contratiempo*) reverse, misfortune;

(= trastorno) upset
5 • a ~ de across; (= por medio de) through • fuimos a ~ del bosque we went through the woods • un árbol caído a ~ de los carriles a tree fallen across the lines • lo sé a ~ de un amigo I heard about it through a friend
6 • al ~ across, crossways • de ~ across, crossways; (= oblicuamente) obliquely; (= de lado) sideways • hubo que introducirlo de ~ it had to be squeezed in sideways • con el sombrero puesto de ~ with his hat on crooked o askew • ir de ~ (Náut) to drift/be blown off course • mirar de ~ to squint • mirar a algn de ~ (lit) to look sideways at sb; (fig) to look askance at sb

travesaño SM 1 (Arquit) crossbeam; (Dep) crossbar
2 [de cama] bolster
3 (CAm, Caribe, Méx) (Ferro) sleeper, tie (EEUU)

travesear ▸ CONJUG 1a VI 1 (= jugar) to play around; (= ser travieso) to play up, be mischievous, be naughty; (pey) to live a dissipated life
2 (= hablar) to talk wittily, sparkle
3 (Méx) [jinete] to show off one's horsemanship

traveseo SM (Méx) display of horsemanship

travesera SF (Mús) flute

travesero ADJ cross (antes de s), slanting, oblique • flauta travesera flute
SM bolster

travesía SF 1 (= calle) side street; [de pueblo] road that passes through a village
2 (= viaje) (Náut) crossing, voyage; (Aer) crossing; (= distancia) distance travelled, distance to be crossed ▸ travesía del desierto (fig) period in the wilderness
3 (= viento) crosswind; (Cono Sur) west wind
4 (en el juego) (= ganancias) amount won; (= pérdidas) amount lost
5 (And, Cono Sur) (= desierto) arid plain, desert region

travesti SMF, **travestí** SMF transvestite; (= artista) drag artist

travestido/a ADJ disguised, in disguise
SM/F = travesti

travestirse ▸ CONJUG 3k VPR to cross-dress

travestismo SM transvestism

travesura SF 1 (= broma) prank, lark • son ~s de niños they're just childish pranks • las ~s de su juventud the wild doings of his youth, the waywardness of his young days
2 (= mala pasada) sly trick
3 (= gracia) wit, sparkle

traviesa SF 1 (Arquit) (= viga) crossbeam
2 (Ferro) sleeper, tie (EEUU)
3 (Min) cross gallery
4 • fuimos (a) campo ~ we went across country

travieso ADJ 1 [niño] naughty, mischievous
2 [adulto] (= inquieto) restless; (= vivo) lively; (= vicioso) dissolute; (= listo) bright, clever, shrewd; (= gracioso) witty

trayecto SM 1 (= distancia) distance • recorrió el ~ en cinco horas she covered the distance in five hours
2 (= viaje) journey • comeremos durante el ~ we'll eat during the journey o on the way • también puedes hacer el ~ en autobús you can also do the journey by bus • final del ~ end of the line
3 [de bala] trajectory

trayectoria SF 1 (= camino) trajectory, path ▸ trayectoria de vuelo flight path
2 (= desarrollo) development, path • la ~ actual del partido the party's present line • la ~ poética de Garcilaso Garcilaso's poetic development ▸ trayectoria profesional career

trayendo etc ▸ traer

traza SF 1 (= aspecto) appearance • este hombre tiene mala ~ this man has an unpleasant appearance • nunca conseguirás trabajo con esas ~s you'll never get a job looking like that • por o según las ~s judging by appearances • esto lleva o tiene ~s de no acabar nunca this looks as though it will never end
2 [de edificio] plan, design; [de ciudad] layout
3 (= habilidad) skill, ability • darse o tener ~ para hacer algo to be skilful o clever at doing sth • para pianista tiene poca ~ she's not much of a pianist
4 (Inform) trace
5 (Cono Sur) (= huella) track, trail

trazable ADJ traceable

trazada SF line, course, direction • cortar la ~ a algn (Aut) to cut in on sb

trazado SM 1 [de carretera] route
2 [de edificio] plan, design; [de ciudad] layout
3 (And) (= cuchillo) machete

trazador(a) ADJ (Mil, Fís) tracer (antes de s) • bala ~a tracer bullet • elemento ~ tracer element
SM/F (= persona) planner, designer
SM 1 (Fís) tracer
2 (Inform) ▸ trazador de gráficos, trazador gráfico plotter ▸ trazador plano flatbed plotter

trazadora SF tracer, tracer bullet

trazar ▸ CONJUG 1f VT 1 (= dibujar) [+ línea] to draw, trace; (Arte) to sketch, outline; (Arquit, Téc) to plan, design
2 [+ fronteras, límites] to mark out; [+ itinerario] to plot; [+ desarrollo, política] to lay down, mark out
3 (= explicar) to outline, describe

trazo SM 1 (= línea) stroke, line ▸ trazo de lápiz pencil line, pencil stroke ▸ trazo discontinuo broken line
2 (= esbozo) sketch, outline
3 trazos [de cara] lines, features • de ~s enérgicos vigorous-looking • de ~s indecisos with an indecisive look about him
4 [de ropaje] fold

TRB SFPL ABR (= toneladas de registro bruto) GRT

TRC SM ABR (= tubo de rayos catódicos) CRT

trébedes SFPL trivet (sing)

trebejos SMPL 1 (= utensilios) equipment (sing), things ▸ trebejos de cocina kitchen utensils, kitchen things
2 (Ajedrez) chessmen

trébol SM 1 (Bot) clover
2 (Arquit) trefoil
3 tréboles (Naipes) clubs

trebolar SM (Cono Sur) clover field, field covered in clover

trece ADJ INV, PRON, SM (gen) thirteen; (ordinal, en la fecha) thirteenth • le escribí el día ~ I wrote to him on the thirteenth • MODISMO: • mantenerse en sus ~ to stand one's ground, stick to one's guns; ▸ seis

treceavo ADJ thirteenth
SM • el ~ the thirteenth • un ~ a thirteenth, a thirteenth part

trecho SM 1 (= tramo) stretch; (= distancia) way, distance; (= tiempo) while • andar un buen ~ to walk a good way • a ~s (= en parte) in parts, here and there; (= cada tanto) intermittently, by fits and starts • de ~ en ~ every so often, at intervals • muy de ~ en ~ very occasionally, only once in a while
2 (Agr) (= parcela) plot, patch
3* (= trozo) bit, part • queda un buen ~ que hacer there's still quite a bit to do • he terminado ese ~ I've finished that bit

trefilar ▸ CONJUG 1a VT [+ alambre] to draw (out)

tregua SF 1 (Mil) truce
2 (= descanso) lull, respite • sin ~ without respite • no dar ~ to give no respite • dar ~s [dolor] to come and go, let up from time to time; [asunto] not to be urgent

treinta ADJ thirty; [fecha] thirtieth; ▸ seis

treintañero/a ADJ thirtysomething*
SM/F thirtysomething*

treintena SF (about) thirty

treintón/ona ADJ thirtysomething*
SM/F thirtysomething*

trekking SM trekking

trematodo SM (Zool) fluke

tremebundo ADJ (= terrible) terrible, frightening; (= amenazador) threatening; (= violento) fierce, savage

tremedal SM quaking bog

tremenda SF • tomarse algo a la ~ to make a great fuss about sth, take sth too seriously

tremendamente ADV tremendously

tremendismo SM 1 [de noticia] stark reality
2 (Arte) use of realism to shock

tremendista ADJ crude, coarsely realistic
SMF 1 (= alarmista) alarmist
2 (= escritor) coarsely realistic writer, writer who shocks by his realism

tremendo ADJ 1* (= grandísimo) tremendous • hay unas diferencias tremendas entre los dos there are tremendous differences between the two of them • le dio una paliza tremenda he gave him a tremendous beating • un error ~ a terrible mistake • me llevé un disgusto ~ I was terribly upset • una roca tremenda de alta a terrifically high rock*
2 (= terrible) terrible, horrific • hemos presenciado escenas tremendas we witnessed terrible o horrific scenes
3* (= divertido) • es ~, ¿eh? he's something else, isn't he?*
4* (= travieso) • esta niña es tremenda this girl is a (little) terror

trementina SF turpentine

tremolar ▸ CONJUG 1a VT 1 [+ bandera] to wave
2 (fig) to show off, flaunt
VI to wave, flutter

tremolina* SF row, fuss, commotion, shindy* • armar una ~ to start a row, make a fuss, to kick up a shindy*

tremotiles SMPL (And, Caribe) tools, tackle (sing)

trémulamente ADV tremulously

trémulo ADJ [voz] tremulous, shaky, quavering; [mano] trembling; [luz] flickering • le contestó trémula de emoción she answered him, trembling o quivering with emotion

tren SM 1 (Ferro) train • cambiar de ~ to change trains, change train • subirse a o tomar o coger un ~ to catch a train • ir en ~ to go by train • MODISMOS: • dejar el ~ a algn (Chile, Ven*) to be left on the shelf • tiene miedo de que la deje el ~ she's scared of being left on the shelf • estar como un ~ (Esp*) to be hot stuff*, be a bit of alright* • llevarse el ~ a algn (Méx*) (= morirse) to kick the bucket*; (= estar furioso) to be in a rage, be incensed • para parar un ~*: • tenemos libros para parar un ~ we've got books coming out of our ears* • recibimos cartas para parar un ~ we got more letters than you could possibly imagine • perder el ~ de algo: • perdimos el ~ de la revolución científica when it came to the scientific revolution, we missed the boat • este país no puede perder una vez más el ~ del cambio this country mustn't get left behind on the road to change • subirse al ~ de algo: • no

han sabido subirse al ~ de la reconversión económica they failed to take the road to economic restructuring • **no era de esos que se empeñaban en subirse al ~ de la unión europea** he was not one of those determined to jump on *o* climb on the European bandwagon ▸ **tren ascendente**† up train ▸ **tren botijo**†* excursion train ▸ **tren correo** mail train ▸ **tren cremallera** cog railway ▸ **tren de alta velocidad** high-speed train ▸ **tren de carga** goods train, freight train (*EEUU*) ▸ **tren de carretera** articulated lorry (*Brit*), articulated truck (*EEUU*) ▸ **tren de cercanías** suburban train, local train ▸ **tren de contenedores** container train ▸ **tren de la bruja** ghost train ▸ **tren de largo recorrido** long-distance train ▸ **tren de mercancías** goods train, freight train (*EEUU*) ▸ **tren de pasajeros** passenger train ▸ **tren descendente**† down train ▸ **tren directo** through train ▸ **tren eléctrico** (= *medio de transporte*) electric train; (= *juguete*) (electric) train set ▸ **tren expreso** express, express train ▸ **tren mixto** passenger and goods train ▸ **tren ómnibus**† stopping train, local train, accommodation train (*EEUU*) ▸ **tren postal** mail train ▸ **tren rápido** express, express train ▸ **tren suplementario** relief train
2 (= *ritmo*) • **ir a buen ~** to go at a good speed • **forzar el ~** to force the pace • **a fuerte ~** fast • MODISMO: • **vivir a todo ~** to live in style ▸ **tren de vida** lifestyle • **no pudo sostener ese ~ de vida** he could not keep up that lifestyle
3 (*Mec*) set (*of gears, wheels*) ▸ **tren de aterrizaje** (*Aer*) undercarriage, landing gear ▸ **tren de bandas en caliente** hot-strip mill ▸ **tren de laminación** rolling-mill ▸ **tren delantero** (*Aut*) front wheel assembly ▸ **tren de lavado** (*Aut*) car wash ▸ **tren trasero** (*Aut*) rear wheel assembly
4 (*en viajes*) (= *equipaje*) luggage; (= *equipo*) equipment ▸ **tren de viaje** equipment for a journey
5 (*Mil*) convoy
6 • **en ~ de** (*LAm*) in the process of • **estamos en ~ de realizarlo** we are in the process of doing it • **estar en ~ de recuperación** to be on the road to recovery
7 (*Caribe*) (= *taller*) workshop; (= *empresa*) firm, company ▸ **tren de lavado** laundry ▸ **tren de mudadas** removal company
8 (*CAm*) **a** (= *trajín*) coming and going
b trenes shady dealings
9 (*Méx*) (= *tranvía*) tram, streetcar (*EEUU*)
10 (*Caribe*) (= *majadería*) cheeky remark

trena‡ SF clink‡, prison, can (*EEUU*‡)
trenca SF duffle-coat
trencilla SF, **trencillo** SM braid
tren-cremallera SM (PL: **trenes-cremallera**) funicular (railway)
trenista SMF **1** (*Caribe*) (= *patrón*) owner of a workshop; (= *gerente*) company manager
2 (*Méx*) (*Ferro*) railway worker, railroad worker (*EEUU*)
Trento SM Trent • **Concilio de ~** Council of Trent
trenza SF **1** [*de pelo*] plait, braid (*EEUU*); (*Cos*) braid; [*de pajas, cintas*] plait; [*de hilos*] twist • MODISMO: • **encontrar a una mujer en ~** to find a woman with her hair down ▸ **trenza postiza** hairpiece
2 (*LAm*) [*de cebollas*] string
3 trenzas (*Caribe*) [*de zapatos*] shoelaces
4 (*Culin*) plait
5 (*Cono Sur*) (= *recomendación*) recommendation, suggestion
6 (*Cono Sur*) (= *pelea*) hand-to-hand fight

trenzado ADJ [*pelo*] plaited, braided (*EEUU*); (*Cos*) braided; (= *entrelazado*) intertwined, twisted together
SM **1** [*de pelo*] plaiting, braiding (*EEUU*); [*de pajas, cintas*] plaiting
2 (*Ballet*) entrechat
trenzar ▷ CONJUG 1f VT [+ *cabello*] to plait, braid (*EEUU*); [+ *pajas, cintas*] to plait; (*Cos*) to braid; [+ *hilo*] to weave, twist (together)
VI [*bailarines*] to weave in and out; [*caballo*] to caper
VPR **trenzarse** (*LAm*) **1*** (= *pelear*) to come to blows
2 • **~se en una discusión** to get involved in an argument
trepa¹ SF **1** (= *subida*) climb, climbing
2 (= *voltereta*) somersault
3 (= *ardid*) trick, ruse
4 (*Caza*) hide, blind (*EEUU*)
5* (= *paliza*) tanning*
SMF* (= *arribista*) social climber; (= *cobista*) creep*
trepa² SF **1** (*Téc*) (*con taladro*) drilling, boring
2 (*Cos*) (= *guarnición*) trimming
3 [*de madera*] grain
trepada SF climb; (*fig*) rise, ascent
trepaderas SFPL (*Caribe, Méx*) climbing irons
trepado SM **1** (*Téc*) drilling, boring
2 [*de sello*] perforation
trepador(a) ADJ **1** [*planta*] climbing; [*rosa*] rambling
2 • **este vino es bien ~** (*And**) this wine goes straight to your head
SM/F* (= *persona*) social climber
SM **1** (*Bot*) climber; (= *rosa*) rambler
2 (*Orn*) nuthatch
3 trepadores (= *garfios*) climbing irons
trepadora SF (*Bot*) climber, rambler
trepanación SF trepanation
trepanar ▷ CONJUG 1a VT to trepan
trepar¹ ▷ CONJUG 1a VI **1** [*persona, animal*] to climb • **~ a un árbol** to climb (up) a tree
2 (*Bot*) to climb (**por** up)
VT • **~ puestos** to climb the ladder
trepar² ▷ CONJUG 1a VT **1** (*Téc*) (= *taladrar*) to drill, bore
2 (*Cos*) to trim
trepe* SM telling-off* • **echar un ~ a algn** to tell sb off*
trepetera* SF (*Caribe*) hubbub, din
trepidación SF vibration, shaking
trepidante ADJ [*ritmo*] frenetic, frantic; [*ruido*] intolerable, ear-splitting; [*frío*] extreme
trepidar ▷ CONJUG 1a VI **1** (= *temblar*) to shake, vibrate
2 (*LAm*) (= *vacilar*) to hesitate, waver • **~ en hacer algo** to hesitate to do sth
treque ADJ (*Caribe*) witty, funny
tres ADJ INV, PRON (*gen*) three; (*ordinal, en la fecha*) third • **las ~** three o'clock • **le escribí el día ~** I wrote to him on the third
• MODISMOS: • **de ~ al cuarto** cheap, poor quality • **como ~ y dos son cinco** as sure as sure can be, as sure as eggs is eggs • **ni a la de ~** on no account, not by a long shot • **no ver ~ en un burro** to be as blind as a bat
SM (= *número*) three; (= *fecha*) third ▸ **tres en raya** (= *juego*) noughts and crosses, tic tac toe (*EEUU*); ▷ **seis**
trescientos/as ADJ, PRON, SM (*gen*) three hundred; (*ordinal*) three hundredth; ▷ **seiscientos**
tresillo SM **1** [*de muebles*] three-piece suite
2 (*Mús*) triplet
tresnal SM (*Agr*) shock, stook
treso ADJ (*Méx*) dirty
treta SF **1** (= *truco*) trick; (= *ardid*) ruse, stratagem; (*Com*) stunt, gimmick ▸ **treta publicitaria** advertising gimmick
2 (*Esgrima*) feint

tri... PREF tri..., three-
tríada SF triad
trial SM (*Dep*) trial
SF trial motorcycle
triangulación SF triangulation
triangular ADJ triangular
VT ▷ CONJUG 1a to triangulate
triángulo SM triangle ▸ **triángulo amoroso** love triangle ▸ **triángulo de aviso** warning triangle ▸ **triángulo de las Bermudas** Bermuda Triangle
triates SMPL (*Méx*) triplets
triatleta SMF triathlete
triatlón SM triathlon
tribal ADJ tribal
tribalismo SM tribalism
tribu SF tribe
tribulación SF tribulation
tribulete* SM trainee journalist
tribuna SF **1** [*de orador*] platform, rostrum; (*en mitin*) platform ▸ **tribuna libre, tribuna pública** (= *debate*) open forum, forum for debate
2 (*Dep*) stand, grandstand ▸ **tribuna cubierta** covered stand ▸ **tribuna de invitados** visitors gallery ▸ **tribuna de prensa** (*Dep*) press box; (*Parl*) press gallery
3 (*Rel*) gallery ▸ **tribuna del órgano** organ loft
4 (*Jur*) ▸ **tribuna del acusado** dock ▸ **tribuna del jurado** jury box
tribunal SM **1** (*Jur*) (= *lugar*) court; (= *conjunto de jueces*) court, bench • **en pleno ~** in open court • **llevar a algn ante los ~es** to take sb to court • **sus actos serán juzgados por el ~ de la opinión pública** public opinion will be the judge of his actions ▸ **Tribunal Constitucional** constitutional court ▸ **Tribunal de Justicia de las Comunidades Europeas, Tribunal de Justicia de la Unión Europea** European Court of Justice ▸ **Tribunal de la Haya** International Court of Justice ▸ **tribunal de primera instancia** court of first instance ▸ **Tribunal Internacional de Justicia** International Court of Justice ▸ **tribunal popular** jury ▸ **Tribunal Supremo** High Court, Supreme Court (*EEUU*) ▸ **tribunal (tutelar) de menores** juvenile court
2 (*Univ*) (= *examinadores*) board of examiners
3 (*Pol*) (= *comisión investigadora*) tribunal
4 (*Cono Sur*) (*Mil*) court martial

TRIBUNAL CONSTITUCIONAL

The role of the Spanish **Tribunal Constitucional** is to see that the 1978 Constitution is adhered to by the organs of government. It has jurisdiction in conflicts of power between the Spanish State and the **Comunidades Autónomas** and between the Autonomous Communities themselves, and it also has powers to safeguard the basic rights of citizens. It consists of 12 members, four nominated by Congress and by Senate, two by the Government and two by the governing body of the Spanish judiciary, the **Consejo General del Poder Judicial**.
▷ **LA CONSTITUCIÓN ESPAÑOLA**

tribuno SM tribune
tributación SF **1** (= *pago*) payment
2 (= *impuesto*) taxation ▸ **tributación directa** direct taxation
tributar ▷ CONJUG 1a VT **1** (*Econ*) to pay
2 [+ *homenaje, respeto etc*] to pay; [+ *gracias, recibimiento*] to give; [+ *afecto etc*] to have, show (**a** for)
VI (= *pagar impuestos*) to pay taxes

tributario ADJ **1** (*Geog, Pol*) tributary (*antes de s*)
2 (*Econ*) tax, taxation (*antes de s*) • **sistema ~** tax system • **privilegio ~** tax concession
SM tributary

tributo SM **1** (= *homenaje*) tribute • **rendir ~** to pay tribute
2 (*Econ*) (= *impuesto*) tax

tricampeón/ona SM/F triple champion, three-times champion

tricentenario SM tercentenary

tricentésimo ADJ three hundredth

tríceps SM (PL: **tríceps**) triceps

trichina SF (*LAm*) trichina

triciclo SM tricycle

tricófero SM (*And, Cono Sur, Méx*) hair restorer

tricola SF (*Cono Sur*) knitted waistcoat

tricolor ADJ tricolour, tricolor (*EEUU*), three-coloured, three-colored (*EEUU*) • **bandera ~** tricolour
SF tricolour

tricornio SM tricorn, three-cornered hat

tricota SF (*LAm*) heavy knitted sweater

tricotar ▹ CONJUG 1a VT to knit • **tricotado a mano** hand-knitted
VI to knit

tricotosa SF knitting machine

tridente SM trident

tridentino ADJ Tridentine, of Trent • **Concilio Tridentino** Council of Trent • **misa tridentina** Tridentine Mass

tridimensional ADJ three-dimensional

trienal ADJ triennial

trienalmente ADV triennially

trienio SM **1** (= *periodo*) period of three years, triennium (*frm*)
2 (= *pago*) *monthly bonus for each three-year period worked with the same employer*

trifásico ADJ (*Elec*) three-phase, triphase
SM • **tener ~*** to have pull, have influence

triforio SM (*Rel*) triforium, clerestory

trifulca* SF row, shindy*

trifulquero* ADJ rowdy, trouble-making

trifurcación SF trifurcation

trifurcarse ▹ CONJUG 1g VPR to divide into three

trigal SM wheat field

trigésimo ADJ thirtieth; ▹ **sexto**

trigo SM **1** (= *cereal*) wheat • **de ~ entero** wholemeal • MODISMO: • **no ser ~ limpio** to be dishonest • **no todo era ~ limpio** it wasn't completely above board, it was a bit fishy*
▸ **trigo blando** soft wheat ▸ **trigo candeal** bread wheat ▸ **trigo duro** hard wheat, durum wheat ▸ **trigo sarraceno** buckwheat
2 trigos (= *campo*) wheat (*sing*), wheat field(s) • MODISMO: • **meterse en ~s ajenos** to meddle in somebody else's affairs
3‡ (= *dinero*) dough*, money

trigonometría SF trigonometry

trigonométrico ADJ trigonometric(al)

trigueño/a ADJ [*cabello*] dark blond, corn-coloured; [*rostro*] olive-skinned, golden-brown; (*LAm*) (*euf*) dark-skinned

triguero/a ADJ wheat (*antes de s*); ▹ **espárrago**
SM/F (= *comerciante*) corn merchant
SM (= *tamiz*) corn sieve

trila SF, **triles** SMPL (game of) "find the lady"

trilateral ADJ, **trilátero** ADJ trilateral, three-sided

trilero SM card-sharp

trilingüe ADJ trilingual

trilita SF trinitrotoluene

trilla SF **1** (*Agr*) threshing
2 (*Caribe, Cono Sur*) (= *paliza*) thrashing, beating
3 (*Méx*) (= *senda*) track
4 (*Caribe*) (= *atajo*) short cut

trillado ADJ **1** (*Agr*) threshed
2 [*camino*] well-trodden
3 [*tema*] (= *gastado*) well-worn, hackneyed; (= *conocido*) well-known
SM **1** (= *investigación*) thorough investigation
2 (*Caribe*) (= *sendero*) path, track

trillador SM thresher

trilladora SF threshing machine

trilladura SF threshing

trillar ▹ CONJUG 1a VT **1** (*Agr*) to thresh
2 [+ *tema etc*] to overuse

trillizo/a SM/F triplet

trillo SM **1** (= *máquina*) threshing machine
2 (*CAm, Caribe*) (= *sendero*) path, track

trillón SM trillion, quintillion (*EEUU*)

trilogía SF trilogy

trimarán SM trimaran

trimestral ADJ quarterly, three-monthly; (*Univ*) term (*antes de s*)

trimestralmente ADV quarterly, every three months

trimestre SM **1** (= *periodo*) (*gen*) quarter, period of three months; (*Univ*) term
2 (*Econ*) (= *pago*) quarterly payment; (= *alquiler*) quarter's rent

trinado SM (*Orn*) song, warble; (*Mús*) trill

trinar ▹ CONJUG 1a VI **1** (*Orn*) to sing, warble, trill; (*Mús*) to trill
2* (= *enfadarse*) to fume, be angry; (*Cono Sur*) (= *gritar*) to shout • **está que trina** he's hopping mad*

trinca SF **1** (= *tres*) group of three, set of three, threesome
2 (*And, Cono Sur*) (= *pandilla*) band, gang; (= *facción*) faction; (= *complot*) plot, conspiracy
3 (*Cono Sur*) (= *canicas*) marbles (*pl*)
4 (*Caribe, Méx*) (= *embriaguez*) drunkenness; ▹ **trinco**

trincar¹ ▹ CONJUG 1g VT **1** (= *atar*) to tie up, bind; (*Náut*) to lash
2 (= *inmovilizar*) to pinion, hold by the arms
3* (= *detener*) to nick*
4‡ (= *matar*) to do in*
5**‡ (= *copular*) to screw**‡
6 (*CAm, Cono Sur, Méx*) (= *exprimir*) to squeeze, press
7 (*Cono Sur**) • **me trinca que ...** I have a hunch that ...
VPR **trincarse** (*CAm, Méx*) • **~se a hacer algo** to start to do sth *o* doing sth, set about doing sth

trincar² ▹ CONJUG 1g VT **1** (= *romper*) to break up
2 (= *cortar*) [+ *carne*] to chop up; [+ *papel*] to tear up

trincar³* ▹ CONJUG 1g VT, VI (= *beber*) to drink
VPR **trincarse** (*Caribe, Méx*) to get drunk

trinchador SM carving knife, carver

trinchante SM **1** (= *cuchillo*) carving knife, carver; (= *tenedor*) meat fork, carving-fork
2 (= *mueble*) side table; (*Cono Sur*) sideboard

trinchar ▹ CONJUG 1a VT **1** (= *cortar*) to carve, cut up
2‡ (= *matar*) to do in*

trinche SM **1** (*LAm*) (= *tenedor*) fork
2 (*And, Cono Sur, Méx*) (= *mueble*) side table
3 (*Méx*) (*Agr*) pitchfork
ADJ • **pelo ~** (*And*) frizzy hair

trinchera SF **1** (= *zanja*) ditch; (*Mil*) trench; (*Ferro*) cutting • **guerra de ~s** trench warfare
2 (= *abrigo*) trench coat
3 (*LAm*) (= *cercado*) fence, stockade
4 (*Méx*) (= *cuchillo*) curved knife

trinchete SM shoemaker's knife; (*And*) table knife

trincho SM (*And*) (= *parapeto*) parapet; (= *zanja*) trench, ditch

trinco/a SM/F (*Caribe, Méx*) drunkard; ▹ **trinca**

trincón‡ ADJ murderous

trineo SM (*pequeño*) sledge, sled (*EEUU*); (*grande*) sleigh ▸ **trineo de balancín** bobsleigh ▸ **trineo de perros** dog sleigh

Trini SF *forma familiar de* **Trinidad**

Trinidad SF **1** (*Rel*) Trinity
2 (*Geog*) Trinidad ▸ **Trinidad y Tobago** Trinidad and Tobago

trinidad SF trio, set of three

trinitaria SF [*de jardín*] pansy; (*silvestre*) heart's-ease

trinitrotolueno SM trinitrotoluene

trino SM (*Orn*) warble, trill; (*Mús*) trill

trinomio ADJ, SM trinomial

trinque* SM liquor, booze*

trinquetada SF (*Caribe*) period of danger; (*And, Méx*) hard times

trinquete¹ SM (*Mec*) pawl, catch; [*de rueda dentada*] ratchet

trinquete² SM **1** (*Náut*) (= *palo*) foremast; (= *vela*) foresail
2 (*Dep*) pelota court

trinquete³ SM (*Méx*) **1** (= *soborno*) bribe; (= *asunto turbio*) shady deal*, corrupt affair
2 • **es un ~ de hombre*** he really is a tough customer
3 (*And*) (= *habitación*) small room

trinquis* SM INV drink, swig*
ADJ (*Méx*) drunk, sloshed*

trío SM trio

tripa SF, **tripas** SFPL **1** (= *intestino*) intestine, gut; (= *vísceras*) guts*, insides*, innards* • **me duele la ~** I have a stomach ache • **quitar las ~s a un pez** to gut a fish • **le gruñían las ~s** his tummy was rumbling* • MODISMOS: • **hacer de ~s corazón** to pluck up courage • **echar las ~s** (= *vomitar*) to retch, vomit violently • **tener malas ~s** to be cruel • **revolver las ~s algn** to turn sb's stomach • **¡te sacaré las ~s!** I'll tear you apart!, I'll rip your guts out!‡
2* (= *barriga*) **a** (*gen*) belly, tummy* • **echar ~** to put on weight, start to get a paunch • **tener mucha ~** to be fat, have a paunch • **llenar la ~ a costa de otro** to eat well at somebody else's expense
b (*Esp*) [*de mujer encinta*] bulge • **dejar a una chica con ~**† to get a girl in the family way • **estar con ~** to be in the family way
3 [*de fruta*] core, seeds (*pl*)
4 • **las ~s*** (= *mecanismo*) the insides*, the works; (= *piezas*) the parts • **sacar las ~s de un reloj** to take out the works of a watch
5 [*de vasija*] belly, bulge
6 (*Com, Jur etc*) (= *expediente*) file, dossier
7 (*Caribe*) [*de neumático*] inner tube

tripartito ADJ tripartite

tripe SM shag

tripear* ▹ CONJUG 1a VI to stuff o.s.*

tripería SM (*And, Méx*) guts (*pl*), entrails (*pl*)

tripero* ADJ greedy

tripi‡ SM LSD, dose of LSD

tripicallos SMPL (*Esp*) (*Culin*) tripe (*sing*)

tripitir ▹ CONJUG 3a VT to repeat again, do a third time

triple ADJ triple; (*de tres capas*) with three layers • **~ salto** triple jump
SM **1** • **el ~: es el ~ de lo que era** it is three times what it was *o* as big as it was • **su casa es el ~ de grande que la nuestra** their house is three times bigger than *o* as big as ours
2 (*Dep*) (= *salto*) triple jump; (*en baloncesto*) three-point basket
SF ▸ **triple vírica** triple vaccine
ADV* • **esta cuerda es ~ gruesa que esa** this string is three times thicker than that one

tripleta SF trio, threesome

triplicado ADJ triplicate • **por ~** in triplicate

triplicar ▸ CONJUG 1g VT to treble, triple • **las pérdidas triplican las ganancias** losses are three times bigger *o* more than the profits
VPR **triplicarse** to treble, triple

triplo SM = **triple**

trípode SM tripod

Trípoli SM Tripoli

tripón/ona* ADJ fat, potbellied
SM/F (*Méx*) little boy, little girl • **los tripones** the kids*

tríptico SM **1** (*Arte*) triptych
2 (= *formulario*) form in three parts; (= *documento*) three-part document; (= *folleto*) three-page leaflet

triptongo SM triphthong

tripudo ADJ fat, potbellied

tripulación SF crew

tripulado ADJ • **vuelo ~** manned flight • **vuelo no ~** unmanned flight • **~ por** manned by, crewed by

tripulante SMF [*de barco, avión*] crew member; **tripulantes** crew (*sing*)

tripular ▸ CONJUG 1a VT **1** [+ *barco, avión*] to crew
2 (*Aut etc*) to drive
3 (*Cono Sur*) to mix (up)

tripulina* SF (*Cono Sur*) row, brawl

trique SM **1** (= *ruido*) crack, sharp noise, swish
2 • **a cada ~** at every moment, repeatedly
3 (*And, Méx*) (= *truco*) trick, dodge
4 triques (*Méx**) things, gear (*sing*), odds and ends; (*And, CAm*) (= *juego*) noughts and crosses, tic tac toe (*EEUU*)

triquina SF trichina

triquinosis SF INV trichinosis

triquiñuela SF trick, dodge • **saber las ~s del oficio** to know the tricks of the trade, know all the dodges • **es un tío ~s*** he's an artful old cuss*

triquis SMPL (*Méx*) = **trique**

triquitraque SM string of fire crackers

trirreactor SM tri-jet

trirreme SM trireme

tris SM INV **1** (= *estallido*) crack; (*al rasgarse*) rip, tearing noise
2 • MODISMOS: • **en un ~** in a trice • **recogimos la mesa en un ~** we cleared the table in no time • **está en un ~** it's touch and go • **estar en un ~ de hacer algo** to be within an inch of doing sth • **estuvo en un ~ que lo perdiera** he very nearly lost it, he was within an inch of losing it • **por un ~**: • **los dos coches evitaron el choque por un ~** the two cars avoided a collision by a hair's breadth
3 (*LAm*) (= *juego*) noughts and crosses (*pl*), tic tac toe (*EEUU*)

trisar ▸ CONJUG 1a VT (*And, Cono Sur*) (= *rajar*) to crack; (= *desportillar*) to chip

trisca SF **1** (= *crujido*) crunch, crushing noise
2 (= *bulla*) uproar, rumpus, row
3 (*Caribe*) (= *mofa*) mockery; (= *chiste*) private joke

triscar ▸ CONJUG 1g VT **1** (= *enredar*) to mix, mingle; (= *confundir*) to mix up
2 [+ *sierra*] to set
3 (*And, Caribe*) (= *mofar*) to mock, joke about; (= *tomar el pelo*) to tease
VI **1** (= *patalear*) to stamp (about)
2 [*corderos etc*] to gambol, frisk about; [*personas*] to romp, play about

triscón ADJ (*And*) hypercritical, overcritical

trisecar ▸ CONJUG 1g VT to trisect

trisemanal ADJ triweekly

trisemanalmente ADV triweekly, thrice weekly

trisilábico ADJ trisyllabic, three-syllable (*antes de s*), three-syllabled

trisílabo ADJ trisyllabic, three-syllable (*antes de s*), three-syllabled
SM trisyllable

trisito SM (*And*) (= *pizca*) pinch; (= *pedacito*) scrap, piece

trismo SM lockjaw

Tristán SM Tristram, Tristan

triste ADJ **1** (= *entristecido*) [*persona*] sad; (= *desgraciado*) miserable; [*carácter*] gloomy, melancholy • **poner ~ a algn** to make sb sad, make sb unhappy, make sb miserable • **me puse muy ~ cuando me enteré de la noticia** I was very sad when I heard the news
2 (= *entristecedor*) [*noticia, canción*] sad; [*paisaje*] dismal, desolate; [*cuarto*] gloomy
3* (= *mustio*) [*flor*] withered
4 (= *lamentable*) sad, sorry • **es ~ verle así** it is sad to see him like that • **es ~ no poder ir** it's a pity *o* shame we can't go • **hizo un ~ papel** he cut a sorry figure • **la ~ verdad es que ...** the sad truth is that ...
5 (= *insignificante*) miserable • **no queda sino un ~ penique** there's just one miserable penny left • **me dieron un ~ trozo de pan para comer** they gave me a miserable piece of bread for lunch
6 (*And*) (= *tímido*) shy, timid
SM (*LAm*) (= *canción*) sad love song

tristemente ADV sadly • **el ~ famoso lugar** the sadly notorious *o* well-known place

tristeza SF **1** [*de persona*] sadness, sorrow
2 (*Bot*) tree virus
3 tristezas (= *sucesos*) unhappy events; (= *noticias*) sad news (*sing*)

tristón ADJ (= *triste*) sad, downhearted; (= *pesimista*) pessimistic, gloomy; (= *depresivo*) given to melancholy

tristura SF (*esp LAm*) = **tristeza**

Tritón SM Triton

tritón SM (*Zool*) newt

trituración SF, **triturado** SM grinding, crushing, trituration (*frm*)

triturador SM, **trituradora** SF (*Téc*) grinder, crushing machine; (*Culin*) mincer, mincing machine ▸ **triturador de basuras** waste-disposal unit ▸ **triturador (de papel)** shredder

triturar ▸ CONJUG 1a VT to grind, crush, triturate (*frm*)

triunfador(a) ADJ [*ejército*] triumphant, victorious; [*equipo, concursante*] winning, victorious
SM/F winner • **es un ~ nato** he's a born winner

triunfal ADJ **1** [*arco, marcha*] triumphal
2 [*grito, sonrisa, recibimiento*] triumphant • **el presidente hizo su entrada ~** the President made his triumphant entrance • **el equipo hizo su entrada ~ en la ciudad** the team entered the city in triumph

triunfalismo SM **1** [*de persona*] (= *optimismo*) euphoria, excessive optimism; (= *petulancia*) smugness, over-confidence, triumphalism • **lo digo sin ~s** I say it without wishing to gloat
2 [*de país*] jingoism

triunfalista ADJ **1** [*persona*] (= *optimista*) euphoric, excessively optimistic; (= *petulante*) smug, over-confident, triumphalist
2 [*país, declaraciones*] jingoistic

triunfalmente ADV triumphantly

triunfante ADJ **1** (= *victorioso*) triumphant • **salir ~** to come out the winner, emerge victorious
2 (= *jubiloso*) jubilant, exultant

triunfar ▸ CONJUG 1a VI **1** (= *ganar, vencer*) to triumph, win • **los socialistas ~on en las elecciones** the socialists triumphed in *o* won the elections • **~ en un concurso** to win a competition • **~ sobre los enemigos** to triumph over one's enemies • **la razón ha triunfado sobre la ignorancia** reason has triumphed over ignorance • **al final triunfó el amor** in the end love conquered all
2 (= *tener éxito*) to be successful, succeed • **ha triunfado en su profesión** she has been successful in her profession • **~ en la vida** to succeed *o* be successful in life
3 (*Naipes*) [*jugador*] to play a trump • **triunfan corazones** hearts are trumps

triunfo SM **1** (= *victoria*) win, victory; (= *éxito*) victory, success • **fue el sexto ~ consecutivo del equipo** it was the team's sixth consecutive win *o* victory • **ha sido un verdadero ~** it has been a real triumph *o* victory • **adjudicarse el ~** to win • MODISMO: • **costar un ~** to be a huge effort • **sacarme la carrera me ha costado un ~** getting a degree has been a huge effort
2 (*Naipes*) trump • **seis sin ~s** six no-trumps • **palo del ~** trump suit • MODISMO: • **tener todos los ~s en la mano** to hold all the trump-cards
3 (= *trofeo*) trophy

triunvirato SM triumvirate

trivial ADJ trivial, trite

trivialidad SF **1** (= *cualidad*) triviality, triteness
2 (= *asunto*) trivial matter; (= *dicho*) trite remark • **~es** trivia, trivialities • **decir ~es** to talk in platitudes

trivialización SF trivializing, minimizing (the importance of), playing-down

trivializar ▸ CONJUG 1f VT to trivialize, minimize (the importance of), play down

trivialmente ADV trivially, tritely

triza SF bit, shred • **hacer algo ~s** (= *rasgar*) to tear sth to shreds; (= *hacer pedazos*) to smash sth to bits • **los críticos hicieron ~s la obra** the critics pulled the play to pieces, the critics tore the play to shreds • **hacer ~s a algn** (= *cansar*) to wear sb out; (= *aplastar*) to flatten sb, crush sb • **estar hecho ~s** [*persona*] to be shattered*

trizar ▸ CONJUG 1f VT (= *rasgar*) to tear to shreds; (= *hacer pedazos*) to smash to bits

troca SF (*Méx*) lorry, truck

trocaico ADJ trochaic

trocar ▸ CONJUG 1g, 1l VT **1** (= *canjear*) barter, to exchange
2 (= *cambiar*) to change • **~ la alegría en tristeza** to change gaiety into sadness
3 (*Cono Sur*) (= *vender*) to sell; (*And*) (= *comprar*) to buy
4 (= *confundir*) to mix up, confuse
5 [+ *comida*] to vomit
VPR **trocarse 1** (= *transformarse*) • **~se en** become, turn into • **las víctimas se ~on en verdugos** the victims became executioners
2 (= *confundirse*) to get mixed up

trocear ▸ CONJUG 1a VT to cut up, cut into pieces

trocha SF **1** (= *senda*) narrow path; (= *atajo*) short cut
2 (*LAm*) (*Ferro*) gauge, gage (*EEUU*) ▸ **trocha normal** standard gauge
3 (*Cono Sur*) (*Aut*) (= *carril*) lane
4 (*And*) (= *trote*) trot
5 (*And*) (= *porción*) portion, helping (*of meat*)

trochar ▸ CONJUG 1a VI (*And*) to trot

troche • **a ~ y moche** ADV [*correr*] helter-skelter, pell-mell; [*desparramar*] all over the place; [*distribuir*] haphazardly • **gastar dinero a ~ y moche** to spend money like water

trochemoche • **a ~** ADV ▸ **troche**

trofeo SM **1** (= *copa*) trophy
2 (= *victoria*) victory, triumph
troglodita SMF **1** (= *cavernícola*) cave dweller, troglodyte
2 (= *bruto*) brute, oaf; (= *huraño*) unsociable individual, recluse
3* (= *glotón*) glutton
troica SF troika
troja SF (*LAm*) granary, barn
troje SF, **troj** SF granary, barn
trol SM **1** (= *duende*) troll
2 (*Internet*) troll
trola[1]* SF fib, lie
trola[2] SF (*And*) (= *jamón*) slice of ham; (= *cuero*) piece of raw hide; (= *corteza*) piece of loose bark
trole SM **1** (*Elec*) trolley, cart (*EEUU*), trolley pole
2†* (= *autobús*) trolley bus
trolear ▸ CONJUG 1a VT (*Internet*) to troll
trolebús SM trolley bus
troleo SM (*Internet*) trolling
trolero/a* SM/F fibber, liar
tromba SF whirlwind • **pasar como una ~** to go by like a whirlwind • **entrar en ~** to come in in a torrent, come rushing in ▸ **tromba de agua** violent downpour ▸ **tromba de polvo** column of dust ▸ **tromba marina** waterspout ▸ **tromba terrestre** whirlwind, tornado
trombo SM clot, thrombus (*frm*)
trombón SM (= *instrumento*) trombone ▸ **trombón de varas** slide trombone
SMF (= *músico*) trombonist
trombonista SMF trombonist
trombosis SF INV thrombosis ▸ **trombosis cerebral** brain haemorrhage, cerebral haemorrhage
trome* ADJ (*And*) bright, smart
trompa SF **1** (*Mús*) horn • MODISMO: • **sonar la ~ marcial** to sound a warlike note ▸ **trompa de caza** hunting horn
2 (= *juguete*) spinning top
3 (*Zool*) [*de elefante*] trunk; [*de insecto*] proboscis
4* (= *nariz*) snout‡, hooter‡; (*LAm*) (= *labios*) thick lips (*pl*), blubber lips (*pl*) • **¡cierra la ~!** (*CAm, Méx*‡) shut your trap!‡
5 (*Anat*) tube, duct • **ligadura de ~s** tubal ligation ▸ **trompa de Eustaquio** Eustachian tube ▸ **trompa de Falopio** Fallopian tube
6 (*Meteo*) = **tromba**
7* (= *borrachera*) • **cogerse** *o* **agarrarse una ~** to get tight*
8 (*Méx*) (*Ferro*) cowcatcher
SMF **1** (*Mús*) horn player
2 (*Cono Sur**) (= *patrón*) boss, chief
ADJ * • **estar ~** to be tight*
trompazo SM, **trompada** SF **1** (= *choque*) bump, bang
2 (= *puñetazo*) punch, swipe
3 (*Méx*) (= *zurra*) thrashing, beating-up*
trompeadura SF (*LAm*) **1** (= *choques*) bumping, banging
2 (= *puñetazos*) series of punches; (= *paliza*) beating-up*
trompear ▸ CONJUG 1a (*LAm*) VT to punch, thump
VPR **trompearse** to fight
trompeta SF **1** (*Mús*) (= *instrumento*) trumpet; (*fig*) clarion
2‡ (= *droga*) reefer*, joint*
3 (*Cono Sur*) (*Bot*) daffodil
SMF (*Mús*) trumpet player; (*Mil*) trumpeter
SM (= *imbécil*) twit*; (= *borracho*) drunk*, old soak*
ADJ (*Méx**) (= *borracho*) sloshed*, tight*
trompetazo SM (*Mús*) trumpet blast; (*fig*) blast, blare
trompetear ▸ CONJUG 1a VI to play the trumpet
trompeteo SM sound of trumpets
trompetero/a SM/F [*de orquesta*] trumpet player; (*Mil*) trumpeter
trompetilla SF **1** (*tb* **trompetilla acústica**) ear trumpet
2 (*Caribe**) (= *ruido*) raspberry*
trompetista SMF trumpet player
trompeto* ADJ (*Méx*) drunk
trompezar ▸ CONJUG 1f VI (*LAm*) = **tropezar**
trompezón SM (*LAm*) = **tropezón**
trompicar ▸ CONJUG 1g VT (= *hacer tropezar*) to trip up
VI (= *tropezarse*) to trip
trompicón SM **1** (= *tropiezo*) trip, stumble • MODISMO: • **a trompicones** in fits and starts
2 (*Caribe*) (= *puñetazo*) blow, punch
trompis* SM INV punch, bash*
trompiza* SF (*And, Méx*) punch-up‡
trompo SM **1** (= *juguete*) spinning top • MODISMO: • **ponerse como un ~*** to stuff o.s.*, eat to bursting point ▸ **trompo de música** humming top
2 (*Aut*) 180 degree turn or skid
3 (*Dep*) spin
4 (*LAm*) (= *desmañado*) clumsy person; (= *bailador*) rotten dancer*
5 (*Esp*‡) (= *dinero*) 1000-peseta note
trompón SM **1*** (= *choque*) bump, bang
2 (= *puñetazo*) hefty punch, vicious swipe
3 (*Bot*) (*tb* **narciso trompón**) daffodil
trompudo ADJ (*LAm*) thick-lipped, blubber-lipped
tron‡ SM = **tronco**[2]
trona SF high chair
tronada SF, **tronadera** SF (*Méx*) thunderstorm
tronado ADJ **1** (= *viejo*) old, useless
2* • **estar ~** (= *loco*) to be potty*; (*LAm*) (= *drogado*) to be high (on drugs)*; (*CAm*) (= *sin dinero*) to be broke*
tronadura SF (*Chile*) (*Min*) blasting
tronamenta SF (*And, Méx*) thunderstorm
tronar ▸ CONJUG 1l VI **1** (*Meteo*) to thunder • MODISMO: • **por lo que pueda ~** just in case, to be on the safe side
2 [*cañones etc*] to boom, thunder
3* (= *enfurecerse*) to rave, rage • **~ contra** to spout forth against, rage *o* thunder against
4* (= *reñir*) • **~ con algn** to fall out with sb
5* (= *arruinarse*) to go broke*; (= *fracasar*) to fail, be ruined
VT **1** (*CAm, Méx**) (= *fusilar*) to shoot
2 • **la tronó** (*Méx**) he blew it*, he messed it up
VPR **tronarse*** **1** (*CAm, Méx*) (= *matarse*) to shoot o.s., blow one's brains out
2 (*LAm*) (= *drogarse*) to take drugs
tronazón SF (*CAm, Méx*) thunderstorm
troncal ADJ • **línea ~** main (trunk) line • **materia ~** core subject
troncar ▸ CONJUG 1g VT = **truncar**
troncha SF **1** (*LAm**) (= *tajada*) slice; (= *pedazo*) piece, chunk
2 (*LAm**) (= *prebenda*) sinecure, soft job
3 (*Méx*) (= *comida*) [*de soldado*] soldier's rations (*pl*); (*escasa*) meagre meal
tronchacadenas SM INV chain cutters (*pl*)
tronchado SM (*Méx*) (= *buen negocio*) gold mine; (= *negocio próspero*) prosperous business
ADJ (*And*) (= *lisiado*) maimed, crippled
tronchante* ADJ hilarious, killingly funny
tronchar ▸ CONJUG 1a VT **1** (= *talar*) to fell, chop down; (= *cortar*) to cut up, cut off; (= *hender*) to split, crack, shatter
2 [*+ vida*] to cut short; [*+ esperanzas*] to dash
3* (= *cansar*) to tire out
VPR **troncharse 1*** (*tb* **troncharse de risa**) to split one's sides laughing
2 [*árbol*] to fall down, split
3* (= *cansarse*) to tire o.s. out
troncho SM **1** (*Bot*) stem, stalk
2 (*Cono Sur*) (= *trozo*) piece, chunk
3 (*And*) (= *enredo*) knot, tangle
4‡* (= *pene*) prick‡*
ADJ (*Cono Sur*) maimed, crippled
tronco[1] SM **1** [*de árbol*] trunk; (= *leño*) log • MODISMO: • **dormir como un ~** to sleep like a log ▸ **tronco de Navidad** (*Culin*) yule log
2 (*Anat*) trunk
3 (= *estirpe*) stock
4 (*Ferro*) main line, trunk line
5‡* (= *pene*) prick‡*
tronco[2]**/a**‡ SM/F **1** (= *tío*) bloke*/bird* • **María y su ~** María and her bloke*
2 (= *amigo*) (*en oración directa*) mate*, pal* • **—oye, ~** "hey, man"*
tronera SF **1** (*Mil*) (= *aspillera*) loophole, embrasure; (*Arquit*) small window
2 (*Billar*) pocket
3 (*Méx*) (= *chimenea*) chimney, flue
SMF* (= *tarambana*) harebrained person
SM* (= *libertino*) rake, libertine
tronido SM **1** (*Meteo*) thunderclap • **~s** thunder (*sing*), booming (*sing*)
2 (= *explosión*) loud report, bang, detonation
tronío SM lavish expenditure, extravagance
trono SM **1** [*de monarca*] (= *asiento*) throne; (= *símbolo*) crown • **heredar el ~** to inherit the crown • **nuestra lealtad al ~** our loyalty to the crown • **subir al ~** to ascend the throne, come to the throne
2 [*de campeón*] crown
tronquista SMF (*LAm*) lorry driver, truck driver (*EEUU*)
tronzar ▸ CONJUG 1f VT **1** (= *cortar*) to cut up; (= *romper*) to split, rend, smash
2 (*Cos*) to pleat
3* [*+ persona*] to tire out
tropa SF **1** (*Mil*) (= *soldados rasos*) rank and file, ordinary soldiers (*pl*); (= *ejército*) army • **las ~s** the troops • **ser de ~** to be in the army ▸ **tropas de asalto, tropa de choque** storm troops
2 (= *multitud*) crowd, troop; (*pey*) mob, troop
3 (*LAm*) (*Agr*) flock, herd
4 (*Cono Sur*) (= *vehículos*) stream of vehicles; (= *coches*) line of cars; (= *carros*) line of carts
5 (*Méx*) (= *maleducado*) rude person; (*Caribe**) (= *tonto*) dope*
tropear ▸ CONJUG 1a VT (*Arg*) to herd
tropecientos* ADJ PL umpteen*
tropel SM **1** (= *gentío*) mob, crowd • **acudir en ~** to crowd in, come in en masse
2 (= *revoltijo*) mess, jumble
3 (= *prisa*) rush, haste
tropelía SF outrage, violent act • **cometer una ~** to commit an outrage
tropero SM **1** (*Arg*) (*Agr*) cowboy, cattle drover
2 (*Méx*) boor
tropezar ▸ CONJUG 1f, 1j VI **1** (*con los pies*) to trip, stumble • **tropezó y por poco se cae** he tripped *o* stumbled and nearly fell • **¡cuidado, no tropieces!** mind you don't trip up! • **ha tropezado con una piedra** she tripped on a stone • **he tropezado con el escalón** I tripped on the step
2 (= *chocar*) • **~ con** *o* **contra algo** to bump into sth • **~ con** *o* **contra un árbol** to bump into a tree
3 (= *enfrentarse*) • **~ con algo** to run into sth, encounter sth • **tropezamos con una dificultad** we ran into *o* encountered a difficulty • **tropezó con muchos obstáculos durante su carrera política** she came up against *o* encountered numerous obstacles in her political career
4 (= *encontrarse*) • **~ con algn** to bump into sb, run into sb • **he tropezado con María en la**

facultad I bumped *o* ran into María in the department
5 (= *reñir*) • **~ con algn** to have an argument with sb
6 (= *cometer un error*) to err, make a mistake • **ha tropezado muchas veces en la vida** she has erred many times *o* made many mistakes in her life
VPR **tropezarse** [*dos personas*] to bump *o* run into each other • **nos tropezamos casi cada día por la calle** we bump *o* run into each other practically every day in the street • **~se con algn** to bump *o* run into sb • **me tropecé con Juan en el banco** I bumped *o* ran into Juan at the bank

tropezón SM **1** (= *traspié*) trip, stumble • **dar un ~** to trip, stumble • **hablar a tropezones** to speak jerkily, speak falteringly • **proceder a ~es** to proceed by fits and starts
2 (= *equivocación*) slip, blunder; (*moral*) lapse
3 tropezones (*Culin*) *small pieces of food added to soup*

tropical ADJ **1** (= *del trópico*) tropical
2 (*Cono Sur*) (= *melodramático*) rhetorical, melodramatic, highly-coloured

tropicalismo SM (*Cono Sur*) rhetoric, melodramatic style, excessive colourfulness

trópico SM **1** (*Geog*) tropic • **los ~s** the tropics ▸ **trópico de Cáncer** Tropic of Cancer ▸ **trópico de Capricornio** Tropic of Capricorn
2 trópicos (*Caribe*) (= *dificultades*) hardships, difficulties • MODISMO: • **pasar los ~s** to suffer hardships, have a hard time

tropiezo SM **1** (= *error*) slip, blunder; (*moral*) moral lapse
2 (= *revés*) (*gen*) setback; (*en el amor*) disappointment in love
3 (= *desgracia*) misfortune, mishap
4 (= *disputa*) argument, quarrel

tropilla SF (*Cono Sur*) drove, team

tropo SM trope

troquel SM die

troquelado SM die cut

troquelar ▹ CONJUG 1a VT **1** [+ *cuero, cartón*] to die-cut; [+ *moneda, medalla*] to strike; [+ *metal*] to die-cast
2 (= *perforar*) to punch

troqueo SM trochee

trosco/a* SM/F Trot*, Trotskyist

trotacalles* SMF INV bum*

trotaconventos SF INV go-between, procuress

trotamundos SMF INV globetrotter

trotar ▹ CONJUG 1a VI **1** [*caballo*] to trot
2* (= *viajar*) to travel about, chase around here and there

trote SM **1** [*de caballo*] trot • **ir al ~** to trot, go at a trot • **irse al ~** to go off in a hurry • **tomar el ~** to dash off
2* (= *uso*) • **de mucho ~** hard-wearing, tough • **chaqueta para todo ~** a jacket for everyday wear
3* (= *ajetreo*) bustle • **el abuelo ya no está para esos ~s** grandad is not up to that sort of thing any more

trotskismo SM Trotskyism

trotskista ADJ, SMF Trotskyist

trova SF ballad

trovador SM troubadour

Troya SF Troy • MODISMOS: • **¡aquí fue ~!** you should have heard the fuss! • **¡arda ~!** press on regardless!, never mind the consequences!

troyano/a ADJ, SM/F Trojan
SM (*Inform*) Trojan horse

troza SF log

trozar ▹ CONJUG 1f VT (*LAm*) to cut up, cut into pieces

trozo SM **1** (= *pedazo*) piece, bit • **un ~ de madera** a piece of wood • **a ~s** in bits • **cortado a ~s** cut into pieces • **vi la película a ~s** I only saw bits of the film • MODISMO: • **es un ~ de pan*** he's a dear, he's a sweetie*
2 (*Literat, Mús*) passage • **~s escogidos** selected passages, selections

trucado ADJ **1** [*baraja*] rigged
2 [*motor*] souped-up

trucaje SM **1** (*Cine*) trick photography
2 (*en el juego*) rigging, fixing

trucar* ▹ CONJUG 1g VT **1** [+ *resultado*] to fix, rig; [+ *baraja*] to tamper with • **las cartas estaban trucadas** (*fig*) the dice were loaded against us
2 (*Aut*) [+ *motor*] to soup up*
VI (*Billar*) to pot the ball, pot

trucha[1] SF **1** (= *pez*) trout ▸ **trucha arco iris** rainbow trout ▸ **trucha marina** sea trout
2 (*Téc*) crane, derrick

trucha[2] SF (*CAm*) (*Com*) (= *puesto*) stall, booth

trucha[3]* SMF (= *persona*) (= *taimado*) tricky individual, wily bird; (= *tramposo*) cheat

truche‡ SM (*And*) snappy dresser*, dude (*EEUU**)

truchero[1]/a SM/F (*CAm*) hawker, vendor

truchero[2] ADJ trout (*antes de s*) • **río ~** trout river

truchimán SM **1** (*Hist*) interpreter
2* rogue, villain

trucho ADJ (*And*) sharp, rascally

truco SM **1** (= *ardid*) trick, dodge; (*Cine*) trick effect, piece of trick photography • **el tío tiene muchos ~s** the fellow is up to all the tricks in the book • **coger el ~ a algn** to see how sb works a trick, catch on to sb's little game • **arte de los ~s** conjuring ▸ **truco de naipes** card trick ▸ **truco publicitario** advertising gimmick
2 (= *habilidad*) knack • **coger el ~** to get the knack, get the hang of it, catch on
3 (*And, Cono Sur*) (= *puñetazo*) punch, bash*
4 (*Cono Sur*) (*Naipes*) *popular card game*
5 trucos (*Billar*) billiards (*sing*), pool (*sing*)

truculencia SF gruesomeness

truculento ADJ gruesome, horrifying

trueco SM = **trueque**

trueno SM **1** (*Meteo*) • **un ~** a clap of thunder, a thunderclap • **~s** thunder (*sing*)
2 (= *ruido*) [*de cañón*] boom, thundering ▸ **trueno gordo*** (*lit*) finale (*of firework display*); (*fig*) big row, major scandal
3* (= *tarambana*) wild youth, madcap; (= *libertino*) rake
4 (*Caribe*) (= *juerga*) binge*, noisy party
5 truenos (*Caribe*) (= *zapatos*) stout shoes

trueque SM **1** (= *cambio*) exchange; (*Com*) barter • **a ~ de** in exchange for • **aun a ~ de perderlo** even if it means losing it
2 trueques (*And*) (*Econ*) change (*sing*)

trufa SF **1** (*Bot*) truffle
2* (= *mentira*) fib, story

trufado ADJ stuffed with truffles

trufar ▹ CONJUG 1a VT **1** (*Culin*) to stuff with truffles
2* (= *estafar*) to take in*, swindle
VI* (= *mentir*) to fib, tell stories

trufi* SM (*And*) taxi

truhán SM **1** (= *pillo*) rogue, crook*, shyster (*EEUU*); (= *estafador*) swindler; (= *charlatán*) mountebank
2 (*Hist*) jester, buffoon

truhanería SF **1** (= *picardía*) roguery; (= *estafa*) swindling
2 (*Hist*) buffoonery

truhanesco ADJ **1** (= *tramposo*) dishonest, crooked*
2 (*Hist*) buffoonish

truísmo SM truism

truja‡ SM fag‡, gasper‡

trujal SM [*de vino*] winepress; [*de aceite*] olive-oil press

trujimán SM = **truchimán**

trujis‡ SM INV fag‡, gasper‡

trulla SF **1** (= *bullicio*) bustle; (= *disturbio*) commotion; (= *ruido*) noise
2 (= *multitud*) crowd, throng
3 (*And*) (= *broma*) practical joke

trullada SF (*Caribe*) crowd, throng

trullo‡ SM nick‡, jail, can (*EEUU‡*)

truncado ADJ (= *reducido*) truncated, shortened; (= *incompleto*) incomplete

truncamiento SM truncation, shortening

truncar ▹ CONJUG 1g VT **1** (= *acortar*) [+ *texto*] to truncate, shorten; [+ *cita*] to mutilate
2 [+ *carrera, vida*] to cut short; [+ *esperanzas*] to dash; [+ *proyecto*] to ruin; [+ *desarrollo*] to stunt, check

trunco ADJ (= *reducido*) truncated, shortened; (= *incompleto*) incomplete

truquero/a (*LAm*) ADJ tricky
SM/F trickster

truqui* SM = **truco**

trusa SF **1** (*And, Méx*) (= *calzoncillos*) underpants (*pl*); (= *bragas*) knickers (*pl*), panties (*pl*) (*EEUU*); [*de bebé*] pants (*pl*)
2 (*Caribe*) (= *bañador*) trunks (*pl*), swimming trunks (*pl*) (*Brit*) ▸ **trusa de baño** trunks (*pl*), swimming trunks (*pl*) (*Brit*)

trust [trus] SM (PL: **trusts** [trus]) (*Econ*) trust, cartel

tsunami SM (PL: **tsunamis** *o* **tsunami**) tsunami

Tte. ABR (= **teniente**) Lieut, Lt

TU SM ABR (= **tiempo universal**) U.T.

tu ADJ POSES your • **han venido tu tía y tus primos** your aunt and your cousins have come • **hágase tu voluntad** (*Rel*) thy will be done

tú PRON PERS **1** you • **cuando tú quieras** whenever you like • **que esto quede entre tú y yo** this is between you and me • **¿yo, gordo? ¿y tú qué?** fat? me? what about you? • **llegamos antes que tú** we arrived before you (did) • **es mucho más alto que tú** he is much taller than you (are) • **en el partido se mantuvo el tú a tú** the game was between equals, the game was an equal struggle • **hablar *o* llamar *o* tratar a algn de tú** to use the "tú" form of address • **nos tratamos de tú** we address each other as "tú" • **háblame de tú, que ahora somos familia** you can address me as "tú", we're family now
2* (*uso vocativo*) • **¡tú! ven aquí** you! come here • **¡oye tú, que me voy a tener que enfadar!** listen, you, I'm going to have to get cross! • **¡tú cállate!** shut up, you!

tualé (*LAm*) SM toilet, bathroom (*EEUU*), lavatory
SF toilet

tuareg ADJ, SMF (PL: **tuareg** *o* **tuaregs**) Tuareg

tuba SF tuba

tubercular ADJ tubercular

tubérculo SM **1** (*Bot*) tuber; (= *patata*) potato
2 (*Anat, Med*) tubercle

tuberculosis SF tuberculosis

tuberculoso/a ADJ tuberculous, tubercular • **estar ~** to suffer from tuberculosis, have tuberculosis
SM/F tuberculosis patient

tubería SF **1** (= *tubo*) pipe
2 (= *conjunto de tubos*) pipes (*pl*), piping

Tubinga SF Tübingen

tubo SM **1** (= *recipiente*) tube • MODISMO: • **pasar por el ~*** to knuckle under ▸ **tubo acústico** speaking-tube ▸ **tubo capilar** capillary ▸ **tubo de chimenea** chimneypot

▸ **tubo de desagüe** (*interior*) waste pipe; (*exterior*) drainpipe ▸ **tubo de ensayo** test tube ▸ **tubo de escape** exhaust (pipe) ▸ **tubo de humo** chimney, flue ▸ **tubo de imagen** television tube ▸ **tubo de lámpara** lamp glass ▸ **tubo de órgano** organ pipe ▸ **tubo de radio** wireless valve, tube (*EEUU*) ▸ **tubo de rayos catódicos** cathode-ray tube ▸ **tubo de respiración** breathing-tube ▸ **tubo de vacío** valve, vacuum tube (*EEUU*) ▸ **tubo digestivo** alimentary canal ▸ **tubo fluorescente** fluorescent tube ▸ **tubo lanzatorpedos** torpedo tube
2 (= *tubería*) pipe
3 • MODISMO: • **por un ~*** loads* • **gastó por un ~** he spent a fortune* • **lo vendió por un ~*** he sold it for a fantastic price*
4 (*LAm*) [*de teléfono*] handset, earpiece
5‡ (= *cárcel*) nick‡, can (*EEUU*‡)

tubular ADJ tubular
SM (= *prenda*) roll-on

tucán SM, **tucano** SM (*LAm*) toucan

Tucídedes SM Thucydides

tuco[1]/a ADJ **1** (*LAm*) (= *mutilado*) maimed, limbless; (= *manco*) with a finger/hand missing
2 (*CAm**) (= *achaparrado*) squat
SM/F (= *persona*) cripple*
SM (*LAm*) (*Anat*) stump

tuco[2] SM (*Cono Sur*) (= *salsa*) pasta sauce; [*de tomate*] tomato sauce

tuco[3] SM (*And, Cono Sur*) (*Entomología*) glow-worm

tuco[4]/a SM/F (*CAm*) (= *tocayo*) namesake

tucura SF **1** (*Cono Sur*) (= *langosta*) locust
2 (*And*) (= *libélula*) dragonfly; (= *mantis*) praying mantis; (= *saltamontes*) grasshopper
3 (= *sacerdote*) corrupt priest

tucuso SM (*Caribe*) hummingbird

tudesco/a ADJ, SM/F German

Tudor SM • **los ~** the Tudors

tuerca SF nut • MODISMO: • **apretar las ~s a algn** to tighten the screws on sb ▸ **tuerca mariposa** wing nut

tuerce‡ SM (*CAm*) misfortune, setback

tuerto/a ADJ **1** (= *con un ojo*) one-eyed; (= *ciego en un ojo*) blind in one eye
2 (= *torcido*) twisted, bent, crooked
3 • **a tuertas** (= *invertido*) upside-down; (= *al revés*) back to front • MODISMO: • **a tuertas o a derechas** (= *con razón o sin ella*) rightly or wrongly; (= *sea como sea*) by hook or by crook; (= *sin pensar*) thoughtlessly, hastily
SM/F (= *persona*) (= *con un ojo*) one-eyed person; (= *ciego en un ojo*) person who is blind in one eye
SM (= *injusticia*) wrong, injustice

tuesta* SF (*Caribe*) binge*

tueste SM roasting

tuétano SM **1** (= *médula*) marrow, squash (*EEUU*) • MODISMO: • **hasta los ~s** through and through, utterly • **mojarse hasta los ~s** to get soaked to the skin • **enamorado hasta los ~s** head over heels in love
2 (= *meollo*) core, essence

tufarada SF (= *olor*) bad smell, foul smell; (= *racha de aire*) gust

tufillas* SMF INV bad-tempered person

tufillo SM slight smell (a of)

tufo[1] SM **1** (= *emanación*) fumes (*pl*)
2 (= *hedor*) (*gen*) stink; [*de cuarto*] fug • MODISMO: • **se le subió el ~ a las narices** he got very cross
3 tufos* (= *vanidad*) swank* (*sing*), conceit (*sing*) • **tener ~s** to be swanky*, be conceited

tufo[2] SM (= *rizo*) curl, sidelock

tugurio SM **1** (= *cafetucho*) den, joint‡; (= *chabola*) hovel, slum, shack; (= *cuartucho*) poky little room; (*Agr*) shepherd's hut
2 tugurios (*And*) shanty town (*sing*)

tuit SM (PL: **tuits**) tweet

tuitear ▸ CONJUG 1a VI, VT to tweet

tuitero/a ADJ Twitter (+ *sustantivo*) • **actividad tuitera** Twitter traffic
SM/F Twitter user

tuja SF (*And*) hide-and-seek

tul SM tulle, net

tulenco ADJ (*CAm*) splay-footed

tulipa SF lampshade

tulipán SM tulip; (*And, Caribe, Méx*) hibiscus

tulipanero SM, **tulipero** SM tulip-tree

tulis SM INV (*Méx*) highway robber, brigand

tullida SF (*Caribe*) (= *truco*) dirty trick

tullido/a ADJ (= *lisiado*) crippled; (= *paralizado*) paralysed
SM/F cripple

tullir ▸ CONJUG 3h VT **1** (= *lisiar*) to cripple, maim; (= *paralizar*) to paralyse
2 (= *cansar*) to wear out, exhaust
3 (= *maltratar*) to abuse, maltreat

tumba[1] SF (= *sepultura*) tomb, grave • MODISMOS: • **hablar a ~ abierta** to speak openly • **llevar a algn a la ~** to carry sb off • **ser (como) una ~** to keep one's mouth shut, not breathe a word to anyone

tumba[2] SF **1** (*LAm*) (= *tala*) felling of timber, clearing of ground; (= *tierra*) ground cleared for sowing; (= *claro*) forest clearing
2 (= *sacudida*) shake, jolt
3 (= *voltereta*) somersault
4 (*Cono Sur*) (= *carne*) *boiled meat of poor quality*

tumba[3] SF (*Caribe, Cono Sur*) (= *tambor*) African drum

tumbaburros* SM INV (*Méx*) dictionary

tumbacuartillos* SM INV old soak‡

tumbacuatro SM (*Caribe*) braggart

tumbadero SM (*Caribe, Méx*) **1** (*Agr*) ground cleared for sowing
2* (= *burdel*) brothel

tumbadora SF (*Caribe*) large conga drum

tumbar ▸ CONJUG 1a VT **1** (= *derribar*) [+ *persona*] to knock down, knock over; [+ *puerta*] (*a golpes*) to batter down; (*a patadas*) to kick down *o* in; [*viento*] to blow down • **tanto alcohol acabó tumbándolo** all that alcohol ended up laying him out • **lo ~on a golpes** they punched him to the ground
2‡ (= *matar*) to do in‡
3* [*olor*] to knock back* • **un olor que te tumba*** an overpowering smell, a smell which knocks you back*
4 (= *impresionar*) to amaze, overwhelm • **el espectáculo me dejó tumbado** the sight overwhelmed me • **su presunción tumbó a todos** his conceit amazed everybody, his conceit knocked everybody sideways
5‡* (= *copular*) to lay‡, screw**
6* (= *suspender*) to fail, flunk (*EEUU*)
7 (*LAm*) [+ *árbol*] to fell; [+ *tierra*] to clear
VI **1** (= *caerse*) to fall down
2 (*Náut*) to capsize
3* (= *impresionar*) • **tiene una desfachatez que tumba de espaldas** his cheek is enough to take your breath away*
VPR **tumbarse 1** (= *acostarse*) to lie down • **estar tumbado** to lie, be lying down
2 [*trigo*] to go flat
3 (= *relajarse*) to decide to take it easy; (= *abandonarse*) to give up (on things), let o.s. go (*after achieving a success etc*)

tumbilla SF (*CAm*) wicker suitcase

tumbo[1] SM **1** (= *sacudida*) shake, jolt • MODISMO: • **dando ~s** with all sorts of difficulties
2 (= *caída*) fall, tumble • **dar un ~** to fall, shake

tumbo[2] SM (*Hist*) monastic cartulary

tumbón* ADJ lazy, bone idle

tumbona SF (= *butaca*) easy chair; [*de playa*] deckchair, beach chair (*EEUU*)

tumefacción SF swelling

tumefacto ADJ swollen

tumescente ADJ tumescent

tumido ADJ swollen, tumid (*frm*)

tumor SM tumour, tumor (*EEUU*), growth ▸ **tumor cerebral** brain tumour ▸ **tumor benigno** benign tumour ▸ **tumor maligno** malignant growth

túmulo SM **1** (= *sepultura*) tumulus, burial mound
2 (*Geog*) mound

tumulto SM turmoil, tumult; (*Pol*) (= *motín*) riot, disturbance ▸ **tumulto popular** popular rising

tumultuario ADJ = **tumultuoso**

tumultuosamente ADV tumultuously; (*pey*) riotously

tumultuoso ADJ tumultuous; (*pey*) riotous, disorderly

tuna[1] SF (*Bot*) prickly pear

tuna[2] SF **1** (*Esp*) (*Mús*) ▸ **tuna estudiantina** student music group
2 (= *vida picaresca*) rogue's life, vagabond life; (*fig*) merry life
3 (*CAm*) (= *embriaguez*) drunkenness

> **TUNA**
> **Tunas**, also known as **estudiantinas**, are groups of students dressed in 17th century costumes who play guitars, lutes and tambourines and who used to go serenading through the streets. More recently, they have been known for making impromptu appearances at weddings and parties singing traditional Spanish songs, often of a bawdy nature, in exchange for drinks or some money.

tunantada SF dirty trick

tunante SM rogue, villain • **¡tunante!** you villain!; (*a un niño*) you young scamp!

tunantería SF **1** (= *vileza*) crookedness, villainy
2 (= *engaño*) dirty trick, villainy

tunar ▸ CONJUG 1a VI to loaf, idle, bum around (*EEUU*)

tunco/a (*CAm, Méx*) ADJ (= *lisiado*) maimed, crippled; (= *manco*) one-armed
SM/F (= *persona*) cripple
SM (*Zool*) pig, hog (*EEUU*)

tunda[1] SF (= *esquileo*) shearing

tunda[2] SF **1** (= *paliza*) beating, thrashing
2 • **darse una ~** to wear o.s. out

tundir[1] ▸ CONJUG 3a VT [+ *pieles*] to shear

tundir[2] ▸ CONJUG 3a VT (= *golpear*) to beat, thrash

tundra SF tundra

tuneado* ADJ customized

tunear ▸ CONJUG 1a VI **1** (= *vivir como pícaro*) to live a rogue's life
2 (= *gandulear*) to loaf, idle; (= *divertirse*) to have a good time
VT* [+ *vehículo*] to tune, to customize

tunecino/a ADJ, SM/F Tunisian

túnel SM **1** (= *paso*) tunnel ▸ **túnel aerodinámico** wind tunnel ▸ **túnel de lavado** car wash ▸ **túnel del Canal de la Mancha** Channel Tunnel ▸ **túnel del tiempo** time warp ▸ **túnel de pruebas aerodinámicas** wind tunnel ▸ **túnel de vestuarios** tunnel leading to the changing rooms ▸ **túnel de viento** wind tunnel
2 (= *crisis*) bad time
3 (*Dep*) nutmeg

tuneladora SF tunnelling machine

tunelar ▸ CONJUG 1a VI to tunnel

tunes SMPL (*And, CAm*) first steps (*of a child*) • **hacer ~** to toddle, start to walk, take one's first steps

Túnez SM (= *país*) Tunisia; (= *ciudad*) Tunis

tungo ADJ (*And*) short, shortened, blunt

SM 1 *(And)* (= *trozo*) bit, chunk
2 *(Cono Sur)* *(Anat)* (= *cuello*) neck
tungsteno SM tungsten
túnica SF 1 *(Hist)* tunic; [*de monje*] robe
2 *(Anat, Bot)* tunic
Tunicia SF Tunisia
túnico SM *(LAm)* shift, long undergarment
túnido SM tuna (fish)
tuning ['tunin] SM car styling, *accessorizing and customizing cars*
tuno/a SM/F (= *pícaro*) rogue, villain • **el muy ~** the old rogue
SM *(Mús)* *member of a student music group*; ▹ TUNA
tunoso ADJ *(And)* prickly
tuntún • **al ~** ADV thoughtlessly, any old how • **juzgar al buen ~** to judge hastily, jump to conclusions
tuntuneco* ADJ *(CAm, Caribe)* stupid, dense*
tuñeco ADJ *(Caribe)* maimed, crippled
tupamaro/a *(Cono Sur)* *(Hist, Pol)* ADJ Tupamaro *(antes de s)*, urban guerrilla *(antes de s)*
SM/F Tupamaro, urban guerrilla
tupé SM 1 (= *mechón*) quiff
2 (= *peluca*) toupée, hairpiece
3* (= *caradura*) nerve*, cheek*
tupí SMF 1 Tupi (Indian)
2 *(esp Para)* = **tupí-guaraní**
SM *(Ling)* Tupi
tupia SF *(And)* dam
tupiar ▹ CONJUG 1b VT *(And)* to dam up
tupición SF 1 *(LAm)* (= *obstrucción*) blockage, obstruction; *(Med)* catarrh
2 *(LAm)* (= *multitud*) dense crowd, throng
3 *(And, Méx)* (= *vegetación*) dense vegetation
4 *(Cono Sur*)* • **una ~ de cosas** a lot of things
5 *(LAm)* (= *confusión*) bewilderment, confusion
tupido ADJ 1 (= *denso*) thick; (= *impenetrable*) impenetrable; [*tela*] close-woven
2 *(LAm)* (= *obstruido*) blocked up, obstructed
3 (= *torpe*) dim*, dense*
4 *(Méx)* (= *frecuente*) common, frequent
ADV *(Méx)* (= *con tesón*) persistently, steadily; (= *a menudo*) often, frequently
tupí-guaraní ADJ Tupi-Guarani
SMF Tupi-Guarani (Indian)
SM *(Ling)* Tupi-Guarani
tupinambo SM Jerusalem artichoke
tupir ▹ CONJUG 3a VT 1 (= *apretar*) to pack tight, press down, compact
2 *(LAm)* (= *obstruir*) to block, stop up, obstruct
VPR **tupirse** 1* (= *comer mucho*) to stuff oneself*
2 *(LAm)* (= *desconcertarse*) to feel silly, get embarrassed
tupperware SM Tupperware®
turba¹ SF (= *combustible*) peat
turba² SF (= *muchedumbre*) crowd, throng; (*en movimiento*) swarm; *(pey)* mob
turbación SF 1 (= *alteración*) disturbance
2 (= *inquietud*) alarm, worry; (= *perplejidad*) bewilderment, confusion; (= *agitación*) trepidation
3 (= *vergüenza*) embarrassment
turbado ADJ 1 (= *alterado*) disturbed
2 (= *inquieto*) alarmed, worried; (= *perplejo*) bewildered
3 (= *avergonzado*) embarrassed
turbador ADJ (= *inquietante*) disturbing, alarming; (= *vergonzoso*) embarrassing
turbal SM peat bog
turbamulta SF mob, rabble
turbante SM 1 (= *prenda*) turban
2 *(Méx)* *(Bot)* gourd, calabash, squash (EEUU)
turbar ▹ CONJUG 1a VT 1 [+ *silencio, reposo, orden*] to disturb • **el ruido turbó su sueño** the noise disturbed her sleep • **nada turbó la buena marcha de las negociaciones** nothing hindered *o* disturbed the smooth progress of the negotiations
2 [+ *agua*] to disturb, stir up
3 (= *alterar*) • **la noticia turbó su ánimo** the news troubled his mind, the news perturbed him • **su llegada inesperada la turbó visiblemente** his unexpected arrival visibly disturbed her
4 (= *avergonzar*) to embarrass • **sus palabras de amor la ~on** his words of love embarrassed her
VPR **turbarse** 1 (= *alterarse*) • **al reconocer a su agresor se turbó enormemente** she was deeply disturbed when she recognized her attacker • **se turbó de tal modo que no pudo responder** he was so disturbed he couldn't reply
2 (= *avergonzarse*) to get embarrassed • **se turbó al ver que ella lo miraba fijamente** when he realized she was staring at him he came over *o* got all embarrassed
turbera SF peat bog
turbiedad SF 1 [*de líquidos*] cloudiness
2 (= *opacidad*) opacity; (= *confusión*) confusion
3 (= *turbulencia*) turbulence
turbina SF turbine ▸ **turbina a *o* de vapor** steam engine ▸ **turbina de gas** gas turbine ▸ **turbina eólica** wind turbine
turbio ADJ 1 [*agua*] cloudy, muddy, turbid *(frm)*
2 [*vista*] dim, blurred; [*mente, pensamientos*] disturbed; [*tema*] unclear, confused
3 [*período*] turbulent, unsettled
4 [*negocio*] shady*; [*método*] dubious
ADV • **ver ~** not to see clearly, to have blurred vision
SMPL **turbios** sediment *(sing)*
turbión SM 1 *(Meteo)* (= *aguacero*) heavy shower, downpour
2 (= *aluvión*) shower, torrent
turbo SM *(Mec)* turbo, turbocharger; (= *coche*) turbocharged car
ADJ INV turbo *(antes de s)*
turbo... PREF turbo...
turboalimentado ADJ turbocharged
turbocompresor SM turbo-compressor; (= *diesel*) turbo-supercharger
turbodiesel ADJ INV, SM turbo diesel
turbohélice SM turboprop, turboprop aeroplane
ADJ INV turboprop *(antes de s)*
turbonada SF *(Cono Sur)* sudden storm, squall
turbopropulsado ADJ turboprop *(antes de s)*
turbopropulsor, turborreactor SM turbojet (aeroplane)
ADJ INV turbojet *(antes de s)*
turbulencia SF 1 *(Meteo)* turbulence
2 [*de río, aguas*] turbulence
3 (= *desorden*) [*de época*] turbulence; [*de reunión*] storminess
4 (= *inquietud*) restlessness
turbulento ADJ 1 [*río, aguas*] turbulent
2 [*período*] troubled, turbulent; [*reunión*] stormy
3 [*carácter*] restless
turca‡ SF piss-up‡, binge* • **coger *o* pillar una ~** to get sozzled*, get pissed‡
turco/a ADJ Turkish
SM/F 1 (= *de Turquía*) Turk • **joven ~** *(Pol)* young Turk
2 *(LAm)* *(pey)* *immigrant from the Middle East*
3 *(LAm)* (= *buhonero*) pedlar, peddler (EEUU), hawker
SM *(Ling)* Turkish
turcochipriota ADJ, SMF Turkish Cypriot
túrdiga SF thong, strip of leather
Turena SF Touraine
turf SM 1 (= *deporte*) • **el ~** the turf, horse-racing
2 (= *pista*) racetrack
turfista ADJ fond of horse-racing
SM/F racegoer
turgencia SF turgidity
turgente ADJ, **túrgido** ADJ turgid, swollen
Turín SM Turin
Turingia SF Thuringia
turismo SM 1 (= *actividad*) tourism; (= *industria*) tourist industry *o* trade • **el ~ constituye su mayor industria** tourism is their biggest industry • **se ha desarrollado mucho el ~ en el norte** tourism has been greatly developed in the north • **ahora se hace más ~ que nunca** numbers of tourists are greater now than ever ▸ **turismo blanco** winter holidays *(pl)*, skiing holidays *(pl)* ▸ **turismo cultural** cultural tourism ▸ **turismo de calidad** quality tourism ▸ **turismo ecológico** eco-tourism ▸ **turismo espacial** space tourism ▸ **turismo interior** domestic tourism ▸ **turismo rural** country holidays *(pl)*, green tourism • **promover el ~ rural** to promote tourism in rural areas • **casas de ~ rural** ≈ holiday cottages ▸ **turismo sexual** sex tourism
2 *(Aut)* car, private car
turista SMF *(gen)* tourist; (= *visitante*) sightseer • **clase ~** economy class, tourist class
turístico ADJ tourist *(antes de s)*
turistizado ADJ touristy
Turkmenistán SM Turkmenistan
turma SF 1 *(Anat)* testicle
2 *(Bot)* truffle; *(And)* potato
túrmix® SM o SF mixer, blender
turnar ▹ CONJUG 1a VI to take turns
VPR **turnarse** to take turns • **se turnan para usarlo** they take it in turns to use it
turné SM tour, trip
turno SM 1 (= *vez*) turn; (*en juegos*) turn, go • **es tu ~** it's your turn • **cuando te llegue el ~** when your turn comes • **espere su ~** wait your turn • **por ~s** in turns, by turns • **estuvo con su querida de ~** he was with his lover of the moment • **el tonto de ~** the inevitable idiot ▸ **turno de preguntas** round of questions
2 [*de trabajo*] shift • **hago el ~ de tarde** I do the afternoon shift • **estar de ~** to be on duty • **farmacia de ~** duty chemist • **médico de ~** duty doctor, doctor on duty • **trabajo por ~s** shiftwork • **trabajar por ~s** to work shifts, do shiftwork ▸ **turno de día** day shift ▸ **turno de noche** night shift ▸ **turno de oficio** spell of court duty ▸ **turno rotativo** rotating shift
turolense ADJ of/from Teruel
SMF native/inhabitant of Teruel • **los ~s** people of Teruel
turón SM polecat
turqueo* SM *(CAm)* fight
turquesa ADJ, SM (= *color*) turquoise
SF turquoise
turquesco ADJ Turkish
turquí ADJ • **color ~** indigo, deep blue
Turquía SF Turkey
turra‡ SF *(Cono Sur)* whore, prostitute
turrón SM 1 (= *dulce*) nougat
2* (= *cargo*) cushy job, sinecure
turulato* ADJ stunned, flabbergasted • **se quedó ~ con la noticia** he was stunned by the news
tururú* ADJ (= *loco*) • **estar ~** to be crazy
EXCL no way!*, you're joking!
tus¹ EXCL (*a un perro*) good dog!, here boy!
tus²* SM • MODISMO: • **no decir tus ni mus**

TURRÓN
Turrón is a type of Spanish sweet rather like nougat that is eaten particularly around Christmas. It has Arabic origins and is made of honey, egg whites, almonds and hazelnuts. There are two traditional varieties: **alicante**, which is hard and contains whole almonds, and **jijona**, which is soft and made from crushed almonds. **Turrón** stalls can also be found at the summer **ferias** in some regions.

to remain silent, say nothing • **sin decir tus ni mus** without saying a word

tusa SF **1** (*And, CAm, Caribe*) [*de maíz*] (= *mazorca*) cob of maize, corncob; (*sin grano*) corn husk, maize husk; (*Caribe*) (= *cigarro*) *cigar rolled in a maize leaf*; (*Cono Sur*) (= *seda*) corn silk
2 (*Cono Sur*) (= *crin*) horse's mane
3 (*Cono Sur*) (= *esquileo*) clipping, shearing
4 (*And*) [*de viruela*] pockmark
5 (*And**) (= *susto*) fright; (= *inquietud*) anxiety
6 (*CAm, Caribe*) (= *mujerzuela*) whore
7 • MODISMO: • **no vale ni una ~** (*CAm, Caribe**) it's worthless

tusar ▷ CONJUG 1a VT (*LAm*) (= *esquilar*) to cut, clip, shear; (= *cortar*) to cut roughly, cut badly

tuse SM (*Cono Sur*) = **tusa**

tuso ADJ **1** (*And, Caribe*) (= *esquilado*) cropped, shorn
2 (*Caribe*) (= *rabón*) docked, tailless
3 (*And, Caribe*) (= *picado de viruelas*) pockmarked

tútano SM (*LAm*) = **tuétano**

tute SM *card game similar to bezique* • MODISMO: • **darse un ~** to work extra hard

tutear ▷ CONJUG 1a VT • **~ a algn** (*lit*) to address sb as "tú" (*2nd person sing*); (*fig*) to be on familiar terms with sb
VPR **tutearse** • **se tutean desde siempre** they have always addressed each other as "tú", they have always been on familiar terms

tutela SF **1** (*Jur*) guardianship • **bajo ~** in ward • **estar bajo ~ jurídica** [*niño*] to be a ward of court
2 (= *protección*) tutelage, protection • **estar bajo la ~ de** (= *amparo*) to be under the protection of; (= *auspicios*) to be under the auspices of

tutelaje SM (*LAm*) = **tutela**

tutelar ADJ tutelary • **ángel ~** guardian angel
VT ▷ CONJUG 1a (= *proteger*) to protect, guard; (= *guiar*) to advise, guide; (= *vigilar*) to supervise, oversee

tuteo SM use of (the familiar) "tú", addressing a person as "tú" • **se ha extendido mucho el ~** the use of "tú" has greatly increased

tutilimundi* SM (*LAm*) everybody

tutiplén†* • **a ~** ADV [*dar*] freely; [*repartir*] haphazardly, indiscriminately; [*comer*] hugely, to excess

tutor(a) SM/F **1** (*Jur*) guardian
2 (*Univ*) tutor ▸ **tutor(a) de curso** (*Escol*) form master/mistress
SM (*Agr*) prop, stake

tutoría SF **1** (*Jur*) guardianship
2 (*Univ*) tutorial (class), section (of a course) (*EEUU*)

tutorial ADJ tutorial

tutorizar ▷ CONJUG 1f VT = **tutelar**

tutsi ADJ Tutsi
SMF Tutsi

tutú SM tutu

tutuma SF (*And, Cono Sur*) **1‡** (= *cabeza*) nut‡, noggin (*EEUU**), head; (= *bollo*) bump; (= *joroba*) hump; (= *cardenal*) bruise
2 (= *fruta*) *type of cucumber*

tutumito SM (*And, CAm*) idiot

tuturuto ADJ **1** (*CAm, Caribe, Méx*) (= *borracho*) drunk
2 (*And, CAm, Caribe*) (= *tonto*) stupid; (= *aturdido*) dumbfounded, stunned
SM (*Cono Sur*) (= *chulo*) pimp

tuve *etc* ▷ **tener**

tuyo/a ADJ POSES yours • **¿es ~ este abrigo?** is this coat yours? • **cualquier amigo ~** any friend of yours
PRON POSES **1** (*gen*) yours • **este es el ~** this one's yours • **la tuya está en el armario** yours is in the cupboard • **mis amigos y los ~s** my friends and yours • **¡adelante, esta es la tuya!** go on, now's your chance! • **¿ya estás haciendo de las tuyas?** are you up to your tricks again? • **lo ~: todo lo ~ me pertenece a mi también** everything that is yours also belongs to me • **he puesto lo ~ en esta caja** I've put your things in this box • **sé que lo ~ con Ana acabó hace tiempo** I know that you and Ana finished a while ago • **la informática no es lo ~** computers are not your thing
2 • **los ~s** (= *tus familiares*) your folks*, your family • **¿echas de menos a los ~s?** do you miss your folks?

tuza SF (*LAm*) (*Zool*) mole

TV SF ABR (= **televisión**) TV

TVE SF ABR = **Televisión Española**

TVP SF ABR (= **trombosis venosa profunda**) (*Med*) DVT

tweed [twi] SM tweed

txistu SM (Basque) flute

txistulari SM (Basque) flute player

Uu

U, u¹ [u] SF (= *letra*) U, u • **doble U** (*Méx*) W • **curva en U** hairpin bend

u² CONJ (*used instead of "o" before o-, ho-*) or • **siete u ocho** seven or eight

U. ABR (= **Universidad**) Univ., U

ualabi SM wallaby

UAM SF ABR **1** (*Esp*) = **Universidad Autónoma de Madrid**
2 (*Méx*) = **Universidad Autónoma Metropolitana**

ubérrimo ADJ exceptionally fertile

ubicación SF **1** (*esp LAm*) (= *posición*) situation, location
2 (= *empleo*) job, position

ubicado ADJ **1** (*esp LAm*) (= *situado*) situated, located • **una tienda ubicada en la calle Lagasca** a shop in Lagasca street • **bien ~** • **ubicadísimo** (*Méx*) well situated *o* located, in a desirable location
2 (*en un trabajo*) working

ubicar ▷ CONJUG 1g VT **1** (*esp LAm*) (= *colocar*) to place, locate; [+ *edificio*] to site
2 (= *encontrar*) **a** • **~ algo** to find sth, locate sth • **no supo ~ Madrid en el mapa** he was unable to find *o* locate Madrid on the map
b (*LAm*) • **~ a algn** to find sb, locate sb • **no hemos podido ~ al jefe** we have been unable to find *o* locate the boss, we have been unable to track down the boss
VPR **ubicarse 1** (= *estar situado*) • **el museo se ubica en el centro de la ciudad** the museum is located *o* situated in the city centre
2 (= *orientarse*) to find one's way around • **a pesar del mapa no consigo ~me** even though I have a map I can't find my way around • **este es el museo, ¿te ubicas ahora?** this is the museum, have you got your bearings now?
3 (*LAm**) (= *colocarse*) to get a job

ubicuidad SF ubiquity • **el don de la ~** the gift for being everywhere at once

ubicuo ADJ ubiquitous

ubre SF udder

ubrera SF (*Med*) thrush

UCD SF ABR (*Esp*) (= **Unión de Centro Democrático**) ▷ LA TRANSICIÓN

UCE SF ABR **1** (*Econ*) (= **Unidad de Cuenta Europea**) ECU
2 (*Esp*) = **Unión de Consumidores de España**

ucedista (*Esp*) ADJ • **política ~** policy of UCD, UCD policy
SMF member of UCD

-ucho, -ucha ▷ Aspects of Word Formation in Spanish 2

uchuvito* ADJ (*And*) drunk, tight*

UCI SF ABR (= **Unidad de Cuidados Intensivos**) ICU

UCM SF ABR (*Esp*) = **Universidad Complutense de Madrid**

-uco, -uca ▷ Aspects of Word Formation in Spanish 2

UCP SF ABR (= **unidad central de proceso**) CPU

UCR SF ABR (*Arg*) = **Unión Cívica Radical**

Ucrania SF Ukraine

ucraniano/a ADJ, SM/F, **ucranio/a** ADJ, SM/F Ukrainian

ucronía SF uchronia, imaginary time

ucrónico ADJ uchronic, imaginary

Ud. PRON ABR = **usted**

-udo ▷ Aspects of Word Formation in Spanish 2

Uds. PRON ABR = **ustedes**

UDV SF ABR (= **unidad de despliegue visual**) VDU

UE SF ABR (= **Unión Europea**) EU

UEFA SF ABR (= **Unión Europea de Fútbol Asociación**) UEFA

UEI SF ABR (= **Unidad Especial de Intervención**) *special force of the Guardia Civil*

-uelo, -uela ▷ Aspects of Word Formation in Spanish 2

UEM SF ABR (= **unión económica y monetaria**) EMU

UEO SF ABR (= **Unión Europea Occidental**) WEU

UEP SF ABR (= **Unión Europea de Pagos**) EPU

UEPS ABR (= **último en entrar, primero en salir**) LIFO

UER SF ABR (= **Unión Europea de Radiodifusión**) EBU

UF SF ABR (*Chile*) (= **Unidad de Fomento**) *changing monetary unit in a fixed dollar system*

uf EXCL (*cansancio*) phew!; (*repugnancia*) ugh!

ufanamente ADV (= *con orgullo*) proudly; (= *con jactancia*) boastfully; (= *con satisfacción*) smugly

ufanarse ▷ CONJUG 1a VPR to boast • **~ con** *o* **de algo** to boast of sth, pride o.s. on sth

ufanía SF **1** (= *orgullo*) pride; (= *jactancia*) boastfulness; (= *satisfacción*) smugness
2 (*Bot*) = **lozanía**

ufano ADJ **1** (= *orgulloso*) proud; (= *jactancioso*) boastful; (= *satisfecho*) smug • **iba muy ~ en el nuevo coche** he was going along so proudly in his new car • **está muy ~ porque le han dado el premio** he is very proud that they have awarded him the prize
2 (*Bot*) = **lozano**

ufología SF ufology, study of unidentified flying objects

ufólogo/a SM/F ufologist

Uganda SF Uganda

ugandés/esa ADJ, SM/F Ugandan

ugetista (*Esp*) ADJ • **política ~** policy of the UGT, UGT policy
SMF member of the UGT

UGT SF ABR (*Esp*) = **Unión General de Trabajadores**

UHF SM ABR (= **ultrahigh frequency**) UHF

UIT SF ABR (= **Unión Internacional para las Telecomunicaciones**) ITU

ujier SM (*en un tribunal*) usher; (= *conserje*) doorkeeper, attendant

-ujo, -uja ▷ Aspects of Word Formation in Spanish 2

újule EXCL (*Méx*) (*para indicar desprecio*) huh!; (*para indicar sorpresa*) wow!, phew!

úlcera SF **1** (*Med*) ulcer, sore ▸ **úlcera de decúbito** bedsore ▸ **úlcera duodenal** duodenal ulcer ▸ **úlcera gástrica** gastric ulcer
2 (*Bot*) rot

ulceración SF ulceration

ulcerar ▷ CONJUG 1a VT to make sore, ulcerate
VPR **ulcerarse** to ulcerate

ulceroso ADJ ulcerous

ule SM (*CAm, Méx*) = **hule¹**

ulerear ▷ CONJUG 1a VT (*Cono Sur*) to roll out

ulero SM (*Cono Sur*) rolling pin

Ulises SM Ulysses

ulluco SM (*And, Cono Sur*) manioc

ulpo SM (*Chile, Perú*) maize gruel

ulterior ADJ **1** [*sitio*] farther, further
2 [*tiempo*] later, subsequent

ulteriormente ADV later, subsequently

ultimación SF completion, conclusion

ultimador(a) SM/F (*LAm*) killer, murderer

últimamente ADV **1** (= *recientemente*) lately, recently • **no lo he visto ~** I haven't seen him lately *o* recently
2 (= *por último*) lastly, finally
3 (= *en último caso*) as a last resort
4 • **¡últimamente!** (*LAm*) well, I'll be damned!, that's the absolute end!

ultimar ▷ CONJUG 1a VT **1** (= *terminar*) [+ *detalles, acuerdo*] to finalize; [+ *proyecto, obra*] to put the finishing *o* final touches to • **el tratado que ultiman estos días ambos gobiernos** the treaty which the two governments have been finalizing over the last few days • **están ultimando la nueva edición del libro** they are putting the finishing *o* final touches to the new edition of the book • **están ultimando los preparativos para la boda** they are making the final preparations for the wedding
2 (*LAm*) (*frm*) (= *matar*) to kill, murder

ultimato SM, **ultimátum** SM (PL: **ultimátums**) ultimatum

ultimizar ▷ CONJUG 1f VT = **ultimar**

último/a ADJ **1** (= *final*) last • **el ~ día del mes** the last day of the month • **la última película que hizo Orson Wells** the last film Orson Wells made • **las últimas Navidades que pasamos allí** the last Christmas we spent there • **la Última Cena** (*Rel*) the Last Supper • **a lo ~*** in the end • **¿y qué ocurre a lo ~?** and what happens in the end? • **estoy a lo ~ del libro** I've nearly finished the book • **por ~** finally, lastly • **por ~, el conferenciante hizo referencia a ...** finally *o* lastly, the speaker mentioned ... • **por última vez** for the last time
2 (= *más reciente*) **a** (*en una serie*) [*ejemplar, moda, novedad*] latest; [*elecciones, periodo*] last • **este coche es el ~ modelo** this car is the latest model • **¿has leído el ~ número de la revista?** have you read the latest issue of the

magazine? • **las últimas noticias** the latest news • **las últimas novedades musicales** the latest music releases • **los dos ~s cuadros que ha hecho no son tan innovadores** his two latest *o* his latest two paintings are not so innovative • **durante la última década** in *o* over the last decade • **en las últimas horas ha aparecido otro posible comprador** in the last few hours another possible buyer has emerged • **volvió a salir elegido en las últimas elecciones** he was reelected at the last election • **la última película que he visto** the last film I saw • **las últimas películas que he visto** the last few films I have seen • **ahora ~** (*Chile*) recently • **su malhumor no es de ahora ~** his bad mood is not a recent thing • **ha estado estudiando más ahora ~** he's been studying more recently • **en los ~s años** in *o* over the last few years, in recent years • **en los ~s tiempos** lately
b (*entre dos*) latter • **de los dos, este ~ es el mejor** of the two, the latter is the best; ▹ **hora**
3 (*en el espacio*) **a** (= *más al fondo*) back • **un asiento en la última fila** a seat in the back row
b (= *más alto*) top • **viven en el ~ piso** they live on the top floor
c (= *más bajo*) bottom, last • **el ~ escalón** the bottom *o* last step • **el equipo en última posición** the team in last *o* bottom place • **ocupan el ~ lugar en el índice de audiencia** they have the lowest viewing figures
d (= *más lejano*) most remote, furthest • **las noticias llegan hasta el ~ rincón del país** news gets to the most remote *o* the furthest parts of the country
4 (= *extremo*) • **solo lo aceptaremos como ~ recurso** we will only accept it as a last resort • **en ~ caso, iría yo** as a last resort *o* if all else fails, I would go • **esta medida tiene como fin ~ reducir el nivel de contaminación** the ultimate aim of this measure is to reduce pollution levels; ▹ **extremo²**, **instancia**, **remedio**
5 (= *definitivo*) • **es mi última oferta** that's my final offer • **dígame cuál es el ~ precio** tell me what your lowest price is • **MODISMO:** • **decir la última palabra** to have the last word
6 • **lo ~* a** (= *lo más moderno*) the latest thing • **lo ~ en pantalones** the latest thing in trousers • **lo ~ en tecnología ofimática** the latest (in) office technology
b (= *lo peor*) the limit • **pedirme eso encima ya es lo ~** for him to ask that of me as well really is the limit
SM/F **1** • **el ~** the last, the last one • **el ~ de la lista** the last (one) on the list • **¿quién es la última?** who's the last in the queue? • **hablar el ~** to speak last • **llegó la última** she arrived last • **ser el ~ en hacer algo** to be the last (one) to do sth • **el ~ en salir que apague la luz** the last one to leave, turn the light off • **MODISMOS:** • **reírse el ~** to have the last laugh • **a la última:** • **estar a la última** to be bang up-to-date* • **siempre va vestida a la última** she's always wearing the latest thing • **zapatos a la última** the latest thing in shoes • **estar en las últimas*** (= *a punto de morir*) to be at death's door, be on one's last legs*; (= *sin dinero*) to be down to one's last penny *o* (*EEUU*) cent • **en últimas** (*Col*) as a last resort; ▹ **vestir**
2* • **¿a qué no sabes la última de Irene?** do you know the latest about Irene?
3 (*Esp*) • **a últimos de mes** towards the end of the month
ADV (*Cono Sur*) in the last position, in the last place

ultra ADJ INV extreme right-wing
SMF neo-fascist
ultra... PREF ultra...
ultracongelación SF (*Esp*) (deep-)freezing
ultracongelado ADJ (*Esp*) deep-frozen
ultracongelador SM (*Esp*) deep-freeze, freezer
ultracongelar ▹ CONJUG 1a VT (*Esp*) to deep-freeze
ultraconservador(a) ADJ, SM/F ultra-conservative
ultracorrección SF hypercorrection
ultracorto ADJ ultra-short
ultraderecha SF extreme right, extreme right-wing
ultraderechista ADJ extreme right(-wing)
SMF extreme right-winger
ultrafino ADJ ultrafine
ultraísmo SM *revolutionary poetic movement of the 1920s (imagist, surrealist etc)*
ultraizquierda SF extreme left(-wing)
ultraizquierdista ADJ extreme left(-wing)
SMF extreme left-winger
ultrajador ADJ, **ultrajante** ADJ (= *ofensivo*) offensive; (= *injurioso*) insulting; (= *descomedido*) outrageous
ultrajar ▹ CONJUG 1a VT **1** (= *ofender*) to offend; (= *injuriar*) to insult, abuse
2 (*liter*) (= *estropear*) to spoil, crumple, disarrange
ultraje SM (= *injuria*) insult; (= *atrocidad*) outrage
ultrajoso ADJ = **ultrajador**
ultraligero ADJ microlight
SM microlight, microlight aircraft
ultramar SM • **de** *o* **en ~** overseas, abroad • **los países de ~** foreign countries • **productos venidos de ~** goods from abroad • **pasó ocho años en ~** he spent eight years overseas
ultramarino ADJ **1** (= *extranjero*) overseas, foreign
2 (*Com*) (= *importado*) imported
SM INV **ultramarinos** (*tb* **tienda de ultramarinos**) grocer's (shop), grocery (store) (*EEUU*)
SMPL **ultramarinos** (= *comestibles*) groceries, foodstuffs
ultramoderno ADJ ultramodern
ultramontanismo SM ultramontanism
ultramontano ADJ, SM ultramontane
ultranza SF • **a ~ 1** (*como adjetivo*) (*Pol etc*) out-and-out, extreme • **un nacionalista a ~** a rabid nationalist • **paz a ~** peace at any price
2 (*como adverbio*) • **luchar a ~** to fight to the death • **lo quiere hacer a ~** he wants to do it at all costs
ultrapotente ADJ extra powerful
ultrarrápido ADJ extra fast
ultrarrojo ADJ = **infrarrojo**
ultrasecreto ADJ top secret
ultrasensitivo ADJ ultrasensitive
ultrasofisticado ADJ highly sophisticated
ultrasónico ADJ ultrasonic
ultrasonido SM ultrasound
ultrasur SMF INV *extremist fan of Real Madrid FC*
ultratumba SF • **la vida de ~** life beyond the grave, life after death • **una voz de ~** a ghostly voice
ultravioleta ADJ INV ultraviolet • **rayos ~** ultraviolet rays
ulular ▹ CONJUG 1a VI [*animal, viento*] to howl, shriek; [*búho*] to hoot, screech
ululato SM [*de animal*] howl, shriek; [*de búho*] hoot, screech
UM SF ABR (*Esp*) = **Unión Mallorquina**
umbilical ADJ umbilical • **cordón ~** umbilical cord

umbral SM **1** [*de entrada*] threshold • **pasar** *o* **traspasar el ~ de algn** to set foot in sb's house • **en los ~es de la muerte** at death's door
2 (= *comienzo*) • **estar en los ~es de algo** to be on the threshold *o* verge of sth • **eso está en los ~es de lo imposible** that borders *o* verges on the impossible
3 (*Com*) ▸ **umbral de la pobreza** poverty line ▸ **umbral de rentabilidad** break-even point
umbralada SF (*And, Cono Sur*), **umbralado** SM (*And, Cono Sur*), **umbraladura** SF (*And*) threshold
umbrío ADJ, **umbroso** ADJ shady
UME SF ABR (= **Unión Monetaria Europea**) EMU
UMI SF ABR (= **unidad de medicina intensiva**) ICU
un(a) ART INDEF **1** (*en singular*) (*refiriéndose a algo no conocido o de forma imprecisa*) a; (*antes de vocal o de h*) an; (*dando mayor énfasis, con expresiones temporales*) one • **una silla** a chair • **un paraguas** an umbrella • **hacía una mañana espléndida** it was a lovely morning • **hay una cosa que me gustaría saber** there is one thing I would like to know • **una mañana me llamó** he called me one morning
2 (*en plural*) **a** (*uso indefinido*) (= *algunos*) some; (= *pocos*) a few • **fui con unos amigos** I went with some friends • **hay unas cervezas en la nevera** there are a few *o* some beers in the fridge • **unas horas más tarde** a few hours later
b (*con partes del cuerpo*) • **tiene unas piernas muy largas** she has very long legs
c (*con objetos a pares*) some • **me he comprado unos zapatos de tacón** I've bought some high-heels • **necesito unas tijeras** I need a pair of scissors
d (*con cantidades, cifras*) about, around • **había unas 20 personas** there were about *o* around 20 people, there were some 20 people • **unos 80 dólares** about *o* around 80 dollars, some 80 dollars • **hacía unos 30 grados** it was about 30 degrees
3 (*enfático*) • **¡se dio un golpe ...!** he banged himself really hard! • **¡había una gente más rara ...!** there were some real weirdos there!* • **¡sois unos vagos!** you're so lazy!
ADJ (*numeral*) one • **solo quiero una hoja** I only want one sheet • **una excursión de un día** a one-day trip, a day trip • **tardamos una mañana entera** it took us a whole morning; ▹ **uno**
una PRON **1** • **es la una** (= *hora*) it's one o'clock • **¡a la una, a las dos, a las tres!** (*antes de empezar algo*) one, two, three!; (*en subasta*) going, going, gone!; (*Dep*) ready, steady, go! • **MODISMOS:** • **una de dos** either one thing or the other • **todos a una** all together
2 (*enfático*) **a** (= *pelea, paliza*) • **armar una** to kick up a fuss • **te voy a dar una que verás** I'm going to give you what for • **MODISMO:** • **no dar una** not to get a single thing right
b (= *mala pasada*) • **hacerle una a algn** to play a dirty trick on sb
3 (*enfático*) • **¡había una de gente!** what a crowd there was!
U.N.A.M. SF ABR (*Méx*) = **Universidad Nacional Autónoma de México**
unánime ADJ unanimous
unánimemente ADV unanimously
unanimidad SF unanimity • **por ~** unanimously
uncial ADJ, SF uncial
unción SF **1** (*Med*) anointing
2 (*Rel*) (*tb fig*) unction
uncir ▹ CONJUG 3b VT to yoke
undécimo ADJ, SM eleventh; ▹ **sexto**

UNED SF ABR (*Esp*) (= **Universidad Nacional de Educación a Distancia**) ≈ OU
UNESCO SF ABR (= **United Nations Educational, Scientific and Cultural Organization**) UNESCO
ungido ADJ anointed • **el Ungido del Señor** the Lord's Anointed
ungir ▸ CONJUG 3c VT **1** (*Med*) to put ointment on, rub with ointment
2 (*Rel*) to anoint
ungüento SM **1** (= *sustancia*) ointment, unguent
2 (= *remedio*) salve, balm
ungulado ADJ ungulate, hoofed
SM ungulate, hoofed animal
uni... PREF uni..., one-..., single-...
únicamente ADV only, solely
unicameral ADJ (*Pol*) single-chamber
unicameralismo SM system of single-chamber government
unicato* SM (*Méx*) sole rule, power monopoly
UNICEF SF ABR (= **United Nations International Children's Emergency Fund**) UNICEF
unicelular ADJ unicellular, single-cell
unicidad SF uniqueness
único ADJ **1** (= *solo*) only • **es el ~ ejemplar que existe** it is the only copy in existence • **fue el ~ sobreviviente** he was the sole *o* only survivor • **hijo ~** only child • **sistema de partido ~** one-party *o* single-party system • **la única dificultad es que ...** the only difficulty is that ... • **es lo ~ que nos faltaba** (*iró*) that's all we needed
2 (= *singular*) unique • **este ejemplar es ~** this specimen is unique • **como pianista es única** as a pianist she is in a class of her own • **¡eres ~! solo a ti se te podía ocurrir algo así** you're amazing! only you could think of something like that
unicolor ADJ one-colour, all one colour
unicornio SM unicorn
unidad SF **1** (= *cohesión*) unity • **defienden la ~ del Estado** they defend the unity of the State • **falta de ~ en la familia** lack of family unity ▸ **unidad de acción** (*Literat*) unity of action; [*de partido, movimiento*] unity ▸ **unidad de lugar** (*Literat*) unity of place ▸ **unidad de tiempo** (*Literat*) unity of time
2 (*Com, Mat*) unit • **precio por ~** unit price • —**¿cuánto es?** —**un euro la ~** "how much is it?"—"one euro each" • **se venden en cajas de seis ~es** they are sold in boxes of six ▸ **unidad de cuenta europea** European currency unit ▸ **unidad de medida** unit of measurement ▸ **unidad monetaria** monetary unit
3 (*Med*) (= *pabellón, sala*) unit ▸ **unidad coronaria** coronary unit ▸ **unidad de cuidados intensivos** intensive care unit ▸ **unidad de quemados** burns unit ▸ **unidad de terapia intensiva** (*Arg, Méx*), **unidad de tratamiento intensivo** (*Chile*), **unidad de vigilancia intensiva** intensive care unit
4 (*Radio, TV*) ▸ **unidad móvil** outside broadcast unit
5 (*Inform*) ▸ **unidad central** mainframe computer ▸ **unidad de control** control unit ▸ **unidad de disco fijo** hard (disk) drive ▸ **unidad de visualización** visual display unit ▸ **unidad periférica** peripheral device
6 (*Ferro*) (= *vagón*) coach, wagon, freight car (*EEUU*)
7 (*Aer*) (= *avión*) aircraft ▸ **unidad de cola** tail unit
8 (*Mil*) unit ▸ **unidad de combate** combat unit ▸ **unidad militar** military unit
unidimensional ADJ one-dimensional
unidireccional ADJ • **calle ~** one-way street
unido ADJ [*amigos, familiares*] close • **una familia muy unida** a very close *o* very close-knit family • **está muy unida a su madre** she's very close to her mother • **mantenerse ~s** to keep together, stick together, stay together
unifamiliar ADJ single-family
unificación SF unification
unificado ADJ [*país, precio*] unified
unificador ADJ unifying, uniting
unificar ▸ CONJUG 1g VT **1** (= *unir*) to unite, unify
2 (= *hacer uniforme*) to standardize
uniformado/a ADJ uniformed
SM/F (*gen*) man/woman in uniform; (= *policía*) policeman/policewoman
uniformar ▸ CONJUG 1a VT **1** (= *hacer uniforme*) to make uniform; (*Téc*) to standardize
2 [+ *persona*] to put into uniform, provide with a uniform
uniforme ADJ [*movimiento, sistema*] uniform; [*superficie*] level, even, smooth; [*velocidad*] steady, uniform
SM uniform ▸ **uniforme de campaña**, **uniforme de combate** battledress ▸ **uniforme de gala** full-dress uniform
uniformemente ADV uniformly
uniformidad SF (*gen*) uniformity; [*de acabado*] evenness, smoothness; [*de velocidad*] steadiness
uniformización SF standardization
uniformizar ▸ CONJUG 1f VT = **uniformar**
Unigénito SM • **el ~** the Only Begotten Son
unilateral ADJ unilateral, one-sided
unilateralismo SM unilateralism
unilateralmente ADV unilaterally
unión SF **1** (= *acción*) **a** [*de puntos, extremos*] joining together; [*de empresas*] merger • **la operación consiste en la ~ de los extremos del hueso fracturado** the operation consists of joining together the two ends of the fractured bone • **crearon el nombre de la empresa mediante la ~ de sus apellidos** the name of the company was created by joining together *o* combining their surnames • **solicitaron su ~ a la OTAN en 1993** they applied to join NATO in 1993
b • **en ~ con** *o* **de** (= *acompañado de*) together with, along with; (= *en asociación con*) in association with, together with • **viajó a París en ~ de sus colegas** he travelled to Paris together with *o* along with his associates • **la construcción del centro fue concedida a Unitex, en ~ con otra empresa** the contract to build the centre was awarded to Unitex, in association with another firm
2 (= *cualidad*) unity • **hemos fracasado por falta de ~** we have failed through lack of unity • **la ~ de los cristianos está muy lejana todavía** Christian unity is still a long way off • REFRÁN: • **la ~ hace la fuerza** united we stand
3 (= *organización*) ▸ **unión aduanera** customs union ▸ **Unión Europea** European Union ▸ **Unión General de Trabajadores** (*Esp*) *socialist union confederation* ▸ **Unión Monetaria (Europea)** (European) Monetary Union ▸ **Unión Panamericana** Pan-American Union ▸ **Unión Soviética** (*Hist*) Soviet Union
4 [*de pareja*] (= *matrimonio*) union • **su ~ en santo matrimonio** their union in holy matrimony ▸ **unión consensual** common-law marriage ▸ **unión de parejas de hecho** civil union ▸ **unión libre** cohabitation
5 (*Mec*) joint • **punto de ~** junction (**entre** between)
unionista (*Pol*) ADJ **1** (*Pol*) unionist
2 (*en Irlanda del Norte*) Unionist
SMF **1** (*Pol*) unionist
2 (*en Irlanda del Norte*) Unionist
unipartidario ADJ one-party
unipartidismo SM one-party system
unipersonal ADJ single, individual
unir ▸ CONJUG 3a VT **1** (= *acercar*) **a** [+ *grupos, tendencias, pueblos*] to unite • **es la persona perfecta para ~ al partido** he is the ideal person to unite the party
b [*sentimientos*] to unite • **los une el mismo amor a la verdad** they are united in their love of the truth • **a nuestros dos países los unen muchas más cosas de las que los dividen** there are far more things that unite our two countries than divide them • **nos une el interés por la ciencia** we share an interest in science • **me une a él una estrecha amistad** I have a very close friendship with him
c [*lazos*] to link, bind • **los lazos que unen ambos países** the ties that bind *o* link both countries
2 (= *atar*) [*contrato*] to bind • **con el periódico me unía un mero contrato** I was bound to the newspaper by nothing more than a simple contract • **el jugador ha rescindido el contrato que lo unía al club** the player has terminated the contract binding him to the club • **~ a dos personas en matrimonio** to join together two people in matrimony
3 (= *asociar, agrupar*) to combine • **uniendo los dos nombres resulta un nuevo concepto** a new concept is created by combining the two nouns • **el esquí de fondo une dos actividades: montañismo y esquí** cross-country skiing combines two activities: mountaineering and skiing • **decidieron ~ sus fuerzas para luchar contra el crimen** they decided to join forces in the fight against crime • **ha logrado ~ su nombre al de los grandes deportistas de este siglo** he has won a place among the great sporting names of this century
4 (= *conectar*) [*carretera, vuelo, ferrocarril*] to link (**con** with) • **la autopista une las dos poblaciones** the motorway links the two towns
5 [+ *objetos, piezas*] (*gen*) to join, join together; (*con pegamento, celo*) to stick together; (*con clavos, puntas*) to fasten together • **~ los bordes con cinta adhesiva** stick the edges together with adhesive tape • **van a tirar el tabique para ~ el salón a la cocina** they are going to knock together the lounge and the kitchen
6 (*Culin*) [+ *líquidos*] to mix; [+ *salsa*] to blend
7 (*Com*) [+ *compañías, intereses*] to merge
VPR **unirse 1** (= *cooperar*) (*para proyectos importantes*) to join together, come together, unite; (*en problemas puntuales*) to join forces • **los sindicatos se han unido en la lucha contra el paro** the trade unions have joined together *o* come together *o* united in the fight against unemployment • **si nos unimos todos, seremos más fuertes** if we all join together *o* come together *o* unite, we will be stronger • **ambas empresas se han unido para distribuir sus productos en Asia** the two companies have joined forces to distribute their products in Asia • **todos los partidos se unieron para mostrar su rechazo a la violencia** all the parties joined together *o* were united in their rejection of violence
2 (= *formar una unidad*) [*empresas, instituciones*] to merge • **tres cajas de ahorro se unen para crear un nuevo banco** three savings banks are merging to make a new bank • **~se en matrimonio** to be joined in matrimony (*frm*), marry
3 • **~se a a** [+ *movimiento, organización,*

expedición] to join • **se unieron al resto del grupo en París** they joined the rest of the group in Paris • **los taxistas se han unido a la huelga de camioneros** the taxi drivers have joined the lorry drivers' strike
b [*problemas, características, estilos*] • **a este atraso económico se une un paro estructural** this economic underdevelopment is compounded by structural unemployment • **a la maravillosa cocina se une un servicio muy eficiente** the wonderful cooking is complemented by very efficient service
c [+ *propuesta, iniciativa*] to support • **me uno a esta propuesta** I support this proposal
4 • **~se con** to join together with, combine with • **se unieron con los demócratas para formar una coalición** they joined together *o* combined with the democrats to form a coalition
5 [*líneas, caminos*] to meet • **se unen las ramas por encima** the branches meet overhead

unisex ADJ INV unisex

unísono ADJ unisonous, unison
SM • **al ~** (*lit*) in unison; (*fig*) in unison, with one voice • **al ~ con** in tune *o* harmony with

unitario/a ADJ **1** (*Pol*) unitary
2 (*Rel*) Unitarian
SM/F **1** (*Arg*) (*Hist*) centralist
2 (*Rel*) Unitarian

unitarismo SM Unitarianism

univalente ADJ univalent

univalvo ADJ univalve

universal ADJ (= *general*) universal; (= *mundial*) world, world-wide • **historia ~** world history • **de fama ~** internationally *o* world famous • **una especie de distribución ~** a species with a world-wide distribution *o* found all over the world

universalidad SF universality

universalizar ▸ CONJUG 1f VT (= *hacer universal*) to universalize; (= *generalizar*) to bring into general use
VPR **universalizarse** to become widespread

universalmente ADV (= *generalmente*) universally; (= *mundialmente*) all over the world

universiada SF university games (*pl*), student games (*pl*)

universidad SF university ▸ **Universidad a Distancia** ≈ Open University ▸ **universidad laboral** polytechnic, technical school *o* institute (EEUU) ▸ **Universidad Nacional de Educación a Distancia** ≈ Open University ▸ **universidad popular** extramural classes (*pl*), extension courses (*pl*)

universitario/a ADJ university (*antes de s*)
SM/F (= *estudiante*) (university) student; (= *licenciado*) university graduate

universo SM **1** (= *cosmos*) universe
2 (= *conjunto*) world • **el ~ poético de Lorca** Lorca's poetic world • **todo un ~ de regalos** a whole world of gifts

unívoco ADJ [*palabra, término*] univocal, monosemous; [*correspondencia*] one-to-one

UNO SF ABR (*Nic*) = **Unión Nacional Opositora**

uno/a PRON **1** (*uso como numeral*) one • **queda solo uno** there's only one left • **trece votos a favor y uno en contra** thirteen votes in favour and one against • **voy a hacer café, ¿quieres uno?** I'm going to make some coffee, do you want one? • **dos maletas grandes y una más pequeña** two large suitcases and a smaller one • **uno es joven y el otro viejo** one (of them) is young and the other is old • **uno a uno** one by one • **cada uno**: • **había tres manzanas para cada uno** there were three apples each • **cada uno a lo suyo** everyone should mind their own business • **de uno en uno** one by one • **Dios es uno** God is one • **la verdad es una** there is only one truth • **uno y otro** both • **el uno y el otro están locos** they're both mad • **el uno le dijo al otro** one said to the other • **uno con otro salen a diez dólares** they average out at ten dollars each • **uno tras otro** one after another, one after the other • **uno por uno** one by one • MODISMOS: • **una y no más** that's the last time I'm doing that • **lo uno por lo otro** what you lose on the swings you gain on the roundabouts • **es todo uno** • **es uno y lo mismo** it's all the same • **comer y sentirse mal fue todo uno** no sooner had she eaten than she fell ill
2 (*uso indefinido*) (= *persona*) **a** (*en singular*) somebody, someone • **uno dijo hace poco que debería estar prohibido** somebody *o* someone said recently that it should be banned • **ha venido una que dice que te conoce** somebody *o* someone came who says she knows you • **más de uno**: • **no gustará a más de uno** there are quite a few (people) who won't like this • **más de uno estaría encantado con esto** most people would be more than happy with this • **para mí es uno de tantos** as far as I'm concerned he's just one of many *o* a very ordinary sort
b (*en plural*) • **llegaron unos y se sentaron** some people arrived and sat down • **unos que estaban allí protestaron** some (of those) who were there protested • **unos me gustan y otros no** some I like, some *o* others I don't • **admirado por unos y odiado por otros** admired by some and hated by others • **los unos dicen que sí y los otros que no** some say yes and some *o* others say no • **unos y otros** all of them
3 (*uso impersonal*) you, one (*frm*) • **uno puede equivocarse** you *o* (*frm*) one can make a mistake • **uno nunca sabe qué hacer** you never know *o* (*frm*) one never knows what to do • **uno no es perfecto** I'm not perfect, one isn't perfect (*frm*) • **uno mismo** yourself, oneself • **es mejor hacerlo uno mismo** it's better to do it yourself *o* oneself • **reírse de uno mismo** to laugh at yourself *o* oneself • **tener confianza en uno mismo** to be self-confident
4 (*uso recíproco*) • **el uno al otro** each other • **se miraban fijamente el uno al otro** they stared at each other • **se interrumpen el uno al otro** they interrupt each other • **unos a otros** each other, one another • **se detestan unos a otros** they hate each other *o* one another
SM (*gen*) one; (*ordinal*) first • **el uno es mi número de la suerte** one is my lucky number • **ciento uno** a hundred and one • **el uno de mayo** the first of May, May the first, 1 May • **planta uno** first floor • **la fila uno** the first row, the front row • **número uno** number one • **este disco ha llegado al número uno** this record has reached number one • **el enemigo público número uno** public enemy number one • **el paro es el problema número uno** unemployment is the number one problem • **es la número uno del tenis mundial** she's the number one tennis player in the world; ▸ **un, seis**

untadura SF **1** (= *acto*) (= *cubrimiento*) smearing, rubbing; (= *engrase*) greasing
2 (= *producto*) (*Med*) ointment; (*Mec etc*) grease, oil
3 (= *mancha*) mark, smear

untar ▸ CONJUG 1a VT **1** (= *cubrir*) to smear, rub (**con, de** with); (*Med*) to anoint, rub (**con, de** with); (*Mec etc*) to grease, oil • **~ su pan en la salsa** to dip *o* soak one's bread in the gravy • **~ el pan con mantequilla** to spread butter on one's bread • **~ los dedos de tinta** to smear ink on one's fingers, smear one's fingers with ink
2* (= *sobornar*) to bribe, grease the palm of
VPR **untarse 1** (= *ensuciarse*) • **~se con** *o* **de** to smear o.s. with
2* (*fraudulentamente*) to have sticky fingers*

unto SM **1** (= *ungüento*) ointment
2 (= *grasa*) grease, animal fat
3 (*Cono Sur*) (= *betún*) shoe polish

untuosidad SF greasiness, oiliness

untuoso ADJ (= *graso*) greasy, oily

untura SF = **untadura**

uña SF **1** (*Anat*) [*de la mano*] nail, fingernail; [*del pie*] toenail; (*Zool*) claw • **comerse las uñas** (*lit*) to bite one's nails; (*fig*) to get very impatient; (*LAm*) (= *ser pobre*) to be really poor • **hacerse las uñas** to have one's nails done, do one's nails • MODISMOS: • **tener las uñas afiladas** to be light-fingered • **ser uña y carne** to be inseparable • **estar de uñas con algn** to be at daggers drawn with sb • **defender algo con uñas y dientes** to defend sth tooth and nail • **dejarse las uñas**: • **se dejó las uñas en ese trabajo** he wore his fingers to the bone at that job • **enseñar las uñas** to show one's claws • **tener las uñas largas** to be light-fingered • **mostrar** *o* **sacar las uñas** to show one's claws ▸ **uña encarnada** ingrowing toenail
2 (= *pezuña*) hoof ▸ **uña de caballo** (*Bot*) coltsfoot • MODISMO: • **escapar a uña de caballo** to ride off at full speed ▸ **uña de vaca** (*Culin*) cow heel
3 [*del alacrán*] sting
4 (*Téc*) claw, nail puller (*EEUU*)
5 [*de ancla*] fluke

uñada SF scratch

uñalarga SMF (*LAm*) thief

uñarada SF = **uñada**

uñero SM **1** (= *panadizo*) whitlow
2 (= *uña encarnada*) ingrowing toenail
3 [*de libro*] thumb notch • **dos tomos con ~** two volumes with thumb index

uñeta SF (*Chile*) plectrum

uñetas* SMF INV (*LAm*) thief

uñetear ▸ CONJUG 1a VT (*Cono Sur*) to steal

uñilargo SM, **uñón** SM (*Perú*) thief

UOE SF ABR (*Esp*) (*Mil*) = **Unidad de Operaciones Especiales**

UP SF ABR **1** (*Chile*) = **Unidad Popular**
2 (*Col*) = **Unión Patriótica**
3 (*Perú*) = **Unión Popular**

upa[1] SM (*And*) idiot

upa[2] EXCL up, up!

UPA SF ABR (= **Unión Panamericana**) PAU

UPAE SF ABR = **Unión Postal de las Américas y España**

upar* ▸ CONJUG 1a VT = **aupar**

UPC SF ABR (= **unidad de procesamiento central**) CPU

uperización SF UHT treatment

uperizado ADJ • **leche uperizada** UHT milk

UPN SF ABR (*Esp*) (= **Unión del Pueblo Navarro**) *Navarrese nationalist party*

UPU SF ABR (= **Unión Postal Universal**) UPU

Urales SMPL (*tb* **montes Urales**) Urals

uralita® SF *corrugated asbestos and cement roofing material*

uranio SM uranium ▸ **uranio enriquecido** enriched uranium

Urano SM Uranus

urbanícola SMF city dweller

urbanidad SF courtesy, politeness, urbanity (*frm*)

urbanificar ▸ CONJUG 1g VT = **urbanizar**

urbanismo SM **1** (= *planificación*) town planning; (= *desarrollo*) urban development

2 (*Caribe*) real-estate development
urbanista SMF town planner
urbanístico ADJ [*problemas*] town-planning (*antes de s*); [*plan, entorno*] urban, city (*antes de s*)
urbanita SMF city dweller, urbanite (*EEUU*)
urbanizable ADJ • **terreno ~** building land • **zona no ~** green belt, land designated as not for building
urbanización SF **1** (= *acto*) urbanization
2 (= *colonia, barrio*) housing development, housing estate
urbanizado ADJ built-up
urbanizadora SF property development company
urbanizar ▷ CONJUG 1f VT **1** [+ *terreno*] to develop, build on, urbanize
2 [+ *persona*] to civilize
urbano ADJ **1** (= *de la ciudad*) urban, town (*antes de s*), city (*antes de s*)
2 (= *educado*) courteous, polite, urbane (*frm*)
urbe SF large city, metropolis; (= *capital*) capital city • **La Urbe** (*Esp*) Madrid, the Capital
urbícola SMF city dweller
urco SM (*And, Cono Sur*) (*gen*) ram; (= *alpaca*) alpaca
urdimbre SF **1** [*de tela*] warp
2 (= *intriga*) scheme, intrigue
urdir ▷ CONJUG 3a VT **1** [+ *tela*] to warp
2 (= *tramar*) to plot
urdu SM (*Ling*) Urdu
urea SF urea
urente ADJ burning, stinging
uréter SM ureter
uretra SF urethra
urgencia SF **1** (= *apresuramiento*) urgency • **con toda ~** with the utmost urgency • **pedir algo con ~** to request sth urgently • **trataron varios asuntos de ~** they dealt with a number of urgent *o* pressing matters
2 (= *emergencia*) emergency • **en caso de ~** in case of (an) emergency, in an emergency • **medida de ~** emergency measure • **déjame entrar en el baño, por favor, que tengo una ~** let me in to the bathroom, please, it's an emergency • **procedimiento de ~** (*Admin*) emergency procedure
3 (*Med*) emergency • **el doctor se ocupará primero de las ~s** the doctor will deal with the emergencies *o* emergency cases first • **servicios de ~** emergency services • **la operaron de ~** she underwent emergency surgery • **"urgencias"** "accident & emergency" • **tuvimos que ir a ~s** we had to go to casualty
urgente ADJ [*mensaje, trabajo*] urgent; [*asunto*] urgent, pressing • **carta ~** special delivery letter • **pedido ~** rush order
urgentemente ADV urgently
urgir ▷ CONJUG 3c VI to be urgent *o* pressing • **urge el dinero** the money is urgently needed • **me urge la respuesta** I need a reply urgently *o* as soon as possible • **el tiempo urge** time presses, time is short • **me urge terminarlo** I must finish it as soon as I can • **me urge partir** I have to leave at once • **"úrgeme vender: dos gatos ..."** "must be sold: two cats ..."
úrico ADJ uric
urinario ADJ urinary
SM urinal, public lavatory
urna SF (= *vasija*) urn; [*de cristal*] glass case; (*Pol*) (*tb* **urna electoral**) ballot box • **acudir a las ~s** to vote, go to the polls
URNG SF ABR (*Guat*) = **Unidad Revolucionaria Nacional Guatemalteca**
uro SM aurochs
urogallo SM capercaillie
urogenital ADJ urogenital
urología SF urology
urológico ADJ urological
urólogo/a SM/F urologist
urpo SM (*Cono Sur*) = **ulpo**
urraca SF **1** (= *ave*) magpie
2* (= *habladora*) chatterbox*; (= *chismosa*) gossip
URSS [urs] SF ABR (*Hist*) (= **Unión de Repúblicas Socialistas Soviéticas**) USSR
ursulina SF **1** (*Rel*) Ursuline nun
2 (*Esp**) goody-goody*
urta SF sea bream
urticaria SF urticaria, nettle rash
urubú SM (*Cono Sur*) black vulture
Uruguay SM (*tb* **el Uruguay**) Uruguay
uruguayismo SM *word or phrase peculiar to Uruguay*
uruguayo/a ADJ, SM/F Uruguayan
USA ADJ INV United States (*antes de s*), American • **dos aviones USA** two US planes
usado ADJ **1** (= *no nuevo*) [*coche*] second-hand, used; [*televisor, ropa*] second-hand; [*sello, billete*] used
2 (= *gastado*) [*pila*] flat; [*ropa, disco*] worn-out • **un diccionario muy ~** a well-thumbed dictionary
usagre SM (*Med*) impetigo; (*Vet*) mange
usanza SF usage, custom • **a ~ india** • **a ~ de los indios** according to Indian custom
usar ▷ CONJUG 1a VT **1** (= *utilizar*) [+ *aparato, transporte, sustancia, expresión*] to use • **solo usan el coche cuando salen al campo** they only use the car when they go to the country • **están dispuestos a ~ la violencia para defender sus ideas** they are prepared to use *o* resort to violence to defend their ideas • **la maleta está sin ~** the suitcase has never been used • **esta herramienta ha de ~se con sumo cuidado** this tool must be used with great care • **no sé ~ este teléfono** I don't know how to use this telephone • **no olvide ~ el cinturón de seguridad** don't forget to wear your seat belt • **~ algo/a algn como** to use sth/sb as • **lo ~on como conejillo de indias** they used him as a guinea pig • **de ~ y tirar** [*envase, producto*] disposable • **literatura que algunos llaman de "~ y tirar"** so-called "pulp fiction"
2 (= *llevar*) [+ *ropa, perfume*] to wear • **el pañuelo que usan los palestinos** the scarf worn by the Palestinians • **esos pantalones están sin ~** these trousers have not been worn • **¿qué número usa?** what size do you take?
3 (= *soler*) • **~ hacer algo** to be in the habit of doing sth
VI • **~ de** [+ *derecho, poder*] to exercise • **~ del derecho al voto** to exercise one's right to vote, use one's vote
VPR **usarse** to be worn • **la chistera ya no se usa** top hats are not worn nowadays, no one wears top hats nowadays
USB SM ABR (*Inform*) (= **universal serial bus**) USB
Usbekia SF, **Usbiekistán** SM Uzbekistan
usía PRON PERS Your Lordship/Your Ladyship
usina SF **1** (*LAm*) factory, plant
2 (*Cono Sur*) [*de electricidad*] power plant; [*de gas*] gasworks; [*de tranvías*] tram depot
uslero SM (*Chile*) rolling pin
USO SF ABR (*Esp*) = **Unión Sindical Obrera**
uso SM **1** (= *utilización*) use • **los médicos desaconsejan el uso indiscriminado de antibióticos** doctors advise against the indiscriminate use of antibiotics • **un mango de plata gastado por el uso** a silver handle worn through use • **una base de datos para uso exclusivo de los científicos** a database for the use of scientists only, a database exclusively for scientists' use • **el uso correcto del pronombre "le"** the correct use of the pronoun "le" • **el uso de la bicicleta no está permitido en autopistas** bicycles are not allowed *o* permitted on motorways • **no está permitido el uso del claxon en las proximidades de un hospital** you cannot hoot your horn in the vicinity of a hospital • **el uso y abuso de un producto/una expresión** the excessive use of a product/an expression • **términos de uso común** terms in common use *o* usage • **un analgésico de uso corriente** a commonly used painkiller • **aparatos de uso doméstico** domestic appliances • **"de uso externo"** (*Med*) "for external use" • **objeto de uso personal** article for personal use, personal item • **jeringuillas de un solo uso** disposable syringes • **estar en uso** to be in use • **tratamientos médicos actualmente en uso** medical treatments currently being used *o* currently in use • **un termino aún hoy en uso** a term still used today • **estar en buen uso** to be in good condition • **está fuera de uso** (= *no se usa*) it is not in use; (= *no funciona*) it is out of order • **hacer uso de** [+ *derecho, privilegio, poder*] to exercise; [+ *armas, fuerza*] to use • **estar en el uso de la palabra** to be speaking, have the floor (*frm*) • **hacer uso de la palabra** to speak ▸ **uso de razón** • **desde que tuvo uso de razón** (*lit*) since he reached the age of reason; (*fig*) for as long as he could remember
2 (= *aplicación*) use • **el mercurio tiene innumerables usos industriales** mercury has countless uses in industry • **esta calculadora tiene varios usos** this calculator has several uses
3 (= *costumbre*) custom • **los usos sociales de nuestro tiempo** the social customs of our time • **los usos más tradicionales de la región** the most traditional customs of the region
4 • **al uso**: • **los tópicos al uso** the usual clichés • **esta no es una guía de turismo al uso** this is not the usual sort of travel guide, this is not a travel guide in the usual sense of the word • **por emplear el tecnicismo al uso** to use the current technical jargon • **las ideas posmodernistas tan al uso en los últimos años** the post-modernist ideas so fashionable in recent years
usted PRON PERS **1** (*en singular*) you (*polite or formal address*) • **esto es para ~** this is for you • **lo haremos sin ~** we'll do it without you • **—muchas gracias —a ~** "thank you very much" — "thank you" • **el coche de ~** your car • **mi coche y el de ~** my car and yours • **hablar** *o* **llamar** *o* **tratar de ~ a algn** to use the "usted" form with sb, address sb using the "usted" form • **no me hables de ~, que no soy tan vieja** you needn't use the "usted" form with me — I'm not that old
2 • **ustedes** you (*polite or formal address in most of Spain and replaces vosotros in Latin America*) • **gracias a todos ~es podremos pagarlo** thanks to all of you we shall be able to pay it • **pasen ~es, por favor** please come in • **a ver, niños ¿~es qué quieren para cenar?** (*esp LAm*) right, what do you children want for tea?
usual ADJ usual, customary
usualmente ADV usually
usuario/a SM/F user • **~ de la vía pública** road user • **~ final** (*Inform*) end user
usufructo SM usufruct, use ▸ **usufructo vitalicio** life interest (**de** in)
usufructuario/a SM/F usufructuary

usura (SF) usury
usurario (ADJ) usurious, extortionate
usurear ▹ CONJUG 1a (VI) (= *prestar*) *to lend money at an exorbitant rate of interest*
usurero/a (SM/F) usurer
usurpación (SF) [*de poder, trono*] usurpation; [*de tierras*] seizure
usurpador(a) (SM/F) usurper
usurpar ▹ CONJUG 1a (VT) [+ *poder, trono*] to usurp; [+ *tierras*] to seize
usuta (SF) (*Arg, Perú*) = **ojota**
utensilio (SM) (= *herramienta*) tool, implement; (*Culin*) utensil • **con los ~s de su oficio** with the tools of his trade ▸ **utensilios de cirujano** surgeon's instruments ▸ **utensilios de pintor** artist's materials ▸ **utensilios para escribir** writing materials ▸ **utensilios para pescar** fishing tackle (*sing*)
uterino (ADJ) uterine • **hermanos ~s** children born of the same mother; ▹ **furor**
útero (SM) womb, uterus ▸ **útero alquilado, útero de alquiler** surrogate motherhood
UTI (ABR) **1** (*Chile*) (= **Unidad de Terapia Intensiva**) ICU, intensive care unit
2 (*Arg, Méx*) (= **Unidad de Tratamiento Intensivo**) ICU, intensive care unit
útil (ADJ) **1** (= *de utilidad*) useful; (= *servible*) usable, serviceable • **es muy ~ saber conducir** it is very useful to be able to drive • **las plantas ~es para el hombre** plants which are useful to man • **el coche es viejo pero todavía está ~** the car is old but it is still serviceable • **es muy ~ tenerlo aquí cerca** it's very handy having it close by here • **¿en qué puedo serle ~?** can I help you?, what can I do for you?
2 • **día ~** (= *hábil*) working day, weekday
3 (*Mil*) • **~ para el servicio** [*persona*] fit for military service; [*vehículo*] operational
(SMPL) **útiles** tools, equipment (*sing*) ▸ **útiles de chimenea** fire irons ▸ **útiles escolares** (*LAm*) school equipment (*sing*) ▸ **útiles de labranza** agricultural implements ▸ **útiles de pesca** fishing tackle (*sing*)
utilería (SF) (*LAm*) props (*pl*)
utilero/a (SM/F) (*LAm*) (*Teat*) property manager, props man
utilidad (SF) **1** (*gen*) usefulness • **no pongo en duda la ~ de tu invento** I'm not questioning the usefulness of your invention • **un método de gran ~ para aprender inglés** a very useful method for learning English • **no lo tires, ya le encontraremos alguna ~** don't throw it away, we'll find some use for it • **un servicio de ~ pública** a public service • **sacar la máxima ~ a algo** to use sth to the full, make full use of sth
2 (*LAm*) (*Com, Econ*) profit ▸ **utilidades ocasionales** windfall profits
3 (*Inform*) utility
utilitario (ADJ) **1** [*persona*] utilitarian
2 [*coche, ropa*] utility (*antes de s*)
(SM) (*Aut*) small car, compact car
utilitarismo (SM) utilitarianism
utilitarista (SMF) utilitarian
utilizable (ADJ) **1** (= *que puede usarse*) usable, serviceable; (= *disponible*) available for use, ready to use
2 (*Téc*) reclaimable
utilización (SF) **1** (= *uso*) use, utilization (*frm*)
2 (*Téc*) reclamation
utilizar ▹ CONJUG 1f (VT) **1** (= *usar*) to use, make use of, utilize (*frm*) • **¿qué medio de transporte utilizas?** which means of transport do you use? • **me dejó ~ su ordenador** she let me use her computer
2 (= *explotar*) [+ *recursos*] to harness; [+ *desperdicios*] to reclaim
utillaje (SM) tools (*pl*), equipment
utillero (SM) **1** (= *ayudante*) plumber's mate
2 (*Ftbl*) kit man
útilmente (ADV) usefully
utopía (SF), **utopia** (SF) Utopia
utópico (ADJ) Utopian
utopista (ADJ), (SMF) Utopian
utrículo (SM) utricle
UV (ABR) (= **ultravioleta**) UV
(SF ABR) (*Esp*) (*Pol*) = **Unió(n) Valenciana**
UVA (ABR) (= **ultravioleta A**) UVA
uva (SF) **1** grape • **las doce uvas** • **las uvas de la suerte** *twelve grapes eaten at midnight on New-Year's Eve* • MODISMOS: • **de uvas a peras** once in a blue moon • **ir de uvas a peras** to change the subject for no reason • **entrar a por uvas** to take the plunge • **estar de mala uva** (*Esp**) to be in a bad mood • **tener muy mala uva** to be a nasty piece of work* • **estar hecho una uva** to be as drunk as a lord ▸ **uva blanca** green grape, white grape ▸ **uva crespa** gooseberry ▸ **uva de Corinto** currant ▸ **uva de gato** (*Bot*) stonecrop ▸ **uva espina** gooseberry ▸ **uva moscatel** muscatel grape ▸ **uva negra** black grape ▸ **uva pasa** raisin ▸ **uvas de mesa** dessert grapes ▸ **uvas verdes** (*fig*) sour grapes
2* (= *vino*) wine; (= *bebida*) drink (*in general*)
3 (*Cono Sur*) (= *beso*) kiss
UVB (SMPL ABR) (= **ultravioleta B**) UVB
uve (SF) (name of the letter) V • **en forma de uve** V-shaped • **escote en uve** V-neck ▸ **uve doble** (name of the letter) W
UVI (SF ABR) (= **unidad de vigilancia intensiva**) ICU ▸ **UVI móvil** mobile intensive care unit
úvula (SF) uvula
uvular (ADJ) uvular
uxoricida (SM) uxoricide, wife-killer
uxoricidio (SM) uxoricide
uzbeko/a (ADJ) Uzbek
(SM/F) Uzbek
-uzo, -uza ▹ **Aspects of Word Formation in Spanish 2**

Vv

V, v ['uβe] [be'korta] (*LAm*) SF (= *letra*) V, v • **en (forma de) V** V-shaped • **escote en V** V-neck ▸ **V chica** (*LAm**) ▸ **V corta** (*LAm**) (the letter) V ▸ **V de la victoria** (*gen*) V for victory; (= *signo*) victory sign, V-sign ▸ **V doble** (*Esp*), **doble V** (*LAm*) (the letter) W

v ABR (*Elec*) (= **voltio(s)**) v

V. ABR **1** = **Usted**
2 = **Véase**
3 (= **Visto**) OK

v. ABR **1** = **ver, véase**
2 (*Literat*) (= **verso**) v

va ▸ **ir**

V.A. ABR = **Vuestra Alteza**

vaca SF **1** (*Zool*) cow • **el mal** *o* **la enfermedad de las ~s locas** mad cow disease • MODISMOS: • **(los años de) las ~s flacas** the lean years • **(los años de) las ~s gordas** the fat years, the boom years • **pasar las ~s gordas** to have a grand time of it* • **ponerse como una ~*** to get as fat as a pig* ▸ **vaca de leche** (*lit*) dairy cow; (*LAm*) (*fig*) good business, profitable deal ▸ **vaca de San Antón** ladybird, ladybug (*EEUU*) ▸ **vaca lechera** dairy cow ▸ **vaca marina** sea cow, manatee ▸ **vaca sagrada** (*tb fig*) sacred cow
2 (*Culin*) beef
3 (= *cuero*) cowhide
4 (*LAm*) (*Com*) *enterprise with profits on a pro rata basis*
5 • MODISMO: • **hacer(se) la ~** (*And*) to play truant, play hooky (*EEUU*)

vacaburra‡ SF boor • **¡vacaburra!** animal!‡

vacación SF, **vacaciones** SFPL holiday(s), vacation (*sing*) (*EEUU*) • **estar de vacaciones** to be (away) on holiday • **irse** *o* **marcharse de vacaciones** to go (away) on holiday, go off on holiday • **hacer vacaciones** to take a day off ▸ **vacaciones escolares** school holidays ▸ **vacaciones pagadas, vacaciones retribuidas** holidays with pay

vacacional ADJ holiday (*antes de s*), vacation (*antes de s*) • **período ~** holiday period

vacacionar ▸ CONJUG 1a VT (*Méx*) to spend one's holidays (*esp Brit*) *o* vacation (*EEUU*)

vacacionista SMF holidaymaker, vacationer (*EEUU*)

vacada SF herd of cows

vacaje SM **1** (*Cono Sur*) (= *vacada*) cows (*pl*), cattle (*pl*); (= *manada*) herd of cows
2 (*Méx*) herd of beef cows

vacante ADJ (*gen*) vacant; [*silla*] empty, unoccupied; [*puesto*] unfilled
SF **1** (= *puesto*) vacancy, (unfilled) post • **hay una ~ en la oficina** there is a vacancy in the office • **proveer una ~** to fill a post
2 (*LAm*) (= *asiento*) empty seat

vacar ▸ CONJUG 1g VI **1** (*gen*) to fall vacant, become vacant; [*puesto*] to remain unfilled
2† [*persona*] (= *cesar*) to cease work; (= *estar inactivo*) to be idle
3† • **~ a** *o* **en** to engage in, devote o.s. to
4† • **~ de** to lack, be without

VACACIONES

¿"Holiday" o "holidays"?

▸ *En inglés británico,* **vacaciones** *se puede traducir tanto por* **holiday** *como por* **holidays** *cuando hablamos de un periodo de tiempo sin colegio o trabajo:*
¿Dónde pasaste las vacaciones?
Where did you spend your holiday(s)?
Larry fue a Londres un par de días durante las vacaciones
Larry went to London for a couple of days during the holiday(s)

▸ **Vacaciones** *se traduce por* **holiday** *cuando se habla de un viaje en particular:*
El año pasado pasamos unas vacaciones maravillosas en Mallorca
We had a lovely holiday in Majorca last year
¿Te lo has pasado bien en las vacaciones?
Did you have a good holiday?
Aquí **holiday** *funciona como un sustantivo contable normal; se añade una "s" cuando se trata de más de un viaje.*

▸ **Estar de vacaciones** *se traduce por* **to be on holiday**. *En este caso* **holiday** *no acepta el plural:*
Estaré de vacaciones dos semanas
I'll be on holiday for a fortnight

Para otros usos y ejemplos ver la entrada.

---

vacarí ADJ cowhide (*antes de s*)

vaccinio SM (*Esp*) bilberry, blueberry (*EEUU*)

vaciadero† SM **1** (= *conducto*) drain
2 (= *vertedero*) rubbish tip, garbage dump (*EEUU*)

vaciado ADJ **1** [*estatua*] cast in a mould, cast in a mold (*EEUU*); [*útiles*] hollow-ground
2 (*Méx*) (= *estupendo*) great*, terrific*
SM **1** [*de objeto*] cast, mould(ing), mold(ing) (*EEUU*) ▸ **vaciado a troquel** die-cast ▸ **vaciado de yeso** plaster cast
2 (= *acto de vaciar*) [*de madera, piedra*] hollowing out; (= *excavación*) excavation; [*de piscina, estanque*] emptying
3 [*de cuchillo*] sharpening
4 (*Aer*) ▸ **vaciado rápido** jettisoning

vaciapatatas SM INV potato scoop

vaciar ▸ CONJUG 1c VT **1** [+ *recipiente, contenido*] to empty; [+ *radiador*] to drain; (= *beber*) to drink up; (*Aer*) to jettison; (*Inform*) to dump • **vacié la nevera para limpiarla** I emptied the fridge to clean it • **vació los bolsillos en la mesa** he emptied out his pockets on to the table • **vació la leche en un vaso** he poured the milk into a glass • **lo vació todo sobre su cabeza** he poured the lot over his head
2 [+ *madera, piedra*] to hollow out; [+ *estatua*] to cast
3 [+ *cuchillo*] to sharpen, grind
4 [+ *tema, teoría*] to expound at length
5 [+ *texto*] to copy out
6* (= *hacer una histerectomía a*) to give a hysterectomy to
VI [*río*] to flow, empty (**en** into)
VPR **vaciarse 1** [*bañera, depósito*] to empty
2* (*tb* **vaciarse por la lengua**) to blab*, spill the beans*

vaciedad SF **1** (= *estado*) emptiness
2 (= *necedad*) (piece of) nonsense • **~es** nonsense (*sing*), rubbish (*sing*), garbage (*sing*) (*EEUU*)

vacila* SM tease, joker

vacilación SF hesitation, vacillation • **sin vacilaciones** unhesitatingly

vacilada SF **1** (*esp CAm, Méx**) (= *broma*) mickey-taking‡; (= *chiste*) joke; (= *chiste verde*) dirty joke • **de ~** as a joke, for a laugh*
2 (*Méx**) (= *borrachera*) binge*, spree
3 (= *truco*) trick

vacilante ADJ **1** [*mano, paso*] unsteady; [*voz*] faltering, halting; [*memoria*] uncertain; [*mueble*] wobbly, tottery
2 [*persona*] (= *inseguro*) hesitant, uncertain; (= *indeciso*) indecisive
3 [*luz*] flickering

vacilar ▸ CONJUG 1a VI **1** (= *dudar*) to hesitate, waver; (= *ser indeciso*) to vacillate; (= *esperar*) to hold back from doing sth • **sin ~** unhesitatingly • **~ en hacer algo** to hesitate to do sth • **~ entre dos posibilidades** to hesitate between two possibilities • **es un hombre que vacila mucho** he is a very indecisive man, he is a man who dithers a lot • **no vaciles en decírmelo** don't hesitate to tell me about it
2 (*por falta de estabilidad*) [*mueble*] to be unsteady, wobble; [*persona*] (*al andar*) to totter, reel; (*al hablar*) to falter; [*memoria*] to fail; [*moralidad*] to be collapsing
3 [*luz*] to flicker
4 (= *variar*) • **un sabor que vacila entre agradable y desagradable** a taste which varies *o* ranges between nice and nasty
5* (= *guasearse*) • **~ con algn** to tease sb, take the mickey out of sb‡
6 (*Méx**) (= *divertirse*) to have fun, lark about*; (= *ir de juerga*) to go on a spree
7* (= *presumir*) to talk big*, show off, swank*
VT **1** (= *burlarse de*) to take the mickey out of‡, make fun of • **¡no me vaciles!** stop messing me about!*
2 (*CAm**) (= *engañar*) to trick

vacile (SM) **1*** (= *guasa*) teasing • **estar de ~** to tease
2 (= *duda*) hesitation
vacilón/ona* (ADJ) **1** (= *guasón*) teasing, jokey • **estar ~** to be in a jokey mood
2 (*CAm, Méx*) (= *juerguista*) fun-loving
3 (= *presumido*) swanky*, stuck-up*
(SM/F) **1** (= *bromista*) tease, joker
2 (*CAm, Méx*) (= *juerguista*) party-goer, reveller
3 (= *presumido*) poser*, show-off*
(SM) (*CAm, Méx*) (= *juerga*) party; (= *diversión*) fun • **andar de ~** to be out on the town
vacío (ADJ) **1** (*gen*) empty; [*puesto, local*] vacant, empty • **el teatro estaba medio ~** the theatre was half empty • **nunca bebo cerveza con el estómago ~** I never drink beer on an empty stomach • **he alquilado un piso ~ porque sale más barato** I've rented an unfurnished flat because it's cheaper • **Madrid queda ~ en agosto** Madrid is empty *o* deserted in August • **de ~: el camión volvió de ~** the lorry came back empty • **lo pedí pero tuve que marcharme de ~** I asked for it but had to go away empty-handed • **MODISMO:** • **irse con las manos vacías** to leave empty-handed
2 (= *superficial*) [*persona*] shallow; [*conversación*] meaningless • **un discurso ~ de contenido** a speech empty *o* devoid of any content
3 (= *sin sentido*) [*existencia*] empty, meaningless
4 (= *vano*) [*esfuerzo*] vain; [*promesa*] empty, hollow
5 • **pan ~** (*And, CAm, Caribe*) dry bread
(SM) **1** (*Fís*) vacuum • **envasar al ~** to vacuum-pack • **envasado al ~** vacuum-packed
2 (= *hueco*) (empty) space, gap • **han dejado un ~ para el nombre** they have left a space for the name • **tener un ~ en el estómago** to have an empty stomach • **MODISMO:** • **hacer el ~ a algn** to send sb to Coventry
3 (= *abismo*) • **el ~** the void, space • **saltó al ~ desde lo alto del acantilado** he jumped from the top of the cliff into space *o* the void • **se arrojó al ~ desde un quinto piso** he threw himself out of a fifth-floor window • **MODISMO:** • **caer en el ~** to fall on deaf ears
4 (= *falta de sentido*) void • **el ~ existencial** the existential void • **su muerte dejó un ~ en nuestras vidas** his death left a void in our lives • **una sensación de ~** a feeling of emptiness
5 (*Jur, Pol*) ▸ **vacío de poder** power vacuum ▸ **vacío legislativo** gap in the legislation ▸ **vacío político** political vacuum
6 (*Mec*) • **marchar en ~** to tick over
7 (*Anat*) side, flank
vacuidad (SF) (*frm*) vacuity (*frm*), vacuousness (*frm*)
vacuna (SF) **1** (= *sustancia*) vaccine • **la ~ de la hepatitis** the hepatitis vaccine • **ponerle una ~ a algn** to vaccinate sb ▸ **vacuna antigripal** flu vaccine
2 (*esp LAm*) (= *acto*) vaccination
vacunación (SF) vaccination
vacunar ▷ CONJUG 1a (VT) **1** (*Med*) to vaccinate (**contra** against)
2 (*ante adversidad, dolor*) (= *preparar*) to prepare; (= *habituar*) to inure; (= *prevenir*) to forearm
(VPR) **vacunarse** to be *o* get vaccinated
vacuno (ADJ) bovine, cow (*antes de s*) • **ganado ~** cattle
(SM) (= *ganado*) cattle (*pl*) • **carne de ~** beef ▸ **vacuno de carne** beef cattle ▸ **vacuno de leche, vacuno lechero** dairy cattle
vacuo (ADJ) **1** (= *vacío*) empty
2 [*comentario, comportamiento*] vacuous (*frm*), frivolous
vade† (SM) = **vademécum**
vadeable (ADJ) **1** [*río*] fordable, crossable
2 [*problema*] not impossible, not insuperable
vadear ▷ CONJUG 1a (VT) **1** [+ *río*] (= *atravesar*) to ford; (*a pie*) to wade across; [+ *agua*] to wade through
2 [+ *dificultad*] to surmount, overcome
3 [+ *persona*] to sound out
(VI) to wade • **cruzar un río vadeando** to wade across a river • **llegar a tierra vadeando** to wade ashore
vademécum (SM) (PL: **vademécums**)
1 (= *libro*) vade mecum
2 (*Escol*) satchel, schoolbag
vadera (SF) wide ford
vade retro (EXCL) (*hum*) go away! • **¡~, Satanás!** get thee behind me (Satan)!
vado (SM) **1** [*de río*] ford
2 (*Esp*) (*Aut*) garage entrance • **"vado permanente"** "garage entrance", "keep clear"
3† (*fig*) (= *salida*) way out, solution • **no hallar ~** to see no way out, find no solution • **tentar el ~** to look into possible solutions
4† (*fig*) (= *descanso*) respite
vagabundaje (SM) vagrancy
vagabundear ▷ CONJUG 1a (VI) **1** (= *andar sin rumbo*) to wander, rove
2 (*pey*) [*pordiosero*] to be a tramp, be a bum (EEUU)
3 (= *gandulear*) to loaf, idle
vagabundeo (SM) **1** (*sin rumbo*) wandering, roving
2 [*de pordiosero*] tramp's life, bumming (EEUU); (*pey*) vagrancy
3 (= *ganduleo*) loafing, idling
vagabundería (SF) (*Ven*) abuse
vagabundo/a (ADJ) **1** (= *errante*) [*persona*] wandering, roving; [*perro*] stray
2 (= *pordiosero*) vagabond (*frm*); (*pey*) vagrant
(SM/F) **1** (= *persona errante*) wanderer, rover
2 (= *pordiosero*) vagabond (*frm*), tramp, bum (EEUU); (*pey*) vagrant
vagación (SF) (*Mec*) free play
vagamente (ADV) vaguely
vagamundería (SF) (*LAm*) idleness, laziness
vagamundero (ADJ) (*LAm*) idle, lazy
vagancia (SF) **1** (= *pereza*) laziness, idleness
2 (= *vagabundeo*) vagrancy
vagante (ADJ) **1** (*liter*) (= *sin rumbo*) wandering
2 (*Mec*) (= *suelto*) free, loose
vagar ▷ CONJUG 1h (VI) **1** (= *errar*) to wander (about), roam; (= *rondar*) to prowl about; (= *pasear*) to saunter up and down, wander about the streets; (= *entretenerse*) to loiter; (= *gandulear*) to idle, loaf • **~ como alma en pena** to wander about like a lost soul
2 (*Mec*) to be loose, move about
(SM) (= *tiempo libre*) leisure, free time; (= *pereza*) idleness; (= *calma*) lack of anxiety, freedom from worry • **andar de ~** to be at leisure
vagido (SM) cry (*of new-born baby*)
vagina (SF) vagina
vaginal (ADJ) vaginal
vaginitis (SF INV) vaginitis
vago/a (ADJ) **1** (*gen*) vague; (*Arte, Fot*) blurred, ill-defined; (= *indeterminado*) indeterminate
2 [*persona*] (= *perezoso*) lazy, slack; (= *poco fiable*) unreliable; (= *ocioso*) idle, unemployed • **MODISMO:** • **ser más ~ que la chaqueta de un guardia*** to be a lazy devil*
3 [*ojo*] lazy; [*objeto*] idle, unused; [*espacio*] empty
4 (= *errante*) roving, wandering
5† • **en ~** [*mantenerse*] unsteadily; [*esforzarse*] in vain • **dar golpes en ~** to flail about, beat the air
(SM/F) **1** (= *holgazán*) idler, lazybones*; (= *inútil*) useless individual, dead loss • **hacer el ~** to loaf around
2 (= *vagabundo*) tramp, vagrant, bum (EEUU); (= *pobre*) down-and-out
vagón (SM) (*Ferro*) [*de pasajeros*] coach, carriage, passenger car (EEUU); [*de mercancías*] goods *o* freight van, goods *o* freight wagon, freight car (EEUU) ▸ **vagón cama** sleeping car ▸ **vagón cisterna** tanker, tank wagon ▸ **vagón de cola** (*lit*) guard's van, caboose (EEUU); (*fig*) rear, tail end ▸ **vagón de equipajes** luggage van ▸ **vagón de ganado, vagón de hacienda** (*Cono Sur*) cattle truck, stock car (EEUU) ▸ **vagón de primera** first-class carriage ▸ **vagón de reja** (*Cono Sur*) cattle truck, stock car (EEUU) ▸ **vagón de segunda** second-class carriage ▸ **vagón directo** through carriage ▸ **vagón mirador** observation car ▸ **vagón postal** mailcoach, mailcar (EEUU) ▸ **vagón restaurante** dining car ▸ **vagón tanque** tanker, tank wagon ▸ **vagón tolva** hopper
vagonada (SF) truckload, wagonload
vagoneta (SF) light truck
vaguada (SF) watercourse, stream bed
vaguear ▷ CONJUG 1a (VI) to laze around
vaguedad (SF) **1** (= *ambigüedad*) vagueness
2 (= *una vaguedad*) vague remark • **hablar sin ~es** to get straight to the point
vaguería (SF), **vaguitis*** (SF INV) (*Esp*) laziness, idleness, slackness
vaharada (SF) **1** [*de aliento*] puff of breath
2 (= *olor*) smell; (= *ráfaga de olor*) whiff; (= *tufo*) reek
vahear ▷ CONJUG 1a (VI) **1** (= *echar vapor*) to steam
2 (= *humear*) to fume, give off fumes, smoke
3 (= *oler*) smell; (= *atufar*) to reek
vahído (SM) dizzy spell
vaho (SM) **1** (= *vapor*) steam, vapour, vapor (EEUU); (*en cristal*) mist, condensation; (= *aliento*) breath; (= *ráfaga de olor*) whiff
2 vahos (*Med*) inhalation (*sing*)
vaina (SF) **1** [*de espada*] sheath, scabbard; [*de útil*] sheath, case; [*de cartucho*] case
2 (*Bot*) [*de garbanzo, guisante*] pod; [*de nuez*] husk, shell
3 vainas (= *judías*) green beans
4 (= *pega*) problem, snag; (*LAm**) (= *molestia*) nuisance, bore; (= *cosa*) thing • **¡qué ~!** what a nuisance!
5 (*And*) (= *chiripa*) fluke, piece of luck
6 (*Cono Sur*) (= *estafa*) swindle
7 • **MODISMO:** • **echar ~** (*Caribe***) to screw**, fuck**
(SMF)* (= *persona inútil*) twit*, nitwit*, dork (*esp EEUU**)
(ADJ) (*LAm*) (= *enojoso*) annoying
vainica (SF) (*Cos*) hemstitch
vainilla (SF) vanilla
vainillina (SF) vanillin
vainita (SF) (*LAm*) green bean
vais ▷ **ir**
vaivén (SM) **1** (= *balanceo*) swaying; (= *acción de mecerse*) rocking; [*de columpio*] swinging; (= *ir y venir*) to-ing and fro-ing; [*de pistón*] backward and forward motion; (= *sacudidas*) lurching
2 [*de tráfico, circulación*] constant movement
3 [*de la suerte*] change of fortune
4 (*Pol*) swing, seesaw, teeter-totter (EEUU)
5 vaivenes (= *altibajos*) ups and downs, vicissitudes (*frm*)
vaivenear† ▷ CONJUG 1a (VT) (*gen*) to oscillate; (= *mecer*) to rock; (*adelante y atrás*) to move backwards and forwards; (= *balancear*) to swing, sway
vajear ▷ CONJUG 1a (VT) (*CAm, Caribe, Méx*) [+ *culebra*] to fascinate, hypnotize; (= *hechizar*) to bewitch; (= *seducir*) to win over by flattery, seduce
vajilla (SF) (*gen*) crockery, dishes (*pl*); (= *una*

vajilla) service, set • **lavar la ~** to wash up ▸ **vajilla de oro** gold plate ▸ **vajilla de porcelana** chinaware

valdiviano/a ADJ of/from Valdivia
SM/F native/inhabitant of Valdivia • **los ~s** the people of Valdivia
SM *typical Chilean dish of dried meat and vegetables*

valdré *etc* ▹ **valer**

vale[1] SM (*Econ*) (= *pagaré*) promissory note (*frm*), IOU*; (= *recibo*) receipt; (= *cuenta*) bill, check (EEUU); (= *cupón*) voucher, chit ▸ **vale de comida** luncheon voucher ▸ **vale de compra** voucher ▸ **vale de correo** money order ▸ **vale de descuento** discount voucher ▸ **vale de regalo** gift voucher, gift certificate (EEUU) ▸ **vale (de) restaurante** luncheon voucher ▸ **vale postal** money order

vale[2]* EXCL (*Esp*) OK, sure; ▹ **valer**

vale[3]* SM (*LAm*) (= *amigo*) pal*, chum, buddy (EEUU) • **ser ~ con algn** (*And*) to be pals with sb* ▸ **vale corrido** (*Caribe*) old crony

valedero ADJ (= *válido*) valid; (*Jur*) binding • **~ para seis meses** valid for six months • **~ hasta el día 16** valid until the 16th

valedor(a) SM/F **1** (= *protector*) protector, guardian
2 (*LAm*) = **vale**[3]

valedura SF **1** (*Méx*) (= *ayuda*) help; (= *protección*) protection; (= *favor*) favour, favor (EEUU)
2 (*And, Caribe*) (= *propina*) *gift made by a gambler out of his winnings*

valemadrista* (*Méx*) ADJ **1** (= *apático*) indifferent, laid-back*
2 (= *cínico*) cynical
SMF **1** (= *apático*) indifferent person
2 (= *cínico*) cynic

Valencia SF Valencia

valencia SF (*Quím*) valency, valence (EEUU)

valenciana SF (*Méx*) trouser turn-up, trouser cuff (EEUU); ▹ **valenciano**

valencianismo SM **1** (*Ling*) *word/phrase etc peculiar to Valencia*
2 (*culturalmente*) *sense of the differentness of Valencia*; (*Pol*) *doctrine of or belief in Valencian autonomy*

valenciano/a ADJ of/from Valencia
SM/F native/inhabitant of Valencia • **los ~s** the people of Valencia; ▹ **valenciana**

valentía SF **1** (= *valor*) bravery, courage; (= *atrevimiento*) boldness; (= *resolución*) resoluteness
2 (= *jactancia*) boastfulness
3 (= *acto de valor*) brave deed, heroic exploit
4 (*pey*) (= *dicho*) boast, brag

valentón/ona ADJ (= *fanfarrón*) boastful; (= *arrogante*) arrogant; (= *matón*) bullying
SM/F (= *fanfarrón*) braggart; (= *matón*) bully

valentonada SF (= *dicho*) boast, brag; (= *acto*) arrogant act

valer

VERBO TRANSITIVO
VERBO INTRANSITIVO
VERBO PRONOMINAL

▹ CONJUG 2p

Para la frase ***valer la pena***, *ver la otra entrada.*

VERBO TRANSITIVO

1 (= *costar*) to cost • **solo el vuelo ya vale 8.000 euros** the flight alone costs 8,000 euros • **este libro vale cinco dólares** this book costs five dollars • **¿cuánto vale?** • **¿qué vale?** how much is it?, how much does it cost? • **esas valen (a) dos euros el kilo** those are two euros a kilo

2 (= *tener un valor de*) to be worth • **el terreno vale más que la casa** the land is worth more than the house • MODISMOS: • **no vale un higo** *o* **un pimiento** (*Esp**) it's not worth a brass farthing • **vale lo que pesa (en oro)** it's worth its weight in gold

3 (= *ser causa de*) [+ *premio*] to win; [+ *críticas, amenazas*] to earn • **la final histórica que le valió a Brasil la copa del mundo** the famous final in which Brazil won the world cup • **son las cualidades que le valieron el premio** these are the qualities which won him the prize • **esa tontería le valió un rapapolvo** that piece of stupidity got *o* earned him a telling-off • **su ausencia le valió la pérdida del contrato** his absence lost *o* cost him the contract

4 (*Mat*) (= *equivaler a*) to equal • **en ese caso X vale 9** in that case X equals 9 • **el ángulo B vale 38 grados** angle B is 38 degrees

5 (= *proteger*) • **¡válgame (Dios)!** oh, my God!, God help me!

VERBO INTRANSITIVO

1 (= *costar*) • **este coche vale muy caro** this car is very expensive *o* costs a lot of money • **¿vale mucho?** is it very expensive?

2 (= *tener valía*) • **vale mucho como intérprete** he's an excellent *o* first-rate interpreter • **Juan vale más que su hermano** Juan is a better person than his brother • **su última película no vale gran cosa** his latest film is not up to much *o* is not much good • **este coche no vale nada** this car is useless • **hacer ~**: • **hizo ~ su derecho al veto** he exercised his veto • **hizo ~ sus derechos** he asserted his rights • **hizo ~ sus argumentos en la reunión** she got her arguments across during the meeting • **hacerse ~** to assert o.s. • **~ por** (= *equivaler a*) to be worth • **cada cupón vale por un paquete de azúcar** each coupon is worth *o* can be exchanged for one bag of sugar • **cuatro fichas azules valen por una negra** four blue counters equal *o* are worth one black one

3 (= *servir*) **a** [*herramienta, objeto*] to be useful • **todavía puede ~** it might still be useful • **este mismo valdrá** this one will do • **eso no vale** that's no good *o* use • **hay que tirar todo lo que no vale** we must throw out everything that is no use • **ya no me vale** it's no good *o* use to me now • **este destornillador no me vale porque es pequeño** this screwdriver is no good to me, it's too small • **~ para algo**: • **es viejo, pero vale para la lluvia** it's old, but it'll do for when it rains • **este trozo no me vale para hacer la cortina** this piece won't do to make the curtain • **este cuchillo no vale para nada** this knife is useless

b [*ropa*] • **este sombrero me vale aún** I can still wear *o* use this hat • **me vale la ropa de mi hermana** my sister's clothes do for* *o* fit me as well • **a mi hijo no le vale la ropa del año pasado** the clothes my son wore last year are too small for him now

c [*situación*] • **no le vale ser hijo del ministro** being the minister's son is no use to him • **su situación privilegiada no le valió** his privileged position was no help *o* use to him • **no le valdrán excusas** excuses won't help him *o* do him any good

d [*persona*] • **yo no valdría para enfermera** I'd be no good as a nurse • **el chico no vale para el trabajo** the boy is no good *o* not right for the job • **no vales para nada** you're hopeless *o* useless, you're a dead loss*

4 (= *ser válido*) [*documento*] to be valid; [*moneda, billete*] to be legal tender • **este tipo de pasaporte no vale desde hace un mes** they stopped using this type of passport a month ago • **estos billetes ya no valen** these banknotes are no longer legal tender • **es una teoría que no vale ya** it is a theory which no longer holds • **valga la expresión** for want of a better way of putting it • **está un poco chiflado, valga la expresión** he's a bit cracked, for want of a better way of putting it • MODISMO: • **¡no hay ... que valga!**: • **—¡pero querido! —¡no hay querido que valga!** "but darling!" — "don't darling me!"*; ▹ **pero, redundancia**

5 • **más vale**: • **más vale así** it's better this way • **más vale no hacerlo** it would be better not to do it • **más vale mantener esto en secreto** it would be best to keep this quiet • **—mañana te devuelvo el dinero —más te vale** "I'll give you the money back tomorrow" — "you'd better!" • **más vale que me vaya** I'd *o* I had better go • **más vale que te lleves el abrigo** you'd *o* you had better take your coat • **más vale que vayas tú** it would be better if you went • REFRÁN: • **más vale tarde que nunca** better late than never

6 (*Esp*) (= *ser suficiente*) to be enough • **dos terrones valen para endulzarlo** two lumps are enough to sweeten it • **vale ya, que habéis estado gritando toda la tarde** that's enough! you've been shouting all afternoon • **¡vale, vale!, no me eches más azúcar** OK! that's enough! don't put any more sugar in • **—¿subo más la persiana? —no, así ya vale** "shall I put the blind up a bit more?" — "no, it's OK like that"

7* (= *estar permitido*) to be allowed • **—¿puedo darle con la mano? —no, eso no vale** "can I hit it with my hand?" — "no, that's not allowed" • **no vale intentarlo dos veces** you're not allowed to have two goes • **no vale empujar** no pushing!, pushing's not allowed • **—le han dado el trabajo al hijo del jefe —¡pues, eso no vale!** "they've given the job to the boss's son" — "that's not on!"* *o* "they can't do that!"

8 vale (*Esp**) (= *de acuerdo*) all right, OK* • **—¿vamos a tomar algo? —¡vale!** "shall we go for a drink?" — "OK!" *o* "all right!" • **pásate por mi casa esta tarde, ¿vale?** drop by my house this afternoon, OK? • **vale que discutan, pero que se peguen es imperdonable** having an argument is one thing but hitting each other is another matter entirely *o* is inexcusable

9 • MODISMO: • **me vale madre** *o* **sombrilla** (*Méx**) I couldn't care less*, I don't give a damn!*

VERBO PRONOMINAL **valerse**

1 • **~se de** (= *utilizar*) [+ *herramienta, objeto*] to use, make use of; (= *aprovecharse de*) [+ *amistad, influencia*] to use • **se valió de un bastón para cruzar el río** he used a cane to get across the river • **se valió del derecho al veto para frenar el acuerdo** he made use of *o* exercised his veto to put a stop to the agreement • **se valió de su cargo para conseguir la información** she used her position to obtain the information

2 (= *arreglárselas*) • **es muy mayor, pero todavía se vale** she is very old, but she can still do things for herself • **no se vale solo** • **no puede ~se por sí mismo** he can't look after himself *o* manage on his own

valeriana SF valerian

valerosamente ADV bravely, valiantly

valeroso ADJ brave, valiant

valet [ba'le] SM (PL: **valets** [ba'le]) (*Naipes*)

jack, knave
valetudinario/a ADJ, SM/F valetudinarian
valga *etc* ▷ **valer**
Valhala SM Valhalla
valía SF **1** (= *valor*) worth, value • **de gran ~** [*objeto*] very valuable, of great worth; [*persona*] worthy, estimable
2 (= *influencia*) influence
validación SF (*gen*) validation; (*Pol*) ratification
validar ▷ CONJUG 1a VT (*gen*) to validate; (*Pol*) to ratify
validez SF validity • **dar ~ a** (*gen*) to validate; (*Pol*) to ratify
valido SM (*Hist*) (royal) favourite, (royal) favorite (*EEUU*)
válido ADJ **1** [*billete, respuesta*] valid (**hasta** until, **para** for)
2 (*Med*) (= *fuerte*) strong, robust; (= *sano*) fit
valiente ADJ **1** [*persona, acción, decisión*] brave, courageous, valiant (*liter*) • **no te las des de ~ porque sé que tienes miedo** don't pretend to be brave because I know you're frightened
2 (*iró*) (*antes de s*) fine • **¡~ amigo estás tú hecho!** a fine friend *o* some friend you are!* • **¡~ gobierno!** some government!*, what a government!*
SMF brave man/woman • **se hace el ~ porque le están mirando todos** he's pretending to be brave because everyone's looking at him
valientemente ADV bravely, courageously, valiantly (*liter*)
valija SF **1** (= *maleta*) case; (*LAm*) suitcase; (= *portamantas*) valise; (= *cartera*) satchel
2 (*Correos*) mailbag; (= *correspondencia*) mail, post ▸ **valija diplomática** diplomatic bag, diplomatic pouch (*EEUU*)
valijería SF (*Cono Sur*) travel-goods shop
valimiento SM **1** (= *valor*) value; (= *beneficio*) benefit
2 (*Pol*) favour, favor (*EEUU*), protection; (*Hist*) position of royal favourite, status of the royal favourite • **~ con algn** • **~ cerca de algn** influence with sb
valioso ADJ **1** (= *de valor*) valuable; (= *útil*) useful, beneficial; (= *estimable*) estimable (*frm*)
2† (= *rico*) wealthy; (= *poderoso*) powerful
valisoletano/a ADJ, SM/F = **vallisoletano**
valkiria SF Valkyrie
valla SF **1** (= *cercado*) fence; (*Mil*) barricade; (= *empalizada*) palisade, stockade; (*Dep*) hurdle • **400 metros ~s** 400 metres hurdles ▸ **valla de contención** crush barrier ▸ **valla de protección, valla de seguridad** barrier ▸ **valla electrificada** electric fence ▸ **valla publicitaria** hoarding, billboard (*EEUU*)
2 (*fig*) (= *barrera*) barrier; (= *límite*) limit; (= *estorbo*) obstacle, hindrance • **romper** *o* **saltar(se) las ~s** to disregard social conventions
3 (*And, Caribe, Méx*) [*de gallos*] cockpit
4 (*And*) (= *zanja*) ditch
valladar SM **1** = **valla**
2 (= *defensa*) defence, defense (*EEUU*), barrier
vallado ADJ (= *cercado*) fenced
SM **1** = **valla**
2 (*Mil*) defensive wall, rampart
3 (*Méx*) (= *zanja*) deep ditch
Valladolid SM Valladolid
vallar ▷ CONJUG 1a VT to fence in, put (up) a fence round
valle SM **1** (*Geog*) valley ▸ **valle de lágrimas** (*liter*) vale of tears (*liter*)
2 • **energía de ~** off-peak power demand/supply • **horas de ~** off-peak hours
vallero/a (*Méx*) ADJ valley (*antes de s*)
SM/F valley dweller
vallino ADJ (*And*) valley (*antes de s*)
vallisoletano/a ADJ of/from Valladolid
SM/F native/inhabitant of Valladolid • **los ~s** the people of Valladolid
vallista SMF hurdler
vallisto ADJ (*Cono Sur, Méx*) valley (*antes de s*)
vallunco ADJ (*CAm*) rustic, peasant (*antes de s*)
valón/ona ADJ Walloon
SM/F Walloon • **los valones** the Walloons
SM (*Ling*) Walloon
valona SF **1** (*And, Caribe*) [*de caballo*] *artistically trimmed mane* • **hacer la ~** (*Caribe*) to shave
2 (*Méx*) = **valedura**
valonar ▷ CONJUG 1a VT (*And*) to shear
valonearse ▷ CONJUG 1a VPR (*CAm*) to lean from the saddle
valor SM **1** (*Com, Econ*) value • **¿cuál es el ~ real de ese cuadro?** what's this painting worth in real terms?, what's the real value of this painting? • **un documento de gran ~** a very valuable document, a document of great value • **objetos de incalculable ~** priceless objects • **billetes de pequeño ~** small-denomination notes • **el contrato fue declarado nulo y sin ~** the contract was declared null and void • **el ~ del cheque no es correcto** the amount on the cheque is not correct • **de ~** [*joya, obra*] valuable • **objetos de ~** valuables • **por ~ de** to the value of • **importaciones por ~ de un millón de dólares** imports to the value of one million dollars • **un cheque por ~ de 500 euros** a cheque for the sum of *o* to the value of 500 euros • **ha habido pérdidas por ~ de diez millones de euros** there have been losses of ten million euros ▸ **valor adquisitivo** purchasing power ▸ **valor a la par** par value ▸ **valor añadido** added value ▸ **valor catastral** rateable value ▸ **valor comercial** commercial value ▸ **valor contable** asset value ▸ **valor de cambio** exchange value ▸ **valor de compra** purchasing power ▸ **valor de desecho** salvage value ▸ **valor de escasez** scarcity value ▸ **valor de mercado** market value ▸ **valor de rescate** surrender value ▸ **valor desglosado** break-up value ▸ **valor de sustitución** replacement value ▸ **valor de uso** use value ▸ **valor en bolsa** stock market value ▸ **valor en libros** book value ▸ **valor estrella** blue-chip stock, blue-chip share ▸ **valor facial** face value, denomination ▸ **valor nominal** nominal value ▸ **valor por defecto** default value ▸ **valor según balance** book value
2 (= *importancia*) value • **una composición de indudable ~ musical** a composition of undoubted musical value • **una pintura de gran ~ artístico** a painting of great artistic merit *o* value • **este anillo tiene un gran ~ para mí** this ring means a great deal to me, this ring is very valuable to me • **dar ~ a algo**: • **lo que le da ~ musical a este trabajo es su originalidad** it is the originality of this work that gives it its musical worth *o* value • **no dábamos ~ a nuestro patrimonio** we didn't value our heritage highly enough • **no le di ~ a sus palabras** I didn't attach any importance to what he said • **quitar ~ a algo** to minimize the importance of sth ▸ **valor alimenticio** nutritional value, food value ▸ **valor calorífico** calorific value ▸ **valor nutritivo** nutritional value ▸ **valor sentimental** sentimental value
3 valores: **a** (= *principios*) values • **los ~es morales de la sociedad occidental** the moral values of Western society; ▹ **escala, juicio**
b (*Econ*) (= *títulos*) securities, stocks, bonds ▸ **valores de renta fija** fixed-interest securities ▸ **valores de renta variable** variable-yield securities ▸ **valores en cartera** holdings ▸ **valores fiduciarios** fiduciary issue (*sing*), banknotes ▸ **valores habidos** investments ▸ **valores inmuebles** real estate (*sing*)
4 (= *persona famosa*) star • **uno de los nuevos ~es del cine español** one of the rising stars of Spanish cinema
5 (= *validez*) validity • **tener ~** to be valid • **este documento ya no tiene ~** this document is no longer valid
6 (*en una escala*) level • **las temperaturas han alcanzado ~es superiores a los normales** temperatures have reached higher than normal levels • **se han medido ~es de 80 litros por metro cúbico** levels of 80 litres per cubic metre have been recorded
7 (*Mat*) value ▸ **valor absoluto** absolute value
8 (*Mús*) value • **el ~ de una blanca es de dos negras** a minim is worth two crotchets
9 (= *coraje*) bravery, courage • **el ~ de los soldados** the bravery *o* courage of the soldiers • **le dieron una medalla al ~** he was awarded a medal for bravery • **no tuve ~ para decírselo** I didn't have the courage to tell her • **armarse de ~** to pluck up (the) courage ▸ **valor cívico** (sense of) civic duty
10* (= *descaro*) nerve* • **¿cómo puedes tener el ~ de negarlo?** how do you have the nerve to deny it?*
valoración SF **1** (= *tasación*) **a** [*de joya, obra de arte*] valuation • **hacer una ~ de algo** to value sth, give a valuation of sth • **la ~ social del trabajo doméstico** the value that society places on housework, how much society values housework
b [*de daños, pérdidas*] (= *acción*) assessment; (= *resultado*) estimate • **hacer una ~ de algo** to assess sth, give an assessment of sth
2 [*de actuación, situación*] assessment • **¿cuál es su ~ de lo que ha pasado?** what's your assessment of what happened? • **en su ~ de los datos** in assessing the facts, in his assessment of the facts • **hacer una ~ de algo** to make an assessment of sth, assess sth • **no quisieron hacer ninguna ~ de los resultados electorales** they declined to make any assessment of the election results
3 (*Quím*) titration
valorar ▷ CONJUG 1a VT **1** (= *tasar*) [+ *joya, obra de arte*] to value (**en** at); [+ *daños, pérdidas*] to assess (**en** at) • **un cuadro valorado en dos millones** a painting valued at two million • **las pérdidas han sido valoradas en miles de millones** the damage has been estimated *o* assessed at thousands of millions
2 (= *apreciar*) [+ *cualidad*] to value, appreciate • **no sabes ~ la amistad** you don't value *o* appreciate friendship • **un trabajo no valorado por la sociedad** it is a job which is not valued *o* appreciated by society • **valoro mucho la sinceridad** I value honesty highly • **los resultados han sido valorados negativamente** the results were judged negatively • **los jóvenes valoran muy poco a los políticos** young people have a very poor opinion of politicians • **"se ~án los conocimientos de inglés"** "knowledge of English an advantage"
3 (= *revalorizar*) to raise the value of
4 (*Quím*) to titrate
valorización SF **1** (= *tasación*) = **valoración**
2 (*LAm*) (= *aumento*) increase in value
valorizar ▷ CONJUG 1f VT **1** (= *tasar*) = **valorar**

2 (*LAm*) (= *aumentar*) to raise the value of
(VPR) **valorizarse** (*LAm*) to increase in value
Valquiria (SF) Valkyrie
vals (PL: **valses**) (SM) waltz
valsar ▸ CONJUG 1a (VI) to waltz
valse (SM) **1** (*LAm*) (= *vals*) waltz
2 (*Caribe*) *Venezuelan folk dance*
valsear ▸ CONJUG 1a (VI) (*LAm*) to waltz
valuable (ADJ) (*LAm*) **1** (= *valioso*) valuable
2 (= *calculable*) calculable
valuación (SF) = **valoración**
valuador(a) (SM/F) (*LAm*) valuer
valuar ▸ CONJUG 1e (VT) = **valorar**
valumen (SM) **1** (*Cono Sur*) [*de plantas*] luxuriance, rankness
2 (*Méx*) (= *lío*) bundle; (= *masa*) mass, bulk
valumoso (ADJ) **1** (*CAm, Cono Sur*) [*planta*] luxuriant, rank
2 (*And, CAm, Méx*) (= *voluminoso*) bulky
3 (*Caribe*) (= *vanidoso*) vain, conceited
valva (SF) (*Bot, Zool*) valve
válvula (SF) valve ▸ **válvula de admisión** inlet valve ▸ **válvula de escape** (*Mec*) exhaust valve; (*fig*) safety valve ▸ **válvula de purga** vent ▸ **válvula de seguridad** safety valve
vamos ▸ **ir**
vampi* (SF) = **vampiresa**
vampiresa (SF) (*Cine*) vamp, femme fatale
vampirizar ▸ CONJUG 1f (VT) to sap, milk, bleed dry
vampiro (SM) **1** (*Zool, Mit*) vampire
2 (= *explotador*) vampire, bloodsucker
van ▸ **ir**
vanagloria (SF) vainglory
vanagloriarse ▸ CONJUG 1b (VPR)
1 (= *jactarse*) to boast (**de** of) • ~ **de hacer algo** to boast of doing sth
2 (= *envanecerse*) to be vain, be arrogant
vanaglorioso (ADJ) (= *ostentoso*) vainglorious; (= *vano*) vain, boastful, arrogant
vanamente (ADV) **1** (= *inútilmente*) in vain
2 (= *con vanidad*) vainly
vanarse ▸ CONJUG 1a (VPR) (*And, Caribe, Cono Sur*) [*fruto*] to shrivel up; [*negocio*] to fall through, come to nothing, produce no results
vandálico (ADJ) **1** [*acto, comportamiento*] loutish
2 (*Hist*) Vandal, Vandalic
vandalismo (SM) vandalism
vándalo/a (ADJ) loutish
(SM/F) **1** (= *salvaje*) vandal
2 (*Hist*) Vandal
vanguardia (SF) (*Mil*) (*tb fig*) vanguard • **de** ~ (*Arte*) avant-garde; (*Pol*) vanguard (*antes de s*) • **un pintor de** ~ an avant-garde painter • **estar en la** ~ **del progreso** to be in the vanguard of progress • **ir a la** *o* **en** ~ (*lit*) to be in the vanguard; (*fig*) to be at the forefront
vanguardismo (SM) (*Arte, Literat*) avant-garde movement; (= *estilo*) ultramodern manner
vanguardista (ADJ) [*moda, estilo*] avant-garde; [*tecnología*] revolutionary • **un coche de tecnología** ~ a car at the cutting edge of technology
(SMF) avant-garde artist
vanidad (SF) **1** (= *presunción*) vanity • **por pura** ~ out of sheer vanity • **halagar la** ~ **de algn** to play up to sb's vanity
2 (= *irrealidad*) unreality; (= *inutilidad*) uselessness, futility; (= *superficialidad*) shallowness
3 (*Rel*) vanity • ~ **de** ~**es** (*Biblia*) vanity of vanities
vanidoso (ADJ) vain, conceited
vano (ADJ) **1** (= *infundado*) [*ilusión, esperanza*] empty, vain; [*temor, sospecha*] groundless; [*superstición*] foolish
2 (= *inútil*) [*intento*] vain, futile • ~**s esfuerzos** vain *o* futile efforts • **sus esfuerzos fueron** ~**s** their efforts were in vain • **en** ~ in vain • **no en** ~ **se le considera el mejor nadador** not for nothing is he held to be the best swimmer
3 (= *vacío*) [*promesa, excusa*] empty • **no son más que palabras vanas** they are just empty words
4 [*persona*] (= *superficial*) shallow; (= *vanidoso*) vain
5 [*cáscara*] empty, hollow
(SM) (*Arquit*) space, opening
vapor (SM) **1** (*gen*) vapour, vapor (EEUU); (*Téc*) [*de agua*] steam; [*de gas*] fumes (*pl*); (*Meteo*) mist, haze • **verduras al** ~ steamed vegetables • **a todo** ~ (*lit, fig*) at full steam • **de** ~ steam (*antes de s*) • **acumular** ~ to get steam up • **echar** ~ to give off steam, steam ▸ **vapor de agua** water vapour
2 (*Náut*) steamship, steamer ▸ **vapor correo** mail boat ▸ **vapor de paletas, vapor de ruedas** paddle steamer ▸ **vapor volandero** tramp steamer
3 (*Med*) vertigo, giddiness
4 vapores† (= *accesos histéricos*) vapours, vapors (EEUU)
vapora (SF) **1** (= *barco*) steam launch
2 (*Caribe*) (*Ferro*) steam engine
vaporar ▸ CONJUG 1a (VT), (VI) = **vaporear**
vaporear ▸ CONJUG 1a (VT) to evaporate
(VI) to give off vapour
(VPR) **vaporearse** to evaporate
vaporización (SF) vaporization
vaporizador (SM) (*para agua*) vaporizer; (= *pulverizador*) spray
vaporizar ▸ CONJUG 1f (VT) (*gen*) [+ *agua*] to vaporize; [+ *perfume*] to spray
(VPR) **vaporizarse** to vaporize
vaporizo (SM) (*Caribe, Méx*) **1** (= *calor*) strong heat, steamy heat
2 (*Med*) inhalation
vaporoso (ADJ) **1** [*tela*] sheer, diaphanous
2 (*de vapor*) vaporous; (= *brumoso*) misty; (= *lleno de vapor*) steamy, steaming
vapulear ▸ CONJUG 1a (VT) **1** [+ *alfombra, persona*] to beat; (= *azotar*) to beat up*, thrash; (*con látigo*) flog
2 (= *regañar*) to slate*
vapuleo (SM) **1** (= *paliza*) beating, thrashing; (*con látigo*) flogging
2 (= *regañina*) slating*
vaquerear ▸ CONJUG 1a (VI) (*And*) to play truant
vaquería (SF) **1** (= *lechería*) dairy
2 (*LAm*) (= *arte del vaquero*) craft of the cowboy; (= *cuidado de ganado*) cattle farming
3 (*And, Caribe*) (= *cubo*) milking pail; (= *establo*) milking shed
4 (*Caribe*) (= *ganado*) herd of dairy cows
5 (*Caribe*) (= *caza*) hunting with a lasso
6 (*Méx*) (= *baile*) barn dance, country dance
vaqueriza (SF) (= *establo*) cowshed; (= *corral*) cattle yard
vaquerizo/a (ADJ) cattle (*antes de s*)
(SM/F) cowherd
vaquero/a (ADJ) (= *de los pastores*) cowboy (*antes de s*); [*tela, falda*] denim (*antes de s*) • **pantalones** ~**s** jeans
(SM/F) **1** [*de ganado*] cowherd, cowboy/cowgirl
2 (*LAm*) (= *lechero*) milkman/milkwoman
3 (*And*) (= *ausente*) truant
(SM) **1** (*Caribe*) (= *látigo*) rawhide whip
2 vaqueros (= *pantalones*) jeans
vaqueta (SF) **1** (= *cuero*) cowhide, leather
2 (*para afilar*) razor strop
(SM) (*Caribe*) shifty sort*
vaquetón (ADJ) **1** (*Caribe*) (= *poco fiable*) unreliable, shifty
2 (*Méx*) (= *lerdo*) dim-witted; (= *flemático*) phlegmatic, slow
3 (*Méx*) (= *descarado*) barefaced, brazen
vaquetudo (ADJ) (*Caribe, Méx*) = **vaquetón**
vaquilla (SF) **1** (= *ternera*) heifer
2 vaquillas (= *reses*) young calves; (= *fiesta*) (*tb* **corrida de vaquillas**) *bullfight with young bulls*
vaquillona (SF) (*LAm*) heifer
V.A.R. (ABR) (= **Vuestra Alteza Real**) HRH
vara (SF) **1** (= *palo*) stick, pole; (*Mec*) rod, bar; [*de carro, carroza*] shaft; (*Bot*) branch (*stripped of its leaves*); [*de flor*] central stem, main stalk ▸ **vara de las virtudes** magic wand ▸ **vara de medir** yardstick, measuring rod ▸ **vara de oro** goldenrod ▸ **vara de pescar** fishing rod ▸ **vara de San José** goldenrod ▸ **vara mágica** magic wand
2 (*Pol*) (= *insignia*) staff of office • **doblar la** ~ **de la justicia** to pervert (the course of) justice • **empuñar la** ~ to take over, take (up) office (*as mayor etc*) • MODISMO: • **medir las cosas con la misma** ~ to judge things by the same standards ▸ **vara alta** (= *autoridad*) authority, power; (= *peso*) influence; (= *dominio*) dominance • **tener mucha** ~ **alta** to have great influence, be influential ▸ **vara consistorial** staff of office
3 (*esp LAm*) (*Mat*) ≈ yard (= *.836 metres*, = *2.8 feet*)
4 (*Taur*) (= *lanza*) lance, pike; (= *herida*) wound with the lance • **poner** ~**s al toro** to wound the bull with the lance
5 • MODISMO: • **dar la** ~ **a*** to annoy, bother
6†‡ (= *revés*) blow; (= *disgusto*) upset, setback
varada (SF) **1** (*Náut*) beaching
2 (= *lanzamiento*) launching
varadero (SM) dry dock
varado (ADJ) **1** (*Náut*) • **estar** ~ (*en la playa*) to be beached; (*en un banco de arena*) to be grounded
2 (*LAm**) • MODISMO: • **estar** ~ (*Cono Sur*) (= *sin trabajo*) to be without regular work; (*CAm, Cono Sur, Méx*) (= *sin dinero*) to be broke*
(SM) (*Cono Sur*) *man without a regular job*
varadura (SF) stranding, running aground
varajillo (SM) (*Caribe*) liqueur coffee
varal (SM) **1** (= *palo*) long pole; [*de carro, carroza*] shaft; (*Teat*) batten; (= *armazón*) framework of poles; (= *puntal*) strut, support
2* (= *persona*) beanpole*
varapalear ▸ CONJUG 1a (VT) to slate, tear to pieces
varapalo (SM) **1** (= *palo*) long pole
2 (= *golpe*) blow with a stick; (= *paliza*) beating
3 (= *regañina*) dressing-down*
4 (= *disgusto*) disappointment, blow
varar ▸ CONJUG 1a (VT) **1** (= *llevar a la playa*) to beach, run aground
2 (= *botar*) to launch
(VI), (VPR) **vararse 1** (*Náut*) to run aground
2 [*negocio, asunto*] to get bogged down
varayoc (SM) (*And*) Indian chief
varazo (SM) blow with a stick
varazón (SF) (*And, Caribe, Méx*) sticks (*pl*), bunch of sticks
vardasca (SF) green twig, switch
varé†‡ (SM) (*Esp*) 100 pesetas
vareador(a) (SM/F) olive picker, olive harvester
varear ▸ CONJUG 1a (VT) **1** [+ *persona*] to beat, hit; [+ *frutas*] to knock down (*with poles*); [+ *alfombra*] to beat; (*Taur*) to goad (*with the lance*)
2 (*Com*) [+ *paño*] to sell by the yard
3 (*Cono Sur*) [+ *caballo*] to exercise, train
varec (SM) kelp, wrack
varejón (SM) (*Cono Sur*) **1** = **vardasca**
2 (= *palo*) stick, straight branch (*stripped of leaves*)
vareta (SF) **1** (= *ramita*) twig, small stick;

(con liga) lime twig for catching birds
2 (*Cos*) stripe
3 (= *indirecta*) insinuation; (= *pulla*) taunt • **echar ~s** to make insinuations
4 • **MODISMOS**: • **estar de ~** • **irse de ~** to have diarrhoea

varetazo (SM) *(Taur) sideways thrust with the horn*

varga (SF) *steepest part of a slope*

variabilidad (SF) variability

variable (ADJ) (*gen*) variable, changeable; (*Mat, Inform*) variable
(SF) (*Mat, Inform*) variable

variación (SF) (*tb Mús*) variation; (*Meteo*) change • **sin ~** unchanged

variado (ADJ) (*gen*) varied; (= *diverso*) mixed; (= *surtido*) assorted; [*superficie, color*] variegated

variante (ADJ) variant
(SF) **1** [*de palabra, texto*] variant ▸ **variante dialectal** dialectal variant ▸ **variante fonética** phonetic variant, alternative pronunciation ▸ **variante ortográfica** spelling variant, alternative spelling
2 (*Aut*) diversion
3 *(en quiniela) draw or away win*
(SM) **1 variantes** (*Esp*) (*Culin*) pickled vegetables (*as hors d'oeuvres*)
2 (*And*) (= *senda*) path; (= *atajo*) short cut

variar ▹ CONJUG 1C (VT) **1** (= *cambiar*) to change, alter • **han variado el enfoque de la revista** they have changed *o* altered the magazine's focus
2 (= *dar variedad a*) to vary • **intento ~ el menú** I try to vary the menu
(VI) **1** (= *cambiar*) to vary • **los precios varían según el tamaño** prices vary according to size • **~ de opinión** to change one's mind • **~ de precio** to vary in price • **~ de tamaño** to vary in size • **para ~** (*iró*) (just) for a change • **hoy hemos comido sopa, para ~** we had soup today, (just) for a change
2 (= *ser diferente*) to be different, differ • **esto varía de lo que dijo antes** this is different *o* this differs from what he said earlier
(VPR) **variarse** (*Arg, Uru**) to show off

varicela (SF) chickenpox

varicoso (ADJ) **1** [*pierna*] varicose
2 [*persona*] *suffering from varicose veins*

variedad (SF) **1** (= *diversidad*) variety
2 (*Bio*) variety
3 **variedades** (*Teat*) variety show (*sing*) • **teatro de ~es** variety theatre, music hall, vaudeville theater (EEUU)

varietés (SMPL) (*Teat*) = **variedad**

varilla (SF) **1** [*de metal*] (*Mec*) rod, bar; [*de faja, abanico, paraguas*] rib; [*de rueda*] spoke; [*de corsé*] rib, stay; [*de gafas*] sidepiece, earpiece ▸ **varilla del aceite** dipstick ▸ **varilla de zahorí** divining rod
2 (*Anat*) jawbone
3 (*Méx*) (= *baratijas*) cheap wares (*pl*), trinkets (*pl*)
4 (*Caribe*) (= *vaina*) nuisance, bother

varillaje (SM) [*de abanico, paraguas*] ribs (*pl*), ribbing; (*Mec*) rods (*pl*), links (*pl*)

varillar ▹ CONJUG 1A (VT) (*Caribe*) [+ *caballo*] to try out, train

vario (ADJ) **1** (= *variado*) varied; [*color*] variegated, motley
2 (= *cambiable*) varying, changeable; [*persona*] fickle
3 **varios** (= *muchos*) several, a number of • **hay varias posibilidades** there are several *o* a number of *o* various possibilities • **en ~s libros que he visto** in a number of books which I have seen • **los inconvenientes son ~s** there are several drawbacks • **asuntos ~s** (any) other business
(PRON) **varios** (= *unos*) some • **~s piensan que ...** some (people) think that ...

varioloso (ADJ) pockmarked

variopinto (ADJ) **1** (= *de distintos colores*) multi-coloured, multi-colored (EEUU), colourful, colorful (EEUU)
2 (= *diverso*) [*objetos, regalos*] diverse, miscellaneous; [*gente, público*] very mixed

varita (SF) wand ▸ **varita de las virtudes, varita mágica** magic wand

variz (PL: **varices** *o* **várices**) (SF) (*Med*) varix • **tener varices** to have varicose veins

varón (ADJ) male • **hijo ~** son, boy
(SM) **1** (= *niño*) boy; (= *hombre*) man, male; (= *gran hombre*) great man, worthy man • **tuvo cuatro hijos, todos varones** she had four children, all boys • **es un santo ~** (= *hombre bondadoso*) he's a saint; (= *hombre simple*) he's a simple fellow ▸ **varón de Dios** saintly man
2 (*And*) (= *marido*) husband
3 (*Cono Sur, Méx*) (= *vigas*) beams (*pl*), timber

varona (SF), **varonesa** (SF) mannish woman

varonera* (SF) (*Arg, Uru*) tomboy

varonil (ADJ) **1** (= *viril*) manly, virile; (= *enérgico*) vigorous
2 (*Bio*) male
3 (*pey*) [*mujer*] mannish • **una mujer de aspecto ~** a woman of mannish appearance

Varsovia (SF) Warsaw

vas *etc* ▹ **ir**

vasallaje (SM) (*Hist*) vassalage; (*pey*) (= *sumisión*) subjection, serfdom

vasallo (SM) vassal

vasar (SM) kitchen dresser, kitchen cabinet (EEUU)

vasco/a (ADJ) Basque
(SM/F) Basque • **los ~s** the Basques
(SM) (*Ling*) Basque

vascófilo/a (SM/F) expert in Basque studies

vascófono/a (ADJ) Basque-speaking
(SM/F) Basque speaker

vascofrancés/esa (ADJ) • **País Vascofrancés** French Basque Country
(SM/F) French Basque

vascohablante (ADJ) Basque-speaking
(SMF) Basque speaker

Vascongadas (SFPL) • **las ~** the Basque Provinces

vascongado/a (ADJ), (SM/F) = **vasco**

vascuence (SM) (*Ling*) Basque

vascular (ADJ) vascular

vase†† ▹ **ir**

vasectomía (SF) vasectomy

vaselina (SF) **1** Vaseline®, petroleum jelly • **MODISMO**: • **poner ~*** to calm things down, make things go smoothly
2 (*Ftbl*) chip

vasera (SF) kitchen shelf, rack

vasija (SF) (*Hist*) vessel; (*Culin*) pot, dish

vaso (SM) **1** (*para beber*) (*gen*) glass; (*para whisky*) tumbler; (*And*) small cup • **MODISMO**: • **ahogarse en un ~ de agua** to make a mountain out of a molehill ▸ **vaso alto** tall glass ▸ **vaso de vino** (= *recipiente*) wineglass; (= *contenido*) glass of wine
2 (= *cantidad*) glass, glassful
3 (= *recipiente*) (*para flores*) vase; [*de pila*] cell; (*liter*) vase, urn; (*And*) (*Aut*) hubcap ▸ **vaso de engrase** (*Mec*) grease cup ▸ **vaso litúrgico, vaso sagrado** liturgical vessel ▸ **vasos comunicantes** communicating vessels
4 (*Anat*) vessel; (= *canal*) duct, tube ▸ **vaso capilar** capillary ▸ **vaso sanguíneo** blood vessel
5 (*Náut*) (= *barco*) boat, ship; (= *casco*) hull
6 (*Zool*) hoof
7 (= *orinal*) (*tb* **vaso de noche**†) chamber pot

vasoconstrictor (ADJ) vasoconstrictor (*antes de s*), vasoconstrictive
(SM) vasoconstrictor, vasoconstrictive substance

vasodilatador (ADJ) vasodilator (*antes de s*), vasodilating
(SM) vasodilator

vasquismo (SM) *(culturalmente) sense of the differentness of the Basque Country; (Pol) doctrine of or belief in Basque autonomy*

vasquista (ADJ) that supports *etc* Basque autonomy • **el movimiento ~** the movement for Basque autonomy • **la familia es muy ~** the family strongly supports Basque autonomy
(SMF) supporter *etc* of Basque autonomy

vástago (SM) **1** (*Bot*) shoot
2 (*Mec*) rod ▸ **vástago de émbolo** piston rod
3 (= *hijo, descendiente*) offspring, descendant
4 (*And, CAm, Caribe*) (= *tronco*) trunk of the banana tree

vastedad (SF) vastness, immensity

vasto (ADJ) vast, huge

vataje (SM) wattage

vate (SM) **1** (*Hist*) seer, prophet
2 (*Literat*) poet, bard

váter (SM) lavatory, W.C., restroom (EEUU)

Vaticano (SM) Vatican • **la Ciudad del ~** Vatican City

vaticano (ADJ) (*gen*) Vatican; (= *papal*) papal

vaticinador (SM) (= *profeta*) seer, prophet; [*del tiempo, economía*] forecaster

vaticinar ▹ CONJUG 1A (VT) (= *predecir*) to predict; (= *pronosticar*) to forecast

vaticinio (SM) (= *predicción*) prediction; (= *pronóstico*) forecast

vatio (SM) watt

vaya *etc* ▹ **ir**

VCL (SM ABR) (= **visualizador cristal líquido**) LCD

Vd. (ABR) = **usted**

Vda. (ABR) = **viuda**

Vds. (ABR) = **ustedes**

ve[1] ▹ **ir, ver**

ve[2] (SF) (*LAm*) ▸ **ve chica, ve corta** *name of the letter V* ▸ **ve doble** *name of the letter W*

V.E. (ABR) = **Vuestra Excelencia**

vea *etc* ▹ **ver**

vecinal (ADJ) **1** [*camino*] local; [*impuesto*] local, municipal • **padrón ~** list of residents
2 (*LAm*) (= *vecino*) neighbouring, neighboring (EEUU), adjacent

vecindad (SF) **1** (= *barrio*) neighbourhood, neighborhood (EEUU); (= *cercanía*) vicinity; (*LAm*) (= *barrio pobre*) inner-city slum
2 (= *vecinos*) neighbours (*pl*), neighbors (EEUU) (*pl*), neighbourhood; (= *comunidad local*) local community; (= *residentes*) residents (*pl*)
3 (*Jur*) residence, abode • **declarar su ~** to state where one lives, give one's place of residence

vecindario (SM) (= *barrio*) neighbourhood, neighborhood (EEUU); (= *población*) population, residents (*pl*); (= *comunidad local*) local community

vecino/a (ADJ) **1** (= *cercano*) neighbouring, neighboring (EEUU) • **se fue a vivir a un pueblo ~** he went to live in a neighbouring *o* nearby village
2 (= *contiguo*) • **vive en el edificio ~** he lives in the house next door • **el garaje ~ al mío** the garage next to mine • **las dos fincas son vecinas** the two properties adjoin
3 (*frm*) (= *parecido*) similar • **suertes vecinas** similar fates
(SM/F) **1** [*de edificio, calle*] neighbour, neighbor (EEUU) • **somos ~s** we are neighbours • **el ~ de al lado** the next-door neighbour ▸ **vecino/a de rellano** next-door neighbour (*in a block of flats*)

2 (= *habitante*) [*de un pueblo*] inhabitant; [*de un barrio*] resident • **un pueblo de 800 ~s** a village of 800 inhabitants • **un ~ de la calle Corredera** a resident of *o* a person who lives in Corredera street • **asociación de ~s** residents' association
vector SM vector
Veda SM Veda
veda SF **1** (= *prohibición*) prohibition
2 (= *temporada*) close season, closed season (EEUU)
vedado SM private preserve • **cazar/pescar en ~** to poach, hunt/fish illegally ▸ **vedado de caza** game reserve
vedar ▹ CONJUG 1a VT (= *prohibir*) to prohibit, ban; (= *impedir*) to stop, prevent; [+ *idea, plan*] to veto • **~ a algn hacer algo** to forbid sb to do sth
vedeta SF = **vedette**
vedetismo SM (= *protagonismo*) insistence on being in the forefront, insistence on playing the star role; (= *estrellato*) stardom
vedette [be'ðet] SF **1** [*de revista musical*] (= *artista principal*) star; (*de menor importancia*) starlet
2 [*de fiesta, equipo, acontecimiento*] star
3 (*Méx*) (= *corista*) chorus girl
védico ADJ Vedic
vedija SF **1** (= *lana*) tuft of wool
2 (= *greña*) mat of hair, matted hair
vega SF **1** (= *terreno bajo*) fertile plain, rich lowland area; (= *prado*) water meadows (*pl*); (*And*) *stretch of alluvial soil*
2 (*Caribe*) (= *tabacal*) tobacco plantation
vegano/a ADJ, SM/F vegan
vegetación SF **1** (= *plantas*) vegetation
2 (*Med*) ▸ **vegetaciones adenoideas** adenoids
vegetal ADJ [*aceite, productos*] vegetable (*antes de s*) • **patología ~** plant pathology
SM **1** (= *planta*) plant, vegetable
2 vegetales (*CAm, Méx*) (= *verduras*) vegetables
3 (= *persona*) vegetable
vegetar ▹ CONJUG 1a VI **1** (*Bot*) to grow
2 (*fig*) [*persona*] to vegetate; [*negocio*] to stagnate
vegetarianismo SM vegetarianism
vegetariano/a ADJ, SM/F vegetarian
vegetativo ADJ vegetative • **sistema nervioso ~** vegetative nervous system • **vida vegetativa** vegetative life
vegoso ADJ (*Cono Sur*) [*tierra*] soggy, damp
veguero ADJ lowland (*antes de s*), low-lying
SM **1** (= *agricultor*) lowland farmer
2 (*Caribe*) [*de tabaco*] tobacco planter
3 (= *cigarro puro*) coarse cigar; (*Cono Sur*) (= *tabaco cubano*) good-quality Cuban tobacco, good cigar
vehemencia SF vehemence
vehemente ADJ vehement
vehementemente ADV vehemently
vehicular[1] ADJ **lengua ~** common language; **el inglés como lengua ~ en la enseñanza** English as a medium of education
vehicular[2] ▹ CONJUG 1a VT (= *transmitir*) to transmit, convey
vehiculizar ▹ CONJUG 1f VT = **vehicular**[2]
vehículo SM **1** (*Aut*) vehicle ▸ **vehículo a motor** motor vehicle ▸ **vehículo astral** spacecraft ▸ **vehículo automóvil** motor vehicle ▸ **vehículo carretero** road vehicle ▸ **vehículo cósmico** spacecraft ▸ **vehículo de carga** goods vehicle ▸ **vehículo de la empresa** company car ▸ **vehículo de motor** motor vehicle ▸ **vehículo de transporte** goods vehicle ▸ **vehículo espacial** spacecraft ▸ **vehículo industrial** commercial vehicle ▸ **vehículo privado** private vehicle ▸ **vehículo utilitario** commercial vehicle
2 [*de modas, ideas*] vehicle (**de** for)
3 (*Med*) carrier, transmitter (**de** of)
veinte ADJ INV, PRON, SM (*gen*) twenty; (*ordinal, en la fecha*) twentieth • **el siglo ~** the twentieth century • **le escribí el día ~** I wrote to him on the twentieth • **los (años) ~** the twenties; ▹ **seis**
veinteañero/a, veintiañero/a ADJ twentyish, about twenty
SM/F person of about twenty, person in his/her twenties
veintena SF • **una ~** about twenty
veintipocos ADJ PL twenty-odd
veintitantos ADJ PL twenty-odd • **tiene ~ años** he's in his twenties, he's twenty-something*, he's twenty-odd*
veintiuna SF (*Naipes*) pontoon, twenty-one (EEUU)
vejación SF (= *humillación*) humiliation; (= *maltrato*) ill-treatment • **sufrir vejaciones** to suffer humiliation
vejamen SM **1** = **vejación**
2 (= *pasquín*) satire, lampoon; (= *pulla*) shaft, taunt
vejaminoso ADJ (*And, Caribe*) irritating, annoying
vejancón/ona* ADJ, **vejarrón/ona*** ADJ ancient*, doddery*, decrepit
SM/F old chap/dear*, old dodderer*
vejar ▹ CONJUG 1a VT (= *molestar*) to vex, annoy; (= *humillar*) to humiliate; (= *mofarse de*) to scoff at; (= *atormentar*) to harass
vejarano ADJ (*LAm**) ancient*, doddery*, decrepit
vejatorio ADJ (= *molesto*) annoying, vexatious; (= *humillante*) humiliating, degrading; [*comentarios*] hurtful, offensive • **es ~ para él tener que pedirlo** it is humiliating for him to have to beg for it
vejestorio SM (*pey*) old dodderer*, old crock*
vejete* SM old boy*
vejez SF **1** (= *senectud*) old age • MODISMO: • **¡a la ~, viruelas!** fancy that happening at his *etc* age!*
2† (= *cuento*) old story; (= *noticia*) piece of stale news
3 vejeces (= *achaques*) ills of old age; (= *manías, chocheces*) grouchiness (*sing*), grumpiness (*sing*)
vejiga SF **1** (*Anat*) bladder ▸ **vejiga de la bilis** gallbladder ▸ **vejiga natatoria** air bladder, swim bladder
2 (*Med*) blister
3 (*en pintura*) blister
vela[1] SF **1** [*de cera*] candle • MODISMOS: • **estar a dos ~s*** (= *sin enterarse*) to be in the dark; (= *sin dinero*) to be broke* • **encender** *o* **poner una ~ a Dios y otra al diablo** to have it both ways • **¿quién te dio ~ en este entierro?** who asked you to butt in? ▸ **vela de sebo** tallow candle
2 (= *vigilia*) • **estar en ~** to be unable to get to sleep • **pasar la noche en ~** to have a sleepless night
3* (= *moco*) bogey*
4 (*Taur**) horn
5 (= *trabajo nocturno*) night work; (*Mil*) (period of) sentry duty
6 (*LAm*) (= *velorio*) wake
7 (*Cono Sur*) (= *molestia*) nuisance • **¡qué ~!** what a nuisance! • MODISMO: • **aguantar la ~** (= *soportar*) to put up with it; (= *plantar cara*) to face the music*
8 (*Caribe, Méx*) (= *bronca*) telling-off*
vela[2] SF (*Náut*) sail; (= *deporte*) sailing • **barco de ~** sailing ship • **darse** *o* **hacerse a la ~** • **largar las ~s** to set sail, get under way • **hacer ~** to go sailing • **a toda ~** • **a ~s desplegadas** (*lit*) under full sail; (*fig*) vigorously, energetically • MODISMOS: • **arriar** *o* **recoger ~s** (= *retractarse*) to back down; (= *abandonar*) to give up, chuck it in* • **estar a dos ~s*** to be broke*, be skint‡ • **estar entre dos ~s*** • **ir a la ~*** to be half-seas over‡ • **ir como las ~s** (*Cono Sur*) to drive very fast • **plegar ~s** to slow down ▸ **vela balón** spinnaker ▸ **vela mayor** mainsail
velación SF wake, vigil
velada SF (evening) party, soirée ▸ **velada de boxeo** fight night ▸ **velada musical** musical evening
veladamente ADV in a veiled way
velado ADJ (*tb fig*) veiled; (*Fot*) fogged, blurred; [*sonido*] muffled
velador SM **1** (= *mesa*) pedestal table; (*LAm*) (= *mesita*) bedside table, night table (EEUU)
2 (*para velas*) candlestick
3 (*Cono Sur*) (= *lámpara*) night light
4 (*Méx*) (= *pantalla*) lampshade
5 (= *vigilante*) watchman, caretaker; (*Hist*) sentinel
veladora SF **1** (*Méx*) (= *lámpara*) table lamp, bedside lamp
2 (*LAm*) (= *vela*) candle; (*Rel*) paraffin lamp
velamen SM sails (*pl*), canvas
velar[1] ▹ CONJUG 1a VT **1** [+ *enfermo*] to sit up with; [+ *muerto*] to keep vigil over
2 (*Mil*) to watch, keep watch over
3 (*LAm*) (= *codiciar*) to look covetously at
VI **1**† (= *permanecer despierto*) to stay awake, go without sleep
2 • **~ por algo/algn** (= *cuidar*) to look after sth/sb • **velaba por la salud de sus hijos** she looked after her children's health • **nadie vela por mis intereses** nobody watches over my interests • **tendremos que ~ por que esto no se repita** we'll have to see to it *o* ensure that this doesn't happen again
3 (*Rel*) to keep vigil
4 [*arrecife*] to appear
velar[2] ▹ CONJUG 1a VT **1** (*Fot*) to fog
2 (*liter*) (= *cubrir con un velo*) to veil
3 (*liter*) (= *ocultar*) to conceal
VPR **velarse 1** (*Fot*) to fog
2 (*liter*) (= *cubrirse con un velo*) to veil o.s.
velar[3] ADJ (*Ling*) velar
velarizar ▹ CONJUG 1f VT to velarize
velarte SM (*Hist*) broadcloth
velatorio SM wake
Velázquez SM Velázquez, Velasquez
veleidad SF **1** (= *volubilidad, inconstancia*) fickleness, capriciousness
2 (= *capricho*) whim; [*de humor*] unpredictable mood
veleidoso ADJ fickle, capricious
velero ADJ [*barco*] manoeuvrable, maneuverable (EEUU)
SM **1** (*Náut*) (*grande*) sailing ship; (*pequeño*) sailing boat, sailboat (EEUU)
2 (*Aer*) glider
3 (= *persona*) sailmaker
veleta SF **1** [*de edificio*] weather vane, weathercock
2 (*Pesca*) float
SMF (= *persona*) fickle person, weathercock
veletería SF (*Cono Sur*) chopping and changing, fickleness
velís SM (*Méx*) (= *maleta*) suitcase; (= *bolso*) valise, overnight bag
veliz SM (*Méx*) = **velís**
vello SM (*Anat*) fuzz, soft hair; (*Bot*) down; (*en frutas*) bloom; (*en cuerna*) velvet ▸ **vello facial** facial hair
vellocino SM fleece ▸ **Vellocino de Oro** Golden Fleece
vellón[1] SM **1** (= *lana*) fleece; (= *piel*) sheepskin
2 (= *mechón*) tuft of wool
vellón[2] SM **1** (*Téc*) copper and silver alloy
2 (*CAm, Caribe*) (= *moneda*) five-cent coin
vellonera SF (*Caribe*) jukebox
vellosidad SF (= *pelusa*) downiness; (= *pelo fuerte*) hairiness; (= *lanosidad*) fluffiness
velloso ADJ (= *con pelusa*) downy; (*más fuerte*)

hairy; (= *lanoso*) fluffy
velludo ADJ hairy
SM plush, velvet
velo SM **1** [*de tul, gasa*] veil • **tomar el ~** to take the veil • **corramos un tupido ~ sobre esto** let us draw a discreet veil over this
2 (*fig*) (= *cobertura*) veil, light covering; (*Fot*) fog; (*en cristal*) mist; [*de silencio, misterio*] shroud
3 (= *pretexto*) pretext, cloak
4 (= *confusión*) confusion, mental fog
5 (*Anat*) ▸ **velo de paladar** soft palate, velum
velocidad SF **1** (*gen*) speed; (*Téc*) velocity; (*fig*) swiftness, speediness • **de alta ~** high-speed • **a gran ~** at high speed • **a máxima** *o* **toda ~** at full speed, at top speed • **¿a qué ~?** how fast?, at what speed? • **¿a qué ~ ibas?** what speed were you doing? • **cobrar ~** to pick up *o* gather speed • **disminuir** *o* **moderar la ~** • **perder ~** to slow down • **exceder la ~ permitida** to speed, exceed the speed limit • MODISMO: • **confundir la ~ con el tocino*** to get things mixed up
▸ **velocidad adquirida** momentum
▸ **velocidad de crucero** cruising speed
▸ **velocidad de despegue** takeoff speed
▸ **velocidad del sonido** speed of sound
▸ **velocidad de obturación, velocidad de obturador** shutter speed ▸ **velocidad de transferencia** transfer rate ▸ **velocidad económica** cruising speed ▸ **velocidad máxima** maximum speed, top speed
▸ **velocidad máxima de impresión** (*Inform*) maximum print speed ▸ **velocidad punta** maximum speed, top speed
2 (*Mec*) gear, speed • **primera ~** • **~ corta** low gear, bottom gear, first gear • **segunda/tercera/cuarta ~** second/third/top gear • **meter la segunda ~** to change into second gear • **cuatro ~es hacia adelante** four forward gears ▸ **velocidades de avance** forward gears
velocímetro SM speedometer
velocípedo SM velocipede
velocista SMF sprinter
velódromo SM cycle track
velomotor SM moped
velón SM **1** (= *lámpara*) oil lamp
2 (*And, Cono Sur, Méx*) (= *vela*) thick tallow candle
3 (*CAm*) (= *parásito*) sponger*, parasite
4 (*And, Caribe*) *person who casts covetous glances*
velorio¹ SM **1** (= *fiesta*) party, celebration; (*And, Caribe, Cono Sur*) dull party, flat affair
2 (*esp LAm*) (= *velatorio*) funeral wake, vigil for the dead ▸ **velorio del angelito** *wake for a dead child*
velorio² SM (*Rel*) *ceremony of taking the veil*
veloz ADJ [*tren, coche, barco*] fast; [*movimiento*] quick, swift • **~ como un relámpago** as quick as lightning
velozmente ADV fast, quickly, swiftly
ven ▸ **venir**
vena SF **1** (*Anat*) vein • **abrirse** *o* **cortarse las ~s** to slit one's wrists • **inyectar en ~** to inject into a vein ▸ **vena yugular** jugular vein
2 (*Min*) vein, seam
3 (*en piedra, madera*) grain
4 (*Bot*) vein, rib
5 [*de humor, ánimo*] mood • **le dio la ~ por hacer eso** he had a notion to do that • **coger a algn de** *o* **en ~** to catch sb in the right mood • **estar de** *o* **en ~** (= *tener ganas*) to be in the mood (**para** for); (= *estar en forma*) to be in good form ▸ **vena de locura** streak of madness
6 (= *talento*) talent, promise • **tiene ~ de pintor** he has the makings of a painter, he shows a talent for painting
7 (*Geog*) underground stream

venablo SM dart • MODISMO: • **echar ~s** to burst out angrily
venado SM **1** (= *ciervo*) deer; (*macho*) stag
2 (*Culin*) venison
3 (*Caribe*) (= *piel*) deerskin
4 (*Caribe*) (= *prostituta*) whore
5 (*And*) (= *contrabando*) contraband
6 • MODISMO: • **correr** *o* **pintar el ~** (*CAm, Méx*) to play truant, play hookey (*EEUU*)
venal¹ ADJ (*Anat*) venous
venal² ADJ (*frm*) **1** (= *vendible*) vendible (*frm*), saleable, salable (*EEUU*)
2 (*pey*) (= *sobornable*) venal (*frm*), corrupt
venalidad SF venality, corruptness
venático ADJ crazy, mad
venatorio ADJ hunting (*antes de s*)
vencedor(a) ADJ [*equipo, partido*] winning, victorious (*frm*); [*general, país*] victorious
SM/F (= *ganador*) [*de una competición, elecciones*] winner; [*de una guerra*] victor • **una guerra sin ~es ni vencidos** a war with neither victor nor vanquished
vencejo¹ SM (*Orn*) swift
vencejo² SM (*Agr*) straw plait, string (*used in binding sheaves*)
vencer ▸ CONJUG 2b VT **1** (= *derrotar*) [+ *enemigo, rival*] to defeat, beat; [+ *enfermedad, dolor*] to beat, overcome • **vencieron al equipo visitante por 3 a 2** they defeated *o* beat the visiting team 3-2 • **nuestro sistema inmunológico es capaz de ~ al virus** our immune system is capable of beating *o* overcoming the virus • **a decir tonterías nadie le vence** when it comes to talking rubbish he's in a class of his own, no one beats him when it comes to talking rubbish • **vence a todos en elegancia** he outdoes them all in style, he beats them all for style
2 (= *controlar*) [+ *miedo, tentación*] to overcome; [+ *pasión*] to control • **consiguió ~ la tentación de fumar** he managed to overcome the temptation to smoke
3 (= *prevalecer*) [*miedo, sueño*] to overcome • **por fin lo venció el sueño** sleep finally overcame him • **me venció el pánico cuando tuve que hablarle** panic got the better of me *o* I was overcome with panic when I had to speak to him
4 (*Dep*) [+ *obstáculo*] to overcome; [+ *prueba*] to complete; [+ *distancia*] to do, complete; [+ *montaña*] to conquer • **vencieron los 15km en dos horas** they did *o* completed the 15km in two hours • **no consiguió ~ todas las pruebas** he didn't manage to complete all the heats
5 (= *hacer ceder*) [+ *soporte, rama*] to break • **el peso de los libros ha vencido el estante** the shelf gave way under the weight of the books, the weight of the books broke the shelf • **conseguimos ~ la puerta** we managed to break the door down
VI **1** (*en batalla, partido, elecciones*) to win • **hemos vencido por dos a cero** we won two nil • **¡~emos!** we shall win *o* overcome! • **dejarse ~ (por)** to give in(to) • **no te dejes ~ y sigue adelante** keep going and don't give in • **por fin se dejó ~ por la curiosidad** he finally gave in to his curiosity, he finally let (his) curiosity get the better of him • **no te dejes ~ por las dificultades** don't give up in the face of difficulties, don't let difficulties get the better of you
2 (*liter*) [*amor, pasión*] to triumph, be triumphant
3 (*Com*) [*documento, póliza, pasaporte*] to expire; [*inversión*] to mature • **su contrato vence a final de año** his contract runs out *o* expires at the end of the year • **el plazo para pagar el alquiler vence mañana** the deadline for paying the rent is tomorrow, the rent is due tomorrow • **el plazo para la entrega de solicitudes vence mañana** the closing date for applications is tomorrow • **la semana que viene me vence el primer plazo del ordenador** I have to pay my first instalment on the computer next week, my first instalment on the computer is due next week
VPR **vencerse 1** (= *ceder*) [*muelle, estante, soporte*] to give way • **la cama se venció con tanto peso** the bed gave way under the weight • **la mesa se vence hacia un lado** the table leans to one side • **la cabeza se le vencía hacia un lado** his head hung *o* leaned to one side
2 (*LAm*) [*pasaporte, permiso*] to expire • **cómetelo antes de que se venza** eat it before the use-by date • **se venció el plazo** the time's up
3 (*Cono Sur, Méx*) [*elástico, resorte*] to wear out; [*costura*] to come apart
4 (= *dominarse*) [*persona*] to control o.s.
vencido/a ADJ **1** (= *derrotado*) [*ejército, general*] defeated; [*equipo, jugador*] losing • **darse por ~** to give up, give in • **ir de ~** [*persona*] to be all in, be on one's last legs • **la enfermedad va de vencida** the illness is past its worst • **la tormenta va de vencida** the worst of the storm is over
2 (= *combado*) [*tabla, viga de madera*] sagging • **la estantería estaba vencida con tanto peso** the shelves were sagging under the weight
3 (*Com*) [*intereses, deuda*] due, payable • **con los intereses ~s** with the interest which is due *o* payable • **le pagan por meses ~s** he is paid at the end of the month
4 (*LAm*) [*boleto, permiso*] out of date; [*medicamento, alimento*] past its use-by date
5 (*Cono Sur, Méx*) [*elástico, resorte*] worn out
SM/F (*Dep*) loser • **los ~s** (*Dep*) the losers; (*Mil*) the defeated, the vanquished (*frm*); ▸ **tercero, vencedor**
ADV • **pagar ~** to pay in arrears
vencimiento SM **1** (*Com*) [*de plazo, contrato*] expiry, expiration (*frm*); [*de inversión, préstamo*] expiry date, date of expiration (*frm*); [*de deuda*] maturity • **al ~ del título** on expiry of the title *o* when the title expires • **con ~ el 1 de marzo** expiring on 1 March
2 [*de estantería, viga*] (*al combarse*) sagging; (*al romperse*) collapse
3 [*de dificultad*] • **tras el ~ de los primeros obstáculos** after overcoming the first few obstacles
venda SF bandage ▸ **venda elástica** elastic bandage
vendaje¹ SM (*Med*) dressing, bandaging
▸ **vendaje compresivo** support bandage
▸ **vendaje provisional** first-aid bandage
vendaje² SM **1** (*Com*) commission
2 (*LAm*) (= *plus*) bonus, perk*
vendar ▸ CONJUG 1a VT **1** [+ *herida*] to bandage, dress; [+ *ojos*] to cover, blindfold
2 (*fig*) (= *enceguecer*) to blind • MODISMO: • **~ los ojos a algn** to hoodwink sb
vendaval SM (= *ventarrón*) gale, strong wind; (*fig*) storm
vendedor(a) ADJ selling; (*Econ*) • **corriente ~a** selling tendency, tendency to sell
SM/F (*gen*) seller, vendor; (*en tienda*) shop assistant, sales assistant, sales clerk (*EEUU*); (= *minorista*) retailer; [*de empresa*] sales representative, salesman/saleswoman
▸ **vendedor(a) a domicilio** door-to-door salesman/saleswoman ▸ **vendedor(a) ambulante** hawker, pedlar, peddler (*EEUU*)
▸ **vendedor(a) de seguros** insurance salesman/saleswoman
vendeja† SF **1** (= *venta*) public sale

V

2 (= *géneros*) *collection of goods offered for sale*

vendepatrias SMF INV traitor

vender ▸ CONJUG 2a VT **1** [+ *producto*] to sell • **venden la bicicleta a mitad de precio** they are selling the bicycle at half price • **lo vendieron por 50 euros** they sold it for 50 euros • **~le algo a algn** to sell sb sth, sell sth to sb • **me ha vendido un ordenador** he sold me a computer • **~ al contado** to sell for cash • **~ al por mayor** to sell wholesale • **~ al por menor** to sell retail • **este coche está sin ~** this car remains unsold • **MODISMO**: • **¡a mí que las vendo!** I'm not falling for that one!
2 (= *traicionar*) [+ *amigo*] to betray, sell out*; [+ *cómplice*] to shop*
VI to sell • **los buenos productos siempre venden** a good product will always sell • **vendemos a precios inmejorables** our prices are unbeatable
VPR **venderse 1** [*producto*] to sell, be sold • **este artículo se vende muy bien** this item is selling very well • **se vende en farmacias** it is sold in chemists' • **el cuadro se vendió por cuatro millones** the painting sold *o* was sold for four million • **se vendían a diez euros en el mercado** they were selling at *o* for ten euros in the market • **es buen político, pero no sabe ~se** he's a good politician but he doesn't know how to sell himself • **"se vende"** "for sale" • **"se vende coche"** "car for sale" • **MODISMO**: • **~se caro** to play hard to get
2 (= *dejarse corromper*) to sell out; (= *dejarse sobornar*) to accept a bribe • **le acusaron de ~se a las multinacionales** they accused him of selling out to the multinationals • **el árbitro se vendió** the referee accepted a bribe
3 (= *traicionarse*) to give o.s. away

vendetta [ben'ðeta] SF vendetta

vendí SM certificate of sale

vendibilidad SF (*gen*) saleability; (*Com*) marketability

vendible ADJ (*gen*) saleable; (*Com*) marketable

vendido ADJ • **MODISMO**: • **ir** *o* **estar ~ a algo/algn*** to be at the mercy of sth/sb

vendimia SF **1** [*de uvas*] grape harvest, wine harvest; (*relativo a calidad, año*) year • **la ~ de 1985** the 1985 vintage
2 (= *provecho*) big profit, killing

vendimiador(a) SM/F vintager

vendimiar ▸ CONJUG 1b VT **1** [+ *uvas*] to harvest, pick
2 (*fig*) to squeeze a profit out of, make a killing out of*
3†‡ (= *matar*) to bump off‡

vendré *etc* ▸ **venir**

venduta SF **1** (*LAm*) (= *subasta*) auction, public sale
2 (*Caribe*) (= *frutería*) greengrocer's (shop), fruiterer's (shop); (= *abacería*) small grocery store
3 (*Caribe*) (= *estafa*) swindle

vendutero SM **1** (*LAm*) (*en subasta*) auctioneer
2 (*Caribe*) (= *comerciante*) greengrocer, produce dealer (*EEUU*)

Venecia SF Venice

veneciano/a ADJ of/from Venice
SM/F native/inhabitant of Venice • **los ~s** the people of Venice

veneno SM (*gen*) poison; [*de serpiente*] venom

venenoso ADJ [*animal*] poisonous, venomous; [*planta, sustancia*] poisonous; [*palabras, lengua*] venomous

venera SF (*Zool*) scallop; (= *concha*) scallop shell; ▸ **CAMINO DE SANTIAGO**

venerable ADJ venerable

veneración SF (*gen*) worship; (*Rel*) veneration

venerando ADJ venerable

venerar ▸ CONJUG 1a VT (*gen*) to worship, revere; (*Rel*) to venerate

venéreo ADJ venereal • **enfermedad venérea** venereal disease

venero SM **1** (*Min*) lode, seam
2 (= *fuente*) spring
3 (*fig*) source, origin ▸ **venero de datos** mine of information

venezolanismo SM *word or phrase peculiar to Venezuela*

venezolano/a ADJ Venezuelan
SM/F Venezuelan • **los ~s** the Venezuelans

Venezuela SF Venezuela

venga *etc* ▸ **venir**

vengador(a) ADJ avenging
SM/F avenger

venganza SF revenge, vengeance • **lo hizo con espíritu de ~** he did it in a spirit of revenge *o* vengeance • **mintió por** *o* **como ~** she lied out of revenge *o* vengeance • **jurar ~ a algn** to swear vengeance on sb • **clamar ~** (*frm*) to cry for vengeance (*frm*)

vengar ▸ CONJUG 1h VT to avenge
VPR **vengarse** to take revenge, get one's revenge • **~se de algn** to take revenge on sb • **~se de una ofensa** to take revenge for an offence

vengativo ADJ [*persona, espíritu*] vengeful, vindictive; [*acto*] retaliatory

vengo *etc* ▸ **venir**

venia SF **1** (= *perdón*) pardon, forgiveness
2 (= *permiso*) permission, consent • **con su ~** by your leave, with your permission • **casarse sin la ~ de sus padres** to marry without the consent of one's parents
3 (*LAm*) (*Mil*) salute

venial ADJ venial

venialidad SF veniality

venida SF **1** (*gen*) coming; (= *llegada*) arrival; (= *vuelta*) return
2† (= *ímpetu*) impetuosity, rashness

venidero ADJ coming, future • **en lo ~** in (the) future • **los ~s** posterity, future generations

venir

VERBO INTRANSITIVO
VERBO PRONOMINAL

▸ CONJUG 3r

Para las expresiones ***venir al caso, venir de lejos, venir a las manos, venir a menos, venir a pelo, venir de perlas, venirse abajo, venirse encima,*** *ver la otra entrada.*

VERBO INTRANSITIVO

1 (*a un lugar*) to come • **vino a Córdoba desde Barcelona** he came to Córdoba from Barcelona • **¡ven acá** *o* **aquí!** come (over) here! • **vino en taxi** he came by taxi • **~ a** (+ *infin*): • **vinieron a verme al hospital** they came to see me in hospital • **me vienen a recoger en coche** they're coming to pick me up in the car • **¿y todo esto a qué viene?** what's all this in aid of? • **¿a qué vienen tantos llantos?** what's all this crying about? • **¿y ahora a qué vienes?** what do you want now? • **hacer ~ a algn**: • **le hicieron ~ desde Londres** they had him come (all the way) from London • **hicieron ~ al médico** they sent for the doctor, they called out the doctor • **~ (a) por algn/algo** to come for sb/sth • **vinieron (a) por el enfermo** they came to pick up the patient, they came for the patient • **han venido (a) por el coche** they've come to pick up the car, they've come for the car • **MODISMO**: • **~le a algn con**: • **no me vengas con historias** don't give me any of your stories

2 (= *volver*) • **¡enseguida** *o* **ahora vengo!** I'll be right back!* • **cuando vinimos de las vacaciones todo estaba sucio** when we got back from our holiday everything was dirty

3 (= *estar*) to be • **la noticia venía en el periódico** the news was in the paper • **viene en la página 47** it's on page 47 • **esta palabra no viene en el diccionario** this word isn't in the dictionary • **el texto viene en castellano** the text is (written) in Spanish • **viene en varios colores** it comes in several colours

4 (= *ocurrir*) to come • **la guerra y todo lo que vino después** the war and everything that happened *o* came afterwards • **ahora viene lo mejor de la película** this is the best bit in the film, the best bit in the film is coming up now • **lo veía ~** I could see it coming • **MODISMOS**: • **(estar) a verlas ~** to wait and see what happens • **venga lo que venga** come what may • **~ rodado** to go smoothly • **REFRÁN**: • **las desgracias nunca vienen solas** it never rains but it pours

5 **venir de** (= *provenir*) to come from • **esta palabra viene del árabe** this word comes from the Arabic • **esta especia viene de oriente** this spice comes from the East • **la fortuna le viene de su padre** his fortune comes from his father • **de ahí vienen muchos problemas** it is the cause of many problems • **la honestidad le viene de familia** honesty runs in her family

6 (= *sobrevenir*) • **de repente le vinieron muchos problemas** a lot of problems suddenly cropped up • **le vino un gran dolor de cabeza** he got a terrible headache • **le vino la idea de salir** he had the idea of going out • **me vinieron ganas de llorar** I felt like crying • **MODISMO**: • **como te** *o* **le venga en gana** just as you wish

7 (= *quedar*) • **la falda me viene ancha** the skirt is too loose (for me) • **el abrigo te viene algo pequeño** the coat is rather small on *o* for you • **te viene estrecho en la espalda** it's too tight round your shoulders • **este puesto de trabajo me viene grande** *o* **ancho** this job is beyond me, this job is too much for me • **~ bien**: • **¿te viene bien el sábado?** is Saturday all right for you? • **hoy no me viene bien** today is not convenient for me • **eso vendrá bien para el invierno** that will come in handy for the winter* • **me vendría bien una copita** I could do with a drink* • **~ mal**: • **mañana me viene mal** tomorrow is inconvenient • **no me vendría mal un descanso** I could do with a rest

8 **por venir** (= *futuro*) • **las generaciones por ~** future generations, generations to come • **lo peor está por ~** the worst is yet *o* still to come
que viene (= *próximo*) next • **el mes que viene** next month • **lo estudiaremos el curso que viene** we'll be studying it next year
venga a (*con sentido reiterativo*) • **yo estoy nerviosísimo y ella venga a mirarme** I'm really nervous and she won't stop staring at me • **yo no tenía dinero y el niño venga a pedir chucherías** I didn't have any money and my boy was always *o* forever asking for little treats • **tenía mucha prisa y los periodistas venga a preguntas** I was in a real hurry and the journalists wouldn't stop asking questions

9 (*como auxiliar*) **a** • **~ a** (+ *infin*) • **el desastre vino a turbar nuestra tranquilidad** the disaster upset our peaceful existence • **viene a llenar**

un gran vacío it fills a big gap • **vino a parar** *o* **dar a la cárcel** he ended up in jail • **~ a ser**: • **viene a ser 84 en total** it comes to 84 all together • **viene a ser lo mismo** it comes to *o* amounts to the same thing
b (+ *gerund*) • **eso lo vengo diciendo desde hace tiempo** that's what I've been saying all along
c (+ *participio*) • **vengo cansado** I'm tired • **venía hecho polvo*** he was shattered*
10 ¡venga! (*Esp**) • **¡venga, vámonos!** come on, let's go! • **¡venga, una canción!** let's have a song! • **préstame cinco euros, venga** go on, lend me five euros • **—¿quieres que lo hagamos juntos? —¡venga!** "shall we do it together?" — "come on, then" • **—¡hasta luego! —¡venga!** "see you later!" — "O.K.!" *o* "right!" • **¡venga ya, no seas pesado!** come on, don't be such a bore! • **—me ha tocado la lotería —¡venga ya!** "I've won the lottery" — "you're kidding! "*
(VERBO PRONOMINAL) **venirse**
1 (*= llegar*) to come • **el niño se vino solo** the child came here all on his own
2 (*= volver*) to come back • **se vino de la fiesta porque estaba aburrido** he came back from the party because he was bored
3 (*= fermentar*) [*vino*] to ferment; [*masa*] to prove
4 (*= convenirse*) • **lo que se ha venido en llamar** ... what we have come to call ...
5 (CAm)** (*sexualmente*) to come**

VENIR

Aunque **venir** *y* **come** *generalmente dan una idea de movimiento en dirección al hablante, e* **ir** *y* **go** *implican que hay un movimiento en dirección opuesta al hablante, tenemos que distinguir algunos casos en los que hay diferencias entre los dos idiomas.*

▷ *En español no solemos describir el movimiento de una acción desde el punto de vista de la otra persona, mientras que en inglés sí. Por ejemplo, si alguien nos llama, respondemos:*
Ya voy
I'm coming

▷ *Si estamos organizando algo por teléfono, por carta, o en una conversación:*
Iré a recogerte a las cuatro
I'll come and pick you up at four
¿Voy contigo?
Shall I come with you?

▷ *Por lo tanto, tenemos que traducir* **ir** *por* **come** *cuando, si vamos a algún sitio, nos unimos a alguien o a un grupo que va o ya está en ese sitio.*

Para otros usos y ejemplos ver la entrada.

venoso (ADJ) **1** [*sangre*] venous
2 [*hoja*] veined, ribbed
venpermutar ▷ CONJUG 1a (VT) (*Col*) to offer for sale or exchange
venta (SF) **1** (*Com*) sale • **han prohibido la ~ de armas** the sale of arms has been banned • **a la ~** on sale • **estar a la ~** to be on sale • **poner algo a la ~** to put sth on *o* up for sale • **salir a la ~** to go on sale • **de ~**: • **de ~ únicamente en farmacias** available only at chemists' • **en ~**: • **estar en ~** to be (up) for sale, be on the market • **"en venta"** "on sale" ▸ **venta a domicilio** door-to-door selling ▸ **venta al contado** cash sale ▸ **venta al detalle** retail ▸ **venta al por mayor** wholesale ▸ **venta al por menor** retail ▸ **venta a plazos** hire purchase, installment plan (*EEUU*) ▸ **venta callejera** peddling, hawking ▸ **venta de garaje** (*esp Méx*) garage sale ▸ **venta de liquidación** clearance sale ▸ **venta directa** direct selling ▸ **venta piramidal** pyramid selling ▸ **venta por balance** stocktaking sale ▸ **venta por catálogo** mail-order selling ▸ **venta por correo** mail-order selling ▸ **venta por cuotas** hire purchase, installment plan (*EEUU*) ▸ **venta por inercia** inertia selling ▸ **venta posbalance** stocktaking sale ▸ **venta pública** public sale, auction ▸ **ventas a término** forward sales ▸ **ventas brutas** gross sales ▸ **ventas de exportación** export sales ▸ **ventas por teléfono** telephone sales
2† (*= posada*) country inn
3 (*Caribe, Méx*) (*= tienda*) small shop, stall; (*Cono Sur*) [*de feria, exposición*] stall, booth
ventada (SF) gust of wind
ventaja (SF) **1** (*= beneficio*) advantage • **tiene la ~ de que está cerca de casa** it has the advantage of being close to home • **es un plan que tiene muchas ~s** it is a plan that has many advantages • **llevar ~ a algn** to have the advantage over sb, be ahead of sb, be one up on sb • **la ~ que A le lleva a B es grande** A has a big advantage over B • **sacar ~ de algo** (*= aprovechar*) to derive profit from sth; (*pey*) to use sth to one's own advantage
2 (*Dep*) (*en carrera*) start, advantage; (*Tenis*) advantage; (*en las apuestas*) odds (*pl*) • **me dio una ~ de cuatro metros** • **me dio cuatro metros de ~** he gave me a four metre start • **me dio una ~ de 20 puntos** he gave me an advantage of 20 points • **llevar ~** (*en carrera*) to be leading *o* ahead • **llevaba una ~ de varios segundos sobre su rival** he was several seconds ahead of his rival • **llevan una ~ de 1-0** they are 1-0 up *o* ahead
3 ventajas (*en empleo*) extras, perks*
▸ **ventajas supletorias** fringe benefits
ventajear ▷ CONJUG 1a (VT) (*And, CAm*)
1 (*= rebasar*) to outstrip, surpass; (*= llevar ventaja a*) to get the advantage of
2 (*= mejorar*) to better, improve on
3 (*= preferir*) to prefer, give preference to
4 • **~ a algn** (*pey*) to beat sb to it, get the jump on sb*
ventajero/a (ADJ), (SM/F) (*LAm*) = **ventajista**
ventajismo (SM) **1** (*= oportunismo*) opportunism
2 (*LAm*) cheek*, nerve*
ventajista (ADJ) (*= poco escrupuloso*) unscrupulous; (*= egoísta*) self-seeking, grasping; (*= taimado*) sly, treacherous
(SMF) (*= oportunista*) opportunist
ventajosamente (ADV) (*gen*) advantageously; (*Econ*) profitably • **estar ~ colocado** to be well placed
ventajoso (ADJ) **1** (*gen*) advantageous; (*Econ*) profitable
2 (*LAm*) = **ventajista**
ventana (SF) **1** (*Constr*) window • **doble ~** double-glazed window • **tirar algo por la ~** (*lit*) to throw sth out of the window; (*fig*) to throw sth away, fail to make any use of sth
▸ **ventana aislante** double-glazed window
▸ **ventana de guillotina** sash window
▸ **ventana salediza** bay window ▸ **ventana vidriera** picture window ▸ **ventanas dobles** double glazing (*sing*)
2 [*de nariz*] nostril
3 (*Inform*) window ▸ **ventana emergente** (*Inform*) pop-up (window)
4 (*And*) (*= claro de bosque*) forest clearing, glade
ventanaje (SM) windows (*pl*)
ventanal (SM) large window
ventanear ▷ CONJUG 1a (VI) to be always at the window, be forever peeping out
ventanilla (SF) **1** [*de vehículo*] window • **si tienes calor baja la ~** open the window if you're hot
2 (*en cine, teatro*) box office; (*en oficina*) window • **recoja sus entradas en la ~** pick your tickets up at the box office • **para abonar en cuenta pase por ~** please make deposits at the cash desk • **me tuvieron todo el día de ~ en ~** they gave me the runaround all day* • **programa de ~ única** *programme to simplify bureaucratic procedures*
3 [*de sobre*] window
4 (*Anat*) (*tb* **ventanilla de la nariz**) nostril
ventanillero/a (SM/F) counter-clerk
ventanillo (SM) (*= ventana*) small window; (*= mirilla*) peephole
ventarrón (SM) (*= viento*) gale, strong wind; (*= ráfaga*) blast
ventear ▷ CONJUG 1a (VT) **1** [*perro*] to sniff
2 [*+ ropa*] (*= airear*) to air; (*= secar*) to put out to dry
3 (*LAm*) [*+ animal*] to brand
4 (*LAm*) (*= abanicar*) to fan
5 (*Cono Sur*) [*+ adversario*] to get far ahead of, leave far behind
6 (*LAm*) (*Agr*) to winnow
(VI) (*= curiosear*) to snoop, pry; (*= investigar*) to inquire, investigate
(VPR) **ventearse 1** (*= henderse*) to split, crack; (*= ampollarse*) to blister; (*= secarse*) to get too dry, spoil
2 (*= ventosear*) to break wind
3 (*And, Caribe, Cono Sur*) (*= estar mucho fuera*) to be outdoors a great deal
4 (*And, Caribe*) (*= engreírse*) to get conceited
ventero/a (SM/F) innkeeper
ventilación (SF) **1** [*de habitación, edificio*] ventilation; (*= abertura*) opening for ventilation • **sin ~** unventilated
▸ **ventilación mecánica** artificial respiration
2 (*= corriente*) draught, draft (*EEUU*)
3 [*de problema, asunto*] airing
ventilado (ADJ) draughty, drafty (*EEUU*), breezy
ventilador (SM) **1** (*gen, de coche*) fan
2 (*= abertura*) air vent, ventilator
3 (*Med*) ventilator
ventilar ▷ CONJUG 1a (VT) **1** (*= airear*) [*+ cuarto*] to air, ventilate; [*+ ropa*] to air
2* (*= resolver*) to sort (out)* • **han ventilado el problema en dos horas** they sorted (out) the problem in two hours*
3 (*= hacer público*) [*+ intimidades, secreto*] to air • **ha estado ventilando los detalles íntimos de su relación** he's been airing the intimate details of their relationship
(VPR) **ventilarse 1** (*= airearse*) [*ropa*] to air • **abre la ventana para que se ventile la habitación** open the window to air *o* ventilate the room
2 (*frm*) (*= tomar aire*) [*persona*] to get some (fresh) air
3* [*+ comida, bebida, trabajo*] to polish off* • **se ventiló la botella de whisky en un día** he polished off the bottle of whisky in one day*
4* (*= matar*) • **~se a algn** to do sb in*
5 (*Esp***) • **~se a algn** (*= copular con*) to shag sb**, screw sb**
ventisca (SF) blizzard, snowstorm
ventiscar ▷ CONJUG 1g (VI), **ventisquear** ▷ CONJUG 1a (VI) (*= nevar*) to blow a blizzard, snow with a strong wind; [*nieve*] to drift
ventisquero (SM) **1** (*= tormenta*) blizzard, snowstorm
2 (*= montículo*) snowdrift; (*= barranco*) *gully/slope where the snow lies*
vento‡ (SM) (*Cono Sur*) dough‡

V

ventolada SF (*LAm*) strong wind, gale
ventolera SM **1** (= *ráfaga*) gust of wind, blast
2 (= *juguete*) windmill
3* (= *capricho*) whim, wild idea • **le dio la ~ de comprarlo** he had a sudden notion to buy it
4 (= *vanidad*) vanity, conceit; (= *satisfacción*) smugness; (= *arrogancia*) arrogance; (= *jactancia*) boastfulness • **tiene mucha ~** she's terribly big-headed*
ventolina SF **1** (*LAm*) (= *ráfaga*) sudden gust of wind
2 (*Náut*) light wind
ventorrillo SM **1** (= *taberna*) small inn, roadhouse
2 (*Caribe, Méx*) (= *tienda*) small shop
ventosa SF **1** (= *agujero*) vent, air hole
2 (*Zool*) sucker
3 (*Med*) cupping glass
4 (*Téc*) suction pad
ventosear ▷ CONJUG 1a VI to break wind
ventosidad SF wind, flatulence (*frm*)
ventoso ADJ **1** (*Meteo*) windy
2 (= *flatulento*) windy, flatulent (*frm*)
SM (*Esp‡*) (= *ladrón*) burglar
ventral ADJ ventral
ventregada SF brood, litter
ventrículo SM ventricle
ventrílocuo/a SM/F ventriloquist
ventriloquia SF ventriloquism
ventrudo ADJ potbellied
ventura SF **1** (= *dicha*) happiness
2 (= *suerte*) luck, (good) fortune; (= *casualidad*) chance • **mala ~** bad luck • **por su mala ~** as bad luck would have it • **por ~** (*frm*) (= *por suerte*) fortunately; (= *por casualidad*) by (any) chance • **¿piensas ir, por ~?** are you by any chance thinking of going? • **echar la buena ~ a algn** to tell sb's fortune • **probar ~** to try one's luck • **~ te dé Dios** I wish you luck
• MODISMO: • **a la ~** at random • **ir a la ~** to go haphazardly, go without a fixed plan • **vivir a la ~** to live in a disorganized way • **todo lo hace a la ~** he does it all in a hit-or-miss fashion • REFRÁN: • **viene la ~ a quien la procura** God helps those who help themselves
venturero ADJ (*Méx*) **1** [*cosecha*] out of season
2 [*trabajo*] temporary, casual
venturoso ADJ **1** (= *afortunado*) lucky, fortunate; (= *exitoso*) successful
2 (= *dichoso*) happy
ventuta SF (*Col*) garage sale
Venus SF (*Mit*) Venus
SM (*Astron*) Venus
venus SF (= *mujer*) goddess
venusiano/a ADJ, SM/F Venusian
veo-veo SM (= *juego*) I spy (with my little eye)

ver

VERBO TRANSITIVO
VERBO INTRANSITIVO
VERBO PRONOMINAL
SUSTANTIVO MASCULINO

▷ CONJUG 2u

Para las expresiones ***ver visiones, no ver tres en un burro****, ver el sustantivo.*

VERBO TRANSITIVO

1 (= *percibir*) **a** [+ *persona, objeto*] to see • **te vi en el parque** I saw you in the park • **desde aquí lo verás mejor** you can see it better from here • **lo he visto con mis propios ojos** I saw it with my own eyes • **me acuerdo como si lo estuviera viendo** I remember it as if I were seeing it now, I remember it as if it were yesterday • **¡vieran qué casa!** (*Méx*) • **¡hubieran visto qué casa!** (*Méx*) you should have seen the house! • **dejarse ver**: • **este año Pedro no se ha dejado ver por aquí** we haven't seen much of Pedro this year
• MODISMOS: • **no veo ni jota** I can't see a thing • **si te he visto no me acuerdo**: • **le pedí que me ayudara, pero si te he visto no me acuerdo** I asked him to help me but he (just) didn't want to know • **ver algn/algo venir**: • **—¿que ha dimitido? —eso ya lo veía venir** "he's resigned?" — "well, you could see it coming" • **ya te veo venir, ¿a que quieres que te preste el coche?** I know what you're after, you want to borrow the car, don't you?
b (+ *gerund*) • **los vi paseando por el parque** I saw them walking in the park
c (+ *infin*) • **la vi bajar la escalera** I saw her come downstairs • **eso lo he visto hacer aquí muchas veces** I have often seen that done here
d (+ *adj*) • **te veo muy triste** you look very sad • **esta casa la veo pequeña para tanta gente** I think this house is too small for so many people
2 (= *mirar*) [+ *televisión, programa, partido*] to watch • **anoche vi una película en la tele** I saw *o* watched a film on TV last night • **es (digno) de ver** it's worth seeing • MODISMO: • **no poder (ni) ver a algn**: • **no lo puedo (ni) ver** I can't stand him
3 (*en saludos*) • **¡cuánto tiempo sin verte!** I haven't seen you for ages! • **¡hasta más ver!** see you again!
4 (= *visitar*) to see • **ayer fui a ver a tu hermano** I went to see your brother yesterday • **tendré que ir a ver al abogado** I shall have to go to *o* and see my solicitor • **el médico todavía no la ha visto** the doctor hasn't seen her yet
5 (= *imaginar*) to see, imagine • **lo estoy viendo de almirante** I can just see *o* imagine him as an admiral
6 (= *vivir*) to live through • **yo he visto dos guerras mundiales** I have lived through two world wars • MODISMOS: • **y usted que lo vea** • **y tú que lo veas**: • **—¡a celebrarlo con salud el año próximo! — ¡y usted que lo vea!** "many happy returns!" — "thank you!"
7 (= *examinar*) to look at • **este tema lo veremos en la próxima clase** we'll be looking at this subject in the next lesson
8 (= *comprobar*) to see • **¡verás como al final te caerás!** you'll fall, you just wait and see! • **ya verás como al final tengo que hacerlo yo** I'll end up doing it myself, you'll see • **habrá que ver**: • **habrá que ver lo que les habrá contado** we'll have to see what he's told them • **voy a ver si está en su despacho** I'll see if he's in his office
9 (= *notar*) to see • **no veo la diferencia entre uno y otro** I can't see the difference between them • **ya veo que tendré que hacerlo yo solo** I can see I'll have to do it myself • **—¿ves que no son iguales? —pues, no lo veo** "can't you see they're not the same?" — "no, I can't" • **—gana más de cien mil al mes —¡ya ves!** "she earns more than 100,000 a month" — "well, there you go!" • **dejarse ver**: • **los efectos de la crisis se dejaron ver meses después** the effects of the crisis were felt months later • **la preocupación se dejaba ver en su cara** the worry showed in his face • **echar de ver algo** to notice sth • **por lo que veo** from what I can see
10 (= *entender*) to see • **ahora veo la importancia del problema** I see how serious the problem is now • **¿no ves que ...?** don't *o* can't you see that ...? • **no veo muy claro para qué lo quiere** I can't really see what he wants it for • **hacer ver algo a algn** to point sth out to sb
11 (= *encontrar*) to see • **no veo nada en contra de eso** I see nothing against it • **no le veo solución al conflicto** I can't see a solution to the conflict • **yo este tema no lo veo así** I don't see this issue that way
12 (*Jur*) [+ *pleito*] to hear, try • **el proceso se verá en mayo** the case will be heard in May
13 tener que ver • **—es demasiado pequeño —¿y eso qué tiene que ver?** "it's too small" — "what's that got to do with it?" • **esto tiene que ver con lo que estudiamos ayer** this has to do with what we were looking at yesterday • **yo no tuve nada que ver en la venta del terreno** I had nothing to do with the sale of the land
14 a ver • **a ver niños, ¿cuál es la capital de Francia?** now, children, what is the capital of France? • **—mira, tú sales en la foto —¿a ver?** "look, you're in the photo" — "let's have a look" *o* "let's see" • **a ver ese niño, que no se quede solo** don't leave that child on his own • **a ver qué dicen las noticias sobre el robo** let's see if there's anything about the robbery on the news • **a ver qué está pasando** let's see what's happening • **—estás estudiando mucho —¡a ver, no queda más remedio!** "you're doing a lot of studying" — "well, I haven't got much choice!" • **¡a ver, cállate ya!** shut up, will you! • **¿a ver?** (*And*) (*Telec*) hello? • **a ver si ...**: • **a ver si acabas pronto** see if you can finish this off quickly • **¡a ver si te crees que no lo sé!** surely you don't think I don't know about it!

VERBO INTRANSITIVO

1 (= *percibir*) to see • **no veo muy bien con el ojo derecho** I can't see very well with my right eye • **como vimos ayer en la conferencia** as we saw in the lecture yesterday • **como veremos más adelante** as we shall see later • **eso está por ver** that remains to be seen
• MODISMOS: • **que no veo***: • **tengo un hambre que no veo** I'm famished! • **que no veas***: • **hay un ruido que no veas** there's a hell of a racket!* • **un coche que no veas** an amazing car • **ver y callar**: • **no digas nada, tú solo ver y callar** you'd better keep your mouth shut about this • **ver para creer** seeing is believing
2 (= *comprobar*) to see • **según voy viendo...** as I am beginning to see... • **—¿quién ha venido? —no sé, voy a ver** "who is it?" —"I don't know, I'll go and see" • **—al final siempre me toca hacerlo a mi —ya veo** "in the end it's always me that has to do it" — "so I see"
3 (= *entender*) to see • **¿ves?, así es mucho más fácil** you see? it's much easier like this • **a mi modo de ver** as I see it, the way I see it • **¿viste?** (*Cono Sur*) right?, are you with me?
4 • **ver de hacer algo** to see about doing sth, try to do sth • **tenemos que ver de solucionar este problema** we must try to *o* and find a solution to this problem • **veremos de salir temprano** we'll see if we can leave early, we'll try to *o* and leave early
5 (*otras locuciones*) • **¡hay que ver!**: • **¡hay que ver lo que te pareces a tu madre!** gosh! how like your mother you are *o* look! • **¡hay que ver lo que ha cambiado la ciudad!** it's incredible *o* you wouldn't believe how much the town has changed! • **¡para que veas!**: • **ha aprobado todas las asignaturas, ¡para que veas!** she passed all her exams, how about that! • **no solo no perdí, sino que arrasé, ¡para que veas!** not only did I not lose, but I won by a mile, so there! • **lo dijo por ver**

(*Caribe*) • **lo dijo de por ver** (*Cono Sur*) he was just trying it on* • **quedar en veremos** (*LAm*): • **todo quedó en veremos** it was all left in the air • **eso está** *o* **queda en veremos** it's not certain yet • **vamos a ver** let's see ..., let me see ... • **—¿esto tiene arreglo? —no sé, vamos a ver** "can this be repaired?" — "I don't know, let's see *o* let me see" • **¿por qué no me llamaste, vamos a ver?** why didn't you call me, I'd like to know? • **ya veremos** we'll see • **—¿podré ir a la fiesta? —ya veremos** "can I go to the party?" — "we'll see"

VERBO PRONOMINAL **verse**

1 *reflexivo* to see o.s. • **no quiere verse en el espejo** she doesn't want to see herself in the mirror • **se vio reflejado en el espejo** he saw his reflection in the mirror

2 *recíproco* (= *saludarse, visitarse*) to see each other; (= *citarse*) to meet • **ahora apenas nos vemos** we hardly see (anything of) each other nowadays • **¡luego nos vemos!** see you later! • **¡nos estamos viendo!** (*LAm*) see you (later)! • **quedamos en vernos en la estación** we arranged to meet at the station • **verse con algn** to see sb

3 *= percibirse* • **desde aquí no se ve** you can't see it from here • **se le veía mucho en el parque** he was often to be seen in the park • **se le veían las bragas** you could see her knickers • **no se ha visto un lío parecido** you never saw such a mess • **¿cuándo se vio nada igual?** have you ever seen anything like it! • **es digno de verse** it's worth seeing • **¡habráse visto!** of all the cheek!*, well I like that! • **eso ya se verá** that remains to be seen

4 *= mirar* • **véase la página 9** see page 9

5 *= notarse* • **—ahora estoy muy feliz —ya se ve** "I'm very happy now" — "I can see that" • **se ve que no tiene idea de informática** he obviously hasn't got a clue about computers • **se ve que sí** so it seems • **¡qué se vean los forzudos!** let's see how tough you are!

6 *= imaginarse* to see o.s., imagine o.s. • **yo ya me veía en la cárcel** I could see myself going to jail

7 *LAm** (= *parecer*) to look • **te ves divina** you look wonderful • **te ves cansado** you look tired • **te vas a ver precioso así** you'll look lovely like that

8 *= estar, encontrarse* to find o.s., be • **verse en un apuro** to find o.s. *o* be in a jam* • **se veía en la cumbre de la fama** he was at the height of his fame

9 **vérselas** • **me las vi y me las deseé para hacerlo*** it was a real sweat to get it done*, it was a tough job to get it done* • **vérselas con algn**: • **tendrá que vérselas con mi abogado** he'll have my solicitor to deal with

SUSTANTIVO MASCULINO

1 *= aspecto* • **de buen ver** good-looking • **tener buen ver** to be good-looking

2 *= opinión* • **a mi ver** as I see it, the way I see it

vera SF (*gen*) edge, verge, berm (*EEUU*); [*de río*] bank • **a la ~ de** (*poét*) near, next to • **a la ~ del camino** beside the road, at the roadside • **se sentó a mi ~** he sat down beside me

veracidad SF truthfulness, veracity (*frm*)

veracruzano/a ADJ of/from Veracruz SM/F native/inhabitant of Veracruz • **los ~s** the people of Veracruz

veragua SF (*CAm*) mildew (*on cloth*)

veranda SF veranda(h)

veraneante SMF holidaymaker, (summer) vacationer (*EEUU*)

veranear ▷ CONJUG 1a VI to spend the summer (holiday), spend the summer vacation (*EEUU*), holiday • **veranean en Jaca** they go to Jaca for the summer • **es un buen sitio para ~** it's a nice place for a summer holiday

veraneo SM summer holiday, summer vacation (*EEUU*) • **lugar de ~** summer resort, holiday resort • **estar de ~** to be away on (one's summer) holiday • **ir de ~ a la montaña** to go off to spend one's summer holidays in the mountains

veraniego ADJ **1** (= *del verano*) summer (*antes de s*)
2 (*fig*) trivial

veranillo SM **1** ▸ **veranillo de San Martín** (*en noviembre*) Indian summer ▸ **veranillo de San Miguel** (*en septiembre*) Indian summer
2 (*CAm*) dry spell (*in the rainy season*) ▸ **veranillo de San Juan** (*Cono Sur*) (*en junio*) ≈ Indian summer

verano SM **1** (= *estación calurosa*) summer
2 (*en regiones ecuatoriales*) dry season

veranoso ADJ (*LAm*) dry

veras SFPL **1** (= *cosas serias*) serious things • **entre burlas y ~** half jokingly
2 • **de ~** (= *de verdad*) really, truly; (= *sinceramente*) sincerely; (= *con empeño*) in earnest • **¿de ~?** really?, is that so? • **lo siento de ~** I am truly sorry • **esto va de ~** this is serious • **ahora va de ~ que lo hago** now I really am going to do it • **ahora me duele de ~** now it really does hurt • **esta vez va de ~** this time it's the real thing*

veraz ADJ truthful

verbal ADJ (*gen*) verbal; [*mensaje*] oral

verbalizar ▷ CONJUG 1f VT to verbalize, express

verbalmente ADV [*acordar*] verbally; [*comunicar*] orally

verbena SF **1** (= *fiesta*) fair; [*de santo*] *open-air celebration on the eve of a saint's day*; (= *baile*) open-air dance
2 (*Bot*) verbena

verbenero ADJ of *o* relating to a *verbena* • **persona verbenera** party animal* • **alegría verbenera** fun of the fair • **música verbenera** fairground music

verbigracia ADV for example, e.g.

verbo SM **1** (*Ling*) verb ▸ **verbo activo** active verb ▸ **verbo auxiliar** auxiliary verb ▸ **verbo defectivo** defective verb ▸ **verbo deponente** deponent verb ▸ **verbo finito** finite verb ▸ **verbo intransitivo, verbo neutro** intransitive verb ▸ **verbo reflexivo** reflexive verb ▸ **verbo transitivo** transitive verb
2 (*Literat*) language, diction • **de ~ elegante** elegant in style
3 (= *juramento*) curse, oath • **echar ~s** to swear, curse
4 • **el Verbo** (*Rel*) the Word

verborrea SF, **verborragia** SF verbosity, verbal diarrhoea *o* (*EEUU*) diarrhea*

verborreico ADJ verbose, wordy

verbosidad SF verbosity, wordiness

verboso ADJ verbose, wordy

verdad SF **1** (= *veracidad*) truth • **la pura ~** the plain truth • **no pudo esclarecer la ~ de los hechos** he couldn't establish the truth about what happened • **hay una parte de ~ en todo esto** there is some truth *o* an element of truth in all this • **nadie está en posesión de la ~** no one has an exclusive right to the truth • **decir la ~** to tell the truth • **a decir ~** • **si te digo la ~** to be honest, to tell you the truth • **la ~ sea dicha** if (the) truth be known • **en ~** to be honest, really • **en ~ no sé qué contestarte** to be honest I don't know what to say to you, I really don't know what to say to you • **en ~ os digo que seréis recompensados** (*Biblia*) verily I say unto you, you shall be rewarded • **faltar a la ~** to be untruthful, be economical with the truth (*euf*) • **en honor a la ~** to be perfectly honest, in all honesty • MODISMO: • **ir con la ~ por delante** to be completely open about things; ▷ **hora**
2 • **de ~** (*como adj*) real; (*como adv*) really • **¿son de ~ estas balas?** are those real bullets? • **ese sí que es un torero de ~** he's what I call a real bullfighter • **—mañana vendré a ayudarte —¿de ~?** "I'll come and help you tomorrow" — "really?" *o* "will you?" • **la quiero de ~** I really love her • **esta vez me voy a enfadar de ~** this time I really am going to get angry • **de ~ que no me importa ir** I really don't mind going, I don't mind going, honestly *o* really
3 • **es ~** it's true • **eso no es ~** that's not true • **¿es ~ que a Diego le ha tocado la lotería?** is it true that Diego has won the lottery? • **bien es ~ que** of course • **bien es ~ que es aún pronto para juzgar los resultados** of course, it's too soon to make any judgement about the results • **si bien es ~ que** although, even though • **si bien es ~ que llevamos poco tiempo aquí, ya puedo decir que ...** although *o* even though we haven't been here long, I can already say that ...
4* (*para enfatizar*) • **pues la ~, no sé** to be honest I don't know, I don't really know • **la ~ es que no me gusta mucho** to be honest I don't like it much, I don't really like it much
5 (*para corroborar algo*) • **estás cansado ¿verdad?** *o* **¿no es ~?** you're tired, aren't you? • **hace frío ¿verdad?** *o* **¿no es ~?** it's cold, isn't it? • **no os gustó ¿verdad?** you didn't like it, did you? • **¿~ que sí fuimos?** we went, didn't we?, we did go, didn't we? • **¿~ que has sido tú?** it was you, wasn't it?
6 (= *afirmación verdadera*) truth • **no me gustan las ~es a medias** I don't like half-truths • **lo que acabas de decir es una gran ~** you couldn't have spoken a truer word • **~ científica** scientific truth • **~ objetiva** objective truth • MODISMOS: • **ser una ~ de Perogrullo** to be patently obvious • **ser una ~ como un puño*** to be the bitter *o* painful truth • **ser una ~ como un templo** to be the plain truth • **las ~es del barquero** the plain truths, the simple truths • **decirle cuatro ~es a algn** to give sb a piece of one's mind*

verdaderamente ADV **1** (= *de verdad*) really • **es ~ una pena** it really is a shame
2 (*con adjetivo*) really, truly • **es ~ triste** it's really *o* truly sad • **un hombre ~ bueno** a really *o* truly good man
3 (*para confirmar*) indeed • **y ~, el sitio no es nada especial** and indeed, the place is nothing special

verdadero ADJ **1** (= *auténtico*) [*caso, joya, motivo, nombre*] real; [*historia, versión*] true; [*testimonio*] truthful • **no creo que sea esa la verdadera razón** I don't think that's the real reason • **¿cuál es tu ~ nombre?** what's your real name? • **es un ~ amigo** he's a true friend
2 (*para enfatizar*) real • **es un ~ héroe** he's a real hero • **fue un ~ desastre** it was a real *o* (*frm*) veritable disaster • **es el ~ retrato de su madre** he's the spitting image of his mother
3 (= *sincero*) [*persona*] truthful

verde ADJ **1** (*color*) green • MODISMOS: • **estar ~ de envidia** to be green with envy • **poner ~ a algn*** to run sb down*, slag sb off‡ • **siempre ponen ~ al jefe** they're always

V

running down* *o* slagging off‡ the boss
• **me llamó y me puso ~ por no haberla ayudado** she called me and gave me a piece of her mind for not helping her*
2 [*árbol, planta*] green; [*fruta, verdura*] green, unripe; [*legumbres*] green; [*madera*] unseasoned
3 [*zona, espacio*] green • **faltan zonas ~s en esta ciudad** there are not enough green spaces in this city
4* [*plan, proyecto*] • **el proyecto está muy ~** the project is at a very early stage
5* (= *sin experiencia*) green* • **está muy ~*** he's very green*, he doesn't know a thing
6* [*chiste, canción*] smutty*, blue*, dirty
• **viejo ~** dirty old man*
7 (*Pol*) Green
(SM) 1 (= *color*) green ▸ **verde botella** bottle green ▸ **verde esmeralda** emerald green ▸ **verde lima** lime green ▸ **verde manzana** apple green ▸ **verde oliva** olive green ▸ **verde pistacho** pistachio green
2 (= *hierba*) grass; (= *follaje*) foliage, greenery; (= *forraje*) green fodder • **sentarse en el ~** to sit on the grass • **segar la hierba en ~** to cut the grass while it is still green
3* (= *billete*) [*de mil pesetas*] 1,000-peseta note; [*de un dólar*] dollar bill, buck (*EEUU**), greenback (*EEUU**)
4 • MODISMO: • **darse un ~ de algo**† to have one's fill of sth
5 (*Cono Sur*) (= *mate*) maté
6 (*Cono Sur*) (= *pasto*) grass, pasture
7 (*Cono Sur*) (= *ensalada*) salad
8 (*And*) (= *plátano*) plantain
9 (*Caribe, Méx*) (= *campo*) country, countryside
10 (*Caribe**) (= *policía*) cop*
(SMF) (*Pol*) Green • **los Verdes** the Greens, the Green Party

verdear ▸ CONJUG 1a (VI) 1 (= *tener color*) to look green; (= *tirar a verde*) to be greenish
2 (= *volverse verde*) to go green, turn green
3 (*Cono Sur*) (= *beber mate*) to drink maté
4 (*Cono Sur*) (*Agr*) to graze

verdecer ▸ CONJUG 2d (VI) [*objeto*] to turn green, grow green; [*persona*] to go green

verdegay (ADJ), (SM) light green

verdemar (ADJ), (SM) sea-green

verde-oliva (ADJ INV) olive green

verderón (SM) 1 (*Orn*) greenfinch
2 (*Esp*‡) 1,000-peseta note

verdete (SM) verdigris

verdiazul (ADJ) greenish-blue

verdiblanco (ADJ) light green

verdín (SM) 1 (= *color*) fresh green
2 (*Bot*) (= *verdete*) verdigris; (= *capa*) scum; (= *musgo*) moss
3 (*en la ropa*) green stain

verdinegro (ADJ) dark green

verdino (ADJ) bright green

verdirrojo (ADJ) green and red

verdolaga (SF) • **crecer como la ~** (*CAm*) to spread like wildfire

verdón (ADJ) (*Cono Sur*) 1 (= *verdino*) bright green
2 [*fruta*] slow to ripen
(SM) 1 (*Orn*) = **verderón**
2 (*Cono Sur*) (= *cardenal*) bruise, welt

verdor (SM) 1 (= *color*) greenness
2 (*Bot*) verdure
3† (= *juventud*) youth

verdoso (ADJ) greenish

verdugo (SM) 1 (= *ejecutor*) executioner; (*en la horca*) hangman
2 (= *tirano*) cruel master, tyrant; (= *atormentador*) tormentor
3 (= *látigo*) lash
4 (= *tormento*) torment
5 (= *cardenal*) welt, weal
6 (*Bot*) shoot
7 (= *estoque*) rapier
8 (= *pasamontañas*) balaclava

verdugón (SM) 1 (= *cardenal*) weal, welt
2 (*Bot*) twig, shoot, sprout
3 (*And*) (= *rasgón*) rent, rip

verdulera (SF) (*pey*) fishwife, coarse woman; ▸ **verdulero**

verdulería (SF) greengrocer's (shop)

verdulero/a (SM/F) greengrocer, vegetable merchant (*EEUU*); ▸ **verdulera**

verdura (SF) 1 (*Culin*) greens (*pl*), (green) vegetables (*pl*) • **sopa de ~(s)** vegetable soup
2 (= *color*) greenness; (= *follaje*) greenery, verdure (*liter*)
3† (= *obscenidad*) smuttiness*, scabrous nature

verdusco (ADJ) dark green, dirty green

vereco* (ADJ) (*CAm*) cross-eyed

verecundia (SF) bashfulness, sensitivity, shyness

verecundo (ADJ) bashful, sensitive, shy

vereda (SF) 1 (= *senda*) path, lane
• MODISMOS: • **entrar en ~** [*persona*] to toe the line; [*elemento*] to fall into place, fit into the normal pattern • **hacer entrar en ~ a algn** • **meter en ~ a algn** to bring sb into line, make sb toe the line • **ir por la ~** to do the right thing, keep to the straight and narrow
2 (*LAm*) (= *acera*) pavement, sidewalk (*EEUU*)
3 (*And*) (= *pueblo*) village, settlement; (= *zona*) *section of a village*
4 (*Méx*) (= *raya*) parting, part (*EEUU*)

veredicto (SM) verdict • **emitir ~** to issue *o* give a verdict ▸ **veredicto de culpabilidad** verdict of guilty, guilty verdict ▸ **veredicto de inculpabilidad** verdict of not guilty, not guilty verdict

veredón (SM) (*Cono Sur*) broad pavement, broad sidewalk (*EEUU*)

verga (SF) 1 (= *vara*) rod, stick; (*Náut*) yard(arm), spar
2 (*Zool*) penis; [*de hombre***] prick**, cock**
• MODISMOS: • **me vale ~**** I don't give a toss‡ • **¡ni ~!**** you must be joking!*, no bloody way!**
3 (*CAm**) • MODISMOS: • **a ~** by hook or by crook • **por la ~ grande** at the back of beyond*

vergajo (SM) 1 [*de toro*] pizzle; [*de hombre***] prick**, cock** • **dar un ~**** to have a screw**
2 (= *látigo*) lash, whip
3 (*And**) (= *canalla*) swine*, rat*

vergazo (SM) • **un ~ de** (*CAm**) lots of*, loads of*

vergel (SM) (*liter*) (= *jardín*) garden, yard (*EEUU*); (= *huerto*) orchard

vergonzante (ADJ) 1 (= *que tiene vergüenza*) shamefaced; (= *tímido*) bashful • **pobre ~** *poor but too ashamed to beg openly*
2 (= *que produce vergüenza*) shameful, shaming

vergonzosamente (ADV) 1 (= *con timidez*) bashfully, shyly; (= *con modestia*) modestly
2 (= *deshonrosamente*) shamefully, disgracefully

vergonzoso (ADJ) 1 [*persona*] (= *tímido*) bashful, shy; (= *modesto*) modest
2 [*acto*] shameful, disgraceful • **es ~ que ...** it is disgraceful that ...
3 • **partes vergonzosas** (*euf*) (*Anat*) private parts

vergüenza (SF) 1 (= *azoramiento*) embarrassment • **casi me muero de ~** I almost died of embarrassment • **¡qué ~!** how embarrassing! • **me da ~ decírselo** I feel too embarrassed to tell him • **sentir ~ ajena** to feel embarrassed for sb
2 (= *dignidad*) shame, sense of shame • **si tuviera ~ no lo haría** if he had any (sense of) shame he wouldn't do it • **¡~ debería darte!** you should be ashamed!, shame on you!
• **¡vaya manera de tratar a tu abuela, qué ~!** what a way to treat your grandmother, you should be ashamed *o* shame on you! • **¡qué poca ~ tienes!** you've got no shame!, you're utterly shameless • **perder la ~** to lose all sense of shame • **sacar a algn a la ~**†† (*lit*) to make a public display of sb; (*fig*) to hold sb up to shame
3 (= *escándalo*) disgrace • **el hijo es la ~ de su familia** the son is a disgrace to his family
• **es una ~ que esté tan sucio** it's a disgrace *o* it's disgraceful that it should be so dirty
4 **vergüenzas*** (*euf*) (= *genitales*) privates (*euf*), naughty bits* (*hum*) • **con las ~s al aire** fully exposed (*hum*)

vericuetos (SMPL) 1 (= *terreno escarpado*) rough track (*sing*)
2 (= *complejidades*) • **los ~ del sistema fiscal** the intricacies of the tax system

verídico (ADJ) truthful, true

verificabilidad (SF) verifiability

verificable (ADJ) verifiable

verificación (SF) 1 (= *inspección*) inspection, check; (*Mec*) testing; [*de resultados*] verification; [*de testamento*] proving ▸ **verificación médica** checkup
2 (= *cumplimiento*) fulfilment, fulfillment (*EEUU*)
3 [*de profecía*] realization

verificar ▸ CONJUG 1a (VT) 1 (= *inspeccionar*) to inspect, check; (*Mec*) to test; [+ *resultados*] to check; [+ *hechos*] to verify, establish; [+ *testamento*] to prove
2 (= *realizar*) [+ *inspección*] to carry out; [+ *ceremonia*] to perform; [+ *elección*] to hold
(VPR) **verificarse** 1 [*acontecimiento*] to occur, happen; [*mitin*] to be held, take place
2 [*profecía*] to come true

verificativo (SM) (*Méx*) (*frm*) • **tener ~** to take place

verija (SF) 1 (*Anat*) groin, genital region
2 (*LAm*) [*de caballo*] flank

verijón* (ADJ) (*Méx*) idle, lazy

veringo (ADJ) (*And*) nude, naked

veringuearse ▸ CONJUG 1a (VPR) (*And*) to undress

verismo (SM) (= *realismo*) realism, truthfulness; (*Arte, Literat*) verism

verista (ADJ) (*Arte, Literat*) veristic

verja (SF) (= *puerta*) iron gate; (= *cerca*) railings (*pl*); (= *reja*) grating, grille

vermicida (SM) vermicide

vermicular (ADJ) vermicular

vermífugo (SM) vermifuge

verminoso (ADJ) infected, wormy

vermú (SM) (PL: **vermús** [ber'mu]) = **vermut**

vermut [ber'mu] (SM) (PL: **vermuts** [ber'mus]) 1 (= *bebida*) vermouth
2 (*And, Cono Sur*) (*Cine*) (early evening) cinema matinee

vernáculo (ADJ) vernacular • **lengua vernácula** vernacular

vernal (ADJ) (*poét*) vernal (*poét*), spring (*antes de s*)

Verónica (SF) Veronica

verónica (SF) 1 (*Bot*) veronica, speedwell
2 (*Taur*) *a kind of pass with the cape*

verosímil (ADJ) (= *probable*) likely, probable; (= *creíble*) credible

verosimilitud (SF) 1 (= *probabilidad*) likelihood, probability; (= *credibilidad*) credibility
2 (*Literat*) verisimilitude

verosímilmente (ADV) (= *de modo probable*) in a likely way; (= *de modo creíble*) credibly

verraco (SM) 1 (= *cerdo*) boar, male pig
2 (*And*) (= *carnero*) ram
3 (*Caribe*) (= *jabalí*) wild boar

V

verraquear ▷ CONJUG 1a (VI) **1** (= *gruñir*) to grunt
2 [*niño*] to wail, howl with rage
verraquera (SF) **1** (= *enfado*) fit of rage, tantrum; (= *lloro*) crying spell
2 (*Caribe*) (= *borrachera*) drunken spell
verruga (SF) **1** (*en cara, espalda*) wart; (*en manos, pies*) verruca
2 (*Bot*) wart
3 (= *latoso*) pest, nuisance
4* (= *defecto*) fault
verrugoso (ADJ) warty, covered in warts
versación (SF) (*Cono Sur, Méx*) expertise, skill
versada (SF) (*LAm*) long tedious poem
versado (ADJ) • **~ en** (= *conocedor*) versed in, conversant with; (= *experto*) expert in, skilled in
versal (*Tip*) (ADJ) capital
(SF) capital (letter)
versalitas (SFPL) (*Tip*) small capitals
Versalles (SM) Versailles
versallesco (ADJ) **1** (*Arte, Hist*) Versailles (*antes de s*)
2 [*lenguaje, modales*] extremely refined
versar ▷ CONJUG 1a (VI) **1** • **~ sobre** (= *tratar*) to deal with, be about
2 (= *girar*) to go round, turn
3 (*Caribe*) (= *versificar*) to versify, improvise verses
4 (*Caribe*) (= *charlar*) to chat, talk
5 (*Méx**) (= *guasearse*) to tease, crack jokes
versátil (ADJ) **1** (= *adaptable*) versatile
2 (*pey*) (= *inconstante*) fickle, changeable
3 (*Anat*) mobile, loose
versatilidad (SF) **1** (= *adaptabilidad*) versatility
2 (*pey*) (= *inconstancia*) fickleness
3 (*Anat*) mobility, ease of movement
versículo (SM) verse
versificación (SF) versification
versificador(a) (SM/F) versifier
versificar ▷ CONJUG 1g (VT) to versify, put into verse
(VI) to write verses, versify
versión (SF) (*gen*) version; (= *traducción*) translation; (= *adaptación*) adaptation • **película en ~ original** original version • **película en ~ española** Spanish-language version • **~ (de) concierto** concert performance
versionar ▷ CONJUG 1a (VT) (= *adaptar*) to adapt, make a new version of; (*Mús*) to adapt; (= *grabar*) record a version of; (= *traducir*) to translate
vers.º (ABR) (*Rel*) (= **versículo**) v
verso (SM) **1** (= *género*) verse; (= *línea*) line, verse line; (= *poema*) poem • **teatro en ~** verse drama • **en el segundo ~ del poema** in the second line of the poem • **hacer ~s** to write poetry ▸ **verso libre** free verse ▸ **verso suelto** blank verse
2 • **echar ~** (*Caribe, Méx**) to rabbit on*
versolari (SM) (*País Vasco, Aragón*) *improviser of verse*
versus (PREP) versus, against
vértebra (SF) vertebra
vertebración (SF) **1** (= *apoyo*) support
2 (= *estructuración*) structuring, essential structure
vertebrado (ADJ), (SM) vertebrate
vertebrador (ADJ) • **fuerza ~a** unifying force, force making for cohesion • **columna ~a** central column • **soporte ~** principal support
vertebral (ADJ) vertebral • **columna ~** spinal column, spine
vertebrar ▷ CONJUG 1a (VT) **1** (= *apoyar*) to hold up, support
2 (= *estructurar*) to provide the backbone of, be the essential structure of
vertedero (SM) **1** [*de basura*] rubbish tip, garbage dump (*EEUU*)
2 = **vertedor**
3 (*Cono Sur*) (= *pendiente*) slope, hillside
vertedor (SM) **1** (= *desagüe*) drain, outlet; [*de presa*] spillway
2 (*Náut*) scoop, bailer
3 (= *cuchara, pala*) scoop, small shovel
verter ▷ CONJUG 2g (VT) **1** [+ *contenido*] to pour (out), empty (out); (*sin querer*) to spill, pour; [+ *lágrimas, luz, sangre*] to shed; [+ *basura, residuos*] to dump, tip • **vertió el contenido de la bolsa encima de la mesa** she poured the contents of the bag onto the table • **he vertido el café sobre el mantel** I've spilled my coffee on the tablecloth
2 [+ *recipiente*] (= *vaciar*) to empty (out); (= *invertir*) to tip up; (*sin querer*) to upset
3 (*Ling*) to translate (**a** into)
(VI) [*río*] to flow, run (**a** into); [*declive*] to fall (**a** towards)
vertical (ADJ) [*línea, plano*] vertical; [*postura, piano*] upright • **despegue ~** (*Aer*) vertical take-off • **ponlo ~** put it upright
(SF) **1** (*Téc, Mat*) vertical line, vertical • **descender en ~** to descend vertically • **elevarse en ~** to rise vertically
2 (*Dep*) • **hacer la ~** to do a handstand
(SM) (*Astron*) vertical circle
verticalidad (SF) (= *posición*) vertical position; (= *dirección*) vertical direction
verticalmente (ADV) vertically
vértice (SM) **1** [*de cono, pirámide*] apex, vertex; [*de ángulo*] vertex ▸ **vértice geodésico** bench mark, survey point
2 (*Anat*) crown (of the head)
verticilo (SM) whorl
vertido (SM) **1** (= *acto*) (*accidental*) spillage; (*deliberado*) dumping; [*de líquido*] pouring • **el ~ de residuos nucleares** the dumping of nuclear waste
2 vertidos (= *residuos*) waste (*sing*) • **~s tóxicos** toxic waste (*sing*)
vertiente (SF) **1** [*de montaña, tejado*] slope
2 (= *aspecto*) side, aspect • **sin considerar la ~ ética de la cuestión** without considering the ethical side *o* aspect of the issue • **la ~ humanística del movimiento** the humanistic side of the movement • **el curso tiene una ~ filosófica** the course has a philosophical dimension
3 (*LAm*) (= *manantial*) spring
vertiginosamente (ADV) **1** (= *de manera vertiginosa*) giddily, dizzily, vertiginously (*frm*)
2 (*fig*) (= *excesivamente*) dizzily, excessively; (= *rápidamente*) very rapidly • **los precios suben ~** prices are rising rapidly, prices are spiralling up
vertiginoso (ADJ) **1** (= *que causa vértigo*) giddy, dizzy, vertiginous (*frm*)
2 [*velocidad*] dizzy, excessive; [*alza*] very rapid
vértigo (SM) **1** (*por la altura*) • **mirar hacia abajo me da ~** looking down makes me (feel) dizzy • **no subo porque tengo ~** I'm not going up because I'm afraid of heights
2 (*Med*) vertigo • **tiene ~** he suffers from *o* has vertigo • **las pastillas pueden provocar ~(s)** these tablets may cause giddiness
3 (= *frenesí*) frenzy • **el ~ de la vida en la ciudad** the frenzy of city life • **el ~ de los negocios** the frenzied rush of business • **el ~ de los placeres** the whirl of pleasures
4* • **de ~: iban a una velocidad de ~** they were going at breakneck speed • **tiene un talento de ~** he has a breathtaking talent • **es de ~ cómo crece la ciudad** it's astonishing how quickly the city is growing
vesania (SF) rage, fury; (*Med*) insanity
vesánico (ADJ) raging, furious; (*Med*) insane
vesícula (SF) (*Anat*) vesicle; (= *ampolla*) blister ▸ **vesícula biliar** gall-bladder
vespa® (SF) Vespa®, scooter, motor-scooter
vespertina (SF) (*Col*) (early evening) matinée
vespertino (ADJ) evening (*antes de s*) • **periódico ~** evening paper
(SM) evening paper
vespino (SM) small motorcycle
vesre* (SM) (*Arg*), **vesrre*** (SM) (*Arg*) back slang
vestal (ADJ), (SF) vestal
veste (SF) (*liter*) garb (*liter*)
vestíbulo (SM) [*de casa, hotel*] vestibule (*frm*), lobby, hall; (*Teat*) foyer
vestiditos (SMPL) baby clothes
vestido (ADJ) dressed • **era la mejor vestida de la fiesta** she was the best dressed woman at the party • **me gusta ir bien ~** I like to be well-dressed • **¿cómo iba vestida la novia?** what was the bride wearing? • **~ con algo** wearing sth, dressed in sth • **va ~ con un traje azul** he's wearing a blue suit, he's dressed in a blue suit • **~ de algo** wearing sth, dressed in sth • **siempre va ~ de negro** he always wears black • **mi mayor ilusión es verte vestida de blanco** my greatest wish is to see you all in white • **¡en marzo y ya vas vestida de verano!** it's only March and you're wearing summer clothes already!
(SM) **1** (= *prenda*) [*de mujer*] dress; (*Col*) [*de hombre*] suit ▸ **vestido de debajo**† undergarment (*frm*) ▸ **vestido de encima**† outer garment (*frm*) ▸ **vestido de fiesta** party dress ▸ **vestido de noche** evening dress ▸ **vestido de novia** wedding dress, bridal gown ▸ **vestido isotérmico** wet suit
2 (= *vestimenta*) clothes (*pl*) • **la historia del ~** the history of costume
vestidor (SM) dressing room
vestidura (SF) **1** (*liter*) clothing, apparel
2 vestiduras (= *ropa*) clothes • MODISMO: • **rasgarse las ~s** to tear one's hair
3 vestiduras (*Rel*) vestments ▸ **vestiduras sacerdotales** priestly vestments
vestier (SM) (*Col*) dressing room
vestigial (ADJ) vestigial
vestigio (SM) **1** (= *señal*) trace, vestige • **no quedaba el menor ~ de ello** there was not the slightest trace of it
2 vestigios (= *ruinas*) remains, relics
vestimenta (SF) **1** (= *ropa*) clothing; (*pey*) gear‡, stuff*
2 vestimentas (*Rel*) vestments
vestir ▷ CONJUG 3k (VT) **1** (= *poner la ropa a*) [+ *niño, muñeca*] to dress • **su madre la vistió de novia** her mother helped her dress for the wedding • REFRÁN: • **vísteme despacio, que tengo prisa** more haste less speed; ▷ **santo**
2 (= *disfrazar*) to dress up • **¿de qué lo vas a ~?** what are you going to dress him up as?
3 (= *hacer la ropa a*) • **lo viste un buen sastre** he has his clothes made at a good tailor's • **la modista que la viste cobra muy barato** the dressmaker who makes her clothes is very cheap
4 (= *proporcionar la ropa*) [*persona*] to clothe; [*institución, Estado*] to pay for one's clothing • **tengo una familia que ~ y alimentar** I have a family to feed and clothe • **~ al desnudo** (*Biblia*) to clothe the naked • **lo viste el Ayuntamiento** the Council pays for his clothing
5 (= *llevar puesto*) to wear • **la modelo viste un traje de noche con sombrero** the model is wearing an evening dress with a hat
6 (= *revestir*) [+ *sillón*] to cover, upholster; [+ *pared*] to cover, decorate

V

7 (*liter*) (= *disfrazar*) [+ *defecto*] to conceal • **viste de prudencia su cobardía** he conceals his cowardice behind a pretence of discretion • **vistió de gravedad su rostro** he assumed *o* adopted a serious expression
(VI) **1** (= *llevar ropa*) to dress • **siempre viste a la última moda** she always dresses in *o* wears the latest fashions • **abrió la puerta a medio ~** he opened the door only half-dressed • **¿todavía estás sin ~?** aren't you dressed yet?, haven't you got dressed yet? • **~ bien** to dress well • **~ mal** to dress badly • **~ de:** • **le gusta ~ de gris** he likes to wear grey • **~ de paisano** [*policía*] to be in plain clothes; [*soldado*] to be in civilian clothes *o* in civvies* *o* in mufti* • **~ de sport** to dress casually • **~ de uniforme** [*policía, soldado*] to wear a uniform, be in uniform; [*alumno*] to wear a uniform • **MODISMO:** • **el mismo que viste y calza**† the very same
2 (= *ser elegante*) [*traje, color*] to be elegant • **el negro viste mucho** black is very elegant • **tener un coche así sí que viste*** owning a car like that is really flashy* • **ahora lo que viste es viajar al Caribe*** the Caribbean is the trendy *o* the in place to go these days* • **de ~** [*ropa, zapatos*] smart; [*traje*] formal • **necesito algo un poco más de ~** I need something a bit smarter *o* more formal • **ese traje es de mucho ~** that suit's too dressy* *o* formal • **saber ~** to know how to dress, have good dress sense
(VPR) **vestirse 1** (= *ponerse la ropa*) to get dressed • **no tardo nada en ~me** I get dressed in no time • **me vestí con lo primero que encontré** I put on the first thing I picked up • **¿cómo te vas a ~ para la fiesta?** what are you going to wear to the party? • **~se de algo** to wear sth • **voy a empezar a ~me de verano** I'm going to start wearing my summer clothes • **~se de fiesta** *o* **de gala** [*persona*] to get (all) dressed up; [*ciudad*] to be (all) decked out • **~se de largo** (*para fiesta, recepción*) to wear an evening dress; ▹ **mona**
2 (= *disfrazarse*) • **~se de algo** to dress up as sth • **¿de qué te vas a ~?** what are you going to dress up as? • **me vestí de marinero** I dressed up as a sailor
3 (= *comprar la ropa*) to buy one's clothes • **se viste en las mejores tiendas** she buys her clothes in the best shops
4 (*liter*) (= *cubrirse*) • **~se de algo** to be covered in sth • **toda la ciudad amaneció vestida de blanco** the day dawned on a city entirely covered in white • **el cielo se vistió de nubes** the sky clouded over • **su rostro se vistió de severidad** his face took on a serious expression
5 (*tras enfermedad*) to get up again
(SM) (= *forma de vestir*) • **su elegancia en el ~** the smart way she dresses
vestón (SM) (*Chile*) jacket
vestuario (SM) **1** (*gen*) clothes (*pl*), wardrobe; (*Teat*) wardrobe, costumes (*pl*); (*Mil*) uniform
2 (= *cuarto*) (*Teat*) [*de actor*] dressing room; (= *área*) backstage area; (*Dep*) (*en club*) changing room
3 (*Teat*) (= *guardarropa*) cloakroom
Vesubio (SM) Vesuvius
veta (SF) (*Min*) seam, vein; [*de madera*] grain; (*en piedra, carne*) streak, stripe
vetar ▹ CONJUG 1a (VT) (*gen*) to veto; [+ *socio*] to blackball
vetazo (SM) (*And*) lash
veteada (SF) (*And*) flogging, beating
veteado (ADJ) [*mármol*] veined; [*madera*] grained; [*carne*] streaked (**de** with); [*tocino*] streaky
(SM) [*del mármol*] veining; [*de la madera*] graining; [*de la carne*] streaks (*pl*)

vetear ▹ CONJUG 1a (VT) **1** (*gen*) to grain; [+ *carne*] to streak
2 (*And*) (= *azotar*) to flog, beat
veteranía (SF) (= *estatus*) status *o* dignity *etc* of being a veteran; (= *servicio*) long service; (= *antigüedad*) seniority
veterano/a (ADJ) (*Mil*) veteran • **es veterana en el oficio** she's an old hand*
(SM/F) (*Mil*) veteran; (*fig*) old hand*, old stager*
veterinaria (SF) veterinary medicine, veterinary science
veterinario/a (SM/F) veterinary surgeon, vet, veterinarian (*EEUU*)
vetevé (SM) (*And*) sofa
veto (SM) veto • **poner el ~ a algo** to veto sth • **tener ~** to have a veto
vetulio (SM) (*And*) old man
vetustez (SF) (*liter*) great age, antiquity; (*iró*) hoariness
vetusto (ADJ) ancient, very old; (*iró*) hoary
vez (SF) **1** (= *ocasión*) time • **aquella vez** that time • **por esta vez** this time, this once • **la próxima vez** next time • **a la vez:** • **hablaban todos a la vez** they were all talking at once *o* at the same time • **canta a la vez que toca** she sings and plays at the same time, she sings while she plays • **me fascina a la vez que me repele** I find it both fascinating and revolting at the same time • **¿has estado alguna vez en ...?** have you ever been to ...? • **alguna que otra vez** occasionally, now and again • **las más de las veces** mostly, in most cases • **por primera vez** for the first time • **la primera vez que lo vi** the first time I saw him • **toda vez que ...** since ..., given that ... • **por última vez** for the last time • **¿cuándo lo viste por última vez?** when was the last time you saw him?, when did you see him last?; ▹ **tal**
2 (*indicando frecuencia*) • **lo he hecho cien veces** I've done it hundreds *o* lots of times* • **¿cuántas veces al año?** how many times a year? • **tres veces** three times • **es cinco veces más caro** it's five times more expensive, it costs five times as much • **a veces** • **algunas veces** sometimes, at times • **contadas veces** seldom • **de vez en cuando** now and again, from time to time, occasionally • **¿cuántas veces?** how often?, how many times? • **dos veces** twice • **a una velocidad dos veces superior a la del sonido** at twice the speed of sound • **en ... veces:** • **se fríen las patatas en dos veces** fry the potatoes in two batches • **por enésima vez** for the umpteenth time* • **muchas veces** often • **otra vez** again • **pocas veces** seldom, rarely • **rara vez** • **raras veces** seldom, rarely • **repetidas veces** again and again, over and over again • **una vez** once • **la veo una vez a la semana** I see her once a week • **una vez dice que sí y otra que no** first he says yes and then he says no, one time he says yes, the next he says no • **más de una vez** more than once • **érase** *o* **había una vez una princesa ...** once upon a time there was a princess ... • **"una vez al año no hace daño"** once in a while can't hurt • **una y otra vez** time and (time) again • **varias veces** several times; ▹ **cada**
3 (*otras expresiones*) • **de una vez** (= *en una sola ocasión*) in one go; (= *definitivamente*) once and for all* • **las derribó todas de una vez** she knocked them all down in one go • **¡acabemos de una vez!** let's get it over with (once and for all)!* • **¡cállate de una vez!** for the last time, shut up!* • **¡dilo de una vez!** just say it! • **en vez de** instead of • **hacer las veces de** to serve as • **un vestíbulo que hacía las veces de vestuario** a hall that served as a changing room • **hizo las veces de musa y amante del poeta** she was a muse and lover to the poet • **una vez que** once • **una vez que me lo dijo se fue** once he had told me, he left • **una vez que se hayan marchado todos me iré yo** once they've all left, I'll go too • **de una vez para siempre** • **de una vez por todas** once and for all*, for good
4 (= *turno*) turn, go • **a su vez** in turn • **cuando le llegue la vez** when his turn comes • **ceder la vez** (*gen*) to give up one's turn; (*en cola*) to give up one's place • **pedir la vez** to ask who's last in the queue • **quitar la vez a algn** to push in in front of sb
5 (*Mat*) • **siete veces nueve** seven times nine
veza (SF) vetch
v.g. (ABR), **v.gr.** (ABR) (= **verbigracia**) viz
VHF (SM ABR) (= **very high frequency**) VHF
vía (SF) **1** (= *calle*) road; (*en autopista*) lane • **¡por favor, dejen la vía libre!** please make way! ▸ **vía de abastecimiento** supply route ▸ **vía de acceso** access road ▸ **vía de agua** leak • **se abrió una vía de agua en el barco** the boat sprang a leak ▸ **vía de circunvalación** bypass, ring road, beltway (*EEUU*) ▸ **vía de dirección única** one-way street *o* road ▸ **vía de escape** escape route, way out ▸ **Vía Láctea** Milky Way ▸ **vía libre** • **el gobierno ha dado** *o* **dejado vía libre al proyecto** the government has given the go-ahead to the project • **eso es dar** *o* **dejar la vía libre a la corrupción** that's leaving the way open for corruption ▸ **vía pecuaria** cattle route ▸ **vía pública** public highway, thoroughfare ▸ **vía romana** Roman road
2 (*Ferro*) (= *raíl*) track, line; (= *andén*) platform • **fue arrollado cuando cruzaba la vía** he was run over when he was crossing the track *o* line • **el tren está estacionado en la vía ocho** the train is (standing) at platform eight ▸ **vía ancha** broad gauge • **de vía ancha** broad-gauge (*antes de s*) ▸ **vía doble** double track ▸ **vía estrecha** narrow gauge • **de vía estrecha** narrow-gauge (*antes de s*) ▸ **vía férrea** railway, railroad (*EEUU*) ▸ **vía muerta** (*Ferro*) siding • **el proceso ha entrado en una vía muerta** the process has come to a dead end ▸ **vía única** single track • **de vía única** single-track (*antes de s*)
3 (*Transportes, Correos*) ▸ **vía aérea** airway • **por vía aérea** [*viaje*] by air; [*envío postal*] (by) airmail ▸ **vía de comunicación** communication route ▸ **vía fluvial** waterway ▸ **vía marítima** sea route, seaway • **por vía marítima** by sea ▸ **vía terrestre** overland route • **por vía terrestre** [*viaje*] overland, by land; [*envío postal*] (by) surface mail
4 (*Anat*) tract ▸ **vías digestivas** digestive tract (*sing*) ▸ **vías respiratorias** respiratory tract (*sing*) ▸ **vías urinarias** urinary tract (*sing*)
5 (= *medio, canal*) • **no conseguirán nada por la vía de la violencia** they won't achieve anything through violence *o* by using violence • **por vía arbitral** by (process of) arbitration • **por vía oficial** through official channels • **tercera vía** middle way, compromise ▸ **vía judicial** • **recurrir a la vía judicial** to go to the courts, have recourse to the law ▸ **vías de hecho** (*euf*) physical violence (*sing*), assault and battery (*sing*)
6 (*Med*) • **por vía oral** *o* **bucal** orally • **por vía tópica** topically, externally • **por vía interna** internally • **por vía intravenosa** intravenously
7 • **en vías de: un país en vías de desarrollo** a developing country • **una especie en vías de extinción** an endangered species • **el asunto está en vías de solución** the matter is on its

V

way to being solved
8 (*Rel*) way ▸ **Vía Crucis** Way of the Cross, Stations of the Cross (*pl*)
9 (*Quím*) process
PREP via • **un vuelo a Nueva York vía Londres** a flight to New York via London • **retransmisión vía satélite** satellite broadcast

viabilidad SF **1** [*de un plan*] viability, feasibility
2 (*Aut*) road conditions (*pl*)

viabilizar ▸ CONJUG 1f VT to make viable

viable ADJ viable, feasible

viacrucis SM INV **1** (*Rel*) Way of the Cross, Stations of the Cross (*pl*) • **MODISMO**: • **hacer el ~‡** to go on a pub-crawl*
2 (= *problemas*) load of disasters, heap of troubles

viada SF (*And*) speed

viaducto SM viaduct

viagra® SM Viagra®

viajado ADJ • **ser muy ~** to be well-travelled

viajante SMF ▸ **viajante (de comercio)** commercial traveller, traveling salesman (*EEUU*) ▸ **viajante en jabones** traveller in soap, soap salesman

viajar ▸ CONJUG 1a VI **1** (= *hacer viajes*) to travel • **ha viajado mucho** he has travelled a lot • **~ en coche/autobús** to go by car/bus • **~ por** to travel around, tour
2‡ (= *flipar*) to trip‡

viajazo SM **1** (*Méx*) (= *empujón*) push, shove
2 (*Caribe*) (= *azote*) lash
3 (*CAm*) (= *bronca*) telling-off*

viaje[1] SM **1** (= *desplazamiento*) (*gen*) trip; (*por mar, el espacio*) voyage • **es su primer ~ al extranjero** it's her first trip abroad • **¡buen ~!** have a good trip! • **un ~ en barco** a boat trip • **los ~s** (= *actividad*) travelling, traveling (*EEUU*), travel • **tras dos años de ~s por África** after two years travel in Africa • **agencia de ~s** travel agent's, travel agency • **estar de ~** to be away • **salir de ~** to go away • **se fue de ~ a Perú** she went on a trip to Peru ▸ **viaje de buena voluntad** goodwill trip, goodwill mission ▸ **viaje de Estado** state visit ▸ **viaje de estudios** field trip ▸ **viaje de fin de curso** end-of-year trip ▸ **viaje de ida** outward journey ▸ **viaje de ida y vuelta, viaje redondo** (*LAm*) return trip, round trip ▸ **viaje de negocios** business trip ▸ **viaje de novios** honeymoon ▸ **viaje de recreo** pleasure trip ▸ **viaje organizado** package tour ▸ **viaje relámpago** lightning visit, flying visit
2 (= *trayecto*) journey • **es un ~ muy largo** it's a very long journey
3 (= *carga*) load • **un ~ de leña** a load of wood
4* [*de droga*] trip* • **tuvo un mal ~** she had a bad trip*
5 (*esp Caribe*) (= *vez*) time • **de un ~** all in one go, at one blow • **lo repitió varios ~s** he repeated it several times
6 • **MODISMO**: • **echar un ~ a algn** (*CAm*) to give sb a telling-off*

viaje[2]* SM (= *tajada*) slash (*with a razor*); (= *golpe*) bash*; (= *puñalada*) stab • **tirar un ~ a algn** to take a slash at sb

viajero/a ADJ travelling, traveling (*EEUU*); (*Zool*) migratory
SM/F (*gen*) traveller, traveler (*EEUU*); (= *pasajero*) passenger • **¡señores ~s, al tren!** will passengers kindly board the train!, all aboard!

vial ADJ (*gen*) road (*antes de s*); (*de la circulación*) traffic (*antes de s*) • **circulación ~** road traffic • **fluidez ~** free movement of traffic • **reglamento ~** (= *control*) traffic control; (= *código*) rules (*pl*) of the road, highway code • **seguridad ~** road safety, safety on the road(s)
SM road

vialidad SF highway administration

vianda SF (*tb* **viandas**) **1** (= *comida*) food
2 (*Caribe*) (= *verduras*) vegetables (*pl*)
3 (*And, Cono Sur*) (= *fiambrera*) lunch box, dinner pail (*EEUU*)

viandante SMF (= *peatón*) pedestrian; (= *paseante*) passer-by; (= *viajero*) traveller, traveler (*EEUU*)

viaraza SF (*LAm*) **1** (= *enojo*) fit of anger, fit of temper • **estar con la ~** to be in a bad mood
2 (= *idea*) bright idea

viario ADJ road (*antes de s*) • **red viaria** road network • **sistema ~** transport system, system of communications

viático SM **1** (*Rel*) viaticum
2 (*Hist*) (= *comida*) *food for a journey*
3 **viáticos** (= *estipendio*) travelling *o* (*EEUU*) traveling expenses, travel allowance (*sing*)

víbora SF **1** (*Zool*) viper • **tener lengua de ~** to have a sharp tongue ▸ **víbora de cascabel** (*esp Méx*) rattlesnake
2 (*Méx*) (= *cartera*) money belt

viborear ▸ CONJUG 1a VI **1** (*Cono Sur*) (= *serpentear*) to twist and turn, snake along
2 (*Caribe*) (*Naipes*) to mark the cards

vibración SF **1** (= *temblor*) vibration
2 (*Ling*) roll, trill
3 **vibraciones*** (= *sentimientos*) vibrations, vibes* • **vibraciones negativas** bad vibes*

vibracional ADJ vibratory

vibrador SM vibrator

vibráfono SM vibraphone

vibrante ADJ **1** (= *que vibra*) vibrating
2 (*Ling*) rolled, trilled
3 [*voz*] ringing; [*reunión*] exciting, lively • **~ de** ringing with, vibrant with
SF (*Ling*) vibrant

vibrar ▸ CONJUG 1a VI **1** (= *moverse*) to vibrate; (= *agitarse*) to shake, rattle; (= *pulsar*) to throb, beat, pulsate; [*voz*] to quiver
2 (*Ling*) • **hacer ~ las erres** to roll *o* trill one's r's
VT (= *hacer mover*) to vibrate; (= *agitar*) to shake, rattle

vibratorio ADJ vibratory

viburno SM viburnum

vicaria SF woman priest

vicaría SF vicarage • **pasar por la ~*** to tie the knot*, get hitched‡

vicario SM (*Rel*) curate ▸ **Vicario de Cristo** Vicar of Christ (*the Pope*) ▸ **vicario general** vicar general

vice* SMF vice-president

vice... PREF vice...

vicealcalde/esa SM/F deputy mayor

vicealmirante SMF vice-admiral

vicecampeón/ona SM/F runner-up

vicecanciller SMF **1** (*Univ*) vice-chancellor
2 (*en Alemania, Austria*) vice-chancellor
3 (*LAm*) deputy foreign minister, assistant secretary of state (*EEUU*)

viceconsejero/a SM/F *deputy minister in a regional government*

vicecónsul SMF vice-consul

vicedecanato SM vice-deanship

vicedecano/a SM/F vice-dean

vicedirector(a) SM/F [*de empresa, organismo*] deputy director; (*Escol*) deputy headmaster, deputy headmistress; (*Prensa*) deputy editor

vicegerente SM assistant manager

vicelendakari SMF, **vicelehendakari** SMF *vice-president of the Basque autonomous government*

vicelíder SMF deputy leader

viceministro/a SM/F deputy minister

Vicente SM Vincent

vicepresidencia SF (*Pol*) vice-presidency; [*de empresa, comité*] vice-chairmanship

vicepresidente/a SM/F (*Pol*) vice-president; [*de comité, empresa*] vice-chairman

vicetiple SF chorus-girl

viceversa ADV vice versa

vichadero SM (*Cono Sur*) = **bichadero**

vichear ▸ CONJUG 1a VT (*Cono Sur*), **vichar** ▸ CONJUG 1a VT (*Cono Sur*) = **bichear**

viciado ADJ **1** [*aire*] foul, stale
2 [*costumbres, texto*] corrupt
3 [*comida*] contaminated

viciar ▸ CONJUG 1b VT **1** (= *corromper*) to corrupt, pervert
2 (*Jur*) to nullify, invalidate
3 [+ *texto*] (= *alterar*) to corrupt; (= *interpretar mal*) to interpret erroneously
4 [+ *droga, producto*] to adulterate; [+ *aire*] to pollute; [+ *comida*] to spoil, contaminate
5 [+ *objeto*] to bend, twist; [+ *madera*] to warp
VPR **viciarse 1** (= *corromperse*) to become corrupted; ▸ **enviciar**
2 [*objeto*] to warp, lose its shape
3 [*comida*] to be/become contaminated
4 [*aire, agua*] to be/become polluted

vicio SM **1** (= *corrupción*) vice
2 (= *mala costumbre*) bad habit, vice • **no le podemos quitar el ~** we can't get him out of the habit • **tiene el ~ de no contestar las cartas** he has the bad habit of not

V

VIAJE

¿"Journey", "voyage", "trip" o "travel"?

▸ **Viaje** *se traduce por* **journey** *cuando se refiere a un* **viaje** *en particular, tanto por aire como por tierra:*

El viaje de Londres a Madrid dura unas dos horas
The journey from London to Madrid takes about two hours

▸ *Un largo* **viaje** *por mar se traduce por* **voyage**:

Muchos marineros murieron en el primer viaje de Colón a América
Many sailors died on Columbus's first voyage to America

▸ *Cuando* **viaje** *hace referencia no solo al trayecto de ida y vuelta, sino también a la estancia en un lugar, se suele traducir por* **trip**. *Normalmente se trata de un viaje con un fin concreto o de un viaje corto:*

Fui a Alemania en viaje de negocios
I went to Germany on a business trip

▸ *Como sustantivo incontable,* **travel** *se utiliza solo en lugar de* **travelling** *para traducir la actividad de viajar; también, en muy contadas ocasiones, puede usarse en plural referido a viajes concretos:*

No le gusta nada viajar en barco
He hates travelling by sea *o* He hates sea travel

Colecciona recuerdos en sus viajes al extranjero
He collects souvenirs on his travels abroad

Para otros usos y ejemplos ver la entrada.

answering letters • **de** *o* **por ~** out of sheer habit • **quejarse de ~** to complain for no reason at all • **hablar de ~** to chatter away • **eso tiene mucho ~*** that's very habit-forming* *o* addictive ▸ **vicio inveterado, vicio de origen** ingrained bad habit
3 (= *adicción*) • **el ~** the drug habit, drug addiction • **darse al ~** to take to drugs
4 (= *defecto*) defect, blemish; (*Jur*) error; (*Ling*) mistake, incorrect form • **adolece de ciertos ~s** it has a number of defects
5 [*de superficie*] warp; [*de línea*] twist, bend
6 (*con niño*) excessive indulgence
7 (*Bot*) rankness
8 • **de ~*** (= *estupendo*) great, super*
9 • **estar de ~** (*LAm*) (= *sin trabajar*) to be idle

viciosamente ADV 1 (= *depravadamente*) dissolutely
2 (*Bot*) rankly, luxuriantly

vicioso/a ADJ 1 (= *depravado*) dissolute, depraved
2 (= *mimado*) spoiled
3 (*Mec*) faulty, defective
4 (*Bot*) rank
SM/F 1 (= *depravado*) dissolute person, depraved person
2 (= *adicto*) addict • **soy un ~ del fútbol** I am hooked on football*, I am a football fanatic *o* addict*

vicisitud SF 1 (= *suceso*) vicissitude (*liter*); (= *desgracia*) accident, mishap; (= *cambio*) sudden change
2 **vicisitudes** (= *alternancia*) vicissitudes (*liter*)

víctima SF 1 (*gen*) victim; (*Zool*) prey; [*de accidente*] casualty • **fue ~ de una estafa** she was the victim of a swindle • **no hay que lamentar ~s del accidente** there were no casualties in the accident • **hay pocas ~s mortales** there are not many dead • **falleció ~ de un ataque cardiaco** he died of *o* from a heart attack • **es ~ de alguna neurosis** he is a prey to some neurosis
2 (*Hist*) sacrifice

victimar ▸ CONJUG 1a VT (*LAm*) (= *herir*) to wound; (= *matar*) to kill

victimario/a SM/F 1 (*Hist*) *person who helped the priest during human sacrifices*
2 (*LAm*) (= *asesino*) killer, murderer

victimismo SM *tendency to see oneself as being victimized* • **reaccionó con ~** he claimed he was being victimized

victimizar ▸ CONJUG 1f VT to victimize

Victoria SF Victoria

victoria SF victory; (*Dep*) win, victory • **la ~ del partido conservador** the conservative party's victory • **su primera ~ fuera de casa** (*Dep*) their first away win *o* victory • **MODISMO:** • **cantar ~** to claim victory • **no podemos cantar ~ hasta que acabe el recuento de votos** we can't claim victory until all the votes have been counted ▸ **victoria pírrica** Pyrrhic victory ▸ **victoria por puntos** (*Boxeo*) points victory

victoriano ADJ Victorian

victoriosamente ADV victoriously

victorioso ADJ victorious

victrola SF (*LAm*) gramophone, phonograph (*EEUU*)

vicuña SF vicuna

vid SF vine

vid. ABR (= **vide, ver**) v

vida SF 1 (= *existencia*) life • **he vivido aquí toda mi ~** I've lived here all my life • **está escribiendo la ~ de Quevedo** he is writing the life *o* a life *o* a biography of Quevedo • **¿qué es de tu ~?** what's new?, how's life? • **le va la ~ en ello** his life depends on it • **con ~** alive • **estar con ~** to be still alive • **escapar** *o* **salir con ~** to escape *o* come out alive • **en ~ de:** • **en ~ de mi marido** when my husband was alive, during my husband's lifetime • **¡en la** *o* **mi ~!** never (in all my life)! • **en mi ~ he visto semejante cosa** I've never seen such a thing (in all my life) • **~ o muerte:** • **una operación a ~ o muerte** a life-or-death operation • **es una cuestión de ~ o muerte** it's a matter of life and death • **estar entre la ~ y la muerte** to be at death's door • **debatirse entre la ~ y la muerte** to be fighting for one's life • **la otra ~** the next life • **perder la ~** to lose one's life • **de por ~** for life • **quitar la ~ a algn** to take sb's life • **quitarse la ~** to take one's own life • **rehacer la ~** to start a new life • **sin ~** lifeless • **encontró en el suelo el cuerpo sin ~ de su marido** she found her husband's lifeless body on the floor • **fue hallado sin ~** he was found dead • **un cuerpo sin ~** a (dead) body, a corpse • **toda la ~:** • **un amigo de toda la ~** a lifelong friend • **ya no hay trabajos para toda la ~** there are no jobs for life nowadays ▸ **vida eterna** everlasting life ▸ **vida íntima** private life ▸ **vida nocturna** nightlife ▸ **vida privada** private life ▸ **vida sentimental** love-life; ▹ **esperanza**
2 (= *forma de vivir*) life • **llevan una ~ muy tranquila** they lead a very quiet life • **la ~ airada** (= *modo de vida*) the criminal life; (= *hampa*) the underworld • **de ~ airada** loose-living, immoral • **mujer de ~ alegre** loose woman • **~ arrastrada** wretched life • **la ~ cotidiana** everyday life • **doble ~** double life • **llevar una doble ~** to lead *o* live a double life • **hacer ~ marital** to live together (as man and wife) • **hacer una ~ normal** to lead a normal life • **no hacer ~ social** to have no social life • **hay que dejarles hacer su ~** you must let them live their own life • **mala ~:** • **echarse a la mala ~** to go astray • **llevar mala ~** to have a dissolute lifestyle • **mujer de mala ~** loose woman ▸ **vida de perros, vida perra** dog's life, wretched life
3 (= *sustento*) • **la ~ está muy cara** the cost of living is very high • **tienen la ~ resuelta** they are set up for life • **coste de la ~** cost of living • **ganarse la ~** to earn *o* make one's living • **se gana la ~ haciendo traducciones** he earns *o* makes his living doing translations • **nivel de ~** standard of living; ▹ **buscar**
4 [*de objeto*] • **la ~ de estos edificios es breve** the life of these buildings is short • **la media de ~ de un televisor** the average lifespan of a television set ▸ **vida útil** (*Com*) lifespan; (*Téc*) useful life
5 • **MODISMOS:** • **amargar la ~ a algn** to make sb's life a misery • **así es la ~** that's life, such is life • **¡por ~ del chápiro verde!*** I'll be darned!* • **complicarse la ~** to make life difficult for o.s. • **contar la ~:** • **¡no me cuentes tu ~!** I don't want your life story! • **costarle la ~ a algn:** • **le costó la ~** it cost him his life • **dar ~ a algn:** • **la mujer que me dio la ~** the woman who brought me into the world • **dar ~ a un personaje** to play a part • **darse buena ~** *o* **la ~ padre** to live the life of Riley* • **estar encantado de la ~** to be delighted • **acepté encantada de la ~** I was delighted to accept • **enterrarse en ~** to cut o.s. off from the world • **¡esto es ~!** this is the life! • **hacer por la ~*** to eat • **dar mala ~ a algn** to ill-treat sb, make sb's life a misery • **meterse en ~s ajenas** to pry into other people's affairs, meddle in other people's affairs • **¡hijo de mi ~!** my dear child! • **la ~ y milagros de algn** sb's life story • **cuéntame tu ~ y milagros** tell me all about yourself • **pasarse la ~:** • **se pasa la ~ quejándose** he's forever complaining • **pasar la ~ a tragos*** to have a miserable life • **pasar a mejor ~** (*euf*) to pass away, go to a better place • **pegarse la gran ~** *o* **la ~ padre** to live the life of Riley* • **tener siete ~s como los gatos** (*hum*) to have nine lives • **vender cara la ~** to sell one's life dearly; ▹ **vivir**
6 (= *vitalidad*) • **lleno de ~** [*ojos*] lively; [*persona*] full of life • **sus ojos sin ~** his lifeless eyes • **este sol es la ~** this sunshine is a real tonic • **dar ~ a:** • **la música le da ~ a estas imágenes** the music brings these images to life • **dar ~ a una fiesta** to liven up a party
7 (*apelativo cariñoso*) • **¡vida!** • **¡~ mía!** my love!, my darling!
8 (*euf*) (= *prostitución*) • **una mujer de la ~** a loose woman • **echarse a la ~** to go on the game* • **hacer la ~** to be on the game*

videncia SF clairvoyance

vidente ADJ sighted
SMF 1 (= *no ciego*) sighted person
2 (= *clarividente*) clairvoyant(e); (= *profeta*) seer
3 (*TV*) viewer

vídeo SM (= *sistema*) video; (= *aparato*) video (recorder); (= *cinta*) video, videotape • **cinta de ~** videotape • **película de ~** video film • **registrar** *o* **grabar en ~** to video, (video)tape ▸ **vídeo compuesto** (*Inform*) composite video ▸ **vídeo comunitario** community video ▸ **vídeo doméstico** home video ▸ **vídeo inverso** (*Inform*) reverse video ▸ **vídeo musical** music video ▸ **vídeo promocional** promotional video

vídeo... PREF video ...

videoadicción SF video addiction*

videoadicto/a SM/F video addict*

videoaficionado/a SM/F video fan

videocámara SF video camera

videocasete SM video cassette

videocasetera SF video cassette recorder

videocassette SF video cassette

videocine SM video films (*pl*)

videocinta SF videotape

videoclip SM (PL: **videoclips**) videoclip, video

videoclub SM (PL: **videoclubs** *o* **videoclubes**) video shop, video store

videoconferencia SF videoconference, teleconference

videoconsola SF (video) games console

videocopia SF pirate video

videodisco SM video disc *o* (*EEUU*) disk

videoedición SF video editing

videofilm SM, **videofilme** SM videofilm

videófono SM videophone

videofrecuencia SF video frequency

videograbación SF (= *acto*) videotaping, taping; (= *programa registrado*) recording

videograbador SM (*Arg*) video recorder, video

videograbadora SF video recorder, video

videograbar ▸ CONJUG 1a VT to video, videotape

videográfico ADJ video (*antes de s*)

videograma SM video recording, videogram, video

videojuego SM video game

videojugador(a) SM/F gamer, video gamer

videolibro SM video book

videollamada SF video call

videomarcador SM electronic scoreboard

videopiratería SF video piracy

videopresentación SF video-presentation

videoproyección SF video-screening • **pantalla de ~** video-screen

videoproyector SM video projector

videorregistrador SM video (tape-)recorder

videorrevista SF video magazine

videoteca SF video library

videotelefonía SF videotelephony

videoteléfono SM videophone

videoterminal SM video terminal, visual display unit, VDU

videotex SM Videotex®

videotexto SM videotext

videovigilancia SF video surveillance

vidilla* SF • **dar ~ a algo** to spice sth up, liven sth up • **dar ~ a algn** to liven sb up

vidorra* SF good life, easy life • **pegarse la ~** to live it up*

vidorria SF **1** (*Arg**) (= *vida alegre*) gay life, easy life
2 (*And, Caribe*) (= *vida triste*) miserable life

vidriado ADJ glazed
SM **1** (= *barniz*) glaze, glazing
2 (= *loza*) glazed earthenware

vidriar ▸ CONJUG 1b VT to glaze
VPR **vidriarse** [*objeto*] to become glazed; [*ojos*] to glaze over

vidriera SF **1** (= *puerta*) glass door; (= *ventana*) glass window ▸ **vidriera (de colores)** stained glass window
2 (*LAm*) (= *escaparate*) shop window; (= *vitrina*) showcase
3 (*Caribe*) (= *puesto*) tobacco stall, tobacco kiosk

vidriería SF **1** (= *fábrica*) glassworks
2 (= *objetos*) glassware

vidriero SM glazier

vidrio SM **1** (= *material*) glass; (*esp LAm*) (= *ventana*) window • **bajo ~** under glass • **~s rotos** broken glass (*sing*) • MODISMOS: • **pagar los ~s rotos** to carry the can* • **soplar ~*** to booze* ▸ **vidrio cilindrado** plate glass ▸ **vidrio coloreado, vidrio de colores** stained glass ▸ **vidrio deslustrado, vidrio esmerilado** frosted glass, ground glass ▸ **vidrio inastillable** laminated glass, splinter-proof glass ▸ **vidrio pintado** stained glass ▸ **vidrio plano** sheet glass ▸ **vidrio polarizado** polarized glass ▸ **vidrio tallado** cut glass
2* (= *vaso*) glass • **tomar unos ~s** to have a few drinks
3 (*Cono Sur*) (= *botella*) bottle of liquor
4 (*LAm*) (= *ventanilla*) window

vidrioso ADJ **1** (*gen*) glassy; (= *frágil*) brittle, fragile; (= *como vidrio*) glass-like
2 [*ojo*] glassy; [*expresión*] glazed; [*superficie*] slippery
3 [*persona*] touchy, sensitive
4 [*asunto*] delicate

vidurria SF (*And, Caribe, Cono Sur*) = **vidorria**

vieira SF scallop

vieja SF **1** (= *anciana*) old woman
2* • **la ~** (= *madre*) my mum*; (= *esposa*) my old woman*
3 (*Cono Sur*) (= *petardo*) cracker, squib
4 (*Méx*) [*de cigarro*] cigar stub

viejada SF (*Cono Sur*) group of old people

viejales* SM INV old chap*

viejera SF **1** (*Caribe*) (= *vejez*) old age
2 (*Caribe*) (= *trasto*) bit of old junk

viejito/a* SM/F (*LAm*) **1** (= *anciano*) old person
2 (= *amigo*) friend

viejo/a ADJ **1** (= *de mucha edad*) old • **hacerse** *o* **ponerse ~** to grow old, get old • **de ~ me gustaría vivir junto al mar** when I'm old, I'd like to live by the sea • MODISMOS: • **~ como el mundo** as old as the hills • **más ~ que el cagar**‡ bloody ancient‡
2 (= *envejecido*) old • **está muy ~ para la edad que tiene** he looks very old for his age
3 (= *usado*) old • **tiraré todos los zapatos ~s** I'll throw all my old shoes away • **ropa vieja** old clothes (*pl*); (= *de segunda mano*) secondhand clothes (*pl*) • **librería de ~** secondhand bookshop • **zapatero de ~** cobbler • MODISMO: • **se cae de ~** it's falling to bits *o* pieces
4 (= *antiguo*) old • **un ~ amigo** an old friend • **viejas costumbres** old customs • **mi padre es de la vieja escuela** my father is of the old school
5 • **Plinio el Viejo** Pliny the Elder
SM/F **1** (= *persona mayor*) old man/old woman • **los ~s** the elderly, old people • **el Viejo de Pascua** (*LAm*) Father Christmas; ▸ **verde**
2 (*LAm**) • **mi ~** (= *padre, esposo*) my old man* • **mi vieja** (= *madre, esposa*) my old woman* • **mis ~s** (*esp LAm*) (= *padres*) my parents, my folks*
3 (*LAm**) (*en oración directa*) (= *querido*) darling
4 (*LAm**) (= *chica*) • **las viejas** the chicks*, the birds*
5* (*como excl*) (= *tío, colega*) mate*, pal*, buddy (*EEUU**)

viejón ADJ (*And, Cono Sur*) elderly

Viena SF Vienna

viene *etc* ▸ **venir**

vienés/esa ADJ, SM/F Viennese

viento SM **1** (*Meteo*) wind; (*ligero*) breeze • **corre** *o* **hay** *o* **hace** *o* **sopla (mucho) ~** it is (very) windy • **~ en popa** following wind • MODISMOS: • **beber los ~s por algn** to be crazy about sb • **como el ~** like the wind • **correr malos ~s para algo** to be the wrong moment for sth • **contra ~ y marea** at all costs, come what may • **gritar algo a los cuatro ~s** to shout sth from the rooftops, tell all and sundry about sth • **echar a algn con ~ fresco*** to chuck sb out* • **¡vete con ~ fresco!** go to blazes!* • **lo mandé a tomar ~*** I sent him packing • **ir ~ en popa** to go splendidly, go great guns*; [*negocio*] to prosper • **sorber los ~s por algn** to be crazy about sb • REFRÁN: • **quien siembra ~s recoge tempestades** sow the wind and reap the whirlwind ▸ **viento a favor** tailwind ▸ **viento ascendente** (*Aer*) upcurrent ▸ **viento colado** draught, draft (*EEUU*) ▸ **viento contrario** headwind ▸ **viento de cara** headwind ▸ **viento de cola** tailwind ▸ **viento de costado** crosswind, side wind ▸ **viento de espalda** tailwind ▸ **viento de la hélice** slipstream ▸ **viento de proa** headwind ▸ **viento en contra** headwind ▸ **viento favorable** lead wind; (*en atletismo*) wind assistance ▸ **viento huracanado** hurricane force wind, violent wind ▸ **viento lateral** side wind ▸ **viento portante** prevailing wind ▸ **viento racheado** gusty wind, squally wind ▸ **vientos alisios** trade winds ▸ **vientos nuevos** (*fig*) winds of change ▸ **viento terral** land breeze ▸ **viento trasero** tailwind
2 (*Mús*) wind instruments (*pl*), wind section
3 (*Camping*) guy rope, guy
4 (= *ventosidad*) wind, flatulence (*frm*)
5 (*Caza*) scent
6 [*de perro*] sense of smell, keen scent
7 (= *vanidad*) conceit, vanity • **estar lleno de ~** to be puffed up (with conceit)
8 (*And*) [*de cometa*] strings (*pl*) (*of a kite*)
9 (*CAm*) (= *reuma*) rheumatism

vientre SM **1** (= *estómago*) belly • **bajo ~** lower abdomen
2 (= *matriz*) womb • **llevar un hijo en su ~** to carry a child in one's womb
3 (= *intestino*) bowels (*pl*) • **hacer de ~** • **descargar el ~** • **exonerar el ~** to have a bowel movement, move one's bowels ▸ **vientre flojo** looseness of the bowels
4 [*de animal muerto*] guts (*pl*), entrails (*pl*)
5 (*Zool*) foetus, fetus (*EEUU*)
6 [*de recipiente*] belly, wide part

vier. ABR (= **viernes**) Fri.

viernes SM INV Friday ▸ **Viernes Santo** Good Friday; ▸ **sábado**

Vietnam SM Vietnam ▸ **Vietnam del Norte** North Vietnam ▸ **Vietnam del Sur** South Vietnam

vietnamita[1] ADJ, SMF Vietnamese
SM (*Ling*) Vietnamese

vietnamita[2] SF (= *máquina*) duplicator

viga SF (= *madera*) balk, timber, lumber (*EEUU*); (*Arquit*) [*de madera*] beam, rafter; [*de metal*] girder • MODISMO: • **estar contando las ~s** to be gazing vacantly at the ceiling ▸ **viga maestra** main beam ▸ **viga transversal** crossbeam

vigencia SF **1** (= *validez*) validity, applicability; [*de contrato*] term, life; [*de ley, reglamento*] operation • **entrar en ~** to come into effect, take effect • **estar en ~** to be in force, be valid • **perder ~** to go out of use, be no longer applicable • **tener ~** to be valid, apply
2 (= *norma social*) social convention, norm of society

vigente ADJ [*ley, reglamento*] current, in force; [*tarifa*] current • **según la normativa ~** according to the regulations currently in force • **una costumbre aún ~ en nuestro siglo** a custom which still prevails in our own century

vigésimo ADJ, SM twentieth; ▸ **sexto**

vigía SMF lookout, watchman • **los ~s** (*Náut*) the watch
SF **1** (*Mil*) watchtower
2 (*Geog*) reef, rock

vigilancia SF **1** (= *custodia*) vigilance • **los niños pequeños requieren ~ constante** small children require constant vigilance • **burlaron la ~ de sus guardianes** they evaded the watchful eye of their guards • **tener bajo ~** [+ *paciente*] to keep under observation; [+ *prisionero*] to keep under surveillance ▸ **vigilancia intensiva** (*Med*) intensive care
2 (= *servicio*) security • **la ~ del hotel es excelente** security at the hotel is excellent

vigilante ADJ (*gen*) vigilant, watchful; (= *alerta*) alert
SMF **1** (*en cárcel*) warder, guard (*EEUU*); [*de trabajo*] supervisor; (*en tienda*) store detective; [*de museo*] keeper; (*en piscina*) attendant ▸ **vigilante de noche, vigilante nocturno** night watchman ▸ **vigilante jurado** armed security guard
2 (*Cono Sur*) (= *policía*) policeman

vigilantemente ADV vigilantly, watchfully

vigilar ▸ CONJUG 1a VT **1** [+ *niño, enfermo, equipaje, máquina*] to keep an eye on, watch • **vigila a los niños para que no se hagan daño** keep an eye on *o* watch the children to see they don't get hurt • **vigila el arroz para que no se pegue** keep an eye on the rice to make sure it doesn't stick
2 [+ *trabajo*] to supervise
3 [+ *presos*] to guard; [+ *frontera*] to guard, police • **vigilaban de cerca al sospechoso** they kept a close watch on the suspect
VI to keep watch • **tú vigila fuera mientras yo me escondo** you keep a lookout *o* keep watch outside while I hide • **~ por algo** to watch over sth • **su misión es ~ por la seguridad del Estado** his task is to watch over national security

vigilia SF **1** (= *vela*) wakefulness; (= *vigilancia*) watchfulness • **pasar la noche de ~** to stay awake all night
2 (= *trabajo*) night work, late work; (= *estudio*) night-time study
3 (*Rel*) vigil; (= *víspera*) eve; (= *abstinencia*) abstinence; (= *ayuno*) fast • **día de ~** day of abstinence • **comer de ~** abstain from meat • **potaje de ~** vegetable stew

vigor SM **1** (= *fuerza*) vigour, vigor (*EEUU*); (= *vitalidad*) vitality; (= *resistencia*) toughness, hardiness; (= *empuje*) drive • **con ~** vigorously **2** (= *vigencia*) • **en ~** [*norma*] in force; [*tarifa, horario*] valid, applicable • **entrar en ~** to take effect, come into force • **poner en ~** to put into effect, put into operation; ▸ **mantenerse**

vigorización SF (= *refuerzo*) strengthening; (= *estímulo*) encouragement, stimulation; (= *vitalidad*) revitalization

vigorizador ADJ, **vigorizante** ADJ (*gen*) invigorating; [*frío, viento*] bracing; [*ducha, bebida*] revitalizing; [*medicina*] tonic

vigorizar ▸ CONJUG 1f VT to invigorate; (= *animar, alentar*) to encourage, stimulate; (= *dar fuerza a*) to strengthen; (= *revitalizar*) to revitalize

vigorosamente ADV (*gen*) vigorously; (= *con fuerza*) strongly, forcefully; (= *con dificultad*) strenuously

vigoroso ADJ (*gen*) vigorous; (= *fuerte*) strong, tough; [*esfuerzo*] strenuous; [*protesta*] vigorous, forceful; [*niño*] sturdy

viguería SF (= *vigas*) beams (*pl*), rafters (*pl*); [*de metal*] girders (*pl*), metal framework

vigués/esa ADJ of Vigo SM/F native/inhabitant of Vigo • **los vigueses** the people of Vigo

vigueta SF joist, small beam

VIH SM ABR (= **virus de la inmunodeficiencia humana**) HIV

vihuela SF (*Hist*) *early form of the guitar*

vihuelista SMF (*Hist*) *vihuela player*

vijúa SF (*And*) rock salt

vikingo/a SM/F Viking

vil ADJ [*persona*] low, villainous; [*acto*] vile, rotten; [*conducta*] despicable, mean; [*trato*] unjust, shabby • **el vil metal** filthy lucre

vileza SF **1** (= *cualidad*) vileness, foulness; (= *carácter*) meanness; (= *injusticia*) injustice **2** (= *acción*) vile act, base deed

vilipendiar ▸ CONJUG 1b VT **1** (= *denunciar*) to vilify, revile **2** (= *despreciar*) to despise, scorn

vilipendio SM **1** (= *denuncia*) vilification, abuse **2** (= *desprecio*) contempt, scorn; (= *humillación*) humiliation

vilipendioso ADJ (= *despreciable*) contemptible; (= *humillante*) humiliating

villa SF **1** (= *pueblo*) small town; (*Pol*) borough, municipality • **la Villa (y Corte)** (*Esp*) Madrid ▸ **villa de emergencia** (*Arg*), **villa miseria** (*Arg*), **villa precaria** (*Arg*) shantytown, slum quarter ▸ **villa olímpica** Olympic village **2** (= *casa*) villa

Villadiego SM • **tomar las de ~*** to beat it quick*

villanaje SM **1** (= *estatus*) humble status, peasant condition **2** (= *personas*) peasantry, villagers (*pl*)

villancico SM (Christmas) carol

villanesco ADJ (= *de campesinos*) peasant (*antes de s*); (= *de pueblo*) village (*antes de s*), rustic

villanía SF **1** (= *cualidad*) villainy, baseness **2** (= *acción*) = **vileza** **3** (= *dicho*) obscene expression, filthy remark **4** (*Hist*) humble birth, lowly status

villano/a ADJ **1** (*Hist*) (= *campesino*) peasant (*antes de s*); (= *rústico*) rustic **2** (= *grosero*) coarse **3** (= *vil*) villainous, base SM/F **1** (*Hist*) serf, villein; (= *campesino*) peasant, rustic **2** (= *canalla*) rotter*, rat*; (*Cine*) villain **3** (*LAm*) villain

villero/a SM/F (*Arg*) shantytown dweller

villista SMF (*Méx*) (*Pol*) supporter of Pancho Villa

villorrio SM one-horse town, dump*; (*LAm*) shantytown

vilmente ADV (= *con vileza*) vilely, foully; (= *despreciablemente*) despicably; (= *injustamente*) unjustly

vilo ADV **1** • **en ~** (= *levantado*) into the air; (= *suspenso*) suspended, unsupported • **sostener algo en ~** to hold sth up **2** • **en ~** (= *intranquilo*) on tenterhooks • **estar** *o* **quedar en ~** • **estar con el alma en ~** to be left in suspense, be on tenterhooks • **tener a algn en ~** to keep sb in suspense, keep sb waiting

vilote SM (*LAm*) coward

vinagre SM vinegar ▸ **vinagre de sidra** cider vinegar ▸ **vinagre de vino** wine vinegar

vinagrera SF **1** (= *botella*) vinegar bottle **2 vinagreras** (= *juego*) cruet stand (*sing*) **3** (*LAm*) (*Med*) heartburn, acidity

vinagreta SF (*tb* **salsa vinagreta**) vinaigrette, French dressing

vinagroso ADJ **1** (= *ácido*) vinegary, tart **2** [*persona*] bad-tempered, sour

vinatería SF **1** (= *tienda*) wine shop **2** (= *comercio*) wine trade

vinatero/a SM/F wine merchant, vintner

vinaza SF nasty wine, wine from the dregs

vinazo SM strong wine

vincha SF (*And, Cono Sur*) hairband, headband

vinculación SF **1** (= *relación*) linking, binding; (*fig*) bond, link **2** (*Jur*) entail

vinculante ADJ binding (**para** on)

vincular ▸ CONJUG 1a VT **1** (= *relacionar*) to link, bind (a to) • **~ sus esperanzas a algo** to base one's hopes on sth • **~ su suerte a la de otro** to make one's fate dependent on sb else's • **están estrechamente vinculados entre sí** they are closely bound together **2** (*Jur*) to entail VPR **vincularse** to be linked, link o.s. (a to)

vínculo SM **1** (= *relación, lazo*) link, bond • **los ~s de la amistad** the bonds of friendship • **hay un fuerte ~ histórico** there is a strong historical link ▸ **vínculo de parentesco** family ties (*pl*), ties (*pl*) of blood **2** (*Jur*) entail

vindicación SF **1** (= *defensa*) vindication **2** (= *venganza*) revenge, vengeance

vindicar ▸ CONJUG 1g VT **1** [+ *persona, reputación*] to vindicate; [+ *derecho*] to regain, win back **2** (= *vengar*) to avenge VPR **vindicarse 1** (= *vengarse*) to avenge o.s. **2** (= *justificarse*) to vindicate o.s.

vine *etc* ▸ **venir**

vineo* SM • **ir de ~** to go boozing*

vinería SF (*LAm*) wine shop

vínico ADJ wine (*antes de s*)

vinícola ADJ [*industria*] wine (*antes de s*); [*región*] wine-growing (*antes de s*), wine-making (*antes de s*)

vinicultor(a) SM/F wine grower

vinicultura SF wine growing, wine production

vinificable ADJ that can be made into wine, suitable for wine-making

vinificación SF fermentation

vinílico ADJ vinyl (*antes de s*)

vinillo SM thin wine, weak wine

vinilo SM vinyl

vino SM **1** (= *bebida*) wine • **aguar** *o* **bautizar el ~** to water the wine • MODISMOS: • **dormir el ~** to sleep off a hangover • **echar agua al ~** to water down a statement • **tener buen ~** to be able to handle one's drink • **tener mal ~** to get wild after a few drinks ▸ **vino añejo** mature wine ▸ **vino blanco** white wine ▸ **vino corriente** ordinary wine ▸ **vino de aguja** sparkling wine ▸ **vino de Jerez** sherry ▸ **vino de la casa** house wine ▸ **vino del año** new wine, wine for early drinking ▸ **vino de Málaga** Malaga (wine) ▸ **vino de mesa** table wine ▸ **vino de Oporto** port (wine) ▸ **vino de pasto** ordinary wine ▸ **vino de postre** dessert wine ▸ **vino de reserva** reserve ▸ **vino de solera** vintage wine ▸ **vino espumoso** sparkling wine ▸ **vino peleón** cheap wine, plonk* ▸ **vino rosado** rosé (wine) ▸ **vino tinto** red wine ▸ **vino tranquilo** non-sparkling wine **2** (= *recepción*) drinks (*pl*), reception • **después de la conferencia hubo un ~** there were drinks after the lecture ▸ **vino de honor** official reception; (*Cono Sur*) special wine

vinolento ADJ boozy‡, fond of the bottle

vinoso (*frm*) ADJ [*sabor*] like wine, vinous; [*color*] wine-coloured, wine-colored (*EEUU*)

vinoteca SF collection of wines

vinotería SF (*Méx*) wine-shop

viña SF **1** (= *planta*) vine; (= *lugar*) vineyard **2** (*Méx*) (= *vertedero*) rubbish dump, garbage dump (*EEUU*)

viñador(a) SM/F (= *propietario*) wine grower; (= *trabajador*) vineyard worker

viñal SM (*Cono Sur*) vineyard

viñatero/a SM/F (*And, Cono Sur*) wine grower

viñedo SM vineyard

viñeta SF (*Arte*) (*tb fig*) vignette; (*Prensa*) cartoon, sketch, drawing; (= *emblema*) emblem, device

viola SF **1** (*Bot*) viola **2** (*Mús*) viola; (*Hist*) viol ▸ **viola de gamba** viola da gamba SMF viola player

violáceo ADJ violet

violación SF **1** (*sexual*) rape **2** [*de ley*] infringement; [*de acuerdo, principio*] violation, breach; [*de derecho, territorio*] violation ▸ **violación de contrato** breach of contract ▸ **violación de domicilio** housebreaking **3** (= *profanación*) violation

violado ADJ, SM violet

violador(a) SM rapist SM/F violator, offender (**de** against)

violar ▸ CONJUG 1a VT **1** [+ *persona*] to rape **2** [+ *ley*] to break, infringe (*frm*); [+ *acuerdo, principio*] to violate, breach; [+ *derecho, territorio*] to violate; [+ *domicilio*] to break into, force entry into **3** (= *profanar*) to violate

violatorio ADJ • **ser ~ de** to be in breach *o* violation of

violencia SF **1** (*gen*) violence; (= *fuerza*) force; (*Jur*) assault, violence; (*Pol*) rule by force • **no ~** non-violence • **hacer algo con ~** to do sth violently • **usar ~ para abrir una caja** to force open a box • **no se consigue nada con él usando la ~** you will not achieve anything with him by using force, you won't get anywhere with him if you use force • **amenazar ~** to threaten violence; [*turba*] to turn ugly • **apelar a la ~** to resort to violence, use force • **hacer ~ a** = **violentar** ▸ **violencia de género** gender violence ▸ **violencia doméstica** domestic violence ▸ **violencia machista** male violence against women **2** (= *vergüenza*) embarrassment; (= *situación*) embarrassing situation • **si eso te causa ~** if that makes you feel awkward *o* uncomfortable, if that embarrasses you • **estar con ~** to be *o* feel awkward **3** • **una ~** a damaging act; (= *atrocidad*) an outrage **4** (*Col*) (*Hist, Pol*) • **la Violencia** *long period of civil* *disturbances and killings beginning in 1948*

violentamente ADV **1** (= *con violencia*) violently; (= *con furia*) furiously, wildly
2 (*LAm*) (= *rápidamente*) quickly

violentar ▷ CONJUG 1a VT **1** [+ *puerta, cerradura*] to force; [+ *rama*] to bend, twist (out of shape); [+ *casa*] to break into
2 [+ *persona*] (= *avergonzar*) to embarrass; (= *forzar*) to force, persuade forcibly; (= *maltratar*) to subject to violence; (*Jur*) to assault
3 [+ *principio*] to violate, outrage; [+ *sentido*] to distort, twist
VPR **violentarse** (= *avergonzarse*) to get embarrassed; (= *forzarse*) to force o.s.

violentismo SM (*Chile*) social agitation

violentista ADJ, SMF (*Chile*) (*Pol*) subversive

violento ADJ **1** [*acto, deporte, persona*] violent • **se produjo una violenta explosión** there was a violent explosion • **murió de muerte violenta** he suffered a violent death
2 (= *incómodo*) awkward, uncomfortable • **me fue muy ~ verlo llorar** seeing him cry made me feel very awkward *o* uncomfortable • **me encuentro ~ estando con ellos** I feel awkward *o* I don't feel at ease when I'm with them
3 [*postura*] awkward
4 [*interpretación*] forced
5 (*LAm*) (= *repentino*) quick • **tuvo que hacer un viaje ~** she had to make a sudden trip

violeta SF violet • **conservador a la ~** dyed-in-the-wool conservative ▸ **violeta africana** African violet ▸ **violeta de genciana** gentian violet
ADJ INV violet
SM violet

violín SM **1** (= *instrumento*) violin
2 ▸ **violín de Ingres** *spare-time occupation, art, hobby etc at which one shines*
3 (*Caribe*) (= *mal aliento*) bad breath
4 • **de ~** (*Méx**) gratis, free
5 • MODISMOS: • **embolsar el ~** (*LAm*) to get egg on one's face* • **meter ~ en bolsa** (*Cono Sur**) to be embarrassed • **pintar un ~** (*Méx**) to make a rude sign • **tocar ~** (*And**) to play gooseberry, be a third wheel (EEUU)
SMF (= *persona*) violinist • **primer ~** • **~ primero** (= *concertino*) leader; [*de sección*] first violin • **segundo ~** second violin

violinista SMF violinist, fiddler*

violón SM double bass • MODISMO: • **tocar el ~*** to talk rot
SMF (= *persona*) double bass player

violoncelista SMF cellist

violoncelo SM cello

violonchelista SMF cellist

violonchelo SM cello

vip* SM (PL: **vips**) VIP

viperino ADJ viperish • **lengua viperina** wicked tongue

vira¹ SF (*Mil*) dart

vira² SF [*de zapato*] welt

viracho ADJ (*Cono Sur*) cross-eyed

Viracocha SM **1** (*And, Cono Sur*) (*Hist*) *Inca god*
2 (*And*) (*Hist**) (= *título*) *name given by Incas to the Spanish Conquistadors*

virada SF (*Náut*) tack, tacking

virador SM (*Fot*) toner

virago SF mannish woman

viraje SM **1** (*Náut*) tack; [*de coche*] turn; (*repentino*) swerve; (*en carretera*) bend, curve ▸ **viraje en horquilla** hairpin bend
2 (*fig*) change of direction; (*Pol*) abrupt switch, volte-face; [*de votos*] swing
3 (*Fot*) toning

viral ADJ viral

virar ▷ CONJUG 1a VT **1** (*Náut*) to put about, turn
2 (*Fot*) to tone
3 (*LAm*) (= *dar vuelta a*) to turn (round); (= *invertir*) to turn over, turn upside down
4 (*Caribe*) (= *azotar*) to whip
VI **1** (= *cambiar de dirección*) to change direction, turn; (*Náut*) to tack, go about; [*vehículo*] to turn; (*con violencia*) to swerve • **tuve que ~ a la izquierda para no atropellarle** I had to swerve left to avoid hitting him • **~ en redondo** to turn round completely • **~ a estribor** to turn to starboard • **~ hacia el sur** to turn towards the south
2 (= *cambiar de parecer*) to change one's views; [*voto*] to swing • **el país ha virado a la derecha** the country has swung (to the) right • **~ en redondo** to swing round completely, make a complete volte-face
VPR **virarse** (*Caribe‡*) (= *morirse*) to kick the bucket‡

virgen (PL: **vírgenes**) ADJ [*persona*] virgin; [*cinta*] blank; [*película*] unexposed
SMF virgin; (*Rel*) • **la Virgen** the Virgin • **la Virgen de las Angustias** Our Lady of Sorrows • **la Santísima Virgen** the Blessed Virgin • **¡Santísima Virgen!** by all that's holy! • MODISMOS: • **aparecérsele la Virgen a algn***: • **se le apareció la Virgen** he got his big chance, he struck lucky* • **ser (devoto) de la Virgen del Puño*** to be very tight-fisted • **ser un viva la Virgen***: • **es un viva la Virgen** he doesn't give a damn‡, he doesn't care one bit*

virgencita SF small picture of the Virgin

Vírgenes SFPL • **islas ~** Virgin Islands

virgiliano ADJ Virgilian

Virgilio SM Virgil

virginal ADJ **1** [*cuerpo, doncella*] virginal
2 (*Rel*) *of or relating to the Virgin*

virginiano/a (*LAm*) ADJ Virgo, Virgoan
SM/F Virgo, Virgoan

virginidad SF virginity

Virgo SM (*Astron, Astrol*) Virgo • **es de ~** (*LAm*) he's (a) Virgo, he's a Virgoan

virgo SM virginity
SMF INV (*Astrol*) Virgo, Virgoan • **los ~ son así** that's what Virgos *o* Virgoans are like
ADJ INV (*Astrol*) Virgo, Virgoan • **soy ~** I'm (a) Virgo, I'm a Virgoan

virguería SF **1** (= *adorno*) silly adornment, frill; (= *objeto delicado*) pretty thing, delicately made object
2 (= *maravilla*) wonder, marvel • **es una ~** it's wonderful • **hacer ~s** (*fig*) to work wonders, do clever things • **hacer ~s con algo** to be clever enough to handle sth well

virguero* ADJ **1** (= *bueno*) super*, smashing*
2 (= *elegante*) smart, nattily dressed; (= *exquisito*) pretty, delicately made
3 (= *hábil*) clever, smart

viricida ADJ viricidal
SM viricide

vírico ADJ viral, virus (*antes de s*) • **enfermedad vírica** viral illness

viril ADJ virile, manly • **la edad ~** the prime of life; ▷ **miembro**

virilidad SF **1** (= *cualidad*) virility, manliness
2 (= *estado*) manhood

virilizar ▷ CONJUG 1f VT to make like a man, induce male characteristics in
VPR **virilizarse** to become like a man, acquire male characteristics

viringo ADJ (*And*) **1** (= *desnudo*) bare, naked
2 (= *despellejado*) skinned, skinless

viroca SF (*Cono Sur*) serious mistake

virola SF **1** (= *regatón*) metal tip, ferrule; [*de herramienta, lanza*] collar
2 (*Cono Sur, Méx*) (= *argolla*) silver ring; (= *disco*) metal disc (*fixed to harness etc as an adornment*)

virolento ADJ pockmarked

virolo ADJ (*And*) cross-eyed

virología SF virology

virólogo/a SM/F virologist

virote SM **1** (= *flecha*) arrow
2 (*Méx**) (= *pan*) bread roll
3† (= *señorito*) hooray Henry*
4 (*And, Méx*) (= *tonto*) simpleton

virreinato SM viceroyalty

virrey SM viceroy

virriondo‡ ADJ (*Méx*) **1** [*animal*] (*hembra*) on heat; (*macho*) in rut
2 [*persona*] randy*, horny‡

virtual ADJ **1** (= *potencial*) potential • **el ~ candidato a la presidencia** the potential candidate for president • **tras el partido de hoy son ya los ~es campeones** after today's match they are virtually assured of the championship
2 (*Inform, Fís*) virtual • **memoria ~** virtual memory • **realidad ~** virtual reality

virtualidad SF potentiality • **tiene ciertas ~es** it has certain potentialities

virtualmente ADJ virtually

virtud SF **1** (= *calidad*) virtue • **~ cardinal** cardinal virtue
2 (= *capacidad*) ability, power; (= *eficacia*) efficacy • **en ~ de** by virtue of, by reason of • **tener la ~ de …** (+ *infin*) to have the virtue of … (+ *ger*), have the power to … (+ *infin*) • **una planta que tiene ~ contra varias enfermedades** a plant which is effective against certain diseases • **~es curativas** healing power (*sing*), healing properties
3 (*Caribe***) (= *pene*) prick**; (= *vagina*) cunt**

virtuosamente ADV virtuously

virtuosismo SM virtuosity

virtuosista ADJ virtuoso

virtuoso/a ADJ virtuous
SM/F virtuoso

viruela SF **1** (= *enfermedad*) smallpox
2 viruelas (= *marcas*) pockmarks • **picado de ~s** pockmarked ▸ **viruelas locas** chickenpox (*sing*)

virulé* • **a la ~** ADJ **1** (= *estropeado*) damaged; (= *torcido*) bent, twisted; (= *viejo*) old; (= *raído*) shabby • **ojo a la ~** shiner*
2 [*persona*] cracked, potty*

virulencia SF virulence

virulento ADJ virulent

virus SM INV virus • **enfermedad por ~** viral illness ▸ **virus atenuado** attenuated virus ▸ **virus de inmunodeficiencia humana** human immunodeficiency virus ▸ **virus gripal** flu virus ▸ **virus informático** computer virus

viruta SF **1** [*de madera, metal*] shaving ▸ **virutas de acero** steel wool (*sing*)
2‡ (= *dinero*) bread‡, money
SM carpenter

virutas SM INV carpenter

vis SF • **vis cómica** sense of comedy • **tener vis cómica** to be witty

visa SF (*LAm*) visa ▸ **visa de permanencia** residence permit ▸ **visa de tránsito** transit visa

visado SM visa ▸ **visado de entrada** entry visa ▸ **visado de salida** exit visa ▸ **visado de tránsito** transit visa ▸ **visado de turista**, **visado turístico** tourist visa

visaje SM (wry) face, grimace • **hacer ~s** to pull faces, grimace

visar ▷ CONJUG 1a VT **1** [+ *pasaporte*] to visa
2 [+ *documento*] to endorse, approve

vis a vis ADV face to face
SM (= *reunión*) face to face (meeting); (*en la cárcel*) private visit

visceral ADJ **1** (*Anat*) visceral
2 (= *profundo*) visceral, deep-rooted • **aversión/reacción ~** gut aversion/reaction

• sentimientos ~es gut feelings
visceralmente ADV deeply, viscerally (*frm*)
vísceras SFPL (*Anat*) viscera (*pl*), entrails; (*fig*) guts, bowels
visco SM birdlime
viscosa SF viscose
viscosidad SF **1** (= *cualidad*) viscosity; [*de líquido*] thickness
2 (*Bot, Zool*) (= *sustancia*) slime; (= *secreción*) sticky secretion
viscoso ADJ (*gen*) viscous; [*líquido*] thick; [*secreción*] slimy
visera SF (*Mil*) visor; [*de gorra*] peak; [*de jockey, tenista*] eyeshade; (*Caribe*) [*de caballo*] (horse's) blinkers (*pl*); [*de estadio*] canopy ▸ **visera de béisbol** baseball cap
visibilidad SF visibility • **la ~ es de 20om** there is a visibility of 200m • **la ~ queda reducida a cero** visibility is down to zero • **una curva de escasa ~** (*Aut*) a bend with poor visibility ▸ **visibilidad cero** zero visibility
visible ADJ **1** (= *que se ve*) visible • **es ~ a simple vista** it's visible to the naked eye, it can be seen with the naked eye • **ponlo donde esté bien ~** put it where it can be easily seen, put it where it's clearly visible
2 (= *evidente*) • **dio muestras de ~ disgusto** he was visibly upset • **la miró con ~ enojo** he looked at her, visibly annoyed
3 (= *decente*) decent, presentable • **¿estás ~?** are you decent *o* presentable?
visiblemente ADV visibly
visigodo/a ADJ Visigothic
SM/F Visigoth
visigótico ADJ Visigothic
visillo SM **1** (= *cortina*) lace curtain, net curtain
2 (*en butaca*) antimacassar
visión SF **1** (*Anat*) vision, (eye)sight • **perder la ~ de un ojo** to lose the sight in *o* of one eye ▸ **visión borrosa** blurred vision ▸ **visión de túnel** tunnel vision ▸ **visión doble** double vision ▸ **visión reducida** impaired vision
2 (*Rel*) vision; (= *fantasía*) fantasy; (= *ilusión*) illusion • **ver visiones** to be seeing things, suffer delusions • **se le apareció en ~** it came to him in a vision
3 (= *vista*) view • **un político con ~ de futuro** a farsighted politician ▸ **visión de conjunto** complete picture, overall view
4 (= *punto de vista*) view, point of view • **su ~ del problema** his view of the problem
5 (*pey*) scarecrow, fright* • **ella iba hecha una ~** she looked a real sight* • **han comprado una ~ de cuadro** they've bought an absolutely ghastly picture
visionado SM **1** (= *acción*) viewing, inspection
2 (*TV*) viewing-room
visionadora SF (*Fot*) viewer
visionar ▸ CONJUG 1a VT **1** (*TV*) to view, see; (*por adelantado*) to preview; (*Fot*) to view, have a viewing of
2 (= *entrever*) to glimpse; (= *prever*) to foresee
3 (= *presenciar*) to witness
visionario/a ADJ visionary; (*pey*) deluded, subject to hallucinations
SM/F visionary; (*pey*) deluded person; (= *loco*) lunatic, crazy individual
visir SM vizier • **gran ~** grand vizier
visita SF **1** (= *acción*) visit; (*breve*) call • **horas de ~** visiting hours • **tarjeta de ~** business card, visiting card • **estar de ~ en un lugar** to be on a visit to a place • **ir de ~** to go visiting • **devolver** *o* **pagar una ~** to return a visit • **hacer una ~ a** to visit, pay a visit to ▸ **visita conyugal** conjugal visit ▸ **visita de cortesía, visita de cumplido** formal visit, courtesy call ▸ **visita de despedida** farewell visit ▸ **visita de Estado** state visit ▸ **visita de intercambio** exchange visit ▸ **visita de médico*** very short call, brief visit ▸ **visita de pésame** *visit to express one's condolences* ▸ **visita en grupo** group visit ▸ **visita guiada** guided tour ▸ **visita íntima** conjugal visit ▸ **visita oficial** official visit ▸ **visita relámpago** flying visit
2 (= *persona*) visitor, caller • **hoy tenemos ~** we have visitors today • **"no se admiten ~s"** "no visitors"
3 (*en la aduana*) search • **derecho de ~** right to search
4 (*Internet*) hit
5 (*Caribe*) (*Med*) enema
visitación SF (*Rel*) visitation
visitador(a) SM/F **1** (= *visitante*) frequent visitor
2 (= *inspector*) inspector ▸ **visitador(a) social** (*LAm*) social worker
3 (*Com, Med*) drug company representative, drug-company *o* drug rep* ▸ **visitador(a) médico/a** medical representative, medical rep*
SF (*LAm*) **1** (= *jeringa*) syringe
2 (= *enema*) enema
visitante ADJ visiting
SMF visitor
visitar ▸ CONJUG 1a VT (*gen*) to visit; (*brevemente*) to call on • **fuimos a ~ a mis tíos** we went to visit my aunt and uncle • **5.000 personas han visitado ya la exposición** 5,000 people have already visited the exhibition
VI • **el médico está visitando** the doctor is holding his surgery
VPR **visitarse 1** [*personas*] to visit each other
2 (*Med*) to attend the doctor's surgery
visiteo SM frequent visiting, constant calling
visitero/a ADJ fond of visiting, much given to calling
SM/F frequent visitor, constant caller
visitón* SM long and boring visit, visitation (*hum*)
vislumbrar ▸ CONJUG 1a VT **1** [+ *paisaje, figura*] to glimpse, catch a glimpse of
2 [+ *solución*] to glimpse, begin to see; [+ *futuro*] to get a slight idea of; [+ *hecho desconocido*] to surmise
vislumbre SF **1** (= *vista*) glimpse, brief view
2 (= *brillo*) gleam, glimmer
3 (= *posibilidad*) glimmer, slight possibility; (= *conjetura*) conjecture; (= *noción*) vague idea • **tener ~s de** to get an inkling of, get a vague idea of
viso SM **1** [*de metal*] gleam, glint
2 (= *aspecto*) • **hay un ~ de verdad en esto** there is an element of truth in this • **tenía ~s de nunca acabar** it seemed that it was never going to finish • **tiene ~s de ser puro cuento** it looks like being just a story • MODISMOS: • **a dos ~s** • **de dos ~s** with a double purpose, two-edged
3 (= *ropa*) slip
4 • MODISMO: • **ser persona de ~** to be somebody, be important
5 (*Geog*) viewpoint, vantage point
6 visos [*de tela*] sheen (*sing*), gloss (*sing*) • **negro con ~s azules** black with a bluish sheen, black with bluish lights in it • **hacer ~s** to shimmer
visón SM mink
visor SM **1** (*Aer*) bombsight; (*Mil*) sight ▸ **visor nocturno** night sight ▸ **visor telescópico** telescopic sight
2 (*Fot*) (*tb* **visor de imagen**) viewfinder
víspera SF eve, day before • **la ~ de** • **en ~s de** on the eve of (*tb fig*) • **estar en ~s de hacer algo** to be on the point *o* verge of doing sth ▸ **víspera de Navidad** Christmas Eve
vista SF **1** (= *visión*) sight, eyesight • **hasta donde alcanza la ~** as far as the eye can see • **el coche desapareció de mi ~** the car disappeared from sight • **nublarse la ~**: • **se me nubló la ~** my eyes clouded over • **perder la ~** to lose one's sight • **tener buena/mala ~** to have good/bad eyesight • MODISMO: • **hacer la ~ gorda** to turn a blind eye, pretend not to notice ▸ **vista cansada** (*por defecto*) longsightedness; (*por agotamiento*) eyestrain ▸ **vista corta** short sight ▸ **vista de águila, vista de lince** eagle eye • **tener ~ de águila** *o* **de lince** to have eagle eyes, to have eyes like a hawk *o* a lynx
2 (= *ojos*) **a** (= *órgano*) eyes (*pl*) • **tiene un problema en la ~** she has something wrong with her eyes • **a la altura de la ~** at eye level • **una luz que hiere la ~** a dazzling light, a light that hurts one's eyes • **torcer la ~** to squint
b (= *mirada*) • **¡~ a la derecha!** (*Mil*) eyes right! • **aguzar la ~** (*para ver a lo lejos*) to screw one's eyes up; (*para descubrir algo*) to look sharp • **alzar la ~** to look up • **apartar la ~** to look away • **no apartar la ~ de algo** to keep one's eyes glued to sth • **bajar la ~** to look down, lower one's gaze • **buscar algo con la ~** to look around for sth • **clavar la ~ en algn/algo** to stare at sb/sth, fix one's eyes on sb/sth • **dirigir la ~ a algn/algo** to look towards sb/sth, turn one's gaze on sb/sth • **echar una ~ a algn/algo** to take a look at sb/sth • **fijar la ~ en algn/algo** to stare at sb/sth, fix one's eyes on sb/sth • **medir a algn con la ~** to size sb up • **pasar la ~ por algo** to look over sth, glance quickly at sth • **con la ~ puesta en la pared** with his eyes fixed on the wall • **con la ~ puesta en las elecciones** with a view to the elections • **con la ~ puesta en la futura legislación medioambiental, la compañía ha sacado un nuevo modelo** in the light of the forthcoming environmental legislation, the company has launched a new model • **¡quítate de mi ~!** get out of my sight! • **recorrer algo con la ~** to run one's eye over sth • **seguir algo con la ~** to follow sth with one's eyes • **volver la ~** to look away • **volver la ~ atrás** to look back • MODISMOS: • **comerse** *o* **devorar a algn con la ~** (*con deseo*) to devour sb with one's eyes; (*con ira*) to look daggers at sb* • **perder algo de ~** to lose sight of sth • **no perder a algn de ~** to keep sb in sight • **saltar a la ~**: • **su inteligencia salta a la ~** she is strikingly intelligent • **una cosa que salta a la ~ es …** one thing that immediately hits *o* strikes you is … • **salta a la ~ que …** it's blindingly obvious that …
3 (= *perspicacia*) foresight • **tuvieron ~ para comprar las acciones** they showed foresight in buying the shares, it was shrewd of them to buy the shares • **ha tenido mucha ~ con el piso** he was very far-sighted about the flat • **tener ~ para los negocios** to have good business acumen
4 (= *panorama*) view • **la ~ desde el castillo** the view from the castle • **con ~s a**: • **con ~s a la montaña** with a view of the mountains • **una habitación con ~s al mar** a room with a sea view, a room overlooking the sea • **con ~s al oeste** facing west ▸ **vista anterior, vista frontal** front view
5 (*Fot*) (= *imagen*) view • **una tarjeta con una ~ de Venecia** a card with a view of Venice ▸ **vista de pájaro** bird's-eye view • **observar algo a ~ de pájaro** to get a bird's-eye view of sth ▸ **vista fija** still ▸ **vista frontal** front view

V

6 (*otras expresiones*) **a** • **a la ~** in sight *o* view • **la parte que quedaba a la ~** the part that was visible *o* in view • **no es muy agradable a la ~** it's not a pretty sight, it's not very pleasant to look at • **cuenta a la ~** (*Econ*) instant access account • **a la ~ está (que ...)** it's obvious (that ...), you can see for yourself (that ...) • **no tengo ningún proyecto a la ~** I have no plans in sight • **estaré a la ~ de lo que pase** I will keep an eye on developments • **yo me quedo a la ~ del fuego** I'll keep an eye on the fire • **a la ~, no son pobres** from what you can tell, they're not poor • **a la ~ de todos** in full view (of everyone) • **los resultados están a la ~ de todos** the results are there for everyone to see • **lo fríen a la ~ del cliente** it's fried in front of the customer • **a la ~ de tal espectáculo** at the sight of such a scene • **a la ~ de sus informes** in the light of *o* in view of his reports • **poner algo a la ~** to put sth on view
b • **a ... años/días ~**: • **pagadero a 30 días ~** payable within 30 days • **a un año ~ de las elecciones** (= *antes*) a year before the elections • **a cinco años ~** (= *después*) five years from then • **a dos años ~ de la exposición** two years after the exhibition
c • **con ~s a** with a view to • **con ~s a una solución del problema** with a view to solving the problem • **han modernizado el estadio con ~s al Mundial** they have modernized the stadium ahead of the World Cup • **una medida con ~s al futuro** a measure taken with the future in mind
d • **de ~** by sight • **conocer a algn de ~** to know sb by sight • **en ~ de** in view of • **en ~ de que ...** in view of the fact that ... • **¡hasta la ~!** see you!, so long! • **a primera ~** at first sight, on the face of it • **a simple ~** (= *sin ayuda de aparatos*) to the naked eye; (= *por la primera impresión*) at first sight
7 (= *aspecto*) appearance, looks (*pl*) • **esos plátanos no tienen muy buena ~** those bananas don't look too good • **un coche con una ~ estupenda** a wonderful-looking car • **de ~ poco agradable** not very nice to look at, unprepossessing
8 (*Jur*) hearing • **~ de una causa** hearing of a case ▸ **vista oral** first hearing
9 vistas (*Hist*) meeting (*sing*), conference (*sing*)
(SMF) (*tb* **vista de aduana**) customs official
vistar* ▸ CONJUG 1a (VT) (*LAm*) to have a look at, look over, look round
vistazo (SM) look, glance • **de un ~** at a glance • **echar** *o* **pegar un ~ a*** to glance at, have a (quick) look at
vistillas (SFPL) viewpoint (*sing*)
visto¹ ▸ **vestir**
visto² (PP) *de* **ver**
(ADJ) **1** (= *conocido*) • **no, esa chaqueta no, que la tengo muy vista** no, not that jacket, I wear it all the time • **ese color está muy ~** you see that colour all over the place, everyone is wearing that colour • **no quisiera hacerme demasiado ~ en este bar** I don't want to be seen too much in this bar • **ese chiste ya está más que ~** that joke is as old as the hills • **ser lo nunca ~** to be unheard of • **tres derrotas consecutivas es lo nunca ~ en este estadio** three defeats in a row is unheard of *o* has never happened before in this stadium • **el ministro, cosa nunca vista, hizo unas declaraciones en contra del presidente** the minister spoke out against the president, something which is unheard of • MODISMO: • **más ~ que el tebeo** (*Esp*) as old as the hills
2 (= *considerado*) • **estar bien/mal ~** [*comportamiento*] to be the done thing/be frowned upon; [*persona*] to be well/badly thought of; [*iniciativa, propuesta*] to be welcomed/not welcomed • **lo que está bien ~** the done thing • **estaba mal ~ que una mujer saliera sola** it was not the done thing for a woman to go out alone, it was frowned upon for a woman to go out alone • **no está bien ~ dentro del sindicato** he's not very well thought of *o* highly regarded in the union
3 (= *expuesto*) [*ladrillo*] bare, exposed; [*viga*] exposed • **un edificio de ladrillo ~** a building of bare *o* exposed brick
4 (*Jur*) • **¡visto!** case adjourned • **~ para sentencia** adjourned for sentencing
5 (*en locuciones*) • **está ~ que ...** it is clear *o* obvious that ... • **está ~ que el problema no tiene solución** it is clear *o* obvious that there is no solution to the problem • **estaba ~ que la historia terminaría en boda** you could tell that they would end up getting married, it was clear *o* obvious that they would end up getting married • **por lo ~** apparently • **por lo ~, no les interesa** apparently *o* from what I can see, they are not interested • **—¿no ha venido el cartero todavía? —por lo ~ no** "hasn't the postman come yet?" — "apparently not" *o* "it would appear not" • MODISMOS: • **ni ~ ni oído** like lightning • **~ y no ~**: • **cogió el bolso y salió corriendo, fue ~ y no ~** he grabbed the bag and ran out, one minute he was there and the next minute he was gone • **lo fusilaron ~ y no ~** they shot him just like that • **en un ~ y no ~** in a flash • **en un ~ y no ~ el conejo desapareció de ante nuestros ojos** in a flash the rabbit disappeared before our very eyes
6 • **~ que** since • **~ que no nos hacían caso nos fuimos** since they took no notice of us we left
(SM) ▸ **visto bueno** approval, go-ahead* • **vuestra propuesta no ha recibido el ~ bueno** your proposal has not been approved *o* didn't get the go-ahead* • **dar el ~ bueno a algo** to give sth one's approval, give sth the go-ahead* • **el juez ha dado el ~ bueno para que se investigue el caso** the judge has given his approval *o* given the go-ahead for the case to be investigated* • **dar el ~ bueno a algn para que haga algo** to give one's approval for sb to do sth, give sb the go-ahead to do sth*
vistosamente (ADV) (*gen*) brightly, colourfully, colorfully (EEUU); (*pey*) gaudily
vistosidad (SF) (*gen*) brightness, colourfulness, colorfulness (EEUU); (*pey*) gaudiness; [*de feria, ballet*] spectacular nature
vistoso (ADJ) [*ropa*] bright, colourful, colorful (EEUU); (*pey*) gaudy; [*partido*] spectacular
Vístula (SM) Vistula
visual (ADJ) visual • **campo ~** field of vision • **memoria ~** visual memory
(SF) **1** (= *línea*) line of sight
2* (= *vistazo*) look, glance • **echar una ~** to take a look (**a** at)
visualización (SF) **1** (= *representación*) visualization
2 (*Inform*) display(ing) • **pantalla de ~** display screen, VDU
3 ▸ **visualización radiográfica** (*Med*) scanning
visualizador (SM) (*Inform*) display screen, VDU
visualizar ▸ CONJUG 1f (VT) **1** (= *imaginarse*) to visualize
2 (= *hacer visible*) to visualize
3 (*Inform*) to display
4 (*LAm*) (= *divisar*) to see, make out
5 • **~ radiográficamente** (*Med*) to scan
visualmente (ADV) visually
vital (ADJ) **1** (= *de la vida*) life (*antes de s*) • **fuerza ~** life force • **espacio ~** living space
2 (= *fundamental*) vital • **es ~ que haya unidad en el partido** party unity is vital • **de importancia ~** vitally important
3 (= *enérgico*) vital, full of vitality
4 (*Anat*) vital • **órganos ~es** vital organs
vitaliciamente (ADV) for life
vitalicio (ADJ) life (*antes de s*), for life • **cargo ~** post held for life • **pensión vitalicia** life pension
(SM) life annuity
vitalidad (SF) vitality
vitalismo (SM) **1** (*Fil*) vitalism
2 [*de persona*] vitality
vitalista (ADJ) **1** (*Fil*) vitalist
2 [*persona*] vital, full of life
(SMF) (*Fil*) vitalist
vitalización (SF) vitalization
vitalizador (ADJ) • **acción ~a** • **efecto ~** revitalizing effect
vitalizante (ADJ) revitalizing
vitalizar ▸ CONJUG 1f (VT) (*esp LAm*) to vitalize
vitamina (SF) vitamin
vitaminado (ADJ) with added vitamins
vitaminar ▸ CONJUG 1a (VT) to add vitamins to
vitamínico (ADJ) vitamin (*antes de s*)
vitaminizado (ADJ) with added vitamins
vitando (*frm*) (ADJ) (*gen*) to be avoided; [*crimen*] heinous
vitela (SF) vellum
vitícola (ADJ) [*industria*] grape (*antes de s*), vine (*antes de s*); [*región*] grape-producing, vine-producing
viticultor(a) (SM/F) (= *cultivador*) vine grower; (= *dueño*) proprietor of a vineyard
viticultura (SF) vine growing, viticulture (*frm*)
vitíligo (SM) vitiligo
vitivinicultura (SF) grape and wine-growing
vitoco* (ADJ) (*Caribe*) vain, stuck-up*
vitola (SF) **1** [*de cigarro*] cigar band
2 (= *aspecto*) appearance, looks (*pl*)
3 (*Mec*) calibrator
vitoquear* ▸ CONJUG 1a (VI) (*Caribe*) to be conceited, swank*
vítor (EXCL) hurrah!
(SM) cheer • **entre los ~es de la multitud** among the cheers of the crowd • **dar ~es a** to cheer (on)
vitorear ▸ CONJUG 1a (VT) to cheer, acclaim
Vitoria (SF) Vitoria
vitoriano/a (ADJ) of/from Vitoria
(SM/F) native/inhabitant of Vitoria • **los ~s** the people of Vitoria
vitral (SM) stained-glass window
vítreo (ADJ) **1** [*ojos*] glassy
2 (*Geol, Min*) vitreous
3 (*Anat*) vitreous • **humor ~** vitreous humour, vitreous humor (EEUU) • **membrana vítrea** vitreous membrane
vitrificación (SF) vitrification
vitrificar ▸ CONJUG 1g (VT) to vitrify
(VPR) **vitrificarse** to vitrify
vitrina (SF) **1** [*de tienda*] glass case, showcase; (*en casa*) display cabinet
2 (*LAm*) (= *escaparate*) shop window
vitrinear* ▸ CONJUG 1a (VT) (*And*) to go window-shopping
vitriolo (SM) vitriol
vitro (ADJ), (ADV) ▸ **in vitro**
vitrocerámica (SF) • **placa de ~** glass-ceramic hob
vitrocerámico (ADJ) glass-ceramic
vitrola (SF) (*LAm*) gramophone, phonograph (EEUU)

V

vitualla (SF), **vituallas** (SFPL) provisions (*pl*), victuals (*pl*)
vituperable (ADJ) reprehensible
vituperación (SF) condemnation, censure, vituperation (*frm*)
vituperar ▷ CONJUG 1a (VT) to condemn, censure, vituperate against (*frm*)
vituperio (SM) **1** (= *condena*) condemnation, censure, vituperation (*frm*)
2 (= *deshonra*) shame, disgrace
3 vituperios (= *insultos*) abuse (*sing*), insults
vituperioso (ADJ) (*frm*) vituperative (*frm*), abusive
viuda (SF) **1** ▸ **viuda negra** (= *araña*) black widow (spider)
2 (*And, Cono Sur*) (= *fantasma*) ghost
3 (*And*) (*Culin*) fish stew
4 (*Caribe*) (= *cometa*) large kite; ▷ **viudo**
viudedad (SF) **1** (= *viudez*) [*de mujer*] widowhood; [*de hombre*] widowerhood
2 (*Econ*) widow's pension
viudez (SF) [*de mujer*] widowhood; [*de hombre*] widowerhood
viudo/a (ADJ) **1** [*persona*] widowed • **estar viuda*** (= *sola*) to be a grass widow
2 (*Culin**) • **garbanzos ~s** chickpeas by themselves
(SM/F) widower/widow; ▷ **viuda**
viva (SM) cheer • **dar un ~** to give a cheer • **prorrumpir en ~s** to burst out cheering, start to cheer
vivac (SM) (PL: **vivacs**) bivouac
vivacidad (SF) **1** (= *vigor*) vigour, vigor (*EEUU*)
2 (= *personalidad*) liveliness, vivacity; (= *inteligencia*) sharpness
3 [*de colores*] brightness
vivalavirgen* (ADJ INV) happy-go-lucky*
(SMF INV) happy-go-lucky person*
vivales* (SM INV) wide boy*, punk (*EEUU**), smooth operator
vivamente (ADV) (*gen*) in lively fashion; [*describir, recordar*] vividly; [*protestar*] sharply, strongly; [*sentir*] acutely, intensely • **lo siento ~** I am deeply sorry, I sincerely regret it • **se lo deseo ~** I sincerely hope he gets it
vivaque (SM) bivouac
vivaquear ▷ CONJUG 1a (VI) to bivouac
vivar[1] (SM) **1** (*Zool*) warren
2 (*para peces*) (= *estanque*) fishpond; (*industrial*) fish farm
vivar[2] ▷ CONJUG 1a (VT) (*LAm*) (= *vitorear*) to cheer
vivaracho (ADJ) **1** [*persona*] (= *vivo*) jaunty; (= *vivaz*) vivacious
2 [*ojos*] bright, lively, twinkling
3 (*Méx*) sharp, sly
vivaz (ADJ) **1** [*niño, persona*] (= *vivo*) lively; (= *listo*) keen, sharp
2 (= *de larga vida*) long-lived; (= *duradero*) enduring, lasting; (*Bot*) perennial
3 (= *vigoroso*) vigorous
vivencia (SF) experience
vivencial (ADJ) existential
vivenciar ▷ CONJUG 1b (VT) to experience
víveres (SMPL) provisions; (*esp Mil*) stores, supplies
vivero (SM) **1** [*de plantas*] nursery; (= *semillero*) seedbed; [*de árboles*] tree nursery
2 (*para peces*) (= *estanque*) fishpond; (*Com*) fish farm; (*Zool*) vivarium ▸ **vivero de ostras** oyster bed
3 (*fig*) breeding ground; (*pey*) hotbed • **es un ~ de discordias** it's a hotbed of discord
viveza (SF) [*de ritmo*] liveliness; [*de imagen*] vividness; [*de luz, color*] brightness; [*de mente, movimiento*] sharpness, quickness; [*de sensación*] intensity, acuteness; [*de emoción*] strength, depth • **contestar con ~** to answer with spirit • **la ~ de su inteligencia** the sharpness of his mind • **la ~ de sus sentimientos** the strength of his feelings ▸ **viveza criolla** native wit; (*pey*) low cunning (*pey*)
vividero (ADJ) habitable, inhabitable, that can be lived in
vivido (ADJ) **1** (= *experimentado*) • **los años ~s en Brasil** the years we lived in Brazil • **la crisis vivida por el gobierno** the crisis the government went through *o* experienced • **un episodio ~ por el autor** an episode which the author himself experienced
2 (= *habitado*) lived-in • **la zona más vivida del palacio** the most lived-in part of the palace
vívido (ADJ) vivid, graphic
vividor(a) (ADJ) opportunistic
(SM) (= *aprovechado*) hustler, wide boy*, punk (*EEUU**)
(SM/F) opportunist
vivienda (SF) **1** (= *alojamiento*) housing • **el problema de la ~** the housing problem • **la escasez de (la) ~** the housing shortage
2 (= *casa*) house, home; (= *piso*) flat, apartment (*EEUU*) • **segunda ~** second home • **bloque de ~s** block of flats, apartment block (*EEUU*) ▸ **vivienda de renta limitada** *controlled rent housing* ▸ **vivienda en alquiler** (= *casa*) house to let *o* rent; (= *piso*) flat to let *o* rent ▸ **viviendas de interés social** (*Méx, Perú*), **viviendas de protección oficial** public housing (*sing*), social housing (*sing*), council housing (*sing*) *o* houses (*Brit*)
viviente (ADJ) living • **los ~s** the living
vivificador (ADJ) (*gen*) life-giving; (*fig*) revitalizing
vivificante (ADJ) = **vivificador**
vivificar ▷ CONJUG 1g (VT) **1** [+ *persona*] to give life to, invigorate
2 [+ *industria*] to revitalize, bring new life to
3 [+ *situación, suceso*] to enliven
vivillo (ADJ), (SM) (*Cono Sur*) = **vividor**
vivíparo (ADJ) viviparous
vivir ▷ CONJUG 3a (VI) **1** (= *estar vivo*) to live • **los elefantes viven muchos años** elephants live long lives, elephants live for many years • **mientras yo viva** as long as I live • **todavía vive** he's still alive
2 (= *pasar la vida*) to live • **solo vive para la música** music is her whole life, she only lives for music • **siempre he vivido honradamente** I have always lived an honest life • **ahora ya puedes ~ tranquila** now you can relax • **desde que me subieron el sueldo no vivo tan mal** since I had a pay rise I haven't been that badly off • **vivieron felices y comieron perdices** they lived happily ever after • **~ bien** to live well • **en este país se vive bien** people live well in this country, people have a good life in this country • MODISMOS: • **~ del cuento** to live on *o* by one's wits • **~ para ver** you live and learn; ▷ **cuerpo, Dios**
3 (= *disfrutar de la vida*) • **no vivo de la intranquilidad que tengo** I'm worried to death • **no podía ~ de la vergüenza** the shame of it was killing him • **no dejar ~ a algn**: • **su marido no la deja ~** her husband is always on at her*, her husband doesn't give her a moment's peace • **los dolores no me dejan ~** the pain never lets up • **los celos no la dejan ~** she is eaten up with jealousy • **saber ~** to know how to live • **tú sí que sabes ~** you really know how to live
4 (= *habitar*) to live • **en esa casa no vive nadie** nobody lives in that house • **estuve viviendo un año en Londres** I lived in London for a year • **¿vives sola?** do you live on your own? • **viven juntos** (*como pareja*) they live together; (*compartiendo casa*) they live together, they share a house (together)
5 (= *subsistir*) • **con lo que gano no me llega para ~** what I earn is not enough to live on • **la fotografía no me da para ~** I can't make *o* earn a living from photography, photography doesn't give me enough to live on • **viven por encima de sus posibilidades** they live beyond their means • **~ de algo** to live on sth • **vive de la caridad** he lives on charity • **yo vivo de mi trabajo** I work for a living • **vive de ilusiones** he lives in a dream world • **~ al día** to live from day to day • **~ de la pluma** to live by one's pen • **~ de las rentas** (*lit*) to have a private income • **publicó un libro hace años y desde entonces vive de las rentas** years ago he published a book and he's lived off it *o* lived on the strength of it ever since; ▷ **aire**
6 (= *durar*) [*recuerdo*] to live, live on; [*prenda, objeto*] to last • **su recuerdo siempre ~á en nuestra memoria** his memory will always be with us, his memory will live on in our minds • **esa chaqueta ya no ~á mucho tiempo** that jacket won't last much longer
7 (*Mil*) • **¿quién vive?** who goes there? • **pedir el quién vive a algn** to challenge sb
8 (*como exclamación*) • **¡viva!** hurray! • **¡viva el rey!** long live the king! • **¡vivan los novios!** (here's) to the bride and groom!
(VT) **1** (= *experimentar*) [+ *guerra, periodo difícil*] to live through, go through • **nosotros no vivimos la época del comunismo** we didn't live through the communist era • **la época que nos ha tocado ~** the age in which we happen to live • **ha vivido momentos de verdadera angustia** she went through moments of real agony • **tú dedícate a ~ la vida** go ahead and live life to the full *o* get the most out of life
2 (= *sentir*) to experience • **yo vivo la música de una forma distinta** I experience music in a different way • **parece que estoy viviendo ese momento otra vez** it's as if I were *o* was experiencing that moment all over again
(SM) (= *forma de vida*) (way of) life • **el buen ~** the good life • **de mal ~**: • **una mujer de mal ~** a loose woman • **gente de mal ~** undesirable people
vivisección (SF) vivisection
vivisector(a) (SM/F) vivisectionist
vivito (ADJ) • **estar ~ y coleando** to be alive and kicking
vivo/a (ADJ) **1** (= *con vida*) **a** [*persona, animal*] (*tras sustantivo*) living; (*tras verbo*) alive • **los seres ~s** living beings • **lo quemaron ~** he was burned alive • **"se busca vivo o muerto"** "wanted, dead or alive" • **venden los cebos ~s** they sell live bait
b [*piel*] raw • **tenía la piel en carne viva** his skin was raw • **me dio *o* hirió en lo más ~** it cut me to the quick • MODISMO: • **a lo ~**: • **le quitó la muela a lo ~** he just pulled the tooth clean out • **lo explica a lo ~** he explains it very expressively • **describir algo a lo ~** to describe sth very realistically; ▷ **cal, fuerza, lágrima, lengua**
2 (*TV, Radio*) • **en ~** (= *en directo*) live; (= *en persona*) in person • **una transmisión en ~ desde el estadio** a live broadcast from the stadium • **un espectáculo con música en ~** a live music show, a show with live music • **¿has visto en ~ a algún famoso?** have you ever seen anyone famous in the flesh?
3 (= *intenso*) [*descripción*] vivid, graphic; [*imaginación, mirada, ritmo*] lively; [*movimiento, paso*] quick, lively; [*color*] bright; [*sensación*] acute; [*genio*] ready; [*inteligencia*] sharp, keen; [*filo*] sharp • **su recuerdo siempre seguirá ~ entre nosotros** her memory will always be with us, her memory will live on in our minds

V

• MODISMO: • **ser la viva imagen** *o* **el ~ retrato de algn** to be the spitting image of sb; ▹ **rojo, voz**
4 [*persona*] (= *listo*) clever; (= *astuto*) sharp; (= *animado*) lively • **pasarse de ~** to be too clever by half*
SM/F **1*** (= *aprovechado*) • **es un ~** he's a clever one*, he's a sly one*
2 • **los ~s** the living
SM (*Cos*) edging, border

vizacha SF (*LAm*) (*Zool*) viscacha
vizcaíno/a ADJ of/from Biscay
SM/F native/inhabitant of Biscay • **los ~s** the people of Biscay
Vizcaya SF Biscay (*Spanish province*) • **el golfo de ~** the Bay of Biscay
vizcondado SM viscounty
vizconde SM viscount
vizcondesa SF viscountess
V.M. ABR = **Vuestra Majestad**
v.m.†† ABR (= **vuesa merced**) *courtesy formula*
V.O. ABR (*Cine*) = **versión original**
Vº.Bº. ABR (= **visto bueno**) OK
vocablo SM (*frm*) word, term • **jugar del ~** to pun, play on words
vocabulario SM vocabulary
vocación SF vocation, calling • **errar la ~** to miss one's vocation • **tener ~ por** to have a vocation for
vocacional ADJ vocational
SF (*Méx*) (*Educ*) technical college
vocal ADJ [*cuerdas*] vocal
SMF [*de comité, tribunal*] member; (= *director*) director, member of the board of directors; (= *portavoz*) chairperson
SF (*Ling*) vowel
vocalía SF committee
vocálico ADJ vocalic, vowel (*antes de s*)
vocalismo SM vowel system
vocalista SMF vocalist, singer
vocalizar ▹ CONJUG 1f VI **1** (= *pronunciar*) to vocalize
2 (*Mús*) (= *canturrear*) to hum; (= *hacer prácticas*) to sing scales, practise, practice (EEUU)
VPR **vocalizarse** to vocalize
vocalmente ADV vocally
vocativo SM vocative
voceado ADJ vaunted, much-trumpeted
voceador ADJ loud, loud-mouthed
SM **1** (= *pregonero*) town crier
2 (*LAm*) [*de periódicos*] news vendor, newspaper seller
vocear ▹ CONJUG 1a VT **1** [+ *mercancías*] to cry
2 (= *llamar*) to call loudly to, shout to
3 (= *dar vivas a*) to cheer, acclaim
4 [+ *secreto*] to shout to all and sundry, shout from the rooftops
5 (= *manifestar*) to proclaim • **su cara voceaba su culpabilidad** his face proclaimed his guilt
6* (= *jactarse*) to boast about, lay public claim to
VI to yell, bawl
vocejón SM loud voice, big voice
voceo SM shouting, yelling, bawling
voceras‡ SM INV loudmouth
vocería SF **1** (= *griterío*) shouting, yelling; (= *escándalo*) hullabaloo*, uproar
2 (*esp LAm*) (= *cargo*) position of spokesperson
vocerío SM = **vocería**
vocero/a SM/F (*esp LAm*) spokesman/spokeswoman, spokesperson
vociferación SF shouting
vociferador ADJ vociferous
vociferante ADJ vociferous
vociferar ▹ CONJUG 1a VT **1** (= *gritar*) to yell, shout
2 (= *jactarse*) to proclaim boastfully
VI to yell, shout, vociferate (*frm*)
vocinglería SF **1** (= *griterío*) shouting; (= *escándalo*) hubbub, uproar
2 (= *cualidad*) [*del vociferador*] loudness, noisiness; [*del hablador*] garrulousness
vocinglero ADJ **1** (= *vociferador*) loud-mouthed
2 (= *hablador*) garrulous
vodevil SM music hall, variety show *o* theatre, vaudeville (EEUU)
vodevilesco ADJ music-hall (*antes de s*), vandeville (*antes de s*) (EEUU)
vodka SM vodka
vodú SM (*LAm*) voodoo
voduísmo SM (*LAm*) voodooism
vol. ABR (= **volumen**) vol.
volada SF **1** (= *vuelo*) short flight, single flight
2 (*LAm*) (*diversos sentidos*) = **bolada**
voladizo ADJ (*Arquit*) projecting
volado ADJ **1** (*Tip*) superior, raised • **letra volada** *o* **voladita** superscript
2 • **estar ~*** (= *loco*) to be crazy*; (= *intranquilo*) to be worried; (= *drogado*) to be high*; (*Méx, Caribe*) (= *soñando*) to be in a dreamy state
3 (*Chile**) (= *despistado*) absent-minded
4 (*LAm**) (*de genio*) quick-tempered
5 (*Arquit*) [*balcón, cornisa*] projecting
SM **1** (*Méx*) (*con una moneda*) • **echar un ~** to toss a coin
2 (*Méx*) (= *aventura*) affair
3 (*CAm*) (= *mentira*) fib, lie
4 (*Caribe, Cono Sur*) (*Cos*) flounce
ADV (*And, CAm, Méx*) in a rush, hastily • **ir ~** to go off in a hurry
volador ADJ flying (*antes de s*)
SM **1** (= *pez*) flying fish; (= *calamar*) *species of squid*
2 (= *cohete*) rocket
3 (*And, CAm*) (= *molinillo*) toy windmill
4 (*Caribe*) (= *cometa*) kite
voladura SF **1** (= *derribo*) blowing up; (*Min*) blasting ▸ **voladura controlada** controlled explosion
2 (*Cos*) flounce, ruffle
volandas ADV **1** • **en ~** (= *por el aire*) through the air • **¡voy en ~!** (*hum*) I must fly!*
2* • **en ~** (= *con rapidez*) like lightning
volandera SF **1** (= *piedra*) millstone, grindstone
2 (*Mec*) washer
3* (= *mentira*) fib
volandero ADJ **1** [*pieza*] loose, shifting; [*cuerda, hoja*] loose; [*dolor*] that moves about
2 (= *al azar*) random, casual; (= *imprevisto*) unexpected
3 (*Orn*) fledged, ready to fly; [*persona*] restless
volanta SF **1** (*And, Caribe*) (= *rueda*) large wheel
2 (*Caribe*) (= *carro*) break
volantazo SM (*Aut*) sharp turn; (*fig*) sudden switch, sudden change of direction
volante ADJ **1** (= *volador*) flying
2 (= *itinerante*) [*estudio, sede*] travelling, traveling (EEUU); ▹ **meta**
3 (= *inquieto*) [*persona*] unsettled
SM **1** (*Aut*) steering wheel • **se puso un rato al ~** she took the wheel for a while • **ir al ~** to be at the wheel, be driving
2 (*Téc*) (*en motor*) flywheel; (*en reloj*) balance wheel
3 (*tb* **papel volante**) (= *nota*) note; (*LAm*) [*de propaganda*] pamphlet; ▹ **hoja**
4 (*Esp*) (*Med*) referral note • **me dieron un ~ para el oftalmólogo** I was referred to *o* I was given a referral to the ophthalmologist
5 (*Bádminton*) (= *pelota*) shuttlecock; (= *juego*) badminton
6 (*Cos*) flounce
SMF (*Chile*) **1** (*Ftbl*) (= *jugador*) winger
2 (= *conductor*) driver; [*de carreras*] racing driver
volantín ADJ loose, unattached
SM **1** (= *sedal*) fishing line
2 (*LAm*) (= *cometa*) kite
3 (*And*) (= *cohete*) rocket
4 (*LAm*) (= *voltereta*) somersault
volantista SM (*Aut*) driver; [*de carreras*] (racing) driver; (*pey*) road hog
volantón ADJ fledged, ready to fly
SM fledgling
volantusa SF (*LAm*) prostitute
volantuzo* SM (*And*) snappy dresser*
volapié SM (*Taur*) wounding thrust • **a ~** [*ave*] half walking and half flying
• MODISMO: • **de ~*** in a split second
volar ▹ CONJUG 1l VI **1** (= *en el aire*) [*avión, pájaro, persona*] to fly • **nunca he volado en helicóptero** I've never flown in *o* been in a helicopter • **¿a qué hora vuelas mañana?** what time is your flight tomorrow?, what time do you fly tomorrow? • **los papeles salieron volando por la ventana** the papers blew out of the window • **el balón pasó volando por encima de nosotros** the ball flew over our heads • **"vuela con Iberia"** "fly (with) Iberia" • **echar a ~** [+ *pájaro*] to set free, let go; [+ *globo, cometa*] to fly; [+ *noticia*] to spread • **echarse a ~** [*pájaro*] (*por primera vez*) to (begin to) fly; (= *levantar el vuelo*) to take off • **~ en globo** to balloon • **dejar ~ la imaginación** to let one's imagination run riot • MODISMOS: • **~ alto**: • **este joven escritor ~á alto** this young writer will go far • **ese político quiere ~ demasiado alto** that politician is too ambitious • **en su última novela vuela alto** in his latest novel he reaches new heights • **~ solo** to go it alone • **un sindicato que hoy vuela solo** a trade union which nowadays is going it alone • **empezó a ~ solo en su último libro** in his latest book he branched out on his own • **desde pequeño se le notaban las ganas de ~ solo** since he was a child you could see how much he wanted to do things his own way; ▹ **burro**
2 • **hacer ~ algo/a algn** to blow sth/sb up • **una bomba hizo ~ el automóvil** a bomb blew up the car • **el choque le hizo ~ por los aires a más de dos metros de la carretera** he was thrown more than two metres from the road by the impact • **hacer ~ algo en pedazos** to blow sth to pieces *o* to smithereens
3 • **volando: ¡venga, volando, que nos vamos!** come on, get a move on, we're going!* • **¡voy para allá volando!** I'll be right there!* • **me preparó la cena volando** he made my dinner in double-quick time* • **hice las maletas volando y me fui** I packed my bags as quick as I could and left* • **pasó volando en la moto** he whizzed *o* sped past on his motorbike • **el deportivo iba volando por la autopista** the sports car sped down the motorway • **~ a hacer algo** to rush to do sth • **voló a decírselo a todo el mundo** he rushed to tell everybody • **me voy volando a echar esta carta** I must rush to post this letter
4 (= *pasar rápido*) [*noticia*] to travel fast; [*tiempo*] to fly; [*días, semanas, meses*] to fly by • **las buenas noticias vuelan** good news travels fast • **¡cómo vuela el tiempo!** (how) time flies! • **los meses vuelan y pronto llegará el verano** the months are flying by and summer will soon be here
5* (= *desaparecer*) [*objeto, persona*] to go, disappear • **cuando me di cuenta, el bolso ya había volado** before I knew it, the bag was gone *o* had gone *o* had disappeared • **en una**

semana ~on las diez botellas the ten bottles went *o* disappeared in the space of a week • **cuando llegó la policía los ladrones ya habían volado** when the police arrived the robbers had vanished *o* disappeared • **el tabaco parece que vuela en esta casa** cigarettes seem to sprout legs in this house*
6 (*Arquit*) to stick out
7 (*Méx**) [*alcohol, diluyente*] to evaporate
8* (*con drogas*) to trip*, get high*
VT 1 (= *hacer volar*) [+ *cometa, globo*] to fly; (*Caza*) [+ *pájaro*] to flush out • **se pasa el día volando aviones de papel** he spends the day flying paper aeroplanes
2 (= *hacer explotar*) [+ *edificio, vehículo*] to blow up; [+ *caja fuerte*] to blow (open) • **~on la entrada de la mina** they blasted open the entrance to the mine • **le ~on la cabeza de un disparo** they blew his head off with one shot
3 (*Tip*) [+ *letra, número*] to put in superscript
4 (*Chile, Méx, Ven**) (= *robar*) to pinch*, nick*
5 (*LAm**) (= *irritar*) [+ *persona*] to irritate
6 (*CAm*) • MODISMOS: • **~ diente** to eat • **~ lengua** to talk, speak • **~ máquina** to type • **~ pata** to walk
VPR **volarse 1** (= *irse por el aire*) [*papel, paraguas*] to blow away; [*globo*] to fly away, fly off; [*sombrero*] to blow off • **se me ~on todos los papeles** all my papers blew away • **con el viento se me ha volado el paraguas** the wind has blown my umbrella away • **se le voló el sombrero** his hat blew off
2* (= *escaparse*) [*persona*] to run off • **el marido se voló con su amante** the husband ran off with his lover
3 (*LAm**) (= *desaparecer*) to go, disappear
4 (*LAm**) (= *enfadarse*) to lose one's temper, blow up*

volate SM 1 (*And*) (= *confusión*) confusion, mess
2 (*And*) (= *objetos*) lot of odd things
3 • **echar ~** (*Caribe**) (= *desesperarse*) to throw up one's hands in despair

volatería SF 1 (= *cetrería*) hawking, falconry
2 (*Orn*) (= *pájaros*) birds (*pl*), flock of birds; (= *aves*) fowls (*pl*)
3 (= *pensamientos*) random thoughts (*pl*), formless collection of ideas
4 (*And*) (= *fuegos artificiales*) fireworks (*pl*)

volatero SM (*And*) rocket

volátil ADJ 1 (*Quím*) volatile
2 [*carácter, situación*] volatile, changeable

volatilidad SF 1 (*Quím*) volatility, volatile nature
2 [*de carácter, situación*] volatility, changeableness

volatilizar ▷ CONJUG 1f VT (*Quím*) to volatilize
VPR **volatilizarse 1** (*Quím*) to volatilize
2 (= *esfumarse*) to vanish into thin air • **¡volatilízate!‡** get lost!‡

volatín SM 1 (= *acrobacia*) acrobatics (*pl*)
2 = volatinero

volatinero/a SM/F tightrope walker

volcado SM ▸ **volcado de memoria** (*Inform*) dump

volcán SM 1 (*Geog*) volcano • MODISMO: • **estar sobre un ~** to be sitting on top of a powder keg ▸ **volcán apagado** extinct volcano ▸ **volcán de lodo** mud volcano ▸ **volcán inactivo** dormant volcano
2 (*And, Cono Sur*) (= *torrente*) summer torrent; (= *avalancha*) avalanche
3 (*CAm*) (= *montón*) pile, heap • **un ~ de cosas** a lot of things, a whole heap of things
4 (*Caribe*) (= *estrépito*) deafening noise; (= *confusión*) confusion, hubbub

volcanada SF (*Cono Sur*) whiff

volcanarse ▷ CONJUG 1a VPR (*And*) to break down

volcánico ADJ volcanic

volcar ▷ CONJUG 1g, 1l VT 1 (= *tirar*) [+ *vaso*] to upset, knock over; [+ *contenido*] to empty out, tip out; [+ *carga*] to dump; [+ *coche, camión*] to overturn; [+ *barco*] to overturn, capsize
2 • **estar volcado a un cometido** to be dedicated to a task
3 • **~ a algn**† (= *marear*) to make sb dizzy, make sb's head swim; (= *convencer*) to force sb to change his mind
4† (= *irritar*) to irritate, exasperate; (= *desconcertar*) to upset; (= *embromar*) to tease
VI [*coche, camión*] to overturn
VPR **volcarse 1** (= *voltearse*) [*recipiente*] to be upset, get overturned; [*contenido*] to tip over; [*coche, camión*] to overturn; [*barco*] to capsize
2 (= *desvivirse*) to bend over backwards*, to go out of one's way • **~se para *o* por conseguir algo** to do one's utmost to get sth • **~se por complacer a algn** to bend over backwards to satisfy sb*
3 (= *entregarse*) • **~se en una actividad** to throw o.s. into an activity

volea SF volley • **media ~** half volley

volear ▷ CONJUG 1a VT, VI to volley • **~ por alto** to lob

voleibol SM volleyball

voleiplaya SM beach ball, beach volleyball

voleo SM 1 (= *volea*) volley • MODISMOS: • **de un ~** • **del primer ~** (= *rápidamente*) quickly; (= *bruscamente*) brusquely, suddenly; (= *de un golpe*) at one blow • **sembrar a *o* al ~** to scatter the seed • **repartir algo a *o* al ~** to distribute sth haphazardly
2* (= *golpe*) punch, bash*

volframio SM wolfram

Volga SM Volga

volibol SM volleyball

volición SF volition

volido SM (*LAm*) flight • **de un ~** quickly, at once

volitivo ADJ volitional, volitive • **capacidad volitiva** willpower

volován SM vol-au-vent

volqueta SF, **volquete** SM (*Aut*) dumper, dumping lorry, dump truck (*EEUU*); (= *carro*) tipcart

voltaico ADJ voltaic

voltaje SM voltage

voltario ADJ (*Cono Sur*) 1 (= *cambiable*) fickle, changeable
2 (= *voluntarioso*) wilful, headstrong
3 (= *pulcro*) spruce, dapper

volteada SF 1 (*Cono Sur*) (*Agr*) roundup
2 (*CAm, Cono Sur, Méx*) (*Pol*) defection

volteado SM 1 (= *volcado*) turn-over, turning over
2 (*And*) (*Mil*) deserter; (*Pol*) turncoat

volteador(a) SM/F acrobat

voltear ▷ CONJUG 1a VT 1 (*esp LAm*) (= *volver al revés*) to turn over, turn upside down; (= *dar la vuelta a*) to turn round; (= *lanzar al aire*) to toss
2 • **~ la espalda** (*LAm*) (= *dar la espalda*) to turn one's back
3 (*esp Cono Sur, Méx*) (= *volcar*) to knock, knock over
4 [+ *campanas*] to peal
5 (*esp LAm*) [+ *lazo*] to whirl, twirl
6 • **~ a algn** (*And, Caribe*) to force sb to change his mind
7 (*Caribe*) (= *buscar*) to search all over for
VI 1 (= *dar vueltas*) to roll over, go rolling over and over; (= *dar una voltereta*) to somersault
2 (*LAm*) (= *torcer*) to turn • **~ a la derecha** to turn right; (= *volverse*) to turn round
3 (*LAm*) • **~ a hacer algo** to do sth again • **volteó a decirlo** he said it again
4 (*Caribe‡*) • **volteó con mi amiga** he went off with my girlfriend
VPR **voltearse** (*LAm*) 1 (= *dar la vuelta*) to turn round; (*Pol*) (= *cambiar de lado*) to change one's allegiance, go over to the other side
2 (= *volcarse*) to overturn, tip over

voltereta SF (= *de acróbata, gimnasta*) (*hacia delante*) somersault; (*hacia los lados*) cartwheel; (*por caída*) roll, tumble • **dar ~s** (*hacia delante*) to turn somersaults; (*hacia los lados*) to do cartwheels ▸ **voltereta lateral** cartwheel ▸ **voltereta sobre las manos** handspring

voltímetro SM voltmeter

voltio SM 1 (*Fís*) volt
2* (= *vuelta, paseo*) stroll • **darse un ~** to go for *o* take a stroll

volubilidad SF (= *inconstancia*) fickleness, changeableness; (= *imprevisibilidad*) unpredictability; (= *inestabilidad*) instability

voluble ADJ 1 [*persona*] (= *inconstante*) fickle, changeable; (= *imprevisible*) erratic, unpredictable; (= *inestable*) unstable
2 (*Bot*) twining, climbing

volumen SM (PL: **volúmenes**) 1 [*de cuerpo*] volume • **el ~ de un líquido** the volume of a liquid • **cajas de gran ~** large *o* bulky boxes ▸ **volumen atómico** atomic volume ▸ **volumen molecular** molecular volume
2 [*de sonido*] volume • **bajar el ~** to turn the volume down • **subir el ~** to turn the volume up • **puso la radio a todo ~** he turned the radio full up
3 (*Com*) volume • **el ~ de las exportaciones** the volume of exports ▸ **volumen de contratación** trading volume ▸ **volumen de negocios, volumen de operaciones** turnover
4 (= *tomo*) volume
5 [*de cabello*] body • **esta espuma da ~ y brillo a su cabello** this foam gives your hair body and shine

volumétrico ADJ volumetric

voluminoso ADJ (*gen*) voluminous; [*paquete*] bulky

voluntad SF 1 (= *capacidad decisoria*) will • **no tiene ~ propia** he has no will of his own • **por ~ propia** of one's own volition *o* free will
2 (= *deseo*) wish • **su ~ es hacerse misionero** his wish is to become a missionary • **no lo dije con ~ de ofenderle** I did not say it with any wish to offend you, I had no desire to offend you • **última ~** last wish; (*Jur*) last will and testament • **lo hizo contra mi ~** he did it against my will • **tienen ~ de ganar** they have the will to win • **hágase tu ~** (*Rel*) Thy will be done • **por causas ajenas a mi ~** for reasons beyond my control • **hace siempre su santa ~** he always does exactly as he pleases ▸ **voluntad divina** divine will ▸ **voluntad popular** will of the people
3 (= *determinación*) (*tb* **fuerza de voluntad**) willpower • **le cuesta, pero tiene mucha ~** it's difficult for him, but he has a lot of willpower *o* a strong will • **no tiene ~ para dejar de beber** he hasn't the willpower to give up drinking • **es una chica con mucha ~** she's a very strong-willed girl • **hace falta ~ para escucharlo hasta el final** you need a strong will to listen to it right through ▸ **voluntad débil** weak will ▸ **voluntad de hierro, voluntad férrea** iron will
4 (= *disposición*) will • **buena ~**: • **lo solucionaremos con un poco de buena ~** with a bit of good will we'll find a solution

• **lo sugerí con buena ~** I suggested it with the best of intentions, I suggested it in good faith • **los hombres de buena ~** (*Rel*) men of goodwill • **mala ~**: • **hay muy mala ~ contra el presidente** there is a lot of ill will against the president • **MODISMO**: • **ganar(se) la ~ de algn** to win sb over
5 • **a ~** at will • **se abre a ~** it opens at will • **se puede beber a ~** you can drink as much as you like
6 • **la ~** (= *dinero*): • **un mendigo le pidió la ~** a beggar asked him if he could spare some money • **cada uno da la ~ para contribuir al regalo** everyone is free to contribute what they want towards the present • **—¿cuánto es? —la ~** "how much is it?" — "as much as you think it's worth"
7† (= *afecto*) fondness, affection • **tener ~ a algn** to be fond of sb, feel affection for sb
voluntariado (SM) (= *trabajo*) voluntary work; (= *trabajadores*) voluntary workers (*pl*)
voluntariamente (ADV) voluntarily
voluntariedad (SF) wilfulness, unreasonableness
voluntario/a (ADJ) **1** (= *no obligado*) voluntary
2 (*Mil*) voluntary; [*fuerza*] volunteer (*antes de s*)
(SM/F) volunteer • **alistarse** *u* **ofrecerse ~** to volunteer (**para** for)
voluntariosamente (ADV) **1** (= *con buenas intenciones*) dedicatedly, in a well-intentioned way
2 (= *tercamente*) wilfully
voluntarioso (ADJ) **1** (= *dedicado*) dedicated, willing
2 (= *terco*) headstrong, wilful, willful (*EEUU*)
voluntarismo (SM) (= *terquedad*) headstrong nature, wilfulness; (= *arbitrariedad*) arbitrariness
voluntarista (ADJ) (= *terco*) headstrong, wilful; (= *arbitrario*) arbitrary
voluptuosamente (ADV) voluptuously
voluptuosidad (SF) voluptuousness
voluptuoso/a (ADJ) voluptuous
(SM/F) voluptuary
voluta (SF) **1** (*Arquit*) scroll, volute
2 [*de humo*] spiral, column
volvedor (ADJ) (*And, Caribe*) • **este caballo es ~** this horse always finds its way home
(SM) **1** (= *llave inglesa*) wrench; (= *destornillador*) screwdriver
2 (*And*) (= *plus*) bonus, extra
volver ▷ CONJUG 2h (PP: **vuelto**) (VT) **1** (= *dar la vuelta a*) [+ *cabeza*] to turn; [+ *colchón, tortilla, enfermo*] to turn over; [+ *jersey, calcetín*] to turn inside out; [+ *página*] to turn, turn over • **~ la espalda** to turn away • **me volvió la espalda** he turned his back on me • **~ la esquina** to go round *o* turn the corner • **MODISMO**: • **tener a algn vuelto como un calcetín** *o* **una media** to have sb wrapped round one's little finger
2 (= *cambiar la orientación de*) to turn • **volvió el arma contra sí mismo** he turned the gun on himself • **~ la vista atrás** to look back • **~ los ojos al pasado** to look back • **volvieron los ojos a épocas más recientes** they looked to more recent times • **vuelve sus ojos ahora hacia uno de sus grandes compositores** she now turns to one of her favourite composers • **~ el pensamiento a Dios** to turn one's thoughts to God • **~ la proa al viento** to turn the bow into the wind
3* (= *devolver*) [+ *compra*] to return; [+ *comida*] to bring up; [+ *imagen*] to reflect; [+ *objeto lanzado*] to send back, return; [+ *visita*] to return • **~ algo a su lugar** to return sth to its place, put sth back (in its place) • **~ la casa a su estado original** to return *o* restore the house to its original condition • **~ bien por mal** to return good for evil
4 (= *enrollar*) [+ *manga*] to roll up
5 (+ *adj*) to make • **el accidente lo volvió inservible** the accident left it useless • **el ácido lo vuelve azul** the acid turns it blue, the acid makes it go blue • **vuelve fieras a los hombres** it turns men into wild beasts • **~ loco a algn** to drive sb mad
6 (*Ling*) to translate (**a** into)
(VI) **1** (= *regresar*) (*a donde se está*) to come back, return; (*a donde se estaba*) to go back, return (**a** to, **de** from) • **déjalas aquí y luego vuelves a por ellas** leave them here and come back for them later • **~ victorioso** to come back victorious, return in triumph • **no he vuelto por allí** I've never gone back there • **volvió muy cansado** he got back very tired • **volviendo a lo que decía** ... going back *o* returning to what I was saying ... • **~ atrás** to go back, turn back • **~ a una costumbre** to revert to a habit
2 • **~ a hacer algo** to do sth again • **~ a empezar** to start (over) again • **me he vuelto a equivocar** I've made a mistake again, I've made another mistake • **he vuelto a salir con ella** I've started going out with her again • **volvió a casarse** she remarried, she (got) married again • **volví a poner en marcha el motor** I restarted the engine • **~ a hacerlo** to redo it • **~ a pintar algo** to repaint sth
3 • **~ en sí** to come to, come round • **~ sobre sí** to change one's mind
4 [*camino*] to turn (**a** to)
(VPR) **volverse 1** (= *darse la vuelta*) **a** [*persona*] to turn, turn round • **se volvió a mí** he turned to me • **se volvió para mirarlo** he turned (round) to look at it • **~se atrás** (*en camino*) to turn back; (*en decisión*) to back out; (*en negociaciones*) to withdraw • **a última hora se han vuelto atrás** they pulled out *o* backed out at the last minute • **si pudiese ~me atrás en el tiempo** ... if I could go back in time ...
b [*objeto*] (*boca abajo*) to turn upside down; (*de dentro a fuera*) to turn inside out • **se le volvió el paraguas** his umbrella turned inside out • **MODISMO**: • **~se (en) contra (de) algn** to turn against sb • **todo se le vuelve en contra** everything is turning against him • **todo se le vuelven dificultades** troubles come thick and fast for him
2 (= *regresar*) to turn back, go back • **empezó a llover y nos volvimos** it started to rain and we turned back • **vuélvete a buscarlo** go back and look for it
3 (+ *adj*) • **se ha vuelto muy cariñoso** he's become very affectionate • **en el ácido se vuelve más oscuro** it turns *o* goes darker in the acid • **~se loco** to go mad
4 [*leche*] to go off, turn sour
vomitado (ADJ) [*persona*] sickly
vomitar ▷ CONJUG 1a (VT) **1** (= *devolver*) to vomit, bring up • **~ sangre** to spit blood
2 [+ *humo, llamas*] to belch, belch forth; [+ *lava*] to spew; [+ *injurias*] to hurl (**contra** at)
3 [+ *secreto*] to tell reluctantly, finally come out with; [+ *ganancias*] to disgorge, shed
(VI) **1** (= *devolver*) to vomit, be sick
2 (*fig*) • **eso me da ganas de ~** that makes me sick, that makes me want to puke*
vomitera (SF), **vomitina** (SF) vomiting, retching
vomitivo (ADJ) **1** (*Med*) emetic
2 (*fig*) disgusting; [*chiste*] sick-making, repulsive
(SM) **1** (*Med*) emetic
2 (*Cono Sur*) (= *fastidio*) nuisance, bore
vómito (SM) **1** (= *acto*) vomiting, being sick
▸ **vómito de sangre** spitting of blood
2 (= *materia*) vomit, sick
3 (*LAm*) ▸ **vómito negro** yellow fever
vomitona* (SF) bad turn*
vomitorio (SM) vomitorium, vomitory
voquible (SM) (*hum*) word
voracear ▷ CONJUG 1a (VT) (*Cono Sur*) to challenge in a loud voice
voracidad (SF) voracity, voraciousness
vorágine (SF) [*de mar, río*] whirlpool, vortex, maelstrom (*frm*); [*de odio, destrucción, confusión*] maelstrom; [*de actividad, publicidad*] whirl
voraz (ADJ) **1** (= *devorador*) voracious, ravenous; (*pey*) greedy
2 [*fuego*] raging, fierce
3 (*Méx*) (= *audaz*) bold
vorazmente (ADV) (*gen*) voraciously, ravenously; (*pey*) greedily
vórtice (SM) **1** (= *remolino*) [*de agua*] whirlpool, vortex; [*de viento*] whirlwind
2 [*de ciclón*] eye
vos* (PRON PERS) **1** (*esp Cono Sur**) you (*sing*)
2†† you, ye††
vosear* ▷ CONJUG 1a (VT) (*esp Cono Sur*) to address as "vos"
voseo* (SM) (*esp Cono Sur*) *addressing a person as "vos", the familiar usage*
Vosgos (SMPL) Vosges
vosotros/as (PRON) (*esp Esp*) **1** (*sujeto*) you (*familiar form of address*) • **~ vendréis conmigo** you'll come with me • **hacedlo ~ mismos** do it yourselves
2 (*después de prep, en comparaciones*) you • **lo he comprado para ~** I've bought it for you • **¿no pedís nada para ~?** aren't you going to ask for anything for yourselves? • **lo han hecho mejor que vosotras** they've done it better than you • **irán sin ~** they'll go without you
votación (SF) (= *acto*) voting; (= *votos*) ballot, vote • **por ~ popular** by popular vote • **por ~ secreta** by secret ballot • **someter algo a ~** to put sth to the vote, take a vote on sth • **la ~ ha sido nutrida** voting has been busy
▸ **votación a mano alzada** show of hands
▸ **votación por poder** voting by proxy
▸ **votación táctica** tactical voting
▸ **votación unánime** unanimous vote
votante (ADJ) voting
(SMF) voter
votar ▷ CONJUG 1a (VT) **1** (*Pol*) [+ *candidato, partido*] to vote for; [+ *moción, proyecto de ley*] to pass, approve (by vote) • **Pérez fue el más votado** Pérez received the highest number of votes, Pérez got most votes
2 (*Rel*) to vow, promise (**a** to)
(VI) **1** (*Pol*) to vote (**por** for)
2 (*Rel*) to vow, take a vow
3 (= *echar pestes*) to curse, swear
votivo (ADJ) votive
voto (SM) **1** (*Pol*) vote • **dar su ~** to cast one's vote, give one's vote (a for) • **emitir su ~** to cast one's vote • **ganar por siete ~s** to win by seven votes • **hubo 13 ~s a favor y 11 en contra** there were 13 votes for and 11 against • **tener ~** to have a vote ▸ **voto afirmativo** vote in favour ▸ **voto bloque** block vote ▸ **voto cautivo** captive vote ▸ **voto de calidad** casting vote ▸ **voto de castigo** protest vote ▸ **voto de censura** vote of censure, vote of no confidence ▸ **voto decisivo** casting vote ▸ **voto de conciencia** free vote ▸ **voto de confianza** vote of confidence ▸ **voto de desconfianza** vote of no confidence ▸ **voto de gracias** vote of thanks ▸ **voto de los indecisos** floating vote ▸ **voto en blanco** blank vote ▸ **voto fluctuante** floating vote ▸ **voto grupo** card vote ▸ **voto nulo** spoiled ballot paper ▸ **voto por correo** postal vote ▸ **voto secreto** secret vote, secret ballot
2 (*Rel*) (= *promesa*) vow; (= *ofrenda*) ex voto

• **hacer ~ de** (+ *infin*) to take a vow to (+ *infin*) ▸ **voto de castidad** vow of chastity ▸ **voto de obediencia** vow of obedience ▸ **voto de pobreza** vow of poverty ▸ **voto de silencio** vow of silence ▸ **votos monásticos** monastic vows
3 (= *juramento*) oath, curse; (= *palabrota*) swearword
4 votos (= *deseos*) wishes, good wishes • **hacer ~s por el restablecimiento de algn** to wish sb a quick recovery, hope that sb will get well soon • **hago ~s para que se remedie pronto** I pray that it will be speedily put right, I earnestly hope that something will soon be done about it • **mis mejores ~s por su éxito** my best wishes for its success

vox populi ADJ vox populi • **ser ~** to become common knowledge

voy ▹ **ir**

voyeur [bo'jer] SM voyeur

voyeurismo [boje'rismo] SM voyeurism

voyeurista ADJ voyeuristic

vóytelas EXCL (*Méx*) wow!*

voz SF **1** (= *sonido humano*) voice • **con la voz entrecortada** *o* **empañada** in a voice choked with emotion • **me temblaba la voz** my voice was trembling *o* shaking • **aclararse la voz** to clear one's throat • **ahuecar la voz** to deepen one's voice • **en voz alta** (= *de forma audible*) aloud, out loud; (= *con tono potente*) loudly • **leyó el poema en voz alta** he read the poem aloud *o* out loud • **soñar en voz alta** to think aloud *o* out loud • **¿me lo puedes repetir en voz alta?** can you say that again louder? • **en voz baja** in a low voice, in a whisper • **me lo dijo en voz baja** she whispered it to me, she told me in a whisper *o* in a low voice • **algunos comentaban, en voz baja, que sería mejor que dimitiera** some were whispering that it would be best if he resigned • **le canta en voz baja para que se duerma** he sings softly to her to put her to sleep • **está empezando a cambiar** *o* **mudar la voz** his voice is beginning to break • **forzar la voz** to strain one's voice • **a media voz** in a whisper • **estábamos hablando a media voz en la oscuridad** we were whispering in the dark • **perder la voz** • **quedarse sin voz** (*temporalmente*) to lose one's voice; (*definitivamente*) to lose the power of speech • **tener la voz tomada** to be hoarse • **a una voz** with one voice • **de viva voz** aloud • **la votación se realizó de viva voz** people voted aloud • **me lo dijo de viva voz** he told me himself *o* personally *o* in person • **MODISMOS**: • **decir algo a voz en cuello** *o* **a voz en grito** to shout sth at the top of one's voice • **ser la voz de su amo** to speak with one's master's voice ▸ **voz argentina** silvery voice ▸ **voz en off** (*TV, Cine*) voice-over ▸ **voz humana** human voice; ▹ **anudar, desanudar, levantar, torrente**
2 (*Mús*) **a** (= *sonido*) [*de instrumento*] sound • **la voz del órgano** the sound *o* (*liter*) the strains of the organ
b (= *persona*) voice • **canción a cuatro voces** song for four voices, four-part song • **cantar a dos voces** to sing a duet • **llevar la voz cantante** (*en un grupo de pop, rock*) to be the lead singer; (*en un concierto clásico*) to be the lead soprano/tenor *etc*; (*fig*) to call the tune
c (= *habilidad para el canto*) voice • **tiene muy buena voz** she has a very good voice • **estar en voz** to be in good voice
3 (= *aviso*) voice • **la voz de la conciencia** the promptings *o* voice of conscience • **hay que escuchar también la voz del corazón** you must listen to your heart as well • **dar la voz de alarma** to raise the alarm • **los consumidores han dado la voz de alarma** consumers have raised the alarm • **dar una voz a algn** to give sb a shout • **cuando hayas terminado, dame una voz** give me a shout when you've finished* ▸ **voz de mando** (*Mil*) command • **formaron a la voz de mando** they lined up at the command • **Patricia parece llevar la voz de mando en este asunto** Patricia is the boss when it comes to this matter
4 (= *rumor*) rumour, rumor (*EEUU*) • **circula** *o* **corre la voz de que ...** there is a rumour going round that ..., the word is that ... • **hacer circular** *o* **correr la voz de que ...** to spread the rumour *o* word that ... ▸ **voz común** hearsay, gossip
5 (*Pol*) (= *opinión*) voice • **la voz del pueblo** the voice of the people • **tener voz y voto** to have full voting rights • **miembro con voz y voto** full member • **nosotros no tenemos ni voz ni voto en este asunto** we have no say whatsoever in this matter • **MODISMO**: • **no tener voz en capítulo** to have no say in a matter ▸ **voz pública** public opinion • **sus equivocaciones no suelen salir a la voz pública** their mistakes are never made public
6 voces (= *gritos*) shouting (*sing*) • **se oían voces a lo lejos** there was shouting in the distance • **a voces**: • **discutir a voces** to argue noisily *o* loudly • **estuve llamando a voces pero no me abrieron la puerta** I called out *o* shouted but they didn't open the door • **su boda es un secreto a voces** their marriage is a well-known secret • **dar** *o* **pegar voces** to shout • **MODISMO**: • **dar cuatro voces a algn** to take sb to task; ▹ **pedir**
7 (*en el juego*) call
8 (*Ling*) **a** (= *vocablo*) word • **una voz de origen árabe** a word of Arabic origin
b [*del verbo*] voice ▸ **voz activa** active voice ▸ **voz media** middle voice ▸ **voz pasiva** passive voice

vozarrón SM booming voice

VP ABR (= **Vice-Presidente**) V.P.

VPO SF ABR = **vivienda de protección oficial**

vra. ABR = **vuestra**

vro. ABR = **vuestro**

vs. ABR (= **versus**) vs

vto. ABR (*Com*) = **vencimiento**

vudú SM voodoo

vuduísmo SM voodooism

vuela *etc* ▹ **volar**

vuelapluma • **a ~** ADV quickly, without much thought

vuelco SM **1** (= *acción*) upset, spill • **dar un ~** [*coche*] to overturn; [*barco*] to capsize
2 • **mi corazón dio un ~** my heart missed a beat
3 (*fig*) catastrophe • **este negocio va a dar un ~** this business is heading for catastrophe

vuelillo SM lace adornment, frill

vuelo[1] ▹ **volar**

vuelo[2] SM **1** [*de ave, avión*] flight • **se servirá un desayuno durante el ~** breakfast will be served during the flight • **alzar** *o* **levantar el ~** (= *echar a volar*) to fly off; (= *marcharse*) to dash off; (= *independizarse*) to leave the nest • **remontar el ~**: **la cigüeña remontó el ~** the stork soared (up) into the sky, the stork took the sky • **la economía empieza a remontar el ~** the economy is beginning to take off • **MODISMOS**: • **captar** *o* **cazar** *o* **coger algo al ~** to be quick to understand sth • **cazarlas al ~** to be quick on the uptake* • **de** *o* **en un ~** rapidly • **no se oía ni el ~ de una mosca** you could have heard a pin drop • **tomar ~** to grow, develop ▸ **vuelo a baja cota** low-level flying ▸ **vuelo a vela** gliding ▸ **vuelo chárter** charter flight ▸ **vuelo con ala delta** hang-gliding ▸ **vuelo con motor** powered flight ▸ **vuelo de bajo coste** low-cost flight ▸ **vuelo de demostración** demonstration flight ▸ **vuelo de instrucción** training flight ▸ **vuelo de órbita** orbital flight ▸ **vuelo de prueba(s)** test flight ▸ **vuelo de reconocimiento** reconnaissance flight ▸ **vuelo directo** direct flight, non-stop flight ▸ **vuelo en picado** dive ▸ **vuelo espacial** space flight ▸ **vuelo interior** internal flight, domestic flight ▸ **vuelo libre** hang-gliding ▸ **vuelo nacional** domestic flight ▸ **vuelo rasante** low-level flying ▸ **vuelo regular** scheduled flight ▸ **vuelo sin escalas, vuelo sin etapas** non-stop flight ▸ **vuelo sin motor** gliding
2 (*Orn*) (= *plumas*) flight feathers (*pl*); (= *alas*) wings (*pl*) • **tirar al ~** to shoot at birds on the wing • **MODISMOS**: • **cortar los ~s a algn** to clip sb's wings • **de altos ~s** [*plan*] important; [*ejecutivo*] high-flying
3 [*de falda, capa*] • **el ~ de la falda** the spread *o* swirl of the skirt • **falda de mucho ~** full *o* wide skirt
4 (*Arquit*) projection

vuelta

SUSTANTIVO FEMENINO

1 (= *giro*) • **una ~ de la tierra** one revolution of the earth • **el documento dio la ~ por toda la oficina** the document went all round the office • **¡media ~!** (*Mil*) about turn!, about face! (*EEUU*) • **los soldados dieron media ~** the soldiers did an about-turn *o* (*EEUU*) an about-face • **estaba cerrado y tuvimos que darnos media ~** it was closed so we had to turn round and go back • **la ~ al mundo** (= *viaje*) a round-the-world trip • **quiere dar la ~ al mundo** she wants to go round the world ▸ **vuelta al ruedo** (*Taur*) *circuit of the ring made by a triumphant bullfighter* • **dar la ~ al ruedo** to go round the ring ▸ **vuelta atrás** backward step ▸ **vuelta de campana** • **el coche dio una ~ de campana en el aire** the car turned right over in mid-air ▸ **vuelta de tuerca** turn of the screw ▸ **vuelta en redondo** complete turn
dar la vuelta (= *volverse*) to turn round • **al final del callejón tienes que dar la ~** you'll have to turn round at the end of the street • **dar la ~ a** [+ *llave, manivela*] to turn; [+ *página*] to turn (over)
dar vueltas • **el camión dio dos ~s y cayó boca abajo** the lorry turned over twice and landed upside down • **dar ~s sobre un eje** to turn on *o* spin round an axis • **he estado dando ~s en la cama toda la noche** I've been tossing and turning (in bed) all night • **el avión dio ~s y más ~s antes de aterrizar** the plane circled round and round before landing • **he tenido que dar muchas ~s para encontrarlo** I had to go all over the place to find it • **dar ~s alrededor de un planeta** to go *o* revolve round a planet
dar vueltas a algo • **el cinturón le daba dos ~s a la cintura** the belt went twice round her waist • **le dimos tres ~s al parque corriendo** we ran three times round the park
darle vueltas a algn • **me da ~s la cabeza** my head is spinning • **estaba mareado y todo me daba ~s** I was dizzy and everything was going *o* spinning round
darse la vuelta (*de pie*) to turn round; (*tumbado*) to turn over • **date la ~ para que te pueda peinar** turn round so I can do your hair • **me di la ~ porque me estaba**

quemando la espalda I turned over because my back was getting burnt
2 (*= otro lado*) [*de hoja*] back, other side; [*de tela*] wrong side • **a la ~ de la página** on the next page, overleaf • **lo escribió a la ~ del sobre** he wrote it on the back of the envelope • **dar la ~ a** [*+ disco*] to turn over • **dale la ~ al jersey** (*= ponlo del derecho*) turn the jumper the right way out; (*= ponlo del revés*) turn the jumper inside out • **dale la ~ al vaso** (*= ponlo boca arriba*) turn the glass the right way up; (*= ponlo boca abajo*) turn the glass upside down • **a la ~ de la esquina** around the corner • **la tienda está a la ~ de la esquina** the shop is just around the corner • **las elecciones están ya a la ~ de la esquina** the elections are almost upon us *o* just around the corner
3 (*= regreso*) **a** (*= acción*) • **¿para cuándo tenéis prevista la ~?** when do you expect to be back? • **¡hasta la ~!** see you when I/you get back • **este acuerdo supone una ~ a la normalidad** the agreement means that things should get back to normal • **la ~ al colegio** (*en septiembre*) the new school year • **"~ al colegio"** "back to school" • **a ~ de correo** by return (of post) • **de ~** on the way back • **de ~, iremos a verlos** we'll go and see them on the way back • **de ~ al trabajo** back to work • **estar de ~** (*lit*) to be back • **estaremos de ~ el domingo** we'll be back on Sunday • **¿meterme en política? a mi edad uno ya está de ~ de todo** go into politics? I'm too old for that sort of thing • **el público ya está de ~ de todo** the public has seen it all before
b (*en transportes*) • **si cierras la ~ el billete sale más barato** the ticket is cheaper if you specify the return date • **billete de ida y ~** return ticket • **el viaje de ~** the return journey
4 (*= paseo*) (*a pie*) stroll; (*en coche, bicicleta*) ride • **dar una ~**: • **dimos una ~ por el parque** we went for a stroll in the park • **después de estudiar me voy a dar una ~** I'm going out for a bit when I've finished studying • **salieron a dar una ~ en la bici** they went out for a ride on their bikes • **nos dio una ~ en su coche** he gave us a ride in his car, he took us for a spin in his car* • **si quieres ver pobreza date una ~ por esta zona** if you want to see poverty take a walk round here
5 (*en camino, ruta*) • **una carretera con muchas ~s** a road with lots of bends *o* twists and turns in it • **el camino da muchas ~s hasta llegar a la cima** the road twists and turns up to the summit • **por este camino se da mucha más ~** it's much further this way, this is a much longer way round
6 (*a un circuito, pista*) lap; (*Golf*) round • **di tres ~s a la pista** I did three laps of the track
▸ **vuelta de honor** lap of honour
7 (*Ciclismo*) tour ▸ **vuelta ciclista** cycle tour • **la ~ ciclista a España** the Tour of Spain
8 (*= ronda*) [*de elección, torneo, bebidas*] round • **el presidente ganó en la segunda ~** the president won in the second round • **la segunda ~ de la competición** the second round of the competition • **partido de ~** return match • **me tocó pagar la primera ~** I had to pay the first round
9 (*= dinero suelto*) change • **quédese con la ~** keep the change
10 (*= cambio*) • **las ~s de la vida** the ups and downs of life • **este acontecimiento dio la ~ a las negociaciones** this event changed the direction of the talks completely
11 (*= cabo, fin*) • **a la ~ de tres años** after three years
12 (*de cuerda*) loop ▸ **vuelta de cabo** (*Náut*) hitch
13 (*Cos*) [*de puntos*] row; [*de pantalón*] turn-up, cuff (*EEUU*)
14 • **MODISMOS**: • **a ~s con algo**: • **¡ya estamos otra vez a ~s con la guerra!** not the war again! • **siempre están a ~s con lo mismo** they're always going on about the same thing • **buscar las ~s a algn** to try to catch sb out • **dar cien (mil) ~s a algn***: • **te da cien (mil) ~s** she can run rings round you, she's miles better than you • **dar la ~ a algn** (*CAm**) to con sb* • **darle ~s a algo**: • **darle ~s a un asunto** to think a matter over • **no le des más ~s a lo que dijo** stop worrying about what he said • **no tiene ~ de hoja**: • **esto es así y no tiene más ~ de hoja** that's how it is and that's all there is to it • **tenemos que hacerlo ya y no hay más ~ de hoja** we've got to do it now, there are no two ways about it *o* there's no alternative • **poner a algn de ~ y media*** (*= insultar*) to lay into sb; (*= reprender*) to give sb a dressing-down* • **sacar la ~ a algn** (*And*) to cuckold sb • **dar la ~ a la tortilla** to change things completely

vueltero (ADJ) (*Cono Sur*) [*persona*] difficult
vueltita* (SF) (*LAm*) (short) stroll *o* walk; (*en coche*) (short) drive
vuelto (PP) *de* **volver**
(SM) (*LAm*) = **vuelta**
vuelva *etc* ▹ **volver**
vuestro/a (*esp Esp*) (ADJ POSES) your (*familiar form of address*); (*después de sustantivo*) of yours • **~ perro** your dog • **~s hijos** your children • **una idea vuestra** an idea of yours, one of your ideas • **un amigo ~** a friend of yours
(PRON POSES) yours (*familiar form of address*) • **—¿de quién es esto? —es ~** "whose is this?" — "it's yours" • **este es el ~** this one's yours • **la vuestra está en el jardín** yours is in the garden • **mis amigos y los ~s** my friends and yours • **¡ánimo, esta es la vuestra!** come on, this is your big chance! • **lo ~**: • **lo ~ también le pertenece a ella** what is yours also belongs to her • **he puesto lo ~ en la caja** I have put your things in the box • **¿ya se han enterado de lo ~?** do they know about you two yet? • **lo ~ es jugar al fútbol** playing football is your thing* • **los ~s** (*= vuestra familia*) your folks*; (*= vuestro equipo*) your lot*, your side • **es (uno) de los ~s** he's one of you
vulcanita (SF) vulcanite
vulcanización (SF) vulcanization
vulcanizadora (SF) (*Chile, Méx*) tyre *o* (*EEUU*) tire repair shop
vulcanizar ▹ CONJUG 1f (VT) to vulcanize
Vulcano (SM) Vulcan
vulcanología (SF) vulcanology
vulcanólogo/a (SM/F) vulcanologist
vulgar (ADJ) **1** (*= no refinado*) [*lengua, gusto, vestido*] vulgar; [*modales, rasgos*] coarse
2 (*= común, corriente*) [*persona, físico*] ordinary, common; [*suceso, vida*] ordinary, everyday • **~ y corriente** ordinary • **el hombre ~** the ordinary man, the common man
3 (*= no técnico*) common • **"glóbulo blanco" es el nombre ~ del leucocito** "white blood cell" is the common name for leucocyte
vulgaridad (SF) **1** (*= cualidad*) vulgarity, coarseness
2 (*= frase*) vulgar *o* coarse expression
3 vulgaridades (*= trivialidades*) banalities, platitudes; (*= necedades*) inanities
vulgarismo (SM) vulgarism
vulgarización (SF) **1** (*= popularización*) popularization • **obra de ~** popular work
2 (*Ling*) translation into the vernacular
vulgarizar ▹ CONJUG 1f (VT) **1** (*= hacer popular*) to popularize
2 (*Ling*) to translate into the vernacular
vulgarmente (ADV) commonly, ordinarily; (*pey*) vulgarly • **los nevus, ~ llamados "lunares"** naevi, commonly *o* popularly known as "moles"
Vulgata (SF) Vulgate
vulgo (SM) common people; (*pey*) lower orders (*pl*), common herd
(ADV) • **el mingitorio, ~ "meadero"** the urinal, commonly *o* popularly known as the "bog"
vulnerabilidad (SF) vulnerability
vulnerable (ADJ) vulnerable (**a** to)
vulneración (SF) infringement, contravention
vulnerar ▹ CONJUG 1a (VT) **1** (*= perjudicar*) [*+ fama*] to damage, harm; [*+ costumbre, derechos*] to interfere with, affect seriously
2 (*Jur, Com*) to violate, break
vulpeja (SF) vixen
vulpino (ADJ) (*Zool*) vulpine; (*fig*) foxy
vulva (SF) vulva

Ww

W, w ['uβe 'doβle], (*LAm*) ['doβle be] SF (= *letra*) W, w
W ABR, **w** ABR (= **vatio**) w
wachimán SM (*LAm*) = **guachimán**
wagneriano ADJ Wagnerian
walkie ['walki] SM, **walky** ['walki] SM walkie-talkie
walki-talki [walki'talki] SM walkie-talkie
Walkman® ['walkman] SM Walkman®
walquiria [bal'kirja] SF Valkyrie
wamba® ['bamba] SF plimsoll, sneaker (*EEUU*)
WAP ADJ WAP
SM WAP ▸ **teléfono WAP** WAP phone
wasap* SM (PL: **wasaps**) WhatsApp®, WhatsApp® message
wasapear* ▸ conjug 1a VI to be on Whatsapp®
VT to whatsapp
wat SM, **watt** SM [bat, wat] (PL: **wats, watts**) watt
wáter ['bater] SM toilet, lavatory
waterpolista SMF water polo player
waterpolo SM water polo
web SM O SF (= *página*) website; (= *red*) (World Wide) Web ▸ **web site** website
webcam [web'kam] SF webcam
webinario SM webinar
weblog ['weblog] SM (PL: **weblogs**) (*Inform*) weblog
webmaster ['webmaster, web'master] SMF webmaster
webring SM (*Inform*) web ring
wedge [weʒ] SM wedge
welter SM, **wélter** SM ['belter] welterweight
western SM western
whiskería SF bar (*specializing in whisky*)
whisky SM, **whiskey** SM ['wiski, 'gwiski] whisky, whiskey ▸ **whisky de malta** malt whisky
wi-fi ADJ, SM wi-fi
wikén SM (*Chile*) weekend
Winchester SM • **disco ~** Winchester disk
windsurf ['winsurf] SM windsurfing • **hacer ~** to go windsurfing
windsurfista [winsur'fista] SMF windsurfer
wisquería SF bar (*specializing in whisky*)
wok SM wok
wolfram ['bolfram] SM, **wolframio** [bol'framjo] SM wolfram
wonderbra® SM, **wonderbrá** SM Wonderbra®

Xx

X, x ['ekis] (SF) (= *letra*) X, x
xantofila (SF) xanthophyll
XDG (SF ABR) (*Esp*) (*Pol*) = **Xunta Democrática de Galicia**
xeno (SM) xenon
xenofilia (SF) xenophilia
xenófilo/a (ADJ) xenophilic
(SM/F) xenophile
xenofobia (SF) xenophobia
xenófobo/a (ADJ) xenophobic
(SM/F) xenophobe
xenón (SM) xenon
xenotransplante (SM) xenograft, xenotransplant
xerocopia (SF) photocopy
xerocopiar ▸ CONJUG 1b (VT) to photocopy
xerófito (ADJ) xerophytic
xerografía (SF) xerography
xerografiar ▸ CONJUG 1b (VT) to xerograph
xilófono (SM) xylophone
xilografía (SF) **1** (= *arte*) xylography
2 (= *impresión*) xylograph, wood engraving
xilográfico (ADJ) xylographic
Xto. (ABR) = **Cristo**
Xunta (SF) *Galician autonomous government*

Yy

Y, y [i'ɣrjeɣa] SF (= *letra*) Y, y

y CONJ **1** (*uso copulativo*) and • **fuimos a Málaga y a Granada** we went to Malaga and Granada • **una isla exótica y de gran belleza** an exotic, tremendously beautiful island • **treinta y uno** thirty-one • **un kilo y cuarto** one and a quarter kilos

2 (*al comienzo de una pregunta*) • **—ya ha llegado el primer grupo —¿y los demás?** "the first group has already arrived" — "(and) what about the others?" • **a mí no me apetece ir, ¿y a ti?** I don't feel like going, what about you? • **—id vosotros —¿y tú, qué vas a hacer?** "you go" — "but what are you going to do?" • **¿y Max? no lo veo por ninguna parte** where's Max? I can't see him anywhere • **—he decidido dejar de estudiar —¿y eso?** "I've decided to stop studying" — "why's that then?" • **¿y qué?** (*con desinterés, desprecio*) so (what)?; (*con interés*) and? • **no, no me han aceptado, ¿y qué?** they haven't accepted me, who cares *o* so what? • **—ya tengo las notas —¿y qué?, ¿has aprobado?** "I've just got the marks" — "and, did you pass?"

3 (*uso adversativo*) • **¡él viviendo en una mansión y su hermano en la calle!** he's living in a mansion while his brother's on the streets! • **¿dices que no quieres tarta y te la comes entera?** you say you don't want any cake and then you eat a whole one?

4 (*esp LAm*) (*en repetición*) • **estuvo llora y llora** he was crying and crying

5 (*esp Arg, Uru*) (*en respuestas*) • **—lo lamento mucho —y bueno, habrá que aceptarlo** "I'm very sorry" — "well, we just have to accept it"

ya ADV **1** (*con acción pasada*) already • **lo hemos visto ya** we've seen it already • **ya han dado las diez** it's past ten already • **¿ya has terminado?** have you finished already? • **¿ya habías estado antes en Valencia?** had you been to Valencia before? • **ya me lo suponía** I thought as much • **ya se acabó** it's all over now • **ya en el siglo X** as early as the tenth century

2 (*con verbo en presente*) **a** (*con una acción esperada*) • **ya es la hora** time's up • **ya es hora de irnos** it's time for us to go now • **ya está aquí** he's here already • **ya viene el autobús** here's the bus • **ya puedes irte** you can go now • **ya podéis ir pasando al comedor** you can start going through into the dining room now • **estos zapatos ya me están pequeños** these shoes are too small for me now • **¿ya anda?** is she walking yet?

b (*expresando sorpresa*) • **¿ya te vas?** are you leaving already?

c (= *ahora*) now • **lo quiero ya** I want it (right) now • **¡cállate ya!** oh, shut up! • **¡ya voy!** coming! • **desde ya (mismo)** (*Esp*): • **lo que quiero es empezar desde ya** I want to start right now *o* away • **una estrategia que empiezo a poner en marcha desde ya mismo** a strategy which I will start to adopt as of now *o* as of this very moment • **ya mismo** (*esp Cono Sur**) (= *en seguida*) at once; (= *claro*) of course, naturally

3 (*con acción futura*) • **ya te llegará el turno a ti** you'll get your turn • **ya lo arreglarán** it'll get fixed sometime • **ya iré cuando pueda** I'll try and make it when I can • **ya verás como todo se arregla** it'll all work out, don't you worry • **ya veremos** we'll see (about that)

4 • **ya no** not any more, no longer • **ya no vive aquí** he doesn't live here any more, he no longer lives here • **ya no viene a visitarnos** he doesn't come to see us any more, he no longer comes to see us • **ya no quiero más** I don't want any more • **ya no lo volverás a ver** you won't see it any more • **Javier ya no es tan alto como su hermano** Javier isn't as tall as his brother any more, Javier is no longer as tall as his brother

5 (*expresando que se ha entendido o se recuerda algo*) • **ya entiendo** I see • **¡ya lo sé!** I know! • **—¿no te acuerdas de ella? es la hija de Ricardo —¡ah, ya!** "don't you remember her? she's Ricardo's daughter" — "oh yes, of course!"

6 (*expresando acuerdo o incredulidad*) • **ya, pero ...** yes, but ... • **¡ya, ya!** (*iró*) yes, yes!, oh, yes!, oh, sure! • **ya, y luego viste un burro volando ¿no?** (*iró*) sure, and pigs might fly! • **esto ya es un robo** this really is robbery

7 (*con valor enfático*) • **pues ya gasta ¿eh?** he really does spend a lot, doesn't he? • **¿una hora tardas en llegar al trabajo? pues ya está lejos ¿eh?** it takes you an hour to get to work? it must be quite some way away! • **ya lo creo que estuvimos allí** you bet we were there • **¿que no se ha casado? ya lo creo que sí** you say she hasn't got married? I think you'll find she has • **es más pobre que Haití, que ya es decir** it's poorer than Haiti, and that's saying something • **¡murió con 104 años, que ya es decir!** she was 104 when she died, which is no mean achievement! • **pues si él no viene, ya me dirás qué hacemos** you tell me what we'll do if he doesn't come • **¡ya está!** that's it! • **rellena el impreso y ya está** fill in the form and that's it • **¡ya está bien!** that's (quite) enough! • **¡ya me gustaría a mí poder viajar!** I wouldn't mind being able to travel either! • **¡ya era hora!** about time too! • **¡ya podían haber avisado de que venían!** they could have said they were coming! • **¡ya puedes ir preparando el dinero!** you'd better start getting the money ready!

CONJ **1** (*uso distributivo*) • **ya por una razón, ya por otra** whether for one reason or another • **ya te vayas, ya te quedes, me es igual** whether you go or stay is all the same to me • **ya dice que sí, ya dice que no** first he says yes, then he says no, one minute he says yes, the next he says no • **no ya** not only • **no ya aquí, sino en todas partes** not only here, but everywhere • **debes hacerlo, no ya por los demás, sino por ti mismo también** you should do it, not just for everyone else's sake but for your own sake too

2 • **ya que** (seeing) as, since • **ya que no viene, iremos nosotros** (seeing) as *o* since she's not coming, we'll go • **ya que ha dejado de llover, ¿por qué no salimos a dar una vuelta?** (seeing) as *o* since it's stopped raining, why don't we go for a walk? • **ya que no estudia, por lo menos podía ponerse a trabajar** seeing as she isn't studying, the least she could do is get a job

yac [jak] SM (PL: **yacs**) yak

yacaré SM (*LAm*) alligator

yacente ADJ reclining, recumbent

yacer ▷ CONJUG 2X VI **1** (= *estar tendido*) to lie • **los heridos yacían sobre el asfalto** the injured were lying on the tarmac • **libros y papeles yacían en confuso montón** books and papers lay in a confused heap

2 (= *estar enterrado*) to lie • **aquí yace Pedro Núñez** here lies Pedro Núñez

3†† (= *fornicar*) • **~ con** to lie with (*liter*)

yacija SF **1** (= *cama*) bed; (*mala*) rough bed • **ser de mala ~** (= *dormir mal*) to sleep badly, be a restless sleeper; (*fig*) be a ne'er-do-well

2 (= *sepultura*) grave, tomb

yacimiento SM (*Geol*) bed, deposit; (*arqueológico*) site ▸ **yacimiento petrolífero** oilfield

yacuzzi® [ja'kusi] SM (PL: **yacuzzis**) Jacuzzi®

yagua SF (*Ven*) (= *palma*) royal palm; (= *tejido*) *fibrous tissue from the wood of the royal palm*

yagual SM (*CAm, Méx*) padded ring (*for carrying loads on the head*)

yaguar SM (*LAm*) jaguar

yaguareté SM (*And, Cono Sur*) jaguar

yaguré SM (*LAm*) skunk

yaíta ADV (*LAm*) = **ya**

yak [jak] SM (PL: **yaks**) yak

Yakarta SF Jakarta

yámbico ADJ iambic

yana ADJ (*And*) black

yanacón/ona SM/F (*And, Cono Sur*) (*Hist*) (= *aparcero*) Indian tenant farmer, Indian sharecropper; (= *criado*) Indian servant

yancófilo ADJ (*LAm*) pro-American, pro-United States

yanomami ADJ, SMF Yanomami

yanqui* ADJ Yankee*
SMF Yank*, Yankee*

yanquilandia SF (*LAm*) (*pey*) the USA

yantar†† ▷ CONJUG 1A VT to eat
VI to have lunch
SM food

yapa* SF **1** (*LAm*) (= *plus*) extra bit; (= *trago*) one for the road, last drink • **dar algo de ~** (*lit*) to throw in a bit extra for free; (*fig*) to add sth for good measure

2 (Caribe, Méx) (= propina) tip
3 (Cono Sur) (Mec) attachment, end piece
yapada SF (LAm) extra bit
yapar ▸ CONJUG 1a VT (LAm) 1 (= dar de más) to throw in as an extra
2 (= extender) to stretch; (= alargar) to add a bit to, lengthen
VI to throw in an extra bit
yarará SF (And, Cono Sur) rattlesnake
yaraví SM (And, Arg) plaintive Indian song
yarda SF yard
yate SM [de vela] yacht; [de motor] pleasure cruiser, motor cruiser
yatista SMF yachtsman/yachtswoman
yaya[1]* SF nan, nana
yaya[2] SM 1 (LAm) (= herida) minor wound; (= cicatriz) scar; (= dolor) slight pain
2 (Caribe) (= bastón) stick, walking stick
yayo/a* SM/F grandpa*/grandma*
yaz SM jazz
yazca etc ▸ **yacer**
yda ABR (= **yarda**) yd
ye... (para ciertas palabras) ▸ **hie...**
yedra SF ivy
yegua SF 1 (= animal) mare ▸ **yegua de cría** brood mare
2 (And, Cono Sur*) (pey) old bag*; (= puta) whore (pey)
3 (And, CAm) [de cigarro] cigar stub
ADJ 1 (CAm, Caribe) (= tonto) stupid; (= ordinario) rough, coarse
2 (Cono Sur) (= grande) big, huge
yeguada SF 1 (= rebaño) herd of horses; (= caballeriza) stud; (Cono Sur) (= yeguas) group of breeding mares
2 (CAm, Caribe) (= burrada) stupid thing, foolish act
yeguarizo SM (Cono Sur) 1 [de cría] stud, group of breeding mares
2 (= caballos) horses (pl)
yegüerío SM (CAm, Caribe) = **yeguarizo**
yeísmo SM pronunciation of Spanish "ll" as "y"
yelmo SM helmet
yema SF 1 [del huevo] yolk; (LAm) (= huevo) egg ▸ **yema mejida** egg flip
2 (Bot) leaf bud
3 (Anat) ▸ **yema del dedo** fingertip
4 (Culin) sweet made with egg yolk and sugar
5 (= lo mejor) best part
6 (= medio) middle • **dar en la ~** to hit the nail on the head • **en la ~ del invierno** in the middle of winter
7 (= dificultad) snag
Yemen SM • ~ Yemen
yemení ADJ, SMF, **yemenita** ADJ, SMF Yemeni
yen SM (PL: **yens** o **yenes**) yen
yendo ▸ **ir**
yerba SF 1 = **hierba**
2 • ~ **(de) mate** maté
3* (= marihuana) grass‡
yerbabuena SF (LAm) mint
yerbal SM (Cono Sur), **yerbatal** SM (And) maté plantation
yerbatero/a (LAm) ADJ of o pertaining to maté
SM/F 1 (= herbolario) herbalist; (= curandero) quack doctor
2 (= comerciante) maté dealer; (= cultivador) maté grower
yerbear ▸ CONJUG 1a VI (Cono Sur) to drink maté
yerbera SF (Cono Sur) maté (leaves) container
yerbero/a SM/F (LAm) = **yerbatero**
yerga etc ▸ **erguir**
yermar ▸ CONJUG 1a VT to lay waste
yermo ADJ (= inhabitado) uninhabited; (= estéril) barren
SM wasteland
yerna* SF (And, Caribe) daughter-in-law
yerno SM son-in-law
yernocracia* SF nepotism
yeros SMPL lentils
yerre etc ▸ **errar**
yerro SM error, mistake
yersey SM (LAm), **yersi** SM (LAm) jersey
yerto ADJ stiff, rigid • ~ **de frío** frozen stiff*
yesca SF 1 (= materia inflamable) tinder; (Cono Sur) (= piedra) flint • **caja de ~** tinderbox • **arder como si fuera ~** to burn like tinder
2 (fig) (= pábulo) fuel; (= situación) inflammable situation; (= grupo) group which is easily inflamed
3 (fig) (Culin) thirst-making food
4 (And) (Econ) debt
yesería SF plastering, plasterwork
yesero SM plasterer
yeso SM 1 (Geol) gypsum
2 (Arquit) plaster • **dar de ~ a una pared** to plaster a wall ▸ **yeso mate** plaster of Paris
3 (Med) (= material) plaster; (= molde) plaster cast
4 (Arte) plaster cast
5 (= tiza) chalk
yesquero SM (LAm) cigarette lighter
yeta* SF (LAm) bad luck
yetar* ▸ CONJUG 1a VT (Cono Sur) to put a jinx on*, jinx*
yeti SM yeti
yetudo* ADJ (Arg, Uru) jinxed
ye-yé†* ADJ groovy*, trendy • **música ye-yé** sixties pop music
SMF groover*, trendy
yídish SM, **yíddish** SM ['jidiʃ] Yiddish
yihad [ji'ad] SF o SM jihad
yihadismo SM jihadism
yihadista ADJ, SMF jihadist
yincana SM 1 (= competición por equipos) event at which teams compete in a series of races, quizzes and other light-hearted activities
2 (= búsqueda del tesoro) treasure hunt
3 (motorista, ecuestre) gymkhana
yip SM (LAm) jeep
yira‡ SF (Arg, Uru) prostitute, hooker‡
yirante‡ SF (Cono Sur) prostitute, hooker‡
yirar‡ ▸ CONJUG 1a VI (Arg, Uru) to be on the game*
yo PRON PERS 1 (sujeto) I • **Carlos y yo no fuimos** Carlos and I didn't go • **yo no soy de los que exageran** I'm not one to exaggerate • **¡y yo que confiaba en ti!** and to think that I trusted you! • **yo que tú** if I were you • **—¿quién es? —soy yo** "who is it?" — "it's me" • **—¿quién lo dijo? —yo no** "who said that?" — "not me" • **lo hice yo misma** I did it myself
2 (en comparaciones, después de prep) me • **es más delgada que yo** she is slimmer than me o than I am • **que esto quede entre tú y yo** this is between you and me • **nos lo comeremos entre tú y yo** we'll eat it between us
SM (Psic) • **el yo** the self, the ego
y/o ABR (= **y o**) and/or
yod SF yod
yodado ADJ iodized, with added iodine • **sal yodada** iodized salt
yodo SM iodine
yodoformo SM iodoform
yoga[1] SM yoga
yoga[2] SF (Méx) (= daga) dagger
yogui SM yogi
yogur SM 1 (= alimento) yoghurt • **mal ~** (euf) = **mala leche** ▸ **leche** ▸ **yogur descremado, yogur desnatado** low-fat yoghurt
2 (Esp‡) (= coche de policía) police car, squad car
yogurtera SF 1 (= electrodoméstico) yoghurt-maker
2 (Esp‡) (= coche) police car, squad car
yol SM yawl
yola SF yawl; (= yate) sailing boat; [de carreras] (racing) shell
yonque* SM (Méx) scrap metal • **estar para el ~** to be ready for the scrap heap
yonqui* SMF junkie*
yoquei SM = **yóquey**
yoquepierdismo* SM (CAm) self-interest, I'm-all-right-Jack attitude*
yóquey SMF (PL: **yóqueis**) jockey
yoyó SM (PL: **yoyós**), **yo-yo** SM (PL: **yo-yos**) yo-yo
YPF SMPL ABR (Arg) = **Yacimientos Petrolíferos Fiscales**
YPFB SMPL ABR (Bol) = **Yacimientos Petrolíferos Fiscales Bolivianos**
yuca SF 1 (Bot) yucca; (LAm) manioc root, cassava
2 (Caribe) (= pobreza) poverty • **pasar ~** to be poor
3 (And) (= comida) food
4 (And) (= pierna) leg
5 (And, CAm) (= mentira) lie
ADJ (CAm‡) (= difícil) tough, hard
yucateco/a ADJ of/from Yucatan
SM/F native/inhabitant of Yucatan • **los ~s** the people of Yucatan
yudo SM judo
yugar* ▸ CONJUG 1a VI (CAm) to slog away*
yugo SM yoke • **sacudir el ~** (fig) to throw off the yoke ▸ **yugo del matrimonio** marriage tie
Yugoslavia SF, **Yugoeslavia** SF (Hist) Yugoslavia
yugoslavo/a, yugoeslavo/a (Hist) ADJ Yugoslavian
SM/F Yugoslav
yuguero SM ploughman, plowman (EEUU)
yugular ADJ jugular • MODISMOS: • **encontrar la ~ de algn** to find sb's weak spot • **lanzarse a la ~** to go for the jugular
yuju EXCL yipee!
yungas SFPL (And, Cono Sur) (Geog) hot tropical valleys
yungla SF jungle
yunque SM 1 [de metal] anvil
2 (Anat) anvil • MODISMO: • **hacer** o **servir de ~** to have to put up with hardships o abuse
3 (= persona) (paciente) stoical person; (trabajador) tireless worker
yunta SF 1 [de bueyes] yoke, team (of oxen)
2 (Chile) [de personas] couple, pair
3 **yuntas** (LAm) (= botones) cufflinks
yuntero SM ploughman, plowman (EEUU)
yuppie ['jupi] ADJ, SMF yuppie
yuta SF 1 (Cono Sur) (Bio) slug
2 • **hacer la ~** (And, Cono Sur) to play truant
yute SM jute
yuxtaponer ▸ CONJUG 2q VT to juxtapose
yuxtaposición SF juxtaposition
yuxtapuesto PP de **yuxtaponer**
yuyal SM (Cono Sur) scrub(land)
yuyerío SM (And, Cono Sur) (= malas hierbas) weeds (pl); (= plantas silvestres) wild plants (pl)
yuyero/a SM/F (Cono Sur) herbalist
yuyo (LAm) SM 1 (= planta silvestre) weed; (= planta medicinal) herb, medicinal plant; (= condimento) herb flavouring o (EEUU) flavoring; (And) cooking herb • MODISMO: • **estar como un ~** (Cono Sur) to be wet*
2 (And) (= emplasto) herbal poultice
3 **yuyos** (CAm) (= ampollas) blisters on the feet

Zz

Z, z ['θeta], (*esp LAm*) ['seta] SF (*= letra*) Z, z
zabordar ▷ CONJUG 1a VI to run aground
zabullir ▷ CONJUG 3h VT = **zambullir**
zacapela SF, **zacapella** SF rumpus*, row
zacatal SM (*CAm*) pasture
zacate SM **1** (*CAm*) (*= hierba*) grass; (*= heno*) hay, fodder; (*CAm, Méx*) (*= paja*) straw, thatch
2 (*Méx*) (*= trapo*) dishcloth
zacatear ▷ CONJUG 1a (*CAm*) VT to beat
VI to graze
zacatera SF (*CAm*) (*= pasto*) pasture; (*= almiar*) haystack
zafacoca* SF **1** (*LAm*) (*= pelea*) brawl
2 (*Méx*) (*= paliza*) beating
3 (*Caribe*) (*= disturbio*) riot
zafacón SM (*Caribe*) wastepaper basket, waste basket (*EEUU*)
zafado* ADJ (*LAm*) **1** (*= loco*) mad, crazy
2 (*= descarado*) cheeky*, cute (*EEUU**)
zafadura SF (*LAm*) dislocation
zafaduría* SF (*LAm*) **1** (*= descaro*) cheek*, nerve*
2 (*= acción*) bit of cheek*
zafante PREP (*Caribe*) except (for)
zafar ▷ CONJUG 1a VT **1** (*= soltar*) to untie
2 (*= desembarazar*) [*+ barco*] to lighten; [*+ superficie*] to clear, free
3 (*LAm*) (*= excluir*) to exclude
VPR **zafarse 1** (*= escaparse*) to escape, run away; (*= irse*) to slip away; (*= soltarse*) to break loose; (*= ocultarse*) to hide o.s. away
2 (*Téc*) to slip off, come off
3 • **~se de** [*+ persona*] to get away from; [*+ trabajo*] to get out of; [*+ dificultad*] to get round; [*+ acuerdo*] to get out of, wriggle out of
4* • **~se con algo** (*= robar*) to pinch sth*; (*= librarse*) to get away with sth
5 (*LAm*) • **~se un brazo** to dislocate one's arm
6 (*CAm, Cono Sur*) (*= esquivar*) to dodge
7 (*And*) (*= volverse loco*) to go a bit crazy, lose one's marbles*
zafarrancho SM **1** (*Náut*) clearing for action ▸ **zafarrancho de combate** call to action stations
2 (*= desastre*) havoc • **hacer un ~** to cause havoc
3* (*= riña*) fracas, row
zafio ADJ coarse, uncouth
zafiro SM sapphire
zafo ADJ **1** (*Náut*) clear
2 (*= ileso*) unharmed; (*= intacto*) undamaged, intact • **salir ~ de algo** to come out of sth unscathed
3 (*LAm*) (*= libre*) free
PREP (*CAm*) (*= excepto*) except (for)
zafón SM (*And*) slip, error
zafra¹ SF oil jar, oil container
zafra² SF (*LAm*) (*= cosecha*) sugar harvest; (*= fabricación*) sugar making
zaga SF **1** (*= parte trasera*) rear • **a la ~** behind, in the rear • **A ha quedado muy a la ~ de B** A is well behind B • **A no le va a la ~ a B** A is every bit as good as B • **no le va a la ~ a nadie** he is second to none • **dejar en ~** to leave behind
2 (*Dep*) defence, defense (*EEUU*)
zagal(a) SM/F (*= muchacho*) boy/girl, lad/lass; (*Agr*) shepherd/shepherdess
zagalejo/a SM/F (*= muchacho*) lad/lass; (*Agr*) shepherd boy/girl
zagalón/ona SM/F strapping young lad/lass
zagual SM paddle
zaguán SM **1** (*= entrada*) hallway, entrance hall
2 (*CAm*) (*= garaje*) garage
zaguero/a ADJ **1** (*= trasero*) rear, back (*antes de s*) • **equipo ~** bottom team
2 [*carro*] *too heavily laden at the back*
3 (*= retrasado*) slow
SM/F (*Ftbl*) defender; (*Rugby*) full back
zahareño ADJ **1** (*= salvaje*) wild
2 (*= arisco*) unsociable
zaherimiento SM (*= crítica*) criticism; (*= reprimenda*) reprimand
zaherir ▷ CONJUG 3i VT (*= criticar*) to criticize sharply, attack; (*= herir*) to wound, hurt; (*= reprender*) to upbraid, reprimand
zahiriente ADJ wounding, hurtful
zahones SMPL chaps
zahorí SMF **1** (*= vidente*) clairvoyant; (*que busca agua*) water diviner
2 (*= persona perspicaz*) highly perceptive person
zahúrda SF **1** (*Agr*) pigsty
2* (*= tugurio*) hovel, shack
zahurra SF (*And*) din, hullabaloo*
zaino¹ ADJ [*caballo*] chestnut; [*vaca*] black
zaino² ADJ (*= pérfido*) treacherous; [*animal*] vicious • **mirar a lo** *o* **de ~** to look sideways
zainoso ADJ (*Cono Sur*) treacherous
Zaire SM Zaire
zaireño/a ADJ, SM/F Zairean
zalagarda SF **1** (*Mil*) ambush, trap; (*Caza*) trap; (*= escaramuza*) skirmish; (*= ardid*) ruse
2 (*= alboroto*) row, din; (*= riña*) noisy quarrel; (*= jaleo*) shindy*
zalamerear ▷ CONJUG 1a VI (*And*) to flatter
zalamería SF (*tb* **zalamerías**) flattery • **no me vengas con ~s** stop trying to butter me up*
zalamero/a ADJ (*= lisonjero*) flattering; (*= relamido*) suave; (*pey*) slimy
SM/F flatterer; (*pey*) slimeball*
zalea SF sheepskin
zalema SF **1** (*= reverencia*) salaam, deep bow
2 = zalamería
zalenco ADJ (*Caribe*) lame
zalenquear ▷ CONJUG 1a VI (*And*) to limp
zamacuco/a SM/F crafty person
zamarra SF (*= piel*) sheepskin; (*= chaqueta*) sheepskin jacket
zamarrazo SM (*= golpe*) blow; (*= revés*) setback
zamarrear ▷ CONJUG 1a VT **1** [*perro*] to shake
2 (*= sacudir*) to shake; (*= empujar*) to shove around
3* (*en discusión*) to corner*
zamarro SM **1** (*= piel*) sheepskin; (*= chaqueta*) sheepskin jacket
2 zamarros (*And*) (*= pantalones*) chaps
3* (*= rústico*) boor, yokel; (*= taimado*) sly person
zamba SF *Argentinian handkerchief dance*; ▹ **zambo**
zambada SF (*And*) group of half-breeds
zambardo (*Cono Sur*) SM **1** (*= desmañado*) clumsy person
2 (*= desmaña*) clumsiness; (*= daño*) damage, breakage
3 (*= chiripa*) fluke
zambeque (*Caribe*) ADJ silly
SM **1** (*= idiota*) idiot
2 (*= jaleo*) uproar, hullabaloo*
zambequería SF (*Caribe*) silliness
zamberío SM (*And*) half-breeds (*pl*)*
Zambeze SM Zambesi
Zambia SF Zambia
zambiano/a ADJ, SM/F Zambian
zambo/a ADJ* knock-kneed
SM/F (*LAm*) person of mixed race (*esp of black and Indian parentage*); ▹ **zamba**
zambomba SF **1** (*= tambor*) *kind of rustic drum*
2 (*como excl*) • **¡zambomba!*** wow!
zambombazo SM **1** (*= estallido*) bang, explosion
2 (*= golpe*) blow, punch
zambombo SM boor, yokel
zambra SF **1** (*= baile*) gipsy *o* (*EEUU*) gypsy dance
2* (*= alboroto*) uproar
zambrate SM (*CAm*), **zambrera** SF (*Caribe*) row, commotion
zambucar ▷ CONJUG 1g VT to hide, tuck away
zambuir ▷ CONJUG 3g VI (*And*) = **zambullir**
zambullida SF dive, plunge
zambullir ▷ CONJUG 3h VT (*en el agua*) to plunge (**en** into); (*debajo del agua*) to duck (**en** under)
VPR **zambullirse 1** (*en el agua*) to dive (**en** into); (*debajo del agua*) to duck (**en** under)
2 (*= ocultarse*) to hide
zambullón SM (*And*) = **zambullida**
Zamora SF Zamora
zamorano/a ADJ of/from Zamora
SM/F native/inhabitant of Zamora • **los ~s** the people of Zamora
zampa SF (*Arquit*) pile
zampabollos* SMF INV **1** (*= glotón*) greedy pig*, glutton
2 (*= grosero*) coarse individual
zampar* ▷ CONJUG 1a VT **1** (*= esconder*) to put away hurriedly (**en** in)
2 (*= sumergir*) to plunge (**en** into)
3 (*= arrojar*) to hurl, dash (**en** against, to) • **lo zampó en el suelo** he hurled *o* dashed it to the floor
4 (*= comer*) to wolf down
5 (*LAm*) • **~ una torta a algn** to wallop sb*

VI to gobble
VPR **zamparse 1** (= *lanzarse*) to bump, crash • **se zampó en medio del corro** he thrust himself roughly into the circle
2 (*en fiesta, reunión*) to gatecrash, go along uninvited
3 • **~se en** to dart into, shoot into • **se zampó en el cine** he shot into the cinema
4 (= *comerse*) • **~se algo** to wolf sth down • **se zampó cuatro porciones enteras** he wolfed down four whole helpings

zampatortas* SMF INV = **zampabollos**

zampón* ADJ greedy

zampoña SF shepherd's pipes (*pl*), rustic flute

zampuzar ▹ CONJUG 1f VT **1** = **zambullir**
2 = **zampar**

zamuro SM (*Ven*) turkey vulture, turkey buzzard (*EEUU*)

zanahoria SF carrot; ▹ **palo**
SMF (*Cono Sur**) (= *imbécil*) idiot, nitwit*; (= *desmañado*) clumsy oaf; (= *pobre*) poor wretch

zanahorio* ADJ (*Col*) (= *mojigato*) strait-laced; (= *anticuado*) unhip*

zanate SM (*CAm, Méx*) rook

zanca SF **1** [*de ave*] shank
2 [*de persona*] (*hum*) shank

zancada SF stride • **alejarse a grandes ~s** to stride away • **en dos ~s** (= *rápidamente*) in a couple of ticks; (= *fácilmente*) very easily

zancadilla SF (*para derribar a algn*) trip; (= *trampa*) trick • **echar la ~ a algn** (*lit*) to trip sb up; (*fig*) to put the skids under sb*

zancadillear ▹ CONJUG 1a VT (*lit*) to trip (up); (*fig*) to put the skids under*

zancajear ▹ CONJUG 1a VI to rush around

zancajo SM **1** (= *talón*) heel • **A no le llega a los ~s a B** A can't hold a candle to B
2* (= *persona*) dwarf, runt

zancajón ADJ (*Méx*) **1** (= *alto*) tall, lanky
2 (= *torpe*) clumsy

zancarrón SM **1** [*de la pierna*] leg bone
2†* (= *viejo*) old bag of bones
3†* (= *profesor*) poor teacher

zanco SM stilt • MODISMO: • **estar en ~s** to be high up

zancón ADJ **1** (= *de piernas largas*) long-legged
2 (*CAm*) (= *alto*) lanky
3 (*LAm*) [*vestido*] too short

zancudero SM (*CAm, Caribe*) swarm of mosquitoes

zancudo ADJ long-legged; ▹ **ave**
SM (*LAm*) mosquito

zanfona SF hurdy-gurdy

zangamanga* SF trick

zanganada SF stupid remark, silly thing (to say)

zanganear* ▹ CONJUG 1a VI **1** (= *gandulear*) to idle, loaf about; (= *hacer el tonto*) to fool around
2 (= *decir disparates*) to make stupid remarks

zángano/a SM/F **1*** (= *holgazán*) idler, slacker
2* (= *pícaro*) rogue
3* (= *pesado*) bore
SM (= *insecto*) drone

zangarriana SF **1** (*Med*) (= *jaqueca*) severe headache, migraine; (= *trastorno leve*) minor upset
2 (= *abatimiento*) blues (*pl*), depression

zangolotear ▹ CONJUG 1a VT to shake
VI to buzz about uselessly
VPR **zangolotearse 1** [*ventana*] to rattle, shake
2 [*persona*] to fidget

zangoloteo SM (= *sacudida*) shaking; [*de persona*] fidgeting; [*de ventana*] rattling

zangolotino ADJ • **niño ~** (= *infantil*) big kid*; (= *tonto*) silly child

zangón SM big lazybones, lazy lump*

zanguanga* SF fictitious illness • **hacer la ~** to swing the lead*, malinger

zanguango/a* ADJ idle, slack
SM/F slacker, shirker

zanja SF **1** (= *fosa*) ditch; (= *hoyo*) pit; (= *tumba*) grave • **abrir las ~s** (*Arquit*) to lay the foundations (**de** for)
2 (*LAm*) (= *barranco*) gully, watercourse
3 (*And*) (= *límite*) fence, low wall

zanjar ▹ CONJUG 1a VT **1** (= *abrir una zanja*) to dig a trench in
2 (= *acabar*) [+ *dificultad*] to get around; [+ *conflicto*] to resolve, clear up; [+ *discusión*] to settle

zanjón SM **1** (= *zanja profunda*) deep ditch
2 (*Caribe, Cono Sur*) (= *risco*) cliff; (= *barranco*) gully, ravine

zanquear ▹ CONJUG 1a VT (*CAm, Caribe, Méx*) to hunt for
VI **1** (= *andar mal*) to waddle
2 (= *ir rápidamente*) to stride along
3 (= *trajinar*) to rush about, bustle about

zanquilargo ADJ long-legged, leggy

zanquivano ADJ spindly-legged

Zanzíbar SM Zanzibar

zapa¹ SF **1** (= *pala*) spade
2 (*Mil*) sap, trench

zapa² SF sharkskin, shagreen

zapador SM sapper

zapallada SF **1** (*Cono Sur*) (= *chiripa*) fluke; (= *suerte*) lucky break; (= *conjetura*) lucky guess
2 (*And*) (= *comentario*) silly remark

zapallito SM (*Cono Sur*) courgette, zucchini (*EEUU*)

zapallo SM **1** (*LAm*) (= *calabaza*) gourd, pumpkin
2 (*Cono Sur*) = **zapallada**
3 (*And*) (= *gordo*) fat person
4 (*And, CAm*) (= *tonto*) dope*, fool
5 (*Cono Sur‡*) (= *cabeza*) nut‡

zapallón* ADJ (*And, Cono Sur*) chubby, fat

zapapico SM pick, pickaxe, pickax (*EEUU*)

zapar ▹ CONJUG 1a VT, VI to sap, mine

zaparrazo SM scratch

zapata SF **1** (= *calzado*) half-boot
2 (*Mec*) shoe ▸ **zapata de freno, zapata de frenos** brake shoe

zapatazo SM **1** (= *golpe dado con zapato*) blow with a shoe; (= *caída, ruido*) thud • **tratar a algn a ~s*** to ride roughshod over sb
2 (*Dep*) fierce kick, hard shot
3 (*Náut*) violent flap of a sail

zapateado SM **1** (= *claqué*) tap dance
2 (= *baile típico español*) zapateado

zapatear ▹ CONJUG 1a VI **1** (= *dar golpecitos*) to tap one's feet; (= *bailar*) to tap-dance
2 [*conejo*] to thump
3 [*vela*] to flap violently
VT **1** (= *dar golpecitos en*) to tap with one's foot
2 (= *patear*) to boot*
3 (= *maltratar*) to ill-treat, treat roughly

zapateo SM tapping ▸ **zapateo americano** (*Arg, Uru*) tap dancing

zapatería SF **1** (= *tienda*) shoeshop; (= *fábrica*) shoe factory, footwear factory
2 (= *oficio*) shoemaking

zapatero/a ADJ **1** [*industria*] shoemaking (*antes de s*)
2 [*legumbres, patatas*] hard, undercooked
SM/F shoemaker • REFRÁN: • **~, a tus zapatos** the cobbler should stick to his last ▸ **zapatero de viejo, zapatero remendón** cobbler
SM (= *mueble*) shoe rack

zapatiesta* SF set-to*, shindy*

zapatilla SF **1** (*para casa*) slipper; (*Dep*) training shoe ▸ **zapatillas de ballet** ballet shoes ▸ **zapatillas de clavos** running shoes, spikes ▸ **zapatillas de deporte** sports shoes, trainers, sneakers (*EEUU*) ▸ **zapatillas de tenis** tennis shoes
2 (*Mec*) washer

zapatista ADJ, SMF *Zapatista*

zapato SM shoe • MODISMOS: • **estaban como tres en un ~** they were packed in like sardines • **meter a algn en un ~** to bring sb to heel • **saber dónde aprieta el ~** to know the score* ▸ **zapato náutico** boat shoe ▸ **zapatos de cordones** lace-up shoes ▸ **zapatos de golf** golf shoes ▸ **zapatos de goma** (*LAm*), **zapatos de hule** (*Méx*) tennis shoes ▸ **zapatos de plataforma** platform shoes ▸ **zapatos de salón** court shoes, pumps (*EEUU*) ▸ **zapatos de tacón, zapatos de tacones altos** high-heeled shoes ▸ **zapatos de tacón de aguja** stilettos; ▹ PANTALONES, ZAPATOS, GAFAS, **niño**

zapatón SM (*LAm*) overshoe, galosh

zape EXCL **1** (*a animal*) shoo!
2 (*sorpresa*) good gracious!

zapear ▹ CONJUG 1a VI (*TV*) to channel-hop
VT **1** [+ *gato*] to shoo, scare away; [+ *persona*] to shoo away, get rid of
2 (*And, CAm*) (= *espiar*) to spy on, watch

zapeo SM channel-hopping

zaperoco* SM (*Caribe*) muddle, mess

zapote SM (*CAm, Méx*) (= *planta*) sapodilla, sapota; (= *fruta*) sapodilla plum, sapota

zapoteca ADJ, SMF Zapotec

zapping ['θapin] SM channel-hopping • **hacer ~** to channel-hop

zaque SM **1** [*de vino*] wineskin
2‡ (= *borracho*) boozer‡, old soak‡

zaquizamí SM **1** (= *buhardilla*) attic, garret
2 (= *cuartucho*) poky little room, hole; (= *tugurio*) hovel

zar SM tsar, czar (*esp EEUU*)

zarabanda SF **1** (*Hist*) sarabande
2 (= *movimiento*) rush, whirl
3 (*Méx*) (= *paliza*) beating

zaragata SM **1*** (= *ajetreo*) bustle; (= *jaleo*) hullabaloo*; (= *riña*) row, set-to*
2 zaragatas (*Caribe*) (= *zalamerías*) flattery (*sing*)

zaragate* SM **1** (*LAm*) (= *malvado*) rogue, rascal; (= *entrometido*) busybody
2 (*Caribe*) (= *zalamero*) flatterer, creep‡

zaragatero* ADJ (= *bullicioso*) rowdy, noisy; (= *peleador*) quarrelsome
SM rowdy, hooligan

Zaragoza SF Saragossa

zaragozano/a ADJ of/from Saragossa
SM/F native/inhabitant of Saragossa • **los ~s** the people of Saragossa

zaragüelles SMPL *baggy trousers that form part of the traditional dress of Valencia and Murcia*

zaramullo ADJ **1** (*And, CAm, Caribe*) (= *afectado*) affected; (= *engreído*) conceited; (= *delicado*) finicky
2 (*And, Caribe*) (= *divertido*) amusing, witty
SM (*And*) **1** (= *tontería*) silly thing
2 (= *entrometido*) busybody; (= *tonto*) fool

zaranda SF **1** (= *tamiz*) sieve
2 (*Méx*) (= *carrito*) wheel barrow
3 (*Caribe*) (= *juguete*) spinning top; (*Mús*) horn

zarandajas* SFPL trifles, odds and ends, little things

zarandear ▹ CONJUG 1a VT **1** (= *sacudir*) to shake vigorously; (= *empujar*) to jostle, push around
2* (= *dar prisa a*) to keep on the go
3 (= *cribar*) to sieve, sift
4 (*LAm*) (= *balancear*) to swing, push to and fro
5 (= *insultar*) to abuse publicly
VPR **zarandearse 1** (*esp LAm*) (= *pavonearse*) to strut about

2 (= *ir y venir*) to keep on the go

zarandeo SM **1** (= *sacudida*) shaking
2 (*por el tamiz*) sieving

zarandillo SM (= *persona enérgica*) active person; (= *persona inquieta*) fidget • MODISMO: • **llevar a algn como un ~** to keep sb on the go

zarape SM (*CAm, Méx*) *brightly-coloured striped blanket*

zarapito SM (*tb* **zarapito real**) curlew

zaraza SF chintz, printed cotton cloth

zarazas SFPL rat poison (*sing*)

zarazo ADJ (*LAm*) **1** [*fruta*] underripe
2* (= *bebido*) tipsy, tight*

zarcillo SM **1** (= *pendiente*) earring
2 (*Bot*) tendril
3 (*Cono Sur, Méx*) (*Agr*) earmark

zarco ADJ light blue

zarigüeya SF opossum, possum

zarina SF tsarina, czarina (*esp EEUU*)

zarista ADJ, SMF tsarist, czarist (*esp EEUU*)

zaroche SM (*LAm*) = **soroche**

zarpa SF **1** [*de león, tigre*] paw; [*de persona**] paw, mitt • **echar la ~ a algo** to get one's hands on sth
2 [*de barro*] splash of mud

zarpada SF = **zarpazo**

zarpar ▹ CONJUG 1a VI to weigh anchor, set sail

zarpazo SM **1** [*de animal*] • **el gato me dio un ~** the cat scratched me • **el oso me dio un ~** the bear hit me with its paw
2 (= *desgracia*) blow

zarpear ▹ CONJUG 1a VT (*CAm, Méx*) to splash with mud

zarrapastroso ADJ, **zarrapastrón** ADJ [*persona*] scruffy; [*ropa*] shabby

zarria SF **1** (= *salpicadura*) splash of mud
2 (= *harapo*) rag, tatter

zarza SF bramble, blackberry (bush)

zarzal SM bramble patch

zarzamora SF blackberry

zarzaparrilla SF sarsaparilla

zarzo SM **1** (*Agr*) hurdle; (*para construir*) wattle
2 (*And*) (= *buhardilla*) attic

zarzuela SF **1** *Spanish light opera*
2 ▸ **zarzuela de mariscos** (*Esp*) seafood casserole
3 • **(Palacio de) la Zarzuela** *royal palace in Madrid*

ZARZUELA
Zarzuelas, named after the Zarzuela Palace where they were first performed in the 17th century for the entertainment of Philip IV, are a kind of Spanish comic folk opera. They are usually in three acts, and their chief ingredients include stock characters, traditional scenes and a mixture of dialogue, music and traditional song. After a decline in popularity in the 18th century, interest in this very Spanish genre was rekindled as part of the 19th century revival of Spanish nationalism.

zarzuelista SMF *composer of Spanish light opera*

zas EXCL bang!, crash! • **le pegó un porrazo ... ¡zas! ... que ...** he gave him a swipe ... bang! ... which ... • **apenas habíamos puesto la radio y ... ¡zas! ... se cortó la corriente** we had only just switched on the radio when "click!" and off went the current • **cayó ¡zas! al agua** she fell into the water with a big splash

zasca EXCL **1** bang!, crash!
2 (*como adv*) all of a sudden

zascandil* SM ne'er-do-well

zascandilear ▹ CONJUG 1a VI to buzz about uselessly, fuss around

zaya SF (*Caribe*) whip

zeda SF (name of the) letter z

zen ADJ INV, SM Zen

Zenón SM Zeno

zenzontle SM (*CAm, Méx*) mockingbird

zepelín SM zeppelin

zeta SF the (name of the) letter z
SM (*Aut*) Z-car, police car

Zetlandia SF • **islas de ~** Shetland Isles *o* Islands, Shetland

Zeus SM Zeus

zigoto SM zygote

zigzag SM (PL: **zigzagues** *o* **zigzags**) zigzag • **relámpago en ~** forked lightning

zigzagueante ADJ zigzag (*antes de s*)

zigzaguear ▹ CONJUG 1a VI to zigzag

zigzagueo SM zigzagging

Zimbabue SM, **Zimbabwe** SM Zimbabwe

zimbabuo/a ADJ, SM/F Zimbabwean

zinc SM zinc

zíngaro/a ADJ, SM/F = **cíngaro**

zíper SM (*Méx*) zip, zipper (*EEUU*)

zipizape* SM set-to*, rumpus* • **armar un ~** to start a rumpus • **los dos están siempre de ~** the two of them are always squabbling

zócalo SM **1** (*Arquit*) (= *pedestal*) plinth, base
2 [*de pared*] skirting board, baseboard (*EEUU*)
3 (*Méx*) (= *plaza*) main square; (= *bulevar*) walk, boulevard; (= *parque*) park

zocato/a ADJ **1** [*fruta, legumbre*] hard
2 [*persona*] left-handed
SM/F left-handed person
SM (*And*) (= *pan*) stale bread

zoclo SM = **zueco**

zoco¹/a ADJ **1** (= *zurdo*) left-handed
2 (*And*) (= *manco*) one-armed; (*And, Caribe, Cono Sur*) (= *mutilado*) maimed
SM/F **1** (= *zurdo*) left-handed person
2 (*Caribe*) (= *tonto*) fool
SM (*Cono Sur*) (= *puñetazo*) hefty punch

zoco² SM (*Arab*) market, souk

zocotroco SM (*And, Cono Sur*) chunk, big lump • **~ de hombre*** hefty man*

zodiaco SM, **zodíaco** SM zodiac

zollenco ADJ (*Méx*) big and tough

zollipar* ▹ CONJUG 1a VI to sob

zombi SMF zombie

zona SF **1** (*en país, región*) area • **las ~s afectadas por las inundaciones** the areas affected by flooding • **las ~s más ricas/remotas/deprimidas del país** the richest/remotest/most depressed areas *o* parts of the country • **la ~ norte/sur/este/oeste de la isla** the northern/southern/eastern/western part of the island • **comimos en uno de los restaurantes típicos de la ~** we ate in a restaurant typical of the area, we ate in a typical local restaurant • **~s costeras** coastal areas • **~ montañosa** *o* **de montaña** mountainous area, mountainous region • **~s rurales** rural areas • **~s turísticas** tourist areas • **~s urbanas** urban areas ▸ **zona catastrófica** disaster area ▸ **zona de combate** combat zone ▸ **zona de conflicto** (*Mil*) conflict zone ▸ **zona de desarrollo** development area ▸ **zona de exclusión (aérea)** (air) exclusion zone ▸ **zona de guerra** war zone ▸ **zona de influencia** area of influence ▸ **zona de libre comercio** free-trade zone, free-trade area ▸ **zona de peligro** danger zone, danger area ▸ **zona de picnic** picnic area ▸ **zona de seguridad** security zone ▸ **zona desnuclearizada** nuclear-free zone ▸ **zona euro** Eurozone • **los países de la ~ euro** the Eurozone countries ▸ **zona franca** duty-free zone ▸ **zona fronteriza** (*gen*) border area; (*Mil*) border zone ▸ **zona húmeda** wetland ▸ **zona industrial** industrial area ▸ **zona militar** military zone, military area ▸ **zona roja** (*Esp*) Republican territory ▸ **zona segura** safe zone
2 (*en ciudad*) area ▸ **zona azul** (*Esp*) (*Aut*) ≈ pay-and-display area ▸ **zona centro** centre • **los aparcamientos de la ~ centro** city centre car parks ▸ **zona cero** Ground Zero • **~ comercial** (*para negocios en general*) commercial district; (*solo de tiendas*) shopping area • **~ de copas**: • **¿dónde está la ~ de copas?** where do people go out to drink? ▸ **zona de ensanche** development area • **~ edificada** built-up area ▸ **zona marginada** (*CAm*) slum area ▸ **zona peatonal** pedestrian precinct ▸ **zona residencial** residential area ▸ **zona roja** (*LAm*) red-light district ▸ **zona rosa** (*Méx*) *partly pedestrianized zone, so called because of its pink paving stones* ▸ **zona verde** green space
3 (*en edificio, recinto*) area • **las ~s comunes de la prisión** the communal areas of the prison • **~ de no fumadores** no smoking area ▸ **zona ancha** (*Dep*) midfield ▸ **zona de castigo** (*Dep*) sin bin ▸ **zona de penumbra, zona de sombra** (*lit*) shaded area; (*fig*) area of secrecy ▸ **zona oscura** • **las ~s oscuras de la personalidad** the hidden areas of the personality • **las ~s oscuras de la política** the shady *o* murky areas of politics ▸ **zona técnica** technical area
4 (*Geog*) zone ▸ **zona glacial** glacial zone ▸ **zona templada** temperate zone ▸ **zona tórrida** torrid zone
5 (*Anat, Med*) area • **las ~s próximas a la columna vertebral** the areas around the spinal column • **sentí un dolor por la ~ del hombro** I felt a pain around my shoulder ▸ **zona erógena** erogenous zone ▸ **zona lumbar** lumbar region
6 (*Baloncesto*) free-zone lane

zonación SF zoning

zonal ADJ zonal

zoncear ▹ CONJUG 1a VI (*LAm*) to behave stupidly

zoncera SF, **zoncería** SF **1** (*LAm*) (= *cualidad*) silliness, stupidity
2 (*Cono Sur*) mere trifle • **costar una ~** to cost next to nothing • **comer una ~** to have a bite to eat

zonchiche SM (*CAm, Méx*) buzzard

zonda SF (*Arg*) hot northerly wind

zonificar ▹ CONJUG 1g VT to zone, divide into zones

zonzo/a ADJ **1** (*LAm*) (= *tonto*) silly, stupid; (= *pesado*) boring
2 (*Méx*) (= *aturdido*) dazed
SM/F (*LAm*) (= *tonto*) idiot; (= *pesado*) bore

zonzoneco ADJ (*CAm*), **zonzoreco** ADJ (*CAm*), **zonzoreno** ADJ (*CAm*) stupid

zoo SM zoo

zoo... PREF zoo...

zoofilia SF bestiality

zoología SF zoology

zoológico ADJ zoological
SM zoo

zoólogo/a SM/F zoologist

zoom [θum] SM (= *objetivo*) zoom lens; (= *toma*) zoom shot

zoomórfico ADJ zoomorphic

zoomorfo SM zoomorph

zooplancton SM zooplankton

zoo-safari SM safari park

zope SM (*CAm*) vulture

zopenco/a* ADJ dull, stupid
SM/F clot*, nitwit*

zopilote SM (*CAm, Méx*) **1** (= *ave*) vulture
2* (= *ladrón*) thief

zopilotear* ▹ CONJUG 1a VT (*CAm, Méx*) **1** (= *comer*) to wolf down

2 (= *robar*) to pinch*, nick*
zopo ADJ crippled, maimed
zoquetada SF (*LAm*) stupidity
zoquetazo SM (*Cono Sur, Méx*) swipe, punch
zoquete SMF* (= *zopenco*) blockhead; (= *patán*) lout, oaf
SM 1 [*de madera*] block
2 [*de pan*] crust
3 (*LAm*) (= *suciedad*) body dirt, human dirt
4 (*Caribe, Méx*) (= *puñetazo*) punch; (= *trompada*) smack in the face
zoquetillo SM shuttlecock
zorenco ADJ (*CAm*) stupid
Zoroastro SM Zoroaster
zorongo SM (*Mús*) *popular song and dance of Andalusia*
zorra SF 1 (= *animal*) vixen
2** (= *prostituta*) whore (*pey*), tart‡, slut‡ • **¡zorra!** you slut!‡
3* (= *borrachera*) • **pillar una ~** to get sloshed*
ADJ‡ (= *puñetero*) bloody‡ • **no tengo ni ~ idea** I haven't a bloody clue‡ • **toda la ~ noche** the whole bloody night‡; ▹ **zorro**
zorral ADJ 1 (*And, CAm*) (= *molesto*) annoying
2 (*And*) (= *obstinado*) obstinate
zorrear* ▹ CONJUG 1a VI to be up to one's tricks again, be up to no good
zorrera SF 1 (= *madriguera*) foxhole; (*fig*) smoky room
2 (= *turbación*) worry, anxiety
3 (= *modorra*) drowsiness
zorrería SF 1 (= *astucia*) foxiness, craftiness
2 (= *acción*) sly trick
zorrero ADJ foxy, crafty
zorrillo SM (*Cono Sur*), **zorrino** SM (*Cono Sur*) skunk
zorro ADJ foxy, crafty
SM 1 (= *animal*) fox ▸ **zorro gris** grey fox
2 (= *piel*) fox fur, fox skin ▸ **zorro plateado** silver fox (fur)
3 (= *persona*) (= *taimado*) crafty, old fox; (= *gandúl*) slacker, shirker • MODISMOS: • **estar hecho un ~** to be very drowsy • **estar hecho unos ~s*** [*habitación*] to be in an awful state; [*persona*] to be all in; ▹ **zorra**
zorrón* ADJ sluttish
zorruno ADJ foxy, fox-like
zorrupia‡ SF tart‡, whore (*pey*)
zorzal SM 1 (= *ave*) thrush
2 (= *hombre listo*) shrewd man; (= *hombre taimado*) sly fellow
3 (*Cono Sur*) (= *tonto*) simpleton; (= *inocente*) dupe, naïve person
zorzalear* ▹ CONJUG 1a VI (*Cono Sur*) to sponge*
zorzalero* ADJ (*Cono Sur*) sponging*, parasitical
zorzalino* ADJ • **la vida zorzalina** the easy life
zosco SM (*Caribe*) idiot
zotal® SM disinfectant
zote* ADJ dim, stupid
SMF dimwit*
zozobra SF 1 (*Náut*) capsizing, overturning
2 (= *inquietud*) worry, anxiety; (= *nerviosismo*) jumpiness
zozobrar ▹ CONJUG 1a VI 1 [*barco*] (= *hundirse*) to founder, sink; (= *volcar*) to capsize, overturn; (= *peligrar*) to be in danger
2 (= *fracasar*) [*plan*] to fail, founder; [*negocio*] to be ruined
3 [*persona*] to be anxious, worry
zueco SM clog, wooden shoe
zulla* SF human excrement
zullarse* ▹ CONJUG 1a VPR (= *ensuciarse*) to dirty o.s.; (= *ventosear*) to fart‡, break wind
zullón* SM fart‡
zulo SM [*de armas*] cache; [*de documentos*] hiding place
zulú ADJ 1 Zulu
2† (*pey*) brutish
SMF 1 Zulu
2† (*pey*) brute
Zululandia SF Zululand
zumaque SM sumac(h)
zumba SF 1 (= *burla*) teasing • **dar** *o* **hacer ~ a algn** to tease sb
2 (*LAm**) (= *paliza*) beating
3 (*Méx*) drunkenness
4 (*Dep*) Zumba®
zumbado* ADJ • **estar ~** to be crazy, be off one's head*
zumbador SM 1 (*Elec*) buzzer
2 (*Caribe, Méx*) (= *ave*) hummingbird
zumbar ▹ CONJUG 1a VI 1 (= *sonar*) [*insecto*] to buzz; [*máquina*] to hum, whirr; [*oídos*] to ring, buzz • **~le a algn los oídos: me zumban los oídos** my ears are ringing, I have a buzzing in my ears • **le estarán zumbando los oídos** his ears must be burning
2 • MODISMO: • **salir zumbando*** to shoot off* • **salió zumbando cuando vio a la policía** he shot off as soon as he caught sight of the police* • **tengo que salir zumbando para no perder el tren** I must rush so I don't miss the train
3* (= *quedar cerca*) to be very close • **no está en peligro ahora, pero le zumba** he's not actually in danger now but it's not far away
VT 1 (= *burlar*) to tease
2 (= *golpear*) to beat, hit
3 (*LAm**) (= *tirar*) to chuck*
4‡ (= *robar*) to nick‡
5** (= *copular con*) to fuck**
VPR **zumbarse 1** (= *burlarse*) • **~se de algn** to tease sb, poke fun at sb
2 (*And, Caribe*) (= *marcharse*) to clear off*
3 (*Caribe*) (= *pasarse*) to overstep the mark
4 (= *copular con*) • **~se a algn**** to fuck sb**
5 (= *masturbarse*) • **zumbársela**** to wank**
zumbido SM 1 [*de insecto*] buzz(ing); [*de máquina*] hum(ming), whirr(ing) ▸ **zumbido de oídos** buzzing in the ears, ringing in the ears
2* (= *puñetazo*) punch, biff*
zumbo[1] SM (*And, CAm*) gourd, calabash
zumbo[2] SM = **zumbido**
zumbón/ona ADJ [*persona*] waggish, funny; [*tono*] teasing; (*pey*) sarcastic
SM/F joker, tease
zumiento ADJ juicy
zumo SM 1 [*de frutas, verduras*] juice ▸ **zumo de naranja** orange juice
2 (= *provecho*) • **sacar el ~ a algo** to get the most out of sth
zumoso ADJ juicy
zuncho SM metal band, metal hoop
zupia SF 1 (= *heces*) dregs (*pl*); (= *vino*) muddy wine; (= *brebaje*) nasty drink, evil-tasting liquid
2 (= *gentuza*) dregs (*pl*)
3 (*And*) (= *aguardiente*) rough liquor
zurcido SM 1 (= *acto*) darning, mending
2 (= *remiendo*) darn, mend
zurcidura SF = **zurcido**
zurcir ▹ CONJUG 3b VT 1 (= *coser*) to darn, mend
2 (= *juntar*) to join, put together; [+ *mentiras*] to concoct, think up
3 • MODISMOS: • **¡que las zurzan!*** to hell with them!* • **¡que te zurzan!*** get lost!*
zurdazo SM (= *golpe*) left-handed punch; (= *tiro*) left-footed shot
zurdear ▹ CONJUG 1a VT (*LAm*) to do with the left hand
zurdo/a ADJ [*mano*] left; [*persona*] left-handed • **a zurdas** (*lit*) with the left hand; (*fig*) the wrong way, clumsily • MODISMO: • **no es ~** he's no fool
SM/F 1 (= *persona*) (*gen*) left-handed person; (*Tenis*) left-hander
2 (*Cono Sur*) (*Pol*) (*pey*) lefty*, left-winger
zurear ▹ CONJUG 1a VI to coo
zureo SM coo, cooing
zuri‡ SM • **darse el ~** to clear out*
zurito SM small glass (*of beer*)
zuro SM cob, corncob
zurra SF 1* (= *paliza*) hiding*
2* (= *trabajo*) hard grind*, drudgery
3* (= *pelea*) roughhouse*
4 [*de pieles*] dressing
zurrador SM dresser
zurrapa SF 1 (= *mancha*) smudge, smear; (*en calzoncillos, bragas*) skidmark*; (= *hilo*) thread, stream (*of dirt*); **zurrapas** (= *posos*) dregs
2 (= *cosa despreciable*) trash, rubbish
zurraposo ADJ full of dregs, muddy
zurrar ▹ CONJUG 1a VT 1* (= *pegar*) to wallop*, give a hiding*
2* (*en discusión*) to flatten
3* (= *criticar*) to lash out at, lay into*
4 [+ *pieles*] to dress
zurria* SF 1 (*And, CAm*) (= *paliza*) hiding*
2 (*And*) (= *multitud*) lot, crowd
zurriaga SF whip, lash
zurriagar ▹ CONJUG 1h VT to whip, lash
zurriagazo SM 1 (= *azote*) lash, stroke
2 (= *desgracia*) stroke of bad luck; (= *revés*) severe blow; (= *mal trato*) piece of unjust *o* harsh treatment
zurriago SM whip, lash
zurribanda* SF = **zurra**
zurriburri* SM 1 (= *confusión*) turmoil, confusion; (= *lío*) mess, mix-up; (= *ruido*) hubbub
2 (= *persona despreciable*) worthless individual
3 (= *pandilla*) gang; (= *turba*) rabble
zurrón SM pouch, bag
zurullo SM, **zurullón** SM 1 (*en líquido*) lump
2** (= *excremento*) turd**
3‡ (= *persona*) lout, hooligan
zurumato ADJ (*Méx*) (= *turulato*) light-headed, woozy*; (= *estúpido*) stupid
zurumbanco ADJ (*CAm, Méx*) 1 = **zurumato**
2* (= *medio borracho*) half-drunk, half cut*
zurumbático ADJ • **estar ~** to be stunned, be dazed
zurumbo ADJ (*CAm*) 1 = **zurumato**
2* (= *medio borracho*) half-drunk, half cut*
zutano/a SM/F (Mr *etc*) So-and-so • **si se casa fulano con zutana** if Mr X marries Miss Y; ▹ **fulano**

Language in Use

Lengua y Uso

by

Beryl T. Atkins and Hélène M. A. Lewis

Teresa Álvarez García   Diana Feri   José Miguel Galván Déniz   Cordelia Lilly

Language in Use

Contents

Spanish-English

		Page
	Introduction	5
1	Suggestions	6
2	Advice	6
3	Offers	7
4	Requests	7
5	Comparisons	8
6	Opinions	9
7	Likes, dislikes and preferences	10
8	Intentions and desires	10
9	Permission	11
10	Obligation	12
11	Agreement	13
12	Disagreement	13
13	Approval	14
14	Disapproval	15
15	Certainty, probability, possibility and capability	15
16	Doubt, improbability, impossibility and incapability	16
17	Explanations	17
18	Apologies	18
19	Job applications	18
20	Commercial correspondence	20
21	General correspondence	22
22	Thanks	25
23	Best wishes	25
24	Announcements	25
25	Invitations	26
26	Essay writing	27
27	The telephone	33
27a	E-mail	35

Lengua y Uso

Índice de materias

Inglés-Español

		Página
	Introducción	5
27	El teléfono	33
27a	Correo electrónico	36
28	Sugerencias	37
29	Consejos	37
30	Propuestas	38
31	Peticiones	38
32	Comparaciones	39
33	Opiniones	40
34	Gustos y preferencias	40
35	Intenciones y deseos	41
36	Permiso	42
37	Obligación	43
38	Acuerdo	44
39	Desacuerdo	44
40	Aprobación	45
41	Desaprobación	46
42	Certeza, probabilidad, posibilidad y capacidad	46
43	Incertidumbre, improbabilidad, imposibilidad e incapacidad	47
44	Explicaciones	48
45	Disculpas	49
46	Solicitudes de trabajo	49
47	Correspondencia comercial	51
48	Correspondencia de carácter general	53
49	Agradecimientos	56
50	Saludos de cortesía y felicitaciones	56
51	Notas y avisos de sociedad	56
52	Invitaciones	57
53	Redacción	58

Corpus acknowledgements

We would like to acknowledge the assistance of the many hundreds of individuals and companies who have kindly given permission for copyright material to be used in The Bank of English. The written sources include many national and regional newspapers in Britain and overseas; magazine and periodical publishers in Britain, the United States and Australia. Extensive spoken data has been provided by radio and television broadcasting companies; research workers at many universities and other institutions; and individual numerous contributors. We are grateful to them all.

Agradecimientos

Agradecemos especialmente la valiosa colaboración de los periódicos EL MUNDO y ABC, así como del Laboratorio de Lingüística Informática de la Universidad Autónoma de Madrid, en el que se realizó el 'Corpus de Referencia de la Lengua Española Contemporánea: corpus oral centro-peninsular' dirigido por el Prof. Dr. Francisco A. Marcos-Marín.

Introduction to Language in Use

Our aim in writing **Language in Use** has been to help non-native speakers find fluent, natural ways of expressing themselves in the foreign language, without risk of the native-language distortion that sometimes results from literal translation.

To achieve this, we have identified a number of essential language functions, such as *agreement, suggestions* and *apologies,* and provided a wealth of examples to show typical ways of expressing them. Users can select phrases to meet their needs using either their knowledge of the foreign language alone or by looking at the translations of the key elements.

The authentic examples in this section are taken from Collins' vast computerized databases of modern English and Spanish. These databases, updated every month, consist of millions of English and Spanish words from a variety of modern written and spoken sources: literature, magazines, newspapers, letters, radio and television.

The layout is designed to make consultation even easier. Clear headings and subdivisions enable you to find the topic of your choice at a glance. We have given style guidance, where appropriate, so that you can be confident that the phrase you have chosen is as assertive, tentative, direct or indirect as you want it to be.

Since Spanish forms of address corresponding to the English *you* vary according to the formality of the relationship, we have tried to reflect this in a consistent manner. As a general rule, *tú/te* has been shown in everyday one-to-one situations where there is no evidence of formality. Where the situation or language suggests a more formal relationship, *usted/le* has been used. Where more than one person is addressed, *vosotros/as* and *ustedes/les* have been used in a similar way. Nevertheless, as usage of *tú/usted* and *vosotros/ustedes* varies depending on which variety of Spanish is being spoken and the age of the speakers, you should be prepared to make adjustments accordingly.

Lengua y Uso – Introducción

Nuestro objetivo al escribir este suplemento de **Lengua y Uso** ha sido ayudar a los estudiantes de ambas lenguas a encontrar formas de expresarse con naturalidad en el idioma extranjero y evitar así las distorsiones que a veces resultan de una traducción literal.

Para ello, se ha analizado el acto de la comunicación partiendo de ciertas funciones del tipo *consejos, permiso* o *posibilidad,* para agrupar toda una serie de frases y expresiones bajo las secciones correspondientes. De esta manera el lector puede seleccionar la frase que le hace falta gracias tanto a sus conocimientos pasivos del idioma extranjero como a la traducción dada a su propia lengua de dichas frases.

Aquí hacemos uso de ejemplos de la lengua hablada y escrita tomados de la base de datos electrónica de la que dispone Collins para su labor lexicográfica: un corpus actualizado mensualmente de millones de palabras en inglés y español, recogidas de libros, revistas, periódicos, cartas, programas de radio y televisión.

La presentación gráfica tiene como objetivo facilitar aún más la labor de consulta. La claridad de los encabezamientos y subdivisiones permite encontrar en un momento el tema buscado. Además, se da una orientación de estilo en los casos apropiados para que pueda saberse con seguridad si la frase se usa de forma más o menos directa, o en un contexto más o menos familiar etc.

En cuanto al tratamiento de *tú* o *usted* en las frases en español y en las traducciones de este suplemento, se ha decidido usar como norma general el *tuteo,* excepto en los ejemplos de situaciones que requieren un trato más formal y por lo tanto el uso de *usted.*

1 SUGGESTIONS

1.1 Making suggestions

Using direct questions

- **¿Quieres que** ponga la maceta en la ventana?
  = *would you like me to*
- **¿Te apetece que** vayamos a verle esta tarde?
  = *do you fancy going*
- **¿Por qué no** lo dejas hasta que volvamos a casa?
  = *why don't you*
- **¿Y si** organizáramos una fiesta para darle una sorpresa?
  = *what if we*
- **¿Te parece bien** que la invitemos a la fiesta?
  = *do you think we should*
- **¿Qué te parece** decírselo por carta?
  = *what do you think about*
- **¿No se te ha ocurrido que** el mejor regalo no es siempre el más caro?
  = *hasn't it ever occurred to you that*
- **¿No cree que sería mejor** hacerlo ahora?
  = *mightn't it be better to*
- **¿Puedo hacerle una propuesta** que quizá le parezca interesante?
  = *may I make a suggestion*

Assertively

- **Yo que tú** no haría nada por ahora
  = *if I were you*
- **Lo que sugiero es lo siguiente**: por ahora no cambiemos los planes
  = *what I suggest is that*
- **Lo que deberíamos hacer es no** preocuparnos demasiado de los demás
  = *what we should not do is*
- **Propongo que** busquemos ayuda profesional
  = *I suggest that*
- **Lo mejor sería no** involucrarse en un conflicto en el que no tenemos ni arte ni parte
  = *it would be best not to*
- **No se olvide de** avisarme en cuanto llegue
  = *don't forget to*
- **Yo propondría que** la actual reforma de la ley se negocie buscando el consenso de todos
  = *I would suggest that*
- **Les sugeriría que** llamaran antes por teléfono
  = *I would advise you to*
- **Quisiera hacer una propuesta para** mejorar el servicio
  = *I should like to make a suggestion to*
- **Si se me permite una sugerencia**, yo creo que debemos trazar un plan de actuación detallado
  = *if I may make a suggestion*

Tentatively

- **Sería cuestión de** hacer una prueba para ver si funciona
  = *we/you would have to*
- **Si le parece bien, podemos** enviárselo por correo urgente
  = *if you agree, we could*
- **Lo que podríamos hacer es** hablar con él antes de que se marche a Italia
  = *what we could do is*
- **Sería mejor que** el ganador del premio fuera un escritor novel
  = *it would be best if*
- **Sería buena idea** aprovechar la atención que va a atraer el acontecimiento
  = *it would be a good idea to*
- **No sería mala idea** levantarse un poco más temprano
  = *it mightn't be a bad idea to*
- **Quizás habría que** ser un poco más firmes con ellos
  = *perhaps you/we should*
- En estas circunstancias **sería muy poco aconsejable** enviar más tropas a la zona
  = *it would be very inadvisable to*
- **Sería preferible** tener mejor calidad de vida para nuestra población
  = *it would be preferable to*
- **Convendría** encontrar una alternativa más sencilla
  = *it would be advisable to*
- **Convendría que** recurriera a los servicios de un especialista
  = *you would do well to*
- **Sería conveniente que** acudieran a un abogado con la documentación
  = *it would be advisable for ... to*

1.2 Asking for suggestions

- **¿Alguna idea**?
  = *any ideas?*
- **¿Tú qué dices**?
  = *what do you think?*
- **¿Cómo lo ves**?
  = *what do you think?*
- **¿Tú qué harías**?
  = *what would you do?*
- **¿Qué hacemos ahora**?
  = *what shall we do now?*
- **¿A ti qué te parece que podemos** hacer ahora?
  = *what do you think we can*
- **Si se le ocurre algo** ...
  = *if you have any ideas*
- **¿Qué haría usted en mi lugar**?
  = *what would you do if you were me?*
- **¿Tiene usted alguna sugerencia** al respecto?
  = *have you any suggestions?*

2 ADVICE

2.1 Asking for advice

- **¿Tú qué me aconsejas**?
  = *what would you advise me to do?*
- **¿Tú qué harías (si estuvieras) en mi lugar**?
  = *what would you do if you were me?*
- **¿Te puedo pedir un consejo**?
  = *can I ask your advice about something?*
- **¿Tú crees que a estas alturas sirve de algo que** desconvoquen la huelga?
  = *do you think there is any point in ...at this late stage?*
- **Necesito que alguien me aconseje**
  = *I need some advice*
- **¿Qué es lo más recomendable** en esta situación?
  = *what would be advisable*
- **Quería pedirle un consejo**
  = *I'd like to ask your advice about something*
- **¿Usted qué me aconsejaría que** hiciera?
  = *what would you advise me to*
- **Le agradecería que me asesorase sobre** ese asunto
  = *I would be grateful for your advice on*

2.2 Giving advice

- **Yo que tú** no haría nada por ahora
  = *if I were you*
- **Yo en tu lugar** no lo dudaría
  = *if I were you*

- **Hay que** tomarse las cosas con más calma
  = *you must*
- **Te interesa más** comprar acciones de la otra empresa
  = *you would be better to*
- **Deberías** mostrarte más abierto y sincero en tu relación
  = *you should*
- **Lo que ella debería hacer es** cambiar su imagen ligeramente
  = *what she should do is*
- **Harías bien en** visitar a un especialista
  = *you would do well to*
- **Más vale no** decir nada por el momento
  = *it would be better or best not to*
- **Mi consejo es que** te sinceres con ellos y les digas la verdad
  = *my advice would be to*
- **Habría que** sopesar los pros y los contras antes de tomar una decisión definitiva
  = *we/you ought to*
- **Lo que habría que hacer es** consultarlo con quien sepa sobre el tema
  = *what we/you ought to do is*
- **Lo que haría falta es que** instalaran un nuevo sistema de refrigeración
  = *what they should do is*
- **Lo mejor que puede hacer es** dirigirse a la oficina central
  = *the best thing you can do is*
- **Le recomiendo que** abandone el hábito del cigarrillo si quiere mejorar su estado de salud
  = *I would advise you to*
- **Sería totalmente desaconsejable** intervenir ahora
  = *it would be extremely inadvisable to*
- **Permítanme ustedes que insista en la necesidad de** presionar a la compañía
  = *I'd like to emphasize the need to*
- **Me permito sugerirle que** corrija dichos errores, para mejorar aún más si cabe la calidad de su periódico
  = *I should like to suggest that you*

More tentatively

- **¿Y si** fueras a verle y le pidieras perdón?
  = *what if you*
- **Yo te aconsejaría** un cambio de aires
  = *I'd recommend*
- **Quizás habría que** preparar unos planes más detallados
  = *perhaps we should*
- **Yo le diría que** fuera prudente a la hora de tomar una decisión
  = *I would advise you to*
- **No sería mala idea** enviarlo todo exprés
  = *it wouldn't be a bad idea to*
- **Sería prudente** llamar antes por teléfono, por si acaso está fuera
  = *it would be wise to*

2.3 Warnings

- **Os advierto que** no vamos a dar ninguna información
  = *I should warn you that*
- **Debo advertirle que** esa agencia no es de fiar
  = *I must warn you that*
- **Si no** pides disculpas ahora, **deberás atenerte a las consecuencias**
  = *if you don't ... you must accept the consequences*
- **Corremos el riesgo de** perder toda credibilidad
  = *we run the risk of*
- **Que sirva de advertencia:** si continuáis con esa actitud, las consecuencias pueden ser nefastas
  = *be warned:*
- **Sería cosa de locos** *or* **una locura** proseguir en estas pésimas condiciones
  = *it would be madness to*

- **Es necesario** cambiar de rumbo **antes de que sea demasiado tarde**
  = *we need to ... before it is too late*
- **Es absolutamente indispensable que** modifiquemos nuestra política de ventas
  = *it is absolutely vital that*

3 OFFERS

3.1 Using direct questions

- ¿**Te ayudo**?
  = *can I help (you)?*
- ¿**Cierro** la ventana?
  = *shall I close*
- ¿**Quieres que** vaya a recoger al niño al colegio?
  = *would you like me to*
- ¿**Necesitas ayuda**?
  = *do you need any help?*
- ¿**Me dejas que te eche una mano con** los preparativos?
  = *can I lend (you) a hand with*
- ¿**Puedo ayudarle en algo**?
  = *can I do anything to help?*
- ¿**Me permite que le ofrezca mi colaboración** de cara al proyecto?
  = *perhaps you will allow me to offer some help*

3.2 Direct offers

- No te preocupes, **ya lo hacemos nosotros**
  = *we'll do it*
- **Si quieres** te acompaño
  = *... if you like*
- **Puedo ir yo si** no hay nadie disponible
  = *I could go if*
- **Déjeme que le ayude**
  = *let me help you*
- **Estoy para lo que haga falta**
  = *I'm ready and willing to do whatever's needed*
- **Estoy dispuesto a** hacer todo lo que sea necesario
  = *I'm prepared to*
- **No dude en venir a mí si** le surge algún problema
  = *don't hesitate to come back to me if*
- **Permítame usted por lo menos que** le lleve a la estación
  = *at least let me*
- **Me tiene a su entera disposición** para todo lo que necesite
  = *I'm entirely at your disposal*
- **Sería un placer** poder servirle en todo lo que haga falta
  = *it would be a pleasure to*

4 REQUESTS

4.1 Using direct questions

- ¿**Me traes** un vaso de agua?
  = *would you fetch me*
- ¿**Me dejas** tu chaqueta?
  = *can I borrow*
- ¿**Quieres** cambiarme el turno?
  = *would you mind*
- ¿**Te importa** echar esta carta al correo?
  = *would you mind*
- ¿**Te puedo pedir un favor**?
  = *would you do me a favour?*
- ¿**Podría decirme** qué pone en ese cartel, **por favor**?
  = *could you tell me ..., please?*

- **¿Le importaría** cerrar un poco la ventana?
  = *would you mind*
- **¿Sería tan amable de** enseñármelo usted mismo?
  = *would you be so kind as to*
- **¿Podría** aclararme unas dudas sobre su patrimonio, **si tiene la bondad**?
  = *would you mind*

Assertively

- **Déjame el coche, anda**, sólo por una noche
  = *lend me the car, won't you*
- **Por favor, házmelo** cuanto antes
  = *please can you do it for me*
- **Solo te pido que** bajes un poco la voz
  = *I'm only asking you to*
- **Alcánzame** las gafas, **si me haces el favor**
  = *pass me ..., will you?*
- **Haga el favor de no** poner los pies en el asiento
  = *please don't*
- Vuelva a llamar en cinco minutos, **si es tan amable**
  = *if you don't mind*
- **Le ruego que** se apresure en responder
  = *please*

More tentatively

- **Si no es mucho pedir**, mándame un listado de direcciones
  = *please ..., if it isn't too much trouble*
- **Nos vendría bien** saberlo mañana, antes de la reunión
  = *it would be good if we could*
- **Preferiría que no** lo utilizara a partir de las ocho
  = *I would rather you didn't*
- **Si no es demasiada molestia, ¿podrías** comentarnos cómo es el panorama musical en tu ciudad?
  = *if it isn't too much trouble, could you*
- **Le agradecería que** me ayudara a resolver el problema
  = *I'd be grateful if you would*

In writing

- **Tenga la amabilidad de** presentarse en nuestras oficinas en horario laboral
  = *please*
- **Agradeceríamos su colaboración en** cualquier aspecto de nuestra investigación
  = *we should be grateful if you would help us in*
- **Les quedaríamos muy agradecidos si** se pudieran poner en contacto con nuestros representantes
  = *we should be very grateful if*
- **Tengan a bien** comunicarnos la respuesta por e-mail
  = *please*

5 COMPARISONS

5.1 Constrasting facts

- Las carreteras están **relativamente** tranquilas para esta época del año
  = *comparatively*
- Las nuestras son producciones modestas, **comparadas con** las más "aparatosas" de otros teatros
  = *compared with*
- **En comparación con** el interior del país, el clima en la costa **no es tan** extremo
  = *in comparison with ... is not so*
- **Si comparamos** el actual estado del río **y** *or* **con** el anterior, podemos observar un aumento en el grado de contaminación
  = *if we compare ... and or with*
- Los países desarrollados consumen en exceso, **mientras que** los del Tercer Mundo no llegan a cubrir las necesidades básicas
  = *while*

5.2 Comparing similar things

- Estos dos cuadros **son igualitos**
  = *are just the same*
- Su programa político **es igual que** el de la oposición
  = *is the same as*
- En nuestras carreteras se producen **casi tantos** accidentes **como** en las de Grecia y Portugal
  = *almost as many ... as*
- El paisaje es **tan** bello **como** lo describió el poeta
  = *as ... as*
- García Márquez se limita a transcribir la realidad **tal como es**
  = *just as or like it is*
- Ambos coches valen **exactamente lo mismo**
  = *exactly the same*
- Ha vuelto a suceder **lo mismo que** hace unos años
  = *the same thing as*
- **Al igual que sucede** en el reino animal, las plantas también luchan por su supervivencia
  = *just as happens*
- Los dos hermanos **se parecen mucho** físicamente
  = *are very alike*
- Las temperaturas aquí **son muy parecidas** *or* **similares a** las de mi tierra
  = *are very similar to*
- Esto **equivale a** veinte horas de trabajo
  = *is equivalent to*

5.3 Comparing dissimilar things

- Los pros **son (muchos) más que** los contras
  = *there are (far) more ... than*
- En su tierra se le aprecia **(muchísimo) menos que** en el extranjero
  = *(far) less than*
- Es aún **(mucho) más** nacionalista **que** su hermano
  = *(far) more ... than*
- Un coche nuevo contamina **bastante menos que** uno viejo
  = *considerably less than*
- Al contribuyente se le cobra **mucho menos de lo que** cuestan los servicios
  = *much less than*
- Lo que diga una revista del corazón **no es lo mismo que** las manifestaciones públicas de un presidente
  = *is not the same as*
- Esa canción ya **no** suena **tanto como** el año pasado
  = *not ... as much as*
- **No se parece en nada a** su padre
  = *he is not at all like*
- **¡Hay diferencia entre** este vino y el otro ...!
  = *there's quite some difference between*
- Un modelo **se diferencia** *or* **distingue del** otro en el número de extras que lleva incorporados
  = *the difference between ... and ... lies in*
- La realidad **es muy diferente** *or* **distinta de** lo que teníamos creído
  = *is very different from*

5.4 Comparing favourably

- Me encuentro **muchísimo mejor** ahora que me han operado
  = *much better*
- Este vino **es muy superior** al otro
  = *is vastly superior to*

5.5 Comparing unfavourably

- Para muchos perder su cargo público resulta **mucho peor que**

perder la dignidad
= *much worse than*

- Las posibilidades que ofrecía un teléfono hace 10 años **no tienen (ni punto de) comparación con** las prestaciones actuales
  = *between ... and*
- Este premio **no es tan** importante **como** el que consiguió hace unos años
  = *is not as ... as*
- Como deportista, Juan **no le llega ni a la suela de los zapatos**
  = *isn't a patch on him*

5.6 Increasing and decreasing

- Estos juegos **tienen cada vez más aceptación entre** los estudiantes
  = *are becoming more and more popular with*
- Las desigualdades **son cada vez mayores**
  = *are becoming greater and greater*
- A decir verdad, yo escribo **cada vez menos**, y acabaré sin duda por dejar de escribir
  = *less and less*
- **Son cada vez menos los que** se casan antes de los 29 años
  = *fewer and fewer people*
- **Cuanto más** madura un vino, **más** añejo es su sabor
  = *the more ..., the more*

6 OPINIONS

6.1 Asking for someone's opinion

- ¿**Qué piensas de** su actitud?
  = *what do you think of*
- ¿**Qué te parece** mi trabajo?
  = *what do you think of*
- ¿**Crees que** le gustará el regalo?
  = *do you think that*
- ¿**Piensas que** se puede estudiar en estas condiciones?
  = *do you think that*
- ¿**Qué opina usted de** la exportación de animales vivos?
  = *what do you think of or about*
- ¿**Qué opinión tiene usted de** sus compatriotas?
  = *what is your opinion of*
- ¿**Qué opinión le merece** la subida del precio de los carburantes?
  = *what is your opinion of*
- ¿**Nos puede ofrecer su opinión sobre** la liberalización del mercado?
  = *could you give us your opinion on*
- **Quisiera saber lo que opina sobre** el informe publicado en la prensa
  = *I should like to know what you think about*
- **Me interesaría conocer su opinión en torno a** la nueva política exterior del gobierno
  = *I should be interested to know your opinion of*

6.2 Expressing your opinion

- **Creo que** le va a encantar tu visita
  = *I think that*
- **Me parece que** le has caído muy bien a todos
  = *I think that*
- **Para ser sincero**, su obra no me apasiona
  = *to be honest*
- **En mi opinión**, fue un error no haberle contratado antes
  = *in my opinion*
- **A mi parecer** *or* **A mi manera de ver**, las cosas se deberían hacer de otro modo
  = *in my view*
- **Mi opinión personal es que** se debería nombrar un comité al respecto
  = *my personal opinion is that*
- **Yo considero que** eso no es perjudicial para el sistema democrático
  = *it is my belief that*
- **Personalmente, creo que** es un gasto innecesario
  = *personally, I think that*
- **Debo reconocer** *or* **admitir que** nuestra posición se ha visto debilitada
  = *I must admit that*
- **Mi posición al respecto** difiere de la suya
  = *my position on the matter*
- **En mi calidad de** *or* **Como** Premio Nobel de la Paz, **quiero reafirmar** mi apoyo inequívoco a una solución pacífica y negociada
  = *as ..., I should like to reaffirm*
- **Si me permite que le dé mi opinión, me parece que** esa oferta es un engaño
  = *if I may be allowed to offer my opinion, I think that*

With more conviction

- **Lo que es yo**, no lo veo necesario
  = *personally*
- **Si quieres mi opinión**, déjame que te diga que no tienes de qué quejarte
  = *if you want my opinion*
- **Si quieren que les dé mi opinión**, hay necesidades más importantes en las que gastar el dinero
  = *if you want my opinion*
- **Tengo que decir que** no me gusta nada
  = *I must say that*
- **Estoy totalmente seguro de que** nos lo van a devolver
  = *I'm quite sure that*
- **Estoy convencida de que** no cuentan con fondos suficientes
  = *I'm convinced that*
- **No puedo menos que pensar que** es un acto deliberado
  = *I can't help thinking that*

More tentatively

- **Me da que** no va a venir
  = *I suspect that*
- **Me da la sensación de que** no va a dar resultado
  = *I have a (funny) feeling that*
- **Tengo la impresión de que** algo marcha mal
  = *I have the impression that*
- **Supongo que** es una posibilidad tan buena como cualquier otra
  = *I suppose that*
- Los padres, **imagino que** también tendrán que contribuir a ello
  = *I suppose that*
- **Con el debido respeto, debo decirle que** eso no es así
  = *with all due respect, I have to tell you that*

6.3 Replying without giving an opinion

- **No sabría decir**
  = *I couldn't say*
- **Preferiría reservarme la opinión**
  = *I would rather reserve judgement*
- **Es difícil dar una opinión** sin conocer las circunstancias
  = *it's difficult to give an opinion*
- **No puedo opinar sobre** un tema del que no tengo conocimiento
  = *I can't express an opinion on*
- **No deseamos ofrecer ninguna opinión hasta que** la situación se haya aclarado
  = *we would rather not express an opinion until*
- **No estoy en posición de hacer declaraciones** al respecto
  = *I'm not in a position to make a statement*

- **No puedo pronunciarme a favor de** ninguna de las opciones
  = *I cannot say I am in favour of*
- **No me es posible emitir una opinión objetiva sobre** este asunto
  = *I cannot give an objective opinion on*

7 LIKES, DISLIKES AND PREFERENCES

7.1 Asking people what they like

- **¿Te gusta** el yogur de fresa?
  = *do you like*
- **¿Cuál de** las tres camisas **te gusta más**?
  = *which of ... do you like best?*
- **¿Le gustaría** viajar a otra época?
  = *would you like to*
- De las dos posibilidades, **¿cuál prefiere**?
  = *which do you prefer?*
- **Quería saber si prefieren** salir ahora **o** después de comer
  = *I wanted to know if you would prefer to ... or*
- **¿Podrían darme su parecer sobre** el nuevo programa?
  = *could you give me your opinion on*

7.2 Saying what you like

- **Me agrada que** hayan venido a verme desde tan lejos
  = *it was good of them to*
- **A todos nos gusta que** nos reconozcan un trabajo bien hecho
  = *we all like it when*
- **Me ha gustado mucho el regalo** que me has enviado
  = *I was delighted with the present*
- A mí los turistas que vienen por aquí **me caen (muy) bien**
  = *I (really) like ...*
- **Lo que más me gusta es** observar a la gente
  = *what I like (doing) best is*
- **Disfruto** charlando con los niños
  = *I enjoy*
- **Disfruto con** sus atrevidos comentarios en televisión
  = *I enjoy*
- **Me seduce la idea de** viajar a Finlandia, no sé por qué
  = *the idea of ... really appeals to me*
- Para muchos ver la televisión **es su pasatiempo favorito**
  = *is their favourite pastime*
- **Soy muy aficionado a** la danza contemporánea
  = *I'm very keen on*
- **Me encanta** el mar y navegar a vela
  = *I love*
- **Me fascina observar** el firmamento en una noche clara
  = *I love watching*
- **Me apasiona** la luminosidad del paisaje mediterráneo
  = *I love*
- **Siento verdadera debilidad por** los postres cremosos
  = *I have a weakness for*

7.3 Saying what you dislike

- **No me gusta** comer fuera de casa
  = *I don't like*
- Sus canciones **no son nada del otro mundo**
  = *aren't anything to write home about*
- **Me cuesta tener que** criticarle en público
  = *I find it hard to have to*
- **No me gusta nada que** me mientan
  = *I don't like ... at all*
- **No me resulta nada agradable** ir a trabajar a estas horas de la noche
  = *I'm not at all keen on*
- **Me molesta** el olor de las sardinas asadas
  = *I find ... very unpleasant*
- Mis nuevos vecinos **me caen muy mal** *or* **no me caen nada bien**
  = *I don't like ... at all*
- **Le he cogido manía a** ese chico
  = *I've really taken a dislike to*
- **No soporto que** me hagan esperar
  = *I can't stand*
- **Lo que más me fastidia es que** suban tanto el volumen
  = *what really annoys me is when*
- **Si hay algo que no aguanto es que** cambien la programación sin avisar
  = *if there's one thing I can't bear, it's when*
- **Detesto** cualquier tipo de violencia
  = *I hate*
- **Me horrorizan** las corridas de toros
  = *I really hate*

7.4 Saying what you prefer

- **Prefiero la** lectura **a** la televisión
  = *I prefer ... to*
- **Prefiero que** llegues tarde **a que** no vengas
  = *I'd rather you ... than*
- **Es mejor** *or* **preferible** hablar en el idioma del cliente
  = *it's better to*
- **Preferiría que** nadie me acompañara
  = *I would rather*
- **Nos vendría mejor** *or* **Nos convendría más** salir antes para evitar la hora de más tráfico
  = *we would do better to*
- **Tengo especial predilección por** la música de Falla
  = *I am particularly fond of*

7.5 Expressing indifference

- Vamos a esperar hasta encontrar la persona idónea, **no pasa nada porque** no haya titular durante un tiempo
  = *it doesn't matter if*
- **Me da igual** *or* **Me da lo mismo** vivir aquí **que** allí
  = *it's all the same to me whether ... or*
- **Me es (completamente) indiferente** que salga de presidente uno **u** otro
  = *it makes (absolutely) no difference to me whether ... or*
- **Si** no lo veo hoy **no importa**
  = *it doesn't matter if*
- **No tiene (la mayor) importancia que** se demoren unos minutos
  = *it doesn't matter (in the slightest) if*

8 INTENTIONS AND DESIRES

8.1 Asking what someone intends or plans to do

- **¿Qué piensas hacer**?
  = *what do you intend to do?*
- **¿Qué vas a hacer** con las plantas estas vacaciones?
  = *what are you going to do*
- **¿Qué planes tienes** para la familia?
  = *what plans have you got*
- **¿Qué intentas hacer**?
  = *what are you trying to do?*
- **¿Qué esperan ustedes conseguir con** esta propuesta?
  = *what do you hope to achieve with*
- **Quisiera saber cómo piensa** actuar en lo referente al tema que nos ocupa
  = *I'd like to know how you intend to*

8.2 Talking about intentions

- **Voy a** tomar el tren de las siete
  = *I'm going to*

- **Pienso** marcharme cuando me haya recuperado por completo
  = *I intend to*
- **Haremos** los preparativos para la fiesta la noche antes
  = *we shall*
- **Tengo la intención de** empezar una serie de conciertos para niños
  = *I plan or intend to*
- **Mi intención no es otra que** explicar que la promoción de la salud es el objetivo principal de la salud pública
  = *my sole aim is to*
- **Me propongo** alcanzar la cima en un tiempo récord
  = *my aim is to*
- **Tienen previsto** casarse coincidiendo con las vacaciones
  = *they are planning to*
- Los vecinos **tienen pensado** denunciar la situación a las autoridades
  = *are planning to*
- **El objetivo de** la directiva **es** remodelar los estatutos del partido
  = *the aim of ... is to*
- El médico **está decidido a** salvar la vida del niño como sea
  = *is determined to*
- **Está resuelta a no** dejarlo hasta que acabe
  = *she is determined not to*
- La presidencia alemana **se ha planteado unos objetivos muy ambiciosos**
  = *has set itself some very ambitious goals*
- **Desconozco sus intenciones**
  = *I don't know what he is intending to do*

8.3 Saying what you would like

- **Me gustaría** saber qué se propone hacer como nuevo director
  = *I'd like to*
- **Me gustaría que** el partido tuviera una actitud más realista
  = *I'd like ... to*
- **Mi único deseo es** volver a mi hogar
  = *all I want is to*
- **Nuestro deseo es que**, de una vez por todas, se nos tome en serio
  = *what we want is for ... to*
- Como actriz, **me encantaría poder** trabajar con un director como él
  = *I'd love to be able to*
- **Ojalá no lloviera** tanto para poder salir más a menudo
  = *if only it didn't rain*
- **Esperemos que** todo salga bien
  = *let's hope that*
- **Es de esperar que** las negociaciones lleguen a buen puerto
  = *it's to be hoped that*
- **Quisiera** dedicar una canción a mi hija Gemma, que cumple mañana 12 años
  = *I should like to*
- **Querría que** mis cuadros estuviesen colgados junto a los de los grandes maestros
  = *I'd like ... to*
- **Desearía que** se le prestara mayor atención a los desamparados
  = *I should like ... to*
- **Sueña con** llegar a ser modelo
  = *her dream is to*

8.4 Saying what you don't intend or don't want to do

- **No quiero que vayan** a pensar otra cosa
  = *I don't want you to*
- Por ahora **no me planteo** hacer una película sobre temas tan delicados
  = *I'm not considering*
- Convocar elecciones anticipadas **no entraba en nuestros planes**
  = *was not on our agenda*
- **No se trata de** hablar otra vez con ellos, sino de que acepten lo que hemos propuesto ya varias veces
  = *it's not a question of*
- **No desearíamos** causarles molestias
  = *we would not wish to*

With more determination

- **No pienso** hacerle caso
  = *I do not intend to*
- **No tenía la más mínima intención de** dimitir
  = *he didn't have the slightest intention of*
- **Jamás haría** una cosa así
  = *I would never do*
- **Me niego (rotundamente) a** entrar en la polémica
  = *I (categorically) refuse to*

9 PERMISSION

9.1 Asking for permission

- ¿**Puedo** pasar?
  = *may I*
- ¿**Me dejas que** lo use yo antes?
  = *will you let me ... please?*
- ¿**Se puede** aparcar aquí?
  = *can I*
- ¿**Te importa si** subo la tele un poco?
  = *do you mind if I*
- ¿**Podría** hacerle unas preguntas?
  = *could I*
- ¿**Le importaría que** me sentara?
  = *would you mind if I*
- ¿**Les molesta que** abra la ventana?
  = *do you mind if I*
- **Con su permiso** vamos a cerrar el tema de una vez
  = *... if you don't mind*
- ¿**Sería mucha molestia** dejarlo para más tarde?
  = *would it be an awful nuisance if*
- ¿**Me permite** usar su teléfono?
  = *may I*
- ¿**Tendrían inconveniente en que** tomáramos unas fotografías?
  = *would you mind if*
- **Espero que no les importe que** hagamos uso de esta información
  = *I hope you don't mind if*

9.2 Giving permission

- ¡**Naturalmente que** puedes ir!
  = *of course*
- **Puede** escoger otro modelo, si le conviene más
  = *you can (always)*
- **Les autorizamos a que** actúen como estimen más conveniente
  = *you have our permission to*
- **Tiene mi autorización para** llevar a cabo el proyecto
  = *you have my authorization to*
- **No tengo ningún inconveniente en** responder a sus preguntas
  = *I don't have any objection to*

9.3 Refusing permission

- ¿Es que piensas que te voy a dejar el coche? ¡**Ni pensarlo**!
  = *no way!*
- **No puedo dejarte** ir de excursión con el tiempo tan malo que hace
  = *I can't let you*
- ¡**No consiento** ese tipo de lenguage en esta casa!
  = *I will not tolerate*
- **No se puede** fumar aquí
  = *you can't*
- **Me opongo a que se les permita** acudir a la reunión
  = *I am opposed to their being allowed to*

- **Eso es imposible, porque no lo permite** el decreto de 2015
  = *that's impossible because ... doesn't allow it*
- **Lo siento, pero no está permitido** entrar si no se pertenece a la organización
  = *I'm sorry, but you aren't allowed to*
- **Le prohíbo (terminantemente) que** se dirija a mí de esa manera
  = *I absolutely forbid you to*

9.4 Saying that permission is granted

- **Le dejan** acostarse a la hora que quiera
  = *he's allowed to*
- **Me dijo que podía** venir cuando quisiera
  = *she said I could*
- Nuestros padres **nos dieron permiso para** organizar una fiesta
  = *gave us permission to*
- **Nos han concedido** la licencia de importación
  = *we have been granted*
- El alcohol es la única droga cuyo consumo público **está permitido**
  = *is allowed*
- **Tengo autorización para** firmar en nombre del Consejo de Administración
  = *I am authorized to*

9.5 Saying that permission is refused

- **No me dejan** participar en la carrera por problemas de salud
  = *I'm not allowed to*
- **Me han denegado** la beca de estudios que necesitaba
  = *I've been refused*
- **No nos han otorgado la autorización necesaria**
  = *we haven't been given the necessary authorization*
- **No nos está permitido** hablar del tema con la prensa
  = *we aren't allowed to*
- **No estoy autorizado para** hacer declaraciones de ningún tipo
  = *I'm not authorized to*
- **No tengo autorización para** darles acceso a las instalaciones
  = *I'm not authorized to*
- El médico **me ha prohibido** fumar
  = *has forbidden me to*
- **Tengo totalmente prohibido** el alcohol, a causa de problemas hepáticos
  = *I'm not allowed*

10 OBLIGATION

10.1 Saying what someone must do

- **Tenemos que** levantarnos a primera hora de la mañana
  = *we have to*
- Hagas lo que hagas, **no te olvides de** avisarme si tienes problemas
  = *don't forget to*
- **No le queda más remedio que** *or* **No tiene más remedio que** soportar la afrenta con dignidad
  = *he has no option but to*
- **Me han encargado que** realice esta inspección
  = *I've been given the job of*
- En nombre del gobierno **debo** hacer la siguiente declaración: ...
  = *I must*
- Las circunstancias políticas **me obligaron a** salir de mi país
  = *forced me to*
- Todos **estamos obligados a** *or* **tenemos la obligación de** actuar con un gran sentido de la responsabilidad
  = *have a duty to*
- Por razones de seguridad a bordo **nos vemos obligados a** limitar el equipaje de mano de nuestros pasajeros
  = *we are obliged to*
- **Tengo el deber de informarles de que** su petición ha sido rechazada
  = *it is my duty to inform you that*
- Aquí **hace falta que alguien** ponga un poco de orden
  = *what we need is someone to*
- En verano **hay que** proteger la piel contra las radiaciones solares
  = *you must*
- Para viajar a Copiapó **es preciso** atravesar desiertos de arena y riscos áridos
  = *you have to*
- **Es obligatorio que** figure en el envase la fecha de elaboración
  = *it is compulsory for ... to*
- **Es esencial** *or* **imprescindible** *or* **indispensable** devolver el agua al medio natural sin contaminaciones
  = *it is essential to*
- **Para que sea** válida la renuncia al puesto **se requiere que** esté hecha libremente
  = *in order to be ... must*
- La ley **estipula que hay que** superar los dieciséis años para solicitar una licencia
  = *stipulates that you have to*
- Es un país donde **se exige que** los automóviles lleven un nivel de equipamiento y automatización muy alto
  = *are required to*
- **Se exige** experiencia en ventas
  = *... required*
- **Es requisito indispensable tener** un nivel de competencia avanzado
  = *it is essential to have*

10.2 Enquiring if someone is obliged to do something

- ¿**De verdad tengo que** pagar para entrar?
  = *do I really have to*
- ¿**Qué debo hacer para** empezar a escribir novelas?
  = *what must I do in order to*
- ¿**Se necesita** carnet de conducir?
  = *do I need*
- ¿**Estoy obligada a** atenerme a estas normas?
  = *do I have to*
- ¿**Tiene** un ciudadano **la obligación de** demostrar su identidad si así lo requiere la policía?
  = *is ... obliged to*

10.3 Saying what someone is not obliged to do

- **No vale** *or* **merece la pena que** te molestes en acompañarme
  =*there's no need for ... to*
- Los ciudadanos europeos **no necesitan** pedir un permiso de trabajo
  = *do not need to*
- **No hace falta que** tomen las comidas en el hotel **si no quieren**
  = *you needn't ... if you don't want to*
- **No está obligada a** contestar si no quiere
  = *you're not obliged to*
- **No tiene por qué** aceptar una oferta que no le interesa
  = *there is no reason why you should*
- **No es obligatorio** llevar el pasaporte
  = *it is not compulsory to*
- **No es necesario** hacer trasbordo para ir a Barcelona
  = *you don't need to*
- Los militares de reemplazo **no tendrán obligación de** obedecer órdenes si no están de servicio
  = *will not be under any obligation to*
- **No es indispensable que** lleguemos antes de las ocho
  = *we don't absolutely have to*
- **No se sientan obligados a** aceptar la propuesta de la Delegación del Gobierno
  = *don't feel obliged to*

10.4 Saying what someone must not do

- **No puedes** presentarte a votar en nombre de otra persona
  = *you cannot*
- **No se puede** solicitar permiso de residencia **hasta que** no se tenga un contrato de trabajo
  = *you cannot ... until you have*
- **No me hable** más del tema
  = *would you mind not saying*
- **No le permito que** hable a los clientes de ese modo
  = *I won't have you*
- **No tiene usted derecho a** tratarme como si fuera un esclavo
  = *you have no right to*
- **Le prohíbo** nombrar al director para nada
  = *I forbid you to*
- **Está prohibido** pisar el césped en los parques
  = *you are not allowed to*
- El régimen ha advertido que **no tolerará que critiquen** abiertamente al Gobierno
  = *it will not tolerate any ... criticism*

11 AGREEMENT

11.1 Agreeing with a statement

- **Claro que** la colección más importante de bonsais es la del Palacio Imperial Japonés
  = *of course*
- **¡Exacto!** Ahí está la raíz del problema
  = *exactly*
- **Naturalmente**. Esa es la única forma de acabar con la corrupción política
  = *of course*
- **Yo también pienso lo mismo**. Nuestro equipo no tiene posibilidades en el campeonato
  = *I agree*
- **Estoy de acuerdo contigo en lo que dices del** machismo
  = *I agree with what you say about*
- **Por supuesto que** no hay derecho a que nos traten así
  = *of course*
- Todo el pueblo cree todavía hoy que está vivo. **Y puede que tengan razón**
  = *they may be right*
- **En eso tienes** *or* **te doy toda la razón**, el emigrante trabaja mucho y nunca se queja
  = *you are quite right there*
- **Te entiendo perfectamente**: yo he pasado por lo mismo hace años
  = *I know exactly what you mean*
- Mi maestra **tenía razón** al decir que para ser bailarín profesional hay que ser bueno
  = *was right*
- **Es cierto que** es un tema que nunca se ha tratado en serio
  = *it is true that*
- **Comprendo muy bien que** es un asunto muy delicado
  = *I quite understand that*
- **Admito que** estaba equivocado
  = *I admit that*
- Los dos **somos del mismo parecer** *or* **de la misma opinión**
  = *are of the same opinion*
- **Compartimos la misma opinión** *or* **el mismo punto de vista**
  = *we share the same view*
- **En eso coincido totalmente con** usted
  = *I entirely agree with ... on that*
- **Estamos en completo acuerdo**
  = *we are in complete agreement*
- **Ningún experto podrá refutar** dicho principio
  = *no one could argue with*

11.2 Agreeing to a proposal

- **¡Me apunto!**
  = *count me in!*
- **¡Claro!** Podéis venir cuando queráis
  = *of course*
- **¡Vale!** Nos vemos a las cuatro
  = *fine*
- **De acuerdo**: publicaremos el artículo en el próximo número de la revista
  = *agreed*
- **Perfecto**. Allí estaremos
  = *fine*
- **Me parece bien que** le invites a cenar
  = *I think it's a good idea (for you) to*
- **Me parece una idea estupenda**
  = *I think it's a great idea*
- **Tengo que reconocer** *or* **admitir que la idea me gusta**
  = *I must admit that I like the idea*
- **Estamos conformes con** el precio que piden
  = *we agree to*
- **Apoyaremos su propuesta** ante el consejo ejecutivo
  = *we will back your proposal*
- **Acepto con mucho gusto** su invitación a visitarle en México
  = *I am very pleased to accept*
- El parlamento **está dispuesto a aceptar** la nueva ley reguladora
  = *is willing to accept*
- La asamblea de accionistas **aprobó el plan** presentado por la junta directiva
  = *approved the plan*
- **Tendré en cuenta sus consejos** a la hora de firmar el acuerdo
  = *I'll bear your advice in mind*
- **Quiero expresarle mi total conformidad con** su plan de actuación para los próximos meses
  = *I should like to say that I wholeheartedly endorse*

11.3 Agreeing to a request

- **¡Claro, hombre! ¡Para eso están los amigos!**
  = *of course! That's what friends are for!*
- ¿Que si puedo echar una mano mañana? **¡Por supuesto que sí!**
  = *of course I will*
- **Sí**, mujer, **faltaría más**, úsalo cuando quieras
  = *but of course*
- **Bueno**. Mañana estaré libre si me necesitas
  = *fine*
- Las fechas que propones **me vienen bien**
  = *are fine for me*
- **Si me necesitas, no tienes más que avisarme**
  = *if you need me, just let me know*
- **Puedes contar con** nuestro apoyo
  = *you can count on*
- **Estaré encantado de** participar en ese intercambio
  = *I'll be delighted to*
- El famoso cantante **accedió a que** la prensa estuviera presente
  = *agreed to*
- **No tengo ningún inconveniente en** que se haga público el informe judicial
  = *I have no objection to*

12 DISAGREEMENT

12.1 Disagreeing with what someone has said

- ¿5.000? No, **¡qué va!**, 10.000 por lo menos
  = *no way!*

- ¿Madridista yo? ¡**Pero que dices, hombre**! Yo del Real Betis y nadie más
  = *you must be joking!*
- **Yo no lo veo así**
  = *that's not how I see it*
- **¿No lo dirás en serio**?
  = *you can't be serious*
- **En eso te equivocas** *or* **estás equivocado**
  = *you're wrong there*
- **No estoy de acuerdo contigo en** ese punto
  = *I disagree with you on*
- **Estamos en contra de** toda clase de extremismos
  = *we are against*
- **No entiendo tu actitud** ante el problema
  = *I can't understand your attitude*
- **No se trata de** *or* **No es cuestión de** hacer nuevas leyes, **sino de** poner en práctica las que ya existen
  = *it's not a question of ... but of*
- **Yo personalmente me inclino por** la segunda opción
  = *personally, I favour*
- Sus críticas **no tienen justificación alguna**
  = *there is absolutely no justification for*
- **Deseo expresar mi total disconformidad con** esta medida
  = *I should like to express my total disagreement with*

More tentatively

- **Yo opino de manera distinta**
  = *I see it differently*
- En lo que se refiere al tema de la seguridad social tengo **una opinión muy distinta** a la suya
  = *I take a very different view*
- **Siento (tener que) contradecirte** *or* **llevarte la contraria, pero** las cosas son como son
  = *I'm sorry to (have to) contradict you, but*
- **No comparto tu opinión** al respecto
  = *I do not share your view*
- **No coincidimos con** su planteamiento
  = *we do not agree with*

12.2 Disagreeing with what someone proposes

- ¡**Vaya ocurrencia**!
  = *what a ridiculous idea!*
- **Me parece una idea descabellada** el cambiar ahora de táctica
  = *I think it would be madness to*
- **No estamos dispuestos a aceptar** sus planteamientos
  = *we are not prepared to accept*
- **Resulta (más que) discutible que** sea la única solución
  = *it's (highly) debatable whether*
- **Me niego a** votar sin estar debidamente informado
  = *I refuse to*
- **No podemos adherirnos a la propuesta del** portavoz de la oposición
  = *we cannot agree to the proposal made by*
- **No podemos suscribir** el ultimátum dado por la OTAN
  = *we cannot support*

More tentatively

- **No lo veo muy claro**
  = *I'm not sure*
- **No me hace mucha gracia** levantarme tan temprano
  = *I'm not keen on (the idea of)*
- **Lo de** introducirnos en el mercado extranjero **no nos convence**
  = *we're not keen on the idea of*
- **Me es imposible apoyar** su solicitud
  = *I cannot give you my support for*
- Su plan **no nos parece factible**
  = *does not seem feasible to us*
- **Me temo que no me será posible** aceptar su proyecto
  = *I'm afraid I shall not be able to*

12.3 Refusing a request

- ¡**Ni pensarlo**!
  = *it's out of the question*
- **No puede ser**. Ya no hay tiempo para cambiar el procedimiento
  = *it's impossible*
- **Lo siento, pero no estamos en condiciones de** aceptar su propuesta en este momento
  = *I'm sorry, but we are not in a position to*
- **Es totalmente imposible** reducir el personal de la empresa
  = *... is out of the question*
- **No accederemos jamás a** introducir la semana de 32 horas
  = *we shall never agree to*

More tentatively

- **Me gustaría, pero no voy a poder**
  I'd like to, but I can't
- **Lo sentimos, pero no podemos atender su petición**
  we regret that we cannot grant your request
- **Por desgracia** *or* **Desgraciadamente, su demanda no puede ser atendida**
  unfortunately, your request cannot be granted
- **Aun sintiéndolo mucho, he de negarme a** hacer lo que nos piden
  I'm very sorry, but I must refuse to
- **Lamentamos comunicarle que** su petición ha sido denegada
  we are sorry to have to inform you that

13 APPROVAL

- Y si se quieren casar, **pues muy bien**, que se casen
  fine
- ¡**Así se hace**!
  = *well done!*
- ¡**Estupendo**!, por mi ahora mismo
  = *great!*
- **Me parece perfecto**. Podemos empezar cuando queráis
  = *that seems fine to me*
- ¡**Buena idea**! Yo también me voy a bañar
  = *good idea!*
- **No hay problema**. Dame tu dirección y te lo mando por correo urgente
  = *no problem*
- **Conforme**: No tomaremos ninguna medida hasta previo aviso
  = *agreed*
- **Trato hecho**
  = *it's a deal*
- **Sigue así** *or* **por ese camino**
  = *carry on just as you are doing*
- **Has hecho bien en** decírmelo
  = *you were right to*
- **Me parece muy bien que** te estés tomando las cosas con tranquilidad
  = *I think it's great that*
- **Me alegro mucho de que** tomes un paso tan importante
  = *I'm so pleased that*
- **Estoy muy contento con** el rendimiento de los jugadores
  = *I'm very pleased with*
- Todos **han dado por bueno** el resultado del referéndum que se convocó el pasado mes de diciembre
  = *has welcomed*

More formally

- **Estoy satisfecho con** la decisión del organismo mundial
  = *I am satisfied with*
- **Nos parece una idea excelente que** haya decidido usted encargarse del asunto
  = *we think it is excellent that*
- Cualquier propuesta **será bien recibida**
  = *will be welcomed*
- **Celebro que** se hayan desmentido los rumores
  = *I am delighted that*
- **Será un placer** colaborar con ustedes
  = *I shall be delighted to*

14 DISAPPROVAL

- Pero ¿**qué dices**, Pedro Morán el mejor corredor del mundo?
  = *what are you on about?*
- **Solo a ti se te ocurre una cosa así**
  = *trust you to come up with something like that!*
- ¡**Menuda ocurrencia**!
  = *what a ridiculous idea!*
- ¿**Cómo voy a aprobar su conducta si** va en contra de mis principios?
  = *how could I possibly approve of such behaviour when*
- **Me parece fatal que** la gente fume en su casa
  = *I think it's terrible when*
- **Lo que me parece mal es que** se hagan inversiones desmesuradas a costa de otras zonas mucho más necesitadas
  = *what I think is wrong is that*
- **De ninguna manera** deben paralizarse las obras
  = *under no circumstances*
- Hay capítulos que **no deberían haber sido** publicados
  = *should not have been*
- Muchos de los encuestados **no están nada contentos con** el rumbo actual de la economía
  = *are unhappy with*
- ¿**Con qué derecho se atreven a** prohibirme que hable?
  = *who do they think they are to*
- ¡**Eso no se puede tolerar**!
  = *this cannot be tolerated*
- **No estoy dispuesto a tolerar** tales afirmaciones
  = *I am not prepared to put up with*
- **Es intolerable que** no se haya llegado a un acuerdo definitivo todavía
  = *it is intolerable that*
- **Es inconcebible que** en los albores del siglo XXI se sigan produciendo este tipo de intoxicaciones
  = *it is unbelievable that*
- Todas las instituciones democráticas **condenan** la violencia
  = *condemn*
- **Deseamos protestar contra** la severidad de la pena impuesta por el juez
  = *we should like to protest against*
- El gobierno **expresó su más enérgica repulsa por** el atentado cometido ayer
  = *expressed its strongest condemnation of*

More tentatively

- **No estamos conformes con** el tono en que se expuso el informe
  = *we are not happy about*
- Los profesores universitarios **están poco satisfechos con** las instituciones para las que trabajan
  = *are unhappy with*
- **Me decepciona que** no haya conseguido su objetivo todavía
  = *I am disappointed that*
- **Nos disgusta** el tratamiento que algunas tertulias radiofónicas dan a Cataluña y el catalán
  = *we are unhappy about*
- **Es deplorable que** ocurran cosas de esta naturaleza
  = *it is deplorable that*

15 CERTAINTY, PROBABILITY, POSSIBILITY AND CAPABILITY

15.1 Expressing certainty

- **Seguro que** no está en casa
  = *I'm sure*
- **Está claro que** lo que pretende la publicidad de estos productos es satisfacer el deseo de muchos de perder unos kilos
  = *it is obvious that*
- **Salta a la vista que** no son del lugar ... por la vestimenta, digo
  = *it's patently obvious that*
- **Estoy segura de que** ésa es la fecha exacta de su nacimiento
  = *I'm sure that*
- **Estamos convencidos de que** los coches se roban para venderlos
  = *we are convinced that*
- **Es obvio que** *or* **Es evidente que** se va a convertir en el principal tema de conversación en los próximos días
  = *it is clear that*
- **Por supuesto que** siempre va a haber alguien que se crea eso
  = *of course*
- La fecha de inicio **será, casi con toda** *or* **total seguridad**, el primer domingo de septiembre
  = *will almost certainly be*
- **Se tiene la certeza de que** los secuestradores fueron como máximo tres
  = *we know for certain that*
- **Sin lugar a dudas** *or* **Sin duda alguna**, esta nueva victoria es un gran aliciente para el equipo
  = *without a doubt*
- **No cabe la menor duda de que** sus condiciones de vida eran infrahumanas
  = *there can't be the slightest doubt that*
- **Es innegable que** determinadas melodías perdurarán siempre
  = *it is undeniable that*

15.2 Expressing probability

- Aquí en este barrio **es fácil que** te atraquen
  = *you are quite likely to be*
- **Ya verás como** todo sale bien
  = *you'll see how*
- **Seguramente** se ha retrasado por el camino
  = *... probably ...*
- **Debe (de) haberse** olvidado de su compromiso
  = *he must have*
- **Lo más seguro** *or* **probable es que** esa no fuera su verdadera intención
  = *... probably ...*
- **Es muy posible** *or* **probable que** lleguemos a nuestro destino dentro del horario previsto
  = *it seems very likely that*
- **(Muy) posiblemente** *or* **probablemente** se trate de una falsa alarma
  = *... (very) probably ...*
- **Parece ser que** la autoridad monetaria podría tomar la decisión de subir los tipos de interés el próximo día 23
  = *it seems that*
- **No sería de extrañar que** *or* **No sería extraño que** los animales fueran al final los más perjudicados
  = *it wouldn't be surprising if*
- **No me sorprendería que** el ciclista francés ganara la etapa de hoy
  = *I shouldn't be surprised if*

- Según la agencia meteorológica, **hay muchas** *or* **grandes posibilidades de que** se produzcan nuevas erupciones
  = *it is very likely that*
- **Todavía tiene mucha** *or* **una buena chance de** ganar la carrera (*LAm*)
  = *he still has a good chance of*
- **Todo lleva a suponer** *or* **Todo parece indicar que** las rupturas matrimoniales seguirán en aumento
  = *all the indications are that*

15.3 Expressing possibility

- **Igual** no tengo suerte y suspendo
  = *I may*
- **A lo mejor** hago escala en Tenerife de camino a Montevideo
  = *maybe*
- **Quizá(s)** tengamos que volver antes de lo previsto
  = *perhaps*
- **Tal vez** nuestras sospechas son infundadas
  = *perhaps*
- **Puede que** la situación se convierta en irreversible
  = *... may*
- Dicho comando **podría ser** el autor de diversos atentados terroristas cometidos en la región desde octubre
  = *could be*
- **Siempre existe la posibilidad de que** el nivel de precios aumente
  = *there's always the possibility that*
- **Cabe la posibilidad de que** los afectados hayan bebido agua contaminada
  = *it is possible that*
- **Cabe pensar que** el error haya sido a propósito
  = *it is possible that*

15.4 Expressing capability

- **¿Sabes** escribir al tacto?
  = *can you*
- **¿Sabes** usar la nueva impresora?
  = *do you know how to*
- **Hablo** francés y **entiendo** el italiano
  = *I can speak ... I can understand*
- **Puedo** invertir hasta trece millones en las obras
  = *I can*
- Se exigen **conocimientos básicos de** mecánica
  = *a basic knowledge of*
- El niño **tiene aptitudes para** la física y las matemáticas
  = *has an aptitude for*
- El ser humano **tiene la capacidad del** raciocinio
  = *has the capacity for*

16 DOUBT, IMPROBABILITY, IMPOSSIBILITY AND INCAPABILITY

16.1 Expressing doubt

- **No sé si** debemos discutir ese tema ahora
  = *I don't know whether*
- **No estoy seguro de cuáles son** sus condiciones
  = *I'm not sure what ... are*
- **No es seguro que** el viaje de vuelta sea en el mismo tren
  = *it isn't certain that*
- **No está claro quién** va a salir más perjudicado de la situación
  = *it isn't clear who*
- **No tengo muy claro que** sirva de algo el que vayamos a la huelga
  = *I'm not very sure that*
- **Me pregunto si** realmente merece la pena trabajar fuera
  = *I wonder whether*
- **No estoy (plenamente) convencido de que** su propuesta sea la solución más acertada
  = *I'm not (entirely) convinced that*
- **Dudo que** vuelva a haber otra oferta similar
  = *I doubt whether*
- **Todavía quedan dudas sobre** las circunstancias en que acontecieron los hechos
  = *doubts still remain about*
- **No hay ninguna seguridad de que** el proyecto esté finalizado el mes que viene
  = *we cannot be certain that*
- **Ya veremos si** conviene o no meterse en ese tipo de aventuras
  = *we shall see in due course whether*
- **No se sabe con certeza si** es una enfermedad hereditaria
  = *no one knows for certain whether*

16.2 Expressing improbability

- **Es difícil que** el número uno español participe en el campeonato el próximo año
  = *... is unlikely to*
- **Dudo mucho que** el cambio se traduzca en una mejora de la calidad
  = *I very much doubt whether*
- **Es bastante dudoso que** se convoque el referéndum
  = *it is rather doubtful whether*
- **No parece que** vaya a hacer buen tiempo
  = *it doesn't look as if*
- **Me extrañaría** *or* **Me sorprendería (mucho) que** la fruta madurara en esas condiciones
  = *I should be (very) surprised if*
- **Es (muy) poco probable que** una subida de las multas se traduzca en un descenso del número de infracciones
  = *... is (very) unlikely to*
- **No parece muy probable que** se logre desarrollar una vacuna eficaz
  = *it doesn't seem very likely that*
- **Es (muy/bastante) improbable que** ocurra un accidente en una central nuclear moderna
  = *... is (very/pretty) unlikely to*
- Quien pierde su empleo **cada vez tiene menos probabilidades de** encontrar uno nuevo a corto plazo
  = *has less and less chance of*

16.3 Expressing impossibility

- No, no estuve en París. **¡Qué más quisiera yo!**
  = *chance would be a fine thing!*
- A estas horas **no puede ser** el cartero
  = *it can't be*
- **No es posible que se trate** de la misma persona
  = *it can't be*
- **Es totalmente** *or* **completamente imposible que** la vegetación crezca en unas condiciones tan adversas
  = *... can't possibly*
- **Me resulta (materialmente) imposible** despedirme de todos en persona
  = *it would be (physically) impossible for me to*
- El camino de la negociación **tiene escasas posibilidades de** éxito
  = *has very little chance of*
- **No hay** *or* **No existe ninguna posibilidad de que** los sindicatos lleguen a un acuerdo con el gobierno en tan poco tiempo
  = *there isn't the slightest chance of*
- **Me es imposible** llamarle hasta mañana
  = *I can't*
- **No parece factible que** el delantero uruguayo vaya a fichar por el Barcelona
  = *it doesn't seem feasible that*

- Se ha demostrado que el plan de regulación del tráfico **es poco viable**
  = *is not very practicable*

16.4 Expressing incapability

- **No veo nada** desde aquí
  = *I can't see anything*
- **No sé cómo explicar** lo que vi
  = *I can't explain*
- **Apenas se podía uno** mover de la cantidad de gente que había
  = *one could hardly*
- Muchos industriales de nuestro país **no se sienten capaces de** competir de igual a igual con los extranjeros
  = *feel incapable of*
- **Yo soy (totalmente) incapaz de** montar escenas en público porque soy muy pudorosa
  = *I am (quite) incapable of*
- Este chico **no sirve para** este trabajo
  = *is no good at*
- **Carece de las aptitudes necesarias para** una misión de tal envergadura
  = *he hasn't the necessary aptitude for*
- Muy a menudo la policía **se ve imposibilitada para** actuar con una mayor efectividad
  = *find themselves unable to*

17 EXPLANATIONS

17.1 Emphasizing the reason for something

- Tuvimos que marcharnos **porque** se puso a llover
  = *because*
- **Como** tardabas en llegar, decidimos irnos
  = *as*
- Las plantas se han marchitado **por** exceso de riego
  = *due to*
- Tiene 10.000 acciones **gracias a** los ahorros de toda la vida
  = *thanks to*
- **Con** la nevada que ha caído no hay correo
  = *what with*
- **Es que** llevamos tanto tiempo agarrados al kalashnikov que no podemos soltarlo fácilmente
  = *it's just that*
- Ha tenido muy mala suerte. **Por eso** le tengo tanta lástima
  = *that's why*
- Habla tan bajo que a menudo parece que susurrara. **Por eso mismo** le aconsejaron que interviniera lo menos posible en mítines populares
  = *that's why*
- El fenómeno **tiene muchísimo que ver con** las nuevas formas de vida que aíslan cada vez más al hombre de la ciudad
  = *has a great deal to do with*
- No toleraba flores junto a ella **por miedo a que** la intoxicaran
  = *for fear that*
- **No es** la religión **la causa de** tanta guerra
  = *it is not ... that causes*
- **En vista de que** el fuego había provocado una densa humareda, se decidió la evacuación del recinto
  = *seeing that*

More formally

- El problema es grave, **ya que** el consumo anual es mayor que la producción
  = *for*
- Se recomienda ir pronto, **puesto que** se forman colas importantes
  = *since*
- La cuantía de las donaciones no era demasiado elevada, **pues** únicamente había monedas de bajo valor
  = *as*
- La evacuación del edificio se vio dificultada **a causa del** bloqueo de una de las salidas de emergencia
  = *because of*
- En todo el mundo se ha desencadenado una gran competencia por las áreas de pesca. **Por este motivo** han surgido grandes problemas
  = *for this reason*
- El absentismo entre los eurodiputados es muy preocupante, **dado que** el Parlamento europeo toma cada vez más decisiones
  = *given that*
- **Por razones de seguridad**, aparcamos el automóvil lejos de la casa
  = *for ... reasons*
- **Sus motivos para** abrir una nueva oficina **son** de orden económico
  = *his reasons for ... are*
- La capital se hallaba ayer prácticamente paralizada **a consecuencia de** la huelga general
  = *as a result of*
- **Como consecuencia de** la crisis económica, las ventas se redujeron en un porcentaje considerable
  = *as a result of*
- **Como resultado de** las acciones emprendidas, los trabajadores lograron parte de sus reivindicaciones
  = *as a result of*
- **Debido a** condiciones meteorológicas adversas, nos vemos obligados a suspender la celebración anunciada
  = *owing to*
- Los problemas de suciedad en la zona **se deben a** una mala gestión municipal
  = *are due to*
- La falta de lluvias **ha ocasionado** una grave sequía al sur del país
  = *has caused*
- Su especial percepción de la atmósfera parisina **arranca de** una infancia llena de vivencias
  = *dates back to*
- Dicha teoría sostiene que la evolución **resulta de** una interacción entre la variación y la selección
  = *is a result of*
- El descenso de la competitividad **procede principalmente de** los elevados costes y del declive de la productividad
  = *is mainly due to*
- La fuerza de esta poesía **radica en** su brillante capacidad verbal
  = *lies in*
- **Ocurre que** a veces a algunos les da por hablar en un tono ofensivo
  = *what happens is that*
- La explosión, **provocada por** una bomba, ha causado un alto número de heridos
  = *which was caused by*
- Yo personalmente **lo atribuyo a** un error del conductor
  = *I attribute it to*

17.2 Emphasizing the result of something

- No quería ir con el estómago vacío, **así que** me preparé un sandwich previo
  = *so*
- Me atrae **tanto** lo que hago **que** no me merece la pena restarle tiempo para dedicarlo a otras cosas
  = *so much that*
- Salieron temprano, **de modo que** cuando él llegó se encontró la casa vacía
  = *so that*
- El recuerdo del hambre infantil le marcó **de tal manera que** siempre devoraba grandes cantidades de pan
  = *in such a way that*

- No fabrican anticuerpos **y por lo tanto** no pueden inmunizarse contra los parásitos y los virus
  = *and therefore*

18 APOLOGIES

18.1 Apologizing

- **Perdona**, me había olvidado de ti
  = *I'm sorry*
- **Perdona que** no avisara con tiempo suficiente
  = *I'm sorry*
- No consigo acordarme del autor. **Lo siento**
  = *I'm sorry*
- **Siento mucho no haber podido** conseguir la información
  = *I'm so sorry that I wasn't able to*
- **Pido perdón a** la familia **por** lo que hicimos
  = *I ask ... to forgive*
- Cualquiera que se atreva a hacer una cosa así es, **con perdón**, un perfecto imbécil
  = *if you'll forgive me for saying so*
- **Lo lamento**. A veces me cuesta reprimirme
  = *I am very sorry*

More formally

- El escritor **pidió disculpas por** su ausencia en el acto inaugural
  = *apologized for*
- En cualquier caso **acepte mis disculpas, por favor**
  = *please accept my apologies*
- **Disculpen si** les he causado alguna molestia
  = *I apologize if*
- **Rogamos disculpen las molestias que** esta deficiencia pueda causarles
  = *we apologize for any inconvenience that*
- **Espero que** el avisado lector **excuse** estas generalidades que seguramente conoce
  = *I hope that ... will excuse*
- **Espero dispensen lo ocurrido**
  = *I hope you'll forgive us/me for this unfortunate incident*
- **Lamentamos profundamente que** haya ocurrido este incidente
  = *we are very sorry that*

18.2 Apologizing for being unable to do something

- **Por desgracia** la empresa **no puede** atender su petición en estos instantes
  = *unfortunately or I'm afraid ... is unable to*
- **Sentimos comunicarle que** a partir de la fecha dejaremos de abonar el importe correspondiente al seguro de las pólizas
  = *we regret to inform you that*
- **Desgraciadamente** *or* **Lamentablemente, nos es imposible** aceptar su propuesta
  = *unfortunately, we are unable to*
- **Muy a nuestro pesar nos vemos obligados a** prescindir de sus servicios a partir de hoy
  = *we very much regret that we are obliged to*

18.3 Admitting responsibility

- **Es culpa mía**. Me lo he buscado
  = *it's my fault*
- **Reconozco que estaba equivocado**
  = *I admit I was wrong*
- **Sé que** mis palabras de anoche **no tienen perdón**
  = *I know that ... was unforgivable*
- **Debo confesar que** el error **fue culpa mía**
  = *I must confess that ... was my fault*
- **Me responsabilizo plenamente de** lo ocurrido
  = *I take full responsibility for*
- **Admitimos que** existen defectos en la organización
  = *we admit that*
- **Asumimos plenamente nuestra responsabilidad**
  = *we fully accept our responsibility*

18.4 Disclaiming responsibility

- De verdad que **no lo hice a posta**
  = *I didn't do it on purpose*
- **Ha sido sin querer**
  = *it was an accident*
- **Lo dijeron sin mala intención**
  = *they didn't mean any harm*
- **No era mi intención ofenderle**: hablaba en broma
  = *I didn't mean to offend you*
- **Pensé que hacía bien en** dirigirme a ellos directamente
  = *I thought I was doing the right thing in*
- **Teníamos entendido que** ellos estaban de acuerdo
  = *we thought that*
- Habría querido actuar de otro modo, **pero no tenía otra salida**
  = *but I had no alternative*
- **Espero que comprenda usted** lo difícil de nuestra situación
  = *I hope you will understand*

18.5 Replying to an apology

- **No pasa nada**, hombre: si se ha roto me compro otro y ya está
  = *don't worry about it*
- **No te preocupes**. ¿Qué culpa tienes tú?
  = *don't worry*
- Fue un lapsus: **no se hable más**
  = *we won't say any more about it*
- **No importa**, ya lo sabíamos
  = *it doesn't matter*
- **No te guardo (ningún) rencor**
  = *I don't bear you any grudge*
- **No es ninguna molestia**
  = *it's no trouble*
- El retraso **no tiene (ninguna) importancia**
  = *is of no importance*
- **Aceptamos de buen grado sus disculpas**
  = *we are happy to accept your apologies*

19 JOB APPLICATIONS

19.1 Starting your letter

- **En referencia al anuncio publicado en** la edición de hoy de La Gaceta, **le agradecería que me enviara los datos y la documentación pertinente** al puesto anunciado
  = *with reference to your advertisement in ..., I should be grateful if you would send me details of*
- **En respuesta a su anuncio de hoy en** Noticias, **les agradecería que me considerasen para el puesto de** jefe de ventas
  = *in response to your advertisement in today's ..., I should be grateful if you would consider me for the position of*
- **Me permito enviarles mis detalles para que los tomen en consideración** en el caso de que necesiten los servicios de alguien con mis cualificaciones/mi experiencia
  = *I am writing to you with my particulars in the hope that you may consider them*

19.2 Detailing your experience and giving your reasons for applying

- **Soy licenciado en Ciencias de la Información y llevo seis meses trabajando en** la redacción de un periódico local, **donde estoy al**

Julia Guedes Tola
Paseo Buenos Aires 141, 5° A
07052 Alicante

12 de julio, 2016

Sr. Director Gerente
INFOCOMP, Sistemas informáticos
C/ Primero de Mayo 73, 1°
46002 VALENCIA

Muy Señor mío:

Me dirijo a usted para solicitar el puesto de Director de ventas anunciado en EL PAIS el día 9 de este mes.

Como podrá ver en la copia del currículum vitae que adjunto, tengo considerable experiencia en el sector comercial, además de numerosas relaciones con empresas de la zona, sin duda de gran utilidad para un puesto como el que solicito.

Adjunto también toda la documentación justificativa que se exige.

Quedo a su disposición para cualquier aclaración que necesite y le agradezco la atención prestada.

Atentamente,

Julia Guedes

CURRICULUM VITAE

NOMBRE Y APELLIDOS **Julia Guedes Tola**
DOMICILIO Paseo Buenos Aires 141, 5° A
07052 Alicante
TELÉFONO (965) 93 15 58
FECHA DE NACIMIENTO 5 de septiembre de 1986
ESTADO CIVIL soltera

ESTUDIOS [1]

2004–2009 : Licenciatura en Ciencias Empresariales, Universidad de Valencia
2008 marzo-junio : Universidad de Dublín, intercambio Erasmus
2003–04 : COU, Instituto Salzillo, Murcia

EXPERIENCIA PROFESIONAL

Desde mayo 2014 : Directora de Ventas, ELECTRÓNICA COSTA BLANCA, Alicante
Febrero 2010 – marzo 2014 : Encargada de Administración, Agencia de Publicidad PLENA PLANA, Castellón
Veranos 2008 y 2009 : Profesora de matemáticas, Academia ESTUDIOS, Alcoy
Enero – marzo 2009 : Prácticas laborales en INTER-CHIP, Valencia

INFORMACIÓN COMPLEMENTARIA

Idiomas: inglés, uso habitual en el entorno laboral. Numerosos contactos empresariales en toda la Costa Blanca. Asesoramiento empresarial ofrecido con regularidad a pequeñas y medianas empresas de la industria turística. Destreza en el uso y aprovechamiento de recursos informáticos en la empresa.

[1] People with British, American or other qualifications applying for jobs in Spanish-speaking countries might use some form of wording to explain their qualifications such as *"equivalente al bachillerato superior español/mexicano"* etc. (3 A-levels), *"equivalente a una licenciatura en Letras/Ciencias"* etc. (B.A. B.Sc. etc) etc. Alternatively, *"Licenciado en Lenguas Clásicas"* etc. might be used.

cargo de la sección de sucesos
= *I have a degree in Media Studies and for the last six months have been working on ... where I am in charge of*

- **Tengo dos años de experiencia como** auxiliar administrativo **en** una empresa de importación-exportación
= *I have two years' experience as ... in*
- Además del inglés, mi lengua materna, **hablo español con fluidez** *or* **soltura, tengo conocimientos de francés y entiendo el italiano escrito**
= *I speak Spanish fluently, have a working knowledge of French, and can understand written Italian*
- **Aunque no tengo experiencia previa en** este tipo de trabajo, **he desempeñado otros trabajos eventuales durante las vacaciones de verano**. Si lo desean, puedo darles los nombres de las entidades en las que he estado empleado
= *although I have no previous experience of ..., I have had other holiday jobs*
- **Mi sueldo actual es de** ... euros **al año, e incluye cuatro semanas de vacaciones remuneradas**
= *my current salary is ... a year, with four weeks paid holiday*
- **Desearía trabajar en su país** durante algún tiempo **con objeto de perfeccionar mis conocimientos de español y adquirir experiencia en** el sector hotelero
= *I should like to work in your country ... so as to improve my Spanish and gain experience in*
- He terminado recientemente mis estudios de Filología Hispánica y **estoy muy interesado en usar mis conocimientos de español dentro de un entorno laboral**
= *I am very keen to use my Spanish in a work environment*
- **Tengo extremo interés en trabajar con** una empresa de su prestigio
= *I should very much like to work for*

19.3 Closing the letter

- **Estoy a su entera disposición para ofrecerles cualquier información complementaria que necesiten**
= *I should be happy to supply any further information that you may need*
- **Podría incorporarme a su empresa a partir de** primeros de junio
= *I would be available for work from*
- **Tendré mucho gusto en entrevistarme con ustedes** cuando lo consideren conveniente
= *I should be delighted to attend for interview*
- **Le agradezco la atención prestada y quedo a la espera de su respuesta**
= *thanking you for your kind attention, I look forward to hearing from you*

19.4 Asking for and giving references

- **Le ruego se sirva comunicarnos** cuánto tiempo lleva trabajando la Sra. Fernández en su empresa, cuáles eran sus responsabilidades **y qué opinión le merece su capacidad profesional para el puesto que solicita. Trataremos su respuesta con la mayor reserva y confidencialidad**
= *please would you let us know ... what you think of her suitability for the post that she has applied for. We shall treat your reply in the strictest confidence*
- **Durante los cinco años que** la Sra. Díaz **ha trabajado en nuestra empresa, siempre ha demostrado** gran constancia, sentido de la responsabilidad y capacidad de organización. **No dudo en recomendarla para el puesto mencionado**
= *in the five years ... has worked for us, she has shown ... I have no hesitation in recommending her for the post in question*

19.5 Accepting and refusing

- **Acudiré con mucho gusto a sus oficinas** de la calle Rato **para una entrevista** el próximo día 15 de octubre a las 10 de la mañana
= *I shall be delighted to attend for interview at your offices*
- **Deseo confirmar mi aceptación del puesto** que me han ofrecido y la fecha de mi incorporación al mismo
= *I am writing to confirm my acceptance of the post*
- **Antes de tomar una decisión, les agradecería que discutiéramos algunos puntos** de su oferta
= *before coming to a decision, I should be grateful if we could discuss a few points*
- **Tras considerarla detenidamente, lamento tener que rechazar** su oferta de trabajo
= *after much consideration, I am sorry to have to decline*

20 COMMERCIAL CORRESPONDENCE

20.1 Enquiries

- **Hemos visto en el último número de** nuestro boletín industrial **su oferta especial en** artículos de oficina
= *having seen your special offer on ... in the last issue of*
- **Les agradeceríamos que nos enviaran información más detallada sobre** los productos que anuncian, **incluyendo descuentos por pedidos al por mayor, forma de pago y fechas de entrega**
= *we should be grateful if you would send us details of ..., including wholesale discounts, payment terms and delivery times*

20.2 ... and replies

- **Acusamos recibo de su carta con fecha de** 10 de febrero, **interesándose por** nuestros equipos. **Adjunto encontrará** nuestro catálogo general y lista de precios en vigor
= *thank you for your letter of ..., inquiring about .... Please find enclosed*
- **En respuesta a su consulta del** 20 del corriente, **nos complace enviarle los detalles que nos solicitaba**
= *in reply to your inquiry of ..., we are pleased to send you the information you requested*

20.3 Orders

- **Les rogamos nos envíen por avión los siguientes artículos a la mayor brevedad**
= *please send us the following items by airmail as soon as possible*
- **Les agradeceríamos que tomaran nota de nuestro pedido** núm. 1.443 **y nos confirmen su aceptación a vuelta de correo**
= *we should be grateful if you would note our order ... and confirm acceptance by return of post*
- **Adjunta le remitimos nota de pedido núm.** 8.493, **que esperamos se sirva cumplimentar con la mayor urgencia**
= *please find enclosed order no ..., which we hope can be executed with all possible speed*
- **Tengan la amabilidad de efectuar la entrega dentro del plazo especificado. De no ser así nos reservamos el derecho a rechazar la mercancía**
= *please ensure that delivery is within the specified time. Otherwise, we must reserve the right to refuse the merchandise*

20.4 ... and replies

- **Acusamos recibo de su pedido núm.** 7721
= *we acknowledge receipt of your order no.*
- **Le agradecemos su pedido con fecha del** 3 de septiembre, **al que daremos salida** tan pronto como nos sea posible
= *thank you for your order of ..., which we will dispatch*
- **La entrega se efectuará en un plazo no superior** a veinte días
= *you should allow 20 days for delivery*

20.5 Deliveries

- **Efectuaremos entrega de los productos en cuanto** recibamos sus instrucciones
= *orders will be dispatched as soon as*
- **No nos responsabilizamos de los daños que la mercancía pueda sufrir en tránsito**
= *we cannot accept responsibility for goods damaged in transit*
- **Sírvanse enviar acuse de recibo**
= *please confirm receipt*

TODOLIBRO S.A.

EDITORES – DISTRIBUIDORES

Av. del Guadalquivir, 144 - 41005 Sevilla
Tel (954) 34 34 90 - Fax (954) 34 00 39

West Distribution Services Ltd
14 St David's Place
Birmingham B12 5TS

Sevilla, 12 de octubre de 2016

Estimados señores:

Acusamos recibo de su carta del 20 de septiembre, en la que nos sugieren la posibilidad de que su representante el Sr. John Kirk nos visite en Sevilla aprovechando su próximo viaje por España, al objeto de establecer una relación más estrecha entre nuestras respectivas casas.

Tendremos, naturalmente, mucho gusto en recibirle y en principio sugerimos la fecha del lunes 24 de octubre para nuestro primer contacto, que podría tener lugar en nuestras oficinas a las 10 de la mañana.

Sin otro particular, quedamos a la espera de sus noticias.

Atentamente,

J. J. Rodriguez

Juan José Rodriguez
Director Comercial

Calzados la Mallorquina
Casa fundada en 1928

Carretera de la Finca, s/n - 07034 Palma de Mallorca - Teléfono (971) 100303

Palma, 2 de marzo de 2016

Dña Ana Hernández
Import-Export. S.A.
Mellado 38
28034 Madrid

Estimada Sra. Hernández:

Con referencia a su carta del 19-2-16, sobre la liquidación de nuestra factura núm 86-109876, le informo que aún existe un saldo pendiente de 800 euros, debido al parecer a que han deducido una nota de crédito por dicha cantidad de la que no tenemos conocimiento.

Sin duda se trata de un error fácilmente subsanable, por lo que le rogamos que revisen sus cálculos con el fin de aclarar su cuenta y podamos continuar nuestras transacciones como de costumbre.

Reciba un atento saludo,

Andrés Carbonell

Andrés Carbonell
Jefe de Ventas

- Le informamos que **la mercancía ha sido despachada según lo acordado**
  = *the goods were dispatched as agreed*

20.6 Payments

- Cumpliendo su encargo, **le remitimos adjunta factura por valor de** 900 euros, **con vencimiento a** diez días **vista**
  = *please find enclosed our invoice for the sum of .... Payment is due within ... of receipt*
- **El importe total se eleva a** 650 euros
  = *the final total amounts to*
- **Sírvase remitirnos el pago a vuelta de correo**
  = *please send payment by return*
- **Adjuntamos cheque por valor de** 150 euros **en liquidación de su factura**
  = *please find enclosed our cheque for the sum of ... in settlement of your invoice*

20.7 Complaints

- **Les comunicamos que no hemos recibido nuestro pedido del 4 de julio dentro del plazo acordado.** Les rogamos que hagan las indagaciones pertinentes
  = *please note that we have not received our order of ... within the agreed time*
- **Nos permitimos recordarle que estamos a la espera del pago de nuestra factura** núm. 43.809, **cuyo plazo venció** el 2 del corriente. Le rogamos se ponga en contacto con nosotros a la mayor brevedad
  = *we should like to remind you that we are awaiting payment for invoice no. ... which fell due on*
- **Hemos apreciado un error de suma en su factura** núm. 7.787, por lo que les rogamos se sirvan remitirnos rectificación
  = *we have found an addition error in invoice*

21 GENERAL CORRESPONDENCE

21.1 Starting a letter

To a friend or acquaintance

- **Como hace tanto tiempo que no sé de ti me he decidido a** mandarte unas líneas ...
  = *as it's been so long since I had news of you, I decided to*
- **Me alegró mucho recibir noticias tuyas**, después de tanto tiempo
  = *it was lovely to hear from you*
- **Gracias por la amable carta** que me enviaste
  = *thank you for the very nice letter*
- **Perdona que no te haya escrito antes pero** mis ocupaciones profesionales me dejan poco tiempo para más
  = *please forgive me for not having written before but*

In formal correspondence

- **Me dirijo a ustedes para solicitar mayor información sobre** los cursos de verano organizados por su entidad
  = *I am writing to ask for further information on*
- **Les ruego que me envíen** los números de abril y mayo pasados de su revista. Adjunto el cupón con detalles de mi tarjeta de crédito
  = *please send me*
- **Le agradecería que me informara si** han encontrado una chaqueta negra que creo haber olvidado en la habitación que ocupamos en su hotel
  = *I should be grateful if you would let me know if*

... and replies

- **En contestación a su carta del** 19 de noviembre, **he de informarle que** no hemos encontrado los documentos por los que se interesa
  = *in answer to your letter of ..., I regret to inform you that*
- **Acusamos recibo de su carta, en la que pregunta por** nuestros cursos de verano
  = *thank you for your letter inquiring about*
- **He recibido su carta en la que solicita** autorización para reproducir uno de mis cuadros en la portada de su revista
  = *I have received your letter asking for*
- **Gracias por su carta del** 29 de enero y disculpe la tardanza en responder
  = *thank you for your letter of*
- **En referencia a su petición para que** se reforme el reglamento del club, **tengo el gusto de comunicarle que** ya ha sido remitida a órgano de dirección
  = *with reference to your request for ..., I am pleased to advise you that*

21.2 Ending a letter

- **Espero que tardes menos en escribirme esta vez**
  = *I hope that this time you won't take so long to write to me*
- **No te olvides de darle mis recuerdos a** todos por ahí
  = *do give my best wishes to*
- **A ver si podemos vernos** pronto
  = *let's see if we can get together*
- **Recuerdos de parte de** mi madre
  = *... sends her best wishes*

In formal correspondence

- **Quedo a la espera de sus noticias**
  = *I look forward to hearing from you*
- **No dude en ponerse en contacto con nosotros si requiere más información**
  = *don't hesitate to contact us if you need further information*
- **Muchas gracias de antemano por su colaboración**
  = *thanking you in advance for your help*

21.3 Travel plans

- **¿Disponen ustedes de un listado de cámpings de** la región?
  = *do you have a list of campsites for*
- **Sírvanse enviarme su guía de actividades deportivas** y lista de precios
  = *please would you send me your guide to sports activities*
- **¿Podría decirme si quedan plazas para** el viaje por el Marruecos interior que anuncian en el número de este mes de su revista?
  = *please could you tell me if there are any places left for*

21.4 Bookings

- Me han recomendado encarecidamente su hotel, por lo que **les agradeceré que me reserven** dos **habitaciones individuales con cuarto de baño** para la primera semana de junio
  = *I should be grateful if you would reserve me ... single rooms with en suite bathroom ...*
- **Deseo confirmar mi reserva. Tenga la amabilidad de decirme si requiere el pago por adelantado**
  = *I should like to confirm my booking. Please would you let me know if you require payment in advance*
- Por circunstancias ajenas a mi voluntad, **me veo obligado a cancelar la reserva hecha** la semana pasada
  = *I am obliged to cancel the booking I made*

Santander, 10 de marzo de 2016

Querido César:

Recibí la carta que nos escribiste hace unos meses. Siento no haberte contestado hasta ahora, aunque ya te imaginarás que no se debe a que no nos hayamos acordado de ti, simplemente hemos estado demasiado ocupados con el traslado.

Tanto Rosa como yo tenemos recuerdos muy agradables de la temporada que pasamos en tu casa de Puebla. En realidad, el objeto principal de esta carta es invitarte a pasar unas semanas con nosotros este verano. Sabemos lo mucho que te gustaría visitar nuestra tierra y en estas fechas nosotros vamos a poder respirar por fin tras unos meses de intensa actividad.

Espero que te encuentres bien y que podamos verte pronto.

Un saludo muy afectuoso de Rosa y un abrazo de

José

Liverpool, 5 de noviembre de 2016

Sra. Dña. Agustina Martos
Dpto de Historia Moderna
Facultad de Filosofía y Letras
Universidad de Salamanca
C/ Fray Luís de León
37002 SALAMANCA
Spain

Estimada señora:

Me dirijo a usted para solicitarle su inestimable colaboración sobre un tema del que tengo entendido que es una gran experta.

Estoy realizando una investigación sobre el comercio durante el reinado de los Reyes Católicos para una futura tesis doctoral y tenía pensado pasar unos meses en España para estudiar el asunto con detenimiento a partir de las fuentes. Un amigo me recomendó que me pusiera en contacto con usted, de ahí esta carta.

En principio mi idea era visitar el Archivo de Simancas, pero antes quisiera saber su opinión; si me aconseja que empiece mis investigaciones en otros archivos o bibliotecas y si debería realizar algún trámite previo para acceder a los mismos.

A pesar de llevar poco tiempo estudiando este periodo de la historia, ha llegado ya a apasionarme y, si no es inconveniente, le estaría inmensamente agradecido si me permitiera visitarla en algún momento de mi viaje a España.

Una vez más, le agradezco de antemano cualquier ayuda que pueda prestarme.

Atentamente,

J. Hamilton

Standard opening and closing formulae

When the person is known to you

OPENING FORMULAE	CLOSING FORMULAE
(fairly formal)	
Estimado señor (García):[1]	Reciba un cordial saludo de
Estimada señorita (González):[1]	
Estimado colega:	Un cordial saludo
Estimada Carmen:	
[1] *the forms Sr., Sra., Srta. can be used before the surname*	
(fairly informal)	
Mi apreciado amigo:	Afectuosamente
Mi apreciada amiga:	
Mi querido amigo:	Un afectuoso saludo de
Mi querida amiga:	

Writing to a firm or an institution (see also 20)

OPENING FORMULAE	CLOSING FORMULAE
Muy señor mío:[1] *(esp Sp)*	Le saluda atentamente
Muy señores míos:[2]	Les saluda atentamente
Estimados señores:[2]	Atentamente
De nuestra consideración: *(LAm)*	
[1] *if the addressee's job title etc is given*	
[2] *if not naming individual addressee*	

When the recipient is not personally known to you

OPENING FORMULAE	CLOSING FORMULAE
Muy señor mío: *(esp Sp)*	Reciba un respetuoso saludo de
Distinguido señor:	
Distinguida señora: *More formal*	
Estimado señor:	Atentamente
Estimada señora:	Le saluda(n[1]) atentamente
	[1] *if the signatory is more than one person*

To close friends and family

OPENING FORMULAE	CLOSING FORMULAE
Querido Juan:	Recibe un fuerte abrazo de
Querida Elvira:	Muchos besos y abrazos de
Mi querido Pepe:	Tu amigo que no te olvida
Mis queridos primos:	
Queridísima Julia:	Con mucho cariño

To a person in an important position

OPENING FORMULAE	CLOSING FORMULAE
Señor Director:	Respetuosamente le saluda
Señor Secretario General:	

22 THANKS

- **Gracias por todo**
  = *thank you for everything*
- **Te escribo esta nota para darte las gracias por** haber ayudado tanto a mi hija a superar sus problemas
  = *I am writing to thank you for*
- **Te agradezco mucho** las molestias que te has tomado
  = *I am very grateful to you for*
- **Te estoy muy agradecido por** el interés que has demostrado
  = *I am very grateful to you for*
- **Ha sido muy amable de su parte** acompañarme durante tan grata visita
  = *it was very kind of you to*
- **Le estamos profundamente agradecidos por** las atenciones que ha mostrado con nosotros
  = *we are very grateful to you for*
- **Quisiera expresarles mi más sincero agradecimiento por** la inestimable ayuda que nos han prestado
  = *I should like to express my heartfelt gratitude for*
- **Le ruego que transmita a** sus colegas **nuestro reconocimiento por** el interés que mostraron en nuestras propuestas
  = *please would you convey our thanks to ... for*

23 BEST WISHES

23.1 For any occasion

- **Les deseamos un feliz** fin de semana
  = *have a good*
- **Le deseo una feliz** estancia en nuestra compañía
  = *I wish you a happy*
- **Le deseamos lo mejor en** estas fechas tan señaladas
  = *all best wishes on*
- **Un cariñoso saludo de** todos nosotros
  = *very best wishes from*
- **Espero que se encuentren todos bien y que podamos tener el placer de volver a verlos pronto**
  = *I hope you are all well and that we shall have the pleasure of seeing you again soon*
- **Transmita mis mejores deseos al** Sr. Giménez **por** su candidatura
  = *please convey my best wishes to ... for*

23.2 Season's greetings

- **Feliz Navidad y Próspero Año Nuevo**
  = *Merry Christmas and a Happy New Year*
- **Felices Pascuas**
  = *Happy Christmas*
- **Les deseamos unas Felices Navidades y lo mejor para el año entrante**
  = *best wishes for a Merry Christmas and a Happy, Prosperous New Year*
- **Felices Fiestas** a todos
  = *Happy Christmas to you all*

23.3 Birthdays and saint's day

- ¡**Felicidades**!
  = *Happy Birthday!*
- ¡**Feliz cumpleaños**!/¡**Feliz aniversario**! (*CAm*)
  = *Happy Birthday!*
- **Te deseamos muchas felicidades** y que cumplas muchos más
  = *Happy Birthday and Many Happy Returns of the Day*
- **Muchísimas felicidades en el día de tu santo**
  = *With All Best Wishes on your Saint's Day*
- ¡Feliz **onomástico**! (*LAm*)
  = *Happy Saint's Day!*

23.4 Get well wishes

- **Que te mejores pronto**
  = *get well soon*
- **Espero que te pongas bien cuanto antes**
  = *I hope that you'll be better soon*
- **Le deseamos una pronta recuperación**
  = *we hope that you'll soon be better*

23.5 Wishing someone luck

- ¡**Suerte**!
  = *good luck!*
- ¡**Buena suerte con** tu nuevo trabajo!
  = *good luck with*
- Adiós y **muchísima suerte**
  = *the best of luck*
- **Te deseo toda la suerte del mundo** en el examen
  = *the very best of luck*
- **Espero que te salga todo bien**
  = *I hope that everything goes well for you*
- **Os deseamos mucho éxito para** el estreno de la obra
  = *we wish you every possible success for*

23.6 Congratulations

- **Felicidades por tu reciente paternidad**, Antonio
  = *congratulations on becoming a father*
- ¡**Enhorabuena** (*Sp*) por la noticia!
  = *congratulations!*
- **Mi más cordial** *or* **calurosa enhorabuena** (*Sp*)
  = *many congratulations*
- Ha estado usted inmejorable. ¡**Le felicito**!
  = *congratulations!*
- **Reciba mis más sinceras felicitaciones por** el premio
  = *warmest congratulations on*

NB: In Spain and South America, births, engagements and marriages are not usually announced in the formal way that they are in English-speaking countries

24 ANNOUNCEMENTS

24.1 Announcing a birth and responding

- El matrimonio Rodríguez García **se complace en anunciar el nacimiento de su hijo** Guillermo el 10 de julio de 2016 en Edimburgo
  = *are pleased to announce the birth of their son*
- **Me alegra comunicarte que** Lola y Fernán **han sido padres de una niña**, que nació el 25 de septiembre y que recibirá el nombre de Emma. Tanto la madre como la niña se encuentran en perfecto estado de salud
  = *I am very glad to tell you that ... have had a daughter*
- **Nuestra más cordial felicitación por el nacimiento de su hijo**, con nuestro deseo de una vida llena de salud y prosperidad
  = *warmest congratulations on the birth of your son*
- **Nos ha dado una gran alegría recibir las noticias del nacimiento de** Ana y les felicitamos de todo corazón
  = *we were delighted to learn of the birth of ...*

24.2 Announcing an engagement and responding

- Los señores de Ramírez López y Ortega de los Ríos **se complacen en anunciar el compromiso matrimonial de** sus hijos Roberto y María José
  = *are happy to announce the engagement of*
- **Deseamos participarte que** Ana y Manolo **se han prometido**. Como es natural, **nos alegramos mucho de que** hayan tomado esta decisión
  = *we wanted to let you know that ... have got engaged .... We are delighted that*

- Hemos sabido que se ha anunciado su compromiso matrimonial con la Srta. Gil de la Casa y **aprovechamos esta oportunidad para darle la enhorabuena** (*Sp*) *or* **felicitarle** en tan dichosa ocasión
  = *we should like to take this opportunity to offer you our very best wishes and congratulations*
- Me he enterado de que se ha formalizado el compromiso de boda. **Me alegro enormemente y les deseo lo mejor** a los novios
  = *it is splendid news and I should like to send ... my very best wishes*

24.3 Announcing a change of address

- **Deseamos comunicarles nuestra nueva dirección a partir del** 1 de marzo: Fernández de la Hoz, 25, 2° derecha, 28010 Madrid. Teléfono 543 43 43
  = *please be advised that from ... our address will be*

24.4 Announcing a wedding

See also **INVITATIONS**

- Helena Pérez Cantillosa y Antonio Fayos de la Cuadra **tienen el placer de anunciar el próximo enlace matrimonial de su hija** María de los Angeles **con** Pedro Carbonell i Trueta, **que se celebrará** en la parroquia de Santa María la Grande el próximo día 3 de mayo a las doce del mediodía
  = *are pleased to announce the forthcoming marriage of their daughter ... and ... which will take place*
- **Me alegra comunicarles que la boda de** mi hijo Juan y Carmen **se celebró** el pasado día 4 en el Juzgado Municipal (*Sp*) *or* Registro Civil (*LAm*)
  = *I am pleased to be able to tell you that ... were married on*

24.5 Announcing a death and responding

- Dña. Juana Gómez Rivero, viuda de Tomás Alvarez Ramajo, **falleció en el día de ayer a la edad de 72 años después de recibir los Santos Sacramentos** y la bendición apostólica. **D.E.P.** Sus hijos, hermanos, y demás familia **ruegan a** sus amistades y personas piadosas **una oración por su alma. El funeral por su eterno descanso tendrá lugar mañana** a las diez de la mañana en la Iglesia de Nuestra Señora de los Remedios
  = *... passed away yesterday aged 72, having received the Holy Sacrament. R.I.P. ... would ask ... to pray for her .... the funeral will take place tomorrow*
- **Con gran dolor anunciamos que** nuestro querido padre, D. Carlos Delgado, ha fallecido en la madrugada del día 10. Rogamos una oración por su alma
  = *it is with deepest sorrow that we have to announce that*
- **Deseamos expresarle nuestro más sentido pésame por tan dolorosa pérdida, y hacemos votos para que logren hacer frente a estos difíciles momentos con la mayor entereza**
  = *we should like to extend our deepest sympathy to you on your sad loss and to say that we very much hope you will be able to find the strength to bear up in this sad time*
- **Me he enterado con gran tristeza de la muerte de** tu hermano Carlos. De verdad **lo siento en el alma. Comprendo que estas palabras no te servirán de consuelo, pero ya sabes que puedes contar conmigo para lo que necesites**....
  = *I was very sad to learn of the death of ... I am so very sorry. Words are of little comfort, but you know you can count on me if there is anything you need*

25 INVITATIONS

25.1 Marriages

- Las familias Herrera Martínez y Gil Pérez **tienen el placer de comunicarles el próximo enlace matrimonial de** sus hijos Cristina y Andrés. **La ceremonia religiosa tendrá lugar el** 5 de junio en la Iglesia de San Francisco de Villalta, a la una de la tarde **y a continuación se dará un almuerzo en** el hotel Las Encinas
  = *... are pleased to announce the marriage of .... The ceremony will take place on ... and there will be a reception afterwards at*

... and replies

- **Tenemos sumo gusto en aceptar su amable invitación a** la boda de su hija. **Aprovechamos la ocasión para felicitar sinceramente a los novios**
  = *we are delighted to accept your kind invitation to ..., and we should like to offer our warmest congratulations to the happy couple*

25.2 Other formal receptions

- María Luisa Gómez y Roberto Espinedo **tienen el gusto de invitarles al bautizo de su hija** Leticia, **que se celebrará** el domingo día 3 a las once de la mañana en la Iglesia parroquial de S. Marcos. **La recepción tendrá lugar en** el restaurante "Los Molinos", Calle de S. Juan 27
  = *request the pleasure of your company at the christening of their daughter ..., which will take place .... A reception will be held afterwards at*
- A la atención de la Srta. Marta Goikoetxea: El Decano de la Facultad de Estudios Empresariales de la Universidad de Donosti **se complace en invitarla a la cena que tendrá lugar el** 3 de julio **con motivo del** décimo aniversario de su incorporación a nuestra facultad. **S.R.C.**
  = *requests the pleasure of your company at a dinner on ... to celebrate the ... R.S.V.P.*
- En Ediciones Frontera **celebramos** el lanzamiento de nuestra nueva colección "Letras históricas" **con un cóctel en** la Galería de Arte de Carmen Villarroel el martes a las ocho de la tarde. **Esperamos que le sea posible acudir** al mismo
  = *we are having a cocktail party to celebrate .... We hope you will be able to attend*

... and replies

- **Agradecemos su amable invitación, que aceptamos con mucho gusto**
  = *thank you very much for your kind invitation, which we are delighted to accept*
- **Gracias por su invitación a** la cena de homenaje del Presidente de la Asociación, **a la que acudiré encantada**
  = *thank you for your invitation to .... shall be delighted to attend*
- **He recibido su invitación, pero lamento no poder asistir, como hubiera sido mi deseo, por tener un compromiso previo**
  = *thank you for your invitation. I greatly regret that, owing to a prior engagement, I shall not be able to attend*

25.3 Less formal invitations

- **Quisiéramos corresponder de alguna forma a su amabilidad al** tener en su casa a nuestra hija el verano pasado, **por lo que hemos pensado que podrían pasar con nosotros** las vacaciones de Semana Santa, si les viene bien
  = *we should like to do something to show our appreciation for your kindness in ... and we wondered if you would be able to spend ... with us*
- **Nos gustaría mucho que** María Teresa y tú **vinierais a cenar con nosotros** el viernes por la noche
  = *we should be so glad if ... would come to dinner*
- **Quedas invitado a una fiesta que damos** el sábado a las nueve de la noche **y a la que esperamos que puedas venir**
  = *you are invited to a party ... and we very much hope you can come*
- **Vamos a reunirnos unos cuantos amigos** en casa el sábado por la tarde para tomar unas copas y picar algo **y nos encantaría que pudieras venir tú también**, sola o acompañada, como prefieras
  = *we are having a little gathering with some friends ... and we should be delighted if you could come too*
- Pascual y yo normalmente pasamos todo el mes de agosto en el apartamento de Gandía, pero en julio **lo tienes a tu disposición. No tienes más que avisar si quieres** pasar allí una temporada
  = *you would be very welcome to use it. Just let us know if you would like to*

... and replies

- **Le agradezco enormemente su amabilidad al invitarme a** pasar unos días con ustedes. **Estoy deseando que lleguen** las vacaciones para ponerme en marcha
  = *it was extremely kind of you to invite me to .... I'm so much looking forward to*
- **Muchas gracias por tu invitación** para el viernes. María Teresa y yo **acudiremos con mucho gusto**
  = *thank you very much for your invitation .... would be delighted to come*
- **Lo siento en el alma pero no me es posible** cenar contigo el domingo
  = *I am extremely sorry but I am unable to*

26 ESSAY WRITING

26.1 The broad outline of the essay

Introductory remarks

- **Hoy es un hecho bien sabido que** ciertas corrientes vanguardistas de la Europa de entreguerras tuvieron especial eco en Canarias
  = *nowadays, it is a well-known fact that*
- **La historia ha sido testigo en repetidas ocasiones de** la ambición de las naciones dominantes
  = *throughout history there have been repeated examples of*
- **Una actitud muy extendida hoy día es la de considerar que** nada tiene valor permanente
  = *the attitude that ... is very widespread these days*
- **Hoy en día todo el mundo está de acuerdo en que** el progreso significa un aumento del nivel de vida. **Sin embargo, cabe preguntarse si** esta mejora repercute por igual en todos los sectores de la población
  = *nowadays, everyone agrees that .... However, we should perhaps ask ourselves whether*
- **Normalmente, al hablar de** "cultura", **nos referimos al** sentido antropológico de la palabra
  = *when we talk about ..., we usually mean*
- **Se suele afirmar que** la televisión tiene una influencia excesiva en el comportamiento de los más jóvenes. **Convendría analizar esta afirmación a la luz de** nuevas investigaciones psicológicas
  = *it is often said that .... This statement needs to be examined in the light of*
- **Uno de los temas que más preocupa a la opinión pública es el de** la seguridad ciudadana
  = *one of the issues which the public is particularly concerned about is*
- **Existe una gran divergencia de opiniones sobre** la dirección que ha de tomar la reforma educativa
  = *there are many different opinions about*
- **Un tema que se ha planteado reiteradamente es el de** la presencia de la mujer en el mundo empresarial
  = *one issue which has often been raised is*
- **Se debate con frecuencia en nuestros días el problema de** los cambios estructurales en la familia
  = *a problem which is often discussed these days is*

Explaining the aim of the essay

- **En el presente informe vamos a abordar** la influencia que el turismo puede haber ejercido en el desarrollo de la España contemporánea
  = *in this paper we shall examine*
- **En este trabajo trataremos de averiguar si** las bacterias deberían incluirse en el reino animal o vegetal
  = *in this essay we shall try to establish whether*
- **Este ensayo es un intento de dar respuesta a una pregunta de crucial importancia**: ¿a qué se debe que la industria de la defensa sea la única que no esté recorrida por los aires desreguladores del liberalismo?
  = *this essay is an attempt to answer a fundamental question*
- **Nuestro propósito es** hacer justicia a la obra de España en América, tantas veces criticada entre nosotros
  = *our aim is to*
- **Este trabajo tiene como objetivo** aclarar las circunstancias que llevaron a este pueblo a ser una fuerza invasora
  = *the aim of this essay is to*
- **Con objeto de** profundizar el papel que ciertos productos tienen en el desarrollo de las alergias, se ha llevado a cabo un estudio en dos escuelas de la ciudad
  = *with the aim of*

Developing the argument

- **Empecemos diciendo que** ninguna filosofía se puede considerar la panacea de todos los problemas
  = *let us begin by saying that*
- **Para comenzar, debemos hacer hincapié en** la diferencia entre adictos y consumidores ocasionales de drogas
  = *first of all, ... must be emphasized*
- **Damos por sentado que** la situación económica del país en el siglo pasado dificultaba la adopción de las nuevas tendencias artísticas
  = *we are assuming that*
- **Centrémonos primero en el problema de** la congestión en el centro de las grandes ciudades
  = *first, let us concentrate on the problem of*
- **En primer lugar conviene examinar si** existe algún uso o costumbre que no permita la agrupación de accionistas
  = *first, we need to consider whether*
- **Como punto de partida hemos tomado** la situación inmediatamente anterior al estallido del conflicto
  = *we have taken as a starting-point*
- **Si partimos del principio del** equilibrio del ecosistema, **podremos comprender cómo** muchas de nuestras actividades lo rompen constantemente
  = *if we start from the principle of ..., we shall be able to see how*
- Los que abogan por una disminución de la actividad pesquera esgrimen varios argumentos de peso. **El primero que vamos a analizar es** la reducción acelerada de los bancos de pesca
  = *the first ... that we shall examine is*

Connecting elements

- **Pero debemos concentrar la atención en** el aspecto realmente importante del problema
  = *however, we should now focus our attention on*
- **Pasemos ahora a considerar otro aspecto del** tema que nos ocupa
  = *let us move on to another aspect of*
- **Dirijamos la atención al segundo aspecto que** apuntábamos
  = *let us turn our attention to the second point that*
- **A continuación trataremos un punto estrechamente relacionado**
  = *next, we shall look at another closely related issue*
- **Nos ocupamos seguidamente de** los detalles que muchos críticos han ignorado
  = *next, we shall consider*
- **Continuemos con** una mención detallada de los distintos apartados de la declaración
  = *let us now move on to*
- **Pero volvamos de nuevo al asunto** que nos ocupa
  = *but, to return to the issue*
- **Examinemos con más detalle** los orígenes de la situación
  = *let us look in greater detail at*

The other side of the argument

- **Pero pasemos al segundo argumento planteado, según el cual** tener el dinero inutilizado en una cuenta corriente perjudica al

Tesoro, pero beneficia al banco emisor
= *now let us move on to the second argument, according to which*

- **Consideremos ahora lo que ocurriría si** contáramos con un aparato que pudiese grabar cada acto de nuestra existencia de manera que tuviéramos un rápido acceso a todo lo que nos ha sucedido
= *now let us consider what would happen if*
- **Pero existe otro factor sin el cual no se puede comprender la importancia de** la ingeniería genética para la naciente bioindustria
= *but there is another factor that should be taken into account if we are to understand the importance of*
- **Un segundo enfoque consiste en decidir si** las limitaciones impuestas a los extranjeros que quieran participar en las empresas privatizadas se adapta a la normativa comunitaria
= *a second approach would be to decide whether*
- **Sin embargo, también merece atención el planteamiento de quienes aseguran que** el transporte es un servicio social subvencionado
= *however, it is also worthwhile considering the view of those who maintain that*
- **Es preciso advertir, no obstante, que** esta biografía es muy elemental y está orientada a lectores con mínimos conocimientos sobre el asunto
= *it should be pointed out, however, that*
- **Lo que digo sobre** la poesía oriental **puede ser aplicado igualmente a** la poesía occidental, tanto la europea como la americana
= *my comments on ... can equally well be applied to*
- **En contrapartida, la creencia de que** es bueno romper estereotipos hace que nuestro estilo de diálogo aparente ser más violento que en otras culturas
= *on the other hand, the belief that*
- **Ante tal afirmación se puede objetar que** uno debe votar a aquéllos ante los cuales se siente más representado
= *such an assertion can be countered with the argument that*

In conclusion

- **En resumen**, los servicios ferroviarios del país necesitan una planificación seria y a largo plazo
= *in short*
- **En definitiva**, la búsqueda de lo absoluto es esencial en su obra
= *in the final analysis*
- **Se trata, en suma, de** desarrollar un método de diseño que permita que la arquitectura aproveche las posibilidades tecnológicas en beneficio de todos
= *in short, it is a question of*
- **Todos los argumentos vistos aquí llevan a la misma conclusión**: se tardarán tantos años en recuperar la biodiversidad perdida que es importante que empecemos a conservarla ya
= *all the arguments set out here lead to the same conclusion*
- **De todo lo que antecede se deduce que** durante algunos años al menos, no se puede esperar llegar a un acuerdo sobre este tema a nivel universal
= *from what has been said, it can be seen that*
- **Todo ello demuestra** la inviabilidad de los sistemas de reparto del trabajo como método de reducir el paro
= *all of this demonstrates*
- **Llegamos así a la conclusión de que** la responsabilidad recae en los países desarrollados
= *we are therefore drawn to the conclusion that*
- **En conclusión**, existe un grave problema de vivienda en la ciudad, que debemos intentar resolver cuanto antes
= *in conclusion*
- **Para concluir, diremos que** los argumentos con los que nos hallamos más de acuerdo son aquellos refrendados por la investigación científica
= *let us conclude by saying that*
- **Como colofón, hagamos mención de** lo que decía el dramaturgo: "Y los sueños, sueños son"
= *finally, let us remember*

26.2 Constructing a paragraph

Ordering elements

- **Ante todo**, entendemos por escalada libre la progresión por una pared sin emplear más que la roca, los pies y las manos
= *first and foremost*
- En esta discusión median poderosas razones políticas; **primero**, porque el tradicional apoyo a la iniciativa privada del Gobierno de Estados Unidos influye también en las actividades culturales; **en segundo lugar**, porque la cultura europea ha estado siempre sujeta al Estado y no es fácil separarlas de repente
= *firstly ...; secondly*
- **Pero antes de examinar esta cuestión, veamos primeramente** cuáles son las enfermedades hereditarias que podrían beneficiarse de esta terapia y cuáles son los equipos que trabajan en este campo
= *before examining this question in detail, let us look at*
- **Finalmente**, habría que pedir con urgencia a todos los responsables públicos que se comiencen a discutir los temas de bioética con la mayor transparencia
= *finally*
- **Por último**, hay que resaltar que la obra hace gala de un estilo que rebasa la simple eficacia
= *lastly*

Connecting elements

- La tendencia de las sociedades humanas es a endiosar mitos y anatemizar diablos. De **los primeros** se esperan milagrosas salvaciones; contra **los segundos** se descargan las miserias
= *the former ... the latter*
- **No sólo** *or* **solamente** se ha creado la esperanza de una paz duradera **sino que también** *or* **además** se han sentado las bases para que así ocurra
= *not only ... but also*
- **En relación con** *or* **En conexión con** lo expuesto anteriormente, hemos de añadir la falta de previsión
= *in connection with*
- **A este respecto hay que destacar que** las enfermedades de transmisión sexual están más extendidas entre los hombres que entre las mujeres
= *in this regard we should point out that*
- **Tanto** la forma **como** el contenido muestran una estructura simétrica
= *both ... and*
- El estudio determina, **por otra parte**, la relación de causa-efecto que se da en la construcción española entre la crisis que padece y su efecto multiplicador
= *moreover*
- El libro tiene dos virtudes. **Por una parte**, reúne toda la información sobre los maltratos a menores **y por otra**, pone sobre la mesa lo que está pasando
= *on the one hand ... and on the other*
- **Si por un lado** en sus mejores obras consigue una trascendentalización del arte, **por otro**, en las más repetitivas, se reduce a una mera manifestación convencional
= *while on the one hand ..., on the other*
- Las operaciones se llevaron a cabo, **bien** por negligencia de los supervisores, **bien** por astucia del perpetrante
= *either ... or*
- **Ni** sus colegas **ni** sus ayudantes, **ni siquiera** los más allegados, tenían idea de lo que el artista se proponía lograr
= *neither ... nor ... nor even*

Adding elements

- Un ajuste de tal magnitud afectaría, **además**, a otras empresas estatales
= *moreover*
- **Además de** los instrumentos señalados para el fomento de la investigación científica por parte de la Administración, **existen** otras

medidas indirectas que pueden tomar diferentes Ministerios
= *in addition to ..., there are*

- **Otro dato a tener en cuenta es** la aprobación de un comunicado conjunto
= *another factor to take into account is*
- **Otro acontecimiento que tuvo también gran importancia fue** la firma de un acuerdo de cooperación entre ambos países
= *another very important event was*
- **Y no sólo eso** *or* **eso no es todo**: tales medidas no compensan a los afectados de ninguna manera
= *and that is not all*
- Todo ejercicio aeróbico estresa el sistema central. **Es más**, el corazón no puede saber qué ejercicio está realizando
= *moreover*
- **Cabe destacar igualmente** que la transferencia genética se ha empleado con éxito en células de mamífero
= *it should also be noted that*
- **Por lo que respecta a** las novedades de producto, la gama todo terreno se ha ampliado con la llegada de tres nuevas versiones
= *as far as ... are concerned*
- **En cuanto a** las tendencias para los 12 meses siguientes, el gasto en software se incrementará en el 59,9% de las empresas
= *as for*

Introducing one's own point of view

- **Soy de la opinión de que** es mejor que los medios de comunicación estén en manos de los propietarios de la edición y de la comunicación que controlados por los propietarios de entes financieros
= *I am of the opinion that*
- La exposición más destacada del pintor aragonés fue, **a mi criterio**, la exhibida en el Casón del Buen Retiro a principios de los sesenta
= *to my mind*
- Para muchos la diferencia es simplemente administrativa, **y yo lo suscribo totalmente**
= *and I would agree wholeheartedly*
- Hasta cierto punto **comparto esta opinión**
I share that view
- **Nuestra hipótesis es que** el pintor busca plasmar la fugacidad, aunque tal vez nos equivoquemos
= *our hypothesis is that*
- **Podemos afirmar que** las raíces del levantamiento armado hay que buscarlas en las condiciones de vida de la población indígena
= *it is true to say that*
- **Vaya por delante mi firme convicción de que**, en un tiempo razonable, vamos a ser capaces de relanzar el arte de nuestra tierra hasta volverle a situar en lugar destacado dentro de Europa
= *first and foremost I am convinced that*
- El problema, **desde mi punto de vista**, reside en que aún no se ha conseguido sintetizar culturalmente una nueva idea de España, como comunidad de pueblos o nación de naciones
= *as I see it*
- **Basta** comenzar a leer la obra **para sentirse** transportado a la época
= *you only need to ... to feel*

Introducing someone else's point of view

- Tras ellos el arte posmodernista **- según concluye el autor -** ha terminado por ser un barrio de Disneylandia, un paraíso de masas
= *as the author concludes*
- Esta y otras consideraciones, **como señala el autor**, deben estimular a nuevas y específicas investigaciones y debates
= *as the author points out*
- **Como afirmó Platón**, ningún hombre puede aspirar al conocimiento total de la verdad absoluta
= *as Plato stated*
- Parece que fue una clara agresión, **a juzgar por los comentarios de** la prensa y de algunas personas
= *judging by the comments of*
- La comisión que investiga el caso **mantiene la teoría de** la existencia de "un poder político paralelo sin cuyo concurso no hubiera sido posible el fraude masivo detectado"
= *the theory supported by ... is that*
- El proponente **reiteró su tesis sobre** la inadmisibilidad de la tortura en ningún supuesto
= *repeated his argument about*
- El museo **asegura que** la retirada del logotipo había sido decidida en la etapa del ministro anterior
= *maintains that*

Introducing an example

- **Sirva de ejemplo** la situación descrita por uno de los viajeros
= *as an example, let us take*
- **Y mencionaré como ejemplo de ello** el episodio independiente compuesto por unas jornadas de cacería en las que el protagonista participa
= *and I shall take as an example*
- **Podemos hacer uso de un ejemplo gráfico**
= *to give a graphic example:*
- **Pongamos por caso** *or* **Supongamos que** uno de los rivales decide retirarse
= *let us suppose that*
- **Procederé a ilustrar con algunos ejemplos** la idea de que se ha producido un desfase entre la ciencia económica y la sociedad
= *with the help of some examples, I shall move on to*
- Las autoridades arguyen que la medida supone un importante ahorro de energía, pero yo disiento. **Veamos un ejemplo**
= *let us look at an example*

Introducing a quotation or source

- **Ya lo dice el refrán**, "Dime con quién andas y te diré quién eres"
= *as the saying goes*
- Tal convicción animó al Realismo decimonónico, **que, en palabras de** Clarín, exigía del novelista la facultad de "saber ver y copiar"
= *which, in the words of*
- **Según la frase atribuida al** famoso pintor, "Yo no busco, encuentro"
= *as ... is supposed to have said*
- **Ya dice** d'Ors **que** el dandismo de Valle-Inclán "no es sino el uniforme de los estudiantes de Coimbra y Santiago, perpetuado toda una vida"
= *as ... says*
- **Podemos citar un pasaje que ilustra** esta posibilidad
= *let us take a passage which illustrates*
- **Tomemos como referencia el momento en que** todo se descubre
= *let us take as our point of reference the moment when*

26.3 The mechanics of the argument

Stating facts

- **La característica más destacada del problema es** su universalidad
= *the most notable aspect of the problem is*
- **A medida que se avanza** en la lectura de la obra, **se abren nuevas perspectivas**
= *as one progresses ..., new perspectives open up*
- **Podemos observar que**, en estos momentos, **existe** una clara tendencia común en los ejecutivos europeos
= *it can be seen that ... there is*
- **Se puede constatar que** hay un gran índice del alcoholismo en la isla
= *it can be seen that*
- **Es un hecho que** la industria está demostrando interés por este

tipo de buques ya que se han hecho varios pedidos de barcos porta-barcazas
= *it is a fact that*

- **Si partimos de la base de que** las corrientes que se engloban bajo el título de "Nuevas tecnologías" nunca han tenido un especial prestigio en este país ...
  = *if we start from the premise that*

Making a supposition

- Por los documentos que existen **podemos suponer que** Ferri sea valenciano, descendiente tal vez de Féliz Ferri, pintor levantino del siglo XVIII
  = *it can be assumed that*
- Esta novedad **permite pensar que** será posible un tratamiento de afecciones neuromusculares humanas en un futuro próximo
  = *leads us to believe that*
- La ruptura entre ambos **podría interpretarse como** una celosa competencia de naturaleza literaria
  = *could be interpreted as*
- **Me atrevo a pensar que** aquellos años fueron los más felices en su matrimonio, como así lo pude constatar en dos ocasiones en que fui a visitarle
  = *I would venture to suggest that*
- **Podría quizá pensarse que** la física da una respuesta clara al problema de la naturaleza del tiempo, pero nada más alejado de la verdad, como observan los dos libros objeto del presente comentario
  = *one might (be tempted to) think that*
- La simplicidad del método **hace suponer que** se continuará empleando en el futuro
  = *suggests that*
- **Especulemos con la hipótesis de** un descenso acelerado de la temperatura del planeta
  = *let us take the hypothetical situation in which there is*

Expressing a certainty

- **Lo cierto es que** los mecanismos de lucha contra el terrorismo no sólo no han mejorado, sino que se encuentran en uno de sus peores momentos
  = *one thing is certain:*
- La salida de presos preventivos produce una sensación de inseguridad en los ciudadanos, pero **está claro que** la justicia debe predominar sobre todo
  = *it is clear that*
- **Es indudable que** Chigorin fue un precursor del nuevo ajedrez, que sería creado en el primer cuarto de este siglo por la llamada escuela hipermoderna
  = *without a doubt*
- **No hay duda de que** esta nueva medida del gobierno supone un peligro para la libertad de expresión
  = *there can be no doubt that*
- **No se puede negar que** el yogur es el derivado lácteo preferido por los españoles
  = *it cannot be denied that*
- **Todos coinciden en que** hay argumentos de peso para defender la filosofía como pilar básico de la formación académica
  = *everyone agrees that*
- **Es evidente que** si la informática y las telecomunicaciones no pudiesen ser utilizadas para reforzar el poder existente, habrían sido dejadas totalmente de lado
  = *it is clear that*
- Más allá de la guerra de cifras, **es incontestable que** la convocatoria de huelga tuvo un seguimiento mayoritario en el sector industrial
  = *unquestionably*
- Un político dimite - **como es obvio en cualquier democracia** - por sentido de la responsabilidad y no por disciplina de partido
  = *as is the case in any normal democracy*

Expressing doubt

- **Es improbable que** un académico empleara la forma "andase"
  = *it is unlikely that*
- **Resulta difícil creer que** una obra de tal celebridad pueda ser vendida en el mercado secreto del arte robado
  = *it is hard to believe that*
- Y aún **cabría preguntarse si** la auténtica literatura no ha sido siempre la manifestación de lo individual e incluso de lo íntimo
  = *the question arises as to whether*
- **Todavía está por ver**, sin embargo, cuáles van a ser las tendencias en las subastas de arte cuando cese la actual recesión
  = *it still remains to be seen*
- Su parecido físico con el autor del crimen, **introduce un elemento de duda** en la identificación
  = *introduces an element of doubt*
- Un nuevo atraco **pone en cuestión** la seguridad de los furgones blindados
  = *raises doubts about*

Conceding a point

- España, que debe considerarse un país desarrollado en el conjunto occidental, no tiene, **sin embargo**, una política medioambiental integral
  = *nevertheless*
- Todavía no estamos en situación de valorar su trabajo, **aunque** sí creemos que es un autor con mucho que decir
  = *although*
- Asegura que lo que le interesa es la felicidad. Habría que saber, **no obstante**, en qué consiste para ella ese concepto tan abstracto
  = *however*
- **Aunque** hayan surgido escépticos por todas partes, el acuerdo de paz entre ambos países se irá construyendo poco a poco
  = *even if*
- Es la operación más importante que haya pactado nunca una empresa española quisiera aclarar en el exterior. **Pero** amenaza también con convertirse en la más controvertida
  = *however*
- **A pesar de que** la obre carece de la unidad que poseen otras "semióperas" de Purcell, el conjunto es de una frescura, una variedad y un encanto admirables
  = *in spite of the fact that*
- **Por mucho que se complique** el lenguaje de la clase política, existe una gran masa de población capaz de descifrarlo
  = *however complicated ... becomes*
- El hombre es capaz de mantener su temperatura corporal en unos límites muy estrechos, **sea cual sea** la temperatura ambiental
  = *whatever ... is*
- Estos viajes cuasidiplomáticos al extranjero por parte de un candidato de la oposición durante el año electoral son, **como mínimo**, insólitos
  = *to say the least*
- No se puede caer en la tentación, comprensible **hasta cierto punto**, de disminuir los precios de los productos petrolíferos a los usuarios
  = *up to a point*
- En el plano social, **hay que reconocer que** los resultados obtenidos a lo largo de más de una década de aplicación de esta ley son, en términos generales, muy satisfactorios
  = *it must be recognized that*
- **Hemos de admitir que** el turismo también ha afectado negativamente a la zona
  = *it must be admitted that*

Emphasizing particular points

- **Ante todo debemos subrayar que** esta obra es muy superior a las anteriores
  = *first and foremost, it should be stressed that*

- **Conviene también precisar que** el hecho de pasar unas vacaciones en la nieve no tiene por qué suponer obligatoriamente pasarse el día exclusivamente esquiando
  = *it should also be pointed out that*
- De todos modos, es evidente que fue un pionero, **no sólo** en lo ideológico, **sino también** en lo que se refiere a la acción social
  = *not only ... but also*
- La gente no le ha apoyado en parte por las sospechas que levanta su personalidad. **Pero un factor aún más importante es** que su discurso democrático hace temblar a una región poco democrática
  = *but an even more important factor is*
- En cuanto al tema de la corrupción, **sería preciso matizar que** no son sólo los cargos públicos los culpables, ya que también se han beneficiado individuos de la sociedad civil
  = *it should be pointed out that*
- **La cuestión fundamental es que** la lucha de los ecologistas no está únicamente encaminada a salvar a tal o cual animal, sino a recuperar el equilibrio entre el hombre y la Tierra
  = *the fact is that*
- La poesía explica el tiempo, y **yo diría incluso que** la poesía no tiene tiempo, que la poesía "es" el tiempo
  = *I would go as far as to say that*
- **Es precisamente** la teoría cuántica, aun con sus paradojas, la que hace posible la creación de una máquina del tiempo
  = *it is precisely ...*

Moderating a statement

- **Sería deseable** la implantación de un impuesto verde que gravase las energías contaminantes
  = *... would be desirable*
- Quizás muchos tan sólo relacionen al director con aquellos años de apertura erótica, **pero sería injusto** condicionar toda su obra a esa etapa transitoria
  = *but it would be unfair to*
- Probablemente por ello se han vertido inexactitudes que, **sin ánimo polémico**, quisiera aclarar
  = *without wishing to be controversial*
- **La cuestión no tendría más importancia si no fuera porque** ese dinero procede de los fondos de ayuda al desarrollo teóricamente destinados a financiar proyectos en países del Tercer Mundo
  = *this would not be particularly important were it not for the fact that*
- **A pesar de ser** una tesis bien construida, **se hace necesario en cierta medida cuestionarse** su validez en el mundo de hoy
  = *although it is ..., should perhaps be questioned*

Indicating agreement

- Por lo que conocemos del autor, bastantes de los episodios aquí narrados son, **efectivamente**, autobiográficos
  = *in fact*
- **Nada más cierto que** la afirmación que la autora hace al final del libro: "Saber dialogar es una asignatura pendiente en la sociedad democrática"
  = *... is absolutely right*
- Debido a la actual necesidad de prudencia, **sí parece justificada** la lentitud del Consejo en la toma de decisiones
  = *does indeed seem justified*
- **Es cierto que** el poder consultar los microfilmes indexados por temas y fechas ayuda considerablemente al historiador
  = *it is true that*
- **Soy partidario del** acuerdo, porque el diálogo y la concordia son siempre armas justas
  = *I am in favour of*
- Como reacción contra ese concepto de realismo, que el autor da **justamente** como extinguido, se alzó el contrario
  = *rightly*

- La exposición del problema que realizó el nuevo presidente de la organización parece **razonable y convincente**
  = *reasonable and convincing*

Indicating disagreement

- En cambio, lo que sí **resulta altamente discutible** es la atención morbosa con que los medios de comunicación han seguido el caso
  = *is highly questionable*
- El resultado de sus obras **es poco convincente**
  = *is not very impressive*
- Pero el trabajo tiene inconvenientes metodológicos que **lo ponen en tela de juicio**
  = *raise doubts about it*
- Con la debida humildad, **expreso mis reservas sobre** lo radical de dicha revisión
  = *I should like to express my doubts about*
- Esas interpretaciones **carecen de base sólida**
  = *there are no real grounds for ...*
- Las soluciones por ellos aportadas **distan mucho de ser indiscutibles**
  = *are questionable, to say the least*
- **Pecaríamos de ingenuos si creyéramos que** ése es el único argumento válido
  = *it would be extremely naïve to believe that*
- El punto de vista antropocentrista que pretende que somos los únicos hombres del universo **es** hoy día **totalmente inaceptable**
  = *is totally unacceptable*
- **Sería un grave error** acabar con el cinturón de dunas en el que se ubicaría la urbanización
  = *it would be a serious mistake to*
- **Es de todo punto absurdo mantener que** los acontecimientos del este de Europa no han repercutido sobre los nacionalismos de los países occidentales
  = *it is completely absurd to suggest that*

Making a correction

- El segundo lienzo de la subasta estaba valorado en 4-6 millones y fue vendido por 3.500.000; **en realidad**, 3.920.000
  = *or, to be precise*
- La idea de este proyecto es difundir el conocimiento de las Reales Academias. **No se trata propiamente de** una historia de las Academias, **sino de** una presentación de las mismas
  = *it is not really ..., but rather*
- Si rechazan escribir sobre literatura **no es porque** tengan mucho que ocultar sobre el proceso de la escritura. **Me parece más bien que** carecen de una sólida cultura literaria
  = *it is not because ..., but rather, it seems to me, because*
- **Tal vez sería más adecuado hablar de** problemas por resolver **que de** inconvenientes, dado que con el ritmo de desarrollo actual los problemas analizados a continuación tendrán solución a corto o medio plazo
  = *perhaps it would be better to talk about ... rather than*
- La transexualidad **tiene más de** conflicto **que de** la perversión sexual que algunos le atribuyen
  = *is more a question of ... than of*

Indicating the reason for something

- La tierra está agotada **debido a** la agricultura y a la ganadería intensiva que practicó la cooperativa durante años
  = *owing to*
- En estas tierras habría habido una ruptura total con el pasado anterior, **lo cual explica** la inexistencia de siervos y libertos y el clima de libertad personal de la época medieval
  = *which explains*
- El descubrimiento fue posible **gracias a** los grandes progresos técnicos que pusieron el radiotelescopio a disposición de los astrónomos
  = *thanks to*

- Y si quienes conocían el manuscrito no concedieron importancia a esas disquisiciones, **es, sin duda, porque** nada en ellas les resultaba digno de especial mención
  = *it is doubtless because*
- Ambas pinturas necesitan ser restauradas, **dado que** su estado de conservación no es bueno
  = *since*
- En la semiótica de entrada cabe todo, **puesto que** todo es signo, o signo de un signo
  = *since*
- El estudio ha demostrado que esta enfermedad **es el motivo de** baja laboral de un 8%
  = *is responsible for*
- **Si** no se observan distorsiones, **es porque** los rayos viajan una distancia corta y bajo un ángulo demasiado empinado para que se curven apreciablemente
  = *if ..., it is because*

Indicating the consequences of something

- El informe prevé una reactivación en la demanda de pisos, **lo que llevará a** un ligero aumento de los precios
  = *which will lead to*
- La enmienda fue aprobada por unanimidad, **lo que significa** que irá directamente al Congreso Federal del partido sin que sea debatida por el pleno
  = *which means that*
- Las galas televisivas recaudan centenares de millones, **por lo que** la ayuda final superará fácilmente los mil millones de pesetas
  = *for which reason*
- La industria auxiliar de la automoción atraviesa una fuerte crisis **como consecuencia de** la recesión en las ventas de automóviles
  = *as a result of*
- El carácter documental de sus libros, unido a la técnica literaria de los mismos, **daba como resultado** una fórmula muy bien acogida por la industria editorial y su público
  = *resulted in*
- El uso de la mitad del arsenal atómico mundial existente **provocaría** en el hemisferio Norte un largo invierno nuclear y la desaparición de la vida humana
  = *would cause*
- Este insecto-palo, carece de alas y es idéntico a una ramita seca. **De ahí que** resulte tan difícil distinguirlo entre la maleza
  = *that is why*
- Tendrán que perfeccionar su producto y seguir las tendencias del mercado, **lo que implica** producir coches para todos los niveles adquisitivos
  = *which involves*

Contrasting or comparing

- Las ciencias sociales se verán severamente afectadas con la reforma universitaria, **por el contrario** las ciencias aplicadas y las carreras técnicas serán muy favorecidas
  = *whereas*
- Las causas clásicas de mortalidad tienden a disminuir en los países desarrollados, **en cambio**, las enfermedades hereditarias toman cada vez mayor relieve
  = *whereas*
- El olfato humano está muy poco desarrollado **en comparación con** el de algunos animales
  = *in comparison with*
- La exportación mantuvo ritmos positivos de crecimiento, **en contraste con** el comportamiento medio de los países de la OCDE
  = *in contrast with*
- **En contraposición al** descenso que se observa en la venta de libros a Europa,las exportaciones a otros países han experimentado un aumento respecto al año anterior
  = *unlike*
- En *La Riqueza de las Naciones*, de Adam Smith, se puede ver **la diferencia entre** la tradición liberal **y** el neoliberalismo actual
  = *the difference between ... and*
- Esta zona posee la mayoría de los yacimientos de crudo **mientras que** en Esmeralda está la principal refinería y puerto de exportación del crudo
  = *while*
- La organización se ha gastado una suma **muy superior a** la prevista
  = *far higher ... than*
- Este material se compone de microfibras con un diámetro **diez veces inferior al de** las fibras de poliéster corriente
  = *ten times smaller than*

27 EL TELÉFONO

Para obtener un número

Could you get me 043 65 27 82, please?
(o-four-three six-five two-seven eight-two)

Could you give me directory enquiries *(Brit)* *o* directory assistance *(EEUU)* please?

Can you give me the number of Europost of 54 Broad Street, Newham?

It's not in the book

What is the code for Exeter?

How do I make an outside call?

You omit the '0' when dialling England from Spain

Diferentes tipos de llamadas

It's a local call

It's a long-distance call

I want to make an international call

I want to make a reverse charge call to a London number *(Brit)* *o* I want to call a London number collect *(EEUU)*

I'd like an alarm call for 7.30 tomorrow morning

Habla el telefonista

What number do you want? *o* What number are you calling?

Where are you calling from?

You can dial the number direct

Replace the receiver and dial again

There's a Mr Campbell calling you from Canberra and wishes you to pay for the call. Will you accept it?

Go ahead, caller

(Información) There's nothing listed under that name

There's no reply from 45 77 57 84

Hold the line, please

All lines are engaged - please try later

I'm trying it for you now

It's ringing for you now

The line is engaged *(Brit)* *o* busy *(EEUU)*

Cuando contestan

Could I have extension 516? *o* Can you give me extension 516?

Is that Mr Lambert's phone?

Could I speak to Mr Swinton, please? *o* Is Mr Swinton there?

Who's speaking?

I'll call back in half an hour

I'm ringing from a callbox *(Brit)* *o* I'm calling from a pay station *o* payphone *(EEUU)*

Could you ask him to ring me when he gets back?

Could you tell him I called?

27 THE TELEPHONE

Getting a number

¿Por favor, me puede poner con el 043 65 27 82?
(cero cuarenta y tres, sesenta y cinco, veintisiete, ochenta y dos)

¿Me pone con Información (Urbana/Interurbana), por favor?

¿Me puede decir el número de Europost? La dirección es Plaza Mayor, 34, Carmona, provincia de Sevilla

No está en la guía

¿Cuál es el prefijo de León?

¿Qué hay que hacer para obtener línea?

No marque el cero del prefijo cuando llame a Londres desde España

Different types of call

Es una llamada local *or* urbana

Es una llamada interurbana

Deseo llamar al extranjero

Quisiera hacer una llamada a cobro revertido a Londres

Por favor, ¿me podrían avisar por teléfono mañana por la mañana a las siete y media?

The operator speaks

¿Con qué número desea comunicar?

¿Desde dónde llama usted?

Puede marcar el número directamente

Cuelgue y vuelva a marcar

Hay una llamada para usted del Sr. Lopez, que telefonea desde Bilbao y desea hacerlo a cobro revertido. ¿Acepta usted la llamada?

Ya puede hablar, señor/señora/señorita or ¡Hable(, por favor)!

(Directory Enquiries) Ese nombre no figura en la guía

El 45 77 57 84 no contesta

No se retire(, señor/señora/señorita)

Las líneas están saturadas; llame más tarde, por favor

Le pongo *(Sp)* *or* Le estoy conectando *(LAm)*

Está sonando *or* llamando

Está comunicando

When your number answers

¿Me da la extensión *or* el interno *(S. Cone)* 516?

¿Es éste el número del señor Lambert?

Por favor, ¿podría hablar con Carlos García? *or* Quisiera hablar con Carlos García, por favor *or* ¿Está Carlos García?

¿De parte de quién? *or* ¿Quién le/la llama?*or* ¿Quién habla?

Llamaré otra vez dentro de media hora

Llamo desde una cabina (telefónica)

¿Puede decirle que me llame cuando vuelva?

¿Podría decirle que llamé?

Contesta la centralita o el conmutador (LAm)

Queen's Hotel, can I help you?
Who is calling, please?
Do you know his extension number?
I am connecting you now *o* I'm putting you through now
I have a call from Tokyo for Mrs Thomas
Sorry to keep you waiting
There's no reply
You're through
Would you like to leave a message?

Para contestar

Hello?

Hello, this is Anne speaking
(Is that Anne?) Speaking
Would you like to leave a message?
Put the phone down and I'll call you back
This is a recorded message
Please speak after the tone

En caso de dificultad

I can't get through
The number is not ringing
I'm getting 'number unobtainable'
Their phone is out of order
We were cut off
I must have dialled the wrong number
We've got a crossed line
I got the wrong extension
This is a very bad line
I can't get a signal here
You're breaking up
I've run out of credit

The switchboard operator speaks

Hotel Castellana, ¿dígame?
¿Me puede decir quién llama?
¿Sabe usted qué extensión *or* interno *(S. Cone)* es?
Le pongo *(Sp) or* Le conecto *or* Le paso
Hay una llamada de Tokio para la Sra. Martínez
Perdone la demora, pero no se retire
No contesta
Ya tiene línea
¿Quiere dejar un recado?

Answering the telephone

¿Diga? *or* ¿Dígame? *or* ¿Aló? *(LAm) or* ¿Bueno? *(Mex) or* ¿Hola? *(S. Cone)*
Sí, soy Ana, ¿dígame?
(¿Es Ana?) Sí, soy yo *or* Sí, aquí Ana *or* Al aparato
¿Quiere dejar un recado?
Cuelgue y le llamaré yo
Este es el contestador automático de ...
Deje su mensaje después de la señal

In case of difficulty

No consigo comunicar
El teléfono no suena
Me sale la señal de línea desconectada
Ese teléfono está estropeado
Nos han cortado (la comunicación)
Debo de haberme equivocado de número
Hay un cruce de líneas
Me han dado una extensión que no era la que yo quería
Se oye muy mal *or* La línea está muy mal
No tengo cobertura
No te oigo
Se me ha acabado el crédito

27a E-MAIL

Sending messages

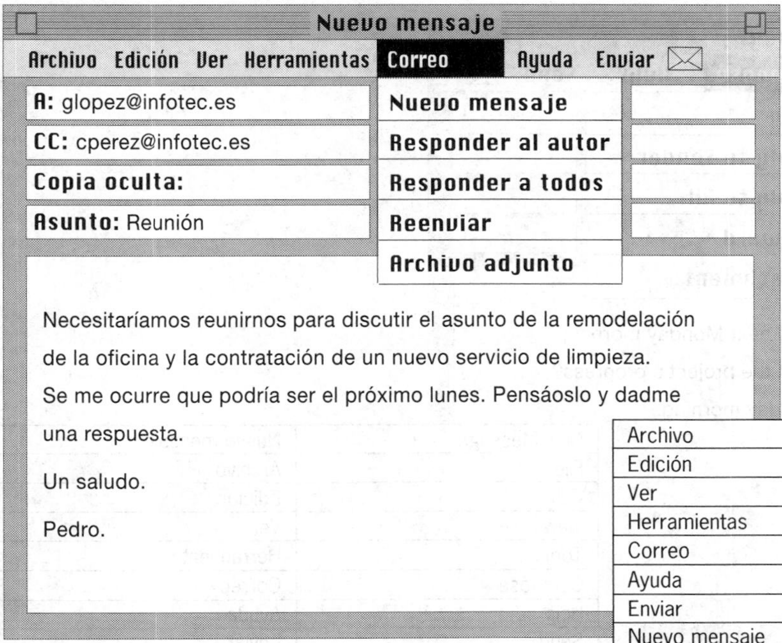
Nuevo mensaje
Archivo Edición Ver Herramientas Correo Ayuda Enviar
A: glopez@infotec.es
CC: cperez@infotec.es
Copia oculta:
Asunto: Reunión
Nuevo mensaje
Responder al autor
Responder a todos
Reenviar
Archivo adjunto
Necesitaríamos reunirnos para discutir el asunto de la remodelación de la oficina y la contratación de un nuevo servicio de limpieza. Se me ocurre que podría ser el próximo lunes. Pensáoslo y dadme una respuesta.
Un saludo.
Pedro.

Archivo	File
Edición	Edit
Ver	View
Herramientas	Tools
Correo	Compose
Ayuda	Help
Enviar	Send
Nuevo mensaje	New
Responder al autor	Reply to Sender

Receiving messages

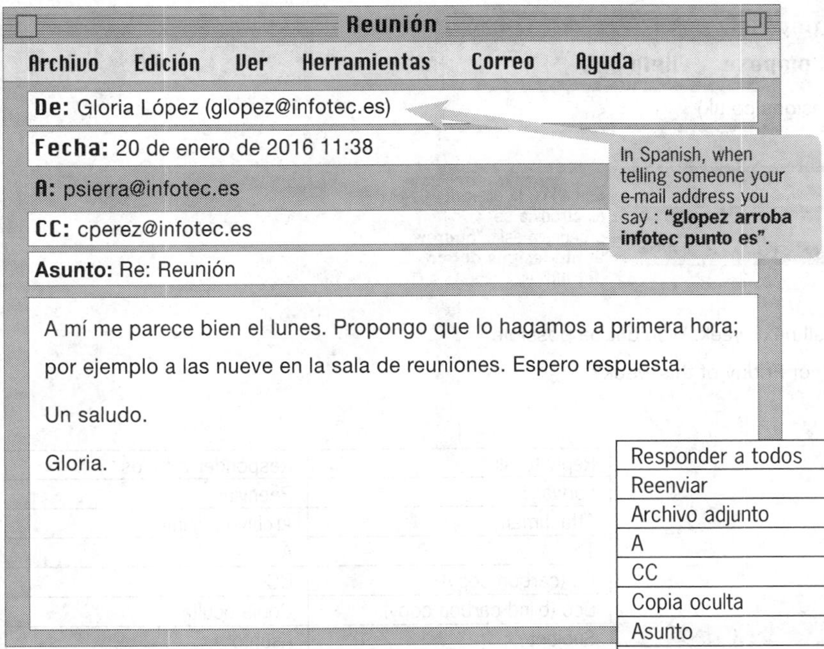
Reunión
Archivo Edición Ver Herramientas Correo Ayuda
De: Gloria López (glopez@infotec.es)
Fecha: 20 de enero de 2016 11:38
A: psierra@infotec.es
CC: cperez@infotec.es
Asunto: Re: Reunión
A mí me parece bien el lunes. Propongo que lo hagamos a primera hora; por ejemplo a las nueve en la sala de reuniones. Espero respuesta.
Un saludo.
Gloria.
In Spanish, when telling someone your e-mail address you say : **"glopez arroba infotec punto es"**.

Responder a todos	Reply to all
Reenviar	Forward
Archivo adjunto	Attachment
A	To
CC	CC
Copia oculta	BCC (blind carbon copy)
Asunto	Subject
De	From
Fecha	Sent

27a CORREO ELECTRÓNICO

Enviar mensajes

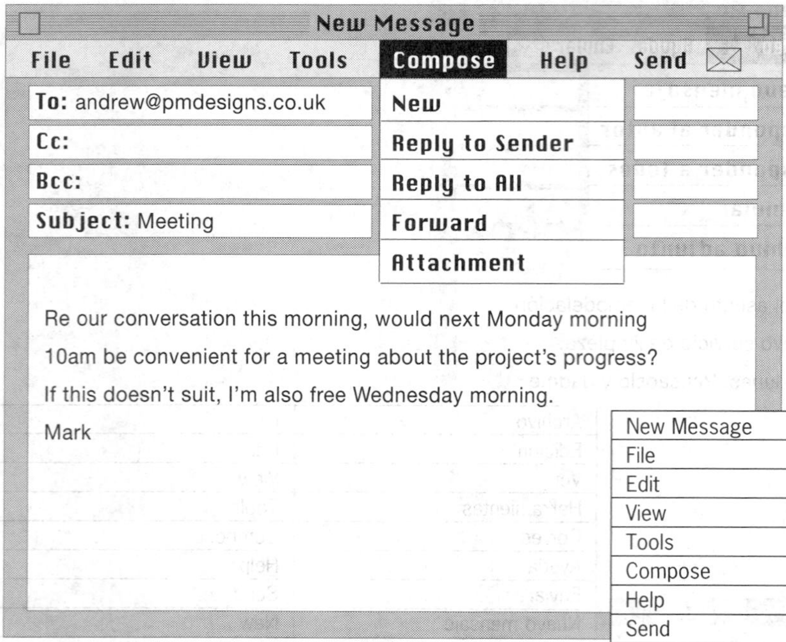

New Message	Nuevo mensaje
File	Archivo
Edit	Edición
View	Ver
Tools	Herramientas
Compose	Correo
Help	Ayuda
Send	Enviar
New	Nuevo mensaje
Reply to Sender	Responder al autor

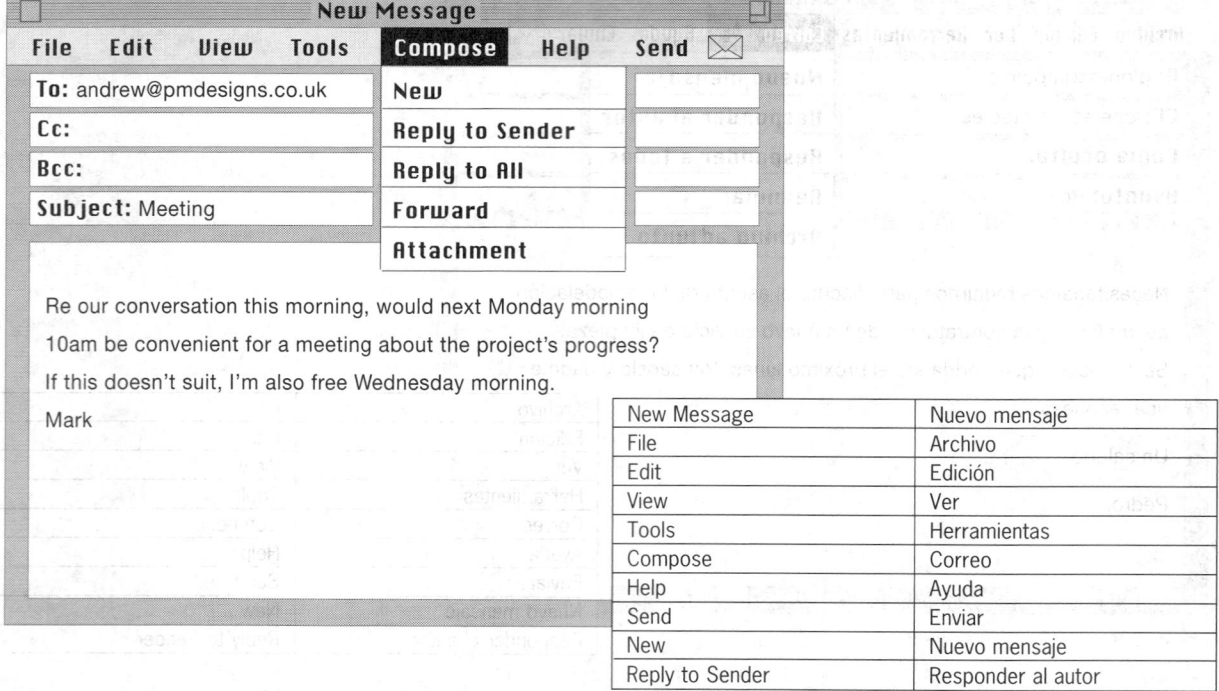

Recibir mensajes

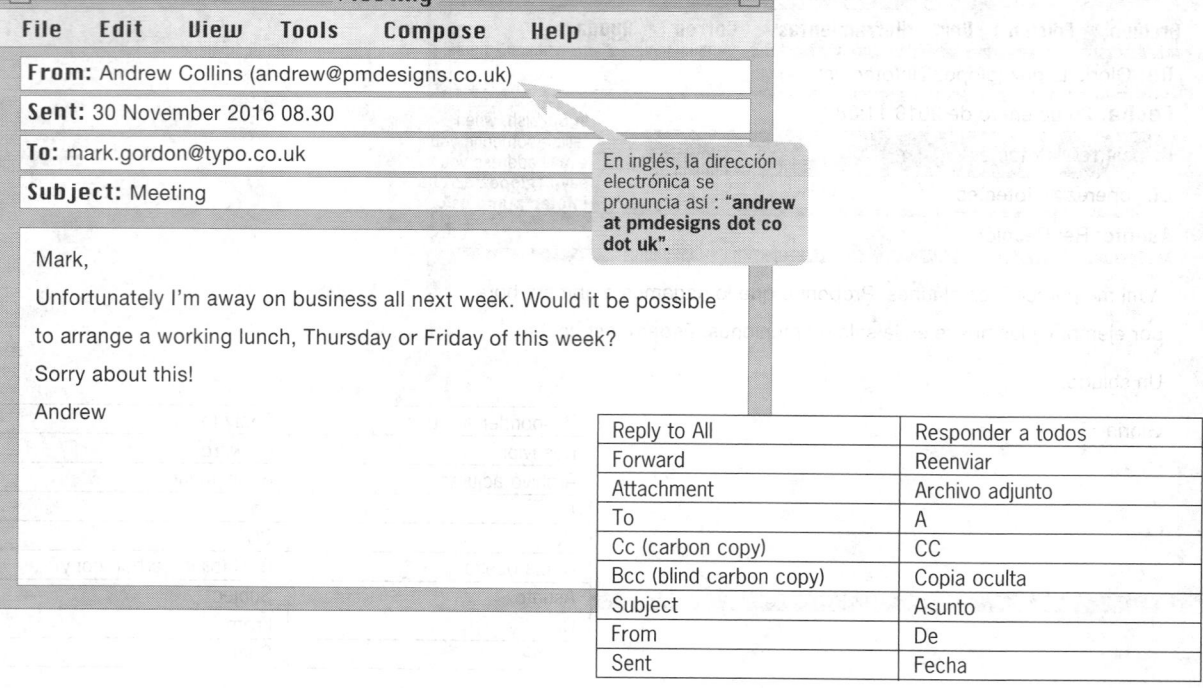

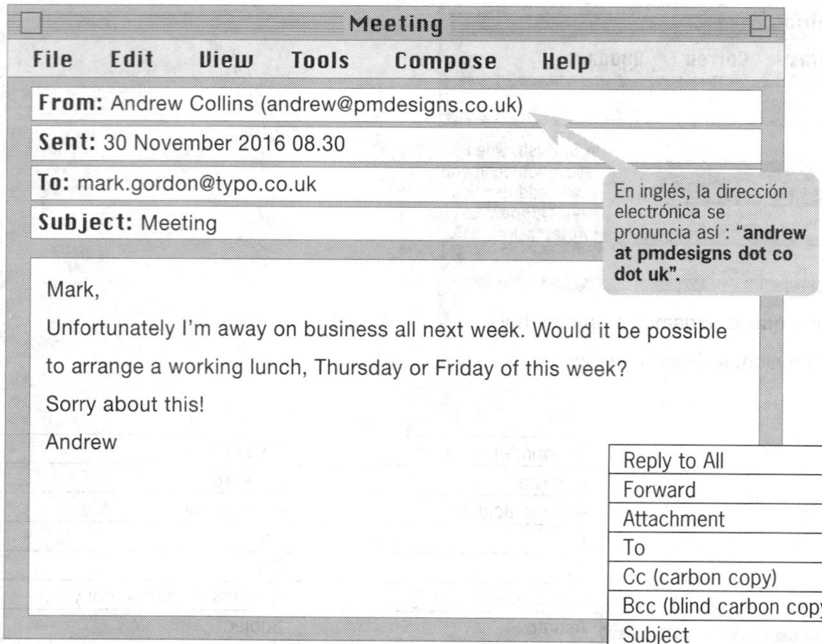

Reply to All	Responder a todos
Forward	Reenviar
Attachment	Archivo adjunto
To	A
Cc (carbon copy)	CC
Bcc (blind carbon copy)	Copia oculta
Subject	Asunto
From	De
Sent	Fecha

28 SUGERENCIAS

28.1 Para hacer sugerencias

- **You might like to** think it over before giving me your decision
  = *tal vez quiera*
- **If you were to** give me the negative, **I could** get copies made
  = *si me diera ... yo podría*
- **You could** help me clear out my office, **if you don't mind**
  = *podría ... si no le importa*
- **We could** stop off in Venice for a day or two, **if you like**
  = *podríamos ... si te apetece*
- I've got an idea - **let's organize** a surprise birthday party for Megan!
  = *vamos a organizar*
- **If you've no objection(s), I'll** speak to them personally
  = *si no tienes inconveniente, hablaré*
- **If I were you, I'd** go
  = *yo que tú, iría*
- **If you ask me, you'd better** take some extra cash
  = *en mi opinión, más vale que*
- **I'd be very careful not to** commit myself at this stage
  = *tendría cuidado de no*
- **I would recommend (that) you** discuss it with him before making a decision
  = *te recomendaría que*
- **It could be in your interest to** have a word with the owner first
  = *te convendría*
- **There's a lot to be said for** living alone
  = *... tiene muchas ventajas*
- Go and see Pompeii - **it's a must!**
  = *no dejes de ir a ver*

Más directamente

- **I suggest that you** go to bed and try to sleep
  = *te sugiero que*
- **I'd like to suggest that you** seriously consider taking a long holiday
  = *te sugeriría*
- **We propose that** half the fee be paid in advance, and half on completion
  = *proponemos que*
- **It is very important that** you take an interest in what he is trying to do
  = *es muy importante que*
- **I am convinced that** this would be a dangerous step to take
  = *estoy convencido de que*
- I cannot put it too strongly: **you really must** see a doctor
  = *de verdad, tienes que*

Menos directamente

- **Say you were to** approach the problem from a different angle
  = *y si*
- In these circumstances, **it might be better to** wait
  = *quizás sería mejor*
- **It might be a good thing** *o* **a good idea to** warn her about this
  = *estaría bien*
- **Perhaps it would be as well to** change the locks
  = *quizás convendría*
- **Perhaps you should** take up a sport
  = *tal vez deberías*
- **If I may make a suggestion,** a longer hemline might suit you better
  = *si me permite una sugerencia*
- **Might I be allowed to offer a little advice?** - talk it over with a solicitor before you go any further
  = *¿me permite que le dé un pequeño consejo?*
- **If I might be permitted to suggest something,** installing bigger windows would make the office much brighter
  = *si se me permite hacer una sugerencia*

Haciendo una pregunta

- **How do you fancy** a holiday in Australia?
  = *¿te apetece ...?*
- I was thinking of going for a drink later. **How about it?**
  = *¿qué te parece?*
- **What would you say to** a trip up to town next week?
  = *¿qué te parecería ...?*
- **Would you like to** stay in Paris for a couple of nights?
  = *¿te gustaría ...?*
- **What if** you try ignoring her and see if that stops her complaining?
  = *¿y si ...?*
- What you need is a change of scene. **Why not** go on a cruise?
  = *¿por qué no ...?*
- **Suppose** *o* **Supposing** you left the kids with your mother for a few days?
  = *¿y si ...?*
- **How would you feel about** taking calcium supplements?
  = *¿qué te parecería ...?*
- **Have you ever thought of** starting up a magazine of your own?
  = *¿no se te ha ocurrido ...?*
- **Would you care to** have lunch with me?
  = *¿querría ...?*

28.2 Para pedir sugerencias

- **What would you do if you were me?**
  = *¿qué harías tú en mi lugar?*
- **Have you any idea how I should** go about it to get the best results?
  = *¿tienes idea cómo debería ...?*
- I've no idea what to call our new puppy: **have you any suggestions?**
  = *¿se te ocurre algo?*
- I can only afford to buy one of them: **which do you suggest?**
  = *¿cuál me aconsejas?*
- **I wonder if you could suggest** where we might go for a few days?
  = *¿podría sugerirnos ...?*
- **I'm a bit doubtful about** where to start
  = *no estoy muy seguro de*

29 CONSEJOS

29.1 Para pedir consejo

- What would you do **if you were me?**
  = *en mi lugar*
- Would a pear tree grow in this spot? If not, **what would you recommend?**
  = *qué recomendaría usted*
- **Do you think I ought to** tell the truth if he asks me where I've been?
  = *crees que debería*
- **What would you advise me to do** in the circumstances?
  = *¿qué me aconsejaría que hiciera?*
- **Would you advise me to** seek promotion within this firm or apply for another job?
  = *¿me aconsejaría usted que ...?*
- **I'd like** *o* **I'd appreciate your advice on** personal pensions
  = *me gustaría que me aconsejara sobre*
- **I'd be grateful if you could advise me on** how to treat this problem
  = *le agradecería que me aconsejara sobre*

29.2 Para aconsejar

De manera impersonal

- **It might be wise** *o* **sensible to** consult a specialist
  = *quizás sería prudente*
- **It might be a good idea to** seek professional advice
  = *quizás sería buena idea*
- **It might be better to** think the whole thing over before taking any decisions
  = *sería mejor*
- **You'd be as well to** state your position at the outset, so there is no mistake
  = *más te valdría*
- **You would be well-advised to** invest in a pair of sunglasses if you're going to Spain
  = *haría bien en*
- **You'd be ill-advised to** have any dealings with this firm
  = *sería poco aconsejable que*
- **It would certainly be advisable to** book a table
  = *se aconseja*
- **It is in your interest** *o* **your best interests to** keep your dog under control if you don't want it to be reported
  = *le conviene*
- **Do be sure to** read the small print before you sign anything
  = *asegúrate de*
- **Try to avoid** upsetting her; she'll only make your life a misery
  = *intenta evitar*
- **Whatever you do, don't** drink the local schnapps
  = *no se te ocurra*

De manera más personal

- **If you ask me, you'd better** take some extra cash
  = *para mí que es mejor que lleves*
- **If you want my advice, you should** steer well clear of them
  = *si quieres un consejo, aléjate*
- **If you want my opinion, I'd** go by air to save time
  = *si quieres mi opinión, yo iría*
- **In your shoes** *o* **If I were you, I'd** be thinking about moving on
  = *yo que tú, me pondría a pensar*
- **Take my advice** and don't rush into anything
  = *hazme caso*
- **I'd be very careful not to** commit myself at this stage
  = *yo tendría mucho cuidado de no*
- **I think you ought to** *o* **should** seek professional advice
  = *creo que deberías*
- **My advice would be to** have nothing to do with them
  = *yo te aconsejaría que*
- **I would advise you to** pay up promptly before they take you to court
  = *yo te aconsejaría que*
- **I would advise against** calling in the police unless he threatens you
  = *yo aconsejaría no*
- **I would strongly advise you to** reconsider this decision
  = *yo le aconsejo que*
- **I would urge you to** reconsider selling the property
  = *le ruego encarecidamente que*
- **Might I be allowed to offer a little advice?** - talk it over with a solicitor before going any further
  = *¿me permite que le dé un consejo?*

29.3 Para hacer una advertencia

- It's really none of my business but **I don't think you should** get involved
  = *creo que no deberías*
- **A word of caution:** watch what you say to him if you want it to remain a secret
  = *una advertencia:*
- **I should warn you that** he's not an easy customer to deal with
  = *te advierto que*
- **Take care not to** lose the vaccination certificate
  = *ten cuidado de no*
- **Watch you don't** trip over your shoelaces
  = *cuidado no*
- **Make sure that** *o* **Mind that** *o* **See that you don't** say anything they might find offensive
  = *ten cuidado de no*
- **I'd think twice about** sharing a flat with him
  = *me lo pensaría dos veces antes de*
- **It would be sheer madness to** attempt to drive without your glasses
  = *sería una auténtica locura*
- **You risk** a long delay in Amsterdam **if** you come back by that route
  = *corre el riesgo de ... si*

30 PROPUESTAS

De manera directa

- **I would be delighted to** help out, if I may
  = *me encantaría*
- **It would give me great pleasure to** show you round the city
  = *sería un placer*
- **We would like to offer you** the post of Sales Director
  = *quisiéramos ofrecerle*
- **I hope you will not be offended if I offer** a contribution towards your expenses
  = *espero que no se ofenda si le ofrezco*
- **Do let me know if I can** help in any way
  = *avísame si puedo*
- **If we can** be of any further assistance, **please do not hesitate to** contact us
  = *si podemos ... no dude en*

Haciendo una pregunta

- **Say we were to** offer you a 5% rise, **how would that sound?**
  = *¿qué le parecería si le ofreciéramos ...?*
- **What if I were to** call for you in the car?
  = *¿y si yo ...?*
- **Could I** give you a hand with your luggage?
  = *¿puedo ...?*
- **Shall I** do the photocopies for you?
  = *¿te hago ...?*
- **Is there anything I can do to** help you find suitable accommodation?
  = *¿puedo hacer algo para ...?*
- **May** o **Can I offer you** a drink?
  = *¿le pongo ...?*
- **Would you like me to** find out more about it for you?
  = *¿quieres que ...?*
- **Would you allow me to** pay for dinner, at least?
  = *¿me deja que ...?*
- **You will let me** show you around Glasgow, **won't you**?
  = *¿me dejarás que ... ¿no?*

31 PETICIONES

- **Please would you** drop by on your way home and pick up the papers you left here?
  = *¿puedes ...?*
- **Would you please** try to keep the noise down while I'm studying?
  = *haced el favor de*

- **Would you mind** looking after Hannah for a couple of hours tomorrow?
  = *¿te importaría ...?*
- **Could I ask you to** watch out for anything suspicious in my absence?
  = *¿podrías ...?*

Por escrito

- **I should be grateful if you could** confirm whether it would be possible to increase my credit limit to £5000
  = *le agradecería que confirmara*
- **We would ask you not to** use the telephone for long-distance calls
  = *le pedimos que no*
- **You are requested to** park at the rear of the building
  = *se ruega*
- **We look forward to** receiving confirmation of your order within 14 days
  = *quedamos a la espera de*
- **Kindly inform us if** you require alternative arrangements to be made
  = *tenga la amabilidad de comunicarnos si*

De manera más indirecta

- **I would rather you didn't** breathe a word to anyone about this
  = *preferiría que no*
- **I would appreciate it if you could** let me have copies of the best photos
  = *te agradecería que*
- **I was hoping that you might** have time to visit your grandmother
  = *esperaba que tendrías*
- **I wonder whether you could** spare a few pounds till I get to the bank?
  = *¿te sería posible ...?*
- **I hope you don't mind if I** borrow your exercise bike for half an hour
  = *espero que no te importe que ...*
- **It would be very helpful** *o* **useful if you could** have everything ready beforehand
  = *nos vendría muy bien si*
- **If it's not too much trouble, would you** pop my suit into the dry cleaners on your way past?
  = *si no es mucha molestia, podrías*
- **You won't forget** to lock up before you leave, **will you?**
  = *no te olvidarás de ..., ¿no?*

32 COMPARACIONES

32.1 Objetivas

- The streets, though wide for China, are narrow **compared with** English ones
  = *comparadas con*
- The bomb used to blow the car up was small **in** *o* **by comparison with** those often used nowadays
  = *en comparación con*
- **If you compare** the facilities we have here **with** those in other towns, you soon realize how lucky we are
  = *si se comparan ... con*
- It is interesting to note **the similarities and the differences between** the two approaches
  = *las semejanzas y las diferencias entre*
- **In contrast to** the opulence of the Kirov, the Northern Ballet Theatre is a modest company
  = *en contraste con*
- Only 30% of the females died **as opposed to** 57% of the males
  = *frente a*
- **Unlike** other loan repayments, those to the IMF cannot simply be rescheduled
  = *a diferencia de*
- The quality of the paintings is disappointing **beside** that of the sculpture section
  = *al lado de*
- **Whereas** burglars often used to make off only with video recorders, they now also tend to empty the fridge
  = *mientras que*
- **What differentiates these wines from** a good champagne is their price
  = *lo que diferencia ... de*

32.2 Comparaciones favorables

- Orwell was, indeed, **far superior to** him intellectually
  = *muy superior a*
- Personally I think high-speed trains **have the edge over** both cars and aircraft for sheer convenience
  = *aventajan a*
- Michaela was astute beyond her years and altogether **in a class of her own**
  = *única en su género*

32.3 Comparaciones desfavorables

- Matthew's piano playing **is not a patch on** his sister's
  = *no le llega a la suela del zapato a*
- My old chair **was nowhere near as** comfortable **as** my new one
  = *no era ni mucho menos tan ... como*
- The parliamentary opposition **is no match for** the government, which has a massive majority
  = *no puede con*
- Commercially made ice-cream **is far inferior to** the home-made variety
  = *es muy inferior a*
- The sad truth was that **he was never in the same class as** his friend
  = *no estaba a la misma altura que*
- Ella doesn't rate anything **that doesn't measure up to** Shakespeare
  = *que no esté al nivel de*
- Her brash charms **don't bear comparison with** Marlene's sultry sex appeal
  = *no tienen comparación con*
- The Australians are far bigger and stronger than us - **we can't compete with** their robot-like style of play
  = *no podemos competir con*

32.4 Para destacar el parecido

- The new computerized system costs **much the same as** a more conventional one
  = *prácticamente lo mismo que*
- When it comes to performance, **there's not much to choose between** them
  = *no hay mucha diferencia entre*
- The impact was **equivalent to** 250 hydrogen bombs exploding
  = *equivalente a*
- English literature written by people these days **is** clearly **on a par with** the writings of the great authors of the past
  = *está al mismo nivel que*
- In Kleinian analysis, the psychoanalyst's role **corresponds to** that of mother
  = *corresponde a*
- The immune system **can be likened to** *o* **compared to** a complicated electronic network
  = *se le puede comparar con*
- **There was a close resemblance between** her **and** her son
  = *había un gran parecido entre ... y*
- **It's swings and roundabouts** - what you win in one round, you lose in another
  = *al final viene a ser lo mismo*

32.5 Para destacar el contraste

- **You cannot compare** a small local library **with** a large city one
  = *no se puede comparar con*
- Homemade clothes **just cannot compare with** bought ones
  = *no se pueden comparar con*
- **There's no comparison between** the sort of photos I take **and** those a professional could give you
  = *no hay comparación entre ... y*
- His books **have little in common with** those approved by the Party
  = *tienen poco en común con*
- We might be twins, but **we have nothing in common**
  = *no tenemos nada en común*
- The modern army **bears little resemblance to** the army of 1940
  = *se parece poco a*

33 OPINIONES

33.1 Para pedir la opinión de alguien

- **What do you think of** the new Managing Director?
  = *¿qué piensas de ...?*
- **What is your opinion on** women's rights?
  = *¿qué opinas sobre ...?*
- **What are your thoughts on** the way forward?
  = *¿cuál es su opinión sobre ...?*
- **What is your attitude to** people who say there is no such thing as sexual inequality?
  = *¿cuál es su actitud hacia ...?*
- **What are your own feelings about** the way the case was handled?
  = *¿qué opina usted acerca de ...?*
- **How do you see** the next stage **developing**?
  = *¿cómo ve el desarrollo de ...?*
- **How do you view** an event like the Birmingham show in terms of the cultural life of the city?
  = *¿cóme ve ...?*
- **I would value your opinion on** how best to set this all up
  = *apreciaría su opinión sobre*
- **I'd be interested to know what your reaction is to** the latest report on food additives
  = *me interesaría conocer su reacción ante*

33.2 Para expresar la opinión propia

- **In my opinion**, eight years as President is quite enough for anyone
  = *en mi opinión*
- **As I see it**, everything depended on Karlov being permitted to go to Finland
  = *según lo veo yo*
- **I feel that** there is an epidemic of fear about cancer which is not helped by all the publicity about the people who die of it
  = *pienso que*
- **Personally, I believe** the best way to change a government is through the electoral process
  = *personalmente, creo que*
- **It seems to me that** the successful designer leads the public
  = *a mi parecer*
- **I am under the impression that** he is essentially a man of peace
  = *mi impresión es que*
- **I have an idea that** you are going to be very successful
  = *presiento que*
- **I am of the opinion that** the rules should be looked at and refined
  = *soy de la opinión de que*
- **I'm convinced that** we all need a new vision of the future
  = *estoy convencido de que*
- **I daresay** there are so many names that you get them mixed up once in a while
  = *me figuro que*
- We're prepared to prosecute the company, which **to my mind** has committed a criminal offence
  = *a mi parecer*
- **From my point of view** activities like these should not be illegal
  = *desde mi punto de vista*
- **As far as I'm concerned**, Barnes had it coming to him
  = *en lo que a mí respecta*
- It's a matter of common sense, nothing more. **That's my view of the matter**
  = *Esa es mi opinión sobre el tema*
- **It is our belief that** to be proactive is more positive than being reactive
  = *nosotros creemos que*
- **If you ask me**, there's something a bit strange going on
  = *para mí que*
- **If you want my opinion**, if you don't do it soon you'll lose the opportunity altogether
  = *si quiere mi opinión*

33.3 Para responder sin expresar una opinión

- Would I say she had been a help? **It depends what you mean by** help
  = *depende de lo que quiera decir con*
- It could be seen as a triumph for capitalism but **it depends on your point of view**
  = *depende de su punto de vista*
- **It's hard** o **difficult to say whether** she has benefited from the treatment or not
  = *resulta difícil decir si*
- **I'm not in a position to comment on whether** the director's accusations are well-founded
  = *no estoy en situación de comentar si*
- **I'd prefer not to comment on** operational decisions taken by the service in the past
  = *preferiría no pronunciarme sobre*
- **I'd rather not commit myself** at this stage
  = *preferiría no comprometerme*
- **I don't have any strong feelings about which of the two** companies we decide to use for the job
  = *no tengo una opinión firme sobre cuál de las dos compañías*
- **This isn't something I've given much thought to**
  = *es algo en lo que no me he parado a pensar*
- **I know nothing about** fine wine
  = *no sé nada sobre*

34 GUSTOS Y PREFERENCIAS

34.1 Para preguntarle a alguien sus preferencias

- **Would you like to** visit the castle, while you are here?
  = *¿te gustaría ...?*
- **How would you feel about** Simon joining us?
  = *¿qué te parecería si ...?*
- **What do you like doing best** when you're on holiday?
  = *¿qué es lo que más te gusta hacer ...?*
- **What's your favourite** film?
  = *¿cuál es tu ... preferida?*
- **Which of the two** proposed options **do you prefer?**
  = *¿cuál de las dos ... prefiere?*
- We could either go to Rome or stay in Florence - **which would you rather** do?
  = *¿qué preferirías ...?*

34.2 Para expresar gustos

- **I'm very keen on** gardening
  = *me gusta mucho*

- **I'm very fond of** white geraniums and blue petunias
  = me gustan mucho
- **I really enjoy** a good game of squash after work
  = disfruto con
- **There's nothing I like more than** a quiet night in with a good book
  = no hay nada que me guste más que
- **I have a weakness for** rich chocolate gateaux
  siento debilidad por
- **I've always had a soft spot for** the Dutch
  = siempre he sentido debilidad por

34.3 Para decir lo que a uno no le gusta

- Acting **isn't really my thing** - I'm better at singing
  = no es lo mío
- Watching football on television **isn't my favourite** pastime
  = no es mi ... preferido
- Some people might find it funny but **it's not my kind of** humour
  = no es mi tipo de
- I enjoy playing golf, although this type of course **is not my cup of tea**
  = no es plato de mi gusto
- Sitting for hours on motorways **is not my idea of fun**
  = no es lo que yo llamo divertirse
- The idea of walking home at 10 or 11 o'clock at night **doesn't appeal to me**
  = no me resulta nada atractiva
- **I've gone off the idea of** cycling round Holland
  = se me han quitado las ganas de
- **I can't stand** *o* **can't bear** the thought of seeing him
  = no soporto
- **I am not enthusiastic about** shopping in large supermarkets
  = no me entusiasma
- **I'm not keen on** seafood
  = no me entusiasma
- **I don't like the fact that** he always gets away with not helping out in the kitchen
  = no me gusta que
- **What I hate most is** waiting in queues for buses
  = lo que más detesto es
- **I dislike** laziness since I'm such an energetic person myself
  = me desagrada
- **There's nothing I dislike more than** having to go to work in the dark
  = no hay nada que me guste menos que
- **I have a particular aversion to** the religious indoctrination of schoolchildren
  = siento una aversión especial por
- **I find it intolerable that** people like him should have so much power
  = me resulta intolerable que

34.4 Para decir lo que uno prefiere

- **I'd prefer to** *o* **I'd rather** wait until I have enough money to go by air
  = preferiría
- **I'd prefer not to** *o* **I'd rather not** talk about it just now
  = prefiero no
- **I'd prefer you to** give *o* **I'd rather you** gave me your comments in writing
  = prefiero que
- **I'd prefer you not to** *o* **I'd rather you didn't** invite him
  = prefiero que no lo invites
- **I like** the blue curtains **better than** the red ones
  = ... me gustan más que ...
- **I prefer** red wine **to** white wine
  = prefiero ... a

34.5 Para expresar indiferencia

- **It makes no odds whether you have** a million pounds or nothing, we won't judge you on your wealth
  = da lo mismo que tengas
- **I really don't care what** you tell her as long as you tell her something
  = me trae sin cuidado lo que
- **It's all the same to me whether** he comes **or** not
  = me da igual que ... o que
- **I don't mind at all** - let's do whatever is easiest
  = me da exactamente lo mismo
- **It doesn't matter which** method you choose to use
  = no importa qué
- **I don't feel strongly about** the issue of privatization
  = no tengo una opinión definida sobre
- **I have no particular preference**
  = no tengo preferencias

35 INTENCIONES Y DESEOS

35.1 Para preguntar a alguien lo que piensa hacer

- **Will you** take the job?
  = ¿vas a ...?
- **What do you intend to do?**
  = ¿qué piensas hacer?
- **Did you mean to** *o* **intend to** tell him about it, or did it just slip out?
  = ¿tenías intención de ...?
- **What do you propose to do** with the money?
  = ¿qué piensas hacer ...?
- **What did you have in mind for** the rest of the programme?
  = ¿qué tenías pensado ...?
- **Have you anyone in mind for** the job?
  = ¿tienes a alguien pensado para ...?

35.2 Para expresar las propias intenciones

- **We're toying with the idea of** releasing a compilation album
  = le estamos dando vueltas a la posibilidad de
- **I'm thinking of** retiring next year
  = estoy pensando en
- **I'm hoping to** go and see her when I'm in Paris
  = espero
- I studied history, **with a view to** becoming a politician
  = con vistas a
- We bought the land **in order to** farm it
  = para
- We do not penetrate foreign companies **for the purpose of** collecting business information
  = con el fin de
- **We plan to** move *o* **We are planning on** moving next year
  = estamos planeando
- **Our aim** *o* **Our object in** buying the company **is to** provide work for the villagers
  = nuestro propósito al ... es
- **I aim to** reach Africa in three months
  = pretendo

Con mayor convicción

- **I am going to** sell the car as soon as possible
  = voy a
- **I intend to** put the house on the market
  = tengo la intención de
- **I have made up my mind to** *o* **I have decided to** go to Japan
  = he decidido

- **I went to Rome with the intention of** visiting her, but she had gone away
  = *con intención de*
- **We have every intention of** winning a sixth successive championship
  = *estamos decididos a*
- **I have set my sights on** recapturing the title
  = *mi objetivo es volver a ganar*
- **My overriding ambition is to** get into politics
  = *mi gran ambición es*
- **I resolve to** do everything in my power to help you
  = *estoy resuelto a*

35.3 Para expresar lo que no se piensa hacer

- **I don't mean to** offend you, but I think you're wrong
  = *no es mi intención*
- **I don't intend to** pay unless he completes the job
  = *no es mi intención*
- **I have no intention of** accepting the post
  = *no tengo intención de*
- **We are not thinking of** taking on more staff
  = *no tenemos previsto*
- **We do not envisage** making changes at this late stage
  = *no contemplamos*

35.4 Para expresar lo que se desea hacer

- **I'd like to** see the Sistine Chapel some day
  = *me gustaría*
- **I want to** work abroad when I leave college
  = *quiero*
- **We want her to** be an architect when she grows up
  = *queremos que sea*
- **I'm keen to** develop the business
  = *tengo mucho interés en*

Con gran entusiasmo

- **I'm dying to** leave home
  = *me muero de ganas de*
- **My ambition is to** become an opera singer
  = *lo que ambiciono es*
- **I long to** go to Australia but I can't afford it
  = *tengo el anhelo de*
- **I insist on** speaking to the manager
  = *insisto en*

35.5 Para expresar lo que no se quiere hacer

- **I would prefer not to** o **I would rather not** have to speak to her about this
  = *preferiría no*
- **I wouldn't want to** have to change my plans just because of her
  = *no quisiera*
- **I don't want to** take the credit for something I didn't do
  = *no quiero*
- **I have no wish** o **desire to** become rich and famous
  = *no tengo ningún deseo de*
- **I refuse to** be patronized by the likes of her
  = *me niego a*

36 PERMISO

36.1 Para pedir permiso

- **Can I** o **Could I borrow** your car this afternoon?
  = *¿me dejas ...?*
- **Can I** use the telephone, please?
  = *¿puedo ...?*
- **Can I have the go-ahead to** order the supplies?
  = *¿me das luz verde para ...?*
- **Are we allowed to** say what we're up to or is it top secret at the moment?
  = *¿podemos ...?*
- **Would it be all right if** I arrived on Monday instead of Tuesday?
  = *¿te importaría que ...?*
- **Would it be possible for us to** leave the car in your garage for a week?
  = *¿nos sería posible dejar ...?*
- We leave tomorrow. **Is that all right by you**?
  = *¿te parece bien?*
- **Do you mind if** I come to the meeting next week?
  = *¿te importa que ...?*
- **Would it bother you if** I invited him?
  = *¿te molestaría que lo invitara ...?*
- **Would you let me** come into partnership with you?
  = *¿me dejaría ...?*
- **Would you have any objection to** sailing at once?
  = *¿tiene algún inconveniente en ...?*
- **With your permission, I'd like to** ask some questions
  = *con su permiso, quisiera*

Con más cautela

- **Is there any chance of** borrowing your boat while we're at the lake?
  = *¿nos sería posible ...?*
- **I wonder if I could possibly** use your telephone?
  = *¿podría ...?*
- **Might I be permitted to** suggest the following ideas?
  = *¿me permitirían que ...?*
- **May I be allowed to** set the record straight?
  = *¿me dejan que ...?*

36.2 Para dar permiso

- **You can** have anything you want
  = *puedes*
- **You are allowed to** visit the museum, as long as you apply in writing to the Curator first
  = *puedes*
- **It's all right by me if** you want to skip the Cathedral visit
  = *por mí puedes ... si*
- **You have my permission to** be absent for that week
  = *te doy permiso para*
- **I've nothing against her** going there with us
  = *no me opongo a que*
- The Crown **was agreeable to** having the case called on March 23
  = *dio su consentimiento para que*
- **I do not mind if** my letter is forwarded to the lady concerned
  = *no veo inconveniente en que*
- **You have been authorized to** use all necessary force to protect relief supply routes
  = *está autorizado a*
- **We should be happy to allow you to** inspect the papers here
  = *no tenemos inconveniente en que*

Con más insistencia

- If you need to keep your secret, **of course you must keep it**
  = *guárdalo, claro*
- **By all means** charge a reasonable consultation fee
  = *por supuesto*
- **I have no objection at all to your** quoting me in your article
  = *no tengo ningún inconveniente en que*

- **We would be delighted to** have you
  = *sería un placer*

36.3 Para denegar permiso

- **You can't** *o* **you mustn't** go anywhere near the research lab
  = *no puedes*
- **I don't want you to** see that man again
  = *no quiero que*
- **I'd rather you didn't** give them my name
  = *preferiría que no*
- **You're not allowed to** leave the ship until relieved
  = *no tienes permiso para*
- **I've been forbidden to** swim for the moment
  = *me han prohibido que*
- **I've been forbidden** alcohol **by** my doctor
  = *... me ha prohibido*
- **I couldn't possibly allow you to** pay for all this
  = *¿cómo te voy a dejar ...?*
- **You must not** enter the premises without the owners' authority
  = *no se le autoriza a*
- **We cannot allow** the marriage **to** take place
  = *no podemos permitir que*

Con más insistencia

- **I absolutely forbid you to** take part in any further search
  = *te prohíbo terminantemente*
- **You are forbidden to** contact my children
  = *tienes prohibido*
- Smoking **is strictly forbidden** at all times
  = *está terminantemente prohibido*
- **It is strictly forbidden to** carry weapons in this country
  = *está terminantemente prohibido*
- **We regret that it is not possible for you to** visit the castle at the moment, owing to the building works (*por escrito*)
  = *lamentamos informarle que no se puede*

37 OBLIGACIÓN

37.1 Para explicar lo que se está obligado a hacer

- **You've got to** *o* **You have to** be back before midnight
  = *tienes que*
- **You must** have an address in Prague before you can apply for the job
  = *tienes que*
- **You need to** have a valid passport if you want to leave the country
  = *hay que*
- I have no choice: this is how **I must** live and I cannot do otherwise
  = *debo*
- **He was forced to** ask his family for a loan
  = *se vio obligado a*
- Jews **are obliged to** accept the divine origin of the Law
  = *están obligados a*
- A degree **is indispensable** for future entrants to the profession
  = *es indispensable*
- Party membership **is an essential prerequisite of** a successful career
  = *es un requisito indispensable para*
- **It is essential to** know what the career options are before choosing a course of study
  = *es esencial*
- Wearing the kilt **is compulsory for** all those taking part
  = *es obligatorio para*
- One cannot admit defeat, **one is driven to** keep on trying
  = *algo te empuja a*
- **We have no alternative but to** fight
  = *no nos queda otro remedio más que*
- Three passport photos **are required**
  = *se necesitan*
- Club members **must not fail to** observe the regulations about proper behaviour
  = *han de*
- **You will** go directly to the headmaster's office and wait for me there
  = *vete*

37.2 Para saber si se está obligado a hacer algo

- **Do I have to** *o* **Have I got to** be home by midnight?
  = *¿tengo que ...?*
- **Does one have** to *o* **need to** book in advance?
  = *¿hay que ...?*
- **Is it necessary to** go into so much detail?
  = *¿es necesario ...?*
- **Ought I to** tell my colleagues?
  = *¿debería ...?*
- **Should I** call the police?
  = *¿debería ...?*
- **Am I meant to** *o* **Am I expected to** *o* **Am I supposed to** fill in this bit of the form?
  = *¿tengo que ...?*

37.3 Para explicar lo que no se está obligado a hacer

- **I don't have to** *o* **I haven't got to** be home so early now the nights are lighter
  = *no tengo que*
- **You don't have to** *o* **You needn't** go there if you don't want to
  = *no hace falta que*
- **You are not obliged to** *o* **You are under no obligation to** invite him
  = *no estás obligado*
- **It is not compulsory** *o* **obligatory to** have a letter of acceptance but it does help
  = *no es obligatorio*
- The Council **does not expect you to** pay all of your bill at once
  = *no espera que*

37.4 Para explicar lo que no se debe hacer

- **On no account must you** be persuaded to give up the cause
  = *no debes de ninguna manera*
- **You are not allowed to** sit the exam more than three times
  = *no puedes*
- Smoking **is not allowed** in the dining room
  = *no se puede*
- **You mustn't** show this document to any unauthorized person
  = *no debe*
- These are tasks **you cannot** ignore, delegate or bungle
  = *no puedes*
- **You're not supposed to** *o* **meant to** use this room unless you are a club member
  = *no puede*
- **I forbid you to** return there
  = *te prohíbo que*

De forma menos directa

- **It is forbidden to** bring cameras into the gallery
  = *está prohibido*
- **You are forbidden to** talk to anyone while the case is being heard
  = *le está prohibido*
- Smoking **is prohibited** *o* **is not permitted** in the dining room
  = *está prohibido*

38 ACUERDO

38.1 Para expresar acuerdo con lo que se dice

- **I fully agree with you** *o* **I totally agree with you** on this point
  = *estoy* *totalmente* *de* *acuerdo* *contigo*
- **We are in complete agreement** on this
  = *estamos totalmente de acuerdo*
- **I entirely take your point about** the extra vehicles needed
  = *tienes toda la razón en que*
- I think **we see completely eye to eye** on this issue
  = *pensamos exactamente lo mismo*
- I talked it over with the chairman and **we are both of the same mind**
  = *ambos somos de la misma opinión*
- **You're quite right in** pointing at distribution as the main problem
  = *tienes razón en*
- **We share your views** on the proposed expansion of the site
  = *compartimos su opinión*
- **My own experience** certainly **bears out** *o* **confirms** what you say
  = *mi experiencia personal confirma*
- **It's true that** you had the original idea but many other people worked on it
  = *es verdad que*
- **As you have quite rightly pointed out**, this will not be easy
  = *como bien dijo usted*
- **I have to concede that** the results are quite eye-catching
  = *he de reconocer que*
- **I have no objection to** this being done
  = *no tengo inconveniente en que*
- **I agree in theory**, but in practice it's never quite that simple
  = *en principio estoy de acuerdo*
- **I agree up to a point**
  = *estoy de acuerdo hasta cierto punto*

De forma más familiar

- Go for a drink instead of working late? **Sounds good to me!**
  = *me parece estupendo*
- **That's a lovely idea**
  = *¡qué buena idea!*
- **I'm all for** encouraging a youth section in video clubs such as ours
  = *soy partidario de*
- **I couldn't agree with you more**
  = *estoy totalmente de acuerdo contigo*

De forma menos directa

- **I am delighted to wholeheartedly endorse** your campaign
  = *me complace dar mi incondicional apoyo a*
- **Our conclusions are entirely consistent with** your findings
  = *nuestras conclusiones confirman ... totalmente*
- Independent statistics **corroborate** those of your researcher
  = *corroboran*
- **We applaud** the group's decision to stand firm on this point
  = *celebramos*

38.2 Para expresar acuerdo con lo propuesto

- This certainly **seems the right way to go about it**
  = *parece ser la forma correcta de proceder*
- **I will certainly give my backing to** such a scheme
  = *cuenta con todo mi apoyo*
- **It makes sense to** enlist helping hands for the final stages
  = *tiene sentido*
- **We certainly welcome** this development
  = *nos alegra*

De forma más familiar

- **It's a great idea**
  = *es una idea estupenda*
- Cruise control? **I like the sound of that**
  = *suena bien*
- **I'll go along with** Ted's proposal that we open the club up to women
  = *apoyo*

De forma menos directa

- This solution **is most acceptable** to us
  = *nos parece muy aceptable*
- The proposed scheme **meets with our approval**
  = *aprobamos*
- This is a proposal which **deserves our wholehearted support**
  = *merece nuestro apoyo incondicional*
- I shall do my best to **fall in with** her wishes
  = *acceder a*

38.3 Para expresar acuerdo con lo que pide alguien

- Of course **I'll be happy to** organize it for you
  = *estaré encantado de*
- **I'll do as you suggest** and send him the documents
  = *seguiré tu consejo*
- **There's no problem about** getting tickets for him
  = *podemos/puedo ... sin problema*

De forma menos directa

- Reputable builders **will not object to** this reasonable request
  = *no podrán reparos a*
- **We should be delighted to** cooperate with you in this enterprise
  = *con mucho gusto*
- An army statement said it **would comply with** the ceasefire
  = *respetaría*
- **I consent to** the performance of such procedures as are considered necessary
  = *accedo a*

39 DESACUERDO

39.1 Para mostrarse en desacuerdo con lo que se ha dicho

- There must be some mistake - **it can't possibly** cost as much as that
  = *no es posible que*
- I'm afraid he **is quite wrong** if he has told you that
  = *se equivoca*
- **You're wrong in thinking that** I haven't understood
  = *te equivocas al pensar que*
- The article **is mistaken in** claiming that debating the subject is a waste of public money
  = *comete un error al*
- Surveys **do not bear out** Mrs Fraser's assumption that these people will return to church at a later date
  = *no confirman*
- **I cannot agree with you** on this point
  = *no estoy de acuerdo contigo*
- **We cannot accept the view that** the lack of research and development explains the decline of Britain
  = *no aceptamos la opinión de que*
- To say we should forget about it, no **I cannot go along with that**
  = *no puedo aceptar eso*
- **We must agree to differ on this one**
  = *habrá que aceptar que nunca nos pondremos de acuerdo en este punto*

Con más insistencia

- **This is most emphatically not the case**
  = *insisto en que no es así*
- **I entirely reject** his contentions
  = *rechazo totalmente*
- **I totally disagree with** the previous two callers
  = *no estoy en absoluto de acuerdo con*
- This is your view of the events: **it is certainly not mine**
  = *yo desde luego no lo veo así*
- **I cannot support you** on this matter
  = *no puedo apoyarte*
- **Surely you can't believe that** he'd do such a thing?
  = *¿no creerás que ...?*

39.2 Para mostrarse en desacuerdo con lo que se ha propuesto

Con decisión

- **I'm dead against** this idea
  = *estoy totalmente en contra de*
- **Right idea, wrong approach**
  = *es una buena idea, pero mal enfocado*
- **I will not hear of** such a thing
  = *no quiero ni oír hablar de*
- **It is not feasible to** change the schedule at this late stage
  = *no es viable*
- This **is not a viable alternative**
  = *no es una alternativa viable*
- Trade sanctions will have an immediate effect but it **is the wrong approach**
  = *no es forma de hacer las cosas*

Con menos insistencia

- **I'm not too keen on** this idea
  = *no me convence mucho*
- **I don't think much of** this idea
  = *no me convence mucho*
- **This doesn't seem to be the right way of dealing** with the problem
  = *esta no parece la mejor forma de*
- While we are grateful for the suggestion, **we are unfortunately unable to** implement this change
  = *por desgracia nos es imposible*
- **I regret that I am not in a position to** accept your kind offer
  = *lamento no hallarme en condiciones de*

39.3 Para mostrarse en desacuerdo con lo que se ha pedido

- **I wouldn't dream of** doing a thing like that
  = *no se me ocurriría*
- I'm sorry but **I just can't** do it
  = *es que no puedo*
- **I cannot in all conscience** leave those kids in that atmosphere
  = *en conciencia no puedo*

Con más decisión

- **This is quite out of the question** for the time being
  = *no puede ser*
- **I won't agree to** any plan that involves your brother
  = *no voy a apoyar*
- **I refuse point blank to** have anything to do with this affair
  = *me niego rotundamente*

De forma menos directa

- **I am afraid I must refuse**
  = *lo siento pero he de negarme*
- **I cannot possibly comply with** this request
  = *me es imposible acceder a*
- **It is unfortunately impracticable for us to** commit ourselves at this stage
  = *nos es, por desgracia, imposible*
- In view of the proposed timescale, **I must reluctantly decline to** take part
  = *aun sintiéndolo, me veo obligado a declinar*

40 APROBACIÓN

40.1 Para aprobar lo que se ha dicho

- **I couldn't agree** (with you) **more**
  = *Estoy totalmente de acuerdo (contigo)*
- **I couldn't have put it better myself**
  = *tal y como lo hubiera dicho yo mismo*
- We must oppose terrorism, whatever its source. - **Hear, hear!**
  = *¡sí, señor!*
- **I endorse** his feelings regarding the condition of the Simpson memorial
  = *suscribo*

40.2 Para aprobar una propuesta

- **It's just the job!**
  = *¡perfecto!*
- **This is just the sort of thing I wanted**
  = *es justo lo que quería*
- **This is exactly what I had in mind**
  = *es justo lo que yo tenía pensado*
- Thank you for sending the draft agenda: **I like the look of it very much**
  = *me ha causado muy buena impresión*
- **We are all very enthusiastic about** o **very keen on** his latest set of proposals
  = *estamos todos entusiasmados con*
- **I shall certainly give it my backing**
  = *por supuesto que lo voy a apoyar*
- Any game which is as clearly enjoyable as this **meets with my approval**
  = *tiene mi aprobación*
- Skinner's plan **deserves our total support** o **our wholehearted approval**
  = *merece todo nuestro apoyo*
- **There are considerable advantages** in the alternative method you propose
  = *... comporta numerosas ventajas*
- **We recognize the merits** of this scheme
  = *reconocemos los méritos de*
- **We view** your proposal to extend the site **favourably**
  = *... nos merece una opinión favorable*
- This project **is worthy of our attention**
  = *merece de nuestra atención*

40.3 Para aprobar una idea

- **You're quite right to** wait before making such an important decision
  = *tienes toda la razón al*
- **I entirely approve of** the idea
  = *apruebo totalmente*
- **I'd certainly go along with that!**
  = *estoy totalmente de acuerdo*
- **I'm very much in favour of** that sort of thing
  = *soy muy partidario de*
- **What an excellent idea!**
  = *¡Qué idea tan estupenda!*

40.4 Para aprobar una acción

- **I applaud** Noble's perceptive analysis of the problems
  = *... merece un aplauso*
- **I have a very high opinion of** their new teaching methods
  = *tengo muy buena opinión de*
- **I have a very high regard for** the work of the Crown Prosecution Service
  = *tengo muy buen concepto de*
- **I think very highly of** the people who have been leading thus far
  = *... me merecen muy buena opinión*
- **I certainly admire** his courage in telling her what he thought of her
  = *siento gran admiración por*
- **I must congratulate you on** the professional way you handled the situation
  = *debo felicitarle por*
- **I greatly appreciated** the enormous risk that they had all taken
  = *les agradecí mucho*
- **I can thoroughly recommend** the event to field sports enthusiasts
  = *recomiendo plenamente*

41 DESAPROBACIÓN

- **This doesn't seem to be the right way of** going about it
  no parece ésta la mejor manera de
- **I don't think much of** what this government has done so far
  no tengo muy buena opinión de
- **I can't say I'm pleased about** what has happened
  no es que esté muy contento con
- The police **took a dim view of** her attempt to help her son break out of jail
  veía ... con malos ojos
- **We have a low** *o* **poor opinion of** opportunists like him
  sentimos poca estima por
- They **should not have refused to** give her the money
  no deberían haberse negado a

Más directamente

- **I'm fed up with** having to wait so long for payments to be made
  = *estoy hasta la coronilla de*
- **I've had (just) about enough of** this whole supermodel thing
  = *... (ya) me tiene harto*
- **I can't bear** *o* **stand** people who smoke in restaurants
  = *no soporto*
- **How dare he** say that!
  = *¡cómo se atreve a ...!*
- **He was quite wrong to** repeat what I said about her
  = *hizo muy mal en*
- **I cannot approve of** *o* **support** any sort of testing on live animals
  = *me resulta inaceptable*
- **We are opposed to** all forms of professional malpractice
  = *nos oponemos a*
- **We condemn** any intervention which could damage race relations
  = *condenamos*
- **I must object to** the tag "soft porn actress"
  = *tengo que protestar contra*
- **I'm very unhappy about** your (idea of) going off to Turkey on your own
  = *me hace muy poca gracia*
- **I strongly disapprove of** such behaviour
  = *desapruebo totalmente*

42 CERTEZA, PROBABILIDAD, POSIBILIDAD Y CAPACIDAD

42.1 Certeza

- **She was bound to** discover that you and I had talked
  = *era de esperar que*
- **It is inevitable that they will** get to know of our meeting
  = *es inevitable que se enteren*
- **I'm sure** *o* **certain (that)** he'll keep his word
  = *estoy seguro de que*
- **I'm positive** *o* **convinced (that)** it was your mother I saw
  = *estoy convencido de que*
- **We now know for certain** *o* **for sure that** the exam papers were seen by several students before the day of the exam
  = *sabemos ya con seguridad*
- **I made sure** *o* **certain that** no one was listening to our conversation
  = *me aseguré de que*
- From all the evidence **it is clear that** they were planning to sell up
  = *está claro que*
- **What is indisputable is that** a diet of fruit and vegetables is healthier
  = *lo que es indiscutible es que*
- **It is undeniable that** racial tensions in Britain have been increasing
  = *no se puede negar que*
- **There is no doubt that** the talks will be long and difficult
  = *no hay ninguna duda de que*
- **There can be no doubt about** the objective of the animal liberationists
  = *no cabe ninguna duda acerca de*
- This crisis has demonstrated **beyond all (possible) doubt** that effective political control must be in place before the creation of such structures
  = *sin lugar a dudas*
- Her pedigree **is beyond dispute** *o* **question**
  = *está fuera de dudas*
- **You have my absolute assurance that** this is the case
  = *tiene mi garantía absoluta de que*
- **I can assure you that** I have had nothing to do with any dishonest trading
  = *puedo asegurarle que*
- **Make no mistake about it** - I will return when I have proof of your involvement
  = *que quede bien claro*

42.2 Probabilidad

- **There is a good** *o* **strong chance that** they will agree to the deal
  = *hay bastantes probabilidades de que*
- **It seems highly likely that** it was Bert who told Peter what had happened
  = *parece muy probable que*
- **The chances** *o* **the odds are that** he will play safe in the short term
  = *lo más probable es que*
- **The probability is that** your investment will be worth more in two years' time
  = *lo más probable es que*
- The child's hearing will, **in all probability,** be severely affected
  = *con toda probabilidad*
- You will **very probably** be met at the airport by one of our men
  = *es muy probable que*
- **It is highly probable that** American companies will face retaliation abroad
  = *es muy probable que*
- **It is quite likely that** you will get withdrawal symptoms at first
  = *es bastante probable que*

- **The likelihood is that** the mood of mistrust and recrimination will intensify
  = *lo más probable es que*
- The person indicted is, **in all likelihood**, going to be guilty as charged
  = *con toda probabilidad*
- **There is reason to believe that** the books were stolen from the library
  = *hay motivo para creer que*
- **He must** know of the paintings' existence
  = *debe de*
- The talks **could very well** spill over into tomorrow
  = *podrían muy bien*
- The cheque **should** reach you by Saturday
  = *debería*
- **It wouldn't surprise me** o **I wouldn't be surprised if** he was working for the Americans
  = *no me sorprendería que*

42.3 Posibilidad

- The situation **could** change from day to day
  = *podría*
- Britain **could perhaps** play a more positive role in developing policy
  = *podría quizá*
- **I venture to suggest (that)** a lot of it is to do with his political ambitions
  = *me atrevería a sugerir que*
- **It is possible that** psychological factors play some unknown role in the healing process
  = *es posible que*
- **It is conceivable that** the economy is already in recession
  = *cabe la posibilidad de que*
- **It is well within the bounds of possibility that** England could be beaten
  = *no se puede descartar la posibilidad de que*
- **It may be that** the whole battle will have to be fought over again
  = *puede ser que*
- **It may be (the case) that** they got your name from the voters' roll
  = *puede ser que*
- **There is an outside chance that** the locomotive may appear in the Gala
  = *hay una remota posibilidad de que*
- **There is a small chance that** your body could reject the implants
  = *existe una pequeña posibilidad de que*

42.4 Para expresar lo que alguien es capaz de hacer

- Our Design and Print Service **can** supply envelopes and package your existing literature
  = *pueden*
- Applicants must **be able to** use a computer
  = *saber*
- **He is qualified to** teach physics
  = *tiene titulación para*

43 INCERTIDUMBRE, IMPROBABILIDAD, IMPOSIBILIDAD E INCAPACIDAD

43.1 Incertidumbre

- **I doubt if** o **It is doubtful whether** he knows where it came from
  = *dudo que*
- **There is still some doubt surrounding** his exact whereabouts
  = *sigue habiendo dudas acerca de*
- **I have my doubts about** replacing private donations with taxpayers' cash
  = *tengo mis dudas sobre la sustitución de*
- **It isn't known for sure** o **It isn't certain** where she is
  = *no se sabe con certeza*
- **No one can say for sure** how any child will develop
  = *no se puede decir con seguridad*
- It's all still up in the air - **we won't know for certain** until next week
  = *no lo sabremos con seguridad*
- You're asking why I should do such an extraordinary thing and **I'm not sure** o **certain that** I really know the answer
  = *no estoy seguro de*
- **I'm not convinced that** you can really teach people who don't want to learn
  = *no estoy convencido de que*
- **We are still in the dark about** where the letter came from
  = *seguimos sin saber*
- How long this muddle can last **is anyone's guess**
  = *cualquiera sabe*
- Sterling is going to come under further pressure. **It is touch and go whether** base rates will have to go up
  = *está por ver si*
- **I'm wondering if** I should offer to help?
  = *no sé*

43.2 Improbabilidad

- You have **probably not** yet seen the document I am referring to
  = *seguramente no*
- **It is highly improbable that** there will be a challenge for the party leadership in the near future
  = *hay poquísimas probabilidades de que*
- **It is very doubtful whether** the expedition will reach the summit
  = *es muy dudoso que*
- **In the unlikely event that** the room was bugged, the music would drown out their conversation
  = *si se diera el caso poco probable de que*
- **It was hardly to be expected that** democratization would be easy
  = *apenas cabía esperar que*

43.3 Imposibilidad

- **There can be no** changes in the schedule
  = *no puede haber*
- Nowadays Carnival **cannot** happen **without** the police telling us where to walk and what direction to walk in
  = *no puede ... sin que*
- People said prices would inevitably rise; **this cannot be the case**
  = *esto es imposible*
- **I couldn't possibly** invite George and not his wife
  = *¿cómo voy a ...?*
- The report **rules out any possibility of** exceptions, and amounts to little more than a statement of the obvious
  = *descarta cualquier posibilidad de*
- **There is no question of** us getting this finished on time
  = *es imposible que*
- A West German spokesman said **it was out of the question that** these weapons would be based in Germany
  = *que ... de ninguna manera*
- **There is not (even) the remotest chance that** o **There is absolutely no chance that** he will succeed
  = *no existe la más remota posibilidad de que*
- The idea of trying to govern twelve nations from one centre **is unthinkable**
  = *es impensable*
- Since we had over 500 applicants, **it would be quite impossible to** interview them all
  = *sería del todo imposible*

43.4 Para expresar lo que uno es incapaz de hacer

- **I can't** drive, I'm afraid
  = *no sé*

- **I don't know how to** use a smartphone
  = *no sé*
- The army **has been unable to** suppress the political violence in the area
  = *no ha podido*
- The congress had shown itself **incapable of** real reform
  = *incapaz de*
- His fellow-directors **were not up** to running the business without him
  = *no eran capaces de*
- We hoped the sales team would be able to think up new marketing strategies, but they **were** unfortunately **not equal to the task**
  = *no fueron capaces de hacerlo*
- I'm afraid the task **proved** (to be) **beyond his capabilities**
  = *resultó demasiado para él*
- I'd like to leave him but sometimes I feel that such a step **is beyond me**
  = *es superior a mis fuerzas*
- **He simply couldn't cope with** the stresses of family life
  = *es que no podía con*
- Far too many women accept that they're **hopeless at** *o* **no good at** managing money
  = *no sirven para controlar*
- **I'm not in a position to** say now how much substance there is in the reports
  = *no estoy en situación de*
- **It is quite impossible for me to** describe the confusion and horror of the scene
  = *me resulta casi imposible*

44 EXPLICACIONES

44.1 Para dar las razones de algo

- He was sacked **for the simple reason that** he just wasn't up to it any more
  = *por la sencilla razón de que*
- **The reason that** we admire him is that he knows what he is doing
  = *la razón de que*
- He said he could not be more specific **for** security **reasons**
  = *por razones de*
- The students were arrested **because of** suspected dissident activities
  = *por*
- Parliament has prevaricated, **largely because of** the unwillingness of the main opposition party to support the changes
  = *sobre todo a causa de*
- Teachers in the eastern part of Germany are assailed by fears of mass unemployment **on account of** their communist past
  = *a causa de*
- Morocco has announced details of the austerity package it is adopting **as a result of** pressure from the International Monetary Fund
  = *como consecuencia de*
- They are facing higher costs **owing to** rising inflation
  = *debido a*
- The full effects will be delayed **due to** factors beyond our control
  = *debido a*
- **Thanks to** their generosity, the charity can afford to buy new equipment
  = *gracias a*
- What also had to go was the notion that some people were born superior to others **by virtue of** their skin colour
  = *en virtud de*
- Both companies became profitable again **by means of** severe cost-cutting
  = *mediante*
- He shot to fame **on the strength of** a letter he had written to the papers
  = *a raíz de*
- The King and Queen's defence of old-fashioned family values has acquired a poignancy **in view of** their inability to have children
  = *en vista de*
- The police have put considerable pressure on the Government to toughen its stance **in the light of** recent events
  = *a la luz de*
- **In the face of** this continued disagreement, the parties have asked for the polling to be postponed
  = *ante*
- His soldiers had been restraining themselves **for fear of** harming civilians
  = *por temor a herir*
- A survey by the World Health Organization says that two out of every five people are dying prematurely **for lack of** food or health care
  = *por falta de*
- **Babies have died for want of** *o* **for lack of** proper medical attention
  = *por falta de*
- I refused her a divorce, **out of** spite I suppose
  = *por*
- The warder was freed unharmed **in exchange for** the release of a colleague
  = *a cambio de*
- The court had ordered his release, **on the grounds that** he had already been acquitted of most of the charges against him
  = *basándose en que*
- I am absolutely in favour of civil disobedience **on** moral **grounds**
  = *por motivos*
- It is unclear why they initiated this week's attack, **given that** negotiations were underway
  = *dado que*
- **Seeing that** he had a police escort, the only time he could have switched containers was on the way to the airport
  = *dado que*
- **As** he had been up since 4 a.m., he was doubtless very tired
  = *como*
- International intervention was appropriate **since** tensions had reached the point where there was talk of war
  = *ya que*
- She could not have been deaf, **for** she started at the sound of a bell (*literario*)
  = *pues*
- I cannot accept this decision. **So** I confirm it is my intention to appeal to a higher authority
  = *así que*
- What the Party said was taken to be right, **therefore** anyone who disagreed must be wrong
  = *por lo tanto*
- **Following** last weekend's rioting in central London, Conservatives say some left-wing Labour MPs were partly to blame
  = *tras*
- **The thing is that** once you've retired there's no going back
  = *lo que pasa es que*

44.2 Para explicar la causa o el origen de algo

- The serious dangers to your health **caused by** *o* **brought about by** cigarettes are now better understood
  = *provocados por*
- When the picture was published recently, **it gave rise to** *o* **led to** speculation that the three were still alive and being held captive
  = *dio lugar a*
- The army argues that security concerns **necessitated** the demolitions
  = *hacían necesarias*

- This lack of recognition **was at the root of** the dispute
  = *fue la razón fundamental de*
- **I attribute** all this mismanagement **to** the fact that the General Staff in London is practically non-existent
  = *atribuyo ... a*
- This unrest **dates from** colonial times
  = *data de*
- The custom **goes back to** pre-Christian days
  = *se remonta a*

45 DISCULPAS

45.1 Para disculparse

- **I'm really sorry**, Steve, **but** we won't be able to come on Saturday
  = *de verdad lo siento ... pero*
- **I'm sorry that** your time has been wasted
  = *siento que*
- **I am sorry to have to** say this to you but you're no good
  = *siento tener que*
- **Apologies if** I wasn't very good company last night
  = *disculpa si*
- **I must apologize for** what happened. Quite unforgivable, and the man responsible has been disciplined
  = *le ruego disculpe*
- **I owe you an apology**. I didn't think you knew what you were talking about
  = *te debo una disculpa*
- The general back-pedalled, saying that **he had not meant to** offend the German government
  = *no había sido su intención ofender*
- **Do forgive me for** being a little abrupt
  = *le ruego me perdone que haya sido*
- **Please forgive me for** behaving so badly
  = *perdóname por haberme comportado*
- **Please accept our apologies** if this has caused you any inconvenience
  = *les rogamos acepten nuestras disculpas*

45.2 Para aceptar responsabilidad de algo

- **I admit** I overreacted, but someone needed to speak out against her
  = *admito que*
- **I have no excuse for** what happened
  = *no tengo excusa para explicar*
- **It is my fault that** our marriage is on the rocks
  = *es culpa mía que*
- The Government **is not entirely to blame for** the crisis
  = *no tiene toda la culpa de*
- **I should never have** let him rush out of the house in anger
  = *no tenía que haber*
- Oh, but **if only I hadn't** lost the keys
  = *ojalá no hubiera*
- I hate to admit that the old man was right, but **I made a stupid mistake**
  = *fue un fallo tonto*
- **My mistake was in** failing to push my concerns and convictions as hard as I could have done
  = *mi error fue no conseguir*
- **My mistake was to** arrive wearing a jacket and polo-neck jumper
  = *cometí el error de*
- In December and January the markets raced ahead, and I missed out on that. **That was my mistake**
  = *ese fue mi error*

45.3 Para expresar lo que se lamenta

- **I'm very upset about** her decision but I accept she needs to move on to new challenges
  = *estoy muy disgustado por*
- **It's a shame that** the press gives so little coverage to these events
  = *es una pena que*
- **I feel awful about** saying this but you really ought to spend more time with your children
  = *me sabe mal*
- **I'm afraid I can't** help you very much
  = *(me temo que) no puedo*
- **It is a pity that** my profession can make a lot of money out of the misfortunes of others
  = *es una lástima que*
- **It is unfortunate that** the matter should have come to a head just now
  = *es de lamentar que*
- David and I **very much regret that** we have been unable to reach an agreement
  = *lamentamos mucho*
- The accused **bitterly regrets** this incident and it won't happen again
  = *lamenta de corazón*
- **We regret to inform you that** the post of Editor has now been filled
  = *lamentamos tener que informarle que*

45.4 Para rechazar toda responsabilidad

- **I didn't do it on purpose**, it just happened
  = *no lo hice a propósito*
- Sorry, Nanna. **I didn't mean to** upset you
  = *no era mi intención*
- Sorry about not coming to the meeting **I was under the impression that** it was just for managers
  = *tenía idea de que*
- **We are simply trying to** protect the interests of local householders
  = *intentamos sencillamente*
- I know how this hurt you but **I had no choice**. I had to put David's life above all else
  = *no me quedaba otro remedio*
- **We were obliged to** accept their conditions
  = *nos vimos obligados a*
- We are unhappy with 1.5%, but under the circumstances **we have no alternative but to** accept
  = *no nos queda otra alternativa que*
- **I had nothing to do with** the placing of any advertisement
  = *no tuve nada que ver con*
- A spokesman for the club assured supporters that **it was a genuine error** and **there was no intention to** mislead them
  = *se trataba de un error auténtico y que no hubo intención de*

46 SOLICITUDES DE TRABAJO

46.1 Para empezar la carta

- **In reply to your advertisement** for a Trainee Manager in today's *Guardian*, I would be grateful if you would send me further details of the post
  = *en respuesta a su anuncio*
- **I wish to apply for the post of** bilingual correspondent, as advertised in this week's *Euronews*
  = *desearía que se me considerara para el puesto de*
- **I am writing to ask if there is any possibility of work in your company**
  = *le ruego me informe si existe alguna posibilidad de empleo dentro de su empresa*

89 Short Street
Glossop
Derby SK13 4AP

The Personnel Director
Norton Manufacturing Ltd
Sandy Lodge Industrial Estate
Northants NN10 8QT

3 February 2016

Dear Sir or Madam[1]

With reference to your advertisement in *The Guardian* of 2 February 2016, I wish to apply for the post of Export Manager in your company.

I am currently employed as Export Sales Executive for United Engineering Ltd. My main role is to develop our European business by establishing contact with potential new distributors and conducting market research both at home and abroad.

I believe I could successfully apply my sales and marketing skills to this post and therefore enclose my curriculum vitae for your consideration. Please do not hesitate to contact me if you require further details. I am available for interview at any time.

I look forward to hearing from you.

Yours faithfully

Janet Lilly

CURRICULUM VITAE

Name: Margaret Sinclair

Address: 12 Poplar Avenue, Leeds LS12 9DT, England

Telephone: 0113 246 6648

Date of Birth: 2.2.91

Marital Status: Single

Nationality: British

Qualifications[2]:
Diploma in Business Management, Liverpool College of Business Studies (2015)
B.A. Honours in French with Hispanic Studies (Upper 2nd class), University of York (2014)
A-Levels: English (B), French (A), Spanish (A), Geography (C) (2009)
GCSEs: in 8 subjects (2007)

Employment History:
Assistant Manager, Biblio Bookshop, York (October 2015 to present)
Sales Assistant, Langs Bookshop, York (summer 2015)
English Assistant, Lycée Victor Hugo, Nîmes, France (2012–13)
Campsite courier, Peñíscola, Spain (summer 2010)

Other Information:
I enjoy reading, the cinema, skiing and amateur dramatics.
I hold a clean driving licence and am a non-smoker.

References:

Mr John Jeffries	Ms Teresa González
Manager	Department of Spanish
Biblio Bookshop	University of York
York	York
YT5 2PS	YT4 3DE

[1] Cuando no se sabe si el destinatario es hombre o mujer, se debe usar esta fórmula. Por otra parte, si se conoce la identidad del destinatario se puede utilizar una de estas formas al escribir el nombre y dirección:

Mr Derek Balder
Mrs Una Claridge
Ms Nicola Stokes
o
Personnel Director
Messrs. J.M. Kenyon Ltd. *etc.*

En el encabezamiento de la carta, las fórmulas correspondientes serían: "Dear Mr Balder", "Dear Mrs Claridge" etc, "Dear Sir/ Madam" (según corresponda, si se sabe si es hombre o mujer), "Dear Sir or Madam" (si no se sabe).

Las cartas que comienzan con el nombre de la persona en el encabezamiento (e.g. "Dear Mr Balder") pueden terminar con la fórmula de despedida "Yours sincerely"; las que empiezan con "Dear Sir/ Madam" normalmente acaban con "Yours faithfully", seguido de la firma.

[2] Si se solicita un puesto en el extranjero se puede emplear una frase que explique el título académico que se posee, p.ej. "Spanish/ Mexican etc. equivalent of A-Levels (bachillerato superior)", "equivalent to a degree in English Studies etc. (licenciatura en Filología Inglesa etc)".

- **I am writing to enquire about the possibility of joining your company on work placement** for a period of 3 months
  = *le agradecería me informara sobre la posibilidad de efectuar prácticas de trabajo en su empresa*

46.2 Para hablar de la experiencia profesional propia

- **I have** three **years' experience of** office work
  = *tengo ... años de experiencia en*
- **I am familiar with** translation tools
  = *tengo experiencia con*
- **As well as speaking fluent** English, **I have a working knowledge of** German
  = *además de hablar ... con fluidez, tengo buenos conocimientos de*
- **As you will see from my CV,** I have worked in Belgium before
  = *como verá en mi currículum*
- **Although I have no experience of** this type of work, I have had other holiday jobs and can supply references from my employers, if you wish
  = *a pesar de carecer de experiencia en*
- **My current salary is** ... per annum and I have four weeks' paid leave
  = *mi sueldo actual es de*

46.3 Para exponer las motivaciones propias

- **I would like to make better use of my languages**
  = *quisiera hacer más uso de los idiomas que conozco*
- **I am keen to work in** public relations
  = *tengo mucho interés en trabajar en*

46.4 Para terminar la carta

- **I will be available from** the end of April
  = *estaré libre a partir de*
- **I am available for interview** at any time
  = *me tendrá a su disposición para una entrevista personal*
- **Please do not hesitate to contact me** for further information
  = *no dude en ponerse en contacto conmigo*
- **Please do not contact my current employers**
  = *le rogaría que no se comunicara con mi empresa*
- **I enclose** a stamped addressed envelope for your reply
  = *adjunto*

46.5 Como pedir y redactar referencias

- In my application for the position of lecturer, I have been asked to provide the names of two referees and **I wondered whether you would mind if I gave your name** as one of them
  = *le agradecería me permitiera dar su nombre*
- Ms Lee has applied for the post of Marketing Executive with our company and has given us your name as a reference. **We would be grateful if you would let us know whether you would recommend her for this position**
  = *le agradeceríamos nos informase si merece su recomendación para tal puesto*
- **Your reply will be treated in the strictest confidence**
  = *su respuesta será tratada con absoluta reserva*
- I have known Mr Chambers for four years in his capacity as Sales Manager and **can warmly recommend him for the position**
  = *me complace recomendarlo para el puesto*

46.6 Para aceptar o rechazar una propuesta de empleo

- Thank you for your letter of 20 March. **I will be pleased to attend for interview** at your Manchester offices on Thursday 7 April at 10am
  = *con mucho gusto me presentaré a la entrevista personal que me solicitan*
- **I would like to confirm my acceptance of** the post of Marketing Executive
  = *deseo confirmar que acepto*
- **I would be delighted to accept this post. However,** would it be possible to postpone my starting date until 8 May?
  = *aceptaría encantado el puesto. Sin embargo,*
- **I would be glad to accept your offer; however,** the salary stated is somewhat lower than what I had hoped for
  = *aceptaría con mucho gusto su oferta; sin embargo*
- Having given your offer careful thought, **I regret that I am unable to accept**
  = *lamento no poder aceptarla*

47 CORRESPONDENCIA COMERCIAL

47.1 Peticiones de información

- **We see from** your advertisement in the Healthy Holiday Guide that you are offering cut-price holidays in Scotland, and **would be grateful if you would send us** details
  = *hemos visto ... Les agradeceríamos que nos enviaran*
- I read about the Happy Pet Society in the NCT newsletter and would be very interested to learn more about it. **Please send me details of** membership
  = *les agradecería que me enviaran información detallada sobre*

... y cómo responder

- **In response to your enquiry of** 8 March, **we have pleasure in enclosing** full details on our activity holidays in Cumbria, **together with** our price list, valid until October 2017
  = *en respuesta a su consulta del ... adjuntamos ... acompañados de*
- **Thank you for your enquiry about** the Society for Wildlife Protection. **I enclose** a leaflet explaining our beliefs and the issues we campaign on. **Should you wish** to join, a membership application form is also enclosed
  = *le agradecemos el interés mostrado por ... Le envío ... Si se decidiera a*

47.2 Pedidos y cómo responder

- **We would like to place an order for** the following items, in the sizes and quantities specified below
  = *desearíamos hacer un pedido de*
- **Please find enclosed our order no.** 3011 for ...
  = *adjunto encontrará nuestro pedido n°*
- **The enclosed order** is based on your current price list, assuming our usual discount
  = *el pedido adjunto*
- **I wish to order** a can of "Buzz off!" wasp repellent, as advertised in the July issue of Gardeners' Monthly, **and enclose a cheque for** £5.50
  = *desearía encargar ... para lo que adjunto un cheque por valor de*
- **Thank you for your order of** 3 May, which will be dispatched within 30 days
  = *le agradecemos su pedido de fecha*
- **We acknowledge receipt of your order no.** 3570 and advise that the goods will be dispatched within 7 working days
  = *acusamos recibo de su pedido n°*
- **We regret that the goods you ordered are temporarily out of stock**
  = *lamentamos tener que informarle que los artículos solicitados se hallan agotados temporalmente*
- **Please allow** 28 days **for delivery**
  = *la entrega se efectuará en un plazo de*

47.3 Entregas

- **Our delivery time is** 60 days from receipt of order
  = *nuestro plazo de entrega es de*
- **We await confirmation of your order**
  = *quedamos a la espera de confirmación de su pedido*

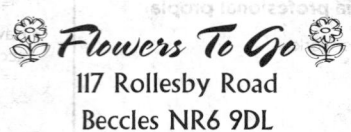

Flowers To Go
117 Rollesby Road
Beccles NR6 9DL
☎ 61 654 31 71

Ms Sharon McNeillie
41 Courthill Street
Beccles NR14 8TR

18 January 2016

Dear Ms McNeillie

Special Offer! 5% discount on orders received in January!

Thank you for your recent enquiry. We can deliver fresh flowers anywhere in the country at very reasonable prices. Our bouquets come beautifully wrapped, with satin ribbons, attractive foil backing, a sachet of plant food and, of course, your own personalized message. For that special occasion, we can even deliver arrangements with a musical greeting, the ideal surprise gift for birthdays, weddings or Christmas!

Whatever the occasion, you will find just what you need to make it special in our latest brochure, which I have pleasure in enclosing, along with our current price list. All prices include delivery within the UK.

During the promotion, a discount of 5% will apply on all orders received before the end of January, so hurry!

We look forward to hearing from you.

Yours sincerely

Daisy Duckworth

Daisy Duckworth
Promotions Assistant

Carrick Foods Ltd
Springwood Industrial Estate
Alexandra Road
Sheffield S11 5GF

Ms J Birkett
Department of English
Holyrood High School
Mirlees Road
Sheffield S19 7KL

14 April 2016

Dear Ms Birkett

Thank you for your letter of 7 April enquiring if it would be possible to arrange a group visit to our factory. We would of course be delighted to invite you and your pupils to take part in a guided factory tour. You will be able to observe the process from preparation through to canning, labelling and packaging of the final product ready for dispatch. Our factory manager will be available to answer pupils' questions at the end of the tour.

I would be grateful if you could confirm the date of your proposed visit, as well as the number of pupils and teachers in the party, at your earliest convenience.

Thank you once again for your interest in our company. I look forward to meeting you.

Yours sincerely

George Whyte

George Whyte

We confirm that the goods were dispatched on 4 September
= *confirmamos que el envío de la mercancía tuvo lugar el*

- **We cannot accept responsibility for** goods damaged in transit
= *lamentamos no poder responsabilizarnos de*

47.4 Para hacer una reclamación

- **We have not yet received** the items ordered on 6 May (ref. order no. 541)
= *no hemos recibido aún*
- **Unfortunately**, the goods were damaged in transit
= *desgraciadamente*
- **The goods received differ significantly from the description** in your catalogue.
= *los artículos recibidos difieren sustancialmente de los descritos*
- If the goods are not received by 20 October, **we shall have to cancel our order**
= *nos veremos obligados a anular nuestro pedido*

47.5 Pagos

- **The total amount outstanding is ...**
= *el importe pendiente se eleva a*
- **We would be grateful if you would attend to this account** immediately
= *les agradeceríamos que nos enviaran liquidación de esta cuenta*
- **Please remit payment by return**
= *sírvase remitirnos el pago a vuelta de correo*
- Full payment **is due within** 14 working days from receipt of goods
= *vence en un plazo de*
- **We enclose** a cheque for ... **in settlement of your invoice no.** 2003L/58
= *adjuntamos ... como liquidación de su factura n°*
- We must point out an error in your account and **would be grateful if you would adjust your invoice** accordingly
= *les agradeceríamos que rectificaran su factura*
- This mistake was due to an accounting error, and **we enclose a credit note for** the sum involved
= *abonamos*
- **Thank you for your cheque for** ... in settlement of our invoice
= *le agradecemos su cheque por valor de*
- **We look forward to doing further business with you** in the near future
= *Esperamos poder volver a servirles*

48 CORRESPONDENCIA DE CARÁCTER GENERAL

48.1 Para comenzar una carta

Para escribir a alguien que se conoce

- **Thank you** o **Thanks for your letter**, which arrived yesterday
= *gracias por tu carta*
- **It was good** o **nice** o **lovely to hear from you**
= *me alegró recibir noticias tuyas*
- It's such a long time since we were last in touch that **I felt I must write a few lines** just to say hello
= *pensé que tenía que escribirte unas líneas*
- **I'm sorry I haven't written for so long**, and hope you'll forgive me; I've had a lot of work recently and ...
= *perdona que no te haya escrito desde hace tanto tiempo*

Para escribir a una organización

- **I am writing to ask whether** you have in stock a book entitled ...
= *el motivo de mi carta es preguntarles si*
- **Please send me** ... I enclose a cheque for ...
= *les ruego me envíen*
- When I left your hotel last week, I think I may have left a red coat in my room. **Would you be so kind as to** let me know whether it has been found?
= *si fueran tan amables, ¿podrían ...?*
- **I** have seen the details of your summer courses, and **wish to know whether** you still have any vacancies on the Beginners' Swedish course
= *desearía saber si*

48.2 Para terminar el cuerpo de la carta (antes de la despedida)

A un conocido

- **Gerald joins me in sending very best wishes to you all**
= *Gerald y yo os deseamos lo mejor a todos*
- **Please remember me to** your wife – I hope she is well
= *dele mis recuerdos a*
- **I look forward to hearing from you**
= *quedo a la espera de tu respuesta*

A un amigo

- **Say hello to Martin for me**
= *saluda a Martin de mi parte*
- **Give my warmest regards to Vincent**
= *un abrazo para Vincent*
- **Do write** when you have a minute
= *escríbeme*
- **Hoping to hear from you before too long**
= *esperando recibir noticias tuyas pronto*

A amigos íntimos

- Rhona **sends her love**/Ray **sends his love**
= *abrazos/besos de parte de*
- **Give my love to** Daniel and Laura, and tell them how much I miss them
= *abrazos/besos a*
- Jodie and Carla **send you a big hug**
= *te mandan un muy fuerte abrazo*

48.3 Preparativos de viaje

Para reservar una habitación

- **Please send me details of** your prices
= *sírvanse enviarme información detallada sobre*
- **Please let me know by return of post if** you have one single room with bath, half board, for the week commencing 3 October
= *sírvanse informarme a vuelta de correo si*
- **I would like to book** bed-and-breakfast accommodation with you
= *desearía reservar*

48.4 Para confirmar o anular una reserva

- **Please consider this a firm booking** and hold the room until I arrive, however late in the evening
= *le ruego considere esta como una reserva en firme*
- **Please confirm the following by e-mail**: one single room with shower for the nights of 20-23 April 2017
= *sírvanse confirmarme por e-mail los siguientes datos*
- **We expect to arrive** in the early evening, unless something unforeseen happens
= *esperamos llegar*
- **I am afraid I must ask you to alter my booking from** 25 August **to** 3 September. I hope this will not cause too much inconvenience
= *me veo obligado a solicitarle que cambie mi reserva del ... al*
- Owing to unforseen circumstances, **I am afraid (that) I must cancel the booking** made with you for the week beginning 5 September
= *lamento tener que anular la reserva*

226 Wilton Street
Leicester LE8 7SP

20th November 2015

Dear Hannah,

Sorry I haven't been in touch for a while. It's been hectic since we moved house and we're still unpacking! Anyway, it's Leah's first birthday on the 30th and I wondered if you and the kids would like to come to her party that afternoon. We were planning to start around 4 o'clock and finish around 5.30 or so. I've invited a clown and a children's conjurer, mainly for the entertainment of the older ones. With a bit of luck, you and I might get a chance to catch up on all our news!

Drop me a line or give me a ring if you think you'll be able to make it over on the 30th. It would be lovely if you could all come!

Hoping to hear from you soon. Say hello to Danny, Paul and Jonathan for me.

Love,
Jackie

14 Apsley Grove
Aberdeen AB4 7LP
Scotland

14th April 2016

Dear Paloma and Paco,

How are you? I hope you and the children enjoyed Montse's birthday party yesterday. I wish I could have been there too.

My flight from Madrid was delayed, so we didn't reach Gatwick till after midnight last night. I am a bit tired, but at least I have the weekend ahead to recover before going back to work on Monday!

You were so kind to me and I can't thank you enough for all your warmth and hospitality. It was a truly unforgettable stay. I took lots of photographs, as you know, and I intend to have them online as soon as possible so we can all look at them.

Remember that you are only too welcome to come and stay with me any time. It would be lovely to see you both and to have the opportunity to do something for you at last.

Keep in touch and take care!

With love from
Sandra

Fórmulas de saludo y de despedida

El esquema siguiente proporciona ejemplos de fórmulas de saludo y de despedida que se usan a menudo en la correspondencia. Dentro de cada sección son posibles las permutaciones:

A alguien conocido personalmente

FÓRMULAS DE SALUDO	FÓRMULAS DE DESPEDIDA
Dear Mr Brown Dear Mrs Drake Dear Mr & Mrs Charlton Dear Miss Baker Dear Ms Black Dear Dr Armstrong Dear Professor Lyons Dear Sir Gerald Dear Lady MacLeod Dear Andrew Dear Margaret	Yours sincerely With all good wishes, Yours sincerely[1] With kindest regards, Yours sincerely[1] [1] *tratamiento más cordial*

A un(a) amigo(a), a un pariente

FÓRMULAS DE SALUDO	FÓRMULAS DE DESPEDIDA
Dear Victoria Dear Aunt Eleanor Dear Granny and Grandad Dear Mum and Dad My dear Elizabeth My dear Albert Dearest Norman My dearest Mother My dearest Lucy My darling Peter	With love from Love from Love to all[1] Love from us all[1] Yours[1] All the best[1] With much love from[2] Lots of love from[2] Much love, as always[2] All my love[2] [1] *tratamiento familiar* [2] *tratamiento afectuoso*

A un conocido o un(a) amigo(a)

FÓRMULAS DE SALUDO	FÓRMULAS DE DESPEDIDA
Dear Alison Dear Annie and George Dear Uncle Eric Dear Mrs Newman Dear Mr and Mrs Jones My dear Miss Armitage	Yours sincerely With best wishes, Yours sincerely[1] With kindest regards, Yours sincerely[1] All good wishes, Yours sincerely[1] With best wishes, *(etc)* Yours ever[2] Kindest regards,[2] Best wishes[2] With best wishes, As always[2] [1] *tratamiento más cordial* [2] *tratamiento familiar*

Cartas comerciales (véase también 47)

FÓRMULAS DE SALUDO	FÓRMULAS DE DESPEDIDA
Dear Sirs[1] Dear Sir[2] Dear Madam[3] Dear Sir or Madam[4] [1] *para dirigirse a una empresa* [2] *para dirigirse a un hombre* [3] *para dirigirse a una mujer* [4] *cuando no se sabe si se dirige uno a un hombre o una mujer*	Yours faithfully

49 AGRADECIMIENTOS

- **Just a line to say thanks for** the lovely book which arrived today
  = *sólo unas letras para darle las gracias por*
- **I can't thank you enough for** finding my watch
  = *no se cómo darle las gracias por*
- **(Would you) please thank him from me**
  = *dele las gracias de mi parte*
- **We greatly appreciated** your support during our recent difficulties
  = *agradecemos enormemente*
- Your advice and understanding **were much appreciated**
  = *le quedamos muy reconocidos por*
- **I am writing to thank you** *o* **to say thank you for** allowing me to quote your experience in my article on multiple births
  = *me dirijo a usted para darle las gracias por permitirme*
- **Please accept our sincere thanks for** all your help and support
  = *le damos nuestro más sincero agradecimiento por*
- **A big thank you to everyone** involved in the show this year
  = *muchísimas gracias a todos*
- **We would like to express our appreciation to** the University of Durham Research Committee for providing a grant
  = *queremos expresar nuestro reconocimiento a*

De parte de un grupo

- **Thank you on behalf of** the Manx Operatic Society **for** all your support
  = *gracias en nombre de ... por*
- **I am instructed by** our committee **to convey our sincere thanks for** your assistance at our recent Valentine Social
  = *... me ha encomendado que les transmitiera nuestro sincero agradecimiento por*

50 SALUDOS DE CORTESÍA Y FELICITACIONES

50.1 Expresiones para cualquier ocasión

- **I hope you have** a lovely holiday
  = *espero que tengas*
- **With love and best wishes for** your wedding anniversary
  = *os deseo un feliz*
- **(Do) give my best wishes to** your mother **for** a happy and healthy retirement
  = *dile a ... que le deseo lo mejor en*
- Len **joins me in sending you our very best wishes for** your future career
  = *... y yo te deseamos lo mejor en*

50.2 En Navidad y Año Nuevo

- **Merry Christmas and a happy New Year**
  = *Feliz Navidad y Próspero Año Nuevo*
- **With season's greetings and very best wishes from** (+ *firma*)
  = *les deseamos unas felices fiestas*
- **May I send you all our very best wishes for** 2017
  = *quisiera desearles a todos un feliz*

50.3 Para un cumpleaños

- **All our love and best wishes on your** 21st **birthday**, from Simon, Liz, Kerry and the cats
  = *te deseamos muchísimas felicidades en tu 21 cumpleaños. Con todo nuestro cariño*
- I am writing to wish you **many happy returns (of the day)**. Hope your birthday brings you everything you wished for
  = *muchas felicidades (en el día de tu cumpleaños)*

50.4 Para desear una pronta recuperación

- Sorry (to hear) you're ill - **get well soon!**
  = *que te mejores pronto*
- I was very sorry to learn that you were ill, and **send you my best wishes for a speedy recovery**
  = *le deseo una pronta recuperación*

50.5 Para desear buena suerte

- **Good luck in your** driving test. I hope things go well for you on Friday
  = *buena suerte en el*
- Sorry to hear you didn't get the job - **better luck next time!**
  = *¡que haya más suerte la próxima vez!*
- **We all wish you the best of luck in** your new job
  = *te deseamos mucha suerte con*

50.6 Para felicitar a alguien

- You're expecting a baby? **Congratulations!** When is the baby due? (*hablado*)
  = *¡enhorabuena! (esp Sp), ¡felicitaciones! (esp LAm)*
- You've finished the job already? **Well done!** (*hablado*)
  = *¡muy bien!*
- **We all send you our love and congratulations on** such an excellent result (*escrito*)
  = *enhorabuena de parte de todos por*
- **This is to send you our warmest congratulations and best wishes on** your engagement (*escrito*)
  = *recibe nuestra más cordial enhorabuena por*

51 NOTAS Y AVISOS DE SOCIEDAD

51.1 Para anunciar un nacimiento

- Julia Archer **gave birth to** a 6lb 5oz **baby son**, Andrew, last Monday. **Mother and baby are doing well**
  = *... dio a luz un niño. Tanto la madre como el niño se encuentran en perfecto estado*
- Ian and Zoë Pitt **are delighted to announce the birth of a daughter**, Laura, on 1st May, 2016, at Minehead Hospital (*en una carta o periódico*)
  = *se complacen en anunciar el nacimiento de su hija*
- At the Southern General Hospital, on 1st December, 2015, **to Paul and Diane Kelly (née Smith) a son, John Alexander,** a brother for Helen (*en un periódico*)
  = *Paul y Diane Kelly tienen el placer de anunciar el nacimiento de su hijo, John Alexander*

... y para responder

- **Congratulations on the birth of** your son
  = *enhorabuena por el nacimiento de*
- **We were delighted to hear about the birth of** Stephanie, and send our very best wishes to all of you
  = *nos alegró mucho saber del nacimiento de*

51.2 Para anunciar un compromiso matrimonial

- I'm sure you'll be pleased to hear that Jim and I **got engaged** yesterday
  = *estamos prometidos desde*
- **It is with much pleasure that the engagement is announced between** Michael, younger son of Professor and Mrs Perkins, York, **and** Jennifer, only daughter of Dr and Mrs Campbell, Hucknall (*en un periódico*)
  = *nos complace anunciar el compromiso matrimonial entre ... y*

... y para responder

- **Congratulations to you both on your engagement**, and very best wishes for a long and happy life together
  = *enhorabuena a los dos por vuestro compromiso*
- **I was delighted to hear of your engagement**, and wish you both all the best for your future together
  = *me ha alegrado mucho saber de su compromiso*

51.3 Para anunciar una boda

- **I'm getting married** in June, to a wonderful man named Lester Thompson
  = *me caso*
- **At Jurby Church, on 1st June, 2016, Eve, daughter of Ian and Mary Jones, Jurby, to John, son of Ray and Myra Watt, Ayr** *(en un periódico)*
  = *El 1 de junio de 2016 tuvo lugar el enlace matrimonial de Eve Jones, hija de Ian y Mary Jones, vecinos de Jurby, con John Watt, hijo de Ray y Myra Watt de Ayr. La ceremonia fue celebrada en la Iglesia de Jurby*

... y para responder

- **Congratulations on your marriage, and best wishes to you both for your future happiness**
  = *enhorabuena por vuestra boda. Os deseamos lo mejor para el futuro*
- **We were delighted to hear about your daughter's marriage to** Iain, and wish them both all the best for their future life together
  = *nos hemos alegrado mucho de saber de la boda de su hija con*

51.4 Para anunciar un fallecimiento

- My husband **died suddenly** in March
  = *murió de repente*
- **It is with great sadness that I have to tell you that** Joe's father **passed away** three weeks ago
  = *con gran dolor tengo que comunicarte el fallecimiento*
- **Suddenly**, at home, in Newcastle-upon-Tyne, on Saturday 2nd July, 2016, Alan, aged 77 years, **the beloved husband of** Helen and **loving father of** Matthew *(en un periódico)*
  = *... falleció repentinamente ... dejando a su desconsolada esposa ... e hijo*

... y para responder

- My husband and I **were greatly saddened to learn of the passing of** Dr Smith, and send (*o* offer) you and your family our most sincere condolences
  = *nos entristeció enormemente enterarnos del fallecimiento de*
- **We wish to extend our deepest sympathy for your sad loss to you and your wife**
  = *queremos expresarle nuestro más sentido pésame a su mujer y a usted por su dolorosa pérdida*

51.5 Para anunciar el cambio de dirección

- We are moving house next week. **Our new address** as of 4 May 2016 **will be ...**
  = *las nuevas señas ... son*

52 INVITACIONES

52.1 Invitaciones oficiales

- Mr and Mrs James Waller **request the pleasure of your company at the marriage of** their daughter Mary Elizabeth to Mr Richard Hanbury at St Mary's Church, Frampton on Saturday, 20th August, 2016 at 2 o'clock and afterwards at Moor House, Frampton
  = *tienen el placer de invitarles al enlace de*
- The Chairman and Governors of Hertford College, Oxford **request the pleasure of the company of** Miss Charlotte Young and partner **at a dinner** to mark the anniversary of the founding of the College
  = *tienen el placer de invitar a ... a la cena*

... y para responder

- **We thank you for your kind invitation to** the marriage of your daughter Annabel on 20th November, **and have much pleasure in accepting**
  = *gracias por su amable invitación a ..., que aceptamos con mucho gusto*
- Mr and Mrs Ian Low **thank** Dr and Mrs Green for **their kind invitation to** the marriage of their daughter Ann on 21st July **and are delighted to accept**
  = *agradecen su amable invitación a ... y aceptan encantados*
- **We regret that we are unable to accept your invitation to** the marriage of your daughter on 6th May
  = *sentimos no poder aceptar su invitación a*

52.2 Invitaciones a fiestas

- **We are celebrating Rosemary's engagement to David** by holding a dinner dance at the Central Hotel on Friday 12th February, 2016, **and very much hope that you will be able to join us**
  = *celebramos el compromiso matrimonial de Rosemary y David ... y esperamos que podáis acompañarnos*
- **We are giving a dinner party** next Saturday, **and would be delighted if you and your wife could come**
  = *damos una cena ... y nos encantaría que vinierais tu mujer y tú*
- **I'm having a party** next week for my 18th - **come along, and bring a friend**
  = *voy a hacer una fiesta ... te espero. Y puedes traer a un amigo*

52.3 Para quedar con alguien

- **Would you and Gordon like to come** to dinner next Saturday?
  = *¿os gustaría venir a ti y a Gordon ...?*
- **Would you be free for** lunch next Tuesday?
  = *¿tienes tiempo para ...?*
- **Perhaps we could** meet for coffee some time next week?
  = *podíamos*

52.4 Para aceptar una invitación

- **Yes, I'd love to meet up with you** tomorrow
  = *sí, me encantaría verte*
- **It was good of you to invite me,** I've been longing to do something like this for ages
  = *me alegro de que me hayas invitado*
- **Thank you for your invitation to** dinner - **I look forward to it very much**
  = *gracias por su invitación a ... iré con mucho gusto*

52.5 Para declinar una invitación

- **I'd love to come, but I'm afraid** I'm already going out that night
  = *me encantaría ir, pero*
- **I wish I could come, but unfortunately** I have something else on
  = *ojalá pudiera ir, pero por desgracia*
- It was very kind of you to invite me to your dinner party next Saturday. **Unfortunately I will not be able to accept**
  = *desgraciadamente no voy a poder aceptar*
- **Much to our regret, we are unable to accept**
  = *sentimos tener que decirle que nos es imposible aceptar*

52.6 Sin dar una respuesta concreta

- **I'm not sure** what I'm doing that night, but I'll let you know later
  = *no estoy seguro de*
- **It all depends on whether** I can get a sitter for Rosie at short notice
  = *depende de si*
- **I'm afraid I can't really make any definite plans** until I know when Alex will be able to take her holidays
  = *el problema es que no puedo planear nada definitivamente*

53 REDACCIÓN

53.1 El argumento en líneas generales

Para introducir un tema

De manera impersonal

- **It is often said** *o* **claimed that** teenagers get pregnant in order to get council accommodation
  = *se suele afirmar que*
- **It is a cliché** *o* **a commonplace (to say) that** American accents are infinitely more glamorous than their British counterparts
  = *es un tópico (decir) que*
- **It is undeniably true that** Gormley helped to turn his union members into far more sophisticated workers
  = *es innegable que*
- **It is a well-known fact that** in this age of technology, it is computer screens which are responsible for many illnesses
  = *es un hecho de sobra conocido que*
- **It is sometimes forgotten that** much Christian doctrine comes from Judaism
  = *a veces se olvida que*
- **It would be naïve to suppose that** in a radically changing world these 50-year-old arrangements can survive
  = *sería ingenuo suponer que*
- **It would hardly be an exaggeration to say that** the friendship of both of them with Britten was among the most creative in the composer's life
  = *se puede decir sin temor a exagerar que*
- **It is hard to open a newspaper nowadays without reading that** TV is going to destroy reading and that electronic technology has made the written word obsolete
  = *hoy en día resulta difícil abrir un periódico en el que no leamos que*
- **First of all, it is important to try to understand** some of the systems and processes involved in order to create a healthier body
  = *en primer lugar, es importante intentar comprender*
- **It is in the nature of** sociological theory **to** make broad generalizations about such things as the evolution of society
  = *es un rasgo característico de*
- **It is often the case that** early interests lead on to a career
  = *suele suceder que*

De manera personal

- **By way of introduction, let me** summarize the background to this question
  = *a modo de introducción, voy a*
- **I would like to start with** a very sweeping statement which can be easily challenged
  = *comenzaré con*
- **Before going specifically into the issue of** criminal law, **I wish first to summarize** how Gewirth derives his principles of morality and justice
  = *antes de entrar en el tema concreto de ... quisiera resumir*
- **Let us look at** what self-respect in your job actually means
  = *examinemos*
- **We commonly think of** people **as** isolated individuals but, in fact, few of us ever spend more than an hour or two of our waking hours alone
  = *normalmente consideramos a ... como*
- **What we are mainly concerned with here is** the conflict between what the hero says and what he actually does
  = *nuestra principal preocupación aquí es*
- **We live in a world in which** the word "equality" is liberally bandied about
  = *en el mundo en que vivimos*

Para incluir conceptos y problemas

- **The concept of** controlling harmful insects by genetic means isn't new
  = *el concepto de*
- **The idea of** getting rich without too much effort has universal appeal
  = *la idea de*
- **The question of whether** Hamlet was really insane has long occupied critics
  = *que ... es una cuestión que*
- Why they were successful where their predecessors had failed **is a question that has been much debated**
  = *es una cuestión muy debatida*
- **One of the most striking aspects of this issue is** the way (in which) it arouses strong emotions
  = *uno de los aspectos más notables de este tema*
- **There are a number of issues** on which China and Britain openly disagree
  = *hay una serie de puntos*

Para hacer generalizaciones

- **People who** work outside the home **tend to believe that** parenting is an easy option
  = *la gente que ... tiende a creer que*
- **There's** always **a tendency for people to** exaggerate their place in the world
  = *hay una tendencia entre la gente a*
- Many gardeners **have a tendency to** treat plants like humans
  = *tienen tendencia a*
- Viewed psychologically, it would seem that **we all have the propensity for** such traits
  = *todos somos propensos a*
- **For the (vast) majority of people**, literature is a subject which is studied at school but which has no relevance to life as they know it
  = *para la (inmensa) mayoría de la gente*
- **For most of us**, housework is a necessary but boring task
  = *para la mayoría de nosotros*
- History **provides numerous examples** *o* **instances of** misguided national heroes who did more harm than good in the long run
  = *aporta numerosos ejemplos*

Para ser más preciso

- The impact of these theories on the social sciences, and economics **in particular**, was extremely significant
  = *en concreto*
- **One particular issue** raised by Butt was, suppose Hughes at the time of his conviction had been old enough to be hanged, what would have happened?
  = *un punto en concreto*
- **A more specific point** relates to using this insight as a way of challenging our hidden assumptions about reality
  = *un aspecto más concreto*
- **More specifically**, he accuses Western governments of continuing to supply weapons and training to the rebels
  = *más en concreto*

53.2 Para presentar una tesis

Para introducirla

- **First of all, let us consider** the advantages of urban life
  = *en primer lugar, consideremos*
- **Let us begin with an examination of** the social aspects of this question
  = *comencemos con un examen de*
- **The first thing that needs to be said is that** the author is presenting a one-sided view
  = *lo primero que hay que decir es que*

- **What should be established at the very outset is that** we are dealing here with a practical issue rather than a philosophical one
  = *antes de nada debemos dejar claro que*

Para delimitar el debate

- **In the next section, I will pursue the question of** whether the expansion of the Dutch prison system can be explained by Box's theory
  = *en la próxima sección me centraré en la cuestión de*
- **I will then deal with the question of** whether or not the requirements for practical discourse are compatible with criminal procedure
  = *a continuación me ocuparé de la cuestión de*
- We must distinguish between the psychic and the spiritual, and **we shall see how** the subtle level of consciousness is the basis for the spiritual level
  = *veremos cómo*
- **I will confine myself to** giving an account of certain decisive facts in my militant career with Sartre
  = *me limitaré a*
- In this chapter, **I shall largely confine myself to** a consideration of those therapeutic methods that use visualization as a part of their procedures
  = *me limitaré en gran medida a*
- **We will not concern ourselves here with** the Christian legend of St James
  = *no nos vamos a ocupar aquí de*
- **Let us now consider** to what extent the present municipal tribunals differ from the former popular tribunals in the above-mentioned points
  = *pasemos a considerar ahora*
- **Let us now look at** the ideal types of corporatism that neo-corporatist theorists developed to clarify the concept
  = *pasemos a examinar*

Para exponer los puntos

- **The main issue under discussion is** how the party should re-define itself if it is to play any future role in Hungarian politics
  = *el principal punto de debate es*
- **A second, related problem is** that business ethics has mostly concerned itself with grand theorizing
  = *otro problema relacionado con esto es*
- **The basic issue at stake is this**: is research to be judged by its value in generating new ideas?
  = *el punto básico en cuestión es éste:*
- **An important aspect of** Milton's imagery **is** the play of light and shade
  = *un aspecto importante de ... es*
- **It is worth mentioning here that** when this was first translated, the opening reference to Heidegger was entirely deleted
  = *cabe mencionar aquí que*
- **Finally, there is the argument that** watching too much television may stunt a child's imagination
  = *por último, está el argumento de que*

Para poner un argumento en duda

- World leaders appear to be taking a tough stand, but **is there any real substance in what's been agreed**?
  = *¿se ha decidido algo concreto?*
- This is a question which **merits close(r) examination**
  = *merece un estudio (más) detallado*
- The unity of the two separate German states **has raised fundamental questions** for Germany's neighbours
  = *ha planteado interrogantes fundamentales para*
- The failure to protect our fellow Europeans in Bosnia **raises fundamental questions on** the role of the armed forces
  = *plantea problemas fundamentales sobre*

- **This raises once again the question of** whether a government's right to secrecy should override the public's right to know
  = *... lo que plantea, una vez más, la cuestión de*
- **This poses the question of** whether these measures are really helping the people they were intended to help
  = *la cuestión que esto plantea es*

Para ofrecer un análisis de la cuestión

- **It is interesting to consider why** this scheme has been so successful
  = *es interesante examinar porqué*
- **On the question of** whether civil disobedience is likely to help end the war, Chomsky is deliberately diffident
  = *en lo que concierne a*
- **We are often faced with the choice between** our sense of duty **and** our own personal inclinations
  = *solemos vernos ante la necesidad de escoger entre ... y*
- **When we speak of** realism in music, **we do not at all have in mind** the illustrative bases of music
  = *al hablar de ..., no tenemos presente en absoluto*
- **It is reasonable to assume that** most people living in industrialized societies are to some extent contaminated by environmental poisons
  = *está dentro de lo razonable suponer que*

Para aportar un argumento

- **An argument in support of** this approach **is that** it produces ...
  = *un argumento a favor de ... es que*
- **In support of his theory**, Dr Gold notes that most oil contains higher-than-atmospheric concentrations of helium-3
  = *para apoyar su teoría*
- **This is the most telling argument in favour of** an extension of the right to vote
  = *éste es el argumento más convincente a favor de*
- **The second reason for advocating** this course of action **is that** it benefits the community at large
  = *la segunda razón para mostrarse partidario de ... es que*
- **The third, more fundamental, reason for** looking to the future **is that** even the angriest investors realize they need a successful market
  = *la tercera razón, más fundamental, para ... es que*
- Despite communism's demise, confidence in capitalism seems to be at an all-time low. **The fundamental reason for** this contradiction seems to me quite simple
  = *la razón fundamental de*

53.3 Para presentar una antítesis

Para criticar u oponerse a algo

- **In actual fact, the idea of** there being a rupture between a so-called old criminology and an emergent new criminology **is somewhat misleading**
  = *de hecho, la idea de ... es en cierto modo engañoso*
- In order to argue this, **I will show that** Wyeth**'s position is**, in actual fact, **untenable**
  = *voy a demostrar que la postura de ... es ... insostenible*
- **It is claimed, however,** that the strict Leboyer method is not essential for a less traumatic birth experience
  = *se afirma, sin embargo,*
- **This need not mean that** we are destined to suffer for ever. **Indeed, the opposite may be true**
  = *esto no significa que .... De hecho quizá sea lo contrario*
- Many observers, though, **find it difficult to share his opinion that** it could mean the end of the Tamil Tigers
  = *les resulta difícil compartir su opinión de que*
- **On the other hand**, there are more important factors that should be taken into consideration
  = *por otra parte*

- The judgement made **may well be true but** the evidence given to sustain it is unlikely to convince the sceptical
  = *bien puede ser* *cierto* *pero*
- Reform **is all very well, but** it is pointless if the rules are not enforced
  = *está muy bien, pero*
- The case against the use of drugs in sport rests primarily on the argument that .... **This argument is weak,** for two reasons
  = *este argumento carece de solidez*
- According to one theory, the ancestors of vampire bats were fruit-eating bats. But **this idea does not hold water**
  = *esta idea no se sostiene*
- Their claim to be a separate race **does not stand up to** historical scrutiny
  = *no resiste*
- **This view does not stand up** if we examine the known facts about John
  = *esta opinión no se sostiene*
- **The trouble with this idea is not that** it is wrong, **but rather that** it is uninformative
  = *el problema no es que esta idea ... sino que*
- **The difficulty with this view is that** he bases the principle on a false premise
  = *el problema que plantea esta opinión radica en que*
- **The snag with** such speculations **is that** too much turns on one man or event
  = *la pega de ... es que*
- But removing healthy ovaries **is entirely unjustified in my opinion**
  no tiene, en mi opinión, justificación alguna

Para proponer una alternativa

- **Another approach may be to** develop substances capable of blocking the effects of the insect's immune system
  = *otro planteamiento posible es*
- **Another way** to reduce failure is to improve vocational education
  = *otra forma de*
- **However, the other side of the coin is** the fact that an improved self-image really can lead to prosperity
  = *sin embargo, la otra cara de la moneda es*
- **It is more accurate to speak of** a plurality of new criminologies rather than of a single new criminology
  = *es más preciso hablar de*
- **Paradoxical as it may seem**, computer models of mind can be positively humanizing
  = *aunque parezca paradójico*

53.4 Para presentar la síntesis argumental

Para evaluar los argumentos expuestos

- **How can we reconcile** these two apparently contradictory viewpoints?
  = *¿cómo reconciliar ...?*
- **On balance**, making money honestly is more profitable than making it dishonestly
  = *al fin y al cabo*
- Since such vitamins are more expensive, **one has to weigh up the pros and cons**
  = *hay que sopesar los pros y los contras*
- **We need to look at the pros and cons of** normative theory as employed by Gewirth and Phillips
  = *es necesario examinar los pros y contras de*
- **The benefits of** partnership in a giant trading market **will** almost certainly **outweigh the disadvantages**
  = *los beneficios de ... pesarán más que los inconvenientes*
- **The two perspectives are not mutually exclusive**
  = *las dos perspectivas no se excluyen mutuamente*

Para decantarse por uno de los argumentos

- Dr Meaden's theory **is the most convincing explanation**
  = *es la explicación más convincente*
- **The truth** *o* **fact of the matter is that** in a free society you can't turn every home into a fortress
  = *lo cierto es que*
- But **the truth is that** Father Christmas has a rather mixed origin
  = *lo cierto es que*
- Although this operation sounds extremely dangerous, **in actual fact** it is extremely safe
  = *en realidad*
- **When all is said and done, it must be acknowledged that** a purely theoretical approach to social issues is sterile
  = *a fin de cuentas, se debe reconocer que*

Para resumir los argumentos

- In this chapter, **I have demonstrated** *o* **shown that** the Cuban alternative has been undergoing considerable transformations
  = *he demostrado que*
- **This shows how**, in the final analysis, adhering to a particular theory on crime is at best a matter of reasoned choice
  = *esto demuestra cómo*
- **The overall picture shows that** prison sentences were relatively frequent, but not particularly severe
  = *la visión de conjunto demuestra que*
- **To recap** *o* **To sum up, then, (we may conclude that)** there are in effect two possible solutions to this problem
  = *en resumen, (se puede concluir que)*
- **To sum up this chapter** I will offer two examples ...
  = *para resumir este capítulo*
- **To summarize**, we have seen that the old staple industries in Britain had been hit after the First World War by a deteriorating international competitive position
  = *en resumen*
- Habermas's argument, **in a nutshell**, is as follows
  = *en suma*
- But **the key to the whole argument is** a single extraordinary paragraph
  = *la clave del problema ... se encuentra en*
- **To round off this section on** slugs, gardeners may be interested to hear that there are three species of predatory slugs in the British Isles
  = *para terminar esta sección sobre*

Para extraer conclusiones

- **From all this, it follows that** it is impossible to extend those kinds of security measures to all potential targets of terrorism
  = *de todo esto se deduce que*
- This, of course, **leads to the logical conclusion that** those who actually produce do have a claim to the results of their efforts
  = *nos lleva a la conclusión lógica de que*
- **There is only one logical conclusion we can reach**, which is that we ask our customers what is the Strategic Reality that they perceive in our marketing programme
  = *sólo podemos llegar a una conclusión lógica*
- **The inescapable conclusion is that** the criminal justice system does not simply reflect the reality of crime; it helps create it
  = *la conclusión ineludible es que*
- **We must conclude that** there is no solution to the problem of defining crime
  = *debemos decir, a modo de conclusión, que*
- **In conclusion**, because interpersonal relationships are so complex, there can be no easy way of preventing conflict
  = *en conclusión*
- **The upshot of all this is that** treatment is unlikely to be available
  la consecuencia de todo esto es que

- **So it would appear that** butter is not significantly associated with heart disease after all
  = *parece, pues, que*
- **This only goes to show that** a good man is hard to find
  = *esto demuestra*
- **The lesson to be learned** from this **is that** you cannot hope to please everyone all of the time
  = *la lección que se puede aprender es*
- **At the end of the day**, the only way the drug problem will be beaten is when people are encouraged not to take them
  = *al fin y al cabo*
- **Ultimately, then**, while we may have some sympathy for these young criminals, we must do our utmost to protect society from them
  = *en definitiva*

53.5 La estructura del párrafo

Para añadir información

- **In addition**, the author does not really empathize with his hero
  = *además*
- This award-winning writer, **in addition to** being a critic, biographer and poet, has written 26 crime novels
  = *además de ser*
- But this is only part of the picture. **Added to this are** fears that a major price increase would cause riots
  = *hay que añadir*
- **An added** complication **is** that the characters are not aware of their relationship to one another
  = *una ... más es*
- **Also**, there is the question of language
  = *además*
- **The question also arises as to** how this idea can be put into practice
  = *también se plantea la cuestión de*
- Politicians, **as well as** academics and educationalists, tend to feel strongly about the way history is taught
  = *al igual que*
- But, **over and above that**, each list contains fictitious names and addresses
  = *además de eso*
- **Furthermore**, ozone is, like carbon dioxide, a greenhouse gas
  = *además*

Para comparar

- **Compared with** the heroine, Alison is an insipid character
  = *comparada con*
- **In comparison with** the Czech Republic, the culture of Bulgaria is less westernized
  = *en comparación con*
- This is a high percentage for the English Midlands but low **by comparison with** some other parts of Britain
  = *si se compara con*
- **On the one hand**, there is no longer a Warsaw Pact threat. **On the other (hand)**, the positive changes could have negative side-effects
  = *por una parte ... por otra*
- **Similarly**, a good historian is not obsessed by dates
  = *del mismo modo*
- There can only be one total at the bottom of a column of figures and **likewise** only one solution to any problem
  = *del mismo modo*
- What others say of us will translate into reality. **Equally**, what we affirm as true of ourselves will likewise come true
  = *de igual manera*
- There will now be a change in the way we are regarded by our partners, and, **by the same token**, the way we regard them
  = *del mismo modo*
- **There is a fundamental difference between** adequate nutrient intake **and** optimum nutrient intake
  = *hay una diferencia fundamental entre ... y*

Para unir dos elementos

- **First of all** *o* **Firstly**, I would like to outline the benefits of the system
  = *en primer lugar*
- In music we are concerned **first and foremost** with the practical application of controlled sounds relating to the human psyche
  = *ante todo*
- **In order to understand** the conflict between the two nations, **it is first of all necessary to** know something of the history of the area
  = *para comprender ... es necesario ante todo*
- **Secondly**, it might be simpler to develop chemical or even nuclear warheads for a large shell than for a missile
  = *en segundo lugar*
- **In the first/second/third place**, the objectives of privatization were contradictory
  = *en primer/segundo/tercer lugar*
- **Finally,** there is the argument that watching too much television may stunt a child's imagination
  = *por último*

Para expresar una opinión personal

- **In my opinion**, the government is underestimating the scale of the epidemic
  = *en mi opinión*
- **My personal opinion is that** the argument lacks depth
  = *mi opinión personal es que*
- This is a popular viewpoint, but **speaking personally**, I cannot understand it
  = *yo personalmente*
- **Personally**, I think that no one can appreciate ethnicity more than black or African people themselves
  = *yo personalmente*
- **For my part**, I cannot agree with the leadership on this question
  = *por mi parte*
- **My own view is that** what largely determines the use of non-national workers are economic factors rather than political ones
  = *mi opinión personal es que*
- **In my view**, it only perpetuates the very problem that it sets out to address
  = *a mi parecer*
- Although the author argues the case for patriotism, **I feel that** he does not do it with any great personal conviction
  = *creo que*
- **I believe that** people do understand that there can be no quick fix for Britain's economic problems
  = *yo creo que*
- **It seems to me that** what we have is a political problem that needs to be solved at a political level
  = *a mi parecer*
- **I would maintain that** we have made a significant effort to ensure that the results are made public
  = *yo afirmaría que*

Para expresar la opinión de otra persona

- **He claims** *o* **maintains that** intelligence is conditioned by upbringing
  = *mantiene que*
- Bukharin **asserts that** all great revolutions are accompanied by destructive internal conflict
  = *afirma que*
- The communiqué **states that** some form of nuclear deterrent will continue to be needed for the foreseeable future
  = *manifiesta que*

- **What he is saying is that** the time of the old, highly structured political party is over
  = *lo que dice es que*
- His admirers **would have us believe that** watching this film is more like attending a church service than having a night at the pictures
  = *quieren hacernos creer*
- **According to** the report, poverty creates a climate favourable to violence
  = *según*

Para dar un ejemplo

- **To take another example**: many thousands of people have been condemned to a life of sickness and pain because ...
  = *para poner otro ejemplo*
- Let us consider, **for example** *o* **for instance**, the problems faced by immigrants arriving in a strange country
  = *por ejemplo*
- His meteoric rise **is the most striking example yet of** voters' disillusionment with the record of the previous government
  = *es el ejemplo más claro de ... hasta ahora*
- The case of Henry Howey Robson **serves to illustrate** the courage exhibited by young men in the face of battle
  = *sirve para ilustrar*
- Just consider, **by way of illustration**, the difference in amounts accumulated if interest is paid gross, rather than having tax deducted
  = *a modo de ejemplo*
- **A case in point is** the decision to lift the ban on contacts with the republic
  = *un ejemplo que viene al caso es*
- **Take the case of** the soldier returning from war
  = *tomemos el caso de*
- **As** the Prime Minister **remarked** recently, the Channel Tunnel will greatly benefit the whole of the European Community
  = *tal y como ha señalado ...*

53.6 Los mecanismos del debate

Para presentar una suposición

- They have telephoned the president to put pressure on him. **And that could be interpreted as** trying to gain an unconstitutional political advantage
  = *y eso se podría interpretar como*
- Retail sales rose sharply last month. This was higher than expected and **could be taken to mean that** inflationary pressures remain strong
  = *podría hacernos suponer*
- In such circumstances, **it might well be prudent** to diversify your investments
  = *quizá sería prudente*
- These substances do not remain effective for very long. **This is possibly because** they work against the insects' natural instinct to feed
  = *posiblemente se deba a que*
- His wife had become an embarrassment to him and therefore **it is not beyond the bounds of possibility that** he may have contemplated murdering her
  = *no está fuera de lo posible que*
- Mr Fraser's assertion **leads one to suppose that** he is in full agreement with Catholic teaching as regards marriage
  = *nos lleva a suponer*
- **It is probably the case that** all long heavy ships are vulnerable
  = *probablemente*
- After hearing nothing from the taxman for so long, most people **might reasonably assume that** their tax affairs were in order
  = *podría suponerse lógicamente que*
- **One could be forgiven for thinking that** because the substances are chemicals they'd be easy to study
  = *es comprensible que se piense que*
- **I venture to suggest that** very often when people like him talk about love, they actually mean lust
  = *me atrevo a sugerir que*

Para expresar certeza

Véase también la sección 42 CERTEZA

- **It is clear that** any risk to the human foetus is very low
  = *está claro que*
- Benn is **indisputably** a fine orator, one of the most compelling speakers in politics today
  = *indiscutiblemente*
- British universities are **undeniably** good, but they are not turning out enough top scientists
  = *no se puede negar que*
- **There can be no doubt that** the Earth underwent a dramatic cooling which destroyed the environment and life style of these creatures
  = *no cabe duda alguna de que*
- **It is undoubtedly true that** over the years there has been a much greater emphasis on safer sex
  = *es indudable que*
- **As we all know**, adultery is far from uncommon, particularly in springtime
  = *como todos sabemos*
- **One thing is certain**: the party is far from united
  = *lo que es cierto es que*
- **It is (quite) certain that** unless peace can be brought to this troubled land no amount of aid will solve the long-term problems of the people
  = *está (muy) claro que*

Para expresar dudas

Véase también la sección 43 DUDAS

- **It is doubtful whether**, in the present repressive climate, anyone would be brave or foolish enough to demonstrate publicly
  = *es dudoso que*
- **It remains to be seen whether** the security forces will try to intervene
  = *queda por ver si*
- **I have a few reservations about** the book
  = *tengo ciertas reservas acerca de*
- The judges are expected to endorse the recommendation, but **it is by no means certain that** they will make up their minds today
  = *no hay ninguna seguridad de que*
- **It is questionable whether** media coverage of terrorist organizations actually affects terrorism
  = *es discutible que*
- **This raises the whole question of** exactly when men and women should retire
  = *esto plantea la cuestión de*
- The crisis **puts a question mark against** the Prime Minister's stated commitment to intervention
  = *abre un interrogante acerca de*
- **Both these claims are true up to a point** and they need to be made. But they are limited in their significance
  = *ambas afirmaciones son ciertas hasta cierto punto*

Para mostrarse de acuerdo

Véase también la sección 38 ACUERDO

- **I agree wholeheartedly with** the opinion that smacking should be outlawed
  = *coincido totalmente con*
- **One must acknowledge that** their history will make change more painful
  = *hay que reconocer que*

- **It cannot be denied that** there are similarities between the two approaches
  = *no se puede negar que*
- Courtney - **rightly in my view** - is strongly critical of the snobbery and élitism that is all too evident in these circles
  = *pienso que con toda la razón*
- Preaching was considered an important activity, **and rightly so** in a country with a high illiteracy rate
  = *y con mayor razón*
- You may dispute the Pope's right to tell people how to live their lives, **but it is hard to disagree with** his picture of modern society
  = *pero es difícil no coincidir con*

Para mostrarse en desacuerdo

Véase también la sección 39 DESACUERDO

- **I must disagree with** Gordon's article on criminality: it is dangerous to suggest that to be a criminal one must look like a criminal
  = *debo mostrar mi desacuerdo con*
- As a former teacher **I find it hard to believe that** there is no link at all between screen violence and violence on the streets
  = *me cuesta creer que*
- The strength of their feelings **is scarcely credible**
  = *es poco verosímil*
- Her claim to have been the first to discover the phenomenon **lacks credibility**
  = *carece de toda credibilidad*
- Nevertheless, **I remain unconvinced by** Milton
  = *... sigue sin convencerme*
- Many do not believe that water contains anything remotely dangerous. Sadly, **this is far from the truth**
  = *dista mucho de ser cierto*
- To say that everyone requires the same amount of a vitamin is as stupid as saying we all have blonde hair and blue eyes. **It simply isn't true**
  = *sencillamente no es cierto*
- His remarks **were** not only highly offensive to black and other ethnic minorities but **totally inaccurate**
  = *totalmente erróneos*
- Stomach ulcers are often associated with good living and a fast-moving lifestyle. **(But) in reality** there is no evidence to support this theory
  = *pero en realidad*
- This version of a political economy **does not stand up to close scrutiny**
  = *no resiste un análisis pormenorizado*

Para resaltar uno de los argumentos

- Nowadays, **there is clearly** less stigma attached to unmarried mothers
  = *está claro que hay*
- Evidence shows that ..., so once again **the facts speak for themselves**
  = *los hechos hablan por sí solos*
- **Few will argue with the principle that** such a fund should be set up
  = *apenas hay quien discuta el principio*
- Hyams **supports this claim** by looking at sentences produced by young children learning German
  = *apoya esta afirmación*
- **The most important thing is to** reach agreement from all sides
  = *lo más importante es*
- Perhaps **the most important aspect of** cognition is the ability to manipulate symbols
  = *el aspecto más importante de*

Para destacar un punto en concreto

- **It would be impossible to exaggerate the importance of** these two volumes for anyone with a serious interest in the development of black gospel music
  = *no se puede exagerar la importancia de*
- The symbolic importance of Jerusalem for both Palestinians and Jews **is almost impossible to overemphasize**
  = *nunca se insistirá demasiado en*
- **It is important to be clear that** Jesus does not identify himself with Yahweh
  = *es importante dejar claro que*
- **It is significant that** Mandalay seems to have become the central focus in this debate
  = *resulta revelador que*
- **It should not be forgotten that** many of those now in exile were close to the centre of power until only one year ago
  = *no hay que olvidar que*
- **It should be stressed that** the only way pet owners could possibly contract such a condition from their pets is by eating them
  = *habría que recalcar que*
- **There is a very important point here and that is that** the accused claims that he was with Ms Martins all evening on the night of the crime
  = *lo que resulta importante aquí es que*
- At the beginning of his book Mr Stone **makes a telling point**. The Balkan peoples, he notes, are for the first time ...
  = *hace un comentario revelador*
- Suspicion is **the chief feature of** Britain's attitude to European theatre
  = *el rasgo primordial de*
- **In order to focus attention on** Hobson's distinctive contributions to macroeconomics, these wider issues are neglected here
  = *con objeto de centrarnos en*
- **These statements are interesting in that** they illustrate different views
  = *estas afirmaciones son interesantes porque*

DICCIONARIO
INGLÉS-ESPAÑOL

ENGLISH-SPANISH
DICTIONARY

Aa

A, a[1] [eɪ] (N) **1** (= *letter*) A, a *f* • **A for Andrew** A de Antonio • **to get from A to B** ir de A a B • **No. 32A** (= *house*) núm. 32 bis, núm. 32 duplicado • **the A-Z of Management Techniques** el manual básico de Técnicas de Gestión, Técnicas de Gestión de la A a la Z • IDIOM: • **to know sth from A to Z** conocer algo de pe a pa *or* de cabo a rabo
2 (*Mus*) • A la *m* • **A major/minor** la mayor/menor • **A sharp/flat** la sostenido/bemol
3 (*Scol*) sobresaliente *m*
(CPD) ▸ **A level** (*Brit*) (*Scol*) (= **Advanced level**) ≈ bachillerato *m* • **to take three A levels** presentarse como candidato en tres asignaturas de *A level* • **she has an A level in chemistry** tiene un título de *A level* en química ▸ **A road** (*Brit*) ≈ carretera *f* nacional ▸ **"A" shares** acciones *fpl* de clase A ▸ **A side** [*of record*] cara *f* A ▸ **A to Z**® (= *map book*) callejero *m*

A LEVELS
Al terminar la educación secundaria obligatoria, los estudiantes de Inglaterra, Gales e Irlanda del Norte pueden estudiar otros dos años en el centro escolar, normalmente para preparar **AS (Advanced Subsidiary) levels** en tres o cinco asignaturas el primer año y completar los **A (Advanced) levels** el segundo año. Cada universidad determina el número de **A levels** y la calificación necesaria para acceder a ella.
En Escocia los exámenes equivalentes son los **Highers** y luego los **Advanced Highers**. A diferencia de Inglaterra, Gales e Irlanda del Norte, los estudiantes pueden ir a la universidad tras hacer los **Highers** el primer año, sin necesidad de obtener los **Advanced Highers**, siempre y cuando consigan la calificación que requiera la universidad.
▷ GCSE

a[2] [eɪ] [ə] (INDEF ART) (BEFORE VOWEL OR SILENT H: **an** [æn] [ən] [n]) **1** un(a) *m/f*; (+ *fem noun starting with stressed a or ha*) un • **a book** un libro • **an apple** una manzana • **a soul** un alma • **an eagle** un águila • **an axe** un hacha
2 (*article often omitted in translation*) **a** (*with professions*) • **he is an engineer** es ingeniero • **I am not a doctor** yo no soy médico • **he's a brilliant scientist** es un excelente científico • **that child's a thief!** ¡ese niño es un ladrón!
b (*after tener/buscar if singular object the norm*) • **I have a wife and six children** tengo mujer y seis hijos • **have you got a passport?** ¿tiene usted pasaporte? • **I haven't got a car** no tengo coche • **she's looking for a secretary** busca secretaria • **she has a daughter** tiene una hija • **they have a lovely house** tienen una casa preciosa; ▷ LOOK FOR
c (*after negatives*) • **you don't stand a chance** no tienes posibilidad alguna • **without a doubt** sin duda • **without saying a word** sin decir palabra
d (*in expressions*) • **half an hour** media hora • **a fine excuse!** ¡bonita disculpa! • **what an idiot!** ¡qué idiota! • **a hundred pounds** cien libras • **a drink would be nice** me gustaría algo de beber
e (*apposition*) • **Patrick, a lecturer at Glasgow University, says that ...** Patrick, profesor de la Universidad de Glasgow, dice que ... • **the Duero, a Spanish river** el Duero, un río español
3 (= *a certain*) un(a) tal • **a Mr Smith called to see you** vino a verte un tal señor Smith
4 (= *each, per*) por • **two apples a head** dos manzanas por persona • **£80 a week** 80 libras por semana • **50 kilometres an hour** 50 kilómetros por hora • **30 pence a kilo** 30 peniques el kilo • **once a week/three times a month** una vez a la semana/tres veces al mes

A. (ABBR) (= **answer**) R
a. (ABBR) = **acre**
a... (PREFIX) a... • **atonal** atonal • **atypical** atípico
a- (PREFIX) (*liter*) • **everyone came a-running** todos acudieron corriendo • **it was a-snowing hard** estaba nevando mucho
A1 ['eɪ'wʌn] (ADJ) de primera clase, de primera categoría • **to feel A1** estar muy bien
A2 [eɪ'tuː] (N ABBR) (*Brit*) (*Scol*) *segunda parte de los estudios de los "A levels"*
A3 ['eɪ'θriː] (ADJ) • **A3 paper** • **A3-size paper** papel *m* tamaño A3, doble folio *m*
A4 ['eɪ'fɔːʳ] (ADJ) • **A4 paper** • **A4-size paper** papel *m* tamaño A4, papel *m* tamaño folio, folios *mpl*
AA (N ABBR) **1** (= **Alcoholics Anonymous**) A.A.
2 (*Brit*) (= **Automobile Association**) ≈ RACE *m*
3 (*US*) (*Univ*) = **Associate in Arts**
4 (*Mil*) = **anti-aircraft**
AAA (N ABBR) **1** = **Amateur Athletics Association**
2 (*US*) (= **American Automobile Association**) ≈ RACE *m*
Aachen ['ɑːxən] (N) Aquisgrán *m*
AAF (N ABBR) = **American Air Force**
AAIB (N ABBR) (*Brit*) = **Air Accident Investigation Branch**
AAM (N ABBR) = **air-to-air missile**
A & E [ˌeɪən'diː] (N ABBR) (= **Accident and Emergency**) ≈ Urgencias *fpl*
A & R [ˌeɪən'ɑːʳ] (N ABBR) = **artists and repertoire** • **an A & R man** un descubridor de talentos
AAR (ABBR) = **against all risks**
aardvark ['ɑːdvɑːk] (N) (*Zool*) cerdo *m* hormiguero
Aaron ['ɛərən] (N) Aarón
AARP [ˌeɪeɪɑːʳ'piː] (N ABBR) (= **American Association of Retired Persons**) *asociación nacional de jubilados de los Estados Unidos*
AAU (N ABBR) (*US*) = **Amateur Athletic Union**
AAUP (N ABBR) (*US*) (*Univ*) = **American Association of University Professors**
AB (ABBR) **1** (*Naut*) = **able(-bodied) seaman**
2 (*US*) (*Univ*) (= **Bachelor of Arts**) Lic. en Fil. y Let.
3 (*Canada*) = **Alberta**
ABA (N ABBR) **1** = **Amateur Boxing Association**
2 (*US*) = **American Bankers Association**
3 (*US*) = **American Bar Association**
aback [ə'bæk] (ADV) • **to take ~** desconcertar, sorprender • **to be taken ~** quedarse desconcertado, sorprenderse • **I was quite taken ~ by the news** la noticia me causó gran sorpresa, la noticia me dejó desconcertado
abacus ['æbəkəs] (N) (PL: **abacuses, abaci** ['æbəsaɪ]) ábaco *m*
abaft [ə'bɑːft] (*Naut*) (ADV) a popa, en popa
(PREP) detrás de
abalone [ˌæbə'ləʊnɪ] (N) oreja *f* marina, oreja *f* de mar
(CPD) ▸ **abalone shell** concha *f* de oreja marina, concha *f* de mar
abandon [ə'bændən] (VT) **1** (= *desert*) [+ *car, family*] abandonar, dejar • **to ~ sb to his fate** abandonar a algn a su suerte • **~ ship!** ¡evacuar el barco!
2 (= *give up*) [+ *plan, attempt*] renunciar a; [+ *game*] anular • **the game was ~ed after 20 minutes' play** después de 20 minutos de juego se anuló el partido • **~ all hope ye who ...** abandonad toda esperanza aquellos que ... • **to ~ o.s. to sth** entregarse *or* abandonarse a algo
(N) • **to dance with wild ~** bailar desenfrenadamente; ▷ **gay**
abandoned [ə'bændənd] (ADJ) **1** (= *deserted*) [*house, building*] abandonado, desierto; [*child*] abandonado, desamparado; [*vehicle, pet*] abandonado
2 (= *unrestrained*) [*manner*] desinhibido, desenfrenado • **in an ~ fashion** con abandono, desenfrenadamente
3† (= *dissolute*) • **an ~ woman** una mujer perdida *or* de conducta dudosa
abandonment [ə'bændənmənt] (N)
1 (= *state*) abandono *m*; (= *act*) acto *m* de desamparar, el abandonar
2 (*moral*) = **abandon**
abase [ə'beɪs] (VT) [+ *person*] humillar, rebajar • **to ~ o.s. (so far as to)** (+ *infin*) rebajarse (hasta el punto de (+ *infin*))
abasement [ə'beɪsmənt] (N) (= *humiliation*) humillación *f*, degradación *f*; (= *moral decay*) depravación *f*, envilecimiento *m*
abashed [ə'bæʃt] (ADJ) (= *shy*) tímido, retraído; (= *ashamed*) avergonzado • **to be ~ at sth** avergonzarse de algo • **he carried on not a bit ~** siguió como si tal cosa
abate [ə'beɪt] (VI) [*wind, storm*] amainar; [*fever*] bajar; [*flood*] retirarse, bajar; [*noise*] disminuir; [*anger*] aplacarse; [*pain, symptoms*] remitir; [*enthusiasm*] moderarse • **inflationary pressures are abating** ceden *or* remiten las presiones inflacionistas
(VT) (*Jur*) [+ *noise, pollution*] (= *eliminate*)

eliminar; (= *reduce*) disminuir
abatement [əˈbeɪtmənt] (N) **1** (= *reduction*) [*of wind, storm*] amaine *m*; [*of fever, flood*] bajada *f*; [*of anger*] aplacamiento *m*; [*of enthusiasm*] moderación *f*; [*of pain, symptoms*] remisión *f*
2 (*Jur*) [*of noise, pollution*] (= *elimination*) eliminación *f*; (= *reduction*) disminución *f*, moderación *f*
abattoir [ˈæbətwɑːʳ] (N) matadero *m*
abbacy [ˈæbəsɪ] (N) abadía *f*
abbé [ˈæbeɪ] (N) abate *m*
abbess [ˈæbɪs] (N) abadesa *f*
abbey [ˈæbɪ] (N) abadía *f* • **Westminster Abbey** la Abadía de Westminster
(CPD) ▸ **abbey church** iglesia *f* abacial, iglesia *f* de abadía
abbot [ˈæbət] (N) abad *m*
abbr., abbrev. (ABBR) = **abbreviation, abbreviated**
abbreviate [əˈbriːvɪeɪt] (VT) abreviar
abbreviated [əˈbriːvɪeɪtɪd] (ADJ) [*word, document*] abreviado
abbreviation [əˌbriːvɪˈeɪʃən] (N) **1** (= *short form*) abreviatura *f*
2 (= *act of shortening*) abreviación *f*
ABC [ˈeɪbiːˈsiː] (N ABBR) **1** (= *alphabet*) abecé *m* • **it's as easy** *or* **simple as ABC*** es coser y cantar*, es facilísimo • **the ABC of Politics** (*as title*) el Abecé de la Política
2 (*US*) = **American Broadcasting Company**
3 (*Australia*) = **Australian Broadcasting Commission**
abdicate [ˈæbdɪkeɪt] (VT) **1** [+ *throne*] abdicar
2 [+ *responsibility, right*] renunciar a
(VI) abdicar (**in favour of** en, en favor de)
abdication [ˌæbdɪˈkeɪʃən] (N) **1** [*of monarch*] abdicación *f*
2 [*of responsibility, right*] renuncia *f* (**of** a)
abdomen [ˈæbdəmen], (*Med*) [æbˈdəʊmen] (N) (*Anat*) abdomen *m*, vientre *m*; [*of insect*] abdomen *m*
abdominal [æbˈdɒmɪnl] (ADJ) abdominal
(N) **abdominals** (= *muscles*) abdominales *mpl*
abducent [æbˈdjuːsənt] (ADJ) abductor
abduct [æbˈdʌkt] (VT) raptar, secuestrar
abduction [æbˈdʌkʃən] (N) rapto *m*, secuestro *m*
abductor [æbˈdʌktəʳ] (N) raptor(a) *m/f*, secuestrador(a) *m/f*
abeam [əˈbiːm] (ADV) (*Naut*) en ángulo recto con la quilla
abed†† [əˈbed] (ADV) en cama, acostado
Aberdonian [ˌæbəˈdəʊnɪən] (ADJ) de Aberdeen
(N) nativo/a *m/f* de Aberdeen, habitante *mf* de Aberdeen
aberrant [əˈberənt] (ADJ) (*Bio*) aberrante; [*behaviour*] anormal
aberration [ˌæbeˈreɪʃən] (N) aberración *f* • **mental ~** enajenación *f* mental
abet [əˈbet] (VT) [+ *criminal*] incitar; [+ *crime*] instigar • **to ~ sb in a crime** ser cómplice de algn en un delito; ▷ **aid**
abetment [əˈbetmənt] (N) incitación *f*, instigación *f*; (*Jur*) complicidad *f*
abetter, abettor [əˈbetəʳ] (N) instigador(a) *m/f*, fautor(a) *m/f*; (*esp Jur*) cómplice *mf*
abeyance [əˈbeɪəns] (N) • **to be in ~** estar en desuso • **to fall into ~** caer en desuso
abhor [əbˈhɔːʳ] (VT) aborrecer, abominar
abhorrence [əbˈhɒrəns] (N) **1** (= *feeling*) aborrecimiento *m*, repugnancia *f* • **violence fills me with ~** aborrezco la violencia • **to hold in ~** aborrecer, detestar
2 (= *object*) abominación *f*
abhorrent [əbˈhɒrənt] (ADJ) aborrecible, detestable • **it's totally ~ to me** lo detesto totalmente
abidance [əˈbaɪdəns] (N) (*frm*) • **~ by the rules/laws** acatamiento *m* de las normas/leyes
abide [əˈbaɪd] (PT, PP: **abode** *or* **abided**) (VT) (*neg only*) aguantar, soportar • **I can't ~ him** no lo aguanto *or* soporto, no lo puedo ver • **I can't ~ a coward** aborrezco los cobardes • **I can't ~ tea** me da asco el té
(VI) † (= *dwell*) morar; (= *stay*) permanecer, continuar
▸ **abide by** (VI + PREP) [+ *rules, law*] atenerse a, acatar; [+ *promise*] cumplir con; [+ *decision*] respetar, atenerse a
abiding [əˈbaɪdɪŋ] (ADJ) (*liter*) permanente, perdurable
ability [əˈbɪlɪtɪ] (N) **1** (= *capacity*) aptitud *f*, capacidad *f* • **~ to pay** solvencia *f*, recursos *mpl* • **his ~ in French** su aptitud para el francés • **to the best of my ~** lo mejor que pueda *or* sepa • **my ~ to do it depends on …** el que yo lo haga depende de …
2 (= *talent*) • **a boy of ~** un chico de talento • **he has great ~** tiene un gran talento; **abilities** talento *m*, dotes *fpl*
ab initio [ˌæbɪˈnɪʃɪəʊ] (ADV) ab initio, desde el principio
(ADJ) • **~ learner** principiante *mf*
abiotic [ˌeɪbaɪˈɒtɪk] (ADJ) abiótico
abject [ˈæbdʒekt] (ADJ) **1** (= *wretched*) [*condition*] deplorable; [*state*] lamentable • **England's ~ performance in the World Cup** la pésima actuación de Inglaterra en el Mundial
2 (= *grovelling*) sumiso • **an ~ slave to fashion** un esclavo sumiso de la moda • **he sounded ~** su tono era sumiso y arrepentido • **we received an ~ apology from the travel company** recibimos una carta de la agencia de viajes deshaciéndose en disculpas
3 (*as intensifier*) [*misery, failure*] absoluto; [*stupidity*] supino; [*cowardice*] abyecto, vil (*liter*); [*surrender*] indigno • **to live in ~ poverty** vivir en la miseria más absoluta
abjectly [ˈæbdʒektlɪ] (ADV) [*fail*] de la forma más indigna, miserablemente • **he apologized ~** se deshizo en disculpas • **~ miserable** sumamente desgraciado • **to be ~ poor** vivir en la miseria más absoluta
abjectness [ˈæbdʒektnɪs] (N)
1 (= *wretchedness*) [*of conditions*] lo miserable; [*of position*] lo indigno • **the ~ of the conditions in which they live** lo miserable de las condiciones en que viven • **we were shocked at the ~ of their performance** nos dejó horrorizados lo mal que lo hicieron
2 (= *grovelling quality*) • **the ~ of his apology** el tono sumiso y arrepentido de su disculpa
abjure [əbˈdʒʊəʳ] (VT) (*frm*) renunciar a, abjurar de
Abkhaz [æbˈkɑːz], **Abkhazi** [æbˈkɑːzɪ], **Abkhazian** [æbˈkɑːzɪən] (ADJ) abjasio
(N) (PL: **Abkhaz**) **1** (= *person*) abjasio/a *m/f*
2 (*Ling*) abjasio *m*
Abkhazia [æbˈkɑːzɪə] (N) Abjazia *f*
ablative [ˈæblətɪv] (*Ling*) (ADJ) ablativo
(N) (*also* **ablative case**) ablativo *m* • **in the ~** en ablativo
(CPD) ▸ **ablative absolute** ablativo *m* absoluto
ablaze [əˈbleɪz] (ADV) **1** (= *on fire*) en llamas, ardiendo • **the cinema was ~ in five minutes** en cinco minutos el cine estaba en llamas *or* ardiendo • **to set sth ~** prender fuego a algo
2 (*fig*) • **the house was ~ with light** la casa resplandecía de luz • **the garden was ~ with colour** el jardín resplandecía de color • **to be ~ with indignation** estar indignadísimo *or* encolerizado
able [ˈeɪbl] (ADJ) **1** • **to be ~ to do sth** (*of acquired skills*) saber hacer algo; (*other contexts*) poder hacer algo • **the child isn't ~ to walk (yet)** el niño no sabe andar (todavía) • **he's not ~ to walk** no puede andar • **come as soon as you are ~** ven en cuanto puedas • **I was eventually ~ to escape** por fin pude escaparme, por fin logré escaparme • **~ to pay** solvente
2 (= *capable*) [*person*] capaz; [*piece of work*] sólido • **she is one of our ~st pupils** es una de nuestras alumnas más capaces
(CPD) ▸ **able seaman** marinero *m* de primera *or* patentado

ABLE, CAN

Poder *and* **saber** *can both translate* **to be able to, can** *and* **could**.

Skills

▷ *Use* **saber** *when* **to be able to, can** *and* **could** *mean "know how to":*
Can you type?
¿Sabes escribir a máquina?
His wife couldn't drive
Su mujer no sabía conducir

Other contexts

▷ *Generally, use* **poder**:
He can stay here
Puede quedarse aquí
We have not been able to persuade them
No hemos podido convencerlos

When **can** *and* **could** *are followed by* **find** *or a verb of perception -* **see, hear, feel, taste** *or* **smell** *- they are usually not translated:*
I can't find it
No lo encuentro
What can you see?
¿Qué ves?

Alternatives to "poder"

▷ *When* **to be able** *means "to be capable of", you can often use* **ser capaz de** *as an alternative to* **poder**:
I don't think he'll be able to resist it
No creo que sea capaz de *or* pueda resistirlo

For further uses and examples, see **able, can**

...able (SUFFIX) ...able
able-bodied [ˈeɪblˈbɒdɪd] (ADJ) sano
(CPD) ▸ **able-bodied seaman** marinero *m* de primera, marinero *m* patentado
abloom [əˈbluːm] (ADJ) (*poet, liter*) • **to be ~** [*flower, tree*] estar en flor
ablution [əˈbluːʃən] (N) **1** (*Rel*) ablución *f* • **to perform one's ~s** (*hum*) lavarse • **to be at one's ~s** (*hum*) estar en el lavabo
2 ablutions (*Mil**) servicios *mpl*
ably [ˈeɪblɪ] (ADV) hábilmente, con mucha habilidad • **~ assisted by** hábilmente ayudado por, con la experta colaboración de
ABM (N ABBR) = **anti-ballistic missile**
abnegate [ˈæbnɪgeɪt] (VT) (*frm*) [+ *responsibility*] eludir, rehuir; [+ *one's religion*] abjurar • **to ~ one's rights** renunciar a sus derechos
abnegation [ˌæbnɪˈgeɪʃən] (N) (*frm*) abnegación *f*
abnormal [æbˈnɔːməl] (ADJ) anormal; [*shape*] irregular
abnormality [ˌæbnɔːˈmælɪtɪ] (N) (= *condition*) anormalidad *f*; (= *instance*) anormalidad *f*, desviación *f*
abnormally [æbˈnɔːməlɪ] (ADV)

1 irregularmente • **an ~ formed bone** un hueso de formación anormal
2 (*= exceptionally*) de modo anormal, anormalmente • **an ~ large sum** una cantidad descomunal
Abo** ['æbəʊ] N (*Australia*) (*pej*) = **Aborigine**
aboard [ə'bɔːd] ADV (*Naut*) a bordo • **to go ~** embarcar, subir a bordo • **to take ~** embarcar, cargar • **all ~!** (*Rail*) ¡viajeros, al tren! • **life ~ is pleasant** es agradable la vida de a bordo
PREP • **~ the ship** a bordo del barco • **~ the train** en el tren
abode [ə'bəʊd] PT, PP *of* **abide**
N (*esp Jur*) morada *f*, domicilio *m* • **place of ~** domicilio *m* • **right of ~** derecho *m* a domiciliarse • **of no fixed ~** sin domicilio fijo • **to take up one's ~** domiciliarse, establecerse
abolish [ə'bɒlɪʃ] VT abolir, suprimir
abolishment [ə'bɒlɪʃmənt] N = **abolition**
abolition [,æbəʊ'lɪʃən] N abolición *f*, supresión *f*
abolitionist [,æbəʊ'lɪʃənɪst] N (*Hist*) abolicionista *mf*
A-bomb ['eɪbɒm] N ABBR (= **atom(ic) bomb**) bomba *f* atómica
abominable [ə'bɒmɪnəbl] ADJ abominable, detestable; [*taste, workmanship*] detestable, pésimo
CPD ▸ **the abominable snowman** el abominable hombre de las nieves
abominably [ə'bɒmɪnəblɪ] ADV abominablemente, pésimamente • **to behave ~** comportarse abominablemente *or* pésimamente • **he writes ~** escribe pésimamente • **to be ~ rude to sb** ser terriblemente grosero con algn
abominate [ə'bɒmɪneɪt] VT (*frm*) abominar (de), detestar
abomination [ə,bɒmɪ'neɪʃən] N 1 (*= feeling*) aversión *f*
2 (*= detestable act, thing*) escándalo *m*
Aboriginal [,æbə'rɪdʒənl] ADJ (*= Australian*) aborigen
N (*= Australian*) aborigen *mf* (*australiano*)
aboriginal [,æbə'rɪdʒənl] ADJ (*= indigenous*) aborigen, indígena
N (*= indigenous inhabitant*) aborigen *mf*, indígena *mf*
Aborigine [,æbə'rɪdʒɪnɪ] N (*in Australia*) aborigen *mf* (*australiano*)
aborigine [,æbə'rɪdʒɪnɪ] N (*= indigenous inhabitant*) aborigen *mf*, indígena *mf*
aborning [ə'bɔːnɪŋ] (*US*) ADV • **to die ~** [*project, idea*] morir antes de nacer
ADJ • **to be ~** nacer
abort [ə'bɔːt] VI 1 (*Med*) abortar
2 (*Comput*) abandonar
3 (*= fail*) [*plan, project, negotiations*] fracasar, malograrse
VT 1 (*Med*) abortar • **~ed foetuses** *or* (*US*) **fetuses** fetos *mpl* de abortos
2 (*= abandon*) [*+ mission, operation*] suspender; [*+ deal, agreement*] anular; [*+ plan*] abandonar; [*+ landing, takeoff*] abortar
3 (*= cause to fail*) malograr • **the bad weather ~ed plans for an air display** el mal tiempo malogró los planes de llevar a cabo una exhibición aérea
4 (*Comput*) abandonar
abortifacient [ə,bɔːtɪ'feɪʃənt] ADJ abortivo
N abortivo *m*
abortion [ə'bɔːʃən] N 1 (*Med*) **a** (*= termination*) aborto *m* (provocado) • **illegal ~** aborto *m* ilegal • **to have an ~** hacerse un aborto, abortar (*no de forma espontánea*) • **to perform** *or* **carry out an ~** practicar un aborto
b (*frm*) (*also* **spontaneous abortion**) aborto *m* (espontáneo)
2* (*= failure*) fracaso *m*, malogro *m*
CPD ▸ **abortion clinic** clínica *f* donde se practican abortos ▸ **abortion law** ley *f* del aborto ▸ **abortion pill** píldora *f* abortiva
abortionist [ə'bɔːʃənɪst] N abortista *mf*
abortive [ə'bɔːtɪv] ADJ 1 (*= failed*) [*attempt, plan*] fracasado, frustrado
2 (*Med*) [*method, medicine*] abortivo
abortively [ə'bɔːtɪvlɪ] ADV [*try, attempt*] en vano • **the negotiations ended ~** las negociaciones fracasaron
abound [ə'baʊnd] VI (*= exist in great quantity*) abundar • **to ~ in** *or* **with** (*= have in great quantity*) estar lleno de, abundar en
about [ə'baʊt]

> When **about** is an element in a phrasal verb, eg **bring about, come about, turn about, wander about**, look up the verb.

ADV 1 (*= approximately*) más o menos, aproximadamente, alrededor de • **~ £20** unas 20 libras, 20 libras más o menos • **there were ~ 25 guests** había unos 25 invitados, había como 25 invitados (*esp LAm*) • **~ seven years ago** hace unos siete años • **at ~ two o'clock** a eso de las dos, sobre las dos • **it's ~ two o'clock** son las dos, más o menos • **he must be ~ 40** tendrá alrededor de 40 años • **that's ~ all I could find** eso es más o menos todo lo que podía encontrar • **that's ~ it** eso es(, más o menos) • **it's just ~ finished** está casi terminado • **that's ~ right** eso es(, más o menos) • **he's ~ the same** sigue más o menos igual • **it's ~ time you stopped** ya es hora de que lo dejes
2 (*place*) • **is anyone ~?** ¿hay alguien? • **is Mr Brown ~?** ¿está por aquí el Sr. Brown? • **to be ~ again** (*after illness*) estar levantado • **we were ~ early** nos levantamos temprano • **all ~** (*= everywhere*) por todas partes • **there's a lot of measles ~** hay mucho sarampión, está dando el sarampión • **there isn't much money ~** hay poco dinero, la gente tiene poco dinero • **to run ~** correr por todas partes • **he must be ~ somewhere** debe de andar por aquí • **there's a thief ~** por aquí anda un ladrón • **to walk ~** pasearse
3 • **to be ~ to do sth** estar a punto de *or* (*LAm*) por hacer algo • **nobody is ~ to sell it** nadie tiene la más mínima intención de venderlo • **I'm not ~ to do all that for nothing** no pienso hacer todo eso gratis
PREP 1 (*= relating to*) de, acerca de, sobre • **a book ~ gardening** un libro de jardinería, un libro sobre la jardinería • **I can tell you nothing ~ him** no le puedo decir nada acerca de él • **I'm phoning ~ tomorrow's meeting** llamo por la reunión de mañana • **they fell out ~ money** riñeron por cuestión de dinero • **~ the other night, I didn't mean what I said** respecto a la otra noche, no iba en serio cuando dije esas cosas • **do something ~ it!** ¡haz algo! • **there's nothing I can do ~ it** no puedo hacer nada al respecto • **how** *or* **what ~ this one?** ¿qué te parece este? • **he was chosen out of 200, how** *or* **what ~ that!** entre 200 lo eligieron a él, ¡quién lo diría! *or* ¡fíjate! • **how** *or* **what ~ coming with us?** ¿por qué no vienes con nosotros? • **how** *or* **what ~ a drink?** ¿vamos a tomar una copa? • **how** *or* **what ~ a song?** ¿por qué no nos cantas algo? • **how** *or* **what ~ it?** (*= what do you say?*) ¿qué te parece?; (*= what of it?*) ¿y qué? • **how** *or* **what ~ me?** y yo, ¿qué? • **what's that book ~?** ¿de qué trata ese libro? • **what did she talk ~?** ¿de qué habló? • **what's all this noise ~?** ¿a qué se debe todo este ruido? • **"I want to talk to you" — "what ~?"** —quiero hablar contigo —¿acerca de qué?
2 (*= particular to*) • **there's something ~ him (that I like)** tiene un no sé qué (que me gusta) • **there's something ~ a soldier** los soldados tienen un no sé qué • **he had a mysterious air ~ him** tenía un cierto aire misterioso • **there's something odd ~ it** aquí hay algo raro
3 (*= doing*) • **while you're ~ it can you get me a beer?** ya que estás en ello ¿me traes una cerveza? • **and while I'm ~ it I'll talk to your father** y de paso hablaré con tu padre • **you've been a long time ~ it** has tardado bastante en hacerlo; ▹ **go about**
4 (*= intending*) • **I can't imagine what he was ~ when he did that** no entiendo lo que pretendía con eso
5 (*= around*) • **to do jobs ~ the house** (*= repairs*) hacer arreglos en la casa • **I had no money ~ me** no llevaba dinero encima • **he looked ~ him** miró a su alrededor • **somewhere ~ here** por aquí cerca • **to wander ~ the town** deambular por la ciudad
about-face [ə,baʊt'feɪs], **about-turn** [ə,baʊt'tɜːn] N 1 (*Mil*) media vuelta *f*
2 (*fig*) cambio *m* radical de postura, giro *m* (brusco)
VI 1 (*Mil*) dar media vuelta
2 (*fig*) cambiar radicalmente de postura
above [ə'bʌv]

> When **above** is an element in a phrasal verb, eg **get above**, look up the verb.

ADV 1 (*= overhead*) arriba • **seen from ~** visto desde arriba • **the flat ~** el piso de arriba
2 (*referring to heaven*) • **from ~** del cielo, de lo alto • **God, who is in heaven ~** Dios en las alturas, Dios que vive en el reino de los cielos • **the gods ~** los dioses en las alturas
3 (*in status*) de más categoría • **those ~** los de más categoría • **orders from ~** órdenes *fpl* superiores *or* de arriba
4 (*in text*) arriba, más arriba • **see ~** véase (más) arriba • **as set out ~** según lo arriba expuesto • **as I said ~** como ya he dicho
5 (*= more*) • **boys of five and ~** los niños mayores de cinco años • **seats are available at £5 and ~** las entradas cuestan a partir de 5 libras
PREP 1 (*= higher than, over*) encima de • **there was a picture ~ the fireplace** había un cuadro encima de la chimenea • **~ the clouds** encima de las nubes • **~ ground: they were trapped 150ft ~ ground** estaban atrapados a una altura de 150 pies sobre el nivel del suelo • **vegetables that grow ~ ground** las verduras que crecen en la superficie • **2,000 metres ~ sea level** 2.000 metros sobre el nivel del mar • **I couldn't hear ~ the din** no podía oír con tanto ruido
2 (*= upstream of*) • **the Thames ~ London** el Támesis más arriba de Londres
3 (*of rank*) • **he is ~ me in rank** tiene una categoría superior a la mía, tiene un rango superior al mío; (*of priority*) • **~ all** sobre todo • **he values honesty ~ all else** ante todo valora la honestidad • **he was, ~ all else, a musician** era, ante todo, un músico; ▹ **station**
4 (*= morally superior*) • **he's ~ that sort of thing** está muy por encima de esas cosas • **he's not ~ a bit of blackmail** es capaz hasta del chantaje • **to get ~ o.s.** pasarse (de listo)
5 (*= beyond*) • **it's ~ me** es demasiado complicado para mí
6 (*numbers*) más de, superior a • **there were not ~ 40 people** no había más de 40 personas • **any number ~ 12** cualquier número superior a 12 • **she can't count ~ ten** no sabe contar más allá de diez • **children ~**

seven years of age los niños mayores de siete años • **temperatures ~ 40 degrees** temperaturas *fpl* por encima de los 40 grados • **temperatures well ~ normal** temperaturas *fpl* muy superiores a las normales • **wage rises of 3% ~ inflation** aumentos *mpl* de sueldo de un 3% por encima del nivel de inflación; ▹ **average**
ADJ [*fact, place*] sobredicho, arriba mencionado; [*photo, illustration*] de arriba
N • **the ~ is a photo of …** lo anterior *or* lo que se ve arriba es una foto de … • **please translate the ~** por favor traduzca lo anterior

above-board [əˈbʌvˈbɔːd] ADV abiertamente, sin rebozo
ADJ legítimo, honrado

above-ground [əˌbʌvˈgraʊnd] ADJ [*car park*] exterior; [*pool*] al aire libre

above-mentioned [əˈbʌvˈmenʃənd] ADJ [*fact, point, place*] sobredicho, arriba mencionado; [*person*] susodicho

above-named [əˈbʌvˈneɪmd] ADJ = **above-mentioned**

Abp ABBR (= **Archbishop**) Arz., Arzpo.

abracadabra [ˌabrəkəˈdæbrə] N abracadabra *m*

abrade [əˈbreɪd] VT (*frm*) raer, raspar

Abraham [ˈeɪbrəhæm] N Abrahán, Abraham

abrasion [əˈbreɪʒən] N (= *act, injury*) abrasión *f*, escoriación *f*

abrasive [əˈbreɪsɪv] ADJ **1** [*substance, surface*] abrasivo
2 (*fig*) [*personality*] desabrido, brusco; [*tone*] áspero, desabrido
N abrasivo *m*

abrasively [əˈbreɪsɪvlɪ] ADV [*say, reply*] ásperamente, con tono áspero *or* desabrido

abrasiveness [əˈbreɪsɪvnɪs] N **1** [*of surface, substance*] lo abrasivo
2 (*fig*) [*of person, tone*] torpeza *f*, desabrimiento *m*

abreaction [ˌæbrɪˈækʃən] N (*Psych*) abreacción *f*

abreast [əˈbrest] ADV **1** (= *side by side*) • **to march four ~** marchar en columna de cuatro en fondo • **streets so narrow that two can barely walk ~** calles tan estrechas que dos personas difícilmente pueden andar hombro con hombro • **to come ~ of sth/sb** llegar a la altura de algo/algn
2 (= *aware of*) • **to be/keep ~ of sth** estar/mantenerse al corriente de algo • **to keep ~ of the news** mantenerse al día *or* al corriente

abridge [əˈbrɪdʒ] VT [+ *book*] resumir, compendiar; (= *cut short*) abreviar, acortar

abridged [əˈbrɪdʒd] ADJ [*book*] resumido, compendiado

abridgement [əˈbrɪdʒmənt] N
1 (= *shortened version*) resumen *m*, compendio *m*
2 (= *act*) abreviación *f*

abroad [əˈbrɔːd] ADV **1** (= *in foreign country*) en el extranjero • **to live ~** vivir en el extranjero • **to go ~** ir al extranjero • **he had to go ~** (*fleeing*) tuvo que salir del país • **when the minister is ~** cuando el ministro está fuera del país • **our army ~** nuestro ejército en el extranjero • **our debts ~** nuestras deudas en el exterior • **troops brought in from ~** tropas traídas del extranjero
2 (*frm*) (= *about*) • **there is a rumour ~ that …** corre el rumor de que … • **how did the news get ~?** ¿cómo se divulgó la noticia?
3† (= *outside*) fuera • **there were not many ~ at that hour** había poca gente por las calles a aquella hora

abrogate [ˈæbrəʊgeɪt] VT (*frm*) abrogar

abrogation [ˌæbrəʊˈgeɪʃən] N (*frm*) abrogación *f*

abrupt [əˈbrʌpt] ADJ **1** (= *sudden*) [*change, rise*] brusco; [*departure*] repentino; [*resignation, dismissal*] repentino, súbito • **to come to an ~ end** terminar de repente • **to come to an ~ halt** *or* **stop** (*lit*) pararse bruscamente *or* en seco; (*fig*) terminarse de repente
2 (= *brusque*) [*person*] brusco, cortante; [*question*] brusco; [*comment, reply*] cortante • **he was ~ to the point of rudeness** estuvo tan brusco *or* cortante que resultaba hasta grosero • **he was very ~ with me** estuvo muy brusco *or* cortante conmigo • **I was taken aback by her ~ manner** me chocó su brusquedad
3 (= *steep*) [*hillside, precipice*] abrupto, escarpado

abruptly [əˈbrʌptlɪ] ADV **1** (= *suddenly*) [*stop, end, leave*] bruscamente, repentinamente; [*brake*] bruscamente
2 (= *brusquely*) [*say, ask*] bruscamente
3 (= *steeply*) abruptamente • **a cliff rose ~ before them** frente a ellos se alzaba abruptamente un acantilado

abruptness [əˈbrʌptnɪs] N **1** (= *suddenness*) lo repentino • **we were taken aback by the ~ of his departure** nos sorprendió lo repentino de su marcha • **we were shocked by the ~ of his dismissal** nos dejó horrorizados que lo despidieran tan de repente
2 (= *brusqueness*) brusquedad *f*
3 (= *steepness*) lo escarpado

ABS N ABBR (= **antilock braking system**) ABS *m*
CPD ▸ **ABS brakes** frenos *mpl* ABS

abs* [æbz] NPL (= *abdominal muscles*) abdominales *mpl*

abscess [ˈæbsɪs] N absceso *m*

abscond [əbˈskɒnd] VI fugarse; (*with funds*) huir

absconder [əbˈskɒndəʳ] N (*from prison*) fugitivo/a *m/f*, evadido/a *m/f*

absconding [əbˈskɒndɪŋ] ADJ en fuga

abseil [ˈæbsaɪl] VI (*Brit*) (*Sport*) (*also* **abseil down**) hacer rappel, bajar en la cuerda • **he ~ed down the rock** hizo rappel roca abajo

abseiling [ˈæbsaɪlɪŋ] N (*Brit*) (*Sport*) rappel *m*

absence [ˈæbsəns] N [*of person*] ausencia *f*; [*of thing*] falta *f* • **in the ~ of** [+ *person*] en ausencia de; [+ *thing*] a falta de • **after an ~ of three months** tras una ausencia de tres meses • **to be sentenced in one's ~** ser condenado en ausencia • **~ of mind** distracción *f*, despiste *m* • PROVERB: • **~ makes the heart grow fonder** la ausencia es al amor lo que el viento al aire, que apaga el pequeño y aviva el grande

absent ADJ [ˈæbsənt] **1** (= *not present*) [*person, thing*] ausente • **"to ~ friends!"** (*toast*) "¡por los amigos ausentes!" • **to be ~** faltar (**from** a) • **to be ~ from school** faltar al colegio • **he has been ~ from his desk for two weeks** lleva dos semanas sin aparecer por el despacho • **~ without leave** (*Mil*) ausente sin permiso • **to go ~ without leave** ausentarse sin permiso
2 (= *absent-minded*) ausente, distraído • **she was ~, preoccupied** estaba ausente *or* distraída, preocupada • **an ~ stare** una mirada ausente *or* distraída
3 (= *lacking*) • **a spirit of compromise was noticeably ~ from the meeting** en la reunión la voluntad de llegar a un acuerdo brilló por su ausencia
VT [æbˈsent] • **to ~ o.s.** ausentarse (**from** de)

absentee [ˌæbsənˈtiː] N (*from school, work*) ausente *mf*
CPD ▸ **absentee ballot** (*US*) voto *m* por correo ▸ **absentee landlord** propietario/a *m/f* absentista ▸ **absentee rate** nivel *m* de absentismo ▸ **absentee voter** (*US*) votante *mf* por correo

absenteeism [ˌæbsənˈtiːɪzəm] N absentismo *m*

absentia [æbˈsentɪə] ▹ **in absentia**

absently [ˈæbsəntlɪ] ADV distraídamente

absent-minded [ˈæbsəntˈmaɪndɪd] ADJ (*momentarily*) distraído, ausente; (*habitually*) despistado, distraído • **an absent-minded professor** un profesor despistado *or* distraído

absent-mindedly [ˈæbsəntˈmaɪndɪdlɪ] ADV distraídamente

absent-mindedness [ˈæbsəntˈmaɪndɪdnɪs] N (*momentary*) distracción *f*; (*habitual*) despiste *m*

absinth, absinthe [ˈæbsɪnθ] N **1** (= *drink*) absenta *f*
2 (*Bot*) ajenjo *m*

absolute [ˈæbsəluːt] ADJ **1** (= *complete, unqualified*) [*certainty, confidence, majority, need*] absoluto; [*support*] incondicional, total; [*refusal*] rotundo; [*prohibition, command*] terminante; [*proof*] irrefutable; [*denial*] rotundo, categórico; [*right*] incuestionable • **he's an ~ beginner** es un auténtico principiante • **it's an ~ fact that …** es indiscutible el hecho de que … • **the divorce was made ~** concedieron el divorcio por sentencia firme • **~ monopoly** monopolio *m* total • **it was the ~ truth, I promise** era la pura verdad, se lo prometo • **~ veto** veto *m* total
2 (= *unlimited*) [*power, monarch*] absoluto
3 (= *not relative*) [*value*] absoluto • **in ~ terms** en términos absolutos • **the quest for ~ truth** la búsqueda de la verdad absoluta
4 (*as intensifier*) [*liar, villain*] redomado • **the party was an ~ disaster** la fiesta fue un completo desastre • **it's an ~ disgrace** es una auténtica vergüenza • **it's the ~ end!** ¡es el colmo! • **she wore an expression of ~ hatred** la expresión de su cara estaba llena de odio • **the man's an ~ idiot** es completamente idiota • **it's ~ rubbish!** ¡es puro disparate!
5 (*Gram*) absoluto
N (*Philos*) • **the ~** lo absoluto
CPD ▸ **absolute alcohol** alcohol *m* puro ▸ **absolute liability** (*Econ, Jur*) responsabilidad *f* total ▸ **absolute majority** mayoría *f* absoluta • **to win an ~ majority** obtener la mayoría absoluta ▸ **absolute pitch** (*Mus*) oído *m* absoluto • **to have ~ pitch** tener oído absoluto ▸ **absolute temperature** temperatura *f* absoluta ▸ **absolute zero** cero *m* absoluto

absolutely [ˈæbsəluːtlɪ] ADV **1** (= *completely*) [*clear, impossible, alone, untrue*] completamente, totalmente; [*hilarious, beautiful, wonderful*] realmente; [*exhausted, horrible*] totalmente; [*necessary*] absolutamente • **it's ~ boiling in here!** ¡aquí dentro hace un calor infernal! • **he's ~ delighted at being a father again** está contentísimo de volver a ser padre • **the food was ~ disgusting** la comida era verdaderamente asquerosa • **punctuality is ~ essential** la puntualidad es de vital importancia • **~ everybody** absolutamente todo el mundo • **~ everything** absolutamente todo • **I've looked ~ everywhere for it** lo he buscado absolutamente por todas partes • **your hands are ~ filthy** tienes las manos sucísimas *or* verdaderamente sucias • **it is ~ forbidden to** (+ *infin*) queda

terminantemente prohibido (+ *infin*) • **it's ~ freezing in here!** ¡aquí dentro hace un frío que pela! • **it makes ~ no difference** no cambia nada en absoluto • **~ nobody/ nothing** nadie/nada en absoluto • **to be ~ right** tener toda la razón • **to lie ~ still** permanecer tumbado completamente quieto • **are you ~ sure?** ¿estás completamente seguro? • **it's ~ true** es la pura verdad, es totalmente cierto
2 (= *unconditionally*) [*refuse, deny*] rotundamente; [*believe*] firmemente • **I agree ~** estoy totalmente de acuerdo
3* (= *certainly*) desde luego • **"it's worrying, isn't it?" — "absolutely"** —es preocupante ¿verdad? —desde luego • **~ not!** ¡de ninguna manera! • **"does this affect your attitude to your work?" — "~ not"** —¿afecta esto a su actitud hacia su trabajo? —no, en absoluto
4 (*Gram*) • **adverbs used ~** adverbios de uso absoluto

absolution [ˌæbsəˈluːʃən] N (*Rel*) absolución *f* • **to give ~ to sb** dar la absolución a algn, absolver a algn

absolutism [ˈæbsəluːtɪzəm] N absolutismo *m*

absolutist [ˈæbsəluːtɪst] ADJ absolutista
N absolutista *mf*

absolve [əbˈzɒlv] VT (= *free*) absolver (**from** de)

absorb [əbˈzɔːb] VT 1 [+ *liquid*] absorber; [+ *heat, sound, shock, vibrations, radiation*] amortiguar
2 (*fig*) [+ *information*] asimilar; [+ *time, energy*] ocupar, absorber • **the business ~s most of his time** el negocio absorbe *or* le lleva la mayor parte de su tiempo • **the parent company ~s the losses made by the subsidiary** la empresa matriz absorbe las pérdidas de la filial • **the country ~ed 1,000 refugees** el país dio entrada a *or* acogió a 1.000 refugiados
3 (= *engross*) • **to be ~ed in** estar absorto en, estar ensimismado con • **she was ~ed in a book** estaba absorta en *or* ensimismada con un libro • **to get ~ed in** centrarse *or* meterse de lleno en

absorbable [əbˈzɔːbəbl] ADJ absorbible

absorbency [əbˈzɔːbənsɪ] N absorbencia *f*

absorbent [əbˈzɔːbənt] ADJ absorbente
CPD ▸ **absorbent cotton** (*US*) algodón *m* hidrófilo

absorber [əbˈzɔːbəʳ] N ▹ **shock absorber**

absorbing [əbˈzɔːbɪŋ] ADJ [*study etc*] (= *fascinating*) apasionante; (= *engrossing*) absorbente • **I find history very ~** me apasiona la historia, encuentro la historia apasionante

absorption [əbˈzɔːpʃən] N (*Comm*) (*also fig*) absorción *f*
CPD ▸ **absorption costing** cálculo *m* del costo de absorción

abstain [əbˈsteɪn] VI 1 (= *refrain*) abstenerse (**from** de) • **to ~ from comment** no ofrecer comentario
2 (= *not vote*) abstenerse
3 (= *not drink*) abstenerse de las bebidas alcohólicas

abstainer [əbˈsteɪnəʳ] N 1 (= *non-voter*) abstencionista *mf*
2 (= *teetotaller*) (*also* **total abstainer**) abstemio/a *m/f*

abstemious [əbˈstiːmɪəs] ADJ [*person*] abstemio; [*meal*] sin alcohol

abstemiousness [əbˈstiːmɪəsnɪs] N sobriedad *f*, moderación *f*

abstention [əbˈstenʃən] N abstención *f* • **there were 20 ~s** hubo 20 abstenciones

abstentionist [əbˈstenʃənɪst] N abstencionista *mf*
ADJ abstencionista

abstinence [ˈæbstɪnəns] N abstinencia *f* (**from** de) • **total ~** abstinencia *f* total (*esp* de bebidas alcohólicas)
CPD ▸ **abstinence syndrome** síndrome *m* de abstinencia

abstinent [ˈæbstɪnənt] ADJ abstinente

abstract ADJ [ˈæbstrækt] abstracto
N [ˈæbstrækt] 1 (= *summary*) resumen *m*, sumario *m*
2 (*Art*) pintura *f* abstracta
3 • **in the ~** en abstracto
VT [æbˈstrækt] 1 (= *remove*) quitar; (*Chem*) extraer
2 (= *steal*) sustraer, robar
3 (= *summarize*) [+ *book, article*] resumir
4 • **to ~ o.s.** abstraerse (**from** de), ensimismarse
CPD [ˈæbstrækt] ▸ **abstract art** arte *m* abstracto ▸ **abstract expressionism** expresionismo *m* abstracto ▸ **abstract noun** nombre *m* abstracto

abstracted [æbˈstræktɪd] ADJ distraído, ensimismado

abstractedly [æbˈstræktɪdlɪ] ADV • **she listened ~** escuchaba distraída

abstraction [æbˈstrækʃən] N 1 (= *act*) abstracción *f*
2 (= *absent-mindedness*) distraimiento *m*, ensimismamiento *m*

abstractly [ˈæbstræktlɪ] ADV de manera abstracta

abstractness [ˈæbstræktnɪs] N carácter *m* abstracto

abstruse [æbˈstruːs] ADJ recóndito, abstruso

abstruseness [æbˈstruːsnɪs] N lo recóndito, carácter *m* abstruso

absurd [əbˈsɜːd] ADJ [*idea, plan*] absurdo; [*appearance*] ridículo • **don't be ~!** ¡no digas tonterías! • **how ~!** ¡qué ridículo! • **you look ~ in that hat** con ese sombrero estás ridículo
N • **the ~** el absurdo • **the theatre of the ~** el teatro del absurdo

absurdist [əbˈsɜːdɪst] ADJ [*play, novel*] del absurdo

absurdity [əbˈsɜːdɪtɪ] N 1 (= *quality*) lo absurdo
2 (= *act of madness*) locura *f*, disparate *m* • **it would be an ~ to try** sería una locura *or* un disparate intentarlo • **it would be an ~ to say that** sería absurdo decir eso

absurdly [əbˈsɜːdlɪ] ADV [*long, complicated*] absurdamente, ridículamente • **they were all laughing ~** todos se estaban riendo de una forma ridícula

ABTA [ˈæbtə] N ABBR (= **Association of British Travel Agents**) ≈ AEDAVE *f*

Abu Dhabi [ˌæbʊˈdɑːbɪ] N Abu Dhabi *m*

abulia [əˈbuːlɪə] N (*Psych*) abulia *f*

abundance [əˈbʌndəns] N abundancia *f* • **in ~** en abundancia, en cantidad, en grandes cantidades • **we have a great ~ of plums** tenemos ciruelas en abundancia • **we had an ~ of rain** llovió copiosamente

abundant [əˈbʌndənt] ADJ abundante • **a country ~ in minerals** un país rico en minerales

abundantly [əˈbʌndəntlɪ] ADV abundantemente • **he made it ~ clear to me that ...** me dejó meridianamente claro que ...

abuse N [əˈbjuːs] 1 (= *insults*) insultos *mpl*, improperios *mpl* (*more frm*) • **to heap ~ on sb** • **hurl ~ at sb** llenar a algn de improperios
2 (= *misuse*) abuso *m* • **~ of trust/power** abuso de confianza/poder • **open to ~** abierto al abuso; ▹ **child, drug, sexual**
VT [əˈbjuːz] 1 (= *insult*) insultar, injuriar • **he roundly ~d the government** dijo mil improperios contra el gobierno
2 (= *mistreat*) [+ *child*] (*physically*) maltratar; (*sexually*) abusar de
3 (= *misuse*) [+ *position, privilege*] abusar de

abuser [əˈbjuːzəʳ] N (*physical*) *culpable de malos tratos*; (*sexual*) *culpable de abusos deshonestos* • **she killed her ~** mató al que la abusaba; ▹ **child, drug**

Abu Simbel [ˌæbʊˈsɪmbl] N Abu Simbel *m*

abusive [əbˈjuːsɪv] ADJ 1 (= *offensive*) ofensivo, insultante; [*language*] lleno de insultos, injurioso • **to be ~ to sb** ser grosero a algn, decir cosas injuriosas a algn (*more frm*) • **to become ~** ponerse grosero
2 (*physically*) [*person*] que maltrata; [*relationship*] de malos tratos
3 (*sexually*) [*person*] que abusa (sexualmente); [*relationship*] de abuso sexual
4 [*practice*] abusivo

abusively [əbˈjuːsɪvlɪ] ADV [*speak, refer*] de manera insultante *or* desconsiderada

abusiveness [əbˈjuːsɪvnɪs] N (= *rudeness*) [*of person*] grosería *f* • **a critic should not descend to mere ~** un crítico no debería rebajarse a simples insultos

abut [əˈbʌt] VI • **to ~ on sth** [*land*] lindar con algo, confinar con algo; [*house, building*] estar contiguo con algo, colindar con algo
VT • **to ~ sth** [*land*] lindar con algo, confinar con algo; [*house, building*] estar contiguo con algo, colindar con algo

abutment [əˈbʌtmənt] N (*Archit*) estribo *m*, contrafuerte *m*; (*Carpentry*) empotramiento *m*

abutting [əˈbʌtɪŋ] ADJ contiguo, colindante

abuzz [əˈbʌz] ADJ • **the whole office was ~ with the news** toda la oficina comentaba la noticia

ABV ABBR (= **alcohol by volume**) volumen *m* de alcohol

abysmal [əˈbɪzməl] ADJ 1 (= *very bad*) [*result, performance*] pésimo • **the play was ~** la representación fue pésima
2 (= *very great*) [*ignorance*] abismal • **to live in ~ poverty** vivir en la mayor miseria

abysmally [əˈbɪzməlɪ] ADV [*play, sing*] pésimamente; [*bad, low*] terriblemente; [*fail*] rotundamente

abyss [əˈbɪs] N (*lit*) abismo *m*, sima *f*; (*fig*) abismo *m*

Abyssinia [ˌæbɪˈsɪnɪə] N Abisinia *f*

Abyssinian [ˌæbɪˈsɪnɪən] ADJ abisinio
N abisinio/a *m/f*

AC N ABBR 1 (*Elec*) (= **alternating current**) C.A. *f*
2 (*Aer*) = **aircraftman**
3 (*US*) (*Sport*) (= **Athletic Club**) C.A. *m*

a/c ABBR 1 (= **account**) c/, c.ta
2 (*US*) (= **account current**) c/c

acacia [əˈkeɪʃə] N acacia *f*

Acad ABBR = **academy, academic**

academe [ˈækədiːm], **academia** [ˌækəˈdiːmɪə] N (*liter*) mundo *m* académico

academic [ˌækəˈdemɪk] ADJ 1 (*Scol, Univ*) [*ability, qualifications, achievement*] académico • **~ standards were high** los niveles académicos eran buenos • **in ~ circles** en círculos universitarios • **~ freedom** libertad *f* de cátedra • **~ journal** revista *f* dirigida a académicos • **~ staff** profesorado *m*, personal *m* docente • **the ~ world** el mundo académico
2 (= *scholarly*) intelectualmente dotado • **an exam for ~ children** un examen para niños intelectualmente dotados
3 (= *theoretical*) [*question*] (puramente) teórico, sin interés práctico; [*debate*] (puramente) teórico • **that's all quite ~** eso no tiene ninguna trascendencia • **it is of ~**

interest only solo tiene interés teórico
N académico/a *m/f*, profesor(a) *m/f* universitario/a
CPD ▸ **academic advisor** (*US*) jefe *mf* de estudios ▸ **academic dean** (*US*) decano/a *m/f* ▸ **academic dress** vestidura *f* universitaria ▸ **academic gown** toga *f* ▸ **academic officers** (*US*) personal *m* docente ▸ **academic rank** (*US*) rango *m* académico ▸ **academic year** (*Univ*) año *m* académico; (*Scol*) año *m* escolar

academically [ˌækəˈdemɪkəlɪ] ADV **1** (*Scol, Univ*) • **an ~ gifted child** un niño con grandes dotes intelectuales • **~, the boy is below average** en los estudios el chico está por debajo del promedio • **she's outstanding ~** es muy brillante desde el punto de vista académico • **an ~ renowned professor** un catedrático de renombre en círculos universitarios • **an ~ sound argument** un argumento sólido desde el punto de vista intelectual
2 (= *theoretically*) • **to argue ~** dar razones puramente teóricas

academicals [ˌækəˈdemɪkəlz] NPL vestidura *fsing* universitaria

academician [əˌkædəˈmɪʃən] N académico/a *m/f*

academy [əˈkædəmɪ] N **1** (= *private college*) academia *f*; (*Scot*) instituto *m* (de segunda enseñanza), colegio *m* • **~ of music** conservatorio *m* • **~ for young ladies** colegio *m* para señoritas; ▹ **military, naval**
2 (= *learned society*) academia *f* • **the Spanish Academy** la Real Academia Española; ▹ **royal**
CPD ▸ **Academy Award** (*Cine*) galardón *m* de la Academia de Hollywood, Oscar *m*

acanthus [əˈkænθəs] N (PL: **acanthuses, acanthi**) acanto *m*

ACAS [ˈeɪkæs] N ABBR (*Brit*) (= **Advisory Conciliation and Arbitration Service**) ≈ IMAC *m*

acc. ABBR **1** (*Econ*) (= **account**) c/, c.[ta]
2 (*Ling*) = **accusative**

accede [ækˈsiːd] VI • **to ~ to 1** (= *assent to*) [+ *request*] acceder a; [+ *suggestion*] aceptar
2 (= *gain, enter into*) [+ *office, post*] tomar posesión de; [+ *party*] adherirse a; [+ *throne*] acceder a, subir a; [+ *treaty*] adherirse a

accelerate [ækˈseləreɪt] VT acelerar, apresurar • **~d depreciation** depreciación *f* acelerada • **~d program** (*US*) (*Univ*) curso *m* intensivo
VI (*esp Aut*) acelerar

acceleration [ækˌseləˈreɪʃən] N (*esp Aut*) aceleración *f*
CPD ▸ **acceleration clause** (*Econ*) provisión *f* para el vencimiento anticipado de una deuda

accelerator [ækˈseləreɪtəʳ] N (*Aut*) acelerador *m* • **to step on the ~** pisar el acelerador
CPD ▸ **accelerator pedal** pedal *m* del acelerador

accent N [ˈæksənt] **1** (*written*) acento *m* • **put an ~ on the "o"** pon un acento sobre la "o" • **acute ~** acento *m* agudo • **written ~** acento *m* ortográfico
2 (= *pronunciation*) acento *m* • **he has a French ~** tiene acento francés • **with a strong Andalusian ~** con (un) fuerte acento andaluz
3 (= *emphasis*) (*fig*) • **to put the ~ on** subrayar (la importancia de), recalcar • **the minister put the ~ on exports** el ministro recalcó la importancia de la exportación • **this year the ~ is on bright colours** (*Fashion*) este año están de moda los colores vivos
4 (*liter*) (= *tone*) • **in ~s of some surprise** en cierto tono de asombro
VT [ækˈsent] **1** [+ *syllable, word*] acentuar
2 [+ *need, difference*] recalcar, subrayar
3 [+ *colour, feature*] realzar
CPD [ˈæksənt] ▸ **accent mark** acento *m* ortográfico

accented [ækˈsentɪd] ADJ [*syllable*] acentuado; [*voice*] con acento

accentual [ækˈsentjʊəl] ADJ acentual

accentuate [ækˈsentjʊeɪt] VT **1** (*lit*) [+ *syllable, word*] acentuar
2 (*fig*) [+ *need, difference etc*] recalcar, subrayar; [+ *colour, feature*] realzar

accentuation [ækˌsentjʊˈeɪʃən] N acentuación *f*

accept [əkˈsept] VT **1** [+ *gift, invitation, apology, offer*] aceptar; [+ *report*] aprobar; (*Med*) [+ *transplant*] tolerar • **the Academy ~ed the word in 1970** la Academia admitió la palabra en 1970
2 [*machine*] [+ *coin*] admitir
3 (*Comm*) [+ *cheque, orders*] aceptar
4 (= *acknowledge*) reconocer, admitir; [+ *person*] admitir, acoger • **it is ~ed that …** se reconoce *or* admite que … • **I do not ~ that way of doing it** no apruebo ese modo de hacerlo • **to ~ responsibility for sth** asumir la responsabilidad de algo • **he was ~ed as one of us** se lo admitió *or* acogió como a uno de nosotros
VI aceptar, asentir

acceptability [əkˌseptəˈbɪlətɪ] N aceptabilidad *f*

acceptable [əkˈseptəbl] ADJ [*behaviour, plan, offer*] aceptable; [*gift*] grato • **that would not be ~ to the government** eso no le resultaría aceptable al gobierno • **that kind of behaviour is not socially ~** ese tipo de comportamiento no es socialmente aceptable

acceptably [əkˈseptəblɪ] ADV **1** (= *in the accepted manner*) [*behave, phrase*] de manera aceptable
2 (= *satisfactorily*) [*play, sing*] razonablemente bien • **inflation is now ~ low** la inflación es ahora lo suficientemente baja

acceptance [əkˈseptəns] N **1** [*of gift, invitation, apology, offer, cheque*] aceptación *f*
2 (= *approval*) aprobación *f*, acogida *f* • **to meet with general ~** tener una buena acogida general • **to win ~** lograr la aprobación
CPD ▸ **acceptance credit** crédito *m* de aceptación ▸ **acceptance speech** discurso *m* de recepción, discurso *m* de aceptación

acceptation [ˌæksepˈteɪʃən] N acepción *f*

accepted [əkˈseptɪd] ADJ [*fact, idea, practice*] reconocido, establecido • **it's the ~ thing** es lo establecido, es la norma • **he's an ~ expert** es un experto reconocido (como tal) • **it is not a socially ~ habit** es una costumbre que no es socialmente aceptable

accepting [əkˈseptɪŋ] ADJ • **to be ~ of sth/sb** aceptar algo/a algn

acceptor [əkˈseptəʳ] N aceptador(a) *m/f*; (*Comm*) aceptante *mf*

access [ˈækses] N **1** (= *entry etc*) acceso *m* • **a road was built to improve ~ to the property** se construyó una carretera para facilitar el acceso a la propiedad • **of easy ~** de fácil acceso • **to gain ~ (to)** (*lit*) lograr entrar (en) • **to gain ~ to sb** conseguir libre acceso a algn • **to give ~ to a room** comunicar con *or* dar acceso a una habitación • **this gives ~ to the garden** por aquí se sale al jardín • **to have ~ to sb** tener libre acceso a algn • **the house has ~ onto the park** la casa tiene salida al parque • **he had ~ to the family papers** tuvo acceso a los papeles de la familia, se le facilitaron los papeles de la familia • **to obtain legal ~ to a property** conseguir una autorización legal para entrar en una propiedad
2 (*Jur*) (*in divorce*) derecho *m* de visita
3 (*Comput*) acceso *m*
4 (= *sudden outburst*) acceso *m*, arrebato *m* • **he had a sudden ~ of generosity** tuvo un repentino acceso *or* arrebato de generosidad • **in an ~ of rage** en un arrebato *or* acceso de cólera
VT (*Comput*) [+ *file*] conseguir acceso a
CPD ▸ **access code** código *m* de acceso ▸ **access course** (*Brit*) curso *m* de acceso ▸ **access point** (*to place*) acceso *m*; (*to network, internet*) punto *m* de acceso ▸ **access provider** (*to internet*) proveedor *m* de acceso ▸ **access road** vía *f* de acceso ▸ **access time** (*Comput*) tiempo *m* de acceso ▸ **access visit** (*to child by parent*) visita *f*

accessary [ækˈsesərɪ] N = **accessory**

accessibility [ækˌsesɪˈbɪlɪtɪ] N [*of place*] facilidad *f* de acceso; [*of person*] lo asequible, carácter *m* abordable; [*of art, language*] accesibilidad *f* • **they want to increase the ~ of art to ordinary people** quieren hacer que el arte sea más accesible al ciudadano medio

accessible [ækˈsesəbl] ADJ **1** [*place*] accesible
2 (= *approachable*) [*person*] accesible, asequible
3 (= *understandable*) [*art, language*] accesible (**to** para)
4 (= *able to be influenced*) • **he is not ~ to reason** no escucha la razón, hace oídos sordos a la razón

accession [ækˈseʃən] N (*frm*) **1** (= *elevation*) (*to office, post*) entrada *f* en posesión (**to** de); [*of king, queen*] subida *f*, ascenso *m* (**to the throne** al trono) • **~ to power** subida *f or* ascenso *m* al poder
2 (= *consent*) (*to treaty*) accesión *f*, adherencia *f* (**to** a)
3 (= *entry, admission*) entrada *f* (**to** en)
4 (= *increase*) aumento
5 (*in library, museum*) (= *acquisition*) (nueva) adquisición *f*

accessorize [əkˈsesəˌraɪz] VT (*US*) [+ *dress*] comprar el bolso y los zapatos a juego con

accessory [ækˈsesərɪ] ADJ **1** (= *additional*) accesorio, secundario
2 (*Jur*) • **to be ~ to** ser cómplice de
N **1 accessories** (*Aut etc*) accesorios *mpl*; (*to outfit*) complementos *mpl*, accesorios *mpl* • **kitchen/bathroom accessories** accesorios *or* artículos *mpl* de cocina/baño
2 (*Jur*) cómplice *mf* (**to** de) • **~ after the fact** cómplice *mf* encubridor(a) • **~ before the fact** cómplice *mf*

accidence [ˈæksɪdəns] N accidentes *mpl*

accident [ˈæksɪdənt] N **1** (= *mishap*) accidente *m* • **to meet with** *or* **have an ~** tener *or* sufrir un accidente • IDIOM: • **it's an ~ waiting to happen** es un peligro en potencia • PROVERB: • **~s will happen** son cosas que pasan; ▹ **road**
2 (= *unforeseen event*) casualidad *f* • **by ~** (= *by chance*) por *or* de casualidad; (= *unintentionally*) sin querer, involuntariamente • **by some ~ I found myself there** me encontré allí por accidente • **more by ~ than design** más por casualidad que por intención • **I'm sorry, it was an ~** lo siento, lo hice sin querer • **it's no ~ that …** no es casualidad *or* casual que …
3 (*Geol, Philos*) accidente *m*
CPD ▸ **Accident and Emergency Department, accident and emergency** (*in hospital*) Urgencias *fpl* ▸ **accident black spot** punto *m* negro, punto *m* de alta siniestralidad ▸ **(road) accident figures** cifras *fpl* de accidentes (en carretera)

▸ **accident insurance** seguro *m* contra accidentes ▸ **accident prevention** prevención *f* de accidentes ▸ **(road) accident statistics** estadísticas *fpl* de accidentes (en carretera)

accidental [ˌæksɪˈdentl] ADJ **1** (= *by chance*) casual, fortuito • **~ death** muerte *f* por accidente
2 (= *unintentional*) imprevisto • **I didn't do it deliberately, it was ~** no lo hice adrede, fue sin querer
N (*Mus*) accidente *m*

accidentally [ˌæksɪˈdentəlɪ] ADV **1** (= *by chance*) por casualidad • **we met quite ~** nos encontramos por pura casualidad
2 (= *unintentionally*) sin querer, involuntariamente • **he was ~ killed** fue muerto por accidente • **the liquids were ~ mixed** los líquidos se mezclaron por descuido • IDIOM: • **~ on purpose*** sin querer y no tan sin querer

accident-prone [ˈæksɪdəntˌprəʊn] ADJ propenso a los accidentes • **he's very accident-prone** es muy propenso a los accidentes

acclaim [əˈkleɪm] VT **1** (= *praise*) aclamar, alabar • **the play was ~ed** la obra fue aclamada
2 (= *proclaim*) aclamar • **he was ~ed king** lo aclamaron rey
N (= *praise*) alabanza *f*, aclamación *f*; (= *applause*) aplausos *mpl* • **the book met with great ~** el libro tuvo una extraordinaria acogida, el libro recibió encendidos elogios

acclaimed [əˈkleɪmd] ADJ [*person, artist, work of art*] célebre • **highly ~** muy célebre

acclamation [ˌækləˈmeɪʃən] N **1** (= *approval*) aclamación *f*
2 (= *applause*) aplausos *mpl*, vítores *mpl* (*more frm*) • **amid the ~s of the crowd** entre los aplausos *or* (*more frm*) vítores de la multitud • **to be chosen by ~** ser elegido por aclamación

acclimate [əˈklaɪmət] VT, VI (*US*) = **acclimatize**

acclimation [ˌæklaɪˈmeɪʃən] N (*US*) = **acclimatization**

acclimatization [əˌklaɪmətaɪˈzeɪʃən], **acclimation** (*US*) [ˌæklaɪˈmeɪʃən] N aclimatación *f*

acclimatize [əˈklaɪmətaɪz], **acclimate** (*US*) [əˈklaɪmət] VT aclimatar (**to** a) • **to ~ o.s.** aclimatarse (**to** a)
VI aclimatarse (**to** a)

acclivity [əˈklɪvɪtɪ] N subida *f*, cuesta *f*

accolade [ˈækəʊleɪd] N **1** (= *praise*) elogio *m* entusiasta; (= *honour*) honor *m*; (= *award*) galardón *m*, premio *m*
2 (*Hist*) acolada *f*, espaldarazo *m*

accommodate [əˈkɒmədeɪt] VT **1** (= *lodge, put up*) [+ *person*] alojar, hospedar • **can you ~ four people in July?** ¿tiene usted habitaciones para cuatro personas en julio?
2 (= *have space for*) tener cabida para • **this car ~s six** este coche tiene cabida *or* asientos para seis personas • **can you ~ two more in your car?** ¿caben dos más en tu coche?
3 (= *reconcile*) [+ *differences*] acomodar, concertar; [+ *quarrel*] poner fin a; [+ *quarrellers*] reconciliar
4 (= *adapt*) acomodar, adaptar (**to** a)
5 (= *supply*) proveer (**with** de) • **to ~ sb with a loan** facilitar un préstamo a algn
6 (= *oblige*) complacer, hacer un favor a
VI [*eye*] adaptarse (**to** a)

accommodating [əˈkɒmədeɪtɪŋ] ADJ (= *helpful*) servicial, complaciente; (= *easy to deal with*) acomodadizo, acomodaticio

accommodation [əˌkɒməˈdeɪʃən] N **1** (*also US* **accommodations**) (= *lodging*) alojamiento *m*; (= *rooms*) habitaciones *fpl* • **have you any ~ available?** ¿tiene usted habitaciones disponibles? • **to book ~ in a hotel** reservar una habitación en un hotel • **"accommodation to let"** "se alquilan habitaciones"
2 (= *space*) lugar *m*, cabida *f* • **there is ~ for 20 passengers** hay lugar para 20 pasajeros • **there is standing ~ only** hay sitio solamente para estar de pie • **the plane has limited ~** el avión tiene un número limitado de plazas
3 (= *agreement*) acuerdo *m* • **to reach an ~ with creditors** llegar a un acuerdo con los acreedores
4 (= *adaptation*) acomodación *f*, adaptación *f*
5 (= *loan*) crédito *m*, préstamo *m*
CPD ▸ **accommodation address** domicilio *f* postal ▸ **accommodation bill** (*Comm*) pagaré *m* de favor ▸ **accommodation bureau** oficina *f* de hospedaje ▸ **accommodation note** = **accommodation bill** ▸ **accommodation train** (*US*) tren *m* de cercanías

accompaniment [əˈkʌmpənɪmənt] N (*also Mus*) acompañamiento *m* • **they marched to the ~ of a military band** desfilaban al compás de una banda militar

accompanist [əˈkʌmpənɪst] N (*Mus*) acompañante/a *m/f*

accompany [əˈkʌmpənɪ] VT **1** (= *escort*) acompañar • **to be accompanied by sb** ir acompañado de algn
2 (*fig*) acompañar • **accompanied by** acompañado de • **he accompanied this with a grimace** esto lo dijo acompañado de una mueca, al decir esto hizo una mueca
3 (*Mus*) acompañar (**on the violin/piano** con el violín/al piano) • **to ~ o.s. on the piano** acompañarse al piano

accompanying letter [əˌkʌmpənɪɪŋˈletəʳ] N carta *f* adjunta

accompli [əˈkɒmpliː] ▹ **fait accompli**

accomplice [əˈkʌmplɪs] N cómplice *mf*

accomplish [əˈkʌmplɪʃ] VT **1** (= *achieve*) efectuar, lograr; [+ *task, mission*] llevar a cabo; [+ *purpose, one's design*] realizar
2 (= *finish*) terminar, concluir

accomplished [əˈkʌmplɪʃt] ADJ **1** [*pianist etc*] experto, consumado; [*performance*] logrado
2 [*fact*] consumado

accomplishment [əˈkʌmplɪʃmənt] N **1** (= *achievement*) logro *m* • **a great ~** un gran logro • **it's quite an ~ to** (+ *infin*) exige mucho talento (+ *infin*) • **her ~ in finishing the film although ill** su logro de terminar la película a pesar de estar enferma
2 (= *completion, fulfilment*) realización *f* • **difficult of ~** de difícil consecución
3 (= *skill*) talento *m*; **accomplishments** talento *m*, dotes *fpl*

accord [əˈkɔːd] N **1** (= *harmony*) acuerdo *m*, armonía *f* • **with one ~** de *or* por común acuerdo • **to be in ~** estar de acuerdo (**with** con), estar en armonía (**with** con) • **of his/her own ~** espontáneamente, (de) motu proprio
2 (= *treaty*) acuerdo *m*
VT [+ *welcome, praise*] dar (**to** a); [+ *honour*] conceder (**to** a)
VI concordar, armonizar (**with** con)

accordance [əˈkɔːdəns] N • **in ~ with** conforme a, de acuerdo con

according [əˈkɔːdɪŋ] ADV **1** • **~ to** según; (= *in accordance with*) conforme a, de acuerdo con • **~ to him ...** según él ... • **~ to what he told me** según me dijo • **it went ~ to plan** salió conforme a *or* de acuerdo con nuestros *etc* planes • **classified ~ to size** clasificado por *or* según tamaños • **to play the game ~ to the rules** jugar siguiendo las reglas
2 • **~ as** según que, a medida que

accordingly [əˈkɔːdɪŋlɪ] ADV
1 (= *correspondingly*) • **it is a difficult job and he should be paid ~** es un trabajo difícil y debería recibir un pago acorde • **to act ~** actuar en consecuencia
2 (= *therefore*) por consiguiente, por lo tanto • **the text was too long and the editor ~ cut it by 20%** el texto era demasiado largo y por consiguiente *or* por lo tanto el editor lo acortó un 20%

accordion [əˈkɔːdɪən] N acordeón *m*

accordionist [əˈkɔːdɪənɪst] N acordeonista *mf*

accost [əˈkɒst] VT abordar • **he ~ed me in the street** me abordó en la calle, se dirigió a mí en la calle • **he ~ed me for a light** se acercó a mí para pedir fuego

accouchement [əˈkuːʃmɑ̃ːŋ] N (*frm*) parto *m*

account [əˈkaʊnt] N **1** (*Comm, Econ*) (*at shop*) cuenta *f*; (= *invoice*) factura *f*; (= *bank account*) cuenta *f* (bancaria) • **they have the Blotto ~** (*Advertising*) ellos hacen la publicidad de Blotto • **cash or ~?** ¿en metálico o a cuenta? • **to charge sth to sb's ~** cargar algo en cuenta a algn • **to close an ~** liquidar una cuenta • **payment on ~** pago *m* a cuenta • **to get £50 on ~** recibir 50 libras anticipadas • **to put £50 down on ~** cargar 50 libras a la cuenta • **to buy sth on ~** comprar algo a cuenta • **to open an ~** abrir una cuenta • **~ payable** cuenta *f* por pagar • **"~ payee only"** "únicamente en cuenta del beneficiario" • **~ receivable** cuenta *f* por cobrar • **to render an ~** pasar factura • **~ rendered** cuenta *f* pasada • **to settle an ~** liquidar una cuenta • **to settle ~s (with)** (*fig*) ajustar cuentas (con) • **statement of ~** estado *m* de cuenta • **the Account** (*St Ex*) periodo *m* (de 15 días) al fin del cual se ajustan las cuentas; ▹ **current, deposit, joint**
2 accounts (*Comm*) (= *calculations*) cuentas *fpl*; (= *department*) (sección *f* de) contabilidad *f* • **to keep the ~s** llevar las cuentas
3 (= *report*) informe *m* • **by all ~s** a decir de todos, según se dice • **by** *or* **according to her own ~** por lo que dice ella • **to give an ~ of** dar cuenta de, informar sobre • **to keep an ~ of** [+ *events*] guardar relación de; [+ *amounts*] llevar cuentas de
4 (= *consideration*) consideración *f* • **on no ~** • **not on any ~** de ninguna manera, bajo ningún concepto • **on that ~** por eso • **on his ~** por él, en su nombre • **on his own ~** por cuenta propia • **on ~ of** (= *because of*) a causa de; (*esp US**) (= *because*) porque, debido a que • **I couldn't do it on ~ of my back's sore*** no he podido hacerlo porque me duele la espalda • **to leave sth out of ~** no tomar algo en consideración *or* cuenta • **to take ~ of sth** • **take sth into ~** tener algo en cuenta *or* consideración, tener algo presente • **to take no ~ of** no tomar *or* no tener en cuenta
5 (= *importance*) importancia *f* • **of no** *or* **little** *or* **small ~** de poca importancia • **of some ~** de cierta importancia, de alguna consideración
6 (= *explanation*) • **to bring** *or* **call sb to ~** pedir cuentas a algn • **to give an ~ of o.s.** justificar su conducta • **to give a good ~ of oneself** (= *perform well*) tener una buena actuación; (= *make good impression*) causar buena impresión • **to be held to ~ for sth** ser obligado a rendir cuentas por algo
7 (= *benefit*) • **to put** *or* **turn sth to (good) ~** aprovechar algo, sacar provecho de algo
VT (*frm*) considerar, creer • **I ~ him a fool** lo

considero un tonto • **I ~ myself lucky** me considero afortunado • **he is ~ed an expert** se le considera un experto • **I should ~ it a favour if ...** agradecería que ...
CPD ▸ **account balance** saldo *m* de la cuenta ▸ **account book** libro *m* de cuentas ▸ **account day** día *m* de liquidación ▸ **account holder** titular *mf* de cuenta, cuentahabiente *mf* (*Mex*) ▸ **account number** (*at bank etc*) número *m* de cuenta ▸ **accounts department** sección *f* or departamento *m* de contabilidad
▸ **account for** VI + PREP **1** (= *explain*) explicar, justificar • **how do you ~ for it?** ¿cómo lo explica *or* justifica usted? • **I cannot ~ for it** no me lo explico • **that ~s for it** esa es la razón *or* la explicación • IDIOM: • **there's no ~ing for taste(s)** sobre gustos no hay nada escrito
2 (= *give reckoning of*) [+ *actions, expenditure*] dar cuenta de, responder de • **everything is now ~ed for** ya se ha dado cuenta de todo, todo está completo ya • **many are still not ~ed for** aún se desconoce la suerte que han corrido muchas personas
3 (= *represent*) representar, suponer • **children ~ for 5% of the audience** los niños representan *or* suponen el 5 por ciento de la audiencia
4 (= *destroy, kill*) acabar con • **one bomb ~ed for the power station** una bomba acabó con la central eléctrica • **they ~ed for three stags** mataron tres ciervos • **the ship ~ed for three enemy aircraft** el barco derribó tres aviones enemigos
accountability [əˌkaʊntəˈbɪlətɪ] N responsabilidad *f*
accountable [əˈkaʊntəbl] ADJ responsable (**for** de, **to** ante) • **not ~ for one's actions** no responsable de los propios actos • **he is ~ only to himself** solo se da cuentas a sí mismo, solo se siente responsable ante sí mismo
accountancy [əˈkaʊntənsɪ] N contabilidad *f*
accountant [əˈkaʊntənt] N contable *mf*, contador(a) *m/f* (*LAm*); (*in bank etc*) economista *mf* • **~'s office** contaduría *f*; ▹ **chartered**
accounting [əˈkaʊntɪŋ] N contabilidad *f*
CPD ▸ **accounting department** (*US*) departamento *m* de contabilidad, sección *f* de contabilidad ▸ **accounting period** periodo *m* contable, ejercicio *m* financiero
accoutred, accoutered (*US*) [əˈkuːtəd] PP, ADJ (*liter*) equipado (**with** de)
accoutrements [əˈkuːtrəmənts], **accouterments** (*US*) [əˈkuːtəmənts] NPL (*frm*) equipo *msing*, avíos *mpl*
accredit [əˈkredɪt] VT **1** (= *credit*) atribuir (**to** a) • **to ~ a quality to sb** • **~ sb with a quality** atribuir una cualidad a algn
2 (= *recognize*) [+ *qualification*] reconocer (oficialmente); [+ *representative, body*] autorizar, acreditar
3 (= *appoint*) acreditar • **to ~ an ambassador to** acreditar a algn como embajador en
accreditation [əˌkredɪˈteɪʃən] N reconocimiento *m* (oficial); (*US*) (*Scol, Univ*) habilitación *f* de enseñanza
CPD ▸ **accreditation officer** (*US*) (*Scol*) inspector(a) *m/f* de enseñanza
accredited [əˈkredɪtɪd] ADJ [*source, supplier, agent*] autorizado
accretion [əˈkriːʃən] N aumento *m*, acrecentamiento *m*
accrual [əˈkruəl] N acumulación *f*
CPD ▸ **accrual rate** tasa *f* de acumulación
accrue [əˈkruː] (*frm*) VI (= *mount up*) acumularse (*also Fin*) • **to ~ from** proceder de • **to ~ to** corresponder a • **some benefit will ~ to you from this** de esto resultará algo a beneficio de usted
CPD ▸ **accrued charges** gastos *mpl* vencidos ▸ **accrued income** renta *f* acumulada ▸ **accrued interest** interés *m* acumulado
acct ABBR (= **account**) c/, c.[ta]
acculturate [əˈkʌltʃəˌreɪt] VT (*frm*) aculturar
acculturation [əˌkʌltʃəˈreɪʃən] N (*frm*) aculturación *f*
accumulate [əˈkjuːmjʊleɪt] VT acumular
VI acumularse
CPD ▸ **accumulated depreciation** depreciación *f* acumulada
accumulation [əˌkjuːmjʊˈleɪʃən] N
1 (= *amassing*) acumulación *f*, acopio *m*
2 (= *mass*) montón *m*
accumulative [əˈkjuːmjʊlətɪv] ADJ acumulativo
accumulator [əˈkjuːmjʊleɪtəʳ] N **1** (*Elec, Comput*) acumulador *m*
2 (*Brit*) (= *bet*) apuesta *f* múltiple acumulativa
accuracy [ˈækjʊrəsɪ] N [*of measurement, figures, clock*] exactitud *f*; [*of instrument*] precisión *f*; [*of translation, copy, words, description*] fidelidad *f*, exactitud *f*; [*of forecast*] lo acertado; [*of aim, shot*] lo certero • **~ is very important for a good typist** no cometer errores es muy importante para un buen mecanógrafo • **they were impressed by the typist's ~** estaban impresionados por la falta de errores en el trabajo del mecanógrafo
accurate [ˈækjʊrɪt] ADJ [*number, measurement, figure, calculation*] exacto; [*instrument, scales*] preciso; [*translation, copy, information, description, memory*] fiel, exacto; [*observation, answer, forecast*] acertado; [*instructions*] preciso; [*shot, aim*] certero; [*missile*] de gran precisión; [*typist*] que no comete errores • **is that clock ~?** ¿tiene ese reloj la hora exacta? • **~ spelling is important** escribir sin faltas es muy importante • **it was his father or, to be ~, his stepfather** era su padre o, para ser exacto, su padrastro • **to be strictly ~ ...** para ser más preciso *or* exacto ... • **the newspaper has been ~ in its reports** el periódico ha informado fielmente de los hechos en sus reportajes • **the tests are 90% ~ in identifying future victims** los análisis aciertan al detectar futuras víctimas en un 90 por ciento de los casos • **clocks that are ~ to one second in 40 million years** relojes que no pierden ni ganan más de un segundo en 40 millones de años • **the scales are ~ to half a gram** la balanza tiene un margen de error de solo medio gramo
accurately [ˈækjʊrɪtlɪ] ADV [*measure*] con exactitud; [*calculate*] exactamente; [*reflect, translate, copy, draw*] fielmente, exactamente; [*inform, describe*] fielmente, con exactitud; [*predict*] con exactitud; [*shoot, aim*] certeramente
accursed†, **accurst**† [əˈkɜːst] ADJ (*liter*) maldito; (= *ill-fated*) infausto, desventurado • **~ be he who ...!** ¡maldito sea quien ...!, ¡mal haya quien ...!
accusal [əˈkjuːzl] N (*Jur*) acusación *f*
accusation [ˌækjʊˈzeɪʃən] N (= *charge*) acusación *f*
accusative [əˈkjuːzətɪv] (*Ling*) ADJ acusativo
N (*also* **accusative case**) acusativo *m* • **in the ~** en acusativo
accusatorial [əˌkjuːzəˈtɔːrɪəl] ADJ = **accusatory**
accusatory [əˈkjuːzətərɪ] ADJ [*remark*] acusatorio; [*glance, gesture, manner*] acusador
accuse [əˈkjuːz] VT • **to ~ sb (of)** acusar a algn (de) • **he stands ~d of ...** se le acusa de ...
accused [əˈkjuːzd] N • **the ~** (*Jur*) (*sing*) el/la acusado/a; (*pl*) los/las acusados/as
accuser [əˈkjuːzəʳ] N acusador(a) *m/f*
accusing [əˈkjuːzɪŋ] ADJ [*look, eyes*] acusador • **in an ~ voice** en tono acusador • **to point an ~ finger at sb** (*lit*) señalar a algn con un dedo acusador; (*fig*) acusar a algn
accusingly [əˈkjuːzɪŋlɪ] ADV [*say*] en tono acusador • **she looked at me ~** me lanzó una mirada acusadora • **she pointed at Derek ~** señaló a Derek con un dedo acusador
accustom [əˈkʌstəm] VT acostumbrar, habituar (**to** a) • **to ~ sb to (doing) sth** acostumbrar a algn a (hacer) algo • **to ~ o.s. to (doing) sth** acostumbrarse a (hacer) algo • **to be ~ed to (doing) sth** estar acostumbrado a (hacer) algo • **to get ~ed to (doing) sth** acostumbrarse a (hacer) algo
accustomed [əˈkʌstəmd] ADJ acostumbrado, usual
AC/DC [ˌeɪsɪːˈdiːsiː] N ABBR = **alternating current/direct current**
ADJ • **he's ~‡** es bisexual
ACE N ABBR (*US*) = **American Council on Education**
ace [eɪs] N **1** (*Cards*) as *m* • IDIOMS: • **to be within an ace of** estar a punto *or* a dos dedos de • **to keep an ace up one's sleeve** • **have an ace in the hole** (*US**) guardar un triunfo en la mano, guardarse un as en la manga • **to play one's ace** jugar su triunfo • **to hold all the aces** tener la sartén por el mango
2 (*Tennis*) ace *m*
3 (= *pilot, racing driver etc*) as *m* • **he's aces** (*US**) es fenomenal*
ADJ* estupendo*, de aúpa* • **ace player** as *m*
CPD ▸ **Ace bandage**® (*US*) venda *f* elástica
acephalous [əˈsefələs] ADJ acéfalo
acerbic [əˈsɜːbɪk] ADJ **1** [*taste*] acre, acerbo
2 (*fig*) mordaz, cáustico
acerbity [əˈsɜːbɪtɪ] N **1** [*of taste*] acritud *f*, aspereza *f*
2 (*fig*) mordacidad *f*
acetate [ˈæsɪteɪt] N acetato *m*
acetic [əˈsiːtɪk] ADJ acético
CPD ▸ **acetic acid** ácido *m* acético
acetone [ˈæsɪtəʊn] N acetona *f*
acetylene [əˈsetɪliːn] N acetileno *m*
CPD ▸ **acetylene burner** soplete *m* oxiacetilénico ▸ **acetylene lamp** lámpara *f* de acetileno ▸ **acetylene torch** soplete *m* oxiacetilénico ▸ **acetylene welding** soldadura *f* oxiacetilénica
ache [eɪk] N (= *pain*) dolor *m* • **I have an ~ in my side** me duele el costado • **full of ~s and pains** lleno de achaques *or* goteras* • IDIOM: • **with an ~ in one's heart** con mucho pesar
VI **1** (= *hurt*) doler • **my head ~s** me duele la cabeza • **it makes my head ~** me da dolor de cabeza • **I'm aching all over** me duele todo
2 (*fig*) • **it was enough to make your heart ~** era para romperle a uno el alma • **my heart ~s for you** lo siento en el alma
3 (= *yearn*) desear, suspirar (**for** por) • **I am aching for you** suspiro por ti • **I am aching to see you again** me muero por volver a verte • **I ~d to help** me moría por ayudar
achievable [əˈtʃiːvəbl] ADJ alcanzable • **an aim readily ~** un propósito fácil de alcanzar
achieve [əˈtʃiːv] VT (= *reach*) conseguir, alcanzar; (= *complete*) llevar a cabo; (= *accomplish*) realizar • **he will never ~ anything** él no hará nunca nada • **what do you hope to ~ by that?** ¿qué esperas lograr con eso?
VI (= *be successful*) avanzar, hacer progresos

• **the children are not achieving as they should** los niños no avanzan *or* hacen los progresos que debieran

achievement [ə'tʃi:vmənt] (N) **1** (= *act*) realización *f*, consecución *f*
2 (= *thing achieved*) logro *m*, éxito *m* • **that's quite an ~** es todo un logro *or* éxito, es toda una hazaña • **among his many ~s** entre los muchos éxitos *or* las muchas hazañas en su haber
3 (*Scol*) • **the level of ~** el nivel de rendimiento escolar; ▷ **record**

achiever [ə'tʃi:vəʳ] (N) (*also* **high achiever**) *persona que realiza su potencial or que llega muy alto*

Achilles [ə'kɪli:z] (N) Aquiles
(CPD) ▸ **Achilles heel** talón *m* de Aquiles ▸ **Achilles tendon** tendón *m* de Aquiles

aching ['eɪkɪŋ] (ADJ) **1** [*tooth, feet*] dolorido, que duele
2 (*fig*) • **with an ~ heart** con mucho pesar
(N) dolor *m*

achingly ['eɪkɪŋlɪ] (ADV) • **she sang three ~ beautiful ballads** cantó tres baladas de una belleza imposible de creer • **her progress has been ~ slow** su progreso ha sido de una lentitud exasperante

achromatic [,ækrəʊ'mætɪk] (ADJ) acromático

achy* ['eɪkɪ] (ADJ) dolorido • **to feel ~** sentirse dolorido • **I feel ~ all over** me duele todo

acid ['æsɪd] (N) **1** (*Chem*) ácido *m*
2‡ (= *drug*) ácido* *m* • **to drop ~** consumir ácido
(ADJ) **1** (= *not alkaline*) [*soil, food, conditions*] ácido
2 (= *sharp, bitter*) [*fruit, taste*] ácido
3 (*fig*) [*remark, tone*] mordaz; [*voice*] agrio, mordaz • **to have an ~ tongue** tener la lengua viperina
(CPD) ▸ **acid drops** (*Brit*) caramelos *mpl* ácidos ▸ **acid green** verde *m* limón ▸ **acid head**‡ (*Drugs*) adicto/a *m/f* al ácido ▸ **acid house (music)** música *f* acid ▸ **acid house party** fiesta *f* acid ▸ **acid rain** lluvia *f* ácida ▸ **acid rock** (*Mus*) rock *m* acid ▸ **the acid test** (*fig*) la prueba de fuego, la prueba decisiva ▸ **acid yellow** amarillo *m* limón

acidic [ə'sɪdɪk] (ADJ) ácido

acidifier [ə'sɪdɪfaɪəʳ] (N) acidulante *m*

acidify [ə'sɪdɪfaɪ] (VT) acidificar
(VI) acidificarse

acidity [ə'sɪdɪtɪ] (N) acidez *f*

acidly ['æsɪdlɪ] (ADV) [*comment, reply*] mordazmente

acidophilous [,æsɪ'dɒfɪləs] (ADJ) acidófilo

acid-proof ['æsɪdpru:f], **acid-resisting** ['æsɪdrɪ'zɪstɪŋ] (ADJ) a prueba de ácidos

acidulant [ə'sɪdjʊlənt] (N) acidulante *m*

acidulous [ə'sɪdjʊləs] (ADJ) acídulo

ack-ack* ['æk'æk] (N) (= *gunfire*) fuego *m* antiaéreo; (= *guns*) artillería *f* antiaérea
(CPD) ▸ **ack-ack fire** fuego *m* antiaéreo ▸ **ack-ack gun** cañón *m* antiaéreo

acknowledge [ək'nɒlɪdʒ] (VT) **1** (= *admit*) reconocer; [+ *claim, truth*] admitir; [+ *crime*] confesarse culpable de • **I ~ that ...** reconozco que ... • **to ~ defeat** darse por vencido • **to ~ that sb is superior** • **~ sb as superior** reconocer que algn es mejor • **to ~ sb as leader** reconocer a algn como jefe • **I ~ myself the loser** reconozco que he perdido • **she ~d herself in the wrong** reconoció que estaba equivocada
2 (= *thank for*) [+ *favour, gift*] agradecer, dar las gracias por
3 (*also* **acknowledge receipt of**) [+ *letter*] acusar recibo de
4 (= *greet*) [+ *person*] saludar; (= *reply to*) [+ *greeting*] contestar a

acknowledged [ək'nɒlɪdʒd] (ADJ) • **an ~ expert** un experto reconocido como tal • **a generally ~ fact** un hecho generalmente reconocido

acknowledgement [ək'nɒlɪdʒmənt] (N) **1** (= *admission*) admisión *f*; (= *recognition*) reconocimiento *m* • **in ~ of** en reconocimiento de, en agradecimiento a • **I wish to make public ~ of the help** quiero agradecer públicamente la ayuda • **to make ~s** expresar su agradecimiento
2 (*Comm*) [*of letter etc*] acuse *m* de recibo
3 [*of greeting*] contestación *f*
4 • **to quote sb without ~** citar a algn sin mencionar la fuente; **acknowledgements** (*in book*) menciones *fpl*
(CPD) ▸ **acknowledgement slip** acuse *m* de recibo

ACLU (N ABBR) = **American Civil Liberties Union**

> **ACLU**
> La **American Civil Liberties Union** o **ACLU** es una organización no partidista que se fundó en 1920 para proteger los derechos de los ciudadanos estadounidenses tal y como lo establece la Constitución. La **ACLU** presta su apoyo en los tribunales cuando se trata de casos de violación de las libertades del ciudadano, especialmente en circunstancias de discriminación por motivos de religión, raza, color o sexo, o en casos relacionados con la libertad de expresión. Esta organización jugó un papel importante en la lucha contra la segregación racial. Sin embargo, debido a su defensa de la libertad total, también ha apoyado marchas del Partido Nazi Americano y del Ku Klux Klan, decisiones que han creado mucha polémica.

acme ['ækmɪ] (N) colmo *m*, cima *f* • **the ~ of perfection** la suma perfección, el colmo de la perfección • **he is the ~ of good taste** es el buen gusto en persona

acne ['æknɪ] (N) acné *m*
(CPD) ▸ **acne rosacea** acné *m* rosáceo

acolyte ['ækəʊlaɪt] (N) **1** (*Rel*) acólito *m*, monaguillo *m*
2 (*fig*) acólito/a *m/f*

aconite ['ækənaɪt] (N) acónito *m*

acorn ['eɪkɔ:n] (N) bellota *f*

acoustic [ə'ku:stɪk] (ADJ) acústico
(CPD) ▸ **acoustic coupler** acoplador *m* acústico ▸ **acoustic guitar** guitarra *f* acústica ▸ **acoustic nerve** nervio *m* auditivo ▸ **acoustic screen** panel *m* acústico ▸ **acoustic shock** (*Telec*) choque *m or* shock *m* acústico

acoustically [ə'ku:stɪklɪ] (ADV) [*poor, perfect*] desde el punto de vista acústico; [*record*] acústicamente

acoustics [ə'ku:stɪks] (N) **1** (*with sing vb*) (*Phys*) acústica *f*
2 (*with pl vb*) [*of hall etc*] acústica *f*

ACPO ['ækpəʊ] (N ABBR) (*Brit*) = **Association of Chief Police Officers**

acquaint [ə'kweɪnt] (VT) **1** (= *inform*) • **to ~ sb with sth** informar a algn de *or* sobre algo • **to ~ o.s. with sth** informarse sobre algo
2 (= *know*) • **to be ~ed** conocerse • **to be ~ed with** [+ *person*] conocer; [+ *fact*] saber; [+ *situation*] estar enterado *or* al corriente de • **to become ~ed with** [+ *person*] (llegar a) conocer; [+ *fact*] saber; [+ *situation*] ponerse al tanto de

acquaintance [ə'kweɪntəns] (N) **1** (*with person*) relación *f*; (*with subject etc*) conocimiento *m* • **to make sb's ~** conocer a algn • **I am very glad to make your ~** tengo mucho gusto en conocerlo • **a plumber of my ~** un fontanero que conozco • **I don't have the honour of her ~** no tengo el honor de conocerla • **it improves on ~** mejora a medida que lo vas conociendo • **on closer** *or* **further ~ it seems less attractive** al conocerlo mejor tiene menos atracción • **to renew (one's) ~ with sb** reanudar la amistad con algn; ▷ **nod**
2 (= *person*) conocido/a *m/f* • **an ~ of mine** un conocido mío • **we're just ~s** nos conocemos ligeramente nada más • **we're old ~s** nos conocemos desde hace tiempo • **to have a wide circle of ~s** conocer a muchas personas
(CPD) ▸ **acquaintance rape** *violación en la que la víctima conoce al violador*

acquaintanceship [ə'kweɪntənsʃɪp] (N) **1** (*between two people*) relaciones *fpl*
2 (= *knowledge*) conocimiento *m* (**with** de), familiaridad *f* (**with** con)

acquiesce [,ækwɪ'es] (VI) (= *agree*) consentir (**in** en), conformarse (**in** con); (*unwillingly*) someterse, doblegarse

acquiescence [,ækwɪ'esns] (N) aquiescencia *f* (**in** a, en), consentimiento *m* (**in** para)

acquiescent [,ækwɪ'esnt] (ADJ) conforme, aquiescente • **he was perfectly ~** se mostró completamente conforme • **he is ~ by nature** por su naturaleza se conforma con todo

acquire [ə'kwaɪəʳ] (VT) [+ *possessions*] (= *get*) adquirir, obtener; (= *manage to get*) conseguir; [+ *habit, reputation, native language*] adquirir; [+ *foreign language*] aprender; [+ *territory*] tomar posesión de; [+ *colour, tint*] adquirir, tomar • **where did you ~ that?** ¿dónde conseguiste eso? • **I seem to have ~d a strange umbrella** parece que he tomado el paraguas de otro • **to ~ a name for honesty** ganarse fama de honrado; ▷ **taste**

acquired [ə'kwaɪəd] (ADJ) adquirido • **an ~ taste** un gusto adquirido
(CPD) ▸ **acquired immune deficiency syndrome** síndrome *m* de inmunodeficiencia adquirida

acquirement [ə'kwaɪəmənt] (N) **1** [*of possessions*] adquisición *f*, obtención *f*
2 acquirements (*frm*) (= *skills*) conocimientos *mpl*

acquirer [ə'kwaɪərəʳ] (N) (*Comm, Econ*) adquirente *mf*

acquisition [,ækwɪ'zɪʃən] (N) **1** (= *act, purchased object*) adquisición *f*
2 (*Comm*) [*of company*] absorción *f*

acquisitive [ə'kwɪzɪtɪv] (ADJ) codicioso • **the ~ society** la sociedad de consumo

acquisitiveness [ə'kwɪzɪtɪvnɪs] (N) codicia *f*

acquit [ə'kwɪt] (VT) **1** (*Jur*) • **to ~ sb (of)** absolver *or* exculpar a algn (de) • **he was ~ted on all charges** lo absolvieron de todas las acusaciones
2 • **to ~ o.s.: how did he ~ himself?** ¿cómo se desenvolvió? • **to ~ o.s. well** defenderse bien • **to ~ o.s. of** [+ *duty*] desempeñar

acquittal [ə'kwɪtl] (N) (*Jur*) absolución *f*, exculpación *f*

acre ['eɪkəʳ] (N) acre *m* (*4.047 metros cuadrados*) • **the family's broad** *or* **rolling ~s** las extensas fincas de la familia • **there are ~s of space for you to play in*** hay la mar de espacio para que juguéis* • **I've got ~s of weeds*** tengo un montón de malas hierbas*

acreage ['eɪkərɪdʒ] (N) superficie *f* medida en acres, extensión *f* medida en acres • **the 1990 wheat ~** el área sembrada de trigo en 1990 • **what ~ do you have here?** ¿cuánto miden estos terrenos?, ¿qué extensión tiene esta tierra? • **they farm a large ~** cultivan unos terrenos muy extensos

a

acrid ['ækrɪd] (ADJ) **1** (*lit*) [*smell, taste*] acre, punzante
2 (*fig*) áspero, mordaz
Acrilan® ['ækrɪlæn] (N) acrilán® *m*
acrimonious [,ækrɪ'məʊnɪəs] (ADJ) [*argument*] reñido, enconado; [*debate, meeting, exchange*] reñido; [*divorce, break-up*] amargo; [*remark*] mordaz, cáustico
acrimoniously [,ækrɪ'məʊnɪəslɪ] (ADV) [*argue*] enconadamente; [*end, break up*] amargamente; [*say*] mordazmente
acrimony ['ækrɪmənɪ] (N) acritud *f*, acrimonia *f* • **there has been no ~ between us** no ha habido acritud *or* acrimonia entre nosotros • **their first meeting ended in ~** su primera reunión acabó en una disputa enconada
acrobat ['ækrəbæt] (N) acróbata *mf*
acrobatic [,ækrəʊ'bætɪk] (ADJ) acrobático
acrobatics [,ækrəʊ'bætɪks] (NPL) acrobacia *fsing*; (*as profession*) acrobacia *fsing*, acrobatismo *msing*; (*Aer*) vuelo *msing* acrobático • **mental/verbal ~** malabarismos *mpl* mentales/verbales
acronym ['ækrənɪm] (N) sigla(s) *f(pl)*, acrónimo *m*
Acropolis [ə'krɒpəlɪs] (N) • **the ~** la Acrópolis
across [ə'krɒs]

When ***across*** *is an element in a phrasal verb, eg* ***come across, run across***, *look up the verb.*

(PREP) **1** (= *from one side to other of*) a través de • **a tree had fallen ~ the road** había caído un árbol a través de la carretera • **to go ~ a bridge** atravesar *or* cruzar un puente • **to run ~ a road** cruzar una calle corriendo • **the bridge ~ the Tagus** el puente sobre el Tajo • **with arms folded ~ his chest** con los brazos cruzados sobre el pecho
2 (= *on the other side of*) al otro lado de • **~ the street from our house** al otro lado de la calle enfrente de nuestra casa • **the lands ~ the sea** las tierras más allá del mar • **from ~ the sea** desde más allá del mar
3 (*in measurements*) • **it is 12km ~ the strait** el estrecho tiene 12km de ancho
4 (= *crosswise over*) a través de; ▷ **board**
(ADV) **1** (= *from one side to the other*) a través, al través • **don't go around, go ~** no des la vuelta, ve al través • **shall I go ~ first?** ¿paso yo el primero? • **to run ~** (*over bridge*) atravesar *or* cruzar corriendo • **to swim ~** atravesar a nado • **to cut sth ~** cortar algo por (el) medio • **a plank had been laid ~** habían colocado una tabla encima • **he helped an old lady ~** ayudó a una señora mayor a cruzar la calle
2 (= *on opposite side*) • **it's ~ from the Post Office** está enfrente de Correos • **he sat down ~ from her** se sentó frente a ella
3 (*in measurements*) • **the lake is 12km ~** el lago tiene 12km de ancho • **the plate is 30cm ~** el plato tiene un diámetro de 30cm • **how far is it ~?** (*river*) ¿cuántos metros tiene de ancho?
4 (= *crossways*) a través, en cruz, transversalmente
across-the-board [ə'krɒsðə'bɔːd] (ADJ) [*increase*] global, general
acrostic [ə'krɒstɪk] (N) acróstico *m*
acrylic [ə'krɪlɪk] (ADJ) acrílico
(CPD) ▸ **acrylic fibre** fibra *f* acrílica
acrylonitrile [,ækrɪləʊ'naɪtraɪl] (N) acrilonitrilo *m*
ACT (N ABBR) (*US*) (= **American College Test**) *examen que se hace al término de los estudios secundarios*
act [ækt] (N) **1** (= *deed*) acto *m*, acción *f* • **to catch sb in the act** sorprender a algn en el acto • **I was in the act of writing to him** justamente le estaba escribiendo
2 (*Parl*) ley *f*
3 (*Theat*) (= *division*) acto *m*; (= *performance*) número *m* • IDIOMS: • **it's a hard** *or* **tough act to follow** es muy difícil de igualar • **to get into** *or* **in on the act*** introducirse en el asunto, lograr tomar parte • **to get one's act together*** organizarse, arreglárselas
4 (*fig*) (= *pretence*) cuento *m*, teatro *m* • **to put on an act** fingir, hacer teatro*
(VT) (*Theat*) [+ *play*] representar • **to act the part of** (*lit*) hacer el papel de • **he really acted the part** (*fig*) la verdad es que daba el papel • IDIOM: • **to act the fool** hacerse el tonto
(VI) **1** (= *perform*) (*Theat*) hacer teatro; (*Cine*) hacer cine • **I acted in my youth** de joven fui actor • **she's away acting in the provinces** está actuando en provincias • **to act in a film** tener un papel en una película • **have you ever acted?** ¿has actuado alguna vez?, ¿tienes experiencia como actor? • **who's acting in it?** ¿quién actúa?
2 (= *pretend*) • **he's only acting** lo está fingiendo (nada más) • **to act ill** fingirse enfermo; ▷ **stupid**
3 (= *behave*) actuar, comportarse • **he is acting strangely** está actuando *or* se está comportando de una manera rara • **she acted as if she was unwell** actuaba *or* se comportaba como si estuviera enferma
4 (= *take action*) obrar, tomar medidas • **to act with caution** obrar con precaución • **he acted to stop it** tomó medidas para impedirlo • **now is the time to act** hay que ponerse en acción ahora mismo • **he declined to act** se negó a actuar • **he acted for the best** hizo lo que mejor le parecía
5 (= *work*) • **he was acting as ambassador** hacía de embajador • **acting in my capacity as chairman** en mi calidad de presidente • **to act for sb** representar a algn
6 (= *function*) [*thing*] funcionar • **to act as sth** servir de algo • **it acts as a deterrent** sirve para disuadir, sirve de disuasión • **it acts as a safety valve** funciona como válvula de seguridad
7 (= *take effect*) [*drug*] surtir efecto, actuar • **the medicine is slow to act** la medicina tarda en surtir efecto *or* actuar • **it acts by stimulating the immune system** actúa estimulando el sistema inmunológico
(CPD) ▸ **act of contrition** acto *m* de contrición ▸ **act of faith** acto *m* de fe ▸ **act of folly** locura *f* ▸ **act of God** (caso *m* de) fuerza *f* mayor • **we're not insured against acts of God** no estamos asegurados en casos de fuerza mayor *or* no estamos asegurados contra fuerzas mayores ▸ **act of justice** acto *m* de justicia ▸ **Act of Parliament** ley *f* (*aprobada por el Parlamento*) ▸ **act of treason** traición *f* • **an act of treason** una traición ▸ **act of war** acción *f* de guerra ▸ **the Acts of the Apostles** los Hechos de los Apóstoles
▸ **act on** (VI + PREP) = **act upon**
▸ **act out** (VT + ADV) representar • **to act out a macabre drama** (*fig*) representar (hasta el final) un drama macabro • **she is given to acting out her fantasies** tiene tendencia a hacer vivir sus fantasías en la realidad
▸ **act up*** (VI + ADV) [*person*] portarse mal; [*knee, back, injury*] molestar, doler; [*machine*] fallar, estropearse
▸ **act upon** (VI + PREP) **1** [+ *advice, suggestion*] seguir; [+ *order*] obedecer • **to act upon the evidence** obrar de acuerdo con los hechos
2 (= *affect*) afectar (a) • **the drug acts upon the brain** la droga afecta al cerebro

ACT OF PARLIAMENT

A una ley ya aprobada por el Parlamento británico se la denomina **Act of Parliament**. Antes, cuando todavía es un proyecto de ley (**bill**), puede ser modificado tanto por la Cámara de los Comunes como por la de los Lores. Si ambas cámaras lo aprueban, se envía al monarca para que dé su aprobación (**Royal Assent**), aunque esto es una mera formalidad. Tras ello la ley ya es oficialmente un **Act of Parliament**, y pasa a formar parte de la legislación británica, reemplazando cualquier ley consuetudinaria (**common law**) que hubiera sobre ese asunto.
▷ **COMMON LAW**

actable ['æktəbl] (ADJ) representable
acting ['æktɪŋ] (ADJ) [*headmaster, president etc*] interino, suplente
(N) (*Theat*) (= *performance*) interpretación *f*, actuación *f*; (= *profession*) profesión *f* de actor, teatro *m* • **what was his ~ like?** ¿qué tal hizo el papel? • **this is ~ as it should be** esto se llama realmente ser actor *or* actriz, así es el teatro de verdad • **~ is not in my line** yo no soy actor • **she has done some ~** tiene alguna experiencia como actriz • **to go in for ~** hacerse actor
actinic [æk'tɪnɪk] (ADJ) actínico
actinium [æk'tɪnɪəm] (N) actinio *m*
action ['ækʃən] (N) **1** (= *activity*) • **the time has come for ~** ha llegado el momento de hacer algo *or* de actuar • **when shall we get some ~ on this?** ¿cuándo se va a hacer algo al respecto? • **into ~**: • **they went into ~ to rescue the climbers** intervinieron para rescatar a los alpinistas • **to put a plan into ~** poner un plan en práctica *or* en marcha • **emergency procedures will be put into ~** las medidas de emergencia serán puestas en marcha • **a man of ~** un hombre de acción • **to be out of ~** [*machinery*] no funcionar, estar averiado • **the lifts are out of ~** los ascensores no funcionan *or* están averiados • **"out of action"** "no funciona", "fuera de servicio" • **he was out of ~ for months** estuvo sin poder hacer nada durante meses • **the illness put him out of ~ for six months** la enfermedad lo dejó seis meses fuera de combate • **~ stations!** ¡a sus puestos!; ▷ **disciplinary, freedom, industrial**
2 (= *steps*) medidas *fpl* • **emergency ~** medidas *fpl* de emergencia • **to take ~ against sb/sth** tomar medidas contra algn/algo • **their advice is to take no ~** aconsejan no hacer nada
3 (= *deed*) acto *m* • **he wasn't responsible for his ~s** no era responsable de sus actos • **to judge sb by his ~s** juzgar a algn por sus actos *or* acciones • IDIOM: • **to suit the ~ to the word** unir la acción a la palabra • PROVERB: • **~s speak louder than words** obras son amores, que no buenas razones
4* (= *excitement*) animación *f*, marcha* *f* • **they were hoping to find some ~** esperaban encontrar algo de animación, esperaban encontrar algo de marcha* • **where's the ~ in this town?** ¿dónde está la marcha en este pueblo?* • **he likes to be where the ~ is** le gusta estar en medio del meollo* • IDIOM: • **a piece** *or* **slice of the ~*** una tajada*, una parte de los dividendos
5 (*Mil*) (= *intervention*) intervención *f*; (= *engagement*) contienda *f*, enfrentamiento *m* • **we are trying to avoid military ~** estamos tratando de evitar la intervención militar • **we didn't know how many men we had lost until the ~ was over** no supimos cuántos hombres habíamos

perdido hasta que terminó la contienda *or* el enfrentamiento • **to go into ~** [*person, unit*] entrar en acción *or* en combate; [*army, battleship*] entrar en acción • **wounded/killed in ~** herido/muerto en acción (de guerra) *or* en combate • **to see ~** luchar
6 (= *mechanism*) [*of piano*] transmisión *f*; [*of clock*] mecanismo *m*
7 (= *motion*) (*gen*) movimiento *m*; [*of horse*] marcha *f*
8 (= *effect, operation*) [*of acid, drug, elements*] efecto *m* • **stones worn smooth by the ~ of water** piedras *fpl* erosionadas por efecto del agua
9 (*Jur*) (= *measures*) acción *f* judicial; (= *lawsuit*) proceso *m* judicial • **the police are not taking any ~** la policía no va a emprender ninguna acción judicial • **to bring an ~ against sb** comenzar un proceso judicial contra algn • **~ for damages** demanda *f* por daños y perjuicios; ▹ **court, legal, libel**
10 (*Theat, Cine*) [*of play*] acción *f* • **the ~ (of the play) takes place in Greece** la acción (de la obra) se desarrolla en Grecia • **~!** (*Cine*) ¡acción!
11 (*Phys*) acción *f*
(VT) poner en práctica, poner en marcha
(CPD) ▸ **action committee** comité *m* de acción ▸ **action film** película *f* de acción ▸ **action group** grupo *m* de acción ▸ **action hero** (*in film*) héroe *m* de películas de acción ▸ **action man** (*esp hum*) hombre *m* de acción ▸ **action movie** (*US*) película *f* de acción ▸ **action painting** tachismo *m* ▸ **action plan** plan *m* de acción ▸ **action point** punto *m* a seguir, acción *f* a tomar ▸ **action replay** (*TV*) repetición *f* (de la jugada); (*fig*) repetición *f* ▸ **action shot** (= *sequence in film*) escena *f* de acción; (= *photograph*) foto *f* de movimiento

actionable [ˈækʃnəbl] (ADJ) (*Jur*) justiciable, procesable

action-packed [ˈækʃnpækt] (ADJ) [*film, book*] lleno de acción; [*holiday, life*] muy movido

activate [ˈæktɪveɪt] (VT) activar

activation [ˌæktɪˈveɪʃən] (N) activación *f*
(CPD) ▸ **activation order** (*Mil*) orden *f* de activación

activator [ˈæktɪˌveɪtəʳ] (N) activador *m*

active [ˈæktɪv] (ADJ) **1** (= *lively*) [*person, brain*] activo; [*imagination*] vivo • **he has an ~ mind** tiene una mente muy activa
2 (= *busy*) [*life, day, period*] de mucha actividad, muy movido
3 (= *not passive*) [*member, population*] activo • **guerrilla groups are ~ in the province** grupos de guerrilleros están luchando en la provincia • **animals which are ~ at night** los animales que desarrollan su actividad por la noche • **we are giving it ~ consideration** lo estamos estudiando en serio • **to take an ~ interest in sth** interesarse vivamente por algo • **after 17 years' ~ involvement in the party** después de 17 años de militar activamente en el partido • **to play** *or* **take an ~ part in sth** participar activamente en algo • **he withdrew from ~ participation in the project** dejó de participar activamente en el proyecto • **to be politically ~** • **to be ~ in politics** militar políticamente • **he played an ~ role in bringing about a ceasefire** desempeñó un papel activo a la hora de conseguir el alto al fuego • **to be sexually ~** tener relaciones sexuales • **the government must take ~ steps to bring down inflation** el gobierno debe tomar medidas directas para bajar la inflación
4 (= *not extinct*) [*volcano*] en actividad
5 (*Chem, Phys, Electronics*) activo • **the ~ ingredient** el ingrediente activo
6 (*Econ, Comm*) [*trading, market*] activo • **~ assets** activo *msing* productivo • **~ balance** saldo *m* activo • **~ money** dinero *m* activo, dinero *m* disponible • **~ partner** socio/a *m/f* activo/a • **~ trade balance** balanza *f* comercial favorable, balanza *f* comercial acreedora
7 (*Mil*) • **~ service** *or* (*US*) **duty** servicio *m* activo • **to be on ~ service** *or* **duty** estar en activo • **to die on ~ service** morir en acto de servicio • **he saw ~ service in Italy and Germany** estuvo en servicio activo en Italia y Alemania
8 (*Ling, Gram*) • **~ vocabulary** vocabulario *m* activo • **the ~ voice** la voz activa • **in the ~ voice** en voz activa
(N) (*Gram*) • **the ~** la voz activa
(CPD) ▸ **active birth** (*Med*) parto *m* natural ▸ **active file** (*Comput*) fichero *m* activo ▸ **the active list** la reserva activa • **to be on the ~ list** estar en la reserva activa ▸ **active suspension** (*Aut*) suspensión *f* activa

actively [ˈæktɪvlɪ] (ADV) [*encourage, promote, campaign, support,*] enérgicamente; [*seek, consider*] seriamente • **to be ~ involved in sth** tomar parte activa en algo, participar activamente en algo

activewear [ˈæktɪvwɛəʳ] (N) (= *sports clothes*) ropa *f* de deporte

activism [ˈæktɪvɪzəm] (N) activismo *m*

activist [ˈæktɪvɪst] (N) activista *mf*

activity [ækˈtɪvɪtɪ] (N) [*of person*] actividad *f*; (*in port, town*) movimiento *m*, actividad *f* • **business activities** actividades *fpl* comerciales • **leisure activities** pasatiempos *mpl* • **social activities** actividades *fpl* sociales • **terrorist activities** actividades *fpl* terroristas
(CPD) ▸ **activity book** (*accompanying text book*) libro *m* de actividades, cuaderno *m* de actividades; (= *book of games*) libro *m* de pasatiempos ▸ **activity holiday** *vacaciones con actividades ya programadas*

actor [ˈæktəʳ] (N) (*male*) actor *m*; (*female*) actriz *f*

actress [ˈæktrɪs] (N) actriz *f*

actressy [ˈæktrɪsɪ] (ADJ) (*pej*) teatral

ACTT (N ABBR) (*Brit*) = **Association of Cinematographic, Television and Allied Technicians**

actual [ˈæktjʊəl] (ADJ) **1** (= *real*) real • **the ~ number is much higher than that** el número real es mucho más alto • **the film was based on ~ events** la película estaba basada en hechos reales • **let's take an ~ case/example** tomemos un caso/ejemplo concreto • **there is no ~ contract** no hay contrato propiamente dicho • **you met an ~ film star?** ¿has conocido a una estrella de cine de verdad? • **in ~ fact** en realidad • **~ size** tamaño *m* real
2 (= *precise*) [*amount, figure*] exacto; [*words*] exacto, textual • **I don't remember the ~ figures** no recuerdo las cifras exactas • **what were his ~ words?** ¿cuáles fueron sus palabras exactas *or* textuales?
3 (= *very*) • **they couldn't find the ~ gun that was used** no encontraron el arma que se utilizó • **the film used the ~ people involved as actors** la película utilizó como actores a los implicados
4 (= *proper*) • **the ~ wedding procession starts at eleven** el desfile de boda propiamente dicho empieza a las once • **on the ~ day somebody will carry that for you** ese día alguien lo llevará por ti
(CPD) ▸ **actual bodily harm** (*Jur*) daños *mpl* físicos, lesiones *fpl* corporales ▸ **actual loss** (*Comm*) pérdida *f* efectiva

actuality [ˌæktjʊˈælɪtɪ] (N) realidad *f* • **in ~** en realidad

actualize [ˈæktjʊəlaɪz] (VT) **1** (= *make real*) realizar
2 (= *represent*) representar de manera realista, describir con realismo

actually [ˈæktjʊəlɪ] (ADV) **1** (= *really*) en realidad, realmente • **she didn't ~ see the accident** en realidad no vio el accidente, no vio el accidente realmente • **no one ~ died** en realidad no murió nadie • **can computers ~ create language?** ¿pueden realmente crear un idioma los ordenadores? • **inflation has ~ fallen** la inflación de hecho ha bajado • **I never thought you'd ~ do it!** ¡jamás pensé que lo harías de verdad!
2 (*correcting, clarifying*) • **that's not true, ~** bueno, eso no es cierto • **~, I don't know him at all** pues la verdad, no lo conozco de nada • **~, you were quite right** pues mira, de hecho tenías razón • **"he earns £30,000 a year" — "£30,500, actually"** —gana 30.000 libras al año —30.500 libras para ser exactos • **~, I didn't come here just to help you** en realidad, no he venido sólo para ayudarte
3 (= *exactly*) exactamente • **what did he ~ say?** ¿qué es lo que dijo exactamente?
4 (*for emphasis*) • **we ~ caught a fish!** ¡incluso *or* hasta pescamos un pez! • **I was so bored I ~ fell asleep!** ¡me aburría tanto que de hecho me quedé dormido! • **you only pay for the electricity you ~ use** solo pagas la electricidad que consumes

actuarial [ˌæktjʊˈɛərɪəl] (ADJ) actuarial
(CPD) ▸ **actuarial tables** tablas *fpl* actuariales

actuary [ˈæktjʊərɪ] (N) actuario/a *m/f* de seguros

actuate [ˈæktjʊeɪt] (VT) **1** [+ *person*] mover, motivar • **he was ~d by envy** estaba movido *or* motivado por la envidia • **a statement ~d by malice** una declaración movida *or* motivada por el rencor
2 (*Mech*) impulsar, accionar

acuity [əˈkjuːɪtɪ] (N) acuidad *f*, agudeza *f*

acumen [ˈækjʊmen] (N) perspicacia *f*, tino *m*, agudeza *f*

acupressure [ˈækjʊˌpreʃəʳ] (N) acupresión *f*, digitopuntura *f*
(CPD) ▸ **acupressure point** punto *m* de acupresión

acupuncture [ˈækjʊpʌŋktʃəʳ] (N) acupuntura *f*
(CPD) ▸ **acupuncture needle** aguja *f* de acupuntura

acupuncturist [ˈækjʊˈpʌŋktʃərɪst] (N) acupuntor(a) *m/f*, acupunturista *mf*

acute [əˈkjuːt] (ADJ) **1** (= *intense*) [*crisis, shortage, problem*] grave; [*anxiety, joy*] profundo, intenso; [*pain*] agudo; [*discomfort*] fuerte • **the report has caused the government ~ embarrassment** el informe ha puesto en una situación de lo más embarazosa al gobierno • **to become ~** [*shortage, problem*] agravarse
2 (= *keen*) [*hearing*] fino, agudo; [*sense of smell*] fino • **to have ~ powers of observation** tener agudas *or* grandes dotes de observación
3 (= *shrewd*) [*person, mind, comment*] agudo, perspicaz • **that was very ~ of you!** ¡qué perspicaz!, ¡eres un lince!
4 (*Med*) [*illness, case, appendicitis*] agudo
5 (*Geom*) [*angle*] agudo
6 (*Ling*) [*accent*] agudo • **e ~** e con acento agudo

acutely [əˈkjuːtlɪ] (ADV) **1** (= *intensely*) [*feel, suffer*] intensamente; [*embarrassing, uncomfortable*] sumamente • **I am ~ aware that …** me doy perfecta cuenta de que …, me doy cuenta perfectamente de que …, soy

a

perfectamente consciente de que ... • **they were ~ aware of the difficulties involved** tenían plena consciencia de todas las dificultades que suponía
2 (= *shrewdly*) perspicazmente
acuteness [əˈkjuːtnɪs] (N) **1** (= *keenness*) [*of vision, hearing, observation, analysis*] agudeza *f*
2 (= *shrewdness*) perspicacia *f*, agudeza *f*
3 (*Med*) gravedad *f*
AD (ADV ABBR) (= **Anno Domini**) d. de C., d.C.
(N ABBR) (*US*) (*Mil*) = **active duty**
ad* [æd] (N ABBR) = **advertisement**
(CPD) ▸ **ad agency** agencia *f* de publicidad ▸ **ad campaign** campaña *f* publicitaria
a.d. (ABBR) = **after date**
A/D (ABBR) = **analogue-digital**
adage [ˈædɪdʒ] (N) adagio *m*, refrán *m*
adagio [əˈdɑːdʒɪəʊ] (N) adagio *m*
Adam [ˈædəm] (N) Adán • IDIOMS: • **I don't know him from ~*** no lo conozco en absoluto • **to be as old as ~** ser de tiempos de Maricastaña, ser más viejo que el mundo
(CPD) ▸ **Adam's ale** agua *f* ▸ **Adam's apple** nuez *f* (de la garganta)
adamant [ˈædəmənt] (ADJ) (*fig*) firme, inflexible • **he was ~ in his refusal** se mantuvo firme *or* inflexible en su negativa
adamantine [ˌædəˈmæntaɪn] (ADJ) adamantino
adamantly [ˈædəməntlɪ] (ADV) [*refuse*] rotundamente, terminantemente • **to be ~ opposed to sth** oponerse terminantemente *or* firmemente a algo
adapt [əˈdæpt] (VT) **1** [+ *machine*] ajustar, adaptar; [+ *building*] remodelar • **it is perfectly ~ed to its environment** está adaptado perfectamente a su ambiente • **to ~ o.s. to sth** adaptarse a algo, ajustarse a algo
2 [+ *text*] adaptar • **~ed from the Spanish** adaptado del español • **~ed for the screen** adaptado para el cine *or* la pantalla • **his novel was ~ed for television** su novela fue adaptada para la televisión • **a novel ~ed by H. Campbell** una novela en versión de H. Campbell
(VI) adaptarse
adaptability [əˌdæptəˈbɪlɪtɪ] (N) adaptabilidad *f*, capacidad *f* para adaptarse *or* acomodarse
adaptable [əˈdæptəbl] (ADJ) [*vehicle etc*] adaptable; [*person*] capaz de acomodarse, adaptable • **he's very ~** se adapta *or* se acomoda con facilidad a las circunstancias
adaptation [ˌædæpˈteɪʃən] (N) (*Bio*) adaptación *f*; [*of text*] versión *f*
adapter, **adaptor** [əˈdæptəʳ] (N) (*gen*) adaptador *m*; (*Brit*) (*Elec*) enchufe *m* múltiple, ladrón *m*
adaption [æˈdæpʃən] (N) = **adaptation**
adaptive [əˈdæptɪv] (ADJ) • **the human body is remarkably ~** el cuerpo humano tiene una gran adaptabilidad *or* una gran capacidad de adaptación • **an ~ reaction to an intolerable situation** una reacción de adaptación a una situación intolerable
ADC (N ABBR) **1** = **aide-de-camp**
2 (*US*) = **Aid to Dependent Children**
3 = **analogue-digital converter**
ADD (N ABBR) = **attention deficit disorder**
add [æd] (VT) **1** (*Math*) sumar
2 (= *join*) añadir, agregar (*esp LAm*) (**to** a) • **there is nothing added** no hay nada añadido • **"add salt to taste"** "añadir sal al gusto" • IDIOM: • **to add insult to injury** para colmo de males
3 (= *say further*) añadir, agregar • **he added that ...** añadió que ..., agregó que ... • **there's nothing to add** no hay nada que añadir, no hay nada más que decir
(VI) (= *count*) sumar
▸ **add in** (VT + ADV) añadir, incluir
▸ **add on** (VT + ADV) añadir • **we added two rooms on** hicimos construir *or* añadimos dos habitaciones más • **you have to add 15 dollars on for service** hay que añadir 15 dólares por el servicio
▸ **add to** (VI + PREP) aumentar, acrecentar • **it only added to our problems** no hizo sino aumentar nuestros problemas • **then, to add to our troubles ...** luego, para colmo de desgracias ..., luego, para más desgracias ...
▸ **add together** (VT + ADV) sumar
▸ **add up** (VT + ADV) **1** [+ *figures*] sumar
2 [+ *benefits, advantages*] calcular
(VI + ADV) **1** [*figures*] sumar • **it doesn't add up** (*Math*) no cuadra
2 (*fig*) (= *make sense*) tener sentido • **it all adds up** es lógico, tiene sentido • **it's all beginning to add up** la cosa empieza a aclararse • **it just doesn't add up** no tiene sentido
▸ **add up to** (VI + PREP) **1** (*Math*) sumar, ascender a • **it adds up to 25** suma 25, asciende a 25
2 (*fig*) (= *mean*) querer decir, venir a ser • **what all this adds up to is ...** lo que quiere decir *or* significa todo esto es que ... • **it doesn't add up to much** es poca cosa, no tiene gran importancia
added [ˈædɪd] (ADJ) añadido, adicional • **with ~ emphasis** con mayor énfasis, con más énfasis aún • **it's an ~ problem** es un problema más • **~ to which ...** y además ..., por si fuera poco ...
(CPD) ▸ **added time** (*Sport*) tiempo *m* adicional ▸ **added value** valor *m* añadido
addendum [əˈdendəm] (N) (PL: **addenda** [əˈdendə]) ad(d)enda *f*, adición *f*, artículo *m* suplementario
adder [ˈædəʳ] (N) víbora *f*
addict [ˈædɪkt] (N) **1** (*addicted to drugs etc*) adicto/a *m/f*
2* (= *enthusiast*) entusiasta *mf* • **I'm a detective story ~*** yo soy un entusiasta de la novela policíaca • **a telly ~*** un(a) teleadicto/a
addicted [əˈdɪktɪd] (ADJ) (*lit*) adicto • **to be ~ to sth** ser adicto a algo (*also fig*) • **I'm ~ to chocolate** soy adicto al chocolate • **to be ~ to drugs** ser drogadicto • **to be ~ to heroin** ser heroinómano • **I went through four years of being ~ to video games** pasé cuatro años enganchado a los videojuegos • **to become ~ to** [+ *drugs etc*] enviciarse con • **she had become ~ to golf** se envició con el golf, se convirtió en una apasionada del golf, se había vuelto una apasionada del golf
addiction [əˈdɪkʃən] (N) **1** (*to drugs, alcohol*) adicción *f*, dependencia *f* • **his ~ to drugs** su adicción a *or* dependencia de las drogas, su drogodependencia • **heroin ~** adicción *f* a *or* dependencia *f* de la heroína, heroinomanía *f*
2 (*fig*) adicción *f* • **his ~ to TV soaps** su adicción a las telenovelas
addictive [əˈdɪktɪv] (ADJ) **1** (*lit*) [*drug*] que crea adicción, adictivo; [*personality*] propenso a las adicciones • **cigarettes are highly ~** los cigarros son muy adictivos *or* crean una fuerte adicción • **an ~ habit** un vicio que crea adicción
2 (*fig*) • **to be ~** ser como una droga, ser adictivo, ser un vicio* • **rock climbing is ~** el alpinismo es como una droga, el alpinismo es adictivo, el alpinismo es un vicio* • **movie-making can quickly become ~** el hacer películas puede convertirse pronto en una adicción
adding machine [ˈædɪŋməʃiːn] (N) sumadora *f*
Addis Ababa [ˈædɪsˈæbəbə] (N) Addis Abeba *m*
addition [əˈdɪʃən] (N) **1** (*Math*) adición *f*, suma *f* • **if my ~ is correct** si he sumado bien • **to do ~** hacer sumas
2 (= *act*) adición *f* • **in ~** además • **in ~ to** además de • **with the ~ of a cardigan, it makes the perfect summer outfit** añadiendo una chaqueta, es el conjunto perfecto para el verano
3 (= *thing added*) • **these are our new ~s** estas son nuestras nuevas adquisiciones • **this is a welcome ~ to our books on agriculture** este aumenta valiosamente nuestra colección de libros sobre agricultura • **we made ~s to our stocks** aumentamos nuestras existencias • **an ~ to the family** un nuevo miembro de la familia
(CPD) ▸ **addition sign** signo *m* de sumar
additional [əˈdɪʃənl] (ADJ) [*cost, payment*] adicional, extra; [*troops, men*] más • **the US is sending ~ troops to the region** los Estados Unidos van a mandar más tropas a la región • **it is an ~ reason to** (+ *infin*) es razón de más para (+ *infin*) • **this gave him ~ confidence** esto aumentó su confianza • **~ charge** cargo *m* adicional
additionality [əˌdɪʃəˈnælɪtɪ] (N) adicionalidad *f*
additionally [əˈdɪʃənlɪ] (ADV) **1** (= *even more*) [*worry*] aún más • **this makes it ~ difficult for me** esto me lo hace aún más difícil, esto aumenta (aún más) mis dificultades
2 (= *moreover*) además
additive [ˈædɪtɪv] (N) aditivo *m*
additive-free [ˈædɪtɪvˈfriː] (ADJ) sin aditivos
addle [ˈædəl] (VT) **1** [+ *brain*] confundir
2 [+ *egg*] pudrir
(VI) [*egg*] pudrirse
addle-brained [ˈædəlˌbreɪnd] (ADJ) de ideas confusas
addled [ˈædld] (ADJ) **1** (= *rotten*) huero, podrido
2 (= *confused*) [*brain*] confuso, débil
add-on [ˈædɒn] (N) (*Comput*) componente *m* *or* dispositivo *m* adicional
(ADJ) [*product, part*] adicional
address [əˈdres] (N) **1** [*of house etc*] dirección *f*, señas *fpl* • **she isn't at this ~ any more** ya no vive en esta casa; ▹ **business, forwarding, home**
2 (= *speech*) discurso *m*; (= *lecture*) conferencia *f* • **election ~** (= *speech*) discurso *m* electoral; (= *leaflet*) carta *f* de propaganda electoral; ▹ **public**
3 (*Parl etc*) petición *f*, memorial *m*
4 (= *title*) • **form of ~** tratamiento *m*
5 (*Comput*) dirección *f* • **absolute/relative ~** dirección *f* absoluta/relativa
6† (= *skill*) destreza *f*, habilidad *f*
7†† (= *manners*) modales *mpl*; (= *behaviour*) conducta *f*, comportamiento *m*
8 • **to pay one's ~es to**† hacer la corte a, pretender a
(VT) **1** [+ *letter*] (= *direct*) dirigir (**to** a); (= *put address on*) poner la dirección en • **the letter was ~ed to the editor** la carta iba dirigida al director • **I ~ed it to your home** lo mandé a tu casa • **this is ~ed to you** esto viene con *or* a su nombre • **this letter is wrongly ~ed** esta carta lleva la dirección equivocada • **I haven't ~ed it yet** todavía no le he puesto la dirección
2 [+ *person*] **a** (= *speak to*) dirigirse a • **are you ~ing me?** ¿se está usted dirigiendo a mí? • **the judge ~ed the jury** el juez se dirigió al jurado
b (= *make a speech to*) [+ *audience*] pronunciar un discurso ante • **to ~ the House** (*Parl*) pronunciar un discurso en el Parlamento

c • **to ~ sb as "tú"** tratar a algn de "tú", tutear a algn • **to ~ sb by his proper title** dar el debido tratamiento a algn
d • **to ~ o.s. to** [+ *person*] dirigirse a; [+ *problem, task*] aplicarse a
3 [+ *remarks*] dirigir • **please ~ your complaints to the manager** se ruega dirijan sus reclamaciones al director
4 [+ *problem*] abordar
CPD ▸ **address book** librito *m* de direcciones, agenda *f* ▸ **address commission** (*Comm*) *comisión que se paga al agente fletador por su tarea de embarque* ▸ **address label** etiqueta *f* para la dirección

addressee [ˌædreˈsiː] N destinatario/a *m/f*; (*Comm*) consignatario/a *m/f* • **"postage to be paid by the ~"** "a franquear en destino"

addressing [əˈdresɪŋ] N (*Comput*) direccionamiento *m*
CPD ▸ **addressing machine** máquina *f* de direcciones

Addressograph® [əˈdresəʊgrɑːf] N máquina *f* de direcciones *or* para dirigir sobres

adduce [əˈdjuːs] VT (*frm*) alegar, aducir

adductor [əˈdʌktəʳ] N (*Anat*) aductor *m*

Adelaide [ˈædəleɪd] N Adelaida *f*

Aden [ˈeɪdn] N Adén *m* • **Gulf of ~** golfo *m* de Adén

adenoidal [ˈædɪnɔɪdl] ADJ adenoideo • **he has an ~ tone** tiene una voz gangosa

adenoids [ˈædɪnɔɪdz] NPL vegetaciones *fpl* adenoideas

adenoma [ˌædɪˈnəʊmə] N (PL: **adenomas** *or* **adenomata** [ˌædɪˈnəʊmətə]) (*Med*) adenoma *m*

adept ADJ [əˈdept] experto, hábil, ducho (**at, in en**)
N [ˈædept] experto/a *m/f*, maestro/a *m/f* • **to be an ~ at sth/at doing sth** ser experto *or* maestro en algo/en hacer algo

adeptly [əˈdeptlɪ] ADV con acierto *or* habilidad

adequacy [ˈædɪkwəsɪ] N [*of income, explanation, facilities*] lo aceptable; [*of punishment, reward, diet*] lo apropiado; [*of person*] capacidad *f*, competencia *f*

adequate [ˈædɪkwɪt] ADJ **1** (= *sufficient*) [*funds*] suficiente • **an ~ supply of food** suficientes alimentos • **one teaspoonful should be ~** una cucharadita bastará *or* será suficiente • **I didn't think the sentence was ~** la sentencia no me pareció correcta
2 (= *satisfactory*) [*diet*] equilibrado, apropiado; [*income, standard*] aceptable; [*housing, facilities*] adecuado, apropiado • **he failed to provide an ~ explanation for the delay** no fue capaz de dar una explicación convincente de su retraso • **is she the most ~ person to do it?** ¿es la persona más adecuada *or* idónea para hacerlo? • **there are no words ~ to express my gratitude** no hay palabras que expresen adecuadamente mi gratitud • **to be ~ for sb** [*housing*] ser adecuado para algn • **my income is quite ~ for my needs** mis ingresos cubren bien mis necesidades • **this saw should be ~ for the job** este serrucho valdrá para ese trabajo • **this typewriter is perfectly ~** esta máquina de escribir me sirve perfectamente • **to feel ~ to a task** sentirse capacitado para una tarea
3 (*pej*) (= *passable*) [*performance, essay*] aceptable, pasable • **the pay was ~ but hardly out of this world** el sueldo era aceptable *or* pasable, pero desde luego, nada del otro mundo

adequately [ˈædɪkwɪtlɪ] ADV [*prepared, trained, protected*] suficientemente; [*punish*] de forma apropiada; [*respond*] apropiadamente; [*perform*] de forma aceptable • **this has never been ~ explained** esto nunca se ha explicado con claridad • **he speaks the language ~** habla el idioma de forma aceptable

ADHD N ABBR = **attention deficit hyperactivity disorder**

adhere [ədˈhɪəʳ] VI (= *stick*) adherirse, pegarse (**to a**)
▸ **adhere to** VI + PREP (= *observe*) [+ *party, policy*] adherirse a; [+ *rule*] observar; (= *stand by*) [+ *belief*] aferrarse a; (= *fulfil*) [+ *promise*] cumplir

adherence [ədˈhɪərəns] N **1** (*lit*) adherencia *f* (**to a**)
2 (*fig*) (*to policy*) adhesión *f*; (*to rule*) observancia *f* (**to de**)

adherent [ədˈhɪərənt] ADJ adhesivo, adherente
N (= *person*) partidario/a *m/f*

adhesion [ədˈhiːʒən] N = **adherence**

adhesive [ədˈhiːzɪv] ADJ adhesivo
N adhesivo *m*, pegamento *m*
CPD ▸ **adhesive plaster** esparadrapo *m* ▸ **adhesive tape** (= *stationery*) cinta *f* adhesiva, Scotch® *m*, celo *m*; (*Med*) esparadrapo *m*

ad hoc [ˌædˈhɒk] ADJ [*decision*] para el caso; [*committee*] formado con fines específicos

adieu [əˈdjuː] EXCL ¡adiós!
N (PL: **adieus** *or* **adieux** [əˈdjuːz]) (*frm*) adiós *m* • **to bid ~ to** [+ *person*] despedirse de; [+ *thing*] renunciar a, abandonar • **to say one's adieus** *or* **adieux** despedirse

ad infinitum [ˌædɪnfɪˈnaɪtəm] ADV hasta el infinito, ad infinitum • **and so on ~** y así hasta el infinito *or* ad infinitum • **it just carries on ~** es inacabable, es cosa de nunca acabar • **it varies ~** tiene un sinfín de variaciones

ad interim [ˈædˈɪntərɪm] ADV en el ínterin, interinamente
ADJ interino

adipose [ˈædɪpəʊs] ADJ adiposo

adiposity [ˌædɪˈpɒsɪtɪ] N adiposidad *f*

adjacent [əˈdʒeɪsənt] ADJ contiguo; [*angle*] adyacente • **~ to** contiguo a

adjectival [ˌædʒekˈtaɪvəl] ADJ adjetivo, adjetival

adjectivally [ˌædʒekˈtaɪvəlɪ] ADV adjetivamente

adjective [ˈædʒektɪv] N adjetivo *m*

adjoin [əˈdʒɔɪn] VT estar contiguo a, lindar con, colindar con
VI estar contiguo, colindar

adjoining [əˈdʒɔɪnɪŋ] ADJ contiguo, colindante (*more frm*) • **the ~ house** la casa contigua, la casa de al lado, la casa colindante (*more frm*) • **two ~ countries** dos países vecinos, dos países colindantes (*more frm*) • **in an ~ room** en un cuarto contiguo

adjourn [əˈdʒɜːn] VT **1** (= *suspend*) suspender; (= *postpone*) aplazar • **to ~ a discussion for a week** aplazar un debate por una semana • **I declare the meeting ~ed** se levanta la sesión • **to stand ~ed** estar en suspenso
2 (*Jur*) • **the court is ~ed** se levanta la sesión
VI **1** [*meeting*] aplazarse; (*Parl*) disolverse • **the court then ~ed** entonces el tribunal levantó la sesión
2 (= *move*) • **to ~ to** [+ *sitting-room, verandah*] pasar a • **they ~ed to the pub** se trasladaron al bar

adjournment [əˈdʒɜːnmənt] N (= *period*) suspensión *f*; (= *postponement*) aplazamiento *m*

Adjt. ABBR = **adjutant**

adjudge [əˈdʒʌdz] VT **1** (= *pronounce, declare*) declarar • **he was ~d the winner** se lo declaró ganador, se le concedió la victoria • **to ~ that …** estimar que …, considerar que …
2 (*Jur*) [+ *costs, damages*] adjudicar • **to ~ sb guilty** declarar culpable a algn

adjudicate [əˈdʒuːdɪkeɪt] VT [+ *contest*] arbitrar, hacer de árbitro en; [+ *claim*] decidir sobre
VI arbitrar • **to ~ on a matter** arbitrar en un asunto

adjudication [əˌdʒuːdɪˈkeɪʃən] N adjudicación *f* • **~ of bankruptcy** (*Jur*) adjudicación *f* de quiebra
CPD ▸ **adjudication order** (*Jur*) orden *f* de adjudicación

adjudicator [əˈdʒuːdɪkeɪtəʳ] N juez *mf*, árbitro *mf*

adjunct [ˈædʒʌŋkt] N adjunto/a *m/f*, accesorio/a *m/f*

adjuration [ˌædʒʊəˈreɪʃən] N (*liter*) súplica *f*

adjure [əˈdʒʊəʳ] VT (*frm*) • **to ~ sb to do sth** (= *order*) ordenar solemnemente a algn que haga algo; (= *implore*) suplicar *or* implorar a algn que haga algo

adjust [əˈdʒʌst] VT **1** (= *regulate*) [+ *height, temperature, speed, knob, dial*] regular; [+ *machine, engine, brakes*] ajustar • **she ~ed her wing mirror** ajustó el retrovisor exterior • **this chair can be ~ed** esta silla se puede regular • **"do not adjust your set"** "no modifique los controles de su aparato"
2 (= *correct*) [+ *figures*] ajustar; [+ *salaries, wages, prices*] reajustar • **~ed gross income** ingresos *mpl* brutos ajustados • **the seasonally ~ed unemployment total** la tasa de desempleo desestacionalizada • **we have ~ed all salaries upwards/downwards** hemos hecho un reajuste de todos los salarios al alza/a la baja
3 (= *change, adapt*) [+ *terms*] modificar • **I tried to ~ my eyes to the darkness** intenté que los ojos se me acostumbrasen a la oscuridad • **to ~ o.s. to a new situation** adaptarse a una nueva situación
4 (= *arrange*) [+ *hat, tie, clothes*] arreglar; [+ *straps*] ajustar • **she ~ed her headscarf** se arregló la pañoleta
5 (*Insurance*) [+ *claim*] liquidar, tasar
VI [*person*] adaptarse; [*machine, device*] ajustarse • **the boy is having trouble in ~ing** el niño está teniendo dificultades para adaptarse • **to ~ to sth** [*person*] acostumbrarse a algo, adaptarse a algo; [*eyes, body*] acostumbrarse a algo • **the seat ~s to various heights** el asiento se puede regular a distintas alturas

adjustability [əˌdʒʌstəˈbɪlɪtɪ] N adaptabilidad *f*

adjustable [əˈdʒʌstəbl] ADJ ajustable, regulable • **the date is ~** podemos cambiar la fecha
CPD ▸ **adjustable spanner** llave *f* inglesa

adjusted [əˈdʒʌstɪd] ADJ • **well ~** equilibrado

adjuster [əˈdʒʌstəʳ] N **1** (= *device*) ajustador *m*, tensor *m*
2 ▹ **loss**

adjustment [əˈdʒʌstmənt] N **1** (= *regulation*) [*of temperature, height, knob, dial*] regulación *f*; [*of machine, engine, brakes*] ajuste *m*
2 (= *rearrangement*) [*of clothing*] arreglo *m*
3 (= *alteration*) modificación *f*, cambio *m* • **we can always make an ~** siempre podemos cambiarlo • **to make an ~ to one's plans** modificar sus planes
4 (= *adaptation*) [*of person*] adaptación *f* • **social ~** adaptación *f* social
5 (*Econ*) ajuste *m*, reajuste *m* • **~ of prices** ajuste *m* de precios • **~ of wages** reajuste *m* salarial • **after ~ for inflation** después de los ajustes *or* reajustes debidos a la inflación
6 (*Insurance*) [*of claim*] liquidación *f*, tasación *f*

a

adjutant ['ædʒətənt] (N) ayudante *mf*
(CPD) ▸ **Adjutant General** *general responsable del aparato administrativo*

Adlerian [,æd'lɪərɪən] (ADJ) (*Psych*) adleriano

ad lib [æd'lɪb] (ADV) [*perform, speak*] improvisando; [*continue*] a voluntad, a discreción
(ADJ) [*production, performance, speech*] improvisado
(VT) [*+ music, words etc*] improvisar
(VI) [*actor, speaker etc*] improvisar

Adm. (ABBR) **1** = **Admiral**
2 = **Admiralty**

adman* ['ædmæn] (N) (PL: **admen** ['ædmen]) profesional *m* de la publicidad, publicista *m*

admass ['ædmæs] (N) *la masa influenciable por la publicidad*

admin* ['ædmɪn] (N ABBR) (*Brit*) (= **administration**) administración *f*

administer [əd'mɪnɪstəʳ] (VT) **1** (= *manage*) [*+ company, estate, funds, finances*] administrar; [*+ country*] gobernar
2 (= *dispense*) [*+ medicine, sacrament*] administrar; [*+ justice, laws, punishment*] administrar, aplicar • **to ~ an oath to sb** tomar juramento a algn

administered [əd'mɪnɪstəd] (CPD) ▸ **administered price** precio *m* fijado por el fabricante (*y que no puede ser variado por el detallista*)

administrate [əd'mɪnɪstreɪt] (VT) administrar, dirigir

administration [əd,mɪnɪs'treɪʃən] (N) **1** [*of company, estate, finances*] administración *f*; [*of country*] gobierno *m* • **a lot of time is spent on ~** se emplea mucho tiempo en la administración • **the job involves a lot of routine ~** el trabajo comprende bastantes tareas rutinarias de administración • **business ~** administración *f* de empresas
2 [*of medicine, sacrament*] administración *f*, dispensa *f*; [*of justice, punishment*] administración *f*, aplicación *f* • **~ of an oath** toma *f* de juramento
3 (= *governing body*) [*of company, institution*] administración *f* • **the college ~** la administración del colegio
4 (*esp US*) (*Pol*) (= *government*) gobierno *m*, administración *f* • **the Reagan ~** el gobierno de Reagan, la administración de Reagan

administrative [əd'mɪnɪstrətɪv] (ADJ) **1** [*work, officer, system*] administrativo; [*costs, expenses*] de administración, administrativo • **~ assistant** ayudante *mf* administrativo/a • **~ law** derecho *m* administrativo • **~ skills** dotes *fpl* administrativas • **~ staff** personal *m* de administración
2 (*US*) (*Jur*) • **~ court** tribunal *m* administrativo • **~ machinery** maquinaria *f* administrativa, aparato *m* administrativo

administratively [əd'mɪnɪstrətɪvlɪ] (ADV) desde el punto de vista administrativo

administrator [əd'mɪnɪstreɪtəʳ] (N) administrador(a) *m/f*; (*Jur*) albacea *mf*

admirable ['ædmərəbl] (ADJ) admirable, digno de admiración

admirably ['ædmərəblɪ] (ADV) admirablemente, de una manera digna de admiración

admiral ['ædmərəl] (N) almirante *mf*

Admiralty ['ædmərəltɪ] (N) (*Brit*) Ministerio *m* de Marina, Almirantazgo *m* • **First Lord of the ~** Ministro *m* de Marina
(CPD) ▸ **Admiralty court** (*US*) tribunal *m* marítimo

admiration [,ædmə'reɪʃən] (N) admiración *f*

admire [əd'maɪəʳ] (VT) (*gen*) admirar; (= *express admiration for*) elogiar • **she was admiring herself in the mirror** se estaba admirando en el espejo

admirer [əd'maɪərəʳ] (N) admirador(a) *m/f*

admiring [əd'maɪərɪŋ] (ADJ) [*look, glance, tone, voice*] (lleno) de admiración, admirativo • **his ~ fans** sus admiradores

admiringly [əd'maɪərɪŋlɪ] (ADV) [*say, describe*] con admiración • **to speak ~ of sb** hablar con admiración de algn • **he looked at her ~** le lanzó una mirada (llena) de admiración, le lanzó una mirada admirativa

admissibility [əd,mɪsə'bɪlɪtɪ] (N) admisibilidad *f*

admissible [əd'mɪsəbl] (ADJ) admisible, aceptable

admission [əd'mɪʃən] (N) **1** (*to building*) entrada *f* • **~ is free on Sundays** la entrada es gratuita los domingos • **"admission free"** "entrada gratis" • **"no admission"** "prohibida la entrada", "se prohíbe la entrada" • **we gained ~ by a window** logramos entrar por una ventana
2 (*to institution as member*) ingreso *m* (**to** en)
3 (= *acknowledgement*) confesión *f*, reconocimiento *m* • **it would be an ~ of defeat** sería un reconocimiento de la derrota, sería reconocer la derrota • **by** *or* **on his own ~** él mismo lo reconoce • **he made an ~ of guilt** hizo una confesión de culpabilidad, se confesó culpable
(CPD) ▸ **admission charge** (*to club*) cuota *f* de admisión; (*to museum, concert*) precio *m* de entrada ▸ **admission fee** cuota *f* de entrada ▸ **admission price** (*to club, organization*) cuota *f* de admisión; (*to museum, concert*) precio *m* de entrada ▸ **admissions form** (*US*) (*Univ*) impreso *m* de matrícula ▸ **admissions office** (*US*) (*Univ*) secretaría *f* ▸ **admissions tutor** [*of university*] ≈ persona responsable de las admisiones a una facultad o universidad

admit [əd'mɪt] (VT) **1** (= *allow to enter*) [*+ person*] dejar entrar; [*+ patient*] (*to hospital*) ingresar; [*+ air, light*] dejar pasar, dejar entrar • **"children not admitted"** "se prohíbe la entrada a los menores de edad" • **"this ticket admits two"** "entrada para dos personas" • **to be ~ted to the Academy** ingresar en la Academia • **to be ~ted to hospital** ingresar en el hospital • **~ting office** (*US*) (*Med*) oficina *f* de ingresos
2 (= *acknowledge*) reconocer; [*+ crime*] confesar; [*+ error*] reconocer • **it is hard, I ~** es difícil, lo reconozco • **it must be ~ted that ...** hay que reconocer que ... • **I ~ nothing!** ¡no tengo nada que confesar!
▸ **admit of** (VI + PREP) (*frm*) admitir • **it ~s of no other explanation** no cabe otra explicación
▸ **admit to** (VI + PREP) [*+ crime*] confesarse culpable de • **she ~s to doing it** confiesa haberlo hecho • **I ~ to feeling a bit ill** confieso que me siento algo mal

admittance [əd'mɪtəns] (N) entrada *f* • **to gain ~** conseguir entrar • **he was refused ~** se le negó la entrada • **"no admittance"** "se prohíbe la entrada", "prohibida la entrada"

admittedly [əd'mɪtɪdlɪ] (ADV) • **it's only a theory, ~, but ...** reconozco que solo es una teoría, pero ..., es verdad que *or* de acuerdo que solo es una teoría, pero ...
• **~, economists often disagree among themselves** hay que reconocer que *or* hay que admitir que *or* es verdad que los economistas a menudo no están de acuerdo entre ellos

admixture [əd'mɪkstʃəʳ] (N) mezcla *f*, adición *f*; (*fig*) dosis *f inv*

admonish [əd'mɒnɪʃ] (VT) (*frm*)
1 (= *reprimand*) reprender, amonestar (**for** por)
2 (= *warn*) advertir, prevenir
3 (= *advise*) aconsejar (**to do** hacer)

admonishment [əd'mɒnɪʃmənt] (N) = **admonition**

admonition [,ædməʊ'nɪʃən] (N) (*frm*) (= *reproof*) reprensión *f*; (= *warning*) amonestación *f*, advertencia *f*; (= *advice*) consejo *m*, recomendación *f*

admonitory [əd'mɒnɪtərɪ] (ADJ) (*frm*) admonitorio

ad nauseam [,æd'nɔːsɪæm] (ADV) hasta la saciedad

adnominal [,aed'nɒmɪnəl] (ADJ) adnominal
(N) adnominal *m*

ado [ə'duː] (N) • **without further** *or* **more ado** sin más (ni más) • IDIOM: • **much ado about nothing** mucho ruido y pocas nueces

adobe [ə'dəʊbɪ] (N) adobe *m*

adolescence [,ædəʊ'lesns] (N) adolescencia *f*

adolescent [,ædəʊ'lesnt] (ADJ) adolescente
(N) adolescente *mf*

Adolf ['ædɒlf], **Adolphus** [ə'dɒlfəs] (N) Adolfo

Adonis [ə'dəʊnɪs] (N) Adonis

adopt [ə'dɒpt] (VT) **1** [*+ child*] adoptar
2 [*+ report*] aprobar; [*+ suggestion*] seguir, aceptar; (*Pol*) [*+ candidate*] elegir

adopted [ə'dɒptɪd] (ADJ) [*child*] adoptivo, adoptado (*Mex*)

adoptee [ə,dɒp'tiː] (N) (*esp US*) hijo/a *m/f* adoptado/a

adopter [ə'dɒptəʳ] (N) adoptante *mf*

adoption [ə'dɒpʃən] (N) adopción *f* • **they have two children by ~** tienen dos hijos adoptivos • **country of ~** patria *f* adoptiva
(CPD) ▸ **adoption agency** agencia *f* de adopción ▸ **adoption papers** documentos *mpl* de adopción

adoptive [ə'dɒptɪv] (ADJ) adoptivo

adorable [ə'dɔːrəbl] (ADJ) adorable, encantador

adorably [ə'dɔːrəblɪ] (ADV) de manera adorable *or* encantadora

adoration [,ædɔː'reɪʃən] (N) adoración *f*

adore [ə'dɔːʳ] (VT) (= *love*) adorar • **I ~ your new flat** me encanta tu nuevo piso

adorer [ə'dɔːrəʳ] (N) (= *worshipper, admirer*) adorador(a) *m/f*

adoring [ə'dɔːrɪŋ] (ADJ) [*look*] lleno de adoración; [*parent etc*] cariñoso

adoringly [ə'dɔːrɪŋlɪ] (ADV) con adoración

adorn [ə'dɔːn] (VT) adornar, embellecer

adornment [ə'dɔːnmənt] (N) **1** (= *act*) [*of body, person*] adorno *m*, embellecimiento *m*; [*of building, room*] decoración *f*
2 (= *object*) adorno *m*

ADP (N ABBR) = **Automatic Data Processing**

adrenal [ə'driːnl] (ADJ) suprarrenal
(CPD) ▸ **adrenal gland** glándula *f* suprarrenal

adrenalin, adrenaline [ə'drenəlɪn] (N) adrenalina *f* • **I feel the ~ rising** (*fig*) siento que me sube la adrenalina
(CPD) ▸ **adrenalin rush, adrenaline rush** subida *f* de adrenalina

Adriatic [,eɪdrɪ'ætɪk] (ADJ) adriático
(N) • **the ~ (Sea)** el (mar) Adriático

adrift [ə'drɪft] (ADV) **1** (*esp Naut*) a la deriva • **to be cast ~** (*lit*) (*accidentally*) irse a la deriva; (*deliberately*) (*also fig*) ser arrojado a la deriva • **to come ~** [*boat*] soltarse, irse a la deriva; [*wire, rope*] soltarse, desprenderse • **to be cut ~** ser soltado a la deriva • **to be set ~** ser dejado a la deriva
2 (= *directionless*) perdido • **she felt ~ and isolated** se sentía perdida y aislada
3 (= *awry*) • **profits can be as much as £5m ~** los beneficios pueden estar hasta 5

millones de libras por debajo de lo esperado • **to go ~** [*plan, scheme*] fallar, irse al garete*
4 (*Sport*) • **to be five points/seconds ~ of** estar a cinco puntos/segundos de, ir cinco puntos/segundos a la zaga de

adroit [əˈdrɔɪt] (ADJ) diestro, hábil

adroitly [əˈdrɔɪtlɪ] (ADV) diestramente, hábilmente

adroitness [əˈdrɔɪtnɪs] (N) destreza *f*, habilidad *f*

ADSL (N ABBR) (*Comput*) (= **asynchronous digital subscriber line**) ADSL *m*

adsorb [ədˈsɔːb] (VT) adsorber

adsorption [ædˈsɔːpʃən] (N) adsorción *f*

ADT (N ABBR) (*US, Canada*) = **Atlantic Daylight Time**

adulate [ˈædjʊleɪt] (VT) adular

adulation [ˌædjʊˈleɪʃən] (N) adulación *f*

adulatory [ˌædjuˈleɪtərɪ], (*US*) [ˈædʒələtɔːrɪ] (ADJ) adulador

adult [ˈædʌlt] (ADJ) **1** [*person*] adulto, mayor; [*animal*] adulto
2 (= *explicit*) [*film, book*] para adultos
3 (= *mature*) maduro, adulto • **to be ~ about sth** comportarse como una persona adulta/como personas adultas con respecto a algo
(N) adulto/a *m/f* • **"adults only"** (*Cine*) "autorizado para mayores de 18 años"
(CPD) ▸ **adult education** educación *f* para adultos ▸ **adult literacy classes** clases *fpl* de alfabetización de adultos

adulterate [əˈdʌltəreɪt] (VT) adulterar

adulteration [əˌdʌltəˈreɪʃən] (N) adulteración *f*

adulterer [əˈdʌltərəʳ] (N) adúltero *m*

adulteress [əˈdʌltərɪs] (N) adúltera *f*

adulterous [əˈdʌltərəs] (ADJ) adúltero

adultery [əˈdʌltərɪ] (N) adulterio *m*

adulthood [ˈædʌlthʊd] (N) adultez *f*, mayoría *f* de edad, edad *f* adulta

adumbrate [ˈædʌmbreɪt] (VT) (*frm*) bosquejar; (= *foreshadow*) presagiar, anunciar

adumbration [ˌædʌmˈbreɪʃən] (N) (*frm*) bosquejo *m*; (= *foreshadowing*) presagio *m*, anuncio *m*

ad val. (ADJ ABBR), (ADV ABBR) (*Comm*) = **ad valorem**

ad valorem [ædvəˈlɔːrəm] (ADV) conforme a su valor, por avalúo
(CPD) ▸ **ad valorem tax** impuesto *m* según valor

advance [ədˈvɑːns] (N) **1** (= *forward movement*) avance *m* • **the rapid ~ of the Russian army** el rápido avance de las tropas rusas
2 (= *progress*) (*in science, technology*) avance *m*, adelanto *m*; [*of disease*] avance *m* • **an important scientific ~** un importante avance *or* adelanto científico • **the rapid ~ of modern industrial society** el vertiginoso desarrollo de la sociedad industrial moderna • **with the ~ of old age** según se va/iba envejeciendo
3 [*of money*] **a** (= *initial payment*) anticipo *m*, adelanto *m* • **she was paid a £530,000 ~ for her next novel** le dieron un anticipo *or* adelanto de 530.000 libras por su próxima novela
b (*on salary*) • **could you give me an ~?** ¿me podría dar un anticipo? • **she got an ~ on her salary** consiguió que le anticiparan parte del sueldo
c (= *loan*) préstamo *m*
4 (= *rise*) (*in prices*) alza *f*, aumento *m* • **any ~ on £15?** (*in auction*) ¿alguien ofrece más de 15 libras?, 15 libras ¿alguien da más?
5 advances (*amorous*) insinuaciones *fpl*; (*Pol*) intentos *mpl* de acercamiento • **to make ~s to** *or* **toward(s) sb** (*amorous*) insinuarse a algn, hacer insinuaciones a algn • **she accused him of making unwanted sexual ~s** lo acusó de insinuaciones sexuales indebidas • **she rejected his ~s** no hizo caso de sus insinuaciones
6 • **in ~: to let sb know a week in ~** avisar a algn con ocho días de antelación • **to book in ~** reservar con antelación • **the dish may be made in ~** el plato puede prepararse con anterioridad • **in ~ of:** • **to arrive in ~ of sb** llegar antes que algn • **to be in ~ of one's time** adelantarse a su época, estar por delante de su época • **to pay in ~** pagar por adelantado • **to send sb on in ~** mandar a algn por delante • **thanking you in ~** agradeciéndole de antemano
(VT) **1** (= *move forward*) [+ *time, date, clock*] adelantar; (*Mil*) [+ *troops*] avanzar • **it ~s the ageing process** acelera el envejecimiento
2 (= *further*) [+ *plan, knowledge*] potenciar; [+ *interests*] promover, fomentar; [+ *career*] promocionar; [+ *cause, claim*] promover; [+ *person*] (*in career*) ascender (**to a**) • **he has done much to ~ our understanding of music** ha contribuido mucho a potenciar nuestros conocimientos musicales
3 (= *put forward*) [+ *idea, opinion, theory*] proponer, sugerir; [+ *suggestion*] hacer; [+ *proposal*] presentar; [+ *opinion*] expresar • **he ~d the theory that …** propuso *or* sugirió la teoría de que …
4 (= *hand over*) [+ *money*] (*as initial fee*) adelantar, anticipar; (*as early wages*) adelantar; (*as loan*) prestar
(VI) **1** (= *move forward*) avanzar • **the advancing enemy army** el ejército enemigo que avanza • **she ~d across the room** avanzó hacia el otro lado de la habitación • **to ~ on sth/sb** (*gen*) acercarse a algo/algn, avanzar hacia algo/algn • **to ~ on sth** (*Mil*) avanzar sobre algo
2 (= *progress*) [*science, technology*] progresar, adelantarse; [*work, society*] avanzar; [*career*] progresar; [*person, pupil*] hacer progresos, progresar; (*in rank*) ascender (**to a**) • **her film career was advancing nicely** su carrera cinematográfica progresaba bien *or* iba por muy buen camino • **despite his advancing years he was a good player** a pesar de su edad (avanzada) era un buen jugador • **with advancing years one forgets** con el paso de los años uno se olvida
3 (*Econ*) (= *rise*) [*price*] subir
(CPD) ▸ **advance booking** reserva *f* anticipada, reserva *f* por anticipado • **"advance booking advisable"** "se recomienda que reserven por adelantado" ▸ **advance booking office** (*Brit*) taquilla *f* (de reservas *or* venta anticipada) ▸ **advance copy** [*of book*] ejemplar *m* de muestra; [*of speech*] copia *f* (del discurso) ▸ **advance guard** (= *reconnaissance group*) avanzada *f*; (= *lookouts*) avanzadilla *f*; (= *mobile unit*) brigada *f* móvil ▸ **advance man** (*US*) (*Pol*) *responsable de una campaña política* ▸ **advance notice** aviso *m* previo • **meals can be provided with ~ notice** con aviso previo, se preparan comidas ▸ **advance party** (= *reconnaissance group*) avanzada *f*; (= *lookouts*) avanzadilla *f* ▸ **advance payment** anticipo *m* ▸ **advance publicity** promoción *f* (antes del estreno, lanzamiento etc) ▸ **advance warning** aviso *m* previo

advanced [ədˈvɑːnst] (ADJ) **1** (= *developed*) [*civilization, society*] avanzado
2 (= *not elementary*) [*course, level, studies*] avanzado, superior; [*student*] (de nivel) avanzado • **~ mathematics** matemáticas *fpl* avanzadas *or* superiores
3 (= *precocious*) adelantado • **her youngest child is very ~ for his age** su hijo menor es muy adelantado para su edad
4 (= *modern*) [*ideas*] avanzado
5 (*in time*) [*stage*] avanzado; [*disease*] de grado avanzado • **the talks are at an ~ stage** las negociaciones están muy avanzadas • **women in ~ stages of pregnancy** mujeres *fpl* en los últimos meses del embarazo • **the research is well ~** la investigación está muy adelantada • **patients with ~ cancer** los pacientes con cáncer de grado avanzado • **she became a mother at the ~ age of 44** tuvo su primer hijo a la avanzada edad de 44 años • **a man of ~ years** un hombre entrado en años, un hombre de edad avanzada • **to be ~ in years** estar entrado en años
(CPD) ▸ **advanced gas-cooled reactor** reactor *m* avanzado refrigerado por gas ▸ **Advanced Level** (*Brit*) (*Scol*) (*frm*) ≈ bachillerato *m* • **she has an Advanced level in chemistry** tiene un título de *Advanced Level* en química ▸ **advanced photo system** sistema *m* avanzado de fotografía

advancement [ədˈvɑːnsmənt] (N)
1 (= *furthering*) fomento *m*
2 (= *improvement*) progreso *m*
3 (*in rank*) ascenso *m*

advantage [ədˈvɑːntɪdʒ] (N) **1** ventaja *f* • **it's no ~ to play first** el jugar primero no es una ventaja • **"languages and shorthand an ~"** (*in job advert*) "serán méritos *or* se valorarán idiomas y taquigrafía" • **to have an ~ over sb** llevar ventaja a algn • **I'm sorry, you have the ~ of me** (*fig*) lo siento, pero no recuerdo su nombre • **to have an ~ in numbers** llevar ventaja en cuanto al número • **he has the ~ of youth** tiene la ventaja de ser joven • **the plan has many ~s** el proyecto tiene muchas ventajas • **to show sth off to best ~** hacer que algo se vea bajo la luz más favorable • **to take ~ of sb** (*unfairly*) aprovecharse de algn, sacar partido de algn; (*sexually*) abusar de algn • **to take ~ of an opportunity** aprovechar una oportunidad • **it's to our ~** es ventajoso para nosotros • **to turn sth to (one's) ~** sacar buen partido de algo
2 (*Sport*) • **~ González** (*Tennis*) ventaja González

advantaged [ədˈvɑːntɪdʒd] (NPL) • **the ~** los privilegiados, los favorecidos

advantageous [ˌædvənˈteɪdʒəs] (ADJ) [*offer, position*] ventajoso, provechoso • **to be ~ to sb** ser ventajoso *or* provechoso para algn, beneficiar a algn

advantageously [ˌædvənˈteɪdʒəslɪ] (ADV) ventajosamente, provechosamente

advent [ˈædvənt] (N) **1** (= *arrival*) advenimiento *m*
2 (*Rel*) • **Advent** Adviento *m*
(CPD) ▸ **Advent calendar** calendario *m* de Adviento ▸ **Advent Sunday** domingo *m* de Adviento

adventitious [ˌædvenˈtɪʃəs] (ADJ) (*frm*) adventicio

adventure [ədˈventʃəʳ] (N) aventura *f* • **the spirit of ~** el espíritu de aventura, el espíritu aventurero
(CPD) ▸ **adventure holiday** (*Brit*) vacaciones *fpl* de aventura ▸ **adventure park** parque *m* de aventuras ▸ **adventure playground** (*Brit*) parque *m* infantil ▸ **adventure story** novela *f* de aventuras

adventurer [ədˈventʃərəʳ] (N) **1** (= *explorer*) aventurero/a *m/f*
2 (*pej*) (= *opportunist*) desaprensivo/a *m/f*

adventuresome [ədˈventʃəsəm] (ADJ) (*US*) [*person*] aventurero; [*day*] lleno de aventuras

adventuress [ədˈventʃərɪs] (N) aventurera *f*

adventurism [ədˈventʃərɪzəm] (N)

aventurismo *m*

adventurist [əd'ventʃərɪst] ADJ aventurista
N aventurista *mf*

adventurous [əd'ventʃərəs] ADJ [*person*] aventurero; [*enterprise*] peligroso, arriesgado; [*style*] innovador, atrevido; [*journey*] (= *intrepid*) intrépido; (= *eventful*) lleno de incidentes • **we had a very ~ time getting here** el viaje para llegar aquí ha estado repleto de incidentes • **we need a more ~ slogan** necesitamos un eslogan más llamativo

adventurously [əd'ventʃərəslɪ] ADV (= *intrepidly*) con espíritu aventurero *or* emprendedor; (= *boldly*) atrevidamente

adventurousness [əd'ventʃərəsnɪs] N [*of person*] carácter *m* aventurero; [*of style*] atrevimiento *m*; [*of journey*] carácter *m* intrépido

adverb ['ædvɜ:b] N adverbio *m*

adverbial [əd'vɜ:bɪəl] ADJ adverbial

adversarial [,ædvɜ:'seərɪəl] ADJ [*role*] de antagonista; [*relationship*] de enfrentamiento, conflictivo
CPD ▸ **adversarial procedure** procedimiento *m* de confrontación ▸ **the adversarial system** (*Jur*) el sistema acusatorio

adversary ['ædvəsərɪ] N adversario/a *m/f*, contrario/a *m/f*

adverse ['ædvɜ:s] ADJ [*criticism, decision, effect, wind*] adverso, contrario; [*conditions*] adverso, desfavorable • **to be ~ to** ser contrario a, estar en contra de

adversely ['ædvɜ:slɪ] ADV desfavorablemente, negativamente • **to affect ~** perjudicar

adversity [əd'vɜ:sɪtɪ] N infortunio *m*, desgracia *f* • **in times of ~** en tiempos difíciles • **he knew ~ in his youth** de joven conoció la miseria • **companion in ~** compañero *m* de desgracias

advert[1] [əd'vɜ:t] VI (*frm*) • **to ~ to** referirse a

advert[2]* ['ædvɜ:t] N ABBR (*Brit*) = **advertisement**

advertise ['ædvətaɪz] VT **1** (*Comm etc*) anunciar • **"as ~d on TV"** "anunciado en TV"
2 (= *draw attention to*) [+ *weakness etc*] exponer, revelar públicamente
VI [*company*] hacer publicidad, hacer propaganda; (*in newspaper etc*) poner un anuncio; (*on TV*) hacer publicidad • **it pays to ~** la publicidad siempre rinde • **to ~ for** buscar por medio de anuncios

advertisement [əd'vɜ:tɪsmənt] N anuncio *m* (**for** de) • **to put an ~ in a newspaper** poner un anuncio en un periódico • **it's not much of an ~ for the place*** no dice mucho en favor de la ciudad/del hotel *etc*
CPD ▸ **advertisement column** (*Brit*) columna *f* or sección *f* de anuncios ▸ **advertisement rates** tarifas *fpl* de anuncios

advertiser ['ædvətaɪzəʳ] N anunciante *mf*

advertising ['ædvətaɪzɪŋ] N **1** (= *business*) publicidad *f* • **my brother's in ~** mi hermano se dedica a la publicidad
2 (= *advertisements collectively*) anuncios *mpl*
CPD ▸ **advertising agency** agencia *f* de publicidad ▸ **advertising campaign** campaña *f* publicitaria ▸ **advertising manager** jefe/a *m/f* de publicidad ▸ **advertising medium** medio *m* de publicidad ▸ **advertising rates** tarifa *fsing* de anuncios

advertorial [,ædvə'tɔ:rɪəl] N (*Press*) publirreportaje *m*

advice [əd'vaɪs] N **1** (*gen*) consejos *mpl* • **he ignored my ~** ignoró mis consejos • **it was good ~** *or* **a good piece of ~** fue un buen consejo • **her doctor's ~ was to rest** el médico le aconsejó descansar • **he did it against the ~ of friends** lo hizo en contra de lo que le aconsejaron sus amigos • **to follow sb's ~** seguir el consejo *or* los consejos de algn • **let me give you some ~** permíteme que te dé un consejo, permíteme que te aconseje • **if you want my ~ ...** si quieres (seguir) mi consejo ... • **my ~ to you is not to say anything** te aconsejo no decir nada, mi consejo es que no digas nada • **I need your ~** necesito que me aconsejes • **on the ~ of sb** siguiendo el consejo *or* los consejos de algn • **a piece of ~** un consejo • **to take sb's ~** seguir el consejo *or* los consejos de algn, hacer caso a algn • **take my ~ and stay away from him!** ¡sigue mi consejo y no te metas con él!, ¡hazme caso y no te metas con él! • **when I want your ~ I'll ask for it** cuando quiera que me aconsejes te lo pediré, cuando quiera tu consejo te lo pediré
2 (= *professional help, information*) asesoramiento *m* • **you need expert ~** necesitas el asesoramiento de un experto, necesitas hacerte asesorar por un experto • **the tourist office will give us ~ on places to visit** la oficina de turismo nos asesorará sobre qué lugares visitar • **to seek sb's ~** consultar a algn, hacerse asesorar por algn • **to seek professional/medical ~** consultar a *or* hacerse asesorar por un profesional/médico • **to take legal ~** consultar a un abogado, asesorarse con un abogado
3 (*Comm*) aviso *m*, notificación *f*
CPD ▸ **advice column** (*gen*) consultorio *m*; (*agony aunt's*) consultorio *m* sentimental ▸ **advice columnist** (*US*) (*gen*) redactor(a) *m/f* de consultorio; (= *agony aunt*) redactor(a) *m/f* de consultorio sentimental ▸ **advice line** servicio *m* de asesoramiento por teléfono ▸ **advice note** nota *f* de aviso ▸ **advice service** servicio *m* de asesoramiento

advisability [əd,vaɪzə'bɪlɪtɪ] N conveniencia *f*, prudencia *f*

advisable [əd'vaɪzəbl] ADJ aconsejable, conveniente • **it would be ~ to** (+ *infin*) sería aconsejable (+ *infin*), sería conveniente (+ *infin*) • **if you think it ~** si le parece bien

advise [əd'vaɪz] VT **1** (= *recommend*) [+ *action*] aconsejar, recomendar • **he ~s caution** aconseja *or* recomienda prudencia • **I'd ~ leaving the car here** aconsejaría que dejáramos el coche aquí • **to ~ sb to do sth** aconsejar a algn que haga algo • **what would you ~ me to do?** ¿qué me aconsejas (que haga)? • **you would be ill ~d to go** no sería prudente que fueras, harías mal yendo *or* en ir • **you would be well ~d to go** sería prudente que fueras, harías bien yendo *or* en ir; ▹ **ill-advised**
2 (= *give advice to*) aconsejar; (= *help and inform professionally*) asesorar • **can you ~ me on the best route?** ¿me puede aconsejar cuál es la mejor ruta? • **he ~s them on investment** les asesora en sus inversiones • **she will ~ you what to do** ella te dirá lo que tienes que hacer
3 (*frm*) (= *inform*) informar; (*officially*) notificar • **to ~ sb of sth** informar a algn de algo; (*officially*) notificar algo a algn • **he wrote to ~ me of his decision** me escribió para informarme de *or* notificarme su decisión • **please ~ us of a convenient date** le ruego nos notifique una fecha conveniente • **to keep sb ~d of** *or* **about sth** mantener a algn al corriente *or* informado de algo
4 (= *warn*) advertir • **they were ~d that it would look bad** les advirtieron (de) que causaría una mala impresión • **to ~ sb against doing sth** aconsejar a algn que no haga algo • **they ~d me against selling the house** me aconsejaron que no vendiera la casa • **the doctor ~d me against it** el médico me lo desaconsejó • **no one had ~d him of the possible consequences** nadie lo había advertido de las posibles consecuencias
VI (= *make recommendations*) dar consejos • **I would ~ against it** yo te lo desaconsejaría, yo no te lo aconsejaría • **he ~d against going** nos aconsejó que no fuéramos • **to ~ on sth** (= *give information on*) informar *or* dar información sobre algo; [*lawyer, accountant*] asesorar sobre algo • **job centres will ~ on training courses** en las oficinas de empleo informan *or* dan información sobre cursillos de formación

advisedly [əd'vaɪzɪdlɪ] ADV deliberadamente • **to speak ~** hablar con conocimiento de causa • **I say so ~** lo digo después de pensarlo bien

advisement [əd'vaɪzmənt] (*US*) N consulta *f*, deliberación *f* • **to take sth under ~** (= *think over*) estudiar algo; (= *get expert advice on*) consultar algo con expertos, someter algo a la deliberación de expertos
CPD ▸ **advisement counseling** guía *f* vocacional

adviser, **advisor** [əd'vaɪzəʳ] N (*in business, politics etc*) asesor(a) *m/f*, consejero/a *m/f* • **legal ~** abogado/a *m/f*, asesor(a) *m/f* jurídico/a • **spiritual ~** consejero *m* espiritual

advisory [əd'vaɪzərɪ] ADJ [*body*] consultivo • **in an ~ capacity** como asesor(a)
N (*esp US*) nota *f* oficial, anuncio *m* público
CPD ▸ **advisory board** junta *f* consultiva ▸ **advisory committee** (*US*) (*Pol*) comité *m* consultivo ▸ **advisory opinion** (*US*) (*Jur*) opinión *f* consultiva *or* asesora ▸ **advisory service** servicio *m* consultivo

advocacy ['ædvəkəsɪ] N **1** (= *support*) apoyo *m* (activo)
2 (*Jur*) defensa *f*
CPD ▸ **advocacy group**, **advocacy organization** (*US*) (= *lobby*) grupo *m* de presión

advocate VT ['ædvəkeɪt] (= *be in favour of*) abogar por, ser partidario de • **what do you ~?** ¿qué nos aconsejas? • **I ~ doing nothing** yo recomiendo no hacer nada
N ['ædvəkɪt] defensor(a) *m/f*, partidario/a *m/f*; (*Scot*) (*Jur*) abogado/a *m/f*; ▹ **devil**, LAWYERS, QC/KC

advocator ['ædvəkeɪtəʳ] N = **advocate**

advt ABBR = **advertisement**

adze, **adz** (*US*) [ædz] N azuela *f*

AEA N ABBR **1** (*Brit*) (= **Atomic Energy Authority**) ≈ JEN *f* (*Sp*)
2 (= **Association of European Airlines**) AAE *f*

AEC N ABBR (*US*) (= **Atomic Energy Commission**) ≈ JEN *f* (*Sp*)

AEEU N ABBR (*Brit*) = **Amalgamated Engineering and Electrical Union**

AEF N ABBR (*US*) = **American Expeditionary Forces**

Aegean [i:'dʒi:ən] N • **the ~** el Egeo
CPD ▸ **Aegean Islands** • **the ~ Islands** las islas del Egeo ▸ **Aegean Sea** • **the ~ Sea** el mar Egeo

aegis, **egis** (*US*) ['i:dʒɪs] N • **under the ~ of** (= *protection*) bajo la tutela de; (= *patronage*) patrocinado por, bajo los auspicios *or* (*frm*) la égida de

aegrotat [i:'grəʊtæt] N (*Brit*) *título universitario que se concede al candidato que por enfermedad no ha podido presentarse a los exámenes*

Aeneas [i:'ni:əs] N Eneas *m*

Aeneid ['i:nɪɪd] N Eneida *f*

aeon ['i:ən] N **1** (*Astron*) eón *m*
2 (*fig*) eternidad *f*

a

aerate [ˈɛəreɪt] (VT) [+ *liquid*] gasificar; [+ *blood*] oxigenar • **~d water** agua *f* con gas
aeration [ɛəˈreɪʃən] (N) aireación *f*
aerial [ˈɛərɪəl] (ADJ) aéreo
(N) (*Brit*) (*Rad, TV*) antena *f*; (*also* **aerial mast**) torre *f* de antena • **indoor ~** antena *f* interior
(CPD) ▸ **aerial input*** (*US*) mensaje *m* recibido por antena ▸ **aerial ladder** (*US*) escalera *f* de bomberos ▸ **aerial photograph** aerofoto *f*, fotografía *f* aérea ▸ **aerial photography** fotografía *f* aérea ▸ **aerial railway** teleférico *m* ▸ **aerial survey** reconocimiento *m* aéreo ▸ **aerial tanker** transportador *m* aéreo
aerialist [ˈɛərɪəlɪst] (N) (*US*) (*on trapeze*) trapecista *mf*; (*on high wire*) funambulista *mf*
aerie [ˈɛərɪ] (N) (*US*) = **eyrie**
aero... [ˈɛərəʊ] (PREFIX) aero...
aerobatic [ˌɛərəʊˈbætɪk] (ADJ) [*display*] de acrobacia aérea
aerobatics [ˌɛərəʊˈbætɪks] (NPL) acrobacia *fsing* aérea
aerobic [ɛəˈrəʊbɪk] (ADJ) [*shoes, dance*] de *or* para aerobic; [*exercise*] aeróbico
aerobics [ɛəˈrəʊbɪks] (NPL) aerobic *msing* • **I do ~** hago aerobic
aerodrome [ˈɛərədrəʊm] (N) (*esp Brit*) aeródromo *m*
aerodynamic [ˈɛərəʊdaɪˈnæmɪk] (ADJ) aerodinámico
aerodynamically [ˈɛərəʊdaɪˈnæmɪklɪ] (ADV) desde el punto de vista aerodinámico, aerodinámicamente
aerodynamics [ˈɛərəʊdaɪˈnæmɪks] (N) aerodinámica *fsing*
aero-engine [ˈɛərəʊˌendʒɪn] (N) motor *m* de aviación
aerofoil [ˈɛərəʊfɔɪl], **airfoil** (*US*) [ˈɛəˌfɔɪl] (N) plano *m* aerodinámico
aerogram, aerogramme [ˈɛərəʊgræm] (N) **1** (= *air-letter*) aerograma *m* **2** (= *radio message*) radiograma *m*
aerolite [ˈɛərəlaɪt] (N) aerolito *m*
aeromodelling [ˈɛərəʊˈmɒdlɪŋ] (N) aeromodelismo *m*
aeronaut [ˈɛərənɔːt] (N) aeronauta *mf*
aeronautic [ˌɛərəˈnɔːtɪk] (ADJ) = **aeronautical**
aeronautical [ˌɛərəˈnɔːtɪk] (ADJ) aeronáutico
aeronautics [ˌɛərəˈnɔːtɪks] (N) aeronáutica *fsing*
aeroplane [ˈɛərəpleɪn] (N) (*Brit*) avión *m*; ▹ **model**
aeroponics [ˌɛərəˈpɒnɪks] (NSING) cultivo *m* aeropónico
aerosol [ˈɛərəsɒl] (N) aerosol *m*, atomizador *m*
(CPD) ▸ **aerosol spray** pulverizador *m*, aerosol *m*
aerospace [ˈɛərəʊspeɪs] (ADJ) aeroespacial • **the ~ industry** la industria aeroespacial
Aertex® [ˈɛəteks] (N) *tejido ligero de algodón usado especialmente para prendas deportivas*
Aeschylus [ˈiːskɪləs] (N) Esquilo
Aesop [ˈiːsɒp] (N) Esopo • **~'s Fables** Fábulas *fpl* de Esopo
aesthete, esthete (*US*) [ˈiːsθiːt] (N) esteta *mf*
aesthetic, esthetic (*US*) [iːsˈθetɪk] (ADJ) estético
aesthetical, esthetical (*US*) [iːsˈθetɪkəl] (ADJ) = aesthetic
aesthetically, esthetically (*US*) [iːsˈθetɪkəlɪ] (ADV) estéticamente
aestheticism, estheticism (*US*) [iːsˈθetɪsɪzəm] (N) esteticismo *m*
aesthetics, esthetics (*US*) [iːsˈθetɪks] (N) estética *fsing*
aetiological, etiological (*US*) [ˌiːtɪəˈlɒdʒɪkəl] (ADJ) (*Med*) (*also fig*) etiológico
aetiology [ˌiːtɪˈɒlədʒɪ] (N) etiología *f*
AEU (N ABBR) (*Brit*) (*formerly*) = **Amalgamated Engineering Union**
a.f. (N ABBR) **1** = **audio frequency** **2** (*Comm*) = **advance freight**
AFA (N ABBR) (*Brit*) = **Amateur Football Association**
afaik (ABBR) (*in text message etc*) (= **as far as I know**) que yo sepa
afar [əˈfɑːʳ] (ADV) (*liter*) lejos • **from ~** desde lejos • **~ off** a lo lejos, en lontananza (*liter*)
AFB (N ABBR) (*US*) (*Mil*) = **Air Force Base**
AFC (N ABBR) **1** (*Brit*) = **Amateur Football Club** **2** (*Brit*) = **Association Football Club** **3** = **automatic frequency control**
AFDC (N ABBR) (*US*) (*Admin*) = **Aid to Families with Dependent Children**
affability [ˌæfəˈbɪlɪtɪ] (N) afabilidad *f*
affable [ˈæfəbl] (ADJ) [*person, mood*] afable
affably [ˈæfəblɪ] (ADV) afablemente
affair [əˈfɛəʳ] (N) **1** (= *business*) asunto *m* • **the government has mishandled the ~** el gobierno ha llevado mal el asunto
2 affairs (= *matters*) asuntos *mpl* • **you will have to put your ~s in order** tendrás que aclarar tus asuntos • **she runs my business ~s** ella se encarga de lo relacionado con mis negocios • **~s of the heart** asuntos *mpl* del corazón • **a man of ~s** un hombre de negocios • **~s of state** asuntos *mpl* de estado
3 (= *event*) ocasión *f* • **it will be a big ~** será una ocasión importante, será todo un acontecimiento • **the minister's visit will be a purely private ~** la visita del ministro tendrá un carácter puramente privado • **dinner was a gloomy ~** la cena no fue una ocasión muy alegre
4 (= *case*) caso *m*, asunto *m* • **the Watergate ~** el caso Watergate, el asunto (de) Watergate
5 (= *concern*) asunto *m* • **that's my ~** eso es asunto mío *or* cosa mía, eso solo me concierne a mí • **if he wants to make a fool of himself, that's his ~** si quiere hacer el ridículo, es asunto suyo *or* allá él
6 (= *love affair*) aventura *f* (amorosa), affaire *m*, lío *m* (amoroso)* • **he had an ~ with a French girl** tuvo una aventura *or* un affaire con una chica francesa, tuvo un lío *or* estuvo liado con una chica francesa* • **they're having an ~** están liados
7* (= *thing*) • **the bed was an iron ~ with brass knobs** la cama era un trasto de hierro con adornos de bronce • **the house was a ramshackle, wooden ~** la casa era un destartalado cobertizo de madera
affect [əˈfekt] (VT) **1** (= *have effect on*) afectar, influir en • **it did not ~ my decision** no influyó en mi decisión
2 (= *concern*) afectar, tener que ver con • **this will ~ everybody** esto afectará a todos
3 (= *harm*) perjudicar
4 (*Med*) • **a wound ~ing the right leg** una herida que afecta a la pierna derecha • **his whole left side was ~ed** tenía todo el costado izquierdo afectado
5 (= *move emotionally*) conmover, afectar • **he seemed much ~ed** parecía muy conmovido *or* afectado
6 (= *feign*) • **he ~ed indifference** afectó *or* aparentó indiferencia, fingió ser indiferente • **she ~ed to cry** ella fingió llorar
7 (*frm*) (= *like*) • **she ~s bright colours** a ella le gustan los colores claros
(N) (*Psych*) afecto *m*, estado *m* afectivo
affectation [ˌæfekˈteɪʃən] (N) afectación *f*, falta *f* de naturalidad; **affectations** afectación *fsing*
affected [əˈfektɪd] (ADJ) **1** (= *pretentious*) [*person, manner, accent*] afectado
2 (= *feigned*) [*remorse, enthusiasm*] fingido
3 (= *suffering effects*) [*area, region, part of body*] afectado • **the worst ~ areas of Central China** las zonas peor afectadas de China Central
affectedly [əˈfektɪdlɪ] (ADV) de manera afectada, con afectación
affecting [əˈfektɪŋ] (ADJ) conmovedor, enternecedor
affection [əˈfekʃən] (N) afecto *m* (**for a, towards** hacia), cariño *m* • **to transfer one's ~s** dar su amor a otro/a
affectionate [əˈfekʃənɪt] (ADJ) **1** cariñoso, afectuoso
2 (*in letter endings*) • **with ~ greetings** cariñosamente, afectuosamente • **your ~ nephew** con abrazos de tu sobrino
affectionately [əˈfekʃənɪtlɪ] (ADV) **1** afectuosamente, cariñosamente
2 (*in letter endings*) • **~ yours** • **yours ~** un abrazo cariñoso
affective [əˈfektɪv] (ADJ) afectivo
affectivity [ˌæfekˈtɪvətɪ] (N) afectividad *f*
affiance [əˈfaɪəns] (VT) (*frm*) prometer en matrimonio (**to a**) • **to be ~d** estar prometido (**to a**) • **to ~ o.s. to** prometerse a
affidavit [ˌæfɪˈdeɪvɪt] (N) (*Jur*) declaración *f* jurada, afidávit *m* • **to swear an ~ (to the effect that)** hacer una declaración jurada (que)
affiliate (VI) [əˈfɪlɪeɪt] • **to ~ to** • **to ~ with** afiliarse a
(N) [əˈfɪlɪɪt] (= *organization*) filial *f*; (= *person*) afiliado/a *m/f*
affiliated [əˈfɪlɪeɪtɪd] (ADJ) [*member, society*] afiliado (**to, with** a) • **~ company** empresa *f* filial *or* subsidiaria
affiliation [əˌfɪlɪˈeɪʃən] (N) **1** (= *connection*) afiliación *f* • **political ~s** filiación *fsing* política
2 (*Jur*) paternidad *f*
(CPD) ▸ **affiliation order** decreto *m* relativo a la paternidad ▸ **affiliation proceedings** proceso *m* para determinar la paternidad
affinity [əˈfɪnɪtɪ] (N) **1** (= *similarity, relationship*) afinidad *f* • **A has certain affinities with B** entre A y B existe cierta afinidad
2 (= *liking*) simpatía *f* • **I feel no ~ whatsoever with** *or* **for him** no siento ninguna simpatía por él
(CPD) ▸ **affinity card** *tarjeta de crédito mediante cuyo uso un porcentaje de cada transacción se destina a una entidad benéfica*
affirm [əˈfɜːm] (VT) (= *state*) afirmar, aseverar; (= *confirm*) confirmar
affirmation [ˌæfəˈmeɪʃən] (N) afirmación *f*, aseveración *f*
affirmative [əˈfɜːmətɪv] (ADJ) afirmativo
(N) • **to answer in the ~** dar una respuesta afirmativa, contestar afirmativamente
(CPD) ▸ **affirmative action** (*US*) (*Pol*) medidas *fpl* a favor de las minorías

AFFIRMATIVE ACTION

Affirmative action es el término estadounidense que hace referencia al tratamiento privilegiado que reciben las minorías étnicas y las mujeres en lo que concierne al empleo o la educación. La administración del presidente Kennedy puso en marcha esta política en los años sesenta, estableciendo cuotas para asegurar más puestos de trabajo y plazas universitarias a aquellos colectivos con baja representación, lo cual se garantizó gracias a la Ley de Igualdad de Oportunidades Laborales (**Equal Employment Opportunities Act**), de 1972. Esta discriminación positiva fue para muchos la causa de que fueran a su vez discriminados los colectivos no minoritarios, por ejemplo, los hombres de raza blanca, por lo que la aplicación estricta de los cupos se ha relajado un tanto desde entonces.

affirmatively [ə'fɜ:mətɪvlɪ] ADV afirmativamente

affix VT [ə'fɪks] [+ *signature*] poner, añadir; [+ *stamp*] poner, pegar; [+ *seal*] imprimir • **to ~ a notice to the wall** pegar un anuncio en la pared
N ['æfɪks] (*Ling*) afijo *m*

afflict [ə'flɪkt] VT afligir • **the ~ed** los afligidos • **to be ~ed with** *or* **by** sufrir de, estar aquejado de

affliction [ə'flɪkʃən] N **1** (= *suffering*) aflicción *f*, congoja *f*
2 (*bodily*) mal *m* • **the ~s of old age** los achaques de la vejez
3 (= *misfortune*) desgracia *f*, infortunio *m* • **it's a terrible ~** es una desgracia tremenda

affluence ['æflʊəns] N riqueza *f*, opulencia *f* • **to live in ~** vivir con lujo

affluent ['æflʊənt] ADJ acaudalado, rico • **the ~ society** la sociedad de la abundancia
N **1** • **the ~** los ricos
2 (*Geog*) afluente *m*

afflux ['æflʌks] N afluencia *f*; (*Med*) aflujo *m*

afford [ə'fɔ:d] VT **1** (= *pay for*) • **we can ~ it** podemos permitírnoslo • **we can't ~ such things** no podemos permitirnos tales cosas, tales cosas no están a nuestro alcance • **we can't ~ to go on holiday** no podemos permitirnos el lujo de ir de vacaciones • **how much can you ~?** ¿cuánto puedes gastar?
2 (= *spare, risk*) • **I can't ~ the time** no tengo tiempo • **I can't ~ to be idle** no puedo permitirme el lujo de no hacer nada • **I can't ~ not to do it** no puedo permitirme el lujo de no hacerlo • **we can ~ to wait** nos podemos permitir esperar • **an opportunity you cannot ~ to miss** una ocasión que no puedes desperdiciar • **can we ~ the risk?** ¿podemos arriesgarnos?
3 (*frm*) (= *provide*) [+ *opportunity*] proporcionar, dar • **it ~s shade** da sombra • **that ~ed me some relief** eso me proporcionó cierto alivio • **this ~s me a chance to speak** esto me da la oportunidad de hablar

affordability [ə,fɔ:də'bɪlɪtɪ] N [*of goods, car, holiday, price, rent*] asequibilidad *f*

affordable [ə'fɔ:dəbl] ADJ [*goods, car, holiday, price, rent*] asequible; [*purchase*] posible

afforest [æ'fɒrɪst] VT poblar de árboles, poblar con árboles

afforestation [æ,fɒrɪs'teɪʃən] N forestación *f*

afforested [æ'fɒrɪstɪd] ADJ [*land*] poblado de árboles

affray [ə'freɪ] N (*frm*) refriega *f*, reyerta *f*

affreightment [ə'freɪtmənt] N fletamento *m*

affricate ['æfrɪkət] ADJ africado
N africada *f*

affright†† [ə'fraɪt] VT (*poet*) asustar, espantar

affront [ə'frʌnt] N afrenta *f*, ofensa *f* • **to be an ~ to** afrentar a
VT ofender, afrentar • **to be ~ed** ofenderse

Afghan ['æfgæn] ADJ afgano
N **1** (= *person*) afgano/a *m/f*
2 (*Ling*) afgano *m*
3 (= *dog*) perro/a *m/f* afgano/a

Afghani [æf'gænɪ] N (= *person*) afgano/a *m/f*
ADJ afgano

Afghanistan [æf'gænɪstæn] N Afganistán *m*

aficionado [ə,fɪsjə'nɑ:dəʊ] N aficionado/a *m/f*

afield [ə'fi:ld] ADV • **far ~** muy lejos • **countries further ~** países más lejanos • **you'll have to go further ~ for that** para eso hará falta buscar más lejos

afire [ə'faɪəʳ] ADJ (*liter*) • **to be ~** arder, estar en llamas • **to be ~ to help** anhelar ardientemente ayudar

aflame [ə'fleɪm] ADJ (*liter*) en llamas

AFL-CIO N ABBR (*US*) = **American Federation of Labor and Congress of Industrial Organizations**

afloat [ə'fləʊt] ADJ a flote • **the oldest ship ~** el barco más viejo que sigue a flote • **by a miracle we were still ~** quedamos a flote de milagro • **the largest navy ~** la mayor marina del mundo • **to spend one's life ~** pasar toda la vida a bordo • **to keep sth ~** (*lit, fig*) mantener algo a flote • **to stay** *or* **keep ~** (*lit, fig*) mantenerse a flote • **to get a business ~** lanzar un negocio

aflutter [ə'flʌtəʳ] ADJ • **to set sb's heart ~** hacer que el corazón de algn se acelere

afoot [ə'fʊt] ADV • **there is something ~** algo se está tramando • **there is a plan ~ to remove him** existe un plan para apearlo • **to set a scheme ~** poner un proyecto en marcha, poner una idea en movimiento

afore†† [ə'fɔ:ʳ] CONJ (*esp Scot*) antes (de) que

aforementioned [ə,fɔ:'menʃənd], **aforenamed** [ə'fɔ:neɪmd], **aforesaid** [ə'fɔ:sed] ADJ susodicho, mencionado

aforethought [ə'fɔ:θɔ:t] ADJ • **with malice ~** con premeditación

afoul [ə'faʊl] ADV **1** • **to run ~ of sb** ponerse a malas *or* indisponerse con algn
2 • **to run ~ of a ship** chocar con un barco

AFP, afp N ABBR (= **alpha-fetoprotein**) AFP *f*

afraid [ə'freɪd] ADJ **1** (= *frightened*) • **to be ~** tener miedo • **don't be ~** no tengas miedo • **I was ~ that nobody would believe me** tenía miedo de que nadie me creyera, temía que nadie me creyera • **I was ~ to ask** me daba miedo preguntar, tenía miedo de preguntar • **to be ~ for sb** temer por algn • **to be ~ for sb's life** temer por la vida de algn • **she suddenly looked ~** de repente parecía asustada • **to be ~ of sth/sb** tener miedo de algo/a algn, temer algo/a algn (*more frm*) • **they're ~ of you** te tienen miedo • **he was ~ of losing his job** tenía miedo de perder su trabajo, temía perder su trabajo (*more frm*) • **she's ~ of flying** le da miedo volar • **I'm ~ of dogs** los perros me dan miedo, les tengo miedo a los perros • **you have nothing to be ~ of** no tienes nada que temer • **he's not ~ of hard work** el trabajo duro no le asusta • **I was ~ of that** me lo temía • IDIOM: • **to be ~ of one's own shadow** tener miedo hasta de su propia sombra
2 (= *sorry*) • **I'm ~ he's out** lo siento, pero no está • **it's a bit stuffy in here, I'm ~** me temo que el aire aquí dentro está muy cargado • **I'm ~ not** me temo que no, no, lo siento • **I'm ~ so** me temo que sí, sí, lo siento

afresh [ə'freʃ] ADV de nuevo, otra vez • **to do sth ~** volver a hacer algo • **to start ~** volver a empezar

Africa ['æfrɪkə] N África *f*

African ['æfrɪkən] ADJ africano
N africano/a *m/f*

African-American [,æfrɪkənə'merɪkən] ADJ afroamericano
N afroamericano/a *m/f*

African-Caribbean [,æfrɪkənkærə'bi:ən] ADJ afrocaribeño
N afrocaribeño/a *m/f*

Afrikaans [,æfrɪ'kɑ:ns] N afrikaans *m*

Afrikaner [,æfrɪ'kɑ:nəʳ] ADJ afrikaner
N afrikaner *mf*

Afro ['æfrəʊ] N (*also* **Afro hairstyle**) peinado *m* afro

Afro... ['æfrəʊ] PREFIX afro...

Afro-American [,æfrəʊə'merɪkən] ADJ afroamericano
N afroamericano/a *m/f*

Afro-Asian [,æfrəʊ'eɪʃən] ADJ afroasiático
N afroasiático/a *m/f*

Afro-Caribbean [,æfrəʊkærɪ'bi:ən] ADJ afrocaribeño
N afrocaribeño/a *m/f*

AFT N ABBR (*US*) = **American Federation of Teachers**

aft [ɑ:ft] ADV (*Naut*) en popa • **to go aft** ir a popa

after ['ɑ:ftəʳ]

> *When* **after** *is an element in a phrasal verb, eg* **ask after**, **look after**, **take after**, *look up the verb.*

PREP **1** (*in time*) después de • **soon ~ eating it** poco después de comerlo • **I'll have a shower ~ you** me ducharé después que tú • **it was twenty ~ three** (*US*) eran las tres y veinte
2 (*in position, order*) detrás de, tras • **day ~ day** día tras día • **one ~ the other** uno tras otro • **excuse ~ excuse** • **one excuse ~ another** excusas y más excusas • **~ you!** ¡pase usted!, ¡usted primero! • **~ you with the salt** pásame la sal cuando acabes • **our biggest customer ~ the US** nuestro mayor cliente después de Estados Unidos
3 (= *behind*) • **close the door ~ you** cierra la puerta al salir *or* cuando salgas • **I'm tired of cleaning up ~ you** estoy cansado de ir detrás de ti limpiándolo todo • **he ran ~ me with my umbrella** corrió tras de mí con mi paraguas
4 (= *seeking*) • **the police are ~ him** la policía lo está buscando *or* está detrás de él • **I have been ~ that for years** eso lo busco desde hace años • **she's ~ a special dress** busca un vestido especial • **she's ~ a husband** va en pos de un marido • **they're all ~ the same thing** todos van a por lo mismo • **what is he ~?** ¿qué pretende? • **I see what you're ~** ya caigo, ya comprendo lo que quieres decir; (*hostile*) ya te he calado
5 (= *in the manner of*) • **this is ~ Goya** esto se pintó según el estilo de Goya • **~ the English fashion** a la (manera) inglesa; ▹ **heart**
6 (= *in honour of*) • **he is named ~ Churchill** se le llamó así por Churchill
7 (= *in view of*) después de • **~ all I've done for you** después de *or* con todo lo que he hecho por ti • **he can't go back ~ what he's done** después de lo que ha hecho no puede volver • **~ all** después de todo
ADV **1** (= *afterward*) después • **for weeks ~** durante varias semanas después • **long ~** mucho tiempo después • **soon ~** poco después
2 (= *behind*) detrás
CONJ después de que, después que* • **we ate ~ they'd gone** comimos después de que ellos se marcharon • **I went out ~ I'd eaten** salí después de comer • **we'll eat ~ you've gone** comeremos cuando te hayas ido
ADJ **1** • **in ~ years** (*frm*) en los años siguientes, años después
2 (*Naut*) de popa

after- ['ɑ:ftəʳ] PREFIX • **an after-show supper** una cena a la salida de un espectáculo; ▹ **after-dinner, after-effect** *etc*

afterbirth ['ɑ:ftəbɜ:θ] N secundinas *fpl*, placenta *f*

afterburner ['ɑ:ftə,bɜ:nəʳ] N dispositivo *m* de poscombustión

aftercare ['ɑ:ftəkɛəʳ] N (*Med*) asistencia *f* postoperatoria; [*of prisoners*] asistencia *f* (para ex-prisioneros)

afterdeck ['ɑ:ftədek] N cubierta *f* de popa

after-dinner ['ɑ:ftə'dɪnəʳ] ADJ de sobremesa • **after-dinner speech** discurso *m* de sobremesa • **after-dinner drink** copa *f* de después de la cena

AFTER

Time

Preposition

▹ *You can usually translate* **after** *referring to a point in time using* **después de**:

Please ring after six
Por favor, llama después de las seis
I'll phone you after the match
Te llamaré después del partido
... Francoism after Franco ...
... el franquismo después de Franco ...

▹ *To translate* **after** *+ period of time, you can also use* **al cabo de** *in more formal Spanish:*

After a year in the army, he had had enough
Después de (estar) un año en el ejército *or* Al cabo de un año en el ejército, no lo soportaba más

NOTE: *Use* **más tarde que** *or* **después que** *with names of people and personal pronouns when they stand in for a verb:*

He got there half an hour after us *or* **after we did**
Llegó allí media hora más tarde que nosotros *or* después que nosotros

▹ *Translate* **after** *+ -ing using* **después de** *+ infinitive:*

Don't go swimming immediately after eating
No te bañes justo después de comer

Conjunction

▹ *When the action in the* **after** *clause has already happened, and the subjects of the two clauses are different, you can generally translate* **after** *using* **después de que**. *This can be followed either by the indicative or, especially in formal or literary Spanish, by the subjunctive:*

I met her after she had left the company
La conocí después de que dejó *or* dejara la empresa

▹ *When the action in the* **after** *clause has not happened yet or had not happened at the time of speaking,* **cuando** *is more common than* **después de que**, *though both translations are possible. In both cases, use the subjunctive:*

We'll test the brakes after you've done another thousand miles
Comprobaremos los frenos cuando *or* después de que haya recorrido mil millas más

▹ *If the subject of both clauses is the same,* **después de** *+ infinitive is usually used rather than* **después de que**:

He wrote to me again after he retired
Me volvió a escribir después de jubilarse

This construction is also sometimes used in colloquial Spanish even when the subjects are different:

After you left, the party ended
Después de irte tú, se terminó la fiesta

For further uses and examples, see main entry.

after-effect [ˈɑːftərɪfekt] (N) consecuencia *f*; **after-effects** [*of treatment*] efectos *mpl* secundarios; [*of illness, operation, accident*] secuelas *fpl*

afterglow [ˈɑːftəgləʊ] (N) **1** (*in sky*) arrebol *m*, resplandor *m* crepuscular
2 (*bodily*) sensación *f* de bienestar

after-hours [ˈɑːftəˈaʊəz] (ADV) fuera de horas
(ADJ) • **after-hours dealings** transacciones *fpl* fuera de horas

afterlife [ˈɑːftəlaɪf] (N) vida *f* de ultratumba

aftermarket [ˈɑːftəˌmɑːkɪt] (N) **1** (*for cars*) mercado *m* de accesorios
2 (*St Ex*) (*for shares and bonds*) mercado *m* secundario

aftermath [ˈɑːftəmæθ] (N) consecuencias *fpl*, secuelas *fpl* • **in the ~ of the war** en el periodo de posguerra

afternoon [ˈɑːftəˈnuːn] (N) tarde *f* • **good ~!** ¡buenas tardes! • **in the ~** por la tarde • **(in the) ~s he's generally out** por las tardes en general no está
(CPD) ▸ **afternoon performance** función *f* de la tarde ▸ **afternoon tea** (*Brit*) ≈ merienda *f*

afterpains [ˈɑːftəˌpeɪnz] (NPL) dolores *mpl* de posparto

afters* [ˈɑːftəz] (NPL) (*Brit*) postre *msing* • **what's for ~?** ¿qué hay de postre?

after-sales [ˈɑːftəseɪlz] (CPD) ▸ **after-sales service, after-sales support** servicio *m* posventa, asistencia *f* posventa

after-school [ˈæftəskuːl] (ADJ) [*activities*] extraescolar
(N) *centro educativo donde se imparten actividades extraescolares*

aftershave [ˈɑːftəʃeɪv] (N) (*also* **aftershave lotion**) aftershave *m inv*, loción *f* para después del afeitado
(CPD) ▸ **aftershave balm** bálsamo *m* para después del afeitado

aftershock [ˈɑːftəʃɒk] (N) [*of earthquake*] réplica *f*

aftersun, after-sun [ˈɑːftəˌsʌn] (N) crema *f* para después del sol
(ADJ) [*lotion, cream*] para después del sol

aftertaste [ˈɑːftəteɪst] (N) (*lit, fig*) regusto *m*, dejo *m*

after-tax [ˈɑːftəˈtæks] (ADJ) después de impuestos
(CPD) ▸ **after-tax profits** beneficios *mpl* postimpositivos

afterthought [ˈɑːftəθɔːt] (N) ocurrencia *f* tardía, idea *f* adicional • **as an ~** por si acaso

after-treatment [ˈɑːftətriːtmənt] (N) tratamiento *m* postoperatorio

afterward [ˈɑːftəwəd], **afterwards** [ˈɑːftəwədz] (*esp Brit*) (ADV) después, más tarde • **~ we all helped with the washing up** después *or* luego *or* más tarde todos ayudamos a fregar los platos • **I realized ~ that he was right** después *or* luego me di cuenta de que él tenía razón • **immediately ~** inmediatamente después, acto seguido • **long ~** mucho tiempo después • **shortly** *or* **soon ~** poco después, al poco rato • **I didn't remember until ~** no lo recordé hasta después *or* hasta más tarde

afterword [ˈɑftəˈwɜːd] (N) epílogo *m*

afterworld [ˈɑːftəwɜːld] (N) mundo *m* más allá

AG (ABBR) **1 = Adjutant General**
2 (= **Attorney General**) ▹ **attorney**

again [əˈgen] (ADV) **1** (= *once more*) otra vez, de nuevo; (*often translated by* "*volver a*" + *infin*) • **try ~** inténtalo otra vez *or* de nuevo, vuelve a intentarlo • **he climbed up ~** volvió a subir • **would you do it all ~?** ¿lo volverías a hacer? • **come ~ soon** vuelve pronto • **what was that joke ~?** ¿cómo era el chiste aquel (que contaste)? • **what, you ~?** ¿tú otra vez (por aquí)? • **~ and ~** una y otra vez, vez tras vez • **I've told you ~ and ~** te lo he dicho una y otra vez *or* mil veces • **I won't do it ever ~** no lo haré nunca más • **as many ~** otros tantos • **as much ~** otro tanto • **never ~!** ¡nunca más! • **oh no, not ~!** ¡Dios mío, otra vez! • **now and ~** de vez en cuando • **he is as old ~ as I am** me dobla la edad
2 (= *besides, moreover*) • **and again ... • then again ...** (= *on the other hand*) por otra parte ...; (= *moreover*) además ... • **~, we just don't know** por otra parte, realmente no sabemos • **~, it may not be true** por otra parte, puede no ser verdad • **these are different ~** también estos son distintos

against [əˈgenst]

When **against** *is an element in a phrasal verb, eg* **go against, run up against**, *look up the verb.*

(PREP) **1** (= *in opposition to*) [+ *person*] contra, en contra de; [+ *plan*] en contra de • **what have you got ~ me?** ¿qué tiene usted en contra de mí?, ¿qué tiene usted contra mí? • **I spoke ~ the plan** hablé en contra del proyecto • **I see nothing ~ it** no veo nada en contra • **he was ~ it** estaba en contra, se opuso a ello • **he was ~ going** estaba en contra de ir • **it's ~ the law** la ley lo prohíbe, es ilegal • **it's ~ the rules** no lo permiten las reglas • **conditions are ~ us** las condiciones nos son desfavorables • **luck was ~ him** la suerte le era contraria • **to stand** *or* **run ~ sb** (*Pol*) presentarse en contra de algn • IDIOM: • **to be up ~ it** estar en un aprieto • **now we're really up ~ it!** ¡ahora sí tenemos problemas!; ▹ **tide**
2 (= *in contact with*) contra • **he hit his head ~ the wall** se dio con la cabeza contra la pared • **he leant the ladder ~ the wall** apoyó la escalera contra la pared
3 (= *in front of*) contra • **~ the light** contra la luz, a contrasol • **the hills stood out ~ the sunset** las colinas se destacaban sobre la puesta del sol
4 (*in comparisons*) • **(as) ~** contra, en contraste con • **six today, as ~ seven yesterday** seis hoy, en comparación con siete ayer
5 (= *for*) • **refund available ~ this voucher** se devuelve el precio al presentar este comprobante • **everything was ready ~ his arrival** todo estaba listo para su llegada
(ADV) en contra • **well, I'm ~** bueno, yo estoy en contra • **there were 20 votes ~** hubo 20 votos en contra

Agamemnon [ˌægəˈmemnən] (N) Agamenón

agape [əˈgeɪp] (ADJ), (ADV) boquiabierto

agar-agar [ˌeɪgəˈeɪgəʳ] (N) gelatina *f*, agar-agar *m*

agate [ˈægət] (N) ágata *f*

agave [əˈgeɪvɪ] (N) agave *f*, pita *f*, maguey *m* (*LAm*)

age [eɪdʒ] (N) **1** [*of person, animal, building*] edad *f* • **what age is she?** ¿qué edad tiene?, ¿cuántos años tiene? • **when I was your age** cuando tenía tu edad • **I have a daughter your age** *or* **the same age as you** tengo una hija de tu edad *or* de tu misma edad • **he's twice your age** te dobla en edad • **he's half your age** lo doblas en edad • **act your age!** ¡compórtate de acuerdo con tu edad!, ¡no seas niño! • **people of all ages** gente de todas las edades • **at my age** a mi edad • **at the age of 11** a los 11 años, a la edad de 11 años • **from an early age** desde muy pequeño • **to feel one's age** sentirse viejo • **she looks/doesn't look her age** aparenta/no aparenta la edad

que tiene • **60 is no age at all** 60 años no son nada • **he is five years of age** tiene cinco años (de edad) • **they are both of an age** los dos tienen la misma edad • **to be of an age to do sth** tener edad suficiente para hacer algo
2 (= *adulthood*) • **to be of age** ser mayor de edad • **to come of age** (*lit, fig*) llegar a *or* alcanzar la mayoría de edad • **to be under age** ser menor de edad
3 (= *old age*) • **age is beginning to tell on him** los años empiezan a pesar sobre él • **wine improves with age** el vino mejora con el paso del tiempo
4 (= *era*) era *f* • **this is the age of the car** esta es la era del automóvil • **the age we live in** los tiempos que vivimos, los tiempos que corren • **in the age of steam** en la era de las locomotoras de vapor; ▹ **enlightenment, nuclear, reason**
5* (= *long time*) • **we waited an age** *or* **for ages** esperamos una eternidad • **it's ages** *or* **an age since I saw him** hace siglos *or* un siglo que no lo veo • **you took ages** has tardado una eternidad *or* un siglo
VT [+ *person*] envejecer; [+ *wine*] envejecer, criar, añejar • **the experience had aged her terribly** esa experiencia la había envejecido tremendamente
VI [*person*] envejecer; [*wine*] madurar, añejarse • **he has aged a lot** ha envejecido mucho • **she seems to have aged ten years in the last month** parece haber envejecido diez años en el último mes • **to age well** [*wine*] mejorar con los años • **she has aged well** se conserva bien para la edad que tiene, le sientan bien los años
CPD ▸ **age bracket** grupo *m* de edad, grupo *m* etario (*more frm*) ▸ **age difference** diferencia *f* de edad ▸ **age discrimination** discriminación *f* por razón de edad ▸ **age gap** diferencia *f* de edad ▸ **age group** grupo *m* de edad, grupo *m* etario (*more frm*) • **the 40 to 50 age group** el grupo que comprende los de 40 a 50 años, el grupo de edad de 40 a 50 • **children of the same age group** niños de la misma edad ▸ **age limit** límite *m* de edad, edad *f* mínima/máxima • **there is no upper age limit** no hay un límite máximo de edad ▸ **age of consent** edad *f* de consentimiento sexual • **to be under the age of consent** no tener la edad de consentimiento sexual • **to be over the age of consent** tener la edad de consentimiento sexual ▸ **age range** escala *f* de edad • **children in the age range from 12 to 14** niños que van de los 12 a los 14 años

aged ADJ **1** ['eɪdʒɪd] (= *old*) viejo, anciano
2 [eɪdʒd] • **~ 15** de 15 años (de edad), que tiene 15 años
NPL ['eɪdʒɪd] • **the ~** los ancianos *mpl*

ageing ['eɪdʒɪŋ] ADJ [*person*] anciano, envejecido; [*machinery*] anticuado, viejo
N envejecimiento *m*, el envejecer, senescencia *f* • **the ~ process** el proceso de envejecer

ageism ['eɪdʒɪzəm] N discriminación *f* por razón de edad

ageist ['eɪdʒɪst] ADJ (= *discriminatory*) [*policy*] que discrimina en razón de la edad; (= *prejudiced*) [*person*] *con prejuicios por razón de edad*
N *persona con prejuicios por razón de edad*

ageless ['eɪdʒlɪs] ADJ (= *eternal*) eterno; (= *always young*) siempre joven

age-long ['eɪdʒlɒŋ] ADJ multisecular

agency ['eɪdʒənsɪ] N **1** (= *office*) agencia *f*; ▹ **advertising, travel**
2 (= *branch*) delegación *f*
3 (= *institution*) organismo *m* • **International Atomic Energy Agency** Organismo *m* Internacional de Energía Atómica
4 (= *mediation*) • **through the ~ of** por medio de, por la mediación de
CPD ▸ **Agency for International Development** (US) Agencia *f* para el Desarrollo Internacional ▸ **agency nurse** enfermero/a *m/f* de agencia

agenda [ə'dʒendə] N **1** (*at meeting*) orden *m* del día • **on the ~** en el orden del día
2 (*fig*) • **environmental issues are high on the party's ~** los asuntos medioambientales ocupan un lugar prominente en el programa político del partido • **to have one's own ~** tener sus propias prioridades • **to set the ~** marcar la pauta

agent ['eɪdʒənt] N **1** (*for company, sports personality, actor*) agente *mf*, representante *mf*; (*Jur*) apoderado/a *m/f*; (*Pol*) delegado/a *m/f*; (*undercover*) agente *mf* • **his father acts as his ~** su padre actúa como su representante
2 (US) (= *station master*) jefe/a *m/f* de estación
3 (*Chem*) agente *m* • **chemical ~** agente *m* químico
4 (= *catalyst*) • **she has portrayed herself as an ~ of change** se ha descrito a sí misma como agente *or* propulsora *or* motor del cambio

agentive ['eɪdʒəntɪv] N (*Gram*) agentivo *m*

agent provocateur ['æʒɑ̃:prɒvɒkə'tɜ:ʳ] N agente *mf* provocador(a)

age-old ['eɪdʒəʊld] ADJ multisecular, antiquísimo

agglomeration [əˌglɒmə'reɪʃən] N aglomeración *f*

agglutinate [ə'glu:tɪneɪt] VT aglutinar
VI aglutinarse

agglutination [əˌglu:tɪ'neɪʃən] N aglutinación *f*

agglutinative [ə'glu:tɪnətɪv] ADJ aglutinante

aggrandize [ə'grændaɪz] VT (= *increase stature of*) [+ *person*] engrandecer; (= *exaggerate*) agrandar, exagerar • **to ~ o.s.** darse aires (de grandeza)

aggrandizement [ə'grændɪzmənt] N [*of person*] engrandecimiento *m*

aggravate ['ægrəveɪt] VT **1** (= *make worse*) agravar
2* (= *annoy*) irritar, sacar de quicio

aggravated ['ægrəveɪtɪd] ADJ **1** (*Jur*) • **~ assault** agresión *f* con agravante(s) • **~ burglary** robo *m* con fuerza • **~ robbery** robo *m* calificado *or* con agravante(s) • **~ murder** asesinato *m* calificado
2* (= *annoyed*) [*person*] irritado

aggravating ['ægrəveɪtɪŋ] ADJ **1** (*Jur*) agravante
2* (= *annoying*) molesto • **he's an ~ child** es un niño molesto • **it's very ~** es para volverse loco

aggravation [ˌægrə'veɪʃən] N
1 (= *exacerbation*) [*of problem, situation, illness*] agravación *f*, empeoramiento *m*
2* (= *annoyance*) irritación *f*
3 (*Jur*) circunstancia *f* agravante • **robbery with ~** robo *m* agravado

aggregate N ['ægrɪgɪt] **1** (= *total*) conjunto *m* • **on ~** en conjunto • **Scotland won 5-4 on ~** ganó Escocia por 5 a 4 en conjunto • **in the ~** en conjunto, en total
2 (*Geol, Constr*) agregado *m*
ADJ ['ægrɪgɪt] total, global
VT ['ægrɪgeɪt] juntar, sumar; (*Comput*) agregar

aggregator ['ægrɪgeɪtəʳ] N (*Comput*) agregador *m*

aggress [ə'gres] VI comportarse de manera agresiva • **to ~ against sb** (= *be unpleasant to*) comportarse de manera agresiva con algn; (*physically*) agredir a algn
VT agredir

aggression [ə'greʃən] N **1** (= *behaviour*) agresión *f* • **an act of ~** un acto de agresión
2 (= *feeling*) agresividad *f* • **~ is not a solely masculine trait** la agresividad no es una característica únicamente masculina

aggressive [ə'gresɪv] ADJ **1** (= *belligerent*) [*person, animal, behaviour*] agresivo • **he was in a very ~ mood** estaba muy agresivo
2 (= *assertive*) [*salesman, company*] enérgico, agresivo; [*player*] agresivo • **~ marketing techniques** técnicas *fpl* de marketing agresivas

aggressively [ə'gresɪvlɪ] ADV
1 (= *belligerently*) [*behave, react*] agresivamente, de manera agresiva; [*say*] con mucha agresividad
2 (= *assertively*) [*trade, sell*] enérgicamente, con empuje; [*play*] agresivamente

aggressiveness [ə'gresɪvnɪs] N
1 (= *belligerence*) agresividad *f*
2 (= *assertiveness*) empuje *m*

aggressor [ə'gresəʳ] N agresor(a) *m/f*

aggrieved [ə'gri:vd] ADJ ofendido • **the ~ husband** el marido ofendido • **in an ~ tone** en un tono de queja • **he was much ~** se ofendió mucho • **to feel ~** ofenderse, resentirse (**at** por)
CPD ▸ **the aggrieved party** la parte perjudicada *or* agraviada

aggro* ['ægrəʊ] N (*Brit*) **1** (= *violence*) agresividad *f*, violencia *f* • **the crowd was looking for ~** la gente buscaba camorra*
2 (= *hassle*) líos *mpl*, problemas *mpl* • **I'm not going, it's too much ~** no voy, es mucha lata*

aghast [ə'gɑ:st] ADJ horrorizado, pasmado (**at** ante) • **to be ~ at** horrorizarse *or* pasmarse ante

agile ['ædʒaɪl] ADJ ágil

agilely ['ædʒaɪllɪ] ADV ágilmente

agility [ə'dʒɪlɪtɪ] N agilidad *f*

agin [ə'gɪn] PREP (*Scot*) (*also hum*) = **against** • **to be** *or* **take ~ sth** oponerse a algo

aging ['eɪdʒɪŋ] ADJ, N = **ageing**

agitate ['ædʒɪteɪt] VT **1** (= *excite, upset*) inquietar, perturbar
2 (= *shake*) agitar
VI (*Pol*) • **to ~ for sth** hacer campaña en pro de algo • **to ~ against sth** hacer campaña en contra de algo

agitated ['ædʒɪteɪtɪd] ADJ inquieto, perturbado • **in an ~ tone** en tono inquieto • **to be very ~** estar muy inquieto (**about** por)

agitation [ˌædʒɪ'teɪʃən] N **1** (*mental*) inquietud *f*, perturbación *f*
2 (= *shaking*) agitación *f*
3 (*Pol*) agitación *f*

agitator ['ædʒɪteɪtəʳ] N **1** (*Pol*) agitador(a) *m/f*
2 (*Chem*) agitador *m*

agitprop ['ædʒɪtˌprɒp] N propaganda *f* política (*esp de izquierdas*)

aglow [ə'gləʊ] ADJ radiante, brillante • **to be ~ with** brillar de • **to be ~ with happiness** irradiar felicidad

AGM N ABBR (= **annual general meeting**) junta *f* anual

Agnes ['ægnɪs] N Inés

agnostic [æg'nɒstɪk] ADJ agnóstico
N agnóstico/a *m/f*

agnosticism [æg'nɒstɪsɪzəm] N agnosticismo *m*

ago [ə'gəʊ] ADV • **long ago** hace mucho tiempo • **not long ago** no hace mucho (tiempo) • **how long ago was it?** ¿hace cuánto tiempo?, ¿cuánto tiempo hace? • **as long ago as 1978** ya en 1978 • **no longer ago than yesterday** ayer solamente, ayer nada

más • **a week ago** hace una semana • **a little while ago** hace poco • **just a moment ago** hace un momento nada más
agog [əˈgɒg] ADJ • **the country was ~** el país estaba emocionadísimo • **he was ~ to hear the news** tenía enorme curiosidad por saber las noticias • **to set ~** emocionar, crear gran curiosidad a
agonize [ˈægənaɪz] VI atormentarse • **to ~ over a decision** dudar antes de tomar una decisión
agonized [ˈægənaɪzd] ADJ angustioso
agonizing [ˈægənaɪzɪŋ] ADJ *[pain]* atroz, muy agudo; *[indecision, suspense]* angustioso; *[moment]* de angustia; *[reappraisal]* agonizante, doloroso
agonizingly [ˈægənaɪzɪŋlɪ] ADV (= *painfully*) dolorosamente • **it was ~ painful** era atrozmente doloroso • **~ close** angustiosamente cerca • **~ slow** terriblemente *or* desesperantemente lento
agony [ˈægənɪ] N **1** *(physical)* dolor *m* agudo • **I was in ~** sufría dolores horrorosos
2 *(mental)* angustia *f* • **to suffer agonies of doubt** estar atormentado por las dudas • **to be in an ~ of impatience** impacientarse mucho • **it was ~!*** ¡fue fatal!* • **the play was sheer ~*** la obra era una birria*; ▷ **pile on**
3 (= *final agony, death agony*) agonía *f* • **he was in his final** *or* **death ~** estaba agonizando
CPD ▸ **agony aunt*** *(Brit)* columnista *f* del consultorio sentimental ▸ **agony column*** *(Brit)* consultorio *m* sentimental ▸ **agony uncle*** *(Brit)* columnista *m* del consultorio sentimental
agoraphobe [ˈægərəfəʊb] N agorafóbico/a *m/f*
agoraphobia [ˌægərəˈfəʊbɪə] N agorafobia *f*
agoraphobic [ˌægərəˈfəʊbɪk] ADJ agorafóbico
N agorafóbico/a *m/f*
AGR N ABBR = **Advanced Gas-Cooled Reactor**
agrammatical [ˌeɪgrəˈmætɪkəl] ADJ agramatical
agrarian [əˈgrɛərɪən] ADJ agrario
CPD ▸ **agrarian reform** reforma *f* agraria ▸ **agrarian revolution** revolución *f* agraria
agrarianism [əˈgrɛərɪənɪzəm] N agrarismo *m*
agree [əˈgriː] VI **1** (= *consent*) consentir • **eventually he ~d** por fin consintió • **you'll never get him to ~** no lograrás nunca su consentimiento • **to ~ to sth** consentir en *or* aceptar algo • **he'll ~ to anything** se aviene a todo • **I ~ to your marrying my niece** acepto que usted se case con mi sobrina
2 (= *be in agreement*) estar de acuerdo; (= *come to an agreement*) ponerse de acuerdo • **I ~** estoy de acuerdo, estoy conforme • **I quite ~** estoy completamente de acuerdo • **don't you ~?** ¿no está de acuerdo?, ¿no le parece? • **to ~ about** *or* **on sth** (= *be in agreement*) estar de acuerdo sobre algo; (= *come to an agreement*) ponerse de acuerdo sobre algo • **I don't ~ about trying again tomorrow** no estoy de acuerdo con lo de volverlo a intentar mañana • **to ~ with** *[+ person]* estar de acuerdo *or* coincidir con; *[+ policy]* estar de acuerdo con, aprobar
3 (= *accord, coincide*) concordar • **these statements do not ~ (with each other)** estas declaraciones no concuerdan • **his reasoning ~s with mine** su razonamiento concuerda con el mío
4 (= *get on together*) *[people]* congeniar • **we simply don't ~** simplemente no congeniamos
5 • **to ~ with a** (= *approve of*) aprobar • **I don't ~ with women playing football** no apruebo que las mujeres jueguen al fútbol
b (= *be beneficial to*) *[food, climate]* • **garlic/this heat doesn't ~ with me** el ajo/este calor no me sienta bien
6 *(Gram)* concordar (**with** con)
VT **1** (= *consent*) • **to ~ to do sth** consentir en *or* aceptar hacer algo
2 (= *be in agreement, come to an agreement*) • **"it's impossible," she ~d** —es imposible —asintió • **to ~ that** estar de acuerdo en que • **everyone ~s that it is so** todos están de acuerdo en que es así • **it was ~d that …** se acordó que … • **it is ~d that …** *(on legal contracts)* se acuerda que … • **they ~d among themselves to do it** (todos) se pusieron de acuerdo para hacerlo • **it was ~d to** (+ *infin*) se acordó (+ *infin*) • **we ~d to meet up later** quedamos en vernos después • **to ~ to disagree** *or* **differ** estar en desacuerdo amistoso
3 (= *admit*) reconocer • **I ~ that I was too hasty** reconozco que lo hice con precipitación • **I ~ that it was foolish** reconozco que era insensato
4 [+ *plan, statement etc*] aceptar, llegar a un acuerdo sobre; [+ *price*] convenir • **the plan was speedily ~d** el proyecto fue aceptado sin demora • **"salary to be agreed"** "sueldo a convenir" • **at a date to be ~d** en una fecha (que queda) por determinar *or* concertar
agreeable [əˈgriːəbl] ADJ **1** (= *pleasing*) *[sensation, pastime, surprise]* agradable; *[person]* agradable, simpático • **it was ~ having her in the office** era agradable tenerla en la oficina • **she made a point of being ~ to them** se esforzó por ser agradable *or* simpática con ellos
2 *(frm)* (= *acceptable*) • **is that ~ to you?** ¿está de acuerdo?, ¿está conforme? • **a solution that would be ~ to all** una solución satisfactoria para todos
3 *(frm)* (= *willing*) • **get your secretary to do it if she is ~** dáselo a tu secretaria para que lo haga si a ella no le importa • **she is ~ to making the arrangements** no le importa encargarse de los preparativos
agreeably [əˈgriːəblɪ] ADV *[chat, reply]* agradablemente • **they were ~ surprised to discover that …** se llevaron una agradable sorpresa al descubrir que …
agreed [əˈgriːd] ADJ *[time, plan]* convenido • **as ~** según lo convenido • **are we all ~?** ¿estamos todos de acuerdo? • **~!** ¡de acuerdo!, ¡conforme(s)!
agreement [əˈgriːmənt] N
1 (= *understanding, arrangement*) acuerdo *m*; (= *consent*) consentimiento *m*; (= *treaty etc*) acuerdo *m*, pacto *m*; *(Comm)* contrato *m* • **to come to** *or* **reach an ~** llegar a un acuerdo • **to enter into an ~** firmar un contrato • **to enter into an ~ to do sth** firmar un contrato para hacer algo • **by mutual ~** por acuerdo mutuo, de común acuerdo; ▷ **gentleman**
2 (= *shared opinion*) acuerdo *m* • **he nodded in ~** • **he nodded his ~** asintió con la cabeza • **to be in ~ on a plan** estar conformes en un proyecto • **to be in ~ with** [+ *person*] estar de acuerdo con; [+ *decision*] estar de acuerdo con, estar conforme con; (= *consistent with*) concordar con, estar en concordancia con
3 *(Gram)* concordancia *f*
agribusiness [ˈægrɪˌbɪznɪs] N agroindustria *f*, industria *f* agropecuaria
agricultural [ˌægrɪˈkʌltʃərəl] ADJ agrícola
CPD ▸ **agricultural college** escuela *f* de agricultura ▸ **agricultural expert** perito/a *m/f* agrónomo/a ▸ **agricultural run-off** vertidos *mpl* agrícolas ▸ **agricultural show** feria *f* agrícola *or* de campo ▸ **agricultural subsidy** subvención *f* agrícola
agriculturalist [ˌægrɪˈkʌltʃərəlɪst] N
1 (= *farmer*) agricultor(a) *m/f*
2 (= *professional expert*) perito/a *m/f* agrónomo/a
agriculturally [ˌægrɪˈkʌltʃərəlɪ] ADV agrícolamente
agriculture [ˈægrɪkʌltʃəʳ] N agricultura *f* • **Ministry of Agriculture, Fisheries and Food** *(Brit)* ≈ Ministerio *m* de Agricultura, Pesca y Alimentación *(Sp)*
agriculturist [ˌægrɪˈkʌltʃərɪst] N = **agriculturalist**
agritourism, agri-tourism [ˈægrɪˌtʊərɪzəm] N agroturismo *m*
agrobiologist [ˌægrəʊbaɪˈɒlədʒɪst] N agrobiólogo/a *m/f*
agrobiology [ˌægrəʊbaɪˈɒlədʒɪ] N agrobiología *f*
agrobiotechnology [ˌægrəʊˌbaɪəʊtekˈnɒlədʒɪ] N agrobiotecnología *f*
agrochemical [ˌægrəʊˈkemɪkəl] ADJ agroquímico
N (producto *m*) agroquímico *m*
agroforestry, agro-forestry [ˌægrəʊˈfɒrɪstrɪ] N agrosilvicultura *f*
agronomist [əˈgrɒnəmɪst] N agrónomo/a *m/f*
agronomy [əˈgrɒnəmɪ] N agronomía *f*
agroproduct [ˌægrəʊˈprɒdʌkt] N agroproducto *m*
aground [əˈgraʊnd] ADV *(Naut)* • **to be ~** estar encallado *or* varado • **to run ~** encallar • **to run a ship ~** varar un barco, hacer que encalle un barco
agt ABBR *(Comm)* = **agent**
ague†† [ˈeɪgjuː] N fiebre *f* intermitente
AH ABBR (= **anno Hegirae**) (= *from the year of the Hegira*) a.h.
ah [ɑː] EXCL ¡ah!
aha [ɑːˈhɑː] EXCL ¡ajá!
ahead [əˈhed] ADV

*When **ahead** is an element in a phrasal verb, eg **draw ahead, go ahead**, look up the verb.*

1 *(in space, order)* delante • **to be ~** *(in race)* llevar la delantera, ir (por) delante, ir ganando; *(fig)* llevar la ventaja, ir a la cabeza • **to go on ~** ir adelante • **this put Barcelona three points ~** esto dio al Barcelona tres puntos de ventaja • **to send sb ~** enviar a algn por delante; ▷ **straight**
2 *(in time)* antes; *[book]* con anticipación • **there's trouble ~** han de sobrevenir disgustos, ya se prevén dificultades • **there's a busy time ~** tendremos mucha tarea • **to look ~** *(fig)* anticipar • **to plan ~** planificar por adelantado *or* con anticipación • **to think ~** pensar en el futuro
3 • **~ of a** *(in space, order)* delante de • **there were three people ~ of us** había tres personas delante de nosotros • **to be ~ of sb** *(in race, competition)* llevar ventaja a • **to get ~ of sb** *(lit, fig)* adelantarse a algn
b *(in time)* • **you'll get there ~ of us** llegarás antes que nosotros • **he's two hours ~ of the next competitor** lleva dos horas de ventaja sobre el rival más próximo • **share prices rose ~ of the annual report** la cotización subió en anticipación del informe anual • **we are three months ~ of schedule** llevamos tres meses de adelanto sobre la fecha prevista • **to arrive ~ of time** llegar antes de la hora prevista • **to be ~ of one's time** anticiparse a su época • **Wagner was two centuries ~ of his time** Wagner se anticipó en dos siglos a su época • **the plane is ~ of its time** el avión va por delante de su tiempo

ahem [ə'hem] EXCL ¡ejem!

ahold [ə'həʊld] N (*esp US*) **1** • **to get ~ of sb** (= *get in touch with*) contactar con algn; (= *find*) localizar a algn • **to get ~ of sth** (= *obtain*) conseguir *or* obtener algo
2 • **to get ~ of o.s.** (*fig*) controlarse

ahoy [ə'hɔɪ] EXCL • **ship ~!** ¡barco a la vista! • **~ there!** ¡ah del barco!

AHQ N ABBR = **Army Headquarters**

AI N ABBR **1** (= **Amnesty International**) AI *f*
2 (= **artificial intelligence**) IA *f*
3 = **artificial insemination**

AIC ABBR = **agent in charge (of investigation)**

AID N ABBR **1** = **artificial insemination by donor**
2 (*US*) (= **Agency for International Development**) AID *f*
3 (*US*) (*Admin*) = **Aid to Families with Dependent Children**

aid [eɪd] N **1** (= *assistance*) ayuda *f* • **to come/go to sb's aid** (*lit*) acudir en ayuda *or* (*more frm*) en auxilio de algn; (*in argument*) salir en defensa de algn • **a neighbour rushed to his aid** un vecino corrió en su ayuda *or* (*more frm*) en su auxilio • **a charity performance in aid of the blind** una representación benéfica a beneficio de los ciegos • **what's all this in aid of?*** ¿a qué viene todo esto? • **with the aid of** con la ayuda de • **she could only walk with the aid of crutches** solo podía andar con la ayuda *or* ayudándose de unas muletas • **the star can be seen without the aid of a telescope** la estrella se puede ver sin necesidad *or* ayuda de un telescopio
2 (*economic, medical*) ayuda *f* • **to give aid** prestar ayuda; ▹ **food, legal**
3 (= *book, tool*) ayuda *f* • **the book is an invaluable aid to teachers** el libro es una ayuda valiosísima para los profesores; ▹ **audiovisual, deaf, hearing, teaching, visual**
4 (= *person*) asistente *mf*
VT **1** [+ *progress, process, recovery*] (= *speed up*) acelerar; (= *contribute to*) contribuir a
2 [+ *person*] ayudar • **to aid sb to do sth** ayudar a algn a hacer algo • **to aid one another** ayudarse mutuamente • **to aid and abet sb** ser cómplice de algn; (*Jur*) instigar y secundar a algn
VI ayudar • **it aids in the prevention of tooth decay** ayuda a prevenir la caries
CPD ▸ **aid agency** organismo *m* de ayuda ▸ **aid package** dotación *f* de ayuda ▸ **aid programme, aid program** (*US*) programa *m* de ayuda ▸ **aid station** (*US*) puesto *m* de socorro ▸ **aid worker** cooperante *mf*

aide [eɪd] N **1** (*Mil*) edecán *m*
2 (*Pol*) ayudante *mf*

-aided ['eɪdɪd] ADJ (*ending in compounds*) • **state-aided schools** escuelas *fpl* subvencionadas por el estado • **grant-aided factories** fábricas *fpl* subvencionadas • **computer-aided design** diseño *m* asistido por ordenador *or* (*esp LAm*) computador

aide-de-camp [ˌeɪddə'kɑ̃ːŋ] N (PL: **aides-de-camp**) edecán *m*

aide-mémoire ['eɪdmeɪ'mwɑːʳ] N (PL: **aides-mémoire, aide-mémoires**) memorándum *m*

AIDS, Aids [eɪdz] N ABBR (= **Acquired Immune Deficiency Syndrome**) SIDA *m*, sida *m*
CPD ▸ **AIDS campaign** campaña *f* anti-sida ▸ **AIDS clinic** sidatorio *m* ▸ **AIDS sufferer** enfermo/a *m/f* del sida ▸ **AIDS test** prueba *f* del sida ▸ **AIDS victim** víctima *f* del sida

AIDS-related ['eɪdzrɪˌleɪtɪd] ADJ relacionado con el SIDA

AIH N ABBR = **artificial insemination by husband**

ail [eɪl] VT† afligir • **what ails you?** ¿qué tienes?, ¿qué te pasa?
VI (*also* **be ailing**) estar enfermo, estar sufriendo

aileron ['eɪlərɒn] N alerón *m*

ailing ['eɪlɪŋ] ADJ [*person*] enfermo, achacoso; [*industry, economy*] debilitado

ailment ['eɪlmənt] N enfermedad *f*, achaque *m*

AIM N ABBR (*Brit*) (*St Ex*) (= **Alternative Investment Market**) segundo mercado *m*, mercado *m* de títulos no cotizados

aim [eɪm] N **1** (= *purpose, object*) objetivo *m*, propósito *m* • **his one aim was to escape** su único objetivo *or* propósito era escaparse • **to achieve one's aims** conseguir sus propósitos *or* lo que se propone • **I achieved the aim I set myself** conseguí mi propósito, conseguí lo que me había propuesto • **to have no aim in life** no tener un norte *or* una meta en la vida • **with the aim of doing sth** con miras a hacer algo, con la intención de hacer algo
2 (*with gun, arrow*) puntería *f* • **to have a good/poor aim** tener buena/mala puntería • **to miss one's aim** fallar *or* errar el tiro • **to take aim (at sth/sb)** apuntar (a algo/algn) • **he took careful aim** apuntó con cuidado
VT [+ *gun*] apuntar; [+ *camera*] dirigir, enfocar; [+ *blow*] lanzar, intentar dar; [+ *remark, criticism*] dirigir • **he aimed the pistol at me** me apuntó con la pistola • **missiles aimed at the capital** misiles apuntando a la capital • **he aimed a kick at my shins** me lanzó una patada a las canillas, intentó darme una patada en las canillas • **this advertising is aimed at children** esta campaña va dirigida a los niños • **talks aimed at ending the war** conversaciones *fpl or* negociaciones *fpl* encaminadas a la finalización de la guerra
VI **1** (*with weapon*) apuntar • **I aimed at his forehead** le apunté a *or* en la frente • **aim for the centre of the green** intenta lanzar la pelota al centro del green
2 (= *aspire*) • **to aim to do sth** ponerse como objetivo hacer algo • **aim to drink five glasses of water a day** póngase como objetivo beber cinco vasos de agua al día • **we must aim at reducing inflation** debemos aspirar a *or* dirigir nuestros esfuerzos a reducir la inflación • **to aim for sth** aspirar a algo • **it will give you something to aim for** así tendrás algo a lo que aspirar • IDIOM: • **to aim high** picar muy alto, aspirar a mucho
3 (= *intend*) • **to aim to do sth** [*person*] proponerse *or* pretender hacer algo • **I aim to finish it today** me he propuesto *or* me propongo terminarlo hoy, pretendo terminarlo hoy • **the book aims to answer these questions** el libro tiene como objetivo *or* pretende contestar estas preguntas

aimless ['eɪmlɪs] ADJ [*way of life, pursuit*] sin sentido, sin propósito; [*person*] sin objeto, sin propósito • **after hours of ~ wandering he went home** tras pasar horas deambulando sin rumbo (fijo), se fue a casa

aimlessly ['eɪmlɪslɪ] ADV [*wander, drift, walk*] sin rumbo (fijo); [*chat, talk*] por hablar; [*live*] sin propósito

aimlessness ['eɪmlɪsnɪs] N [*of wandering*] falta *f* de rumbo; [*of life*] falta *f* de sentido, falta *f* de propósito; [*of conversation*] falta *f* de objeto

ain't‡ [eɪnt] (*dialect*) = **am not, is not, are not, has not, have not** ▹ **be, have**

air [ɛəʳ] N **1** (*lit*) aire *m* • **I need some air!** ¡necesito un poco de aire! • **by air** [*travel*] en avión; [*send*] por avión, por vía aérea • **(seen) from the air** desde el aire • **to get some fresh air** tomar un poco el aire • **to throw sth (up) in** *or* **into the air** lanzar algo al aire • **the balloon rose (up) in** *or* **into the air** el globo se elevó en el aire • **we let the air out of his tyres** le desinflamos las ruedas • **one can't live on air** no se puede vivir del aire • **the cold night air** el aire frío de la noche • **in the open air** al aire libre • **the air rang with their laughter** su risa resonaba en el aire • **the sea air** el aire del mar • **spring is in the air** ya se siente la primavera • **to take the air**† tomar el fresco, airearse • **to take to the air** [*bird*] alzar *or* levantar el vuelo; [*plane*] despegar • **to fly through the air** volar por el aire *or* por los aires • IDIOMS: • **to be in the air**: • **it's still very much in the air** está todavía en el aire, todavía no es seguro • **there's something in the air** se respira algo • **to leave sth (hanging) in the air** dejar algo en el aire *or* pendiente • **our plans are up in the air** nuestros planes están en el aire • **to be walking** *or* **floating on air** no caber en sí de alegría; ▹ **breath, change, clear, hot, thin**
2 (*Rad, TV*) • **off air** fuera de antena • **the argument continued off air** la discusión continuó fuera de antena • **to go off (the) air** [*broadcaster, station*] cerrar la emisión; [*programme*] finalizar • **to be on (the) air** [*programme, person*] estar en el aire; [*station*] emitir, estar en el aire • **we are on (the) air from six to seven** emitimos de seis a siete, estamos en el aire de seis a siete • **the programme could be on (the) air within a year** el programa podría emitirse dentro de un año • **you're on (the) air** estás en el aire, estamos emitiendo • **would you be prepared to talk about it on (the) air?** ¿estaría dispuesto a hablar de ello durante la emisión del programa?, ¿estaría dispuesto a hablar de ello una vez estemos en el aire? • **to go on (the) air** salir al aire
3 (= *appearance, manner*) aire *m* • **he looked at me with an air of surprise** me miró con aire de sorpresa, me miró algo sorprendido • **he has an air of importance** tiene cierto aire de importancia • **to give o.s. airs** • **put on airs** darse aires (de importancia) • **airs and graces** afectación *fsing*
4 (*Mus*) aire *m*
5† (= *breeze*) brisa *f*
VT **1** (= *ventilate*) [+ *room*] ventilar, airear; [+ *clothes, bed*] airear, orear
2 (= *make public*) [+ *idea, grievance*] airear, hacer público • **it gives them a chance to air their views** les da la oportunidad de airear *or* hacer públicos sus puntos de vista • **he always has to air his knowledge in front of me** siempre tiene que hacer alarde de *or* lucir lo que sabe delante de mí
3 (*US*) (*Rad, TV*) [+ *programme*] emitir
4 (*US*) (= *transport*) transportar por avión, aerotransportar
VI **1** [*clothes*] airearse, orearse • **I hung the blankets out to air** colgué las mantas fuera para que se aireasen *or* se oreasen
2 (*US*) (*TV, Rad*) [*programme*] emitirse
CPD ▸ **air alert** alerta *f* aérea ▸ **air ambulance** (= *plane*) avión *m* sanitario, avión *m* ambulancia; (= *helicopter*) helicóptero *m* sanitario, helicóptero *m* ambulancia ▸ **air attack** ataque *m* aéreo ▸ **air bag** airbag *m*, bolsa *f* de aire ▸ **air base** base *f* aérea ▸ **air bed** colchón *m* inflable ▸ **air bladder** (*Zool*) vejiga *f* natatoria ▸ **air brake** (*Aut, Rail*) freno *m* neumático *or* de aire; (*Aer*) freno *m* aerodinámico ▸ **air brick** ladrillo *m* de ventilación ▸ **air bridge** puente *m* aéreo

▸ **air bubble** burbuja *f* de aire ▸ **air burst** explosión *f* en el aire ▸ **air cargo** carga *f* aérea ▸ **air carrier** aerolínea *f* ▸ **air chamber** cámara *f* de aire ▸ **air chief marshal** (*Brit*) comandante *m* supremo de las Fuerzas Aéreas ▸ **air commodore** (*Brit*) general *m* de brigada aérea ▸ **air conditioner** acondicionador *m* de aire ▸ **air conditioning** aire *m* acondicionado • **a cinema with air conditioning** un cine climatizado ▸ **air corridor** pasillo *m* aéreo, corredor *m* aéreo ▸ **air cover** (*Mil*) cobertura *f* aérea ▸ **air current** corriente *f* de aire ▸ **air cushion** (= *inflatable cushion*) almohada *f* inflable; (*Aer*) colchón *m* de aire ▸ **air cylinder** bombona *f* de aire ▸ **air disaster** catástrofe *f* aérea ▸ **air display** exhibición *f* aérea, desfile *m* aéreo ▸ **air duct** tubo *m* de aire, tubo *m* de ventilación ▸ **air express** (*US*) avión *m* de carga ▸ **air fare** tarifa *f* aérea, precio *m* del billete de avión • **a 10% reduction in air fares** un descuento del 10% en las tarifas aéreas *or* los precios de los billetes de avión • **I'll pay for the air fare** yo pagaré el billete de avión ▸ **air ferry** transbordador *m* aéreo ▸ **air filter** filtro *m* de aire ▸ **air force** fuerzas *fpl* aéreas, ejército *m* del aire ▸ **air force base** (*esp US*) base *f* aérea ▸ **Air Force One** (*US*) avión *m* presidencial ▸ **air freight** (= *transport, charge*) flete *m* aéreo; (= *goods*) carga *f* aérea • **to send sth by air freight** transportar algo por avión ▸ **air freight terminal** terminal *f* de mercancías (*transportadas por aire*) ▸ **air freshener** ambientador *m* ▸ **air guitar** guitarra *f* imaginaria ▸ **air gun** (= *pistol*) pistola *f* de aire (comprimido); (= *rifle*) escopeta *f* de aire (comprimido) ▸ **air hole** respiradero *m* ▸ **air hostess** (*Brit*) azafata *f*, aeromoza *f* (*LAm*), cabinera *f* (*Col*) ▸ **air inlet** entrada *f* de aire, toma *f* de aire ▸ **air intake** (*in engine*) entrada *f* de aire, toma *f* de aire; (*when breathing*) aire *m* inhalado, capacidad *f* pulmonar ▸ **air lane** pasillo *m* aéreo, corredor *m* aéreo ▸ **air letter** aerograma *m* ▸ **air marshal** (*Brit*) mariscal *m* del aire ▸ **air mass** masa *f* de aire ▸ **air mattress** colchón *m* inflable ▸ **air miles** puntos *mpl* (acumulables para viajar) ▸ **air miss** air-miss *m*, aproximación *f* peligrosa entre dos aviones ▸ **air pistol** pistola *f* de aire comprimido ▸ **air pocket** bolsa *f* de aire ▸ **air pollutant** contaminante *m* atmosférico ▸ **air pollution** contaminación *f* del aire, contaminación *f* atmosférica ▸ **air power** fuerza *f* aérea • **the use of air power** el uso de la fuerza aérea ▸ **air pressure** presión *f* atmosférica ▸ **air pump** bomba *f* de aire ▸ **air purifier** purificador *m* de aire ▸ **air rage** síndrome *m* del pasajero alborotador ▸ **air raid** ataque *m* aéreo; ▹ **air-raid** ▸ **air rifle** escopeta *f* de aire (comprimido) ▸ **air shaft** pozo *m* de ventilación ▸ **air show** (*commercial*) feria *f* de la aeronáutica; (= *air display*) exhibición *f* de acrobacia aérea ▸ **air shuttle** puente *m* aéreo ▸ **air sock** manga *f* (de viento) ▸ **air space** espacio *m* aéreo • **Spanish air space** espacio *m* aéreo español ▸ **air steward** auxiliar *m* de vuelo ▸ **air stewardess** auxiliar *f* de vuelo, azafata *f* ▸ **air strike** ataque *m* aéreo ▸ **air superiority** supremacía *f* aérea ▸ **air suspension** (*Aut*) suspensión *f* neumática ▸ **air taxi** aerotaxi *m* ▸ **air terminal** terminal *f* (de aeropuerto) ▸ **air ticket** billete *m* de avión ▸ **air time** (*Rad, TV*) tiempo *m* en antena ▸ **air traffic** tráfico *m* aéreo; ▹ **air-traffic** ▸ **air travel** viajes *mpl* en avión ▸ **air valve** respiradero *m* ▸ **air vent** (*in building*) respiradero *m*; (*in clothing*) abertura *f* (*en prenda de ropa*); (*on dryer*) tobera *f* de aire caliente ▸ **air vice-marshall** (*Brit*) general *m* de división de las Fuerzas Aéreas ▸ **air waybill** hoja *f* de ruta aérea

airborne ['ɛəbɔːn] ADJ **1** [*aircraft*] volando, en el aire • **to become ~** elevarse en los aires, subir • **we shall soon be ~** el avión despegará pronto • **suddenly we were ~** de repente nos vimos en el aire • **we were ~ for eight hours** volamos durante ocho horas
2 (*Mil*) aerotransportado • **~ troops** tropas *fpl* aerotransportadas
3 [*virus, germ, bacteria*] transmitido por el aire; [*seed*] llevado por el aire
CPD ▸ **airborne attack** ataque *m* aéreo

airbrush ['ɛəbrʌʃ] N aerógrafo *m*
VT pintar con aerógrafo

airbus ['ɛəbʌs] N aerobús *m*
CPD ▸ **airbus service** puente *m* aéreo

air-con* ['ɛəkɒn] N (= **air conditioning**) aire *m* acondicionado

air-condition ['ɛəkən,dɪʃən] VT climatizar, refrigerar

air-conditioned ['ɛəkən,dɪʃənd] ADJ [*room, hotel*] climatizado, con aire acondicionado

air-cooled ['ɛəkuːld] ADJ refrigerado por aire

aircraft ['ɛəkrɑːft] N (*pl inv*) avión *m* • **the ~ industry** la industria aeronáutica
CPD ▸ **aircraft carrier** porta(a)viones *m* ▸ **aircraft hangar** hangar *m* de aviones

aircraftman ['ɛəkrɑːftmən] N (PL: **aircraftmen**) (*Brit*) cabo *m* segundo (de las fuerzas aéreas)

aircrew ['ɛəkruː] N tripulación *f* de avión

airdrome ['ɛə,drəʊm] N (*US*) = **aerodrome**

airdrop ['ɛədrɒp] N entrega *f* por paracaídas
VT entregar por paracaídas, lanzar desde el aire

Airedale ['ɛədeɪl] N (*also* **Airedale dog**) perro *m* Airedale

airer ['ɛərə^r] N tendedero *m*

airfield ['ɛəfiːld] N campo *m* de aviación

airflow ['ɛəfləʊ] N corriente *f* de aire, flujo *m* de aire

airfoil ['ɛə,fɔɪl] N (*US*) = **aerofoil**

airframe ['ɛəfreɪm] N armazón *m or f* (*de avión*)

airhead‡ ['ɛəhed] N cabeza *f* de serrín*, chorlito* *m*

airily ['ɛərɪlɪ] ADV [*say*] sin darle importancia; [*dismiss*] muy a la ligera; [*wave, gesture*] despreocupadamente

airiness ['ɛərɪnɪs] N **1** [*of room, building*] (= *spaciousness*) lo espacioso, lo amplio; (= *ventilation*) buena ventilación *f*
2 [*of manner*] ligereza *f*

airing ['ɛərɪŋ] N • **to give sth an ~** [+ *linen, room*] ventilar algo; [+ *idea*] airear algo, someter algo a la discusión; [+ *issue, matter*] ventilar algo; [+ *film on TV*] dar algo, pasar algo, proyectar algo; [+ *play*] poner en escena algo
CPD ▸ **airing cupboard** (*Brit*) armario *m* para oreo

airless ['ɛəlɪs] ADJ [*room*] mal ventilado; [*day*] sin viento • **it's very ~ in here** aquí dentro falta aire

airlift ['ɛəlɪft] N puente *m* aéreo
VT aerotransportar, transportar por avión

airline ['ɛəlaɪn] N línea *f* aérea
CPD ▸ **airline pilot** piloto *mf* de compañía aérea

airliner ['ɛəlaɪnə^r] N avión *m* de pasajeros

airlock ['ɛəlɒk] N (*in pipe*) burbuja *f* de aire; (*in spacecraft etc*) cámara *f* estanca, compartimento *m* estanco; (*accidental*) bolsa *f* de aire

airmail ['ɛəmeɪl] N correo *m* aéreo • **to send a letter (by) ~** mandar una carta por correo aéreo *or* por avión
VT mandar por correo aéreo *or* por avión
CPD ▸ **airmail edition** (*Press*) edición *f* aérea ▸ **airmail letter** carta *f* por correo aéreo ▸ **airmail paper** papel *m* para avión ▸ **airmail sticker** etiqueta *f* de correo aéreo

airman ['ɛəmən] N (PL: **airmen**) aviador *m*, piloto *m*

airplane ['ɛəpleɪn] N (*US*) = **aeroplane**

airplay ['ɛəpleɪ] N (*Rad*) cobertura *f* radiofónica

airport ['ɛəpɔːt] N aeropuerto *m*
CPD ▸ **airport novel** *la típica novela de intriga o aventuras que se vende en los aeropuertos para leer durante el viaje* ▸ **airport tax** impuestos *mpl* de aeropuerto

airproof ['ɛəpruːf] ADJ hermético

air-raid ['ɛəreɪd] CPD ▸ **air-raid precautions** precauciones *fpl* a tomar en caso de ataque aéreo ▸ **air-raid shelter** refugio *m* antiaéreo ▸ **air-raid warden** vigilante *mf* que se encarga de dar la voz de alarma en caso de ataque aéreo ▸ **air-raid warning** alarma *f* antiaérea; ▹ **air**

airscrew ['ɛəskruː] N (*Brit*) hélice *f* de avión

air-sea [ɛə'siː] CPD ▸ **air-sea base** base *f* aeronaval ▸ **air-sea rescue** rescate *m* aeronaval

airship ['ɛəʃɪp] N aeronave *f*

airsick ['ɛəsɪk] ADJ mareado (en avión) • **to be ~** estar mareado (en avión) • **to get ~** marearse (en avión)

airsickness ['ɛəsɪknɪs] N mareo *m* (en avión)

airspace ['ɛəspeɪs] N espacio *m* aéreo

airspeed ['ɛəspiːd] N velocidad *f* aérea
CPD ▸ **airspeed indicator** anemómetro *m*

airstream ['ɛəstriːm] N corriente *f* de aire

airstrip ['ɛəstrɪp] N pista *f* de aterrizaje

airtight ['ɛətaɪt] ADJ **1** (*lit*) [*container, seal*] hermético
2 (= *not open to question*) [*case, argument*] sin fisuras, irrefutable

air-to-air [,ɛətə'ɛə^r] ADJ [*missile*] aire-aire

air-to-ground [,ɛətə'graʊnd] ADJ [*missile*] aire-tierra, aire-superficie

air-to-sea [,ɛətə'siː] ADJ [*missile*] aire-mar

air-to-surface [,ɛətə'sɜːfɪs] ADJ [*missile*] aire-superficie, aire-tierra

air-traffic ['ɛətræfɪk] CPD ▸ **air-traffic control** control *m* del tráfico aéreo ▸ **air-traffic controller** controlador(a) *m/f* aéreo/a; ▹ **air**

airwaves ['ɛəweɪvz] NPL (*Rad, TV*) (= *radio waves*) ondas *fpl* hertzianas; (= *programmes*) programación *f* • **over the airwaves** a través de las ondas, por los medios de comunicación audiovisuales

airway ['ɛəweɪ] N **1** (*Aer*) (= *company*) línea *f* aérea, aerolínea *f*; (= *route*) ruta *f* aérea
2 (*Anat*) vía *f* respiratoria
3 (= *ventilator shaft*) conducto *m* de ventilación

airwoman ['ɛə,wʊmən] N (PL: **airwomen**) aviadora *f*

airworthiness ['ɛə,wɜːðɪnɪs] N buenas condiciones *fpl* para el vuelo

airworthy ['ɛəwɜːðɪ] ADJ en condiciones de volar, en condiciones de vuelo

airy ['ɛərɪ] ADJ (COMPAR: **airier**, SUPERL: **airiest**) **1** [*room, building*] (= *spacious*) espacioso, amplio; (= *well ventilated*) bien ventilado
2 [*fabric, clothing*] (= *lightweight*) ligero; (= *unsubstantial*) etéreo
3 (= *careless, light*) [*remark*] hecho a la ligera; [*gesture, wave*] despreocupado
4 (= *empty*) [*idea, generalization*] ligero • **he's always full of ~ promises** siempre hace promesas a la ligera

airy-fairy* [,ɛərɪ'fɛərɪ] ADJ (*Brit*) [*ideas,*

principles] superficial, vacío; [*plan, promises*] vano, fantasioso; [*person*] insustancial
aisle [aɪl] N (*Rel*) nave *f* (lateral); (*in theatre, plane, train, coach, supermarket*) pasillo *m*
• **~ seat** asiento *m* de pasillo • IDIOMS: • **to walk up** *or* **down the ~ with sb†** llevar al altar a algn • **it had them rolling in the ~s** los tuvo muertos de (la) risa
AISP N ABBR (= **Agricultural Income Subsidies Programme**) PARA *m*
aitch [eɪtʃ] N *nombre de la h inglesa* • **to drop one's ~es** no pronunciar las haches (*indicio clasista o de habla dialectal*)
Aix-la-Chapelle [ˈeɪkslæʃəˈpel] N Aquisgrán *m*
Ajaccio [əˈʒætʃɪəʊ] N Ajaccio *m*
ajar [əˈdʒɑːʳ] ADV entreabierto • **to leave the door ~** dejar entreabierta la puerta, no cerrar completamente la puerta, entrecerrar la puerta (*Mex*)
Ajax [ˈeɪdʒæks] N Áyax
AK ABBR (*US*) (*Post*) = **Alaska**
AKA, aka ABBR (= **also known as**) alias
akimbo [əˈkɪmbəʊ] ADV • **with arms ~** en jarras
akin [əˈkɪn] ADJ **1** parecido (**to** a), semejante (**to** a)
2 (*frm*) (= *related by blood*) consanguíneo • **they are not ~** no tienen parentesco consanguíneo
AL ABBR (*US*) = **Alabama**
ALA N ABBR (*US*) = **American Library Association**
Ala. ABBR (*US*) = **Alabama**
à la [ˈɑːlɑː] PREP a la
alabaster [ˈæləbɑːstəʳ] N alabastro *m*
ADJ alabastrino
alabastrine [ˌæləˈbæstraɪn] ADJ alabastrino
à la carte [ælæˈkɑːt] ADV a la carta
alacrity [əˈlækrɪtɪ] N prontitud *f*, presteza *f* • **with ~** con prontitud *or* presteza
Aladdin [əˈlædɪn] N Aladino
CPD ▸ **Aladdin's cave** (*fig*) cueva *f* de ricos tesoros ▸ **Aladdin's lamp** lámpara *f* de Aladino
Alans [ˈælənz] NPL alanos *mpl*
Alaric [ˈælərɪk] N Alarico
alarm [əˈlɑːm] N **1** (= *warning, bell*) alarma *f*; (= *signal*) señal *f* de alarma • **to raise** *or* **sound the ~** dar la alarma; ▹ **false, fire**
2 (= *fear*) alarma *f*, sobresalto *m* • **there was general ~** cundió la alarma general • **there was some ~ at this** esto produjo cierta inquietud • **to cry out in ~** gritar alarmado • **to cause ~** causar alarma • **~ and despondency** inquietud y desconcierto
3 (*also* **alarm clock**) despertador *m*
VT alarmar • **to be ~ed at** asustarse de • **don't be ~ed** no te asustes, no te inquietes
CPD ▸ **alarm bell** timbre *m* de alarma • **the court's decision has set ~ bells ringing in government** la decisión del tribunal ha hecho cundir la alarma entre el gobierno ▸ **alarm call** (= *wake-up call*) llamada *f* de aviso (para despertar) • **I'd like an ~ call for six a.m., please** llámenme *or* despiértenme a las seis, por favor ▸ **alarm clock** despertador *m* ▸ **alarm signal** señal *f* de alarma ▸ **alarm system** sistema *m* de alarma
alarmed [əˈlɑːmd] ADJ [*voice*] sobresaltado, asustado; ▹ **alarm**
alarming [əˈlɑːmɪŋ] ADJ alarmante
alarmingly [əˈlɑːmɪŋlɪ] ADV de modo alarmante • **~ high numbers** cifras *fpl* alarmantes
alarmist [əˈlɑːmɪst] ADJ alarmista
N alarmista *mf*
alarum†† [əˈlærəm] N = **alarm**
alas [əˈlæs] EXCL (*liter*) ¡ay (de mí)! • **~, it is not so** desafortunadamente, no es así • **I must tell you, ~, that ...** tengo que decirte, y lo siento, que ... • **I have no money, ~** no tengo dinero, y esto es triste • **~ for Poland!** ¡ay de Polonia!
Alas. ABBR (*US*) = **Alaska**
Alaska [əˈlæskə] N Alaska *f*
CPD ▸ **Alaska Highway** carretera *f* de Alaska ▸ **Alaska Range** cordillera *f* de Alaska
Alaskan [əˈlæskən] ADJ de Alaska
N nativo/a *m/f* de Alaska, habitante *mf* de Alaska
alb [ælb] N (*Rel*) alba *f*
Albania [ælˈbeɪnɪə] N Albania *f*
Albanian [ælˈbeɪnɪən] ADJ albanés
N **1** (= *person*) albanés/esa *m/f*
2 (*Ling*) albanés *m*
albatross [ˈælbətrɒs] N **1** (*Orn*) albatros *m inv*
2 (*fig*) (= *burden*) rémora *f* • IDIOM: • **to be an ~ around sb's neck** suponer una rémora para algn
3 (*Golf*) albatros *m inv*, menos tres *m*
albeit [ɔːlˈbiːɪt] CONJ aunque
Albert [ˈælbət] N Alberto
Albigenses [ˌælbɪˈdʒensiːz] NPL albigenses *mpl*
Albigensian [ˌælbɪˈdʒensɪən] ADJ albigense
albinism [ˈælbɪnɪzəm] N albinismo *m*
albino [ælˈbiːnəʊ] ADJ albino
N albino/a *m/f*
Albion [ˈælbɪən] N Albión *f*
album [ˈælbəm] N (= *book, record, CD*) álbum *m* • **autograph/photograph ~** álbum *m* de autógrafos/fotografías
CPD ▸ **album chart** lista *f* de álbumes más vendidos ▸ **album cover** portada *f* del álbum
albumen, albumin [ˈælbjʊmɪn] N (= *egg white*) clara *f* de huevo; (*Bot*) albumen *m*; (*Chem*) albúmina *f*
albuminous [ælˈbjuːmɪnəs] ADJ albuminoso
alchemical [ælˈkemɪkəl] ADJ alquímico, de alquimia
alchemist [ˈælkɪmɪst] N alquimista *mf*
alchemy [ˈælkɪmɪ] N (= *ancient chemistry*) alquimia *f*; (*fig*) (= *mysterious power*) poder *m* mágico
alcohol [ˈælkəhɒl] N (= *drink*) alcohol *m* (*also Chem*) • **I never touch ~** no pruebo el alcohol, soy abstemio
CPD ▸ **alcohol abuse** abuso *m* del alcohol ▸ **alcohol abuser** alcohólico/a *m/f*
alcohol-free [ˈælkəhɒlˌfriː] ADJ sin alcohol
alcoholic [ˌælkəˈhɒlɪk] ADJ alcohólico • **~ drinks** bebidas *fpl* alcohólicas
N alcohólico/a *m/f*, alcoholizado/a *m/f*
alcoholism [ˈælkəhɒlɪzəm] N alcoholismo *m* • **to die of ~** morir alcoholizado
alcopop [ˈælkəʊpɒp] N (*Brit*) *combinado de refresco y alcohol que se vende ya embotellado*
alcove [ˈælkəʊv] N nicho *m*, hueco *m*
Ald. ABBR = **alderman**
al dente [ælˈdenteɪ] ADJ al dente
alder [ˈɔːldəʳ] N aliso *m*
alderman [ˈɔːldəmən] N (PL: **aldermen**) concejal(a) *m/f* (*de categoría superior*)
aldosterone [ælˈdɒstəˌrəʊn] N aldosterona *f*
aldrin [ˈɔːldrɪn] N aldrina *f*
ale [eɪl] N cerveza *f*; ▹ **brown, light², pale¹**
aleatoric [ˌeɪlɪəˈtɒrɪk], **aleatory** [ˈeɪlɪətərɪ] ADJ aleatorio
Alec [ˈælɪk] N *familiar form of* **Alexander**
alec, aleck [ˈælɪk] ▹ **smart alec**
alehouse† [ˈeɪlˌhaʊs] N taberna *f*
alert [əˈlɜːt] ADJ **1** (= *mentally acute*) [*person*] espabilado, despierto; [*expression*] vivo • **they were ~** eran espabilados, tenían la mente despierta • **he's a very ~ baby** es un bebé muy despierto
2 (= *vigilant*) alerta (*inv*), atento • **we must stay ~** hay que estar atentos
3 (= *aware*) • **to be ~ to sth** ser consciente *or* al tanto de algo
N alerta *f* • **to be on the ~** estar alerta • **to put** *or* **place troops on (the) ~** poner a las tropas sobre aviso *or* en situación de alerta; ▹ **red**
VT alertar, poner sobre aviso • **to ~ sb to sth** alertar a algn de algo, poner a algn sobre aviso de algo • **we are now ~ed to the dangers** ahora estamos sobre aviso en cuanto a los peligros
alertly [əˈlɜːtlɪ] ADV prestando mucha atención
alertness [əˈlɜːtnɪs] N (= *mental acuteness*) lo espabilado, lo despierto; (= *vigilance*) vigilancia *f*
Aleutian [əˈluːʃən] ADJ • **the ~ Islands** • **the ~s** las Islas Aleutianas
A-level [ˈeɪˌlevl] N ABBR (*Brit*) (*Scol*) ▹ **A**
Alex [ˈælɪks] N *familiar form of* **Alexander**
Alexander [ˌælɪgˈzɑːndəʳ] N Alejandro • **~ the Great** Alejandro Magno
Alexandria [ˌælɪgˈzɑːndrɪə] N Alejandría *f*
alexandrine [ˌælɪgˈzændraɪn] N alejandrino *m*
ALF N ABBR (*Brit*) (= **Animal Liberation Front**) Frente *m* de Liberación Animal
Alf [ælf] N *familiar form of* **Alfred**
alfalfa [ælˈfælfə] N alfalfa *f*
Alfred [ˈælfrɪd] N Alfredo
alfresco [ælˈfreskəʊ] ADJ al aire libre
ADV al aire libre
alga [ˈælgə] N (PL: **algae** [ˈældʒiː]) alga *f*
algal [ˈælgəl] ADJ de algas
Algarve [ælˈgɑːv] N • **the ~** el Algarve
algebra [ˈældʒɪbrə] N álgebra *f*
algebraic [ˌældʒɪˈbreɪɪk] ADJ algebraico
Algeria [ælˈdʒɪərɪə] N Argelia *f*
Algerian [ælˈdʒɪərɪən] ADJ argelino
N argelino/a *m/f*
algicide [ˈældʒɪsaɪd] N algicida *m*
Algiers [ælˈdʒɪəz] N Argel *m*
algorithm [ˈælgəˌrɪðəm] N algoritmo *m*
algorithmic [ˌælgəˈrɪðmɪk] ADJ algorítmico
alias [ˈeɪlɪəs] N alias *m inv*
ADV • **Smith ~ Stevens** Smith alias Stevens
alibi [ˈælɪbaɪ] N (*in relation to crime*) coartada *f*; (= *excuse**) excusa *f*, pretexto *m*
VT • **to ~ sb** (*US**) proveer de una coartada a algn
VI (*US**) buscar excusas (**for doing sth** por haber hecho algo)
Alice [ˈælɪs] N Alicia • **~ in Wonderland** Alicia en el país de las maravillas • **~ through the Looking-Glass** Alicia en el país del espejo
CPD ▸ **Alice band** (*Brit*) diadema *f*
alien [ˈeɪlɪən] ADJ **1** (= *foreign*) extranjero
2 (= *unfamiliar*) extraño, ajeno • **~ to** ajeno a
3 (= *extraterrestrial*) alienígena, extraterrestre • **~ being** alienígena *mf*, extraterrestre *mf*
N **1** (= *foreigner*) extranjero/a *m/f*
2 (= *extraterrestrial*) alienígena *mf*, extraterrestre *mf*
alienate [ˈeɪlɪəneɪt] VT **1** (= *offend*) [+ *person*] ofender; [+ *sb's sympathies*] perder, enajenar (*frm*) • **to ~ o.s. from sb** alejarse *or* apartarse de algn
2 (*Pol, Philos*) alienar, enajenar
3 (*Jur*) enajenar
alienated [ˈeɪlɪəneɪtɪd] ADJ alienado
alienation [ˌeɪlɪəˈneɪʃən] N **1** (*Pol, Philos*) alienación *f*, enajenación *f* • **feelings of ~ (from society)** sentimientos *mpl* de

a

alienación *or* enajenación (social)
2 (= *estrangement*) [*of friend*] alejamiento *m*
3 (*Jur*) enajenación *f*, traspaso *m*
4 (*Med*) enajenación *f* mental

alienist ['eɪlɪənɪst] (N) (*US*) alienista *mf*

alight¹ [ə'laɪt] (ADJ) **1** (*lit*) • **to be ~** [*fire*] estar ardiendo; [*lamp*] estar encendido *or* (*LAm*) prendido • **to keep a fire ~** mantener un fuego ardiendo • **to set ~** pegar fuego a, incendiar
2 (*fig*) • **~ with** [+ *happiness, enthusiasm*] resplandeciente de

alight² [ə'laɪt] (VI) **1** (*from vehicle*) bajar, apearse (**from** de)
2 (*on branch etc*) [*bird, insect*] posarse (**on** sobre)
▸ **alight on** (VI + PREP) [+ *fact, idea*] caer en la cuenta de, darse cuenta de

align [ə'laɪn] (VT) alinear • **to ~ o.s. with** (*Pol*) (*also fig*) ponerse del lado de

alignment [ə'laɪnmənt] (N) (*lit, fig*) alineación *f* • **to be in ~** estar alineados, estar en línea recta • **to be out of ~ (with)** no estar alineado (con)

alike [ə'laɪk] (ADJ) • **they are very ~** son muy parecidos, se parecen mucho • **you're all ~!** ¡sois todos iguales!, ¡todos son iguales! (*esp LAm*) • **to look ~** parecerse • **they all look ~ to me** yo no veo diferencia entre ellos, para mí todos son iguales
(ADV) **1** (= *in the same way*) del mismo modo, igual • **to think/dress ~** pensar/vestir del mismo modo *or* igual
2 (= *both, equally*) • **men and women ~** tanto los hombres como las mujeres

alimentary [,ælɪ'mentərɪ] (ADJ) alimenticio
(CPD) ▸ **alimentary canal** tubo *m* digestivo

alimony ['ælɪmənɪ] (N) (*Jur*) pensión *f* alimenticia

A-line ['eɪlaɪn] (ADJ) [*vestido*] de línea trapezoide

alive [ə'laɪv] (ADJ) **1** vivo • **to be ~** estar vivo, vivir • **it's good to be ~!** ¡qué bueno es vivir! • **to be still ~** vivir todavía; [*dying person*] estar todavía con vida • **while ~ he did no harm** en vida no hizo daño a nadie • **she plays as well as any pianist ~** toca tan bien como cualquier pianista del mundo • **he's the best footballer ~** es el mejor futbolista del mundo • **to bring a story ~** dar vida a una historia, animar una historia • **to be buried ~** ser enterrado vivo • **to burn sb ~** quemar a algn vivo • **the scene came ~ as she described it** la escena se animaba *or* vivificaba al describirla ella • **we were being eaten ~ by mosquitoes** los mosquitos nos comían vivos • **to keep sb ~** conservar a algn con vida • **to keep a memory ~** guardar vivo *or* fresco un recuerdo, hacer perdurar una memoria • **to keep a tradition ~** mantener viva una tradición • **man ~!†** ¡hombre! • **no man ~ could do better** no lo podría hacer mejor nadie • **he managed to stay ~ on fruit** logró sobrevivir comiendo frutas • **the prisoner must be taken ~** hay que capturar vivo *or* con vida al prisionero; ▹ **dead**
2 (*fig*) (= *lively*) activo, enérgico • **look ~!†*** (= *hurry*) ¡date prisa!, ¡apúrate! (*LAm*) • IDIOM: • **~ and kicking*** vivito y coleando
3 • **~ with** [+ *insects*] lleno de, hormigueante en • **a book ~ with interest** un libro lleno de interés
4 (*frm*) • **~ to** (= *aware of*) consciente de • **I am ~ to the danger** estoy consciente del peligro, me doy cuenta del peligro • **I am fully ~ to the fact that ...** soy consciente de que ..., no ignoro que ... • **I am fully ~ to the honour you do me** soy plenamente consciente del honor que se me hace

alkali ['ælkəlaɪ] (N) (PL: **alkalis, alkalies**) álcali *m*

alkaline ['ælkəlaɪn] (ADJ) alcalino

alkalinity [,ælkə'lɪnɪtɪ] (N) alcalinidad *f*

alkaloid ['ælkəlɔɪd] (ADJ) alcaloideo
(N) alcaloide *m*

alkie‡, alky‡ ['ælkɪ] (N ABBR) (= **alcoholic**) borrachín/ina *m/f*

---

all [ɔːl]

ADJECTIVE
PRONOUN
ADVERB
NOUN
COMPOUNDS

*When **all** is part of a set combination, eg **in all seriousness/probability**, look up the noun. Note that **all right** has an entry to itself.*

(ADJECTIVE)
1 todo • **all my life** toda mi vida • **all my friends** todos mis amigos • **all men** todos los hombres • **they drank all the beer** se bebieron toda la cerveza • **all the others went home** todos los demás se fueron a casa • **it rained all day** llovió todo el día, llovió el día entero • **she hasn't been in all day** no ha estado en todo el día • **all three (of them) were found guilty** los tres fueron declarados culpables • **I'll take all three (of them)** me llevo los tres • **40% of all marriages end in divorce** el 40% de los matrimonios terminan en divorcio • **it would have to rain today, of all days!** ¡tenía que llover hoy justamente! • **for all their efforts, they didn't manage to score** a pesar de todos sus esfuerzos, no lograron marcar un tanto • **they chose him, of all people!** lo eligieron a él, como si no hubiera otros • **all those who disobey will be punished** todos aquellos que desobedezcan serán castigados
all that • **it's not as bad as all that** no es para tanto • **all that is irrelevant now** todo eso ya no importa
and all that y cosas así, y otras cosas por el estilo • **he went on about loyalty and all that** habló sin parar sobre la lealtad y cosas así • **sorry and all that, but that's the way it is** disculpas y todo lo demás, pero así son las cosas
of all the ... • **of all the luck!** ¡vaya suerte! • **of all the tactless things to say!** ¡qué falta de tacto!; ▹ **best, four**
2 (= *any*) • **it has been proved beyond all doubt** se ha probado sin que quepa la menor duda • **the town had changed beyond all recognition** la ciudad había cambiado hasta hacerse irreconocible

(PRONOUN)
1 (*singular*) **a** (= *everything*) todo • **it's all done** está todo hecho • **we did all we could to stop him** hicimos todo lo posible para detenerlo • **it was all I could do not to laugh** apenas pude contener la risa • **all is not lost** (*liter or hum*) aún quedan esperanzas • **all of it** todo • **I didn't read all of it** no lo leí todo *or* entero • **not all of it was true** no todo era cierto • **you can't see all of Madrid in a day** no puedes ver todo Madrid *or* Madrid entero en un día • **I do all of the work** yo hago todo el trabajo • **I do all of the cooking** siempre cocino yo • **it took him all of three hours** (= *at least*) le llevó tres horas enteras; (*iro*) (= *only*) le llevó ni más ni menos que tres horas • **she must be all of 16** (*iro*) debe de tener al menos 16 años • **is that all?** • **will that be all?** ¿es eso todo?, ¿nada más? • **six o'clock? is that all?** ¿las seis? ¿nada más? • **that's all** eso es todo, nada más • **all is well** todo está bien • IDIOM: • **when all is said and done** a fin de cuentas • PROVERB: • **all's well that ends well** bien está lo que bien acaba; ▹ **best, once**
b (= *the only thing*) • **all I can tell you is ...** todo lo que puedo decirte es ..., lo único que puedo decirte es ... • **all I want is to sleep** lo único que quiero es dormir • **that was all that we managed to salvage from the fire** eso fue todo lo que conseguimos rescatar del incendio • **all that matters is that you're safe** lo único que importa es que estás a salvo • **all that he did was laugh** lo único que hizo fue reírse
2 (*plural*) todos *mpl*, todas *fpl* • **they all came with their husbands** todas vinieron con sus maridos • **this concerns all of you** esto os afecta a todos (vosotros) • **his was the worst performance of all** la suya fue la peor actuación de todas • **they all say that** todos dicen lo mismo • **all who knew him loved him** todos los que le conocieron le querían
3 (*in scores*) • **the score is two all** van empatados a dos, el marcador es de empate a dos • **to draw two all** empatar a dos • **it's 30 all** (*Tennis*) treinta iguales
4 (*in set structures*) **above all** sobre todo
after all después de todo
all but • **all but seven/twenty** todos menos siete/veinte
all for nothing • **I rushed to get there, all for nothing** fui a toda prisa, todo para nada, fui a toda prisa, y total para nada
all in all en general • **all in all, things turned out quite well** en general, las cosas salieron bastante bien • **we thought, all in all, it wasn't a bad idea** pensamos que, mirándolo bien, no era una mala idea
all told en total
and all • **what with the rain and all** con la lluvia y todo lo demás • **the dog ate the sausage, mustard and all** el perro se comió la salchicha, mostaza incluida
for all I care • **you can go right now for all I care** por mí como si te vas ahora mismo
for all I know • **for all I know he could be dead** puede que hasta esté muerto, no lo sé • **for all I know, he could be right** igual hasta tiene razón, no lo sé
if (...) at all • **I'll go tomorrow if I go at all** si es que voy, iré mañana • **it rarely rains here, if at all** aquí rara vez llueve, si es que llueve • **I'd like to see him today, if (it's) at all possible** me gustaría verlo hoy, si es del todo posible • **they won't attempt it, if they have any sense at all** si tienen el más mínimo sentido común, no lo intentarán
in all • **50 men in all** 50 hombres en total
it all • **he ate it all** se lo comió todo • **it all happened so quickly** sucedió todo tan rápido • **she seemed to have it all: a good job, a happy marriage** parecía tenerlo todo: un buen trabajo, un matrimonio feliz
it's all or nothing es todo o nada
most of all sobre todo, más que nada
no ... at all • **I have no regrets at all** no me arrepiento en absoluto • **it makes no difference at all** da exactamente igual
not ... at all • **I don't feel at all well** no me siento nada bien • **she wasn't at all apologetic** no se disculpó para nada • **I'm not at all tired** no estoy cansado en lo más mínimo *or* en absoluto • **it was not at all nice** no fue nada agradable • **you mean he didn't cry at all?** ¿quieres decir que no lloró nada? • **did you mention me at all?** ¿mencionaste mi nombre por casualidad?
not at all! (*answer to thanks*) ¡de nada!, ¡no

hay de qué! • **"are you disappointed?" — "not at all!"** —¿estás defraudado? —en absoluto

ADVERB

1 (*= entirely*) todo

Make ***todo*** *agree with the person or thing described:*

• **she went all red** se puso toda colorada • **you're all wet** estás todo mojado • **it's all dirty** está todo sucio • **he was all covered in blood** estaba completamente cubierto de sangre • **the children were all alone** los niños estaban completamente solos • **there were insects all around us** había insectos por todas partes • **I did it all by myself** lo hice completamente solo • **she was dressed all in black** iba vestida completamente de negro • **we shook hands all round** nos estrechamos todos las manos

2 (*in set structures*) **all along** • **all along the street** a lo largo de toda la calle, por toda la calle • **this is what I feared all along** esto es lo que estaba temiendo desde el primer momento *or* el principio

all but (*= nearly*) casi • **he all but died** casi se muere, por poco se muere • **he's all but forgotten now** ya casi no se le recuerda

all for sth • **to be all for sth** estar completamente a favor de algo • **I'm all for it** estoy completamente a favor • **I'm all for giving children their independence** estoy completamente a favor de *or* apoyo completamente la idea de dar independencia a los niños

all in (*= all inclusive*) (*Brit*) todo incluido; (*= exhausted**) hecho polvo* • **the trip cost £200 all in** el viaje costó 200 libras, todo incluido • **after a day's skiing I was all in** después de un día esquiando, estaba hecho polvo* *or* rendido • **you look all in** se te ve rendido, ¡vaya cara de estar hecho polvo!*

all out • **to go all out** (*= spare no expense*) tirar la casa por la ventana; (*Sport*) emplearse a fondo • **to go all out for the prize** volcarse por conseguir el premio • **we must go all out to ensure it** hemos de desplegar todos nuestros medios para asegurarlo

all over • **all over the world you'll find ...** en *or* por todo el mundo encontrarás ... • **he's travelled all over the world** ha viajado por todo el mundo • **you've got mud all over your shoes** tienes los zapatos cubiertos de barro • **I spilled coffee all over my shirt** se me cayó el café encima y me manché toda la camisa • **they were all over him*** le recibieron con el mayor entusiasmo • **I ache all over** me duele (por) todo el cuerpo • **I looked all over for you** te busqué por *or* en todas partes • **it happens all over** ocurre en todas partes • **that's him all over*** eso es muy típico de él

all the more ... • **considering his age, it's all the more remarkable that he succeeded** teniendo en cuenta su edad, es aún más extraordinario que lo haya logrado • **she valued her freedom, all the more so because she had fought so hard for it** valoraba mucho su libertad, tanto más cuanto que había luchado tanto por conseguirla

all too ... • **it's all too true** lamentablemente es cierto • **all too soon, the holiday was over** cuando quisimos darnos cuenta las vacaciones habían terminado • **the evening passed all too quickly** la tarde pasó demasiado rápido

all up with • **it's all up with him** está acabado

all very ... • **that's all very well but ...** todo eso está muy bien, pero ...

not all there • **he isn't all there*** no tiene todos los tornillos bien*, le falta algún tornillo*

not all that ... • **it isn't all that far** no está tan lejos • **it shouldn't be all that difficult** no debería resultar tan difícil; ▹ **all-out, better**

NOUN

(*= utmost*) • **he had given her his all** (*= affection*) se había entregado completamente a ella; (*= possessions*) le había dado todo lo que tenía • **I really didn't give it my all** no di todo lo que podía dar de mí • **I decided to give it my all** decidí echarle el resto • **he puts his all into every game** se da completamente en cada partido, siempre da todo lo que puede de sí en cada partido

COMPOUNDS

▸ **the all clear** (*= signal*) el cese de la alarma, el fin de la alarma; (*fig*) el visto bueno, luz verde • **all clear!** ¡fin de la alerta! • **to be given the all clear** (*to do sth*) recibir el visto bueno, recibir luz verde; (*by doctor*) recibir el alta médica *or* definitiva ▸ **All Fools' Day** ≈ día *m* de los (Santos) Inocentes ▸ **All Hallows' (Day)** día *m* de Todos los Santos ▸ **All Saints' Day** día *m* de Todos los Santos ▸ **All Souls' Day** día *m* de (los) Difuntos (*Sp*), día *m* de (los) Muertos (*LAm*)

all- [ɔ:l] PREFIX • **all-American** típicamente americano, americano cien por cien • **all-leather** todo cuero • **with an all-Chinese cast** con un reparto totalmente chino • **there will be an all-Spanish final** en la final figurarán únicamente españoles • **it's an all-woman show** es un espectáculo enteramente femenino

ALL-AMERICAN

El término **all-American** se usa para referirse a los deportistas universitarios que son seleccionados por su habilidad en un deporte determinado para formar parte de un equipo nacional, equipo que no compite como tal, ya que es solo un título honorífico. De estos equipos, el que recibe mayor publicidad es el de fútbol americano.

Este término se usa también para hacer referencia a una persona que representa el ideal de la clase media norteamericana, como cuando se dice, por ejemplo: **he is a fine, upstanding all-American boy**.

Allah ['ælə] N Alá *m*

all-around [ˌɔ:lə'raʊnd] ADJ (*US*) = **all-round**

allay [ə'leɪ] VT [+ *fears*] aquietar, calmar; [+ *doubts*] despejar; [+ *pain*] aliviar

all-consuming ['ɔ:lkən'sju:mɪŋ] ADJ [*passion, interest*] absorbente

allegation [ˌælɪ'geɪʃən] N alegato *m*

allege [ə'ledʒ] VT 1 (*+ verb/clause*) afirmar (that que) • **she is ~d to have stolen money from a cash box** se afirma que robó dinero del que había en una caja • **he is ~d to be wealthy** según se dice es rico • **he is ~d to be the leader** según se dice él es el jefe

2 (*+ noun*) alegar • **he absented himself alleging illness** se ausentó alegando estar enfermo

alleged [ə'ledʒd] ADJ [*crime, thief, victim, author*] presunto; [*fact, reason*] supuesto • **~ police brutality** presunta brutalidad policial • **his ~ involvement in the scandal** su presunta *or* supuesta relación con el escándalo

allegedly [ə'ledʒɪdlɪ] ADV presuntamente, supuestamente • **the crimes he had ~ committed** los crímenes que presuntamente *or* supuestamente había cometido • **his van ~ struck two people** según se afirma *or* supuestamente, su furgoneta atropelló a dos personas • **~ illegal immigrants** inmigrantes presuntamente ilegales • **his ~ beautiful wife** su esposa, que según se dice es muy bella

allegiance [ə'li:dʒəns] N lealtad *f* • **to owe ~ to** deber lealtad a • **to pledge** *or* **swear ~ to** jurar lealtad a • **oath of ~** (*Brit*) juramento *m* de lealtad *or* fidelidad

allegoric [ˌælɪ'gɒrɪk] ADJ, **allegorical** [ˌælɪ'gɒrɪkəl] ADJ alegórico

allegorically [ˌælɪ'gɒrɪkəlɪ] ADV alegóricamente

allegorize ['ælɪgəraɪz] VT alegorizar

allegory ['ælɪgərɪ] N alegoría *f*

allegro [ə'legrəʊ] N alegro *m*

alleluia [ˌælɪ'lu:jə] N aleluya *f*

all-embracing ['ɔ:lɪm'breɪsɪŋ] ADJ [*survey, study, work, knowledge*] exhaustivo, global; [*hospitality*] generalizado, sin distingos

Allen key ['ælənˌki:], **Allen wrench** (*US*) ['ælənˌrentʃ] N llave *f* (de) Allen

allergen ['ælədʒən] N alérgeno *m*

allergenic [ˌælə'dʒenɪk] ADJ alergénico

allergic [ə'lɜ:dʒɪk] ADJ alérgico • **to be ~ to** (*Med*) (*also hum*) ser alérgico a

allergist ['ælədʒɪst] N alergista *mf*, alergólogo/a *m/f*

allergy ['ælədʒɪ] N alergia *f* (**to a**) • **total ~ syndrome** síndrome *m* de alergia total

CPD ▸ **allergy clinic** clínica *f* de alergias

alleviate [ə'li:vɪeɪt] VT aliviar, mitigar

alleviation [əˌli:vɪ'eɪʃən] N alivio *m*, mitigación *f*

alley ['ælɪ] N 1 (*between buildings*) callejón *m*, callejuela *f*; (*in garden, park*) paseo *m* • IDIOM: • **this is right up my ~*** esto es lo que me va, esto es lo mío

2 (*US*) (*Tennis*) banda *f* lateral para dobles; ▹ **blind, bowling**

CPD ▸ **alley cat** (*also fig*) gato/a *m/f* callejero/a

alleyway ['ælɪweɪ] N = **alley**

all-fired* ['ɔ:lfaɪəd] (*US*) ADJ excesivo • **in an all-fired hurry** con muchísima prisa

ADV a más no poder

alliance [ə'laɪəns] N alianza *f* • **to enter into an ~ with** aliarse con

allied ['ælaɪd] ADJ 1 (*Mil, Pol*) **a** (*= united, in league*) [*troops, countries, parties*] aliado • **~ against sb/sth** aliado en contra de algn/algo • **a group closely ~ to General Pera's faction** un grupo estrechamente ligado a la facción del General Pera • **~ with sth/sb** aliado con algo/algn

b • **Allied** (*Hist*) [*nations, tanks, operation, casualties*] aliado • **the Allied forces** las fuerzas aliadas

2 (*= associated*) [*subjects, products, industries*] relacionado, afín • **~ to sth** relacionado con algo, afín a algo • **lectures on subjects ~ to health** conferencias sobre temas relacionados con *or* afines a la salud

3 (*= coupled*) • **~ to** *or* **with sth** combinado con algo • **his sense of humour ~ to** *or* **with his clean-cut looks** su sentido del humor combinado con su cuidado aspecto

CPD ▸ **allied health professional** (*US*) *profesional de la medicina o la enfermería que trabaja para una mutua*

alligator ['ælɪgeɪtə^r] N caimán *m*

all-important ['ɔ:lɪm'pɔ:tənt] ADJ de primera *or* de suma importancia

all-in ['ɔ:lɪn] ADJ (*Brit*) [*price*] global, con todo incluido; [*insurance policy*] contra todo riesgo

CPD ▸ **all-in wrestling** lucha *f* libre

all-inclusive ['ɔ:lɪn'klu:sɪv] ADJ [*price*] con todo incluido • **all-inclusive insurance policy** póliza *f* de seguro contra todo riesgo

a

all-in-one [,ɔːlɪn'wʌn] (N) (= *piece of equipment*) todo *m* en uno; (= *suit*) traje *m* de una pieza
(ADJ) [*method, solution, design, product*] todo en uno
alliteration [ə,lɪtə'reɪʃən] (N) aliteración *f*
alliterative [ə'lɪtərətɪv] (ADJ) aliterado
all-metal ['ɔːl'metl] (ADJ) enteramente metálico
all-night ['ɔːl'naɪt] (ADJ) [*café, garage*] abierto toda la noche; [*vigil, party*] que dura toda la noche
(CPD) ▸ **all-night pass** (*Mil*) permiso *m* de pernocta ▸ **all-night service** servicio *m* nocturno ▸ **all-night showing** (*Cine*) sesión *f* continua nocturna
all-nighter* ['ɔːl'naɪtəʳ] (N) *espectáculo o fiesta etc que dura hasta la madrugada*
allocate ['æləʊkeɪt] (VT) **1** (= *allot*) asignar (**to** a) • **to ~ funds for a purpose** asignar *or* destinar fondos para un propósito
2 (= *distribute*) repartir (**among** entre)
allocation [,æləʊ'keɪʃən] (N) **1** (= *allotting*) (*also Comput*) asignación *f*
2 (= *distribution*) reparto *m*
3 (= *share, amount*) ración *f*, cuota *f*
allomorph ['æləʊmɔːf] (N) alomorfo *m*
allopathic [,æləʊ'pæθɪk] (ADJ) alopático
allopathy [æ'lɒpəθɪ] (N) alopatía *f*
allophone ['æləʊfəʊn] (N) alófono *m*
allot [ə'lɒt] (VT) **1** (= *assign*) [+ *task, share, time*] asignar (**to** a) • **the space ~ted to each contributor** el espacio asignado a cada colaborador • **we finished in the time ~ted** terminamos en el tiempo previsto • **he was ~ted the role of villain** le dieron el papel de malo
2 (= *distribute*) repartir, distribuir
allotment [ə'lɒtmənt] (N) **1** (= *distribution*) reparto *m*, distribución *f*
2 (= *quota*) asignación *f*, cuota *f*
3 (*Brit*) (= *land*) parcela *f*
all-out ['ɔːl'aʊt] (ADJ) [*effort*] supremo; [*attack*] con máxima fuerza • **all-out strike** huelga *f* general • **all-out war** (*Mil*) guerra *f* total, conflicto *m* bélico generalizado; (*fig*) guerra *f* total • **all out** (*adv*) ▹ **all**
all-over ['ɔːl'əʊvəʳ] (ADJ) [*pattern*] repetido sobre toda la superficie; [*suntan*] completo, integral
allow [ə'laʊ] (VT) **1** (= *permit*) **a** permitir • **smoking is not ~ed** no está permitido fumar • **"no dogs allowed"** "no se admiten perros" • **~ me!** ¡permítame! • **he can't have sweets, he's not ~ed** no puede comer caramelos, no se lo permiten *or* no lo dejan • **to ~ sb to do sth** dejar *or* (*more frm*) permitir a algn hacer algo, dejar *or* (*more frm*) permitir que algn haga algo • **nobody was ~ed to leave** no dejaron *or* permitieron marcharse a nadie, no dejaron *or* permitieron que nadie se marchara • **~ me to introduce you to Dr Amberg** permítame que le presente al Dr Amberg • **we cannot ~ this to happen** no podemos permitir que esto ocurra • **~ the mixture to cool** deje enfriar la mezcla • **he was ~ed home after hospital treatment** le permitieron *or* le dejaron irse a casa tras recibir tratamiento en el hospital • **he is not ~ed visitors** no le permiten visitas
b • **to ~ sb in/out/past** permitir *or* dejar a algn entrar/salir/pasar, permitir *or* dejar a algn que entre/salga/pase • **he's not ~ed out on his own** no le dejan salir *or* que salga solo a la calle, no le permiten salir *or* que salga solo a la calle • **they made holes in the box to ~ air in** hicieron unos agujeros en la caja para que entrara el aire
2 • **to ~ o.s.**: • **to ~ o.s. to be persuaded** dejarse convencer • **he won't ~ himself to fail** hará lo imposible por evitar el fracaso • **she ~ed herself a smile** dejó escapar una sonrisa
3 (= *reckon on*) dejar • **~ 5cms for shrinkage** dejar 5cms por si encoge • **~ (yourself) three hours for the journey** deja *or* calcula tres horas para el viaje • **how much should I ~ for expenses?** ¿cuánto debo prever para los gastos? • **please ~ 28 days for delivery** lo recibirá en su casa en un plazo de 28 días
4 (= *grant*) [+ *money*] asignar; [+ *time*] dar • **the time ~ed has been extended to 28 days** el plazo asignado ha sido ampliado a 28 días • **the judge ~ed him £1,000 costs** el juez le asignó 1.000 libras en concepto de costes • **to ~ sb a discount** aplicar *or* hacer un descuento a algn • **the extra income will ~ me more freedom** el ingreso extra me dará más libertad
5 (*Jur*) (= *admit*) [+ *claim, appeal*] admitir, aceptar; (*Sport*) [+ *goal*] conceder • **to ~ that** reconocer que • **I had to ~ that she was discreet** tuve que reconocer que era discreta
▸ **allow for** (VI + PREP) tener en cuenta • **after ~ing for his costs** después de haber tenido en cuenta sus gastos • **~ for delays on some roads** tengan en cuenta que puede haber retenciones en algunas carreteras • **we have to ~ for that possibility** debemos tener presente esa posibilidad • **we must ~ for the cost of the wood** tenemos que dejar un margen para el coste de la madera
▸ **allow of** (VI + PREP) admitir • **a question that ~s of only one reply** una pregunta que solo admite una respuesta
allowable [ə'laʊəbl] (ADJ) **1** (= *permissible*) permisible, admisible
2 [*expense*] deducible • **~ against tax** desgravable
allowance [ə'laʊəns] (N) **1** (= *payment*) (*from state*) prestación *f*; (*from ex-husband, benefactor*) pensión *f*; (*from parents*) dinero mensual/semanal *etc*; (= *allocated from fund*) asignación *f*; (*esp US*) (= *pocket money*) dinero *m* de bolsillo • **he makes his mother an ~** le concede una pensión a su madre • **he has an ~ of £100 a month** tiene una asignación de 100 libras mensuales; ▹ **family**
2 (= *discount*) descuento *m*, rebaja *f*; (*Tax*) desgravación *f* • **tax ~** desgravación *f* fiscal
3 (= *concession*) concesión *f* • **one must make ~s** hay que hacer concesiones • **to make ~(s) for sb** ser comprensivo con algn, disculpar a algn • **to make ~(s) for the weather** tener en cuenta el tiempo
4 (*Mech*) tolerancia *f*
5 (= *volume, weight*) margen *m*
alloy (N) ['ælɔɪ] (= *metal*) aleación *f*; (*fig*) mezcla *f*
(VT) [ə'lɔɪ] alear, ligar
(CPD) ['ælɔɪ] ▸ **alloy wheels** llantas *fpl* de aleación
all-party [ɔːl'pɑːtɪ] (ADJ) [*group, talks*] multipartidista
all-pervading [,ɔːlpə'veɪdɪŋ], **all-pervasive** [,ɔːlpə'veɪsɪv] (ADJ) omnipresente
all-points bulletin [,ɔːlpɔɪnts'bʊlɪtɪn] (N) (*US*) *boletín difundido por la policía para la búsqueda y captura de un sospechoso*
all-powerful ['ɔːl'paʊəfʊl] (ADJ) omnipotente, todopoderoso
all-purpose ['ɔːl'pɜːpəs] (ADJ) [*tool, cleaner*] multiuso (*inv*), universal; [*vehicle, flour, wine*] para todo uso
all right [,ɔːl'raɪt] (ADJ) **1** (= *satisfactory*) • **it's ~** (= *it's fine*) todo está bien; (= *passable*) no está mal; (= *don't worry*) no te preocupes • **the film was ~** la película no estuvo mal • **yes, that's ~** sí, de acuerdo *or* vale • **are you ~?** ¿estás bien? • **well, he's ~** (= *not bad*) bueno, es regular • **he's ~ as a goalkeeper** como portero vale • **it's ~ by me** yo, de acuerdo, lo que es por mí, no hay problema • **it's ~ for you!** a ti ¿qué te puede importar? • **it's ~ for some!** (*iro*) ¡los hay con suerte! • **it's ~ for you to smile** tú bien puedes sonreír • **is it ~ for me to go at four?** ¿me da permiso para *or* puedo marcharme a las cuatro? • **is it ~ for me to take the dog?** ¿se me permite llevar al perro? • **is that ~ with you?** ¿te parece bien? • **it's ~ with me** yo, de acuerdo, lo que es por mí, no hay problema • **is he ~ with the girls?** ¿se comporta bien con las chicas? • IDIOMS: • **it'll be ~ on the night** todo estará listo para el estreno • **she's a bit of ~‡** ¡está buenísima!*
2 (= *safe, well*) bien • **I'm/I feel ~ now** ya estoy bien • **it's ~, you can come out again now** está bien, puedes salir ya • **do you think the car will be ~ there overnight?** ¿tú crees que le pasará algo al coche allí toda la noche? • **she's ~ again now** está mejor, se ha repuesto ya
3 (= *well-provided*) • **we're ~ for the rest of our lives** no tendremos problemas económicos en el resto de la vida • **are you ~ for cigarettes?** ¿tienes suficiente tabaco? • IDIOM: • **I'm ~, Jack** (*Brit**) mientras yo esté bien, a los demás que los zurzan*
4 (= *available*) • **are you ~ for Tuesday?** ¿te viene bien el martes?
(ADV) **1** (= *satisfactorily, without difficulty*) bien • **everything turned out ~** todo salió bien • **I can see ~, thanks** veo bien, gracias • **he's doing ~ for himself*** no le van nada mal las cosas
2* (= *without doubt*) • **he complained ~!** ¡ya lo creo que se quejó! • **you'll get your money back ~** se te devolverá tu dinero, eso es seguro
(EXCL) (*in approval*) ¡bueno!, ¡muy bien!; (*in agreement*) ¡de acuerdo!, ¡vale!, ¡okey!; (*introducing a new subject*) bueno; (*in exasperation*) ¡se acabó!; (*esp US*) (*in triumph*) ¡olé!, ¡sí señor! • **~, let's get started** bueno, vamos a empezar • **~, who's in charge here?** muy bien ¿quién manda aquí? • **"we'll talk about it later" — "all right"** —lo hablamos después —vale
all-risks ['ɔːl'rɪsks] (CPD) ▸ **all-risks insurance** seguro *m* contra todo riesgo
all-round ['ɔːl'raʊnd] (ADJ) [*success etc*] completo; [*improvement*] general, en todos los aspectos; [*view*] amplio; [*person*] completo, con capacidad para todo
all-rounder ['ɔːl'raʊndəʳ] (N) persona *f* con capacidad para todo
all-singing all-dancing*
[ɔːl'sɪŋɪŋɔːl'dɑːnsɪŋ] (ADJ) por todo lo alto*
allspice ['ɔːlspaɪs] (N) pimienta *f* inglesa, pimienta *f* de Jamaica
all-star ['ɔːl'stɑː] (ADJ) [*cast*] todo estelar • **all-star performance** • **show with an all-star cast** función *f* de primeras figuras, función *f* estelar
all-terrain [,ɔːltə'reɪn] (CPD) ▸ **all-terrain bike** bicicleta *f* todo terreno ▸ **all-terrain vehicle** vehículo *m* todo terreno
all-the-year-round [,ɔːlðə,jɪə'raʊnd] (ADJ) [*sport*] que se practica todo el año; [*resort*] abierto todo el año
all-time ['ɔːl'taɪm] (ADJ) de todos los tiempos • **an all-time record** un récord nunca igualado • **exports have reached an all-time high** las exportaciones han alcanzado cifras nunca conocidas antes • **the pound is at an all-time low** la libra ha caído a su punto más bajo
allude [ə'luːd] (VI) • **to ~ to** aludir a, referirse a

a

allure [əˈljʊəʳ] N atractivo *m*, encanto *m*
VT (*liter*) atraer, cautivar

alluring [əˈljʊərɪŋ] ADJ seductor, atrayente

alluringly [əˈljʊərɪŋlɪ] ADV de manera seductora, de manera atrayente

allusion [əˈluːʒən] N alusión *f*, referencia *f*

allusive [əˈluːsɪv] ADJ alusivo, lleno de alusiones, lleno de referencias

allusively [əˈluːsɪvlɪ] ADV en forma de alusión

alluvial [əˈluːvɪəl] ADJ aluvial

alluvium [əˈluːvɪəm] N (PL: **alluviums, alluvia** [əˈluːvɪə]) aluvión *m*, depósito *m* aluvial

all-weather [ˈɔːlˈweðəʳ] ADJ para todo tiempo

ally [ˈælaɪ] N aliado/a *m/f* • **the Allies** los Aliados
VT [əˈlaɪ] • **to ~ o.s. with** aliarse con, hacer alianza con

all-year-round [ˌɔːljɪəˈraʊnd] ADJ [*sport*] que se practica todo el año; [*resort*] abierto todo el año

alma mater [ˈælməˈmeɪtəʳ] N alma máter *f*

almanac, almanack [ˈɔːlmənæk] N almanaque *m*

almighty [ɔːlˈmaɪtɪ] ADJ **1** (= *omnipotent*) todopoderoso • **Almighty God • God Almighty** Dios Todopoderoso • **the ~ dollar** el todopoderoso dólar
2* (= *tremendous*) tremendo, de mil demonios* • **an ~ din** un ruido tremendo *or* de mil demonios • **I foresee ~ problems** preveo unos enormes problemas • **he's an ~ fool if he believes that!** ¡vaya tonto si cree eso!
N • **the Almighty** el Todopoderoso
ADV* terriblemente, la mar de* • **an ~ loud bang** un estallido terriblemente fuerte

almond [ˈɑːmənd] N (= *nut*) almendra *f*; (= *tree*) almendro *m*
ADJ • **an ~ taste** un sabor a almendra
CPD [*essence, extract*] de almendra(s)
▸ **almond oil** aceite *m* de almendra ▸ **almond paste** pasta *f* de almendras ▸ **almond tree** almendro *m*

almond-eyed [ˈɑːmənd'aɪd] ADJ de ojos almendrados

almond-shaped [ˈɑːməndˌʃeɪpt] ADJ almendrado

almoner† [ˈɑːmənəʳ] N **1** (*Hist*) limosnero *m*
2 (*Brit*) (*Med*) oficial *mf* de asistencia social (adscrito a un hospital)

almost [ˈɔːlməʊst] ADV casi • **it's ~ finished/ready** casi está terminado/listo • **it's ~ midnight** ya es casi medianoche • **he ~ certainly will win** casi seguro que gana • **he ~ fell** casi se cae, por poco no se cae • **I had ~ forgotten about it** casi lo olvido, por poco no lo olvido • **we're ~ there** estamos a punto de llegar, ya nos falta poco para llegar • **"have you finished?" — "almost"** —¿has acabado? —casi

alms [ɑːmz] NPL limosna *fsing*

almsbox [ˈɑːmzbɒks] N cepillo *m* para los pobres

almshouse [ˈɑːmzhaʊs] N hospicio *m*, casa *f* de beneficencia

aloe [ˈæləʊ] N aloe *m*, agave *f*
CPD ▸ **aloe vera** aloe *m* vera

aloft [əˈlɒft] ADV (*liter*) (= *above*) arriba; (= *upward*) hacia arriba; (*Naut*) en *or* a la arboladura

alone [əˈləʊn] ADJ **1** (= *by oneself*) solo • **she lives ~** vive sola • **to be ~** estar solo *or* a solas • **I was left to bring up my two children ~** me quedé sola teniendo que criar a mis dos hijos • **all ~** (completamente) solo • **I feel so ~** me siento tan sola • **am I ~ in thinking so?** ¿soy yo el único que lo cree? • **they are not ~ in their belief** no son los únicos que lo creen, no son ellos solos los que lo creen • **to leave sb ~** dejar solo a algn • **I only left her ~ for a moment** no la dejé sola más que un momento • **don't leave them ~ together** no los dejes solos a los dos • **I won't leave you ~ with him** no te dejaré sola con él • **we spent some time ~ together** pasamos algún tiempo juntos los dos solos • **I was ~ with my thoughts** estaba a solas con mis pensamientos
2 (= *undisturbed*) **a** • **to leave** *or* **let sb ~** dejar a algn en paz • **leave** *or* **let me ~!** ¡déjame en paz!, ¡déjame estar! (*LAm*)
b • **to leave** *or* **let sth ~** no tocar algo • **leave** *or* **let it ~!** ¡déjalo!, ¡no lo toques! • **why can't he leave** *or* **let things ~?** (*fig*) ¿por qué no puede dejar las cosas como están? • **to leave** *or* **let well ~**: • **you'd better leave** *or* **let well ~** mejor no te metas en ese asunto • **don't interfere, just leave** *or* **let well ~** no te entrometas, déjalo estar • **the article doesn't look bad as it is, I would leave** *or* **let well ~** el artículo no está mal tal y como está, yo no lo tocaría
3 (*as conj*) • **let ~**: • **I wouldn't allow her to go with her sister, let ~ by herself** no la dejaría ir con su hermana, y aún menos sola • **he can't read, let ~ write** no sabe leer y aún menos escribir • **he can't change a light bulb, let ~ rewire the house!** no puede ni cambiar una bombilla, ¿cómo va a renovar toda la instalación eléctrica de la casa?
ADV solamente, solo, sólo

> *In the past the standard spelling for* **solo** *as an adverb was with an accent (***sólo***). Nowadays the* **Real Academia Española** *advises that the accented form is only required where there might otherwise be confusion with the adjective* **solo**.

• **you and you ~ can make that decision** tú y solamente *or* solo tú puedes tomar esa decisión, eres el único que puede tomar esa decisión • **the travel ~ cost £600** solamente *or* solo el viaje costó 600 libras • **she spends more money on hats ~ than I do on my entire wardrobe** solo en sombreros se gasta más de lo que yo gasto en ropa, se gasta más en sombreros nomás que lo que yo gasto en toda mi ropa (*LAm*) • **a charm which is hers ~** un encanto que es muy suyo • **she decided to go it ~*** (= *do it unaided*) decidió hacerlo sola, decidió hacerlo por su cuenta; (= *start a company*) decidió establecerse por su cuenta • **the US is prepared to go it ~ as the only nation not to sign the treaty** EEUU está dispuesto a quedarse solo siendo el único país que no firme el tratado • PROVERB: • **man cannot live by bread ~** no solo de pan vive el hombre

along [əˈlɒŋ]

> *When* **along** *is an element in a phrasal verb, eg* **get along, play along, string along**, *look up the verb.*

ADV **1** (= *forward*) • **move ~ there!** ¡circulen, por favor! • **she walked ~** siguió andando
2 (= *with you, us etc*) • **bring him ~ if you like** tráelo, si quieres • **are you coming ~?** ¿tú vienes también?
3 (= *here, there*) • **I'll be ~ in a moment** ahora voy • **she'll be ~ tomorrow** vendrá mañana
4 (*in set expressions*) • **all ~** desde el principio • **he was lying to me all ~** me había mentido desde el principio • **~ with** junto con • **he came, ~ with his friend** él vino, junto con su amigo
PREP por, a lo largo de • **to walk ~ the street** andar por la calle • **the trees ~ the path** los árboles a lo largo del camino • **all ~ the street** todo lo largo de la calle • **the shop is ~ here** la tienda está por aquí • **we acted ~ the lines suggested** hemos obrado de acuerdo con las indicaciones que nos hicieron • **somewhere ~ the way it fell off** en alguna parte del camino se cayó • **somewhere ~ the way** *or* **the line someone made a mistake** (*fig*) en un momento determinado alguien cometió un error

alongside [əˈlɒŋˈsaɪd] PREP **1** (= *next to*) al lado de • **there's a stream ~ the garden** hay un arroyo al lado del jardín • **the car stopped ~ me** el coche se paró a mi lado • **they have to work ~ each other** tienen que trabajar juntos • **how can these systems work ~ each other?** ¿cómo estos sistemas pueden funcionar en colaboración?
2 (*Naut*) al costado de • **to come ~ a ship** atracarse al costado de un buque
ADV (*Naut*) de costado • **to bring a ship ~** acostar un buque • **to come ~** atracar

aloof [əˈluːf] ADJ **1** (= *standoffish*) [*person, manner*] distante • **he was very ~ with me** conmigo se mostró muy distante • **she has always been somewhat ~** ella siempre ha guardado las distancias
2 (= *uninvolved*) • **to hold o.s.** *or* **remain** *or* **stand ~ from sb** guardar *or* mantener las distancias con algn, mantenerse apartado de algn • **to hold o.s.** *or* **remain** *or* **stand ~ from sth** mantenerse al margen de algo

aloofness [əˈluːfnɪs] N actitud *f* distante

alopecia [ˌæləʊˈpiːʃə] N alopecia *f*

aloud [əˈlaʊd] ADV en voz alta • **to think ~** pensar en voz alta

alpaca [ælˈpækə] N alpaca *f*

alpenhorn [ˈælpənhɔːn] N trompa *f* de los Alpes

alpenstock [ˈælpɪnstɒk] N alpenstock *m*, bastón *m* montañero

alpha [ˈælfə] N (= *letter*) alfa *f*; (*Brit*) (*Scol, Univ*) sobresaliente *m*
CPD ▸ **alpha male** (*in group of animals*) macho *m* alfa, macho *m* dominante; (*fig*) cabecilla *m* de la banda ▸ **alpha particle** (*Phys*) partícula *f* alfa ▸ **alpha rhythm, alpha wave** (*Physiol*) ritmo *m* alfa

alphabet [ˈælfəbet] N alfabeto *m*

alphabetic [ˌælfəˈbetɪk] ADJ, **alphabetical** [ˌælfəˈbetɪkəl] ADJ alfabético • **in ~ order** en *or* por orden alfabético

alphabetically [ˌælfəˈbetɪkəlɪ] ADV alfabéticamente, en *or* por orden alfabético

alphabetize [ˈælfəbətaɪz] VT alfabetizar, poner en orden alfabético

alphanumeric [ˌælfənjuːˈmerɪk] ADJ alfanumérico
CPD ▸ **alphanumeric character** carácter *m* alfanumérico ▸ **alphanumeric field** campo *m* alfanumérico

Alphonso [ælˈfɒnsəʊ] N Alfonso

alpine [ˈælpaɪn] ADJ alpino
N planta *f* alpestre

alpinist [ˈælpɪnɪst] N alpinista *mf*

Alps [ælps] NPL • **the ~** los Alpes

al Qaeda [ælkaɪˈiːdə] N Al Qaeda *m or f*

already [ɔːlˈredɪ] ADV ya • **Liz had ~ gone** Liz ya se había ido • **is it finished ~?** ¿ya está terminado? • **that's enough ~!** (*US**) ¡basta!, ¡ya está bien!

alright [ˌɔːlˈraɪt] = **all right**

Alsace [ˈælsæs] N Alsacia *f*

Alsace-Lorraine [ˈælsæsləˈreɪn] N Alsacia-Lorena *f*

Alsatian [ælˈseɪʃən] ADJ alsaciano
N **1** (= *person*) alsaciano/a *m/f*
2 (*Brit*) (*also* **Alsatian dog**) (perro *m*) pastor *m* alemán, perro *m* lobo

also [ˈɔːlsəʊ] ADV **1** (*gen*) también • **her**

cousin ~ came su primo también vino
2 (*as linker*) además • **~, I must explain that ...** además debo aclarar que ...
also-ran ['ɔ:lsəʊræn] (N) **1** (*Sport*) caballo *m* perdedor
2* (= *person*) nulidad *f*
alt. (ABBR) (= **altitude**) alt.
Alta (ABBR) (*Canada*) = **Alberta**
Altamira [,æltə'mi:rə] (N) • **the ~ caves** las cuevas de Altamira
altar ['ɒltəʳ] (N) altar *m* • **high ~** altar *m* mayor • IDIOMS: • **he sacrificed all on the ~ of his ambition** lo sacrificó todo en aras de su ambición • **to lead a girl to the ~** conducir a una chica al altar
(CPD) ▸ **altar boy** acólito *m*, monaguillo *m* ▸ **altar cloth** sabanilla *f*, paño *m* de altar ▸ **altar rail** comulgatorio *m* ▸ **altar stone** piedra *f* del altar ▸ **altar table** mesa *f* del altar
altarpiece ['ɒltəpi:s] (N) retablo *m*
alter ['ɒltəʳ] (VT) **1** (= *change*) [+ *text*] modificar, cambiar; (*esp for the worse*) alterar; [+ *painting, speech*] retocar; [+ *opinion, course*] cambiar de; (*Archit*) reformar; (*Sew*) arreglar • **then that ~s things** entonces la cosa cambia • **it has ~ed things for the better** ha cambiado las cosas para mejor, ha mejorado las cosas • **circumstances ~ cases** el caso depende de las circunstancias • **I see no need to ~ my view** no veo ninguna necesidad de cambiar mi opinión
2 (= *falsify*) [+ *evidence*] falsificar; [+ *document*] alterar
3 (*US*) (= *castrate*) castrar
(VI) [*person, place*] cambiar • **I find him much ~ed** le veo muy cambiado • **to ~ for the better** mejorar, cambiar para mejor • **to ~ for the worse** empeorar, cambiar para peor
alteration [,ɒltə'reɪʃən] (N) **1** (= *change*) (*to text*) modificación *f*, cambio *m*; (*esp for the worse*) alteración *f* (**in, to** de); (*to painting, speech etc*) retoque *m*; (*Sew*) arreglo *m* • **to make ~s to** [+ *building, text*] hacer modificaciones en; [+ *dress*] hacer arreglos a
2 **alterations** (*Archit*) reformas *fpl*
altercation [,ɒltə'keɪʃən] (N) altercado *m*
alter ego ['æltər'i:gəʊ] (N) álter ego *m*
-altering ['ɔ:ltərɪŋ] (SUFFIX) • **life-altering** que cambia la vida • **it will be a life-altering decision for her** será una decisión que le cambiará la vida; ▹ **mind-altering, mood-altering**
alternate (ADJ) [ɒl'tɜ:nɪt] **1** (= *alternating*) alterno • **~ layers of cheese and potatoes** capas alternas de queso y patatas • **we had a week of ~ rain and sunshine** tuvimos una semana en la que se alternaron el sol y las lluvias • **let's read ~ lines** vamos a leer cada uno un renglón
2 (= *every second*) • **on ~ days** cada dos días, un día sí y otro no • **he lives ~ months in Brussels and London** vive un mes en Bruselas y uno en Londres • **to write on ~ lines** escribir en renglones alternos
3 (*Bot, Math*) alterno
4 (*US*) = **alternative**
(N) [ɒl'tɜ:nɪt] (*US*) (*Sport*) (*at conference*) suplente *mf*
(VI) ['ɒltɜ:neɪt] alternar • **an annual cycle of drought alternating with floods** un ciclo anual de sequías alternando con inundaciones • **the temperatures ~ between very hot and extremely cold** las temperaturas oscilan entre un calor y un frío intensos • **he ~s between euphoria and depression** pasa de la euforia a la depresión y vice versa • **they ~ between avoiding us and ignoring us** unas veces nos evitan y otras nos ignoran
(VT) ['ɒltɜ:neɪt] alternar
alternately [ɒl'tɜ:nɪtlɪ] (ADV) • **the meetings took place ~ in France and Germany** las reuniones se celebraron una vez en Francia y la siguiente en Alemania • **he could ~ bully and charm people** un momento podía intimidar a la gente y al siguiente embelesarles • **I lived ~ with my mother and my grandmother** viví unas veces con mi madre y otras con mi abuela • **she became ~ angry and calm** su ánimo iba de la ira a la calma y vice versa • **we have Mondays off ~** nos turnamos para librar el lunes
alternating ['ɒltɜ:neɪtɪŋ] (ADJ) alterno
(CPD) ▸ **alternating current** (*Elec*) corriente *f* alterna
alternation [,ɒltɜ:'neɪʃən] (N) alternación *f* • **in ~** alternativamente
alternative [ɒl'tɜ:nətɪv] (ADJ) **1** [*plan, route*] alternativo, otro • **the only ~ system** el único sistema alternativo • **do you have an ~ candidate?** ¿tienes otro candidato?
2 (= *non-traditional*) alternativo • **the ~ society** la sociedad alternativa
(N) alternativa *f* • **there are several ~s** hay varias alternativas *or* posibilidades • **what ~s are there?** ¿qué alternativas *or* opciones hay? • **I have no ~** no tengo más remedio, no me queda otra alternativa *or* opción • **there is no ~** no hay otro remedio, no queda otra (*LAm*) • **you have no ~ but to go** no tienes más alternativa *or* opción *or* remedio que ir • **fruit is a healthy ~ to chocolate** la fruta es una opción más sana que el chocolate
(CPD) ▸ **alternative comedian** humorista *mf* alternativo/a ▸ **alternative comedy** humorismo *m* alternativo ▸ **alternative energy** energías *fpl* alternativas ▸ **alternative medicine** medicina *f* alternativa ▸ **alternative school** (*US*) *colegio para niños que requieren una atención diferenciada*
alternatively [ɒl'tɜ:nətɪvlɪ] (ADV) • **~, you can use household bleach** si no, puede usar lejía doméstica • **we could go on to the next village, or, alternatively, we could camp here** podemos ir hasta el siguiente pueblo, o podemos acampar aquí
alternator ['ɒltɜ:neɪtəʳ] (N) (*Aut, Elec*) alternador *m*
although [ɔ:l'ðəʊ] (CONJ) aunque • **~ it's raining, there are 20 people here already** aunque está lloviendo, ya hay aquí 20 personas • **~ poor, they were honest** aunque eran pobres, eran honrados
altimeter ['æltɪmi:təʳ] (N) altímetro *m*
altitude ['æltɪtju:d] (N) altitud *f*, altura *f* • **at these ~s** a estas altitudes
(CPD) ▸ **altitude sickness** mal *m* de altura, soroche *m* (*LAm*) ▸ **altitude training** entrenamiento *m* en altitud • **to do ~ training** entrenarse en altitud
alto ['æltəʊ] (N) (= *instrument, male singer*) alto *m*; (= *female singer*) contralto *f*
(ADJ) alto
(CPD) ▸ **alto saxophone** saxofón *m* alto
altocumulus [,æltəʊ'kju:mjʊləs] (N) (PL: **altocumuli** [,æltəʊ'kju:mjʊlaɪ]) altocúmulo *m*
altogether [,ɔ:ltə'geðəʳ] (ADV) **1** (= *in all*) en total • **~, he played in 40 matches** en total, participó en 40 partidos • **how much is that ~?** ¿cuánto es en total? • **~ it was rather unpleasant** en general fue muy desagradable
2 (= *entirely*) [*stop, disappear*] por completo, del todo; [*different, impossible*] totalmente; [*wonderful*] realmente • **he abandoned his work ~** dejó de trabajar por completo *or* del todo • **she looked ~ lovely** estaba realmente encantadora • **I'm not ~ happy with your work** no estoy del todo satisfecho con tu trabajo • **Asia was another matter ~** lo de Asia era un tema totalmente diferente • **"do you believe him?" — "not ~"** —¿le crees? —no del todo • **it's ~ out of the question** es totalmente imposible • **I'm not ~ sure** no estoy del todo seguro, no estoy totalmente seguro • **it's ~ too complicated** es realmente demasiado complicado
(N) • **in the ~*** (= *naked*) en cueros*
altoist ['æltəʊɪst] (N) (= *saxophone player*) saxo *m* alto, saxofonista *mf* alto
altostratus [,æltəʊ'streɪtəs] (N) (PL: **altostrati** [,æltəʊ'streɪtaɪ]) altostrato *m*
altruism ['æltrʊɪzəm] (N) altruismo *m*
altruist ['æltrʊɪst] (N) altruista *mf*
altruistic [,æltrʊ'ɪstɪk] (ADJ) altruista
ALU (N ABBR) (= **Arithmetical Logic Unit**) ULP *f*
alum ['æləm] (N) alumbre *m*
aluminium [,æljʊ'mɪnɪəm], **aluminum** (*US*) [ə'lu:mɪnəm] (N) aluminio *m*
(CPD) ▸ **aluminium foil** papel *m* de aluminio, aluminio *m* doméstico
alumnus [ə'lʌmnəs] (N) (PL: **alumni** [ə'lʌmnaɪ]), **alumna** [ə'lʌmnə] (N) (PL: **alumnae** [ə'lʌmni:]) (*esp US*) graduado/a *m/f* • **~ association** asociación *f* de graduados
alveolar [æl'vɪələʳ] (ADJ) alveolar
alveolus [æl'vɪələs] (N) (PL: **alveoli** [æl'vɪəlaɪ]) alvéolo *m*, alveolo *m*
always ['ɔ:lweɪz] (ADV) siempre • **as ~** como siempre • **nearly ~** casi siempre • **he's ~ late** siempre llega tarde • **he's ~ moaning** siempre está quejándose • **you can ~ go by train** también puedes ir en tren
always-on [,ɔ:lweɪz'ɒn] (ADJ) [*internet connection*] permanente
Alzheimer's ['æltshaɪməz], **Alzheimer's disease** (N) (enfermedad *f* de) Alzheimer *m*
AM (N ABBR) **1** (= **amplitude modulation**) A.M. *f*
2 (*US*) (= **Artium Magister, Master of Arts**) ▹ **MA**
3 (*Welsh Pol*) (= **Assembly Member**) parlamentario/a *m/f*
Am (ABBR) **1** = **America**
2 = **American**
am [æm] (VB) *1st pers sing present of* **be**
a.m. (ADV ABBR) (= **ante meridiem**) a.m. • **at four ~** a las cuatro de la mañana
AMA (N ABBR) (*US*) = **American Medical Association**
amalgam [ə'mælgəm] (N) amalgama *f* (**of** de)
(CPD) ▸ **amalgam filling** amalgama *f* dental
amalgamate [ə'mælgəmeɪt] (VT) [+ *texts*] amalgamar; [+ *companies*] fusionar
(VI) [*organizations*] amalgamarse, unirse; [*companies*] fusionarse
amalgamation [ə,mælgə'meɪʃən] (N) amalgamiento *m*; (*Comm*) fusión *f*
amanita [,æmə'naɪtə] (N) amanita *f*
amanuensis [ə,mænjʊ'ensɪs] (N) (PL: **amanuenses** [ə,mænju'ensi:z]) amanuense *mf*
Amaryllis [,æmə'rɪlɪs] (N) Amarilis
amaryllis [,æmə'rɪlɪs] (N) amarilis *f inv*
amass [ə'mæs] (VT) [+ *wealth, information*] acumular
amateur ['æmətəʳ] (N) **1** (*lit*) (= *non-professional*) amateur *mf*; (= *hobbyist*) aficionado/a *m/f* • **he boxed first as an ~ then as a professional** boxeó primero como amateur y después como profesional • **an enthusiastic ~** un amateur entusiasta • **I love gardening but I'm just an ~** me encanta la jardinería, pero no soy más que un aficionado
2 (*pej*) chapucero/a *m/f* • **those guys are ~s!***

a

¡esos tipos son unos chapuceros!
ADJ **1** (= *not professional*) [*athlete, actor, production*] amateur; [*club, competition*] para amateurs, para aficionados • **~ athletics/photography** atletismo/fotografía para amateurs • **an ~ photographer** un aficionado a la fotografía, un fotógrafo aficionado • **an ~ detective** un detective aficionado • **I have an ~ interest in pottery** me interesa la cerámica como aficionado • **~ status** condición *f* de amateur
2 (*pej*) [*production, performance*] de aficionados, chapucero • **it was a very ~ performance** fue una actuación de aficionados *or* muy chapucera
CPD ▸ **amateur dramatics** teatro *m* amateur, teatro *m* de aficionados

amateurish ['æmətərɪʃ] ADJ (*pej*) poco profesional, inexperto

amateurishly ['æmətərɪʃlɪ] ADV (*pej*) de manera poco profesional

amateurishness ['æmətərɪʃnɪs] N (*pej*) [*of performance, work*] carácter *m* poco profesional

amateurism ['æmətərɪzəm] N **1** (= *amateur status*) lo amateur
2 (*pej*) falta *f* de profesionalidad

amatory ['æmətərɪ] ADJ (*frm*) (*liter*) amatorio, erótico

amaze [ə'meɪz] VT pasmar, asombrar • **to be ~d (at)** quedar pasmado (de) • **I was ~d that I managed to do it** estaba asombrado de haberlo conseguido • **you ~ me!** ¡me admiras!, ¡me dejas patidifuso!*

amazed [ə'meɪzd] ADJ [*glance, expression*] asombrado, lleno de estupor

amazement [ə'meɪzmənt] N asombro *m* • **the news caused general ~** la noticia causó sorpresa generalizada *or* un asombro general • **they looked on in ~** miraron asombrados • **to my ~** para mi gran asombro *or* sorpresa

amazing [ə'meɪzɪŋ] ADJ **1** (= *astonishing*) asombroso • **that's ~ news!** ¡es una noticia asombrosa!
2 (= *wonderful*) extraordinario • **Kay's an ~ cook** Kay es una cocinera extraordinaria

amazingly [ə'meɪzɪŋlɪ] ADV
1 (= *astonishingly*) asombrosamente • **it was ~ easy** asombraba lo fácil que era, era asombrosamente fácil • **~ enough** por increíble que parezca, aunque parece mentira • **~, nobody was killed** por milagro, no hubo víctimas
2 (= *wonderfully*) extraordinariamente • **she is ~ generous** es extraordinariamente generosa • **he is ~ fit for his age** su estado físico es extraordinario para un hombre de su edad • **he did ~ well** tuvo un éxito formidable

Amazon ['æməzən] N **1** (*Geog*) Amazonas *m*
2 (*Myth*) amazona *f*; (*fig*) (*also* **amazon**) amazona *f*; (*US*) (*pej*) marimacho *m*
CPD ▸ **Amazon basin** cuenca *f* del Amazonas ▸ **Amazon jungle, Amazon rain forest** selva *f* del Amazonas, selva *f* amazónica

Amazonia [,æmə'zəʊnɪə] N Amazonia *f*

Amazonian [,æmə'zəʊnɪən] ADJ amazónico

ambassador [æm'bæsədə^r] N embajador(a) *m/f*; (*fig*) embajador(a) *m/f*, representante *mf* (**for** de) • **the Spanish ~** el embajador de España

ambassadorial [æm,bæsə'dɔ:rɪəl] ADJ de embajador

ambassadorship [æm'bæsədəʃɪp] N embajada *f*

ambassadress† [æm'bæsədrɪs] N embajadora *f*

amber ['æmbə^r] N ámbar *m* • **at** *or* **on ~** (*Brit*) (*Aut*) en ámbar
ADJ **1** [*jewellery*] de ámbar; [*colour*] ambarino
2 (*Brit*) (*Aut*) • **~ light** luz *f* ámbar

ambergris ['æmbəgri:s] N ámbar *m* gris

ambi… ['æmbɪ] PREFIX ambi…

ambiance ['æmbɪəns] = **ambience**

ambidextrous [,æmbɪ'dekstrəs] ADJ ambidiestro, ambidextro

ambience ['æmbɪəns] N ambiente *m*, atmósfera *f*

ambient ['æmbɪənt] ADJ ambiental
CPD ▸ **ambient music** música *f* ambiental

ambiguity [,æmbɪ'gjʊɪtɪ] N (= *lack of clarity*) ambigüedad *f*; [*of meaning*] doble sentido *m*

ambiguous [æm'bɪgjʊəs] ADJ [*remark, meaning*] ambiguo

ambiguously [æm'bɪgjʊəslɪ] ADV ambiguamente, de forma ambigua

ambiguousness [æm'bɪgjʊəsnɪs] N ambigüedad *f*

ambit ['æmbɪt] N ámbito *m* • **within the ~ of** dentro del *or* en el ámbito de

ambition [æm'bɪʃən] N ambición *f* • **to achieve one's ~** realizar su ambición • **he has no ~** no tiene ambición • **to have an ~ to be a doctor** ambicionar ser médico • **his ~ is to …** ambiciona …

ambitious [æm'bɪʃəs] ADJ [*person, plan, goal*] ambicioso • **he was not an ~ man** no era un hombre ambicioso • **perhaps you're being too ~** quizá estés intentando abarcar demasiado • **if you feel a bit more ~ you could try this recipe** si te sientes con ganas de probar algo más difícil, puedes intentar esta receta • **to be ~ for** *or* **of sth** (*frm*) ambicionar algo • **to be ~ for sb** ambicionar grandes cosas para algn • **he was ~ to be the boss** aspiraba a *or* ambicionaba ser el jefe • **his ~ reform programme** su ambicioso programa de reforma • **that's rather ~, isn't it?** eso es bastante ambicioso, ¿no? • **starting with this could be a little ~** empezar con eso podría ser querer abarcar demasiado *or* podría ser un poco ambicioso

ambitiously [æm'bɪʃəslɪ] ADV ambiciosamente • **a book ~ titled …** un libro con el ambicioso título de … • **next Keith will ~ attempt to name all Shakespeare's plays in two minutes** ahora Keith llevará a cabo su ambicioso intento de nombrar todas las obras de Shakespeare en dos minutos • **he decided, perhaps rather ~, to build the extension himself** decidió, quizás sobrevalorando sus posibilidades *or* intentando abarcar demasiado, construir la extensión él mismo • **he had ~ hoped to finish the job in a month** había esperado poder terminar el trabajo en un mes, lo que era mucho esperar

ambitiousness [æm'bɪʃəsnɪs] N ambición *f*

ambivalence [æm'bɪvələns] N ambivalencia *f*

ambivalent [æm'bɪvələnt] ADJ ambivalente

ambivalently [æm'bɪvələntlɪ] ADV [*feel, respond*] de manera ambivalente

amble ['æmbl] VI [*person*] andar sin prisa; [*horse*] amblar, ir a paso de andadura • **to ~ along** andar sin prisa, pasearse despacio • **the bus ~s along at 40kph** el autobús va tranquilamente a 40kph • **he ~d into my office at ten o'clock** entró tranquilamente en mi oficina a las diez • **he ~d up to me** se me acercó a paso lento
N [*of horse*] ambladura *f*, paso *m* de andadura • **to walk at an ~** [*person*] andar sin prisa, pasearse despacio

Ambrose ['æmbrəʊz] N Ambrosio

ambrosia [æm'brəʊzɪə] N ambrosía *f*

ambulance ['æmbjʊləns] N ambulancia *f*
CPD ▸ **ambulance chaser*** (*esp US*) (*pej*) *abogado sin escrúpulos a la caza de personas accidentadas cuyos casos reporten jugosos beneficios* ▸ **ambulance chasing** *práctica de abogados sin escrúpulos, a la caza de personas accidentadas cuyos casos reporten jugosos beneficios* ▸ **ambulance crew** personal *m* de ambulancia ▸ **ambulance driver** conductor(a) *m/f* de ambulancia, ambulanciero/a *m/f* ▸ **ambulance man** ambulanciero *m* ▸ **ambulance service** • **the ~ service** el servicio de ambulancia ▸ **ambulance woman** ambulanciera *f*

ambulatory [,æmbjʊ'leɪtərɪ] ADJ (*US*) (*Med*) no encamado

ambush ['æmbʊʃ] N emboscada *f* • **to set** *or* **lay an ~ for** tender una emboscada a • **to lie in ~** estar emboscado (**for** para coger)
VT cazar por sorpresa, agarrar por sorpresa (*LAm*) • **to be ~ed** caer en una emboscada, ser cazado por sorpresa

am-dram ['æmdræm] N ABBR (= **amateur dramatics**) teatro *m* amateur

ameba [ə'mi:bə] N (*US*) = **amoeba**

ameliorate [ə'mi:lɪəreɪt] (*frm*) VT mejorar
VI mejorar, mejorarse

amelioration [ə,mi:lɪə'reɪʃən] N (*frm*) mejora *f*, mejoramiento *m*

amen ['ɑ:'men] EXCL amén • **~ to that** así sea, ojalá sea así
N amén *m*

amenable [ə'mi:nəbl] ADJ **1** (= *responsive*) • **~ to argument** flexible, que se deja convencer • **~ to discipline** sumiso, dispuesto a dejarse disciplinar • **~ to reason** dispuesto a entrar en razón • **~ to treatment** susceptible de ser curado, curable • **I'd like to visit you at home if you're ~** me gustaría hacerle una visita en su casa, si le parece bien
2 (*Jur*) responsable (**for** de)

amend [ə'mend] VT [+ *law*] enmendar; [+ *text, wording*] corregir

amendment [ə'mendmənt] N **1** (*to law*) enmienda *f* (**to a**) • **the Fifth Amendment** (*US*) la Quinta Enmienda (*a la Constitución de los Estados Unidos*) • **to invoke** *or* **plead** *or* **take the Fifth (Amendment)** (*US*) acogerse a la quinta, negarse a dar testimonio bajo la protección de la Quinta Enmienda (*relativa a la autoincriminación*)
2 (*to text*) corrección *f*

FIFTH AMENDMENT

La Quinta Enmienda a la Constitución de los Estados Unidos establece varios principios legales fundamentales que protegen al ciudadano frente al poder del Estado. Entre estos derechos están el de que una persona no sea encarcelada o sus bienes sean embargados sin juicio previo, así como el derecho a no ser procesada dos veces por el mismo delito, o a no ser obligada a aportar pruebas contra sí misma. Al hecho de negarse a aportar pruebas autoincriminatorias se le conoce como **taking the fifth** (acogerse a la quinta) y, durante las investigaciones anticomunistas que el senador McCarthy realizó en la década de los años 50, aquellos que se acogían a esta quinta enmienda eran generalmente acusados de llevar a cabo actividades antiamericanas.

amends [ə'mendz] NPL • **to make ~ (to sb) for sth** (= *apologize*) dar satisfacción (a algn) por algo; (= *compensate*) compensar (a algn) por algo • **I'll try to make ~ in future** trataré de dar satisfacción en el futuro

amenity [ə'mi:nɪtɪ] N **1** (= *quality*) amenidad *f*
2 (= *thing*) (*gen pl*) **amenities** comodidades *fpl* • **the amenities of life** las cosas agradables de la vida • **a house with all amenities** una casa con todas las comodidades *or* todo confort • **the hotel has very good amenities** el hotel tiene excelentes servicios e instalaciones • **the town has many amenities** la ciudad ofrece gran variedad de servicios • **we are trying to improve the city's amenities** nos esforzamos por mejorar las instalaciones de la ciudad
CPD ▸ **amenity bed** (*Brit*) (*Med*) habitación *f* privada ▸ **amenity society** (*Brit*) asociación *f* para la conservación del medio ambiente

amenorrhoea, **amenorrhea** (*US*) [eɪ,menə'rɪə] N amenorrea *f*

Amerasian [,æmə'reɪʃn] N amerasiático/a *m/f*
ADJ amerasiático

America [ə'merɪkə] N (= *continent*) América *f*; (= *USA*) Estados *mpl* Unidos

American [ə'merɪkən] ADJ (= *of USA*) norteamericano, estadounidense; [*continent*] americano • **the ~ dream** el sueño americano • IDIOM: • **as ~ as apple pie** genuinamente americano
N **1** (= *person*) (*from USA*) norteamericano/a *m/f*, americano/a *m/f*; (*from continent*) americano/a *m/f*
2 (*Ling**) inglés *m* americano
CPD ▸ **American English** inglés *m* americano ▸ **American football** fútbol *m* americano ▸ **American Indian** amerindio/a *m/f* ▸ **American leather** cuero *m* artificial ▸ **American Legion** *organización de veteranos de las dos guerras mundiales*; ▷ LEGION ▸ **American plan** (*US*) (*in hotel*) (habitación *f* con) pensión *f* completa ▸ **American sign language** lenguaje *m* americano por signos, lenguaje *m* gestual americano ▸ **American Spanish** español *m* de América

AMERICAN DREAM

El término **American Dream** (el sueño americano), se refiere a los valores y creencias que para muchos estadounidenses son característicos de su modo de entender la vida como nación y que encuentran su materialización en la Declaración de Independencia de 1776. Con este término se pone especial énfasis en el individualismo, la importancia de trabajar duro, el hecho de que todos podemos mejorar y que la libertad y la justicia han de ser universales. Para muchos el "sueño americano" era una oportunidad para hacer fortuna.

El término también se usa de forma irónica para referirse al contraste entre estos ideales y las actitudes materialistas que caracterizan a la sociedad estadounidense actual.

Americana [ə,merɪ'kɑ:nə] N *objetos, documentos etc pertenecientes a la herencia cultural norteamericana*

Americanism [ə'merɪkənɪzəm] N americanismo *m*

Americanization [ə,merɪkənaɪ'zeɪʃən] N americanización *f*

Americanize [ə'merɪkənaɪz] VT americanizar

Americanized [ə'merɪkənaɪzd] ADJ [*country, culture, language*] americanizado • **to become ~** americanizarse

americium [,æmə'rɪsɪəm] N americio *m*

Amerind ['æmərɪnd] N amerindio/a *m/f*

Amerindian [,æmə'rɪndɪən] ADJ amerindio
N amerindio/a *m/f*

amethyst ['æmɪθɪst] N amatista *f*

Amex ['æmeks] N ABBR (*US*) **1** ® (= **American Express**®) American Express® • **~ card** tarjeta *f* de American Express®
2 (*US*) = **American Stock Exchange**

amiability [,eɪmɪə'bɪlɪtɪ] N amabilidad *f*, afabilidad *f*

amiable ['eɪmɪəbl] ADJ amable, afable

amiably ['eɪmɪəblɪ] ADV amablemente, afablemente

amicable ['æmɪkəbl] ADJ amistoso, amigable • **to reach an ~ settlement** llegar a un acuerdo amistoso

amicably ['æmɪkəblɪ] ADV amistosamente, amigablemente

amid [ə'mɪd] PREP en medio de, entre

amidships [ə'mɪdʃɪps] ADV en medio del barco

amidst [ə'mɪdst] PREP (*frm*) en medio de, entre

amino-acid [ə'mi:nəʊ,æsɪd] N aminoácido *m*

amir [ə'mɪəʳ] = **emir**

Amish ['ɑ:mɪʃ] N • **the ~** los amish (*secta religiosa menonita*)

amiss [ə'mɪs] ADJ • **there's something ~** pasa algo • **something is ~ in your calculations** algo falla en tus cálculos • **have I said something ~?** ¿he dicho algo inoportuno? • **there was nothing ~ that I could see** por lo que vi, todo estaba bien
ADV • **don't take it ~, will you?** no lo tomes a mal, no te vayas a ofender • **a lick of paint wouldn't go** *or* **come ~** una mano de pintura no vendría mal • **a little politeness wouldn't go** *or* **come ~** un poco de educación no estaría de más, no vendría mal un poco de educación

amity ['æmɪtɪ] N (*frm*) concordia *f*, amistad *f*

AMM N ABBR = **antimissile missile**

Amman [ə'mɑ:n] N Ammán *m*

ammeter ['æmɪtəʳ] N amperímetro *m*

ammo* ['æməʊ] N ABBR = **ammunition**

ammonal ['æmənəl] N amonal *m*

ammonia [ə'məʊnɪə] N amoníaco *m* • **liquid ~** amoníaco *m* líquido

ammonium [ə'məʊnɪəm] N amonio *m*
CPD ▸ **ammonium hydroxide** hidróxido *m* amónico ▸ **ammonium sulphate** sulfato *m* amónico

ammunition [,æmjʊ'nɪʃən] N **1** (*lit*) munición *f*
2 (*fig*) argumentos *mpl*
CPD ▸ **ammunition belt** cartuchera *f*, canana *f* ▸ **ammunition clip** cargador *m* ▸ **ammunition depot, ammunition dump** depósito *m* de municiones, polvorín *m* ▸ **ammunition pouch** cartuchera *f* ▸ **ammunition store** depósito *m* de municiones, polvorín *m*

amnesia [æm'ni:zɪə] N amnesia *f*

amnesiac [æm'ni:zɪæk] ADJ amnésico
N amnésico/a *m/f*

amnesty ['æmnɪstɪ] N amnistía *f* • **to grant an ~ to** amnistiar (a), conceder una amnistía a
VT amnistiar

Amnesty International [,æmnɪstɪɪntə'næʃnəl] N Amnistía *f* Internacional

amnio* ['æmnɪəʊ] N = **amniocentesis**

amniocentesis [,æmnɪəʊsen'ti:sɪs] N (PL: **amniocenteses** [,æmnɪəʊsən'ti:si:z]) amniocentesis *f*

amniotic [,æmnɪ'ɒtɪk] ADJ amniótico • **~ fluid** líquido *m* amniótico • **~ sac** saco *m* amniótico

amoeba [ə'mi:bə] N (PL: **amoebas, amoebae** [ə'mi:bi:]) ameba *f*, amiba *f*

amoebic [ə'mi:bɪk] ADJ amébico
CPD ▸ **amoebic dysentery** disentería *f* amébica

amok [ə'mɒk] ADV • **to run ~** enloquecerse, desbocarse

among [ə'mʌŋ], **amongst** [ə'mʌŋst] PREP entre, en medio de • **from ~** de entre • **~ the Yanomami it is deemed a virtue** entre los yanomami se considera una virtud • **he is ~ those who ...** es de los que ... • **it is not ~ the names I have** no figura entre los nombres que tengo • **this is ~ the possibilities** esa es una de las posibilidades • **they quarrelled ~ themselves** riñeron entre sí • **one can say that ~ friends** eso se puede decir entre amigos • **share it ~ yourselves** repartíoslo entre vosotros

amoral [eɪ'mɒrəl] ADJ amoral

amorality [,eɪmɒ'rælɪtɪ] N amoralidad *f*

amorous ['æmərəs] ADJ [*person, look*] apasionado • **to feel ~** sentirse apasionado • **he made ~ advances to his secretary** se le insinuó a su secretaria

amorously ['æmərəslɪ] ADV [*look, embrace*] apasionadamente

amorphous [ə'mɔ:fəs] ADJ amorfo

amorphousness [ə'mɔ:fəsnɪs] N carácter *m* amorfo

amortizable [ə'mɔ:tɪzəbl] ADJ amortizable
CPD ▸ **amortizable loan** préstamo *m* amortizable

amortization [ə,mɔ:tɪ'zeɪʃən] N amortización *f*

amortize [ə'mɔ:taɪz] VT amortizar

amount [ə'maʊnt] N **1** (= *quantity*) cantidad *f* • **a huge ~ of rice** una cantidad enorme de arroz • **there is quite an ~ left** queda bastante • **any ~ of** cualquier cantidad de • **I have any ~ of time** tengo mucho tiempo • **we have had any ~ of trouble** hemos tenido un sinnúmero de problemas • **no ~ of arguing will help** es totalmente inútil discutir • **in small ~s** en pequeñas cantidades • **the total ~** el total, la cantidad total
2 (= *sum of money*) cantidad *f*, suma *f* • **a large ~ of money** una gran cantidad *or* suma de dinero
3 (= *total value*) valor *m* • **a bill for the ~ of** una cuenta por importe *or* valor de • **check in the ~ of 50 dollars** (*US*) cheque *m* por valor de 50 dólares • **to the ~ of** por valor de • **debts to the ~ of £100** deudas *fpl* por valor de 100 libras

▸ **amount to** VI + PREP **1** (= *add up to*) [*sums, figures, debts*] sumar, ascender a
2 (= *be equivalent to*) equivaler a, significar • **it ~s to the same thing** es igual, viene a ser lo mismo • **this ~s to a refusal** esto equivale a una negativa
3 (= *be worth*) • **it doesn't ~ to much** apenas es significativo, viene a ser poca cosa • **he'll never ~ to much** nunca dejará de ser nadie

amour† [ə'mʊəʳ] N (*liter*) amorío *m*, aventura *f* amorosa

amour-propre ['æmʊə'prɒpr] N amor *m* propio

amp [æmp] N **1** (*also* **ampere**) amperio *m* • **a 13-amp plug** un enchufe de 13 amperios
2* (*also* **amplifier**) ampli* *m*, amplificador *m*

amperage ['æmpərɪdʒ] N amperaje *m*

ampere, ampère ['æmpɛəʳ] N amperio *m*
CPD ▸ **ampere-hour** amperio-hora *m*

ampersand ['æmpəsænd] N el signo & (= *and*)

amphetamine [æm'fetəmi:n] N anfetamina *f*

amphibia [æm'fɪbɪə] NPL anfibios *mpl*

amphibian [æm'fɪbɪən] N anfibio *m*
ADJ anfibio

amphibious [æmˈfɪbɪəs] ADJ [*animal, vehicle*] anfibio
amphitheatre, amphitheater (US) [ˈæmfɪˌθɪətəʳ] N anfiteatro *m*
Amphitryon [æmˈfɪtrɪən] N Anfitrión
amphora [ˈæmfərə] N (PL: **amphoras, amphorae** [ˈæmfəˌriː]) ánfora *f*
ample [ˈæmpl] ADJ (COMPAR: **ampler**, SUPERL: **amplest**) **1** (= *plentiful, more than sufficient*) **a** (*before noun*) [*evidence, proof, resources*] abundante; [*time, space*] de sobra • **to have ~ time (to do sth)** tener tiempo de sobra (para hacer algo) • **there is ~ space for a desk in this room** hay sitio de sobra para un escritorio en esta habitación • **she has ~ means** tiene medios más que suficientes • **there'll be ~ opportunity to relax** habrá oportunidades de sobra para relajarse • **an ~ supply of jars** una abundante cantidad de tarros • **there was an ~ supply of food** había comida en abundancia • **to make ~ use of sth** usar algo en abundancia • **she was given ~ warning that ...** se le avisó con tiempo de sobra de que ...
b • **to be ~** ser más que suficiente • **eight hours' sleep should be ~** ocho horas de sueño deberían ser más que suficientes • **one cupful of rice is ~ for two people** una taza de arroz es más que suficiente para dos personas • **thanks, I have ~** gracias, tengo bastante
2 (= *generous*) [*garment*] amplio, grande; [*waist*] ancho, generoso; [*portion, bosom*] generoso • **his ~ stomach** su enorme *or* prominente barriga • **his ~ chin** su papada
amplification [ˌæmplɪfɪˈkeɪʃən] N **1** [*of sound*] amplificación *f*
2 (*fig*) (= *elaboration*) desarrollo *m*, explicación *f*
amplifier [ˈæmplɪfaɪəʳ] N amplificador *m*
amplify [ˈæmplɪfaɪ] VT **1** [+ *sound*] amplificar; (*also Rad*) aumentar
2 (*fig*) [+ *statement etc*] desarrollar • **he refused to ~ his remarks** se negó a hacer más comentarios
amplitude [ˈæmplɪtjuːd] N amplitud *f*
amply [ˈæmplɪ] ADV **1** (= *sufficiently*) [*demonstrate, illustrate*] ampliamente, suficientemente • **we were ~ rewarded** fuimos ampliamente recompensados • **we were ~ justified** estuvimos plenamente justificados
2 (= *generously*) • **she is ~ proportioned** es de proporciones generosas
ampoule, ampule (US) [ˈæmpuːl] N ampolla *f*
amputate [ˈæmpjʊteɪt] VT amputar
amputation [ˌæmpjʊˈteɪʃən] N amputación *f*
amputee [ˌæmpjʊˈtiː] N *persona cuya pierna o cuyo brazo ha sido amputada/o*
Amsterdam [ˌæmstəˈdæm] N Amsterdam *m*
amt ABBR (= **amount**) impte
Amtrak [ˈæmtræk] N (US) *empresa nacional de ferrocarriles de los EEUU*
amuck [əˈmʌk] ADV = **amok**
amulet [ˈæmjʊlɪt] N amuleto *m*
amuse [əˈmjuːz] VT **1** (= *cause mirth to*) divertir • **the thought seemed to ~ him** la idea parecía divertirle • **this ~d everybody** divirtió *or* hizo reír a todos • **we are not ~d** (*hum*) no nos hace gracia • **to be ~d at** *or* **by** divertirse con • **with an ~d expression** con una mirada risueña
2 (= *entertain*) distraer, entretener • **to keep sb ~d** entretener a algn • **this should keep them ~d for years** esto deberá ocupar su atención por muchos años • **to ~ o.s.** distraerse • **run along and ~ yourselves** marchaos y a pasarlo bien
amusement [əˈmjuːzmənt] N **1** (= *mirth*) • **with a look of ~** con mirada risueña • **there was general ~ at this** al oír esto se rieron todos • **much to my ~** con gran regocijo mío • **to conceal one's ~** ocultar sus ganas de reír, aguantarse la risa
2 (= *entertainment*) distracción *f*, diversión *f* • **they do it for ~ only** para ellos es un pasatiempo nada más
3 amusements (= *pastimes*) diversiones *fpl*, distracciones *fpl*; (*Brit*) (*in fairground*) atracciones *f*; (*in amusement arcade*) máquinas *fpl* electrónicas, máquinas *fpl* tragaperras • **a town with plenty of ~s** una ciudad que ofrece muchas diversiones
CPD ▸ **amusement arcade** (*Brit*) sala *f* de juegos recreativos ▸ **amusement park** (*esp US*) parque *m* de atracciones ▸ **amusement ride** atracción *f* (*en parque de atracciones*)
amusing [əˈmjuːzɪŋ] ADJ **1** (= *funny*) gracioso, divertido • **I found it ~** me pareció gracioso *or* divertido • **I didn't find it ~** no le vi la gracia
2 (= *entertaining*) entretenido
amusingly [əˈmjuːzɪŋlɪ] ADV **1** (= *funnily*) de forma divertida • **~ written** escrito con gracia
2 (= *entertainingly*) de forma entretenida
an [æn] [ən] [n] INDEF ART ▹ **a**
ANA N ABBR (US) **1** = **American Newspaper Association**
2 = **American Nurses' Association**
anabolic [ˌænəˈbɒlɪk] ADJ anabólico • **~ steroid** esteroide *m* anabolizante
anachronism [əˈnækrənɪzəm] N anacronismo *m*
anachronistic [əˌnækrəˈnɪstɪk] ADJ anacrónico
anacoluthon [ˌænəkəˈluːθɒn] N (PL: **anacolutha** [ˌænəkəˈluːθə]) anacoluto *m*
anaconda [ˌænəˈkɒndə] N anaconda *f*
Anacreon [əˈnækrɪən] N Anacreonte
anaemia, anemia (US) [əˈniːmɪə] N anemia *f*
anaemic, anemic (US) [əˈniːmɪk] ADJ (*Med*) anémico; (*fig*) (= *weak*) débil
anaerobic [ˌænɛəˈrəʊbɪk] ADJ anaerobio
CPD ▸ **anaerobic digester** digestor *m* anaerobio ▸ **anaerobic digestion** digestión *f* anaerobia
anaesthesia, anesthesia (US) [ˌænɪsˈθiːzɪə] N anestesia *f*
anaesthetic, anesthetic (US) [ˌænɪsˈθetɪk] N anestésico *m* • **local/general ~** anestesia *f* local/total • **to be under (an) ~** estar anestesiado • **to give sb an ~** • **put sb under (an) ~** anestesiar a algn
ADJ anestésico
anaesthetist, anesthetist (US) [æˈniːsθɪtɪst] N anestesista *mf*
anaesthetize, anesthetize (US) [æˈniːsθɪtaɪz] VT anestesiar
anagram [ˈænəgræm] N anagrama *m*
anal [ˈeɪnəl] ADJ anal
CPD ▸ **anal retentive** (*Psych*) persona estancada en la fase anal; (= *fussy person**) quisquilloso/a *m/f*, puñetero/a *m/f* ▸ **anal sex** sexo *m* anal
analgesia [ˌænælˈdʒiːzɪə] N analgesia *f*
analgesic [ˌænælˈdʒiːsɪk] ADJ analgésico
N analgésico *m*
analog [ˈænəlɒg] N (US) = **analogue**
analogical [ˌænəˈlɒdʒɪkəl] ADJ analógico
analogous [əˈnæləgəs] ADJ análogo (**to, with a**)
analogue [ˈænəlɒg] N análogo *m*
CPD analógico ▸ **analogue computer** ordenador *m* analógico
analogy [əˈnælədʒɪ] N analogía *f*; (= *similarity*) semejanza *f* • **by ~ with** • **on the ~ of** por analogía con • **to argue from** *or* **by ~** razonar por analogía • **to draw an ~ between** señalar una semejanza entre
analysand [əˈnælɪˌsænd] N (*Psych*) sujeto *m* analizado, analizando *m*
analyse, analyze (US) [ˈænəlaɪz] VT **1** (= *study*) analizar
2 (*Psych*) psicoanalizar
analyser, analyzer (US) [ˈænəlaɪzəʳ] N (*Tech*) analizador *m*
analysis [əˈnælɪsɪs] N (PL: **analyses** [əˈnælɪsiːz]) **1** (= *study*) análisis *m inv* • **in the final** *or* **last** *or* **ultimate ~** a fin de cuentas
2 (*Psych*) psicoanálisis *m*
analyst [ˈænəlɪst] N **1** (*Chem etc*) analista *mf*
2 (*Psych*) psicoanalista *mf*
analytic [ˌænəˈlɪtɪk] ADJ = **analytical**
analytical [ˌænəˈlɪtɪkəl] ADJ analítico • **an ~ mind** una mente analítica
CPD ▸ **analytical psychology** psicología *f* analítica
analytically [ˌænəˈlɪtɪklɪ] ADV [*think, question*] de manera analítica
analyze [ˈænəlaɪz] VT (US) = **analyse**
analyzer [ˈænəlaɪzəʳ] N (US) = **analyser**
anapaest, anapest [ˈænəpiːst] N anapesto *m*
anaphoric [ˌænəˈfɒrɪk] ADJ anafórico
anaphylactic shock [ˌænəfɪlæktɪkˈʃɒk] N choque *m* anafiláctico
anarchic [æˈnɑːkɪk] ADJ anárquico
anarchical [æˈnɑːkɪkəl] ADJ = **anarchic**
anarchism [ˈænəkɪzəm] N anarquismo *m*
anarchist [ˈænəkɪst] N anarquista *mf*
ADJ anarquista
anarchistic [ˌænəˈkɪstɪk] ADJ anarquista
anarcho- [æˈnɑːkəʊ-] PREFIX anarco- • **anarcho-punk** anarcopunk *mf*; ▹ **anarcho-syndicalism**
anarcho-syndicalism [ˌænɑːkəʊ-ˈsɪndɪkəlɪzəm] N anarcosindicalismo *m*
anarchy [ˈænəkɪ] N **1** (*Pol*) anarquía *f*
2* (= *chaos*) anarquía *f*
anathema [əˈnæθɪmə] N **1** (*Rel*) anatema *m*
2 (*fig*) • **he is ~ to me** no lo puedo ver, para mí es inaguantable • **the idea is ~ to her** para ella la idea es una abominación, la idea le resulta odiosa
anathematize [əˈnæθɪmətaɪz] VT anatematizar
anatomical [ˌænəˈtɒmɪkəl] ADJ anatómico
anatomically [ˌænəˈtɒmɪklɪ] ADV anatómicamente
anatomist [əˈnætəmɪst] N anatomista *mf*
anatomize [əˈnætəmaɪz] VT (*Bio*) anatomizar; (*fig*) analizar minuciosamente, diseccionar
anatomy [əˈnætəmɪ] N **1** (*Med*) anatomía *f*
2 (*hum*) (= *body*) anatomía *f*
3 (*frm*) (= *analysis*) análisis *m inv* minucioso, disección *f*
anatto [əˈnætəʊ] N achiote *m*, bija *f*
ANC N ABBR (= **African National Congress**) CNA *m*
ancestor [ˈænsɪstəʳ] N **1** (= *person*) antepasado/a *m/f*
2 (*fig*) [*of machine, idea, organization*] antecesor(a) *m/f*, predecesor(a) *m/f*
ancestral [ænˈsestrəl] ADJ ancestral
CPD ▸ **ancestral home** casa *f* solariega
ancestress† [ˈænsɪstrɪs] N antepasada *f*
ancestry [ˈænsɪstrɪ] N (= *lineage*) ascendencia *f*, linaje *m*; (= *noble birth*) abolengo *m*
anchor [ˈæŋkəʳ] N **1** (*Naut*) ancla *f* • **to be** *or* **lie** *or* **ride at ~** estar al ancla, estar anclado • **to cast** *or* **drop ~** echar anclas • **~s aweigh!** ¡leven anclas!; ▹ **weigh**

2 (*fig*) seguridad *f*, sostén *m*; (= *person*) pilar *m*
3 = **anchorman, anchorwoman**
VT **1** (*Naut*) anclar
2 (*fig*) sujetar (**to** a), afianzar (**to** en)
3 (*esp US*) (*TV, Rad*) presentar
VI (*Naut*) anclar

anchorage [ˈæŋkərɪdʒ] N ancladero *m*, fondeadero *m*
CPD ▸ **anchorage dues, anchorage fee** anclaje *m*

anchorite [ˈæŋkəraɪt] N anacoreta *mf*

anchorman [ˈæŋkəmæn] N (PL: **anchormen**) (*TV, Rad*) presentador *m*; (*fig*) hombre clave

anchorwoman [ˈæŋkəˌwʊmən] N (PL: **anchorwomen**) (*TV, Rad*) presentadora *f*

anchovy [ˈæntʃəvɪ] N (*live, fresh*) boquerón *m*; (*salted, tinned*) anchoa *f*
CPD ▸ **anchovy paste** pasta *f* de anchoas

ancient [ˈeɪnʃənt] ADJ **1** (= *old, classical*) antiguo • **~ Greek** griego *m* antiguo • **~ history** historia *f* antigua • **that's ~ history!*** ¡eso pertenece a la historia! • **in ~ days** en la antigüedad, hace muchísimo tiempo • **~ monument** (*Brit*) monumento *m* histórico • **~ Rome** la Roma antigua • **remains of ~ times** restos *mpl* de la antigüedad
2* (*hum*) [*person*] viejo, anciano; [*clothing, object*] antiquísimo, de los tiempos de Maricastaña* • **we went in his ~ car** fuimos en su antiquísimo coche • **he's getting pretty ~** va para viejo; ▹ **OLD**

ancients [ˈeɪnʃənts] NPL • **the ~** los antiguos

ancillary [ænˈsɪlərɪ] ADJ **1** (= *secondary*) subordinado (**to** a)
2 (= *supporting*) [*staff, workers*] auxiliar; [*services*] complementario
3 (= *additional*) [*charges, costs*] adicional

and [ænd] [ənd] [nd] [ən] CONJ **1** y; (*before i-, hi- but not hie-*) e • **you and me** tú y yo • **French and English** francés e inglés • **and?** ¿y?, ¿y qué más? • **and how!*** ¡y (no veas) cómo! • **and/or** y/o
2 (+ *compar adj*) • **better and better** cada vez mejor • **more and more** cada vez más • **more and more difficult** cada vez más difícil
3 (*in numbers*) • **one and a half** uno y medio • **a hundred and one** ciento uno • **two hundred and ten** doscientos diez • **five hours and 20 minutes** cinco horas y 20 minutos • **ten dollars and 50 cents** diez dólares y *or* con 50 centavos
4 (*negative sense*) ni • **without shoes and socks** sin zapatos ni calcetines • **you can't buy and sell here** aquí no se permite comprar ni vender
5 (*repetition, continuation*) • **she cried and cried** no dejaba de llorar, lloraba sin parar • **I rang and rang** llamé muchas veces • **he talked and talked** habló sin parar *or* (*LAm*) cesar
6 (*before infin*) • **try and do it** trata de hacerlo • **please try and come!** ¡procura venir! • **wait and see** espera y verás • **come and see me** ven a verme
7 (*implying a distinction*) • **there are lawyers and lawyers!** hay abogados y abogados
8 (*implying a conditional*) • **one move and you're dead!** ¡como te muevas disparo!, ¡un solo movimiento y disparo!

> **AND**
>
> *In order to avoid two "i" sounds coming together,* **and** *is translated by* **e** *not* **y** *before words beginning with* **i** *and* **hi** *and before the letter* **y** *used on its own:*
>
> **... Spain and Italy ...**
> ... España e Italia ...
> **... grapes and figs ...**
> ... uvas e higos ...
> **... words ending in S and Y ...**
> ... palabras terminadas en S e Y ...
>
> *Words beginning with* **hie** *are preceded by* **y**, *since* **hie** *is not pronounced "i":*
>
> **... coal and iron mines ...**
> ... minas de carbón y hierro ...

Andalusia [ˌændəˈluːzɪə] N Andalucía *f*

Andalusian [ˌændəˈluːzɪən] ADJ andaluz
N **1** (= *person*) andaluz(a) *m/f*
2 (*Ling*) andaluz *m*

andante [ænˈdæntɪ] ADV (*musical indication*) andante
N (= *piece of music*) andante *m*

Andean [ˈændɪən] ADJ andino
CPD ▸ **Andean high plateau** altiplanicie *f* andina, altiplano *m* (*LAm*) andino

Andes [ˈændiːz] NPL • **the ~** los Andes

andiron [ˈændaɪən] N morillo *m*

Andorra [ˌænˈdɔːrə] N Andorra *f*

Andorran [ˌænˈdɔːrən] ADJ andorrano
N andorrano/a *m/f*

Andrew [ˈændruː] N Andrés

androcentric [ˌændrəʊˈsentrɪk] ADJ androcéntrico

androcentricity [ˌændrəʊsenˈtrɪsɪtɪ] N androcentrismo *m*

androgen [ˈændrədʒən] N andrógeno *m*

androgenic [ˈændrəˈdʒenɪk] ADJ androgénico

androgynous [ænˈdrɒdʒɪnəs] ADJ andrógino

androgyny [ænˈdrɒdʒɪnɪ] N androginia *f*

android [ˈændrɔɪd] N androide *m*

Andromache [ænˈdrɒməkɪ] N Andrómaca

Andromeda [ænˈdrɒmɪdə] N Andrómeda

androsterone [ænˈdrɒstəˌrəʊn] N androsterona *f*

Andy [ˈændɪ] N *familiar form of* **Andrew**

anecdotal [ˌænɪkˈdəʊtəl] ADJ anecdótico

anecdote [ˈænɪkdəʊt] N anécdota *f*

anemia [əˈniːmɪə] N (*US*) = **anaemia**

anemic [əˈniːmɪk] ADJ (*US*) = **anaemic**

anemone [əˈnemənɪ] N (*Bot*) anémona *f*, anemone *f*; (= *sea anemone*) anémona *f*

aneroid [ˈænərɔɪd] ADJ aneroide
CPD ▸ **aneroid barometer** barómetro *m* aneroide

anesthesia [ˌænɪsˈθiːzɪə] N (*US*) = **anaesthesia**

anesthesiologist [ˌænɪsˌθiːzɪˈɒlədʒɪst] N (*US*) anestesista *mf*

anesthetic [ˌænɪsˈθetɪk] ADJ, N (*US*) = **anaesthetic**

anesthetist [æˈniːsθɪtɪst] N (*US*) = **anaesthetist**

anesthetize [æˈniːsθɪtaɪz] VT (*US*) = **anaesthetize**

aneurism, aneurysm [ˈænjərɪzəm] N aneurisma *m*

anew [əˈnjuː] ADV (*liter*) de nuevo, otra vez • **to begin ~** comenzar de nuevo, volver a empezar

angel [ˈeɪndʒəl] N **1** (*Rel*) ángel *m* • **Angel of Darkness** ángel *m* de las tinieblas • **the Angel of Death** el ángel exterminador • IDIOMS: • **I'm on the side of the ~s** yo estoy de parte de los ángeles • **speak** *or* **talk of ~s!** hablando del ruin de Roma (por la puerta asoma) • **to rush in where ~s fear to tread** meterse en la boca del lobo; ▹ **fool, guardian**
2* (= *person*) • **she's an ~** es un ángel • **be an ~ and give me a cigarette** ¿me das un pitillo, amor?
3 (*esp Theat**) caballo *m* blanco*, promotor(a) *m/f*
CPD ▸ **angel dust*** (*Drugs*) polvo *m* de ángel ▸ **angel food cake** (*US*) *bizcocho muy esponjoso hecho sin las yemas de huevo* ▸ **angel investor** inversor(a) *m/f* providencial ▸ **angels on horseback** (*Brit*) (*Culin*) *rollitos de beicon rellenos de ostras y servidos sobre pan tostado*

Angeleno [ˌændʒəˈliːnəʊ] N habitante *mf* de Los Angeles

angelfish [ˈeɪndʒəlfɪʃ] N (PL: **angelfish**) angelote *m*, pez *m* ángel

angelic [ænˈdʒelɪk] ADJ angélico

angelica [ænˈdʒelɪkə] N angélica *f*

angelical [ænˈdʒelɪkəl] ADJ = **angelic**

angelically [ænˈdʒelɪklɪ] ADV angelicalmente, como los ángeles

angelus [ˈændʒɪləs] N ángelus *m*

anger [ˈæŋgəʳ] N ira *f* • **red with ~** rojo de ira • **to move** *or* **rouse sb to ~** provocar la ira de algn • **to speak in ~** hablar indignado • **words spoken in ~** palabras pronunciadas en un momento de enfado (*Sp*), palabras pronunciadas en un momento de enojo (*LAm*)
VT enfadar (*Sp*), enojar (*LAm*) • **to be easily ~ed** enfadarse fácilmente (*Sp*), enojarse fácilmente (*LAm*)
CPD ▸ **anger management** control *m* de la ira, manejo *m* de la ira

angina [ænˈdʒaɪnə] N (*Med*) (*also* **angina pectoris**) angina *f* (de pecho)

angiogram [ˈændʒɪəʊgræm] N angiograma *m*

angioplasty [ˈændʒɪəˌplæstɪ] N (*Med*) angioplastia *f*

angiosperm [ˈændʒɪəˌspɜːm] N angiosperma *f*

Angle [ˈæŋgl] N anglo/a *m/f*

angle¹ [ˈæŋgl] N **1** (*Math, Geom etc*) ángulo *m* • **at an ~ of 80 degrees** • **at an 80 degree ~** con un ángulo de 80 grados • **an iron bar stuck out at an ~** una barra de hierro sobresalía formando un ángulo • **he wore his hat at an ~** llevaba el sombrero ladeado, llevaba el sombrero hacía un lado • **hold the knife at an ~** coge el cuchillo inclinado • **cut the bread at an ~** corte el pan en diagonal • **to be at an ~ to sth** formar ángulo con algo • **to look at a building from a different ~** contemplar un edificio desde otro ángulo • **photographed from a low ~** fotografiado desde un ángulo inferior • **a high-/low-angle shot** (*Phot*) una toma desde un ángulo superior/inferior • **~ of approach** (*Aer*) ángulo *m* de aterrizaje • **~ of climb** (*Aer*) ángulo *m* de subida; ▹ **right**
2 (*fig*) **a** (= *point of view*) punto *m* de vista • **what's your ~ on this?** ¿cuál es tu punto de vista al respecto?, ¿tú qué opinas de esto? • **from the parents' ~** desde el punto de vista *or* la perspectiva de los padres
b (= *aspect*) componente *m* • **the director decided to play down the love ~** el director decidió restar importancia al componente amoroso
c (= *focus*) perspectiva *f*, ángulo *m* • **to look at sth from a different ~** enfocar algo desde otra perspectiva *or* desde otro ángulo • **to look at a problem from all ~s** estudiar un problema desde todas las perspectivas, estudiar un problema desde todos los ángulos *or* puntos de vista • **this article gives a new ~ on the question** este artículo da un nuevo enfoque a la cuestión
VT **1** [+ *object*] orientar; (*Sport*) [+ *shot*] sesgar, ladear • **he ~d the lamp towards his**

a

desk orientó la luz de la lámpara hacia la mesa • **an ~d header** un cabezazo sesgado *or* ladeado *or* de lado
2 (*fig*) **a** (= *aim*) dirigir • **this article is ~d towards non-specialists** este artículo va dirigido al lector no especializado
b (= *bias*) sesgar • **the report was ~d so as to present them in a bad light** el informe estaba sesgado de forma que daba una mala impresión de ellos
VI (= *turn*) desviarse, torcerse • **the path ~d sharply to the left** el camino se desviaba *or* torcía de pronto hacia la izquierda
CPD ▸ **angle bracket** (= *support*) escuadra *f*; (*Typ*) corchete *m* agudo ▸ **angle grinder** esmeril *m* angular ▸ **angle iron** (*Constr*) hierro *m* angular

angle² [ˈæŋgl] VI **1** (= *fish*) pescar (con caña) • **to ~ for trout** pescar truchas
2 (*fig*) • **to ~ for sth** (*gen*) andar buscando algo; (*for votes, for job*) andar a la caza de algo • **he's just angling for sympathy** solo anda buscando compasión

Anglepoise® [ˈæŋglpɔɪz] N (*Brit*) (*also* **Anglepoise lamp**) lámpara *f* de estudio

angler [ˈæŋgləʳ] N pescador(a) *m/f* (de caña)

anglerfish [ˈæŋgləfɪʃ] N rape *m*

Angles [ˈæŋglz] NPL anglos *mpl*

Anglican [ˈæŋglɪkən] ADJ anglicano
N anglicano/a *m/f*

Anglicanism [ˈæŋglɪkənɪzəm] N anglicanismo *m*

anglicism [ˈæŋglɪsɪzəm] N anglicismo *m*, inglesismo *m*

anglicist [ˈæŋglɪsɪst] N anglicista *mf*

anglicize [ˈæŋglɪsaɪz] VT dar forma inglesa a, anglicanizar

anglicized [ˈæŋglɪsaɪzd] ADJ [*name, version, person*] anglicanizado • **to become ~** anglicanizarse

angling [ˈæŋglɪŋ] N pesca *f* con caña

Anglo* [ˈæŋgləʊ] N blanco/a *m/f*, americano/a *m/f* (de origen no hispano)

Anglo- [ˈæŋgləʊ] PREFIX anglo... • **Anglo-Spanish** angloespañol • **an Anglo-French project** un proyecto anglofrancés

Anglo-American [ˈæŋgləʊəˈmerɪkən] ADJ angloamericano
N angloamericano/a *m/f*

Anglo-Asian [ˈæŋgləʊˈeɪʃn] ADJ angloasiático
N angloasiático/a *m/f*

Anglo-Catholic [ˈæŋgləʊˈkæθlɪk] ADJ anglocatólico
N anglocatólico/a *m/f*

Anglo-Catholicism [ˈæŋgləʊkəˈθɒlɪsɪzəm] N anglocatolicismo *m*

Anglo-French [ˌæŋgləʊˈfrentʃ] ADJ anglofrancés

Anglo-Indian [ˈæŋgləʊˈɪndɪən] ADJ angloindio
N angloindio/a *m/f*

Anglo-Irish [ˈæŋgləʊˈaɪərɪʃ] ADJ angloirlandés
N angloirlandés/esa *m/f*

Anglo-Norman [ˌæŋgləʊˈnɔːmən] ADJ anglonormando
N **1** (= *person*) anglonormando/a *m/f*
2 (*Ling*) anglonormando *m*

anglophile [ˈæŋgləʊfaɪl] N anglófilo/a *m/f*

anglophobe [ˈæŋgləʊfəʊb] N anglófobo/a *m/f*

anglophobia [ˌæŋgləʊˈfəʊbjə] N anglofobia *f*

anglophone [ˈæŋgləʊfəʊn] ADJ anglófono
N anglófono/a *m/f*

Anglo-Saxon [ˈæŋgləʊˈsæksən] ADJ anglosajón
N **1** (= *person*) anglosajón/ona *m/f*
2 (*Ling*) anglosajón *m*

> **ANGLO-SAXON**
>
> La lengua anglosajona, **Anglo-Saxon**, también llamada **Old English**, se extendió en Inglaterra tras las invasiones de pueblos germánicos en el siglo V y continuó usándose hasta la conquista normanda de la isla. Hoy en día sigue siendo una parte importante del idioma inglés. Como ejemplos de palabras de origen anglosajón que aún se usan tenemos **man**, **child**, **eat**, **love** o **harvest**.
>
> El término se usa también para describir el mundo angloparlante, sobre todo si tiene su origen o está muy influido por costumbres inglesas, si bien hay personas de origen escocés, irlandés, galés o minorías étnicas que prefieren no usarlo.

Angola [æŋˈgəʊlə] N Angola *f*

Angolan [æŋˈgəʊlən] ADJ angoleño
N angoleño/a *m/f*

angora [æŋˈgɔːrə] N angora *f* • **an ~ sweater** un jersey *or* suéter de angora

angostura [ˌæŋgəˈstjʊərə] N angostura *f*
CPD ▸ **angostura bitters®** bíter *msing* de angostura

Angoulême [ɑːŋgʊˈlem] N Angulema *f*

angrily [ˈæŋgrɪlɪ] ADV [*react, speak*] con ira • **"I tried!" he said ~** —¡lo intenté! —dijo enfadado *or* (*LAm*) enojado • **he protested ~** protestó airadamente

angry [ˈæŋgrɪ] ADJ (COMPAR: **angrier**, SUPERL: **angriest**) **1** (= *cross*) [*person*] enfadado (*Sp*), enojado (*LAm*); [*voice*] de enfado (*Sp*), de enojo (*LAm*); [*letter, reply*] airado • **to be ~** estar enfadado (**with** con) • **he was very ~** estaba muy enfadado • **you won't be ~, will you?** no te vas a enfadar *or* (*LAm*) enojar ¿verdad? • **to be ~ about** *or* **at sth** estar enfadado por algo • **he was very ~ about** *or* **at being dismissed** estaba furioso porque lo habían despedido • **to get ~** enfadarse (*Sp*), enojarse (*LAm*) • **she gave me an ~ look** me miró enfadada • **your father looks very ~** tu padre parece estar muy enfadado • **this sort of thing makes me ~** estas cosas me sacan de quicio* • **don't make me ~!** ¡no me hagas enfadar! • **there were ~ scenes when it was announced that ...** hubo escenas airadas cuando se anunció que ... • **~ young man** (*Brit*) joven *m* airado
2 (*liter*) [*sky*] tormentoso, borrascoso; [*sea*] bravo
3 (*Med*) [*wound, rash*] inflamado • **the blow left an ~ mark on his forehead** el golpe dejó una marca de un rojo encendido en su frente

angst [æŋst] N angustia *f*

angst-ridden [ˈæŋst,rɪdn] ADJ angustiado

angstrom [ˈæŋstrʌm] N angstrom *m*

anguish [ˈæŋgwɪʃ] N (*physical*) tormentos *mpl*; (*mental*) angustia *f* • **to be in ~** (*physically*) padecer tormentos, sufrir lo indecible; (*mentally*) estar angustiado

anguished [ˈæŋgwɪʃt] ADJ (*physically*) atormentado de dolor; (*mentally*) angustiado

angular [ˈæŋgjʊləʳ] ADJ [*shape, lines*] angular; [*face, features*] anguloso

angularity [ˌæŋgjʊˈlærətɪ] N [*of shape, lines*] angularidad *f*; [*of face, features*] angulosidad *f*

aniline [ˈænɪliːn] N anilina *f*
CPD ▸ **aniline dye** colorante *m* de anilina

anima [ˈænɪmə] N (*Psych*) ánima *f*, alma *f*

animal [ˈænɪməl] N **1** (= *not plant*) animal *m* • **man is a political ~** el hombre es un animal político
2 (*fig*) (= *thing*) cosa *f* • **there's no such ~** no existe tal cosa • **they are two different ~s** son cosas bien distintas
3* (*pej*) (= *person*) animal* *mf*, bestia* *mf* • **you ~!** ¡animal!*, ¡bestia!*
ADJ animal
CPD ▸ **animal cracker** (*US*) galletita *f* de animales ▸ **animal experiment** experimento *m* con animales ▸ **animal fats** grasas *fpl* de animal ▸ **animal husbandry** cría *f* de animales ▸ **animal instinct** instinto *m* animal ▸ **the animal kingdom** el reino animal ▸ **Animal Liberation Front** (*Brit*) Frente *m* de Liberación Animal ▸ **animal liberationist** miembro *mf* del Frente de Liberación de los Animales ▸ **animal lover** amante *mf* de los animales ▸ **animal magnetism** [*of person*] atracción *f* animal, magnetismo *m* salvaje ▸ **animal rights** derechos *mpl* de los animales ▸ **animal rights campaigner** activista *mf* por los derechos de los animales ▸ **animal rights movement** movimiento *m* por los derechos de los animales ▸ **animal sanctuary** centro *m* de acogida para animales ▸ **animal spirits** vitalidad *f* ▸ **animal testing** pruebas *fpl* de laboratorio con animales ▸ **animal welfare** protección *f* de los animales

animalcule [ˌænɪˈmælkjuːl] N (*frm*) animálculo *m*

animality [ˌænɪˈmælətɪ] N animalidad *f*

animate ADJ [ˈænɪmɪt] vivo
VT [ˈænɪmeɪt] animar, estimular

animated [ˈænɪmeɪtɪd] ADJ **1** (= *lively*) [*person, discussion*] animado • **to become ~** animarse
2 (*Cine*) • **~ cartoon** dibujos *mpl* animados

animatedly [ˈænɪmeɪtɪdlɪ] ADV [*talk, behave*] animadamente

animation [ˌænɪˈmeɪʃən] N **1** (= *liveliness*) vivacidad *f*, animación *f*
2 (*Cine*) (= *process*) animación *f*; (= *film*) película *f* de animación, dibujos *mpl* animados

animator [ˈænɪmeɪtəʳ] N (*Cine*) animador(a) *m/f*

animatronics [ˌænɪməˈtrɒnɪks] N (*Cine*) animación *f* por ordenador

anime [ˈænɪmeɪ] N anime *m*

animism [ˈænɪmɪzəm] N animismo *m*

animist [ˈænɪmɪst] ADJ animista
N animista *mf*

animosity [ˌænɪˈmɒsɪtɪ] N animosidad *f*, rencor *m*

animus [ˈænɪməs] N **1** (= *animosity*) odio *m*
2 (*Psych*) animus *m*, alma *f*

anise [ˈænɪs] N anís *m*

aniseed [ˈænɪsiːd] N (= *flavour*) anís *m*; (= *seed*) grano *m* de anís
CPD ▸ **aniseed ball** bolita *f* de anís

anisette [ˌænɪˈzet] N anisete *m*, anís *m*

Anjou [ɑːŋˈʒuː] N Anjeo *m*

Ankara [ˈæŋkərə] N Ankara *f*

ankle [ˈæŋkl] N tobillo *m* • **I've twisted my ~** me he torcido el tobillo
CPD ▸ **ankle boot** botín *m* ▸ **ankle bracelet** brazalete *m* para el tobillo ▸ **ankle joint** articulación *f* del tobillo ▸ **ankle sock** (*Brit*) calcetín *m* tobillero ▸ **ankle strap** tirita *f* tobillera

anklebone [ˈæŋklbəʊn] N hueso *m* del tobillo

ankle-deep [ˈæŋklˈdiːp] ADV • **to be ankle-deep in water** estar metido hasta los tobillos en el agua • **the water is only ankle-deep** el agua llega a los tobillos nada más

anklet [ˈæŋklɪt] N brazalete *m* para el tobillo, ajorca *f* para el pie; (*US*) calcetín *m* corto

ankylosis [ˌæŋkɪˈləʊsɪs] N anquilosis *f*

Ann [æn] N Ana • **Ann Boleyn** Ana Bolena

ann ABBR **1** = **annual**
2 (*Econ*) = **annuity**

annalist ['ænəlɪst] (N) analista *mf*, cronista *mf*
annals ['ænəlz] (NPL) anales *mpl* • **in all the ~ of crime** en toda la historia del crimen • **never in the ~ of human endeavour** nunca en la historia de los esfuerzos humanos
annatto [ə'nætəʊ] (N) achiote *m*, bija *f*
Anne [æn] (N) Ana
anneal [ə'ni:l] (VT) templar
annex (VT) [ə'neks] **1** [+ *territory*] anexar, anexionar (**to a**)
2 [+ *document*] adjuntar, añadir (**to a**)
(N) ['æneks] (*US*) = **annexe**
annexation [ˌænek'seɪʃən] (N) anexión *f*
annexe ['æneks] (N) **1** (= *building*) edificio *m* anexo
2 (= *document*) anexo *m*
annihilate [ə'naɪəleɪt] (VT) aniquilar
annihilation [əˌnaɪə'leɪʃən] (N) aniquilación *f*, aniquilamiento *m*
anniversary [ˌænɪ'vɜ:sərɪ] (N) aniversario *m* • **wedding ~** aniversario *m* de bodas • **golden/silver wedding ~** bodas *fpl* de oro/plata • **the Góngora ~ dinner** el banquete para festejar el aniversario de Góngora
Anno Domini ['ænəʊ'dɒmɪnaɪ] (N) (*frm*) • **~ 43** el año 43 después de Jesucristo • **the third century ~** el siglo tercero de Cristo
annotate ['ænəʊteɪt] (VT) anotar, comentar
annotation [ˌænəʊ'teɪʃən] (N) (= *act*) anotación *f*; (= *instance*) anotación *f*, apunte *m*
announce [ə'naʊns] (VT) **1** (*gen*) anunciar • **we regret to ~ the death of …** lamentamos tener que anunciar la muerte de …
2 (= *inform*) comunicar, hacer saber • **it is ~d from London that …** se comunica desde Londres que …
3 (= *declare*) declarar • **he ~d that he wasn't going** declaró que no iba
announcement [ə'naʊnsmənt] (N) (*gen*) anuncio *m*; (= *declaration*) declaración *f* • **~ of birth** (aviso *m*) natalicio *m* • **~ of death** (nota *f*) necrológica *f* • **I'd like to make an ~** tengo algo que anunciar
announcer [ə'naʊnsəʳ] (N) **1** (*TV, Rad*) locutor(a) *m/f*
2 (*at airport etc*) el *or* la que hace anuncios
annoy [ə'nɔɪ] (VT) molestar, fastidiar • **he's just trying to ~ you** lo que quiere es molestarte *or* fastidiarte • **is this man ~ing you, madam?** ¿le está molestando este hombre, señora? • **don't be ~ed if I can't come** no te enfades si no puedo venir • **to be ~ed about** *or* **at sth** estar enfadado *or* molesto por algo • **to be ~ed with sb** estar enfadado *or* molesto con algn • **to get ~ed** enfadarse • **it's no good getting ~ed with me** de nada sirve enfadarte conmigo
annoyance [ə'nɔɪəns] (N) **1** (= *displeasure*) irritación *f*; (= *anger*) enfado *m*, enojo *m* (*LAm*) • **to my ~ I find that …** con gran disgusto mío descubro que …
2 (= *annoying thing*) molestia *f*
annoying [ə'nɔɪɪŋ] (ADJ) [*habit, noise*] molesto, irritante; [*person*] irritante, pesado • **the ~ thing about it is that …** lo que más me fastidia del asunto es que … • **how ~!** ¡qué fastidio! • **it's ~ to have to wait** es un fastidio tener que esperar • **he's such an ~ person!** ¡qué hombre más irritante *or* pesado! • **I find her very ~** me resulta muy pesada • **I find it very ~** me molesta mucho
annoyingly [ə'nɔɪɪŋlɪ] (ADV) [*behave, act*] de modo irritante • **and then, ~ enough, she wasn't at home** y encima no estaba en casa, lo que me fastidió mucho • **~, I shan't be able to be there** me da mucha rabia, pero no voy a poder ir • **the radio was ~ loud** la radio estaba tan alta que molestaba • **she was ~ vague** era tan distraída que sacaba de quicio* • **he has an ~ loud voice** tiene un vozarrón de lo más irritante
annual ['ænjʊəl] (ADJ) anual
(N) **1** (= *publication*) anuario *m*; (= *children's comic book*) *cómic para niños que se publica en forma de libro normalmente por Navidad*
2 (*Bot*) planta *f* anual
(CPD) ▸ **annual general meeting** (*Brit*) junta *f* general anual ▸ **annual income** ingresos *mpl* anuales ▸ **annual report** informe *m* anual
annually ['ænjʊəlɪ] (ADV) anualmente, cada año • **£500 ~** 500 libras al año
annuity [ə'nju:ɪtɪ] (N) anualidad *f*
(CPD) ▸ **annuity payment** anualidad *f*
annul [ə'nʌl] (VT) [+ *judgment, contract, marriage*] anular; [+ *law*] revocar, abrogar
annulment [ə'nʌlmənt] (N) [*of marriage*] anulación *f*; [*of law*] revocación *f*, abrogación *f*
annum ['ænəm] (N) ▹ **per**
Annunciation [əˌnʌnsɪ'eɪʃən] (N) Anunciación *f*
anode ['ænəʊd] (N) ánodo *m*
anodize ['ænədaɪz] (VT) anodizar
anodyne ['ænəʊdaɪn] (ADJ) (*Med*) analgésico; (*fig*) anodino
(N) (*Med*) analgésico *m*; (*fig*) remedio *m*
anoint [ə'nɔɪnt] (VT) **1** (*with oil etc*) ungir (**with de**)
2 (*fig*) (= *nominate*) designar, nombrar
anointing [ə'nɔɪntɪŋ] (N) unción *f* • **~ of the sick** (*Rel*) unción *f* de los enfermos
anointment [ə'nɔɪntmənt] (N) ungimiento *m*
anomalous [ə'nɒmələs] (ADJ) anómalo
anomaly [ə'nɒməlɪ] (N) anomalía *f*
anomie, anomy ['ænəʊmɪ] (N) anomia *f*
anon¹ [ə'nɒn] (ADV) **1** luego, dentro de poco • **I'll see you ~** nos veremos luego
2†† • **ever and ~** de vez en cuando
anon² [ə'nɒn] (ABBR) = **anonymous**
anonymity [ˌænə'nɪmɪtɪ] (N) anonimato *m* • **to preserve one's ~** permanecer en el anonimato • **the ~ of rented rooms** lo anónimo de las habitaciones de alquiler
anonymous [ə'nɒnɪməs] (ADJ) **1** (= *unnamed*) [*caller, writer, phone call, poem*] anónimo; [*ballot*] secreto • **he received an ~ letter** recibió un anónimo • **Alcoholics Anonymous** Alcohólicos *mpl* Anónimos • **he wishes to remain ~** quiere permanecer en el anonimato
2 (= *unmemorable*) [*place, room*] anónimo, sin ninguna seña de identidad • **~-looking people** gente de apariencia anónima
anonymously [ə'nɒnɪməslɪ] (ADV) [*send, give, speak*] anónimamente, de manera anónima; [*live*] en el anonimato; [*publish*] de forma anónima, sin el nombre del autor • **the book came out ~** el libro salió de forma anónima *or* sin el nombre del autor
anorak ['ænəræk] (N) **1** (*esp Brit*) (= *coat*) anorak *m*
2 (*Brit**) (*pej*) (= *person*) pelmazo/a *m/f*, petardo/a *m/f*
anorectic [ˌænə'rektɪk] = **anorexic**
anorexia [ˌænə'reksɪə] (N) (*Med*) anorexia *f*
(CPD) ▸ **anorexia nervosa** anorexia *f* nerviosa
anorexic [ˌænə'reksɪk] (ADJ) anoréxico
(N) anoréxico/a *m/f*
another [ə'nʌðəʳ] (ADJ) **1** (= *additional*) otro • **would you like ~ beer?** ¿quieres otra cerveza? • **have ~ one** toma *or* coge otro • **we need ~ two men** necesitamos dos hombres más, necesitamos otros dos hombres • **not ~ minute!** ¡ni un minuto más! • **there are ~ two months to go** faltan otros dos meses *or* dos meses más • **~ two kilometres** dos kilómetros más • **without ~ word** sin decir ni una palabra más • **there's not ~ painting like it** no existe otro cuadro como este • **I don't think he'll be ~ Mozart** no creo que llegue a ser otro Mozart • **I've discovered yet ~ problem** he descubierto otro problema más • **take ~ five** coge cinco más *or* otros cinco, toma cinco más *or* otros cinco (*LAm*)
2 (= *different*) otro • **do it ~ time** hazlo en otra ocasión • **that's quite ~ matter** eso es otra cosa totalmente distinta, eso es otro cantar
(PRON) otro/a *m/f* • **help yourself to ~** sírvete otro • **in one form or ~** de una forma u otra • **what with one thing and ~** entre una cosa u otra • **if not this time then ~** si no esta vez, pues otra; ▸ **one**
A.N. Other [ˌeɪˌen'ʌðəʳ] (N) fulano* *m*, un tipo cualquiera* • **"A.N. Other"** (*on list*) "a concretar"
anoxia [ə'nɒksɪə] (N) anoxia *f*
anoxic [ə'nɒksɪk] (ADJ) anóxico
Ansaphone® ['ɑ:nsəfəʊn] (N) = **answerphone**
ANSI (N ABBR) (*US*) = **American National Standards Institute**
answer ['ɑ:nsəʳ] (N) **1** (= *reply*) respuesta *f*, contestación *f* • **he has an ~ for everything** tiene respuesta *or* contestación para todo • **I never got an ~ to my question** nunca me respondieron *or* contestaron (a) la pregunta • **he smiled in ~** como respuesta esbozó una sonrisa • **in ~ to your letter** en respuesta a su carta • **in ~ to your question** en *or* como respuesta a su pregunta, para responder *or* contestar (a) su pregunta • **there's no ~** (*Telec*) no contestan • **I knocked but there was no ~** llamé a la puerta pero no hubo respuesta *or* no abrieron • **there's no ~ to that** no existe una respuesta para eso • **I made no ~** no respondí • **her only ~ was to smile** respondió simplemente con una sonrisa, como respuesta se limitó a sonreír • **it was the ~ to my prayers** fue la solución a todos mis problemas • IDIOMS: • **to know all the ~s** tener respuesta para todo, saberlo todo • **he's not exactly the ~ to a maiden's prayer** no es precisamente un príncipe azul
2 (= *solution*) solución *f* • **we have the ~ to your problem** tenemos la solución a su problema • **prison is not the ~** la cárcel no es solución • **there is no easy ~** no hay una solución fácil
3 (= *equivalent*) • **cachaça is Brazil's ~ to tequila** la cachaça es el tequila brasileño • **Belgium's ~ to Sylvester Stallone** el Sylvester Stallone belga
4 (*in exam, quiz*) **a** (= *correct response*) (*to question*) respuesta *f*; (*to problem*) solución *f*
b (= *individual response*) respuesta *f* • **write your ~s on the sheets provided** escriba las respuestas en las hojas que se le han proporcionado
5 (*Jur*) contestación *f* a la demanda, réplica *f*
(VT) **1** (= *reply to*) [+ *person*] contestar a, responder a; [+ *question*] contestar (a), responder (a); [+ *letter*] contestar (a); [+ *criticism*] responder a • **~ me** contéstame, respóndeme • **to ~ your question, I did see him** contestando *or* respondiendo a tu pregunta, (te diré que) sí lo vi • **she never ~ed my letters** nunca contestaba (a) mis cartas • **he ~ed not a word** no dijo (ni una) palabra • **to ~ that …** responder que …, contestar que … • **"not yet," he ~ed** —aún no —respondió • **to ~ a call for help** acudir a una llamada de socorro • **to ~ the door** (ir a) abrir la puerta, atender la puerta (*LAm*) • **our prayers have been ~ed** nuestras súplicas

han sido escuchadas • **to ~ the telephone** contestar el teléfono
2 (= *fulfil*) [+ *needs*] satisfacer; [+ *description*] responder a • **two men ~ing the description of the suspects** dos hombres que respondían a la descripción de los sospechosos • **it ~s the purpose** sirve para su propósito, cumple su cometido
3 (*Jur*) • **to ~ a charge** responder a una acusación, responder a un cargo
4 (*Naut*) • **to ~ the helm** obedecer al timón
(VI) contestar, responder • **she didn't ~ immediately** tardó en contestar *or* responder • **if the phone rings, let someone else ~** si suena el teléfono, deja que conteste otro • **the doorbell rang but I didn't ~** sonó el timbre pero no abrí
(CPD) ▸ **answer machine** contestador *m* automático ▸ **answer paper** hoja *f* de respuestas
▸ **answer back** (VI + ADV) 1 (= *be cheeky*) (*on one occasion*) replicar, contestar; (*habitually*) ser respondón/ona • **don't ~ back!** ¡no repliques!
2 (= *defend o.s.*) defenderse (*contra las críticas*)
▸ **answer for** (VI + PREP) 1 (= *take responsibility for*) [+ *actions*] responder de • **I'll not ~ for the consequences** no respondo de las consecuencias, no me responsabilizo de las consecuencias • **to ~ for the truth of sth** responder de la veracidad de algo • **to ~ for sb's safety** responder de la seguridad de algn • **he's got a lot to ~ for** tiene la culpa de muchas cosas • **he must be made to ~ for his crimes** le tienen que hacer pagar por sus crímenes
2 (= *reply for*) responder por • **I can't ~ for the others, but ...** no puedo responder por los demás, pero ... • **can't she ~ for herself?** ¿no sabe responder ella sola?
3 (= *serve as*) servir de
▸ **answer to** (VI + PREP) 1 (= *be accountable to*) • **to ~ to sb** responder ante algn • **I ~ to nobody** no tengo que darle cuentas a nadie
2 (= *respond to*) • **the steering ~s to the slightest touch** la dirección responde *or* es sensible al más mínimo roce
3 (= *be called*) • **the dog ~s to the name of Kim** el perro atiende por Kim
4 (= *fit*) [+ *description*] responder a • **he ~s to the description circulated by police** responde a la descripción que ha hecho circular la policía
answerable ['ɑːnsərəbl] (ADJ) 1 (= *accountable*) responsable • **to be ~ to sb (for sth)** ser responsable ante algn (de algo) • **he's not ~ to anyone** no tiene que dar cuentas a nadie
2 [*question*] que tiene respuesta • **the question is not readily ~** la pregunta no tiene respuesta fácil
answering ['ɑːnsərɪŋ] (CPD) ▸ **answering machine** contestador *m* (automático)
▸ **answering service** (*live*) servicio *m* telefónico de contestación; (*with answerphone*) servicio *m* de contestador automático
answerphone ['ɑːnsəˌfəʊn] (N) contestador *m* (automático)
ant [ænt] (N) hormiga *f* • IDIOM: • **to have ants in one's pants*** tener avispas en el culo*
ANTA (N ABBR) (*US*) = **American National Theater and Academy**
antacid ['ænt'æsɪd] (ADJ) antiácido
(N) antiácido *m*
antagonism [æn'tægənɪzəm] (N) (*towards sb*) hostilidad *f*; (*between people*) rivalidad *f*, antagonismo *m*
antagonist [æn'tægənɪst] (N) antagonista *mf*, adversario/a *m/f*
antagonistic [ænˌtægə'nɪstɪk] (ADJ)
1 (= *hostile*) [*person, attitude*] hostil, antagonista
2 (= *opposed*) [*ideas, views*] antagónico, opuesto • **I am not in the least ~ to the idea** yo no me opongo en lo más mínimo a la idea
antagonize [æn'tægənaɪz] (VT) • **I don't want to ~ him** no quiero contrariarle • **he managed to ~ everybody** logró ponerse a malas con todos, logró suscitar el antagonismo de todos
Antarctic [ænt'ɑːktɪk] (ADJ) antártico
(N) • **the ~** el Antártico
(CPD) ▸ **the Antarctic Circle** el círculo Polar Antártico ▸ **the Antarctic Ocean** el Océano Antártico
Antarctica [ænt'ɑːktɪkə] (N) Antártida *f*
ante ['æntɪ] (*esp US*) (N) (*Cards*) apuesta *f*
• IDIOM: • **to raise** *or* **up the ~*** (*Cards*) subir la apuesta; (*fig*) elevar las demandas
(VT) apostar
(VI) poner su apuesta
▸ **ante up*** (VI + ADV) (*US*) pagar, apoquinar*
ante... ['æntɪ] (PREFIX) ante...
anteater ['æntˌiːtəʳ] (N) (*Zool*) oso *m* hormiguero
antebellum ['æntɪ'beləm] (ADJ) prebélico (*particularmente referido a la guerra civil norteamericana*)
antecedent [ˌæntɪ'siːdənt] (N) antecedente *m*; **antecedents** (= *past history*) antecedentes *mpl*; (= *ancestors*) antepasados *mpl*
(ADJ) precedente, que precede (**to** a)
antechamber ['æntɪˌtʃeɪmbəʳ] (N) antecámara *f*, antesala *f*
antedate ['æntɪ'deɪt] (VT) 1 (= *precede*) preceder, ser anterior a • **text A ~s B by 50 years** el texto A es anterior a B en 50 años • **this building ~s the Norman conquest** este edificio data de antes de *or* es anterior a la conquista normanda
2 [+ *cheque*] antedatar
antediluvian ['æntɪdɪ'luːvɪən] (ADJ) (*Rel*) (*also fig*) antediluviano
antelope ['æntɪləʊp] (N) (PL: **antelope, antelopes**) antílope *m*
antenatal ['æntɪ'neɪtl] (ADJ) prenatal
• **~ exercises** ejercicios *mpl* para mujeres embarazadas
(N) = **antenatal examination**
(CPD) ▸ **antenatal care** asistencia *f* prenatal ▸ **antenatal clinic** clínica *f* prenatal ▸ **antenatal examination** reconocimiento *m* prenatal
antenna [æn'tenə] (N) (PL: **antennas** *or* **antennae** [æn'teniː]) 1 [*of insect, animal*] antena *f*
2 (*TV*) antena *f*
antepenult [ˌæntɪpɪ'nʌlt] (N) sílaba *f* antepenúltima
antepenultimate ['æntɪpɪ'nʌltɪmɪt] (ADJ) antepenúltimo
anterior [æn'tɪərɪəʳ] (ADJ) anterior (**to** a)
anteroom ['æntɪrʊm] (N) antesala *f*
ant-heap ['ænthiːp] (N) hormiguero *m*
anthem ['ænθəm] (N) himno *m*; (*Rel*) antífona *f*; ▸ **national**
anther ['ænθəʳ] (N) antera *f*
anthill ['ænthɪl] (N) hormiguero *m*
anthologist [æn'θɒlədʒɪst] (N) antologista *mf*
anthologize [æn'θɒlədʒaɪz] (VT) [+ *works*] hacer una antología de; [+ *poem, author*] incluir en una antología
anthology [æn'θɒlədʒɪ] (N) antología *f*
Anthony ['æntənɪ] (N) Antonio
anthracite ['ænθrəsaɪt] (N) antracita *f*
anthrax ['ænθræks] (N) ántrax *m*
anthropo... [ˌænθrəʊpɒ] (PREFIX) antropo...
anthropocentric [ˌænθrəʊpəʊ'sentrɪk] (ADJ) antropocéntrico
anthropoid ['ænθrəʊpɔɪd] (ADJ) antropoide
(N) antropoide *mf*
anthropological [ˌænθrəpə'lɒdʒɪkəl] (ADJ) antropológico
anthropologist [ˌænθrə'pɒlədʒɪst] (N) antropólogo/a *m/f*
anthropology [ˌænθrə'pɒlədʒɪ] (N) antropología *f*
anthropometry [ˌænθrə'pɒmɪtrɪ] (N) antropometría *f*
anthropomorphic [ˌænθrəpəʊ'mɔːfɪk] (ADJ) antropomórfico
anthropomorphism [ˌænθrəʊpə'mɔːfɪzəm] (N) antropomorfismo *m*
anthropomorphist [ˌænθrəpəʊ'mɔːfɪst] (ADJ) antropomorfista
(N) antropomorfista *mf*
anthropomorphous [ˌænθrəʊpə'mɔːfəs] (ADJ) antropomorfo
anthropophagi [ˌænθrəʊ'pɒfəgaɪ] (NPL) antropófagos *mpl*
anthropophagous [ˌænθrəʊ'pɒfəgəs] (ADJ) antropófago
anthropophagy [ˌænθrəʊ'pɒfədʒɪ] (N) antropofagia *f*
anthroposophical [ˌænθrəpə'sɒfɪkəl] (ADJ) antroposófico
anti ['æntɪ] (PREP) • **she is ~ the whole idea*** ella está completamente en contra de la idea
(ADJ) • **he's rather ~*** está más bien opuesto
anti... ['æntɪ] (PREFIX) anti...
anti-abortion [ˌæntɪə'bɔːʃən] (ADJ) • **anti-abortion campaign** campaña *f* en contra del aborto, campaña *f* antiabortista
anti-abortionist [ˌæntɪə'bɔːʃənɪst] (N) antiabortista *mf*
anti-aircraft [ˌæntɪ'ɛəkrɑːft] (ADJ) [*gun*] antiaéreo
(CPD) ▸ **anti-aircraft defence, anti-aircraft defense** (*US*) defensa *f* antiaérea
anti-allergenic [ˌæntɪælə'dʒenɪk] (ADJ) antialergénico
anti-apartheid [ˌæntɪə'pɑːteɪt] (ADJ) anti-apartheid
anti-authority [ˌæntɪɔː'θɒrɪtɪ] (ADJ) [*speeches, attitude*] antiautoritario, contestatario
anti-bacterial [ˌæntɪbæk'tɪərɪəl] (ADJ) bactericida
anti-ballistic [ˌæntɪbə'lɪstɪk] (ADJ) antibalístico • **anti-ballistic missile** misil *m* antibalístico
antibiotic [ˌæntɪbaɪ'ɒtɪk] (N) antibiótico *m*
(ADJ) antibiótico
antibody ['æntɪˌbɒdɪ] (N) anticuerpo *m*
antic ['æntɪk] (N) ▸ **antics**
anticancer, anti-cancer [ˌæntɪ'kænsəʳ] (CPD) [*treatment, therapy*] anticanceroso ▸ **anticancer drug** medicamento *m* anticanceroso
antichoice [ˌæntɪ'tʃɔɪs] (ADJ) antiabortista
Antichrist ['æntɪkraɪst] (N) Anticristo *m*
anticipate [æn'tɪsɪpeɪt] (VT) 1 (= *expect*) [+ *trouble, pleasure*] esperar, contar con • **this is worse than I ~d** esto es peor de lo que esperaba • **the police ~d trouble** la policía esperaba disturbios, la policía contaba con que hubiera disturbios • **I ~ seeing him tomorrow** espero *or* cuento con verlo mañana • **as ~d** según se esperaba, como esperábamos • **the ~d audience did not materialize** no apareció el público que se esperaba *or* con que se había contado • **an eagerly-anticipated event** un acontecimiento muy esperado • **to ~ that ...** prever que ..., calcular que ... • **do you ~ that this will be easy?** ¿crees que esto va a

resultar fácil? • **we ~ that he will come in spite of everything** contamos con que *or* esperamos que venga a pesar de todo
2 (= *foresee*) [+ *event*] prever; [+ *question, objection, wishes*] anticipar • **~d cost** (*Comm*) coste *m* previsto • **~d profit** beneficios *mpl* previstos
3 (= *forestall*) [+ *person*] anticiparse a, adelantarse a; [+ *event*] anticiparse a, prevenir • **you have ~d my wishes** usted se ha anticipado *or* adelantado a mis deseos • **you have ~d my orders** (*wrongly*) usted ha actuado sin esperar mis órdenes
VI (= *act too soon*) anticiparse

anticipation [æn,tɪsɪ'peɪʃən] N
1 (= *expectation*) expectativa *f* • **in ~** (= *ahead of time*) de antemano • **in ~ of a fine week** esperando una semana de buen tiempo • **I bought it in ~ of her visit** lo compré en previsión de su visita • **thanking you in ~** en espera de sus noticias
2 (= *excitement*) ilusión *f* • **we waited in great ~** esperábamos con gran ilusión
3 (= *foresight*) previsión *f*, anticipación *f* • **to act with ~** obrar con previsión
4 (= *foretaste*) anticipo *m*, adelanto *m*

anticipatory [æn'tɪsɪpeɪtərɪ] ADJ anticipador • **~ breach of contract** violación *f* anticipadora de contrato

anticlerical ['æntɪ'klerɪkl] ADJ anticlerical
N anticlerical *mf*

anticlericalism ['æntɪ'klerɪklɪzəm] N anticlericalismo *m*

anticlimactic ['æntɪklaɪ'mæktɪk] ADJ decepcionante

anticlimax ['æntɪ'klaɪmæks] N
1 (= *disappointment*) decepción *f* • **what an ~!** ¡qué decepción! • **the book ends in ~** la novela termina de modo decepcionante • **the game came as an ~** el partido no correspondió con lo que se esperaba
2 (*Rhetoric*) anticlímax *m inv*

anticlockwise ['æntɪ'klɒkwaɪz] (*Brit*) ADJ en sentido contrario al de las agujas del reloj
ADV en sentido contrario al de las agujas del reloj

anticoagulant ['æntɪkəʊ'ægjʊlənt] ADJ anticoagulante
N anticoagulante *m*

anticonvulsant [,æntɪkən'vʌlsənt] N antiepiléptico *m*
ADJ antiepiléptico

anticorrosive ['æntɪkə'rəʊzɪv] ADJ anticorrosivo

antics ['æntɪks] NPL [*of clown etc*] payasadas *fpl*; [*of child, animal etc*] gracias *fpl*; (= *pranks*) travesuras *fpl* • **he's up to his old ~ again** (*pej*) ya está haciendo de las suyas otra vez

anticyclone ['æntɪ'saɪkləʊn] N anticiclón *m*

anticyclonic [,æntɪsaɪ'klɒnɪk] ADJ anticiclónico, anticiclonal

anti-dandruff [,æntɪ'dændrəf] ADJ anticaspa (*inv*)

antidazzle [,æntɪ'dæzl] ADJ antideslumbrante

antidepressant [,æntɪdɪ'presnt] ADJ antidepresivo
N antidepresivo *m*

antidoping [,æntɪ'dəʊpɪŋ] ADJ antidóping (*inv*)

antidote ['æntɪdəʊt] N (*Med*) antídoto *m* (**for, to** contra); (*fig*) remedio *m* (**for, to** contra, para)

anti-dumping [,æntɪ'dʌmpɪŋ] ADJ [*duty, measures*] anti-dumping (*inv*)

anti-Establishment ['æntɪɪs'tæblɪʃmənt] ADJ en contra del sistema

anti-fascism [,æntɪ'fæʃɪzəm] N movimiento *m* antifascista

antifeminism [,æntɪ'femɪnɪzəm] N antifeminismo *m*

antifeminist [,æntɪ'femɪnɪst] ADJ antifeminista
N antifeminista *mf*

antifreeze ['æntɪ'fri:z] N anticongelante *m*

anti-friction [,æntɪ'frɪkʃən] ADJ antifriccional, contrafricción (*inv*)

antigen ['æntɪdʒən] N antígeno *m*

anti-glare [,æntɪ'gleəʳ] ADJ antideslumbrante

anti-globalization [,æntɪ,gləʊbəlaɪ'zeɪʃən] N antiglobalización *f* • **anti-globalization protesters** manifestantes *mfpl* antiglobalización

Antigone [æn'tɪgənɪ] N Antígona

Antigua [æn'ti:gə] N Antigua *f*

anti-hero ['æntɪ,hɪərəʊ] N (PL: **antiheroes**) antihéroe *m*

anti-heroine ['æntɪ,herəʊɪn] N antiheroína *f*

antihistamine [,æntɪ'hɪstəmɪn] ADJ antihistamínico
N antihistamínico *m*

anti-inflammatory [,æntɪɪn'flæmətərɪ] ADJ antiinflamatorio
N antiinflamatorio *m*

anti-inflationary [,æntɪɪn'fleɪʃnərɪ] ADJ antiinflacionista

anti-knock ['æntɪ'nɒk] ADJ antidetonante

Antilles [æn'tɪli:z] NPL Antillas *fpl*

anti-lock ['æntɪ'lɒk] ADJ [*device, brakes*] antibloque (*inv*)

antilogarithm [,æntɪ'lɒgərɪðəm] N antilogaritmo *m*

antimacassar ['æntɪmə'kæsəʳ] N antimacasar *m*

antimagnetic [,æntɪmæg'netɪk] ADJ antimagnético

antimalarial [,æntɪmə'leərɪəl] ADJ antipalúdico

anti-marketeer [,æntɪ,mɑ:kə'tɪəʳ] N (*Brit*) (*Pol*) persona *f* contraria al Mercado Común

antimatter ['æntɪ,mætəʳ] N antimateria *f*

antimissile [,æntɪ'mɪsaɪl] ADJ antimisil

antimony ['æntɪmənɪ] N antimonio *m*

anti-motion sickness [,æntɪ'məʊʃən,sɪknɪs] ADJ [*pill*] contra el mareo

antinomy [æn'tɪnəmɪ] N antinomia *f*

antinuclear [,æntɪ'nju:klɪəʳ] ADJ antinuclear

antinuke* [,æntɪ'nju:k] ADJ antinuclear

Antioch ['æntɪɒk] N Antioquía *f*

antioxidant [,æntɪ'ɒ:ksɪdənt] N antioxidante *m*

antiparasitic [,æntɪ,pærə'sɪtɪk] ADJ antiparasitario

antipasto [,æntɪ'pæstəʊ] N antipasto *m*

antipathetic [,æntɪpə'θetɪk] ADJ hostil (**to a**)

antipathy [æn'tɪpəθɪ] N (*between people*) antipatía *f* (**between** entre, **towards, to** hacia); (*to thing*) aversión *f* (**towards, to** hacia, por)

antipersonnel [,æntɪpɜ:sə'nel] ADJ (*Mil*) destinado a causar bajas

antiperspirant [,æntɪ'pɜ:spərənt] ADJ antitranspirante
N antitranspirante *m*

antiphon ['æntɪfən] N antífona *f*

antiphony [æn'tɪfənɪ] N canto *m* antifonal

Antipodean, antipodean [æn,tɪpə'di:ən] ADJ de las antípodas; (*Brit*) (*hum*) (= *Australian*) australiano
N habitante *mf* de las antípodas; (*Brit*) (*hum*) (= *Australian*) australiano/a *m/f*

antipodes [æn'tɪpədi:z] NPL antípodas *fpl* • **the Antipodes** (*Brit*) (*esp hum*) Australia *f* (y Nueva Zelanda *f*)

antipope ['æntɪpəʊp] N antipapa *m*

antiprotectionist [,æntɪprə'tekʃənɪst] ADJ antiproteccionista

antiquarian [,æntɪ'kweərɪən] ADJ anticuario
N (= *collector*) coleccionista *mf* de antigüedades; (= *dealer*) anticuario/a *m/f*
CPD ▸ **antiquarian bookseller** librero/a *m/f* de viejo ▸ **antiquarian bookshop** librería *f* de viejo ▸ **antiquarian collection** colección *f* de antigüedades

antiquary ['æntɪkwərɪ] N = **antiquarian**

antiquated ['æntɪkweɪtɪd] ADJ (*pej*) anticuado

antique [æn'ti:k] ADJ **1** [*furniture, vase*] de época; [*bracelet*] antiguo
2 (= *ancient*) antiguo, de la antigüedad; (*pej*) anticuado
N antigüedad *f*
CPD ▸ **antique dealer** anticuario/a *m/f* ▸ **antique shop, antique store** (*US*) tienda *f* de antigüedades ▸ **antiques fair** mercado *m* de antigüedades

antiqued [æn'ti:kt] ADJ [*furniture*] envejecido

antiquity [æn'tɪkwɪtɪ] N **1** (= *age, ancient times*) antigüedad *f* • **of great ~** muy antiguo • **high ~** remota antigüedad • **in ~** en la antigüedad, en el mundo antiguo
2 antiquities antigüedades *fpl*

anti-racism [,æntɪ'reɪsɪzəm] N antirracismo *m*

anti-racist [,æntɪ'reɪsɪst] ADJ antirracista
N antirracista *mf*

anti-religious [,æntɪrɪ'lɪdʒəs] ADJ antirreligioso

anti-retroviral [,æntɪretrəʊ'vaɪərəl] N antirretroviral *m*
ADJ antirretroviral

anti-riot [,æntɪ'raɪət] ADJ [*police, troops*] antidisturbios

anti-roll [,æntɪ'rəʊl] CPD ▸ **anti-roll bar** barra *f* estabilizadora, barra *f* antivuelco ▸ **anti-roll device** estabilizador *m*

antirrhinum [,æntɪ'raɪnəm] N antirrino *m*

anti-rust [,æntɪ'rʌst] ADJ antioxidante

anti-segregationist [,æntɪsegrə'geɪʃənɪst] ADJ antisegregacionista

anti-semite [,æntɪ'si:maɪt] N antisemita *mf*

anti-semitic ['æntɪsɪ'mɪtɪk] ADJ antisemita

anti-semitism [,æntɪ'semɪtɪzəm] N antisemitismo *m*

antiseptic [,æntɪ'septɪk] ADJ antiséptico
N antiséptico *m*

anti-skid [,æntɪ'skɪd] ADJ antideslizante

anti-slavery [,æntɪ'sleɪvərɪ] ADJ en contra de la esclavitud

antislip [,æntɪ'slɪp] ADJ [*floor*] antideslizante

anti-smoking [,æntɪ'sməʊkɪŋ] ADJ antitabaco

antisocial [,æntɪ'səʊʃəl] ADJ **1** (= *offensive*) [*behaviour, tendency*] antisocial
2 (= *unsociable*) insociable

antistatic [,æntɪ'stætɪk] ADJ antiestático

anti-strike [,æntɪ'straɪk] ADJ antihuelga

anti-submarine [,æntɪsʌbmə'ri:n] ADJ antisubmarino

anti-tank [,æntɪ'tæŋk] ADJ antitanque

antitechnological [,æntɪteknə'lɒdʒɪkəl] ADJ antitecnológico

anti-terrorist [,æntɪ'terərɪst] ADJ antiterrorista

anti-theft [,æntɪ'θeft] CPD ▸ **anti-theft device** sistema *m* antirrobo

antithesis [æn'tɪθɪsɪs] N (PL: **antitheses** [æn'tɪθɪsi:z]) antítesis *f inv*

antithetic [,æntɪ'θetɪk] ADJ, **antithetical** [,æntɪ'θetɪkəl] ADJ antitético

antithetically [,æntɪ'θetɪkəlɪ] ADV

a

por antítesis
antitoxic [ˌæntɪˈtɒksɪk] (ADJ) antitóxico
antitoxin [ˌæntɪˈtɒksɪn] (N) antitoxina *f*
anti-trust [ˌæntɪˈtrʌst] (ADJ) (*US*) antimonopolista
(CPD) ▸ **anti-trust law** ley *f* antimonopolios ▸ **anti-trust legislation** legislación *f* antimonopolios
antivirus [ˌæntɪˈvaɪərəs] (ADJ) [*program, software, company*] antivirus (*inv*)
antivivisection [ˈæntɪˌvɪvɪˈsekʃən] (N) antiviviseccionismo *m*
(CPD) ▸ **antivivisection movement** movimiento *m* antiviviseccionista
antivivisectionism [ˌæntɪvɪvɪˈsekʃənɪzəm] (N) antiviviseccionismo *m*
antivivisectionist [ˌæntɪvɪvɪˈsekʃənɪst] (N) antiviviseccionista *mf*
anti-war [ˌæntɪˈwɔːʳ] (ADJ) antibelicista, pacifista
anti-wrinkle [ˌæntɪˈrɪŋkl] (ADJ) antiarrugas
antler [ˈæntləʳ] (N) cuerna *f*, asta *f*; **antlers** cornamenta *fsing*
Antony [ˈæntənɪ] (N) Antonio
antonym [ˈæntənɪm] (N) antónimo *m*
antonymy [ænˈtɒnɪmɪ] (N) antonimia *f*
antsy‡ [ˈæntsɪ] (ADJ) (*US*) nervioso, inquieto
Antwerp [ˈæntwɜːp] (N) Amberes *m*
anus [ˈeɪnəs] (N) ano *m*
anvil [ˈænvɪl] (N) yunque *m*
anxiety [æŋˈzaɪətɪ] (N) **1** (= *concern*) preocupación *f*, inquietud *f* • **he expressed his anxieties about the future** expresó su preocupación *or* inquietud por el futuro • **we've had a lot of ~ over the children's health** hemos estado muy preocupados por la salud de los niños • **it is a great ~ to me** me preocupa mucho
2 (= *keenness*) ansia *f*, afán *m* • **~ to do sth** ansia *or* afán de hacer algo • **in his ~ to leave, he forgot his case** estaba tan ansioso por irse que olvidó su maleta
3 (*Med, Psych*) ansiedad *f*, angustia *f*
(CPD) ▸ **anxiety attack** ataque *m* de ansiedad ▸ **anxiety neurosis** neurosis *f inv* de ansiedad
anxious [ˈæŋkʃəs] (ADJ) **1** (= *worried*) [*person*] preocupado, inquieto; [*expression*] de preocupación, de inquietud; [*face, eyes*] angustiado • **you'd better go home, your mother will be ~** es mejor que te vayas a casa, tu madre estará preocupada *or* inquieta • **to be ~ about sth** estar preocupado por algo • **he was ~ about starting his new job** le preocupaba empezar en el nuevo trabajo • **I'm very ~ about you** me tienes muy preocupado • **to become** *or* **get ~** ponerse nervioso • **to feel ~** estar preocupado, estar inquieto • **with an ~ glance** con una mirada llena de preocupación *or* inquietud • **in an ~ voice** en un tono angustiado
2 (= *worrying*) [*situation, wait*] angustioso; [*hours, days*] lleno de ansiedad, angustioso • **it's been a very ~ time for me** ha sido un periodo muy angustioso para mí, he pasado un periodo lleno de ansiedad • **it was an ~ moment** fue un momento angustioso
3 (= *keen*) • **he's ~ that nothing should go wrong** no quiere que exista el más mínimo riesgo de que algo salga mal, no quiere de ninguna manera que nada vaya mal • **I am very ~ that he should go** quiero que vaya a toda costa • **she is ~ to see you before you go** tiene muchas ganas de verte antes de que te vayas • **I'm not very ~ to go** tengo pocas ganas de ir • **~ to please her mother, she cleaned the house** deseosa de *or* deseando agradar a su madre, limpió la casa • **to be ~ for reform** desear *or* ansiar una reforma • **he is ~ for results** está deseoso de *or* ansioso por ver resultados • **to be ~ for promotion/success** ansiar *or* ambicionar un ascenso/el éxito • **he was ~ for her to leave** estaba impaciente por que ella se marchara, tenía muchas ganas de que ella se marchara
4 (*Med, Psych*) [*feeling*] de angustia; [*person*] que padece de ansiedad • **to be ~** padecer ansiedad
anxiously [ˈæŋkʃəslɪ] (ADV) **1** (= *worriedly*) [*look, wait*] con preocupación, con inquietud • **"am I boring you?" she said, ~** —¿te aburro? —dijo con ansiedad
2 (= *keenly, eagerly*) ansiosamente, con ansiedad
anxiousness [ˈæŋkʃəsnɪs] (N) **1** (= *concern*) preocupación *f*, inquietud *f*; (= *fear*) (*also Med, Psych*) ansiedad *f*, angustia *f*
2 (= *keenness*) ansia *f*, afán *m* • **~ to do sth** ansia *or* afán de hacer algo

any [ˈenɪ]

ADJECTIVE
PRONOUN
ADVERB

ADJECTIVE

1 (*in questions*)

*When **any** modifies an uncountable noun in questions it is usually not translated:*

• **have you got any money?** ¿tienes dinero?
• **is there any sugar?** ¿hay azúcar?

*When **any** modifies a plural noun in questions it is often not translated. However, if a low number is expected in response, **algún/alguna** + singular noun is used:*

• **are there any tickets left?** ¿quedan entradas? • **did they find any survivors?** ¿hubo supervivientes? • **do you speak any foreign languages?** ¿hablas algún idioma extranjero? • **do you have any questions?** ¿alguna pregunta?

2 (*+ negative, implied negative*)

*When **any** modifies an uncountable noun it is usually not translated:*

• **I haven't any money** no tengo dinero
• **I have hardly any money left** casi no me queda dinero

*When the translation is countable, **ningún/ninguna** + singular noun can be used:*

• **you haven't any excuse** no tienes ninguna excusa • **she accepted without any hesitation** aceptó sin ninguna duda • **we got him home without any problem** lo llevamos a casa sin ningún problema

*When **any** modifies a plural noun, it is either left untranslated or, for greater emphasis, translated using **ningún/ninguna** + singular noun:*

• **he hasn't got any friends** no tiene amigos
• **I can't see any cows** no veo ninguna vaca
• **I won't do any such thing!** ¡no voy a hacer una cosa semejante!

3 (*in conditional constructions*)

***Any** + plural noun is often translated using **algún/alguna** + singular noun:*

• **if there are any problems let me know** si hay algún problema, me lo dices • **if there are any tickets left** si queda alguna entrada • **if he had any decency he would apologize** si tuviera un poco de decencia, se disculparía • **if it is in any way inconvenient to you ...** si por cualquier razón le resultara inconveniente ...

4 (= *no matter which*) cualquier • **any teacher will tell you** te lo dirá cualquier profesor • **bring me any (old) book** tráeme un libro cualquiera • **buy any two tins of soup and get one free** por cada dos latas de sopa cualesquiera que compre le regalamos otra • **wear any hat (you like)** ponte el sombrero que quieras • **he's not just any violinist** no es un violinista cualquiera • **take any one you like** tome cualquiera, tome el que quiera • **it could have happened to any one of us** le podría haber pasado a cualquiera de nosotros • **it's much like any other seaside resort** es muy parecido a cualquier otro sitio costero • **come at any time** ven cuando quieras • **we can cater for up to 300 guests at any one time** podemos proveer hasta a 300 invitados en cada ocasión • **any person who** *or* **that breaks the rules will be punished** se castigará a toda persona que no acate las reglas; ▹ **day, minute, moment, case, rate**

5 (*in set expressions*) • **any amount of:** • **they'll spend any amount of money to get it** se gastarán lo que haga falta para conseguirlo • **any number of:** • **there must be any number of people in my position** debe haber gran cantidad de personas en mi situación • **I've told you any number of times** te lo he dicho montones de veces

PRONOUN

1 (*in questions*)

*When **any** refers to an uncountable noun in questions it is usually not translated:*

• **I fancy some soup, have we got any?** me apetece sopa, ¿tenemos? • **is there any milk left?** ¿queda (algo de) leche?

*When **any** refers to a plural noun in questions it is often translated using **alguno/alguna** in the singular:*

• **I need a stamp, have you got any?** necesito un sello, ¿tienes alguno? • **do any of you know the answer?** ¿sabe alguno (de vosotros) la respuesta? • **have any of them arrived?** ¿ha llegado alguno (de ellos)?

2 (*+ negative, implied negative*)

*When **any** refers to an uncountable noun it is usually not translated:*

• **"can I have some bread?" — "we haven't any"** —¿hay pan? —no nos queda nada *or* no tenemos

*When **any** refers to a plural noun, it is either left untranslated or, for greater emphasis, translated using **ningún/ninguna** in the singular:*

• **"did you buy the oranges?" — "no, there weren't any"** ¿compraste (las) naranjas? —no, no había *or* no tenían • **she has two brothers but I haven't got any** tiene dos hermanos pero yo no tengo ninguno • **I don't like any of them** no me gusta ninguno • **I don't believe any of them has done it** no creo que lo haya hecho ninguno de ellos • **he hasn't done any of his homework** no ha hecho nada de deberes

3 (*in conditional constructions*) • **if any of you knows how to drive** si alguno de vosotros sabe conducir • **few, if any, survived** pocos, si alguno, sobrevivió
4 (= *no matter which*) cualquiera • **any of those books will do** cualquiera de esos libros servirá • **it's better than any of his other films** es mejor que cualquiera de sus otras películas
ADVERB
1 (*in questions*) • **would you like any more soup?** ¿quieres más sopa? • **is he any better?** ¿está (algo) mejor?
2 (+ *negative*) • **don't wait any longer** no esperes más (tiempo) • **I don't love him any more** ya no le quiero • **I couldn't do that any more than I could fly** yo puedo hacer eso tanto como volar • **the room didn't look any too clean** la habitación no parecía muy limpia
3 (*esp US*)* (= *at all*) • **it doesn't help us any** eso no nos ayuda para nada • **does she sing any?** ¿sabe cantar de una forma u otra?

anybody ['enɪbɒdɪ] PRON **1** (*in questions, conditional constructions*) alguien • **did you see ~?** ¿viste a alguien? • **has ~ got a pen?** ¿tiene alguien un bolígrafo? • **is this ~'s seat?** ¿es de alguien *or* alguno este asiento?, ¿está *or* hay alguien sentado aquí? • **is there ~ else I can talk to?** ¿hay alguien más con quien pueda hablar? • **if ~ calls, I'm not in** si llama alguien, no estoy • **if ~ can do it, he can** si alguien lo puede hacer, es él
2 (+ *negative, implied negative*) nadie • **I can't see ~** no veo a nadie • **she doesn't like ~ contradicting her** no le gusta que nadie la contradiga • **I didn't ask ~ else** no se le pregunté a nadie más • **hardly ~ came** apenas vino nadie • **there was hardly ~ there** casi no había nadie
3 (= *no matter who*) cualquiera • **I need a volunteer, ~ will do** necesito un voluntario, cualquier persona *or* cualquiera sirve • **~ will tell you the same** cualquiera te diría lo mismo, todos te dirán lo mismo • **~ would have thought he had lost!** cualquiera habría pensado que había perdido • **it's ~'s race** esta carrera la podría ganar cualquiera • **it would have defeated ~ but Jane** habría desanimado a cualquiera *or* a todos menos a Jane • **~ else would have laughed** cualquier otro se hubiera reído • **that's ~'s guess** ¡quién sabe! • **it's not available to just ~** no está a disposición de cualquier persona *or* cualquiera • **I'm not going to marry just ~** yo no me caso con cualquiera • **he's not just ~, he's the boss** no es cualquiera, es el jefe • **bring ~ you like** trae a quien quieras • **~ who *or* that wants to go back should go now** si alguno quiere volver, que lo haga ahora • **I'll shoot ~ who *or* that moves** al primero que se mueva le disparo • **~ who *or* that invests in this** todo el que invierta en esto • **~ with any sense would know that!** ¡cualquiera con (algo de) sentido común sabría eso!
4 (= *person of importance*) alguien • **she knows everybody who's ~** conoce a todo el mundo que es alguien *or* importante

anyhow ['enɪhaʊ] ADV **1** = anyway
2* (= *carelessly, haphazardly*) de cualquier modo, de cualquier manera • **he leaves things just ~** deja las cosas de cualquier modo *or* manera • **the books were all ~, on the floor** los libros estaban por el suelo de cualquier modo *or* manera • **I came in late and finished my essay off ~** volví tarde y terminé mi ensayo sin pensarlo mucho

anymore [ˌenɪ'mɔːʳ] ADV ▷ any
anyone ['enɪwʌn] PRON = anybody
anyplace* ['enɪpleɪs] PRON (*US*) = anywhere
anyroad‡ ['enɪrəʊd] ADV (*Brit*) = anyway
anything ['enɪθɪŋ] PRON **1** (*in questions, conditional constructions*) algo, alguna cosa • **do you need ~?** ¿necesitas algo *or* alguna cosa? • **would you like ~ to eat?** ¿quieres algo *or* alguna cosa de comer? • **is there ~ inside?** ¿hay algo *or* alguna cosa dentro? • **can ~ be done?** ¿se puede hacer algo *or* alguna cosa? • **are you doing ~ tonight?** ¿haces algo *or* alguna cosa esta noche?, ¿tienes algún plan para esta noche? • **is there ~ more boring than ...?** ¿puede haber algo más aburrido que ...? • **did you see ~ interesting?** ¿viste algo de interés? • **if ~ should happen to me** si algo me ocurriera • **if I hear ~ I'll tell you** si oigo algo, te lo diré • **think before you say ~** piensa antes de decir nada • **~ else?** (*in shop etc*) ¿algo más?, ¿alguna cosa más? • **if ~ it's much better** es mucho mejor si cabe • **if ~ it's larger** si acaso, es algo más grande • **is there ~ in what he says?** ¿hay algo de verdad en lo que dice? • **have you heard ~ of them?** ¿tienes alguna noticia de ellos?
2 (+ *negative, implied negative*) nada • **I can't see ~** no veo nada • **you haven't seen ~ yet** todavía no has visto nada • **can't ~ be done?** ¿no se puede hacer nada? • **I didn't see ~ interesting** no vi nada de interés • **we can't do ~ else** no podemos hacer otra cosa, no podemos hacer nada más • **hardly ~** casi nada • **I don't think there's ~ more annoying than ...** no creo que haya nada más irritante que ... • IDIOM: • **not for ~ in the world** por nada del mundo
3 (*no matter what*) cualquier cosa • **~ could happen** puede pasar cualquier cosa • **they'll eat ~** comen de todo, comen cualquier cosa (*pej*) • **he will give you ~ (that) you ask for** te dará lo que pidas • **~ but that** todo menos eso • **"was she apologetic?" — "~ but!"** —¿se disculpó? —¡nada de eso! • **it was ~ but pleasant** fue cualquier cosa menos agradable, era de todo menos agradable • **their friendship was more important than ~ else** su amistad era más importante que todo lo demás • **~ else would be considered unacceptable** todo lo demás se consideraría inaceptable • **she wanted more than ~ else to be an actress** ella quería ser actriz por encima de todo • **he did it more out of pity than ~ else** más que nada lo hizo por compasión • **I'm not buying just ~** yo no compro cualquier cosa • **sing ~ you like** canta lo que quieras, canta cualquier cosa • **it could take ~ up to three months** podría llevar hasta tres meses • IDIOM: • **I'd give ~ to know** daría cualquier cosa por saberlo
4 (*in guesses, estimates*) • **he must have ~ between 15 and 20 apple trees** debe de tener entre 15 y 20 manzanos
5 (*in set expressions*) • **as ~***: • **she was as white as ~** estaba más pálida que todo, estaba de lo más pálida • **it's as clear as ~ what they want** lo que quieren está tan claro como el agua*, está muy claro lo que quieren • **as much as ~**: • **I'm in it for the publicity as much as ~** más que nada estoy en esto por la publicidad • **it was a matter of principle as much as ~** era una cuestión de principios más que nada • **he ran like ~*** corrió hasta más no poder, corrió como loco* • **she cried like ~*** lloró como una descosida* • **or ~** (= *or anything like it*): • **did she say who she was or ~?** ¿dijo quién era ella o algo por el estilo? • **he's not a minister or ~** no es ministro ni nada por el estilo • **he's not ugly or ~, just strange** no es feo ni nada por el estilo, solo raro

anytime ['enɪtaɪm] ADV ▷ time
anyway ['enɪweɪ], **anyways*** ['enɪweɪz] (*US*) ADV **1** (= *in any event*) de todas formas, de todos modos • **~, you're here** de todas formas *or* de todos modos, estás aquí • **~, it's not my fault** de todas formas *or* de todos modos, yo no tengo la culpa • **he doesn't want to go out and ~ he's not allowed** no quiere salir y de todas formas *or* de todos modos no le dejan • **whose money is this ~?** de todas formas *or* de todos modos, ¿de quién es el dinero? • **who needs men ~?** de todas formas *or* de todos modos, ¿quién necesita a los hombres? • **~, why invite somebody you never speak to?** de todas formas *or* de todos modos ¿por qué invitar a alguien con quien nunca hablas?
2 (= *regardless*) de todas formas, de todos modos • **I shall go ~** iré de todas formas *or* de todos modos • **he's not supposed to drink but he does ~** se supone que no debe beber, pero lo hace de todas formas *or* de todos modos
3 (= *at least*) al menos • **it's not a good idea, I don't think so ~** no es buena idea, al menos eso es lo que yo pienso
4 (= *incidentally*) por cierto • **why are you going ~?** por cierto ¿por qué te vas?
5 (*continuing what has been said*) en fin • **~, as I was saying ...** en fin, como decía antes ... • **so ~, this policeman came up to me and said ...** en fin, este policía se me acercó y dijo ...

anywhere ['enɪweəʳ] ADV **1** (*in questions*) (*location*) en alguna parte, en algún lugar *or* sitio; (*direction*) a alguna parte, a algún lugar *or* sitio • **have you seen my coat ~?** ¿has visto mi abrigo en *or* por alguna parte?, ¿has visto mi abrigo por algún sitio? • **can you see him ~?** ¿le ves por alguna parte *or* por algún sitio? • **did you visit ~ else?** ¿visitasteis algún otro sitio?
2 (+ *negatives, implied negatives*) (*location*) por *or* en ninguna parte, por *or* en ningún sitio; (*direction*) a ninguna parte, a ningún sitio • **I can't find it ~** no lo encuentro por *or* en ninguna parte, no lo encuentro por *or* en ningún sitio • **I'm not going ~** no voy a ninguna parte, no voy a ningún sitio • **we didn't go ~ special** no fuimos a ningún sitio especial • **he was first and the rest didn't come ~** él se clasificó primero y los demás quedaron muy por debajo • **it's not available ~ else** no lo tienen en ningún otro sitio, no lo tienen en ninguna otra parte • **I wouldn't live ~ else** no viviría en ninguna otra parte, no viviría en ningún otro sitio • **I'm not going to live just ~** yo no voy a vivir en cualquier sitio • **it isn't ~ near Castroforte** está bastante lejos de Castroforte • **the house isn't ~ near big enough*** la casa no es ni por asomo lo bastante grande • **it isn't ~ near enough*** (*sum of money*) con eso no hay suficiente ni mucho menos • IDIOM: • **that won't get you ~*** así no conseguirás nada
3 (*in affirmative sentences*) en cualquier parte • **put the books down ~** pon los libros en cualquier parte *or* donde sea • **~ you go you'll see the same** dondequiera que vayas verás lo mismo, verás lo mismo en cualquier parte a donde vayas • **sit ~ you like** siéntate donde quieras • **she leaves her things just ~** deja sus cosas en cualquier parte • **you can buy stamps almost ~** se pueden comprar sellos casi en cualquier sitio • **she could have been ~ between 30 and 50 years old** podría haber tenido desde 30 hasta 50 años • **it would be the same ~ else** sería lo mismo

en cualquier otra parte • **~ from 200 to 300** (*US*) entre 200 y 300 • **~ in the world** en cualquier parte del mundo
PRON • **we haven't found ~ else to live** no hemos encontrado ningún otro sitio para vivir • **it's miles from ~** está completamente aislado • **a plane ticket to ~ in the world** un billete de avión a cualquier parte del mundo

Anzac ['ænzæk] N ABBR = **Australia-New Zealand Army Corps**

AOB ABBR (= **any other business**) ruegos *mpl* y preguntas

AOCB ABBR (= **any other competent business**) ruegos *mpl* y preguntas

AONB N ABBR (*Brit*) (= **Area of Outstanding Natural Beauty**) ≈ Paraje *m* Natural

aorist ['ɛərɪst] N aoristo *m*

aorta [eɪ'ɔːtə] N (PL: **aortas, aortae** [eɪ'ɔːtiː]) aorta *f*

aortic [eɪ'ɔːtɪk] ADJ aórtico

AP N ABBR = **Associated Press**

apace [ə'peɪs] ADV (*frm*) aprisa, rápidamente

apache [ə'pætʃɪ] N apache *m*

apart [ə'pɑːt]

When **apart** *is an element in a phrasal verb, eg* **fall apart, tear apart**, *look up the verb.*

ADV **1** (= *separated*) • **it was the first time we had been ~** era la primera vez que estábamos separados • **with one's feet ~** con los pies apartados • **the two towns are 10km ~** los dos pueblos están a 10km el uno del otro • **their birthdays are two days ~** sus cumpleaños se separan por dos días • **posts set equally ~** postes espaciados con regularidad *or* colocados a intervalos iguales • **to hold o.s. ~** mantenerse aparte • **to keep ~** separar, mantener aislado (**from** de) • **he lives ~ from his wife** vive separado de su mujer • **they have lived ~ for six months** viven separados desde hace seis meses • **we live three doors ~** vivimos a tres puertas de ellos • **the house stands somewhat ~** la casa está algo aislada • **they stood a long way ~** estaban muy apartados (el uno del otro) • **he stood ~ from the others** se mantuvo apartado de los otros • **I can't tell them ~** no puedo distinguir el uno del otro; ▹ **set apart**
2 (= *in pieces*) • **to come** *or* **fall ~** romperse, deshacerse • **to take sth ~** desmontar algo; ▹ **fall apart, take apart, tear apart**
3 (= *aside*) • **joking ~ …** en serio … • **these problems ~ …** aparte de estos problemas …, estos problemas aparte …
4 • **~ from a** (= *excluding*) aparte de • **~ from the fact that …** aparte del hecho de que … • **but quite ~ from that …** pero aparte de eso …
b (= *except for*) • **he ate everything ~ from the meat** comió todo menos *or* excepto la carne • **they all voted against ~ from John** todos votaron en contra aparte de John

apartheid [ə'pɑːteɪt] N apartheid *m*

aparthotel [ə'pɑːthəʊ,tel] N aparthotel *m*

apartment [ə'pɑːtmənt] N **1** (*US*) (= *flat*) piso *m* (*Sp*), apartamento *m* (*LAm*), departamento *m* (*Arg*)
2 (*Brit*) (= *room*) cuarto *m*, aposento *m* (*liter*)
CPD ▸ **apartment building, apartment block** (*US*) bloque *m* de pisos (*Sp*), bloque *m* de apartamentos (*LAm*), bloque *m* de departamentos (*Arg*) ▸ **apartment complex** complejo *m* de pisos (*Sp*), complejo *m* de apartamentos (*LAm*), complejo *m* de departamentos (*Arg*) ▸ **apartment hotel** (*US*) aparthotel *m* ▸ **apartment house** (*US*) casa *f* de apartamentos

apathetic [,æpə'θetɪk] ADJ apático • **to be ~ towards sth** ser indiferente hacia algo, no mostrar interés alguno en algo

apathetically [,æpə'θetɪkəlɪ] ADV con apatía, con indiferencia

apathy ['æpəθɪ] N apatía *f*, indiferencia *f* • **~ towards sth** indiferencia hacia algo, falta *f* de interés en algo

APB N ABBR (*US*) (= **all points bulletin**) *frase usada por la policía por "descubrir y aprehender"*

APC N ABBR = **armo(u)red personnel carrier**

ape [eɪp] N **1** (*Zool*) mono *m*, simio *m*, antropoide *mf* • IDIOM: • **to go ape** (*US*‡) (= *lose one's temper*) ponerse como un energúmeno*, ponerse hecho una fiera*; (= *go crazy*) ponerse como una moto‡
2* (*pej*) (= *person*) • **you (great) ape!** ¡bestia!*
VT imitar, remedar

APEC ['eɪpek] N ABBR = **Asia Pacific Economic Co-operation**

Apennines ['æpɪnaɪnz] NPL Apeninos *mpl*

aperient [ə'pɪərɪənt] ADJ laxante
N laxante *m*

aperitif [ə,perɪ'tiːf] N aperitivo *m*

aperture ['æpətʃjʊəʳ] N **1** (= *crack*) rendija *f*, resquicio *m*
2 (*Phot*) abertura *f*

apeshit** ['eɪpʃɪt] ADJ (*esp US*) • IDIOM: • **to go ~** (= *lose one's temper*) ponerse como un energúmeno*, ponerse hecho una fiera*; (= *go crazy*) ponerse como una moto‡

APEX ['eɪpeks] N ABBR **1** (*Brit*) = **Association of Professional, Executive, Clerical and Computer Staff**
2 (*also* **apex**) = **Advance Purchase Excursion** • **~ ticket** billete *m* APEX

apex ['eɪpeks] N (PL: **apexes, apices** ['eɪpɪsiːz]) **1** (*Math*) vértice *m*
2 (*fig*) cumbre *f*, cima *f*

aphasia [æ'feɪzɪə] N afasia *f*

aphid ['eɪfɪd] N áfido *m*

aphis ['eɪfɪs] N (PL: **aphides** ['eɪfɪdiːz]) áfido *m*

aphonic [,eɪ'fɒnɪk] ADJ afónico

aphorism ['æfərɪzəm] N aforismo *m*

aphoristic [,æfə'rɪstɪk] ADJ aforístico

aphrodisiac [,æfrəʊ'dɪzɪæk] ADJ afrodisiaco
N afrodisiaco *m*

Aphrodite [,æfrəʊ'daɪtɪ] N Afrodita

API N ABBR (*US*) = **American Press Institute**

apiarist ['eɪpɪərɪst] N apicultor(a) *m/f*

apiary ['eɪpɪərɪ] N colmenar *m*

apices ['eɪpɪsiːz] NPL *of* **apex**

apiculture ['eɪpɪkʌltʃəʳ] N apicultura *f*

apiece [ə'piːs] ADV (= *for each person*) cada uno/a; (= *for each thing*) cada uno/a • **they had a gun ~** tenía cada uno un revólver • **he gave them an apple ~** dio una manzana a cada uno • **the rule is a dollar ~** la regla es un dólar por cabeza *or* persona

aplastic anaemia, aplastic anemia (*US*) [eɪ'plæstɪkə'niːmɪə] N anemia *f* aplástica

aplenty [ə'plentɪ] ADV (*liter*) • **there was food ~** había comida abundante, había abundancia de comida

aplomb [ə'plɒm] N (*liter*) aplomo *m* • **with great ~** con gran aplomo *or* serenidad

APO N ABBR (*US*) = **Army Post Office**

Apocalypse [ə'pɒkəlɪps] N Apocalipsis *m*

apocalyptic [ə,pɒkə'lɪptɪk] ADJ apocalíptico

apocopate [ə'pɒkəpeɪt] VT apocopar

apocope [ə'pɒkəpɪ] N apócope *f*

Apocrypha [ə'pɒkrɪfə] NPL libros *mpl* apócrifos de la Biblia, Apócrifos *mpl*

apocryphal [ə'pɒkrɪfəl] ADJ apócrifo

apodosis [ə'pɒdəsɪs] N apódosis *f*

apogee ['æpədʒiː] N apogeo *m*

apolitical [,eɪpə'lɪtɪkəl] ADJ apolítico

Apollo [ə'pɒləʊ] N Apolo

apologetic [ə,pɒlə'dʒetɪk] ADJ [*look, smile, letter, tone*] de disculpa • **he came in with an ~ air** entró como pidiendo disculpas • **he didn't seem in the least ~** no parecía sentirlo en absoluto • **"oh, I'm sorry," said the girl, immediately ~** —ay, lo siento —dijo la niña disculpándose rápidamente • **twenty minutes late, a profusely ~ Mrs Perks arrived** la Sra. Perks llegó con veinte minutos de retraso disculpándose profusamente • **he was very ~** se deshizo en disculpas • **to be ~ about sth** disculparse por algo

apologetically [ə,pɒlə'dʒetɪkəlɪ] ADV • **he smiled ~** sonrió como pidiendo disculpas • **"it's my fault," he said ~** —es culpa mía —dijo en tono de disculpa • **he came in ~** entró como pidiendo perdón

apologetics [ə,pɒlə'dʒetɪks] NSING apologética *f*

apologia [,æpə'ləʊdʒɪə] N apología *f*

apologist [ə'pɒlədʒɪst] N apologista *mf*

apologize [ə'pɒlədʒaɪz] VI disculparse, pedir perdón; (*for absence etc*) presentar las excusas • **there's no need to ~** no hay de qué disculparse • **I ~!** ¡lo siento! • **to ~ to sb (for sth)** disculparse con algn (por algo) • **he ~d for being late** se disculpó por llegar tarde • **to ~ for sb** disculparse *or* pedir perdón por algn • **never ~!** disculpas, ¡nunca!

apologue ['æpəlɒg] N apólogo *m*

apology [ə'pɒlədʒɪ] N **1** (= *expression of regret*) disculpa *f* • **letter of ~** carta *f* de disculpa • **I demand an ~** exijo una disculpa • **to make** *or* **offer an ~** disculparse, presentar sus excusas (**for** por) • **to make no ~** *or* **apologies for sth** no tener reparo en algo • **I make no apologies for being blunt** no tengo ningún reparo en serle franco • **please accept my apologies** le ruego me disculpe • **I owe you an ~** te debo una disculpa • **to send an ~** (*at meeting*) presentar sus excusas • **there are apologies from Gerry and Jane** se han excusado Gerry y Jane
2 (*Literat*) apología *f*
3 (*pej*) • **an ~ for a stew** una birria de guisado • **this ~ for a letter** esta que apenas se puede llamar carta

apophthegm ['æpəθem] N apotegma *m*

apoplectic [,æpə'plektɪk] ADJ **1** (*Med*) apoplético
2* (= *very angry*) furioso • **to get ~** enfurecerse

apoplexy ['æpəpleksɪ] N **1** (*Med*†) apoplejía *f*
2 (= *rage*) cólera *f*, ira *f*

apostasy [ə'pɒstəsɪ] N apostasía *f*

apostate [ə'pɒstɪt] N apóstata *mf*

apostatize [ə'pɒstətaɪz] VI apostatar (**from** de)

a posteriori ['eɪpɒs,terɪ'ɔːraɪ] ADJ, ADV a posteriori

apostle [ə'pɒsl] N **1** (*Rel*) apóstol *m*
2 (*fig*) apóstol *m*, paladín *m*

apostolate [ə'pɒstəlɪt] N apostolado *m*

apostolic [,æpəs'tɒlɪk] ADJ apostólico • **the ~ coalition** la coalición apostólica
CPD ▸ **apostolic succession** sucesión *f* apostólica

apostrophe [ə'pɒstrəfɪ] N **1** (*Ling*) apóstrofo *m*
2 (= *address*) apóstrofe *m*

apostrophize [ə'pɒstrəfaɪz] VT apostrofar

apothecary† [ə'pɒθɪkərɪ] N boticario *m*

apotheosis [ə,pɒθɪ'əʊsɪs] N (PL: **apotheoses** [ə,pɒθɪ'əʊsiːz]) apoteosis *f*

app [æp] N ABBR (= *application*) app *f*, aplicación *f*

appal, appall (*US*) [ə'pɔːl] VT horrorizar

Appalachia [ˌæpəˈleɪtʃɪə] N *región de los (montes) Apalaches*

Appalachian Mountains [ˌæpəˌleɪtʃənˈmaʊntɪnz] NPL • **the ~** los (montes) Apalaches

Appalachians [ˌæpəˈleɪtʃənz] NPL (montes *mpl*) Apalaches *mpl*

appalled [əˈpɔːld] ADJ (= *horrified*) horrorizado; (= *dismayed*) consternado • **everyone was ~** (*horrified*) se horrorizaron todos; (*dismayed*) todos quedaron consternados • **we were ~ at** *or* **by the plan to demolish the church** el plan para demoler la iglesia nos dejó consternados • **they were ~ that he had escaped a prison sentence** se quedaron consternados al saber que había evitado una pena de cárcel • **I was ~ by the news** me horrorizó la noticia

appalling [əˈpɔːlɪŋ] ADJ [*sight, behaviour, weather, destruction*] espantoso, horroroso; [*suffering, crime, conditions*] atroz, espantoso; [*spelling, mistake, headache, smell*] espantoso • **he has ~ taste in clothes** tiene un gusto pésimo para la ropa • **her first novel was ~** su primera novela fue un horror

appallingly [əˈpɔːlɪŋlɪ] ADV **1** (= *badly*) [*sing, play*] pésimamente; [*treat*] espantosamente mal, terriblemente mal; [*suffer*] horriblemente, terriblemente • **he had behaved ~** se había portado fatal *or* terriblemente mal • **the situation has deteriorated ~** la situación ha empeorado de forma terrible
2 (= *extremely*) [*difficult, selfish, ignorant*] terriblemente • **the film was ~ bad** la película era pésima

apparatchik [ˌæpəˈrættʃɪk] N **1** (*in Communist country*) miembro *m* del aparato del partido comunista, apparatchik *m*
2 (*in organization*) funcionario/a *m/f*, burócrata *mf*

apparatus [ˌæpəˈreɪtəs] (PL: **apparatus, apparatuses**) N **1** (*Anat, Mech*) aparato *m*; (= *set of instruments*) equipo *m*
2 (*fig*) (= *system*) sistema *m*, aparato *m*

apparel [əˈpærəl] N **1** (*Brit†*) atuendo *m*; (*hum*) atavío *m*
2 (*US*) ropa *f*
VT vestir (**in** de); (*hum*) trajear, ataviar (**in** de)

apparent [əˈpærənt] ADJ **1** (= *clear*) claro • **to be ~ that** estar claro que • **it was ~ that there were problems** estaba claro que había problemas • **it was immediately ~ that he was lying** enseguida se vio claramente que mentía • **to become ~** hacerse patente • **it became ~ that he was not coming** se hizo patente que no venía • **it is becoming ~ that we will have to find larger premises** ya se está viendo que vamos a tener que encontrar un local más grande • **this attitude is ~ in some of the things they say** esta actitud queda patente *or* se ve claramente en algunas de las cosas que dicen • **for no ~ reason** sin motivo aparente • **it was ~ to me that there were problems** veía claro *or* me resultaba obvio que había problemas
2 (= *seeming*) [*success, contradiction, interest*] aparente • **more ~ than real** más aparente que real
3 ▹ **heir**

apparently [əˈpærəntlɪ] ADV **1** (= *it appears*) por lo visto, según parece • **~, they're getting a divorce** por lo visto *or* según parece, se van a divorciar • **"is she the new teacher?" — "apparently"** —¿es ella la nueva profesora? —por lo visto *or* eso parece • **"I thought they were coming" — "apparently not"** —pensé que venían —por lo visto no *or* parece que no
2 (= *seemingly, on the surface*) aparentemente • **to be ~ calm** estar aparentemente tranquilo • **an ~ harmless question** una pregunta aparentemente inocente • **the murders follow an ~ random pattern** los asesinatos parecen seguir un esquema aleatorio

apparition [ˌæpəˈrɪʃən] N **1** (= *ghost*) aparecido *m*, fantasma *m*
2 (= *appearance*) aparición *f*

appeal [əˈpiːl] N **1** (*requesting sth*) **a** (= *call*) llamamiento *m*, llamado *m* (*LAm*); (= *request*) petición *f*, solicitud *f* • **he made an ~ for calm** hizo un llamamiento a la calma • **to issue an ~ for aid for sb** hacer un llamamiento solicitando ayuda para algn • **the police repeated their ~ for witnesses to contact them** la policía volvió a hacer un llamamiento a posibles testigos del hecho para que se pusieran en contacto con ellos • **an ~ to arms/reason** un llamamiento a las armas/la cordura • **our ~ for volunteers** la petición *or* solicitud que hicimos de voluntarios
b (= *entreaty*) súplica *f* • **he was deaf to all ~s** hacía oídos sordos a todas las súplicas
c (= *campaign for donations*) • **they launched a £5 million ~ for cancer research** realizaron una campaña para la recaudación de 5 millones de libras para la lucha contra el cáncer • **an ~ on behalf of a mental health charity** una petición de ayuda para una organización benéfica de salud mental
d (*Jur*) apelación *f*, recurso *m* (de apelación) • **his ~ was successful** su apelación *or* recurso (de apelación) dio resultado • **there is no ~ against his decision** su fallo es inapelable • **she won/lost the case on ~** ganó/perdió el caso en la apelación *or* en segunda instancia • **right of** *or* **to ~** derecho *m* de apelación, derecho *m* a apelar • **their lands were forfeit without ~** sus tierras fueron confiscadas sin posibilidad de apelación; ▹ **court**
2 (= *attraction*) atractivo *m*, encanto *m* • **the party's new name was meant to give it greater public ~** el nuevo nombre del partido tenía como objetivo atraer a más público • **the idea held little ~** la idea no le resultaba muy atrayente; ▹ **sex**
VI **1** • **to ~ for** (= *call publicly for*) [+ *peace, tolerance, unity*] hacer un llamamiento a; (= *request*) solicitar, pedir • **the authorities ~ed for calm** las autoridades hicieron un llamamiento a la calma • **the police have ~ed to the public for information** la policía ha hecho un llamamiento al público pidiendo información • **to ~ for funds** solicitar *or* pedir fondos • **he ~ed for silence** rogó silencio
2 (= *call upon*) • **to ~ to sb's finer feelings/sb's generosity** apelar a los sentimientos nobles/la generosidad de algn • **to ~ to the country** (*Pol*) recurrir al arbitrio de las urnas
3 (*Jur*) apelar • **to ~ against** [+ *sentence, ruling*] apelar contra *or* de, recurrir (contra) • **they have ~ed to the Supreme Court to stop her extradition** han apelado *or* recurrido al Tribunal Supremo para detener su proceso de extradición
4 (= *be attractive*) • **that sort of comedy doesn't ~ any more** ese tipo de humor ya no gusta • **to ~ to sb** [*idea, activity*] atraer a algn, resultar atrayente a algn • **I don't think this will ~ to the public** no creo que esto le atraiga al público, no creo que esto le resulte atrayente al público • **it ~s to the child in everyone** hace salir al niño que llevamos dentro
VT (*US*) (*Jur*) • **to ~ a decision/verdict** apelar contra *or* de una decisión/un veredicto, recurrir (contra) una decisión/un veredicto
CPD ▸ **appeal(s) committee** comité *m* de apelación ▸ **appeal court** tribunal *m* de apelación ▸ **appeal judge** juez *mf* de apelación, jueza *f* de apelación ▸ **appeal(s) procedure** procedimiento *m* de apelación ▸ **appeal(s) process** proceso *m* de apelación ▸ **appeal(s) tribunal** tribunal *m* de apelación

appealable [əˈpiːləbl] ADJ (*Jur*) • **the decision is ~** se puede entablar un recurso de apelación contra la decisión

appealing [əˈpiːlɪŋ] ADJ **1** (= *attractive*) [*idea*] atractivo, atrayente • **the idea would be very ~ to Britain** la idea resultaría muy atractiva *or* atrayente para Gran Bretaña • **the book is especially ~ to the younger reader** el libro es de especial interés para el lector joven • **they are trying to make the party more ~ to younger voters** intentan hacer que el partido atraiga al electorado joven
2 (= *beseeching*) [*look, eyes*] suplicante

appealingly [əˈpiːlɪŋlɪ] ADV **1** (= *attractively*) • **a lock of hair fell ~ across his forehead** un mechón de pelo le caía sobre la frente de modo que resultaba muy atractivo *or* atrayente • **he found her ~ stubborn** su terquedad le resultaba atractiva *or* atrayente
2 (= *beseechingly*) de modo suplicante

appear [əˈpɪəʳ] VI **1** (= *arrive, become visible*) [*person, graffiti*] aparecer; [*ghost*] aparecerse; [*spot, stain, crack*] aparecer, salir; [*symptom*] aparecer, presentarse • **Trudy ~ed at last** por fin apareció Trudy • **he ~ed briefly to address his supporters** hizo una breve aparición para dirigirse a sus seguidores • **he ~ed without a tie** se presentó sin corbata • **he ~ed from nowhere** salió *or* apareció de la nada • **where did you ~ from?** ¿de dónde has salido? • **the sun ~ed from behind a cloud** el sol salió de detrás de una nube • **to ~ in public** aparecer en público • **to ~ to sb** (*as vision*) aparecerse a algn • **he ~ed to me in a dream** se me apareció en sueños
2 (*Theat, TV*) salir • **she ~ed in "Fuenteovejuna"** salió *or* hizo un papel en "Fuenteovejuna" • **she ~ed as Ophelia** hizo (el papel) de Ofelia • **to ~ on stage** aparecer en escena • **to ~ on television** salir en *or* por televisión
3 (*Jur*) **a** [*defendant*] comparecer • **to ~ before sb** comparecer ante algn • **to ~ in court** comparecer ante el tribunal *or* los tribunales • **to ~ on a charge of murder** comparecer acusado de homicidio
b [*lawyer*] • **to ~ for** *or* **on behalf of sb** representar a algn • **to ~ for the defence/the prosecution** representar a la defensa/la acusación
4 (= *be published*) salir, publicarse • **the book ~ed in 1960** el libro salió *or* se publicó en 1960 • **the term first ~ed in print in 1530** el primer testimonio escrito del término se remonta a 1530 • **it was her life's ambition to ~ in print** la ilusión de su vida era ver su nombre impreso
5 (= *seem*) parecer • **he ~s tired** parece cansado • **how does it ~ to you?** ¿qué impresión le da? • **it ~s to me that they are mistaken** me da la impresión de que *or* me parece que están equivocados • **they ~ not to like each other** parece que no se gustan, no parece que se gusten • **there ~s to be a mistake** parece que hay un error • **she ~ed not to notice** no pareció darse cuenta • **we must ~ to be fair** debemos dar la impresión de ser justos • **it ~s not** • **it would ~ not**

a

parece que no • **"he came then?" — "so it would ~"** —¿entonces él ha venido? —eso parece • **she got the job, or so it would ~** le dieron el trabajo, según parece
6 (= *become apparent*) • **as will ~ in due course** según se verá a su debido tiempo

appearance [ə'pɪərəns] (N) **1** (= *act of showing o.s.*) aparición *f* • **to make an ~** aparecer, dejarse ver • **to make a personal ~** aparecer en persona • **to put in an ~** hacer acto de presencia
2 (*Theat, TV*) aparición *f* • **to make one's first ~** hacer su primera aparición, debutar • **his ~ as Don Mendo** su actuación en el papel de Don Mendo • **his ~ in "Don Mendo"** su actuación en "Don Mendo" • **cast in order of ~** personajes *mpl* en orden de aparición en escena
3 (*Jur*) comparecencia *f* • **to make an ~ in court** comparecer ante el tribunal
4 [*of book etc*] publicación *f*
5 (= *look*) aspecto *m* • **she takes great care over her ~** cuida mucho su aspecto • **at first ~** a primera vista • **to have a dignified ~** tener aspecto solemne • **he had the ~ of an executive** parecía ejecutivo, tenía aspecto de ejecutivo • **in ~** de aspecto
6 appearances apariencias *fpl* • **~s can be deceptive** las apariencias engañan • **to** *or* **by all ~s** al parecer • **contrary to all ~s** en contra de las apariencias • **you shouldn't go by ~s** no hay que fiarse de las apariencias • **to judge by ~s, ...** a juzgar por las apariencias, ... • **to keep up ~s** guardar las apariencias • **for the sake of ~s** • **for ~s' sake** para guardar las apariencias
(CPD) ▸ **appearance fee, appearance money** *honorario que cobra una personalidad célebre por hacer una aparición pública, por ejemplo por televisión*

appease [ə'pi:z] (VT) **1** (= *pacify*) [+ *person*] apaciguar, calmar; [+ *anger*] aplacar
2 (= *satisfy*) [+ *person*] satisfacer; [+ *hunger*] saciar; [+ *curiosity*] satisfacer, saciar
3 (*Pol*) apaciguar, contemporizar con

appeasement [ə'pi:zmənt] (N)
1 (= *pacification*) [*of person*] apaciguamiento *m*; [*of anger*] aplacamiento *m*
2 (*Pol*) contemporización *f*, entreguismo *m*

appeaser [ə'pi:zəʳ] (N) (*Pol*) conciliador(a) *m/f*

appellant [ə'pelənt] (N) apelante *mf*

appellate [ə'pelɪt] (ADJ) • **~ court** (*US*) (*Jur*) tribunal *m* de apelación

appellation [ˌæpe'leɪʃən] (N) (= *name*) nombre *m*; (= *title*) título *m*; [*of wine*] denominación *f* de origen

append [ə'pend] (*frm*) (VT) **1** (= *add*) [+ *signature*] añadir; [+ *note*] agregar, añadir
2 (= *attach*) adjuntar
3 (*Comput*) anexionar (al final)

appendage [ə'pendɪdʒ] (N) **1** (*frm*) (= *adjunct*) apéndice *m*
2 (*fig*) pegote* *m*

appendectomy [ˌæpen'dektəmɪ] (N) apendectomía *f*

appendices [ə'pendɪsi:z] (*esp Brit*) (NPL) *of* **appendix**

appendicitis [əˌpendɪ'saɪtɪs] (N) apendicitis *f inv* • **to have ~** tener apendicitis • **acute ~** apendicitis *f* aguda

appendix [ə'pendɪks] (N) (PL: **appendixes, appendices** [ə'pendɪsi:z]) **1** (*Anat*) apéndice *m* • **to have one's ~ out** hacerse extirpar el apéndice
2 [*of book*] apéndice *m*

apperception [ˌæpə'sepʃən] (N) (*frm*) percepción *f*
(CPD) ▸ **apperception test** (*US*) test *m* de percepción

appertain [ˌæpə'teɪn] (VI) • **to ~ to** relacionarse con, tener que ver con

appetite ['æpɪtaɪt] (N) **1** (*for food*) apetito *m* • **to eat with an ~** comer con buen apetito *or* con ganas • **to have a good ~** tener buen apetito • **to have no ~** no tener apetito; ▹ **suppressant**
2 (*fig*) deseo *m*, anhelo *m* (**for** de) • **they had no ~ for further fighting** ya no les apetecía seguir luchando, no tenían más ganas de luchar • **it spoiled their ~ for going abroad** eso les quitó las ganas de ir al extranjero

appetizer ['æpɪtaɪzəʳ] (N) (= *drink*) aperitivo *m*; (= *food*) aperitivo *m*, tapas *fpl* (*Sp*), botanas *fpl* (*Mex*), bocaditos *mpl* (*Peru*)

appetizing ['æpɪtaɪzɪŋ] (ADJ) apetitoso

appetizingly ['æpɪtaɪzɪŋlɪ] (ADV) de manera atractiva

Appian Way ['æpɪən'weɪ] (N) Vía *f* Apia

applaud [ə'plɔ:d] (VT) **1** [*audience, spectators*] aplaudir
2 (*fig*) [+ *decision, efforts*] aplaudir
(VI) aplaudir

applaudable [ə'plɔ:dəbl] (ADJ) digno de aplauso

applause [ə'plɔ:z] (N) **1** (= *clapping*) aplausos *mpl* • **a round of ~ for Peter!** ¡un aplauso para Peter! • **there was loud ~** sonaron fuertes aplausos
2 (= *approval*) aprobación *f*; (= *praise*) alabanza *f*, aplauso *m* • **to win the ~ of** ganarse la aprobación de

apple ['æpl] (N) (= *fruit*) manzana *f*; (= *tree*) manzano *m* • **~ of discord** manzana *f* de la discordia • IDIOMS: • **~s and pears** (*Brit*‡) (= *stairs*) escalera *f* • **the Big Apple** (*US**) la Gran Manzana, Nueva York *f*; ▹ CITY NICKNAMES • **the ~ of one's eye** la niña de los ojos de algn • **one bad** *or* **rotten ~ can spoil the whole barrel** manzana podrida echa ciento a perder
(CPD) ▸ **apple blossom** flor *f* del manzano ▸ **apple brandy** licor *m* de manzana ▸ **apple core** corazón *m* de manzana ▸ **apple dumpling** *postre a base de manzana asada y masa* ▸ **apple fritter** manzana *f* rebozada ▸ **apple orchard** manzanar *m*, manzanal *m* ▸ **apple pie** pastel *m* de manzana, pay *m* de manzana (*LAm*); ▹ **apple-pie** ▸ **apple sauce** (*Culin*) compota *f* de manzana; (*US**) (= *hokum*) tonterías *fpl* ▸ **apple tart** tarta *f* de manzana ▸ **apple tree** manzano *m* ▸ **apple turnover** empanada *f* de manzanas

applecart ['æplkɑ:t] (N) • IDIOM: • **to upset** *or* **overturn the ~** echarlo todo a rodar, desbaratar los planes

apple-green ['æplgri:n] (ADJ) verde manzana (*inv*)
(N) verde *m* manzana

applejack ['æpldʒæk] (N) (*US*) licor *m* de manzana

apple-pie ['æpl'paɪ] (ADJ) • **in apple-pie order** en perfecto orden • **to make sb an apple-pie bed** (*Brit*) hacerle la petaca a algn; ▹ **apple**

applet ['æplɪt] (N) applet *m*

appliance [ə'plaɪəns] (N) **1** (= *device*) aparato *m* • **electrical ~** (aparato *m*) electrodoméstico *m*
2 (= *application*) [*of skill, knowledge*] aplicación *f*
3 (*Brit*) (*also* **fire appliance**) coche *m* de bomberos

applicability [ˌæplɪkə'bɪlɪtɪ] (N) aplicabilidad *f*

applicable [ə'plɪkəbl] (ADJ) aplicable, pertinente (**to** a) • **delete what is not ~** táchese lo que no proceda • **this law is also ~ to foreigners** esta ley es aplicable *or* se refiere también a los extranjeros • **a rule ~ to all** una regla que se extiende a todos

applicant ['æplɪkənt] (N) **1** (*for job etc*) aspirante *mf*, candidato/a *m/f* (**for a post** a un puesto)
2 (*for money, assistance*) solicitante *mf*
3 (*Jur*) suplicante *mf*

application [ˌæplɪ'keɪʃən] (N) **1** [*of ointment etc*] aplicación *f* • **"for external application only"** "para uso externo"
2 (= *request*) solicitud *f*, petición *f* (**for** de) • **~ for shares** solicitud *f* de acciones • **~s in triplicate** las solicitudes por triplicado • **to make an ~ for** solicitar • **to make an ~ to** dirigirse a • **prices on ~** los precios, a solicitud • **details may be had on ~ to the office** los detalles pueden obtenerse mediante solicitud a nuestra oficina • **are you going to put in an ~?** ¿te vas a presentar? • **to submit one's ~** presentar su solicitud
3 (= *diligence*) aplicación *f* • **he lacks ~** le falta aplicación
(CPD) ▸ **application form** solicitud *f* ▸ **applications package** (*Comput*) paquete *m* de programas de aplicación ▸ **application(s) program** (*Comput*) programa *m* de aplicación *or* aplicaciones ▸ **application(s) software** (*Comput*) paquete *m* de aplicación *or* aplicaciones

applicator ['æplɪkeɪtəʳ] (N) aplicador *m*

applied [ə'plaɪd] (ADJ) aplicado • **~ linguistics** lingüística *fsing* aplicada • **~ mathematics** matemáticas *fpl* aplicadas • **~ science** ciencias *fpl* aplicadas
(CPD) ▸ **applied arts** artes *fpl* decorativas

appliqué [æ'pli:keɪ] (N) (*also* **appliqué lace, appliqué work**) encaje *m* de aplicación

appliquéd [ə'pli:keɪd] (ADJ) [*cushion, bedspread*] aplicado • **an appliquéd design** *or* **motif** un aplique

apply [ə'plaɪ] (VT) **1** [+ *ointment, paint etc*] aplicar (**to** a) • **to ~ heat to a surface** (*Tech*) exponer una superficie al calor; (*Med*) calentar una superficie • **to ~ a match to sth** prender fuego a algo con una cerilla
2 (= *impose*) [+ *rule, law*] aplicar, emplear
3 (= *use*) • **to ~ the brakes** frenar • **to ~ pressure on sth** ejercer presión sobre algo • **to ~ pressure on sb** (*fig*) presionar a algn
4 (= *dedicate*) • **to ~ one's mind to a problem** dedicarse a resolver un problema • **to ~ o.s. to a task** dedicarse *or* aplicarse a una tarea
(VI) **1** (= *be relevant*) ser aplicable, ser pertinente • **cross out what does not ~** táchese lo que no proceda • **to ~ to** (= *be applicable to*) ser aplicable a, referirse a • **the law applies to everybody** la ley es aplicable a *or* de obligado cumplimiento para todos • **this rule doesn't ~ to us** esta norma no nos afecta
2 (*for job, audition*) presentarse • **are you ~ing?** ¿te vas a presentar? • **"please apply at the office"** "diríjanse a la oficina" • **to ~ to sb** dirigirse a algn, acudir a algn • **to ~ for** [+ *scholarship, grant, assistance*] solicitar, pedir; [+ *job*] solicitar, presentarse a • **"patent applied for"** "patente en trámite" • **to ~ to sb for sth** solicitar algo a algn; ▹ **within**

appoggiatura [əˌpɒdʒə'tʊərə] (N) (PL: **appoggiaturas, appoggiature** [əˌpɒdʒə'tʊərɪ]) apoyatura *f*

appoint [ə'pɔɪnt] (VT) **1** (= *nominate*) nombrar (**to** a) • **they ~ed him chairman** le nombraron presidente • **they ~ed him to do it** le nombraron para hacerlo
2 (*frm*) [+ *time, place*] fijar, señalar (**for** para) • **at the ~ed time** a la hora señalada

appointee [əpɔɪn'ti:] (N) persona *f* nombrada

appointive [ə'pɔɪntɪv] (ADJ) • **~ position** (*US*) *puesto que se cubre por nombramiento*

appointment [ə'pɔɪntmənt] (N)

1 (= *arrangement to meet*) **a** (*with client, bank manager etc*) cita *f* • **to meet sb by ~** reunirse con algn mediante cita previa • **I have an ~ at ten** tengo cita a las diez • **do you have an ~?** (*to caller*) ¿tiene usted cita? • **to keep an ~** acudir a una cita • **to make an ~ (with sb)** concertar una cita (con algn) • **to make an ~ for three o'clock** pedir (una) cita para las tres
b (*with dentist, doctor, hairdresser etc*) hora *f* • **I have an ~ at ten** tengo hora a las diez • **do you have an ~?** ¿tiene usted hora? • **to make an ~ (with sb)** pedir hora (con algn) • **to make an ~ for three o'clock** pedir hora para las tres
2 (*to a job*) nombramiento *m* (**to** para); (= *job*) puesto *m*, empleo *m* • **there are still several ~s to be made** todavía hay varios nombramientos por hacer • **"by appointment to HRH"** "proveedores oficiales de S.A.R." • **"appointments (vacant)"** (*Press*) "oferta de empleo"
3 appointments (*frm*) (= *furniture etc*) mobiliario *msing*
CPD ▸ **appointments board, appointments service** (*Univ etc*) oficina *f* de colocación ▸ **appointments bureau** agencia *f* de colocaciones

apportion [ə'pɔːʃən] VT [+ *resources etc*] repartir, distribuir; [+ *blame*] asignar • **the blame is to be ~ed equally** todos tienen la culpa por partes iguales

apportionment [ə'pɔːʃənmənt] N **1** [*of resources etc*] reparto *m*, distribución *f*
2 (*US*) (*Pol*) delimitación *f* de distritos *or* condados

apposite ['æpəzɪt] ADJ apropiado (**to** para)

apposition [ˌæpə'zɪʃən] N **1** [*of position*] yuxtaposición *f*
2 (*Gram*) aposición *f* • **in ~** en aposición

appositional [ˌæpə'zɪʃənl] ADJ aposicional

appraisal [ə'preɪzəl] N **1** (= *valuation*) tasación *f*, valoración *f*
2 [*of worth, importance*] estimación *f*, apreciación *f*; [*of situation, employee*] evaluación *f*

appraise [ə'preɪz] VT **1** (= *value*) [+ *property, jewellery*] tasar, valorar
2 (= *assess*) [+ *worth, importance*] estimar, apreciar; [+ *situation*] evaluar; [+ *staff*] evaluar
3 (*US*) (= *price*) tasar

appraiser [ə'preɪzəʳ] N (*US*) (*Comm, Econ*) tasador(a) *m/f*

appraising [ə'preɪzɪŋ] ADJ [*look etc*] apreciativo

appreciable [ə'priːʃəbl] ADJ **1** (= *noticeable*) apreciable • **an ~ difference** una diferencia apreciable
2 (= *large*) importante, considerable • **an ~ sum** una cantidad importante *or* considerable

appreciably [ə'priːʃəblɪ] ADV [*change, grow*] sensiblemente, perceptiblemente • **he is ~ older than his brother** es considerablemente mayor que su hermano • **the weather had turned ~ colder** el tiempo se había vuelto bastante más frío

appreciate [ə'priːʃɪeɪt] VT **1** (= *be grateful for*) agradecer • **I ~d your help** agradecí tu ayuda • **I ~ the gesture** agradezco el detalle • **we should much ~ it if ...** agradeceríamos mucho que (+ *subjun*)
2 (= *value, esteem*) apreciar, valorar • **he does not ~ music** no sabe apreciar *or* valorar la música • **I am not ~d here** aquí no se me aprecia *or* valora • **we much ~ your work** tenemos un alto concepto de su trabajo
3 (= *understand*) [+ *problem, difference*] comprender • **I ~ your wishes** comprendo sus deseos • **yes, I ~ that** sí, lo comprendo • **to ~ that ...** comprender que ... • **we fully ~ that ...** comprendemos perfectamente que ...
4 (= *be sensitive to*) percibir • **the smallest change can be ~d on this machine** en esta máquina se percibe el más leve cambio
VI [*property etc*] revalorizarse, aumentar(se) en valor

appreciation [əˌpriːʃɪ'eɪʃən] N
1 (= *understanding*) comprensión *f*; [*of art etc*] aprecio *m* • **he showed no ~ of my difficulties** no reconoció mis dificultades • **you have no ~ of art** no sabes apreciar el arte, no entiendes de arte
2 (= *gratitude*) gratitud *f*, agradecimiento *m*; (= *recognition*) apreciación *f*, reconocimiento *m* • **as a token of my ~** en señal de mi gratitud *or* agradecimiento • **she smiled her ~** sonrió agradecida
3 (= *report*) informe *m*; (= *obituary*) nota *f* necrológica, necrológica *f*; (*Literat*) crítica *f*, comentario *m*
4 (= *rise in value*) revalorización *f*, aumento *m* en valor

appreciative [ə'priːʃɪətɪv] ADJ **1** (= *grateful*) [*person*] agradecido; [*smile*] de agradecimiento; [*look*] lleno de agradecimiento • **to be ~ of** [+ *kindness, efforts*] mostrarse agradecido por, agradecer • **he was very ~ of what I had done** se mostró muy agradecido por lo que yo había hecho, agradeció mucho lo que yo había hecho
2 (= *admiring*) [*person*] apreciativo; [*comment*] elogioso; [*look, whistle*] de admiración • **it's rewarding to act before an ~ audience** es gratificante actuar ante un público que sabe apreciar la calidad de lo que ve *or* ante un público apreciativo • **to be ~ of** [+ *art, music, good food*] saber apreciar
3 (= *aware*) • **to be ~ of** [+ *danger, risk*] ser capaz de apreciar • **they were not fully ~ of the danger that lay ahead** no eran capaces de apreciar del todo el peligro que les acechaba

appreciatively [ə'priːʃɪətɪvlɪ] ADV • **he accepted the gift ~** aceptó el regalo agradecido • **the audience clapped** *or* **applauded ~** el público aplaudió agradecido • **she smiled ~** sonrió con admiración, sonrió agradecida

apprehend [ˌæprɪ'hend] (*frm*) VT **1** (= *arrest*) detener, aprehender
2 (= *understand*) comprender
3 (= *fear*) recelar, recelar de

apprehension [ˌæprɪ'henʃən] N **1** (= *fear*) aprensión *f*, temor *m* • **she was filled with ~ at the prospect** le invadía el temor ante esa perspectiva • **my chief ~ is that ...** mi mayor temor es que (+ *subjun*)
2 (*frm*) (= *awareness*) comprensión *f*
3 (*frm*) (= *arrest*) detención *f*

apprehensive [ˌæprɪ'hensɪv] ADJ inquieto • **I was feeling a little ~** sentía cierta aprensión, me sentía inquieto • **he is ~ that he might fail the exam** teme *or* le preocupa suspender el examen • **she is ~ that some accident might befall her children** teme que *or* le preocupa que sus hijos puedan tener un accidente • **to be ~ about sth** estar inquieto por algo • **everyone is ~ about the ordeals to come** todos están inquietos por los terribles momentos que puedan avecinarse • **I'm a bit ~ about the trip** el viaje me tiene inquieto • **they're a little ~ about coming** les inquieta un poco la idea de venir • **we were both ~ about the reaction of the other players** ambos temíamos la reacción de los otros jugadores • **to grow ~** inquietarse • **he gave her an ~ look** la miró aprensivo *or* inquieto, le dirigió una mirada de aprensión *or* inquietud

apprehensively [ˌæprɪ'hensɪvlɪ] ADV con aprensión, con temor

apprentice [ə'prentɪs] N **1** (= *learner*) aprendiz(a) *m/f*
2 (= *beginner*) principiante *mf*
VT • **to ~ sb to** colocar a algn de aprendiz con • **to be ~d to** estar de aprendiz con
CPD ▸ **apprentice electrician** aprendiz(a) *m/f* de electricista

apprenticeship [ə'prentɪʃɪp] N aprendizaje *m* • **to serve one's ~** hacer el aprendizaje

apprise [ə'praɪz] VT (*frm*) informar • **to ~ sb of sth** informar a algn de algo • **to be ~d of** estar al corriente de • **I was never ~d of your decision** no se me comunicó su decisión, no me informaron de su decisión

appro* ['æprəʊ] ABBR (*Comm*) = **approval** • **on ~** a prueba

approach [ə'prəʊtʃ] VT **1** (= *come near*) [+ *place*] acercarse a, aproximarse a; [+ *person*] abordar, dirigirse a • **he ~ed the house** se acercó *or* aproximó a la casa • **a man ~ed me in the street** un hombre me abordó en la calle
2 (*with request etc*) dirigirse a; (= *speak to*) hablar con • **have you tried ~ing the mayor?** ¿has probado a dirigirte al alcalde? • **have you ~ed your bank manager about the loan?** ¿has hablado con el gerente del banco sobre el préstamo? • **he is difficult to ~** no es fácil abordarle
3 (= *tackle*) [+ *subject, problem, job*] abordar • **we must ~ the matter with care** tenemos que abordar el asunto con mucho cuidado • **I ~ it with an open mind** me lo planteo sin ningún prejuicio • **it all depends on how we ~ it** depende de cómo lo enfoquemos
4 (= *approximate to*) (*in quality*) aproximarse a; (*in appearance*) parecerse a • **here the colour ~es blue** aquí el color tira a azul • **it was ~ing midnight** era casi medianoche • **the performance ~ed perfection** la interpretación rayaba en la perfección • **he's ~ing 50** se acerca a los 50 • **no other painter ~es him** (*fig*) no hay otro pintor que se le pueda comparar
VI acercarse
N **1** (= *act*) acercamiento *m*, aproximación *f* • **at the ~ of the enemy** al acercarse *or* aproximarse el enemigo • **at the ~ of Easter** al acercarse la Pascua • **at the ~ of night** al caer la noche • **we observed his ~** lo vimos acercarse
2 (*to problem, subject*) enfoque *m*, planteamiento *m* • **a new ~ to maths** un nuevo enfoque *or* planteamiento sobre las matemáticas • **I don't like your ~ to this matter** no me gusta tu modo de enfocar esta cuestión • **we must think of a new ~** tenemos que idear otro método
3 (= *offer*) oferta *f*, propuesta *f*; (= *proposal*) proposición *f*, propuesta *f* • **to make ~es to sb** dirigirse a algn • **to make amorous ~es to sb** (*liter*) requerir de amores a algn
4 (= *access*) acceso *m* (**to** a); (= *road*) vía *f* de acceso, camino *m* de acceso • **~es** accesos *mpl*; (*Mil*) aproches *mpl* • **the northern ~es of the city** los accesos *or* las vías de acceso a la ciudad por el norte
5 (*Golf*) aproximación *f*, golpe *m* de aproximación
CPD ▸ **approach light** (*Aer*) baliza *f* de aproximación ▸ **approach road** vía *f* de acceso, entrada *f* ▸ **approach shot** (*Golf*) golpe *m* de aproximación

approachability [əˌprəʊtʃə'bɪlɪtɪ] N [*of place*] accesibilidad *f*; [*of person*] carácter *m* accesible

approachable [ə'prəʊtʃəbl] ADJ [*person*]

a

accesible, abordable; [*place*] accesible; [*text, idea, work*] asequible

approaching [ə'prəʊtʃɪŋ] (ADJ) próximo, venidero; [*car, vehicle*] que se acerca en dirección opuesta, que viene en dirección contraria • **the ~ elections** las próximas elecciones

approbation [,æprə'beɪʃən] (N) aprobación *f*

appropriate (ADJ) [ə'prəʊprɪɪt] [*time, place, method, response*] apropiado, adecuado; [*moment*] oportuno, apropiado, adecuado; [*authority, department*] competente, correspondiente • **it is ~ that ...** resulta apropiado *or* adecuado que ... • **it may be ~ to discuss this with your solicitor** quizá sería conveniente que discutiera esto con su abogado • **she's the most ~ person to present the award** es la persona más indicada *or* más adecuada para presentar el premio • **to take ~ action** tomar las medidas apropiadas *or* adecuadas *or* pertinentes • **choose A, B or C as ~** elija A, B o C según corresponda • **this treatment was very ~ for our son** este tratamiento resultó ser muy apropiado *or* adecuado para nuestro hijo • **it would not be ~ for me to discuss individual cases** no sería apropiado que comentara casos concretos • **to take ~ precautions** tomar las debidas precauciones • **it seemed ~ to end with a joke** parecía apropiado terminar con un chiste • **words ~ to the occasion** palabras apropiadas *or* adecuadas para la ocasión • **a job ~ to his talents** un trabajo que se adecúa a sus aptitudes • **A, and where ~, B** A, y en su caso, B • **you will be answering queries, and, where ~, demonstrating our software** dará información a quien la pida y, si se presta, hará demostraciones de nuestro software
(VT) [ə'prəʊprɪeɪt] **1** (= *steal*) apropiarse de
2 (= *set aside*) [+ *funds*] asignar, destinar (**for** a)

appropriately [ə'prəʊprɪɪtlɪ] (ADV) [*dress*] apropiadamente; [*respond*] apropiadamente, adecuadamente; [*act*] debidamente • **~ dressed for the occasion** vestido apropiadamente para la ocasión, vestido acorde con la ocasión • **it's entitled, ~ enough, "Art for the Nation"** se titula, muy apropiadamente, "Arte para la Nación" • **they have committed a crime and they must be punished ~** han cometido un crimen y deben recibir el correspondiente castigo

appropriateness [ə'prəʊprɪɪtnɪs] (N) lo apropiado

appropriation [ə,prəʊprɪ'eɪʃən] (N)
1 (= *confiscation*) apropiación *f* • **illegal ~** apropiación *f* indebida
2 (= *allocation*) asignación *f*
3 (= *funds assigned*) fondos *mpl*; (*US*) crédito *m*
(CPD) ▸ **appropriation account** cuenta *f* de asignación ▸ **appropriation bill** (*US*) (*Pol*) proyecto *m* de ley de presupuestos ▸ **Appropriation Committee** (*US*) (*Pol*) Comisión *f* de gastos de la Cámara de Representantes ▸ **appropriation fund** fondo *m* de asignación

approval [ə'pru:vəl] (N) (= *consent*) aprobación *f*, visto *m* bueno • **does this have your ~?** ¿le da usted su aprobación *or* visto bueno a esto? • **to meet with sb's ~** obtener la aprobación de algn • **a look of ~** una mirada de aprobación • **on ~** (*Comm*) a prueba • **he nodded his ~** asintió con la cabeza
(CPD) ▸ **approval rating** cota *f* de popularidad

approve [ə'pru:v] (VT) [+ *plan, decision, legislation, expenditure, minutes*] aprobar; [+ *drug, medicine, method*] autorizar • **the council has ~d the construction of a hotel** el ayuntamiento ha dado su aprobación para *or* ha aprobado la construcción de un hotel
(VI) **1** (= *be in favour*) • **I think she'll ~** creo que estará de acuerdo, creo que le parecerá bien • **he's not allowed sweets, his mother doesn't ~** no le dejan comer caramelos, a su madre no le gusta
2 (= *give authorization*) dar su aprobación • **if Congress ~s, the project will go ahead next year** si el Congreso da su aprobación *or* lo aprueba, el proyecto se llevará a cabo el año que viene

▸ **approve of** (VI + PREP) **1** • **to ~ of sth: not everyone ~s of the festival** no todo el mundo está de acuerdo con la celebración del festival • **he doesn't ~ of drinking** no le parece bien *or* no le gusta que se beba alcohol • **I don't ~ of her going** no me parece bien *or* no me gusta que vaya
2 • **to ~ of sb: they don't ~ of my fiancé** no les parece bien mi novio

approved (ADJ) (= *accredited*) acreditado • **the ~ method of cleaning** el método de limpieza aconsejado por las autoridades
(CPD) ▸ **approved school** (*Brit*) correccional *m*, reformatorio *m*

approving [ə'pru:vɪŋ] (ADJ) [*words, look*] aprobatorio, de aprobación • **several people gave her ~ glances** varias personas le lanzaron miradas aprobatorias *or* de aprobación

approvingly [ə'pru:vɪŋlɪ] (ADV) con aprobación • **he looked at her ~** la miró con aprobación • **he nodded ~** hizo un gesto de aprobación con la cabeza

approx [ə'prɒks] (ABBR) (= **approximately**) aprox.

approximate (ADJ) [ə'prɒksɪmɪt] aproximado
(VI) [ə'prɒksɪmeɪt] • **to ~ to** aproximarse a, acercarse a

approximately [ə'prɒksɪmɪtlɪ] (ADV) aproximadamente, más o menos • **the film lasts three hours ~** la película dura aproximadamente tres horas, la película dura tres horas (poco) más o menos

approximation [ə,prɒksɪ'meɪʃən] (N) aproximación *f*

appt. (ABBR) (*US*) = **appointment**

appurtenance [ə'pɜ:tɪnəns] (N) (= *appendage*) dependencia *f*; (= *accessory*) accesorio *m* • **the house and its ~s** la casa con sus dependencias

APR, apr (N ABBR) (= **annual(ized) percentage rate**) TAE *f*

Apr (ABBR) (= **April**) ab., abr.

après-ski [,æpreɪ'ski:] (N) après-ski *m*
(ADJ) de après-ski

apricot ['eɪprɪkɒt] (N) **1** (= *fruit*) albaricoque *m*, chabacano *m* (*Mex*), damasco *m* (*LAm*)
2 (= *tree*) albaricoquero *m*, chabacano *m* (*Mex*), damasco *m* (*LAm*)
(CPD) ▸ **apricot jam** mermelada *f* de albaricoque, mermelada *f* de chabacano (*Mex*), mermelada *f* de damasco (*LAm*)

April ['eɪprəl] (N) abril *m*; ▸ **July**
(CPD) ▸ **April Fool** (= *trick*) ≈ inocentada *f* • **~ Fool!** ≈ ¡inocente! ▸ **April Fools' Day** ≈ día *m* de los (Santos) Inocentes (*en el Reino Unido y los EEUU, el 1 abril*) ▸ **April showers** lluvias *fpl* de abril

APRIL FOOLS' DAY

El 1 de abril es **April Fools' Day** en la tradición anglosajona. En ese día se les gastan bromas a los desprevenidos, quienes reciben la denominación de **April Fool** (inocente), y tanto la prensa escrita como la televisión difunden alguna historia falsa con la que sumarse al espíritu del día.

a priori [eɪpraɪ'ɔ:raɪ] (ADV) a priori
(ADJ) apriorístico

apron ['eɪprən] (N) **1** (= *garment*) delantal *m*; (*workman's, mason's etc*) mandil *m*
2 (*Aer*) plataforma *f* de estacionamiento
3 (*Theat*) proscenio *m*
(CPD) ▸ **apron stage** (*Theat*) escena *f* saliente ▸ **apron strings** (*fig*) • **he's tied to his mother's/wife's ~ strings** está pegado a las faldas de su madre/esposa

apropos [,æprə'pəʊ] (ADV) a propósito
(PREP) • **~ of** a propósito de
(ADJ) oportuno

APS (N ABBR) (= **Advanced Photo System**) APS *m*
(ADJ ABBR) APS

apse [æps] (N) ábside *m*

APT (N ABBR) (*Brit*) (*formerly*) (= **Advanced Passenger Train**) ≈ TGV *m*, ≈ AVE *m* (*Sp*)

apt [æpt] (ADJ) (COMPAR: **apter**, SUPERL: **aptest**) **1** (= *suitable*) [*name, title*] acertado, apropiado; [*description*] acertado, atinado; [*remark*] acertado, oportuno • **how apt that he should have been jailed on the anniversary of his crime!** ¡qué oportuno que lo hayan encerrado en el aniversario de su delito!
2 (= *liable*) • **to be apt to do sth** tener tendencia a hacer algo, tender a hacer algo • **we are apt to forget that ...** nos olvidamos fácilmente de que ..., tenemos tendencia *or* tendemos *or* somos propensos a olvidarnos de que ... • **he's apt to be late** tiene tendencia a *or* tiende a *or* suele llegar tarde • **I am apt to be out on Mondays** los lunes no suelo estar • **this is apt to occur** esto tiene tendencia *or* tiende a ocurrir, hay propensión a que esto ocurra
3 (= *clever*) capaz • **he has proved himself an apt pupil** ha demostrado ser un alumno capaz

apt. (ABBR) (= **apartment**) apto.

aptitude ['æptɪtju:d] (N) (= *ability*) aptitud *f*, talento *m*; (= *tendency*) inclinación *f* • **to have an ~ for sth** tener aptitud(es) *or* talento para algo
(CPD) ▸ **aptitude test** prueba *f* de aptitud

aptly ['æptlɪ] (ADV) [*describe, remark*] acertadamente • **he was ~ described by his biographer as ...** fue descrito acertadamente por su biógrafo como ... • **an ~ named plant** una planta con un nombre muy acertado *or* apropiado • **I always felt he had been ~ named** siempre me pareció que su nombre era muy acertado *or* apropiado

aptness ['æptnɪs] (N) [*of name, description*] lo acertado, lo apropiado; [*of remark*] lo acertado, lo oportuno

Apuleius [,æpjə'lɪəs] (N) Apuleyo

aqua ['ækwə] (N) (= *colour*) aguamarina *f*
(ADJ) (*in colour*) aguamarina (*inv*)

aqua-aerobics ['ækwəɛə'rəʊbɪks] (N) aerobic *msing* acuático

aquaculture ['ækwə,kʌltʃə^r] (N) acuicultura *f*

aquafarming ['ækwə,fɑ:mɪŋ] (N) piscicultura *f*

aqualung ['ækwəlʌŋ] (N) escafandra *f* autónoma

aquamarine [,ækwəmə'ri:n] (ADJ) aguamarina (*inv*)
(N) aguamarina *f*

aquanaut ['ækwənɔ:t] (N) submarinista *mf*

aquaplane ['ækwəpleɪn] (N) tabla *f* de esquí acuático
(VI) (*Brit*) (*Aut*) patinar

aquaplaning ['ækwəpleɪnɪŋ] (N) **1** esquí *m* acuático
2 (*Brit*) (*Aut*) aquaplaning *m*

Aquarian [ə'kwɛərɪən] (N) acuario *mf* • **I'm**

an ~ soy acuario

aquarium [ə'kwɛərɪəm] N (PL: **aquariums** *or* **aquaria** [ə'kwɛərɪə]) (= *tank, building*) acuario *m*

Aquarius [ə'kwɛərɪəs] N **1** (= *sign, constellation*) Acuario *m*
2 (= *person*) acuario *mf* • **she's (an) ~** es acuario

aquatic [ə'kwætɪk] ADJ acuático
N **1** (*Bot*) planta *f* acuática
2 (*Zool*) animal *m* acuático

aquatics [ə'kwætɪks] N (*Sport*) deportes *mpl* acuáticos

aquatint ['ækwətɪnt] N acuatinta *f*

aqueduct ['ækwɪdʌkt] N acueducto *m*

aqueous ['eɪkwɪəs] ADJ acuoso, ácueo (*frm*)

aquifer ['ækwɪfəʳ] N acuífero *m*

aquiferous [ə'kwɪfərəs] ADJ acuífero

aquiline ['ækwɪlaɪn] ADJ • **an ~ nose** una nariz aguileña *or* aquilina

Aquinas [ə'kwaɪnəs] N Aquino • **St Thomas ~** Santo Tomás de Aquino

AR ABBR **1** (*Comm*) = **account rendered**
2 (*for tax*) = **annual return**
3 (*report*) = **annual return**
4 (*US*) = **Arkansas**

A/R ABBR = **against all risks**

ARA N ABBR (*Brit*) = **Associate of the Royal Academy**

Arab ['ærəb] ADJ árabe
N **1** (= *person*) árabe *mf*
2 (= *horse*) caballo *m* árabe
CPD ▸ **Arab League** Liga *f* Árabe ▸ **Arab Spring** Primavera *f* árabe

arabesque [,ærə'besk] N arabesco *m*

Arabia [ə'reɪbɪə] N Arabia *f*

Arabian [ə'reɪbɪən] ADJ árabe, arábigo • **the ~ Desert** el desierto Arábigo • **the ~ Gulf** el golfo Arábigo • **the ~ Sea** el mar de Omán • **The ~ Nights** Las mil y una noches
N árabe *mf*

Arabic ['ærəbɪk] ADJ árabe
N (*Ling*) árabe *m*
CPD ▸ **Arabic numerals** numeración *fsing* arábiga

Arabist ['ærəbɪst] N arabista *mf*

Arabization [,ærəbaɪ'zeɪʃən] N arabización *f*

Arabize ['ærəbaɪz] VT arabizar

arable ['ærəbl] ADJ cultivable, arable (*esp LAm*) • **~ farm** granja *f* agrícola • **~ farming** agricultura *f* • **~ land** tierra *f* de cultivo *or* cultivable
N tierra *f* de cultivo, tierra *f* cultivable
CPD ▸ **arable farmer** agricultor(a) *m/f*

arachnid [ə'ræknɪd] N arácnido *m*

arachnophobia [ə,ræknə'fəʊbɪə] N aracnofobia *f*

Aragon ['ærəgən] N Aragón *m*

Aragonese [,ærəgə'ni:z] ADJ aragonés
N **1** (= *person*) aragonés/esa *m/f*
2 (*Ling*) aragonés *m*

ARAM N ABBR (*Brit*) = **Associate of the Royal Academy of Music**

Aramaic [,ærə'meɪɪk] N arameo *m*

arbiter ['ɑ:bɪtəʳ] N **1** (= *adjudicator*) árbitro/a *m/f*
2 (*fig*) • **to be an ~ of taste/style** ser un árbitro del buen gusto/de la moda

arbitrage [,ɑ:bɪ'trɑ:ʒ] N arbitraje *m*

arbitrager ['ɑ:bɪ,trɑ:ʒəʳ] N arbitrajista *mf*

arbitrageur [,ɑ:bɪtrɑ:'ʒɜ:ʳ] N arbitrajista *mf*

arbitrarily ['ɑ:bɪtrərɪlɪ] ADV arbitrariamente

arbitrariness ['ɑ:bɪtrərɪnɪs] N arbitrariedad *f*

arbitrary ['ɑ:bɪtrərɪ] ADJ arbitrario

arbitrate ['ɑ:bɪtreɪt] VT resolver, juzgar
VI arbitrar, mediar (**between** entre)

arbitration [,ɑ:bɪ'treɪʃən] N arbitraje *m* • **they went to ~** recurrieron al arbitraje • **the question was referred to ~** se confió el asunto a un tribunal de arbitraje

arbitrator ['ɑ:bɪtreɪtəʳ] N árbitro/a *m/f*, mediador(a) *m/f*

arbor ['ɑ:bəʳ] N (*US*) = **arbour**

arboreal [ɑ:'bɔ:rɪəl] ADJ arbóreo

arboretum [,ɑ:bə'ri:təm] N (PL: **arboretums, arboreta** [,ɑ:bə'ri:tə]) arboreto *m*, jardín *m* botánico arbóreo

arboriculture ['ɑ:bərɪ,kʌltʃəʳ] N arboricultura *f*

arborist ['ɑ:bərɪst] N arboricultor(a) *m/f*

arbour, arbor (*US*) ['ɑ:bəʳ] N cenador *m*, pérgola *f*

arbutus [ɑ:'bju:təs] N madroño *m*

ARC N ABBR **1** (*Med*) = **AIDS-related complex**
2 = **American Red Cross**

arc [ɑ:k] N arco *m*
VI arquearse, formar un arco
CPD ▸ **arc lamp** lámpara *f* de arco; (*in welding*) arco *m* voltaico ▸ **arc light** luz *f* de arco ▸ **arc welding** soldadura *f* por arco

arcade [ɑ:'keɪd] N **1** (= *shopping precinct*) galería *f* comercial; (*round public square*) soportales *mpl*, pórtico *m*; (*in building*) galería *f* interior; (*in church*) claustro *m*
2 (*Brit*) (*also* **amusement arcade**) sala *f* de juegos, salón *m* de juegos
3 (*Archit*) (= *arch*) bóveda *f*; (= *passage*) arcada *f*
CPD ▸ **arcade game** videojuego *m*

Arcadia [ɑ:'keɪdɪə] N Arcadia *f*

Arcadian [ɑ:'keɪdɪən] ADJ árcade, arcádico
N árcade *mf*, arcadio/a *m/f*

Arcady ['ɑ:kədɪ] N Arcadia *f*

arcane [ɑ:'keɪn] ADJ arcano

arch¹ [ɑ:tʃ] N **1** (*Archit*) arco *m*; (= *vault*) bóveda *f*
2 [*of foot*] puente *m* • **fallen ~es** pies *mpl* planos
3 (*dental*) arcada *f*, arco *m*
VT [+ *back, body etc*] arquear • **to ~ one's eyebrows** arquear las cejas
VI **1** arquearse, formar un arco
2 • **to ~ over** (*Archit*) abovedar

arch² [ɑ:tʃ] ADJ **1** (= *superior*) [*look*] de superioridad; [*remark*] en tono de superioridad
2 (= *mischievous*) malicioso
3 (= *cunning*) [*glance, person*] astuto

arch³ [ɑ:tʃ] ADJ (= *great*) • **an ~ criminal** un consumado delincuente • **an ~ hypocrite** un consumado hipócrita, un hipócrita de primer orden; ▷ **arch-enemy**

archaeological, archeological (*esp US*) [,ɑ:kɪə'lɒdʒɪkəl] ADJ arqueológico

archaeologist, archeologist (*esp US*) [,ɑ:kɪ'ɒlədʒɪst] N arqueólogo/a *m/f*

archaeology, archeology (*esp US*) [,ɑ:kɪ'ɒlədʒɪ] N arqueología *f*

archaic [ɑ:'keɪɪk] ADJ arcaico

archaism ['ɑ:keɪɪzəm] N arcaísmo *m*

archangel ['ɑ:k,eɪndʒəl] N arcángel *m*

archbishop ['ɑ:tʃbɪʃəp] N arzobispo *m* • **the Archbishop of Canterbury** el Arzobispo de Canterbury

archbishopric [ɑ:tʃ'bɪʃəprɪk] N arzobispado *m*

archdeacon ['ɑ:tʃ'di:kən] N arcediano *m*

archdiocese ['ɑ:tʃ'daɪəsɪs] N archidiócesis *f inv*

archduchess ['ɑ:tʃ'dʌtʃɪs] N archiduquesa *f*

archduchy ['ɑ:tʃ'dʌtʃɪ] N archiducado *m*

archduke ['ɑ:tʃ'dju:k] N archiduque *m*

arched [ɑ:tʃt] ADJ [*roof, window, doorway*] abovedado; [*bridge*] con arcos, con arcadas; [*brow*] arqueado

arch-enemy ['ɑ:tʃ'enɪmɪ] N archienemigo/a *m/f*

archeological [,ɑ:kɪə'lɒdʒɪkəl] ADJ (*esp US*) = **archaeological**

archeologist [,ɑ:kɪ'ɒlədʒɪst] N (*esp US*) = **archaeologist**

archeology [,ɑ:kɪ'ɒlədʒɪ] N (*esp US*) = **archaeology**

archer ['ɑ:tʃəʳ] N arquero/a *m/f*

archery ['ɑ:tʃərɪ] N tiro *m* con arco

archetypal [ɑ:kɪ'taɪpl] ADJ arquetípico

archetypally [,ɑ:kɪ'taɪpəlɪ] ADV arquetípicamente

archetype ['ɑ:kɪtaɪp] N **1** (= *original*) arquetipo *m*
2 (= *epitome*) modelo *m*, arquetipo *m*

archetypical [,ɑ:kɪ'tɪpɪkəl] ADJ = **archetypal**

archiepiscopal [,ɑ:kɪɪ'pɪskəpəl] ADJ arzobispal

Archimedes [,ɑ:kɪ'mi:di:z] N Arquímedes • **~' screw** rosca *f* de Arquímedes

archipelago [,ɑ:kɪ'pelɪgəʊ] N (PL: **archipelagos, archipelagoes**) archipiélago *m*

archiphoneme ['ɑ:kɪ,fəʊni:m] N archifonema *m*

architect ['ɑ:kɪtekt] N **1** (= *professional*) arquitecto/a *m/f*
2 (*fig*) artífice *mf* • **the ~ of victory** el artífice de la victoria

architectonic [,ɑ:kɪtek'tɒnɪk] ADJ arquitectónico

architectural [,ɑ:kɪ'tektʃərəl] ADJ arquitectónico

architecturally [,ɑ:kɪ'tektʃərəlɪ] ADV arquitectónicamente • **an ~ striking building** un edificio impresionante desde el punto de vista arquitectónico

architecture ['ɑ:kɪtektʃəʳ] N arquitectura *f*

architrave ['ɑ:kɪtreɪv] N arquitrabe *m*

archival [ɑ:'kaɪvəl] ADJ [*material*] de archivo

archive ['ɑ:kaɪv] N (*gen*) archivo *m*; (*Comput*) archivo *m*, fichero *m*
VT archivar
CPD ▸ **archive file** (*Comput*) fichero *m* archivado ▸ **archive film** imágenes *fpl* de archivo ▸ **archive material** material *m* de archivo

archivist ['ɑ:kɪvɪst] N archivero/a *m/f*, archivista *mf* (*LAm*)

archly [ɑ:tʃlɪ] ADV **1** (= *in a superior way*) con aire de superioridad
2 (= *mischievously*) maliciosamente
3 (= *cunningly*) con astucia

archness ['ɑ:tʃnɪs] N **1** (= *air of superiority*) aire *m* de superioridad
2 (= *mischievousness*) malicia *f*
3 (= *cunning*) astucia *f*

archpriest ['ɑ:tʃ'pri:st] N arcipreste *m*

archway ['ɑ:tʃweɪ] N (= *passage*) pasaje *m*

> **ARCHBISHOP**
> En la Iglesia Anglicana (**Church of England**) existen dos arzobispos: **Archbishop of York** y **Archbishop of Canterbury**, siendo este el jefe espiritual de la Iglesia. Ambos arzobispos, que ocupan un escaño en la Cámara de los Lores, son nombrados por el monarca con el asesoramiento del Primer Ministro y los representantes de la Iglesia Anglicana. El Arzobispo de Canterbury es quien corona al nuevo monarca británico en la ceremonia de la coronación (**Coronation Ceremony**) y oficia en las bodas reales. Los dos arzobispos ejercen autoridad administrativa sobre el clero en sus respectivos arzobispados (**provinces**).
> ▷ **CHURCHES OF ENGLAND/SCOTLAND**

abovedado; (= *arch*) arco *m*

ARCM N ABBR (*Brit*) = **Associate of the Royal College of Music**

arctic ['ɑ:ktɪk] ADJ **1** (*Geog*) ártico
2 (*fig*) (= *cold*) glacial, gélido
N • **the Arctic** el Ártico
CPD ▸ **Arctic Circle** Círculo *m* Polar Ártico ▸ **arctic fox** zorro *m* polar ▸ **Arctic Ocean** océano *m* Ártico

ARD N ABBR (*US*) = **acute respiratory disease**

Ardennes [ɑ:'denz] NPL Ardenas *fpl*

ardent ['ɑ:dənt] ADJ **1** (= *enthusiastic*) [*supporter, admirer, opponent*] apasionado, ferviente; [*feminist, nationalist*] acérrimo; [*desire*] ardiente, ferviente; [*belief, plea*] ferviente • **she is ~ in her opposition to the proposals** se opone ardientemente a las propuestas
2 (= *passionate*) [*lover, lovemaking*] apasionado

ardently ['ɑ:dəntlɪ] ADV **1** (= *enthusiastically*) [*support, defend, desire*] ardientemente, fervientemente; [*speak*] con vehemencia
2 (= *passionately*) [*kiss*] apasionadamente

ardour, ardor (*US*) ['ɑ:dəʳ] N **1** (*for sth*) (= *love*) pasión *f*; (= *fervour, eagerness*) fervor *m*, ardor *m*
2 (*romantic*) ardor *m*, pasión *f*

arduous ['ɑ:djʊəs] ADJ [*work, task*] arduo; [*climb, journey*] arduo, penoso; [*conditions*] riguroso, duro

arduously ['ɑ:djʊəslɪ] ADV [*work*] arduamente; [*climb*] con dificultad, penosamente

arduousness ['ɑ:djʊəsnɪs] N [*of work, task*] lo arduo; [*of climb, journey*] lo arduo, lo penoso; [*of conditions*] lo riguroso, lo duro

are [ɑ:ʳ] PRESENT *2nd pers sing, 1st, 2nd, 3rd pers pl of* **be**

area ['ɛərɪə] N **1** (= *surface measure*) superficie *f*, extensión *f*, área *f* • **the lake is 130 square miles in ~** el lago tiene 130 millas cuadradas de superficie *or* de extensión, el lago se extiende sobre una superficie *or* área de 130 millas cuadradas; ▹ **surface**
2 (= *region*) [*of country*] zona *f*, región *f*; [*of city*] zona *f*; (*Admin, Pol*) zona *f*, área *f* • **in mountainous ~s of Europe and Asia** en las zonas *or* regiones montañosas de Europa y Asia • **an ~ of outstanding natural beauty** una zona de una belleza natural excepcional • **an ~ of high unemployment** una zona con un alto índice de desempleo • **the London ~** la zona *or* el área de Londres • **rural/urban ~s** zonas *fpl* rurales/urbanas; ▹ **catchment, disaster, sterling**
3 (= *extent, patch*) zona *f* • **the blast caused damage over a wide ~** la explosión causó daños en una extensa zona • **there is an ~ of wasteland behind the houses** hay un terreno baldío detrás de las casas • **when applying the cream avoid the ~ around the eyes** evite aplicarse la crema en la zona que rodea los ojos
4 (= *space*) zona *f* • **communal ~** zona *f* comunitaria • **dining ~** comedor *m* • **picnic ~** merendero *m* • **play ~** zona *f* recreativa • **reception ~** recepción *f* • **slum ~** barrio *m* bajo • **smoking ~s are provided** se han habilitado zonas para fumadores • **waiting ~** zona *f* de espera
5 (*Sport*) (*also* **penalty area**) área *f* de penalti, área *f* de castigo; ▹ **goal**
6 (*Brit*) (= *basement courtyard*) patio *m*
7 (= *sphere*) [*of knowledge*] campo *m*, terreno *m*; [*of responsibility*] esfera *f* • **I am not a specialist in this ~** no soy especialista en este campo *or* terreno • **~ of study** campo *m* de estudio • **that is not my ~ of competence** eso no es competencia mía • **it affects all ~s of our lives** afecta a todos los sectores de nuestra vida • **it's a potential ~ of concern** puede llegar a ser motivo de preocupación • **there are still some ~s of disagreement** aún existen discrepancias sobre algunos puntos • **one of the problem ~s is lax security** una cuestión problemática es la falta de seguridad; ▹ **grey**
CPD ▸ **area code** (*US*) (*Telec*) prefijo *m* (local), código *m* territorial ▸ **area manager** jefe/a *m/f* de zona ▸ **area office** oficina *f* regional ▸ **area representative** representante *mf* de zona

arena [ə'ri:nə] N **1** (= *stadium*) estadio *m*
2 (= *circus*) pista *f*
3 (*Bullfighting*) (= *building*) plaza *f*; (= *pit*) ruedo *m*
4 (*fig*) (= *stage*) palestra *f* • **the political ~** el ruedo político

aren't [ɑ:nt] = **are not**

areola [ə'rɪələ] N (PL: **areolas** *or* **areolae** [ə'rɪəli:]) aureola *f*, areola *f*

Argentina [,ɑ:dʒən'ti:nə] N Argentina *f*

Argentine ['ɑ:dʒəntaɪn] ADJ argentino
N **1** (= *person*) argentino/a *m/f*
2 • **the ~** la Argentina

Argentinian [,ɑ:dʒən'tɪnɪən] ADJ argentino
N argentino/a *m/f*

Argie‡ ['ɑ:dʒɪ] N (*pej*) = **Argentinian**

argon ['ɑ:gɒn] N argón *m*

Argonaut ['ɑ:gənɔ:t] N argonauta *m*

argot ['ɑ:gəʊ] N argot *m*

arguable ['ɑ:gjʊəbl] ADJ discutible • **it is ~ whether ...** no está probado que ... • **it is ~ that ...** se puede decir que ...

arguably ['ɑ:gjʊəblɪ] ADV • **he is ~ the best player in the world** se podría mantener que es el mejor jugador del mundo

argue ['ɑ:gju:] VI **1** (= *disagree*) discutir; (= *fight*) pelearse • **his parents were always arguing** sus padres estaban siempre discutiendo *or* peleándose • **he started arguing with the referee** empezó a discutir con el árbitro • **to ~ (with sb) about** *or* **over sth** discutir *or* pelearse (con algn) por algo • **they were arguing about what to do next** estaban discutiendo sobre qué hacer después • **she achieved it, you can't ~ with that** lo logró, eso es indiscutible • **I didn't dare ~** no me atreví a llevar la contraria • **just get in and don't ~ (with me)!** ¡entra y no (me) discutas!
2 (= *reason*) • **he ~s well** presenta sus argumentos de modo convincente, razona bien • **to ~ against sth** dar razones en contra de algo • **to ~ against doing sth** dar razones para que no se haga algo • **to ~ for sth** abogar por algo • **he ~d for the president's powers to be restricted** abogó en favor de que se limitaran los poderes del presidente • **he ~s from a deeply religious conviction** sus argumentos parten de una profunda convicción religiosa
3 (= *indicate*) • **his lack of experience ~s against him** su falta de experiencia es un factor en su contra • **it ~s well for him** es un elemento a su favor
VT **1** (= *debate*) discutir • **I won't ~ that point** no voy a discutir ese punto; ▹ **toss**
2 (= *persuade*) • **he ~d me into/out of going** me convenció de que fuera/no fuera • **he ~d his way out of getting the sack** consiguió que no lo despidieran con buenos razonamientos
3 (= *maintain*) sostener • **to ~ that** sostener que • **he ~d that it couldn't be done** sostenía que no se podía hacer • **it could be ~d that we are not doing enough** se podría decir que no estamos haciendo lo suficiente
4 (= *cite, claim*) (*esp Jur*) alegar • **the defence ~d diminished responsibility** la defensa alegó un atenuante de responsabilidad
5 • **to ~ a case a** (*Jur*) presentar un pleito, exponer un pleito
b (*fig*) • **a well ~d case** un argumento bien expuesto • **to ~ the case for sth** abogar en favor de algo
6 (= *suggest*) indicar • **it ~s a certain lack of feeling** indica cierta falta de sentimientos
▸ **argue out** VT + ADV [+ *problem*] discutir a fondo • **they ~d the whole thing out over dinner** discutieron a fondo todo el asunto durante la cena

argument ['ɑ:gjʊmənt] N **1** (= *disagreement*) discusión *f*; (= *fight*) pelea *f* • **I don't want any ~ (about it)** no quiero discutir, no hay discusión que valga • **to get into an ~ (with sb)** empezar a discutir (con algn) • **to have an ~ (with sb)** discutir (con algn); (*more heatedly*) pelearse (con algn) • **we had an ~ about money** tuvimos una discusión *or* discutimos por razones de dinero • **let's not have an ~ about it** no discutamos • **there was an ~ over the missing plate** hubo una discusión sobre el plato que faltaba • **you've only heard one side of the ~** tú solo conoces una cara del asunto • IDIOM: • **he had an ~ with a wall** (*hum*) se dio contra la pared
2 (= *debate*) polémica *f* • **there is some ~ as to whether or not it's possible** hay bastante polémica sobre si es posible o no • **she is open to ~** está dispuesta a discutirlo • **the conclusion is open to ~** la conclusión se presta a discusión *or* es discutible • **to win/lose an ~** ganar/perder (en) un enfrentamiento; ▹ **sake**
3 (= *case*) argumento *m*, razones *fpl* • **there is a strong ~ for** *or* **in favour of doing nothing** existen argumentos *or* razones de peso para *or* en favor de no hacer nada • **an ~ could be made for government intervention** se podrían alegar razones para la intervención del gobierno
4 (= *reasoning*) razonamiento *m* • **if you take this ~ one step further** si llevas el razonamiento un poco más allá • **his ~ is that ...** él sostiene que ...; ▹ **line¹**
5 (= *synopsis*) argumento *m*, resumen *m*
6 (*Jur*) • **opening ~** exposición *f* inicial • **closing ~** conclusiones *fpl* finales

argumentation [,ɑ:gjʊmən'teɪʃən] N argumentación *f*, argumentos *mpl*

argumentative [,ɑ:gjʊ'mentətɪv] ADJ [*person*] amigo de las discusiones, discutidor

Argus ['ɑ:gəs] N Argos

argy-bargy* ['ɑ:dʒɪ'bɑ:dʒɪ] N (*Brit*) pelotera* *f*, altercado *m*

aria ['ɑ:rɪə] N aria *f*

Arian ['ɛərɪən] ADJ arriano
N arriano/a *m/f*

Arianism ['ɛərɪənɪzəm] N arrianismo *m*

ARIBA [ə'ri:bə] N ABBR (*Brit*) = **Associate of the Royal Institute of British Architects**

arid ['ærɪd] ADJ (*lit, fig*) árido

aridity [ə'rɪdɪtɪ] N (*lit, fig*) aridez *f*

Arien ['ɛərɪən] N aries *mf* • **I'm an ~** soy aries

Aries ['ɛəri:z] N **1** (= *sign, constellation*) Aries *m*
2 (= *person*) aries *mf* • **I'm (an) ~** soy aries

aright [ə'raɪt] ADV correctamente, acertadamente • **if I heard you ~** si le oí bien • **if I understand you ~** si le entiendo correctamente • **to set ~** rectificar

arise [ə'raɪz] (PT: **arose** [ə'rəʊz]) (PP: **arisen** [ə'rɪzn]) VI **1** (= *occur*) surgir, presentarse • **difficulties have ~n** han surgido *or* se han presentado dificultades • **a storm arose** (*liter*) se levantó una tormenta • **a great clamour arose** (*liter*) se produjo un tremendo clamor • **should the need ~** de ser

necesario • **should the occasion ~** si se presenta la ocasión • **the question does not ~** no hay tal problema, la cuestión no viene al caso • **the question ~s whether …** se plantea el problema de si …
2 (= *result*) surgir • **there are problems arising from his attitude** surgen problemas a raíz de su actitud • **matters arising (from the last meeting)** asuntos pendientes (de la última reunión) • **arising from this, can you say …?** partiendo de esta base, ¿puede usted decir …?
3† (= *get up*) levantarse, alzarse • **arise!** (*slogan*) ¡arriba!

arisen [ə'rɪzn] PP *of* arise
aristo* ['ærɪstəʊ] N (*Brit*) aristócrata *mf*
aristocracy [,ærɪs'tɒkrəsɪ] N (= *nobility*) aristocracia *f*
aristocrat ['ærɪstəkræt] N aristócrata *mf*
aristocratic [,ærɪstə'krætɪk] ADJ aristocrático
Aristophanes [,ærɪs'tɒfəni:z] N Aristófanes
Aristotelian [,ærɪstə'ti:lɪən] ADJ aristotélico
Aristotelianism [,ærɪstə'ti:lɪənɪzəm] N aristotelismo *m*
Aristotle ['ærɪstɒtl] N Aristóteles
arithmetic N [ə'rɪθmətɪk] aritmética *f*; ▹ **mental**
ADJ [,ærɪθ'metɪk] aritmético
• **~ progression** progresión *f* aritmética
CPD [,ærɪθ'metɪk] ▸ **arithmetic mean** media *f* aritmética
arithmetical [,ærɪθ'metɪkəl] ADJ = **arithmetic**
arithmetician [ə,rɪθmə'tɪʃən] N aritmético/a *m/f*
Ariz. ABBR (*US*) = **Arizona**
ark [ɑ:k] N arca *f* • **Noah's Ark** el Arca *f* de Noé • **Ark of the Covenant** Arca *f* de la Alianza • IDIOM: • **it's out of the Ark*** viene del año de la nana*
Ark. ABBR (*US*) = **Arkansas**
arm[1] [ɑ:m] N **1** (*Anat*) brazo *m* • **with one's arms folded** con los brazos cruzados • **to give sb one's arm** dar el brazo a algn • **to hold sth/sb in one's arms** coger algo/a algn en brazos • **arm in arm**: • **he walked arm in arm with his wife** iba cogido del brazo de su mujer • **they were walking along arm in arm** iban cogidos del brazo • **they rushed into each other's arms** corrieron a echarse uno en brazos del otro • **this pushed them into the arms of the French** esto les obligó a buscar el apoyo de los franceses • **he held it at arm's length** (*lit*) lo sujetaba con el brazo extendido; ▹ **to keep sb at arm's length** • **she came in on her father's arm** entró del brazo de su padre • **with his coat over his arm** con el abrigo sobre el brazo • **to put one's arm(s) round sb** abrazar a algn • **within arm's reach** al alcance de la mano • **to take sb's arm** coger a algn del brazo • **to take sb in one's arms** tomar a algn en sus brazos • **to throw one's arms round sb's neck** echar los brazos al cuello a algn • **he had a parcel under his arm** llevaba un paquete debajo del brazo *or* bajo el brazo • IDIOMS: • **to cost an arm and a leg*** costar un ojo de la cara* • **to keep sb at arm's length** (*fig*) mantener las distancias con algn • **a list as long as your arm** una lista kilométrica • **the (long *or* strong) arm of the law** el brazo de la ley • **to welcome sth/sb with open arms** recibir algo/a algn con los brazos abiertos • **to put the arm on sb** (*US**) presionar a algn • **I'd give my right arm to own it** daría mi brazo derecho por que fuera mío; ▹ **babe, chance, fold[2], twist**
2 (= *part*) **a** [*of chair, river, crane, pick-up*] brazo *m*; [*of spectacles*] patilla *f*; [*of coat*] manga *f* • **arm of the sea** brazo *m* de mar
b [*of organization, company, also Mil*] (= *division*) división *f*; (= *section*) sección *f*; (*Pol*) brazo *m* • **the military arm of the Western alliance** el brazo armado de la alianza occidental • **the political arm of a terrorist group** el brazo político de un grupo terrorista; ▹ **fleet**
arm[2] [ɑ:m] VT [+ *person, ship, nation*] armar, proveer de armas; [+ *missile*] equipar • **to arm sb with sth** (*lit*) armar a algn de *or* con algo; (*fig*) proveer a algn de algo • **to arm o.s. with sth** (*lit*) armarse de *or* con algo; (*fig*) armarse de algo • **she had armed herself with a rifle** se había armado de *or* con un rifle • **I armed myself with all the information I would need** me armé de toda la información que necesitaría
VI armarse (**against** contra); ▹ **arms**
armada [ɑ:'mɑ:də] N flota *f*, armada *f* • **the Armada** (*Hist*) la (Armada) Invencible
armadillo [,ɑ:mə'dɪləʊ] N armadillo *m*
Armageddon [,ɑ:mə'gedn] N (*Bible*) la batalla de Armagedón; (*fig*) la guerra del fin del mundo
armament ['ɑ:məmənt] N armamento *m* • **~s** (= *weapons*) armamento *msing*
CPD ▸ **the armaments industry** la industria de armamento, la industria armamentista *or* armamentística
armature ['ɑ:mətjʊə^{r}] N **1** (*Bot, Elec, Zool*) armadura *f*; [*of dynamo*] inducido *m*
2 (= *supporting framework*) armazón *f*
armband ['ɑ:mbænd] N brazalete *m*
armchair ['ɑ:mtʃɛə^{r}] N sillón *m*
CPD ▸ **armchair general** general *mf* de salón ▸ **armchair strategist** estratega *mf* de salón, estratega *mf* de café
armed [ɑ:md] PT, PP *of* **arm[2]**
ADJ [*conflict, struggle, resistance*] armado • **their men were not ~** sus hombres no iban armados • **their men were heavily ~** sus hombres iban bien provistos de armas • **~ guards** guardias *mpl* armados • **the ~ forces** las fuerzas armadas • **~ robbery** robo *m* a mano armada • **~ with sth** (*lit, fig*) armado de *or* con algo • **they were ~ with machine guns** iban armados de *or* con ametralladoras • **she came ~ with reams of statistics** vino armada de *or* con páginas y páginas de estadísticas • **the missile was ~ with a conventional warhead** el misil estaba equipado de *or* con una cabeza convencional • IDIOM: • **~ to the teeth** armado hasta los dientes
CPD ▸ **armed intervention** intervención *f* armada • **they want to avoid ~ intervention** quieren evitar la intervención armada ▸ **armed response unit** unidad *f* de respuesta armada ▸ **armed response vehicle** vehículo *m* de respuesta armada
-armed [ɑ:md] ADJ (*ending in compounds*) de brazos … • **strong-armed** de brazos fuertes • **one-armed** manco
Armenia [ɑ:'mi:nɪə] N Armenia *f*
Armenian [ɑ:'mi:nɪən] ADJ armenio
N **1** (= *person*) armenio/a *m/f*
2 (*Ling*) armenio *m*
armful ['ɑ:mfʊl] N brazada *f*
armhole ['ɑ:mhəʊl] N sobaquera *f*, sisa *f*
armistice ['ɑ:mɪstɪs] N armisticio *m*
CPD ▸ **Armistice Day** Día *m* del Armisticio
armlet ['ɑ:mlɪt] N brazal *m*
armload ['ɑ:mləʊd] N (= *armful*) brazada *f* • **he arrived carrying an ~ of firewood** llegó cargando una brazada de leña • **he was carrying an ~ of books** llevaba un montón de libros en los brazos
armlock ['ɑ:m'lɒk] N llave *f* de brazo • **to hold sb in an ~** inmovilizar a algn con una llave
armor ['ɑ:mə^{r}] N (*US*) = **armour**
armored ['ɑ:məd] ADJ (*US*) = **armoured**
armorer ['ɑ:mərə^{r}] N (*US*) = **armourer**
armorial [ɑ:'mɔ:rɪəl] ADJ heráldico • **~ bearings** escudo *m* de armas
armor-piercing ['ɑ:mə,pɪəsɪŋ] ADJ (*US*) = **armour-piercing**
armor-plated ['ɑ:mə'pleɪtɪd] ADJ (*US*) = **armour-plated**
armory ['ɑ:mərɪ] N (*US*) = **armoury**
armour, armor (*US*) ['ɑ:mə^{r}] N **1** (*Mil, Zool*) (*also fig*) armadura *f*; (= *steel plates*) blindaje *m*
2 (= *tank forces*) divisiones *fpl* acorazadas, fuerzas *fpl* blindadas
VT blindar, acorazar
CPD ▸ **armour plate** blindaje *m* ▸ **armour plating** = **armour plate**
armour-clad ['ɑ:məklæd] ADJ = **armoured**
armoured, armored (*US*) ['ɑ:məd] ADJ acorazado, blindado • **~ car** carro *m* blindado • **~ column** columna *f* blindada • **~ personnel carrier** vehículo *m* blindado para el transporte de tropas
armourer, armorer (*US*) ['ɑ:mərə^{r}] N armero *m*
armour-piercing, armor-piercing (*US*) ['ɑ:mə,pɪəsɪŋ] ADJ [*shell*] perforante
armour-plated, armor-plated (*US*) ['ɑ:mə'pleɪtɪd] ADJ = **armoured**
armoury, armory (*US*) ['ɑ:mərɪ] N **1** (*lit, fig*) (= *arsenal*) arsenal *m*
2 (*US*) (= *arms factory*) fábrica *f* de armas
armpit ['ɑ:mpɪt] N **1** (*Anat*) sobaco *m*, axila *f*
2* (= *unpleasant place*) cloaca *f*
armrest ['ɑ:mrest] N [*of chair*] brazo *m*; (*in bus, plane etc*) apoyo *m* para el brazo, apoyabrazos *m inv*
arms [ɑ:mz] NPL **1** (= *weapons*) armas *fpl* • **to bear ~** portar armas • **to lay down one's ~** deponer *or* rendir las armas • **order ~!** ¡descansen armas! • **present ~!** ¡presenten armas! • **shoulder ~!** • **slope ~!** ¡sobre el hombro, armas! • **to take up ~ (against sth/sb)** tomar las armas (contra algo/algn) • **by 1809 Britain had 817,000 men under ~** en 1809 Gran Bretaña tenía 817.000 hombres en sus filas *or* en las fuerzas armadas • IDIOM: • **to be up in ~ about sth**: • **environment groups are up in ~ about the plan** los grupos ecologistas están oponiéndose al plan enfurecidamente • **no need to get up in ~ over such a small thing** no hace falta poner el grito en el cielo *or* ponerse así por una cosa tan insignificante; ▹ **rise**
2 (= *coat of arms*) escudo *msing* de armas, blasón *msing*
CPD ▸ **arms control** control *m* de armamento(s) ▸ **arms dealer** traficante *mf* de armas ▸ **arms embargo** embargo *m* de armas ▸ **arms factory** fábrica *f* de armas ▸ **arms inspection** inspección *f* de armamentos ▸ **arms inspector** inspector(a) *m/f* de armamentos ▸ **arms limitation** límite *m* armamentístico ▸ **arms manufacturer** fabricante *mf* de armas ▸ **the arms race** la carrera armamentística, la carrera de armamentos ▸ **arms reduction** reducción *f* de armas ▸ **arms trade** tráfico *m* de armas
arm-twisting* ['ɑ:m,twɪstɪŋ] N presión *f*
arm-wrestle ['ɑ:mresl] VI • **to arm-wrestle with sb** echar un pulso a algn
arm-wrestling ['ɑ:m,reslɪŋ] N pulso *m*, pulseada *f* (*S. Cone*)
army ['ɑ:mɪ] N **1** (*Mil*) ejército *m* • **to be in the ~** ser militar • **to join the ~** alistarse
2 (*fig*) ejército *m*, multitud *f*
CPD ▸ **army base** base *f* militar ▸ **army**

chaplain capellán *m* castrense ▸ **army corps** cuerpo *m* del ejército ▸ **army doctor** médico/a *m/f* militar ▸ **army life** vida *f* militar ▸ **Army List** lista *f* de oficiales del ejército ▸ **army officer** oficial *mf* del ejército ▸ **army of occupation** ejército *m* de ocupación ▸ **army slang** argot *m* militar ▸ **army surplus** excedentes *mpl* del ejército

army-issue [ˈɑ:mɪ,ɪʃu:] ADJ del ejército, proporcionado por el ejército

arnica [ˈɑ:nɪkə] N árnica *f*

aroma [əˈrəʊmə] N aroma *m* (**of** de, a)

aromatherapist [əˈrəʊməˈθerəpɪst] N aromaterapeuta *mf*

aromatherapy [əˈrəʊməˈθerəpɪ] N aromaterapia *f*

CPD ▸ **aromatherapy massage** masaje *m* de aromaterapia ▸ **aromatherapy oil** aceite *m* esencial de aromaterapia

aromatic [,ærəʊˈmætɪk] ADJ aromático

arose [əˈrəʊz] PT *of* **arise**

around [əˈraʊnd]

When ***around*** *is an element in a phrasal verb, eg* ***look around, move around, potter around****, look up the verb.*

ADV alrededor, en los alrededores • **is he ~?** ¿está por aquí? • **there's a lot of flu ~** hay mucha gripe por ahí • **all ~** por todos lados • **she's been ~*** (= *travelled*) ha viajado mucho, ha visto mucho mundo; (*pej*) (= *experienced*) se las sabe todas • **~ here** por aquí • **is there a chemist's ~ here?** ¿hay alguna farmacia por aquí? • **we're looking ~ for a house** estamos buscando casa • **for miles ~** en muchas millas a la redonda • **he must be somewhere ~** debe de estar por aquí

PREP **1** alrededor de • **she wore a scarf ~ her neck** llevaba una bufanda alrededor del cuello • **she ignored the people ~ her** ignoró a la gente que estaba a su alrededor • **to wander ~ the town** pasearse por la ciudad • **there were books all ~ the house** había libros en todas partes de la casa *or* por toda la casa • **to go ~ the world** dar la vuelta al mundo; ▹ **round, corner**

2 (= *approximately*) aproximadamente, alrededor de • **it costs ~ £100** cuesta alrededor de *or* aproximadamente 100 libras • **~ 50** 50 más o menos • **he must be ~ 50** debe de tener unos 50 años • **~ 1950** alrededor de 1950, hacia 1950 • **~ two o'clock** a eso de las dos

arousal [əˈraʊzəl] N (*sexual*) excitación *f* (sexual)

arouse [əˈraʊz] VT **1** (*frm*) (= *awaken from sleep*) despertar

2 (= *stimulate*) [+ *suspicion, curiosity*] despertar, suscitar • **it ~d great interest** despertó *or* suscitó mucho interés • **to ~ the appetite** abrir el apetito • **it should ~ you to greater efforts** debería incitarte a esforzarte más

3 (*sexually*) excitar

aroused [əˈraʊzd] ADJ (*sexually*) excitado

arousing [əˈraʊzɪŋ] ADJ (*sexually*) excitante

ARP NPL ABBR = **air-raid precautions**

arpeggio [ɑ:ˈpedʒɪəʊ] N arpegio *m*

arr. ABBR **1** (*on timetable*) = **arrives, arrival**

2 (*Mus*) (= **arranged**) *adaptación de*

arrack [ˈærək] N arac *m*, aguardiente *m* de palma *or* caña *etc*

arraign [əˈreɪn] VT procesar, acusar (**before** ante)

arraignment [əˈreɪnmənt] N (*Jur*) ≈ lectura *f* del acta de acusación

arrange [əˈreɪndʒ] VT **1** (= *put into order*) [+ *books, thoughts*] ordenar; [+ *hair, flowers*] arreglar • **to ~ one's affairs** poner sus asuntos en orden • **how did we ~ matters last time?** ¿cómo lo organizamos la última vez?

2 (= *place*) [+ *furniture, chairs*] disponer, colocar • **how is the room ~d?** ¿qué disposición tienen los muebles?

3 (= *plan*) planear, fijar; [+ *meeting*] organizar; [+ *schedule, programme*] acordar • **to ~ a party** organizar una fiesta • **everything is ~d** todo está arreglado • **"to be ~d"** "por determinar" • **it was ~d that ...** se quedó en que ... • **have you anything ~d for tomorrow?** ¿tienes planes para mañana?, ¿tienes algún compromiso mañana? • **a marriage has been ~d between ...** se ha concertado la boda de ... • **I've ~d a surprise for tonight** he preparado una sorpresa para esta noche • **to ~ a time for** fijar una hora para • **what did you ~ with him?** ¿en qué quedaste con él?

4 (*Mus*) adaptar, hacer los arreglos de

VI • **to ~ to do sth** quedar en hacer algo • **I ~d to meet him at the cafe** quedé en verlo *or* quedé con él en el café • **I have ~d to see him tonight** quedamos en vernos esta noche, he quedado con él esta noche • **to ~ with sb to** (+ *infin*) ponerse de acuerdo con algn para que (+ *subjun*) • **to ~ with sb that** convenir con algn en que (+ *subjun*) • **I have ~d for you to go** lo he arreglado para que vayas • **can you ~ for my luggage to be sent up?** por favor, (haga) que me suban el equipaje • **can you ~ for him to replace you?** ¿puedes arreglarlo para que te sustituya?

arranged [əˈreɪndʒd] ADJ [*marriage*] concertado (*por los padres*)

CPD ▸ **arranged marriage** matrimonio *m* concertado

arrangement [əˈreɪndʒmənt] N **1** (= *order*) orden *m*

2 (*Mus*) arreglo *m*

3 (= *agreement*) acuerdo *m* • **prices by ~** precios a convenir • **larger orders by ~** los pedidos de mayor cantidad previo acuerdo • **by ~ with Covent Garden** con permiso de Covent Garden • **to come to an ~ (with sb)** llegar a un acuerdo (con algn) • **we have an ~ with them** tenemos un acuerdo con ellos • **he has an ~ with his secretary** (*amorous*) se entiende con su secretaria

4 (= *plan*) plan *m* • **if this ~ doesn't suit you** si este plan no le viene bien

5 arrangements (= *plans*) planes *mpl*; (= *preparations*) preparativos *mpl* • **what are the ~s for your holiday?** ¿qué plan *or* planes tienes para las vacaciones? • **we must make ~s to help** debemos ver cómo podemos ayudar • **to make one's own ~s** obrar por cuenta propia • **if she doesn't like the idea she must make her own ~s** si no le gusta la idea que se las arregle sola • **all the ~s are made** todo está arreglado • **Pamela is in charge of the travel ~s** Pamela se encarga de los preparativos para el viaje

CPD ▸ **arrangement fee** (*for a loan*) gastos *mpl* de gestión

arranger [əˈreɪndʒəʳ] N **1** (*Mus*) arreglista *mf*

2 (= *organizer*) organizador(a) *m/f*

arrant [ˈærənt] ADJ (*frm*) [*knave, liar etc*] consumado • **~ nonsense** puro disparate *m*

array [əˈreɪ] N **1** (*Mil*) formación *f*, orden *m* • **in battle ~** en orden *or* formación de batalla • **in close ~** en filas apretadas

2 (= *collection*) colección *f*; (= *series*) serie *f* • **a fine ~ of flowers** un bello conjunto de flores • **a great ~ of hats** una magnífica colección de sombreros

3 (= *dress*) atavío *m*

4 (*Comput*) matriz *f*, tabla *f*

VT (*frm*) **1** (= *arrange, display*) disponer

2 (= *line up*) desplegar (**against** ante), formar (**against** contra)

3 (= *dress*) ataviar, engalanar (**in** con, de)

arrayed [əˈreɪd] ADJ **1** (= *arranged*) [*objects, goods*] dispuesto, colocado

2 • **to be ~ against sb** (*Mil*) estar desplegado ante algn

3 (*liter*) (= *dressed, clad*) ataviado • **to be ~ in sth** ir ataviado con algo

arrears [əˈrɪəz] NPL **1** [*of money*] atrasos *mpl* • **rent ~** atrasos *mpl* de alquiler • **to be in ~** (*with rent*) ir atrasado en los pagos • **to get into ~** atrasarse en los pagos • **to pay one month in ~** pagar con un mes de retraso *or* a mes vencido • **to be in ~ with one's correspondence** tener correspondencia atrasada

2 (*Sport*) • **to be in ~** ir retrasado

arrest [əˈrest] N [*of person*] detención *f*; [*of goods*] secuestro *m* • **to make an ~** hacer una detención • **to be under ~** estar detenido • **you're under ~** queda usted detenido • **to put** *or* **place sb under ~** detener *or* arrestar a algn

VT **1** [+ *criminal*] detener

2 [+ *attention*] atraer

3 [+ *progress, decay etc*] (= *halt*) detener, parar; (= *hinder*) obstaculizar • **measures to ~ inflation** medidas para detener la inflación

CPD ▸ **arrest warrant** orden *f* de detención

arrestable [əˈrestəbəl] ADJ [*offence*] que puede causar detención

arrested development [ə,restɪddɪˈveləpmənt] N atrofia *f*, desarrollo *m* atrofiado

arresting [əˈrestɪŋ] ADJ llamativo, que llama la atención

arrhythmia [əˈrɪðmɪə] N (*Med*) arritmia *f*

arrival [əˈraɪvəl] N **1** [*of person, letter etc*] llegada *f*, arribo *m* (*esp LAm*) • **"Arrivals"** (*Aer*) "Llegadas" • **on ~** al llegar • **dead on ~** ingresó cadáver

2 (= *person*) persona *f* que llega • **Jim was the first ~ at the party** Jim fue el primero en llegar a la fiesta • **a new ~** (= *newcomer*) un recién llegado; (= *baby*) un recién nacido

CPD ▸ **arrival board** (*US*), **arrivals board** panel *m* de llegadas ▸ **arrivals hall, arrivals lounge** sala *f* de llegadas

arrive [əˈraɪv] VI **1** [*person, taxi, letter, meal etc*] llegar, arribar (*esp LAm*); [*time, winter, event etc*] llegar • **to ~ (up)on the scene** entrar en escena

2 [*baby*] nacer, llegar

3* (= *succeed in business etc*) triunfar, alcanzar el éxito

▸ **arrive at** VI + PREP [+ *decision, solution*] llegar a; [+ *perfection*] lograr, alcanzar • **we finally ~d at a price** por fin convenimos (en) un precio • **they finally ~d at the idea of doing ...** finalmente llegaron a la conclusión de hacer ... • **how did you ~ at this figure?** ¿cómo has llegado a esta cifra?

arriviste [,ærɪˈvi:st] N arribista *mf*

arrogance [ˈærəgəns] N arrogancia *f*, prepotencia *f* (*esp LAm*)

arrogant [ˈærəgənt] ADJ arrogante, prepotente (*esp LAm*)

arrogantly [ˈærəgəntlɪ] ADV con arrogancia, con prepotencia (*esp LAm*)

arrogate [ˈærəʊgeɪt] VT • **to ~ sth to o.s.** arrogarse algo

arrow [ˈærəʊ] N (= *weapon, sign*) flecha *f*

arrowhead [ˈærəʊhed] N punta *f* de flecha

arrowroot [ˈærəʊru:t] N arrurruz *m*

arse‡* [ɑ:s] (*Brit*) N culo‡ *m* • **get (up) off your ~!** ¡mueve el culo!‡ • **move** *or* **shift your ~!** (= *move over*) córrete para allá; (= *hurry up*) ¡mueve el culo!‡ • IDIOM: • **he can't tell his ~ from his elbow** no tiene ni puñetera *or* puta idea‡, confunde la velocidad con el tocino*

VT • **I can't be ~d** no me apetece un huevo‡

a

▸ **arse about****, **arse around**** VI + ADV hacer el ganso *or* idiota*
arsehole** ['ɑ:sheʊl] N (*Brit*) **1** (= *person*) gilipollas** *mf inv*, pendejo/a *m/f* (*LAm**), huevón/ona *m/f* (*S. Cone**)
2 (*Anat*) culo‡ *m*
arsenal ['ɑ:sɪnl] N arsenal *m*
arsenic ['ɑ:snɪk] N arsénico *m*
arsenical [ɑ:'senɪkl] ADJ arsénico, arsenical
arson ['ɑ:sn] N incendio *m* premeditado
arsonist ['ɑ:sənɪst] N incendiario/a *m/f*, pirómano/a *m/f*
art[1] [ɑ:t] N **1** (= *painting etc*) arte *m* • **the arts** las bellas artes • **art for art's sake** el arte por el arte • **work of art** obra *f* de arte
2 (= *skill*) arte *m*, habilidad *f*, destreza *f*; (= *technique*) técnica *f*; (= *knack*) maña *f*; (= *gift*) don *m*, facilidad *f* • **the art of embroidery** el arte del bordado • **the art of persuasion/ seduction** el arte de la persuasión/la seducción; ▹ **fine**[1]
3 (*Univ*) • **Arts** Filosofía *f* y Letras • **Faculty of Arts** Facultad *f* de Filosofía y Letras; ▹ **bachelor, master**
4 (= *cunning*) arte *m*
CPD ▸ **art collection** colección *f* de arte ▸ **art college** escuela *f* de Bellas Artes ▸ **art dealer** marchante *mf* ▸ **art deco** art decó *m* ▸ **art director** director(a) *m/f* artístico/a ▸ **art exhibition** exposición *f* de arte ▸ **art form** medio *m* de expresión artística ▸ **art gallery** (*state-owned*) museo *m* (de arte); (*private*) galería *f* de arte ▸ **art lover** aficionado/a *m/f* al arte ▸ **art nouveau** modernismo *m* ▸ **art paper** papel *m* cuché ▸ **arts and crafts** artesanías *fpl* ▸ **art school** escuela *f* de Bellas Artes ▸ **Arts Council** (*Brit*) *institución pública encargada de la promoción de la cultura y de las actividades artísticas* ▸ **Arts degree** licenciatura *f* en Letras ▸ **Arts student** estudiante *mf* de Letras ▸ **art student** estudiante *mf* de Bellas Artes; ▹ **performance**
art[2]†† [ɑ:t] PRESENT *thou form of* **be**
artefact ['ɑ:tɪfækt] N **1** (= *object*) artefacto *m*
2 (*fig*) (= *product*) producto *m*; (= *accident*) accidente *m*
arterial [ɑ:'tɪərɪəl] ADJ [*blood*] arterial • ~ **road** arteria *f*
arteriosclerosis [ɑ:'tɪərɪəʊsklɪə'rəʊsɪs] N arteriosclerosis *f inv*
artery ['ɑ:tərɪ] N **1** (*Anat*) arteria *f*
2 (= *road*) arteria *f*
artesian [ɑ:'ti:zɪən] ADJ • ~ **well** pozo *m* artesiano
artful [ɑ:tfʊl] ADJ **1** (= *cunning*) [*person, trick*] astuto, taimado, ladino (*esp LAm*)
2 (= *skilful*) ingenioso • **an ~ way of doing sth** una forma ingeniosa de hacer algo
artfully ['ɑ:tfəlɪ] ADV **1** (= *cunningly*) con mucha maña, astutamente
2 (= *skilfully*) [*arranged, constructed, designed*] ingeniosamente
artfulness ['ɑ:tfʊlnɪs] N **1** (= *cunning*) maña *f*, astucia *f*
2 (= *skill*) ingenio *m*
art-house ['ɑ:thaʊs] ADJ [*film*] de autor, de arte y ensayo • **art-house cinema** (= *films*) cine *m* de autor, cine *m* de arte y ensayo; (= *place*) cine *m* de arte y ensayo
arthritic [ɑ:'θrɪtɪk] ADJ artrítico
arthritis [ɑ:'θraɪtɪs] N artritis *f inv*
arthropod ['ɑ:θrəpɒd] N artrópodo *m*
Arthur ['ɑ:θəʳ] N Arturo • **King ~** el Rey Arturo
Arthurian [ɑ:'θjʊərɪən] ADJ artúrico
artic* [ɑ:'tɪk] N (*Brit*) (*Aut*) = **articulated lorry**
artichoke ['ɑ:tɪtʃəʊk] N **1** (= *globe artichoke*) alcachofa *f*, alcaucil *m*
2 (= *Jerusalem artichoke*) aguaturma *f*, cotufa *f* (*LAm*)
article ['ɑ:tɪkl] N **1** (= *item, product*) artículo *m*; (= *object*) objeto *m*, cosa *f* • **~s of value** objetos *mpl* de valor • **~s of clothing** prendas *fpl* de vestir
2 (*in newspaper etc*) artículo *m*; ▹ **leading**
3 (*Ling*) artículo *m* • **definite/indefinite ~** artículo *m* definido/indefinido, artículo *m* determinado/indeterminado
4 (*Admin, Jur*) artículo *m*, cláusula *f*
VT (*Brit*) • **to be ~d to sb** estar de aprendiz con algn
CPD ▸ **article of faith** artículo *m* de fe ▸ **article of partnership** contrato *m* de asociación ▸ **articles of apprenticeship** (*Brit*) contrato *msing* de aprendizaje ▸ **articles of association** (*Comm*) estatutos *mpl* sociales ▸ **articles of war** (*US*) (*Mil Hist*) código *msing* militar
articled clerk ['ɑ:tɪkld,klɑ:k] N (*Brit*) pasante *mf*
articulacy [ɑ:'tɪkjʊləsɪ] N [*of person*] elocuencia *f*; [*of speech*] articulación *f*; [*of description*] precisión *f*
articulate ADJ [ɑ:'tɪkjʊlɪt] **1** [*speech, account*] articulado; [*person*] elocuente, que se expresa bien • **she's very** *or* **highly ~** se expresa muy bien • **he's not very ~** le cuesta expresarse
2 (*Anat*) articulado
VT [ɑ:'tɪkjʊleɪt] **1** (= *express*) [+ *thoughts, feelings*] expresar
2 (= *pronounce*) [+ *word, sentence*] articular
articulated [ɑ:'tɪkjʊleɪtɪd] ADJ • ~ **lorry** camión *m* articulado
articulately [ɑ:'tɪkjʊlɪtlɪ] ADV [*speak, express o.s.*] con facilidad, fluidamente; [*pronounce*] articulando bien
articulation [ɑ:,tɪkjʊ'leɪʃən] N **1** (= *expression*) [*of thoughts, feelings*] expresión *f*
2 (= *pronunciation*) [*of word, sentence*] articulación *f*
3 (*Anat*) articulación *f*
articulatory [ɑ:'tɪkjʊlətərɪ] ADJ articulatorio
artifact ['ɑ:tɪfækt] N (*esp US*) = **artefact**
artifice ['ɑ:tɪfɪs] N **1** (= *cunning*) habilidad *f*, ingenio *m*
2 (= *trick*) artificio *m*, ardid *m*; (= *strategem*) estratagema *f*
artificial [,ɑ:tɪ'fɪʃəl] ADJ **1** (= *synthetic*) [*light, flower, lake, leg, limb*] artificial; [*leather*] sintético; [*jewel*] de imitación; [*hair*] postizo
2 (*fig*) [*person, manner*] artificial, afectado; [*smile*] forzado; [*situation*] artificial
CPD ▸ **artificial additive** aditivo *m* artificial • **"no artificial additives"** (*on food packaging*) "sin aditivos artificiales" ▸ **artificial horizon** horizonte *m* artificial ▸ **artificial insemination** inseminación *f* artificial ▸ **artificial intelligence** inteligencia *f* artificial ▸ **artificial manure** abono *m* químico ▸ **artificial respiration** respiración *f* artificial ▸ **artificial silk** seda *f* artificial, rayón *m* ▸ **artificial sweetener** edulcorante *m*
artificiality [,ɑ:tɪfɪʃɪ'ælɪtɪ] N **1** (*lit*) (= *synthetic nature*) artificialidad *f*
2 (*fig*) [*of person, manner*] artificialidad *f*, afectación *f*, falta *f* de naturalidad
artificially [,ɑ:tɪ'fɪʃəlɪ] ADV **1** (= *by synthetic means*) artificialmente
2 (*fig*) con afectación
artillery [ɑ:'tɪlərɪ] N (= *guns, troops etc*) artillería *f*
artilleryman [ɑ:'tɪlərɪmən] N (PL: **artillerymen**) artillero *m*
artisan ['ɑ:tɪzæn] N artesano/a *m/f*
artisanal [ɑ:'tɪzənəl] ADJ [*skills, groups, clothes*] artesanal
artist ['ɑ:tɪst] N artista *mf*
artiste [ɑ:'ti:st] N (*esp Brit*) (*Theat*) artista *mf* (del espectáculo); (*Mus*) intérprete *mf*
artistic [ɑ:'tɪstɪk] ADJ [*ability, design, temperament, freedom*] artístico • **to be ~** [*person*] tener dotes artísticas • **an ~ flower arrangement** un arreglo floral muy artístico
CPD ▸ **artistic director** director(a) *m/f* artístico/a
artistically [ɑ:'tɪstɪkəlɪ] ADV [*arranged, presented*] con mucho arte, artísticamente • **~ gifted children** niños con dotes artísticas • **to be ~ inclined** tener dotes artísticas • **~, the photographs are stunning** desde el punto de vista artístico, las fotografías son sensacionales
artistry ['ɑ:tɪstrɪ] N (= *skill*) arte *m*, habilidad *f*
artless ['ɑ:tlɪs] ADJ **1** (= *straightforward*) [*beauty*] natural; [*person, smile, comment*] ingenuo, sin malicia; [*book, story, film*] sencillo, sin artificios
2 (= *naïve*) simple
3 (= *clumsy*) torpe
artlessly ['ɑ:tlɪslɪ] ADV **1** (= *innocently*) ingenuamente
2 (= *clumsily*) torpemente
artlessness ['ɑ:tlɪsnɪs] N
1 (= *straightforwardness*) [*of beauty*] naturalidad *f*; [*of person, behaviour, comment*] ingenuidad *f*, falta *f* de malicia
2 (= *clumsiness*) torpeza *f*
artsy* ['ɑ:tsɪ] (*esp US*) = **arty**
artsy-craftsy* ['ɑ:tsɪ'krɑ:ftsɪ] ADJ (*US*) = **arty-crafty**
artsy-fartsy‡ ['ɑ:tsɪ'fɑ:tsɪ] ADJ (*US*) = **arty-farty**
artwork ['ɑ:twɜ:k] N material *m* gráfico
arty* ['ɑ:tɪ] ADJ [*style*] con pretensiones artísticas, seudoartístico; [*clothing*] afectado, extravagante; [*person*] de gusto muy afectado, que se las da de muy artista • **she looks ~** • **she is ~-looking** tiene pinta de cultureta
arty-crafty* ['ɑ:tɪ'krɑ:ftɪ], **artsy-craftsy*** (*US*) ['ɑ:tsɪ'krɑ:ftsɪ] ADJ [*style*] con pretensiones artísticas; [*person*] (= *creative*) con inclinación por las manualidades, muy manitas (*inv*); (= *keen on craftware*) metido a artesano, enamorado de la artesanía
arty-farty‡ ['ɑ:tɪ'fɑ:tɪ], **artsy-fartsy*** (*US*) ['ɑ:tsɪ'fɑ:tsɪ] ADJ pretencioso, con pretensiones artísticas
ARV N ABBR (*US*) (= **American Revised Version**) *versión norteamericana de la Biblia*
arvee* [ɑ:'vi:] N (*US*) = **recreational vehicle**
Aryan ['ɛərɪən] ADJ ario
N ario/a *m/f*
AS ABBR (*US*) **1** = **Associate in Sciences**
2 = **American Samoa**

as [æz] [əz]

CONJUNCTION
PREPOSITION
ADVERB

For set combinations in which **as** *is not the first word, eg* **such ... as, the same ... as, dressed as, acknowledge as***, look up the other word.*

CONJUNCTION
1 *in time clauses*

You can usually use **cuando** *when the* **as** *clause simply tells you when an event happened:*

cuando • **as I was passing the house** cuando pasaba por delante de la casa • **he came in as I was leaving** entró cuando yo salía

Alternatively, use **al** *+ infinitive:*

• **he came in as I was leaving** entró al salir yo • **he tripped as he was coming out of the bank** tropezó al salir *or* cuando salía del banco • **as the car drew level with us, I realized Isabel was driving** al llegar el coche a nuestra altura *or* cuando el coche llegó a nuestra altura, me di cuenta de que lo conducía Isabel

Translate **as** *using* **mientras** *for longer actions which are happening at the same time:*

(= *while*) mientras • **as we walked, we talked about the future** mientras caminábamos, hablábamos del futuro

In the context of two closely linked actions involving parallel development, translate **as** *using* **a medida que** *or* **conforme**. *Alternatively, use* **según va** *etc + gerund:*

• **as one gets older, life gets more and more difficult** a medida que se envejece *or* conforme se envejece *or* según va uno envejeciendo, la vida se hace cada vez más difícil • **as he got older he got deafer** a medida que *or* conforme envejeció se fue volviendo más sordo, según fue envejeciendo se fue volviendo más sordo

2 (*in reason clauses*)

When **as** *means "since" or "because", you can generally use* **como**, *provided you put it at the beginning of the sentence. Alternatively, use the more formal* **puesto que** *either at the beginning of the sentence or between the clauses or* **ya que** *especially between the clauses.*

como; (*more frm*) puesto que, ya que • **as you're here, I'll tell you** como estás aquí *or* puesto que estás aquí, te lo diré • **he didn't mention it as he didn't want to worry you** como no quería preocuparte, no lo mencionó, no lo mencionó puesto que no quería preocuparte • **he couldn't come as he had an appointment** no pudo asistir porque *or* puesto que *or* ya que tenía un compromiso • **patient as she is, she'll probably put up with it** con lo paciente que es, seguramente lo soportará

3 (*describing way, manner*) como • **leave things as they are** dejad las cosas como están • **I'm okay as I am** estoy bien tal como estoy • **knowing him as I do, I'm sure he'll refuse** conociéndolo como lo conozco, estoy seguro de que no aceptará • **the village, situated as it is near a motorway, …** el pueblo, situado como está cerca de una autopista, … • **as I've said before …** como he dicho antes … • **as I was saying …** como iba diciendo … • **her door is the first as you go up** su puerta es la primera según se sube • **she is very gifted, as is her brother** tiene mucho talento, al igual que su hermano • **you'll have it by noon as agreed** lo tendrá antes del mediodía, tal como acordamos • **it's not bad, as hotels go** no está mal, en comparación con otros hoteles • **as in all good detective stories** como en toda buena novela policíaca • **as you know** como sabe • **Arsenal are playing as never before!** ¡Arsenal está jugando mejor que nunca! • **as often happens** como suele ocurrir • **he performed brilliantly, as only he can** actuó de maravilla, como solo él sabe hacerlo • **as you were!** (*Mil*) ¡descansen! • **do as you wish** haga lo que quiera

4 (*= though*) aunque • **tired as he was, he went to the party** aunque estaba cansado, asistió a la fiesta • **interesting as the book is, I don't think it will sell very well** el libro es interesante, pero aún así no creo que se venda bien, aunque el libro es interesante, no creo que se venda bien • **try as she would** *or* **might, she couldn't lift it** por más que se esforzó no pudo levantarlo • **unlikely as it may seem …** por imposible que parezca …

5 (*in set structures*) **as if** *or* **as though** como si • **it was as if** *or* **as though he were still alive** era como si estuviera todavía vivo • **he looked as if** *or* **as though he was ill** parecía como si estuviera enfermo • **it isn't as if** *or* **as though he were poor** no es que sea pobre, que digamos • **as if she knew!** ¡como si ella lo supiera!

as if to • **the little dog nodded his head, as if to agree** el perrito movió la cabeza, como asintiendo

as in • **it's spelled with V as in Valencia** se escribe con V de Valencia

as it is • **as it is, it doesn't make much difference** en realidad, casi da lo mismo • **as it is we can do nothing** en la práctica *or* tal y como están las cosas no podemos hacer nada • **I've got quite enough to do as it is** tengo ya bastante trabajo

as it were • **I'd understood the words, but I hadn't understood the question, as it were** había entendido las palabras, pero no había comprendido la pregunta, por así decirlo • **I have become, as it were, two people** me he convertido como en dos personas • **he was as it were tired and emotional** estaba de alguna forma cansado y con los nervios a flor de piel

as was • **that's the headmistress, the deputy as was** esa es la directora, que antes era la subdirectora

PREPOSITION

1 (*= while*) • **she was often ill as a child** de pequeña se ponía enferma con frecuencia

2 (*= in the capacity of*) como • **he succeeded as a politician** tuvo éxito como político • **I don't think much of him as an actor** como actor, no me gusta mucho • **she treats me as her equal** me trata de igual a igual • **we're going as tourists** vamos en plan de turismo • **he was there as adviser** estaba allí en calidad de asesor • **Gibson as Hamlet** (*Theat*) Gibson en el papel de Hamlet • **he works as a waiter** trabaja de camarero; ▹ **such**

ADVERB

1 (*in comparisons*) **as … as** tan … como • **I am as tall as him** soy tan alto como él • **this tree can grow as tall as 50 feet** este árbol puede llegar a medir 50 pies de alto • **as big as a house** (tan) grande como una casa • **she hit him as hard as she could** lo golpeó lo más fuerte que pudo, lo golpeó tan fuerte como pudo • **he was writing as long ago as 1945** en 1945 ya escribía • **she doesn't walk as quickly** *or* **as fast as me** no camina tan rápido como yo • **walk as quickly** *or* **as fast as you can** camina lo más rápido que puedas • **he ate as quickly as possible** comió lo más rápido posible • **it was still being done by hand as recently as 1960** en 1960 todavía seguía haciéndose a mano • **the fresh snow was as white as white could be** la nieve fresca era todo lo blanca que podía ser • **is it as far as that?** ¿tan lejos está? • **is it as big as all that?** ¿es de verdad tan grande?

as little as • **by saving as little as ten pounds a month** ahorrando tan solo diez libras al mes

as many … as tantos/as … como • **I haven't got as many pairs of shoes as you** no tengo tantos pares de zapatos como tú • **I've got a lot of tapes but I haven't got as many as him** *or* **as he has** tengo muchas cintas, pero no tantas como él • **she gets as many as eight thousand letters a month** llega a recibir hasta ocho mil cartas al mes

as much • **she thought he was an idiot, and said as much** pensaba que era un idiota, y así lo expresó

as much … as tanto/a … como • **I haven't got as much energy as you** no tengo tanta energía como tú • **you've got as much as she has** tienes tanto como ella • **you spend as much as me** *or* **as I do** tú gastas tanto como yo • **it didn't cost as much as I had expected** no costó tanto como yo me esperaba • **it can cost as much as $2,000** puede llegar a costar 2.000 dólares

as one • **they all stood up as one** se levantaron todos a la vez

half/twice/three times as … • **it's half as expensive** es la mitad de caro • **it's twice as expensive** es el doble de caro • **it's three times as expensive** es tres veces más caro • **she's twice as nice as her sister** es el doble de simpática que su hermana • **her coat cost twice as much as mine** su abrigo costó el doble que el mío

without as *or* **so much as** • **she gave me back the book without as much as an apology** me devolvió el libro sin pedirme siquiera una disculpa

2 (*in set structures*) **as for** • **as for the children, they were exhausted** en cuanto a los niños, estaban rendidos, los niños, por su parte, estaban rendidos • **as for that …** en cuanto a esto …

as from • **as from tomorrow** a partir de mañana

as of • **as of yesterday/now** a partir de ayer/ahora

as to • **as to that I can't say** en lo que a eso se refiere, no lo sé • **as to her mother …** en cuanto a su madre … • **to question sb as to his intentions** preguntar a algn sus intenciones • **they make decisions as to whether students need help** deciden si los alumnos necesitan ayuda • **he inquired as to what the problem was** preguntó cuál era el problema

as yet hasta ahora, hasta el momento; ▹ **regard**

ASA (N ABBR) **1** (*Brit*) = **Advertising Standards Authority**
2 (*Brit*) = **Amateur Swimming Association**
3 (*US*) = **American Standards Association**

ASA/BS (ABBR) = **American Standards Association/British Standard**

a.s.a.p.* (ADV ABBR) (= **as soon as possible**) lo antes posible, lo más pronto posible

asbestos [æz'bestəs] (N) amianto *m*, asbesto *m*

asbestosis [ˌæzbes'təʊsɪs] (N) asbestosis *f inv*

ASBO ['æzbəʊ] (N ABBR) (*Brit*) (= **Antisocial Behaviour Order**) *orden por comportamiento antisocial*

ascend [ə'send] (VT) (*frm*) [+ *stairs*] subir; [+ *mountain*] subir a; [+ *throne*] ascender a, subir a
(VI) (= *rise*) subir, ascender; (= *slope up*) elevarse

ascendancy [ə'sendənsɪ] (N) ascendiente *m*, dominio *m*

ascendant [ə'sendənt] (N) • **to be in the ~** estar en auge, ir ganando predominio
ascendency [ə'sendənsɪ] (N) = **ascendancy**
ascender [ə'sendəʳ] (N) (*Typ*) ascendiente *m*
ascending [ə'sendɪŋ] (ADJ) ascendente • **in ~ order** en orden ascendente
ascension [ə'senʃən] (N) ascensión *f*
(CPD) ▸ **Ascension Day** día *m* de la Ascensión ▸ **Ascension Island** isla *f* Ascensión
ascent [ə'sent] (N) **1** (= *climb, way up*) subida *f*; (*in plane*) ascenso *m*
2 (= *slope*) pendiente *f*, cuesta *f*
3 (*fig*) ascenso *m*
ascertain [,æsə'teɪn] (VT) determinar, establecer (**that** que)
ascertainable [,æsə'teɪnəbl] (ADJ) determinable
ascertainment [,æsə'teɪnmənt] (N) determinación *f*
ascetic [ə'setɪk] (ADJ) ascético
(N) asceta *mf*
asceticism [ə'setɪsɪzəm] (N) ascetismo *m*
ASCII ['æski:] (N ABBR) (= **American Standard Code for Information Interchange**) ASCII *m*
(CPD) ▸ **ASCII file** fichero *m* ASCII
ascorbic [ə'skɔ:bɪk] (ADJ) • **~ acid** ácido *m* ascórbico

ASCOT
Ascot o **Royal Ascot** es una competición de carreras de caballos que dura cuatro días y se celebra en junio en el hipódromo de Ascot, cerca del castillo de Windsor, en el sur de Inglaterra. Es uno de los acontecimientos más importantes en el calendario hípico británico, y también lo es a nivel social, pues a él acuden miembros de la realeza y la clase alta británica. La familia real hace acto de presencia en carruajes, y sigue las carreras desde una zona reservada llamada **Royal Enclosure**. Se considera un gran honor ser invitado a ella y los invitados han de observar estrictas normas de etiqueta. En el día conocido como **Ladies Day** (el Día de las Damas), es tradicional que las mujeres vayan a las carreras luciendo sombreros y vestidos espectaculares.

ascribable [əs'kraɪbəbl] (ADJ) atribuible (**to** a)
ascribe [ə'skraɪb] (VT) • **to ~ sth to sb/sth** atribuir algo a algn/algo
ascription [ə'skrɪpʃən] (N) atribución *f*
ASCU (N ABBR) (*US*) = **Association of State Colleges and Universities**
ASE (N ABBR) (*US*) = **American Stock Exchange**
ASEAN (N ABBR) = **Association of South-East Asian Nations**
aseptic [eɪ'septɪk] (ADJ) aséptico
asexual [eɪ'seksjʊəl] (ADJ) asexual
asexually [eɪ'seksjʊəlɪ] (ADV) de forma asexual
ASH [æʃ] (N ABBR) (*Brit*) = **Action on Smoking and Health**
ash¹ [æʃ] (N) **1** (*also* **ash tree**) fresno *m*
2 (= *wood*) (madera *f* de) fresno *m*
(ADJ) de madera de fresno • **a black ash table** una mesa negra (de madera) de fresno
ash² [æʃ] (N) (*from fire, cigarette*) ceniza *f* • **ashes** (*gen, mortal remains*) cenizas *fpl* • **to burn** *or* **reduce sth to ashes** reducir algo a cenizas • **ashes to ashes, dust to dust** (*Rel*) las cenizas a las cenizas, el polvo al polvo • **the Ashes** (*Cricket*) *trofeo de los partidos de críquet Australia-Inglaterra* • **IDIOM:** • **to rise out of the ashes of sth** surgir de las cenizas de algo
(CPD) ▸ **ash bin, ash can** (*US*) cubo *m* or (*LAm*) bote *m* or (*LAm*) tarro *m* de la basura ▸ **Ash Wednesday** miércoles *m inv* de Ceniza; ▹ **ash blond(e)**
ashamed [ə'ʃeɪmd] (ADJ) **1** (= *remorseful*) avergonzado, apenado (*LAm*) • **he was/felt ~ about what had happened** estaba/se sentía avergonzado por lo que había pasado • **she was in tears, saying how ~ she felt** estaba llorando y diciendo lo avergonzada *or* arrepentida que se sentía *or* estaba • **she was ~ that she had been so nasty** • **she was ~ about having been so nasty** estaba avergonzada *or* se avergonzaba *or* se arrepentía de haber sido tan cruel • **to be ~ of o.s.** estar avergonzado de sí mismo • **you ought to be ~ of yourself!** ¡debería darte vergüenza *or* (*LAm*) pena!, ¡no te da vergüenza!
2 (= *embarrassed*) • **I was ~ to ask for money** me daba vergüenza *or* (*LAm*) pena pedir dinero • **I've done nothing, I'm ~ to say** me da vergüenza *or* (*LAm*) pena reconocerlo pero no he hecho nada • **I was too ~ to tell anyone** me sentía demasiado avergonzado como para decírselo a nadie • **it's nothing to be ~ of** no hay por qué avergonzarse *or* (*LAm*) apenarse • **I'm ~ of you** me avergüenzo de ti • **I felt ~ that the money spent on my education had been wasted** me daba vergüenza pensar que el dinero que se había gastado en mi educación no había servido para nada
ash blond, ash blonde [æʃ'blɒnd] (ADJ) rubio ceniza
(N) rubio/a *m/f* ceniza
ash-coloured, ash-colored (*US*) ['æʃkʌləd] (ADJ) **1** (*lit*) color ceniza (*inv*), ceniciento
2 (= *pale*) pálido
ashen ['æʃn] (ADJ) **1** (= *greyish*) ceniciento
2 (= *pale*) pálido
3 (= *ashwood*) de fresno
ashen-faced [,æʃən'feɪst] (ADJ) ceniciento, pálido
Ashkenazi [,æʃkə'nɑ:zɪ] (ADJ) askenazí
(N) (PL: **Ashkenazim** [,æʃkə'nɑ:zɪm]) askenazí *mf*
ashlar ['æʃləʳ] (N) **1** sillar *m*
2 (*also* **ashlar work**) sillería *f*
ashman ['æʃmæn] (N) (PL: **ashmen**) (*US*) basurero *m*
ashore [ə'ʃɔ:ʳ] (ADV) en tierra • **to be ~** estar en tierra • **to go/come ~** desembarcar • **to put sb ~** desembarcar a algn, poner a algn en tierra • **to run ~** encallar
ashpan ['æʃpæn] (N) cenicero *m*, cajón *m* de la ceniza
ashram ['æʃrəm] (N) ashram *m*
ashtray ['æʃtreɪ] (N) cenicero *m*
ashy ['æʃɪ] (ADJ) lleno de ceniza
Asia ['eɪʃə] (N) Asia *f*
(CPD) ▸ **Asia Minor** Asia *f* Menor
Asian ['eɪʃn] (ADJ) asiático • **~ flu** gripe *f* asiática
(N) asiático/a *m/f*
Asian-American ['eɪʃnə'merɪkən] (ADJ) asiático-americano
(N) asiático-americano/a *m/f*
Asiatic [,eɪsɪ'ætɪk] (ADJ), (N) asiático/a *m/f*
A-side ['eɪsaɪd] (N) cara *f* A
aside [ə'saɪd]

When ***aside*** *is an element in a phrasal verb, eg* ***brush aside, cast aside, put aside, stand aside,*** *look up the verb.*

(ADV) **1** (= *to one side*) a un lado • **to set** *or* **put sth ~** apartar algo • **to cast ~** desechar, echar a un lado • **to step ~** hacerse a un lado • **joking ~** bromas aparte
2 • **~ from** (= *as well as*) aparte de, además de; (= *except for*) aparte de
(N) (*Theat*) aparte *m* • **to say sth in an ~** decir algo aparte
asinine ['æsɪnaɪn] (ADJ) **1** (*frm*) (= *ass-like*) asnal
2 (= *stupid*) estúpido

ask [ɑ:sk]

TRANSITIVE VERB
INTRANSITIVE VERB
PHRASAL VERBS

TRANSITIVE VERB
1 (= *inquire*) preguntar • **"how is Frank?" he asked** —¿cómo está Frank? —preguntó • **to ask sb sth** preguntar algo a algn • **I asked him his name/the time** le pregunté su nombre/la hora • **to ask o.s. sth** preguntarse algo • **did you ask him about the job?** ¿le has preguntado por el trabajo?; (*in more detail*) ¿le has preguntado acerca del trabajo? • **I've been meaning to ask you about that** llevo tiempo queriendo *or* hace tiempo que quiero preguntarte acerca de eso • **ask her about her plans for Christmas** pregúntale qué planes tiene para la Navidad • **ask me another!** ¡no tengo ni idea! • **don't ask me!*** ¡yo qué sé!*, ¡qué sé yo! (*esp LAm**) • **I ask you!*** (*despairing*) ¿te lo puedes creer? • **ask him if he has seen her** pregúntale si la ha visto • **if you ask me, I think she's crazy** para mí que está loca • **and where have you been, may I ask?** ¿y dónde has estado, si se puede saber? • **to ask (sb) a question** hacer una pregunta (a algn) • **I asked the teacher what to do next** le pregunté al profesor lo que tenía que hacer después • **ask them what time the party is** pregúntales a qué hora es la fiesta • **who asked you?*** ¿quién te ha preguntado a ti? • **ask her why she didn't come** pregúntale por qué no vino
2 (= *request*) pedir • **to ask sb a favour** • **ask a favour of sb** pedir un favor a algn • **how much are they asking for the car?** ¿cuánto piden por el coche? • **they are asking £200,000 for the house** piden 200.000 libras por la casa • **that's asking the impossible** eso es pedir lo imposible • **it's not a lot to ask** no es mucho pedir • **that's asking a lot** eso es mucho pedir • **what more can you ask?** ¿qué más se puede pedir? • **to ask sth of sb:** • **he did everything asked of him** hizo todo lo que se le pidió • **all he asked of us was that we tell people about his plight** solo nos pidió que habláramos a la gente de la difícil situación en que se encontraba • **to ask that sth be done** pedir que se haga algo • **all I'm asking is that you keep an open mind** solo te pido que *or* lo único que pido es que mantengas una actitud abierta • **to ask to do sth: I asked to see the director** pedí ver al director • **he asked to go on the picnic** preguntó si podía ir (con ellos) de picnic • **to ask sb to do sth** pedir a algn que haga algo • **we had to ask him to leave** tuvimos que decirle *or* pedirle que se marchara • **that's asking too much** eso es pedir demasiado • **I think she's asking too much** creo que está exigiendo demasiado; ▹ **permission**
3 (= *invite*) invitar • **have you been asked?** ¿te han invitado? • **to ask sb to dinner** invitar a algn a cenar

INTRANSITIVE VERB
1 (= *inquire*) preguntar • **he was too shy to ask** le dio vergüenza preguntar • **ask about our reduced rates for students** pregunta por *or* infórmate sobre nuestros descuentos para

estudiantes • **he was asking about the Vikings** preguntaba acerca de *or* sobre los vikingos • **I asked about the possibility of staying on** pregunté acerca de *or* sobre la posibilidad de quedarme más tiempo, pregunté si era posible que me quedara más tiempo • **he was asking about you** estaba preguntando por ti • **"what's the matter?" — "don't ask"** —¿qué pasa? —más te vale no saberlo • **now you're asking!*** (= *what a difficult question*) ¡vaya con la preguntita!*; (= *who knows*) ¡quién sabe!; (= *wouldn't we all like to know*) ¡eso quisiera saber yo!* • **I was only asking** era solo una pregunta • **"what has he gone and done now?" — "you may well ask!"** —¿qué es lo que ha hecho ahora? —¡buena pregunta!

2 (= *make request*) pedir • **if you need anything, just ask** si quieres algo no tienes más que pedirlo • **the asking price** el precio que se pide/pedía *etc* • **I offered £5,000 below the asking price** les ofrecí 5.000 libras menos de lo que pedían • **it's yours for the asking** no tienes más que pedirlo y es tuyo

▸ **ask after** (VI + PREP) [+ *person*] preguntar por; [+ *sb's health*] preguntar por, interesarse por • **Jane was asking after you** Jane (me) preguntaba por ti

▸ **ask along** (VT + ADV) invitar • **ask him along if you like** si quieres, dile que venga, invítale si quieres

▸ **ask around** (VI + ADV) preguntar por ahí • **ask around to find out which are the best schools** pregunta por ahí y entérate de cuáles son las mejores escuelas

▸ **ask back** (VT + ADV) (*for second visit*) volver a invitar; (*on reciprocal visit*) devolver la invitación a • **she asked me back to her house after the show** me invitó a su casa después del espectáculo

▸ **ask for** (VI + PREP) **1** (= *request*) pedir, solicitar (*more frm*) • **he wrote asking for help** escribió pidiendo *or* (*more frm*) solicitando ayuda • **to ask for sth back** pedir que se devuelva algo

2 (= *look for*) • **to ask for sb** preguntar por algn • **there's someone asking for you at reception** hay alguien en recepción que pregunta por ti

3 (*in idiomatic phrases*) • **he is all I could ask for in a son** tiene todo lo que podría pedirle a un hijo • **he asked for it!** ¡él se lo ha buscado! • **you're asking for a good smack!** ¡si sigues así, te vas a ganar una buena bofetada! • **it's just asking for trouble** eso no es otra cosa que buscarse problemas

(VT + PREP) • **to ask sb for sth** pedir algo a algn

▸ **ask in** (VT + ADV) invitar a entrar, invitar a pasar • **to ask sb in for a drink** invitar a algn a que pase a tomar algo

▸ **ask out** (VT + ADV) invitar a salir • **they never ask her out** no la invitan nunca a salir (con ellos) • **he asked her out to dinner** la invitó (a salir) a cenar

▸ **ask over** (VT + ADV) invitar (a casa)

▸ **ask round** (VT + ADV) invitar (a casa) • **they've asked us round for drinks** nos han invitado (a su casa) a tomar unas copas

ASK

▸ *Translate* **ask** *by* **preguntar** *only in contexts where information is being sought:*

I'll ask him
Voy a preguntárselo
Ask her what she thinks
Pregúntale qué le parece
We asked everywhere
Preguntamos en todas partes

▸ *Use* **pedir** *when* **ask** *means "request" or "demand":*

No one asked to see my passport
Nadie me pidió el pasaporte
We asked them to be here before five
Les pedimos que estuviesen *or* estuvieran aquí antes de las cinco
He was asked to explain his behaviour
Le pidieron que explicara su comportamiento

NOTE: **Pedir que** *is followed by the subjunctive.*

For further uses and examples, see **ask, ask about, ask for** *etc*

askance [əˈskɑːns] (ADV) • **to look ~ at sb** mirar a algn con recelo *or* desconfianza • **to look ~ at sth** ver algo con recelo *or* desconfianza

askew [əˈskjuː] (ADJ) ladeado • **the picture is ~** el cuadro está torcido
(ADV) de lado

asking price [ˈɑːskɪŋˌpraɪs] (N) precio *m* solicitado

ASL [ˌeɪesˈel] (N ABBR) (= **American Sign Language**) lenguaje *m* americano por signos, lenguaje *m* gestual americano

aslant [əˈslɑːnt] (ADV) a través, oblicuamente
(PREP) a través de

asleep [əˈsliːp] (ADJ) **1** (= *not awake*) dormido • **to be ~** estar dormido • **to be fast** *or* **sound ~** estar profundamente dormido • **to fall ~** dormirse, quedarse dormido

2 (= *numb*) adormecido • **my foot's ~** se me ha (quedado) dormido el pie

ASLEF [ˈæzlef] (N ABBR) (*Brit*) = **Associated Society of Locomotive Engineers and Firemen**

AS level [ˌeɪˈeslevl] (N) (*Brit*) (= **Advanced Subsidiary level**) *certificado académico que se hace después de los GCSEs y que cuenta para los A levels*; ▸ **GCSE**

ASM (N ABBR) **1** (*Mil*) = **air-to-surface missile**
2 (*Theat*) = **assistant stage manager**

asocial [eɪˈsəʊʃəl] (ADJ) **1** (= *solitary*) asocial, insociable
2 (= *antisocial*) antisocial

asp¹ [æsp] (N) áspid(e) *m*

asp² [æsp] = **aspen**

ASP (ABBR) = **American Selling Price**

asparagus [əsˈpærəgəs] (N) (= *plant*) espárrago *m*; (= *food*) espárragos *mpl*
(CPD) ▸ **asparagus tips** puntas *fpl* de espárrago

aspartame [əˈspɑːˌteɪm] (N) aspartamo *m*

ASPCA (N ABBR) (*US*) = **American Society for the Prevention of Cruelty to Animals**

aspect [ˈæspekt] (N) **1** [*of situation*] aspecto *m* • **to study all ~s of a question** estudiar un asunto bajo todos sus aspectos • **seen from this ~** desde este punto de vista

2 [*of building, room*] • **a house with a northerly ~** una casa orientada hacia el norte

3 (*Gram*) aspecto *m*

aspen [ˈæspən] (N) álamo *m* temblón

asperity [æsˈperɪtɪ] (N) aspereza *f*

aspersion [əsˈpɜːʃən] (N) calumnia *f* • **to cast ~s on sb** difamar *or* calumniar a algn

asphalt [ˈæsfælt] (N) **1** (= *material*) asfalto *m*

2 (= *surface, ground*) pista *f* asfaltada, recinto *m* asfaltado
(VT) asfaltar
(CPD) ▸ **asphalt jungle** jungla *f* de asfalto

asphodel [ˈæsfəˌdel] (N) asfódelo *m*

asphyxia [æsˈfɪksɪə] (N) asfixia *f*

asphyxiate [æsˈfɪksɪeɪt] (VT) asfixiar
(VI) asfixiarse, morir asfixiado

asphyxiation [æsˌfɪksɪˈeɪʃən] (N) asfixia *f*

aspic [ˈæspɪk] (N) gelatina *f* (*de carne etc*)

aspidistra [ˌæspɪˈdɪstrə] (N) aspidistra *f*

aspirant [ˈæspɪrənt] (N) aspirante *mf*, candidato/a *m/f* (**to** a)

aspirate (ADJ) [ˈæspərɪt] aspirado
(N) [ˈæspərɪt] aspirada *f*
(VT) [ˈæspəreɪt] aspirar • **~d H** H *f* aspirada

aspiration [ˌæspəˈreɪʃən] (N) (*also Ling*) aspiración *f*

aspirational [ˌæspəˈreɪʃənl] (ADJ) [*person*] con aspiraciones; [*product*] que viste mucho, que queda muy bien

aspire [əsˈpaɪəʳ] (VI) • **to ~ to sth** aspirar a algo • **we can't ~ to that** no aspiramos a tanto, nuestras pretensiones son más modestas • **he ~s to a new car** anhela tener un coche nuevo • **to ~ to do sth** aspirar a hacer algo, ambicionar hacer algo

aspirin [ˈæsprɪn] (N) (PL: **aspirin, aspirins**) (= *substance, tablet*) aspirina *f*

aspiring [əsˈpaɪərɪŋ] (ADJ) (= *ambitious*) ambicioso; (= *budding*) en potencia, en ciernes • **this is good news for any ~ politician** eso es bueno para cualquier político en potencia *or* en ciernes

ass¹ [æs] (N) **1** (*Zool*) asno *m*, burro *m*
2* (= *fool*) imbécil *mf* • **the man's an ass** es un imbécil • **don't be an ass!** ¡no seas imbécil! • **what an ass I am!** ¡soy un imbécil!, ¡qué burro soy!* • IDIOM: • **to make an ass of o.s.** quedar en ridículo

ass²‡‡ [æs] (*US*) (N) culo‡ *m* • **a piece of ass** (= *girl*) un bombón* • **to have a piece of ass** (= *sex*) echar un polvo‡‡

assail [əˈseɪl] (VT) (*frm*) **1** (= *attack*) (*lit*) acometer, atacar; (*fig*) atacar • **he was ~ed by critics** le atacaron los críticos • **a sound ~ed my ear** un ruido penetró (en) mis oídos

2 (= *bombard*) • **to ~ sb with questions** asaltar *or* bombardear a algn a preguntas, freír a algn a preguntas* • **they ~ed her with questions** la asaltaron *or* bombardearon a preguntas, la frieron a preguntas* • **he was ~ed by doubts** • **doubts ~ed him** le asaltaban las dudas

assailant [əˈseɪlənt] (N) asaltante *mf*, agresor(a) *m/f* • **she did not recognize her ~s** no reconoció a los que la agredieron • **there were four ~s** eran cuatro los agresores

Assam [æˈsæm] (N) Assam *m*

assassin [əˈsæsɪn] (N) asesino/a *m/f*

assassinate [əˈsæsɪneɪt] (VT) asesinar

assassination [əˌsæsɪˈneɪʃən] (N) asesinato *m*

assault [əˈsɔːlt] (N) **1** (*Mil*) (*also fig*) asalto *m*, ataque *m* (**on** a) • **to make** *or* **mount an ~ on** asaltar

2 (*Jur*) agresión *f* • **~ and battery** (*Jur*) lesiones *fpl*; ▸ **indecent**
(VT) **1** (*Mil*) asaltar, atacar
2 (*Jur*) asaltar, agredir; (*sexually*) agredir sexualmente; (= *rape*) violar
(CPD) ▸ **assault course** pista *f* americana ▸ **assault craft** barcaza *f* de asalto ▸ **assault rifle** fusil *m* de asalto, rifle *m* de asalto ▸ **assault troops** tropas *fpl* de asalto ▸ **assault weapon** fusil *m* de asalto, rifle *m* de asalto

assay (N) [əˈseɪ] [*of metal, mineral etc*] ensayo *m*; [*of gold*] ensayo *m*,

aquilatamiento *m*
(VT) **1** [+ *metal, mineral etc*] ensayar; [+ *gold*] ensayar, aquilatar; (*fig*) intentar, probar
2†† (= *try*) • **to ~ to** (+ *infin*) intentar (+ *infin*)
(CPD) ▸ **assay mark** señal *f* de ensayo
▸ **assay office** oficina *f* de ensayo

assemblage [əˈsemblɪdʒ] (N) **1** [*of people*] reunión *f*; [*of things*] colección *f*
2 (*Mech*) montaje *m*

assemble [əˈsembl] (VT) **1** (= *bring together*) [+ *people, team, collection*] reunir; [+ *facts, evidence, ideas*] recopilar; (*Parl*) convocar • **the ~d dignitaries** los dignatarios reunidos, la reunión de dignatarios
2 (= *put together*) [+ *device, machine, piece of furniture*] armar, montar
(VI) reunirse

assembler [əˈsembləʳ] (N) **1** (= *worker*) ensamblador(a) *m/f*, montador(a) *m/f*
2 (*Comput*) ensamblador *m*

Assembly [əˈsemblɪ] (N) (= *Parliament*) • **the Welsh ~** el Parlamento del País de Gales • **the Northern Ireland ~** el Parlamento de Irlanda del Norte • **the ~** (*US*) la Asamblea

assembly [əˈsemblɪ] (N) **1** (= *meeting*) reunión *f*, asamblea *f*; (= *people present*) concurrencia *f*, asistentes *mpl* • **the right of ~** el derecho de reunión
2 (*Pol*) asamblea *f*
3 (*Brit*) (*Scol*) reunión *f* general de todos los alumnos
4 (*Tech*) montaje *m*, ensamblaje *m*
(CPD) ▸ **assembly language** (*Comput*) lenguaje *m* ensamblador ▸ **assembly line** cadena *f* de montaje ▸ **assembly line production** producción *f* en cadena ▸ **assembly line worker** trabajador(a) *m/f* en línea *or* cadena de montaje ▸ **assembly plant** planta *f* de montaje, maquiladora *f* (*Mex*) ▸ **assembly room(s)** salón *m* de celebraciones ▸ **assembly shop** taller *m* de montaje

assemblyman [əˈsemblɪmən] (N) (PL: **assemblymen**) (*US*) asambleísta *m*, miembro *m* de una asamblea

assemblywoman [əˈsemblɪwʊmən] (N) (PL: **assemblywomen**) (*US*) asambleísta *f*, miembro *f* de una asamblea

assent [əˈsent] (N) (= *agreement*) asentimiento *m*, consentimiento *m*; (= *approval*) aprobación *f* • **royal ~** aprobación *f* real • **by common ~** de común acuerdo • **to nod one's ~** asentir con la cabeza
(VI) asentir (**to** a), consentir (**to** en)

assert [əˈsɜːt] (VT) **1** (= *declare*) afirmar, aseverar; [+ *innocence*] afirmar
2 (= *insist on*) [+ *rights*] hacer valer
3 (= *establish*) [+ *authority*] imponer
4 • **to ~ o.s.** imponerse

assertion [əˈsɜːʃən] (N) afirmación *f*, aseveración *f*

assertive [əˈsɜːtɪv] (ADJ) [*manner, tone*] firme y enérgico; [*behaviour*] enérgico • **try to be a bit more ~** intenta ser un poco más firme y enérgico, intenta hacerte valer un poco más • **you were very ~ in that meeting** te mostraste muy firme y enérgico en esa reunión • **slowly she began to become more ~** poco a poco empezó a mostrarse más segura de sí misma *or* empezó a hacerse valer más

assertively [əˈsɜːtɪvlɪ] (ADV) [*speak, reply*] con firmeza, con convicción

assertiveness [əˈsɜːtɪvnɪs] (N) firmeza *f*
(CPD) ▸ **assertiveness course** curso *m* de autoafirmación ▸ **assertiveness training** ejercicios *mpl* de reafirmación personal

assess [əˈses] (VT) **1** (= *evaluate*) [+ *damage, property*] valorar, tasar; [+ *situation etc*] valorar • **how do you ~ your chances now?** ¿cómo valora sus posibilidades ahora?
2 (= *calculate*) [+ *value, amount*] calcular (**at** en); [+ *income*] gravar
3 (*Univ, Scol, Ind*) evaluar • **how did you ~ this candidate?** ¿cómo evaluó a este candidato?

assessable [əˈsesəbl] (ADJ) calculable, tasable • **~ income** ingresos *mpl* imponibles • **a theory not readily ~** una teoría difícil de enjuiciar

assessment [əˈsesmənt] (N) **1** (= *evaluation*) [*of damage, property*] valoración *f*, tasación *f*; (= *judgment*) juicio *m*, valoración *f* • **what is your ~ of the situation?** ¿qué juicio *or* valoración le merece la situación?
2 (*Econ, Tax*) • **tax ~** cálculo *m* de los ingresos, estimación *f* de la base impositiva
3 (*Univ, Scol*) (= *appraisal*) evaluación *f*;
▸ **continuous**

assessor [əˈsesəʳ] (N) **1** (*Jur*) perito/a *m/f* asesor(a)
2 (*Insurance*) perito/a *m/f* tasador(a)
3 (*Educ*) examinador(a) *m/f*
4 (*US*) [*of taxes etc*] tasador(a) *m/f*

asset [ˈæset] (N) **1** (= *advantage*) ventaja *f* • **she is a great ~ to the department** es una persona valiosísima en el departamento
2 (*Econ etc*) bien *m*; (= *book-keeping item*) partida *f* del activo • **~s** (*on accounts*) haberes *mpl*, activo *msing* • **personal ~s** bienes *mpl* personales • **real ~s** bienes *mpl* muebles, bienes *mpl* raíces • **~s and liabilities** activo *msing* y pasivo *msing* • **~s in hand** activo *msing* disponible, bienes *mpl* disponibles
(CPD) ▸ **asset stripper** (*Econ*) *especulador que compra empresas en crisis para vender sus bienes* ▸ **asset stripping** (*Econ*) *acaparamiento de activos con vistas a su venta y a la liquidación de la empresa*

asseverate [əˈsevəreɪt] (VT) (*frm*) aseverar

asseveration [əˌsevəˈreɪʃən] (N) (*frm*) aseveración *f*

asshole** [ˈæshəʊl] (*esp US*) (N) **1** (*Anat*) culo‡ *m*
2 (= *person*) gilipollas** *mf inv*

assiduity [ˌæsɪˈdjuːɪtɪ] (N) diligencia *f*

assiduous [əˈsɪdjʊəs] (ADJ) diligente

assiduously [əˈsɪdjʊəslɪ] (ADV) diligentemente

assiduousness [əˈsɪdjʊəsnɪs] (N) diligencia *f*

assign [əˈsaɪn] (VT) **1** (= *allot*) [+ *task*] asignar; [+ *room*] destinar; [+ *date*] señalar, fijar (**for** para) • **which is the room ~ed to me?** ¿qué habitación se me ha destinado?
2 [+ *person*] destinar • **to ~ sb to sth** destinar a algn a algo • **they ~ed him to the Paris embassy** lo destinaron a la embajada de París
3 (= *attribute*) [+ *literary work, sculpture*] atribuir; [+ *reason*] señalar, indicar
4 (*Jur*) [+ *property*] ceder
(N) (*Jur*) cesionario/a *m/f*

assignation [ˌæsɪgˈneɪʃən] (N) **1** (= *meeting*) [*of lovers*] cita *f* secreta
2 (= *allocation*) [*of money, person, responsibility*] asignación *f*

assignee [ˌæsaɪˈniː] (N) (*Jur*) = **assign**

assignment [əˈsaɪnmənt] (N) **1** (= *mission*) misión *f*; (= *task*) tarea *f* • **to be on (an) ~** estar cumpliendo una misión
2 (*Scol, Univ*) trabajo *m*
3 (= *allocation*) asignación *f*

assignor [ˌæsaɪˈnɔːʳ] (N) (*Jur*) cedente *mf*, cesionista *mf*

assimilate [əˈsɪmɪleɪt] (VT) asimilar
(VI) asimilarse

assimilation [əˌsɪmɪˈleɪʃən] (N) asimilación *f*

Assisi [əˈsiːzɪ] (N) Asís *m*

assist [əˈsɪst] (VT) (= *help*) [+ *person*] ayudar; [+ *development, growth etc*] fomentar, estimular • **to ~ sb to do sth** ayudar a algn a hacer algo • **we ~ed him to his car** le ayudamos a llegar a su coche
(VI) (= *help*) ayudar • **to ~ in sth** ayudar en algo • **to ~ in doing sth** ayudar a hacer algo
(N) (*Sport*) asistencia *f*

assistance [əˈsɪstəns] (N) ayuda *f*, auxilio *m* • **to be of ~ to** • **give ~ to** ayudar a, prestar ayuda a • **can I be of any ~?** ¿puedo ayudarle?, ¿le puedo servir en algo? • **to come to sb's ~** acudir en ayuda *or* auxilio de algn

assistant [əˈsɪstənt] (N) ayudante *mf*; (= *language assistant*) lector(a) *m/f*
(CPD) ▸ **assistant director** (*Theat*) ayudante *mf* de dirección ▸ **assistant manager** subdirector(a) *m/f* ▸ **assistant master** (*Brit*) (*Scol*†) profesor *m* de instituto ▸ **assistant mistress** (*Brit*) (*Scol*†) profesora *f* de instituto ▸ **assistant principal** (*Scol*) subdirector(a) *m/f* ▸ **assistant professor** (*US*) profesor(a) *m/f* agregado/a ▸ **assistant referee** (*Ftbl*) árbitro/a *m/f* asistente ▸ **assistant secretary** subsecretario/a *m/f*

assistantship [əˈsɪstəntʃɪp] (N) **1** (*Brit*) (*at school*) lectorado *m*
2 (*US*) (*at college*) agregaduría *f*, puesto *m* de profesor agregado

assisted [əˈsɪstɪd] (ADJ) • **~ passage** pasaje *m* subvencionado • **~ place** (*Brit*) (*Scol*) *plaza de un colegio privado, subvencionada por el gobierno y destinada a alumnos seleccionados que no pueden sufragar las cuotas del mismo* • **~ suicide** suicidio *m* asistido

assizes [əˈsaɪzɪz] (NPL) (*Brit*) (*Jur*) sesiones *fpl* jurídicas (regionales)

assn. (ABBR) = **association**

assoc. (ABBR) **1** = **association**
2 = **associate(d)**

associate (ADJ) [əˈsəʊʃɪɪt] [*company*] asociado
(N) [əˈsəʊʃɪɪt] (= *colleague*) colega *mf*; (*in crime*) cómplice *mf*; (*also* **associate member**) [*of society*] miembro *mf* no numerario/a; [*of professional body*] colegiado/a *m/f*; [*of learned body*] miembro *mf* correspondiente • **Fred Bloggs and Associates** Fred Bloggs y Asociados
(VT) [əˈsəʊʃɪeɪt] **1** (*mentally*) [+ *ideas, things, people*] asociar, relacionar • **to ~ one thing with another** asociar *or* relacionar una cosa con otra • **I always ~ you with Barcelona** siempre te asocio *or* relaciono con Barcelona
2 (= *affiliate, connect*) vincular, asociar • **to be ~d with sth/sb: high blood pressure is ~d with heart disease** se vincula *or* asocia la tensión alta con las enfermedades coronarias • **he was ~d with the communist party** estaba vinculado *or* asociado con el partido comunista • **it is a privilege to be ~d with her** es un privilegio estar relacionado con ella • **I don't wish to be ~d** *or* **to ~ myself with it/him** no quiero tener nada que ver con ello/él
(VI) [əˈsəʊʃɪeɪt] • **to ~ with sb** relacionarse con algn, tratar con algn
(CPD) [əˈsəʊʃɪɪt] ▸ **associate degree** (*US*) licenciatura *f* ▸ **associate director** subdirector(a) *m/f*, director(a) *m/f* adjunto/a ▸ **associate judge** juez *mf* asesor(a) ▸ **Associate Justice** (*US*) juez *mf* asociado/a ▸ **associate member** [*of society*] miembro *mf* no numerario/a; [*of professional body*] colegiado/a *m/f*; [*of learned body*] miembro *mf* correspondiente ▸ **associate producer** (*TV, Cine*) productor(a) *m/f* asociado/a ▸ **associate professor** (*US*) profesor(a) *m/f* adjunto/a ▸ **associate's degree** (*US*) licenciatura *f*

associated [əˈsəʊʃɪeɪtɪd] (ADJ) **1** (= *connected*) asociado, relacionado • **engineering**

problems ~ with aircraft design problemas de ingeniería asociados *or* relacionados con el diseño de aviones
2 (*Comm*) asociado, afiliado
CPD ▸ **associated company** compañía *f* asociada, compañía *f* afiliada

association [əˌsəʊsɪ'eɪʃən] N **1** (= *act, partnership*) asociación *f* • **in ~ with** conjuntamente con • **to form an ~ with** asociarse con
2 (= *organization*) sociedad *f*, asociación *f*
3 (= *connection*) conexión *f* • **~ of ideas** asociación *f* de ideas
4 associations (= *memories*) recuerdos *mpl* • **the name has unpleasant ~s** el nombre trae recuerdos desagradables • **the town has historic ~s** la ciudad posee connotaciones históricas
CPD ▸ **association football** (*Brit*) fútbol *m*

associative [ə'səʊʃɪətɪv] ADJ **1** (*Math*) asociativo
2 (*Comput*) • **~ storage** almacenamiento *m* asociativo

assonance ['æsənəns] N asonancia *f*

assonant ['æsənənt] ADJ asonante
N asonante *f*

assonate ['æsəneɪt] VI asonar

assort [ə'sɔːt] VI concordar (**with** con), convenir (**with** a) • **it ~s ill with his character** no cuadra con su carácter

assorted [ə'sɔːtɪd] ADJ surtido • **~ cakes** pasteles surtidos • **he dined with ~ ministers** cenó con diversos ministros

assortment [ə'sɔːtmənt] N **1** (*Comm*) surtido *m*
2 (= *mixture*) mezcla *f*; (= *collection*) colección *f* • **there was a strange ~ of guests** había una extraña mezcla de invitados • **Peter was there with an ~ of girlfriends** allí estaba Peter con una colección de amigas • **quite an ~!** ¡aquí hay de todo!

asst. ABBR (= **assistant**) ayte.

assuage [ə'sweɪdʒ] VT (*liter*) [+ *feelings, anger*] aplacar; [+ *pain*] calmar, aliviar; [+ *passion*] mitigar, suavizar; [+ *desire*] satisfacer; [+ *appetite*] satisfacer, saciar; [+ *person*] apaciguar, sosegar • **he was not easily ~d** no resultaba fácil apaciguarlo *or* sosegarlo

assume [ə'sjuːm] VT **1** (= *suppose*) suponer • **we may therefore ~ that ...** así, es de suponer que ... • **let us ~ that ...** pongamos por caso *or* supongamos que ... • **assuming that ...** suponiendo que ..., en el supuesto de que ... • **you are assuming a lot** supones demasiado, eso es mucho suponer • **you resigned, I ~** dimitiste, me imagino
2 (= *take on, take over*) [+ *power, control, responsibility*] asumir; [+ *authority*] (*unjustly*) apropiarse, arrogarse
3 (= *adopt*) [+ *name, attitude, look of surprise*] adoptar; [+ *air*] darse

assumed [ə'sjuːmd] ADJ [*name*] falso, fingido • **under an ~ name** bajo *or* con (un) nombre falso

assumption [ə'sʌmpʃən] N **1** (= *supposition*) suposición *f*, supuesto *m* • **on the ~ that** suponiendo que, poniendo por caso que • **we cannot make that ~** no podemos dar eso por sentado • **to start from a false ~** partir de una base falsa
2 (= *taking*) [*of power, responsibility*] asunción *f*
3 • **the Assumption** (*Rel*) la Asunción
CPD ▸ **Assumption Day** Día *m* de la Asunción

assurance [ə'ʃʊərəns] N **1** (= *guarantee*) garantía *f*, promesa *f* • **you have my ~ that ...** les aseguro que ... • **I give you my ~ that ...** le puedo asegurar que ... • **I can give you no ~ about that** no les puedo garantizar nada
2 (= *certainty*) certeza *f*, seguridad *f* • **with the ~ that ...** con la seguridad de que ...
3 (= *confidence*) confianza *f*; (= *self-confidence*) seguridad *f*, aplomo *m* • **he spoke with ~** habló con seguridad *or* aplomo
4 (*esp Brit*) (= *insurance*) seguro *m*; ▹ **life**
CPD ▸ **assurance company** (*esp Brit*) compañía *f* de seguros

assure [ə'ʃʊəʳ] VT **1** (= *ensure*) asegurar, garantizar • **success was ~d** el éxito estaba asegurado • **to ~ o.s. of sth** asegurarse de algo
2 (= *reassure*) asegurar • **I ~d him of my support** le aseguré mi apoyo • **you may rest ~d that ...** • **let me ~ you that ...** tenga la (plena) seguridad de que ... • **it is so, I ~ you** es así, se lo garantizo
3 (*esp Brit*) (*Econ*) asegurar • **his life is ~d for £500,000** su vida está asegurada en 500.000 libras

assured [ə'ʃʊəd] ADJ **1** (= *self-assured*) seguro, confiado
2 (= *certain*) seguro • **you have an ~ future** tienes un porvenir seguro
N • **the ~** (*esp Brit*) (*Econ*) (*sing*) el asegurado/la asegurada; (*pl*) los asegurados/las aseguradas

assuredly [ə'ʃʊərɪdlɪ] ADV **1** (= *without doubt*) sin duda • **she is ~ the ideal person for the job** sin duda es la persona ideal para el puesto, no hay ninguna duda de que es la persona ideal para el puesto • **most ~** con toda seguridad
2 (= *confidently*) con confianza, sin titubeos

assuredness [ə'ʃʊədnɪs] N (= *confidence*) seguridad *f*, confianza *f*

ass-wipe** ['æswaɪp] N (*US*) **1** (= *toilet paper*) papel *m* del wáter*
2 (= *person*) mamón/ona** *m/f*

Assyria [ə'sɪrɪə] N Asiria *f*

Assyrian [ə'sɪrɪən] ADJ asirio
N asirio/a *m/f*

AST N ABBR (*US, Canada*) = **Atlantic Standard Time**

aster ['æstəʳ] N áster *f*

asterisk ['æstərɪsk] N asterisco *m*
VT señalar con un asterisco, poner un asterisco a

astern [ə'stɜːn] ADV (*Naut*) a popa • **to fall ~** quedarse atrás • **to go ~** ciar, ir hacia atrás • **to make a boat fast ~** amarrar un barco por la popa • **~ of** detrás de

asteroid ['æstərɔɪd] N asteroide *m*

asthma ['æsmə] N asma *m or f*

asthmatic [æs'mætɪk] ADJ asmático
N asmático/a *m/f*

astigmatic [ˌæstɪg'mætɪk] ADJ astigmático

astigmatism [æs'tɪgmətɪzəm] N astigmatismo *m*

astir [ə'stɜːʳ] ADJ **1** • **to be ~** (= *on the go*) estar activo, estar en movimiento
2† (= *out of bed*) estar levantado • **we were ~ early** nos levantamos temprano • **nobody was ~ at that hour** a tal hora todos estaban todavía en la cama

ASTM N ABBR (*US*) = **American Society for Testing Materials**

ASTMS N ABBR (*Brit*) = **Association of Scientific, Technical and Managerial Staff**

astonish [ə'stɒnɪʃ] VT asombrar, pasmar • **you ~ me!** (*iro*) ¡no me digas!, ¡vaya sorpresa!

astonished [ə'stɒnɪʃt] ADJ estupefacto, pasmado • **to be ~** asombrarse (**at de**) • **I am ~ that ...** me asombra que ... (+ *subjun*)

astonishing [ə'stɒnɪʃɪŋ] ADJ [*achievement, coincidence, news*] asombroso, pasmoso • **I find it ~ that ...** me asombra *or* pasma que ... (+ *subjun*), me parece increíble que ... (+ *subjun*)

astonishingly [ə'stɒnɪʃɪŋlɪ] ADV asombrosamente • **it was ~ easy** asombraba lo fácil que era, era asombrosamente fácil • **an ~ beautiful young woman** una joven de una belleza asombrosa • **she has ~ blue eyes** tiene unos ojos de un azul increíble • **he learned the language ~ quickly** aprendió la lengua con una rapidez asombrosa, fue asombroso lo rápido que aprendió la lengua • **~ (enough), he was right** por increíble que parezca, tenía razón

astonishment [ə'stɒnɪʃmənt] N asombro *m*; (*stronger*) estupefacción *f* • **a look of ~** una mirada de asombro; (*stronger*) una mirada de estupefacción • **her ~ at my good fortune** su asombro *or* sorpresa ante mi buena suerte • **to my ~** para mi asombro *or* sorpresa

astound [ə'staʊnd] VT asombrar, pasmar

astounded [ə'staʊndɪd] ADJ pasmado, estupefacto • **I am ~** estoy pasmado

astounding [ə'staʊndɪŋ] ADJ asombroso, pasmoso • **~!** ¡esto es asombroso! • **I find it ~ that ...** me asombra *or* pasma que ... (+ *subjun*)

astoundingly [ə'staʊndɪŋlɪ] ADV asombrosamente • **he has done ~ well** le ha ido asombrosamente bien, es asombroso lo bien que le ha ido • **she has ~ blue eyes** tiene unos ojos de un azul increíble • **~, an American won the Tour de France** por asombroso que parezca, un americano ganó el Tour de France

astrakhan [ˌæstrə'kæn] N astracán *m*

astral ['æstrəl] ADJ astral
CPD ▸ **astral projection** viaje *m* astral

astray [ə'streɪ] ADV **1** (*lit*) • **to go ~** (= *get lost*) extraviarse
2 (*fig*) • **to go ~** (= *make a mistake*) equivocarse; (*morally*) ir por mal camino • **to lead sb ~** llevar a algn por mal camino • **I was led ~ by his voice** su voz me despistó

astride [ə'straɪd] ADV a horcajadas
PREP [+ *horse, fence*] a horcajadas sobre

astringency [əs'trɪndʒənsɪ] N **1** (*Med*) astringencia *f*
2 (*fig*) adustez *f*, austeridad *f*

astringent [əs'trɪndʒənt] ADJ **1** (*Med*) astringente
2 (*fig*) adusto, austero
N (*Med*) astringente *m*

astro... [æstrəʊ] PREFIX astro...

astrolabe ['æstrəʊleɪb] N astrolabio *m*

astrologer [əs'trɒlədʒəʳ] N astrólogo/a *m/f*

astrological [ˌæstrə'lɒdʒɪkəl] ADJ astrológico

astrologically [ˌæstrə'lɒdʒɪklɪ] ADV astrológicamente

astrologist [əs'trɒlədʒɪst] N astrólogo/a *m/f*

astrology [əs'trɒlədʒɪ] N astrología *f*

astronaut ['æstrənɔːt] N astronauta *mf*

astronautic [ˌæstrəʊ'nɔːtɪk] ADJ = **astronautical**

astronautical [ˌæstrəʊ'nɔːtɪkəl] ADJ astronáutico

astronautics [ˌæstrəʊ'nɔːtɪks] NSING astronáutica *f*

astronomer [əs'trɒnəməʳ] N astrónomo/a *m/f*

astronomic [ˌæstrə'nɒmɪk] ADJ = **astronomical**

astronomical [ˌæstrə'nɒmɪkəl] ADJ (*lit, fig*) astronómico

astronomically [ˌæstrə'nɒmɪkəlɪ] ADV [*rise, grow, increase*] astronómicamente, exageradamente • **lobster is ~ expensive** la langosta está a precios astronómicos • **they set ~ high standards for their employees** exigen un nivel exageradamente alto a sus empleados

astronomy [əs'trɒnəmɪ] N astronomía *f*
astrophysicist [,æstrəʊ'fɪzɪsɪst] N astrofísico/a *m/f*
astrophysics ['æstrəʊ'fɪzɪks] NSING astrofísica *f*
Astroturf® ['æstrəʊtɜːf] N césped *m* artificial
Asturian [æ'stʊərɪən] ADJ asturiano
N **1** (= *person*) asturiano/a *m/f*
2 (*Ling*) asturiano *m*
Asturias [æ'stʊərɪæs] N Asturias *f*
astute [əs'tjuːt] ADJ [*person, decision*] astuto, sagaz; [*mind*] astuto; [*choice*] inteligente • **that was very ~ of you** en eso has sido muy listo
astutely [əs'tjuːtlɪ] ADV [*decide*] astutamente, sagazmente; [*choose*] inteligentemente
astuteness [əs'tjuːtnɪs] N astucia *f*, sagacidad *f*
asunder [ə'sʌndəʳ] ADV • **to tear ~** (*liter*) hacer pedazos
ASV N ABBR (*US*) (= **American Standard Version**) *traducción americana de la Biblia*
Aswan [æs'wɑːn] N Asuán *f*
CPD ▸ **Aswan High Dam** Presa *f* de Asuán
asylum [ə'saɪləm] N **1** (= *refuge*) asilo *m* • **to seek political ~** pedir asilo político • **to afford** *or* **give ~ to sb** [*place*] servir de asilo a algn; [*person*] dar asilo a algn
2† (= *mental hospital*) manicomio *m*
CPD ▸ **asylum seeker** solicitante *mf* de asilo
asymmetric [,eɪsɪ'metrɪk] ADJ = asymmetrical
asymmetrical [,eɪsɪ'metrɪkəl] ADJ asimétrico
CPD ▸ **asymmetrical bars** (*Sport*) barras *fpl* asimétricas
asymmetry [eɪ'sɪmətrɪ] N asimetría *f*
asymptomatic [æ,sɪmptə'mætɪk] ADJ asintomático
asynchronous [æ'sɪŋkrənəs] ADJ asíncrono
AT N ABBR (= **automatic translation**) TA *f*
at [æt]

> *When* **at** *is an element in a phrasal verb, eg* **look at**, *look up the verb.*

PREP **1** (*position*) **a** (*specifying rough location*) en • **there weren't many people at the party/lecture** no había mucha gente en la fiesta/conferencia • **at the hairdresser's/ supermarket** en la peluquería/el supermercado • **at the office** en la oficina • **at school** en la escuela, en el colegio • **at sea** en el mar • **at table** en la mesa • **at John's** en casa de Juan • IDIOMS: • **where it's at**: • **Glasgow's where it's at** en Glasgow es donde está la movida*, en Glasgow es donde está el rollo (*Sp**) • **where we're at**: • **I'll just run through where we're at** te voy a poner al tanto *or* al corriente de cuál es la situación
b (*specifying position*) • **my room's at the back of the house** mi dormitorio está en la parte de atrás de la casa • **the dress fastens at the back** el vestido se abrocha por detrás • **at the bottom of the stairs** al pie de las escaleras • **to stand at the door** estar de pie *or* (*LAm*) parado en la puerta • **at the edge** en el borde • **my room's at the front of the house** mi dormitorio está en la parte delantera de la casa • **the dress fastens at the front** el vestido se abrocha por delante • **at the top** (*gen*) en lo alto; (*of mountain*) en la cumbre • **to be at the window** estar junto a la ventana • **he came in at the window** entró por la ventana
c (*esp Internet*) (= *name of @ symbol*) arroba *f* • **"my email address is jones at collins dot uk"** (*jones@collins.uk*) —mi dirección electrónica es jones arroba collins punto uk
2 (*direction*) (= *towards*) hacia • **the car was coming straight at us** el coche venía directo hacia nosotros • **to look at sth** mirar algo
3 (*time, age*) a • **at four o'clock** a las cuatro • **at midday** a mediodía • **at 16 he was already a household name** a los 16 años era ya un nombre muy conocido • **at lunchtime** a la hora de la comida, a la hora de almorzar • **at an early age** de pequeño/pequeña • **at Christmas** por *or* en Navidades • **at Easter** en Semana Santa • **at the moment** en este momento • **at that moment the bomb went off** en aquel momento estalló la bomba • **at night** de noche, por la noche • **at a time like this** en un momento como este • **at my time of life** con los años que tengo
4 (*rate*) a • **at 50p a kilo** a 50 peniques el kilo • **at 50p each** (a) 50 peniques cada uno • **at a high price** a un precio elevado • **at 4% interest** al 4% de interés • **two at a time** de dos en dos • **to go at 100km an hour** ir a 100km por hora
5 (*activity*) • **he's good at games** se le dan bien los deportes • **at it**: • **while you're at it*** (= *doing it*) de paso; (= *by the way*) a propósito • **she's at it again*** otra vez con las mismas • **boys at play** muchachos que juegan, los muchachos cuando juegan • **I could tell she'd been at the whisky** se notaba que le había estado dando al whisky* • **at war** en guerra • **to be at work** (= *working*) estar trabajando; (= *in the office*) estar en la oficina
6 (*manner*) • **acting at its best** una actuación de antología • **at peace** en paz • **at a run** corriendo, a la carrera • **at full speed** a toda velocidad
7 (*cause*) • **to awaken at the least sound** despertarse al menor ruido • **at her cries** al escuchar sus gritos • **at my request** a petición mía • **at his suggestion** a sugerencia suya • **I was shocked/surprised at the news** me escandalizó/sorprendió la noticia
atavism ['ætəvɪzəm] N atavismo *m*
atavistic [,ætə'vɪstɪk] ADJ atávico
ataxia [ə'tæksɪə] N ataxia *f*
ataxic [ə'tæksɪk] ADJ atáxico
ATB N = **all-terrain bike**
ATC N ABBR = **Air Training Corps**
ate [et, eɪt] PT *of* **eat**
A-test ['eɪtest] N prueba *f* de bomba atómica
atheism ['eɪθɪɪzəm] N ateísmo *m*
atheist ['eɪθɪɪst] N ateo/a *m/f*
atheistic [,eɪθɪ'ɪstɪk] ADJ ateo, ateísta
Athenian [ə'θiːnɪən] ADJ ateniense
N ateniense *mf*
Athens ['æθɪnz] N Atenas *f*
athirst [ə'θɜːst] ADJ • **to be ~ for** (*liter*) tener sed de
athlete ['æθliːt] N atleta *mf*
CPD ▸ **athlete's foot** (*Med*) pie *m* de atleta ▸ **athletes' village** villa *f* olímpica
athletic [æθ'letɪk] ADJ **1** (*Sport*) [*club, association, event*] de atletismo
2 (= *sporty*) [*person, body*] atlético • **he was tall, with an ~ build** era alto y atlético
CPD ▸ **athletic sports** atletismo *msing*
athletically [æθ'letɪklɪ] ADV **1** (= *agilely*) [*jump, climb*] con agilidad, ágilmente
2 (*Sport*) • **~, she's outstanding** es una atleta excepcional • **~ talented youngsters** jóvenes con talento para el atletismo
athleticism [æθ'letsɪzəm] N atletismo *m*
athletics [æθ'letɪks] NSING (*Brit*) atletismo *m*; (*US*) deportes *mpl*
CPD ▸ **athletics coach** entrenador(a) *m/f* de atletismo ▸ **athletics competition** competición *f* atlética ▸ **athletics meeting** competición *f* atlética, prueba *f* atlética ▸ **athletics track** pista *f* de atletismo
at-home [ət'həʊm] N recepción *f* (*en casa particular*)
athwart [ə'θwɔːt] ADV de través, al través
PREP a través de
atishoo [ə'tɪʃuː] EXCL ¡(h)achís!
Atlantic [ət'læntɪk] ADJ atlántico
N • **the ~ (Ocean)** el (Océano) Atlántico
Atlanticism [ət'læntɪsɪzəm] N atlantismo *m*
Atlanticist [ət'læntɪsɪst] ADJ, N atlantista *mf*
Atlantis [ət'læntɪs] N Atlántida *f*
atlas ['ætləs] N **1** (= *world atlas*) atlas *m inv*; (= *road atlas*) guía *f* de carreteras
2 • **Atlas** (*Myth*) Atlas *m*, Atlante *m*
CPD ▸ **the Atlas Mountains** los Atlas
ATM N ABBR (*US*) (= **Automated Teller Machine**) cajero *m* automático • **ATM card** tarjeta *f* de cajero automático
atmosphere ['ætməsfɪəʳ] N **1** (= *air*) atmósfera *f*
2 (*fig*) ambiente *m*
atmospheric [,ætməs'ferɪk] ADJ **1** (*Met, Phys*) atmosférico
2 (*fig*) [*music, film, book*] evocador
CPD ▸ **atmospheric pollution** contaminación *f* atmosférica ▸ **atmospheric pressure** presión *f* atmosférica
atmospherics [,ætməs'ferɪks] NPL (*Rad*) interferencias *fpl*
ATO N ABBR (= **Australian Taxation Office**) *oficinas de la administración fiscal australiana*
atoll ['ætɒl] N atolón *m*
atom ['ætəm] N **1** (*Phys*) átomo *m*
2 (*fig*) pizca *f* • **there is not an ~ of truth in it** eso no tiene ni pizca de verdad • **if you had an ~ of sense** si tuvieras una gota de sentido común • **to smash sth to ~s** hacer algo añicos
CPD ▸ **atom bomb** bomba *f* atómica ▸ **atom smasher** acelerador *m* de partículas atómicas, rompeátomos *m inv*
atomic [ə'tɒmɪk] ADJ atómico
CPD ▸ **atomic age** era *f* atómica *or* nuclear ▸ **atomic bomb** bomba *f* atómica ▸ **atomic clock** reloj *m* atómico ▸ **atomic energy** energía *f* atómica *or* nuclear ▸ **Atomic Energy Authority** (*Brit*), **Atomic Energy Commission** (*US*) Consejo *m* de Energía Nuclear ▸ **atomic nucleus** núcleo *m* atómico ▸ **atomic number** número *m* atómico ▸ **atomic particle** partícula *f* atómica ▸ **atomic physics** física *f* atómica ▸ **atomic pile** pila *f* atómica ▸ **atomic power** (= *nation*) potencia *f* nuclear ▸ **atomic power station**† central *f* nuclear ▸ **atomic structure** estructura *f* atómica ▸ **atomic theory** teoría *f* de los átomos ▸ **atomic warfare** guerra *f* atómica ▸ **atomic warhead** cabeza *f* atómica ▸ **atomic weight** peso *m* atómico
atomic-powered [ə'tɒmɪk'paʊəd] ADJ impulsado por energía atómica
atomize ['ætəmaɪz] VT atomizar, pulverizar
atomizer ['ætəmaɪzəʳ] N atomizador *m*, pulverizador *m*
atonal [æ'təʊnl] ADJ atonal
atone [ə'təʊn] VI • **to ~ for** expiar
atonement [ə'təʊnmənt] N expiación *f* • **to make ~ for** enmendar, desagraviar • **Day of Atonement** Día *m* de la Expiación
atonic [æ'tɒnɪk] ADJ átono
atop [ə'tɒp] ADV encima
PREP (= *on*) encima de, sobre; [+ *mountain*] en la cumbre de, en la cima de • **he climbed**

~ a tank subió encima de un tanque

ATP N ABBR = **Association of Tennis Professionals**

atria ['eɪtrɪə] NPL *of* **atrium**

at-risk [ət'rɪsk] ADJ *[group]* en peligro
CPD ▸ **at-risk register** *(Brit) (Social Work)* ≈ registro *m* de delitos de violencia familiar *or* doméstica

atrium ['eɪtrɪəm] (PL: **atria** *or* **atriums**) N atrio *m*

atrocious [ə'trəʊʃəs] ADJ **1** *(= shocking) [crime, treatment]* atroz
2* *(= very bad) [film, food, spelling]* pésimo, espantoso; *[weather]* espantoso

atrociously [ə'trəʊʃəslɪ] ADV **1** *(= shockingly) [treat]* atrozmente • **he was ~ bad-tempered** tenía un genio atroz
2 *(= badly) [sing, spell, behave]* pésimamente, espantosamente

atrocity [ə'trɒsɪtɪ] N atrocidad *f*

atrophy ['ætrəfɪ] N *(Med)* atrofia *f*
VI atrofiarse
VT atrofiar

att. ABBR **1** *(Comm)* = **attached**
2 = **attorney**

attaboy* ['ætə,bɔɪ] EXCL *(esp US)* ¡bravo!, ¡dale!

attach [ə'tætʃ] VT **1** *(= fasten)* sujetar; *(= stick)* pegar; *(= tie)* atar, amarrar *(LAm)*; *(with pin etc)* prender; *(= join up) [+ trailer etc]* acoplar; *(= put on) [+ seal]* poner • **you ~ it to the wall with rings** se sujeta a la pared con argollas • **to ~ o.s. to** *[+ group]* agregarse a, unirse a • **he ~ed himself to us** *(pej)* se pegó a nosotros
2 *(in letter)* adjuntar • **the document is ~ed** enviamos adjunto el documento • **the ~ed letter** la carta adjunta • **please find ~ed details of ...** les adjuntamos detalles de ...
3 *(= attribute) [+ importance, value]* dar, atribuir **(to a)**
4 *(= associate, connect)* • **to ~ conditions (to sth)** imponer condiciones (a algo); ▹ **string**
5 *(Jur) [+ property]* incautar, embargar
VI **1** • **to ~ to** *(= correspond to)* corresponder a, pertenecer a • **certain duties ~ to this post** ciertas responsabilidades corresponden a este puesto • **no blame ~es to you** no tienes culpa alguna
2 *(Chem) [compound, atom]* unirse **(to a)**

attachable [ə'tætʃəbl] ADJ • **to be ~** poder adjuntarse

attaché [ə'tæʃeɪ] N agregado/a *m/f*; ▹ **cultural**
CPD ▸ **attaché case** maletín *m*

attached [ə'tætʃt] ADJ **1** *(= close)* • **they are very ~ (to each other)** se quieren mucho • **to be ~ to** *(= fond of) [+ person]* tener cariño a; *[+ theory]* estar apegado a • **to become ~ to sb** *(fig)* encariñarse con algn
2 • **to be ~*** *(= married, spoken for)* no estar libre
3 *(= associated)* • **the salary ~ to the post is ...** el sueldo que corresponde al puesto es ... • **to be ~ to an embassy** estar agregado a una embajada • **commission ~ to the Ministry of ...** comisión que depende del Ministerio de ...

attachment [ə'tætʃmənt] N **1** *(= accessory)* accesorio *m*, dispositivo *m*
2 *(Comput) (= document)* archivo *m* adjunto
3 *(= act of attaching)* unión *f*
4 *(to company, department etc)* adscripción *f* temporal • **to be on ~ (to)** estar adscrito temporalmente (a)
5 *(= affection)* cariño *m* **(to por)**; *(= loyalty)* adhesión *f*
6 *(Jur)* incautación *f*, embargo *m*

attack [ə'tæk] N **1** *(Mil, Sport) (also fig)* ataque *m* **(on a, contra, sobre)**; *(= assault)* atentado *m*, agresión *f* • **an ~ on sb's life** un atentado contra la vida de algn • **an ~ on the security of the state** un atentado contra la seguridad del estado • **to launch an ~** *(Mil) (also fig)* lanzar un ataque • **to leave o.s. open to ~** dejarse expuesto a un ataque • **to return to the ~** volver al ataque • **surprise ~** ataque por sorpresa • **to be/come under ~** ser atacado • PROVERB: • **~ is the best form of defence** la mejor defensa es el ataque
2 *(Med) (gen)* ataque *m*; *(= fit)* acceso *m*, crisis *f inv* • **an ~ of pneumonia** una pulmonía • **an ~ of nerves** un ataque de nervios, una crisis nerviosa; ▹ **heart**
VT **1** *(Mil, Sport, Med) (also fig)* atacar; *(= assault)* agredir; *[bull etc]* embestir • **it ~s the liver** ataca al hígado • **they mercilessly ~ed his Marxist approach** atacaron despiadadamente su enfoque marxista
2 *(= tackle) [+ job, problem]* enfrentarse con; *(= combat)* combatir • **we must ~ poverty** debemos combatir la pobreza
3 *(Chem)* atacar
VI atacar
CPD ▸ **attack dog** perro *m* de presa

attackable [ə'tækəbl] ADJ atacable, expuesto al ataque

attacker [ə'tækə^r] N agresor(a) *m/f*, atacante *mf*

attacking [ə'tækɪŋ] ADJ *(Sport) [style]* agresivo, de ataque

attagirl* ['ætə,gɜːl] EXCL *(esp US)* ¡bravo!, ¡dale!

attain [ə'teɪn] VT *(= achieve, reach) [+ knowledge]* lograr; *[+ happiness]* lograr, conquistar; *[+ goal, aim]* lograr, conseguir, alcanzar; *[+ age, rank]* llegar a, alcanzar; *(= get hold of)* conseguir
VI *(frm)* • **to ~ to** llegar a

attainable [ə'teɪnəbl] ADJ alcanzable

attainder [ə'teɪndə^r] N *(Jur)* extinción *f* de los derechos civiles de un individuo

attainment [ə'teɪnmənt] N **1** *(= achieving) [of knowledge]* logro *m*; *[of happiness]* logro *m*, conquista *f*; *[of independence, freedom]* conquista *f*, consecución *f*; *[of goal, aim]* logro *m*, consecución *f* • **difficult of ~** de difícil consecución, de difícil realización
2 *(= accomplishment)* logro *m*
3 attainments *(= skill)* talento *msing* **(in para)**; *(= knowledge)* conocimientos *mpl* **(in de)**
CPD ▸ **attainment target** *(Brit) (Scol)* nivel *m* básico estipulado

attempt [ə'tempt] N **1** *(= try)* intento *m* • **we'll do it or die in the ~** lo haremos o moriremos en el intento • **at the first ~** en el primer intento • **this is my first ~** es la primera vez que lo intento • **after several ~s they gave up** tras varios intentos *or* varias tentativas, se dieron por vencidos • **we had to give up the ~** tuvimos que renunciar a la empresa • **it was a good ~** fue un esfuerzo digno de alabanza • **to make an ~ to do sth** hacer una tentativa de hacer algo, intentar hacer algo • **he made no ~ to help** ni siquiera intentó ayudar • **he made two ~s at it** lo intentó dos veces • **to make an ~ on the record** tratar de batir el récord • **to make an ~ on the summit** tratar de llegar a la cumbre
2 *(= attack)* atentado *m* • **to make an ~ on sb's life** atentar contra la vida de algn
VT **1** *[+ task]* intentar realizar; *[+ exam question]* intentar responder a • **to ~ a reply** intentar responder, tratar de responder • **to ~ a smile** intentar sonreír • **to ~ suicide** intentar suicidarse
2 *(= try)* • **to ~ to do sth** tratar de *or* intentar *or* *(esp LAm)* procurar hacer algo • **the pilot ~ed to land** el piloto trató de aterrizar

attempted [ə'temptɪd] ADJ • **~ murder** tentativa *f* de asesinato, intento *m* de asesinato • **~ suicide** intento *m* de suicidio

attend [ə'tend] VT **1** *(= be present at) [+ meeting, school etc]* asistir a, acudir a; *(regularly) [+ school, church]* ir a
2 *(= wait upon) [waiter]* servir, atender; *[servant, helper]* ocuparse de; *(Med)* atender, asistir; *(= accompany)* acompañar • **~ed by six bridesmaids** acompañada por seis damas de honor
3 *(frm) (fig)* • **a method ~ed by many risks** un método que comporta muchos riesgos • **the policy was ~ed by many difficulties** la política tropezó con muchas dificultades
VI **1** *(= be present)* asistir, acudir
2 *(= pay attention)* prestar atención, poner atención *(LAm)*

▸ **attend on**† VI + PREP = **attend upon**

▸ **attend to** VI + PREP **1** *(= pay attention to) [+ words, work, lesson, speech]* prestar atención a, poner atención en *(LAm)*; *[+ advice]* seguir
2 *(= deal with) [+ task, business]* ocuparse de, atender; *(Comm) [+ order]* tramitar • **to ~ to one's work** ocuparse de su trabajo
3 *(= give help to)* servir a • **to ~ to a customer** atender a un(a) cliente • **are you being ~ed to?** *(in shop)* ¿le atienden? • **I'll ~ to you in a moment** un momentito y estoy con usted

▸ **attend upon**† VI + PREP *[+ person]* servir; *[servant, helper]* ocuparse de

attendance [ə'tendəns] N **1** *(= presence)* asistencia *f* **(at a)** • **is my ~ necessary?** ¿debo asistir?, ¿es preciso que asista yo? • **to be in ~** asistir • **to be in ~ on the minister** acompañar al ministro, formar parte del séquito del ministro; ▹ **dance**
2 *(= those present)* concurrencia *f* • **a large ~** una numerosa concurrencia • **what was the ~ at the meeting?** ¿cuántos asistieron a la reunión? • **we need an ~ of 1,000** hace falta atraer a un público de 1.000 personas
3 *(Med)* asistencia *f*
CPD ▸ **attendance centre** *(Brit) (Jur)* centro *m* de régimen abierto ▸ **attendance fee** honorarios *mpl* por asistencia ▸ **attendance figures** *(at match, concert)* número *m* de espectadores ▸ **attendance money** pago *m* por asistencia ▸ **attendance officer** *(Brit) (Scol)* encargado/a *m/f* del control de asistencia ▸ **attendance order** *(Brit) (Scol) orden que exige a los padres la asistencia de sus hijos a la escuela* ▸ **attendance record** historial *m* de asistencia • **his ~ record is poor** su historial de asistencia deja que desear ▸ **attendance sheet** hoja *f* de asistencia

attendant [ə'tendənt] N **1** *(in car park, museum)* guarda *mf*, celador(a) *m/f*; *(Theat)* acomodador(a) *m/f*; *(at wedding etc)* acompañante *mf*
2 *(= servant)* sirviente/a *m/f* • **the prince and his ~s** el príncipe y su séquito
ADJ **1** *(frm) (= associated)* relacionado, concomitante • **the ~ circumstances** las circunstancias concomitantes • **the ~ difficulties** las dificultades intrínsecas • **old age and its ~ ills** la vejez y los achaques correspondientes • **the risks ~ on the exploration of the unknown** los riesgos que conlleva la exploración de lo desconocido
2 *(= accompanying)* de compañía • **the ~ crowd** la gente que asistía • **to be ~ (up)on sb** atender a algn

attendee [ə,ten'diː] N *(esp US)* asistente *mf*

attention [ə'tenʃən] N **1** atención *f* • **(your) ~ please!** ¡atención por favor! • **to attract sb's ~** llamar la atención de algn • **to call** *or* **draw sb's ~ to sth** hacer notar algo a algn • **it has come to my ~ that ...** me he enterado de que ... • **it requires daily ~** hay que atenderlo

a diario • **it will have my earliest ~** lo atenderé lo antes posible • **for the ~ of Mr. Jones** a la atención del Sr. Jones • **to pay ~ (to)** prestar atención (a) • **he paid no ~** no hizo caso (**to that** de eso) • **to pay special ~ to** fijarse de modo especial en, prestar especial atención a • **to turn one's ~ to** pasar a considerar, pasar a estudiar
2 (*Mil*) • **~!** ¡firme(s)! • **to come to ~** ponerse firme(s) • **to stand at** *or* **to ~** estar firme(s)
3 attentions [*of would-be suitor, media*] atenciones *fpl*
(CPD) ▸ **attention deficit disorder** trastorno *m* de déficit de atención ▸ **attention deficit hyperactivity disorder** trastorno *m* hiperactivo de déficit de atención ▸ **attention span** capacidad *f* de concentración

attention-grabbing [ə'tenʃən,græbɪŋ] (ADJ) [*campaign, headline*] que llama la atención, atrayente

attention-seeking [ə'tenʃən,si:kɪŋ] (ADJ) que busca *or* intenta llamar la atención

attentive [ə'tentɪv] (ADJ) **1** (= *alert*) [*audience, pupil*] atento • **he isn't very ~ in class** no está muy atento en la clase • **to be ~ to sth/sb** prestar atención a algo/algn • **you have to be ~ to the customers' needs** tienes que estar pendiente de *or* prestar atención a las necesidades de los clientes
2 (= *considerate, polite*) atento • **to be ~ to sb** ser atento con algn

attentively [ə'tentɪvlɪ] (ADV) (= *alertly, considerately*) atentamente

attentiveness [ə'tentɪvnɪs] (N) **1** (= *alertness*) atención *f*
2 (= *consideration*) atención *f*

attenuate [ə'tenjʊeɪt] (VT) atenuar

attenuating [ə'tenjʊeɪtɪŋ] (ADJ) atenuante

attenuation [ə,tenjʊ'eɪʃən] (N) atenuación *f*, disminución *f*

attest [ə'test] (VT) atestiguar; [+ *signature*] legalizar • **to ~ that …** atestiguar que …
(VI) • **to ~ to** dar fe de, dar testimonio de

attestation [ætes'teɪʃən] (N) (= *evidence*) testimonio *m*, atestación *f*; (= *authentication*) confirmación *f*, autenticación *f*

attested herd [ə,testɪd'hɜ:d] (N) (*Brit*) (*Agr*) ganado *m* certificado

attic ['ætɪk] (N) desván *m*, altillo *m* (*LAm*), entretecho *m* (*LAm*)
(CPD) ▸ **attic room** desván *m*, altillo *m* (*LAm*), entretecho *m* (*LAm*)

Attila ['ætɪlə] (N) Atila

attire [ə'taɪəʳ] (*frm*) (N) atavío *m*
(VT) ataviar (**in** de)

attired [ə'taɪəd] (ADJ) (*frm*) ataviado • **~ in** ataviado con *or* de

attitude ['ætɪtju:d] (N) **1** (= *way of behaving*) actitud *f* • **you won't get anywhere with that ~** no vas a conseguir nada con esa actitud • **I don't like your ~** no me gusta tu actitud • **his ~ towards** *or* **to me has changed** su actitud con respecto a mí ha cambiado • **if that's your ~** si te pones en ese plan • **~ of mind** disposición *f* de ánimo
2 (= *position, posture*) **a** (*mental*) postura *f* • **the government's ~ is negative** la postura del gobierno es negativa • **what's your ~ to this?** ¿cuál es tu postura a este respeto?
b (*physical*) (= *posture*) postura *f*, pose *f* • **to strike** *or* **adopt an ~** adoptar una pose
3 (*esp US**) (= *spirit*) • **women with ~** mujeres *fpl* con carácter, mujeres *f* con personalidad • **don't give me ~, girl!** ¡no te me pongas de morros, guapa!*
(CPD) ▸ **attitude problem** • **to have an ~ problem** tener un problema de actitud

attitudinal [,ætɪ'tju:dɪnl] (ADJ) [*change, difference*] de actitud

attitudinize [,ætɪ'tju:dɪnaɪz] (VI) tomar posturas afectadas *or* teatrales

Attn, **attn** (ABBR) = **(for the) attention (of)**

attorney [ə'tɜ:nɪ] (N) **1** (*US*) (*also* **attorney-at-law**) abogado/a *m/f*; ▸ **district**
2 (= *representative*) apoderado/a *m/f* • **power of ~** procuración *f*, poderes *mpl*
(CPD) ▸ **Attorney General** (PL: **Attorney Generals** *or* **Attorneys General**) (*US*) ≈ ministro/a *m/f* de justicia, ≈ procurador(a) *m/f* general (*LAm*); (*Brit*) ≈ fiscal *mf* general del Estado

> **ATTORNEY**
> En Estados Unidos un **attorney** puede defender a sus clientes tanto en las cortes federales como en las estatales. En ocasiones solo cobran sus honorarios si ganan el caso (**no win, no fee**), lo cual les permite representar a clientes con pocos recursos sin cobrarles, si se trata de casos de gran repercusión social, con la esperanza de obtener beneficios considerables si lo ganan. Ésta es la razón por la que las compensaciones que se piden por daños y perjuicios suelen ser tan altas y llegan tantos casos a los tribunales. También existe la figura del abogado de oficio, que recibe el nombre de **public defender**.
> ▸ **LAWYERS**

attract [ə'trækt] (VT) **1** [+ *publicity, visitors*] atraer; [+ *interest*] atraer, suscitar; [+ *attention*] llamar
2 (= *cause to like*) atraer • **to be ~ed to sb** sentirse atraído por algn
3 (*Phys*) [*magnet*] atraer

attraction [ə'trækʃən] (N) **1** (*between people, also Phys*) atracción *f* • **sexual ~** atracción *f* sexual • **I felt an instant ~ towards him** inmediatamente me sentí atraída por él
2 (= *attractive feature*) encanto *m*, atractivo *m*; (= *inducement*) aliciente *m* • **city life has no ~ for me** para mí la vida en la ciudad no tiene ningún encanto *or* atractivo, no me atrae la vida en *or* de la ciudad • **one of the ~s of the quiet life** uno de los encantos *or* atractivos de la vida retirada • **one of the ~s was a free car** uno de los alicientes era un coche gratis • **the ~ of the plan is that …** el atractivo del plan está en que …, lo atractivo del plan es que … • **spring ~s in Madrid** las diversiones de la primavera madrileña • **the main ~ at the party was Cindy** el interés de la fiesta se cifraba en Cindy • **the film has the special ~ of featuring Nicola Kidd** la película tiene la atracción especial de presentar a Nicola Kidd

attractive [ə'træktɪv] (ADJ) **1** (= *appealing to senses*) [*woman, picture, house, features*] atractivo; [*voice, smile, personality*] atractivo, atrayente; [*name*] bonito; [*sound*] agradable • **to find sb ~** encontrar atractivo a algn • **he was immensely ~ to women** las mujeres lo encontraban muy atractivo, a las mujeres les parecía muy atractivo
2 (= *interesting*) [*price, salary, offer*] atractivo; [*option, plan, prospect*] atrayente • **the idea was ~ to her** la idea la atraía
3 (*Phys*) • **~ power** fuerza *f* de atracción

attractively [ə'træktɪvlɪ] (ADV) **1** (= *appealingly*) [*smile, laugh*] de manera atrayente; [*arranged, presented, packaged*] de manera atractiva; [*dressed, furnished*] con buen gusto • **an ~ illustrated guidebook** una guía con bonitas ilustraciones • **an ~ designed garden** un jardín de trazado atractivo
2 (= *interestingly*) • **the books are ~ priced** los libros tienen un precio que resulta atractivo • **it is an ~ simple solution** es una solución que resulta atractiva por su sencillez

attractiveness [ə'træktɪvnɪs] (N) [*of person, place, voice, price, offer*] lo atractivo

attributable [ə'trɪbjʊtəbl] (ADJ) • **~ to** atribuible a

attribute (N) ['ætrɪbju:t] atributo *m*
(VT) [ə'trɪbju:t] (*also Literat, Art*) atribuir (**to** a); [+ *blame*] atribuir, achacar (**to** a) • **to what would you ~ this?** ¿a qué atribuyes *or* achacas tú esto?

attribution [,ætrɪ'bju:ʃən] (N) atribución *f*

attributive [ə'trɪbjʊtɪv] (ADJ) (*Ling*) atributivo

attributively [ə'trɪbjʊtɪvlɪ] (ADV) como atributo

attrit [ə'trɪt] (VT), **attrite** [ə'traɪt] (VT) desgastar, agotar

attrition [ə'trɪʃən] (N) **1** (= *wearing away*) desgaste *m* • **war of ~** guerra *f* de desgaste
2 (*Ind, Univ*) amortización *f* de puestos

attune [ə'tju:n] (VT) • **to be ~d to sth** (= *in touch with*) estar sensibilizado a algo; (= *in keeping with*) estar acorde con algo • **she is deeply ~d to the needs of the land** está profundamente sensibilizada a las necesidades del terreno • **a style of campaigning that is completely ~d to the electorate** un estilo de campaña que está totalmente en consonancia con el electorado • **he is so well ~d to her thoughts and moods that …** está tan compenetrado con sus pensamientos y cambios de humor que … • **to ~ o.s. to** • **become ~d to** (= *start understanding*) sensibilizarse a; (= *get used to*) adaptarse a, acostumbrarse a

atty (ABBR) (*US*) = **attorney**

Atty Gen. (ABBR) = **Attorney General**

ATV (N ABBR) = **all-terrain vehicle**

atypical [,eɪ'tɪpɪkəl] (ADJ) atípico

atypically [,eɪ'tɪpɪklɪ] (ADV) atípicamente, de manera atípica

aubergine ['əʊbəʒi:n] (N) **1** (*esp Brit*) (*Bot*) berenjena *f*
2 (= *colour*) (color *m*) berenjena *f*
(ADJ) color berenjena (*inv*)

auburn ['ɔ:bən] (ADJ) [*hair*] color castaño rojizo (*inv*)

auction ['ɔ:kʃən] (N) **1** [*of goods etc*] subasta *f*, remate *m* (*LAm*) • **to put up for ~** subastar, poner en pública subasta • **to sell at ~** vender en pública subasta
2 (*Bridge*) subasta *f*
(VT) (*also* **auction off**) subastar, rematar (*LAm*)
(CPD) ▸ **auction bridge** bridge-remate *m* ▸ **auction house** casa *f* de subastas ▸ **auction room** sala *f* de subastas ▸ **auction sale** subasta *f*, remate *m* (*LAm*) ▸ **auction site** (*on the internet*) sitio *m* de subastas (*por Internet*)

auctioneer [,ɔ:kʃə'nɪəʳ] (N) subastador(a) *m/f*, rematador(a) *m/f*

aud. (ABBR) = **audit, auditor**

audacious [ɔ:'deɪʃəs] (ADJ) **1** (= *bold*) audaz, osado
2 (= *impudent*) atrevido, descarado

audaciously [ɔ:'deɪʃəslɪ] (ADV) **1** (= *boldly*) audazmente, con audacia
2 (= *impudently*) con atrevimiento, descaradamente, con descaro

audacity [ɔ:'dæsɪtɪ] (N) **1** (= *boldness*) audacia *f*, osadía *f*
2 (= *impudence*) atrevimiento *m*, descaro *m* • **to have the ~ to do sth** tener el descaro de hacer algo

audibility [,ɔ:dɪ'bɪlɪtɪ] (N) audibilidad *f*

audible ['ɔ:dɪbl] (ADJ) audible • **his voice was scarcely ~** apenas se podía oír su voz, su voz era apenas perceptible • **there was an ~ gasp**

a

se oyó un grito ahogado
audibly ['ɔːdɪblɪ] ADV de forma audible
audience ['ɔːdɪəns] N **1** (= *gathering*) público *m*; (*in theatre etc*) público *m*, auditorio *m* • **there was a big ~** asistió un gran público • **those in the ~** los que formaban/forman *etc* parte del público *or* de la audiencia • **TV ~s** telespectadores *mpl*
2 (= *interview*) audiencia *f* (**with** con) • **to have an ~ with** tener audiencia con, ser recibido en audiencia por • **to grant sb an ~** dar audiencia *or* conceder (una) audiencia a algn • **to receive sb in ~** recibir a algn en audiencia
CPD ▸ **audience appeal** • **it's got ~ appeal** tiene gancho con el público ▸ **audience chamber** sala *f* de audiencias ▸ **audience participation** participación *f* del público ▸ **audience rating** (*TV, Rad*) índice *m* de audiencia ▸ **audience research** (*TV, Rad*) sondeo *m* de opiniones
audio ['ɔːdɪəʊ] ADJ de audio
N audio *m*
CPD ▸ **audio book** audiolibro *m* ▸ **audio cassette** cassette *f*, cinta *f* de audio ▸ **audio equipment** equipo *m* de audio ▸ **audio frequency** audiofrecuencia *f* ▸ **audio recording** grabación *f* en audio ▸ **audio system** sistema *m* audio; ▹ **audiotape**
audio... ['ɔːdɪəʊ] PREFIX audio...
audioguide ['ɔːdɪəʊˌgaɪd] N audioguía *f*
audiometer [ˌɔːdɪ'ɒmɪtəʳ] N audiómetro *m*
audiotape ['ɔːdɪəʊˌteɪp] N **1** (= *magnetic tape*) cinta *f* magnética de audio
2 (*US*) (= *cassette*) casete *f*
VT (*US*) grabar en casete • **an ~d recording of family members' discussions** una grabación en casete de las conversaciones de los miembros de la familia
audiotronic [ˌɔːdɪəʊ'trɒnɪk] ADJ audio-electrónico
audiotyping ['ɔːdɪəʊˌtaɪpɪŋ] N mecanografía *f* por dictáfono
audiotypist ['ɔːdɪəʊˌtaɪpɪst] N mecanógrafo/a *m/f* de dictáfono
audiovisual [ˌɔːdɪəʊ'vɪzjʊəl] ADJ audiovisual • **~ aids** medios *mpl* audiovisuales • **~ equipment** equipo *m* audiovisual • **~ method** método *m* audiovisual
audit ['ɔːdɪt] N auditoría *f*, revisión *f* de cuentas
VT **1** (*Econ*) auditar, realizar una auditoría de, revisar
2 (*US*) • **to ~ a course** asistir a un curso como oyente
auditing ['ɔːdɪtɪŋ] N • **~ of accounts** auditoría *f*, revisión *f* de cuentas
audition [ɔː'dɪʃən] N (*Theat, Cine, TV*) prueba *f*, audición *f* • **to give sb an ~** (*Theat*) hacer una prueba a algn, ofrecer una audición a algn
VI • **he ~ed for the part** hizo una prueba *or* audición para el papel
VT hacer una prueba a, hacer una audición a • **he was ~ed for the part** le hicieron una prueba *or* audición para el papel
auditor ['ɔːdɪtəʳ] N **1** (*Comm, Econ*) auditor(a) *m/f* • **~'s report** informe *m* de auditoría
2 (*US*) (*Univ*) oyente *mf*, estudiante *mf* libre
auditorium [ˌɔːdɪ'tɔːrɪəm] N (PL: **auditoriums, auditoria** [ˌɔːdɪ'tɔːrɪə]) auditorio *m*, sala *f*
auditory ['ɔːdɪtərɪ] ADJ auditivo
Audubon ['ɔːdəbɒn] N • **the ~ Society** (*US*) *sociedad para la conservación de la naturaleza*, ≈ ICONA *m*, ≈ ADENA *f*
AUEW N ABBR (*Brit*) = **Amalgamated Union of Engineering Workers**
au fait [əʊ'feɪ] ADJ • **to be ~ with sth** estar al corriente *or* al tanto de algo
Aug ABBR (= **August**) ag.
Augean Stables [ɔː'dʒiːən'steɪblz] NPL establos *mpl* de Augias
aught†† [ɔːt] N algo, alguna cosa; (+ *negation*) nada • **if there is ~ I can do** si puedo hacer algo, si puedo ayudarles de algún modo • **for ~ I care he can ...** igual me da si él ... • **for ~ I know** que yo sepa
augment [ɔːg'ment] VT aumentar
VI aumentar(se)
augmentation [ˌɔːgmen'teɪʃən] N aumento *m*
augmentative [ɔːg'mentətɪv] ADJ aumentativo
au gratin [əʊ'grætɛ̃] ADJ (*Culin*) gratinado
augur ['ɔːgəʳ] VT augurar, pronosticar • **it ~s no good** esto no promete nada bueno
VI • **it ~s well/ill** es un buen/mal augurio (**for** para)
augury ['ɔːgjʊrɪ] N augurio *m*, presagio *m* • **to take the auguries**†† consultar los augurios
August ['ɔːgəst] N agosto *m*; ▹ **July**
august [ɔː'gʌst] ADJ (*frm*) augusto
Augustan [ɔː'gʌstən] ADJ de Augusto • **the ~ age** (*Latin Literat*) el siglo de Augusto; (*English Literat*) la época neoclásica (del siglo XVIII)
Augustine [ɔː'gʌstɪn] N Agustín
Augustinian [ɔːgə'stɪnɪən] ADJ agustino
N agustino/a *m/f*
Augustus [ɔː'gʌstəs] N Augusto
auk [ɔːk] N alca *f* • **little auk** mérgulo *m* marino
auld [ɔːld] ADJ (*Scot*) = **old** • **~ lang syne** tiempos *mpl* antiguos, los buenos tiempos de antaño • **Auld Reekie** Edimburgo *m*

> **AULD LANG SYNE**
> **Auld Lang Syne** es el título de una canción tradicional escocesa que se canta en todo el Reino Unido y en EE.UU. al final de algunas fiestas y celebraciones sociales, y en especial para dar la bienvenida al Año Nuevo, a las doce de la noche de fin de año. Con la canción se intenta hacernos recordar los tiempos pasados para que se tengan presentes en esos momentos. Unos versos bien conocidos son: **Should auld acquaintance be forgot, And never brought to mind? ... We'll tak' a cup o' kindness yet, For the sake of auld lang syne.**
> ▹ **HOGMANAY**

aunt [ɑːnt] N tía *f* • **my ~ and uncle** mis tíos *mpl*
CPD ▸ **Aunt Sally** blanco *m* (*de insultos, críticas etc*)
auntie*, **aunty*** ['ɑːntɪ] N **1** (= *relative*) tía *f*
2 • **Auntie** (*Brit*) (*hum*) la BBC
au pair ['əʊ'pɛəʳ] ADJ • **~ girl** au pair *f*
N (PL: **au pairs**) au pair *mf*
VI • **to ~ (for sb)** hacer de au pair (para algn)
aura ['ɔːrə] N (PL: **auras, aurae** ['ɔːriː]) (= *atmosphere*) aura *f*, halo *m*; (*Rel*) aureola *f* • **a mystic ~** un halo místico • **an ~ of doom** un halo fatídico
aural ['ɔːrəl] ADJ del oído • **~ exam** examen *m* de comprensión oral
aureole ['ɔːrɪəʊl] N aureola *f*
au revoir [ˌəʊrə'vwɑːʳ] ADV hasta la vista
auricle ['ɔːrɪkl] N aurícula *f*
auricular [ɔː'rɪkjʊləʳ] ADJ (*Anat*) (= *of ear, heart*) auricular
CPD ▸ **auricular nerve** nervio *m* auricular
aurochs ['ɔːrɒks] N uro *m*, aurochs *m*
aurora borealis [ɔː'rɔːrəbɔːrɪ'eɪlɪs] N aurora *f* boreal
auscultation [ˌɔːskəl'teɪʃən] N auscultación *f*
auspices ['ɔːspɪsɪz] NPL • **under the ~ of** bajo los auspicios de
auspicious [ɔːs'pɪʃəs] ADJ (*frm*) [*day, time*] propicio; [*sign*] de buen augurio; [*occasion, moment*] feliz • **it was an ~ start to their election campaign** fue un comienzo lleno de buenos auspicios para su campaña electoral • **to make an ~ start** comenzar felizmente *or* con buenos auspicios
auspiciously [ɔːs'pɪʃəslɪ] ADV con buenos auspicios, propiciamente • **to start ~** comenzar felizmente *or* con buenos auspicios
Aussie* ['ɒzɪ] = **Australian**
austere [ɒs'tɪəʳ] ADJ austero, severo
austerely [ɒs'tɪəlɪ] ADV austeramente
austerity [ɒs'terɪtɪ] N austeridad *f*
Australasia [ˌɔːstrə'leɪzɪə] N Australasia *f*
Australasian [ˌɔːstrə'leɪzɪən] ADJ australasiano
N australasiano/a *m/f*
Australia [ɒs'treɪlɪə] N Australia *f*
Australian [ɒs'treɪlɪən] ADJ australiano
N australiano/a *m/f*
CPD ▸ **Australian Rules Football** fútbol *m* australiano
Austria ['ɒstrɪə] N Austria *f*
Austrian ['ɒstrɪən] ADJ austriaco, austríaco
N austriaco/a *m/f*, austríaco/a *m/f*
Austro- ['ɒstrəʊ] PREFIX austro- • **Austro-Hungarian** austro-húngaro
AUT N ABBR (*Brit*) = **Association of University Teachers**
aut ABBR = **automatic**
autarchy ['ɔːtɑːkɪ] N autarquía *f*
auteur [ɔː'tɜːʳ] N (= *film director*) *director de cine cuya influencia es tal en una película que se le considera al mismo nivel de su autor* • **film d'~** film d'auteur
authentic [ɔː'θentɪk] ADJ **1** (= *genuine*) [*document, painting, data*] auténtico • **the ~ taste of Italy** el auténtico sabor de Italia
2 (= *realistic*) [*scene, atmosphere*] realista
authentically [ɔː'θentɪkəlɪ] ADV **1** (= *genuinely*) auténticamente • **~ Chinese dishes** auténticos *or* genuinos platos de China
2 (= *realistically*) [*furnished, restored*] fielmente
authenticate [ɔː'θentɪkeɪt] VT autentificar, autenticar
authentication [ɔːˌθentɪ'keɪʃən] N autentificación *f*, autenticación *f*
authenticity [ˌɔːθen'tɪsɪtɪ] N **1** (= *genuineness*) [*of text, painting*] autenticidad *f*
2 (= *realistic quality*) [*of decor, furniture*] realismo *m*
author ['ɔːθəʳ] N **1** (= *writer*) autor(a) *m/f* • **~! ~!** (*Theat*) ¡que salga el autor! • **~'s copy** (*signed by author*) ejemplar *m* autógrafo; (*belonging to author*) ejemplar *m* del autor
2 (*fig*) [*of plan, trouble etc*] autor(a) *m/f*, creador(a) *m/f*
VT (*esp Brit*) escribir, componer
authoress ['ɔːθərɪs] N autora *f*
authorial [ɔː'θɔːrɪəl] ADJ del autor
authoring ['ɔːθərɪŋ] N (*Comput*) [*of web document*] edición *f*
authoritarian [ˌɔːθɒrɪ'tɛərɪən] ADJ autoritario
N autoritario/a *m/f*
authoritarianism [ˌɔːθɒrɪ'tɛərɪənɪzəm] N autoritarismo *m*
authoritative [ɔː'θɒrɪtətɪv] ADJ **1** (= *reliable*) [*account, book, writer, professor*] de gran autoridad, acreditado; [*source, statement,*

information, study] autorizado; [*newspaper*] serio
2 (= *commanding*) [*person, voice, manner*] autoritario
authoritatively [ɔː'θɒrɪtətɪvlɪ] ADV
1 (= *reliably*) [*speak, write*] con autoridad
2 (= *commandingly*) [*say, nod, behave*] de manera autoritaria, autoritariamente
authority [ɔː'θɒrɪtɪ] N **1** (= *power*) autoridad *f* • **those in ~** los que tienen la autoridad • **who is in ~ here?** ¿quién manda aquí? • **to be in ~ over** tener autoridad sobre
2 (= *authorization*) • **to give sb the ~ to do sth** autorizar a algn a hacer algo, autorizar a algn para que haga algo • **to have ~ to do sth** tener autoridad *or* estar autorizado para hacer algo • **on one's own ~** por su propia autoridad • **to do sth without ~** hacer algo sin tener autorización
3 (= *official body*) autoridad *f* • **the authorities** las autoridades • **the customs authorities** las autoridades aduaneras • **to apply to the proper authorities** dirigirse a la autoridad competente; ▸ **health, local, regional**
4 (= *expert*) autoridad *f* • **he's an ~ (on)** es una autoridad (en)
5 (= *expert opinion*) autoridad *f* • **on the ~ of Plato** con la autoridad de Platón • **I have it on good ~ that ...** sé de buena fuente que ...
6 (= *authoritativeness*) autoridad *f* • **to speak with ~** hablar con autoridad *or* con conocimiento de causa
authorization [,ɔːθəraɪ'zeɪʃən] N autorización *f*
authorize ['ɔːθəraɪz] VT (= *empower*) autorizar; (= *approve*) aprobar • **to ~ sb to do sth** autorizar a algn a hacer algo • **to be ~d to do sth** estar autorizado para hacer algo, tener autorización para hacer algo
authorized ['ɔːθəraɪzd] ADJ autorizado • **~ agent** agente *mf* oficial • **~ biography** biografía *f* oficial • **~ capital** (*Comm*) capital *m* autorizado, capital *m* escriturado • **~ distributor** distribuidor *m* autorizado • **Authorized Version** Versión *f* Autorizada (de la Biblia)
authorship ['ɔːθəʃɪp] N **1** [*of book etc*] autoría *f* • **of unknown ~** de autor desconocido
2 (= *profession*) profesión *f* de autor
autism ['ɔːtɪzəm] N autismo *m*
autistic [ɔː'tɪstɪk] ADJ autista
auto ['ɔːtəʊ] (*US*) N coche *m*, automóvil *m* (*frm*), carro *m* (*LAm*), auto *m* (*S. Cone*)
CPD ▸ **auto repair** reparación *f* de automóviles ▸ **auto show** feria *f* del automóvil ▸ **auto worker** trabajador(a) *m/f* de la industria automovilística *or* del automóvil
auto... ['ɔːtəʊ] PREFIX auto...
autobahn ['ɔːtəʊbɑːn] N (*in Germany etc*) autopista *f*
autobank ['ɔːtəʊbæŋk] N cajero *m* automático
autobiographic ['ɔːtəʊ,baɪəʊ'græfɪk] ADJ = **autobiographical**
autobiographical ['ɔːtəʊ,baɪəʊ'græfɪkəl] ADJ autobiográfico
autobiography [,ɔːtəʊbaɪ'ɒgrəfɪ] N autobiografía *f*
autocade ['ɔːtəʊkeɪd] N caravana *f* de automóviles
autochthonous [ɔː'tɒkθənəs] ADJ autóctono
autocracy [ɔː'tɒkrəsɪ] N autocracia *f*
autocrat ['ɔːtəʊkræt] N autócrata *mf*
autocratic [,ɔːtəʊ'krætɪk] ADJ autocrático
autocross ['ɔːtəʊkrɒs] N autocross *m*
autocue ['ɔːtəʊkjuː] N (*Brit*) (*TV*) autocue *m*, chuleta* *f*
autocycle ['ɔːtəʊsaɪkl] N ciclomotor *m*
auto-da-fe, auto-da-fé ['ɔːtəʊdɑː'feɪ] N (PL: **autos-da-fe**) auto *m* de fe
autodidact ['ɔːtəʊ,daɪdækt] N (*frm*) autodidacta *mf*
autodrome† ['ɔːtəʊdrəʊm] N autódromo *m*
autoeroticism [,ɔːtəʊɪ'rɒtɪsɪzəm] N autoerotismo *m*
autofocus ['ɔːtəʊfəʊkəs] N (*Phot*) autofoco *m*, autoenfoque *m*
autogiro ['ɔːtəʊ'dʒaɪərəʊ] N autogiro *m*
autograph ['ɔːtəgrɑːf] N **1** (= *signature*) autógrafo *m*
2 (= *manuscript*) autógrafo *m*
VT (= *sign*) firmar; [+ *book, photo*] dedicar
CPD ▸ **autograph album** álbum *m* de autógrafos ▸ **autograph hunter** cazador(a) *m/f* de autógrafos
autohypnosis ['ɔːtəʊhɪp'nəʊsɪs] N autohipnosis *f inv*
auto-immune [,ɔːtəʊɪ'mjuːn] ADJ autoinmune
automaker ['ɔːtəʊmeɪkə^r] N (*US*) (= *car manufacturer*) fabricante *m* de coches, fabricante *m* de automóviles (*frm*), fabricante *m* de carros (*LAm*), fabricante *m* de autos (*S. Cone*)
automat ['ɔːtəmæt] N **1** (*Brit*) máquina *f* expendedora
2 (*US*) restaurante *m* de autoservicio
automata [ɔː'tɒmətə] NPL *of* **automaton**
automate ['ɔːtəmeɪt] VT automatizar
automated ['ɔːtə,meɪtɪd] ADJ automatizado
CPD ▸ **automated teller, automated telling machine** cajero *m* automático
automatic [,ɔːtə'mætɪk] ADJ (*Tech*) (*gen*) automático • **disqualification is ~** la descalificación es automática
N (= *pistol*) pistola *f* automática; (= *car*) coche *m* automático; (= *washing machine*) lavadora *f*
CPD ▸ **automatic data processing** (*Comput*) proceso *m* automático de datos ▸ **automatic pilot** (*Aer*) piloto *m* automático • **to be on ~ pilot** (*fig*) ir como un/una autómata ▸ **automatic ticketing machine** máquina *f* de venta automática de billetes, máquina *f* de venta automática de boletos (*LAm*) ▸ **automatic transmission** (*Aut*) transmisión *f* automática
automatically [,ɔːtə'mætɪkəlɪ] ADV automáticamente
automation [,ɔːtə'meɪʃən] N automatización *f*
automatism [ɔː'tɒmətɪzəm] N automatismo *m*
automaton [ɔː'tɒmətən] N (PL: **automatons, automata**) autómata *m*
automobile ['ɔːtəməbiːl] (*US*) N coche *m*, automóvil *m* (*frm*), carro *m* (*LAm*), auto *m* (*S. Cone*)
CPD ▸ **automobile industry** industria *f* del automóvil
automotive [ɔːtə'məʊtɪv] ADJ automotor (*f*: automotora, automotriz)
autonomous [ɔː'tɒnəməs] ADJ autónomo
autonomously [ɔː'tɒnəməslɪ] ADV [*operate*] de manera autónoma
autonomy [ɔː'tɒnəmɪ] N autonomía *f*
autopilot ['ɔːtəʊpaɪlət] N (*Aer*) piloto *m* automático • **to be on ~** (*fig*) ir como un/una autómata
autopsy ['ɔːtɒpsɪ] N autopsia *f*
auto-reverse ['ɔːtəʊrɪ'vɜːs] N rebobinado *m* automático, autorreverse *m*
auto-suggestion ['ɔːtəʊsə'dʒestʃən] N (auto)sugestión *f*
auto-teller ['ɔːtəʊ,telə^r] N cajero *m* automático
auto-timer ['ɔːtəʊ,taɪmə^r] N programador *m* automático
autumn ['ɔːtəm] N (*esp Brit*) otoño *m* • **in ~** en otoño • **I like to go walking in (the) ~** me gusta salir a pasear en otoño • **in the ~ of 1998** en el otoño de 1998 • **in early/late ~** a principios/a finales del otoño • **an ~ day** un día de otoño
CPD ▸ **autumn equinox** equinoccio *m* otoñal, equinoccio *m* de otoño
autumnal [ɔː'tʌmnəl] ADJ otoñal, de(l) otoño
Auvergne [əʊ'vεən] N Auvernia *f*
auxiliary [ɔːg'zɪlɪərɪ] ADJ auxiliar • **~ police** (*US*) cuerpo *m* de policía auxiliar • **~ staff** (*Brit*) (*Scol*) profesores *mpl* auxiliares
N **1** (*Med*) ayudante *mf*
2 (*Mil*) **auxiliaries** tropas *fpl* auxiliares
3 (*also* **auxiliary verb**) verbo *m* auxiliar
AV N ABBR (= **Authorized Version**) *traducción inglesa de la Biblia*
ABBR = **audiovisual**
Av. ABBR (= **Avenue**) Av., Avda.
av. ABBR (= **average**) prom.
a.v., a/v ABBR = **ad valorem**
avail [ə'veɪl] (*liter*) N • **it is of no ~** es inútil • **to be of little ~** ser de poco provecho • **of what ~ is it to ...?** ¿de qué sirve ...? • **to no ~** en vano
VT valer • **to ~ o.s. of** aprovechar(se de), valerse de
VI • **it ~s nothing to** (+ *infin*) de nada sirve (+ *infin*)
availability [ə,veɪlə'bɪlɪtɪ] N **1** [*of goods, tickets*] disponibilidad *f* • **the high crime rate is due to the easy ~ of guns** el alto índice de criminalidad se debe a la fácil disponibilidad de armas *or* a lo fácil que es conseguir armas • **..., subject to ~ (*goods*)** ..., siempre que haya existencias
2 [*of person*] • **this depends on your ~ for work** esto depende de si estás disponible para trabajar
available [ə'veɪləbl] ADJ **1** [*object, service*] **a** (+ *verb*) • **to be ~**: • **application forms are ~ here** las solicitudes se pueden conseguir aquí • **it's ~ in other colours** también viene en otros colores • **this item is not ~ at the moment** no disponemos de *or* no tenemos este artículo en este momento • **television isn't yet ~ here** la televisión aún no ha llegado aquí • **to become ~**: • **new treatments are becoming ~** están apareciendo nuevos tratamientos • **a place has become ~ on the course/flight** ha quedado una plaza libre en el curso/el vuelo • **~ for sth/sb**: • **a car park is ~ for the use of customers** hay un aparcamiento a la disposición de los clientes • **there are three boats ~ for hire** hay tres botes que se pueden alquilar • **to be freely ~** ser fácil de conseguir • **the guide is ~ from all good bookshops** la guía se puede encontrar en todas las buenas librerías • **this service is ~ from all good travel agents** cualquier agencia de viaje de calidad le ofrecerá este servicio • **tickets are ~ from the box office** las entradas están a la venta en taquilla • **to make sth ~ to sb** [+ *resources*] poner algo a la disposición de algn
b (+ *noun*) disponible • **according to the ~ information** según la información disponible *or* de que se dispone • **we did what we could in the time ~** hicimos lo que pudimos en el tiempo disponible *or* del que disponíamos • **I have very few days ~ at the moment** en este momento tengo muy pocos días libres • **he tried every ~ means to find her** hizo todo lo posible para encontrarla • **I'd like a seat on the first ~ flight** quiero

a

una plaza en el primer vuelo que haya • **the money ~ for spending** el dinero disponible para gastos • **~ to sb:** • **the information ~ to us** la información de la que disponemos
2 [*person*] **a** (= *free, at hand*) libre • **are you ~ next Thursday?** ¿estás libre el jueves que viene? • **I'm ~ on this number** me puedes localizar en este número • **counsellors are ~ to talk to anyone who needs advice** los orientadores están a la disposición de *or* están disponibles para hablar con cualquiera que necesite consejo • **there's no-one ~ to take your call** no hay nadie que pueda atender a su llamada • **the Minister is not ~ for comment** el Ministro no se dispone a hacer comentarios • **to make o.s. ~:** • **he made himself ~ in case anybody had any questions** se puso a disposición de cualquiera que tuviese preguntas
b (= *unattached*) [*man, woman*] soltero y sin compromiso

avalanche ['ævəlɑ:nʃ] (N) avalancha *f*; (*fig*) torrente *m*, avalancha *f*

avant-garde ['ævɑ:ŋ'gɑ:d] (ADJ) vanguardista, de vanguardia
(N) vanguardia *f*

avarice ['ævərɪs] (N) avaricia *f*

avaricious [ˌævə'rɪʃəs] (ADJ) avaro

avatar ['ævətɑ:ʳ] (N) **1** [*of deity*] avatar *m*
2 (*in video games*) avatar *m*

avdp (ABBR) = **avoirdupois**

Ave (ABBR) (= **avenue**) Av., Avda.

avenge [ə'vendʒ] (VT) vengar • **to ~ o.s.** vengarse (**on sb** en algn)

avenger [ə'vendʒəʳ] (N) vengador(a) *m/f*

avenging [ə'vendʒɪŋ] (ADJ) vengador

avenue ['ævənju:] (N) **1** (= *road*) avenida *f*, paseo *m*
2 (*fig*) vía *f*, camino *m* • **to explore every ~** explorar todas las vías *or* todos los caminos

aver [ə'vɜ:ʳ] (VT) afirmar, asegurar

average ['ævərɪdʒ] (ADJ) **1** (*Math, Statistics*) [*age, wage, price, speed*] medio, promedio (*inv*)
2 (= *normal, typical*) medio • **the ~ American drives 10,000 miles per year** el americano medio hace unas 10.000 millas al año con su coche • **an ~ thirteen-year-old child could understand it** un niño de trece años de inteligencia media podría entenderlo • **that's ~ for a woman of your age** eso es lo normal para una mujer de tu edad • **of ~ ability** de capacidad media • **of ~ height** de estatura mediana *or* media • **the ~ man** el hombre medio • **he's not your ~ footballer*** no es el típico futbolista
3 (= *mediocre*) mediocre • **a very ~ novel** una novela bastante mediocre • **an ~ piece of work** un trabajo de una calidad mediana • **"how was the film?" — "average"** —¿qué tal fue la película? —nada del otro mundo
(N) media *f*, promedio *m* • **to do an ~ of 150kph** hacer una media *or* un promedio de 150kph • **it takes an ~ of ten weeks for a house sale to be completed** como promedio la venta de una casa se lleva a término en unas diez semanas • **above ~** superior a la media *or* al promedio, por encima de la media *or* del promedio • **below ~** inferior a la media *or* al promedio, por debajo de la media *or* del promedio • **on ~** como promedio, por término medio • **a rough ~** una media aproximada • **to take an ~ of sth** calcular la media *or* el promedio de algo
(VT) **1** (*also* **average out**) (= *calculate average of*) calcular la media de, calcular el promedio de
2 (= *reach an average of*) • **pay increases are averaging 9.75%** los aumentos de sueldo son, como media *or* promedio, del 9,75% • **we ~ eight hours' work a day** trabajamos por término medio unas ocho horas diarias, trabajamos una media *or* un promedio de unas ocho horas diarias • **the sales ~ 200 copies a week** el promedio de ventas es de unos 200 ejemplares a la semana • **the temperature ~d 13 degrees over the month** la temperatura media *or* promedio fue de unos 13 grados a lo largo del mes, la temperatura alcanzó una media *or* un promedio de unos 13 grados a lo largo del mes • **he ~d 140kph all the way** (*Aut*) hizo un promedio *or* una media de 140kph en todo el recorrido
(ADV)* regular • **she did ~ in the oral exam** el examen oral le fue regular
▸ **average down** (VT + ADV) • **to ~ sth down** sacar el promedio *or* la media de algo tirando hacia abajo
▸ **average out** (VT + ADV) calcular la media de, calcular el promedio de
(VI + ADV) • **it'll ~ out in the end** al final una cosa compensará por la otra • **to ~ out at** salir a un promedio *or* una media de • **it ~s out at 50p a glass** sale a un promedio *or* una media de 50 peniques el vaso • **our working hours ~ out at eight a day** trabajamos un promedio *or* una media de ocho horas al día
▸ **average up** (VT + ADV) • **to ~ sth up** sacar el promedio *or* la media de algo tirando hacia arriba

> **AVERAGE, HALF**
>
> **Position of "medio"**
>
> *You should generally put* **medio** *after the noun when you mean "average" and before the noun when you mean "half":*
>
> **... the average citizen ...**
> ... el ciudadano medio ...
> **... the average salary ...**
> ... el salario medio ...
> **... half a kilo of tomatoes ...**
> ... medio kilo de tomates ...
>
> *For further uses and examples, see* **average, half**

averagely ['ævərɪdʒlɪ] (ADV) regular • **she did ~ (well) in the oral exam** el examen oral le fue regular • **he performed very ~ at school** en los estudios le iba bastante regular • **we scored only ~** las puntuaciones que obtuvimos no pasaron de ser regulares

averse [ə'vɜ:s] (ADJ) • **to be ~ to sth** sentir repugnancia por algo • **to be ~ to doing sth** ser reacio a hacer algo • **he is ~ to getting up early** es reacio a levantarse temprano • **would you be ~ to having the meeting at your house?** ¿estarías dispuesto a celebrar la reunión en tu casa? • **I'm not ~ to an occasional drink** no me opongo a tomar una copa de vez en cuando

aversion [ə'vɜ:ʃən] (N) **1** (= *dislike*) aversión *f* (**to, for** hacia) • **I have an ~ to garlic/cooking** el ajo/la cocina me repugna, tengo aversión por el ajo/la cocina • **I have an ~ to him** me repugna, le tengo aversión • **I took an ~ to it** empezó a repugnarme
2 (= *hated thing*) cosa *f* aborrecida • **it is one of my ~s** es una de las cosas que me repugnan
(CPD) ▸ **aversion therapy** terapia *f* por aversión, terapia *f* aversiva

avert [ə'vɜ:t] (VT) **1** (= *turn away*) [+ *eyes, thoughts*] apartar (**from** de); [+ *suspicion*] desviar (**from** de); [+ *possibility*] evitar
2 (= *prevent*) [+ *accident, danger etc*] prevenir
3 (= *parry*) [+ *blows*] desviar

aviary ['eɪvɪərɪ] (N) pajarera *f*

aviation [ˌeɪvɪ'eɪʃən] (N) aviación *f*
(CPD) ▸ **aviation fuel** combustible *m* de aviación ▸ **aviation industry** industria *f* de la aviación ▸ **aviation spirit** gasolina *f* de aviación

aviator ['eɪvɪeɪtəʳ] (N) aviador(a) *m/f*

avid ['ævɪd] (ADJ) [*collector, viewer*] ávido; [*supporter, fan*] ferviente • **an ~ reader** un ávido lector • **to be ~ for sth** estar ávido de algo

avidity [ə'vɪdɪtɪ] (N) avidez *f*

avidly ['ævɪdlɪ] (ADV) ávidamente, con avidez • **to read ~** leer con avidez

Avignon ['ævɪnjɔ̃] (N) Aviñón *m*

avionics [ˌeɪvɪ'ɒnɪks] (NSING) aviónica *f*

avocado [ævə'kɑ:dəʊ] (N) (PL: **avocados**)
1 (*also* **avocado pear**) aguacate *m*, palta *f* (*And, S. Cone*)
2 (= *tree*) aguacate *m*, palto *m* (*LAm*)

avocation [ˌævəʊ'keɪʃən] (N) (*frm*) (= *minor occupation*) diversión *f*, distracción *f*; (= *employment*) vocación *f*

avoid [ə'vɔɪd] (VT) [+ *obstacle*] evitar, esquivar; [+ *argument, question, subject*] evitar, eludir; [+ *duty*] eludir; [+ *danger*] salvarse de • **are you trying to ~ me?** ¿me estás evitando *or* esquivando? • **I try to ~ him** procuro no tener nada que ver con él • **he ~s all his friends** huye de todos sus amigos • **this way we ~ London** por esta ruta evitamos pasar por Londres • **to ~ sb's eye** esquivar la mirada de algn • **to ~ tax** (*legally*) evitar pagar impuestos; (*illegally*) defraudar al fisco • **to ~ doing sth** evitar hacer algo • **he managed to ~ (hitting) the tree** logró esquivar el árbol • **I'm trying to ~ being seen by Jeremy** estoy intentando evitar que me vea Jeremy, estoy intentando que Jeremy no me vea • IDIOM: • **it's to be ~ed like the plague** de esto hay que huir como de la peste

avoidable [ə'vɔɪdəbl] (ADJ) evitable

avoidance [ə'vɔɪdəns] (N) • **the ~ of fatty foods** el evitar los alimentos grasos • **you can improve your health by the ~ of stress** uno puede mejorar su salud evitando el estrés; ▹ **tax**

avoirdupois [ˌævədə'pɔɪz] (N) *sistema de pesos usado, aunque cada vez menos, en países de habla inglesa (1 libra = 16 onzas = 453,50 gramos)*

avow [ə'vaʊ] (VT) (*frm*) **1** (= *recognize*) reconocer, admitir, confesar • **many men ~ they find blondes insipid and cold** muchos hombres admiten *or* reconocen *or* confiesan que las rubias les parecen frías e insípidas • **he ~ed himself beaten** reconoció *or* admitió que había perdido
2 (= *affirm*) afirmar, declarar

avowal [ə'vaʊəl] (N) (*frm*) **1** (= *recognition*) reconocimiento *m*, admisión *f*, confesión *f*
2 (= *affirmation*) afirmación *f*, declaración *f*

avowed [ə'vaʊd] (ADJ) (*frm*) [*purpose, opponent, supporter*] declarado • **their ~ aim is to disrupt society** su objetivo declarado es causar problemas en la sociedad

avowedly [ə'vaʊɪdlɪ] (ADV) (*frm*) declaradamente, abiertamente

AVP (N ABBR) (*US*) = **assistant vice-president**

avuncular [ə'vʌŋkjʊləʳ] (ADJ) como de tío • **~ advice** consejos *mpl* amistosos

aw [ɔ:] (EXCL) ¡ay!

AWACS [eɪ'wæks] (N ABBR) (= **Airborne Warning and Control System**) AWACS *m*

await [ə'weɪt] (VT) **1** (= *wait for*) esperar, aguardar • **we ~ your instructions** esperamos *or* aguardamos sus instrucciones • **we ~ your reply with interest** aguardamos su respuesta con interés
2 (= *be in store for*) esperar, aguardar • **the fate that ~s him** la suerte que le espera • **a surprise ~s him** le espera *or* le aguarda una sorpresa

awake [əˈweɪk] (PT: **awoke** *or* **awaked**, PP: **awoken** *or* **awaked**) ADJ despierto • **to be ~** estar despierto • **fully ~** totalmente despierto • **I was still only half ~** aún estaba medio dormido • **coffee keeps me ~** (= *keeps me alert*) el café me mantiene despierto; (= *stops me sleeping*) el café me desvela • **the noise kept me ~** el ruido no me dejó dormir • **to lie ~**: • **he lay ~ all night, thinking about his new job** no pudo dormir en toda la noche *or* estuvo desvelado toda la noche, pensando en su nuevo trabajo • **I'm not really ~ yet** aún no estoy despierto del todo • **to stay ~** mantenerse despierto, no dormirse • **I found it difficult to stay ~** me costaba mantenerme despierto, me costaba no dormirme • **I'm not going to stay ~ all night worrying about that** no voy a pasarme toda la noche en vela preocupándome por eso • **to be ~ to sth** (*fig*) ser consciente de algo • **wide ~** totalmente despierto
VT **1** (= *wake up*) despertar
2 (= *arouse*) [+ *suspicion, curiosity*] despertar; [+ *hope*] hacer nacer; [+ *memories*] reavivar, resucitar
VI **1** (*liter*) (= *wake up*) despertar • **I awoke from a deep sleep** desperté de un sueño profundo • **when are we going to ~ from this nightmare?** ¿cuándo vamos a despertar de esta pesadilla? • **she awoke to a lovely, sunny day** despertó y el día era precioso, soleado • **he awoke to find himself in hospital** al despertar(se) vio que se hallaba en el hospital
2 (= *become aware*) • **to ~ to sth** darse cuenta de algo • **she awoke to the fact that ...** se dio cuenta de que ... • **he finally awoke to his responsibilities** finalmente tomó conciencia de sus responsabilidades
awaked† [əˈweɪkt] PT, PP *of* awake
awaken [əˈweɪkən] VT despertar • **to ~ sb to a danger** alertar a algn de un peligro
VI (*also* **to awaken from sleep**) despertar • **to ~ from one's illusions** desilusionarse, quitarse las ilusiones • **to ~ to a danger** darse cuenta de un peligro
awakening [əˈweɪknɪŋ] ADJ (*fig*) naciente
N despertar *m* • **he got a rude ~** tuvo una desagradable sorpresa
award [əˈwɔːd] N **1** (= *prize*) premio *m*; (*Mil*) (= *medal*) condecoración *f*
2 (*Jur*) (= *ruling*) fallo *m*, sentencia *f*; (= *sum of money*) (*punitive*) sanción *f*; (= *damages*) concesión *f* • **a record ~ for sexual harassment** una sanción récord por acoso sexual • **they are appealing against the ~ of £350,000 to Violet Bush** van a recurrir contra la concesión de £350.000 a Violet Bush
3 (= *act of awarding*) entrega *f*, concesión *f*; ▷ **pay**
VT **1** [+ *prize, medal*] conceder, otorgar • **the prize is not being ~ed this year** este año el premio se ha declarado desierto
2 (*Jur*) [+ *damages*] adjudicar
3 (*Sport*) • **to ~ a penalty (against sb)** pitar *or* señalar (un) penalti (contra algn) • **to ~ sb a penalty** conceder un penalti a algn
CPD ▸ **award(s) ceremony** ceremonia *f* de entrega de premios ▸ **award winner** premiado/a *m/f*, galardonado/a *m/f*
award-winning [əˈwɔːdˌwɪnɪŋ] ADJ premiado, galardonado
aware [əˈwɛəʳ] ADJ **1** (= *cognizant*) • **to be ~ that ...** saber que ..., ser consciente de que ... • **I am fully ~ that ...** tengo plena conciencia de que ... • **to be ~ (of)** ser consciente (de) • **we are ~ of what is happening** somos conscientes de lo que ocurre • **our employees are ~ of this advertisement** los empleados de la empresa han sido informados de este anuncio • **not that I am ~ (of)** que yo sepa, no • **to become ~ of** enterarse de • **to make sb ~ of sth** hacer que algn se dé cuenta de algo
2 (= *knowledgeable*) • **politically ~** con conciencia política • **sexually ~** enterado de lo sexual • **socially ~** sensibilizado con los temas sociales
3 (= *alert*) despierto
awareness [əˈwɛənɪs] N conciencia *f*, conocimiento *m* • **sexual ~ in the young** la conciencia sexual *or* los conocimientos sexuales de los jóvenes
awash [əˈwɒʃ] ADJ **1** (*with water*) inundado • **the house was ~** la casa estaba inundada • **the deck is ~** la cubierta está a flor de agua
2 (*fig*) • **we are ~ with applicants** estamos inundados de solicitudes
away [əˈweɪ]

> *When* ***away*** *is an element in a phrasal verb, eg* ***boil away, die away, get away***, *look up the verb.*

ADV **1** (= *at or to a distance*) • **far ~** • **a long way ~** lejos • **~ in the distance** a lo lejos • **it's ten miles ~ (from here)** está a diez millas (de aquí) • **~ from the noise** lejos del ruido • **keep the child ~ from the fire** no dejes que el niño se acerque al fuego • **White won with Peters only two strokes ~** ganó White con Peters a solo dos golpes de distancia • **~ back in 1066** allá en 1066
2 (= *absent*) • **to be ~** estar fuera, estar ausente • **to be ~ (from home)** estar fuera, estar ausente • **she's ~ today** hoy está fuera • **he's ~ for a week** está fuera una semana • **he's ~ in Bognor** está en Bognor • **she was ~ before I could shout** se fue antes de que yo pudiese gritar • **I must ~** (*liter or hum*) tengo que marcharme • **~ with you!*** (= *go away!*) ¡vete!, ¡fuera de aquí!; (*expressing disbelief*) ¡venga ya!, ¡anda ya!; (*joking*) ¡no digas bobadas! • **~ with him!** ¡fuera!, ¡que se lo lleven de aquí!
3 (*Sport*) fuera (de casa) • **they have won only two games ~** han ganado solamente dos partidos fuera (de casa) • **to play ~** (*Sport*) jugar fuera • **Chelsea are ~ to Everton on Saturday** el Chelsea juega fuera, en campo del Everton, el sábado
4 (*after vb*) (= *continuously*) sin parar • **to talk ~** no parar de hablar, seguir hablando • **I could hear her talking ~** la oía hablar sin parar • **to work ~** seguir trabajando, trabajar sin parar • **he was working ~ in the garden** estaba dale que te pego en el jardín, estaba trabajando sin parar en el jardín • **he was grumbling ~** no paraba de refunfuñar
ADJ • **the ~ team** el equipo de fuera • **~ match** partido *m* fuera de casa • **~ win** victoria *f* fuera de casa
CPD ▸ **away day** (*for training etc*) *día de entrenamiento para un grupo de empleados, que normalmente tiene lugar fuera de la oficina* ▸ **away game** (*Sport*) partido *m* fuera de casa ▸ **away goal** (*Sport*) gol *m* marcado fuera de casa ▸ **away match** = **away game**
awe [ɔː] N (= *fear*) pavor *m*; (= *wonder*) asombro *m*; (= *reverence*) temor *m* reverencial • **to go** *or* **be in awe of** • **hold in awe** tener temor reverencial a
VT (= *impress*) impresionar; (= *frighten*) atemorizar • **in an awed voice** con un tono de respeto y temor
awe-inspiring [ˈɔːɪnˌspaɪərɪŋ] ADJ = **awesome**
awesome [ˈɔːsəm] ADJ **1** (= *impressive*) [*sight, beauty*] impresionante, imponente; [*achievement*] impresionante
2 (= *huge*) [*task, responsibility*] abrumador
3 (*esp US**) (= *excellent*) formidable
awesomely [ˈɔːsəmlɪ] ADV • **he is ~ talented** tiene un talento impresionante • **the scenery is ~ beautiful** el paisaje es de una belleza imponente
awe-struck [ˈɔːstrʌk] ADJ pasmado, atemorizado
awful [ˈɔːfəl] ADJ **1** (= *dreadful*) [*weather*] horrible, espantoso; [*clothes, crime*] horroroso, espantoso; [*smell, dilemma*] terrible • **what ~ weather!** ¡qué tiempo más horrible *or* espantoso! • **we met and I thought he was ~** le conocí y me cayó fatal • **you are ~!** (= *wicked*) ¡qué malo eres!, ¡qué mala idea tienes! • **to feel ~** (= *embarrassed, guilty*) sentirse fatal; (= *ill*) encontrarse *or* sentirse fatal • **I felt ~ about what had happened** me sentía fatal por lo que había ocurrido • **I have an ~ feeling something's going to happen** tengo la terrible sospecha de que va a pasar algo • **how ~!** ¡qué horror! • **how ~ for you!** ¡qué mal rato habrás pasado! • **to look ~** tener muy mal aspecto • **you look ~, are you feeling all right?** tienes muy mala cara *or* tienes muy mal aspecto, ¿te encuentras bien? • **for one ~ moment I thought I'd broken it** ¡fue horrible! por un momento pensé que se me había roto • **it smells ~** huele fatal • **prices have gone up something ~**‡ los precios han subido cosa mala* • **they beat him up something ~**‡ le dieron una tremenda paliza • **what an ~ thing to happen!** ¡qué cosa tan horrible *or* terrible! • **the ~ thing is that he thought we were joking** lo peor (del caso) es que él pensó que estábamos de broma • **you said some pretty ~ things** hiciste algunos comentarios muy hirientes • **I learned the ~ truth** supe la amarga verdad
2 (= *bad, poor*) • **his English is ~** habla inglés fatal
3 (= *awesome*) imponente, tremendo
4* (*as intensifier*) • **there were an ~ lot of people** había un montón de gente* • **I've got an ~ lot of work to do** tengo un montón de trabajo* • **it's an ~ nuisance** es una molestia terrible • **he's an ~ bore** es terriblemente pesado • **she's got an ~ cheek!** ¡tiene una cara increíble!* • **it seems an ~ waste** parece un desperdicio terrible
ADV (*esp US**) • **ten years is an ~ long time** diez años es un montón de tiempo* • **it's an ~ long way to go** está lejísimo • **it's ~ cold outside** fuera hace un frío horroroso*
awfully* [ˈɔːflɪ] ADV **1** (*as intensifier*) • **he's ~ nice** es majísimo • **it's ~ hard** *or* **difficult** es terriblemente difícil • **she works ~ hard** trabaja durísimo • **it was ~ hot** hacía un calor espantoso • **that's ~ good of you** es muy amable de su parte • **I'm ~ sorry** lo siento muchísimo • **would you mind ~ if we didn't go?** ¿te molestaría mucho que no fuéramos? • **thanks ~!**† ¡muchísimas gracias!
2 (= *badly*) [*play, sing*] pésimamente, fatal
awfulness [ˈɔːfʊlnɪs] N **1** (= *dreadfulness*) lo terrible • **the ~ of the situation kept coming back to him** lo terrible de la situación se le venía insistentemente a la cabeza • **he had to serve 18 years because of the ~ of his crimes** sus crímenes fueron tan horrorosos que tuvo que servir una condena de 18 años
2 (= *poor quality*) • **it gets mentioned, if only for its ~** se habla de eso, aunque solo sea por lo malo que es
awhile [əˈwaɪl] (*esp US*) ADV un rato, algún tiempo • **not yet ~** todavía no
awkward [ˈɔːkwəd] ADJ **1** (= *inconvenient, difficult*) [*moment, time*] malo; [*shape*]

a

incómodo, poco práctico; [*corner*] peligroso • **have I called at an ~ moment?** ¿he llamado en mal momento? • **this scandal comes at an ~ moment for the government** este escándalo llega en un momento difícil *or* en un mal momento para el gobierno • **to be at an ~ age** estar en una edad difícil • **he's being ~ about it** está poniendo inconvenientes • **he's an ~ customer*** es un tipo difícil*, es un sujeto de cuidado* • **Thursday is ~ for me** el jueves no me viene bien • **to make things ~ for sb** poner las cosas difíciles a algn, crear dificultades a algn • **it would be ~ to postpone my trip again** sería difícil volver a aplazar mi viaje • **it's not far, but it's ~ to get to by public transport** no está lejos, pero es complicado llegar en transporte público • **it's very ~ to carry** es muy difícil de llevar
2 (= *embarrassing, uncomfortable*) [*silence*] embarazoso; [*problem, question*] delicado, difícil; [*situation*] delicado, violento; [*matter, subject*] delicado • **to feel ~** sentirse incómodo • **he had always felt ~ with Clara** siempre se había sentido incómodo con Clara, nunca se había sentido a gusto con Clara • **I felt ~ about asking her for a rise** me resultaba violento pedirle un aumento de sueldo • **there was an ~ moment when ...** hubo un momento violento *or* embarazoso cuando ... • **to put sb in an ~ position** poner a algn en una situación embarazosa *or* delicada, poner a algn en un compromiso
3 (= *clumsy*) [*person, gesture, movement*] torpe; [*phrasing*] poco elegante, torpe • **to sleep in an ~ position** dormir en mala posición

awkwardly ['ɔ:kwədlɪ] (ADV)
1 (= *uncomfortably*) [*say, shake hands*] con embarazo • **there was an ~ long silence** hubo un silencio largo y embarazoso • **Sonia patted her shoulder ~** Sonia, violenta *or* incómoda, le dio unas palmaditas en el hombro
2 (= *clumsily*) [*move, walk, dance*] torpemente, con torpeza; [*translate*] con poca fluidez • **he expresses himself ~** se expresa mal, le cuesta expresarse • **he fell ~** cayó en mala postura • **the keyhole is ~ placed under the handle** el ojo de la cerradura está colocado bajo el picaporte, lo cual resulta incómodo

awkwardness ['ɔ:kwədnɪs] (N) **1** (= *difficult nature*) [*of problem*] lo delicado; [*of situation*] lo delicado, lo violento; [*of person*] falta *f* de colaboración; [*of shape, design*] lo incómodo, lo poco práctico
2 (= *embarrassment, discomfort*) embarazo *m*
3 (= *clumsiness*) torpeza *f*

awl [ɔ:l] (N) lezna *f*

awning ['ɔ:nɪŋ] (N) toldo *m*

awoke [ə'wəʊk] (PT) *of* awake

awoken [ə'wəʊkən] (PP) *of* awake

AWOL ['eɪwɒl] (ABBR) (*Mil*) (= **absent without leave**) ausente sin permiso

awry [ə'raɪ] (ADV) • **to be ~** estar de través, estar al sesgo, estar mal puesto • **to go ~** salir mal, fracasar • **with his hat on ~** con el sombrero torcido *or* ladeado

axe, ax (*US*) [æks] (N) (= *tool*) hacha *f*
• IDIOMS: • **when the axe fell** cuando se descargó el golpe • **to have an axe to grind** tener un interés creado • **I have no axe to grind** no tengo ningún interés personal • **to get** *or* **be given the axe** [*employee*] ser despedido; [*project*] ser cancelado
(VT) [+ *budget*] recortar; [+ *project, service*] cancelar; [+ *jobs*] reducir; [+ *staff*] despedir

axes ['æksi:z] (NPL) *of* axis

axial ['æksɪəl] (ADJ) axial

axiom ['æksɪəm] (N) axioma *m*

axiomatic [,æksɪəʊ'mætɪk] (ADJ) axiomático

axis ['æksɪs] (N) (PL: **axes** ['æksi:z]) **1** (*Geom etc*) eje *m*
2 (*Anat*) axis *m inv*
3 • **the Axis** (*Hist*) el Eje
(CPD) ▸ **axis of evil** eje *m* del mal

axle ['æksl] (N) eje *m*, árbol *m*, flecha *f* (*Mex*)
(CPD) ▸ **axle shaft** palier *m*

ay [aɪ] (ADV), (N) = **aye¹**

ayatollah [aɪə'tɒlə] (N) ayatolá *m*, ayatollah *m*

aye¹ [aɪ] (ADV) (*esp Scot, N Engl*) sí • **aye, aye sir!** sí, mi capitán
(N) sí *m* • **to vote aye** votar sí • **the ayes have it** se ha aprobado la moción • **there were 50 ayes and 3 noes** votaron 50 a favor y 3 en contra

aye²† [aɪ] (ADV) • **for ever and aye** (*Scot*) por siempre jamás

AYH (N ABBR) (*US*) = **American Youth Hostels**

Aymara [,aɪmə'rɑ:] (ADJ) aimara, aimará
(N) **1** (= *person*) aimara *mf*, aimará *mf*
2 (*Ling*) aimara *m*, aimará *m*

Ayurveda [,ɑ:jʊə'veɪdə] (N) ayurveda *m*

Ayurvedic [,ɑ:jʊə'veɪdɪk] (ADJ) ayurvédico

AZ (ABBR) (*US*) = **Arizona**

azalea [ə'zeɪlɪə] (N) (*Bot*) azalea *f*

Azerbaijan [,æzəbaɪ'dʒɑ:n] (N) Azerbaiyán *m*

Azerbaijani [,æzəbaɪ'dʒɑ:nɪ] (ADJ) azerbaiyano
(N) azerbaiyano/a *m/f*

Azeri [ə'zεərɪ] (ADJ) azerí
(N) **1** (= *person*) azerí *mf*
2 (*Ling*) azerí *m*

Azores [ə'zɔ:z] (NPL) Azores *fpl*

AZT (N ABBR) (= **azidothymidine**) AZT *m* (*medicina antisida*)

Aztec ['æztek] (ADJ) azteca
(N) azteca *mf*

azure ['eɪʒə^r] (ADJ) celeste, azul celeste (*inv*)
(N) **1** (= *colour*) celeste *m*, azul *m* celeste
2 (*Heraldry*) azur *m*

Bb

B, b [biː] (N) **1** (= *letter*) B *f*, b *f* • **B for Bertie** B de Burgos • **number 7b** (*in house numbers*) número 7b
2 (*Mus*) • **B** si *m* • **B major/minor** si mayor/menor • **B sharp/flat** si sostenido/bemol
3 (*Scol*) notable *m*
(CPD) ▸ **B road** (*Brit*) ≈ carretera *f* comarcal *or* secundaria

b. (ABBR) (= **born**) n

B2B [ˌbiːtəˈbiː] (= **business to business**)
(N ABBR) B2B *m*
(ADJ ABBR) B2B, entre empresas

B2C [ˌbiːtəˈsiː] (= **business to consumer**)
(N ABBR) B2C *m*
(ADJ ABBR) B2C

B4 [bɪˈfɔːʳ] (ABBR) (*in text message, email*) (= **before**) antes

BA (N ABBR) **1** (*Univ*) (= **Bachelor of Arts**) Lic. en Fil. y Let.; ▸ DEGREE
2 = **British Academy**
3 = **British Association (for the Advancement of Science)**
(ABBR) (*Geog*) (= **Buenos Aires**) Bs.As.

BAA (N ABBR) = **British Airports Authority**

baa [bɑː] (N) balido *m*
(EXCL) ¡be!
(VI) balar

baa-lamb* [ˈbɑːlæm] (N) corderito *m*, borreguito *m*

babble [ˈbæbl] (N) [*of baby*] balbuceo *m*; [*of stream*] murmullo *m*; (= *small talk**) cháchara *f* • **a ~ of voices arose** se oyó un murmullo de voces
(VI) **1** [*person*] (= *talk to excess*) parlotear*; (= *gossip*) chismorrear*, cotillear*
2 [*baby*] balbucear; [*stream*] murmurar
(VT) decir balbuceando
▸ **babble away, babble on** (VI + ADV) hablar sin parar

babbling [ˈbæblɪŋ] (ADJ) [*person*] hablador; [*baby*] balbuceante; [*stream*] que murmura, músico
(N) = **babble**

babe [beɪb] (N) **1** (*liter†*) criatura *f*
2 (*esp US**) chica *f*; (*in direct address*) nena* *f*
(CPD) ▸ **babe in arms** niño/a *m/f* de pecho

babel [ˈbeɪbəl] (N) babel *m or f* • **Tower of Babel** Torre *f* de Babel

baboon [bəˈbuːn] (N) babuino *m*

Babs [bæbz] (N) *familiar form of* **Barbara**

baby [ˈbeɪbɪ] (N) **1** (= *infant*) bebé *mf*, bebe/a *m/f* (*Arg*), guagua *f* (*And*); (= *small child*) nene/a *m/f*, niño/a *m/f* • **she's having a ~ in May** va a tener un niño en mayo • **she's having the ~ in hospital** va a dar a luz en el hospital • **the ~ of the family** el benjamín/la benjamina • **don't be such a ~!** ¡no seas niño/niña!
• IDIOMS: • **I was left holding the ~*** me tocó cargar con el muerto • **to throw out the ~ with the bathwater** actuar con exceso de celo, pasarse*
2 (*US‡*) (= *girlfriend*) chica* *f*; (*in direct address*) nena* *f*, cariño *m*; (= *boyfriend*) chico* *m*; (*in direct address*) cariño
3* (*fig*) **a** (= *special responsibility*) • **the new system was his ~** el nuevo sistema fue obra suya • **that's not my ~** eso no es cosa mía
b (*esp US*) (= *thing*) • **that ~ cost me a fortune** ese chisme me costó una fortuna*
(VT) mimar, consentir
(ADJ) **1** (= *for a baby*) de niño • **~ clothes** ropita *f* de niño
2 (= *young*) • **~ hedgehog** cría *f* de erizo • **~ rabbit** conejito *m*
3 (= *small*) pequeño • **~ car** coche *m* pequeño • **~ sweetcorn** mazorca *f* pequeña
(CPD) ▸ **baby bath** (= *bowl, bath*) bañera *f* para bebé; (= *gel*) gel *m* de baño para bebé ▸ **baby batterer** *persona que maltrata a los niños* ▸ **baby battering** maltrato *m* de los niños ▸ **baby bed** (*US*) cuna *f* ▸ **baby blues*** (= *depression*) depresión *fsing* posparto ▸ **baby bonds** (*US*) bonos *mpl* depreciados ▸ **baby boom** boom *m* de natalidad ▸ **baby boomer** niño/a *m/f* nacido/a en época de un boom de natalidad (*esp de los años 60*) ▸ **Baby bouncer**® columpio *m* para bebés ▸ **baby boy** nene *m* ▸ **baby break** interrupción *f* de las actividades profesionales por maternidad ▸ **baby brother** hermano *m* pequeño ▸ **baby buggy** cochecito *m* (de bebé) ▸ **baby carriage** (*US*) cochecito *m* (de bebé) ▸ **baby clothes** ropita *fsing* de niño ▸ **baby doll** (= *toy*) muñeca *f* (*en forma de bebé*); (= *nightdress*) baby doll *m* (*camisón*) ▸ **baby doll nightie** baby doll *m* (*camisón*) ▸ **baby face** cara *f* de niño ▸ **baby food(s)** comida *f* para bebés, potitos *mpl* (*Sp**) ▸ **baby girl** nena *f* ▸ **baby grand** (*Mus*) piano *m* de media cola ▸ **baby lotion** loción *f* para bebé ▸ **baby milk** (*powdered*) leche *f* maternizada ▸ **baby minder** niñera *f* ▸ **baby monitor** monitor *m* de bebés ▸ **baby oil** aceite *m* para bebés ▸ **baby seat** (*Aut*) sillita *f or* asiento *m* de seguridad para bebés ▸ **baby shower** (*US*) *fiesta con entrega de regalos a la madre y al recién nacido* ▸ **baby sister** hermana *f* pequeña ▸ **baby snatcher** mujer *f* que roba un bebé ▸ **baby talk** habla *f* infantil ▸ **baby tender** (*US*) canguro *mf* ▸ **baby tooth*** diente *m* de leche ▸ **baby walker** andador *m*, tacatá *m* (*Sp**) ▸ **baby wipe** toallita *f* húmeda

baby-doll pyjamas [ˌbeɪbɪdɒlpɪˈdʒɑːməz] (NPL) picardía *f* (*camisón corto con pantalones a juego*)

baby-faced [ˈbeɪbɪˌfeɪst] (ADJ) [*person*] con cara aniñada

Babygro® [ˈbeɪbɪˌgrəʊ] (N) (PL: **Babygros**) pijama *m* de una pieza

babyhood [ˈbeɪbɪhʊd] (N) primera infancia *f*

babyish [ˈbeɪbɪɪʃ] (ADJ) infantil

Babylon [ˈbæbɪlən] (N), **Babylonia** [ˌbæbɪˈləʊnɪə] (N) Babilonia *f*

Babylonian [ˌbæbɪˈləʊnɪən] (ADJ) babilónico; [*person*] babilonio
(N) babilonio/a *m/f*

baby-sit [ˈbeɪbɪsɪt] (VI) cuidar niños, hacer de canguro (*Sp*)
(VT) cuidar, hacer de canguro a (*Sp*)

baby-sitter [ˈbeɪbɪˌsɪtəʳ] (N) babysitter *mf*, canguro *mf* (*Sp*)

baby-sitting [ˈbeɪbɪˌsɪtɪŋ] (N) • **I can't pay for baby-sitting** no puedo pagar un/una babysitter *or* un/una canguro • **I hate baby-sitting** no me gusta nada hacer de babysitter *or* canguro

baccalaureate [ˌbækəˈlɔːrɪɪt] (N) bachillerato *m*

baccarat [ˈbækərɑː] (N) bacará *m*, bacarrá *m*

bacchanalia [ˌbækəˈneɪlɪə] (NPL) bacanales *fpl*; (*fig*) bacanal *f*

bacchanalian [ˌbækəˈneɪlɪən] (ADJ) bacanal, báquico

Bacchic [ˈbækɪk] (ADJ) báquico

Bacchus [ˈbækəs] (N) Baco

baccy* [ˈbækɪ] (N) tabaco *m*

bachelor [ˈbætʃələʳ] (N) **1** (= *unmarried man*) soltero *m* • **confirmed ~** solterón *m*
2 (*Univ*) • **Bachelor of Arts/Science** (= *degree*) licenciatura *f* en Filosofía y Letras/Ciencias; (= *person*) licenciado/a *m/f* en Filosofía y Letras/Ciencias • **~'s degree** licenciatura *f*; ▸ DEGREE
(CPD) ▸ **bachelor flat** piso *m or* (*LAm*) departamento *m* de soltero ▸ **bachelor girl** (*US*) soltera *f* ▸ **Bachelor of Arts degree** Licenciatura *f* en Filosofía y Letras ▸ **Bachelor of Science degree** Licenciatura *f* en Ciencias ▸ **bachelor pad** piso *m or* (*LAm*) departamento *m* de soltero ▸ **bachelor party** fiesta *f* para solteros

bachelordom [ˈbætʃələdəm] (N) soltería *f*

bachelorhood [ˈbætʃələhʊd] (N) soltería *f*

bacillary [bəˈsɪlərɪ] (ADJ) bacilar

bacillus [bəˈsɪləs] (N) (PL: **bacilli** [bəˈsɪlaɪ]) bacilo *m*

back [bæk]

NOUN
ADVERB
TRANSITIVE VERB
INTRANSITIVE VERB
ADJECTIVE
COMPOUNDS
PHRASAL VERBS

When **back** *is an element in a phrasal verb, eg* **come back, go back, put back,** *look up the verb.*

NOUN

1 (= *part of body*) **a** [*of person*] espalda *f*; [*of animal*] lomo *m* • **I've got a bad ~** tengo la espalda mal, tengo un problema de espalda • **to shoot sb in the ~** disparar a algn por la espalda • **he was lying on his ~** estaba tumbado boca arriba • **to carry sth/sb on one's ~** llevar algo/a algn a la espalda • **to**

have one's ~ to sth/sb estar de espaldas a algo/algn • **with his ~ to the light** de espaldas a la luz • **sitting ~ to ~** sentados espalda con espalda

b • IDIOMS: • **behind sb's ~** a espaldas de algn • **they laughed at her behind her ~** se rieron de ella a sus espaldas • **she has been seeing David behind my ~** ha estado viendo a David a mis espaldas • **to break the ~ of sth*** (= *do the difficult part*) hacer la peor parte de algo; (= *do the main part*) hacer lo más gordo de algo*, hacer la mayor parte de algo • **to get off sb's ~*** dejar a algn en paz • **to get sb's ~ up*** poner negro a algn*, mosquear a algn‡ • **to live off the ~ of sb** vivir a costa de algn • **to be on sb's ~*** estar encima de algn • **my boss is always on my ~** mi jefe siempre está encima mío • **on the ~ of sth** a consecuencia de algo • **shares rose on the ~ of two major new deals** las acciones subieron a consecuencia de dos nuevos e importantes tratos • **to put one's ~ into sth** poner mucho esfuerzo *or* empeño en algo • **to put one's ~ into doing sth*** esforzarse a tope por hacer algo*, emplearse a fondo en hacer algo • **to put sb's ~ up*** poner negro a algn*, mosquear a algn‡ • **to see the ~ of sb**: • **I was glad to see the ~ of him** me alegró deshacerme de él • **the moment** *or* **as soon as your ~ is turned ...** en cuanto te descuidas ... • **to have one's ~ to the wall** estar entre la espada y la pared; ▹ **flat, stab**

2 (= *reverse side*) [*of cheque, envelope*] dorso *m*, revés *m*; [*of hand*] dorso *m*; [*of head*] parte *f* de atrás, parte *f* posterior (*more frm*); [*of dress*] espalda *f*; [*of medal*] reverso *m* • **write your name on the ~** escriba su nombre en el reverso • **the ~ of the neck** la nuca • IDIOM: • **to know sth like the ~ of one's hand**: • **I know Naples like the ~ of my hand** conozco Nápoles como la palma de la mano

3 (= *rear*) [*of room, hall*] fondo *m*; [*of car*] parte *f* trasera, parte *f* de atrás; [*of book*] (= *back cover*) tapa *f* posterior; (= *spine*) lomo *m* • **there was damage to the ~ of the car** la parte trasera *or* de atrás del coche resultó dañada • **at the ~ (of)** [+ *building*] en la parte de atrás (de); [+ *cupboard, hall, stage*] en el fondo (de) • **there's a car park at the ~** hay un aparcamiento en la parte de atrás • **be quiet at the ~!** ¡los de atrás guarden silencio! • **they sat at the ~ of the bus** se sentaron en la parte de atrás del autobús, se sentaron al fondo del autobús • **he's at the ~ of all this trouble** él está detrás de todo este lío* • **ambition is at the ~ of it** la ambición es lo que ha causado todo esto* • **this idea had been at the ~ of his mind for several days** esta idea le había estado varios días rondándole la cabeza • **the ship broke its ~** el barco se partió por la mitad • **~ to front** al revés • **you've got your sweater on ~ to front** te has puesto el jersey al revés • **in ~ of the house** (*US*) detrás de la casa • **in the ~ of the car** en la parte trasera del coche • **I'll sit in the ~** yo me sentaré detrás • **the toilet's out the ~** el baño está fuera en la parte de atrás • **they keep the car round the ~** dejan el coche detrás de la casa; ▹ **beyond, mind**

4 (*Sport*) (= *defender*) defensa *mf* • **the team is weak at the ~** la defensa del equipo es débil • **left ~** defensa *mf* izquierdo/a • **right ~** defensa *mf* derecho/a

ADVERB

1 (*in space*) atrás • **stand ~!** ¡atrás! • **keep (well) ~!** (= *out of danger*) ¡quédate ahí atrás! • **keep ~!** (= *don't come near me*) ¡no te acerques! • **meanwhile, ~ in London/~ at the airport** mientras, en Londres/en el aeropuerto • **he little suspected how worried they were ~ at home** qué poco sospechaba lo preocupados que estaban en casa • **~ and forth** de acá para allá • **to go ~ and forth** [*person*] ir de acá para allá • **there were phone calls ~ and forth** se hicieron un montón de llamadas el uno al otro • **~ from the road** apartado de la carretera

2 (*in time*) • **some months ~** hace unos meses • **~ in the 12th century** allá en el siglo XII • **it all started ~ in 1980** todo empezó ya en 1980, todo empezó allá en 1980 (*liter*) • **I saw her ~ in August** la vi el agosto pasado

3 (= *returned*) • **to be ~** volver • **when/what time will you be ~?** ¿cuándo/a qué hora vuelves?, ¿cuándo/a qué hora estarás de vuelta? • **he's not ~ yet** aún no ha vuelto, aún no está de vuelta • **the electricity is ~** ha vuelto la electricidad • **black is ~ (in fashion)** vuelve (a estar de moda) el negro, se vuelve a llevar el negro • **he went to Paris and ~** fue a París y volvió • **30 kilometres there and ~** 30 kilómetros ida y vuelta • **you can go there and ~ in a day** puedes ir y volver en un día • **she's now ~ at work** ya ha vuelto al trabajo • **the kids will be ~ at school tomorrow** los niños vuelven al colegio mañana • **I'll be ~ by 6** estaré de vuelta para las 6 • **I'd like it ~** quiero que me lo devuelvan • **full satisfaction or your money ~** si no está totalmente satisfecho, le devolvemos el dinero • **everything is ~ to normal** todo ha vuelto a la normalidad • **I want it ~** quiero que me lo devuelvan; ▹ **hit back**

TRANSITIVE VERB

1 (= *reverse*) [+ *vehicle*] dar marcha atrás a • **she ~ed the car into the garage** entró el coche en el garaje dando marcha atrás • **he ~ed the car into a wall** dio marcha atrás y chocó con un muro

2 (= *support*) **a** (= *back up*) [+ *plan, person*] apoyar • **they found a witness to ~ his claim** encontraron un testigo que apoyó lo que decía

b (= *finance*) [+ *person, enterprise*] financiar

c (*Mus*) [+ *singer*] acompañar

3 (= *bet on*) [+ *horse*] apostar por • **I'm ~ing Manchester to win** yo apuesto por que va a ganar el Manchester • **to ~ the wrong horse** (*lit*) apostar por el caballo perdedor • **Russia ~ed the wrong horse in him** (*fig*) Rusia se ha equivocado al apoyar a él • **to ~ a winner** (*lit*) apostar por el ganador • **he is confident that he's ~ing a winner** (*fig*) (*person*) está seguro de que está dando su apoyo a un ganador; (*idea, project*) está seguro de que va a funcionar bien

4 (= *attach backing to*) [+ *rug, quilt*] forrar

INTRANSITIVE VERB

1 (*person*) **a** (*in car*) dar marcha atrás • **she ~ed into me** dio marcha atrás y chocó conmigo

b (= *step backwards*) echarse hacia atrás, retroceder • **he ~ed into a table** se echó hacia atrás y se dio con una mesa, retrocedió y se dio con una mesa

2 (= *change direction*) [*wind*] cambiar de dirección (*en sentido contrario a las agujas del reloj*)

ADJECTIVE

1 (= *rear*) [*leg, pocket, wheel*] de atrás, trasero • **the ~ row** la última fila

2 (= *previous, overdue*) [*rent, tax, issue*] atrasado

COMPOUNDS

▸ **back alley** callejuela *f* (*que recorre la parte de atrás de una hilera de casas*) ▸ **back boiler** caldera *f* pequeña (*detrás de una chimenea*) ▸ **back burner** quemador *m* de detrás • IDIOMS: • **to put sth on the ~ burner** posponer algo, dejar algo para más tarde ▸ **back catalogue** (*Mus*) catálogo *m* de grabaciones discográficas ▸ **back copy** (*Press*) número *m* atrasado ▸ **the back country** (*US*) zona *f* rural (*con muy baja densidad de población*); ▹ **back-country** ▸ **back cover** contraportada *f* ▸ **back door** puerta *f* trasera • **to do sth by** *or* **through the ~ door** hacer algo de forma encubierta ▸ **back flip** voltereta *f* hacia atrás ▸ **back formation** (*Ling*) derivación *f* regresiva ▸ **back garden** (*Brit*) jardín *m* trasero ▸ **back lot** (*Cine*) exteriores *mpl* (del estudio); [*of house, hotel, company premises*] solar *m* trasero ▸ **back marker** (*Brit*) (*Sport*) competidor(a) *m/f* rezagado/a ▸ **back matter** [*of book*] apéndices *mpl* ▸ **back number** [*of magazine, newspaper*] número *m* atrasado ▸ **back page** contraportada *f* ▸ **back pain** dolor *m* de espalda, dolor *m* lumbar ▸ **back passage** (*Brit*) (*euph*) recto *m* ▸ **back pay** atrasos *mpl* ▸ **back rest** respaldo *m* ▸ **back road** carretera *f* comarcal, carretera *f* secundaria ▸ **back room** cuarto *m* interior; (*fig*) *lugar donde se hacen investigaciones secretas* ▸ **back rub** (= *massage*) masaje *m* en la espalda • **to give sb a ~ rub** masajearle la espalda a algn, darle un masaje a algn en la espalda ▸ **back seat** asiento *m* trasero, asiento *m* de atrás • IDIOM: • **to take a ~ seat** mantenerse en un segundo plano ▸ **back somersault** salto *m* mortal hacia atrás ▸ **back stop** (*Sport*) *red que se coloca alrededor de una cancha para impedir que se escapen las pelotas* ▸ **back talk*** (*US*) = **backchat** ▸ **back tooth** muela *f* ▸ **back view** • **the ~ view of the hotel is very impressive** el hotel visto desde atrás es impresionante, la parte de atrás del hotel es impresionante ▸ **back vowel** (*Ling*) vocal *f* posterior

▸ **back away** (VI + ADV) **1** (*lit*) retroceder (**from** ante)

2 (*fig*) (*from promise, pledge, statement*) echarse atrás, dar marcha atrás (**from** en) • **the government have been ~ing away from making such a commitment** el gobierno ha estado tratando de evitar comprometerse a tal cosa

▸ **back down** (VI + ADV) echarse atrás, dar marcha atrás • **to ~ down on sth** echarse atrás en algo, dar marcha atrás en algo

▸ **back off** (VI + ADV) (= *stop exerting pressure*) echarse atrás, dar marcha atrás (**from** en); (= *withdraw*) retirarse • **~ off!** ¡déjame en paz!, ¡déjame estar! • **she asked him to ~ off and give her some space** le pidió que no le estuviera encima y la dejara respirar • **the government has ~ed off from its decision** el gobierno se ha echado atrás *or* el gobierno ha dado marcha atrás en su decisión

▸ **back on to** (VI + PREP) • **the house ~s on to the golf course** por atrás la casa da al campo de golf

▸ **back out** (VI + ADV) **1** (*lit*) [*vehicle, driver*] salir marcha atrás (**of** de); [*person*] salir hacia atrás (**of** de)

2 (*fig*) [*person*] (*of team*) retirarse (**of** de); (*of deal, duty*) echarse atrás (**of** en) • **they are threatening to ~ out of the deal** amenazan con echarse atrás en el trato

(VT + ADV) [+ *vehicle*] sacar marcha atrás

▸ **back up** (VT + ADV) **1** (= *support*) [+ *person*] apoyar, respaldar

2 (= *confirm*) [+ *claim, theory*] respaldar

3 (= *reverse*) [+ *car*] dar marcha atrás a, hacer retroceder

4 (*Comput*) [+ *file*] hacer una copia de seguridad *or* de reserva de

5 (= *delay*) • **the traffic was ~ed up for two miles** había una caravana (de tráfico) de dos millas, había retenciones (de tráfico) de dos millas

(VI + ADV) **1** (*in car*) (= *reverse*) dar marcha atrás

2 (= *queue*) • **traffic is ~ing up for miles behind**

the accident hay una caravana (de tráfico) de varias millas desde el lugar del accidente, hay retenciones (de tráfico) de varias millas desde el lugar del accidente

backache ['bækeɪk] N dolor *m* de espalda
backbench ['bæk'bentʃ] ADJ [*committee, revolt*] de los diputados sin cargo oficial; [*MP*] sin cargo oficial
backbencher [,bæk'bentʃəʳ] N (*Brit*) (*Parl*) *diputado sin cargo oficial en el gobierno o la oposición*

BACKBENCHER
Se conoce como **backbencher** al parlamentario británico que no se sienta en los escaños (**benches**) de las primeras filas de la Cámara de los Comunes (**House of Commons**) junto al líder de su partido, por no pertenecer al Gobierno o a su equivalente en la oposición. Al no ser titulares de ningún cargo, les resulta más fácil hablar o votar en contra de la política oficial del partido. Se los conoce también colectivamente como los **backbenches**.
▸ FRONT BENCH

backbenches [,bæk'bentʃəz] NPL (*Brit*) (*Parl*) *escaños de los diputados sin cargo oficial en el gobierno o la oposición* • **the Tory ~** los diputados conservadores sin cargo oficial
backbite ['bækbaɪt] VI murmurar
VT [+ *absent person*] hablar mal de
backbiting ['bækbaɪtɪŋ] N murmuración *f*
backboard ['bækbɔːd] N (*US*) (*Sport*) tablero *m*
backbone ['bækbəʊn] N **1** (*Anat*) columna *f* vertebral, espina *f* dorsal • **a patriot to the ~** un patriota hasta la médula
2 (*fig*) (= *courage*) agallas *fpl*; (= *strength*) resistencia *f* • **the ~ of the organisation** el pilar de la organización
back-breaking ['bækbreɪkɪŋ] ADJ deslomador, matador
backchat ['bæktʃæt] N réplicas *fpl* (insolentes)
backcloth ['bækklɒθ] N (*Brit*) (*Theat*) (*also fig*) telón *m* de fondo
backcomb ['bækkəʊm] VT (*Brit*) [+ *hair*] cardar
back-country ['bæk,kʌntrɪ] ADJ (= *rural*) rural • **back-country jeep expeditions** expediciones *fpl* en jeep al campo
backdate ['bæk'deɪt] VT [+ *cheque*] poner fecha anterior a, antedatar; [+ *pay rise*] dar efecto retroactivo a • **a pay rise ~d to April** un aumento salarial con efecto retroactivo desde abril
backdoor ['bæk,dɔːʳ] ADJ (= *underhand*) [*deal, increase, privatization etc*] subrepticio
backdrop ['bækdrɒp] N = **backcloth**
-backed [bækt] ADJ (*ending in compounds*)
1 • **low-backed chair** silla *f* de respaldo bajo
2 • **rubber-backed carpet** alfombra *f* con refuerzo de caucho
backer ['bækəʳ] N **1** (*Comm*) (= *guarantor*) fiador(a) *m/f*; (= *financier*) promotor(a) *m/f*, patrocinador(a) *m/f*
2 (*Pol*) (= *supporter*) partidario/a *m/f*
3 (= *one who bets*) apostante *mf*
backfire ['bæk'faɪəʳ] N (*Aut*) petardeo *m*
VI (*Aut*) petardear • **their plan ~d** (*fig*) les salió el tiro por la culata*
backgammon ['bæk,gæmən] N backgammon *m*
background ['bækgraʊnd] N **1** [*of picture etc*] fondo *m*; (*fig*) ambiente *m* • **on a red ~** sobre un fondo rojo • **in the ~** al *or* en el fondo; (*fig*) en segundo plano, en la sombra • **to stay in the ~** mantenerse en segundo plano, no buscar publicidad
2 [*of person*] formación *f*, educación *f* • **she comes from a wealthy ~** proviene de una familia acaudalada • **what is his ~?** ¿cuáles son sus antecedentes?
3 [*of situation, event*] antecedentes *mpl* • **the ~ to the crisis** los antecedentes de la crisis • **to fill in the ~ for sb** poner a algn en antecedentes
CPD ▸ **background check** verificación *f* de antecedentes • **they are calling for fingerprinting and ~ checks for airport employees** están pidiendo la verificación de antecedentes y la toma de huellas digitales de los empleados de aeropuerto • **you have to have a ~ check before you can buy a gun** para comprar una pistola tienen que verificar tus antecedentes ▸ **background music** música *f* de fondo ▸ **background noise** ruido *m* de fondo ▸ **background reading** lecturas *fpl* de fondo, lecturas *fpl* preparatorias ▸ **background report** (*Jur*) *informe de los peritos sobre la vida de alguien* ▸ **background studies** estudios *mpl* del ambiente histórico (*en que vivió un autor etc*) ▸ **background task** (*Comput*) tarea *f* secundaria
backhand ['bækhænd] ADJ [*blow*] de revés • **~ drive/shot/stroke** (*Tennis*) revés *m* • **~ volley** (*Tennis*) volea *f* de revés
N (*Tennis*) revés *m*
backhanded ['bæk'hændɪd] ADJ **1** [*blow*] de revés
2 (*fig*) [*compliment*] ambiguo, equívoco
backhander* ['bæk'hændəʳ] N (*Brit*)
1 (= *blow*) revés *m*
2 (= *bribe*) soborno *m*, mordida *f* (*CAm, Mex*), coima *f* (*And, S. Cone*)
backing ['bækɪŋ] N **1** (= *support*) apoyo *m*; (*Comm*) respaldo *m* (financiero)
2 (*Mus*) acompañamiento *m*
3 (= *protective layer*) refuerzo *m*
CPD ▸ **backing group** (*Mus*) grupo *m* de acompañamiento ▸ **backing singer** (*Mus*) corista *mf* ▸ **backing store** (*Comput*) memoria *f* auxiliar ▸ **backing vocals** (*Mus*) coros *mpl*
backlash ['bæklæʃ] N (*fig*) reacción *f* en contra; (*Pol*) reacción *f* violenta • **the male ~** la violenta reacción masculina, el contraataque de los hombres
backless ['bæklɪs] ADJ [*dress*] sin espalda, muy escotado por detrás
back-line player ['bæklaɪn,pleɪəʳ] N (*US*) defensa *mf*
backlist ['bæklɪst] N fondo *m* editorial
backlog ['bæklɒg] N • **because of the ~ (of work/orders)** por el trabajo acumulado *or* atrasado/el volumen de pedidos pendientes • **a ~ of cases** un montón de casos atrasados
backpack ['bækpæk] N mochila *f*
VI hacer excursionismo de mochila
backpacker ['bæk,pækəʳ] N mochilero/a *m/f*
backpacking ['bæk,pækɪŋ] N • **to go ~** hacer excursionismo de mochila
back-pedal ['bæk'pedl] VI (*on bicycle*) pedalear hacia atrás; (*fig*) echarse atrás, dar marcha atrás
back-pedalling ['bæk,pedəlɪŋ] N • **back-pedalling is his speciality** (*fig*) echarse atrás *or* dar marcha atrás es su especialidad
backplate ['bækpleɪt] N (*US*) sesos *mpl* de cerdo
backroom ['bækrʊm] ADJ **1** (*pej*) [*deal, negotiations*] entre bastidores
2 (*referring to people*) • **Mr Smith's ~ staff** los empleados desconocidos que trabajan para el Sr. Smith • **~ team** equipo que trabaja en la sombra
CPD ▸ **backroom boy** *persona que colabora en un proyecto de investigación sin obtener reconocimiento público*
backscratching* ['bæk,skrætʃɪŋ] N (*fig*) compadreo *m*
back-seat driver [,bæksiːt'draɪvəʳ] N *pasajero que siempre está dando consejos al conductor*
backshift ['bækʃɪft] N (*Brit*) (*Ind*) turno *m* de tarde
backside* ['bæk'saɪd] N trasero* *m*
backslapping ['bæk,slæpɪŋ] N espaldarazos *mpl* • **mutual ~** bombo *m* mutuo
backslash ['bækslæʃ] N (*Typ*) barra *f* inversa
backslide ['bæk'slaɪd] (PT, PP: **backslid**) VI reincidir, recaer
backslider ['bæk'slaɪdəʳ] N reincidente *mf*
backsliding ['bæk'slaɪdɪŋ] N reincidencia *f*, recaída *f*
backspace ['bækspeɪs] (*Typ*) VI retroceder
N retroceso *m*, tecla *f* de retroceso
backspin ['bækspɪn] N (*Tennis, Cricket*) efecto *m* cortado; (*Billiards, Snooker*) efecto *m* bajo, efecto *m* de retroceso • **to give a ball ~** • **put ~ on a ball** (*Tennis, Cricket*) cortar una pelota; (*Billiards, Snooker*) picar una bola
backstage ['bæk'steɪdʒ] N (= *off-stage*) bastidores *mpl*, espacio *m* entre bastidores; (= *dressing-rooms*) camarines *mpl*
ADJ entre bastidores
ADV entre bastidores • **to go ~** ir a los camarines
CPD ▸ **backstage pass** pase *m* backstage (*para los bastidores*)
backstairs ['bæk'steəz] NPL escalera *f* de servicio
CPD [*staff*] de servicio; [*work*] doméstico; (*fig*) [*gossip, plot*] clandestino, subrepticio
backstitch ['bækstɪtʃ] N pespunte *m*
VT pespuntar
backstreet ['bækstriːt] N • **the ~s** (*lit*) las callejuelas; (*quiet*) las calles tranquilas *or* apartadas del centro; (*poor*) las calles de los barrios bajos
CPD [*hotel, shop*] de barrio ▸ **backstreet abortion** aborto *m* clandestino ▸ **backstreet abortionist** abortista *mf* clandestino/a
backstretch ['bækstretʃ] N (*Sport*) estiramiento *m* hacia atrás
backstroke ['bækstrəʊk] N espalda *f* • **the 100 metres ~** los 100 metros espalda
backswing ['bækswɪŋ] N (*Sport*) backswing *m*, swing *m* hacia atrás
backtalk ['bæktɔːk] N (*US*) = **backchat**
back-to-back ['bæktə'bæk] ADJ
• **back-to-back credit** créditos *mpl* contiguos
• **back-to-back houses** (*Brit*) casas *fpl* adosadas (*por la parte trasera*)
ADV • **to sit back-to-back** sentarse *or* estar sentados espalda con espalda • **they showed two episodes back-to-back** echaron dos capítulos seguidos
backtrack ['bæktræk] VI **1** (*on route, journey*) desandar el camino, dar marcha atrás
2 (*fig*) (*in account, explanation*) ir más atrás, retroceder; (= *renege*) (*on promise, decision*) echarse atrás, dar marcha atrás (**on** en)
backtracking ['bæktrækɪŋ] N = **back-pedalling**
backup ['bækʌp] N **1** (= *support*) apoyo *m*
2 (*US*) [*of traffic*] embotellamiento *m*
3 (*Comput*) (*also* **backup file**) copia *f* de seguridad
CPD [*train, plane*] suplementario; (*Comput*) [*disk, file*] de seguridad ▸ **backup copy** (*Comput*) copia *f* de seguridad ▸ **backup lights** (*US*) luces *fpl* de marcha atrás ▸ **backup operation** operación *f* de apoyo ▸ **backup plan** plan *m* alternativo ▸ **backup**

services servicios *mpl* auxiliares
backward ['bækwəd] ADJ **1** [*motion, glance*] hacia atrás • **~ and forward movement** movimiento *m* de vaivén
2 [*pupil, country*] atrasado
3 (= *reluctant*) tímido • **he wasn't ~ in claiming the money** no se mostró tímido a la hora de reclamar el dinero • **he's not ~ in coming forward** (*iro*) no peca de tímido
ADV **1** [*look*] atrás, hacia atrás; [*move*] hacia atrás • **to walk/fall ~** andar/caer hacia atrás • **to go ~ and forward** ir y venir, ir de acá para allá • **this is a step ~** (*fig*) esto supone un paso atrás; ▷ **bend over**
2 (= *in reverse*) al revés • **to read sth ~** leer algo para atrás • IDIOM: • **to know sth ~*** saberse algo al dedillo *or* de pe a pa
CPD ▸ **backward roll** voltereta *f* hacia atrás ▸ **backward somersault** (*on ground*) voltereta *f* hacia atrás; (*in mid-air*) salto *m* mortal hacia atrás
backwardation [,bækwə'deɪʃən] N (*St Ex*) retraso *m* en la entrega de acciones; (= *fee*) prima *f* pagada por retraso en la entrega de acciones
backward-compatible ['bækwədkəm'pætɪbl] ADJ (*Comput, Tech*) *compatible con el modelo, sistema etc anterior*
backward-looking ['bækwəd,lʊkɪŋ] ADJ retrógrado
backwardness ['bækwədnɪs] N [*of country*] atraso *m*; [*of person*] (*socially*) timidez *f*; (*mentally*) retraso *m*
backwards ['bækwədz] ADV (*esp Brit*) = **backward**
backwards-compatible ['bækwədzkəm'pætɪbl] ADJ = **backward-compatible**
backwash ['bækwɒʃ] N **1** (*Naut*) agua *f* de rechazo
2 (*fig*) reacción *f*, repercusiones *fpl*
backwater ['bækwɔːtəʳ] N **1** [*of river*] remanso *m*
2 (*fig*) lugar *m* atrasado
backwoods ['bækwʊdz] NPL región *f* apartada, ≈ Las Batuecas
CPD ▸ **backwoods community** comunidad *f* rústica
backwoodsman ['bækwʊdzmən] N (PL: **backwoodsmen**) **1** (*lit*) campesino/a *m/f*; (*pej*) patán *m*
2 (*fig*) (= *reactionary*) reaccionario/a *m/f*; (*Brit*) (*Pol*) *par que asiste con muy poca frecuencia a las sesiones de la Cámara de los Lores*
backyard ['bæk'jɑːd] N (*Brit*) patio *m* trasero; (*US*) jardín *m* trasero • **in one's own ~** en su misma puerta, delante de sus narices* • **"not in my ~"** (*slogan*) "no lo quiero en mi patio" (*residuos tóxicos etc*)
bacon ['beɪkən] N beicon *m* (*Sp*), tocino *m* (*LAm*), panceta *f* (*Arg*) • **~ and eggs** huevos *mpl* con tocino • IDIOMS: • **to bring home the ~*** (= *earn one's living*) ganarse las habichuelas* • **to save sb's ~*** salvar el pellejo a algn*
bacteria [bæk'tɪərɪə] NPL bacterias *fpl*
bacterial [bæk'tɪərɪəl] ADJ bacteriano, bacterial
bacteriological [bæk,tɪərɪə'lɒdʒɪkəl] ADJ bacteriológico
bacteriologist [bæk,tɪərɪ'ɒlədʒɪst] N bacteriólogo/a *m/f*
bacteriology [bæk,tɪərɪ'ɒlədʒɪ] N bacteriología *f*
bacteriophage [bæk'tɪərɪəfeɪdʒ] N bacteriófago *m*
bacteriosis [,bæktɪərɪ'əʊsɪs] N bacteriosis *f*
bacterium [bæk'tɪərɪəm] N (PL: **bacteria**) bacteria *f*
bad [bæd] ADJ (COMPAR: **worse**, SUPERL: **worst**) **1** (= *disagreeable*) malo • **I've had a bad day at work** he tenido un mal día en el trabajo • **to taste bad** saber mal, no saber bueno • **she looked as if she had a bad smell under her nose** parecía como si algo le oliera mal • **to go from bad to worse** ir de mal en peor; ▷ **mood²**, **temper**, **time**
2 (= *poor, inferior*) malo • **her English is bad** habla inglés mal • **his handwriting is bad** tiene mala letra • **business is bad** el negocio va mal • **to be bad at sth** ser malo para algo • **I was bad at sports** era muy malo para los deportes, los deportes se me daban mal • **he was a bad driver** era un mal conductor • **that's not a bad idea** esa no es una mala idea • **I'm a bad liar** no sé mentir • **bad light stopped play** se suspendió el partido debido a la falta de luz • **it would make me look bad in the press** daría una mala imagen de mí en la prensa • **he wasn't bad-looking** no estaba mal • **bad management** mala administración • **this wine's not bad at all** este vino no está nada mal • **too bad**: • **it's too bad you couldn't get tickets** es una pena *or* una lástima que no hayas podido conseguir entradas • **"that was my drink!" — "too bad!"** —¡ésa era mi bebida! —¡qué le vamos a hacer! • **if you don't like it, (that's) too bad!** si no te gusta, ¡peor para ti! • **the firm has had a bad year** la empresa ha tenido un mal año
3 (= *serious, severe*) [*accident, mistake*] grave; [*headache*] fuerte • **she's got a bad cold** está muy resfriada, tiene un resfriado fuerte • **the traffic was bad today** hoy había mucho tráfico
4 (= *unfavourable*) malo • **the plane was diverted due to bad weather** el avión fue desviado debido al mal tiempo • **you've come at a bad time** vienes en un mal momento • **things are looking bad for the government** las cosas se están poniendo feas para el gobierno • **it'll look bad if we don't go** quedará mal que no vayamos; ▷ **book**
5 (= *harmful*) malo • **he was a bad influence** era una mala influencia • **to be bad for sth/sb**: • **smoking is bad for you** *or* **for your health** fumar es malo *or* perjudicial para la salud, fumar perjudica la salud • **soap is bad for the skin** el jabón no es bueno para la piel
6 (= *wicked*) [*person, behaviour*] malo • **you bad boy!** ¡qué niño más malo eres! • **they're a bad lot*** no son buena gente • **he said a bad word** ha dicho una palabrota • **it's too bad of you!** ¿no te da vergüenza? • **it's really too bad of him!** ¡realmente no tiene vergüenza!; ▷ **language**
7 • **to feel bad about sth** (= *sorry*): • **I feel bad about hurting his feelings** me sabe mal haber herido sus sentimientos; (= *guilty*) • **are you trying to make me feel bad?** ¿estás intentando hacer que me sienta culpable? • **don't feel bad (about it), it's not your fault** no te preocupes, no es culpa tuya
8 (= *ailing*) • **I feel bad** me siento mal • **he has a bad back** está mal de la espalda • **to be in a bad way**: • **the economy is in a bad way** la economía va mal • **he looked in a bad way** tenía mal aspecto
9 (= *rotten*) [*food*] podrido; [*milk*] cortado; [*tooth*] picado • **to go bad** pasarse, estropearse; ▷ **blood**
10 (*Econ*) [*cheque*] sin fondos • **a bad debt** una deuda incobrable *or* de pago dudoso
N lo malo • **parents can have a powerful influence for good or bad** los padres pueden tener mucha influencia para lo bueno y para lo malo • **there's good and bad in this news** esta noticia tiene su lado bueno y su lado malo • **there is both good and bad in every human being** hay una parte buena y una parte mala en cada ser humano • **to take the bad with the good** aceptar tanto lo bueno como lo malo
ADV* • **he's hurt bad** está malherido • **she took it bad** se lo tomó a mal • **if you want it that bad you can pay for it yourself** si tanto lo quieres, cómpratelo tú • **to need sth real bad** necesitar algo desesperadamente • **the way she looks at him, you can tell she's got it bad** por la forma en que lo mira, se nota que está colada por él* • **to be in bad with sb**: • **he's in bad with the law** tiene problemas con la ley
CPD ▸ **bad apple** (= *person*) manzana *f* podrida ▸ **bad guy*** (= *baddy*) (*in film, story*) malo *m*; (= *criminal*) delincuente *m* ▸ **bad hair day*** (= *bad day*) mal día *m* • **to have a bad hair day** (*bad day*) tener un mal día; (*with messy hair*) tener el pelo todo revuelto

BAD

"Malo" shortened to "mal"

▷ **Malo** *must be shortened to* **mal** *before a masculine singular noun:*
He was in a bad mood
Estaba de mal humor

Position of "malo"

▷ **Mal/Mala** *etc precedes the noun in general comments. Here, there is no comparison, implied or explicit, with something better:*
I'm afraid I have some bad news for you
Me temo que traigo malas noticias para usted
I've had a bad day today
Hoy he tenido un mal día

▷ **Malo/Mala** *etc follows the noun when there is an implicit or explicit comparison with something good:*
... his only bad day in the race ...
... su único día malo en la carrera ...

Ser/Estar malo

▷ *Use* **malo** *with* **ser** *to describe inherent qualities and characteristics:*
Smoking is bad for your health
Fumar es malo para la salud
This is a very bad film
Esta película es malísima

▷ *Use* **malo** *with* **estar** *to describe unpleasant food or else to mean "unwell":*
The food was really bad
La comida estaba malísima
He's been unwell lately
Ha estado malo últimamente

Estar mal

▷ *Use* **estar** *with the adverb* **mal** *to give a general comment on a situation that seems bad or wrong:*
Cheating in your exams is really bad
Está muy mal que copies en los exámenes
In the space of an hour I've signed fifty books. Not bad
En una hora he firmado cincuenta libros. No está mal
I managed to come second, which wasn't bad
He conseguido acabar segundo, lo que no estuvo mal

For further uses and examples, see main entry.

baddie*, **baddy*** ['bædɪ] (N) (*Cine*) (*often hum*) malo *m*
baddish ['bædɪʃ] (ADJ) bastante malo, más bien malo
bade [bæd] (PT) *of* **bid**
badge [bædʒ] (N) **1** (= *emblem*) insignia *f*; (*sewn on coat*) distintivo *m*; (*Brit*) (*metal*) chapa *f* • **~ of office** distintivo *m or* insignia *f* de su función
2 (*fig*) señal *f*
badger ['bædʒəʳ] (N) tejón *m*
(VT) acosar, atormentar (**for** para obtener) • **to ~ sb into doing sth** acosar a algn hasta que haga algo • **stop ~ing me!** ¡deja ya de fastidiarme!
(CPD) ▸ **badger baiting** *lucha de perros contra tejones*
badinage ['bædɪnɑːʒ] (N) chanzas *fpl*, bromas *fpl*
badlands ['bædlændz] (NPL) (*US*) tierras *fpl* malas, *región yerma, esp en los estados de Nebraska y Dakota del Sur*
badly ['bædlɪ] (ADV) **1** (= *poorly*) mal • **he did ~ in his exams** los exámenes le fueron mal • **things are going ~** las cosas van mal • **we came off ~ in the deal** salimos mal parados del negocio • **~ made/written/designed** mal hecho/escrito/diseñado • **to sleep ~** dormir mal; ▸ **pay**
2 (= *seriously, severely*) gravemente • **he was ~ injured** estaba gravemente herido • **they were ~ beaten** (*in contest*) sufrieron una seria derrota; (*physically*) les dieron una paliza tremenda • **to be ~ mistaken** estar muy equivocado • **it was a gamble that went ~ wrong** se corría un riesgo y salió muy mal • **the building was ~ damaged in the explosion** en la explosión el edificio resultó muy dañado
3 (= *unfavourably*) • **to speak/think ~ of sb** hablar/pensar mal de algn • **to reflect ~ on sb** dejar mal a algn • **"how did he take it?" — "badly"** —¿qué tal se lo tomó? —fatal
4 (= *wrongly*) • **to treat sb ~** tratar mal a algn • **to behave ~** portarse mal
5 (= *very much*) [*want, need*] • **~-needed medical supplies** medicamentos *mpl* que se necesitan desesperadamente • **it ~ needs painting** hace mucha falta pintarlo • **he ~ needs help** necesita ayuda a toda costa • **they ~ wanted a child** estaban desesperados por tener un niño • **we ~ need another assistant** nos hace muchísima falta otro ayudante
6 • **to be ~ off** (= *poor*) andar *or* estar mal de dinero • **we are ~ off for coal** andamos mal de carbón • **you're not that ~ off, you only have to work 20 hours a week** no estás tan mal, solo tienes que trabajar 20 horas por semana
badman ['bædmæn] (PL: **badmen**) (N) (*esp US*) gángster *m*
bad-mannered ['bæd'mænəd] (ADJ) maleducado, grosero
badminton ['bædmɪntən] (N) bádminton *m*
badmouth* ['bæd,maʊθ] (VT) hablar pestes de*
badness ['bædnɪs] (N) **1** (= *wickedness*) maldad *f*
2 (= *poor quality*) mala calidad *f*
bad-tempered ['bæd'tempəd] (ADJ) [*person*] (*temporarily*) de mal humor; (*permanently*) de mal genio, de mal carácter; [*argument*] fuerte; [*tone etc*] áspero, malhumorado
Bae (N ABBR) (= **British Aerospace**) ≈ CASA *f*
Baffin ['bæfɪn] (N) • **~ Bay** Bahía *f* de Baffin • **~ Island** Tierra *f* de Baffin
baffle ['bæfl] (VT) **1** (= *perplex*) desconcertar • **at times you ~ me** a veces me desconciertas • **the problem ~s me** el problema me tiene perplejo, no le veo solución alguna al problema • **the police are ~d** la policía está desconcertada *or* perpleja
2 (*frm*) (= *frustrate*) [+ *progress*] impedir; [+ *plan, attempt*] frustrar • **it ~s description** es imposible describirlo
(N) (*also* **baffle board, baffle plate**) deflector *m*; (*Rad*) pantalla *f* acústica
bafflement ['bæflmənt] (N) desconcierto *m*, perplejidad *f*
baffling ['bæflɪŋ] (ADJ) [*action*] incomprensible, desconcertante; [*crime*] misterioso; [*problem*] dificilísimo
BAFTA ['bæftə] (N ABBR) = **British Academy of Film and Television Arts**
bag [bæg] (N) **1** [*of paper, plastic*] bolsa *f*; (= *large sack*) costal *m*; (= *handbag*) bolso *m*, cartera *f* (*LAm*); (= *suitcase*) maleta *f*, valija *f* (*LAm*), veliz *m* (*Mex*); (*carried over shoulder*) zurrón *m*, mochila *f* • **a bag of sweets/chips** una bolsa de caramelos/patatas fritas • **to pack one's bags** hacer las maletas • **they threw him out bag and baggage** lo pusieron de patitas en la calle • **he was like a bag of bones** estaba como un esqueleto • **it's a mixed bag*** hay un poco de todo • **the whole bag of tricks*** todo el rollo* • IDIOMS: • **to be left holding the bag** (*US**) cargar con el muerto* • **to be in the bag***: • **it's in the bag** es cosa segura, está en el bote (*Sp**) • **we had the game nearly in the bag** el partido estaba casi ganado, teníamos el partido casi en el bote (*Sp**) • **not to be sb's bag** (*US**): • **it's not his bag** no es lo suyo
2 (*Hunting*) cacería *f*, piezas *fpl* cobradas • **a good day's bag** una buena cacería
3 bags (= *baggage*) equipaje *m*; (*Brit**) (= *trousers*) pantalones *mpl* • **bags under the eyes** ojeras *fpl*
4 • **bags of** (*Brit**) (= *lots*) un montón de • **we've bags of time** tenemos tiempo de sobra
5 (= *woman*) • **old bag*** bruja* *f*
(VT) **1** (*also* **bag up**) [+ *goods, groceries*] meter en una bolsa/en bolsas
2 (*Hunting*) cazar; (= *shoot down*) derribar
3* (= *get possession of*) pillar*, hacerse con; (*Brit*) (= *claim in advance*) reservarse • **I bags that** eso pa' mí
(VI) **1** (*also* **bag out**) [*garment*] hacer bolsas
(CPD) ▸ **bag lady*** indigente *f* vagabunda ▸ **bag snatcher** ladrón/a *m/f* de bolsos
bagatelle [,bægə'tel] (N) **1** (= *trifle*) bagatela *f*
2 (= *board game*) bagatelle *f*
3 (*Billiards*) billar *m* romano
4 (*Mus*) bagatela *f*
bagel ['beɪgl] (N) (*US*) *especie de bollo en forma de aro*
bagful ['bægfʊl] (N) bolsa *f* (lleno)
baggage ['bægɪdʒ] (N) **1** (= *luggage*) equipaje *m*; (*Mil*) bagaje *m*
2 (*fig*) (*Psych*) bagaje *m*
3†* (= *woman*) bruja* *f*
(CPD) ▸ **baggage allowance** límite *m* de equipaje ▸ **baggage car** (*US*) furgón *m* de equipajes ▸ **baggage carousel** (*at airport*) cinta *f* de equipajes ▸ **baggage check** talón *m* de equipaje ▸ **baggage (check)room** (*US*) consigna *f* ▸ **baggage hall** (*at airport*) sala *f* de equipajes ▸ **baggage handler** despachador(a) *m/f* de equipaje ▸ **baggage handling** (*at airport*) handling *m* de equipajes ▸ **baggage locker** consigna *f* automática ▸ **baggage (re)claim** recogida *f* de equipaje ▸ **baggage screening** (*at airport*) control *m* de equipajes ▸ **baggage train** tren *m* de equipajes
bagging ['bægɪŋ] (N) (= *material*) material *m* usado para hacer bolsas
baggy ['bægɪ] (ADJ) (COMPAR: **baggier**, SUPERL: **baggiest**) ancho; [*trousers*] (*at the knees*) con bolsas en las rodillas; (= *wide*) abombachado
Baghdad [,bæg'dæd] (N) Bagdad *m*
bagpiper ['bægpaɪpəʳ] (N) gaitero *m*
bagpipes ['bægpaɪps] (NPL) gaita *fsing*
bag-snatching ['bæg,snætʃɪŋ] (N) tirón *m* (de bolsos)
baguette [bæ'get] (N) baguette *f*, barrita *f* de pan
bah [bɑː] (EXCL) ¡bah!
Bahamas [bə'hɑːməz] (NPL) • **the ~** las Bahamas
Bahamian [bə'heɪmɪən] (ADJ) bahamés
(N) bahamés/esa *m/f*
Bahrain [bɑː'reɪn] (N) Bahrein *m*
Bahraini [bɑː'reɪnɪ] (ADJ) bahreiní
(N) bahreiní *mf*
bail¹ [beɪl] (*Jur*) (N) (*Jur*) fianza *f* • **on ~** bajo fianza • **he's out on ~** está libre bajo fianza • **to be released on ~** ser puesto en libertad bajo fianza • **to jump ~*** fugarse estando bajo fianza • **to go** *or* **stand ~ for sb** pagar la fianza de algn
(VT) (*Jur*) (*also* **bail out**) pagar la fianza de
(CPD) ▸ **bail bandit*** (*Brit*) *persona que comete un delito estando en libertad bajo fianza* ▸ **bail bond** (*US*) fianza *f*
▸ **bail out** (VT + ADV) • **to ~ sb out** (*Jur*) pagar la fianza de algn; (*fig*) echar un cable a algn
bail² [beɪl] (N) (*Cricket*) palito *m* corto
bail³ [beɪl] (VT) (*Naut*) achicar
▸ **bail out** (VI + ADV) (*Aer*) lanzarse *or* tirarse en paracaídas
(VT + ADV) (*US*) = **bale out**
bailable ['beɪləbl] (ADJ) (*Jur*) susceptible de fianza
bailee [beɪ'liː] (N) (*Jur*) depositario/a *m/f*, consignatario/a *m/f*
bailiff ['beɪlɪf] (N) **1** (*Jur*) alguacil *m*
2 (*on estate*) administrador(a) *m/f*
bailiwick ['beɪlɪwɪk] (N) **1** (*Jur*) alguacilazgo *m*
2 (*esp US*) (*fig*) (= *speciality*) ámbito *m* de actuación
bailor ['beɪləʳ] (N) (*Jur*) fiador(a) *m/f*
bain-marie [bɛ̃mə'riː] (N) (PL: **bains-marie**) baño *m* (de) María
bairn [bɛən] (N) (*Scot, N Engl*) niño/a *m/f*
bait [beɪt] (N) (*Fishing, Hunting*) cebo *m*; (*fig*) anzuelo *m*, cebo *m* • IDIOMS: • **to rise to the ~**: • **he didn't rise to the ~** no picó • **to swallow the ~** (*lit*) picar; (*fig*) morder el anzuelo, caer en la trampa
(VT) **1** [+ *hook, trap*] cebar
2 (= *torment*) [+ *person, animal*] atormentar
baize [beɪz] (N) paño *m* • **green ~** tapete *m* verde
bake [beɪk] (VT) **1** [+ *food*] cocer (al horno); [+ *bricks etc*] cocer • **to ~ one's own bread** hacer el pan en casa • **~d beans** judías *fpl* en salsa de tomate • **~d potato** patata *f or* (*LAm*) papa *f* al horno
2 (= *harden*) endurecer
(VI) **1** [*person*] • **I love to ~** me gusta hacer pasteles/pan *etc* al horno
2 [*bread, cake*] hacerse en el horno
3 (*fig*) (= *swelter*) • **we were baking in the heat** nos asábamos de calor
(N) (*Brit*) (*Culin*) *pastel salado cocinado al horno esp con verduras o pescado*
bakehouse ['beɪkhaʊs] (N) tahona *f*, panadería *f*
Bakelite® ['beɪkəlaɪt] (N) baquelita *f*
baker ['beɪkəʳ] (N) panadero/a *m/f*; [*of cakes*] pastelero/a *m/f* • **~'s (shop)** (*for bread*) panadería *f*; (*for cakes*) pastelería *f* • **~'s dozen** docena *f* de fraile
bakery ['beɪkərɪ] (N) (*for bread*) panadería *f*; (*for cakes*) pastelería *f*

b

bakeware ['beɪkweəʳ] (N) fuentes *fpl* de horno
Bakewell tart [,beɪkwəl'tɑːt] (N) *tarta hecha a base de almendras, mermelada y azúcar en polvo*
baking ['beɪkɪŋ] (N) **1** (= *activity*) • **she does the ~ on Monday** los lunes hace el pan/los pasteles *etc*
2 (= *batch*) hornada *f*
(ADJ)* (= *hot*) • **it's ~ (hot) in here** esto es un horno • **a ~ hot day** un día de calor asfixiante
(CPD) ▸ **baking chocolate** (*US*) chocolate *m* fondant ▸ **baking dish** fuente *f* para el horno ▸ **baking mitt** (*US*) guante *m* para el horno, manopla *f* para el horno ▸ **baking pan** = baking tin ▸ **baking powder** Royal® *m*, levadura *f* en polvo (*Sp*) ▸ **baking sheet** = baking tray ▸ **baking soda** bicarbonato *m* de soda ▸ **baking tin** molde *m* (para el horno) ▸ **baking tray** bandeja *f* de horno
baksheesh ['bækʃiːʃ] (N) propina *f*
bal. (ABBR) = balance
balaclava [,bælə'klɑːvə] (N) (*also* **balaclava helmet**) pasamontañas *m inv*
balalaika [,bælə'laɪkə] (N) balalaica *f*
balance ['bæləns] (N) **1** (= *equilibrium*) equilibrio *m* • **a nice ~ of humour and pathos** un sutil equilibrio entre el humor y el patetismo • **the ~ of his mind was disturbed** (*frm*) su mente estaba desequilibrada • **in ~** en equilibrio, equilibrado • **to keep one's ~** mantener el equilibrio • **to lose one's ~** perder el equilibrio • **the ~ of nature** el equilibrio de la naturaleza • **off ~**: • **he's a bit off ~** (*mentally*) está un poco desequilibrado • **to catch sb off ~** pillar a algn desprevenido • **to throw sb off ~** (*lit*) hacer que algn pierda el equilibrio; (*fig*) desconcertar a algn • **on ~** (*fig*) teniendo *or* tomando en cuenta todos los factores, una vez considerados todos los factores (*frm*) • **to be out of ~** [*mechanism, wheel*] estar desequilibrado • **~ of power** (*Mil, Comm*) equilibrio *m* de poder; (*Phys*) equilibrio *m* de fuerzas • **to redress the ~** restablecer el equilibrio • **he has no sense of ~** no tiene sentido del equilibrio • **to strike a ~** conseguir *or* establecer un equilibrio
2 (= *scales*) balanza *f* • **to be** *or* **hang in the ~** (*fig*) estar pendiente de un hilo
3 (*Comm*) saldo *m* • **what's my ~?** ¿qué saldo tengo? • **to pay off the ~ of an account** liquidar el saldo de una cuenta • **bank ~** saldo *m* • **~ carried forward** balance *m* a cuenta nueva • **closing ~** saldo *m* de cierre • **credit/debit ~** saldo *m* acreedor/deudor • **~ of payments/trade** balanza *f* de pagos/comercio
4 (= *remainder*) [*of items*] resto *m*; [*of money*] saldo *m* • **~ due** saldo *m* deudor • **~ outstanding** saldo *m* pendiente
5 (*Audio*) balance *m*
(VT) **1** (= *place in equilibrium*) [+ *weight*] equilibrar; [+ *object*] poner/mantener en equilibrio; (*Aut*) [+ *wheel*] nivelar • **he ~d the glass on top of the books** puso el vaso en equilibrio sobre los libros • **the seal ~d the ball on its nose** la foca mantenía la pelota en equilibrio sobre su hocico • **he ~d himself on one foot** se mantuvo en equilibrio sobre un pie • **cats use their tails to ~ themselves** los gatos utilizan el rabo para equilibrarse
2 (= *compare*) comparar, sopesar; (= *make up for*) compensar • **this increase must be ~d against the rate of inflation** hay que sopesar este aumento y la tasa de inflación
3 (*Comm*) • **to ~ an account** hacer el balance de una cuenta • **to ~ the books** hacer balance, hacer cuadrar las cuentas • **to ~ the budget** nivelar el presupuesto • **to ~ the cash** hacer caja
(VI) **1** (= *keep equilibrium*) mantener el equilibrio, mantenerse en equilibrio
2 (*Comm*) [*accounts*] cuadrar
(CPD) ▸ **balance of payments deficit** déficit *m* en la balanza de pagos • **our ~ of payments deficit has improved slightly** nuestro déficit en la balanza de pagos ha mejorado ligeramente ▸ **balance of terror** equilibrio *m* del terror ▸ **balance sheet** balance *m*, hoja *f* de balance ▸ **balance transfer** (*on credit card*) transferencia *f* de saldo ▸ **balance weight** contrapeso *m*
▸ **balance out** (VT + ADV) (*fig*) compensar • **the two things ~ each other out** las dos cosas se compensan mutuamente
(VI + ADV) • **the profits and losses ~ out** las ganancias y las pérdidas se compensan
▸ **balance up** (VT + ADV) finiquitar, saldar
balanced ['bælənst] (ADJ) [*meal, view, person, budget*] equilibrado • **evenly ~** • **well ~** bien equilibrado • **a ~ diet** una dieta equilibrada
balancing ['bælənsɪŋ] (N) **1** (= *equilibrium*) • **~ on a high wire is not easy** mantener el equilibrio en la cuerda floja no es fácil
2 (*Comm, Econ*) • **~ of accounts** balance *m* de cuentas • **~ of the books** balance *m* de los libros
(CPD) ▸ **balancing act** • IDIOM: • **to do a ~ act (between)** hacer malabarismos (con)
balcony ['bælkənɪ] (N) balcón *m*; (*interior*) (*Theat*) galería *f*; (*large*) terraza *f* • **first/second ~** (*US*) (*Theat*) primer/segundo piso *m*
bald [bɔːld] (ADJ) (COMPAR: **balder**, SUPERL: **baldest**) **1** (= *hairless*) [*person, head*] calvo; (= *shaven*) pelado • **~ patch** (*on head*) calva *f*, claro *m*; (*on animal*) calva *f* • **he can't spend much on the barber's, with that ~ head of his** con lo calvo que está no puede gastar mucho en peluquería • **to go ~** quedarse calvo • IDIOM: • **(as) ~ as an egg** *or* **a coot** más calvo que una bola de billar
2 (= *worn*) [*tyre*] desgastado, gastado; [*lawn*] pelado • **~ patches on the lawn/carpet** calvas *fpl* en el césped/la alfombra
3 (= *unadorned*) [*statement*] directo, sin rodeos; [*style*] escueto • **these are the ~ facts** estos son los hechos sin más
(CPD) ▸ **bald eagle** águila *f* de cabeza blanca
balderdash ['bɔːldədæʃ] (N) tonterías *fpl*
bald-headed ['bɔːld'hedɪd] (ADJ) calvo • IDIOM: • **to go bald-headed into*** lanzarse ciegamente a
balding ['bɔːldɪŋ] (ADJ) parcialmente calvo
baldly ['bɔːldlɪ] (ADV) (*fig*) [*state*] sin rodeos
baldness ['bɔːldnɪs] (N) **1** [*of person*] calvicie *f*
2 [*of tyre*] desgaste *m*
3 [*of statement*] lo directo; [*of style*] lo escueto
baldy* ['bɔːldɪ] (N) calvo *m*
bale¹ [beɪl] (N) [*of cloth*] bala *f*; [*of hay*] fardo *m*, bala *f*
bale² [beɪl] ▹ **bale out**
▸ **bale out** (VT + ADV) (*Naut*) [+ *water*] achicar; [+ *ship*] achicar *or* sacar el agua de
Bâle [bɑːl] (N) Basilea *f*
Balearic [,bælɪ'ærɪk] (ADJ) • **the ~ Islands** las islas Baleares
Balearics [,bælɪ'ærɪks] (NPL) • **the ~** las Baleares
baleful ['beɪlfʊl] (ADJ) [*influence, presence*] funesto, siniestro; [*look, stare*] torvo, hosco • **to give sb a ~ look** dirigir a algn una mirada torva *or* hosca, mirar a algn de forma torva *or* hosca
balefully ['beɪlfəlɪ] (ADV) [*stare, look, say*] siniestramente, con hostilidad
baler ['beɪləʳ] (N) (*Agr*) empacadora *f*, enfardadora *f*
balk [bɔːk] (N) **1** (*Agr*) caballón *m*
2 (*Billiards*) cabaña *f*
3 (= *building timber*) viga *f*
(VT) (= *thwart*) impedir; (= *miss*) perder, no aprovechar • **we were ~ed of the chance to see it** perdimos la oportunidad de verlo
(VI) • **to ~ (at)** [*horse*] plantarse (ante); (*fig*) [*person*] • **some students ~ at carrying out animal experiments** algunos estudiantes se muestran reacios *or* se resisten a llevar a cabo experimentos con animales
Balkan ['bɔːlkən] (ADJ) balcánico
(N) • **the ~s** los Balcanes
balkanization ['bɔːlkənaɪ'zeɪʃən] (N) balcanización *f*
Balkanize, balkanize ['bɔːlkənaɪz] (VT) balcanizar
ball¹ [bɔːl] (N) **1** (*Tennis, Cricket, Golf etc*) pelota *f*; (*Ftbl*) balón *m*; (= *sphere*) bola *f* • **to play ~ (with sb)** (*lit*) jugar a la pelota (con algn); (*fig*) cooperar (con algn) • **to roll (o.s.) up into a ~** hacerse un ovillo • **the ~ is with you** *or* **in your court** (*fig*) te corresponde a ti dar el siguiente paso • **that's the way the ~ bounces** (*US**) así es la vida, así son las cosas • **the whole ~ of wax** (*US**) (*fig*) toda la historia* • IDIOMS: • **to be behind the eight ~** (*US*) estar en apuros • **to be on the ~** estar al tanto, ser muy despabilado • **you have to be on the ~ for this** para esto hay que estar al tanto • **to have a lot on the ~** (*US**) tener mucho talento • **to keep one's eye on the ~** no perder de vista lo principal • **to start/keep the ~ rolling** poner/mantener la cosa en marcha • **to be a ~ of fire**: • **he's a real ~ of fire** es muy dinámico • **he's not exactly a ~ of fire** no es que sea muy dinámico que digamos • **to keep several ~s in the air** hacer varias cosas al mismo tiempo • **to pick up** *or* **take the ~ and run with it** tomar el testigo e intentarlo
2 (*Mil*) bala *f* • **~ and chain** (*lit*) grillete *m* con bola; (*fig*) atadura *f*
3 [*of wool*] ovillo *m*
4 (*Anat*) [*of foot*] pulpejo *m*; [*of thumb*] base *f*
5‡ (= *testicle*) cojón‡ *m*, huevo‡ *m* • IDIOM: • **to break** *or* **bust sb's ~s** joder la existencia a algn
6 balls (*Brit*‡) (= *nonsense*) pavadas* *fpl*, huevadas *fpl* (*And, Chile*‡); (= *courage*) cojones‡ *mpl*, pelotas‡ *fpl*‡
(VT) **1** (*also* **ball up**) [+ *handkerchief etc*] hacer una bola con
2 (*esp US*‡) (= *have sex with*) echarse un polvo con‡, tirarse‡
(VI) **1** (*also* **ball up**) [*fist etc*] hacerse una bola
2 (*esp US*‡) (= *have sex*) echarse un polvo‡, follar (*Sp*‡), chingar (*Mex*‡)
(CPD) ▸ **ball and socket joint** junta *f* articulada ▸ **ball bearing** cojinete *m* de bolas, balero *m* (*Mex*), rulemán *m* (*S. Cone*) ▸ **ball boy** (*Tennis*) recogedor *m* de pelotas ▸ **ball control** (*Ftbl*) dominio *m* del balón ▸ **ball game** (*US*) partido *m* de béisbol • **this is a different ~ game*** (*fig*) esto es otro cantar*, esto es algo muy distinto • **it's a whole new ~ game*** (*fig*) las cosas han cambiado totalmente; ▹ BASEBALL ▸ **ball girl** (*Tennis*) recogedora *f* de pelotas ▸ **ball joint** junta *f* articulada ▸ **ball lightning** (*Met*) relámpago *m* en bola *or* en globo
▸ **ball up** (VT + ADV) **1** = ball
2 (*US*‡) estropear, joder‡
(VI + ADV) = ball
▸ **balls up** (VT + ADV) estropear, joder‡
ball² [bɔːl] (N) **1** (= *dance*) baile *m* de etiqueta
2* (= *good time*) • **we had a ~** lo pasamos en grande*
ballad ['bæləd] (N) balada *f*; (*Spanish*) romance *m*, corrido *m* (*Mex*)
ballade [bæ'lɑːd] (N) (*Mus*) balada *f*
ballast ['bæləst] (N) (*Naut*) (*also fig*) lastre *m*; (*Rail*) balasto *m* • **in ~** en lastre

(VT) (*Naut*) lastrar; (*Rail*) balastar
ballcock ['bɔ:lkɒk] (N) llave *f* de bola *or* de flotador
ballerina [,bælə'ri:nə] (N) bailarina *f* (de ballet) • **prima ~** primera bailarina *f*
ballet ['bæleɪ] (N) ballet *m*
(CPD) ▸ **ballet dancer** bailarín/ina *m/f* (de ballet) ▸ **ballet school** escuela *f* de ballet ▸ **ballet shoes** zapatillas *fpl* de ballet ▸ **ballet skirt** falda *f* de bailarina *or* de ballet
balletic [bæ'letɪk] (ADJ) [*grace, movements*] de bailarina, de ballet
ballgown ['bɔ:lgaʊn] (N) traje *m* de fiesta, vestido *m* de gala
ballistic [bə'lɪstɪk] (ADJ) balístico • IDIOM: • **to go ~*** subirse por las paredes*
(CPD) ▸ **ballistic missile** misil *m* balístico
ballistics [bə'lɪstɪks] (NSING) balística *f*
balloon [bə'lu:n] (N) globo *m*; (*in cartoons*) bocadillo *m* • **then the ~ went up*** luego se armó la gorda* • IDIOM: • **to go down like a lead ~***: • **that went down like a lead ~** eso cayó muy mal, eso cayo fatal*
(VI) **1** [*injury*] hincharse (como un tomate)
2 (*also* **balloon out**) [*sail*] hincharse como un globo; [*skirt*] inflarse
ballooning [bə'lu:nɪŋ] (N) • **to go ~** montar en globo
balloonist [bə'lu:nɪst] (N) ascensionista *mf*, aeronauta *mf*
ballot ['bælət] (N) (= *voting*) votación *f*; (= *paper*) papeleta *f* (de voto) • **on the first ~** a la primera votación • **to take a ~ on sth** someter algo a votación • **there will be a ~ for the remaining places** se sortearán las plazas restantes • **to vote by secret ~** votar en secreto
(VT) • **to ~ the members on a strike** someter la huelga a votación entre los miembros
(VI) **1** (= *vote*) votar
2 (= *draw lots*) • **to ~ for** [+ *tickets*] rifar, sortear • **to ~ for a place** sortear un puesto
(CPD) ▸ **ballot box** urna *f* ▸ **ballot box stuffing** (*US*) fraude *m* electoral, pucherazo* *m* ▸ **ballot paper** papeleta *f* (de voto) ▸ **ballot rigging** fraude *m* electoral
balloting ['bælətɪŋ] (N) votación *f*
ballpark ['bɔ:lpɑ:k] (N) (*US*) estadio *m* de béisbol • IDIOM: • **to be in the same ~**: • **it's in the same ~** está en la misma categoría; ▹ BASEBALL
(CPD) ▸ **ballpark estimate** cálculo *m* aproximado ▸ **ballpark figure, ballpark number** cifra *f* aproximada
ballplayer, ball player ['bɔ:l,pleɪəʳ] (N) (*US*) (*Baseball*) jugador(a) *m/f* de béisbol; (*Basketball*) baloncestista *mf*; (*Ftbl*) jugador(a) *m/f* de fútbol americano
ballpoint ['bɔ:lpɔɪnt], **ballpoint pen** (N) bolígrafo *m*, birome *m or f* (*S. Cone*)
ballroom ['bɔ:lrʊm] (N) salón *m or* sala *f* de baile
(CPD) ▸ **ballroom dancer** bailarín/ina *m/f* de salón ▸ **ballroom dancing** baile *m* de salón
balls-up** ['bɔ:lzʌp], **ball-up**** ['bɔ:lʌp] (*US*) (N) cagada** *f* • **he made a balls-up of the job** lo jodió todo**
ballsy‡ ['bɔ:lzɪ] (ADJ) de armas tomar*, con agallas*
ball-tampering ['bɔ:l,tæmpərɪŋ] (N) (*Cricket*) *manipulación de la bola*
bally‡ ['bælɪ] (ADJ) (*Brit*) puñetero‡
ballyhoo* [,bælɪ'hu:] (N) (= *publicity*) bombo* *m*, propaganda *f* estrepitosa
balm [bɑ:m] (N) (*also fig*) bálsamo *m*
balmy ['bɑ:mɪ] (ADJ) (COMPAR: **balmier**, SUPERL: **balmiest**) **1** (*liter*) (= *soothing*) balsámico
2 (= *mild*) [*breeze, air*] suave, cálido
3* = **barmy**
balneotherapy [,bælnɪə'θerəpɪ] (N) balneoterapia *f*
baloney* [bə'ləʊnɪ] (N) (*esp US*) tonterías *fpl*, chorradas *fpl* (*Sp**)
BALPA ['bælpə] (N ABBR) (= **British Airline Pilots' Association**) ≈ SEPLA *m*
balsa ['bɔ:lsə] (N) (*also* **balsa wood**) (madera *f* de) balsa *f*
balsam ['bɔ:lsəm] (N) bálsamo *m*
balsamic [bɔ:l'sæmɪk] (ADJ) [*vinegar*] balsámico
balti ['bɔ:ltɪ] (N) (*Culin*) *especialidad de comida india con verduras o carne cocinadas en una cazuela de fondo cóncavo*
Baltic ['bɔ:ltɪk] (ADJ) báltico • **the ~ states** los estados bálticos • **one of the ~ ports** uno de los puertos del mar Báltico
(N) • **the ~ (Sea)** el mar Báltico
baltic* ['bɔ:ltɪk] (ADJ) (= *very cold*) • **it's ~ in here!** ¡aquí hace un frío polar!
balustrade [,bæləs'treɪd] (N) balaustrada *f*, barandilla *f*
bamboo [bæm'bu:] (N) (= *cane, plant*) bambú *m*
(CPD) ▸ **the Bamboo Curtain** el Telón de Bambú ▸ **bamboo shoots** brotes *mpl* de bambú
bamboozle* [bæm'bu:zl] (VT) enredar, engatusar • **she was ~d into buying it** la enredaron *or* engatusaron para que lo comprara
ban [bæn] (N) prohibición *f* (on de) • **to be under a ban** estar prohibido • **to put a ban on sth** prohibir algo • **to lift the ban on sth** levantar la prohibición de algo
(VT) [+ *activity, book*] prohibir; [+ *person*] excluir (**from** de) • **Ban the Bomb Campaign** Campaña *f* contra la Bomba Atómica • **he was banned from the club** le prohibieron la entrada en el club, lo excluyeron del club • **he was banned from driving** le retiraron el carnet de conducir • **the bullfighter was banned for three months** al torero le prohibieron torear durante tres meses
banal [bə'nɑ:l] (ADJ) banal
banality [bə'nælɪtɪ] (N) banalidad *f*
banana [bə'nɑ:nə] (N) (= *fruit*) plátano *m*, banana *f* (*LAm*); (= *tree*) platanero *m*, banano *m* (*LAm*)
(CPD) ▸ **banana boat** barco *m* bananero ▸ **banana peel** (*US*) piel *f* de plátano ▸ **banana republic** república *f* bananera ▸ **banana skin** piel *f* de plátano; (*fig*) problema *m* no previsto ▸ **banana split** banana split *m inv* ▸ **banana tree** platanero *m*, banano *m* (*LAm*)
bananas* [bə'nɑ:nəz] (ADJ) chalado* • **to go ~** perder la chaveta* (**over** por)
band¹ [bænd] (N) **1** (= *strip of material*) faja *f*, tira *f*; (= *ribbon*) cinta *f*; (= *edging*) franja *f*; [*of cigar*] vitola *f*, faja *f*; [*of wheel*] fleje *m*; (= *ring*) anillo *m*, sortija *f* (*LAm*); (= *armband*) brazalete *m*; (= *hatband*) cintillo *m*; [*of harness*] correa *f*; (= *stripe*) raya *f*, franja *f*; [*of territory*] faja *f*; ▹ **rubber¹**
2 (*Rad*) (= *waveband*) banda *f*
3 [*of statistics, tax etc*] banda *f*
(VT) [+ *tax, property*] dividir en bandas
(CPD) ▸ **band saw** sierra *f* de cinta
band² [bænd] (N) **1** (*Mus*) orquesta *f*, conjunto *m*; (*Mil*) (= *brass band*) banda *f*; (= *pop group*) grupo *m* • **then the ~ played** (*US**) (*fig*) y se armó la gorda*
2 (= *group of people*) cuadrilla *f*, grupo *m*; (*pej*) (= *gang*) pandilla *f*
(CPD) ▸ **band practice** ensayo *m* del grupo
▸ **band together** (VI + ADV) juntarse, asociarse; (*pej*) apandillarse
bandage ['bændɪdʒ] (N) venda *f*
(VT) (*also* **bandage up**) vendar • **with a ~d hand** con una mano vendada
Band-Aid® ['bændeɪd] (N) (*esp US*) tirita *f* (*Sp*), curita *f* (*LAm*)
bandana, bandanna [bæn'dænə] (N) pañuelo *m*
B & B (N ABBR) (= **bed and breakfast**) *alojamiento y desayuno*; ▹ BED AND BREAKFAST
bandbox ['bændbɒks] (N) sombrerera *f*
-banded [-bændɪd] (SUFFIX) • **gold-banded** con franjas doradas • **red-banded** con franjas rojas
banding ['bændɪŋ] (N) (*Brit*) (*Scol*) calificaciones *fpl* por letras
bandit ['bændɪt] (N) bandido *m*; ▹ **one-armed**
banditry ['bændɪtrɪ] (N) bandolerismo *m*, bandidismo *m*
bandleader ['bændli:dəʳ] (N) líder *mf* de banda
bandmaster ['bændmɑ:stəʳ] (N) director *m* de banda
bandolier [,bændə'lɪəʳ] (N) bandolera *f*
bandsman ['bændzmən] (N) (PL: **bandsmen**) músico *m* (de banda)
bandstand ['bændstænd] (N) quiosco *m* de música
bandwagon ['bænd,wægən] (N) • IDIOM: • **to jump** *or* **climb on the ~** subirse al carro *or* al tren
bandwidth ['bændwɪdθ] (N) ancho *m* de banda
bandy¹ ['bændɪ] (VT) [+ *jokes, insults*] cambiar, intercambiar • **don't ~ words with me!** ¡no discuta conmigo!
▸ **bandy about, bandy around** (VT + ADV) • **the story was bandied about that ...** se rumoreaba que ... • **to ~ sb's name about** circular el nombre de algn
bandy² ['bændɪ], **bandy-legged** ['bændɪ'legd] (ADJ) estevado
bane [beɪn] (N) (*liter*) (= *poison*) veneno *m*; (*fig*) plaga *f*, azote *m* • **it's the ~ of my life** me amarga la vida
baneful ['beɪnfʊl] (ADJ) (*liter*) (= *poisonous*) nocivo; (= *destructive*) funesto, fatal
banefully ['beɪnfəlɪ] (ADV) (*liter*) (= *poisonously*) nocivamente; (= *destructively*) funestamente, fatalmente
bang [bæŋ] (N) (= *noise*) [*of explosion*] estallido *m*; [*of door*] portazo *m*; [*of blow*] porrazo *m*, golpe *m* • **the door closed with a ~** la puerta se cerró de golpe • IDIOMS: • **to go with a ~***: • **it went with a ~** fue todo un éxito • **not with a ~ but a whimper** no con un estallido sino con un sollozo • **to get more ~ for the buck** *or* **more ~s for your bucks** (*esp US**) llevarse más por el mismo precio
(ADV) **1** • **to go ~** hacer ¡pum!, estallar • **~ went £10*** adiós 10 libras
2* justo, exactamente • **~ in the middle** justo en (el) medio • **I ran ~ into a traffic jam** me encontré de repente en un embotellamiento • **it hit him ~ on the ear** le dio justo en la oreja, le dio en toda la oreja* • **~ on!** ¡acertado! • **the answer was ~ on** (*Brit*) la respuesta dio en el blanco • **~ on time** (*Brit*) a la hora justa • **it was ~ on target** (*Brit*) dio justo en el blanco • **~ up to date** totalmente al día • **to keep ~ up to date** mantenerse totalmente al día • **this production is ~ up to date** este montaje está de rabiosa actualidad
(VT) **1** (= *strike*) golpear • **to ~ the door** dar un portazo • **to ~ one's head (on sth)** dar con la cabeza (contra algo) • **he ~ed himself against the wall** se dio contra la pared • **to ~ one's fist on the table** dar un puñetazo en la mesa
2** (= *have sex with*) echarse un polvo con**, tirarse**
(VI) (= *explode*) explotar, estallar; (= *slam*)

b

[*door*] cerrarse de golpe • **downstairs a door ~ed** abajo se cerró de golpe una puerta • **to ~ at** *or* **on sth** dar golpes en algo
(EXCL) ¡pum!; (*of a blow*) ¡zas!
▸ **bang about, bang around** (VI + ADV) moverse ruidosamente
▸ **bang away** (VI + ADV) [*guns*] disparar estrepitosamente; [*workman*] martillear • **she was ~ing away on the piano** aporreaba el piano
▸ **bang down** (VT + ADV) [+ *receiver*] colgar de golpe • **he ~ed it down on the table** lo arrojó violentamente sobre la mesa
▸ **bang into** (VI + PREP) (= *collide with*) chocar con, darse contra
▸ **bang on*** (VI + ADV) (*Brit*) • **to ~ on about sth** dar la tabarra con algo*
▸ **bang out** (VT + ADV) [+ *tune*] tocar ruidosamente
▸ **bang together** (VT + ADV) [+ *heads*] hacer chocar • **I'll ~ your heads together!** ¡voy a dar un coscorrón a los dos! • **the leaders should have their heads ~ed together** hay que obligar a los jefes a que lleguen a un acuerdo
▸ **bang up‡** (VT + ADV) (*Brit*) [+ *prisoner*] encerrar (en su celda)

banger* ['bæŋəʳ] (*Brit*) (N) **1** (= *sausage*) salchicha *f*
2 (= *firework*) petardo *m*
3 (= *old car*) armatoste* *m*, cacharro* *m*

banging‡ ['bæŋɪŋ] (ADJ) (*US*) • **that girl is ~** esa tía está buenísima

Bangkok [bæŋ'kɒk] (N) Bangkok *m*

Bangladesh [ˌbæŋglə'deʃ] (N) Bangladesh *m*

Bangladeshi [ˌbæŋglə'deʃɪ] (ADJ) bangladesí
(N) bangladesí *mf*

bangle ['bæŋgl] (N) brazalete *m*, pulsera *f*

bangs [bæŋz] (NPL) (*US*) (= *fringe*) flequillo *m*

bang-up‡ ['bæŋʌp] (ADJ) (*US*) tope, guay (*Sp*‡)

banish ['bænɪʃ] (VT) [+ *person*] expulsar, desterrar; (*fig*) [+ *thought, fear*] desterrar, apartar (**from** de) • **to ~ a topic from one's conversation** desterrar un tema de la conversación

banishment ['bænɪʃmənt] (N) destierro *m*

banister ['bænɪstəʳ] (N), **banisters** ['bænɪstəz] (NPL) barandilla *fsing*, pasamanos *m inv*

banjax‡ ['bændʒæks] (VT) dar una paliza a

banjaxed‡ ['bændʒækst] (ADJ) destrozado

banjo ['bændʒəʊ] (N) (PL: **banjoes, banjos**) banjo *m*

bank¹ [bæŋk] (N) **1** [*of river etc*] orilla *f*; (= *small hill*) loma *f*; (= *embankment*) terraplén *m*; (= *sandbank*) banco *m*; (= *escarpment*) escarpa *f*; [*of clouds*] grupo *m*; [*of snow*] montículo *m*; [*of switches*] batería *f*, serie *f*; [*of phones*] equipo *m*, batería *f*; [*of oars*] hilera *f*
2 (*Aer*) inclinación *f* lateral
(VT) **1** (*also* **bank up**) [+ *earth, sand*] amontonar, apilar; [+ *fire*] alimentar (*con mucha leña o carbón*)
2 (*Aer*) ladear
(VI) **1** (*Aer*) ladearse
2 • **to ~ up** [*clouds etc*] acumularse

bank² [bæŋk] (*Comm, Econ*) (N) (*Econ*) banco *m*; (*in games*) banca *f*; (*also* **savings bank**) caja *f* de ahorros • **Bank of England** Banco *m* de Inglaterra • **Bank of International Settlements** (*US*) Banco *m* Internacional de Pagos • **Bank of Spain** Banco *m* de España • IDIOM: • **to break the ~** hacer saltar *or* quebrar la banca
(VT) [+ *money*] depositar en un/el banco, ingresar
(VI) • **we ~ with Smith** tenemos la cuenta en el banco Smith
(CPD) ▸ **bank acceptance** letra *f* de cambio ▸ **bank account** cuenta *f* bancaria ▸ **bank balance** saldo *m* • **this won't be good for my ~ balance** esto no será bueno para mi situación financiera ▸ **bank bill** (*Brit*) letra *f* de cambio; (*US*) billete *m* de banco ▸ **bank book** libreta *f* (de depósitos); (*in savings bank*) cartilla *f* ▸ **bank card** tarjeta *f* bancaria ▸ **bank charges** (*Brit*) comisión *f* ▸ **bank clerk** (*Brit*) empleado/a *m/f* de banco ▸ **bank credit** crédito *m* bancario ▸ **bank deposits** depósitos *mpl* bancarios ▸ **bank draft** letra *f* de cambio ▸ **bank giro** giro *m* bancario ▸ **bank holiday** (*Brit*) fiesta *f*, día *m* festivo, (día *m*) feriado *m* (*LAm*) ▸ **bank loan** préstamo *m* bancario ▸ **bank manager** director(a) *m/f* de banco ▸ **bank raid** (= *bank robbery*) atraco *m* a un banco ▸ **bank rate** tipo *m* de interés bancario ▸ **bank robber** (= *armed robber*) atracador(a) *m/f* de banco; (*involving break-in*) ladrón/ona *m/f* de banco ▸ **bank robbery** (= *hold-up*) atraco *m* a un banco; (= *break-in*) robo *m* de un banco ▸ **bank run** (*US*) asedio *m* de un banco ▸ **bank statement** estado *m* de cuenta ▸ **bank transfer** transferencia *f* bancaria ▸ **bank vault** cámara *f* acorazada de un banco
▸ **bank on** (VI + PREP) contar con • **don't ~ on it** sería prudente no contar con eso, no puedes estar tan seguro de eso
▸ **bank up** (VT) [+ *earth, sand*] amontonar, apilar; [+ *fire*] alimentar (*con mucha leña o carbón*)

BANK HOLIDAY
El término **bank holiday** se aplica en el Reino Unido a todo día festivo oficial en el que cierran bancos y comercios, que cae normalmente en lunes. Los más destacados coinciden con Navidad, Semana Santa, finales de mayo y finales de agosto. Al contrario que en los países de tradición católica, no se celebran las festividades dedicadas a los santos.

bankable ['bæŋkəbl] (ADJ) [*idea*] válido, valedero; [*person*] taquillero

banked ['bæŋkt] (ADJ) **1** [*road, track*] inclinado
2 (= *piled*) • **~ with** amontonado con

banker ['bæŋkəʳ] (N) **1** (*Econ*) banquero/a *m/f* • **to be ~** (*in game*) tener la banca
2 (*Betting*) apuesta *f* fija
(CPD) ▸ **banker's card** tarjeta *f* bancaria ▸ **banker's draft** efecto *m* bancario ▸ **banker's order** (*Brit*) orden *f* bancaria ▸ **banker's reference** referencia *f* bancaria

banking¹ ['bæŋkɪŋ] (N) [*of earth*] terraplén *m*, rampas *fpl*

banking² ['bæŋkɪŋ] (N) (*Comm, Econ*) banca *f*
(CPD) bancario ▸ **banking account** cuenta *f* bancaria ▸ **banking hours** horas *fpl* bancarias ▸ **banking house** casa *f* de banca

banknote ['bæŋknəʊt] (N) billete *m* de banco

bankroll ['bæŋkrəʊl] (*esp US*) (N) recursos *mpl* económicos
(VT) financiar

bankrupt ['bæŋkrʌpt] (ADJ) **1** (*Jur*) en quiebra • **to be ~** estar en quiebra • **to go ~** ir a la bancarrota, quebrar • **to be declared ~** declararse en quiebra
2 (*fig*) **a*** (= *penniless*) sin un duro (*Sp**), sin un peso (*LAm**)
b (= *deficient*) • **spiritually/morally ~** en franca decadencia espiritual/moral • **to be ~ of ideas** estar totalmente falto de ideas
(N) (*Jur*) quebrado/a *m/f*
(VT) **1** (*Jur*) llevar a la quiebra
2* (*fig*) (= *impoverish*) arruinar • **to ~ o.s. buying pictures** arruinarse comprando cuadros
(CPD) ▸ **bankrupt's estate** activo *m or* masa *f* de la quiebra

bankruptcy ['bæŋkrəptsɪ] (N) **1** (*Jur*) quiebra *f*
2 (*fig*) falta *f* (**of** de) • **moral ~** decadencia *f* moral
(CPD) ▸ **bankruptcy court** (*Brit*) tribunal *m* de quiebras ▸ **bankruptcy proceedings** juicio *m* de insolvencia

banned substance [ˌbænd'sʌbstəns] (N) (*Sport*) sustancia *f* prohibida

banner ['bænəʳ] (N) (= *flag*) bandera *f*; (= *placard*) pancarta *f*
(CPD) ▸ **banner ad*** (*Internet*) banner *m* ▸ **banner headlines** grandes titulares *mpl*

banning ['bænɪŋ] (N) [*of activity, smoking, alcohol, advertising*] prohibición *f* • **the ~ of sth** la prohibición de algo

bannister ['bænɪstəʳ] (N) = **banister**

banns [bænz] (NPL) amonestaciones *fpl* • **to put up** *or* **call the ~** correr las amonestaciones

banquet ['bæŋkwɪt] (N) banquete *m*
(VI) banquetear
(VT) [+ *person*] dar un banquete en honor de

banqueting hall ['bæŋkwɪtɪŋˌhɔːl] (N) comedor *m* de gala, sala *f* de banquetes

banquette [bæŋ'ket] (N) banqueta *f* alargada

banshee ['bæn'ʃiː] (N) (*Irl*) *hada que anuncia una muerte en la familia*

bantam ['bæntəm] (N) gallina *f* bántam

bantamweight ['bæntəmweɪt] (N) (*Sport*) (= *boxer*) peso *m* gallo • **the ~ champion** el campeón de los pesos gallos

banter ['bæntəʳ] (N) bromas *fpl*, guasa *f*
(VI) bromear

bantering ['bæntərɪŋ] (ADJ) [*tone*] de chanza
(N) = **banter**

Bantu [ˌbæn'tuː] (ADJ) bantú
(N) **1** (PL: **Bantu** *or* **Bantus**) (= *person*) bantú *mf* • **the bantu(s)** los bantú, los bantúes
2 (*Ling*) bantú *m*

BAOR (N ABBR) = **British Army of the Rhine**

bap [bæp] (N) (*Brit*) bollo *m* pequeño de pan

baptism ['bæptɪzəm] (N) (*in general*) bautismo *m*; (= *ceremony*) bautizo *m* • **~ of fire** bautismo *m* de fuego

baptismal [bæp'tɪzməl] (ADJ) bautismal

Baptist ['bæptɪst] (N) baptista *mf*, bautista *mf* • **St John the ~** San Juan Bautista
(CPD) ▸ **Baptist church** Iglesia *f* Bautista

baptize [bæp'taɪz] (VT) bautizar • **he was ~d John** lo bautizaron con el nombre de Juan

bar¹ [bɑːʳ] (N) **1** (= *piece*) [*of wood, metal*] barra *f*; [*of soap*] pastilla *f*; [*of chocolate*] tableta *f*
2 (= *lever*) palanca *f*; (*on electric fire*) resistencia *f*; [*of window, cage etc*] reja *f*; (*on door*) tranca *f* • **behind bars** entre rejas • **to put sb behind bars** encarcelar a algn • **to spend three years behind bars** pasar tres años entre rejas
3 (= *hindrance*) obstáculo *m* (**to** para) • **it is a bar to progress** es un obstáculo para el progreso
4 (= *ban*) prohibición *f* (**on** de)
5 (= *pub*) bar *m*, cantina *f* (*esp LAm*); (= *counter*) barra *f*, mostrador *m*
6 (*Jur*) • **the Bar** (= *persons*) el colegio de abogados; (= *profession*) la abogacía, la Barra (*Mex*) • **the prisoner at the bar** el/la acusado/a • **to be called** *or* (*US*) **admitted to the Bar** recibirse de abogado, ingresar en la abogacía; ▸ **read**
7 (*Brit*) (*Mus*) (= *measure, rhythm*) compás *m*
(VT) **1** (= *obstruct*) [+ *way*] obstruir
2 (= *prevent*) [+ *progress*] impedir
3 (= *exclude*) excluir (**from** de); (= *ban*) prohibir • **to be barred from a club** ser excluido de un club • **to bar sb from doing sth** prohibir a algn hacer algo
4 (= *fasten*) [+ *door, window*] atrancar

CPD ▸ **bar billiards** (*Brit*) billar *m* americano ▸ **bar chart** cuadro *m* de barras ▸ **bar code** código *m* de barras ▸ **bar food** (= *pub food*) comida *f* de pub ▸ **bar girl*** (*US*) camarera *f* de barra ▸ **bar graph** (*esp US*) gráfico *m* de barras ▸ **bar meal** comida *f* en el pub • **to go for a bar meal** ir a comer al pub ▸ **bar stool** taburete *m* (de bar)

bar² [bɑ:ʳ] PREP salvo, con excepción de • **all bar two** todos salvo *or* con excepción de dos • **bar none** sin excepción • **it was all over bar the shouting** (*fig*) en realidad ya estaba concluido el asunto

barb [bɑ:b] N **1** [*of arrow, hook*] lengüeta *f*; [*of feather*] barba *f*; (*Zool*) púa *f*
2 (*fig*) dardo *m*
CPD ▸ **barb wire** = **barbed wire**

Barbadian [bɑ:ˈbeɪdɪən] ADJ de Barbados
N nativo/a *m/f or* habitante *mf* de Barbados

Barbados [bɑ:ˈbeɪdɒs] N Barbados *m*

barbarian [bɑ:ˈbɛərɪən] ADJ bárbaro
N bárbaro/a *m/f*

barbaric [bɑ:ˈbærɪk] ADJ bárbaro

barbarically [bɑ:ˈbærɪkəlɪ] ADV salvajemente

barbarism [ˈbɑ:bərɪzəm] N **1** (= *cruelty*) barbarie *f*
2 (*Gram*) barbarismo *m*

barbarity [bɑ:ˈbærɪtɪ] N barbaridad *f*

barbarous [ˈbɑ:bərəs] ADJ bárbaro

barbarously [ˈbɑ:bərəslɪ] ADV bárbaramente

Barbary [ˈbɑ:bərɪ] N Berbería *f*
CPD ▸ **Barbary ape** macaco *m* ▸ **the Barbary Coast** la costa berebere

barbecue [ˈbɑ:bɪkju:] N (= *grill*) barbacoa *f*; (= *party*) parrillada *f*, barbacoa *f*, asado *m* (*LAm*)
VT asar a la parrilla
CPD ▸ **barbecue grill** (= *device*) parrilla *f* de barbacoa ▸ **barbecue pit** barbacoa *f* (*utensilio*) ▸ **barbecue sauce** salsa *f* picante

barbed [bɑ:bd] ADJ **1** [*arrow etc*] armado de lengüetas
2 (*fig*) [*criticism*] incisivo, mordaz
CPD ▸ **barbed wire** alambre *m* de púas *or* de espino • **~-wire fence** cercado *m* de alambrada *or* de alambre de espino *or* (*LAm*) de alambrado

barbel [ˈbɑ:bəl] N **1** (*Anat*) barbilla *f*, cococha *f*
2 (= *fish*) barbo *m*

barbell [ˈbɑ:bel] N (*Sport*) haltera *f*, pesas *fpl*

barber [ˈbɑ:bəʳ] N peluquero *m*, barbero *m* • **at/to the ~'s (shop)** en/a la peluquería *or* barbería • **The Barber of Seville** El Barbero de Sevilla

barbershop [ˈbɑ:bəʃɒp] (*US*) N barbería *f*
CPD ▸ **barbershop quartet** *cuarteto vocal armónico de hombres que se especializa en canciones sentimentales de los años 20 y 30*

barbican [ˈbɑ:bɪkən] N barbacana *f*

barbie* [ˈbɑ:bɪ] N (*Brit, Australia*) (= **barbecue**) (= *event, equipment*) barbacoa *f*

Barbie doll® [ˈbɑ:bɪdɒl] N muñeca *f* Barbie®

barbitone [ˈbɑ:bɪtəʊn] N barbitúrico *m*

barbiturate [bɑ:ˈbɪtjʊrɪt] N barbitúrico *m*

Bar-B-Q [ˈbɑ:bɪkju:] N ABBR = **barbecue**

barbs‡ [bɑ:bz] NPL (*Drugs*) barbitúricos *mpl*

barcarole, barcarolle [ˌbɑ:kəˈrəʊl] N barcarola *f*

Barcelona [ˌbɑ:səˈləʊnə] N Barcelona *f*

bard [bɑ:d] N (*liter*) bardo *m*, vate *m* • **the Bard** (= *Shakespeare*) el Vate • **the Bard of Avon** el Cisne del Avon

bardic [ˈbɑ:dɪk] ADJ [*poetry etc*] de los bardos

bare [bɛəʳ] ADJ (COMPAR: **barer**, SUPERL: **barest**) **1** (= *uncovered*) [*body, skin, shoulders, person*] desnudo; [*head*] descubierto; [*feet*] descalzo; [*landscape*] pelado; [*tree*] sin hojas; [*ground*] árido, sin vegetación; [*floorboards*] sin alfombrar; (*Elec*) [*wire*] pelado, sin protección • **~ to the waist** desnudo hasta la cintura • **to sleep on ~ boards** dormir en una tabla • **in one's ~ feet** descalzo • **he put his ~ hand in the flame** puso la mano directamente en la llama • **he killed the lion with his ~ hands** mató al león solo con las manos *or* sin armas • **to lay sth ~** [+ *flaw, mistake*] poner algo de manifiesto; [+ *intentions, plans*] poner algo al descubierto • **to lay ~ one's heart to sb** abrir el corazón a algn • **to lay ~ a secret** revelar un secreto • **~ of sth** desprovisto de algo • **~ patch** (*on lawn, carpet*) calva *f*
2 (= *empty, unadorned*) [*room*] sin muebles; [*wall*] desnudo; [*statement*] escueto • **the food cupboard was ~** la despensa estaba vacía • **they only told us the ~ facts** se limitaron a contarnos estrictamente los hechos
3 (= *meagre*) [*majority*] escaso • **the ~ bones** (*fig*) lo esencial • **to strip sth down to the ~ bones** reducir algo a lo esencial • **the ~ essentials** *or* **necessities** lo estrictamente indispensable • **to earn a ~ living** ganar lo justo para vivir • **the ~ minimum** lo justo, lo indispensable
4 (= *mere*) • **the match lasted a ~ 18 minutes** el partido duró apenas 18 minutos • **sales grew at a ~ 2% a year** las ventas ascendieron apenas a un 2% al año
VT [+ *body*] desnudar; [+ *wire*] pelar; [+ *sword*] desenvainar • **to ~ one's head** descubrirse • **to ~ one's soul to sb** abrir el corazón a algn • **the dog ~d its teeth** el perro enseñó *or* mostró los dientes

bareback [ˈbɛəbæk] ADV a pelo, sin silla • **to ride ~** montar a pelo

bare-bones [ˈbɛəˈbeʊnz] ADJ (*esp US*) muy limitado

barefaced [ˈbɛəfeɪst] ADJ descarado • **a ~ lie** una mentira descarada • **it's ~ robbery** es un robo descarado

barefoot [ˈbɛəˈfʊt], **barefooted** [ˈbɛəˈfʊtɪd] ADJ descalzo
ADV descalzo

bareheaded [ˈbɛəˈhedɪd] ADJ con la cabeza descubierta

barelegged [ˈbɛəˈlegɪd] ADJ con las piernas descubiertas

barely [ˈbɛəlɪ] ADV **1** (= *scarcely*) apenas • **he can ~ read** apenas puede leer • **he looked around him with ~ concealed horror** miró a su alrededor disimulando apenas su horror • **there was ~ enough room for all of us** apenas había sitio para todos nosotros • **there was ~ anyone there** allí no había casi nadie • **I had ~ closed the door when the phone rang** apenas había cerrado la puerta cuando sonó el teléfono
2 (= *scantily*) • **a ~ furnished room** una habitación escasamente amueblada

bareness [ˈbɛənɪs] N **1** (= *nakedness*) desnudez *f*
2 (= *emptiness*) [*of room*] lo vacío; [*of wall, tree*] desnudez *f*; [*of landscape*] desnudez *f*, lo pelado

Barents Sea [ˈbærənts'si:] N • **the ~** el mar de Barents

barf‡ [bɑ:f] VI (*US*) vomitar, arrojar*

barfly* [ˈbɑ:flaɪ] N (*US*) ≈ culo *m* de café*

bargain [ˈbɑ:gɪn] N **1** (= *agreement*) trato *m*; (= *transaction*) negocio *m*; (= *advantageous deal*) negocio *m* ventajoso • **it's a ~!** ¡trato hecho!, ¡de acuerdo! • **into the ~** (*fig*) para colmo • **you drive a hard ~** sabes regatear • **to make** *or* **strike a ~** cerrar un trato • **I'll make a ~ with you** hagamos un trato
2 (= *cheap thing*) ganga *f* • **~s** (*Comm*) artículos *mpl* de ocasión, oportunidades *fpl* • **it's a real ~** es una verdadera ganga
VI **1** (= *negotiate*) negociar (**about** sobre, **for** para obtener, **with** con)
2 (= *haggle*) regatear
CPD de ocasión ▸ **bargain basement, bargain counter** sección *f* de ofertas *or* oportunidades ▸ **bargain hunter** cazador(a) *m/f* de ofertas *or* oportunidades • **she's a real ~ hunter** siempre va a la caza de ofertas *or* oportunidades ▸ **bargain hunting** caza *f* de ofertas *or* oportunidades • **to go ~ hunting** ir en busca de gangas • **I enjoy ~ hunting** me gusta ir de rebajas ▸ **bargain offer** oferta *f* especial ▸ **bargain price** precio *m* de ganga ▸ **bargain sale** saldo *m*
▸ **bargain for** VI + PREP • **I wasn't ~ing for that** yo no contaba con eso • **he got more than he ~ed for** resultó peor de lo que esperaba
▸ **bargain on** VI + PREP (= *count on*) contar con

bargainer [ˈbɑ:gɪnəʳ] N (= *negotiator*) negociador(a) *m/f* • **to be a hard ~** ser un duro negociador

bargaining [ˈbɑ:gɪnɪŋ] N (= *negotiation*) negociación *f*; (= *haggling*) regateo *m*
CPD ▸ **bargaining chip, bargaining counter** baza *f* a jugar, moneda *f* de cambio ▸ **bargaining power** poder *m* de negociación ▸ **bargaining table** mesa *f* de negociaciones

barge [bɑ:dʒ] N (*Naut*) barcaza *f*; (*towed*) lancha *f* a remolque, gabarra *f*; (*ceremonial*) falúa *f*
VT (= *push*) empujar; (*Sport*) cargar contra
VI • **to ~ through a crowd** abrirse paso a empujones entre una multitud • **to ~ past sb** apartar a algn de un empujón
CPD ▸ **barge pole** bichero *m* • **I wouldn't touch it with a ~ pole** (*Brit**) (*fig*) yo no lo querría ni regalado
▸ **barge about, barge around** VI + ADV moverse pesadamente, dar tumbos
▸ **barge in** VI + ADV **1** (= *enter*) irrumpir
2 (*fig*) (= *interrupt*) meterse • **to ~ in on a conversation** entrometerse en una conversación
▸ **barge into** VI + PREP **1** [+ *person*] chocar contra; [+ *room*] irrumpir en
2 (*fig*) (= *interrupt*) interrumpir

bargee [bɑ:ˈdʒi:] N (*Brit*) gabarrero *m*

bar-hopping [ˈbɑ:ˌhɒpɪŋ] N (*US*) • **to go bar-hopping** ir de bar en bar, ir de copeo*

baritone [ˈbærɪtəʊn] N barítono *m*
CPD [*voice*] de barítono ▸ **baritone saxophone** saxofón *m* barítono

barium [ˈbɛərɪəm] N bario *m*
CPD ▸ **barium meal** sulfato *m* de bario

bark¹ [bɑ:k] N [*of tree*] corteza *f*
VT [+ *tree*] descortezar; [+ *skin*] raer, raspar • **to ~ one's shins** desollarse las espinillas
CPD ▸ **bark chippings** virutas *fpl* de corteza

bark² [bɑ:k] N [*of dog*] ladrido *m* • IDIOM: • **his ~ is worse than his bite** perro ladrador, poco mordedor
VI **1** [*dog*] ladrar (**at** a); [*fox*] aullir • IDIOM: • **to be ~ing up the wrong tree** ir muy descaminado
2 (= *speak sharply*) vociferar (**at** a)
VT (*also* **bark out**) [+ *order*] escupir, gritar

bark³ [bɑ:k] N (*liter, poet*) (= *boat*) barco *m*

barkeeper [ˈbɑ:ˌki:pəʳ] N (*US*) tabernero/a *m/f*

barker [ˈbɑ:kəʳ] N voceador(a) *m/f*, charlatán/ana *m/f* de feria

barking [ˈbɑ:kɪŋ] N [*of dog*] ladrido *m*; [*of fox*] aullido *m*
ADJ (*Brit**) • **~ (mad)** chiflado*, como una regadera*

barley [ˈbɑ:lɪ] N cebada *f*

CPD ▸ **barley sugar** azúcar *m* cande ▸ **barley water** (*esp Brit*) hordiate *m*

barleycorn ['bɑːlɪkɔːn] N grano *m* de cebada

barleyfield ['bɑːlɪfiːld] N cebadal *m*

barmaid ['bɑːmeɪd] N (*esp Brit*) camarera *f*, moza *f* (*LAm*)

barman ['bɑːmən] N (PL: **barmen**) bárman *m*, camarero *m*

Bar Mitzvah, bar mitzvah [bɑː'mɪtsvə] N Bar Mitzvah *m*

barmy* ['bɑːmɪ] ADJ (COMPAR: **barmier**, SUPERL: **barmiest**) (*Brit*) chiflado*, chalado* • **you must be ~!** ¿estás loco?

barn [bɑːn] N granero *m*; (= *raised barn*) troje *f*; (*US*) (*for horses*) cuadra *f*; (*for cattle*) establo *m*; (*for buses etc*) parque *m*, garaje *m* • **a great ~ of a house** una casa enorme, un caserón
CPD ▸ **barn conversion** (= *building project*) reconversión *f* de un granero; (= *building*) granero *m* reconvertido ▸ **barn dance** baile *m* campesino ▸ **barn door** puerta *f* de granero ▸ **barn owl** lechuza *f*

barnacle ['bɑːnəkl] N percebe *m*

barney* ['bɑːnɪ] N (*Brit*) (= *quarrel*) bronca *f*, agarrada* *f*

barnstorm ['bɑːnstɔːm] VI (*US*) *hacer una campaña electoral por las zonas rurales*

barnstorming ['bɑːnstɔːmɪŋ] ADJ (*Brit*) arrollador, arrasador

barnyard ['bɑːnjɑːd] N corral *m*
CPD ▸ **barnyard fowl(s)** aves *fpl* de corral

barometer [bə'rɒmɪtəʳ] N barómetro *m*

barometric [ˌbærəʊ'metrɪk] ADJ barométrico
CPD ▸ **barometric pressure** presión *f* barométrica

baron ['bærən] N **1** (= *member of nobility*) barón *m*; (*fig*) magnate *m*
2 • **~ of beef** solomillo *m*

baroness ['bærənɪs] N baronesa *f*

baronet ['bærənɪt] N baronet *m*

baronetcy ['bærənɪtsɪ] N dignidad *f* del baronet

baronial [bə'rəʊnɪəl] ADJ baronial

barony ['bærənɪ] N baronía *f*

baroque [bə'rɒk] ADJ (*Archit, Art, Mus*) barroco (*also fig*)
N barroco *m*

barque [bɑːk] N = **bark³**

barrack (*esp Brit*) ['bærək] VT abuchear

barracking ['bærəkɪŋ] (*esp Brit*) N abucheo *m*

barrack-room ['bærəkrʊm] N dormitorio *m* de tropa
CPD cuartelero ▸ **barrack-room ballad** canción *f* cuartelera ▸ **barrack-room lawyer** protestón/ona *m/f*

barracks ['bærəks] NPL **1** (*Mil*) cuartel *msing* • **confined to ~** arrestado en cuartel
2 (= *house*) caserón *m* • **a great ~ of a place** (*Brit*) una casa enorme, un caserón

barrack-square ['bærək'skwɛəʳ] N plaza *f* de armas

barracuda [ˌbærə'kjuːdə] N (PL: **barracuda** *or* **barracudas**) barracuda *f*

barrage ['bærɑːʒ] N **1** (= *dam*) presa *f*
2 (*Mil*) cortina *f* de fuego; [*of balloons etc*] aluvión *m*
3 (*fig*) • **a ~ of noise** un estrépito • **a ~ of questions** una lluvia de preguntas • **there was a ~ of protests** se produjo un aluvión de protestas
VT • **to be ~d by sb** (*fig*) verse asediado por algn • **he was ~d by phone calls** se vio desbordado por un aluvión de llamadas
CPD ▸ **barrage balloon** globo *m* de barrera

barre [bar] N (*Ballet*) barra *f* • **at the ~** en la barra

barred [bɑːʳd] ADJ [*window etc*] enrejado, con reja

barrel ['bærəl] N **1** (*gen*) barril *m*, tonel *m*; [*of oil*] barril *m*; (*for rain*) tina *f*; (*Tech*) tambor *m* • IDIOMS: • **to have sb over a ~*** tener a algn con el agua al cuello* • **to scrape the (bottom of the) ~** rebañar las últimas migas
2 [*of gun, pen*] cañón *m*
CPD ▸ **barrel organ** organillo *m* ▸ **barrel vault** bóveda *f* de cañón

barrel-chested ['bærəl'tʃestɪd] ADJ de pecho fuerte y grueso

barrelful ['bærəlˌfʊl] N barril *m*

barrelhouse ['bærəlˌhaʊs] N (*US*) **1** (= *bar*) bar *m*
2 (= *jazz*) *estilo primitivo de jazz*

barren ['bærən] ADJ [*soil*] árido; [*plant, woman*] estéril • **~ of** falto de, desprovisto de

barrenness ['bærənnɪs] N [*of soil*] aridez *f*; [*of woman*] esterilidad *f*

barrette [bə'ret] N (*US*) pasador *m* (para el pelo)

barricade [ˌbærɪ'keɪd] N barricada *f*
VT cerrar con barricadas • **to ~ o.s. in a house** hacerse fuerte en una casa

barrier ['bærɪəʳ] N barrera *f*, valla *f*; (*Rail*) (*in station*) barrera *f*; (= *crash barrier*) valla *f* protectora; (*fig*) barrera *f*, obstáculo *m* (**to** para)
CPD ▸ **barrier cream** crema *f* protectora ▸ **barrier method** método *m* (de) barrera

barring ['bɑːrɪŋ] PREP excepto, salvo • **we shall be there ~ accidents** iremos a menos que suceda algo imprevisto

barrio ['bɑːrɪəʊ] N (*esp US*) barrio *m* hispano

barrister ['bærɪstəʳ] N (*Brit*) abogado/a *m/f*; ▷ LAWYERS, QC/KC

bar-room ['bɑːˌrʊm] N (*US*) bar *m*, taberna *f*
CPD ▸ **bar-room brawl** pelea *f* de taberna

barrow¹ ['bærəʊ] N (= *wheelbarrow*) carretilla *f*; (= *market stall*) carreta *f*
CPD ▸ **barrow boy** (*Brit*) vendedor *m* callejero

barrow² ['bærəʊ] N (*Archeol*) túmulo *m*

Bart ABBR (*Brit*) = **Baronet**

bartender ['bɑːtendəʳ] N bárman *m*, camarero *m*

barter ['bɑːtəʳ] N trueque *m*
VT • **to ~ sth (for sth)** trocar *or* cambiar algo (por algo)
VI • **to ~ with sb (for sth)** negociar con algn (por algo)
▸ **barter away** VT + ADV [+ *rights, freedom*] malvender

Bartholomew [bɑː'θɒləmjuː] N Bartolomé

barytone ['bærɪtəʊn] N viola *f* de bordón

basal ['beɪsl] ADJ **1** (*lit, fig*) básico
2 (*Physiol*) basal

basalt ['bæsɔːlt] N basalto *m*

base¹ [beɪs] N **1** (= *bottom, support*) [*of wall*] base *f*; [*of column*] base *f*, pie *m*; [*of vase, lamp*] pie *m*
2 (= *basis, starting point*) base *f*
3 (*Mil*) base *f*; [*of organization, company*] sede *f*; (= *residence*) lugar *m* de residencia; (= *workplace*) base *f*
4 (*Baseball*) base *f* • IDIOMS: • **to get to** *or* **reach first ~** (*esp US*) (*Baseball*) llegar a la primera base; (*fig*) alcanzar la primera meta • **to touch ~ with sb** (*esp US*) ponerse en contacto con algn • **to touch** *or* **cover all (the) ~s** (*esp US*) abarcarlo todo • **to be off ~** (*US**): • **he's way off ~** está totalmente equivocado
5 (*Math*) base *f*
6 (*Drugs**) cocaína *f* (para fumar)
VT **1** (= *post, locate*) • **to ~ sb at** [+ *troops*] estacionar a algn en • **we were ~d on Malta** nos estacionaron en Malta • **the job is ~d in London** el trabajo tiene su base en Londres • **where are you ~d now?** ¿dónde estás ahora?
2 (= *found*) [+ *opinion, relationship*] • **to ~ sth on** basar *or* fundar algo en • **to be ~d on** basarse *or* fundarse en • **a story ~d on fact** una historia basada en la realidad • **I ~ myself on the following facts** me apoyo en los hechos siguientes
CPD ▸ **base camp** campo *m* base ▸ **base coat** [*of paint*] primera capa *f* ▸ **base form** (*Ling*) base *f* derivativa ▸ **base jumping** *salto en paracaídas realizado ilegalmente desde rascacielos, puentes etc* ▸ **base lending rate** tipo *m* de interés base ▸ **base period** período *m* base ▸ **base rate** tipo *m* de interés base ▸ **base station** (*Telec*) base *f*; (*Rad*) estación *f* base

base² [beɪs] (COMPAR: **baser**, SUPERL: **basest**) ADJ **1** [*action, motive*] vil, bajo
2 [*metal*] bajo de ley
3 (*US*) = **bass¹**

baseball ['beɪsbɔːl] N (= *sport*) béisbol *m*; (= *ball*) pelota *f* de béisbol
CPD ▸ **baseball cap** gorra *f* de béisbol ▸ **baseball mitt** guante *m* de béisbol ▸ **baseball player** jugador(a) *m/f* de béisbol

BASEBALL

El **baseball** es el deporte nacional norteamericano. Dos equipos de nueve jugadores se enfrentan en un campo de cuatro bases que forman un rombo. El bateador (**batter**) intenta dar a la pelota que le ha tirado el lanzador (**pitcher**) y enviarla fuera del alcance de los fildeadores (**fielders**) para después correr alrededor del rombo de base en base y volver a su punto inicial. Existen dos ligas importantes en los Estados Unidos: la **National League** y la **American League**. Los equipos ganadores de estas dos ligas juegan después otra serie de partidos que se denominan **World Series**.

Algunos aspectos de este deporte, tales como la camaradería y el espíritu de competición tanto entre equipos como entre miembros de un mismo equipo se usan a menudo en el cine como metáforas del modo de vida americano. Culturalmente el béisbol ha aportado, además de conocidas prendas de vestir como las botas o las gorras de béisbol, ciertas expresiones idiomáticas como **a ballpark figure** (una cifra aproximada) o **a whole new ball game** (una situación completamente distinta).

baseboard ['beɪsbɔːd] N (*US*) rodapié *m*

-based [beɪst] ADJ (*ending in compounds*) • **coffee-based** basado en el café • **shore-based** con base en tierra • **sea-/land-based missile** misil *m* situado en una base marítima/terrestre • **to be London-based** [*person, job*] tener su base en Londres; [*organization, company*] tener su sede en Londres

Basel ['bɑːzəl] N Basilea *f*

baseless ['beɪslɪs] ADJ infundado

baseline ['beɪslaɪn] N **1** (*Tennis*) línea *f* de saque *or* de fondo
2 (*Survey*) línea *f* de base
3 (*fig*) (*on scale*) punto *m* de referencia

basely ['beɪslɪ] ADV vilmente, de forma despreciable

baseman ['beɪsmən] N (PL: **basemen**) (*Baseball*) hombre *m* de base

basement ['beɪsmənt] N sótano *m*
CPD ▸ **basement flat** (*Brit*), **basement apartment** (*US*) (apartamento *m* or (*LAm*) departamento *m* de) sótano *m*

baseness ['beɪsnɪs] N bajeza *f*, vileza *f*

bases¹ ['beɪsiːz] NPL *of* **basis**

bases[2] ['beɪsɪz] NPL *of* **base**[1]
bash* [bæʃ] N **1** (= *knock*) porrazo* *m*, golpe *m*
2 (*Brit*) (= *attempt*) intento *m* • **I'll have a ~ (at it)** lo intentaré • **go on, have a ~!** ¡venga, inténtalo!
3 (= *party*) fiesta *f*, juerga *f*
VT [+ *table, door*] golpear; [+ *person*] pegar; (*also* **bash about**) dar una paliza a
VI • **to ~ away** = **bang away**
▸ **bash in*** VT + ADV [+ *door*] echar abajo; [+ *hat, car*] abollar; [+ *lid, cover*] forzar a golpes, cargarse a golpes* • **to ~ sb's head in** romper la crisma a algn*
▸ **bash on*** VI + ADV continuar (a pesar de todo) • **~ on!** ¡adelante!
▸ **bash out*** VT + ADV (= *produce quickly*) sacar cantidad de*, sacar en cantidades industriales*
▸ **bash up*** VT + ADV [+ *car*] estrellar; (*Brit*) [+ *person*] pegar una paliza a
bashed in ['bæʃtɪn] ADJ [*head*] hundido
bashful ['bæʃfʊl] ADJ tímido, vergonzoso
bashfully ['bæʃfʊlɪ] ADV tímidamente
bashfulness ['bæʃfʊlnɪs] N timidez *f*
bashing* ['bæʃɪŋ] N tunda *f*, paliza *f* • **to give sb a ~** dar una paliza a algn • **the team took a real ~** el equipo recibió una paliza*
-bashing* [-bæʃɪŋ] SUFFIX • **union-bashing** ataques *mpl* contra los sindicatos • **queer-bashing**** ataques *mpl* contra homosexuales
BASIC, Basic ['beɪsɪk] N ABBR (*Comput*) (= **Beginner's All-purpose Symbolic Instruction Code**) BASIC *m*
basic ['beɪsɪk] ADJ **1** (= *fundamental*) [*reason, idea, problem*] básico, fundamental; [*knowledge*] básico, elemental; [*skills, vocabulary, needs*] básico • **~ French** francés *m* básico *or* elemental • **a ~ knowledge of Russian** unos conocimientos básicos *or* elementales de ruso • **a ~ right** un derecho fundamental • **~ to sth** básico *or* fundamental para algo
2 (= *forming starting point*) [*salary, working hours*] base • **the ~ rate of income tax** el tipo impositivo *or* de gravamen básico
3 (= *rudimentary*) [*equipment, furniture*] rudimentario; [*cooking*] muy sencillo, muy poco elaborado • **the hotel was extremely ~** el hotel era sumamente sencillo
4 (*Chem*) básico • **~ salt** sal *f* básica • **~ slag** escoria *f* básica
NPL • **~s such as bread and milk** alimentos básicos como el pan y la leche • **the ~s** los principios básicos • **to get back to ~s** volver a empezar por los principios básicos • **to get down to (the) ~s** ir a lo importante • **they had forgotten everything and we had to go back to ~s** lo habían olvidado todo y tuvimos que volver a empezar por los principios
CPD ▸ **basic airman** (*US*) soldado *m* raso de la fuerzas aéreas ▸ **basic rate** (*Econ*) tipo *m* de interés base ▸ **basic training** (*Mil*) entrenamiento *m* básico ▸ **basic wage** salario *m* base
basically ['beɪsɪklɪ] ADV básicamente, fundamentalmente • **~ we agree** básicamente *or* fundamentalmente estamos de acuerdo • **it's ~ the same** es básicamente *or* fundamentalmente lo mismo • **he's ~ lazy** más que nada es perezoso, básicamente *or* fundamentalmente es perezoso • **it's ~ simple** en el fondo es sencillo • **well, ~, all I have to do is ...** bueno, básicamente *or* en pocas palabras, todo lo que tengo que hacer es ...
basil ['bæzl] N albahaca *f*
basilica [bə'zɪlɪkə] N basílica *f*
basilisk ['bæzɪlɪsk] N basilisco *m*
basin ['beɪsn] N **1** (*Culin*) bol *m*, cuenco *m*
2 (= *washbasin*) palangana *f*; (*in bathroom*) lavabo *m*; [*of fountain*] taza *f*
3 (*Geog*) cuenca *f*; [*of port*] dársena *f*
basinful ['beɪsnfʊl] N (= *bowlful*) palangana *f*
basis ['beɪsɪs] N (PL: **bases**) (= *foundation*) base *f* • **on a daily ~** diariamente, a base diaria • **on the ~ of what you've said** en base a lo que ha dicho
CPD ▸ **basis point** (*Econ*) punto *m* base *or* básico
bask [bɑːsk] VI • **to ~ in the sun** tomar el sol • **to ~ in the heat** disfrutar del calor • **to ~ in sb's favour** disfrutar del favor de algn; ▹ **reflect**
basket ['bɑːskɪt] N **1** (*big*) cesto *m*; (*two-handled*) canasta *f*; (*two-handled, for earth etc*) espuerta *f*; (= *hamper*) canasta *f*; (= *pannier*) sera *f*, serón *m*; [*of balloon*] barquilla *f*
2 (*Basketball*) canasta *f* • **to score a ~** encestar, meter una canasta
3 • **a ~ of currencies** (*Econ*) una cesta de monedas (*nacionales*), una canasta de divisas (*LAm*)
CPD ▸ **basket case**** (= *person*) chalado/a* *m/f*, majareta *mf* (*Sp**); (= *country, organization*) caso *m* perdido ▸ **basket chair** silla *f* de mimbre
basketball ['bɑːskɪtbɔːl] N (= *sport*) baloncesto *m*; (= *ball*) balón *m* de baloncesto
CPD ▸ **basketball player** jugador(a) *m/f* de baloncesto
basketful ['bɑːskɪtfʊl] ADJ • **a ~ of food** una cesta de comida
basketry ['bɑːskɪtrɪ] N = **basketwork**
basketwork ['bɑːskɪtwɜːk] N cestería *f*
Basle [bɑːl] N Basilea *f*
basmati rice [bəz'mætɪ'raɪs] N arroz *m* basmati (*arroz de grano largo*)
Basque [bæsk] ADJ vasco
N **1** (= *person*) vasco/a *m/f*
2 (*Ling*) euskera *m*, vascuence *m*
CPD ▸ **the Basque Country** el País Vasco, Euskadi *f* ▸ **the Basque Provinces** las Vascongadas
bas-relief ['bæsrɪ,liːf] N bajorrelieve *m*
bass[1] [beɪs] (*Mus*) ADJ bajo
N (= *voice, singer, guitar*) bajo *m*; (= *double bass*) contrabajo *m*
CPD ▸ **bass baritone** barítono *m* bajo ▸ **bass clef** clave *f* de fa ▸ **bass drum** bombo *m* ▸ **bass flute** flauta *f* contralto ▸ **bass guitar** bajo *m* ▸ **bass guitarist** bajista *mf* ▸ **bass horn** trompa *f* baja ▸ **bass strings** instrumentos *mpl* de cuerda bajos ▸ **bass trombone** trombón *m* bajo ▸ **bass tuba** tuba *f* ▸ **bass viol** viola *f* de gamba baja
bass[2] [bæs] N (= *fish*) róbalo *m*
basset ['bæsɪt] N (*also* **basset hound**) basset *m*
bassist ['beɪsɪst] N (*Mus*) bajista *mf*, bajo *m*
bassoon [bə'suːn] N bajón *m*, fagot *m*
bassoonist [bə'suːnɪst] N fagot *mf*, fagotista *mf*
basso profundo [,bæsəʊprə'fʊndəʊ] N bajo *m* profundo
bastard ['bɑːstəd] ADJ (= *illegitimate*) bastardo
N **1** (= *illegitimate child*) bastardo/a *m/f*
2** (*pej*) cabrón/ona** *m/f*, hijo/a *m/f* de puta**, hijo/a *m/f* de la chingada (*Mex***) • **you ~!** ¡cabrón!** • **you old ~!** ¡hijoputa!** • **that silly ~** ese idiota* • **this job is a real ~** este trabajo es muy jodido**
CPD ▸ **bastard daughter** hija *f* bastarda ▸ **bastard son** hijo *m* bastardo
bastardized ['bɑːstədaɪzd] ADJ [*language*] corrupto
bastardy ['bɑːstədɪ] N (*Jur*) bastardía *f*
baste [beɪst] VT **1** (*Culin*) pringar
2 (*Sew*) hilvanar
3* (= *beat*) dar una paliza a
basting ['beɪstɪŋ] N **1** (*Sew*) hilván *m*
2* (= *beating*) paliza *f*, zurra *f*
bastion ['bæstɪən] N (*also fig*) baluarte *m*
Basutoland [bə'suːtəʊlænd] N (*formerly*) Basutolandia *f*
BASW N ABBR = **British Association of Social Workers**
bat[1] [bæt] N (*Zool*) murciélago *m* • **old bat*** (= *old woman*) bruja* *f* • IDIOMS: • **to be bats** • **have bats in the belfry*** estar más loco que una cabra* • **to go like a bat out of hell*** ir como alma que lleva el diablo, ir a toda hostia (*Sp**)
bat[2] [bæt] N **1** (*in ball games*) paleta *f*, pala *f*; (*in cricket, baseball*) bate *m* • IDIOMS: • **off one's own bat*** por cuenta propia • **right off the bat** (*US**) de repente
2* (= *blow*) golpe *m*
VI (*Sport*) batear • IDIOM: • **to go (in) to bat for sb** (= *support*) dar la cara por algn, salir en apoyo de algn
VT* (= *hit*) golpear, apalear • **to bat sth around** (*US**) (= *discuss*) discutir acerca de algo
bat[3] [bæt] VT • **he didn't bat an eyelid** (*Brit*) • **he didn't bat an eye** (*US*) ni pestañeó • **without batting an eyelid** (*Brit*) • **without batting an eye** (*US*) sin pestañear, sin inmutarse
batch [bætʃ] N **1** [*of goods etc*] lote *m*, remesa *f*; [*of papers*] pila *f*; [*of people*] grupo *m*; [*of bread*] hornada *f*
2 (*Comput*) lote *m*
CPD ▸ **batch file** (*Comput*) fichero *m* BAT ▸ **batch mode** (*Comput*) • **in ~ mode** en tratamiento por lotes ▸ **batch processing** (*Comput*) tratamiento *m* por lotes ▸ **batch production** (*Ind*) producción *f* por lotes
bated ['beɪtɪd] ADJ • **with ~ breath** sin respirar
bath [bɑːθ] N (PL: **baths** [bɑːðz]) **1** (*esp Brit*) (*also* **bathtub**) bañera *f*, tina *f* (*LAm*), bañadera *f* (*S. Cone*)
2 (= *act*) baño *m* • **to have** *or* **take a ~** darse un baño, bañarse • **to give sb a ~** dar un baño a algn, bañar a algn
3 (*Chem, Phot*) baño *m*
4 baths (*Brit*) (= *swimming pool*) piscina *f*, alberca *f* (*Mex*), pileta *f* (*S. Cone*)
VT (*Brit*) bañar, dar un baño a
VI (*Brit*) bañarse
CPD ▸ **bath bomb** bomba *f* de baño ▸ **bath chair** silla *f* de ruedas ▸ **bath cube** cubo *m* de sales para el baño ▸ **bath oil** aceite *m* para el baño ▸ **bath salts** sales *fpl* de baño ▸ **bath sheet, bath towel** toalla *f* de baño
bathe [beɪð] N (*Brit*) (= *swim*) baño *m* • **to go for a ~** ir a bañarse
VT **1** [+ *wound etc*] lavar
2 (*esp US*) bañar • **to ~ the baby** bañar al niño
3 (*fig*) • **~d in light** bañado de luz • **~d in tears/sweat** bañado en lágrimas/sudor
VI **1** (*Brit*) (= *swim*) bañarse • **to go bathing** ir a bañarse
2 (*US*) (= *take bath*) bañarse
bather ['beɪðəʳ] N bañista *mf*
bathetic [bə'θetɪk] ADJ que pasa de lo sublime a lo trivial
bathhouse ['bɑːθhaʊs] N (PL: **bathhouses** ['bɑːθhaʊzɪz]) baño *m*
bathing ['beɪðɪŋ] N el bañarse • **"no bathing"** "prohibido bañarse"
CPD ▸ **bathing beauty** sirena *f or* belleza *f* de la playa ▸ **bathing cap** (*US*) gorro *m* de baño ▸ **bathing costume** (*Brit*) traje *m* de baño, bañador *m*, malla *f* (*S. Cone*) ▸ **bathing hut** caseta *f* de playa ▸ **bathing machine**

b

(*Hist*) caseta *f* de playa movible ▸ **bathing suit** (*US*) = **bathing costume** ▸ **bathing trunks** bañador *m* (*de hombre*) ▸ **bathing wrap** albornoz *m*

bathmat ['bɑ:θmæt] (N) alfombra *f* de baño

bathos ['beɪθɒs] (N) paso *m* de lo sublime a lo trivial

bathrobe ['bɑ:θrəʊb] (N) albornoz *m*

bathroom ['bɑ:θrʊm] (N) cuarto *m* de baño; (*US*) (= *toilet*) servicio *m*, baño *m* (*esp LAm*) • **to go to** *or* **use the ~** (*US*) ir al servicio
(CPD) ▸ **bathroom cabinet** armario *m* de aseo ▸ **bathroom fittings** aparatos *mpl* sanitarios ▸ **bathroom scales** báscula *f* de baño

bathtub ['bɑ:θtʌb] (N) (*esp US*) bañera *f*, tina *f* (*LAm*), bañadera *f* (*S. Cone*)

bathwater ['bɑ:θwɔ:tə^r] (N) agua *f* del baño

bathysphere ['bæθɪsfɪə^r] (N) batisfera *f*

batik [bə'ti:k] (N) (= *process, cloth*) batik *m*

batiste [bæ'ti:st] (N) batista *f*

batman ['bætmən] (N) (PL: **batmen**) (*Brit*) (*Mil*) ordenanza *m*

baton ['bætən] (N) (*Mus*) batuta *f*; (*Mil*) bastón *m*; [*of policeman*] porra *f*; (*in race*) testigo *m* • IDIOMS: • **to hand on** *or* **pass the ~ to sb** entregar el testigo a algn • **to pick up the ~** recoger el testigo
(CPD) ▸ **baton charge** carga *f* con bastones ▸ **baton round** bala *f* de goma

batrachian [bə'treɪkɪən] (N) batracio *m*

batsman ['bætsmən] (N) (PL: **batsmen**) (*Cricket*) bateador *m*

battalion [bə'tælɪən] (N) batallón *m*

batten ['bætn] (N) (*Brit*) (*Carpentry*) listón *m*; (*Naut*) junquillo *m*, sable *m*
(VT) [+ *roof, shutters*] sujetar con listones • **to ~ down the hatches** (*also fig*) atrancar las escotillas
▸ **batten on** (VI + PREP) explotar, aprovecharse de

batter¹ ['bætə^r] (N) (*Culin*) mezcla *f* para rebozar • **in ~** rebozado

batter² ['bætə^r] (N) (*Baseball, Cricket*) bateador(a) *m/f*; ▹ BASEBALL, CRICKET
(VT) **1** [+ *person*] apalear; [+ *wife, baby*] maltratar; [*boxer*] magullar; [*wind, waves*] azotar; (*Mil*) cañonear, bombardear
2 (*verbally etc*) criticar ásperamente, poner como un trapo*
▸ **batter at, batter away at** (VI + PREP) dar grandes golpes en
▸ **batter down, batter in** (VT + ADV) [+ *door*] derribar a golpes

battered ['bætəd] (ADJ) (= *bruised*) magullado; [*hat*] estropeado; [*car*] abollado
(CPD) ▸ **battered baby** niño/a *m/f* maltratado/a ▸ **battered wife** mujer *f* maltratada

batterer ['bætərə^r] (N) *persona que maltrata físicamente a su mujer o marido e hijos* • **wife-batterer** marido *m* violento

battering ['bætərɪŋ] (N) (= *blows*) paliza *f*; (*Mil*) bombardeo *m* • **the ~ of the waves** el golpear de las olas • **he got a ~ from the critics** los críticos fueron muy duros con él, los críticos lo pusieron como un trapo*
(CPD) ▸ **battering ram** ariete *m*

battery ['bætərɪ] (N) **1** (*Elec*) (*dry*) pila *f*; (*wet*) batería *f*
2 (*Mil*) batería *f*
3 (= *series*) [*of tests*] serie *f*; [*of lights*] batería *f*, equipo *m*; [*of questions*] descarga *f*, sarta *f*
4 (*Agr*) batería *f*
5 (*Jur*) violencia *f*, agresión *f*
(CPD) ▸ **battery charger** (*Elec*) cargador *m* de baterías ▸ **battery farm** (*Brit*) granja *f* (avícola) de cría intensiva ▸ **battery farming** (*Brit*) cría *f* (avícola) intensiva ▸ **battery fire** (*Mil*) fuego *m* de batería ▸ **battery hen** (*Brit*) gallina *f* de criadero ▸ **battery set** (*Rad*) radio *f* de pilas, transistor *m*

battery-operated [ˌbætərɪ'ɒpəreɪtɪd] (ADJ) a pilas

battle ['bætl] (N) **1** (*Mil*) batalla *f* • **to do ~** librar batalla (**with** con) • **to fight a ~** luchar • **the ~ was fought in 1346** la batalla se libró en 1346 • **to join ~** (*frm*) trabar batalla
2 (*fig*) lucha *f* (**for control of** por el control de, **to control** por controlar) • **to do ~ for** luchar por • **a ~ of wills** un duelo de voluntades • **a ~ of wits** un duelo de ingenio • **that's half the ~*** (con eso) ya hay medio camino andado* • **the ~ lines are drawn** (*fig*) todo está listo para la batalla • IDIOMS: • **to fight a losing ~** luchar por una causa perdida • **to win the ~ but lose the war** ganar la batalla pero perder la guerra
(VI) **1** (*Mil*) • **the two armies ~d all day** los dos ejércitos se batieron durante todo el día
2 (*fig*) luchar (**against** contra **for** por **to do** por hacer) • **to ~ against the wind** luchar contra el viento • **to ~ for breath** esforzarse por respirar
(VT) (*esp US*) luchar contra, librar batalla contra
(CPD) ▸ **battle array** • **in ~ array** en formación *or* en orden de batalla ▸ **battle bus** (*Brit*) (*in election campaign*) autobús *m* de campaña ▸ **battle cruiser** crucero *m* de batalla ▸ **battle cry** (*Mil*) grito *m* de combate; (*fig*) lema *m*, consigna *f* ▸ **battle dress** traje *m* de campaña ▸ **battle fatigue** *trastorno mental postraumático provocado por el combate militar* ▸ **battle fleet** flota *f* de guerra ▸ **battle order** = **battle array** ▸ **battle royal** batalla *f* campal ▸ **battle zone** zona *f* de batalla
▸ **battle on** (VI + ADV) seguir luchando
▸ **battle out** (VT + ADV) • **to ~ it out** enfrentarse

battle-axe, battle-ax (*US*) ['bætlæks] (N) **1** (= *weapon*) hacha *f* de guerra
2* (*pej*) (= *woman*) arpía *f*

battledore ['bætldɔ:^r] (N) raqueta *f* de bádminton • **~ and shuttlecock** *antiguo juego predecesor del bádminton*

battlefield ['bætlfi:ld] (N), **battleground** ['bætlgraʊnd] (N) campo *m* de batalla

battle-hardened ['bætlˌhɑ:dənd] (ADJ) endurecido por la lucha

battlements ['bætlmənts] (NPL) almenas *fpl*

battler ['bætlə^r] (N) luchador(a) *m/f*

battle-scarred ['bætlˌskɑ:d] (ADJ) (*gen*) marcado por la lucha; (*hum*) deteriorado

battleship ['bætlʃɪp] (N) **1** (*Mil*) acorazado *m*
2 • **~s** (= *game*) los barquitos (*juego*)

Battn (ABBR) (= **battalion**) Bón.

batty* ['bætɪ] (ADJ) (COMPAR: **battier**, SUPERL: **battiest**) (*esp Brit*) chiflado*, chalado*

bauble ['bɔ:bl] (N) chuchería *f*

baud [bɔ:d] (*Comput*) (N) baudio *m*
(CPD) ▸ **baud rate** velocidad *f* (de transmisión) en baudios

baulk [bɔ:lk] (VI) ▹ **balk**

bauxite ['bɔ:ksaɪt] (N) bauxita *f*

Bavaria [bə'vɛərɪə] (N) Baviera *f*

Bavarian [bə'vɛərɪən] (ADJ) bávaro
(N) bávaro/a *m/f*

bawbee [bɔ:'bi:] (N) (*Scot*) (*hum*) medio penique *m*

bawd†† [bɔ:d] (N) alcahueta *f*

bawdiness ['bɔ:dɪnɪs] (N) lo verde

bawdy ['bɔ:dɪ] (ADJ) (COMPAR: **bawdier**, SUPERL: **bawdiest**) subido de tono, verde*, colorado (*Mex**)

bawdyhouse†† ['bɔ:dɪhaʊs] (N) (PL: **bawdyhouses** ['bɔ:dɪhaʊzɪz]) mancebía *f*

bawl [bɔ:l] (VI) **1** (= *cry*) berrear
2 (= *shout*) chillar • **to ~ at sb** gritar a algn
▸ **bawl out** (VT + ADV) **1** vocear, vociferar
2* (= *scold*) • **to ~ sb out** echar una bronca a algn*

bay¹ [beɪ] (N) (*Geog*) bahía *f*; (*small*) abra *f*; (*very large*) golfo *m* • **the Bay of Biscay** el golfo de Vizcaya

bay² [beɪ] (N) **1** (*Archit*) (*between two walls*) crujía *f*; (*also* **bay window**) ventana *f* salediza
2 (*for parking*) parking *m*, área *f* de aparcamiento *or* (*LAm*) estacionamiento; (*for loading*) área *f* de carga
3 (*Rail*) nave *f*
(CPD) ▸ **bay window** ventana *f* salediza

bay³ [beɪ] (VI) [*dog*] aullar (**at** a) • IDIOMS: • **to bay for blood** (*Brit*) clamar venganza • **to bay for sb's blood** (*Brit*) pedir la cabeza de algn
(N) **1** (= *bark*) aullido *m*
2 • **at bay** (*Hunting*) acorralado (*also fig*) • **to keep** *or* **hold sth/sb at bay** (*fig*) mantener algo/a algn a raya • **to bring to bay** (*Hunting*) acorralar (*also fig*)

bay⁴ [beɪ] (ADJ) [*horse*] bayo
(N) caballo *m* bayo

bay⁵ [beɪ] (N) (*Bot*) laurel *m*
(CPD) ▸ **bay leaf** (hoja *f* de) laurel *m* ▸ **bay rum** ron *m* de laurel *or* de malagueta

bayonet ['beɪənɪt] (N) bayoneta *f* • **with fixed ~s** con las bayonetas caladas • **at ~ point** a punta de bayoneta
(VT) herir/matar con la bayoneta
(CPD) ▸ **bayonet bulb** (*Elec*) bombilla *f* or (*LAm*) foco *m* de bayoneta ▸ **bayonet charge** carga *f* a la bayoneta ▸ **bayonet practice** ejercicios *mpl* con bayoneta, prácticas *fpl* de bayoneta

Bayonne [baɪ'jɒn] (N) Bayona *f*

bayou ['baɪju:] (N) (*US*) pantanos *mpl*

bazaar [bə'zɑ:^r] (N) bazar *m*

bazooka [bə'zu:kə] (N) bazuca *f*

BB (N ABBR) (= **Boys' Brigade**) *organización parecida a los Boy Scouts*
(CPD) ▸ **BB gun** (*US*) *carabina de aire comprimido*

BBA (N ABBR) (*US*) (*Univ*) = **Bachelor of Business Administration**

BBB (N ABBR) (*US*) = **Better Business Bureau**

BBC (N ABBR) = **British Broadcasting Corporation** • **the BBC** la BBC; ▹ OPEN UNIVERSITY

BBFC (N ABBR) = **British Board of Film Classification**

bbl (ABBR) = **barrels**

BBQ (N ABBR) = **barbecue**

BBS (N ABBR) (*Comput*) = **bulletin board system**

BC (ADV ABBR) (= **Before Christ**) a. de C., a.C., A.C.
(N ABBR) (*Canada*) = **British Columbia**

BCD (N ABBR) (*Comput*) = **binary-coded decimal**

BCG (N ABBR) (= **Bacillus Calmette-Guérin**) BCG *m*

BCom [bi:'kɒm] (N ABBR) = **Bachelor of Commerce**

BD (N ABBR) (*Univ*) = **Bachelor of Divinity**
(ABBR) = **bills discounted**

bd (ABBR) (*Econ*) = **bond**

B/D (ABBR) = **bank draft**

b/d (ABBR) (*Econ*) = **brought down**

BDD (N ABBR) (= **body dysmorphic disorder**) trastorno *m* dismórfico corporal, dismorfofobia *f*

BDS (N ABBR) (*Univ*) = **Bachelor of Dental Surgery**

BE (N ABBR) (*Econ*) (= **bill of exchange**) L/C

be [bi:]

INTRANSITIVE VERB
AUXILIARY VERB
MODAL VERB

(PRESENT: **am, is, are**, PT: **was, were**, PP: **been**)

INTRANSITIVE VERB

1 (*linking nouns, noun phrases, pronouns*) ser • **he's a pianist** es pianista • **he wants to be a doctor** quiere ser médico • **Monday's a holiday** el lunes es fiesta • **two and two are four** dos y dos son cuatro • **it's me!** ¡soy yo! • **it was me** fui yo • **who wants to be Hamlet?** ¿quién quiere hacer de *or* ser Hamlet? • **you be the patient and I'll be the doctor** tú eres el enfermo y yo seré el médico • **if I were you ...** yo en tu lugar ..., yo que tú ...*

2 (*possession*) ser • **she's his sister** es su hermana • **it's mine** es mío

3 (*characteristics seen as inherent*) ser • **the sky is blue** el cielo es azul • **it's (made of) plastic** es de plástico • **they're English** son ingleses • **he's tall** es alto • **it's round/enormous** es redondo/enorme • **she is boring** es aburrida • **I used to be poor but now I'm rich** antes era pobre pero ahora soy rico • **if I were rich** si fuera rico • **I'm from the south** soy del sur • **the book is in French** el libro es en francés

Use ***estar*** *with past participles used as adjectives describing the results of an action or process:*

• **it's broken** está roto • **he's dead** está muerto

4 (*changeable or temporary state*) estar • **it's dirty** está sucio • **she's bored/ill** está aburrida/enferma • **how are you?** ¿cómo estás?, ¿qué tal estás? • **how are you now?** ¿qué tal te encuentras ahora? • **I'm very well, thanks** estoy muy bien, gracias

In certain expressions where English uses ***be*** *+ adjective to describe feelings (****be cold/hot/hungry/thirsty****), Spanish uses* ***tener*** *with a noun:*

• **I'm cold/hot** tengo frío/calor • **my feet are cold** tengo los pies fríos • **I'm hungry/thirsty** tengo hambre/sed • **be good!** ¡pórtate bien! • **you're late** llegas tarde; ▹ **afraid, sleepy, right**

5 (*age*) • **"how old is she?" — "she's nine"** —¿cuántos años tiene? —tiene nueve años • **she will be two tomorrow** mañana cumple dos años • **when I'm old** cuando sea viejo • **when I was young** cuando era joven

6 (*= take place*) ser • **the meeting's today** la reunión es hoy • **the service will be at St Ninian's Church** el oficio será en la iglesia de San Ninian

7 (*= be situated*) estar • **Edinburgh is in Scotland** Edimburgo está en Escocia • **it's on the table** está sobre *or* en la mesa • **where is the Town Hall?** ¿dónde está *or* queda el ayuntamiento? • **it's 5 km to the village** el pueblo está *or* queda a 5 kilómetros • **he won't be here tomorrow** mañana no estará aquí • **we've been here for ages** hace mucho tiempo que estamos aquí, llevamos aquí mucho tiempo, estamos aquí desde hace mucho tiempo • **here you are(, take it)** aquí tienes(, tómalo) • **there's the church** ahí está la iglesia

8 (*impersonal use*) **a** (*referring to weather*) hacer • **it's hot/cold** hace calor/frío • **it's too hot** hace demasiado calor • **it's fine** hace buen tiempo; ▹ **windy, sunny, foggy** *etc*

b (*referring to time, date etc*) ser • **it's eight o'clock** son las ocho • **it's morning in New York now** en Nueva York ahora es por la mañana • **wake up, it's morning** despierta, es de día • **what's the date (today)?** ¿qué fecha es hoy? • **it's 3 May** *or* **the 3rd of May** es 3 de mayo • **it's Thursday today** hoy es jueves

But note the following alternatives with ***estar****:*

• **it's 3 May** *or* **the 3rd of May** estamos a 3 de mayo • **it's Thursday today** hoy estamos a jueves

c (*asking and giving opinion*) ser • **is it certain that ...?** ¿es verdad *or* cierto que ...? • **it is easy to make a mistake** es fácil cometer un fallo • **is it fair that she should be punished while ...?** ¿es justo que se la castigue mientras que ...? • **it is possible that he'll come** es posible que venga, puede (ser) que venga • **it is impossible to study all the time** es imposible estar siempre estudiando • **it is unbelievable that ...** es increíble que ... • **it's not clear whether ...** no está claro si ... • **it would be wrong for us to do that** no estaría bien que nosotros hiciésemos eso

d (*emphatic*) ser • **it's me who does all the work** soy yo quien hace todo el trabajo • **it was Peter who phoned** fue Peter quien llamó • **why is it that she's so successful?** ¿cómo es que tiene tanto éxito?, ¿por qué tiene tanto éxito? • **it was then that ...** fue entonces cuando ...

9 (*= exist*) haber • **there is/are** hay • **what is (there) in that room?** ¿qué hay en esa habitación? • **there is nothing more beautiful** no hay nada más bello • **is there anyone at home?** ¿hay alguien en casa? • **there were six road accidents here last year** el año pasado hubo seis accidentes de tráfico aquí • **there must be an explanation** debe de haber una explicación • **there being no alternative solution ...** al no haber *or* no habiendo otra solución ... • **let there be light!** ¡hágase la luz! • **there are three of us** somos tres • **there were three of them** eran tres • **after the shop there's the bus station** después de la tienda está la estación de autobuses; ▹ THERE IS, THERE ARE

10 (*= cost*) • **how much was it?** ¿cuánto costó? • **the book is £20** el libro vale *or* cuesta 20 libras • **how much is it?** ¿cuánto es?; (*when paying*) ¿qué le debo? (*frm*)

11 (*= visit*) • **has the postman been?** ¿ha venido el cartero? • **he has been and gone** vino y se fue • **I have been to see my aunt** he ido a ver a mi tía • **have you ever been to Glasgow?** ¿has estado en Glasgow alguna vez? • **I've been to China** he estado en China

12 (*in noun compounds*) futuro • **mother to be** futura madre *or* mamá *f* • **my wife to be** mi futura esposa

13 (*in set expressions*) • **to be or not to be** ser o no ser • **been and***: • **you've been and done it now!** ¡buena la has hecho!* • **that dog of yours has been and dug up my flowers!** ¡tu perro ha ido y me ha destrozado las flores! • **you're busy enough as it is** estás bastante ocupado ya con lo que tienes, ya tienes suficiente trabajo • **as things are** tal como están las cosas • **be that as it may** sea como fuere • **if it hadn't been for ...**: • **if it hadn't been for you** *or* (*frm*) **had it not been for you, we would have lost** si no hubiera sido por ti *or* de no haber sido por ti, habríamos perdido • **let me be!** ¡déjame en paz! • **if that's what you want to do, then so be it** si eso es lo que quieres hacer, adelante • **what is it to you?*** ¿a ti qué te importa? • **what's it to be?** (*in bar etc*) ¿qué va a ser?, ¿qué vas a tomar?

AUXILIARY VERB

1 (*forming passive*) ser • **the house was destroyed by an earthquake** la casa fue destruida por un terremoto

The passive is not used as often in Spanish as in English, active and reflexive constructions often being preferred:

• **the box had been opened** habían abierto la caja • **these cars are produced in Spain** estos coches se fabrican en España • **it is said that ...** dicen que ..., se dice que ... • **he was killed by a terrorist** lo mató un terrorista • **she was killed in a car crash** murió en un accidente de coche, resultó muerta en un accidente de coche (*frm*) • **what's to be done?** ¿qué hay que hacer? • **it's a film not to be missed** es una película que no hay que perderse • **we searched everywhere for him, but he was nowhere to be seen** lo buscamos por todas partes pero no lo encontramos en ningún sitio

2 (*forming continuous*) estar • **it's raining** está lloviendo • **what are you doing?** ¿qué estás haciendo?, ¿qué haces? • **don't distract me when I'm driving** no me distraigas cuando estoy conduciendo • **he's always grumbling** siempre está quejándose • **he was studying until the early hours** estuvo estudiando hasta la madrugada

Use the present simple to talk about planned future events and the ***ir a*** *construction to talk about intention:*

• **they're coming tomorrow** vienen mañana • **"it's a pity you aren't coming with us" — "but I am coming!"** —¡qué pena que no vengas con nosotros! —¡sí que voy! • **will you be seeing her tomorrow?** ¿la verás *or* la vas a ver mañana? • **will you be needing more?** ¿vas a necesitar más? • **I shall be seeing him** voy a verlo • **I'll be seeing you** hasta luego, nos vemos (*esp LAm*)

The imperfect tense can be used for continuous action in the past:

• **he was driving too fast** conducía demasiado rápido; ▹ **for, since**

3 (*verb substitute*) **a** • **he's older than you are** es mayor que tú • **he isn't as happy as he was** no está tan contento como antes • **"he's going to complain about you" — "oh, is he?"** —va a quejarse de ti —¿ah, sí? • **"I'm worried" — "so am I"** —estoy preocupado —yo también • **"I'm not ready" — "neither am I"** —no estoy listo —yo tampoco • **"you're tired" — "no, I'm not"** —estás cansado —no, ¡qué va! • **"you're not eating enough" — "yes I am"** —no comes lo suficiente —que sí • **"they're getting married" — "oh, are they?"** (*showing surprise*) —se casan —¿ah, sí? *or* —¡no me digas! • **"he isn't very happy" — "oh, isn't he?"** —no está muy contento —¿ah, no? • **"he's always late, isn't he?" — "yes, he is"** —siempre llega tarde, ¿verdad? —(pues) sí • **"is it what you expected?" — "no, it isn't"** —¿es esto lo que esperabas? —(pues) no • **"she's pretty" — "no, she isn't"** —es guapa —¡qué va!

b (*in question tags*) • **he's handsome, isn't he?** es guapo, ¿verdad?, es guapo, ¿no?, es guapo, ¿no es cierto? • **it was fun, wasn't it?** fue divertido, ¿verdad?, fue divertido, ¿no? • **she wasn't happy, was she?** no era feliz, ¿verdad? • **so he's back again, is he?** así que ha vuelto, ¿eh? • **you're not ill, are you?** ¿no estarás enfermo?

b

MODAL VERB (*with infinitive construction*)
1 (= *must, have to*) • **you're to put on your shoes** tienes que ponerte los zapatos • **he's not to open it** no debe abrirlo, que no lo abra • **I am to do it** he de hacerlo yo, soy yo el que debe hacerlo • **I am not to speak to him** no tengo permiso para hablar con él • **I wasn't to tell you his name** no podía *or* debía decirte su nombre
2 (= *should*) deber • **he is to be congratulated on his work** debemos felicitarlo por su trabajo • **am I to understand that ...?** ¿debo entender que ...? • **she wrote "My Life", not to be confused with Bernstein's book of the same name** escribió "Mi Vida", que no debe confundirse con la obra de Bernstein que lleva el mismo título • **he was to have come yesterday** tenía que *or* debía haber venido ayer • **he is to be pitied** es digno de lástima
3 (= *will*) • **the talks are to start tomorrow** las conversaciones darán comienzo mañana • **her house is to be sold** su casa se pondrá a la venta • **they are to be married in the summer** se casarán en el verano
4 (= *can*) • **these birds are to be found all over the world** estos pájaros se encuentran por todo el mundo • **little traffic was to be seen** había poco tráfico • **you weren't to know** no tenías por qué saberlo
5 (*expressing destiny*) • **this was to have serious repercussions** esto iba a tener serias repercusiones • **they were never to return** jamás regresaron • **it was not to be** no quiso el destino que así fuera
6 (*in conditional sentences*) • **you must work harder if you are to succeed** debes esforzarte más si quieres triunfar • **if it was** *or* **were to snow** ... si nevase *or* nevara ... • **if I were to leave the job, would you replace me?** si yo dejara el puesto, ¿me sustituirías?

B/E (N ABBR) **1** (*Econ*) (= **bill of exchange**) L/C
2 (*Econ*) = **Bank of England**

be- [bɪ] (PREFIX) • **bespectacled** con gafas • **bejewelled** enjoyado

beach [biːtʃ] (N) playa *f*
(VT) [+ *boat*] varar; [+ *whale*] embarrancar, encallar
(CPD) ▸ **beach babe*** mujer *f* espectacular (*en la playa*) ▸ **beach ball** balón *m* de playa ▸ **beach barbecue** barbacoa *f* en la playa ▸ **beach buggy** buggy *m* ▸ **beach bum*** playero/a *m/f* (de mucho cuidado)* ▸ **beach chair** (*US*) tumbona *f* ▸ **beach hut** caseta *f* de playa ▸ **beach pyjamas** pijama *m* de verano ▸ **beach towel** toalla *f* de playa ▸ **beach umbrella** sombrilla *f* ▸ **beach volleyball** voley-playa *m*, voleibol-playa *m* ▸ **beach wrap** batín *m* (de playa)

beachcomber [ˈbiːtʃˌkəʊməʳ] (N) raquero/a *m/f*

beachfront [ˈbiːtʃfrʌnt] (ADJ) [*house, shop,*

BE

"Ser" or "estar"?

You can use "ser":

▹ *when defining or identifying by linking two nouns or noun phrases:*
Paris is the capital of France
París es la capital de Francia
He was the most hated man in the village
Era el hombre más odiado del pueblo

▹ *to describe essential or inherent characteristics (e.g. colour, material, nationality, race, shape, size etc):*
His mother is German
Su madre es alemana
She was blonde
Era rubia

▹ *with most impersonal expressions not involving past participles:*
It is important to be on time
Es importante llegar a tiempo

Está claro que *is an exception:*
It is obvious you don't understand
Está claro que no lo entiendes

▹ *when telling the time or talking about time or age:*
It is ten o'clock
Son las diez
It's very late. Let's go home
Es muy tarde. Vamos a casa
He lived in the country when he was young
Vivió en el campo cuando era joven

▹ *to indicate possession or duty:*
It's mine
Es mío
This is your responsibility
Este asunto es responsabilidad tuya

▹ *with events in the sense of "take place":*
The 1992 Olympic Games were in Barcelona
Los Juegos Olímpicos de 1992 fueron en Barcelona
"Where is the exam?" - "It's in Room 1"
"¿Dónde es el examen?" - "Es en el Aula Número 1"

NOTE: Compare this usage with that of **estar** *(see below) to talk about location of places, objects and people.*

You can use "estar":

▹ *to talk about location of places, objects and people:*
"Where is Zaragoza?" - "It's in Spain"
"¿Dónde está Zaragoza?" - "Está en España"
Your glasses are on the bedside table
Tus gafas están en la mesilla de noche

NOTE: But use **ser** *with events in the sense of "take place" (see above).*

▹ *to talk about changeable state, condition or mood:*
The teacher is ill
La profesora está enferma
The coffee's cold
El café está frío
How happy I am!
¡Qué contento estoy!

NOTE: **Feliz**, *however, which is seen as more permanent than* **contento**, *is used mainly with* **ser**.

▹ *to form progressive tenses:*
We're having lunch. Is it ok if I call you later?
Estamos comiendo. Te llamaré luego, ¿vale?

Both "ser" and "estar" can be used with past participles

▹ *Use* **ser** *in passive constructions:*
This play was written by Lorca
Esta obra fue escrita por Lorca
He was shot dead (by a terrorist group)
Fue asesinado a tiros (por un grupo terrorista)

NOTE: The passive is not used as often in Spanish as it is in English.

▹ *Use* **estar** *with past participles to describe the results of a previous action or event:*
We threw them away because they were broken
Los tiramos a la basura porque estaban rotos
He's dead
Está muerto

▹ *Compare the use of* **ser** *+ past participle which describes action and* **estar** *+ past participle which describes result in the following:*
The window was broken by the firemen
La ventana fue rota por los bomberos
The window was broken
La ventana estaba rota
It was painted around 1925
Fue pintado hacia 1925
The floor is painted a dark colour
El suelo está pintado de color oscuro

▹ **Ser** *and* **estar** *are both used in impersonal expressions with past participles. As above, the use of* **ser** *implies action while the use of* **estar** *implies result:*
It is understood that the work was never finished
Es sabido que el trabajo nunca se llegó a terminar
It is a proven fact that vaccinations save many lives
Está demostrado que las vacunas salvan muchas vidas

"Ser" and "estar" with adjectives

▹ *Some adjectives can be used with both* **ser** *and* **estar** *but the meaning changes completely depending on the verb:*
Es listo
He's clever
¿Estás listo?
Are you ready?
La química es aburrida
Chemistry is boring
Estoy aburrido
I'm bored

▹ *Other adjectives can also be used with both verbs but the use of* **ser** *describes a characteristic while the use of* **estar** *implies a change:*
Es muy guapo
He's very handsome
Estás muy guapa con ese vestido
You look great in that dress!
Es delgado
He's slim
¡Estás muy delgada!
You're (looking) very slim

For further uses and examples, see main entry.

hotel etc] en primera línea de playa

beachhead ['bi:tʃhed] N cabeza *f* de playa

beachwear ['bi:tʃwɛəʳ] N ropa *f* de playa

beacon ['bi:kən] N **1** (*in port*) faro *m*; (*on aerodrome*) baliza *f*, aerofaro *m*; (*Rad*) radiofaro *m*; (= *fire*) almenara *f*
2 (= *hill*) hacho *m*
CPD ▸ **beacon light** luz *f* de faro ▸ **beacon school** ≈ colegio *m* modelo

bead [bi:d] N **1** (*gen*) cuenta *f*; [*of glass*] abalorio *m*; **beads** (= *necklace*) collar *m*; (*Rel*) rosario *m* • **to tell one's ~s** rezar el rosario
2 [*of dew, sweat*] gota *f*
3 [*of gun*] mira *f* globular • **to draw a ~ on** apuntar a

beaded ['bi:dɪd] ADJ [*dress, cushion*] bordado con cuentas • **his forehead was ~ with sweat** su frente estaba salpicada con gotas de sudor

beading ['bi:dɪŋ] N **1** (*Archit*) astrágalo *m*, contero *m*
2 (*Carpentry*) moldura *f*
3 (*on garment*) canutillo *m*, adorno *m* de cuentas

beadle ['bi:dl] N **1** (*Brit*) (*Univ*) bedel *m*
2 (*Rel*) pertiguero *m*

beady ['bi:dɪ] ADJ • **~ eyes** ojos *mpl* pequeños y brillantes

beady-eyed ['bi:dɪ'aɪd] ADJ de ojos pequeños y brillantes

beagle ['bi:gl] N sabueso *m*, beagle *m*

beak [bi:k] N **1** [*of bird*] pico *m*; (= *nose**) napia* *f*
2 (*Naut*) rostro *m* • **~ of land** promontorio *m*
3 (*Brit**) (= *judge*) magistrado/a *m/f*

beaked [bi:kt] ADJ picudo

beaker ['bi:kəʳ] N vaso *m*; (*Chem*) vaso *m* de precipitación

be-all ['bi:'ɔ:l] N (*also* **be-all and end-all**) único objeto *m*, única cosa *f* que importa • **he is the be-all of her life** él es el único objeto de su vida • **money is not the be-all** el dinero no es lo único que importa

beam [bi:m] N **1** (*Archit*) viga *f*, travesaño *m*; [*of plough*] timón *m*; [*of balance*] astil *m*; (*Mech*) balancín *m*
2 (*Naut*) (= *timber*) bao *m*; (= *width*) manga *f*; ▹ **broad**
3 [*of light, laser*] rayo *m*; (*from beacon, lamp*) haz *m* de luz; (*from radio beacon*) haz *m* de radiofaro • **to drive on full** *or* **main ~** conducir con luz de carretera *or* con luces largas • IDIOMS: • **to be on the ~*** seguir el buen camino • **to be (way) off ~** (*Brit**) andar (totalmente) descaminado
4 (= *smile*) sonrisa *f* radiante • **with a ~ of pleasure** con una sonrisa de placer
5 (*Sport*) barra *f* fija
VT **1** (= *transmit*) [+ *signal*] emitir
2 (= *smile*) • **she ~ed her thanks at me** me lanzó una mirada de agradecimiento
VI **1** (= *shine*) brillar
2 (= *smile*) sonreír satisfecho • **~ing with pride** radiante de orgullo
CPD ▸ **beam lights** (*Aut*) luces *fpl* largas
▸ **beam down** (*Science Fiction*) VT + ADV teletransportar
VI + ADV teletransportarse
▸ **beam up** (*Science Fiction*) VT + ADV teletransportar
VI + ADV teletransportarse

beam-ends [,bi:m'endz] NPL (*Naut*) cabezas *fpl* de los baos (de un buque) • **she was on her beam-ends** (*Naut*) el buque escoraba peligrosamente • IDIOM: • **they are on their beam-ends** están en un grave aprieto, no tienen donde caerse muertos

beaming ['bi:mɪŋ] ADJ sonriente, radiante

bean [bi:n] N **1** (*gen*) frijol *m*, alubia *f* (*Sp*); (*kidney*) frijol *m*, judía *f* (*Sp*), poroto *m* (*S. Cone*); (*broad, haricot*) haba *f*; (*green*) habichuela *f*, judía *f* verde (*Sp*), ejote *m* (*Mex*), poroto *m* verde (*S. Cone*); (*coffee*) grano *m* • **not a ~!*** ¡nada en absoluto! • **I haven't a ~** (*Brit**) estoy pelado*, no tengo un duro (*Sp**), no tengo un peso (*LAm**) • **I didn't make a ~ on the deal*** no saqué ni un céntimo del negocio • IDIOMS: • **to be full of ~s** (*Brit**) estar lleno de vida • **to know how many ~s make five** (*Brit*†*) saber cuántas son dos y dos • **he doesn't know ~s about it** (*US**) no sabe ni papa de eso*, no tiene ni zorra idea (*Sp**) • **not to amount to a hill** *or* **row of ~s*** no valer nada; ▹ **spill¹**
2 (*as form of address*) • **hello, old ~!** (*Brit*†*) ¡hola, macho! (*Sp**), ¡hola, viejo! (*LAm**)
3 (*US**) (= *head, brain*) coco* *m*
CPD ▸ **bean counter*** (*pej*) *contable o gerente obsesionado por los números* ▸ **bean curd** tofu *m*

beanbag ['bi:nbæg] N (*for throwing*) *saquito que se usa para realizar ejercicios gimnásticos*; (= *chair*) *asiento en forma de bolsa rellena de bolitas de poliestireno*

beanburger ['bi:n,bɜ:gəʳ] N *hamburguesa vegetariana preparada con alubias*

beaner‡ ['bi:nəʳ] N (*pej*) *bola lanzada deliberadamente a la cabeza del bateador*

beanery* ['bi:nərɪ] N (*US*) cafetería *f*

beanfeast* ['bi:nfi:st] N, **beano*** ['bi:nəʊ] N (*Brit*) (= *party*) fiesta *f*, juerga *f*; (= *meal*) comilona* *f*

beanpole ['bi:npəʊl] N emparrado *m* • **he's a real ~*** (*fig*) está como un espárrago*

beanshoots ['bi:nʃu:ts] NPL,

beansprouts ['bi:nspraʊts] NPL (*Culin*) brotes *mpl* de soja

beanstalk ['bi:nstɔ:k] N judía *f*

bear¹ [bɛəʳ] N **1** (= *animal*) oso/a *m/f*; (*fig*) (= *man*) grandullón* *m* • **he was a huge ~ of a man** era un hombre grande como un oso • **the Great/Little Bear** la Osa Mayor/Menor • IDIOMS: • **to be like a ~ with a sore head*** estar de un humor de perros* • **to be loaded for ~** (*US**) estar dispuesto para el ataque; ▹ **brown, grizzly, polar**
2 (*also* **teddy bear**) osito *m* de peluche
3 (*Econ*) (= *pessimistic trader*) bajista *mf*
CPD ▸ **bear baiting** *espectáculo en el que se azuzan a unos perros contra un oso* ▸ **bear cub** osezno *m* ▸ **bear garden** (*fig*) manicomio *m*, casa *f* de locos ▸ **bear hug** fuerte abrazo *m*
▸ **bear market** (*Econ*) mercado *m* bajista
▸ **bear pit** (*fig*) manicomio *m*, casa *f* de locos

bear² [bɛəʳ] (PT: **bore**, PP: **borne**) VT
1 (= *support*) [+ *weight*] aguantar, sostener; ▹ **-bearing**
2 (= *take on*) [+ *cost*] correr con, pagar; [+ *responsibility*] cargar con; (*fig*) [+ *burden*] soportar • **the government ~s some responsibility for this crisis** el gobierno tiene parte de responsabilidad en esta crisis • **he bore no responsibility for what had happened** no era responsable de lo que había pasado • **they ~ most of the responsibility for elderly relatives** cargan con la mayor parte de la responsabilidad de atender a familiares ancianos
3 (= *endure*) [+ *pain, suspense*] soportar, aguantar • **I can't ~ the suspense** no puedo soportar *or* aguantar el suspense • **I can't ~ him** no lo puedo ver, no lo soporto *or* aguanto • **the dog can't ~ being shut in** el perro no soporta estar encerrado • **I can't ~ to look** no puedo mirar • **he can't ~ to talk about it** no puede hablar de ello • **he can't ~ to see her suffer** no soporta verla sufrir; ▹ **brunt**
4 (= *bring*) [+ *news, gift*] traer • **a letter ~ing important news** una carta que trae/traía importantes noticias
5 (= *carry*) llevar, portar (*liter*) • **protesters ~ing placards** manifestantes *mfpl* llevando *or* portando pancartas • **to ~ arms** (*frm*) portar armas (*frm*) • **he bore himself like a soldier** (*posture*) tenía un porte soldadesco; (*behaviour*) se comportó como un verdadero soldado • **there was dignity in the way he bore himself** había dignidad en su porte
6 (= *have, display*) [+ *signature, date, message, title*] llevar; [+ *mark, scar*] conservar • **his ideas bore little relation to reality** sus ideas no tenían mucha relación con la realidad • **she bore no resemblance to the girl I knew 20 years ago** no se parecía en nada a la chica que había conocido 20 años atrás • **the room bore all the signs of a violent struggle** el cuarto conservaba todas las huellas de una riña violenta • **to ~ a grudge** guardar rencor • **she ~s him no ill-will** (*grudge*) no le guarda rencor; (*hostility*) no siente ninguna animadversión hacia él; ▹ **witness, mind**
7 (= *stand up to*) [+ *examination*] resistir • **her story won't ~ scrutiny** su historia no resistirá un análisis • **it doesn't ~ thinking about*** da horror solo pensarlo • **the film ~s comparison with far more expensive productions** la película puede compararse con producciones mucho más caras
8 (*liter*) (= *produce*) [+ *fruit*] dar; (*frm*) [+ *child*] dar a luz a; (*Econ*) [+ *interest*] devengar • **her hard work bore fruit when she was promoted** sus esfuerzos dieron fruto cuando la ascendieron • **she bore him a daughter** le dio una hija
VI **1** (= *move*) • **to ~ (to the) right/left** torcer *or* girar a la derecha/izquierda
2 • **to ~ on sth** (= *relate to*) guardar relación con algo, tener que ver con algo; (= *influence*) influir en algo; ▹ **bring**
3 (= *afflict*) • **his misdeeds bore heavily on his conscience** sus fechorías le pesaban en la conciencia
▸ **bear away** VT + ADV llevarse • **injured people were borne away in ambulances** se llevaron a los heridos en ambulancias • **the wreckage was borne away by** *or* **on the tide** los restos del naufragio fueron arrastrados por la corriente
▸ **bear down** VI + ADV **1** (= *come closer*) • **to ~ down on sth/sb** echarse encima a algo/algn • **the ferry was ~ing down on us** el ferry se nos echaba encima
2 (= *press down*) presionar • **you have to ~ down hard on the screw** hay que apretar fuerte el tornillo
3 (= *push*) (*in childbirth*) empujar
▸ **bear in on, bear in upon** VI + ADV + PREP (*frm*) • **after half an hour it was borne in (up)on him that no one was listening** después de media hora cayó en la cuenta de que *or* se percató de que nadie le estaba escuchando
▸ **bear off** VT + ADV = **bear away**
▸ **bear on** VI + PREP [+ *person*] interesar; [+ *subject*] tener que ver con
▸ **bear out** VT + ADV confirmar • **the facts seem to ~ out her story** los hechos parecen confirmar su historia • **their prediction was not borne out by events** sus predicciones no se vieron confirmadas por los sucesos • **perhaps you can ~ me out on this, Alan?** Alan, ¿me puedes confirmar que estoy en lo cierto?
▸ **bear up*** VI + ADV • **how are you ~ing up?** ¿qué tal ese ánimo? • **she's ~ing up well under the circumstances** lo está llevando bien dadas las circunstancias • **"how are you?" — "~ing up!"** —¿qué tal? —¡voy aguantando! • **~ up! it's nearly over** ¡ánimo,

que ya queda poco! • **the children bore up well during the visit to the museum** los niños aguantaron bien la vista al museo
▸ **bear with** (VI + PREP) tener paciencia con • **thank you for ~ing with us during this difficult time** gracias por tener paciencia con nosotros en estos tiempos difíciles • **if I repeat myself, please ~ with me** les ruego que tengan paciencia si me repito • **~ with it, it gets better** ten un poco de paciencia *or* aguanta un poco, ya verás como mejora • **if you'll ~ with me, I'll explain** si esperas un poco, te explico

bearable [ˈbɛərəbl] (ADJ) soportable

beard [bɪəd] (N) **1** barba *f* • **to have** *or* **wear a ~** llevar barba
2 (*Bot*) arista *f*
(VT) desafiar

bearded [ˈbɪədɪd] (ADJ) (*gen*) con barba; (*heavily*) barbudo

beardless [ˈbɪədlɪs] (ADJ) barbilampiño, lampiño; [*youth*] imberbe

bearer [ˈbɛərəʳ] (N) **1** (= *bringer*) [*of tradition, culture, idea*] poseedor(a) *m/f*; [*of burden*] porteador(a) *m/f*, portador(a) *m/f*; [*of letter, news*] portador(a) *m/f* • **I hate to be the ~ of bad news** siento traer malas noticias, siento ser portador de malas noticias (*frm*)
2 (= *possessor*) [*of cheque*] portador(a) *m/f*; [*of title*] poseedor(a) *m/f*; [*of credentials, office, passport*] titular *mf*
3 (= *servant*) porteador *m*; (*also* **pallbearer**) portador(a) *m/f* del féretro; (*also* **stretcher-bearer**) camillero/a *m/f*; ▹ **flag, standard**
(CPD) ▸ **bearer bond** título *m* al portador

bearing [ˈbɛərɪŋ] (N) **1** (= *relevance*) relación *f* • **this has no ~ on the matter** esto no tiene relación *or* no tiene nada que ver con el asunto • **this has a direct ~ on our future** esto influye directamente en nuestro futuro
2 (*in navigation*) rumbo *m* • **to take a ~ (on sth)** tomar una demora (de algo) • **to find** *or* **get one's ~s** (*fig*) orientarse • **to lose one's ~s** (*fig*) desorientarse
3 (= *posture*) porte *m*; (= *behaviour*) comportamiento *m*, modales *mpl*
4 (*Mech*) cojinete *m*; ▹ **ball**
5 (*Heraldry*) blasón *m*; ▹ **armorial**

-bearing [ˈbɛərɪŋ] (ADJ) (*ending in compounds*) • **oil-bearing rock** roca *f* que contiene petróleo • **malaria-bearing mosquitos** mosquitos *mpl* portadores de malaria • **a large fruit-bearing tree** un gran árbol frutal • **non-weight-bearing exercise, such as swimming and cycling** un ejercicio que no implique cargar peso, como la natación o el ciclismo; ▹ **interest-bearing, load-bearing**

bearish [ˈbɛərɪʃ] (ADJ) [*person, attitude*] pesimista; [*market*] (de tendencia) bajista

bearskin [ˈbɛəskɪn] (N) **1** piel *f* de oso • **a ~ rug** una alfombra de piel de oso
2 (*Mil*) *gorro militar de piel de oso*

beast [biːst] (N) **1** (= *animal*) bestia *f* • **~ of burden** bestia *f* de carga • **the king of the ~s** el rey de los animales • **the Beast** (*Rel*) la Bestia • **the mark of the Beast** (*Rel*) la marca de la Bestia; ▹ **wild**
2* (= *person*) bestia* *mf* • **that ~ of a policeman** aquel bestia de policía* • **what a ~ he is!** ¡qué bruto *or* bestia es!* • **you ~!** ¡animal!*
3* (= *thing*) • **it's a ~ of a day** es un día horrible* • **it's a ~ of a job** es un trabajo de chinos* • **a good thriller is a rare ~ indeed** escasean las buenas novelas/películas de suspense • **this is quite a different ~** esto ya es otra cosa

beastliness [ˈbiːstlɪnɪs] (N) bestialidad *f*

beastly [ˈbiːstlɪ] (ADJ) (COMPAR: **beastlier**, SUPERL: **beastliest**) **1**†* (= *horrid*) espantoso • **that was a ~ thing to do** eso sí que fue cruel • **you were ~ to me** te portaste muy mal conmigo • **where's that ~ book?** ¿dónde está el maldito libro ese?
2†† (= *animal*) bestial
(ADV) (*Brit*†*) • **it's ~ awkward** es terriblemente difícil • **it's ~ cold** hace un frío de muerte

beat [biːt] (VB: PT: **beat**, PP: **beaten**) (N)
1 (= *stroke, blow*) [*of drum*] redoble *m*; [*of heart*] latido *m* • **her heart missed** *or* **skipped a ~** le dio un vuelco el corazón • **he replied without missing a ~** (*fig*) contestó sin alterarse
2 (= *beating*) [*of drums*] redoble *m*; [*of waves, rain*] batir *m* • **the ~ of wings** el batir de alas; ▹ **drum**
3 (*Mus*) (= *rhythm*) compás *m*, ritmo *m*; (= *rhythmic unit*) tiempo *m*; [*of conductor*] • **his ~ is not very clear** no marca el compás con mucha claridad
4 (= *route*) [*of policeman*] ronda *f* • **he had spent 20 years on the ~** había hecho la ronda durante 20 años • **we need more officers on the ~** deberíamos tener más agentes haciendo la ronda • **that's rather off my ~** (*fig*) no es lo mío; ▹ **pound**
5 (*also* **beatnik**) beatnik *mf*
(VT) **1** (= *strike, thrash*) [+ *surface*] golpear, dar golpes en; [+ *drum*] tocar; [+ *carpet*] sacudir; [+ *metal*] batir; (*Culin*) [+ *eggs, cream*] batir; (*Hunting*) (*to raise game*) batir • **to ~ sth flat** aplanar algo a golpes • **I had Latin ~en into me at school** en el colegio me enseñaron latín a fuerza de golpes • **he ~ his fists on the table** aporreó la mesa con los puños, dio golpes con los puños en la mesa • **they had to ~ a path through the jungle** tuvieron que abrirse paso a través de la jungla; ▹ **breast, path, retreat, track**
2 (= *beat up*) [+ *person*] pegar • **he was badly ~en** le habían dado una buena paliza • **to ~ sb's brains out*** partir la crisma a algn*, partir la cabeza a algn • **to ~ sb to death** matar a algn a golpes *or* de una paliza
3 (= *flap*) [+ *wings*] batir
4 (*Mus*) • **to ~ time** marcar el compás
5 (= *defeat*) [+ *team, adversary*] ganar a; [+ *problem*] superar • **he ~ Smith by five seconds** le ganó a Smith por cinco segundos • **Arsenal ~ Leeds 5-1** el Arsenal ganó 5-1 contra el Leeds, el Arsenal derrotó al Leeds 5-1 • **she was easily ~en into third place** fue fácil ganarla haciéndola quedar en el tercer puesto • **she doesn't know when she's ~en** no sabe reconocer que ha perdido • **our prices cannot be ~en** nuestros precios son insuperables *or* imbatibles • **we've got to ~ inflation** tenemos que superar la inflación • **"how did he escape?" — "(it) ~s me!"*** —¿cómo escapó? —¡no me lo explico! *or* —¡(no tengo) ni idea! • IDIOM: • **if you can't ~ them, join them** si no puedes con ellos, únete a ellos; ▹ **hollow**
6 (= *better*) [+ *record*] batir • **he ~ his own previous best time** batió su propio récord • **it ~s sitting at home doing nothing*** es mejor que estar en casa sin hacer nada • **you can't ~ a nice cup of tea*** no hay nada mejor que una buena taza de té • **coffee ~s tea any day*** el café da cien vueltas al té • **that ~s everything!*** ¡eso es el colmo! • **can you ~ it** *or* **that?*** ¿has visto cosa igual? • **~ it!*** ¡lárgate!*
7 (= *pre-empt*) adelantarse • **if we leave early, we can ~ the rush hour** si salimos temprano, nos evitamos la hora punta • **I'll ~ you to that tree** ¿a que llego antes que tú a aquel árbol?, te echo una carrera hasta aquel árbol • **they determined to be the first to get there but the other team ~ them to it (by 36 hours)** estaban decididos a llegar los primeros pero el otro equipo les ganó *or* se les adelantó (en 36 horas) • **I could see she was about to object but I ~ her to it** me di cuenta de que iba a poner objeciones pero me adelanté
(VI) **1** (= *hit*) • **to ~ on** *or* **against** *or* **at sth** [*rain, waves*] azotar algo; [*person*] dar golpes en algo, golpear algo • **the waves ~ against the harbour wall** las olas azotaban el muro del puerto • **someone was ~ing on the door** alguien estaba dando golpes en *or* golpeando *or* aporreando la puerta • **she began ~ing at the flames with a pillow** empezó a apagar las llamas a golpes con una almohada
2 (= *sound rhythmically*) [*heart*] latir; [*drum*] redoblar; [*wings*] batir
3 (*Hunting*) (*to raise game*) batir • IDIOM: • **to ~ about the bush** andarse con rodeos • **let's not ~ about the bush** no nos andemos con rodeos • **stop ~ing about the bush!** ¡deja de andarte con rodeos!
(ADJ)* **1** (= *exhausted*) rendido, molido*; ▹ **dead**
2 (= *defeated*) • **the problem has me ~** me doy por vencido con este problema • **Gerald had him ~ on the practical side of things** Gerald le daba mil vueltas en el aspecto práctico de las cosas
(CPD) ▸ **beat box** caja *f* de ritmos ▸ **beat generation** generación *f* beat ▸ **beat music** *música rock de las décadas de los cincuenta y sesenta*
▸ **beat back** (VT + ADV) **1** (= *fight off*) [+ *attack*] rechazar • **England won 4-1, ~ing back challenges from the U.S. and France** Inglaterra ganó 4-1 frente al reto que suponían EEUU y Francia
2 (= *force back*) hacer retroceder • **they were ~en back by smoke and flames** el humo y las llamas les hicieron retroceder
▸ **beat down** (VT + ADV) **1** [+ *door*] derribar a golpes
2 [+ *seller*] • **he tried to ~ me down on the price** intentó que le rebajase el precio, intentó que se lo dejase más barato • **I ~ him down to £20** conseguí que me lo rebajara a 20 libras
(VI + ADV) [*sun*] caer a plomo; [*rain*] caer con fuerza • **the rain was ~ing down outside** fuera la lluvia caía con fuerza
▸ **beat off** (VT + ADV) **1** [+ *competition*] • **they ~ off competition from other companies to win the contract** derrotaron a otras compañías que competían por conseguir el contrato
2 [+ *attack, challenge*] = **beat back**
▸ **beat out** (VT + ADV) **1** [+ *flames*] apagar (a golpes)
2 (*Mus*) [+ *rhythm*] marcar; [+ *tune*] tocar (con mucho ritmo)
3 (*US*) (= *defeat*) [+ *person*] derrotar
4 [+ *dent*] quitar (a golpes)
▸ **beat up** (VT + ADV) **1** [+ *person*] dar una paliza a, pegar
2 (*Culin*) batir
▸ **beat up on** (VI + ADV + PREP) (*US**) (= *hit*) dar una paliza a, pegar; (= *bully*) intimidar; (= *criticize*) arremeter contra

beatable [ˈbiːtəbəl] (ADJ) • **to be ~** [*team, opponent*] no ser invencible

beaten [ˈbiːtn] (PP) *of* **beat**
(ADJ) **1** (= *shaped, compacted*) [*metal, earth*] batido • IDIOM: • **off the ~ track** (= *isolated*) apartado, retirado; (= *unfrequented*) fuera de los lugares donde va todo el mundo • **to get off the ~ track** apartarse de los lugares donde va todo el mundo

b

2 (= *defeated*) [*person*] derrotado • **he was a ~ man** era un hombre derrotado
beaten-up* ['bi:tn'ʌp] (ADJ) [*car*] hecho un cacharro*; [*clothes*] hecho polvo*
beater ['bi:təʳ] (N) **1** (*Culin*) batidora *f*; (*also* **carpet beater**) sacudidor *m*; ▹ **panel, wife, world**
2 (*Hunting*) ojeador(a) *m/f*, batidor(a) *m/f*
beatific [,bi:ə'tɪfɪk] (ADJ) beatífico • **a ~ smile** una sonrisa beatífica
beatifically [,bi:ə'tɪfɪklɪ] (ADV) beatíficamente
beatification [bi:,ætɪfɪ'keɪʃən] (N) beatificación *f*
beatify [bi:'ætɪfaɪ] (VT) beatificar
beating ['bi:tɪŋ] (N) **1** (= *striking*) [*of drum*] redoble *m*; [*of heart*] latido *m*, pulsación *f* • **the ~ of wings** el batir de alas • **the ~ of the rain/the waves** el batir *or* el azote de la lluvia/las olas
2 (= *punishment*) paliza *f*, golpiza *f* (*LAm*) • **to get a ~** recibir una paliza • **to give sb a ~** dar una paliza a algn • **to take a ~: our team took a ~** a nuestro equipo le dieron una paliza*, nuestro equipo recibió una paliza* • **the dollar is taking a ~ on the currency markets** le están dando una paliza al dólar en los mercados de divisas*
3 (= *bettering*) • **that score will take some ~** será difícil superar esa puntuación
4 (*Hunting*) batida *f*
beating-up [,bi:tɪŋ'ʌp] (N) paliza *f*
beatitude [bi:'ætɪtju:d] (N) beatitud *f* • **the Beatitudes** las Bienaventuranzas
beatnik ['bi:tnɪk] (N) beatnik *mf*
Beatrice ['bɪətrɪs] (N) Beatriz
beat-up* ['bi:tʌp] (ADJ) hecho polvo*, de perras*
beau [bəʊ] (N) (PL: **beaus, beaux** [bəʊz]) (= *fop*) petimetre *m*, dandy *m*; (= *ladies' man*) galán *m*; (= *suitor*) pretendiente *m*; (= *sweetheart*) novio *m*
(ADJ) • **~ ideal** lo bello ideal; (= *person*) tipo *m* ideal
Beaufort scale ['bəʊfət,skeɪl] (N) escala *f* Beaufort
beaut* [bju:t] (N) • **it's a ~** es sensacional, es pistonudo (*Sp**)
beauteous ['bju:tɪəs] (ADJ) (*poet*) bello
beautician [bju:'tɪʃən] (N) esteticista *mf*
beautiful ['bju:tɪfʊl] (ADJ) hermoso, bello, lindo (*esp LAm*) • **what a ~ house!** ¡qué casa más preciosa! • **the ~ people** la gente guapa
(CPD) ▸ **beautiful game** (= *football*) • **the ~ game** el fútbol
beautifully ['bju:tɪflɪ] (ADV) (= *wonderfully*) maravillosamente; (= *precisely*) perfectamente • **she plays ~** toca a la perfección • **that will do ~** así sirve perfectamente
beautify ['bju:tɪfaɪ] (VT) embellecer
beauty ['bju:tɪ] (N) **1** (= *quality*) belleza *f*, hermosura *f* • **the ~ of it is that ...** lo mejor de esto es que ... • **that's the ~ of it** eso es lo que tiene de bueno • PROVERBS: • **~ is in the eye of the beholder** todo es según el cristal con que se mira • **~ is only skin-deep** la belleza no lo es todo, la belleza es algo solo superficial
2 (= *person, thing*) belleza *f*, preciosidad *f* • **isn't he a little ~?** (= *child*) ¡mira qué rico es el niño! • **she's no ~** no es ninguna belleza • **Beauty and the Beast** la Bella y la Bestia • **it's a ~** es una preciosidad • **that was a ~!** (= *stroke etc*) ¡qué golpe más fino!
3 beauties (= *attractions*) maravillas *fpl* • **the beauties of Majorca** las maravillas de Mallorca
(CPD) ▸ **beauty competition, beauty contest** concurso *m* de belleza ▸ **beauty consultant** esteticista *mf* ▸ **beauty cream** crema *f* de belleza ▸ **beauty editor** directora *f* de la sección de belleza ▸ **beauty pageant** (*US*) concurso *m* de belleza ▸ **beauty parlour, beauty parlor** (*US*) salón *m* de belleza ▸ **beauty product** producto *m* de belleza ▸ **beauty queen** reina *f* de la belleza ▸ **beauty salon** salón *m* de belleza ▸ **beauty shop** (*US*) salón *m* de belleza ▸ **beauty sleep** (*hum*) primer sueño *m* • **I need my ~ sleep** necesito dormir mis horas (para luego estar bien) ▸ **beauty spot** (*on face*) lunar *m* postizo; (*in country*) lugar *m* pintoresco
beaver ['bi:vəʳ] (N) **1** castor *m*
2 (*esp US***) coño** *m*
▸ **beaver away*** (VI + ADV) trabajar con empeño
bebop ['bi:bɒp] (N) bebop *m*
becalmed [bɪ'kɑ:md] (ADJ) **1** [*ship*] al pairo
2 (*fig*) [*economy, team*] estancado • **to remain ~** permanecer estancado
became [bɪ'keɪm] (PT) *of* **become**
because [bɪ'kɒz] (CONJ) porque • **I came ~ you asked me to** vine porque me lo pediste • **~ he was ill he couldn't go** no pudo ir por estar enfermo • **just ~ he has two cars he thinks he's somebody** solo porque tiene dos coches se cree todo un personaje • **~ of** (*prep*) por • **I did it ~ of you** lo hice por ti • **many families break up ~ of a lack of money** muchas familias se deshacen por *or* debido a la falta de dinero
bechamel [,beɪʃə'mel] (N) (*also* **bechamel sauce**) besamel *f*
beck¹ [bek] (N) • IDIOM: • **to be at the ~ and call of** estar siempre a disposición de
beck² [bek] (N) (*N Engl*) arroyo *m*, riachuelo *m*
beckon ['bekən] (VT) **1** (= *signal*) llamar con señas, hacer señas a • **he ~ed me in/over** me hizo señas para que entrara/me acercara
2 (= *attract*) llamar, atraer
(VI) **1** (= *signal*) • **to ~ to sb** llamar a algn con señas, hacer señas a algn
2 (= *be attractive*) [*bright lights, fame*] ejercer su atracción
3 (= *loom*) avecinarse, estar a la vuelta de la esquina
become [bɪ'kʌm] (PT: **became**, PP: **become**)
(VI) **1** (= *grow to be*) • **to ~ famous** hacerse famoso • **to ~ sad** ponerse triste • **to ~ ill** ponerse enfermo, enfermar • **to ~ old** hacerse *or* volverse viejo • **to ~ angry** enfadarse • **to ~ red** ponerse rojo, enrojecerse • **we became very worried** empezamos a inquietarnos muchísimo • **he became blind** (se) quedó ciego • **this is becoming difficult** esto se está poniendo difícil • **to ~ accustomed to sth** acostumbrarse a algo • **it became known that ...** se supo que ..., llegó a saberse que ... • **when he ~s 21** cuando cumpla los 21 años
2 (= *turn into*) convertirse en, transformarse en • **the building has ~ a cinema** el edificio se ha convertido *or* transformado en cine • **the gas ~s liquid** el gas se convierte en líquido
3 (= *acquire position of*) (*through study*) hacerse; (*by promotion etc*) llegar a ser • **to ~ a doctor** hacerse médico • **to ~ professor** llegar a ser catedrático • **he became king in 1911** subió al trono en 1911 • **later this lady became his wife** esta dama llegó a ser su esposa más tarde • **to ~ a father** convertirse en padre
(IMPERS VB) • **what has ~ of him?** ¿qué ha sido de él? • **what will ~ of me?** ¿qué será de mí? • **whatever can have ~ of that book?** ¿dónde estará ese libro?
(VT) (= *look nice on*) favorecer, sentar bien • **that thought does not ~ you** ese pensamiento es indigno de ti; ▹ BECOME
becoming† [bɪ'kʌmɪŋ] (ADJ) **1** (= *fetching*) [*clothes, hairstyle, hat*] favorecedor, sentador (*LAm*) • **that dress is very ~** ese vestido es muy favorecedor, ese vestido te sienta muy bien
2 (= *suitable*) [*conduct, language*] apropiado • **it is not ~ for young ladies to speak like that** no es apropiado que las señoritas hablen así, no es propio de señoritas hablar así
becomingly† [bɪ'kʌmɪŋlɪ] (ADV)
1 (= *fetchingly*) [*blush, smile*] de forma encantadora; [*dress*] de modo favorecedor
2 (= *suitably*) apropiadamente
becquerel [,bekə'rel] (N) becquerelio *m*
BECTU ['bektu] (N ABBR) (*Brit*) = **Broadcasting, Entertainment, Cinematographic and Theatre Union**
BEd [bi:'ed] (N ABBR) = **Bachelor of Education**
bed [bed] (N) **1** (= *furniture*) cama *f* • **I was in bed** estaba en la cama • **could you give me a bed for the night?** ¿me puede hospedar *or* alojar esta noche? • **to get into bed** meterse en la cama • **to get sb into bed** (= *have sex*) llevarse a algn a la cama • **to get into bed with sb** (*fig*) (= *agree to work together*) aliarse con algn • **to go to bed** acostarse • **to go to bed with sb** acostarse con algn • **to make the bed** hacer la cama • **to put a child to bed** acostar a un niño • **to put a paper to bed** terminar la redacción de un número • **to stay in bed** (*because ill*) guardar cama; (*because lazy*) quedarse en la cama • **to take to one's bed** irse a la cama • IDIOMS: • **to get out of bed (on) the wrong side** (*Brit*) • **get up (on) the wrong side of the bed** (*US*) levantarse con el pie izquierdo • **you've made your bed, now you must lie in** *or* **on it** quien mala cama hace en ella se yace
2 [*of animal*] lecho *m*
3 [*of river*] cauce *m*, lecho *m*; [*of sea*] fondo *m*
4 (= *flower bed*) arriate *m*, parterre *m*; (= *vegetable bed*) arriate *m*; (= *oyster bed*) banco *m*, vivero *m* • IDIOM: • **his life's no bed of roses** su vida no es un lecho de rosas
5 (= *layer*) [*of coal, ore*] estrato *m*, capa *f*; (*in road-building*) capa *f*; (*Archit, Tech*) base *f* • **served on a bed of lettuce/rice** servido sobre una base de lechuga/arroz
(VT) **1** (*Archit etc*) fijar, engastar
2†* [+ *woman*] llevar a la cama, acostarse con
(CPD) ▸ **bed and board** comida *f* y cama, pensión *f* completa ▸ **bed and breakfast** pensión *f* (con desayuno) ▸ **bed bath** (*Med*) • **they gave her a bed bath** la lavaron en la cama ▸ **bed jacket** mañanita *f* ▸ **bed linen** ropa *f* de cama ▸ **bed of nails** cama *f* de clavos ▸ **bed rest** reposo *m* en cama ▸ **bed settee** sofá-cama *m*
▸ **bed down** (VI + ADV) (= *go to bed*) acostarse
(VT + ADV) [+ *children*] acostar; [+ *animals*] hacer un lecho para
▸ **bed out** (VT + ADV) [+ *plants*] plantar en un macizo

BED AND BREAKFAST
Se llama **Bed and Breakfast** a una casa particular de hospedaje tanto en el campo como en la ciudad, que ofrece cama y desayuno a tarifas inferiores a las de un hotel. El servicio se suele anunciar con carteles colocados en las ventanas del establecimiento, en el jardín o en la carretera y en ellos aparece a menudo únicamente el símbolo **B&B**.

bedaub [bɪ'dɔ:b] (VT) embadurnar
bedazzle [bɪ'dæzəl] (VT) deslumbrar, encandilar • **many people are ~d by fame** mucha gente está deslumbrada por la fama

BECOME, GO, GET

The translation of **become/go/get** *depends on the context and the type of change involved and how it is regarded. Very often there is more than one possible translation, or even a special verb to translate* **get** *+ adjective (e.g.* **get angry - enfadarse**), *but here are some general hints.*

Become *etc* **+ adjective**

▹ *Use* **ponerse** *to talk about temporary but normal changes:*

I got quite ill
Me puse muy malo
He went pale
Se puso blanco
You've got very brown
Te has puesto muy moreno
He got very angry
Se puso furioso

▹ *Use* **volverse** *to refer to sudden, longer-lasting and unpredictable changes, particularly those affecting the mind:*

He has become very impatient in the last few years
Se ha vuelto muy impaciente estos últimos años
She went mad
Se volvió loca

▹ *Use* **quedar(se)** *especially when talking about changes that are permanent, involve deterioration and are due to external circumstances. Their onset may or may not be sudden:*

He went blind
(Se) quedó ciego
Goya went deaf
Goya (se) quedó sordo

Quedar(se) *is also used to talk about pregnancy:*

She became pregnant
(Se) quedó embarazada

▹ *Use* **hacerse** *for states resulting from effort or from a gradual, cumulative process:*

They became very famous
Se hicieron muy famosos
The pain became unbearable
El dolor se hizo insoportable

▹ *Use* **llegar a ser** *to suggest reaching a peak:*

The heat became stifling
El calor llegó a ser agobiante

Become *etc* **+ noun**

▹ *Use* **hacerse** *for career goals and religious or political persuasions:*

He became a lawyer
Se hizo abogado
I became a Catholic in 1990
Me hice católico en 1990
He became a member of the Green Party
Se hizo miembro del Partido Verde

▹ *Use* **llegar a** *+ noun and* **llegar a ser** *+ phrase for reaching a peak after a period of gradual change. This construction is often used to talk about professional accomplishments:*

If you don't make more effort, you'll never get to be a teacher
Si no te esfuerzas más, no llegarás a profesor
Castelar became one of the most important politicians of his time
Castelar llegó a ser uno de los políticos más importantes de su época
Football became an obsession for him
El fútbol llegó a ser una obsesión para él

▹ *Use* **convertirse en** *for long-lasting changes in character, substance and kind which take place gradually:*

Those youngsters went on to become delinquents
Aquellos jóvenes se convirtieron después en delincuentes
Over the years I have become a more tolerant person
Con los años me he convertido en una persona más tolerante
Water turns into steam
El agua se convierte en vapor

▹ *Use* **quedar(se)** *+ adjective to talk about changes, particularly when they are permanent, for the worse and due to external circumstances. Their onset may or may not be sudden:*

She became a widow
(Se) quedó viuda

▹ *To translate* **have turned into** *or* **have become** *etc + noun in emphatic phrases particularly about people, you can use* **estar hecho un(a)** *+ noun:*

Juan has become a really good pianist
Juan está hecho todo un pianista

For further uses and examples, see **become, go, get, turn**

bedazzled [bɪ'dæzəld] (ADJ) deslumbrado
bedbug ['bedbʌg] (N) chinche *m or f*
bedchamber† ['bed,tʃeɪmbəʳ] (N) cámara *f*, aposentos *mpl*
bedclothes ['bedkləʊðz] (NPL) ropa *fsing* de cama
bedcover ['bedkʌvəʳ] (N) = **bedspread**
bedcovers ['bedkʌvəz] (NPL) mantas *fpl*, frazadas *fpl* (*LAm*)
-bedded ['bedɪd] (ADJ) (*ending in compounds*) • **twin-bedded room** habitación *f* doble
bedding ['bedɪŋ] (N) ropa *f* de cama; (*for animal*) cama *f*
(CPD) ▸ **bedding plant** planta *f* de parterre
Bede [bi:d] (N) Beda • **the Venerable ~** el venerable Beda
bedeck [bɪ'dek] (VT) engalanar, adornar
bedecked [bɪ'dekt] (ADJ) • **to be ~ with** estar engalanado con • **flower-bedecked** engalanado con flores
bedevil [bɪ'devəl] (VT) • **to be ~led by problems** [*project*] estar plagado de problemas • **the team has been ~led by injuries** el equipo ha sufrido muchas lesiones • **an industry ~led by rising costs** una industria aquejada por el aumento de los costes
bedfellow ['bedfeləʊ] (N) compañero/a *m/f* de cama • **they are** *or* **make strange ~s** (*fig*) forman una extraña pareja
bedframe ['bedfreɪm] (N) bastidor *m* de la cama
bedhead ['bedhed] (N) testero *m*, cabecera *f*
bedlam ['bedləm] (N) **1** (= *uproar*) alboroto *m* • **it was sheer ~** la confusión era total • **~ broke out** se armó la de San Quintín*
2 (*Hist*) (= *asylum*) manicomio *m*
bedmate ['bedmeɪt] (N) = **bedfellow**
Bedouin ['bedʊɪn] (ADJ) beduino
(N) (PL: **Bedouin** *or* **Bedouins**) beduino/a *m/f*
bedpan ['bedpæn] (N) bacinilla *f* (de cama)
bedpost ['bedpəʊst] (N) columna *f or* pilar *m* de cama
bedraggled [bɪ'drægld] (ADJ) [*person*] desaliñado; [*hair, feathers, fur*] enmarañado; [*flowers*] mustio
bedridden ['bedrɪdn] (ADJ) postrado en la cama
bedrock ['bedrɒk] (N) (*Geol*) lecho *m* de roca; (*fig*) lo fundamental, base *f*
bedroll ['bedrəʊl] (N) petate *m*
bedroom ['bedrʊm] (N) dormitorio *m*, habitación *f*, recámara *f* (*CAm, Mex*) • **three-bedroom flat** piso *m or* (*LAm*) departamento *m* de tres dormitorios
(CPD) ▸ **bedroom eyes*** ojos *mpl* seductores ▸ **bedroom farce** comedia *f* de alcoba ▸ **bedroom slippers** pantuflas *fpl*, zapatillas *fpl* (*Sp*) ▸ **bedroom suburb** (*US*) ciudad *f* dormitorio ▸ **bedroom suite** juego *m* de muebles para dormitorio ▸ **bedroom tax*** (*Brit*) *reducción en el subsidio de la vivienda de aquellos que tienen más habitaciones de las que el gobierno estima necesarias*
-bedroomed ['bedrʊmd] (ADJ) (*ending in compounds*) • **a five-bedroomed house** una casa con cinco dormitorios
Beds [beds] (N ABBR) (*Brit*) = **Bedfordshire**
bedside ['bedsaɪd] (N) cabecera *f* • **to wait at the ~ of** esperar a la cabecera de
(CPD) ▸ **bedside lamp** lámpara *f* de noche ▸ **bedside manner** • **to have a good ~ manner** tener mucho tacto con los enfermos ▸ **bedside rug** alfombrilla *f* de cama ▸ **bedside table** mesilla *f* de noche
bedsit* ['bedsɪt] (N), **bedsitter** ['bed'sɪtəʳ] (N), **bedsitting room** ['bed'sɪtɪŋrʊm] (N) (*Brit*) *habitación amueblada, cuyo alquiler incluye cocina y baño comunes*
bedsocks ['bedsɒks] (NPL) calcetines *mpl* de cama
bedsore ['bedsɔːʳ] (N) úlcera *f* de decúbito
bedspread ['bedspred] (N) colcha *f*, cubrecama *m*
bedstead ['bedsted] (N) cuja *f*, armazón *m or f* de cama
bedstraw ['bedstrɔː] (N) (*Bot*) cuajaleche *m*, amor *m* de hortelano
bedtime ['bedtaɪm] (N) hora *f* de acostarse • **it's past your ~** ya deberías estar acostado • **ten o'clock is my usual ~** normalmente me voy a la cama a las diez • **bedtime!** ¡a la cama!
(CPD) ▸ **bedtime story** cuento *m* (*para dormir a un niño*)
bed-wetting ['bedwetɪŋ] (N) incontinencia *f* nocturna, enuresis *f* (*frm*)
bedworthy* ['bed,wɜːðɪ] (ADJ) atractivo
bee [bi:] (N) **1** (*Zool*) abeja *f* • IDIOMS: • **to have a bee in one's bonnet about sth** tener algo metido entre ceja y ceja • **he thinks he's the bee's knees*** se cree la mar de listo *or* de elegante* *etc*
2 (*esp US*) círculo *m* social; ▸ **spelling**
(CPD) ▸ **bee eater** (*Orn*) abejaruco *m* ▸ **bee sting** picadura *f* de abeja
Beeb* [bi:b] (N) • **the ~** (*Brit*) la BBC
beech [bi:tʃ] (N) (= *tree*) haya *f*; (= *wood*) hayedo *m*
(CPD) ▸ **beech grove** hayal *m* ▸ **beech tree** haya *f*
beechmast ['bi:tʃmɑ:st] (N) hayucos *mpl*
beechnut ['bi:tʃnʌt] (N) hayuco *m*
beechwood ['bi:tʃwʊd] (N) **1** (= *group of trees*) hayedo *m*, hayal *m*
2 (= *material*) (madera *f* de) haya *f*
beef [bi:f] (N) **1** (*Culin*) carne *f* de vaca *or* (*LAm*) de res • **roast ~** rosbif *m*, carne *f* asada (*LAm*)
2* (= *brawn*) músculos *mpl*
3 (*esp US**) (= *complaint*) queja *f*
(VI)* (= *complain*) quejarse (**about** de)

b

CPD ▸ **beef cattle** ganado *m* vacuno ▸ **beef olive** *picadillo envuelto en una lonja de carne y cocinado en salsa* ▸ **beef sausage** salchicha *f* de carne de vaca ▸ **beef tea** caldo *m* de carne (*para enfermos*)
▸ **beef up*** VT + ADV [+ *essay, speech*] reforzar, fortalecer
beefburger ['bi:f,bɜ:gəʳ] N hamburguesa *f*
beefcake* ['bi:fkeɪk] N (*hum*) cachas* *m inv*
beefeater ['bi:f,i:təʳ] N (*Brit*) alabardero *m* de la Torre de Londres
beefsteak ['bi:fsteɪk] N biftec *m*, bistec *m*, bife *m* (*S. Cone*)
beefy* ['bi:fɪ] ADJ (COMPAR: **beefier**, SUPERL: **beefiest**) (= *brawny*) fornido
beehive ['bi:haɪv] N colmena *f*
beekeeper ['bi:ki:pəʳ] N apicultor(a) *m/f*, colmenero/a *m/f*
beekeeping ['bi:,ki:pɪŋ] N apicultura *f*
beeline ['bi:laɪn] N • IDIOM: • **to make a ~ for sth/sb** ir directo *or* derecho a algo/algn
Beelzebub [bi:'elzɪbʌb] N Belcebú
been [bi:n] PP *of* **be**
beep [bi:p] N (*Brit*) pitido *m* • **please leave a message after the ~** deje un mensaje después de la señal
VI sonar
VT [+ *horn*] tocar
beeper ['bi:pəʳ] N localizador *m*, busca* *m*
beer [bɪəʳ] N cerveza *f* • **draught ~** cerveza *f* de barril • **light/dark ~** cerveza *f* rubia/negra • **we're only here for the ~** (*hum*) venimos en plan de diversión • IDIOM: • **life isn't all ~ and skittles** (*Brit*) la vida no es un lecho de rosas, la vida no es todo Jauja*; ▹ **small**
CPD ▸ **beer barrel** barril *m* de cerveza ▸ **beer belly*** panza* *f* (*de beber cerveza*) ▸ **beer bottle** botella *f* de cerveza ▸ **beer can** bote *m or* lata *f* de cerveza ▸ **beer garden** terraza *f* de verano, jardín *m* (de un bar) ▸ **beer glass** jarra *f* de cerveza ▸ **beer gut*** = **beer belly** ▸ **beer mug** jarra *f* de cerveza
beerfest ['bɪəfest] N (*US*) festival *m* cervecero
beermat ['bɪəmæt] N posavasos *m inv*
beery ['bɪərɪ] ADJ [*smell*] a cerveza; [*person*] muy aficionado a la cerveza; [*party*] donde se bebe mucha cerveza • **it was a ~ affair** allí se bebió una barbaridad
beeswax ['bi:zwæks] N cera *f* de abejas
beet [bi:t] N **1** (= *crop*) remolacha *f* forrajera **2** (*US*) = **beetroot**
CPD ▸ **beet sugar** azúcar *m* de remolacha
beetle ['bi:tl] N escarabajo *m*
▸ **beetle off*** VI + ADV (*Brit*) marcharse
beetle-browed ['bi:tl'braʊd] ADJ cejialto, de cejas muy espesas
beetroot ['bi:tru:t] N (*Brit*) remolacha *f*, betabel *m* (*Mex*), betarraga *f* (*Chile, Bol*)
befall [bɪ'fɔ:l] (PT: **befell**, PP: **befallen**) (*liter*)
VT acontecer a, suceder a
VI acontecer, suceder • **whatever may ~** pase lo que pase
befallen [bɪ'fɔ:lən] PP *of* **befall**
befell [bɪ'fel] PT *of* **befall**
befit [bɪ'fɪt] VT (*frm*) corresponder a • **he writes beautifully, as ~s a poet** escribe con gran belleza, como corresponde a un poeta • **it ill ~s him to speak thus** no es la persona más indicada para decir eso • **they offered him a post ~ting his experience** le ofrecieron un puesto acorde a su experiencia
befitting [bɪ'fɪtɪŋ] ADJ (*frm*) apropiado
befog [bɪ'fɒg] VT (*liter*) (= *confuse*) [+ *issue etc*] entenebrecer; [+ *person*] ofuscar, confundir
before [bɪ'fɔ:ʳ]

*When **before** is an element in a phrasal verb, eg **come before**, **go before**, look up the verb.*

BEFORE

Time

Adverb

▹ *When **before** is an adverb, you can usually translate it using **antes**:*
Why didn't you say so before?
¿Por qué no lo has dicho antes?
I had spoken to her before
Había hablado con ella antes

▹ *But the **before** in **never before** and **ever before** is often not translated:*
I've never been to Spain before
Nunca he estado en España
I had never been to a police station before
Nunca había estado (antes) en una comisaría
It's not true that the working class is earning more money than ever before
No es cierto que la clase obrera gane más dinero que nunca

▹ *The **day/night/week** etc **before** should usually be translated using **el día/la noche/la semana** etc **anterior**:*
The night before, he had gone to a rock concert
La noche anterior había ido a un concierto de rock

▹ *In more formal contexts, where **before** could be substituted by **previously**, **anteriormente** is another option:*
As I said before ...
Como he dicho antes *or* anteriormente ...

▹ *When **before** is equivalent to **already**, translate using **ya** (**antes**) or, in questions about whether someone has done what they are doing now before, using **¿es la primera vez que ...?**:*
"How about watching this film?" — "Actually, I've seen it before"
—¿Vemos esa película? —Es que ya la he visto
I had been to Glasgow a couple of times before
Ya había estado (antes) en Glasgow un par de veces
Have you been to Spain before?
¿Has estado ya en España? *or* ¿Es la primera vez que vienes a España?

▹ *Translate period of time + **before** using **hacía** + period of time:*
They had married nearly 40 years before
Se habían casado hacía casi 40 años

NOTE: ***Hacía** is invariable in this sense.*

Preposition

▹ *When **before** is a preposition, you can usually translate it using **antes de**:*
Please ring before seven
Por favor, llama antes de las siete
Shall we go for a walk before dinner?
¿Nos vamos a dar un paseo antes de cenar?

▹ *But use **antes que** with names of people and personal pronouns when they stand in for a verb:*
If you get there before me *or* before I do, wait for me in the bar
Si llegas antes que yo, espérame en el bar

▹ *Translate **before** + -ing using **antes de** + infinitive:*
He said goodbye to the children before leaving
Se despidió de los niños antes de irse

Conjunction

▹ *When **before** is a conjunction, you can usually translate it using **antes de que** + subjunctive:*
I'll ask Peter about it before he goes away on holiday
Se lo preguntaré a Peter antes de que se vaya de vacaciones
We reached home before the storm broke
Llegamos a casa antes de que empezara la tormenta

▹ *If the subject of both clauses is the same, **antes de** + infinitive is usually used rather than **antes de que**:*
Give me a ring before you leave the office
Llámame antes de salir de la oficina

This construction is also sometimes used in colloquial Spanish when the subjects are different:
Before you arrived she was very depressed
Antes de llegar tú, estaba muy deprimida

For further uses and examples, see main entry.

PREP **1** (*in time, order, rank*) antes de • **~ Christ** antes de Cristo • **the week ~ last** hace dos semanas • **~ long** (*in future*) antes de poco; (*in past*) poco después • **~ going, would you ...** antes de marcharte, quieres ... • **income ~ tax** renta *f* bruta *or* antes de impuestos • **profits ~ tax** beneficios *mpl* preimpositivos **2** (*in place*) delante de; (= *in the presence of*) ante, delante de, en presencia de • **they were married ~ a judge** se casaron en presencia de un juez **3** (= *facing*) • **the question ~ us** (*in meeting*) el asunto que tenemos que discutir • **the problem ~ us is ...** el problema que se nos plantea es ... • **the task ~ us** la tarea que tenemos por delante • **we still have two hours ~ us** tenemos todavía dos horas por delante • **a new life lay ~ him** una vida nueva se abría ante él **4** (= *rather than*) • **I should choose this one ~ that** yo escogería este antes que aquel • **death ~ dishonour!** ¡antes la muerte que el deshonor!
ADV **1** (*time*) antes • **a moment ~** un momento antes • **the day ~** el día anterior • **~, it used to be different** antes, todo era distinto • **on this occasion and the one ~** en esta ocasión y la anterior **2** (*place, order*) delante, adelante • **~ and behind** por delante y por detrás • **that chapter and the one ~** ese capítulo y el anterior
CONJ (*time*) antes de que; (*rather than*) antes que
beforehand [bɪ'fɔ:hænd] ADV de antemano, con antelación
befoul [bɪ'faʊl] VT (*liter*) ensuciar
befriend [bɪ'frend] VT entablar amistad con, hacerse amigo de
befuddle [bɪ'fʌdl] VT (= *confuse*) atontar,

b

confundir; (= *make tipsy*) atontar

befuddled [bɪ'fʌdld] ADJ (= *confused*) aturdido • **~ with drink** atontado por la bebida

beg [beg] VT **1** (= *implore*) rogar, suplicar • **I beg you!** ¡te lo suplico! • **to beg forgiveness** suplicar *or* implorar perdón • **he begged my help** suplicó mi ayuda • **to beg sb for sth** suplicar algo a algn • **he begged me to help him** me suplicó que le ayudara • **I beg to inform you** (*frm*) tengo el honor de informarle • **I beg to differ** siento tener que disentir • IDIOM: • **to beg the question**: • **some definitions of mental illness beg the question of what constitutes normal behaviour** algunas definiciones de enfermedad mental dan por sentado lo que constituye un comportamiento normal
2 [*beggar*] [+ *food, money*] pedir • **he begged a pound** pidió una libra
VI **1** (= *implore*) • **to beg for** [+ *forgiveness, mercy*] implorar
2 [*beggar*] mendigar, pedir limosna • **there's some cake going begging*** queda un poco de tarta, ¿no la quiere nadie?
▸ **beg off*** VI + ADV (*US*) dar una excusa

began [bɪ'gæn] PT *of* **begin**

beget [bɪ'get] (PT: **begot, begat** [bɪ'gæt]) (PP: **begotten**) VT (*frm*) engendrar (*also fig*)

begetter [bɪ'getəʳ] N (*frm*) creador(a) *m/f*, instigador(a) *m/f*

beggar ['begəʳ] N **1** mendigo/a *m/f*, pordiosero/a *m/f* • PROVERB: • **~s can't be choosers** a buen hambre no hay pan duro
2* (= *fellow*) tío/a* *m/f* • **lucky ~!** ¡qué suerte tiene el tío/la tía!* • **poor little ~!** ¡pobrecito!
VT **1** (= *ruin*) arruinar
2 (*fig*) (= *exceed*) excederse a • **it ~s description** es imposible describirlo • **it ~s belief** resulta totalmente inverosímil

beggarly ['begəlɪ] ADJ miserable

beggary ['begərɪ] N (*frm*) mendicidad *f* • **to reduce to ~** reducir a la miseria

begging ['begɪŋ] N mendicidad *f*
CPD ▸ **begging bowl** platillo *m* para limosnas • **to hold out a ~ bowl** (*fig*) pasar el platillo ▸ **begging letter** *carta en la que se pide dinero*

begin [bɪ'gɪn] (PT: **began**, PP: **begun**) VT
1 (= *start*) empezar, comenzar • **to ~ doing sth** • **~ to do sth** empezar a hacer algo • **it's ~ning to rain** está empezando a llover • **he ~s the day with a glass of orange juice** empieza el día con un zumo de naranja • **I can't ~ to thank you** no encuentro palabras para agradecerle • **it doesn't ~ to compare with …** no puede ni compararse con … • **this skirt began life as an evening dress** esta falda empezó siendo un traje de noche
2 (= *undertake*) emprender; (= *set in motion*) iniciar; [+ *discussion*] entablar • **I was foolish ever to ~ it** hice mal en emprenderlo
VI **1** (= *start*) empezar, comenzar, iniciarse (*frm*) • **the work will ~ tomorrow** el trabajo empezará *or* comenzará mañana • **the teacher began by writing on the board** el profesor empezó escribiendo en la pizarra • **let me ~ by saying …** quiero comenzar diciendo … • **~ning from Monday** a partir del lunes • **to ~ on sth** emprender algo • **to ~ with sth** comenzar por *or* con algo • **to ~ with, I'd like to know …** en primer lugar, quisiera saber … • **to ~ with there were only two of us** al principio solo éramos dos
2 (= *originate*) [*river*] nacer; [*rumour, custom*] originarse

beginner [bɪ'gɪnəʳ] N principiante *mf* • **it's just ~'s luck** es la suerte del principiante

beginning [bɪ'gɪnɪŋ] N **1** [*of speech, book, film etc*] principio *m*, comienzo *m* • **at the ~ of** al principio de • **at the ~ of the century** a principios de siglo • **the ~ of the end** el principio del fin • **right from the ~** desde el principio • **from ~ to end** de principio a fin, desde el principio hasta el final • **in the ~** al principio • **to make a ~** empezar
2 (= *origin*) origen *m* • **from humble ~s** de orígenes modestos • **Buddhism had its ~s …** el budismo tuvo sus orígenes … • **he had the ~s of a beard** tenía un asomo de barba

begone†† [bɪ'gɒn] EXCL (*liter*) ¡fuera de aquí!

begonia [bɪ'gəʊnɪə] N begonia *f*

begot [bɪ'gɒt] PT *of* **beget**

begotten [bɪ'gɒtn] VB *pp of* **beget** • **God gave His only Begotten Son** Dios entregó a su Unigénito

begrime [bɪ'graɪm] VT (*liter*) tiznar, ensuciar

begrudge [bɪ'grʌdʒ] VT **1** (= *envy*) • **to ~ sb sth** envidiar algo a algn • **I don't ~ him his success** no le envidio su éxito
2 (= *give reluctantly*) dar de mala gana • **I don't ~ all the money I've spent** no me duele todo el dinero que he gastado

begrudging [bɪ'grʌdʒɪŋ] ADJ reacio

begrudgingly [bɪ'grʌdʒɪŋlɪ] ADV de mala gana, a regañadientes

beguile [bɪ'gaɪl] VT **1** (= *deceive*) • **to ~ sb into doing sth** engatusar a algn para que haga algo
2 (= *enchant*) seducir, cautivar
3 (*liter*) (= *pass*) [+ *time*] pasar (*de manera entretenida*)

beguiling [bɪ'gaɪlɪŋ] ADJ seductor, persuasivo

begun [bɪ'gʌn] PP *of* **begin**

behalf [bɪ'hɑːf] N • **on** *or* (*US*) **in ~ of** en nombre de, de parte de • **a collection on ~ of orphans** una colecta en beneficio de los huérfanos, una colecta para los huérfanos • **I interceded on his ~** intercedí por él • **don't worry on my ~** no te preocupes por mí

behave [bɪ'heɪv] VI **1** [*person*] portarse (**to, towards** con), comportarse • **he ~d like an idiot** se comportó como un idiota • **to ~ (o.s.)** portarse bien • **did the children ~ themselves?** ¿se portaron bien los niños? • **~ (yourself)!** ¡compórtate!, ¡pórtate bien! • **if you ~ (yourself)** si te portas bien, si te comportas debidamente
2 (*Mech etc*) funcionar

behaviour, behavior (*US*) [bɪ'heɪvjəʳ] N
1 [*of person*] conducta *f*, comportamiento *m* • **good ~** buena conducta *f* • **to be on one's best ~** comportarse lo mejor posible • **you must be on your best ~** tienes que portarte lo mejor posible
2 (*Mech etc*) funcionamiento *m*
CPD ▸ **behaviour pattern** patrón *m* de conducta

behavioural, behavioral (*US*) [bɪ'heɪvjərəl] ADJ [*problems, changes*] conductual; [*theory, science*] conductista

behaviourism, behaviorism (*US*) [bɪ'heɪvjərɪzəm] N conductismo *m*, behaviorismo *m*

behaviourist, behaviorist (*US*) [bɪ'heɪvjərɪst] ADJ conductista, behaviorista
N conductista *mf*, behaviorista *mf*

behead [bɪ'hed] VT decapitar

beheld [bɪ'held] PT, PP *of* **behold**

behemoth [bɪ'hiːmɒθ] N (*liter*) (= *monster*) gigante *m*

behest [bɪ'hest] N (*frm*) • **at his ~** a petición suya

behind [bɪ'haɪnd]

> *When **behind** is an element in a phrasal verb, eg **fall behind**, **stay behind**, look up the verb.*

PREP **1** (= *to the rear of*) detrás de • **~ the door** detrás de la puerta • **look ~ you!** ¡cuidado atrás! • **with his hands ~ his back** las manos en la espalda
2 (= *responsible for*) detrás de • **what's ~ all this?** ¿qué hay detrás de todo esto?
3 (= *less advanced than*) • **Hill is nine points ~ Schumacher** Hill tiene nueve puntos menos que Schumacher • **we're well ~ them in technology** nos dejan muy atrás *or* estamos muy a la zaga de ellos en tecnología
4 (= *supporting*) • **his family is ~ him** tiene el apoyo de su familia
5 (= *in the past of*) • **it's all ~ us now** todo eso ha quedado ya atrás
6 (= *to one's credit*) • **she has four novels ~ her** tiene cuatro novelas en el haber
ADV **1** (= *in or at the rear*) detrás, atrás • **to come from ~** venir desde atrás • **to follow close ~** seguir muy de cerca • **to attack sb from ~** atacar a algn por la espalda • **to leave sth ~** olvidar algo
2 (= *behind schedule*) • **to be a bit ~** estar algo atrasadillo • **to be ~ with the rent** tener atrasos de alquiler • **to be ~ with one's work** estar atrasado en el trabajo
3 (= *less advanced*) • **Pepe won with Paco only two strokes ~** ganó Pepe con Paco a solo dos golpes de distancia
N* trasero *m*

behindhand [bɪ'haɪndhænd] ADV atrasado, con retraso

behold [bɪ'həʊld] (PT, PP: **beheld**) VT (*liter*) contemplar • **behold!** ¡mire! • **~ the results!** ¡he aquí los resultados!; ▹ **lo**

beholden [bɪ'həʊldən] ADJ (*frm*) • **to be ~ to sb** tener obligaciones con algn

beholder [bɪ'həʊldəʳ] N espectador(a) *m/f*, observador(a) *m/f*

behove [bɪ'həʊv], **behoove** (*US*) [bɪ'huːv] IMPERS VT (*frm*) • **it ~s him to** (+ *infin*) le incumbe (+ *infin*)

beige [beɪʒ] ADJ (*color*) beige (*inv*)
N beige *m*

Beijing ['beɪ'dʒɪŋ] N Pekín *m*

being ['biːɪŋ] N **1** (= *existence*) existencia *f* • **in ~** existente • **to come** *or* **be brought into ~** nacer
2 (= *creature*) ser *m*; ▹ **human**
CPD ▸ **being from outer space** extraterrestre *mf*

Beirut [beɪ'ruːt] N Beirut *m*

bejewelled, bejeweled (*US*) [bɪ'dʒuːəld] ADJ enjoyado

belabour, belabor (*US*) [bɪ'leɪbəʳ] VT†
(= *beat*) apalear; (*fig*) (*with insults*) atacar; (*with questions*) asediar (**with** con)

Belarus [belə'rʊs] N Bielorrusia *f*

Belarussian [ˌbelə'rʌʃən] ADJ bielorruso
N **1** (= *person*) bielorruso/a *m/f*
2 (*Ling*) bielorruso *m*

belated [bɪ'leɪtɪd] ADJ tardío, atrasado

belatedly [bɪ'leɪtɪdlɪ] ADV con retraso

belay [bɪ'leɪ] VT amarrar (*dando vueltas en una cabilla*)

belch [beltʃ] N eructo *m*
VI eructar
VT (*also* **belch out**) [+ *smoke, flames*] arrojar, vomitar

beleaguered [bɪ'liːgəd] ADJ **1** [*city*] asediado
2 (*fig*) (= *harassed*) atormentado, acosado

Belfast ['belfɑːst] N Belfast *m*

belfry ['belfrɪ] N campanario *m*

Belgian ['beldʒən] ADJ belga
N belga *mf*

Belgium ['beldʒəm] N Bélgica *f*

Belgrade [bel'greɪd] N Belgrado *m*

belie [bɪ'laɪ] VT (= *fail to justify*) [+ *hopes etc*] defraudar; (= *prove false*) [+ *words*]

contradecir, desmentir
belief [bɪ'li:f] N **1** (= *tenet, doctrine*) creencia *f*; (= *trust*) confianza *f*; (= *opinion*) opinión *f* • **contrary to popular ~** … al contrario de lo que muchos creen … • **a man of strong ~s** un hombre de firmes convicciones • **to the best of my ~** según mi leal saber y entender • **it is my ~ that** … estoy convencido de que … • **I did it in the ~ that** … lo hice creyendo que … • **it's beyond ~** es increíble (**that** que) • **wealthy beyond ~** de una fortuna increíble
2 (*no pl*) (= *faith*) fe *f* • **his ~ in God** su fe en Dios
believable [bɪ'li:vəbl] ADJ creíble, verosímil
believe [bɪ'li:v] VT **1** (= *think*) creer • **I ~ so** creo que sí • **I ~ not** creo que no • **he is ~d to be abroad** se cree que está en el extranjero
2 [+ *story, evidence, person*] creer • **don't you ~ it!** ¡no te lo creas! • **~ it or not, she bought it** aunque parezca mentira, lo compró • **it was hot, ~ (you) me** hacía calor, ¡y cómo! • **I couldn't ~ my eyes** no podía dar crédito a mis ojos • **do you really ~ the threat?** ¿crees de veras en la amenaza? • **I would never have ~d it of him** jamás le hubiera creído capaz de eso
VI creer • **to ~ in God** creer en Dios • **I don't ~ in corporal punishment** no soy partidario del castigo corporal • **we don't ~ in drugs** no aprobamos el uso de las drogas
believer [bɪ'li:vəʳ] N **1** (*Rel*) creyente *mf*, fiel *mf*
2 (= *advocate*) partidario/a *m/f* • **to be a great ~ in** … ser muy partidario de … • **I am a ~ in letting things take their course** soy partidario de dejar que las cosas sigan su propio curso
Belisha beacon† [bɪ,liʃə'bi:kən] N poste *m* luminoso (*de cruce de peatones*)
belittle [bɪ'lɪtl] VT (= *demean*) menospreciar; (= *minimize*) quitar importancia a, minimizar
Belize [be'li:z] N Belice *m*
Belizean [be'li:zɪən] ADJ beliceño
N beliceño/a *m/f*
bell [bel] N **1** (= *church bell*) campana *f*; (= *handbell*) campanilla *f*; (= *doorbell, electric bell*) timbre *m*; (*for cow*) cencerro *m*; (*for cat, on toy, dress etc*) cascabel *m* • **two/eight** *etc* **~s** (*Naut*) *las medias horas de cada guardia marítima* • IDIOMS: • **to ring a ~**: • **that rings a ~** eso me suena • **it doesn't ring a ~ with me** no me suena • **he was saved by the ~** (*lit*) (*Boxing*) le salvó la campana; (*fig*) se salvó por los pelos*
2 [*of trumpet*] pabellón *m*; [*of flower*] campanilla *f*
3 (*Brit**) (= *phone call*) • **I'll give you a ~** te llamaré
CPD ▸ **bell glass, bell jar** fanal *m*, campana *f* de cristal ▸ **bell pepper** (*esp US*) pimiento *m* morrón ▸ **bell pull** campanilla *f* ▸ **bell push** pulsador *m* de timbre ▸ **bell rope** cuerda *f* de campana ▸ **bells and whistles*** (*esp Comput*) elementos *mpl* accesorios; (*pej*) florituras *fpl* ▸ **bell tent** pabellón *m* ▸ **bell tower** campanario *m*
belladonna [,belə'dɒnə] N (*Bot, Med*) belladona *f*
CPD ▸ **belladonna lily** azucena *f* rosa
bell-bottomed ['bel'bɒtəmd] ADJ [*trousers*] acampanado
bell-bottoms ['be'bɒtəmz] NPL pantalones *mpl* de campana
bellboy ['belbɔɪ] N botones *m inv*
bellbuoy ['belbɔɪ] N boya *f* de campana
belle [bel] N • **the ~ of the ball** la reina del baile
belles-lettres ['bel'letr] NPL bellas letras *fpl*
bellflower ['bel,flaʊəʳ] N (*Bot*) campanilla *f*
bellhop ['belhɒp] N (*US*) botones *m inv*
bellicose ['belɪkəʊs] ADJ belicoso
bellicosity [,belɪ'kɒsɪtɪ] N belicosidad *f*
belligerence [bɪ'lɪdʒərəns] N, **belligerency** [bɪ'lɪdʒərənsɪ] N agresividad *f*
belligerent [bɪ'lɪdʒərənt] ADJ beligerante
N parte *f* beligerante
belligerently [bɪ'lɪdʒərəntlɪ] ADV agresivamente
bellow ['beləʊ] N [*of bull etc*] bramido *m*; [*of person*] rugido *m*
VI [*animal*] bramar; [*person*] rugir
VT (*also* **bellow out**) [+ *order, song*] gritar
bellows ['beləʊz] NPL fuelle *msing* • **a pair of ~** un fuelle
bell-ringer ['bel,rɪŋəʳ] N campanero/a *m/f*; (*as hobby*) campanólogo/a *m/f*
bell-ringing ['bel,rɪŋɪŋ] N campanología *f*
bell-shaped ['belʃeɪpt] ADJ acampanado
bellwether ['belweðəʳ] N (*esp US*) (= *indication*) barómetro *m*
belly ['belɪ] N **1** (= *abdomen*) barriga* *f*, guata *f* (*Chile**)
2 [*of vessel*] barriga *f*
VI (*also* **belly out**) [*sail*] hincharse
CPD ▸ **belly button*** ombligo *m* ▸ **belly dance** danza *f* del vientre ▸ **belly dancer** danzarina *f* del vientre ▸ **belly flop** panzazo* *m* • **to do a ~ flop** dar(se) un panzazo* ▸ **belly landing** (*Aer*) aterrizaje *m* de panza • **to make a ~ landing** aterrizar de panza ▸ **belly laugh** carcajada *f* (grosera) ▸ **belly of pork** falda *f* de cerdo
bellyache* ['belɪeɪk] N dolor *m* de barriga*
VI (= *complain*) renegar, echar pestes* (**at** de)
bellyaching* ['belɪ,eɪkɪŋ] N quejas *fpl* constantes
bellyful* ['belɪfʊl] N (*fig*) • **I've had a ~ (of)** estoy hasta la coronilla *or* las narices (de)*
belly-up* [,belɪ'ʌp] ADV • **to go belly-up** [*company, scheme*] irse al garete*, irse al traste
belong [bɪ'lɒŋ] VI **1** (= *be possession*) • **to ~ to sb** pertenecer a algn • **who does this ~ to?** ¿a quién pertenece esto?, ¿de quién es esto? • **the house/the book doesn't ~ to you** la casa/el libro no te pertenece • **the land ~s to him** la tierra es de su propiedad, la tierra le pertenece
2 (= *be product*) ser • **the handwriting ~s to a male** la letra es de hombre
3 (= *be member*) • **I used to ~ to the Labour Party** estuve afiliado a *or* fui miembro del partido laborista • **do you ~ to a church?** ¿perteneces a alguna iglesia? • **to ~ to a club** ser socio de un club
4 (= *be appropriate*) • **we truly ~ together** estamos verdaderamente hechos el uno para el otro • **those ideas ~ in the middle ages** esas ideas son de la edad media • **the future ~s to technology** el futuro está en manos de la tecnología
5 (= *fit in*) • **I feel I ~ here** aquí me siento en casa • **he feels the need to ~** siente la necesidad de ser parte de algún grupo • **I don't ~ here** este no es mi sitio
6 (= *have rightful place*) • **it ~s on the shelf** va en el estante • **your toys don't ~ in the living room** el sitio de tus juguetes no es el salón, tus juguetes no deberían estar en el salón • **go back home where you ~** vuelve a casa, que es donde está tu sitio
7 (= *be part*) ser • **that top ~s to this bottle** ese tapón es el de esta botella • **it ~s to the rodent family** pertenece a *or* es de la familia de los roedores • **Henry and I ~ to different generations** Henry y yo pertenecemos a distintas generaciones *or* somos de dos generaciones diferentes
belonging [bɪ'lɒŋɪŋ] N • **sense of ~** (*to country, community*) sentimiento *m* de pertenecer a algo
belongings [bɪ'lɒŋɪŋz] NPL pertenencias *fpl*; ▹ **personal**
Belorussia [,bjeləʊ'rʌʃə] N = **Belarus**
Belorussian [,beləʊ'rʌʃən] ADJ, N = **Belarussian**
beloved [bɪ'lʌvɪd] ADJ querido (**by, of** por) • **my dearly ~ brethren** … mis queridos hermanos …
N querido/a *m/f*, amado/a *m/f*
below [bɪ'ləʊ]

> *When* **below** *is an element in a phrasal verb, eg* **go below**, *look up the verb.*

PREP **1** (= *under*) debajo de, bajo • **~ the bed** debajo de la cama, bajo la cama • **the room ~ this is my study** la habitación que está debajo de esta es mi estudio • **her skirt reaches well ~ her knees** la falda le llega muy por debajo de las rodillas • **their readership has dropped to ~ 18,000** el número de lectores que tenían ha descendido por debajo de los 18.000 • **to be ~ sb in rank** ser inferior a algn en rango • **~ average** inferior al promedio, inferior a *or* por debajo de la media • **~ freezing (point)** bajo cero • **~ (the) ground** bajo tierra • **temperatures ~ normal** temperaturas inferiores a las normales • **~ sea level** por debajo del nivel del mar • **~ the surface** por debajo de la superficie, bajo la superficie • **~ zero** bajo cero • **five degrees ~ zero** cinco grados bajo cero
2 (*Geog*) (= *downstream of*) más abajo de • **the Thames ~ Oxford** el Támesis más abajo de Oxford
ADV **1** (= *beneath*) abajo • **~, we could see the valley** abajo podíamos ver el valle • **the flat ~** el piso de abajo • **they live two floors ~** viven dos pisos más abajo • **decisions occur at departmental level or ~** las decisiones se toman a nivel de departamento o a un nivel inferior • **her name was written ~** su nombre estaba escrito debajo • **it was five (degrees) ~** hacía cinco grados bajo cero • **down ~** abajo • **far ~** mucho más abajo • **from ~** desde abajo • **here ~** (*lit*) aquí abajo; (= *not in sky*) aquí en la tierra; (= *in this life*) en este mundo • **immediately ~** justamente debajo
2 (*in document*) • **see ~** véase más abajo • **as stated ~** como se indica más abajo
3 (*Naut*) (*also* **below deck**) abajo • **to go ~** bajar
below-the-belt [bɪ,ləʊðə'belt] ADJ [*tactics*] desleal; [*question, comment*] malintencionado; ▹ **belt**
below-the-line promotion [bɪ'ləʊðəlaɪn prə'məʊʃən] N (*Comm*) campaña *f* BTL
Belshazzar [bel'ʃæzəʳ] N Baltasar • **~'s Feast** la Cena de Baltasar
belt [belt] N **1** (= *garment*) cinturón *m*, fajo *m* (*Mex*); (= *seat belt*) cinturón *m* de seguridad • IDIOMS: • **to tighten one's ~** apretarse el cinturón • **that was below the ~** ese fue un golpe bajo • **he has three novels under his ~** tiene tres novelas en su haber • **it was a ~-and-braces job*** se tomaron todas las precauciones posibles
2 (*Tech*) (= *conveyor belt etc*) correa *f*, cinta *f*
3 (*Geog*) (= *zone*) zona *f* • **industrial ~** cinturón *m* industrial
VT* (= *thrash*) zurrar (con correa) • **he ~ed me one** (= *slap*) me dio una torta*; (= *punch*) me dio un mamporro*

b

(VI) (*Brit**) (= *rush*) • **he ~ed into the room** entró pitando en la habitación* • **he ~ed down the street** salió pitando por la calle abajo* • **to ~ past** pasar como una bala
(CPD) ▸ **belt bag** riñonera *f* ▸ **belt loop** trabilla *f*
▸ **belt along*** (VI + ADV) ir como una bala
▸ **belt down*** (VT + ADV) (*US*) [+ *drink*] cepillarse*
▸ **belt off*** (VI + ADV) salir pitando*
▸ **belt out*** (VT + ADV) [+ *song*] cantar a pleno pulmón
(VI + ADV) (*also* **come belting out**) salir disparado
▸ **belt up** (VI + ADV) **1** (*Aut*) abrocharse el cinturón
2 (*Brit*‡) (= *be quiet*) cerrar el pico*, callarse la boca‡ • **~ up!** ¡cállate la boca!‡
belted ['beltɪd] (ADJ) [*jacket, coat*] con cinturón
belter* ['beltəʳ] (N) **1** (= *singer*) • **she's a ~** qué pulmones tiene; (= *song*) *canción cantada a pleno pulmón*
2 (= *party*) bombazo* *m*
belting* ['beltɪŋ] (ADJ) (*Brit*) (= *brilliant*) espectacular
beltway ['beltweɪ] (N) (*US*) carretera *f* de circunvalación
bemoan [bɪ'məʊn] (VT) lamentar
bemuse [bɪ'mju:z] (VT) aturdir, confundir
bemused [bɪ'mju:zd] (ADJ) perplejo, aturdido
bemusedly [bɪ'mju:zɪdlɪ] (ADV) [*look, stare*] con aire perplejo
bemusement [bɪ'mju:zmənt] (N) (= *puzzlement*) perplejidad *f*
Ben [ben] (N) *familiar form of* **Benjamin**
ben [ben] (N) (*Scot*) (= *mountain*) montaña *f*; (= *room*) cuarto *m* interior
bench [bentʃ] (N) **1** (= *seat, workbench*) banco *m*; (*Sport*) banquillo *m*; (= *court*) tribunal *m* • **the Bench** (*Jur*) la magistratura • **to be on the ~** (*Jur*) ser juez, ser magistrado; (*Sport*) estar en el banquillo
2 benches (*Brit*) (*Parl*) • **on the Tory/Labour ~es** en los escaños conservadores/laboristas
bencher ['bentʃəʳ] (N) (*Brit*) (*Jur*) *miembro de la junta de gobierno de uno de los cuatro colegios de formación de magistrados*
benchmark ['bentʃmɑ:k] (N) cota *f*
(CPD) ▸ **benchmark price** precio *m* de referencia
benchmarking ['bentʃmɑ:kɪŋ] (*Comm*) (N) benchmarking *m*
benchwarmer* ['bentʃ,wɔ:məʳ] (N) (*US*) (*Sport*) calientabanquillos *m*
bend [bend] (VB: PT, PP: **bent**) (N) **1** (*gen*) curva *f*; (*in pipe etc*) ángulo *m*; (= *corner*) recodo *m*; (*Naut*) gaza *f* • **"dangerous bend"** "curva peligrosa" • IDIOM: • **he's round the ~!** (*Brit**) ¡está chiflado!* • **to go round the ~** volverse loco • **to drive sb round the ~** volver loco a algn*
2 • **the ~s** (*Med*) la enfermedad de descompresión
3 (*Heraldry*) banda *f*
(VT) **1** (= *make curved*) [+ *wire*] curvar, doblar; (= *cause to sag*) combar; [+ *arm, knee*] doblar; [+ *sail*] envergar • **on ~ed knee** de rodillas • **to ~ the rules for sb** adaptar las normas a beneficio de algn • **to ~ sb to one's will** doblar a algn a su voluntad • IDIOM: • **to ~ sb's ear*** marear a algn*
2 (= *incline*) [+ *body, head*] inclinar
3 (= *direct*) [+ *efforts, steps etc*] dirigir (**to a**) • **to ~ one's mind to a problem** aplicarse a un problema; ▹ **bent**
(VI) **1** [*branch*] doblarse; [*wire*] torcerse; [*arm, knee*] doblarse; [*road, river*] torcer (**to the left** a la izquierda)
2 [*person*] (= *stoop*) inclinarse, doblarse
▸ **bend back** (VT + ADV) doblar hacia atrás
▸ **bend down** (VT + ADV) [+ *branch*] doblar; [+ *head*] inclinar
(VI + ADV) [*person*] agacharse
▸ **bend over** (VT + ADV) doblar
(VI + ADV) [*person*] inclinarse • IDIOM: • **to ~ over backwards (to do sth)** hacer lo imposible (por hacer algo)
bender ['bendəʳ] (N) **1** • **to go on a ~‡** ir de juerga*, ir de borrachera*
2* (= *tent*) choza *f*
bendy ['bendɪ] (ADJ) (= *flexible*) [*toy, wire*] flexible; [*river*] sinuoso
(CPD) ▸ **bendy bus** autobús *m* articulado
beneath [bɪ'ni:θ] (PREP) **1** (= *below*) debajo de, bajo
2 (*fig*) inferior a, por debajo de • **it would be ~ him to do such a thing** hacer tal cosa sería indigno de él • **she married ~ her** se casó con un hombre de clase inferior • **~ contempt** despreciable
(ADV) abajo, debajo
Benedict ['benɪdɪkt] (N) Benito; (= *pope*) Benedicto
Benedictine [,benɪ'dɪktɪn] (ADJ) benedictino
(N) benedictino *m*
benediction [,benɪ'dɪkʃən] (N) bendición *f*
benefaction [,benɪ'fækʃən] (N) (*frm*) (= *gift*) beneficio *m*
benefactor ['benɪfæktəʳ] (N) bienhechor(a) *m/f*, benefactor(a) *m/f*
benefactress ['benɪfæktrɪs] (N) bienhechora *f*, benefactora *f*
benefice ['benɪfɪs] (N) beneficio *m*
beneficence [bɪ'nefɪsəns] (N) (*frm*) beneficencia *f*
beneficent [bɪ'nefɪsənt] (ADJ) (*frm*) benéfico
beneficial [,benɪ'fɪʃəl] (ADJ) **1** (= *advantageous*) beneficioso • **~ to the health** beneficioso para la salud • **the change will be ~ to you** el cambio te resultará beneficioso
2 (*Jur*) • **~ owner** verdadero/a propietario/a *m/f*
beneficially [,benɪ'fɪʃəlɪ] (ADV) beneficiosamente
beneficiary [,benɪ'fɪʃərɪ] (N) (*Jur*) beneficiario/a *m/f*; (*Rel*) beneficiado *m*
benefit ['benɪfɪt] (N) **1** (= *advantage*) beneficio *m*, provecho *m* • **to give sb the ~ of the doubt** dar a algn el beneficio de la duda • **for the ~ of one's health** en beneficio de la salud • **I'll try it on for your ~** lo probaré en tu honor • **to have the ~ of** tener la ventaja de • **to be of ~ to sb** beneficiar a algn • **to reap the ~ of** sacar el fruto de • **to be to the ~ of** ser provechoso a • **without ~ of** sin la ayuda de • **to marry without ~ of clergy** casarse por lo civil
2 (*Admin*) (= *money*) ayuda *f*; (*also* **unemployment benefit**) subsidio *m* de desempleo
3 (*Theat, Sport*) (= *charity performance*) beneficio *m*
(VI) beneficiar(se), sacar provecho • **to ~ by/from** sacar provecho de
(VT) beneficiar
(CPD) ▸ **benefit association** (*esp US*) sociedad *f* de beneficencia ▸ **benefit concert** (*to raise money for charity*) concierto *m* benéfico ▸ **benefit fraud** fraude *m* en las prestaciones sociales ▸ **benefit match** partido *m* con fines benéficos ▸ **benefit payment** pago *m* de la prestación ▸ **benefit performance** función *f* benéfica ▸ **benefits agency** oficina *f* de prestaciones sociales ▸ **benefit society** = **benefit association** ▸ **benefits package** paquete *m* de beneficios
Benelux ['benɪlʌks] (N) Benelux *m* • **the ~ countries** los países del Benelux
benevolence [bɪ'nevələns] (N) benevolencia *f*
benevolent [bɪ'nevələnt] (ADJ) **1** (= *kind*) benévolo, benevolente • **a ~ smile** una sonrisa benévola *or* benevolente
2 (= *charitable*) [*organization, society*] benéfica, de beneficencia
(CPD) ▸ **benevolent fund** fondos *mpl* benéficos
benevolently [bɪ'nevələntlɪ] (ADV) con benevolencia, benévolamente
BEng [,bi:'eŋ] (N ABBR) (*Univ*) = **Bachelor of Engineering**
Bengal [beŋ'gɔ:l] (ADJ) bengalí
(N) Bengala *f*
(CPD) ▸ **Bengal tiger** tigre *m* de Bengala
Bengalese [,beŋgə'li:z] (ADJ) bengalí
Bengali [beŋ'gɔ:lɪ] (ADJ) bengalí
(N) (= *person*) bengalí *mf*; (*Ling*) bengalí *m*
Benghazi [ben'gɑ:zɪ] (N) Bengasi *m*
benighted [bɪ'naɪtɪd] (ADJ) (*liter*) (*fig*) ignorante
benign [bɪ'naɪn] (ADJ) **1** (= *kind*) [*person, view*] benevolente; [*smile, gesture*] benévolo, benevolente • **a policy of ~ neglect of the economy** una política en que, por su propio interés, se deja que la economía siga su curso sin interferir
2 (= *favourable*) [*substance, influence*] benéfico; [*conditions*] favorable; [*climate*] benigno
3 (*Med*) [*tumour, growth*] benigno
benignant [bɪ'nɪgnənt] (ADJ) benigno (*also Med*); (= *healthy*) saludable
benignly [bɪ'naɪnlɪ] (ADV) **1** (= *kindly*) [*smile, say*] benévolamente, con benevolencia
2 (= *favourably*) con benignidad, benignamente
Benjamin ['bendʒəmɪn] (N) Benjamín
benny†‡ ['benɪ] (N) (*Drugs*) bencedrina® *f*
bent [bent] (PT), (PP) *of* **bend**
(ADJ) **1** [*wire, pipe*] doblado; (= *twisted*) torcido
2 (*esp Brit*‡) (*pej*) (= *dishonest*) pringado (*Sp**), chueco (*LAm**), corrupto
3 (*Brit*‡) (*pej*) (= *homosexual*) del otro bando*, invertido
4 • **to be ~ on doing sth** (*fig*) (= *determined*) estar resuelto a *or* empeñado en hacer algo • **to be ~ on a quarrel** estar resuelto a *or* empeñado en provocar una riña • **to be ~ on pleasure** estar resuelto a *or* empeñado en divertirse
(N) (= *inclination*) inclinación *f*; (= *aptitude*) facilidad *f* • **of an artistic ~** con una inclinación artística, con inclinaciones artísticas • **to follow one's ~** seguir su inclinación • **he has a ~ for annoying people** tiene una facilidad para molestar a la gente
benumb [bɪ'nʌm] (VT) (*with cold*) entumecer; (= *frighten, shock*) paralizar
benumbed [bɪ'nʌmd] (ADJ) (= *cold*) [*person, fingers*] entumecido; (= *frightened, shocked*) paralizado
Benzedrine® ['benzɪdri:n] (N) bencedrina® *f*
benzene ['benzi:n] (N) benceno *m*
benzine ['benzi:n] (N) bencina *f*
bequeath [bɪ'kwi:ð] (VT) legar
bequest [bɪ'kwest] (N) legado *m*
berate [bɪ'reɪt] (VT) regañar
Berber ['bɜ:bəʳ] (ADJ) bereber
(N) bereber *mf*
bereave [bɪ'ri:v] (PT, PP: **bereft**) (VT) privar (**of de**)
bereaved [bɪ'ri:vd] (ADJ) afligido • **the ~** los familiares del difunto/de la difunta • **with the thanks of his ~ family** con el agradecimiento de su afligida familia
bereavement [bɪ'ri:vmənt] (N) (= *loss*) pérdida *f*; (= *mourning*) duelo *m*; (= *sorrow*) pesar *m*

CPD ▸ **bereavement counselling** (*Brit*), **bereavement counseling** (*US*) apoyo *m* psicológico (*a personas que han sufrido la pérdida de alguien querido*) • **she's been going for ~ counselling since the death of her husband** ha estado recibiendo apoyo psicológico desde la muerte de su marido ▸ **bereavement counsellor** (*Brit*), **bereavement counselor** (*US*) consejero *m/f* (*que acompaña a personas que han sufrido la pérdida de alguien querido*)

bereft [bɪ'reft] ADJ (*frm*) • **to be ~ of** (*= not have to hand*) estar desprovisto de; (*= not possess*) estar falto de; (*= be robbed*) ser despojado de

beret ['bereɪ] N boina *f* • **the Red Berets** (*Mil*) los boinas rojas

berg [bɜ:g] N = **iceberg**

bergamot ['bɜ:gəmɒt] N bergamota *f*

beriberi ['berɪ,berɪ] N beriberi *m*

Bering Sea ['berɪŋ'si:] N mar *m* de Bering

berk‡ [bɜ:k] N (*Brit*) imbécil* *mf*, gilipollas *mf* (*Sp*‡), huevón/ona *m/f* (*LAm*‡)

berkelium [bɜ:'ki:lɪəm] N berkelio *m*

Berks [bɑ:ks] N ABBR (*Brit*) = **Berkshire**

Berlin [bɜ:'lɪn] N Berlín *m* • **East/West ~** Berlín Este/Oeste
CPD berlinés ▸ **the Berlin Wall** el Muro de Berlín

Berliner [bɜ:'lɪnəʳ] N berlinés/esa *m/f*

berm [bɜ:m] N (*US*) arcén *m*

Bermuda [bɜ:'mju:də] N las Bermudas
CPD ▸ **Bermuda shorts** bermudas *fpl* ▸ **the Bermuda Triangle** el triángulo de las Bermudas

Bern [bɜ:n] N Berna *f*

Bernard ['bɜ:nəd] N Bernardo

Bernese [bɜ:'ni:z] ADJ bernés
CPD ▸ **Bernese Alps, Bernese Oberland** Alpes *mpl* Berneses

berry ['berɪ] N baya *f* • IDIOM: • **brown as a ~** morenísimo

berrying ['berɪɪŋ] N • **to go ~** ir a coger bayas

berserk [bə'sɜ:k] ADJ desquiciado • **to drive sb ~** desquiciar a algn • **to go ~** perder los estribos, ponerse hecho una furia*

Bert [bɜ:t] N *familiar form of* **Albert, Herbert** *etc*

berth [bɜ:θ] N **1** (*on ship, train*) (*= cabin*) camarote *m*; (*= bunk*) litera *f*
2 (*Naut*) (*at wharf*) amarradero *m*; (*in marina etc*) punto *m* de atraque • IDIOM: • **to give sb a wide ~** evitar el encuentro con algn
VI (*Naut*) atracar
VT (*Naut*) atracar

berthed ['bɜ:θt] ADJ [*ship*] atracado

beryl ['berɪl] N berilo *m*

beryllium [be'rɪljəm] N berilio *m*

beseech [bɪ'si:tʃ] (PT, PP: **besought**) VT • **to ~ sb to do sth** suplicar a algn que haga algo

beseeching [bɪ'si:tʃɪŋ] ADJ [*look*] suplicante; [*tone*] suplicante, de súplica

beseechingly [bɪ'si:tʃɪŋlɪ] ADV en tono suplicante *or* de súplica • **to look at sb ~** mirar a algn suplicante

beset [bɪ'set] (PT, PP: **beset**) VT [*+ person*] acosar • **he was ~ with** *or* **by fears** le acosaban los temores • **a policy ~ with dangers** una política plagada de peligros • **a path ~ with obstacles** (*fig*) un camino plagado de obstáculos

besetting [bɪ'setɪŋ] ADJ [*vice, failing*] grande • **his ~ sin** su gran pecado

beside [bɪ'saɪd] PREP **1** (*= at the side of*) al lado de, junto a; (*= near*) cerca de • **to be ~ o.s.** (*with anger*) estar fuera de sí; (*with joy*) estar loco de alegría • **that's ~ the point** eso no tiene nada que ver con el asunto, eso no viene al caso
2 (*= compared with*) comparado con • **what is that ~ victory?** ¿y eso qué importa comparado con la victoria?
3 (*= in addition to*) además de, aparte de; (*= apart from*) aparte de

besides [bɪ'saɪdz] PREP **1** (*= in addition to*) además de, aparte de • **there were three of us ~ Mary** éramos tres además de *or* aparte de Mary • **there are others ~ ourselves who might be interested** además de nosotros *or* aparte de nosotros hay otros que pueden estar interesados • **~ which he was unwell** aparte de eso estaba malo, además estaba malo
2 (*= apart from*) aparte de • **no one ~ you has the key** nadie, aparte de ti, tiene la llave • **Thomas was the only blond in the family, ~ the mother** Thomas era el único rubio de la familia, aparte de la madre
ADV **1** (*= in addition*) además • **he wrote a novel and several short stories ~** escribió una novela y además varias narraciones cortas • **and much more ~** y mucho más todavía
2 (*= anyway*) además • **I didn't want to invite him, and ~, he said he was busy** no quería invitarlo, además dijo que estaba ocupado

besiege [bɪ'si:dʒ] VT (*Mil*) (*also fig*) asediar • **we were ~d with inquiries** nos inundaron con solicitudes de información • **we are ~d with calls** nos están llamando incesantemente

besieger [bɪ'si:dʒəʳ] N sitiador(a) *m/f*

besmear [bɪ'smɪəʳ] VT embarrar, embadurnar

besmirch [bɪ'smɜ:tʃ] VT manchar, mancillar

besom ['bi:zəm] N escoba *f*

besotted [bɪ'sɒtɪd] ADJ **1** (*= infatuated*) • **he is ~ with her** anda loco por ella • **they are ~ with love** están enamoradísimos
2 (*= foolish*) atontado, entontecido
3 • **~ with drink** embrutecido por la bebida

besought [bɪ'sɔ:t] PT, PP *of* **beseech**

bespatter [bɪ'spætəʳ] VT salpicar (**with** de)

bespeak† [bɪ'spi:k] (PT: **bespoke**, PP: **bespoken** *or* **bespoke**) VT **1** (*= be evidence of*) indicar
2 (*= order*) [*+ goods*] encargar, reservar

bespectacled [bɪ'spektɪkld] ADJ con gafas

bespoke [bɪ'spəʊk] PT, PP *of* **bespeak**
ADJ (*Brit*) [*garment*] hecho a la medida; [*tailor*] que confecciona a la medida

bespoken [bɪ'spəʊkən] PP *of* **bespeak**

besprinkle [bɪ'sprɪŋkl] VT (*with liquid*) salpicar, rociar (**with** de); (*with powder*) espolvorear (**with** de)

Bess [bes], **Bessie, Bessy** ['besɪ] N (*familiar forms of* **Elizabeth**) Isabelita • **Good Queen ~** (*Brit*) (*Hist*) la buena reina Isabel

best [best] ADJ (*superl of* **good**) el/la mejor • **to be ~** ser el/la mejor • **she wore her ~ dress** llevaba su mejor vestido • **the ~ pupil in the class** el/la mejor alumno/a de la clase • **the ~ one of all** el/la mejor de todos • **"~ before 20 June"** "consumir preferentemente antes del 20 de junio" • **to know what is ~ for sb** saber lo que más le conviene a algn • **my ~ friend** mi mejor amigo/a • **may the ~ man win!** ¡que gane el mejor! • **for the ~ part of the year** durante la mayor parte del año • **the ~ thing to do is …** lo mejor que se puede hacer es …
ADV (*superl of* **well**) mejor • **John came off ~** Juan salió ganando • **as ~ I could** lo mejor que pude • **she did ~ of all in the test** hizo el test mejor que nadie • **you had ~ leave now** lo mejor es que te vayas ahora • **I had ~ go** más vale que vaya • **I had ~ see him at once** lo mejor sería verlo en seguida • **you know ~** tú sabes mejor • **when it comes to hotels I know ~** en cuestión de hoteles yo soy el que más sabe • **Mummy knows ~** estas cosas las decide mamá, mamá sabe lo que más conviene
N lo mejor • **he deserves the ~** se merece lo mejor • **all the ~!** (*as farewell*) ¡que tengas suerte! • **all the ~** • **my ~** (*US*) (*ending letter*) un abrazo • **all the ~ to Jim!** ¡recuerdos para Jim! • **at ~** en el mejor de los casos • **he wasn't at his ~** no estaba en plena forma • **the garden is at its ~ in June** en junio es cuando el jardín luce más • **at the ~ of times** en las mejores circunstancias • **to do one's ~ (to do sth)** hacer todo lo posible (para *or* por hacer algo) • **is that the ~ you can do?** ¿y eso es todo lo que puedes hacer? • **I acted for the ~** lo hice con la mejor intención • **it's all for the ~** todo conduce al bien a la larga • **to be the ~ of friends** ser muy amigos • **to get the ~ of it** salir ganando • **in order to get the ~ out of the car** para obtener el máximo rendimiento del coche • **we have had the ~ of the day** el buen tiempo se acabó por hoy • **let's hope for the ~** esperemos lo mejor • **to look one's ~** tener un aspecto inmejorable • **she's not looking her ~** está algo desmejorada • **to make the ~ of it** sacar el mayor partido posible • **the ~ of it is that …** lo mejor del caso es que … • **to play (the) ~ of three** jugar al mejor de tres • **I try to think the ~ of him** procuro conservar mi buena opinión de él • **to the ~ of my knowledge** que yo sepa • **I'll do it to the ~ of my ability** lo haré lo mejor que pueda • **she can dance with the ~ of them** sabe bailar como la que más • IDIOMS: • **to get the ~ of the bargain** llevarse la mejor parte, salir ganando • **to have the ~ of both worlds** tenerlo todo • **to make the ~ of a bad job** sacar el mejor partido posible
VT (*= defeat, win over*) vencer
CPD ▸ **best boy** (*Cine*) ayudante *mf* (*de rodaje*) ▸ **best man** (*at wedding*) padrino *m* de boda ▸ **best practice** mejores prácticas *fpl*

> **BEST MAN**
> En una boda tradicional el novio (**bridegroom**) va acompañado del **best man**, un amigo íntimo o un pariente cercano que tiene la responsabilidad de asegurarse de que todo marche bien en el día de la boda (**wedding day**). No hay pues, madrina. El **best man** se encarga, entre otras cosas, de los anillos de boda, de llevar al novio a la iglesia a tiempo y de dar la bienvenida a los invitados. En el banquete de boda (**wedding reception**) lee los telegramas enviados por los que no han podido asistir, presenta los discursos que vayan a dar algunos invitados, da su propio discurso, casi siempre en clave de humor y sobre el novio, y propone un brindis por la pareja de recién casados (**newly-weds**).

best-before date [bestbɪ'fɔ:deɪt] N (*Comm*) fecha *f* de consumo preferente

bestial ['bestɪəl] ADJ bestial

bestiality [,bestɪ'ælɪtɪ] N (*= behaviour*) bestialidad *f*; (*sexual*) bestialismo *m*

bestiary ['bestɪərɪ] N bestiario *m*

bestir [bɪ'stɜ:ʳ] VT (*liter*) • **to ~ o.s.** menearse

bestow [bɪ'stəʊ] VT [*+ title, honour*] conferir (**on** a); [*+ affections*] ofrecer (**on** a); [*+ compliment*] hacer (**on** a)

bestowal [bɪ'stəʊəl] N [*of title, honour*] otorgamiento *m*; [*of money, gifts*] donación *f*; [*of affections*] ofrecimiento *m*

bestraddle [bɪ'strædl] VT [*+ horse*] montar a horcajadas, estar a horcajadas sobre

b

bestrew [bɪ'stru:] (PT: **bestrewed**, PP: **bestrewed** *or* **bestrewn**) VT (*liter*) [+ *things*] desparramar, esparcir; [+ *surface*] sembrar, cubrir (**with** de)

bestridden [bɪ'strɪdn] PP *of* **bestride**

bestride [bɪ'straɪd] (PT: **bestrode**, PP: **bestridden**) VT [+ *horse*] montar a horcajadas; [+ *stream etc*] cruzar de un tranco; (*fig*) dominar

bestrode [bɪ'strəʊd] PT *of* **bestride**

bestseller ['best'seləʳ] N best-seller *m*, éxito *m* de ventas

best-selling ['best'selɪŋ] ADJ • **our best-selling line** nuestro producto de mayor venta • **for years it was our best-selling car** durante años fue el coche que más se vendió

bet [bet] (PT, PP: **bet**) VI **1** (= *place bet*) apostar • **I'm not a betting man** no me gusta apostar • **to bet against sb** apostar que algn va a perder • **to bet on sth/sb** apostar a *or* por algo/por algn • **I bet on the wrong horse** aposté por el *or* al caballo que no debía • **they are forbidden to bet on their own races** tienen prohibido apostar en sus propias carreras
2 (= *be certain*) • **don't bet on it!** • **I wouldn't bet on it!** ¡no estés tan seguro! • **(do you) want to bet?*** ¿qué te apuestas *or* juegas? • **"are you going?" — "you bet!"*** —¿vas a ir? —¡hombre, claro! *or* (*LAm*) —¡cómo no! • **"I'm so relieved it's all over" — "I'll bet"*** —es un alivio que todo haya pasado —ya me lo imagino
VT **1** (= *stake*) [+ *money*] apostar, jugar • **I bet £10 on a horse called Premonition** aposté 10 libras a *or* por un caballo llamado Premonition, jugué 10 libras a un caballo llamado Premonition • **he bet them (that) they would lose** hizo una apuesta con ellos a que perdían • **he bet them £500 that they would lose** les apostó *or* jugó 500 libras a que perdían
2* (= *predict*) apostar, jugarse • **I bet you anything** *or* **any money he won't come** te apuesto *or* me juego lo que quieras a que no viene • **you can bet she'll be there** puedes tener por seguro que estará allí • **"I bet I can jump over that stream" — "I bet you can't!"** —¡a que puedo saltar ese arroyo! —¡a que no! • **"it wasn't easy" — "I bet it wasn't"** —no fue fácil —ya me imagino que no • **you can bet your bottom dollar** *or* **your life that ...*** puedes apostarte lo que quieras a que ... • **"did you tell him off?" — "you bet your life I did!"** —¿le reñiste? —¡ya lo creo!
N **1** (= *stake*) apuesta *f* • **a £5 bet** una apuesta de 5 libras • **I had a bet on that horse** había apostado por ese caballo • **I've made a bet with him that he can't do it** le he hecho una apuesta a que no puede hacerlo • **(do you) want a bet?*** ¿qué te apuestas *or* juegas? • **they placed bets on who could get her to talk** apostaron a ver quién podía hacerla hablar • **place your bets!** ¡hagan sus apuestas! • **to take bets** aceptar apuestas; ▹ **hedge**
2 (= *prediction*) • **it's my bet he's up to no good** apuesto a que está tramando algo • **it's a fair** *or* **good bet that interest rates will go up** es muy posible que los tipos de interés van a subir • **he's a good bet for president** es el que más posibilidades tiene de conseguir la presidencia
3* (= *option*) • **it's our best bet** es la mejor opción que tenemos • **your best** *or* **safest bet is to keep quiet about it** lo mejor que puedes hacer es no decir nada • **these companies are a safe bet for investors** estas compañías no presentan ningún riesgo para los inversores

beta ['bi:tə] N beta *f*
CPD ▸ **beta blocker** (*Med*) betabloqueador *m* ▸ **beta carotene** betacaroteno *m*

betake [bɪ'teɪk] (PT: **betook**, PP: **betaken**) VT (*liter*) • **to ~ o.s. to** dirigirse a, trasladarse a

betaken [bɪ'teɪkən] PP *of* **betake**

betel ['bi:təl] N betel *m*
CPD ▸ **betel nut** betel *m*

bête noire ['beɪt'nwɑ:ʳ] N bestia *f* negra, pesadilla *f*

bethink [bɪ'θɪŋk] (PT, PP: **bethought**) VT (*liter*) • **to ~ o.s. of** acordarse de

Bethlehem ['beθlɪhem] N Belén *m*

bethought [bɪ'θɔ:t] PT, PP *of* **bethink**

betide [bɪ'taɪd] (*liter*) VT acontecer; ▹ **woe**
VI acontecer

betimes [bɪ'taɪmz] ADV (*liter*) (= *early*) temprano, al alba; (= *quickly*) rápidamente; (= *in good time*) a tiempo

betoken [bɪ'təʊkən] (*liter*) VT presagiar, anunciar

betook [bɪ'tʊk] PT *of* **betake**

betray [bɪ'treɪ] VT **1** (= *be disloyal to*) [+ *person, country, principles*] traicionar
2 (= *inform on*) delatar • **to ~ sb to the enemy** entregar a algn al enemigo
3 (= *reveal*) [+ *secret*] revelar; [+ *ignorance, fear*] delatar, revelar • **his accent ~s him** su acento lo delata • **his accent ~s him as a foreigner** su acento revela su origen extranjero • **his face ~ed a certain surprise** su cara delataba *or* revelaba cierto asombro

betrayal [bɪ'treɪəl] N **1** [*of person, country*] traición *f* • **a ~ of trust** un abuso de confianza
2 [*of secret, plot*] revelación *f*
3 [*of feelings, intentions*] descubrimiento *m*

betrayer [bɪ'treɪəʳ] N traidor(a) *m/f* • **she killed her ~** mató a quien la traicionó

betroth [bɪ'trəʊð] VT (*liter*) prometer en matrimonio (**to a**) • **to be ~ed** (= *act*) desposarse; (= *state*) estar desposado

betrothal [bɪ'trəʊðəl] N (*liter*) desposorios *mpl*

betrothed [bɪ'trəʊðd] (*liter, hum*) ADJ prometido
N INV prometido/a *m/f*

better[1] ['betəʳ] ADJ (*compar of* **good**) mejor • **he is ~ than you** es mejor que tú • **he's much ~** (*Med*) está mucho mejor • **that's ~!** ¡eso es! • **it is ~ to** (+ *infin*) más vale (+ *infin*) • **~ and ~** cada vez mejor • **she is ~ at dancing than her sister** se le da mejor bailar a ella que a su hermana • **it couldn't be ~** no podría ser mejor • **these products are ~ for the environment** estos productos son mejores para el medio ambiente • **to get ~** mejorar; (*Med*) mejorar(se), reponerse • **he's no ~ than a thief** no es más que un ladrón • **she's no ~ than she ought to be†** es una mujer que tiene historia • **to go one ~** hacer mejor todavía (**than que**) • **it lasted the ~ part of a year** duró la mayor parte del año • **the sooner the ~** cuanto antes mejor • **it would be ~ to go now** sería mejor irse ya; ▹ **half, nature, day**
ADV (*compar of* **well**) mejor • **all the ~** tanto mejor • **so you're both coming — all the ~!** así es que venís los dos, ¡tanto mejor! • **I feel all the ~ for having confided in someone** me siento mucho mejor después de haberme confiado a alguien • **he was all the ~ for it** le hizo mucho bien • **it would be all the ~ for a drop of paint** no le vendría mal una mano de pintura • **I had ~ go** más vale que me vaya, mejor me vaya (*esp LAm*) • **he thinks he knows ~** cree que se lo sabe todo • **at his age he ought to know ~** a la edad que tiene debería tener más juicio • **but he knew ~ than to ...** pero sabía que no se debía ... • **he knows ~ than the experts** sabe más que los expertos • **they are ~ off than we are** están mejor de dinero que nosotros • **you'd be ~ off staying where you are** te convendría más quedarte • **so much the ~** tanto mejor • **write to her or, ~ still, go and see her** escríbele o, mejor aún, vete a verla • **they withdrew, the ~ to resist** se retiraron para poder resistir mejor • **to think ~ of it** cambiar de parecer; ▹ **late**
N **1** el/la mejor • **it's a change for the ~** es una mejora • **to get the ~ of** (= *beat*) vencer, quedar por encima de • **for ~ or worse** para bien o mal
2 • **my ~s** mis superiores
VT mejorar; [+ *record, score*] superar • **to ~ o.s.** (*financially*) mejorar su posición; (*culturally, educationally*) superarse

better[2] ['betəʳ] N (= *gambler*) apostador(a) *m/f*

betterment ['betəmənt] N mejora *f*, mejoramiento *m*

betting ['betɪŋ] N • **the ~ is that they'll divorce** se da casi por sentado que van a divorciarse • **what's the ~ he won't come back?** ¿qué te apuestas a que no vuelve? • **the latest ~ is ...** las últimas apuestas son ...
CPD ▸ **betting man** (= *gambler*) jugador *m* • **are you a ~ man, Mr Day?** ¿le gusta apostar, Sr. Day? ▸ **betting office, betting shop** (*Brit*) casa *f* de apuestas ▸ **betting slip** (*Brit*) boleto *m* de apuestas ▸ **betting tax** impuesto *m* sobre las apuestas

bettor ['betəʳ] N (*US*) = **better**[2]

Betty ['betɪ] N (*familiar form of* **Elizabeth**) Isabelita

between [bɪ'twi:n] PREP **1** entre • **the shops are shut ~ two and four o'clock** las tiendas cierran de dos a cuatro • **~ now and May** de ahora a mayo • **I sat (in) ~ John and Sue** me senté entre John y Sue • **it's ~ five and six metres long** mide entre cinco y seis metros de largo
2 (= *amongst*) entre • **we shared it ~ us** nos lo repartimos entre los dos • **just ~ you and me** • **just ~ ourselves** entre nosotros • **we only had £5 ~ us** teníamos solo 5 libras entre todos • **we did it ~ the two of us** lo hicimos entre los dos
ADV (*also* **in between**) (*time*) mientras tanto; (*place*) en medio, entre medio

betweentimes [bɪ'twi:ntaɪmz] ADV, **betweenwhiles** [bɪ'twi:nwaɪlz] ADV mientras, entretanto

betwixt [bɪ'twɪkst] ADV • **~ and between** entre lo uno y lo otro, entre las dos cosas
PREP †† (*liter*) = **between**

bevel ['bevəl] ADJ biselado
N (= *tool*) (*also* **bevel edge**) cartabón *m*, escuadra *f* falsa; (= *surface*) bisel *m*
VT biselar

bevel-edged [,bevl'edʒd] ADJ biselado

bevelled, beveled (*US*) ['bevəld] ADJ [*edge*] biselado

beverage ['bevərɪdʒ] N bebida *f*

bevvy* ['bevɪ] N (*Brit*) **1** (= *drink*) trago* *m* • **he's back on the ~** ha vuelto a la bebida
2 (= *drinking session*) • **to go out on the ~** ir a emborracharse

bevy ['bevɪ] N [*of girls, women*] grupo *m*; [*of birds*] bandada *f*

bewail [bɪ'weɪl] VT lamentar

beware [bɪ'wɛəʳ] VI • **to ~ of sth/sb** tener cuidado con algo/algn • **beware!** ¡cuidado! • **"beware of the dog!"** "¡cuidado con el perro!" • **"beware of pickpockets!"** "¡ojo con

los carteristas!" • **"beware of imitations!"** (*Comm*) "desconfíe de las imitaciones"
bewhiskered [bɪ'wɪskəd] ADJ bigotudo
bewigged [bɪ'wɪgd] ADJ con peluca
bewilder [bɪ'wɪldəʳ] VT desconcertar, dejar perplejo
bewildered [bɪ'wɪldəd] ADJ [*person*] desconcertado, perplejo • **he gave me a ~ look** me miró perplejo
bewildering [bɪ'wɪldərɪŋ] ADJ desconcertante
bewilderingly [bɪ'wɪldərɪŋlɪ] ADV de modo desconcertante • **a ~ complicated matter** un asunto de una complejidad increíble
bewilderment [bɪ'wɪldəmənt] N perplejidad *f*, desconcierto *m* • **to look around in ~** mirar alrededor perplejo *or* desconcertado
bewitch [bɪ'wɪtʃ] VT (= *cast a spell on*) hechizar; (= *seduce*) seducir, cautivar; (= *enchant*) encantar
bewitching [bɪ'wɪtʃɪŋ] ADJ cautivador
bewitchingly [bɪ'wɪtʃɪŋlɪ] ADV cautivadoramente • **~ beautiful** de una belleza cautivadora
beyond [bɪ'jɒnd] PREP **1** (*in space*) (= *further than*) más allá de; (= *on the other side of*) al otro lado de • **you can't go ~ the barrier** no se puede cruzar la barrera • **~ the convent walls** tras los muros del convento • **~ the seas** allende los mares
2 (*in time*) • **she won't stay much ~ a month** no se quedará mucho más de un mes • **we can't see ~ 2010** no podemos ver más allá de 2010 • **it was ~ the middle of June** era más de mediados de junio • **~ 12 o'clock** pasadas las 12 • **it's ~ bedtime** ya se ha pasado la hora de irse a la cama
3 (= *surpassing, exceeding*) • **the situation was ~ her control** la situación estaba fuera de su control • **what he has done is ~ my comprehension** lo que ha hecho me resulta incomprensible • **it's ~ me why ...*** no alcanzo a ver por qué ... • **this is getting ~ me** se me está haciendo imposible esto • **it's ~ belief** es increíble • **it's ~ doubt that ...** no cabe duda de que ... • **that's ~ a joke** eso es el colmo • **that job was ~ him** ese trabajo era demasiado para él *or* era superior a sus fuerzas • **his interests extend ~ the fine arts to philosophy** sus intereses se extienden más allá de las bellas artes a la filosofía • **~ repair** irreparable
4 (= *apart from*) aparte de • **I knew nothing ~ a few random facts** no sabía nada, aparte de algunos hechos aislados • **he has no personal staff, ~ a secretary** no tiene personal, aparte de una secretaria
ADV más allá • **next year and ~** el año que viene y después
N • **the (great) ~** el más allá • **to live at the back of ~*** vivir en el quinto pino, vivir en el quinto infierno*
bezique [bɪ'zi:k] N *juego de cartas que se juega con dos barajas*
BF* N ABBR = **bloody fool**
b/f ABBR = **brought forward**
BFPO N ABBR (*Brit*) (*Mil*) = **British Forces Post Office**
b/fwd ABBR = **b/f**
bhaji ['bɑ:dʒɪ] N *verduras rebozadas típicas de la cocina india*
bhangra, Bhangra ['bæŋgrə] N *música folclórica hindú muy popular en el Reino Unido*
bhp N ABBR = **brake horsepower**
Bhutan [bu:'tɑ:n] N Bután *m*
bi... [baɪ] PREFIX bi...
Biafra [bɪ'æfrə] N Biafra *f*
Biafran [bɪ'æfrən] ADJ de Biafra
N nativo/a *m/f* *or* habitante *mf* de Biafra
biannual [baɪ'ænjʊəl] ADJ semestral
biannually ['baɪ'ænjʊəlɪ] ADV semestralmente, dos veces al año
bias ['baɪəs] N **1** (= *inclination*) propensión *f*, predisposición *f* (**to, towards** a) • **a course with a practical ~** un curso orientado a la práctica • **a right-wing ~** una tendencia derechista
2 (= *prejudice*) prejuicio *m* (**against** contra), parcialidad *f*
3 [*of material*] sesgo *m*, bies *m* • **to cut sth on the ~** cortar algo al sesgo *or* al bies
VT influir en • **to ~ sb for/against sth** predisponer a algn en pro/en contra de algo • **to be ~(s)ed in favour of** estar predispuesto a *or* en favor de • **to be ~(s)ed against** tener prejuicio contra
CPD ▸ **bias binding** (*Sew*) bies *m*, ribete *m* al bies
biased, biassed ['baɪəst] ADJ parcial
biathlon [baɪ'æθlən] N biatlón *m*
bib [bɪb] N (*for child*) babero *m*; (*on dungarees*) peto *m* • IDIOM: • **in one's best bib and tucker*** acicalado
Bible ['baɪbl] N Biblia *f* • **the Holy ~** la Santa Biblia
CPD ▸ **the Bible Belt** (*US*) *los estados ultraprotestantes de EEUU* ▸ **Bible class** (*for confirmation etc*) ≈ catequesis *f inv* ▸ **Bible college** (*US*) colegio *m* evangelista ▸ **Bible reading** (= *passage*) pasaje *m* de la biblia • **today's ~ reading** la lectura de la Biblia de hoy ▸ **Bible school** (*US*) escuela *f* de enseñanza de la Biblia ▸ **Bible story** historia *f* de la Biblia ▸ **Bible study** estudio *m* de la Biblia ▸ **Bible thumper*** *creyente muy celoso de la Biblia*
biblical ['bɪblɪkəl] ADJ bíblico
biblio... ['bɪblɪəʊ] PREFIX biblio...
bibliographer [,bɪblɪ'ɒgrəfəʳ] N bibliógrafo/a *m/f*
bibliographic [,bɪblɪə'græfɪk] ADJ = **bibliographical**
bibliographical [,bɪblɪə'græfɪkəl] ADJ bibliográfico
bibliography [,bɪblɪ'ɒgrəfɪ] N bibliografía *f*
bibliomania [,bɪblɪəʊ'meɪnɪə] N bibliomanía *f*
bibliometric [,bɪblɪəʊ'metrɪk] ADJ bibliométrico
bibliometry [,bɪblɪ'ɒmɪtrɪ] N bibliometría *f*
bibliophile ['bɪblɪəʊfaɪl] N bibliófilo/a *m/f*
bibulous ['bɪbjʊləs] ADJ bebedor, borrachín
bicameral [baɪ'kæmərəl] ADJ bicameral
bicarb* ['baɪkɑ:b] N = **bicarbonate of soda**
bicarbonate of soda [baɪ'kɑ:bənɪtəv'səʊdə] N bicarbonato *m* de soda
bicentenary [,baɪsen'ti:nərɪ] N bicentenario *m*
CPD (de) bicentenario ▸ **bicentenary celebrations** celebraciones *fpl* de(l) bicentenario
bicentennial [baɪsen'tenɪəl] N, CPD (*US*) = **bicentenary**
biceps ['baɪseps] N bíceps *m inv*
bicker ['bɪkəʳ] VI discutir, reñir
bickering ['bɪkərɪŋ] N riñas *fpl*, discusiones *fpl*
bickie* ['bɪkɪ] N (*Brit*) (*esp baby talk*) galleta *f*
bicuspid [baɪ'kʌspɪd] ADJ bicúspide
N bicúspide *m*
bicycle ['baɪsɪkl] N bicicleta *f* • **to ride a ~** ir *or* montar en bicicleta
VI ir en bicicleta • **to ~ to Dover** ir en bicicleta a Dover
CPD ▸ **bicycle chain** cadena *f* de bicicleta ▸ **bicycle clip** pinza *f* para ir en bicicleta ▸ **bicycle kick** (*Ftbl*) chilena *f* ▸ **bicycle lane** carril *m* para ciclistas ▸ **bicycle path** pista *f* de ciclismo ▸ **bicycle pump** bomba *f* de bicicleta ▸ **bicycle rack** (*on floor, ground*) aparcamiento-bici *m*; (*on car roof*) portabicicletas *m inv* ▸ **bicycle shed** cobertizo *m* para bicicletas ▸ **bicycle touring** cicloturismo *m* ▸ **bicycle track** pista *f* de ciclismo
bicyclist† ['baɪsɪklɪst] N ciclista *mf*
bid [bɪd] N **1** (*at auction*) oferta *f*, puja *f*; (*Econ*) oferta *f* • **the highest bid** la mejor oferta *or* puja • **to raise one's bid** subir su puja
2 (= *attempt*) tentativa *f*, intento *m* • **in a bid to** en un intento de • **to make a bid for freedom/power** hacer un intento para conseguir la libertad/el poder • **to make a bid to do sth** hacer un intento para hacer algo
3 (*Cards*) marca *f* • **no bid** paso
VT **1** (PT, PP: **bid**) (*at auction etc*) pujar • **to bid £10 for** ofrecer 10 libras por
2 (PT: **bad(e)**, PP: **bidden†**) (*also poet*) (= *order*) mandar • **to bid sb to do sth** mandar a algn hacer algo
3 (PT: **bad(e)**, PP: **bidden**) • **to bid sb good morning** dar los buenos días a algn; ▹ **adieu**
VI (PT, PP: **bid**) **1** (*at auction etc*) • **to bid (for)** pujar (por), hacer una oferta (por) • **to bid against sb** pujar contra algn
2 (= *try*) • **to bid for power/fame** intentar alcanzar el poder/la fama • **to bid to do sth** intentar hacer algo
3 (*Cards*) marcar, declarar
4 (*liter*) • **to bid fair to** (+ *infin*) prometer (+ *infin*), dar esperanzas de (+ *infin*)
CPD ▸ **bid price** precio *m* de oferta
▸ **bid up** VT + ADV [+ *item*] ofrecer más por • **to bid up the price (of sth)** ofrecer un precio más alto (por algo)
biddable ['bɪdəbl] ADJ **1** [*person*] obediente, sumiso
2 (*Cards*) marcable
bidden ['bɪdn] PP *of* **bid**
bidder ['bɪdəʳ] N **1** (*at auction*) (*also Comm*) postor(a) *m/f* • **the highest ~** el/la mejor postor(a)
2 (*Cards*) declarante *mf*
bidding ['bɪdɪŋ] N **1** (*at auction*) ofertas *fpl*, puja *f* • **the ~ opened at £5** la primera puja fue de 5 libras • **there was keen ~ for the picture** hubo una rápida serie de ofertas por el cuadro • **to raise** *or* **up the ~** subir la puja
2 (*Cards*) declaración *f* • **to open the ~** abrir la declaración
3 (*frm*) (= *order*) orden *f*, mandato *m* • **they did it at her ~** lo hicieron cumpliendo sus órdenes • **to do sb's ~** cumplir las órdenes *or* el mandato de algn
4 (*Rel*) (*also* **bidding prayers**) oraciones *fpl* de los fieles
biddy* ['bɪdɪ] N • **old ~** viejecita *f*
bide [baɪd] VT • **to ~ one's time** esperar la hora propicia
bidet ['bi:deɪ] N bidet *m*, bidé *m*
bidirectional [baɪdɪ'rekʃənl] ADJ bidireccional
biennial [baɪ'enɪəl] ADJ **1** (= *every two years*) bienal
2 (*Bot*) bianual
N (= *plant*) planta *f* bienal
biennially [baɪ'enɪəlɪ] ADV bienalmente, cada dos años
bier [bɪəʳ] N andas *fpl* (*para el féretro*)
biff* [bɪf] N bofetada *f*
VT dar una bofetada a
bifocal ['baɪ'fəʊkəl] ADJ bifocal
N **bifocals** gafas *fpl* bifocales
bifurcate ['baɪfəkeɪt] VI bifurcarse
big [bɪg] ADJ (COMPAR: **bigger**, SUPERL: **biggest**) **1** (*in size*) [*house, book, city*] grande • **a big car** un coche grande • **a big stick** un

b

palo grande • **this dress is too big for me** este vestido me queda demasiado grande • **how big is the wardrobe?** ¿cómo es de grande el armario? • **he was a big man** era un hombre corpulento • **a big woman** (= *heavily-built*) una mujer grande *or* grandota; (*euph*) (= *fat*) una mujer de grandes dimensiones • **there's a big backlog of applications** hay un montón de solicitudes atrasadas • **to take a big bite out of sth** dar un buen bocado a algo • **the big city** la gran ciudad • **I'm not a big eater*** no soy de mucho comer • **to get** *or* **grow big(ger)** crecer • **he gave me a big kiss** me dio un besote *or* un beso fuerte • **he likes using big words** le gusta usar palabras difíciles; ▹ GREAT, BIG, LARGE

2 (= *significant, serious*) [*change, problem*] grande • **the biggest problem at the moment is unemployment** el mayor problema de hoy día es el desempleo • **the big question is, will he accept?** la cuestión es: ¿aceptará? • **it makes a big difference** eso cambia mucho las cosas • **you're making a big mistake** estás cometiendo un grave error • **a tragedy? that's rather a big word** ¿una tragedia? eso es llevar las cosas un poco lejos

3 (= *important*) [*company, bank*] importante, grande • **he's one of our biggest customers** es uno de nuestros clientes más importantes, es uno de nuestros mayores clientes • **this is her big day** hoy es su gran día, hoy es un día muy importante para ella • **to be big in publishing/plastics** ser muy conocido en el mundo editorial/la industria del plástico • **the big match** el partido más importante

4* (*in age*) [*girl, boy*] grande • **my big brother/sister** mi hermano/a mayor • **big boys don't cry** los niños grandes no lloran • **you're a big girl now!** ¡ahora ya eres mayorcita!

5* (*as intensifier*) • **he's a big cheat/bully/liar** es un tramposo/un abusón/un mentiroso de marca mayor

6 (*in phrases*) • **the big eight/ten** (*US*) (*Univ*) *las ocho/diez mayores universidades del centro oeste de EE.UU.* • **to have a big heart** tener un gran corazón • **what's the big hurry?*** ¿a qué viene tanta prisa? • **what's the big idea?*** ¿a qué viene eso? • **to have big ideas** hacerse ilusiones • **don't get any big ideas** no te hagas muchas ilusiones • **there's big money in tourism** se puede ganar mucho dinero con el turismo • **to make** *or* **earn big money** ganar mucho dinero • **to have a big mouth*** (*fig*) ser un bocazas* • **why don't you keep your big mouth shut!*** ¡no seas bocazas!* • **me and my big mouth!*** ¡quién me manda decir nada! • **Mr Big*** el número uno • **it was big of you to lend them the money** fue muy generoso de tu parte prestarles el dinero • **(that's) big of you!*** (*iro*) ¡qué generosidad la tuya! (*iro*) • **to be big on sth/sb*** ser un fanático de algo/algn • **a big one** (*US**) un billete de mil dólares • **we're onto something big!** ¡hemos dado con algo gordo! • **to do sth/things in a big way*** hacer algo/las cosas a lo grande • **I think boxing will take off in a big way here*** pienso que el boxeo va a tener una aceptación buenísima aquí • **the big wide world** el ancho mundo • IDIOM: • **he's too big for his boots*** tiene muchos humos • **you're getting too big for your boots, young lady!*** se te están subiendo mucho los humos, señorita; ▹ **deal**[1], GREAT, BIG, LARGE

ADV * • **to act big** fanfarronear • **to go down big** tener muchísimo éxito, ser un verdadero éxito • **to make it big** triunfar • **she could have made it big as a singer** podría haber triunfado como cantante • **to talk big** darse mucha importancia, fanfarronear • **to think big** planear a lo grande, ser ambicioso

CPD ▸ **the Big Apple** la Gran Manzana, Nueva York *f*; ▹ CITY NICKNAMES ▸ **big band** *orquesta grande que tocaba música de jazz o de baile y que fue muy popular entre los años 30 y 50* ▸ **the big bang** (*Astron*) el big bang, la gran explosión • **the big bang theory** la teoría del big bang *or* de la gran explosión ▸ **Big Ben** (*Brit*) Big Ben *m* ▸ **Big Brother** (*Pol*) (*also fig*) • **Big Brother is watching you** el Gran Hermano te vigila ▸ **big business** (*Ind, Comm*) las grandes empresas • **tourism is big business in Thailand** el turismo es un gran negocio en Tailandia ▸ **the big cats** (*Zool*) los grandes felinos ▸ **big dipper** (*at fair*) montaña *f* rusa • **the Big Dipper** (*US*) (*Astron*) la Osa Mayor ▸ **the Big Easy** Nueva Orleans ▸ **big end** (*Aut*) cabeza *f* de biela ▸ **big fish*** (*fig*) (= *person*) pez *m* gordo* ▸ **big game** caza *f* mayor • **big game hunter** cazador(a) *m/f* de caza mayor • **big game hunting** caza *f* mayor ▸ **the big hand** (*used to or by children*) (*on clock*) la aguja grande ▸ **big night** (= *important evening*) gran noche *f* ▸ **The Big Issue** (*Brit*) *revista vendida por personas sin hogar*, ≈ La Farola (*Sp*) ▸ **big name*** figura *f* importante ▸ **big noise***, **big shot*** pez *m* gordo* ▸ **big talk** fanfarronadas *fpl* ▸ **the big time*** el estrellato, el éxito • **to make the big time** alcanzar el éxito, triunfar; ▹ **big-time** ▸ **big toe** dedo *m* gordo (del pie) ▸ **big top** (= *circus*) circo *m*; (= *main tent*) carpa *f* principal ▸ **big wheel** (*at fair*) noria *f*; (= *person**) personaje *m*, pez *m* gordo*

bigamist [ˈbɪɡəmɪst] N bígamo/a *m/f*

bigamous [ˈbɪɡəməs] ADJ bígamo

bigamy [ˈbɪɡəmɪ] N bigamia *f*

big-boned [ˌbɪɡˈbəʊnd] ADJ de huesos grandes, huesudo

biggie* [ˈbɪɡɪ] N (= *song, film*) gran éxito *m*; (= *person, company*) uno/a *m/f* de los grandes • **some ~ in drugs** uno de los grandes en lo de las drogas • **the film is this summer's box-office ~** esta película es el gran éxito de taquilla de este verano

biggish [ˈbɪɡɪʃ] ADJ bastante grande

bighead* [ˈbɪɡhed] N creído/a* *m/f*, engreído/a *m/f*

big-headed* [ˈbɪɡˈhedɪd] ADJ creído*, engreído

big-hearted [ˈbɪɡˈhɑːtɪd] ADJ generoso

bight [baɪt] N **1** (*Geog*) ensenada *f*, cala *f*; (= *bend*) recodo *m*

2 [*of rope*] gaza *f*, laza *f*

bigmouth* [ˈbɪɡmaʊθ] N (PL: **bigmouths** [ˈbɪɡmaʊðz]) (= *loudmouth*) bocazas* *mf*; (= *gossipy person*) cotilla* *mf*

big-mouthed [ˈbɪɡˈmaʊθt] ADJ **1** de boca grande

2* (= *loudmouthed*) bocazas*; (= *gossipy*) cotilla*

bigot [ˈbɪɡət] N intolerante *mf*

bigoted [ˈbɪɡətɪd] ADJ intolerante

bigotry [ˈbɪɡətrɪ] N intolerancia *f*

big-ticket [ˈbɪɡˌtɪkɪt] ADJ (*US*) • **big-ticket item** compra *f* importante

big-time* [ˈbɪɡtaɪm] ADJ • **big-time football/politics** fútbol *m*/política *f* de alto nivel • **a big-time politician/actor** un político/actor de primera línea • **a big-time banker** un banquero de categoría

ADV • **he has tasted success big-time** ha conocido el éxito con mayúsculas* • **they screwed (things) up big-time** metieron la pata bien hondo* • **America lost big-time** el equipo americano se llevó una soberana paliza*

bigwig* [ˈbɪɡwɪɡ] N gerifalte *mf*, pez *m* gordo*

bijou [ˈbiːʒuː] ADJ • **"bijou residence for sale"** (*Brit*) "se vende vivienda, verdadera monada"

bike* [baɪk] N (= *bicycle*) bici* *f*; (= *motorcycle*) moto *f* • **to ride a ~** (= *bicycle*) ir *or* montar en bici; (= *motorcycle*) ir en moto • **on your ~!** (*Brit**) ¡largo de aquí!*, ¡andando!*

VI ir en bici • **I ~d 10km** hice 10km en bici

CPD ▸ **bike hire** alquiler *m* de bicicletas ▸ **bike lane** carril *m* de bicicleta, carril *m* bici ▸ **bike rack** (*on floor, ground*) aparcamiento-bici *m*; (*on car roof*) portabicicletas *m inv* ▸ **bike ride** vuelta *f* en bicicleta • **to go on a ~ ride** dar una vuelta en bicicleta ▸ **bike shed** cobertizo *m* para bicicletas ▸ **bike shop** tienda *f* de bicicletas

biker* [ˈbaɪkəʳ] N motociclista *mf*

bikeway [ˈbaɪkweɪ] N (= *lane*) carril *m* de bicicletas; (= *track*) pista *f* de ciclismo

bikini [bɪˈkiːnɪ] N bikini *m* (*f in Arg*)

CPD ▸ **bikini bottom(s)** parte *f* de abajo del bikini, bragas *fpl* del bikini ▸ **bikini briefs** bragas *fpl* del bikini, parte *f* de abajo del bikini ▸ **bikini line** entrepierna *f* ▸ **bikini top** parte *f* de arriba del bikini

bilabial [baɪˈleɪbɪəl] ADJ bilabial

N bilabial *f*

bilateral [baɪˈlætərəl] ADJ bilateral

bilaterally [baɪˈlætərəlɪ] ADV bilateralmente

bilberry [ˈbɪlbərɪ] N arándano *m*

bile [baɪl] N **1** (*Med*) bilis *f*

2 (*fig*) (= *anger*) mal genio *m*, displicencia *f*

bilestone [ˈbaɪlˌstəʊn] N cálculo *m* biliar

bilge [bɪldʒ] N **1** (*Naut*) pantoque *m*; (*also* **bilge water**) aguas *fpl* de pantoque

2‡ (= *nonsense*) tonterías *fpl*

CPD ▸ **bilge pump** (*Naut*) bomba *f* de achique ▸ **bilge water** aguas *fpl* de pantoque

bilharzia [bɪlˈhɑːzɪə] N, **bilharziasis** [ˌbɪlhɑːˈzaɪəsɪs] N bilharzia *f*, bilharziosis *f*, bilharciosis *f*

bilingual [baɪˈlɪŋɡwəl] ADJ bilingüe

bilingualism [baɪˈlɪŋɡwəlɪzəm] N bilingüismo *m*

bilious [ˈbɪlɪəs] ADJ **1** (= *horrid*) [*colour*] bilioso

2 (= *sick*) [*person*] bilioso

3 (= *irritable*) bilioso

4 (*Med*) • **to be** *or* **feel ~** sentirse revuelto

CPD ▸ **bilious attack** cólico *m* bilioso

biliousness [ˈbɪlɪəsnɪs] N (*Med*) trastornos *mpl* biliares

bilk* [bɪlk] VT (*US*) estafar, defraudar • **to ~ sb out of sth** estafar algo a algn

bill[1] [bɪl] N **1** (*esp Brit*) (*in restaurant, hotel etc*) cuenta *f*, adición *f* (*S. Cone*) • **can we have the ~, please?** ¿nos trae la cuenta, por favor? • **to pay the ~** pagar la cuenta • **put it on my ~, please** póngalo en mi cuenta • IDIOM: • **to foot the ~ (for sth)** correr con los gastos (de algo), pagar (algo)

2 (*Comm, Econ*) (= *invoice*) factura *f* • **the gas ~** la factura del gas • **wage(s) ~** (*in industry*) gastos *mpl* de nómina *or* salariales • **~s discounted** efectos *mpl* descontados • **~s payable** efectos *mpl* a pagar • **~s receivable** efectos *mpl* a cobrar

3 (*Parl*) proyecto *m* de ley • **the ~ passed the Commons** (*Brit*) el proyecto de ley fue aprobado en la Cámara de los Comunes

4 (*US*) (= *banknote*) billete *m* • **a 5-dollar ~** un billete de 5 dólares

5 (= *notice*) cartel *m* • **"stick no bills"** "prohibido fijar carteles"

6 (*Theat*) programa *m* • **to head** *or* **top the ~** ser la atracción principal, encabezar el reparto • IDIOM: • **that fills** *or* **fits the ~** eso cumple los requisitos

VT **1** (*Theat*) anunciar, presentar • **he is ~ed to appear next week** figura en el programa de la semana que viene • **it is ~ed as Britain's most interesting museum** lo presentan como el museo más interesante de Gran Bretaña

2 (*Comm*) • **to ~ sb for sth** extender *or* pasar a algn la factura de algo • **you've ~ed me for five instead of four** me ha puesto cinco en vez de cuatro en la factura

CPD ▸ **bill of exchange** letra *f* de cambio ▸ **bill of fare** carta *f*, menú *m* ▸ **bill of health** • **the doctor gave him a clean ~ of health** el médico le aseguró que estaba perfectamente ▸ **bill of lading** conocimiento *m* de embarque ▸ **bill of rights** declaración *f* de derechos ▸ **bill of sale** escritura *f* de venta

bill[2] [bɪl] N **1** [*of bird*] pico *m*
2 [*of anchor*] uña *f*
3 (*Agr*) podadera *f*, podón *m*
4 (*Geog*) promontorio *m*

VI • **to ~ and coo** [*birds*] arrullarse; (*fig*) [*lovers*] arrullarse, hacerse arrumacos

BILL OF RIGHTS

El conjunto de las diez enmiendas (**amendments**) originales a la Constitución de los Estados Unidos, en vigor desde 1791, recibe el nombre de **Bill of Rights**. Aquí se enumeran los derechos que tiene todo ciudadano norteamericano y se definen algunos de los poderes de los gobiernos estatales y federal. Se incluyen, por ejemplo, el derecho a la libertad de culto, de asociación y de prensa (**First Amendment**), el derecho a llevar armas (**Second Amendment**) y el derecho a un juicio justo (**Sixth Amendment**). Entre las enmiendas hechas a la Constitución después de 1791 están el derecho a la igualdad de protección legal para todos los ciudadanos (**Fourteenth Amendment**) y el derecho al voto (**Fifteenth Amendment**).

▷ FIFTH AMENDMENT

Bill [bɪl] N **1** *familiar form of* **William**
2 (*Brit*‡) • **the (Old) ~** la poli*, la pasma (*Sp*‡)

billabong ['bɪlə,bɒŋ] N (*Australia*) [*of river*] brazo *m*; (= *pool*) poza *f*

billboard ['bɪlbɔ:d] N cartelera *f*

billet[1] ['bɪlɪt] N (*Mil*) alojamiento *m*
VT (*Mil*) • **to ~ sb (on sb)** alojar a algn (en casa de algn)

billet[2] ['bɪlɪt] N (= *wood*) leño *m*

billet-doux ['bɪleɪ'du:] N (PL: **billets-doux** ['bɪleɪ'du:]) carta *f* amorosa

billeting ['bɪlətɪŋ] N acantonamiento *m*
CPD ▸ **billeting officer** oficial *mf* de acantonamiento

billfold ['bɪlfəʊld] N (*US*) billetero *m*, cartera *f*

billhook ['bɪlhʊk] N podadera *f*, podón *m*

billiard ['bɪljəd] ADJ de billar
CPD ▸ **billiard ball** bola *f* de billar ▸ **billiard cue** taco *m* (de billar) ▸ **billiard hall** sala *f* de billar, billares *mpl* ▸ **billiard table** mesa *f* de billar

billiards ['bɪljədz] NSING billar *msing*

billing[1] ['bɪlɪŋ] N (*Theat*) • **to get top ~** ser la atracción principal, encabezar el reparto

billing[2] ['bɪlɪŋ] N • **~ and cooing** (*fig*) besuqueo *m*, caricias *fpl*

billion ['bɪlɪən] N (PL: **billion** *or* **billions**) (= *thousand million*) mil millones *mpl*; (*Brit*†) (= *million million*) billón *m* • **I've told you a ~ times** te lo he dicho infinidad de veces

billionaire [,bɪlɪə'neəʳ] N billonario/a *m/f*

billionth ['bɪljənθ] ADJ (= *thousand millionth*) milmillonésimo; (*Brit*†) (= *million millionth*) billonésimo
N milmillonésima *f*; (*Brit*†) billonésima *f*

billow ['bɪləʊ] N oleada *f* • **the ~s** (*liter*) las olas, el mar
VI [*smoke*] salir en nubes; [*sail*] ondear
▸ **billow out** VI + ADV hincharse (*de viento etc*)

billowy ['bɪləʊɪ] ADJ [*sea, waves, smoke*] ondulante; [*sail*] ondeante

billposter ['bɪl,pəʊstəʳ], **billsticker** ['bɪl,stɪkəʳ] N pegador(a) *m/f* de carteles

Billy ['bɪlɪ] N *familiar form of* **William**

billy ['bɪlɪ] N (*US*) (*also* **billy club**) porra *f*

billycan ['bɪlɪkæn] N cazo *m*

billy goat ['bɪlɪgəʊt] N macho *m* cabrío

billy-o, billy-oh* ['bɪlɪəʊ], **billy-ho*** ['bɪlɪhəʊ] ADV (*Brit*) • **like billy-o** a todo tren*, a más no poder • **it's raining like billy-o** llueve a más no poder

BIM N ABBR = **British Institute of Management**

bimbo* ['bɪmbəʊ] N (PL: **bimbos** *or* **bimboes**) (*pej*) *mujer guapa y tonta*, tía *f* buena sin coco (*Sp**)

bimonthly ['baɪ'mʌnθlɪ] ADJ (= *every two months*) bimestral; (= *twice monthly*) bimensual, quincenal
ADV (= *every two months*) bimestralmente; (= *twice monthly*) bimensualmente, quincenalmente
N (= *two monthly publication*) revista *f* bimestral; (= *fortnightly publication*) revista *f* bimensual *or* quincenal

bin [bɪn] N (*for bread*) panera *f*; (*for coal*) carbonera *f*; (= *rubbish bin, dustbin*) cubo *m* de la basura, tarro *m* de la basura (*LAm*); (= *litter bin*) papelera *f*
VT* (= *throw away*) tirar
CPD ▸ **bin bag, bin liner** bolsa *f* de la basura

binary ['baɪnərɪ] ADJ binario
CPD ▸ **binary code** código *m* binario ▸ **binary notation** notación *f* binaria ▸ **binary number** número *m* binario ▸ **binary system** sistema *m* binario

bind [baɪnd] (PT, PP: **bound**) VT **1** (= *tie together*) atar; (= *tie down, make fast*) sujetar; (*fig*) unir (**to** a) • **bound hand and foot** atado de pies y manos
2 (= *encircle*) rodear (**with** de), ceñir (**with** con, de)
3 [+ *wound, arm etc*] vendar; [+ *bandage*] enrollar
4 (*Sew*) [+ *material, hem*] ribetear; (*Agr*) [+ *corn*] agavillar
5 [+ *book*] encuadernar
6 (= *oblige*) • **to ~ sb to sth** obligar a algn a cumplir con algo • **to ~ sb to do sth** obligar a algn a hacer algo • **to ~ sb as an apprentice to** poner a algn de aprendiz con; ▷ **bound**[1]
7 (*Culin*) unir, trabar
VI [*cement etc*] cuajarse; [*parts of machine*] trabarse
N (*Brit**) (= *nuisance*) lata* *f* • **it's a ~** es una lata* • **what a ~!** ¡qué lata!* • **to be in a ~** estar en apuros • **the ~ is that ...** el problema es que ...
▸ **bind on** VT + ADV prender
▸ **bind over** VT + ADV (*Brit*) (*Jur*) obligar a comparecer ante el magistrado • **to ~ sb over for six months** conceder a algn la libertad bajo fianza durante seis meses • **to ~ sb over to keep the peace** exigir a algn legalmente que no reincida
▸ **bind together** VT + ADV (*lit*) atar; (*fig*) unir
▸ **bind up** VT + ADV **1** [+ *wound*] vendar
2 • **to be bound up in** [+ *work, research etc*] estar absorto en • **to be bound up with** (= *connected to*) estar estrechamente ligado *or* vinculado a

binder ['baɪndəʳ] N **1** (= *file*) carpeta *f*
2 (*Agr*) agavilladora *f*
3 [*of book*] encuadernador(a) *m/f*

bindery ['baɪndərɪ] N taller *m* de encuadernación

binding ['baɪndɪŋ] N **1** [*of book*] encuadernación *f*
2 (*Sew*) ribete *m*
3 (*on skis*) ataduras *fpl*
ADJ **1** [*agreement, contract, decision*] vinculante; [*promise*] que hay que cumplir • **to be ~ on sb** ser obligatorio para algn
2 (*Med*) que estriñe

bindweed ['baɪndwi:d] N convólvulo *m*, enredadera *f*

binge* [bɪndʒ] N [*of drinking*] borrachera *f*; [*of eating*] comilona* *f*, atracón* *m* • **to go on a ~** ir de juerga • **to go on a spending ~** salir de compras a despilfarrar el dinero
VI (*gen*) correrse un exceso; (*eating*) darse una comilona*, darse un atracón* • **to ~ on chocolate** darse un atracón *or* ponerse hasta arriba de chocolate*
CPD ▸ **binge drinker** *persona que se emborracha con regularidad* ▸ **binge drinking** borracheras *fpl* ▸ **binge eating** (*by person with eating disorder*) hiperfagia *f*

bingo ['bɪŋgəʊ] N bingo *m*
EXCL ¡premio!
CPD ▸ **bingo caller** locutor(a) *m/f* de bingo ▸ **bingo hall** bingo *m*

binman ['bɪn,mæn] N (PL: **binmen**) (*Brit*) basurero *m*

binnacle ['bɪnəkl] N bitácora *f*

binocular [bɪ'nɒkjuləʳ] ADJ binocular

binoculars [bɪ'nɒkjuləz] NPL gemelos *mpl*, prismáticos *mpl*; (*Mil*) anteojo *m* de campaña

binomial [baɪ'nəʊmɪəl] ADJ de dos términos
N binomio *m*

bint‡ [bɪnt] N (*Brit*) (*pej*) tía *f* (*Sp**), tronca‡ *f*, titi‡ *f*

binuclear [baɪ'nju:klɪəʳ] ADJ binuclear

bio... ['baɪəʊ] PREFIX bio...

bioactive [,baɪəʊ'æktɪv] ADJ bioactivo

biobank ['baɪəʊbæŋk] N biobanco *m*

biochemical [,baɪəʊ'kemɪkəl] ADJ bioquímico

biochemist ['baɪəʊ'kemɪst] N bioquímico/a *m/f*

biochemistry [,baɪəʊ'kemɪstrɪ] N bioquímica *f*

biodegradable [,baɪəʊdɪ'greɪdəbl] ADJ biodegradable

biodegradation [,baɪəʊ,degrə'deɪʃən] N biodegradación *f*

biodegrade [,baɪəʊdɪ'greɪd] VT biodegradar
VI biodegradarse

biodiesel ['baɪəʊ,di:zəl] N biodiésel *m*

biodiversity [,baɪəʊdaɪ'vɜ:sɪtɪ] N biodiversidad *f*

biodynamic ['baɪəʊdaɪ'næmɪk] ADJ biodinámico

bioengineering ['baɪəʊendʒɪ'nɪərɪŋ] N bioingeniería *f*

bioethanol [,baɪəʊ'eθənɒl] N bioetanol *m*

bioethics [,baɪəʊ'eθɪks] NSING bioética *f*

biofeedback [,baɪəʊ'fi:dbæk] N biofeedback *m*

biofuel ['baɪəʊfjʊəl] N combustible *m* biológico

biogas ['baɪəʊgæs] N biogás *m*

biogenesis [,baɪəʊ'dʒenɪsɪs] N biogénesis *f*

biogenetics [,baɪəʊdʒɪ'netɪks] NSING biogenética *f*

biographee [baɪ,ɒgrə'fi:] N biografiado/a *m/f*

biographer [baɪ'ɒgrəfəʳ] N biógrafo/a *m/f*

biographic [,baɪəʊ'græfɪk] ADJ

= biographical
biographical [ˌbaɪəʊˈgræfɪkəl] ADJ biográfico
biography [baɪˈɒgrəfɪ] N biografía *f*
biohazard [ˌbaɪəʊˈhæzəd] N biorriesgo *m*, riesgo *m* biológico
bioinformatics [ˌbaɪəʊˌɪnfəˈmætɪks] NSING bioinformática *f*
biol. ABBR (= **biology**) biol.
biological [ˌbaɪəˈlɒdʒɪkəl] ADJ biológico
CPD ▸ **biological clock** reloj *m* biológico, reloj *m* interno ▸ **biological diversity** = **biodiversity** ▸ **biological soap powder** detergente *m* biológico ▸ **biological warfare** guerra *f* biológica ▸ **biological weapons** armas *fpl* biológicas
biologically [ˌbaɪəˈlɒdʒɪkəlɪ] ADV [*active, programmed, determined*] biológicamente; [*different*] desde el punto de vista biológico • **~ speaking it provides a source of variation** desde el punto de vista biológico proporciona una fuente de variación
biologist [baɪˈɒlədʒɪst] N biólogo/a *m/f*
biology [baɪˈɒlədʒɪ] N biología *f*
biomass [ˈbaɪəʊˌmæs] N biomasa *f*
biome [ˈbaɪəʊm] N biomedio *m*
biomechanics [ˌbaɪəʊmɪˈkænɪks] NSING biomecánica *f*
biomedical [ˌbaɪəʊˈmedɪkl] ADJ biomédico
biometric [ˌbaɪəˈmetrɪk] ADJ [*data, technology, device*] biométrico
biometrics [ˌbaɪəˈmetrɪks] NSING, **biometry** [baɪˈɒmətrɪ] N biometría *f*
bionic [baɪˈɒnɪk] ADJ biónico
bionics [baɪˈɒnɪks] NSING electrónica *f* biológica
bio-organic [ˌbaɪəʊɔːˈgænɪk] ADJ bioorgánico
CPD ▸ **bio-organic chemistry** química *f* bioorgánica
biophysical [ˌbaɪəʊˈfɪzɪkəl] ADJ biofísico
biophysicist [ˌbaɪəʊˈfɪzɪsɪst] N biofísico/a *m/f*
biophysics [ˌbaɪəʊˈfɪzɪks] NSING biofísica *f*
biopic* [ˈbaɪəʊˌpɪk] N biografía *f* cinematográfica
biopiracy [ˌbaɪəʊˈpaɪərəsɪ] N biopiratería *f*
bioprospecting [ˌbaɪəʊprəsˈpektɪŋ] N bioprospección *f*
ADJ [*company*] bioprospector
biopsy [ˈbaɪɒpsɪ] N biopsia *f*
biorhythm [ˈbaɪəʊrɪðəm] N biorritmo *m*
bioscopy [baɪˈɒskəpɪ] N bioscopia *f*
biosecurity [ˈbaɪəʊsɪˌkjʊərɪtɪ] N bioseguridad *f*
ADJ [*measures, programme, advice*] de bioseguridad
biosensor [ˈbaɪəʊˈsensəʳ] N biosensor *m*
biosphere [ˈbaɪəˌsfɪəʳ] N biosfera *f*
biostatistics [ˌbaɪəʊstəˈtɪstɪks] NPL bioestadística *f*
biosynthesis [ˌbaɪəʊˈsɪnθɪsɪs] N biosíntesis *f*
biosynthetic [ˌbaɪəʊˌsɪnˈθetɪk] ADJ biosintético
biotech* [ˈbaɪəʊtek] N biotecnología *f*
ADJ [*industry, company*] biotecnológico, de biotecnología; [*shares*] biotecnológico
biotechnological [ˌbaɪəʊˌteknəˈlɒdʒɪkəl] ADJ biotecnológico
biotechnologist [ˌbaɪəʊtekˈnɒlədʒɪst] N biotecnólogo/a *m/f*
biotechnology [ˌbaɪəʊtekˈnɒlədʒɪ] N biotecnología *f*
bioterror [ˌbaɪəʊˈterəʳ] N bioterrorismo *m*
ADJ [*attack*] bioterrorista
bioterrorism [ˌbaɪəʊˈterərɪzəm] N bioterrorismo *m*
bioterrorist [ˌbaɪəʊˈterərɪst] ADJ bioterrorista
N bioterrorista *mf*
biotic [baɪˈɒtɪk] ADJ biótico
biotope [ˈbaɪəˌtəʊp] N biotopo *m*
biotype [ˈbaɪəˌtaɪp] N biotipo *m*
biowarfare [ˈbaɪəʊˈwɔːfɛəʳ] N guerra *f* bacteriológica
bioweapon [ˈbaɪəʊˌwepən] N arma *f* biológica
bipartisan [ˌbaɪˈpɑːtɪzæn] ADJ bipartidario
bipartite [baɪˈpɑːtaɪt] ADJ (= *consisting of two parts*) [*structure*] bipartido; [*treaty*] bipartito
biped [ˈbaɪped] N bípedo *m*
biplane [ˈbaɪpleɪn] N biplano *m*
bipolar [baɪˈpəʊləʳ] ADJ bipolar
CPD ▸ **bipolar disorder** trastorno *m* bipolar
bipolarize [baɪˈpəʊləraɪz] VT bipolarizar
birch [bɜːtʃ] N (= *tree, wood*) abedul *m*; (*for whipping*) vara *f*
VT (= *punish*) castigar con la vara
CPD ▸ **birch tree** abedul *m*
birching [ˈbɜːtʃɪŋ] N azotamiento *m* (con la vara)
birchwood [ˈbɜːtʃwʊd] N (= *forest*) bosque *m* de abedules; (= *material*) abedul *m*
bird [bɜːd] N **1** (*gen small*) pájaro *m*; (*Zool, Culin*) ave *f* • **~ of ill omen** (*liter*) pájaro *m* de mal agüero • **a little ~ told me*** (*hum*) me lo dijo un pajarito • **the ~ has flown** (*fig*) el pájaro ha volado • IDIOMS: • **they haven't yet told her about the ~s and the bees** todavía no le han explicado las cosas de la vida • **to kill two ~s with one stone** matar dos pájaros de un tiro • **to be strictly for the ~s*** ser cosa de poca monta *or* de tontos • **they're ~s of a feather** son lobos de una camada • PROVERBS: • **~s of a feather flock together** Dios los cría y ellos se juntan • **a ~ in the hand is worth two in the bush** más vale pájaro en mano que ciento volando; ▹ **early**
2 (*Brit*) (*Theat**) • IDIOMS: • **to get the ~** ganarse un abucheo, ser pateado • **to give sb the ~** abuchear a algn, patear a algn
3 (*Brit**) (= *girl*) chica *f*, pollita *f*, niña *f* (*LAm*); (= *girlfriend*) chica *f*, amiguita *f*
4* (= *fellow*) tipo* *m*, tío *m* (*Sp**) • **he's a queer ~** es un bicho raro
5‡ (= *imprisonment*) • **to do two years ~** pasar dos años a la sombra‡
CPD ▸ **bird bath** pila *f* para pájaros ▸ **bird brain*** casquivano/a *m/f* ▸ **bird call** reclamo *m* ▸ **bird dog** (*US*) perro *m* de caza ▸ **bird fancier** criador(a) *m/f* de pájaros ▸ **bird feeder** comedero *m* para pájaros ▸ **bird flu** gripe *f* aviar ▸ **bird food** comida *f* para pájaros ▸ **bird nesting** • **to go ~ nesting** ir a buscar nidos ▸ **bird of paradise** ave *f* del paraíso ▸ **bird of passage** ave *f* de paso ▸ **bird of prey** ave *f* de rapiña ▸ **bird sanctuary** reserva *f* de pájaros ▸ **bird's nest** nido *m* de pájaro ▸ **bird table** *mesita de jardín para poner comida a los pájaros*
bird-brained* [ˈbɜːdbreɪnd] ADJ casquivano
birdcage [ˈbɜːdkeɪdʒ] N jaula *f* de pájaro; (*large, outdoor*) pajarera *f*
birder [ˈbɜːdəʳ] N aficionado/a *m/f* a la observación de aves, observador(a) *m/f* de aves
birdhouse [ˈbɜːdhaʊs] N (*in garden*) caja *f* nido; (*in zoo*) pajarera *f*
birdie [ˈbɜːdɪ] N **1** (*Golf*) birdie *m*, menos uno *m*
2 (*baby talk*) pajarito *m* • **watch the ~!** (*Phot**) ¡mira el pajarito!
VT (*Golf*) • **to ~ a hole** hacer birdie *or* uno bajo par en un hoyo
bird-like [ˈbɜːdlaɪk] ADJ como un pájaro
birdlime [ˈbɜːdlaɪm] N liga *f*
birdseed [ˈbɜːdsiːd] N alpiste *m*
bird's-eye view [ˌbɜːdzaɪˈvjuː] N vista *f* de pájaro
birdshot [ˈbɜːdʃɒt] N perdigones *mpl*
birdsong [ˈbɜːdsɒŋ] N canto *m* de los pájaros
bird-watcher [ˈbɜːdwɒtʃəʳ] N observador(a) *m/f* de aves
bird-watching [ˈbɜːdˌwɒtʃɪŋ] N observación *f* de aves • **to go bird-watching** realizar observación de aves
biretta [bɪˈretə] N birrete *m*
Biro® [ˈbaɪrəʊ] N (*Brit*) bolígrafo *m*, birome *f* (*S. Cone*)
birth [bɜːθ] N (*gen*) nacimiento *m*; (*Med*) parto *m*; (*fig*) nacimiento *m*, surgimiento *m* • **at ~** al nacer • **French by ~** francés de nacimiento • **of humble ~** de origen humilde • **place of ~** lugar *m* de nacimiento • **to give ~ to** (*lit*) dar a luz a; (*fig*) dar origen a • **to be in at the ~ of** (*fig*) asistir al nacimiento de • **the ~ of an idea** el origen de una idea
CPD ▸ **birth canal** canal *m* uterino ▸ **birth certificate** partida *f* de nacimiento ▸ **birth control** control *m* de la natalidad • **method of ~ control** método *m* anticonceptivo ▸ **birth control pill** píldora *f* anticonceptiva ▸ **birth defect** defecto *m* congénito, defecto *m* de nacimiento ▸ **birth mother** madre *f* biológica ▸ **birth pill** = **birth control pill** ▸ **birth plan** [*of pregnant woman*] plan *m* para el parto ▸ **birth rate** tasa *f or* índice *m* de natalidad ▸ **birth sign** (= *sign of the zodiac*) signo *m* del zodiaco • **what's your ~ sign?** ¿de qué signo eres? ▸ **birth weight** [*of newborn baby*] peso *m* al nacer
birthdate [ˈbɜːθdeɪt] N fecha *f* de nacimiento
birthday [ˈbɜːθdeɪ] N [*of person*] cumpleaños *m inv*; [*of event etc*] aniversario *m* • **on my 21st ~** el día en que cumplo/cumplí 21 años • **happy ~!** ¡feliz cumpleaños!
CPD ▸ **birthday bash*** fiesta *f* de cumpleaños ▸ **birthday boy** cumpleañero *m* ▸ **birthday cake** tarta *f* de cumpleaños ▸ **birthday card** tarjeta *f* de cumpleaños ▸ **birthday girl** cumpleañera *f* ▸ **birthday party** fiesta *f* de cumpleaños ▸ **birthday present** regalo *m* de cumpleaños ▸ **birthday suit*** • **in one's ~ suit** (*hum*) en cueros*
birthing [ˈbɜːθɪŋ] ADJ [*pool, centre etc*] de partos, para el parto
birthmark [ˈbɜːθmɑːk] N antojo *m*, marca *f* de nacimiento
birthplace [ˈbɜːθpleɪs] N lugar *m* de nacimiento
birthright [ˈbɜːθraɪt] N derechos *mpl* de nacimiento; (*fig*) patrimonio *m*, herencia *f* • **it is the ~ of every Englishman** pertenece por derecho natural a todo inglés, es el patrimonio de todo inglés • IDIOM: • **to sell one's ~ for a mess of pottage** vender su primogenitura por un plato de lentejas
birthstone [ˈbɜːθstəʊn] N piedra *f* natalicia
biryani [ˌbɪrɪˈɑːnɪ] N *plato típico de la comida hindú preparado con arroz, carne o verdura y condimentado con azafrán o cúrcuma*
BIS N ABBR (*US*) (= **Bank of International Settlements**) BIP *m*
Biscay [ˈbɪskeɪ] N Vizcaya *f*
biscuit [ˈbɪskɪt] N (*Brit*) galleta *f*; (*US*) magdalena *f* • IDIOM: • **that takes the ~!‡** ¡eso es el colmo!*
CPD ▸ **biscuit barrel** galletero *m* ▸ **biscuit tin** (*Brit*) caja *f* de galletas
bisect [baɪˈsekt] VT bisecar
bisection [baɪˈsekʃən] N (*Math*) bisección *f*, división *f* en dos partes; (= *angle*) bisección *f*
bisector [baɪˈsektəʳ] N bisector *m*

b

bisexual ['baɪ'seksjʊəl] (ADJ) bisexual (N) bisexual *mf*

bisexuality [baɪˌseksjʊ'ælɪtɪ] (N) bisexualidad *f*

bishop ['bɪʃəp] (N) **1** (*Rel*) obispo *m* • **yes, Bishop** sí, Ilustrísima
2 (*Chess*) alfil *m*

bishopric ['bɪʃəprɪk] (N) obispado *m*

bismuth ['bɪzməθ] (N) bismuto *m*

bison ['baɪsən] (N) (PL: **bison, bisons**) bisonte *m*

bisque [bɪsk] (N) (*Culin*) sopa *f* de mariscos; (*Sport*) ventaja *f*; (*Pottery*) bizcocho *m*, biscuit *m*

bistable [baɪ'steɪbl] (ADJ) (*Comput*) biestable

bistro ['biːstrəʊ] (N) bistro(t) *m*

bit¹ [bɪt] (N) **1** (= *piece*) trozo *m*, pedazo *m* • **bits of paper** trozos *mpl* or pedazos *mpl* de papel • **have you got a bit of paper I can write on?** ¿tienes un trozo de papel para escribir? • **he washed off every bit of dirt** se lavó hasta la última mancha de suciedad • **in bits** (= *broken*) hecho pedazos; (= *dismantled*) desmontado, desarmado • **who owns this bit of land?** ¿a quién pertenece este trozo *or* pedazo de tierra? • **bits and pieces** (= *items*) cosas *fpl*; (= *possessions*) cosas *fpl*, trastos* *mpl*; [*of fabric*] retales *mpl*, retazos *mpl* • **to bits: to blow sth to bits** hacer saltar algo en pedazos, volar algo en pedazos • **to come to bits** (= *break*) hacerse pedazos; (= *be dismantled*) desmontarse, desarmarse • **to smash sth to bits** hacer algo añicos *or* pedazos • **to tear sth to bits** [+ *letter, document*] romper algo en pedazos • **the dogs tear the fox to bits** los perros destrozan al zorro • **she tore the argument to bits** hizo pedazos el argumento • IDIOMS: • **to love sb to bits*** querer un montón a algn* • **the professor pulled his essay to bits** el profesor destrozó su trabajo • **he was thrilled to bits with the present** estaba que no cabía en sí (de alegría) con el regalo, el regalo le hizo muchísima ilusión
2 • **a bit of a** (= *some*) un poco de • **with a bit of luck** con un poco de suerte • **a bit of advice** un consejo • **I need a bit of peace and quiet** necesito un poco de paz y tranquilidad • **what you say won't make a bit of difference** digas lo que digas no va a cambiar nada • **this is a bit of all right!*** ¡esto está muy bien!, ¡esto no está nada mal! • **he's a bit of all right*** ese está buenísimo *or* para comérselo*
b (= *rather*) • **he's a bit of a liar** es bastante *or* un poco mentiroso • **it was a bit of a shock** fue un golpe bastante duro • **I've got a bit of a cold** estoy un poco resfriado • **I'm a bit of a socialist** yo tengo algo de socialista • **quite a bit of** bastante • **they have quite a bit of money** tienen bastante dinero • **I've been seeing quite a bit of her** la he estado viendo bastante
3 (*adverbial uses*) • **a bit** un poco • **a bit bigger/smaller** un poco más grande/pequeño • **a bit later** poco después, un poco más tarde • **that sounds a bit technical** eso suena un poco técnico • **it's a bit awkward just now** ahora no es buen momento • **bit by bit** poco a poco • **our performance was every bit as good as theirs** nuestra actuación fue tan buena como la suya en todos los aspectos • **she swept into the room, every bit the actress** entró majestuosamente en la habitación, muy en su papel de actriz • **he looked every bit the angelic child** tenía toda la pinta *or* todo el aspecto de un niño angelical • **a good bit** bastante • **it's a good bit further than we thought** queda bastante más lejos de lo que creíamos • **a good bit bigger/cheaper** bastante más grande/barato • **would you like a little bit more?** ¿quieres un poquito más? • **that's a bit much!** ¡eso pasa de castaño oscuro! • **it's a bit much expecting you to take the blame** es demasiado esperar que tú asumas la culpa • **not a bit:** • **I'm not a bit surprised** no me sorprende lo más mínimo *or* en absoluto • **"wasn't he embarrassed?" — "not a bit of it"** —¿y no le daba vergüenza? —qué va* *or* —en absoluto • **quite a bit** bastante • **they're worth quite a bit** valen bastante • **he's quite a bit older than me** es bastante mayor que yo • **I've had a bit too much to eat** me he pasado un poco comiendo, he comido un poco más de la cuenta
4 (= *part*) parte *f* • **he'd just got to the exciting bit** acababa de llegar a la parte emocionante • **to enjoy every bit of sth** disfrutar algo totalmente
5 (*Brit**) (= *role*) • **she's doing the prima donna bit** está haciendo su papel de diva • **it's important not to overdo the motherly bit** es importante no ser excesivamente maternal • **to do one's bit** aportar su granito de arena • **we must all do our bit to put an end to starvation in the Third World** para erradicar el hambre en el Tercer Mundo todos debemos aportar nuestro granito de arena • **he did his bit in the war** durante la guerra cumplió con su deber • **I've done my bit** yo he hecho mi parte *or* lo que me tocaba
6 (= *moment*) rato *m*, momento *m* • **I'll see you in a bit** te veo dentro de un momento *or* dentro de un ratito • **I waited quite a bit** esperé bastante tiempo *or* un buen rato
7 (= *coin*) (*Brit*) moneda *f*; (*US*) (= *12.5 cents*) doce centavos y medio • **a tuppenny bit** una moneda de dos peniques • **two bits** (*US*) 25 centavos • **for two bits I'd throw it all in** por dos duros lo dejaría todo • **he was always throwing in his two bits about how he'd put the economy to rights** siempre estaba dando su opinión *or* echando su cuarto a espadas sobre cómo arreglaría la economía
8 (*Comput*) bit *m*
9 (*Brit‡*) (*pej*) (= *woman*) tía *f* (*Sp**); ▷ side
(CPD) ▸ **bit part** (*Cine, Theat*) papel *m* de poca importancia, papel *m* pequeño

bit² [bɪt] (N) **1** [*of drill*] broca *f*
2 (*for horse*) freno *m*, bocado *m* • IDIOMS: • **to be champing** *or* **chomping at the bit:** • **I expect you're champing** *or* **chomping at the bit** supongo que te devora la impaciencia • **they were champing** *or* **chomping at the bit to get started** no veían la hora de poner manos a la obra • **to get the bit between one's teeth:** • **once she gets the bit between her teeth, there's no stopping her** una vez que se pone en marcha no hay quien la pare

bit³ [bɪt] (PT) *of* **bite**

bitch [bɪtʃ] (N) **1** [*of canines*] hembra *f*; [*of dog*] perra *f*
2‡ (= *woman*) bruja* *f* • **you ~!** ¡(tía) cerda!*, ¡lagarta! (*Sp**)
3‡ • **this car is a ~** este coche es una lata* • **it's a ~ of a problem** es un problema que se las trae* • **life's a ~ (and then you die)** esta vida es un asco*, esta vida es una mierda‡
4 (*esp US‡*) (= *complaint*) queja *f* • **what's your ~?** ¿de qué coño te quejas tú?‡
(VI)* (= *complain*) quejarse (**about** de)

bitchiness* ['bɪtʃɪnɪs] (N) mala leche* *f*

bitchy* ['bɪtʃɪ] (ADJ) (COMPAR: **bitchier**, SUPERL: **bitchiest**) [*person*] malicioso; [*remark*] malintencionado, de mala leche (*Sp**) • **to be ~ to sb** ser malicioso con algn • **that was a ~ thing to do** eso fue una puñalada trapera*, eso fue una guarrada (*Sp**)

bitcoin ['bɪtkɔɪn] (N) bitcoin *m*

bite [baɪt] (VB: PT: **bit**, PP: **bitten**) (N) **1** (= *act*) mordisco *m*; (= *wound*) [*of dog, snake etc*] mordedura *f*; [*of insect*] picadura *f*; (= *toothmark*) dentellada *f* • **to take a ~ at** morder • **the dog took a ~ at him** el perro intentó morderlo • **to take a ~ out of** [+ *apple etc*] dar un mordisco a; (*esp US*) (*fig*) [+ *savings, budget*] llevarse un pellizco de • IDIOMS: • **he wants another** *or* **a second ~ at the cherry** quiere otra oportunidad, quiere probar otra vez • **to put the ~ on sb** (*US**) hacer cerrar el pico a algn*
2* [*of food*] bocado *m* • **I've not had a ~ to eat** no he probado bocado • **do you fancy a ~ (to eat)?** ¿te apetece algo (de comer)? • **I'll get a ~ (to eat) on the train** tomaré algo en el tren
3 (*Fishing*) • **are you getting any ~s?** ¿están picando?
4 (*fig*) (= *sharpness*) mordacidad *f*; [*of food, drink*] fuerza *f* • **a novel with ~** una novela mordaz • **a speech with ~** un discurso mordaz *or* incisivo • **without any ~** sin garra • **there's a ~ in the air** hace un frío cortante
(VT) **1** [*dog, person*] morder; [*bird, fish, insect*] picar • **it won't ~ (you)!*** ¡no te va a morder!, ¡no muerde! • **to ~ sth in two** partir algo en dos de un mordisco • **to ~ one's nails** comerse *or* morderse las uñas • **what's biting you?*** ¿qué mosca te ha picado?* • **to get bitten*** (= *be cheated*) dejarse timar • **to be bitten with the desire to do sth*** tener el gusanillo de hacer algo* • IDIOMS: • **to ~ the bullet** enfrentarse al toro • **to ~ the dust** (= *die*) morder el polvo; (= *fail*) venirse abajo • **it's the old story of biting the hand that feeds you** ya sabes "cría cuervos (y te sacarán los ojos)" • **to ~ one's lip** *or* **tongue** morderse la lengua • PROVERB: • **once bitten twice shy** el gato escaldado del agua fría huye
2 [*acid*] corroer; (*Mech*) asir, trabar
(VI) **1** [*dog, person*] morder; [*insect, fish*] picar • **to ~ at** tratar de morder
2 (*fig*) [*cuts, inflation etc*] hacerse sentir • **the strike is beginning to ~** la huelga empieza a hacer mella

▸ **bite back** (VT + ADV) [+ *words*] dejar sin decir, tragarse*
(VI + ADV) • **the dog bit back** el perro mordió a su vez

▸ **bite into** (VI + PREP) [*person*] meter los dientes en; [*acid*] corroer

▸ **bite off** (VT + ADV) arrancar con los dientes • IDIOMS: • **to ~ off more than one can chew** abarcar demasiado • **to ~ sb's head off** echar una bronca a algn*

▸ **bite on** (VI + PREP) morder

▸ **bite through** (VI + PREP) [+ *string, thread*] cortar con los dientes; [+ *tip, one's tongue*] morderse • **he fell and bit through his tongue** se cayó y se mordió la lengua

biter ['baɪtəʳ] (N) • IDIOM: • **the ~ bit** el cazador cazado

bite-size* ['baɪtsaɪz], **bite-sized*** ['baɪtsaɪzd] (ADJ) **1** (*lit*) [*food*] cortado a taquitos *or* en dados • **bite-sized pieces of ham** taquitos *mpl* de jamón
2 (*fig*) [*information*] en cantidades digeribles, en pequeñas dosis

biting ['baɪtɪŋ] (ADJ) [*cold, wind*] cortante; [*criticism etc*] mordaz

bitmap ['bɪtmæp] (*Comput*) (N) **1** (= *bit array*) mapa *m* de bits
2 (= *bitmap image*) imagen *f* en mapa de bits
(ADJ) [*graphics*] en mapa de bits
(VT) (= *convert*) convertir en mapa de bits

bitmapped ['bɪtmæpt] (ADJ) (*Comput*) en mapa de bits • **~ graphics** gráficos en mapa de bits • **~ maps require huge storage space** los mapas en mapa de bits requieren mucho espacio para almacenamiento

bit-player ['bɪt,pleɪəʳ] N actor *m* secundario, actriz *f* secundaria

bitten ['bɪtn] PP *of* bite

bitter ['bɪtəʳ] ADJ **1** (*in taste*) [*drink, medicine*] amargo • **it tasted ~** sabía amargo • IDIOM: • **a ~ pill to swallow** un trago amargo
2 (= *icy*) [*weather, winter*] gélido, glacial; [*wind*] cortante, gélido • **it's ~ today!** hoy hace un frío gélido *or* glacial
3 (= *fierce*) [*enemy, hatred*] implacable; [*battle*] encarnizado • **a ~ struggle** una lucha enconada
4 (= *resentful*) [*person*] amargado, resentido; [*protest*] amargo • **to feel ~ about sth** estar amargo *or* resentido por algo
5 (= *painful*) [*disappointment*] amargo • **to carry on to the ~ end** continuar hasta el final (cueste lo que cueste) • **to shed ~ tears** llorar lágrimas amargas
N **1** (*Brit*) (= *beer*) cerveza *f* amarga
2 bitters *licor amargo hecho con extractos de plantas*
CPD ▸ **bitter aloes** áloes *mpl* amargos ▸ **bitter lemon** (= *drink*) refresco *m* de limón ▸ **bitter orange** (= *drink*) refresco *m* de naranja

bitterly ['bɪtəlɪ] ADV **1** (= *icily*) • **it's ~ cold** hace un frío gélido *or* glacial • **a ~ cold day** un día gélido *or* glacial
2 (= *fiercely*) [*oppose*] implacablemente; [*hate*] implacablemente, a muerte; [*fight*] a muerte; [*criticize*] duramente • **a ~ contested match** un partido muy reñido
3 (= *deeply*) [*regret, resent*] amargamente; [*resentful, jealous, ashamed*] terriblemente • **I was ~ disappointed** sufrí una terrible *or* amarga decepción, quedé terriblemente decepcionado
4 (= *resentfully*) [*say, reply*] con rencor; [*speak, think*] amargamente, con rencor; [*complain*] amargamente • **she spoke ~ of her experiences** habló amargamente *or* con rencor de sus experiencias
5 (= *sorrowfully*) [*weep, cry*] amargamente

bittern ['bɪtɜːn] N avetoro *m* (común)

bitterness ['bɪtənɪs] N **1** (= *taste*) amargor *m*
2 (= *iciness*) crudeza *f*
3 (= *fierceness*) [*of struggle, fight*] lo enconado; [*of hatred*] lo implacable
4 (= *resentfulness*) amargura *f*, rencor *m* • **I accepted it without ~** lo acepté sin amargura *or* sin rencor • **I have no ~ towards you** no le guardo rencor • **a look of ~** una mirada de amargura
5 (= *depth*) [*of disappointment*] amargura *f*

bittersweet ['bɪtəswiːt] ADJ (*lit, fig*) agridulce

bitty* ['bɪtɪ] ADJ **1** (COMPAR: **bittier**, SUPERL: **bittiest**) (= *disconnected*) deshilvanado
2 (*US*) (= *small*) pequeñito

bitumen ['bɪtjʊmɪn] N betún *m*

bituminous [bɪ'tjuːmɪnəs] ADJ bituminoso

bivalent ['baɪ'veɪlənt] ADJ bivalente

bivalve ['baɪvælv] ADJ bivalvo
N (molusco *m*) bivalvo *m*

bivouac ['bɪvʊæk] (VB: PT, PP: **bivouacked**)
N vivaque *m*
VI vivaquear

bi-weekly ['baɪ'wiːklɪ] ADJ **1** (= *fortnightly*) quincenal
2 (= *twice weekly*) bisemanal
ADV **1** (= *fortnightly*) quincenalmente
2 (= *twice weekly*) bisemanalmente
N **1** (= *fortnightly*) revista *f* quincenal
2 (= *twice weekly*) revista *f* bisemanal

biz* [bɪz] N ABBR = **business**

bizarre [bɪ'zɑːʳ] ADJ (= *strange*) extraño, raro; [*dress, appearance etc*] estrafalario

bizarrely [bɪ'zɑːlɪ] ADV [*dress*] de forma estrafalaria • **she dressed ~** se vistió de forma estrafalaria • **both films, ~, include excerpts from the same news report** las dos películas, qué extraño, incluyen fragmentos de la misma noticia • **~, death is not a disqualification for voting although non-attendance at party meetings is** es extraño, porque mientras que la muerte no impide votar, la falta de asistencia a reuniones del partido, sí

bk ABBR **1** (= **book**) l., lib.
2 (= **bank**) Bco., B.

bkcy ABBR = **bankruptcy**

bkg ABBR = **banking**

bkpt ABBR = **bankrupt**

BL N ABBR **1** = **British Library**
2 = **Bachelor of Law**

B/L ABBR = **bill of lading**

blab* [blæb] VT (*also* **blab out**) [+ *secret*] soplar*
VI (= *chatter*) chismorrear*, cotillear (*Sp**); (*to police etc*) cantar*

blabber* ['blæbəʳ] VI (*also* **blabber on**) charlotear, parlar

blabbermouth* ['blæbə,maʊθ] N (*pej*) bocazas* *mf*, cotilla *mf* (*Sp**)

black [blæk] ADJ (COMPAR: **blacker**, SUPERL: **blackest**) **1** (*in colour*) negro • **(accident) ~ spot** (*Aut*) punto *m* negro • **~ and white photo** foto *f* en blanco y negro • **~ and white TV** TV *f* monocromo • **his face was ~ and blue** tenía la cara amoratada • **with a face as ~ as thunder** con cara de pocos amigos • IDIOM: • **to swear ~ and blue** jurar por todo lo más santo (**that** que)
2 (*of race*) negro • **~ man** negro *m* • **~ woman** negra *f*
3 (= *dark*) oscuro, tenebroso • **as ~ as pitch** • **as ~ as your hat** oscuro como boca de lobo
4 (= *dirty*) sucio; (*with smoke*) negro, ennegrecido
5 (*Brit*) (*trade union parlance*) • **to declare a product ~** boicotear un producto
6 (*fig*) [*day, event*] negro, funesto, aciago; [*outlook*] negro; [*forecast*] pesimista; [*thought*] malévolo; [*rage*] negro; [*look*] ceñudo, de desaprobación • **a ~ day on the roads** una jornada negra en las carreteras • **he is not as ~ as he is painted** no es tan malo como lo pintan • **things look pretty ~** la situación es desconsoladora • **things were looking ~ for him** la situación se le presentaba muy difícil
N **1** (= *colour*) negro *m*, color *m* negro • **a film in ~ and white** un film en blanco y negro • IDIOM: • **in ~ and white**: • **I should like it in ~ and white** quisiera tenerlo por escrito • **there it is in ~ and white!** ¡ahí lo tiene en letras de molde!
2 (= *person*) negro/a *m/f*
3 (= *mourning*) luto *m* • **to be in ~** • **wear ~** estar de luto
4 (= *darkness*) oscuridad *f*, noche *f*
5 • **to stay in the ~** estar en números negros
VT **1** ennegrecer; [+ *shoes*] limpiar, lustrar • **to ~ sb's eye** poner a algn el ojo amoratado, poner a algn el ojo a la funerala (*Sp**)
2 (*Brit*) (*trade union parlance*) boicotear
CPD ▸ **Black Africa** el África negra ▸ **black arts** magia *f* negra ▸ **black bass** perca *f* negra, perca *f* truchada ▸ **black belt** (*Sport*) cinturón *m* negro ▸ **black box** (*Aer*) caja *f* negra ▸ **black cab** (*Brit*) taxi *m* negro (*el típico británico*) ▸ **black coffee** café *m* solo, tinto *m* (*Col*); (*large*) café *m* americano ▸ **black college** (*US*) *universidad para gente de color* ▸ **black comedy** comedia *f* negra ▸ **Black Country** *región industrial al noroeste de Birmingham (Inglaterra)* ▸ **Black Death** peste *f* negra ▸ **black economy** economía *f* negra ▸ **Black English** (*US*) *inglés hablado por los negros americanos* ▸ **black eye** ojo *m* amoratado, ojo *m* a la funerala (*Sp**) ▸ **Black Forest** Selva *f* Negra ▸ **Black Forest gâteau** *pastel de chocolate, nata y guindas* ▸ **black goods** géneros *mpl* sujetos a boicoteo ▸ **black grouse** gallo *m* lira ▸ **black hole** (*Astron*) agujero *m* negro ▸ **black humour** humor *m* negro ▸ **black ice** *hielo invisible en la carretera* ▸ **black line** raya *f* en negro ▸ **black magic** magia *f* negra ▸ **Black Maria** (*Brit*) coche *m or* furgón *m* celular ▸ **black mark** señal *f* roja; (*fig*) nota *f* adversa, punto *m* negativo ▸ **black market** mercado *m* negro, estraperlo *m* (*Sp*) ▸ **black marketeer** estraperlista *mf* (*Sp*) ▸ **Black Moslem** musulmán *m* negro ▸ **Black Nationalism** nacionalismo *m* negro ▸ **Black Panthers** Panteras *fpl* negras ▸ **black pepper** pimienta *f* negra ▸ **Black Power** poder *m* negro ▸ **black pudding** (*Brit*) morcilla *f*, moronga *f* (*Mex*) ▸ **Black Rod** (*Brit*) (*Parl*) *dignatario de la Cámara de los Lores encargado de reunir a los Comunes en la apertura del Parlamento* ▸ **Black Sea** mar *m* Negro ▸ **black sheep (of the family)** oveja *f* negra ▸ **Black Studies** (*US*) *estudios de la cultura negra americana* ▸ **black tie** corbata *f* de lazo, corbata *f* de smoking • **"~ tie"** (*on invitation*) "de etiqueta" ▸ **black tie dinner** cena *f* de etiqueta ▸ **Black Watch** (*Brit*) (*Mil*) *regimiento escocés* ▸ **black widow (spider)** viuda *f* negra
▸ **black out** VT + ADV (= *obliterate with ink etc*) suprimir • **to ~ out a house** apagar las luces de una casa, hacer que no sean visibles por fuera las luces de una casa • **the screen was ~ed out by the strike** (*TV*) debido a la huelga no había programas en la pantalla • **the storm ~ed out the city** la tormenta causó un apagón en la ciudad
VI + ADV (= *faint*) desmayarse, perder el conocimiento

blackball ['blækbɔːl] VT (= *vote against*) dar bola negra a, votar en contra de; (= *exclude*) dejar fuera
N (= *ball*) bola *f* negra; (= *vote*) voto *m* en contra

blackberry ['blækbərɪ] N (= *fruit*) zarzamora *f*, mora *f*; (= *plant*) zarza *f*
CPD ▸ **blackberry bush** zarza *f*

blackberrying ['blæk,berɪɪŋ] N • **to go ~** ir a coger zarzamoras

blackbird ['blækbɜːd] N mirlo *m*

blackboard ['blækbɔːd] N pizarra *f*, encerado *m*

blackcap ['blækkæp] N (*Orn*) curruca *f* capirotada

blackcock ['blækkɒk] N gallo *m* lira

blackcurrant [,blæk'kʌrənt] N (= *fruit*) grosella *f* negra; (= *bush*) grosellero *m* negro, casis *f inv*
CPD ▸ **blackcurrant bush** grosellero *m* negro, casis *f inv*

blacken ['blækən] VT **1** ennegrecer; (*by fire*) calcinar; [+ *face*] tiznar de negro
2 (*fig*) [+ *reputation*] manchar
VI ennegrecerse

blackfly ['blækflaɪ] N *tipo de mosquito de pequeño tamaño*

blackguard† ['blægɑːd] N canalla* *mf*
VT vilipendiar

blackguardly† ['blægɑːdlɪ] ADJ vil, canallesco

blackhead ['blækhed] N espinilla *f*

black-headed gull [,blækhedɪd'gʌl] N gaviota *f* de cabeza negra

black-hearted [,blæk'hɑːtɪd] ADJ malvado, perverso

blacking ['blækɪŋ] N betún *m*

blackish ['blækɪʃ] ADJ negruzco; (*wine parlance*) aguindado

b

blackjack ['blækdʒæk] N (*esp US*)
1 (= *truncheon*) cachiporra *f* con puño flexible
2 (= *flag*) bandera *f* pirata
3 (*Cards*) veintiuna *f*

blackleg ['blækleg] (*Brit*) (*Ind*) N esquirol *mf*
VI ser esquirol, trabajar durante una huelga

blacklegging ['blæk,legɪŋ] N (*Brit*) (*Ind*) esquirolaje *m*

blacklist ['blæklɪst] N lista *f* negra
VT poner en la lista negra

blackly ['blæklɪ] ADV (= *gloomily*) con tristeza

blackmail ['blækmeɪl] N chantaje *m* • **it's sheer ~!** ¡es un chantaje!
VT chantajear • **to ~ sb into doing sth** chantajear a algn para que haga algo • **he was ~ed into it** lo hizo obligado por el chantaje

blackmailer ['blækmeɪləʳ] N chantajista *mf*

blackness ['blæknɪs] N negrura *f*; (= *darkness*) oscuridad *f*, tinieblas *fpl*

blackout ['blækaʊt] N 1 (*Elec*) apagón *m*
2 (*Med*) desmayo *m*
3 (*of news*) bloqueo *m* informativo, apagón *m* informativo • **there was a media ~ at the request of the police** hubo un bloqueo informativo en los medios de comunicación a petición de la policía
CPD ▸ **blackout curtains** cortinas *fpl* opacas

blackshirt ['blækʃɜːt] N (*Pol*) camisa negra *mf*

blacksmith ['blæksmɪθ] N herrero/a *m/f* • **~'s (forge)** herrería *f*

blackthorn ['blækθɔːn] N endrino *m*

blacktop ['blæktɒp] (*US*) N (= *substance, road*) asfalto *m*
VT asfaltar

bladder ['blædəʳ] N (*Anat*) vejiga *f*; [*of football etc*] cámara *f* de aire
CPD ▸ **bladder cancer** cáncer *m* de (la) vejiga

bladdered* ['blædəd] ADJ (= *drunk*) mamado • **to get ~** cogerse una tajada

blade [bleɪd] N 1 (= *cutting edge*) [*of knife, tool*] filo *m*; (= *flat part*) [*of weapon, razor etc*] hoja *f*; [*of skate*] cuchilla *f*
2 [*of propeller*] paleta *f*; [*of oar*] pala *f*; (*Aut*) [*of wiper*] rasqueta *f*
3 [*of grass etc*] brizna *f*
4† (= *gallant*) • **(young) ~** galán *m*, joven *m* apuesto

blading* ['bleɪdɪŋ] N (= *inline skating*) patinar *m* con patines en línea

blaeberry ['bleɪbərɪ] N arándano *m*

blag‡ [blæg] N (= *robbery*) atraco *m*, robo *m* a mano armada
VT (*Brit*) [+ *ticket*] sacar de gorra* • **to ~ one's way into a club** colarse de gorra en una discoteca*

blagger‡ ['blægəʳ] N (*Brit*) 1 (= *cadger*) gorrón/ona *m/f*; (= *cheater*) tramposo/a* *m/f*
2 (= *robber*) ladrón/ona *m/f*

blah* [blɑː] ADJ (*US*) poco apetitoso
N 1 (= *words*) paja *f*, palabrería *f* • **and there was a lot more ~, ~, ~** y hubo mucho más bla, bla, bla
2 • **the ~s** (*US*) la depre*

Blairite ['bleəraɪt] N, ADJ (*Brit*) (*Pol*) blairista *mf*

blamable ['bleɪməbl] ADJ censurable, culpable

blame [bleɪm] N culpa *f* • **to bear** *or* **take the ~** asumir la culpa • **to lay** *or* **put the ~ (for sth) on sb** echar a algn la culpa (de algo)
VT 1 (= *hold responsible*) culpar, echar la culpa a • **to ~ sb (for sth)** echar a algn la culpa (de algo), culpar a algn (de algo) • **to ~ sth on sb** culpar de algo a algn • **to be to ~ for** tener la culpa de • **I am not to ~** yo no tengo la culpa • **who's to ~?** ¿quién tiene la culpa? • **you have only yourself to ~** la culpa la tienes tú
2 (= *reproach*) censurar • **and I don't ~ him** y con toda la razón, y lo comprendo perfectamente
CPD ▸ **blame culture** cultura *f* de la culpa

blameless ['bleɪmlɪs] ADJ (= *innocent*) inocente; (= *irreproachable*) intachable

blamelessly ['bleɪmlɪslɪ] ADV (= *innocently*) inocentemente; (= *irreproachably*) intachablemente

blameworthy ['bleɪmwɜːðɪ] ADJ [*action*] censurable, reprobable; [*person*] culpable

blanch [blɑːntʃ] VI [*person*] palidecer
VT (*Culin*) blanquear; (= *boil*) escaldar • **~ed almonds** almendras *fpl* peladas

blancmange [blə'mɒnʒ] N (*Brit*) crema *f* (de vainilla *etc*)

bland [blænd] ADJ (COMPAR: **blander**, SUPERL: **blandest**) 1 (*pej*) (= *dull*) [*food, taste*] soso, insípido; [*smile, expression*] insulso; [*music, book, film*] soso, anodino; [*statement*] anodino • **it tastes rather ~** tiene un sabor bastante soso
2 (= *mild*) [*person, action*] suave, afable; [*diet*] blando

blandish ['blændɪʃ] VT engatusar, halagar

blandishments ['blændɪʃmənts] NPL halagos *mpl*, lisonjas *fpl*

blandly ['blændlɪ] ADV (*pej*) [*say, reply*] débilmente; [*smile*] de manera insulsa

blandness ['blændnɪs] N [*of taste, food, diet*] carácter *m* insípido; [*of book, film, person*] sosería *f*; [*of expression, look, smile*] carácter *m* insulso

blank [blæŋk] ADJ 1 [*paper, space etc*] en blanco; [*tape*] virgen, sin grabar; [*wall*] liso, sin adorno • **the screen went ~** se fue la imagen de la pantalla
2 [*expression etc*] vacío, vago • **a ~ look** una mirada vacía *or* vaga • **a look of ~ amazement** una mirada de profundo asombro • **when I asked him he looked ~** cuando se lo pregunté se quedó mirando con una expresión vaga • **my mind went ~** se me quedó la mente en blanco
3 (= *unrelieved*) • **in a state of ~ despair** en un estado de desesperación total
N 1 (= *void*) vacío *m*; (*in form*) espacio *m* en blanco • **my mind was a complete ~** no pude recordar nada • IDIOM: • **to draw a ~** no llegar a ninguna parte
2 (*Mil*) cartucho *m* de fogueo • **to fire ~s** usar municiones de fogueo
VT (*Brit**) (= *snub*) dar de lado a
CPD ▸ **blank cartridge** cartucho *m* de fogueo ▸ **blank cheque, blank check** (*US*) cheque *m* en blanco • **to give sb a ~ cheque** dar a algn un cheque en blanco; (*fig*) dar carta blanca a algn (**to** para) ▸ **blank verse** verso *m* blanco *or* suelto
▸ **blank out** VT + ADV [+ *feeling, thought*] desechar

blanket ['blæŋkɪt] N manta *f*, frazada *f* (*LAm*), cobija *f* (*LAm*); (*fig*) [*of snow*] manto *m*; [*of smoke, fog*] capa *f*; ▹ **security, wet**
ADJ [*statement, agreement*] general; [*ban*] global; [*coverage*] exhaustivo • **this insurance policy gives ~ cover** esta póliza de seguro es a todo riesgo
VT (*fig*) cubrir (**in, with** de, con), envolver (**by, in, with** en)
CPD ▸ **blanket bath** = **bed bath** ▸ **blanket stitch** punto *m* de festón

blankly ['blæŋklɪ] ADV • **he looked at me ~** me miró sin comprender

blankness ['blæŋknɪs] N [*of expression, eyes*] vacuidad *f*

blare [bleəʳ] N [*of music, siren*] estruendo *m*; [*of trumpet*] trompetazo *m*
VT (*also* **blare out**) [+ *words, order*] vociferar; [+ *music*] tocar muy fuerte
VI (*also* **blare out**) [*music, siren*] sonar a todo volumen, resonar

blarney* ['blɑːnɪ] N labia* *f*
VT dar coba a*, engatusar
CPD ▸ **Blarney Stone** *piedra del castillo de Blarney, al sudoeste de Irlanda, que se dice que transmite el don de la galantería al que la besa* • IDIOM: • **to kiss the Blarney Stone** aprender a tener labia*

blasé ['blɑːzeɪ] ADJ [*attitude*] indiferente • **she's very ~ about the risks involved** le traen sin cuidado los riesgos que el asunto conlleva • **he's won so many Oscars he's become ~ about it** ha ganado tantos óscars que ya está de vuelta de ello *or* le da igual

blaspheme [blæs'fiːm] VI (= *swear*) blasfemar

blasphemer [blæs'fiːməʳ] N blasfemador(a) *m/f*, blasfemo/a *m/f*

blasphemous ['blæsfɪməs] ADJ blasfemo

blasphemously ['blæsfɪməslɪ] ADV [*act, argue*] blasfemamente • **to speak/curse ~** blasfemar

blasphemy ['blæsfɪmɪ] N blasfemia *f*

blast [blɑːst] N 1 [*of air, steam, wind*] ráfaga *f*; [*of sand, water*] chorro *m* • **(at) full ~** (*fig*) a toda marcha
2 (= *sound*) [*of whistle etc*] toque *m*; [*of bomb*] explosión *f* • **at each ~ of the trumpet** a cada trompetazo
3 (= *shock wave*) [*of explosion etc*] sacudida *f*, onda *f* expansiva
4 [*of criticism etc*] tempestad *f*, oleada *f*
5* (= *fun*) • **it was a ~** fue el desmadre* • **we got a real ~ out of the party** nos lo pasamos de miedo en la fiesta*
VT 1 (= *tear apart*) (*with explosives*) volar; (*by lightning*) derribar; (*Mil*) bombardear • **to ~ open** abrir con carga explosiva
2 (*Bot*) marchitar; (*with blight*) añublar; (*fig*) [+ *hopes, future*] malograr, echar por tierra
3 (= *shoot*) pegar un tiro a, abrir fuego contra
4 (= *criticize*) [+ *person*] emprenderla con; [+ *film, novel, report*] poner por los suelos
5 (*Sport*) [+ *ball*] estrellar
6 (= *send out*) [+ *air, water*] lanzar
VI (*also* **blast out**) [*music, siren*] sonar a todo volumen, resonar
EXCL (*Brit‡*) ¡maldita sea!* • **~ it!** ¡maldita sea!*
CPD ▸ **blast furnace** alto horno *m*
▸ **blast away** VT + ADV [+ *rocks etc*] volar, quitar con explosivos
VI + ADV [*gun*] seguir disparando • **they were ~ing away at the town** seguían bombardeando el pueblo
▸ **blast off** VI + ADV [*spacecraft*] despegar
▸ **blast out** VT + ADV [*DJ*] [+ *music*] poner a todo volumen; [*group*] [+ *tune*] tocar a todo volumen

blasted ['blɑːstɪd] ADJ 1‡ (= *wretched*) condenado*, maldito*
2 (*liter*) [*landscape*] inhóspito

blasting ['blɑːstɪŋ] N 1 (*Tech*) voladura *f* • **"blasting in progress"** "explosión controlada en curso"
2* (= *rebuke*) • **to give sb a ~ for (having done) sth** echar una bronca *or* abroncar a algn por (haber hecho) algo*

blast-off ['blɑːstɒf] N [*of spacecraft*] despegue *m*

blat* [blæt] VI (*esp US*) [*sheep*] balar

blatancy ['bleɪtənsɪ] N (= *obviousness*) [*of injustice, lie, error*] lo flagrante • **the ~ of their disregard for ...** lo descarado de su menosprecio por ...

blatant ['bleɪtənt] ADJ [*injustice, lie*] flagrante; [*bully, coward, thief, liar*] descarado • **he's not only racist, but he's ~ about it** no solo es un racista sino que además no lo disimula • **he was quite ~ about cheating in the exam** copió en el examen con todo descaro *or* sin ningún disimulo

blatantly ['bleɪtəntlɪ] ADV **1** (= *glaringly*) [*untrue, unfair*] descaradamente, obviamente • **its faults are ~ obvious** sus defectos saltan a la vista • **it's ~ obvious that ...** es a todas luces evidente que ...
2 (= *flagrantly*) [*ignore, encourage, disregard*] descaradamente, abiertamente; [*sexist, racist*] descaradamente

blather* ['blæðəʳ] N disparates *mpl*
VI charlatanear, decir tonterías • **to ~ (on) about sth** enrollarse con algo*, dar la tabarra con algo*

blaze¹ [bleɪz] N **1** (= *fire*) (*in hearth*) fuego *m*; (= *flare-up*) llamarada *f*; [*of buildings etc*] incendio *m*; (= *bonfire*) hoguera *f*; (= *glow*) [*of fire, sun etc*] resplandor *m*
2 (= *display*) derroche *m* • **a ~ of colour** un derroche de color
3 (= *outburst*) arranque *m* • **in a ~ of anger** en un arranque de cólera • **in a ~ of publicity** en medio de un gran despliegue publicitario
4†‡ • **like ~s** hasta más no poder • **what the ~s ...?** ¿qué diablos ...?* • **go to ~s!** ¡vete a la porra!*
VI **1** [*fire*] arder; [*light*] resplandecer • **the sun was blazing** el sol brillaba implacablemente • **all the lights were blazing** brillaban todas las luces
2 [*eyes*] centellear • **to ~ with anger** estar muy indignado, echar chispas*
VT • **the news was ~d across the front page** la noticia venía en grandes titulares en la primera plana
▸ **blaze abroad** VT + ADV (*liter*) [+ *news etc*] proclamar a voz en grito
▸ **blaze away** VI + ADV [*soldiers*] disparar continuamente
▸ **blaze down** VI + ADV • **the sun was blazing down** el sol brillaba implacablemente
▸ **blaze forth** VI + ADV (*liter*) [*sun*] aparecer súbitamente; (*fig*) [*anger*] estallar
▸ **blaze out** VI + ADV [*fire*] llamear; [*sun*] resplandecer, relucir; [*light*] relucir; (*fig*) [*anger, hatred*] estallar
▸ **blaze up** VI + ADV [*fire*] llamear; (*fig*) [*feelings*] estallar

blaze² [bleɪz] N (*on animal*) mancha *f* blanca; (*on tree*) señal *f*
VT [+ *tree*] marcar • **to ~ a trail** (*also fig*) abrir camino

blazer ['bleɪzəʳ] N (= *jacket*) chaqueta *f* de sport, blazer *m*

blazing ['bleɪzɪŋ] ADJ **1** [*building etc*] en llamas; [*fire*] llameante; [*sun*] abrasador, ardiente; [*light*] brillante; [*eyes*] centelleante
2* [*row, anger*] violento

blazon ['bleɪzn] N blasón *m*
VT (*fig*) proclamar

bldg ABBR = **building**

bleach [bli:tʃ] N lejía *f*
VT [+ *clothes*] blanquear; [+ *hair*] aclarar, decolorar
VI blanquearse

bleached [bli:tʃt] ADJ [*hair*] decolorado, (teñido de) rubio platino; [*clothes*] descolorido

bleachers ['bli:tʃəz] NPL (*US*) gradas *fpl*

bleaching ['bli:tʃɪŋ] N decoloración *f*
CPD ▸ **bleaching agent** decolorante *m*
▸ **bleaching powder** polvos *mpl* de blanqueo

bleak [bli:k] ADJ (COMPAR: **bleaker**, SUPERL: **bleakest**) [*landscape*] desolado, inhóspito; [*weather*] desapacible, crudo; [*smile, voice*] lúgubre, sombrío; [*future*] sombrío; [*welcome*] poco hospitalario; [*room*] lúgubre • **it was a ~, lonely existence out there** allá la vida era triste y desoladora • **it looks** *or* **things look rather ~ for him** las cosas no se le presentan muy alentadoras
N (= *fish*) breca *f*, albur *m*

bleakly ['bli:klɪ] ADV [*look*] desoladamente; [*smile*] lúgubremente, con aire sombrío; [*speak*] con desaliento, en tono sombrío

bleakness ['bli:knɪs] N [*of landscape*] desolación *f*; [*of room, furnishings*] lo lúgubre; [*of weather*] crudeza *f*, desapacibilidad *f*; [*of prospects, future*] lo sombrío

blearily ['blɪərɪlɪ] ADV [*look*] con ojos de sueño

bleary ['blɪərɪ] ADJ (COMPAR: **blearier**, SUPERL: **bleariest**) (*with sleep*) con cara de sueño; (*with tears*) lloroso; (= *tired*) agotado

bleary-eyed ['blɪərɪaɪd] ADJ con cara de sueño

bleat [bli:t] N **1** [*of sheep, goat*] balido *m*
2* (= *complaint*) queja *f*
VI **1** [*sheep, goat*] balar
2* (= *complain*) quejarse (**about** de), gimotear

bled [bled] PT, PP *of* **bleed**

bleed [bli:d] (PT, PP: **bled**) VI **1** (*from cut, wound*) sangrar; [*tree*] exudar • **his nose is ~ing** le sangra la nariz • **to ~ to death** morir desangrado • **my heart ~s for him** (*iro*) ¡qué pena me da!
2 [*colours*] diluirse (**into** en), correrse (**into** en)
VT **1** (*Med*) sangrar
2 [+ *brakes, radiator*] desaguar, sangrar
3* (= *exploit*) desangrar, sacar los cuartos a (*Sp**) • IDIOMS: • **to ~ sb dry** *or* **white** chupar la sangre a algn • **to ~ a country dry** *or* **white** explotar despiadadamente un país

bleeder ['bli:dəʳ] N **1** (*Med**) hemofílico/a *m/f*
2 (*Brit*‡) tipo/a* *m/f*, tío/a *m/f* (*Sp**) • **poor ~!** ¡pobre desgraciado! • **he's a lucky ~!** ¡qué suerte tiene el tío! (*Sp**), ¡qué suertudo es! (*LAm**)

bleeding ['bli:dɪŋ] ADJ **1** [*wound etc*] sangrante; (*fig*) [*heart*] dolorido
2 (*Brit*‡) condenado*, puñetero‡
ADV (*Brit*‡) • **~ awkward** condenadamente difícil*
N (= *medical procedure*) sangría *f*; (= *blood loss*) desangramiento *m*, hemorragia *f*
CPD ▸ **bleeding edge** (= *cutting edge*) vanguardia *f*

bleeding-edge [ˌbli:dɪŋ'edʒ] ADJ (= *cutting-edge*) [*technology*] de vanguardia

bleeding-heart [ˌbli:dɪŋ'hɑ:t] ADJ (*fig*) • **bleeding-heart liberal** liberal *mf* de gran corazón

bleep [bli:p] N (*Rad, TV*) pitido *m*
VI [*transmitter*] emitir pitidos
VT* (*in hospital etc*) llamar por el busca(personas)

bleeper ['bli:pəʳ] N (= *pager*) busca* *m inv*, buscapersonas *m inv*

blemish ['blemɪʃ] N (*on fruit*) mancha *f*; (*on complexion*) imperfección *f*; (*fig*) (*on reputation*) tacha *f*
VT (= *spoil*) estropear

blemished ['blemɪʃt] ADJ [*skin, fruit*] con manchas

blench [blentʃ] VI (= *flinch*) acobardarse; (= *pale*) palidecer

blend [blend] N mezcla *f*
VT [+ *teas, food etc*] mezclar; [+ *colours*] mezclar, combinar
VI (= *harmonize*) armonizar (**with** con) • **to ~ in with** armonizarse con • **to ~ into** [*colour*] fundirse con

blended ['blendɪd] ADJ mezclado

blender ['blendəʳ] N **1** (*Culin*) licuadora *f*
2 (= *person*) catador(a) *m/f* • **tea ~** catador(a) *m/f* de té

bless [bles] VT **1** [*God, priest*] bendecir • **God ~ you!** ¡Dios te bendiga! • **God ~ the Pope!** ¡Dios guarde al Papa! • **~ you!** ¡qué cielo eres!; (*after sneezing*) ¡Jesús! • **and Paul, ~ him** *or* **~ his heart, had no idea that ...** y Paul, el pobre, no tenía ni idea de que ... • **to ~ o.s.** santiguarse
2 (*fig*) • **they were never ~ed with children** Dios jamás les dio la bendición de los hijos • **she is ~ed with every virtue** la adornan mil virtudes • **I ~ the day I bought it** bendigo el día que lo compré • **well I'm ~ed!** • **God ~ my soul!**†* ¡vaya por Dios! • **I'm ~ed if I know** (*Brit**) no tengo ni idea

blessed ['blesɪd] ADJ **1** (*Rel*) (= *holy*) bendito, santo; (= *beatified*) beato • **the Blessed Virgin** la Santísima Virgen • **the Blessed Sacrament** el Santísimo Sacramento • **~ be Thy Name** bendito sea Tu Nombre • **of ~ memory** que Dios lo/la tenga en su gloria
2 (*liter*) (= *joyous*) feliz, maravilloso • **a day of ~ calm** un día de bendita tranquilidad
3 (*Brit*‡) (= *wretched*) santo*, dichoso* • **the whole ~ day** todo el santo día* • **where's that ~ book?** ¿dónde está ese dichoso libro?* • **we didn't find a ~ thing** no encontramos nada de nada*
NPL • **the Blessed** los bienaventurados

blessedly ['blesɪdlɪ] ADV (= *gloriously*) [*empty*] gloriosamente, maravillosamente; (= *fortunately*) [*brief, short*] afortunadamente

blessedness ['blesɪdnɪs] N (*Rel*) bienaventuranza *f*, santidad *f*; (= *happiness*) dicha *f*, felicidad *f*

blessing ['blesɪŋ] N **1** (*Rel*) bendición *f*
2 (= *advantage*) beneficio *m* • **the ~s of electricity** los beneficios de la electricidad • **the ~s of science** los adelantos de la ciencia • IDIOMS: • **it's a ~ in disguise** no hay mal que por bien no venga • **it's a mixed ~** tiene sus pros y sus contras • **to count one's ~s** agradecer lo que se tiene • **you can count your ~s that ...** tienes que estar agradecido de que ...

blest [blest] ADJ, PP *of* **bless**

blether ['bleðəʳ] (*Scot*) = **blather**

blethering* ['bleðərɪŋ] N (*Scot*) disparates *fpl*

blew [blu:] PT *of* **blow²**

blight [blaɪt] N **1** (*Bot*) [*of plants, cereals, fruit, trees*] roya *f*
2 (*fig*) plaga *f* • **urban ~** desertización *f* urbana • **to cast a ~ on** *or* **over** arruinar
VT **1** (*Bot*) (= *wither*) marchitar
2 (*fig*) (= *spoil*) arruinar; (= *frustrate*) frustrar; [+ *urban scene*] desertizar

blighter†* ['blaɪtəʳ] N (*Brit*) tipo/a* *m/f*, tío/a *m/f* (*Sp**) • **you ~!** (*hum*) ¡menudo canalla estás hecho!*, ¡qué cabrito! (*Sp**) • **what a lucky ~!** ¡qué suerte tiene el tío! (*Sp**), ¡qué suertudo es! (*LAm**)

Blighty†* ['blaɪtɪ] N (*Brit*) (*Mil*) Inglaterra *f*

blimey‡ ['blaɪmɪ] EXCL (*Brit*) ¡caray!

blimp [blɪmp] N **1** (*esp US*) (= *airship*) zepelín *m*, dirigible *m*
2 (*Brit**) (= *person*) reaccionario/a *m/f*, militarista *mf*, patriotero/a *m/f* • **a (Colonel) Blimp** ≈ un carpetovetónico

blimpish ['blɪmpɪʃ] ADJ (*Brit*) reaccionario

blind [blaɪnd] ADJ **1** (*lit*) (= *sightless*) ciego • **a ~ man** un ciego, un hombre ciego • **to go ~** quedar(se) ciego • **~ in one eye** tuerto • **the accident left him ~** el accidente lo dejó ciego • **to be ~ with tears** estar cegado por las lágrimas • IDIOMS: • **(as) ~ as a bat*** más ciego que un topo • **to turn a ~ eye (to sth)**

hacer la vista gorda (con algo);
▸ **colour-blind**
2 (*fig*) (= *unable to see*) ciego • **you've got to be ~ not to see that it's a trick** hay que estar ciego para no darse cuenta de que es un engaño • **I was so in love that I was ~** estaba tan enamorado que no podía ver claro • **to be ~ to sth** no poder ver algo • **he is ~ to her true character** no puede ver su verdadero carácter • **to be ~ to sb's faults** no ver los defectos de algn • **to be ~ to the consequences of one's actions** no ver las consecuencias de las acciones de uno • **I am not ~ to those considerations** no ignoro esas consideraciones • PROVERB: • **love is ~** el amor es ciego
3 (= *irrational*) [*rage, panic, faith*] ciego • **a ~ guess** una respuesta al azar • **to be ~ with rage** estar cegado por la ira, estar ciego de ira
4 • **a ~ bit of sth***: • **it won't make a ~ bit of difference** va a dar exactamente lo mismo • **he didn't take a ~ bit of notice** no hizo ni caso • **it isn't a ~ bit of use** no sirve absolutamente para nada
5 (*Aer*) [*landing, flying*] guiándose solo por los instrumentos
6 (= *without openings*) [*building, wall*] ciego; [*window*] condenado
(N) 1 • **the ~** los ciegos • IDIOM: • **it's a case of the ~ leading the ~** es como un ciego llevando a otro ciego
2 (= *shade*) persiana *f* • **Venetian ~** persiana *f* veneciana
3 (= *pretence*) pretexto *m*, subterfugio *m* • **it's all a ~** no es más que un pretexto *or* subterfugio
(ADV) (= *fly, land*) guiándose solo por los instrumentos • **to bake pastry ~** cocer una masa en blanco *or* sin relleno • **to be ~ drunk*** estar más borracho que una cuba* • **he swore ~ that …** juró y perjuró que …
(VT) 1 (= *render sightless*) dejar ciego, cegar • **to be ~ed in an accident** quedar ciego después de un accidente
2 (= *dazzle*) [*sun, light*] deslumbrar, cegar • **to ~ sb with science** deslumbrar a algn con conocimientos
3 (*fig*) cegar • **to be ~ed by anger/hate** estar cegado por la ira/el odio, estar ciego de ira/odio • **her love ~ed her to his faults** su amor no le dejaba ver sus faltas
(CPD) ▸ **blind alley** callejón *m* sin salida ▸ **blind corner** curva *f* sin visibilidad ▸ **blind date** (= *meeting*) cita *f* a ciegas • **to go on a ~ date with sb** tener una cita a ciegas con algn ▸ **blind man's buff** gallina *f* ciega ▸ **blind spot** (*Aut*) ángulo *m* muerto; (*Med*) punto *m* ciego • **I have a ~ spot about computers** • **computers are a ~ spot with me** los ordenadores no son mi punto fuerte ▸ **blind test** (*Marketing*) prueba *f* a ciegas ▸ **blind trust** (*Comm*) fideicomiso *m* ciego

blinder ['blaɪndəʳ] (N) 1 • **to play a ~ (of a match)** (*Brit**) jugar de maravilla
2 **blinders** (*US*) (= *blinkers*) anteojeras *fpl*

blindfold ['blaɪndfəʊld] (ADJ) con los ojos vendados; [*game of chess*] a la ciega • **I could do it ~** podría hacerlo con los ojos vendados
(N) venda *f*
(VT) vendar los ojos a

blinding ['blaɪndɪŋ] (ADJ) [*light, glare*] cegador, deslumbrante • **I've got a ~ headache** tengo un dolor de cabeza que no veo

blindingly ['blaɪndɪŋlɪ] (ADV) • **a ~ obvious fact** un hecho de claridad meridiana • **it is ~ obvious that …** es a todas luces evidente que …

blindly ['blaɪndlɪ] (ADV) 1 (= *unseeingly*) [*grope, stumble*] a ciegas, a tientas; [*shoot*] a ciegas • **she stared ~ at the wall** se quedó mirando obnubilada a la pared
2 (= *unquestioningly*) [*follow, accept, obey*] ciegamente

blindness ['blaɪndnɪs] (N) ceguera *f* • **~ to the truth** ceguera frente a la verdad

blindside ['blaɪndsaɪd] (VT) (*US*) sorprender

blindworm ['blaɪndwɜːm] (N) lución *m*

bling* ['blɪŋ], **bling bling*** ['blɪŋ'blɪŋ] (N) (= *jewellery*) joyas *fpl* (*muy llamativas*)
(ADJ) • **~-bling jewellery** joyas (*muy llamativas*)

blini ['blɪnɪ] (N) panqueque *m* ruso

blink [blɪŋk] (N) [*of eyes*] parpadeo *m*; (= *gleam*) destello *m* • IDIOMS: • **in the ~ of an eye** en un abrir y cerrar de ojos • **to be on the ~*** (*TV etc*) estar averiado
(VT) [+ *eyes*] cerrar
(VI) [*eyes*] parpadear, pestañear; [*light*] parpadear
▸ **blink at** (VI + PREP) (= *ignore*) pasar por alto

blinkered ['blɪŋkəd] (*Brit*) (ADJ) [*horse*] con anteojeras; (*fig*) [*person*] estrecho de miras; [*view*] miope, estrecho

blinkers ['blɪŋkəz] (NPL) 1 (*Brit*) [*of horse*] anteojeras *fpl*
2 (*Aut*) intermitentes *mpl*, direccionales *mpl* (*Mex*)

blinking* ['blɪŋkɪŋ] (ADJ) (*Brit*) maldito • **you ~ idiot!** ¡imbécil!*

blip [blɪp] (N) 1 = **bleep**
2 (*fig*) (= *aberration*) irregularidad *f* momentánea • **this is just a ~** es un problema pasajero

bliss [blɪs] (N) 1 (*Rel*) (= *happy state*) dicha *f* • PROVERB: • **ignorance is ~** ojos que no ven, corazón que no siente
2* (*fig*) éxtasis *m*, arrobamiento *m* • **the concert was ~!** ¡el concierto fue una gloria! • **what ~!** ¡qué gustazo!* • **isn't he ~?** ¡qué encanto de hombre!
▸ **bliss out**‡ (VT + ADV) (*esp US*) • **to be ~ed out** flipar de gusto‡, estar en la gloria

blissful ['blɪsfʊl] (ADJ) 1 (= *happy*) dichoso • **in ~ ignorance** feliz en la ignorancia
2* (= *wonderful*) maravilloso, estupendo

blissfully ['blɪsfəlɪ] (ADV) [*sigh, lounge*] con felicidad • **~ happy** sumamente feliz • **~ ignorant** feliz en la ignorancia

blister ['blɪstəʳ] (N) (*on skin*) ampolla *f*; (*on paintwork*) burbuja *f*
(VT) ampollar
(VI) [*skin*] ampollarse; [*paintwork*] formar burbujas
(CPD) ▸ **blister pack** envase *m* en lámina al vacío

blistered ['blɪstəd] (ADJ) • **to be ~** estar lleno de ampollas • **to have ~ feet** tener los pies llenos de ampollas • **~ paint** pintura con burbujas

blistering ['blɪstərɪŋ] (ADJ) 1 [*heat etc*] abrasador
2 [*criticism*] feroz, devastador
3 [*pace, speed*] frenético

blister-packed ['blɪstəˌpækt] (ADJ) envasado en lámina al vacío

blithe [blaɪð] (ADJ) (*liter*) alegre

blithely ['blaɪðlɪ] (ADV) (*liter*) [*continue, ignore*] alegremente

blithering* ['blɪðərɪŋ] (ADJ) • **~ idiot** imbécil* *mf*

BLitt [ˌbiːˈlɪt] (N ABBR) (*Univ*) = **Bachelor of Letters**

blitz [blɪts] (N) 1 (*Mil*) guerra *f* relámpago; (*Aer*) bombardeo *m* aéreo • **the Blitz** (*Brit*) (*Hist*) *el bombardeo alemán de Gran Bretaña en 1940 y 1941*
2* (*fig*) campaña *f* (**on** contra) • **I'm going to have a ~ on ironing tomorrow** mañana voy a atacar la plancha*
(VT) (*Mil*) bombardear

blitzed‡ [blɪtst] (ADJ) (= *drunk*) mamado‡, borracho como una cuba*

blitzkrieg ['blɪtskriːg] (N) 1 (*Mil*) guerra *f* relámpago
2* (*fig*) (= *attack*) arremetida *f*

blizzard ['blɪzəd] (N) ventisca *f*; (*fig*) [*of letters, bills etc*] aluvión *m*, avalancha *f*

BLM (N ABBR) (*US*) = **Bureau of Land Management**

bloated ['bləʊtɪd] (ADJ) 1 (= *swollen*) [*stomach*] hinchado; [*face*] hinchado, abotargado • **to feel ~** sentirse hinchado
2 (*fig*) [*bureaucracy*] excesivo; [*budget, ego*] inflado • **~ with pride** henchido de orgullo

bloater ['bləʊtəʳ] (N) arenque *m* ahumado

bloating ['bləʊtɪŋ] (N) (= *swelling*) hinchazón *f*

blob [blɒb] (N) (= *drop*) [*of ink etc*] gota *f*; (= *lump*) [*of mud etc*] grumo *m*; (= *stain*) mancha *f*

bloc [blɒk] (N) 1 (*Pol*) bloque *m*
2 • **en ~** en bloque

block [blɒk] (N) 1 [*of stone*] bloque *m*; [*of wood*] zoquete *m*, tarugo *m*; (*for paving*) adoquín *m*; (*butcher's, executioner's*) tajo *m*; (= *toy*) (*also* **building block**) cubo *m*; [*of brake*] zapata *f*; [*of cylinder*] bloque *m* • IDIOM: • **on the ~** (*US**) con dinero contante y sonante*, a tocateja (*Sp**); ▸ **chip**
2 (= *building*) bloque *m*; (*esp US*) (= *group of buildings*) manzana *f*, cuadra *f* (*LAm*) • **~ of flats** (*Brit*) bloque *m* de pisos (*Sp*), edificio *m* de departamentos (*LAm*) • **to walk around the ~** dar la vuelta a la manzana • **three ~s from here** (*esp US*) a tres manzanas de aquí
3 (= *section*) [*of tickets, stamps*] serie *f* • **~ of seats** grupo *m* de asientos • **~ of shares** paquete *m* de acciones
4 (= *blockage*) (*in pipe*) (*gen*) atasco *m*; (*Med*) bloqueo *m* • **writer's ~** bloqueo *m* de escritor • **to have a mental ~** tener un bloqueo mental
5 (*Brit*) (*Typ*) molde *m*; (= *writing pad*) bloc *m*
6 (*Sport*) **blocks** (*also* **starting blocks**) tacos *mpl* de salida • **to be first/last off the ~s** ser el más rápido/lento en la salida; (*fig*) ser el más/menos madrugador
7 (*Comput*) bloque *m*
8* (= *head*) • IDIOM: • **to knock sb's ~ off*** romper la crisma a algn*
(VT) 1 (= *obstruct*) [+ *road, gangway*] bloquear; [+ *traffic, progress*] estorbar, impedir; [+ *pipe*] obstruir; (*Parl*) [+ *bill*] bloquear; (*Comm*) [+ *account*] bloquear; (*Sport*) bloquear, parar • **to ~ sb's way** cerrar el paso a algn • **he stopped in the doorway, ~ing her view** se paró en la entrada, tapándole la vista • **am I ~ing your view?** ¿te estoy tapando? • **the road is ~ed in four places** el camino está cortado en cuatro lugares • **"road blocked"** "cerrado (por obras)" • **my nose is ~ed** tengo la nariz taponada
2 (*Comput*) agrupar
(VI) (*Sport*) bloquear, parar
(CPD) ▸ **block and tackle** (*Tech*) aparejo *m* de poleas ▸ **block booking** reserva *f* en bloque ▸ **block capitals** (letras *fpl*) mayúsculas *fpl* • **in ~ capitals** en mayúsculas, en letra *or* caracteres de imprenta ▸ **block diagram** diagrama *m* de bloques ▸ **block grant** subvención *f* en bloque ▸ **block letters** = **block capitals** ▸ **block release** (*Brit*) (*Scol*) exención *f* por estudios ▸ **block vote** voto *m* por representación
▸ **block in** (VT + ADV) (= *sketch roughly*) esbozar
▸ **block off** (VT + ADV) [+ *road etc*] cortar; (*accidentally*) bloquear
▸ **block out** (VT + ADV) 1 (= *suppress*) [+ *thought, idea*] desechar, apartar de la mente

b

2 (= *obscure*) [+ *light*] tapar; (= *erase*) borrar
3 (= *sketch roughly*) [+ *scheme, design*] esbozar
▸ **block up** VT + ADV **1** (= *obstruct*) [+ *passage*] obstruir; [+ *pipe*] atascar • **my nose is all ~ed up** tengo la nariz taponada
2 (= *fill in*) [+ *gap*] cerrar

blockade [blɒˈkeɪd] N (*Mil, Ind*) bloqueo *m* • **to run a ~** burlar un bloqueo • **under ~** bloqueado
VT [+ *traffic*] bloquear

blockage [ˈblɒkɪdʒ] N (= *obstruction*) (*Med*) obstrucción *f*; (*in pipe*) atasco *m*

blockbuster* [ˈblɒkˌbʌstəʳ] N **1** (= *film*) exitazo* *m*, gran éxito *m* de taquilla; (= *book*) exitazo* *m*, best-seller *m*
2 (*Mil*) bomba *f* revientamanzanas

blockhead* [ˈblɒkhed] N (*pej*) zopenco/a* *m/f* • **you ~!** ¡imbécil!*

blockhouse [ˈblɒkhaʊs] N (PL: **blockhouses** [ˈblɒkhaʊzɪz]) blocao *m*

blog [blɒg] N blog *m*
VI bloguear

blogger [ˈblɒgəʳ] N bloguero/a *m/f*, blogger *mf inv*

blogging [ˈblɒgɪŋ] N • **surfing and ~ on the internet can be a substitute for real life** navegar y bloguear en Internet pueden ser un sustituto de la vida real

blogosphere [ˈblɒgəsfɪər] N blogosfera *f*

blogpost [ˈblɒgpəʊst] N entrada *f* del blog, post *m*

blogspace [ˈblɒgspeɪs] N blogosfera *f*

bloke* [bləʊk] N (*Brit*) (= *man*) tipo* *m*, tío *m* (*Sp**); (= *boyfriend*) amigo *m*

blokeish, blokish* [ˈbləʊkɪʃ] = **blokey**

blokey* [ˈbləʊkɪ] ADJ (*Brit*) [*man*] machote*, tío*; [*manners, gestures*] hombruno

blond, blonde [blɒnd] ADJ (COMPAR: **blonder**, SUPERL: **blondest**) rubio, güero (*CAm, Mex*), catire (*Carib*)
N rubio/a *m/f*, güero/a *m/f* (*CAm, Mex*), catire/a *m/f* (*Carib*)
CPD ▸ **blond(e) bombshell*** rubia *f* explosiva*

blood [blʌd] N **1** (*lit*) sangre *f* • **to be after sb's ~** tenérsela jurada a algn* • **it makes my ~ boil** me saca de quicio*, hace que me hierva la sangre • **it makes my ~ boil to think how ...** me hierve la sangre solo de pensar que ... • **in cold ~** a sangre fría • **to donate** *or* **give ~** donar *or* dar sangre • **to draw ~** (= *wound*) hacer sangre; (*Med*) sacar sangre • **to draw first ~** (*fig*) abrir el marcador, anotarse el primer tanto • **a ~ and guts film** una película sangrienta *or* violenta • **acting was in his ~** llevaba la profesión de actor en la sangre • **to sweat ~** (= *work hard*) sudar tinta *or* sangre*; (= *worry*) sudar la gota gorda* • **~ and thunder** (= *melodrama*) melodrama *m* • IDIOMS: • **to have sb's ~ on one's hands** tener las manos manchadas con la sangre de algn • **to make one's ~ run cold**: • **the look in his eyes made her ~ run cold** su mirada hizo que se le helara la sangre (en las venas) • **to get ~ out of a stone** sacar agua de las piedras • **getting her to talk is like trying to get ~ out of a stone** hacer que hable es como sacar agua de las piedras; ▹ **bay[3]**, **flesh**
2 (= *family, ancestry*) sangre *f* • **of noble/royal ~** de sangre noble/real • PROVERB: • **~ is thicker than water** la sangre tira; ▹ **blue**
3 (*fig*) **a** (= *people*) • **fresh** *or* **new** *or* **young ~** savia *f* nueva
b (= *feeling*) • **bad ~** hostilidad *f* • **there had always been bad ~ between him and his in-laws** siempre había existido hostilidad entre él y la familia de su mujer
CPD ▸ **blood alcohol, blood alcohol content** alcoholemia *f* ▸ **blood alcohol level** nivel *m* de alcoholemia ▸ **blood bank** banco *m* de sangre ▸ **blood blister** ampolla *f* de sangre ▸ **blood brother** hermano *m* de sangre ▸ **blood cell** glóbulo *m* ▸ **blood clot** coágulo *m* de sangre ▸ **blood corpuscle** glóbulo *m* sanguíneo ▸ **blood count** hemograma *m*, recuento *m* sanguíneo *or* globular ▸ **blood diamond** diamante *m* de sangre ▸ **blood disorder** enfermedad *f* de la sangre ▸ **blood donor** donante *mf* de sangre ▸ **blood feud** enemistad *f* mortal (*entre clanes, familias*) ▸ **blood flow** flujo *f* sanguíneo • **~ flow to the feet** el flujo sanguíneo a los pies ▸ **blood group** grupo *m* sanguíneo ▸ **blood heat** temperatura *f* del cuerpo ▸ **blood loss** pérdida *f* de sangre ▸ **blood money** dinero *m* manchado de sangre (*en pago por asesinato*); (*as compensation*) *indemnización que se paga a la familia de alguien que ha sido asesinado* ▸ **blood orange** naranja *f* sanguina ▸ **blood plasma** plasma *m* sanguíneo ▸ **blood poisoning** septicemia *f*, envenenamiento *m* de la sangre ▸ **blood pressure** tensión *f or* presión *f* arterial, presión *f* sanguínea • **to have high/low ~ pressure** tener la tensión alta/baja, tener hipertensión/hipotensión • **to take sb's ~ pressure** tomar la tensión a algn ▸ **blood product** producto *m* sanguíneo ▸ **blood pudding** morcilla *f* ▸ **blood relation, blood relative** • **she is no ~ relation to him** ella y él no son de la misma sangre, ella y él no son (parientes) cosanguíneos (*frm*) ▸ **blood relationship** consanguinidad *f*, lazo *m* de parentesco ▸ **blood sample** muestra *f* de sangre • **to take a ~ sample** obtener una muestra de sangre • **to give a ~ sample** dar una muestra de sangre ▸ **blood sausage** (*US*) = **blood pudding** ▸ **blood sport** *deporte en el que se matan animales* ▸ **blood sugar (level)** nivel *m* de azúcar en la sangre ▸ **blood supply** riego *m* sanguíneo ▸ **blood test** análisis *m inv* de sangre ▸ **blood transfusion** transfusión *f* de sangre ▸ **blood type** = **blood group** ▸ **blood vessel** vaso *m* sanguíneo

blood-and-thunder [ˈblʌdənˈθʌndəʳ] ADJ melodramático

bloodbath [ˈblʌdbɑːθ] N (PL: **bloodbaths** [ˈblʌdbɑːðz]) carnicería *f*, baño *m* de sangre

bloodcurdling [ˈblʌdˌkɜːdlɪŋ] ADJ espeluznante

bloodhound [ˈblʌdhaʊnd] N **1** (= *dog*) sabueso *m*
2* (= *detective*) detective *mf* privado/a

bloodily [ˈblʌdɪlɪ] ADV • **the rebellion was ~ put down** reprimieron la rebelión de forma sangrienta • **a man was dying ~ on the floor** un hombre moría en el suelo en un baño de sangre *or* moría desangrado en el suelo

bloodiness [ˈblʌdɪnɪs] N (*lit*) lo sangriento • **the ~ of his deeds** el carácter sangriento de sus actos

bloodless [ˈblʌdlɪs] ADJ **1** (= *pale*) (*gen*) pálido; (*due to blood loss*) exangüe • **her face was ~** su rostro no tenía color, su rostro estaba pálido; (*due to blood loss*) su rostro estaba exangüe • **her lips were ~** sus labios apenas tenían color *or* eran casi blancos; (*due to accident, death*) sus labios estaban exangües
2 (= *without bloodshed*) [*revolution, coup*] incruento, sin derramamiento de sangre
3 (= *characterless*) [*film, novel, style*] soso, anodino; [*person*] sin sangre en las venas, con sangre de horchata

bloodlessly [ˈblʌdlɪslɪ] ADV sin derramamiento de sangre

bloodletting [ˈblʌdˌletɪŋ] N (*Med*) sangría *f*; (*fig*) carnicería *f*, baño *m* de sangre

bloodline [ˈblʌdlaɪn] N línea *f* de sangre, línea *f* de parentesco por consanguinidad • **the Celtic royal ~ descended through the mother's side** la línea de sangre de la realeza celta venía por parte de la madre

blood-lust [ˈblʌdlʌst] N sed *f* de sangre

blood-red [ˈblʌdˈred] ADJ [*fabric, paint, car*] de color rojo sangre, rojo sangre; [*sun, sky, sunset*] de un rojo encendido; [*flower*] encarnado

bloodshed [ˈblʌdʃed] N derramamiento *m* de sangre • **an act of mindless ~** un derramamiento de sangre sin sentido

bloodshot [ˈblʌdʃɒt] ADJ [*eye*] (*from crying, lack of sleep*) rojo, enrojecido; (*from anger*) inyectado en sangre

bloodstain [ˈblʌdsteɪn] N mancha *f* de sangre

bloodstained [ˈblʌdsteɪnd] ADJ manchado de sangre

bloodstock [ˈblʌdstɒk] N caballos *mpl* de pura sangre, purasangres *mpl*

bloodstone [ˈblʌdstəʊn] N restañasangre *m*, sanguinaria *f*

bloodstream [ˈblʌdstriːm] N • **the ~** la corriente sanguínea, el flujo sanguíneo

bloodsucker [ˈblʌdsʌkəʳ] N (*Zool*) (*also fig*) sanguijuela *f*

bloodthirstiness [ˈblʌdˌθɜːstɪnɪs] N [*of person, animal*] sed *f* de sangre, carácter *m* sanguinario; [*of film, book*] lo sangriento

bloodthirsty [ˈblʌdθɜːstɪ] ADJ (COMPAR: **bloodthirstier**, SUPERL: **bloodthirstiest**) (= *brutal*) sanguinario; (= *gory*) [*film, book*] sangriento

bloody [ˈblʌdɪ] ADJ (COMPAR: **bloodier**, SUPERL: **bloodiest**) **1** (*lit*) (= *bloodstained*) [*hands, dress*] ensangrentado, manchado de sangre; (= *cruel*) [*battle*] sangriento, cruento (*frm*); [*steak*] sanguinolento • **her fingers were cracked and ~** sus dedos estaban agrietados y sangraban • **to give sb a ~ nose** romper la nariz a algn
2 (*Brit‡*) • **shut the ~ door!** ¡cierra la puerta, coño!**, ¡me cago en diez, cierra esa puerta!‡ • **that ~ dog!** ¡ese puñetero perro!‡ • **you ~ idiot!** ¡maldito imbécil!* • **I'm a ~ genius!** ¡la leche, soy un genio!‡, ¡joder, qué genio soy!** • **~ hell!** ¡maldita sea!*, ¡joder!**
ADV (*Brit‡*) • **not ~ likely!** ¡ni hablar!, ¡ni de coña!‡ • **he can ~ well do it himself!** ¡que lo haga él, leche!‡, ¡que lo haga él, coño!** • **that's no ~ good!** ¡me cago en la mar, eso no vale para nada!‡, ¡eso no vale para nada, joder!** • **it's a ~ awful place** es un sitio asqueroso, es un sitio de mierda** • **he runs ~ fast** corre que se las pela*, corre (de) la hostia**
VT • **he had bloodied his knee when he fell** se había hecho sangre en la rodilla al caer • **she stared at her bloodied hands** se miró las manos manchadas de sangre • **he was bloodied but unbowed** (*fig*) había sufrido pero no se daba por vencido
CPD ▸ **Bloody Mary** bloody mary *m*

bloody-minded* [ˈblʌdɪˈmaɪndɪd] ADJ (*Brit*) **1** (= *stubborn*) terco, empecinado • **the bloody-minded conservatism of some groups** el terco conservadurismo de algunos grupos
2 (= *awkward*) atravesado, difícil • **you're just being bloody-minded** son ganas de ser atravesado *or* difícil, son ganas de fastidiar • **he didn't really want a replacement, he was just being bloody-minded about it** no quería realmente un sustituto, lo hacía sólo para fastidiar

bloody-mindedness* [ˈblʌdɪˈmaɪndɪdnɪs] (*Brit*) N **1** (= *stubbornness*) terquedad *f*
2 (= *awkwardness*) • **it's just bloody-mindedness on his part** son ganas de

fastidiar *or* de ser atravesado • **he did it out of sheer bloody-mindedness** lo hizo sólo para fastidiar

bloom [blu:m] (N) **1** (= *flower*) flor *f*; (*on fruit*) vello *m*, pelusa *f* • **in ~** en flor • **in full ~** en plena floración • **in the full ~ of youth** en la flor de la juventud • **to come into ~** florecer
2 (*fig*) (*on complexion*) rubor *m*
(VI) [*flower*] abrirse; [*tree*] florecer; (*fig*) [*economy, industry*] prosperar

bloomer ['blu:məʳ] (N) **1*** (= *mistake*) planchazo* *m*, metedura *f* de pata* • **to make a ~** llevarse un planchazo*, meter la pata*
2 • **to be a late ~** (*fig*) ser una flor tardía, tardar en desarrollarse

bloomers ['blu:məz] (NPL) bombachos *mpl*, pantaletas *fpl* (*LAm*)

blooming ['blu:mɪŋ] (ADJ) **1** [*tree*] floreciente, en flor
2 (*fig*) (= *flourishing*) radiante • **to be ~ with health** • **be in ~ health** estar rebosante de *or* rebosar salud
3 (*Brit**) • **the ~ car wouldn't start** el maldito coche no arrancaba* • **get that ~ thing out of the way!** ¡quita eso de ahí, hombre!*
(ADV) (*Brit**) • **I think it's ~ marvellous** a mí me parece genial* • **we had to lift this ~ great box** tuvimos que levantar un pedazo de caja enorme *or* una caja de agárrate y no te menees*

blooper* ['blu:pəʳ] (N) (*esp US*) = **bloomer**

blossom ['blɒsəm] (N) (= *collective*) flores *fpl*; (= *single*) flor *f* • **in ~** en flor
(VI) [*tree*] florecer; (*fig*) florecer, llegar a su apogeo • **it ~ed into love** se transformó en amor

▸ **blossom out** (VI + ADV) (*fig*) [*person*] alcanzar su plenitud, florecer

blossoming ['blɒsəmɪŋ] (N) florecimiento *m*

blot [blɒt] (N) [*of ink*] borrón *m*, mancha *f*; (*fig*) (*on reputation etc*) tacha *f*, mancha *f* • **the chimney is a ~ on the landscape** la chimenea afea el paisaje • IDIOM: • **a ~ on the family escutcheon** una mancha en el honor de la familia
(VT) **1** (= *spot*) (*with ink*) manchar; (*fig*) [+ *reputation*] desacreditar • IDIOM: • **to ~ one's copybook** (*Brit*) manchar su reputación
2 (= *dry*) (*with blotter*) [+ *ink, writing*] secar
(VI) [*pen*] echar borrones; [*ink*] correrse

▸ **blot out** (VT + ADV) **1** (*lit*) [+ *words*] borrar
2 (*fig*) [*mist, fog*] [+ *view*] tapar, ocultar; [+ *memories*] borrar

▸ **blot up** (VT + ADV) [+ *ink*] secar

blotch [blɒtʃ] (N) [*of ink, colour*] mancha *f*; (*on skin*) mancha *f*, erupción *f*

blotched ['blɒtʃt] (ADJ) (= *marked*) manchado

blotchy ['blɒtʃɪ] (ADJ) (COMPAR: **blotchier**, SUPERL: **blotchiest**) manchado, lleno de manchas

blotter ['blɒtəʳ] (N) **1** (= *blotting paper*) secante *m*
2 (*US*) (= *notebook*) registro *m*

blotting-pad ['blɒtɪŋ,pæd] (N) secante *m*

blotting paper ['blɒtɪŋ,peɪpəʳ] (N) papel *m* secante

blotto‡ ['blɒtəʊ] (ADJ) • **to be ~** (= *drunk*) estar mamado‡, estar como una cuba*

blouse [blaʊz] (N) **1** (= *woman's garment*) blusa *f* • **he's a big girl's ~*** es un mariquita*
2 (*US*) (*Mil*) guerrera *f*

blouson ['blu:zɒn] (N) cazadora *f*

blow¹ [bləʊ] (N) **1** (= *hit*) golpe *m*; (= *slap*) bofetada *f* • **a ~ with a hammer/fist/elbow** un martillazo/un puñetazo/un codazo • **at one ~** de un solo golpe • **a blow-by-blow account** una narración pormenorizada • **to cushion** *or* **soften the ~** (*lit*) amortiguar el golpe; (*fig*) disminuir los efectos (*de un desastre etc*) • **to deal** *or* **strike sb a ~** dar *or* asestar un golpe a algn • **to strike a ~ for freedom** (*fig*) dar un paso más hacia la libertad • **without striking a ~** sin violencia • **to come to ~s** (*lit, fig*) llegar a las manos
2 (*fig*) (= *setback*) golpe *m* • **it is a cruel ~ for everybody** es un golpe cruel para todos • **the news came as a great ~** la noticia fue un duro golpe • **that's a ~!** ¡qué lástima! • **the affair was a ~ to his pride** la cosa le hirió en el amor propio • **it was the final ~ to our hopes** acabó de echar por tierra nuestras esperanzas

blow² [bləʊ] (PT: **blew**, PP: **blown**) (VT)
1 (= *move by blowing*) [*wind etc*] [+ *leaves papers*] hacer volar • **the wind blew the ship towards the coast** el viento llevó *or* empujó el barco hacia la costa • **the wind has ~n dust all over it** el viento lo ha cubierto de polvo • **the wind blew the door shut** el viento cerró la puerta de golpe • **to ~ sb a kiss** enviar *or* tirar un beso a algn
2 [+ *trumpet, whistle*] tocar, sonar; [+ *glass*] soplar; [+ *egg*] vaciar (soplando) • **to ~ bubbles** (*soap*) hacer pompas; (*gum*) hacer globos • **to ~ one's nose** sonarse (la nariz) • **to ~ smoke in sb's face** *or* **eyes** (*lit*) echar el humo en la cara *or* los ojos a algn; (*US*) (*fig*) engañar a algn • **to ~ smoke rings** hacer anillos *or* aros de humo • IDIOMS: • **to ~ smoke up sb's ass** (*US***) lamer el culo a algn**, dar coba a algn* • **to ~ one's own trumpet** • **~ one's own horn** (*US*) darse bombo* • **to ~ the whistle on sth/sb** dar la voz de alarma sobre algo/algn
3 (= *burn out, explode*) [+ *fuse*] fundir, quemar; [+ *tyre*] reventar; [+ *safe etc*] volar • **to ~ sth sky-high** volar algo en mil pedazos • **to ~ a theory sky-high** echar por tierra una teoría • **to ~ a matter wide open** destapar un asunto • IDIOMS: • **to ~ the lid off sth** sacar a la luz algo, dejar algo al descubierto • **to ~ sb's mind*** dejar alucinado a algn* • **to ~ one's top** • **~ one's cork** *or* **stack** (*US*) reventar, estallar • **to ~ sth out of the water** echar por tierra algo, dar al traste con algo
4 (= *spoil, ruin*) • **to ~ one's chance of doing sth*** echar a perder *or* desperdiciar la oportunidad de hacer algo • **to ~ sb's cover** desenmascarar a algn • **to ~ it*** pifiarla* • **now you've ~n it!*** ¡ahora sí que la has pifiado!* • **to ~ one's lines** (*US*) (*Theat**) perder el hilo, olvidar el papel • **to ~ a secret** revelar un secreto; ▹ **gaff³**
5 • **to ~ money on sth*** malgastar dinero en algo
6 (*esp US***) (= *fellate*) mamársela a**, hacer una mamada a**
7 (*Drugs*) • **to ~ grass‡** fumar hierba
8* (*in exclamations*) • **~ me!** • **~ it!** • **well I'm ~ed!** ¡caramba! • **~ this rain!** ¡dichosa lluvia!* • **I'll be ~ed if ...** que me cuelguen si ...* • **~ the expense!** ¡al cuerno el gasto!*
(VI) **1** [*wind, whale*] soplar; [*person*] (*from breathlessness*) jadear • **to ~ on one's fingers** soplarse los dedos • **to ~ on one's soup** enfriar la sopa soplando • **it's ~ing a gale** hace muchísimo viento; ▹ **hot, wind¹**
2 [*leaves etc*] (*with wind*) volar • **the door blew open/shut** se abrió/cerró la puerta con el viento
3 (= *make sound*) [*trumpet, siren*] sonar • **the referee blew for a foul** el árbitro pitó falta
4 [*fuse etc*] fundirse, quemarse; [*tyre*] reventar
5‡ (= *leave*) largarse*, pirarla (*Sp**) • **I must ~** tengo que largarme*
(N) **1** [*of breath*] soplo *m*
2 (*Brit‡*) (= *marijuana*) maría‡ *f*; (*US*) (= *cocaine*) coca‡ *f*, perico‡ *m*
(CPD) ▸ **blow drier, blow dryer** secador *m* de pelo ▸ **blow job**** mamada** *f* • **to give sb a ~ job** mamársela *or* chupársela a algn**

▸ **blow about** (VT + ADV) [+ *leaves etc*] llevar de acá para allá
(VI + ADV) [*leaves etc*] moverse de acá para allá por el viento

▸ **blow away** (VI + ADV) [*hat*] salir volando, volarse
(VT + ADV) **1** [*wind*] [+ *leaves, rubbish*] hacer volar
2‡ (= *kill*) cargarse a*, liquidar*
3* (= *defeat*) machacar*
4* (= *impress*) dejar pasmado*

▸ **blow down** (VT + ADV) derribar
(VI + ADV) venirse abajo

▸ **blow in** (VI + ADV) **1** (= *collapse*) venirse abajo
2* (= *enter*) entrar de sopetón* • **look who's ~n in!** ¡mira quién ha caído del cielo!*

▸ **blow off** (VI + ADV) **1** [*hat*] salir volando, volarse
2 (*Brit‡*) tirarse un pedo‡
(VT + ADV) [+ *gas*] dejar escapar • IDIOM: • **to ~ off steam** desfogarse
(VT + PREP) • **to ~ the dust off a table** quitar el polvo de una mesa soplando

▸ **blow out** (VT + ADV) **1** (= *extinguish*) [+ *candle*] apagar (con un soplo) • **the next day the storm had ~n itself out** al día siguiente la tormenta se había calmado
2 (= *swell out*) [+ *cheeks*] hinchar
3 • **to ~ one's brains out*** pegarse un tiro, levantarse *or* volarse la tapa de los sesos* • **to ~ sb's brains out*** pegar un tiro a algn, levantar *or* volar la tapa de los sesos a algn*
(VI + ADV) **1** [*candle etc*] apagarse
2 [*tyre*] reventar; [*window*] romperse (*con la fuerza del viento etc*)

▸ **blow over** (VT + ADV) derribar, tumbar
(VI + ADV) **1** [*tree etc*] caer
2 [*storm*] pasar
3 (*fig*) [*dispute*] olvidarse

▸ **blow up** (VT + ADV) **1** (= *explode*) [+ *bridge etc*] volar
2 (= *inflate*) [+ *tyre etc*] inflar, hinchar (*Sp*)
3 (= *enlarge*) [+ *photo*] ampliar
4 (= *exaggerate*) [+ *event etc*] exagerar • **they blew it up out of all proportion** se exageró una barbaridad sobre eso, se sacó totalmente de quicio
5* (= *reprimand*) • **the boss blew the boy up** el jefe puso al chico como un trapo*
(VI + ADV) **1** [*explosive*] estallar, explotar; [*container*] estallar, reventar • **his allegations could ~ up in his face** con esas acusaciones le podría salir el tiro por la culata*
2 [*storm*] levantarse • **it's ~ing up for rain** con este viento tendremos lluvia
3 (*fig*) **a** [*row etc*] estallar • **now something else has ~n up** ahora ha surgido otra cosa
b* (*in anger*) salirse de sus casillas* • **to ~ up at sb** perder los estribos con algn

blowback ['bləʊ,bæk] (N) (*Tech, Mil*) retroceso *m*

blow-dry ['bləʊ,draɪ] (N) (= *hairstyle*) • **I'd like a cut and blow-dry** quisiera un corte y secado a mano
(VT) [+ *style*] secar a mano

blower* ['bləʊəʳ] (N) (*Brit*) (= *telephone*) teléfono *m* • **who's on the ~?** ¿con quién hablas? • **get on the ~ to them** dales un toque (por teléfono)

blowfly ['bləʊflaɪ] (N) moscarda *f*, mosca *f* azul

blowgun ['bləʊgʌn] (N) (*US*) cerbatana *f*

blowhard* ['bləʊhɑ:d] (N) (*esp US*) fanfarrón/ona *m/f*

blowhole ['bləʊhəʊl] (N) **1** [*of whale*] orificio *m* nasal
2 (*in ice*) brecha *f*, orificio *m* (*para respirar*)

b

blowlamp ['bləʊlæmp] N soplete *m*
blown [bləʊn] PP *of* **blow²**
ADJ [*flower*] marchito
blow-out ['bləʊaʊt] N **1** (*Aut*) (= *burst tyre*) reventón *m*, pinchazo *m*, ponchada *f* (*Mex*)
2 (*Elec*) [*of fuse*] apagón *m*
3 [*of oil well*] explosión *f*
4‡ (= *big meal*) comilona* *f*, atracón* *m*
blowpipe ['bləʊpaɪp] N (= *weapon*) cerbatana *f*
blowsy ['blaʊzɪ] ADJ = **blowzy**
blowtorch ['bləʊtɔːtʃ] N soplete *m*
blow-up ['bləʊʌp] N **1** (*Phot*) ampliación *f*
2* riña *f*, pelea *f* (**between** entre)
blowy* ['bləʊɪ] ADJ [*day*] de mucho viento • **on a ~ day in March** un día de marzo de mucho viento • **it's ~ here** aquí hay mucho viento
blowzy ['blaʊzɪ] ADJ (COMPAR: **blowzier**, SUPERL: **blowziest**) [*woman*] desaliñado; (= *red in face*) coloradote*
BLS N ABBR (*US*) = **Bureau of Labor Statistics**
BLT N ABBR = **bacon, lettuce and tomato** • **a BLT sandwich** *un sándwich de bacon, lechuga y tomate*
blub* [blʌb] VI (*Brit*) lloriquear
blubber¹ ['blʌbəʳ] N [*of whale, seal*] grasa *f*
blubber²* ['blʌbəʳ] N lloriqueo *m* • **she just wanted to have a good ~** tenía ganas de llorar
VI (= *weep*) lloriquear • **stop ~ing!** ¡deja ya de lloriquear!
VT decir lloriqueando
blubberer* ['blʌbərəʳ] N llorica *mf**
blubbery ['blʌbərɪ] ADJ (= *fat*) fláccido, fofo • **~ lips** labios *mpl* carnosos
bludgeon ['blʌdʒən] N cachiporra *f*
VT aporrear • **to ~ sb into doing sth** (*fig*) coaccionar *or* forzar a algn a hacer algo
blue [bluː] ADJ (COMPAR: **bluer**, SUPERL: **bluest**) **1** azul; [*body, bruise*] amoratado • **~ with cold** amoratado de frío • IDIOMS: • **once in a ~ moon** de Pascuas a Ramos • **you can shout till you're ~ in the face*** puedes gritar hasta hartarte • **to go like a ~ streak** (*US**) ir como un rayo • **to talk like a ~ streak** (*US**) hablar muy deprisa
2* (= *obscene*) verde, colorado (*LAm*) • **~ film** película *f* porno
3* (= *sad*) triste, deprimido • **to feel ~** estar deprimido, estar tristón* • **to look ~** tener aspecto triste
4 (*Pol*) conservador
N **1** (= *colour*) azul *m*
2 (*Pol*) conservador(a) *m/f*; ▹ **true-blue**
3 (*Chem*) añil *m*
4 • **the ~** (= *sky*) el cielo; (= *sea*) el mar • IDIOM: • **to come out of the ~** [*money, good news*] venir como cosa llovida del cielo, bajar del cielo; [*bad news*] caer como una bomba • **he said out of the ~** dijo de repente, dijo inesperadamente
5 blues (*Mus*) blues *m*; (= *feeling*) melancolía *f*, tristeza *f* • **he's got the ~s** está deprimido
6 • **Dark/Light Blue** (*Brit*) (*Univ*) deportista *mf* representante de Oxford/Cambridge
VT **1** [+ *washing*] añilar, dar azulete a
2 (*Brit**) (= *squander*) despilfarrar
CPD ▸ **blue baby** niño/a *m/f* azul, niño/a *m/f* cianótico/a ▸ **blue beret** casco *m* azul ▸ **blue blood** sangre *f* azul ▸ **blue book** (*US*) (*Scol*) cuaderno *m* de exámenes ▸ **blue cheese** queso *m* de pasta verde ▸ **blue chips** = **blue-chip securities** ▸ **blue jeans** tejanos *mpl*, vaqueros *mpl* ▸ **blue pencil** lápiz *m* negro (en la censura); ▹ **blue-pencil** ▸ **Blue Peter** (*Naut*) bandera *f* de salida ▸ **blues band** banda *f* de blues ▸ **blues guitar** guitarra *f* de blues ▸ **blue shark** tiburón *m* azul ▸ **blue whale** ballena *f* azul ▸ **blue whiting** bacaladilla *f*
Bluebeard ['bluːbɪəd] N Barba Azul
bluebell ['bluːbel] N campánula *f* azul; (*Scot*) (= *harebell*) campanilla *f*
blueberry ['bluːbərɪ] N arándano *m*
bluebird ['bluːbɜːd] N pájaro *m* azul, azulejo *m* (de América)
blue-black [ˌbluː'blæk] ADJ azul oscuro (*inv*)
blue-blooded ['bluː'blʌdɪd] ADJ de sangre azul
bluebottle ['bluːˌbɒtl] N moscarda *f*
blue-chip ['bluː'tʃɪp] ADJ [*company*] de primera (categoría); [*investment*] asegurado
CPD ▸ **blue-chip securities** fianzas *fpl* fiables
blue-collar ['bluːˌkɒləʳ] ADJ [*job*] manual
CPD ▸ **blue-collar worker** obrero/a *m/f*, trabajador(a) *m/f* manual
blue-eyed ['bluːˌaɪd] ADJ de ojos azules
CPD ▸ **blue-eyed boy** (*fig*) consentido *m*, niño *m* mimado
bluegrass ['bluːgrɑːs] N (*US*) (*Bot*) *hierba norteamericana usada como forraje*
CPD ▸ **bluegrass music** *música folk de Kentucky*
blueish ['bluːɪʃ] ▹ **bluish**
bluejacket ['bluːˌdʒækɪt] N marinero *m* (de buque de guerra)
bluejay ['bluːdʒeɪ] N (*US*) arrendajo *m* azul
blueness ['bluːnɪs] N azul *m*, lo azul
blue-pencil ['bluː'pensl] VT tachar con lápiz negro (en la censura); ▹ **blue**
blueprint ['bluːprɪnt] N (= *plan*) proyecto *m*, anteproyecto *m*; (= *drawing*) cianotipo *m*
blue-sky ['bluːskaɪ] ADJ [*project, research*] sin límites • **we need to do some blue-sky thinking** tenemos que ponernos a pensar sin ningún tipo de límite • **blue-sky laws** (*US*) legislación *f* para regular la emisión y venta de valores
bluestocking† ['bluːˌstɒkɪŋ] N (= *scholarly woman*) literata *f*, marisabidilla *f*
bluesy ['bluːzɪ] ADJ (*Mus*) de blues
bluetit ['bluːtɪt] N herrerillo *m* (común)
Bluetooth® ['bluːtuːθ] ADJ • **~ technology** tecnología *f* Bluetooth®
blue-water ['bluː'wɔːtəʳ] ADJ (*Naut*) [*navy, ship*] de altura, pelágico
bluey* ['bluːɪ] ADJ azulado
bluff¹ [blʌf] ADJ **1** [*cliff etc*] escarpado
2 [*person*] franco, directo
N (*Geog*) risco *m*, peñasco *m*
bluff² [blʌf] N (= *act of bluffing*) farol *m*, bluff *m* • IDIOM: • **to call sb's ~** poner a algn en evidencia
VT (= *deceive by pretending*) engañar, embaucar • **to ~ it out by ...** salvar la situación haciendo creer que ...
VI farolear, tirarse un farol (*Sp**)
bluffer ['blʌfəʳ] N farolero/a *m/f*
bluish ['bluːɪʃ] ADJ azulado, azulino
blunder ['blʌndəʳ] N metedura *f* de pata*, plancha *f* (*Sp**) • **to make a ~** meter la pata*, tirarse una plancha (*Sp**)
VI **1** (= *err*) cometer un grave error, meter la pata*
2 (= *move clumsily*) • **to ~ about** andar dando tumbos • **to ~ into sth/sb** tropezar con algo/algn • **to ~ into sth** [+ *trap*] caer en algo; (*fig*) caer *or* meterse en algo
blunderbuss ['blʌndəbʌs] N trabuco *m*
blunderer ['blʌndərəʳ] N metepatas* *mf*
blundering ['blʌndərɪŋ] ADJ [*person*] torpe, que mete la pata*; [*words, act*] torpe
N torpeza *f*
blunt [blʌnt] ADJ **1** (= *not sharp*) [*edge*] desafilado; [*point*] despuntado • **with a ~ instrument** con un instrumento contundente
2 (= *outspoken*) [*manner, person*] directo, franco; [*statement*] terminante • **I will be ~ with you** voy a hablarte con franqueza • **he was very ~ with me** no se mordió la lengua conmigo
VT [+ *blade, knife*] desafilar; [+ *pencil*] despuntar; (*fig*) debilitar, mitigar
bluntly ['blʌntlɪ] ADV [*speak*] francamente, directamente
bluntness ['blʌntnɪs] N **1** [*of blade etc*] falta *f* de filo, lo poco afilado
2 (= *outspokenness*) franqueza *f*
blur [blɜːʳ] N (= *shape*) contorno *m* borroso • **everything is a ~ when I take off my glasses** todo se vuelve borroso cuando me quito los lentes • **the memory is just a ~** es un recuerdo muy vago • **my mind was a ~** todo se volvió borroso en mi mente
VT **1** (= *obscure*) [+ *writing*] borrar, hacer borroso; [+ *outline*] desdibujar; [+ *sight*] oscurecer, empañar • **my eyes were ~red with tears** las lágrimas me enturbiaban la vista
2 (*fig*) [+ *memory*] enturbiar; [+ *judgment*] ofuscar
VI (= *be obscured*) desdibujarse, volverse borroso • **her eyes ~red with tears** las lágrimas le enturbiaban la vista
Blu-ray ['bluːreɪ] N Blu-ray *m*
CPD ▸ **Blu-ray disc** disco *m* Blu-ray ▸ **Blu-ray movie** película *f* Blu-ray ▸ **Blu-ray release** lanzamiento *m* en Blu-ray
blurb [blɜːb] N propaganda *f*
blurred [blɜːd] ADJ **1** [*outline etc*] borroso, poco nítido • **a ~ photo** una foto movida *or* desenfocada
2 (*fig*) [*memory*] borroso • **to be/become ~** estar/volverse borroso • **class distinctions are becoming ~** las diferencias de clase se están difuminando
blurry ['blɜːrɪ] ADJ (= *blurred*) [*vision, image*] borroso
blurt [blɜːt] VT • **to ~ out** [+ *secret*] dejar escapar; [+ *whole story*] contar de buenas a primeras
blush [blʌʃ] N **1** (*from embarrassment*) rubor *m*, sonrojo *m*; (= *glow*) tono *m* rosáceo • **the first ~ of dawn** la primera luz del alba • **in the first ~ of youth** en la inocencia de la juventud • **at first ~** a primera vista • **to bring a ~ to sb's face** hacer sonrojar a algn • **to spare** *or* **save his ~es** para que no se ruborice • **spare my ~es!** ¡qué cosas dices!
2 (*US*) (= *make-up*) colorete *m*
VI ruborizarse, sonrojarse (**at** por, **with** de) • **to make sb ~** hacer que algn se ruborice *or* se sonroje • **I ~ for you** siento vergüenza por ti • **I ~ to even think about it** me avergüenzo de solo pensarlo • **she ~ed to the roots of her hair** se puso colorada como un tomate
blusher ['blʌʃəʳ] N colorete *m*
blushing ['blʌʃɪŋ] ADJ ruboroso; [*bride*] candoroso
bluster ['blʌstəʳ] N (= *empty threats*) fanfarronadas *fpl*, bravatas *fpl*
VI [*wind*] soplar con fuerza, bramar
VT • **to ~ it out** defenderse echando bravatas, baladronear
blusterer ['blʌstərəʳ] N fanfarrón/ona *m/f*
blustering ['blʌstərɪŋ] ADJ [*person*] jactancioso, fanfarrón
blustery ['blʌstərɪ] ADJ [*wind*] tempestuoso; [*day*] de mucho viento
Blu-Tack® ['bluːtæk] N Blu-Tack® *m*
Blvd ABBR (= **boulevard**) Blvr
BM N ABBR **1** = **British Museum**
2 (*Univ*) = **Bachelor of Medicine**
BMA N ABBR = **British Medical Association**
BMC N ABBR = **British Medical Council**
BMI N ABBR (= **body mass index**) IMC *m*

b

BMJ N ABBR = **British Medical Journal**
B-movie ['bi:,mu:vɪ] N película *f* de la serie B
BMus N ABBR (*Univ*) = **Bachelor of Music**
BMX N ABBR (= **bicycle motocross**) ciclocross *m*
CPD ▸ **BMX bike** bicicleta *f* de ciclocross
bn ABBR = **billion**
BNFL N ABBR = **British Nuclear Fuels Limited**
BNP N ABBR (= **British National Party**) *partido político de la extrema derecha*
BO N ABBR **1** (= **body odour**) olor *m* a sudor
2 (*US*) = **box office**
b.o. ABBR (*Comm*) = **buyer's option**
B/O ABBR (*Econ*) = **brought over**
boa ['bəʊə] N **1** (*also* **boa constrictor**) boa *f*
2 (= *garment*) boa *f* (de plumas)
Boadicea [,bəʊədɪ'sɪə] N Boadicea
boar [bɔ:ʳ] N (= *male pig*) cerdo *m*, verraco *m* • **wild ~** jabalí *m*
board [bɔ:d] N **1** [*of wood*] tabla *f*, tablón *m*; (= *table*) mesa *f*; (*for chess etc*) tablero *m*; (= *ironing board*) tabla *f* de planchar; (= *notice board*) tablón *m*; (*in bookbinding*) cartón *m*; (*Comput*) placa *f*, tarjeta *f* • **above ~** (= *legitimate*) legítimo; (= *in order*) en regla, legal • **an increase across the ~** un aumento global *or* general • **to go by the ~** (= *go wrong*) ir al traste; (= *be abandoned*) abandonarse • **in ~s** (*book*) en cartoné • IDIOM: • **to sweep the ~** ganar todas las bazas; (*in election*) copar todos los escaños
2 (= *provision of meals*) comida *f* • **full ~** pensión *f* completa • **half ~** media pensión *f* • **~ and lodging** (*Brit*) casa *f* y comida
3 (*Naut, Aer*) • **on ~** a bordo • **on ~ (the) ship** a bordo del barco • **to go on ~** embarcarse, subir a bordo • IDIOM: • **to take sth on ~** [+ *idea*] adoptar algo, asimilar algo
4 (= *group of officials*) junta *f*, consejo *m*
5 (*gas, water etc*) comisión *f*
6 • **the ~s** (*Theat*) las tablas • IDIOM: • **to tread the ~s** (*as profession*) ser actor/actriz; (= *action*) salir a escena
VT **1** [+ *ship, plane*] subir a bordo de, embarcarse en; [+ *enemy ship*] abordar; [+ *bus, train*] subir a
2 (*also* **board up**) (= *cover with boards*) entablar
3 (= *feed, lodge*) hospedar, dar pensión (completa) a
VI • **to ~ with** hospedarse en casa de
CPD ▸ **board chairman** presidente/a *m/f* del consejo de administración ▸ **board game** juego *m* de tablero ▸ **board meeting** reunión *f* de la junta directiva *or* del consejo de administración ▸ **board member** (= *member of board of directors*) miembro *m* de la junta directiva, miembro *m* del consejo de administración ▸ **board of directors** junta *f* directiva, consejo *m* de administración ▸ **board of education** (*esp US*) *consejo supervisor del sistema educativo* ▸ **board of governors** (*Brit*) (*Scol*) consejo *m* (*de un colegio, instituto etc*) ▸ **board of inquiry** comisión *f* investigadora ▸ **Board of Trade** (*Brit*) (*formerly*) Departamento *m* de Comercio y Exportación; (*US*) Cámara *f* de Comercio
▸ **board in** VT + ADV = board up
▸ **board out** VT + ADV [+ *person*] buscar alojamiento a • **he is ~ed out with relatives** vive con unos parientes (*pagando la pensión*)
▸ **board up** VT + ADV [+ *door, window*] entablar
boarder ['bɔ:dəʳ] N (*in house*) huésped(a) *m/f*; (*Brit*) (*Scol*) interno/a *m/f*
boarding ['bɔ:dɪŋ] N entablado *m*
CPD ▸ **boarding card** tarjeta *f* de embarque, pase *m* de embarque (*LAm*) ▸ **boarding house** pensión *f*, casa *f* de huéspedes, residencial *f* (*S. Cone*) ▸ **boarding party** pelotón *m* de abordaje ▸ **boarding pass** = boarding card ▸ **boarding school** internado *m*
boardroom ['bɔ:drʊm] N sala *f* de juntas
CPD ▸ **boardroom level** • **at ~ level** (*in company*) en la junta directiva ▸ **boardroom pay** (= *directors' pay*) remuneración *f* de los consejeros
boardwalk ['bɔ:dwɔ:k] N (*US*) paseo *m* marítimo entablado
boast [bəʊst] N alarde *m* • **it is his ~ that ...** se jacta de que ... • **to be the ~ of** ser el orgullo de
VT (*frm*) (= *pride o.s. on*) ostentar, jactarse de
VI presumir, alardear • **he ~s about** *or* **of his strength** presume de fuerte • **that's nothing to ~ about** eso no es motivo para vanagloriarse
boasted ['bəʊstɪd] ADJ alardeado, cacareado
boaster ['bəʊstəʳ] N jactancioso/a *m/f*, fanfarrón/ona *m/f*
boastful ['bəʊstfʊl] ADJ jactancioso, fanfarrón
boastfully ['bəʊstfʊlɪ] ADV jactanciosamente, con fanfarronería
boastfulness ['bəʊstfʊlnɪs] N jactancia *f*, fanfarronería *f*
boasting ['bəʊstɪŋ] N jactancia *f*, fanfarronadas *fpl*
boat [bəʊt] N (*gen*) barco *m*; (= *large ship*) buque *m*, navío *m*; (*small*) barca *f*; (= *rowing boat*) barca *f*, bote *m* (de remo); (= *racing eight, ship's boat*) bote *m* • **to go by ~** ir en barco • **to launch** *or* **lower the ~s** botar los botes al agua • IDIOMS: • **to burn one's ~s** quemar las naves • **to miss the ~** perder el tren • **to push the ~ out*** tirar la casa por la ventana* • **to rock the ~** hacer olas • **we're all in the same ~*** estamos todos en la misma situación
CPD ▸ **boat deck** cubierta *f* de botes ▸ **boat hook** bichero *m* ▸ **boat people** *refugiados que huyen en barco* ▸ **boat race** regata *f* • **the Boat Race** (*Brit*) *carrera anual de remo entre Oxford y Cambridge* ▸ **boat ride** paseo *m* en barco ▸ **boat shoes** marinos *mpl* ▸ **boat train** tren *m* que enlaza con el barco ▸ **boat trip** (= *excursion*) excursión *f* en barco
boatbuilder ['bəʊt,bɪldəʳ] N constructor(a) *m/f* de barcos • **~'s (yard)** astillero *m*
boatbuilding ['bəʊt,bɪldɪŋ] N construcción *f* de barcos
boater ['bəʊtəʳ] N (= *hat*) canotié *m*
boatful ['bəʊtfʊl] N (*goods*) cargamento *m* • **the refugees arrived in ~s** llegaron barcos llenos de refugiados
boathouse ['bəʊthaʊs] N cobertizo *m* para botes
boating ['bəʊtɪŋ] N • **to go ~** ir a dar un paseo en barca
CPD ▸ **boating holiday** vacaciones *fpl* en barca ▸ **boating lake** (*in park*) lago *m* para barcos ▸ **boating trip** paseo *m* en barca
boatload ['bəʊtləʊd] N barcada *f*
boatman ['bəʊtmən] N (PL: **boatmen**) barquero *m*
boatswain ['bəʊsn] N contramaestre *m*
boatyard ['bəʊtjɑ:d] N astillero *m*
Bob [bɒb] N *familiar form of* **Robert** • IDIOM: • **Bob's your uncle!** (*Brit**) ¡y se acabó!, ¡y listo!
bob¹ [bɒb] N (= *jerk*) [*of head etc*] sacudida *f*, meneo *m*; (= *curtsy*) reverencia *f*
VI (= *jerk*) [*person*] menearse; [*animal*] moverse, menearse • **to bob to sb** (= *curtsy*) hacer una reverencia a algn
▸ **bob about** VI + ADV (*in wind etc*) bailar; (*on water*) balancearse, mecerse
▸ **bob down** VI + ADV (= *duck*) agacharse
▸ **bob up** VI + ADV aparecer; (*fig*) (= *appear*) surgir, presentarse • **to bob up and down** [*cork*] subir y bajar; [*boat*] cabecear; [*person*] levantarse y sentarse repetidas veces
bob² [bɒb] N (= *hairstyle*) pelo *m* a lo garçon
VT [+ *hair*] cortar a lo garçon
bob³* [bɒb] N (*pl inv*) (*Brit*) (*formerly*) (= *shilling*) chelín *m* • **that must be worth a few bob** eso tiene que valer un buen pico* *or* un dineral • **he's not short of a few bob** está forrado*
bob⁴ [bɒb] N (= *bobsleigh*) bob *m*, bobsleigh *m*
bobbed [bɒbd] ADJ [*hair*] cortado a lo garçon
bobbin ['bɒbɪn] N (*Tech*) carrete *m*, bobina *f*; (*Sew*) [*of cotton*] canilla *f*
bobble ['bɒbl] N **1** (*Brit*) (*on hat*) borla *f*
2 (*US**) (= *mistake*) pifia* *f*
VI [*ball etc*] saltar, moverse de un lado para otro
VT (*US**) (= *handle ineptly*) pifiarla con*
CPD ▸ **bobble hat** (*Brit*) gorro *m* con borla
Bobby ['bɒbɪ] N *familiar form of* **Robert**
bobby* ['bɒbɪ] N (*Brit*) (= *policeman*) poli* *m*
bobby pin ['bɒbɪ,pɪn] N (*US*) horquilla *f*, prendedor *m*
bobbysocks*, **bobbysox*** ['bɒbɪsɒks] NPL (*US*) escarpines *mpl*
bobbysoxer* ['bɒbɪsɒksəʳ] N (*US*) tobillera *f*
bobcat ['bɒbkæt] N (*US*) lince *m*
bobsled ['bɒbsled] N (*US*) bob *m*, bobsleigh *m*
bobsleigh ['bɒbsleɪ] N (*Brit*) bob *m*, bobsleigh *m*
bobtail ['bɒbteɪl] N (= *tail*) cola *f* corta; (= *animal*) animal *m* de cola corta, animal *m* rabón
bobtailed ['bɒbteɪld] ADJ rabicorto
Boccaccio [bɒ'kætʃɪəʊ] N Bocacio
Boche [bɒʃ] ADJ (*pej*) alemán, tudesco
N (*pej*) boche *m*, alemán *m* • **the ~** los alemanes
bock beer ['bɒk,bɪəʳ] N (*US*) cerveza *f* alemana
bod* [bɒd] N **1** (*Brit*) (= *person*) tipo/a* *m/f*, tío/a *m/f* (*Sp**)
2 (= *body*) cuerpo *m*
bodacious‡ [bəʊ'deɪʃəs] ADJ (*US*) tremendo*, fabuloso*
bode [bəʊd] (*liter*) VT presagiar • **it ~s no good** no promete nada bueno
VI • **it ~s well/ill** es de buen/mal agüero
bodega [bəʊ'deɪgə] N (= *grocery shop*) almacén *m*, tienda *f* de ultramarinos
bodge* [bɒdʒ] VT (*Brit*) = **botch**
bodice ['bɒdɪs] N [*of dress*] canesú *m*
bodice-ripping* ['bɒdɪsrɪpɪŋ] ADJ [*film, novel*] romanticón
-bodied ['bɒdɪd] ADJ (*ending in compounds*) de cuerpo ... • **small-bodied** de cuerpo pequeño • **full-bodied** [*cry*] fuerte; [*wine*] de mucho cuerpo
bodiless ['bɒdɪləs] ADJ sin cuerpo
bodily ['bɒdɪlɪ] ADJ [*scar, injury*] en el cuerpo; [*comfort*] del cuerpo; [*pain*] corporal; [*fluid*] corporal, del cuerpo • **~ functions** funciones *fpl* fisiológicas • **~ needs** necesidades *fpl* corporales • **actual ~ harm** (*Jur*) daños *mpl* físicos, lesiones *fpl* corporales • **grievous ~ harm** (*Jur*) daños *mpl* físicos graves, lesiones *fpl* corporales graves
ADV • **to lift sb ~** levantar a algn totalmente • **he hurled himself ~ at the Prince** se lanzó con todo su peso sobre el Príncipe • **the audience moved ~ to the front** el público se abalanzó en masa hacia la parte delantera
bodkin ['bɒdkɪn] N **1** (*Sew*) aguja *f* de jareta

b

2 (*Typ*) punzón *m*
3†† (= *for hair*) espadilla *f*
body [ˈbɒdɪ] (N) **1** [*of person, animal*] cuerpo *m*, tronco *m* • **~ and soul** (*as adv*) de todo corazón, con el alma • **to belong to sb ~ and soul** pertenecer a algn en cuerpo y alma • IDIOMS: • **over my dead ~!*** ¡en sueños!, ¡ni pensarlo! • **to keep ~ and soul together** ir tirando • **her salary hardly keeps ~ and soul together** apenas se gana para vivir
2 (= *corpse*) cadáver *m*
3 (= *external structure*) armazón *m or f*, casco *m*; (*Aut*) (*also* **bodywork**) carrocería *f*
4 (= *core*) [*of argument*] meollo *m* • **the main ~ of his speech** la parte principal *or* el meollo de su discurso
5 (= *mass, collection*) [*of information, literature*] conjunto *m*, grueso *m*; [*of people*] grupo *m*; [*of water*] masa *f* • **a large ~ of people** un nutrido grupo de personas • **the student ~** [*of school*] el alumnado; [*of university*] el estudiantado • **the ~ politic** (*frm*) el estado • **a fine ~ of men** un buen grupo de hombres • **a large ~ of evidence** un buen conjunto de pruebas • **there is a ~ of opinion that ...** hay buen número de gente que opina que ... • **in a ~** todos juntos, en masa
6 (= *organization*) organismo *m*, órgano *m*
7 [*of wine*] cuerpo *m*; [*of hair*] volumen *m*, cuerpo *m* • **to give one's hair ~** dar volumen *or* cuerpo al cabello
8 (*Astron, Chem*) cuerpo *m*; ▹ **foreign, heavenly**
9†* (= *person*) tipo/a* *m/f*, tío/a *m/f* (*Sp**)
10 = **body stocking**
(CPD) ▸ **body armour, body armor** (*US*) *equipo de protección corporal* ▸ **body art** arte *m* corporal ▸ **body bag** bolsa *f* para restos humanos ▸ **body blow** (*fig*) golpe *m* duro, revés *m* ▸ **body clock** reloj *m* biológico ▸ **body count** (*US*) número *m or* balance *m* de las víctimas • **to do a ~ count** [*of those present*] hacer un recuento de la asistencia; [*of dead*] hacer un recuento de los muertos ▸ **body double** (*Cine, TV*) doble *mf* ▸ **body dysmorphic disorder** trastorno *m* dismórfico corporal, dismorfofobia *f* ▸ **body fascism** discriminación *f* por el (aspecto) físico ▸ **body fat** grasa *f* corporal, grasa *f* (del cuerpo) ▸ **body fluids** fluidos *mpl* corporales ▸ **body hair** vello *m* corporal ▸ **body image** imagen *f* corporal • **women with a poor ~ image** mujeres que tienen una pobre imagen de sus cuerpos ▸ **body language** lenguaje *m* corporal, lenguaje *m* del cuerpo ▸ **body lotion** loción *f* corporal ▸ **body mass** (= *ratio of weight to height*) masa *f* corporal ▸ **body mass index** índice *m* de masa corporal ▸ **body mike*** micro *m* de solapa* ▸ **body odour, body odor** (*US*) olor *m* corporal ▸ **body piercing** piercing *m* ▸ **body repairs** (*Aut*) reparación *f* de la carrocería ▸ **body repair shop** (*Aut*) taller *m* de reparaciones (*de carrocería*) ▸ **body scanner** escáner *m* ▸ **body scrub** exfoliante *m* corporal ▸ **body search** registro *m* de la persona; ▹ **body-search** ▸ **body shop** (*Aut*) taller *m* de reparaciones (*de carrocería*) ▸ **body snatcher** (*Hist*) ladrón/a *m/f* de cadáveres ▸ **body stocking** body *m*, bodi *m* ▸ **body suit** = **body stocking** ▸ **body swerve** (*Sport*) finta *f*, regate *m* ▸ **body temperature** temperatura *f* corporal ▸ **body warmer** chaleco *m* acolchado ▸ **body weight** peso *m* (del cuerpo)
bodybuilder [ˈbɒdɪˌbɪldəʳ] (N) culturista *mf*
bodybuilding [ˈbɒdɪˌbɪldɪŋ] (N) culturismo *m*
(CPD) ▸ **bodybuilding exercises** ejercicios *mpl* de musculación
bodycheck [ˈbɒdɪˌtʃek] (N) (*Sport*) blocaje *m*
bodyguard [ˈbɒdɪɡɑːd] (N) (= *one person*) guardaespaldas *mf inv*, guarura *mf* (*Mex*); (= *group*) escolta *f*, guardia *f* personal; (*royal*) guardia *f* de corps
body-search [ˈbɒdɪsɜːtʃ] (VT) registrar (la persona de); ▹ **body**
bodyshell [ˈbɒdɪʃel] (N) (*Aut*) carrocería *f*
bodywork [ˈbɒdɪwɜːk] (N) (*Aut*) carrocería *f*
Boer [ˈbəʊəʳ] (ADJ) bóer
(N) bóer *mf*
(CPD) ▸ **Boer War** Guerra *f* Bóer, Guerra *f* del Transvaal
B. of E. (N ABBR) = **Bank of England**
boffin* [ˈbɒfɪn] (N) (*Brit*) cerebrito* *mf*
bog [bɒɡ] (N) **1** (= *swamp*) pantano *m*, ciénaga *f*
2 (*Brit*‡) (= *toilet*) retrete *m*, meadero‡ *m*
(CPD) ▸ **bog paper**‡ (*Brit*) papel *m* de wáter ▸ **bog roll**‡ (*Brit*) rollo *m* de papel de wáter
▸ **bog down** (VT + ADV) • **to get bogged down (in)** quedar atascado (en), hundirse (en); (*fig*) empantanarse *or* atrancarse (en)
▸ **bog off**‡ (VI + ADV) irse al pedo* • **bog off, Sonia!** ¡vete al pedo, Sonia!*
bogey [ˈbəʊɡɪ] (N) **1** (= *goblin*) duende *m*, trasgo *m*; (= *bugbear*) pesadilla *f* • **that is our ~ team** ese es nuestro equipo pesadilla*
2 (*Golf*) bogey *m*, más uno *m*
3 (*Brit*‡) (*in nose*) moco *m*
4 (*Brit**) (= *policeman*) poli* *m*
5 (*Rail*) bogie *m*, boga *f*
(VT) (*Golf*) • **to ~ a hole** hacer bogey *or* uno sobre par en un hoyo
bogeyman [ˈbəʊɡɪˌmæn] (N) (PL: **bogeymen**) coco* *m*
boggle* [ˈbɒɡl] (VI) pasmarse, quedarse patidifuso* • **to ~ (at)** (= *hesitate*) quedarse patidifuso (ante)*; (= *be afraid*) quedarse helado (ante) • **don't just stand and ~** no te quedes ahí parado con la boca abierta • **the imagination ~s** se queda uno alucinado* • **the mind ~s!** te quedas helado *or* patidifuso*
(VT) • **it ~s the mind** te deja alucinado*
boggy [ˈbɒɡɪ] (ADJ) (COMPAR: **boggier**, SUPERL: **boggiest**) pantanoso
bogie [ˈbəʊɡɪ] (N) = **bogey**
Bogotá [ˌbɒɡəʊˈtɑː] (N) Bogotá *m*
bog-standard* [ˈbɒɡˈstændəd] (ADJ) (*Brit*) normalito*, común y corriente
bogtrotter‡ [ˈbɒɡˌtrɒtəʳ] (N) (*pej*) irlandés/esa *m/f*
bogus [ˈbəʊɡəs] (ADJ) [*claim*] falso, fraudulento; [*interest*] fingido; [*doctor, policeman*] falso
bogy [ˈbəʊɡɪ] (N) = **bogey**
Bohemia [bəʊˈhiːmɪə] (N) Bohemia *f*
Bohemian [bəʊˈhiːmɪən] (ADJ) (*Geog*) (*also fig*) bohemio
(N) (*Geog*) (*also fig*) bohemio/a *m/f*
Bohemianism [bəʊˈhiːmɪənɪzəm] (N) bohemia *f*, vida *f* bohemia
boho* [ˈbəʊhəʊ] (ADJ) bohemio
(N) bohemio/a *m/f*
boil¹ [bɔɪl] (N) (*Med*) divieso *m*, furúnculo *m*, chupón *m* (*And*), postema *f* (*Mex*)
boil² [bɔɪl] (N) • **to be on the ~** estar hirviendo; (*fig*) [*situation*] estar a punto de estallar; [*person*] estar furioso • **to bring to the ~** • **bring to a ~** (*US*) calentar hasta que hierva, llevar a ebullición • **to come to the ~** • **come to a ~** (*US*) comenzar a hervir; (*fig*) entrar en ebullición • **to go off the ~** dejar de hervir
(VT) hervir, hacer hervir, calentar hasta que hierva; (*Culin*) [+ *liquid*] hervir; [+ *vegetables, meat*] herventar, cocer; [+ *egg*] pasar por agua
(VI) **1** hervir • **to ~ dry** quedarse sin caldo/agua
2 (*fig*) • **it makes me ~** me hace rabiar • **to ~ with rage** estar furioso • **to ~ with indignation** estar indignado; ▹ **blood**
▸ **boil away** (VI + ADV) (= *evaporate completely*) evaporarse, reducirse (por ebullición)
▸ **boil down** (VT + ADV) [+ *sauce etc*] reducir por cocción; (*fig*) reducir a forma más sencilla
▸ **boil down to** (VI + ADV) reducirse a • **it all ~s down to this** la cosa se reduce a lo siguiente
▸ **boil over** (VI + ADV) **1** [*liquid*] irse, rebosar
2 (*fig*) desbordarse
▸ **boil up** (VI + ADV) (*lit*) [*milk*] hervir, subir • **anger was ~ing up in him** estaba a punto de estallar de ira • **they are ~ing up for a real row** se están enfureciendo de verdad
boiled [bɔɪld] (ADJ) hervido
(CPD) ▸ **boiled egg** huevo *m* pasado por agua, huevo *m* a la copa (*And, S. Cone*) ▸ **boiled potatoes** patatas *fpl* cocidas al agua ▸ **boiled shirt** camisa *f* de pechera ▸ **boiled sweet** (*Brit*) caramelo *m* con sabor a frutas
boiler [ˈbɔɪləʳ] (N) **1** (*for central heating*) caldera *f*; (*in ship, engine*) calderas *fpl*; (*Brit*) (*for washing clothes*) caldero *m*, calefón *m* (*S. Cone*)
2 (*Culin*) gallina *f* vieja
(CPD) ▸ **boiler room** sala *f* de calderas ▸ **boiler suit** (*Brit*) mono *m*, overol *m* (*LAm*), mameluco *m* (*S. Cone*)
boilerhouse [ˈbɔɪləhaʊs] (N) (PL: **boilerhouses** [ˈbɔɪləhaʊzɪz]) edificio *m* de la caldera
boilermaker [ˈbɔɪləˌmeɪkəʳ] (N) calderero/a *m/f*
boilermaking [ˈbɔɪləˌmeɪkɪŋ] (N) fabricación *f* de calderas
boilerman [ˈbɔɪləˌmæn] (N) (PL: **boilermen**) calderero *m*
boiling [ˈbɔɪlɪŋ] (ADJ) **1** (*gen*) hirviendo
2* (*fig*) **a** (= *very hot*) • **I'm ~** estoy asado* • **it's ~ in here** aquí hace un calor terrible
b (= *angry*) echando chispas*
(ADV)* • **it's ~ hot** (*weather*) hace un calor espantoso • **on a ~ hot day** un día de mucho calor • **I'm ~ hot** estoy asado*
(CPD) ▸ **boiling point** punto *m* de ebullición
boil-in-the-bag meal [ˌbɔɪlɪnðəˌbæɡˈmiːl] (N) *plato precocinado empaquetado en bolsas para cocción*
boisterous [ˈbɔɪstərəs] (ADJ) **1** (= *unrestrained*) [*person*] bullicioso, escandaloso; [*crowd*] bullicioso, alborotado; [*meeting*] bullicioso, tumultuoso
2 (= *in high spirits*) [*child, game*] bullicioso, alborotado; [*party*] bullicioso, muy animado
3 (= *rough*) [*sea, waves*] embravecido; [*wind*] tempestuoso
boisterously [ˈbɔɪstərəslɪ] (ADV) [*play*] bulliciosamente, alborotadamente; [*laugh*] escandalosamente
bold [bəʊld] (ADJ) (COMPAR: **bolder**, SUPERL: **boldest**) **1** (= *brave*) [*person, attempt, plan*] atrevido, audaz
2 (= *forward*) [*child, remark*] atrevido, descarado • **if I may be** *or* **make so ~** (*frm*) si me permite el atrevimiento (*frm*) • **to make ~ with sth** (*frm*) servirse de algo como si fuera suyo • IDIOM: • **(as) ~ as brass** más fresco que una lechuga*
3 (= *striking*) [*colour, clothes, design*] llamativo; [*brush stroke, handwriting, move*] enérgico; [*shape, relief, contrast*] marcado
4 (*Typ*) [*letters*] en negrita
(N) (*Typ*) negrita *f*
(CPD) ▸ **bold type** negrita *f*
boldface [ˈbəʊldfeɪs] (*Typ*) (N) negrita *f*
(ADJ) en negrita • **in ~ type** en negrita
boldly [ˈbəʊldlɪ] (ADV) **1** (= *bravely*) [*speak, behave*] audazmente • **you must act ~ and confidently** debes actuar con audacia y

seguridad en ti mismo • **to ~ go where no man has gone before** atreverse a ir donde ningún otro hombre ha estado antes
2 (= *forwardly*) [*stare, announce, claim*] descaradamente, con atrevimiento
3 (= *strikingly*) [*painted, drawn, written*] con energía • **he signed his name ~ at the bottom** firmó enérgicamente al pie • **a ~ designed airport** un aeropuerto con un diseño atrevido • **a ~ patterned fabric** una tela con un estampado llamativo • **a ~ coloured shirt** una camisa de color llamativo

boldness ['bəʊldnɪs] N **1** (= *daring*) audacia *f*
2 (= *forwardness*) atrevimiento *m*, descaro *m*
3 (= *striking quality*) [*of design, colours, clothes*] lo llamativo; [*of lines, strokes*] lo enérgico; [*of contrast*] lo marcado

bole [bəʊl] N tronco *m*

bolero [bə'lɛərəʊ] N bolero *m*

boletus [bəʊ'li:təs] N (PL: **boletuses** *or* **boleti** [bəʊ'li:,taɪ]) seta *f*

Bolivia [bə'lɪvɪə] N Bolivia *f*

Bolivian [bə'lɪvɪən] ADJ boliviano
N boliviano/a *m/f*

boll [bəʊl] N (*Bot*) cápsula *f*

bollard ['bɒləd] N (*Brit*) (*at roadside*) baliza *f*; (*Naut*) noray *m*, bolardo *m*

bollocking** ['bɒləkɪŋ] N (*Brit*) • **to give sb a ~** echar una bronca a algn*, poner a algn como un trapo*

bollocks** ['bɒləks] (*Brit*) NPL cojones** *mpl*
N (= *nonsense*) pavadas* *fpl*, huevadas *fpl* (*And, Chile***)

Bollywood* ['bɒlɪwʌd] N (*hum*) *la industria cinematográfica de la India*

Bologna [bə'ləʊnjə] N Bolonia *f*

bologna [bə'ləʊnjə], **bologna sausage** N (*Culin*) *tipo de salchicha*

bolognese [bɒlə'njeɪz] ADJ • **~ sauce** salsa *f* boloñesa

boloney [bə'ləʊnɪ] N **1*** = **baloney**
2 (*US*) (= *sausage*) *tipo de salchicha*

Bolshevik ['bɒlʃəvɪk] ADJ bolchevique
N bolchevique *mf*

Bolshevism ['bɒlʃəvɪzəm] N bolchevismo *m*

Bolshevist ['bɒlʃəvɪst] ADJ bolchevista
N bolchevista *mf*

bolshie*, **bolshy*** ['bɒlʃɪ] (*Brit*) N (*Pol*) bolchevique *mf*
ADJ (*Pol*) bolchevique; (*fig*) rebelde, protestón

bolster ['bəʊlstəʳ] N (= *pillow*) cabezal *m*, almohadón *m* (*con forma cilíndrica*); (*Tech*) cojín *m*
VT (*fig*) (*also* **bolster up**) reforzar; [+ *morale etc*] levantar

bolt [bəʊlt] N **1** (*on door, gun*) cerrojo *m*; [*of crossbow*] cuadrillo *m*; [*of lock*] pestillo *m*; (*Tech*) perno *m*, tornillo *m* • IDIOM: • **he's shot his ~** ha quemado su último cartucho
2 [*of cloth*] rollo *m*
3 (= *dash*) salida *f* repentina; (= *flight*) fuga *f* • **to make a ~ for it** echar a correr • **he made a ~ for the door** se lanzó hacia la puerta
4 [*of lightning*] rayo *m*, relámpago *m* • IDIOM: • **it came like a ~ from the blue** cayó como una bomba
ADV • **~ upright** rígido, muy erguido • **to sit ~ upright** incorporarse de golpe
VT **1** [+ *door etc*] echar el cerrojo a; (*Tech*) sujetar con tornillos, empernar • **to ~ two things together** unir dos cosas con pernos
2 (*also* **bolt down**) [+ *food*] engullir, tragar (*LAm*)
VI **1** (= *escape*) escaparse, huir; [*horse*] desbocarse
2 (= *rush*) echar a correr • **to ~ past** pasar como un rayo
3 (*US*) (*Pol*) separarse del partido
CPD ▸ **bolt cutter** cizalla *f* ▸ **bolt hole** (*Brit*) refugio *m*
▸ **bolt in** VI + ADV (= *rush in*) entrar precipitadamente
▸ **bolt on** VT + ADV (*Tech*) asegurar con perno
▸ **bolt out** VI + ADV (= *rush out*) salir de golpe
VT + ADV (= *lock out*) • **to ~ sb out** dejar fuera a algn echando el cerrojo

bomb [bɒm] N bomba *f* • **the Bomb** la bomba atómica • IDIOMS: • **to go like a ~** (*Brit**): • **it went like a ~** [*party, event*] resultó fenomenal*, fue un éxito • **this car goes like a ~** este coche va como un bólido* • **to cost a ~** (*Brit**) costar un ojo de la cara* • **to make a ~** (*Brit**) ganarse un fortunón*
VT **1** [+ *target*] bombardear
2 (*US**) (= *fail*) suspender
VI (*US**) (= *fail*) fracasar • **the show ~ed** el espectáculo fracasó
CPD ▸ **bomb alert** aviso *m* de bomba ▸ **bomb attack** atentado *m* con bomba ▸ **bomb bay** compartimento *m* de bombas ▸ **bomb belt** cinturón *m* bomba ▸ **bomb blast** explosión *f* ▸ **bomb crater** cráter *m* de bomba ▸ **bomb damage** daños *mpl* provocados por los bombardeos ▸ **bomb disposal** desactivación *f* *or* neutralización *f* de bombas ▸ **bomb disposal expert** artificiero/a *m/f*, experto/a *m/f* en desactivar bombas ▸ **bomb disposal squad**, **bomb disposal unit** brigada *f* de bombas ▸ **bomb explosion** explosión *f* ▸ **bomb factory** *local clandestino de fabricación de bombas* ▸ **bomb hoax** falso aviso *m* de bomba ▸ **bomb scare** amenaza *f* de bomba ▸ **bomb shelter** refugio *m* antiaéreo ▸ **bomb site** *lugar en el que ha estallado una bomba* ▸ **bomb warning** aviso *m* de bomba
▸ **bomb along*** VI + ADV ir a toda marcha*, ir a toda hostia (*Sp**) • **we were ~ing along at 150** íbamos a 150
▸ **bomb out** VT + ADV [+ *house*] volar • **the family was ~ed out** (*by terrorists*) a la familia les volaron la casa; (*by planes*) a la familia les bombardearon la casa

bombard [bɒm'bɑ:d] VT (*Mil*) bombardear (**with con**) • **I was ~ed with questions** me acosaron *or* bombardearon a preguntas

bombardier [,bɒmbə'dɪəʳ] N bombardero *m*

bombardment [bɒm'bɑ:dmənt] N (*Mil*) bombardeo *m*

bombast ['bɒmbæst] N (= *pomposity*) ampulosidad *f*, rimbombancia *f*; (= *words*) palabras *fpl* altisonantes, rimbombancia *f*; (= *boasts*) bravatas *fpl*

bombastic [bɒm'bæstɪk] ADJ [*language, manner, style*] ampuloso, rimbombante; [*person*] pomposo

bombastically [bɒm'bæstɪklɪ] ADV rimbombantemente

Bombay [bɒm'beɪ] N Bombay *m*
CPD ▸ **Bombay duck** (*Culin*) *pescado seco utilizado en la elaboración del curry*

bombed-out [,bɒmd'aʊt] ADJ [*building*] destruido por las bombas

bomber ['bɒməʳ] N **1** (= *aircraft*) bombardero *m*
2 (= *person*) terrorista *mf* que coloca bombas
CPD ▸ **bomber command** jefatura *f* de bombardeo ▸ **bomber jacket** chaqueta *f* *or* (*Sp*) cazadora *f* (*tipo aviador*) ▸ **bomber pilot** piloto *m* de bombardero

bombing ['bɒmɪŋ] N bombardeo *m*
CPD ▸ **bombing campaign** (*in war*) campaña *f* de bombardeos; (*by terrorists*) campaña *f* de atentados con bomba ▸ **bombing mission** (*in war*) misión *f* de bombardeo

bomblet ['bɒmlɪt] N *bomba de pequeño tamaño, dentro de una bomba de fragmentación*

bombproof ['bɒmpru:f] ADJ a prueba de bombas

bombshell ['bɒmʃel] N **1** (*Mil*) (*formerly*) obús *m*, granada *f*
2 (*fig*) [*of news etc*] bomba *f* • **it fell like a ~** cayó como una bomba
3* (= *attractive woman*) • **she was a real ~** era todo un bombón*; ▹ **blond(e)**

bombsight ['bɒmsaɪt] N mira *f* *or* visor *m* de bombardeo

bona fide ['bəʊnə'faɪdɪ] ADJ (= *genuine*) auténtico; (= *legal*) legal

bona fides ['bəʊnə'faɪdɪz] N [*of person*] buena fe *f*

bonanza [bə'nænzə] N (*fig*) (*in profits*) bonanza *f*

bonbon ['bɒnbɒn] N *tipo de caramelo*

bonce* [bɒns] N (*Brit*) coco* *m*

bond [bɒnd] N **1** (= *link*) lazo *m*, vínculo *m* • **a ~ of friendship** un vínculo de amistad • **his word is as good as his ~** es un hombre de palabra, es de fiar; ▹ **marriage**
2 bonds (= *chains etc*) cadenas *fpl*
3 (*Econ*) bono *m*; ▹ **premium**
4 (*Jur*) (= *bail*) fianza *f*
5 (*Comm*) • **in ~** en depósito bajo fianza • **to put goods into ~** depositar mercancías en el almacén aduanero • **to take goods out of ~** retirar mercancías del almacén aduanero
6 (= *adhesion*) unión *f*
7 (*Chem etc*) enlace *m*
VT **1** (*Tech*) [+ *materials*] (*also* **bond together**) unir, pegar
2 (*Psych*) unir
VI **1** (*Tech*) adherirse (**with a**)
2 (*Psych*) establecer lazos *or* vínculos afectivos • **she was having difficulty ~ing with the baby** no conseguía establecer vínculos afectivos con su bebé
CPD ▸ **bond washing** (*Econ*) lavado *m* de bonos

bondage ['bɒndɪdʒ] N **1** (= *enslavement*) esclavitud *f*, cautiverio *m* • **to be in ~ to sth** ser esclavo de algo
2 (= *sexual practice*) bondage *m*

bonded ['bɒndɪd] ADJ unido, vinculado; (*Comm*) en aduana
CPD ▸ **bonded goods** mercancías *fpl* en almacén aduanero ▸ **bonded warehouse** almacén *m* aduanero *or* de depósito

bondholder ['bɒnd,həʊldəʳ] N obligacionista *mf*, titular *mf* de bonos

bonding ['bɒndɪŋ] N (*Psych*) vinculación *f* afectiva

bone [bəʊn] N **1** [*of human, animal etc*] hueso *m*; [*of fish*] espina *f* • **~s** [*of dead*] huesos *mpl*; (*more respectfully*) restos *mpl* mortales • **~ of contention** manzana *f* de la discordia • **chilled** *or* **frozen to the ~** congelado de frío • **to cut costs to the ~** reducir los gastos al mínimo • **I feel it in my ~s** tengo esa corazonada, me da en la nariz (*Sp**) • **he won't make old ~s** no llegará a viejo • IDIOMS: • **close to the ~** (*joke*) subido de tono • **I have a ~ to pick with you** tenemos una cuenta que ajustar • **to make no ~s about doing sth** no vacilar en hacer algo • **he made no ~s about it** no se anduvo con rodeos • **to work one's fingers to the ~** trabajar como un esclavo
2 (= *substance*) hueso *m*
VT [+ *meat*] deshuesar; [+ *fish*] quitar las espinas a
CPD ▸ **bone china** porcelana *f* fina ▸ **bone density** densidad *f* ósea ▸ **bone marrow** médula *f* ósea ▸ **bone marrow donor** donante *mf* de médula ósea ▸ **bone marrow transplant** transplante *m* de médula ósea

▸ **bone up*** (VI + ADV) quemarse las cejas (**on** estudiando), empollar (**on** sobre)
boned [bəʊnd] (ADJ) **1** [*meat*] deshuesado; [*fish*] sin espinas
2 [*corset*] de ballenas
bone-dry [ˌbəʊn'draɪ] (ADJ) completamente seco
bonehead* ['bəʊnhed] (N) tonto/a *m/f*
boneheaded* ['bəʊn'hedɪd] (ADJ) estúpido
bone-idle* [ˌbəʊn'aɪdl] (ADJ) gandul, holgazán, flojo (*LAm*)
boneless ['bəʊnlɪs] (ADJ) **1** (*Anat*) sin hueso(s), deshuesado
2 (*fig*) sin carácter, débil
bonemeal ['bəʊnmiːl] (N) harina *f* de huesos
boner ['bəʊnəʳ] (N) **1** (*US**) (= *blunder*) metedura *f* de pata*, plancha *f* (*Sp**) • **to pull a ~** meter la pata*, tirarse una plancha (*Sp**)
2‡ (= *erection*) erección *f* • **to have a ~** tenerla dura‡
boneshaker* ['bəʊnʃeɪkəʳ] (N) (*Aut etc*) armatoste* *m*, rácano* *m*; (= *bicycle*) *bicicleta antigua con ruedas sólidas y sin muelles*
boneyard* ['bəʊnjɑːd] (N) (*for cars*) cementerio *m* de coches
bonfire ['bɒnfaɪəʳ] (N) (*for celebration*) hoguera *f*; (*for rubbish*) fogata *f*
bongo ['bɒŋgəʊ] (N) (*also* **bongo drum**) bongó *m*
bonhomie ['bɒnɒmiː] (N) afabilidad *f*
boniness ['bəʊnɪnɪs] (N) delgadez *f*
bonk [bɒŋk] (N) **1*** (= *hit*) golpe *m* • **it went ~*** hizo ¡pum!, se oyó un ruido sordo
2 (*Brit‡*) (= *sex*) • **to have a ~** echarse un polvo**‡*, follar (*Sp*‡*)
(VI) (*Brit‡*) (= *have sex*) echarse un polvo**‡*, follar (*Sp*‡*)
(VT) **1*** (= *hit*) golpear, pegar
2 (*Brit‡*) (= *have sex with*) tirarse a**‡*, echarse un polvo con**‡*
bonkers* ['bɒŋkəz] (ADJ) (*esp Brit*) • **to be ~** estar chalado*, estar como una cabra* • **to go ~** perder la chaveta*
bonking‡ ['bɒŋkɪŋ] (N) (*Brit*) (= *sex*) joder**‡* *m*
bon mot ['bɒn'məʊ] (N) agudeza *f*
Bonn [bɒn] (N) Bonn *m*
bonnet ['bɒnɪt] (N) **1** (*woman's*) gorra *f*; (*large, showy*) papalina *f*, toca *f*; (*esp Scot*) (*man's*) gorra *f* escocesa; (*baby's*) gorro *m*
2 (*Brit*) (*Aut*) capó *m*, cofre *m* (*Mex*)
bonny ['bɒnɪ] (ADJ) (COMPAR: **bonnier**, SUPERL: **bonniest**) (*esp Scot*) (= *pretty*) [*child*] hermoso, lindo (*esp LAm*); [*dress*] bonito, lindo (*esp LAm*)
bonsai ['bɒnsaɪ] (N) bonsai *m*
bonus ['bəʊnəs] (N) **1** (*on wages*) prima *f*, bonificación *f*; (*insurance etc*) gratificación *f*; (*to shareholders*) dividendo *m* adicional
2 (*fig*) ventaja *f*
(CPD) ▸ **bonus ball** (*in lottery*) (número *m*) complementario *m* ▸ **bonus point** (*in game, quiz*) punto *m* extra ▸ **bonus question** (*in quiz*) pregunta *f* bonus ▸ **bonus scheme** plan *m* de incentivos ▸ **bonus shares** acciones *fpl* gratuitas
bon voyage ['bɒnvɔɪ'ɑːʒ] (EXCL) ¡buen viaje!
bony ['bəʊnɪ] (ADJ) (COMPAR: **bonier**, SUPERL: **boniest**) **1** (= *having bones*) huesudo; [*fish*] espinoso, lleno de espinas
2 (= *like bone*) óseo
3 (= *thin*) [*person*] flaco, delgado
bonzer* ['bɒnzəʳ] (ADJ) (*Australia*) guay*
boo [buː] (N) rechifla *f*, abucheo *m* • IDIOM: • **he wouldn't say boo to a goose*** es incapaz de matar una mosca
(EXCL) ¡uh!
(VT) [+ *actor, referee*] abuchear, silbar • **he was booed off the stage** la rechifla le obligó a abandonar el escenario
(VI) silbar
boob [buːb] (N) **1** (*Brit**) (= *mistake*) metedura *f* de pata* • **to make a ~** meter la pata*
2‡ (= *breast*) teta* *f*
(VI)* meter la pata*
(CPD) ▸ **boob job*** operación *f* de senos • **to have a ~ job** operarse los senos • **she denies having had a ~ job** niega que se haya operado los senos ▸ **boob tube** (= *garment*) camiseta-tubo *f*; (*US*) (= *TV set*) televisor *m*
booboo* ['buːbuː] (N) (*US*) metedura *f* de pata*
booby ['buːbɪ] (N) **1** (= *fool*) bobo/a *m/f*
2 boobies‡ tetas* *fpl*
(CPD) ▸ **booby hatch‡** (*US*) (= *mental hospital*) casa *f* de locos ▸ **booby prize** premio *m* al último ▸ **booby trap** trampa *f*; (*Mil etc*) trampa *f* explosiva, bomba *f* cazabobos
booby-trap ['buːbɪtræp] (VT) poner trampa explosiva a • **the house had been booby-trapped** habían puesto una trampa explosiva en la casa • **booby-trapped car** coche-bomba *m* • **booby-trapped door** puerta *f* con sorpresa
boogie* ['buːgɪ] (N) (= *dance*) bailoteo* *m* • **to go for a ~** irse de marcha*, darle marcha (al cuerpo)‡
(VI) bailotear*, dar marcha (al cuerpo)‡
boogie-woogie ['buːgɪˌwuːgɪ] (N) bugui-bugui *m*
boo-hoo* [ˌbuː'huː] (EXCL) ¡bua!
booing ['buːɪŋ] (N) abucheo *m*
book [bʊk] (N) **1** (= *publication*) libro *m* • **by the ~** según las reglas • **to play it** *or* **to go by the ~** seguir las reglas • **economics/her life is a closed ~ to me** la economía/su vida es un misterio para mí • **the ~ of Genesis** el libro del Génesis • **the Good Book** la Biblia • **in my ~** (*fig*) tal como yo lo veo, a mi modo de ver • **a ~ on politics** un libro de política • **that's one for the ~** eso es digno de mención • **his mind is an open ~** su mente es un libro abierto • IDIOMS: • **to bring sb to ~** pedir cuentas a algn • **those who planned the murder were never brought to ~** nunca se les pidió cuentas a los que planearon el asesinato • **to be in sb's good/bad ~s:** • **I'm in his bad ~s at the moment** en este momento estoy en su lista negra • **I was trying to get back in her good ~s** estaba intentando volver a congraciarme con ella • **to read sb like a ~:** • **I know where he's off to, I can read him like a ~** sé dónde va, a mí no me engaña • **to suit sb's ~:** • **it suits his ~ to play the easy-going liberal** le viene bien hacerse el liberal poco exigente, se hace el liberal poco exigente porque le conviene • **to throw the ~ at sb** castigar severamente a algn; ▹ **leaf, trick, turn-up**
2 (*also* **notebook**) libreta *f*, librito *m*; (*also* **exercise book**) cuaderno *m*
3 (*also* **telephone book**) guía *f* • **I'm in the ~** estoy en la guía
4 (= *set*) [*of tickets, cheques*] talonario *m*; [*of matches*] estuche *m*; [*of stamps*] librito *m*; [*of samples*] muestrario *m*
5 books: a (*Comm*) • **the ~s** las cuentas, la contabilidad • **to keep the ~s** llevar las cuentas *or* los libros *or* la contabilidad; ▹ **cook**
b (= *register of members*) registro *msing* • **they had less than 30 members on their ~s** tenían menos de 30 miembros en el registro • **to take sb's name off the ~s** borrar a algn del registro • **he was the most expensive player on the ~s** era el jugador más caro que tenían fichado
6 (*Jur*) (*also* **statute book**) código *m*; ▹ **statute**
7 (*Gambling*) • **to make a ~ on sth** aceptar apuestas a algo • **to open** *or* **start a ~ on sth** empezar a aceptar apuestas a algo
8 (*US*) (*Mus*) (= *libretto*) libreto *m*
(VT) **1** (*Brit*) (= *reserve*) [+ *ticket, seat, room, table, flight*] reservar • **we ~ed the hotel rooms in advance** reservamos habitaciones en el hotel por adelantado • **all the restaurants are fully ~ed** todos los restaurantes están llenos • **have you ~ed your holiday yet?** ¿ya has reservado las vacaciones?
2 (= *arrange*) [+ *appointment, time*] pedir • **I've ~ed an appointment with the dentist** he pedido hora con el dentista • **can we ~ a time to meet soon?** ¿podemos quedar un día de estos?
3 (= *engage*) [+ *performer, artiste*] contratar
4* (= *take name of*) **a** [*police*] • **he was ~ed for speeding** lo multaron por exceso de velocidad • **they took him to the station and ~ed him for assault** lo llevaron a la comisaría y lo acusaron de agresión
b (*Sport*) [+ *player*] amonestar
5 (= *note down*) [+ *order*] anotar
(VI) (*Brit*) hacer una reserva, reservar • **to ~ into a hotel** hacer una reserva *or* reservar en un hotel
(CPD) ▸ **book club** club *m* del libro, club *m* de lectores ▸ **book cover** cubierta *f* de libro ▸ **book fair** feria *f* del libro ▸ **book jacket** sobrecubierta *f* ▸ **book learning** aprendizaje *m* (a través) de los libros, saber *m* libresco (*frm*) • **~ learning is only part of school life** el aprendizaje de los libros es solo una parte de la vida escolar ▸ **book post** correo *m* de libros ▸ **book price** [*of car*] precio *m* de catálogo ▸ **book review** crítica *f* *or* reseña *f* de un libro ▸ **book signing** (*by author*) firma *f* de libros ▸ **book token** vale *m* para libros, cheque *m* regalo para libros ▸ **book value** valor *m* contable *or* en libros
▸ **book in** (*Brit*) (VI + ADV) (= *record arrival*) registrarse; (= *reserve a room*) reservar habitación • **they ~ed in under false names** reservaron habitación bajo un nombre falso
(VT + ADV) • **they're ~ed in at the White Swan** tienen reservada una habitación en el White Swan • **I've ~ed you in with Dr Stuart for four o'clock** te he conseguido hora con el Dr. Stuart para las cuatro • **make sure you're ~ed in for antenatal care** asegúrate de que estás apuntada para la asistencia previa al parto
▸ **book up** (VT + ADV) (*esp Brit*) **1** [+ *holiday*] hacer reserva de
2 • **to be ~ed up a** [*hotel, restaurant, flight*] • **we are ~ed up all summer** no tenemos nada libre en todo el verano, lo tenemos todo reservado para todo el verano • **the hotel is ~ed up** el hotel está completo, todas las habitaciones del hotel están reservadas • **all the flights were ~ed up** todos los vuelos estaban completos, no quedaban plazas en ningún vuelo
b [*performer*] • **the orchestra is ~ed up until 2010** la orquestra tiene un programa de actuaciones completo hasta 2010
c [*person*] • **I'm ~ed up for tonight** tengo muchos compromisos para esta noche • **I'm ~ed up all next week** la semana que viene tengo un programa muy apretado
bookable ['bʊkəbl] (ADJ) (*Brit*) **1** (= *reservable*) [*seat*] que se puede reservar • **"seats bookable in advance"** "las entradas pueden reservarse con antelación"
2 (*Sport*) [*offence*] sujeto a tarjeta amarilla
bookbinder ['bʊkˌbaɪndəʳ] (N) encuadernador(a) *m/f*
bookbinding ['bʊkˌbaɪndɪŋ] (N) encuadernación *f*
bookcase ['bʊkkeɪs] (N) librería *f*,

estantería *f*, librero *m* (*Mex*)

bookend ['bʊkend] (N) sujetalibros *m inv*

> **BOOKER PRIZE**
> **Booker Prize**, o mejor dicho **Man Booker Prize**, es el nombre de un premio literario que se concede anualmente a una obra de ficción escrita originalmente en inglés y publicada en el Reino Unido. El premio, que viene otorgándose desde 1969 y es uno de los más conocidos en el Reino Unido, estaba financiado por la empresa **Booker McConnell** hasta 2002, cuando la administración del premio pasó a la **Booker Prize Foundation**, y el **Man Group** se convirtió en su patrocinador. La entrega de premios, en la que se anuncia el ganador, provoca un considerable interés en los medios de comunicación.

bookie* ['bʊkɪ] (N) = **bookmaker**

booking ['bʊkɪŋ] (N) **1** [*of hotel, holiday, restaurant*] reserva *f*; [*of performers*] contratación *f* • **to make a ~** hacer una reserva • **telephone ~** reserva *f* por teléfono; ▹ **block**
2 (= *engagement*) • **the band has a ~ next week** han contratado al grupo para la semana que viene
3 (*Sport*) [*of player*] • **he had nine ~s last year** el año pasado recibió tarjeta amarilla nueve veces
(CPD) ▸ **booking clerk** taquillero/a *m/f* ▸ **booking conditions** condiciones *fpl* de reserva ▸ **booking fee** suplemento *m* por hacer la reserva ▸ **booking form** formulario *m* de reserva ▸ **booking office** (*Rail*) despacho *m* de billetes *or* (*LAm*) boletos; (*Theat*) taquilla *f*

bookish ['bʊkɪʃ] (ADJ) [*learning*] basado en libros, libresco (*frm*); [*person*] estudioso • **her dowdy, ~ image** su imagen aburrida, de ratón de biblioteca*

bookkeeper ['bʊk,ki:pər] (N) contable *mf*, tenedor(a) *m/f* de libros, contador(a) *m/f* (*LAm*)

bookkeeping ['bʊk,ki:pɪŋ] (N) contabilidad *f*, teneduría *f* de libros

booklet ['bʊklɪt] (N) folleto *m*

book-lover ['bʊk,lʌvər] (N) bibliófilo/a *m/f*, amante *mf* de los libros

bookmaker ['bʊkmeɪkər] (N) corredor *m* de apuestas; ▹ GREYHOUND RACING

bookmaking ['bʊkmeɪkɪŋ] (N) apuestas *fpl*, correduría *f* de apuestas • **a ~ firm** una casa de apuestas

bookmark ['bʊkmɑ:k] (N) **1** (*for book*) marcador *m*, señalador *m*
2 (*Internet*) marcador *m*, favorito *m*
(VT) (*Internet*) marcar como sitio favorito, agregar a favoritos

bookmobile ['bʊkməʊ,bi:l] (N) (*US*) biblioteca *f* ambulante, bibliobús *m* (*Sp*)

bookplate ['bʊkpleɪt] (N) ex libris *m*

bookrest ['bʊkrest] (N) atril *m*

bookseller ['bʊk,selər] (N) librero/a *m/f* • **a ~'s** una librería

bookselling ['bʊk,selɪŋ] (N) venta *f* de libros

bookshelf ['bʊkʃelf] (N) (PL: **bookshelves**) estante *m* (para libros) • **bookshelves** estantería *fsing*

bookshop ['bʊkʃɒp] (N) (*esp Brit*) librería *f*

bookstall ['bʊkstɔ:l] (N) (*at station*) quiosco *m* (de libros); (*at fair*) puesto *m* de libros

bookstand ['bʊkstænd] (N) (*US*) **1** (= *bookrest*) atril *m*
2 (= *bookcase*) librería *f*, estantería *f*
3 (= *bookstall*) (*at station, airport*) quiosco *m* de prensa • **to hit the ~s** salir publicado

bookstore ['bʊkstɔ:r] (N) (*esp US*) librería *f*

bookworm ['bʊkwɜ:m] (N) (*fig*) ratón *m* de biblioteca*

Boolean ['bu:lɪən] (ADJ) booleano
(CPD) ▸ **Boolean algebra** álgebra *f* de Boole ▸ **Boolean logic** lógica *f* booleana

boom[1] [bu:m] (N) **1** (*Naut*) botalón *m*, botavara *f*
2 (*across harbour*) barrera *f*
3 [*of crane*] aguilón *m*; [*of microphone*] jirafa *f*

boom[2] [bu:m] (N) [*of guns*] estruendo *m*, estampido *m*; [*of thunder*] retumbo *m*, trueno *m*
(VI) [*voice, radio*] (*also* **boom out**) resonar, retumbar; [*sea*] bramar; [*gun*] tronar, retumbar
(VT) (*also* **boom out**) tronar
(CPD) ▸ **boom box*** (*US*) radiocasete *m* portátil (*muy grande*)

boom[3] [bu:m] (N) (*in an industry*) auge *m*, boom *m*; (= *period of growth*) expansión *f* • **in ~ conditions** en condiciones de prosperidad repentina
(VI) [*prices*] estar en alza; [*commodity*] tener mucha demanda; [*industry, town*] gozar de un boom, estar en auge • **business is ~ing** el negocio está en auge
(CPD) ▸ **boom economy** economía *f* de alza ▸ **boom market** mercado *m* de alza ▸ **boom town** ciudad *f* beneficiaria del auge

boom-bust ['bu:m'bʌst], **boom-and-bust** ['bu:mənd'bʌst] (ADJ) (*Econ*) [*economy, market*] con grandes altibajos

boomerang ['bu:məræŋ] (N) bumerang *m*
(ADJ) contraproducente, contrario a lo que se esperaba
(VI) (*fig*) (= *backfire*) resultar contraproducente, tener el efecto contraproducente al buscado (**on para**) • **it ~ed on him** le salió el tiro por la culata*

booming[1] ['bu:mɪŋ] (ADJ) [*voice*] resonante, retumbante

booming[2] ['bu:mɪŋ] (ADJ) (*Comm etc*) próspero, que goza de un boom, floreciente

boon [bu:n] (N) (= *blessing*) gran ayuda *f* • **it would be a ~ if he went** nos ayudaría muchísimo que él fuera • **it would be a ~ to humanity** sería un gran beneficio para la humanidad
(CPD) ▸ **boon companion** compañero/a *m/f* inseparable

boondocks* ['bu:ndɒks] (NPL) (*US*) • **out in the ~** en el quinto pino

boondoggle* ['bu:ndɒgl] (VI) (*US*) enredar*

boons* [bu:nz] (NPL) (*US*) = **boondocks**

boor [bʊər] (N) palurdo/a *m/f*

boorish ['bʊərɪʃ] (ADJ) [*manners*] grosero

boorishly ['bʊərɪʃlɪ] (ADV) [*behave, speak*] groseramente

boorishness ['bʊərɪʃnɪs] (N) grosería *f*

boost [bu:st] (N) **1** (= *encouragement*) estímulo *m*, aliento *m* • **to give a ~ to** estimular, alentar
2 (= *upward thrust*) (*to person*) empuje *m*, empujón *m*; (*to rocket*) impulso *m*, propulsión *f*
(VT) **1** (= *increase*) [+ *sales, production*] fomentar, incrementar; [+ *confidence, hopes*] estimular • **to ~ sb's morale** levantar la moral a algn
2 (= *promote*) [+ *product*] promover, hacer publicidad de; [+ *person*] dar bombo a
3 (*Elec*) [+ *voltage*] elevar; [+ *radio signal*] potenciar
4 (*Space*) propulsar, lanzar

booster ['bu:stər] (N) **1** (= *encouragement*) estímulo *m*
2 (*TV, Rad*) repetidor *m*
3 (*Elec*) elevador *m* de tensión
4 (*Space*) (*also* **booster rocket**) cohete *m* secundario
5 (*Aer*) impulsor *m*, impulsador *m*
6 (*Mech*) aumentador *m* de presión
7 (*Med*) dosis *f inv* de refuerzo *or* recuerdo
(CPD) ▸ **booster injection** dosis *f inv* de refuerzo *or* recuerdo, revacunación *f* ▸ **booster rocket** cohete *m* secundario ▸ **booster seat** (*for child*) (asiento *m*) elevador *m* ▸ **booster shot** = **booster injection** ▸ **booster station** (*TV, Rad*) repetidor *m*

boot[1] [bu:t] (N) **1** bota *f*; (= *ankle boot*) borceguí *m* • IDIOMS: • **to die with one's ~s on** morir con las botas puestas • **now the ~ is on the other foot** (*Brit*) ahora se ha dado vuelta a la tortilla • **to give sb the ~*** despedir a algn, poner a algn en la calle* • **to get** *or* **be given the ~*** ser despedido • **he was quaking** *or* **shaking** *or* **trembling in his ~s** le temblaban las piernas • **to lick sb's ~s** hacer la pelotilla a algn* • **to put the ~ in** (*Brit**) emplear la violencia; (*fig*) obrar decisivamente; ▹ **big**
2 (*Brit*) (*Aut*) maletero *m*, baúl *m* (*S. Cone*), maletera *f* (*And, Chile*), cajuela *f* (*Mex*)
3 (*US*) (*Aut*) (*also* **Denver boot**) cepo *m*
(VT) **1*** (= *kick*) dar un puntapié a • **to ~ sb out*** poner a algn de patitas en la calle*
2 (*Comput*) (*also* **boot up**) cebar, inicializar
(VI) (*Comput*) (*also* **boot up**) cebar, inicializar
(CPD) ▸ **boot boy*** (*Brit*) camorrista *m* ▸ **boot camp** (*in army*) campamento *m* militar; (= *prison*) *prisión civil con régimen militar* ▸ **boot polish** betún *m* ▸ **boot sale** (*Brit*) (*also* **car boot sale**) mercadillo *m* (*en el que se exponen las mercancías en el maletero del coche*)

boot[2] [bu:t] • **to ~** (*adv*) (*liter*) además, por añadidura

bootblack ['bu:tblæk] (N) limpiabotas *mf inv*, bolero/a *m/f* (*Mex*), embolador(a) *m/f* (*Col*)

bootee [bu:'ti:] (N) (*baby's*) bota *f* de lana; (*woman's*) borceguí *m*

booth [bu:ð] (N) (*at fair*) puesto *m*; (*in restaurant*) reservado *m*; (*phone, interpreter's, voting*) cabina *f*

booting-up [,bu:tɪŋ'ʌp] (N) (*Comput*) operación *f* de cargo, iniciación *f*
(CPD) ▸ **booting-up switch** tecla *f* de iniciación

bootlace ['bu:tleɪs] (N) cordón *m*

bootleg ['bu:tleg] (ADJ) (= *illicit*) [*alcohol*] de contrabando; [*tape, edition*] pirata
(N) (*Mus*) grabación *f* pirata
(VI) contrabandear con licores
(VT) [+ *tape, recording*] grabar y vender ilegalmente

bootlegger ['bu:t,legər] (N) [*of alcohol*] contrabandista *mf*; [*of tapes, recordings*] productor(a) *m/f* de copias pirata

bootless ['bu:tlɪs] (ADJ) (*liter*) infructuoso

bootlicker* ['bu:tlɪkər] (N) lameculos‡ *m*

bootlicking* ['bu:tlɪkɪŋ] (ADJ) pelotillero*
(N) pelotilleo* *m*

bootmaker ['bu:tmeɪkər] (N) zapatero/a *m/f* que hace botas

boots [bu:ts] (NSING) (*Brit*) limpiabotas *mf inv* (de un hotel)

bootstrap ['bu:tstræp] (N) oreja *f* • IDIOM: • **to pull oneself up by one's ~s** reponerse gracias a sus propios esfuerzos

booty ['bu:tɪ] (N) botín *m*

booze* [bu:z] (N) bebida *f* • **to go on the ~** darse a la bebida • **to be off the ~** haber dejado la bebida
(VI) (= *get drunk*) empinar el codo*; (= *go out drinking*) salir a beber
(VT) beber

boozer‡ ['bu:zər] (N) **1** (= *person*) bebedor(a) *m/f*, tomador(a) *m/f* (*LAm*)
2 (*Brit*) (= *pub*) bar *m*

booze-up‡ ['bu:z,ʌp] (N) (*Brit*) *reunión social donde se bebe mucho alcohol*

b

boozy‡ ['bu:zɪ] ADJ [person] aficionado a la bebida, borracho; [party] donde se bebe bastante; [song etc] tabernario

bop¹* [bɒp] (Mus) N bop m
VI menear el esqueleto*

bop²* [bɒp] VT (esp US) (= hit) cascar*

bo-peep [bəʊ'pi:p] N • **to play bo-peep** jugar tapándose la cara y descubriéndola de repente • **Little Bo-peep** *personaje de una poesía infantil, famoso por haber perdido sus ovejas*

boraces ['bɔ:rə,si:z] NPL *of* **borax**

boracic [bə'ræsɪk] ADJ bórico

borage ['bɒrɪdʒ] N borraja f

borax ['bɔ:ræks] N (PL: **boraxes** *or* **boraces**) bórax m

Bordeaux [bɔ:'dəʊ] N **1** (Geog) Burdeos m
2 (= wine) burdeos m

bordello [bɔ:'deləʊ] N casa f de putas

border ['bɔ:də^r] N **1** (= edge) (as decoration) borde m, margen m; (as boundary) límite m
2 (= frontier) frontera f • **the Borders** (Brit) *la frontera entre Inglaterra y Escocia*
3 (Sew) orilla f, cenefa f
4 (in garden) arriate m, parterre m
VT **1** (= adjoin) bordear, lindar con • **it is ~ed on the north by ...** linda al norte con ...
2 (Sew) ribetear, orlar
CPD [area, ballad] fronterizo; [guard] de la frontera ▸ **border dispute** disputa f fronteriza ▸ **border incident** incidente m fronterizo ▸ **border patrol** (US) patrulla f de fronteras ▸ **border post** puesto m fronterizo ▸ **border town** pueblo m fronterizo
▸ **border on, border upon** VI + PREP **1** [+ area, country] lindar con, limitar con
2 (fig) (= come near to being) rayar en • **with a self-confidence ~ing on arrogance** con una confianza en sí mismo que raya en la arrogancia

bordering ['bɔ:dərɪŋ] ADJ contiguo

borderland ['bɔ:dəlænd] N zona f fronteriza

borderline ['bɔ:dəlaɪn] N (between districts) límite m, línea f divisoria • **on the ~** (between classes) a medio camino; (in exam etc) en el límite
CPD ▸ **borderline case** (= situation, thing, person) caso m dudoso

bore¹ [bɔ:^r] N **1** (= tool) taladro m, barrena f; (Geol) sonda f
2 (also **bore hole**) perforación f
3 (= diameter) agujero m, barreno m; [of gun] calibre m; [of cylinder] alesaje m • **a 12-bore shotgun** una escopeta del calibre 12
VT [+ hole, tunnel] hacer, perforar • **to ~ a hole in** hacer *or* perforar un agujero en • **to ~ one's way through** abrirse camino por • **wood ~d by insects** madera f carcomida
VI • **to ~ for oil** hacer perforaciones en busca de petróleo

bore² [bɔ:^r] N **1** (= person) pesado/a m/f, pelmazo/a* m/f • **what a ~ he is!** ¡qué hombre más pesado!, ¡es más pesado que el plomo!*
2 (= event, task) lata* f • **it's such a ~** es una lata*, es un rollo (Sp*) • **what a ~!** ¡qué lata!*, ¡qué rollo! (Sp*)
VT aburrir • **to be ~d** • **get ~d** aburrirse • **he's ~d to death** *or* **tears** • **he's ~d stiff*** está aburrido como una ostra*, está muerto de aburrimiento • **to be ~d with** estar aburrido *or* harto de

bore³ [bɔ:^r] PT *of* **bear²**

bore⁴ [bɔ:^r] N (= tidal wave) marea f

boredom ['bɔ:dəm] N aburrimiento m

borehole ['bɔ:həʊl] N perforación f

borer ['bɔ:rə^r] N **1** (Tech) taladro m, perforadora f
2 (= insect) carcoma f

Borgia ['bɔ:dʒjə] N Borja m

boric acid [,bɔ:rɪk'æsɪd] N ácido m bórico

boring ['bɔ:rɪŋ] ADJ (= tedious) aburrido, pesado • **she's so ~** es muy aburrida *or* pesada

boringly ['bɔ:rɪŋlɪ] ADV de forma aburrida

born [bɔ:n] VB (pp *of* **bear²**) nacido • **to be ~** (lit) nacer; (fig) [idea] surgir, nacer • **I was ~ in 1955** nací en 1955 • **a daughter was ~ to them** les nació una hija • **to be ~ again** renacer, volver a nacer • **evil is ~ of idleness** la pereza es madre de todos los vicios • **he wasn't ~ yesterday!*** ¡no se chupa el dedo!*
ADJ [actor, leader] nato • **he is a ~ liar** es mentiroso por naturaleza • **a Londoner ~ and bred** londinense de casta y cuna • **in all my ~ days** en mi vida

-born [bɔ:n] ADJ (ending in compounds) • **British-born** británico de nacimiento

born-again ['bɔ:nə,gen] ADJ renacido, vuelto a nacer

borne [bɔ:n] PP *of* **bear²**

-borne [-bɔ:n] ADJ (ending in compounds) llevado por, traído por

Borneo ['bɔ:nɪəʊ] N Borneo m

boron ['bɔ:rɒn] N boro m

borough ['bʌrə] N municipio m; (in London, New York) distrito m

borrow ['bɒrəʊ] VT pedir prestado (**from,** **of** a), tomar prestado; [+ idea etc] adoptar, apropiarse; [+ word] tomar (**from** de) • **may I ~ your car?** ¿me prestas el coche? • **you can ~ it till I need it** te lo presto hasta que lo necesite

borrower ['bɒrəʊə^r] N **1** [of money] prestatario/a m/f • PROVERB: • **neither a ~ nor a lender be** ni prestes ni pidas prestado
2 (in library) usuario/a m/f

borrowing ['bɒrəʊɪŋ] N préstamo(s) m(pl) (**from** de)
CPD ▸ **borrowing power(s)** capacidad f de endeudamiento

borstal ['bɔ:stl] N (Brit) correccional m de menores
CPD ▸ **borstal boy** joven m delincuente (que ha pasado por el correccional)

borzoi ['bɔ:zɔɪ] N galgo m ruso

Bosch [bɒʃ] N El Bosco

bosh* [bɒʃ] N tonterías fpl

bo's'n ['bəʊsən] N = **boatswain**

Bosnia ['bɒznɪə] N Bosnia f

Bosnia Herzegovina ['bɒznɪə,hɜ:tsəgə'vi:nə] N Bosnia Herzegovina f

Bosnian ['bɒznɪən] ADJ bosnio
N bosnio/a m/f

bosom ['bʊzəm] N [of woman] seno m, pecho m; [of garment] pechera f • **in the ~ of the family** en el seno de la familia • IDIOM: • **to take sb to one's ~** acoger amorosamente a algn
CPD ▸ **bosom friend** amigo/a m/f íntimo/a *or* entrañable

bosomy ['bʊzəmɪ] ADJ tetuda‡, de pecho abultado

Bosphorus ['bɒsfərəs] N Bósforo m

boss¹ [bɒs] N (gen) jefe/a m/f; (= owner, employer) patrón/ona m/f; (= manager) gerente mf; (= foreman) capataz m; [of gang] cerebro m; (US) (Pol) cacique m • **I like to be my own ~** quiero mandar en mis asuntos, quiero controlar mis propias cosas • **I'm the ~ here** aquí mando yo • **OK, you're the ~** vale, tú mandas
VT mangonear*, dar órdenes a
ADJ (US*) chulo*
▸ **boss about, boss around** VT + ADV mangonear*, dar órdenes a

boss² [bɒs] N (= bulge) protuberancia f; (= stud) clavo m, tachón m; [of shield] ombligo m; (Archit) llave f de bóveda

BOSS N ABBR (in South Africa) = **Bureau of State Security**

boss-eyed [,bɒs'aɪd] ADJ bizco

bossiness ['bɒsɪnɪs] N carácter m mandón, tiranía f

bossy ['bɒsɪ] ADJ (COMPAR: **bossier**, SUPERL: **bossiest**) [person] mandón

Bostonian [bɒs'təʊnɪən] N bostoniano/a m/f

bosun ['bəʊsən] N = **boatswain**

bot [bɒt] N robot m

botanic [bə'tænɪk] ADJ, **botanical** [bə'tænɪkəl] ADJ [gardens] botánico

botanist ['bɒtənɪst] N botánico/a m/f, botanista mf

botanize ['bɒtənaɪz] VI herborizar

botany ['bɒtənɪ] N botánica f

botch* [bɒtʃ] N (= crude repair) chapuza* f • **to make a ~ of** ▹ VT
VT (also **botch up**) hacer una chapuza de* • **to ~ it** estropearlo

botched [bɒtʃt] ADJ [attempt, robbery, rescue] chapucero • **a ~ job** una chapuza*

botch-up* ['bɒtʃʌp] N chapuza f

both [bəʊθ] ADJ ambos/as, los/las dos • **~ (the) boys** los dos *or* ambos chicos
PRON ambos/as mpl/fpl, los/las dos mpl/fpl • **~ of them** los dos • **~ of us** nosotros dos, los dos • **we ~ went** fuimos los dos • **they were ~ there** • **~ of them were there** estaban allí los dos
ADV a la vez • **she was ~ laughing and crying** reía y lloraba a la vez • **I find it ~ impressive and vulgar** encuentro que es impresionante y vulgar a la vez • **he ~ plays and sings** canta y además toca • **~ you and I saw it** lo vimos tanto tú como yo, lo vimos los dos

bother ['bɒðə^r] N **1** (= nuisance) molestia f, lata* f • **what a ~!** ¡qué lata!* • **it's such a ~ to clean** es una lata limpiarlo*, es muy incómodo limpiarlo
2 (= problems) problemas mpl • **I found the street without any ~** encontré la calle sin problemas • **do you have much ~ with your car?** ¿tienes muchos problemas con el coche? • **he had a spot of ~ with the police** tuvo un pequeño problema con la policía
3 (= trouble) molestia f • **it isn't any ~** • **it's no ~** no es ninguna molestia • **I went to the ~ of finding one** me tomé la molestia de buscar uno
4 (Brit*) (= violence) • **to go out looking for ~** salir a buscar camorra*
VT **1** (= worry) preocupar; (= annoy) molestar, fastidiar • **does the noise ~ you?** ¿le molesta el ruido? • **does it ~ you if I smoke?** ¿le molesta que fume? • **his leg ~s him** le duele la pierna • **to ~ o.s. about/with sth** molestarse *or* preocuparse por algo
2 (= inconvenience) molestar; (= pester) dar la lata a* • **I'm sorry to ~ you** perdona la molestia • **don't ~ me!** ¡no me molestes!, ¡no fastidies!, ¡no me friegues! (LAm*) • **please don't ~ me about it now** le ruego que no me moleste con eso ahora
VI (= take trouble) tomarse la molestia (**to do** de hacer) • **to ~ about/with** molestarse *or* preocuparse por • **don't ~** no te molestes, no te preocupes • **he didn't even ~ to write** ni siquiera se molestó en escribir
EXCL ¡porras!*

botheration†* [,bɒðə'reɪʃən] EXCL ¡porras!*

bothered ['bɒðəd] ADJ **1** • **I can't be ~** me da pereza, no tengo ganas, me da flojera (LAm) • **I can't be ~ to go** me da pereza ir, no tengo ganas de ir, me da flojera ir (LAm)
2 • **"shall we stay in or go out?" — "I'm not ~"** —¿salimos o nos quedamos? —me da igual
3 (= disconcerted) • **to get ~** desconcertarse, ponerse nervioso; ▹ **hot**

BOTH

Pronoun and adjective

▷ *When* **both** *is a pronoun or an adjective you can usually translate it using* **los/las dos:**

We're both climbers, Both of us are climbers
Los dos somos alpinistas
I know both of them
I know them both
Los conozco a los dos
Both (of the) sisters were blind
Las dos hermanas eran ciegas

▷ *Alternatively, in more formal speech, use* **ambos/ambas:**

We both liked it
Nos gustó a ambos
Both (of the) regions are autonomous
Ambas regiones son autónomas

NOTE: Don't use the article with **ambos.**

"both ... and"

▷ **Both ... and** *can be translated in a variety of ways, depending on what is referred to. If it relates to two individuals, you can usually use the invariable* **tanto ... como.** *Alternatively, you can often use* **los/las dos**, *though this may involve changing the syntax:*

Both Mary and Peter will be very happy here
Tanto Mary como Peter van a ser muy felices aquí, Mary y Peter van a ser los dos muy felices aquí

Both Mike and Clare could see something was wrong
Tanto Mike como Clare veían que algo iba mal

▷ *When talking about two groups or things use* **tanto ... como** *or, if* **both ... and** *is equivalent to "at one and the same time", use* **a la vez:**

The course is directed at both piano and violin teachers
El curso está dirigido a profesores tanto de piano como de violín, El curso está dirigido a la vez a profesores de piano y de violín

▷ **Tanto ... como** *can also be used with adverbs:*

He was a weak man both physically and mentally
Era un hombre débil, tanto física como mentalmente

When adverbs ending in **-mente** *are linked together with a conjunction as here, only the last retains the* **-mente.**

▷ *When* **both ... and** *relates to verbs, you can usually use* **y además:**

He both paints and sculpts
Pinta y además hace esculturas

▷ *Use* **a la vez** *to comment on descriptions which are both true at the same time:*

The book is both interesting and depressing
El libro es interesante y deprimente a la vez

For further uses and examples, see main entry.

bothersome ['bɒðəsəm] (ADJ) molesto

Bothnia ['bɒθnɪə] (N) • **Gulf of ~** golfo *m* de Botnia

Botox® ['bəʊtɒks] (N) Botox *m* • **~ injections** inyecciones *fpl* de Botox

Botswana [bɒ'tswa:nə] (N) Botsuana *f*

bottle ['bɒtl] (N) **1** (*gen*) botella *f*; (*empty*) envase *m*; [*of ink, scent*] frasco *m*; (*baby's*) biberón *m* • IDIOM: • **to hit** *or* **take to the ~*** darse a la bebida
2 (*Brit**) (= *courage*) • **it takes a lot of ~ to ...** hay que tener muchas agallas para ...* • **to lose one's ~** rajarse*
(VT) **1** [+ *wine*] embotellar; [+ *fruit*] envasar, enfrascar
2 (*Brit*‡) • **he ~d it** se rajó*
(CPD) ▸ **bottle bank** contenedor *m* de vidrio ▸ **bottle brush** escobilla *f*, limpiabotellas *m inv*; (*Bot*) callistemon *m* ▸ **bottle opener** abrebotellas *m inv*, destapador *m* (*LAm*) ▸ **bottle party** *fiesta a la que cada invitado contribuye con una botella* ▸ **bottle top** (*gen*) tapón *f*; (= *crown cork*) chapa *f*
▸ **bottle out**‡ (VI + ADV) (*Brit*) rajarse* • **they ~d out of doing it** se rajaron y no lo hicieron*
▸ **bottle up** (VT + ADV) [+ *emotion*] reprimir, contener

bottled ['bɒtld] (ADJ) • **~ beer** cerveza *f* de botella • **~ gas** gas *m* de bombona • **~ water** agua *f* embotellada

bottle-fed ['bɒtlfed] (ADJ) alimentado con biberón

bottle-feed ['bɒtl,fi:d] (VT) (PT, PP: **bottle-fed**) criar con biberón

bottle-green ['bɒtl'gri:n] (ADJ) verde botella (*adj inv*)
(N) verde *m* botella

bottleneck ['bɒtlnek] (N) (*on road*) embotellamiento *m*, atasco *m*; (*fig*) obstáculo *m*

bottler ['bɒtlə^r] (N) (= *person*) embotellador(a) *m/f*; (= *company*) embotelladora *f*

bottling ['bɒtlɪŋ] (N) embotellado *m*

bottom ['bɒtəm] (N) **1** [*of box, cup, sea, river, garden*] fondo *m*; [*of stairs, page, mountain, tree*] pie *m*; [*of list, class*] último/a *m/f*; [*of foot*] planta *f*; [*of shoe*] suela *f*; [*of chair*] asiento *m*; [*of ship*] quilla *f*, casco *m* • **at the ~ (of)** [+ *page, hill, ladder*] al pie (de); [+ *road*] al fondo (de) • **the ~ has fallen out of the market** el mercado se ha venido abajo • **the ~ fell** *or* **dropped out of his world** se le vino el mundo abajo • **to knock the ~ out of** desfondar • **on the ~ (of)** (= *underside*) [+ *box, case etc*] en la parte inferior (de), en el fondo (de); [+ *shoe*] en la suela (de); [+ *sea, lake etc*] en el fondo (de) • **to go to the ~** (*Naut*) irse a pique • **to send a ship to the ~** hundir un buque • **to touch ~** (*lit*) tocar fondo; (*fig*) tocar fondo, llegar al punto más bajo • **~s up!*** ¡salud!; ▷ **false**
2 (= *buttocks*) trasero *m*
3 (*fig*) (= *deepest part*) • **at ~** en el fondo • **he's at the ~ of it** él está detrás de esto • IDIOMS: • **to get to the ~ of sth** llegar al fondo de algo • **from the ~ of my heart** de todo corazón
4 (*also* **bottoms**) [*of tracksuit, pyjamas*] pantalón *m*, parte *f* de abajo; [*of bikini*] braga *f*, parte *f* de abajo
(ADJ) (= *lowest*) más bajo; (= *last*) último; ▷ **dollar**
(CPD) ▸ **bottom drawer** ajuar *m* ▸ **bottom floor** planta *f* baja ▸ **bottom gear** (*Aut*) primera *f* (marcha) ▸ **bottom half** parte *f* de abajo, mitad *f* inferior ▸ **bottom line** (= *minimum*) mínimo *m* aceptable; (= *essential point*) lo fundamental • **the ~ line is he has to go** a fin de cuentas tenemos que despedirlo ▸ **bottom price** precio *m* más bajo ▸ **bottom step** primer peldaño *m* ▸ **bottom team** colista *m* ▸ **bottom feeder*** (= *person*) aprovechador(a) *m/f*
▸ **bottom out** (VI + ADV) [*figures etc*] tocar fondo

-bottomed [-'bɒtəmd] (SUFFIX) • **a loose-bottomed cake tin** un molde con el fondo suelto • **a glass-bottomed boat** un barco con el fondo de cristal

bottomless ['bɒtəmlɪs] (ADJ) [*pit*] sin fondo, insondable; [*supply*] interminable

bottommost ['bɒtəmməʊst] (ADJ) más bajo, último

botulism ['bɒtjʊlɪzəm] (N) botulismo *m*

bouclé ['bu:kleɪ] (N) lana *f or* ropa *f* rizada
(ADJ) de lana rizada

boudoir ['bu:dwa:^r] (N) tocador *m*

bouffant ['bu:fɒŋ] (ADJ) [*hairdo*] crepado

bougainvillea [,bu:gən'vɪlɪə] (N) buganvilla *f*

bough [baʊ] (N) rama *f*

bought [bɔ:t] (PT), (PP) *of* **buy**

bouillon ['bu:jɔ:ŋ] (N) caldo *m*
(CPD) ▸ **bouillon cube** cubito *m* de caldo

boulder ['bəʊldə^r] (N) canto *m* rodado

boules ['bu:l] (NSING) petanca *f*

boulevard ['bu:ləva:^r] (N) bulevar *m*, zócalo *m* (*Mex*)

bounce [baʊns] (N) **1** [*of ball*] (re)bote *m* • **to catch a ball on the ~** agarrar una pelota de rebote
2 (= *springiness*) [*of hair, mattress*] elasticidad *f*
3 (*fig*) (= *energy*) energía *f*, dinamismo *m* • **he's got plenty of ~** tiene mucha energía
(VT) **1** [+ *ball*] hacer (re)botar • **to ~ a baby on one's knee** hacer el caballito a un niño pequeño • **to ~ radio waves off the moon** hacer rebotar las ondas radiofónicas en la luna • **to ~ one's ideas off sb** exponer las ideas a algn para que dé su opinión
2* [+ *cheque*] rechazar
3* (= *eject*) plantar en la calle*, poner de patitas en la calle*
4 • **I will not be ~d into it** no lo voy a hacer bajo presión, no voy a dejar que me presionen para hacerlo
(VI) **1** [*ball*] (re)botar
2* [*cheque*] ser rechazado
3 (= *bound*) dar saltos • **he ~d up out of his chair** se levantó de la silla de un salto • **he ~d in** irrumpió alegremente
4 (= *be returned*) [*email message*] ser devuelto
▸ **bounce back** (VI + ADV) (*fig*) [*person*] recuperarse

bouncer* ['baʊnsə^r] (N) gorila* *m*

bouncing ['baʊnsɪŋ] (ADJ) • **~ baby** niño/a *m/f* sanote

bouncy ['baʊnsɪ] (ADJ) (COMPAR: **bouncier**, SUPERL: **bounciest**) **1** [*ball*] con mucho rebote; [*hair*] con mucho cuerpo; [*mattress*] elástico
2 (*fig*) [*person*] enérgico, dinámico
(CPD) ▸ **bouncy castle** castillo *m* inflable

bound¹ [baʊnd] (N) **bounds** (= *limits*) límite *msing* • **out of ~s** zona *f* prohibida • **it's out of ~s to civilians** los civiles tienen la entrada prohibida • **to put a place out of ~s** prohibir la entrada a un lugar • **his ambition knows no ~s** su ambición no tiene límites • **to set ~s to one's ambitions** poner límites a sus ambiciones • **to keep sth within ~s** tener algo a raya • **it is within the ~s of possibility** cabe dentro de los límites de lo posible
(VT) (*gen passive*) limitar, rodear • **a field ~ed by woods** un campo rodeado de bosque • **on one side it is ~ed by the park** por un lado limita *or* linda con el parque

bound² [baʊnd] (N) (= *jump*) salto *m* • **at a ~** • **in one ~** de un salto

b

(VI) [person, animal] saltar; [ball] (re)botar • **to ~ forward** avanzar a saltos • **he ~ed out of bed** se levantó de la cama de un salto • **his heart ~ed with joy** su corazón daba brincos de alegría
(VT) saltar por encima de

bound³ [baʊnd] (PT), (PP) *of* **bind**
(ADJ) **1** (= *tied*) [*prisoner*] atado • **~ hand and foot** atado de pies y manos • **the problems are ~ together** existe una estrecha relación entre los problemas • **they are ~ up in each other** están absortos el uno en el otro • **he's ~ up in his work** está muy absorbido por su trabajo • **to be ~ up with sth** estar estrechamente ligado a algo
2 (= *sure*) • **to be ~ to: we are ~ to win** seguro que ganamos, estamos seguros de ganar • **he's ~ to come** es seguro que vendrá, no puede dejar de venir • **it's ~ to happen** tiene forzosamente que ocurrir • **they'll regret it, I'll be ~** se arrepentirán de ello, estoy seguro
3 (= *obliged*) obligado • **he's ~ to do it** tiene que hacerlo • **you're not ~ to go** no estás obligado a ir • **I'm ~ to say that ...** me siento obligado a decir que ..., siento el deber de decir que ... • **I feel ~ to tell you that ...** me veo en la necesidad de decirte que ... • **I feel ~ to him by gratitude** la gratitud hace que me sienta en deuda con él • **to be ~ by contract to sb** tener obligaciones contractuales con algn; ▹ **honour**

bound⁴ [baʊnd] (ADJ) • **where are you ~ (for)?** ¿adónde se dirige usted? • **~ for** [*train, plane*] con destino a; [*ship, person*] con rumbo a • **he's ~ for London** se dirige a Londres; ▹ **homeward**

-bound [-baʊnd] (ADJ) (*ending in compounds*) • **to be London-bound** [*person*] ir rumbo a Londres • **a Paris-bound flight/plane** un vuelo/avión con destino a París • **the south-bound carriageway** la calzada dirección sur

boundary ['baʊndərɪ] (N) **1** (= *border*) límite *m* • **to make ~ changes** (*Brit*) (*Pol*) hacer cambios en las circunscripciones
2 (*Cricket*) banda *f*
(CPD) ▸ **boundary dispute** disputa *f* territorial ▸ **boundary fence** cerca *f* divisoria ▸ **boundary line** límite *m*, frontera *f* ▸ **boundary stone** mojón *m*

bounden† ['baʊndən] (ADJ) • **~ duty** obligación *f* ineludible

bounder†* ['baʊndəʳ] (N) (*Brit*) sinvergüenza *m*, granuja *m*

boundless ['baʊndlɪs] (ADJ) (*fig*) ilimitado, sin límite

bounteous ['baʊntɪəs], **bountiful** ['baʊntɪfʊl] (ADJ) [*crop etc*] abundante; [*person*] generoso, munífico

bounty ['baʊntɪ] (N) **1** (= *generosity*) generosidad *f*, munificencia *f*
2 (= *reward*) recompensa *f*; (*Mil*) premio *m* de enganche
(CPD) ▸ **bounty hunter** cazarrecompensas *mf inv*

bouquet [bʊ'keɪ] (N) **1** [*of flowers*] ramo *m*, ramillete *m*
2 [*of wine*] buqué *m*
(CPD) ▸ **bouquet garni** ramillete *m* de hierbas aromáticas

Bourbon ['bʊəbən] (*Hist*) (N) Borbón *m*
(ADJ) borbónico

bourbon ['bʊəbən] (N) Borbón *m*; (*US*) (*also* **bourbon whiskey**) whisky *m* americano, bourbon *m*
(ADJ) borbónico

bourgeois ['bʊəʒwɑː] (ADJ) burgués
(N) burgués/esa *m/f*

bourgeoisie [ˌbʊəʒwɑː'ziː] (N) burguesía *f*

bourse ['bʊəs] (N) (= *stock exchange*) bolsa *f*

bout [baʊt] (N) **1** [*of illness*] ataque *m*
2 (= *period*) [*of work*] tanda *f* • **drinking ~** juerga *f*, farra *f* (*LAm**)
3 (= *boxing match*) combate *m*, encuentro *m*; (*Fencing*) asalto *m*

boutique [buː'tiːk] (N) boutique *f*, tienda *f* de ropa
(CPD) ▸ **boutique hotel** hotel *m* boutique

bovine ['bəʊvaɪn] (ADJ) bovino; (*fig*) lerdo, estúpido

bovver‡ ['bɒvəʳ] (N) (*Brit*) camorra* *f*
(CPD) ▸ **bovver boots** *botas de suela gruesa usadas por los cabezas rapadas*

bow¹ [bəʊ] (N) **1** (= *weapon*) (*also Mus*) arco *m* • **bow and arrow** arco *m* y flechas
2 (= *knot*) lazo *m* • **to tie a bow** hacer un lazo
(CPD) ▸ **bow legs** piernas *fpl* arqueadas ▸ **bow tie** pajarita *f* ▸ **bow window** mirador *m*, ventana *f* saledіza

bow² [baʊ] (N) (= *greeting*) reverencia *f* • **to make a bow** inclinarse (**to** delante de), hacer una reverencia (**to** a) • **to make one's bow** presentarse, debutar • **to take a bow** salir a agradecer los aplausos, salir a saludar
(VT) **1** (= *lower*) [+ *head*] inclinar, bajar
2 (= *bend*) [+ *back*] encorvar, doblar; [+ *branches*] inclinar, doblar
3 • **to bow one's thanks** inclinarse en señal de agradecimiento
(VI) **1** (*in greeting*) inclinarse (**to** delante de), hacer una reverencia (**to** a) • IDIOM: • **to bow and scrape** mostrarse demasiado solícito
2 (= *bend*) [*branch etc*] arquearse, doblarse • **to bow beneath** (*fig*) estar agobiado por
3 (*fig*) (= *yield*) inclinarse *or* ceder (**to** ante) • **to bow to the inevitable** resignarse a lo inevitable
▸ **bow down** (VT + ADV) (*lit, fig*) doblegar
(VI + ADV) (*lit, fig*) doblegarse
▸ **bow out** (VI + ADV) (*fig*) retirarse, despedirse

bow³ [baʊ] (N) (*Naut*) (*also* **bows**) proa *f* • **on the port/starboard bow** a babor/estribor • IDIOM: • **a shot across the bows** un cañonazo de advertencia
(CPD) ▸ **bow doors** portón *m* de proa ▸ **bow wave** *ola causada por un barco al desplazarse por el agua*

Bow Bells [ˌbəʊ'belz] (NPL) *famoso campanario de Londres* • **born within the sound of ~** nacido en la zona alrededor de Bow Bells (*definición del puro Cockney londinense*)

bowdlerization [ˌbaʊdləraɪ'zeɪʃən] (N) expurgación *f*

bowdlerize ['baʊdləraɪz] (VT) [+ *book*] expurgar

bowed¹ ['bəʊd] (ADJ) (= *curved*) [*legs*] arqueado

bowed² ['baʊd] (ADJ) (= *bent forward*) encorvado

bowel ['baʊəl] (N) **1** intestino *m*
2 **bowels** (*Anat*) intestinos *mpl*, vientre *msing*; (*fig*) entrañas *fpl* • **the ~s of the earth/ship** las entrañas de la tierra/del barco • **the ~s of compassion** (*liter*) la compasión
(CPD) ▸ **bowel movement** evacuación *f* (del vientre) ▸ **bowel obstruction** obstrucción *f* intestinal

bower ['baʊəʳ] (N) emparrado *m*, enramada *f*

bowing ['bəʊɪŋ] (N) (*Mus*) técnica *f* del arco; (*marked on score*) inicio *m* del golpe de arco • **his ~ was sensitive** su uso del arco era sensible • **to mark the ~** indicar *or* marcar los movimientos del arco

bowl¹ [bəʊl] (N) **1** (= *large cup*) tazón *m*, cuenco *m*; (= *dish*) (*for soup*) plato *m* sopero; (*for washing up*) palangana *f*, barreño *m*; (*for salad*) fuente *f*, ensaladera *f* • IDIOM: • **life isn't a ~ of cherries for her right now** actualmente su vida no es un camino de rosas *or* no es de color de rosa
2 (= *amount*) plato *m*
3 (= *hollow*) [*of lavatory*] taza *f*; [*of spoon*] cuenco *m*; [*of pipe*] cazoleta *f*; [*of fountain*] tazón *m*
4 (*US*) (= *stadium*) estadio *m*
5 (*Geog*) cuenca *f*

bowl² [bəʊl] (N) **1** (= *ball*) bola *f*, bocha *f*
2 • **~s** (= *game*) (*Brit*) (*on green*) bochas *fpl*; (= *tenpin bowling*) bolos *mpl*, boliche *m*
(VT) (*Cricket*) [+ *ball*] lanzar, arrojar; (*also* **bowl out**) [+ *batsman*] eliminar
(VI) **1** (*Cricket*) lanzar
2 • **to go ~ing** (*Brit*) ir a jugar a las bochas; (*US*) ir a jugar al boliche
3 • **we were ~ing down Knightsbridge** (*on foot*) caminábamos por Knightsbridge a toda prisa; (*in vehicle*) íbamos por Knightsbridge a toda velocidad
▸ **bowl along** (VI + ADV) (*on foot*) caminar a toda prisa; (*in vehicle*) ir a toda velocidad
▸ **bowl over** (VT + ADV) **1** (= *knock down*) tumbar, derribar
2 (*fig*) desconcertar, dejar atónito • **we were quite ~ed over by the news** la noticia nos desconcertó *or* sorprendió bastante • **she ~ed him over** ella lo dejó patidifuso*

bow-legged ['bəʊ'legɪd] (ADJ) [*person*] estevado, que tiene las piernas en arco; [*stance*] con las piernas en arco

bowler¹ ['bəʊləʳ] (N) **1** (*Cricket, Rounders etc*) lanzador(a) *m/f*; ▹ CRICKET
2 (*US*) (*Sport*) jugador(a) *m/f* de bolos

bowler² ['bəʊləʳ] (N) (*Brit*) (*also* **bowler hat**) bombín *m*, sombrero hongo *m*

bowlful ['bəʊlfʊl] (N) tazón *m*, cuenco *m*

bowline ['bəʊlɪn] (N) bolina *f*

bowling ['bəʊlɪŋ] (N) **1** (*also* **tenpin bowling**) bolos *mpl*, boliche *m*
2 (*on green*) bochas *fpl*
3 (*Cricket*) lanzamiento *m*
(CPD) ▸ **bowling alley** bolera *f*, boliche *m* ▸ **bowling green** campo *m* de bochas ▸ **bowling match** (*Brit*) concurso *m* de bochas

bowman ['bəʊmən] (N) (PL: **bowmen**) (= *archer*) arquero *m*; (*with crossbow*) ballestero *m*

bowsprit ['bəʊsprɪt] (N) bauprés *m*

bowstring ['bəʊstrɪŋ] (N) cuerda *f* de arco

bow-wow ['baʊ'waʊ] (N) (*baby talk*) (= *dog*) guau-guau *m*
(EXCL) ¡guau!

box¹ [bɒks] (N) **1** (*gen*) caja *f*; (= *large*) cajón *m*; (= *chest etc*) arca *f*, cofre *m*; (*for money etc*) hucha *f*; (*for jewels etc*) estuche *m* • **cardboard box** caja *f* de cartón • **box of matches** caja *f* de cerillas • **wine box** *caja de cartón revestida de plástico por dentro y con una llave en el exterior por la que se vierte el vino* • IDIOMS: • **to be out of one's box** (*Brit‡*) (*from drugs*) estar volado‡, estar colocado (*Sp**); (*from alcohol*) estar como una cuba* • **to think out of** *or* **outside the box** pensar de forma diferente
2 (*in theatre, stadium*) palco *m*
3 • **the box** (*Brit**) (= *television*) la caja boba*, la tele* • **we saw it on the box*** lo vimos en la tele*
4 (*Brit*) (= *road junction*) parrilla *f*
5 (*on form, to be filled in*) casilla *f*
6 (*Sport*) (= *protection*) protector *m*
7 (*also* **post-office box**) apartado *m* de correos, casilla *f* de correo (*LAm*)
8 (*Typ*) (*surrounding table, diagram*) recuadro *m*
(VT) poner en una caja • **a boxed set of six cups and saucers** un juego de seis tazas y platillos envasado en una caja de cartón • **to box the compass** cuartear la aguja
(CPD) ▸ **box camera** cámara *f* de cajón ▸ **box file** archivador *m*, archivo *m* ▸ **box girder**

viga *f* en forma de cajón, vigas *fpl* gemelas ▸ **box junction** (*Brit*) (*Aut*) cruce *m* con parrilla ▸ **box kite** *cometa en forma de cubo, abierto por dos lados* ▸ **box lunch** (*US*) bolsa *f* de sándwiches *or* (*Sp*) bocadillos ▸ **box number** apartado *m* de correos, casilla *f* de correo (*LAm*) ▸ **box office** taquilla *f*, boletería *f* (*LAm*) • **to be good box office** ser taquillero; ▹ box-office ▸ **box pleat** (*Sew*) tablón *m* ▸ **box seat** (*US*) (*Theat*) asiento *m* de palco ▸ **box set** caja *f* ▸ **box spring** muelle *m*

▸ **box in** VT + ADV **1** (= *fix wooden surround to*) [+ *bath*] tapar *or* cerrar con madera
2 (= *shut in*) [+ *car*] encajonar • **to get boxed in** (*Sport*) encontrarse tapado
3 (*fig*) • **to box sb in** acorralar a algn • **to feel boxed in** sentirse acorralado

▸ **box off** VT + ADV compartimentar

▸ **box up** VT + ADV poner en una caja; (*fig*) constreñir

box[2] [bɒks] N (= *blow*) • **a box on the ear** un cachete *m*
VT (*Sport*) boxear contra • **to box sb's ears**† guantear a algn, dar un mamporro a algn*
VI boxear • IDIOM: • **to box clever** (*Brit**) andarse listo, montárselo bien*

box[3] [bɒks] N (*Bot*) boj *m*

boxcar ['bɒks,kɑːʳ] N (*US*) furgón *m*

boxer ['bɒksəʳ] N **1** (*Sport*) boxeador(a) *m/f*
2 (= *dog*) bóxer *mf*
CPD ▸ **boxer shorts** calzones *mpl*

boxing ['bɒksɪŋ] N boxeo *m*, box *m* (*LAm*)
CPD ▸ **Boxing Day** (*Brit*) día *m* de San Esteban (*26 de diciembre*) ▸ **boxing gloves** guantes *mpl* de boxeo ▸ **boxing match** combate *m* de boxeo ▸ **boxing promoter** promotor(a) *m/f* de boxeo ▸ **boxing ring** cuadrilátero *m*, ring *m*

> **BOXING DAY**
> El día después de Navidad es **Boxing Day**, fiesta en todo el Reino Unido, aunque si el 26 de diciembre cae en domingo el día de descanso se traslada al lunes. El nombre proviene de una costumbre del siglo XIX, cuando en dicho día se daba un aguinaldo o pequeño regalo (**Christmas box**) a los comerciantes, carteros etc. En la actualidad es una fecha en la que se celebran importantes encuentros deportivos.

box-office ['bɒksɒfɪs] ADJ taquillero
CPD ▸ **box-office receipts** ingresos *mpl* de taquilla ▸ **box-office success** éxito *m* de taquilla; ▹ box

boxroom ['bɒksrʊm] N (*Brit*) trastero *m*

boxwood ['bɒkswʊd] N boj *m*

boxy ['bɒksɪ] ADJ (*pej*) [*building*] amazacotado; [*car*] cuadrado

boy [bɔɪ] N **1** (= *small*) niño *m*; (= *young man*) muchacho *m*, chico *m*, joven *m* (*LAm*); (= *son*) hijo *m* • **oh boy!** ¡vaya! • **I have known him from a boy** lo conozco desde chico • IDIOMS: • **to send a boy to do a man's job** mandar a un muchacho a hacer un trabajo de hombre • **boys will be boys** ¡los hombres, ya se sabe, son como niños!; ▹ old
2* (= *fellow*) chico *m*, hijo *m* • **that's the boy!** • **that's my boy!** ¡bravo! • **but my dear boy!** ¡pero hijo!, ¡pero hombre! • **García and his boys in the national team** García y sus muchachos del equipo nacional • **he's out with the boys** ha salido con los amigos • **he's one of the boys now** ahora es un personaje • **the boys in blue** (*Brit**) la policía; ▹ job
3 (= *servant*) criado *m*
CPD ▸ **boy band** (*Brit*) (*Mus*) *grupo de música pop masculino* ▸ **boy racer*** (*Brit*) (*pej*) loco *m* del volante ▸ **boy scout** (muchacho *m or* niño *m*) explorador *m* ▸ **boy wonder*** niño *m* prodigio, joven promesa *m*

boycott ['bɔɪkɒt] N boicot *m*
VT [+ *firm, country*] boicotear

boyfriend ['bɔɪfrend] N amigo *m*; (= *fiancé etc*) novio *m*, pololo *m* (*Chile**)

boyhood ['bɔɪhʊd] N niñez *f*; (*as teenager*) adolescencia *f*

boyish ['bɔɪɪʃ] ADJ [*appearance, manner*] juvenil; (= *tomboyish*) (*of girl*) de muchacho, de chico; (*of small girl*) de niño

boyishly ['bɔɪɪʃlɪ] ADV como un joven

boy-meets-girl ['bɔɪmiːts'gɜːl] ADJ • **a boy-meets-girl story/film** una historia/película de amor entre un chico y una chica

boyo* ['bɔɪəʊ] N (*Brit*) (*often in direct address*) joven *m*, muchacho *m*

bozo‡ ['bəʊzəʊ] N (*esp US*) imbécil* *mf*

BP N ABBR **1** = **British Petroleum**
2 (= **blood pressure**) TA

Bp ABBR (= **Bishop**) ob., obpo.

B/P, b/p ABBR (*Comm*) = **bills payable**

bpi ABBR (*Comput*) = **bits per inch**

BPOE N ABBR (*US*) (= **Benevolent and Protective Order of Elks**) *organización benéfica*

bps ABBR (*Comput*) = **bits per second**

BR N ABBR (= **British Rail**) (*formerly*) *ferrocarriles británicos*, ≈ RENFE *f* (*Sp*)

Br ABBR **1** (= **Brother**) H., Hno.
2 = **British**

B/R ABBR = **bills receivable**

bra [brɑː] N sostén *m*, sujetador *m*, corpiño *m* (*Arg*)

brace [breɪs] N **1** (*Constr*) (= *strengthening piece*) abrazadera *f*, refuerzo *m*; (*Archit*) riostra *f*, tirante *m*; (*Naut*) braza *f*; (= *tool*) berbiquí *m* • **~ and bit** berbiquí *m* y barrena *f*
2 (*also* **braces**) (*for teeth*) corrector *msing*, aparato *msing*
3 braces (*Brit*) tirantes *mpl*, suspensores *mpl* (*LAm*)
4 (*Mus*) corchete *m*
5 (*Typ*) corchete *m*
6 (*pl inv*) (= *pair*) par *m*
VT (= *strengthen*) [+ *building*] asegurar, reforzar • **to ~ o.s.** prepararse (*para resistir una sacudida etc*); (*fig*) fortalecer su ánimo • **to ~ o.s. for** prepararse para • **to ~ o.s. against** agarrarse a

bracelet ['breɪslɪt] N pulsera *f*, brazalete *m*

bracing ['breɪsɪŋ] ADJ [*air, activity*] vigorizante

bracken ['brækən] N helecho *m*

bracket ['brækɪt] N **1** (*gen*) soporte *m*; (= *angle bracket*) escuadra *f*; (*Archit*) ménsula *f*, repisa *f*
2 (*Typ*) (*usu pl*) (*round*) paréntesis *m inv*; (*also* **square bracket**) corchete *m*; (*angled*) corchete *m* (agudo); (*curly*) corchete *m*, llave *f* • **in ~s** entre paréntesis; ▹ angle[1], square
3 (= *group*) clase *f*, categoría *f* • **he's in the £200,000 a year ~** pertenece a la categoría de los que ganan 200,000 libras al año • **income ~** nivel *m* de ingresos
VT **1** (*Constr*) (= *join by brackets*) asegurar con soportes/escuadras
2 (*Typ*) poner entre paréntesis/corchetes
3 (*fig*) (*also* **bracket together**) agrupar, poner juntos • **to ~ sth with sth** agrupar algo con algo

▸ **bracket off** VT + ADV separar, poner aparte

brackish ['brækɪʃ] ADJ [*water*] salobre

bract [brækt] N bráctea *f*

brad [bræd] N puntilla *f*, clavito *m*

brae [breɪ] N (*Scot*) ladera *f* de monte, pendiente *f*

brag [bræg] VI jactarse, fanfarronear (**about, of** de, **that** de que)
N (= *boast*) fanfarronada *f*, bravata *f*

braggart ['brægət] N fanfarrón/ona *m/f*, jactancioso/a *m/f*

bragging ['brægɪŋ] N fanfarronadas *fpl*

Brahman ['brɑːmən] N (PL: **Brahmans**), **Brahmin** ['brɑːmɪn] N (PL: **Brahmin** *or* **Brahmins**) brahmán/ana *m/f*

Brahmaputra ['brɑːmə'puːtrə] N Brahmaputra *m*

braid [breɪd] N **1** (*on dress, uniform*) galón *m* • **(gold) ~** galón *m* de oro
2 (*esp US*) [*of hair*] trenza *f*
VT (*esp US*) [+ *hair*] trenzar, hacer trenzas en; [+ *material*] galonear

braided ['breɪdɪd] ADJ [*garment*] con galones • **girls with ~ hair** chicas con trenzas

Braille [breɪl] N Braille *m*
CPD ▸ **Braille library** biblioteca *f* Braille

brain [breɪn] N **1** (*Anat*) cerebro *m* • IDIOMS: • **he's got politics on the ~** tiene la política metida en la cabeza • **to get one's ~ into gear*** poner la mente a carburar*
2 brains: **a** (*Anat, Culin*) sesos *mpl* • IDIOMS: • **to beat sb's ~s out*** romper la crisma a algn* • **to blow one's ~s out*** volarse *or* levantarse la tapa de los sesos*
b* (= *intelligence*) inteligencia *fsing*, cabeza *fsing* • **he's got ~s** es muy listo, tiene mucha cabeza • **he's the ~s of the family** es el listo de la familia; ▹ pick, rack[1]
VT‡ romper la crisma a*
CPD ▸ **brain cell** (*Anat*) célula *f* cerebral ▸ **brain damage** lesión *f* cerebral *or* medular ▸ **brain death** muerte *f* clínica *or* cerebral ▸ **brain drain** fuga *f* de cerebros ▸ **brain haemorrhage, brain hemorrhage** (*US*) hemorragia *f* cerebral ▸ **brain scan** exploración *f* cerebral mediante escáner ▸ **brain scanner** escáner *m* cerebral ▸ **brains trust, brain trust** (*US*) grupo *m* de peritos; (*TV etc*) jurado *m* de expertos ▸ **brain surgeon** neurocirujano/a *m/f* ▸ **brain teaser** rompecabezas *m inv* ▸ **brain tumour, brain tumor** (*US*) tumor *m* cerebral

brainbox* ['breɪn,bɒks] N (*hum*) cerebro *m*

brainchild ['breɪntʃaɪld] N parto *m* del ingenio, invento *m*

brain-damaged ['breɪn,dæmɪdʒd] ADJ • **he was brain-damaged by meningitis** sufrió lesiones cerebrales por la meningitis • **the child was brain-damaged for life** el niño quedó con lesiones medulares de por vida

brain-dead ['breɪn,ded] ADJ **1** (*Med*) clínicamente muerto
2* (= *stupid*) subnormal*, tarado*

-brained [-breɪnd] SUFFIX • **a scatter-brained professor** un profesor atolondrado • **hare-brained** disparatado, descabellado

brainiac* ['breɪnɪæk] N pitagorín *m*

brainless ['breɪnlɪs] ADJ estúpido, tonto

brainpower ['breɪn,paʊəʳ] N fuerza *f* intelectual

brainstorm ['breɪnstɔːm] N **1** (*Brit*) (*fig*) ataque *m* de locura, frenesí *m*
2 (*US*) = **brainwave**
VI *hacer una puesta en común de ideas y sugerencias*
VT [+ *ideas*] poner en común

brainstorming ['breɪnstɔːmɪŋ] N puesta *f* en común, brainstorming *m*
CPD ▸ **brainstorming session** reunión *f* para hacer una puesta en común

brainwash ['breɪnwɒʃ] VT lavar el cerebro a • **to ~ sb into doing sth** convencer a algn para que haga algo

brainwashing ['breɪn,wɒʃɪŋ] N lavado *m* de cerebro

brainwave ['breɪnweɪv] N **1** (*Brit**) idea *f* luminosa*, idea *f* genial*
2 brainwaves (*Med*) ondas *fpl* cerebrales

brainwork ['breɪnwɜːk] N trabajo *m*

intelectual
brainy* ['breɪnɪ] ADJ (COMPAR: **brainier**, SUPERL: **brainiest**) listo, inteligente
braise [breɪz] VT (*Culin*) cocer a fuego lento, estofar
brake¹ [breɪk] N (*Aut etc*) freno *m* • **to put the ~s on** (*Aut*) frenar • **to put the ~s on sth** (*fig*) poner freno a algo
VI frenar
VT frenar
CPD ▸ **brake block** pastilla *f* de frenos ▸ **brake cable** [*of vehicle*] cable *m* del freno ▸ **brake drum** tambor *m* de freno ▸ **brake fluid** líquido *m* de frenos ▸ **brake horsepower** potencia *f* al freno ▸ **brake lever** palanca *f* de freno ▸ **brake light** luz *f* de freno ▸ **brake lining** forro *m* *or* guarnición *f* del freno ▸ **brake pad** pastilla *f* de frenos ▸ **brake pedal** pedal *m* de freno ▸ **brake shoe** zapata *f* del freno ▸ **brake van** (*Brit*) (*Rail*) furgón *m* de cola
brake² [breɪk] N (= *vehicle*) break *m*; (= *estate car*) rubia *f*
brake³ [breɪk] N (*Bot*) helecho *m*; (= *thicket*) soto *m*
brakesman ['breɪksmən] N (PL: **brakesmen**) encargado *m* del montacargas de la mina
braking ['breɪkɪŋ] N (*Aut etc*) frenado *m*
CPD ▸ **braking distance** distancia *f* de parada ▸ **braking power** potencia *f* de freno
bramble ['bræmbl] N zarza *f*
bran [bræn] N salvado *m*
CPD ▸ **bran tub** (*Brit*) sorteo *m* de regalos
branch [brɑːntʃ] N **1** [*of tree*] rama *f*; (*fig*) [*of science*] rama *f*; [*of government, police*] sección *f*; [*of industry*] ramo *m*
2 (*Comm*) [*of company, bank*] sucursal *f*
3 (*in road, railway, pipe*) ramal *m*
4 [*of river*] brazo *m*; (*US*) [*of stream*] arroyo *m*
5 [*of family*] rama *f*
VI [*road etc*] bifurcarse
CPD ▸ **branch line** (*Rail*) ramal *m*, línea *f* secundaria ▸ **branch manager** director(a) *m/f* de sucursal ▸ **branch office** sucursal *f*
▸ **branch off** VI + ADV • **after a few miles, a small road ~es off to the right** después de unas cuantas millas hay una carretera pequeña que sale hacia la derecha • **we ~ed off before reaching Madrid** tomamos un desvío antes de llegar a Madrid • **we ~ed off at Medina** tomamos el desvío de la carretera principal en Medina
▸ **branch out** VI + ADV (*fig*) extenderse
brand [brænd] N **1** (*Comm*) marca *f* (de fábrica)
2 (*Agr*) (= *mark*) marca *f*; (= *iron*) hierro *m* de marcar
3 (= *burning wood*) tizón *m*, tea *f*
VT **1** [+ *cattle*] marcar (con hierro candente)
2 (*fig*) • **to ~ sb as** tildar a algn de • **to ~ sth as** calificar algo de • **to be ~ed as a liar** ser tildado de mentiroso • **it is ~ed on my memory** lo tengo grabado en la memoria
3 • **~ed goods** (*Comm*) artículos *mpl* de marca
CPD ▸ **brand awareness** conciencia *f* de marca ▸ **brand image** imagen *f* de marca ▸ **brand leader** marca *f* líder ▸ **brand loyalty** fidelidad *f* a una marca ▸ **brand name** nombre *m* de marca
branding ['brændɪŋ] N [*of product*] imagen *f* de marca
branding iron ['brændɪŋ,aɪən] N hierro *m* (de marcar)
brandish ['brændɪʃ] VT [+ *weapon*] blandir
brand-name goods [,brændneɪm'gʊdz] NPL (*US*) artículos *mpl* de marca
brand-new ['brænd'njuː] ADJ [*car, motorbike*] salido de fábrica, flamante; [*house, sofa*] completamente nuevo; [*boyfriend, TV series*] nuevo
brandy ['brændɪ] N coñac *m*, brandy *m*
CPD ▸ **brandy butter** mantequilla *f* al coñac ▸ **brandy snap** *barquillo con sabor a jengibre y generalmente relleno de nata*
brash [bræʃ] ADJ (COMPAR: **brasher**, SUPERL: **brashest**) **1** (= *over-confident*) presuntuoso; (= *rash*) impetuoso
2 (= *crude*) [*colour*] chillón; [*taste*] vulgar
brashly ['bræʃlɪ] ADV **1** [*act*] (= *over-confidently*) presuntuosamente; (= *rashly*) impetuosamente
2 (*with adj*) [*intrusive*] descaradamente
brashness ['bræʃnɪs] N (= *over-confidence*) presunción *f*; (= *rashness*) impetuosidad *f*
Brasilia [brə'zɪljə] N Brasilia *f*
brass [brɑːs] N **1** (= *metal*) latón *m*; ▹ **bold**
2 (= *plate*) placa *f* conmemorativa; (*Rel*) plancha *f* sepulcral (de latón) • **to clean the ~es** pulir los bronces
3 • **the ~ a** (*Mus*) los metales
b (*Mil*) los jefazos; ▹ **top**
4 (*Brit‡*) (= *money*) pasta* *f*
5‡ (= *impudence*) cara* *f* • **he had the ~ to ask me for it** tuvo la cara de pedírmelo*
ADJ (= *made of brass*) (hecho) de latón
• IDIOMS: • **not to be worth a ~ farthing** no valer un ardite • **it's cold enough to freeze the balls off a ~ monkey** • **it's ~ monkey weather** (*Brit‡*) ¡hace un frío que pela!* • **to get down to ~ tacks*** ir al grano*
CPD ▸ **brass band** banda *f* de metal ▸ **brass hat*** (*Mil*) jefazo/a* *m/f* ▸ **brass knuckles** (*US*) nudilleras *fpl* ▸ **brass neck*** cara(dura)* *f*, valor *m* ▸ **brass rubbing** (= *art, object*) calco *m* de plancha sepulcral (de latón) ▸ **the brass section** (*Mus*) los metales
▸ **brass off*** VT + ADV fastidiar
brassed off* ['brɑːst'ɒf] ADJ (*Brit*) • **to be ~ with** estar hasta la coronilla *or* las narices de*
brasserie ['brɑːsərɪ] N brasserie *f*
brassica ['bræsɪkə] N brassica *f*, crucífera *f*
brassiere ['bræsɪəʳ] N sostén *m*, sujetador *m*, corpiño *m* (*Arg*)
brassy ['brɑːsɪ] ADJ (COMPAR: **brassier**, SUPERL: **brassiest**) **1** (= *like brass*) (*in colour*) dorado, de color dorado; (= *cheap*) ordinario
2 (= *harsh*) [*sound*] estridente; (= *metallic*) metálico
3 [*person*] descarado
brat* [bræt] N (*pej*) mocoso/a* *m/f*
CPD ▸ **brat pack** (*pej*) (= *actors etc*) *generación de jóvenes artistas con éxito*
bravado [brə'vɑːdəʊ] N (PL: **bravados** *or* **bravadoes**) bravatas *fpl*, baladronadas *fpl*
• **a piece of ~** una bravata • **out of sheer ~** de puro bravucón
brave [breɪv] ADJ (COMPAR: **braver**, SUPERL: **bravest**) **1** (= *courageous*) [*person, deed*] valiente, valeroso • **be ~!** ¡sé valiente! • **that was very ~ of you** has demostrado mucho valor al hacer eso • **she went in with a ~ smile** entró sonriendo valientemente • **try to put on a ~ smile** intenta sonreír aunque te cueste • **to make a ~ attempt to do sth** intentar valientemente hacer algo • IDIOM: • **as ~ as a lion** más fiero que un león; ▹ **face**
2 (*liter*) (= *splendid*) magnífico (*liter*) • **a Brave New World** un mundo feliz
N **1** • **the ~** los valientes • **the ~st of the ~** los más valientes entre los valientes
2 (= *Indian*) guerrero *m*
VT [+ *weather*] afrontar, hacer frente a; [+ *death*] desafiar • **to ~ the storm** (*fig*) capear el temporal • **to ~ sb's anger** afrontar *or* hacer frente a la ira de algn
▸ **brave out** VT + ADV • **to ~ it out** afrontar la situación
bravely ['breɪvlɪ] ADV valientemente, con valor • **she smiled ~** sonrió valiente *or* valientemente • **the flag was flying ~** la bandera ondeaba magnífica
bravery ['breɪvərɪ] N valentía *f*, valor *m*
bravo ['brɑː'vəʊ] EXCL (PL: **bravoes** *or* **bravos**) ¡bravo!, ¡olé!
bravura [brə'vʊərə] N **1** arrojo *m*, brío *m*
2 (*Mus*) virtuosismo *m*
CPD [*display, performance*] brillante
brawl [brɔːl] N pelea *f*, reyerta *f*
VI pelear, pegarse
brawling ['brɔːlɪŋ] ADJ pendenciero, alborotador
N peleas *fpl*, alboroto *m*
brawn [brɔːn] N **1** (*Brit*) (*Culin*) carne *f* en gelatina
2 (= *strength*) fuerza *f* muscular
brawny ['brɔːnɪ] ADJ (COMPAR: **brawnier**, SUPERL: **brawniest**) fornido, musculoso
bray [breɪ] N [*of ass*] rebuzno *m*; (= *laugh*) carcajada *f*
VI [*ass*] rebuznar; [*trumpet*] sonar con estrépito
braze [breɪz] VT soldar
brazen ['breɪzn] ADJ **1** (= *shameless*) descarado • **I couldn't do anything so ~ as that** yo nunca podría hacer algo con tanto descaro • **a ~ hussy** una desvergonzada, una descarada
2 (= *made of brass*) de latón
VT • **to ~ it out** echar cara (a la situación)
brazenly ['breɪznlɪ] ADV descaradamente, con descaro
brazenness ['breɪzənnɪs] N descaro *m*
brazier ['breɪzɪəʳ] N brasero *m*
Brazil [brə'zɪl] N Brasil *m*
CPD ▸ **Brazil nut** nuez *f* del Brasil
Brazilian [brə'zɪlɪən] ADJ brasileño
N brasileño/a *m/f*
BRCS N ABBR = **British Red Cross Society**
breach [briːtʃ] N **1** (= *violation*) [*of law etc*] violación *f*, infracción *f* • **to be in ~ of a rule** incumplir una regla
2 (= *gap*) (*in wall, Mil*) brecha *f* • IDIOMS: • **to fill the ~** • **step into the ~** llenar el vacío
3 (= *estrangement*) ruptura *f*; (*between friends*) (= *act*) rompimiento *m* de relaciones; (= *state*) desavenencia *f* • **to heal the ~** hacer las paces
VT **1** [+ *defences, wall*] abrir brecha en
2 [+ *security*] poner en peligro
VI [*whale*] salir a la superficie
CPD ▸ **breach of confidence** abuso *m* de confianza ▸ **breach of contract** incumplimiento *m* de contrato ▸ **breach of faith** abuso *m* de confianza ▸ **breach of the peace** (*Jur*) perturbación *f* del orden público ▸ **breach of privilege** (*Parl*) abuso *m* del privilegio parlamentario ▸ **breach of promise** incumplimiento *m* de la palabra de casamiento ▸ **breach of security** fallo *m* de seguridad ▸ **breach of trust** abuso *m* de confianza
bread [bred] N **1** (= *food*) pan *m* • **white/brown/rye/wholemeal ~** pan *m* blanco/moreno/de centeno/integral • **~ and butter** pan *m* con mantequilla; (*fig**) (= *living*) pan de cada día* • **to be on ~ and water** estar a pan y agua • **the ~ and wine** (*Rel*) el pan y el vino • IDIOMS: • **to break ~ with** sentarse a la mesa con • **to cast one's ~ on the waters** hacer el bien sin mirar a quién • **to earn one's daily ~** ganarse el pan • **to know which side one's ~ is buttered (on)** saber dónde aprieta el zapato • **to take the ~ out of sb's mouth** quitar el pan de la boca de algn
• PROVERB: • **man cannot live by ~ alone** no solo de pan vive el hombre;
▹ **bread-and-butter**

2‡ (= *money*) pasta* *f*, lana *f* (*LAm**), plata *f* (*LAm**)
CPD ▸ **bread grains** granos *mpl* panificables ▸ **bread pudding** pudín *m* de leche y pan ▸ **bread roll** panecillo *m* ▸ **bread sauce** salsa *f* de pan

bread-and-butter ['bredən'bʌtəʳ] ADJ (*fig*) [*issues, needs*] básico, primario; [*product*] de más venta; [*customer*] más asiduo
CPD ▸ **bread-and-butter letter** carta *f* de agradecimiento (*a una señora en cuya casa el invitado ha pasado varios días*)
▸ **bread-and-butter pudding** pudín *m* de pan y mantequilla

breadbasket ['bred,bɑːskɪt] N
1 (= *container*) cesto *m* para el pan
2 (*fig*) (= *country, area*) granero *m*
3‡ (= *stomach*) panza* *f*, tripa *f* (*Sp**)

breadbin ['bredbɪn] N panera *f*

breadboard ['bredbɔːd] N (*in kitchen*) tabla *f* para cortar el pan; (*Comput*) circuito *m* experimental

breadbox ['bredbɒks] N (*US*) = **breadbin**

breadcrumb ['bredkrʌm] N 1 miga *f*, migaja *f*
2 **breadcrumbs** (*Culin*) pan *m* rallado • **fish in ~s** pescado *m* empanado

breaded ['bredɪd] ADJ empanado

breadfruit ['bredfruːt] N (PL: **breadfruit** *or* **breadfruits**) fruto *m* del árbol del pan
CPD ▸ **breadfruit tree** árbol *m* del pan

breadknife ['brednaɪf] N (PL: **breadknives**) cuchillo *m* para cortar pan

breadline ['bredlaɪn] N (*US*) cola *f* del pan • IDIOM: • **on the ~** (*Brit*) en la miseria

breadstick ['bredstɪk] N piquito *m*, palito *m*

breadth [bretθ] N 1 (= *width*) anchura *f*, ancho *m* • **to be two metres in ~** tener dos metros de ancho
2 (*fig*) [*of experience, knowledge*] amplitud *f*

breadthwise ['bretθwaɪz] ADV de lado a lado

breadwinner ['bred,wɪnəʳ] N sostén *m* de la familia

break [breɪk] (VB: PT: **broke**, PP: **broken**) N
1 (= *fracture*) rotura *f*; (*in bone*) fractura *f*; (*fig*) (*in relationship*) ruptura *f* • **to make a ~ with** romper con
2 (= *gap*) (*in wall etc*) abertura *f*, brecha *f*; (= *crack*) grieta *f*; (*Typ*) (*on paper etc*) espacio *m*, blanco *m*; (*Elec*) (*in circuit*) corte *m* • **a ~ in the clouds** un claro entre las nubes
3 (= *pause*) (*in conversation*) interrupción *f*, pausa *f*; (*in journey*) descanso *m*, pausa *f*; (= *stop*) parada *f*; (= *holiday*) vacaciones *fpl*; (= *rest*) descanso *m*; (= *tea break*) descanso *m* para tomar el té, once(s) *f(pl)* (*LAm*); (*Brit*) (*Scol*) recreo *m* • **a ~ in continuity** una solución de continuidad • **give me a ~!** ¡dame un respiro!; (*impatient*) ¡déjame, anda! • **to have** *or* **take a ~** descansar, tomarse un descanso • **to take a weekend ~** hacer una escapada de fin de semana • **with a ~ in her voice** con la voz entrecortada • **a ~ in the weather** un cambio del tiempo • **without a ~** sin descanso *or* descansar
4* (= *chance*) oportunidad *f* • **to give sb a ~** dar una oportunidad a algn • **lucky ~** golpe *m* de suerte, racha *f* de buena suerte
5 (= *break-out*) fuga *f* • **to make a ~ for it*** tratar de fugarse
6 • **at ~ of day** (*liter*) al amanecer
7 (*Tennis*) ruptura *f* • **two ~s of service** dos servicios rotos
8 (*Billiards, Snooker*) tacada *f*, serie *f*
9 (= *vehicle*) break *m*, volanta *f* (*LAm*)
VT 1 (= *smash*) [+ *glass etc*] romper; [+ *branch, stick*] romper, quebrar (*LAm*); [+ *ground*] roturar; [+ *code*] descifrar; [+ *conspiracy*] deshacer; [+ *drugs ring etc*] desarticular • **to ~ one's back** romperse la columna • **I'm not going to ~ my back to finish it today** no me voy a matar para terminarlo hoy • **to ~ sb's heart** romper *or* partir el corazón a algn • **to ~ one's leg** romperse la pierna • **~ a leg!*** (*Theat*) ¡buena suerte! • **to ~ surface** [*submarine, diver*] emerger, salir a la superficie • IDIOM: • **to ~ the ice** romper el hielo; ▹ **spirit**
2 (= *surpass*) [+ *record*] batir, superar
3 (= *fail to observe*) [+ *law, rule*] violar, quebrantar; [+ *appointment*] no acudir a • **he broke his word/promise** faltó a su palabra/promesa • **to ~ a date** faltar a una cita
4 (= *weaken, destroy*) [+ *resistance, spirits*] quebrantar, quebrar (*LAm*); [+ *health*] quebrantar; [+ *strike*] romper, quebrar (*LAm*); [+ *habit*] perder; [+ *horse*] domar, amansar; [+ *bank*] (*in gambling*) quebrar, hacer quebrar; [+ *person*] (*financially*) arruinar; (*morally*) abatir, vencer • **to ~ sb of a habit** quitar una costumbre a algn
5 (= *interrupt*) [+ *silence, spell*] romper; [+ *journey*] interrumpir; [+ *electrical circuit*] cortar, interrumpir
6 (= *soften*) [+ *force*] mitigar, contener; [+ *impact, fall*] amortiguar
7 (= *disclose*) [+ *news*] comunicar (**to** a)
8 (= *leave*) • **to ~ camp** levantar el campamento • **to ~ cover** salir al descubierto • **to ~ ranks** romper filas
9 • **to ~ sb's serve** *or* **service** (*Tennis*) romper el servicio de algn
10 (*Naut*) [+ *flag*] desplegar
11 (*US**) • **can you ~ me a 100-dollar bill?** ¿me puede cambiar un billete de 100 dólares?
VI 1 (= *smash*) [*window, glass*] romperse; (*into pieces*) hacerse pedazos
2 (= *be fractured*) [*chair*] romperse, partirse; [*branch, twig*] romperse, quebrarse (*LAm*); [*limb*] fracturarse; [*boil*] reventar; (*fig*) [*heart*] romperse, partirse
3 (= *cease to function*) [*machine*] estropearse
4 (= *arrive*) [*dawn, day*] apuntar, rayar; [*news*] darse a conocer; [*story*] revelarse; [*storm*] estallar; [*wave*] romper
5 (= *give way*) [*health, spirits*] quebrantarse; [*weather*] cambiar; [*heat wave*] terminar; [*boy's voice*] mudarse; [*singing voice*] cascarse; [*bank*] quebrar
6 (= *pause*) • **let's ~ for lunch** vamos a hacer un descanso para comer
7 • **to ~ free** (*from chains, ropes etc*) soltarse; (*fig*) liberarse • **to ~ loose** desatarse, escaparse; (*fig*) desencadenarse
8 • **to ~ even** cubrir los gastos
9 (*Boxing*) separarse
10 (*Billiards, Snooker*) abrir el juego
11 (*Sport*) [*ball*] torcerse, desviarse
CPD ▸ **break dancer** bailarín/ina *m/f* de break ▸ **break dancing** break *m* ▸ **break point** (*Tennis*) punto *m* de break, punto *m* de ruptura; (*Comput*) punto *m* de interrupción

▸ **break away** VI + ADV 1 [*piece*] desprenderse, separarse
2 (*Ftbl etc*) escapar, despegarse
3 • **to ~ away from** [+ *guard*] evadirse de; [+ *group*] (= *leave*) separarse de; (*from disagreement*) romper con

▸ **break down** VT + ADV 1 (= *destroy*) [+ *door etc*] echar abajo, derribar; [+ *resistance*] vencer, acabar con; [+ *suspicion*] disipar
2 (= *analyse*) [+ *figures*] analizar, desglosar; [+ *substance*] descomponer
VI + ADV [*machine*] estropearse, malograrse (*Peru*), descomponerse (*LAm*); (*Aut*) averiarse, descomponerse (*LAm*); [*person*] (*under pressure*) derrumbarse; (*from emotion*) romper *or* echarse a llorar; [*health*] quebrantarse; [*talks etc*] fracasar; [*chemicals, waste*] descomponerse

▸ **break forth** VI + ADV [*light, water*] surgir; [*storm*] estallar • **to ~ forth into song** ponerse a cantar

▸ **break in** VT + ADV 1 [+ *door*] forzar, echar abajo
2 (= *train*) [+ *horse*] domar, amansar; [+ *recruit*] formar
3 [+ *shoes*] domar, acostumbrarse a
VI + ADV 1 [*burglar*] forzar la entrada
2 (= *interrupt*) (*on conversation*) interrumpir

▸ **break into** VI + PREP 1 [+ *house*] entrar a robar en, allanar; [+ *safe*] forzar
2 (*Comm etc*) • **to ~ into a new market** introducirse en un mercado nuevo • **to ~ into films** introducirse en el mundo cinematográfico
3 (= *begin suddenly*) echar a, romper a • **to ~ into a run** echar *or* empezar a correr • **to ~ into song** ponerse a cantar

▸ **break off** VT + ADV 1 [+ *piece etc*] partir
2 (= *end*) [+ *engagement, talks*] romper; (*Mil*) [+ *action*] terminar
VI + ADV 1 [*piece of rock, ice, handle*] desprenderse; [*twig, segment of orange*] desgajarse
2 (= *stop*) interrumpirse, pararse

▸ **break out** VI + ADV 1 [*prisoners*] fugarse, escaparse
2 (= *begin*) [*fire, war, epidemic*] estallar; [*discussion, fighting, argument*] producirse
3 • **he broke out in spots** le salieron granos • **he broke out in a sweat** quedó cubierto de sudor
VT + ADV [+ *champagne etc*] descorchar

▸ **break through** VI + ADV [*sun*] salir; [*water etc*] abrirse paso, abrirse (un) camino • **to ~ through to** [+ *new seam*] [*miners*] llegar a, abrir un camino hasta
VI + PREP [+ *defences, barrier*] atravesar; [+ *crowd*] abrirse paso entre

▸ **break up** VT + ADV 1 [+ *rocks etc*] hacer pedazos, deshacer; [+ *ship*] desguazar
2 (*fig*) [+ *crowd*] dispersar, disolver; [+ *meeting, organization*] disolver; [+ *gang*] desarticular; [+ *marriage*] deshacer; [+ *estate*] parcelar; [+ *industry*] desconcentrar; [+ *fight*] intervenir en • **~ it up!** ¡basta ya!
3 (*US**) (= *cause to laugh*) hacer reír a carcajadas
VI + ADV 1 [*ship*] hacerse pedazos; [*ice*] deshacerse
2 (*fig*) [*partnership*] deshacerse, disolverse; [*marriage*] deshacerse; [*federation*] desmembrarse; [*group*] disgregarse; [*weather*] cambiar; [*crowd, clouds*] dispersarse • **they broke up after ten years of marriage** se separaron después de diez años de matrimonio
3 (= *divide*) dividirse, desglosarse (**into** en)
4 (*Brit*) [*pupils*] empezar las vacaciones; [*session*] levantarse, terminar • **the school ~s up tomorrow** las clases terminan mañana
5 (*US**) (= *laugh*) reír a carcajadas
6 (*Telec*) • **the line's** *or* **you're ~ing up** no hay cobertura, no te oigo *or* no se te oye bien

▸ **break with** VI + PREP • **to ~ with sth/sb** romper con algo/algn

breakable ['breɪkəbl] ADJ (= *brittle*) quebradizo; (= *fragile*) frágil
N **breakables** objetos *mpl* frágiles

breakage ['breɪkɪdʒ] N (= *act of breaking*) rotura *f*; (= *thing broken*) destrozo *m*

breakaway ['breɪkəweɪ] ADJ [*group etc*] disidente
N (*Sport*) escapada *f*
CPD ▸ **breakaway state** (*Pol*) estado *m* independizado

breakbeat [ˈbreɪk͵biːt] N (*Mus*) breakbeat *m*

breakdown [ˈbreɪkdaʊn] N **1** (= *failure*) [*of system, electricity*] fallo *m*; [*of negotiations, marriage*] fracaso *m*; [*of vehicle, machine*] avería *f*, descompostura *f* (*LAm*)
2 (*fig*) [*of talks*] ruptura *f*
3 (*Med*) colapso *m*, crisis *f inv* nerviosa
4 (= *analysis*) [*of numbers etc*] análisis *m inv*, desglose *m*; (*Chem*) descomposición *f*; (= *report*) informe *m* detallado
CPD ▸ **breakdown cover** (*Insurance*) asistencia *f* mecánica ▸ **breakdown service** (*Brit*) (*Aut*) servicio *m* de asistencia en carretera ▸ **breakdown truck**, **breakdown van** (*Brit*) (*Aut*) (camión *m*) grúa *f*

breaker [ˈbreɪkəʳ] N (= *wave*) ola *f* grande

break-even [͵breɪkˈiːvən] ADJ • **break-even chart** gráfica *f* del punto de equilibrio • **break-even point** punto *m* de equilibrio

breakfast [ˈbrekfəst] N desayuno *m* • **to have ~** desayunar
VI desayunar • **to ~ off** *or* **on eggs** desayunar huevos
CPD ▸ **breakfast bar** barra *f* para el desayuno ▸ **breakfast cereal** cereales *mpl* para el desayuno ▸ **breakfast cup** taza *f* de desayuno ▸ **breakfast room** habitación *f* del desayuno ▸ **breakfast show** (*Rad, TV*) programa *m* matinal ▸ **breakfast table** mesa *f* del desayuno ▸ **breakfast television** televisión *f* matinal ▸ **breakfast time** hora *f* del desayuno ▸ **breakfast TV** tele(visión) *f* matinal

break-in [ˈbreɪk͵ɪn] N robo *m* (con allanamiento de morada)

breaking [ˈbreɪkɪŋ] N **1** rotura *f*, rompimiento *m*
2 • **~ and entering** (*Jur*) violación *f* de domicilio, allanamiento *m* de morada
CPD ▸ **breaking news** noticia *fsing* de última hora ▸ **breaking point** punto *m* de máxima tensión tolerable; (*fig*) [*of person*] límite *m* • **to reach ~ point** llegar al límite ▸ **breaking story** noticia *f* de última hora

breaking-up [͵breɪkɪŋˈʌp] N [*of meeting etc*] disolución *f*, levantamiento *m* (de la sesión); [*of school, college*] fin *m* de las clases, fin *m* de curso

breakneck [ˈbreɪknek] ADJ • **at ~ speed** a una velocidad vertiginosa

break-out [ˈbreɪkaʊt] N fuga *f*, evasión *f*

breakthrough [ˈbreɪkθruː] N (*Mil*) avance *m*; (*in research etc*) adelanto *m* muy importante • **to achieve** *or* **make a ~** conseguir *or* hacer un adelanto muy importante

break-up [ˈbreɪkʌp] N [*of partnership*] disolución *f*; [*of couple*] separación *f*
CPD ▸ **break-up value** (*Comm*) valor *m* en liquidación

breakwater [ˈbreɪk͵wɔːtəʳ] N rompeolas *m inv*

bream [briːm] N (= *sea bream*) besugo *m*

breast [brest] N (= *chest*) pecho *m*; [*of woman*] seno *m*, pecho *m*; (*Culin*) [*of bird*] pechuga *f*; (*fig*) corazón *m* • **to beat one's ~** darse golpes de pecho • IDIOM: • **to make a clean ~ of** confesar con franqueza • **to make a clean ~ of it** confesarlo todo, descargar la conciencia
VT **1** [+ *waves*] hacer cara a, arrostrar
2 (*Sport*) [+ *finishing tape*] romper
CPD ▸ **breast cancer** cáncer *m* de mama ▸ **breast enhancement** (*Med*) aumento *m* mamario, aumento *m* de los pechos • **to have ~ enhancement** aumentarse los pechos ▸ **breast implant** implante *m* mamario • **silicone ~ implants** implantes mamarios de silicona ▸ **breast lump** bulto *m* en el pecho ▸ **breast milk** leche *f* materna ▸ **breast pocket** bolsillo *m* de pecho ▸ **breast screening** mamografías *fpl* preventivas

breastbone [ˈbrestbəʊn] N esternón *m*

-breasted [ˈbrestɪd] SUFFIX
1 • **large-breasted** [*woman*] de grandes pechos
2 (*Zool*) • **red-breasted** pechirrojo

breast-fed [ˈbrestfed] ADJ criado a pecho

breast-feed [ˈbrestfiːd] (PT, PP: **breast-fed**) VT amamantar, criar a los pechos

breast-feeding [ˈbrest͵fiːdɪŋ] N amamantamiento *m*, cría *f* a los pechos

breastplate [ˈbrestpleɪt] N peto *m*

breaststroke [ˈbreststrəʊk] N braza *f* de pecho • **to swim** *or* **do the ~** nadar a la braza

breastwork [ˈbrestwɜːk] N parapeto *m*

breath [breθ] N **1** (*lit*) (= *respiration*) aliento *m* • **you could smell the whisky on his ~** estaba claro que el aliento le olía a whisky • **without pausing for ~** sin detenerse ni un momento para recobrar el aliento *or* la respiración • **to have bad ~** tener mal aliento • **he stopped running to catch his ~** dejó de correr para recobrar el aliento *or* la respiración • **the pain made her catch her ~** el dolor hizo que se le cortara la respiración • **to draw ~** (*lit*) respirar; (*liter*) (= *exist*) • **he was one of the meanest people who ever drew ~** era una de las personas más mezquinas que jamás ha visto este mundo • **to draw one's first ~** (*liter*) venir al mundo • **to draw one's last ~** (*liter*) exhalar el último suspiro (*liter*) • **to get one's ~ back** recobrar el aliento *or* la respiración • **to hold one's ~** (*lit*) contener la respiración; (*fig*) • **the whole world is holding its ~** el mundo entero está en vilo • **"he said he would be here" — "well, I wouldn't hold your ~"** —dijo que vendría —sí, pues yo le esperaría sentado* • **to lose one's ~** perder el aliento • **to be/get out of ~** estar/quedar sin aliento • **in the same** *or* **next ~** acto seguido • **she felt hot and short of ~** tenía calor y se ahogaba • **he was short of ~ after the climb** estaba sin aliento después de la escalada • **she has asthma and sometimes gets short of ~** tiene asma y a veces se ahoga *or* le falta el aliento • **she sucked in her ~** tomó aliento, aspiró • **to take a ~** respirar • **he took a deep ~** respiró hondo • **to take one's ~ away** dejar a uno sin habla • **he muttered something under his ~** dijo algo entre dientes *or* en voz baja • **to waste one's ~*** gastar saliva (en balde)*; ▹ **bated, save**
2 (*fig*) (= *puff*) soplo *m* • **there wasn't a ~ of wind** no corría ni un soplo de viento • **we must avoid the slightest ~ of scandal** debemos evitar el más mínimo soplo de escándalo • **a ~ of fresh air**: • **we went out for a ~ of fresh air** salimos a tomar el (aire) fresco • **she's like a ~ of fresh air** es como un soplo de aire fresco
CPD ▸ **breath freshener** spray *m* bucal ▸ **breath test** (*Aut*) prueba *f* de alcoholemia; ▹ **breath-test**

breathable [ˈbriːðəbl] ADJ [*air*] respirable, que se puede respirar; [*fabric, garment*] transpirable, que deja pasar el aire

breathalyse, **breathalyze** (*US*) [ˈbreθəlaɪz] VT someter a la prueba de la alcoholemia *or* del alcohol

Breathalyser®, **Breathalyzer** (*US*) [ˈbreθəlaɪzəʳ] N alcoholímetro *m*
CPD ▸ **Breathalyser test** prueba *f* de la alcoholemia

breathe [briːð] VT **1** [+ *air*] respirar • **to ~ air into a balloon** inflar un globo soplando • **he ~d alcohol all over me** el aliento le apestaba a alcohol • IDIOMS: • **to ~ new life into sth** infundir nueva vida a algo • **to ~ one's last** (*liter*) (= *die*) exhalar el último suspiro (*liter*)
2 (= *utter*) [+ *prayer*] decir en voz baja • **to ~ a sigh** suspirar, dar un suspiro • **I won't ~ a word** no diré nada *or* palabra
VI **1** [*person, animal*] respirar; (*noisily*) resollar • **now we can ~ again** (*fig*) ahora podemos respirar tranquilos; ▹ **neck**
2 [*wine*] respirar
3 [*fabric, garment*] transpirar, dejar pasar el aire
▸ **breathe in** VT + ADV, VI + ADV aspirar
▸ **breathe out** VT + ADV exhalar
VI + ADV espirar

breather* [ˈbriːðəʳ] N (= *short rest*) respiro *m*, descanso *m* • **to take a ~** tomarse un respiro *or* descanso • **to give sb a ~** dejar que algn se tome un respiro *or* descanso

breathing [ˈbriːðɪŋ] N respiración *f* • **heavy ~** resuello *m*
CPD ▸ **breathing apparatus** respirador *m* ▸ **breathing exercise** ejercicio *m* respiratorio ▸ **breathing space** (*fig*) respiro *m* ▸ **breathing tube** tubo *m* de respiración

breathless [ˈbreθlɪs] ADJ **1** (*from exertion*) [*voice*] entrecortado • **he arrived ~** llegó sin aliento, llegó jadeando • **she was ~ from climbing the stairs** subir las escaleras la había dejado sin aliento • **it leaves you ~** corta la respiración • **at a ~ pace** a un ritmo acelerado
2 (*with excitement*) • **a ~ silence** un silencio intenso • **she was ~ with excitement** la emoción la había dejado sin aliento • **we were ~ with anticipation** esperábamos ansiosísimos

breathlessly [ˈbreθlɪslɪ] ADV **1** (*lit*) [*say, ask*] entrecortadamente, jadeante; [*walk, climb*] jadeando, con la respiración entrecortada
2 (*fig*) [*watch, wait*] ansiosamente

breathlessness [ˈbreθlɪsnɪs] N falta *f* de aliento, dificultad *f* al respirar

breathtaking [ˈbreθ͵teɪkɪŋ] ADJ [*sight*] imponente, impresionante; [*speed*] vertiginoso; [*effrontery*] pasmoso • **the view is ~** la vista corta la respiración, la vista es imponente *or* impresionante

breathtakingly [ˈbreθ͵teɪkɪŋlɪ] ADV • **~ beautiful** de una belleza impresionante, tan hermoso que corta la respiración • **~ simple** de una sencillez impresionante *or* pasmosa • **to go ~ fast** ir a una velocidad vertiginosa

breath-test [ˈbreθtest] VT someter a la prueba de la alcoholemia *or* del alcohol; ▹ **breath**

breathy [ˈbreθɪ] ADJ [*voice*] entrecortado

bred [bred] PT, PP *of* **breed**

-bred [bred] ADJ (*ending in compounds*) criado, educado • **well-bred** bien educado, formal

breech [briːtʃ] N [*of gun*] recámara *f*
CPD ▸ **breech birth**, **breech delivery** (*Med*) parto *m* de nalgas • **he was a ~ birth** nació de nalgas

breeches [ˈbriːtʃɪz] NPL calzones *mpl* • **riding ~** pantalones *mpl* de montar • IDIOM: • **to wear the ~** llevar los pantalones *or* calzones
CPD ▸ **breeches buoy** (*Naut*) boya *f* pantalón

breechloader [ˈbriːtʃ͵ləʊdəʳ] N arma *f* de retrocarga

breed [briːd] (VB: PT, PP: **bred**) N (*lit*) [*of animal*] raza *f*; [*of plant*] variedad *f*; (*fig*) estirpe *f*
VT **1** [+ *animals*] criar • **town bred** criado en la ciudad • **they are bred for show** se crían para las exposiciones • **we ~ them for hunting** los criamos para la caza
2 (*fig*) [+ *hate, suspicion*] crear, engendrar
VI [*animals*] reproducirse, procrear • **they ~ like flies** *or* **rabbits** se multiplican como conejos

breeder ['bri:dər] (N) **1** (= *person*) criador(a) *m/f*
2 (= *animal*) reproductor(a) *m/f*
3 (*Phys*) (*also* **breeder reactor**) reactor *m*
breeding ['bri:dɪŋ] (N) **1** (*Bio*) reproducción *f*
2 [*of stock*] cría *f*
3 [*of person*] (*also* **good breeding**) educación *f*, crianza *f* • **bad ~** • **ill ~** mala crianza *f*, falta *f* de educación • **he has (good) ~** es una persona educada • **it shows bad ~** muestra una falta de educación
(CPD) ▸ **breeding ground** (*Bio*) lugar *m* de cría; (*fig*) caldo *m* de cultivo (**of, for** de, para)
▸ **breeding pair** pareja *f* reproductora
▸ **breeding season** época *f* de reproducción
▸ **breeding stock** animales *mpl* de cría
breeks [bri:ks] (NPL) (*Scot*) pantalones *mpl*
breeze [bri:z] (N) **1** (= *wind*) brisa *f*
2 • **it's a ~*** es coser y cantar* • **to do sth in a ~** (*US**) hacer algo con los ojos cerrados; ▷ shoot
(VI) • **to ~ in** entrar como si nada • **to ~ through sth*** hacer algo con los ojos cerrados
breeze-block ['bri:zblɒk] (N) (*Brit*) bovedilla *f*
breezeway ['bri:zweɪ] (N) (*US*) pasillo *m* cubierto
breezily ['bri:zɪlɪ] (ADV) (= *cheerfully*) alegremente; (= *nonchalantly*) despreocupadamente
breezy ['bri:zɪ] (ADJ) (COMPAR: **breezier**, SUPERL: **breeziest**) **1** [*day, weather*] de viento; [*spot*] desprotegido del viento • **it's ~** hace viento
2 [*person's manner*] (= *cheerful*) animado, alegre; (= *nonchalant*) despreocupado
Bren carrier ['bren,kærɪər] (N) = **Bren gun carrier**
Bren gun ['bren,gʌn] (N) fusil *m* ametrallador
(CPD) ▸ **Bren gun carrier** vehículo *m* de transporte ligero (con fusil ametrallador)
brethren ['breðrɪn] (NPL) (*irr pl of brother*) (*esp Rel*) hermanos *mpl*
Breton ['bretən] (ADJ) bretón
(N) **1** (= *person*) bretón/ona *m/f*
2 (*Ling*) bretón *m*
breve [bri:v] (N) (*Mus, Typ*) breve *f*
breviary ['bri:vɪərɪ] (N) (*Rel*) breviario *m*
brevity ['brevɪtɪ] (N) (= *shortness*) brevedad *f*; (= *conciseness*) concisión *f* • PROVERB: • **~ is the soul of wit** lo bueno si breve dos veces bueno
brew [bru:] (N) [*of beer*] variedad *f* (de cerveza); [*of tea, herbs*] infusión *f*
(VT) **1** [+ *beer*] elaborar; [+ *tea*] hacer, preparar
2 (*fig*) [+ *scheme, mischief*] tramar
(VI) **1** [*beer*] elaborarse; [*tea*] hacerse
2 (*fig*) [*storm*] avecinarse; [*plot*] tramarse • **there's trouble ~ing** algo se está tramando
▸ **brew up*** (VI + ADV) (*Brit*) preparar el té
brewer ['bru:ər] (N) cervecero/a *m/f*
brewery ['bru:ərɪ] (N) cervecería *f*, fábrica *f* de cerveza
brewing ['bru:ɪŋ] (N) (*of beer*) fabricación *f* (de cerveza)
brew-up ['bru:ʌp] (N) • **let's have a brew-up** (*Brit**) vamos a tomar un té
briar ['braɪər] (N) **1** (= *thorny bush*) zarza *f*; (= *wild rose*) escaramujo *m*, rosa *f* silvestre; (= *hawthorn*) espino *m*; (= *heather*) brezo *m*
2 (= *pipe*) pipa *f* de brezo
bribable ['braɪbəbl] (ADJ) sobornable
bribe [braɪb] (N) soborno *m*, mordida *f* (*CAm, Mex**), coima *f* (*And, S. Cone**) • **to take a ~** dejarse sobornar (**from** por)
(VT) sobornar, comprar* • **to ~ sb to do sth** sobornar a algn para que haga algo
bribery ['braɪbərɪ] (N) soborno *m*, mordida *f* (*CAm, Mex**), coima *f* (*And, S. Cone**)
bric-à-brac ['brɪkəbræk] (N) (*no pl*) chucherías *fpl*, curiosidades *fpl*
brick [brɪk] (N) **1** (*Constr*) ladrillo *m*, tabique *m* (*Mex*) • **~s and mortar** construcción *f*, edificios *mpl* • IDIOMS: • **to come down on sb like a ton of ~s*** echar una bronca de miedo a algn* • **to drop a ~** (*Brit**) meter la pata*, tirarse una plancha (*Sp**) • PROVERB: • **you can't make ~s without straw** sin paja no hay ladrillos
2 (*Brit*) (= *toy*) cubo *m*
3 [*of ice cream*] bloque *m*
4†* (= *person*) • **he's a ~** es buen chico • **be a ~ and lend it to me** préstamelo como buen amigo
(CPD) de ladrillo(s) ▸ **brick kiln** horno *m* de ladrillos ▸ **brick wall** pared *f* de ladrillos • IDIOM: • **to beat one's head against a ~ wall** esforzarse en balde
▸ **brick in** (VT + ADV) [+ *window etc*] tapar con ladrillos *or* (*Mex*) tabiques
▸ **brick up** (VT + ADV) [+ *window etc*] tapar con ladrillos *or* (*Mex*) tabiques
brickbat ['brɪkbæt] (N) trozo *m* de ladrillo; (*fig*) crítica *f*
brick-built ['brɪk,bɪlt] (ADJ) construido de ladrillos
brickie* ['brɪkɪ] (N) (*Brit*) albañil *mf*, paleta *mf* (*Sp**)
bricklayer ['brɪk,leɪər] (N) albañil *mf*
bricklaying ['brɪk,leɪɪŋ] (N) albañilería *f*
brick-red ['brɪkred] (ADJ) rojo ladrillo
(N) rojo *m* ladrillo
brickwork ['brɪkwɜ:k] (N) enladrillado *m*, ladrillos *mpl*
brickworks ['brɪkwɜ:ks] (N), **brickyard** ['brɪk,jɑ:d] (N) ladrillar *m*
bridal ['braɪdl] (ADJ) nupcial
(CPD) ▸ **bridal suite** suite *f* nupcial
bride [braɪd] (N) novia *f* • **the ~ and groom** los novios • **~ of Christ** (*Rel*) esposa *f* de Cristo
bridegroom ['braɪdgrʊm] (N) novio *m*; ▷ BEST MAN
bridesmaid ['braɪdzmeɪd] (N) dama *f* de honor
bridge¹ [brɪdʒ] (N) **1** (*gen*) puente *m* (*also Mus*) • **to build a ~ between two communities** (*fig*) crear un vínculo (de unión) entre dos comunidades • **we must rebuild our ~s** (*fig*) tenemos que restablecer las relaciones • IDIOMS: • **to burn one's ~s** quemar las naves • **we'll cross that ~ when we come to it** trataremos ese problema en su momento • **don't cross your ~s before you come to them** no adelantes los acontecimientos • **much water has flowed under the ~ since then** mucho ha llovido desde entonces
2 (*Naut*) puente *m* de mando
3 [*of nose*] caballete *m*; [*of spectacles*] puente *m*
4 (*Dentistry*) puente *m*
(VT) tender un puente sobre • **to ~ a gap** (*fig*) llenar un vacío
(CPD) ▸ **bridge building** construcción *f* de puentes; (*fig*) restablecimiento *m* de relaciones
bridge² [brɪdʒ] (N) (*Cards*) bridge *m*
(CPD) ▸ **bridge party** reunión *f* de bridge
▸ **bridge player** jugador(a) *m/f* de bridge
▸ **bridge roll** *tipo de bollo pequeño y alargado*
bridgehead ['brɪdʒhed] (N) (*Mil*) cabeza *f* de puente
Bridget ['brɪdʒɪt] (N) Brígida
bridgework ['brɪdʒ,wɜ:k] (N) (*Dentistry*) puente *m*
bridging loan ['brɪdʒɪŋ,ləʊn] (N) (*Brit*) (*Econ*) crédito *m* puente
bridle ['braɪdl] (N) [*of horse*] brida *f*, freno *m*
(VT) [+ *horse*] frenar, detener
(VI) picarse, ofenderse (**at** por)
(CPD) ▸ **bridle path** camino *m* de herradura
bridleway ['braɪdlweɪ] (N) (*Brit*) camino *f* de herradura
Brie, brie [bri:] (N) brie *m*
brief [bri:f] (ADJ) (COMPAR: **briefer**, SUPERL: **briefest**) **1** (= *short*) [*visit, period, career*] breve, corto; [*glimpse, moment, interval*] breve
2 (= *concise*) [*speech, description, statement*] breve • **please be ~** sea breve, por favor • **he was ~ and to the point** fue breve y yendo al grano • **in ~** en resumen, en suma
3 (= *skimpy*) [*panties, bathing costume, shorts*] diminuto, breve
(N) **1** (*Jur*) escrito *m* • **to hold a ~ for sb** (*fig*) ser partidario de algn, abogar por algn • **I hold no ~ for those who …** no soy partidario de los que …, no abogo por los que … • **I hold no ~ for him** no lo defiendo
2 (= *instructions, remit*) instrucciones *fpl* • **his ~ is to negotiate a solution to the conflict** sus instrucciones son solucionar el conflicto mediante negociaciones • **it's not part of my ~ to sort out disputes** no entra dentro de mi competencia solventar disputas
3 **briefs** (*man's*) calzoncillos *mpl*, slip *m*, calzones *mpl* (*LAm*); (*woman's*) bragas *fpl* (*Sp*), calzones *mpl* (*LAm*)
(VT) **1** (*Jur, Mil*) (= *instruct*) dar instrucciones a • **the pilots were ~ed** dieron instrucciones a los pilotos
2 (= *inform, prepare*) informar • **we were ~ed on recent developments** nos informaron sobre los acontecimientos recientes
briefcase ['bri:fkeɪs] (N) cartera *f*, maletín *m*
briefer ['bri:fər] (N) (*esp Mil*) informador(a) *m/f*
briefing ['bri:fɪŋ] (N) (= *meeting*) sesión *f* informativa; (*written*) informe *m*
(CPD) ▸ **briefing paper** nota *f* informativa
briefly ['bri:flɪ] (ADV) **1** (= *for short time*) [*speak, reply, smile, pause*] brevemente • **she visited us ~** nos hizo una breve *or* corta visita • **"good morning," he said, looking up ~** "buenos días," dijo, levantando la vista fugazmente • **I wondered ~ if he were lying** por un momento me pregunté si no estaría mintiendo • **he was ~ detained by the police** la policía lo tuvo detenido durante un corto espacio de tiempo
2 (= *in brief*) [*tell, reply, describe*] en pocas palabras, en resumen • **the facts, ~, are these** los hechos, en pocas palabras *or* en resumen, son estos • **~, we still don't know** en resumen *or* en suma, aún no lo sabemos
briefness ['bri:fnɪs] (N) brevedad *f*
brier ['braɪər] (N) = **briar**
brig [brɪg] (N) (*Naut*) bergantín *m*
Brig. (ABBR) = **Brigadier**
brigade [brɪ'geɪd] (N) (*Mil*) brigada *f*; (*fire etc*) cuerpo *m* • **one of the old ~** un veterano
brigadier [,brɪgə'dɪər] (N) general *mf* de brigada
(CPD) ▸ **brigadier general** (*US*) general *mf* de brigada
brigand ['brɪgənd] (N) bandido *m*, bandolero *m*
brigandage ['brɪgəndɪdʒ] (N) bandidaje *m*, bandolerismo *m*
Brig. Gen. (ABBR) (*US*) Gral. de Brigada
bright [braɪt] (ADJ) (COMPAR: **brighter**, SUPERL: **brightest**) **1** (= *vivid, shining*) [*light, sun, reflection*] brillante, luminoso; [*star, metal*] brillante; [*surface*] resplandeciente; [*fire*] luminoso; [*uniform, bird, flower*] lleno de colorido; [*eyes*] brillante; [*colour*] fuerte, vivo • **~ red** rojo fuerte • **her eyes were ~ with excitement** sus ojos brillaban de excitación
2 (= *sunny*) [*day, weather*] radiante, soleado;

[*room, house*] luminoso, con mucha luz • **a ~ October day** un radiante *or* soleado día de octubre • **a ~, sunny day** un día de sol radiante • **the outlook is ~er for tomorrow** (*Met*) la previsión meteorológica para mañana es que hará mejor tiempo
3 (= *cheerful*) [*person*] alegre, animado; [*face, expression, smile*] radiante; [*voice*] lleno de animación • **~ and breezy** radiante y lleno de vida • IDIOM: • **to look on the ~ side** ver el lado positivo de las cosas
4 (= *clever*) [*person*] listo, inteligente; [*idea*] brillante, genial • **was it your ~ idea to let the children do the washing-up?** (*iro*) ¿ha sido tuya la brillante *or* genial idea de dejar que los niños laven los platos? • **whose ~ idea was that?** (*iro*) ¿quién tuvo *or* de quién fue esa brillante idea? • IDIOM: • **as ~ as a button** más listo que el hambre
5 (= *promising*) [*future*] brillante, prometedor; [*outlook, prospects, start*] prometedor • **the future looks ~ (for him)** el futuro se le presenta brillante *or* prometedor • **I can see a ~ future ahead of you** te auguro un futuro brillante • **the outlook is ~er** las perspectivas son más prometedoras
(ADV) • **to get up ~ and early** levantarse tempranito
(CPD) ▸ **bright lights** (*US*) (*Aut*) luces *fpl* largas • **he was attracted by the ~ lights of the big city** (*fig*) se sentía atraído por las luces de neón de la gran ciudad ▸ **bright spark*** (*iro*) listillo/a *m/f* • **you're a ~ spark, aren't you!** ¡te has pasado de listo!

brighten ['braɪtn] (*also* **brighten up**) (VT)
1 (= *make lighter*) [+ *room*] dar más luz a, iluminar más; (*TV*) [+ *picture*] dar brillo a
2 (= *make more cheerful*) [+ *room*] alegrar; [+ *situation*] mejorar
(VI) **1** [*person*] animarse, alegrarse; [*eyes*] iluminarse, brillar
2 [*weather*] despejarse; [*prospects*] mejorar

bright-eyed ['braɪt'aɪd] (ADJ) de ojos vivos

brightly ['braɪtlɪ] (ADV) **1** (= *brilliantly*) [*shine*] intensamente, con intensidad; [*burn*] con intensidad • **~ lit** radiantemente iluminado
2 (= *vividly*) • **~ coloured flowers** flores *fpl* de colores vivos • **~ painted pictures** cuadros *mpl* pintados con llamativos colores • **~ patterned shawls** mantones *mpl* con unos diseños llamativos
3 (= *cheerily*) [*smile, say, answer*] alegremente

brightness ['braɪtnɪs] (N) **1** [*of light, sun, fire, eyes, metal*] brillo *m*, resplandor *m*; [*of morning, day*] claridad *f*, luminosidad *f*; [*of colour*] viveza *f*
2 (= *cheerfulness*) alegría *f*, animación *f*
3 (= *cleverness*) inteligencia *f*
4 (= *promise*) [*of future, prospects*] lo prometedor
(CPD) ▸ **brightness control** (*TV*) botón *m* de ajuste del brillo

brill[1] [brɪl] (N) (PL: **brill** *or* **brills**) rodaballo *m* menor

brill[2]* [brɪl] (ADJ) (*Brit*) (= *brilliant*) genial*, fenómeno*
(EXCL) ¡fantástico!*

brilliance ['brɪljəns] (N), **brilliancy** ['brɪljənsɪ] (N) **1** (= *brightness*) [*of light*] resplandor *m*, brillo *m*; [*of colour*] luminosidad *f*; [*of gemstone*] resplandor *m*, fulgor *m*, brillo *m*
2 (= *cleverness*) [*of student, scientist*] brillantez *f*, genialidad *f*

brilliant ['brɪljənt] (ADJ) **1** (= *bright*) [*sunshine*] resplandeciente, radiante; [*light*] brillante; [*colour*] brillante, luminoso; [*smile*] radiante • **his teeth were (a) ~ white** tenía los dientes de un blanco reluciente
2 (= *clever*) [*person, idea, mind*] brillante, genial; [*thesis*] brillante
3 (= *outstanding*) [*career, future*] brillante; [*success, victory*] rotundo • **the party was a ~ success** la fiesta fue un éxito rotundo *or* total
4* (= *wonderful*) [*book, film, restaurant*] genial*, buenísimo • **we had a ~ time in Spain** lo pasamos fenomenal *or* genial en España* • **she's ~ with children** se le dan fenomenal los niños* • **she's ~ at making cakes** se le da fenomenal hacer pasteles* • **brilliant!** ¡fantástico!, ¡genial!*
(N) (= *diamond*) brillante *m*

brilliantine ['brɪljənti:n] (N) brillantina *f*

brilliantly ['brɪljəntlɪ] (ADV) **1** (= *brightly*) [*shine*] intensamente, con intensidad • **~ lit** *or* **illuminated** radiantemente iluminado • **a ~ sunny morning** una mañana de sol radiante • **~ coloured** de colores vivos *or* brillantes
2 (= *superbly*) [*play, perform, act*] brillantemente; [*written, executed*] con brillantez • **she played ~** tocó brillantemente, tocó genial* • **the strategy worked ~** la estrategia funcionó a la perfección • **he succeeded ~ in politics** tuvo una brillante carrera política • **a ~ simple idea** una idea brillante y sencilla • **he was ~ successful** tuvo un éxito rotundo *or* total

Brillo pad® ['brɪləʊ,pæd] (N) estropajo *m* de aluminio

brim [brɪm] (N) [*of cup*] borde *m*; [*of hat*] ala *f*
(VI) (*also* **brim over**) rebosar, desbordarse • **to ~ with** rebosar de

brimful ['brɪm'fʊl] (ADJ) lleno hasta el borde • **~ of** *or* **with confidence** lleno *or* rebosante de confianza

-brimmed ['brɪmd] (SUFFIX) • **wide-brimmed** de ala ancha • **floppy-brimmed** flexible

brimstone ['brɪmstəʊn] (N) azufre *m*

brindled ['brɪndld] (ADJ) manchado, mosqueado

brine [braɪn] (N) (*for preserving*) salmuera *f*; (*liter*) (= *sea*) piélago *m* (*liter*), mar *m or f*

bring [brɪŋ] (PT, PP: **brought**) (VT) **1** [*person, object*] [+ *news, luck etc*] traer; [+ *person*] llevar, conducir • **~ it over here** tráelo para acá • **~ it closer** acércalo • **to ~ sth to an end** terminar con algo • **to ~ a matter to a conclusion** concluir un asunto, llevar un asunto a su desenlace • **it brought us to the verge of disaster** nos llevó al borde del desastre • **I was not brought into the matter at any stage** no me dieron voz en este asunto en ningún momento; ▹ **book**
2 (= *cause*) traer • **the hot weather ~s storms** el calor trae tormenta • **to ~ influence/pressure to bear (on)** ejercer influencia/presión (sobre) • **you ~ nothing but trouble** no haces más que causarme problemas • **it brought tears to her eyes** hizo que se le llenaran los ojos de lágrimas • **this brought him to his feet** esto hizo que se levantara • **he brought it upon himself** se lo buscó él mismo
3 (*Jur*) [+ *charge*] hacer, formular; [+ *suit*] entablar • **no charges will be brought** no se hará ninguna acusación • **the case was brought before the judge** la causa fue vista por el juez
4 (= *yield*) [+ *profit etc*] dar, producir • **to ~ a good price** alcanzar un buen precio
5 (= *induce*) • **to ~ sb to do sth** hacer que algn haga algo • **he was brought to see his error** le hicieron ver su error • **it brought me to realize that ...** me hizo comprender que ... • **he couldn't ~ himself to tell her/touch it** no se sentía con el valor suficiente para decírselo/tocarlo

▸ **bring about** (VT + ADV) **1** [+ *change*] provocar; [+ *crisis, death, war*] ocasionar, provocar
2 [+ *boat*] virar, dar la vuelta a

▸ **bring along** (VT + ADV) traer consigo, llevar consigo

▸ **bring around** (VT + ADV) **1** (= *persuade*) convencer
2 (= *steer*) [+ *conversation*] llevar, dirigir
3 [+ *unconscious person*] hacer volver en sí, reanimar

▸ **bring away** (VT + ADV) llevarse

▸ **bring back** (VT + ADV) (*lit*) [+ *person, object*] traer de vuelta; [+ *thing borrowed*] devolver; [+ *monarchy etc*] restaurar; (*to life*) devolver la vida a • **she brought a friend back for coffee** trajo una amiga a casa a tomar café • **it ~s back memories** trae recuerdos

▸ **bring down** (VT + ADV) **1** (= *lower*) [+ *prices*] bajar
2 (*Mil, Hunting*) abatir, derribar
3 (= *topple*) [+ *opponent*] derribar; [+ *government*] derrocar

▸ **bring forth** (VT + ADV) [+ *child*] dar a luz a; (*fig*) [+ *protests, criticism*] dar lugar a, suscitar (*frm*)

▸ **bring forward** (VT + ADV) **1** [+ *evidence, idea*] presentar; [+ *argument*] exponer; [+ *suggestion*] proponer; [+ *offer*] hacer
2 (= *advance time of*) [+ *date, meeting*] adelantar
3 (*Book-keeping*) pasar a otra cuenta • **brought forward** saldo *m* anterior

▸ **bring in** (VT + ADV) **1** [+ *person*] hacer entrar, hacer pasar; [+ *object*] traer; [+ *heavy object*] entrar; [+ *meal*] servir; [+ *harvest*] recoger; [+ *suspect*] detener, llevar a la comisaría • **to ~ in the police** pedir la intervención de la policía • **~ him in!** ¡que entre!, ¡que pase!
2 (= *yield*) [+ *income*] producir, proporcionar; [+ *wages*] sacar
3 (= *introduce*) [+ *fashion, custom*] introducir; (*Pol*) [+ *bill*] presentar, introducir • **to ~ in a verdict** (*Jur*) pronunciar un veredicto
4 (= *attract*) atraer • **this should ~ in the masses** esto debería atraer a las masas

▸ **bring off** (VT + ADV) **1** [+ *plan*] lograr, conseguir; [+ *success*] obtener • **he didn't ~ it off*** no le salió*
2 [+ *people from wreck*] rescatar

▸ **bring on** (VT + ADV) **1** (= *cause*) [+ *illness, quarrel*] producir, causar
2 (= *stimulate*) [+ *crops*] hacer crecer *or* madurar; [+ *flowers*] hacer florecer; [+ *growth*] estimular, favorecer
3 (*Theat, Sport*) [+ *performer*] presentar; [+ *player*] sacar (de la reserva), hacer salir

▸ **bring out** (VT + ADV) **1** (= *take out*) sacar; [+ *argument*] sacar a relucir
2 (= *introduce*) [+ *product, model*] sacar, lanzar al mercado; [+ *book*] publicar, sacar
3 (= *reveal*) [+ *colour, meaning*] realzar • **to ~ out the best in sb** sacar a la luz lo mejor que hay en algn
4 (= *develop*) [+ *quality*] sacar a la luz, despertar
5 (= *give confidence to*) [+ *person*] ayudar a adquirir confianza

▸ **bring over** (VT + ADV) **1** [+ *person, object*] ir a buscar
2 (= *convert*) [+ *person*] convertir, convencer

▸ **bring round** (VT + ADV) **1** (= *persuade*) convencer
2 (= *steer*) [+ *conversation*] llevar, dirigir
3 [+ *unconscious person*] hacer volver en sí, reanimar

▸ **bring to** (VT + ADV) **1** [+ *unconscious person*] hacer volver en sí, reanimar
2 (*Naut*) pairear, poner al pairo

▸ **bring together** (VT + ADV) reunir; [+ *enemies*] reconciliar

▸ **bring under** (VT + ADV) (= *subjugate*) someter
▸ **bring up** (VT + ADV) **1** (= *carry*) subir; [*person*] hacer subir
2 (= *rear*) [+ *child*] criar, educar • **a well brought up child** un niño bien educado • **she was badly brought up** la criaron de manera poco satisfactoria • **he was brought up to believe that ...** lo educaron en la creencia de que ... • **where were you brought up?** (*iro*) ¡cómo se ve que no has ido a colegios de pago!
3 [+ *subject*] sacar a colación, sacar a relucir; (*in meeting*) plantar
4 (= *vomit*) devolver, vomitar
5 • **to ~ sb up short** parar a algn en seco
6 • **to ~ up the rear** (*Mil*) cerrar la marcha
7 • **to ~ sb up in court** (*Jur*) hacer comparecer a algn ante el magistrado
bring-and-buy sale [ˌbrɪŋəndˈbaɪseɪl] (N) (*Brit*) *venta de objetos usados con fines benéficos*
bringer [ˈbrɪŋəʳ] (N) (*liter*) portador(a) *m/f*
brink [brɪŋk] (N) (*lit, fig*) borde *m* • **on the ~ of sth** al borde de algo • **to be on the ~ of doing sth** estar a punto de hacer algo
brinkmanship [ˈbrɪŋkmənʃɪp] (N) política *f* arriesgada
briny [ˈbraɪnɪ] (ADJ) salado, salobre
(N) • **the ~**† (*also hum*) el mar
brio [ˈbriːəʊ] (N) (= *vigour*) brío *m*
brioche [brɪˈɒʃ] (N) brioche *m*
briquette [brɪˈket] (N) briqueta *f*
brisk [brɪsk] (ADJ) (COMPAR: **brisker**, SUPERL: **briskest**) [*walk*] enérgico; [*person, voice, movement*] enérgico, dinámico; [*manner*] brusco; [*wind, day*] fresco; [*trade*] activo • **at a ~ pace** con paso brioso *or* enérgico • **business is ~** (*in shop etc*) el negocio lleva un buen ritmo • **trading was ~ today** (*St Ex*) hoy hubo mucho movimiento en la bolsa, hoy el mercado estuvo muy dinámico
brisket [ˈbrɪskɪt] (N) carne *f* de pecho (para asar)
briskly [ˈbrɪsklɪ] (ADV) [*speak, say*] enérgicamente; [*walk, trot, march*] con brío, con paso enérgico • **these goods are selling ~** estos artículos se están vendiendo mucho
briskness [ˈbrɪsknɪs] (N) [*of walk, movement*] brío *m*; [*of manner*] brusquedad *f*; [*of trade*] dinamismo *m*
brisling [ˈbrɪzlɪŋ] (N) espadín *m* (noruego)
bristle [ˈbrɪsl] (N) [*of brush, on animal*] cerda *f*; [*of beard*] • **~(s)** barba *f* (incipiente)
(VI) **1** [*hair etc*] erizarse, ponerse de punta • **to ~ with** (*fig*) estar erizado de • **he ~d with anger** se enfureció
2 (*fig*) [*person*] resentirse (**at** de)
(CPD) ▸ **bristle brush** cepillo *m* de púas
bristling [ˈbrɪslɪŋ] (ADJ) **1** [*moustache, beard, eyebrows*] hirsuto
2 (= *energetic*) enérgico
bristly [ˈbrɪslɪ] (ADJ) (COMPAR: **bristlier**, SUPERL: **bristliest**) [*beard, hair*] erizado • **to have a ~ chin** tener la barba crecida
Bristol [ˈbrɪstəl] (N) • **~ board** cartulina *f*; ▹ shipshape
bristols‡ [ˈbrɪstəlz] (NPL) (*Brit*) (= *breasts*) tetas* *fpl*
Brit* [brɪt] (N) británico/a *m/f*; (*loosely*) inglés/esa *m/f*
Britain [ˈbrɪtən] (N) (*also* **Great Britain**) Gran Bretaña *f*; (*loosely*) Inglaterra *f*
Britannia [brɪˈtænɪə] (N) Britania *f* (*figura que representa simbólicamente a Gran Bretaña*); ▹ RULE BRITANNIA
Britannic [brɪˈtænɪk] (ADJ) • **His/Her ~ Majesty** su Majestad Británica
britches [ˈbrɪtʃəz] (NPL) = **breeches**
Briticism [ˈbrɪtɪsɪzəm] (N) (*US*) modismo *m* *or* vocablo *m* *etc* del inglés británico
British [ˈbrɪtɪʃ] (ADJ) (*gen*) británico; (*loosely*) inglés • **the best of ~ (luck)!*** ¡y un cuerno!*
(NPL) • **the ~** los británicos; (*loosely*) los ingleses
(CPD) ▸ **British Asian** británico/a *m/f* de origen asiático ▸ **the British Broadcasting Corporation** la BBC ▸ **British Columbia** Columbia *f* Británica ▸ **British Council** (*in other countries*) Consejo *m* Británico ▸ **the British disease** (*hum*) *la falta de motivación laboral de los años 60-70 en el Reino Unido* ▸ **British English** inglés *m* británico ▸ **the British Isles** las islas Británicas ▸ **British Legion** *organización de veteranos de las dos guerras mundiales*; ▹ LEGION ▸ **British Museum** Museo *m* Británico ▸ **British Rail** *la antigua compañía estatal de ferrocarriles británicos, privatizada en 1993*, ≈ RENFE *f* (*Sp*) ▸ **British Sign Language** lenguaje *m* de signos británico ▸ **British Summer Time** *hora de verano en Gran Bretaña* ▸ **British Thermal Unit** unidad *f* térmica británica

BRITAIN

A veces se usa el término **England** para referirse a la totalidad del país, aunque no es un término usado con precisión; sin embargo, mucha gente confunde a menudo los nombres **Britain**, **Great Britain**, **United Kingdom** y **British Isles**.

Se denomina **Great Britain** a la isla que comprende Inglaterra, Escocia y Gales. Desde el punto de vista administrativo, el término también incluye las islas menores cercanas, a excepción de la isla de Man (**Isle of Man**) y las islas Anglonormandas o islas del Canal de la Mancha (**Channel Islands**).

United Kingdom (of Great Britain and Northern Ireland), o **UK**, es la unidad política que comprende Gran Bretaña e Irlanda del Norte.

British Isles es el término geográfico que abarca Gran Bretaña, Irlanda, la isla de Man y las islas Anglonormandas. En lo político, el término comprende dos estados soberanos: el Reino Unido y la República de Irlanda.

El término **Britain** se utiliza fundamentalmente para referirse al Reino Unido, y en algunas ocasiones también a la isla, a Gran Bretaña.

BRITISH COUNCIL

El **British Council** se creó en 1935 para fomentar la cultura británica en el extranjero y actualmente tiene delegaciones en más de 100 países. Sus principales cometidos son la organización de actividades culturales, tales como exposiciones y conferencias, con el fin de dar a conocer el arte, la ciencia y la literatura del país, así como la enseñanza del inglés, además de ayudar a aquellos que desean estudiar en el Reino Unido.

Britisher [ˈbrɪtɪʃəʳ] (N) (*US*) británico/a *m/f*, natural *mf* de Gran Bretaña
Briton [ˈbrɪtən] (N) británico/a *m/f*; (*loosely*) inglés/esa *m/f*
Britpop [ˈbrɪtpɒp] (N) Britpop *m*
Brittany [ˈbrɪtənɪ] (N) Bretaña *f*
brittle [ˈbrɪtl] (ADJ) (COMPAR: **brittler**, SUPERL: **brittlest**) quebradizo
brittle-bone disease [ˌbrɪtlˈbəʊndɪziːz] (N) osteogénesis *f* imperfecta
brittleness [ˈbrɪtlnɪs] (N) lo quebradizo
Bro. (ABBR) (= **Brother**) H., Hno.
broach [brəʊtʃ] (VT) **1** [+ *cask*] espitar; [+ *bottle etc*] abrir
2 [+ *subject*] abordar, sacar a colación • **he didn't ~ the subject** no sacó el tema a colación, no abordó ese tema
broad [brɔːd] (ADJ) (COMPAR: **broader**, SUPERL: **broadest**) **1** (= *wide*) [*road*] ancho, amplio; [*shoulders*] ancho; [*forehead*] despejado, amplio; [*smile*] de oreja a oreja, abierto (*liter*) • **it is three metres ~** tiene tres metros de ancho • **a ~ expanse of lawn** una amplia extensión de césped • **to be ~ in the shoulder** [*person*] ser ancho de hombros *or* de espaldas; [*garment*] ser ancho de hombros
• IDIOMS: • **to be ~ in the beam*** (*pej*) [*person*] tener un buen trasero*, tener buenas posaderas* • **it's as ~ as it's long*** lo mismo da
2 (= *general, extensive*) [*outline, objectives, view*] general • **in ~ terms** en términos generales • **the ~ outlines of sth** las líneas generales de algo • **to be in ~ agreement** estar de acuerdo en líneas generales
3 (= *wide-ranging*) [*education, syllabus*] amplio; [*range, spectrum*] amplio, extenso; [*mind*] abierto • **a ~ spectrum of opinion** un amplio espectro de opiniones • **a film with ~ appeal** una película que atrae a una amplia gama de público • **it has ~er implications** tiene repercusiones en más aspectos • **in its ~est sense** en su sentido más amplio
4 (= *unsubtle*) [*hint*] claro
5 (= *strong*) [*accent*] cerrado • **(in) ~ Scots/Yorkshire** (con) un acento escocés/de Yorkshire cerrado
6 (= *coarse*) • **~ humour** humor *m* ordinario *or* basto • **a ~ joke** una broma ordinaria *or* grosera
7 • **in ~ daylight** en plena luz del día
(N) **1** (*US**) tipa* *f*, tía *f* (*Sp**)
2 (= *widest part*) • **the ~ of the back** la parte más ancha de la espalda • **the (Norfolk) Broads** (*Geog*) *área de estuarios en Norfolk*
(CPD) ▸ **broad bean** (*esp Brit*) haba *f* gruesa ▸ **broad church** (= *organization*) organización *f* abierta *or* liberal ▸ **broad jump** (*US*) salto *m* de longitud
broadband [ˈbrɔːdbænd] (N) banda *f* ancha
(CPD) ▸ **broadband access** acceso *m* de banda ancha
broad-based [ˈbrɔːdˈbeɪst] (ADJ) = **broadly-based**
broad-brimmed [ˈbrɔːdˈbrɪmd] (ADJ) [*hat*] de ala ancha
broad-brush [ˌbrɔːdˈbrʌʃ] (ADJ) [*strategy, approach*] muy general
broadcast [ˈbrɔːdkɑːst] (VB: PT, PP: **broadcast**) (N) (*Rad, TV*) emisión *f*, programa *m*
(VT) **1** (*TV*) [+ *match, event*] transmitir; (*Rad*) emitir, radiar
2 (*Agr*) sembrar a voleo
3 (*fig*) [+ *news, rumour*] divulgar, difundir
(VI) (*TV, Rad*) [*station*] transmitir, emitir; [*person*] hablar por la radio/televisión
(ADV) [*sow*] a voleo
(CPD) (*Agr*) [*seed*] sembrado a voleo ▸ **broadcast journalism** periodismo *m* de radio y televisión ▸ **broadcast journalist** periodista *mf* de radio y televisión ▸ **broadcast media** medios *mpl* de radiodifusión y teledifusión ▸ **broadcast news** noticias *fpl* de radio y televisión ▸ **broadcast satellite** satélite *m* de retransmisiones
broadcaster [ˈbrɔːdkɑːstəʳ] (N) (*Rad, TV*) locutor(a) *m/f*
broadcasting [ˈbrɔːdkɑːstɪŋ] (N) (*TV*) teledifusión *f*, transmisión *f*; (*Rad*) radiodifusión *f*
(CPD) ▸ **broadcasting station** emisora *f*

b

broadcloth ['brɔːdklɒθ] (N) velarte *m*
broaden ['brɔːdn] (VT) [+ *road*] ensanchar; [+ *horizons, outlook*] ampliar • **travel ~s the mind** los viajes son muy educativos
(VI) (*also* **broaden out**) ensancharse
broadleaved ['brɔːd'liːvd] (ADJ) de hoja ancha
broadloom ['brɔːdluːm] (ADJ) • **~ carpet** alfombra *f* sin costuras
broadly ['brɔːdlɪ] (ADV) **1** (= *by and large*) [*agree, accept*] en líneas generales • **~ similar** parecido en líneas generales • **~ speaking** en general, hablando en términos generales • **it is ~ true that ...** en líneas generales es verdad que ...
2 (= *widely*) [*smile, grin*] abiertamente, de oreja a oreja
3 (= *unsubtly*) [*hint*] claramente
broadly-based ['brɔːdlɪ,beɪst] (ADJ) que cuenta con una base amplia • **a broadly-based coalition** una coalición que representa gran diversidad de intereses
broad-minded ['brɔːd'maɪndɪd] (ADJ) tolerante, de miras amplias
broad-mindedness ['brɔːd'maɪndɪdnɪs] (N) amplitud *f* de criterio, tolerancia *f*
broadness ['brɔːdnɪs] (N) **1** (*in dimension*) anchura *f*, extensión *f*
2 [*of accent*] lo cerrado
broadsheet ['brɔːdʃiːt] (N) periódico *m* de gran formato; ▷ BROADSHEETS AND TABLOIDS

BROADSHEETS AND TABLOIDS

En el Reino Unido se utilizan los términos **broadsheet** y **tabloid** para referirse tanto a dos formatos distintos de periódicos como a dos géneros diferentes de prensa. Dado que la prensa seria empleaba tradicionalmente el formato grande, **broadsheet** se convirtió en sinómino de calidad y seriedad en la información. Por otro lado, la prensa más popular empleaba el formato tabloide, más pequeño, con lo que el término **tabloids** se asociaba a las noticias sensacionalistas, los escándalos y los cotilleos de la prensa rosa. En la actualidad, la mayor parte de los periódicos de calidad británicos han adoptado también el formato más pequeño, pero debido a las connotaciones negativas o sensacionalistas que todavía tiene la palabra **tabloid**, la prensa seria prefiere definir su nuevo formato como **compact** (compacto).
En Estados Unidos, el término **standard-sized newspapers** es el equivalente a **broadsheet**.

broad-shouldered ['brɔːd'ʃəʊldəd] (ADJ) ancho de espaldas
broadside ['brɔːdsaɪd] (N) (*Naut*) (= *side*) costado *m*; (= *shots*) (*also fig*) andanada *f* • **to fire a ~** (*lit, fig*) soltar *or* disparar una andanada • **~ on** (*as adv*) de costado
(ADV) • **to be moored ~ to sth** estar amarrado de costado a algo
broad-spectrum [,brɔːd'spektrəm] (ADJ) [*antibiotic, vaccine, herbicide, pesticide*] de amplio espectro
broadsword ['brɔːd,sɔːd] (N) sable *m*
Broadway ['brɔːd,weɪ] (N) Broadway *m* (*calle de Nueva York famosa por sus teatros*); ▷ OFF-BROADWAY
(CPD) [*musical, theatre*] de Broadway
broadways ['brɔːdweɪz] (ADV), **broadwise** ['brɔːdwaɪz] (ADV) a lo ancho, por lo ancho • **~ on to the waves** de costado a las olas
brocade [brəʊ'keɪd] (N) brocado *m*
brocaded [brəʊ'keɪdɪd] (ADJ) con brocado
broccoli ['brɒkəlɪ] (N) brécol *m*, brócoli *m*
brochure ['brəʊʃjʊəʳ] (N) folleto *m*
brock [brɒk] (N) (*Brit*) (*liter*) tejón *m*

brogue¹ [brəʊg] (N) (= *shoe*) zapato *m* grueso de cuero
brogue² [brəʊg] (N) (= *accent*) acento *m* regional (*sobre todo irlandés*)
broil [brɔɪl] (VT) (*US*) (*Culin*) asar a la parrilla
broiler ['brɔɪləʳ] (N) **1** (= *chicken*) pollo *m* para asar
2 (*US*) (= *grill*) parrilla *f*, grill *m*
(CPD) ▸ **broiler house** batería *f* de engorde
broiling ['brɔɪlɪŋ] (ADJ) [*sun*] achicharrante • **it's ~ hot** hace un calor achicharrante
broke [brəʊk] (PT) *of* **break**
(ADJ) **1*** (*incorrect usage*) (= *broken*) estropeado • IDIOM: • **if it ain't ~, don't fix it*** no hay que complicar las cosas *or* complicarse la vida sin necesidad
2* (= *penniless*) pelado* • **I'm ~** estoy pelado*, estoy sin un duro (*Sp**), estoy sin un peso (*LAm**) • **to go ~** arruinarse • IDIOM: • **to go for ~** jugarse el todo por el todo; ▷ **flat**
broken ['brəʊkən] (PP) *of* **break**
(ADJ) **1** [*object*] roto, quebrado (*LAm*); [*bone*] roto, fracturado; [*skin*] cortado • **"do not use on ~ skin"** "no aplicar si hay cortes o heridas en la piel" • **he sounds like a ~ record** parece un disco rallado
2 (= *not working*) [*machine*] estropeado, averiado
3 (= *uneven*) [*road surface*] accidentado
4 (= *ruined*) [*health, spirit*] quebrantado; [*heart*] roto, destrozado • **to die of a ~ heart** morir de pena • **~ in health** deshecho, muy decaído • **a ~ man** un hombre deshecho • **a ~ reed** (*fig*) una persona quemada
5 (= *interrupted*) [*line*] quebrado; [*voice*] entrecortado; [*sleep*] interrumpido; [*cloud*] fragmentario • **he speaks ~ English** chapurrea el inglés • **she had a ~ night** durmió mal, despertándose a cada momento
6 (= *failed*) [*marriage*] deshecho • **a ~ home** una familia dividida
7 [*promise*] roto, quebrantado
broken-down ['brəʊkən'daʊn] (ADJ) [*machine, car*] averiado, estropeado, descompuesto (*Mex*); [*house*] destartalado, desvencijado
broken-hearted ['brəʊkən'hɑːtɪd] (ADJ) con el corazón destrozado *or* partido
brokenly ['brəʊkənlɪ] (ADV) [*say etc*] en tono angustiado, con palabras entrecortadas
broker ['brəʊkəʳ] (N) (*Comm*) agente *mf*; (= *stockbroker*) corredor(a) *m/f* de bolsa, bolsista *mf*
(VT) [+ *deal, agreement*] negociar
brokerage ['brəʊkərɪdʒ] (N) corretaje *m*
broking ['brəʊkɪŋ] (N) = **brokerage**
brolly* ['brɒlɪ] (N) (*Brit*) paraguas *m inv*
bromance* ['brəʊmæns] (N) *amistad íntima entre hombres*
bromide ['brəʊmaɪd] (N) **1** (*Chem, Typ*) bromuro *m*
2 (*fig*) (= *platitude*) perogrullada *f*
bromine ['brəʊmiːn] (N) bromo *m*
bronchi ['brɒŋkaɪ] (NPL) *of* **bronchus**
bronchial ['brɒŋkɪəl] (ADJ) bronquial
(CPD) ▸ **bronchial asthma** asma *f* bronquial ▸ **bronchial tubes** bronquios *mpl*
bronchitic [brɒŋ'kɪtɪk] (ADJ) bronquítico
bronchitis [brɒŋ'kaɪtɪs] (N) bronquitis *f*
bronchopneumonia [,brɒŋkəʊnjuː'məʊnɪə] (N) bronconeumonía *f*
broncho-pulmonary ['brɒŋkəʊ'pʌlmənərɪ] (ADJ) broncopulmonar
bronchus ['brɒŋkəs] (N) (PL: **bronchi** ['brɒŋkaɪ]) bronquio *m*
bronco ['brɒŋkəʊ] (N) (*US*) potro *m* cerril
broncobuster* ['brɒŋkəʊ,bʌstəʳ] (N) (*US*) domador *m* de potros cerriles, domador *m* de caballos

brontosaurus [,brɒntə'sɔːrəs] (N) (PL: **brontosauruses** *or* **brontosauri** [,brɒntə'sɔːraɪ]) brontosaurio *m*
Bronx cheer* [,brɒŋks'tʃɪəʳ] (N) (*US*) pedorreta‡ *f*
bronze [brɒnz] (N) **1** (= *metal, sculpture*) bronce *m*
2 [*of skin*] bronceado *m*
(VI) [*person*] broncearse
(VT) [+ *skin*] broncear
(ADJ) (= *made of bronze*) de bronce; [*colour*] color de bronce
(CPD) ▸ **the Bronze Age** la Edad de Bronce ▸ **bronze medal** medalla *f* de bronce ▸ **bronze medallist** medallero/a *m/f* de bronce
bronzed [brɒnzd] (ADJ) [*person*] bronceado
bronzer ['brɒnzəʳ] (N) **1** (= *make-up*) base *f* bronceadora
2 (*for tanning*) bronceador *m* artificial
bronzing ['brɒnzɪŋ] (ADJ) [*powder, gel*] bronceador
brooch [brəʊtʃ] (N) prendedor *m*, broche *m*; (*ancient*) fíbula *f*
brood [bruːd] (N) (*gen*) cría *f*, camada *f*; [*of chicks*] nidada *f*; [*of insects etc*] generación *f*; (*hum*) [*of children*] prole *f*
(VI) **1** [*bird*] empollar
2 (*fig*) [*person*] ponerse melancólico • **to ~ on** *or* **over** dar vueltas a • **you mustn't ~ over it** no debes darle tantas vueltas • **disaster ~ed over the town** se cernía el desastre sobre la ciudad
(CPD) ▸ **brood mare** yegua *f* de cría
brooding ['bruːdɪŋ] (ADJ) [*evil, presence etc*] siniestro, amenazador
broodings ['bruːdɪŋs] (NPL) meditaciones *fpl*
broody ['bruːdɪ] (ADJ) (COMPAR: **broodier**, SUPERL: **broodiest**) **1** [*hen*] clueca; [*woman**] con ganas de tener hijos
2 (= *pensive*) triste, melancólico
brook¹ [brʊk] (N) (= *stream*) arroyo *m*
brook² [brʊk] (VT) (*frm*) (= *tolerate*) tolerar, admitir • **he ~s no opposition** no admite oposición
brooklet ['brʊklɪt] (N) arroyuelo *m*
broom [bruːm, brʊm] (N) **1** (= *brush*) escoba *f* • **new ~** (*fig*) escoba *f* nueva • PROVERB: • **a new ~ sweeps clean** escoba nueva barre bien
2 (*Bot*) retama *f*, hiniesta *f*
(CPD) ▸ **broom closet** (*US*), **broom cupboard** (*Brit*) armario *m* de los artículos de limpieza
broomstick ['brʊmstɪk] (N) palo *m* de escoba
Bros. (ABBR) (= **Brothers**) Hnos
broth [brɒθ] (N) caldo *m*
brothel ['brɒθl] (N) burdel *m*, prostíbulo *m*
brother ['brʌðəʳ] (N) (*also Rel*) hermano *m*; (*Trade Union etc*) compañero *m* • **hey, ~!*** ¡oye, colega!*, ¡oye, tío! (*Sp**) • **oh, ~!*** ¡vaya hombre!
(CPD) ▸ **brother workers** colegas *mpl*
brotherhood ['brʌðəhʊd] (N) **1** fraternidad *f* • **the ~ of man** la fraternidad humana
2 (= *group*) hermandad *f*
brother-in-arms ['brʌðəɪn'ɑːmz] (N) (PL: **brothers-in-arms**) compañero *m* de armas
brother-in-law ['brʌðərɪnlɔː] (N) (PL: **brothers-in-law**) cuñado *m*, hermano *m* político
brotherly ['brʌðəlɪ] (ADJ) fraterno, fraternal
brougham [bruːm] (N) break *m*
brought [brɔːt] (PT), (PP) *of* **bring**
brouhaha* ['bruːhɑːhɑː] (N) barullo *m*
brow [braʊ] (N) **1** (= *forehead*) frente *f*; (*also* **eyebrow**) ceja *f*; ▷ **knit**
2 [*of hill*] cumbre *f*, cima *f*; [*of cliff*] borde *m*
browbeat ['braʊbiːt] (PT: **browbeat**, PP: **browbeaten**) (VT) intimidar, convencer con amenazas • **to ~ sb into doing sth** intimidar

a algn para que haga algo
brown [braʊn] ADJ (COMPAR: **browner**, SUPERL: **brownest**) **1** (*gen*) marrón, color café (*LAm*); [*hair*] castaño; [*leather*] marrón
2 (= *tanned*) moreno, bronceado; [*skin*] moreno • **to go ~** ponerse moreno, broncearse • IDIOM: • **as ~ as a berry** muy moreno, bronceadísimo
N marrón *m*, color *m* café (*LAm*); [*of eyes, hair*] castaño *m*
VT **1** [*sun*] [+ *person*] broncear, poner moreno
2 (*Culin*) dorar
VI **1** [*leaves etc*] volverse de color marrón
2 [*skin*] ponerse moreno, broncearse
3 (*Culin*) dorarse
CPD ▸ **brown ale** cerveza *f* oscura *or* negra ▸ **brown bear** oso *m* pardo ▸ **brown belt** (*in judo, karate*) cinturón *m* marrón ▸ **brown bread** pan *m* negro, pan *m* moreno (*Sp*) ▸ **brown egg** huevo *m* moreno ▸ **brown goods** (productos *mpl* de) línea *f* marrón, (productos *mpl* de) gama *f* marrón ▸ **brown owl** (*Orn*) autillo *m* ▸ **brown paper** papel *m* de estraza ▸ **brown rice** arroz *m* integral ▸ **brown sauce** (*Brit*) *salsa de condimento, con sabor agridulce* ▸ **brown study** • IDIOM: • **to be in a ~ study**† estar absorto en sus pensamientos, estar en Babia* ▸ **brown sugar** azúcar *m* moreno
▸ **brown off*** VT + ADV (*Brit*) fastidiar
browned-off* [ˌbraʊnd'ɒf] ADJ (*Brit*) • **I'm browned-off** estoy harto *or* hasta las narices* (**with** de)
brownfield ['braʊnfi:ld] ADJ [*site, land*] previamente urbanizado
brownie ['braʊnɪ] N **1** (= *fairy*) duende *m*
2 (*also* **Brownie Guide**) niña *f* exploradora • IDIOM: • **to earn** *or* **win Brownie points** (*hum*) apuntarse tantos a favor, hacer méritos
3 (*US*) (= *cookie*) pastelillo *m* de chocolate y nueces
browning ['braʊnɪŋ] N (*Brit*) (*Culin*) aditamento *m* colorante
brownish ['braʊnɪʃ] ADJ pardusco, que tira a moreno
brown-nose‡ ['braʊnˌnəʊz] (*US*) N lameculos** *mf inv*
VT lamer el culo a**
brown-nosing‡ ['braʊnˌnəʊzɪŋ] N • **they have to do some brown-nosing** tienen que lamer el culo a unas cuantas personas**
brownout ['braʊnaʊt] N (*esp US*) (= *drop in voltage*) oscilación *f*
Brownshirt ['braʊnʃɜ:t] N (*Hist*) *soldado de las SA en la Alemania nazi*
brownstone ['braʊnstəʊn] N (*US*) (casa *f* construida con) piedra *f* caliza de color rojizo
browse [braʊz] VI **1** (*in shop*) echar una ojeada, curiosear • **to spend an hour browsing in a bookshop** pasar una hora hojeando los libros en una librería
2 [*animal*] pacer
3 (*Internet*) curiosear
VT **1** (*also* **browse through**) [+ *book*] hojear; [+ *clothes*] mirar, echar un vistazo a
2 [*animal*] [+ *grass*] pacer; [+ *trees*] ramonear
N • **to have a ~ (around)** echar una ojeada *or* un vistazo
▸ **browse on** VI + PREP [*animal*] pacer
browser ['braʊzəʳ] N **1** (*in shop*) *persona que entra a una tienda a curiosear*
2 (*Internet*) navegador *m*
brucellosis [ˌbru:sə'ləʊsɪs] N brucelosis *f*
Bruges [bru:ʒ] N Brujas *f*
bruise [bru:z] N (*on person*) cardenal *m*, moretón *m* (*esp LAm*); (*on fruit*) maca *f*, magulladura *f*
VT **1** [+ *leg etc*] magullar, amoratar (*esp LAm*); [+ *fruit*] magullar, dañar
2 (*fig*) [+ *feelings*] herir
VI • **I ~ easily** me salen cardenales *or* moretones con facilidad
bruised ['bru:zd] ADJ magullado, amoratado (*esp LAm*)
bruiser* ['bru:zəʳ] N gorila* *m*
bruising ['bru:zɪŋ] ADJ [*experience*] doloroso, penoso; [*match*] durísimo, violento
bruit† [bru:t] VT • **to ~ about** (*US*) (*liter*) rumorear
Brum* [brʌm] N (*Brit*) = **Birmingham**
Brummie* ['brʌmɪ] N (*Brit*) nativo/a *m/f or* habitante *mf* de Birmingham
brunch [brʌntʃ] N desayuno-almuerzo *m*
Brunei [bru:'naɪ] N Brunei *m*
brunette [bru:'net] N morena *f*, morocha *f* (*LAm*), prieta *f* (*Mex*)
ADJ moreno
brunt [brʌnt] N • **the ~ of the attack** lo más fuerte del ataque • **the ~ of the work** la mayor parte del trabajo • **to bear the ~ of sth** aguantar lo más recio *or* duro de algo
bruschetta [bru:'sketə] N bruschetta *f*
brush [brʌʃ] N **1** (*gen*) cepillo *m*; (= *sweeping brush*) cepillo *m*, escobilla *f*; (= *scrubbing brush*) cepillo *m* de cerda; (= *shaving brush, decorator's*) brocha *f*; (= *paint brush*) (*artist's*) pincel *m*; (*Elec*) (= *contact*) escobilla *f* • **shoe ~** cepillo *m* para zapatos
2 (= *act of brushing*) cepillado *m* • **give your coat a ~** cepíllate el abrigo • **let's give it a ~** vamos a pasar el cepillo
3 (= *tail*) [*of fox*] rabo *m*, hopo *m*
4 (= *skirmish*) roce *m* • **to have a ~ with the police** tener un roce con la policía
5 (= *light touch*) toque *m*
6 (= *undergrowth*) maleza *f*, broza *f*
VT **1** (= *clean*) [+ *floor*] cepillar; [+ *clothes, hair*] cepillar • **to ~ one's shoes** limpiarse los zapatos • **to ~ one's teeth** lavarse los dientes, cepillarse los dientes
2 (= *touch lightly*) rozar
▸ **brush against** VI + PREP rozar (al pasar)
▸ **brush aside** VT + ADV (*fig*) no hacer caso de, dejar a un lado
▸ **brush away** VT + ADV (*gen*) quitar (con cepillo *or* la mano *etc*)
▸ **brush down** VT + ADV cepillar, limpiar; [+ *horse*] almohazar
▸ **brush off** VT + ADV **1** [+ *mud*] quitar (con cepillo *or* la mano *etc*)
2 (*fig*) (= *dismiss*) no hacer caso de
VI + ADV • **the mud ~es off easily** el barro sale *or* se quita fácilmente
▸ **brush past** VT + ADV rozar al pasar
VI + ADV pasar muy cerca
▸ **brush up** VT + ADV **1** [+ *crumbs*] recoger
2 (= *improve, revise*) (*also* **brush up on**) repasar, refrescar
brushed [brʌʃt] ADJ [*nylon, denim etc*] afelpado
CPD ▸ **brushed cotton** felpa *f*
brush-off* ['brʌʃɒf] N • **to give sb the brush-off** mandar a algn a paseo*, zafarse de algn
brushstroke ['brʌʃstrəʊk] N pincelada *f* • **in broad ~s** (*fig*) a grandes rasgos
brush-up ['brʌʃʌp] N • **to have a wash and brush-up** lavarse y arreglarse
brushwood ['brʌʃwʊd] N maleza *f*, monte *m* bajo; (= *faggots*) broza *f*, leña *f* menuda
brushwork ['brʌʃwɜ:k] N pincelada *f*, técnica *f* del pincel • **Turner's ~** la pincelada de Turner, la técnica del pincel de Turner
brusque [bru:sk] ADJ (COMPAR: **brusquer**, SUPERL: **brusquest**) [*comment, manner etc*] brusco, áspero; [*person*] brusco • **he was very ~ with me** me trató con poca cortesía *or* con aspereza
brusquely ['bru:sklɪ] ADV bruscamente, con brusquedad, abruptamente
brusqueness ['bru:sknɪs] N brusquedad *f*, aspereza *f*
Brussels ['brʌslz] N Bruselas *f*
CPD ▸ **Brussels sprout** col *f* de Bruselas
brutal ['bru:tl] ADJ **1** (= *savage*) [*person, murder, attack*] brutal; [*tone, remark*] cruel • **the government's ~ treatment of political prisoners** la brutalidad *or* la crueldad con la que el gobierno trata a los prisioneros políticos
2 (= *stark*) [*honesty, frankness*] descarnada; [*reality*] crudo; [*change*] brutal
3 (= *harsh*) [*weather, climate*] crudo, riguroso
brutalism ['bru:təlɪzəm] N (*Archit*) brutalismo *m*
brutality [bru:'tælɪtɪ] N [*of person*] brutalidad *f*; [*of murder*] salvajismo *m*, crueldad *f*; ▹ **police**
brutalize ['bru:təlaɪz] VT brutalizar
brutally ['bru:təlɪ] ADV **1** (= *savagely*) [*attack, murder, suppress*] de manera brutal, brutalmente
2 (= *starkly*) [*say, reply, expose*] crudamente, descarnadamente • **let me be ~ honest/frank with you** voy a serte tremendamente sincero/franco • **the talks had been ~ frank** las conversaciones habían sido francas y crudas • **a ~ competitive world** un mundo despiadadamente competitivo • **the choice is ~ clear** la elección es de una claridad cruel *or* despiadada
brute [bru:t] N (= *animal*) bestia *f*; (= *person*) bruto/a *m/f*, bestia *mf* • **you ~!** ¡bestia!, ¡animal!* • **it's a ~ of a problem*** es un problema de los más feos
ADJ [*force, strength*] bruto; [*fact*] crudo; [*emotion*] tosco
brutish ['bru:tɪʃ] ADJ bruto
Brutus ['bru:təs] N Bruto
Brylcreem® ['brɪlkri:m] N gomina *f*, fijador *m* (*de pelo*)
VT engominar, echarse gomina en
BS N ABBR **1** (= **British Standard**) *norma de calidad*
2 (*US*) (*Univ*) (= **Bachelor of Science**) ▹ DEGREE
3 (*esp US‡*) = **bullshit**
bs N ABBR **1** (*Comm*) = **bill of sale**
2 (*Comm, Econ*) = **balance sheet**
BSA N ABBR (*US*) = **Boy Scouts of America**
BSB N ABBR (= **British Sky Broadcasting**) *emisora de televisión por satélite*
BSC N ABBR = **Broadcasting Standards Council**
BSc N ABBR (*Univ*) (= **Bachelor of Science**) ▹ DEGREE
BSE N ABBR = **bovine spongiform encephalopathy**
BSI N ABBR (*Brit*) (= **British Standards Institution**) *organismo que fija niveles de calidad de los productos*
B-side ['bi:saɪd] N cara *f* B
BSL N ABBR (= **British Sign Language**) lenguaje *m* de signos británico
BST N ABBR (*Brit*) = **British Summer Time**
BT N ABBR (= **British Telecom**) ≈ Telefónica *f* (*Sp*)
Bt ABBR = **Baronet**
bt ABBR (= **beat**) derrotó
BTA N ABBR = **British Tourist Authority**
BTEC ['bi:tek] N ABBR (*Brit*) = **Business and Technology Education Council**
1 (= *organization*) *institución responsable de los estudios de ciencia y tecnología empresarial*
2 (= *diploma*) *estudios de ciencia y tecnología empresarial*
bt fwd ABBR = **brought forward**

BTU, **btu** (N ABBR) = **British Thermal Unit**
BTW* (ABBR) (= **by the way**) por cierto
bub* [bʌb] (N) (US) colega* *m*
bubble ['bʌbl] (N) (*in liquid*) burbuja *f*; (*in paint*) ampolla *f*; (= *soap bubble*) pompa *f*; (*in cartoon*) bocadillo *m*, globo *m* • **to blow ~s** (*with soap*) hacer pompas; (*with bubble gum*) hacer globos • **the ~ burst** (*fig*) se deshizo la burbuja
(VI) [*champagne, bath water*] burbujear; (= *bubble forth*) borbotar
(CPD) ▸ **bubble and squeak** (*Brit*) (*Culin*) *carne picada frita con patatas y col* ▸ **bubble bath** gel *m* de baño ▸ **bubble car** coche-cabina *m*, huevo *m* ▸ **bubble gum** chicle *m* (de globo) ▸ **bubble memory** memoria *f* de burbuja ▸ **bubble pack** envasado *m* en lámina ▸ **bubble wrap** envoltorio *m* de plástico con burbujas
▸ **bubble over** (VI + ADV) [*boiling liquid*] derramarse; (*fig*) (*with happiness etc*) rebosar (with de)
▸ **bubble up** (VI + ADV) [*liquid*] burbujear, borbotear
bubblehead‡ ['bʌblhed] (N) (*esp US*) (*pej*) cabeza *mf* de chorlito*
bubblejet printer ['bʌbldʒet'prɪntəʳ] (N) impresora *f* de inyección de burbujas
bubbler ['bʌbləʳ] (N) (*US, Australia*) (= *drinking fountain*) fuente *f*, bebedero *m*
bubbly ['bʌblɪ] (ADJ) (COMPAR: **bubblier**, SUPERL: **bubbliest**) (*lit*) burbujeante, con burbujas; (*fig**) [*person*] lleno de vida, dicharachero
(N)* (= *champagne*) champaña *f*
bubonic plague [bju:ˌbɒnɪk'pleɪg] (N) peste *f* bubónica
buccaneer [ˌbʌkə'nɪəʳ] (N) (*Hist*) bucanero *m*; (*fig*) emprendedor(a) *m/f*
(VI) piratear
buccaneering [ˌbʌkə'nɪərɪŋ] (ADJ) (*fig*) aventurero
Bucharest [ˌbu:kə'rest] (N) Bucarest *m*
buck [bʌk] (N) **1** (= *male*) [*of deer*] ciervo *m* (macho); [*of rabbit*] conejo *m* (macho); (= *antelope*) antílope *m*
2 (*US**) (= *dollar*) dólar *m* • **to make a ~** hacer dinero • **to make a fast** *or* **quick ~** hacer dinero fácil
3 • IDIOMS: • **to pass the ~*** escurrir el bulto*, pasar la pelota* • **to pass the ~ to sb** cargar el muerto a algn*, pasar la pelota a algn* • **the ~ stops here** yo soy el responsable/nosotros somos los responsables
4 (*in gym*) potro *m*
5 (*US**) • **young ~** joven *m*
6† (= *dandy*) galán *m*, dandy *m*
(ADJ) (= *male*) macho
(ADV) • **~ naked** (*US**) en cueros*
(VI) **1** [*horse*] corcovear
2 (*US*) (= *move violently*) • **she ~ed against her captor** se volvió con fuerza contra su captor • **the revolver ~ed violently upwards** el revólver dio una sacudida hacia arriba • **to ~ against** (*fig*) [+ *rules, authority*] rebelarse contra
3 • **to ~ for sth** (*US**) buscar algo
(VT) **1** (*esp US*) [+ *rider*] derribar, desarzonar
2 • **to ~ the market** (*Econ*) ir en contra del mercado • **to ~ the system** rebelarse contra el sistema • **to ~ the trend** ir en contra de la tendencia
(CPD) ▸ **buck nigger** (*Hist*) negrazo *m* ▸ **buck private** (*US*) (*Mil*) soldado *mf* raso ▸ **buck rabbit** conejo *m* (macho) ▸ **buck sergeant** (*US*) (*Mil*) sargento *mf* chusquero ▸ **buck's fizz** *sangría hecha con champán u otro vino espumoso y zumo de naranja* ▸ **buck teeth** dientes *mpl* salientes
▸ **buck up*** (VI + ADV) **1** (= *cheer up*) animarse, levantar el ánimo • **~ up!** ¡ánimo!
2 (= *hurry up*) espabilarse, apurarse (*LAm*) • **~ up!** ¡espabílate!, ¡date prisa!
(VT + ADV) **1** (= *cheer up*) animar, dar ánimos a • **we were very ~ed up by what he said** lo que dijo nos levantó mucho el ánimo
2 (= *hurry up*) dar prisa a
3 • **you'll have to ~ your ideas up** tendrás que moverte, tendrás que ponerte a trabajar en serio
buckboard ['bʌkbɔ:d] (N) (*US*) carreta *f*
bucket ['bʌkɪt] (N) cubo *m*, balde *m* (*LAm*); (*child's*) cubito *m*; [*of waterwheel etc*] cangilón *m* • **a ~ of water** un cubo *or* (*LAm*) un balde de agua • IDIOMS: • **to rain ~s*** llover a cántaros • **to weep ~s*** llorar a mares; ▸ **kick**
(VI) **1*** (= *hurtle*) ir a toda velocidad, ir a toda pastilla (*Sp**)
2 • **the rain is ~ing down*** • **it's ~ing (down)*** está lloviendo a cántaros
(CPD) ▸ **bucket seat** asiento *m* envolvente ▸ **bucket shop** (*Econ*) agencia *f* de bolsa fraudulenta; (*Brit*) (*for air tickets*) agencia *f* de viajes que vende barato
bucketful ['bʌkɪtfʊl] (N) cubo *m* (lleno), balde *m* (lleno) (*LAm*) • **by the ~** a cubos; (*fig*) a montones, en grandes cantidades
Buckingham Palace [ˌbʌkɪŋəm'pælɪs] (N) palacio *m* de Buckingham
buckle ['bʌkl] (N) [*of shoe, belt*] hebilla *f*
(VT) **1** [+ *shoe, belt*] abrochar
2 (= *warp*) [+ *wheel, girder*] combar, torcer
3 [+ *knees*] doblar
(VI) [*wheel, girder*] combarse, torcerse; [*knees*] doblarse
▸ **buckle down** (VI + ADV) ponerse a trabajar • **to ~ down to a job** dedicarse en serio a una tarea
▸ **buckle in** (VT + ADV) • **to ~ a baby in** abrochar el cinturón de un niño
▸ **buckle on** (VT + ADV) [+ *armour, sword*] ceñirse
▸ **buckle to** (VI + ADV) ponerse a trabajar
▸ **buckle up** (VI + ADV) (*US*) ponerse el cinturón de seguridad
buckled ['bʌkəld] (ADJ) [*shoes*] abrochado
buckra ['bʌkrə] (N) (*US*) (*pej*) blanco *m*
buckram ['bʌkrəm] (N) bucarán *m*
Bucks [bʌks] (N ABBR) (*Brit*) = **Buckinghamshire**
bucksaw ['bʌksɔ:] (N) sierra *f* de arco
buckshee‡ [bʌk'ʃi:] (*Brit*) (ADJ) gratuito
(ADV) gratis
buckshot ['bʌkʃɒt] (N) perdigón *m*, posta *f*
buckskin ['bʌkskɪn] (N) (cuero *m* de) ante *m*
buckthorn ['bʌkθɔ:n] (N) espino *m* cerval
buck-toothed ['bʌk'tu:θt] (ADJ) de dientes salientes, dientudo (*LAm**)
buckwheat ['bʌkwi:t] (N) alforfón *m*, trigo *m* sarraceno
bucolic [bju:'kɒlɪk] (ADJ) bucólico
(N) • **the Bucolics** las Bucólicas
bud¹ [bʌd] (N) [*of flower*] capullo *m*; (*on tree, plant*) brote *m*, yema *f* • **in bud** [*tree*] en brote; ▸ **nip**¹
(VI) [*flower, tree*] brotar, echar brotes
(VT) (*Hort*) injertar de escudete
bud²* [bʌd] (N) (*US*) = **buddy**
Budapest [ˌbju:də'pest] (N) Budapest *m*
Buddha ['bʊdə] (N) Buda *m*
Buddhism ['bʊdɪzəm] (N) budismo *m*
Buddhist ['bʊdɪst] (ADJ) budista
(N) budista *mf*
budding ['bʌdɪŋ] (ADJ) (*fig*) [*talent*] en ciernes
buddleia ['bʌdlɪə] (N) budleia *f*
buddy ['bʌdɪ] (N) (*esp US*) amigo *m*, amigote* *m*, compadre *m* (*LAm*), cuate *m* (*Mex**), pata *m* (*Peru**); (*in direct address*) hermano* *m*, macho *m* (*Sp**)
(CPD) ▸ **buddy movie** *película en la que los personajes centrales son un par de amigotes* ▸ **buddy system*** • **they use the ~ system** emplean el amiguismo, se ayudan mutuamente
budge [bʌdʒ] (VT) (= *move*) mover, hacer que se mueva • **I couldn't ~ him an inch** (*fig*) no lo pude convencer
(VI) (= *move*) moverse; (*fig*) ceder, rendirse • **he didn't dare to ~** no se atrevía a moverse • **he won't ~ an inch** (*fig*) no cede lo más mínimo
▸ **budge up** (VI + ADV) moverse un poco, correrse a un lado
budgerigar ['bʌdʒərɪgɑ:ʳ] (N) periquito *m*
budget ['bʌdʒɪt] (N) presupuesto *m* • **the Budget** (*Brit*) (*Pol*) los Presupuestos Generales del Estado • **my ~ won't stretch** *or* **run to steak** mi presupuesto no me permite comprar bistec
(VI) planear el presupuesto
(VT) [+ *sum*] asignar • **the movie is only ~ed at 10m dollars** a la película se le ha asignado un presupuesto de solo 10 millones de dólares • **~ed costs** costos *mpl* presupuestados
(CPD) (*Econ*) presupuestario; (= *cut-price*) [*holiday, prices*] económico ▸ **budget account** cuenta *f* presupuestaria ▸ **budget day** día *m* de la presentación de los Presupuestos Generales del Estado ▸ **budget deficit** déficit *m* presupuestario ▸ **budget plan** plan *m* presupuestario ▸ **budget speech** discurso *m* en el que se presentan los Presupuestos Generales del Estado
▸ **budget for** (VI + PREP) hacer un presupuesto para • **we hadn't ~ed for the price increase** no habíamos contado con el aumento de precios

BUDGET
Cuando el Ministro de Economía y Hacienda británico (**Chancellor of the Exchequer**) presenta los presupuestos generales del Estado al Parlamento, en el país se refieren a ellos simplemente como **the Budget**, el cual suele incluir cambios en los impuestos y en las prestaciones sociales. Su discurso se televisa en su totalidad, para que los ciudadanos se enteren por sí mismos de cómo afectarán los cambios a su declaración de la renta, así como al precio de artículos tales como la gasolina, el alcohol o el tabaco.

-budget [-bʌdʒɪt] (SUFFIX) • **low-budget** de bajo presupuesto • **big-budget** de gran presupuesto
budgetary ['bʌdʒɪtrɪ] (ADJ) [*control, deficit, policy, year*] presupuestario
budgeting ['bʌdʒɪtɪŋ] (N) elaboración *f* de un presupuesto, presupuesto *m* • **with careful ~** con buena administración
budgie* ['bʌdʒɪ] (N) = **budgerigar**
Buenos Aires [ˌbwenəs'aɪərɪz] (N) Buenos Aires *msing*
(ADJ) bonaerense, porteño (*Arg**)
buff¹ [bʌf] (ADJ) [*colour*] de color de ante
(N) piel *f* de ante • **in the ~*** en cueros*
(VT) (*also* **buff up**) lustrar, pulir
buff²* [bʌf] (N) aficionado/a *m/f*, entusiasta *mf* • **film ~** cinéfilo/a *m/f*
buffalo ['bʌfələʊ] (N) (PL: **buffalo** *or* **buffaloes**) **1** búfalo *m*
2 (*esp US*) (= *bison*) bisonte *m*
buffer¹ ['bʌfəʳ] (N) (*Brit*) (*Rail*) (*on carriage*) tope *m*; (*in station*) parachoques *m inv*, amortiguador *m* (de choques); (*US*) (*Aut*) parachoques *m inv*; (*Comput*) memoria *f* intermedia • IDIOM: • **the plan suddenly hit**

the ~s el plan frenó de golpe
VT (*fig*) (= *protect*) proteger
CPD ▸ **buffer state** estado *m* tapón ▸ **buffer zone** zona *f* parachoques
buffer[2]* [ˈbʌfəʳ] N • **old ~** (*Brit*) mastuerzo *m*, carca* *m*
buffering [ˈbʌfərɪŋ] N (*Comput*) almacenamiento *m* en memoria intermedia
buffet[1] [ˈbʌfɪt] N (= *blow*) golpe *m*
VT (= *hit*) abofetear; [*sea, wind*] zarandear
buffet[2] [ˈbʊfeɪ] N (*for refreshments*) cantina *f*, cafetería *f*; (= *meal*) buffet *m* (libre), comida *f* buffet
CPD ▸ **buffet car** (*Brit*) (*Rail*) coche-restaurante *m* ▸ **buffet lunch** almuerzo *m* buffet ▸ **buffet meal** buffet *m* (libre), comida *f* buffet ▸ **buffet supper** cena *f* buffet
buffeting [ˈbʌfɪtɪŋ] N [*of sea etc*] el golpear • **to get a ~ from** sufrir los golpes de
buffoon [bəˈfuːn] N bufón *m*, payaso *m*
buffoonery [bəˈfuːnərɪ] N bufonadas *fpl*
bug [bʌg] N **1** (*Zool*) chinche *mf*; (*esp US**) (= *any insect*) bicho *m*
2* (= *germ*) microbio *m*; (*fig*) (= *obsession*) gusanillo *m* • **flu bug** virus *m inv* de la gripe • **there's a bug going around** hay un virus que corre por ahí • **I've got the travel bug** me ha picado el gusanillo de los viajes
3* (= *hidden microphone*) micrófono *m* oculto
4 (*esp US**) (= *defect, snag*) traba *f*, pega *f*
5 (*Comput*) virus *m inv*
6 (*US**) (= *small car*) coche *m* compacto
7 (*US**) (= *enthusiast*) aficionado/a *m/f*, entusiasta *mf*
VT **1*** [+ *telephone*] intervenir, pinchar*; [+ *room*] poner un micrófono oculto en; [+ *person*] escuchar clandestinamente a, pinchar el teléfono de* • **my phone is bugged** mi teléfono está pinchado* • **do you think this room is bugged?** ¿crees que en esta habitación hay un micro oculto?
2* (= *annoy*) fastidiar, molestar • **don't bug me!** ¡deja de molestar(me) *or* fastidiar! • **what's bugging you?** ¿qué mosca te ha picado?*
CPD ▸ **bug hunter*** entomólogo/a *m/f*
▸ **bug out**‡ VI + ADV (*US*) largarse*
bugaboo [ˈbʌgəbuː] N (*US*) espantajo *m*, coco *m*
bugbear [ˈbʌgbɛəʳ] N pesadilla *f*
bug-eyed* [ˌbʌgˈaɪd] ADJ • **to be bug-eyed** mirar con los ojos saltones
bug-free* [ˈbʌgˈfriː] ADJ (*Comput*) libre de virus, sin virus
bugger [ˈbʌgəʳ] N **1** (*Jur*) sodomita *mf*
2 (*Brit***) (= *person*) hijo/a *m/f* de puta‡, gilipollas *mf* (*Sp*‡) • **he's a lucky ~!** ¡qué suerte tiene el cabrón!‡ • **that silly ~** ese cabrón‡, ese gilipollas (*Sp*‡) • **some poor ~** algún desgraciado* • **I don't give a ~!** ¡me importa un carajo!‡ • **don't play silly ~s!** ¡deja de hacer pendejadas!‡, ¡no des el coñazo! (*Sp*‡)
3 (*Brit***) (= *nuisance, annoyance*) • **it's a ~** es jodidísimo**
EXCL (*Brit*) • **~ (it** *or* **me)!**** ¡mierda!**
VT **1** (*Jur*) cometer sodomía con
2 (*Brit***) • **(well) I'll be ~ed!** ¡no me jodas!** • **lawyers be ~ed!** ¡que se jodan los abogados!** • **I'll be ~ed if I will** paso de hacerlo ¡qué coño!**
▸ **bugger about****, **bugger around**** (*Brit*) VT + ADV • **to ~ sb about** joder a algn** VI + ADV hacer pendejadas‡, hacer el gilipollas (*Sp*‡)
▸ **bugger off**** (*Brit*) VI + ADV largarse* • **~ off!** ¡vete a la mierda!**, ¡vete a tomar por culo! (*Sp***), ¡chinga tu madre! (*Mex***)
▸ **bugger up**** (*Brit*) VT + ADV • **to ~ sth up** joder algo**

bugger-all** [ˈbʌgəˌɔːl] N (*Brit*) nada
buggery [ˈbʌgərɪ] N sodomía *f*
bugging [ˈbʌgɪŋ] N (*Telec*) intervención *f*
CPD ▸ **bugging device** micrófono *m* oculto
buggy [ˈbʌgɪ] N **1** (*also* **baby buggy**) (*Brit*) (= *pushchair*) sillita *f* de paseo; (*US*) (= *pram*) cochecito *m* (de niño)
2 (*horse-drawn*) calesa *f*
3 (*Golf*) cochecito *m*; ▹ **beach, moon**
bughouse‡ [ˈbʌghaʊs] N (PL: **bughouses** [ˈbʌghaʊzɪz]) (*US*) (= *asylum*) casa *f* de locos, manicomio *m*
bugle [ˈbjuːgl] N corneta *f*, clarín *m*
bugler [ˈbjuːgləʳ] N corneta *mf*
bug-ridden [ˈbʌgˌrɪdn] ADJ • **this house is bug-ridden** esta casa está llena de bichos
build [bɪld] (VB: PT, PP: **built**) N (= *physique*) figura *f*, tipo *m* • **of powerful ~** fornido
VT **1** [+ *house*] construir, hacer; [+ *ship*] construir; [+ *nest*] hacer; [+ *fire*] preparar • **to ~ a mirror into a wall** empotrar un espejo en la pared • **a house built into the hillside** una casa construida en la ladera • **this car wasn't built for speed** este coche no está hecho para correr • **built to last** hecho para durar; ▹ **castle**
2 (*fig*) [+ *empire, organization*] levantar; [+ *relationship*] establecer; [+ *trust, confidence*] cimentar; [+ *self-confidence*] desarrollar; [+ *words, sequence*] formar
VI **1** (*Constr*) edificar, construir
2 (= *increase*) [*pressure, sound, speed*] aumentar; [*excitement*] crecer
▸ **build in** VT + ADV **1** [+ *cupboard*] empotrar; (*Mech*) incorporar
2 [+ *safeguards*] incluir, incorporar
▸ **build on** VT + ADV (= *add*) añadir • **to ~ a garage on to a house** añadir un garaje a una casa • **the garage is built on to the house** la casa tiene un garaje anexo
VI + PREP (*fig*) • **now we have a base to ~ on** ahora tenemos una base sobre la que podemos construir
▸ **build up** VT + ADV **1** [+ *area, town etc*] urbanizar • **the area was built up years ago** la zona fue urbanizada hace años
2 (= *establish*) [+ *business, firm*] levantar; [+ *reputation*] labrarse; [+ *impression*] crear • **to ~ up a lead** tomar la delantera • **he had built up a picture in his mind of what she was like** se había formado una imagen mental de cómo era ella
3 (= *increase*) [+ *stocks etc*] acumular; [+ *sales, numbers*] incrementar • **to ~ up one's strength** fortalecerse • **to ~ up one's hopes** hacerse ilusiones • **to ~ up sb's confidence** dar más confianza en sí mismo a algn • **to ~ up one's (self-)confidence** desarrollar la confianza en sí mismo
VI + ADV (= *increase*) [*pressure, sound, speed*] aumentar; (*Econ*) [*interest*] acumularse; [*excitement*] crecer
builder [ˈbɪldəʳ] N (= *company*) constructor(a) *m/f*; (= *worker*) albañil *mf*; (= *contractor*) contratista *mf*; (*fig*) fundador(a) *m/f*
building [ˈbɪldɪŋ] N **1** (= *house, office etc*) edificio *m*; (*at exhibition*) pabellón *m*
2 (= *activity*) construcción *f*
CPD ▸ **building block** (= *toy*) bloque *m* de construcción; (*fig*) elemento *m* esencial, componente *m* básico ▸ **building contractor** contratista *mf* de construcciones ▸ **the building industry** la industria de la construcción ▸ **building land** tierra *f* para construcción, terrenos *mpl* edificables ▸ **building lot** solar *m* (para construcción) ▸ **building materials** material *msing* de construcción ▸ **building permit** permiso *m* de obras ▸ **building plot** = **building lot** ▸ **building site** obra *f* ▸ **building society** (*Brit*)

sociedad *f* de crédito hipotecario ▸ **the building trade** la industria de la construcción ▸ **building worker** obrero/a *m/f* *or* trabajador(a) *m/f* de la construcción ▸ **building works** obras *fpl* de construcción
build-up [ˈbɪldʌp] N **1** [*of pressure, tension, traffic*] aumento *m*; [*of gas*] acumulación *f*, concentración *f*; [*of forces*] concentración *f*
2 (= *publicity*) propaganda *f* • **to give sth/sb a good build-up** hacer mucha propaganda a favor de algo/algn
built [bɪlt] PT, PP *of* **build**
ADJ • **heavily/slightly ~** [*person*] fornido/menudo
-built [bɪlt] ADJ (*ending in compounds*) • **American-built** de construcción americana • **brick-built** construido de ladrillos
built-in [ˈbɪltˈɪn] ADJ [*wardrobe, mirror*] empotrado; (*as integral part of*) incorporado
CPD ▸ **built-in obsolescence** caducidad *f* programada *or* controlada
built-up [ˈbɪltˈʌp] N • **built-up area** zona *f* urbanizada
bulb [bʌlb] N **1** (*Bot*) bulbo *m*, camote *m* (*Mex*); [*of garlic*] cabeza *f*
2 (*Elec*) bombilla *f*, bombillo *m* (*LAm*), foco *m* (*LAm*)
3 [*of thermometer*] cubeta *f*, ampolleta *f*
bulbous [ˈbʌlbəs] ADJ [*shape*] bulboso
Bulgar [ˈbʌlgəʳ] N (*Hist*) búlgaro/a *m/f*
Bulgaria [bʌlˈgɛərɪə] N Bulgaria *f*
Bulgarian [bʌlˈgɛərɪən] ADJ búlgaro
N **1** (= *person*) búlgaro/a *m/f*
2 (*Ling*) búlgaro *m*
bulge [bʌldʒ] N **1** (*in surface, of curve*) abombamiento *m*, protuberancia *f*; (*in pocket*) bulto *m*
2 (*in birth rate, sales*) alza *f*, aumento *m* • **the postwar ~ in the birth rate** la explosión demográfica de la posguerra
VI [*pocket etc*] estar abultado; [*eyes*] saltarse • **his pockets ~d with apples** iba con los bolsillos repletos de manzanas • **their eyes ~d at the sight** se les saltaron los ojos al verlo
bulging [ˈbʌldʒɪŋ] ADJ [*pocket*] muy lleno; [*suitcase*] que está para reventar; [*eyes*] saltón
bulgur wheat [ˈbʌlgəˌwiːt] N trigo *m* de bulgur
bulimia [bjuːˈlɪmɪə] N bulimia *f*
bulimic [bjuːˈlɪmɪk] ADJ bulímico
N bulímico/a *m/f*
bulk [bʌlk] N **1** (= *size*) [*of thing*] bulto *m*; [*of person*] corpulencia *f*, masa *f* • **the enormous ~ of the ship** la enorme mole del buque • **he set his full ~ down in a chair** dejó caer todo el peso de su cuerpo en un sillón
2 (= *main part*) • **the ~ of** la mayoría de • **the ~ of the work** la mayor parte del trabajo • **the ~ of the army** el grueso del ejército
3 (*Comm*) • **to buy in ~** (= *in large quantities*) comprar al por mayor • **in ~** (= *not pre-packed*) suelto, a granel
VI • **to ~ large** tener un puesto importante, ocupar un lugar importante
CPD ▸ **bulk buying** compra *f* al por mayor ▸ **bulk carrier** (buque *m*) granelero *m* ▸ **bulk goods** mercancías *fpl* a granel ▸ **bulk purchase** compra *f* al por mayor
bulk-buy [ˈbʌlkbaɪ] VI [*individual*] comprar en grandes cantidades; [*company, organization, retailer*] comprar al por mayor
bulkhead [ˈbʌlkhed] N (*Naut*) mamparo *m*
bulkiness [ˈbʌlkɪnɪs] N volumen *m*, lo abultado
bulky [ˈbʌlkɪ] ADJ (COMPAR: **bulkier**, SUPERL: **bulkiest**) [*parcel*] abultado; [*person*] corpulento
bull[1] [bʊl] N **1** (*Zool*) toro *m*; (= *male*) [*of*

elephant, seal] macho *m* • IDIOMS: • **like a ~ in a china shop** como un elefante en una cristalería • **to take the ~ by the horns** coger *or* (*LAm*) agarrar el toro por los cuernos; ▹ red
2 (*Econ*) alcista *mf*
3‡ (= *nonsense*) sandeces* *fpl*, chorradas *fpl* (*Sp**) • **to talk a lot of ~** decir sandeces*, decir chorradas (*Sp**)
4 (*Mil*‡) trabajos *mpl* rutinarios
(ADJ) (*Zool*) macho
(VT) (*Econ*) • **to ~ the market** hacer subir el mercado comprando acciones especulativamente
(CPD) ▸ **bull bars** (*Aut*) defensa *fsing* (delantera *or* frontal) ▸ **bull calf** (*Zool*) becerro *m* ▸ **bull dyke**‡ (*pej*) camionera* *f* ▸ **bull market** (*Econ*) mercado *m* en alza *or* alcista ▸ **bull neck** cuello *m* de toro ▸ **bull terrier** bulterrier *m*

bull² [bʊl] (N) (*Rel*) bula *f*

bulldog [ˈbʊldɒg] (N) dogo *m*, buldog *m*
(CPD) ▸ **the bulldog breed** los ingleses (*con su aspecto heroico y porfiado*) ▸ **Bulldog ® clip** pinza *f*

bulldoze [ˈbʊldəʊz] (VT) **1** (*Constr*) [+ *site*] nivelar (con motoniveladora); [+ *building*] arrasar (con motoniveladora)
2 (*fig*) [+ *opposition*] arrollar • **I was ~d into doing it** me forzaron a hacerlo • **the government ~d the bill through parliament** el gobierno hizo presiones para que se aprobara el proyecto de ley en el parlamento

bulldozer [ˈbʊldəʊzəʳ] (N) motoniveladora *f*, bulldozer *m*

bullet [ˈbʊlɪt] (N) bala *f* • **to go by like a ~** pasar como (una) bala *or* un rayo • IDIOM: • **to bite the ~** enfrentarse al toro
(CPD) ▸ **bullet hole** agujero *m* de bala ▸ **bullet point** (= *important point*) punto *m* importante; (= *symbol*) topo *m* ▸ **bullet train** tren *m* de gran velocidad (*japonés*) ▸ **bullet wound** balazo *m*

bulletin [ˈbʊlɪtɪn] (N) (= *statement*) comunicado *m*, parte *m*; (= *journal*) boletín *m*
(CPD) ▸ **bulletin board** (*US*) tablón *m* de anuncios; (*Comput*) tablero *m* de noticias

bulletproof [ˈbʊlɪtpruːf] (ADJ) antibalas, a prueba de balas
(CPD) ▸ **bulletproof glass** vidrio *m* antibalas *or* a prueba de balas ▸ **bulletproof vest** chaleco *m* antibalas *or* a prueba de balas

bullfight [ˈbʊlfaɪt] (N) corrida *f* (de toros)

bullfighter [ˈbʊlfaɪtəʳ] (N) torero/a *m/f*

bullfighting [ˈbʊlfaɪtɪŋ] (N) toreo *m*, tauromaquia *f* • **I hate ~** odio los toros

bullfinch [ˈbʊlfɪntʃ] (N) camachuelo *m*

bullfrog [ˈbʊlfrɒg] (N) rana *f* toro

bullheaded [ˈbʊlˈhedɪd] (ADJ) [*person*] terco

bullhorn [ˈbʊlhɔːn] (N) (*US*) megáfono *m*

bullion [ˈbʊljən] (N) oro *m*/plata *f* en barras *or* en lingotes

bullish [ˈbʊlɪʃ] (ADJ) optimista; (*Econ*) (de tendencia) alcista

bull-necked [ˈbʊlˈnekt] (ADJ) de cuello de toro

bullock [ˈbʊlək] (N) buey *m*

bullpen* [ˈbʊlpen] (N) (*US*) **1** (*Baseball*) (= *area*) *área en la que calientan los pitchers reservas*; (= *players*) pitchers *mpl*
2 (= *office*) oficina *f* abierta
3 (= *cell*) calabozo *m*

bullring [ˈbʊlrɪŋ] (N) plaza *f* de toros

bull's-eye [ˈbʊlzaɪ] (N) **1** [*of target*] blanco *m* • **to hit the bull's-eye** • **score a bull's-eye** (*lit, fig*) dar en el blanco
2 (= *sweet*) caramelo *m* de menta
3 (= *lantern*) linterna *f* sorda
4 (*Naut*) ojo *m* de buey

bullshit** [ˈbʊlʃɪt] (N) (= *nonsense*) sandeces* *fpl*, chorradas *fpl* (*Sp**)
(VI) decir sandeces*, decir chorradas (*Sp**)
(VT) • **don't ~ me now** no me vengas ahora con sandeces *or* chorradas*

bullshitter** [ˈbʊlˈʃɪtəʳ] (N) fanfarrón/ona *m/f*

bullwhip [ˈbʊlwɪp] (N) látigo *m* de cuero trenzado

bully¹ [ˈbʊlɪ] (N) **1** (= *person*) matón/ona *m/f*, peleón/ona *m/f*
2 (*Brit*) (*Hockey*) (*also* **bully-off**) saque *m*
(VT) (*also* **bully around**) intimidar • **to ~ sb into doing sth** intimidar a algn para que haga algo
▸ **bully off** (VI + ADV) (*Brit*) (*Hockey*) sacar

bully²* [ˈbʊlɪ] (ADJ) † (= *first-rate*) de primera
(EXCL) • **~ for you!** ¡bravo!

bully³* [ˈbʊlɪ] (N) (*Mil*) (*also* **bully beef**) carne *f* de vaca conservada en lata

bully-boy* [ˈbʊlɪˌbɔɪ] (N) matón *m*, esbirro *m*
(CPD) ▸ **bully-boy tactics** táctica *fsing* de matón

bullying [ˈbʊlɪɪŋ] (ADJ) [*person*] matón, valentón; [*attitude*] amedrentador, propio de matón
(N) intimidación *f*, abuso *m*
(CPD) ▸ **bullying tactics** tácticas *fpl* intimidatorias

bulrush [ˈbʊlrʌʃ] (N) espadaña *f*

bulwark [ˈbʊlwək] (N) (*Mil*) (*also fig*) baluarte *m*; (*Naut*) borda *f*

bum¹* [bʌm] (N) (*Brit*) (*Anat*) culo* *m* • IDIOM: • **to put bums on seats** (*Theat etc*) llenar el teatro *or* cine etc
(CPD) ▸ **bum bag** riñonera *f* ▸ **bum boy**** (*Brit*) (*pej*) maricón‡ *m*

bum²* [bʌm] (N) (*esp US*) (= *idler*) holgazán/ana *m/f*, vago/a *m/f*; (= *tramp*) vagabundo/a *m/f*; (= *scrounger*) gorrón/ona* *m/f*; (*as term of general disapproval*) vago/a *m/f* • IDIOMS: • **to go** *or* **live on the bum** [*scrounger*] vivir de gorra; [*tramp*] vagabundear • **to give sb the bum's rush** echar a algn a patadas*
(ADJ) **1** (= *worthless*) sin ningún valor
2 (*esp US*) (= *false*) falso
(VT) [+ *money, food*] gorrear* • **he bummed a cigarette off me** me gorreó un pitillo*
(CPD) ▸ **bum deal** • **I knew I was getting a bum deal** sabía que se estaban aprovechando de mí ▸ **bum rap** acusación *f* falsa ▸ **bum steer** bulo *m*
▸ **bum around*** (VI + ADV) holgazanear

bumble [ˈbʌmbl] (VI) (= *walk unsteadily*) andar de forma vacilante, andar a tropezones; (*fig*) trastabillar

bumblebee [ˈbʌmblbiː] (N) abejorro *m*

bumbling [ˈbʌmblɪŋ] (ADJ) (= *inept*) inepto, inútil; (= *muttering*) que habla a tropezones
(N) divagación *f*

bumf* [bʌmf] (N) **1** (*Brit*) (*pej*) (= *papers, information*) papeleo* *m*, papeles *mpl*
2 (= *lavatory paper*) papel *m* higiénico

bummer‡ [ˈbʌməʳ] (N) (= *nuisance*) latazo* *m*; (= *disaster*) desastre *m* • **what a ~!** ¡vaya desastre!

bump [bʌmp] (N) **1** (= *blow, noise*) choque *m*, topetazo *m*; (= *jolt of vehicle*) sacudida *f*; (*Aer*) rebote *m*; (*in falling*) batacazo *m* • **things that go ~ in the night** cosas que hacen ruidos misteriosos en la noche • IDIOM: • **to come down to earth with a ~** volver a la realidad de un golpe
2 (= *swelling*) bollo *m*, abolladura *f*; (*on skin*) chichón *m*, hinchazón *f*; (*on road etc*) bache *m*
(VT) [+ *car*] chocar contra • **to ~ one's head** darse un golpe en la cabeza • **to ~ one's head on a door** dar con la cabeza contra una puerta
(VI) • **to ~ along** (= *move joltingly*) avanzar dando sacudidas • **the economy continues to ~ along the bottom** (*Brit*) la economía continúa arrastrándose por los suelos
▸ **bump against** (VI + PREP) chocar contra, topetar, dar contra
▸ **bump into** (VI + PREP) **1** [+ *person, vehicle*] chocar contra, dar con *or* contra
2* (= *meet*) tropezar con, toparse con • **fancy ~ing into you!** ¡qué casualidad encontrarte aquí!
▸ **bump off*** (VT + ADV) (= *kill*) cargarse a*
▸ **bump up*** (VT + ADV) **1** (= *increase*) [+ *price*] subir, aumentar
2 • **he was ~ed up to first-class on his flight home** en el viaje de vuelta lo pusieron en primera clase
▸ **bump up against** (VI + PREP) = bump into

bumper¹ [ˈbʌmpəʳ] (N) (*Brit*) (*Aut*) parachoques *m inv* • **traffic is ~ to ~ as far as the airport** hay una caravana que llega hasta el aeropuerto
(CPD) ▸ **bumper car** auto *m* de choque ▸ **bumper sticker** pegatina *f* de parachoques

bumper² [ˈbʌmpəʳ] (N) (= *glass*) copa *f* llena
(ADJ) [*crop, harvest*] abundante
(CPD) ▸ **bumper issue** edición *f* especial

bumph* [bʌmf] (N) (*Brit*) = **bumf**

bumpiness [ˈbʌmpɪnɪs] (N) [*of surface, road, drive*] lo accidentado; [*of flight*] lo agitado

bumpkin [ˈbʌmpkɪn] (N) (*also* **country bumpkin**) (*pej*) pueblerino/a *m/f*, paleto/a *m/f* (*Sp**)

bump-start [ˈbʌmpstɑːt] (N) • **to give a car a bump-start** empujar un coche para que arranque
(VT) [+ *car*] empujar para que arranque

bumptious [ˈbʌmpʃəs] (ADJ) engreído, presuntuoso

bumpy [ˈbʌmpɪ] (ADJ) (COMPAR: **bumpier**, SUPERL: **bumpiest**) [*surface, road, drive*] accidentado; [*journey, flight*] agitado, con mucho traqueteo

bun [bʌn] (N) **1** (*Culin*) bollo *m*, magdalena *f*; (*Brit*) (= *cake*) pastel *m* • IDIOM: • **to have a bun in the oven**‡ estar en estado
2 (= *hairstyle*) moño *m* • **to wear one's hair in a bun** recogerse el pelo en un moño
3 buns (*esp US*‡) (= *buttocks*) trasero* *msing*
(CPD) ▸ **bun fight*** *merienda servida para mucha gente*

bunch [bʌntʃ] (N) **1** [*of flowers*] ramo *m*; (*small*) ramillete *m*; [*of bananas, grapes*] racimo *m*; [*of keys*] manojo *m* • **to wear one's hair in ~es** (*Brit*) llevar coletas • **the best** *or* **pick of the ~*** (*fig*) el/la mejor de todos
2* (= *set of people*) grupo *m*, pandilla *f* • **they're an odd ~** son gente rara • **they're a ~ of traitors** son una panda de traidores • IDIOM: • **the best of a bad ~** entre malos, los mejores; ▹ mixed
3 (*US**) • **a ~ of** (= *several, many*) un montón de • **a ~ of times** un montón de veces
4 • **thanks a ~!*** (*iro*) ¡hombre, pues te lo agradezco!, ¡gracias mil!
(VT) [+ *objects*] agrupar, juntar
▸ **bunch together** (VT + ADV) agrupar, juntar
(VI + ADV) [*people*] agruparse, apiñarse
▸ **bunch up** (VT + ADV) **1** [+ *dress, skirt*] arremangar
2 • **they sat ~ed up on the bench** se apretujaban en el banco
(VI + ADV) apretujarse

bundle [ˈbʌndl] (N) **1** [*of clothes, rags*] bulto *m*, fardo *m*, lío *m*; [*of sticks*] haz *m*; [*of papers*] legajo *m* • **~ of joy** (= *baby*) bebé *mf* • **he's a ~ of nerves** es un manojo de nervios • **he's not exactly a ~ of laughs** no es muy divertido que digamos
2‡ (= *money*) • **to make a ~** ganarse un

dineral*, ganarse un pastón (*Sp*‡) • **it cost a ~** costó un dineral *or* una millonada*
3 (= *large number*) montón *m* • **to go a ~ on**‡ volverse loco por*
4 (*Comput*) paquete *m*
(VT) **1** (*also* **bundle up**) [+ *clothes*] atar en un bulto
2 (= *put hastily*) guardar sin orden • **the body was ~d into the car** metieron el cadáver en el coche a la carrera
(CPD) ▸ **bundled software** (*Comput*) paquete *m* de software
▸ **bundle off** (VT + ADV) [+ *person*] despachar • **they ~d him off to Australia** lo despacharon a Australia
▸ **bundle out** (VT + ADV) • **to ~ sb out** echar a algn • **they ~d him out into the street** lo pusieron de patitas en la calle*
▸ **bundle up** (VT + ADV) [+ *clothes, belongings*] liar, atar
bung [bʌŋ] (N) **1** [*of cask*] tapón *m*
2 (*Brit**) (= *bribe*) soborno *m*
(VT) (*Brit*) **1** (*also* **bung up**) [+ *pipe, hole*] tapar, taponar • **to be ~ed up** [*sink, pipe*] estar atascado, estar obstruido • **my nose is ~ed up*** tengo la nariz tapada
2‡ (= *throw*) echar; (= *put*) poner, meter • **~ it over** échalo para acá
▸ **bung in*** (VT + ADV) (= *include*) añadir
▸ **bung out*** (VT + ADV) tirar, botar
bungalow [ˈbʌŋɡələʊ] (N) chalé *m*, bungalow *m*
bungee jumping [ˈbʌndʒiːˈdʒʌmpɪŋ] (N) bungee *m*, banyi *m*; (*from bridge*) puenting *m*, puentismo *m* • **to go ~** hacer bungee *or* banyi; (*from bridge*) hacer puenting *or* puentismo
bunghole [ˈbʌŋhəʊl] (N) piquera *f*, boca *f* (de tonel)
bungle [ˈbʌŋɡl] (N) chapuza* *f*
(VT) [+ *work*] hacer chapuceramente • **to ~ it** hacer una chapuza*, amolarlo (*Mex**) • **to ~ an opportunity** desperdiciar una oportunidad
bungled [ˈbʌŋɡld] (ADJ) • **a ~ job** una chapuza* • **a ~ operation** una operación mal ejecutada
bungler [ˈbʌŋɡləʳ] (N) chapucero/a *m/f*
bungling [ˈbʌŋɡlɪŋ] (ADJ) torpe, desmañado
bungy jumping [ˈbʌndʒiːˈdʒʌmpɪŋ] (N) = **bungee jumping**
bunion [ˈbʌnjən] (N) (*Med*) juanete *m*
bunk¹ [bʌŋk] (N) (*Naut*) litera *f*, camastro *m*; (*Rail*) (*child's*) litera *f*; (= *bed**) cama *f*
(CPD) ▸ **bunk bed** litera *f*
bunk²* [bʌŋk] (*Brit*) (N) • **to do a ~** ▹ VI
(VI) largarse*, escaquearse (*Sp**)
▸ **bunk off*** (*Brit*) (VI + ADV) (*from school, work*) escaquearse (*Sp**)
(VI + PREP) • **to ~ off school** hacer novillos *or* rabona
bunk³* [bʌŋk] (N) (= *nonsense*) bobadas* *fpl* • **~!** ¡bobadas!* • **history is ~** la historia son bobadas*
bunker [ˈbʌŋkəʳ] (N) **1** (= *coal bunker*) carbonera *f*; (*Naut*) pañol *m* del carbón
2 (*Mil*) refugio *m* antiaéreo/antinuclear, búnker *m*
3 (*Golf*) búnker *m*
(VT) **1** (*Naut*) proveer de carbón
2 • **to be ~ed** (*Golf*) tener la pelota en un búnker; (*fig**) estar en un atolladero
bunkhouse [ˈbʌŋkhaʊs] (N) (PL: **bunkhouses** [ˈbʌŋkhaʊzɪz]) (*US*) casa *f* de dormitorios (para trabajadores de hacienda)
bunkmate* [ˈbʌŋkmeɪt] (N) compañero *m* de cuarto
bunkum* [ˈbʌŋkəm] (N) bobadas* *fpl*
bunk-up* [ˌbʌŋkˈʌp] (N) • **to give sb a bunk-up** ayudar a algn a subir
bunny [ˈbʌnɪ] (N) **1** (*baby talk*) (= *rabbit*) conejito *m*
2 (*US**) (= *pretty girl*) bombón* *m*, tía *f* buena (*Sp**)
(CPD) ▸ **bunny girl** conejita *f* ▸ **bunny hill** (*US*) (= *ski slope*) pista *f* de principiantes
▸ **bunny rabbit** (*baby talk*) conejito *m*
▸ **bunny slope** (*US*) (= *ski slope*) pista *f* de principiantes
Bunsen burner [ˌbʌnsnˈbɜːnəʳ] (N) mechero *m* Bunsen
bunting¹ [ˈbʌntɪŋ] (N) (*Orn*) escribano *m*
bunting² [ˈbʌntɪŋ] (N) (= *decoration*) banderitas *fpl*, empavesado *m*; (= *cloth*) lanilla *f*
buoy [bɔɪ], (*US*) [ˈbuːɪ] (N) boya *f*
(VT) [+ *channel*] aboyar, señalar con boyas
▸ **buoy up** (VT + ADV) (*lit*) [+ *person, boat*] mantener a flote; (*fig*) [+ *spirits etc*] levantar; [+ *person*] animar, alentar
buoyancy [ˈbɔɪənsɪ] (N) **1** (*Phys*) [*of ship, object*] capacidad *f* para flotar, flotabilidad *f*; [*of liquid*] sustentación *f* hidráulica; (*Aer*) fuerza *f* ascensional
2 (*fig*) optimismo *m*
3 (*Econ*) [*of market, prices*] tendencia *f* al alza
buoyant [ˈbɔɪənt] (ADJ) **1** (*Phys*) [*ship, object*] flotante, boyante (*Tech*) • **fresh water is not so ~ as salt water** en el agua dulce no se flota tanto como en la salada
2 (= *bouncy*) [*mood, person*] optimista; [*step*] ligero
3 (*Econ*) [*market, prices*] con tendencia al alza
buoyantly [ˈbɔɪəntlɪ] (ADV) [*walk*] con paso ligero; [*recover, return*] con optimismo
BUPA [ˈbuːpə] (N ABBR) (= **British United Provident Association**) *seguro médico privado*
buppie*, **buppy*** [ˈbʌpɪ] (N ABBR) (= **black upwardly mobile professional**) *yuppie negro*
bur [bɜːʳ] (N) = **burr**
burble [ˈbɜːbl] (VI) **1** [*baby*] hacer gorgoritos; [*stream*] burbujear
2 (*pej*) [*person*] (= *talk*) farfullar
burbot [ˈbɜːbət] (N) lota *f*
burbs*, **'burbs*** [bɜːbz] (NPL) (*US*) = **suburbs**
burden [ˈbɜːdn] (N) **1** (= *load*) carga *f*; (= *weight*) peso *m*
2 (*fig*) [*of taxes, years*] peso *m*, carga *f* • **the ~ of proof lies with him** él lleva la carga de la prueba • **to be a ~ to sb** ser una carga para algn • **he carries a heavy ~** tiene que cargar con una gran responsabilidad • **to make sb's life a ~** amargar la vida a algn
3 (*Naut*) arqueo *m*
4 (= *chief theme*) [*of speech etc*] tema *m* principal
5 (= *chorus*) [*of song*] estribillo *m*
(VT) cargar (**with con**) • **to be ~ed with** tener que cargar con • **don't ~ me with your troubles** no me vengas con tus problemas
burdensome [ˈbɜːdnsəm] (ADJ) gravoso, oneroso
burdock [ˈbɜːdɒk] (N) (*Bot*) bardana *f*
bureau [ˈbjʊərəʊ] (N) (PL: **bureaus** *or* **bureaux** [ˈbjʊərəʊz]) **1** (= *organization*) **a** (= *travel/employment agency*) agencia *f*, oficina *f*
b (*US*) (= *government department*) departamento *m*; ▹ **federal**
2 (= *piece of furniture*) **a** (*Brit*) (= *desk*) buró *m*, escritorio *m*
b (*US*) (= *chest of drawers*) cómoda *f*
(CPD) ▸ **bureau de change** caja *f* de cambio
▸ **Bureau of Indian affairs** (*US*) Departamento *m* de Asuntos Indios
▸ **bureau of standards** (*US*) oficina *f* de pesos y medidas

BUREAU OF INDIAN AFFAIRS

La agencia del gobierno estadounidense denominada **Bureau of Indian Affairs** (**Departamento de Asuntos Indios**) se encarga de todos los asuntos relacionados con los indios nativos norteamericanos. Este organismo, fundado en 1824 como parte del Ministerio de Guerra, llevaba en un principio la gestión de las reservas indias. Hoy en día trabaja conjuntamente con los indios para tratar de mejorar su situación, elaborando programas de salud y bienestar social y dando facilidades para la educación y el empleo. Desde la década de los sesenta viene proporcionando también asistencia técnica y formación para que puedan gestionar sus tierras y recursos.

bureaucracy [bjʊəˈrɒkrəsɪ] (N) burocracia *f*; (*pej*) papeleo* *m*, trámites *mpl*
bureaucrat [ˈbjʊərəʊkræt] (N) burócrata *mf*
bureaucratic [ˌbjʊərəʊˈkrætɪk] (ADJ) burocrático
burg* [bɜːɡ] (N) (*US*) (*esp hum, pej*) (= *town*) burgo *m*
burgeon [ˈbɜːdʒən] (VI) (*Bot*) retoñar; (*fig*) empezar a prosperar (rápidamente); [*trade etc*] florecer
burgeoning [ˈbɜːdʒənɪŋ] (ADJ) [*industry, market*] en vías de expansión, que empieza a prosperar *or* florecer; [*career*] que empieza a prosperar *or* florecer; [*population*] en aumento
burger [ˈbɜːɡəʳ] (N) hamburguesa *f*
(CPD) ▸ **burger bar** hamburguesería *f*
burgess [ˈbɜːdʒɪs] (N) (*Brit*) ciudadano/a *m/f*; (*Parl*††) diputado/a *m/f*
burgh [ˈbʌrə] (N) (*Scot*) villa *f*
burgher†† [ˈbɜːɡəʳ] (N) (= *bourgeois*) burgués/esa *m/f*; (= *citizen*) ciudadano/a *m/f*
burglar [ˈbɜːɡləʳ] (N) ladrón/ona *m/f*
(CPD) ▸ **burglar alarm** alarma *f* antirrobo
burglarize [ˈbɜːɡləraɪz] (VT) (*US*) robar (de una casa *etc*)
burglar-proof [ˈbɜːɡləpruːf] (ADJ) a prueba de ladrones
burglary [ˈbɜːɡlərɪ] (N) robo *m* (*en una casa*); (*Jur*) allanamiento *m* de morada
burgle [ˈbɜːɡl] (VT) (*Brit*) robar (*de una casa etc*)
Burgundian [bɜːˈɡʌndɪən] (ADJ) borgoñón
(N) borgoñón/ona *m/f*
Burgundy [ˈbɜːɡəndɪ] (N) **1** (*Geog*) Borgoña *f*
2 (= *wine*) vino *m* de Borgoña
burgundy [ˈbɜːɡəndɪ] (ADJ) [*jacket, curtains*] burdeos (*inv*)
(N) (= *colour*) burdeos *m*
burial [ˈberɪəl] (N) entierro *m* • **I like the idea of ~ at sea** me gusta la idea de que mi cadáver sea arrojado al mar
(CPD) ▸ **burial ground** cementerio *m*, camposanto *m*, panteón *m* (*LAm*) ▸ **burial mound** túmulo *m* ▸ **burial place** lugar *m* de sepultura ▸ **burial service** funerales *mpl*
▸ **burial vault** panteón *m* familiar, cripta *f*
Burkina-Faso [bɜːˈkiːnəˈfæsəʊ] (N) Burkina Faso *f*
burlap [ˈbɜːlæp] (N) (*esp US*) arpillera *f*
burlesque [bɜːˈlesk] (ADJ) burlesco
(N) **1** (= *parody*) parodia *f*
2 (*US*) (*Theat*) revista *f* de estriptise
(VT) parodiar
(CPD) ▸ **burlesque show** (*US*) revista *f* de estriptise
burly [ˈbɜːlɪ] (ADJ) (COMPAR: **burlier**, SUPERL: **burliest**) fornido, fuerte
Burma [ˈbɜːmə] (N) Birmania *f*
Burmese [bɜːˈmiːz] (ADJ) birmano
(N) birmano/a *m/f*
burn¹ [bɜːn] (VB: PT, PP: **burned**, **burnt**) (N)

1 (*Med*) quemadura *f*
2 (*Space*) [*of rocket*] fuego *m*
(VT) **1** (*gen*) quemar; [*+ house, building*] incendiar; [*+ corpse*] incinerar; [*+ mouth, tongue*] quemar, escaldar • **to ~ a house to the ground** incendiar y arrasar una casa • **to ~ a hole in sth** hacer un agujero en algo quemándolo • **to ~ sth to ashes** reducir algo a cenizas • **to be ~ed alive** ser quemado vivo • **to be ~t to death** morir abrasado • **to ~ one's finger/hand** quemarse el dedo/la mano • **I've ~t myself!** ¡me he quemado!, ¡me quemé! (*LAm*) • **I ~t the toast** se me ha quemado la tostada • IDIOMS: • **to ~ one's boats** *or* **bridges** quemar las naves • **to ~ the candle at both ends** hacer de la noche día • **to ~ one's fingers** • **get one's fingers ~ed** pillarse los dedos • **money ~s a hole in his pocket** el dinero le quema las manos
2 [*sun*] [*+ person, skin*] tostar; [*+ plants*] abrasar • **with a face ~ed by the sun** con la cara tostada al sol
3 [*+ fuel*] consumir, usar
4 [*+ CD, DVD*] tostar
(VI) **1** [*fire, building etc*] arder, quemarse; (*= catch fire*) incendiarse • **to ~ to death** morir abrasado
2 [*skin*] (*in sun*) quemarse, tostarse
3 [*meat, pastry etc*] quemarse
4 [*light, gas*] estar encendido
5 (*fig*) • **to ~ with anger/passion** *etc* arder de rabia/pasión *etc* • **to ~ with desire for** desear ardientemente • **to ~ with impatience** consumirse de impaciencia • **to ~ to do sth** desear ardientemente hacer algo
(CPD) ▸ **burns unit** unidad *f* de quemados
▸ **burn away** (VT + ADV) quemar
(VI + ADV) **1** (*= be consumed*) consumirse
2 (*= go on burning*) seguir ardiendo, arder bien
▸ **burn down** (VT + ADV) [*+ building*] incendiar
(VI + ADV) **1** [*house*] incendiarse
2 [*candle, fire*] apagarse
▸ **burn off** (VT + ADV) [*+ paint etc*] quitar con soplete; [*+ weeds*] quemar
▸ **burn out** (VT + ADV) **1** (*= destroy*) [*+ building*] reducir a cenizas; (*criminally*) incendiar
2 [*+ person*] incendiar la casa de
3 (*Elec*) fundir, quemar
4 • **the fire had ~t itself out** (*in hearth*) el fuego se había apagado; [*forest fire*] el incendio se había extinguido • **he's ~t himself out** (*fig*) está quemado
(VI + ADV) **1** [*fuse*] fundirse
2 [*candle, fire*] apagarse
▸ **burn up** (VI + ADV) **1** [*fire*] echar llamas, arder más
2 [*rocket etc*] desintegrarse
(VT + ADV) **1** [*+ rubbish etc*] quemar; [*+ crop*] abrasar
2 (*= consume*) [*+ calories, energy*] quemar
3 (*US**) (*= make angry*) sacar de quicio*

burn² [bɜːn] (N) (*Scot*) arroyo *m*, riachuelo *m*

burned-out [ˌbɜːndˈaʊt] (ADJ) quemado

burner [ˈbɜːnəʳ] (N) (*on cooker etc*) quemador *m*; ▹ **back**

burning [ˈbɜːnɪŋ] (N) **1** (*= singeing*) • **there's a smell of ~** huele a quemado • **I can smell ~** huelo a quemado
2 (*= setting on fire*) quema *f* • **the ~ (down) of the Embassy during the riots** la quema de la embajada durante los disturbios
(ADJ) **1** (*= on fire*) [*building, forest*] en llamas; [*coals, flame*] ardiente; [*candle*] encendido • **the ~ bush** (*Bible*) la zarza ardiente, la zarza que ardía sin consumirse
2 (*= hot*) [*sun*] abrasador, ardiente; [*sand*] ardiente; [*desert*] infernal; [*face, skin*] ardiendo; [*thirst, fever*] abrasador; [*sensation*] de ardor, de escozor • **they drank some water to cool their ~ throats** bebieron agua para refrescar sus ardientes gargantas • **with a ~ face** (*through embarrassment, shame*) con la cara ardiendo de vergüenza
3 (*= intense*) [*desire, passion, eyes*] ardiente; [*ambition*] que quema; [*hatred*] violento; [*question, topic*] candente
(ADV) • **~ hot** • **his forehead was ~ hot** su frente estaba ardiendo • **don't touch that, it's ~ hot!** ¡no toques eso! ¡está ardiendo! • **phew, it's ~ hot today!** ¡uf! ¡hoy hace un calor abrasador!

burnish [ˈbɜːnɪʃ] (VT) **1** [*+ metal*] bruñir
2 (*fig*) [*+ image*] mejorar

burnished [ˈbɜːnɪʃt] (ADJ) (*liter*) (*= polished*) bruñido

burnoose, burnous, burnouse [bɜːˈnuːz] (N) albornoz *m*

burnout* [ˈbɜːnaʊt] (N) agotamiento *m*, fatiga *f*

Burns Night (N) *noche en que se conmemora el nacimiento del poeta escocés Robert Burns*

> **BURNS NIGHT**
> En la noche del 25 de enero, **Burns Night**, se celebra el aniversario del nacimiento del poeta escocés Robert Burns (1759-1796). Los escoceses de todo el mundo se reúnen para celebrar su vida y obra haciendo una cena en su honor (**Burns Supper**), en la que, al son de la gaita, se sirve **haggis** (asaduras de cordero, avena y especias cocidas en las tripas del animal) con patatas y puré de nabos. Después de la cena se cantan canciones de Burns, se leen sus poemas y se hacen discursos de carácter festivo relacionados con ellos.

burnt [bɜːnt] (PT), (PP) *of* **burn**
(ADJ) quemado • PROVERB: • **a ~ child dreads the fire** el gato escaldado del agua fría huye • **it has a ~ taste** sabe a quemado
(CPD) ▸ **burnt almonds** almendras *fpl* tostadas ▸ **burnt offering** (*Rel*) holocausto *m* • **I forgot to turn off the oven and we had a ~ offering for dinner** (*hum*) se me olvidó apagar el horno y tuvimos carbón para cenar ▸ **burnt orange** (*= colour*) naranja *m* oscuro ▸ **burnt sienna** (*= colour*) siena *f* tostada ▸ **burnt sugar** azúcar *m* quemado ▸ **burnt umber** (*= colour*) siena *m* tostado

burnt-out [ˌbɜːntˈaʊt] (ADJ) [*person*] quemado

burp* [bɜːp] (N) eructo *m*
(VI) eructar
(VT) [*+ baby*] hacer eructar

burqa [ˈbɜːkə] (N) burqa *m*, burka *m*

burr [bɜːʳ] (N) (*Bot*) erizo *m*

burrow [ˈbʌrəʊ] (N) [*of animal*] madriguera *f*; [*of rabbit*] conejera *f*
(VT) [*+ hole*] cavar • **to ~ one's way** abrirse camino cavando (**into** en)
(VI) [*animal*] hacer una madriguera • **to ~ into** hacer madrigueras en, horadar; (*fig*) investigar minuciosamente • **he ~ed under the bedclothes** se metió debajo de la ropa de cama

bursar [ˈbɜːsəʳ] (N) (*Univ etc*) tesorero/a *m/f*; [*of school*] administrador(a) *m/f*

bursary [ˈbɜːsərɪ] (N) (*Brit*) (*Univ*) beca *f*

burst [bɜːst] (VB: PT, PP: **burst**) (N) **1** (*in pipe*) reventón *m*
2 [*of shell etc*] estallido *m*, explosión *f*; [*of shots*] ráfaga *f* • **a ~ of activity** un arranque repentino de actividad • **in a ~ of anger** en un arranque de cólera • **a ~ of applause** una salva de aplausos • **a ~ of laughter** una carcajada • **he put on a ~ of speed** aceleró bruscamente
(ADJ) • **a ~ blood vessel** un derrame • **a ~ pipe** una tubería reventada • **a ~ tyre** un neumático reventado, una llanta pinchada (*LAm*)
(VT) [*+ pipe, balloon, bag, tyre, bubble*] reventar; [*+ banks, dam*] romper • **the river has ~ its banks** el río se ha desbordado • **to ~ open a door** abrir una puerta de golpe
(VI) [*balloon, tyre, boil, boiler, bubble, pipe*] reventar(se); [*dam*] romperse; [*shell, firework*] explotar, estallar; [*storm*] desatarse, desencadenarse; (*fig*) [*heart*] partirse • **~ing at the seams** lleno a reventar • **I'm ~ing for the loo** (*Brit**) estoy que reviento*, tengo que ir al wáter • **the door ~ open** la puerta se abrió de golpe • **I was ~ing to tell you*** reventaba de ganas de decírtelo • **to be ~ing with pride** no caber dentro de sí de orgullo • **he was ~ing with impatience** reventaba de impaciencia • **London is ~ing with young people** Londres está que bulle de juventud
▸ **burst forth** (VI + ADV) [*plants, buds*] brotar; [*water*] salir a chorro; [*sun*] aparecer de repente; [*anger, violence*] estallar
▸ **burst in** (VI + ADV) entrar violentamente • **he ~ in on the meeting** irrumpió en la reunión
▸ **burst into** (VI + PREP) **1** • **to ~ into a room** irrumpir en un cuarto
2 • **to ~ into flames** estallar en llamas • **to ~ into song** romper *or* ponerse a cantar • **to ~ into tears** echarse a llorar
▸ **burst out** (VI + ADV) **1** • **to ~ out of a room** salir repentinamente de un cuarto • **to be ~ing out of a dress*** no caber en un vestido
2 • **to ~ out laughing** echarse a reír • **to ~ out singing** romper *or* ponerse a cantar • **"no!" he ~ out** —¡no!, —gritó con pasión
▸ **burst through** (VI + PREP) [*+ barrier*] romper (violentamente) • **the sun ~ through the clouds** el sol apareció de repente entre las nubes

bursting [ˈbɜːstɪŋ] (N) (*Comput*) separación *f* de hojas
(CPD) ▸ **bursting point** • **filled to ~ point** lleno a reventar

burthen†† [ˈbɜːðən] = **burden**

burton* [ˈbɜːtn] (*Brit*) (N) • **it's gone for a ~** (*= broken etc*) se ha ido al traste*; (*= lost*) se ha perdido • **he's gone for a ~** (*Brit**) [*pilot, driver*] estiró la pata*, la palmó (*Sp‡*)

Burundi [bəˈrʊndɪ] (N) Burundi *m*

bury [ˈberɪ] (VT) **1** [*+ body, treasure*] enterrar; (*fig*) [*+ memory, matter*] echar tierra sobre • **buried by an avalanche** sepultado por una avalancha • **he wanted to be buried at sea** quería que su cadáver fuera arrojado al mar • **to be buried alive** ser enterrado vivo • IDIOMS: • **to ~ the hatchet** • **~ the tomahawk** (*US*) enterrar el hacha de guerra
2 (*= conceal*) • **he buried his face in his hands** escondió la cara entre las manos • **it's buried away in the library** está en algún rincón de la biblioteca • **to ~ o.s. in the country** perderse en la campiña • **the bullet buried itself in a tree** la bala se empotró en un árbol
3 (*= engross*) • **buried in thought** ensimismado, absorto en sus pensamientos • **she buried herself in her book** se ensimismó en la lectura, se enfrascó en el libro
4 (*= plunge*) [*+ claws, knife*] clavar (**in** en) • **to ~ a dagger in sb's heart** clavar un puñal en el corazón de algn
5 (*Sport**) (*= defeat*) aplastar*

bus [bʌs] (PL: **buses,** (*US*) **buses** *or* **busses**) (N) **1** (*= city bus*) autobús *m*, colectivo *m* (*Ven, Arg*), micro *m* (*Chile, Bol*), camión *m* (*Mex*); (*= coach*) autocar *m*, flota *f* (*Bol, Col*) • **to come/go by bus** venir/ir en autobús • IDIOM: • **to miss the bus** perder el tren

2‡ (= *car*) cacharro* *m*; (= *plane*) avión *m* viejo
3 (*Comput*) bus *m*
VT llevar en autobús • **the children are bussed to school** los niños van al colegio en autobús
VI 1 (= *go by bus*) ir en autobús
2 (*US**) (*in cafe*) quitar los platos de la mesa
CPD ▸ **bus company** empresa *f* de autobús ▸ **bus conductor** cobrador(a) *m/f* ▸ **bus conductress** cobradora *f* ▸ **bus depot** cochera *f* de autobuses ▸ **bus driver** conductor(a) *m/f* de autobús ▸ **bus fare** (= *ticket price*) tarifa *f* del autobús, precio *m* del autobús; (= *bus money*) dinero *m* del autobús ▸ **bus lane** (*Brit*) carril *m* de autobuses, carril-bus *m* ▸ **bus pass** (*Brit*) abono *m* de autobús ▸ **bus route** recorrido *m* del autobús • **the house is on a bus route** pasa un autobús por delante de la casa ▸ **bus service** servicio *m* de autobuses ▸ **bus shelter** marquesina *f* de autobús ▸ **bus station** estación *f* de autobuses ▸ **bus stop** parada *f*, paradero *m* (*LAm*) ▸ **bus ticket** billete *m* de autobús; ▹ **bus**

busbar [ˈbʌzbɑːʳ] N 1 (*Comput*) bus *m*
2 (*Tech*) barra *f* ómnibus

busboy [ˈbʌsbɔɪ] N (*US*) ayudante *m* de camarero

busby [ˈbʌzbɪ] N (*Brit*) gorro *m* alto de piel negra

bush[1] [bʊʃ] N 1 (= *shrub*) arbusto *m*, mata *f*; (= *thicket*) (*also* **bushes**) matorral *m* • IDIOM: • **to beat about the ~** andarse con rodeos *or* por las ramas
2 (*in Africa, Australia*) • **the ~** el monte
CPD ▸ **bush baby** (*Zool*) lemúrido *m* ▸ **bush fire** incendio *m* de monte ▸ **bush telegraph*** (*fig*) teléfono *m* árabe*

bush[2] [bʊʃ] N (*Tech*) cojinete *m*

bushed [bʊʃt] ADJ 1* (= *exhausted*) agotado, hecho polvo*; (= *puzzled*) perplejo, pasmado
2 (*Australia*) perdido en el monte

bushel [ˈbʊʃl] N *medida de áridos (Brit = 36,37 litros; US = 35,24 litros)*

bushland [ˈbʊʃlænd] N monte *m*

bush-league* [ˈbʊʃˌliːg] ADJ (*US*) (*Baseball*) de calidad mediocre

bushman [ˈbʊʃmən] N (PL: **bushmen**) bosquimano *m*, bosquimán *m*

bushmeat [ˈbʊʃmiːt] N *carne de animales silvestres o salvajes*

bushranger [ˈbʊʃˌreɪndʒəʳ] N (*Australia*) bandido *m*

bushwhack [ˈbʊʃˌwæk] (*US*) VI abrirse camino por el bosque
VT (= *ambush*) tender una emboscada a

bushwhacker [ˈbʊʃˌwækəʳ] N (*US*) pionero/a *m/f*, explorador(a) *m/f*

bushy [ˈbʊʃɪ] ADJ (COMPAR: **bushier**, SUPERL: **bushiest**) [*plant*] parecido a un arbusto; [*ground*] lleno de arbustos; [*hair*] espeso, tupido; [*beard, eyebrows*] poblado

bushy-tailed [ˌbʊʃɪˈteɪld] ADJ • **bright-eyed and bushy-tailed** rebosante de energía y entusiasmo

busily [ˈbɪzɪlɪ] ADV afanosamente • **he was ~ engaged in painting it** lo estaba pintando afanosamente • **everyone was ~ writing** todos escribían con ahínco

business [ˈbɪznɪs] N 1 (= *commerce*) negocios *mpl*, comercio *m* • **~ is good at the moment** el negocio va bien por el momento • **~ is ~** los negocios son los negocios • **~ as usual** (= *general slogan*) aquí no ha pasado nada; (= *notice outside shop*) "seguimos atendiendo al público durante las reformas" • **~ before pleasure** primero es la obligación que la devoción • **to carry on ~ as** tener un negocio de • **to do ~ with** negociar con • **he's in ~** se dedica al comercio • **he's in ~ in London** trabaja en una empresa comercial de Londres • **he's in the selling ~** se dedica al comercio • **now we're in ~*** ya caminamos • **if we can find a car we're in ~*** si encontramos un coche empezamos a rodar • **to go into ~** dedicarse al comercio • **the shop is losing ~** la tienda está perdiendo clientela • **he means ~** habla en serio • **I'm here on ~** estoy (en viaje) de negocios • **to go abroad on ~** ir al extranjero en viaje de negocios • **to go out of ~** quebrar • **to put sb out of ~** hacer que algn quiebre • **to set up in ~ as** montar un negocio de • **to set sb up in ~** montar un negocio a algn • **to get down to ~** ir al grano
2 (= *firm*) negocio *m*, empresa *f* • **it's a family ~** es una empresa familiar
3 (= *trade, profession*) oficio *m*, ocupación *f* • **what ~ are you in?** ¿a qué se dedica usted? • **he's got the biggest laugh in the ~** tiene la risa más fuerte que hay por aquí
4 (= *task, duty, concern*) asunto *m*, responsabilidad *f* • **to send sb about his ~** echar a algn con cajas destempladas • **the ~ before the meeting** (*frm*) los asuntos a tratar • **I have ~ with the minister** tengo asuntos que tratar con el ministro • **what ~ have you to intervene?** ¿con qué derecho interviene usted? • **we're not in ~ to** (+ *infin*) no tenemos por costumbre (+ *infin*) • **we are not in the ~ of subsidizing scroungers** no tenemos por costumbre costearles la vida a los gorrones • **mind your own ~!** • **none of your ~!*** ¡y a ti qué te importa!, ¡no te metas!* • **that's my ~** eso es cosa mía • **it is my ~ to** (+ *infin*) me corresponde (+ *infin*) • **I will make it my ~ to tell him** yo me encargaré de decírselo • **it's no ~ of mine** yo no tengo nada que ver con eso, no es cosa mía • **you had no ~ doing that** no tenías derecho a hacerlo • **they're working away like nobody's ~** están trabajando como locos • **it's none of his ~** no es asunto suyo • **any other ~** (*on agenda*) ruegos *mpl* y preguntas
5* (= *affair, matter*) asunto *m*, cuestión *f* • **the Suez ~** el asunto de Suez, la cuestión Suez • **it's a nasty ~** es un asunto feo • **finding a flat can be quite a ~** encontrar piso *or* (*LAm*) un departamento puede ser muy difícil • **did you hear about that ~ yesterday?** ¿te contaron algo de lo que pasó ayer? • **I can't stand this ~ of doing nothing** no puedo con este plan de no hacer nada • **what a ~ this is!** ¡vaya lío!
6 (*Theat*) acción *f*, gag *m*
7 • **the dog did its ~*** el perro hizo sus necesidades
8 • **he's/it's the ~*** es fantástico
CPD ▸ **business account** cuenta *f* comercial, cuenta *f* empresarial ▸ **business address** dirección *f* comercial *or* profesional ▸ **business administration** (*as course*) administración *f* de empresas ▸ **business agent** agente *mf* de negocios ▸ **business angel** (= *backer*) inversor(a) *m/f* providencial ▸ **business associate** socio/a *m/f*, asociado/a *m/f* ▸ **business card** tarjeta *f* de visita ▸ **business centre, business center** (*US*) centro *m* financiero ▸ **business class** (*Aer*) clase *f* preferente ▸ **business college** escuela *f* de administración de empresas ▸ **business consultancy** asesoría *f* empresarial ▸ **business consultant** asesor(a) *m/f* de empresas ▸ **business deal** trato *m* comercial ▸ **business district** zona *f* comercial ▸ **business end*** (*fig*) [*of tool, weapon*] punta *f* ▸ **business expenses** gastos *mpl* (comerciales) ▸ **business hours** horas *fpl* de oficina ▸ **business language** lenguaje *m* comercial ▸ **business letter** carta *f* de negocios, carta *f* comercial ▸ **business loan** préstamo *m* comercial ▸ **business lunch** comida *f* de negocios ▸ **business machines** máquinas *fpl* para la empresa ▸ **business management** dirección *f* empresarial ▸ **business manager** (*Comm, Ind*) director(a) *m/f* comercial, gerente *mf* comercial; (*Theat*) secretario/a *m/f* ▸ **business park** parque *m* industrial ▸ **business partner** socio/a *m/f* ▸ **business people** gente *f* de negocios, profesionales *mpl* ▸ **business person** hombre/mujer *m/f* de negocios, profesional *mf* ▸ **business plan** plan *m* de empresa ▸ **business practice** práctica *f* empresarial ▸ **business premises** local *msing* comercial ▸ **business school** = business college ▸ **business sense** cabeza *f* para los negocios ▸ **business Spanish** español *m* comercial ▸ **business studies** ciencias *fpl* empresariales, empresariales *fpl* ▸ **business titan** gigante *m* empresarial ▸ **business use** uso *m* empresarial • **for ~ use only** solo para uso empresarial • **the ~ use of sth** el uso de algo con fines empresariales • **you can claim a certain amount for ~ use of your home** puedes deducir una cierta cantidad por el uso con fines empresariales de tu casa ▸ **business venture** empresa *f* comercial • **his first ~ venture** su primera empresa comercial ▸ **(Faculty of) Business Studies** (Facultad *f* de) Ciencias *fpl* Empresariales ▸ **business suit** traje *m* de oficina *or* de calle ▸ **business trip** viaje *m* de negocios

businesslike [ˈbɪznɪslaɪk] ADJ [*approach, transaction, firm, person, manner*] formal, serio

businessman [ˈbɪznɪsmæn] N (PL: **businessmen**) (*gen*) hombre *m* de negocios; (= *trader*) empresario *m*; ▹ **small**

businesswoman [ˈbɪznɪsˌwʊmən] N (PL: **businesswomen**) mujer *f* de negocios; (= *trader*) empresaria *f*

busing [ˈbʌsɪŋ] N = bussing

busk [bʌsk] VI (*Brit*) tocar música (en la calle)

busker [ˈbʌskəʳ] N (*Brit*) músico/a *m/f* callejero/a

busload [ˈbʌsləʊd] N autobús *m* lleno • **they came by the ~** (*fig*) vinieron en masa, vinieron en tropel

busman [ˈbʌsmən] N (PL: **busmen**) conductor *m*/cobrador *m* de autobús • **~'s holiday** (*fig*) *ocupación del ocio parecida a la del trabajo diario*

bussing [ˈbʌsɪŋ] N (*US*) transporte *m* escolar

bust[1] [bʌst] N 1 (*Art*) busto *m*
2 (= *bosom*) pecho *m*
CPD ▸ **bust measurement** talla *f* de pecho

bust[2] [bʌst] ADJ 1* (= *broken*) estropeado, escacharrado (*Sp**)
2* (= *bankrupt*) • **to go ~** [*business*] quebrar, irse a pique*; [*person*] arruinarse
N 1 (*Police*‡) (= *raid*) redada *f*
2 (*US**) (= *failure*) pifia* *f*
VT 1* (= *break*) destrozar, escacharrar (*Sp**) • IDIOMS: • **to ~ a gut**‡ echar los bofes* • **to ~ one's ass** (*US**‡) ir de culo‡
2 (*Police*‡) (= *arrest*) agarrar, trincar (*Sp**); (= *raid*) hacer una redada en • **the police ~ed him for drugs** la policía lo agarró por cuestión de drogas, la policía lo trincó por cuestión de drogas (*Sp**) • **the police ~ed the place** la policía hizo una redada en el local
3 (*esp US**) (= *demote*) [+ *police officer*] degradar
VI* romperse, estropearse • **New York or ~!** ¡o Nueva York o nada!
▸ **bust up*** VT + ADV [+ *marriage, friendship*] romper
VI + ADV [*friends*] reñir, pelearse • **to ~ up with sb** (= *quarrel*) reñir *or* pelearse con algn; (= *break up*) romper con algn

bustard ['bʌstəd] (N) avutarda *f*
buster* ['bʌstəʳ] (N) (*in direct address*) macho *m* (*Sp**), tío *m* (*Sp**)
-buster ['bʌstəʳ] (N) (*ending in compounds*) • **sanctions-buster** infractor(a) *m/f* de sanciones • **crime-buster** *persona que esclarece crímenes*
bustier ['bu:stɪeɪ] (N) bustier *m*
-busting ['bʌstɪŋ] (SUFFIX) • **inflation-busting** (*used as noun*) combate *m* a la inflación; (*used as adjective*) de combate a la inflación • **crime-busting** (*noun*) combate *m* a la delincuencia; (*adjective*) de combate a la delincuencia
bustle¹ ['bʌsl] (N) (= *activity*) ajetreo *m*, bullicio *m*; (= *haste*) prisa *f*
(VI) (*also* **bustle about**) ir y venir • **to ~ in/out** entrar/salir afanosamente • **bustling with activity** rebosante de actividad
bustle² ['bʌsl] (N) (*Hist*) [*of dress*] polisón *m*
bustling ['bʌslɪŋ] (ADJ) [*streets*] animado, lleno de movimiento; [*crowd*] animado, afanoso
bust-up* ['bʌstʌp] (N) (= *quarrel*) riña *f*, bronca* *f*; (= *break-up*) ruptura *f*
busty* ['bʌstɪ] (ADJ) tetuda*
busway ['bʌsweɪ] (N) (*US*) carril *m* de autobuses, carril-bus *m*
busy ['bɪzɪ] (ADJ) (COMPAR: **busier**, SUPERL: **busiest**) **1** [*person*] ocupado • **are you ~?** ¿está ocupado? • **he's a ~ man** es un hombre muy ocupado • **to be ~ doing sth** estar ocupado haciendo algo • **she's ~ studying/cooking** está ocupada estudiando/cocinando • **to be ~ at** *or* **on** *or* **with** estar ocupado en *or* con • **he's ~ at his work** está ocupado en su trabajo • **to get ~** empezar a trabajar; (= *hurry*) menearse, darse prisa • **let's get ~** ¡a trabajar! • **to keep ~** mantenerse ocupado • **to keep sb ~** ocupar a algn • IDIOM: • **as ~ as a bee** ocupadísimo, atareadísimo
2 [*day, time*] activo, ajetreado • **the busiest season is the autumn** la época de mayor actividad es el otoño
3 [*place, town*] concurrido; [*scene*] animado, lleno de movimiento
4 [*telephone, line*] comunicando, ocupado
(VT) • **to ~ o.s. with/doing sth** ocuparse con/en hacer algo
(CPD) ▸ **Busy Lizzie** (*Bot*) alegría *f* de la casa ▸ **busy signal** (*esp US*) (*Telec*) señal *f* de comunicando, tono *m* (de) ocupado
busybody ['bɪzɪbɒdɪ] (N) entrometido/a *m/f*
but [bʌt] (CONJ) **1** (*contrasting*) pero • **she was poor but she was honest** era pobre pero honrada • **I want to go but I can't afford it** quiero ir, pero no tengo el dinero • **but it does move!** ¡pero sí se mueve!
2 (*in direct contradiction*) sino • **he's not Spanish but Italian** no es español sino italiano • **he didn't sing but he shouted** no cantó sino que gritó
3 (*subordinating*) • **we never go out but it rains** nunca salimos sin que llueva • **I never go there but I think of you** nunca voy allá sin pensar en ti • PROVERB: • **it never rains but it pours** llueve sobre mojado
4 (*as linker*) • **but then he couldn't have known** por otro lado, no podía saber *or* haberlo sabido • **but then you must be my cousin!** ¡entonces tú debes ser mi primo!
(ADV) (= *only*) solo, sólo, solamente; (= *no more than*) no más que

> *In the past the standard spelling for* **solo** *as an adverb was with an accent* (**sólo**). *Nowadays the* **Real Academia Española** *advises that the accented form is only required where there might otherwise be confusion with the adjective* **solo**.

> **BUT**
>
> *There are three main ways of translating the conjunction* **but**: **pero**, **sino** *and* **sino que**.
>
> **Contrasting**
>
> ▹ *To introduce a contrast or a new idea, use* **pero**:
> **Strange but interesting**
> Extraño pero interesante
> **I thought he would help me but he refused**
> Creí que me ayudaría, pero se negó
>
> ▹ *In informal language,* **pero** *can be used at the start of a comment:*
> **But where are you going to put it?**
> Pero ¿dónde lo vas a poner?
>
> NOTE: *In formal language,* **sin embargo** *or* **no obstante** *may be preferred:*
> **But, in spite of the likely benefits, he still opposed the idea**
> Sin embargo *or* No obstante, a pesar de las probables ventajas, todavía se oponía a la idea
>
> **Correcting a previous negative**
>
> ▹ *When* **but** *or* **but rather** *introduces a noun phrase, prepositional phrase or verb in the infinitive which corrects a previous negative, translate* **but** *using* **sino**:
> **Not wine, but vinegar**
> No vino, sino vinagre
> **They aren't from Seville, but from Bilbao**
> No son de Sevilla, sino de Bilbao
> **His trip to London was not to investigate the case but to hush it up**
> Su viaje a Londres no fue para investigar el caso sino para taparlo
>
> ▹ *When* **but** *or* **but rather** *introduces a verb clause (or requires a verb clause in Spanish) which corrects a previous negative, translate using* **sino que**:
> **He's not asking you to do what he says but (rather) to listen to him**
> No te pide que hagas lo que él dice, sino que le escuches
>
> **Not only ... but also**
>
> ▹ *When the* **but also** *part of this construction contains subject + verb, translate using* **no solo** *or* **no sólo** *or* **no solamente ... sino que también** *or* **sino que además**:
> **It will not only cause tension, but it will also damage the economy**
> No solo *or* No sólo *or* No solamente provocará tensiones, sino que además *or* sino que también dañará la economía
>
> ▹ *When the* **but also** *part does not contain subject + verb, translate using* **no solo** *or* **no sólo** *or* **no solamente ... sino también** *or* **sino además**:
> **Not only rich but also powerful**
> No solo *or* No sólo *or* No solamente rico sino también *or* sino además poderoso
> **We don't only want to negotiate but also to take decisions**
> No queremos solo *or* sóloor solamente negociar, sino también tomar decisiones
>
> *For further uses and examples, see main entry.*

• **if I could but speak to him** si solamente *or* solo pudiese hablar con él • **you can but try** con intentar no se pierde nada • **one cannot but admire him** no se puede sino admirarle • **she's but a child** no es más que una niña • **all but naked** casi desnudo • **had I but known** de haberlo sabido (yo), si lo hubiera sabido
(PREP) (= *except*) menos, excepto, salvo • **anything but that** cualquier cosa menos eso • **everyone but him** todos menos él • **but for you** si no fuera por ti • **the last but one** el/la penúltimo/a • **the last but three** el tercero antes del último • **there is nothing for it but to pay up** no hay más remedio que pagar • **who but she could have said something like that?** ¿quién sino ella podría haber dicho semejante cosa?
(N) pero *m*, objeción *f* • **no buts about it!** ¡no hay pero que valga! • **come on, no buts, off to bed with you!** ¡vale ya! no hay pero que valga, ¡a la cama!
butane ['bju:teɪn] (N) butano *m*; (*US*) (*for camping*) camping gas *m*
(CPD) ▸ **butane gas** gas *m* butano
butch‡ [bʊtʃ] (ADJ) [*woman*] marimacho; [*man*] macho
(N) (= *woman*) marimacho *m or f*; (= *man*) macho *m*
butcher ['bʊtʃəʳ] (N) **1** (*also fig*) carnicero/a *m/f* • **~'s (shop)** carnicería *f* • **at the ~'s** en la carnicería
2 (*US*) vendedor(a) *m/f* de dulces
3 • IDIOM: • **let's have a ~'s** (*Brit‡*) déjame verlo; ▹ RHYMING SLANG
(VT) [+ *animal*] matar; (*fig*) hacer una carnicería con, masacrar
butchery ['bʊtʃərɪ] (N) (*lit*) carnicería *f*; (*fig*) matanza *f*, carnicería *f*
butler ['bʌtləʳ] (N) mayordomo *m*
butt¹ [bʌt] (N) (= *barrel*) tonel *m*; (*for rainwater*) tina *f*, aljibe *m*
butt² [bʌt] (N) **1** (*also* **butt-end**) cabo *m*, extremo *m*; [*of gun*] culata *f*; [*of cigar*] colilla *f*
2 (*US**) (= *cigarette*) colilla *f*
3 (*esp US‡*) (= *bottom*) trasero* *m*, culo‡ *m* • IDIOM: • **to work one's ~ off** romperse los cuernos*
(CPD) ▸ **butt cheeks‡** (*US*) nalgas *fpl*
butt³ [bʌt] (N) **1** (*Archery, Shooting*) (= *target*) blanco *m* • **the ~s** el campo de tiro al blanco
2 (*fig*) blanco *m* • **she's the ~ of his jokes** ella es el blanco de sus bromas
butt⁴ [bʌt] (N) (= *push with head*) cabezazo *m*; [*of goat*] topetazo *m*
(VT) [*goat*] topetar; [*person*] dar un cabezazo a • **to ~ one's head against** dar un cabezazo contra • **to ~ one's way through** abrirse paso a cabezazos
▸ **butt in** (VI + ADV) (= *interrupt*) interrumpir; (= *meddle*) meterse
▸ **butt into** (VI + PREP) [+ *conversation*] meterse en; [+ *meeting*] interrumpir
▸ **butt out‡** (VI + ADV) (*US*) no entrometerse • **~ out!** ¡no te metas donde no te importa!
butter ['bʌtəʳ] (N) mantequilla *f*, manteca *f* (*Arg*) • IDIOM: • **~ wouldn't melt in his mouth** es una mosquita muerta*
(VT) [+ *bread*] untar con mantequilla
(CPD) ▸ **butter bean** *tipo de frijol blanco o judía blanca* ▸ **butter dish** mantequera *f* ▸ **butter icing** glaseado *m* de mantequilla ▸ **butter knife** cuchillo *m* de mantequilla
▸ **butter up*** (VT + ADV) (*Brit*) dar jabón a*
butterball* ['bʌtəbɔ:l] (N) (*US*) gordo/a *m/f*
buttercup ['bʌtəkʌp] (N) ranúnculo *m*
butter-fingered* ['bʌtə,fɪŋgəd] (ADJ) torpe
butterfingers* ['bʌtə,fɪŋgəz] (N) manazas*

b

mf • ~! ¡premio!
butterfly ['bʌtəflaɪ] (N) **1** (*Zool*) mariposa *f*
• IDIOM: • **I've got butterflies (in my stomach)** tengo los nervios en el estómago, estoy nerviosísimo
2 (*Swimming*) mariposa *f*
(CPD) ▸ **butterfly effect** efecto *m* mariposa ▸ **butterfly knot** nudo *m* de lazo ▸ **butterfly mind** mentalidad *f* frívola ▸ **butterfly net** manga *f* de mariposas ▸ **butterfly nut** tuerca *f* de mariposa ▸ **butterfly stroke** braza *f* de mariposa
buttermilk ['bʌtəmɪlk] (N) suero *m* de leche, suero *m* de manteca
butterscotch ['bʌtəskɒtʃ] (N) *dulce de azúcar terciado con mantequilla*
buttery ['bʌtərɪ] (N) despensa *f*
butt-naked* [ˌbʌt'neɪkɪd] (ADJ) (*esp US*) en bolas*
buttocks ['bʌtəks] (NPL) nalgas *fpl*
button ['bʌtn] (N) **1** (*on garment, machine*) botón *m* • **on the ~*** [*arrive*] en punto; (= *absolutely exact*) exacto • IDIOM: • **to press** *or* **push the right ~** dar en la tecla
2 (*US*) (= *badge*) insignia *f*
3 • **Buttons** (*esp Brit*) (*in hotel*) botones *m inv*
(VT) (*also* **button up**) abrochar, abotonar
• IDIOM: • **to ~ one's lip*** no decir ni mu*
(VI) abrocharse • **it ~s in front** se abrocha por delante
(CPD) ▸ **button lift** telesquí *m* ▸ **button mushroom** champiñón *m* pequeño
button-down ['bʌtndaʊn] (ADJ) [*shirt*] con cuello de botones; [*collar*] de botones
buttoned-up* ['bʌtndˌʌp] (ADJ) reservado
buttonhole ['bʌtnhəʊl] (N) **1** [*of garment*] ojal *m*
2 (*Brit*) (= *flower*) *flor que se lleva en el ojal*
(VT) (*fig*) enganchar • **I was ~d by Brian** Brian me enganchó y no me dejaba irme
buttonhook ['bʌtnhʊk] (N) abotonador *m*
button-through dress [ˌbʌtnθruː'dres] (N) vestido *m* abrochado por delante
buttress ['bʌtrɪs] (N) **1** (*Archit*) contrafuerte *m*
2 (*fig*) apoyo *m*, sostén *m*
(VT) **1** (*Archit*) apuntalar
2 (*fig*) reforzar, apoyar
butty* ['bʌtɪ] (N) (*Brit*) bocadillo *m*
buxom ['bʌksəm] (ADJ) con mucho pecho
buy [baɪ] (VB: PT, PP: **bought**) (N) compra *f*
• **a bad buy** una mala compra • **a good buy** una buena compra • **this month's best buy** la mejor oferta del mes
(VT) **1** (= *purchase*) comprar • **to buy sth for sb** • **buy sb sth** comprar algo a algn • **he bought me a bracelet** me compró una pulsera • **let me buy it for you** deja que te lo compre • **to buy sth from sb** comprar algo a algn
• **I bought it from my brother/the shop on the corner** se lo compré a mi hermano/lo compré en la tienda de la esquina • **I can't get anyone to buy it off me*** no consigo que me lo compre nadie • **you can buy them cheaper in the supermarket** en el supermercado los venden más baratos
• **money couldn't buy it** no se puede comprar con dinero • **their victory was dearly bought** la victoria les costó cara
2 (= *bribe*) sobornar, comprar*
3* (= *believe*) creer, tragar • **he won't buy that explanation** no se va a tragar esa explicación*
• **all right, I'll buy it** bueno, te creo
4 • **he bought it‡** (= *died*) estiró la pata*
▸ **buy back** (VT + ADV) volver a comprar
▸ **buy in** (VT + ADV) (*Brit*) [+ *food*] proveerse *or* abastecerse de; (*St Ex*) comprar; (*Econ*) comprar (por cuenta del dueño)
▸ **buy into** (VI + PREP) **1** [+ *company*] comprar acciones de
2 (*fig**) [+ *idea*] apoyar
▸ **buy off*** (VT + ADV) (= *bribe*) sobornar, comprar*
▸ **buy out** (VT + ADV) (*Comm*) [+ *business, partner*] comprar su parte de • **to buy o.s. out of the army** *pagar una suma de dinero para dejar el ejército antes del periodo acordado*
▸ **buy up** (VT + ADV) [+ *property*] acaparar; [+ *stock*] comprar todas las existencias de
buy-back ['baɪbæk] (N) [*of shares*] recompra *f*
(CPD) ▸ **buy-back option** opción *f* de recompra
buyer ['baɪəʳ] (N) comprador(a) *m/f*
(CPD) ▸ **buyer's market** mercado *m* favorable al comprador ▸ **buyer's remorse** arrepentimiento *m* del comprador
buying ['baɪɪŋ] (N) compra *f*
(CPD) ▸ **buying power** poder *m* adquisitivo
buy-out ['baɪaʊt] (N) compra *f* de la totalidad de las acciones • **management buy-out** compra *f* de acciones por los gerentes • **workers' buy-out** compra *f* de una empresa por los trabajadores
(CPD) ▸ **buy-out clause** cláusula *f* de rescisión
buzz [bʌz] (N) **1** [*of insect, device*] zumbido *m*; [*of conversation*] rumor *m*
2* (= *telephone call*) llamada *f* (telefónica), telefonazo* *m* • **to give sb a ~** dar un telefonazo a algn*, dar un toque a algn (*Sp**)
3* (= *thrill*) • **to get a ~ from sth** gozar con algo • **driving fast gives me a ~** conducir a toda velocidad me entusiasma
4* (= *rumour*) rumor *m*
(VT) **1*** (= *call by buzzer*) llamar por el interfono; (*US*) (*Telec*) dar un telefonazo *or* (*Sp*) un toque a*
2 (*Aer*) [+ *plane, building, ship*] pasar rozando
(VI) **1** [*insect*] zumbar
2 [*ears, crowd*] zumbar • **my head is ~ing** me zumba la cabeza
3 (*fig*) • **the school ~ed with the news** todo el colegio comentaba la noticia
(CPD) (= *trendy*) [*phrase, topic*] de moda ▸ **buzz bomb** bomba *f* volante ▸ **buzz saw** sierra *f* circular
▸ **buzz about, buzz around*** (VI + ADV) [*person*] trajinar
▸ **buzz off‡** (VI + ADV) (*esp Brit*) largarse* • ~ **off!** ¡largo de aquí!*
buzzard ['bʌzəd] (N) (*Brit*) águila *f* ratonera; (*US*) buitre *m*, gallinazo *m* (*LAm*), zopilote *m* (*CAm, Mex*)
buzzer ['bʌzəʳ] (N) **1** (= *intercom*) portero *m* automático, interfono *m*
2 (= *factory hooter*) sirena *f*
3 (*electronic*) (*on cooker, timer etc*) timbre *m*
buzzing ['bʌzɪŋ] (N) zumbido *m*
buzzkill* ['bʌzkɪl] (N) (= *person*) aguafiestas *mf inv* • **it was a real ~** nos/les *etc* bajó la moral
buzzword* ['bʌzwɜːd] (N) palabra *f* que está de moda, cliché *m*
b.v. (ABBR) = **book value**
BVM (N ABBR) = **Blessed Virgin Mary**
b/w (ABBR) (= **black and white**) b/n

by [baɪ]

PREPOSITION
ADVERB

When **by** *is the second element in a phrasal verb, eg* **go by**, **stand by**, *look up the verb. When it is part of a set combination, eg* **by chance**, **by degrees**, **by half**, *look up the other word.*

PREPOSITION

1 (= *close to*) al lado de, junto a • **the house by the church** la casa que está al lado de *or* junto a la iglesia • **come and sit by me** ven y siéntate a mi lado *or* junto a mí • **I've got it by me** lo tengo a mi lado • **"where's the bank?" — "it's by the post office"** —¿dónde está el banco? —está al lado de *or* junto a la oficina de correos • **the house by the river** la casa que hay junto al río • **a holiday by the sea** unas vacaciones en la costa
2 (= *via*) por • **he came in by the back door/by the window** entró por la puerta de atrás/por la ventana • **which route did you come by?** ¿por dónde *or* por qué camino *or* por qué ruta viniste? • **I went by Dover** fui por Dover
3 (= *past*) por delante de • **she walked by me** pasó por delante de mí • **he rushed by me without seeing me** pasó deprisa por delante de mí sin verme • **we drove by the cathedral** pasamos con el coche por delante de la catedral
4 (= *during*) • **by day** de día • **by night** de noche • **by day he's a bank clerk and by night he's a security guard** de día es un empleado de banco y de noche es guarda de seguridad • **a postcard of London by night** una postal nocturna de Londres
5 (*in expressions of time*) **a** (= *not later than*) para • **we must be there by four o'clock** tenemos que estar allí para las cuatro • **can you finish it by tomorrow?** ¿puedes terminarlo para mañana? • **I'll be back by midnight** estaré de vuelta antes de *or* para la medianoche
• **applications must be submitted by 21 April** las solicitudes deben presentarse antes del 21 de abril • **by the time I got there it was too late** cuando llegué ya era demasiado tarde
• **it'll be ready by the time you get back** estará listo para cuando regreses • **by that time** *or* **by then I knew** para entonces ya lo sabía
b (*in year, on date, on day*) • **by tomorrow/Tuesday, I'll be in France** mañana/el martes ya estaré en Francia • **by yesterday it was clear that ...** ayer ya se veía claro que ... • **by 30 September we had spent £500** a 30 de septiembre habíamos gastado 500 libras
• **by 1998 the figure had reached ...** en 1998 la cifra había llegado a ... • **by 2010 the figure will have reached ...** hacia el año 2010 la cifra habrá llegado a ...
6 (*indicating amount or rate*) • **to reduce sth by a third** reducir algo en una tercera parte • **to rent a house by the month** alquilar una casa por meses • **letters were arriving by the sackload** las cartas llegaban a montones • **it seems to be getting bigger by the minute/day** parece que va creciendo minuto a minuto/día a día • **to sell sth by the dozen** vender algo por docenas • **we get paid by the hour** nos pagan por horas • **we sell by the kilo** vendemos por kilos • **we charge by the kilometre** cobramos por kilómetro • **little by little** poco a poco • **one by one** uno tras otro, uno a uno • **two by two** de dos en dos
7 (*indicating agent, cause*) por • **the thieves were caught by the police** los ladrones fueron capturados por la policía, la policía capturó a los ladrones • **surrounded by enemies** rodeado de enemigos • **a painting by Picasso** un cuadro de Picasso • **who's that song by?** ¿de quién es esa canción? • **he had a daughter by his first wife** tuvo una hija con su primera mujer
8 (*indicating transport, method etc*) • **by air** [*travel*] en avión; [*send*] por avión, por vía aérea • **by bus/car** en autobús/coche • **to pay by cheque** pagar con cheque • **made by hand** hecho a mano • **by land** por tierra • **by the light of the moon/a candle** a la luz de la luna/de una vela • **by rail** *or* **train** en tren • **by sea** por mar

9 (*with gerund*) • **by working hard** a fuerza de mucho trabajar, trabajando mucho • **he ended by saying that** … terminó diciendo que …
10 (*= according to*) según • **by my watch it's five o'clock** según mi reloj son las cinco • **by my calculations** según mis cálculos • **to call sth by its proper name** llamar algo por su nombre • **it's all right by me** por mí no hay problema *or* está bien • **if that's okay by you** si no tienes inconveniente
11 (*measuring difference*) • **she missed the plane by a few minutes** perdió el avión por unos minutos • **we beat them to Joe's house by five minutes** llegamos a casa de Joe cinco minutos antes que ellos • **broader by a metre** un metro más ancho • **she's lighter than her brother by only a couple of pounds** pesa solo un par de libras menos que su hermano • **it's too short by a metre** es un metro más corto de lo que tendría que ser • **it missed me by inches** no me dio por un pelo, me pasó rozando
12 (*in measurements, sums*) • **a room 3 metres by 4** una habitación de 3 metros por 4 • **to divide by** dividir por *or* entre • **to multiply by** multiplicar por
13 • **by oneself** solo • **he was all by himself** estaba solo • **I did it all by myself** lo hice yo solo • **don't leave the two of them alone by themselves** no los dejes solos
14 (*with compass point*) • **north by northeast** nornordeste • **south by southwest** sudsudoeste, sursuroeste
15 (*in oaths*) por • **I swear by Almighty God** juro por Dios Todopoderoso • **by heaven*** por Dios

ADVERB
1 (*= past*) • **a train hurtled by** pasó un tren a toda velocidad • **they wouldn't let me by** no me dejaban pasar • **she rushed by without stopping** pasó a toda prisa, sin pararse
2 (*in set expressions*) • **by and by**: • **I'll be with you by and by** enseguida estoy contigo • **you'll be sorry by and by** no tardarás en arrepentirte • **by and by we heard voices** al poco rato oímos unas voces • **close** *or* **hard by** muy cerca • **by and large** en general, por lo general • **to put sth by** poner algo a un lado

---

bye[1]* [baɪ] (EXCL) (*= goodbye*) adiós, hasta luego, chao *or* chau (*esp LAm*) • **bye for now!** ¡hasta luego!
bye[2] [baɪ] (N) **1** (*Sport*) bye *m* • **to have a bye** pasar a la segunda eliminatoria por sorteo
2 • **by the bye** por cierto, a propósito
bye-bye* [ˌbaɪˈbaɪ] (EXCL) ¡adiós!, ¡hasta luego!, chao *or* chau (*esp LAm*)
bye-byes [ˈbaɪˌbaɪz] (NPL) (*baby talk*) • **to go bye-byes** dormirse, quedar dormido • **it's time to go bye-byes** es hora de acostarte
bye-law [ˈbaɪlɔː] (N) = **by-law**
by-election, bye-election [ˈbaɪɪˌlekʃən] (N) elección *f* parcial; ▹ MARGINAL SEAT

BY-ELECTION
Se denomina **by-election** en el Reino Unido y otros países de la **Commonwealth** a las elecciones convocadas con carácter excepcional cuando un escaño queda desierto por fallecimiento o dimisión de un parlamentario (**Member of Parliament**). Dichas elecciones tienen lugar únicamente en el área electoral representada por el citado parlamentario, su **constituency**.

Byelorussia [ˌbjeləʊˈrʌʃə] (N) Bielorrusia *f*
Byelorussian [ˌbjeləʊˈrʌʃən] (ADJ) bielorruso
(N) **1** (*= person*) bielorruso/a *m/f*
2 (*Ling*) bielorruso *m*
bygone [ˈbaɪgɒn] (ADJ) [*days, times*] pasado
(N) • IDIOM: • **to let ~s be ~s** olvidar el pasado • **let ~s be ~s** lo pasado, pasado está
by-law [ˈbaɪlɔː] (N) ordenanza *f* municipal
by-line [ˈbaɪlaɪn] (N) (*Press*) pie *m* de autor
by-name [ˈbaɪneɪm] (N) sobrenombre *m*; (*= nickname*) apodo *m*, mote *m*
BYOB (ABBR) (= **bring your own bottle**) trae botella
BYOD (ABBR) (= **bring your own device**) tráete tu dispositivo
bypass [ˈbaɪpɑːs] (N) **1** (*= road*) (carretera de) circunvalación *f*
2 (*Elec*) desviación *f*
3 (*Med*) (operación *f* de) by-pass *m* • **a heart ~** un by-pass de corazón • **to have a humour/charisma ~** (*hum*) no tener ni gota de sentido del humor/carisma
(VT) **1** [*+ town*] evitar entrar en
2 (*fig*) [*+ person, difficulty*] evitar
(CPD) ▸ **bypass operation** (operación *f* de) by-pass *m* ▸ **bypass surgery** cirugía *f* de by-pass
by-play [ˈbaɪpleɪ] (N) (*Theat*) acción *f* aparte, escena *f* muda
by-product [ˈbaɪˌprɒdəkt] (N) (*Chem etc*) subproducto *m*, derivado *m*; (*fig*) consecuencia *f*, resultado *m*
byre [ˈbaɪəʳ] (N) establo *m*
by-road [ˈbaɪrəʊd] (N) camino *m* vecinal, carretera *f* secundaria
bystander [ˈbaɪˌstændəʳ] (N) (*= spectator*) espectador(a) *m/f*; (*= witness*) testigo *mf* • **an innocent ~** un transeúnte que pasaba/pasa *etc* por allí
byte [baɪt] (N) (*Comput*) byte *m*, octeto *m*
byway [ˈbaɪweɪ] (N) camino *m* poco frecuentado • **the ~s of history** los aspectos poco conocidos de la historia
byword [ˈbaɪwɜːd] (N) **1** sinónimo *m* • **his name is a ~ for success** su nombre es sinónimo de éxito
2 (*= slogan*) palabra *f* de moda
by-your-leave [ˌbaɪjɔːˈliːv] (N) • **without so much as a by-your-leave** sin siquiera pedir permiso, sin más ni más
Byzantine [baɪˈzæntaɪn] (ADJ) bizantino
(N) bizantino/a *m/f*
Byzantium [baɪˈzæntɪəm] (N) Bizancio *m*

Cc

C

C[1], **c**[1] [siː] (N) 1 (= *letter*) C, c *f* • **C for Charlie** C de Carmen
2 (*Mus*) • **C** do *m* • **C major/minor** do mayor/menor • **C sharp/flat** do sostenido/bemol
C[2] (ABBR) 1 (*Literat*) (= **chapter**) cap., c., c/
2 (*Geog*) = **Cape**
3 (= **Celsius, Centigrade**) C
4 (*Pol*) = **Conservative**
c[2] (ABBR) 1 (*US*) (*Econ*) (= **cent**) c
2 (= **century**) S.
3 (= **circa**) (= *about*) h.
4 (*Math*) = **cubic**
5 (= **carat**) qts., quil.
c. (ABBR) (= **chapter**) cap., c., c/
C14 (N ABBR) (= **carbon 14**) C-14
(CPD) ▸ **C14 dating** datación *f* por C-14
C4 (ABBR) (*Brit*) (*TV*) = **Channel Four**
CA (N ABBR) 1 = **Central America**
2 = **chartered accountant**
3 (*US*) = **California**
4 (*Brit*) (= **Consumers' Association**) ≈ OCU *f* (*Sp*)
ca. (ABBR) (= **circa**) h.
C/A (ABBR) 1 (= **current account**) cta. cte., c/c
2 = **credit account**
3 = **capital account**
CAA (N ABBR) 1 (*Brit*) (= **Civil Aviation Authority**) ≈ Aviación *f* Civil
2 (*US*) = **Civil Aeronautics Authority**
CAB (N ABBR) (*Brit*) (= **Citizens' Advice Bureau**) *oficina que facilita información gratuita sobre materias legales*; ▸ CITIZENS' ADVICE BUREAU
cab [kæb] (N) 1 (= *taxi*) taxi *m*, colectivo *m* (*LAm*)
2 [*of lorry etc*] cabina *f*
3†† (*horse-drawn*) cabriolé *m*, coche *m* de caballos
(CPD) ▸ **cab driver** taxista *mf* ▸ **cab rank, cab stand** parada *f* de taxis
cabal [kəˈbæl] (N) (= *clique*) contubernio *m*, camarilla *f*; (= *conspiracy*) conspiración *f*
cabala [kəˈbɑːlə] (N) = **cabbala**
cabaret [ˈkæbəreɪ] (N) cabaret *m*
cabbage [ˈkæbɪdʒ] (N) 1 (*Bot*) col *f*, repollo *m*
2 (*fig*) (= *person*) vegetal *m*
(CPD) ▸ **cabbage white (butterfly)** mariposa *f* de la col
cabbala [kəˈbɑːlə] (N) cábala *f*
cabbalistic [ˌkæbəˈlɪstɪk] (ADJ) cabalístico
cabbie*, **cabby*** [ˈkæbɪ] (N) [*of taxi*] taxista *mf*; [*of horse-drawn cab*††] cochero *m*
caber [ˈkeɪbəʳ] (N) (*Scot*) tronco *m*; ▸ TOSS, HIGHLAND GAMES
cabin [ˈkæbɪn] (N) 1 (= *hut*) cabaña *f*
2 (*Naut*) camarote *m*; [*of lorry, plane*] cabina *f*
(CPD) ▸ **cabin boy** grumete *m* ▸ **cabin class** (*Naut*) segunda clase *f* ▸ **cabin crew** (*Aer*) tripulación *f* de pilotaje ▸ **cabin cruiser** yate *m* de crucero (a motor) ▸ **cabin fever** (= *claustrophobic feeling*) claustrofobia *f*, agobio *m* (*por estar encerrado*) ▸ **cabin trunk** baúl *m*
cabinet [ˈkæbɪnɪt] (N) 1 (= *cupboard*) armario *m*; (*for display*) vitrina *f*; (*for medicine*) botiquín *m*; (*Rad, TV*) caja *f*
2 (*Pol*) (*also* **Cabinet**) consejo *m* de ministros, gabinete *m* ministerial
(CPD) ▸ **cabinet crisis** crisis *f inv* del gobierno ▸ **cabinet meeting** consejo *m* de ministros ▸ **Cabinet Minister** ministro/a *m/f* (del Gabinete)

CABINET
El Consejo de Ministros británico (**Cabinet**) se compone de unos veinte ministros, escogidos por el Primer Ministro (**Prime Minister**). Su función es la de planificar la legislación importante y defender la política del Gobierno en los debates.
En Estados Unidos el **Cabinet** tiene meramente carácter consultivo, su función es aconsejar al Presidente. Sus miembros, escogidos por él y nombrados con el consentimiento del Senado (**Senate**), son jefes de departamentos ejecutivos o altos cargos del gobierno, pero no pueden ser miembros del Congreso (**Congress**). Existe otro grupo de asesores del Presidente, que actúan a un nivel menos oficial, que se conoce como **kitchen cabinet**.

cabinetmaker [ˈkæbɪnɪtˌmeɪkəʳ] (N) ebanista *mf*
cabinetmaking [ˈkæbɪnɪtˌmeɪkɪŋ] (N) ebanistería *f*
cable [ˈkeɪbl] (N) 1 (= *wire, rope, cablegram, pattern*) cable *m*
2 = **cable television**
(VT) 1 [+ *news, money*] mandar por cable, cablegrafiar; [+ *person*] mandar un cable a
2 (*TV*) [+ *city, homes*] instalar la televisión por cable en
(CPD) ▸ **cable address** dirección *f* cablegráfica ▸ **cable car** teleférico *m*, funicular *m* ▸ **cable railway** (*aerial*) teleférico *m*; (*funicular*) funicular *m* aéreo ▸ **cable stitch** punto *m* de trenza ▸ **cable television** televisión *f* por cable ▸ **cable transfer** (*Econ*) transferencia *f* por cable
cablecast [ˈkeɪblˌkɑːst] (N) emisión *f* de televisión por cable
(VT) emitir por cable
cablegram [ˈkeɪblgræm] (N) cablegrama *m*
cable-knit [ˈkeɪblˌnɪt] (ADJ) [*sweater*] de patrón de cable
cableway [ˈkeɪblweɪ] (N) teleférico *m*, funicular *m* aéreo
cabling [ˈkeɪblɪŋ] (N) (*Elec*) (= *cables*) red *f* de cables, cableado *m*; (= *process*) cableado *m*
cabman [ˈkæbmən] (N) (PL: **cabmen**) 1 (= *taxi driver*) taxista *m*
2†† [*of horse-drawn cab*] cochero *m*
caboodle [kəˈbuːdl] (N) • **the whole (kit and) ~*** todo el rollo*, toda la pesca*
caboose [kəˈbuːs] (N) (*US*) furgón *m* de cola
cabrio* [ˈkæbrɪəʊ] (N) descapotable *m*
cabriolet [ˌkæbrɪəʊˈleɪ] (N) descapotable *m*
cacao [kəˈkɑːəʊ] (N) cacao *m*
cache [kæʃ] (N) 1 (= *stores*) víveres *mpl* escondidos; [*of contraband, arms, explosives*] alijo *m*
2 (*Comput*) = **cache memory**
(VT) (= *hide*) esconder, ocultar; (= *hoard*) acumular
(CPD) ▸ **cache memory** (*Comput*) (memoria *f*) cache *m or f*
cachet [ˈkæʃeɪ] (N) caché *m*, cachet *m*
cack‡ [kæk] (N) (*Brit*) (*lit, fig*) mierda‡ *f*
cack-handed* [ˌkækˈhændɪd] (ADJ) (*esp Brit*) (= *clumsy*) [*person*] patoso*, desmañado; [*attempt, version*] chapucero*, torpe
cackle [ˈkækl] (N) [*of hen*] cacareo *m*; (= *laugh*) risa *f* aguda; (= *chatter*) parloteo *m* • **cut the ~!*** ¡corta el rollo!*
(VI) [*hen*] cacarear; [*person*] reírse a carcajada limpia, carcajearse
CACM (N ABBR) (= **Central American Common Market**) MCCA *m*
cacophonous [kəˈkɒfənəs] (ADJ) cacofónico
cacophony [kæˈkɒfənɪ] (N) cacofonía *f*
cactus [ˈkæktəs] (PL: **cactuses, cacti** [ˈkæktaɪ]) (N) cacto *m*, cactus *m inv*
CAD [kæd] (N ABBR) (= **computer-aided design**) DAO *m*, DAC *m* (*LAm*)
cad†* [kæd] (N) canalla *m*, sinvergüenza *m* • **you cad!** ¡canalla!*
cadaster, cadastre [kəˈdæstəʳ] (N) catastro *m*
cadaver [kəˈdeɪvəʳ] (N) (*esp US*) cadáver *m*
cadaverous [kəˈdævərəs] (ADJ) cadavérico
CADCAM [ˈkædˌkæm] (N ABBR) = **computer-aided design and manufacture**
caddie [ˈkædɪ] (*Golf*) (N) caddie *mf*
(VI) • **to ~ for sb** hacer de caddie a algn
caddis fly [ˈkædɪsflaɪ] (N) frígano *m*
caddish†* [ˈkædɪʃ] (ADJ) desvergonzado, canallesco • **~ trick** canallada *f*
caddy[1] [ˈkædɪ] (N) = **caddie**
caddy[2] [ˈkædɪ] (N) 1 (*also* **tea caddy**) cajita *f* para té
2 (*US*) (= *shopping trolley*) carrito *m* de la compra
cadence [ˈkeɪdəns] (N) (*Mus*) [*of voice*] cadencia *f*; (= *rhythm*) ritmo *m*, cadencia *f* • **the ~s of prose** el ritmo de la prosa
cadenza [kəˈdenzə] (N) cadencia *f*
cadet [kəˈdet] (N) 1 (*Mil etc*) cadete *m*
2 (= *younger son*) hijo *m* menor
(CPD) ▸ **cadet corps** (*Brit*) (*in school*) cuerpo *m* de alumnos que reciben entrenamiento militar; (*Police*) cuerpo *m* de cadetes ▸ **cadet school** escuela *f* en la que se ofrece instrucción militar
cadge* [kædʒ] (*Brit*) (VT) [+ *money, cigarette etc*] gorronear*, sablear* • **could I ~ a lift from you?** ¿me puedes llevar?, ¿me das un aventón? (*Mex*)
(VI) gorronear*, vivir de gorra* • **you can't ~ off me** no te molestes en pedirme nada

cadger* ['kædʒəʳ] N (*Brit*) gorrón/ona* *m/f*, sablista* *mf*
Cadiz [kə'dɪz] N Cádiz *m*
cadmium ['kædmɪəm] N cadmio *m*
cadre ['kædrɪ] N (*Mil etc*) cuadro *m*; (*Pol*) (= *worker, official*) delegado/a *m/f*
CAE N ABBR (= **computer-aided engineering**) IAO *f*, IAC *f* (*LAm*)
caecum, cecum (*US*) ['si:kəm] N (PL: **caeca** ['si:kə]) (intestino *m*) ciego *m*
Caesar ['si:zəʳ] N César
CPD ▸ **Caesar salad** ensalada *f* césar
Caesarean, Cesarean (*US*) [si:'zɛərɪən] N (*also* **Caesarean operation** *or* **section**) (operación *f* de) cesárea *f*
caesium, cesium (*US*) ['si:zɪəm] N cesio *m*
caesura [sɪ'zjʊərə] N (PL: **caesuras** *or* **caesurae** [sɪ'zjʊəri:]) cesura *f*
CAF, c.a.f. N ABBR (= **cost and freight**) C y F
café ['kæfeɪ] N café *m*
CPD ▸ **café bar** café *m* bar ▸ **café society** la gente de moda
cafeteria [,kæfɪ'tɪərɪə] N (restaurante *m* de) autoservicio *m*; (*in factory, office*) cafetería *f*, comedor *m*
cafetière [,kæfə'tjɛəʳ] N (*with plunger*) cafetera *f* de émbolo
caff‡ [kæf] N (*Brit*) = **café**
caffein, caffeine ['kæfi:n] N cafeína *f*
caffeine-free [,kæfi:n'fri:] ADJ [*beverage*] sin cafeína
caftan ['kæftæn] N caftán *m*
cage [keɪdʒ] N jaula *f*; (*in mine*) jaula *f* de ascensor
VT enjaular • **like a ~d tiger** como una fiera enjaulada
CPD ▸ **cage(d) bird** pájaro *m* de jaula
cagey ['keɪdʒɪ] (COMPAR: **cagier**, SUPERL: **cagiest**) ADJ (= *reserved*) reservado; (= *cautious*) cauteloso • **he was very ~ about it** en eso se anduvo con mucha reserva • **Michael was ~ about his plans after resigning** Michael mantenía celosamente en secreto sus planes tras dimitir
cagily ['keɪdʒɪlɪ] ADV [*say*] cautelosamente, con cautela
caginess ['keɪdʒɪnɪs] N [*of person, reply*] cautela *f*
cagoule [kə'gu:l] N chubasquero *m*; (*without zip*) canguro *m*
cahoots* [kə'hu:ts] NPL • IDIOM: • **to be in ~ with sb** estar conchabado con algn*
CAI N ABBR (= **computer-aided instruction**) IAO *f*
caiman ['keɪmən] N caimán *m*
Cain [keɪn] N Caín • IDIOM: • **to raise ~*** armar la gorda, protestar enérgicamente
cairn [kɛən] N montón *m* de piedras colocadas como señal
Cairo ['kaɪərəʊ] N El Cairo
caisson ['keɪsən] N (*Mech*) cajón *m* hidráulico; (*Naut*) cajón *m* de suspensión; [*of dry-dock*] puerta *f* de dique; (*Mil*) cajón *m* de municiones
cajole [kə'dʒəʊl] VT engatusar, camelar • **to ~ sb into doing sth** engatusar a algn para que haga algo
cajolery [kə'dʒəʊlərɪ] N zalamerías *fpl*
Cajun ['keɪdʒən] ADJ cajún • **~ cookery** cocina *f* tipo cajún
N **1** (= *person*) cajún *mf*
2 (*Ling*) cajún *m*

cake [keɪk] N **1** (*large*) tarta *f*, pastel *m*, torta *f* (*LAm*); (*small*) pastel *m*, queque *m* (*LAm*); (*sponge, plain*) bizcocho *m*, pan *m* dulce • **the way the national ~ is divided** (*fig*) la forma en que está repartida la tarta *or* está repartido el pastel nacional • IDIOMS: • **it's a piece of ~*** es pan comido, está tirado* • **to go** *or* **sell like hot ~s*** venderse como rosquillas • **to have one's ~ and eat it**: • **he wants to have his ~ and eat it** quiere nadar y guardar la ropa • **that takes the ~!*** ¡es el colmo!
2 (= *bar*) [*of chocolate*] barra *f*; [*of soap*] pastilla *f*
VT • **~d with mud** embarrado, cubierto de barro seco
VI [*blood*] coagularse; [*mud*] endurecerse
CPD ▸ **cake mix** polvos *mpl* para hacer pasteles ▸ **cake pan** (*US*) bizcochera *f* ▸ **cake shop** pastelería *f* ▸ **cake tin** (*for baking*) bizcochera *f*; (*for storing*) caja *f* de pastel
caked [keɪkt] PT, PP *of* **cake**
ADJ ▹ **cake**
cakewalk ['keɪkwɔ:k] N (= *dance*) cake-walk *m* (*baile y música afroamericanos*) • IDIOM: • **to be a ~** ser coser y cantar • **winning this case will be a ~** ganar este caso será coser y cantar
Cal. ABBR = **California**
cal. N ABBR = **calorie**
calabash ['kæləbæʃ] N calabaza *f*
calaboose* ['kæləbu:s] N (*US*) jaula *f*; (= *prison*) cárcel *f*
calamine ['kæləmaɪn] N (*also* **calamine lotion**) (loción *f* de) calamina *f*
calamitous [kə'læmɪtəs] ADJ calamitoso, desastroso
calamity [kə'læmɪtɪ] N calamidad *f*, desastre *m*
calcareous [kæl'kɛərɪəs] ADJ calcáreo
calcicole ['kælsɪ,kəʊl] N calcícola *f*
calcicolous [kæl'sɪkələs] ADJ calcícola
calcification [,kælsɪfɪ'keɪʃən] N calcificación *f*
calcified ['kælsɪfaɪd] ADJ calcificado
calcifugous [kæl'sɪfjəgəs] ADJ calcífugo
calcify ['kælsɪfaɪ] VT calcificar
VI calcificarse
calcium ['kælsɪəm] N calcio *m*
CPD ▸ **calcium carbonate** carbonato *m* de calcio ▸ **calcium chloride** cloruro *m* de calcio
calculable ['kælkjʊləbl] ADJ calculable
calculate ['kælkjʊleɪt] VT **1** (= *measure*) [+ *weight, speed, number, distance*] calcular
2 (= *judge*) [+ *effects, consequences, risk*] calcular
3 (= *intend*) • **his words were ~d to cause pain** había planeado expresamente sus palabras para hacer daño • **this is ~d to give him a jolt** el propósito de esto es darle una sacudida • **a move ~d to improve his popularity** una operación diseñada *or* pensada para darle mayor popularidad
VI (*Math*) calcular, hacer cálculos
▸ **calculate on** VI + PREP (= *count on*) contar con
calculated ['kælkjʊleɪtɪd] ADJ (= *deliberate*) [*insult, action*] deliberado, intencionado • **(to take) a ~ risk** (correr) un riesgo calculado
calculating ['kælkjʊleɪtɪŋ] ADJ (= *scheming*) [*person*] calculador
CPD ▸ **calculating machine** calculadora *f*, máquina *f* de calcular

calculation [,kælkjʊ'leɪʃən] N (*Math*) (= *estimation*) cálculo *m* • **to make** *or* **do a ~** realizar un cálculo
calculator ['kælkjʊleɪtəʳ] N (= *machine*) calculadora *f*
calculus ['kælkjʊləs] N (PL: **calculuses** *or* **calculi** ['kælkjʊlaɪ]) (*Math*) cálculo *m* • **integral/differential ~** cálculo *m* integral/diferencial
Calcutta [kæl'kʌtə] N Calcuta *f*
caldron ['kɔ:ldrən] = **cauldron**
Caledonia [,kælə'dəʊnɪə] N Caledonia *f*
Caledonian [,kælɪ'dəʊnɪən] ADJ caledoniano
N caledoniano/a *m/f*
calendar ['kæləndəʳ] N **1** (= *chart*) calendario *m*
2 (= *year*) calendario *m* • **the Church ~** el calendario eclesiástico • **the university ~** (*Brit*) el calendario universitario • **the most important event in the sporting ~** el acontecimiento más importante del año *or* calendario deportivo
3 (*Jur*) lista *f* (de pleitos)
CPD ▸ **calendar month** mes *m* civil ▸ **calendar year** año *m* civil
calf[1] [kɑ:f] N (PL: **calves**) **1** (= *young cow*) becerro/a *m/f*, ternero/a *m/f*; (= *young seal, elephant etc*) cría *f*; (= *young whale*) ballenato *m* • **the cow is in** *or* **with ~** la vaca está preñada • IDIOM: • **to kill the fatted ~** celebrar una fiesta de bienvenida
2 = **calfskin**
CPD ▸ **calf love** amor *m* juvenil
calf[2] [kɑ:f] N (PL: **calves**) (*Anat*) pantorrilla *f*, canilla *f* (*esp LAm*)
calfskin ['kɑ:fskɪn] N piel *f* de becerro
caliber ['kælɪbəʳ] N (*US*) = **calibre**
calibrate ['kælɪbreɪt] VT [+ *gun*] calibrar; [+ *scale of measuring instrument*] graduar
calibrated ['kælɪbreɪtɪd] ADJ calibrado
calibration [,kælɪ'breɪʃən] N [*of gun etc*] calibración *f*; [*of measuring instrument*] graduación *f*
calibre, caliber (*US*) ['kælɪbəʳ] N **1** [*of rifle*] calibre *m*
2 [*of person*] calibre *m*, talla *f* • **a man of his ~** un hombre de su calibre *or* talla • **then he showed his real ~** luego demostró su verdadero valor *or* su verdadera talla • **the high ~ of the research staff** el alto nivel de los investigadores
calico ['kælɪkəʊ] N (PL: **calicoes** *or* **calicos**) calicó *m*, percal *m*
ADJ [*jacket, shirt etc*] de percal
Calif. ABBR = **California**
California [,kælɪ'fɔ:nɪə] N California *f*
Californian [,kælɪ'fɔ:nɪən] ADJ californiano
N californiano/a *m/f*
californium [,kælɪ'fɔ:nɪəm] N californio *m*
calipers ['kælɪpəz] NPL (*US*) = **callipers**
caliph ['keɪlɪf] N califa *m*
caliphate ['keɪlɪfeɪt] N califato *m*
calisthenics [,kælɪs'θenɪks] NSING (*US*) = **callisthenics**
CALL [kɔ:l] N ABBR = **computer-assisted language learning**
call [kɔ:l] N **1** (= *cry*) llamada *f*, llamado *m* (*LAm*); (= *shout*) grito *m*; [*of bird*] canto *m*, reclamo *m*; (*imitating bird's cry*) reclamo *m*; (*imitating animal's cry*) chilla *f* • **they came at my ~** acudieron a mi llamada • **please give me a ~ at seven** (*in hotel*) despiérteme a las siete, por favor; (*at friend's*) llámame a las siete • **within ~** al alcance de la voz
2 (*Telec*) llamada *f* • **long-distance ~** conferencia *f* • **to make a ~** llamar (por teléfono), hacer una llamada, telefonear (*esp LAm*)

CAJUN
A los habitantes del sur de Luisiana que hablan un dialecto francés se les llama **Cajuns**. Son los descendientes de los canadienses franceses expulsados de Nueva Escocia por los británicos en 1755, llamada entonces Acadia (**Cajun** es la forma acortada de **Acadian**). El dialecto combina francés arcaico con inglés y español, junto con algunas palabras y frases hechas indias. Tanto su comida picante como su música se conocen hoy en el mundo entero.

3 (= *appeal, summons, invitation*) llamamiento *m*, llamado (*LAm*); (*Aer*) (*for flight*) anuncio *m*; (*Theat*) (*to actor*) llamamiento *m* • **a ~ went to the fire brigade** se llamó a los bomberos • **he's had a ~ to the Palace** le han llamado a palacio • **to answer the ~** (*Rel*) acudir al llamamiento • **the boat sent out a ~ for help** el barco emitió una llamada de socorro • **there were ~s for the Minister's resignation** hubo quienes pidieron la dimisión del ministro • **a ~ for a strike** una convocatoria de huelga • **a ~ for congress papers** una convocatoria de ponencias para un congreso • **to be on ~** (= *on duty*) estar de guardia; (= *available*) estar disponible • **money on ~** dinero *m* a la vista • **the minister sent out a ~ to the country to remain calm** el ministro hizo un llamamiento al país para que conservara la calma
4 (= *lure*) llamada *f* • **the ~ of duty** la llamada del deber • **to answer the ~ of nature** (*euph*) hacer sus necesidades fisiológicas • **the ~ of the sea** la llamada del mar • **the ~ of the unknown** la llamada de lo desconocido
5 (= *visit*) (*also Med*) visita *f* • **the boat makes a ~ at Vigo** el barco hace escala en Vigo • **to pay a ~ on sb** ir a ver a algn, hacer una visita a algn • **port of ~** puerto *m* de escala
6 (= *need*) motivo *m* • **you had no ~ to say that** no tenías motivo alguno para decir eso • **there is no ~ for alarm** no tienen por qué asustarse
7 (= *demand*) demanda *f* (**for** de) • **there isn't much ~ for these now** hay poca demanda de estos ahora
8 (= *claim*) • **to have first ~ on sth** (*resources etc*) tener prioridad en algo; (*when buying it*) tener opción de compra sobre algo • **there are many ~s on my time** hay muchos asuntos que requieren mi atención • **the UN has many ~s on its resources** la ONU reparte sus recursos en muchos frentes
9 (*Bridge*) marca *f*, voz *f* • **whose ~ is it?** ¿a quién le toca declarar?
10 • IDIOM: • **to have a close ~** escapar por un pelo, salvarse de milagro • **that was a close ~** eso fue cosa de milagro
(VT) **1** (= *shout out*) [+ *name, person*] llamar, gritar • **did you ~ me?** ¿me llamaste? • **they ~ed me to see it** me llamaron para que lo viese; ▹ **attention, halt, name, shot, tune**
2 (= *summon*) [+ *doctor, taxi*] llamar; [+ *meeting, election*] convocar • **to be ~ed to the Bar** (*Brit*) (*Jur*) licenciarse como abogado, recibirse de abogado (*LAm*) • **he felt ~ed to serve God** se sentía llamado a servir al Señor • **to ~ a strike** convocar una huelga • **to ~ sb as a witness** citar a algn como testigo
3 (*Telec*) llamar (por teléfono) • **I'll ~ you tomorrow** te llamo mañana • **London ~ed you this morning** esta mañana le llamaron desde Londres • **don't ~ us, we'll ~ you** no se moleste en llamar, nosotros le llamaremos
4 (= *announce*) [+ *flight*] anunciar
5 (= *waken*) despertar, llamar • **please ~ me at eight** me llama *or* despierta a las ocho, por favor
6 (= *name, describe*) llamar • **to be ~ed** llamarse • **I'm ~ed Peter** me llamo Peter • **what are you ~ed?** ¿cómo te llamas? • **they ~ each other by their surnames** se llaman por los apellidos • **what are they ~ing him?** ¿qué nombre le van a poner? • **they're ~ing the boy John** al niño le van a llamar John • **I ~ed him a liar** lo llamé mentiroso • **are you ~ing me a liar?** ¿me está diciendo que soy un mentiroso?, ¿me está llamando mentiroso?
7 (= *consider*) • **I ~ it an insult** para mí eso es un insulto • **let's ~ it £50** quedamos en 50 libras • **I had nothing I could ~ my own** no tenía más que lo puesto • **what time do you ~ this?** (*iro*) ¿qué hora crees que es? • **~ yourself a friend?** (*iro*) ¿y tú dices que eres un amigo? • IDIOM: • **let's ~ it a day*** ya basta por hoy
8 [+ *result*] (*of election, race*) hacer público, anunciar • **it's too close to ~** la cosa está muy igualada *or* reñida
9 (*Bridge*) declarar • **to ~ three spades** declarar tres picas
10 (*US*) (*Sport*) [+ *game*] suspender
(VI) **1** (= *shout*) [*person*] llamar; (= *cry, sing*) [*bird*] cantar • **did you ~?** ¿me llamaste? • **to ~ to sb** llamar a algn
2 (*Telec*) • **who's ~ing?** ¿de parte de quién?, ¿quién (le) llama? • **London ~ing** (*Rad*) aquí Londres
3 (= *visit*) pasar (a ver) • **please ~ again** (*Comm*) gracias por su visita
(CPD) ▸ **call centre** (*Brit*) (*Telec*) centro *m* de atención al cliente, call centre *m* ▸ **call girl** prostituta *f* (*que concierta citas por teléfono*) ▸ **call letters** (*US*) (*Telec*) letras *fpl* de identificación, indicativo *m* ▸ **call loan** (*Econ*) préstamo *m* cobrable a la vista ▸ **call money** (*Econ*) dinero *m* a la vista ▸ **call number** (*US*) [*of library book*] número *m* de catalogación ▸ **call option** (*St Ex*) opción *f* de compra a precio fijado ▸ **call sign** (*Rad*) (señal *f* de) llamada *f* ▸ **call signal** (*Telec*) código *m* de llamada

▸ **call aside** (VT + ADV) [+ *person*] llamar aparte

▸ **call at** (VI + PREP) [+ *house*] visitar, pasar por; [+ *port*] hacer escala en

▸ **call away** (VT + ADV) • **he was ~ed away** tuvo que salir *or* marcharse, se vio obligado a ausentarse (*frm*) (**from** de) • **to be ~ed away on business** tener que ausentarse por razones de trabajo *or* asuntos de negocios

▸ **call back** (VT + ADV) **1** (*Telec*) (= *call again*) volver a llamar a; (= *return call*) devolver la llamada a
2 (= *recall*) hacer volver
(VI + ADV) **1** (*Telec*) (= *call again*) volver a llamar; (= *return call*) devolver la llamada • **can you ~ back later? I'm busy just now** ¿puede volver a llamar dentro de un rato? ahora no puedo atenderlo
2 (= *return*) volver, regresar (*LAm*) • **I'll ~ back later** volveré más tarde

▸ **call down** (VT + ADV) **1** (*liter*) [+ *blessings*] pedir (**on** para) • **to ~ curses down on sb** maldecir a algn, lanzar maldiciones contra algn
2 (*US**) (= *scold*) echar la bronca a*, poner verde a*

▸ **call for** (VI + PREP) **1** (= *summon*) [+ *wine, bill*] pedir • **to ~ for help** pedir auxilio
2 (= *demand*) [+ *courage, action*] exigir, requerir • **this ~s for firm measures** esto exige *or* requiere unas medidas contundentes • **this ~s for a celebration!** ¡esto hay que celebrarlo!
3 (= *collect*) [+ *person*] pasar a buscar; [+ *goods*] recoger
4 (*US*) (= *predict*) pronosticar, prever

▸ **call forth** (VT + ADV) sacar; [+ *remark*] inspirar; [+ *protest*] motivar, provocar

▸ **call in** (VT + ADV) **1** (= *summon*) hacer entrar; [+ *doctor, expert, police*] llamar a
2 (*Comm etc*) (= *withdraw*) [+ *faulty goods, currency*] retirar; [+ *book, loan*] pedir la devolución de
(VI + ADV) venir, pasar • **to ~ in on sb** pasar a ver a algn • **we can ~ in on James on the way home** podemos pasar a ver a James de camino a casa • **~ in any time** ven cuando quieras, pasa por aquí cuando quieras

▸ **call off** (VT + ADV) **1** (= *cancel*) [+ *meeting, race*] cancelar, suspender; [+ *deal*] anular; [+ *search*] abandonar, dar por terminado • **the strike was ~ed off** se desconvocó la huelga
2 [+ *dog*] llamar (*para que no ataque*)

▸ **call on** (VI + PREP) **1** (= *visit*) pasar a ver
2 (*also* **call upon**) (= *appeal*) • **to ~ (up)on sb for help** pedir ayuda a algn, acudir a algn pidiendo ayuda • **to ~ (up)on sb to do sth** (= *appeal*) apelar a algn para que haga algo; (= *demand*) exigir a algn que haga algo • **he ~ed (up)on the nation to be strong** hizo un llamamiento a la nación para que se mostrara fuerte
3 (*also* **call upon**) (= *invite to speak*) ceder *or* pasar la palabra a • **I now ~ (up)on Mr Brown to speak** cedo la palabra al Sr. Brown

▸ **call out** (VT + ADV) **1** (= *shout out*) [+ *name*] gritar
2 (= *summon*) [+ *doctor, rescue services*] llamar; [+ *troops*] hacer intervenir • **to ~ workers out on strike** llamar a los obreros a la huelga
(VI + ADV) (*in pain, for help etc*) gritar

▸ **call out for** (VI + PREP) (= *require*) pedir; (= *summon, ask for*) llamar • **to ~ out for help** pedir ayuda • **the situation ~s out for an urgent solution** la situación exige una solución urgente • **to ~ out for sb to do sth** pedir a algn que haga algo

▸ **call over** (VT + ADV) llamar

▸ **call round** (VI + ADV) pasar por casa • **I'll ~ round in the morning** pasaré por ahí por la mañana • **to ~ round to see sb** ir de visita a casa de algn

▸ **call together** (VT + ADV) convocar, reunir

▸ **call up** (VT + ADV) **1** (*Mil*) llamar para el servicio militar
2 (*Telec*) llamar (por teléfono)
3 [+ *memories*] traer a la memoria

▸ **call upon** (VI + PREP) (*frm*) ▹ **call on**

callable ['kɔːləbəl] (ADJ) (*Econ*) redimible, amortizable

callback ['kɔːlbæk] (N) (*Comm*) retirada *f* (*de productos con defecto de origen*)

callbox ['kɔːlbɒks] (N) (*Brit*) cabina *f* (telefónica)

callboy ['kɔːlbɔɪ] (N) (*Theat*) traspunte *m*; (*in hotel*) botones *m inv*

callcard ['kɔːlkɑːd] (N) (*esp Irl*) tarjeta *f* telefónica

called-up capital [ˌkɔːldʌp'kæpɪtl] (N) capital *m* desembolsado

caller ['kɔːlə^r] (N) **1** (= *visitor*) visita *f* • **the first ~ at the shop** el primer cliente de la tienda
2 (*Brit*) (*Telec*) persona *f* que llama • **~, please wait** espere por favor
(CPD) ▸ **caller display, caller ID display** identificación *f* de llamada entrante

calligrapher [kə'lɪgrəfə^r] (N) calígrafo/a *m/f*

calligraphic [ˌkælɪ'græfɪk] (ADJ) caligráfico

calligraphy [kə'lɪgrəfɪ] (N) caligrafía *f*

call-in ['kɔːlɪn] (N) (*also* **call-in program**) (*US*) (programa *m*) coloquio *m* (por teléfono)

calling ['kɔːlɪŋ] (N) (= *vocation*) vocación *f*, profesión *f*
(CPD) ▸ **calling card** (*esp US*) tarjeta *f* de visita comercial

callipers, calipers (*US*) ['kælɪpəz] (NPL) (*Med*) soporte *msing* ortopédico; (*Math*) calibrador *msing*

callisthenics, calisthenics (*US*) [ˌkælɪs'θenɪks] (NSING) calistenia *f*

callosity [kæ'lɒsɪtɪ] (N) callo *m*, callosidad *f*

callous ['kæləs] (ADJ) **1** [*person, remark*] insensible, cruel; [*treatment, murder, crime, attack*] despiadado, cruel • **his ~ disregard for their safety** su cruel indiferencia ante su seguridad
2 (*Med*) calloso

N (*Med*) callo *m*

calloused ['kæləsd] ADJ [*fingers, hands*] encallecido, calloso

callously ['kæləslɪ] ADV despiadadamente, cruelmente

callousness ['kæləsnɪs] N insensibilidad *f*, crueldad *f*

call-out charge ['kɔːlaʊt,tʃɑːdʒ], **call-out fee** ['kɔːlaʊt,fiː] N gastos *mpl* de desplazamiento

callow ['kæləʊ] ADJ (= *immature*) [*youth*] imberbe, bisoño

call-up ['kɔːlʌp] N **1** (*Mil*) llamada *f* al servicio militar; [*of reserves*] movilización *f*; (= *conscription*) servicio *m* militar obligatorio
2 (*Sport*) convocatoria *f* • **to get a call-up into a squad** ser convocado para jugar con un equipo
CPD ▸ **call-up papers** (*Mil*) notificación *fsing* de llamada a filas

callus ['kæləs] N (PL: **calluses**) = **callous**

callused ['kæləst] ADJ = **calloused**

calm [kɑːm] ADJ (COMPAR: **calmer**, SUPERL: **calmest**) **1** (= *unruffled*) [*person, voice, place*] tranquilo • **to grow ~** tranquilizarse, calmarse • **to keep** *or* **remain ~** mantener la calma • **keep ~!** ¡tranquilo(s)!, ¡calma! • **on ~er reflection, she decided that it would be a mistake** tras un periodo de calma y reflexión, decidió que sería un error • **(cool,) ~ and collected** tranquilo y con dominio de sí mismo • **I feel ~er now** ahora estoy más tranquilo *or* calmado
2 (= *still*) [*sea, lake, water, weather*] en calma; [*day, evening*] sin viento • **the sea was dead ~** el mar estaba en calma chicha
3 (*Econ*) [*market, trading*] sin incidencias
N calma *f*, tranquilidad *f* • **the ~ before the storm** (*lit, fig*) la calma antes de la tormenta; (*Naut*) • **a dead ~** una calma chicha
VT (*also* **calm down**) [+ *person*] calmar, tranquilizar • **to ~ o.s.** calmarse, tranquilizarse • **~ yourself!** ¡cálmate!, ¡tranquilízate! • **to ~ sb's fears** tranquilizar a algn
VI [*sea, wind*] calmarse
▸ **calm down** VT + ADV = **calm**
VI + ADV [*person*] tranquilizarse, calmarse; [*wind*] amainar, calmarse • **~ down!** ¡cálmate!, ¡tranquilízate!; (*to excited child*) ¡tranquilízate!

calming ['kɑːmɪŋ] ADJ tranquilizante, calmante

calmly ['kɑːmlɪ] ADV [*walk*] tranquilamente; [*speak, discuss, reply*] con calma, tranquilamente; [*react, think*] con calma

calmness ['kɑːmnɪs] N [*of person, voice*] calma *f*, tranquilidad *f*; [*of weather, sea*] calma *f*

Calor gas® ['kælə,gæs] N (*Brit*) butano *m*

caloric [,kə'lɒrɪk] ADJ calórico, térmico
CPD ▸ **caloric energy** energía *f* calórica *or* térmica

calorie ['kælərɪ] N caloría *f* • **she's very ~-conscious** es muy cuidadosa con la línea • **a ~-controlled diet** un régimen de bajo contenido calórico

-calorie [-'kælərɪ] SUFFIX • **low-calorie** bajo en calorías • **reduced-calorie** con menos calorías • **low-calorie product** producto *m* bajo en calorías

calorific [,kælə'rɪfɪk] ADJ calorífico
CPD ▸ **calorific value** (*Phys*) valor *m* calorífico

calque [kælk] N calco *m* (**on** de)

calumniate [kə'lʌmnɪeɪt] VT (*frm*) calumniar

calumny ['kæləmnɪ] N (*frm*) calumnia *f*

Calvados ['kælvə,dɒs] N Calvados *m*

Calvary ['kælvərɪ] N Calvario *m*

calve [kɑːv] VI parir

calves [kɑːvz] NPL *of* **calf**

Calvin ['kælvɪn] N Calvino

Calvinism ['kælvɪnɪzəm] N calvinismo *m*

Calvinist ['kælvɪnɪst] ADJ calvinista
N calvinista *mf*

Calvinistic [,kælvɪ'nɪstɪk] ADJ calvinista

calypso [kə'lɪpsəʊ] N calipso *m*

calyx ['keɪlɪks] N (PL: **calyxes** *or* **calyces** ['keɪlɪsiːz]) cáliz *m*

cam¹ [kæm] N leva *f*

cam²* [kæm] N ABBR = **camera**

CAM [kæm] N ABBR (= **computer-aided manufacture**) FAO *f*

camaraderie [,kæmə'rɑːdərɪ] N compañerismo *m*

camber ['kæmbəʳ] N (*in road*) combadura *f*
VT combar, arquear
VI combarse, arquearse

Cambodia [kæm'bəʊdɪə] N Camboya *f*

Cambodian [kæm'bəʊdɪən] ADJ camboyano
N camboyano/a *m/f*

cambric ['keɪmbrɪk] N batista *f*

Cambs ABBR (*Brit*) = **Cambridgeshire**

camcorder ['kæmkɔːdəʳ] N videocámara *f*, filmadora *f* (*LAm*)

came [keɪm] PT *of* **come**

camel ['kæməl] N **1** (= *animal*) camello *m*
2 (= *colour*) color *m* camello
CPD ▸ **camel coat** (*also* **camelhair coat**) abrigo *m* de pelo de camello ▸ **camel hair** pelo *m* de camello

camellia [kə'miːlɪə] N camelia *f*

cameo ['kæmɪəʊ] N **1** (= *jewellery*) camafeo *m*
2 (*Cine*) (*also* **cameo role**) cameo *m*
CPD ▸ **cameo appearance** cameo *m* ▸ **cameo brooch** camafeo *m*

camera ['kæmərə] N **1** (*Phot*) cámara *f*, máquina *f* fotográfica; (*Cine, TV*) cámara *f* • **on ~** delante de la cámara, en cámara • **to be on ~** estar enfocado
2 (*Jur*) • **in ~** a puerta cerrada
CPD ▸ **camera angle** ángulo *m* de la cámara ▸ **camera crew** equipo *m* de cámara ▸ **camera phone** móvil *m* con cámara (*Sp*), celular *m* con cámara (*LAm*) ▸ **camera-ready copy** material *m* preparado para la cámara

cameraman ['kæmərəmæn] N (PL: **cameramen**) cámara *m*, operador *m*

camera-shy ['kæmərəʃaɪ] ADJ • **to be camera-shy** cohibirse en presencia de la cámara

camerawoman ['kæmərə,wʊmən] N (PL: **camerawomen**) cámara *f*, operadora *f*

camerawork ['kæmərə,wɜːk] N (*Cine*) manejo *m* de la cámara

Cameroon, **Cameroun** [,kæmə'ruːn] N Camerún *m*

Cameroonian [,kæmə'ruːnɪən] ADJ camerunés, camerunense
N camerunés/esa *m/f*, camerunense *mf*

camiknickers ['kæmɪ,nɪkəz] NPL *especie de body holgado o camisón y braga de una sola pieza*

camisole ['kæmɪsəʊl] N camisola *f*

camomile ['kæməʊmaɪl] N camomila *f*
CPD ▸ **camomile tea** manzanilla *f*

camouflage ['kæməflɑːʒ] N camuflaje *m*
VT camuflar

camp¹ [kæmp] N **1** (= *collection of tents*) campamento *m*; (= *organized site*) camping *m* • **to make** *or* **pitch ~** poner *or* montar el campamento, acampar • **to break** *or* **strike ~** levantar el campamento
2 (*Pol etc*) bando *m*, facción *f* • IDIOM: • **to have a foot in both ~s** tener intereses en ambos bandos
VI **1** (*in tent*) acampar • **to go ~ing** ir de camping
2* (= *stay*) alojarse temporalmente
CPD ▸ **camp bed** cama *f* de campaña, cama *f* plegable, catre *m* (*LAm*) ▸ **camp chair** silla *f* plegable ▸ **camp counselor** (*US*) animador(a) *m/f* (*de camping*) ▸ **camp follower** (= *sympathizer*) simpatizante *mf*; (*Mil*) (= *prostitute*) prostituta *f*; (= *civilian worker*) trabajador(a) *m/f* civil ▸ **camp site** camping *m* ▸ **camp stool** taburete *m* plegable ▸ **camp stove** camping gas® *m*
▸ **camp out** VI + ADV pasar la noche al aire libre • **to ~ out on the beach** pasar la noche en la playa

camp² [kæmp] ADJ **1** (= *affected, theatrical*) amanerado, afectado
2 (= *effeminate*) afeminado • IDIOM: • **to be as ~ as a row of tents*** tener mucha pluma*, ser mariquita perdido*
N **1** (*Theat*) (*also* **high camp**) amaneramiento *m*
2 (= *effeminacy*) lo afeminado
VT • **to ~ it up*** parodiarse a sí mismo

campaign [kæm'peɪn] N (*Mil*) (*also fig*) campaña *f* • **election ~** campaña *f* electoral
VI (*Mil*) (*also fig*) hacer campaña • **to ~ for/against** hacer campaña a favor de/en contra de
CPD ▸ **campaign trail** recorrido *m* electoral ▸ **campaign worker** colaborador(a) *m/f* en una campaña política

campaigner [kæm'peɪnəʳ] N **1** (*Mil*) • **old ~** veterano/a *m/f*
2 (= *supporter*) defensor(a) *m/f*, partidario/a *m/f* • **a ~ for sth** un partidario *or* defensor de algo • **environmental ~s** defensores del medio ambiente • **a ~ against sth** un luchador contra algo

campanile [,kæmpə'niːlɪ] N campanario *m*

campanologist [,kæmpə'nɒlədʒɪst] N campanólogo/a *m/f*

campanology [,kæmpə'nɒlədʒɪ] N campanología *f*

camper ['kæmpəʳ] N **1** (= *person*) campista *mf*; (*in holiday camp*) veraneante *mf*
2 (*also* **camper van**) caravana *f*, autocaravana *f*

campfire ['kæmp'faɪə] N hoguera *f* de campamento; [*of scouts*] reunión *f* alrededor de la hoguera

campground ['kæmpgraʊnd] N (*US*) camping *m*

camphone ['kæmfəʊn] N móvil *m* con cámara (*Sp*), celular *m* con cámara (*LAm*)

camphor ['kæmfəʳ] N alcanfor *m*

camphorated ['kæmfəreɪtɪd] ADJ alcanforado

camping ['kæmpɪŋ] N camping *m*
CPD ▸ **Camping gas**® (*Brit*) (= *gas*) gas *m* butano; (*US*) (= *stove*) camping gas® *m* ▸ **camping ground**, **camping site** (terreno *m* de) camping *m* ▸ **camping stove** camping gas® *m* ▸ **camping van** caravana *f*, autocaravana *f*

campion ['kæmpɪən] N colleja *f*

campus ['kæmpəs] N (PL: **campuses**) (*Univ*) (= *district*) ciudad *f* universitaria; (= *internal area*) recinto *m* universitario, campus *m inv*

campy* ['kæmpɪ] ADJ = **camp²**

CAMRA ['kæmrə] N ABBR (*Brit*) (= **Campaign for Real Ale**) *organización para la defensa y promoción de la cerveza tradicional*

camshaft ['kæmʃɑːft] N (*Aut*) árbol *m* de levas

can¹ [kæn] MODAL VB (NEG: **cannot**, **can't**, CONDIT, PT: **could**) **1** (= *be able to*) poder • **he can do it if he tries hard** puede hacerlo si se esfuerza • **I can't** *or* **cannot go any further** no puedo seguir • **I'll tell you all I can** te diré todo lo que pueda • **he will do all he can to**

help you hará lo posible por ayudarte • **you can but ask** con preguntar no se pierde nada • **they couldn't help it** ellos no tienen la culpa • **"have another helping" — "I really couldn't"** —¿otra ración? —no puedo
2 (= *know how to*) saber • **he can't swim** no sabe nadar • **can you speak Italian?** ¿sabes (hablar) italiano?
3 (= *may*) poder • **can I use your telephone?** ¿puedo usar su teléfono? • **can I have your name?** ¿me dice su nombre? • **could I have a word with you?** ¿podría hablar contigo un momento? • **can't I come too?** ¿puedo ir también?
4 (*with verbs of perception: not translated*) • **I can hear it** lo oigo • **I couldn't see it anywhere** no lo veía en ninguna parte • **I can't understand why** no comprendo por qué
5 (*expressing disbelief, puzzlement*) • **that cannot be!** ¡eso no puede ser!, ¡es imposible! • **he can't have said that** no puede haber dicho eso • **they can't have left already!** ¡no es posible que ya se han ido! • **how could you lie to me!** ¿cómo pudiste mentirme? • **how can you say that?** ¿cómo te atreves a decir eso? • **you can't be serious!** ¿lo dices en serio? • **it can't be true!** ¡no puede ser! • **what can he want?** ¿qué querrá? • **where on earth can she be?** ¿dónde demonios puede estar?
6 (*expressing possibility, suggestion etc*) • **he could be in the library** puede que esté en la biblioteca • **you could try telephoning his office** ¿por qué no le llamas a su despacho? • **they could have forgotten** puede (ser) que se hayan olvidado • **you could have told me!** ¡podías habérmelo dicho! • **it could have been a wolf** podía ser un lobo • **I reckon you could have got a job last year** creo que podías obtener un trabajo el año pasado
7 (= *want to*) • **I'm so happy I could cry** soy tan feliz que me dan ganas de llorar *or* que me voy a echar a llorar • **I could have cried** me daban ganas de llorar • **I could scream!** ¡es para volverse loco!
8 (= *be occasionally capable of*) • **she can be very annoying** a veces te pone negro • **it can get very cold here** aquí puede llegar a hacer mucho frío
9 (*in comparisons*) • **I'm doing it as well as I can** lo hago lo mejor que puedo • **as cheap as can be** lo más barato posible • **as big as big can be** lo más grande posible • **she was as happy as could be** estaba de lo más feliz
10 • **could do with: I could do with a drink** ¡qué bien me vendría una copa! • **we could do with a bigger house** nos convendría una casa más grande; ▹ **ABLE, CAN**

can² [kæn] (N) **1** (= *container*) (*for foodstuffs*) bote *m*, lata *f*; (*for oil, water etc*) bidón *m* • **a can of beer** una lata de cerveza • **IDIOMS:** • **a can of worms*** un asunto peliagudo • **to open a can of worms*** abrir la caja de Pandora • **(to be left) to carry the can** (*Brit**) pagar el pato
2 (*esp US*) (= *garbage can*) cubo *m or* (*LAm*) bote *m or* tarro *m* de la basura
3 (*Cine*) [*of film*] lata *f* • **IDIOM:** • **it's in the can*** está en el bote*
4 (*US‡*) (= *prison*) chirona* *f*
5 (*US‡*) (= *toilet*) wáter *m*
6 (*US‡*) (= *buttocks*) culo‡ *m*
(VT) **1** [+ *food*] enlatar, envasar • **IDIOM:** • **can it!** (*US‡*) ¡cállate!
2 (*US**) (= *dismiss*) [+ *employee*] despedir
(CPD) ▸ **can opener** abrelatas *m inv*

Canaan ['keɪnən] (N) Canaán *m*

Canaanite ['keɪnənaɪt] (N) canaanita *mf*

Canada ['kænədə] (N) Canadá *m*

Canadian [kə'neɪdɪən] (ADJ) canadiense
(N) canadiense *mf*
(CPD) ▸ **Canadian French** (= *language*) francés *m* de Canadá

canal [kə'næl] (N) **1** (*for barge*) canal *m*
2 (*Anat*) tubo *m*
(CPD) ▸ **canal boat** barcaza *f* ▸ **the Canal Zone** (*US*) (= *Panama*) (*formerly*) la zona del Canal de Panamá

canalization [ˌkænəlaɪ'zeɪʃən] (N) canalización *f*

canalize ['kænəlaɪz] (VT) canalizar

canapé ['kænəpeɪ] (N) (*Culin*) canapé *m*

canard [kæ'nɑːd] (N) bulo *m*, chisme *m*

Canaries [kə'nɛərɪz] (NPL) • **the ~** las Canarias

canary [kə'nɛərɪ] (N) canario *m*
(CPD) ▸ **the Canary Islands** las islas Canarias ▸ **canary seed** alpiste *m* ▸ **canary yellow** amarillo *m* canario

canary-yellow [kəˌnɛərɪ'jeləʊ] (ADJ) (de color) amarillo canario (*inv*)

canasta [kə'næstə] (N) canasta *f*

Canberra ['kænbərə] (N) Canberra *f*

cancan ['kænkæn] (N) cancán *m*

cancel ['kænsəl] (PT, PP: **cancelled**, (*US*) **canceled**) (VT) **1** [+ *reservation, taxi*] anular, cancelar; [+ *room*] anular la reserva de; [+ *holiday, party, plans*] suspender; [+ *flight, train, performance*] suspender, cancelar; [+ *order, contract*] anular; [+ *permission etc*] retirar; (*Aut*) [+ *indicator*] quitar
2 (= *mark, frank*) [+ *stamp*] matar; [+ *cheque*] anular
3 (= *delete*) [+ *name, word*] borrar, suprimir
4 (*Math*) anular
(VI) [*tourist etc*] cancelar la reserva/el vuelo *etc*
(CPD) ▸ **cancel key** tecla *f* de anulación
▸ **cancel out** (VT + ADV) (*Math*) anular; (*fig*) contrarrestar, compensar • **they ~ each other out** (*Math*) se anulan mutuamente; (*fig*) se contrarrestan, una cosa compensa la otra • **the disadvantages ~ out the benefits** las desventajas anulan los beneficios • **the reduction in noise would be ~led out by the extra traffic** la reducción del ruido se vería neutralizada *or* contrarrestada por el tráfico adicional
(VI + ADV) (*Math*) anularse

cancellation [ˌkænsə'leɪʃən] (N) **1** [*of reservation, taxi*] anulación *f*, cancelación *f*; [*of room*] anulación *f* de reserva; [*of holiday, party, plans*] cancelación *f*; [*of flight, train, performance*] suspensión *f*, cancelación *f*; [*of order, contract*] anulación *f* • **"cancellations will not be accepted after ..."** (*for travel, hotel*) "no se admiten cancelaciones de reserva después del ..."; (*for theatre etc*) "no se admite la devolución de localidades después del ..."
2 (*Post*) (= *mark*) matasellos *m inv*; (= *act*) inutilización *f*
(CPD) ▸ **cancellation fee** tarifa *f* por cancelación

Cancer ['kænsəʳ] (N) **1** (= *sign, constellation*) (*also Geog*) Cáncer *m*; ▹ **tropic**
2 (= *person*) cáncer *mf* • **I'm (a) ~** soy cáncer

cancer ['kænsəʳ] (N) (*Med*) cáncer *m*
(CPD) ▸ **cancer patient** enfermo/a *m/f* de cáncer ▸ **cancer research** investigación *f* del cáncer ▸ **cancer specialist** cancerólogo/a *m/f*, oncólogo/a *m/f* ▸ **cancer stick‡** (*Brit*) pito* *m*, fumata‡ *m*

cancer-causing ['kænsəˌkɔːzɪŋ] (ADJ) cancerígeno

Cancerian [kæn'sɪərɪən] (N) cáncer *mf* • **to be a ~** ser cáncer

cancerous ['kænsərəs] (ADJ) canceroso • **to become ~** cancerarse

candelabra [ˌkændɪ'lɑːbrə] (N) (PL: **candelabra** *or* **candelabras**) candelabro *m*

C and F [ˌsiːənd'ef] (*Comm*) (ABBR) (= **Cost and Freight**) (*Comm*) C y F

candid ['kændɪd] (ADJ) [*person, interview, remark, statement*] franco, sincero • **to be quite ~ ...** hablando con franqueza ... • **he is delightfully ~ about his business affairs** es increíblemente franco *or* sincero acerca de sus negocios
(CPD) ▸ **candid camera** cámara *f* indiscreta

candida ['kændɪdə] (N) (*Med*) afta *f*

candidacy ['kændɪdəsɪ] (N) (*esp US*) candidatura *f*

candidate ['kændɪdeɪt] (N) (*for job*) aspirante *mf* (**for** a), solicitante *mf* (**for** de); (*for election, examination*) candidato/a *m/f* (**for** a); (*in competitive examination*) opositor(a) *m/f* (**for a post** a un puesto) • **the overweight are prime ~s for heart disease** los obesos son los que presentan más riesgo de padecer enfermedades cardiacas

candidature ['kændɪdətʃəʳ] (N) (*Brit*) candidatura *f*

candidly ['kændɪdlɪ] (ADV) francamente, con franqueza

candidness ['kændɪdnɪs] (N) franqueza *f*

candied ['kændɪd] (ADJ) azucarado
(CPD) ▸ **candied fruit** fruta *f* escarchada ▸ **candied peel** piel *f* almibarada

candle ['kændl] (N) vela *f*, candela *f*; (*in church*) cirio *m* • **IDIOMS:** • **to hold a ~ to sb:** • **you can't hold a ~ to him** no le llegas ni a la suela de los zapatos • **it's not worth the ~** no merece *or* vale la pena; ▹ **burn¹**
(CPD) ▸ **candle end** cabo *m* de vela ▸ **candle grease** cera *f* derretida ▸ **candle holder** = **candlestick**

candlelight ['kændllaɪt] (N) luz *f* de una vela • **by ~** a la luz de las velas

candlelit ['kændllɪt] (ADJ) alumbrado por velas • **a ~ supper for two** una cena para dos a la luz de las velas
(CPD) ▸ **candlelit dinner** cena *f* a la luz de las velas

Candlemas ['kændlməs] (N) Candelaria *f* (*2 febrero*)

candlepower ['kændlˌpaʊəʳ] (N) bujía *f*

candlestick ['kændlstɪk] (N) (*single*) candelero *m*; (*low, with handle*) palmatoria *f*; (*large, ornamental*) candelabro *m*; (*in church*) cirial *m*

candlewick ['kændlwɪk] (N) **1** (= *cloth*) tela *f* de algodón afelpada, chenille *f*
2 (= *wick of candle*) pabilo *m*, mecha *f* (de vela)

can-do* [ˌkæn'duː] (ADJ) (*US*) [*person, organization*] dinámico

candour, candor (*US*) ['kændəʳ] (N) franqueza *f*, sinceridad *f*

C & W [ˌsiːən'dʌbljuː] (N ABBR) (= **Country and Western**) ▹ **country**

candy ['kændɪ] (N) **1** (= *sugar candy*) azúcar *m* cande
2 (*US*) (= *sweets*) golosinas *fpl*, caramelos *mpl*, dulces *mpl* • **IDIOM:** • **it's like taking ~ from a baby** es coser y cantar
(VT) [+ *fruit*] escarchar
(CPD) ▸ **candy bar** (*US*) barrita *f* de caramelo; (*chocolate*) chocolatina *f* ▸ **candy store** (*US*) confitería *f*, bombonería *f* • **IDIOM:** • **like a kid in a ~ store** (*esp US*) como el rey/la reina del mambo, como si fuera el amo/ama del mundo

candyfloss ['kændɪflɒs] (*Brit*) (N) algodón *m* de azúcar; (*pej*) (*fig*) morralla *f*

candy-striped ['kændɪˌstraɪpt] (ADJ) a rayas de colores

cane [keɪn] (N) **1** (*Bot*) caña *f*; (*for baskets, chairs etc*) mimbre *m*
2 (= *stick*) (*for walking*) bastón *m*; (*for punishment*) vara *f*, palmeta *f* • **to get the ~** (*Scol*) ser castigado con la vara *or* palmeta
(VT) [+ *pupil*] castigar con la vara *or* palmeta
(CPD) ▸ **cane chair** silla *f* de mimbre ▸ **cane**

liquor caña *f* ▸ **cane sugar** azúcar *m* de caña
canine ['kænaɪn] ADJ canino
N **1** (= *dog*) canino *m*
2 (*also* **canine tooth**) colmillo *m*, diente *m* canino
caning ['keɪnɪŋ] N • **to give sb a ~** castigar a algn con la vara *or* palmeta; (*fig**) dar una paliza a algn*
canister ['kænɪstəʳ] N (*for tea, coffee*) lata *f*, bote *m*; [*of gas*] bombona *f*; (*for film*) lata *f*
canker ['kæŋkəʳ] N (*Med*) úlcera *f* en la boca; (*Bot*) cancro *m*; (= *scourge*) cáncer *m*
VT (*Med*) ulcerar
VI (*Med*) ulcerarse
cankerous ['kæŋkərəs] ADJ ulceroso
cannabis ['kænəbɪs] N (*Bot*) cáñamo *m* (índico); (= *drug*) cannabis *m*
CPD ▸ **cannabis resin** resina *f* de hachís
canned [kænd] PT, PP *of* **can²**
ADJ **1** [*food*] enlatado, en lata • **~ foods** conservas *fpl* alimenticias
2* (= *recorded*) [*music*] grabado, enlatado • **~ laughter** (*TV, Rad*) risas *fpl* grabadas
3‡ (= *drunk*) mamado, tomado (*LAm*)
cannelloni [ˌkænɪ'ləʊnɪ] NPL canelones *mpl*
cannery ['kænərɪ] N fábrica *f* de conservas
cannibal ['kænɪbəl] ADJ antropófago
N caníbal *mf*, antropófago/a *m/f*
cannibalism ['kænɪbəlɪzəm] N canibalismo *m*
cannibalistic [ˌkænɪbə'lɪstɪk] ADJ canibalesco
cannibalization [ˌkænɪbəlaɪ'zeɪʃən] N [*of machine, product*] canibalización *f*
cannibalize ['kænɪbəlaɪz] VT [*+ car etc*] desguazar, desmontar
cannily ['kænɪlɪ] ADV (= *cleverly*) astutamente
canning ['kænɪŋ] N enlatado *m*
CPD ▸ **canning factory** fábrica *f* de conservas ▸ **canning industry** industria *f* conservera
cannon ['kænən] N (PL: **cannon** *or* **cannons**) **1** (*Mil*) cañón *m*; (*collectively*) artillería *f*
2 (*Brit*) (*Billiards*) carambola *f*
VI (*Brit*) (*Billiards*) hacer carambola
CPD ▸ **cannon fodder** carne *f* de cañón ▸ **cannon shot** cañonazo *m*, disparo *m* de cañón; (= *ammunition*) bala *f* de cañón • **within ~-shot** a tiro de cañón
▸ **cannon into** VI + PREP chocar con *or* contra
▸ **cannon off** VI + PREP rebotar contra
cannonade [ˌkænə'neɪd] N cañoneo *m*
cannonball ['kænənbɔːl] N bala *f* de cañón
cannot ['kænɒt] NEG *of* **can¹**
cannula ['kænjʊlə] N (PL: **cannulae, cannuli**) cánula *f*
canny ['kænɪ] ADJ (COMPAR: **cannier**, SUPERL: **canniest**) astuto
canoe [kə'nuː] N canoa *f*; (*Sport*) piragua *f*
VI ir en canoa
canoeing [kə'nuːɪŋ] N piragüismo *m*
canoeist [kə'nuːɪst] N piragüista *mf*
canon ['kænən] N **1** (*Rel etc*) (= *decree*) canon *m*; (= *rule, norm*) canon *m*, norma *f*
2 (= *priest*) canónigo *m*
3 (*Mus*) canon *m*
4 (*Literat*) [*of single author*] bibliografía *f* autorizada, catálogo *m* autorizado de obras; (*more broadly*) corpus *m inv*
CPD ▸ **canon law** (*Rel*) derecho *m* canónico
canonical [kə'nɒnɪkəl] ADJ canónico
canonization [ˌkænənaɪ'zeɪʃən] N canonización *f*
canonize ['kænənaɪz] VT canonizar
canonry ['kænənrɪ] N canonjía *f*
canoodle* [kə'nuːdl] VI (*esp Brit*) besuquearse*
canopy ['kænəpɪ] N **1** (= *outside shop*) toldo *m*
2 (*of cockpit*) cubierta *f* exterior de la cabina
3 (*above bed, throne*) dosel *m*; (*over king, pope, bishop*) palio *m*; (*over altar*) baldaquín *m*; (*over tomb*) doselete *m* • **a ~ of stars** un manto *or* un firmamento de estrellas • **a ~ of leaves** un manto de hojas
cant¹ [kænt] N (= *slope*) inclinación *f*, sesgo *m*; [*of crystal etc*] bisel *m*
VT inclinar, sesgar
VI inclinarse, ladearse
▸ **cant over** VI + ADV volcar
cant² [kænt] N **1** (= *hypocrisy*) hipocresía(s) *f(pl)*
2 (= *jargon*) jerga *f*
VI camandulear
can't [kɑːnt] NEG *of* **can¹**
Cantab [kæn'tæb] ADJ ABBR (*Brit*) = **Cantabrigiensis, of Cambridge**
Cantabrian [kæn'tæbrɪən] ADJ cantábrico
cantaloup ['kæntəluːp] N cantalupo *m*
cantankerous [kæn'tæŋkərəs] ADJ cascarrabias (*inv*), gruñón
cantata [kæn'tɑːtə] N cantata *f*
canteen [kæn'tiːn] N **1** (= *restaurant*) cantina *f*, comedor *m*
2 (= *bottle*) cantimplora *f*
3 • **a ~ of cutlery** un juego de cubiertos
canter ['kæntəʳ] N medio galope *m* • **to go for a ~** ir a dar un paseo a caballo • **at a ~** a medio galope • IDIOM: • **to win in** *or* **at a ~** (*Brit*) (*fig*) ganar fácilmente
VI ir a medio galope
Canterbury ['kæntəbərɪ] N Cantórbery *m*
CPD ▸ **Canterbury Tales** Cuentos *mpl* de Cantórbery
cantharides [kæn'θærɪdiːz] NPL polvo *m* de cantárida
canticle ['kæntɪkl] N cántico *m* • **the Canticles** el Cantar de los Cantares
cantilever ['kæntɪliːvəʳ] N viga *f* voladiza
CPD ▸ **cantilever bridge** puente *m* voladizo
canting ['kæntɪŋ] ADJ hipócrita
canto ['kæntəʊ] N canto *m*
canton ['kæntɒn] N (*Admin, Pol*) cantón *m*
cantonal ['kæntənl] ADJ cantonal
Cantonese [ˌkæntə'niːz] ADJ cantonés
N **1** (= *person*) cantonés/esa *m/f*
2 (*Ling*) cantonés *m*
cantonment [kən'tuːnmənt] N acantonamiento *m*
Canuck‡ [kə'nʊk] N (*pej*) (= *Canadian, French Canadian*) canuck *mf*
Canute [kə'njuːt] N Canuto
canvas ['kænvəs] N **1** (= *cloth*) lona *f*; (*Naut*) velas *fpl*, velamen *m* • **under ~** en tienda de campaña, en carpa (*LAm*); (*Naut*) con el velamen desplegado
2 (*Art*) lienzo *m*
CPD ▸ **canvas chair** silla *f* de lona ▸ **canvas shoes** zapatos *mpl* de lona; (*rope-soled*) alpargatas *fpl*
canvass ['kænvəs] VT **1** (*Pol*) [*+ district*] hacer campaña en; [*+ voters*] solicitar el voto de; [*+ votes*] solicitar
2 (*US*) [*+ votes*] escudriñar
3 (*Comm*) [*+ district, opinions*] sondear; [*+ orders*] solicitar; [*+ purchaser*] solicitar pedidos de
4 (= *discuss*) [*+ possibility, question*] discutir, someter a debate
VI **1** (*Pol*) solicitar votos, hacer campaña (**for** a favor de)
2 (*Comm*) buscar clientes
N **1** (*Pol*) (*for votes*) solicitación *f* • **to make a door-to-door ~** ir solicitando votos de puerta en puerta
2 (*Comm*) (= *inquiry*) sondeo *m*
canvasser, canvaser (*US*) ['kænvəsəʳ] N **1** (*Pol*) persona *f* que hace campaña electoral para un partido en una zona concreta
2 (*Comm*) promotor(a) *m/f*
canvassing ['kænvəsɪŋ] N solicitación *f* (de votos) • **to go out ~** salir a solicitar votos
canyon ['kænjən] N cañón *m*
canyoning ['kænjənɪŋ] N (*Sport*) barranquismo *m*
CAP N ABBR (*Pol*) (= **Common Agricultural Policy**) PAC *f*
cap [kæp] N **1** (= *hat*) gorra *f*; (*soldier's*) gorra *f* militar; (*for swimming*) gorro *m* de baño; (*servant's etc*) cofia *f*; (*Univ*) bonete *m* • **cap and gown** (*Univ*) toga *f* y bonete • IDIOMS: • **to go cap in hand** ir con el sombrero en la mano • **if the cap fits, wear it** el que se pica, ajos come • **to set one's cap at sb†** proponerse conquistar a algn • **to put on one's thinking cap** ponerse a pensar detenidamente • **I must put on my thinking cap** tengo que meditarlo
2 (*Brit*) (*Sport*) • **he's got his cap for England** • **he's an England cap** forma parte de la selección nacional inglesa, juega con la selección nacional inglesa
3 (= *lid, cover*) [*of bottle*] tapón *m*; (*made of metal*) chapa *f*, tapón *m*; [*of pen*] capuchón *m*
4 [*of gun*] cápsula *f* (fulminante)
5 [*of mushroom*] sombrerete *m*, sombrerillo *m*
6 [*of tooth*] (*artificial*) funda *f*
7 (*Mech*) casquete *m*; (*Aut*) (= *radiator/petrol cap*) tapón *m*
8 (= *contraceptive*) diafragma *m*
9 (= *percussion cap*) cápsula *f* (fulminante)
VT **1** [*+ bottle etc*] tapar; [*+ tooth*] enfundar; [*+ oil-well*] encapuchar, tapar
2 (= *surpass*) [*+ story, joke*] • **see if you can cap that story** a ver si cuentas un chiste mejor que ese • **I can cap that** yo sé algo mejor sobre el mismo asunto • **and to cap it all, he ...** y para colmo, él ...
3 (= *complete*) coronar, completar
4 (= *limit*) [*+ expenditure*] restringir; [*+ council etc*] imponer un límite presupuestario a
5 (*Brit*) (*Sport*) [*+ player*] seleccionar (para el equipo nacional), incluir en la selección nacional
cap. ABBR (*Typ*) (= **capital (letter)**) may
capability [ˌkeɪpə'bɪlɪtɪ] N (= *competence*) competencia *f*; (= *potential ability*) capacidad *f* • **to have the ~ to do sth** ser capaz de hacer algo, tener capacidad para hacer algo • **the ~ for rational thought** la capacidad de raciocinio • **within/beyond one's capabilities** dentro de/más allá de sus posibilidades • **military/nuclear ~** potencial *m* militar/nuclear
capable ['keɪpəbl] ADJ **1** (= *competent*) competente, capaz • **she's a very ~ speaker** es una oradora muy competente *or* capaz • **she's very ~** es muy competente *or* capaz • **I can leave the matter in your very ~ hands** si te confío a ti el asunto, estará en buenas manos
2 (= *able to*) capaz; (= *predisposed towards*) susceptible • **sports cars ~ of reaching 150mph** coches deportivos que pueden alcanzar *or* que son capaces de alcanzar las 150 millas por hora • **it's ~ of some improvement** (*frm*) se puede mejorar algo • **such men are ~ of anything** hombres así son capaces de cualquier cosa
capably ['keɪpəblɪ] ADV competentemente
capacious [kə'peɪʃəs] ADJ [*room*] amplio, espacioso; [*container*] de mucha cabida, grande; [*dress*] ancho, holgado
capacitance [kə'pæsɪtəns] N (*Elec*) capacitancia *f*
capacitor [kə'pæsɪtəʳ] N (*Elec*) capacitor *m*
capacity [kə'pæsɪtɪ] N **1** [*of container etc*]

capacidad *f*; (= *seating capacity*) cabida *f*, aforo *m*; (*Aut*) cilindrada *f*; (= *carrying capacity*) capacidad *f* de carga • **what is the ~ of this hall?** ¿cuántos caben en esta sala? • **filled to ~** al completo
2 (= *position*) calidad *f* • **in my ~ as Chairman** en mi calidad de presidente • **in what ~ were you there?** ¿en calidad de qué estabas allí? • **I've worked for them in various capacities** he trabajado para ellos desempeñando distintas funciones
3 (= *ability*) capacidad *f* • **her capacities** su capacidad *or* aptitud • **her ~ for research** su capacidad *or* aptitud para la investigación • **to work at full ~** [*machine, factory*] funcionar a pleno rendimiento
CPD ▸ **capacity audience** lleno *m* • **there was a ~ audience in the theatre** hubo un lleno en el teatro ▸ **capacity booking** reserva *f* total ▸ **capacity crowd** = **capacity audience**

caparison [kəˈpærɪsn] N caparazón *m*, gualdrapa *f*; [*of person*] vestido *m* rico, galas *fpl*; (= *harness etc*) equipo *m*
VT engualdrapar • **gaily ~ed** brillantemente enjaezado; (*fig*) brillantemente vestido

cape¹ [keɪp] N (*Geog*) cabo *m* • **the Cape** (= *Cape Province*) la provincia del Cabo; (= *Cape of Good Hope*) el cabo de Buena Esperanza
CPD ▸ **Cape Canaveral** Cabo *m* Cañaveral ▸ **Cape Cod** Cape Cod ▸ **Cape Coloureds** *personas de padres racialmente mixtos (que habitan en la provincia del Cabo)* ▸ **Cape gooseberry** uvilla *f*, aguaymanto *m*, alquequenje *m*, uchuva *f* (*And*), capulí *m* (*And*) ▸ **cape honeysuckle** madreselva *f* siempreviva, bignonia *f* del Cabo ▸ **Cape Horn** cabo *m* de Hornos ▸ **Cape of Good Hope** cabo *m* de Buena Esperanza ▸ **Cape Province** Provincia *f* del Cabo ▸ **Cape Town** El Cabo, Ciudad *f* del Cabo ▸ **Cape Verde Islands** islas *fpl* de cabo Verde

cape² [keɪp] N (= *garment*) capa *f*; (*short*) capotillo *m*, esclavina *f*; [*of policeman, cyclist*] chubasquero *m*; (*Bullfighting*) capote *m*

caper¹ [ˈkeɪpəʳ] N (*Culin*) alcaparra *f*
CPD ▸ **caper sauce** salsa *f* de alcaparras

caper² [ˈkeɪpəʳ] N **1** [*of horse*] cabriola *f* • **to cut ~s** hacer cabriolas
2 (= *escapade*) travesura *f*; (= *business**) lío *m*, embrollo *m* • **that was quite a ~** eso sí que fue un número* • **I don't bother with taxes and all that ~** no me molesto con impuestos y cosas así • **how did your Spanish ~ go?** ¿qué tal el viajecito por España?
VI **1** [*horse*] hacer cabriolas; [*other animal*] brincar, corcovear; [*child*] juguetear, brincar • **to ~ about** brincar, juguetear
2* (= *go*) ir, correr • **he went ~ing off to Paris** se marchó a París como si tal cosa

capercaillie [ˌkæpəˈkeɪlɪ] N urogallo *m*

capful [ˈkæpfʊl] N • **one ~ to four litres of water** un tapón por cada cuatro litros de agua

capillarity [ˌkæpɪˈlærɪtɪ] N capilaridad *f*

capillary [kəˈpɪlərɪ] ADJ capilar
N capilar *m*

capital [ˈkæpɪtl] ADJ **1** (*Jur*) capital
2 (= *chief*) capital
3 (= *essential*) capital, primordial • **of ~ importance** de capital importancia
4 [*letter*] mayúsculo • **~ Q** Q *f* mayúscula • **he's Conservative with a ~ C** es conservador con mayúscula
5†* (= *splendid*) magnífico, estupendo • **~!** ¡magnífico!, ¡estupendo!
N **1** (*also* **capital letter**) mayúscula *f* • **~s** (*large*) mayúsculas *fpl*, versales *fpl*; (*small*) versalitas *fpl* • **please write in ~s** escribir en letras de imprenta
2 (*also* **capital city**) capital *f*
3 (*Econ*) capital *m* • **to make ~ out of sth** (*fig*) sacar provecho de algo
4 (*Archit*) capitel *m*
CPD ▸ **capital account** cuenta *f* de capital ▸ **capital allowance** desgravación *f* sobre bienes de capital ▸ **capital assets** activo *msing* fijo ▸ **capital equipment** bienes *mpl* de equipo ▸ **capital expenditure** inversión *f* de capital ▸ **capital formation** formación *f* de capital ▸ **capital gain(s)** plusvalía *f* ▸ **capital gains tax** impuesto *m* sobre las plusvalías ▸ **capital goods** bienes *mpl* de equipo ▸ **capital growth** aumento *m* del capital ▸ **capital investment** inversión *f* de capital ▸ **capital levy** impuesto *m* sobre el capital ▸ **capital offence, capital offense** (*US*) delito *m* capital ▸ **capital outlay** desembolso *m* de capital ▸ **capital punishment** pena *f* de muerte ▸ **capital reserves** reservas *fpl* de capital ▸ **capital sentence** condena *f* a la pena de muerte ▸ **capital ship** acorazado *m* ▸ **capital spending** capital *m* adquisitivo ▸ **capital stock** (= *capital*) capital *m* social *or* comercial; (= *shares*) acciones *fpl* de capital ▸ **capital sum** capital *m* ▸ **capital transfer tax** (*Brit*) impuesto *m* sobre plusvalía de cesión

capital-intensive [ˌkæpɪtlɪnˈtensɪv] ADJ de utilización intensiva de capital

capitalism [ˈkæpɪtəlɪzəm] N capitalismo *m*

capitalist [ˈkæpɪtəlɪst] ADJ capitalista
N capitalista *mf*

capitalistic [ˌkæpɪtəˈlɪstɪk] ADJ capitalista

capitalization [kəˌpɪtəlaɪˈzeɪʃən] N capitalización *f*

capitalize [ˈkæpɪtəlaɪz] VT **1** (*Fin*) capitalizar
2 [+ *letter, word*] escribir con mayúscula
VI • **to ~ on** sacar provecho de, aprovechar

capitation [ˌkæpɪˈteɪʃən] N (= *act*) capitación *f*; (= *tax*) impuesto *m* por cabeza
CPD ▸ **capitation grant** subvención *f* por capitación

Capitol [ˈkæpɪtɒl] N (*US*) Capitolio *m*

> **CAPITOL**
>
> El Capitolio (**Capitol**), situado en la ciudad de Washington, es el edificio en el que se reúne el Congreso de los Estados Unidos (**Congress**). Al estar situado en la colina llamada **Capitol Hill**, también se suele hacer referencia a él con ese nombre en los medios de comunicación.
>
> Por otra parte a menudo se llama **Capitol**, por extensión, al edificio en el que tienen lugar las sesiones parlamentarias de la cámara de representantes de muchos estados.

capitulate [kəˈpɪtjʊleɪt] VI (*Mil*) (= *surrender*) rendirse, capitular (**to** ante); (*fig*) claudicar, capitular (**to** ante)

capitulation [kəˌpɪtjʊˈleɪʃən] N (*Mil*) (*also fig*) capitulación *f*, rendición *f*

capo [ˈkæpəʊ] N (*on guitar*) cejilla *f*

capon [ˈkeɪpən] N capón *m*

cappuccino [ˌkæpəˈtʃiːnəʊ] N capuchino *m*

caprice [kəˈpriːs] N capricho *m*, antojo *m*

capricious [kəˈprɪʃəs] ADJ caprichoso, antojadizo

capriciously [kəˈprɪʃəslɪ] ADV caprichosamente

capriciousness [kəˈprɪʃəsnɪs] N carácter *m* caprichoso

Capricorn [ˈkæprɪkɔːn] N **1** (= *sign, constellation*) (*also Geog*) Capricornio *m*; ▹ **tropic**
2 (= *person*) capricornio *mf* • **she's (a) ~** es capricornio

Capricornean [kæprɪˈkɔːnɪən] N capricornio *mf* • **to be a ~** ser capricornio

caps [kæps] NPL ABBR (*Typ*) (= **capitals, capital letters**) may.

capsicum [ˈkæpsɪkəm] N pimiento *m*

capsize [kæpˈsaɪz] VT volcar; (*Naut*) hacer zozobrar, tumbar
VI volcarse, dar una vuelta de campana; (*Naut*) zozobrar

capstan [ˈkæpstən] N cabrestante *m*

capsule [ˈkæpsjuːl] N (*all senses*) cápsula *f*
ADJ [*version, summary*] conciso, sucinto

Capt. ABBR (*Mil*) = **Captain**

captain [ˈkæptɪn] N (*Mil, Naut, Sport*) capitán/ana *m/f*; (*Aer*) comandante *mf*; (*US*) (*Police*) comisario/a *m/f* de distrito • **~ of industry** magnate *mf* de la industria, gran industrial *mf*
VT [+ *team*] capitanear

captaincy [ˈkæptənsɪ] N capitanía *f*

captcha [ˈkæptʃə] N (= *Completely Automated Public Turing test to tell Computers and Humans Apart*) captcha *m*

caption [ˈkæpʃən] N (= *heading*) título *m*, titular *m*; (*on photo, cartoon*) leyenda *f*, pie *m*; (*in film*) subtítulo *m*
VT [+ *essay, article*] titular; [+ *photo, cartoon*] poner una leyenda a

captious [ˈkæpʃəs] ADJ (*liter*) criticón, reparón

captivate [ˈkæptɪveɪt] VT encantar, cautivar

captivating [ˈkæptɪveɪtɪŋ] ADJ cautivador, fascinante

captive [ˈkæptɪv] ADJ [*animal, bird, market*] cautivo • **to take sb ~** hacer prisionero a algn • **to hold sb ~** tener *or* mantener prisionero *or* cautivo a algn • **he had a ~ audience** la gente no tenía más remedio que escucharle
N cautivo/a *m/f*, preso/a *m/f*
CPD ▸ **captive breeding** cría *f* en cautividad

captivity [kæpˈtɪvɪtɪ] N cautiverio *m*, cautividad *f* • **bred in ~** criado en cautividad • **to hold** *or* **keep sb in ~** tener a algn en cautividad *or* en cautiverio

captor [ˈkæptəʳ] N captor(a) *m/f*, apresador(a) *m/f*

capture [ˈkæptʃəʳ] N **1** [*of animal, soldier, escapee*] captura *f*, apresamiento *m*; [*of city etc*] toma *f*, conquista *f*
2 (*Comput*) captura *f*, recogida *f*
3 (= *thing caught*) presa *f*
VT **1** [+ *animal*] apresar; [+ *soldier, escapee*] capturar, apresar; [+ *city etc*] tomar, conquistar; (*Comm*) [+ *market*] conquistar, acaparar; [+ *leadership*] apoderarse de
2 (= *attract*) [+ *attention, interest*] captar • **a film that has ~d the imagination of teenagers** una película que ha cautivado la imaginación de los adolescentes • **this phenomenon has ~d the attention of many scientists** este fenómeno ha llamado la atención de muchos científicos • **the woman who has ~d his heart** la mujer que le ha arrebatado el corazón
3 (= *convey, evoke*) captar, reflejar • **to ~ sth on film** captar algo con la cámara
4 [+ *data*] capturar, recoger

capuchin [ˈkæpjʊʃɪn] N **1** (= *cowl*) capucho *m*
2 (*Zool*) mono *m* capuchino
3 • **Capuchin** (*Rel*) capuchino *m*

car [kɑːʳ] N **1** (*Aut*) coche *m*, automóvil *m* (*frm*), carro *m* (*LAm*), auto *m* (*S. Cone*) • **by car** en coche
2 (*esp US*) [*of train*] vagón *m*, coche *m*
3 (= *tramcar*) tranvía *m*
4 [*of cable railway*] coche *m*; [*of lift*] caja *f*; [*of balloon etc*] barquilla *f*

CPD ▸ **car accident** accidente *m* de coche, accidente *m* de tráfico ▸ **car alarm** alarma *f* de coche ▸ **car allowance** extra *m* por uso de coche propio ▸ **car bomb** coche-bomba *m* ▸ **car bombing** atentado *m* con coche bomba ▸ **car boot sale** (*Brit*) mercadillo *m* (*en el que se exponen las mercancías en el maletero del coche*) ▸ **car chase** persecución *f* de coches • **there followed a car chase along the motorway** se persiguió luego al coche por la autopista ▸ **car crash** accidente *m* de coche, accidente *m* de tráfico ▸ **car ferry** transbordador *m* para coches ▸ **car hire** alquiler *m* de coches • **car-hire firm** empresa *f* de alquiler de coches ▸ **car industry** industria *f* del automóvil ▸ **car insurance** seguro *m* de automóvil ▸ **car journey** viaje *m* en coche ▸ **car keys** llaves *fpl* del coche ▸ **car licence** permiso *m* de conducir ▸ **car licence plate** (*Brit*), **car license plate** (*US*) matrícula *f* ▸ **car maker** fabricante *m* de coches ▸ **car number** (*Brit*) matrícula *f* ▸ **car park** aparcamiento *m*, parking *m*, (playa *f* de) estacionamiento *m* (*LAm*) ▸ **car phone** teléfono *m* móvil (de coche) ▸ **car pool** [*of company*] parque *m* móvil; (= *sharing*) uso *m* compartido de coches ▸ **car radio** radio *f* de coche, autorradio *f* ▸ **car rental** = **car hire** ▸ **car sharing** (= *sharing rides*) *uso compartido del coche*; (*with hire-car scheme*) *uso de coches que pueden ser alquilados por periodos cortos de tiempo* ▸ **car sharing scheme** (*involving shared journeys*) *acuerdo para compartir el coche para ir al trabajo y otros trayectos*; (*involving hire cars*) *plan de alquiler de coches por cortos periodos de tiempo* ▸ **car sickness** *mareo al viajar en coche* • **he's prone to car sickness** se suele marear en el coche • **it helps prevent car sickness** ayuda a evitar los mareos en el coche ▸ **car wash** tren *m or* túnel *m* de lavado (de coches) ▸ **car worker** trabajador(a) *m/f* de la industria del automóvil

CAR BOOT SALE
En los mercadillos británicos llamados **car boot sales** la gente vende todo tipo de objetos usados de los que quiere deshacerse, como ropa, muebles, libros etc, que exhiben en los maleteros de sus coches o en mesas cercanas a ellos. Normalmente tienen lugar en aparcamientos u otros espacios abiertos y los propietarios de los vehículos han de pagar una pequeña tarifa por aparcar. Los mercadillos más importantes atraen también a comerciantes y en ellos se venden tanto artículos usados como nuevos. En otras ocasiones se organizan para recaudar dinero con fines benéficos. En Estados Unidos hay ventas parecidas, que se llaman **garage sales**.

Caracas [kəˈrækəs] N Caracas *m*

carafe [kəˈræf] N garrafa *f*

caramel [ˈkærəməl] N caramelo *m*
CPD ▸ **caramel cream, caramel custard** flan *m*

caramelize [ˈkærəməlaɪz] VT caramelizar, acaramelar
VI caramelizarse, acaramelarse

carapace [ˈkærəpeɪs] N carapacho *m*

carat [ˈkærət] N quilate *m* • **24-carat gold** oro *m* de 24 quilates

caravan [ˈkærəvæn] N **1** (*Brit*) (*Aut*) remolque *m*, caravana *f*, tráiler *m* (*LAm*); (*gipsies'*) carromato *m*
2 (*in desert*) caravana *f*
VI • **to go ~ning** ir de vacaciones en una caravana
CPD ▸ **caravan site** camping *m* para caravanas

caravanette [ˌkærəvəˈnet] N (*Brit*) caravana *f* pequeña

caravanning [ˈkærəvænɪŋ] N caravaning *m* • **to go ~** ir de vacaciones en una caravana

caravanserai, caravansary [ˌkærəˈvænsəraɪ, ˌkærəˈvænsərɪ] N caravasar *m*

caravel [kærəˈvel] N carabela *f*

caraway [ˈkærəweɪ] N alcaravea *f*
CPD ▸ **caraway seeds** carvis *mpl*

carb* [ˈkɑːb] N (= *carbohydrate*) carbohidrato *m* • **a low-carb diet** una dieta baja en carbohidratos

carbide [ˈkɑːbaɪd] N carburo *m*

carbine [ˈkɑːbaɪn] N carabina *f*

carbohydrate [ˈkɑːbəʊˈhaɪdreɪt] N (*Chem*) hidrato *m* de carbono; (= *starch in food*) fécula *f*

carbolic [kɑːˈbɒlɪk] N (*also* **carbolic acid**) ácido *m* carbólico *or* fénico; (*also* **carbolic soap**) jabón *m* con fenol

carbon [ˈkɑːbən] N **1** (*Chem*) carbono *m*
2 (*Elec*) carbón *m*
3 (= *carbon paper*) papel *m* de calco, papel *m* carbón, papel *m* carbónico (*S. Cone*)
CPD ▸ **carbon capture** captura *f* de carbono ▸ **carbon capture and storage** captura *f* y almacenamiento de carbono ▸ **carbon copy** (*typing*) copia *f* hecha con papel de carbón; (*fig*) vivo retrato *m* • **he's a ~ copy of my uncle** es el vivo retrato de mi tío, es calcado a mi tío ▸ **carbon credit** crédito *m* de carbono ▸ **carbon cycle** ciclo *m* del carbono ▸ **carbon dating** datación *f* utilizando carbono 14 ▸ **carbon dioxide** bióxido *m* de carbono ▸ **carbon emissions** emisiones *fpl* de dióxido de carbono ▸ **carbon fibre** fibra *f* de carbono ▸ **carbon footprint** huella *f* ecológica ▸ **carbon monoxide** monóxido *m* de carbono ▸ **carbon paper** papel *m* de calco, papel *m* carbón, papel *m* carbónico (*S. Cone*) ▸ **carbon ribbon** cinta *f* mecanográfica de carbón ▸ **carbon sink** secuestro *m* de carbono ▸ **carbon tax** impuesto *m* sobre el carbono ▸ **carbon tetrachloride** tetracloruro *m* de carbono ▸ **carbon trading** comercio *m* de derechos de emisión

carbonaceous [ˌkɑːbəˈneɪʃəs] ADJ carbonoso

carbonate [ˈkɑːbənɪt] N carbonato *m*

carbonated [ˈkɑːbəneɪtɪd] ADJ [*water*] con gas • **~ drink** bebida *f* gaseosa

carbon-date [ˌkɑːbənˈdeɪt] VT datar mediante la prueba del carbono 14

carbonic acid [kɑːˌbɒnɪkˈæsɪd] N ácido *m* carbónico

carboniferous [ˌkɑːbəˈnɪfərəs] ADJ carbonífero

carbonization [ˌkɑːbənaɪˈzeɪʃən] N carbonización *f*

carbonize [ˈkɑːbənaɪz] VT carbonizar
VI carbonizarse

carbonless paper [ˈkɑːbənlɪsˈpeɪpəʳ] N papel *m* autocopiativo

carbon-neutral [ˌkɑːbənˈnjuːtrəl] ADJ neutral en carbono • **to become** *or* **go carbon-neutral** convertirse en neutral en carbono

carborundum [ˌkɑːbəˈrʌndəm] N carborundo *m*

carboy [ˈkɑːbɔɪ] N garrafón *m*

carbuncle [ˈkɑːbʌŋkl] N **1** (*Med*) carbunc(l)o *m*
2 (= *ruby*) carbúnculo *m*, carbunco *m*

carburation [ˌkɑːbjʊˈreɪʃən] N carburación *f*

carburettor, carburetor (*US*) [ˌkɑːbjʊˈretəʳ] N carburador *m*

carcass, carcase [ˈkɑːkəs] N **1** [*of animal*] res *f* muerta; (= *body*) cuerpo *m*; (= *dead body*) cadáver *m* • IDIOM: • **to save one's ~** salvar el pellejo
2 [*of building, vehicle*] carcasa *f*, armazón *m or f*

carcinogen [kɑːˈsɪnədʒen] N carcinógeno *m*

carcinogenic [ˌkɑːsɪnəˈdʒenɪk] ADJ cancerígeno, carcinógeno

carcinoma [ˌkɑːsɪˈnəʊmə] N (PL: **carcinomas** *or* **carcinomata** [ˌkɑːsɪˈnəʊmətə]) carcinoma *m*

card¹ [kɑːd] N **1** (= *greetings card, visiting card etc*) tarjeta *f*; (= *membership card, press card*) carnet *m*, carné *m*
2 (= *index card*) ficha *f*
3 (= *playing card*) carta *f*, naipe *m* • **a pack of ~s** una baraja • **to play ~s** jugar a las cartas *or* los naipes • **to lose money at ~s** perder el dinero jugando a las cartas
4 (*at dance, race*) programa *m*
5 (= *thin cardboard*) cartulina *f*
6†* (= *person*) • **isn't he a ~?** ¡qué gracia tiene el tío!, ¡qué tipo más salado!
7 • IDIOMS: • **to ask for one's ~s** (*Brit**) dejar su puesto, renunciar • **to get one's ~s** (*Brit**) ser despedido • **to have a ~ up one's sleeve** guardarse una carta bajo la manga • **to hold all the ~s** tener los triunfos en la mano • **to lay one's ~s on the table** poner las cartas sobre la mesa *or* boca arriba • **it's on** *or* (*US*) **in the ~s** es probable • **it's quite on** *or* (*US*) **in the ~s that ...** es perfectamente posible que ... (+ *subjun*) • **to play** *or* **keep one's ~s close to one's chest** *or* (*US*) **close to the vest** no soltar prenda • **to play one's ~s right** jugar bien sus cartas; ▹ **Christmas, house**
VT (*US**) • **to ~ sb** verificar los papeles de identidad de algn
CPD ▸ **card catalogue** fichero *m*, catálogo *m* de fichas ▸ **card game** juego *m* de naipes *or* cartas ▸ **card index** fichero *m*; ▹ **card-index** ▸ **card player** jugador(a) *m/f* de cartas ▸ **card reader** lector *m* de fichas ▸ **card stacker** depósito *m* de descarga de fichas ▸ **card table** mesa *f* de juego ▸ **card trick** truco *m* de cartas ▸ **card vote** voto *m* por delegación

card² [kɑːd] (*Tech*) N carda *f*
VT cardar

cardamom [ˈkɑːdəməm] N cardamomo *m*

cardboard [ˈkɑːdbɔːd] N cartón *m*; (*thin*) cartulina *f*
CPD ▸ **cardboard box** caja *f* de cartón ▸ **cardboard city*** *área en la que los vagabundos duermen a la intemperie*, ≈ zona *f* de chabolas ▸ **cardboard cut-out** figura *f* de cartón

card-carrying member [ˌkɑːdˌkærɪɪŋˈmembəʳ] N miembro *mf* con carnet

cardholder [ˈkɑːdˌhəʊldəʳ] N [*of political party, organization*] miembro *mf* con carnet; [*of credit card*] titular *mf* (de tarjeta de crédito); [*of library*] socio *mf* (de una biblioteca); [*of restaurant etc*] asiduo/a *m/f*

cardiac [ˈkɑːdɪæk] ADJ cardíaco
CPD ▸ **cardiac arrest** paro *m* cardíaco

cardie* [ˈkɑːdɪ] N ABBR (*Brit*) = **cardigan**

cardigan [ˈkɑːdɪgən] N chaqueta *f* de punto, rebeca *f*

cardinal [ˈkɑːdɪnl] ADJ cardinal • **a ~ rule** una regla primordial *or* fundamental • **of ~ importance** de capital importancia
N (*Rel*) cardenal *m*
CPD ▸ **cardinal number** (*Math*) número *m* cardinal ▸ **cardinal point** punto *m* cardinal ▸ **cardinal sin** (*Rel*) pecado *m* capital ▸ **cardinal virtue** virtud *f* cardinal

card-index [ˌkɑːdˈɪndeks] VT fichar, catalogar

cardio... ['kɑːdɪəʊ] PREFIX cardio...
cardiogram ['kɑːdɪəʊ,græm] N cardiograma *m*
cardiograph ['kɑːdɪəʊ,græf] N cardiógrafo *m*
cardiological [,kɑːdɪə'lɒdʒɪkəl] ADJ cardiológico
cardiologist [,kɑːdɪ'ɒlɪdʒɪst] N cardiólogo/a *m/f*
cardiology [,kɑːdɪ'ɒlədʒɪ] N cardiología *f*
cardiopulmonary ['kɑːdɪəʊ'pʌlmənərɪ] ADJ cardiopulmonar
cardiorespiratory ['kɑːdɪəʊ'respərətɔːrɪ] ADJ cardiorrespiratorio
cardiovascular [,kɑːdɪəʊ'væskjʊləʳ] ADJ cardiovascular
cardphone ['kɑːd,fəʊn] N (*Brit*) teléfono *m* de tarjeta
Cards ABBR (*Brit*) = **Cardiganshire**
cardsharp ['kɑːd,ʃɑːp] N, **cardsharper** ['kɑːd,ʃɑːpəʳ] N fullero/a *m/f*, tahúr *m*
CARE [kɛəʳ] N ABBR (*US*) (= **Cooperative for American Relief Everywhere**) *sociedad benéfica*
care [kɛəʳ] N **1** (= *anxiety*) preocupación *f*, inquietud *f* • **he has many ~s** hay muchas cosas que le preocupan • **full of ~s** lleno de inquietudes • **he hasn't a ~ in the world** no le preocupa nada
2 (= *carefulness*) cuidado *m*, atención *f* • **have a ~, sir!†** ¡mire usted lo que está diciendo! • **to take ~** tener cuidado • **take ~!** (*as warning*) ¡cuidado!, ¡ten cuidado!; (*as good wishes*) ¡cuídate! • **to take ~ to** (+ *infin*) cuidar de que (+ *subjun*), asegurarse de que (+ *subjun*) • **to take ~ not to** (+ *infin*) guardarse de (+ *infin*) • **take ~ not to drop it!** ¡cuidado no lo vayas a dejar caer!, ¡procura no soltarlo! • **"with ~"** "¡atención!", "¡con cuidado!"; (*on box*) "frágil" • **convicted of driving without due ~ and attention** declarado culpable de conducir sin la debida precaución
3 (= *charge*) cargo *m*, cuidado *m*; (*Med*) asistencia *f*, atención *f* médica • **to be in the ~ of** estar bajo la custodia de • **he is in the ~ of Dr Wood** le asiste *or* atiende el doctor Wood • **the parcel was left in my ~** dejaron el paquete a mi cargo *or* cuidado • **the child has been taken into ~** pusieron al niño en un centro de protección de menores • **Mr López ~ of** (*abbr* **c/o**) **Mr Jones** (*on letter*) Sr. Jones, para (entregar al) Sr. López • **to take ~ of** (= *take charge of*) encargarse de, ocuparse de; (= *look after*) cuidar a • **that takes ~ of that** con eso todo queda arreglado • **that can take ~ of itself** eso se resolverá por sí mismo • **I'll take ~ of him!*** ¡yo me encargo de él! • **she can take ~ of herself** sabe cuidar de sí misma • **I'll take ~ of this** (*bill etc*) esto corre de mi cuenta • **to take good ~ of o.s.** cuidarse mucho
VI (= *be concerned*) preocuparse (**about** por), interesarse (**about** por) • **we need more people who ~** necesitamos más gente que se preocupe por los demás, necesitamos más personas que se interesen por el prójimo • **I don't ~** no me importa, me da igual *or* lo mismo • **I don't ~ either way** me da lo mismo • **for all I ~, you can go** por mí, te puedes ir • **that's all he ~s about** es lo único que le interesa • **as if I ~d!** ¿y a mí qué? • **to ~ deeply about** [+ *person*] querer mucho a; [+ *thing*] interesarse mucho por • **who ~s?** ¿qué me importa?, ¿y qué?
VT **1** (= *be concerned*) • **I don't ~ what you think** no me importa tu opinión • **what do I ~?** ¿a mí qué me importa? • **I don't ~ twopence** *or* **a fig** *or* **a hoot!** ¡me importa un comino! • **I couldn't ~ less what people say** (*Brit*) me importa un bledo lo que diga la gente • **I couldn't ~ less** • **I could ~ less** (*US*) eso me trae sin cuidado
2 (*frm*) (= *like*) • **to ~ to**: • **I shouldn't ~ to meet him** no me gustaría conocerle • **if you ~ to** si quieres • **would you ~ to tell me?** ¿quieres decírmelo? • **would you ~ to take a walk?** ¿te apetece dar un paseo? • **would you ~ to come this way?** si no tiene inconveniente en pasar por aquí, por aquí si es tan amable *or* (*LAm*) si gusta
CPD ▸ **care assistant** (*Brit*) auxiliar *mf* de enfermería ▸ **care giver** (*professional*) cuidador(a) *m/f* (*de atención domiciliaria*); (= *relative, friend*) *persona que cuida de un incapacitado* ▸ **care home** hogar *m* de acogida ▸ **care label** (*on garment*) etiqueta *f* de instrucciones de lavado ▸ **care order** (*Brit*) (*Jur, Social Work*) *orden judicial para la puesta de un niño bajo tutela estatal* ▸ **care plan** programa *m* de ayuda ▸ **care worker** asistente *mf* social, cuidador(a) *m/f*
▸ **care for** VI + PREP **1** (= *look after*) [+ *people*] cuidar a; [+ *things*] cuidar de • **well ~d for** (bien) cuidado, bien atendido
2 (= *like*) tener afecto a, sentir cariño por; (*amorously*) sentirse atraído por • **I don't much ~ for him** no me resulta simpático • **she no longer ~s for him** ya no le quiere • **I know he ~s for you a lot** sé que te tiene mucho cariño • **I don't ~ for coffee** no me gusta el café • **I don't ~ for the idea** no me hace gracia la idea • **would you ~ for a drink?** ¿te apetece una copa?
careen [kə'riːn] VT carenar
VI inclinarse, escorar
career [kə'rɪəʳ] N (= *occupation*) profesión *f*; (= *working life*) carrera *f* profesional • **he made a ~ (for himself) in advertising** se dedicó a la publicidad, desarrolló su carrera profesional en el campo de la publicidad
VI correr a toda velocidad • **to ~ down the street** correr calle abajo • **to ~ into a wall** estrellarse contra un muro
CPD [*diplomat, soldier*] de carrera; [*criminal*] profesional ▸ **career girl** mujer *f* de carrera ▸ **career guidance** (*US*) orientación *f* profesional ▸ **career move** cambio *m* (en la trayectoria) profesional • **a good/bad ~ move** una buena/mala decisión para la trayectoria profesional ▸ **career prospects** perspectivas *fpl* profesionales ▸ **careers advisor** (*Brit*), **careers counselor** (*US*) (*Scol*) *persona encargada de la guía vocacional de los alumnos* ▸ **careers guidance** (*Brit*) guía *f* vocacional ▸ **careers office** oficina *f* de guía vocacional ▸ **careers officer** consejero/a *m/f* de orientación profesional ▸ **careers service** servicio *m* de orientación profesional ▸ **careers teacher** (*Brit*) (*Scol*) = **careers advisor** ▸ **career woman** mujer *f* de carrera
careerist [kə'rɪərɪst] N ambicioso/a *m/f*, arribista *mf*
carefree ['kɛəfriː] ADJ despreocupado, alegre
careful ['kɛəfʊl] ADJ **1** (= *taking care, cautious*) **a** cuidadoso, cauteloso • **he's a ~ driver** es un conductor prudente, conduce con prudencia *or* cuidado
b • **to be ~** tener cuidado • **(be) ~!** ¡(ten) cuidado! • **she's very ~ about what she eats** pone mucho cuidado en *or* es muy prudente con lo que come • **be ~ of the dog** ten cuidado con el perro • **be ~ that he doesn't hear you** procura que no te oiga, ten cuidado de que no te oiga • **be ~ to shut the door** no te olvides de cerrar la puerta • **he was ~ to point out that ...** se cuidó de señalar que ... • **he was ~ not to offend her** tuvo cuidado de no ofenderle • **be ~ not to drop it** • **be ~ (that) you don't drop it** procura que no se te caiga, ten cuidado de que no se te caiga • **we have to be very ~ not to be seen** tenemos que tener mucho cuidado de que no nos vean • **you can't be too ~** todos las precauciones son pocas • **be ~ what you say to him** (ten) cuidado con lo que le dices • **to be ~ with sth** tener cuidado con algo • **be ~ with the glasses** cuidado con los vasos • **he's very ~ with his money** es muy ahorrador; (*pej*) es muy tacaño
2 (= *painstaking*) [*work*] cuidadoso, esmerado; [*writer*] cuidadoso, meticuloso; [*planning, examination*] meticuloso, cuidadoso • **after ~ consideration of all the relevant facts** después de considerar todos los datos cuidadosamente • **after weeks of ~ preparation** después de semanas de cuidadosos *or* intensos preparativos • **we have made a ~ study of the report** hemos estudiado el informe cuidadosamente *or* detenidamente • **after giving this problem ~ thought, I believe that ...** después de pensar detenidamente sobre este problema, creo que ...
carefully ['kɛəfəlɪ] ADV **1** (= *cautiously*) [*drive, step*] con cuidado; [*choose*] con cuidado, cuidadosamente; [*reply*] con cautela • **he chose his words ~** escogió con cuidado *or* cuidadosamente sus palabras • **I have to spend ~** tengo que tener cuidado a la hora de gastar dinero • **she ~ avoided looking at him** tuvo cuidado de no mirarlo • **think ~ before you answer** piénsalo bien antes de contestar • **to go** *or* **tread ~** (*lit, fig*) andar con cuidado
2 (= *painstakingly*) (*gen*) cuidadosamente; [*listen*] atentamente
carefulness ['kɛəfəlnɪs] N cuidado *m*
caregiver ['kɛəgɪvəʳ] N (*esp US*) = **care giver**
careless ['kɛəlɪs] ADJ **1** (= *negligent*) [*person*] descuidado; [*appearance*] descuidado, desaliñado; [*handwriting*] poco cuidado • **~ driving** conducción *f* negligente • **~ driver** conductor(a) *m/f* negligente • **a ~ mistake** una falta de atención, un descuido • **she was producing work that was ~** no ponía cuidado en el trabajo que hacía • **it was ~ of her to do that** no fue muy prudente de *or* por su parte hacer eso • **how ~ of me!** ¡qué descuido! • **his spelling is ~** no pone cuidado en la ortografía • **you shouldn't be so ~ with money** deberías tener más cuidado con el dinero, deberías mirar más el dinero
2 (= *thoughtless*) [*remark, comment*] desconsiderado • **she is ~ of others** no le importan los demás, es desconsiderada con los demás
3 (= *carefree*) [*existence, days*] despreocupado
carelessly ['kɛəlɪslɪ] ADV **1** (= *negligently*) [*write, leave, handle*] sin cuidado, sin la debida atención; [*drive*] imprudentemente, con negligencia
2 (= *casually*) [*say, reply*] a la ligera; [*drop, toss*] despreocupadamente
carelessness ['kɛəlɪsnɪs] N **1** (= *negligence*) falta *f* de atención, falta *f* de cuidado • **through sheer ~** por simple falta de atención *or* cuidado • **the ~ of his work** la falta de atención *or* cuidado con la que hace su trabajo
2 (= *casualness*) despreocupación *f*
carer ['kɛərəʳ] N (*professional*) cuidador(a) *m/f* (*de atención domiciliaria*); (= *relative, friend*) *persona que cuida de un incapacitado*
caress [kə'res] N caricia *f*
VT acariciar
caret ['kærət] N signo *m* de intercalación
caretaker ['kɛə,teɪkəʳ] N **1** (*Brit*) [*of school, flats etc*] portero/a *m/f*, conserje *mf*; (= *watchman*) vigilante *m*

2 (*US*) (= *care giver*) cuidador(a) *m/f* (*de atención domiciliaria*)
CPD ▸ **caretaker government** gobierno *m* de transición ▸ **caretaker manager** (*Sport*) entrenador(a) *m/f* provisional *or* suplente
careworn [ˈkɛəwɔːn] ADJ [*person*] agobiado; [*face, frown*] preocupado, lleno de ansiedad
carfare [ˈkɑːfeəʳ] N (*US*) pasaje *m*, precio *m* (del billete)
cargo [ˈkɑːgəʊ] N (PL: **cargoes** *or* (*esp US*) **cargos**) cargamento *m*, carga *f*
CPD ▸ **cargo boat** buque *m* de carga, carguero *m* ▸ **cargo plane** avión *m* de carga ▸ **cargo ship** buque *m* de carga, carguero *m*
carhop [ˈkɑːhɒp] N (*US*) camarero/a *m/f* de un restaurante "drive-in"
Caribbean [ˌkærɪˈbiːən] ADJ caribe • **the ~ (Sea)** el (Mar) Caribe
caribou [ˈkærɪbuː] N (PL: **caribous** *or* **caribou**) caribú *m*
caricature [ˈkærɪkətjʊəʳ] N caricatura *f*; (*in newspaper*) dibujo *m* cómico • **it was a ~ of a ceremony** (*fig*) fue una parodia de ceremonia
VT caricaturizar
caricaturist [ˌkærɪkəˈtjʊərɪst] N caricaturista *mf*
CARICOM [ˈkærɪˌkɒm] N ABBR (= **Caribbean Community and Common Market**) CMCC *f*
caries [ˈkɛəriːz] NSING caries *f inv*
carillon [kəˈrɪljən] N carillón *m*
caring [ˈkɛərɪŋ] ADJ afectuoso, bondadoso • **the ~ professions** las profesiones humanitarias • **the ~ society** la sociedad humanitaria
N (= *care*) cuidado *m*; (= *affection*) afecto *m*, cariño *m*; (= *help*) ayuda *f*, auxilio *m*
carious [ˈkɛərɪəs] ADJ cariado
car-jacker [ˈkɑːˌdʒækəʳ] N *ladrón que asalta a sus víctimas en sus propios automóviles*
carjacking [ˈkɑːˌdʒækɪŋ] N *asalto generalmente acompañado de robo e intimidación a una persona en su propio automóvil*
Carlism [ˈkɑːlɪzəm] N carlismo *m*
Carlist [ˈkɑːlɪst] ADJ carlista
N carlista *mf*
Carmelite [ˈkɑːməlaɪt] ADJ carmelita
N carmelita *mf*
carmine [ˈkɑːmaɪn] ADJ carmín, de carmín
N carmín *m*
carnage [ˈkɑːnɪdʒ] N matanza *f*, carnicería *f*
carnal [ˈkɑːnl] ADJ (*frm*) carnal • **to have ~ knowledge of** tener conocimiento carnal de
carnation [kɑːˈneɪʃən] N clavel *m*
carnival [ˈkɑːnɪvəl] N carnaval *m*; (*US*) parque *m* de atracciones
CPD ▸ **carnival queen** reina *f* del carnaval *or* de la fiesta
carnivore [ˈkɑːnɪvɔːʳ] N **1** (*Zool*) carnívoro/a *m/f*
2 (*hum*) (= *non-vegetarian*) carnívoro/a *m/f*, no vegetariano/a *m/f*
carnivorous [kɑːˈnɪvərəs] ADJ **1** [*animal*] carnívoro
2 (*hum*) (= *non-vegetarian*) carnívoro, no vegetariano
carob [ˈkærəb] N (= *bean*) algarroba *f*; (= *tree*) algarrobo *m*
carol [ˈkærəl] N (*also* **Christmas carol**) villancico *m*
VI (*liter*) cantar alegremente
CPD ▸ **carol singer** *persona que canta villancicos en Navidad*
Carolingian [kærəˈlɪnʒɪən] ADJ carolingio
carotene [ˈkærətiːn] N caroteno *m*
carotid [kəˈrɒtɪd] N (*also* **carotid artery**) carótida *f*
carousal [kəˈraʊzəl] N (*liter*) jarana *f*, parranda *f*
carouse [kəˈraʊz] VI (*liter*) ir de juerga *or* jarana
carousel [ˌkæruːˈsel] N **1** (*US*) (= *merry-go-round*) tiovivo *m*, carrusel *m*
2 (*Phot*) bombo *m* de diapositivas
3 (*at airport*) cinta *f* de equipajes
carp¹ [kɑːp] N (PL: **carp** *or* **carps**) (= *fish*) carpa *f*
carp² [kɑːp] VI (= *complain*) quejarse, poner pegas • **to ~ at** criticar
carpal [ˈkɑːpl] ADJ carpiano
N (*also* **carpal bone**) carpo *m*
CPD ▸ **carpal tunnel syndrome** síndrome *m* del túnel carpiano
Carpathians [kɑːˈpeɪθɪənz] NPL • **the ~** los montes Cárpatos
carpenter [ˈkɑːpɪntəʳ] N carpintero/a *m/f*
carpentry [ˈkɑːpɪntrɪ] N carpintería *f*
carpet [ˈkɑːpɪt] N alfombra *f*; (*small*) tapete *m*; (*fitted*) moqueta *f* • **a ~ of leaves** (*fig*) una alfombra de hojas • IDIOMS: • **to be on the ~*** tener que aguantar un rapapolvo* • **to roll out the red ~ for sb** recibir a algn con todos los honores, ponerle a algn la alfombra roja • **they tried to sweep it under the ~** quisieron echar tierra sobre el asunto, trataron de esconder los trapos sucios
VT **1** [+ *floor*] (*wall to wall*) enmoquetar; (*with individual rugs*) alfombrar (**with** de)
2* (= *scold*) • **to ~ sb** echar un rapapolvo a algn*
CPD ▸ **carpet bag** (*US*) maletín *m*, morral *m* ▸ **carpet bombing** bombardeo *m* de arrasamiento ▸ **carpet slippers** zapatillas *fpl* ▸ **carpet square, carpet tile** loseta *f* ▸ **carpet sweeper** escoba *f* mecánica
carpetbagger [ˈkɑːpɪtˌbægəʳ] N **1** (*US*) (*Pol*) aventurero/a *m/f* político/a
2 (*Econ*) (*pej*) *oportunista que trata de sacar beneficio de una operación de conversión de una sociedad de crédito hipotecario en entidad bancaria*
carpet-bomb [ˈkɑːpɪtˌbɒm] VT arrasar con bombas
carpeted [ˈkɑːpɪtɪd] ADJ [*floor*] alfombrado • **~ with** (*fig*) cubierto de
carpeting [ˈkɑːpɪtɪŋ] N alfombrado *m*, tapizado *m*; (*wall to wall*) moqueta *f*
carping [ˈkɑːpɪŋ] ADJ criticón, reparón
N quejas *fpl* constantes
carpooling [ˈkɑːˌpuːlɪŋ] N *uso compartido de coches*
car-pool lane [ˈkɑːpuːlˌleɪn] N (*US*) carril *m* para vehículos con más de un pasajero
carport [ˈkɑːpɔːt] N cochera *f*
carrel, **carrell** [ˈkærəl] N (*in library*) (= *desk*) mesa *f* de estudio; (= *room*) sala *f* de estudio
carriage [ˈkærɪdʒ] N **1** (*Brit*) (*Rail*) vagón *m*, coche *m*
2 (*horse-drawn*) coche *m*, carruaje *m*
3 [*of typewriter*] carro *m*; (= *gun carriage*) cureña *f*
4 (= *bearing*) [*of person*] porte *m*
5 (*Comm*) (= *transportation*) transporte *m*, flete *m*; (= *cost*) porte *m*, flete *m* • **~ forward** porte debido • **~ free** franco de porte • **~ inwards/outwards** gastos *mpl* de transporte a cargo del comprador/vendedor • **~ paid** portes pagados
CPD ▸ **carriage clock** reloj *m* de mesa ▸ **carriage drive** calzada *f* ▸ **carriage return** (*on typewriter etc*) tecla *f* de retorno ▸ **carriage trade** (*US*) sector *m* de transporte de mercancías
carriageway [ˈkærɪdʒweɪ] N (*Brit*) (*Aut*) calzada *f*; ▸ **dual**
carrier [ˈkærɪəʳ] N **1** (*Comm*) (= *person*) transportista *mf*; (= *company*) empresa *f* de transportes
2 (= *airline*) aerotransportista *m*, aerolínea *f*
3 (*Med*) [*of disease*] portador(a) *m/f*
4 (*also* **aircraft carrier**) portaaviones *m inv*; (*also* **troop carrier**) (*Aer*) avión *m* de transporte de tropas; (*Naut*) (= *troopship*) barco *m* de transporte de tropas
5 (= *basket etc*) portaequipajes *m inv*; (*on cycle*) cesta *f*
6 (*Brit*) (*also* **carrier bag**) bolsa *f* (de papel *or* plástico)
CPD ▸ **carrier bag** bolsa *f* (de papel *or* plástico) ▸ **carrier pigeon** paloma *f* mensajera
carrion [ˈkærɪən] N carroña *f*
CPD ▸ **carrion crow** corneja *f* negra
carrot [ˈkærət] N zanahoria *f* • IDIOM: • **to dangle a ~ in front of sb** *or* **offer sb a ~** ofrecer un incentivo a algn
CPD ▸ **carrot cake** pastel *m* de zanahoria
carrot-and-stick [ˈkærətəndˈstɪk] ADJ • **a carrot-and-stick policy** la política del palo y la zanahoria
carroty [ˈkærətɪ] ADJ [*hair*] pelirrojo
carrousel [ˌkæruːˈsel] N (*US*) = **carousel**
carry [ˈkærɪ] VT **1** (= *take*) llevar • **I carried the tray into the kitchen** llevé la bandeja a la cocina • **he carries our lives in his hands** nuestras vidas están en sus manos • **to ~ sth around with one** llevar algo consigo • **I've been ~ing your umbrella around since last week** llevo cargando con tu paraguas desde la semana pasada • **as fast as his legs could ~ him** tan rápido como le permitían sus piernas, a todo correr • **to ~ one's audience with one** (*fig*) ganarse al público • **to ~ sth in one's head** tener algo en mente • **he carries his drink well** aguanta mucho bebiendo
2 (= *support*) [+ *burden*] sostener • **it's too heavy to ~** pesa mucho para llevarlo encima *or* para cargar con ello
3 (= *have on one's person*) [+ *money, documents*] llevar (encima) • **he always carries a gun** siempre lleva pistola (encima) • **are you ~ing any money?** ¿llevas dinero (encima)?
4 (= *transport*) [+ *goods*] transportar; [+ *passengers, message*] llevar • **the train does not ~ passengers** el tren no lleva pasajeros • **this bus carries 60 passengers** este autobús tiene asientos para 60 personas • **the wind carried the sound to him** el viento llevó el sonido hasta él
5 (*Comm*) (= *stock*) [+ *goods*] tener, tratar en
6 (*Med*) [+ *disease*] transmitir, ser portador de
7 (= *involve*) [+ *consequence*] acarrear; [+ *responsibility*] conllevar; [+ *interpretation*] encerrar, llevar implícito; [+ *meaning*] tener; [+ *authority etc*] revestir • **the offence carries a £50 fine** la infracción será penalizada con una multa de 50 libras • **a crime which carries the death penalty** un delito que lleva aparejada la pena de muerte
8 (= *have, be provided with*) [+ *guarantee*] tener, llevar; [+ *warning*] llevar
9 [*newspaper etc*] [+ *story*] traer, imprimir • **both papers carried the story** ambos periódicos traían la noticia • **this journal does not ~ reviews** esta revista no tiene reseñas
10 (= *extend*) extender, prolongar • **to ~ sth too far** (*fig*) llevar algo demasiado lejos
11 (*Math*) [+ *figure*] llevarse; (*Econ*) [+ *interest*] llevar
12 (= *approve*) [+ *motion*] aprobar; [+ *proposition*] hacer aceptar • **the motion was carried** la moción fue aprobada
13 (= *win*) [+ *election, point*] ganar; (*Parl*) [+ *seat*] ganar • IDIOMS: • **to ~ the day** triunfar • **to ~ all** *or* **everything before one** arrasar con todo
14 • **to ~ o.s.** portarse • **he carries himself like a soldier** se comporta como un soldado • **she carries herself well** se mueve con garbo
15 [*pregnant woman*] [+ *child*] estar encinta de

(VI) **1** [*sound*] oírse • **she has a voice which carries** tiene una voz que se oye bastante lejos
2 [*pregnant woman*] • **she's ~ing†** está embarazada
(N) [*of ball, shot*] alcance *m*
▸ **carry along** (VT + ADV) llevar; [*flood, water*] arrastrar
▸ **carry away** (VT + ADV) **1** (*lit*) llevarse
2 (*fig*) entusiasmar • **to get carried away by sth** entusiasmarse con algo
▸ **carry back** (VT + ADV) **1** (*lit*) [+ *object*] traer
2 (*fig*) • **that music carries me back to the 60s** esa música me hace recordar los 60
3 (*Econ*) cargar (sobre cuentas anteriores)
▸ **carry down** (VT + ADV) bajar
▸ **carry forward** (VT + ADV) (*Math, Econ*) pasar a la página/columna siguiente • **carried forward** suma y sigue
▸ **carry off** (VT + ADV) **1** (*lit*) llevarse
2 (*fig*) (= *seize, win*) llevarse; [+ *prize*] alzarse con, arramblar con; [+ *election*] ganar • **he carried it off very well** salió muy airoso de la situación
3 (= *kill*) matar, llevar a la tumba
▸ **carry on** (VT + ADV) **1** (= *continue*) [+ *tradition etc*] seguir, continuar
2 (= *conduct*) [+ *conversation*] mantener; [+ *business, trade*] llevar (adelante)
(VI + ADV) **1** (= *continue*) continuar, seguir • **if you ~ on like that** si sigues así • **we ~ on somehow** de algún modo vamos tirando • **~ on!** ¡siga!; (*in talking*) ¡prosigue! • **to ~ on doing sth** seguir haciendo algo
2* (= *make a fuss*) montar un número*, armarla* • **to ~ on about sth** machacar sobre algo • **how he carries on!** ¡no para nunca!, ¡está dale que dale! • **don't ~ on so!** ¡no hagas tanto escándalo!
3* (= *have an affair*) tener un lío* (**with sb** con algn)
▸ **carry out** (VT + ADV) **1** (= *accomplish etc*) [+ *plan*] llevar a cabo; [+ *threat, promise, order*] cumplir • **he never carried out his intention to write to her** tenía intención de escribirla, pero nunca lo hizo
2 (= *perform, implement*) [+ *idea, search etc*] realizar; [+ *test, experiment*] verificar; [+ *work*] realizar, llevar a cabo • **to ~ out repairs** hacer reparaciones
▸ **carry over** (VT + ADV) **1** (= *postpone*) posponer
2 (= *pass on*) transmitir • **a tradition carried over from one generation to the next** una tradición transmitida de generación en generación
3 (*Comm*) pasar a cuenta nueva
▸ **carry through** (VT + ADV) **1** (= *accomplish*) [+ *task*] llevar a término
2 (= *sustain*) [+ *person*] sostener
(VT + PREP) • **to ~ sb through a crisis** ayudar a algn a superar una crisis • **we have enough food to ~ us through the winter** tenemos comida suficiente para pasar todo el invierno
▸ **carry up** (VT + ADV) subir

carryall [ˈkærɪɔːl] (N) (*US*) = **holdall**

carry-back [ˈkærɪbæk] (N) (*Econ*) traspaso *m* al período anterior

carrycot [ˈkærɪkɒt] (N) (*Brit*) cuna *f* portátil, capazo *m*

carrying charge [ˈkærɪɪŋ,tʃɑːdʒ] (N) (*Comm*) costo *m* de géneros no en venta (*almacenados etc*)

carrying-on [ˈkærɪɪŋˈɒn] (N) **1** [*of work, business etc*] continuación *f*
2 carryings-on* (= *romantic intrigues*) plan *m*, relaciones *fpl* amorosas (ilícitas)

carry-on* [ˌkærɪˈɒn] (N) (= *fuss*) jaleo* *m*, lío* *m*, follón* *m* • **what a carry-on!** ¡qué jaleo or follón!* • **there was a great carry-on about the tickets** se armó un tremendo lío a causa de los billetes* • **did you ever see such a carry-on?** ¿se ha visto un jaleo igual?*
(CPD) ▸ **carry-on bag** bolsa *f* de mano
▸ **carry-on luggage** equipaje *m* de mano

carry-out [ˈkærɪˌaʊt] (ADJ) [*meal etc*] para llevar
(N) (= *food*) comida *f* para llevar; (*esp Scot*) (= *drink*) bebida *f* para llevar

carry-over [ˈkærɪˈəʊvəʳ] (N) (= *surplus*) remanente *m*, sobrante *m*; (*Comm*) suma *f* anterior (para traspasar), suma *f* que pasa de una página (de cuenta) a la siguiente; (*St Ex*) aplazamiento *m* de pago hasta el próximo día de ajuste de cuentas

carshare [ˈkɑːʃɛəʳ] (VI) (= *take turns to drive*) *turnarse para usar un coche u otro para ir al trabajo o al colegio con los colegas y amigos*; (*by booking slots for car use*) *usar coches de alquiler disponibles por cortos periodos de tiempo*

car-sick [ˈkɑːˌsɪk] (ADJ) • **to be/get car-sick** marearse (en el coche)

carsickness [ˈkɑːˌsɪknɪs] (N) *mareo al viajar en coche* • **he's prone to ~** se suele marear en el coche • **it helps prevent ~** ayuda a evitar los mareos en el coche

cart [kɑːt] (N) (*horse-drawn*) carro *m*; (*heavy*) carretón *m*; (= *hand cart*) carretilla *f*, carro *m* de mano; (*US*) (*for shopping*) carrito *m*; (*US*) (*motorized*) cochecito *m* • IDIOM: • **to put the ~ before the horse** empezar la casa por el tejado
(VT)* llevar, acarrear • **I had to ~ his books about all day** tuve que cargar con sus libros todo el día
(CPD) ▸ **cart track** (= *rut*) carril *m*, rodada *f*; (= *road*) camino *m* (para carros)
▸ **cart away***, **cart off*** (VT + ADV) llevarse

cartage [ˈkɑːtɪdʒ] (N) acarreo *m*, porte *m*

carte blanche [ˌkɑːtˈblɑːntʃ] (N) carta *f* blanca • **to give sb ~** dar carta blanca a algn

cartel [kɑːˈtel] (N) (*Comm*) cartel *m*

carter [ˈkɑːtəʳ] (N) carretero *m*

Cartesian [kɑːˈtiːzɪən] (ADJ) cartesiano
(N) cartesiano/a *m/f*

Carthage [ˈkɑːθɪdʒ] (N) Cartago *f*

Carthaginian [ˌkɑːθəˈdʒɪnɪən] (ADJ) cartaginés
(N) cartaginés/esa *m/f*

carthorse [ˈkɑːthɔːs] (N) caballo *m* de tiro

Carthusian [kɑːˈθjuːzɪən] (ADJ) cartujo
(N) cartujo/a *m/f*

cartilage [ˈkɑːtɪlɪdʒ] (N) cartílago *m*

cartilaginous [ˌkɑːtɪˈlædʒɪnəs] (ADJ) cartilaginoso

cartload [ˈkɑːtləʊd] (N) carretada *f* (*also fig*) • **by the ~** a carretadas, a montones

cartographer [kɑːˈtɒɡrəfəʳ] (N) cartógrafo/a *m/f*

cartographic [ˌkɑːtəʊˈɡræfɪk] (ADJ) cartográfico

cartographical [ˌkɑːtəʊˈɡræfɪkəl] (ADJ) = **cartographic**

cartography [kɑːˈtɒɡrəfɪ] (N) cartografía *f*

cartomancy [ˈkɑːtəmænsɪ] (N) cartomancia *f*

carton [ˈkɑːtən] (N) [*of milk*] envase *m* de cartón, caja *f*; [*of ice-cream, yogurt*] vasito *m*; [*of cigarettes*] cartón *m*

cartoon [kɑːˈtuːn] (N) **1** (*in newspaper etc*) viñeta *f*, chiste *m*; (= *comic strip*) historieta *f*
2 (*Art*) (= *sketch for fresco etc*) cartón *m*
3 (*Cine, TV*) dibujos *mpl* animados
(CPD) ▸ **cartoon character** (*on TV*) personaje *m* de dibujos animados; (*in comic strip*) personaje *m* de tebeo ▸ **cartoon strip** (= *strip cartoon*) (*esp Brit*) historieta *f*

cartoonist [ˌkɑːˈtuːnɪst] (N) dibujante *mf*

cartridge [ˈkɑːtrɪdʒ] (N) (*also Comput*) cartucho *m*; (*for pen*) recambio *m*
(CPD) ▸ **cartridge belt** cartuchera *f*, canana *f* ▸ **cartridge case** cartucho *m* ▸ **cartridge paper** papel *m* de dibujo ▸ **cartridge player** lector *m* de cartucho

cartwheel [ˈkɑːtwiːl] (N) **1** (= *wheel*) rueda *f* de carro
2 (*Gymnastics*) voltereta *f* lateral, rueda *f* • **to do** *or* **turn a ~** dar una voltereta lateral, hacer la rueda

cartwright [ˈkɑːtraɪt] (N) carretero/a *m/f*

carve [kɑːv] (VT) (*Culin*) [+ *meat*] trinchar; [+ *stone, wood*] tallar, esculpir; [+ *name on tree etc*] grabar • **to ~ one's way through the crowd** (*fig*) abrirse camino a la fuerza por entre la multitud
(VI) (*Culin*) trinchar la carne
▸ **carve out** (VT + ADV) [+ *piece of wood*] tallar; [+ *piece of land*] limpiar; [+ *statue, figure*] esculpir; [+ *tool*] tallar • **to ~ out a career for o.s.** abrirse camino
▸ **carve up** (VT + ADV) **1** [+ *meat*] trinchar
2 (*fig*) [+ *country*] repartirse; [+ *person**] coser a puñaladas

carver [ˈkɑːvəʳ] (N) **1** (= *knife*) cuchillo *m* de trinchar, trinchante *m*; **carvers** cubierto *m* de trinchar
2 (*Culin*) (= *person*) trinchador(a) *m/f*

carvery [ˈkɑːvərɪ] (N) restaurante *m* que se especializa en asados

carve-up* [ˈkɑːvˌʌp] (N) (= *division*) división *f*, repartimiento *m*; (*Pol etc*) arreglo *m*

carving [ˈkɑːvɪŋ] (N) (= *act*) tallado *m*; (= *ornament*) talla *f*, escultura *f*
(CPD) ▸ **carving knife** cuchillo *m* de trinchar, trinchante *m*

caryatid [ˌkærɪˈætɪd] (N) (PL: **caryatids** *or* **caryatides** [ˌkærɪˈætɪdiːz]) cariátide *f*

Casablanca [ˌkæsəˈblæŋkə] (N) Casablanca *f*

Casanova [ˌkæsəˈnəʊvə] (N) (*fig*) casanova *m*, conquistador *m*

cascade [kæsˈkeɪd] (N) cascada *f*, salto *m* de agua; (*fig*) [*of sparks*] cascada *f*; [*of letters*] aluvión *m*; [*of stones*] lluvia *f*
(VI) caer en cascada

cascara [kæsˈkɑːrə] (N) (*Pharm*) cáscara *f* sagrada

case¹ [keɪs] (N) **1** (*Brit*) (= *suitcase*) maleta *f*, valija *f* (*S. Cone*), veliz *m* (*Mex*); (= *briefcase*) cartera *f*, maletín *m*, portafolio(s) *m* (*LAm*); (= *packing case*) cajón *m*; [*of drink*] caja *f*; (*for jewellery*) joyero *m*, estuche *m*; (*for camera, guitar, gun etc*) funda *f*; (*for spectacles*) (*soft*) funda *f*; (*hard*) estuche *m*; (*for watch*) caja *f*; (= *display case*) vitrina *f*; [*of window*] marco *m*, bastidor *m*; [*of cartridge*] funda *f*, cápsula *f*
2 (*Typ*) caja *f* • **lower ~** minúscula *f* • **upper ~** mayúscula *f*
(VT) **1** (= *encase*) • **her leg was ~d in plaster** tenía la pierna escayolada *or* enyesada • **~d in concrete** revestido de hormigón
2 • **to ~ the joint‡** estudiar el terreno para un robo

case² [keɪs] (N) **1** (*gen*) (*also Med*) caso *m* • **it's a sad ~** es un caso triste • **it's a hopeless ~** (*Med*) es un caso de desahucio • **a fever ~** un caso de fiebre • **he's working on the train-robbery ~** está investigando el caso del robo del tren • **as the ~ may be** según el caso • **it's a ~ for the police** este es asunto para la policía, esto es cosa de la policía • **it's a ~ of ...** se trata de ... • **it's a clear ~ of murder** es un claro caso de homicidio • **a ~ in point** un ejemplo al respecto *or* que hace al caso • **if that is the ~** en ese caso
2 (*Jur*) (*gen*) caso *m*, proceso *m*; (= *particular dispute*) causa *f*, pleito *m*; (= *argument*) argumento *m*, razón *f* • **the Dreyfus ~** el proceso de Dreyfus; (*more loosely*) el asunto Dreyfus • **there is no ~ to answer** no hay

acusación para contestar • **there's a strong ~ for reform** hay buenos fundamentos para exigir una reforma • **there's a ~ for saying that ...** puede decirse razonablemente que ... • **there is a ~ for that attitude** hay argumentos en favor de esa actitud • **the ~ for the defence** la defensa • **the ~ for the prosecution** la acusación • **to have a good** *or* **strong ~** tener buenos argumentos *or* buenas razones • **to make (out) a ~ for sth** dar razones para algo, presentar argumentos en favor de algo • **to make the ~ for doing nothing** exponer las razones para no hacer nada • **to put** *or* **state one's ~** presentar sus argumentos, exponer su caso • **to rest one's ~** terminar la presentación de su alegato

3 (*with "in"*) • **(just) in ~** por si acaso, por si las moscas* • **in ~ he comes** por si viene, (en) caso de que venga • **in your ~** en tu caso • **in any ~** de todas formas, en cualquier caso, en todo caso • **in most ~s** en la mayoría de los casos • **in no ~** en ningún caso, de ninguna manera • **in ~ of emergency** en caso de emergencia • **as in the ~ of** como en el caso de • **in such a ~** en tal caso • **in that ~** en ese caso

4 (*Ling*) caso *m*

5* (= *eccentric person*) • **he's a ~** es un tipo raro*, es un caso

6‡ • **get off my ~!** ¡déjame ya en paz! • **to be on sb's ~** estar siempre encima de algn • **to get on sb's ~** meterse en la vida de algn

(CPD) ▸ **case file** historial *m* ▸ **case grammar** gramática *f* de caso ▸ **case history** (*Med*) historial *m* médico *or* clínico • **what is the patient's ~ history?** ¿cuál es el historial del enfermo? • **I'll give you the full ~ history** le contaré la historia con todos los detalles ▸ **case law** jurisprudencia *f* ▸ **case study** estudio *m* de casos ▸ **case system** (*Ling*) sistema *m* de casos

casebook [ˈkeɪsbʊk] (N) diario *m*, registro *m*

case-by-case [ˈkeɪsbaɪkeɪs] (ADJ) [*basis, approach*] caso por caso

case-hardened [ˈkeɪs,hɑːdnd] (ADJ) (*Tech*) cementado; (*fig*) [*person*] insensible, poco compasivo

caseload [ˈkeɪsləʊd] (N) *número de encargos asignados a un(a) profesional*

casement [ˈkeɪsmənt] (N) (*also* **casement window**) ventana *f* de bisagras; (= *frame*) marco *m* de ventana

case-sensitive [ˈkeɪs,sensɪtɪv] (ADJ) (*Comput*) capaz de distinguir mayúsculas de minúsculas

casework [ˈkeɪswɜːk] (N) (*Sociol*) asistencia *f* *or* trabajo *m* social individualizado

caseworker [ˈkeɪs,wɜːkəʳ] (N) asistente *mf* social

cash [kæʃ] (N) **1** (= *coins, notes*) (dinero *m* en) efectivo *m*, metálico *m* • **to pay (in) ~** pagar al contado *or* en efectivo • **~ on delivery** envío *m* *or* entrega *f* contra reembolso • **~ down** al contado • **to pay ~ (down) for sth** pagar algo al contado • **~ in hand** efectivo en caja; ▹ **hard**

2* (= *money*) dinero *m*, pasta *f* (*Sp**), plata *f* (*LAm**) • **to be short of ~** andar mal de dinero • **I haven't any ~ on me** no llevo dinero encima

(VT) [+ *cheque*] cobrar, hacer efectivo • **to ~ sb a cheque** cambiarle a algn un cheque

(CPD) ▸ **cash account** cuenta *f* de caja ▸ **cash advance** adelanto *m* ▸ **cash bar** bar *m* privado (*sin barra libre*) ▸ **cash box** caja *f* para el dinero, alcancía *f* ▸ **cash card** tarjeta *f* de cajero automático ▸ **cash cow** producto *m* muy rentable ▸ **cash crop** cultivo *m* comercial ▸ **cash deficit** déficit *m* de caja ▸ **cash desk** caja *f* ▸ **cash discount** descuento *m* por pago al contado ▸ **cash dispenser** (*Brit*) cajero *m* automático ▸ **cash flow** flujo *m* de caja, movimiento *m* de efectivo • **~-flow problems** problemas *mpl* de cash-flow ▸ **cash income** ingresos *mpl* al contado ▸ **cash machine** cajero *m* automático ▸ **cash offer** oferta *f* de pago al contado ▸ **cash order** orden *f* de pago al contado ▸ **cash payment** pago *m* al contado ▸ **cash price** precio *m* al contado ▸ **cash prize** premio *m* en metálico ▸ **cash ratio** coeficiente *m* de caja ▸ **cash receipts** total *m* cobrado ▸ **cash reduction** = **cash discount** ▸ **cash register** caja *f* registradora ▸ **cash reserves** reserva *fsing* en efectivo ▸ **cash sale** venta *f* al contado ▸ **cash squeeze** restricciones *fpl* económicas ▸ **cash terms** = **cash payment** ▸ **cash value** valor *m* en dinero

▸ **cash in** (VT + ADV) [+ *investment, insurance policy*] cobrar

▸ **cash in on*** (VI + PREP) • **to ~ in on sth** sacar partido *or* provecho de algo

▸ **cash up** (VI + ADV) (*Brit*) contar el dinero recaudado

cash-and-carry [ˈkæʃənˈkærɪ] (N) (= *shop*) autoservicio *m* mayorista

(ADJ) [*goods, business*] de venta al por mayor

cashback [ˈkæʃbæk] (N) **1** (= *discount*) devolución *f*

2 (*at supermarket etc*) *retirada de dinero en efectivo de un establecimiento donde se ha pagado con tarjeta; también dinero retirado*

cashbook [ˈkæʃbʊk] (N) libro *m* de caja

cashew [kæˈʃuː] (N) (*also* **cashew nut**) anacardo *m*

cashier [kæˈʃɪəʳ] (N) cajero/a *m/f*

(VT) (*Mil*) separar del servicio, destituir

(CPD) ▸ **cashier's check** (*US*) cheque *m* bancario ▸ **cashier's desk** (*US*) caja *f*

cashless [ˈkæʃlɪs] (ADJ) • **the ~ society** la sociedad sin dinero

cashmere [kæʃˈmɪəʳ] (N) cachemir *m*, cachemira *f*

(CPD) de cachemir, de cachemira

cashpoint [ˈkæʃ,pɔɪnt] (N) (*Brit*) cajero *m* automático

cash-strapped [ˈkæʃ,stræpt] (ADJ) escaso de dinero • **to be cash-strapped** estar *or* andar escaso de dinero

casing [ˈkeɪsɪŋ] (N) (*Tech*) (*gen*) cubierta *f*; [*of boiler*] revestimiento *m*; [*of cylinder*] camisa *f*; [*of tyre*] llanta *f*; [*of window*] marco *m*

casino [kəˈsiːnəʊ] (N) casino *m*

cask [kɑːsk] (N) (*for wine*) cuba *f*; (*large*) tonel *m*

casket [ˈkɑːskɪt] (N) (*for jewels*) estuche *m*, cofre *m*; (*esp US*) (= *coffin*) ataúd *m*

Caspian Sea [ˈkæspɪən,siː] (N) mar *m* Caspio

Cassandra [kəˈsændrə] (N) Casandra

cassava [kəˈsɑːvə] (N) mandioca *f*

casserole [ˈkæsərəʊl] (N) (= *utensil*) cacerola *f*, cazuela *f*; (= *food*) guiso *m*, cazuela *f*

(VT) hacer un guiso de

cassette [kæˈset] (N) casete *m*, cassette *m*

(CPD) ▸ **cassette deck** platina *f*, pletina *f* ▸ **cassette player** casete *m*, cassette *m* ▸ **cassette recorder** casete *m*, cassette *m* ▸ **cassette tape** = **cassette**

cassis [kæˈsiːs] (N) cassis *m*

Cassius [ˈkæsɪəs] (N) Casio

cassock [ˈkæsək] (N) sotana *f*

cassowary [ˈkæsəwɛərɪ] (N) casuario *m*

cast [kɑːst] (VB: PT, PP: **cast**) (N) **1** (= *throw*) [*of net, line*] lanzamiento *m*

2 (= *mould*) molde *m*; (*Med*) (= *plaster cast*) escayola *f*; [*of worm*] forma *f* • **leg in ~** pierna *f* enyesada *or* escayolada • **~ of features** facciones *fpl*, fisonomía *f* • **~ of mind** temperamento *m*

3 (*Tech*) (= *metal casting*) pieza *f* fundida

4 [*of play etc*] reparto *m* • **~ (and credits)** (*Cine, TV*) reparto *m*

5 (*Med*) (= *squint*) estrabismo *m* • **to have a ~ in one's eye** tener estrabismo en un ojo

(VT) **1** (= *throw*) echar, lanzar; [+ *net, anchor etc*] echar

2 (*fig*) [+ *shadow*] proyectar; [+ *light*] arrojar (on sobre); [+ *blame, glance, spell*] echar; [+ *horoscope*] hacer • **to ~ doubt upon sth** poner algo en duda • **to ~ one's eyes over sth** echar una mirada a algo • **to ~ lots** echar a suertes • **to ~ one's vote** votar, dar su voto

3 (= *shed*) [+ *horseshoe*] mudar • **the snake ~ its skin** la culebra mudó la piel

4 [+ *metal*] fundir; [+ *statue, clay*] moldear, vaciar

5 (*Theat*) [+ *part, play*] hacer el reparto de • **to ~ an actor in the part of** dar a un actor el papel de • **he was ~ as Macbeth** le dieron el papel de Macbeth • **we shall ~ the play on Tuesday** haremos el reparto de los papeles de la obra el martes

(VI) (*Fishing*) lanzar, arrojar

(CPD) ▸ **cast iron** hierro *m* fundido *or* colado; ▹ **cast-iron**

▸ **cast about for, cast around for** (VI + PREP) [+ *job, answer*] buscar, andar buscando

▸ **cast aside** (VT + ADV) (= *reject*) descartar, desechar

▸ **cast away** (VT + ADV) **1** (= *throw away*) desechar, tirar

2 (*Naut*) • **to be ~ away** naufragar • **to be ~ away on an island** naufragar y llegar a una isla

▸ **cast back** (VT + ADV) • **to ~ one's thoughts back** to rememorar

▸ **cast down** (VT + ADV) **1** (= *lower*) [+ *eyes*] bajar

2 (*fig*) desanimar • **to be ~ down** estar deprimido

▸ **cast in** (VT + ADV), (VI + ADV) • **to ~ in (one's lot) with sb** compartir el destino de algn

▸ **cast off** (VT + ADV) **1** (*lit*) desechar, abandonar; [+ *burden*] deshacerse de, quitarse de encima; [+ *clothing*] quitarse; [+ *wife*] repudiar; [+ *mistress*] dejar • **the slaves ~ off their chains** los esclavos se deshicieron de sus cadenas

2 (*Naut*) soltar las amarras de, desamarrar

3 (*Knitting*) [+ *stitch*] cerrar

(VI + ADV) **1** (*Naut*) soltar amarras

2 (*Knitting*) cerrar

▸ **cast on** (VT + ADV), (VI + ADV) (*Knitting*) montar

▸ **cast out** (VT + ADV) (*liter*) expulsar

▸ **cast up** (VT + ADV) **1** (*lit*) echar

2 (*Math, Econ*) [+ *account*] sumar

3 (*fig*) (= *reproach*) • **to ~ sth up to** *or* **at sb** echar en cara algo a algn

castanets [,kæstəˈnets] (NPL) castañuelas *fpl*

castaway [ˈkɑːstəweɪ] (N) náufrago/a *m/f*

caste [kɑːst] (N) casta *f* • IDIOM: • **to lose ~** desprestigiarse

(ADJ) de casta

(CPD) ▸ **caste mark** marca *f* de casta ▸ **caste system** sistema *m* de castas

castellated [ˈkæstəleɪtɪd] (ADJ) almenado

caster [ˈkɑːstəʳ] (N) = **castor**

(CPD) ▸ **caster sugar** (*Brit*) azúcar *m* extrafino, azúcar *m* lustre

castigate [ˈkæstɪɡeɪt] (VT) (*frm*) reprobar, censurar

castigation [,kæstɪˈɡeɪʃən] (N) (*frm*) reprobación *f*, censura *f*

Castile [kæsˈtiːl] (N) Castilla *f*

Castilian [kæs'tɪlɪən] ADJ castellano
N 1 (= person) castellano/a m/f
2 (Ling) castellano m

casting ['kɑ:stɪŋ] N 1 (Tech) pieza f fundida, pieza f de fundición
2 (Cine, Theat) reparto m
CPD ▸ **casting couch** (Cine) (hum) diván m del director (del reparto) ▸ **casting director** director(a) m/f de casting ▸ **casting vote** voto m decisivo, voto m de calidad

cast-iron ['kɑ:st,aɪən] ADJ 1 (lit) (hecho) de hierro fundido
2 (fig) [will] inquebrantable, férreo; [case] irrebatible; [excuse] frente a la que no se puede decir nada

castle ['kɑ:sl] N 1 (= building) castillo m
• IDIOM: • **to build ~s in the air** or (Brit) **in Spain** construir castillos en el aire
2 (Chess) torre f
VI (Chess) enrocar

castling ['kɑ:slɪŋ] N (Chess) enroque m

cast-off ['kɑ:stɒf] ADJ [clothing etc] de desecho, en desuso
N **cast-offs** (= garments) ropa f de desecho, ropa f que ya no se pone • **our players are mostly cast-offs from the first team** la mayoría de nuestros jugadores vienen descartados del primer equipo • **society's cast-offs** los marginados de la sociedad
CPD ▸ **cast-off clothes** (unwanted) ropa f de desecho, ropa f que ya no se pone; (pej) (old and out-moded) trapos mpl viejos

castor ['kɑ:stəʳ] N 1 (on furniture) ruedecilla f
2 (= sifter) (for sugar) azucarero m
CPD ▸ **castor oil** aceite m de ricino ▸ **castor oil plant** ricino m ▸ **castor sugar** = caster sugar

castrate [kæs'treɪt] VT castrar

castration [kæs'treɪʃən] N castración f

castrato [kæs'trɑ:təʊ] N (PL: **castrato** or **castrati** [kæs'trɑ:tɪ]) castrato m

Castroism ['kæstrəʊɪzəm] N castrismo m

Castroist ['kæstrəʊɪst] ADJ castrista
N castrista mf

casual ['kæʒjʊəl] ADJ 1 (= not planned) [walk, stroll] sin rumbo fijo, al azar; [meeting, encounter] fortuito; [caller] ocasional • **it was just a ~ conversation between strangers** no era más que una conversación para pasar el rato entre extraños • **to the ~ eye** a simple vista • **he ran a ~ eye down the page** le echó un vistazo a la página • **a ~ glance** una ojeada • **to the ~ observer** para el observador ocasional • **a ~ remark** un comentario hecho a la ligera • **she gave him a ~ wave** lo saludó informalmente con la mano
2 (= offhand) [attitude] despreocupado, poco serio; [manner] informal; [tone] informal, poco serio • **he tried to appear/sound ~** intentó parecer/sonar relajado • **he was very ~ about it** no le dio mucha importancia • **to assume a ~ air** hacer como si nada
3 (= informal) [discussion] informal; [clothing] de sport, informal • **~ wear** ropa de sport, ropa informal
4 (= occasional) [drinker, drug user, relationship] esporádico • **he's just a ~ acquaintance** es un conocido nada más • **~ sex** relaciones fpl sexuales promiscuas
5 (= temporary) [labour, work, employment] eventual • **on a ~ basis** temporalmente, eventualmente • **~ worker** (in office, factory) trabajador(a) m/f eventual; (on farm) trabajador(a) m/f temporero/a, jornalero/a m/f
N **casuals** (= shoes) zapatos mpl de sport; (= clothes) ropa f de sport, ropa f informal

casualization [,kæʒjʊəlaɪ'zeɪʃən] (Brit) N [of labour, employment] precarización f

casualize ['kæʒjʊəlaɪz] (Brit) VT [+ workforce, employees] precarizar

casually ['kæʒjʊəlɪ] ADV 1 (= offhandedly) [walk, lean] con aire despreocupado, despreocupadamente; [look, wave] despreocupadamente; [mention, say, ask] de pasada • **I said it quite ~** lo dije sin darle importancia
2 (= informally) [dress] de manera informal; [talk] informalmente • **they were smartly but ~ dressed** iban vestidos de manera informal pero elegante

casualness ['kæʒjuəlnɪs] N
1 (= offhandedness) despreocupación f
2 (= informality) informalidad f, naturalidad f

casualty ['kæʒjʊəltɪ] N 1 (Mil) (dead) baja f; (wounded) herido/a m/f • **there were heavy casualties** hubo muchas bajas
2 (in accident) (dead) víctima f; (wounded) herido/a m/f • **Casualty** (= hospital department) Urgencias • **fortunately there were no casualties** por fortuna no hubo víctimas or heridos
3 (fig) • **a ~ of modern society** una víctima de la sociedad moderna
CPD ▸ **casualty department** (servicio m de) urgencias fpl ▸ **casualty list** (Mil) lista f de bajas; (in accident) lista f de víctimas ▸ **casualty ward** sala f de urgencias

casuist ['kæzjʊɪst] N (frm) casuista mf; (pej) sofista mf

casuistry ['kæzjʊɪstrɪ] N (frm) casuística f; (pej) sofismas mpl, razonamiento m falaz

CAT ['kæt] N ABBR 1 = **computer-aided teaching**
2 (= **computerized axial tomography**) TAC m or f
3 (= **computer-assisted translation**) TAO f
4 = **College of Advanced Technology**
CPD ▸ **CAT scan** escáner m TAC • **to have a CAT scan: I'm going to have a CAT scan** me van a hacer un (escáner) TAC

cat [kæt] N 1 (domestic) gato/a m/f; (= lion etc) felino/a m/f • IDIOMS: • **to put** or **set the cat among the pigeons:** • **that's put** or **set the cat among the pigeons!** ¡eso ha puesto a los perros en danza!, ¡ya se armó la gorda!* • **something the cat has brought** or **dragged in:** • **he looked like something the cat had brought** or **dragged in*** estaba hecho un desastre • **look what the cat brought** or **dragged in!*** (iro) (expressing dislike) ¡vaya facha or pinta que traes!; (as greeting) ¡anda, mira quién viene por aquí! • **to let the cat out of the bag** irse de la lengua • **the cat's out of the bag** se ha descubierto todo el pastel • **to be like a cat on hot bricks** or **on a hot tin roof** estar sobre ascuas • **to look like the cat that ate the canary** or (Brit) **that got the cream** estar más ancho que largo, no caber en sí de satisfacción • **to fight like cat and dog** llevarse como el perro y el gato • **to play a game of cat and mouse** or **a cat-and-mouse game with sb** jugar al gato y ratón con algn • **not to have a cat in hell's chance*** no tener la más mínima posibilidad • **to see which way the cat jumps** esperar a ver de qué lado caen las peras • **the cat's pyjamas** or **whiskers***: • **he thinks he's the cat's pyjamas** or **whiskers*** se cree la mar de listo* • **there isn't room to swing a cat** aquí no cabe un alfiler • **(has the) cat got your tongue?*** ¿te ha comido la lengua el gato? • PROVERBS: • **when the cat's away, the mice will play** cuando el gato no está, bailan los ratones • **cats have nine lives** los gatos tienen siete vidas; ▹ **curiosity, fat, rain, skin, scald**
2 (US‡) (= person) tío/a* m/f, tipo/a* m/f • **he's a real cool cat** es un tío la mar de chulo*
3†† (= cat-o'-nine-tails) azote m
4* (= catalytic converter) catalizador m
CPD ▸ **cat basket** (for carrying) cesto m para llevar al gato; (for sleeping) cesto m del gato ▸ **cat burglar** (ladrón/ona m/f) balconero/a m/f ▸ **cat's cradle** (juego m de la) cuna f ▸ **cat flap** gatera f ▸ **cat food** comida f para gatos ▸ **cat litter** arena f higiénica (para gatos) ▸ **cat's whisker** (Rad) cable m antena

cataclysm ['kætəklɪzəm] N cataclismo m

cataclysmic [,kætə'klɪzmɪk] ADJ de cataclismo

catacombs ['kætəku:mz] NPL catacumbas fpl

catafalque ['kætəfælk] N catafalco m

Catalan ['kætəlæn] ADJ catalán
N 1 (= person) catalán/ana m/f
2 (Ling) catalán m

catalepsy ['kætlepsɪ] N catalepsia f

cataleptic [,kætə'leptɪk] ADJ cataléptico
N cataléptico/a m/f

catalogue, catalog (US) ['kætəlɒg] N catálogo m; (also **card catalogue**) fichero m; (US) (= pamphlet, prospectus) folleto m
• **a whole ~ of complaints** (fig) toda una serie de quejas
VT catalogar, poner en un catálogo • **it is not catalog(u)ed** no consta en el catálogo

Catalonia [,kætə'ləʊnɪə] N Cataluña f

Catalonian [,kætə'ləʊnɪən] = **Catalan**

catalyse, catalyze (US) ['kætəlaɪz] VT catalizar

catalysis [kə'tælɪsɪs] N (PL: **catalyses** [kə'tælə,si:z]) catálisis f

catalyst ['kætəlɪst] N (Chem) (also fig) catalizador m

catalytic [,kætə'lɪtɪk] ADJ catalítico
CPD ▸ **catalytic converter** (Aut) catalizador m

catamaran [,kætəmə'ræn] N catamarán m

catapult ['kætəpʌlt] N 1 (Brit) (= slingshot) tirador m, tirachinas m inv
2 (Aer, Mil) catapulta f
VT 1 (Aer) catapultar
2 (fig) • **he was ~ed to fame** fue catapultado a la fama
VI (fig) • **his record ~ed to number one** su disco subió catapultado al número uno

cataract ['kætərækt] N 1 (= waterfall) catarata f
2 (Med) catarata f

catarrh [kə'tɑ:ʳ] N catarro m

catarrhal [kə'tɑ:rəl] ADJ catarral

catastrophe [kə'tæstrəfɪ] N catástrofe f

catastrophic [,kætə'strɒfɪk] ADJ catastrófico

catastrophically [,kætə'strɒfɪklɪ] ADV catastróficamente

catatonic [,kætə'tɒnɪk] ADJ catatónico
N catatónico/a m/f

catbird ['kætbɜ:d] N • IDIOM: • **to be (sitting) in the ~ seat** (US*) sentirse seguro

catcall ['kætkɔ:l] (Theat etc) N **catcalls** silbido msing
VI silbar

catch [kætʃ] (VB: PT, PP: **caught**) N 1 [of ball etc] cogida f, parada f; [of trawler] pesca f; [of single fish] presa f, pesca f, captura f • **good ~!** (Sport) ¡la cogiste! ¡bien hecho!, ¡bien agarrada! (LAm) • **he's a good ~*** (as husband etc) es un buen partido
2 (= fastener) cierre m; (Brit) (on door) pestillo m; (Brit) (on box, window) cerradura f; (= small flange) fiador m
3 (= trick) trampa f; (= snag) pega f • **where's the ~?** ¿cuál es la trampa? • **there must be a ~ here somewhere** aquí debe de haber trampa • **a question with a ~ to it** una pregunta capciosa or de pega • **the ~ is that ...** la dificultad es que ...
4 • **with a ~ in one's voice** con la voz

entrecortada
5 (= *game*) catch-can *m*, lucha *f*
VT 1 (= *grasp*) asir; [+ *ball*] coger, agarrar (*LAm*); [+ *fish*] pescar; [+ *thief*] coger, atrapar • **~!** ¡cógelo!, ¡toma! • **to be caught between two alternatives** estar entre la espada y la pared, no saber a qué carta quedarse • **a toaster with a tray to ~ the breadcrumbs** un tostador con una bandeja para recoger las migas • **to ~ sb's attention** *or* **eye** llamar la atención de algn • IDIOM: • **to be caught like a rat in a trap** estar atrapado como un ratón
2 (= *take by surprise*) pillar *or* coger *or* (*LAm*) tomar de sorpresa • **to ~ sb doing sth** sorprender *or* pillar a algn haciendo algo • **to ~ o.s. doing sth** sorprenderse a sí mismo haciendo algo • **you won't ~ me doing that** yo sería incapaz de hacer eso, nunca me verás haciendo eso • **they caught him in the act** le cogieron *or* pillaron con las manos en la masa • **we never caught them at it** no los sorprendimos nunca in fraganti • **we won't get caught like that again** no volveremos a caer en esta trampa • **he got caught in the rain** la lluvia lo pilló desprevenido • **you've caught me at a bad moment** me has pillado en un mal momento • IDIOM: • **he was caught off stride** *or* **off balance*** lo cogieron con la guardia baja
3 (= *contact, get hold of*) • **I tried to ~ you on the phone** traté de hablar contigo por teléfono • **when can I ~ you next?** ¿cuándo podemos quedar otra vez para esto? • **(I'll) ~ you later!*** ¡nos vemos!
4 [+ *bus, train etc*] coger, tomar (*LAm*) • **we only just caught the train** por poco perdimos el tren • **hurry if you want to ~ it** date prisa si quieres llegar a tiempo
5 (= *hear*) oír; (= *understand*) comprender, entender • **I didn't quite ~ what you said** no oí bien lo que dijiste
6 (= *see, hear, visit*) [+ *TV programme, film*] ver; [+ *radio programme*] oír, escuchar; [+ *exhibition, concert*] ir a • **to ~ the post** (= *be in time for*) llegar antes de la recogida del correo
7 (*Med*) [+ *disease*] coger, pillar, contagiarse de • **to ~ (a) cold** resfriarse • **you'll ~ your death (of cold)!*** ¡(te) vas a agarrar un buen resfriado! • IDIOM: • **to ~ a cold*** (*in business deal etc*) tener un tropiezo económico
8 (= *capture*) [+ *atmosphere, likeness*] saber captar, plasmar • **the painter has caught her expression** el pintor ha sabido captar su expresión • **to ~ the mood of the times** definir el espíritu de la época
9 (= *trap*) • **I caught my fingers in the door** me pillé los dedos en la puerta • **I caught my coat on that nail** mi chaqueta se enganchó en ese clavo
10 (= *hit*) • **to ~ sb a blow** pegar un golpe a algn • **the punch caught him on the arm** recibió el puñetazo en el brazo • **I caught my head on that beam** me di con la cabeza en esa viga • **she caught me one on the nose*** me pegó en la nariz
11 (= *receive, come into contact with*) • **this room ~es the morning sun** este cuarto recibe el sol de la mañana • **her brooch caught the light** su broche reflejaba la luz • **the light was ~ing her hair** la luz brillaba en su pelo
12 • **to ~ one's breath** contener la respiración
13 • **to ~ it*** merecerse una regañina (**from** de) • **you'll ~ it!*** ¡las vas a pagar!, ¡te va a costar caro! • **he caught it good and proper*** le cayó una buena
VI 1 (= *hook*) engancharse (**on** en); (= *tangle*) enredarse • **her dress caught in the door** se pilló el vestido con la puerta • **her dress caught on a nail** se le enganchó el vestido en un clavo
2 [*fire, wood*] prender, encenderse; (*Culin*) [*rice, vegetables etc*] quemarse
CPD ▸ **catch cry** slogan *m*, eslogan *m* ▸ **catch phrase** muletilla *f*, frase *f* de moda ▸ **catch question** pregunta *f* capciosa, pregunta *f* de pega
▸ **catch at** VI + PREP [+ *object*] tratar de coger *or* (*LAm*) agarrar; [+ *opportunity*] aprovechar
▸ **catch on** VI + ADV 1 (= *become popular*) cuajar, tener éxito • **it never really caught on** no logró establecerse de verdad
2 (= *understand*) caer en la cuenta; (= *get the knack*) coger el truco • **to ~ on to** comprender
▸ **catch out** VT + ADV (*esp Brit*) (*with trick question*) hundir • **to ~ sb out** sorprender *or* pillar a algn • **you won't ~ me out again like that** no me vas a pillar así otra vez • **we were caught out by the rise in the dollar** la subida del dólar nos cogió desprevenidos
▸ **catch up** VT + ADV 1 • **to ~ sb up** (*walking, working etc*) alcanzar a algn
2 (= *enmesh*) • **we were caught up in the traffic** nos vimos bloqueados por el tráfico • **a society caught up in change** una sociedad afectada por cambios • **to be caught up in the excitement** participar de la emoción
3 (= *grab*) [+ *weapon, pen etc*] recoger, agarrar
VI + ADV • **to ~ up (on** *or* **with one's work)** ponerse al día (en el trabajo) • **to ~ up on one's sleep** recuperar el sueño atrasado • **to ~ up with** [+ *person*] alcanzar; [+ *news etc*] ponerse al corriente de • **the police finally caught up with him in Vienna** al final la policía dio con él *or* lo localizó en Viena • **the truth has finally caught up with him** ya no le queda más remedio que enfrentarse a la verdad
catch-22 [ˌkætʃˌtwentɪˈtuː] N • **a catch-22 situation** un callejón sin salida, un círculo vicioso
catch-all [ˈkætʃˌɔːl] ADJ [*regulation, clause etc*] general; [*phrase*] para todo
N *algo que sirve para todo*
catcher [ˈkætʃəʳ] N (*Baseball*) apañador(a) *m/f*, receptor(a) *m/f*
catching [ˈkætʃɪŋ] ADJ 1 (*Med*) contagioso
2 (*fig*) [*enthusiasm, laughter*] contagioso
catchment [ˈkætʃmənt] N [*of river*] cuenca *f* hidrográfica
CPD ▸ **catchment area** (*Brit*) zona *f* de captación ▸ **catchment basin** cuenca *f*
catchpenny [ˈkætʃˌpenɪ] ADJ llamativo (y barato), hecho para venderse al instante • **~ solution** solución *f* atractiva (pero poco recomendable)
catchup [ˈkætʃəp] N (*US*) = **ketchup**
catchword [ˈkætʃwɜːd] N (= *catch phrase*) [*of person*] muletilla *f*; (*Pol*) eslogan *m*; (*Typ*) reclamo *m*
catchy [ˈkætʃɪ] ADJ (COMPAR: **catchier**, SUPERL: **catchiest**) [*tune, slogan*] pegadizo; [*name, title*] fácil de recordar, con gancho
catechism [ˈkætɪkɪzəm] N (= *instruction*) catequesis *f inv*, catequismo *m*; (= *book*) catecismo *m*
catechist [ˈkætɪkɪst] N catequista *mf*
catechize [ˈkætɪkaɪz] VT catequizar
categoric [ˌkætɪˈgɒrɪk] ADJ = **categorical**
categorical [ˌkætɪˈgɒrɪkəl] ADJ categórico, terminante; [*refusal*] rotundo
categorically [ˌkætɪˈgɒrɪkəlɪ] ADV [*state etc*] de modo terminante; [*refuse*] rotundamente
categorization [ˌkætɪgəraɪˈzeɪʃən] N categorización *f*
categorize [ˈkætɪgəraɪz] VT clasificar • **to ~ sth as** calificar algo de, clasificar algo como
category [ˈkætɪgərɪ] N categoría *f*
CPD ▸ **Category A prisoner** (*Brit*) preso/a *m/f* peligroso/a
cater [ˈkeɪtəʳ] VI 1 (= *provide food*) proveer de comida (**for** a)
2 (*fig*) • **to ~ for** *or* (*US*) **to** atender a, ofrecer (sus) servicios a • **we ~ for group bookings** (*Brit*) nos ocupamos de las reservas de grupos • **to ~ for** *or* (*US*) **to sb's needs** atender las necesidades de algn • **to ~ for** *or* (*US*) **to all tastes** atender a todos los gustos • **this magazine ~s for** *or* (*US*) **to the under-21's** esta revista está dirigida a gente por debajo de los 21 años
cater-cornered [ˈkeɪtəˈkɔːnəd] (*US*) ADJ diagonal
ADV diagonalmente
caterer [ˈkeɪtərəʳ] N proveedor(a) *m/f* de catering
catering [ˈkeɪtərɪŋ] N servicio *m* de comidas • **a career in ~** una carrera en la hostelería • **who did the ~?** ¿quién se encargó del servicio de comidas?
CPD ▸ **catering college** escuela *f* de cocina ▸ **catering company** empresa *f* de hostelería ▸ **catering industry, catering trade** hostelería *f*, restauración *f*
caterpillar [ˈkætəpɪləʳ] N 1 (*Zool*) oruga *f*
2 (*also* **Caterpillar tractor®**) tractor *m* de oruga
CPD ▸ **Caterpillar track®** rodado *m* de oruga
caterwaul [ˈkætəwɔːl] VI [*person*] aullar; [*cat*] maullar
caterwauling [ˈkætəˌwɔːlɪŋ] N [*of person*] chillidos *mpl*, aullidos *mpl*; [*of cat*] maullidos *mpl*
catfight [ˈkætfaɪt] N (*between women*) pelea *f* de mujeres
catfish [ˈkætfɪʃ] N (PL: **catfish** *or* **catfishes**) siluro *m*, bagre *m*
catgut [ˈkætgʌt] N cuerda *f* de tripa; (*Med*) catgut *m*
Cath. ABBR 1 = **Cathedral**
2 = **Catholic**
Catharine [ˈkæθərɪn] N Catalina
catharsis [kəˈθɑːsɪs] N (PL: **catharses**) catarsis *f*
cathartic [kəˈθɑːtɪk] ADJ 1 (*Med*) catártico, purgante
2 (*fig*) catártico
N (*Med*) purgante *m*
cathedral [kəˈθiːdrəl] N catedral *f*
CPD ▸ **cathedral choir** coro *m* catedralicio ▸ **cathedral church** iglesia *f* catedral ▸ **cathedral city** ciudad *f* episcopal
Catherine [ˈkæθərɪn] N Catalina
CPD ▸ **Catherine wheel** (= *firework*) girándula *f*
catheter [ˈkæθɪtəʳ] N catéter *m*
catheterize [ˈkæθɪtəˌraɪz] VT [+ *bladder, person*] entubar
cathode [ˈkæθəʊd] N cátodo *m*
CPD ▸ **cathode ray** rayo *m* catódico ▸ **cathode ray tube** tubo *m* de rayos catódicos
catholic [ˈkæθəlɪk] ADJ 1 • **(Roman) Catholic** católico • **the Catholic Church** la Iglesia Católica
2 (= *wide-ranging*) [*tastes, interests*] católico
N • **Catholic** católico/a *m/f*
Catholicism [kəˈθɒlɪsɪzəm] N catolicismo *m*
cathouse‡ [ˈkæthaʊs] N (PL: **cathouses** [ˈkæthaʊzɪz]) (*US*) casa *f* de putas
Cathy [ˈkæθɪ] N *familiar form of* **Catharine, Catherine**
catkin [ˈkætkɪn] N amento *m*, candelilla *f*
cat-lick* [ˈkætlɪk] N mano *f* de gato • **to give o.s. a cat-lick** lavarse a lo gato
catlike [ˈkætlaɪk] ADJ felino, gatuno
catmint [ˈkætmɪnt] N hierba *f* gatera,

nébeda *f*
catnap* [ˈkætnæp] N siestecita *f*, sueñecito *m* • **to take a ~** echarse una siestecita *or* un sueñecito
VI echarse una siestecita, echarse un sueñecito
catnip [ˈkætnɪp] N (*US*) = **catmint**
Cato [ˈkeɪtəʊ] N Catón
cat-o'-nine-tails [ˈkætəˈnaɪnteɪlz] N azote *m* (con nueve ramales)
Catseye®, cat's-eye [ˈkætsaɪ] N (*Brit*) (*on road*) catadióptrico *m*
cat's-paw [ˈkætspɔː] N (*fig*) instrumento *m*
catsuit [ˈkætsuːt] N traje *m* de gato
catsup [ˈkætsəp] N (*US*) catsup *m*, salsa *f* de tomate
cattery [ˈkætərɪ] N residencia *f* para gatos
cattiness [ˈkætɪnɪs] N malicia *f*, rencor *m*
cattle [ˈkætl] NPL ganado *msing*
CPD ▸ **cattle breeder** criador(a) *m/f* de ganado ▸ **cattle breeding** crianza *f* de ganado ▸ **cattle crossing** paso *m* de ganado ▸ **cattle drive** (*US*) recogida *f* de ganado ▸ **cattle egret** garcilla *f* bueyera ▸ **cattle farm** granja *f* de ganado ▸ **cattle grid** (*Brit*), **cattle guard** (*US*) paso *m* canadiense ▸ **cattle market** mercado *m* ganadero *or* de ganado; (*also fig*) feria *f* de ganado ▸ **cattle prod** picana *f* ▸ **cattle raising** ganadería *f* ▸ **cattle ranch** finca *f* ganadera, estancia *f* (*LAm*) ▸ **cattle rustler** (*US*) ladrón *m* de ganado, cuatrero *m* ▸ **cattle shed** establo *m* ▸ **cattle show** feria *f* de ganado ▸ **cattle truck** (*Aut*) camión *m* de ganado; (*Brit*) (*Rail*) vagón *m* para ganado
cattleman [ˈkætlmæn] N (PL: **cattlemen**) ganadero *m*
catty* [ˈkætɪ] ADJ (COMPAR: **cattier**, SUPERL: **cattiest**) [*person, remark*] malicioso
Catullus [kəˈtʌləs] N Catulo
CATV N ABBR = **community antenna television**
catwalk [ˈkætwɔːk] N pasarela *f*
Caucasian [kɔːˈkeɪzɪən] ADJ (*by race*) caucásico; (*Geog*) caucasiano
N (*by race*) caucásico/a *m/f*; (*Geog*) caucasiano/a *m/f*
Caucasus [ˈkɔːkəsəs] N Cáucaso *m*
caucus [ˈkɔːkəs] N (PL: **caucuses**) (*Brit*) camarilla *f* (política), junta *f* secreta; (*US*) (= *meeting*) junta *f* ejecutiva; (= *committee*) comité *m* ejecutivo, comisión *f* ejecutiva
VI reunirse (para tomar decisiones)
caudal [ˈkɔːdl] ADJ caudal
caught [kɔːt] PT, PP *of* **catch**
cauldron [ˈkɔːldrən] N caldera *f*, calderón *m* • **a ~ of unrest** (*fig*) una caldera *or* olla a presión
cauliflower [ˈkɒlɪflaʊəʳ] N coliflor *f*
CPD ▸ **cauliflower cheese** coliflor *f* con queso ▸ **cauliflower ear** oreja *f* deformada por los golpes
caulk [kɔːk] VT calafatear
causal [ˈkɔːzəl] ADJ causal
causality [kɔːˈzælɪtɪ] N causalidad *f*
causally [ˈkɔːzəlɪ] ADV causalmente • **they are ~ related** guardan una relación de causa y efecto
causation [kɔːˈzeɪʃən] N causalidad *f*
causative [ˈkɔːzətɪv] ADJ causativo
cause [kɔːz] N **1** (= *origin*) causa *f*; (= *reason*) motivo *m*, razón *f* • **~ and effect** (relación de) causa y efecto • **with good ~** con razón • **to be the ~ of** ser causa de • **there's no ~ for alarm** no hay por qué inquietarse • **to give ~ for complaint** dar motivo de queja • **you have ~ to be worried** usted tiene motivo para estar preocupado • **to show ~** (*frm*) aducir argumentos convincentes
2 (= *purpose*) causa *f* • **in the ~ of justice** por la justicia • **to make common ~ with** hacer causa común con • **it's all in a good ~** se está haciendo por una buena causa • **to die in a good ~** morir por una causa noble • **to take up sb's ~** apoyar la campaña de algn; ▹ **lost**
3 (*Jur*) causa *f*, pleito *m*
VT causar, provocar; [+ *accident, trouble*] causar • **I don't want to ~ you any inconvenience** no quisiera causarle ninguna molestia • **to ~ sb to do sth** hacer que algn haga algo
CPD ▸ **cause célèbre** pleito *m or* caso *m* célebre
'cause*, cause* [kəz] [kɒz] CONJ (= *because*) porque
causeway [ˈkɔːzweɪ] N calzada *f or* carretera *f* elevada; (*in sea*) arrecife *m*
caustic [ˈkɔːstɪk] ADJ **1** (*Chem*) cáustico
2 (*fig*) [*remark etc*] mordaz, sarcástico
CPD ▸ **caustic soda** sosa *f* cáustica
caustically [ˈkɔːstɪklɪ] ADV [*say, remark, observe*] de forma cáustica
cauterization [ˌkɔːtəraɪˈzeɪʃən] N (*Med*) cauterización *f*
cauterize [ˈkɔːtəraɪz] VT cauterizar
caution [ˈkɔːʃən] N **1** (= *care*) cautela *f*, prudencia *f* • **"caution!"** (*Aut*) "¡cuidado!", "¡precaución!" • **proceed with ~** actúe con precaución • IDIOM: • **to throw ~ to the winds** abandonar la prudencia
2 (= *warning*) advertencia *f*, aviso *m*; (*Brit*) (*Police*) amonestación *f*
3 • **he's a ~†*** (= *amusing*) es un tío divertidísimo; (= *odd*) es un tío muy raro
VT • **to ~ sb** (*Brit*) (*Police*) amonestar a algn • **to ~ sb against doing sth** advertir a algn que no haga algo
cautionary [ˈkɔːʃənərɪ] ADJ [*tale*] de escarmiento, aleccionador • **to sound a ~ note** recomendar precaución
cautious [ˈkɔːʃəs] ADJ (= *careful*) cuidadoso; (= *wary*) cauteloso, prudente • **to make a ~ statement** hacer una declaración prudente • **to play a ~ game** jugar con mucha prudencia
cautiously [ˈkɔːʃəslɪ] ADV cautelosamente, con cautela • **~ optimistic** moderadamente *or* prudentemente optimista
cautiousness [ˈkɔːʃəsnɪs] N cautela *f*, prudencia *f*
cavalcade [ˌkævəlˈkeɪd] N cabalgata *f*; (*fig*) desfile *m*
cavalier [ˌkævəˈlɪəʳ] N caballero *m*; (= *escort††*) galán *m*; (*Brit*) (*Hist*) *partidario del Rey en la Guerra Civil inglesa (1641-49)*
ADJ (*pej*) (= *offhand*) desdeñoso
cavalierly [ˌkævəˈlɪəlɪ] ADV (*pej*) desdeñosamente
cavalry [ˈkævəlrɪ] N caballería *f*
CPD ▸ **cavalry charge** carga *f* de caballería ▸ **cavalry officer** oficial *m* de caballería ▸ **cavalry twill** *tela asargada utilizada para confeccionar pantalones*
cavalryman [ˈkævəlrɪmən] N (PL: **cavalrymen**) soldado *m* de caballería
cave¹ [keɪv] N cueva *f*, caverna *f*
CPD ▸ **cave dweller** cavernícola *mf*, troglodita *mf* ▸ **cave painting** pintura *f* rupestre
▸ **cave in** VI + ADV **1** [*ceiling*] derrumbarse, desplomarse; [*ground*] hundirse
2* (*fig*) (= *submit*) ceder, rendirse
cave²†* [ˈkeɪvɪ] EXCL (*Brit*) (*Scol*) • **~!** ¡ojo!, ¡ahí viene! • **to keep ~** estar a la mira
caveat [ˈkævɪæt] N advertencia *f*; (*Jur*) advertencia *f* de suspensión • **to enter a ~** hacer una advertencia
cave-in [ˈkeɪvɪn] N [*of roof etc*] derrumbe *m*, derrumbamiento *m*; [*of pavement etc*] socavón *m*
caveman [ˈkeɪvmæn] N (PL: **cavemen**) **1** (*Anthropology*) hombre *m* de las cavernas, cavernícola *m*, troglodita *m*; (*more loosely*) hombre *m* prehistórico
2* (*hum*) (*aggressively masculine*) machote* *m*
caver [ˈkeɪvəʳ] N espeleólogo/a *m/f*
cavern [ˈkævən] N caverna *f*
cavernous [ˈkævənəs] ADJ [*eyes, cheeks*] hundido; [*pit, darkness*] cavernoso
cavewoman [ˈkeɪvwʊmən] N (PL: **cavewomen**) mujer *f* de las cavernas, cavernícola *f*, troglodita *f*; (*more loosely*) mujer *f* prehistórica
caviar, caviare [ˈkævɪɑːʳ] N caviar *m*
cavil [ˈkævɪl] (PT, PP: **cavilled**, (*US*) **caviled**)
N reparo *m*
VI poner peros *or* reparos (**at** a)
caving [ˈkeɪvɪŋ] N espeleología *f* • **to go ~** (*gen*) hacer espeleología; (*on specific occasion*) ir en una expedición espeleológica
cavity [ˈkævɪtɪ] N cavidad *f*; (*in tooth*) caries *f inv* • **nasal cavities** fosas *fpl* nasales
CPD ▸ **cavity wall** pared *f* con cámara de aire, doble pared *f* ▸ **cavity wall insulation** aislamiento *m* con cámara de aire
cavort [kəˈvɔːt] VI dar *or* hacer cabriolas, dar brincos; (*fig*) divertirse ruidosamente
cavy [ˈkeɪvɪ] N conejillo *m* de Indias, cobaya *m*
caw [kɔː] N graznido *m*
VI graznar
cawing [ˈkɔːɪŋ] N graznidos *mpl*, el graznar
cay [keɪ] N (= *island*) cayo *m*
cayenne [ˈkeɪen] N (*also* **cayenne pepper**) pimentón *m* picante
cayman [ˈkeɪmən] N caimán *m*
CPD ▸ **the Cayman Islands** las islas Caimán
CB N ABBR **1** (= **Citizens' Band Radio**) BC *f*
2 (= **Companion (of the Order) of the Bath**) *título honorífico británico*
ABBR (*Mil*) = **confined to barracks**
CPD ▸ **CB Radio** radio *f* de BC, BC *f*
CBC N ABBR = **Canadian Broadcasting Corporation**
CBE N ABBR (= **Commander (of the Order) of the British Empire**) *título honorífico británico*
CBI N ABBR (= **Confederation of British Industry**) ≈ CEOE *f*
CBS N ABBR (*US*) (= **Columbia Broadcasting System**) *cadena de televisión*
CBT N ABBR = **cognitive behavioural therapy**
CC N ABBR (*Brit*) (*formerly*) (= **County Council**) gobierno *m* de un condado
cc ABBR **1** (= **cubic centimetre(s)**) cc, cm^3
2 = **carbon copy, carbon copies**
CCA N ABBR (*US*) = **Circuit Court of Appeals**
CCC N ABBR (*US*) = **Commodity Credit Corporation**
CCTV N ABBR = **closed-circuit television**
CPD ▸ **CCTV camera** cámara *f* de circuito cerrado de televisión, cámara *f* de videovigilancia
CCU N ABBR (*US*) (*Med*) = **coronary care unit**
CD N ABBR **1** (= **compact disc**) CD *m*
2 (= **Corps Diplomatique**) C.D.
3 = **Civil Defence (Corps)**
4 (*US*) (*Pol*) = **Congressional District**
5 (*Pol*) = **Conference on Disarmament**
CPD ▸ **CD burner, CD writer** grabadora *f* de CD ▸ **CD drive** unidad *f* de CD ▸ **CD player** lector *m* de CD ▸ **CD rack** estante *m* para CDs, torre *m* para CDs ▸ **CD recorder** grabadora *m* de CD
CDC N ABBR (*US*) = **Centers for Disease Control and Prevention**
CD-I® ADJ ABBR (= **compact disc interactive**) CD-I *m*
CD-R N ABBR (= **compact disc - recordable**)

CD-R *m inv*

Cdr. ABBR (*Brit*) (*Naut, Mil*) (= **commander**) Cdte. • **~ R. Thomas** (*on envelope*) Cdte. R. Thomas

CD-ROM [ˌsiːdiːˈrɒm] N ABBR (= **compact disc read-only memory**) CD-ROM *m*
CPD ▸ **CD-ROM drive** unidad *f* de CD-ROM

CD-RW N ABBR (= **compact disc - rewritable**) CD-RW *m*

CDT N ABBR **1** (*US*) = **Central Daylight Time**
2 (*Brit*) (*Scol*) = **Craft, Design and Technology**

CDTV N ABBR = **compact disc television**

CDV, CD-video N ABBR = **compact disc video**

CDW N ABBR = **collision damage waiver**

CE N ABBR = **Church of England**

cease [siːs] VT (= *stop*) cesar, parar; (= *suspend*) suspender; (= *end*) terminar • **to ~ work** suspender el trabajo, terminar de trabajar • **~ fire!** ¡alto el fuego!
VI cesar (**to do, doing** de hacer) • **to ~ from doing sth** dejar de hacer algo, cesar de hacer algo

ceasefire [ˌsiːsˈfaɪəʳ] N alto *m* el fuego, cese *m* de hostilidades
CPD ▸ **ceasefire line** línea *f* del alto el fuego

ceaseless [ˈsiːslɪs] ADJ incesante, continuo

ceaselessly [ˈsiːslɪslɪ] ADV incesantemente, sin cesar

Cecil [ˈsesl] N Cecilio

Cecily [ˈsɪsɪlɪ] N Cecilia

cecum [ˈsiːkəm] N (PL: **ceca**) (*US*) = **caecum**

CED N ABBR (*US*) = **Committee for Economic Development**

cedar [ˈsiːdəʳ] N cedro *m*
ADJ [*wood, table etc*] de cedro

cede [siːd] VT [+ *territory*] ceder (**to** a); [+ *argument*] reconocer, admitir

cedilla [sɪˈdɪlə] N cedilla *f*

CEEB N ABBR (*US*) = **College Entry Examination Board**

ceilidh [ˈkeɪlɪ] N *baile con música y danzas tradicionales escocesas o irlandesas*

ceiling [ˈsiːlɪŋ] N **1** [*of room*] techo *m*; (*Archit*) cielo *m* raso; ▹ **hit**
2 (*Aer*) techo *m*
3 (*fig*) (= *upper limit*) límite *m*, tope *m* • **to fix a ~ for** • **put a ~ on** fijar el límite de
CPD ▸ **ceiling fan** ventilador *m* de techo
▸ **ceiling price** precio *m* tope

celandine [ˈseləndaɪn] N celidonia *f*

celeb* [sɪˈleb] N famoso/a *m/f*

celebrant [ˈselɪbrənt] N celebrante *m*

celebrate [ˈselɪbreɪt] VT **1** [+ *birthday, special occasion*] celebrar; (*with a party*) festejar; [+ *anniversary etc*] conmemorar • **what are you celebrating?** ¿qué festejáis?, ¿cuál es el motivo de esta fiesta? • **we're celebrating his arrival** estamos celebrando su llegada • **he ~d his birthday by scoring two goals** celebró su cumpleaños marcando dos goles
2 [+ *mass*] celebrar, decir; [+ *marriage*] celebrar
VI divertirse, festejar

celebrated [ˈselɪbreɪtɪd] ADJ célebre, famoso

celebration [ˌselɪˈbreɪʃən] N **1** (= *act*) celebración *f*, festejo *m* • **in ~ of** para celebrar
2 (= *party*) fiesta *f*, guateque *m*; (= *festivity*) festividad *f* • **we must have a ~** hay que celebrarlo *or* festejarlo, hay que hacer una fiesta • **the jubilee ~s** las conmemoraciones *or* los festejos del aniversario

celebratory [ˌselɪˈbreɪtərɪ] ADJ [*event etc*] de celebración • **let's have a ~ dinner** vamos a ofrecer una cena para celebrarlo

celebrity [sɪˈlebrɪtɪ] N **1** (= *person*) (*famous*) persona *f* famosa, famoso/a *m/f*; (*well-known*) persona *f* conocida
2 (= *fame*) celebridad *f*
CPD ▸ **celebrity couple** pareja *f* de famosos ▸ **celebrity culture** famoseo *m* ▸ **celebrity guest** (*at party, on show*) invitado/a *m/f* famoso/a; (*in hotel*) huesped *mf* famoso/a ▸ **celebrity interview** entrevista *f* con famosos ▸ **celebrity magazine** revista *f* del corazón ▸ **celebrity show** programa *m* del corazón ▸ **celebrity status** (= *prominence*) condición *f* de famoso ▸ **celebrity wedding** boda *f* de famosos

celeriac [səˈlerɪæk] N apio-nabo *m*

celerity [sɪˈlerɪtɪ] N (*frm*) celeridad *f*

celery [ˈselərɪ] N apio *m* • **head/stick of ~** cabeza *f*/tallo *m* de apio

celestial [sɪˈlestɪəl] ADJ (*lit, fig*) celestial

celibacy [ˈselɪbəsɪ] N celibato *m*

celibate [ˈselɪbɪt] ADJ célibe
N célibe *mf*

cell [sel] N **1** (*in prison, monastery etc*) celda *f*
2 (*Bio, Pol*) célula *f*
3 (*Elec*) pila *f*
4 (*US*) (= *cellphone*) móvil *m* (*Sp*), celular *m* (*LAm*)
CPD ▸ **cell biology** biología *f* celular ▸ **cell division** (*Bio*) división *f* celular ▸ **cell site, cell tower** (*US*) (*Telec*) antena *f* de telefonía móvil

cellar [ˈseləʳ] N sótano *m*; (*for wine*) bodega *f* • **to keep a good ~** tener buena bodega

cellist [ˈtʃelɪst] N violoncelista *mf*, violonchelista *mf*

cellmate [ˈselmeɪt] N compañero/a *m/f* de celda

cello [ˈtʃeləʊ] N violoncelo *m*, violonchelo *m*

Cellophane® [ˈseləfeɪn] N celofán *m*

cellphone [ˈselˌfəʊn] N móvil *m* (*Sp*), celular *m* (*LAm*)

cellular [ˈseljʊləʳ] ADJ (*Bio*) celular
CPD ▸ **cellular blanket** manta *f* con tejido muy suelto ▸ **cellular phone, cellular telephone** teléfono *m* móvil (*Sp*), teléfono *m* celular (*LAm*)

cellulite [ˈseljʊlaɪt] N celulitis *f*

cellulitis [ˌseljuˈlaɪtɪs] N celulitis *f*

celluloid [ˈseljʊlɔɪd] N celuloide *m* • **on ~** (*Cine*) en el celuloide, en el cine
ADJ (*Cine*) del celuloide, cinematográfico

cellulose [ˈseljʊləʊs] N celulosa *f*

Celsius [ˈselsɪəs] ADJ celsius, centígrado • **20 degrees ~** 20 grados centígrados

Celt [kelt, selt] N celta *mf*

Celtiberia [ˌkeltaɪˈbɪərɪ] N Celtiberia *f*

Celtiberian [ˌkeltaɪˈbɪərɪən] ADJ celtibérico
N celtíbero/a *m/f*

Celtic [ˈkeltɪk, ˈseltɪk] ADJ celta, céltico
N (*Ling*) celta *m*

cembalo [ˈtʃembələʊ] N (PL: **cembalos** *or* **cembali** [ˈtʃembəlɪ]) clavicordio *m*, clave *m*

cement [səˈment] N cemento *m*; (= *glue*) cola *f*
VT **1** (*Constr*) cementar, cubrir de cemento
2 (*fig*) cimentar
CPD ▸ **cement mixer** hormigonera *f*
▸ **cement over** VT + ADV (= *cover with cement*) recubrir de cemento

cementation [ˌsiːmenˈteɪʃən] N cementación *f*

cemetery [ˈsemɪtrɪ] N cementerio *m*

cenotaph [ˈsenətɑːf] N cenotafio *m*

censer [ˈsensəʳ] N incensario *m*

censor [ˈsensəʳ] N censor(a) *m/f*
VT censurar

censorious [senˈsɔːrɪəs] ADJ (*frm*) hipercrítico

censorship [ˈsensəʃɪp] N censura *f*

censurable [ˈsenʃərəbl] ADJ censurable

censure [ˈsenʃəʳ] N censura *f* • **vote of ~** voto *m* de censura
VT censurar

census [ˈsensəs] N (PL: **censuses**) censo *m* • **to take a ~ of** levantar el censo de
CPD ▸ **census data** datos *mpl* de empadronamiento ▸ **census taker** (*US*) encuestador(a) *m/f* del censo

cent [sent] N (= *division of dollar*) centavo *m*; (= *division of euro*) céntimo *m* • **I haven't a ~** (*US**) no tengo ni un céntimo *or* (*LAm*) ni un peso

cent. ABBR **1** (= **centigrade**) C
2 = **central**
3 (= **century**) s

centaur [ˈsentɔːʳ] N centauro *m*

centenarian [ˌsentɪˈnɛərɪən] ADJ centenario
N centenario/a *m/f*

centenary [senˈtiːnərɪ] (*esp Brit*) N centenario *m* • **the ~ celebrations for ...** las festividades para celebrar el centenario de ...

centennial [senˈtenɪəl] ADJ centenario
N (*US*) = **centenary**

center *etc* [ˈsentəʳ] (*US*) = **centre** *etc*

centesimal [senˈtesɪməl] ADJ centesimal

centigrade [ˈsentɪgreɪd] ADJ centígrado • **30 degrees ~** 30 grados centígrados

centigram, centigramme [ˈsentɪgræm] N centigramo *m*

centilitre, centiliter (*US*) [ˈsentɪˌliːtəʳ] N centilitro *m*

centime [ˈsɑ̃ːntiːm] N céntimo *m*

centimetre, centimeter (*US*) [ˈsentɪˌmiːtəʳ] N centímetro *m*

centipede [ˈsentɪpiːd] N ciempiés *m inv*

central [ˈsentrəl] ADJ **1** (= *in the middle*) central • **the houses are arranged around a ~ courtyard** las casas están distribuidas alrededor de un patio central
2 (= *near the centre of town*) [*house, office, location*] céntrico • **I'm looking for somewhere more ~** busco algo más céntrico • **his flat is very ~** su piso está muy céntrico • **it's in ~ Paris** está en el centro de París
3 (= *principal*) [*figure, problem, idea, fact*] central, fundamental; [*role*] fundamental; [*aim*] principal • **of ~ importance** de la mayor importancia, primordial • **the issue of Aids is ~ to the plot of the film** el tema del SIDA es fundamental en el argumento de la película • **it is ~ to our policy** es un punto clave de nuestra política
4 (*Admin, Pol*) [*committee, planning, control etc*] central
N (*US*) (= *exchange*) central *f* telefónica
CPD ▸ **Central America** Centroamérica *f*, América *f* Central ▸ **Central Asia** Asia *f* Central ▸ **central bank** banco *m* central
▸ **central casting** (*Cine*) departamento *m* de reparto *or* casting • **a Texan farmer straight from** *or* **out of ~ casting** (*hum*) un granjero tejano de pura cepa *or* con toda la barba
▸ **Central Daylight Time** (*US*) horario *m* de verano de la zona central (de Estados Unidos) ▸ **Central Europe** Europa *f* Central
▸ **central government** gobierno *m* central
▸ **central heating** calefacción *f* central
▸ **central locking** (*Aut*) cierre *m* centralizado
▸ **central nervous system** sistema *m* nervioso central ▸ **central processing unit** (*Comput*) unidad *f* central de proceso
▸ **central reservation** (*Brit*) (*Aut*) mediana *f*
▸ **Central Standard Time** (*US*) horario *m* de la zona central (de Estados Unidos);
▹ **Central African, Central American, Central Asian, Central European**

Central African [ˌsentrəlˈæfrɪkən] ADJ centroafricano
CPD ▸ **Central African Republic** República *f* Centroafricana

Central American [ˌsentrələˈmerɪkən] N centroamericano/a *m/f*
ADJ centroamericano, de América Central

Central Asian [ˌsentrəlˈeɪʃn] ADJ centroasiático, de Asia Central

Central European [ˌsentrəljʊərəˈpiːən] N centroeuropeo/a *m/f*
ADJ centroeuropeo, de Europa Central
CPD ▸ **Central European Time** horario *m* de la zona central europea

centralism [ˈsentrəlɪzəm] N (*Pol*) centralismo *m*

centralist [ˈsentrəlɪst] ADJ centralista

centrality [senˈtrælɪtɪ] N (*frm*) centralidad *f*

centralization [ˌsentrəlaɪˈzeɪʃən] N centralización *f*

centralize [ˈsentrəlaɪz] VT centralizar

centralized [ˈsentrəlaɪzd] ADJ centralizado

centrally [ˈsentrəlɪ] ADV [*positioned, located*] en el centro, en un sitio céntrico • **~ heated** con calefacción central • **~ planned economy** economía *f* de planificación central • **he lives ~** vive en el centro

centre, center (*US*) [ˈsentəʳ] N **1** (= *middle*) centro *m*; [*of chocolate*] relleno *m* • **in the ~** en el centro • **the man at the ~ of the controversy** el hombre sobre el que gira la polémica
2 (= *focus*) centro *m* • **the ~ of attention** el centro de atención • **the ~ of attraction** el centro de atracción • **a ~ of intrigue** un centro de intrigas
3 (= *place for specific activity*) centro *m* • **health ~** centro *m* de salud, centro *m* médico
4 (*Pol*) centro *m*
5 (*Sport*) (= *player, kick*) centro *m*
VT **1** (= *place in centre*) centrar
2 (*Sport*) [+ *ball*] pasar al centro, centrar
3 (= *concentrate*) concentrar (**on** en)
VI • **to ~ (a)round/in/on** concentrarse en; [*hopes etc*] cifrarse en
CPD ▸ **centre court** (*Tennis*) pista *f* central ▸ **centre forward** (*Sport*) (delantero/a *m/f*) centro *mf* ▸ **centre ground** (*in politics*) centro *m* • **to occupy the ~ ground** [*political party*] ser de centro ▸ **centre of gravity** centro *m* de gravedad ▸ **centre party** (*Pol*) partido *m* centrista ▸ **centre spread** (*Brit*) (*Press*) páginas *fpl* centrales ▸ **centre stage** (*Theat*) centro *m* del escenario • **to take ~ stage** adquirir protagonismo, pasar a un primer plano

centre-back [ˈsentəˈbæk] N (*Sport*) defensa *mf* centro, escoba *m*

centreboard, centerboard (*US*) [ˈsentəbɔːd] N orza *f* de deriva

centred, centered (*US*) [ˈsentəd] ADJ • **to feel ~** (*mentally*) estar centrado • **to be ~ in** [*earth tremor*] tener el epicentro en

-centred, -centered (*US*) [ˈsentəd] ADJ (*ending in compounds*) centrado en, basado en • **home-centred** centrado en el hogar

centrefold, centerfold (*US*) [ˈsentəˌfəʊld] N póster *m* central, encarte *m* central

centre-half [ˌsentəˈhɑːf] N (PL: **centre-halves** [ˌsentəˈhɑːvz]) (*Sport*) medio *mf* centro

centrepiece, centerpiece (*US*) [ˈsentəpiːs] N centro *m* de mesa; (*fig*) atracción *f* principal

centrifugal [senˈtrɪfjʊgəl] ADJ centrífugo

centrifuge [ˈsentrɪfjuːʒ] N centrifugadora *f*
VT centrifugar

centripetal [senˈtrɪpɪtl] ADJ centrípeto

centrism [ˈsentrɪzəm] N centrismo *m*

centrist [ˈsentrɪst] ADJ centrista
N centrista *mf*

centuries-old [ˈsentjʊrɪzˌəʊld] ADJ secular

centurion [senˈtjʊərɪən] N centurión *m*

century [ˈsentjʊrɪ] N **1** (= *100 years*) siglo *m* • **in the 20th ~** en el siglo veinte
2 (*Cricket*) cien puntos *mpl*, cien carreras *fpl*

CEO N ABBR (*US*) = **Chief Executive Officer**

cep [sep] N (*Bot*) boleto *m* comestible

ceramic [sɪˈræmɪk] ADJ de cerámica
CPD ▸ **ceramic hob** vitrocerámica *f*

ceramics [sɪˈræmɪks] N (= *art*) cerámica *fsing*; (= *objects*) cerámicas *fpl*

cereal [ˈsɪərɪəl] ADJ cereal
N (= *crop*) cereal *m*; (= *breakfast cereal*) cereales *mpl*

cerebellum [ˌserɪˈbeləm] N (PL: **cerebellums** *or* **cerebella** [ˌserɪˈbelə]) cerebelo *m*

cerebral [ˈserɪbrəl], (*US*) [səˈriːbrəl] ADJ
1 (*Med*) cerebral
2 (= *intellectual*) cerebral, intelectual
CPD ▸ **cerebral cortex** córtex *m* (cerebral) ▸ **cerebral palsy** parálisis *f* cerebral

cerebration [ˌserɪˈbreɪʃən] N (*frm*) meditación *f*, actividad *f* mental

cerebrum [ˈserəbrəm] N (PL: **cerebrums** *or* **cerebra** [ˈserəbrə]) cerebro *m*

ceremonial [ˌserɪˈməʊnɪəl] ADJ [*rite*] ceremonial; [*dress*] de ceremonia, de gala
N ceremonial *m*

ceremonially [ˌserɪˈməʊnɪəlɪ] ADV con ceremonia

ceremonious [ˌserɪˈməʊnɪəs] ADJ ceremonioso

ceremoniously [ˌserɪˈməʊnɪəslɪ] ADV ceremoniosamente

ceremony [ˈserɪmənɪ] N ceremonia *f*
• IDIOM: • **to stand on ~** andarse con ceremonias *or* cumplidos • **let's not stand on ~** dejémonos de ceremonias *or* cumplidos

cerise [səˈriːz] ADJ (de) color de cereza
N cereza *f*

CERN [sɜːn] N ABBR = **Conseil Européen pour la Recherche Nucléaire**

cert* [sɜːt] N ABBR (*Brit*) = **certainty** • **it's a (dead) ~** es cosa segura • **he's a (dead) ~ for the job** sin duda le darán el puesto

cert. ABBR **1** = **certificate**
2 = **certified**

certain [ˈsɜːtən] ADJ **1** (= *convinced*) • **to be ~** [*person*] estar seguro • **I'm ~ he's hiding something** estoy seguro de que está ocultando algo • **to be ~ about sth** estar seguro de algo • **to feel ~** estar seguro • **to be ~ of sth** estar seguro de algo • **I am ~ of it** estoy seguro de ello • **you don't sound very ~** no pareces estar muy seguro
2 (= *sure*) • **for ~**: • **I can't say for ~** no puedo decirlo con seguridad *or* a ciencia cierta • **we don't know for ~ what caused the accident** no sabemos con seguridad *or* a ciencia cierta lo que causó el accidente • **he's up to something, that's for ~** trama algo, de eso no hay duda *or* eso es seguro • **to make ~ of sth** asegurarse de algo • **you should make ~ of your facts** debes asegurarte de que los datos son ciertos • **to make ~ that** asegurarse de que • **I wanted to make absolutely ~ that this was the right number** quería asegurarme del todo de que este número era el correcto • **I made ~ that he kept his promise** me aseguré de que cumpliese su promesa
3 (= *definite, guaranteed*) [*defeat, death, winner*] seguro; [*cure*] definitivo; [*fact*] cierto, seguro • **one thing is ~ ...** una cosa es segura ... • **it is ~ that ...** es seguro que ... • **it's almost ~ that her husband is dead** es casi seguro que *or* se tiene la casi completa seguridad de que su marido está muerto • **the hospital is facing almost ~ closure** el hospital se enfrenta al cierre casi inevitable • **it is far from ~ that they can win this election** no es ni mucho menos seguro *or* no está nada claro que puedan ganar estas elecciones • **he has been there four times to my ~ knowledge** me consta que *or* sé con certeza que ha estado allí cuatro veces • **in the ~ knowledge that ...** con la seguridad *or* certeza de que ... • **nothing's ~ in this world** no hay nada seguro en este mundo
4 (+ *infin*) • **be ~ to tell her** no dejes *or* olvides de decírselo • **he is ~ to be there** (es) seguro que estará allí • **there's ~ to be an argument** con seguridad se producirá una discusión; (*less formal*) seguro que habrá una discusión • **there's ~ to be strong opposition to these proposals** está garantizado que estas propuestas se enfrentarán a una fuerte oposición • **the plans are almost ~ to go ahead** los planes se llevarán a cabo casi con toda seguridad
5 (= *particular*) cierto • **on a ~ day in May** cierto día de mayo • **a ~ Mr/Mrs Smith** un tal Señor/una tal Señora Smith • **of a ~ age** de cierta edad • **in ~ circumstances** en ciertas *or* determinadas circunstancias • **a ~ number of people/years** un cierto número de personas/años • **a ~ person told me that ...** cierta persona me dijo que ... • **she has a ~ something** tiene algo *or* un no sé qué • **at ~ times of the day/month/year** en ciertos momentos del día/ciertos días del mes/ciertas épocas del año
6 (= *slight*) [*impatience, bitterness, courage*] cierto • **there's a ~ amount of confusion about the arrangements** existe una cierta confusión *or* un cierto grado de confusión sobre los preparativos • **to a ~ degree** *or* **extent** hasta cierto punto
PRON (*frm*) ciertos/as *mpl/fpl*, algunos/as *mpl/fpl* • **~ of our leaders** ciertos líderes nuestros, algunos de nuestros líderes

certainly [ˈsɜːtənlɪ] ADV **1** (= *undoubtedly*) con toda certeza, sin duda alguna • **if nothing is done there will ~ be an economic crisis** si no se hace nada, con toda certeza *or* sin duda alguna se producirá una crisis económica • **your answer is almost ~ right** casi seguro que *or* casi con seguridad tu respuesta está bien • **it is ~ true that ...** desde luego es verdad *or* cierto que ...
2 (= *definitely*) • **something should ~ be done about that** decididamente, deberían hacer algo al respecto • **I will ~ get it finished by tomorrow** definitivamente lo termino para mañana • **it's ~ better** desde luego es mucho mejor • **this computer is ~ an improvement on the old one** este ordenador es sin ninguna duda mejor que el antiguo • **it ~ impressed me** ya lo creo que me impresionó • **I shall ~ be there** no faltaré, seguro que estaré • **you ~ did that well** desde luego eso lo hiciste bien • **I would ~ like to try** desde luego (que) me gustaría probar • **such groups most ~ exist** esos grupos existen con toda seguridad
3 (*in answer to questions, requests*) • **"could you give me a lift?" — "certainly!"** —¿me podrías llevar? —¡claro (que sí)! *or* ¡por supuesto! *or* ¡faltaría más! • **~ madam!** ¡con mucho gusto, señora!, ¡por supuesto, señora! • **"wouldn't you agree?" — "oh, ~"** —¿estás de acuerdo? —sí, desde luego • **"had you forgotten?" — "~ not"** —¿se le había olvidado? —por supuesto que no *or* claro que no • **"would you ever eat snake?" — "~ not!"** —¿comerías serpiente? —¡qué va! • **"will you accept his offer?" — "~ not!"** —¿vas a aceptar su oferta? —¡qué va! *or* ¡de ninguna manera! • **"can I go on my own?" — "~ not!"** —¿puedo ir sola? —¡de eso nada! *or* ¡ni hablar!

4 (= *granted*) • **~, she has potential, but ...** desde luego tiene posibilidades, pero ..., no hay duda de que tiene posibilidades, pero ...
certainty ['sɜːtəntɪ] N 1 (*no pl*) (= *conviction*) certeza *f*, seguridad *f* • **I can't say with any ~ that this will happen** no puedo decir con ninguna certeza *or* seguridad que esto vaya a suceder
2 (= *sure fact*) • **faced with the ~ of disaster** ante la seguridad *or* lo inevitable del desastre • **we know for a ~ that ...** sabemos a ciencia cierta que ... • **it's a ~** es cosa segura • **there are no certainties in modern Europe** en la Europa moderna no hay nada seguro, pocas cosas son seguras en la Europa moderna • **there is no ~ that they will be alive** no existe la seguridad *or* la certeza de que vayan a estar vivos
Cert. Ed. N ABBR = **Certificate of Education**
certifiable [,sɜːtɪ'faɪəbl] ADJ 1 [*fact, claim*] certificable
2 (*Med*) declarado demente; (= *mad**) loco, demente
certificate [sə'tɪfɪkɪt] N certificado *m*; (*Univ etc*) diploma *m*, título *m* • **birth/death/marriage ~** partida *f* de nacimiento/defunción/matrimonio • **~ of airworthiness** certificado *m* de aeronavegabilidad • **~ of deposit** certificado *m* de depósito • **~ of incorporation** escritura *f* de constitución (*de una sociedad anónima*) • **~ of origin** certificado *m* de origen • **Certificate of Secondary Education** (*Brit*) (*Scol*) (*formerly*) ≈ Título *m* de BUP • **X ~** (*Cine*) (para) mayores de 18 años
certificated [sə'tɪfɪkeɪtɪd] ADJ titulado, diplomado
certification [,sɜːtɪfɪ'keɪʃən] N certificación *f*
certified ['sɜːtɪfaɪd] ADJ 1 [*cheque*] certificado; [*translation*] confirmado, jurado
2 [*person*] (*in profession*) titulado, diplomado; (= *declared insane*) demente
CPD ▸ **certified copy** copia *f* certificada
▸ **certified letter** (*US*) carta *f* certificada
▸ **certified mail** (*US*) correo *m* certificado
▸ **certified public accountant** (*US*) contable *mf* diplomado/a
certify ['sɜːtɪfaɪ] VT 1 (= *confirm*) certificar • **certified as a true copy** confirmada como copia auténtica • **to ~ that...** declarar que...
2 (*Med*) • **to ~ sb (insane)** certificar que algn no está en posesión de sus facultades mentales • **you ought to be certified!*** (*esp hum*) ¡estás como una cabra!, ¡estás para que te encierren!
certitude ['sɜːtɪtjuːd] N certidumbre *f*
cerumen [sɪ'ruːmen] N cerumen *m*
cervical ['sɜːvɪkəl] ADJ cervical
CPD ▸ **cervical cancer** cáncer *m* cervical *or* del cuello del útero ▸ **cervical screening** cribado *m* del cáncer de cuello de útero
▸ **cervical smear** frotis *m* cervical, citología *f*
cervix ['sɜːvɪks] N (PL: **cervixes** *or* **cervices** [sə'vaɪsiːz]) cuello *m* del útero
Cesarean [siː'zeərɪən] N (*US*) = **Caesarean**
cesium ['siːzɪəm] N (*US*) = **caesium**
cessation [se'seɪʃən] N (*frm*) cese *m*, suspensión *f* • **~ of hostilities** cese *m* de hostilidades
cession ['seʃən] N cesión *f*
cesspit ['sespɪt], **cesspool** ['sespuːl] N pozo *m* negro; (*fig*) sentina *f*
CET N ABBR = **Central European Time**
cetacean [sɪ'teɪʃɪən] ADJ cetáceo
N cetáceo *m*
Cetnik ['tʃetnɪk] ADJ, N chetnik *mf*
Ceylon [sɪ'lɒn] N (*Hist*) Ceilán *m*
CPD ▸ **Ceylon tea** té *m* de Ceilán
Ceylonese [sɪlɒ'niːz] (*Hist*) ADJ ceilanés
N ceilanés/esa *m/f*
CF, cf¹ N ABBR (= **cost and freight**) C y F
cf² ABBR (= **confer, compare**) cfr., cf.
C/F, c/f, c/fwd ABBR = **carried forward**
CFC N ABBR (= **chlorofluorocarbon**) CFC *m*
CFE N ABBR (*Brit*) = **college of further education**
NPL ABBR = **Conventional Forces in Europe**
CFO N ABBR = **chief financial officer**
CFS N ABBR (= **chronic fatigue syndrome**) (= *ME*) SFC *m*, síndrome *m* de fatiga crónica
CG N ABBR = **coastguard**
cg ABBR (= **centigram(s), centigramme(s)**) cg
CGA N ABBR (*Comput*) = **colour graphics adaptor**
CGI N ABBR (= **computer-generated imagery**) imágenes *fpl* generadas por ordenador
CH N ABBR (*Brit*) (= **Companion of Honour**) *título honorífico*
ch ABBR 1 (*Literat*) (= **chapter**) cap., c., c/
2 (*Econ*) (= **cheque**) ch.
3 (*Rel*) = **church**
Ch. ABBR (= **chapter**) cap., c., c/
c.h. ABBR (= **central heating**) cal.cen.
cha-cha ['tʃɑːtʃɑː], **cha-cha-cha** ['tʃɑːtʃɑː'tʃɑː] N cha-cha-chá *m*
Chad [tʃæd] N Chad *m* • **Lake ~** lago *m* Chad
ADJ chadiano
chador ['tʃʌdəʳ] N chador *m*
chafe [tʃeɪf] VT 1 (= *rub against*) [+ *skin etc*] rozar, raspar
2 (= *warm*) calentar frotando
VI 1 (= *become sore*) irritar • **to ~ against sth** rozar *or* raspar algo
2 (*fig*) impacientarse *or* irritarse (**at** por)
chaff [tʃɑːf] N 1 (= *husks*) cascarilla *f*, ahechaduras *fpl*; (= *animal food*) pienso *m*, forraje *m*; ▹ **wheat**
2 (*fig*) paja *f*
VT zumbarse de, tomar el pelo a
chaffinch ['tʃæfɪntʃ] N pinzón *m* (vulgar)
chafing dish ['tʃeɪfɪŋdɪʃ] N calientaplatos *m inv*
chagrin ['ʃægrɪn] N (= *anger*) disgusto *m*; (= *disappointment*) desilusión *f*, desazón *f* • **to my ~** con gran disgusto mío
VT mortificar, disgustar
chagrined ['ʃægrɪnd] ADJ (= *upset*) disgustado
chain [tʃeɪn] N 1 (*lit*) cadena *f* • **to pull the ~** [*of lavatory*] tirar de la cadena
2 **chains** (= *fetters*) cadenas *fpl*, grillos *mpl*; (*Aut*) cadenas *fpl* • **in ~s** encadenado
3 (*fig*) • **~ of mountains** cordillera *f* • **~ of shops** cadena *f* de tiendas • **~ of command** cadena *f* de mando • **~ of events** serie *f* de acontecimientos • **to form a human ~** formar una cadena humana
4 (= *measure*) *medida de longitud equivalente a 22 yardas o 20,12 metros*
VT encadenar • **he was ~ed to the wall** estaba encadenado a la pared
CPD ▸ **chain gang** (*US*) cadena *f* de presidiarios ▸ **chain letter** carta *f* que circula en cadena (*con promesa de una ganancia cuantiosa para los que siguen las indicaciones que da*) ▸ **chain lightning** relámpagos *mpl* en zigzag ▸ **chain mail** cota *f* de malla ▸ **chain pump** bomba *f* de cangilones ▸ **chain reaction** reacción *f* en cadena ▸ **chain smoker** fumador(a) *m/f* empedernido/a
▸ **chain stitch** (*Sew*) punto *m* de cadeneta, cadeneta *f* ▸ **chain store** tienda *f* que pertenece a una cadena
▸ **chain up** VT + ADV encadenar
chain-link fence [,tʃeɪnlɪŋk'fens] N valla *f* de tela metálica
chainsaw ['tʃeɪn,sɔː] N sierra *f* de cadena
chain-smoke ['tʃeɪn,sməʊk] VI fumar un pitillo tras otro
chair [tʃeəʳ] N 1 (*gen*) silla *f*; (= *armchair*) sillón *m*, butaca *f*; (= *wheelchair*) silla *f* (de ruedas); (= *seat*) lugar *m*, asiento *m* • **please take a ~** siéntese *or* tome asiento por favor
2 (*Univ*) cátedra *f*
3 [*of meeting*] presidencia *f*; (= *chairman*) presidente *m* • **to be in the ~** • **take the ~** presidir • **to address the ~** dirigirse al presidente
4 • **the ~** (*US*) (= *electric chair*) la silla eléctrica
VT 1 [+ *person*] llevar a hombros • **they ~ed him off the ground** le sacaron del campo a hombros
2 [+ *meeting*] presidir
chairback ['tʃeəbæk] N respaldo *m*
chairbound ['tʃeəbaʊnd] ADJ en silla de ruedas
chairlift ['tʃeəlɪft] N telesilla *m or f*, teleférico *m*
chairman ['tʃeəmən] N (PL: **chairmen**) presidente/a *m/f* • **~'s report** informe *m* del presidente
chairmanship ['tʃeəmənʃɪp] N (= *post*) presidencia *f*; (= *art*) arte *m* de presidir reuniones
chairoplane ['tʃeərəʊ,pleɪn] N silla *f* colgante
chairperson ['tʃeə,pɜːsn] N presidente/a *m/f*
chairwarmer* ['tʃeə,wɔːməʳ] N (*US*) calientasillas *mf inv*
chairwoman ['tʃeə,wʊmən] N (PL: **chairwomen**) presidenta *f*
chaise longue ['ʃeɪz'lɒŋ] N (PL: **chaise-longues**) tumbona *f*
chakra ['tʃækrə] N chakra *m*
chalet ['ʃæleɪ] N chalet *m*, chalé *m*
chalice ['tʃælɪs] N (*Rel*) cáliz *m*; ▹ **poison**
chalk [tʃɔːk] N (*Geol*) creta *f*; (*for writing*) tiza *f*, gis *m* (*Mex*) • **a (piece of) ~** una tiza *f*, un gis *m* (*Mex*) • IDIOMS: • **by a long ~** (*Brit**) de lejos • **not by a long ~** (*Brit**) ni con mucho, ni mucho menos • **to be as different as ~ and cheese** ser como el día y la noche
VT [+ *message*] escribir con tiza; [+ *luggage*] marcar con tiza
CPD ▸ **chalk dust** polvo *m* de tiza
▸ **chalk up** VT + ADV (*lit*) apuntar; (*fig*) [+ *success, victory*] apuntarse
chalkboard ['tʃɔːkbɔːd] N (*US*) pizarra *f*
chalkface ['tʃɔːkfeɪs] N • **the teacher at the ~** el maestro en su clase, el profesor delante de la pizarra • **those at the ~** los que enseñan
chalkpit ['tʃɔːkpɪt] N cantera *f* de creta
chalktalk* ['tʃɔːktɔːk] N (*US*) charla *f* ilustrada en la pizarra
chalky ['tʃɔːkɪ] ADJ (COMPAR: **chalkier**, SUPERL: **chalkiest**) (*Geol*) cretáceo
challenge ['tʃælɪndʒ] N 1 (*to game, fight etc*) desafío *m*, reto *m*; [*of sentry*] alto *m* • **to issue a ~ to sb** desafiar a algn • **to rise to the ~** ponerse a la altura de las circunstancias • **to take up a ~** aceptar un desafío
2 (= *bid*) (*for leadership etc*) intento *m* (**for** por) • **Vigo's ~ for the league leadership** la tentativa que hace el Vigo para hacerse con el liderato de la liga
3 (*fig*) desafío *m*, reto *m* • **this task is a great ~** esta tarea representa un gran desafío • **the ~ of the 21st century** el reto del siglo XXI • **the ~ of new ideas** el reto de las nuevas ideas
4 (*Jur*) recusación *f*
VT 1 (*to duel*) desafiar, retar; [*sentry*] dar el alto a
2 [+ *speaker*] hablar en contra de • **to ~ sb to do sth** desafiar *or* retar a algn a que haga algo

3 (= *dispute*) [+ *fact, point*] poner en duda • **I ~ that conclusion** dudo que esa conclusión sea acertada
4 (*Jur*) recusar
-challenged ['tʃælɪndʒd] ADJ (*ending in compounds*) (*esp hum*) • **vertically-challenged** no muy alto • **intellectually-challenged** no muy listo
challenger ['tʃælɪndʒəʳ] N desafiador(a) *m/f*; (= *competitor*) aspirante *mf*; (= *opponent*) contrincante *mf*
challenging ['tʃælɪndʒɪŋ] ADJ
1 (= *provocative*) [*remark, look, tone*] desafiante
2 (= *stimulating*) [*book*] estimulante, provocador; (= *demanding*) [*job, task*] que supone un desafío *or* un reto
challengingly ['tʃælɪndʒɪŋlɪ] ADV
1 (= *defiantly*) [*say*] en tono desafiante; [*act*] con una actitud desafiante, provocadoramente
2 (= *demandingly*) [*difficult*] de forma que supone un desafío *or* un reto
chamber ['tʃeɪmbəʳ] N 1 [*of parliament*] cámara *f*; (= *esp bedroom*†) aposento† *m*; **chambers** [*of judge*] despacho *m*; [*of barrister*] bufete *m* • **the Upper/Lower Chamber** (*Pol*) la Cámara Alta/Baja • **~ of commerce** cámara *f* de comercio
2 [*of gun*] recámara *f*
CPD ▸ **chamber choir** coro *m* de cámara ▸ **chamber concert** concierto *m* de cámara ▸ **chamber music** música *f* de cámara ▸ **chamber of horrors** cámara *f* de los horrores ▸ **chamber orchestra** orquesta *f* de cámara ▸ **chamber pot** orinal *m*
chamberlain ['tʃeɪmbəlɪn] N chambelán *m*, gentilhombre *m* de cámara
chambermaid ['tʃeɪmbəmeɪd] N (*in hotel*) camarera *f*
chambray ['tʃæmbreɪ] N (*US*) = **cambric**
chameleon [kə'miːlɪən] N camaleón *m*
chamfer ['tʃæmfəʳ] N chaflán *m*, bisel *m*
VT chaflanar, biselar
chammy ['ʃæmɪ] N gamuza *f*
chamois N 1 ['ʃæmwɑː] (*Zool*) gamuza *f*
2 ['ʃæmɪ] (*also* **chamois leather**) gamuza *f*
chamomile ['kæməʊmaɪl] N = **camomile**
champ¹ [tʃæmp] VI • **to ~ at** morder, mordiscar; [+ *bit*] tascar, morder • IDIOM: • **to be ~ing at the bit (to do sth)** estar impaciente (por hacer algo)
champ²* [tʃæmp] N = **champion**
Champagne [ʃæm'peɪn] N (= *region*) Champaña *f*
champagne [ʃæm'peɪn] N champán *m*, champaña *m*
CPD ▸ **champagne breakfast** desayuno *m* con champán ▸ **champagne cork** corcho *m* de champán • **~ corks are popping** los corchos del champán saltan ▸ **champagne flute** copa *f* alta (*de champán*) ▸ **champagne glass** copa *f* de champán
champers* ['ʃæmpəz] N (*hum*) champán *m*
champion ['tʃæmpɪən] N campeón/ona *m/f*; [*of cause*] defensor(a) *m/f*, paladín *m* • **boxing ~** campeón *m* de boxeo • **world ~** campeón *m* mundial
ADJ 1 (= *award-winning*) campeón • **a ~ athlete** un campeón de atletismo
2* magnífico, estupendo • **~!** ¡magnífico!, ¡estupendo!
VT defender, abogar por
championship ['tʃæmpɪənʃɪp] N
1 (= *contest*) campeonato *m*
2 [*of cause*] defensa *f*
CPD ▸ **championship point** (*in tennis*) punto *m* de campeonato
chance [tʃɑːns] N 1 (= *fate*) azar *m*; (= *coincidence*) casualidad *f* • **by ~** por casualidad • **we met by ~ in Paris** nos encontramos por casualidad en París • **do you have a room available, by any ~?** ¿no tendrá por casualidad una habitación libre?, ¿por casualidad tiene una habitación libre? • **to leave nothing to ~** no dejar nada al azar *or* a la casualidad, no dejar ningún cabo suelto *or* por atar • **to trust sth to ~** dejar algo al azar; ▹ **game¹**
2 (= *opportunity*) oportunidad *f*, ocasión *f* • **~ would be a fine thing!*** ¡ojalá!, ¡ya quisiera yo! • **you'll never get another ~ like this** nunca se te presentará otra oportunidad *or* ocasión como esta • **all those eligible will get a ~ to vote** todas las personas que cumplan los requisitos podrán votar • **to give sb a ~:** • **he didn't give me a ~ to say anything** no me dio (la) oportunidad de decir nada • **give me a ~, I've only just got here!** ¡espera un ratito, acabo de llegar! • **he never had a ~ in life** nunca tuvo suerte en la vida • **given half a ~ he'd eat the lot*** si se le dejara, se lo comería todo • **you always wanted to ride a horse, and here's your ~** siempre quisiste montar a caballo, ahora tienes la oportunidad • **to jump** *or* **leap at the ~** aprovechar la oportunidad *or* ocasión, no dejar escapar la oportunidad *or* ocasión • **it's the ~ of a lifetime** es la oportunidad de mi/tu/su *etc* vida • **to have an eye on** *or* **to the main ~*** (*pej*) estar a la que salta* • **to miss one's ~** perder la *or* su oportunidad • **she's gone out, now's your ~!** ha salido, ¡ésta es tu oportunidad! • **they decided to give me a second ~** decidieron darme una segunda oportunidad
3 (= *possibility*) posibilidad *f* • **his ~s of survival are slim** tiene escasas posibilidades de sobrevivir, sus posibilidades de sobrevivir son escasas • **the ~s are that ...** lo más probable es que ... • **it has a one in 11,000 ~ (of winning)** tiene una posibilidad entre 11.000 (de ganar) • **to have a good ~ of success** tener bastantes posibilidades de éxito • **to be in with a ~** (*Brit**) tener muchas posibilidades • **I had very little ~ of winning** tenía muy pocas posibilidades de ganar • **he has no ~ of winning** no tiene ninguna posibilidad de ganar, no tiene posibilidad alguna de ganar • **no ~!*** (*refusing*) ¡ni hablar!*; (*dismissing a possibility*) ¡qué va!* • **there is a slight ~ she may still be there** puede que exista una pequeña posibilidad de que todavía esté allí • **they don't stand a ~ (of winning)** no tienen ninguna posibilidad *or* posibilidad alguna (de ganar) • **he never stood a ~, the truck went straight into him** no pudo hacer nada, el camión se fue derecho a él; ▹ **fat**
4 (= *risk*) riesgo *m* • **I'll take that ~** correré ese riesgo, me arriesgaré • **I'm not taking any ~s** no quiero arriesgarme • **you shouldn't take any ~s where your health is concerned** no deberías correr riesgos *or* arriesgarte cuando se trata de tu salud • **we decided to take a ~ on the weather** decidimos arriesgarnos con el tiempo
VT 1 (= *run the risk of*) [+ *rejection, fine*] arriesgarse a • **to ~ doing sth** arriesgarse a hacer algo • **to ~ it*** jugársela, arriesgarse • IDIOM: • **to ~ one's arm** *or* **one's luck** probar suerte
2 (*frm*) (= *happen*) • **to ~ to do sth** hacer algo por casualidad • **she ~d to look up at that moment** en ese momento dio la casualidad de que levantó la vista *or* levantó la vista por casualidad • **I ~d to catch sight of her as she passed** la vi por casualidad cuando pasaba
CPD ▸ **chance meeting** encuentro *m* fortuito *or* casual ▸ **chance remark** comentario *m* casual
▸ **chance on, chance upon** VI + PREP [+ *object*] tropezar(se) con, encontrar por casualidad; [+ *person*] tropezar(se) con, encontrarse por casualidad con
chancel ['tʃɑːnsəl] N coro *m* y presbiterio
chancellery ['tʃɑːnsərɪ] N cancillería *f*
chancellor ['tʃɑːnsələʳ] N 1 (*Pol*) (= *head of government*) canciller *mf* • **Lord Chancellor** *jefe de la administración de la justicia en Inglaterra y Gales, y presidente de la Cámara de los Lores* • **Chancellor** (*Brit*) = **Chancellor of the Exchequer**
2 (*Univ*) rector(a) *m/f* honorario/a
CPD ▸ **Chancellor of the Exchequer** (*Brit*) Ministro/a *m/f or* (*LAm*) Secretario/a *m/f* de Economía y Hacienda
chancellorship ['tʃɑːnsələʃɪp] N 1 (*Pol*) cancillería *f*
2 (*Univ*) rectorado *m* honorario
chancer* ['tʃænsəʳ] N (*Brit*) trepa* *mf*
chancery ['tʃɑːnsərɪ] N 1 (*Brit*) (*Jur*) (*also* **Chancery Division**) *sala del High Court que se ocupa de causas de derecho privado* • **ward in ~** *pupilo/a bajo la protección del tribunal*
2 (*US*) = **chancellery**
3 (*US*) (*Jur*) (*also* **Court of Chancery**) tribunal *m* de equidad
chancre ['ʃæŋkəʳ] N chancro *m*
chancy* ['tʃɑːnsɪ] ADJ (COMPAR: **chancier**, SUPERL: **chanciest**) arriesgado
chandelier [ʃændə'lɪəʳ] N araña *f* (de luces)
chandler ['tʃɑːndləʳ] N velero *m*
change [tʃeɪndʒ] N 1 (*gen*) cambio *m*; (= *transformation*) transformación *f*; (= *alteration*) modificación *f*; (= *variation*) variación *f*; [*of skin*] muda *f* • **the day out made a refreshing ~** el día fuera de casa nos dio un buen cambio de aire • **to resist ~** resistirse a las innovaciones • **~ of address** cambio *m* de domicilio • **to have a ~ of air** cambiar de aires • **the ~ of air has done me good** el cambio de aires me ha sentado bien • **a ~ for the better** un cambio para bien • **a ~ of clothes** ropa para cambiarse; (= *underclothes*) una muda • **just for a ~** para variar • **~ of heart** cambio *m* de idea • **he's had a ~ of heart** ha cambiado de idea • **~ of horses** relevo *m* de los tiros • **a ~ in policy** un cambio de política • **the ~ of life** (*Med*) la menopausia • **~ of ownership** cambio *m* de dueño • **~ of scene** cambio *m* de aires • **a ~ for the worse** un cambio para mal • IDIOM: • **to get no ~ out of sb** no conseguir sacar nada a algn • PROVERB: • **a ~ is as good as a rest** un cambio de aires da fuerzas para seguir; ▹ **ring²**
2 (= *small coins*) cambio *m*, suelto *m*, sencillo *m*, feria *f* (*Mex**); (*for a larger coin*) cambio *m*; (= *money returned*) vuelta *f*, vuelto *m* (*LAm*) • **can you give me ~ for one pound?** ¿tiene cambio de una libra?, ¿puede cambiarme una moneda de una libra? • **keep the ~** quédese con la vuelta • **you won't get much ~ out of a pound if you buy sugar** con una libra no te va a sobrar mucho si compras azúcar
VT 1 (*by substitution*) [+ *address, name etc*] cambiar; [+ *clothes, colour*] cambiar de • **to ~ trains/buses/planes (at)** hacer transbordo (en), cambiar de tren/autobús/avión (en) • **to ~ gear** (*Aut*) cambiar de marcha • **to get ~d** cambiarse • **to ~ hands** cambiar de mano *or* de dueño • **he wants to ~ his job** quiere cambiar de trabajo • **to ~ one's mind** cambiar de opinión *or* idea • **to ~ places** cambiar de sitio • **I'm going to ~ my shoes** voy a cambiarme de zapatos • **let's ~ the subject** cambiemos de tema
2 (= *exchange*) (*in shop*) cambiar (**for** por) • **can I ~ this dress for a larger size?** ¿puedo

cambiar este vestido por otro de una talla mayor?
3 (= *alter*) [+ *person*] cambiar; (*fig*) evolucionar; (= *transform*) transformar (**into** en) • **I find him much ~d** le veo muy cambiado • **the prince was ~d into a frog** el príncipe se transformó en rana
4 [+ *money*] cambiar • **to ~ pounds into dollars** cambiar libras en dólares • **can you ~ this note for me?** ¿me hace el favor de cambiar este billete?
5 (= *put fresh nappy on*) [+ *baby*] cambiar (el pañal de)
VI 1 (= *alter*) cambiar • **you've ~d!** ¡cómo has cambiado!, ¡pareces otro! • **you haven't ~d a bit!** ¡no has cambiado en lo más mínimo!
2 (= *be transformed*) transformarse (**into** en)
3 (= *change clothes*) cambiarse, mudarse • **she ~d into an old skirt** se cambió y se puso una falda vieja
4 (= *change trains*) hacer transbordo, cambiar de tren; (= *change buses*) hacer transbordo, cambiar de autobús • **all ~!** ¡fin de trayecto!
CPD ▸ **change machine** máquina *f* de cambio ▸ **change management** (*Comm*) gestión *f* del cambio empresarial ▸ **change purse** (*US*) monedero *m*
▸ **change around** VT + ADV (= *rearrange*) cambiar de posición
VI + ADV cambiar
▸ **change down** VI + ADV (*Brit*) (*Aut*) cambiar a una velocidad inferior
▸ **change over** VI + ADV (*from sth to sth*) cambiar (**to** a); [*players etc*] cambiar(se)
VT + ADV cambiar
▸ **change round** ▹ change around
▸ **change up** VI + ADV (*Brit*) (*Aut*) cambiar a una velocidad superior

changeability [ˌtʃeɪndʒəˈbɪlɪtɪ] N [*of situation, weather*] variabilidad *f*, lo cambiante; [*of person*] volubilidad *f*, lo cambiante

changeable [ˈtʃeɪndʒəbl] ADJ [*situation, weather*] variable; [*person*] voluble, inconstante

changeless [ˈtʃeɪndʒlɪs] ADJ inmutable

changeling [ˈtʃeɪndʒlɪŋ] N *niño sustituido por otro*

changeover [ˈtʃeɪndʒˌəʊvəʳ] N cambio *m*

changing [ˈtʃeɪndʒɪŋ] ADJ cambiante • **a ~ world** un mundo en perpetua evolución
N • **the ~ of the Guard** el cambio *or* relevo de la Guardia
CPD ▸ **changing room** (*Brit*) vestuario *m*

channel [ˈtʃænl] N (= *watercourse, TV channel*) canal *m*; (= *strait*) estrecho *m*; (= *deepest part of river*) cauce *m*; (*fig*) [*of communication*] vía *f* • **irrigation ~** acequia *f*, canal *m* de riego • **green/red ~** (*Customs*) pasillo *m* verde/rojo • **to go through the usual ~s** seguir las vías normales • **the (English) Channel** el canal (de la Mancha) • **~ of distribution** vía *f or* canal *m* de distribución
VT (= *hollow out*) [+ *course*] acanalar; (= *direct*) [+ *river*] encauzar; (*fig*) [+ *interest, energies*] encauzar, dirigir (**into** a)
CPD ▸ **Channel crossing** travesía *f* del canal de la Mancha ▸ **Channel ferry** (*Brit*) ferry *m or* transbordador *m* que cruza el canal de la Mancha ▸ **the Channel Islands** las islas Anglonormandas *or* del canal de la Mancha ▸ **Channel port** puerto *m* del canal de la Mancha ▸ **the Channel Tunnel** el túnel del canal de la Mancha
▸ **channel off** VT + ADV (*lit, fig*) [+ *water, energy, resources*] canalizar

channel-hop [ˈtʃænlhɒp] VI (*Brit*) (*TV*) hacer zapping

channel-hopping [ˈtʃænlˈhɒpɪŋ] N (*Brit*) (*TV*) zapping *m*

channel-surf [ˈtʃænlˌsɜːf] (*US*) = **channel-hop**

channel-surfing [ˈtʃænlˌsɜːfɪŋ] (*US*) = **channel-hopping**

chant [tʃɑːnt] N (*Mus, Rel*) canto *m*; [*of crowd*] grito *m*, consigna *f*; (*fig*) (*monotonous*) sonsonete *m* • **plain ~** (*Rel*) canto *m* llano
VT (*Mus, Rel*) cantar; [+ *slogan*] gritar (rítmicamente), corear; (*fig*) salmodiar, recitar en tono monótono
VI (*Mus, Rel*) cantar; (*at demonstration etc*) gritar (rítmicamente)

chanterelle [ˌtʃæntəˈrel] N rebozuelo *m*

chantey [ˈʃæntɪ] N (*US*) saloma *f*

Chanukah [ˈhɑːnʊkɑː] N (= *Hanukkah*) Janucá *f*

chaos [ˈkeɪɒs] N caos *m* • **to be in ~** [*house*] estar en completo desorden; [*country*] estar en el caos; ▹ **organized**
CPD ▸ **chaos theory** teoría *f* del caos

chaotic [keɪˈɒtɪk] ADJ caótico

chaotically [keɪˈɒtɪklɪ] ADV caóticamente

chap¹ [tʃæp] N (*on lip*) grieta *f*
VT agrietar
VI agrietarse

chap²* [tʃæp] N (= *man*) tío* *m*, tipo* *m* • **a ~ I know** un tío que conozco • **he's a nice ~** es buen chico, es buena persona • **he's very deaf, poor ~** es muy sordo, el pobre • **how are you, old ~?** ¿qué tal, amigo *or* (*S. Cone*) viejo? • **be a good ~ and say nothing** sé buen chico y no digas nada • **poor little ~** pobrecito *m*

chap³ [tʃæp] N (*Anat*) mandíbula *f*; (= *cheek*) mejilla *f*

chap. ABBR (= **chapter**) cap., c., c/

chapati, chapatti [tʃəˈpætɪ, tʃəˈpɑːtɪ] N (PL: **chapat(t)i** *or* **chapat(t)is** *or* **chapat(t)ies**) chapatti *m* (*en la cocina india, pan de forma achatada, sin levadura*)

chapel [ˈtʃæpəl] N 1 (= *part of church*) capilla *f*; (= *nonconformist church*) templo *m*
2 (*as adj*) • **it doesn't matter whether they're church or ~** no importa si son protestantes de la Iglesia Anglicana o de fuera de ella
3 [*of union*] división *f* sindical

chaperon, chaperone [ˈʃæpərəʊn] N acompañante *f* (de señoritas), carabina *mf* (*Sp**)
VT acompañar a, hacer de carabina a (*Sp**)

chaplain [ˈtʃæplɪn] N capellán *m* • **~ general** (*Mil*) vicario *m* general castrense

chaplaincy [ˈtʃæplənsɪ] N capellanía *f*

chaplet [ˈtʃæplɪt] N guirnalda *f*, corona *f* de flores; (= *necklace*) collar *m*; (*Rel*) rosario *m*

chapped [tʃæpt] ADJ [*skin*] agrietado

chappy* [ˈtʃæpɪ] N = **chap²**

chaps [tʃæps] NPL (*US*) zahones *mpl*, chaparreras *fpl*

chapter [ˈtʃæptəʳ] N 1 [*of book*] capítulo *m* • IDIOM: • **~ and verse** con pelos y señales, con todo lujo de detalles • **he can quote you ~ and verse** él te lo puede citar textualmente
2 (*Rel*) cabildo *m*
3 (= *branch of society, organization*) sección *f*
4 (*fig*) (= *period*) • **a ~ of accidents** una serie de desgracias
CPD ▸ **chapter house** sala *f* capitular

char¹ [tʃɑːʳ] VT (= *burn black*) carbonizar
VI carbonizarse

char² [tʃɑːʳ] N (= *charwoman*) = **charlady**
VI limpiar, trabajar como asistenta

char³‡ [tʃɑːʳ] N (*Brit*) té *m*

charabanc† [ˈʃærəbæŋ] N (*Brit*) autobús *m*, autocar *m* (*Sp*)

character [ˈkærɪktəʳ] N 1 (= *nature*) [*of thing*] carácter *m*, naturaleza *f*; [*of person*] carácter *m*, personalidad *f* • **a man of good ~** un hombre de buena reputación • **to bear a good ~** tener buena reputación • **that is more in ~ for him** eso es más típico de él • **his sudden concern for me was completely out of ~ (for him)** su inesperado interés por mí no era nada típico de él
2 (*in novel, play*) (= *person*) personaje *m*; (= *role*) papel *m* • **chief ~** protagonista *mf*
3 (= *energy, determination*) carácter *m* • **a man of ~** un hombre de carácter • **he lacks ~** le falta carácter
4* (= *person*) tipo/a* *m/f*, individuo/a *m/f* • **he's a very odd ~** es un tipo muy raro* • **he's quite a ~** es todo un personaje
5 (*Comput, Typ, Bio*) carácter *m*
CPD ▸ **character actor** actor *m* de carácter ▸ **character actress** actriz *f* de carácter ▸ **character assassination** difamación *f* ▸ **character code** (*Comput*) código *m* de caracteres ▸ **character development** (*in a novel, play, film*) evolución *f* de los personajes ▸ **character part** (*Theat*) papel *m* de carácter ▸ **character recognition** (*Comput*) reconocimiento *m* de caracteres ▸ **character recognition software** software *m* de reconocimiento de caracteres ▸ **character reference** informe *m*, referencia *f* ▸ **character set** (*Typ*) juego *m* de caracteres ▸ **character sketch** esbozo *m* de carácter ▸ **character space** (*Typ*) espacio *m* (de carácter) ▸ **character trait** (= *characteristic*) rasgo *m* de carácter ▸ **character witness** *testigo de la defensa que atestigua el buen carácter del acusado*

character-building [ˈkærɪktəbɪldɪŋ] ADJ [*activity*] que fortalece la personalidad • **to be character-building** fortalecer la personalidad

characterful [ˈkærɪktəfʊl] ADJ [*wine, singer*] con (mucho) carácter

characteristic [ˌkærɪktəˈrɪstɪk] ADJ característico (**of** de)
N característica *f*

characteristically [ˌkærɪktəˈrɪstɪkəlɪ] ADV característicamente, de modo característico • **he was in ~ jovial mood** como es típico de él, estaba de muy buen talante

characterization [ˌkærɪktəraɪˈzeɪʃən] N (*in novel*) caracterización *f*

characterize [ˈkærɪktəraɪz] VT (= *be characteristic of*) caracterizar; (= *describe*) calificar (**as** de)

characterless [ˈkærɪktəlɪs] ADJ sin carácter

charade [ʃəˈrɑːd] N (*frm, pej*) payasada *f*, farsa *f*; **charades** (= *game*) charada *f*

charcoal [ˈtʃɑːkəʊl] N carbón *m* vegetal; (*Art*) carboncillo *m*
CPD ▸ **charcoal drawing** dibujo *m* al carbón *or* al carboncillo

charcoal-burner [ˈtʃɑːkəʊlˌbɜːnəʳ] N carbonero *m*

charcoal-grey [ˌtʃɑːkəʊlˈgreɪ] ADJ gris marengo (*inv*)

chard [tʃɑːd] N (*also* **Swiss chard**) acelgas *fpl*

charge [tʃɑːdʒ]

NOUN
TRANSITIVE VERB
INTRANSITIVE VERB
COMPOUNDS

NOUN

1 (= *accusation*) (*Jur*) cargo *m*, acusación *f*; (*fig*) acusación *f* • **the ~s were dropped** retiraron los cargos *or* la acusación • **what is the ~?** ¿de qué se me acusa? • **the ~ was murder** lo acusaron de asesinato • **to lay o.s. open to**

C

the ~ of ... exponerse a que le acusen de ... • **to bring a ~ against sb** formular *or* presentar cargos contra algn • **he will appear in court on a ~ of murder** *or* **murder ~** comparecerá ante el tribunal acusado de asesinato • **he was arrested on a ~ of murder** *or* **murder ~** lo detuvieron bajo acusación de asesinato; ▹ **press**
2 (*Mil*) • **to put sb on a ~** arrestar a algn
3 (= *fee*) precio *m*; (*professional*) honorarios *mpl*; (*Telec*); **charges** tarifa *fsing* • **~ for admission** precio *m* de entrada • **is there a ~?** ¿hay que pagar (algo)? • **is there a ~ for delivery?** ¿se paga el envío? • **there's no ~** es gratis • **"no charge for admission"** "entrada gratis", "entrada gratuita" • **extra ~** recargo *m*, suplemento *m* • **free of ~** gratis • **interest ~s** cargos *mpl* en concepto de interés • **to make a ~ for (doing) sth** cobrar por (hacer) algo • **for a small ~, we can supply ...** por una pequeña cantidad, podemos proporcionarle ...; ▹ **prescription, reverse, service**
4 (*US*) (= *charge account*) • **cash or ~?** ¿al contado o a crédito?
5 (= *responsibility*) • **I've been given ~ of this class** han puesto a esta clase a mi cargo • **to have ~ of sb/sth** hacerse cargo de algn/algo • **the patients under her ~** los pacientes a su cargo
in charge • **the person in ~** el/la encargado/a • **who is in ~ here?** ¿quién es el encargado aquí? • **look, I'm in ~ here!** ¡oye, aquí mando yo!
in charge of • **to be in ~ of** [+ *department, operation*] estar al frente *or* al cargo de • **he's in ~ of the shop when I'm out** se encarga de la tienda cuando yo no estoy • **it is illegal for anyone under 16 to be left in ~ of young children** es ilegal dejar a niños pequeños a cargo *or* al cuidado de alguien menor de 16 años
to put sb in charge of [+ *department, operation*] poner a algn al frente *or* al cargo de; [+ *ship, plane*] poner a algn al mando de • **to put sb in ~ of doing sth** encargar a algn que haga algo
to take charge (*of firm, project*) hacerse cargo (of de) • **he took ~ of the situation at once** se hizo cargo de la situación inmediatamente • **will you take ~ of the situation while I'm away?** ¿te puedes hacer cargo de la situación mientras no esté yo?
6 (= *person*) • **the teacher and her ~s** la maestra y los alumnos a su cargo • **the nurse and her ~s** la enfermera y los enfermos a su cargo
7 (*electrical*) carga *f* • **there is no ~ left in the battery** la batería está descargada • IDIOM: • **to get a ~ out of sth:** • **I got a big ~ out of working with the Philharmonic Orchestra** disfruté muchísimo trabajando con la Orquesta Filarmónica
8 (= *explosive*) carga *f*
9 (= *attack*) (*by people, army*) carga *f*, ataque *m*; (*by bull*) embestida *f*; ▹ **sound**
10 (= *financial burden*) carga *f* • **to be a ~ on ...** ser una carga para ...
11 (*Heraldry*) blasón *m*
TRANSITIVE VERB
1 (*Jur*) (*also fig*) (= *accuse*) acusar (**with** de) • **he was ~d with stealing a car** lo acusaron del robo de un coche • **to find sb guilty/not guilty as ~d** declarar a algn culpable/ inocente de los delitos que se le imputan • **he ~d the minister with lying about the economy** acusó al ministro de mentir acerca de la economía • **to ~ that** (*US*) alegar que
2 (= *ask for*) [+ *price*] cobrar • **what did they ~ you for it?** ¿cuánto te cobraron? • **what are they charging for the work?** ¿cuánto cobran *or* piden por el trabajo? • **to ~ 3% commission** cobrar un 3% de comisión
3 (= *record as debt*) • **to ~ sth (up) to sb** • **~ sth (up) to sb's account** cargar algo en la cuenta de algn • **~ it (up) to my card** cárguelo a mi tarjeta
4 (= *attack*) [*person, army*] cargar contra, atacar; [*bull etc*] embestir
5 (*Elec*) (*also* **charge up**) [+ *battery*] cargar
6 (= *order*) • **to ~ sb to do sth** ordenar a algn hacer *or* que haga algo • **to ~ sb with a mission** confiar una misión a algn • **I am ~d with the task of modernizing the company** me han encargado la tarea de modernizar la empresa
7 (*US*) (*in library*) • **to ~ a book** [*reader*] rellenar la ficha del préstamo; [*librarian*] registrar un libro como prestado
INTRANSITIVE VERB
1 (= *ask for a fee*) cobrar • **they'll mend it but they'll ~!** lo arreglarán, pero ¡te va a salir caro!
2 (= *attack*) [*person, army*] atacar; [*bull*] embestir • **~!** ¡a la carga! • **he ~d into the room** irrumpió en la habitación
3 (*Elec*) (*also* **charge up**) [*battery*] cargarse • **leave the battery to ~ (up) for a couple of hours** deja que la batería se cargue durante un par de horas
COMPOUNDS
▸ **charge account** (*US*) cuenta *f* de crédito
▸ **charge card** (*Brit*) (*Comm*) tarjeta *f* (de) cliente; (*US*) (= *credit card*) tarjeta *f* de crédito
▸ **charge nurse** (*Brit*) enfermero/a *m/f* jefe

chargeable [ˈtʃɑːdʒəbl] (ADJ) **1** (*Jur*) [*offence*] imputable • **to be ~ with** [*person*] ser susceptible de ser acusado de
2 • **to be ~ to** [+ *person*] correr a cargo de; [+ *account*] cargarse a
charge-cap [ˈtʃɑːdʒkæp] (VT) (*Brit*) [+ *local authority*] fijar un tope a los impuestos de
charged [tʃɑːdʒd] (ADJ) (*Elec*) cargado, con carga
chargé d'affaires [ˈʃɑːʒeɪdæˈfɛəʳ] (PL: **chargés d'affaires**) (N) encargado *m* de negocios
chargehand [ˈtʃɑːdʒhænd] (N) (*Brit*) capataz *m*
charger [ˈtʃɑːdʒəʳ] (N) (*Elec*) cargador *m*; (= *warhorse*) corcel *m*, caballo *m* de guerra
char-grilled [ˌtʃɑːʳˈgrɪld] (ADJ) a la brasa
charily [ˈtʃɛərɪlɪ] (ADV) (= *warily*) cautelosamente; (= *sparingly*) parcamente, con parquedad
chariot [ˈtʃærɪət] (N) carro *m* (*romano, de guerra etc*)
charioteer [ˌtʃærɪəˈtɪəʳ] (N) auriga *m*
charisma [kæˈrɪzmə] (N) carisma *m*
charismatic [ˌkærɪzˈmætɪk] (ADJ) carismático
(CPD) ▸ **charismatic church** iglesia *f* carismática
charitable [ˈtʃærɪtəbl] (ADJ) **1** (= *helping needy*) [*organization, society, institution, donation*] benéfico • **~ trust** fundación *f* benéfica • **to have ~ status** tener categoría de organización benéfica • **~ work** obras *fpl* benéficas, obras *fpl* de beneficiencia
2 (= *kindly*) [*person, deed, gesture*] benévolo, caritativo; [*remark, view*] comprensivo • **to be ~ to sb** mostrarse benévolo con algn • **to take a ~ view of sth** tener una visión comprensiva de algo, adoptar un punto de vista comprensivo sobre algo
charitably [ˈtʃærɪtəblɪ] (ADV) [*say, act*] caritativamente, con benevolencia
charity [ˈtʃærɪtɪ] (N) **1** (= *goodwill*) caridad *f* • **out of ~** por caridad • PROVERB: • **~ begins at home** la caridad bien entendida empieza por uno mismo
2 (= *financial relief*) obras *fpl* benéficas; (= *alms*) limosnas *fpl* • **all proceeds go to ~** todo lo recaudado se destinará a obras benéficas • **he gave the money to ~** donó el dinero a una organización benéfica • **to live on ~** vivir de la caridad • **to raffle sth for ~** rifar algo para fines benéficos
3 (= *organization*) organización *f* benéfica
4 (= *act*) • **it would be a ~ if ...** sería una obra de caridad si ...
(CPD) ▸ **charity appeal** cuestación *f* para obras benéficas ▸ **charity shop** (*Brit*) *tienda de artículos de segunda mano que dedica su recaudación a causas benéficas* ▸ **charity work** trabajo *m* voluntario (*para una organización benéfica*)
charlady [ˈtʃɑːleɪdɪ] (N) (*Brit*) mujer *f* de la limpieza, asistenta *f*
charlatan [ˈʃɑːlətən] (N) charlatán/tana *m/f*
Charlemagne [ˈʃɑːləmeɪn] (N) Carlomagno
Charles [tʃɑːlz] (N) Carlos
charleston [ˈtʃɑːlstən] (N) charlestón *m*
charley horse* [ˈtʃɑːlɪhɔːs] (N) (*US*) calambre *m*
Charlie* [ˈtʃɑːlɪ] (N) **1** (*Brit*†) (= *fool*) imbécil *m* • **I felt a right ~!** ¡me sentí como un idiota! • **he must have looked a right ~!** ¡debía parecer un verdadero imbécil!*
2 (*familiar form of* **Charles**) Carlitos • **~ Chaplin** Charlot
charlie* [ˈtʃɑːlɪ] (N) (= *cocaine*) coca* *f*
Charlotte [ˈʃɑːlət] (N) Carlota
charm [tʃɑːm] (N) **1** (= *attractiveness*) encanto *m*, atractivo *m*; (= *pleasantness*) simpatía *f* • **he has great ~** es verdaderamente encantador, tiene un fuerte atractivo • **to turn on the ~** ponerse fino • **to fall victim to sb's ~s** sucumbir a los encantos de algn
2 (= *magic spell*) hechizo *m*; (*recited*) ensalmo *m* • **it worked like a ~** funcionó a las mil maravillas
3 (= *object*) dije *m*, amuleto *m*
(VT) **1** (= *delight*) encantar • **we were ~ed by Granada** nos encantó Granada
2 (= *entice with charm*) • **to ~ one's way out of a situation** utilizar su encanto para salir de un apuro • IDIOM: • **he could ~ the birds out of the trees** con su encanto es capaz de conseguir todo lo que se propone
3 (= *bewitch*) encantar, hechizar • **~ed circle** círculo *m* privilegiado • IDIOM: • **to lead a ~ed life** tener suerte en todo
(CPD) ▸ **charm bracelet** pulsera *f* amuleto *or* de dijes ▸ **charm offensive** ofensiva *f* amistosa • **to launch a ~ offensive** lanzar una ofensiva amistosa ▸ **charm school*** = **finishing school**
▸ **charm away** (VT + ADV) hacer desaparecer como por magia, llevarse misteriosamente
charmer [ˈtʃɑːməʳ] (N) persona *f* encantadora
charming [ˈtʃɑːmɪŋ] (ADJ) [*place*] encantador; [*person*] encantador, simpático • **how ~ of you!** ¡qué detalle! • **~!** (*iro*) ¡qué simpático! (*iro*)
charmingly [ˈtʃɑːmɪŋlɪ] (ADV) de modo encantador • **a ~ simple dress** un vestido sencillo pero muy mono • **as you so ~ put it** (*iro*) como tú tan finamente has indicado (*iro*)
charmless [ˈtʃɑːmlɪs] (ADJ) [*place*] sin encanto, poco atractivo; [*person*] sin atractivo, sin chispa*
charnel-house [ˈtʃɑːnlhaʊs] (N) (PL: **charnel-houses** [ˈtʃɑːnlhaʊzɪz]) osario *m*
charred [tʃɑːd] (ADJ) carbonizado
chart [tʃɑːt] (N) **1** (= *table*) tabla *f*, cuadro *m*;

(= *graph*) gráfica *f*, gráfico *m*; (*Met*) mapa *m*; (*Naut*) (= *map*) carta *f* (de navegación) • **weather ~** mapa meteorológico
2 (*Mus*) • **the ~s*** la lista de éxitos • **to be in the ~s** [*record, pop group*] estar en la lista de éxitos
VT (= *plot*) [+ *course*] trazar; (= *record on graph*) [+ *sales, growth etc*] hacer una gráfica de, representar gráficamente; (= *follow*) [+ *progress*] reflejar • **the book ~s the rise and fall of the empire** el libro describe la grandeza y decadencia del imperio • **the diagram ~s the company's progress** el diagrama muestra *or* refleja el progreso de la compañía
CPD ▸ **chart music** (= *songs in the charts*) la lista *f* de éxitos ▸ **chart topper*** éxito *m* discográfico

charter ['tʃɑːtəʳ] N 1 (= *authorization*) carta *f*; [*of city*] fuero *m*; [*of organization*] estatutos *mpl*; [*of company*] escritura *f* de constitución • **royal ~** cédula *f* real
2 (= *hire*) (*Naut*) alquiler *m*; (*Aer*) fletamento *m* • **this boat is available for ~** este barco se alquila
VT 1 [+ *organization*] aprobar los estatutos de; [+ *company*] aprobar la escritura de constitución de
2 [+ *bus*] alquilar; [+ *ship, plane*] fletar
CPD ▸ **charter flight** vuelo *m* chárter ▸ **charter plane** avión *m* chárter

chartered ['tʃɑːtəd] ADJ [*surveyor*] colegiado; [*librarian*] diplomado (*con un mínimo de dos años de experiencia*); [*company*] legalmente constituido • **~ accountant** (*Brit, Canada*) censor(a) *m/f* jurado/a de cuentas, contador(a) *m/f* público/a (*LAm*)

charterer ['tʃɑːtərəʳ] N fletador(a) *m/f*

Chartism ['tʃɑːtɪzəm] N (*Hist*) cartismo *m*

Chartist ['tʃɑːtɪst] N • **the ~s** (*Hist*) los cartistas

charwoman ['tʃɑːˌwʊmən] N (PL: **charwomen**) mujer *f* de la limpieza, asistenta *f*

chary ['tʃɛərɪ] ADJ (COMPAR: **charier**, SUPERL: **chariest**) 1 (= *wary*) cauteloso • **he's ~ of getting involved** evita inmiscuirse
2 (= *sparing*) • **she's ~ in her praise** no se prodiga en alabanzas

chase¹ [tʃeɪs] N persecución *f* • **the ~** (= *hunting*) la caza • **a car ~** una persecución de coches • **to give ~ to** dar caza a, perseguir • **to join in the ~ for sth** unirse a los que buscan algo
VT (= *pursue*) perseguir • **he's started chasing girls*** ya anda detrás de las chicas • **to ~ sb for money** reclamar dinero a algn
VI correr • **I've been chasing all over the place looking for you** te he estado buscando por todas partes • **to ~ after sb** (= *pursue*) correr tras algn; (= *seek out*) ir *or* andar a la caza de algn
▸ **chase away, chase off** VT + ADV ahuyentar
▸ **chase down** VT + ADV 1 (= *track down*) localizar
2 (*US*) (= *catch*) recabar, tratar de localizar
▸ **chase out** VT + ADV echar fuera
▸ **chase up** VT + ADV [+ *information*] recabar, tratar de localizar; [+ *person*] buscar; [+ *matter*] investigar • **I'll ~ him up about it** se lo voy a recordar • **I'll ~ it up for you** investigaré lo que está pasando con lo tuyo • **to ~ up debts** reclamar el cobro de las deudas

chase² [tʃeɪs] VT [+ *metal*] grabar, adornar grabando, cincelar

chaser ['tʃeɪsəʳ] N *bebida tomada inmediatamente después de otra distinta, p.ej., una copita de licor después de una cerveza*

chasm ['kæzəm] N (*Geol*) sima *f*; (*fig*) abismo *m*

chassis ['ʃæsɪ] N (PL: **chassis**) 1 (*Aut*) chasis *m inv*
2 (*Aer*) tren *m* de aterrizaje

chaste [tʃeɪst] ADJ casto

chastely ['tʃeɪstlɪ] ADV castamente

chasten ['tʃeɪsn] VT castigar, escarmentar

chastened ['tʃeɪsnd] PT, PP *of* **chasten**
ADJ (*by experience*) escarmentado; [*tone*] sumiso • **they seemed much ~** parecían haberse arrepentido

chasteness ['tʃeɪstnɪs] N castidad *f*

chastening ['tʃeɪsnɪŋ] ADJ [*experience*] aleccionador

chastise [tʃæs'taɪz] VT (= *scold*) regañar; (= *punish*) castigar

chastisement ['tʃæstɪzmənt] N castigo *m*

chastity ['tʃæstɪtɪ] N castidad *f*
CPD ▸ **chastity belt** cinturón *m* de castidad

chasuble ['tʃæzjʊbl] N casulla *f*

chat [tʃæt] N charla *f*, plática *f* (*CAm*) • **to have a ~ with** (*gen*) charlar con, platicar con (*CAm*); (= *discuss*) hablar con • **I'll have a ~ with him about it** hablaré con él de *or* sobre ello
VI 1 (= *talk*) charlar, platicar (*CAm*) (**with, to** con)
2 (*Internet*) chatear
CPD ▸ **chat room** (*Internet*) canal *m* de charla, foro *m* de discusión, chat *m* ▸ **chat show** programa *m* de entrevistas ▸ **chat show host** presentador *m* de programa de entrevistas ▸ **chat show hostess** presentadora *f* de programa de entrevistas
▸ **chat up*** VT + ADV (*Brit*) (= *try to pick up*) tratar de ligar*; [+ *influential person*] dar jabón a*

château ['ʃætəʊ] N (PL: **châteaux** ['ʃætəʊz]) (*in France*) castillo *m*

chatline ['tʃætlaɪn] N *servicio telefónico que permite a los que llaman conversar unos con otros sobre distintos temas*

chattels ['tʃætlz] NPL bienes *mpl* muebles; (*loosely*) cosas *fpl*, enseres *mpl*; ▹ **goods**

chatter ['tʃætəʳ] N (*gen*) charla *f*; (*excessive*) cháchara *f*, cotorreo *m*; [*of birds, monkeys*] parloteo *m*
VI [*person*] (*gen*) charlar; (*excessively*) estar de cháchara, cotorrear; [*birds, monkeys*] parlotear • **her teeth were ~ing** le castañeteaban los dientes • **she does ~ so** es muy habladora • **stop ~ing!** ¡silencio!

chatterbox* ['tʃætəbɒks], **chatterer** ['tʃætərəʳ] N charlatán/ana* *m/f*, parlanchín/ina* *m/f*, platicón/ona *m/f* (*Mex**)

chattering ['tʃætərɪŋ] N [*of person*] parloteo *m*; (*excessive*) charloteo *m*; [*of birds, monkeys*] parloteo *m*; [*of teeth*] castañeteo *m*
CPD ▸ **the chattering classes*** (*Brit*) (*pej*) los intelectualoides*

chatty ['tʃætɪ] ADJ (COMPAR: **chattier**, SUPERL: **chattiest**) [*person*] hablador; [*letter*] afectuoso y lleno de noticias; [*style*] informal

chat-up line ['tʃætʌpˌlaɪn] N • **a good chat-up line** una buena frase para entrarle a algn*

chauffeur ['ʃəʊfəʳ] N chófer *mf*, chofer *mf* (*LAm*)
VT llevar en coche (**to the station** a la estación) • **I had to ~ him all over town** (*iro*) tuve que hacer de chófer y llevarle de una punta a otra de la ciudad
VI hacer de chófer (**for para**)

chauffeur-driven ['ʃəʊfəˌdrɪvən] ADJ • **chauffeur-driven car** coche *m* con chófer *or* (*LAm*) chofer

chauvinism ['ʃəʊvɪnɪzəm] N (= *male chauvinism*) machismo *m*; (= *nationalism*) chovinismo *m*, patriotería *f*

chauvinist ['ʃəʊvɪnɪst] N (= *male chauvinist*) machista *m*; (= *nationalist*) chovinista *mf*, patriotero/a *m/f*
ADJ (= *male chauvinist*) machista; (= *nationalist*) chovinista, patriotero • **(male) ~ pig*** (*pej*) machista asqueroso (*pej*)

chauvinistic [ˌʃəʊvɪ'nɪstɪk] ADJ = **chauvinist**

chav* ['tʃæv] N ≈ chico/a *m/f* de barrio, *adolescente que suele vestir con gorra, chandal y zapatillas de deporte y que se dedica a vaguear por las calles del barrio*

CHE ABBR = **Campaign for Homosexual Equality**

ChE ABBR (*esp US*) 1 = **Chemical Engineer**
2 = **Chief Engineer**

cheap [tʃiːp] ADJ (COMPAR: **cheaper**, SUPERL: **cheapest**) 1 (= *inexpensive*) [*goods, labour, shop, ticket*] barato; [*imports*] a bajo precio; [*loan, credit*] a bajo interés • **it's ten pence ~er** es diez peniques más barato • **it's ~er to buy than to rent** sale más económico *or* barato comprar que alquilar • **gas cookers are ~er to run** las cocinas de gas salen *or* resultan más económicas • **these cars are very ~ to produce** la fabricación de estos coches sale muy barata • **~ labour** mano *f* de obra barata • **~ money** dinero *m* barato • **dresses at ridiculously ~ prices** vestidos a unos precios regalados • **it's ~ at the price*** está bien de precio, es barato para lo que es • **that's ~ at half the price!*** ¡es más que regalado! • **~ rate** tarifa *f* reducida • IDIOM: • **~ and cheerful** bueno, bonito y barato; ▹ **dirt-cheap**
2 (= *poor-quality*) [*product*] barato, corriente • **beware of ~ imitations!** ¡esté al tanto de imitaciones baratas! • **~ and nasty** ordinario, chabacano
3 (= *vulgar, mean*) [*joke*] ordinario, chabacano; [*behaviour, tactics*] rastrero; [*remark, question*] de mal gusto; [*opportunism, sensationalism*] barato; [*promises*] fácil • **a ~ laugh** la risa fácil • **~ thrills** placeres *mpl* baratos • **a ~ trick** una mala pasada
4 (= *not deserving respect*) bajo, indigno • **to feel ~** sentirse humillado • **they hold life ~ there** allí la vida no vale nada • **to look ~** parecer ordinario, tener un aspecto ordinario • **to make o.s. ~** rebajarse, humillarse
ADV [*buy, sell*] barato • **it's going ~** se vende barato • **quality doesn't come ~** la calidad hay que pagarla
N • **on the ~*** (*pej*) [*decorate, travel*] en plan barato* • **to do sth on the ~** hacer algo en plan barato* • **to buy** *or* **get sth on the ~** comprar algo por poco dinero *or* a bajo precio
CPD ▸ **cheap shot** golpe *m* bajo

cheapen ['tʃiːpən] VT (= *make cheaper*) [+ *cost*] abaratar; (*fig*) (= *debase*) [+ *sb's name, work*] degradar • **to ~ o.s.** hacer cosas indignas, rebajarse
VI abaratarse

cheapie* ['tʃiːpɪ] ADJ de barato*
N (= *ticket, meal etc*) ganga *f*

cheap-jack ['tʃiːpdʒæk] ADJ [*product*] de bajísima calidad, malísimo; [*furniture*] muy mal hecho; [*person*] chapucero
N (= *person*) chapucero/a *m/f*, baratillero *m*

cheaply ['tʃiːplɪ] ADV [*buy, sell*] barato, a bajo precio; [*produce goods*] a bajo precio; [*live, eat, decorate, furnish*] con poco dinero • **two can live as ~ as one** dos pueden vivir por el mismo dinero que uno

cheapness ['tʃiːpnɪs] N 1 (= *low cost*) lo barato, baratura *f*
2 (= *poor quality*) lo corriente, ordinariez *f*

cheapo* ['tʃiːpəʊ] ADJ baratejo

cheapshot* ['tʃi:pʃɒt] VT • **to ~ sb** (*US*) hablar mal de algn

cheapskate* ['tʃi:pskeɪt] N tacaño/a *m/f*, roñoso/a* *m/f*

cheat [tʃi:t] N **1** (= *person*) tramposo/a *m/f*; (*at cards*) tramposo/a *m/f*, fullero/a *m/f*
2 (= *fraud*) estafa *f*, fraude *m*; (= *trick*) trampa *f* • **it was a ~** fue una estafa *or* un timo, hubo trampa
VT (= *swindle*) estafar, timar; (= *trick*) engañar • **to ~ sb out of sth** estafar algo a algn • **to feel ~ed** sentirse defraudado
VI hacer trampa(s); (*in exam*) copiar
▸ **cheat on** VI + PREP (*esp US*) [+ *person*] engañar

cheater ['tʃi:təʳ] N (*esp US*) (= *person*) = **cheat**

cheating ['tʃi:tɪŋ] N trampa *f*; (*at cards*) trampas *fpl*, fullerías *fpl* • **that's ~** eso es trampa • **no ~!** ¡sin hacer trampas!

Chechen ['tʃetʃən] ADJ checheno
N (PL: **Chechen** *or* **Chechens**) checheno/a *m/f*

Chechnya [tʃɪtʃ'njɑ:] N Chechenia *f*

check [tʃek] N **1** (= *inspection*) control *m*, inspección *f*, chequeo *m*; (*Mech*) revisión *f*; (*Med*) chequeo *m* • **he has regular ~s on his blood pressure** le controlan la tensión con regularidad • **security ~** control *m* de seguridad • **to keep a ~ on sth/sb** controlar algo/a algn, vigilar algo/a algn • **to run** *or* **make a ~ on sth** comprobar *or* revisar algo • **to run** *or* **make a ~ on sb** hacer averiguaciones *or* indagaciones sobre algn
2 (= *restraint*) • **~s and balances** (*US*) (*Pol*) *mecanismo de equilibrio de poderes* • **to act as a ~ on sth** poner freno a algo, servir de freno a algo • **to hold** *or* **keep sth in ~** tener algo controlado *or* bajo control • **population growth must be held in ~** hay que tener *or* mantener el crecimiento demográfico bajo control • **she kept her temper in ~** controlaba *or* contenía su genio • **to hold** *or* **keep sb in ~** controlar a algn, mantener a algn a raya
3 (*Chess*) jaque *m* • **~!** ¡jaque! • **to be in ~** estar (en) jaque • **to put sb in ~** dar *or* hacer jaque a algn
4 (= *square*) cuadro *m*; (= *fabric*) tela *f* a cuadros, tela *f* de cuadros • **a red and white ~ dress** un vestido rojo y blanco a *or* de cuadros
5 (*US*) (= *bill*) cuenta *f*
6 (*US*) = **cheque**
7 (*US*) (= *tick*) marca *f*, señal *f* • **~!** ¡vale!*
8 (*US*) (= *tag, ticket*) resguardo *m*
VT **1** (= *examine*) [+ *ticket, passport*] controlar, revisar; [+ *merchandise, premises*] inspeccionar, controlar; [+ *tyres, oil*] revisar, comprobar; [+ *temperature, pressure*] controlar • **he ~ed his watch every hour** miraba el reloj cada hora • **he stopped to ~ his map** se detuvo para leer *or* mirar el mapa • **~ each item for flaws** compruebe todos los artículos para ver que no tengan defectos • **~ the phone book for local suppliers** mire en la guía telefónica para encontrar proveedores en su zona
2 (= *confirm, verify*) [+ *facts, figures*] comprobar • **please ~ the number and dial again** por favor, compruebe que el número es el correcto y vuelva a marcar • **~ the seasoning** pruébelo para ver que esté sazonado a su gusto • **~ that he's gone before you do it** asegúrate de que *or* comprueba que se ha ido antes de hacerlo • **to ~ sth against sth** comparar *or* cotejar algo con algo
3‡ (= *look at*) (*also* **check out**) mirar • **wow, ~ that car!** ¡hala! ¡mira *or* fíjate qué coche!
4 (= *hold back*) [+ *attack, advance, progress*] detener, frenar • **to ~ the spread of AIDS** detener *or* frenar la propagación del SIDA • **to ~ o.s.** contenerse, refrenarse
5 (*US*) (= *tick*) marcar, señalar
6 (*US*) [+ *luggage*] (*at airport*) facturar, chequear (*LAm*); (*at station*) dejar en consigna; [+ *clothes, property*] (*in cloakroom*) dejar (en el guardarropa)
7 (*Chess*) [+ *king*] dar jaque a
VI **1** (= *confirm*) comprobar, chequear (*esp LAm*) • **I'm not sure he's here, I'll just ~** no estoy seguro de que esté aquí, iré a comprobar(lo) *or* iré a mirar • **I'll need to ~ with the manager** lo tendré que consultar con el encargado
2 (= *examine*) • **to ~ for sth**: • **they ~ed for broken bones** lo examinaron para ver si tenía algún hueso roto • **~ periodically for wear and tear** compruebe periódicamente el deterioro • **he ~ed on her several times during the night** fue a verla varias veces durante la noche para asegurarse de que estaba bien
3 (= *hesitate*) pararse en seco, pararse de repente
4 (*US*) (= *agree*) concordar (**with** con)
CPD ▸ **check mark** (*US*) (= *tick*) señal *f* ▸ **check suit** traje *m* a *or* de cuadros
▸ **check in** VI + ADV **1** (= *register*) (*at airport*) facturar *or* (*LAm*) chequear (el equipaje); (*at hotel*) registrarse; (*at clinic, hospital*) ingresar
2 (*US*) (= *communicate*) • **he ~s in with us by phone every week** se pone en contacto con nosotros *or* nos llama por teléfono todas las semanas
VT + ADV [+ *luggage*] facturar, chequear (*LAm*); [+ *person*] (*at hotel*) registrar; (*at airport*) facturar el equipaje de • **go to that desk and someone will ~ you in** vaya a ese mostrador y allí le facturarán el equipaje
▸ **check off** VT + ADV • **to ~ items off on a list** comprobar puntos en una lista
▸ **check on** VI + ADV [+ *information, time etc*] verificar • **to ~ on sb** investigar a algn
▸ **check out** VI + ADV **1** (*of hotel*) (pagar y) marcharse (**of** de)
2 (*US*) (= *agree*) cuadrar • **their credentials ~ out** sus credenciales cuadran • **his alibi ~s out** su coartada concuerda (con los hechos)
VT + ADV **1** (= *investigate*) • **the police had to ~ out the call** la policía tuvo que investigar la llamada
2 (= *confirm*) [+ *facts, statement*] comprobar, verificar
3* (= *look at*) mirar • **~ out the girl in the pink shirt!** ¡mira a esa chica con la camisa rosa!
4 [+ *purchases*] [*customer*] pagar; [*cashier*] pasar por la caja
▸ **check over** VT + ADV revisar, escudriñar
▸ **check up** VT + ADV • **can you ~ up what time the film starts?** ¿puedes confirmar *or* mirar a qué hora empieza la película? • **they never ~ up to see how much it costs** nunca comprueban *or* miran cuánto cuesta
▸ **check up on** VI + PREP **1** (= *confirm*) [+ *story*] comprobar, verificar • **he phoned me to ~ up on some facts** me llamó para comprobar *or* verificar cierta información
2 (= *investigate*) • **we've ~ed up on you and it seems you are telling the truth** hemos hecho indagaciones *or* averiguaciones sobre usted y parece que nos está diciendo la verdad • **I'm sure he knew I was ~ing up on him** estoy seguro de que sabía que lo estaba espiando *or* vigilando

checkbook ['tʃekbʊk] N (*US*) = **chequebook**

checked [tʃekt] ADJ [*tablecloth, shirt, pattern*] a cuadros, de cuadros

checker ['tʃekəʳ] N **1** (= *examiner*) verificador(a) *m/f*
2 (*US*) (*in supermarket*) cajero/a *m/f*; (*in cloakroom*) encargado/a *m/f* de guardarropa

checkerboard ['tʃekəbɔ:d] N (*US*) tablero *m* de damas

checkered ['tʃekəd] ADJ (*US*) = **chequered**

checkers ['tʃekəz] NPL (*US*) damas *fpl*

check-in ['tʃekɪn] N (*also* **check-in desk**) (*at airport*) mostrador *m* de facturación • **your check-in time is an hour before departure** la facturación es una hora antes de la salida

checking ['tʃekɪŋ] N control *m*, comprobación *f*
CPD ▸ **checking account** (*US*) cuenta *f* corriente

checking-in [ˌtʃekɪŋ'ɪn] N (*Aer*) facturación *f*

checklist ['tʃeklɪst] N lista *f* de control (*con la que se coteja algo*)

checkmate ['tʃek'meɪt] N (*in chess*) mate *m*, jaque *m* mate; (*fig*) callejón *m* sin salida • **~!** ¡jaque mate!
VT **1** (*in chess*) dar mate a
2 (*fig*) poner en un callejón sin salida a • **to be ~d** estar en un callejón sin salida

checkout ['tʃekaʊt] N (*in supermarket*) (*also* **checkout counter**) caja *f*; (*in hotel*) = **checkout time**
CPD ▸ **checkout girl** cajera *f* (de supermercado) ▸ **checkout time** hora *f* a la que hay que dejar libre la habitación

checkpoint ['tʃekpɔɪnt] N (punto *m* de) control *m*, retén *m* (*LAm*)

checkroom ['tʃekrʊm] N (*US*) guardarropa *m*; (*Rail*) consigna *f*; (*euph*) lavabo *m*

checkup ['tʃekʌp] N (*Med*) (*at doctor's*) reconocimiento *m* general, chequeo *m*; (*at dentist's*) revisión *f*; (*Aut*) [*of vehicle*] revisión *f*

cheddar ['tʃedəʳ] N (*also* **cheddar cheese**) queso *m* cheddar

cheek [tʃi:k] N **1** (*Anat*) mejilla *f*, carrillo *m*; (= *buttock*) nalga *f* • **they were dancing ~ to ~** bailaban muy apretados • IDIOMS: • **~ by jowl (with)** codo a *or* con codo (con) • **to turn the other ~** poner la otra mejilla
2* (= *impudence*) descaro *m*, cara* *f*, frescura *f* • **what a ~!** • **of all the ~!** ¡qué cara!*, ¡qué caradura!*, ¡qué frescura! • **to have the ~ to do sth** tener la cara de hacer algo
VT* portarse como un fresco con*

cheekbone ['tʃi:kbəʊn] N pómulo *m*

cheekily* ['tʃi:kɪlɪ] ADV descaradamente, con frescura

cheekiness* ['tʃi:kɪnɪs] N descaro *m*, frescura *f*

cheeky ['tʃi:kɪ] ADJ (COMPAR: **cheekier**, SUPERL: **cheekiest**) [*person*] descarado, fresco; [*question*] indiscreto, descarado; [*grin*] malicioso • **don't be ~!** ¡no seas descarado!

cheep [tʃi:p] N [*of bird*] pío *m*
VI piar

cheer [tʃɪəʳ] N **1** (= *applause*) ovación *f*, aclamación *f*; (= *hurrah*) vítor *m*, viva *m* • **a ~**

CHECKS AND BALANCES

El sistema de **checks and balances** es uno de los principios de gobierno de Estados Unidos, cuyo objetivo es prevenir abusos de poder por parte de uno de los tres poderes del Estado. Para garantizar la libertad dentro del marco constitucional, los padres de la Constitución estadounidense crearon un sistema por el que tanto el poder del Presidente, como el del Congreso, el de los Tribunales o el de los gobiernos de cada estado puede ser sometido a debate o, si fuera necesario, controlado por el resto de los poderes.

went up from the crowd la multitud prorrumpió en ovaciones *or* vítores • **there were loud ~s at this** esto fue muy aplaudido • **three ~s for the president!** ¡viva el presidente!, ¡tres hurras por el presidente!
2 (= *comfort*) consuelo *m* • **the inflation figures offer little ~ to the government** el nivel de inflación brinda poco consuelo al gobierno
3 (= *state of mind*) • **be of good ~** (*liter*) ¡ánimo!
(EXCL) • **~s!** (= *toast*) ¡salud!; (*Brit**) (= *thank you*) ¡gracias!; (= *goodbye*) ¡hasta luego!
(VT) **1** (= *applaud*) [+ *winner etc*] aclamar, vitorear
2 (*also* **cheer up**) (= *gladden*) alegrar, animar • **I was much ~ed by the news** me alegró mucho la noticia
(VI) (= *shout*) dar vivas, dar vítores
▸ **cheer on** (VT + ADV) animar (*con aplausos or gritos*)
▸ **cheer up** (VI + ADV) animarse, alegrarse • **~ up!** ¡anímate!, ¡ánimo!
(VT + ADV) alegrar, animar; [+ *person*] levantar el ánimo a

cheerful [ˈtʃɪəfʊl] (ADJ) [*person, expression, voice, atmosphere*] alegre, jovial; [*occasion*] feliz; [*place*] alegre, animado; [*colour*] alegre, vivo; [*fire*] acogedor; [*news, prospect, outlook*] alentador • **to be ~ about sth** alegrarse de *or* por algo • **she felt she had nothing to be ~ about** sintió que no tenía nada por lo que alegrarse • **she was very ~ about moving into her new flat** la idea de mudarse al nuevo piso la alegraba mucho • **to feel ~** • **be in a ~ mood** estar de buen humor; ▹ **cheap**

cheerfully [ˈtʃɪəfʊlɪ] (ADV) **1** (= *cheerily*) [*smile, say, greet*] alegremente, jovialmente • **the nursery is ~ painted** la guardería está pintada con colores alegres
2 (= *blithely*) alegremente, tranquilamente • **he ~ ignored the doctor's advice** ignoró alegremente *or* tranquilamente los consejos del médico
3 (= *gladly*) • **I could ~ strangle him** con mucho gusto lo estrangularía • **she ~ agreed to try using his method** aceptó de buena gana probar su método

cheerfulness [ˈtʃɪəfʊlnɪs] (N) [*of person, smile*] alegría *f*, jovialidad *f*; [*of place*] alegría *f*, animación *f*

cheerily [ˈtʃɪərɪlɪ] (ADV) alegremente, jovialmente

cheering [ˈtʃɪərɪŋ] (ADJ) [*news*] bueno, esperanzador; [*prospect*] alentador
(N) ovaciones *fpl*, vítores *mpl*

cheerio* [ˈtʃɪərɪˈəʊ] (EXCL) (*Brit*) ¡hasta luego!, ¡chau! (*LAm*)

cheerleader [ˈtʃɪəˌliːdəʳ] (N) (*esp US*) animador(a) *m/f*

cheerless [ˈtʃɪəlɪs] (ADJ) triste, sombrío

cheery [ˈtʃɪərɪ] (ADJ) (COMPAR: **cheerier**, SUPERL: **cheeriest**) [*person*] alegre, jovial; [*room, atmosphere*] acogedor; [*voice*] risueño, alegre; [*letter*] alegre

cheese [tʃiːz] (N) **1** (= *dairy product*) queso *m* • **say ~!** (*Phot*) ¡a ver, una sonrisa! • **hard ~!*** ¡mala pata!
2* (= *person*) • **big ~** pez *m* gordo
(VT) (*Brit**) • **I'm ~d off with this** estoy hasta las narices de esto*
(CPD) ▸ **cheese and wine, cheese and wine party** *fiesta en casa en la que se suelen degustar distintos tipos de vino y de queso* ▸ **cheese dish** tabla *f* de quesos ▸ **cheese grater** rallador *m* de queso ▸ **cheese sauce** salsa *f* de queso, ≈ salsa *f* Mornay

cheeseboard [ˈtʃiːzbɔːd] (N) tabla *f* de quesos

cheeseburger [ˈtʃiːzˌbɜːgəʳ] (N) hamburguesa *f* con queso

cheesecake [ˈtʃiːzkeɪk] (N) tarta *f or* (*LAm*) pay *m* de queso; (*fig**) *fotos, dibujos etc de chicas atractivas en traje o actitud incitante*

cheesecloth [ˈtʃiːzklɒθ] (N) estopilla *f*

cheeseparing [ˈtʃiːzˌpɛərɪŋ] (ADJ) tacaño
(N) economías *fpl* pequeñas

cheesy [ˈtʃiːzɪ] (ADJ) **1** [*taste, smell*] a queso; [*socks, feet*] maloliente
2* horrible, sin valor
3 [*grin*] de hiena

cheetah [ˈtʃiːtə] (N) guepardo *m*

chef [ʃef] (N) cocinero/a *m/f* jefe/a, chef *m*

chef-d'oeuvre [ʃeɪˈdɜːvrə] (N) (PL: **chefs-d'oeuvre** [ʃeɪˈdɜːvrə]) obra *f* maestra

Chekhov [ˈtʃekɒf] (N) Chejov

chemical [ˈkemɪkəl] (ADJ) químico
(N) sustancia *f* química, producto *m* químico
(CPD) ▸ **chemical engineer** ingeniero/a *m/f* químico/a ▸ **chemical engineering** ingeniería *f* química ▸ **chemical warfare** guerra *f* química ▸ **chemical weapon** arma *f* química

chemically [ˈkemɪkəlɪ] (ADV) químicamente; [*do, carry out*] por medios químicos • **~ dependent** toxicodependiente

chemise [ʃəˈmiːz] (N) blusa *f* camisera

chemist [ˈkemɪst] (N) **1** (= *scientist*) químico/a *m/f*; (*Brit*)
2 (= *pharmacist*) (*Brit*) farmacéutico/a *m/f* • **~'s (shop)** farmacia *f* • **all-night ~'s** farmacia *f* de turno *or* de guardia

chemistry [ˈkemɪstrɪ] (N) química *f* • **the ~ between them is right** (*fig*) están muy compenetrados
(CPD) ▸ **chemistry laboratory** laboratorio *m* de química ▸ **chemistry set** juego *m* de química

chemo* [ˈkiːməʊ] (N) (= *chemotherapy*) quimio* *f*

chemotherapy [ˈkiːməʊˈθerəpɪ] (N) quimioterapia *f*

chenille [ʃəˈniːl] (N) felpilla *f*

Chennai [tʃɪˈnaɪ] (N) Chennai *f*

cheque, check (*US*) [tʃek] (N) (*Brit*) cheque *m*, talón *m* (bancario) (*Sp*) • **a ~ for £20** un cheque por *or* de 20 libras • **to make out** *or* **write a ~ (for £100/to Rodríguez)** extender un cheque (de 100 libras/a favor de Rodríguez) • **to pay by ~** pagar con cheque • **bad ~** cheque *m* sin fondos *or* sin provisión
(CPD) ▸ **cheque account** (*Brit*) cuenta *f* cheque ▸ **cheque card** (*also* **cheque guarantee card**) tarjeta *f* de identificación bancaria ▸ **cheque stub** (*Brit*) talón *m* del cheque

chequebook, checkbook (*US*) [ˈtʃekbʊk] (N) talonario *m* de cheques, chequera *f* (*LAm*) • **~ journalism** periodismo *m* a golpe de talonario

chequerboard [ˈtʃekəbɔːd] (N) (*Brit*) = **checkerboard**

chequered, checkered (*US*) [ˈtʃekəd] (ADJ) **1** (= *checked*) [*tablecloth, shirt, pattern*] a cuadros, de cuadros
2 (= *varied*) • **a ~ career** una carrera accidentada *or* llena de altibajos
(CPD) ▸ **chequered flag** (*Motor racing*) bandera *f* a cuadros

chequers [ˈtʃekəz] (N) damas *fpl*

cherish [ˈtʃerɪʃ] (VT) [+ *person*] querer, apreciar; [+ *hope*] abrigar, acariciar; [+ *memory*] conservar

cherished [ˈtʃerɪʃt] (ADJ) [*memory*] precioso, entrañable; [*possession*] preciado; [*privilege*] apreciado • **it's a long-cherished dream of mine to go to Florence** ir a Florencia es un sueño que llevo albergando desde hace tiempo

cheroot [ʃəˈruːt] (N) puro *m* (cortado en los dos extremos)

cherry [ˈtʃerɪ] (N) (= *fruit*) cereza *f*; (= *tree, wood*) cerezo *m*
(CPD) [*pie, jam*] de cereza ▸ **cherry blossom** flor *f* de cerezo ▸ **cherry brandy** aguardiente *m* de cerezas ▸ **cherry orchard** cerezal *m* ▸ **cherry red** rojo *m* cereza ▸ **cherry tree** cerezo *m*

cherry-pick [ˈtʃerɪpɪk] (VT) (*fig*) escoger cuidadosamente, seleccionar cuidadosamente

cherry-red [ˌtʃerɪˈred] (ADJ) (de) color rojo cereza

cherub [ˈtʃerəb] (N) (PL: **cherubs**)
1 querubín *m*, angelito *m*
2 (*Rel*) (PL: **cherubim** [ˈtʃerəbɪm]) querubín *m*

cherubic [tʃeˈruːbɪk] (ADJ) querúbico

chervil [ˈtʃɜːvɪl] (N) perifollo *m*

Ches (ABBR) (*Brit*) = **Cheshire**

Cheshire cat [ˈtʃeʃəˈkæt] (N) • IDIOM: • **to grin like a ~** sonreír de oreja a oreja

chess [tʃes] (N) ajedrez *m*
(CPD) ▸ **chess club** club *m* de ajedrez ▸ **chess piece** pieza *f* de ajedrez ▸ **chess player** jugador(a) *m/f* de ajedrez, ajedrecista *mf* ▸ **chess set** (juego *m* de) ajedrez *m* ▸ **chess tournament** torneo *m* de ajedrez

chessboard [ˈtʃesbɔːd] (N) tablero *m* de ajedrez

chessman [ˈtʃesmæn] (N) (PL: **chessmen**) pieza *f* de ajedrez

chest [tʃest] (N) **1** (*Anat*) pecho *m* • **to have ~ trouble** tener problemas respiratorios, padecer de los bronquios • **to have a cold on the ~** tener el pecho resfriado • IDIOM: • **to get sth off one's ~*** desahogarse
2 (= *box*) cofre *m*, arca *f* • **~ of drawers** cómoda *f*
(CPD) [*pain*] de pecho ▸ **chest cold** resfriado *m* de pecho ▸ **chest expander** tensor *m*, extensor *m* ▸ **chest freezer** congelador *m* de arcón ▸ **chest infection** infección *f* de las vías respiratorias ▸ **chest measurement, chest size** anchura *f* de pecho; [*of clothes*] talla *f* (*de chaqueta etc*) ▸ **chest specialist** especialista *mf* de las vías respiratorias ▸ **chest X-ray** radiografía *f* torácica

-chested [ˈtʃestɪd] (SUFFIX) • **to be bare-chested** estar con el torso desnudo; ▹ **flat-chested**

chesterfield [ˈtʃestəfiːld] (N) (*esp US*) sofá *m*

chestnut [ˈtʃesnʌt] (N) **1** (= *fruit*) castaña *f*; (= *tree, colour*) castaño *m*
2 (= *horse*) caballo *m* castaño
3* (= *story*) historia *f* • **not that old ~!** ¡ya estamos con la misma historia de siempre!
(ADJ) (*also* **chestnut brown**) [*hair*] (de color) castaño (*inv*)
(CPD) ▸ **chestnut tree** castaño *m*

chesty* [ˈtʃestɪ] (ADJ) (COMPAR: **chestier**, SUPERL: **chestiest**) (*Brit*) [*cough*] de pecho; [*person*] que tiene el pecho cargado *or* congestionado • **you sound a bit ~** por la voz parece que tienes el pecho cargado *or* congestionado

Chetnik [ˈtʃetnɪk] (ADJ) chetnik
(N) chetnik *mf*

cheval glass [ʃəˈvælglɑːs] (N) psique *f*

chevron [ˈʃevrən] (N) (*Mil*) galón *m*; (*Heraldry*) cheurón *m*

chew [tʃuː] (N) **1** (= *action*) • **to give sth a ~** masticar algo
2 (*Brit*) (= *sweet*) caramelo *m* masticable; (= *dog treat*) golosina *f* para perros
(VT) [+ *food etc*] mascar, masticar • **the goats had ~ed off all the flower heads** las cabras se habían comido todas las flores • IDIOMS: • **to ~ sb's ass** (*US***) poner verde a algn* • **to ~**

the fat *or* rag‡ estar de palique*, dar a la lengua*, charlar
▸ **chew on** VI + PREP (= *consider*) considerar, rumiar; (= *reflect on*) dar vueltas a
▸ **chew out** VT + ADV (*US*) = **chew up**
▸ **chew over** VT + ADV (= *consider*) rumiar, considerar; (= *reflect on*) dar vueltas a
▸ **chew up** VT + ADV **1** [+ *food*] masticar bien **2** (= *damage*) estropear • **this cassette player is ~ing up all my tapes** este casete está estropeando todas mis cintas **3*** (= *scold*) echar una bronca a
chewing gum [ˈtʃuːɪŋɡʌm] N chicle *m*, goma *f* de mascar
chewy [ˈtʃuːɪ] ADJ (COMPAR: **chewier**, SUPERL: **chewiest**) difícil de masticar; [*meat*] fibroso, correoso; [*sweet*] masticable
chiaroscuro [kɪˌɑːrəsˈkʊərəʊ] N claroscuro *m*
chic [ʃiːk] ADJ elegante
N chic *m*, elegancia *f*
chicane [ʃɪˈkeɪn] N (*Sport*) chicane *f*
chicanery [ʃɪˈkeɪnərɪ] N embustes *mpl*, sofismas *mpl* • **a piece of ~** una triquiñuela
Chicano [tʃɪˈkɑːnəʊ] ADJ chicano
N chicano/a *m/f*
chichi [ˈʃiːʃiː] ADJ afectado, cursi*
chick [tʃɪk] N **1** (= *baby bird*) pajarito *m*; (= *baby hen*) pollito *m*, polluelo *m*
2‡ (= *woman*) chica *f*, chavala *f* (*Sp*)
CPD ▸ **chick flick*** comedia *f* romántica
▸ **chick lit*** *género literario en tono humorístico que trata de la vida cotidiana y amorosa de mujeres jóvenes, sobre todo solteras y de la clase media urbana*
chickadee [ˈtʃɪkədiː] N carbonero *m*
chicken [ˈtʃɪkɪn] N (= *hen*) gallina *f*; (= *cock*) pollo *m*; (*as food*) pollo; (= *coward**) gallina *mf* • **roast ~** pollo *m* asado • IDIOMS: • **to be ~*** dejarse intimidar, acobardarse • **to play ~*** jugar a quién es más valiente • **it's a ~ and egg situation** es aquello de la gallina y el huevo • **the ~s are coming home to roost** ahora se ven las consecuencias • PROVERB: • **don't count your ~s before they're hatched** no hagas las cuentas de la lechera; ▹ **spring**
CPD ▸ **chicken breast** pechuga *f* de pollo
▸ **chicken drumstick** muslo *m* de pollo
▸ **chicken farmer** avicultor(a) *m/f* ▸ **chicken farming** avicultura *f* ▸ **chicken feed** (*lit*) pienso *m* para gallinas • **it's ~ feed to him** para él es una bagatela ▸ **chicken liver** hígado *m* de pollo ▸ **chicken nuggets** nuggets *mpl* de pollo ▸ **chicken run** corral *m*
▸ **chicken wing** alita *f* de pollo ▸ **chicken wire** tela *f* metálica, alambrada *f*
▸ **chicken out*** VI + ADV rajarse • **to ~ out of sth/doing sth: he ~ed out of the audition** se rajó y no se presentó a la prueba • **he ~ed out of asking her to dinner** se rajó y no la invitó a cenar, no se atrevió a invitarla a cenar
chicken-hearted [ˈtʃɪkɪnˌhɑːtɪd] ADJ cobarde, gallina
chickenpox [ˈtʃɪkɪnpɒks] N varicela *f*
chickenshit‡ [ˈtʃɪkɪnʃɪt] N (*US*) **1** (= *coward*) gallina‡ *mf*
2 • **to be ~** (= *worthless*) no valer un pimiento*
chickpea [ˈtʃɪkpiː] N garbanzo *m*
chickweed [ˈtʃɪkwiːd] N pamplina *f*
chicory [ˈtʃɪkərɪ] N (*in coffee*) achicoria *f*; (*as salad*) escarola *f*
chide [tʃaɪd] (PT: **chid**, PP: **chidden**, **chid**) VT (*liter*) reprender
chief [tʃiːf] ADJ (= *principal*) [*reason etc*] principal, mayor; (*in rank*) jefe, de más categoría
N [*of organization*] jefe/a *m/f*; [*of tribe*] jefe/a *m/f*, cacique *m*; (= *boss**) jefe/a *m/f*, patrón/ona *m/f* • **yes, ~!** ¡sí, jefe! • **Chief of Staff** (*Mil*) Jefe del Estado Mayor • **... in ~** ... en jefe
CPD ▸ **chief assistant** primer(a) ayudante *m/f* ▸ **chief constable** (*Brit*) jefe/a *m/f* de policía ▸ **chief executive** (*Brit*) (*local government*) director(a) *m/f*; [*of company*] (*also* **chief executive officer**) presidente *mf*
▸ **chief financial officer** director(a) *m/f* financiero/a ▸ **chief inspector** (*Brit*) (*Police*) inspector(a) *m/f* jefe ▸ **chief justice** (*US*) presidente/a *m/f* del Tribunal Supremo
▸ **chief of police** ≈ jefe/a *m/f* de policía
▸ **chief operating officer** director(a) *m/f* general, presidente *mf* del consejo de administración ▸ **chief superintendent** (*Brit*) (*Police*) comisario/a *m/f* jefe/a
chiefly [ˈtʃiːflɪ] ADV principalmente, sobre todo
chieftain [ˈtʃiːftən] N jefe/a *m/f*, cacique *m* (*LAm*)
chiffchaff [ˈtʃɪftʃæf] N mosquitero *m* común
chiffon [ˈʃɪfɒn] N gasa *f*
CPD de gasa
chignon [ˈʃiːnjɔːŋ] N moño *m*
chihuahua [tʃɪˈwɑːwɑː] N chihuahua *m*
chilblain [ˈtʃɪlbleɪn] N sabañón *m*
child [tʃaɪld] N (PL: **children**) niño/a *m/f*; (= *son/daughter*) hijo/a *m/f*; (*Jur*) (= *non-adult*) menor *mf* • **I have known him since he was a ~** lo conozco desde niño • **to be with ~**† estar encinta • **to get sb with ~**† dejar a algn encinta • **it's ~'s play** es un juego de niños
CPD ▸ **child abduction** secuestro *m* de menores ▸ **child abuse** (*with violence*) malos tratos *mpl* a niños; (*sexual*) abuso *m* sexual de niños ▸ **child abuser** (*with violence*) *persona que maltrata a un niño*; (*sexual*) *persona que abusa sexualmente de un niño* ▸ **child actor** niño *m* actor, niña *f* actriz ▸ **child benefit** subsidio *m* familiar (por hijos) ▸ **child bride** (*lit*) novia *f* niña • **I was a ~ bride for my much older husband** (*fig*) era una niña para mi marido, que era mucho mayor que yo ▸ **child cruelty** crueldad *f* con los niños ▸ **child development** desarrollo *m* del niño ▸ **child genius** (= *prodigy*) niño/a *m/f* prodigio ▸ **child guidance** psicopedagogía *f* ▸ **child guidance centre** centro *m* psicopedagógico ▸ **child labour**, **child labor** (*US*) trabajo *m* de menores ▸ **child lock** (*on door*) cerradura *f* de seguridad para niños ▸ **child prodigy** niño/a *m/f* prodigio ▸ **child psychologist** psicólogo/a *m/f* infantil ▸ **child rearing** educación *f* de los niños ▸ **children's home** centro *m* de acogida de menores ▸ **children's literature** literatura *f* infantil ▸ **child restraint** dispositivo *m* de seguridad para niños
▸ **child seat** (*in car*) asiento *m* para niños
▸ **child sex abuser** autor(a) *m/f* de delitos sexuales contra menores ▸ **child star** artista *mf* infantil ▸ **child welfare** protección *f* a *or* de la infancia

CHILDREN IN NEED

La organización benéfica **Children in Need** (Niños Necesitados), fundada por la **BBC** en 1972, recauda dinero en beneficio de los niños necesitados en el Reino Unido y en el extranjero. Se la conoce sobre todo por los **telethons** (telemaratones) que organiza anualmente: los programas de TV en los que se invita a los televidentes a llamar para hacer donativos y a organizar sus propias campañas de ayuda para niños enfermos, minusválidos, pobres etc

childbearing [ˈtʃaɪldˌbeərɪŋ] N (= *act*) parto *m*; (*as statistic*) natalidad *f*
ADJ • **~ women** las mujeres fecundas, las mujeres que producen hijos • **women of ~ age** las mujeres en edad de tener hijos
childbed [ˈtʃaɪldbed] N parturición *f*
childbirth [ˈtʃaɪldbɜːθ] N parto *m* • **to die in ~** morir de parto
childcare [ˈtʃaɪldkɛəʳ] N cuidado *m* de los niños
CPD ▸ **childcare facilities** guarderías *fpl*
▸ **childcare provider** (= *person*) cuidador(a) *m/f* de niños; (= *organization*) organización *f* que cuida de niños
childhood [ˈtʃaɪldhʊd] N niñez *f*, infancia *f* • **from ~** desde niño • IDIOM: • **to be in one's second ~** estar en su segunda infancia; ▹ **sweetheart**
childish [ˈtʃaɪldɪʃ] ADJ **1** (*esp pej*) infantil, pueril • **don't be ~!** ¡no seas niño!
2 [*disease*] infantil, de la infancia • **~ ailment** enfermedad *f* infantil *or* de la infancia
childishly [ˈtʃaɪldɪʃlɪ] ADV de modo infantil *or* pueril, como un niño
childishness [ˈtʃaɪldɪʃnɪs] N infantilismo *m*, puerilidad *f*
childless [ˈtʃaɪldlɪs] ADJ sin hijos
childlike [ˈtʃaɪldlaɪk] ADJ de niño • **with a ~ faith** con una confianza ingenua
Childline [ˈtʃaɪldlaɪn] N (*Brit*) ≈ Teléfono del Menor (*Sp*), ≈ Teléfono de la Infancia (*Sp*), *servicio telefónico al cual niños y adolescentes pueden llamar para pedir ayuda en situaciones de maltrato o abuso, o para obtener información*
childminder [ˈtʃaɪldˌmaɪndəʳ] N (*Brit*) niñera *f*
childminding [ˈtʃaɪldˌmaɪndɪŋ] N (*Brit*) cuidado *m* de niños
childproof [ˈtʃaɪldˌpruːf] ADJ a prueba de niños • **child-proof (door) lock** cerradura *f* de seguridad para niños
children [ˈtʃɪldrən] NPL *of* **child**
child-resistant [ˈtʃaɪldrɪˌzɪstənt] ADJ = **childproof**
Chile [ˈtʃɪlɪ] N Chile *m*
Chilean [ˈtʃɪlɪən] ADJ chileno
N chileno/a *m/f*
chili [ˈtʃɪlɪ] N = **chilli**
chill [tʃɪl] N (= *coldness*) frío *m*; (*Med*) resfriado *m*; (= *mild fever*) escalofrío *m*
• **there's a ~ in the air** hace fresco • **to catch a ~** (*Med*) resfriarse • **to cast a ~ over** enfriar el ambiente de • **to take the ~ off** [+ *room*] calentar un poco, templar; [+ *wine*] templar
ADJ [*wind*] frío
VT [+ *wine*] enfriar; [+ *food*] refrigerar
• **serve ~ed** sírvase bien frío • **to ~ sb's blood** (*fig*) helarle la sangre en las venas a algn • **to be ~ed to the bone** estar helado hasta los huesos
VI* = **chill out**
▸ **chill out*** VI + ADV (*esp US*) tranquilizarse, relajarse • **~ out, man!** ¡tranqui tronco!*
chillax* [tʃɪˈlæks] VI relajarse
chilled out* [ˌtʃɪldˈaʊt] ADJ (= *relaxed*) relajado, desestresado*
chiller [ˈtʃɪləʳ] N (= *film*) película *f* de terror
chilli [ˈtʃɪlɪ] N (PL: **chillies**) (*also* **chilli pepper**) chile *m*, ají *m* (*S. Cone*), guindilla *f* (*Sp*) • **~ con carne** chile con carne • **~ powder** chile *m* en polvo • **~ sauce** salsa *f* de ají
chilliness [ˈtʃɪlɪnɪs] N frío *m*; (*fig*) frialdad *f*
chilling [ˈtʃɪlɪŋ] ADJ (*fig*) escalofriante
chillingly [ˈtʃɪlɪŋlɪ] ADV (= *frighteningly*) [*similar, familiar*] escalofriantemente
chillness [ˈtʃɪlnɪs] N = **chilliness**
chill-out* [ˈtʃɪlaʊt] ADJ [*music*] relajante
chilly [ˈtʃɪlɪ] ADJ (COMPAR: **chillier**, SUPERL: **chilliest**) **1** (= *cold*) [*weather, water, day, room*] frío • **to be** *or* **feel ~** [*person*] tener frío • **I feel a bit ~** tengo un poco de frío • **it's ~ today** hace fresquito hoy
2 (= *unfriendly*) frío
chime [tʃaɪm] N (= *sound*) [*of church bells*]

repique *m*; [*of clock*] campanada *f*; (= *set*) juego *m* de campanas, carillón *m* • **a ~ of bells** un carillón
VT [+ *bell*] tocar
VI repicar, sonar • **the clock ~d six** el reloj dio las seis
▸ **chime in*** VI + ADV (= *butt in*) meter baza; (= *say*) decir • **to ~ in with** (*in conversation*) meter baza hablando de; (= *harmonize*) estar en armonía con

C

chimera [kaɪˈmɪərə] N quimera *f*
chimerical [kaɪˈmerɪkəl] ADJ quimérico
chiming [ˈtʃaɪmɪŋ] ADJ • **~ clock** reloj *m* de carillón
N [*of church bells*] repiqueteo *m*; [*of clock*] campanadas *fpl*
chimney [ˈtʃɪmnɪ] N **1** [*of building*] chimenea *f*
2 [*of lamp*] tubo *m*
3 (*Mountaineering*) olla *f*, chimenea *f*
CPD ▸ **chimney breast** (*Brit*) campana *f* de chimenea ▸ **chimney corner** rincón *m* de la chimenea ▸ **chimney pot** cañón *m* de chimenea ▸ **chimney stack** fuste *m* de chimenea ▸ **chimney sweep** deshollinador(a) *m/f*
chimneypiece [ˈtʃɪmnɪ,piːs] N (*Brit*) repisa *f* de chimenea
chimp* [tʃɪmp] N = **chimpanzee**
chimpanzee [,tʃɪmpænˈziː] N chimpancé *m*
chin [tʃɪn] N barbilla *f*, mentón *m* • **double ~** papada *f* • IDIOMS: • **to keep one's ~ up*** no desanimarse • **(keep your) ~ up!** ¡no te desanimes!, ¡ánimo! • **to take it on the ~*** encajar el golpe; (*fig*) (= *put up with*) soportarlo
VT (*Brit**) (= *punch*) dar una hostia a*; (= *reprimand*) echar un rapapolvo a*
VI (*US**) charlar; ▹ **chuck**[1]
China [ˈtʃaɪnə] N China *f*
CPD ▸ **China Sea** mar *m* de China ▸ **China tea** té *m* de China
china[1] [ˈtʃaɪnə] N (= *crockery*) loza *f*, vajilla *f*; (= *fine china*) porcelana *f*
CPD [*cup, plate etc*] de porcelana ▸ **china cabinet** vitrina *f* de la porcelana ▸ **china clay** caolín *m* ▸ **china doll** muñeca *f* de porcelana
china[2]†* [ˈtʃaɪnə] N amigo *m*, compinche *m* • **here you are, my old ~** toma, macho*
Chinaman†††‡ [ˈtʃaɪnəmən] N (PL: **Chinamen**) chino *m*
Chinatown [ˈtʃaɪnətaʊn] N barrio *m* chino
chinaware [ˈtʃaɪnəweəʳ] N porcelana *f*
chinch [ˈtʃɪntʃ], **chinch bug** N (*US*) chinche *m* or *f* de los cereales
chinchilla [tʃɪnˈtʃɪlə] N chinchilla *f*
chin-chin†* [,tʃɪnˈtʃɪn] EXCL ¡chin-chin!
Chinese [,tʃaɪˈniːz] ADJ chino • **a ~ man** un chino • **a ~ woman** una china
N **1** (= *person*) chino/a *m/f* • **the ~** (= *people*) los chinos
2 (*Ling*) chino *m*
CPD ▸ **Chinese chequers** damas *fpl* chinas ▸ **Chinese lantern** farolillo *m* chino ▸ **Chinese leaves** col *fsing* china
Chink*‡ [tʃɪŋk] N (*offensive*) chino/a *m/f*
chink[1] [tʃɪŋk] N (= *slit*) (*in wall*) grieta *f*, hendidura *f*; (*in door*) resquicio *m* • **a ~ of light** un hilo de luz • IDIOM: • **it's the ~ in his armour** es su punto débil *or* su talón de Aquiles
chink[2] [tʃɪŋk] N (= *sound*) sonido *m* metálico, tintineo *m*
VT [+ *metal*] hacer sonar; [+ *glass*] hacer tintinear
VI [*metal*] sonar; [*glass*] tintinear
chinless [ˈtʃɪnlɪs] ADJ (*fig*) (= *spineless*) apocado

chinos [ˈtʃiːnəʊz] NPL chinos *mpl* (*pantalones de algodón a veces con pinzas*)
chintz [tʃɪnts] N cretona *f*
chintzy [ˈtʃɪntsɪ] ADJ **1** [*style*] coqueto
2 (*US*) (= *poor-quality*) basto, ordinario
chin-ups [ˈtʃɪnʌps] NPL • **to do chin-ups** hacer flexiones (de brazos) (*en barra o espalderas*)
chinwag* [ˈtʃɪnwæg] N • **to have a ~** charlar, darle al palique
chip [tʃɪp] N **1** (= *piece*) pedacito *m*; (= *splinter*) [*of glass, wood*] astilla *f*; (= *stone*) lasca *f* • IDIOMS: • **he's a ~ off the old block** de tal palo tal astilla • **to have a ~ on one's shoulder** ser un resentido
2 (*Culin*) **chips** (*Brit*) (= *French fries*) patatas *fpl* fritas, papas *fpl* fritas (*esp LAm*); (*US*) (= *crisps*) patatas *fpl* (fritas) de bolsa, chips *mpl*
3 (= *break, mark*) mella *f*; (*on rim of vessel*) desportilladura *f*
4 (*Gambling*) ficha *f* • IDIOMS: • **he's had his ~s*** se le acabó la suerte • **to hand** *or* **cash in one's ~s*** palmarla* • **when the ~s are down** cuando llega el momento de la verdad
5 (*Comput*) chip *m*
6 (*Golf*) (= *chip shot*) chip *m*
VT [+ *cup, plate*] desconchar, desportillar; [+ *furniture*] desportillar; [+ *surface*] picar; [+ *paint, varnish*] desconchar, desprender
VI [*pottery*] desconcharse, desportillarse; [*paint, varnish*] desconcharse
CPD ▸ **chip and PIN** *tecnología de identificación del usuario mediante una tarjeta chip que debe ir acompañada por un número PIN* ▸ **chip and PIN card** tarjeta *f* chip con número PIN ▸ **chip basket** (*Brit*) (*for deep-fat fryer*) cubeta *f* ▸ **chip pan** (*Brit*) sartén *f* ▸ **chip shop*** pescadería *f* (*donde se vende principalmente pescado rebozado y patatas fritas*)
▸ **chip away** VT + ADV [+ *paint, varnish*] desconchar
VI + ADV [*paint, varnish*] desconcharse • **to ~ away at** [+ *lands*] ir usurpando; [+ *authority*] ir minando *or* debilitando • **they ~ped away at her resistance** fueron debilitando su resistencia
▸ **chip in*** VI + ADV **1** (= *contribute*) contribuir (**with** con); (= *share costs*) compartir los gastos
2 (= *interrupt*) interrumpir (**with** diciendo)
▸ **chip off** VI + ADV [*paint etc*] desconcharse, desprenderse (en escamas)
VT + ADV [+ *paint etc*] desconchar, desprender
chip-based [ˈtʃɪp,beɪst] ADJ • **chip-based technology** tecnología *f* a base de microchips
chipboard [ˈtʃɪpbɔːd] N madera *f* aglomerada, aglomerado *m*
chipmunk [ˈtʃɪpmʌŋk] N ardilla *f* listada
chipolata [,tʃɪpəˈlɑːtə] N (*Brit*) salchicha *f* fina
chipped [ˈtʃɪpt] ADJ [*bone, tooth*] astillado; [*mug, glass, paint*] desconchado, desportillado; [*enamel*] picado
chipper* [ˈtʃɪpəʳ] ADJ alegre, contento
chippings [ˈtʃɪpɪŋz] NPL gravilla *fsing* • **"loose chippings"** "gravilla suelta"
chippy* [ˈtʃɪpɪ] N **1** (*US*) tía* *f*, fulana* *f*
2 (*Brit*) *tienda que vende pescado frito con patatas fritas*
chiromancer [ˈkaɪərəmænsəʳ] N quiromántico/a *m/f*, quiromante *mf*
chiropodist [kɪˈrɒpədɪst] N (*Brit*) podólogo/a *m/f*, pedicuro/a *m/f*
chiropody [kɪˈrɒpədɪ] N (*Brit*) podología *f*, pedicura *f*
chiropractic [,kaɪərəʊˈpræktɪk] ADJ quiropráctico
N quiropráctica *f*

chiropractor [ˈkaɪrəʊ,præktəʳ] N quiropráctico *m*
chirp [tʃɜːp] N [*of birds*] pío *m*, gorjeo *m*; [*of crickets*] chirrido *m*, canto *m*
VI [*birds*] piar, gorjear; [*crickets*] chirriar, cantar
chirping [ˈtʃɜːpɪŋ] N [*of bird*] pío *m*, gorjeo *m*; [*of grasshopper*] chirrido *m*, canto *m*
chirpy* [ˈtʃɜːpɪ] ADJ (COMPAR: **chirpier**, SUPERL: **chirpiest**) alegre, animado
chirrup [ˈtʃɪrəp] N, VI ▹ **chirp**
chisel [ˈtʃɪzl] (VB: PT, PP: **chiselled** (*Brit*) *or* **chiseled** (*US*)) N (*for wood*) formón *m*, escoplo *m*; (*for stone*) cincel *m*
VT **1** (*also* **chisel out**) [+ *wood*] tallar; [+ *stone*] cincelar; (= *carve*) tallar, labrar • **~led features** (*fig*) facciones *fpl* marcadas
2* (= *swindle*) timar, estafar
chiseller, **chiseler** (*US*) [ˈtʃɪzləʳ] N gorrón *m*
chit[1] [tʃɪt] N (= *note*) vale *m*
chit[2] [tʃɪt] N • **a ~ of a girl** una muchachita no muy crecida
chitchat [ˈtʃɪttʃæt] N (= *gossip*) chismes *mpl*, habladurías *fpl*; (= *chatter*) • **"what did you talk about?" - "oh, nothing in particular, just ~"** —¿de qué hablasteis? —de nada en particular, solo estuvimos dándole al palique
chitlings [ˈtʃɪtlɪŋz] NPL, **chitlins** [ˈtʃɪtlɪnz] NPL, **chitterlings** [ˈtʃɪtəlɪŋz] NPL menudos *mpl* de cerdo (comestibles)
chitty [ˈtʃɪtɪ] N = **chit**[1]
chiv‡ [tʃɪv] N chori‡ *m*, navaja *f*
chivalresque [ʃɪvəlˈresk] ADJ, **chivalric** [ʃɪˈvælrɪk] ADJ caballeresco
chivalrous [ˈʃɪvəlrəs] ADJ caballeroso
chivalrously [ˈʃɪvəlrəslɪ] ADV caballerosamente
chivalry [ˈʃɪvəlrɪ] N (= *courteousness*) caballerosidad *f*; (*in medieval times*) caballería *f*
chives [tʃaɪvz] NPL cebollinos *mpl*
chivvy* [ˈtʃɪvɪ] VT (*Brit*) perseguir, acosar • **to ~ sb into doing sth** no dejar en paz a algn hasta que hace algo
▸ **chivvy up*** VT + ADV [+ *person*] espabilar
chlamydia [klæmˈɪdɪə] N clamidia *f*
chloral [ˈklɔːrəl] N cloral *m*
chlorate [ˈklɔːreɪt] N clorato *m*
chloric [ˈklɔːrɪk] ADJ clórico
CPD ▸ **chloric acid** ácido *m* clórico
chloride [ˈklɔːraɪd] N cloruro *m*
CPD ▸ **chloride of lime** cloruro *m* de cal
chlorinate [ˈklɒrɪneɪt] VT clorar, tratar con cloro
chlorinated [ˈklɒrɪneɪtɪd] ADJ • **~ water** agua *f* clorinada
chlorination [,klɔːrɪˈneɪʃən] N cloración *f*, tratamiento *m* con cloro
chlorine [ˈklɔːriːn] N cloro *m*
CPD ▸ **chlorine monoxide** monóxido *m* de cloro ▸ **chlorine nitrate** nitrato *m* de cloro
chlorofluorocarbon [,klɔːrə,flʊərəˈkɑːbən] N clorofluorocarbono *m*
chloroform [ˈklɒrəfɔːm] N cloroformo *m*
VT cloroformizar, cloroformar (*LAm*)
chlorophyll [ˈklɒrəfɪl] N clorofila *f*
choc* [tʃɒk] N = **chocolate**
chocaholic* [,tʃɒkəˈhɒlɪk] N adicto/a *m/f* al chocolate
choc-ice [ˈtʃɒkaɪs] N (*Brit*) helado *m* cubierto de chocolate
chock [tʃɒk] N (= *wedge*) calzo *m*, cuña *f*
VT calzar, poner un calzo *or* una cuña a
chock-a-block* [ˈtʃɒkəˈblɒk] ADJ de bote en bote, hasta los topes • **chock-a-block of** *or* **with** atestado de, totalmente lleno de
chocker‡ [ˈtʃɒkəʳ] ADJ • **to be ~** estar harto (**with** de)

chock-full* ['tʃɒk'fʊl] (ADJ) atestado, lleno a rebosar

chocolate ['tʃɒklɪt] (N) chocolate *m*; (= *individual sweet*) bombón *m* • **hot** *or* **drinking ~** chocolate *m* caliente • **a box of ~s** una caja de bombones *or* chocolatinas
(CPD) [*biscuit, cake, egg*] de chocolate; [*colour*] (*also* **chocolate brown**) (de color) chocolate
▸ **chocolate bar** (*small*) chocolatina *f*; (*big*) tableta *f* de chocolate ▸ **chocolate biscuit** galleta *f* de chocolate ▸ **chocolate chip cookie** galleta *f* con pepitas de chocolate
▸ **chocolate drop** caramelo *m* de chocolate
▸ **chocolate éclair** relámpago *m* de chocolate

chocolate-box ['tʃɒklɪt,bɒks] (ADJ) [*look, picture*] de postal de Navidad

choice [tʃɔɪs] (ADJ) **1** (= *selected*) selecto, escogido; (= *high quality*) de primera calidad
2 (*hum*) [*example, remark*] apropiado, oportuno; [*language*] fino
(N) **1** (= *act of choosing*) elección *f*, selección *f*; (= *right to choose*) opción *f* • **it's your ~** • **the ~ is yours** usted elige • **for ~** preferentemente • **it was not a free ~** no pude elegir libremente • **I did it from ~** lo hice de buena gana • **he did it but not from ~** lo hizo pero de mala gana • **to make one's ~** elegir • **the house of my ~** mi casa predilecta • **the prince married the girl of his ~** el príncipe se casó con la joven que había elegido • **the drug/weapon of ~** la droga/el arma preferida • **to take one's ~** elegir • **take your ~!** ¡elija usted!, ¡escoja usted!
2 (= *thing chosen*) preferencia *f*, elección *f*
• **this book would be my ~** este libro es el que yo escogería
3 (= *variety*) surtido *m* • **we have a wide ~** (*Comm*) tenemos un gran surtido • **you have a wide ~** tienes muchas posibilidades
4 (= *option*) opción *f*, alternativa *f* • **he gave me two ~s** me dio a elegir entre dos opciones • **to have no ~** no tener alternativa, no tener opción • **he had no ~ but to go** no tuvo más remedio que ir

choir ['kwaɪəʳ] (N) **1** (*Mus*) coro *m*, coral *f*
2 (*Archit*) coro *m*
(CPD) ▸ **choir practice** • **to go to ~ practice** ir al coro ▸ **choir school** *escuela primaria para niños cantores* ▸ **choir stall** silla *f* de coro; ▹ **practice**

choirboy ['kwaɪəbɔɪ] (N) niño *m* de coro

choirmaster ['kwaɪə,mɑːstəʳ] (N) director *m* de coro, maestro *m* de coros

choke [tʃəʊk] (N) (*Aut*) (e)stárter *m*, chok(e) *m* (*LAm*); (*Mech*) obturador *m*, cierre *m*
(VT) **1** [+ *person*] ahogar, asfixiar; (*with hands*) estrangular • **in a voice ~d with emotion** con una voz ahogada *or* sofocada por la emoción
2 [+ *pipe etc*] atascar, obstruir • **a canal ~d with weeds** un canal atascado por las hierbas • **a street ~d with traffic** una calle congestionada por el tráfico
(VI) [*person*] ahogarse, asfixiarse • **to ~ to death** morir asfixiado • **to ~ on a fishbone** atragantarse con una espina • **to ~ with laughter** morirse de risa
▸ **choke back** (VT + ADV) [+ *tears*] tragarse; [+ *feelings*] ahogar
▸ **choke down** (VT + ADV) [+ *rage, sobs*] ahogar
▸ **choke off** (VT + ADV) (*fig*) [+ *supply, suggestions etc*] cortar; [+ *discussion*] cortar por lo sano; [+ *person*] cortar
▸ **choke up** (VT + ADV) [+ *pipe, drain*] obstruir
(VI + ADV) **1** [*pipe, drain*] atascarse
2 [*person*] quedarse sin habla

choked ['tʃəʊkt] (ADJ) **1** (= *strangled*) • **a ~ cry** un grito ahogado *or* entrecortado • **in a ~ voice** con voz entrecortada • **~ with emotion** ahogado por la emoción
2 (*Brit**) (= *angry, upset*) disgustado • **I still feel ~ about him leaving** aún me dura el disgusto de que se fuera

choker ['tʃəʊkəʳ] (N) **1** (= *necklace*) gargantilla *f*; (*hum*) cuello *m* alto
2 (*Mech*) obturador *m*
3* (= *disappointment*) fastidio *m*
4 (*esp US**) (= *person*) agobiado/a* *m/f*

choking ['tʃəʊkɪŋ] (ADJ) asfixiador, asfixiante
(N) ahogo *m*, asfixia *f*

choky‡ ['tʃəʊkɪ] (N) (= *prison*) trena‡ *f*; (= *cell*) unidad *f* de aislamiento

cholera ['kɒlərə] (N) cólera *m*

choleric ['kɒlərɪk] (ADJ) colérico

cholesterol [kə'lestərɒl] (N) colesterol *m*

chomp* [tʃɒmp] (VT) mascar
(VI) mascar; ▹ **bit²**

Chomskyan ['tʃɒmskɪən] (ADJ) de Chomsky, chomskiano

choo-choo* ['tʃuːtʃuː] (N) (*Brit*) (*child language*) chu-chu *m*, tren *m*

choose [tʃuːz] (PT: **chose**, PP: **chosen**) (VT)
1 (*gen*) elegir, escoger; (= *select*) [+ *team*] seleccionar; [+ *candidate*] elegir • **he was chosen (as) leader** fue elegido líder • **there is nothing to ~ between them** vale tanto el uno como el otro, no veo la diferencia entre ellos
2 (= *opt*) • **to ~ to do sth** optar por hacer algo
• **if I don't ~ to** si no quiero
(VI) elegir, escoger • **to ~ between** elegir entre • **there are several to ~ from** hay varios entre los que elegir • **as/when I ~** como/cuando me parezca*, como/cuando me dé la gana (*Sp**)

choosey, choosy ['tʃuːzɪ] (ADJ) (COMPAR: **choosier**, SUPERL: **choosiest**) (*gen*) exigente; (*about food*) delicado; (= *touchy*) quisquilloso
• **he's a bit ~ about it** en esto es algo difícil de contentar • **I'm ~ about who I go out with** yo no salgo con un cualquiera • **in his position he can't be ~** su posición no le permite darse el lujo de escoger

chop¹ [tʃɒp] (N) **1** (= *blow*) golpe *m* cortante; (= *cut*) tajo *m*
2 (*Culin*) chuleta *f*
3 (*Brit**) (*fig*) • **to get the ~** [*project*] ser rechazado *or* desechado; [*person*] (= *be sacked*) ser despedido • **to give sb the ~** despedir a algn • **he's for the ~** le van a despedir • **this programme is for the ~** este programa se va a suprimir
(VT) **1** [+ *wood*] cortar, talar; [+ *meat, vegetables*] picar • **to ~ one's way through** abrirse camino a con un machete
2 (*Brit**) [+ *person*] despedir
3 (*Sport*) [+ *ball*] cortar
▸ **chop at** (VI + PREP) tratar de tajar
▸ **chop down** (VT + ADV) [+ *tree*] talar
▸ **chop off** (VT + ADV) **1** (*lit*) cortar de un tajo
• **they ~ped off his head** le cortaron la cabeza
2 (*fig*) recortar, reducir
▸ **chop up** (VT + ADV) desmenuzar; [+ *meat*] picar

chop² [tʃɒp] (VI) (*Brit**) • **to ~ and change** cambiar constantemente de opinión

chopped almonds [,tʃɒpt'ɑːməndz] (NPL) almendras *fpl* picadas

chopper ['tʃɒpəʳ] (N) **1** (= *axe*) hacha *f*; [*of butcher*] tajadera *f*, cuchilla *f*
2* (= *helicopter*) helicóptero *m*; (*Brit*) (= *bicycle*) *bicicleta de manillar alto y asiento alargado*; (*US*) (= *motorbike*) *motocicleta de manillar alto y asiento alargado*

chopping ['tʃɒpɪŋ] (CPD) ▸ **chopping block, chopping board** tajo *m*, tabla *f* de cortar
▸ **chopping knife** tajadera *f*, cuchilla *f*

choppy ['tʃɒpɪ] (ADJ) (COMPAR: **choppier**, SUPERL: **choppiest**) [*sea, weather*] picado, agitado

chops* [tʃɒps] (NPL) (*Anat*) boca *fsing*, labios *mpl* • **to lick one's ~** relamerse, chuparse los dedos

chopsticks ['tʃɒpstɪks] (NPL) palillos *mpl*

chop suey [,tʃɒp'suːɪ] (N) chop suey *m*

choral ['kɔːrəl] (ADJ) coral
(CPD) ▸ **choral society** orfeón *m*

chorale [kɒ'rɑːl] (N) coral *m*

chord [kɔːd] (N) **1** (*Mus*) acorde *m* • IDIOMS:
• **to strike a ~** sonarle (algo a uno) • **we must strike a common ~** tenemos que encontrar un punto en común • **this struck a responsive ~ with everyone** esto produjo una reacción positiva en todos • **to touch the right ~** despertar emociones
2 (*Math, Anat*) cuerda *f*

chore [tʃɔːʳ] (N) faena *f*, tarea *f*; (*pej*) tarea *f* rutinaria • **to do the (household) ~s** hacer los quehaceres domésticos

choreograph ['kɒrɪə,græf] (VT) coreografiar

choreographer [,kɒrɪ'ɒgrəfəʳ] (N) coreógrafo/a *m/f*

choreographic [,kɒrɪəʊ'græfɪk] (ADJ) coreográfico

choreography [,kɒrɪ'ɒgrəfɪ] (N) coreografía *f*

chorister ['kɒrɪstəʳ] (N) corista *mf*; (*US*) director(a) *m/f* de un coro

chortle ['tʃɔːtl] (N) risa *f* alegre
(VI) reírse alegremente • **to ~ over sth** reírse satisfecho por algo

chorus ['kɔːrəs] (N) (PL: **choruses**) **1** [*of singers, play*] coro *m*; (*in musical*) conjunto *m* • **in ~** a coro • **to sing in ~** cantar a coro
2 (= *refrain*) estribillo *m* • **to join in the ~** unirse en el estribillo
3 (*fig*) • **a ~ of praise greeted the book** el libro fue recibido por un coro de aprobación *or* alabanzas • **a ~ of shouts greeted this** esto fue recibido por un coro de exclamaciones
(VT) (= *speak in unison*) decir a coro; (= *answer*) contestar a coro
(CPD) ▸ **chorus girl** corista *f* ▸ **chorus line** línea *f* de coro

chose [tʃəʊz] (PT) *of* choose

chosen ['tʃəʊzn] (PP) *of* choose
(ADJ) preferido, predilecto • **the ~ few** la minoría privilegiada • **the Chosen (People)** el pueblo elegido • **their ~ representative** el representante que han elegido
(N) • **one of the ~** uno de los elegidos

chough [tʃʌf] (N) chova *f* (piquirroja)

choux pastry ['ʃuː'peɪstrɪ] (N) masa *f* de profiteroles

chow¹ [tʃaʊ] (N) (= *dog*) chow-chow *m*, perro *m* chino

chow²‡ [tʃaʊ] (N) (*esp US*) (= *food*) comida *f*

chowder ['tʃaʊdəʳ] (N) (*esp US*) sopa *f* de pescado

chow mein [tʃaʊ'meɪn] (N) *plato de la cocina china de tallarines rehogados con carne o verduras*

Chris [krɪs] (N) *familiar form of* **Christopher**

Christ [kraɪst] (N) Cristo *m*
(EXCL) • **~!**‡ ¡hostia(s)!*, ¡carajo! (*LAm*)
(CPD) ▸ **Christ Child** • **the ~ Child** el Niño *m* Jesús

christen ['krɪsn] (VT) **1** (*Rel*) bautizar
2 (= *name*) bautizar con el nombre de • **they ~ed him Jack after his uncle** le pusieron Jack como su tío
3* (= *use for first time*) estrenar

Christendom ['krɪsndəm] (N) cristiandad *f*

christening ['krɪsnɪŋ] (N) bautizo *m*, bautismo *m*
(CPD) ▸ **christening gown, christening robe** faldón *m* de bautizo

Christian ['krɪstɪən] (ADJ) cristiano
(N) cristiano/a *m/f*
(CPD) ▸ **Christian Democrat** (*Pol*)

democratacristiano/a *m/f*, democristiano/a *m/f* ▸ **Christian Democrat(ic) Party** (*Pol*) partido *m* democratacristiano, partido *m* democristiano ▸ **Christian name** nombre *m* de pila ▸ **Christian Science** Ciencia *f* Cristiana ▸ **Christian Scientist** Científico/a *m/f* Cristiano/a

C

Christianity [ˌkrɪstɪˈænɪtɪ] (N) cristianismo *m*

Christianize [ˈkrɪstɪənaɪz] (VT) cristianizar

Christlike [ˈkraɪstlaɪk] (ADJ) como Cristo

Christmas [ˈkrɪsməs] (N) Navidad *f*; (= *season*) Navidades *fpl* • **at ~** en Navidad, por Navidades • **happy** *or* **merry ~!** ¡Feliz Navidad!, ¡Felices Pascuas!; ▹ **father**
(CPD) [*decorations, festivities*] de Navidad, navideño/a ▸ **Christmas box** (*Brit*) aguinaldo *m* ▸ **Christmas cake** pastel *m* de Navidad, tarta *f* de Navidad ▸ **Christmas card** crismas *m inv*, tarjeta *f* de Navidad ▸ **Christmas carol** villancico *m* ▸ **Christmas club** club *m* de ahorros (*que los reparte por Navidades*) ▸ **Christmas cracker** *tubito con decoración navideña que contiene un pequeño regalo sorpresa y que se abre al tirar dos personas de sus extremos* ▸ **Christmas Day** día *m* de Navidad ▸ **Christmas dinner** comida *f* de Navidad ▸ **Christmas Eve** Nochebuena *f* ▸ **Christmas hamper** cesta *f* de Navidad ▸ **Christmas Island** isla *f* Christmas ▸ **Christmas lights** luces *fpl* de Navidad ▸ **Christmas party** fiesta *f* de Navidad ▸ **Christmas present** regalo *m* de Navidad ▸ **Christmas pudding** (*esp Brit*) pudín *m* de Navidad ▸ **Christmas rose** eléboro *m* negro ▸ **Christmas shopping** • **to do one's ~ shopping** hacer las compras de Navidad ▸ **Christmas stocking** ≈ zapatos *mpl* de Reyes ▸ **Christmas time** Navidades *fpl*, Pascua *f* de Navidad ▸ **Christmas tree** árbol *m* de Navidad

> **CHRISTMAS DINNER**
> La comida de Navidad (**Christmas dinner**) que se celebra en familia el día 25, es un momento central de las celebraciones navideñas. En ella se suele comer pavo relleno asado (**roast turkey with stuffing**) acompañado de coles de Bruselas y patatas asadas. En el Reino Unido el postre tradicional es **Christmas pudding**, un pastel hecho a base de frutas secas, especias y brandy al que se le añade **brandy butter**, una mezcla de mantequilla, azúcar y brandy.

Christmassy* [ˈkrɪsməsɪ] (ADJ) navideño, propio de Navidad

Christopher [ˈkrɪstəfəʳ] (N) Cristóbal

chromatic [krəˈmætɪk] (ADJ) (*Mus, Tech*) cromático
(CPD) ▸ **chromatic scale** (*Mus*) escala *f* cromática

chromatogram [krəʊˈmætəˌgræm] (N) cromatograma *m*

chromatography [ˌkrəʊməˈtɒgrəfɪ] (N) cromatografía *f*

chrome [krəʊm] (N) cromo *m*
(CPD) ▸ **chrome steel** acero *m* al cromo, acerocromo *m* ▸ **chrome yellow** amarillo *m* de cromo

chromium [ˈkrəʊmɪəm] (N) cromo *m*
(CPD) ▸ **chromium plating** cromado *m*

chromium-plated [ˈkrəʊmɪəmˌpleɪtɪd] (ADJ) cromado

chromosomal [ˌkrəʊməˈsəʊməl] (ADJ) cromosomático, cromosómico

chromosome [ˈkrəʊməsəʊm] (N) cromosoma *m*

chronic [ˈkrɒnɪk] (ADJ) **1** [*invalid, disease*] crónico
2 (= *inveterate*) [*smoker*] empedernido; [*liar*] incorregible
3 (*Brit**) [*weather, person*] horrible, malísimo • **I had toothache something ~** me dolían las muelas horriblemente
(CPD) ▸ **chronic fatigue syndrome** síndrome *m* de fatiga crónica ▸ **chronic wasting disease** enfermedad *f* del desgaste crónico

chronically [ˈkrɒnɪkəlɪ] (ADV) • **to be ~ sick** sufrir una enfermedad crónica • **beer is ~ scarce** hay una escasez permanente de cerveza

chronicle [ˈkrɒnɪkl] (N) crónica *f* • **Chronicles** (*Bible*) Crónicas *fpl*
(VT) (= *recount*) hacer una crónica de

chronicler [ˈkrɒnɪkləʳ] (N) cronista *mf*

chronograph [ˈkrəʊnəˌgrɑːf] (N) (= *technical instrument*) cronógrafo *m*; (= *stopwatch*) cronómetro *m*

chronological [ˌkrɒnəˈlɒdʒɪkəl] (ADJ) cronológico • **in ~ order** en orden cronológico

chronologically [ˌkrɒnəˈlɒdʒɪkəlɪ] (ADV) por orden cronológico

chronology [krəˈnɒlədʒɪ] (N) cronología *f*

chronometer [krəˈnɒmɪtəʳ] (N) cronómetro *m*

chrysalis [ˈkrɪsəlɪs] (N) (PL: **chrysalises** [ˈkrɪsəlɪsɪz]) (*Bio*) crisálida *f*

chrysanth* [krɪˈsænθ] (N) (*Brit*) = **chrysanthemum**

chrysanthemum [krɪˈsænθəməm] (N) crisantemo *m*

chub [tʃʌb] (N) (PL: **chub** *or* **chubs**) cacho *m*

chubby [ˈtʃʌbɪ] (ADJ) (COMPAR: **chubbier**, SUPERL: **chubbiest**) [*baby, hands*] rechoncho, regordete; [*face, cheeks*] mofletudo

chuck¹ [tʃʌk] (N) **1*** (= *throw*) tiro *m*, echada *f*
2* • **to get the ~** (*from job*) ser despedido • **to give sb the ~** (*from relationship*) dar la patada a algn*, plantar a algn*
3 • **a ~ under the chin** una palmada cariñosa en la barbilla
(VT) **1*** (= *throw*) tirar, echar
2* (= *throw away*) (*also* **chuck away**) tirar, botar (*LAm*); [+ *money*] tirar; [+ *chance*] desperdiciar
3* (= *give up*) (*also* **chuck up, chuck in**) [+ *job*] dejar, plantar*; [+ *boyfriend, girlfriend*] dar la patada a*, plantar* • **so I had to ~ it** así que tuve que dejarlo • **~ it!** ¡basta ya!, ¡déjalo!
4 • **to ~ sb under the chin** dar una palmada cariñosa bajo la barbilla a algn
▸ **chuck away*** (VT + ADV) [+ *old clothes, books*] tirar, botar (*LAm*); [+ *money*] despilfarrar; [+ *chance*] desperdiciar
▸ **chuck in*** (VT + ADV) abandonar, renunciar a • **I'm thinking of ~ing it in** estoy pensando en mandarlo a paseo
▸ **chuck out*** (VT + ADV) [+ *rubbish*] tirar, botar (*LAm*); [+ *person*] echar (fuera); [+ *employee*] despedir, dar el pasaporte a*
▸ **chuck up** (VT + ADV)* abandonar, renunciar a
(VI + ADV) (*US‡*) (= *vomit*) arrojar*

chuck² [tʃʌk] (N) **1** (*also* **chuck steak**) bistec *m* de pobre
2 (*US‡*) (= *food*) manduca* *f*; ▹ **DUDE RANCH**
(CPD) ▸ **chuck wagon** carromato *m* de provisiones

chuck³ [tʃʌk] = **chock**

chuck⁴ [tʃʌk] (N) (*Tech*) portabrocas *m inv*

chucker-out* [ˈtʃʌkərˈaʊt] (N) (*Brit*) gorila *m* (*en la entrada de un local*)

chuckle [ˈtʃʌkl] (N) risita *f*, risa *f* sofocada • **we had a good ~ over that** nos reímos bastante con eso
(VI) reírse entre dientes, soltar una risita • **to ~ at** *or* **over** reírse con

chuddar [ˈtʃʌdəʳ] (N) chador *m*

chuffed* [tʃʌft] (ADJ) (*Brit*) (= *pleased*) satisfecho, contento • **he was pretty ~ about it** estaba la mar de contento por eso

chug [tʃʌg] (VI) [*steam engine*] resoplar; [*motor*] traquetear • **the train ~ged past** pasó el tren resoplando
▸ **chug along** (VI + ADV) [*car, train*] ir despacio resoplando; (*fig*) ir tirando

chukka, chukker [ˈtʃʌkəʳ] (N) (*Polo*) tiempo *m* de un partido de polo

chum* [tʃʌm] (N) amiguete* *m*, colega *mf*, cuate *mf* (*Mex**), pata *mf* (*Peru**); (= *child*) amiguito/a *m/f*; (*in direct address*) amigo • **to be great ~s** ser íntimos amigos • **to be ~s with sb** ser amigo de algn
▸ **chum up*** (VI + ADV) hacerse amigos • **to ~ up with sb** hacerse amigo de algn

chummy* [ˈtʃʌmɪ] (ADJ) (COMPAR: **chummier**, SUPERL: **chummiest**) muy amigo • **they're very ~** son muy amigos • **he's very ~ with the boss** es muy amigo del jefe • **he got ~ with the boss** se hizo amigo del jefe

chump [tʃʌmp] (N) **1*** (= *idiot*) tonto/a *m/f* • **you ~!** ¡imbécil!
2‡ (= *head*) cabeza *f* • IDIOM: • **to be off one's ~** estar chiflado
(CPD) ▸ **chump chop** (*Brit*) *chuleta gruesa con hueso*

chunder* [ˈtʃʌndəʳ] (VI) devolver, potar*

chunk [tʃʌŋk] (N) [*of bread, cheese etc*] pedazo *m*, trozo *m*; [*of land, time, money**] cantidad *f* considerable

chunky [ˈtʃʌŋkɪ] (ADJ) (COMPAR: **chunkier**, SUPERL: **chunkiest**) [*person*] fornido; [*furniture, mug*] achaparrado; [*knitwear*] grueso, de lana gorda

Chunnel [ˈtʃʌnl] (N) (*hum*) túnel *m* bajo el canal de la Mancha

chunter* [ˈtʃʌntəʳ] (VI) (*Brit*) (*also* **chunter on**) (= *mutter*) murmurar; (= *complain*) gruñir, refunfuñar*

church [tʃɜːtʃ] (N) **1** (= *building*) (*gen*) iglesia *f*; (*Protestant*) templo *m*
2 (= *service*) (*Catholic*) misa *f*; (*Protestant*) oficio *m* • **to go to ~** (*Catholic*) ir a misa; (*Protestant*) ir al oficio • **after ~** después de la misa *or* del oficio
3 (= *institution*) • **the Church** la Iglesia • **Church and State** Iglesia y Estado • **to enter the Church** hacerse cura *or* (*Protestant*) pastor

> **CHURCHES OF ENGLAND/ SCOTLAND**
> La Iglesia Anglicana (**Church of England**) es la iglesia oficial de Inglaterra. Tiene su origen en la ruptura de Enrique VIII con la Iglesia católica en el siglo XVI. En ella se unen aspectos de la tradición católica y de la protestante. Su dirigente oficial es el monarca y su jefe espiritual el Arzobispo de Canterbury. Al clero se le permite contraer matrimonio y, desde 1992, las mujeres pueden ejercer el sacerdocio, cambio al que se opuso radicalmente la corriente conservadora.
> La Iglesia Presbiteriana Escocesa (**Church of Scotland**) es la iglesia nacional de Escocia, pero no depende de ninguna autoridad civil. Sigue la doctrina calvinista y se rige según las normas presbiterianas, lo que significa que está gobernada a nivel local, por **ministers** y dirigentes laicos (**elders**). Tanto hombres como mujeres pueden ejercer el sacerdocio. Hay una reunión anual (**General Assembly**) en la que se discuten asuntos nacionales, presidida por un **Moderator**, que es elegido anualmente.
> ▹ **ARCHBISHOP**

CPD [*doctrine*] de la Iglesia ▸ **Church Fathers** Padres *mpl* de la Iglesia ▸ **church hall** sacristía *f* ▸ **church music** música *f* sacra *or* religiosa ▸ **Church of England** Iglesia *f* Anglicana ▸ **Church of Scotland** Iglesia *f* Presbiteriana Escocesa ▸ **church school** colegio *m* religioso ▸ **church service** oficio *m*, servicio *m* religioso ▸ **church wedding** boda *f* eclesiástica, boda *f* por la iglesia • **they want a ~ wedding** quieren casarse por la iglesia

churchgoer [ˈtʃɜːtʃˌgəʊəʳ] N fiel *mf*

churchgoing [ˈtʃɜːtʃgəʊɪŋ] ADJ • **a ~ family** (*Catholic*) una familia que va a misa; (*Protestant*) una familia que va al oficio

churchman [ˈtʃɜːtʃmən] N (PL: **churchmen**) **1** (= *priest*) sacerdote *m*, eclesiástico *m*
2 (= *member*) fiel *m* practicante

churchwarden [ˈtʃɜːtʃˈwɔːdn] N capillero *m*

churchwoman [ˈtʃɜːtʃˌwʊmən] N (PL: **churchwomen**) fiel *f* practicante

churchy* [ˈtʃɜːtʃɪ] ADJ (*pej*) (= *pious*) beato; (= *churchgoing*) que va mucho a la iglesia, que toma muy en serio las cosas de la iglesia

churchyard [ˈtʃɜːtʃjɑːd] N cementerio *m*, campo *m* santo

churl [tʃɜːl] N (= *person*) patán *m*

churlish [ˈtʃɜːlɪʃ] ADJ (= *rude*) grosero, maleducado; (= *unfriendly*) poco amistoso, arisco; (= *mean*) mezquino • **it would be ~ not to thank him** sería muy grosero *or* maleducado no darle las gracias

churlishly [ˈtʃɜːlɪʃlɪ] ADV (= *rudely*) groseramente, sin educación

churlishness [ˈtʃɜːlɪʃnɪs] N (= *rudeness*) grosería *f*, mala educación *f*; (= *unfriendliness*) conducta *f* poco amistosa; (= *meanness*) mezquindad *f*

churn [tʃɜːn] N (*for butter*) mantequera *f*; (*Brit*) (*for milk*) lechera *f*
VT **1** [+ *butter*] batir *or* hacer en una mantequera
2 (*fig*) (*also* **churn up**) [+ *sea, mud*] revolver, agitar
VI [*sea*] revolverse, agitarse • **her stomach was ~ing** se le revolvía el estómago
▸ **churn out** VT + ADV (*pej*) [+ *books, goods*] producir en serie, producir en masa

chute [ʃuːt] N **1** (*for rubbish*) vertedero *m*
2 (*Brit*) (*in playground, swimming pool*) tobogán *m*
3* (= *parachute*) paracaídas *m inv*

chutney [ˈtʃʌtnɪ] N salsa *f* picante (de frutas y especias)

chutzpa, chutzpah* [ˈxʊtspə] N (*esp US*) cara *f* dura

CI ABBR = **Channel Islands**

C.I. N ABBR = **Consular Invoice**

CIA N ABBR (*US*) (= **Central Intelligence Agency**) CIA *f*

ciabatta [tʃəˈbætə] N chapata *f*

ciao* [tʃaʊ] EXCL ¡chao!

cicada [sɪˈkɑːdə] N (PL: **cicadas** *or* **cicadae** [sɪˈkɑːdiː]) cigarra *f*

Cicero [ˈsɪsərəʊ] N Cicerón

Ciceronian [ˌsɪsəˈrəʊnɪən] ADJ ciceroniano

CID N ABBR (*Brit*) = **Criminal Investigation Department** • **CID man/woman** • **CID officer** policía *mf or* oficial *mf* del Departamento de Investigación Criminal

cider [ˈsaɪdəʳ] N sidra *f*
CPD ▸ **cider apple** manzana *f* de sidra ▸ **cider press** lagar *m* para hacer sidra ▸ **cider vinegar** vinagre *m* de sidra

CIF, c.i.f. N ABBR (= **cost, insurance, freight**) c.s.f.

cig* [sɪg] N (*Brit*) = **cigarette**

cigar [sɪˈgɑːʳ] N puro *m*, cigarro *m*
CPD ▸ **cigar case** cigarrera *f* ▸ **cigar holder** boquilla *f* de puro ▸ **cigar lighter** (*Aut*) encendedor *m* de puro

cigarette [ˌsɪgəˈret] N cigarrillo *m*, cigarro *m* • **he had a ~** (se) fumó un cigarrillo *or* cigarro
CPD ▸ **cigarette ash** ceniza *f* de cigarrillo ▸ **cigarette burn** quemadura *f* de cigarrillo ▸ **cigarette butt** colilla *f* ▸ **cigarette card** cromo *m* (coleccionable) ▸ **cigarette case** pitillera *f*, cigarrera *f* (*LAm*) ▸ **cigarette end** colilla *f* ▸ **cigarette holder** boquilla *f* ▸ **cigarette lighter** encendedor *m*, mechero *m* ▸ **cigarette machine** máquina *f* de tabaco ▸ **cigarette paper** papel *m* de fumar ▸ **cigarette smoke** humo *m* de cigarrillo

cigarillo [ˌsɪgəˈrɪləʊ] N purito *m*

cigar-shaped [sɪˈgɑːʃeɪpt] ADJ en forma de puro

ciggy* [ˈsɪgɪ] N (*Brit*) = **cigarette**

CIM N ABBR (*Comput*) = **computer-integrated manufacturing**

C.-in-C. N ABBR = **Commander-in-Chief**

cinch* [sɪntʃ] N • **it's a ~** (= *easy thing*) está tirado, es pan comido; (= *sure thing*) es cosa segura

cinchona [sɪŋˈkəʊnə] N quino *m*
CPD ▸ **cinchona bark** quina *f*

cinder [ˈsɪndəʳ] N **1** (= *ember*) carbonilla *f* • IDIOM: • **to be burned to a ~** [*food etc*] quedar carbonizado
2 cinders (= *ashes*) cenizas *fpl*
CPD ▸ **cinder block** (*US*) ladrillo *m* de cenizas ▸ **cinder track** (*Sport*) pista *f* de ceniza

Cinderella [ˌsɪndəˈrelə] N Cenicienta *f* • **it's the ~ of the arts** es la hermana pobre de las artes

cine [ˈsɪnɪ] CPD (*Brit*) ▸ **cine camera** cámara *f* cinematográfica ▸ **cine film** película *f* de cine ▸ **cine projector** proyector *m* de películas

cinéaste [ˈsɪnɪæst] N cinéfilo/a *m/f*

cinema [ˈsɪnəmə] (*esp Brit*) N cine *m* • **the silent/talking ~** el cine mudo/sonoro
CPD ▸ **cinema complex** cine *m* multisalas

cinema-going [ˈsɪnəməˌgəʊɪŋ] (*esp Brit*) N • **cinema-going is very popular among the young** el ir al cine es muy popular entre los jóvenes
ADJ • **the cinema-going public** el público aficionado al cine

Cinemascope® [ˈsɪnəməskəʊp] N Cinemascope® *m*

cinematic [ˌsɪnɪˈmætɪk] ADJ cinemático

cinematograph [ˌsɪnɪˈmætəgrɑːf] N (*Brit*) cinematógrafo *m*

cinematographer [ˌsɪnəməˈtɒgrəfəʳ] N cinematógrafo/a *m/f*

cinematography [ˌsɪnəməˈtɒgrəfɪ] N cinematografía *f*

cinephile [ˈsɪnɪfaɪl] N cinéfilo/a *m/f*

cinerary [ˈsɪnərərɪ] ADJ cinerario

cinnabar [ˈsɪnəbɑːʳ] N cinabrio *m*

cinnamon [ˈsɪnəmən] N canela *f*
CPD ▸ **cinnamon stick** rama *f* de canela ▸ **cinnamon toast** ≈ torrija *f*

cipher [ˈsaɪfəʳ] N **1** (= *o, zero*) cero *m*; (= *any number, initials*) cifra *f*; (= *Arabic numeral*) cifra *f*, número *m*
2 (= *secret writing*) cifra *f*, código *m* • **in ~** cifrado, en clave
3 (= *monogram*) monograma *m*
4 (*fig*) (= *person*) • **he's a mere ~** es un cero a la izquierda
VT **1** [+ *code, calculations, communications*] cifrar
2 (*Math*) calcular

circ ABBR (= **circa**) hacia

circa [ˈsɜːkə] PREP hacia • **~ 1500** hacia (el año) 1500

circadian [səˈkeɪdɪən] ADJ circadiano • **~ cycle** ciclo *m* circadiano

circle [ˈsɜːkl] N **1** (*gen*) círculo *m* • **to stand in a ~** formar un corro • IDIOMS: • **to come full ~** volver al punto de partida • **to go round in ~s*** dar vueltas sobre lo mismo, no avanzar • **it had us running round in ~s*** nos tuvo dando vueltas sin orden ni concierto; ▹ **vicious**
2 (= *set of people*) círculo *m*, grupo *m* • **John and his ~** Juan y sus amigos, Juan y su peña • **in certain ~s** en ciertos medios • **in business ~s** en el mundo de los negocios • **the family ~** el círculo familiar • **to move in fashionable ~s** frecuentar los ambientes que están de moda • **an inner ~ of ministers** un grupo de ministros que ostentan mayor poder • **she moves in wealthy ~s** frecuenta la buena sociedad
3 (*Brit*) (*Theat*) anfiteatro *m*
VT **1** (= *surround*) cercar, rodear; (= *move round*) girar alrededor de, dar vueltas alrededor de • **the lion ~d its prey** el león se movió alrededor de la presa • **the cosmonaut ~d the earth** el cosmonauta dio la vuelta a la tierra • **the aircraft ~d the town twice** el avión dio dos vueltas sobre la ciudad
2 (= *draw round*) poner un círculo alrededor de, rodear con un círculo
VI dar vueltas

circlet [ˈsɜːklɪt] N (*worn on head*) diadema *f*; (*worn on finger*) anillo *m*; (*worn on arm*) aro *m*, brazalete *m*

circuit [ˈsɜːkɪt] N **1** (= *route*) circuito *m*; (= *course*) recorrido *m*; (= *long way round*) rodeo *m*; (= *lap by runner*) vuelta *f*
2 (*Brit*) (*Jur*) distrito *m*
3 (*Cine*) cadena *f*
4 (*esp Brit*) (= *sports track*) pista *f*
5 (*Aut, Elec*) circuito *m*; ▹ **short-circuit**
CPD ▸ **circuit board** (*Elec*) tarjeta *f* de circuitos ▸ **circuit breaker** (*Elec*) cortacircuitos *m inv* ▸ **circuit court** (*US*) (*Jur*) tribunal *m* superior ▸ **circuit switching network** (*Elec*) red *f* de conmutación de circuito ▸ **circuit training** (*Sport*) circuito *m* de entrenamiento

circuitous [sɜːˈkjʊɪtəs] ADJ [*route*] tortuoso, sinuoso; [*method*] tortuoso, solapado

circuitry [ˈsɜːkɪtrɪ] N circuitería *f*, sistema *m* de circuitos

circular [ˈsɜːkjʊləʳ] ADJ circular, redondo • **~ motion** movimiento *m* circular • **~ tour** circuito *m*
N (*in firm*) circular *f*; (= *advertisement*) panfleto *m*
CPD ▸ **circular saw** sierra *f* circular

circularity [ˌsɜːkjʊˈlærɪtɪ] N circularidad *f*

circularize [ˈsɜːkjʊləraɪz] VT enviar circulares a

circulate [ˈsɜːkjʊleɪt] VI (*gen*) circular
VT (*gen*) poner en circulación; [+ *letter, papers etc*] hacer circular; [+ *news*] hacer circular

circulating [ˈsɜːkjʊleɪtɪŋ] ADJ circulante
CPD ▸ **circulating assets** activo *msing* circulante ▸ **circulating capital** capital *m* circulante ▸ **circulating library** (*US*) biblioteca *f* circulante ▸ **circulating medium** (*Econ*) medios *mpl* monetarios

circulation [ˌsɜːkjʊˈleɪʃən] N **1** (*gen*) circulación *f* • **to withdraw sth from ~** retirar algo de la circulación • **to put into ~** poner en circulación • **he's back in ~*** se está dejando ver otra vez
2 (= *number of papers printed*) tirada *f*
3 (*Med*) • **she has poor ~** tiene mala

circulación
circulatory [ˌsɜːkjʊˈleɪtərɪ] (ADJ) circulatorio
circum... [ˈsɜːkəm] (PREFIX) circun..., circum...
circumcise [ˈsɜːkəmsaɪz] (VT) circuncidar
circumcision [ˌsɜːkəmˈsɪʒən] (N) circuncisión *f*
circumference [səˈkʌmfərəns] (N) circunferencia *f*
circumflex [ˈsɜːkəmfleks] (N) circunflejo *m*
(CPD) ▸ **circumflex accent** acento *m* circunflejo
circumlocution [ˌsɜːkəmləˈkjuːʃən] (N) circunloquio *m*, rodeo *m*
circumlocutory [ˌsɜːkəmˈlɒkjʊtərɪ] (ADJ) con muchos circunloquios
circumnavigate [ˌsɜːkəmˈnævɪgeɪt] (VT) circunnavegar
circumnavigation [ˈsɜːkəmˌnævɪˈgeɪʃən] (N) circunnavegación *f*
circumnavigator [ˌsɜːkəmˈnævɪgeɪtəʳ] (N) circunnavegador(a) *m/f*
circumscribe [ˈsɜːkəmskraɪb] (VT) (*lit*) circunscribir; (*fig*) (= *limit*) limitar, restringir
circumscription [ˌsɜːkəmˈskrɪpʃən] (N)
1 (= *restriction*) limitación *f*
2 (*on coin*) grafila *f*
circumspect [ˈsɜːkəmspekt] (ADJ) circunspecto, prudente
circumspection [ˌsɜːkəmˈspekʃən] (N) circunspección *f*, prudencia *f*
circumspectly [ˈsɜːkəmspektlɪ] (ADV) prudentemente
circumstance [ˈsɜːkəmstəns] (*usu pl*) (N)
1 circunstancia *f* • **in** *or* **under the ~s** en *or* dadas las circunstancias • **under no ~s** de ninguna manera, bajo ningún concepto • **owing to ~s beyond our control** debido a circunstancias ajenas a nuestra voluntad • **~s alter cases** las circunstancias cambian los casos • **were it not for the ~ that ...** si no se diera la circunstancia de que ... • **a victim of ~** una víctima de las circunstancias; ▹ **pomp**
2 (= *economic situation*) • **to be in easy/poor ~s** estar en buena/mala situación económica • **what are your ~s?** ¿cuál es su situación económica? • **if the family ~s allow it** si lo permite la situación económica de la familia
circumstantial [ˌsɜːkəmˈstænʃəl] (ADJ) [*report, statement*] detallado • **~ evidence** (*Jur*) pruebas *fpl* circunstanciales
circumstantiate [ˌsɜːkəmˈstænʃɪeɪt] (VT) probar refiriendo más detalles, corroborar, confirmar
circumvent [ˌsɜːkəmˈvent] (VT) [+ *law, rule*] burlar; [+ *difficulty, obstacle*] salvar, evitar
circumvention [ˌsɜːkəmˈvenʃən] (N) acción *f* de burlar *or* salvar • **the ~ of this obstacle will not be easy** no va a ser fácil salvar este obstáculo
circus [ˈsɜːkəs] (N) (PL: **circuses**)
1 (= *entertainment*) circo *m*
2 (*in place names*) plaza *f*, glorieta *f*
cirrhosis [sɪˈrəʊsɪs] (N) cirrosis *f*
(CPD) ▸ **cirrhosis of the liver** cirrosis *f* hepática
cirrocumulus [ˌsɪrəʊˈkjuːmjʊləs] (N) (PL: **cirrocumuli** [ˌsɪrəʊˈkjuːmjʊlaɪ]) cirrocúmulo *m*
cirrostratus [ˌsɪrəʊˈstrɑːtəs] (N) (PL: **cirrostrati** [ˌsɪrəʊˈstrɑːtaɪ]) cirrostrato *m*
cirrus [ˈsɪrəs] (N) (PL: **cirri** [ˈsɪraɪ]) cirro *m*
CIS (N ABBR) (= **Commonwealth of Independent States**) CEI *f*
cissy* [ˈsɪsɪ] (N) mariquita* *m*
Cistercian [sɪsˈtɜːʃən] (ADJ) cisterciense • **~ Order** Orden *f* del Císter
(N) cisterciense *m*
cistern [ˈsɪstən] (N) [*of WC*] cisterna *f*; (= *tank*) depósito *m*; (*for hot water*) termo *m*; (*for rainwater*) aljibe *m*, cisterna *f*
citadel [ˈsɪtədl] (N) ciudadela *f*; (*in Spain, freq*) alcázar *m*; (*fig*) reducto *m*
citation [saɪˈteɪʃən] (N) cita *f*; (*US*) (*Jur*) citación *f*; (*Mil*) mención *f*, citación *f*
(CPD) ▸ **citation index** índice *m* de citación
cite [saɪt] (VT) **1** (= *quote*) citar
2 (*Jur*) • **he was ~d to appear in court** lo citaron para que se compareciera ante el tribunal
3 (*Mil*) mencionar, citar
citizen [ˈsɪtɪzn] (N) [*of state*] ciudadano/a *m/f*, súbdito/a *m/f*; [*of city*] habitante *mf*, vecino/a *m/f*
(CPD) ▸ **citizen journalism** periodismo *m* ciudadano ▸ **Citizens' Advice Bureau** (*Brit*) *organización voluntaria británica que asesora legal o financieramente* ▸ **citizen's arrest** *arresto realizado por un ciudadano ordinario* ▸ **Citizens' Band** (*Rad*) banda *f* ciudadana

CITIZENS' ADVICE BUREAU
Las oficinas de información al ciudadano, **Citizens' Advice Bureaux** o **CABs**, se crearon en 1939 para asesorar al pueblo británico sobre las normas que había que cumplir en tiempos de guerra. Después pasaron a ser un servicio de asesoramiento general al público, ofreciendo información gratuita y ayuda en problemas de carácter diverso. Actualmente se encargan de aconsejar en lo concerniente a la vivienda, problemas económicos, prestaciones y servicios sociales y derechos del consumidor. Existen unas 900 oficinas por todo el país, financiadas con dinero público y en las que trabajan normalmente voluntarios dirigidos por una persona que cobra por su trabajo.

citizenry [ˈsɪtɪznrɪ] (N) ciudadanos *mpl*, ciudadanía *f*
citizenship [ˈsɪtɪznʃɪp] (N) ciudadanía *f*
citrate [ˈsɪtreɪt] (N) citrato *m*
citric [ˈsɪtrɪk] (ADJ) • **~ acid** ácido *m* cítrico
citron [ˈsɪtrən] (N) (= *fruit*) cidra *f*; (= *tree*) cidro *m*
citrus [ˈsɪtrəs] (N) (PL: **citruses**) cidro *m*
(CPD) ▸ **citrus fruits** cítricos *mpl*, agrios *mpl*
city [ˈsɪtɪ] (N) ciudad *f* • **the City** (*Brit*) (*Econ*) *el centro financiero de Londres*
(CPD) municipal, de la ciudad ▸ **City and Guilds** (*Brit*) *organismo examinador que concede titulaciones en cursos técnicos y especializados* ▸ **city break** (*Tourism*) viaje *m* de corta duración a una gran ciudad ▸ **city centre**, **city center** (*US*) centro *m* de la ciudad ▸ **city council** concejo *m* municipal, ayuntamiento *m* ▸ **city desk** (*Brit*) (*Press*) sección *f* de noticias financieras (de un periódico); (*US*) (*Press*) sección *f* de noticias de la ciudad (de un periódico) ▸ **city dweller** habitante *mf* de una ciudad ▸ **city editor** redactor(a) *m/f* encargado/a de las noticias financieras ▸ **city fathers** concejales *mpl* ▸ **city hall** palacio *m* municipal; (*US*) ayuntamiento *m* ▸ **city limits** perímetro *msing* urbano ▸ **city manager** administrador(a) *m/f* municipal ▸ **city news** (*Brit*) noticias *fpl* financieras; (*US*) noticias *fpl* de la ciudad ▸ **city page** (*Econ*) sección *f* de información financiera ▸ **city plan** (*US*) plano *m* de la ciudad ▸ **city planner** (*US*) urbanista *mf* ▸ **city planning** (*US*) urbanismo *m* ▸ **city slicker*** (*pej*) capitalino/a* *m/f* ▸ **City Technology College** (*Brit*) ≈ Centro *m* de formación profesional

CITY NICKNAMES
Las ciudades estadounidenses a menudo tienen apodos por los que se las conoce informalmente. Por ejemplo, a Nueva York se la llama **Big Apple**, ya que **apple** en argot significa gran ciudad. Chicago es **Windy City** debido a los fuertes vientos que vienen del lago Michigan. A Nueva Orleans la llaman **Big Easy**, por la tranquilidad con la que se lo toman todo sus habitantes. Detroit tiene el apelativo de **Motown**, que es un compuesto de **Motor** y **Town**, por las fábricas de coches que hay en ella.
A otras ciudades estadounidenses se las conoce por sus iniciales, como por ejemplo, Los Angeles, **LA** y Dallas, **Big D** o por una parte de su nombre como **Vegas**, en lugar de **Las Vegas** o **Corpus** por **Corpus Christi**, en Texas.
También hay veces en las que se usa una versión acortada del nombre, como ocurre en el caso de San Francisco y Philadelphia, a las que se llama **Frisco** y **Philly** respectivamente.

cityscape [ˈsɪtɪskeɪp] (N) paisaje *m* urbano
city-state [ˈsɪtɪˌsteɪt] (N) ciudad-estado *f*
civet [ˈsɪvɪt] (N) algalia *f*
civic [ˈsɪvɪk] (ADJ) [*rights, duty*] cívico; [*authorities*] municipal
(CPD) ▸ **civic centre** (*Brit*) conjunto *m* de edificios municipales; ▹ **pride**
civics [ˈsɪvɪks] (NPL) cívica *fsing*; (*as course*) educación *fsing* cívica
civies* [ˈsɪvɪz] (NPL) (*US*) = **civvies**
civil [ˈsɪvl] (ADJ) **1** (= *societal*) [*strife, conflict*] civil; [*unrest*] social
2 (= *not military*) [*aviation, ship*] civil
3 (= *not religious*) [*ceremony, service, marriage*] civil
4 (*Jur*) (= *not criminal*) [*case, action, proceedings, charge*] civil; [*penalty*] por infracción de la ley; [*court*] de lo Civil
5 (= *polite*) [*person*] cortés, atento; [*behaviour*] cortés • **to be ~ to sb** ser cortés *or* atento con algn • **that's very ~ of you** es usted muy amable; ▹ **tongue**
(CPD) ▸ **Civil Aviation Authority** Aviación *f* Civil ▸ **civil defence**, **civil defense** (*US*) defensa *f* civil ▸ **civil disobedience** desobediencia *f* civil ▸ **civil engineer** ingeniero/a *m/f* civil, ingeniero/a *m/f* de caminos (canales y puertos) (*Sp*) ▸ **civil engineering** ingeniería *f* civil, ingeniería *f* de caminos (canales y puertos) (*Sp*) ▸ **civil law** derecho *m* civil ▸ **civil liberties** libertades *fpl* civiles ▸ **civil list** (*Brit*) *presupuesto de la casa real aprobado por el parlamento* ▸ **civil marriage** matrimonio *m* civil ▸ **civil partner** pareja *f* civil (*del mismo sexo*) ▸ **civil partnership** unión *f* de parejas civiles (*del mismo sexo*) ▸ **civil rights** derechos *mpl* civiles • **~ rights leader** defensor(a) *m/f* de los derechos civiles ▸ **civil rights movement** movimiento *m* pro derechos civiles ▸ **civil servant** funcionario/a *m/f* (del Estado) ▸ **Civil Service** administración *f* pública ▸ **civil status** estado *m* civil ▸ **civil war** guerra *f* civil • **the American Civil War** la guerra de Secesión ▸ **civil wedding** boda *f* civil
civilian [sɪˈvɪlɪən] (ADJ) (= *non-military*) civil • **in ~ clothes** vestido/a de paisano *or* civil • **there were no ~ casualties** no hubo bajas entre la población civil
(N) civil *mf*
civility [sɪˈvɪlɪtɪ] (N) **1** (= *politeness*) cortesía *f*, amabilidad *f*
2 (*usu pl*) (= *polite remark*) cortesía *f*,

cumplido *m*
civilization [ˌsɪvɪlaɪˈzeɪʃən] (N) civilización *f*
civilize [ˈsɪvɪlaɪz] (VT) civilizar
civilized [ˈsɪvɪlaɪzd] (ADJ) **1** (= *socially advanced*) [*society, country, world, people*] civilizado • **to become ~** civilizarse
2 (= *refined, decent*) [*person, manner*] educado; [*behaviour, conversation, company*] civilizado; [*meal, place, tastes*] refinado; [*time of day*] decente • **he never phones at a ~ hour** nunca llama a una hora decente • **how ~! real champagne!** ¡qué refinado *or* cuánto refinamiento! ¡champán de verdad! • **I know we disagree, but we could at least be ~ about it** sé que no estamos de acuerdo, pero vamos a ser civilizados por lo menos
civilizing [ˈsɪvɪlaɪzɪŋ] (ADJ) • **she has had a ~ influence on him** bajo su influencia se ha vuelto más civilizado *or* refinado
civilly [ˈsɪvɪlɪ] (ADV) cortésmente, atentamente
civism [ˈsɪvɪzəm] (N) civismo *m*
civvies* [ˈsɪvɪz] (NPL) traje *msing* civil • **in ~** vestido/a de paisano *or* civil
civvy* [ˈsɪvɪ] (ADJ) • **~ street** (*Brit*) la vida civil
CJ (ABBR) = **chief justice**
CJD (N ABBR) (= **Creutzfeldt-Jakob disease**) *enfermedad de Creutzfeldt-Jakob*
CKD (ADJ ABBR) (= **completely knocked down**) ▸ **knock down**
cl (ABBR) (= **centilitre(s)**) cl
clack [klæk] (VI) (= *chatter*) charlar, chismear • **this will make the tongues ~** esto será tema para los chismosos
clad [klæd] (ADJ) vestido (**in** de)
cladding [klædɪŋ] (N) (*Tech*) revestimiento *m*
claim [kleɪm] (N) **1** (= *demand*) (*for rights, wages*) reivindicación *f*, demanda *f*; (*for damages, on insurance*) reclamación *f*; (*for expenses, benefit*) solicitud *f*; (*Jur*) demanda *f* • **pay** *or* **wage ~** reivindicación *f* salarial • **to file a ~** (*Jur*) presentar *or* interponer una demanda • **she lost her ~ for damages** el tribunal rechazó su demanda de daños y perjuicios • **to make a ~** (*on insurance*) reclamar • **we made a ~ on our insurance** reclamamos al seguro • **have you made a ~ since last year?** (*for benefit*) ¿ha solicitado alguna ayuda estatal desde el año pasado? • **there are many ~s on my time** tengo una agenda muy apretada • **to put in a ~ (for sth)** (*for expenses*) presentar una solicitud (de algo); (*on insurance*) reclamar (algo)
2 (= *right*) (*to property, title*) derecho *m* • **he renounced his ~ to the throne** renunció a su derecho al trono • **they will not give up their ~ to the territory** no renunciarán a su reivindicación del territorio • **the town's main ~ to fame is its pub** este pueblo se destaca más que nada por el bar • **to lay ~ to sth** (*lit*) reclamar algo; (*fig*) atribuirse algo • **he cannot lay ~ to much originality** no puede atribuirse mucha originalidad, no puede presumir de original; ▸ **stake, prior**
3 (= *assertion*) afirmación *f* • **he rejected ~s that he had had affairs with six women** desmintió las afirmaciones de que había tenido seis amantes • **I make no ~ to be infallible** no pretendo ser infalible
(VT) **1** (= *demand as due*) [+ *rights*] reivindicar; [+ *lost property*] reclamar; [+ *allowance, benefit*] (= *apply for*) solicitar; (= *receive*) cobrar • **if you wish to ~ expenses you must provide receipts** si desea que se le reembolsen los gastos debe presentar los recibos • **25% of people who are entitled to ~ State benefits do not do so** el 25% de las personas que tienen derecho a cobrar ayuda del Estado no lo hace • **to ~ damages from sb** demandar a algn por daños y perjuicios • **he ~ed damages for negligence on the part of the hospital** exigió que el hospital le compensara por haber cometido negligencia, demandó al hospital por negligencia
2 (= *state title to*) [+ *territory*] reivindicar; [+ *victory*] atribuirse; [+ *prize*] llevarse; [+ *throne*] reclamar • **neither side can ~ victory in this war** ninguno de los dos bandos puede atribuirse la victoria en esta guerra • **Williams ~ed a fourth Wimbledon title** Williams se llevó su cuarto título de Wimbledon • **~ your prize by ringing the competition hotline** llévese el premio llamando a la línea directa del concurso • **he was too modest to ~ the credit** era demasiado modesto como para atribuirse el mérito • **so far no one has ~ed responsibility for the bomb** hasta ahora nadie ha reivindicado la colocación de de la bomba
3 (= *assert*) • **he ~s a 70% success rate** afirma *or* alega que resuelve satisfactoriamente un 70% de los casos • **to ~ that** afirmar que • **they ~ the police opened fire without warning** afirman que la policía abrió fuego sin previo aviso • **I do not ~ that everyone can do this** no estoy diciendo que todo el mundo pueda hacer esto • **he ~s to have seen her** afirma haberla visto • **these products ~ to be environmentally safe** se afirma que estos productos no dañan el medio ambiente
4 (= *require*) [+ *attention*] requerir, exigir • **something else ~ed her attention** otra cosa requirió *or* exigió su atención
5 (= *take*) [+ *life*] cobrarse • **the accident ~ed four lives** el accidente se cobró cuatro vidas
(VI) (= *make demand*) presentar reclamación • **make sure you ~ within a month of the accident** asegúrese de presentar reclamación antes de un mes desde la fecha del accidente • **to ~ for sth** reclamar (los gastos de) algo • **I ~ed for damage to the carpet after the flood** reclamé los gastos del deterioro de la alfombra tras la inundación
(CPD) ▸ **claim form** (*for benefit*) (impreso *m* de) solicitud *f*; (*for expenses*) impreso *m* de reembolso ▸ **claims adjuster, claims adjustor** (*US*) (= *insurance adjuster*) perito/a *m/f* de siniestros
claimant [ˈkleɪmənt] (N) (*in court*) demandante *mf*; (*Brit*) [*of benefit*] solicitante *mf*; (*to throne*) pretendiente *mf*
clairvoyance [kleəˈvɔɪəns] (N) clarividencia *f*
clairvoyant, clairvoyante [kleəˈvɔɪənt] (ADJ) clarividente, vidente
(N) clarividente *mf*, vidente *mf*
clam [klæm] (N) **1** (*Zool*) almeja *f*
2 (*US*‡) (= *dollar*) dólar *m*
(CPD) ▸ **clam chowder** (*US*) sopa *f* de almejas
▸ **clam up*** (VI + ADV) cerrar el pico*, no decir ni pío
clambake [ˈklæmbeɪk] (N) (*US*) (*Culin*) merienda *f* en la playa *or* en el campo (*en la que se cocinan y comen almejas*); (= *party**) fiesta *f*
clamber [ˈklæmbəʳ] (N) subida *f*
(VI) trepar, subir gateando (**over** sobre, **up** a)
clammy [ˈklæmɪ] (ADJ) (COMPAR: **clammier**, SUPERL: **clammiest**) (= *damp*) frío y húmedo; (= *sticky*) pegajoso
clamor [ˈklæməʳ] (N) (*US*) = **clamour**
clamorous [ˈklæmərəs] (ADJ) clamoroso, vociferante, ruidoso
clamour, clamor (*US*) [ˈklæməʳ] (N) clamor *m*
(VI) clamorear, vociferar • **to ~ for sth** clamar algo, pedir algo a voces
clamp [klæmp] (N) **1** (= *brace*) abrazadera *f*; (*Aut*) (*on parked car*) cepo *m*; (= *laboratory clamp*) grapa *f*; (*on bench*) cárcel *f*
2 (*Agr*) ensilado *m*, montón *m*
(VT) **1** (= *secure*) (*with brace*) afianzar *or* sujetar con abrazadera; (*in laboratory*) afianzar *or* sujetar con grapa; (*on bench*) afianzar *or* sujetar con cárcel • **he ~ed it in his hand** lo agarró con la mano • **he ~ed his hand down on it** lo sujetó firmemente con la mano
2 [+ *car*] poner un cepo en
▸ **clamp down** (VI + ADV) • **to ~ down (on)** [+ *tax evasion, crime etc*] poner frenos (a), tomar fuertes medidas (contra)
clampdown [ˈklæmpdaʊn] (N) restricción *f* (on de), prohibición *f* (**on** en)
clamping [ˈklæmpɪŋ] (N) (= *action*) colocación *f* de cepos
clan [klæn] (N) (*also fig*) clan *m*
clandestine [klænˈdestɪn] (ADJ) clandestino
(CPD) ▸ **clandestine entrant** (= *illegal immigrant*) inmigrante *mf* ilegal
clandestinely [klænˈdestɪnlɪ] (ADV) clandestinamente
clang [klæŋ] (N) ruido *m* metálico fuerte
(VI) sonar mucho, hacer estruendo • **the gate ~ed shut** la puerta se cerró ruidosamente
(VT) hacer sonar
clanger* [ˈklæŋəʳ] (N) (*Brit*) plancha *f* (*Sp**), metedura *f or* (*LAm*) metida *f* de pata* • IDIOM: • **to drop a ~** meter la pata*, tirarse una plancha (*Sp**)
clangor [ˈklæŋgəʳ] (N) (*US*) = **clangour**
clangorous [ˈklæŋgərəs] (ADJ) estrepitoso, estruendoso
clangour, clangor (*US*) [ˈklæŋgəʳ] (N) estruendo *m*
clank [klæŋk] (N) sonido *m* metálico seco
(VI) sonar • **the train went ~ing past** el tren pasó con gran estruendo
(VT) hacer sonar
clannish [ˈklænɪʃ] (ADJ) exclusivista, con fuerte sentimiento de tribu
clansman [ˈklænzmən] (N) (PL: **clansmen**) miembro *m* del clan
clanswoman [ˈklænzˌwʊmən] (N) (PL: **clanswomen**) miembro *f* del clan
clap¹ [klæp] (N) **1** (*on shoulder, of the hands*) palmada *f* • **a ~ of thunder** un trueno
2 (= *applause*) aplauso *m* • **to get a ~** recibir un aplauso • **to give sb a ~** dar un aplauso a algn
(VT) **1** (= *applaud*) [+ *person, play, announcement*] aplaudir • **to ~ one's hands** dar palmadas, batir las palmas • **to ~ sb on the back** dar a algn una palmada en la espalda
2 (= *place*) poner • **he ~ped his hat on** se encasquetó el sombrero • **to ~ a hand over sb's mouth** tapar la boca a algn con la mano • **to ~ eyes on** clavar la vista en • **to ~ sth shut** cerrar algo de golpe • **they ~ped him in prison*** lo metieron en la cárcel
(VI) aplaudir
clap²‡ [klæp] (N) • **the ~** (= *disease*) gonorrea *f*
clapboard [ˈklæpbɔːd] (N) (*US*) chilla *f*, tablilla *f*
clapped-out* [ˌklæptˈaʊt] (ADJ) (*Brit*) [*car, bus etc*] desvencijado; [*person*] para el arrastre
clapper [ˈklæpəʳ] (N) [*of bell*] badajo *m*; (*Cine*) claqueta *f* • IDIOM: • **to run like the ~s** (*Brit**) correr como loco
clapperboard [ˈklæpəˌbɔːd] (N) (*Cine*) claqueta *f*
clapping [ˈklæpɪŋ] (N) (= *applause*) aplausos *mpl*; (= *sound of hands*) palmoteo *m*
claptrap* [ˈklæptræp] (N) (*pej*) burradas *fpl*, disparates *mpl*
claque [klæk] (N) claque *f*
claret [ˈklærət] (N) **1** (= *wine*) vino *m* de

C

Burdeos
2 (= *colour*) burdeos *m*
clarification [,klærɪfɪ'keɪʃən] (N) aclaración *f*
clarified ['klærɪfaɪd] (ADJ) [*butter*] clarificado
clarify ['klærɪfaɪ] (VT) **1** [+ *statement etc*] aclarar, clarificar
2 [+ *liquid, butter*] clarificar
clarinet [,klærɪ'net] (N) clarinete *m*
clarinettist [,klærɪ'netɪst] (N) clarinetista *mf*
clarion ['klærɪən] (N) (toque *m* de) trompeta *f*
(CPD) ▸ **clarion call** llamada *f* fuerte y sonora
clarity ['klærɪtɪ] (N) **1** [*of statement etc*] claridad *f*
2 [*of image, sound*] claridad *f*, nitidez *f*
3 [*of water, glass*] claridad *f*, transparencia *f*; [*of air*] pureza *f*
clash [klæʃ] (N) **1** (= *noise*) estruendo *m*, fragor *m*; [*of cymbals*] ruido *m* metálico
2 [*of armies, personalities*] choque *m*; (= *conflict*) choque *m*, conflicto *m*; (= *confrontation*) enfrentamiento *m*; [*of interests, opinions*] conflicto *m*; [*of dates, programmes*] coincidencia *f*; [*of colours*] desentono *m* • **a ~ with the police** un choque *or* un enfrentamiento con la policía • **a ~ of wills** un conflicto de voluntades
(VT) [+ *cymbals, swords*] golpear
(VI) **1** [*personalities, interests*] oponerse, chocar; [*colours*] desentonar; [*dates, events*] coincidir
2 (= *disagree*) estar en desacuerdo; (= *argue*) pelear; (*Mil*) encontrarse, enfrentarse (**with** con)
clasp [klɑːsp] (N) **1** [*of brooch, necklace*] cierre *m*; [*of belt etc*] broche *m*; [*of book*] broche *m*, manecilla *f*
2 • **with a ~ of the hand** con un apretón de manos
(VT) **1** (= *fasten*) abrochar
2 (= *take hold of*) agarrar; (= *hold hands*) apretar • **to ~ one's hands (together)** juntar las manos • **to ~ sb's hands** apretar las manos a algn, estrechar las manos de algn
3 (= *embrace*) abrazar • **to ~ sb to one's bosom** estrechar a algn contra el pecho
(CPD) ▸ **clasp knife** navaja *f*
class [klɑːs] (N) **1** (*also Scol, Bio, Sociol*) clase *f* • **the ~ of 82** la promoción del 82 • **ruling/middle/working ~** clase *f* dirigente/media/obrera • **first ~** primera clase *f* • **lower ~es** clase *fsing* baja • **upper ~** clase *f* alta
2 (= *category*) categoría *f* • **~ of degree** (*Brit*) (*Univ*) *tipo de título universitario según la nota con que se ha obtenido* • **a good ~ (of) novel** una novela de buena calidad • **it's just not in the same ~** no se puede comparar • **in a ~ of one's own** sin par *or* igual • **it's in a ~ by itself** no tiene par *or* igual, es único en su género
3 (= *style*) • **to have ~** tener clase
(VT) clasificar • **to ~ sb as sth** clasificar a algn de algo
(ADJ) (= *classy*) [*player, actor*] de primera clase
(CPD) ▸ **class action** (*Jur*) querella *f* colectiva ▸ **class background** (= *social class*) clase *f* social ▸ **class conflict** conflicto *m* de clases ▸ **class differences** diferencias *fpl* de clases ▸ **class distinction** (*Sociol*) diferencia *f* de clase ▸ **class list** (*Scol*) lista *f* de clase; (*Univ*) lista *f* de estudiantes aprobados para la licenciatura ▸ **class president** (*US*) ≈ delegado/a *m/f* de clase ▸ **class society** (*Pol*) sociedad *f* formada por clases ▸ **class struggle** (*Sociol*) lucha *f* de clases ▸ **class system** sistema *m* de clases sociales ▸ **class teacher** (*Brit*) tutor(a) *m/f* ▸ **class war(fare)** = class struggle
class-conscious ['klɑːs'kɒnʃəs] (ADJ) con conciencia de clase
class-consciousness ['klɑːs'kɒnʃəsnɪs] (N) conciencia *f* de clase
classic ['klæsɪk] (ADJ) **1** (= *timeless, traditional*) clásico • **she was dressed in a ~ black suit** vestía un clásico traje de chaqueta negro
2* (= *wonderful, memorable*) memorable; (= *hilarious*) genial* • **it was ~** fue genial* • **the film "Casablanca" produced some ~ lines** la película "Casablanca" nos dejó varias frases memorables • **the president came out with a ~ line** el presidente salió con una frase de las que hacen época
(N) **1** (= *book, play*) clásico *m* • **it is a ~ of its kind** es un clásico en su género
2 classics (*Univ*) clásicas *fpl*
3* (= *hilarious remark or event*) • **that was a ~!** ¡fue genial!*
(CPD) ▸ **classic car** coche *m* antiguo (*de coleccionista*)
classical ['klæsɪkəl] (ADJ) [*ballet, style, Greece, Latin*] clásico; [*musician, recording*] de música clásica • **~ music** música *f* clásica • **~ scholar** académico/a *m/f* especializado/a en lenguas clásicas • **~ times** la época clásica
classically ['klæsɪkəlɪ] (ADV) [*educated, trained*] en la tradición clásica • **a ~ trained pianist** un pianista formado en la tradición clásica *or* con una formación clásica • **she is ~ beautiful** es de una belleza clásica • **the ~ undesirable son-in-law** el típico yerno indeseable
classicism ['klæsɪsɪzəm] (N) clasicismo *m*
classicist ['klæsɪsɪst] (N) clasicista *mf*
classifiable ['klæsɪfaɪəbl] (ADJ) clasificable
classification [,klæsɪfɪ'keɪʃən] (N) clasificación *f*
classified ['klæsɪfaɪd] (ADJ) (= *secret*) [*document etc*] confidencial, secreto • **~ information** información *f* confidencial, información *f* secreta
(N) **1** (*Press*) • **late night ~** últimas noticias con los resultados del fútbol
2 classifieds (= *small ads*) anuncios *mpl* por palabras, clasificados *mpl*
(CPD) ▸ **classified ad, classified advertisement** anuncio *m* por palabras, clasificado *m* ▸ **classified results** (*Brit*) (*Sport*) clasificación *fsing* ▸ **classified section** (*Press*) sección *f* de anuncios por palabras
classify ['klæsɪfaɪ] (VT) **1** (= *sort*) clasificar (**in, into en**) • **to ~ sth under the letter B** clasificar algo bajo la letra B
2 (= *restrict access to*) [+ *information*] clasificar como secreto
classiness* ['klɑːsɪnɪs] (N) elegancia *f*
classism ['klɑːsɪzəm] (N) clasismo *m*
classist ['klɑːsɪst] (ADJ) clasista
classless ['klɑːslɪs] (ADJ) [*society*] sin clases
classmate ['klɑːsmeɪt] (N) (*Brit*) compañero/a *m/f* de clase, condiscípulo/a *m/f*
classroom ['klɑːsrʊm] (N) aula *f*, clase *f*
(CPD) ▸ **classroom assistant** ≈ profesor(a) *m/f* de apoyo ▸ **classroom discussion** debate *m* en clase
classy* ['klɑːsɪ] (ADJ) (COMPAR: **classier**, SUPERL: **classiest**) elegante, de buen tono
clatter ['klætəʳ] (N) (= *loud noise*) estruendo *m*; [*of plates*] estrépito *m*; [*of hooves*] trápala *f*; [*of train*] triquitraque *m*; (= *hammering*) martilleo *m*
(VI) [*metal object etc*] hacer estrépito, hacer estruendo; [*hooves*] trapalear • **to ~ in/out** entrar/salir estrepitosamente • **to come ~ing down** caer ruidosamente • **to ~ down the stairs** bajar ruidosamente la escalera
Claudius ['klɔːdɪəs] (N) Claudio
clause [klɔːz] (N) (*Ling*) oración *f*; (*in contract, law*) cláusula *f*; (*in will*) disposición *f*
claustrophobia [,klɔːstrə'fəʊbɪə] (N) claustrofobia *f*
claustrophobic [,klɔːstrə'fəʊbɪk] (ADJ) claustrofóbico
(N) *persona que padece de claustrofobia*
clavichord ['klævɪkɔːd] (N) clavicordio *m*
clavicle ['klævɪkl] (N) clavícula *f*
claw [klɔː] (N) **1** (*Zool*) [*of cat, bird etc*] garra *f*; [*of lobster*] pinza *f*
2 (*Tech*) garfio *m*, gancho *m*
3 claws* (= *fingers*) dedos *mpl*, mano *fsing* • **to get one's ~s into sb** (= *attack*) atacar con rencor a algn; (= *dominate*) dominar a algn • **to get one's ~s on** agarrarse de *or* a • **get your ~s off that!** ¡fuera las manos! • **to show one's ~s** sacar las uñas
(VT) **1** (= *scratch*) arañar; (= *tear*) desgarrar • **to ~ sth to shreds** desgarrar algo completamente, hacer algo trizas
2 • **to ~ one's way somewhere** abrirse camino a toda costa • **to ~ one's way to the top** (*fig*) abrirse paso hasta la cima a toda costa
(CPD) ▸ **claw hammer** martillo *m* de orejas
▸ **claw at** (VI + PREP) (= *scratch*) arañar; (= *tear*) desgarrar
▸ **claw back** (VT + ADV) (*fig*) volver a tomar, tomar otra vez para sí
clawback ['klɔːbæk] (N) (*Econ*) *desgravación fiscal obtenida por devolución de impuestos*
clay [kleɪ] (N) arcilla *f*, barro *m*
(CPD) ▸ **clay court** (*Tennis*) pista *f* de tierra batida ▸ **clay pigeon** plato *m* de barro; (*US*) (*fig*) (= *victim*) víctima *f* ▸ **clay pigeon shooting** tiro *m* al plato, tiro *m* al pichón ▸ **clay pipe** pipa *f* de cerámica ▸ **clay pit** pozo *m* de arcilla
clayey ['kleɪɪ] (ADJ) arcilloso
clean [kliːn] (ADJ) (COMPAR: **cleaner**, SUPERL: **cleanest**) **1** (= *not dirty*) [*clothes, sheets, floor, face*] limpio; [*air, water*] limpio, puro • **he washed the floor ~** fregó el suelo • **the rain washed the streets ~** la lluvia limpió las calles • **to come ~** (*lit*) quedar limpio; (*fig**) confesarlo todo • **to come ~ about sth*** confesar algo • **to have ~ hands** (*lit, fig*) tener las manos limpias • **to wipe sth ~** limpiar algo • IDIOMS: • **to make a ~ breast of it** confesarlo todo • **to make a ~ sweep** (= *complete change*) hacer tabla rasa; (= *win everything*) arrasar • **to make a ~ sweep of sth** (*of prizes, awards*) arrasar con algo • **to make a ~ sweep of the votes** acaparar todos los votos, barrer • **as ~ as a whistle** *or* **new pin*** limpio como los chorros del oro, limpio como la patena
2 (= *fresh*) [*smell*] a limpio; [*taste*] refrescante
3 (= *new, unused*) [*sheet of paper, page*] en blanco, en limpio • **to make a ~ copy** hacer una copia en limpio
4 (= *not indecent*) [*joke*] inocente; [*film, life*] decente • **keep it ~!** ¡no seas indecente! • **~ living** vida *f* sana
5 (= *smooth, even*) [*movement*] fluido; [*shot*] certero; [*cut*] limpio; [*sound*] nítido, claro; [*features, outline*] nítido, bien definido • **a ~ break** (*Med*) una fractura limpia • **a ~ break with the totalitarian past** una ruptura radical con el pasado totalitario • **to make a ~ break** cortar por lo sano • **I need (to make) a ~ break with the past** necesito romper con el pasado totalmente
6 (= *fair*) [*fight, game, match*] limpio; [*player*] que juega limpio
7 (= *untarnished*) [*image, reputation*] bueno, impecable • **they gave him a ~ bill of health** le declararon en perfecto estado de salud • **a ~ driving licence** un carnet de conducir sin infracciones • **to have a ~ record** (*gen*) tener un historial limpio; (*no criminal record*) no tener antecedentes penales • **we have a ~ safety record** nuestro historial de seguridad

está limpio *or* no registra incidentes
8 (= *environmentally friendly*) [*machine, substance, energy*] no contaminante
9 (*Nuclear physics*) (= *uncontaminated*) [*area, person, object*] no contaminado
10 (= *ritually pure*) [*animal*] puro
11 (= *trouble-free*) [*operation, job, getaway*] sin problemas
12‡ (= *innocent*) • **they can't touch me, I'm ~** no me pueden hacer nada, tengo las manos limpias*
13‡ (= *not in possession of drugs, weapon, stolen property*) • **he's ~** no lleva nada encima • **his room was ~** no encontraron nada en su habitación
ADV **1*** (= *completely*) • **he ~ forgot** lo olvidó por completo • **he got ~ away** se escapó sin dejar rastro • **it went ~ through the window** pasó limpiamente por la ventana • **I'm ~ out of them** no me queda ni uno • **he jumped ~ over the fence** saltó la valla limpiamente
2 (= *fairly*) • **to fight/play ~** luchar/jugar limpio
N limpieza *f*, aseo *m* (*LAm*); (= *wash*) lavado *m* • **the windows could do with a ~** no estaría de más limpiar las ventanas • **to give sth a ~** limpiar algo • **to give sth a quick ~** dar una pasada (rápida) a algo • **to give sth a good ~** limpiar algo bien
VT [+ *room, carpet, windows, shoes*] limpiar; [+ *vegetables, clothes*] lavar; [+ *car*] lavar, limpiar; [+ *blackboard*] borrar; [+ *wound, cut*] desinfectar • **to ~ one's teeth** lavarse los dientes
VI **1** (*around the house*) limpiar
2 (= *be cleaned*) • **that floor ~s easily** este suelo es muy fácil de limpiar
▸ **clean down** VT + ADV limpiar
▸ **clean off** VT + ADV [+ *dirt, rust*] limpiar
▸ **clean out** VT + ADV **1** [+ *room, cupboard*] vaciar • **to ~ out a box** limpiar (el interior de) una caja
2* (*fig*) (= *leave penniless*) dejar limpio/a*, dejar pelado/a*; (*in robbery*) limpiar* • **the burglars came back to ~ me out again** los ladrones volvieron para limpiarme (la casa) de nuevo • **we were ~ed out** nos dejaron sin blanca
▸ **clean up** VT + ADV **1** [+ *room, mess*] limpiar, asear • **to ~ o.s. up** lavarse, ponerse decente
2 (*fig*) [+ *city, television etc*] limpiar, quitar lo indecente de; [+ *act, play*] suprimir los pasajes indecentes de
VI + ADV **1** (= *tidy*) limpiar • **to ~ up after a party** limpiar después de una fiesta • **to ~ up after sb** limpiar lo que ha dejado *or* ensuciado otro
2* (= *make profit*) hacer mucho dinero (**on** con) • **he ~ed up on that deal** hizo mucho dinero con ese negocio
clean-break divorce [ˌkliːnˌbreɪkdɪˈvɔːs] N *divorcio en el que se renuncia a la pensión alimenticia por un bien que se puede capitalizar*
clean-cut [ˈkliːnˈkʌt] ADJ **1** (= *clearly outlined*) claro, bien definido; [*outline*] nítido
2 [*person*] de buen parecer; (= *smart*) de aspecto elegante
cleaner [ˈkliːnəʳ] N **1** (= *man*) encargado *m* de la limpieza; (= *woman*) encargada *f* de la limpieza, asistenta *f* • **~'s (shop)** tintorería *f*, lavandería *f* • IDIOM: • **to take sb to the ~'s**: • **we'll take them to the ~'s*** les dejaremos sin blanca*, les dejaremos limpios*; ▸ **vacuum**
2 (= *substance*) producto *m* de limpieza
cleaning [ˈkliːnɪŋ] N limpieza *f*, limpia *f* (*LAm*) • **to do the ~** hacer la limpieza
CPD ▸ **cleaning fluid** líquido *m* de limpieza ▸ **cleaning lady, cleaning woman** señora *f* de la limpieza ▸ **cleaning products** productos *mpl* de limpieza
clean-limbed [ˌkliːnˈlɪmd] ADJ bien proporcionado
cleanliness [ˈklenlɪnɪs] N limpieza *f* • **the importance of personal ~** la importancia del aseo *or* de la higiene personal • PROVERB: • **~ is next to godliness** la limpieza lo es todo
clean-living [ˌkliːnˈlɪvɪŋ] ADJ de vida sana
cleanly¹ [ˈkliːnlɪ] ADV **1** (= *without polluting*) [*burn, operate*] de forma limpia, sin contaminar
2 (= *neatly*) [*cut, break*] limpiamente; [*hit, catch*] con habilidad, con destreza
3 (= *fairly*) [*play, fight*] limpiamente
cleanly² [ˈklenlɪ] ADJ [*person, animal*] limpio, aseado
cleanness [ˈkliːnnɪs] N **1** [*of clothes, sheets etc*] limpieza *f*; [*of air, water*] pureza *f*
2 (= *smoothness*) [*of cut, fracture*] limpieza *f*; [*of outline, features*] nitidez *f*; [*of movement*] fluidez *f*
3 (= *fairness*) [*of fight, game*] limpieza *f*
clean-out [ˈkliːnaʊt] N limpieza *f*
cleanse [klenz] VT [+ *skin*] limpiar (**of** de); (*fig*) [+ *soul etc*] purificar
cleanser [ˈklenzəʳ] N (= *detergent*) detergente *m*; (= *disinfectant*) desinfectante *m*; (= *cosmetic*) leche *f or* crema *f* limpiadora
clean-shaven [ˈkliːnˈʃeɪvn] ADJ (= *beardless*) sin barba ni bigote, totalmente afeitado; (= *smooth-faced*) lampiño
cleansing [ˈklenzɪŋ] ADJ (*for complexion*) limpiador; (*fig*) purificador
N limpieza *f*
CPD ▸ **cleansing cream** crema *f* desmaquilladora ▸ **cleansing department** departamento *m* de limpieza ▸ **cleansing lotion** loción *f* limpiadora
cleanskin* [ˈkliːnˌskɪn] N (= *person*) persona *f* sin antecedentes
clean-up [ˈkliːnʌp] N limpia *f*, limpieza *f*
clear [klɪəʳ] ADJ (COMPAR: **clearer**, SUPERL: **clearest**) **1** (= *unambiguous*) [*meaning, explanation*] claro • **a ~ case of murder** un caso claro de homicidio • **now let's get this ~ ...** vamos a dejar esto claro ... • **to make it ~ that ...** dejar claro *or* bien sentado que ... • **to make o.s. ~** explicarse claramente • **do I make myself ~?** ¿me explico bien? • **he's a ~ thinker** tiene la mente lúcida *or* despejada
2 (= *obvious*) [*motive, consequence*] claro, evidente • **it is (absolutely) ~ to me that ...** no me cabe (la menor) duda de que ... • **it became ~ that ...** empezó a verse claro que ... • **it's not ~ whether ...** no está claro si ... • IDIOMS: • **as ~ as crystal** más claro que el agua • **as ~ as day** más claro que el sol • **as ~ as mud*** nada claro
3 (= *certain*) [*understanding, proof*] seguro, cierto • **he was perfectly ~ that he did not intend to go** dijo claramente *or* tajantemente que no pensaba ir • **are we ~ that we want this?** ¿estamos seguros de que queremos esto? • **I'm not very ~ about this** no tengo una idea muy clara de esto • **I'm not ~ whether ...** no tengo claro si ...
4 (= *transparent*) [*water, glass*] claro, transparente • **a ~ soup** una sopa clara
5 [*sky, weather*] despejado; [*air*] puro • **on a ~ day** en un día despejado
6 (= *bright*) [*light, colour*] claro • **~ blue eyes** ojos azul claro; ▸ **light¹**
7 [*photograph, outline*] claro, preciso; [*complexion*] terso • **to have a ~ head** tener la cabeza despejada
8 (= *distinct*) [*sound, impression, voice*] claro • IDIOM: • **as ~ as a bell**: • **I could hear his voice as ~ as a bell** oía su voz como si estuviera a mi lado, oía su voz con toda claridad
9 (= *unobstructed*) [*road, space*] libre, despejado • **all ~!** ¡vía libre!, ¡adelante! • **to get a ~ look at sb/sth** poder ver algn/algo bien • **to be ~ of sth** (= *free of*) estar libre de algo; (= *away from*) estar lejos de algo • **we had a ~ view** teníamos una buena vista, se veía bien
10 (= *untroubled*) [*conscience*] limpio, tranquilo
11 (*after deductions*) • **a ~ profit** una ganancia neta • **£3 ~ profit** una ganancia neta de 3 libras
12 • **a ~ majority** una mayoría absoluta • **to win by a ~ margin** ganar por un amplio margen • **a ~ winner** un ganador absoluto
13 (= *complete*) • **three ~ days** tres días enteros
14 (= *without commitments*) [*day, afternoon*] libre; [*diary*] despejado
ADV **1** ▸ **loud**
2 (= *completely*) • **he jumped ~ across the river** atravesó el río limpiamente de un salto • **you could hear it ~ across the valley** se oía claramente desde el otro lado del valle
3 (= *free*) • **to get ~ away** escaparse sin dejar rastro alguno • **to get ~ of** (= *get rid of*) deshacerse de • **when we get ~ of London** (= *away from*) cuando estemos fuera de Londres • **to keep ~ of sb/sth**: • **keep ~ of the wall** no te acerques a la pared • **I decided to keep ~ of him** decidí evitarle • **keep ~ of my daughter!** ¡no te acerques a mi hija!, ¡mantente alejado de mi hija! • **to stand ~ of sth** mantenerse apartado de algo • **stand ~ of the doors!** ¡apártense de las puertas!
4 (*Brit*) (*Sport*) (= *ahead*) • **to be seven metres/seconds/points ~ of sb** estar siete metros/segundos/puntos por delante de algn; ▸ **steer¹**
5 (= *net*) • **he'll get £250 ~** sacará 250 libras netas
6 (*esp US*) • **~ to sth** (= *as far as*) hasta algo • **they went ~ to Mexico** llegaron hasta Méjico
N **1** • **to be in the ~** (= *out of debt*) estar libre de deudas; (= *free of suspicion*) quedar fuera de toda sospecha; (= *free of danger*) estar fuera de peligro
2 • **message in ~** mensaje *m* no cifrado
VT **1** (= *remove obstacles etc from*) [+ *place, surface*] despejar; [+ *road, railway track*] dejar libre, despejar; [+ *site*] desmontar; [+ *woodland*] despejar, desbrozar; [+ *court, hall*] desocupar, desalojar (de público *etc*); [+ *pipe*] desatascar; [+ *postbox*] recoger las cartas de • **to ~ one's conscience** descargar la conciencia • **to ~ one's head** despejar la cabeza • **to ~ sth of sth** despejar algo de algo • **to ~ a space for sth/sb** hacer sitio para algo/algn • **to ~ the table** recoger *or* quitar la mesa • **to ~ one's throat** carraspear, aclararse la voz • **to ~ the way for sth** (*fig*) dejar el camino libre para algo • IDIOM: • **to ~ the air** (= *clarify things*) aclarar las cosas; (= *ease tensions*) relajar el ambiente
2 [+ *liquid*] aclarar, clarificar; (*Med*) [+ *blood*] purificar
3 (*Sport*) [+ *ball*] despejar
4 (= *get over*) [+ *fence etc*] salvar, saltar por encima de; (= *get past*) [+ *rocks etc*] pasar sin tocar • **the plane just ~ed the roof** el avión no tocó el tejado por poco, el avión pasó casi rozando el tejado • **to ~ two metres** [*jumper*] saltar dos metros • **this part has to ~ that by at least one centimetre** entre esta pieza y aquella tiene que haber un espacio de un centímetro al menos
5 (= *declare innocent etc*) [+ *person*] absolver, probar la inocencia de • **he was ~ed of murder** fue absuelto de asesinato • **to ~ o.s. of a charge** probar su inocencia de una acusación

C

6 (*= authorize*) • **you will have to be ~ed by Security** será preciso que le acredite la Seguridad • **the plan will have to be ~ed with the director** el plan tendrá que ser aprobado por el director
7 • **to ~ a cheque** (*= accept*) aceptar *or* dar el visto bueno a un cheque; (*= double check*) compensar un cheque
8 (*Comm etc*) [*+ debt*] liquidar, saldar; [*+ profit*] sacar (una ganancia de); [*+ goods etc*] liquidar • **he ~ed £50 on the deal** sacó 50 libras del negocio • **he ~s £250 a week** se saca 250 libras a la semana • **we have just about ~ed our costs** nos ha llegado justo para cubrir los gastos • **"half-price to clear"** "liquidación a mitad de precio"
9 (*Comput*) despejar
VI **1** (*= improve*) [*weather*] (*also* **clear up**) despejarse; [*sky*] despejarse; [*fog*] disiparse
2 [*liquid*] aclararse, clarificarse
3 [*cheque*] ser compensado
4 (*Sport*) despejar
CPD ▸ **clear round** (*Showjumping*) ronda *f* sin penalizaciones
▸ **clear away** VT + ADV [*+ things, clothes etc*] quitar (de en medio); [*+ dishes*] retirar
VI + ADV **1** (*= clear the table*) quitar los platos, quitar la mesa
2 [*mist*] disiparse
▸ **clear off** VT + ADV [*+ debt*] liquidar, saldar
VI + ADV* (*= leave*) largarse*, mandarse mudar (*LAm*) • **~ off!** ¡lárgate!*, ¡fuera de aquí!
▸ **clear out** VT + ADV [*+ room*] ordenar y tirar los trastos de; [*+ cupboard*] vaciar; [*+ objects*] quitar • **he ~ed everyone out of the room** hizo salir a todo el mundo de la habitación • **he ~ed everything out of the room** despejó la habitación de cosas
VI + ADV = **clear off**
▸ **clear up** VT + ADV **1** (*= resolve*) [*+ matter, difficulty*] aclarar; [*+ mystery, crime*] resolver, esclarecer; [*+ doubt*] resolver, aclarar, disipar
2 (*= tidy*) [*+ room, books, toys*] ordenar
VI + ADV **1** [*weather*] despejarse
2 [*illness*] curarse
3 (*= tidy up*) ponerlo todo en orden, ordenar

clearance ['klɪərəns] N **1** (*= act of clearing*) [*of road etc*] despeje *m*; [*of land*] desmonte *m*, roza *f*
2 (*= height, width etc*) margen *m* (*de altura, anchura etc*)
3 (*= authorization*) (*by customs*) despacho *m* de aduana; (*by security*) acreditación *f*; (*Econ*) compensación *f* • **~ for take-off** (*Aer*) pista libre para despegar
4 (*Ftbl*) despeje *m*
CPD ▸ **clearance sale** liquidación *f*, realización *f* (*LAm*)

clear-cut ['klɪə'kʌt] ADJ [*decision, victory*] claro; [*statement*] sin ambages

clear-eyed [ˌklɪər'aɪd] ADJ de ojos claros; (*fig*) clarividente

clear-headed ['klɪə'hedɪd] ADJ lúcido, de mente despejada

clear-headedness ['klɪə'hedɪdnɪs] N lucidez *f*

clearing ['klɪərɪŋ] N **1** (*in wood*) claro *m*
2 (*Econ*) liquidación *f*
CPD ▸ **clearing account** (*Econ*) cuenta *f* de compensación ▸ **clearing bank** (*Brit*) (*Econ*) banco *m* central ▸ **clearing house** (*Econ*) cámara *f* de compensación

clearly ['klɪəlɪ] ADV **1** (*= unambiguously*) [*define, state, forbid*] claramente
2 (*= rationally*) [*think*] con claridad
3 (*= distinctly*) [*see, speak, hear*] claramente, con claridad • **~ visible** claramente visible • **~ marked** marcado claramente
4 (*= obviously*) evidentemente, obviamente • **~, the police cannot break the law in order to enforce it** evidentemente *or* obviamente la policía no puede ir contra la ley para aplicarla • **a very pleasant man, educated and ~ intelligent** un hombre muy agradable, educado y obviamente inteligente • **he was ~ not convinced** estaba claro *or* era evidente que no estaba convencido • **the owner was ~ not expecting us** estaba claro *or* era evidente que el dueño no nos esperaba

clearness ['klɪənɪs] N claridad *f*

clear-out ['klɪəraʊt] N • **to have a good clear-out** limpiarlo todo, despejarlo todo

clear-sighted ['klɪə'saɪtɪd] ADJ clarividente, perspicaz

clear-sightedness ['klɪə'saɪtɪdnɪs] N clarividencia *f*, perspicacia *f*

clear-up rate ['klɪə'rʌpreɪt] N (*Police*) *ratio de casos resueltos por número de denuncias*

clearway ['klɪəweɪ] N (*Brit*) carretera *f* en la que está prohibido parar

cleat [kliːt] N abrazadera *f*, listón *m*, fiador *m*

cleavage ['kliːvɪdʒ] N **1** (*= division, split*) escisión *f*, división *f*
2 [*of woman*] escote *m*

cleave¹ [kliːv] (PT: **clove, cleft**, PP: **cloven, cleft**) VT (*= split*) partir; [*+ water*] surcar

cleave² [kliːv] VI • **to ~ to** adherirse a, no separarse de • **to ~ together** ser inseparables

cleaver ['kliːvəʳ] N cuchilla *f* de carnicero

clef [klef] N (*Mus*) clave *f*

cleft [kleft] PT, PP *of* **cleave¹**
ADJ • **~ chin** barbilla *f* partida • IDIOM: • **to be in a ~ stick** estar entre la espada y la pared
N (*in rock*) grieta *f*, hendidura *f*; (*in chin*) partición *f*
CPD ▸ **cleft palate** fisura *f* del paladar

cleg [kleg] N tábano *m*

clematis ['klemətɪs] N clemátide *f*

clemency ['klemənsɪ] N clemencia *f*

clement ['klemənt] ADJ clemente, benigno

clementine ['klemantaɪn] N clementina *f*

clench [klentʃ] VT [*+ teeth*] apretar; [*+ fist*] cerrar • **to ~ sth in one's hands** apretar algo en las manos • **the ~ed fist** el puño cerrado

Cleopatra [ˌkliːə'pætrə] N Cleopatra

clerestory ['klɪəˌstɔːrɪ] N triforio *m*

clergy ['klɜːdʒɪ] NPL clero *m*

clergyman ['klɜːdʒɪmən] N (PL: **clergymen**) clérigo *m*; (*Anglican*) pastor *m* anglicano; (*Protestant*) pastor *m* protestante

clergywoman ['klɜːdʒɪˌwʊmən] N (PL: **clergywomen**) (*Anglican*) pastora *f* anglicana; (*Protestant*) pastora *f* protestante

cleric ['klerɪk] N eclesiástico *m*, clérigo *m*

clerical ['klerɪkəl] ADJ **1** (*Comm*) [*job*] de oficina • **~ error** error *m* de copia • **~ grades** (*Civil Service etc*) oficinistas *mpl* • **~ staff** personal *m* de oficina • **~ work** trabajo *m* de oficina • **~ worker** oficinista *mf*
2 (*Rel*) clerical • **~ collar** alzacuello(s) *m*

clericalism ['klerɪkaˌlɪzəm] N clericalismo *m*

clerihew ['klerɪhjuː] N *estrofa inglesa de cuatro versos, de carácter festivo*

clerk [klɑːk], (*US*) [klɜːk] N **1** (*Comm*) oficinista *mf*, empleado/a *m/f*; (*in civil service*) funcionario/a *m/f*; (*in bank*) empleado/a *m/f*; (*in hotel*) recepcionista *mf*; (*Jur*) escribano *m*; ▸ **town**
2 (*US*) (*= shop assistant*) dependiente/a *m/f*, vendedor(a) *m/f*
3 (*Rel††*) clérigo *m*
VI (*US*) trabajar como dependiente
CPD ▸ **Clerk of Court** escribano/a *m/f* del tribunal ▸ **clerk of works** (*Brit*) (*Constr*) maestro/a *m/f* de obras

clerkship ['klɑːkʃɪp], (*US*) ['klɜːkʃɪp] N empleo *m* de oficinista; (*Jur*) escribanía *f*

clever ['klevəʳ] ADJ (COMPAR: **cleverer**, SUPERL: **cleverest**) **1** (*= intelligent*) [*person*] inteligente, listo • **~ girl!** ¡qué chica más lista! • **that was ~ of you** ¡qué listo eres! • **that wasn't very ~, was it?*** eso ha sido una metedura de pata ¿no te parece?*
2 (*= skilful*) [*craftsman, sportsman*] hábil, habilidoso; [*piece of work, action*] hábil, ingenioso • **he is very ~ with his hands** es muy mañoso, es muy hábil *or* habilidoso con las manos • **she is very ~ with cars** entiende de coches, tiene mano para los coches • **to be ~ at sth** tener aptitud para algo
3 (*= ingenious*) [*book, idea, design*] ingenioso
4 (*esp pej*) (*= smart, astute*) [*politician, lawyer, criminal*] astuto, listo; [*move, approach, plan*] astuto, ingenioso; [*trick, hoax, technique, advertising*] ingenioso • **he was too ~ for us** fue más listo que nosotros • **he did some ~ book-keeping** hizo la contabilidad con bastante maña • **don't get ~ (with me)!*** ¡no te hagas el listo (conmigo)! • **to be too ~ by half*** pasarse de listo • IDIOMS: • **~ Dick** (*Brit**) • **~ clogs** (*Brit**) sabelotodo *mf inv*, listorro/a* *m/f*; ▹ **half**

clever-clever* ['klevəˌklevəʳ] ADJ sabihondo • **he's very clever-clever** es un siete ciencias

cleverly ['klevəlɪ] ADV **1** (*= intelligently*) [*deduce, work out*] de forma inteligente, con inteligencia • **she ~ worked out the answer** supo averiguar la respuesta de forma inteligente *or* con inteligencia
2 (*= skilfully*) hábilmente, ingeniosamente • **the photographer ~ framed the shot with trees** el fotógrafo encuadró hábilmente *or* ingeniosamente la fotografía entre árboles • **~ constructed** ingeniosamente construido • **it is ~ designed** tiene un diseño ingenioso
3 (*esp pej*) (*= astutely*) [*avoid, plan, disguise*] astutamente, con maña

cleverness ['klevənɪs] N **1** (*= intelligence*) inteligencia *f*
2 (*= skill*) habilidad *f*
3 (*= ingenuity*) ingenio *m*
4 (*= astuteness*) [*of person*] astucia *f*, maña *f*; [*of trick, technique, plan*] lo ingenioso

clew [kluː] N (*US*) = **clue**

cliché ['kliːʃeɪ] N cliché *m*, tópico *m*

cliched, clichéd ['kliːʃeɪd] ADJ [*image, view*] manido, muy visto; [*song*] de siempre

click [klɪk] N [*of camera etc*] golpecito *m* seco, clic *m*; [*of heels*] taconeo *m*; [*of tongue*] chasquido *m*; [*of gun*] piñoneo *m*; [*of typewriter etc*] tecleo *m*
VT [*+ tongue*] chasquear; (*Comput*) hacer clic en • **to ~ one's heels** dar un taconazo
VI **1** [*camera etc*] hacer clic; [*gun*] piñonear; [*typewriter etc*] teclear • **the door ~ed shut** la puerta se cerró con un golpecito seco
2* (*= be understood*) quedar claro/a • **it didn't ~ with me until …** no caí en la cuenta hasta (que) … • **suddenly it all ~ed (into place)** de pronto, todo encajaba (en su sitio)
3* (*= be a success*) [*product, invention*] ser un éxito; [*two people*] congeniar, gustarse inmediatamente • **to ~ with sb** congeniar *or* conectar con algn
4 (*Comput*) hacer clic • **to ~ on an icon** hacer clic en un icono
CPD ▸ **click fraud** fraude *m* de clics

clickable ['klɪkəbl] ADJ (*Comput*) cliqueable

clickbait* ['klɪkbeɪt] N cebo *m* de clics, *contenido diseñado para que las personas hagan clic sobre él*

clicker* ['klɪkəʳ] N (*US*) (*= remote control*) mando *m* a distancia, telemando *m*

clicking ['klɪkɪŋ] N chasquido *m*

clickjacking* ['klɪkdʒækɪŋ] (N) secuestro *m* de clics, clickjacking *m*
client ['klaɪənt] (N) cliente/a *m/f* • **my ~** (*in court*) mi defendido
(CPD) ▸ **client base** clientela *f* habitual
▸ **client state** (*Pol*) estado *m* satélite, estado *m* cliente
clientele [ˌkliːɑ̃ːnˈtel] (N) clientela *f*
cliff [klɪf] (N) (= *sea cliff*) acantilado *m*; [*of mountain etc*] risco *m*, precipicio *m*
(CPD) ▸ **cliff dweller*** (*US*) (*fig*) *persona que habita en un bloque* ▸ **cliff face** pared *f* de acantilado
cliffhanger ['klɪfˌhæŋəʳ] (N) (= *film*) película *f* melodramática, película *f* de suspense • **the match was a real ~** el partido fue un suspense hasta el último momento
cliff-hanging ['klɪfˌhæŋɪŋ] (ADJ) muy emocionante (por su final dudoso y apasionante), que tiene a todos pendientes de su resultado; [*drama*] de suspense
clifftop ['klɪftɒp] (N) lo alto de un acantilado • **I have a beautiful house on a ~** tengo una casa hermosa encima de un acantilado
(ADJ) en *or* por lo alto de un acantilado • **a ~ walk** un paseo por el acantilado
climacteric [klaɪ'mæktərɪk] (ADJ) climactérico
(N) período *m* climactérico
climactic [klaɪ'mæktɪk] (ADJ) culminante
climate ['klaɪmɪt] (N) clima *m*; (*fig*) ambiente *m* • **the ~ of opinion** la opinión general
(CPD) ▸ **climate change** cambio *m* climático
▸ **climate control** (= *air conditioning*) climatizador *m*
climatic [klaɪ'mætɪk] (ADJ) climático
• **~ change** cambio *m* climático
climatological [ˌklaɪmətə'lɒdʒɪkəl] (ADJ) climatológico
climatologist [ˌklaɪmə'tɒlədʒɪst] (N) climatólogo/a *m/f*
climatology [ˌklaɪmə'tɒlədʒɪ] (N) climatología *f*
climax ['klaɪmæks] (N) **1** (= *high point*) punto *m* culminante, apogeo *m*; [*of play etc*] clímax *m inv* • **to reach a ~** llegar a su punto álgido, alcanzar una cima de intensidad
2 (= *sexual climax*) orgasmo *m*
(VI) **1** (= *reach high point*) llegar a un *or* su clímax
2 (= *achieve orgasm*) tener un orgasmo
climb [klaɪm] (N) (*gen*) subida *f*, ascenso *m*; [*of mountain*] escalada *f*; (*fig*) ascenso *m* • **it was a stiff ~** la subida fue penosa
(VT) (*also* **climb up**) [+ *tree, ladder etc*] trepar, subir a; [+ *staircase*] subir (por); [+ *mountain*] escalar; [+ *cliff*] trepar por; [+ *wall*] trepar (a)
(VI) **1** [*person, plant*] trepar, subir • **to ~ along a ledge** subir por un saliente • **to ~ over a wall** franquear *or* saltar una tapia • **to ~ to power** (*fig*) subir al poder
2 [*road*] ascender; [*plane*] elevarse, remontar el vuelo; [*price, sun*] subir • **the path ~s higher yet** la senda llega aún más arriba
▸ **climb down** (VI + PREP) [+ *tree etc*] bajar • **to ~ down a cliff** bajar por un precipicio
(VI + ADV) **1** [*person*] (*from tree etc*) bajar
2 (*fig*) rendirse; (= *retract statement etc*) desdecirse, retractarse
▸ **climb into** (VI + PREP) • **to ~ into an aircraft** subir a un avión • **to ~ into a tree** trepar a un árbol
▸ **climb out** (VI + ADV) salir trepando
▸ **climb out of** (VI + PREP) salir trepando de
▸ **climb up** (VI + PREP) • **to ~ up a rope** trepar por una cuerda • **to ~ up a cliff** trepar por un precipicio
(VI + ADV) subir, trepar
climbdown ['klaɪmdaʊn] (N) vuelta *f* atrás, retroceso *m*
climber ['klaɪməʳ] (N) **1** (= *mountaineer*) montañista *mf*, alpinista *mf*, andinista *mf* (*LAm*)
2 (*Bot*) trepadora *f*, enredadera *f*
3 (*fig*) (*also* **social climber**) arribista *mf*, trepador(a) *m/f*
climbing ['klaɪmɪŋ] (N) (= *rock climbing*) montañismo *m*, alpinismo *m*, andinismo *m* (*LAm*) • **to go ~** hacer montañismo *or* alpinismo, ir de escalada
(CPD) ▸ **climbing accident** accidente *m* de escalada • **his parents were killed in a ~ accident** sus padres murieron mientras escalaban ▸ **climbing boot** bota *f* de montaña ▸ **climbing frame** *estructura metálica en la cual los niños juegan trepando* ▸ **climbing irons** garfios *mpl* ▸ **climbing wall** muro *m* de escalada
clime [klaɪm] (N) (*liter*) (= *climate*) clima *m*; (= *country*) región *f* • **in warmer/sunnier ~s** en tierras *or* regiones más cálidas/soleadas • **he went off to foreign ~s** se marchó a tierras extranjeras
clinch [klɪntʃ] (N) **1** (*Boxing*) clinch *m*
2‡ (= *embrace*) abrazo *m* • **in a ~** abrazados, agarrados (*LAm*) • **to go into a ~** abrazarse, agarrarse (*LAm*)
(VT) **1** (= *secure*) afianzar; [+ *nail*] remachar, roblar
2 (= *settle decisively*) [+ *deal*] cerrar, firmar; [+ *argument*] remachar, terminar; [+ *agreement*] cerrar • **to ~ matters** para acabar de remacharlo • **that ~es it** está decidido, ni una palabra más
clincher* ['klɪntʃəʳ] (N) • **that was the ~** eso fue el punto clave, eso fue el argumento irrebatible
clinching ['klɪntʃɪŋ] (ADJ) [*argument*] decisivo, irrebatible
cling [klɪŋ] (PT, PP: **clung**) (VI) **1** (= *hold on*) (*to person*) pegarse (**to** a); (*affectionately*) agarrarse, aferrarse (**to** a); (*to rope*) agarrarse (**to** a, de); (*to belief, opinion*) aferrarse, seguir fiel (**to** a) • **they clung to one another** no se desprendían de su abrazo
2 (= *stick*) [*clothes*] (*to skin*) pegarse (**to** a) • **a dress that ~s to the figure** un vestido que se pega al cuerpo • **the smell clung to her clothes** la ropa se quedó impregnada del olor
3 (= *stay close*) (*to friend, mother etc*) no separarse (**to** de) • **to ~ together** (*fig*) no separarse (ni un momento)
Clingfilm® ['klɪŋfɪlm] (N) film *m* adherente (para envolver alimentos)
clinging ['klɪŋɪŋ] (ADJ) **1** (*pej*) (= *overdependent*) [*person*] pegajoso • **~ vine** (*US*) (*fig*) lapa* *mf*
2 [*dress*] ceñido
3 [*odour*] tenaz
clingwrap ['klɪŋræp] (N) = **Clingfilm**
clingy* ['klɪŋɪ] (ADJ) **1** [*person*] pegajoso
2 [*clothes*] ceñido
clinic ['klɪnɪk] (N) (*in NHS hospital*) consultorio *m*; (= *private hospital*) clínica *f*; (*for guidance*) consultorio *m*
clinical ['klɪnɪkəl] (ADJ) **1** (*Med*) clínico
2 (= *unemotional, cool*) frío
(CPD) ▸ **clinical depression** depresión *f* clínica ▸ **clinical psychologist** psicólogo/a *m/f* clínico/a ▸ **clinical psychology** psicología *f* clínica ▸ **clinical thermometer** termómetro *m* clínico ▸ **clinical trials** ensayos *mpl* clínicos
clinically ['klɪnɪkəlɪ] (ADV) **1** (*Med*) clínicamente • **~ dead** clínicamente muerto
2 (= *coldly*) fríamente
clinician [klɪ'nɪʃən] (N) médico/a *m/f* de clínica
clink¹ [klɪŋk] (N) [*of coins*] tintín *m*, tintineo *m*; [*of glasses*] choque *m*
(VT) hacer sonar, hacer tintinear • **to ~ glasses with sb** entrechocar la copa con algn
(VI) [*coins*] tintinear
clink²‡ [klɪŋk] (N) (= *jail*) trena‡ *f*
clinker ['klɪŋkəʳ] (N) **1** (= *burnt out coal*) escoria *f* de hulla
2 (= *paving material*) ladrillo *m* duro
3 (*US‡*) (= *gaffe*) metedura *f* de pata; (= *failed film, play*) birria* *f*
clinker-built ['klɪŋkəˌbɪlt] (ADJ) (*Naut*) de tingladillo
clip¹ [klɪp] (N) **1** (= *cut*) tijeretazo *m*, tijeretada *f*; (= *shearing*) esquila *f*, esquileo *m*; (= *wool*) cantidad *f* de lana esquilada
2 (*Cine*) secuencia *f*
3 (= *blow*) golpe *m*, cachete *m* • **at a (fast) ~** (*US*) a toda pastilla
(VT) **1** (= *cut*) cortar; (= *cut to shorten*) acortar; [+ *hedge*] podar; [+ *ticket*] picar; (*also* **clip off**) [+ *wool*] trasquilar, esquilar; [+ *hair*] recortar; (*also* **clip out**) [+ *article from newspaper*] recortar; [+ *words*] comerse, abreviar • IDIOM: • **to ~ sb's wings** cortar las alas a algn
2 (= *hit*) golpear, dar un cachete a
(CPD) ▸ **clip joint*** (*US*) bar *m* (muy caro)
▸ **clip off** (VT + ADV) cortar, quitar cortando
▸ **clip out** (VT + ADV) recortar
clip² [klɪp] (N) (= *clamp*) grapa *f*; (= *paper clip*) sujetapapeles *m inv*, clip *m*, grampa *f* (*S. Cone*); [*of pen*] sujetador *m*; (= *hair clip*) horquilla *f*, clip *m*; (= *brooch*) alfiler *m*, clip *m*, abrochador *m* (*LAm*); [*of cyclist*] pinza *f*
(VT) sujetar
(N) ▸ **clip art** (*Comput*) clip art *m*, objetos *mpl* gráficos
▸ **clip on** (VT + ADV) [+ *brooch*] prender, sujetar; [+ *document*] sujetar con un clip
(VI + ADV) • **it ~s on here** se fija aquí (con clip)
▸ **clip together** (VT + ADV) unir
clipboard ['klɪpˌbɔːd] (N) tablilla *f* con sujetapapeles, carpeta *f* sujetapapeles
clip-clop ['klɪp'klɒp] (N) *ruido de los cascos del caballo*
clip-on ['klɪpɒn] (ADJ) [*badge*] para prender, con prendedor; [*earrings*] de pinza
clipped [klɪpt] (ADJ) [*accent*] entrecortado; [*style*] sucinto; [*hair*] corto
clipper ['klɪpəʳ] (N) (*Naut*) clíper *m*
clippers ['klɪpəz] (NPL) (*for hair*) maquinilla *fsing* (para el pelo); (*for nails*) cortaúñas *msing inv*; (*for hedge*) tijeras *fpl* de podar
clippie†* ['klɪpɪ] (N) (*Brit*) cobradora *f* (de autobús)
clipping ['klɪpɪŋ] (N) (*from newspaper*) recorte *m*
clique [kliːk] (N) camarilla *f*
cliquey ['kliːkɪ] (ADJ) exclusivista
cliquish ['kliːkɪʃ] (ADJ) = **cliquey**
cliquishness ['kliːkɪʃnɪs] (N) exclusivismo *m*
cliquy ['kliːkɪ] (ADJ) = **cliquey**
cliterodectomy [ˌklɪtərɪ'dektəmɪ] (N) clitoridectomía *f*
clitoral ['klɪtərəl] (ADJ) del clítoris
clitoridectomy [ˌklɪtərɪ'dektəmɪ] (N) clitoridectomía *f*
clitoris ['klɪtərɪs] (N) clítoris *m*
Cllr (ABBR) = **Councillor**
cloak [kləʊk] (N) capa *f*, manto *m* • **under the ~ of darkness** (*fig*) al amparo de la oscuridad
(VT) (= *cover*) cubrir (**in, with** de); (*fig*) encubrir, disimular • **a ~ed figure** una silueta envuelta *or* embozada en una capa
cloak-and-dagger ['kləʊkən'dægəʳ] (ADJ) [*activity*] clandestino; [*play*] de capa y espada; [*story*] de agentes secretos
cloakroom ['kləʊkrʊm] (N) **1** (*for coats*) guardarropa *m*, ropero *m*
2 (*Brit*) (*euph*) (= *toilet*) lavabo *m*, servicios *mpl*,

C

baño m (LAm)
CPD ▸ **cloakroom attendant** (for coats) ayudante mf de vestuario ▸ **cloakroom ticket** ticket m de guardarropa

clobber‡ ['klɒbəʳ] N 1 (= clothes) ropa f, traje m
2 (Brit) (= gear) bártulos* mpl, trastos mpl (Sp*)
VT (= beat up, defeat) dar una paliza a*

clobbering* ['klɒbərɪŋ] N (= beating, defeat) paliza* f • **to get a ~** recibir una paliza*

cloche [klɒʃ] N campana f de cristal

clock [klɒk] N 1 (= timepiece) (gen) reloj m; [of taxi] taxímetro m; (= speedometer) velocímetro m; (= milometer) cuentakilómetros m inv • **you can't put the ~ back** (= return to past) no puedes volver al pasado; (= stop progress) no se puede detener el progreso • **to keep one's eyes on** or **watch the ~** mirar mucho el reloj (ansiando abandonar el trabajo) • **to work against the ~** trabajar contra reloj • **alarm ~** despertador m • **grandfather ~** reloj m de pie, reloj m de caja • **30,000 miles on the ~** (Aut) 30.000 millas en el cuentakilómetros • **it's only got 60 miles on the ~** este coche ha hecho solamente 60 millas • **round** or **around the ~** las veinticuatro horas del día • **the garage is open round the ~** el garaje está abierto las veinticuatro horas del día • **we have surveillance round the ~** tenemos vigilancia de veinticuatro horas, tenemos vigilancia permanente • **to sleep round the ~** dormir un día entero
2‡ (= face) jeta f
VT 1 (= time, measure) [+ runner, time] cronometrar • **we ~ed 80mph** alcanzamos una velocidad de 80 millas por hora
2 (Brit*) (= hit) • **he ~ed him one** le dio un bofetón*
CPD ▸ **clock card** tarjeta f de fichar ▸ **clock golf** *variedad del golf que consiste en golpear la pelota desde distintas posiciones en una circunferencia alrededor del agujero* ▸ **clock radio** radio-despertador m ▸ **clock repairer** relojero/a m/f ▸ **clock tower** torre f de reloj ▸ **clock watcher** *persona que mira mucho el reloj ansiando abandonar el trabajo*

▸ **clock in** VI + ADV (= mark card) fichar, picar; (= start work) entrar a trabajar

▸ **clock off** VI + ADV (= mark card) fichar or picar la salida; (= leave work) salir del trabajo

▸ **clock on** VI + ADV = **clock in**

▸ **clock out** VI + ADV = **clock off**

▸ **clock up** VT + ADV (Aut) hacer • **he ~ed up 250 miles** (Aut) hizo 250 millas

clockface ['klɒkfeɪs] N esfera f de reloj

clockmaker ['klɒk,meɪkəʳ] N relojero/a m/f

clockwise ['klɒkwaɪz] ADJ, ADV en el sentido de las agujas del reloj

clockwork ['klɒkwɜːk] N • **to go like ~** funcionar como un reloj
CPD [toy] de cuerda ▸ **clockwork train** tren m de cuerda

clod [klɒd] N 1 [of earth] terrón m
2 (= person) patán m, zoquete mf • **you ~!** ¡bestia!

clodhopper ['klɒd,hɒpəʳ] N patán m

clodhopping ['klɒdhɒpɪŋ] ADJ [person] torpón, desgarbado; [boots] basto, pesado

clog [klɒg] N zueco m, chanclo m
VT (also **clog up**) [+ pipe, drain, machine, mechanism] atascar
VI (also **clog up**) atascarse

cloister ['klɔɪstəʳ] N claustro m; **cloisters** soportales mpl

cloistered ['klɔɪstəd] ADJ • **to lead a ~ life** llevar una vida de ermitaño

clonal ['kləʊnəl] ADJ clónico

clone [kləʊn] N clon m; (Comput) clónico m
VT clonar

cloning ['kləʊnɪŋ] N clonación f, clonaje m

clonk [klɒnk] N (= sound) ruido m hueco
VI (= make sound) hacer un ruido hueco

close¹ [kləʊs] ADV (COMPAR: **closer**, SUPERL: **closest**) cerca • **the shops are very ~** las tiendas están muy cerca • **the hotel is ~ to the station** el hotel está cerca de la estación • **she was ~ to tears** estaba a punto de llorar • **according to sources ~ to the police** según fuentes allegadas a la policía • **~ by** muy cerca • **come ~r** acércate más • **to come ~ to** acercarse a • **we came very ~ to losing the match** estuvimos a punto de perder el partido, faltó poco para que perdiéramos el partido • **that comes ~ to an insult** eso es casi un insulto • **the runners finished very ~** los corredores llegaron casi al mismo tiempo • **to fit ~** ajustarse al cuerpo • **to follow ~ behind** seguir muy de cerca • **to hold sb ~** abrazar fuertemente a algn • **to keep ~ to the wall** ir arrimado a la pared • **he must be ~ on 50** debe andar cerca de los 50 • **it's ~ on six o'clock** son casi las seis • **stay ~ to me** no te alejes or separes de mí • **~ together** juntos, cerca uno del otro • **to look at sth ~ up** mirar algo de cerca
ADJ 1 (= near) [place] cercano, próximo; [contact] directo; [connection] estrecho, íntimo • **~ combat** lucha f cuerpo a cuerpo • **at ~ quarters** de cerca • **to come a ~ second to sb/sth** disputarle la primera posición a algn/algo • **he was the ~st thing to a real worker among us** entre nosotros él tenía más visos de ser un obrero auténtico, de nosotros él era el que tenía más visos de ser un obrero • IDIOM: • **it was a ~ shave*** se salvaron por un pelo or de milagro
2 (= intimate) [relative] cercano; [friend] íntimo • **we have only invited ~ relations** solo hemos invitado a parientes cercanos • **she's a ~ friend of mine** es una amiga íntima mía • **I'm very ~ to my sister** estoy muy unida a mi hermana • **they're very ~ (to each other)** están muy unidos • **a ~ circle of friends** un estrecho círculo de amigos
3 (= almost equal) [result, election, fight] muy reñido; [scores] casi iguales • **it was a very ~ contest** fue una competición muy reñida • **to bear a ~ resemblance to** tener mucho parecido con
4 (= exact, detailed) [examination, study] detallado; [investigation, questioning] minucioso; [surveillance, control] estricto; [translation] fiel, exacto • **to pay ~ attention to sb/sth** prestar mucha atención a algn/algo • **to keep a ~ watch on sb** mantener a algn bajo estricta vigilancia
5 (= not spread out) [handwriting, print] compacto; [texture, weave] compacto, tupido; [formation] cerrado
6 (= stuffy) [atmosphere, room] sofocante, cargado; [weather] pesado, bochornoso • **it's ~ this afternoon** hace bochorno esta tarde
7 (= secretive) reservado; (= mean) tacaño
8 (Ling) [vowel] cerrado
N recinto m
CPD ▸ **close company** (Brit) (Econ) sociedad f exclusiva, compañía f propietaria ▸ **close corporation** (US) = **close company** ▸ **close season** (Hunting, Fishing) veda f; (Ftbl) temporada f de descanso (de la liga de fútbol) ▸ **close work** trabajo m minucioso

close² [kləʊz] N (= end) final m, conclusión f • **at the ~** al final • **at the ~ of day** a la caída de la tarde • **at the ~ of the year** al final del año • **to bring sth to a ~** terminar algo, concluir algo • **to draw to a ~** tocar a su fin, estar terminando
VI 1 (= shut) [shop] cerrar; [door, window] cerrarse • **the doors ~ automatically** las puertas se cierran automáticamente • **the shops ~ at five thirty** las tiendas cierran a las cinco y media • **this window does not ~ properly** esta ventana no cierra bien • **his eyes ~d** se le cerraron los ojos
2 (= end) terminar, terminarse, concluir; (Econ) • **shares ~d at 120p** al cierre las acciones estaban a 120 peniques
VT 1 (= shut) cerrar; [+ hole] tapar • **please ~ the door** cierra la puerta, por favor • **"road closed"** "cerrado el paso" • **to ~ one's eyes** cerrar los ojos • **to ~ one's eyes to sth** (= ignore) hacer la vista gorda a algo • **to ~ the gap between two things** llenar el hueco entre dos cosas • **~ your mouth when you're eating!** ¡no abras la boca comiendo! • **to ~ ranks** cerrar filas
2 (= end) [+ discussion, meeting] cerrar, poner fin a; [+ ceremony] clausurar, dar término a; [+ bank account] liquidar; [+ account] (Comm) saldar; [+ bargain, deal] cerrar

▸ **close down** VI + ADV [business] (gen) cerrarse definitivamente; (by order) clausurarse; (TV, Rad) cerrar (la emisión)
VT + ADV (gen) cerrar definitivamente; (by legal order) clausurar

▸ **close in** VI + ADV [hunters] acercarse rodeando, rodear; [night] caer; [darkness, fog] cerrarse • **the days are closing in** los días son cada vez más cortos • **night was closing in** caía ya la noche
VT + ADV [+ area] cercar, rodear

▸ **close in on** VI + ADV + PREP • **to ~ in on sb** rodear a algn, cercar a algn

▸ **close off** VT + ADV [+ road] cerrar al tráfico, cerrar al público; [+ supply] cortar; [+ access] bloquear

▸ **close on** VI + PREP 1 (= get nearer to) acercarse a
2 (US) = **close in on**

▸ **close out** VT + ADV (US) (Econ) liquidar

▸ **close round** VI + PREP • **the crowd ~d round him** la multitud se agolpó en torno suyo • **the clouds ~d round the peak** las nubes envolvieron la cumbre • **the waters ~d round it** lo envolvieron las aguas

▸ **close up** VI + ADV [flower] cerrarse del todo; [people in queue] arrimarse; [ranks] apretarse; [wound] cicatrizarse • **~ up, please** arrímense, por favor
VT + ADV [+ building] cerrar (del todo); [+ pipe, opening] tapar, obstruir; [+ wound] cerrar

▸ **close with** VI + PREP (= begin to fight) enzarzarse con

close-cropped ['kləʊs'krɒpt] ADJ (cortado) al rape, rapado

closed [kləʊzd] ADJ (gen) cerrado; [hearing, meeting] a puerta cerrada • **her eyes were ~** tenía los ojos cerrados • **sociology is a ~ book to me** la sociología es un misterio para mí • **the case is ~** (Jur) el caso está cerrado • **behind ~ doors** (fig) a puerta cerrada • **to have a ~ mind** ser de miras estrechas, ser de mente cerrada • **it's ~ on Sundays** los domingos está cerrado, cierra los domingos • **the road is ~ to traffic** la carretera está cerrada al tráfico • **the door was ~ to us** (fig) para nosotros las puertas estaban cerradas
CPD ▸ **closed primary** (US) (Pol) *elección primaria reservada a los miembros de un partido* ▸ **closed season** (Hunting, Fishing) veda f; (Ftbl, Rugby) temporada f de descanso (de la liga de fútbol) ▸ **closed session** (Jur) sesión f a puerta cerrada • **in ~ session** en sesión a puerta cerrada ▸ **closed shop** (Ind) *empresa con todo el personal afiliado obligatoriamente a un solo sindicato*

closed-circuit ['kləʊzd,sɜːkɪt] CPD ▸ **closed-circuit television** televisión f por circuito cerrado ▸ **closed-circuit television**

camera cámara *f* de circuito cerrado de televisión, cámara *f* de videovigilancia
closed-door ['kləʊzd,dɔːʳ] ADJ (US) [*meeting, session*] a puerta cerrada
close-down ['kləʊzdaʊn] N cierre *m*
close-fisted ['kləʊs'fɪstɪd] ADJ tacaño
close-fitting ['kləʊs'fɪtɪŋ] ADJ ceñido, ajustado
close-grained [,kləʊs'greɪnd] ADJ tupido
close-harmony [,kləʊs,hɑːmənɪ] CPD
▸ **close-harmony singing** canto *m* en estrecha armonía
close-knit ['kləʊsnɪt] ADJ muy unido
closely ['kləʊslɪ] ADV **1** (= *carefully*) [*look, examine*] atentamente, de cerca • **to watch ~** fijarse, prestar mucha atención • **to listen ~** escuchar con atención, escuchar atentamente • **a ~ guarded secret** un secreto celosamente guardado
2 (= *nearly*) • **to resemble sth/sb ~** parecerse mucho a algo/algn • **~ related/connected** estrechamente relacionado/unido • **~ contested** muy reñido • **~ packed** [*case*] repleto • **this will be a ~ fought race** será una carrera muy reñida
closeness ['kləʊsnɪs] N **1** (= *nearness*) proximidad *f*; [*of resemblance*] parecido *m*; [*of translation*] fidelidad *f*
2 [*of friendship*] intimidad *f*
3 [*of weather, atmosphere*] pesadez *f*, bochorno *m*; [*of room*] mala ventilación *f*
4 [*of election*] lo muy reñido
5 (= *secretiveness*) reserva *f*; (= *meanness*) tacañería *f*
close-run [,kləʊs'rʌn] ADJ • **close-run race** carrera *f* muy reñida
close-set ['kləʊs,set] ADJ [*eyes*] muy juntos
close-shaven [,kləʊs'ʃeɪvən] ADJ muy bien afeitado
closet ['klɒzɪt] N **1** (= *toilet*) wáter *m*, lavabo *m*
2 (US) (= *cupboard*) armario *m*, placar(d) *m* (*LAm*); (*for clothes*) ropero *m* • **to come out of the ~** (*fig*) anunciarse públicamente
VT • **to be ~ed with sb** estar encerrado con algn
CPD [*fascist, racist*] secreto/a, no declarado/a
▸ **closet gay** gay *m* no declarado
close-up ['kləʊsʌp] N primer plano *m* • **in close-up** en primer plano
CPD ▸ **close-up lens** teleobjetivo *m*
closing ['kləʊzɪŋ] ADJ último, final • **~ speech** discurso *m* de clausura • **in the ~ stages** en las últimas etapas • **when is ~ time?** ¿a qué hora cierran? • **his ~ words were …** sus palabras finales fueron …
CPD ▸ **closing date** fecha *f* tope, fecha *f* límite ▸ **closing down** cierre *m* ▸ **closing down sale** liquidación *f* por cierre ▸ **closing entry** (*in account*) asiento *m* de cierre
▸ **closing price** (*St Ex*) cotización *f* de cierre
▸ **closing time** (*Brit*) hora *f* de cerrar
closure ['kləʊʒəʳ] N **1** (= *close-down*) cierre *m*
2 (= *end*) fin *m*, conclusión *f*
3 (*Parl*) clausura *f*
clot [klɒt] N **1** (*Med*) embolia *f*; [*of blood*] coágulo *m* • **~ on the brain** embolia *f* cerebral
2* (= *fool*) papanatas *mf inv*, tonto/a *m/f* del bote • **you ~!** ¡bobo!
VI (*Med*) coagularse
cloth [klɒθ] N **1** (= *material*) paño *m*, tela *f* • **bound in ~** encuadernado en tela
2 (*for cleaning*) trapo *m*
3 (= *tablecloth*) mantel *m* • **to lay the ~** poner la mesa
4 (*Rel*) • **the ~** el clero • **a man of the ~** un clérigo
CPD ▸ **cloth cap** (*Brit*) gorra *f* de paño
clothbound ['klɒθ,baʊnd] ADJ • **~ book** libro *m* encuadernado en tela
clothe [kləʊð] VT **1** [+ *family*] vestir (**in, with** de)
2 (*fig*) cubrir, revestir (**in, with** de)
cloth-eared ['klɒθɪəd] ADJ sordo como una tapia
clothed [kləʊðd] ADJ vestido
clothes [kləʊðz] NPL ropa *fsing*, vestidos *mpl* • **to put one's ~ on** vestirse, ponerse la ropa • **to take one's ~ off** quitarse la ropa, desvestirse
CPD ▸ **clothes basket** canasta *f* de la ropa sucia ▸ **clothes brush** cepillo *m* de la ropa
▸ **clothes drier, clothes dryer** secadora *f*
▸ **clothes hanger** percha *f*, gancho *m* (*LAm*)
▸ **clothes horse** tendedero *m* plegable; (*US**) (= *model*) modelo *mf* • **she's a ~ horse** (*US**) está obsesionada con los trapos* ▸ **clothes line** cuerda *f* para (tender) la ropa ▸ **clothes moth** polilla *f* ▸ **clothes peg, clothes pin** (*US*) pinza *f* de la ropa ▸ **clothes rack** tendedero *m* ▸ **clothes rope** = **clothes line**
▸ **clothes shop** tienda *f* (de ropa)
clothespole ['kləʊðzpəʊl], **clothesprop** ['kləʊðzprɒp] N palo *m* de tendedero
clothier ['kləʊðɪəʳ] N ropero *m*; (= *tailor*) sastre *m* • **~'s (shop)** pañería *f*, ropería *f*; (= *tailor's*) sastrería *f*
clothing ['kləʊðɪŋ] N ropa *f*, vestimenta *f* • **article of ~** prenda *f* de vestir
CPD ▸ **clothing allowance** extra *m* para ropa de trabajo ▸ **clothing industry** industria *f* textil ▸ **the clothing trade** la industria de la confección
clotted cream [,klɒtɪd'kriːm] N (*Culin*) nata *f* cuajada
clotting agent ['klɒtɪŋ,eɪdʒənt] N agente *m* coagulante
cloture ['kləʊtʃəʳ] N (*US*) (*Pol*) clausura *f*
CPD ▸ **cloture rule** control del tiempo de intervención (*en un debate*)
cloud [klaʊd] N nube *f* (*also fig, Comput*) • **a ~ of dust/smoke/gas/insects** una nube de pol vo/humo/gases/insectos • IDIOMS: • **to be under a ~** (= *under suspicion*) estar bajo sospecha; (= *resented*) estar desacreditado • **to have one's head in the ~s** estar en las nubes • **to be on ~ nine** estar en el séptimo cielo • PROVERB: • **every ~ has a silver lining** no hay mal que por bien no venga
VT **1** (= *make cloudy*) [+ *vision*] nublar; [+ *liquid*] enturbiar; [+ *mirror*] empañar
2 (*fig*) (= *confuse*) aturdir • **to ~ the issue** complicar el asunto
VI (*also* **cloud over**) nublarse (*also fig*)
CPD ▸ **cloud computing** informática *f* en la nube ▸ **cloud cover** capa *f* de nubes
▸ **cloud over** VI + ADV nublarse
cloud-based ['klaʊdbeɪst] ADJ (*Comput*) en la nube
cloudberry ['klaʊdbərɪ] N (*US*) camemoro *m*
cloudburst ['klaʊdbɜːst] N chaparrón *m*
cloud-cuckoo-land [,klaʊd'kʊkuː,lænd], **cloudland** ['klaʊdlænd] (*US*) N • **to be in cloud-cuckoo-land** estar en babia, estar con la cabeza en el aire (*LAm*)
cloudiness ['klaʊdɪnɪs] N **1** (*Met*) lo nublado, lo nuboso
2 (= *murkiness*) lo turbio
cloudless ['klaʊdlɪs] ADJ sin nubes, despejado
cloudy ['klaʊdɪ] ADJ (COMPAR: **cloudier**, SUPERL: **cloudiest**) **1** (*Met*) [*sky*] nublado, cubierto de nubes; [*day, weather*] nublado • **it's ~ today** hoy está nublado
2 (= *murky*) [*liquid*] turbio
3 (= *unclear*) [*policy, ideas, memory*] confuso
4 (= *misty*) [*eyes, glass*] empañado
clout¹ [klaʊt] N **1** (= *blow*) tortazo *m*
2 (= *influence, power*) influencia *f*, peso *m*, palanca *f* (*LAm*)
VT dar un tortazo a
clout² [klaʊt] N • PROVERB: • **ne'er cast a ~ till May be out** hasta el cuarenta de mayo no te quites el sayo
clove¹ [kləʊv] N **1** (= *spice*) clavo *m*
2 • **~ of garlic** diente *m* de ajo
clove² [kləʊv] PT *of* **cleave¹**
CPD ▸ **clove hitch** ballestrinque *m*
cloven ['kləʊvn] PP *of* **cleave¹**
cloven-footed [,kləʊvn'fʊtɪd] ADJ [*animal*] de pezuña hendida; [*devil*] con pezuña
cloven hoof [,kləʊvn'huːf] N pata *f* hendida
clover ['kləʊvəʳ] N trébol *m* • IDIOM: • **to be in ~*** vivir a cuerpo de rey
cloverleaf ['kləʊvəliːf] N (PL: **cloverleaves**)
1 (*Bot*) hoja *f* de trébol
2 (*Aut*) cruce *m* en trébol
clown [klaʊn] N **1** (*in circus*) payaso/a *m/f*, clown *mf* • **to make a ~ of o.s.** hacer el ridículo
2* patán *m*, zoquete *mf*
VI (*also* **clown about** *or* **around**) hacer el payaso • **stop ~ing!** ¡déjate de tonterías!
clowning ['klaʊnɪŋ] N payasadas *fpl*
clownish ['klaʊnɪʃ] ADJ [*person*] cómico; [*behaviour*] de payaso; [*sense of humour*] de payaso, tonto
cloy [klɔɪ] VI empalagar
cloying ['klɔɪɪŋ] ADJ empalagoso
cloyingly ['klɔɪɪŋlɪ] ADV empalagosamente • **~ sweet** tan dulce que empalaga, empalagosamente dulce
cloze test ['kləʊz,test] N *test consistente en rellenar los espacios en blanco de un texto*
CLU N ABBR (*US*) = **Chartered Life Underwriter**
club [klʌb] N **1** (= *stick*) porra *f*, cachiporra *f*
2 (= *golf club*) palo *m*
3 clubs (*Cards*) (*in Spanish pack*) bastos *mpl*; (*in conventional pack*) tréboles *mpl*
4 (= *association*) club *m*; (= *gaming club*) casino *m*; (= *building*) centro *m*, club *m* • **a golf ~** un club de golf • **the youth ~** el club juvenil • **join the ~!** (*fig*) ¡ya somos dos! • **to be in the ~** (*hum*) estar en estado • **he put her in the ~** él la dejó en estado
5 (= *disco*) discoteca *f*
VT [+ *person*] aporrear, dar porrazos a • **to ~ sb to death** matar a algn a porrazos
VI • **to ~ together** (*esp Brit*) (= *join forces*) unir fuerzas • **we all ~bed together to buy him a present** le compramos un regalo entre todos
CPD ▸ **club car** (*US*) (*Rail*) coche *m* club
▸ **club class** clase *f* club ▸ **club foot** pie *m* zopo ▸ **club member** socio/a *m/f* del club
▸ **club sandwich** *bocadillo vegetal con pollo y beicon* ▸ **club soda** (*US*) agua *f* de soda ▸ **club steak** (*US*) bistec *m* culer
clubbable* ['klʌbəbl] ADJ sociable
clubber ['klʌbəʳ] N discotequero/a *m/f*
clubbing* ['klʌbɪŋ] N (*Brit*) ir de discotecas • **to go ~** ir de discotecas
club-footed ['klʌb,fʊtɪd] ADJ con el pie zopo
clubhouse ['klʌbhaʊs] N (PL: **clubhouses**) sede *f* de un club
clubland ['klʌblænd] N (*esp Brit*) *zona de las discotecas de moda*
clubman ['klʌbmən] N • **he isn't much of a ~** no le interesan mucho los clubs
clubroom ['klʌbrʊm] N salón *m*, sala *f* de reuniones
cluck [klʌk] N **1** [*of hen*] cloqueo *m*
2 (*with tongue*) chasquido *m* (de la lengua)
VI **1** [*hen*] cloquear
2 [*person*] chasquear con la lengua
▸ **cluck over** VI + PREP • **she ~ed over the children** con los niños estaba como la

gallina con sus polluelos
clue, **clew** (US) [klu:] N (*in guessing game*) pista *f*; (*in a crime*) pista *f*, indicio *m*; [*of crossword*] indicación *f* • **an important ~** una pista importante • **I haven't a ~*** no tengo ni idea • **can you give me a ~?** ¿me das una pista?
VT • **to ~ sb up*** informar a algn
clued up* [,klu:d'ʌp] ADJ • **~ (on)** al tanto (de), al corriente (de)
clueless* ['klu:lɪs] ADJ despistado, que no tiene ni idea
clump¹ [klʌmp] N [*of trees, shrubs*] grupo *m*; [*of flowers, grass*] mata *f*; [*of earth*] terrón *m*
clump² [klʌmp] N [*of feet*] pisada *f* fuerte
VI • **to ~ about** caminar dando pisadas fuertes
clumpy ['klʌmpɪ] ADJ (COMPAR: **clumpier**, SUPERL: **clumpiest**) [*shoes*] grandón, grandote
clumsily ['klʌmzɪlɪ] ADV **1** (= *awkwardly*) [*walk, express, apologize*] con torpeza, torpemente
2 (= *roughly*) [*produced*] toscamente, chapuceramente
clumsiness ['klʌmzɪnɪs] N (= *awkwardness*) torpeza *f*; (= *tactlessness*) falta *f* de tacto
clumsy ['klʌmzɪ] ADJ (COMPAR: **clumsier**, SUPERL: **clumsiest**) **1** (= *awkward*) [*person, action*] torpe, patoso; [*movement*] torpe, desgarbado; [*remark, apology*] torpe, poco delicado; [*tool*] pesado, difícil de manejar
2 (= *crudely made*) [*painting, forgery*] tosco, chapucero
clung [klʌŋ] PT, PP *of* **cling**
Cluniac ['klu:nɪæk] ADJ cluniacense
N cluniacense *m*
clunk [klʌŋk] N **1** (= *sound*) sonido *m* metálico sordo
2 (US‡) cabeza *mf* hueca
VI (= *make sound*) sonar a hueco
clunker‡ ['klʌŋkəʳ] N (US) cacharro* *m*
clunky ['klʌŋkɪ] ADJ (COMPAR: **clunkier**, SUPERL: **clunkiest**) macizo
cluster ['klʌstəʳ] N [*of trees, houses, people, stars*] grupo *m*; [*of flowers*] macizo *m*; [*of plants*] mata *f*; [*of fruit*] racimo *m*
VI [*people, things*] agruparse, apiñarse; [*plants*] arracimarse • **to ~ round sb/sth** apiñarse en torno a algn/algo
CPD ▸ **cluster bomb** bomba *f* de dispersión, bomba *f* de racimo
clutch¹ [klʌtʃ] N **1** (*Aut*) embrague *m*, cloche *m* (*LAm*); (= *pedal*) (pedal *m* del) embrague *m* *or* cloche *m* • **to let the ~ in** embragar • **to let the ~ out** desembragar
2 (= *grasp*) • **to make a ~ at sth** tratar de agarrar algo • **to fall into sb's ~es** caer en las garras de algn • **to get sth out of sb's ~es** hacer que algn ceda la posesión *or* se desprenda de algo
3 (US*) (= *crisis*) crisis *f inv*
VT (= *catch hold of*) asir, agarrar (*esp LAm*); (= *hold tightly*) apretar, agarrar • **she ~ed my arm and begged me not to go** se me agarró al brazo y me suplicó que no me marchara
VI • **to ~ at** tratar de agarrar; (*fig*) aferrarse a • **he ~ed at my hand** trató de agarrarme la mano • **to ~ at a hope** aferrarse a una esperanza • IDIOM: • **to ~ at straws** aferrarse a cualquier esperanza
CPD ▸ **clutch bag** bolso *m* (*sin asas*) ▸ **clutch pedal** [*of car*] (pedal *m* del) embrague *m*
clutch² [klʌtʃ] N [*of eggs*] nidada *f*
clutter ['klʌtəʳ] N desorden *m*, confusión *f* • **in a ~** en desorden, en un montón
VT atestar • **to ~ up a room** amontonar cosas en un cuarto • **to be ~ed up with sth** estar atestado de algo
CM ABBR (US) = **North Mariana Islands**

cm ABBR (= **centimetre(s)**) cm
Cmdr ABBR (*Mil*) (= **Commander**) Cdte
CNAA N ABBR (*Brit*) (= **Council for National Academic Awards**) *organismo no universitario que otorga diplomas*
CND N ABBR = **Campaign for Nuclear Disarmament**
CNN N ABBR (US) (= **Cable News Network**) *agencia de noticias*
CO N ABBR **1** (*Mil*) = **Commanding Officer**
2 (*Brit*) (*Admin*) (= **Commonwealth Office**) *Ministerio de Relaciones con la Commonwealth*
3 = **conscientious objector**
4 (US) = **Colorado**
co- [kəʊ] PREFIX co-
Co. ABBR **1** [keʊ] (*Comm*) (= **company**) Cía., S.A. • **Joe and Co.*** Joe y compañía
2 = **county**
c/o ABBR **1** (= **care of**) c/d, a/c
2 (*Comm*) = **cash order**
coach [kəʊtʃ] N **1** (*esp Brit*) (= *bus*) autobús *m*, autocar *m* (*Sp*), coche *m* de línea, pullman *m* (*LAm*), camión *m* (*Mex*), micro *m* (*Arg*); (*Brit*) (*Rail*) coche *m*, vagón *m*, pullman *m* (*Mex*); (*horse-drawn*) diligencia *f*; (*ceremonial*) carroza *f*
2 (*Sport*) (= *trainer*) entrenador(a) *m/f* • **the Spanish ~** el entrenador del equipo español
3 (= *tutor*) profesor(a) *m/f* particular
VT [+ *team*] entrenar, preparar; [+ *student*] enseñar, preparar • **to ~ sb in French** enseñar francés a algn • **to ~ sb in a part** preparar a algn para un papel
CPD ▸ **coach building** (*Brit*) construcción *f* de carrocerías ▸ **coach class** (US) (= *economy class*) clase *f* turista ▸ **coach driver** (*Brit*) conductor(a) *m/f* de autobús, conductor(a) *m/f* de autocar (*Sp*) ▸ **coach operator** compañía *f* de autobuses, compañía *f* de autocares (*Sp*) ▸ **coach park** (*Brit*) aparcamiento *m* para autobuses, aparcamiento *m* para autocares (*Sp*) ▸ **coach party** (*Brit*) grupo *m* que viaja en autobús *or* (*Sp*) autocar ▸ **coach station** estación *f* de autobuses ▸ **coach tour** (*Brit*) gira *f* en autocar, viaje *m* en autocar ▸ **coach transfer** (*Brit*) traslado *m* en autobús, traslado *m* en autocar (*Sp*) ▸ **coach trip** (*Brit*) excursión *f* en autobús, excursión *f* en autocar (*Sp*)
coachbuilder ['kəʊtʃ,bɪldəʳ] N (*Brit*) (*Aut*) carrocero *m*
coaching ['kəʊtʃɪŋ] N **1** (*Sport*) (= *training*) entrenamiento *m*
2 (*esp US*) (= *tuition*) enseñanza *f* particular
coachload ['kəʊtʃləʊd] N (*Brit*) autobús *m* (lleno), autocar *m* (lleno) (*Sp*) • **they came by the ~** vinieron en masa
coachman ['kəʊtʃmən] N (PL: **coachmen**) cochero *m*
coachwork ['kəʊtʃwɜ:k] N (*Brit*) carrocería *f*
coagulant [kəʊ'ægjʊlənt] N coagulante *m*
coagulate [kəʊ'ægjʊleɪt] VT coagular
VI coagularse
coagulation [kəʊ,ægjʊ'leɪʃən] N coagulación *f*
coal [kəʊl] N carbón *m*; (*soft*) hulla *f*
• IDIOMS: • **to carry ~s to Newcastle** llevar leña al monte *or* agua al mar • **to haul sb over the ~s** echarle una bronca a algn • **to heap ~s of fire on sb's head** avergonzar a algn devolviéndole bien por mal
VI (*Naut*) tomar carbón
CPD ▸ **coal bunker** carbonera *f* ▸ **coal cellar** carbonera *f* ▸ **coal dust** polvillo *m* de carbón, carbonilla *f* ▸ **coal fire** chimenea *f* de carbón ▸ **coal gas** gas *m* de hulla ▸ **coal hod** cubo *m* de carbón ▸ **coal industry** industria *f* del carbón ▸ **coal measures** depósitos *mpl* de carbón ▸ **coal merchant** carbonero *m* ▸ **coal mine** mina *f* de carbón ▸ **coal miner** minero/a *m/f* del carbón ▸ **coal mining** minería *f* del carbón ▸ **coal oil** (US) parafina *f* ▸ **coal pit** mina *f* de carbón, pozo *m* de carbón ▸ **coal scuttle** cubo *m* para carbón ▸ **coal shed** carbonera *f* ▸ **coal strike** huelga *f* de mineros ▸ **coal tar** alquitrán *m* mineral ▸ **coal tit** carbonero *m* garrapinos ▸ **coal yard** patio *m* del carbón
coal-black ['kəʊl'blæk] ADJ negro como el carbón
coal-burning ['kəʊl,bɜ:nɪŋ] ADJ que quema carbón
coalesce [,kəʊə'les] VI (= *merge, blend*) fundirse; (= *join together*) unirse, incorporarse
coalescence [,kəʊə'lesəns] N (= *merging*) fusión *f*; (= *joining together*) unión *f*, incorporación *f*
coalface ['kəʊlfeɪs] N frente *m* donde empieza la veta de carbón
coalfield ['kəʊlfi:ld] N yacimiento *m* de carbón, cuenca *f* minera
coal-fired [,kəʊl'faɪəd] ADJ que quema carbón
coalition [,kəʊə'lɪʃən] N (*Pol*) coalición *f*
CPD ▸ **coalition government** gobierno *m* de coalición
coalman ['kəʊlmən] N (PL: **coalmen**) carbonero *m*
coarse [kɔ:s] ADJ (COMPAR: **coarser**, SUPERL: **coarsest**) **1** (= *rough*) [*texture*] basto, áspero; [*sand*] grueso; [*skin*] áspero
2 (= *badly made*) burdo, tosco
3 (= *vulgar*) [*character, laugh, remark*] ordinario, tosco; [*joke*] verde
CPD ▸ **coarse fishing** pesca *f* de agua dulce (*excluyendo salmón y trucha*)
coarse-grained ['kɔ:sgreɪnd] ADJ de grano grueso; (*fig*) tosco, basto
coarsely ['kɔ:slɪ] ADV **1** (= *crudely*) [*made*] toscamente
2 (= *vulgarly*) [*laugh, say*] groseramente
coarsen ['kɔ:sn] VT [+ *person*] embrutecer; [+ *skin*] curtir
VI [*person*] embrutecerse; [*skin*] curtirse
coarseness ['kɔ:snɪs] N **1** (= *roughness*) [*of texture*] aspereza *f*; [*of fabrication*] tosquedad *f*
2 (= *lack of refinement*) falta *f* de finura, falta *f* de elegancia
3 (= *vulgarity*) [*of person, remark*] ordinariez *f*, tosquedad *f*; [*of joke*] lo verde
coast [kəʊst] N (= *shore*) costa *f*; (= *coastline*) litoral *m* • **it's on the west ~ of Scotland** está en la costa oeste de Escocia • IDIOM: • **the ~ is clear** (= *there is no one about*) no hay moros en la costa; (= *the danger is over*) pasó el peligro
VI (*also* **coast along**) (*Aut*) ir en punto muerto; (*on sledge, cycle*) deslizarse cuesta abajo; (*fig*) avanzar sin esfuerzo
coastal ['kəʊstəl] ADJ costero • **~ defences** defensas *fpl* costeras • **~ traffic** (*Naut*) cabotaje *m*
coaster ['kəʊstəʳ] N **1** (*Naut*) buque *m* costero, barco *m* de cabotaje; (US) trineo *m*
2 (= *small mat for drinks*) posavasos *m inv*
coastguard ['kəʊstgɑ:d] N (= *person*) guardacostas *mf inv*; (= *organization*) servicio *m* de guardacostas
CPD ▸ **coastguard station** puesto *m* de guardacostas ▸ **coastguard vessel** guardacostas *m*
coastline ['kəʊstlaɪn] N litoral *m*
coast-to-coast ['kəʊstə'kəʊst] (US) ADJ de costa a costa
ADV de costa a costa
coat [kəʊt] N **1** (= *winter/long coat*) abrigo *m*; (= *jacket*) chaqueta *f* (*Sp*), americana *f*, saco *m* (*LAm*); (*chemist's*) bata *f* • IDIOM: • **to cut one's ~ according to one's cloth** adaptarse a las

circunstancias
2 (*animal's*) (= *hide*) pelo *m*, pelaje *m*; (= *wool*) lana *f*
3 (= *layer*) capa *f* • **a ~ of paint** una mano de pintura
4 • **~ of arms** escudo *m* (de armas)
(VT) cubrir, revestir (**with** de); (*with a liquid*) bañar (**with** en) • **to ~ sth with paint** dar una mano de pintura a algo
(CPD) ▸ **coat hanger** percha *f*, gancho *m* (*LAm*)
coated [ˈkəʊtɪd] (ADJ) [*tongue*] saburral
coating [ˈkəʊtɪŋ] (N) capa *f*, baño *m*; [*of paint*] mano *f*
coatstand [ˈkəʊtstænd] (N) perchero *m*
coattails [ˈkəʊtteɪlz] (NPL) faldón *msing* • **IDIOM**: • **to ride on sb's ~** salir adelante gracias al favor de algn, lograr el éxito a la sombra de algn
co-author [ˈkəʊ,ɔːθəʳ] (N) coautor(a) *m/f*
(VT) (*US*) escribir conjuntamente
coax [kəʊks] (VT) • **to ~ sth out of sb** sonsacar algo a algn (engatusándolo) • **to ~ sb into/out of doing sth** engatusar a algn para que haga/no haga algo • **to ~ sb along** mimar a algn
coaxial [,kəʊˈæksɪəl] (ADJ) coaxial • **~ cable** (*Comput*) cable *m* coaxial
coaxing [ˈkəʊksɪŋ] (ADJ) mimoso
(N) mimos *mpl*, halagos *mpl*
coaxingly [ˈkəʊksɪŋlɪ] (ADV) mimosamente
cob [kɒb] (N) **1** (= *swan*) cisne *m* macho
2 (= *horse*) jaca *f* fuerte
3 (= *loaf*) pan *m* redondo
4 (= *nut*) avellana *f*
5 (= *maize*) mazorca *f*
cobalt [ˈkəʊbɒlt] (N) cobalto *m*
(CPD) ▸ **cobalt blue** azul *m* cobalto ▸ **cobalt bomb** bomba *f* de cobalto
cobber* [ˈkɒbəʳ] (N) (*Australia*) amigo *m*, compañero *m*; (*in direct address*) amigo
cobble [ˈkɒbl] (N) = **cobblestone**
(VT) **1** (*also* **cobble up**) [+ *shoes*] remendar
2 [+ *street*] empedrar, adoquinar
▸ **cobble together** (VT + ADV) (*pej*) hacer apresuradamente
cobbled [ˈkɒbld] (ADJ) • **~ street** calle *f* empedrada, calle *f* adoquinada
cobbler [ˈkɒbləʳ] (N) zapatero/a *m/f* (remendón/ona)
cobblers [ˈkɒbləz] (NPL) (*Brit*) **1** (*Anat***) cojones** *mpl*
2‡ (*fig*) chorradas* *fpl*
cobblestone [ˈkɒblstəʊn] (N) adoquín *m*
COBOL [ˈʊʃθkəʊbɒl] (N) (*Comput*) COBOL *m*
cobra [ˈkəʊbrə] (N) cobra *f*
cobweb [ˈkɒbweb] (N) telaraña *f* • **to blow away the ~s** (*fig*) despejar la mente
cobwebbed [ˈkɒbwebd] (ADJ) cubierto de telarañas, lleno de telarañas
coca [ˈkəʊkə] (N) coca *f*
cocaine [kəˈkeɪn] (N) cocaína *f*
(CPD) ▸ **cocaine addict** cocainómano/a *m/f* ▸ **cocaine addiction** adicción *f* a la cocaína
coccyx [ˈkɒksɪks] (N) (PL: **coccyges** [kɒkˈsaɪdʒiːz]) cóccix *m inv*
cochineal [ˈkɒtʃɪniːl] (N) cochinilla *f*
cochlea [ˈkɒklɪə] (N) (PL: **cochleae** [ˈkɒklɪiː]) cóclea *f*, caracol *m* óseo
cock [kɒk] (N) **1** (*esp Brit*) (= *rooster*) gallo *m*; (= *other male bird*) macho *m* • **old ~!*** ¡amigo!, ¡viejo! • **IDIOM**: • **~ of the walk** gallito *m* del lugar
2 (= *tap*) (*also* **stopcock**) llave *f* de paso
3** (= *penis*) polla** *f*
4 [*of gun*] martillo *m* • **to go off at half ~** (*fig*) [*plan*] ponerse en práctica sin la debida preparación
(VT) **1** [+ *gun*] amartillar; [+ *head*] ladear • **to ~ one's eye at** mirar con intención a, guiñar el ojo a • **IDIOM**: • **to ~ a snook at sb/sth** (*Brit*) (*fig*) burlarse de algn/algo
2 (*also* **cock up**) [+ *ears*] aguzar • **to keep one's ears ~ed** mantenerse alerta, aguzar el oído *or* la oreja
(CPD) ▸ **cock sparrow** gorrión *m* macho ▸ **cock teaser**** calientapollas** *f inv*
▸ **cock up**** (VT + ADV) • **to ~ sth up** (*Brit*) joder algo**
cockade [kɒˈkeɪd] (N) escarapela *f*
cock-a-doodle-doo [ˈkɒkəduːdlˈduː] (EXCL) ¡quiquiriquí!
cock-a-hoop [ˈkɒkəˈhuːp] (ADJ) contentísimo
cockamamie*, **cockamamy*** [,kɒkəˈmeɪmɪ] (ADJ) (*US*) que no tiene ni pies ni cabeza*
cock-and-bull [ˈkɒkənˈbʊl] (ADJ) • **cock-and-bull story** cuento *m* chino
cockatiel [,kɒkəˈtɪəl] (N) cocatil *m*
cockatoo [,kɒkəˈtuː] (N) cacatúa *f*
cockchafer [ˈkɒk,tʃeɪfəʳ] (N) abejorro *m*
cockcrow [ˈkɒkkrəʊ] (N) • **at ~** al amanecer
cocked [kɒkt] (ADJ) • **~ hat** sombrero *m* de tres picos • **IDIOM**: • **to knock sth into a ~ hat** ser muy superior a algo
cocker [ˈkɒkəʳ] (N) (*also* **cocker spaniel**) cocker *m*
cockerel [ˈkɒkrəl] (N) gallito *m*, gallo *m* joven
cockeyed [ˈkɒkaɪd] (ADJ) **1** (= *crooked*) torcido, chueco (*LAm*)
2 (= *absurd*) disparatado
cockfight [ˈkɒkfaɪt] (N) pelea *f* de gallos
cockfighting [ˈkɒk,faɪtɪŋ] (N) la pelea de gallos, peleas *fpl* de gallos
cockily* [ˈkɒkɪlɪ] (ADV) chulescamente
cockiness* [ˈkɒkɪnɪs] (N) engreimiento *m*
cockle [ˈkɒkl] (N) (*Zool*) berberecho *m* • **IDIOM**: • **to warm the ~s of sb's heart** llenar a algn de ternura
cockleshell [ˈkɒklʃel] (N) **1** (= *shell*) concha *f* de berberecho
2 (= *boat*) cascarón *m* de nuez
cockney [ˈkɒknɪ] (N) **1** (= *person*) *persona nacida en el este de Londres y especialmente de clase obrera*
2 (= *dialect*) dialecto *m* de esa zona
(ADJ) *del este de Londres y especialmente de clase obrera*; ▹ **RHYMING SLANG**

> **COCKNEY**
> Se llama **cockneys** a las personas de la zona este de Londres conocida como **East End**, un barrio tradicionalmente obrero, aunque según la tradición un **cockney** auténtico ha de haber nacido dentro del área en la que se oye el repique de las campanas de la iglesia de **St Mary-le-Bow**, en la **City** londinense. Este término también hace referencia al dialecto que se habla en esta parte de Londres, aunque a veces también se aplica a cualquier acento de la clase trabajadora londinense. El actor Michael Caine es un **cockney** famoso.
> ▹ **RHYMING SLANG**

cockpit [ˈkɒkpɪt] (N) **1** (*Aer*) cabina *f*
2 (*for cockfight*) reñidero *m*
cockroach [ˈkɒkrəʊtʃ] (N) cucaracha *f*
cockscomb [ˈkɒkskəʊm] (N) cresta *f* de gallo
cocksucker** [ˈkɒk,sʌkəʳ] (N) cabrón‡ *m*, mamón‡ *m*
cocksure [ˈkɒkˈʃʊəʳ] (ADJ) creído, engreído
cocktail [ˈkɒkteɪl] (N) (= *drink*) combinado *m*, cóctel *m* • **fruit ~** macedonia *f* de frutas • **prawn ~** cóctel *m* de gambas
(CPD) ▸ **cocktail bar** (*in hotel*) bar *m* (*de cócteles*), coctelería *f* ▸ **cocktail cabinet** mueble-bar *m* ▸ **cocktail dress** vestido *m* de fiesta ▸ **cocktail lounge** salón *m* de fiestas ▸ **cocktail onion** cebolla *f* perla ▸ **cocktail party** cóctel *m* ▸ **cocktail sausage** salchichita *f* de aperitivo ▸ **cocktail shaker** coctelera *f* ▸ **cocktail stick** palillo *m* (de madera)
cockup‡ [ˈkɒkʌp] (N) (*Brit*) • **what a ~!** ¡qué lío!, ¡qué desmadre! • **to make a ~ of sth** fastidiar algo, joder algo** • **there's been a ~ over my passport** me han armado un follón con el pasaporte*
cocky* [ˈkɒkɪ] (ADJ) (COMPAR: **cockier**, SUPERL: **cockiest**) (*pej*) chulo, creído
cocoa [ˈkəʊkəʊ] (N) cacao *m*; (= *drink*) chocolate *m* • **a cup of ~** una taza de chocolate
(CPD) ▸ **cocoa bean** grano *m* de cacao ▸ **cocoa butter** mantequilla *f* de cacao ▸ **cocoa powder** cacao *m* en polvo
coconut [ˈkəʊkənʌt] (N) **1** (= *nut*) coco *m*
2 (= *tree*) cocotero *m*
(CPD) ▸ **coconut matting** estera *f* de fibra de coco ▸ **coconut milk** leche *f* de coco ▸ **coconut oil** aceite *m* de coco ▸ **coconut palm** cocotero *m* ▸ **coconut shy** tiro *m* al coco ▸ **coconut tree** cocotero *m*
cocoon [kəˈkuːn] (N) capullo *m*
(VT) envolver
COD (ABBR) **1** (*Brit*) (= **cash on delivery**) C.A.E.
2 (*US*) (= **collect on delivery**) C.A.E.
cod [kɒd] (N) (PL: **cod** *or* **cods**) bacalao *m*
coda [ˈkəʊdə] (N) coda *f*
coddle [ˈkɒdl] (VT) **1** (*also* **mollycoddle**) consentir, mimar
2 (*Culin*) • **~d eggs** *huevos cocidos a fuego lento*
code [kəʊd] (N) **1** (= *cipher*) clave *f*, cifra *f* • **in ~** en clave, cifrado • **it's written in ~** está cifrado *or* escrito en clave
2 (*Telec*) prefijo *m*, código *m*; (*Comput*) código *m* • **what is the ~ for London?** ¿cuál es el prefijo *or* código de Londres? • **postal ~** código *m* postal, distrito *m* postal
3 [*of laws*] código *m* • **~ of behaviour** código *m* de conducta • **~ of practice** código *m* profesional; ▹ **highway**
(VT) [+ *message*] poner en clave, cifrar
(CPD) ▸ **code book** libro *m* de códigos ▸ **code dating** fechación *f* en código ▸ **code letter** letra *f* de código ▸ **code name** alias *m inv*, nombre *m* en clave; (*Pol*) nombre *m* de guerra; ▹ **code-name** ▸ **code number** (*Tax*) ≈ número *m* de identificación fiscal ▸ **code of conduct** código *m* de conducta ▸ **code of honour** código *m* de honor ▸ **code word** palabra *f* en clave
coded [ˈkəʊdɪd] (ADJ) en cifra, en clave (*also fig*)
codeine [ˈkəʊdiːn] (N) (*Pharm*) codeína *f*
code-name [ˈkəʊdneɪm] (VT) dar nombre en clave a • **the operation was code-named Albert** la operación tuvo el nombre en clave de Albert
co-dependency [,kəʊdɪˈpendənsɪ] (N) codependencia *f*
co-dependent [,kəʊdɪˈpendənt] (ADJ) [*person*] codependiente
(N) codependiente *mf*
codex [ˈkəʊdeks] (N) (PL: **codices**) códice *m*
codfish [ˈkɒdfɪʃ] (N) (PL: **codfish** *or* **codfishes**) bacalao *m*
codger* [ˈkɒdʒəʳ] (N) (*also* **old codger**) sujeto *m*, vejete *m*
codices [ˈkɒdɪ,siːz] (NPL) *of* **codex**
codicil [ˈkɒdɪsɪl] (N) codicilo *m*
codification [,kəʊdɪfɪˈkeɪʃən] (N) [*of laws*] codificación *f*
codify [ˈkəʊdɪfaɪ] (VT) codificar
coding [ˈkəʊdɪŋ] (N) codificación *f*
(CPD) ▸ **coding sheet** hoja *f* de programación
cod-liver oil [ˈkɒdlɪvərˈɔɪl] (N) aceite *m* de

hígado de bacalao

codpiece [ˈkɒdpiːs] N (*Hist*) bragueta *f*

co-driver [ˈkəʊdraɪvəʳ] N (*Aut*) copiloto *mf*

codswallop‡ [ˈkɒdzwɒləp] N (*Brit*) chorradas* *fpl*

coed* [ˈkəʊˈed] ADJ mixto
N **1** (*US*) (= *female student*) alumna *f* de un colegio mixto
2 (*Brit*) (= *school*) colegio *m* mixto
ADJ, ABBR = **coeducational**

co-edit [kəʊˈedɪt] VT [+ *book*] coeditar

co-edition [ˈkəʊɪˌdɪʃən] N edición *f* conjunta

co-editor [kəʊˈedɪtəʳ] N coeditor(a) *m/f*

coeducation [ˈkəʊˌedjʊˈkeɪʃən] N enseñanza *f* mixta

coeducational [ˈkəʊˌedjʊˈkeɪʃənl] ADJ mixto

coefficient [ˌkəʊɪˈfɪʃənt] N coeficiente *m*

coelacanth [ˈsiːləkænθ] N celacanto *m*

coerce [kəʊˈɜːs] VT obligar, coaccionar • **to ~ sb into doing sth** obligar a algn a hacer algo, coaccionar a algn para que haga algo

coercion [kəʊˈɜːʃən] N coacción *f* • **under ~** obligado a ello, a la fuerza

coercive [kəʊˈɜːsɪv] ADJ coactivo, coercitivo

coeval [kəʊˈiːvəl] ADJ coetáneo (**with** de), contemporáneo (**with** de)
N coetáneo/a *m/f*, contemporáneo/a *m/f*

coexist [ˈkəʊɪgˈzɪst] VI coexistir (**with** con)

coexistence [ˈkəʊɪgˈzɪstəns] N coexistencia *f*

coexistent [ˈkəʊɪgˈzɪstənt] ADJ coexistente

co-extensive [ˌkəʊɪkˈstensɪv] ADJ de la misma extensión (**with** que)

C of C N ABBR = **Chamber of Commerce**

C of E [ˌsiːəvˈiː] N ABBR (= **Church of England**) Iglesia *f* anglicana • **to be ~*** ser anglicano

coffee [ˈkɒfɪ] N café *m* • **a cup of ~** una taza de café, un café • **white ~** (*milky*) café *m* con leche; (*with dash of milk*) café *m* cortado • **black ~** café *m* solo, tinto *m* (*Col*); (*large*) café *m* americano • **two white ~s, please** dos cafés con leche, por favor
CPD ▸ **coffee bar** café *m*, cafetería *f* ▸ **coffee bean** grano *m* de café ▸ **coffee break** descanso *m* (para tomar café) ▸ **coffee cake** (*Brit*) pastel *m* de café ▸ **coffee cup** taza *f* para café, tacita *f*, pocillo *m* (*LAm*) ▸ **coffee filter** filtro *m* de café ▸ **coffee granules** gránulos *mpl* de café ▸ **coffee grinder** molinillo *m* de café ▸ **coffee grounds** poso *msing* de café ▸ **coffee house** café *m* ▸ **coffee machine** (*small*) máquina *f* de café, cafetera *f*; (= *vending machine*) máquina *f* expendedora de café ▸ **coffee maker** máquina *f* de hacer café, cafetera *f* ▸ **coffee mill** molinillo *m* de café ▸ **coffee morning** tertulia *f* formada para tomar el café por la mañana ▸ **coffee percolator** = **coffee maker** ▸ **coffee plantation** cafetal *m* ▸ **coffee service**, **coffee set** servicio *m* de café ▸ **coffee shop** café *m* ▸ **coffee spoon** cucharilla *f* de café ▸ **coffee table** mesita *f* para servir el café ▸ **coffee whitener** leche *f* en polvo

coffee-coloured, **coffee-colored** (*US*) [ˈkɒfɪˌkʌləd] ADJ (de) color café

coffeepot [ˈkɒfɪpɒt] N cafetera *f*

coffee-table book [ˈkɒfɪteɪblˌbʊk] N libro *m* de gran formato (*bello e impresionante*)

coffer [ˈkɒfəʳ] N **1** (= *chest*) cofre *m*, arca *f*; **coffers** (*fig*) tesoro *msing*, fondos *mpl*
2 (*Archit*) (= *sunken panel*) artesón *m*
3 = **cofferdam**

cofferdam [ˈkɒfədæm] N ataguía *f*

coffin [ˈkɒfɪn] N ataúd *m*

C of I [ˌsiːəvˈaɪ] N ABBR = **Church of Ireland**

co-founder [ˌkəʊˈfaʊndəʳ] N cofundador(a) *m/f*

C of S [ˌsiːəvˈes] N ABBR **1** (*Rel*) = **Church of Scotland**
2 (*Mil*) = **Chief of Staff**

cog [kɒg] N diente *m* (de rueda dentada) • IDIOM: • **just a cog in the wheel** una pieza del mecanismo, nada más

cogency [ˈkəʊdʒənsɪ] N convicción *f*, contundencia *f*

cogent [ˈkəʊdʒənt] ADJ convincente, contundente

cogently [ˈkəʊdʒəntlɪ] ADV de modo convincente, de forma contundente

cogitate [ˈkɒdʒɪteɪt] VI meditar, reflexionar

cogitation [ˌkɒdʒɪˈteɪʃən] N meditación *f*, reflexión *f*

cognac [ˈkɒnjæk] N coñac *m*

cognate [ˈkɒgneɪt] ADJ cognado (**with** con), afín
N cognado *m*

cognisance [ˈkɒgnɪzəns] (*Brit*) = **cognizance**

cognisant [ˈkɒgnɪzənt] (*Brit*) = **cognizant**

cognition [kɒgˈnɪʃən] N cognición *f*

cognitive [ˈkɒgnɪtɪv] ADJ cognitivo, cognoscitivo • **~ modelling** modelización *f* cognoscitiva
CPD ▸ **cognitive behavioural therapy** terapia *f* cognitivo-conductual

cognizance [ˈkɒgnɪzəns] N conocimiento *m* • **to be within one's ~** ser de la competencia de uno • **to take ~ of** tener en cuenta

cognizant [ˈkɒgnɪzənt] ADJ • **to be ~ of** saber, estar enterado de

cognomen [kɒgˈnəʊmen] N (*frm*) (PL: **cognomens** *or* **cognomina**) (= *surname*) apellido *m*; (= *nickname*) apodo *m*

cognoscenti [ˌkɒnəʊˈʃentɪ] NPL expertos *mpl*, peritos *mpl*

cogwheel [ˈkɒgwiːl] N rueda *f* dentada

cohabit [kəʊˈhæbɪt] VI cohabitar (**with sb** con algn)

cohabitation [ˌkəʊhæbɪˈteɪʃən] N cohabitación *f*

cohere [kəʊˈhɪəʳ] VI adherirse, pegarse; [*ideas*] formar un conjunto sólido, ser consecuentes

coherence [kəʊˈhɪərəns] N coherencia *f*

coherent [kəʊˈhɪərənt] ADJ [*person, theory, argument, behaviour*] coherente, congruente; [*account, speech*] coherente • **incapable of ~ speech** incapaz de hablar coherentemente

coherently [kəʊˈhɪərəntlɪ] ADV [*think, speak, argue, act*] coherentemente, de manera coherente, con coherencia; [*behave*] coherentemente, de manera coherente

cohesion [kəʊˈhiːʒən] N cohesión *f*

cohesive [kəʊˈhiːsɪv] ADJ (*Sci*) cohesivo; (*fig*) cohesionado

cohesively [kəʊˈhiːsɪvlɪ] ADV (*Sci*) cohesivamente; (*fig*) [*write, argue*] cohesionadamente

cohesiveness [kəʊˈhiːsɪvnɪs] N cohesión *f*

cohort [ˈkəʊhɔːt] N cohorte *f*

COHSE [ˈkəʊzɪ] N ABBR (*Brit*) (*formerly*) = **Confederation of Health Service Employees**

COI N ABBR (*Brit*) = **Central Office of Information**

coif [kɔɪf] N cofia *f*

coiffed [ˈkwɑːft] ADJ (*frm*) peinado

coiffeur [kwɒˈfɜːʳ] N peluquero *m*

coiffure [kwɒˈfjʊəʳ] N peinado *m*

coiffured [kwɒˈfjʊəd] ADJ (*frm*) peinado

coil [kɔɪl] N **1** (= *roll*) rollo *m*; (= *single loop*) vuelta *f*; [*of hair*] rizo *m*; [*of snake*] anillo *m*; [*of smoke*] espiral *f*
2 (*Aut, Elec*) bobina *f*, carrete *m*
3 (= *contraceptive*) espiral *f*, DIU *m*
VT arrollar, enrollar • **to ~ sth up** enrollar algo • **to ~ sth round sth** enrollar algo alrededor de algo
VI **1** [*snake*] enroscarse • **to ~ up (into a ball)** hacerse un ovillo • **to ~ round sth** enroscarse alrededor de algo
2 [*smoke*] subir en espiral

coiled [kɔɪld] ADJ arrollado, enrollado

coin [kɔɪn] N moneda *f* • **a 20p ~** una moneda de 20 peniques • **to toss a ~** echar una moneda al aire, jugárselo a cara o cruz • IDIOM: • **to pay sb back in his own ~** pagar a algn en *or* con la misma moneda
VT [+ *money*] acuñar; (*fig*) [+ *word*] inventar, acuñar • **he must be ~ing money*** debe de estar haciéndose de oro • **to ~ a phrase** (*hum*) para decirlo así, si me permite la frase

coinage [ˈkɔɪnɪdʒ] N (= *system*) moneda *f*, sistema *m* monetario; (= *act*) acuñación *f*; (*fig*) [*of word*] invención *f*

coinbox [ˈkɔɪnbɒks] N (*Telec*) depósito *m* de monedas

coincide [ˌkəʊɪnˈsaɪd] VI **1** (= *happen at same time*) coincidir • **to ~ with** coincidir con
2 (= *agree*) estar de acuerdo • **to ~ with** estar de acuerdo con

coincidence [kəʊˈɪnsɪdəns] N coincidencia *f*, casualidad *f* • **what a ~!** ¡qué coincidencia!, ¡qué casualidad!

coincident [kəʊˈɪnsɪdənt] ADJ
1 (= *simultaneous*) [*events*] coincidente • **~ with her marriage ...** al mismo tiempo que su boda ...
2 (= *identical*) [*ideas, opinions*] coincidente • **to be ~ with** coincidir con

coincidental [kəʊˌɪnsɪˈdentl] ADJ **1** (= *by chance*) fortuito, casual
2 (= *simultaneous*) coincidente

coincidentally [ˌkəʊɪnsɪˈdentəlɪ] ADV por casualidad, casualmente • **not ~, we arrived at the same time** no es una casualidad que llegáramos al mismo tiempo

coin-op* [ˈkɔɪnˌɒp] N ABBR (= **coin-operated laundry**) *lavandería que funciona con monedas*

coin-operated [ˈkɔɪnˈɒpəreɪtɪd] ADJ [*machine, laundry*] que funciona con monedas

coinsurance [ˌkəʊɪnˈʃʊərəns] N coaseguro *m*, seguro *m* copartícipe

coinsurer [ˌkəʊɪnˈʃʊərəʳ] N coasegurador(a) *m/f*

coir [ˈkɔɪəʳ] N coco *m*
CPD ▸ **coir matting** fibra *f* de coco

coital [ˈkɔɪtəl] ADJ (*frm*) coital; ▹ **post-coital**

coitus [ˈkɔɪtəs] N coito *m* • **~ interruptus** coitus *m* interruptus

Coke® [kəʊk] N Coca-Cola® *f*

coke [kəʊk] N **1** (= *fuel*) coque *m*
2‡ (= *cocaine*) coca *f*

Col ABBR **1** (*Mil*) (= **Colonel**) Cnel., Cor. • **Col. T. Richard** (*on envelope*) Cnel. T. Richard, Cor. T. Richard
2 (*US*) = **Colorado**

col. ABBR **1** (= **column**) col, col.ª
2 = **colour**

col [kɒl] ABBR (= **column**) col

COLA [ˈkəʊlə] N ABBR (*US*) (*Econ*) = **cost-of-living adjustment**

cola [ˈkəʊlə] N (= *drink*) cola *m*

colander [ˈkʌləndəʳ] N colador *m*, escurridor *m*

cold [kəʊld] ADJ (COMPAR: **colder**, SUPERL: **coldest**) **1** (= *lacking heat*) frío • **a ~ buffet** un buffet frío • **to be ~** [*person*] tener frío; [*thing*] estar frío • **I'm ~** tengo frío • **my hands are ~** tengo las manos frías • **it was ~** • **the weather was ~** hacía frío • **the house was ~** la casa estaba fría, en la casa hacía frío • **to get ~** [*food, coffee*] enfriarse • **your dinner's getting ~** se te está enfriando la cena • **the nights are getting ~er** está haciendo más frío por las noches • **I'm getting ~** me está

entrando frío • **no, no, you're getting ~er** (*in game*) no, no, cada vez más frío • **to go ~**: • **your coffee's going ~** se te está enfriando el café • **I went ~ at the very thought** solo de pensarlo me entraron escalofríos • **the trail went ~ in Athens** las huellas desaparecieron en Atenas • IDIOM: • **to pour** *or* **throw ~ water on** *or* **over sth** poner pegas *or* trabas a algo; ▹ **comfort, foot**
2 (= *hostile*) [*look, voice, person*] frío • **to get** *or* **receive a ~ reception** [*person*] tener un recibimiento frío; [*proposal*] tener una acogida fría • **to give sb a ~ reception** recibir a algn con frialdad • **to give sth a ~ reception** acoger algo con frialdad • **the proposal was given a ~ reception by the banks** los bancos acogieron la propuesta con frialdad • **to be ~ to** *or* **with sb** mostrarse frío con algn
3* (= *indifferent*) • IDIOM: • **to leave sb ~** dejar frío a algn • **his music leaves me ~** su música me deja frío
4 (= *dispassionate*) • **he approached everything with ~ logic** lo enfocaba todo con fría lógica • **the ~ facts** la cruda realidad; ▹ **blood, light¹**
5 [*colour, light*] frío
6 • **from ~** en frío • **I can't sing it from ~** no puedo cantarlo en frío
7 (= *unconscious*) ▹ **out**
(N) **1** (= *cold weather*) frío *m* • **her hands were blue with ~** tenía las manos moradas del frío • **come in out of the ~!** ¡entra, que hace frío! • **to feel the ~** ser friolento *or* (*Sp*) friolero • IDIOM: • **to leave sb out in the ~** (*fig*) dejar a algn al margen, dar a algn a un lado • **she felt left out in the ~** sintió que la habían dejado al margen *or* dado de lado
2 (*Med*) resfriado *m*, catarro *m*, constipado *m*, resfrío *m* (*LAm*) • **I've got a ~** estoy resfriado *or* acatarrado *or* constipado • **to catch a ~** resfriarse, constiparse • **to have a chest ~** tener el pecho congestionado *or* cargado • **you'll catch your death of ~*** vas a pillar un resfriado de muerte • **to get a ~** resfriarse, constiparse • **to give sb a/one's ~** contagiar *or* pegar un/el resfriado a algn • **to have a head ~** estar resfriado *or* constipado
(ADV) **1** (= *abruptly*) • **she turned him down ~** lo rechazó rotundamente • **he stopped ~ in his tracks** se paró en seco
2 (= *without preparation*) • **he played his part ~** representó su papel en frío *or* sin haberse preparado de antemano • **to come to sth ~** llegar a algo frío *or* sin preparación
(CPD) ▸ **cold calling** venta *f* en frío ▸ **cold cream** crema *f* hidratante ▸ **cold cuts** (*US*) = **cold meats** ▸ **cold fish** (*fig*) persona *f* seca ▸ **cold frame** vivero *m* para plantas ▸ **cold front** (*Met*) frente *m* frío ▸ **cold meats** fiambres *fpl*, embutidos *mpl* ▸ **cold snap** ola *f* de frío ▸ **cold sore** herpes *m inv* labial, pupa* *f* ▸ **cold start** (*Aut*) arranque *m* en frío ▸ **cold storage** conservación *f* en cámaras frigoríficas • **to put sth into ~ storage** [+ *food*] refrigerar algo;* (*fig*) [+ *project*] aparcar algo* ▸ **cold store** cámara *f* frigorífica ▸ **cold sweat** sudor *m* frío • **he broke into a ~ sweat** le entró un sudor frío ▸ **cold turkey*** mono* *m*, síndrome *m* de abstinencia • **to go ~ turkey** dejar la droga en seco • **he quit smoking ~ turkey** dejó de fumar a base de aguantarse el mono* ▸ **cold war** guerra *f* fría

cold-blooded ['kəʊld'blʌdɪd] (ADJ) (*Zool*) de sangre fría; (*fig*) desalmado, despiadado
cold-bloodedly ['kəʊld'blʌdɪdlɪ] (ADV) a sangre fría
cold-hearted ['kəʊld'hɑːtɪd] (ADJ) insensible, cruel
coldly ['kəʊldlɪ] (ADV) (*fig*) fríamente, con frialdad
coldness ['kəʊldnɪs] (N) **1** (*lit*) (= *lack of heat*) frío *m*
2 (*fig*) (= *hostility*) frialdad *f*
cold-shoulder ['kəʊld'ʃəʊldəʳ] (VT) (= *rebuff*) volver la espalda a
coleslaw ['kəʊlslɔː] (N) *ensalada de col, zanahoria, cebolla y mayonesa*
coley ['kəʊlɪ] (N) abadejo *m*
colic ['kɒlɪk] (N) (*esp of horses, children*) cólico *m*
colicky ['kɒlɪkɪ] (ADJ) [*baby*] que padece de cólicos; [*pain*] de cólico • **to be ~** tener un cólico
Coliseum [ˌkɒlɪ'siːəm] (N) Coliseo *m*
colitis [kɒ'laɪtɪs] (N) colitis *f*
collaborate [kə'læbəreɪt] (VI) (*also Pol*) colaborar • **to ~ on sth/in doing sth** colaborar en algo • **to ~ with sb** colaborar con algn
collaboration [kəˌlæbə'reɪʃən] (N) colaboración *f*; (*Pol*) colaboracionismo *m* • **in ~** en colaboración (**with** con)
collaborationist [kə'læbə'reɪʃənɪst] (ADJ) colaboracionista
collaborative [kə'læbərətɪv] (ADJ) • **by a ~ effort** por un esfuerzo común, ayudándose unos a otros • **it's a ~ work** es un trabajo de colaboración
collaboratively [kə'læbərətɪvlɪ] (ADV) en colaboración
collaborator [kə'læbəreɪtəʳ] (N) colaborador(a) *m/f*; (*Pol*) colaboracionista *mf*
collage [kɒ'lɑːʒ] (N) collage *m*
collagen ['kɒlədʒən] (N) colágeno *m*
collapse [kə'læps] (N) (*Med*) colapso *m*; [*of building, roof, floor*] hundimiento *m*, desplome *m*; [*of government*] caída *f*; [*of plans, scheme*] fracaso *m*; (*financial*) ruina *f*; [*of civilization, society*] ocaso *m*; (*Comm*) [*of business*] quiebra *f*; [*of prices*] hundimiento *m*, caída *f*
(VI) **1** [*person*] (*Med*) sufrir un colapso; (*with laughter*) morirse (de risa); [*building, roof, floor*] hundirse, desplomarse; [*civilization, society*] desaparecer, extinguirse; [*government*] caer; [*scheme*] fracasar; [*business*] quebrar; [*prices*] hundirse, bajar repentinamente • **the bridge ~d during the storm** el puente se vino abajo durante la tormenta • **the deal ~d** el negocio fracasó • **the company ~d** la compañía quebró *or* se hundió
2 (= *fold down*) plegarse, doblarse
collapsible [kə'læpsəbl] (ADJ) plegable
collar ['kɒləʳ] (N) **1** [*of coat, shirt*] cuello *m* • IDIOM: • **to get hot under the ~** sulfurarse
2 (= *necklace*) collar *m*
3 (*for dog*) collar *m*
4 (*Med*) collarín *m*
5 (*Tech*) (*on pipe etc*) collar *m*
(VT)* [+ *person*] abordar, acorralar; [+ *object*] (= *get for o.s.*) apropiarse
(CPD) ▸ **collar button** (*US*) botón *m* de camisa ▸ **collar size** medida *f* del cuello
collarbone ['kɒləbəʊn] (N) clavícula *f*
collarless ['kɒləlәs] (ADJ) [*shirt, jacket*] sin cuello
collarstud ['kɒləstʌd] (N) (*Brit*) botón *m* de camisa
collate [kɒ'leɪt] (VT) cotejar
collateral [kɒ'lætərəl] (N) **1** (*Econ*) garantía *f* subsidiaria
2 (= *person*) colateral *mf*
(CPD) ▸ **collateral damage** daños *mpl* colaterales ▸ **collateral loan** préstamo *m* colateral ▸ **collateral security** garantía *f* colateral
collation [kə'leɪʃən] (N) **1** [*of texts*] cotejo *m*
2 (= *meal*) colación *f*
colleague ['kɒliːg] (N) colega *mf*
collect [kə'lekt] (VT) **1** (= *assemble*) reunir, juntar; [+ *facts, documents*] recopilar, reunir; (= *collect in*) recoger • **the teacher ~ed the exercise books** el maestro recogió los cuadernos • **to ~ o.s.** *or* **one's thoughts** (*fig*) reponerse, recobrar el dominio de uno mismo
2 (*as hobby*) [+ *stamps, valuables*] coleccionar
3 (= *call for, pick up*) [+ *person*] recoger, pasar por (*LAm*); [+ *post, rubbish*] recoger; [+ *books*] coger, recoger; [+ *subscriptions, rent*] cobrar; [+ *taxes*] recaudar; [+ *ticket*] recoger • **I'll ~ you at eight** vengo a recogerte a las ocho • **their mother ~s them from school** su madre los recoge del colegio, su madre los pasa a buscar por el colegio • **I'll go and ~ the mail** voy por el correo
4 (= *gather*) [+ *dust, water*] acumular, retener
(VI) **1** (= *gather*) [*people*] reunirse, congregarse; [*water*] estancarse; [*dust*] acumularse
2 (= *collect money*) hacer una colecta • **I'm ~ing for UNICEF** estoy haciendo una colecta para la UNICEF • **to ~ for charity** recaudar *or* recolectar fondos con fines benéficos
3 (= *pick up*) • **~ on delivery** (*US*) contra reembolso
(ADV) • **to call ~** (*US*) (*Telec*) llamar a cobro revertido
(CPD) ▸ **collect call** (*US*) llamada *f* a cobro revertido
collectable [kə'lektəbl] (N) coleccionable *m*
collected [kə'lektɪd] (ADJ) **1** (= *cool*) sosegado, tranquilo
2 (= *compiled*) • **the ~ works of Shakespeare** las obras completas de Shakespeare
collectible [kə'lektəbl] (N) coleccionable *m*
collecting [kə'lektɪŋ] (N) coleccionismo *m*, el coleccionar
(CPD) ▸ **collecting box, collecting tin** bote *m* de cuestación, lata *f* petitoria
collection [kə'lekʃən] (N) **1** (= *act of collecting*) [*of post, rubbish*] recogida *f*; [*of taxes*] recaudación *f* • **to await ~** estar listo para ser recogido
2 (= *things collected*) [*of pictures, stamps*] colección *f*; (*pej*) montón *m* • **my CD ~** mi colección de CDs
3 (= *money*) colecta *f* • **a ~ for charity** una colecta para obras benéficas • **to make a ~ for** hacer una colecta a beneficio de
4 (= *group of people*) grupo *m*
(CPD) ▸ **collection box** (*for donations*) hucha *f* de las limosnas ▸ **collection charges** (*Econ, Comm*) gastos *mpl* de recogida ▸ **collection plate** cepillo *m*, platillo *m* ▸ **collection point** (*in large store*) punto *m* de recogida de las compras
collective [kə'lektɪv] (N) **1** (= *co-operative*) colectivo *m*
2 (*also* **collective noun**) (*Ling*) colectivo *m*
(ADJ) colectivo
(CPD) ▸ **collective bargaining** negociación *f* del convenio colectivo ▸ **collective farm** granja *f* colectiva ▸ **collective noun** sustantivo *m* colectivo, nombre *m* colectivo ▸ **collective ownership** propiedad *f* colectiva ▸ **collective security** seguridad *f* colectiva ▸ **collective unconscious** subconsciente *m* colectivo
collectively [kə'lektɪvlɪ] (ADV) colectivamente
collectivism [kə'lektɪvɪzəm] (N) colectivismo *m*
collectivist [kə'lektɪvɪst] (ADJ) colectivista
collectivization [kəˌlektɪvaɪ'zeɪʃən] (N) colectivización *f*
collectivize [kə'lektɪvaɪz] (VT) colectivizar
collector [kə'lektəʳ] (N) [*of taxes*]

recaudador(a) *m/f*; [*of stamps*] coleccionista *mf* • **~'s item** *or* **piece** pieza *f* de coleccionista; ▹ **ticket**

colleen ['kɒliːn] N (*Irl*) muchacha *f*

college ['kɒlɪdʒ] N (= *part of university*) colegio *m* universitario, escuela *f* universitaria; (*US*) [*of university*] ≈ facultad *f*; [*of agriculture, technology*] escuela *f*; [*of music*] conservatorio *m*; (= *body*) colegio *m* • **College of Advanced Technology** (*Brit*) politécnico *m* • **College of Further Education** Escuela *f* de Formación Profesional • **to go to ~** seguir estudios superiores

CPD ▸ **college graduate** (*after 3-year course*) diplomado/a *m/f*; (*after longer course*) licenciado/a *m/f* ▸ **college professor** profesor(a) *m/f* de universidad ▸ **college student** (= *university student*) estudiante *mf* universitario/a

> **COLLEGE**
> En el Reino Unido los **colleges** pueden ser centros universitarios en los que se estudian carreras en materias como arte o música, o bien centros de formación profesional. En algunas universidades como Oxford y Cambridge, los **colleges** son facultades en las que además de formación se da alojamiento al alumnado.
>
> En las universidades estadounidenses, un **college** es una institución similar a una facultad en la que se pueden estudiar carreras de cuatro años para obtener el título de **bachelor's degree**, mientras que los cursos de postgrado se imparten en **graduate schools**. Por otra parte, existen también los **junior colleges** o **community colleges** en los que se imparten clases de formación a estudiantes y trabajadores y en los que, después de un curso de dos años, se obtiene un diploma llamado **associate degree**.
>
> ▹ **DEGREE**

college-bound ['kɒlɪdʒbaʊnd] ADJ (*US*) • **college-bound student** estudiante *mf* que se prepara para la universidad

collegiate [kə'liːdʒɪɪt] ADJ **1** (*Rel*) colegial, colegiado • **~ church** iglesia *f* colegial
2 (*Univ*) que tiene colegios, organizado a base de colegios

collide [kə'laɪd] VI • **to ~ (with)** (*lit, fig*) chocar (con), colisionar (con)

collie ['kɒlɪ] N perro *m* pastor escocés, collie *m*

collier ['kɒlɪəʳ] N **1** (= *miner*) minero *m* (de carbón)
2 (= *ship*) barco *m* carbonero

colliery ['kɒlɪərɪ] N (*Brit*) mina *f* de carbón

collision [kə'lɪʒən] N choque *m*, colisión *f* • **to come into ~ with** chocar con, colisionar con

CPD ▸ **collision course** • **to be on a ~ course** (*fig*) ir camino del enfrentamiento ▸ **collision damage waiver** cobertura *f* parcial de daños por colisión

collocate ['kɒləkət] (*Ling*) N colocador *m*
VI ['kɒləkeɪt] • **to ~ with** colocarse con

collocation [ˌkɒlə'keɪʃən] N colocación *f*

colloquia [kə'ləʊkwɪə] NPL *of* **colloquium**

colloquial [kə'ləʊkwɪəl] ADJ coloquial, familiar

colloquialism [kə'ləʊkwɪəlɪzəm] N (= *word*) palabra *f* familiar; (= *expression*) expresión *f* familiar; (= *style*) estilo *m* familiar

colloquially [kə'ləʊkwɪəlɪ] ADV coloquialmente

colloquium [kə'ləʊkwɪəm] N (PL: **colloquiums** *or* **colloquia**) coloquio *m*

colloquy ['kɒləkwɪ] N coloquio *m*

collude [kə'luːd] VI confabularse (**with** con)

collusion [kə'luːʒən] N confabulación *f*, connivencia *f* • **to be in ~ with** confabular *or* conspirar con

collusive [kə'luːsɪv] ADJ (*frm*) [*behaviour*] colusivo, connivente

collywobbles* ['kɒlɪˌwɒblz] N (*fig*) nerviosismo *m*, ataque *m* de nervios

Colo. ABBR (*US*) = **Colorado**

Cologne [kə'ləʊn] N Colonia *f*

cologne [kə'ləʊn] N (*also* **eau de cologne**) agua *f* de colonia, colonia *f*

Colombia [kə'lɒmbɪə] N Colombia *f*

Colombian [kə'lɒmbɪən] ADJ colombiano
N colombiano/a *m/f*

colon[1] ['kəʊlən] N (PL: **colons** *or* **cola**) (*Anat*) colon *m*
CPD ▸ **colon cancer** cáncer *m* de colon

colon[2] ['kəʊlən] N (PL: **colons**) (*Typ*) dos puntos *mpl*

colonel ['kɜːnl] N coronel *m*

colonial [kə'ləʊnɪəl] ADJ colonial • **the ~ power** el poder colonizador
N colono *m*

colonialism [kə'ləʊnɪəlɪzəm] N colonialismo *m*

colonialist [kə'ləʊnɪəlɪst] N colonialista *mf*

colonic [kəʊ'lɒnɪk] ADJ de colon
CPD ▸ **colonic irrigation** lavado *m* de colon

colonist ['kɒlənɪst] N (= *pioneer*) colonizador(a) *m/f*; (= *inhabitant*) colono *m*

colonization [ˌkɒlənaɪ'zeɪʃən] N colonización *f*

colonize ['kɒlənaɪz] VT colonizar

colonized ['kɒlənaɪzd] ADJ colonizado

colonizer ['kɒlənaɪzəʳ] N colonizador(a) *m/f*

colonnade [ˌkɒlə'neɪd] N columnata *f*, galería *f*

colonnaded [ˌkɒlə'neɪdɪd] ADJ [*building*] con columnas

colony ['kɒlənɪ] N (PL: **colonies**) colonia *f*

colophon ['kɒləfən] N colofón *m*, pie *m* de imprenta

color *etc* ['kʌləʳ] N, VT, VI (*US*) = **colour** *etc*

Colorado beetle [ˌkɒlə'rɑːdəʊ'biːtl] N escarabajo *m* de la patata, dorífora *f*

colorant ['kʌlərənt] N (*US*) = **colourant**

coloration [ˌkʌlə'reɪʃən] N colorido *m*, colores *mpl*, coloración *f*

coloratura [ˌkɒlərə'tʊərə] N **1** (= *passage*) coloratura *f*
2 (= *singer*) soprano *f* de coloratura

colorcast ['kʌləkɑːst] (*US*) N programa *m* de TV en color
VT transmitir en color

colossal [kə'lɒsl] ADJ colosal, descomunal

colossally [kə'lɒsəlɪ] ADV colosalmente, descomunalmente

colossus [kə'lɒsəs] N (PL: **colossi** *or* **colossuses**) coloso *m*

colostomy [kə'lɒstəmɪ] N colostomía *f*
CPD ▸ **colostomy bag** bolsa *f* de colostomía

colostrum [kə'lɒstrəm] N colostro *m*, calostro *m*

colour, color (*US*) ['kʌləʳ] N **1** (= *shade*) color *m* • **what ~ is it?** ¿de qué color es? • **they come in different ~s** los hay de varios colores • **to change ~** cambiar *or* mudar de color • **it was green in ~** era de color verde • **as time goes by my memories take on a different ~** (*fig*) con el paso de los años mis recuerdos van tomando otro color • IDIOM: • **let's see the ~ of your money!** (*hum*) ¡a ver la pasta!*
2 (= *colourfulness*) color *m* • **splashes of ~** salpicones *fpl or* notas *fpl* de color • **what this room needs is a touch of ~** lo que este cuarto necesita es un toque de color • **in ~** (*TV, Cine*) en color
3 (= *dye, paint, pigment*) color *m* • **the latest lip and eye ~s** los últimos colores para labios y ojos
4 (= *complexion*) color *m* • **the ~ drained from his face** palideció, se le fue el color de la cara • **the ~ rose to her face** se le subieron los colores • **to put the ~ back in sb's cheeks** devolverle el color *or* los colores a algn • IDIOM: • **to be off ~** estar indispuesto
5 (= *race*) color *m* • **people of ~** (*US*) personas *fpl* de color
6 colours [*of country, team*] colores *mpl*; (= *flag*) bandera *f*; (*Mil*) estandarte *m* • **the Hungarian national ~s** los colores húngaros; (= *flag*) la bandera húngara • **to salute the ~s** saludar a la bandera • **the battalion's ~s** el estandarte del batallón • **he was wearing the team's ~s** vestía los colores del equipo • IDIOMS: • **with flying ~s**: • **she passed her exams with flying ~s** aprobó los exámenes con unas notas excelentes • **he has come out of all the tests with flying ~s** ha salido airoso de todas las pruebas • **to nail one's ~s to the mast**: • **he nailed his ~s to the mast** hizo constar sus opiniones • **to show one's true ~s** • **show o.s. in one's true ~s** demostrar cómo se es de verdad; ▹ **flying**
7 (= *authenticity, vividness*) color *m*, colorido *m* • **an article full of local ~** un artículo lleno de colorido local
8 (= *pretext*) • **under the ~ of …** bajo la apariencia de …
9 (*Mus*) (*also* **tone colour**) timbre *m*
VT **1** (= *apply colour to*) [+ *picture*] (*with paint*) pintar; (*with crayons*) colorear
2 (= *dye, tint*) teñir • **to ~ one's hair** teñirse *or* tintarse el pelo
3 (= *influence*) influir en • **his politics are ~ed by his upbringing** sus opiniones políticas están influenciadas por su educación • **you must not allow it to ~ your judgement** no debes permitir que influya en tu juicio
VI **1** (= *blush*) ponerse colorado, sonrojarse
2 (= *change colour*) tomar color • **fry the onion until it begins to ~** fría la cebolla hasta que empiece a coger color
3 (*with crayons*) [*child*] colorear
CPD [*film, photograph, slide*] en *or* (*LAm*) a color ▸ **colour bar** barrera *f* racial ▸ **colour blindness** daltonismo *m* ▸ **colour chart** carta *f* de colores ▸ **colour filter** (*Phot*) filtro *m* de color ▸ **colour guard** (*Mil*) portaestandarte *mf* ▸ **colour line** barrera *f* de color ▸ **colour match** coordinación *f* de colores ▸ **colour prejudice** prejuicio *m* racial ▸ **colour scheme** combinación *f* de colores ▸ **colour sergeant** (*Mil*) sargento *mf* portaestandarte ▸ **colour supplement** (*Journalism*) suplemento *m* a color ▸ **colour television** televisión *f* en color, televisión *f* a color (*LAm*)
▸ **colour in** VT + ADV (*with crayons*) colorear; (*with paint*) pintar

colourant, colorant (*US*) ['kʌlərənt] N colorante *m*

colour-blind, color-blind (*US*) ['kʌləblaɪnd] ADJ daltónico

colour-coded, color-coded (*US*) ['kʌlə'kəʊdɪd] ADJ con código de colores

coloured, colored (*US*) ['kʌləd] ADJ **1** [*pencils, glass, chalk, beads*] de colores • **brightly ~ silks** sedas *fpl* de colores vivos
2 (= *biased*) parcial • **a highly ~ tale** una historia de lo más parcial
3†** (= *black*) [*person*] de color
N **1**†** (= *black*) persona *f* de color
2 (*in South Africa*) *persona de padres racialmente mixtos*

3 coloureds (= *clothes*) ropa *fsing* de color
-coloured, **-colored** (*US*) [ˌkʌləd] ADJ (*ending in compounds*) • **rust-coloured** de color de herrumbre, color herrumbre • **gold-coloured** (de color) dorado • **straw-coloured** (de) color paja • **coffee-coloured** (de) color café
colourfast, **colorfast** (*US*) [ˈkʌləfɑːst] ADJ no desteñible
colourful, **colorful** (*US*) [ˈkʌləfəl] ADJ
1 (= *bright*) [*display, image*] lleno de color, lleno de colorido; [*procession*] lleno de colorido; [*clothes, design, pattern*] de colores vivos • **a bunch of ~ flowers** un ramo de flores de vistosos colores
2 (= *picturesque*) [*figure, character, story, history*] pintoresco; [*description, account, style*] colorista; [*scene*] vivo, animado • **her ~ past** (*euph*) su movidito pasado*
3 (*euph*) (= *vulgar*) [*language*] subido de tono
colourfully, **colorfully** (*US*) [ˈkʌləfʊlɪ] ADV
1 (= *brightly*) [*decorated, painted*] con colores muy vivos; [*dressed*] de forma muy vistosa
2 (= *in picturesque terms*) [*describe*] con mucho colorido • **he swore ~** utilizó expresiones muy subidas de tono
colouring, **coloring** (*US*) [ˈkʌlərɪŋ] N (*gen*) colorido *m*; (= *substance*) colorante *m*; (= *complexion*) tez *f* • **"no artificial colouring"** "sin colores artificiales" • **food ~** colorante *m* • **high ~** sonrojamiento *m*
CPD ▸ **colouring book** libro *m* (con dibujos) para colorear
colourist, **colorist** (*US*) [ˈkʌlərɪst] N
1 (= *artist*) colorista *mf*
2 (= *hairdresser*) *peluquero especializado en tintes*
colourless, **colorless** (*US*) [ˈkʌləlɪs] ADJ sin color, incoloro; (*fig*) (= *dull*) [*person*] soso • **a ~ liquid** un líquido transparente
colourway [ˈkʌləweɪ] N (*Brit*) combinación *f* de colores
colt [kəʊlt] N potro *m*
coltish [ˈkəʊltɪʃ] ADJ juguetón, retozón
coltsfoot [ˈkəʊltsfʊt] N (PL: **coltsfoots**) uña *f* de caballo, fárfara *f*
Columbia [kəˈlʌmbɪə] N • **(District of) ~** (*US*) Distrito *m* de Columbia
Columbine [ˈkɒləmbaɪn] N Columbina
columbine [ˈkɒləmbaɪn] N aguileña *f*
Columbus [kəˈlʌmbəs] N Colón
CPD ▸ **Columbus Day** Día *m* de la Raza
column [ˈkɒləm] N (*gen*) columna *f*; (*in newspaper*) columna *f*, sección *f* • **fifth ~** quinta columna *f* • **spinal ~** (*Anat*) columna *f* vertebral
CPD ▸ **column inch** • **they gave the news only two ~ inches** dieron solo dos pulgadas de columna a la noticia
columnist [ˈkɒləmnɪst] N columnista *mf*, articulista *mf*
colza [ˈkɒlzə] N colza *f*
coma [ˈkəʊmə] N coma *m* • **to be in a ~** estar en (estado de) coma
comatose [ˈkəʊmətəʊs] ADJ comatoso
comb [kəʊm] N **1** (*for hair*) peine *m*; (*ornamental*) peineta *f*; (*for horse*) almohaza *f* • **to run a ~ through one's hair** peinarse, pasarse un peine
2 [*of fowl*] cresta *f*
3 (= *honeycomb*) panal *m*
4 (*Tech*) carda *f*
VT **1** [+ *hair*] peinar • **to ~ one's hair** peinarse
2 (= *search*) [+ *countryside*] registrar a fondo, peinar • **we've been ~ing the town for you** te hemos buscado por toda la ciudad
3 (*Tech*) [+ *wool*] cardar
▸ **comb out** VT + ADV [+ *hair*] desenmarañar • **they ~ed out the useless members of the staff** se deshicieron de los miembros del personal inútiles
combat [ˈkɒmbæt] N **1** (= *action*) combate *m*
2 combats* (= *trousers*) pantalones *mpl* de combate
VT (*fig*) combatir, luchar contra
CPD ▸ **combat boots** botas *fpl* de combate ▸ **combat duty** servicio *m* de frente ▸ **combat fatigues**, **battle fatigues** uniforme *m* de combate ▸ **combat gear** ropa *f* de combate ▸ **combat jacket** guerrera *f* ▸ **combat troops** tropas *fpl* de combate ▸ **combat trousers** pantalones *mpl* de camuflaje ▸ **combat zone** zona *f* de combate
combatant [ˈkɒmbətənt] N combatiente *mf*
combative [ˈkɒmbətɪv] ADJ combativo
combativeness [ˈkɒmbətɪvnɪs] N combatividad *f*
combe [kuːm] N = **coomb**
combination [ˌkɒmbɪˈneɪʃən] N **1** (*gen*) combinación *f*; (= *mixture*) mezcla *f* • **a ~ of circumstances** un conjunto *or* una combinación de circunstancias
2 [*of safe*] combinación *f*
3 combinations (= *undergarment*) combinación *f*
CPD ▸ **combination lock** cerradura *f* de combinación ▸ **combination skin** piel *f* mixta
combinatory [ˌkɒmbɪˈneɪtərɪ] ADJ combinacional
combine VT [kəmˈbaɪn] • **to ~ (with)** combinar (con) • **the film ~s humour with suspense** la película combina el humor con el suspense • **to ~ business with pleasure** combinar los negocios con el placer • **expertise ~d with charm** la pericia combinada con la simpatía • **he ~s all the qualities of a leader** reúne todas las cualidades de un líder • **it's difficult to ~ a career with a family** es difícil compaginar la profesión con la vida familiar • **a ~d effort** un esfuerzo conjunto • **a ~d operation** (*Mil*) una operación conjunta
VI [kəmˈbaɪn] **1** (= *join together*) combinarse, unirse • **to ~ with** aunarse con • **to ~ against sth/sb** unirse en contra de algo/algn
2 (*Chem*) • **to ~ (with)** combinarse (con), mezclarse (con)
N [ˈkɒmbaɪn] **1** (*Comm*) asociación *f*
2 (*also* **combine harvester**) cosechadora *f*
CPD [ˈkɒmbaɪn] ▸ **combine harvester** cosechadora *f*
combined assets [kəmˌbaɪndˈæsets] NPL capital *m* común
combined honours [kəmˌbaɪndˈɒnəz] N (*Brit*) (= *degree course*) • **to do ~** (*in any two subjects*) hacer dos carreras; (*in related subjects*) hacer dos especialidades
combings [ˈkəʊmɪŋz] NPL peinaduras *fpl*
combo* [ˈkɒmbəʊ] N (PL: **combos**) **1** (*Mus*) grupo *m*, conjunto *m*
2 (= *clothes*) conjunto *m*
combs* [kɒmz] NPL combinación *f*
combustibility [kəmˌbʌstɪˈbɪlɪtɪ] N combustibilidad *f*
combustible [kəmˈbʌstɪbl] ADJ combustible
N combustible *m*
combustion [kəmˈbʌstʃən] N combustión *f*; ▹ **internal**
CPD ▸ **combustion chamber** cámara *f* de combustión
come [kʌm] (PT: **came**, PP: **come**) VI **1** (*gen*) venir; (= *arrive*) llegar • **we have ~ to help you** hemos venido a ayudarte • **when did he ~?** ¿cuándo llegó? • **they came late** llegaron tarde • **the letter came this morning** la carta llegó esta mañana • **(I'm) coming!** ¡voy!, ¡ya voy! • **he came running/dashing** *etc* **in** entró corriendo/volando *etc* • **the day/time will ~ when …** ya llegará el día/la hora (en) que … • **it will be two years ~ March** en marzo hará dos años • **a week ~ Monday** ocho días a partir del lunes • **we'll ~ after you** te seguiremos • **~ and see us soon** ven a vernos pronto • **it may ~ as a surprise to you …** puede que te asombre *or* (*LAm*) extrañe … • **it came as a shock to her** le afectó mucho • **to ~ for sth/sb** venir por *or* (*LAm*) pasar por algo/algn • **to ~ from** (= *stem from*) [*word, custom*] venir de, proceder de, provenir de; (= *originate from*) [*person*] ser de • **she has just ~ from London** acaba de venir *or* (*LAm*) regresar de Londres • **I ~ from Wigan** soy de Wigan • **where do you ~ from?** ¿de dónde eres? • **this necklace ~s from Spain** este collar es de España • **I don't know where you're coming from** (*US**) no alcanzo a comprender la base de tu argumento • **to ~ and go** ir y venir • **people were coming and going all day** la gente iba y venía todo el día • **the pain ~s and goes** el dolor va y viene • **the picture ~s and goes** (*TV*) un momento tenemos imagen y al siguiente no • **~ home** ven a casa • **it never came into my mind** no pasó siquiera por mi mente • **we came to a village** llegamos a un pueblo • **to ~ to a decision** llegar a una decisión • **the water only came to her waist** el agua le llegaba solo hasta la cintura • **it came to me that there was a better way to do it** se me ocurrió que había otra forma mejor de hacerlo • **when it ~s to choosing, I prefer wine** si tengo que elegir, prefiero vino • **when it ~s to mathematics …** en cuanto a *or* en lo que se refiere a las matemáticas … • **when your turn ~s** cuando llegue tu turno • **they have ~ a long way** (*lit*) han venido desde muy lejos; (*fig*) han llegado muy lejos • **~ with me** ven conmigo
2 (= *have its place*) venir • **May ~s before June** mayo viene antes de junio • **it ~s on the next page** viene en la pagina siguiente • **work ~s before pleasure** primero el trabajo, luego la diversión • **the adjective ~s before the noun** el adjetivo precede al sustantivo • **he came third** llegó en tercer lugar
3 (= *happen*) pasar, ocurrir • **recovery came slowly** la recuperación fue lenta • **how does this chair ~ to be broken?** ¿cómo es que esta silla está rota? • **how ~?*** ¿cómo es eso?, ¿cómo así?, ¿por qué? • **how ~ you don't know?*** ¿cómo es que no lo sabes? • **no good will ~ of it** de eso no saldrá nada bueno • **nothing came of it** todo quedó en nada • **that's what ~s of being careless** eso es lo que pasa *or* ocurre por la falta de cuidado • **no harm will ~ to him** no le pasará nada • **~ what may** pase lo que pase
4 (= *be, become*) • **I have ~ to like her** ha llegado a caerme bien • **I came to think it was all my fault** llegué a la conclusión de que era culpa mía • **now I ~ to think of it** ahora que lo pienso, pensándolo bien • **it came to pass that …** (*liter*) aconteció que … • **those shoes ~ in two colours** esos zapatos vienen en dos colores • **the button has ~ loose** el botón se ha soltado • **it ~s naturally to him** lo hace sin esfuerzo, no le cuesta nada hacerlo • **it'll all ~ right in the end** al final, todo se arreglará • **my dreams came true** mis sueños se hicieron realidad
5‡ (= *have orgasm*) correrse (*Sp***), acabar (*LAm***)
6 (*in phrases*) • **~ again?*** ¿cómo (dice)? • **he's as good as they ~** es bueno como él solo • **he's as stupid as they ~** es tonto de remate • **I like my tea just as it ~s** me gusta el té hecho de cualquier modo • **they don't ~ any**

better than that mejores no los hay • **to ~ between two people** (= *interfere*) meterse *or* entrometerse entre dos personas; (= *separate*) separar a dos personas • **nothing can ~ between us** no hay nada que sea capaz de separarnos • **cars like that don't ~ cheap** los coches así no son baratos • **come, come!** ¡vamos! • **the new ruling ~s into force next year** la nueva ley entra en vigor el año que viene • **I don't know whether I'm coming or going** no sé lo que me hago • **he had it coming to him*** se lo tenía bien merecido • **if it ~s to it** llegado el caso • **oh, ~ now!** ¡vamos! • **I could see it coming** lo veía venir • **~ to that …** si vamos a eso … • **in (the) years to ~** en los años venideros

(VT) • **don't ~ that game with me!*** ¡no me vengas con esos cuentos! • **that's coming it a bit strong** eso me parece algo exagerado, no es para tanto

▸ **come about** (VI + ADV) suceder, ocurrir • **how did this ~ about?** ¿cómo ha sido esto?

▸ **come across** (VI + ADV) **1** (= *make an impression*) • **to ~ across well/badly** causar buena/mala impresión • **she ~s across as a nice girl** da la impresión de ser una chica simpática • **it didn't ~ across like that** no lo entendimos en ese sentido, no es esa la impresión que nos produjo

2 (*US*) (= *keep one's word*) cumplir la palabra

(VI + PREP) (= *find*) dar con, topar con, encontrarse con • **I came across a dress that I hadn't worn for years** di con *or* me encontré un vestido que hacía años que no me ponía

▸ **come across with** (VI + PREP) [+ *money*] apoquinar* • **to ~ across with the information** soltar prenda

▸ **come along** (VI + ADV) **1** • **~ along!** (*in friendly tone*) ¡vamos!, ¡venga!, ¡ándale! (*esp Mex*), ¡ándele! (*Mex*); (*impatiently*) ¡date prisa!, ¡apúrate! (*LAm*)

2 (= *accompany*) acompañar • **are you coming along?** ¿vienes?, ¿nos acompañas? • **you'll have to ~ along with me to the station** usted tendrá que acompañarme a la comisaría

3 (= *progress*) ir • **how is the book coming along?** ¿qué tal va el libro? • **it's coming along nicely** va bien

4 (= *arrive*) [*chance*] presentarse • **then who should ~ along but Alex** entonces se presentó nada más ni nada menos que Alex

▸ **come apart** (VI + ADV) deshacerse, caer en pedazos

▸ **come around** (VI + ADV) = **come round**

▸ **come at** (VI + PREP) **1** [+ *solution*] llegar a

2 (= *attack*) atacar, precipitarse sobre

▸ **come away** (VI + ADV) **1** (= *leave*) marcharse, salir • **~ away from there!** ¡sal *or* quítate de ahí!

2 (= *become detached*) separarse, desprenderse

▸ **come back** (VI + ADV) **1** (= *return*) volver, regresar (*LAm*) • **my brother is coming back tomorrow** mi hermano vuelve mañana • **would you like to ~ back for a cup of tea?** ¿quieres volver a casa a tomar un té? • **to ~ back to what we were discussing …** volviendo a lo anterior … • **it all ~s back to money** todo viene a ser cuestión de dinero

2* (= *reply*) • **can I ~ back to you on that one?** ¿te importa si dejamos ese punto para mas tarde? • **when accused, he came back with a counter-accusation** cuando le acusaron, respondió con una contraacusación

3 (= *return to mind*) • **it's all coming back to me** ahora sí me acuerdo

▸ **come before** (VI + PREP) (*Jur*) [*person*] comparecer ante • **his case came before the courts** su caso llegó a los tribunales

▸ **come by** (VI + PREP) (= *obtain*) conseguir, adquirir • **how did she ~ by that name?** ¿cómo adquirió ese nombre?

(VI + ADV) **1** (= *pass*) pasar • **could I ~ by please?** ¿me permite?, ¿se puede?

2 (= *visit*) visitar, entrar a ver • **next time you ~ by** la próxima vez que vengas por aquí

▸ **come down** (VI + PREP) bajar • **to ~ down the stairs** bajar las escaleras

(VI + ADV) **1** (= *descend*) [*person, prices, temperature*] bajar (**from** de, **to** a); [*rain*] caer; [*plane*] (= *land*) aterrizar; (= *crash*) estrellarse • **to ~ down in the world** venir a menos • **to ~ down hard on sb** ser duro con algn • **she came down on them like a ton of bricks** se les echó encima • **to ~ down against a policy** declararse en contra de una política • **so it ~s down to this** así que se reduce a esto • **if it ~s down to it, we'll have to move** si es necesario habrá que mudarse • **to ~ down on sb's side** tomar partido por algn • **if it ~s down heads** [*coin*] si sale cara

2 (= *be transmitted*) [*heirloom*] pasar; [*tradition*] ser transmitido

3 [*building*] (= *be demolished*) ser derribado/a; (= *fall down*) derrumbarse

▸ **come down with** (VI + PREP) **1** (= *become ill from*) caer enfermo de, enfermar de • **to ~ down with flu** caer enfermo *or* enfermar de gripe

2* (= *pay out*) apoquinar

▸ **come forward** (VI + ADV) **1** (= *advance*) avanzar

2 (= *volunteer*) ofrecerse, presentarse • **to ~ forward with a suggestion** ofrecer una sugerencia

3 (= *respond*) responder

▸ **come in** (VI + ADV) [*person*] entrar; [*train, person in race*] llegar; [*tide*] crecer • **~ in!** ¡pase!, ¡entre!, ¡siga! (*LAm*) • **the Tories came in at the last election** en las últimas elecciones, ganaron los conservadores • **where do I ~ in?** y yo ¿qué hago?, y yo ¿qué pinto? • **they have no money coming in** no tienen ingresos *or* (*LAm*) entradas • **he has £500 coming in each week** tiene ingresos *or* (*LAm*) entradas de 500 libras por semana • **he came in last** (*in race*) llegó el último • **it will ~ in handy** vendrá bien • **to ~ in for criticism/praise** ser objeto de críticas/elogios • **to ~ in on a deal** tomar parte en un negocio

▸ **come into** (VI + PREP) **1** (= *inherit*) [+ *legacy*] heredar • **he came into a fortune** heredó una fortuna, le correspondió una fortuna

2 (= *be involved in*) tener que ver con, ser parte de • **melons don't ~ into it** los melones no tienen que ver, los melones no hacen al caso

▸ **come of** (VI + PREP) • **to ~ of a good family** ser de buena familia; ▹ **age**

▸ **come off** (VI + ADV) **1** [*button*] caerse; [*stain*] quitarse • **does this lid ~ off?** ¿se puede quitar esta tapa?

2 (= *take place, come to pass*) tener lugar, realizarse

3 (= *succeed*) tener éxito, dar resultados • **to ~ off well/badly** (= *turn out*) salir bien/mal

4 (= *acquit o.s.*) portarse • **to ~ off best** salir mejor parado, salir ganando

5 (*Theat*) • **the play came off in January** la obra dejó de figurar en la cartelera en enero

(VI + PREP) **1** (= *separate from*) • **she came off her bike** se cayó de la bicicleta • **the car came off the road** el coche se salió de la carretera • **the label came off the bottle** la etiqueta se desprendió de la botella • **~ off it!*** ¡vamos, anda!, ¡venga ya! • **I told him to ~ off it** le dije que dejase de hacer el tonto

2 (= *give up*) dejar • **it's time you came off the pill** es hora de dejar la píldora

▸ **come on** (VI + ADV) **1** • **~ on!** (*expressing encouragement*) ¡vamos!, ¡venga!, ¡ándale! (*esp Mex*), ¡ándele! (*Mex*); (*urging haste*) ¡date prisa!, ¡apúrate! (*LAm*); (*expressing disbelief*) ¡venga ya!

2 (= *progress*) ir; [*plant*] crecer, desarrollarse • **how is the book coming on?** ¿qué tal va el libro? • **it's coming on nicely** va bien

3 (= *start*) empezar • **winter is coming on now** ya está empezando el invierno • **I feel a cold coming on** me está entrando un catarro; ▹ **come on to**

4 (*Theat*) salir a escena

5 [*light*] encenderse

6 (*US*) (*fig*) • **he came on sincere** fingía ser sincero

(VI + PREP) = **come upon**

▸ **come on to** (VI + PREP) **1** (= *start discussing*) [+ *question, topic, issue*] pasar a • **I'll ~ on to that in a moment** • **I'm coming on to that next** de eso hablaré en seguida

2 (*esp US**) (*sexually*) tirar los tejos a*, insinuarse a

▸ **come out** (VI + ADV) **1** (= *emerge*) [*person, object, sun, magazine*] salir (**of** de); [*qualities*] mostrarse; [*news*] divulgarse, difundirse; [*scandal*] descubrirse, salir a la luz; [*film*] estrenarse • **we came out of the cinema at ten** salimos del cine a las diez • **her book ~s out in May** su libro sale en mayo • **the idea came out of an experiment** la idea surgió a raíz de un experimento • **he came out of it with credit** salió con honor; ▹ **closet**

2 (= *open*) [*flower*] abrirse, florecer

3 (*into the open*) [*debutante*] ser presentada en sociedad, ponerse de largo; [*homosexual*] declararse • **to ~ out on strike** declararse en huelga; (*fig*) • **to ~ out for/against sth** declararse en pro/en contra de algo

4 [*stain*] (= *be removed*) quitarse; [*dye*] (= *run*) desteñirse • **I don't think this stain will ~ out** no creo que esta mancha se vaya a quitar

5 (= *become covered with*) • **he came out in a rash** le salió un sarpullido • **he came out in spots** le salieron granos • **I came out in a sweat** empecé a sudar, me cubrí de sudor

6 (*in conversation*) • **to ~ out with a remark** salir con un comentario • **you never know what he's going to ~ out with next!*** ¡nunca se sabe por dónde va a salir!

7 (= *turn out*) salir • **it all came out right** todo salió bien • **none of my photos came out** no salió ninguna de mis fotos • **you always ~ out well in photos** siempre sales bien en las fotos • **it ~s out at £5 a head** sale a 5 libras por cabeza

▸ **come over** (VI + ADV) **1** (*lit*) venir, venirse • **they came over to England for a holiday** se vinieron a Inglaterra de vacaciones • **you'll soon ~ over to my way of thinking** (*fig*) ya me darás la razón

2* (= *feel suddenly*) ponerse • **she came over quite ill** se puso bastante mala • **he came over all shy** de repente le dio vergüenza • **I came over all dizzy** me mareé

3 (= *give impression*) • **how did he ~ over?** ¿qué impresión produjo? • **to ~ over well/badly** causar buena/mala impresión • **her speech came over very well** su discurso causó buena impresión • **to ~ over as** dar la impresión de ser, dar una imagen de

(VI + PREP) • **I don't know what's ~ over him!** ¡no sé lo que le pasa! • **a feeling of weariness came over her** le invadió una sensación de cansancio • **a change came over him** se operó en él un cambio

▸ **come round** (VI + ADV) **1** (= *visit*) • **~ round whenever you like** pasa por la casa cuando quieras • **he is coming round to see us tonight** viene a vernos *or* pasará a vernos esta noche

2 (= *occur regularly*) llegar • **I shall be glad**

when payday ~s round ya estoy esperando el día de pago
3 (= *make detour*) dar un rodeo, desviarse • **I had to ~ round by the Post Office to post a letter** tuve que desviarme hasta Correos para echar una carta
4 (= *change one's mind*) dejarse convencer • **she'll soon ~ round to my way of thinking** no tardará en darme la razón • **he came round to our view** adoptó nuestra opinión
5 (= *throw off bad mood*) tranquilizarse, calmarse; (= *cheer up*) animarse • **leave him alone, he'll soon ~ round** déjalo en paz, ya se calmará
6 (= *regain consciousness, esp after anaesthetic*) volver en sí • **he came round after about ten minutes** volvió en sí después de unos diez minutos

▸ **come through** (VI + ADV) **1** (= *survive*) sobrevivir; (= *recover*) recuperarse • **he's badly injured, but he'll ~ through all right** está malherido, pero se recuperará *or* se pondrá bien
2 [*telephone call*] llegar • **the call came through from France at 10p.m.** a las 10 de la noche lograron comunicar desde Francia
(VI + PREP) **1** (= *survive*) [+ *war, danger*] sobrevivir; (*uninjured*) salir ileso/a de; [+ *illness*] recuperarse de
2 (= *pass*) [+ *test*] superar

▸ **come through with** (VI + PREP) (*US*) = **come up with**

▸ **come to** (VI + PREP) [*amount*] ascender a, sumar • **how much does it ~ to?** ¿cuánto es en total?, ¿a cuánto asciende? • **it ~s to £15 altogether** en total son 15 libras • **so it ~s to this** así que viene a ser esto • **what are we coming to?** ¿adónde va a parar todo esto?
(VI + ADV) (= *regain consciousness, esp after accidental knock-out*) recobrar el conocimiento • **he came to in hospital** recobró el conocimiento en el hospital

▸ **come together** (VI + ADV) (= *assemble*) reunirse, juntarse • **great qualities ~ together in his work** en su obra se dan cita grandes cualidades • **it's all coming together now** [*project, plan*] parece que ya empieza a tomar forma

▸ **come under** (VI + PREP) • **it ~s under the heading of vandalism** se puede clasificar de vandalismo • **he came under the teacher's influence** cayó bajo la influencia del profesor • **to ~ under attack** sufrir un ataque, verse atacado

▸ **come up** (VI + ADV) **1** (= *ascend*) [*person*] subir; [*sun*] salir; [*plant*] aparecer • **~ up here!** ¡sube aquí! • **he has ~ up in the world** ha subido mucho en la escala social
2 (= *crop up*) [*difficulty*] surgir; [*matters for discussion*] plantearse, mencionarse • **something's ~ up so I'll be late home** ha surgido algo, así es que llegaré tarde a casa • **to ~ up for sale** ponerse a la venta
3 (*Jur*) [*accused*] (= *appear in court*) comparecer; [*lawsuit*] (= *be heard*) oírse, presentarse • **to ~ up before the judge** comparecer ante el juez • **his case ~s up tomorrow** su proceso se verá mañana
4 (*Univ*) matricularse • **he came up to Oxford last year** (*Brit*) se matriculó en la universidad de Oxford el año pasado
(VI + PREP) subir • **to ~ up the stairs** subir las escaleras

▸ **come up against** (VI + PREP) [+ *problem*] tropezar con; [+ *enemy*] tener que habérselas con • **she came up against complete opposition to her proposals** tropezó con una oposición total ante sus propuestas

▸ **come upon** (VI + PREP) (= *find*) [+ *object, person*] topar(se) con, encontrar

▸ **come up to** (VI + PREP) **1** (= *reach*) llegar hasta • **the water came up to my waist** el agua me llegaba hasta la cintura
2 (= *approach*) acercarse a • **she came up to me and kissed me** se me acercó y me besó
3 (*fig*) estar a la altura de, satisfacer • **it didn't ~ up to our expectations** no estuvo a la altura de lo que esperábamos • **the goods didn't ~ up to the required standard** la mercancía no satisfacía el nivel de calidad requerido; ▸ **scratch**

▸ **come up with** (VI + PREP) **1** (= *suggest, propose*) [+ *idea, plan*] proponer, sugerir; [+ *suggestion*] hacer; [+ *solution*] ofrecer, sugerir
2 (= *find*) [+ *money*] encontrar • **eventually he came up with the money** por fin encontró el dinero

> **COME, GO**
>
> *Although* **come** *and* **venir** *usually imply motion towards the speaker while* **go** *and* **ir** *imply motion away from them, there are some differences between the two languages. In English we sometimes describe movement as if from the other person's perspective. In Spanish, this is not the case.*
>
> ▹ *For example when someone calls you:*
> **I'm coming**
> Ya voy
>
> ▹ *Making arrangements over the phone or in a letter:*
> **I'll come and pick you up at four**
> Iré a recogerte a las cuatro
> **Can I come too?**
> ¿Puedo ir yo también?
> **Shall I come with you?**
> ¿Voy contigo?
>
> ▹ *So, use* **ir** *rather than* **venir** *when going towards someone else or when joining them to go on somewhere else.*
>
> ▹ *Compare:*
> **Are you coming with us?** (*viewed from the speaker's perspective*)
> ¿(Te) vienes con nosotros?
>
> *For further uses and examples, see* **come, go**

comeback ['kʌmbæk] (N) **1** (= *reaction*) (*usually adverse*) reacción *f*
2 (*US*) (= *response*) réplica *f*; (*witty*) respuesta *f* aguda
3 (= *return*) • **to make a ~** (*Theat*) volver a las tablas; (*Cine*) volver a los platós • **he is making a ~ to professional football** está listo para volver al fútbol profesional • **butter has made a ~ in the British diet** la mantequilla ha recobrado su importancia en la dieta británica
4 (= *redress*) • **to have no ~** no poder pedir cuentas, no poder reclamar

Comecon ['kɒmɪkɒn] (N ABBR) (*formerly*) (= **Council for Mutual Economic Aid**) COMECON *m*

comedian [kə'miːdɪən] (N) humorista *mf*, cómico/a *m/f*

comedic [kə'miːdɪk] (ADJ) (*frm*) [*moment, performance*] cómico

comedienne [kə,miːdɪ'en] (N) humorista *f*, cómica *f*

comedown ['kʌmdaʊn] (N) (= *humiliation*) humillación *f* • **the house is a bit of a ~ from the mansion she is used to** la casa representa un cierto bajón de nivel en comparación con la mansión a la que ha estado acostumbrada

comedy ['kɒmɪdɪ] (N) (*gen*) comedia *f*; (= *humour of situation*) comicidad *f* • **~ of manners** comedia *f* de costumbres
(CPD) ▸ **comedy club** *local nocturno donde hay actuaciones de monologuistas, magos etc* ▸ **comedy show** (*TV*) programa *m* de humor

come-hither ['kʌm'hɪðəʳ] (ADJ) [*look*] insinuante, provocativo

comeliness ['kʌmlɪnɪs] (N) (*liter*) gracia *f*, encanto *m*, donaire† *m*

comely ['kʌmlɪ] (ADJ) (COMPAR: **comelier**, SUPERL: **comeliest**) (*liter*) lindo

come-on* ['kʌm,ɒn] (N) **1** (= *enticement*) insinuación *f*, invitación *f* • **to give sb the come-on** insinuársele a algn
2 (*Comm*) truco *m*, señuelo *m*

comer ['kʌməʳ] (N) • **the first ~** el primero/la primera en llegar • **he has defended his title against all ~s** ha defendido su título contra todos los contendientes

comestible [kə'mestɪbl] (ADJ) (*frm*) comestible

comestibles [kə'mestɪblz] (NPL) (*frm*) comestibles *mpl*

comet ['kɒmɪt] (N) cometa *m*

comeuppance [,kʌm'ʌpəns] (N) • IDIOM: • **to get one's ~** llevarse su merecido

COMEX ['kɒmeks] (N ABBR) (*US*) = **Commodities Exchange**

comfort ['kʌmfət] (N) **1** (= *solace*) consuelo *m* • **you're a great ~ to me** eres un gran consuelo para mí • **if it's any ~ to you** si te sirve de consuelo • **that's cold** *or* **small ~** eso no me consuela nada • **the exam is too close for ~** el examen está demasiado cerca para que me sienta tranquilo • **to give ~ to the enemy** dar aliento al enemigo • **to take ~ from sth** consolarse con algo • **I take ~ in** *or* **from the fact/knowledge that …** me consuelo sabiendo que …
2 (= *well-being*) confort *m*, comodidad *f*; (= *facility*) comodidad *f* • **to live in ~** vivir cómodamente • **with every modern ~** con todo confort, con toda comodidad • **he likes his home ~s** le gusta rodearse de las comodidades del hogar
(VT) (= *give solace*) consolar, confortar
(CPD) ▸ **comfort blanket** mantita *f* (*para dormir*) ▸ **comfort eating, comfort food** *comida como terapia contra la depresión* ▸ **comfort station** (*US*) servicios *mpl*, aseos *mpl*, baño *m* (*LAm*) ▸ **comfort zone** zona *f* de confort

comfortable ['kʌmfətəbl] (ADJ) **1** (*physically*) [*chair, shoes, position*] cómodo; [*room, house, hotel*] confortable, cómodo; [*temperature*] agradable • **are you ~, sitting there?** ¿estás cómodo sentado ahí? • **you don't look very ~** no pareces estar muy cómodo • **I'm not ~ in these shoes** no estoy *or* voy cómodo con estos zapatos • **to make o.s. ~** ponerse cómodo
2 (*mentally, emotionally*) cómodo, a gusto • **I'm not ~** *or* **I don't feel ~ at formal dinners** no me siento cómodo *or* a gusto en las cenas formales • **she wasn't ~ about giving him the keys** no se sentía a gusto dejándole las llaves • **to feel ~ with sb/sth** sentirse cómodo *or* a gusto con algn/algo • **he came closer to the truth than was ~** se acercó de manera inquietante a la verdad
3 (*financially*) [*income*] bueno, suficiente; [*life, lifestyle*] holgado • **he's ~** está en buena posición económica
4 (= *easy*) [*lead, majority, margin*] amplio, holgado • **a ~ job** un buen empleo, un empleo cómodo y bien pagado • **he was elected with a ~ majority** fue elegido por una amplia mayoría, fue elegido por una mayoría holgada • **to have a ~ win over sb**

vencer a algn fácilmente
5 (*Med*) estable • **he was described as ~ in hospital last night** anoche el hospital describió su condición como estable
comfortably ['kʌmfətəblɪ] ADV **1** (*physically*) [*sit, rest, lie*] cómodamente; [*sleep*] confortablemente • **sitting ~** cómodamente sentado • **~ furnished** amueblado confortablemente • **these shoes fit ~** voy muy cómodo con estos zapatos • **we are settled ~ in our new home** ya nos hemos acomodado en la casa nueva
2 (*financially*) [*live*] holgadamente, con desahogo • **to be ~ off** vivir holgadamente *or* con desahogo, disfrutar de una posición acomodada *or* desahogada (*frm*)
3 (= *easily*) [*manage*] sin problemas; [*win, defeat*] fácilmente, sin problemas; [*afford*] sin problemas, cómodamente • **the desk fits ~ into this corner** el escritorio cabe holgadamente *or* de sobra en esta esquina
comforter ['kʌmfətə^r] N **1** (*baby's*) chupete *m*, chupón *m* (*LAm*)
2 (*US*) (= *blanket*) edredón *m*
3 (= *scarf*) bufanda *f*
comforting ['kʌmfətɪŋ] ADJ consolador, (re)confortante; [*words*] de consuelo
comfortingly ['kʌmfətɪŋlɪ] ADV [*say*] de manera reconfortante
comfortless ['kʌmfətlɪs] ADJ incómodo, sin comodidad
comfrey ['kʌmfrɪ] N consuelda *f*
comfy* ['kʌmfɪ] ADJ (COMPAR: **comfier**, SUPERL: **comfiest**) [*chair, room*] cómodo; [*bed*] cómodo y calentito • **I'm nice and ~ here** estoy súper a gusto *or* súper cómoda aquí*
comic ['kɒmɪk] ADJ cómico; (= *amusing*) gracioso, divertido
N **1** (= *person*) cómico/a *m/f*
2 (*esp Brit*) (= *paper*) cómic *m*; (*children's*) revista *f* de historietas, tebeo *m* (*Sp*)
3 comics (*US*) = **comic strip**
CPD ▸ **comic book** (*esp US*) libro *m* de cómics ▸ **comic opera** ópera *f* bufa *or* cómica ▸ **comic relief** toque *m* humorístico *or* cómico (*en una obra dramática*) ▸ **comic strip** historieta *f*, tira *f* cómica ▸ **comic verse** poesía *f* humorística *or* cómica

COMIC RELIEF
Comic Relief es una campaña con fines benéficos organizada por actores y humoristas para recaudar dinero y paliar así la pobreza, especialmente en África. La cadena de televisión **BBC** le dedica cada dos años una noche entera y en el programa actores, humoristas y famosos hacen números cómicos, informando a la vez sobre proyectos para luchar contra la pobreza e invitando al público a que llame y haga donativos. Como muestra de apoyo mucha gente lleva narices rojas de plástico (**red noses**) o las ponen en la parte frontal del coche.

comical ['kɒmɪkəl] ADJ cómico, gracioso
comically ['kɒmɪkəlɪ] ADV de manera cómica, graciosamente
coming ['kʌmɪŋ] ADJ **1** (= *approaching*) [*weeks, months, years*] próximo, venidero (*frm*) • **in the ~ weeks** en las próximas semanas, en las semanas venideras (*frm*) • **the ~ year** el año que viene, el próximo año • **this ~ Friday** el viernes que viene, el próximo viernes • **the ~ election** las próximas elecciones • **~ generations** las generaciones venideras (*frm*)
2 (= *promising*) [*politician, actor*] prometedor • **it's the ~ thing*** es lo que se va a poner de moda, es lo que se va a llevar
N llegada *f* • **the ~ of spring** la llegada de la primavera • **the ~ of Christ** el advenimiento de Cristo • **~ of age** (llegada *f* a la) mayoría *f* de edad • **the ~s and goings of the guests** las idas y venidas de los invitados • **there was too much ~ and going** había demasiado ir y venir de gente; ▹ **second¹**
coming-out ['kʌmɪŋ'aʊt] N presentación *f* en sociedad
Comintern ['kɒmɪntɜːn] N ABBR (*Pol*) (= **Communist International**) Comintern *f*
comm. ABBR **1** = **commerce**
2 = **commercial**
3 = **committee**
comma ['kɒmə] N coma *f*; ▹ **inverted**
command [kə'mɑːnd] N **1** (= *order*) (*esp Mil*) orden *f*; (*Comput*) orden *f*, comando *m* • **he gave the ~ (to attack/retreat)** dio la orden (de atacar/retirarse) • **his ~s were obeyed at once** sus órdenes se cumplieron de inmediato • **at** *or* **by the ~ of sb** por orden de algn • **by royal ~** por real orden
2 (= *control*) [*of army, ship*] mando *m* • **to be at sb's ~** [*resources, money, troops*] estar a la disposición de algn; [*men*] estar a las órdenes de algn, estar bajo el mando de algn • **to have at one's ~** [+ *resources, money, troops*] disponer de, tener a su disposición; [+ *men*] tener a sus órdenes, estar al mando de • **to have ~ of sth** estar al mando de algo • **to be in ~ (of sth)** estar al mando (de algo) • **who is in ~ here?** ¿quién manda aquí? • **to be in ~ of one's faculties** estar en posesión de sus facultades • **to be in ~ of the situation** ser dueño de la situación • **to take ~ of sth** asumir el mando de algo • **under the ~ of** bajo el mando de
3 (= *mastery*) dominio *m* • **his ~ of English** su dominio del inglés • **to have a good ~ of English** dominar el inglés • **~ of the seas** dominio de los mares
4 (= *authority*) (*Mil, Naut*) mando *m*, jefatura *f* • **second in ~** segundo *m*; (*Naut*) segundo *m* de a bordo; ▹ **high**
VT **1** (= *order*) • **to ~ sb to do sth** mandar *or* ordenar a algn que haga algo • **to ~ sth to be done** mandar *or* ordenar que se haga algo
2 (= *be in control of*) [+ *soldiers, army*] mandar, estar al mando de; [+ *ship*] comandar
3 (= *have at one's disposal*) [+ *resources, money, services*] disponer de, contar con
4 (= *deserve and get*) [+ *attention*] ganarse; [+ *respect*] imponer; [+ *sympathy*] merecerse, hacerse acreedor de; [+ *price*] venderse a, venderse por; [+ *fee*] exigir
5 (= *overlook*) [+ *area*] dominar; [+ *view*] tener, disfrutar de
CPD ▸ **command economy** economía *f* planificada ▸ **command key** (*Comput*) tecla *f* de comando ▸ **command language** (*Comput*) lenguaje *m* de comandos ▸ **command line** (*Comput*) orden *f*, comando *m* ▸ **command module** (*on a space rocket*) módulo *m* de mando ▸ **command performance** gala *f* (a petición) real ▸ **command post** puesto *m* de mando
commandant [,kɒmən'dænt] N comandante *mf*
commandeer [,kɒmən'dɪə^r] VT **1** (= *requisition*) [+ *building, stores, ship etc*] requisar, expropiar; [+ *men*] reclutar a la fuerza
2* tomar, apropiarse (de)
commander [kə'mɑːndə^r] N (*Mil*) comandante *mf*; (*Hist*) [*of chivalric order*] comendador *m*; (*Naut*) capitán *m* de fragata
commander-in-chief [kə'mɑːndərɪn'tʃiːf] N (PL: **commanders-in-chief**) jefe/a *m/f* supremo/a, comandante/a *m/f* en jefe
commanding [kə'mɑːndɪŋ] ADJ [*appearance*] imponente; [*tone of voice*] autoritario, imperioso; [*lead*] abrumador; [*position*] dominante
CPD ▸ **commanding officer** (*Mil*) comandante *mf*
commandingly [kə'mɑːndɪŋlɪ] ADV [*speak*] de forma autoritaria, imperiosamente
commandment [kə'mɑːndmənt] N (*Bible*) mandamiento *m* • **the Ten Commandments** los diez mandamientos
commando [kə'mɑːndəʊ] N (PL: **commandos** *or* **commandoes**) (= *man, group*) comando *m*
commemorate [kə'meməreɪt] VT conmemorar
commemoration [kə,memə'reɪʃən] N conmemoración *f* • **in ~ of** en conmemoración de
CPD [*service, ceremony*] de conmemoración
commemorative [kə'memərətɪv] ADJ conmemorativo
N (*US*) (= *stamp*) sello *m* conmemorativo; (= *coin*) moneda *f* conmemorativa
commence [kə'mens] (*frm*) VT comenzar • **to ~ doing** *or* **to do sth** comenzar a hacer algo • **to ~ proceedings (against sb)** (*Jur*) entablar demanda (a algn)
VI comenzar
commencement [kə'mensmənt] N **1** (*frm*) (= *start*) comienzo *m*, principio *m*
2 (*US*) (*Univ*) (ceremonia *f* de) graduación *f*, (ceremonia *f* de) entrega *f* de diplomas
commend [kə'mend] VT **1** (= *praise*) elogiar • **to ~ sb for** *or* **on sth** elogiar a algn por algo • **to ~ sb for his action** elogiar la acción de algn • **her entry was highly ~ed** (*in competition*) su participación recibió una mención elogiosa *or* especial
2 (= *recommend*) recomendar • **I ~ him to you** se lo recomiendo • **it has little to ~ it** poco se puede decir en su favor • **the plan does not ~ itself to me** el proyecto no me resulta aceptable
3 (= *entrust*) encomendar (**to** a) • **to ~ sb's/one's soul to God** encomendar el alma de algn/su alma a Dios
4† (*frm*) • **~ me to Mr White** (= *give respects*) presente mis respetos al Sr. White (*frm*)
commendable [kə'mendəbl] ADJ encomiable, loable
commendably [kə'mendəblɪ] ADV • **it was ~ short** tuvo el mérito de ser breve • **you have been ~ prompt** le felicito por la prontitud
commendation [,kɒmen'deɪʃən] N **1** (= *praise*) elogio *m*, encomio *m*; (*Mil*) distinción *f*
2 (= *recommendation*) recomendación *f*
commendatory [kə'mendətrɪ] ADJ elogioso
commensurable [kə'menʃərəbl] ADJ conmensurable, comparable (**with** con)
commensurate [kə'menʃərɪt] ADJ • **~ with** en proporción a, que corresponde a • **"salary commensurate with experience"** "sueldo según experiencia"
commensurately [kə'menʃərɪtlɪ] ADV [*high, modest*] proporcionalmente; [*increase, grow, fall*] en proporción • **~ with** en proporción a
comment ['kɒment] N (= *remark*) (*written or spoken*) comentario *m*, observación *f*; (= *gossip*) comentarios *mpl* • **no ~** sin comentarios • **to make a ~** hacer un comentario *or* una observación • **she made the ~ that ...** observó que ... • **he made no ~** no hizo ningún comentario • **to cause ~** (= *cause gossip*) provocar comentarios
VI hacer observaciones *or* comentarios, comentar • **to ~ on** [+ *text*] comentar, hacer

un comentario de; [+ *subject*] hacer observaciones *or* comentarios acerca de; (*to the press*) hacer declaraciones sobre
(VT) (*in conversation*) observar • **to ~ that ...** observar que ...
commentary ['kɒməntərɪ] (N) (*gen*) comentario *m*; (*Rad, TV*) (*on sporting event*) crónica *f*; (*on text*) comentario *m* (de texto)
(CPD) ▸ **commentary box** cabina *f* de prensa
commentate ['kɒmənteɪt] (*Rad, TV*) (VT) hacer la crónica de
(VI) hacer la crónica, comentar
commentator ['kɒmənteɪtəʳ] (N) (*Rad, TV*) comentarista *mf*
commerce ['kɒmɜːs] (N) comercio *m*
• **Chamber of Commerce** Cámara *f* de Comercio
commercial [kə'mɜːʃəl] (ADJ) comercial
(N) (*TV*) (= *advert*) anuncio *m*, spot *m* publicitario
(CPD) ▸ **commercial art** arte *m* publicitario ▸ **commercial artist** dibujante *mf* publicitario/a ▸ **commercial bank** banco *m* comercial, banco *m* mercantil ▸ **commercial break** (*TV*) espacio *m* publicitario, pausa *f* publicitaria ▸ **commercial centre** centro *m* comercial ▸ **commercial college** escuela *f* de secretariado ▸ **commercial exploitation** explotación *f* comercial ▸ **commercial law** derecho *m* mercantil ▸ **commercial paper** (*esp US*) efectos *mpl* negociables, papel *m* comercial ▸ **commercial property** propiedad *f* comercial ▸ **commercial radio** radio *f* comercial ▸ **commercial television** televisión *f* privada ▸ **commercial traveller**, **commercial traveler** (*US*) viajante *mf* (de comercio) ▸ **commercial value** valor *m* comercial • **"no commercial value"** "sin valor comercial" ▸ **commercial vehicle** vehículo *m* comercial
commercialism [kə'mɜːʃəlɪzəm] (N) comercialismo *m*, mercantilismo *m*
commercialization [kə,mɜːʃəlaɪ'zeɪʃən] (N) comercialización *f*
commercialize [kə'mɜːʃəlaɪz] (VT) comercializar
commercialized [kə'mɜːʃəlaɪzd] (ADJ) (*pej*) [*art, festival, place*] comercial, explotado comercialmente
commercially [kə'mɜːʃəlɪ] (ADV) [*viable, competitive, produced*] comercialmente • **it is not ~ available** no puede adquirirse en el mercado
commie* ['kɒmɪ] (ADJ) rojo
(N) rojo/a *m/f*
commiserate [kə'mɪzəreɪt] (VI) • **friends called to ~ when they found out I hadn't got the job** cuando me rechazaron para el trabajo mis amigos me llamaron para decirme lo mucho que lo sentían • **"I know how you feel," he ~d** —sé cómo te sientes —le dijo a modo de consuelo
commiseration [kə,mɪzə'reɪʃən] (N) conmiseración *f* • **my ~s to the runner-up** lo siento mucho por el que ha llegado segundo
commissar ['kɒmɪsɑːʳ] (N) comisario/a *m/f*
commissariat [,kɒmɪ'seərɪət] (N) comisaría *f*
commissary ['kɒmɪsərɪ] (N) **1** comisario/a *m/f* político/a
2 (*US*) (= *shop*) economato *m*
commission [kə'mɪʃən] (N) **1** (= *committee*) comisión *f* • **~ of inquiry** comisión *f* investigadora
2 (= *order for work, esp of artist*) comisión *f*
3 (*for salesman*) comisión *f* • **to sell things on ~** *or* **on a ~ basis** vender cosas a comisión • **I get 10% ~** me dan el 10 por ciento de comisión
4 (*Mil*) (= *position*) graduación *f* de oficial; (= *warrant*) nombramiento *m*
5 (= *use, service*) servicio *m* • **to put into ~** poner en servicio • **to be out of ~** estar fuera de servicio • **to put out of ~** inutilizar • **to take out of ~** retirar del servicio
6 [*of crime*] perpetración *f*
(VT) **1** [+ *artist etc*] hacer un encargo a; [+ *picture*] encargar, comisionar (*esp LAm*); [+ *article*] encargar • **to ~ sb to do sth** encargar a algn que haga algo
2 (*Mil*) [+ *officer*] nombrar; [+ *ship*] poner en servicio • **~ed officer** oficial *mf*
(CPD) ▸ **commission agent** comisionista *mf* ▸ **Commission for Racial Equality** (*Brit*) *comisión para la igualdad racial*
commissionaire [kə,mɪʃə'nɛəʳ] (N) (*Brit, Canada*) portero *m*, conserje *m*
commissioner [kə'mɪʃənəʳ] (N) (= *official*) comisario/a *m/f*; (= *member of commission*) comisionado/a *m/f* • **~ for oaths** (*Brit*) notario/a *m/f* público/a • **~ of police** inspector(a) *m/f* jefe de policía
commissioning editor [kə'mɪʃənɪŋ'edɪtəʳ] (N) jefe(a) *m/f* de sección, responsable *mf* de departamento
commit [kə'mɪt] (VT) **1** [+ *crime, sin, error*] cometer • **to ~ suicide** suicidarse; ▹ **perjury**
2 (= *consign*) [+ *resources*] asignar, destinar; [+ *troops*] enviar; (*Parl*) [+ *bill*] remitir a una comisión • **to ~ sb** (*to mental hospital*) internar a algn • **to ~ sth to sb's charge** confiar algo a algn • **to ~ sth to the flames** arrojar algo al fuego • **to ~ sth to memory** aprender algo de memoria • **to ~ sth to paper** poner algo por escrito • **to ~ sb to prison** encarcelar a algn • **to ~ sb for trial** remitir a algn al tribunal • **to ~ sth to writing** poner algo por escrito
3 (= *pledge*) comprometer • **accepting this offer does not ~ you to anything** aceptar esta oferta no le compromete a nada • **I am ~ted to help him** me he comprometido a ayudarle • **he is ~ted to change** está dedicado a buscar una forma de cambiar • **we are deeply ~ted to this policy** creemos firmemente en esta política
4 • **to ~ o.s. (to)** comprometerse (a) • **I can't ~ myself** no puedo comprometerme • **without ~ting myself** sin compromiso por mi parte
(VI) • **to ~ to sb/sth** comprometerse con algn/a algo
commitment [kə'mɪtmənt] (N)
1 (= *obligation*) obligación *f* • **he has heavy teaching ~s** tiene muchas obligaciones como profesor • **family ~s** obligaciones familiares
2 (= *pledge*) • **to give a ~ to do sth** comprometerse a hacer algo • **she would give no ~** no quiso comprometerse
3 (= *devotion*) entrega *f*, devoción *f*
committal [kə'mɪtl] (N) **1** (*Jur*) • **~ for trial** (auto *m* de) procesamiento *m* • **~ to prison** encarcelamiento *m*, (auto *m* de) prisión *f*
2 (*to mental asylum*) reclusión *f*
3 (= *burial*) entierro *m*
committed [kə'mɪtɪd] (ADJ) comprometido
• **a ~ writer** un escritor comprometido
committee [kə'mɪtɪ] (N) comité *m*, comisión *f* • **to be** *or* **sit on a ~** ser miembro de un comité • **~ of inquiry** (*Parl*) comisión *f* investigadora; ▹ **executive**, **management**
(CPD) ▸ **committee meeting** reunión *f* del comité ▸ **committee member** miembro *mf* del comité ▸ **committee stage** (*Parl*) *fase en la que un proyecto de ley está siendo estudiado por un comité*
commode [kə'məʊd] (N) (*with chamber pot*) silla *f* con orinal; (= *chest of drawers*) cómoda *f*
commodify [kə'mɒdɪfaɪ] (VT) cosificar
commodious [kə'məʊdɪəs] (ADJ) grande, espacioso
commodity [kə'mɒdɪtɪ] (N) artículo *m* (de consumo *or* de comercio), producto *m*, mercancía *f*, mercadería *f* (*LAm*); (*Econ, St Ex*) materia *f* prima
(CPD) ▸ **commodity exchange** bolsa *f* de artículos de consumo ▸ **commodity markets** mercados *mpl* de materias primas ▸ **commodity trade** comercio *m* de materias primas
commodore ['kɒmədɔːʳ] (N) comodoro *m*
common ['kɒmən] (ADJ) **1** (= *usual, ordinary*) [*event, experience, name, species*] común, corriente; [*misconception, mistake*] común, frecuente • **this butterfly is ~ in Spain** esta mariposa es común *or* corriente en España • **it is ~ for these animals to die young** es corriente *or* frecuente que estos animales mueran jóvenes • **it is a ~ belief that ...** es una creencia extendida *or* generalizada que ... • **~ belief has it that ...** según la opinión generalizada ... • **it's (just) ~ courtesy** es una cortesía elemental • **the ~ man** el hombre de la calle, el hombre medio • **it's a ~ occurrence** es corriente que suceda • **in ~ parlance** en lenguaje corriente • **the ~ people** la gente corriente • **it is ~ practice in the USA** es una práctica común en EE.UU. • **pigeons are a ~ sight in London** es corriente *or* frecuente ver palomas en Londres • **the ~ soldier** el soldado raso • **to have the ~ touch** saber tratar con la gente corriente • **in ~ use** de uso corriente • IDIOM: • **~ or garden** (*esp Brit**) común y corriente, normal y corriente
2 (= *shared*) [*cause, aim, language*] común • **to work for a ~ aim** cooperar para un mismo fin *or* para un objetivo común • **by ~ agreement** *or* **consent** de común acuerdo • **for the ~ good** para el bien común, para el bien de todos • **~ ground** (*fig*) puntos *mpl* en común, puntos *mpl* de confluencia *or* acuerdo • **they discussed several issues of ~ interest** hablaron de varios asuntos de interés común *or* de interés mutuo • **it is ~ knowledge that ...** es del dominio público que ... • **the desire for freedom is ~ to all people** todo el mundo comparte el deseo de la libertad
3 (*pej*) (= *vulgar*) [*person, behaviour, speech*] ordinario, basto • IDIOM: • **as ~ as muck*** de lo más ordinario, más basto que la lija (del cuatro)
4 (*Zool, Bot*) común • **the ~ house fly** la mosca común
(N) **1** (= *land*) campo *m* comunal, ejido *m*
2 (*Brit*) (*Pol*) • **the Commons** (la Cámera de) los Comunes; ▹ **House**
3 • **in ~: we have a lot in ~ (with other people)** tenemos mucho en común (con otra gente) • **we have nothing in ~** no tenemos nada en común • **in ~ with many other companies, we advertise in the local press** al igual que otras muchas empresas, nos anunciamos en la prensa local
(CPD) ▸ **the Common Agricultural Policy** la Política Agrícola Común ▸ **common cold** resfriado *m* común ▸ **common core** (*Scol*) (*also* **common-core syllabus**) asignaturas *fpl* comunes ▸ **common currency** • **to become/be ~ currency** [*idea, belief*] convertirse en/ser moneda corriente ▸ **common denominator** (*Math*) común denominador *m* • **lowest ~ denominator** mínimo común denominador *m* ▸ **Common Entrance** (*Brit*) (*Scol*) *examen de acceso a un colegio de enseñanza privada* ▸ **common factor** (*Math*) factor *m* común ▸ **common land** propiedad *f* comunal ▸ **common law** (*Jur*) (*established by custom*) derecho *m*

consuetudinario; (*based on precedent*) jurisprudencia *f*; ▹ **common-law** ▸ **the Common Market** el Mercado Común ▸ **common noun** nombre *m* común ▸ **common ownership** (*= joint ownership*) copropiedad *f*; (*Pol*) (*= collective ownership*) propiedad *f* colectiva ▸ **the Book of Common Prayer** la liturgia de la Iglesia Anglicana ▸ **common room** (*esp Brit*) (*for students*) sala *f* de estudiantes; (*for teachers*) sala *f* de profesores ▸ **common salt** sal *f* común ▸ **common sense** sentido *m* común; ▹ **commonsense** ▸ **common stock** (*US*) (*St Ex*) acciones *fpl* ordinarias ▸ **common time** (*Mus*) cuatro *m* por cuatro ▸ **common wall** pared *f* medianera

COMMON LAW

Se llama **common law** o **case law** (derecho consuetudinario o jurisprudencia), al conjunto de leyes basadas en el fallo de los tribunales, a diferencia de las leyes establecidas por escrito en el Parlamento. El derecho consuetudinario inglés se desarrolló después de la conquista normanda, cuando los jueces basaban sus decisiones en la tradición o en el precedente judicial. La jurisprudencia sigue usándose como base del sistema legal anglosajón, aunque va perdiendo vigencia por el desarrollo del derecho escrito.

▹ **ACT OF PARLIAMENT, CONSTITUTION**

commonality [ˌkɒməˈnælɪtɪ], **commonalty** [ˈkɒmənəltɪ] N **1** (*frm*) (*= things in common*) cosas *fpl* en común • **there is a ~ of interests between them** tienen muchos intereses en común
2 • **the ~** (*= ordinary people*) el común de la gente, la plebe

commoner [ˈkɒmənəʳ] N **1** (*= not noble*) plebeyo/a *m/f*
2 (*at Oxford Univ etc*) estudiante *mf* que no tiene beca del colegio

common-law [ˈkɒmənˌlɔː] ADJ [*marriage*] consensual
CPD ▸ **common-law husband** pareja *f* de hecho ▸ **common-law wife** pareja *f* de hecho

commonly [ˈkɒmənlɪ] ADV **1** (*= usually, frequently*) [*called*] comúnmente; [*prescribed*] frecuentemente • **more ~ known as ...** más comúnmente conocido como ... • **anorexia is more ~ found among women** la anorexia es más común *or* corriente entre las mujeres • **an orchid which is not ~ found in this country** una orquídea que no es corriente encontrar *or* que no se encuentra frecuentemente en este país • **it is ~ the case that ...** es corriente que ..., frecuentemente se da el caso de que ... • **acupuncture is ~ used in China** la acupuntura es una práctica muy común en China
2 (*= generally*) • **the ~ held view** la opinión extendida *or* generalizada • **it is ~ accepted as the best in the world** es aceptado por todos como el mejor del mundo • **it is ~ believed that ...** es una creencia extendida *or* generalizada que ... • **the disease is ~ thought to be caused by a virus** es una creencia extendida *or* generalizada que esta enfermedad está causada por un virus
3 (*= vulgarly*) [*behave, speak, dress*] ordinariamente, vulgarmente

commonness [ˈkɒmənnɪs] N **1** (*= frequency*) frecuencia *f*
2 (*= vulgarity*) ordinariez *f*

commonplace [ˈkɒmənpleɪs] ADJ (*= normal*) común, normal, corriente; (*pej*) vulgar, ordinario • **it is ~ to see this sort of thing** es frecuente *or* corriente ver este tipo de cosas
N (*= event*) cosa *f* común y corriente; (*= statement*) tópico *m*, lugar *m* común

Commons [ˈkɒmənz] NPL (*Pol*) = **common**

commonsense [ˈkɒmənˌsens] ADJ racional, lógico • **the ~ thing to do is ...** lo lógico es ...

Commonwealth [ˈkɒmənwelθ] N • **the ~** la Commonwealth, la Comunidad Británica de Naciones; (*Brit*) (*Hist*) la república de Cromwell • **the ~ of Independent States** la Comunidad de Estados Independientes • **the ~ of Kentucky** el estado de Kentucky • **the ~ of Puerto Rico** el estado de Puerto Rico
CPD ▸ **Commonwealth of Australia** Mancomunidad *f* de Australia

COMMONWEALTH

La **Commonwealth** (Comunidad Británica de Naciones) es una asociación de estados soberanos, la mayoría de los cuales eran colonias británicas en el pasado, establecida para fomentar el comercio y los lazos de amistad entre ellos. Actualmente se compone de más de cincuenta estados miembros, entre los cuales se encuentran el Reino Unido, Australia, Canadá, la India, Jamaica, Kenia, Nueva Zelanda, Nigeria, Pakistán y Sudáfrica. Los países miembros reconocen al soberano británico como **Head of the Commonwealth** y se reúnen anualmente para debatir asuntos políticos y económicos. Además, cada cuatro años uno de los países miembros es el anfitrión de la competición deportiva conocida como **Commonwealth Games**.

commonwealth [ˈkɒmənwelθ] N [*of nations*] mancomunidad *f*

commotion [kəˈməʊʃən] N (*= noise*) alboroto *m*; (*= activity*) jaleo *m*, tumulto *m*, confusión *f*; (*civil*) disturbio *m* • **to cause a ~** provocar *or* causar un alboroto • **to make a ~** (*= noise*) armar un alboroto; (*= fuss*) armar un lío* • **there was a ~ in the crowd** se armó un lío entre los espectadores • **what a ~!** ¡qué alboroto!

comms [ˈkɒmz] (= **communications**) NPL ABBR contacto *msing*
ADJ [*software, package, program*] de comunicación

communal [ˈkɒmjuːnl] ADJ [*property, ownership*] comunal; [*living room, dining room, facilities*] común; [*activities*] comunitario

communally [ˈkɒmjuːnəlɪ] ADV [*live, eat*] en comunidad • **to act ~** obrar como comunidad • **the property is held ~** la propiedad pertenece a la comunidad

communard [ˈkɒmjʊnɑːd] N miembro *m* de la comuna

commune [ˈkɒmjuːn] N (*= group*) comuna *f*
VI [kəˈmjuːn] **1** (*Rel*) (*esp US*) comulgar
2 • **to ~ with** estar en contacto con • **to ~ with nature/one's soul** estar en contacto con la naturaleza/su alma

communicable [kəˈmjuːnɪkəbl] ADJ (*gen*) comunicable; [*disease*] transmisible

communicant [kəˈmjuːnɪkənt] N (*Rel*) comulgante *mf*

communicate [kəˈmjuːnɪkeɪt] VT • **to ~ sth (to sb)** [*+ thoughts, information*] comunicar algo (a algn); (*frm*) [*+ disease*] transmitir algo (a algn)
VI (*= speak*) comunicarse (**with** con) • **we ~ by letter/telephone** mantenemos correspondencia/estamos en contacto telefónico • **they just can't ~** no se entienden en absoluto

communicating [kəˈmjuːnɪkeɪtɪŋ] ADJ • **~ rooms** habitaciones *fpl* que se comunican

communication [kəˌmjuːnɪˈkeɪʃən] N
1 (*= verbal or written contact*) contacto *m*; (*= exchange of information*) comunicación *f* • **to be in/get into ~ with** (*frm*) estar/ponerse en contacto con • **there has been a breakdown of** *or* **in ~ between the police and the community** el diálogo entre la policía y la comunidad ha sufrido un deterioro
2 (*= message*) mensaje *m*, comunicación *f*
3 communications comunicaciones *fpl* • **good/poor ~s** buenas/malas comunicaciones
CPD ▸ **communication breakdown** problema *m* de comunicación ▸ **communication channels** canales *mpl* de comunicación • **to keep ~ channels open** mantener abiertos los canales de comunicación ▸ **communication cord** (*Rail*) timbre *m* *or* palanca *f* de alarma ▸ **communication problem** (*personal*) problema *m* de expresión; (*within organization*) problema *m* de comunicación ▸ **communication skills** habilidad *f* *or* aptitud *f* para comunicarse ▸ **communications network** red *f* de comunicaciones ▸ **communications satellite** satélite *m* de comunicaciones ▸ **communications software** paquete *m* de comunicaciones

communicative [kəˈmjuːnɪkətɪv] ADJ comunicativo

communicator [kəˈmjuːnɪkeɪtəʳ] N (*= person*) comunicador(a) *m/f* • **to be a good/bad ~** saber/no saber comunicarse

communion [kəˈmjuːnɪən] N (*Rel*) comunión *f* • **to take** *or* **receive ~** comulgar
CPD ▸ **communion rail** comulgatorio *m* ▸ **communion service** comunión *f* ▸ **communion table** mesa *f* de comunión ▸ **communion wine** (*in church*) vino *m* sacro

communiqué [kəˈmjuːnɪkeɪ] N comunicado *m*

communism [ˈkɒmjʊnɪzəm] N comunismo *m*

communist [ˈkɒmjʊnɪst] ADJ comunista
N comunista *mf*
CPD ▸ **Communist party** partido *m* comunista

community [kəˈmjuːnɪtɪ] N **1** (*= people at large*) comunidad *f*, sociedad *f*; (*= people locally*) comunidad *f* • **the local ~** el vecindario
2 (*cultural etc*) comunidad *f*, colectividad *f* • **the black ~** la población negra • **the artistic ~** el mundillo artístico • **the English ~ in Rome** la colectividad *or* colonia inglesa de Roma
3 • **the Community** (*= EEC*) la Comunidad
CPD ▸ **community action** actuación *f* de la comunidad ▸ **community care** (*Brit*) política *f* de integración social de enfermos y ancianos ▸ **community care programme** *programa cuyo objetivo es ayudar a integrar a pacientes con problemas mentales en la comunidad en vez de enviarlos a residencias especiales* ▸ **community centre** centro *m* social ▸ **community charge** (*Brit*) (*Admin*) (*formerly*) (contribución *f* de) capitación *f* ▸ **community chest** (*US*) fondo *m* para beneficencia social ▸ **community college** (*US*) *establecimiento docente de educación terciaria donde se realizan cursos de dos años* ▸ **community health centre** centro *m* médico comunitario ▸ **Community law** derecho *m* comunitario ▸ **community leader** representante *mf* de una comunidad ▸ **community life** vida *f* comunitaria ▸ **community policeman** policía *m* de barrio ▸ **community policewoman** policía *f* de barrio

▸ **community policing** *política policial de acercamiento a la comunidad* ▸ **Community policy** (EC) política *f* comunitaria ▸ **community politics** política *f* local ▸ **Community regulations** normas *fpl* comunitarias ▸ **community service** trabajo *m* comunitario (*prestado en lugar de cumplir una pena de prisión*) ▸ **community singing** canto *m* colectivo ▸ **community spirit** sentimiento *m* de comunidad, civismo *m* ▸ **community worker** asistente *mf* social

communize ['kɒmju:naɪz] VT comunizar

commutable [kə'mju:təbl] ADJ (*also Jur*) conmutable

commutation [,kɒmjʊ'teɪʃən] N (*also Fin*) conmutación *f*; (*US*) (*Rail etc*) uso *m* de un billete de abono
CPD ▸ **commutation ticket** (*US*) billete *m* de abono

commutator ['kɒmjʊ,teɪtəʳ] N (*Elec*) conmutador *m*

commute [kə'mju:t] VI viajar diariamente (de la casa al trabajo) • **I live in Brighton but I ~ to London** vivo en Brighton pero voy todos los días a trabajar a Londres • **she ~s between Oxford and London** para ir al trabajo viaja *or* se desplaza diariamente de Oxford a Londres
VT [+ *payment*] conmutar (**for/into** por/en); [+ *sentence*] conmutar (**to** por)
N viaje *m* diario al trabajo

commuter [kə'mju:təʳ] N *persona que viaja cada día de su casa a su trabajo*
CPD ▸ **the commuter belt** zona *f* de los barrios exteriores ▸ **commuter line** (*on railway network*) línea *f* de cercanías (*utilizada principalmente para ir y venir del trabajo*) ▸ **commuter services** servicios *mpl* de cercanías ▸ **commuter town** ciudad *f* dormitorio ▸ **commuter traffic** (= *people going to work*) gente *f* que va al trabajo; (= *people returning from work*) gente *f* que vuelve del trabajo • **earlier on protesters had stopped ~ traffic** con anterioridad, manifestantes habían parado el tráfico de gente yendo al trabajo ▸ **commuter train** tren *m* de cercanías

commuting [kə'mju:tɪŋ] N • **~ is very stressful** el viajar para ir al trabajo provoca mucho estrés

compact[1] ADJ [kəm'pækt] (= *small*) compacto; (= *dense*) apretado, sólido; [*style*] breve, conciso
VT [kəm'pækt] [+ *snow, earth*] compactar (**into** en); (= *condense*) [+ *text, activities*] condensar
VI [kəm'pækt] [*snow*] comprimirse
N ['kɒmpækt] **1** (*also* **powder compact**) polvera *f*
2 (*US*) (*Aut*) (*also* **compact car**) utilitario *m*
CPD ['kɒmpækt] ▸ **compact car** (*US*) utilitario *m* ▸ **compact disc** disco *m* compacto, compact *m* ▸ **compact disc player** lector *m* de discos compactos

compact[2] ['kɒmpækt] N (= *agreement*) pacto *m*, convenio *m*

compacted [kəm'pæktɪd] ADJ (= *compressed*) [*earth, soil*] compactado

compaction [kəm'pækʃən] N (= *compression*) compresión *f*

compactly [kəm'pæktlɪ] ADV (= *in a neat way*) de modo compacto; (= *tightly*) apretadamente, sólidamente; (= *concisely*) brevemente, concisamente

compactness [kəm'pæktnɪs] N [*of house, room*] compacidad *f*; [*of style*] concisión *f*

companion [kəm'pænjən] N
1 (= *accompanying person*) compañero/a *m/f*; (*lady's*) señora *f* de compañía • **travelling ~** compañero/a *m/f* de viaje
2 (= *book*) guía *f*, manual *m*
3 (= *one of pair of objects*) compañero *m*, pareja *f*
4 (*Naut*) lumbrera *f*; (= *companionway*) escalerilla *f* (que conduce a los camarotes)
CPD ▸ **companion volume** tomo *m* complementario

companionable [kəm'pænjənəbl] ADJ [*person*] sociable, amigable • **they sat in ~ silence** estaban sentados en amigable silencio

companionably [kəm'pænjənəblɪ] ADV amigablemente

companionship [kəm'pænjənʃɪp] N (= *company*) compañía *f*; (= *friendship, friendliness*) compañerismo *m*

companionway [kəm'pænjənweɪ] N (*Naut*) escalerilla *f* (que conduce a los camarotes)

company ['kʌmpənɪ] N **1** (= *companionship*) compañía *f* • **it's ~ for her** le hace compañía • **he's good/poor ~** es/no es muy agradable estar con él • **to keep sb ~** hacer compañía a algn, acompañar a algn • PROVERB: • **two's ~(, three's a crowd)** dos es compañía, tres es multitud
2 (= *group, friends*) • **to keep bad ~** andar en malas compañías • **to get into bad ~** tener malas compañías • **to be in good ~** (*fig*) estar bien acompañado • **to join ~ with** reunirse con • **to part ~ separarse** (**with** de); (*fig*) (= *come apart, unstuck*) desprenderse, soltarse (**with** de) • **present ~ excepted** mejorando lo presente, salvando a los presentes • PROVERB: • **a man is known by the ~ he keeps** dime con quién andas y te diré quién eres
3 (*no pl*) (= *guests*) visita *f*, invitados *mpl* • **we have ~** tenemos visita *or* invitados • **are you expecting ~?** ¿esperas visita?
4 (*Comm*) (= *firm*) compañía *f*, empresa *f*; (= *association*) sociedad *f* • **Smith and Company** Smith y Compañía • **he's a ~ man** se desvive por la empresa • **in ~ time** en horas de trabajo; ▹ **limited**
5 (*Mil*) compañía *f*, unidad *f* • **ship's ~** tripulación *f*
6 (*Theat*) compañía *f* (de teatro)
CPD ▸ **company car** coche *m* de la empresa ▸ **company commander** capitán *m* de compañía ▸ **company director** director(a) *m/f* de empresa ▸ **company law** derecho *m* de compañías ▸ **company lawyer** (*Brit*) (*Jur*) abogado *mf* empresarial; (*working within company*) abogado *mf* de la compañía ▸ **company logo** logotipo *m* de la empresa ▸ **company pension** pensión *f* de la empresa ▸ **company pension scheme** plan *m* de pensiones de la empresa ▸ **company policy** política *f* de la empresa ▸ **company secretary** administrador(a) *m/f* de empresa ▸ **company union** (*US*) sindicato *m* de empresa

comparability [kɒmpərə'bɪlɪtɪ] N comparabilidad *f*

comparable ['kɒmpərəbl] ADJ comparable • **~ to** *or* **with** comparable a *or* con • **a ~ case** un caso análogo • **they are not ~** no se los puede comparar

comparably ['kɒmpərəblɪ] ADV • **salaries in line with ~ qualified professions** sueldos a la par con los de las profesiones similares

comparative [kəm'pærətɪv] ADJ
1 (= *relative*) relativo • **before becoming famous she had lived in ~ obscurity** había vivido en relativa oscuridad antes de hacerse famosa
2 [*study*] comparativo, comparado
3 (*Gram*) comparativo
N (*Gram*) comparativo *m*
CPD ▸ **comparative literature** literatura *f* comparada

comparatively [kəm'pærətɪvlɪ] ADV (= *relatively*) relativamente; [*consider, view*] desde un punto de vista relativo • **the books can be studied ~** se puede hacer un estudio comparado de los libros

comparator [kəm'pærətəʳ] N elemento *m* de comparación

compare [kəm'pɛəʳ] VT **1** (*gen*) comparar; (= *put side by side*) [+ *texts*] cotejar • **to ~ sth/sb with** *or* **to sth/sb** comparar algo/a algn con *or* a algo/algn • **Oxford is small ~d with London** Oxford es pequeño en comparación a *or* comparado con Londres • **as ~d with** comparado con • IDIOM: • **to ~ notes with sb** cambiar impresiones con algn
2 (*Gram*) formar los grados de comparación de
VI • **she can't ~ with you** no se la puede comparar contigo • **it doesn't ~ with yours** no se lo puede comparar al tuyo, no tiene comparación con el tuyo • **how do they ~?** ¿cuáles son sus cualidades respectivas? • **how do they ~ for speed?** ¿cuál tiene mayor velocidad? • **how do the prices ~?** ¿qué tal son los precios en comparación? • **it ~s favourably with the other** no pierde por comparación con el otro, supera al otro • **it ~s poorly with the other** es inferior al otro
N • **beyond ~** (*poet*) incomparable, sin comparación, sin par

comparison [kəm'pærɪsn] N **1** (*between things, people*) comparación *f* • **there's no ~ (between them)** no hay comparación (entre ellos), no se puede comparar (el uno con el otro) • **in** *or* **by ~ (with)** en comparación (con) • **this one is large in ~** este es grande en comparación • **to draw a ~** establecer una comparación • **it will bear** *or* **stand ~ with the best** se puede comparar con los mejores
2 (*Gram*) comparación *f*

compartment [kəm'pɑ:tmənt] N compartimiento *m*; (*Brit*) (*Rail*) compartimiento *m*

compartmentalization [,kɒmpɑ:t,mentəlaɪ'zeɪʃən] N compartimentación *f*

compartmentalize [,kɒmpɑ:t'mentəlaɪz] VT dividir en categorías; (*pej*) aislar en compartimientos estancos, compartimentar

compartmentalized [,kɒmpɑ:t'mentəlaɪzd] ADJ compartimentado

compass ['kʌmpəs] N **1** (*Naut etc*) brújula *f*
2 (*Math*) (*usu pl*) compás *m* • **a pair of ~es** un compás
3 (*frm*) (= *range*) alcance *m*; (= *area*) ámbito *m* • **beyond my ~** fuera de mi alcance • **within the ~ of the plan** dentro de lo abarcado por el plan
VT (*frm*) (= *cover, take in*) abarcar; (*liter*) (= *surround*) rodear
CPD ▸ **compass card** (*Naut*) rosa *f* de los vientos ▸ **compass course** ruta *f* magnética ▸ **compass point** punto *m* cardinal ▸ **compass rose** = compass card

compassion [kəm'pæʃən] N compasión *f* • **to have ~ for sth/for** *or* **on sb** tener compasión por *or* de algo/algn, compadecerse de algo/algn • **to feel ~ for sb** sentir compasión por *or* de algn • **to move sb to ~** mover a algn a la compasión
CPD ▸ **compassion fatigue** (*in emergency workers*) desgaste *m* por empatía; (*in desensitized public*) insensibilización *f*

compassionate [kəm'pæʃənɪt] ADJ [*person*] compasivo • **on ~ grounds** por compasión
CPD ▸ **compassionate leave** permiso *m*

por motivos familiares

compassionately [kəmˈpæʃənɪtlɪ] ADV compasivamente, con compasión

compatibility [kəmˌpætəˈbɪlɪtɪ] N compatibilidad *f*

compatible [kəmˈpætɪbl] ADJ compatible • **we weren't really ~** la verdad es que no éramos compatibles • **to be ~ with sth/sb** ser compatible con algo/algn • **an IBM-compatible computer** un ordenador compatible con IBM
N (*Comput*) compatible *m* • **an IBM-compatible** un compatible con IBM

compatriot [kəmˈpætrɪət] N compatriota *mf*

compel [kəmˈpel] VT **1** (= *oblige*) obligar • **to ~ sb to do sth** obligar a algn a hacer algo, compeler a algn a hacer algo (*frm*) • **I feel ~led to say that ...** me veo obligado a decir que ...
2 (= *command*) [+ *respect, obedience*] imponer; [+ *admiration*] ganarse

compellable [kəmˈpeləbl] ADJ (*Jur*) [*witness*] competente (*y que puede ser obligado a testificar*)

compelling [kəmˈpelɪŋ] ADJ **1** (= *convincing*) [*argument, evidence*] convincente; [*curiosity*] irresistible • **I went there for ~ reasons** fui porque tenía razones de peso • **to make a ~ case for sth** exponer unos argumentos convincentes a favor de algo
2 (= *riveting*) [*account, film, book*] fascinante, apasionante • **his new novel makes ~ reading** su nueva novela es fascinante *or* apasionante

compellingly [kəmˈpelɪŋlɪ] ADV [*write, tell*] de manera convincente, de modo convincente; [*attractive*] irresistiblemente; [*persuasive*] terriblemente

compendia [kəmˈpendɪə] NPL *of* **compendium**

compendious [kəmˈpendɪəs] ADJ compendioso

compendium [kəmˈpendɪəm] N (PL: **compendiums** *or* **compendia**) compendio *m* • **~ of games** juegos *mpl* reunidos

compensate [ˈkɒmpənseɪt] VT
1 compensar; (*for loss, damage*) indemnizar, resarcir • **to ~ sb for sth** compensar a algn por algo; (*for loss, damage*) indemnizar a algn por algo, resarcir a algn de algo
2 (= *reward*) recompensar
VI • **to ~ for sth** compensar algo

compensation [ˌkɒmpənˈseɪʃən] N (= *award etc*) compensación *f*; (*for loss, damage*) indemnización *f*, resarcimiento *m*; (= *reward*) recompensa *f* • **they got £2,000 ~** recibieron 2.000 libras de indemnización • **in ~ (for)** en compensación (por)
CPD ▸ **compensation award** daños *mpl* y perjuicios ▸ **compensation fund** fondo *m* de compensación ▸ **compensation package** daños *mpl* y perjuicios ▸ **compensation payout** pago *m* de una indemnización

compensatory [ˌkɒmpənˈseɪtərɪ] ADJ compensatorio
CPD ▸ **compensatory damages** indemnización *fsing* por daños y perjuicios ▸ **compensatory finance** financiación *f* compensatoria

compere, **compère** [ˈkɒmpɛəʳ] N presentador(a) *m/f*, animador(a) *m/f*
VT [+ *show*] presentar
VI actuar de presentador

compete [kəmˈpiːt] VI (*as rivals*) competir (**against, with** con, **for** por); (= *take part*) tomar parte (**in** en), presentarse (**in** a); (*Comm*) competir, hacer la competencia • **there are 50 students competing for six places** hay 50 estudiantes compitiendo por seis puestos • **there are many firms competing for a share in the market** hay muchas empresas compitiendo por una participación en el mercado • **his poetry can't ~ with Eliot's** no se puede comparar su poesía con la de Eliot • **I can't ~ with that racket*** no puedo hablar por encima de esa bulla*

competence [ˈkɒmpɪtəns], **competency** [ˈkɒmpɪtənsɪ] N **1** (= *ability*) competencia *f*, capacidad *f* • **her ~ as a nurse** su competencia *or* capacidad como enfermera • **he has achieved a certain level of ~ in reading** ha conseguido un cierto nivel de competencia en la lectura
2 (= *jurisdiction*) competencia *f* • **that is not within my ~** eso está fuera de mi competencia, eso no me compete

competent [ˈkɒmpɪtənt] ADJ **1** (= *proficient*) [*person, pilot, nurse*] competente, capaz • **to be ~ at sth** ser competente en algo • **students must be ~ in five basic subjects** los estudiantes tienen que ser competentes en *or* dominar cinco asignaturas fundamentales • **to feel ~ to do sth** sentirse capacitado para hacer algo
2 (= *satisfactory*) [*work, performance*] aceptable • **his work is ~, but not very original** su trabajo es aceptable pero no muy original • **a ~ knowledge of the language** un conocimiento *or* dominio suficiente del idioma • **he did a very ~ job** hizo su trabajo muy bien • **a highly ~ piece of work** un trabajo muy bien hecho
3 (*Jur*) [*court*] competente; [*witness*] hábil

competently [ˈkɒmpɪtəntlɪ] ADV [*handle, perform, play*] competentemente, de forma muy competente

competing [kəmˈpiːtɪŋ] ADJ [*product, bid, offer*] rival; [*interests*] conflictivo • **there are ~ claims on my time** hay muchas cosas que requieren mi tiempo

competition [ˌkɒmpɪˈtɪʃən] N
1 (= *competing*) competencia *f*, rivalidad *f* • **in ~ with** en competencia con • **there was keen ~ for the prize** se disputó reñidamente el premio
2 (*Comm*) competencia *f* • **unfair ~** competencia desleal
3 (= *contest*) concurso *m*; (*eg for Civil Service posts*) oposición *f*; (*Sport*) competición *f* • **to go in for a ~** • **enter a ~** inscribirse en *or* presentarse a un concurso • **60 places to be filled by ~** 60 vacantes a cubrir por oposición

competitive [kəmˈpetɪtɪv] ADJ [*person*] competitivo; [*spirit*] competitivo, de competencia; [*exam, selection*] por concurso *or* oposiciones; (*Comm*) competitivo • **we must make ourselves more ~** tenemos que hacernos más competitivos • **we must improve our ~ position** tenemos que mejorar nuestras posibilidades de competir • **the technology has given them a ~ advantage** la tecnología les ha dado una ventaja competitiva • **~ sports** deportes *mpl* competitivos; ▹ **edge**

competitively [kəmˈpetɪtɪvlɪ] ADV [*think, behave*] con espíritu competidor; [*swim, run, play etc*] a nivel de competición • **~ priced** a precio competitivo • **their products are ~ priced** sus productos tienen precios competitivos

competitiveness [kəmˈpetɪtɪvnɪs] N [*of person*] espíritu *m* competitivo, espíritu *m* de competencia; [*of prices*] competitividad *f*

competitor [kəmˈpetɪtəʳ] N (= *rival*) competidor(a) *m/f*, rival *mf*; (*in contest*) concursante *mf*; (*Sport*) competidor(a) *m/f*, participante *mf*; (*eg for Civil Service post*) opositor(a) *m/f*; (*Comm*) competidor(a) *m/f* • **our ~s beat us to it** se nos adelantó la competencia

compilation [ˌkɒmpɪˈleɪʃən] N (= *act*) [*of list, catalogue*] compilación *f*; [*of information*] recopilación *f*; (= *document*) compilación *f*
CPD ▸ **compilation album** (*Mus*) álbum *m* recopilatorio

compile [kəmˈpaɪl] VT [+ *list, catalogue*] compilar (*also Comput*); [+ *information*] recopilar

compiler [kəmˈpaɪləʳ] N [*of catalogue, list, dictionary*] compilador(a) *m/f* (*also Comput*); [*of information*] recopilador(a) *m/f*

complacency [kəmˈpleɪsənsɪ] N, **complacence** [kəmˈpleɪsns] N autosuficiencia *f*, satisfacción *f* de sí mismo *or* consigo

complacent [kəmˈpleɪsənt] ADJ [*person*] (demasiado) pagado de sí mismo • **a ~ look** una expresión de autosatisfacción • **we can't afford to be ~** no podemos permitirnos el lujo de confiarnos, no podemos dormirnos en los laureles

complacently [kəmˈpleɪsəntlɪ] ADV de modo satisfecho • **he looked at me ~** me miró con expresión de autosatisfacción

complain [kəmˈpleɪn] VI **1** (= *grumble*) quejarse (**about, of** de, **to** a) • **to ~ that** quejarse de que • **they ~ed to the neighbours** se quejaron a los vecinos • **I can't ~** yo no me quejo
2 (= *make a formal complaint*) reclamar (**about** por, **to** ante) • **we're going to ~ to the manager** vamos a reclamar al director • **you should ~ to the police** tendrías que denunciarlo a la policía
3 (*Med*) • **to ~ of** quejarse de

complainant [kəmˈpleɪnənt] N (*Jur*) demandante *mf*, querellante *mf*

complainer [kəmˈpleɪnəʳ] N **1** (= *moaner*) quejica *mf*
2 (*Jur*) = **complainant**

complaint [kəmˈpleɪnt] N **1** (= *statement of dissatisfaction*) queja *f*; (*to manager of shop etc*) reclamación *f*; (*to police*) denuncia *f* • **I had no ~s about the service** no tenía ninguna queja del servicio • **to have cause for ~** tener motivo de queja • **to make** *or* **lodge a ~** reclamar, formular una queja
2 (= *cause of dissatisfaction*) motivo *m* de queja
3 (*Med*) (= *illness*) mal *m*, dolencia *f*
CPD ▸ **complaints book** libro *m* de reclamaciones ▸ **complaints department** sección *f* de reclamaciones ▸ **complaints procedure** procedimiento *m* para presentar reclamaciones

complaisance [kəmˈpleɪzəns] N (*liter*) complacencia *f*, sumisión *f*

complaisant [kəmˈpleɪzənt] ADJ (*gen*) servicial, cortés; [*wife, husband*] consentido, sumiso

-complected [kəmˈplektɪd] ADJ (*ending in compounds*) (*US*) = **-complexioned**

complement N [ˈkɒmplɪmənt] **1** (*gen*) complemento *m* • **to be a ~ to** complementar a • **this wine is the perfect ~ to smoked salmon** este vino complementa perfectamente al salmón ahumado
2 [*of staff*] (*esp on ship*) dotación *f*, personal *m* • **the orchestra did not have its full ~ of brass** la orquesta no contaba con su sección de metales completa
VT [ˈkɒmplɪment] complementar

complementarity [ˌkɒmplɪmenˈtærɪtɪ] N complementariedad *f*

complementary [ˌkɒmplɪˈmentərɪ] ADJ complementario • **the skirt and jacket are ~** la falda y la chaqueta son del mismo traje
CPD ▸ **complementary medicine** medicina *f* complementaria

complementation [ˌkɒmplɪmenˈteɪʃən] (N) (*Gram*) complementación *f*

complete [kəmˈpliːt] (ADJ) **1** (= *whole*) entero • **a ~ office block was burnt to the ground** un bloque de oficinas entero quedó reducido a cenizas
2 (= *finished*) terminado • **the work of restoring the farmhouse is ~** la restauración de la granja está terminada
3 (= *total*) [*control, lack*] total, absoluto; [*change*] total; [*surprise*] auténtico • **in ~ agreement** totalmente de acuerdo, en completo acuerdo • **in ~ contrast to sth/sb** todo lo contrario que algo/algn • **it's a ~ disaster** es un completo desastre, es un desastre total • **the man's a ~ idiot** es un auténtico idiota • **it is a ~ mistake to think that ...** es totalmente erróneo pensar que ... • **he is the ~ opposite of me** no nos parecemos en nada • **to my ~ satisfaction** para mi completa *or* total satisfacción
4 (= *full*) [*list, set, group*] completo • **the Complete Works of Shakespeare** las Obras Completas de Shakespeare • **at last her happiness was ~** por fin, su dicha era completa • **no garden is ~ without a bed of rose bushes** ningún jardín puede considerarse completo si no tiene un arriate de rosales
5 (= *all-round*) [*novelist, footballer*] completo, perfecto • **he is the ~ film-maker** es el director de cine completo *or* perfecto
6 • **~ with:a mansion ~ with swimming pool** una mansión con piscina y todo • **he arrived ~ with equipment** llegó con todo su equipo • **the diary comes ~ with a ballpoint pen** la agenda viene con bolígrafo incluido • **it comes ~ with instructions** viene con sus correspondientes instrucciones
(VT) **1** (= *make up*) [+ *set, collection, team*] completar; [+ *misfortune, happiness*] colmar • **a grey silk tie ~d the outfit** una corbata de seda gris completaba el conjunto
2 (= *finish*) [+ *work*] terminar, acabar; [+ *contract*] cumplir, llevar a cabo • **the course takes three years to ~** se tarda tres años en hacer el curso • **to ~ a prison sentence** cumplir una pena de cárcel
3 (= *fill in*) [+ *form, questionnaire*] rellenar • **~ the application form** rellene la solicitud

completely [kəmˈpliːtlɪ] (ADV) completamente, totalmente • **something ~ different** algo completamente *or* totalmente diferente • **~ and utterly ridiculous** total y absolutamente ridículo • **almost ~** casi completamente, casi por completo • **I'm sorry, I ~ forgot** lo siento, me olvidé completamente *or* totalmente *or* por completo • **she's not ~ recovered yet** aún no está completamente *or* totalmente *or* del todo recuperada

completeness [kəmˈpliːtnɪs] (N) [*of report, study, information*] lo completo • **at varying stages of ~** en diferentes fases de finalización

completion [kəmˈpliːʃən] (N) finalización *f*, terminación *f*, conclusión *f* • **to be nearing ~** estar a punto de finalizarse *or* terminarse *or* concluirse, estar llegando a su finalización *or* conclusión • **on ~ of contract** cuando se cumpla el contrato
(CPD) ▸ **completion date** (*Jur*) (*for work*) fecha *f* de cumplimiento; (*in house-buying*) fecha *f* de entrega (de llaves)

complex [ˈkɒmpleks] (ADJ) (= *difficult*) complejo, complicado; (= *consisting of different parts*) complejo; (*Ling*) compuesto
(N) **1** (*Psych*) complejo *m* • **inferiority/Oedipus ~** complejo *m* de inferioridad/Edipo • **he's got a ~ about his nose** está acomplejado por su nariz, su nariz lo acompleja
2 [*of buildings*] complejo *m* • **sports ~** complejo *m* deportivo • **housing ~** colonia *f* de viviendas, urbanización *f* • **shopping ~** complejo *m* comercial

complexion [kəmˈplekʃən] (N) tez *f*, cutis *m*; (*in terms of colour*) tez *f*, piel *f*; (*fig*) cariz *m*, aspecto *m* • **that puts a different ~ on it** eso le da otro cariz *or* aspecto

-complexioned [kəmˈplekʃnd] (ADJ) (*ending in compounds*) de piel ... • **dark-complexioned** de piel morena • **light-complexioned** de piel blanca

complexity [kəmˈpleksɪtɪ] (N) complejidad *f*, lo complejo

compliance [kəmˈplaɪəns] (N) (*with rules etc*) conformidad *f*; (= *submissiveness*) sumisión *f* (**with** a) • **in ~ with** conforme a, en conformidad con

compliant [kəmˈplaɪənt] (ADJ) sumiso

complicate [ˈkɒmplɪkeɪt] (VT) complicar

complicated [ˈkɒmplɪkeɪtɪd] (ADJ) complicado • **to become ~** • **get ~** complicarse

complication [ˌkɒmplɪˈkeɪʃən] (N) complicación *f* • **it seems there are ~s** parece que han surgido complicaciones *or* dificultades

complicit [kəmˈplɪsɪt] (ADJ) [*person*] cómplice • **to be ~ in sth** ser cómplice de algo

complicity [kəmˈplɪsɪtɪ] (N) complicidad *f* (in en)

compliment (N) [ˈkɒmplɪmənt] **1** (= *respect*) cumplido *m*; (= *flirtation*) piropo *m*; (= *flattery*) halago *m* • **what a nice ~!** ¡qué detalle! • **that was meant as a ~** lo dije con buena intención • **to pay sb a ~** (*respectful*) hacer cumplidos a algn; (*amorous*) echar piropos a algn; (= *flatter*) halagar a algn • **to return the ~** devolver el cumplido • **I take it as a ~ that ...** me halaga (el) que ...
2 compliments (= *greetings*) saludos *mpl* • **my ~s to the chef** mi enhorabuena al cocinero • **the ~s of the season** felicidades *fpl* • **to send one's ~s to sb** enviar saludos a algn • **"with ~s"** "con un atento saludo" • **with the ~s of the management** obsequio de la casa • **with the ~s of Mr Pearce** con un atento saludo del Sr. Pearce, de parte del Sr. Pearce • **with the author's ~s** homenaje *m* *or* obsequio *m* del autor
(VT) [ˈkɒmplɪment] • **to ~ sb on sth/on doing sth** felicitar a algn por algo/por conseguir algo • **they ~ed me on my Spanish** me felicitaron por mi español
(CPD) [ˈkɒmplɪmənt] ▸ **compliment(s) slip** nota *f* de saludo, saluda *m* (*Admin*)

complimentary [ˌkɒmplɪˈmentərɪ] (ADJ) **1** [*remark etc*] elogioso • **he was very ~ about the play** habló de la obra en términos muy favorables
2 (= *free*) [*copy of book etc*] de obsequio • **~ ticket** invitación *f*

complin, compline [ˈkɒmplɪn] (N) completas *fpl*

comply [kəmˈplaɪ] (VI) • **to ~ with** [+ *rules*] cumplir; [+ *laws*] acatar; [+ *orders*] obedecer; [+ *wishes, request*] acceder a

component [kəmˈpəʊnənt] (ADJ) componente • **its ~ parts** (*of structure, device*) las piezas que lo integran; (*of organization, concept*) las partes que lo integran
(N) (= *part*) componente *m*; (*Tech*) pieza *f*
(CPD) ▸ **components factory** fábrica *f* de componentes, maquiladora *f* (*LAm*)

comport [kəmˈpɔːt] (*frm*) (VI) • **to ~ with** concordar con
(VT) • **to ~ o.s.** comportarse

comportment [kəmˈpɔːtmənt] (N) (*frm*) comportamiento *m*

compose [kəmˈpəʊz] (VT) **1** [+ *music*] componer; [+ *poetry, letter*] escribir • **to be ~d of** constar de, componerse de
2 • **to ~ o.s.** calmarse, serenarse

composed [kəmˈpəʊzd] (ADJ) tranquilo, sereno

composedly [kəmˈpəʊzɪdlɪ] (ADV) tranquilamente, serenamente

composer [kəmˈpəʊzəʳ] (N) compositor(a) *m/f*

composite [ˈkɒmpəzɪt] (ADJ) compuesto
(CPD) ▸ **composite motion** moción *f* compuesta

composition [ˌkɒmpəˈzɪʃən] (N) **1** (*Mus*) (= *act of composing, thing composed*) composición *f*; (*Literat*) redacción *f*
2 (*Art*) (= *make-up*) composición *f*

compositional [ˌkɒmpəˈzɪʃənl] (ADJ) [*skill, style*] de composición

compositor [kəmˈpɒzɪtəʳ] (N) cajista *mf*

compos mentis [ˈkɒmpɒsˈmentɪs] (ADJ) • **to be ~** estar en su sano *or* entero juicio; (*Jur*) estar en pleno uso de sus facultades mentales • **he normally takes a good hour to become ~** generalmente no es persona *or* no se espabila hasta que no pasa más de una hora

compost [ˈkɒmpɒst] (N) compost *m*, fertilizante *m* orgánico
(CPD) ▸ **compost bin** (*in garden*) cubo *m* de compost ▸ **compost heap** montón *m* de desechos para formar el compost

composting [ˈkɒmpɒstɪŋ] (N) compostación *f*

composure [kəmˈpəʊʒəʳ] (N) calma *f*, serenidad *f* • **to recover** *or* **regain one's ~** recobrar la calma

compote [ˈkɒmpəʊt] (N) compota *f*

compound (N) [ˈkɒmpaʊnd] **1** (*Chem*) compuesto *m*
2 (= *word*) palabra *f* compuesta
3 (= *enclosed area*) recinto *m* (cercado)
(ADJ) [ˈkɒmpaʊnd] **1** (*Chem*) compuesto
2 [*number, sentence, tense*] compuesto
3 [*fracture*] múltiple
(VT) [kəmˈpaʊnd] (*fig*) [+ *problem, difficulty*] agravar • **to ~ a felony** aceptar dinero para no entablar juicio
(VI) [kəmˈpaʊnd] (*Jur etc*) • **to ~ with** capitular con
(CPD) [ˈkɒmpaʊnd] ▸ **compound interest** interés *m* compuesto

compounding [ˈkɒmpaʊndɪŋ] (N) composición *f*

comprehend [ˌkɒmprɪˈhend] (VT) **1** (= *understand*) comprender, entender
2 (= *include*) comprender, abarcar
(VI) comprender

comprehensible [ˌkɒmprɪˈhensəbl] (ADJ) comprensible

comprehensibly [ˌkɒmprɪˈhensəblɪ] (ADV) comprensiblemente, de modo comprensible

comprehension [ˌkɒmprɪˈhenʃən] (N) **1** (= *understanding*) comprensión *f* • **it is beyond ~** es incomprensible
2 (*Scol*) (= *exercise*) prueba *f* de comprensión
(CPD) ▸ **comprehension test** test *m* de comprensión

comprehensive [ˌkɒmprɪˈhensɪv] (ADJ) **1** (= *complete*) [*list, guide, range*] completo; [*report, description, study*] exhaustivo; [*account, view*] de conjunto, integral; [*knowledge*] extenso; [*training*] completo, exhaustivo; [*victory, defeat*] aplastante
2 (*Brit*) (*Scol*) • **~ education** *sistema de enseñanza secundaria que abarca a alumnos de todos los niveles de aptitud* • **~ school** instituto *m* (de segunda enseñanza)

3 (*Insurance*) (*also* **fully comprehensive**) [*insurance, policy, cover*] a todo riesgo
(N) (*also* **comprehensive school**) instituto *m* (de segunda enseñanza)
(CPD) ▸ **comprehensive insurance policy** seguro *m* a todo riesgo

> **COMPREHENSIVE SCHOOLS**
> En los años sesenta se crearon en el Reino Unido las **comprehensive schools**, centros estatales de enseñanza secundaria no selectivos orientados a cubrir las necesidades educativas de alumnos con distintas habilidades, para fomentar la igualdad de oportunidades y acabar con la división tradicional entre los centros selectivos de enseñanzas teóricas (**grammar schools**) y otros de enseñanza básicamente profesional (**secondary modern schools**). Aunque durante años fueron los centros educativos más habituales, en la actualidad muchos se han convertido en centros especializados, que incluso seleccionan parte de su alumnado. Estos reciben el nombre de **academies** o **specialist schools**.
> ▹ GRAMMAR SCHOOL

comprehensively [ˌkɒmprɪˈhensɪvlɪ] (ADV) (= *thoroughly*) de forma exhaustiva • **the book is ~ illustrated** el libro está ampliamente ilustrado • **they were ~ beaten by the Italian champions** sufrieron una derrota aplastante frente a *or* ante los campeones italianos

comprehensiveness [ˌkɒmprɪˈhensɪvnɪs] (N) carácter *m* exhaustivo • **the ~ of his report** lo exhaustivo de su informe

compress (VT) [kəmˈpres] (*gen*) comprimir; [+ *text etc*] condensar
(N) [ˈkɒmpres] (*Med*) compresa *f*

compressed [kəmˈprest] (ADJ) comprimido
(CPD) ▸ **compressed air** aire *m* comprimido ▸ **compressed charge** (*US*) precio *m* inclusivo

compression [kəmˈpreʃən] (N) compresión *f*

compressor [kəmˈpresəʳ] (N) compresor *m*
(CPD) ▸ **compressor unit** unidad *f* de compresión

comprise [kəmˈpraɪz] (VT) (= *include*) comprender; (= *be made up of*) constar de, consistir en

compromise [ˈkɒmprəmaɪz] (N)
1 (= *agreement*) arreglo *m*, solución *f* intermedia • **to reach a ~ (over sth)** llegar a un arreglo (sobre algo)
2 (= *giving in*) transigencia *f* • **there can be no ~ with treason** no transigimos con la traición
(VI) **1** (= *reach an agreement*) llegar a un arreglo • **so we ~d on seven** así que, ni para uno ni para otro, convinimos en siete
2 (= *give in*) transigir, transar (*LAm*) • **to ~ with sb over sth** transigir con algn sobre algo • **to agree to ~ (with sb)** avenirse a transigir (con algn) • **in the end I agreed to ~** terminé dando mi brazo a torcer
(VT) **1** (= *endanger safety of*) poner en peligro
2 (= *bring under suspicion*) [+ *reputation, person*] comprometer • **to ~ o.s.** comprometerse
(CPD) [*decision, solution*] intermedio

compromising [ˈkɒmprəmaɪzɪŋ] (ADJ) [*situation*] comprometedor; [*mind, spirit*] acomodaticio

comptometer [kɒmpˈtɒmɪtəʳ] (N) máquina *f* de calcular

comptroller [kənˈtrəʊləʳ] (N) interventor(a) *m/f*

compulsion [kəmˈpʌlʃən] (N) **1** (= *urge*) compulsión *f*
2 (= *force*) • **under ~** a la fuerza, bajo coacción • **you are under no ~** no tienes ninguna obligación

compulsive [kəmˈpʌlsɪv] (ADJ) compulsivo; ▹ **viewing**

compulsively [kəmˈpʌlsɪvlɪ] (ADV) compulsivamente

compulsorily [kəmˈpʌlsərɪlɪ] (ADV) por fuerza, forzosamente

compulsory [kəmˈpʌlsərɪ] (ADJ) obligatorio
(CPD) ▸ **compulsory liquidation** liquidación *f* obligatoria ▸ **compulsory purchase** expropiación *f* ▸ **compulsory purchase order** orden *f* de expropiación ▸ **compulsory redundancy** despido *m* forzoso

compunction [kəmˈpʌŋkʃən] (N) escrúpulo *m* • **without ~** sin escrúpulo

computation [ˌkɒmpjʊˈteɪʃən] (N) **1** (*gen*) (*often pl*) cómputo *m*, cálculo *m*
2 (*Comput*) computación *f*

computational [ˌkɑmpjʊˈteɪʃənl] (ADJ) computacional
(CPD) ▸ **computational linguistics** lingüística *f* computacional

compute [kəmˈpjuːt] (VT) computar, calcular

computer [kəmˈpjuːtəʳ] (N) ordenador *m* (*Sp*), computador *m* (*LAm*), computadora *f* (*LAm*) • **we do it by ~ now** ahora lo hacemos con el ordenador • **the records have all been put on ~** todos los registros han entrado en (el) ordenador • **she's in ~s** se dedica a la informática, trabaja en algo de informática
(CPD) ▸ **computer animation** animación *f* por ordenador ▸ **computer buff** as *mf* de la informática ▸ **computer chip** chip *m* informático ▸ **computer crime** delitos *mpl* informáticos ▸ **computer dating service** agencia *f* matrimonial por ordenador ▸ **computer disk** (= *hard disk*) disco *m* duro ▸ **computer error** error *m* informático ▸ **computer expert** experto/a *m/f* en ordenadores ▸ **computer game** videojuego *m* ▸ **computer graphics** gráficas *fpl* por ordenador ▸ **computer language** lenguaje *m* de ordenador ▸ **computer literacy** competencia *f* en la informática ▸ **computer model** modelo *m* informático ▸ **computer operator** operador(a) *m/f* de ordenador ▸ **computer peripheral** periférico *m* ▸ **computer printout** impresión *f* (de ordenador) ▸ **computer program** programa *m* de ordenador ▸ **computer programmer** programador(a) *m/f* de ordenadores ▸ **computer programming** programación *f* de ordenadores ▸ **computer science** informática *f* ▸ **computer scientist** informático/a *m/f* ▸ **computer screen** pantalla *f* de ordenador ▸ **computer simulation** simulación *f* por ordenador ▸ **computer skills** conocimientos *mpl* de informática ▸ **computer software** software *m* informático ▸ **computer studies** = **computer science** ▸ **computer system** sistema *m* informático ▸ **computer terminal** terminal *m* de ordenador ▸ **computer typesetting** composición *f* por ordenador ▸ **computer user** usuario/a *m/f* de ordenador ▸ **computer virus** virus *m* informático

computer-aided [kəmˈpjuːtərˈeɪdɪd], **computer-assisted** [kəmˈpjuːtərəˈsɪstɪd] (ADJ) asistido por ordenador *or* (*LAm*) computador *or* computadora

computerate [kəmˈpjuːtərət] (ADJ) • **to be ~** tener conocimientos de informática

computer-controlled [kəmˈpjuːtə kənˈtrəʊld] (ADJ) controlado por ordenador *or* (*LAm*) computador *or* computadora

computerese [kəmˌpjuːtəˈriːz] (N) jerga *f* informática

computer-generated [kəmˌpjuːtə ˈdʒenəreɪtɪd] (ADJ) [*graphics, images*] realizado *or* creado por ordenador *or* (*LAm*) computador *or* computadora

computerization [kəmˌpjuːtəraɪˈzeɪʃən] (N) computerización *f*, computarización *f*

computerize [kəmˈpjuːtəraɪz] (VT) [+ *company, hospital, system, accounts*] informatizar; [+ *data, information, records*] computerizar, computarizar, informatizar • **we're ~d now** ya nos hemos informatizado

computerized [kəmˈpjuːtəraɪzd] (ADJ)
1 [*system, process, business*] informatizado
2 [*information, data, records*] computerizado

computer-literate [kəmˌpjuːtəˈlɪtərɪt] (ADJ) • **to be computer literate** tener conocimientos de informática

computer-operated [kəmˌpjuːtər ˈɒpəreɪtɪd] (ADJ) operado por ordenador *or* (*LAm*) computador *or* computadora, computerizado

computing [kəmˈpjuːtɪŋ] (N) informática *f*
(CPD) ▸ **computing problem** problema *m* de cómputo ▸ **computing task** tarea *f* de computar

comrade [ˈkɒmrɪd] (N) compañero/a *m/f*, camarada *mf*; (*Pol*) camarada *mf*

comrade-in-arms [ˈkɒmrɪdɪnˈɑːmz] (N) compañero *m* de armas

comradely [ˈkɒmreɪdlɪ] (ADJ) de camarada • **I gave him some ~ advice** le di unos consejos de camarada • **we did it in a ~ spirit** lo hicimos como camaradas

comradeship [ˈkɒmrɪdʃɪp] (N) compañerismo *m*, camaradería *f*

con[1]* [kɒn] (VT) estafar, timar • **I've been conned!** ¡me han estafado! • **to con sb into doing sth** engañar a algn para que haga algo
(N) estafa *f*, timo *m* • **it was all a big con** no fue más que una estafa
(CPD) ▸ **con artist*** estafador(a) *m/f*, timador(a) *m/f* ▸ **con game*** estafa *f*, timo *m* ▸ **con man*** estafador(a) *m/f*, timador(a) *m/f* ▸ **con trick*** estafa *f*, timo *m*

con[2] [kɒn] (N) (= *disadvantage*) contra *m* • **the pros and cons** los pros y los contras

con[3]‡ [kɒn] (N) (= *prisoner*) preso/a *m/f*

Con. (ABBR) (*Brit*) **1** = **Conservative**
2 = **constable**

conc. (ABBR) = **concessions** • **admission £5 (~ £4)** entrada: 5 libras (tarifa reducida: 4 libras) (*para jubilados, estudiantes etc*)

concatenate [kɒnˈkætɪˌneɪt] (VT) (*frm*) concatenar

concatenation [kɒnˌkætɪˈneɪʃən] (N) (*frm*) concatenación *f*

concave [ˈkɒnˈkeɪv] (ADJ) cóncavo

concavity [kɒnˈkævɪtɪ] (N) concavidad *f*

conceal [kənˈsiːl] (VT) [+ *object, news*] ocultar; [+ *emotions, thoughts*] disimular; (*Jur*) encubrir • **~ed lighting** luces *fpl* indirectas • **~ed turning** (*Aut*) cruce *m* poco visible

concealment [kənˈsiːlmənt] (N) [*of object*] ocultación *f*; [*of emotion*] disimulación *f*; (*Jur*) encubrimiento *m* • **place of ~** escondrijo *m*

concede [kənˈsiːd] (VT) [+ *point, argument*] reconocer, conceder; [+ *game, territory*] ceder • **to ~ that** admitir que • **to ~ defeat** darse por vencido
(VI) ceder, darse por vencido

conceit [kənˈsiːt] (N) **1** (= *pride*) vanidad *f*, presunción *f*, engreimiento *m*
2 (*Literat*) concepto *m*

conceited [kənˈsiːtɪd] (ADJ) vanidoso, engreído • **to be ~ about** envanecerse con *or* de *or* por

conceitedly [kənˈsiːtɪdlɪ] (ADV) con vanidad *or* engreimiento

conceivable [kən'si:vəbl] ADJ imaginable, concebible

conceivably [kən'si:vəblɪ] ADV • **you may ~ be right** es posible que tenga razón • **it cannot ~ be true** no es posible que sea verdad • **more than one could ~ need** más de lo que se podría imaginar como necesidad

conceive [kən'si:v] VT **1** [+ *child*] concebir
2 (= *imagine*) concebir • **to ~ a dislike for sth/sb** cobrar antipatía a algo/algn
VI **1** (= *become pregnant*) concebir
2 (= *think*) • **to ~ of sth** imaginar algo • **to ~ of doing sth** imaginarse haciendo algo • **I cannot ~ of anything worse** no me puedo imaginar nada peor • **I cannot ~ why** no entiendo porqué

concelebrant [kən'selɪˌbrənt] N (*frm*) concelebrante *m*

concelebrate [kən'selɪbreɪt] VT (*frm*) [+ *mass*] concelebrar

concentrate ['kɒnsəntreɪt] VT **1** [+ *efforts, thoughts*] concentrar • **to ~ one's efforts on sth/on doing sth** centrar *or* concentrar los esfuerzos en algo/en hacer algo • **he ~d his mind on the task ahead** se concentró *or* se centró en la tarea que tenía por delante
2 (= *group together*) [+ *troops etc*] concentrar, reunir • **heavy industry is ~d in the north of the country** la industria pesada se concentra en el norte del país
VI **1** (= *pay attention*) concentrarse • **I couldn't ~** no me podía concentrar • **~!** ¡concéntrate! • **to ~ on sth** concentrarse en algo • **I was concentrating on my homework** me estaba concentrando en los deberes
2 (= *focus on*) • **to ~ on sth** centrarse en algo • **the talks are expected to ~ on practical issues** se espera que las conversaciones se centren en *or* giren en torno a cuestiones prácticas • **to ~ on doing sth** concentrarse *or* centrarse en hacer algo
3 (= *come together*) [*troops, crowd*] concentrarse, reunirse
N (*Chem*) concentrado *m*

concentrated ['kɒnsənˌtreɪtɪd] ADJ concentrado

concentration [ˌkɒnsən'treɪʃən] N concentración *f*
CPD ▸ **concentration camp** campo *m* de concentración ▸ **concentration span** [*of person*] capacidad *f* de concentración • **he has a short attention span** le cuesta mucho mantenerse concentrado

concentric [kən'sentrɪk] ADJ concéntrico

concept ['kɒnsept] N concepto *m* • **have you any ~ of how hard it is?** ¿tienes idea de lo difícil que es?
CPD ▸ **concept album** (*Mus*) volumen *m* monográfico

conception [kən'sepʃən] N **1** [*of child, idea*] concepción *f*; ▷ **immaculate**
2 (= *idea*) concepto *m* • **a bold ~** un concepto grandioso • **he has not the remotest ~ of ...** no tiene ni la menor idea de ...

conceptual [kən'septjʊəl] ADJ conceptual
CPD ▸ **conceptual art** arte *m* conceptual

conceptualization [kənˌseptjʊəlaɪ'zeɪʃən] N conceptualización *f*

conceptualize [kən'septjʊəlaɪz] VT conceptualizar

conceptually [kən'septjʊəlɪ] ADV conceptualmente, como concepto • **~, the idea made sense** como concepto, la idea podía funcionar

concern [kən'sɜ:n] N **1** (= *business*) asunto *m* • **it's no ~ of yours** no es asunto tuyo • **technical aspects were the ~ of the army** de los aspectos técnicos se encargaba el ejército, los aspectos técnicos eran asunto del ejército • **if they want to go ahead, that's their ~** si quieren seguir adelante, es asunto suyo • **what ~ is it of yours?** ¿qué tiene que ver contigo?
2 (= *anxiety*) preocupación *f* • **his health is giving cause for ~** su salud está dando motivo de preocupación • **to express ~ about sth** expresar preocupación por algo • **it is a matter for ~ that ...** es motivo de preocupación el (hecho de) que ... • **with an expression** *or* **a look of ~** con cara preocupada *or* de preocupación • **there is ~ that ...** preocupa que ...
3 (= *interest, regard*) interés *m* • **my main ~ is the welfare of my children** mi interés principal *or* lo que más me preocupa es el bienestar de mis hijos • **it's of no ~ to me** me tiene sin cuidado, a mí no me importa • **out of ~ for her feelings, I didn't say anything** no dije nada por no herir sus sentimientos • **out of ~ for the public's safety** por la seguridad pública
4 (= *firm*) negocio *m*, empresa *f* • **a family ~** un negocio familiar • **a going ~** un negocio próspero, una empresa próspera • **the farm is not a going ~** la granja no es un buen negocio
VT **1** (= *affect*) afectar, concernir • **it ~s me directly** me afecta *or* concierne directamente • **it doesn't ~ you at all** no te afecta *or* concierne para nada
2 (= *interest, involve*) • **please contact the department ~ed** póngase en contacto con la sección correspondiente • **it is best for all ~ed** es lo mejor para todas las partes interesadas • **as far as I am ~ed** por *or* en lo que a mí se refiere, por *or* en lo que a mí respecta • **she can go to hell as far as I'm ~ed** por mí se puede ir a la porra*, por *or* en lo que a mí respecta se puede ir a la porra* • **I was just another student as far as he was ~ed** para él yo no era más que otra estudiante • **to ~ o.s. with sth** • **I didn't ~ myself with politics** no me metí en política • **don't ~ yourself with things you can do nothing about** no te preocupes por cosas que están fuera de tu alcance • **those ~ed** los interesados • **to whom it may ~** (*frm*) a quien corresponda • **to be ~ed with sth** • **essential reading for anyone ~ed with children** lecturas fundamentales para cualquiera al que le interesen los niños • **they are mainly ~ed with maximizing profits** su interés principal es maximizar los beneficios
3 (= *be about*) • **my question ~s money** mi pregunta hace referencia al dinero • **chapter two is ~ed with the civil war** el capítulo dos trata de la guerra civil
4 (= *worry*) preocupar • **it ~s me that ...** me preocupa el hecho de que ...

concerned [kən'sɜ:nd] ADJ **1** (= *worried*) preocupado • **to be ~ about sth/sb** estar preocupado por algo/algn • **I'm not nagging, I'm ~ about you** no es que quiera darte la lata, estoy preocupado por ti *or* me preocupas • **to be ~ at** *or* **by sth** estar preocupado por algo • **doctors are ~ at his slow recovery** los médicos están preocupados por *or* a los médicos les preocupa la lentitud con la que se está recuperando • **to be ~ for sth/sb** estar preocupado por algo/algn • **he was ~ for his son's happiness** le preocupaba la felicidad de su hijo • **he sounded very ~** parecía estar muy preocupado • **he was ~ that he might have hurt her** le preocupaba que pudiera haberle hecho daño
2 • **to be ~ to do sth** poner mucho interés en hacer algo • **Britain was ~ to avoid war** Gran Bretaña puso mucho interés en evitar la guerra; ▷ **concern**

concerning [kən'sɜ:nɪŋ] PREP **1** (= *with regard to*) con respecto a, con relación a, en lo que se refiere a (*frm*) • **~ your last remark, ...** con respecto *or* relación a su último comentario, ..., en lo que se refiere a su último comentario, ...
2 (= *about*) sobre, acerca de • **theories ~ evolution** teorías sobre *or* acerca de la evolución • **something ~ his mother** algo que tenía que ver con su madre, algo relacionado con su madre

concert N ['kɒnsət] concierto *m* • **to give a ~** dar un concierto • **in ~** (*Mus*) en concierto • **in ~ with** (*Mus*) en concierto con; (*fig*) (= *in agreement with*) de común acuerdo con
VT [kən'sɜ:t] concertar
CPD ['kɒnsət] ▸ **concert grand** piano *m* de cola ▸ **concert hall** sala *f* de conciertos ▸ **concert party** (*Theat*) grupo *m* de artistas de revista; (*Econ*) *conjunto de inversores que se pone de acuerdo en secreto para adquirir la mayoría de las acciones de una empresa* ▸ **concert performer** concertista *mf* ▸ **concert pianist** pianista *mf* de concierto ▸ **concert pitch** diapasón *m* normal • **at ~ pitch** (*fig*) en plena forma, en un momento excelente ▸ **concert promoter** promotor(a) *m/f* de conciertos ▸ **concert ticket** entrada *f* de concierto ▸ **concert tour** gira *f* de conciertos ▸ **concert venue** (= *site of performance*) lugar *m* del concierto; (= *concert hall*) sala *f* de conciertos; (*for open-air performances*) auditorio *m*

concerted [kən'sɜ:tɪd] ADJ [*campaign, attack*] coordinado, organizado; [*attempt*] coordinado, concertado • **to make a ~ effort (to do sth)** aunar *or* coordinar los esfuerzos (por hacer algo)

concertgoer ['kɒnsətˌgəʊə^r] N aficionado/a *m/f* a los conciertos • **we are regular ~s** vamos con regularidad a los conciertos

concertina [ˌkɒnsə'ti:nə] N concertina *f*
VI • **the vehicles ~ed into each other** los vehículos quedaron hechos un acordeón
CPD ▸ **concertina crash** (*Aut*) choque *m or* colisión *f* en cadena

concertmaster ['kɒnsətˌmɑ:stə^r] N (*US*) primer violín *m*

concerto [kən'tʃɛətəʊ] N (PL: **concertos, concerti** [kən'tʃɛəti:]) concierto *m*

concession [kən'seʃən] N **1** (= *reduction*) concesión *f*; (*on tax*) desgravación *f*, exención *f* • **price ~** reducción *f*
2 (= *franchise*) concesión *f*; (= *exploration rights*) (*for oil*) derechos *mpl* de exploración

concessionaire [kənˌseʃə'nɛə^r] N (*esp US*) concesionario/a *m/f*

concessionary [kən'seʃənərɪ] ADJ [*ticket, fare*] reducido
N concesionario/a *m/f*

concessioner [kən'seʃənə^r] (*US*) N concesionario *m*

conch [kɒntʃ] N (PL: **conchs** *or* **conches**)
1 (= *shell*) caracola *f*
2 (*Archit*) cóclea *f*

concierge [ˌkɔ̃:nsɪ'ɛəʒ] N conserje *m*

conciliate [kən'sɪlɪeɪt] VT conciliar

conciliation [kənˌsɪlɪ'eɪʃən] N conciliación *f*
CPD ▸ **conciliation service** servicio *m* de conciliación ▸ **conciliation talks** negociaciones *fpl* de conciliación

conciliator [kən'sɪlɪeɪtə^r] N conciliador(a) *m/f*; (*Ind*) árbitro *mf*

conciliatory [kən'sɪlɪətərɪ] ADJ conciliador

concise [kən'saɪs] ADJ conciso

concisely [kən'saɪslɪ] ADV concisamente, con concisión

conciseness [kən'saɪsnɪs] N, **concision** [kən'sɪʒən] N concisión *f*

conclave ['kɒnkleɪv] N cónclave *m*

C

conclude [kən'klu:d] (VT) **1** (= *end*) acabar, concluir • **"to be ~d"** [*serial*] "terminará en el próximo episodio"
2 (= *finalize*) [+ *treaty*] concertar, pactar; [+ *agreement*] llegar a, concertar; [+ *deal*] cerrar
3 (= *infer*) concluir • **it was ~d that …** se concluyó que … • **what are we to ~ from that?** ¿que conclusión se saca de eso? • **from your expression I ~ that you are angry** por tu expresión deduzco que estás enfadado
4 (*US*) (= *decide*) decidir (**to do sth** hacer algo)
(VI) (= *end*) terminar, concluir • **he ~d by saying** terminó diciendo • **the judge ~d in his favour** el juez decidió a su favor • **to ~ I must say …** para concluir *or* terminar, debo decir …
concluding [kən'klu:dɪŋ] (ADJ) final
conclusion [kən'klu:ʒən] (N) **1** (= *end*) conclusión *f*, término *m* • **to reach a happy ~** llegar a feliz término • **in ~** para concluir *or* terminar, en conclusión • **to bring sth to a ~** concluir algo
2 (= *signing*) [*of treaty, agreement, deal*] firmar *m*
3 (= *inference*) conclusión *f* • **to come to the ~ that** llegar a la conclusión de que • **draw your own ~s** extraiga usted las conclusiones oportunas • **to jump to ~s** sacar conclusiones precipitadas; ▹ **foregone**
conclusive [kən'klu:sɪv] (ADJ) [*answer, victory*] concluyente, decisivo; [*proof*] concluyente
conclusively [kən'klu:sɪvlɪ] (ADV) concluyentemente
concoct [kən'kɒkt] (VT) [+ *food, drink*] confeccionar; [+ *lie, story*] inventar; [+ *plot*] tramar, fraguar
concoction [kən'kɒkʃən] (N) **1** (= *food*) mezcla *f*, mejunje *m*; (= *drink*) brebaje *m*
2 (= *act*) [*of food, drink*] confección *f*; [*of story*] invención *f*
concomitant [kən'kɒmɪtənt] (*frm*) (ADJ) concomitante
(N) hecho *m* concomitante
concord ['kɒŋkɔ:d] (N) **1** (= *harmony*) concordia *f*
2 (= *treaty*) acuerdo *m*
3 (*Mus, Gram*) concordancia *f*
concordance [kən'kɔ:dəns] (N)
1 (= *agreement*) concordancia *f*
2 (= *index, book*) concordancias *fpl*
concordant [kən'kɔ:dənt] (ADJ) concordante
concordat [kɒn'kɔ:dæt] (N) concordato *m*
Concorde ['kɒŋkɔ:d] (N) Concorde *m* • **to fly by ~** volar en Concorde
concourse ['kɒŋkɔ:s] (N) **1** [*of people*] concurrencia *f*; [*of rivers*] confluencia *f*
2 (*in building, station*) explanada *f*
concrete ['kɒnkri:t] (ADJ) **1** (= *not abstract*) concreto
2 (*Constr*) de hormigón *or* (*LAm*) concreto
(N) hormigón *m*
(VT) • **to ~ a path** cubrir un sendero de hormigón
(CPD) ▸ **concrete jungle** jungla *f* de asfalto ▸ **concrete mixer** hormigonera *f* ▸ **concrete noun** nombre *m* concreto
concretely ['kɒŋkri:tlɪ] (ADV) concretamente
concretion [kən'kri:ʃən] (N) concreción *f*
concretize ['kɒnkrɪtaɪz] (VT) concretar
concubine ['kɒŋkjʊbaɪn] (N) concubina *f*
concupiscence [kən'kju:pɪsəns] (N) (*frm*) concupiscencia *f*
concupiscent [kən'kju:pɪsənt] (ADJ) (*frm*) concupiscente
concur [kən'kɜ:ʳ] (VI) **1** (= *agree*) estar de acuerdo (**with** con)
2 (= *happen at the same time*) concurrir
concurrence [kən'kʌrəns] (N) **1** (*frm*) (= *consent*) conformidad *f*
2 (= *coincidence*) concurrencia *f*
concurrent [kən'kʌrənt] (ADJ) concurrente • **~ with** concurrente con
(CPD) ▸ **concurrent processing** procesamiento *m* concurrente
concurrently [kən'kʌrəntlɪ] (ADV) al mismo tiempo, simultáneamente
concuss [kən'kʌs] (VT) (*Med*) producir una conmoción cerebral a
concussed [kən'kʌst] (ADJ) • **to be ~** sufrir una conmoción cerebral
concussion [kən'kʌʃən] (N) (*Med*) conmoción *f* cerebral
condemn [kən'dem] (VT) (= *sentence, censure*) condenar; [+ *building*] declarar en ruina; [+ *food*] declarar insalubre • **to ~ sb to death** condenar a algn a muerte • **the ~ed cell** la celda de los condenados a muerte • **the ~ed man** el reo de muerte • **such conduct is to be ~ed** tal conducta es censurable
condemnation [ˌkɒndem'neɪʃən] (N) (= *sentencing*) condena *f*; (= *censure*) censura *f*
condemnatory [ˌkɒndem'neɪtərɪ] (ADJ) condenatorio
condensation [ˌkɒnden'seɪʃən] (N)
1 (= *vapour*) vaho *m*
2 (= *summary*) resumen *m*
condense [kən'dens] (VT) **1** [+ *vapour*] condensar • **~d milk** leche *f* condensada
2 [+ *text*] abreviar, resumir
(VI) condensarse
condensed [kən'denst] (ADJ) **1** (= *abridged*) [*version, book*] abreviado
2 (= *concentrated*) [*soup, liquid*] concentrado, condensado
condenser [kən'densəʳ] (N) condensador *m*
condescend [ˌkɒndɪ'send] (VI) • **to ~ to sb** tratar a algn con condescendencia • **to ~ to do sth** dignarse (a) hacer algo, condescender a hacer algo
condescending [ˌkɒndɪ'sendɪŋ] (ADJ) [*attitude, tone, smile*] condescendiente • **in a ~ way** de manera condescendiente • **he's very ~** tiene una actitud muy condescendiente, se cree muy superior • **they were so ~** su actitud fue tan condescendiente • **to be ~ to** *or* **towards sb** tratar a algn con condescendencia
condescendingly [ˌkɒndɪ'sendɪŋlɪ] (ADV) con condescendencia • **to treat people ~** tratar a la gente con condescendencia • **he ~ agreed to do it** accedió hacerlo como si de un favor se tratara
condescension [ˌkɒndɪ'senʃən] (N) condescendencia *f*
condiment ['kɒndɪmənt] (N) condimento *m*
condition [kən'dɪʃən] (N) **1** (= *state*) condición *f*, estado *m* • **in good ~** en buenas condiciones, en buen estado • **to keep o.s. in ~** mantenerse en forma • **living ~s** condiciones de vida • **to be in no ~ to do sth** no estar en condiciones de hacer algo • **to be out of ~** no estar en forma • **physical ~** estado físico • **physical ~s** condiciones físicas • **in poor ~** en malas condiciones • **weather ~s** estado del tiempo • **working ~s** condiciones de trabajo
2 (= *stipulation*) condición *f* • **on ~ that a** condición de que • **on no ~** bajo ningún concepto • **I'll do it on one ~** lo haré, con una condición • **on this ~** con esta condición • **~s of sale** condiciones de venta
3 (= *circumstance*) circunstancia *f* • **under existing ~s** en las circunstancias actuales
4 (= *disease*) enfermedad *f*, padecimiento *m* • **he has a heart ~** tiene una afección cardíaca
5 (*social*) clase *f* • **of humble ~** de clase humilde
(VT) **1** (= *make healthy*) [+ *hair*] condicionar
2 (= *determine*) determinar • **to be ~ed by** depender de
3 (*Psych*) (= *train*) condicionar
conditional [kən'dɪʃənl] (ADJ) condicional • **~ offer** oferta *f* condicional • **~ tense/clause** tiempo *m*/oración *f* condicional • **to be ~ upon** depender de
(N) condicional *m*
(CPD) ▸ **conditional discharge** (*Brit*) (*Jur*) descargo *f* bajo reserva
conditionally [kən'dɪʃnəlɪ] (ADV) condicionalmente, con reservas
conditioned [kən'dɪʃənd] (ADJ) condicionado
(CPD) ▸ **conditioned reflex** reflejo *m* condicionado
conditioner [kən'dɪʃənəʳ] (N) (*for hair*) suavizante *m*, acondicionador *m* (*LAm*), enjuague *m* (*LAm*); (*for skin*) crema *f* suavizante; (= *fabric conditioner*) suavizante *m*
conditioning [kən'dɪʃənɪŋ] (ADJ) • **~ shampoo** champú *m* acondicionador
(N) (*social*) condicionamiento *m*; ▹ **air**
condo* ['kɒndəʊ] (N) (*US*) = **condominium**
condole [kən'dəʊl] (VI) (*frm*) • **to ~ with sb** condolerse de algn
condolence [kən'dəʊləns] (N) (*usu pl*) pésame *m* • **to send one's ~s** dar el pésame • **please accept my ~s** le acompaño en el sentimiento
condom ['kɒndəm] (N) condón *m*, preservativo *m*
condominium [ˌkɒndə'mɪnɪəm] (N) (PL: **condominiums**) **1** (*US*) (= *building*) bloque *m* de pisos, condominio *m* (*LAm*) (*en copropiedad de los que lo habitan*); (= *apartment*) piso *m or* apartamento *m* (en propiedad), condominio *m* (*LAm*)
2 (*Pol*) condominio *m*
condone [kən'dəʊn] (VT) consentir, tolerar
condor ['kɒndɔ:ʳ] (N) cóndor *m*
conduce [kən'dju:s] (VI) • **to ~ to** conducir a
conducive [kən'dju:sɪv] (ADJ) • **~ to** conducente a
conduct (N) ['kɒndʌkt] (= *behaviour*) comportamiento *m*, conducta *f*; [*of business etc*] dirección *f*, manejo *m*
(VT) [kən'dʌkt] **1** (= *guide*) llevar, conducir • **~ed tour** visita *f* con guía • **we were ~ed to the interview room** nos llevaron *or* condujeron a la sala de entrevistas • **we were ~ed round by Lord Rice** Lord Rice actuó de guía
2 [+ *heat, electricity*] conducir
3 [+ *campaign*] dirigir, llevar; [+ *legal case*] presentar; (*Mus*) dirigir • **I don't like the way they ~ business** no me gusta la forma en que llevan los negocios, no me gusta la forma de hacer negocios que tienen • **to ~ a correspondence with sb** estar en correspondencia con algn, cartearse con algn
4 (= *behave*) • **to ~ o.s.** comportarse
(VI) [kən'dʌkt] (*Mus*) dirigir
(CPD) ['kɒndʌkt] ▸ **conduct report** (*Scol*) informe *m* de conducta
conduction [kən'dʌkʃən] (N) (*Elec*) conducción *f*
conductive [kən'dʌktɪv] (ADJ) conductivo
conductivity [ˌkɒndʌk'tɪvɪtɪ] (N) conductividad *f*
conductor [kən'dʌktəʳ] (N) **1** (*Mus*) director(a) *m/f*; (*on bus*) cobrador(a) *m/f*; (*US*) (*Rail*) revisor(a) *m/f*
2 (*Phys*) [*of heat, electricity*] conductor *m*; (*also* **lightning conductor**) pararrayos *m inv*
conductress [kən'dʌktrɪs] (N) cobradora *f*
conduit ['kɒndɪt] (N) conducto *m*
cone [kəʊn] (N) **1** (*Math*) cono *m* • **traffic ~**

cono *m* señalizador
2 (*Bot*) piña *f*
3 (*also* **ice cream cone**) cucurucho *m*
▸ **cone off** (VT + ADV) [*+ road*] cerrar *or* cortar con conos
coney ['kəʊnɪ] (N) (*US*) conejo *m*
confab* ['kɒnfæb] (N) = **confabulation**
confabulate [kən'fæbjʊleɪt] (VI) conferenciar
confabulation [kən,fæbjʊ'leɪʃən] (N) conferencia *f*
confection [kən'fekʃən] (N) **1** (*Culin*) dulce *m*, confite *m*
2 (= *thing produced*) creación *f*
3 (= *manufacture*) confección *f*, hechura *f*
confectioner [kən'fekʃənəʳ] (N) confitero/a *m/f* • **~'s (shop)** confitería *f*, dulcería *f* (*LAm*) • **~'s sugar** (*US*) azúcar *m* glas(eado)
confectionery [kən'fekʃənərɪ] (N) (= *sweets*) dulces *mpl*, golosinas *fpl*; (*Brit*) (= *cakes*) pasteles *mpl*
confederacy [kən'fedərəsɪ] (N) (= *alliance*) confederación *f*; (= *plot*) complot *m* • **the Confederacy** (*US*) los Estados Confederados
confederate (ADJ) [kən'fedərɪt] confederado
(N) [kən'fedərɪt] **1** (*pej*) (= *accomplice*) cómplice *mf*
2 (*US*) (*Hist*) confederado/a *m/f*
(VT) [kən'fedəreɪt] confederar
(VI) [kən'fedəreɪt] confederarse
confederation [kən,fedə'reɪʃən] (N) confederación *f*
confer [kən'fɜːʳ] (VT) • **to ~ sth on sb** [*+ honour*] conceder *or* otorgar algo a algn; [*+ title*] conferir *or* conceder algo a algn
(VI) conferenciar, estar en consultas • **to ~ with sb** consultar con algn
conferee [,kɒnfɜː'riː] (N) (*US*) congresista *mf*
conference ['kɒnfərəns] (N) (= *discussion, meeting*) reunión *f*, conferencia *f*; (= *assembly*) asamblea *f*, congreso *m*; (*party political, academic*) congreso *m* • **to be in ~** estar en una reunión; ▹ **press, video**
(CPD) ▸ **conference call** conferencia *f* ▸ **conference centre** (= *town*) ciudad *f* de congresos; (= *building*) palacio *m* de congresos; (*in institution*) centro *m* de conferencias ▸ **conference committee** (*US*) *comité provisional compuesto por miembros del Congreso y del Senado de EE. UU. destinado a una negociación concreta sobre un proyecto de ley* ▸ **conference hall** sala *f* de conferencias *or* congresos ▸ **conference member** congresista *mf* ▸ **conference room** sala *f* de conferencias ▸ **conference system** sistema *m* de conferencias ▸ **conference table** mesa *f* negociadora
conferencing ['kɒnfərənsɪŋ] (N) (*Comput*) conferencia *f*; ▹ **video**
(CPD) ▸ **conferencing system** sistema *m* de conferencias
conferment [kən'fɜːmənt], **conferral** [kən'fɜːrəl] (N) [*of honour*] otorgamiento *m*, concesión *f* (**on** a); [*of title*] concesión *f* (**on** a)
confess [kən'fes] (VT) **1** [*+ crime, sin*] confesar; [*+ guilt, error*] confesar, reconocer • **to ~ that** ... confesar que ... • **to ~ one's guilt** confesar *or* reconocer ser culpable • **to ~ o.s. guilty of** [*+ sin, crime*] confesarse culpable de • **I ~ myself totally ignorant** me confieso totalmente ignorante en eso
2 (*Rel*) • **to ~ sb** confesar a algn
(VI) **1** (= *admit*) confesar • **he ~ed to the murder** se confesó culpable del asesinato, confesó haber cometido el asesinato • **to ~ to doing sth** confesarse culpable de haber hecho algo • **I must ~, I like your car** debo reconocer que me gusta tu coche • **to ~ to a liking for sth** reconocerse aficionado a algo
2 (*Rel*) confesarse

confessed [kən'fest] (ADJ) declarado
confession [kən'feʃən] (N) **1** (= *act, document*) confesión *f* • **to make a ~** confesar, hacer una confesión • **to make a full ~** confesarlo todo, confesar de plano
2 (*Rel*) • **to go to ~** confesarse • **to hear sb's ~** confesar a algn • **~ of faith** profesión *f* de fe
confessional [kən'feʃənl] (N) confesionario *m*
confessor [kən'fesəʳ] (N) (*Rel*) (= *priest*) confesor *m*; (= *adviser*) director *m* espiritual
confetti [kən'fetiː] (N) confeti *m*
confidant [,kɒnfɪ'dænt] (N) confidente *m*
confidante [,kɒnfɪ'dænt] (N) confidenta *f*
confide [kən'faɪd] (VT) (= *tell*) [*+ secret*] confiar • **he ~d to me that** ... me confió que ..., me dijo en confianza que ... • **to ~ sth to sb** confiar algo a algn, contar algo en confianza a algn
(VI) **1** (= *trust*) • **to ~ in sb** confiarse a algn, hacer confidencias a algn • **please ~ in me** puedes fiarte de mí
2 (= *tell secrets*) • **to ~ in sb** confiarse a algn • **to ~ in** *or* **to sb that** ... confiar a algn que ..., confesar a algn en secreto que ...
confidence ['kɒnfɪdəns] (N) **1** (= *trust*) confianza *f* • **to gain sb's ~** ganarse la confianza de algn • **to have (every) ~ in sb** tener (entera) confianza en algn • **to have (every) ~ that** estar seguro de que • **to inspire ~** inspirar confianza • **a motion of no ~** moción *f* de censura • **to put one's ~ in sth/sb** confiar en algo/algn
2 (*also* **self-confidence**) confianza *f* (en sí mismo), seguridad *f* (en sí mismo) • **to gain ~** ganar confianza *or* seguridad (en sí mismo) • **he lacks ~** le falta confianza *or* seguridad (en sí mismo)
3 (= *secrecy*) confianza *f* • **in ~** en confianza • **to tell sb (about) sth in strict ~** decir algo a algn en la más estricta confianza • **"write in ~ to Michelle Davis"** "escriba a Michelle Davis: discreción garantizada" • **to take sb into one's ~** confiarse a algn
4 (= *revelation*) confidencia *f* • **they exchanged ~s** se hicieron confidencias
(CPD) ▸ **confidence man** timador *m*, estafador *m* ▸ **confidence trick, confidence game** (*esp US*) timo *m*, estafa *f* ▸ **confidence trickster** timador(a) *m/f*, estafador(a) *m/f* ▸ **confidence vote** voto *m* de confianza
confident ['kɒnfɪdənt] (ADJ) [*person*] seguro, seguro de sí mismo; [*prediction*] hecho con seguridad, hecho con confianza; [*performance, smile, reply, manner*] lleno de seguridad, lleno de confianza • **to be ~ that** estar seguro de que • **to be ~ of doing sth** confiar en hacer algo • **he is ~ of success** confía en obtener el éxito • **to feel** *or* **be ~ about sth** tener confianza en algo • **the prime minister is in ~ mood** el primer ministro está lleno de confianza
confidential [,kɒnfɪ'denʃəl] (ADJ) [*information, remark*] confidencial, secreto; [*secretary, tone of voice*] de confianza • **"confidential"** (*on letter etc*) "confidencial"
confidentiality [,kɒnfɪ,denʃɪ'ælɪtɪ] (N) confidencialidad *f*
confidentially [,kɒnfɪ'dənʃəlɪ] (ADV) confidencialmente, en confianza
confidently ['kɒnfɪdəntlɪ] (ADV) [*predict, promise*] con seguridad, con confianza; [*smile, stride, enter*] con seguridad; [*speak, reply*] con un tono de seguridad *or* confianza • **"sure," he said ~** —claro —dijo lleno de confianza • **we ~ expect that** ... creemos con toda confianza que ...
confiding [kən'faɪdɪŋ] (ADJ) • **in a ~ tone** en tono de confianza • **he is too ~** es demasiado confiado

confidingly [kən'faɪdɪŋlɪ] (ADV) como disponiéndose a hacer una confidencia
configuration [kən,fɪgjʊ'reɪʃən] (N) configuración *f*
configure [kən'fɪgəʳ] (VT) configurar
confine [kən'faɪn] (VT) **1** (= *imprison*) encerrar (**in, to** en) • **to be ~d to bed** tener que guardar cama • **to be ~d to one's room** no poder dejar su cuarto
2 (= *limit*) limitar • **to ~ o.s. to doing sth** limitarse a hacer algo • **please ~ yourself to the facts** por favor, limítese a los hechos • **the damage is ~d to this part** el daño afecta solo a esta parte • **this bird is ~d to Spain** esta ave existe únicamente en España
3 (*Med*†) • **to be ~d** [*woman*] estar de parto
confined [kən'faɪnd] (ADJ) reducido • **a ~ space** un espacio reducido
confinement [kən'faɪnmənt] (N) **1** (= *imprisonment*) prisión *f*, reclusión *f* • **to be in solitary ~** estar incomunicado, estar en pelota‡ • **~ to barracks** arresto *m* en cuartel
2 (*Med*†) parto *m*
confines ['kɒnfaɪnz] (NPL) confines *mpl*, límites *mpl*
confirm [kən'fɜːm] (VT) **1** (= *prove*) confirmar
2 (*Rel*) confirmar
confirmation [,kɒnfə'meɪʃən] (N) **1** (= *proof*) confirmación *f*
2 (*Rel*) confirmación *f*
confirmed [kən'fɜːmd] (ADJ) [*bachelor, alcoholic*] empedernido; [*atheist*] inveterado, redomado
confiscate ['kɒnfɪskeɪt] (VT) confiscar, incautarse de
confiscation [,kɒnfɪs'keɪʃən] (N) confiscación *f*, incautación *f*
confiscatory [kən'fɪskətərɪ] (ADJ) • **they have ~ powers** tienen poderes para confiscar
confit ['kɒnfiː] (N) confit *m*
conflagration [,kɒnflə'greɪʃən] (N) conflagración *f*, incendio *m*
conflate [kən'fleɪt] (VT) combinar
conflation [kən'fleɪʃən] (N) combinación *f*
conflict (N) ['kɒnflɪkt] conflicto *m* • **to be in ~ with sth/sb** estar en conflicto con algo/algn • **the theories are in ~** las teorías están en conflicto *or* se contradicen • **to come into ~ with** entrar en conflicto con • **~ of interests** conflicto *m* de intereses, incompatibilidad *f* (de intereses) • **~ of evidence** contradicción *f* de testimonios
(VI) [kən'flɪkt] [*ideas, evidence, statements etc*] estar reñido (**with** con); [*interests*] estar en conflicto (**with** con) • **that ~s with what he told me** eso contradice lo que me dijo
(CPD) ▸ **conflict diamond** diamante *m* de sangre
conflicting [kən'flɪktɪŋ] (ADJ) [*reports, evidence*] contradictorio; [*interests*] opuesto
confluence ['kɒnflʊəns] (N) confluencia *f*
conform [kən'fɔːm] (VI) (*to laws*) someterse (**to** a); (*to standards*) ajustarse (**to** a); (*socially*) adaptarse, amoldarse • **he will ~ to the agreement** se ajustará al acuerdo
conformance [kən'fɔːməns] (N) = **conformity**
conformation [,kɒnfə'meɪʃən] (N) conformación *f*, estructura *f*
conformism [kən'fɔːmɪzəm] (N) conformismo *m*
conformist [kən'fɔːmɪst] (ADJ) conformista
(N) conformista *mf*
conformity [kən'fɔːmɪtɪ] (N) conformidad *f* • **in ~ with** conforme a *or* con
confound [kən'faʊnd] (VT) (= *confuse*) confundir; (= *amaze*) pasmar, desconcertar • **~ it!**† ¡demonio! • **~ him!**† ¡maldito sea!*
confounded [kən'faʊndɪd] (ADJ)

condenado*, maldito**††**

confront [kən'frʌnt] VT (= *face squarely*) hacer frente a; (= *face defiantly*) enfrentarse con • **to ~ sb with sth** confrontar a algn con algo • **to ~ sb with the facts** exponer delante de algn los hechos • **the problems which ~ us** los problemas con los que nos enfrentamos • **we were ~ed by the river** estábamos delante el río

confrontation [ˌkɒnfrən'teɪʃən] N enfrentamiento *m*, confrontación *f*

confrontational [ˌkɒnfrən'teɪʃənəl] ADJ [*approach, attitude, style*] confrontacional, agresivo

Confucian [kən'fjuːʃən] ADJ de Confucio
N confuciano/a *m/f*

Confucianism [kən'fjuːʃənɪzəm] N confucianismo *m*, confucionismo *m*

Confucius [kən'fjuːʃəs] N Confucio

confuse [kən'fjuːz] VT **1** (= *perplex*) confundir, desconcertar • **you're just confusing me** no haces más que confundirme, lo único que haces es confundirme más
2 (= *mix up*) confundir • **to ~ the issue** complicar el asunto • **to ~ A and B** confundir A con B

confused [kən'fjuːzd] ADJ **1** [*situation etc*] confuso
2 (= *perplexed*) confuso, confundido, desconcertado • **to be ~** estar confuso *or* confundido • **to get ~** (= *muddled up*) hacerse un lío; (= *perplexed*) confundirse, desconcertarse • **his mind is ~** tiene la cabeza trastornada

confusedly [kən'fjuːzɪdlɪ] ADV confusamente

confusing [kən'fjuːzɪŋ] ADJ [*instructions, message*] confuso • **it's a very ~ situation** la situación es muy confusa • **the traffic signs are ~** las señales de tráfico están poco claras • **it's all very ~** es muy difícil de entender

confusingly [kən'fjuːzɪŋlɪ] ADV [*written, explained*] de manera confusa • **~, two of them had the same name** para mayor confusión, dos de ellos tenían el mismo nombre

confusion [kən'fjuːʒən] N **1** (= *disorder*) desorden *m* • **to be in ~** estar en desorden • **to retire in ~** retirarse en desorden
2 (= *perplexity*) confusión *f*, desorientación *f* • **people were in a state of ~** la gente estaba desorientada
3 (= *commotion*) confusión *f* • **in all the ~ I forgot it** lo olvidé en medio de tanta confusión • **I heard a ~ of voices** oí unas voces confusas
4 (= *embarrassment*) • **to be covered in ~** estar avergonzado

confute [kən'fjuːt] VT refutar

conga ['kɒŋgə] N **1** (= *dance*) conga *f*
2 (*also* **conga drum**) congas *fpl*

congeal [kən'dʒiːl] VT coagular, cuajar
VI coagularse, cuajarse

congenial [kən'dʒiːnɪəl] ADJ (*frm*) [*atmosphere, environment, place*] agradable; [*person, company*] simpático, agradable • **to find sb ~** tener simpatía a algn • **the land proved ~ to farming** la tierra resultó ser buena para la agricultura • **he found few people ~ to him** conoció a pocas personas con las que congeniara

congenital [kən'dʒenɪtl] ADJ congénito

congenitally [kən'dʒenɪtlɪ] ADV congénitamente

conger ['kɒŋgər] N (*also* **conger eel**) congrio *m*

congested [kən'dʒestɪd] ADJ **1** [*street, building etc*] atestado de gente • **to get ~ with** llenarse de, atestarse de • **it's getting very ~ in here** esto se está llenando demasiado
2 (*Med*) congestionado

congestion [kən'dʒestʃən] N **1** [*of traffic*] congestión *f*; [*of people*] aglomeración *f*
2 (*Med*) congestión *f*
CPD ▸ **congestion charge(s)** tasa *fsing* por congestión

congestive [kən'dʒestɪv] ADJ (*Med*) congestivo • **~ heart failure** insuficiencia *f* cardíaca congestiva

conglomerate N [kən'glɒmərɪt] (*Comm*) conglomerado *m*
VT [kən'glɒməreɪt] conglomerar, aglomerar
VI [kən'glɒməreɪt] conglomerarse, aglomerarse

conglomeration [kənˌglɒmə'reɪʃən] N conglomeración *f*

Congo ['kɒŋgəʊ] N • **the ~** el Congo • **Republic of the ~** República *f* del Congo

Congolese [ˌkɒŋgəʊ'liːz] ADJ congoleño
N congoleño/a *m/f*

congrats‡ [kən'græts] EXCL (*esp Brit*) ¡enhorabuena!, ¡felicidades!

congratulate [kən'grætjuleɪt] VT felicitar • **to ~ sb (on sth/on doing sth)** felicitar a algn (por algo/por hacer algo) • **my friends ~d me on passing my test** mis amigos me felicitaron por aprobar el examen

congratulation [kənˌgrætjʊ'leɪʃən] N **1** • **letter of ~** carta *f* de felicitación
2 congratulations felicitaciones *fpl* • **~s on sth** felicitaciones *fpl* por algo
EXCL **congratulations!** ¡enhorabuena!, ¡felicidades! • **~s, you have a healthy baby boy ...** enhorabuena, acaba de tener a un niño sano ... • **~s on ...** enhorabuena por ... • **~s on your new job!** ¡enhorabuena por su nuevo trabajo! • **~s to ...** felicidades a ... • **~s to everybody who sent in their ideas** felicidades a todos los que mandaron sus ideas

congratulatory [kən'grætjʊlətərɪ] ADJ de felicitación

congregant ['kɒŋgrɪgənt] (*esp US*) N fiel *mf*

congregate ['kɒŋgrɪgeɪt] VI reunirse, congregarse

congregation [ˌkɒŋgrɪ'geɪʃən] N **1** (*Rel*) fieles *mpl*, feligreses *mpl*
2 (= *assembly*) reunión *f*

congregational [ˌkɒŋgrɪ'geɪʃənl] ADJ congregacionalista

congregationalist [ˌkɒŋgrɪ'geɪʃənəlɪst] N congregacionalista *mf*

congress ['kɒŋgres] N (= *meeting*) congreso *m* • **Congress** (*Pol*) el Congreso
CPD ▸ **congress member** miembro *mf* del congreso, congresista *mf*; ▹ CABINET, CAPITOL

> **CONGRESS**
> En el Congreso de Estados Unidos (**Congress**) se elaboran y aprueban las leyes federales. Consta de dos cámaras: la Cámara de Representantes (**House of Representatives**), cuyos 435 miembros son elegidos cada dos años por voto popular directo y en número proporcional a los habitantes de cada estado, y el Senado (**Senate**), con 100 senadores (**senators**), dos por estado, elegidos por un período de seis años, aunque alrededor de un tercio de los escaños queda libre cada dos años debido al escalonamiento de las elecciones.

congressional [kɒn'greʃənl] ADJ del congreso

congressman ['kɒŋgresmən] N (PL: **congressmen**) (*US*) diputado *m*, miembro *m* del Congreso

congressperson ['kɒŋgrespɜːsən] N (*US*) (*Pol*) congresista *mf*

congresswoman ['kɒŋgresˌwʊmən] N (PL: **congresswomen**) (*US*) diputada *f*, miembro *f* del Congreso

congruence ['kɒŋgrʊəns] N, **congruency** ['kɒŋgrʊənsɪ] N congruencia *f*

congruent ['kɒŋgrʊənt] ADJ congruente

congruity [kɒŋ'gruːɪtɪ] N congruencia *f* (with con)

congruous ['kɒŋgrʊəs] ADJ congruo (with con)

conic ['kɒnɪk] ADJ cónico
CPD ▸ **conic section** sección *f* cónica

conical ['kɒnɪkəl] ADJ cónico

conifer ['kɒnɪfər] N conífera *f*

coniferous [kə'nɪfərəs] ADJ conífero

conjectural [kən'dʒektʃərəl] ADJ conjetural

conjecture [kən'dʒektʃər] N • **it's only ~** son conjeturas, nada más
VT conjeturar
VI conjeturar

conjoin [kən'dʒɔɪn] (*frm*) VT aunar, unir
VI aunarse, unirse

conjoined twin [kənˌdʒɔɪnd'twɪn] N (gemelo/a *m/f*) siamés/esa *m/f*

conjoint [kɒn'dʒɔɪnt] ADJ (*frm*) conjunto

conjointly ['kɒn'dʒɔɪntlɪ] ADV (*frm*) conjuntamente

conjugal ['kɒndʒʊgəl] ADJ [*rights, bliss*] conyugal • **~ duties** deberes *mpl* conyugales, débito *msing* conyugal (*Jur*) • **~ visit** vis a vis* *m*, visita *f* del cónyuge

conjugate ['kɒndʒʊgeɪt] (*Ling*) VT conjugar
VI conjugarse

conjugation [ˌkɒndʒʊ'geɪʃən] N (*Ling*) conjugación *f*

conjunct [kən'dʒʌŋkt] ADJ (*Astron*) en conjunción

conjunction [kən'dʒʌŋkʃən] N **1** (*Ling*) conjunción *f*
2 • **in ~ with** junto con, juntamente con

conjunctive [kən'dʒʌŋktɪv] ADJ conjuntivo

conjunctivitis [kənˌdʒʌŋktɪ'vaɪtɪs] N conjuntivitis *f*

conjuncture [kən'dʒʌŋktʃər] N coyuntura *f*

conjure¹ ['kʌndʒər] VI hacer juegos de manos • **he ~s with handkerchiefs** hace trucos con pañuelos • **a name to ~ with** un personaje importante, una figura destacada
▸ **conjure away** VT + ADV conjurar, hacer desaparecer
▸ **conjure up** VT + ADV **1** [*conjurer*] [+ *rabbit etc*] hacer aparecer
2 (*fig*) [+ *memories, visions*] evocar; [+ *meal*] preparar en un abrir y cerrar de ojos

conjure² [kən'dʒʊər] VT (*liter*) suplicar • **to ~ sb to do sth** suplicar a algn que haga algo

conjurer, conjuror ['kʌndʒərər] N ilusionista *mf*, prestidigitador(a) *m/f*

conjuring ['kʌndʒərɪŋ] N ilusionismo *m*, prestidigitación *f*
CPD ▸ **conjuring trick** juego *m* de manos

conjuror ['kʌndʒərər] N = **conjurer**

conk* [kɒŋk] N **1** (*Brit*) (= *nose*) narigón* *m*
2 (= *blow*) golpe *m*
3 (*US*) (= *head*) coco* *m*, cholla *f* (*Mex**)
▸ **conk out*** VI + ADV **1** (= *break down*) averiarse, fastidiarse*, descomponerse (*LAm*)
2 (= *die*) estirar la pata*; (= *fall asleep*) dormir como un tronco*

conker* ['kɒŋkər] N (*Brit*) castaña *f* de Indias; **conkers** (= *game*) juego *m* de las castañas

Conn ABBR (*US*) = **Connecticut**

connect [kə'nekt] VT **1** (= *join*) conectar; [+ *road, railway, airline*] unir; [+ *pipes, drains*] empalmar (**to a**) • **to ~ sth (up) to the mains** (*Elec*) conectar algo a la red eléctrica

2 (= *install*) [+ *cooker, telephone*] conectar
3 (*Telec*) [+ *caller*] poner, comunicar (*LAm*) **(with** con) • **please ~ me with Mr Lyons** póngame con el Sr. Lyons, por favor • **"I am trying to ~ you"** "estoy intentando ponerle al habla"
4 (= *associate*) vincular, asociar • **to ~ sth/sb (with)** vincular *or* asociar algo/a algn (con) • **I never ~ed you with that** nunca te vinculé *or* asocié con eso, nunca creí que tuvieras nada que ver con eso
(VI) [*trains, planes*] enlazar (**with** con); [*road, pipes, electricity*] empalmar (**with** con)
connected [kə'nektɪd] (ADJ) 1 (= *related*) [*concepts, events*] relacionado • **to be ~ (to** *or* **with)** estar relacionado (con) • **what firm are you ~ with?** ¿con qué empresa estás conectado *or* relacionado? • **are these matters ~?** ¿tienen alguna relación entre sí estas cuestiones? • **to be well ~** estar bien relacionado
2 (*Bot, Jur*) conexo
3 (*fig*) [*argument etc*] conexo
(CPD) ▸ **connected speech** discurso *m* conexo
connecting [kə'nektɪŋ] (ADJ) [*rooms etc*] comunicado • **bedroom with ~ bathroom** habitación comunicada con el baño
(CPD) ▸ **connecting flight** vuelo *m* de enlace ▸ **connecting rod** biela *f*
connection [kə'nekʃən] (N) 1 (*Rail etc*) enlace *m*; (*Elec, Tech*) conexión *f*, empalme *m*; (*Telec*) línea *f*, comunicación *f* • **we missed our ~** perdimos el enlace • **to make a ~** hacer enlace, empalmar • **our ~s with the town are poor** son malas nuestras comunicaciones con la ciudad • **there's a loose ~** (*Elec*) hay un hilo suelto • **we've got a bad ~** (*Telec*) no se oye bien
2 (= *relationship*) relación *f* (**between** entre, **with** con) • **in ~ with** en relación a, con respecto a • **there's no ~ between the two events** no hay ninguna relación *or* conexión entre los dos sucesos • **in this ~** a este respecto • **"no ~ with any other firm"** "ésta es una firma independiente"
3 **connections** (= *relatives*) parientes *mpl*; (= *business connections*) relaciones *fpl*, contactos *mpl* • **we have ~s everywhere** tenemos relaciones con todas partes • **you have to have ~s** hay que tener buenas relaciones
(CPD) ▸ **connection charge, connection fee** cuota *f* de conexión
connective [kə'nektɪv] (ADJ) conjuntivo
(N) conjunción *f*
(CPD) ▸ **connective tissue** tejido *m* conjuntivo
connectivity [ˌkɒnek'tɪvɪtɪ] (N) conectividad *f*
connector [kə'nektəʳ] (N) (*Elec*) conector *m*
connexion [kə'nekʃən] (N) = **connection**
conning tower ['kɒnɪŋˌtaʊəʳ] (N) [*of submarine*] torre *f* de mando
connivance [kə'naɪvəns] (N) 1 (= *tacit consent*) consentimiento *m* (**at** en), connivencia *f* (*frm*) (**at** en) • **with the ~ of** con el consentimiento *or* (*frm*) la connivencia de
2 (= *conspiracy*) connivencia *f* (*frm*), complicidad *f*
connive [kə'naɪv] (VI) 1 (= *condone*) hacer la vista gorda (**at** a)
2 (= *conspire*) confabularse • **to ~ with sb to do sth** confabularse con algn para hacer algo
conniving [kə'naɪvɪŋ] (ADJ) intrigante, mañoso
connoisseur [ˌkɒnə'sɜːʳ] (N) conocedor(a) *m/f*, entendido/a *m/f* • **an art ~** un entendido en arte • **a wine ~** un entendido en vinos, un enólogo
connotation [ˌkɒnəʊ'teɪʃən] (N) connotación *f*
connotative ['kɒnəˌteɪtɪv] (ADJ) connotativo
connote [kɒ'nəʊt] (VT) connotar
connubial [kə'njuːbɪəl] (ADJ) conyugal, connubial
conquer ['kɒŋkəʳ] (VT) [+ *territory, nation etc*] conquistar; [+ *fear, enemy*] vencer
(VI) triunfar
conquering ['kɒŋkərɪŋ] (ADJ) vencedor, victorioso
conqueror ['kɒŋkərəʳ] (N) conquistador(a) *m/f*
conquest ['kɒŋkwest] (N) conquista *f*
conquistador [kɒn'kwɪstədɔːʳ] (N) conquistador *m*
Cons. (ABBR) (*Brit*) = **Conservative**
consanguinity [ˌkɒnsæŋ'gwɪnɪtɪ] (N) consanguinidad *f*
conscience ['kɒnʃəns] (N) conciencia *f* • **in all ~** en conciencia • **bad ~** mala conciencia • **to have a clear ~** tener la conciencia tranquila *or* limpia • **I have a clear ~ about it** tengo la conciencia tranquila *or* limpia al respecto • **with a clear ~** con la conciencia tranquila *or* limpia • **I have a guilty ~ (about it)** me remuerde la conciencia (por ello) • **I could not in ~ say that** en conciencia no podría decir eso • **the ~ of the nation** la voz de la conciencia del país • **to have sth on one's ~** tener algo pesando sobre la conciencia, tener cargo *or* remordimiento de conciencia por algo • **I have it on my ~** me está remordiendo la conciencia por ello • **social ~** conciencia *f* social • **a doctor with a social ~** un médico socialmente concienciado *or* con conciencia social
(CPD) ▸ **conscience money** *dinero que se paga para descargar la conciencia* ▸ **conscience raising** = **consciousness raising**
conscience-stricken ['kɒnʃənsˌstrɪkən] (ADJ) lleno de remordimientos
conscientious [ˌkɒnʃɪ'enʃəs] (ADJ) concienzudo
(CPD) ▸ **conscientious objector** objetor(a) *m/f* de conciencia
conscientiously [ˌkɒnʃɪ'enʃəslɪ] (ADV) concienzudamente
conscientiousness [ˌkɒnʃɪ'enʃəsnɪs] (N) diligencia *f*, escrupulosidad *f*
conscious ['kɒnʃəs] (ADJ) 1 (= *aware*) • **to be ~ of sth/of doing sth** ser consciente de algo/de hacer algo • **to be ~ that** tener (plena) conciencia de que • **to become ~ of sth** darse cuenta de algo • **to become ~ that** darse cuenta de que • **she became ~ of him looking at her** se dio cuenta de que él la miraba • **environmentally ~** consciente de los problemas medioambientales • **politically ~** con conciencia política
2 (= *deliberate*) [*decision*] deliberado; [*prejudice*] consciente; [*error, irony, insult*] intencional, deliberado • **they made a ~ choice** *or* **decision not to have children** decidieron deliberadamente no tener hijos • **he made a ~ effort to look as though he was enjoying himself** se esforzó deliberadamente por aparentar que se estaba divirtiendo
3 (*Med*) consciente • **to be ~** estar consciente, tener conocimiento • **to be fully ~** estar totalmente consciente • **to become ~** recobrar el reconocimiento, volver en sí
4 (*Psych*) [*memory, thought*] consciente • **the ~ mind** la conciencia • **to remain below the level of ~ awareness** quedarse en el subconsciente • **on a ~ level** conscientemente
(N) (*Psych*) • **the ~** la conciencia • **at a level below the ~** por debajo de los niveles de conciencia
-conscious [-ˌkɒnʃəs] (ADJ) (*ending in compounds*) • **security-conscious** consciente de los problemas relativos a la seguridad
consciously ['kɒnʃəslɪ] (ADV) 1 (= *deliberately*) conscientemente, deliberadamente
2 (= *with full awareness*) [*remember, think*] conscientemente • **to be ~ aware of sth** ser plenamente consciente de algo
consciousness ['kɒnʃəsnɪs] (N)
1 (= *awareness*) conciencia *f*, consciencia *f* (**of** de) • **to raise sb's ~ of sth** concienciar a algn sobre algo (*Sp*), concientizar a algn sobre algo (*LAm*)
2 (*Med*) conocimiento *m* • **to lose ~** perder el conocimiento • **to regain ~** recobrar el conocimiento, volver en sí
(CPD) ▸ **consciousness raising** concienciación *f* (*Sp*), concientización *f* (*LAm*)
conscript (N) ['kɒnskrɪpt] recluta *mf*, conscripto/a *m/f* (*LAm*)
(VT) [kən'skrɪpt] (*Mil*) reclutar, llamar a filas
conscripted [kən'skrɪptɪd] (ADJ) [*labourer etc*] reclutado a la fuerza, forzado • **~ troops** reclutas *mpl*, conscriptos *mpl* (*LAm*)
conscription [kən'skrɪpʃən] (N) servicio *m* militar obligatorio, conscripción *f* (*LAm*)
consecrate ['kɒnsɪkreɪt] (VT) consagrar
consecrated ground ['kɒnsɪkreɪtɪdˌgraʊnd] (N) terreno *m* consagrado
consecration [ˌkɒnsɪ'kreɪʃən] (N) consagración *f*
consecutive [kən'sekjʊtɪv] (ADJ)
1 (= *successive*) consecutivo • **on three ~ days** tres días consecutivos *or* seguidos
2 (*Ling*) consecutivo
consecutively [kən'sekjʊtɪvlɪ] (ADV) consecutivamente
consensual [kən'sensjʊəl] (ADJ) [*approach, decision etc*] consensuado; [*sex*] consentido
consensus [kən'sensəs] (N) consenso *m* • **the ~ of opinion** el consenso general
consent [kən'sent] (N) consentimiento *m* • **with the ~ of** con el consentimiento de • **without his ~** sin su consentimiento • **by common ~** de *or* por común acuerdo • **by mutual ~** de *or* por mutuo acuerdo • **the age of ~** la edad en la que es válido el consentimiento en las relaciones sexuales
(VI) • **to ~ (to sth/to do sth)** consentir (en algo/en hacer algo)
consenting [kən'sentɪŋ] (ADJ) • **~ party** parte *f* que da su consentimiento • **between ~ adults** entre personas de edad para consentir
consequence ['kɒnsɪkwəns] (N) 1 (= *result*) consecuencia *f* • **to take the ~s** aceptar las consecuencias • **in ~** por consiguiente, por lo tanto • **in ~ of (which)** como consecuencia de (lo cual)
2 (= *importance*) importancia *f*, trascendencia *f* • **it is of no ~** no tiene importancia, es de poca trascendencia
consequent ['kɒnsɪkwənt] (ADJ) consiguiente
consequential [ˌkɒnsɪ'kwenʃəl] (ADJ)
1 (= *resulting*) consiguiente, resultante • **the moves ~ upon this decision** las medidas consiguientes a *or* resultantes de esta decisión
2 (= *important*) importante
consequentially [ˌkɒnsɪ'kwenʃəlɪ] (ADV) (= *as a result*) como consecuencia
consequently ['kɒnsɪkwəntlɪ] (ADV) por consiguiente, por lo tanto
conservancy [kən'sɜːvənsɪ] (N) conservación *f*
conservation [ˌkɒnsə'veɪʃən] (N)

conservación *f*, protección *f* • **energy ~** la conservación de la energía
CPD ▸ **conservation area** zona *f* declarada de patrimonio histórico-artístico; (= *nature reserve*) zona *f* protegida; ▹ **nature**

conservationism [ˌkɒnsəˈveɪʃənɪzəm] N conservacionismo *m*

conservationist [ˌkɒnsəˈveɪʃənɪst] N conservacionista *mf*, ecologista *mf*

conservatism [kənˈsɜːvətɪzəm] N conservadurismo *m*

Conservative [kənˈsɜːvətɪv] (*Brit*) ADJ (*Pol*) conservador • **~ Party** Partido *m* Conservador
N (*Pol*) conservador(a) *m/f* • **to vote ~** votar a favor del partido Conservador

conservative [kənˈsɜːvətɪv] ADJ
1 (= *conventional*) [*person, suit, colour, ideas*] conservador
2 (= *cautious*) [*attitude, approach, guess*] prudente, cauteloso • **a ~ estimate** un cálculo prudente *or* cauteloso

conservatively [kənˈsɜːvətɪvlɪ] ADV (= *conventionally*) • **he dresses very ~** es muy conservador en su forma de vestir, viste de forma muy conservadora • **~ minded people** gente con ideas muy conservadoras

conservatoire [kənˈsɜːvətwɑːʳ] N conservatorio *m*

conservator [kənˈsɜːvətəʳ] N restaurador(a) *m/f*

conservatory [kənˈsɜːvətrɪ] N invernadero *m*

conserve [kənˈsɜːv] VT [+ *natural resources, environment, historic buildings*] conservar, preservar; [+ *moisture*] conservar; [+ *energy, water*] ahorrar, conservar • **to ~ one's energies** ahorrar (las) energías
N conserva *f*

consider [kənˈsɪdəʳ] VT **1** (= *think about*) [+ *problem, possibility*] considerar, pensar en • **~ how much you owe him** piensa en *or* considera lo que le debes • **to ~ doing sth: have you ever ~ed going by train?** ¿has pensado alguna vez (en) ir en tren?, ¿has considerado alguna vez ir en tren? • **we ~ed cancelling our holiday** pensamos en cancelar nuestras vacaciones • **would you ~ buying it?** ¿te interesa comprarlo? • **I'm ~ing resigning** estoy pensando en dimitir, estoy considerando la posibilidad de dimitir • **he is being ~ed for the post** lo están considerando para el puesto • **we are ~ing the matter** estamos estudiando el asunto • **it is my ~ed opinion that …** después de haberlo pensado *or* considerado detenidamente, creo que … • **to ~ one's position** (*euph*) (= *consider resigning*) pensar en dimitir, estudiar la conveniencia de dimitir • **he refused even to ~ it** se negó a pensarlo *or* considerarlo siquiera • **I wouldn't ~ it for a moment** yo ni me lo plantearía siquiera
2 (= *take into account*) tomar *or* tener en cuenta • **when one ~s that …** cuando uno toma *or* tiene en cuenta que … • **you must ~ other people's feelings** hay que tomar *or* tener en cuenta los sentimientos de los demás • **all things ~ed** pensándolo bien
3 (= *be of the opinion*) considerar • **I ~ that …** considero que …
4 (= *regard as*) considerar • **I ~ it an honour** lo considero un honor • **I ~ the matter closed** para mí el tema está cerrado • **to ~ o.s.:** • **I ~ myself happy** me considero feliz • **to ~ sb to be intelligent** considerar a algn inteligente • **he is ~ed to be the best** se le considera el mejor • **he ~s it a waste of time** lo considera una pérdida de tiempo • **~ yourself lucky!** ¡date por satisfecho! • **~ yourself dismissed** considérese despedido

considerable [kənˈsɪdərəbl] ADJ considerable • **a ~ number of applicants** un número considerable de solicitudes • **a ~ sum of money** una suma considerable de dinero • **they achieved a ~ degree of success** tuvieron un éxito considerable • **we had ~ difficulty** tuvimos bastante dificultad • **I'd been living in England for a** *or* **some ~ time** llevaba bastante tiempo viviendo en Inglaterra • **to a** *or* **some ~ extent** en gran parte • **the building suffered ~ damage** el edificio sufrió daños de consideración

considerably [kənˈsɪdərəblɪ] ADV bastante, considerablemente

considerate [kənˈsɪdərɪt] ADJ [*person, action*] atento, considerado • **to be ~ towards** ser atento con • **it's most ~ of you** es muy amable de su parte

considerately [kənˈsɪdərɪtlɪ] ADV con consideración

consideration [kənˌsɪdəˈreɪʃən] N
1 (= *thought, reflection*) consideración *f* • **after due ~** tras (darle) la debida consideración • **without due ~** sin (darle) la debida consideración • **we are giving the matter our ~** estamos estudiando *or* considerando la cuestión • **in ~ of** en consideración a • **to take sth into ~** tener *or* tomar algo en cuenta *or* consideración • **taking everything into ~** teniendo en cuenta todo • **after some ~, he decided to …** tras considerarlo, decidió … • **the issue is under ~** la cuestión se está estudiando
2 (= *thoughtfulness*) consideración *f* • **as a mark of my ~** en señal de respeto • **out of ~ for sb/sb's feelings** por consideración a algn/los sentimientos de algn • **to show ~ for sb/sb's feelings** respetar a algn/los sentimientos de algn
3 (= *factor*) • **his age is an important ~** su edad es un factor importante • **that is a ~** eso debe tomarse en cuenta • **money is the main ~** el dinero es la consideración principal • **it's of no ~** no tiene importancia
4 (= *payment*) retribución *f* • **for a ~** por una gratificación

considering [kənˈsɪdərɪŋ] PREP teniendo en cuenta, en vista de • **~ the circumstances** teniendo en cuenta las circunstancias
CONJ (*also* **considering that**) en vista de que, teniendo en cuenta que • **~ (that) it was my fault** teniendo en cuenta que la culpa fue mía
ADV después de todo, a fin de cuentas • **I got a good mark, ~** después de todo *or* a fin de cuentas, saqué buena nota

consign [kənˈsaɪn] VT **1** (*Comm*) (= *send*) enviar, consignar
2 (*frm*) (= *commit, entrust*) confiar • **to ~ to oblivion** sepultar en el olvido

consignee [ˌkɒnsaɪˈniː] N consignatario/a *m/f*

consigner [kənˈsaɪnəʳ] N = **consignor**

consignment [kənˈsaɪnmənt] N envío *m*, remesa *f* • **goods on ~** mercancías *fpl* en consignación
CPD ▸ **consignment note** talón *m* de expedición

consignor [kənˈsaɪnəʳ] N remitente *mf*

consist [kənˈsɪst] VI • **to ~ of** constar de, consistir en • **to ~ in sth/in doing sth** consistir en algo/en hacer algo

consistency [kənˈsɪstənsɪ] N **1** (= *constancy*) [*of person, action, behaviour*] coherencia *f*, uniformidad *f*; [*of results*] lo regular • **the manager was impressed by the ~ of her work** el jefe quedó impresionado por la calidad que caracterizaba todo su trabajo
2 (= *cohesion*) [*of argument*] coherencia *f*, lógica *f* • **their statements lack ~** sus declaraciones no concuerdan
3 (= *density*) [*of paste, mixture*] consistencia *f*

consistent [kənˈsɪstənt] ADJ **1** (= *constant*) [*person, action, behaviour*] consecuente, coherente; [*results*] uniforme; [*work, performance*] de calidad constante
2 (= *cohesive*) [*argument*] coherente, lógico • **he made various statements which were not ~** realizó varias declaraciones que no concordaban • **his actions are not ~ with his beliefs** sus actos no son consecuentes con sus ideas • **that is not ~ with what you told me** eso no encaja *or* no concuerda con lo que me dijiste

consistently [kənˈsɪstəntlɪ] ADV
1 (= *regularly*) [*refuse, deny, oppose, support*] sistemáticamente; [*work, perform*] con un nivel de calidad constante • **the quality of this product has been ~ high over the last few years** el nivel de calidad de este producto se ha mantenido durante los últimos años • **the rate of inflation has been ~ low** el nivel de inflación se ha mantenido bajo • **she has had ~ good marks** en general sus notas han sido buenas • **he ~ achieved marks of over 90%** sus notas estaban habitualmente por encima del 90%
2 (= *logically*) [*argue, behave*] consecuentemente • **to act ~** obrar con consecuencia

consolation [ˌkɒnsəˈleɪʃən] N consuelo *m* • **that's one ~** esto es un consuelo, por lo menos • **if it's any ~ to you** si te consuela de algún modo • **it is some ~ to know that …** me reconforta saber que …
CPD ▸ **consolation prize** premio *m* de consolación

consolatory [kənˈsɒlətərɪ] ADJ consolador

console¹ [kənˈsəʊl] VT consolar • **to ~ sb for sth** consolar a algn por algo

console² [ˈkɒnsəʊl] N (= *control panel*) consola *f*
CPD ▸ **console game** juego *m* para videoconsola

consolidate [kənˈsɒlɪdeɪt] VT
1 (= *strengthen*) [+ *position, influence*] consolidar
2 (= *combine*) concentrar, fusionar
VI **1** (= *strengthen*) consolidarse
2 (= *combine*) concentrarse, fusionarse

consolidated [kənˈsɒlɪdeɪtɪd] ADJ consolidado • **~ accounts** cuentas *fpl* consolidadas • **~ balance sheet** hoja *f* de balance consolidado • **~ fund** fondo *m* consolidado

consolidation [kənˌsɒlɪˈdeɪʃən] N
1 (= *strengthening*) consolidación *f*
2 (= *combining*) concentración *f*, fusión *f*

consoling [kənˈsəʊlɪŋ] ADJ consolador, reconfortante

consols [ˈkɒnsɒlz] NPL (*Brit*) (*Econ*) fondos *mpl* consolidados

consommé [ˈkɒnsɒmeɪ] N consomé *m*, caldo *m*

consonance [ˈkɒnsənəns] N consonancia *f*

consonant [ˈkɒnsənənt] N consonante *f*
ADJ • **~ with** de acuerdo *or* en consonancia con

consonantal [ˌkɒnsəˈnæntl] ADJ consonántico

consort [ˈkɒnsɔːt] N consorte *mf* • **prince ~** príncipe *m* consorte
VI [kənˈsɔːt] • **to ~ with sb** (*esp pej*) asociarse con algn

consortium [kənˈsɔːtɪəm] N (PL: **consortia** [kənˈsɔːtɪə]) consorcio *m*

conspectus [kənˈspektəs] N vista *f* general

conspicuous [kənˈspɪkjʊəs] ADJ
1 (= *attracting attention*) [*clothes*] llamativo; [*person, behaviour*] que llama la atención; [*notice, attempt*] visible • **to be ~ by one's/its absence** brillar por su ausencia • **I felt ~ in**

that ridiculous outfit vestido de aquella manera tan ridícula tenía la impresión de que todo el mundo me miraba *or* tenía la impresión de ser el objeto de atención • **I left the keys in a ~ place** dejé las llaves en un lugar bien visible • **to make o.s. ~** llamar la atención
2 (= *noticeable*) [*bravery*] destacado, manifiesto; [*difference*] manifiesto, notorio • **he was ~ for his courage** destacaba por su valor • **a ~ lack of sth** una carencia manifiesta de algo • **the film was a ~ failure/success** la película fue un fracaso/éxito rotundo
(CPD) ▸ **conspicuous consumption** (*Econ*) consumo *m* ostentoso

conspicuously [kən'spɪkjʊəslɪ] (ADV) **1** (= *so as to attract attention*) [*behave, act*] de modo que llama la atención; [*dressed*] de forma muy llamativa
2 (= *noticeably*) [*worried, uncomfortable, embarrassed*] visiblemente • **to be ~ absent** brillar por su ausencia • **he has remained ~ silent on the issue** de forma ostensible, ha guardado silencio respecto al asunto • **she had been ~ successful** obtuvo un éxito rotundo • **they have ~ failed to solve the problem** es muy evidente que no han conseguido resolver el problema

conspiracy [kən'spɪrəsɪ] (N) (= *plotting*) conspiración *f*, conjuración *f*; (= *plot*) complot *m*, conjura *f*
(CPD) ▸ **conspiracy theorist** persona *f* que formula una teoría de la conspiración ▸ **conspiracy theory** teoría *f* de la conspiración, teoría *f* conspirativa

conspirator [kən'spɪrətəʳ] (N) conspirador(a) *m/f*

conspiratorial [kən,spɪrə'tɔːrɪəl] (ADJ) de conspirador

conspiratorially [kən,spɪrə'tɔːrɪəlɪ] (ADV) [*behave*] con complicidad

conspire [kən'spaɪəʳ] (VI) **1** [*people*] conspirar • **to ~ with sb against sth/sb** conspirar con algn contra algo/algn • **to ~ to do sth** conspirar para hacer algo
2 [*events*] • **to ~ against/to do sth** conjurarse *or* conspirar contra/para hacer algo

constable ['kʌnstəbl] (N) (*Brit*) (*also* **police constable**) agente *mf* de policía, policía *mf*; (*as form of address*) señor(a) policía

constabulary [kən'stæbjʊlərɪ] (N) policía *f*

Constance ['kɒnstəns] (N) Constanza

constancy ['kɒnstənsɪ] (N) **1** (= *regularity*) [*of temperature etc*] constancia *f*
2 (= *faithfulness*) fidelidad *f*

constant ['kɒnstənt] (ADJ) **1** (= *unchanging*) [*temperature, velocity*] constante • **to remain ~** permanecer constante
2 (= *continual*) [*quarrels, interruptions, complaints*] constante, continuo • **to be in ~ use** usarse continuamente • **to be in ~ pain** sufrir dolor continuamente
3 (= *faithful*) [*friend, companion*] leal, fiel
(N) (*Math, Phys*) constante *f*
(CPD) ▸ **constant dollar plan** costo *m* promedio en dólares

Constantine ['kɒnstəntaɪn] (N) Constantine

Constantinople [,kɒnstæntɪ'nəʊpl] (N) Constantinopla *f*

constantly ['kɒnstəntlɪ] (ADV) (= *continuously*) constantemente, continuamente • **to be ~ changing** estar cambiando constantemente *or* continuamente • **she's ~ complaining** se está quejando constantemente *or* continuamente • **"gates constantly in use"** "vado permanente"

constellation [,kɒnstə'leɪʃən] (N) constelación *f*

consternation [,kɒnstə'neɪʃən] (N) consternación *f* • **in ~** consternado • **there was general ~** hubo una consternación general

constipate ['kɒnstɪpeɪt] (VT) estreñir

constipated ['kɒnstɪpeɪtɪd] (ADJ) estreñido • **to be ~** estar estreñido

constipation [,kɒnstɪ'peɪʃən] (N) estreñimiento *m*

constituency [kən'stɪtjʊənsɪ] (N) (= *district*) distrito *m* electoral, circunscripción *f* electoral; (= *people*) electorado *m*
(CPD) ▸ **constituency party** partido *m* local

CONSTITUENCY
En el sistema electoral británico, se denomina **Constituency** al distrito o circunscripción electoral y al grupo de electores registrados en él. Cada circunscripción elige a un diputado (**Member of Parliament**), que se halla disponible para las consultas y peticiones de sus electores durante ciertas horas a la semana. Dicho espacio de tiempo se denomina **surgery**.

constituent [kən'stɪtjʊənt] (N) **1** (= *component*) constitutivo *m*, componente *m*
2 (*Pol*) (= *voter*) elector(a) *m/f*
(ADJ) [*part*] constitutivo, integrante
(CPD) ▸ **constituent assembly** cortes *fpl* constituyentes

constitute ['kɒnstɪtjuːt] (VT) **1** (= *amount to*) significar, constituir; (= *make up*) constituir, componer
2 (*frm*) (= *appoint, set up*) constituir • **to ~ o.s. a judge** constituirse en juez

constitution [,kɒnstɪ'tjuːʃən] (N) **1** (*Pol*) constitución *f*
2 (= *health*) constitución *f*

CONSTITUTION
El Reino Unido no tiene una constitución escrita. La Constitución británica está compuesta por el derecho legislado en el Parlamento (**statute law**) y por el derecho consuetudinario (**common law**), además de aquellas normas y prácticas necesarias para el funcionamiento del gobierno. Las leyes constitucionales pueden ser modificadas o derogadas por el Parlamento como cualquier otra ley.
▸ ACT OF PARLIAMENT, COMMON LAW

constitutional [,kɒnstɪ'tjuːʃənl] (ADJ) constitucional
(N) paseo *m*
(CPD) ▸ **constitutional monarchy** monarquía *f* constitucional ▸ **constitutional reform** reforma *f* constitucional ▸ **constitutional law** derecho *m* político

constitutionality [,kɒnstɪtjuːʃə'nælɪtɪ] (*frm*) (N) constitucionalidad *f*

constitutionally [,kɒnstɪ'tjuːʃənəlɪ] (ADV) según la constitución

constrain [kən'streɪn] (VT) (= *oblige*) obligar • **to ~ sb to do sth** obligar a algn a hacer algo • **to feel/be ~ed to do sth** sentirse/verse obligado a hacer algo

constrained [kən'streɪnd] (ADJ) [*atmosphere*] constrictivo; [*voice, manner, smile*] constreñido

constraint [kən'streɪnt] (N) **1** (= *compulsion*) coacción *f*, fuerza *f* • **under ~** obligado (a ello)
2 (= *limit*) restricción *f* • **budgetary ~s** restricciones presupuestarias
3 (= *restraint*) reserva *f*, cohibición *f* • **to feel a certain ~** sentirse algo cohibido

constrict [kən'strɪkt] (VT) [+ *muscle*] oprimir; [+ *vein*] estrangular; [+ *movements*] restringir

constricted [kən'strɪktɪd] (ADJ) [*space*] limitado, reducido; [*freedom, movement*] restringido; (*Phon*) constrictivo • **to feel ~** (*by clothes etc*) sentirse constreñido • **I feel ~ by these regulations** me siento constreñido por estas reglas

constricting [kən'strɪktɪŋ] (ADJ) [*dress, ideology*] estrecho

constriction [kən'strɪkʃən] (N) [*of vein*] estrangulamiento *m*

constrictive [kən'strɪktɪv] (ADJ) = **constricting**

constrictor [kən'strɪktəʳ] (N) constrictor *f*

construct (VT) [kən'strʌkt] construir
(N) ['kɒnstrʌkt] construcción *f*

construction [kən'strʌkʃən] (N) **1** (= *act, structure, building*) construcción *f* • **under ~** • **in course of ~** en construcción
2 (*fig*) (= *interpretation*) interpretación *f* • **to put a wrong ~ on sth** interpretar algo mal • **it depends what ~ one places on his words** depende de cómo se interpreten sus palabras
3 (*Ling*) construcción *f*
(CPD) ▸ **construction company** compañía *f* constructora ▸ **construction engineer** ingeniero/a *m/f* de la construcción ▸ **construction industry** industria *f* de la construcción ▸ **construction site** obra *f* ▸ **construction worker** trabajador(a) *m/f* de la construcción

constructional [kən'strʌkʃənl] (ADJ) estructural • **~ toy** juguete *m* con que se construyen modelos

constructive [kən'strʌktɪv] (ADJ) constructivo

constructively [kən'strʌktɪvlɪ] (ADV) constructivamente

constructivism [kən'strʌktɪvɪzəm] (N) constructivismo *m*

constructivist [kən'strʌktɪvɪst] (ADJ) constructivista
(N) constructivista *mf*

constructor [kən'strʌktəʳ] (N) constructor *m*

construe [kən'struː] (VT) interpretar

consul ['kɒnsəl] (N) (= *diplomatic official*) cónsul *mf* • **~ general** cónsul *mf* general

consular ['kɒnsjʊləʳ] (ADJ) consular

consulate ['kɒnsjʊlɪt] (N) consulado *m*

consulship ['kɒnsəlʃɪp] (N) consulado *m*

consult [kən'sʌlt] (VT) **1** [+ *book, person, doctor*] consultar
2 (*frm*) (= *show consideration for*) [+ *one's interests*] tener en cuenta
(VI) consultar • **to ~ together** reunirse para hacer consultas • **people should ~ more** la gente debería consultar más entre sí • **to ~ with** (*US*) consultar con, aconsejarse con

consultancy [kən'sʌltənsɪ] (N) (*Comm*) consultoría *f*; (*Med*) puesto *m* de especialista
(CPD) ▸ **consultancy fees** (*Comm*) derechos *mpl* de asesoría; (*Med*) derechos *mpl* de consulta

consultant [kən'sʌltənt] (N) **1** (*gen*) consultor(a) *m/f*, asesor(a) *m/f* • **to act as ~ to** asesorar
2 (*Brit*) (*Med*) especialista *mf*
(CPD) ▸ **consultant engineer** ingeniero *mf* consejero ▸ **consultant paediatrician** especialista *mf* en pediatría ▸ **consultant physician** médico *mf* especialista ▸ **consultant psychiatrist** psiquiatra *mf* especialista

consultation [,kɒnsəl'teɪʃən] (N) (= *act*) consulta *f*; (= *meeting*) negociaciones *fpl* • **in ~ with** tras consultar a
(CPD) ▸ **consultation document**

C

documento *m* de consulta ▸ **consultation period** periodo *m* de consulta

consultative [kənˈsʌltətɪv] (ADJ) consultivo • **~ document** documento *m* consultivo • **I was there in a ~ capacity** yo estuve en calidad de asesor

consulting [kənˈsʌltɪŋ] (ADJ) • **~ hours** (*Brit*) (*Med*) horas *fpl* de consulta • **~ room** (*Brit*) (*Med*) consultorio *m*, consulta *f*

consumable [kənˈsjuːməbl] (ADJ) (*Econ etc*) consumible • **~ goods** bienes *mpl* consumibles, artículos *mpl* de consumo

consumables [kənˈsjuːməblz] (NPL) bienes *mpl* consumibles, artículos *mpl* de consumo

consume [kənˈsjuːm] (VT) **1** (= *eat*) consumir, comerse; (= *drink*) consumir, beber
2 (= *use*) [+ *resources, fuel*] consumir; [+ *space, time etc*] ocupar
3 (= *destroy*) (*by fire*) consumir • **the house was ~d by fire** la casa fue consumida *or* arrasada por las llamas • **to be ~d with envy/grief** estar muerto de envidia/pena

consumer [kənˈsjuːməʳ] (N) consumidor(a) *m/f* • **the ~** el consumidor
(CPD) ▸ **consumer behaviour, consumer behavior** (*US*) comportamiento *m* del consumidor ▸ **consumer choice** libertad *f* del consumidor para elegir ▸ **consumer confidence** confianza *f* de los consumidores ▸ **consumer credit** crédito *m* al consumidor ▸ **consumer demand** demanda *f* de consumo ▸ **consumer durables** bienes *mpl* (de consumo) duraderos ▸ **consumer goods** bienes *mpl* de consumo ▸ **consumer group** asociación *f* de consumidores ▸ **consumer price index** índice *m* de precios al consumo ▸ **consumer product** producto *m* al consumidor ▸ **consumer protection** protección *f* del consumidor ▸ **consumer research** estudios *mpl* de mercado ▸ **consumer resistance** resistencia *f* por parte del consumidor ▸ **consumer rights** derechos *mpl* del consumidor ▸ **the consumer society** la sociedad de consumo ▸ **consumer survey** encuesta *f* sobre consumo; ▹ **product** ▸ **consumer watchdog** organismo *m* para la defensa de los consumidores

consumerism [kənˈsjuːmərɪzəm] (N) consumismo *m*

consumerist [kənˈsjuːmərɪst] (ADJ) (*pej*) [*society*] consumista

consuming [kənˈsjuːmɪŋ] (ADJ) arrollador, apasionado; [*passion*] dominante, avasallador

-consuming [-kənˈsjuːmɪŋ] (SUFFIX) • **oil-consuming** consumidor de petróleo • **space-consuming** que ocupa mucho espacio; ▹ **time-consuming**

consummate (ADJ) [kənˈsʌmɪt] consumado; [*skill*] sumo
(VT) [ˈkɒnsʌmeɪt] consumar

consummately [kənˈsʌmətlɪ] (ADV) [*professional, talented*] extremadamente; [*well-made, performed*] perfectamente

consummation [ˌkɒnsʌˈmeɪʃən] (N) consumación *f*

consumption [kənˈsʌmpʃən] (N) **1** [*of food, fuel etc*] consumo *m* • **not fit for human ~** [*food*] no apto para el consumo humano
2† (= *tuberculosis*) tisis *f*

consumptive [kənˈsʌmptɪv] (*Med*) (ADJ) tísico
(N) tísico/a *m/f*

cont. (ABBR) (= **continued**) sigue

contact [ˈkɒntækt] (N) **1** (= *connection*) contacto *m* • **to come into ~ with** tocar; (*violently*) chocar con
2 (= *communication*) comunicación *f* • **to be in ~ with sth/sb** estar en contacto con algo/algn • **to get into ~ with** ponerse en contacto con • **to lose ~ (with sb)** perder el contacto (con algn) • **to make ~ (with sb)** ponerse en contacto (con algn) • **I seem to make no ~ with him** me resulta imposible comunicar con él; ▹ **radio**
3 (*Elec*) contacto *m* • **to make/break a ~** (*in circuit*) hacer/interrumpir el contacto
4 (= *personal connection*) relación *f*; (*pej*) enchufe *m*, cuña *f* (*LAm*), hueso *m* (*Mex**), muñeca *f* (*S. Cone**); (= *intermediary*) contacto *m* • **he has a lot of ~s** tiene muchas relaciones • **business ~s** relaciones *fpl* comerciales • **he rang up one of his business ~s** llamó a uno de sus colegas comerciales • **you have to have a ~ in the business** hay que tener un buen enchufe en el negocio • **he's got good ~s** tiene buenas relaciones
5 = **contact lens**
(VT) (*gen*) contactar con, ponerse en contacto con; (*by telephone etc*) comunicar con • **where can we ~ you?** ¿cómo podemos ponernos en contacto contigo?, ¿dónde podemos encontrarte?
(CPD) ▸ **contact address** dirección *f* de contacto ▸ **contact adhesive** adhesivo *m* de contacto ▸ **contact breaker** (*Elec*) interruptor *m* ▸ **contact centre** (*Brit*), **contact center** (*US*) centro *m* de contacto ▸ **contact details** información *fsing* de contacto ▸ **contact lens** lente *f* de contacto, lentilla *f* ▸ **contact man** intermediario *m* ▸ **contact number** número *msing* de contacto ▸ **contact print** contact *m* ▸ **contact sport** deporte *m* de contacto

contactless [ˈkɒntæktlɪs] (ADJ) [*card, payment, technology*] sin contacto

contagion [kənˈteɪdʒən] (N) contagio *m*

contagious [kənˈteɪdʒəs] (ADJ) contagioso

contain [kənˈteɪn] (VT) (*all senses*) contener • **to ~ o.s.** contenerse

container [kənˈteɪnəʳ] (N) **1** (= *box, jug etc*) recipiente *m*; (= *package, bottle*) envase *m*
2 (*Comm*) (*for transport*) contenedor *m*, contáiner *m*
(CPD) ▸ **container depot** terminal *f* para portacontenedores ▸ **container lorry** portacontenedores *m inv* ▸ **container port** puerto *m* para contenedores ▸ **container ship** portacontenedores *m inv*, buque *m* contenedor ▸ **container terminal** terminal *f* para portacontenedores ▸ **container train** portacontenedores *m inv* ▸ **container transport** transporte *m* en contenedores

containerization [kənˌteɪnəraɪˈzeɪʃən] (N) transporte *m* en contenedores

containerize [kənˈteɪnəraɪz] (VT) (*Comm*) [+ *goods*] transportar en contenedores, contenerizar

containment [kənˈteɪnmənt] (N) (*Pol*) contención *f*

contaminant [kənˈtæmɪnənt] (N) contaminante *m*

contaminate [kənˈtæmɪneɪt] (VT) **1** (*lit*) contaminar • **to be ~d by** contaminarse con *or* de
2 (*fig*) corromper, contaminar

contaminated [kənˈtæmɪneɪtɪd] (ADJ) contaminado

contamination [kənˌtæmɪˈneɪʃən] (N) contaminación *f*

contango [kənˈtæŋgəʊ] (N) (*St Ex*) *aplazamiento de pago hasta el próximo día de ajuste de cuentas*

contd., cont'd (ABBR) (= **continued**) sigue

contemplate [ˈkɒntempleɪt] (VT) **1** (= *gaze at*) contemplar • **I ~ the future with misgiving** el futuro lo veo dudoso
2 (= *consider*) contemplar; (= *reflect upon*) considerar • **we ~d a holiday in Spain** nos planteamos unas vacaciones en España • **he ~d suicide** pensó en suicidarse • **to ~ doing sth** pensar en hacer algo • **when do you ~ doing it?** ¿cuándo se propone hacerlo?
3 (= *expect*) contar con

contemplation [ˌkɒntemˈpleɪʃən] (N) contemplación *f*, meditación *f*

contemplative [kənˈtemplətɪv] (ADJ) contemplativo

contemplatively [kənˈtemplətɪvlɪ] (ADV) pensativamente

contemporaneous [kənˌtempəˈreɪnɪəs] (ADJ) contemporáneo

contemporaneously [kənˌtempəˈreɪnɪəslɪ] (ADV) contemporáneamente

contemporary [kənˈtempərərɪ] (ADJ) contemporáneo • **~ with** contemporáneo de
(N) contemporáneo/a *m/f*

contempt [kənˈtempt] (N) desprecio *m*, desdén *m* • **to hold sth/sb in ~** despreciar algo/a algn • **it's beneath ~** es más que despreciable • **to bring into ~** desprestigiar, envilecer • **to hold in ~** despreciar; (*Jur*) declarar en rebeldía • **~ of court** (*Jur*) desacato *m* (a los tribunales)

contemptible [kənˈtemptəbl] (ADJ) despreciable, desdeñable

contemptuous [kənˈtemptjʊəs] (ADJ) [*person*] desdeñoso (**of** con); [*manner*] despreciativo, desdeñoso; [*gesture*] despectivo • **to be ~ of** desdeñar, menospreciar

contemptuously [kənˈtemptjʊəslɪ] (ADV) desdeñosamente, con desprecio

contend [kənˈtend] (VT) • **to ~ that** afirmar que, sostener que
(VI) • **to ~ (with sb) for sth** competir (con algn) por algo • **we have many problems to ~ with** se nos plantean muchos problemas • **you'll have me to ~ with** tendrás que vértelas conmigo • **he has a lot to ~ with** tiene que enfrentarse a muchos problemas

contender [kənˈtendəʳ] (N) (= *rival*) competidor(a) *m/f*; (*Sport etc*) contendiente *mf*

contending [kənˈtendɪŋ] (ADJ) rival, opuesto

content¹ [kənˈtent] (ADJ) **1** (= *happy*) contento (**with** con) • **to be ~** estar contento • **he is ~ to watch** se conforma *or* se contenta con mirar
2 (= *satisfied*) satisfecho (**with** con)
(N) (= *happiness*) contento *m*; (= *satisfaction*) satisfacción *f* • **to one's heart's ~** hasta hartarse, a más no poder • **you can complain to your heart's ~** protesta cuanto quieras
(VT) (= *make happy*) contentar; (= *satisfy*) satisfacer • **to ~ o.s. with sth/with doing sth** contentarse *or* darse por contento con algo/con hacer algo

content² [ˈkɒntent] (N) **1 contents** [*of box, packet etc*] contenido *msing*; [*of book*] índice *msing* (de materias)
2 (= *subject matter, amount*) contenido *m*
(CPD) ▸ **content provider** proveedor *m* de contenidos ▸ **contents insurance** seguro *m* de contenido ▸ **contents page** índice *m*

contented [kənˈtentɪd] (ADJ) satisfecho, contento

contentedly [kənˈtentɪdlɪ] (ADV) con satisfacción, contentamente

contentedness [kənˈtentɪdnɪs] (N) contento *m*, satisfacción *f*

contention [kənˈtenʃən] (N) **1** (= *strife*) discusión *f*; (= *dissent*) disensión *f* • **teams in ~** equipos rivales
2 (= *point*) opinión *f*, argumento *m* • **it is our ~ that ...** pretendemos que ..., sostenemos que ...

contentious [kənˈtenʃəs] (ADJ) **1** (= *controversial*) [*issue, view, proposal*]

conflictivo, muy discutido
2 (= *argumentative*) [*person*] que le gusta discutir
contentment [kən'tentmənt] N contento *m*, satisfacción *f*
contest N ['kɒntest] (= *struggle*) contienda *f*, lucha *f*; (*Boxing, Wrestling*) combate *m*; (= *competition, quiz*) concurso *m*; (*Sport*) competición *f* • **beauty ~** concurso *m* de belleza • **a fishing ~** una competición de pesca
VT [kən'test] [+ *argument, will etc*] impugnar, rebatir; [+ *election, seat*] presentarse como candidato/a a; [+ *legal suit*] defender • **I ~ your right to do that** pongo en tela de juicio que usted tenga el derecho de hacer eso • **the seat was not ~ed** no hubo disputa por el escaño, en las elecciones se presentó un solo candidato
VI [kən'test] • **to ~ against** contender con • **they are ~ing for a big prize** se disputan un premio importante
contestant [kən'testənt] N (*in competition*) concursante *mf*; (*Sport etc*) contrincante *mf*, contendiente *mf*
context ['kɒntekst] N contexto *m* • **in/out of ~** en/fuera de contexto • **we must see this in ~** tenemos que ver esto en su contexto • **to put sth in ~** poner algo en su contexto • **it was taken out of ~** fue sacado de su contexto
contextual [kən'tekstjʊəl] ADJ contextual
contextualize [kən'tekstjʊəlaɪz] VT contextualizar
contiguity ['kɒntɪgju:ɪtɪ] N contigüidad *f*
contiguous [kən'tɪgjʊəs] ADJ contiguo (to a)
continence ['kɒntɪnəns] N continencia *f*
continent¹ ['kɒntɪnənt] ADJ continente
continent² ['kɒntɪnənt] N **1** (*Geog*) continente *m*
2 (*Brit*) • **the Continent** el continente europeo, Europa *f* (continental) • **on the Continent** en Europa (continental)
continental [ˌkɒntɪ'nentl] ADJ **1** (*Geog*) continental
2 (*Brit*) (= *European*) continental, europeo
N (*Brit*) europeo/a *m/f* (continental)
CPD ▸ **continental breakfast** desayuno *m* estilo europeo ▸ **continental drift** deriva *f* continental ▸ **continental quilt** edredón *m* ▸ **continental shelf** plataforma *f* continental
contingency [kən'tɪndʒənsɪ] N eventualidad *f*, contingencia *f* • **to provide for every ~** tener en cuenta cualquier eventualidad *or* contingencia • **should the ~ arise** en caso de presentarse la eventualidad • **£50 for contingencies** 50 libras en caso de que surja una eventualidad *or* para gastos imprevistos
CPD ▸ **contingency funds** fondos *mpl* para imprevistos ▸ **contingency planning** planificación *f* para una eventual emergencia ▸ **contingency plans** medidas *fpl* para casos de emergencia
contingent [kən'tɪndʒənt] ADJ • **to be ~ upon** depender de
N **1** (*Mil*) contingente *m*
2 (= *group*) representación *f*
continual [kən'tɪnjʊəl] ADJ (= *continuous*) continuo; (= *persistent*) constante
continually [kən'tɪnjʊəlɪ] ADV continuamente, constantemente
continuance [kən'tɪnjʊəns] N continuación *f*
continuation [kənˌtɪnjʊ'eɪʃən] N
1 (= *maintenance*) prosecución *f*; (= *resumption*) reanudación *f*
2 (= *sth continued*) prolongación *f*; (= *story, episode*) continuación *f*

continue [kən'tɪnju:] VT **1** (= *carry on*) [+ *policy, tradition*] seguir
2 (= *resume*) [+ *story etc*] reanudar, continuar • **~d on page ten** sigue en la página diez • **to be ~d** continuará
VI **1** (= *carry on*) continuar • **"and so," he ~d** —y de este modo —continuó • **to ~ doing** *or* **to do sth** continuar *or* seguir haciendo algo • **she ~d talking to her friend** continuó *or* siguió hablando con su amiga • **to ~ on one's way** seguir su camino • **to ~ with sth** seguir con algo
2 (= *remain*) seguir • **to ~ in office** seguir en su puesto • **to ~ in a place** seguir en un sitio
3 (= *extend*) prolongarse, seguir • **the road ~s for two miles** la carretera se prolonga *or* sigue dos millas más • **the forest ~s to the sea** el bosque se prolonga *or* sigue hasta el mar
continuing [kən'tɪnjʊɪŋ] ADJ [*argument*] irresoluto; [*correspondence*] continuado
CPD ▸ **continuing education** *cursos de enseñanza para adultos*
continuity [ˌkɒntɪ'nju:ɪtɪ] N continuidad *f*
CPD ▸ **continuity announcer** locutor(a) *m/f* de continuidad ▸ **continuity man/girl** (*Cine*) secretario/a *m/f* de rodaje
continuo [kən'tɪnjʊəʊ] N continuo *m*
continuous [kən'tɪnjʊəs] ADJ continuo
CPD ▸ **continuous assessment** evaluación *f* continua ▸ **continuous (feed) paper** papel *m* continuo ▸ **continuous inventory** inventario *m* continuo ▸ **continuous performance** (*in cinema*) sesión *f* continua ▸ **continuous stationery** papel *m* continuo
continuously [kən'tɪnjʊəslɪ] ADV continuamente
continuum [kən'tɪnjʊəm] N (PL: **continuums** *or* **continua**) continuo *m*
contort [kən'tɔ:t] VT retorcer
contortion [kən'tɔ:ʃən] N (= *act*) retorcimiento *m*; (= *movement*) contorsión *f*
contortionist [kən'tɔ:ʃənɪst] N contorsionista *mf*
contour ['kɒntʊə^r] N contorno *m*
CPD ▸ **contour flying** vuelo *m* rasante ▸ **contour line** curva *f* de nivel ▸ **contour map** plano *m* acotado
contoured ['kɒntʊəd] ADJ [*surface, seat*] contorneado
contra... ['kɒntrə] PREFIX contra...
contraband ['kɒntrəbænd] N contrabando *m*
CPD de contrabando
contrabass [ˌkɒntrə'beɪs] N contrabajo *m*
contrabassoon [ˌkɒntrəbə'su:n] N contrafagot *m*
contraception [ˌkɒntrə'sepʃən] N contracepción *f*, anticoncepción *f*
contraceptive [ˌkɒntrə'septɪv] ADJ anticonceptivo
N anticonceptivo *m*, contraceptivo *m*
CPD ▸ **contraceptive pill** píldora *f* anticonceptiva
contract N ['kɒntrækt] **1** (= *document*) contrato *m* • **~ of employment** *or* **service** contrato *m* de trabajo • **breach of ~** incumplimiento *m* de contrato • **by ~** por contrato • **to enter into a ~ (with sb) (to do sth/for sth)** firmar un contrato (con algn) (para hacer algo/de algo) • **to place a ~ with** dar un contrato a • **to sign a ~** firmar un contrato • **to put work out to ~** sacar una obra a contrato • **to be under ~ to do sth** hacer algo bajo contrato • **they are under ~ to X** tienen contrato con X, tienen obligaciones contractuales con X
2 (*fig*) • **there's a ~ out for him** le han puesto precio

VT [kən'trækt] **1** (= *acquire*) [+ *disease, debt*] contraer; [+ *habit*] tomar, adquirir
2 (= *enter into*) [+ *alliance*] entablar, establecer; [+ *marriage*] contraer
3 (*Ling*) (= *shorten*) contraer
VI [kən'trækt] **1** (= *become smaller*) [*metal*] contraerse, encogerse
2 [*muscles, face*] contraerse
3 (*Ling*) [*word, phrase*] contraerse
4 (*Comm*) • **to ~ (with sb) to do sth** comprometerse por contrato (con algn) a hacer algo • **to ~ for** contratar
CPD ['kɒntrækt] ▸ **contract bridge** bridge *m* de contrato ▸ **contract date** fecha *f* contratada, fecha *f* de contrato ▸ **contract killer** asesino *m* a sueldo ▸ **contract killing** asesinato *m* pagado ▸ **contract price** precio *m* contractual, precio *m* contratado ▸ **contract work** trabajo *m* bajo contrato
▸ **contract in** VI + ADV tomar parte (**to** en)
▸ **contract out** VT + ADV • **this work is ~ed out** este trabajo se hace fuera de la empresa con un contrato aparte
VI + ADV (*Brit*) optar por no tomar parte (**of** en)
contracted [kən'træktɪd] ADJ **1** (*Ling*) contraído
2 [*brow*] fruncido
contracting [kən'træktɪŋ] ADJ • **~ party** contratante *mf*
contraction [kən'trækʃən] N contracción *f*
contractor [kən'træktə^r] N contratista *mf*
contractual [kən'træktʃʊəl] ADJ [*duty, obligation*] contractual
CPD ▸ **contractual liability** responsabilidad *f* contractual
contractually [kən'træktʃʊəlɪ] ADV contractualmente • **a ~ binding agreement** un acuerdo vinculante por contrato • **we are ~ bound to finish it** estamos obligados a terminarlo por contrato
contradict [ˌkɒntrə'dɪkt] VT (= *be contrary to*) contradecir; (= *declare to be wrong*) desmentir; (= *argue*) replicar, discutir • **don't ~ me!** ¡no me repliques!
contradiction [ˌkɒntrə'dɪkʃən] N contradicción *f* • **to be a ~ in terms** ser contradictorio
contradictory [ˌkɒntrə'dɪktərɪ] ADJ contradictorio
contradistinction [ˌkɒntrədɪs'tɪŋkʃən] N • **in ~ to** a diferencia de
contraflow ['kɒntrəfləʊ] N (*Brit*) (*Aut*) (*also* **contraflow system**) sistema *m* de contracorriente
CPD ▸ **contraflow lane** carril *m* en sentido contrario
contraindication [ˌkɒntrəˌɪndɪ'keɪʃən] N contraindicación *f*
contralto [kən'træltəʊ] N (PL: **contraltos** *or* **contralti** [kən'træltɪ]) (= *person*) contralto *f*
CPD [*voice*] de contralto
contraption* [kən'træpʃən] N (= *gadget*) artilugio *m*, aparato *m*; (= *vehicle*) armatoste *m*
contrapuntal [ˌkɒntrə'pʌntl] ADJ de contrapunto
contrarian [kən'trɛərɪən] (*frm*) ADJ inconformista
N *persona que deliberadamente lleva la contraria* • **he is by nature a ~** por naturaleza le gusta llevar la contraria
contrarily [kən'trɛərɪlɪ] ADV (= *perversely*) tercamente
contrariness [kən'trɛərɪnɪs] N (= *perverseness*) terquedad *f*
contrariwise [kən'trɛərɪwaɪz] ADV (= *on the contrary*) al contrario; (= *on the other hand*) por otra parte; (= *in opposite direction*) en sentido

contrario; (*= the other way round*) a la inversa

contrary ['kɒntrərɪ] ADJ **1** [*direction*] contrario; [*opinions*] opuesto • **~ to** en contra de, contrario a • **~ to what we thought** en contra de lo que pensábamos
2 [kən'treərɪ] (*= perverse*) terco
N contrario *m* • **on the ~** al contrario, todo lo contrario • **quite the ~** muy al contrario • **he holds the ~** él sostiene lo contrario • **the ~ seems to be true** parece que es al revés • **I know nothing to the ~** yo no sé nada en sentido contrario • **unless we hear to the ~** a no ser que nos digan lo contrario

contrast N ['kɒntrɑːst] (*gen*) contraste *m* • **in ~ to** *or* **with** a diferencia de, en contraste con • **to form a ~ to** *or* **with** contrastar con
VT [kən'trɑːst] • **to ~ with** comparar con, contrastar con
VI [kən'trɑːst] • **to ~ with** contrastar con, hacer contraste con

contrasting [kən'trɑːstɪŋ] ADJ [*opinion*] opuesto; [*colour*] que hace contraste

contrastive [kən'trɑːstɪv] ADJ (*Ling*) contrastivo

contravene [ˌkɒntrə'viːn] VT (*= infringe*) [*+ law*] contravenir; (*= go against*) ir en contra de; (*= dispute*) oponerse a

contravention [ˌkɒntrə'venʃən] N contravención *f*

contretemps ['kɒntrətɒm] N (PL: **contretemps**) contratiempo *m*, revés *m*

contribute [kən'trɪbjuːt] VT [*+ money, ideas*] contribuir, aportar (*esp LAm*); [*+ facts, information etc*] aportar; [*+ help*] prestar; [*+ article to a newspaper*] escribir • **she ~d £10 to the collection** contribuyó con 10 libras a la colecta
VI (*to charity, collection*) contribuir (**to** a); (*to newspaper*) colaborar (**to** en); (*to discussion*) intervenir (**to** en); (*= help in bringing sth about*) contribuir • **everyone ~d to the success of the play** todos contribuyeron al éxito de la obra • **it all ~d to the muddle** todo sirvió para aumentar la confusión

contribution [ˌkɒntrɪ'bjuːʃən] N (*= money*) contribución *f*, aporte *m* (*esp LAm*); (*to journal*) artículo *m*, colaboración *f*; (*to discussion*) intervención *f*, aportación *f*; [*of information etc*] aportación *f*; (*to pension fund*) cuota *f*, cotización *f*

contributor [kən'trɪbjʊtəʳ] N [*of money*] persona *f* que contribuye; [*of taxes*] contribuyente *mf*; (*to journal*) colaborador(a) *m/f*

contributory [kən'trɪbjʊtərɪ] ADJ [*cause, factor*] que contribuye, contribuyente • **~ pension scheme** plan *m* cotizable de jubilación

contrite ['kɒntraɪt] ADJ arrepentido; (*Rel*) contrito

contritely ['kɒntraɪtlɪ] ADV [*say etc*] en tono arrepentido

contrition [kən'trɪʃən] N arrepentimiento *m*; (*Rel*) contrición *f*

contrivance [kən'traɪvəns] N (*= machine, device*) artilugio *m*, aparato *m*; (*= invention*) invención *f*, invento *m*; (*= stratagem*) estratagema *f*

contrive [kən'traɪv] VT [*+ plan, scheme*] inventar, idear • **to ~ a means of doing sth** inventar una manera de hacer algo
VI • **to ~ to do** (*= manage, arrange*) lograr hacer; (*= try*) procurar hacer

contrived [kən'traɪvd] ADJ artificial

control [kən'trəʊl] N **1** (*= command*) control *m* (**over** sobre) • **troops regained ~ of the capital** las tropas recuperaron el control de la capital • **he is giving up ~ of the company** va a ceder el control de la empresa • **to gain ~ of** [*+ company, territory*] hacerse con el control de • **they have no ~ over their pupils** no pueden controlar a sus alumnos • **to be in ~ (of sth)**: • **who is in ~?** ¿quién manda? • **they are in complete ~ of the situation** tienen la situación totalmente controlada *or* dominada • **people feel more in ~ of their lives** la gente se siente más dueña de su vida, la gente siente que tiene mayor control de su vida • **his party has lost ~ of the Senate** su partido perdió el control del Senado • **to take ~ of a company** hacerse con el control de una empresa • **it was time to take ~ of her life again** era hora de volver a tomar las riendas de su vida • **under British ~** bajo dominio *or* control británico • **to be under private ~** estar en manos de particulares
2 (*= power to restrain*) control *m* • **due to circumstances beyond our ~** debido a circunstancias ajenas a nuestra voluntad • **to lose ~ (of o.s.)** perder el control *or* dominio de uno mismo • **he lost ~ of the car** perdió el control del coche • **to be out of ~** estar fuera de control • **the children were getting out of ~** los niños se estaban descontrolando • **the car went out of ~** el coche quedó fuera de control • **everything is under ~** todo está bajo control • **I brought my temper under ~** dominé *or* controlé el genio • **to bring** *or* **get a fire under ~** conseguir dominar *or* controlar un incendio • **to keep sth/sb under ~** mantener algo/a algn bajo control
3 (*= restraint*) restricción *f* • **they want greater ~s on arms sales** quieren mayores restricciones en la venta de armamento • **arms ~** control *m* de armamentos • **birth ~** control *m* de la natalidad • **price/wage ~** reglamentación *f or* control *m* de precios/salarios
4 controls (*Tech*) mandos *mpl* • **to be at the ~s** estar a (cargo de) los mandos • **to take over the ~s** hacerse cargo de los mandos
5 (*= knob, switch*) botón *m* • **volume ~** botón *m* del volumen
6 (*in experiment*) testigo *m*
7 (*= checkpoint*) control *m* • **an agreement to abolish border ~s** un acuerdo para eliminar los controles en las fronteras • **passport ~** control *m* de pasaportes
8 (*Sport*) (*= mastery*) dominio *m* • **his ball ~ is very good** su dominio del balón es muy bueno, domina bien el balón
VT **1** (*= command*) [*+ country, territory, business, organization*] controlar
2 (*= restrain*) [*+ crowd, child, animal, disease*] controlar; [*+ fire, emotions, temper*] controlar, dominar • **to ~ the spread of malaria** contener la propagación de la malaria • **to ~ o.s.** controlarse, dominarse • **~ yourself!** ¡contrólese!, ¡domínese!
3 (*= regulate*) [*+ activity, prices, wages, expenditure*] controlar, regular; [*+ traffic*] dirigir • **legislation to ~ immigration** legislación para controlar *or* regular la inmigración • **he was trying to ~ the conversation** estaba intentando llevar las riendas de la conversación
4 (*= operate*) [*+ machine, vehicle*] manejar, controlar; [*+ horse*] controlar, dominar
CPD ▸ **control column** palanca *f* de mando ▸ **control freak*** • **he's a total ~ freak** tiene la manía de controlarlo todo ▸ **control group** (*in experiment*) grupo *m* testigo ▸ **control key** (*Comput*) tecla *f* de control ▸ **control knob** (*Rad, TV*) botón *m* de mando ▸ **control panel** tablero *m* de control ▸ **control room** (*Mil, Naut*) sala *f* de mandos; (*Rad, TV*) sala *f* de control ▸ **control tower** (*Aer*) torre *f* de control

controllable [kən'trəʊləbl] ADJ controlable

controlled [kən'trəʊld] ADJ **1** (*= restrained*) [*emotion*] contenido • **she was very ~** tenía gran dominio de sí misma • **she spoke in a ~ voice** al hablar, su voz no reveló lo que sentía
2 (*= regulated*) controlado • **~ economy** economía *f* dirigida • **~ explosion** explosión *f* controlada
3 (*= restricted*) [*drug, substance*] *que se dispensa únicamente con receta médica*

-controlled [kən'trəʊld] ADJ (*ending in compounds*) • **a Labour-controlled council** un ayuntamiento laborista *or* gobernado por los laboristas • **a government-controlled organization** una organización bajo control gubernamental • **computer-controlled equipment** equipamiento computerizado

controller [kən'trəʊləʳ] N (*Comm*) interventor(a) *m/f*; (*Aer*) controlador(a) *m/f* • **air-traffic ~** controlador(a) *m/f* aéreo/a

controlling [kən'trəʊlɪŋ] ADJ **1** [*factor*] determinante
2 (*Econ*) • **a ~ interest** una participación mayoritaria

controversial [ˌkɒntrə'vɜːʃəl] ADJ controvertido, polémico • **euthanasia is a ~ subject** la eutanasia es un tema controvertido *or* polémico

controversially [ˌkɒntrə'vɜːʃəlɪ] ADV de forma controvertida, de forma polémica

controversy [kɒn'trɒvəsɪ] N controversia *f*, polémica *f*; (*= debate*) polémica *f* • **there was a lot of ~ about it** hubo mucha controversia *or* polémica en torno a eso • **to cause ~** ocasionar controversia *or* polémica

controvert ['kɒntrəvɜːt] VT contradecir

contumacious [ˌkɒntjʊ'meɪʃəs] ADJ (*frm*) contumaz

contumaciously [ˌkɒntjʊ'meɪʃəslɪ] ADV (*frm*) contumazmente

contumacy ['kɒntjʊməsɪ] N (*frm*) contumacia *f*

contumely ['kɒntjʊmɪlɪ] N (*frm*) contumelia *f*

contuse [kən'tjuːz] VT (*Med*) contusionar

contusion [kən'tjuːʒən] N (*Med*) contusión *f*

conundrum [kə'nʌndrəm] N (*= riddle*) acertijo *m*, adivinanza *f*; (*= problem*) enigma *m*

conurbation [ˌkɒnɜː'beɪʃən] N (*Brit*) conurbación *f*

convalesce [ˌkɒnvə'les] VI convalecer

convalescence [ˌkɒnvə'lesəns] N convalecencia *f*

convalescent [ˌkɒnvə'lesənt] ADJ convaleciente
N convaleciente *mf*
CPD ▸ **convalescent home** clínica *f* de reposo

convection [kən'vekʃən] N convección *f*
CPD ▸ **convection oven** horno *m* de convección

convector [kən'vektəʳ] N (*also* **convector heater, convection heater**) calentador *m* de convección

convene [kən'viːn] VT convocar
VI reunirse

convener [kən'viːnəʳ] N (*esp Brit*) coordinador(a) *m/f* sindical

convenience [kən'viːniəns] N **1** (*= comfort*) comodidad *f*; (*= advantage*) ventaja *f*, provecho *m* • **at your earliest ~** tan pronto como le sea posible • **you can do it at your own ~** puede hacerlo cuando le venga mejor *or* (*LAm*) le convenga • **for your ~ an envelope is enclosed** para facilitar su contestación adjuntamos un sobre • **it is a great ~ to be so**

close resulta muy práctico estar tan cerca
2 (= *amenity*) comodidad *f*, confort *m*;
▷ **public, modern**
CPD ▸ **convenience foods** comidas *fpl* fáciles de preparar; (= *ready-cooked meals*) platos *mpl* preparados ▸ **convenience store** tienda *f* de conveniencia, chino* *m* (*Sp*)
convenient [kən'viːnɪənt] ADJ **1** (= *suitable*) conveniente; [*tool, device*] práctico, útil; [*size*] idóneo, cómodo • **if it is ~ to you** si le viene bien • **when it is ~ for you** cuando le venga bien • **would tomorrow be ~?** ¿le viene bien mañana? • **is it ~ to call tomorrow?** ¿le viene bien llamar mañana? • **it is ~ to live here** resulta práctico vivir aquí • **her death was certainly ~ for him** (*iro*) es cierto que su muerte fue oportuna para él • **at a ~ moment** en un momento oportuno • **we looked for a ~ place to stop** buscamos un sitio apropiado para parar • **it's not a ~ time for me** a esa hora no me viene bien
2 (= *near*) [*place*] bien situado, accesible • **the house is ~ for the shops** la casa está muy cerca de las tiendas • **the hotel is ~ for the airport** el hotel está bien situado con respecto al aeropuerto • **he put it on a ~ chair** lo puso en una silla que estaba a mano
conveniently [kən'viːnɪəntlɪ] ADV (= *handily*) convenientemente; (= *suitably*) [*time*] oportunamente • **the house is ~ situated** la casa está en un sitio muy práctico • **it fell ~ close** cayó muy cerca • **when you ~ can do so** cuando puedas hacerlo sin que te cause molestia • **he very ~ forgot to write it down** (*iro*) muy oportunamente *or* mira por donde, se olvidó de apuntarlo (*iro*)
convenor [kən'viːnəʳ] N = **convener**
convent ['kɒnvənt] N convento *m*
CPD ▸ **convent girl** chica *f* de colegio de monjas ▸ **convent school** colegio *m* de monjas
convention [kən'venʃən] N **1** (= *custom*) convención *f* • **you must follow ~** hay que seguir los convencionalismos
2 (= *meeting*) asamblea *f*, congreso *m*
3 (= *agreement*) convenio *m*, convención *f*
conventional [kən'venʃənl] ADJ [*behaviour, tastes, weapons, method*] convencional; [*person*] tradicional, convencional; [*belief, values*] tradicional; [*style, clothes*] clásico, tradicional • **~ medicine** la medicina tradicional *or* convencional • **she was not beautiful in the ~ sense of the word** no era una belleza en el sentido generalmente aceptado de la palabra • **~ wisdom** (*frm*) la opinión convencional
conventionalism [kən'venʃənəlɪzəm] N convencionalismo *m*
conventionally [kən'venʃənəlɪ] ADV [*dress, behave*] de manera convencional; [*produced, grown*] de manera tradicional • **~ educated students** estudiantes educados de manera convencional *or* tradicional • **~ beautiful women** mujeres con una belleza convencional *or* clásica
conventioneer [kən,venʃə'nɪəʳ] N (*esp US*) asistente *mf* a un congreso, congresista *mf*
converge [kən'vɜːdʒ] VI converger, convergir • **the crowd ~d on the square** la muchedumbre se dirigió a la plaza
convergence [kən'vɜːdʒəns] N convergencia *f*
convergent [kən'vɜːdʒənt], **converging** [kən'vɜːdʒɪŋ] ADJ convergente
conversant [kən'vɜːsənt] ADJ • **~ with** versado en, familiarizado con • **to become ~ with** familiarizarse con
conversation [,kɒnvə'seɪʃən] N conversación *f*, plática *f* (*LAm*) • **we had a long ~** tuvimos una larga conversación • **to have a ~ with sb** conversar *or* (*LAm*) platicar con algn • **what was your ~ about?** ¿de qué hablabas? • **I said it just to make ~** lo dije solo por decir algo
CPD ▸ **conversation class** clase *f* de conversación • **a Spanish ~ class** una clase de conversación en español ▸ **conversation mode** (*Comput*) modo *m* de conversación ▸ **conversation piece** • **it was a ~ piece** fue tema de conversación ▸ **conversation stopper*** • **that was a ~ stopper*** eso nos *etc* dejó a todos sin saber qué decir
conversational [,kɒnvə'seɪʃənl] ADJ [*style, tone*] familiar • **her ~ skills were somewhat lacking** no era muy buena conversadora • **he has the ~ skills of a two-year-old** habla como un niño de dos años
CPD ▸ **conversational mode** (*Comput*) modo *m* de conversación
conversationalist [,kɒnvə'seɪʃnəlɪst] N conversador(a) *m/f* • **to be a good ~** brillar en la conversación • **he's not much of a ~** no es muy buen conversador
conversationally [,kɒnvə'seɪʃnəlɪ] ADV en tono familiar
converse[1] [kən'vɜːs] VI • **to ~ (with sb) (about sth)** conversar *or* (*LAm*) platicar (con algn) (sobre algo) • **to ~ by signs** hablar por señas
converse[2] ['kɒnvɜːs] N (*Math, Logic*) proposición *f* recíproca; (*gen*) inversa *f* • **but the ~ is true** pero la verdad es al revés
ADJ contrario, opuesto; (*Logic*) recíproco
conversely [kɒn'vɜːslɪ] ADV a la inversa
conversion [kən'vɜːʃən] N **1** (*gen*) (*Rel*) conversión *f* (**into** en, **to** a)
2 (= *house conversion*) reforma *f*, remodelación *f*
3 (*Rugby, American Ftbl*) transformación *f*
4 (*Jur*) apropiación *f* ilícita
CPD ▸ **conversion kit** equipo *m* de conversión ▸ **conversion (loan) stock** obligaciones *fpl* convertibles ▸ **conversion table** tabla *f* de equivalencias
convert ['kɒnvɜːt] N converso/a *m/f* • **to become a ~** convertirse, hacerse converso
VT [kən'vɜːt] **1** [+ *appliance*] adaptar; [+ *house*] reformar, convertir (**into** en); (*Econ*) [+ *currency*] convertir (**to, into** en); (*Rel*) convertir (**to** a); (*fig*) convencer (**to** a) • **to ~ sth into** convertir algo en, transformar algo en
2 (*Rugby, US Football*) transformar
3 (*Jur*) apropiarse ilícitamente (**to one's own use** para uso propio)
VI [kən'vɜːt] convertirse (**to** a)
converted [kən'vɜːtɪd] ADJ [*barn, loft*] reformado; ▷ **preach**
converter [kən'vɜːtəʳ] N (*Elec*) convertidor *m*
convertibility [kən,vɜːtə'bɪlɪtɪ] N convertibilidad *f*
convertible [kən'vɜːtəbl] ADJ [*currency*] convertible; [*car*] descapotable; [*settee*] transformable
N (= *car*) descapotable *m*
CPD ▸ **convertible debenture** obligación *f* convertible ▸ **convertible loan stock** obligaciones *fpl* convertibles
convertor [kən'vɜːtəʳ] = **converter**
convex ['kɒn'veks] ADJ convexo
convexity [kɒn'veksɪtɪ] N convexidad *f*
convey [kən'veɪ] VT **1** [+ *goods, oil*] transportar, llevar; [+ *sound, smell*] llevar; [+ *current*] transmitir; (*frm*) [+ *person*] conducir, acompañar (*LAm*)
2 [+ *thanks, congratulations*] comunicar; [+ *meaning, ideas*] expresar • **to ~ to sb that …** comunicar a algn que … • **the name ~s nothing to me** el nombre no me dice nada • **what does this music ~ to you?** ¿qué es lo que te evoca esta música?
3 (*Jur*) traspasar, transferir
conveyance [kən'veɪəns] N **1** (= *act*) (*no pl*) transporte *m*, transmisión *f*; (*Jur*) [*of property*] traspaso *m*
2 (*frm*) (= *vehicle*) vehículo *m*, medio *m* de transporte • **public ~** vehículo *m* de servicio público
3 (*Jur*) (= *deed*) escritura *f* de traspaso
conveyancer [kən'veɪənsəʳ] N (*Brit*) (*Jur*) *persona que formaliza el traspaso de la propiedad de inmuebles*, ≈ notario/a *m/f*
conveyancing [kən'veɪənsɪŋ] N (*Brit*) (*Jur*) preparación *f* de escrituras de traspaso
conveyor [kən'veɪəʳ] N portador *m*, transportador *m*; (= *belt*) = **conveyor belt**
CPD ▸ **conveyor belt** cinta *f* transportadora
convict ['kɒnvɪkt] N (= *prisoner*) presidiario/a *m/f*
VT [kən'vɪkt] declarar culpable (**of** de), condenar • **a ~ed murderer** un asesino convicto y confeso • **he was ~ed of drunken driving** fue condenado por conducir en estado de embriaguez
VI [kən'vɪkt] [*jury*] condenar
CPD ['kɒnvɪkt] ▸ **convict settlement** colonia *f* de presidiarios
conviction [kən'vɪkʃən] N **1** (*Jur*) condena *f* • **there were 12 ~s for theft** hubo 12 condenas por robo • **to have no previous ~s** no tener antecedentes penales
2 (= *belief*) convicción *f*, creencia *f* • **it is my ~ that …** creo firmemente que …
3 (= *persuasion, persuasiveness*) • **he said with ~** dijo con convicción • **without much ~** no muy convencido • **to carry ~** ser convincente • **open to ~** dispuesto a dejarse convencer
convince [kən'vɪns] VT convencer • **to ~ sb (of sth/that)** convencer a algn (de algo/de que) • **I am not ~d** no estoy convencido, no me convence
convinced [kən'vɪnst] ADJ [*Christian etc*] convencido
convincing [kən'vɪnsɪŋ] ADJ convincente
convincingly [kən'vɪnsɪŋlɪ] ADV de forma convincente
convivial [kən'vɪvɪəl] ADJ [*person, company*] sociable, agradable; [*evening, atmosphere*] alegre, agradable
conviviality [kən,vɪvɪ'ælɪtɪ] N alegría *f* y buen humor • **there was an atmosphere of ~** había un ambiente de alegría y buen humor
convocation [,kɒnvə'keɪʃən] N (*frm*) (= *act*) convocación *f*; (= *meeting*) asamblea *f*
convoke [kən'vəʊk] VT convocar
convoluted ['kɒnvə,luːtɪd] ADJ [*shape*] enrollado, enroscado; [*argument*] enrevesado
convolution [,kɒnvə'luːʃən] N circunvolución *f*
convolvulus [kən'vɒlvjʊləs] N (PL: **convolvuluses** *or* **convolvuli** [kən'vɒlvjʊlaɪ]) enredadera *f*
convoy ['kɒnvɔɪ] N (= *procession*) convoy *m*; (= *escort*) escolta *f* • **in/under ~** en convoy
VT convoyar, escoltar
convulse [kən'vʌls] VT **1** (*often pass*) [*earthquake etc*] sacudir; [*war, riot*] convulsionar, conmocionar
2 (*fig*) • **to be ~d with laughter** desternillarse de risa • **to be ~d with anger** estar ciego de ira • **to be ~d with pain** retorcerse de dolor
convulsion [kən'vʌlʃən] N **1** (= *fit, seizure*) convulsión *f* • **to have ~s** tener convulsiones
2 (*fig*) conmoción *f* • **they were in ~s*** [*of laughter*] se desternillaban de risa

C

convulsive [kən'vʌlsɪv] ADJ [*movement*] convulsivo; [*laughter*] incontenible
convulsively [kən'vʌlsɪvlɪ] ADV [*shake, jerk*] convulsivamente
cony ['kəʊnɪ] N (*US*) conejo *m*
COO N ABBR (= **chief operating officer**) director(a) *m/f* general, presidente/a *m/f* del consejo de administración
coo¹ [ku:] VI [*dove*] arrullar; [*baby*] hacer gorgoritos
coo²* [ku:] EXCL (*Brit*) ¡toma!, ¡vaya!
co-occur [ˌkəʊə'kɜ:ʳ] VI coocurrir
co-occurrence [ˌkəʊə'kʌrəns] N coocurrencia *f*
cooee ['ku:i:] EXCL ¡yuju!
VI exclamar "yuju"
cooing ['ku:ɪŋ] N arrullos *mpl*
cook [kʊk] N cocinero/a *m/f* • **PROVERB**: • **too many ~s spoil the broth** demasiadas cocineras estropean el caldo
VT **1** (*Culin*) [+ *rice, vegetables*] cocinar, guisar; (= *boil*) cocer; (= *grill*) asar (a la parrilla); (= *fry*) freír • **to ~ a meal** preparar *or* hacer una comida • **IDIOM**: • **to ~ sb's goose*** hacer la pascua a algn
2* (= *falsify*) [+ *accounts*] falsificar • **IDIOM**: • **to ~ the books** amañar las cuentas
VI **1** [*food*] cocinarse, cocer • **what's ~ing?*** (*fig*) ¿qué se guisa?, ¿qué pasa?
2 [*person*] cocinar, guisar (*esp LAm*) • **can you ~?** ¿sabes cocinar?
▸ **cook up** VT + ADV **1** (*Culin*) preparar
2* [+ *excuse, story*] inventar; [+ *plan*] tramar
cookbook ['kʊkbʊk] N = **cookery book**
cooked [kʊkt] ADJ [*breakfast*] caliente
CPD ▸ **cooked meats** fiambres *fpl*
cooker ['kʊkəʳ] N **1** (*Brit*) (= *stove*) cocina *f*, horno *m* (*esp LAm*); (*US*) olla *f* para cocinar • **gas/electric ~** cocina *f* de gas/eléctrica
2 (= *cooking apple*) manzana *f* para cocer
cookery ['kʊkərɪ] N cocina *f* • **French ~** la cocina francesa • **I'm no good at ~** yo no sé nada de cocina
CPD ▸ **cookery book** (*Brit*) libro *m* de cocina
▸ **cookery course** curso *m* de cocina
cookhouse ['kʊkhaʊs] N cocina *f*; (*Mil*) cocina *f* móvil de campaña
cookie ['kʊkɪ] N **1** (*esp US*) (= *biscuit*) galleta *f* • **that's the way the ~ crumbles*** así es la vida
2* (= *person*) tipo/a* *m/f*, tío/a* *m/f* • **she's a smart ~** es una chica lista • **a tough ~** un tío duro*
3 (*Internet*) cookie *f*
CPD ▸ **cookie cutter** (*US*) molde *m* para galletas
cooking ['kʊkɪŋ] N **1** (= *art*) cocina *f* • **typical Galician ~** la típica cocina gallega • **her ~ is a delight** sus platos son una delicia
2 (= *process*) cocción *f*
CPD [*utensils, salt*] de cocina; [*chocolate*] de hacer ▸ **cooking apple** manzana *f* para cocer
▸ **cooking foil** papel *m* de aluminio
▸ **cooking oil** aceite *m* para cocinar
▸ **cooking salt** sal *f* de cocina ▸ **cooking time** tiempo *m* de cocción
cookout ['kʊkaʊt] N (*US*) barbacoa *f*, comida *f* hecha al aire libre
cooktop ['kʊktɒp] N (*esp US*) placa *f* de cocina
cookware ['kʊkweəʳ] N batería *f* de cocina
cool [ku:l] ADJ (COMPAR: **cooler**, SUPERL: **coolest**) **1** (= *not hot*) [*air, room, skin, drink*] fresco • **it was a ~ day** el día estaba fresco • **it's getting** *or* **turning ~er** está empezando a refrescar • **it's nice and ~ in here** aquí dentro hace fresquito *or* se está fresquito • **"keep in a cool place"** "guardar en un lugar fresco" • **it helps you to keep ~** [*food, drink*] refresca; [*clothing, fan*] ayuda a mantenerse fresco
2 (= *light, comfortable*) [*dress, fabric*] fresco
3 (= *pale*) [*colour, shade, blue*] fresco
4 (= *calm*) [*person, manner, action, tone*] sereno • **his ~ handling of the situation** el aplomo con el que *or* la sangre fría con la que manejó la situación • **~, calm and collected** tranquilo y con dominio de sí mismo • **to keep** *or* **stay ~** no perder la calma • **keep ~!** ¡tranquilo! • **to keep a ~ head** no perder la calma • **to play it ~*** tomárselo con calma, hacer como si nada
5 (*pej*) (= *audacious*) [*behaviour*] fresco, descarado • **did you see the ~ way he asked me to do it?** ¿viste la frescura con la que me pidió que lo hiciese? • **as ~ as you please** más fresco que una lechuga* • **he's a ~ customer*** es un fresco, es un caradura • **we paid a ~ £200,000 for that house*** pagamos la friolera de 200.000 libras por esa casa • **IDIOM**: • **to be as ~ as a cucumber*** estar más fresco que una lechuga*
6 (= *distant, unenthusiastic*) [*person, response*] frío • **a ~ welcome** *or* **reception** un recibimiento frío • **relations were ~ but polite** la relación era fría *or* distante pero correcta • **to be ~ towards** *or* **with sb** mostrarse frío con algn, tratar a algn con frialdad
7‡ (= *trendy, stylish*) [*object, person*] guay (*Sp‡*) • **hey, (that's really) ~!** ¡ala, qué guay!‡, ¡ala, cómo mola! (*Sp‡*) • **it's ~ to say you like computers** queda muy bien decir que te gustan los ordenadores
8‡ (= *acceptable*) • **don't worry, it's ~** tranqui, no pasa nada* • **he's ~** es un tipo legal (*Sp**)
N **1** (= *low temperature*) frescor *m* • **in the ~ of the evening** en el frescor de la tarde • **to keep sth in the ~** guardar algo en un lugar fresco
2 (= *calm*) • **to keep/lose one's ~*** no perder/perder la calma
VT **1** [+ *brow, room*] refrescar; [+ *engine*] refrigerar; [+ *hot food or drink*] dejar enfriar; [+ *wine, soft drink*] poner a enfriar • **IDIOM**: • **to ~ one's heels** esperar impaciente
2 (= *dampen*) [+ *emotions, feelings*] enfriar • **~ it!*** ¡tranquilo!
VI **1** (*also* **cool down**) [*air, liquid*] enfriarse; [*weather*] refrescar • **the air ~s in the evenings here** aquí refresca al atardecer • **the room had ~ed considerably** la habitación estaba mucho más fresca, ahora hacía bastante más fresco en la habitación
2 (= *abate*) [*feeling, emotion*] enfriarse • **her passion for Richard had begun to ~** su pasión por Richard había empezado a enfriarse • **by Monday tempers had ~ed** el lunes los ánimos se habían calmado
CPD ▸ **cool bag** bolsa *f* isotérmica ▸ **cool box** nevera *f* portátil
▸ **cool down** VT + ADV **1** (= *make colder*) enfriar
2 (= *make calmer*) • **to ~ sb down** calmar a algn
VI + ADV **1** (= *become colder*) [*object*] enfriarse; [*person*] refrescarse, tener menos calor
2 (= *become calmer*) [*person, situation*] calmarse • **~ down!** ¡cálmese!
▸ **cool off** VI + ADV (= *become less angry*) calmarse; (= *lose enthusiasm*) perder (el) interés, enfriarse; (= *become less affectionate*) distanciarse, enfriarse
coolant ['ku:lənt] N (*Tech*) (líquido *m*) refrigerante *m*
cooler ['ku:ləʳ] N **1** (= *cool box*) nevera *f* portátil
2‡ (= *prison*) chirona* *f*, trena* *f*
cool-headed ['ku:lˌhedɪd] ADJ sereno, imperturbable
coolie** ['ku:lɪ] N cooli *m*, culi *m*
cooling ['ku:lɪŋ] ADJ refrescante
CPD ▸ **cooling system** sistema *m* de refrigeración ▸ **cooling tower** (*at power station*) torre *f* de refrigeración ▸ **cooling fan** ventilador *m*
cooling-off period [ˌku:lɪŋ'ɒfˌpɪərɪəd] N (*Ind*) plazo *m* de negociación; (*Comm*) plazo *m* de prueba
coolly ['ku:lɪ] ADV **1** (= *calmly*) [*react, behave*] con serenidad, con sangre fría • **he reacted ~ in the midst of the crisis** mostró mucha sangre fría en medio de la crisis • **he very ~ put out his hand and picked up the snake** con una serenidad *or* con una sangre fría increíble alargó la mano y cogió la serpiente
2 (= *unemotionally*) [*say, reply*] con tranquilidad, con sangre fría • **she ~ denied everything** negó todo con una sangre fría increíble
3 (*pej*) (= *audaciously*) descaradamente, con mucha frescura
4 (= *unenthusiastically*) fríamente, con frialdad
coolness ['ku:lnɪs] N **1** (= *coldness*) [*of water, air, weather*] frescor *m*
2 (= *calmness*) tranquilidad *f*, serenidad *f*; (*in battle, crisis*) sangre *f* fría
3 (*pej*) (= *audacity*) frescura *f*, descaro *m*
4 (= *lack of enthusiasm*) [*of welcome, person*] frialdad *f* • **her ~ towards him** su frialdad con él
coomb [ku:m] N garganta *f*, desfiladero *m*
coon [ku:n] N **1** (*Zool*) = **raccoon**
2** (*offensive*) (= *black person*) negro/a *m/f* (*pej*)
coop [ku:p] N gallinero *m*
▸ **coop up** VT + ADV encerrar
co-op* ['kəʊˌɒp] N **1** (= *shop*) = **cooperative**
2 (*US*) = **cooperative apartment**
3 (*US*) (*Univ*) = **cooperative**
cooped up [ˌku:pt'ʌp] ADJ encerrado
cooper ['ku:pəʳ] N tonelero/a *m/f*
cooperage ['ku:pərɪdʒ] N tonelería *f*
cooperate [kəʊ'ɒpəreɪt] VI cooperar, colaborar • **to ~ with sb (in sth/to do sth)** cooperar con algn (en algo/para hacer algo)
cooperation [kəʊˌɒpə'reɪʃən] N cooperación *f*, colaboración *f*
cooperative [kəʊ'ɒpərətɪv] ADJ **1** [*attitude*] colaborador, cooperador; [*person*] servicial, dispuesto a ayudar
2 [*farm etc*] cooperativo
N cooperativa *f*
CPD ▸ **cooperative society** (*Brit*) cooperativa *f*
cooperatively [kəʊ'ɒpərətɪvlɪ] ADV (= *jointly*) en cooperación, en colaboración, conjuntamente; (= *obligingly*) servicialmente
co-opt [kəʊ'ɒpt] VT • **to co-opt sb (onto sth)** nombrar (como miembro) a algn (para algo)
co-option [kəʊ'ɒpʃən] N cooptación *f*
coordinate N [kəʊ'ɔ:dnɪt] **1** (*usu pl*) (*on map*) coordenada *f*
2 coordinates (= *clothes*) coordinados *mpl*
VT [kəʊ'ɔ:dɪneɪt] [+ *movements, work*] coordinar; [+ *efforts*] aunar
coordinated [kəʊ'ɔ:dɪneɪtɪd] [*activity, operation*] ADJ coordinado
coordinating [kəʊ'ɔ:dɪneɪtɪŋ] ADJ [*committee, body, centre*] coordinador; [*fabric, wallpaper, skirt, shoes*] haciendo juego, a juego (*Sp*)
CPD ▸ **coordinating conjunction** conjunción *f* coordinante
coordination [kəʊˌɔ:dɪ'neɪʃən] N coordinación *f*
coordinator [kəʊ'ɔ:dɪneɪtəʳ] N coordinador(a) *m/f*
coot [ku:t] N **1** (*Orn*) focha *f* (común), fúlica *f*

2* (= fool) bobo/a m/f
cootie* ['ku:tɪ] N (US) piojo m
co-owner [,kəʊ'əʊnəʳ] N copropietario/a m/f
co-ownership [,kəʊ'əʊnəʃɪp] N copropiedad f
cop* [kɒp] N **1** (= policeman) poli m (Sp*), cana m (S. Cone*) • **the cops** la pasma (Sp‡), la cana (S. Cone‡) • **cops and robbers** (= game) policías y ladrones
2 (Brit) • **it's not much cop** no es gran cosa • **it's a fair cop!** ¡está bien!
VT **1** (Brit) (= catch) [+ person] pescar, pillar; [+ beating, fine] ganarse • **he copped six months** se cargó seis meses • **you'll cop it!** ¡te la vas a ganar! • **I copped it from the headmaster** el director me puso como un trapo • **cop this!** ¡hay que ver esto! • **cop hold of this** coge (Sp) or toma esto
2 (US) (Jur) • **to cop a plea** declararse culpable de un delito menor para obtener una sentencia más leve
3 (US) [+ drugs] comprar
CPD ▸ **cop car*** (= police car) coche m de policía ▸ **cop shop‡** (Brit) comisaría f
▸ **cop off with*** VI + PREP (Brit) liarse con*, ligar con*, enrollarse con (Sp*)
▸ **cop out*** VI + ADV escabullirse, rajarse
co-partner ['kəʊ'pɑ:tnəʳ] N consocio mf, copartícipe mf
co-partnership ['kəʊ'pɑ:tnəʃɪp] N asociación f, cogestión f, coparticipación f
cope¹ [kəʊp] VI **1** arreglárselas • **he's coping pretty well** se las está arreglando bastante bien • **we shall be able to ~ better next year** podremos arreglarnos mejor el año que viene • **can you ~?** ¿tú puedes con esto? • **how are you coping?** ¿cómo lo llevas?* • **he can't ~ any more** ya no puede más
2 • **to ~ with** [+ task, person] poder con; [+ situation] enfrentarse con; [+ difficulties, problems] (= tackle) hacer frente a, abordar; (= solve) solucionar
cope² [kəʊp] N (Rel) capa f pluvial
Copenhagen [,kəʊpn'heɪgən] N Copenhague m
Copernicus [kə'pɜ:nɪkəs] N Copérnico
copestone ['kəʊpstəʊn] N (piedra f de) albardilla f
copier ['kɒpɪəʳ] N (= photocopier) fotocopiadora f
co-pilot ['kəʊ'paɪlət] N copiloto mf
coping ['kəʊpɪŋ] N (Constr) albardilla f, mojinete m
CPD ▸ **coping stone** = **copestone**
coping mechanism N mecanismo m de supervivencia
copious ['kəʊpɪəs] ADJ copioso, abundante
copiously ['kəʊpɪəslɪ] ADV copiosamente, en abundancia
cop-out* ['kɒpaʊt] N evasión f de responsabilidad
copper ['kɒpəʳ] N **1** (= material) cobre m
2 (= utensil) caldera f de lavar
3 (Brit*) (= coin) perra f (chica), centavo m (LAm); (= penny) penique m • **it costs a few ~s** vale unos peniques
4 (Brit) ▹ **cop**
ADJ **1** (= made of copper) de cobre
2 (= colour) cobrizo
CPD ▸ **copper beech** haya f roja or de sangre ▸ **copper sulphate** sulfato m de cobre ▸ **copper wire** hilo m de cobre
copper-bottomed [,kɒpə'bɒtəmd] ADJ con fondo de cobre; (fig) totalmente fiable, de máxima seguridad
copper-coloured, **copper-colored** (US) ['kɒpə,kʌləd] ADJ cobrizo
copperhead ['kɒpəhed] N víbora f cobriza
copperplate ['kɒpəpleɪt] N (also **copperplate writing**) letra f caligrafiada, caligrafía f
coppersmith ['kɒpəsmɪθ] N cobrero/a m/f
coppery ['kɒpərɪ] ADJ cobreño; [colour] cobrizo
coppice ['kɒpɪs] N soto m, bosquecillo m
copra ['kɒprə] N copra f
co-presidency [kəʊ'prezɪdənsɪ] N copresidencia f
co-president [kəʊ'prezɪdənt] N copresidente/a m/f
co-processor [,kəʊ'prəʊsesəʳ] N coprocesador m • **graphics co-processor** coprocesador m de gráficos
co-produce [,kəʊprə'dju:s] VT coproducir
co-production [,kəʊprə'dʌkʃən] N coproducción f
copse [kɒps] N soto m, bosquecillo m
Copt [kɒpt] N copto/a m/f
'copter*, copter* ['kɒptəʳ] N ABBR (= **helicopter**) helicóptero m
Coptic ['kɒptɪk] ADJ copto
CPD ▸ **the Coptic Church** la Iglesia Copta
copula ['kɒpjʊlə] N (PL: **copulas** or **copulae** ['kɒpjʊli:]) cópula f
copulate ['kɒpjʊleɪt] VI copular
copulation [,kɒpjʊ'leɪʃən] N cópula f
copulative ['kɒpjʊlətɪv] ADJ copulativo
copy ['kɒpɪ] N **1** (gen) (= duplicate) copia f; [of photograph] copia f; [of painting] copia f, imitación f; (= carbon copy) copia f (en papel carbón) • **rough ~** borrador m • **fair ~** copia en limpio • **to make a ~ of** hacer or sacar una copia de
2 [of book, newspaper] ejemplar m; [of magazine] número m
3 (= no pl) (Press) (= written material) original m, manuscrito m • **there's plenty of ~ here** tenemos aquí un material abundante • **a murder is always good ~** un asesinato es siempre un buen tema • **to make good ~** ser una noticia de interés
VT **1** (= imitate) copiar, imitar; (Scol) (= cheat) copiar
2 (= make copy of) (gen) sacar una copia de; (in writing) (also Comput) copiar; (with carbon) sacar una copia/copias al carbón; (= photocopy) fotocopiar • **to ~ from** copiar de • **to ~ and paste** [+ files, words] copiar y pegar
3 (= send a copy to) enviar una copia (**to** a)
4 (Rad, Telec) recibir
CPD ▸ **copy boy** (Press) chico m de los recados de la redacción ▸ **copy editor** editor(a) m/f, corrector(a) m/f de manuscritos ▸ **copy machine** fotocopiadora f ▸ **copy typist** mecanógrafo/a m/f
▸ **copy down** VT + ADV anotar, tomar nota de
▸ **copy out** VT + ADV copiar
copybook ['kɒpɪbʊk] N cuaderno m de escritura • IDIOM: • **to blot one's ~** manchar su reputación
CPD perfecto • **the pilot made a ~ landing** el piloto hizo un aterrizaje de libro
copycat* ['kɒpɪkæt] N imitador(a) m/f
CPD ▸ **copycat crime** crimen m que trata de emular a otros
copy-edit ['kɒpɪ'edɪt] VT editar y corregir
copying ['kɒpɪɪŋ] N **1** (= imitation) • **children learn by ~** los niños aprenden por imitación
2 (Scol) (= cheating) • **~ will be severely punished** el que sea descubierto copiando recibirá un severo castigo
CPD ▸ **copying ink** (for machine use) tinta f de copiar ▸ **copying machine** copiadora f
copyist ['kɒpɪɪst] N copista mf
copyreader ['kɒpɪ,ri:dəʳ] N corrector(a) m/f
copyright ['kɒpɪraɪt] ADJ protegido por los derechos de(l) autor
N derechos mpl de autor, propriedad f literaria • **the book is still in ~** siguen vigentes los derechos del autor de este libro • **it will be out of ~ in 2020** los derechos de(l) autor terminarán en 2020 • **"~ reserved"** "es propiedad", "copyright"
VT registrar como propiedad literaria
copywriter ['kɒpɪ,raɪtəʳ] N escritor(a) m/f de material publicitario
coquetry ['kɒkɪtrɪ] N coquetería f
coquette [kə'ket] N coqueta f
coquettish [kə'ketɪʃ] ADJ coqueta
coquettishly [kə'ketɪʃlɪ] ADV coquetamente, con coquetería
cor‡ [kɔ:ʳ] EXCL (Brit) ¡caramba! • **cor blimey!** ¡Dios mío!*
coracle ['kɒrəkl] N barquilla f de cuero
coral ['kɒrəl] N coral m
CPD de coral, coralino ▸ **coral island** isla f coralina ▸ **coral necklace** collar m de coral ▸ **coral reef** arrecife m de coral ▸ **Coral Sea** mar m del Coral
cor anglais ['kɔ:r'ɔ̃ŋgleɪ] N (PL: **cors anglais**) corno m inglés
corbel ['kɔ:bəl] N ménsula f, repisa f
cord [kɔ:d] N **1** (= thick string) cuerda f; (for pyjamas, curtains, of window) cordón m; (Elec) cable m
2 (also **umbilical cord**) cordón m umbilical • IDIOM: • **to cut** or **sever the ~** soltar amarras; ▹ **spinal, vocal**
3 (= material) pana f; **cords** (= trousers) pantalones mpl de pana
VT atar con cuerdas
cordage ['kɔ:dɪdʒ] N cordaje m, cordería f
cordial ['kɔ:dɪəl] ADJ cordial, afectuoso
N (Brit) (= drink) cordial m; (= liqueur) licor m
cordiality [,kɔ:dɪ'ælɪtɪ] N cordialidad f
cordially ['kɔ:dɪəlɪ] ADV cordialmente, afectuosamente • **I ~ detest him** le odio cordialmente
cordite ['kɔ:daɪt] N cordita f
cordless ['kɔ:dlɪs] ADJ [iron, kettle, tool] sin cable
CPD ▸ **cordless telephone** teléfono m inalámbrico or sin hilos
cordon ['kɔ:dn] N cordón m
VT (also **cordon off**) acordonar
CPD ▸ **cordon sanitaire** (Pol) cordón m sanitario
cordon bleu [,kɔ:dɔ̃n'blɜ:] N cordón m azul; (Culin) cocinero/a m/f de primera clase
CPD de primera clase
Cordova ['kɔ:dəvə] N Córdoba f
Cordovan ['kɔ:dəvən] ADJ cordobés
N cordobés/esa m/f; (= leather) cordobán m
corduroy ['kɔ:dərɔɪ] N pana f; **corduroys** pantalones mpl de pana
CPD ▸ **corduroy road** (US) camino m de troncos
CORE [kɔ:ʳ] N ABBR (US) = **Congress of Racial Equality**
core [kɔ:ʳ] N **1** [of fruit] corazón m; [of earth] centro m, núcleo m; [of cable, nuclear reactor] núcleo m
2 (fig) [of problem etc] esencia f, meollo m; [of group etc] centro m • **English to the ~** inglés hasta los tuétanos • **rotten to the ~** corrompido hasta la médula • **shocked to the ~** profundamente afectado • **a hard ~ of resistance** un núcleo or foco arraigado de resistencia • **the hard ~ of unemployment** los parados que tienen pocas posibilidades de salir de esa situación
VT [+ fruit] deshuesar
CPD ▸ **core business** actividad f principal ▸ **core curriculum** (Scol) asignaturas fpl comunes ▸ **core memory** (Comput) memoria f de núcleos ▸ **core subject** (Scol, Univ) asignatura f común ▸ **core time**

periodo *m* nuclear ▸ **core value** valor *m* central

co-religionist ['kəʊrɪ'lɪdʒənɪst] N correligionario/a *m/f*

corer ['kɔːrəʳ] N (*Culin*) despepitadora *f*

co-respondent ['kəʊrɪs'pɒndənt] N (*Jur*) codemandado/a *m/f*

Corfu [kɔː'fuː] N Corfú *m*

corgi ['kɔːgɪ] N perro/a *m/f* galés/esa

coriander [ˌkɒrɪ'ændəʳ] N culantro *m*, cilantro *m*

Corinth ['kɒrɪnθ] N Corinto *m*

Corinthian [kə'rɪnθɪən] ADJ corintio

cork [kɔːk] N **1** (= *substance*) corcho *m*
2 (= *stopper*) corcho *m*, tapón *m*
VT [+ *bottle*] (*also* **cork up**) tapar con corcho, taponar
CPD de corcho ▸ **cork oak**, **cork tree** alcornoque *m*

corkage ['kɔːkɪdʒ] N *precio que se cobra en un restaurante por abrir una botella traída de fuera*

corked [kɔːkt] ADJ [*wine*] con sabor a corcho

corker (†) ['kɔːkəʳ] N **1** (= *lie*) bola* *f*; (= *story*) historia *f* absurda
2 (*Sport*) (= *shot, stroke*) golpe *m* de primera; (= *good player*) crac* *m*; (= *attractive girl*) tía *f* buena* • **that's a ~!** ¡es cutre!*

corkscrew ['kɔːkskruː] N sacacorchos *m inv*
ADJ en espiral
VI subir en espiral

corm [kɔːm] N (*Bot*) bulbo *m*

cormorant ['kɔːmərənt] N cormorán *m* (grande)

Corn ABBR (*Brit*) = **Cornwall**

corn¹ [kɔːn] N **1** (*Brit*) (= *wheat*) trigo *m*; (*gen term*) cereales *mpl*; (*US*) (= *maize*) maíz *m*; (= *individual grains*) granos *mpl*
2* (= *sentimentality*) sentimentalismo *m*, sensiblería *f*
CPD ▸ **corn bread** (*US*) pan *m* de maíz ▸ **corn exchange** bolsa *f* de granos ▸ **corn meal** (*US*) harina *f* de maíz ▸ **corn oil** aceite *m* de maíz ▸ **corn on the cob** mazorca *f* de maíz, choclo *m* (*And, S. Cone*), elote *m* (*Mex*) ▸ **corn pone** (*US*) pan *m* de maíz ▸ **corn poppy** amapola *f*

corn² [kɔːn] N (*Med*) callo *m* • IDIOM: • **to tread on sb's ~s** (*Brit*) herir las sensibilidades de algn
CPD ▸ **corn plaster** emplasto *m* or parche *m* para callos

cornball* ['kɔːnbɔːl] N (*US*) paleto/a‡ *m/f*

corncob ['kɔːnkɒb] N mazorca *m* de maíz, choclo *m* (*And, S. Cone*), elote *m* (*Mex*)

corncrake ['kɔːnkreɪk] N guión *m* de codornices

cornea ['kɔːnɪə] N (PL: **corneas** or **corneae** ['kɔːnɪiː]) córnea *f*

corneal ['kɔːnɪəl] ADJ corneal

corned beef [ˌkɔːnd'biːf] N carne *f* de vaca en conserva
CPD ▸ **corned beef hash** refrito *m* de picadillo de ternera

cornelian [kɔː'niːlɪən] N cornalina *f*

corner ['kɔːnəʳ] N **1** (= *angle*) [*of object*] (*outer*) ángulo *m*, esquina *f*; (*inner*) rincón *m*; [*of mouth*] comisura *f*; [*of eye*] rabillo *m*; (= *bend in road*) curva *f*, recodo *m*; (*where two roads meet*) esquina *f* • **in the ~ of the room** en un rincón de la habitación • **the ~ of a table/page** la esquina de una mesa/página • **it's just around the ~** está a la vuelta de la esquina • **prosperity is just around the ~** la prosperidad está a la vuelta de la esquina • **to cut a ~** (*Aut*) tomar una curva muy cerrada • **out of the ~ of one's eye** con el rabillo del ojo • **to go round the ~** doblar la esquina • **to turn the ~** doblar la esquina; (*fig*) salir del apuro • **a two-cornered fight** una pelea entre dos • IDIOMS: • **to be in a (tight) ~** estar en un aprieto • **to cut ~s** atajar; (= *save money, effort etc*) ahorrar dinero/trabajo *etc* • **to drive sb into a ~** poner a algn entre la espada y la pared, acorralar a algn • **to paint o.s. into a ~** verse acorralado
2 (*fig*) (= *cranny, place*) • **a picturesque ~ of Soria** un rincón pintoresco de Soria • **in every ~** por todos los rincones • **every ~ of Europe** todos los rincones de Europa • **the four ~s of the world** las cinco partes del mundo • **in odd ~s** en cualquier rincón
3 (*Ftbl*) (*also* **corner kick**) córner *m*, saque *m* de esquina
4 (*Comm*) monopolio *m* • **he made a ~ in peanuts** se hizo con el monopolio de los cacahuetes, acaparó el mercado de los cacahuetes
VT **1** [+ *animal, fugitive*] acorralar, arrinconar; (*fig*) [+ *person*] (= *catch to speak to*) abordar, detener
2 (*Comm*) [+ *market*] acaparar
VI (*Aut*) tomar las curvas
CPD ▸ **corner cupboard** rinconera *f*, esquinera *f* ▸ **corner flag** (*Ftbl*) banderola *f* de esquina ▸ **corner house** casa *f* que hace esquina ▸ **corner kick** (*Ftbl*) córner *m*, saque *m* de esquina ▸ **corner seat** asiento *m* del rincón, rinconera *f* ▸ **corner shop**, **corner store** (*US*) tienda *f* de la esquina, tienda *f* pequeña del barrio ▸ **corner table** mesa *f* rinconera

cornered ['kɔːnəd] ADJ acorralado, arrinconado

cornering ['kɔːnərɪŋ] N • **the new suspension allows much safer ~** (*Aut*) la nueva suspensión proporciona un mayor agarre en las curvas

cornerstone ['kɔːnəstəʊn] N (*lit, fig*) piedra *f* angular

cornet ['kɔːnɪt] N **1** (*Mus*) corneta *f*
2 (*Brit*) (= *ice cream*) cucurucho *m*

corn-fed ['kɔːnfed] ADJ [*chicken*] alimentado con maíz

cornfield ['kɔːnfiːld] N [*of wheat*] trigal *m*, campo *m* de trigo; (*US*) [*of maize*] maizal *m*, milpa *f*

cornflakes ['kɔːnfleɪks] NPL copos *mpl* de maíz, cornflakes *mpl*; (*loosely*) cereales *mpl*

cornflour ['kɔːnflaʊəʳ] N (*Brit*) harina *f* de maíz, maicena *f*

cornflower ['kɔːnflaʊəʳ] N aciano *m*
ADJ (*also* **cornflower blue**) azul aciano (*inv*)

cornice ['kɔːnɪs] N (*Archit*) cornisa *f*

corniche ['kɔːniːʃ, kɔː'niːʃ] N (*also* **corniche road**) corniche *f*

Cornish ['kɔːnɪʃ] ADJ de Cornualles
N (*Ling*) córnico *m*
CPD ▸ **Cornish pasty** empanada *f* de Cornualles (*con cebolla, patata y carne*)

cornmeal ['kɔːnmiːl] N harina *f* de maíz

cornstarch ['kɔːnstɑːtʃ] N (*US*) = **cornflour**

cornucopia [ˌkɔːnjʊ'kəʊpɪə] N cuerno *m* de la abundancia

Cornwall ['kɔːnwəl] N Cornualles *m*

corny* ['kɔːnɪ] ADJ (COMPAR: **cornier**, SUPERL: **corniest**) [*joke, story*] trillado, muy visto; [*film, play*] sensiblero, sentimental

corolla [kə'rɒlə] N corola *f*

corollary [kə'rɒlərɪ] N corolario *m*

corona [kə'rəʊnə] N (PL: **coronas** or **coronae** [kə'rəʊniː]) (*Anat, Astron*) corona *f*; (*Elec*) descarga *f* de corona; (*Archit*) corona *f*, alero *m*

coronary ['kɒrənərɪ] ADJ coronario
N (*also* **coronary thrombosis**) infarto *m*, trombosis *f* coronaria
CPD ▸ **coronary care unit** unidad *f* de cuidados coronarios ▸ **coronary heart disease** enfermedad *f* coronaria

coronation [ˌkɒrə'neɪʃən] N coronación *f*

coroner ['kɒrənəʳ] N juez *mf* de instrucción

coronet ['kɒrənɪt] N corona *f* (de marqués *etc*); (= *diadem*) diadema *f*

Corp ABBR **1** (*Comm, Econ*) (= **Corporation**) S.A.
2 (*Pol*) = **Corporation**
3 (*Mil*) = **Corporal**

corp. ABBR = **corporation**

corpora ['kɔːpərə] NPL *of* **corpus**

corporal ['kɔːpərəl] ADJ corporal
N (*Mil*) cabo *m*
CPD ▸ **corporal punishment** castigo *m* corporal

corporate ['kɔːpərɪt] ADJ (= *joint*) [*ownership, responsibility*] corporativo, colectivo; [*action, effort*] combinado; (= *of company, firm*) [*image, planning, identity, growth*] corporativo
CPD ▸ **corporate body** corporación *f* ▸ **corporate car** (*US*) coche *m* de la empresa ▸ **corporate crime** delito *m* de empresa ▸ **corporate culture** cultura *f* empresarial ▸ **corporate headquarters** sede *f* social ▸ **corporate hospitality** hospitalidad *f* corporativa ▸ **corporate law** derecho *m* de sociedades ▸ **corporate name** nombre *m* social ▸ **corporate strategy** estrategia *f* de la empresa

corporately ['kɔːpərɪtlɪ] ADV corporativamente, como corporación

corporation [ˌkɔːpə'reɪʃən] N **1** (*Comm*) corporación *f*; (*US*) (= *limited company*) sociedad *f* anónima
2 [*of city*] ayuntamiento *m*
3 (*Brit**) (= *paunch*) panza* *f*
CPD corporativo ▸ **corporation tax** (*Brit*) impuesto *m* sobre sociedades

corporatism ['kɔːpərətɪzəm] N corporacionismo *m*

corporatist ['kɔːpərətɪst] ADJ [*theory, tendencies*] corporativista

corporeal [kɔː'pɔːrɪəl] ADJ corpóreo

corps [kɔːʳ] N (PL: **corps** [kɔːz]) (*Mil*) cuerpo *m* (de ejército); ▸ **diplomatic**, **press**
CPD ▸ **corps de ballet** cuerpo *m* de baile

corpse [kɔːps] N cadáver *m*

corpulence ['kɔːpjʊləns] N corpulencia *f*

corpulent ['kɔːpjʊlənt] ADJ corpulento

corpus ['kɔːpəs] N (PL: **corpuses** or **corpora**) cuerpo *m*
CPD ▸ **corpus delicti** cuerpo *m* del delito ▸ **Corpus Christi** Corpus *m*

corpuscle ['kɔːpʌsl] N [*of blood*] glóbulo *m*, corpúsculo *m*

corral [kə'rɑːl] (*US*) N corral *m*
VT acorralar

correct [kə'rekt] ADJ **1** (= *accurate*) correcto • **(that's) ~!** ¡correcto!, ¡exacto! • **is this spelling ~?** ¿está bien escrito esto? • **your suspicions are ~** está en lo cierto con sus sospechas • **"correct fare only"** (*in buses etc*) "importe exacto" • **to be ~** [*person*] tener razón, estar en lo cierto • **am I ~ in saying that ...?** ¿me equivoco al decir que ...?, ¿estoy en lo cierto al decir que ...? • **he was normally ~ in his calculations** normalmente sus cálculos eran exactos • **he was ~ to blame the government** estuvo en lo cierto cuando culpó al gobierno • **the president was ~ to reject the offer** el presidente hizo bien al rechazar la oferta • **it is ~ to say that ...** es acertado decir que ... • **have you got the ~ time?** ¿tiene la hora exacta?
2 (= *appropriate*) adecuado • **the ~ weight for your height and build** el peso adecuado dadas su altura y constitución • **in the ~ place** en su sitio
3 (= *proper*) [*person, behaviour, manners*] correcto; [*dress*] apropiado • **it's the ~ thing to do** es lo correcto
VT **1** (= *put right*) [+ *mistake, habit, exam,*

eyesight] corregir; [+ *person*] corregir, rectificar; [+ *imbalance*] eliminar; [+ *clock*] poner en hora • **"I don't mean tomorrow," she ~ed herself** —no, no mañana —se corrigió • **~ me if I'm wrong** dime si tengo razón o no • **~ me if I'm wrong, but ...** a lo mejor me equivoco, pero ... • **I stand ~ed** reconozco mi error
2 (*frm*) (= *punish*) castigar; (= *admonish*) reprender

correcting fluid [kəˌrektɪŋ'flu:ɪd] N corrector *m*

correction [kə'rekʃən] N **1** (*gen*) corrección *f*, rectificación *f*; (*on page*) tachadura *f* • **I am open to ~ but ...** corregidme si me equivoco, pero ...
2 (*esp US*) (= *punishment*) corrección *f* • **a house of ~†** un correccional, un reformatorio
CPD ▸ **correction fluid** corrector *m*

correctional [kə'rekʃənəl] (*US*) ADJ penitenciario
CPD ▸ **correctional facility** centro *m* penitenciario ▸ **correctional officer** funcionario/a *m/f* de prisiones

corrective [kə'rektɪv] ADJ correctivo
N correctivo *m*
CPD ▸ **corrective glasses** gafas *fpl* correctoras ▸ **corrective surgery** cirugía *f* correctiva

correctly [kə'rektlɪ] ADV **1** (= *accurately, in right way*) [*answer, pronounce, predict*] correctamente • **if I remember ~** si mal no recuerdo • **if I understand you ~** si le he entendido bien
2 (= *respectably, decently*) [*behave, proceed*] correctamente
3 (= *appropriately*) • **she refused, quite ~, to give in to his demands** se negó, con toda la razón, a ceder a sus exigencias • **when an accident happens, quite ~, questions are asked** como debe ser, cuando ocurre un accidente se hacen indagaciones

correctness [kə'rektnɪs] N **1** (= *accuracy*) [*of answer, amount, term, calculation*] exactitud *f*
2 (= *appropriateness*) [*of method, approach*] lo apropiado, lo adecuado
3 (= *decency*) [*of person, behaviour, dress*] corrección *f*

correlate ['kɒrɪleɪt] VT establecer una correlación entre, correlacionar • **to ~ sth with sth** poner algo en correlación con algo
VI tener correlación • **to ~ with** estar en correlación con

correlation [ˌkɒrɪ'leɪʃən] N correlación *f*

correlative [kɒ'relətɪv] ADJ correlativo
N correlativo *m*

correspond [ˌkɒrɪs'pɒnd] VI **1** (= *be in accordance*) corresponder (**with** con); (= *be equivalent*) equivaler (**to** a)
2 (*by letter*) escribirse, mantener correspondencia (**with** con)

correspondence [ˌkɒrɪs'pɒndəns] N **1** (= *agreement*) correspondencia *f*, conexión *f* (**between** entre)
2 (= *letter-writing*) correspondencia *f* • **to be in ~ with sb** mantener correspondencia con algn
3 (= *letters*) correspondencia *f*
CPD ▸ **correspondence college** centro *m* de enseñanza por correspondencia ▸ **correspondence column** (*Press*) (sección *f* de) cartas *fpl* al director ▸ **correspondence course** curso *m* por correspondencia

correspondent [ˌkɒrɪs'pɒndənt] N (*Press*) corresponsal *mf*; (= *letter-writer*) corresponsal *mf* • **I'm a hopeless ~** soy muy mala para escribir cartas

corresponding [ˌkɒrɪs'pɒndɪŋ] ADJ correspondiente

correspondingly [ˌkɒrɪs'pɒndɪŋlɪ] ADV (= *as a result*) por consecuencia; (= *proportionately*) proporcionalmente, en la misma medida

corridor ['kɒrɪdɔ:ʳ] N pasillo *m*, corredor *m* • **the ~s of power** los pasillos del poder

corroborate [kə'rɒbəreɪt] VT corroborar, confirmar

corroboration [kəˌrɒbə'reɪʃən] N corroboración *f*, confirmación *f*

corroborative [kə'rɒbərətɪv] ADJ corroborativo, confirmatorio

corrode [kə'rəʊd] VT (*lit, fig*) corroer
VI corroerse

corroded [kə'rəʊdɪd] ADJ corroído

corrosion [kə'rəʊʒən] N corrosión *f*

corrosive [kə'rəʊzɪv] ADJ corrosivo; (*fig*) destructivo

corrugated ['kɒrəgeɪtɪd] ADJ ondulado
CPD ▸ **corrugated cardboard** cartón *m* ondulado ▸ **corrugated iron** hierro *m* ondulado, calamina *f* (*LAm*) ▸ **corrugated paper** papel *m* ondulado

corrugation [ˌkɒrə'geɪʃən] N ondulación *f*

corrupt [kə'rʌpt] ADJ **1** (= *depraved*) pervertido, depravado
2 (= *dishonest*) corrompido, venal
3 (*Comput*) [*text, file*] corrompido
VT **1** (= *deprave*) pervertir, corromper
2 (= *bribe*) sobornar
3 [+ *language*] corromper; (*Comput*) [+ *text, file*] corromper
CPD ▸ **corrupt practices** (= *dishonesty, bribery*) corrupción *fsing*

corrupted [kə'rʌptɪd] ADJ (*Comput*) [*file*] corrompido

corruptible [kə'rʌptəbl] ADJ corruptible

corruption [kə'rʌpʃən] N **1** (= *depravity*) perversión *f*, corrupción *f*
2 (= *dishonesty*) corrupción *f*, venalidad *f*
3 [*of language*] corrupción *f*; (*Comput*) [*of text, file*] corrupción *f*

corruptly [kə'rʌptlɪ] ADV [*behave, act*] de manera corrupta

corsage [kɔ:'sɑ:ʒ] N (= *flowers*) ramillete *m*; (= *bodice*) cuerpo *m*

corsair ['kɔ:sɛəʳ] N corsario *m*

cors anglais ['kɔ:z'ɔ̃ŋgleɪ] NPL *of* **cor anglais**

corset ['kɔ:sɪt] N faja *f*; (*old style*) corsé *m*

corseted ['kɔ:sɪtɪd] ADJ encorsetado

Corsica ['kɔ:sɪkə] N Córcega *f*

Corsican ['kɔ:sɪkən] ADJ corso
N corso/a *m/f*

cortège [kɔ:'teɪʒ] N (= *procession*) cortejo *m*, comitiva *f*; (= *retinue*) séquito *m*; (= *funeral cortège*) cortejo *m* fúnebre

cortex ['kɔ:teks] N (PL: **cortices** ['kɔ:tɪsi:z]) (*Anat, Bot*) córtex *m*, corteza *f*

corticoids ['kɔ:tɪkɔɪdz] NPL, **corticosteroids** ['kɔ:tɪkəʊ'stɪərɔɪdz] NPL corticoides *mpl*, corticoesteroides *mpl*

cortisone ['kɔ:tɪzəʊn] N cortisona *f*

Corunna [kə'rʌnə] N La Coruña

coruscating ['kɒrəskeɪtɪŋ] ADJ [*humour*] chispeante

corvette [kɔ:'vet] N corbeta *f*

cos¹ [kɒs] N (*Brit*) (*also* **cos lettuce**) lechuga *f* romana

cos² [kɒs] ABBR = **cosine**

cos³‡, 'cos‡ [kɒz] CONJ = **because**

COS, c.o.s. ABBR (*Comm*) = **cash on shipment**

cosh [kɒʃ] (*Brit*) N porra *f*, cachiporra *f*
VT aporrear

cosignatory ['kəʊ'sɪgnətərɪ] N cosignatario/a *m/f*

cosily ['kəʊzɪlɪ] ADV (= *warmly, comfortably*) cómodamente, agradablemente; [*chat*] íntimamente

cosine ['kəʊsaɪn] N coseno *m*

cosiness ['kəʊzɪnɪs] N [*of room*] lo acogedor; (= *intimacy*) intimidad *f*

COSLA ['kɒzlə] N ABBR (*Scot*) = **Convention of Scottish Local Authorities**

cosmetic [kɒz'metɪk] ADJ cosmético • **the changes are merely ~** (*fig*) los cambios son puramente cosméticos
N (*often pl*) cosmético *m*
CPD ▸ **cosmetic preparation** cosmético *m* ▸ **cosmetic surgery** cirugía *f* estética

cosmetician [kɒzmɪ'tɪʃən] N cosmetólogo/a *m/f*

cosmetologist [kɒzme'tɒlədʒɪst] N cosmetólogo/a *m/f*

cosmetology [kɒzme'tɒlədʒɪ] N cosmetología *f*

cosmic ['kɒzmɪk] ADJ cósmico
CPD ▸ **cosmic rays** rayos *mpl* cósmicos

cosmogony [kɒz'mɒgənɪ] N cosmogonía *f*

cosmographer [kɒz'mɒgrəfəʳ] N cosmógrafo/a *m/f*

cosmography [kɒz'mɒgrəfɪ] N cosmografía *f*

cosmological [ˌkɒzmə'lɒdʒɪkəl] ADJ [*science, theorist*] cosmológico

cosmologist [kɒz'mɒlədʒɪst] N cosmólogo *mf*

cosmology [kɒz'mɒlədʒɪ] N cosmología *f*

cosmonaut ['kɒzmənɔ:t] N cosmonauta *mf*

cosmopolitan [ˌkɒzmə'pɒlɪtən] ADJ cosmopolita
N cosmopolita *mf*

cosmos ['kɒzmɒs] N cosmos *m*

co-sponsor ['kəʊ'spɒnsəʳ] N (*esp Advertising*) copatrocinador(a) *m/f*

Cossack ['kɒsæk] ADJ cosaco *m*
N cosaco/a *m/f*

cosset ['kɒsɪt] VT mimar, consentir

cossie* ['kɒzɪ] N (*Brit*) bañador *m*

cost [kɒst] N **1** (= *expense*) (*often pl*) coste *m*, costo *m* (*esp LAm*); (= *amount paid, price*) precio *m* • **at ~** (*Comm*) a (precio de) coste • **at all ~s** • **at any ~** • **whatever the ~** (*fig*) cueste lo que cueste, a toda costa • **she cared for her elderly mother at great ~ to her own freedom** cuidó de su madre anciana pagando un precio muy alto a costa de su propia libertad • **these are solutions that can be implemented at little ~** estas son soluciones que pueden ponerse en práctica y que son poco costosas • **at the ~ of his life/health** a costa de su vida/salud • **to bear the ~ of** (*lit*) pagar *or* correr con los gastos de; (*fig*) sufrir las consecuencias de • **to count the ~ of sth/of doing sth** pensar en los riesgos de algo/de hacer algo • **without counting the ~** sin pensar en los riesgos • **to my ~** a mis expensas
2 costs: **a** (*Jur*) costas *fpl* • **he was ordered to pay ~s** se le condenó a pagar las costas
b (= *expenses*) gastos *mpl*
VT **1** (PT, PP: **cost**) costar, valer • **it ~ £2** costó 2 libras • **how much does it ~?** ¿cuánto cuesta?, ¿cuánto vale?, ¿a cuánto está? • **what will it ~ to have it repaired?** ¿cuánto va a costar repararlo? • **it ~ him a lot of money** le costó mucho dinero • **it'll ~ you*** te va a salir caro • **it ~ him his life/job** le costó la vida/el trabajo • **it ~ me a great deal of time/effort** me robó mucho tiempo/me costó mucho esfuerzo • **it ~s nothing to be polite** no cuesta nada ser educado • **whatever it ~s** • **~ what it may** (*also fig*) cueste lo que cueste • IDIOM: • **to ~ the earth**: • **it ~s the earth*** cuesta un riñón, cuesta un ojo de la cara
2 (PT, PP: **costed**) (*Comm*) [+ *articles for sale*] calcular el coste de; [+ *job*] calcular el

presupuesto de • **the job was ~ed at £5000** se calculó que el coste del trabajo ascendería a 5.000 libras • **it has not been properly ~ed** no se ha calculado detalladamente el coste
(CPD) ▸ **cost accountant** contable *mf* de costes *or* (*esp LAm*) costos ▸ **cost accounting** contabilidad *f* de costes *or* (*esp LAm*) costos ▸ **cost analysis** análisis *m inv* de costes *or* (*esp LAm*) costos ▸ **cost centre** centro *m* (de determinación) de costes *or* (*esp LAm*) costos ▸ **cost control** control *m* de costes *or* (*esp LAm*) costos ▸ **cost of living** coste *m or* (*esp LAm*) costo *m* de la vida • **~-of-living adjustment** ajuste *m* del coste de la vida • **~-of-living allowance** subsidio *m* por coste • **~-of-living bonus** plus *m* de carestía de vida, prima *f* por coste de la vida • **~-of-living increase** incremento *m* según el coste de la vida • **~-of-living index** índice *m* del coste *or* (*LAm*) de (la) vida ▸ **cost price** (*Brit*) precio *m* de coste *or* (*LAm*) costo • **at ~ price** a precio de coste
▸ **cost out** (VT + ADV) presupuestar
co-star ['kəʊstɑːʳ] (N) coprotagonista *mf*, coestrella *mf*
(VI) • **to co-star with sb** figurar con algn como protagonista
(VT) • **the film co-stars A and B** la película presenta como protagonistas a A y B *or* está coprotagonizada por A y B
Costa Rica ['kɒstə'riːkə] (N) Costa Rica *f*
Costa Rican ['kɒstə'riːkən] (ADJ) costarricense
(N) costarricense *mf*
cost-benefit analysis [ˌkɒstˌbenəfɪt ə'næləsɪs] (N) análisis *m* coste-beneficio *or* (*LAm*) costo-beneficio
cost-conscious ['kɒstˌkɒnʃəs] (ADJ) consciente de (los) costes *or* (*LAm*) costos
cost-cutting ['kɒstˌkʌtɪŋ] (N) recorte *m* de costes *or* (*LAm*) costos
cost-effective [ˌkɒstɪ'fektɪv] (ADJ) rentable
cost-effectively [ˌkɒstɪ'fektɪvlɪ] (ADV) [*operate*] de manera rentable
cost-effectiveness [ˌkɒstɪ'fektɪvnɪs] (N) rentabilidad *f*, relación *f* coste-rendimiento *or* (*LAm*) costo-rendimiento
coster ['kɒstəʳ], **costermonger** ['kɒstəˌmʌŋgəʳ] (N) (*Brit*) vendedor *m* ambulante
costing ['kɒstɪŋ] (N) cálculo *m* del coste
costive ['kɒstɪv] (ADJ) estreñido
costliness ['kɒstlɪnɪs] (N) (= *expense*) alto precio *m*, lo caro; (= *opulence*) suntuosidad *f*
costly ['kɒstlɪ] (ADJ) (COMPAR: **costlier**, SUPERL: **costliest**) (= *expensive*) (*lit, fig*) costoso; (= *opulent*) suntuoso
cost-plus [ˌkɒst'plʌs] (N) (*Comm*) precio *m* de coste más beneficio • **on a cost-plus basis** a base de precio de coste más beneficio
costume ['kɒstjuːm] (N) **1** [*of country*] traje *m*; (= *fancy dress*) disfraz *m*; (= *suit*) traje *m* sastre; (= *bathing costume*) bañador *m*, traje *m* de baño
2 costumes (*Theat*) vestuario *msing*
(CPD) ▸ **costume ball** baile *m* de disfraces ▸ **costume department** (*in theatre or television company*) vestuario *m* ▸ **costume designer** (*Cine, TV*) diseñador(a) *m/f* de vestuario ▸ **costume drama** obra *f* dramática de época ▸ **costume jewellery** (*Brit*), **costume jewelry** (*US*) bisutería *f*, joyas *fpl* de fantasía ▸ **costume party** (*US*) = **costume ball** ▸ **costume piece, costume play** = **costume drama**
costumier [kɒs'tjuːmɪəʳ], **costumer** (*esp US*) [kɒs'tjuːməʳ] (N) sastre *m* de teatro
cosy, cozy (*US*) ['kəʊzɪ] (ADJ) (COMPAR: **cosier**, SUPERL: **cosiest**) **1** (= *warm*) [*room, atmosphere*] acogedor; [*clothes*] de abrigo, caliente
2 (= *friendly*) [*chat*] íntimo, personal
3 (*pej*) (= *convenient*) [*arrangement, relationship*] de lo más cómodo; (= *easy, comfortable*) [*life*] holgado
(N) (*for teapot, egg*) *cubierta que se utiliza para mantener el té de una tetera, los huevos etc calientes*
▸ **cosy up***, **cozy up*** (*US*) (VI + ADV) • **to ~ up to sb** (*US*) (*fig*) tratar de quedar bien con algn
cot [kɒt] (N) (*Brit*) (*for baby*) cuna *f*; (*US*) (= *folding bed*) cama *f* plegable, catre *m*
(CPD) ▸ **cot death** (*Brit*) muerte *f* súbita del lactante ▸ **cot death syndrome** síndrome *m* de la muerte súbita del lactante
coterie ['kəʊtərɪ] (N) grupo *m*; (= *clique*) peña *f*, camarilla *f*
coterminous [kəʊ'tɜːmɪnəs] (*frm*) (ADJ) (*Geog*) colindante (**with** con); [*concepts, ideas*] coincidente (**with** con) • **to be ~ with** (*Geog*) colindar con; [*concepts, ideas*] coincidir con
Cotswolds ['kɒtswəʊldz] (NPL) *región montañosa de relieve suave del suroeste de Inglaterra*
cottage ['kɒtɪdʒ] (N) (= *country house*) casita *f* de campo, quinta *f* (*LAm*); (= *humble dwelling*) choza *f*, barraca *f*; (*US*) vivienda *f* campestre, quinta *f*
(CPD) ▸ **cottage cheese** requesón *m* ▸ **cottage garden** pequeño jardín *m* ▸ **cottage hospital** (*Brit*) hospital *m* rural ▸ **cottage industry** industria *f* artesanal *or* casera ▸ **cottage loaf** (*Brit*) pan *m* casero ▸ **cottage pie** (*Brit*) *pastel de carne cubierta de puré de patatas*
cottager ['kɒtɪdʒəʳ] (N) (*Brit*) aldeano/a *m/f*; (*US*) veraneante *mf* (en una casita de campo)
cottaging* ['kɒtɪdʒɪŋ] (*Brit*) (N) (*between homosexual men*) cruising* *m*
cotter ['kɒtəʳ] (N) chaveta *f*
cotton ['kɒtn] (N) (= *cloth*) algodón *m*; (= *plant, industry etc*) algodonero *m*; (*Brit*) (= *thread*) hilo *m* (de algodón); (*US*) = **cotton wool**
(CPD) [*shirt, dress*] de algodón ▸ **cotton belt** (*US*) (*Geog*) zona *f* algodonera ▸ **cotton bud** bastoncillo *m* de algodón ▸ **cotton candy** (*US*) algodón *m* (azucarado) ▸ **the cotton industry** la industria algodonera ▸ **cotton mill** fábrica *f* de algodón ▸ **cotton reel** carrete *m* de hilo, bobina *f* de hilo ▸ **cotton swab** (*US*) = **cotton bud** ▸ **cotton waste** borra *f* de algodón ▸ **cotton wool** (*Brit*) algodón *m* hidrófilo
▸ **cotton on*** (VI + ADV) (*Brit*) • **to ~ on (to sth)** caer en la cuenta (de algo)
cottongrass ['kɒtngrɑːs] (N) algodonosa *f*, algodoncillo *m* (silvestre)
cotton-picking* ['kɒtnˌpɪkɪŋ] (ADJ) (*US*) condenado*
cottonseed oil ['kɒtnsiːdˌɔɪl] (N) aceite *m* de algodón
cottontail ['kɒtnteɪl] (N) (*US*) conejo *m* (de cola blanca)
cottonwood ['kɒtnwʊd] (N) (*US*) álamo *m* de Virginia
cotyledon [ˌkɒtɪ'liːdən] (N) cotiledón *m*
couch [kaʊtʃ] (N) sofá *m*; (*Med*) (*in doctor's surgery*) camilla *f*; (*psychiatrist's*) diván *m*
• IDIOM: • **to be on the ~** (*esp US*) ir al psicoanalista
(VT) expresar • **~ed in jargon** redactado en jerigonza
(CPD) ▸ **couch grass** hierba *f* rastrera ▸ **couch potato*** teleadicto/a *m/f*, *persona que se apalanca en el sofá*
couchette [kuː'ʃet] (N) (*on train, ferry*) litera *f*
couchsurfing* ['kaʊtʃsɜːfɪŋ] (N) alojamiento *m* gratuito en casas de terceros
cougar ['kuːgər] (N) puma *m*
cough [kɒf] (N) tos *f* • **to have a bad ~** tener mucha tos
(VI) **1** toser
2* (= *confess*) cantar*
(CPD) ▸ **cough drop** pastilla *f* para la tos ▸ **cough medicine, cough mixture** jarabe *m* para la tos ▸ **cough sweet** caramelo *m* para la tos ▸ **cough syrup** = **cough mixture**
▸ **cough up** (VT + ADV) **1** [+ *blood, phlegm*] escupir, arrojar; (*Med*) expectorar
2 (*fig**) [+ *money*] soltar
(VI + ADV) (*fig**) soltar la pasta*
coughing ['kɒfɪŋ] (N) toser *m*, toses *fpl* • **fit of ~** acceso *m* de tos • **you couldn't hear the symphony for ~** el público tosía tanto que apenas se oía la sinfonía
could [kʊd] (VB) ▷ **can¹**, ABLE, CAN
couldn't ['kʊdnt] = **could not** ▷ **can¹**
coulomb ['kuːlɒm] (N) culombio *m*
council ['kaʊnsl] (N) **1** (= *committee*) consejo *m*, junta *f*; (*Rel*) concilio *m*; ▷ **security**
2 (*in local government*) concejo *m* municipal • **city/town ~** ayuntamiento *m* • **you should write to the ~ about it** deberías escribir al ayuntamiento acerca de eso • **the ~ should move the rubbish** les corresponde a los servicios municipales recoger la basura
3 (= *meeting*) reunión *f*, sesión *f* • **~ of war** consejo *m* de guerra
(CPD) ▸ **Council of Europe** Consejo *m* de Europa ▸ **council flat** (*Brit*) piso *m or* (*LAm*) departamento *m* de protección oficial ▸ **council house** (*Brit*) casa *f* de protección oficial ▸ **council housing** (*Brit*) viviendas *fpl* de protección oficial ▸ **council (housing) estate** (*Brit*) urbanización *f or* barrio *m* de viviendas de protección oficial ▸ **council meeting** pleno *m* municipal ▸ **Council of Ministers** Consejo *m* de Ministros (*de la Unión Europea*) ▸ **council tax** (*Brit*) *impuesto municipal* ▸ **council tenant** (*Brit*) inquilino/a *m/f* (de una vivienda de protección oficial)
councillor, councilor (*US*) ['kaʊnsɪləʳ] (N) concejal(a) *m/f*
councilman ['kaʊnsɪlmən] (N) (PL: **councilmen**) (*US*) concejal *m*
councilwoman ['kaʊnslˌwʊmən] (N) (PL: **councilwomen**) (*US*) concejala *f*
counsel ['kaʊnsəl] (N) **1** (*frm, liter*) (= *advice*) consejo *m* • **to hold/take ~ (with sb) about sth** consultar *or* pedir consejo (a algn) sobre algo • **to keep one's own ~** guardar silencio • **a ~ of perfection** un ideal imposible
2 (*Jur*) (*pl inv*) abogado/a *m/f* • **~ for the defence** (*Brit*) abogado/a *m/f* defensor(a) • **~ for the prosecution** (*Brit*) fiscal *mf* • **Queen's** *or* **King's Counsel** (*Brit*) abogado/a *m/f* del Estado
(VT) [+ *person*] (*frm*) aconsejar; (*Med etc*) orientar; [+ *prudence etc*] recomendar • **to ~ sb to do sth** aconsejar a algn que haga algo
counselling, counseling (*US*) ['kaʊnsəlɪŋ] (N) (*gen*) (= *advice*) asesoramiento *m*; (*Psych*) asistencia *f* sociopsicológica; (*Brit*) (*Scol*) ayuda *f* psicopedagógica
(CPD) ▸ **counselling service** servicio *m* de orientación; (*Univ*) servicio *m* de orientación universitaria
counsellor, counselor (*US*) ['kaʊnsələʳ] (N) **1** (*Psych*) consejero/a *m/f*; (= *adviser*) asesor(a) *m/f*
2 (*US*) (*Scol*) consejero/a *m/f*, asesor(a) *m/f*
3 (*Irl, US*) (*Jur*) (*also* **counsellor-at-law**) abogado/a *m/f*
count¹ [kaʊnt] (N) **1** (= *act of counting*) recuento *m*; [*of votes*] escrutinio *m*, recuento *m*; (*Boxing*) cuenta *f* • **to keep/lose ~ (of sth)** llevar/perder la cuenta (de algo) • **at the last ~** en el último recuento • **to make** *or* **do a ~ of sth** hacer un recuento de algo • **to be out for the ~** estar fuera de combate

2 (= *total*) recuento *m* • **the final ~** (*in election*) el último recuento • **hold the stretch for a ~ of ten, then relax** estírese y cuente hasta diez, luego relájese; ▹ **pollen, sperm**
3 (*Jur*) cargo *m* • **he was found guilty on all ~s** fue declarado culpable de todos los cargos • **he was indicted on two ~s of murder** le fueron imputados dos cargos por asesinato
4 (= *point*) • **you're wrong on both ~s** estás equivocado en los dos aspectos • **I think she deserves recognition on two ~s** creo que merece reconocimiento por dos motivos
VT **1** (= *add up, check*) contar • **she was ~ing the days until he came home** contaba los días que faltaban para su vuelta • **to ~ the cost of (doing) sth** (*lit*) reparar en el coste de (hacer) algo; (*fig*) reparar en las consecuencias de (hacer) algo; ▹ **chicken, blessing, cost**
2 (= *include*) contar • **not ~ing the children** sin contar a los niños • **ten ~ing him** diez con él, diez contándolo a él
3 (= *consider*) considerar • **I ~ you among my friends** te cuento entre mis amigos, te considero amigo mío • **I ~ myself lucky** me considero feliz • **~ yourself lucky!** ¡date por satisfecho!
VI **1** (= *add up, recite numbers*) contar • **can you ~?** ¿sabes contar? • **~ing from the left** contando de izquierda a derecha • **~ing from today/last Sunday** a partir de hoy/contando desde el domingo pasado • **to ~ (up) to ten** contar hasta diez
2 (= *be considered, be valid*) valer, contar • **that doesn't ~** eso no vale, eso no cuenta • **every second ~s** cada segundo cuenta *or* es importante • **it will ~ against him** irá en su contra • **to ~ as**: • **two children ~ as one adult** dos niños cuentan como un adulto • **a conservatory ~s as an extension** un jardín de invierno cuenta como una ampliación de la casa • **ability ~s for little here** aquí la capacidad que se tenga sirve de muy poco
CPD ▸ **count noun** (*Gram*) sustantivo *m* contable
▸ **count down** VI + ADV • **~ down from ten to one** cuenta hacia atrás del diez al uno • **children tend to ~ down to Christmas** los niños suelen contar los días que quedan para Navidad
▸ **count in*** VT + ADV incluir • **~ me in!** ¡yo me apunto!, ¡cuenta conmigo! • **to ~ sb in on sth** contar con algn para algo
▸ **count on** VI + PREP **1** (= *rely on*) contar con • **we're ~ing on him** contamos con él • **I wouldn't ~ on it!** ¡no contaría con ello! • **he's ~ing on winning** cuenta con ganar • **he can be ~ed on to ruin everything** puedes contar con que él estropeará todo • **I can always ~ on you to cheer me up** siempre puedo contar contigo para que me levantes el ánimo
2 (= *expect*) contar con • **I hadn't ~ed on this** no había contado con esto
▸ **count out** VT + ADV **1** (= *count*) [+ *money*] ir contando; [+ *small objects*] contar (uno por uno)
2 (= *exclude*) [+ *possibility*] descartar • **we can't ~ out the possibility that they'll attack** no podemos descartar la posibilidad de que ataquen
3* • **if that's what I have to do, you can ~ me out** si eso es lo que tengo que hacer, no cuentes conmigo • **(you can) ~ me out of this!** ¡no cuentes conmigo para esto!, ¡déjame fuera de esto!
4 (*Boxing*) • **the referee ~ed him out** el árbitro terminó la cuenta antes de que se levantara • **to be ~ed out** ser declarado fuera de combate

▸ **count toward, count towards** VI + PREP contar para • **this work ~s towards your final degree** este trabajo cuenta para la nota final de la licenciatura • **the time he has already spent in prison will ~ towards his sentence** el tiempo que ya ha pasado en la cárcel se descontará de su condena
▸ **count up** VT + ADV contar
▸ **count upon** VI + PREP = **count on**
count[2] [kaʊnt] N (= *nobleman*) conde *m*
countable ['kaʊntəbl] ADJ contable
• **~ noun** (*Ling*) nombre *m* contable
countdown ['kaʊntdaʊn] N cuenta *f* atrás, cuenta *f* regresiva (*LAm*)
countenance ['kaʊntɪnəns] (*frm*) N **1** (*liter*) (= *face*) semblante *m*, rostro *m* • **to keep one's ~** contener la risa, no perder la serenidad • **to lose ~** desconcertarse • **to be out of ~** estar desconcertado • **to put sb out of ~** desconcertar a algn
2 (*frm*) (*no pl*) (= *approval*) consentimiento *m* • **to give** *or* **lend ~ to** [+ *news*] acreditar
VT (*frm*) (= *permit*) • **to ~ sth** consentir *or* permitir algo • **to ~ sb doing sth** permitir a algn que haga algo
counter[1] ['kaʊntəʳ] N **1** [*of shop*] mostrador *m*; [*of canteen*] barra *f*; (= *position in post office, bank*) ventanilla *f* • **you can buy it over the ~** (*Med*) esto se compra sin receta médica • IDIOM: • **to buy under the ~** comprar de estraperlo *or* bajo mano; ▹ **over-the-counter**
2 (*in game*) ficha *f*
3 (*Tech*) contador *m*
CPD ▸ **counter staff** personal *m* de ventas
counter[2] ['kaʊntəʳ] ADV • **~ to** contrario a, en contra de • **to run ~ to** ir en sentido contrario a, ser contrario a
VT [+ *blow*] responder a, parar; [+ *attack*] contestar a, hacer frente a • **to ~ sth with sth/by doing sth** contestar a algo con algo/haciendo algo
VI • **to ~ with** contestar *or* responder con
counter... ['kaʊntəʳ] PREFIX contra...
counteract [ˌkaʊntə'rækt] VT contrarrestar
counterargument, counter-argument ['kaʊntərˌɑːgjʊmənt] N contraargumento *m*, argumento *m* en contrario
counter-attack ['kaʊntərəˌtæk] N contraataque *m*
VT, VI contraatacar
counter-attraction ['kaʊntərəˌtrækʃən] N atracción *f* rival
counterbalance ['kaʊntəˌbæləns] N contrapeso *m*; (*fig*) compensación *f*
VT contrapesar; (*fig*) compensar
counterbid ['kaʊntəbɪd] N contraoferta *f* • **to make/launch a ~** hacer/presentar una contraoferta
VT, VI contraofertar
counterblast ['kaʊntəblɑːst] N respuesta *f* vigorosa (**to** a)
counterblow ['kaʊntəbləʊ] N contragolpe *m*
countercharge ['kaʊntətʃɑːdʒ] N contraacusación *f*
countercheck ['kaʊntətʃek] N segunda comprobación *f*
VT comprobar por segunda vez
counterclaim ['kaʊntəkleɪm] N (*Jur*) contrademanda *f*
counterclockwise [ˌkaʊntə'klɒkwaɪz] ADV (*US*) en sentido contrario al de las agujas del reloj
counter-culture ['kaʊntəˌkʌltʃəʳ] N contracultura *f*
counter-espionage ['kaʊntər'espɪənɑːʒ] N contraespionaje *m*

counterexample ['kaʊntərɪgˌzɑːmpl] N contraejemplo *m*
counterfeit ['kaʊntəfiːt] ADJ (= *false*) falsificado
N falsificación *f*; (= *coin*) moneda *f* falsa; (= *note*) billete *m* falso
VT falsificar
counterfeiter ['kaʊntəfɪtəʳ] N [*of document, goods, money*] falsificador(a) *m/f*
counterfoil ['kaʊntəfɔɪl] N (*Brit*) matriz *f* (*Sp*), talón *m* (*LAm*)
counter-gambit ['kaʊntəgæmbɪt] N táctica *f* contraataque
counter-indication ['kaʊntərˌɪndɪ'keɪʃən] N contraindicación *f*
counterinflationary [ˌkaʊntərɪn'fleɪʃnərɪ] ADJ (*Econ*) antiinflacionista, contra la inflación
counter-insurgency ['kaʊntərɪn'sɜːdʒənsɪ] N medidas *fpl* antiinsurrectivas
counter-insurgent ['kaʊntərɪn'sɜːdʒənt] N contrainsurgente *mf*
counterintelligence ['kaʊntərɪnˌtelɪdʒəns] N = **counter-espionage**
counterman ['kaʊntəˌmæn] N (PL: **countermen**) (*US*) (*in restaurant*) camarero *m* (*detrás de la barra*)
countermand ['kaʊntəmɑːnd] VT revocar, cancelar
counter-measure ['kaʊntəmeʒəʳ] N contramedida *f*
counter-move ['kaʊntəmuːv] N contrajugada *f*; (*fig*) contraataque *m*; (= *manoeuvre*) contramaniobra *f*
counter-offensive ['kaʊntərə'fensɪv] N contraofensiva *f*
counteroffer ['kaʊntərˌɒfəʳ] N contraoferta *f*
counter-order ['kaʊntərˌɔːdəʳ] N contraorden *f*
counterpane ['kaʊntəpeɪn] N colcha *f*, cubrecama *m*
counterpart ['kaʊntəpɑːt] N (= *equivalent*) equivalente *m*; (= *person*) homólogo/a *m/f*
counterpoint ['kaʊntəpɔɪnt] N (*Mus*) (*also fig*) contrapunto *m*
VT (*fig*) poner el contrapunto a
counterpoise ['kaʊntəpɔɪz] N contrapeso *m*
VT contrapesar
counter-productive [ˌkaʊntəprə'dʌktɪv] ADJ contraproducente
counter-proposal ['kaʊntəprəˌpəʊzəl] N contrapropuesta *f*
counterpunch ['kaʊntəpʌntʃ] N contragolpe *m*
Counter-Reformation ['kaʊntəˌrefə'meɪʃən] N Contrarreforma *f*
counter-revolution ['kaʊntərevə'luːʃən] N contrarrevolución *f*
counter-revolutionary ['kaʊntərevə'luːʃənrɪ] ADJ contrarrevolucionario
N contrarrevolucionario/a *m/f*
countersign ['kaʊntəsaɪn] N (*Mil*) contraseña *f*
VT refrendar
countersignature ['kaʊntəˌsɪgnətʃəʳ] N refrendo *m*
countersink ['kaʊntəsɪŋk] (PT: **countersank** ['kaʊntəsæŋk]) (PP: **countersunk** ['kaʊntəsʌŋk]) VT [+ *hole*] avellanar; [+ *screw*] encastrar
counter-stroke ['kaʊntəstrəʊk] N contragolpe *m*
countersunk ['kaʊntəsʌŋk] ADJ [*screw*] encastrado
countertenor ['kaʊntəˌtenəʳ] N contratenor *m*
CPD [*voice*] de contratenor

c

counterterrorism [ˌkaʊntəˈterərɪzəm] (N) antiterrorismo *m*
(ADJ) [*official, expert, agent*] antiterrorista
counterterrorist [ˌkaʊntəˈterərɪst] (ADJ) antiterrorista
countertop [ˈkaʊntətɒp] (N) (*US*) (= *kitchen work surface*) encimera *f*
countervailing [ˈkaʊntəˌveɪlɪŋ] (ADJ) compensatorio
(CPD) ▸ **countervailing duties** aranceles *mpl* compensatorios
counterweigh [ˌkaʊntəˈweɪ] (VT) contrapesar
counterweight [ˈkaʊntəweɪt] (N) (*lit, fig*) contrapeso *m*
(VT) (*lit*) contrabalancear; (*fig*) contrarrestar, contrabalancear
counterwoman [ˈkaʊntəˌwʊmən] (N) (PL: **counterwomen**) (*US*) (*in restaurant*) camarera *f* (*detrás de la barra*)
countess [ˈkaʊntɪs] (N) condesa *f*
counting [ˈkaʊntɪŋ] (N) cálculo *m*
countless [ˈkaʊntlɪs] (ADJ) incontable, innumerable • **on ~ occasions** infinidad *f* de veces
countrified [ˈkʌntrɪfaɪd] (ADJ) rústico
country [ˈkʌntrɪ] (N) **1** (= *nation*) país *m*; (= *people*) pueblo *m* • **to go to the ~** (*Brit*) (*Pol*) convocar a elecciones generales
2 (= *fatherland*) patria *f* • **to die for one's ~** morir por la patria • **love of ~** amor a la patria
3 (*no pl*) (= *countryside*) campo *m* • **we had to leave the road and go across ~** tuvimos que dejar la carretera e ir a través del campo • **in the ~** en el campo • **to live off the ~** vivir de lo que produce la tierra
4 (*no pl*) (= *terrain, land*) terreno *m*, tierra *f* • **this is good fishing ~** esta es buena tierra para la pesca • **unknown ~** (*also fig*) terreno desconocido • **mountainous ~** región *f* montañosa • **there is some lovely ~ further south** más al sur el paisaje es muy bonito
(CPD) ▸ **country and western (music)** música *f* country, música *f* ranchera (*Mex*) ▸ **country bumpkin** (*pej*) patán *m*, paleto/a *m/f* ▸ **country club** club *m* campestre ▸ **country cottage** casita *f* (en el campo) ▸ **country cousin** (*fig*) pueblerino/a *m/f* ▸ **country dance** baile *m* regional ▸ **country dancing** danza *f* folklórica ▸ **country dweller** persona *f* que vive en el campo ▸ **country folk** gente *f* del campo ▸ **country gentleman** hacendado *m* ▸ **country house** casa *f* de campo, quinta *f*; (= *farm*) finca *f* (*esp LAm*), rancho *m* (*Mex*) ▸ **country lane** camino *m* rural ▸ **country life** vida *f* campestre *or* del campo ▸ **country mile*** • IDIOM: • **to miss sth by a ~ mile** (*US*) quedarse a una legua de algo ▸ **country music** = **country and western (music)** ▸ **country of origin** país *m* de origen ▸ **country park** parque *m* ▸ **country people** = **country folk** ▸ **country road** camino *m* vecinal ▸ **country seat** casa *f* solariega, hacienda *f* (*LAm*) ▸ **country singer** cantante *mf* country
country-born [ˌkʌntrɪˈbɔːn] (ADJ) nacido en el campo
country-bred [ˌkʌntrɪˈbred] (ADJ) criado en el campo
countryman [ˈkʌntrɪmən] (N) (PL: **countrymen**) **1** (= *rural dweller*) hombre *m* del campo, campesino *m*
2 (= *fellow-countryman*) compatriota *mf*
countryside [ˈkʌntrɪsaɪd] (N) campo *m*
countrywide [ˌkʌntrɪˈwaɪd] (ADJ) nacional
countrywoman [ˈkʌntrɪˌwʊmən] (N) (PL: **countrywomen**) **1** (= *rural dweller*) campesina *f*
2 (= *fellow-countrywoman*) compatriota *f*
county [ˈkaʊntɪ] (N) (*Brit*) condado *m*; (*US*) (= *subdivision of state*) comarca *f*, provincia *f*
(CPD) ▸ **county boundary** límite *m* comarcal *or* provincial ▸ **county clerk's office** (*US*) registro *m* civil ▸ **county council, county commission** (*US*) ≈ diputación *f* provincial ▸ **county court** (*Brit*) juzgado *m* de primera instancia ▸ **county cricket** (*Brit*) *partidos de críquet entre los condados* ▸ **county family** (*Brit*) familia *f* aristocrática rural ▸ **county prison** (*US*) centro *m* penitenciario regional ▸ **county recorder's office** (*US*) ≈ registro *m* de la propiedad ▸ **county road** (*US*) ≈ carretera *f* secundaria ▸ **county seat** (*US*) = **county town** ▸ **county town** (*Brit*) capital *f* de condado
coup [kuː] (N) **1** (*Pol*) (*also* **coup d'état**) golpe *m* (de estado)
2 (= *triumph*) éxito *m* • **to bring off a ~** obtener un éxito inesperado
(CPD) ▸ **coup de grace** golpe *m* de gracia ▸ **coup de théâtre** golpe *m* de efecto
coupé [ˈkuːpeɪ] (N) (*Aut*) cupé *m*
couple [ˈkʌpl] (N) **1** (= *pair*) par *m* • **a ~ of** un par de
2 (= *partners*) pareja *f*; (= *married couple*) matrimonio *m* • **young ~** matrimonio *m* joven
3 (= *two or three*) • **just a ~ of minutes** dos minutos nada más • **I know a ~ of lads who can do the job** conozco a un par de chicos que pueden hacer el trabajo • **we had a ~ in a bar*** tomamos un par de copas en un bar
(VT) **1** [+ *names etc*] unir, juntar; [+ *ideas*] asociar • **to ~ sth with sth** unir algo a algo, juntar algo con algo
2 (*Tech*) • **to ~ (on *or* up)** acoplar (a), enganchar (a)
(VI) (*Zool*) copularse
coupledom [ˈkʌpldəm] (N) convivencia *f* en pareja
coupler [ˈkʌpləʳ] (N) (*Comput*) acoplador *m*; (*US*) (*Rail*) enganche *m*; ▹ **acoustic**
couplet [ˈkʌplɪt] (N) pareado *m*
coupling [ˈkʌplɪŋ] (N) **1** (*Tech*) acoplamiento *m*; (*Aut, Rail*) enganche *m*
2 (*sexual*) cópula *f*
coupon [ˈkuːpɒn] (N) (= *voucher in newspaper, advertisement*) cupón *m*; (*for price reduction or gifts*) vale *m*; (= *football pools coupon*) boleto *m* (de quiniela)
courage [ˈkʌrɪdʒ] (N) valor *m*, valentía *f* • **~!** ¡ánimo! • **I haven't the ~ to refuse** no tengo valor para negarme • **to have the ~ of one's convictions** obrar de acuerdo con su conciencia • **to pluck up one's ~** • **take one's ~ in both hands** armarse de valor • **to take ~ from** cobrar ánimos *or* sacar fuerzas de
courageous [kəˈreɪdʒəs] (ADJ) valiente, valeroso
courageously [kəˈreɪdʒəslɪ] (ADV) valientemente
courgette [kʊəˈʒet] (N) (*Brit*) calabacín *m*, calabacita *f*
courier [ˈkʊrɪəʳ] (N) (= *messenger*) mensajero/a *m/f*; (= *tourist guide*) guía *mf* de turismo
course [kɔːs] (N) **1** (= *route, direction*) [*of ship, plane*] rumbo *m*; [*of river*] curso *m*; [*of planet*] órbita *f* • **on a southerly ~** con rumbo sur • **to change ~** (*lit*) cambiar de rumbo • **the government has changed ~ on Europe** el gobierno ha dado un nuevo rumbo *or* giro a su política con respecto a Europa • **to be/go off ~** (*lit, fig*) haberse desviado/desviarse de su rumbo • **the plane was 300 miles off ~** el avión se había desviado 300 millas de su rumbo • **the boat was blown off ~** el viento desvió al barco de su rumbo • **we are on ~ for victory** vamos bien encaminados para la victoria • **to plot a ~ (for Jamaica)** trazar el rumbo (para ir a Jamaica) • **to set (a) ~ for** (*Naut*) poner rumbo a; ▹ **collision**
2 (= *line of action*) • **I'd advise you not to follow that ~** te aconsejaría que no escogieras ese camino • **the best ~ would be to ...** lo mejor sería ... • **we have to decide on the best ~ of action** tenemos que decidir cuáles son las mejores medidas a tomar • **it's the only ~ left open to him** es la única opción que le queda
3 (= *process*) curso *m* • **it changed the ~ of history/of her life** cambió el curso de la historia/de su vida • **in the normal *or* ordinary ~ of events** normalmente • **in the ~ of:** • **in the ~ of my work** en el cumplimiento de mi trabajo • **in the ~ of conversation** en el curso *or* transcurso de la conversación • **in *or* during the ~ of the next few days** en el curso de los próximos días • **in *or* during the ~ of the journey** durante el viaje • **to let things take *or* run their ~** dejar que las cosas sigan su curso; ▹ **due, event, matter**
4 • **of ~** claro, desde luego, por supuesto, cómo no (*esp LAm*), sí pues (*S. Cone*) • **of ~! I should have known** ¡pero si está claro! me lo tenía que haber imaginado • **"can I have a drink?" — "of ~ you can"** —¿puedo tomar algo de beber? —claro *or* desde luego *or* por supuesto que sí • **I've read about her in the papers, of ~** por supuesto, la conozco de los periódicos • **of ~, I may be wrong** claro que puedo estar confundido • **of ~ not!** (*answering*) ¡claro que no!, ¡por supuesto que no! • **"can I go?" — "of ~ not *or* of ~ you can't"** —¿puedo ir? —claro que no *or* ni hablar *or* por supuesto que no
5 (*Scol, Univ*) curso *m* • **to go on a ~** ir a hacer un curso • **a ~ in business administration** un curso de administración de empresas • **short ~** cursillo *m* • **~ of study** (*gen*) estudios *mpl*; (*Univ*) carrera *f*, estudios *mpl* • **to take *or* do a ~ in *or* on sth** hacer un curso de algo
6 (*Med*) (= *regimen*) • **she was put on a ~ of steroids** le recetaron esteroides, le pusieron un tratamiento a base de esteroides • **a ~ of treatment** un tratamiento
7 (*Sport*) (= *distance*) recorrido *m*; (= *surface*) pista *f*; (= *racecourse*) hipódromo *m* • **golf ~** campo *m* or (*S. Cone*) cancha *f* (de golf) • IDIOM: • **to stay the ~** no cejar, aguantar hasta el final; ▹ **obstacle**
8 (*Culin*) plato *m* • **main ~** plato *m* principal • **a three-course meal** una comida de tres platos
9 (*Naut*) (= *sail*) vela *f* mayor
10 (*Constr*) (= *layer*) [*of bricks*] hilada *f*
(VI) [*water, air*] correr; [*tears*] rodar; [*sweat*] caer; (*fig*) [*emotion*] invadir • **it sent the blood coursing through his veins** hacía que la sangre corriera por sus venas • **rage/relief ~d through him** le invadió la ira/una sensación de alivio
(VT) (*Hunting†*) cazar
(CPD) ▸ **course book** manual *m* (del curso) ▸ **course fees** derechos *mpl* de matrícula ▸ **course requirements** *estudios previos requeridos para poder realizar determinado curso* ▸ **course work** trabajos *mpl* (para clase)
courser [ˈkɔːsəʳ] (N) **1** (= *dog*) perro *m* de carreras
2 (*poet*) (= *horse*) corcel *m* (*poet*)
coursing [ˈkɔːsɪŋ] (N) caza *f* con perros
court [kɔːt] (N) **1** (*Jur*) tribunal *m*, juzgado *m*, corte *f* (*esp LAm*); (= *officers and/or public*) tribunal *m* • **he was brought before the ~ on a charge of theft** fue procesado por robo • **in open ~** en pleno tribunal • **to rule sth out of ~** no admitir algo • **to settle (a case) out of ~** llegar a un acuerdo las partes (sin ir a

juicio) • **to take sb to ~ (over sth)** llevar a algn a los tribunales *or* ante el tribunal (por algo); ▹ **crown, high, magistrate, out-of-court, supreme**

2 (*Tennis*) pista *f*, cancha *f* • **hard/grass ~** pista *f or* cancha *f* dura/de hierba

3 (*royal*) (= *palace*) palacio *m*; (= *people*) corte *f* • **at ~** en la corte • **to hold ~** (*fig*) dar audiencia, recibir en audiencia

4 (*Archit*) patio *m*

5 • **to pay ~ to**† hacer la corte a

VT 1 [+ *woman*] pretender *or* cortejar a

2 (*fig*) (= *seek*) [+ *favour*] intentar conseguir; [+ *death, disaster*] buscar, exponerse a • **to ~ favour with sb** intentar congraciarse con algn

VI † ser novios • **are you ~ing?** ¿tienes novio? • **they've been ~ing for three years** llevan tres años de relaciones • **a ~ing couple** una pareja de novios

CPD ▸ **court action** • **she was threatened with ~ action** la amenazaron con llevarla a juicio, la amenazaron con presentar una demanda judicial contra ella ▸ **court appearance** comparecencia *f* ante el tribunal ▸ **court card** (*esp Brit*) figura *f* ▸ **court case** proceso *m* ▸ **court circular** noticiario *m* de la corte ▸ **court hearing** vista *f* oral ▸ **court martial** = **court-martial** ▸ **court of appeal** tribunal *m* de apelación ▸ **court of inquiry** comisión *f* de investigación ▸ **court of justice, court of law** tribunal *m* de justicia ▸ **Court of Session** (*Scot*) Tribunal *m* Supremo de Escocia ▸ **court order** mandato *m* judicial ▸ **court ruling** decisión *f* judicial ▸ **court shoe** (*Brit*) escarpín *m*

Courtelle® [kɔː'tel] N Courtelle® *f*

courteous ['kɜːtɪəs] ADJ cortés, atento

courteously ['kɜːtɪəslɪ] ADV cortésmente

courtesan [ˌkɔːtɪ'zæn] N cortesana *f*

courtesy ['kɜːtɪsɪ] N (= *politeness*) cortesía *f*; (= *polite act*) atención *f*, gentileza *f* • **by ~ of** (por) cortesía de • **to exchange courtesies** intercambiar cumplidos de etiqueta • **will you do me the ~ of ...?** si fuera tan amable de ..., haga el favor de ... • **you might have had the ~ to tell me** podrías haber tenido la gentileza de decírmelo • **I'll do it out of ~** lo haré por cortesía

CPD ▸ **courtesy bus** autobús *m* de cortesía ▸ **courtesy call** visita *f* de cumplido ▸ **courtesy car** coche *m* de cortesía ▸ **courtesy card** (*US*) tarjeta *f* (de visita) ▸ **courtesy coach** (*Brit*) autocar *m or* autobús *m* de cortesía ▸ **courtesy light** (*Aut*) luz *f* interna ▸ **courtesy title** título *m* de cortesía ▸ **courtesy visit** = **courtesy call**

courthouse ['kɔːthaʊs] N (PL: **courthouses** ['kɔːthaʊzɪz]) (*esp US*) (*Jur*) palacio *m* de justicia

courtier ['kɔːtɪəʳ] N cortesano/a *m/f*

courtliness ['kɔːtlɪnɪs] N (= *politeness*) cortesía *f*; (= *refinement*) refinamiento *m*

courtly ['kɔːtlɪ] ADJ cortés, elegante, fino

CPD ▸ **courtly love** amor *m* cortés

court-martial ['kɔːt'mɑːʃəl] N (PL: **courts-martial, court-martials**) consejo *m* de guerra, tribunal *m* militar

VT juzgar en consejo de guerra

courtroom ['kɔːtrʊm] N sala *f* de justicia, sala *f* de tribunal

courtship ['kɔːtʃɪp] N (= *act*) cortejo *m*; (= *period*) noviazgo *m*

courtyard ['kɔːtjɑːd] N patio *m*

couscous ['kuːskuːs] N (= *grain, dish*) cuscús *m*

cousin ['kʌzn] N primo/a *m/f* • **first ~** primo/a *m/f* carnal • **second ~** primo/a *m/f* segundo/a

couth [kuːθ] N (*US*) buenos modales *mpl*

couture [kuː'tjʊəʳ] N alta costura *f*

couturier [kuː'tʊərɪˌeɪ] N modisto *m*

cove¹ [kəʊv] N (*Geog*) cala *f*, ensenada *f*; (*US*) (= *valley*) valle *m*

cove²* [kəʊv] N (*Brit*†) (= *fellow*) tío* *m*

coven ['kʌvən] N aquelarre *m*

covenant ['kʌvɪnənt] N 1 (*legal*) pacto *m*, convenio *m*; (*also* **tax covenant**) (*Brit*) *sistema de contribuciones caritativas con beneficios fiscales para el beneficiario*; ▹ **deed**

2 • **Covenant** (*Bible*) Alianza *f*

VT pactar, concertar • **to ~ £20 a year to a charity** concertar el pago de 20 libras anuales a una sociedad benéfica

VI • **to ~ with sb for sth** pactar algo con algn

covenanter ['kʌvɪnəntəʳ] N (*Scot*) (*Hist*) firmante *mf* de un pacto

Coventry ['kɒvəntrɪ] N • IDIOM: • **to send sb to ~** (*Brit*) hacer el vacío a algn

cover ['kʌvəʳ] N 1 (*gen*) [*of dish, saucepan*] tapa *f*, tapadera *f*; [*of furniture, typewriter*] funda *f*; [*of lens*] tapa *f*; (*for book*) forro *m*; (*for merchandise, on vehicle*) cubierta *f*

2 (= *bedspread*) cubrecama *m*, colcha *f*; (*often pl*) (= *blanket*) manta *f*, frazada *f* (*LAm*), cobija *f* (*LAm*)

3 [*of magazine*] portada *f*; [*of book*] cubierta *f*, tapa *f* • **to read a book from ~ to ~** leer un libro de cabo a rabo

4 (*Comm*) (= *envelope*) sobre *m* • **under separate ~** por separado; ▹ **first-day cover**

5 (*no pl*) (= *shelter*) cobijo *m*, refugio *m*; (*for hiding*) escondite *m*; (= *covering fire*) cobertura *f* • **to break ~** salir al descubierto • **to run for ~** correr a cobijarse; (*fig*) ponerse a buen recaudo • **to take ~ (from)** (*Mil*) ponerse a cubierto (de); (= *shelter*) protegerse *or* resguardarse (de) • **under ~** a cubierto; (= *indoors*) bajo techo • **under ~ of darkness** al amparo de la oscuridad

6 (*no pl*) (*Econ, Insurance*) cobertura *f* • **without ~** (*Econ*) sin cobertura • **full/fire ~** (*Insurance*) cobertura total/contra incendios

7 (*in espionage etc*) tapadera *f* • **to blow sb's ~*** (*accidentally*) poner a algn al descubierto; (*intentionally*) desenmascarar a algn

8 (*frm*) (*at table*) cubierto *m*

9 (*Mus*) = **cover version**

VT 1 • **to ~ sth (with)** [+ *surface, wall*] cubrir algo (con *or* de); [+ *saucepan, hole, eyes, face*] tapar algo (con); [+ *book*] forrar algo (con); [+ *chair*] tapizar algo (con) • **to ~ one's face with one's hands** taparse la cara con las manos • **to be ~ed in** *or* **with snow/dust/chocolate** estar cubierto de nieve/polvo/chocolate • **~ed with confusion/shame** lleno de confusión/muerto de vergüenza • IDIOM: • **to ~ o.s. with glory/disgrace** cubrirse de gloria/hundirse en la miseria

2 (= *hide*) [+ *feelings, facts, mistakes*] ocultar; [+ *noise*] ahogar • **to ~ (up) one's tracks** (*lit, fig*) borrar las huellas

3 (= *protect*) (*Mil, Sport*) cubrir • **to keep sb ~ed** cubrir a algn • **I've got you ~ed!** ¡te tengo a tiro!, ¡te estoy apuntando! • **the soldiers ~ed our retreat** los soldados nos cubrieron la retirada • **he only said that to ~ himself** lo dijo solo para cubrirse • IDIOMS: • **to ~ one's back*** • **~ one's ass**** cubrirse las espaldas

4 (*Insurance*) cubrir • **what does your travel insurance ~ you for?** ¿qué (cosas) cubre tu seguro de viaje? • **the house is ~ed against fire** la casa está asegurada contra incendios

5 (= *be sufficient for*) [+ *cost, expenses*] cubrir, sufragar • **to ~ a loss** cubrir una pérdida • **£10 will ~ everything** con 10 libras será suficiente

6 (= *take in, include*) incluir • **goods ~ed by this invoice** los artículos incluídos en esta factura • **such factories will not be ~ed by this report** tales fábricas no se verán incluídas en este informe • **we must ~ all possibilities** debemos tener en cuenta todas las posibilidades

7 (= *deal with*) [+ *problem, area*] abarcar; [+ *points in discussion*] tratar, discutir • **his speech ~ed most of the points raised** su discurso abarcó la mayoría de los puntos planteados • **his work ~s many different fields** su trabajo abarca muchas especialidades distintas • **no law ~s a situation like this** ninguna ley contempla una situación semejante

8 [+ *distance*] recorrer, cubrir • **we ~ed eight miles in one hour** recorrimos ocho millas en una hora • **to ~ a lot of ground** (*in travel, work*) recorrer mucho trecho; (= *deal with many subjects*) abarcar muchos temas

9 (*Press*) (= *report on*) cubrir • **all the newspapers ~ed the story** todos los periódicos cubrieron el caso • **he was sent to ~ the riots** lo enviaron para que hiciera un reportaje de los disturbios

10 (*Mus*) • **to ~ a song** hacer una versión de una canción

11 (= *inseminate*) [+ *animal*] cubrir

VI • **to ~ for sb** (*at work etc*) suplir a algn; (= *protect*) encubrir a algn

CPD ▸ **cover band** *grupo musical que imita canciones de éxito* ▸ **cover charge** (*in restaurant*) (precio *m* del) cubierto *m* ▸ **cover girl** modelo *f* de portada ▸ **cover letter** (*US*) carta *f* de explicación ▸ **cover note** (*Brit*) (*Insurance*) ≈ seguro *m* provisional ▸ **cover price** precio *m* de venta al público ▸ **cover story** (*Press*) tema *m* de portada; (*in espionage etc*) tapadera *f* ▸ **cover version** (*Mus*) versión *f*

▸ **cover in** VT + ADV cubrir; (= *put roof on*) poner un techo a, techar

▸ **cover over** VT + ADV [+ *surface, object, hole*] cubrir, tapar; [+ *problem*] tapar, esconder

▸ **cover up** VT + ADV 1 [+ *child, object*] cubrir completamente, tapar

2 (*fig*) (= *hide*) [+ *facts*] ocultar; [+ *emotions*] disimular

VI + ADV 1 (*with clothes*) abrigarse, taparse

2 (*fig*) • **to ~ up for sb** encubrir a algn

coverage ['kʌvərɪdʒ] N 1 (*Press*) reportaje *m* • **to give full ~ to an event** (= *report widely*) dar amplia difusión a un suceso; (= *report in depth*) informar a fondo sobre un suceso

2 (*Insurance*) cobertura *f*

coveralls ['kʌvərɔːlz] NPL (*US*) (= *overalls*) mono *msing*

covered ['kʌvəd] ADJ (= *enclosed*) [*area*] cubierto

covered wagon [ˌkʌvəd'wægən] N carreta *f* entoldada

covering ['kʌvərɪŋ] N 1 (= *wrapping*) cubierta *f*, envoltura *f*; (= *dress etc*) abrigo *m*

2 (= *layer*) • **a ~ of snow/dust/icing** una capa de nieve/polvo/azúcar glaseado

CPD ▸ **covering letter** (*Brit*) carta *f* de explicación

coverlet ['kʌvəlɪt] N sobrecama *m*, colcha *f*, cobertor *m*

covert ['kʌvət] ADJ (*gen*) secreto, encubierto; [*glance*] furtivo, disimulado

N soto *m*, matorral *m*

CPD ▸ **covert attack** ataque *m* por sorpresa

covertly ['kʌvətlɪ] ADV [*observe*] encubiertamente

cover-up ['kʌvərʌp] N encubrimiento *m* • **there's been a cover-up** están tratando de encubrir el asunto

covet ['kʌvɪt] VT codiciar

covetable ['kʌvɪtəbl] ADJ codiciable

C

coveted ['kʌvɪtɪd] ADJ [*title, award, prize*] codiciado
covetous ['kʌvɪtəs] ADJ [*person*] codicioso; [*glance*] ávido
covetousness ['kʌvɪtəsnɪs] N codicia *f*
covey ['kʌvɪ] N **1** (*Orn*) nidada *f* (*de perdices*)
2 (*fig*) grupo *m*
cow¹ [kaʊ] N **1** (*Zool*) vaca *f*; (= *female of other species*) hembra *f* • IDIOM: • **till the cows come home** hasta que las ranas críen pelo
2‡ (*pej*) (= *woman*) estúpida *f*, bruja *f*
CPD ▸ **cow dung** excrementos *mpl* de vaca ▸ **cow house** establo *m* ▸ **cow parsley** perejil *m* de monte ▸ **cow town*** (*US*) pueblucho *m* de mala muerte
cow² [kaʊ] VT [+ *person*] intimidar, acobardar • **a cowed look** una mirada temerosa
coward ['kaʊəd] N cobarde *mf*
cowardice ['kaʊədɪs], **cowardliness** ['kaʊədlɪnɪs] N cobardía *f*
cowardly ['kaʊədlɪ] ADJ cobarde
cowbell ['kaʊbel] N cencerro *m*
cowboy ['kaʊbɔɪ] N **1** vaquero *m*, gaucho *m* (*Arg*); (*Cine etc*) cowboy *m* • **~s and Indians** (= *game*) indios *mpl* y americanos
2 (*Brit**) (*pej*) chorizo/a *m/f* (*Sp*) • **he's a real ~** es un auténtico chorizo • **the ~s of the building trade** los piratas de la construcción
CPD ▸ **cowboy boots** botas *fpl* camperas ▸ **cowboy hat** sombrero *m* de cowboy ▸ **cowboy outfit** traje *m* de vaquero
cowcatcher ['kaʊˌkætʃəʳ] N rastrillo *m* delantero, quitapiedras *m inv*
cower ['kaʊəʳ] VI encogerse (de miedo) • **the servants were ~ing in a corner** los criados se habían refugiado medrosos en un rincón
cowgirl ['kaʊgɜːl] N vaquera *f*
cowhand ['kaʊhænd] N vaquero/a *m/f*
cowherd ['kaʊhɜːd] N pastor(a) *m/f* de ganado, vaquero/a *m/f*
cowhide ['kaʊhaɪd] N cuero *m*
cowl [kaʊl] N (= *hood*) capucha *f*; (= *garment*) cogulla *f*; [*of chimney*] sombrerete *m*
cowlick ['kaʊlɪk] N (*US*) chavito *m*, mechón *m*
cowling ['kaʊlɪŋ] N cubierta *f*
cowman ['kaʊmən] N (PL: **cowmen**) vaquero *m*; (= *owner*) ganadero *m*
co-worker ['kəʊ'wɜːkəʳ] N colaborador(a) *m/f*
cowpat ['kaʊpæt] N boñiga *f*
cowpoke* ['kaʊpəʊk] N (*US*) vaquero *m*
cowpox ['kaʊpɒks] N vacuna *f*
cowrie ['kaʊrɪ] N cauri *m*
cowshed ['kaʊʃed] N establo *m*
cowslip ['kaʊslɪp] N (*Bot*) primavera *f*, prímula *f*
cox [kɒks] N timonel *mf*
VT gobernar
VI hacer *or* actuar de timonel
coxcomb ['kɒkskəʊm] N cresta *f* de gallo
coxless pairs [ˌkɒkslɪs'pɛəz] N dos *m* sin timonel
coxswain ['kɒksn] N timonel *mf*
Coy ABBR (*Mil*) = **company**
coy [kɔɪ] ADJ (COMPAR: **coyer**, SUPERL: **coyest**) **1** (= *demure*) [*person, smile*] tímido; (*pej*) (= *coquettish*) coqueta, coquetón
2 (= *evasive*) esquivo, reticente
coyly ['kɔɪlɪ] ADV **1** (= *demurely*) tímidamente; (*pej*) (= *coquettishly*) con coquetería
2 (= *evasively*) con evasivas
coyness ['kɔɪnɪs] N **1** (= *demureness*) timidez *f*; (*pej*) (= *coquettishness*) coquetería *f*
2 (= *evasiveness*) evasivas *fpl*, reticencias *fpl*
coyote [kɔɪ'əʊtɪ] N coyote *m*
coypu ['kɔɪpuː] N (PL: **coypus** *or* **coypu**) coipo *m*
coz* [kɒz] = **cousin**
'coz‡ [kɒz] = **because**
coziness ['kəʊzɪnɪs] N (*US*) = **cosiness**
cozy ['kəʊzɪ] ADJ (*US*) = **cosy**
cozzie* ['kɒzɪ] N (*Brit, Australia*) = **cossie**
CP N ABBR **1** (*Pol*) (= **Communist Party**) PC *m*
2 (*Comm*) (= **carriage paid**) pp
3 = **Cape Province**
cp ABBR (= **compare**) comp
C/P, c/p ABBR (= **carriage paid**) pp
CPA N ABBR **1** (*US*) (*Econ*) = **Certified Public Accountant**
2 = **critical path analysis**
CPI N ABBR (*US*) (= **Consumer Price Index**) IPC *m*
cpi ABBR (*Comput*) = **characters per inch**
Cpl N ABBR (*Mil*) = **Corporal**
CP/M N ABBR (= **Control Program for Microprocessors**) CP/M *m*
CPO N ABBR **1** (*Naut*) = **Chief Petty Officer**
2 = **Crime Prevention Officer**
CPR N ABBR = **cardiopulmonary resuscitation**
cps ABBR (*Comput*) **1** (= **characters per second**) cps
2 = **cycles per second**
CPSA N ABBR (*Brit*) (= **Civil and Public Services Association**) *sindicato de funcionarios*
CPU N ABBR (*Comput*) (= **central processing unit**) UPC *f*, UCP *f*
CPVE N ABBR (*Brit*) = **Certificate of Pre-vocational Education**
Cr ABBR **1** (*Comm*) (= **credit**) H.
2 (*Comm*) (= **creditor**) acr.
3 (*Pol*) = **councillor**
crab [kræb] N **1** (*Zool*) cangrejo *m*, jaiba *f* (*LAm*) • **the Crab** (*Astron*) (la constelación de) Cáncer • IDIOM: • **to catch a ~** (*Rowing*) fallar con el remo, dar una calada
2 crabs (*Med*) ladillas *fpl*
VI • **to ~ (about)** (*US**) quejarse (acerca de)
CPD ▸ **crab apple** (= *fruit*) manzana *f* silvestre; (= *tree*) manzano *m* silvestre ▸ **crab grass** garranchuelo *m* ▸ **crab louse** ladilla *f*
crabbed ['kræbd] ADJ **1** [*writing*] apretado, indescifrable
2 [*mood*] malhumorado, hosco
crabby* ['kræbɪ] ADJ malhumorado, hosco
crabmeat ['kræbmiːt] N carne *f* de cangrejo
crabwise ['kræbˌwaɪz] ADJ [*movement*] como de cangrejo, lateral
ADV [*move*] como cangrejo, lateralmente
crack [kræk] N **1** (= *fracture*) (*in plate, glass*) raja *f*; (*in wall, ceiling, ice*) grieta *f*; (*in skin*) grieta *f*; (*fig*) (*in system, relationship*) grieta *f* • IDIOM: • **to paper over the ~s** (*fig*) disimular las grietas
2 (= *slight opening*) rendija *f* • **I opened the door a ~** abrí un poquito la puerta
3 (= *noise*) [*of twigs*] crujido *m*; [*of whip*] chasquido *m*; [*of rifle*] estampido *m*, estallido *m*; [*of thunder*] estampido *m*, estruendo *m* • IDIOMS: • **to get a fair ~ of the whip** tener la oportunidad de demostrar lo que vale • **to give sb a fair ~ of the whip** dar la oportunidad a algn de demostrar lo que vale
4 (= *blow*) golpe *m* • **he got a nasty ~ on the head** se llevó un buen golpe en la cabeza
5* (= *attempt*) intento *m* • **to have** *or* **take a ~ at sth** intentar algo • **he was anxious to have the first ~ at it** estaba deseoso de ser el primero en intentarlo
6* (= *joke, insult*) comentario *m* burlón • **he made a silly ~ about our new car** hizo un chiste tonto sobre nuestro coche nuevo
7 (= *drug*) crack *m*
8 • **at the ~ of dawn** al romper el alba • **I'm not getting up at the ~ of dawn!*** ¡no me voy a levantar con el canto del gallo!*
9* (= *fun*) • **it's good ~** es muy divertido
ADJ [*team, sportsperson, troops*] de primera • **he's a ~ shot** es un tirador de primera
VT **1** (= *break*) [+ *glass, pottery*] rajar; [+ *wood, ground, wall*] agrietar, resquebrajar; [+ *ice*] resquebrajar; [+ *skin*] agrietar; (*fig**) [+ *person*] derrotar • **to ~ sb's resolve** hacerle perder la determinación a algn
2 (= *break open*) [+ *nut*] cascar; [+ *egg*] cascar, romper; [+ *safe*] forzar; (*fig**) [+ *market*] entrar en, introducirse en; [+ *drugs/spy ring*] desarticular • **to ~ (open) a bottle*** abrir una botella; ▷ **nut**
3 (= *hit*) golpear • **he fell and ~ed his head on the pavement** se cayó y se golpeó la cabeza con la acera
4 (= *cause to sound*) [+ *whip*] chasquear, restallar; [+ *finger joints*] hacer crujir • IDIOM: • **to ~ the whip** apretarle a algn las clavijas
5* (= *tell*) [+ *joke*] contar • **to ~ jokes** bromear, contar chistes
6 (= *solve*) [+ *problem, case*] resolver; [+ *code*] descifrar • **the police think they've ~ed it** la policía cree haberlo resuelto
7 • **to ~ a smile** sonreír
VI **1** (= *break*) [*glass, pottery*] rajarse; [*wall, wood, ground*] agrietarse, resquebrajarse; [*ice*] resquebrajarse; [*skin*] agrietarse
2 [*voice*] (*with emotion*) quebrarse
3 (= *yield, break down*) [*person*] desmoronarse • **I thought his nerve would ~** creía que iba a perder el valor • **to ~ under the strain** [*person*] desmoronarse bajo la presión, sufrir una crisis nerviosa a cause de la presión; [*relationship*] desmoronarse; [*alliance*] desmoronarse *or* quebrantarse bajo la presión
4 (= *make noise*) [*thunder*] retumbar; [*whip*] chasquear; [*dry wood, joints*] crujir
5 • **to get ~ing*** poner manos a la obra • **you'd better get ~ing** más te vale poner manos a la obra • **I promised to get ~ing on** *or* **with the decorating** le prometí que empezaría a pintar inmediatamente
CPD ▸ **crack cocaine** crack *m* ▸ **crack house** (*Drugs*) *lugar donde se vende crack or cocaína dura*
▸ **crack down** VI + ADV • **to ~ down (on sth/sb)** tomar medidas enérgicas *or* duras (contra algo/algn)
▸ **crack on*** VI + ADV (*Brit*) ponerse en marcha, ponerse las pilas*
▸ **crack up*** VI + ADV **1** (= *break down*) [*person*] desmoronarse, sufrir una crisis nerviosa; [*relationship*] desmoronarse; [*alliance*] desmoronarse, quebrantarse
2 (= *laugh*) troncharse de risa*
VT + ADV • **the film's not all it's ~ed up to be** la película no es tan buena como se dice • **he's not all he's ~ed up to be** no es tan maravilloso como lo pintan*
crackajack* ['krækədʒæk] N, ADJ (*US*) = **crackerjack**
crack-brained* ['krækbreɪnd] ADJ loco
crackdown ['krækdaʊn] N campaña *f* (**on** contra), medidas *fpl* enérgicas (**on** contra)
cracked [krækt] ADJ **1** [*cup, plate*] rajado; [*wall*] agrietado; [*lips*] cortado, agrietado; [*skin*] agrietado • **the bone's not really broken, only ~** el hueso no está rota en realidad, solo tiene una fisura pequeña
2 [*voice*] cascado
3* (= *mad*) chiflado*, tarado*
CPD ▸ **cracked wheat** trigo *m* partido
cracker ['krækəʳ] N **1** (= *firework*) buscapiés *m inv*
2 (*also* **Christmas cracker**) *tubito con decoración navideña que contiene un pequeño regalo sorpresa y*

que se abre al tirar dos personas de sus extremos
3 (= *biscuit*) galleta *f* salada, cracker *m*
4 (*Brit**) • **a ~ of a game** un partido fenomenal*
crackerjack* ['krækədʒæk] N (= *person*) as* *m*; (= *thing*) bomba* *f*
ADJ bomba*, súper*
crackers* ['krækəz] ADJ (*Brit*) lelo, chiflado*
crackhead* ['kræk,hed] N adicto/a *m/f* al crack
cracking ['krækɪŋ] N 1 (*Chem*) [*of petroleum*] craqueo *m*
2 (= *cracks*) grietas *fpl*, agrietamiento *m*
ADJ (*Brit**) 1 (= *very fast*) • **at a ~ speed** *or* **pace** a toda pastilla*
2 (= *excellent*) de órdago*
ADV (*Brit**) • **this book is a ~ good read** este libro es superameno
crackle ['krækl] N (*usu no pl*) (= *noise*) [*of twigs burning*] crepitación *f*, chisporroteo *m*; [*of frying*] chisporroteo *m*; [*of dry leaves*] crujido *m*; [*of shots*] traqueteo *m*; (*on telephone*) interferencia *f*
VI [*burning twigs*] crepitar, chisporrotear; [*bacon*] chisporrotear; [*dry leaves*] crujir; [*shots*] traquetear; [*phone line*] tener interferencias
crackling ['kræklɪŋ] N 1 (= *no pl*) (*Culin*) chicharrones *mpl*
2 (= *sound*) chisporroteo *m*; (*on radio, telephone*) interferencias *fpl*
crackly ['krækəlɪ] ADJ [*phone line, noise*] chirriante, chisporroteante
crackpot* ['krækpɒt] ADJ tonto
N chiflado/a* *m/f*, excéntrico/a *m/f*
crack-up ['krækʌp] N (*Med*) crisis *f inv* nerviosa, colapso *m* nervioso; (*Econ etc*) quiebra *f*
cradle ['kreɪdl] N 1 (= *cot, birthplace etc*) cuna *f* • IDIOMS: • **from the ~ to the grave** desde que nació, nacen *etc* hasta que murió, mueren *etc* • **to rob the ~*** casarse con una persona mucho más joven
2 [*of telephone*] soporte *m*, horquilla *f*
3 (*Constr*) andamio *m* volante
VT [+ *child*] mecer, acunar; [+ *object*] abrazar • **to ~ a child in one's arms** mecer un niño en los brazos
CPD ▸ **cradle cap** costra *f* láctea ▸ **cradle snatcher*** • **she's a ~ snatcher** siempre va detrás de los jovencitos
cradlesong ['kreɪdlsɒŋ] N canción *f* de cuna
craft [krɑːft] N 1 (= *trade*) oficio *m*
2 (= *no pl*) (= *skill*) destreza *f*, habilidad *f*
3 (= *handicraft*) artesanía *f* • **arts and ~s** artesanías *fpl*
4 (*pej*) (= *cunning*) astucia *f*, maña *f*
5 (= *boat*) (*pl inv*) barco *m*, embarcación *f*
VT hacer (a mano) • **~ed products** productos *mpl* de artesanía
CPD ▸ **craft centre** centro *m* de artesanía ▸ **craft, design and technology** (*Scol*) diseño *m* y pretecnología ▸ **craft fair** feria *f* de artesanía ▸ **craft knife** cutter *m* ▸ **craft union** sindicato *m* de obreros especializados ▸ **craft work** artesanía *f*
craftily ['krɑːftɪlɪ] ADV astutamente
craftiness ['krɑːftɪnɪs] N astucia *f*
craftsman ['krɑːftsmən] N (PL: **craftsmen**) artesano *m*
craftsmanship ['krɑːftsmənʃɪp] N (*no pl*) (= *skill*) destreza *f*, habilidad *f*; (= *workmanship*) trabajo *m*
craftsperson ['krɑːfts,pɜːsn] N (PL: **craftspeople**) artesano/a *m/f*
craftswoman ['krɑːfts,wʊmən] N (PL: **craftswomen**) artesana *f*
crafty ['krɑːftɪ] ADJ (COMPAR: **craftier**, SUPERL: **craftiest**) 1 [*person*] astuto, vivo; [*action*] hábil
2 [*gadget etc*] ingenioso
crag [kræg] N peñasco *m*, risco *m*
craggy ['krægɪ] ADJ (COMPAR: **craggier**, SUPERL: **craggiest**) [*rock*] rocoso, escarpado; [*features*] hosco, arrugado
craic* [kræk] N (*Irl*) ambiente *m*, marcha *f* • **it's good ~** es muy divertido
crake [kreɪk] N gallareta *f*
cram [kræm] VT 1 (= *stuff*) meter (**into** en) • **we can't ~ any more in** es imposible meter más • **to ~ food into one's mouth** llenarse la boca de comida • **to ~ things into a case** ir metiendo cosas en una maleta hasta que ya no cabe más nada • **she ~med her hat down over her eyes** se enfundó el sombrero hasta los ojos
2 (= *fill*) llenar a reventar (**with** de) • **the hall is ~med** la sala está de bote en bote • **the room was ~med with furniture** la habitación estaba atestada de muebles • **his head is ~med with strange ideas** tiene la cabeza llena de ideas raras • **to ~ o.s. with food** atiborrarse de comida, darse un atracón*
3 (*Scol*) [+ *subject*] empollar, aprender apresuradamente; [+ *pupil*] preparar apresuradamente para un examen
VI 1 [*people*] apelotonarse (**into** en) • **can I ~ in here?** ¿hay un hueco para mí aquí? • **seven of us ~med into the Mini** los siete logramos encajarnos en el Mini
2 [*pupil*] (*for exam*) empollar
cram-full ['kræm'fʊl] ADJ atestado (**of** de), de bote en bote
crammer ['kræməʳ] N (*Scol*) (= *pupil*) empollón/ona *m/f*; (= *teacher*) profesor(a) *m/f* (*que prepara rapidísimamente a sus alumnos para los exámenes*)
cramp¹ [kræmp] N (*Med*) calambre *m* • **writer's ~** calambre *m* en las manos (por escribir mucho)
VT (= *restrict*) [+ *development*] poner obstáculos a, poner trabas a • IDIOM: • **to ~ sb's style** cortar las alas a algn
cramp² [kræmp] N (*Tech*) grapa *f*; (*Archit*) pieza *f* de unión, abrazadera *f*
cramped [kræmpt] ADJ [*position*] encogido, incómodo; [*room etc*] estrecho; [*writing*] menudo, apretado • **to live in ~ conditions** vivir en la estrechez • **they were all ~ together** estaban apiñados • **we are very ~ for space** apenas hay espacio para moverse
crampon ['kræmpən] N garfio *m*; (*Mountaineering*) crampón *m*
cramponning ['kræmpənɪŋ] N (*Mountaineering*) uso *m* de crampones
cranberry ['krænbərɪ] N arándano *m*
CPD ▸ **cranberry juice** zumo *m* de arándanos ▸ **cranberry sauce** salsa *f* de arándanos
crane [kreɪn] N 1 (*Orn*) grulla *f*
2 (*Tech*) grúa *f*
VT 1 • **to ~ one's neck** estirar el cuello
2 (*also* **crane up**) levantar con grúa
VI (*also* **crane forward**) inclinarse estirando el cuello • **to ~ to see sth** estirar el cuello para ver algo
CPD ▸ **crane driver, crane operator** operador(a) *m/f* de grúa
cranefly ['kreɪnflaɪ] N típula *f*
cranesbill ['kreɪnzbɪl] N (*Bot*) geranio *m*
cranial ['kreɪnɪəl] ADJ craneal
CPD ▸ **cranial osteopathy** osteopatía *f* craneal
cranium ['kreɪnɪəm] N (PL: **craniums** *or* **crania** ['kreɪnɪə]) cráneo *m*
crank¹ [kræŋk] N (*Tech*) manivela *f*, manubrio *m*
VT (*also* **crank up**) [+ *engine*] hacer arrancar con la manivela
▸ **crank out*** VT + ADV producir penosamente
▸ **crank up*** VT + ADV 1 [+ *hearing aid*] subir; [+ *music*] poner más fuerte • **to ~ up the volume** subir el volumen
2 (= *intensify*) [+ *campaign, bombing*] intensificar
crank²* [kræŋk] N (= *eccentric person*) excéntrico/a *m/f*; (*US*) (= *bad-tempered person*) ogro* *m*, cascarrabias* *mf inv*
crankcase ['kræŋkkeɪs] N cárter *m*
crankiness* ['kræŋkɪnɪs] N (= *strangeness*) excentricidad *f*; (*US*) (= *bad temper*) mal humor *m*
crankshaft ['kræŋkʃɑːft] N cigüeñal *m*
cranky* ['kræŋkɪ] ADJ (COMPAR: **crankier**, SUPERL: **crankiest**) (= *strange*) [*idea, person*] excéntrico; (*US*) (= *bad-tempered*) malhumorado, enojón (*LAm*)
cranny ['krænɪ] N grieta *f*
crap** [kræp] N 1 (= *faeces*) mierda** *f*
2 (= *nonsense*) estupideces *fpl*, macanas* *fpl*, gilipolleces *fpl* (*Sp*‡), huevadas *fpl* (*Chile, And***), boludeces *fpl* (*S. Cone***) • **that's ~** eso son gilipolleces‡, eso es una chorrada* • **to talk ~** decir gilipolleces‡, decir chorradas*
3 (= *unwanted items*) porquería *f*
ADJ [*joke, job*] pésimo • **the film was ~** la película era una mierda** • **to be ~** ser una mierda** • **I'm ~ at football** yo jugando al fútbol soy una mierda** *or* soy malísimo
VI cagar**
▸ **crap out**** VI + ADV (*US*) 1 (= *back down*) rajarse*
2 (= *fail*) fracasar
crape [kreɪp] N = **crepe**
crappy** ['kræpɪ] ADJ chungo*
craps [kræps] NSING (*US*) (= *game*) dados *mpl* • **to shoot ~** jugar a los dados
crapulous ['kræpjʊləs] ADJ (*frm*) crapuloso, ebrio
crash [kræʃ] N 1 (= *noise*) estrépito *m*; (= *thunder*) estruendo *m*; (= *explosion*) estallido *m*
2 (= *accident*) (*Aut*) choque *m*; (*Aer*) accidente *m* • **to have a ~** (*Aut*) tener un accidente de coche, chocar con el coche • **to be in a car/plane ~** tener un accidente de coche/aviación
3 (*Econ*) [*of stock exchange*] crac *m*; [*of business*] (= *failure*) quiebra *f* • **the 1929 ~** la crisis económica de 1929
VT 1 (= *smash*) [+ *car, aircraft etc*] estrellar (**into** contra) • **he ~ed his head against the wall** se estrelló la cabeza contra la pared
2* (= *gatecrash*) • **to ~ a party** colarse en una fiesta*
VI 1 (= *fall noisily*) caer con estrépito; (= *move noisily*) moverse de manera ruidosa • **to come ~ing down** caer con gran estrépito
2 (= *have accident*) tener un accidente; (*Aer*) estrellarse, caer a tierra; (= *collide*) [*two vehicles*] chocar • **to ~ into/through** chocar *or* estrellarse contra
3 (*Econ*) [*business*] quebrar; [*stock exchange*] sufrir una crisis • **when the stock market ~ed** cuando la bolsa se derrumbó
4 (*Comput*) bloquearse, colgarse (*Sp*)
5‡ (= *sleep*) dormir, pasar la noche
ADV • **he went ~ into a tree** dio de lleno contra un árbol
EXCL ¡zas!, ¡pum!
CPD [*diet etc*] intensivo, acelerado ▸ **crash barrier** (*Brit*) (*Aut*) quitamiedos *m inv*; (*at stadium etc*) valla *f* protectora ▸ **crash course** curso *m* intensivo *or* acelerado ▸ **crash dive** [*of submarine*] inmersión *f* de emergencia ▸ **crash helmet** casco *m* protector ▸ **crash landing** aterrizaje *m* forzoso *or* de

emergencia ▸ **crash pad**‡ guarida *f*, lugar *m* donde dormir ▸ **crash programme** (*Brit*), **crash program** (*US*) programa *m* de urgencia ▸ **crash site** [*of plane, car*] lugar *m* del siniestro, lugar *m* del accidente

▸ **crash out**‡ (VT + ADV) • **to be ~ed out** estar hecho polvo* (VI + ADV) (= *collapse*) caer redondo; (= *sleep*) dormirse

C

crashing† ['kræʃɪŋ] (ADJ) • **a ~ bore** una paliza*, un muermo*

crashingly ['kræʃɪŋlɪ] (ADV)† [*dull, boring*] tremendamente

crash-land ['kræʃlænd] (VT) [+ *aircraft*] poner forzosamente en tierra (VI) aterrizar forzosamente

crass [kræs] (ADJ) (*pej*) (= *extreme*) [*stupidity*] extremo; [*mistake*] craso; (= *coarse*) [*person, behaviour*] grosero, maleducado; [*performance*] malo, desastroso

crassly ['kræslɪ] (ADV) estúpidamente, tontamente

crassness ['kræsnɪs] (N) estupidez *f*

crate [kreɪt] (N) **1** cajón *m* de embalaje, jaula *f*
2* (= *car etc*) armatoste *m*, cacharro* *m*
(VT) (*also* **crate up**) embalar (en cajones)

crater ['kreɪtəʳ] (N) cráter *m*

cratered ['kreɪtəd] (ADJ) [*surface*] lleno de cráteres

cravat, cravate [krə'væt] (N) pañuelo *m*

crave [kreɪv] (VT) **1** (*also* **crave for**) [+ *food*] tener antojo de; [+ *affection, attention*] reclamar
2 (= *beg*) [+ *pardon*] suplicar; [+ *permission*] implorar, rogar

craven ['kreɪvən] (ADJ) (*liter*) cobarde

cravenly ['kreɪvənlɪ] (ADV) (*liter*) cobardemente

cravenness ['kreɪvənnɪs] (N) (*liter*) cobardía *f*

craving ['kreɪvɪŋ] (N) (*for food etc*) antojo *m*; (*for affection, attention*) anhelo *m*, ansias *fpl* • **to get a ~ for sth** encapricharse por algo

craw [krɔː] (N) • IDIOM: • **to stick in one's ~***: • **it really sticks in my ~ that she thinks ...** no trago con que ella piense que ...

crawfish ['krɔːfɪʃ] (N) (PL: **crawfish** *or* **crawfishes**) (*US*) = **crayfish**

crawl [krɔːl] (N) **1** (= *slow pace*) [*of traffic*] • **the traffic went at a ~** la circulación avanzaba a paso de tortuga • **the ~ to the coast** la cola de coches hasta la costa
2 (*Swimming*) crol *m* • **to do the ~** nadar a crol
(VI) **1** (= *drag o.s.*) arrastrarse; [*child*] andar a gatas, gatear • **to ~ in/out** meterse/salirse a gatas • **the fly ~ed up the window** la mosca subió despacito por el cristal
2 (= *move slowly*) [*traffic*] avanzar lentamente, formar caravana; [*time*] alargarse interminablemente • **the cars were ~ing along** los coches avanzaban a paso de tortuga
3* (= *suck up*) • **to ~ to sb** dar coba a algn*, hacer la pelota a algn*
4 • **to be ~ing with vermin** estar plagado *or* cuajado de bichos; ▹ **flesh**
(CPD) ▸ **crawl space** (*US*) (*between floors*) *espacio entre plantas para tuberías o cables*

crawler ['krɔːləʳ] (N) (*Mech*) tractor *m* de oruga
(CPD) ▸ **crawler lane** (*Brit*) (*Aut*) carril *m* (de autopista) para vehículos lentos

crawling ['krɔːlɪŋ] (ADJ) • **to be ~ with** (*pej*) estar atestado de

crayfish ['kreɪfɪʃ] (N) (PL: **crayfish** *or* **crayfishes**) (*freshwater*) cangrejo *m or* (*LAm*) jaiba *f* de río; (*saltwater*) cigala *f*

crayon ['kreɪən] (N) (*Art*) pastel *m*, lápiz *m* de tiza; (*child's*) lápiz *m* de color
(VT) dibujar al pastel

craze [kreɪz] (N) (= *fashion*) moda *f* (**for** de); (= *fad*) manía *f* (**for** por) • **it's the latest ~** es la última moda, es el último grito

crazed [kreɪzd] (ADJ) **1** [*look, person*] loco, demente
2 [*pottery, glaze*] agrietado, cuarteado

-crazed [-kreɪzd] (SUFFIX) • **drug-crazed** enloquecido por la droga • **power-crazed** ebrio de poder

crazily ['kreɪzɪlɪ] (ADV) **1** (= *madly*) [*shout, argue, laugh*] como (un) loco
2 (= *crookedly*) [*tilt, lean*] de modo peligroso, peligrosamente

craziness ['kreɪzɪnɪs] (N) (= *madness*) [*of person*] locura *f*; [*of behaviour, idea*] insensatez *f*

crazy ['kreɪzɪ] (ADJ) (COMPAR: **crazier**, SUPERL: **craziest**) **1** (= *mad*) loco, chiflado* • **you were ~ to do it** fue una locura hacerlo • **you would be ~ to do that** tendrías que estar loco para hacer eso • **it would be ~ for him to give up his job** sería una locura que dejase el trabajo • **to drive sb ~** (= *drive mad*) volver loco a algn; (= *infuriate*) sacar de quicio a algn • **it's enough to drive you ~** es para volverse loco • **to go ~** (= *mad*) volverse loco; (= *excited*) ponerse como loco; (= *angry*) ponerse como un energúmeno • **it was a ~ idea** fue una locura *or* un disparate, era una idea descabellada *or* disparatada • **everyone shouted like ~** todos gritaban como locos • **they were selling like ~** se estaban vendiendo como rosquillas *or* como pan caliente* • **it sounds ~** parece una locura • **~ talk** disparates *mpl*, tonterías *fpl* • **I've done some ~ things in my time** he hecho algunas locuras en mi vida • **~ with grief/anxiety** loco de pena/preocupación • **it's a ~ world** el mundo está loco, es un mundo de locos
2* (= *keen*) • **he's football ~** es un fanático del fútbol • **to be ~ about sb** estar loco por algn • **they're ~ about football** el fútbol les vuelve locos • **I'm not ~ about it** no es que me vuelva loco, no me entusiasma
3 • **to lean at a ~ angle** inclinarse de modo peligroso
(N) (*US**) loco/a *m/f*
(CPD) ▸ **crazy bone** (*US*) hueso *m* del codo ▸ **crazy golf** (*Brit*) minigolf *m* ▸ **crazy house*** (*US*) casa *f* de locos*, manicomio *m* ▸ **crazy paving** pavimento *m* de baldosas irregulares ▸ **crazy quilt** (*US*) edredón *m* de retazos

CRB (N ABBR) (*Brit*) = **Criminal Records Bureau**

CRC (N ABBR) **1** (*US*) = **Civil Rights Commission**
2 = **Camera-Ready Copy**

CRE (N ABBR) (*Brit*) = **Commission for Racial Equality**

creak [kriːk] (N) [*of wood, shoe etc*] crujido *m*; [*of hinge etc*] chirrido *m*, rechinamiento *m*
(VI) crujir; (= *squeak*) chirriar, rechinar

creaky ['kriːkɪ] (ADJ) (COMPAR: **creakier**, SUPERL: **creakiest**) rechinador; (*fig*) poco sólido

cream [kriːm] (N) **1** (*on milk*) nata *f*, crema *f* (*LAm*) • **~ of tartar** crémor *m* tártaro • **~ of tomato soup** sopa *f* de crema de tomate • **~ of wheat** (*US*) sémola *f*; ▹ **double, single, whipped**
2 (*fig*) flor *f* y nata, crema *f* • **the ~ of society** la flor y nata de la sociedad • **the ~ of the crop** lo mejor de lo mejor
3 (= *lotion*) (*for face, shoes etc*) crema *f*, pomada *f* • **shoe ~** betún *m* • **face ~** crema *f* para la cara
(ADJ) **1** (= *cream-coloured*) color crema (*inv*)
2 (= *made with cream*) de nata *or* (*LAm*) crema
(VT) **1** [+ *milk*] desnatar, descremar (*LAm*); [+ *butter*] batir
2 (*also* **cream together**) (= *mix*) batir • **~ed potatoes** puré *msing* de patatas *or* (*LAm*) papas
3 (*US*‡) [+ *enemy, opposing team*] arrollar, aplastar
4 • **to ~ one's pants**** correrse sin querer**
(CPD) ▸ **cream cake** pastel *m* de nata *or* (*LAm*) crema ▸ **cream cheese** queso *m* crema ▸ **cream cracker** galleta *f* de soda ▸ **cream puff** petisú *m*, pastel *m* de nata *or* (*LAm*) crema ▸ **cream soda** gaseosa *f* de vainilla ▸ **cream tea** (*Brit*) *merienda en cafetería que suele constar de té, bollos, mermelada y nata*

▸ **cream off*** (VT + ADV) [+ *best talents, part of profits*] separar lo mejor de

creamer ['kriːməʳ] (N) **1** (= *powder*) sucedáneo *m* de la leche
2 (*esp US*) (= *jug*) jarrita *f* de leche

creamery ['kriːmərɪ] (N) **1** (*on farm*) lechería *f*; (= *butter factory*) fábrica *f* de productos lácteos
2 (= *small shop*) lechería *f*

creaminess ['kriːmɪnɪs] (N) cremosidad *f*

creamy ['kriːmɪ] (ADJ) (COMPAR: **creamier**, SUPERL: **creamiest**) [*taste, texture*] cremoso; [*colour*] color crema (*inv*)

crease [kriːs] (N) **1** (= *fold*) raya *f*; (= *wrinkle*) arruga *f*
2 (*Cricket*) línea *f* de bateo
(VT) [+ *paper*] doblar; (*esp several times*) plegar; [+ *clothes*] arrugar • **to ~ one's trousers** (= *press crease in*) hacer la raya a los pantalones
(VI) arrugarse

▸ **crease up*** (*Brit*) (VT + ADV) • **he was ~d up (with laughter)** se tronchaba (de risa) (VI + ADV) • **he ~d up (with laughter)** se tronchaba (de risa)

creased ['kriːst] (ADJ) [*fabric, garment, paper*] arrugado; [*face, skin*] lleno de arrugas

creaseless ['kriːslɪs], **crease-resistant** ['kriːsrɪˌzɪstənt] (ADJ) inarrugable

create [kriː'eɪt] (VT) **1** (*gen*) (*Comput*) crear; [+ *character*] inventar; [+ *rôle*] encarnar; [+ *fashion*] desarrollar; [+ *fuss, noise*] armar; [+ *problem*] causar, crear • **to ~ an impression** impresionar, causar buena impresión
2 (= *appoint*) nombrar • **he was ~d a peer by the Queen** fue nombrado par por la reina
(VI) (*Brit**) (= *make a fuss*) montar un número*, armar un lío*

creation [kriː'eɪʃən] (N) **1** creación *f* • **the Creation** (*Rel*) la Creación
2 (= *dress etc*) modelo *m*

creationism [kriː'eɪʃənɪzəm] (N) creacionismo *m*

creationist [kriː'eɪʃənɪst] (N) creacionista *mf*

creative [kriː'eɪtɪv] (ADJ) [*person, talent, energy, solution*] creativo • **the ~ use of language** el uso creativo del lenguaje • **~ thinking** creatividad *f*
(CPD) ▸ **creative accounting** contabilidad *f* embellecida ▸ **creative writing** escritura *f* creativa ▸ **creative writing course** taller *m* de escritura creativa, taller *m* de creación literaria

creatively [kriː'eɪtɪvlɪ] (ADV) con creatividad

creativity [ˌkriːeɪ'tɪvɪtɪ] (N) creatividad *f*

creator [krɪ'eɪtəʳ] (N) creador(a) *m/f* • **the Creator** (*Rel*) el Creador

creature ['kriːtʃəʳ] (N) **1** (*gen*) criatura *f*; (= *animal*) animal *m*; (= *insect etc*) bicho *m*
2 (= *person*) • **pay no attention to that ~** no hagas caso de esa individua • **poor ~!** ¡pobrecito! • **wretched ~!** ¡desgraciado! • **~ of habit** esclavo/a *m/f* de la costumbre
3 (*pej*) (= *dependent person*) títere *m*
(CPD) ▸ **creature comforts** comodidades *fpl*

(materiales)
crèche [kreɪʃ] (N) (*Brit*) guardería *f*
cred* [kred] (N) = **street cred**
credence ['kriːdəns] (N) • **to give ~ to** dar crédito a
credentials [krɪ'denʃəlz] (NPL) (= *identifying papers*) credenciales *fpl*; (= *letters of reference*) referencias *fpl*; [*of diplomat*] cartas *fpl* credenciales • **what are his ~ for the post?** ¿qué méritos alega para el puesto?
credibility [,kredə'bɪlɪtɪ] (N) (*no pl*) credibilidad *f*
(CPD) ▸ **credibility gap** falta *f* de credibilidad ▸ **credibility rating** índice *m* de credibilidad
credible ['kredɪbl] (ADJ) (*gen*) creíble, digno de crédito; [*person*] plausible; [*witness*] de integridad
credibly ['kredɪblɪ] (ADV) creíblemente, verosímilmente
credit ['kredɪt] (N) **1** (*Econ*) **a** (*in account*) (= *positive balance*) • **his account is in ~** su cuenta tiene saldo positivo *or* está en números negros • **as long as you stay in ~** *or* **keep your account in ~** mientras pueda mantener un saldo positivo • **you have £10 to your ~** tiene 10 libras en el haber, tiene un saldo a favor de 10 libras; ▹ **letter**
b (*for purchases*) crédito *m* • **they were refused ~** se les denegó un crédito • **is his ~ good?** ¿se le puede dar crédito sin riesgo? • **to give sb ~** conceder un crédito a algn • **interest-free ~** crédito *m* sin intereses • **to buy sth on ~** comprar algo a crédito *or* a plazos • **"no credit given"** "no se fía" • **"credit terms available"** "se vende a plazos", "facilidades de pago"
c (*Accounting*) saldo *m* acreedor, saldo *m* positivo • **on the ~ side** (*lit*) en el haber; (*fig*) entre los aspectos positivos
2 (= *honour*) honor *m* • **he's a ~ to his family** es un orgullo para su familia, honra a su familia • **it does you ~** dice mucho a tu favor, te honra • **with a skill that would have done ~ to an expert** con una habilidad que hubiera sido el orgullo de un experto • **to his ~, I must point out that ...** debo decir en su favor que ...
3 (= *recognition*) mérito *m* • **they deserve ~ for not giving up** merecen que se les reconozca el mérito de no haberse rendido • **~ where it's** *or* **~'s due** a cada uno según sus méritos • **to get the ~ (for sth)** llevarse el mérito (de algo) • **I did the work and he got all the ~** yo hice el trabajo y él se llevó todo el mérito • **to give sb ~ for (doing) sth** reconocer a algn el mérito de (haber hecho) algo • **to take the ~ for (doing) sth** llevarse el mérito de (haber hecho) algo • **it would be wrong for us to take all the ~** no estaría bien que nos llevásemos todo el mérito
4 (= *credence*) • **he's a lot better than people give him ~ for** es bastante mejor de lo que la gente cree • **I gave you ~ for more sense** te creía más sensato • **I have to give some ~ to his story** tengo que reconocer que su historia tiene algo de verdad
5 credits (*Cine, TV*) (= *titles*) títulos *mpl* de crédito, créditos *mpl*; (= *achievements*) logros *mpl* • **she has a long list of stage ~s** cuenta con una larga lista de éxitos *or* logros en escena
6 (*esp US*) (*Univ*) (= *award*) crédito *m*, unidad *f* de valor académico
(VT) **1** (= *believe*) creer • **it's hard to ~ that such things went on** es difícil de creer que pasaran cosas semejantes • **would you ~ it!** ¡parece mentira!
2 (= *attribute*) • **I ~ed him with more sense** le creía más sensato • **~ me with some sense!** ¡no me tomes por idiota! • **he is ~ed with the discovery** se le atribuye a él el descubrimiento • **you don't ~ her with a mind of her own** no te das cuenta de que ella sabe lo que quiere
3 (*Comm*) [+ *money, interest*] abonar, ingresar • **the money was ~ed to his account** el dinero se abonó *or* se ingresó en su cuenta • **we ~ you with the interest monthly** le abonamos *or* ingresamos el interés mensualmente
(CPD) ▸ **credit account** cuenta *f* de crédito ▸ **credit agency** agencia *f* de créditos ▸ **credit balance** saldo *m* acreedor, saldo *m* positivo ▸ **credit bureau** (*US*) oficina *f* de crédito ▸ **credit card** tarjeta *f* de crédito ▸ **credit control** control *m* del crédito ▸ **credit crunch** restricciones *fpl* al crédito ▸ **credit entry** anotación *f* en el haber ▸ **credit facilities** facilidades *fpl* de crédito ▸ **credit history** [*of person*] historial *m* crediticio, informe *m* de solvencia ▸ **credit hour** (*US*) ≈ hora *f* de crédito ▸ **credit limit** límite *m* de crédito ▸ **credit line** línea *f* de crédito ▸ **credit note** nota *f* de crédito ▸ **credit rating** clasificación *f* crediticia; (*fig*) credibilidad *f* • **the government's ~ rating has plummeted** la credibilidad del gobierno ha caído en picado ▸ **credit reference** informe *m* de crédito ▸ **credit risk** • **to be a (bad)~ risk** presentar riesgo crediticio • **to be a good ~ risk** no presentar riesgo crediticio • **to assess ~ risk** evaluar el riesgo crediticio ▸ **credit slip** (*US*) comprobante *m* del crédito ▸ **credit squeeze** restricciones *fpl* de crédito ▸ **credit transfer** transferencia *m* ▸ **credit union** cooperativa *f* de crédito
creditable ['kredɪtəbl] (ADJ) loable, encomiable
creditably ['kredɪtəblɪ] (ADV) de modo loable
creditor ['kredɪtəʳ] (N) acreedor(a) *m/f*
creditworthiness ['kredɪt,wɜːðɪnɪs] (N) solvencia *f*
creditworthy ['kredɪt,wɜːðɪ] (ADJ) solvente
credo ['kreɪdəʊ] (N) credo *m*
credulity [krɪ'djuːlɪtɪ] (N) credulidad *f*
credulous ['kredjʊləs] (ADJ) crédulo
credulously ['kredjʊləslɪ] (ADV) con credulidad
creed [kriːd] (N) (= *religion*) credo *m*, religión *f*; (= *system of beliefs*) credo *m* • **the Creed** (*Rel*) el Credo
creek [kriːk] (N) (*Brit*) (= *inlet*) cala *f*, ensenada *f*; (*US*) (= *stream*) riachuelo *m*
• IDIOM: • **up the ~ (without a paddle)*** (= *in difficulties*) en un lío *or* (*LAm*) aprieto
creel [kriːl] (N) nasa *f*, cesta *f* (de pescador)
creep [kriːp] (PT, PP: **crept**) (VI) **1** [*animal*] deslizarse, arrastrarse; [*plant*] trepar
2 [*person*] (*stealthily*) ir cautelosamente; (*slowly*) ir muy despacio • **to ~ in/out/up/down** entrar/salir/subir/bajar sigilosamente • **to ~ about on tiptoe** andar a *or* de puntillas • **to ~ along** [*traffic*] avanzar a paso de tortuga • **to ~ up on sb** acercarse sigilosamente a algn
3 (*fig*) • **it made my flesh ~** me puso la carne de gallina • **doubts began to ~ in** las dudas empezaron a aparecer • **an error crept in** se deslizó un error • **he felt old age ~ing up on him** sintió como la vida le ganaba años • **fear crept over him** le invadió el terror
(N) **1*** (= *person*) • **what a ~!** ¡qué lameculos es!* • **he's a ~** (= *weird*) ¡qué tipo más raro!, ¡qué bicho!
2 • **it gives me the ~s*** me da miedo, me da escalofríos
creeper ['kriːpəʳ] (N) **1** (*Bot*) enredadera *f*
2 creepers (*US*) (= *rompers*) (*for baby*) pelele *m*
creeping ['kriːpɪŋ] (ADJ) (*Med etc*) progresivo; [*barrage*] móvil
(CPD) ▸ **creeping inflation** inflación *f* progresiva
creepy* ['kriːpɪ] (ADJ) (COMPAR: **creepier**, SUPERL: **creepiest**) horripilante, escalofriante
creepy-crawly* ['kriːpɪ'krɔːlɪ] (N) (*Brit*) bicho *m*
cremate [krɪ'meɪt] (VT) incinerar
cremation [krɪ'meɪʃən] (N) cremación *f*, incineración *f*
crematorium [,kremə'tɔːrɪəm] (N) (PL: **crematoriums** *or* **crematoria** [,kremə'tɔːrɪə]), **crematory** (*US*) ['kremə,tɔːrɪ] crematorio *m*
crème caramel [,kremkærə'mel] (N) flan *m*
crème de la crème ['kremdəlɑː'krem] (N) • **the ~** la crème de la crème, la flor y nata
crème de menthe ['kremdəmɒnθ] (N) licor *m* de crema de menta
crème fraîche [,krem'freʃ] (N) crème *f* fraîche, crema *f* fresca
crenellated ['krenɪleɪtɪd] (ADJ) almenado
crenellations [,krenɪ'leɪʃənz] (NPL) almenas *fpl*
Creole ['kriːəʊl] (ADJ) criollo
(N) **1** (= *person*) criollo/a *m/f*
2 (*Ling*) lengua *f* criolla
creosote ['krɪəsəʊt] (N) creosota *f*, chapote *m* (*Mex*)
(VT) echar creosota a
crepe, crêpe [kreɪp] (N) **1** (= *fabric*) crespón *m*
2 (*also* **crepe rubber**) crepé *m* • **~-soled shoes** zapatos *mpl* de suela de crepé
3 (= *pancake*) crepa *f*
(CPD) ▸ **crepe bandage** venda *f* de crespón ▸ **crepe de Chine** crep(é) *m* de China ▸ **crepe paper** papel *m* crepé ▸ **crepe sole** (*on shoes*) suela *f* de crepé
crept [krept] (PT), (PP) *of* **creep**
crepuscular [krɪ'pʌskjʊləʳ] (ADJ) (*liter*) crepuscular
crescendo [krɪ'ʃendəʊ] (N) (PL: **crescendos** *or* **crescendi** [krɪ'ʃendɪ]) (*Mus*) (*also fig*) crescendo *m*
crescent ['kresnt] (ADJ) creciente
(N) (= *shape*) medialuna *f*; (= *street*) *calle en forma de semicírculo*
(CPD) ▸ **crescent moon** luna *f* creciente
crescent-shaped ['kresənt∫eɪpt] (ADJ) en forma de media luna
cress [kres] (N) berro *m*
crest [krest] (N) [*of bird, wave*] cresta *f*; [*of turkey*] moco *m*; [*of hill*] cima *f*, cumbre *f*; (*on helmet*) penacho *m*; (*Heraldry*) blasón *m*
• IDIOM: • **to be on the ~ of a wave** estar en la cresta de la ola
(VT) [+ *hill*] coronar, alcanzar la cima de
(VI) (*US*) llegar al máximo, alcanzar su punto más alto • **the flood ~ed at two metres** las aguas llegaron a dos metros sobre su nivel normal
crested ['krestɪd] (ADJ) [*bird etc*] crestado, con cresta; [*notepaper*] con escudo
crestfallen ['krest,fɔːlən] (ADJ) cariacontecido
cretaceous [krɪ'teɪʃəs] (ADJ) cretáceo
Cretan ['kriːtən] (ADJ) cretense
(N) cretense *mf*
Crete [kriːt] (N) Creta *f*
cretin* ['kretɪn] (N) (*Med*) cretino/a *m/f*; (*pej*) cretino/a *m/f*, imbécil *mf*
cretinism ['kretɪnɪzəm] (N) (*Med*) cretinismo *m*
cretinous ['kretɪnəs] (ADJ) cretino; (*pej**) imbécil
cretonne [kre'tɒn] (N) cretona *f*
Creutzfeldt-Jakob disease [,krɔɪtsfelt

'jækɒbdɪˌziːz] (N) enfermedad *f* de Creutzfeldt-Jakob
crevasse [krɪ'væs] (N) grieta *f*
crevice ['krevɪs] (N) grieta *f*, hendedura *f*
crew¹ [kruː] (N) **1** (*Aer, Naut*) tripulación *f*; (*Navy*) dotación *f*; (*excluding officers*) marineros *mpl* rasos • **three ~ were drowned** perecieron ahogados tres tripulantes
2 (*Cine, Rowing*) (*gen*) (= *team*) equipo *m*
3 (= *gang*) pandilla *f*, banda *f* • **they looked a sorry ~** daba lástima verlos
(VI) • **to ~ for sb** hacer de tripulación para algn
(VT) tripular
(CPD) ▸ **crew cut** pelado *m* al rape
crew² [kruː] (PT) *of* **crow**
crewman ['kruːmən] (N) (PL: **crewmen**)
1 (*Naut*) tripulante *mf*
2 (*TV etc*) miembro *mf* del equipo (*de cámara etc*)
crew-neck ['kruːnek] (N) cuello *m* de barco; (*also* **crew-neck sweater**) suéter *m* con cuello de barco
crib [krɪb] (N) **1** (*Brit*) (*for infant*) pesebre *m*; (*US*) (*for toddler*) cuna *f*; (*Rel*) Belén *m*; (= *manger*) cuadra *f* • **portable ~** (*US*) cuna *f* portátil
2 (*Scol**) (= *illicit copy*) plagio *m*; (*in exam*) chuleta* *f*; (= *translation*) traducción *f*
(VT) (*Scol**) plagiar, tomar (**from** de)
(VI) (*Scol**) usar una chuleta*
(CPD) ▸ **crib death** (*US*) muerte *f* en la cuna
cribbage ['krɪbɪdʒ] (N) *juego de cartas que se juega utilizando un tablero de puntuación*
crick [krɪk] (N) • **to have a ~ in one's neck/back** tener tortícolis/lumbago
(VT) • **to ~ one's neck** tener tortícolis • **to ~ one's back** tener un ataque de lumbago
cricket¹ ['krɪkɪt] (N) (*Zool*) grillo *m*
cricket² ['krɪkɪt] (N) (= *sport*) críquet *m*, crícket *m* • **that's not ~** (*fig*) es una jugada sucia
(CPD) ▸ **cricket ball** pelota *f* de críquet ▸ **cricket bat** bate *m* de críquet ▸ **cricket match** partido *m* de críquet ▸ **cricket pavilion** caseta *f* de críquet ▸ **cricket pitch** terreno *m* de juego de críquet

CRICKET
El críquet se practica en todo el Reino Unido y los países de la **Commonwealth**, aunque se considera un juego típicamente inglés. Se juega sobre todo en verano al aire libre, sobre hierba y se puede reconocer inmediatamente porque todos los jugadores van vestidos de blanco. Tiene unas reglas un tanto complejas: hay dos equipos de 11 jugadores. En el primer equipo todos los jugadores batean por turnos, mientras que en el otro equipo hay un boleador (**bowler**) y diez fildeadores (**fielders**) en puntos estratégicos del campo. El boleador lanza la pelota al bateador (**batsman**). Éste intenta a su vez lanzarla lo más lejos posible y así tener tiempo para correr de un poste (**wicket**) a otro y conseguir puntos, llamados por ello (**runs**). Los fildeadores del equipo contrario intentan atrapar la pelota lanzada por el bateador para evitar que consiga más puntos. Si atrapan la pelota en el aire o si dan en el **wicket** con ella, el bateador es eliminado. Cuando todos los bateadores del primer equipo han sido eliminados, se cambian los papeles. Un partido puede durar varios días seguidos.
Como ocurre con el béisbol en Estados Unidos, algunas expresiones de críquet han pasado a la lengua cotidiana, entre otras, **a sticky wicket** (una situación difícil).

cricketer ['krɪkɪtəʳ] (N) criquetero/a *m/f*, jugador(a) *m/f* de críquet
cricketing ['krɪkɪtɪŋ] (ADJ) de cricket • **his brief ~ career** su corta trayectoria como jugador de críquet
crier ['kraɪəʳ] (N) ▸ **town**
crikey‡ ['kraɪkɪ] (EXCL) (*Brit*) ¡caramba!
crime [kraɪm] (N) **1** (= *offence*) delito *m*; (*very serious*) crimen *m* • **to commit a ~** cometer un delito • **the scene of the ~** el lugar del delito • **a ~ against humanity** un crimen contra la humanidad • **it's not a ~!** (*fig*) ¡no es para tanto! • **it's a ~ to let that food go to waste** es un crimen echar a perder esa comida
2 (= *activity*) delincuencia *f* • **~ is rising** la delincuencia va en aumento • PROVERB: • **~ doesn't pay** el crimen no compensa
(CPD) ▸ **crime of passion** crimen *m* pasional ▸ **crime prevention** prevención *f* del crimen ▸ **crime rate** índice *m* de criminalidad ▸ **crime scene** lugar *m* del delito, escena *f* del crimen ▸ **Crime Squad** ≈ Brigada *f* de Investigación Criminal (*Sp*) ▸ **crime statistics** estadísticas *fpl* del crimen ▸ **crime wave** ola *f* de crímenes *or* delitos ▸ **crime writer** autor(a) *m/f* de novelas policíacas
Crimea [kraɪ'mɪə] (N) Crimea *f*
Crimean War [kraɪ'mɪən'wɔːʳ] (N) Guerra *f* de Crimea
criminal ['krɪmɪnl] (N) criminal *mf*
(ADJ) **1** (*Jur*) [*act, activity, behaviour*] delictivo; [*investigation, organization*] criminal; [*trial, case*] penal • **he had done nothing ~** no había cometido ningún delito • **to bring ~ charges against sb** formular *or* presentar cargos en contra de algn
2 (= *shameful*) • **it would be ~ to throw them away** sería un crimen tirarlos • **it was a ~ waste of resources** era un crimen desperdiciar recursos así
(CPD) ▸ **criminal assault** intento *m* de violación ▸ **criminal code** código *m* penal ▸ **criminal court** juzgado *m* de lo penal ▸ **criminal damage** delito *m* de daños ▸ **criminal intent** intención *f* dolosa ▸ **Criminal Investigation Department** (*Brit*) ≈ Brigada *f* de Investigación Criminal (*Sp*) ▸ **the criminal justice system** el sistema penal ▸ **criminal law** derecho *m* penal ▸ **criminal lawyer** penalista *mf*, abogado/a *m/f* criminalista ▸ **criminal negligence** negligencia *f* criminal ▸ **criminal offence** delito *m* • **it's a ~ offence** es un delito ▸ **criminal profiling** elaboración *f* de perfiles de delincuentes ▸ **criminal record** antecedentes *mpl* penales • **to have a ~ record** tener antecedentes penales ▸ **Criminal Records Bureau** (*Brit*) *oficina de antecedentes penales* ▸ **criminal wrongdoing** actividades *mpl* delictivas
criminality [ˌkrɪmɪ'nælɪtɪ] (N) criminalidad *f*
criminalization [ˌkrɪmɪnəlaɪ'zeɪʃən] (N) criminalización *f*
criminalize ['krɪmɪnəlaɪz] (VT) criminalizar
criminally ['krɪmɪnəlɪ] (ADV) **1** (*Jur*) • **they are ~ liable** se les puede imputar delito • **the hospital staff had been ~ negligent** el personal del hospital había cometido delito por negligencia • **they are ~ responsible from the age of 16** son responsables desde el punto de vista penal a partir de los 16 años • **the ~ insane** los delincuentes psicóticos
2 (= *shamefully*) vergonzosamente • **the pay was ~ poor** el sueldo era tan bajo que daba vergüenza, el sueldo era vergonzosamente bajo
criminologist [ˌkrɪmɪ'nɒlədʒɪst] (N) criminalista *mf*
criminology [ˌkrɪmɪ'nɒlədʒɪ] (N) criminología *f*
crimp [krɪmp] (VT) [+ *hair*] rizar, encrespar
crimped [krɪmpt] (ADJ) rizado, con rizos, encrespado
Crimplene® ['krɪmpliːn] (N) ≈ crepé *m* de poliéster
crimson ['krɪmzn] (ADJ) carmesí
(N) carmesí *m*
cringe [krɪndʒ] (VI) **1** (= *shrink back*) encogerse (**at** ante) • **to ~ with fear** encogerse de miedo • **to ~ with embarrassment** morirse de vergüenza • **it makes me ~** me da horror
2 (= *fawn*) acobardarse, agacharse (**before** ante)
cringe-making* ['krɪndʒmeɪkɪŋ] (ADJ) (= *embarrassing*) sonrojante, bochornoso
cringing ['krɪndʒɪŋ] (ADJ) servil, rastrero
crinkle ['krɪŋkl] (N) arruga *f*
(VT) arrugar
(VI) arrugarse
crinkle-cut ['krɪŋkl,cʌt] (ADJ) [*chips, crisps*] ondulado
crinkly ['krɪŋklɪ] (ADJ) (COMPAR: **crinklier**, SUPERL: **crinkliest**) [*hair*] (= *very curly*) rizado, crespo; [*paper etc*] (= *having wrinkles, creases*) arrugado; [*leaves etc*] crespado
crinoline ['krɪnəliːn] (N) miriñaque *m*, crinolina *f*
cripes‡ [kraɪps] (EXCL) ¡caramba!*
cripple‡ ['krɪpl] (N) (*lame*) cojo/a *m/f*, lisiado/a *m/f*; (*disabled*) minusválido/a *m/f*; (*maimed*) mutilado/a *m/f* • **he's an emotional ~** tiene serios traumas
(VT) **1** (*physically*) lisiar, mutilar
2 (*fig*) [+ *ship, plane*] inutilizar; [+ *production, exports*] paralizar
crippled ['krɪpld] (ADJ) **1** (= *maimed*) tullido, lisiado; (= *disabled*) minusválido • **he is ~ with arthritis** está paralizado por la artritis
2 (*fig*) [*plane, vehicle*] averiado; [*factory*] (*after bomb etc*) paralizado
(NPL) ‡ • **the ~** (= *maimed*) los tullidos; (= *disabled*) los minusválidos
crippling ['krɪplɪŋ] (ADJ) [*disease*] que conduce a la parálisis; [*blow, defect*] muy grave, muy severo; [*taxes, debts*] abrumador, agobiante
cripplingly ['krɪplɪŋlɪ] (ADV) **1** • **~ high** [*taxes, debts*] agobiante • **~ high prices** precios prohibitivos • **~ high interest rates** tipos de interés prohibitivos
2 • **to be ~ shy** estar bloqueado por la timidez • **to be ~ embarrassed** estar muy cortado*
crisis ['kraɪsɪs] (N) (PL: **crises** ['kraɪsiːz]) crisis *f inv*; (*Med*) punto *m* crítico • **to come to a ~** entrar en crisis • **we've got a ~ on our hands** estamos enfrentándonos a una crisis
(CPD) ▸ **crisis centre** (*Brit*), **crisis center** (*US*) (*for disaster*) ≈ centro *m* coordinador de rescate; (*for personal help*) ≈ teléfono *m* de la esperanza; (*for battered women*) centro *m* de ayuda (*a las mujeres maltratadas*) ▸ **crisis management** gestión *f* de crisis ▸ **crisis of confidence** crisis *f* de confianza
crisp [krɪsp] (ADJ) (COMPAR: **crisper**, SUPERL: **crispest**) **1** (= *fresh, crunchy*) [*lettuce, salad*] fresco; [*apple, snow, bacon, leaves*] crujiente; [*paper*] limpio; [*banknote*] nuevecito; [*linen*] almidonado
2 (= *cold, clear*) [*air*] vivificante, vigorizante; [*day, morning*] frío y despejado • **the weather was clear and ~** el día estaba frío y despejado
3 (= *sharp*) [*voice, sound*] bien definido, nítido; [*image*] nítido
4 (= *tight*) [*curl*] apretado
5 (= *brisk, curt*) [*tone, reply*] seco, tajante; [*statement, phrase*] escueto • **a ~ prose style** una prosa escueta

N (Brit) (also **potato crisp**) patata f frita (de bolsa), papa f (frita) (de bolsa) (LAm) • IDIOM: • **burnt to a ~** [toast etc] chamuscado; [person] (= sunburnt) achicharrado
crispbread ['krɪspbred] N pan m tostado (escandinavo)
crisper ['krɪspəʳ] N (in fridge) cajón m de las verduras (del frigorífico)
crisply ['krɪsplɪ] ADV [pressed, ironed] cuidadosamente; [say, reply] secamente; [speak, write] de manera concisa, de manera sucinta • **~ fried onion rings** crujientes aros de cebolla fritos
crispness ['krɪspnɪs] N **1** (= crunchiness) [of lettuce, salad] frescura f; [of apple, snow, bacon] lo crujiente; [of linen] lo almidonado
2 (= coldness, clarity) [of air] lo vivificante, lo vigorizante; [of weather] lo frío y despejado
3 (= sharpness) [of voice, sound, image] nitidez f
4 (= briskness) [of tone, reply] sequedad f
crispy ['krɪspɪ] ADJ (COMPAR: **crispier**, SUPERL: **crispiest**) [food] crujiente
criss-cross ['krɪskrɒs] ADJ entrecruzado
N • **a criss-cross of paths** veredas fpl entrecruzadas
VI entrecruzarse
criss-crossed ['krɪskrɒst] ADJ entrelazado • **criss-crossed by** surcado de
crit* [krɪt] N [of play, book etc] crítica f
criterion [kraɪ'tɪərɪən] N (PL: **criterions** or **criteria** [kraɪ'tɪərɪə]) criterio m
critic ['krɪtɪk] N (= reviewer) crítico/a m/f; (= faultfinder) criticón/ona m/f
critical ['krɪtɪkəl] ADJ **1** (= important) [factor, element] crítico; [issue] apremiante; [problem] muy serio • **it is ~ to understand what is happening** es de vital importancia entender lo que está ocurriendo • **of ~ importance** de vital importancia • **how you finance a business is ~ to its success** el éxito de un negocio depende de forma crucial de cómo se financie
2 (= decisive) [moment, stage] crítico • **it was a ~ time for the nation** fue un período crítico para la nación • **at a ~ juncture** en una coyuntura crítica
3 (= perilous, serious) [situation, state] crítico
4 (Med) [patient, condition, illness] grave • **to be on the ~ list** estar en la lista de enfermos graves • **to be off the ~ list** estar fuera de peligro
5 (= fault-finding) [attitude, remark, report] crítico • **he's too ~** siempre está criticando, critica demasiado • **to watch sb with a ~ eye** observar a algn con ojo crítico • **to be ~ of sth/sb** criticar algo/a algn
6 (= analytical) [person, reader, analysis] crítico
7 (Cine, Literat, Mus, Theat) crítico • **the film met with ~ acclaim** la película fue aplaudida por la crítica • **to be a ~ success** [book, play etc] ser un éxito de crítica
8 (Phys, Nuclear physics) [temperature, pressure] crítico • **to go ~** empezar una reacción en cadena
CPD ▸ **critical angle** (Aer, Opt) ángulo m crítico ▸ **critical care unit** unidad f de cuidados intensivos, unidad f de terapia intensiva (S. Cone, Mex) ▸ **critical edition** edición f critica ▸ **critical essays** ensayos mpl de crítica ▸ **critical mass** masa f crítica ▸ **critical path analysis** análisis m inv del camino crítico
critically ['krɪtɪkəlɪ] ADV **1** (= crucially) • **~ important** crucial
2 (Med) [ill, injured] gravemente, de gravedad
3 (= seriously) • **we are running ~ low on food supplies** nuestras provisiones de alimentos están quedando reducidas a unos niveles críticos
4 (= disparagingly) [speak, say] con desaprobación, en tono de crítica
5 (= analytically) [study, examine, watch] con ojo crítico, críticamente
6 (Cine, Literat, Mus, Theat) • **the band's ~ acclaimed new album** el nuevo disco del grupo, aclamado por la crítica • **his first two books were ~ acclaimed** sus dos primeros libros tuvieron muy buena acogida por parte de la crítica
criticism ['krɪtɪsɪzəm] N crítica f (also Literat, Cine etc)
criticize ['krɪtɪsaɪz] VT, VI (= review, find fault) criticar • **I don't wish to ~, but ...** no quisiera criticar, pero ...
critique [krɪ'ti:k] N crítica f
VT evaluar • **to ~ sb's work/performance** evaluar el trabajo/la actuación de algn
critter* ['krɪtəʳ] (US) N (= creature) bicho m
croak [krəʊk] N [of raven] graznido m; [of frog] croar m, canto m; [of person] gruñido m
VI **1** [raven] graznar; [frog] croar, cantar; [person] carraspear
2* (= die) estirar la pata*, espicharla*
VT (= say) decir con voz ronca
croaky ['krəʊkɪ] ADJ [voice] ronco
Croat ['krəʊæt] N croata mf
Croatia [krəʊ'eɪʃə] N Croacia f
Croatian [krəʊ'eɪʃən] ADJ croata
N croata mf
crochet ['krəʊʃeɪ] N ganchillo m, croché m
VT hacer en croché, hacer de ganchillo
VI hacer ganchillo or croché
CPD ▸ **crochet hook** aguja f de ganchillo
crock [krɒk] N **1** (= earthenware pot) vasija f de barro • IDIOM: • **it's a ~ of shit** (esp US**) es una sandez*, es una gilipollez (Sp**), es una pendejada (And, Mex‡), es una huevada (And, S. Cone‡)
2* (= person) (also **old crock**) carcamal* m, vejete/a* m/f; (= car etc) cacharro* m
VT lisiar, incapacitar
crockery ['krɒkərɪ] N (Brit) loza f, vajilla f
crocodile ['krɒkədaɪl] N cocodrilo m • **to walk in a ~** andar en doble fila
CPD ▸ **crocodile clip** pinza f de cocodrilo ▸ **crocodile tears** (fig) lágrimas fpl de cocodrilo
crocodile-infested ['krɒkədaɪlɪn,festɪd] ADJ infestado de cocodrilos
crocus ['krəʊkəs] N (PL: **crocuses**) azafrán m
Croesus ['kri:səs] N Creso
croft [krɒft] N (Scot) (= small farm) granja f pequeña
crofter ['krɒftəʳ] N (Scot) arrendatario/a m/f de una granja pequeña
crofting ['krɒftɪŋ] (Scot) N minifundismo m, agricultura f en pequeña escala
CPD [community] de granjas pequeñas
croissant ['kwæsɒŋ] N croissant m, cruasán m, medialuna f (esp LAm)
crone [krəʊn] N bruja f, vieja f
crony* ['krəʊnɪ] N (pej) (= friend) compinche* mf, amigote/a* mf
cronyism ['krəʊnɪɪzəm] N amiguismo m
crook [krʊk] N **1** (shepherd's) cayado m; (bishop's) báculo m; (= hook) gancho m; ▹ **hook**
2 • **the ~ of one's arm** el pliegue del codo
3* (= thief) ladrón/ona m/f; (= villain) maleante mf
4 (= curve) codo m, recodo m
VT (fig) [+ finger] doblar • **to ~ one's arm** empinar el codo
ADJ (Australia*) (= ill) mal
crooked ['krʊkɪd] ADJ **1** (= not straight) torcido, chueco (LAm); (= bent over) encorvado, doblado; [path] sinuoso, tortuoso; [smile] torcido
2* (= dishonest) [deal] sucio; [means] nada honrado; [person] nada honrado, criminal
crookedly ['krʊkɪdlɪ] ADV [smile] con un rictus, torciendo la boca
crookedness ['krʊkɪdnɪs] N **1** (lit) sinuosidad f
2 (fig) criminalidad f
croon [kru:n] VT, VI canturrear, cantar en voz baja
crooner ['kru:nəʳ] N cantante mf melódico/a
crooning ['kru:nɪŋ] N canturreo m, tarareo m
crop [krɒp] N **1** (= species grown) cultivo m; (= produce) [of fruit, vegetables] cosecha f; [of cereals] cereal m; (fig) montón m
2 (Orn) buche m
3 [of whip] mango m; (= riding crop) fusta f, látigo m de montar
VT (= cut) [+ hair] cortar al rape; [animal] [+ grass] pacer
CPD ▸ **crop circle** círculo misterioso en los sembrados ▸ **crop dusting** = **crop spraying** ▸ **crop rotation** rotación f de cultivos ▸ **crop sprayer** (= device) fumigadora f (de cultivos), sulfatadora f; (= plane) avión m fumigador ▸ **crop spraying** fumigación f aérea, aerofumigación f (de cultivos) ▸ **crop top** camiseta f corta (que deja el ombligo al aire)
▸ **crop out** VI + ADV (Geol) aflorar
▸ **crop up** VI + ADV **1** (Geol) aflorar
2 (fig) (= arise) surgir, presentarse • **something must have ~ped up** habrán tenido algún problema, habrá pasado or surgido algo • **the subject ~ped up during the conversation** el tema surgió durante la conversación
cropped ['krɒpt] ADJ [hair, top, trousers] corto
cropper* ['krɒpəʳ] N **1** • IDIOM: • **to come a ~** (= fall) darse un batacazo*, cazar la liebre*; (= fail) [person] llevarse una buena plancha or un buen planchazo*; [project] irse al garete*
2 (Agr) agricultor(a) m/f; ▹ **sharecropper**
croquet ['krəʊkeɪ] N (= game) croquet m
croquette [krəʊ'ket] N (Culin) croqueta f
crosier ['krəʊʒəʳ] N báculo m (pastoral)
cross [krɒs] N **1** (= sign, decoration) cruz f • **to sign with a ~** marcar con una cruz • **to make the sign of the ~** hacer la señal de la cruz (**over** sobre), santiguarse • **the Cross** (Rel) la Cruz • IDIOM: • **to bear a/one's ~**: • **we each have our ~ to bear** cada quien carga su cruz • **it's one of the ~es we women have to bear** es una de las cruces que tenemos las mujeres
2 (Bio, Zool) cruce m, cruzamiento m; (fig) mezcla f • **it's a ~ between a horse and a donkey** es un cruce or cruzamiento de caballo y burro • **the game is a ~ between squash and tennis** el juego es una mezcla de squash y tenis, el juego está a medio camino entre el squash y el tenis
3 (= bias) • **cut on the ~** cortado al bies or al sesgo
4 (Ftbl) centro m, pase m cruzado
ADJ **1** (= angry) enfadado, enojado (LAm); (= vexed) molesto • **to be/get ~ with sb (about sth)** enfadarse or (LAm) enojarse con algn (por algo) • **it makes me ~ when that happens** me da mucha rabia que pase eso • **don't be/get ~ with me** no te enfades or (LAm) enojes conmigo • **they haven't had a ~ word in ten years** no han cruzado palabra en diez años, llevan diez años sin cruzar palabra
2 (= diagonal etc) transversal, oblicuo
VT **1** (= go across) [person] [+ road, room] cruzar; [+ bridge] cruzar, pasar; [+ ditch] cruzar, salvar; [+ river, sea, desert] cruzar, atravesar; [+ threshold] cruzar, traspasar

• **this road ~es the motorway** esta carretera atraviesa la autopista • **the bridge ~es the river here** el puente atraviesa el río por aquí • **it ~ed my mind that …** se me ocurrió que … • **they have clearly ~ed the boundary into terrorism** está claro que han traspasado la frontera que separa del terrorismo • **the word never ~ed his lips** jamás pronunció esa palabra • **a smile ~ed her lips** una sonrisa se dibujó en sus labios, esbozó una sonrisa • **we'll ~ that bridge when we come to it** (*fig*) no anticipemos problemas
2 (= *draw line across*) [+ *cheque*] cruzar • **~ed cheque** (*Brit*) cheque *m* cruzado • **to ~ o.s.** santiguarse • **~ my heart!** (*in promise*) ¡te lo juro! • **to ~ a "t"** poner el rabito a la "t"
3 (= *place crosswise*) [+ *arms, legs*] cruzar • **keep your fingers ~ed for me** ¡deséame suerte! • **I got a ~ed line** (*Telec*) había (un) cruce de líneas • **they got their lines ~ed** (*fig*) hubo un malentendido entre ellos • IDIOMS: • **to ~ sb's palm with silver** dar una moneda de plata a algn • **to ~ swords with sb** cruzar la espada con algn; ▹ **wire**
4 (= *thwart*) [+ *person*] contrariar, ir contra; [+ *plan*] desbaratar • **to be ~ed in love** sufrir un fracaso sentimental
5 [+ *animals, plants*] cruzar
(VI) **1** (= *go to other side*) cruzar, ir al otro lado • **he ~ed from one side of the room to the other to speak to me** cruzó *or* atravesó la sala para hablar conmigo, fue hasta el otro lado de la sala para hablar conmigo • **to ~ from Newhaven to Dieppe** pasar *or* cruzar de Newhaven a Dieppe
2 (= *intersect*) [*roads etc*] cruzarse; ▹ **path**
3 (= *meet and pass*) [*letters, people*] cruzarse
▸ **cross off** (VT + ADV) tachar
▸ **cross out** (VT + ADV) borrar • **"~ out what does not apply"** "táchese lo que no proceda"
▸ **cross over** (VI + ADV) (= *cross the road*) cruzar; (*fig*) (= *change sides*) cambiar de chaqueta, ser un/una tránsfuga
(VI + PREP) cruzar

crossbar ['krɒsbɑːʳ] (N) [*of bicycle*] barra *f*; [*of goalpost*] travesaño *m*, larguero *m*
crossbeam ['krɒsbiːm] (N) viga *f* transversal
cross-bencher ['krɒs'bentʃəʳ] (N) diputado/a *m/f* independiente
crossbill ['krɒsbɪl] (N) piquituerto *m* común
crossbones ['krɒsbəʊnz] (NPL) tibias *fpl* cruzadas; ▹ **skull**
cross-border ['krɒs'bɔːdəʳ] (ADJ) [*conflict*] fronterizo; [*trade*] internacional, transfronterizo; [*raid*] a través de la frontera, fronterizo
(CPD) ▸ **cross-border security** seguridad *f* en la frontera
crossbow ['krɒsbəʊ] (N) ballesta *f*
crossbred ['krɒsbred] (ADJ) cruzado, híbrido
(PT), (PP) of **crossbreed**
crossbreed ['krɒsbriːd] (N) cruce *m*, híbrido *m*
(VT) (PT, PP: **crossbred**) cruzar
crossbreeding ['krɒsbriːdɪŋ] (N) [*of animals*] cruzamiento *m*; [*of plants*] hibridación *f*
cross-Channel ['krɒs,tʃænl] (ADJ) • **cross-Channel services** servicios *mpl* a través del canal de la Mancha • **cross-Channel ferry** ferry *m or* transbordador *m* que cruza el canal de la Mancha
cross-check ['krɒstʃek] (N) comprobación *f* adicional, verificación *f*
(VT) comprobar una vez más *or* por otro sistema, verificar
cross-compiler ['krɒskəm'paɪləʳ] (N) compilador *m* cruzado
cross-country ['krɒs'kʌntrɪ] (ADJ) [*route, walk*] a campo traviesa
(CPD) ▸ **cross-country race** cross *m inv*, campo *m* a través ▸ **cross-country running** cross *m* ▸ **cross-country skiing** esquí *m* de fondo
cross-cultural ['krɒs'kʌltʃərəl] (ADJ) transcultural
cross-current ['krɒs'kʌrənt] (N) contracorriente *f*
cross-disciplinary [,krɒs'dɪsɪplɪnərɪ] (ADJ) multidisciplinario
cross-dress ['krɒsdres] (VI) travestirse
cross-dresser ['krɒsdresəʳ] (N) travesti *mf*, travestido/a *m/f*
cross-dressing [,krɒs'dresɪŋ] (N) travestismo *m*
cross-examination ['krɒsɪg,zæmɪ'neɪʃən] (N) (*Jur*) repreguntas *fpl*; (*fig*) interrogatorio *m*
cross-examine ['krɒsɪg'zæmɪn] (VT) (*Jur*) repreguntar; (*fig*) interrogar (severamente)
cross-eyed ['krɒsaɪd] (ADJ) bizco
cross-fertilize ['krɒs'fɜːtɪlaɪz] (VT) fecundar por fertilización cruzada
crossfield ['krɒsfiːld] (ADJ) • **~ pass** (*Ftbl, Hockey*) cruce *m*
crossfire ['krɒsfaɪəʳ] (N) fuego *m* cruzado • **we were caught in the ~** quedamos atrapados en medio del tiroteo *or* en el fuego cruzado; (*fig*) nos veíamos atacados por ambos lados
cross-grained ['krɒsgreɪnd] (ADJ) de fibras cruzadas
cross-hatching ['krɔːs,hætʃɪŋ] (N) sombreado *m* con rayas
crossing ['krɒsɪŋ] (N) **1** (*esp by sea*) travesía *f*
2 (= *road junction*) cruce *m*; (= *pedestrian crossing*) paso *m* de peatones; (= *level crossing*) paso *m* a nivel
(CPD) ▸ **crossing guard** (*US*) *persona encargada de ayudar a los niños a cruzar la calle* ▸ **crossing point** paso *m*; (*at border*) paso *m* fronterizo
cross-legged ['krɒs'legd] (ADV) • **to sit cross-legged on the floor** sentarse en el suelo con las piernas cruzadas
crossly ['krɒslɪ] (ADV) con enfado *or* (*LAm*) enojo • **"what do you mean!" he said ~** —¿qué quieres decir con eso? —dijo enfadado *or* (*LAm*) enojado
crossover ['krɒsəʊvəʳ] (N) **1** (*Aut etc*) paso *m*
2 (*Mus*) fusión *f*
cross-party ['krɒs'pɑːtɪ] (ADJ) • **cross-party support** apoyo *m* multilateral
crosspatch* ['krɒspætʃ] (N) gruñón/ona *m/f*, cascarrabias *mf*
crosspiece ['krɒspiːs] (N) travesaño *m*
cross-platform [krɒs'plætfɔːm] (ADJ) multiplataforma (*inv*)
cross-ply ['krɒsplaɪ] (ADJ) (*Aut*) [*tyre*] a carcasa diagonal
cross-pollination ['krɒs,pɒlɪ'neɪʃən] (N) polinización *f* cruzada
cross-posting [,krɒs'pəʊstɪŋ] (N) [*of emails*] envío *m* cruzado (*a otros foros*)
cross-purposes ['krɒs'pɜːpəsɪz] (NPL) • **I think we're at cross-purposes** me temo que hemos tenido un malentendido • **we were talking at cross-purposes** hablábamos de cosas distintas
cross-question ['krɒs'kwestʃən] (VT) (*Jur*) repreguntar; (*fig*) interrogar
cross-questioning ['krɒs'kwestʃənɪŋ] (N) (*Jur*) repreguntas *fpl*; (*fig*) interrogación *f*
cross-refer [,krɒsrɪ'fɜːʳ] (VT) remitir (**to** a)
cross-reference ['krɒs'refərəns] (N) remisión *f*
(VT) poner referencia cruzada a • **to cross-reference A to Q** hacer una remisión de A a Q, poner en A una nota que remite al usuario a Q
crossroads ['krɒsrəʊdz] (NSING) cruce *m*, encrucijada *f* • **to be at a ~** (*fig*) estar en una encrucijada
cross-section ['krɒs'sekʃən] (N) (*Bio etc*) corte *m or* sección *f* transversal; [*of population*] muestra *f* (representativa)
cross-stitch ['krɒsstɪtʃ] (N) punto *m* de cruz
(VT) coser en punto de cruz
crosstalk ['krɒstɔːk] (N) (*Brit*) réplicas *fpl* agudas
(CPD) ▸ **crosstalk act** (*Theat*) diálogo *m* ágil salpicado de humor
cross-tie ['krɒs,taɪ] (N) (*US*) durmiente *m*, traviesa *f*
cross-training ['krɒstreɪnɪŋ] (N) formación *f* multidisciplinar
cross-vote [,krɒs'vəʊt] (VI) votar en contra del partido
crosswalk ['krɒs,wɔːk] (N) (*US*) paso *m* de peatones
crosswind ['krɒswɪnd] (N) viento *m* de costado
crosswise ['krɒswaɪz] (ADV) transversalmente
crossword ['krɒswɜːd] (N) • **~ (puzzle)** crucigrama *m*
crotch [krɒtʃ] (N) **1** (*also* **crutch**) (*Anat*) [*of garment*] entrepierna *f*
2 [*of tree*] horquilla *f*
crotchet ['krɒtʃɪt] (N) (*Brit*) (*Mus*) negra *f*
crotchety ['krɒtʃɪtɪ] (ADJ) arisco, malhumorado
crouch [kraʊtʃ] (VI) (*also* **crouch down**) [*person*] agacharse, ponerse en cuclillas; [*animal*] agazaparse
croup¹ [kruːp] (N) (*Med*) crup *m*
croup² [kruːp] (N) [*of horse*] grupa *f*
croupier ['kruːpɪeɪ] (N) crupier *mf*
crouton, croûton ['kruːtɒn] (N) cuscurro *m*, picatoste *m*
crow [krəʊ] (N) **1** (= *bird*) cuervo *m* • **as the ~ flies** en línea recta, a vuelo de pájaro • **stone the ~s!*** ¡caray!*
2 (= *noise*) [*of cock*] cacareo *m*; [*of baby, person*] grito *m* • **a ~ of delight** un gorjeo de placer
(VI) **1** (PT: **crowed, crew**) [*cock*] cacarear, cantar
2 (PT: **crowed**) [*child*] gorjear; (*fig*) jactarse, pavonearse • **to ~ over** *or* **about sth** jactarse de algo, felicitarse por algo • **it's nothing to ~ about** no hay motivo para sentirse satisfecho
crowbar ['krəʊbɑːʳ] (N) palanca *f*
crowd [kraʊd] (N) **1** (= *mass of people*) multitud *f*, muchedumbre *f* • **he disappeared into the ~** desapareció entre la multitud *or* la muchedumbre *or* el gentío • **she lost him in the ~** lo perdió de vista entre la multitud *or* la muchedumbre *or* el gentío • **~s of people** una multitud de gente • **there was quite a ~** había bastante gente • **they always go round in a ~** siempre salen en grupo • **accidents always draw a ~** los accidentes siempre atraen a un gentío • **she's the sort of person who stands out in a ~** es la típica persona que (se) destaca en un grupo de gente
2 (= *spectators*) público *m*, espectadores *mpl* • **a ~ of 10,000 watched the parade** 10.000 espectadores presenciaron el desfile • **the away/home ~** (*Ftbl*) los seguidores del equipo visitante/de casa • **the match drew a big ~** el partido atrajo mucho público • **he certainly draws the ~s** [*performer*] no cabe duda de que atrae mucho público
3* (= *social group*) gente *f* • **I don't like that ~ at all** esa gente no me gusta nada • **she got in with a nice ~ at work** se juntó con (una) gente maja en el trabajo • **all the old ~ have come out for the occasion** la antigua pandilla ha salido para celebrar la ocasión

4 (= *common people*) • **the ~: she's just one of the ~** es del montón • **to follow the ~** (*fig*) dejarse llevar por los demás *or* por la corriente • **he likes to stand out from the ~** le gusta distinguirse de los demás
(VT) **1** (= *fill*) [+ *place*] atestar, llenar • **demonstrators ~ed the streets** los manifestantes atestaron *or* llenaron las calles • **new buildings ~ the narrow lanes of the old town** los nuevos edificios se apiñan en los estrechos callejones del casco viejo • **the thoughts that ~ed her mind** los pensamientos que le inundaban la mente
2 (= *squeeze, force*) apiñar • **they ~ed the prisoners into trucks** apiñaron a los prisioneros en unos camiones
3 (= *press against*) empujar • **they ~ed me against the wall** me empujaron contra la pared
4 (*fig*) (= *harass*) agobiar • **I do things at my own pace, so don't ~ me** deja de agobiarme, me gusta trabajar a mi ritmo
(VI) (= *gather together*) apiñarse • **they ~ed at the window to see him** se apiñaron en la ventana para verlo • **to ~ in** entrar en tropel • **memories ~ed in on me** me inundó una ola de recuerdos • **dense vegetation ~ed in on both sides of the road** la vegetación crecía espesa a ambos lados de la carretera • **I feel as if everything's ~ing in on me** me siento desbordado por todo • **we all ~ed into her little flat** todos nos metimos en su pisito, abarrotándolo de gente • **thousands of people have ~ed into the capital** miles de personas han llegado en tropel a la capital • **to ~ around** *or* **round sth/sb** apiñarse alrededor de algo/algn
(CPD) ▸ **crowd control** control *m* de masas
▸ **crowd scene** (*Cine, Theat*) escena *f* masiva *or* multitudinaria
▸ **crowd out** (VT + ADV) **1** (= *not let in*) desplazar
2 (= *fill*) [*people*] atestar • **the bar was ~ed out** el bar estaba atestado (de gente)

crowded ['kraʊdɪd] (ADJ) [*room*] (*with people*) atestado (de gente), abarrotado (de gente); [*meeting, event*] muy concurrido; [*day*] lleno de actividad • **it's very ~ here** esto está atestado *or* abarrotado (de gente) • **she has a very ~ schedule** tiene una agenda muy apretada • **~ urban areas** zonas *fpl* urbanas muy pobladas • **they live in ~ conditions** viven hacinados • **every room is ~ with furniture** todas las habitaciones están abarrotadas de muebles • **the bar gets very ~ after nine o'clock** el bar se llena de gente a partir de las nueve • **the houses are ~ together** las casas están apiñadas

crowdfunding ['kraʊdfʌndɪŋ] (N) micromecenazgo *m*, crowdfunding *m*

crowd-pleaser ['kraʊd,pli:zəʳ] (N) • **to be a crowd-pleaser** [*person*] ser alguien que complace al público

crowd-puller ['kraʊd,pʊləʳ] (N) gran atracción *f* • **the show is bound to be a crowd-puller** no cabe duda de que este espectáculo atraerá a mucho público

crowdsource ['kraʊdsɔ:s] (VT) obtener de forma colaborativa

crowdsourcing ['kraʊdsɔ:sɪŋ] (N) colaboración *f* participativa *or* abierta

crowfoot ['krəʊfʊt] (N) (PL: **crowfoots**) ranúnculo *m*

crowing ['krəʊɪŋ] (N) [*of cock*] canto *m*, cacareo *m*; [*of child*] gorjeo *m*; (*fig*) cacareo *m*

crown [kraʊn] (N) **1** (= *headdress, monarchy*) corona *f*
2 (*Jur*) • **the Crown** el Estado
3 (*Sport*) (= *title*) campeonato *m*, título *m*
4 (= *top*) [*of hat*] copa *f*; [*of head*] coronilla *f*; [*of hill*] cumbre *f*, cima *f*; [*of tooth*] corona *f* • **the ~ of the road** el centro de la calzada
(VT) **1** [+ *king etc*] coronar • **he was ~ed king** fue coronado rey • **all the ~ed heads of Europe** todos los monarcas europeos
2 (*usu pass*) (= *cap, round off*) coronar, rematar • **and to ~ it all it began to snow** y para colmo (de desgracias) *or* para remate empezó a nevar • **I wouldn't exactly say our efforts were ~ed with success** (*iro*) yo no me atrevería a decir que nuestros esfuerzos se vieron coronados por el éxito
3 [+ *tooth*] poner una corona en
4 (*Draughts*) [+ *piece*] coronar
5* (= *hit*) golpear en la cabeza • **I'll ~ you if you do that again!** ¡como lo vuelves a hacer te rompo la crisma!*
(CPD) ▸ **crown colony** (*Brit*) colonia *f*
▸ **crown court** (*Brit*) (*Jur*) ≈ Audiencia *f* provincial ▸ **crown jewels** joyas *fpl* de la corona ▸ **crown lands** propiedad *f* de la corona ▸ **crown prince** príncipe *m* heredero
▸ **crown princess** princesa *f* heredera
▸ **Crown Prosecution Service** (*Brit*) *fiscalía general británica* ▸ **crown prosecutor** (*Brit*) *fiscal general británico*

crowning ['kraʊnɪŋ] (ADJ) [*achievement*] supremo, máximo • **the house's ~ glory is its garden** el máximo *or* mayor atractivo de la casa es el jardín
(N) (= *ceremony*) coronación *f*

crow's-feet ['krəʊzfi:t] (NPL) (= *wrinkles*) patas *fpl* de gallo

crow's-nest ['krəʊznest] (N) (*Naut*) cofa *f* de vigía

crozier ['krəʊʒəʳ] (N) = crosier

CRT (N ABBR) (= **cathode ray tube**) TRC *m*

crucial ['kru:ʃəl] (ADJ) decisivo, crucial • **the next few weeks will be ~ for this government** las próximas semanas van a ser decisivas *or* cruciales para este gobierno • **their cooperation is ~ to the success of the project** su colaboración resulta crucial para el éxito del proyecto • **to play a ~ role in sth** desempeñar un papel decisivo *or* crucial en algo

crucially ['kru:ʃəlɪ] (ADV) • **to be ~ important** ser de crucial importancia • **their future is ~ dependent** *or* **depends ~ on this decision** su futuro depende de forma crucial de esta decisión • **~, he failed to secure the backing of the banks** lo verdaderamente crucial fue que no logró asegurarse el respaldo de los bancos

cruciate ['kru:ʃɪɪt] (ADJ) cruzado • **~ ligament** ligamento cruzado

crucible ['kru:sɪbl] (N) crisol *m* (*also fig*)

crucifix ['kru:sɪfɪks] (N) crucifijo *m*

crucifixion [,kru:sɪ'fɪkʃən] (N) crucifixión *f*

cruciform ['kru:sɪfɔ:m] (ADJ) cruciforme

crucify ['kru:sɪfaɪ] (VT) **1** (*lit*) crucificar
2 (*fig*) • **he'll ~ me when he finds out!** ¡cuando se entere me mata! • **the newspapers are ~ing him** los periódicos se están ensañando con él

crud‡ [krʌd] (N) (*esp US*) porquería *f*

cruddy‡ ['krʌdɪ] (ADJ) asqueroso

crude [kru:d] (ADJ) (COMPAR: **cruder**, SUPERL: **crudest**) **1** (= *unprocessed*) [*oil*] crudo; [*steel, materials*] bruto; [*sugar*] sin refinar
2 (= *primitive*) [*device, bomb, method, hut*] rudimentario; [*table, door*] tosco, basto; [*drawing, piece of work*] tosco, burdo • **to make a ~ attempt at doing sth** hacer un burdo intento de hacer algo
3 (= *coarse*) [*person, behaviour, language, joke*] grosero, ordinario
(N) (*also* **crude oil**) crudo *m*

crudely ['kru:dlɪ] (ADV) **1** (= *primitively*) [*carved, constructed, drawn*] toscamente, burdamente
2 (= *coarsely*) [*speak, behave, joke, gesture*] groseramente, ordinariamente • **to put it ~** hablando en plata*

crudeness ['kru:dnɪs], **crudity** ['kru:dɪtɪ] (N) **1** (= *primitiveness*) [*of device, bomb, weapon, method, hut*] lo rudimentario; [*of table, drawing, piece of work*] tosquedad *f*
2 (= *coarseness*) [*of language, person, behaviour, joke*] grosería *f*, ordinariez *f*

crudités ['kru:dɪteɪ] (NPL) crudités *mpl*

cruel ['krʊəl] (ADJ) (COMPAR: **crueller**, SUPERL: **cruellest**) cruel • **they were very ~ to her** fueron muy crueles con ella • **it's a ~ fact** es un hecho brutal • PROVERB: • **you have to be ~ to be kind** quien bien te quiere te hará llorar

cruelly ['krʊəlɪ] (ADV) cruelmente

cruelty ['krʊəltɪ] (N) crueldad *f* (**to** con, hacia) • **society for the prevention of ~ to animals** sociedad *f* protectora de los animales

cruet ['kru:ɪt] (N) (= *oil and vinegar*) vinagrera *f*, alcuza *f* (*Bol, Chile*); (= *stand*) vinagreras *fpl*, alcuzas *fpl* (*Bol, Chile*)

cruise [kru:z] (N) crucero *m* • **to go on a ~** hacer un crucero
(VI) **1** [*ship, fleet*] navegar; [*holidaymaker*] hacer un crucero; [*plane*] volar • **the car was cruising (along) at 80km/h** el coche marchaba plácidamente a una velocidad de 80km/h • **we are cruising at an altitude of 33,000 ft** estamos volando a una altura (de crucero) de 33.000 pies • **cruising speed** velocidad *f* de crucero • **cruising altitude** altura *f or* altitud *f* de crucero
2 (*fig*) • **to ~ to victory** vencer fácilmente
3* (= *pick up men/women*) ir de ligue*, ir a ligar*
(VT) [*ship*] [+ *waters, seas*] surcar; [*vehicle*] [+ *streets*] circular por
(CPD) ▸ **cruise control** control *m* de crucero
▸ **cruise missile** misil *m* de crucero
▸ **cruise around** (VI + ADV) (*US*) pasear en coche

cruiser ['kru:zəʳ] (N) (*Naut*) crucero *m*

cruiserweight ['kru:zəweɪt] (N) (*Boxing*) peso *m* semipesado

cruller ['krʌləʳ] (N) (*US*) buñuelo *m*

crumb [krʌm] (N) **1** [*of bread, cake etc*] miga *f* • IDIOM: • **to live off** *or* **on the ~s from sb's table** vivir de las migajas de algn
2 (*fig*) (= *small piece*) migaja *f* • **a ~ of comfort** algo de consuelo • **~s of knowledge/information** fragmentos *mpl* de conocimiento/información

crumble ['krʌmbl] (VT) [+ *bread*] desmigar, desmigajar; [+ *earth, cheese etc*] desmenuzar
(VI) **1** [*bread*] desmigarse, desmigajarse; [*earth, cheese etc*] desmenuzarse; [*building, plaster etc*] desmoronarse
2 (*fig*) [*hopes, power, self-confidence*] desmoronarse, venirse abajo; [*coalition*] venirse abajo, derrumbarse

crumbly ['krʌmblɪ] (ADJ) (COMPAR: **crumblier**, SUPERL: **crumbliest**) [*earth*] quebradizo; [*cheese*] que se desmenuza con facilidad; (*Culin*) [*mixture*] quebradizo; (*US*) [*pastry*] sobado

crummy* ['krʌmɪ] (ADJ) (COMPAR: **crummier**, SUPERL: **crummiest**) **1** (= *bad*) miserable; [*hotel*] de mala muerte* • **you can keep your ~ job** puede usted quedarse su empleo de pacotilla
2 (= *unwell*) fatal* • **I'm feeling ~** me siento fatal*

crumpet ['krʌmpɪt] (N) **1** (*esp Brit*) (*Culin*) ≈ bollo *m* blando para tostar
2 (*Brit‡*) (= *girl*) jai‡ *f*, tía* *f*; (= *girls*) las jais‡, las tías* • **a bit of ~** (*Brit‡*) una jai‡, una tía*

crumple ['krʌmpl] (VT) (*also* **crumple up**)

C

[+ *paper*] estrujar; [+ *clothes*] arrugar
VI [*material*] arrugarse; [*person*] (= *fall*) desplomarse; (= *lose one's nerve*) desmoronarse, venirse abajo • **she ~d to the floor** se desplomó • **he just ~d and lost all his confidence** se desmoronó *or* se vino abajo y perdió toda la confianza • **his face ~d and he started to cry** se le descompuso el rostro y se echó a llorar
CPD ▸ **crumple zone** (*Aut*) zona *f* de deformación absorbente

crumpled [ˈkrʌmpəld] ADJ **1** [*clothes, paper*] arrugado, hecho un higo*
2 [*body*] encogido

crunch [krʌntʃ] N crujido *m*; (*fig*) crisis *f*, punto *m* decisivo • IDIOMS: • **when it comes to the ~** cuando llega el momento de la verdad • **if it comes to the ~** si llega el momento
VT (*with teeth*) mascar, ronzar; [+ *ground etc*] hacer crujir; (*fig*) [+ *numbers*] devorar • **to ~ an apple/a biscuit** mascar *or* ronzar una manzana/una galleta
VI [*gravel, snow, glass*] crujir • **the tyres ~ed on the gravel** la grava crujía bajo el peso de los neumáticos, los neumáticos hacían crujir la grava
CPD [*meeting, match*] decisivo, crucial
▸ **crunch time** momento *m* decisivo

crunchy [ˈkrʌntʃɪ] ADJ (COMPAR: **crunchier**, SUPERL: **crunchiest**) crujiente

crupper [ˈkrʌpəʳ] N [*of horse*] anca *f*, grupa *f*; (= *part of harness*) baticola *f*

crusade [kruːˈseɪd] N cruzada *f*; (*fig*) campaña *f*, cruzada *f*
VI (*fig*) • **to ~ for/against sth** hacer una campaña en pro de/en contra de algo

crusader [kruːˈseɪdəʳ] N cruzado *m*; (*fig*) paladín *m*, campeón/ona *m/f*

crusading [kruːˈseɪdɪŋ] ADJ [*journalist, lawyer, newspaper*] militante

crush [krʌʃ] N **1** (= *crowd*) aglomeración *f*, multitud *f*; [*of cars*] masa *f* • **there was an awful ~** hubo la mar de gente • **there's always a ~ in the tube** el metro va siempre atestado de gente • **I lost my handbag in the ~** perdí el bolso en la aglomeración • **they died in the ~** murieron aplastados
2* (= *infatuation*) enamoramiento *m* • **to have a ~ on sb** estar enamorado de algn, perder la chaveta por algn*
3 (*Brit*) • **orange ~** naranjada *f*
VT **1** (= *squash*) aplastar, apachurrar (*And, CAm*); (= *crumple*) [+ *paper*] estrujar; [+ *clothes*] arrugar; (= *grind, break up*) [+ *stones*] triturar, moler; [+ *grapes*] exprimir, prensar; [+ *garlic*] machacar; [+ *ice*] picar; [+ *scrap metal*] comprimir • **to ~ sth into a case** meter algo a la fuerza en una maleta • **to ~ sth to a pulp** hacer papilla algo
2 (*fig*) [+ *enemy, opposition, resistance*] doblegar, aplastar; [+ *argument*] aplastar, abrumar; [+ *hopes*] defraudar
VI [*clothes*] arrugarse • **can we all ~ in?** ¿habrá sitio para todos?
CPD ▸ **crush barrier** barrera *f* de seguridad

crusher [ˈkrʌʃəʳ] N (*for paper, stone, food*) trituradora *f* • **garlic ~** triturador *m* de ajos

crushing [ˈkrʌʃɪŋ] ADJ [*defeat, blow, reply*] aplastante; [*grief etc*] abrumador; [*argument*] decisivo; [*burden*] agobiador

crushingly [ˈkrʌʃɪŋlɪ] ADV [*dull, familiar*] terriblemente

crush-resistant [ˌkrʌʃrɪˈzɪstənt] ADJ inarrugable

crust [krʌst] N [*of bread etc*] corteza *f*; (= *dry bread*) mendrugo *m*; [*of pie*] pasta *f*; (*Med*) (*on wound, sore*) costra *f*; [*of wine*] depósito *m*, poso *m*; (= *layer*) capa *f*; (*Geol*) corteza *f* • **there were only a few ~s to eat** para comer solo había unos pocos mendrugos • **a thin ~ of ice** una fina capa de hielo • **the earth's ~** la corteza terrestre; ▹ **earn, upper**
VT • **frost ~ed the windscreen** el parabrisas tenía una capa de hielo • **boots ~ed with mud** botas con barro incrustado

crustacean [krʌsˈteɪʃɪən] N crustáceo *m*

crusted [ˈkrʌstɪd] ADJ (= *encrusted*) incrustado

-crusted [-ˌkrʌstɪd] SUFFIX • **ice-crusted** con una costra de hielo • **blood-crusted** cubierto de sangre

crusty [ˈkrʌstɪ] ADJ (COMPAR: **crustier**, SUPERL: **crustiest**) **1** [*bread*] crujiente; [*loaf*] de corteza dura
2* [*person*] arisco, malhumorado

crutch [krʌtʃ] N **1** (*Med*) muleta *f*; (*fig*) (= *support*) apoyo *m*
2 = **crotch**

crux [krʌks] N (PL: **cruxes** *or* **cruces** [ˈkruːsiːz]) • **the ~ of the matter** lo esencial *or* el meollo *or* el quid del asunto

cry [kraɪ] N **1** (= *call, shout*) grito *m*; (= *howl*) [*of animal*] aullido *m*; [*of street vendor*] pregón *m* • **to give a cry of surprise** dar un grito de sorpresa • **"jobs, not bombs" was their cry** su grito de guerra fue —trabajo sí, bombas no • **a cry for help** (*lit*) un grito de socorro *or* auxilio; (*fig*) una llamada de socorro *or* auxilio • **the hounds were in full cry** los perros seguían de cerca la presa • **the crowd was in full cry after him** la multitud lo perseguía con gritos • **the newspapers are in full cry over the scandal** la prensa ha puesto el grito en el cielo por el escándalo; ▹ **far**
2 (= *watchword*) lema *m*, slogan *m*
3 (= *weep*) llanto *m* • **to have a cry** llorar • **she had a good cry** lloró largamente
VI **1** (= *call out, shout*) gritar, llamar (en voz alta) • **they are crying for his resignation** piden a gritos que dimita • **he cried (out) with pain** dio un grito de dolor • **to cry for help/mercy** pedir socorro/clemencia a voces
2 (= *weep*) llorar • **he was crying for his mother** lloraba por su madre • **I cried for joy** lloraba de alegría • **she was crying with rage** lloraba de rabia • **I laughed till I cried** terminé llorando de la risa • **I'll give him something to cry about!*** le voy a dar de qué llorar • **to cry over sth** llorar por algo
• PROVERB: • **it's no good crying over spilt milk** a lo hecho, pecho; ▹ **shoulder**
VT **1** (*also* **cry out**) (= *call*) gritar; [+ *warning*] lanzar a gritos; [+ *wares*] pregonar
2 • **to cry o.s. to sleep** llorar hasta dormirse
▸ **cry down** VT + ADV despreciar, desacreditar
▸ **cry off** VI + ADV (= *withdraw*) retirarse; (= *back out**) rajarse
▸ **cry out** VI + ADV (= *call out, shout*) lanzar un grito, echar un grito • **to cry out against** protestar contra, poner el grito en el cielo por • **the system is crying out for reform** (*fig*) el sistema pide la reforma a gritos *or* necesita urgentemente reformarse • **this car is crying out to be resprayed** este coche está pidiendo a gritos una mano de pintura • **for crying out loud!*** ¡por Dios!
VT + ADV **1** (= *call*) gritar; [+ *warning*] lanzar a gritos
2 • **to cry one's eyes** *or* **heart out** llorar a lágrima viva *or* a moco tendido

crybaby [ˈkraɪˌbeɪbɪ] N llorón/ona *m/f*

crying [ˈkraɪɪŋ] ADJ [*child*] que llora; (= *whining*) llorón; [*need**] urgente • **it's a ~ shame*** (= *pity*) es una verdadera lástima; (= *outrage*) es una auténtica vergüenza
N (= *weeping*) llanto *m*; (= *sobbing*) lloriqueo *m*

cryogenics [ˌkraɪəˈdʒenɪks] N criogenia *f*

cryonics [kraɪˈɒnɪks] N criogenética *f*

cryosurgery [ˌkraɪəʊˈsɜːdʒərɪ] N criocirugía *f*

crypt [krɪpt] N cripta *f*

cryptic [ˈkrɪptɪk] ADJ [*message, clue*] críptico; [*comment*] enigmático, críptico; (= *coded*) en clave
CPD ▸ **cryptic crossword** crucigrama *m* críptico

cryptically [ˈkrɪptɪkəlɪ] ADV enigmáticamente, de forma críptica

crypto- [ˈkrɪptəʊ] PREFIX cripto-

crypto-communist [ˈkrɪptəʊˈkɒmjʊnɪst] N criptocomunista *mf*

cryptogram [ˈkrɪptəʊgræm] N criptograma *m*

cryptographer [krɪpˈtɒgrəfəʳ] N criptógrafo/a *m/f*

cryptographic [ˌkrɪptəˈgræfɪk], **cryptographical** [ˌkrɪptəˈgræfɪkəl] ADJ criptográfico

cryptography [krɪpˈtɒgrəfɪ] N criptografía *f*

crystal [ˈkrɪstl] N cristal *m* • **quartz/rock ~** cristal de roca
ADJ (= *clear*) [*water, lake*] cristalino
CPD [*glass, vase*] de cristal ▸ **crystal ball** bola *f* de cristal ▸ **crystal meth** metanfetamina *f* ▸ **crystal set** (*Rad*) receptor *m* de cristal

crystal-clear [ˈkrɪstlˈklɪəʳ] ADJ (*lit*) [*water*] cristalino; (= *obvious*) evidente, más claro que el agua

crystal-gazing [ˈkrɪstlˌgeɪzɪŋ] N (*fig*) adivinación *f* (*del futuro en la bola de cristal*)

crystalline [ˈkrɪstəlaɪn] ADJ cristalino

crystallization [ˌkrɪstəlaɪˈzeɪʃən] N **1** [*of thoughts, opinions*] cristalización *f*
2 (*Chem*) [*of substance*] cristalización *f*

crystallize [ˈkrɪstəlaɪz] VT (*Chem*) cristalizar; [+ *fruit*] escarchar; (*fig*) cristalizar, resolver • **~d fruits** frutas *fpl* escarchadas
VI (*Chem*) cristalizarse; (*fig*) concretarse, cristalizarse

crystallographer [ˌkrɪstəˈlɒgrəfəʳ] N cristalógrafo/a *m/f*

crystallography [ˌkrɪstəˈlɒgrəfɪ] N cristalografía *f*

CSA N ABBR **1** (*Brit*) = **Child Support Agency**
2 (*US*) = **Confederate States of America**

CSC N ABBR (*Brit*) (= **Civil Service Commission**) *comisión de reclutamiento de funcionarios*

CSE N ABBR (*Brit*) (*Scol*) (= **Certificate of Secondary Education**) ≈ BUP *m* (*Sp*)

CSEU N ABBR (*Brit*) = **Confederation of Shipbuilding and Engineering Unions**

CS gas [ˌsiːˌesˈgæs] N (*Brit*) gas *m* lacrimógeno

CST N ABBR (*US*) = **Central Standard Time**

CSU N ABBR (*Brit*) = **Civil Service Union**

CT ABBR **1** (*Econ*) = **cable transfer**
2 (*US*) = **Connecticut**
3 (= **computerized tomography**) TC
CPD ▸ **CT scanner** escáner *m*

ct ABBR **1** (= **carat**) qts, quil
2 = **cent**

Ct. ABBR (*US*) = **Connecticut**

CTC N ABBR = **City Technology College**

CTT N ABBR (*Brit*) = **Capital Transfer Tax**

cu. ABBR = **cubic**

cub [kʌb] N **1** (= *animal*) cachorro *m* • **wolf/lion cub** cachorro *m* de lobo/león
2 (*also* **cub scout**) lobato *m*, niño *m* explorador
3 (*Brit*†) (= *youngster*) jovenzuelo *m*
CPD ▸ **cub reporter** periodista *mf* novato/a

Cuba [ˈkjuːbə] N Cuba *f*

Cuban ['kju:bən] ADJ cubano
N cubano/a *m/f*
cubbyhole ['kʌbɪhəʊl] N (= *small room*) cuchitril *m*; (= *cupboard*) armario *m* pequeño; (= *pigeonhole*) casilla *f*
cube [kju:b] N **1** (= *solid*) cubo *m*; [*of sugar*] terrón *m*; [*of ice*] cubito *m*; [*of cheese*] dado *m*, cubito *m*
2 (= *number*) • **the ~ of four** cuatro (elevado) al cubo
VT (*Math*) cubicar, elevar al cubo
CPD ▸ **cube root** (*Math*) raíz *f* cúbica
cubic ['kju:bɪk] ADJ cúbico
CPD ▸ **cubic capacity** capacidad *f* cúbica ▸ **cubic foot** pie *m* cúbico ▸ **cubic measure** medida *f* cúbica ▸ **cubic metre** metro *m* cúbico
cubicle ['kju:bɪkəl] N (*in hospital, dormitory*) cubículo *m*; (*in swimming baths*) caseta *f*
cubism ['kju:bɪzəm] N cubismo *m*
cubist ['kju:bɪst] ADJ cubista
N cubista *mf*
cubit ['kju:bət] N codo *m*
cuckold ['kʌkəld] N cornudo *m*
VT poner los cuernos a
cuckoo ['kʊku:] N cuco *m*, cuclillo *m*
ADJ* loco, lelo*
CPD ▸ **cuckoo clock** reloj *m* de cuco, cucú *m*
cuckoopint [,kʊku:'paɪnt] N aro *m*
cucumber ['kju:kʌmbəʳ] N pepino *m*; ▹ **cool**
cud [kʌd] N • **to chew the cud** [*animal*] rumiar; (= *think over*) reflexionar, dar vueltas a las cosas
cuddle ['kʌdl] N abrazo *m*
VT abrazar, apapachar (*Mex**)
VI [*two persons*] abrazarse, estar abrazados
• **to ~ down** [*child in bed*] acurrucarse (en la cama) • **to ~ up to sb** arrimarse a algn
cuddlesome ['kʌdlsəm] ADJ = **cuddly**
cuddly ['kʌdlɪ] ADJ (COMPAR: **cuddlier**, SUPERL: **cuddliest**) [*person*] rico, tierno; [*animal*] cariñoso; [*toy*] de peluche
cudgel ['kʌdʒəl] N porra *f* • IDIOM: • **to take up the ~s for sth/sb** salir a la defensa de algo/algn
VT aporrear
cue [kju:] N **1** (*Billiards*) taco *m*
2 (*Theat*) (*verbal, by signal*) pie *m*, entrada *f*; (*Mus*) (*by signal*) entrada *f* • **to give sb his cue** (*Theat*) dar el pie *or* la entrada a algn; (*Mus*) dar a algn su entrada • **that gave me my cue** (*fig*) eso me sirvió de indicación • **to come in on cue** entrar en el momento justo • **then, right on cue for the photographers, she threw him a kiss** entonces, en el momento justo para los fotógrafos, ella le lanzó un beso • IDIOM: • **to take one's cue from sb** seguir el ejemplo de algn
CPD ▸ **cue ball** (*Billiards*) bola *f* jugadora; (*Snooker*) bola *f* blanca ▸ **cue card** letrero *m* (*apuntando lo que se ha de decir*) ▸ **cue word** palabra *f* clave
▸ **cue in** VT + ADV (*Rad, TV, Mus*) dar la entrada a; (*Theat*) dar el pie a, dar la entrada a • **to cue sb in on sth** (*US**) poner a algn al tanto *or* al corriente de algo
cuff¹ [kʌf] N bofetada *f*
VT abofetear
cuff² [kʌf] N [*of sleeve*] puño *m*; (*US*) [*of trousers*] vuelta *f*; **cuffs*** (= *handcuffs*) esposas *fpl* • IDIOM: • **off the ~** (*as adv*) de improviso; (*as adj*) improvisado; ▹ **off-the-cuff**
cufflinks ['kʌflɪŋks] NPL gemelos *mpl*, mancuernas *fpl* (*CAm, Mex*)
cu.ft. ABBR = **cubic foot, cubic feet**
cu.in. ABBR = **cubic inch(es)**
cuisine [kwɪ'zi:n] N cocina *f*
cul-de-sac ['kʌldə'sæk] (PL: **culs-de-sac, cul-de-sacs**) N (*lit*) calle *f* sin salida, calle *f* cortada; (*fig*) callejón *m* sin salida
culinary ['kʌlɪnərɪ] ADJ culinario
cull [kʌl] VT (= *select*) [+ *fruit*] entresacar; [+ *flowers*] coger; (= *kill selectively*) [+ *deer, seals*] matar selectivamente
N [*of deer, seals*] matanza *f* selectiva • **seal ~** matanza *f* selectiva de focas
culling ['kʌlɪŋ] N [*of animals*] (= *selective killing*) sacrificio *m* selectivo; (= *slaughter*) masacre *f*
culminate ['kʌlmɪneɪt] VI • **to ~ in** culminar en
culminating ['kʌlmɪneɪtɪŋ] ADJ culminante
culmination [,kʌlmɪ'neɪʃən] N culminación *f*, punto *m* culminante • **it is the ~ of a great deal of effort** es la culminación de grandes esfuerzos
culottes [kjʊ:'lɒts] NPL falda *fsing* pantalón
culpability [,kʌlpə'bɪlɪtɪ] N (*frm*) culpabilidad *f*
culpable ['kʌlpəbl] ADJ (*frm*) culpable
CPD ▸ **culpable homicide** homicidio *m* sin premeditación
culprit ['kʌlprɪt] N culpable *mf*; (*Jur*) acusado/a *m/f*
cult [kʌlt] N culto *m* (**of** a) • **to make a ~ of sth** rendir culto a algo
CPD ▸ **cult figure** ídolo *m* ▸ **cult film, cult movie** película *f* de culto
cultivable ['kʌltɪvəbl] ADJ cultivable
cultivar ['kʌltɪvɑ:ʳ] N (*Bot*) variedad *f* cultivada
cultivate ['kʌltɪveɪt] VT **1** [+ *crop, land, friendships*] cultivar
2 (*fig*) [+ *habit*] cultivar
cultivated ['kʌltɪveɪtɪd] ADJ (*fig*) [*person*] cultivado, culto; [*tastes, voice*] refinado
CPD ▸ **cultivated land** tierras *fpl* cultivadas
cultivation [,kʌltɪ'veɪʃən] N **1** (*Agr*) cultivo *m*
2 (*fig*) [*of habit, qualities*] cultivo *m*
cultivator ['kʌltɪveɪtəʳ] N **1** (= *person*) cultivador(a) *m/f*
2 (= *machine*) cultivadora *f*
cultural ['kʌltʃərəl] ADJ cultural
CPD ▸ **cultural attaché** agregado/a *m/f* cultural
culturally ['kʌltʃərəlɪ] ADV [*diverse*] culturalmente, desde el punto de vista cultural • **to be ~ aware/sensitive** estar pendiente de/sensibilizado con la cultura • **~, they have much in common with their neighbours** culturalmente hablando, tienen mucho en común con sus vecinos
culture ['kʌltʃəʳ] N **1** (= *the arts*) cultura *f*; (= *civilization*) civilización *f*, cultura *f*
2 (= *education, refinement*) cultura *f* • **she has no ~** carece de cultura, es una inculta
3 (*Agr*) (= *breeding*) cría *f*; [*of plants etc*] cultivo *m*
VT [+ *tissue etc*] cultivar
CPD ▸ **culture clash** choque *m* de culturas, choque *m* cultural ▸ **culture fluid** caldo *m* de cultivo ▸ **culture gap** vacío *m* cultural ▸ **culture medium** caldo *m* de cultivo ▸ **culture shock** choque *m* cultural ▸ **culture vulture*** (*hum*) cultureta* *mf*
cultured ['kʌltʃəd] ADJ [*person*] culto, cultivado; [*tastes, voice*] refinado
CPD ▸ **cultured pearl** perla *f* cultivada
culvert ['kʌlvət] N alcantarilla *f* (debajo de una carretera)
cum [kʌm] PREP con • **it's a sort of kitchen-cum-library** es algo así como cocina y biblioteca combinadas • **I was butler-cum-gardener to Lady Jane** yo fui mayordomo y jardinero a la vez en el servicio de Lady Jane
cu. m. ABBR (= **cubic metre(s), cubic meter(s)**) m^3
Cumb ABBR (= **Cumberland**) *antigua provincia del noroeste de Inglaterra*
cumbersome ['kʌmbəsəm], **cumbrous** ['kʌmbrəs] ADJ (= *bulky*) voluminoso, de mucho bulto; (= *awkward*) incómodo • **he was muffled in thick and ~ clothing** las abultadas ropas de abrigo casi le tapaban la cara • **the machine was slow and ~ to use** la máquina resultaba lenta y aparatosa *or* lenta e incómoda (de manejar)
• **~ administrative procedures** procedimientos *mpl* administrativos engorrosos
cumin ['kʌmɪn] N comino *m*
cum laude [kʊm'laʊdeɪ] ADJ (*Univ*) cum laude
cummerbund ['kʌməbʌnd] N faja *f*
cumulative ['kju:mjʊlətɪv] ADJ cumulativo
cumulatively ['kju:mjʊlətɪvlɪ] ADV en forma conjunta
cumulonimbus [,kju:mjʊləʊ'nɪmbəs] N (PL: **cumulonimbi** [,kju:mjʊləʊ'nɪmbaɪ]) cumulonimbo *m*
cumulus ['kju:mələs] N (PL: **cumuli** ['kju:mjʊlaɪ]) cúmulo *m*
cuneiform ['kju:nɪfɔ:m] ADJ cuneiforme
cunnilingus [,kʌnɪ'lɪŋgəs] N cunnilingus *m*
cunning ['kʌnɪŋ] ADJ **1** (*pej*) (= *sly*) taimado, vivo (*LAm*)
2 (= *clever*) [*person*] astuto, ingenioso; [*plan, scheme, device*] ingenioso
3 (*US**) (= *cute*) mono, precioso
N (= *slyness*) astucia *f*; (= *cleverness*) ingenio *m*
cunningly ['kʌnɪŋlɪ] ADV **1** (= *slyly*) astutamente
2 (= *cleverly*) [*contrived, designed*] astutamente, sutilmente; [*disguised*] astutamente
cunt** [kʌnt] N **1** (= *genitals*) coño** *m*, concha *f* (*And, S. Cone***)
2 (= *person*) hijo/a *m/f* de puta**
CUP N ABBR = **Cambridge University Press**
cup [kʌp] N (*for tea etc*) taza *f*; (= *amount*) (*also* **cupful**) taza *f*; (*Sport etc*) (= *prize*) copa *f*; (*Rel*) (= *chalice*) cáliz *m*; [*of brassiere*] copa *f* • **a cup of tea** una taza de té, un té • **coffee cup** tacita *f*, pocillo *m* (*LAm*) • **how's your cup?** ¿quieres más té/café *etc*? • **his cup of sorrow was full** le agobiaba el dolor • IDIOMS: • **to be in one's cups** estar borracho • **to be sb's cup of tea***: • **it's not everyone's cup of tea*** no es del gusto de todos • **he's not my cup of tea*** no es de mi agrado, no es santo de mi devoción • **football isn't my cup of tea*** a mí el fútbol no me va; ▹ **paper**
VT • **to cup one's hands** (*for shouting*) formar bocina con las manos; (*for drinking*) ahuecar las manos • **to cup one's hands round sth** rodear algo con las manos
CPD ▸ **cup final** (*Ftbl*) final *m* de copa ▸ **cup tie** (*Ftbl*) partido *m* de copa
cup-bearer ['kʌp,bɛərəʳ] N copero *m*
cupboard ['kʌbəd] N (*free-standing*) armario *m*; (*built-in*) armario *m*, closet/clóset *m* (*LAm*), placar(d) *m* (*S. Cone*)
CPD ▸ **cupboard love** (*Brit*) amor *m* interesado
cupcake ['kʌpkeɪk] N pastelito *m*
cupful ['kʌpfʊl] N taza *f* • **two ~s of milk** dos tazas de leche
Cupid ['kju:pɪd] N Cupido *m*
CPD ▸ **Cupid's arrow** (= *love*) flecha *f* de Cupido ▸ **Cupid's bow** (*also* **Cupid's bow lips**) labios *mpl* en forma de arco de Cupido
cupid ['kju:pɪd] N (= *figurine*) cupido *m*
cupidity [kju:'pɪdɪtɪ] N (*frm*) codicia *f*
cupola ['kju:pələ] N cúpula *f*
cuppa* ['kʌpə] N (*Brit*) taza *f* de té
cur [kɜ:ʳ] N perro *m* de mala raza; (= *person*) canalla *m*

curable ['kjʊərəbl] ADJ curable
curaçao [kjʊərəsəʊ] N curaçao *m*
curacy ['kjʊərəsɪ] N (*as parish priest*) curato *m*; (*as assistant*) coadjutoría *f*
curare [kjʊə'rɑːrɪ] N curare *m*
curate ['kjʊərɪt] N (= *parish priest*) cura *m*; (= *assistant*) coadjutor *m* • IDIOM: • **to be like the ~'s egg**: • **it's like the ~'s egg** (*Brit*) tiene su lado bueno y su lado malo
curative ['kjʊərətɪv] ADJ curativo
curator [kjʊə'reɪtəʳ] N [*of museum*] director(a) *m/f*; [*of museum department*] conservador(a) *m/f*
curatorial [,kjʊərə'tɔːrɪəl] ADJ • **the museum's ~ staff** el equipo de conservadores del museo • **~ expertise** conocimientos *mpl* de conservación
curb [kɜːb] N **1** (*fig*) freno *m* • **to put a ~ on sth** poner freno a algo, refrenar algo
2 (*US*) = **kerb**
VT (*fig*) [+ *temper, impatience etc*] dominar, refrenar; [+ *spending*] restringir; [+ *inflation*] poner freno a, frenar
CPD ▸ **curb crawling** (*US*) = **kerb crawling**
curbstone ['kɜːbstəʊn] N (*US*) = **kerbstone**
curd [kɜːd] N (*usu pl*) cuajada *f*
CPD ▸ **curd cheese** requesón *m*; ▹ **bean**, **lemon**
curdle ['kɜːdl] VT (= *form curds in*) cuajar; (= *separate*) [+ *milk, sauce*] cortar • **it was enough to ~ the blood** fue para helar la sangre a uno
VI (= *form curds*) cuajarse; (= *separate*) [*milk, sauce*] cortarse
curdy ['kɜːdɪ] ADJ (= *coagulated*) coagulado; (= *lumpy*) cuajado
cure [kjʊəʳ] N (= *remedy*) remedio *m*; (= *course of treatment*) cura *f*; (= *process of recovery*) curación *f* • **there is no known ~** no existe curación • **to be beyond ~** [*person*] padecer una enfermedad incurable; [*situation, injustice*] ser irremediable • **to take a ~** (*for illness*) tomar un remedio
VT **1** (*Med*) [+ *disease, patient*] curar; (*fig*) [+ *poverty, injustice, evil*] remediar • **to ~ sb of a habit** quitar a algn un vicio • PROVERB: • **what can't be ~d must be endured** hay cosas que no queda más remedio que aguantar
2 (= *preserve*) (*in salt*) salar; (*by smoking*) curar; (*by drying*) secar; [+ *animal hide*] curtir
cure-all ['kjʊərɔːl] N panacea *f*, curalotodo *m*
cureless ['kjʊəlɪs] ADJ sin cura
curettage [,kjʊə'retɪdʒ] N legrado *m*, raspado *m*
curfew ['kɜːfjuː] N toque *m* de queda
curie ['kjʊərɪ] N curie *m*
curing ['kjʊərɪŋ] N curación *f*; ▹ **cure**
curio ['kjʊərɪəʊ] N curiosidad *f*
curiosity [,kjʊərɪ'ɒsɪtɪ] N **1** (= *inquisitiveness*) curiosidad *f* (**about** por, acerca de) • **out of ~** por curiosidad • PROVERB: • **~ killed the cat** la curiosidad mata al hombre
2 (= *rare thing*) curiosidad *f*
CPD ▸ **curiosity shop** tienda *f* de curiosidades ▸ **curiosity value** • **its only attraction is its ~ value** su único interés es el valor que tiene como rareza
curious ['kjʊərɪəs] ADJ **1** (= *inquisitive*) curioso • **I'd be ~ to know** tengo curiosidad por saberlo • **she was ~ about her sister's new boyfriend** sentía curiosidad por conocer al nuevo novio de su hermana • **"do you want to know for any special reason?" — "no, I'm just ~"** —¿quieres saberlo por alguna razón especial? —no, solo por curiosidad
2 (= *strange*) curioso • **it's ~ that she didn't say why** es curioso que no dijese por qué • **it's ~ how we keep meeting each other** es curioso que siempre nos estemos encontrando
curiously ['kjʊərɪəslɪ] ADV **1** (= *inquisitively*) [*ask, look*] con curiosidad
2 (= *oddly*) [*silent, reticent*] curiosamente • **~, he didn't object** curiosamente, no puso objeciones • **~ shaped** con una forma curiosa • **~ enough, it's true** curiosamente *or* aunque parezca extraño, es cierto
curiousness ['kjʊərɪəsnɪs] N **1** = **curiosity**
2 (= *strangeness*) curiosidad *f*
curl [kɜːl] N [*of hair*] rizo *m*; (= *ringlet*) bucle *m*, sortija *f*; [*of smoke etc*] espiral *m*, voluta *f*
VT [+ *hair*] rizar; [+ *paper*] arrollar • **she ~ed her lip in scorn** hizo una mueca de desprecio
VI [*hair*] rizarse; [*paper*] arrollarse; [*leaf*] abarquillarse; [*waves*] encresparse
▸ **curl up** VI + ADV [*paper, stale bread*] arrollarse; [*leaf*] abarquillarse; [*cat, dog*] hacerse una pelota; [*person*] hacerse un ovillo, acurrucarse • **she lay ~ed up on the bed** estaba acurrucada encima de la cama • **to ~ up into a ball** hacerse un ovillo • **to ~ up with a book** acurrucarse con un libro • **to ~ up with embarrassment/laughter*** morirse de vergüenza/risa
curler ['kɜːləʳ] N (*for hair*) rulo *m*, bigudí *m*, rulero *m* (*S. Cone*)
curlew ['kɜːluː] N zarapito *m*
curlicue ['kɜːlɪkjuː] N floritura *f*, floreo *m*
curling ['kɜːlɪŋ] N (*Sport*) curling *m*
CPD ▸ **curling iron(s)**, **curling tongs** (*for hair*) tenacillas *fpl* de rizar
curl-paper ['kɜːl,peɪpəʳ] N papillote *m*
curly ['kɜːlɪ] ADJ (COMPAR: **curlier**, SUPERL: **curliest**) [*hair, eyelashes, lettuce*] rizado; [*writing*] de trazo ondulado, lleno de florituras
curly-haired [,kɜːlɪ'hɛəd], **curly-headed** [kɜːlɪ'hedɪd] ADJ de pelo rizado
curmudgeon† [kɜː'mʌdʒən] N cascarrabias *mf inv*
curmudgeonly† [kɜː'mʌdʒənlɪ] ADJ [*person*] arisco, cascarrabias; [*attitude*] de viejo cascarrabias
currant ['kʌrənt] N (= *dried grape*) pasa *f* de Corinto; (= *bush*) grosellero *m*; (= *fruit*) grosella *f*
CPD ▸ **currant bun** bollo *m* con pasas, pan *m* de pasas (*LAm*)
currency ['kʌrənsɪ] N **1** (= *monetary system, money*) moneda *f* • **foreign ~** moneda *f* extranjera, divisas *fpl*; ▹ **paper**
2 (*fig*) aceptación *f* • **his theory had wide ~ in America** su teoría tuvo amplia aceptación en América • **these things are the ~ of everyday life** estas cosas son el pan nuestro de cada día • **to gain ~** [*views, ideas*] darse a conocer, difundirse • **it was his writing that gave the term ~** el término se dio a conocer gracias a sus escritos
CPD ▸ **currency market** mercado *m* monetario, mercado *m* de divisas ▸ **currency note** pagaré *m* fiscal, pagaré *m* de tesorería ▸ **currency restrictions** restricciones *fpl* monetarias ▸ **currency snake** serpiente *f* monetaria ▸ **currency trading** operaciones *fpl* en el mercado de divisas ▸ **currency unit** unidad *f* monetaria
current ['kʌrənt] ADJ [*fashion, tendency*] actual; [*price, word*] corriente; [*year, month, week*] presente, en curso • **the ~ month/year** el presente mes/año, el mes/año en curso • **the ~ issue of the magazine** el último número de la revista • **her ~ boyfriend** su novio de ahora • **to be in ~ use** estar en uso corriente • **a word in ~ use** una palabra de uso corriente • **the ~ opinion is that ...** actualmente se cree que ... • **this idea/method is still quite ~** esta idea/este método se usa bastante todavía
N (*all senses*) corriente *f* • **direct/alternating ~** corriente *f* directa/alterna • IDIOMS: • **to go against the ~** ir contra la corriente • **to go with the ~** dejarse llevar por la corriente
CPD ▸ **current account** (*Brit*) cuenta *f* corriente ▸ **current affairs** temas *mpl* de actualidad ▸ **current assets** activo *msing* corriente ▸ **current events** = **current affairs** ▸ **current liabilities** pasivo *msing* corriente
currently ['kʌrəntlɪ] ADV actualmente, en la actualidad
curricle ['kʌrɪkəl] N carro *m*
curricular [kə'rɪkjʊləʳ] ADJ [*activities*] curricular
curriculum [kə'rɪkjʊləm] N (PL: **curriculums** *or* **curricula** [kə'rɪkjʊlə]) [*of school*] plan *m* de estudios; [*of college/university course*] programa *m* de estudios
CPD ▸ **curriculum vitae** (*esp Brit*) curriculum *m* (vitae), historial *m* (profesional)
curried ['kʌrɪd] ADJ al curry
curry¹ ['kʌrɪ] N curry *m*
VT preparar con curry
CPD ▸ **curry powder** curry *m* en polvo
curry² ['kʌrɪ] VT [+ *horse*] almohazar
currycomb ['kʌrɪkəʊm] N almohaza *f*
curse [kɜːs] N **1** (= *malediction, spell*) maldición *f* • **to put a ~ on sb** maldecir a algn • **a ~ on it!** ¡maldito sea!
2 (= *bane*) maldición *f*, azote *m* • **drought is the ~ of Spain** la sequía es el azote de España • **it's been the ~ of my life** me ha amargado la vida, ha sido mi cruz • **the ~ of it is that ...** lo peor (del caso) es que ...
3 (= *oath*) palabrota *f* • **to utter a ~** blasfemar • **~s!*** ¡maldito sea!, ¡maldición!
4* (= *menstruation*) • **the ~** la regla, el período
VT [+ *luck, stupidity*] maldecir; [+ *person*] echar pestes de • **~ it!** ¡maldito sea! • **I ~ the day I met him** maldita sea la hora en que lo conocí • **to be ~d with** padecer, tener que soportar • **he seemed to be ~d with bad luck** parecía que la mala suerte le perseguía • **to ~ o.s.** maldecirse (**for being a fool** por tonto)
VI blasfemar, echar pestes, soltar palabrotas • **to ~ and swear** echar sapos y culebras
cursed ['kɜːsɪd] ADJ maldito
cursive ['kɜːsɪv] ADJ cursivo
cursor ['kɜːsəʳ] N (*Comput*) cursor *m*
CPD ▸ **cursor key** tecla *f* del cursor
cursorily ['kɜːsərɪlɪ] ADV [*glance*] brevemente, de forma somera; [*read*] por encima, de forma somera
cursoriness ['kɜːsərɪnɪs] N superficialidad *f*, carácter *m* somero
cursory ['kɜːsərɪ] ADJ [*examination, inspection*] somero, superficial; [*nod*] brusco • **at a ~ glance** a primera vista • **to give sth a ~ glance** mirar algo brevemente *or* de forma somera
curt [kɜːt] ADJ [*person, tone*] seco, corto; [*nod*] brusco
curtail [kɜː'teɪl] VT (= *restrict*) restringir; (= *cut short*) acortar, abreviar; (= *reduce*) [+ *expenditure*] reducir
curtailment [kɜː'teɪlmənt] N (= *restriction*) restricción *f*; (= *shortening*) acortamiento *m*; [*of expenditure*] reducción *f*
curtain ['kɜːtn] N **1** (*gen*) (*Mil*) cortina *f*; (= *lace, small etc*) visillo *m*; (*Theat*) telón *m* • **to draw the ~s** (*together*) correr las cortinas; (*apart*) abrir las cortinas • **a ~ of fire** (*Mil*) una cortina de fuego • **when the final ~ came down** cuando el telón bajó por última vez • **it'll be ~s for you!*** será el acabóse para ti

• IDIOMS: • **to raise the ~ on sth** dar el pistoletazo de salida a algo • **to bring the ~ down on sth** poner punto final a algo
2 (*fig*) [*of secrecy*] halo *m*; [*of mist*] manto *m*
VT proveer de cortinas
CPD ▸ **curtain call** (*Theat*) llamada *f* a escena ▸ **curtain hook** colgadero *m* de cortina ▸ **curtain pole** = **curtain rod** ▸ **curtain rail** riel *m* (de las cortinas) ▸ **curtain ring** anilla *f* (de las cortinas) ▸ **curtain rod** barra *f* (de las cortinas) ▸ **curtain wall** [*of house, building*] muro *mpl* de cerramiento; [*of castle*] (= *low wall outside*) contramuralla *f*, falsabraga *f*; (*between bastions or towers*) lienzo *m*, muralla *f*
▸ **curtain off** VT + ADV [+ *separate room*] separar con cortina; [+ *bed, area*] encerrar con cortina

curtained ['kɜ:tənd] ADJ [*door etc*] con cortina(s)

curtain-raiser ['kɜ:tn,reɪzəʳ] N pieza *f* preliminar

curtly ['kɜ:tlɪ] ADV [*say, reply*] bruscamente, secamente; [*nod*] bruscamente

curtness ['kɜ:tnɪs] N brusquedad *f*

curtsey, curtsy ['kɜ:tsɪ] N reverencia *f* • **to drop** *or* **make a curts(e)y** hacer una reverencia
VI hacer una reverencia (**to** a)

curvaceous* [kɜ:'veɪʃəs] ADJ [*woman*] de buen cuerpo, curvilíneo

curvature ['kɜ:vətʃəʳ] N **1** (*Math*) curvatura *f*
2 • **~ of the spine** (*Med*) escoliosis *f inv*, desviación *f* de columna

curve [kɜ:v] N (*gen*) curva *f*
VT [+ *spine, back*] encorvar, doblar
VI [*road, line etc*] torcerse, hacer curva; [*surface*] combarse • **the walls ~ inward/outward** las paredes están combadas hacia dentro/fuera • **the road ~s round the mountain** la carretera va haciendo curvas *or* dando vueltas alrededor de la montaña • **the boomerang ~d through the air** el bumerán describió *or* hizo una curva en el aire • **a wide, curving staircase** una amplia escalera en curva
CPD ▸ **curve ball** (*esp US*) • IDIOM: • **to throw sb a ~ ball** poner a algn en un aprieto

curved [kɜ:vd] ADJ curvo, encorvado

curvilinear [,kɜ:vɪ'lɪnɪəʳ] ADJ curvilíneo

curvy ['kɜ:vɪ] ADJ [*line*] curvo; [*road etc*] serpentino, con muchas curvas; [*figure, woman*] curvilíneo

cushion ['kʊʃən] N (*gen*) cojín *m*; [*of chair, for knees etc*] almohadilla *f*; [*of air, moss*] colchón *m*; (= *edge of billiard table*) banda *f*
VT [+ *blow, fall*] amortiguar • **to ~ sb against sth** proteger a algn de algo
CPD ▸ **cushion cover** funda *f* de cojín

cushioning ['kʊʃənɪŋ] N (= *padding*) almohadillado *m*

cushy* ['kʊʃɪ] ADJ (COMPAR: **cushier**, SUPERL: **cushiest**) • **a ~ job** un chollo*, un hueso (*Mex**) • **to have a ~ life** *or* **time** tener la vida arreglada

cusp [kʌsp] N (*Bot, Astron*) cúspide *f*; [*of tooth*] corona *f*; [*of moon*] cuerno *m*

cuspidor ['kʌspɪdɔ:ʳ] N (*US*) escupidera *f*, salivadera *f* (*S. Cone*)

cuss* [kʌs] N (*US*) tipo* *m*, tío* *m*
VT, VI = **curse**

cussed* ['kʌsɪd] ADJ **1** terco, cabezón
2 = **cursed**

cussedness* ['kʌsɪdnɪs] N terquedad *f* • **out of sheer ~*** de puro terco

cussword* ['kʌswɜ:d] N (*US*) palabrota *f*

custard ['kʌstəd] N ≈ natillas *fpl* (*utilizada como acompañante en algunos postres*); (*also* **egg custard**) flan *m*
CPD ▸ **custard apple** (*Bot*) chirimoya *f* ▸ **custard cream** (= *biscuit*) galleta *f* de crema ▸ **custard pie** pastel *m* de natillas; (= *missile*) torta *f* de crema ▸ **custard powder** polvos *mpl* para (hacer) natillas ▸ **custard tart** pastel *m* de crema

custodial [kʌs'təʊdɪəl] ADJ **1** • **~ sentence** condena *f* de prisión
2 • **~ staff** (*in museum etc*) personal *m* de vigilancia

custodian [kʌs'təʊdɪən] N (*gen*) custodio/a *m/f*, guardián/ana *m/f*; [*of museum etc*] conservador(a) *m/f*

custody ['kʌstədɪ] N (*Jur*) [*of children*] custodia *f*; (= *police custody*) detención *f* • **the mother has ~ of the children** la madre tiene la custodia de los hijos • **to be in ~** estar detenido • **to take sb into ~** detener a algn • **in safe ~** bajo custodia, en buenas manos, bajo segura custodia • **in the ~ of** al cargo *or* cuidado de, bajo la custodia de

custom ['kʌstəm] N **1** (= *habit, usual behaviour*) costumbre *f* • **social ~s** costumbres *fpl* sociales • **it is her ~ to go for a walk each evening** tiene la costumbre de *or* tiene por costumbre dar un paseo cada tarde, acostumbra *or* suele dar un paseo cada tarde
2 (*Comm*) clientela *f*; (= *total sales*) caja *f*, ventas *fpl* • **to attract ~** atraer clientela • **to get sb's ~** ganar la clientela de algn • **we've not had much ~ today** hoy hemos tenido pocos clientes • **the shop has lost a lot of ~** la tienda ha perdido muchos clientes; ▷ **customs**
CPD (*esp US*) ▸ **custom-built, custom-made**

customarily ['kʌstəmərɪlɪ] ADV por regla general, normalmente

customary ['kʌstəmərɪ] ADJ [*place, time*] acostumbrado, de costumbre, habitual; [*wit, good humour etc*] acostumbrado, habitual; [*practice*] normal, habitual • **it's ~ to** (+ *infin*) es la costumbre (+ *infin*)

custom-built ['kʌstəm,bɪlt] ADJ hecho de encargo

customer ['kʌstəməʳ] N **1** cliente *mf*
2 (*Brit**) tipo/a* *m/f*, tío/a* *m/f* • **he's an awkward ~** es un tipo *or* un tío difícil* • **ugly ~** antipático/a
CPD ▸ **customer base** clientela *f* habitual ▸ **customer profile** perfil *m* del cliente ▸ **customer relations** (= *relationship with customers*) relaciones *fpl* con la clientela; (*used as sing noun*) (*also* **customer relations department**) departamento *m* de atención al cliente ▸ **customer satisfaction** satisfacción *f* del cliente ▸ **customer service** servicio *m* de atención al cliente ▸ **customer service department** departamento *m* de atención al cliente ▸ **customer services** (= *counter*) mostrador *m* de información y atención al cliente

customhouse ['kʌstəmhaʊs] N (*US*) aduana *f*

customizable ['kʌstə,maɪzəbl] ADJ personalizable

customize ['kʌstəmaɪz] VT [+ *car*] adaptar al gusto del cliente, adaptar por encargo del cliente; [+ *product*] personalizar • **~d software** software *m* a medida del usuario

customized ['kʌstəmaɪzd] ADJ [*product, clothes*] hecho a medida; [*car*] tuneado

custom-made ['kʌstəm'meɪd] ADJ [*furniture, clothing*] a medida, hecho a medida; [*car*] hecho de encargo

customs ['kʌstəmz] NPL aduana *fsing*; (*also* **customs duty**) derechos *mpl* de aduana • **to go through (the) ~** pasar por la aduana • **Customs and Excise** (*Brit*) Aduanas *fpl* y Arbitrios
CPD ▸ **customs clearance** despacho *m* aduanero ▸ **customs declaration** declaración *f* aduanera ▸ **customs house** aduana *f* ▸ **customs inspection** inspección *f* de aduanas ▸ **customs inspector** inspector(a) *m/f* de aduanas, aduanero/a *m/f* ▸ **customs invoice** factura *f* de aduana ▸ **customs officer** oficial *mf* de aduanas, vista *mf* (de aduanas), aduanero/a *m/f* ▸ **customs post** puesto *m* aduanero ▸ **Customs Service** (*US*) aduana *f*, servicio *m* aduanero

cut [kʌt] (VB: PT, PP: **cut**) N **1** (*in skin*) corte *m*, cortadura *f*; (= *wound*) herida *f*; (*Med*) (= *incision*) corte *m*, incisión *f*; (= *slash*) tajo *m*; (*with knife*) cuchillada *f*; (*with whip*) latigazo *m*; (*Cards*) corte *m* • **he's got a cut on his forehead** tiene un corte en la frente • **he had a cut on his chin from shaving** se había hecho un corte *or* se había cortado en la barbilla al afeitarse • **he was treated for minor cuts and bruises** recibió asistencia médica por heridas y hematomas • **there's a cut in his jacket** lleva una raja en la chaqueta • IDIOMS: • **to be a cut above sb**: • **he's a cut above the others** está por encima de los demás • **the cut and thrust of politics** la esgrima política • **the unkindest cut of all** el golpe más duro
2 (= *reduction*) (*in wages, prices, production*) rebaja *f*, reducción *f*; (*in expenditure, budget*) corte *m*, recorte *m*; (*in tax, interest rates*) bajada *f*, rebaja *f*; (*in staff, workforce*) reducción *f*, recorte *f*; (= *deletion*) corte *m*; (= *deleted part*) trozo *m* suprimido; (*Elec*) apagón *m*, corte *m* • **public spending cuts** cortes *mpl* presupuestarios • **wage cuts** rebajas *fpl* de sueldo • **to take a cut in salary** aceptar una reducción de sueldo • **they made some cuts in the text** hicieron algunos cortes en el texto, suprimieron algunas cosas del texto
3 [*of clothes etc*] corte *m*; [*of hair*] corte *m*, peinado *m*
4 [*of meat*] (= *part of animal*) corte *m* (de carne); (= *piece*) trozo *m*; (= *slice*) tajada *f*
5* (= *share*) parte *f*, tajada *f* • **the salesman gets a cut of 5%** el vendedor recibe su parte de 5%
6 (= *woodcut*) grabado *m*; (*US*) foto *f*, diagrama *m*, dibujo *m*
7 • **cut and paste** (*Comput*) cortar y pegar
VT **1** [+ *meat, bread, cards*] cortar • **to cut one's finger** cortarse el dedo • **to cut sb free** (*from wreckage*) liberar a algn; (*when tied up*) desatar *or* soltar a algn • **to cut sth in half** cortar algo por la mitad • **to cut sth open** [+ *fruit, vegetable, body, package*] abrir algo • **I cut my hand open on a tin** me corté la mano en una lata • **he cut his head open** se abrió la cabeza • **to cut sth (in)to pieces** cortar algo en pedazos • **to cut an army to pieces** aniquilar un ejército • **to cut sth to size** cortar algo a la medida • **to cut sb's throat** degollar a algn • **he is cutting his own throat** (*fig*) labra su propia ruina • **to cut sth in two** cortar *or* partir algo en dos • IDIOM: • **you could cut the atmosphere with a knife** se mascaba *or* respiraba la tensión en el ambiente; ▷ **fine¹, ice, loss, tooth**
2 (= *shape*) [+ *stone, glass, jewel*] tallar; [+ *key, hole*] hacer; [+ *channel*] abrir, excavar; [+ *engraving, record*] grabar • **to cut one's way through** abrirse camino por; ▷ **coat**
3 (= *clip, trim*) [+ *hedge, grass*] cortar; [+ *corn, hay*] segar • **to get one's hair cut** cortarse el pelo
4 (= *reduce*) [+ *wages, prices, production*] reducir, rebajar (**by 5%** en un 5 por cien); [+ *expenditure*] reducir, recortar; [+ *taxes, interest rates*] bajar, rebajar; [+ *staff, workforce*] reducir, recortar; [+ *speech, text*] acortar,

hacer cortes en; [+ *film*] cortar, hacer cortes en; (= *delete*) [+ *passage*] suprimir, cortar; (= *interrupt*) interrumpir, cortar • **she cut two seconds off the record** mejoró *or* rebajó la plusmarca en dos segundos • **we cut the journey time by half** reducimos el tiempo de viaje a la mitad • **to cut sth/sb short** interrumpir algo/a algn; ▹ **corner**
5 (*fig*) (= *hurt*) herir • IDIOM: • **to cut sb to the quick**: • **it cut me to the quick** me tocó en lo vivo
6 (= *intersect with*) [*road*] cruzar, atravesar; (*Math*) [*line*] cortar
7 (*esp US**) • **to cut classes** hacer novillos*, ausentarse de clase • **to cut sb dead** negar el saludo *or* (*LAm*) cortar a algn
8 (= *turn off*) [+ *engine*] parar; (= *stop*) [+ *electricity supply*] cortar, interrumpir • **cut all this soft-soaping and tell me what you want*** deja ya de darme coba y dime qué quieres*
9 (= *adulterate*) [+ *cocaine etc*] cortar
10 (= *succeed*) • **he couldn't cut it as a singer** como cantante no daba la talla
VI **1** [*person, knife*] cortar; [*material*] cortarse • **paper cuts easily** el papel se corta fácilmente • **she cut into the melon** cortó el melón • **will that cake cut into six?** ¿se puede dividir el pastel en seis? • IDIOMS: • **to cut loose (from sth)** deshacerse (de algo) • **it cuts both ways** tiene doble filo
2 (*Math etc*) [*lines*] cortarse
3 (= *hurry*) • **I must cut along now** tengo que marcharme ya • IDIOMS: • **to cut and run*** largarse*, escaparse • **to cut to the chase** (*esp US**) ir al grano, dejar de marear la perdiz*
4 (*Cine, TV*) (= *change scene*) cortar y pasar • **they cut from the palace to the castle scene** cortan y pasan del palacio a la escena del castillo • **cut!** ¡corten!
5 (*Cards*) cortar
ADJ [*flowers*] cortado; [*glass*] tallado • **cut price** a precio reducido, rebajado, de rebaja
CPD ▸ **cut and blow-dry** corte *m* y secado con secador

▸ **cut across** VT + PREP **1** atajar por • **to cut across a field** atajar por un campo • **to cut across country** atajar por el campo
2 (*fig*) • **this cuts across the usual categories** esto rebasa las categorías establecidas

▸ **cut along** VI + ADV irse de prisa

▸ **cut away** VT + ADV [+ *unwanted part*] cortar, eliminar

▸ **cut back** VT + ADV **1** (= *prune*) [+ *plant*] podar
2 (= *reduce*) [+ *production, expenditure, staff*] reducir, recortar • **to cut sth back by 50%** reducir algo en un 50 por ciento
VI + ADV **1** (= *make savings*) economizar • **to cut back on** = **cut down**
2 (*Cine*) (= *flash back*) volver (**to a**)

▸ **cut down** VT + ADV **1** [+ *tree*] cortar, talar; [+ *enemy*] matar; [+ *clothes*] acortar
2 (= *reduce*) [+ *consumption*] reducir; [+ *expenditure*] reducir, recortar; [+ *text*] acortar, abreviar • IDIOM: • **to cut sb down to size** bajar los humos a algn
VI + ADV • **you're drinking too much, you really should cut down** bebes demasiado, deberías moderarte • **to cut down on** [+ *fatty food*] reducir el consumo de; [+ *expenditure*] moderar, reducir; [+ *public services*] recortar, reducir • **I'm cutting down on coffee and cigarettes** estoy intentando tomar menos café y fumar menos

▸ **cut in** VI + ADV (*in conversation*) interrumpir; (*Aut*) meterse delante • **to cut in on a conversation** interrumpir una conversación
VT + ADV* • **to cut sb in (on sth)** incluir a algn (en algo)

▸ **cut into** VI + PREP • **to cut into one's holidays** interrumpir sus vacaciones • **we shall have to cut into our savings** tendremos que usar una parte de los ahorros

▸ **cut off** VT + ADV **1** (*with scissors, knife*) cortar; (= *amputate*) amputar, quitar • **they cut off his head** le cortaron la cabeza • IDIOM: • **to cut off one's nose to spite one's face*** tirar piedras contra su propio tejado
2 (= *disconnect*) [+ *telephone, gas*] cortar, desconectar • **we've been cut off** (*Telec*) nos han cortado la comunicación
3 (= *interrupt*) • **to cut sb off in the middle of a sentence** cortar *or* interrumpir a algn en mitad de una frase, no dejar terminar a algn • **to cut off sb's supplies** cortar *or* interrumpir el suministro a algn
4 (= *isolate*) aislar • **I feel very cut off, living out here in the country** me siento muy aislado, viviendo aquí en el campo • **cut off by floods** aislado por las inundaciones • **we were cut off by the snow** quedamos bloqueados por la nieve • **the village was cut off for several days by the snow** la aldea quedó aislada *or* incomunicada por la nieve durante varios días • **to cut o.s. off from sth/sb** aislarse de algo/algn • **to cut off the enemy's retreat** cortar la retirada al enemigo • IDIOM: • **to cut sb off without a penny** desheredar completamente a algn

▸ **cut out** VT + ADV **1** [+ *article, picture*] recortar; [+ *dress, skirt etc*] cortar; [+ *diseased part*] extirpar • IDIOMS: • **to be cut out for sth/to do sth** estar hecho para ser algo/hacer algo • **he's not cut out to be a poet** no tiene madera de poeta • **you'll have your work cut out for you** te va a costar trabajo • **he had his work cut out to finish it** tuvo que trabajar duro para terminarlo
2 (= *exclude*) [+ *unnecessary details*] eliminar, suprimir; [+ *light*] tapar; [+ *intermediary, middleman*] saltarse a, eliminar • **he cut his nephew out of his will** borró de su testamento la mención del sobrino • **you can cut that out for a start!*** ¡para empezar deja de hacer eso! • **cut out the singing!*** ¡basta ya de cantar! • **cut it out!*** ¡basta ya!
3 (= *give up*) [+ *fatty food*] dejar de comer • **to cut out alcohol/cigarettes** dejar de beber/fumar
4 (= *delete*) suprimir
VI + ADV [*car engine*] pararse; (*Elec*) cortarse, interrumpirse

▸ **cut through** VI + PREP **1** (*lit*) [+ *bone, cable*] atravesar, traspasar; [+ *jungle, undergrowth*] abrirse camino a través de
2 (= *take short cut via*) atajar por, cortar por • **to cut through the lane** atajar *or* cortar por el callejón
3 (= *circumvent*) saltarse, sortear • **we have to find a way to cut through all this red tape** hay que encontrar la manera de saltarse *or* sortear todo este papeleo

▸ **cut up** VT + ADV **1** [+ *food, paper, wood*] cortar en pedazos; [+ *meat*] picar; (= *wound*) herir, acuchillar
2* • **to be cut up about sth** (= *hurt*) estar muy afectado por algo; (= *annoyed*) estar muy molesto por algo • **he was very cut up by the death of his son** estaba muy afectado por la muerte de su hijo
VI + ADV • IDIOM: • **to cut up rough*** ponerse agresivo

cut-and-dried [ˌkʌtən'draɪd], **cut-and-dry** [ˌkʌtən'draɪ] ADJ [*answer*] concreto; [*situation, issue*] definido, claro • **this situation is not as cut-and-dried as it may seem** la situación no está tan definida *or* clara como podría parecer

cutaneous [kjuː'teɪnɪəs] ADJ cutáneo

cutback ['kʌtbæk] N **1** (*in expenditure, staff, production*) recorte *m*, reducción *f* • **to make ~s (in sth)** hacer *or* realizar recortes (en algo)
2 (*Cine*) (= *flashback*) flashback *m*

cut-down ['kʌtdaʊn] ADJ reducido

cute [kjuːt] ADJ **1** (= *sweet*) [*face, animal, baby*] lindo, precioso, mono*, rico*; [*person*] guapo • **isn't he ~!** (= *baby*) ¡qué lindo es!, ¡qué mono *or* rico es!*; (= *pet*) ¡qué lindo es!, ¡qué mono *or* rico es!*, ¡es una monada *or* monería!*; (= *man*) ¡es guapísimo!
2 (*esp US*) (= *clever*) listo, vivo (*LAm*); (= *affecting prettiness etc*) presumido

cutesy* ['kjuːtsɪ] ADJ (*pej*) [*person, painting, clothes*] cursi

cut-glass ['kʌt'glɑːs] ADJ de vidrio tallado

cuticle ['kjuːtɪkl] N cutícula *f*
CPD ▸ **cuticle remover** quitacutículas *m inv* ▸ **cuticle stick** palito *m* quitacutículas

cutie* ['kjuːtɪ] N (*US*) monada* *f*, ricura* *f*

cutie pie* ['kjuːtɪpaɪ] N (*US*) = **cutie**

cutlass ['kʌtləs] N alfanje *m*

cutler ['kʌtləʳ] N cuchillero *m*

cutlery ['kʌtlərɪ] N (*Brit*) cubiertos *mpl*, cubertería *f*; ▹ **canteen**
CPD ▸ **cutlery drawer** cajón *m* de la cubertería

cutlet ['kʌtlɪt] N chuleta *f* • **a veal ~** una chuleta de ternera

cutoff ['kʌtɒf] N **1** (*also* **cutoff point**) (= *limit*) límite *m*
2 (*Mech*) (*in pipe or duct*) cierre *m*, corte *m*; (*Elec*) valor *m* límite, corte *m*
3 (*US*) atajo *m*
4 cutoffs tejanos *mpl* cortados, vaqueros *mpl* cortados
ADJ [*jeans*] cortado
CPD ▸ **cutoff date** fecha *f* tope, fecha *f* límite ▸ **cutoff voltage** tensión *f* de corte ▸ **cutoff switch** conmutador *m* de corte, limitador *m* de potencia

cut-out ['kʌtaʊt] N **1** (= *paper, cardboard figure*) recorte *m*, figura *f* recortada; (*child's*) (*for cutting out*) recortable *m*, diseño *m* para recortar
2 (*Elec*) (= *switch*) cortacircuitos *m inv*, automático *m*; (*Mech*) válvula *f* de escape

cut-price ['kʌtpraɪs] ADJ [*goods*] a precio reducido, rebajado, de ocasión; [*shop*] de saldos

cut-rate [ˌkʌt'reɪt] ADJ = **cut-price**

cutter ['kʌtəʳ] N **1** (= *tool*) cortadora *f*; (*for paper, cardboard*) cutter *m* • **wire ~s** cizalla *fsing*, cortaalambres *m*
2 (= *person*) cortador(a) *m/f*
3 (= *boat*) cúter *m*; (*US*) (= *coastguard*) patrullero *m*, guardacostas *m*

cut-throat ['kʌtθrəʊt] N (= *murderer*) asesino/a *m/f*
ADJ (= *fierce*) [*competition*] feroz, encarnizado
CPD ▸ **cut-throat razor** navaja *f* (de afeitar)

cutting ['kʌtɪŋ] N **1** [*of plant*] esqueje *m*
2 (*from newspaper*) recorte *m*; (*Cine*) montaje *m*
3 (*for road, railway*) desmonte *m*, zanja *f*
ADJ (= *sharp*) [*edge, wind etc*] cortante; (*fig*) [*remark*] mordaz
CPD ▸ **cutting board** plancha *f* para cortar ▸ **cutting edge** filo *m*; (*fig*) vanguardia *f* ▸ **cutting room** (*Cine*) sala *f* de montaje

cutting-edge ['kʌtɪŋˌedʒ] ADJ [*research, design*] más vanguardista • **cutting-edge technology** la tecnología más vanguardista

cuttlefish ['kʌtlfɪʃ] N (PL: **cuttlefish** *or* **cuttlefishes**) jibia *f*, sepia *f*

cut-up* [ˌkʌt'ʌp] ADJ (*US*) gracioso

CV N ABBR (= **curriculum vitae**) C.V. *m*

CW (N ABBR) **1** = **chemical weapons**
2 = **chemical warfare**
CWO, **cwo** (ABBR) **1** (*Comm*) = **cash with order**
2 = **chief warrant officer**
CWS (N ABBR) = **Cooperative Wholesale Society**
cwt (ABBR) = **hundredweight(s)**
CYA (ABBR) (= **see you**) (*in text messaging*) ≈ ta luego*
cyanide ['saɪənaɪd] (N) cianuro *m* • **~ of potassium** cianuro *m* potásico
cyanose ['saɪənəʊz] (N) cianosis *f*
cyber- ['saɪbər] (PREFIX) ciber-
cyberattack ['saɪbərə,tæk] (N) ciberataque *m*
cyberbully ['saɪbə,bʊlɪ] (N) ciberacosador(a) *m/f*
cyberbullying ['saɪbə,bʊlɪɪŋ] (N) ciberacoso *m*
cybercafé ['saɪbə,kæfeɪ] (N) cibercafé *m*
cybercrime ['saɪbəkraɪm] (N) ciberdelitos *mpl*
cyberespionage [,saɪbəʳespɪə,nɑːʒ] (N) ciberespionaje *m*
cybermall ['saɪbə,mɔːl] (N) centro *m* comercial virtual
cybernetic [,saɪbə'netɪk] (ADJ) cibernético
cybernetics [,saɪbə'netɪks] (NSING) cibernética *f*
cyberpet ['saɪbə,pet] (N) cibermascota *f*
cyberpunk ['saɪbəpʌŋk] (N) (*Literat*) ciberpunk *m*
cybersecurity [,saɪbəsɪ'kjʊərɪtɪ] (N) ciberseguridad *f*
cybersex ['saɪbəseks] (N) cibersexo *m*
cyberspace ['saɪbəspeɪs] (N) ciberespacios *m pl*
cyberspying ['saɪbə,spaɪɪŋ] (N) ciberespionaje *m*
cybersquatter ['saɪbəskwɒtəʳ] (N) ciberokupa *mf*
cybersquatting ['saɪbəskwɒtɪŋ] (N) piratería *f* de dominios
cyberterrorism ['saɪbə,terərɪsm] (N) ciberterrorismo *m*
cyberterrorist ['saɪbə,terərɪst] (ADJ) ciberterrorista
(N) ciberterrorista *mf*
cyberwarfare [,saɪbə'wɔːfeəʳ] (N) ciberguerra *f*
cyborg ['saɪbɔːg] (N) ciborg *m*, organismo *m* cibernético

cyclamate ['sɪkləmeɪt] (N) ciclamato *m*
cyclamen ['sɪkləmən] (N) ciclamen *m*
cycle ['saɪkl] (N) **1** (= *bicycle*) bicicleta *f* • **racing ~** bicicleta *f* de carreras
2 [*of seasons, poems etc*] ciclo *m* • **life ~** ciclo *m* vital • **menstrual ~** ciclo *m* menstrual • **a 10-second ~** un ciclo de 10 segundos
(VI) (= *travel*) ir en bicicleta • **we ~d to the coast** fuimos en bicicleta a la costa • **I ~ to school** voy al colegio en bicicleta • **can you ~?** ¿sabes montar en bicicleta?
(CPD) ▸ **cycle clip** pinza *f* para ir en bicicleta ▸ **cycle helmet** casco *m* de bicicleta ▸ **cycle hire** (= *business*) alquiler *m* de bicicletas; [*of one bike*] alquiler *m* de una bicicleta ▸ **cycle lane** (*Brit*) carril *m* de bicicleta, carril *m* bici ▸ **cycle path** carril *m* de bicicleta ▸ **cycle race** carrera *f* ciclista ▸ **cycle rack** soporte *m* para bicicletas; (*on car roof*) baca *f* para transportar bicicletas ▸ **cycle ride** paseo *m* en bicicleta • **to go for a ~ ride** ir a dar un paseo en bicicleta ▸ **cycle shed** cobertizo *m* para bicicletas ▸ **cycle track** (*in countryside*) ruta *f* para ciclistas, senda *f* para ciclistas; (*Sport*) pista *f* de ciclismo, velódromo *m*
cycler ['saɪkləʳ] (N) (*US*) ciclista *mf*
cycleway ['saɪklweɪ] (N) ruta *f* para ciclistas
cyclic ['saɪklɪk], **cyclical** ['saɪklɪkəl] (ADJ) cíclico
(CPD) ▸ **cyclical stocks** valores *mpl* cíclicos
cycling ['saɪklɪŋ] (N) ciclismo *m* • **to go ~** ir *or* montar en bicicleta, hacer ciclismo • **the roads round here are ideal for ~** las carreteras de por aquí son ideales para ir *or* montar en bicicleta
(CPD) ▸ **cycling holiday** vacaciones *fpl* en bicicleta ▸ **cycling shorts** culotes *mpl*, culotte(s) *m(pl)*
cyclist ['saɪklɪst] (N) ciclista *mf*
cyclone ['saɪkləʊn] (N) ciclón *m*
cyclonic [saɪ'klɒnɪk] (ADJ) ciclónico
Cyclops ['saɪklɒps] (N) (PL: **Cyclopses** *or* **Cyclopes** [saɪ'kləʊpiːz]) cíclope *m*
cyclostyle ['saɪkləʊstaɪl] (N) ciclostil(o) *m*
(VT) reproducir en ciclostil(o)
cyclostyled ['saɪkləʊstaɪld] (ADJ) en ciclostil(o)
cyclotron ['saɪklətrɒn] (N) ciclotrón *m*
cygnet ['sɪgnɪt] (N) pollo *m* de cisne
cylinder ['sɪlɪndəʳ] (N) **1** (= *shape*) cilindro *m*
2 (*Tech*) cilindro *m* • **a 6-cylinder engine** un motor de 6 cilindros • IDIOM: • **to fire on all ~s** emplearse a fondo, dar el do de pecho
(CPD) ▸ **cylinder block** bloque *m* de cilindros ▸ **cylinder capacity** cilindrada *f* ▸ **cylinder head** culata *f* de cilindro ▸ **cylinder head gasket** junta *f* de culata ▸ **cylinder vacuum cleaner** aspirador *m* de trineo
cylindrical [sɪ'lɪndrɪkəl] (ADJ) cilíndrico
cymbal ['sɪmbəl] (N) (*freq pl*) címbalo *m*, platillo *m*
cynic ['sɪnɪk] (N) cínico/a *m/f*
cynical ['sɪnɪkəl] (ADJ) cínico
cynically ['sɪnɪklɪ] (ADV) cínicamente, con cinismo
cynicism ['sɪnɪsɪzəm] (N) cinismo *m*
cynosure ['saɪnəʃʊəʳ] (N) • **~ of every eye** blanco *m* de todas las miradas
CYO (N ABBR) (*US*) = **Catholic Youth Organization**
cypher ['saɪfəʳ] = **cipher**
cypress ['saɪprɪs] (N) ciprés *m*
Cypriot ['sɪprɪət] (ADJ) chipriota
(N) chipriota *mf*
Cyprus ['saɪprəs] (N) Chipre *f*
Cyrillic [sɪ'rɪlɪk] (ADJ) cirílico
(N) cirílico *m*
(CPD) ▸ **Cyrillic alphabet** alfabeto *m* cirílico
cyst [sɪst] (N) quiste *m*
cystic ['sɪstɪk] (ADJ) cístico
(CPD) ▸ **cystic fibrosis** fibrosis *f* cística
cystitis [sɪs'taɪtɪs] (N) cistitis *f*
cytological [,saɪtə'lɒdʒɪkəl] (ADJ) citológico
cytology [saɪ'tɒlədʒɪ] (N) citología *f*
cytoplasm ['saɪtəʊplæzm] (N) citoplasma *m*
cytotoxic [,saɪtəʊ'tɒksɪk] (ADJ) citotóxico
CZ (ABBR) (*US*) (*Geog*) = **Canal Zone**
czar [zɑːʳ] (N) zar *m*
czarina [zɑː'riːnə] (N) zarina *f*
czarism ['zɑːrɪzəm] (N) zarismo *m*
czarist ['zɑːrɪst] (ADJ), (N) zarista *mf*
Czech [tʃek] (ADJ) checo • **the ~ Republic** la República Checa
(N) **1** (= *person*) checo/a *m/f*
2 (*Ling*) checo *m*
Czechoslovak ['tʃekəʊ'sləʊvæk] (*Hist*) (ADJ) checoslovaco
(N) checoslovaco/a *m/f*
Czechoslovakia ['tʃekəʊslə'vækɪə] (N) (*Hist*) Checoslovaquia *f*
Czechoslovakian ['tʃekəʊslə'vækɪən] (*Hist*) (ADJ) checoslovaco
(N) checoslovaco/a *m/f*

C

Dd

d

D[1], **d**[1] [diː] N **1** (= *letter*) D, d *f* • **D for David** D de Dolores
2 (*Mus*) • **D** re *m* • **D major/minor** re mayor/menor • **D sharp/flat** re sostenido/bemol
D[2] N (*Scol*) (= *mark around 50%*) aprobado *m*, suficiente *m*
ABBR (*US*) (*Pol*) = **Democrat(ic)**
d[2] ABBR **1** (= **date**) fha.
2 (= **daughter**) hija *f*
3 (= **died**) m.
4 (*Rail etc*) = **depart(s)**
5 (*Brit*†) = **penny**
DA N ABBR (*US*) (*Jur*) = **District Attorney**
D/A ABBR = **deposit account**
DAB ['dæb] N ABBR (*Rad*) (= **digital audio broadcasting**) radiodifusión *f* de audio digital
dab[1] [dæb] N **1** (= *light stroke*) toque *m*; (= *blow*) golpecito *m*
2 (= *small amount*) pizca *f*; [*of paint*] ligero brochazo *m*; [*of liquid*] gota *f*
3 dabs (*esp Brit*‡) huellas *fpl* digitales
VT (= *touch lightly*) tocar ligeramente; (*with cream, butter*) untar ligeramente; (*with paint, water*) dar unos toques a • **to dab a stain off** quitar una mancha humedeciéndola • **to dab on** untar ligeramente
▸ **dab at** VI + PREP • **to dab at one's mouth/eyes** limpiarse la boca/los ojos (*dándose toquecitos*)
dab[2] [dæb] N (= *fish*) lenguado *m*
dab[3]* [dæb] ADJ • **IDIOM:** • **to be a dab hand at (doing) sth** (*Brit*) ser un hacha para (hacer) algo
ADV • **dab in the middle** (*US*) en el mismo centro
dabble ['dæbl] VT salpicar, mojar • **to ~ one's hands/feet in water** chapotear con las manos/los pies en el agua
VI (*fig*) • **to ~ in sth** hacer algo/interesarse por algo superficialmente • **to ~ in politics** ser politiquero, politiquear • **to ~ in shares** jugar a la bolsa • **I only ~ in it** para mí es un pasatiempo nada más
dabbler ['dæbləʳ] N (*pej*) aficionado/a *m/f* (*in* a), diletante *mf* • **he's just a ~** es un simple aficionado, para él es un pasatiempo nada más
dabchick ['dæbtʃɪk] N somorgujo *m* menor
Dacca ['dækə] N Dacca *f*
dace [deɪs] N (PL: **dace** *or* **daces**) albur *m*
dacha ['dætʃə] N dacha *f*
dachshund ['dækshʊnd] N perro *m* salchicha
Dacron® ['dækrɒn] N (*US*) Dacrón® *m*
dactyl ['dæktɪl] N dáctilo *m*
dactylic [dæk'tɪlɪk] ADJ dactílico
dad* [dæd] N papá *m*
Dada ['dɑːdɑː] N dada *m*, dadaísmo *m*
ADJ dadaísta
dadaism ['dɑːdɑːɪzəm] N dadaísmo *m*
dadaist ['dɑːdɑːɪst] ADJ dadaísta
N dadaísta *mf*
daddy* ['dædɪ] N = **dad**
daddy-long-legs ['dædɪ'lɒŋlegz] N (*Brit*) típula *f*
dado ['deɪdəʊ] N (PL: **dadoes** *or* **dados**) [*of wall*] friso *m*; (*Archit*) [*of pedestal*] dado *m*
daemon ['diːmən] N demonio *m*
daff* [dæf] N ABBR (*Brit*) = **daffodil**
daffodil ['dæfədɪl] N narciso *m*
daffy* ['dæfɪ] ADJ chiflado*
daft* [dɑːft] ADJ (COMPAR: **dafter**, SUPERL: **daftest**) **1** (= *silly*) [*person*] tonto, bobo, tarado (*S. Cone**); [*idea, action, question*] tonto • **don't be ~** no seas tonto *or* bobo • **he's not as ~ as he looks** no es tan tonto como parece • **if you're ~ enough to pay £600** si eres tan bobo como para pagar 600 libras • **the ~ things some people do!** ¡hay que ver las estupideces que hace la gente! • **IDIOMS:** • **to be ~ in the head*** estar mal de la cabeza*, estar tocado del ala* • **to be as ~ as a brush*** ser más tonto que Abundio*
2 (= *crazy*) • **to be ~ about sb** estar loco por algn • **he's ~ about football** le apasiona el fútbol, el fútbol le vuelve loco
daftness* ['dɑːftnɪs] N estupidez *f*
dagger ['dægəʳ] N **1** (= *knife*) daga *f*, puñal *m* • **IDIOMS:** • **to be at ~s drawn (with sb)** estar a matar (con algn) • **to look ~s at sb** fulminar a algn con la mirada
2 (*Typ*) cruz *f*, obelisco *m*
dago** ['deɪgəʊ] N (PL: **dagos** *or* **dagoes**) *término ofensivo aplicado a españoles, portugueses e italianos*
daguerreotype [də'gerəʊ,taɪp] N daguerrotipo *m*
dahlia ['deɪlɪə] N dalia *f*
Dáil [dɔɪl] N (*also* **Dáil Éireann**) *Cámara baja del Parlamento de la República de Irlanda*
daily ['deɪlɪ] ADJ **1** (= *occurring each day*) diario • **there are ~ flights from Manchester to Munich** hay vuelos diarios de Manchester a Munich, hay vuelos de Manchester a Munich diariamente • **on a ~ basis** (= *every day*) diariamente • **they are paid on a ~ basis** (= *by the day*) les pagan por días *or* por día trabajado; (= *every day*) les pagan cada día • **our ~ bread** el pan nuestro de cada día • **~ newspaper** diario *m*, periódico *m* • **incidents of this kind are a ~ occurrence** este tipo de incidentes ocurre diariamente *or* a diario
2 (= *normal, everyday*) cotidiano • **the ~ grind** la rutina diaria • **the ~ life of a primary school teacher** la vida cotidiana de un profesor de primaria • **we went about our ~ lives as if nothing had happened** continuamos con nuestra vida normal como si nada hubiera pasado • **the ~ round** la rutina diaria
ADV diariamente, a diario • **incidents of this kind happen ~** este tipo de incidentes ocurre diariamente *or* a diario • **the ticket office is open ~** la taquilla abre diariamente *or* todos los días • **twice ~** dos veces al día
N **1** (= *newspaper*) diario *m*, periódico *m*
2 (*esp Brit**) • **~ (help** *or* **woman)** asistenta *f*, chacha* *f*
daintily ['deɪntɪlɪ] ADV [*walk*] elegantemente, con pasos delicados; [*eat*] (= *delicately*) con delicadeza, delicadamente; (= *affectedly*) remilgadamente, melindrosamente • **the fish was ~ served** se sirvió el pescado exquisitamente presentado • **a plate of ~ cut sandwiches** un plato de sandwiches delicadamente cortados
daintiness ['deɪntɪnɪs] N [*of person, hands, vase*] finura *f*, delicadeza *f*; [*of steps*] elegancia *f*, delicadeza *f*; [*of figure*] gracia *f*, delicadeza *f*
dainty ['deɪntɪ] ADJ (COMPAR: **daintier**, SUPERL: **daintiest**) **1** (= *delicate*) [*person, hands, vase*] fino, delicado; [*steps*] elegante, delicado; [*figure*] delicado; [*food, clothes*] exquisito, refinado • **a ~ morsel** un bocado exquisito
2 (= *fastidious*) delicado, melindroso
N bocado *m* exquisito • **dainties** exquisiteces *fpl*
daiquiri ['daɪkɪrɪ] N daiquiri *m*, daiquirí *m*
dairy ['deərɪ] N (= *shop*) lechería *f*; (*on farm*) vaquería *f*
CPD [*products*] lácteo ▸ **dairy butter** mantequilla *f* casera ▸ **dairy cattle, dairy cows** vacas *fpl* lecheras ▸ **dairy farm** granja *f* de productos lácteos ▸ **dairy farmer** ganadero/a *m/f* de vacuno de leche ▸ **dairy farming** industria *f* láctera, industria *f* lactaria ▸ **dairy herd** ganado *m* lechero ▸ **dairy ice cream** helado *m* de nata ▸ **dairy produce** productos *mpl* lácteos
dairying ['deərɪɪŋ] N producción *f* de lácteos
dairymaid ['deərɪmeɪd] N lechera *f*
dairyman ['deərɪmən] N (PL: **dairymen**) lechero *m*
dais ['deɪɪs] N estrado *m*
daisy ['deɪzɪ] N margarita *f* • **IDIOM:** • **to be pushing up the daisies*** criar malvas*
CPD ▸ **daisy chain** (*lit*) guirnalda *f* de margaritas; (*fig*) serie *f*
daisywheel ['deɪzɪ,wiːl] N margarita *f*
CPD ▸ **daisywheel printer** impresora *f* de margarita
Dakar ['dækəʳ] N Dakar *m*
dal [dɑːl] = **dhal**
Dalai Lama ['dælaɪ'lɑːmə] N Dalai Lama *m*
dale [deɪl] N valle *m* • **the (Yorkshire) Dales** los valles de Yorkshire
dalliance ['dælɪəns] N **1** (*liter*) (*amorous*) coqueteo *m*, flirteo *m*
2 (*esp hum*) (*with hobby, politics etc*) escarceos *mpl*
dally ['dælɪ] VI **1** (= *dawdle*) tardar • **to ~ over sth** perder el tiempo con algo; ▹ **dilly-dally**
2 (= *amuse o.s.*) divertirse • **to ~ with** [+ *lover*] coquetear con, tener escarceos amorosos con; [+ *idea*] entretenerse con
Dalmatia [dæl'meɪʃə] N Dalmacia *f*
Dalmatian [dæl'meɪʃən] N (= *person*)

dálmata *mf*
ADJ dálmata
dalmatian [dælˈmeɪʃən] N (= *dog*) perro *m* dálmata
daltonism [ˈdɔːltənɪzəm] N daltonismo *m*
dam¹ [dæm] N (= *wall*) dique *m*, presa *f*; (= *reservoir*) presa *f*, embalse *m*
VT (*also* **dam up**) poner un dique a, represar; (*fig*) reprimir, contener
▸ **dam up** VT + ADV = **dam**
dam²‡ [dæm] ADJ = **damn, damned**
dam³ [dæm] N (*Zool*) madre *f*
damage [ˈdæmɪdʒ] N **1** (*gen*) daño *m*; (*visible, eg on car*) desperfectos *mpl*; (*to building, area*) daños (*pl*) • **to do** *or* **cause ~ to** [+ *building*] causar daños a; [+ *machine*] causar desperfectos en • **the bomb did a lot of ~** la bomba causó muchos daños • **not much ~ was caused to the car** el coche no sufrió grandes desperfectos
2 (*fig*) (*to chances, reputation etc*) perjuicio *m*, daño *m* • **to do** *or* **cause ~ to sth/sb** causar perjuicio a algo/algn, perjudicar algo/a algn • **the ~ is done** el daño ya está hecho • IDIOM: • **what's the ~?*** (= *cost*) ¿cuánto va a ser?, ¿qué se debe?
3 damages (*Jur*) daños *mpl* y perjuicios; ▹ **recover**
VT (= *harm*) dañar; [+ *machine*] averiar, causar desperfectos en; [+ *health, chances, reputation*] perjudicar • **to be ~d in a collision** sufrir daños en un choque
CPD ▸ **damage control** = **damage limitation** ▸ **damage control operation** (*US*) campaña *f* para minimizar los daños
▸ **damage limitation** • **an exercise in ~ limitation** una campaña para minimizar los daños • **to be engaged in ~ limitation** esforzarse en minimizar los daños
▸ **damage limitation exercise** campaña *f* para minimizar los daños
damaged [ˈdæmɪdʒd] ADJ dañado
damaging [ˈdæmɪdʒɪŋ] ADJ (*gen*) dañino; (*fig*) perjudicial (**to** para)
damascene [ˈdæməsiːn] ADJ damasquinado, damasquino
VT damasquinar
Damascus [dəˈmɑːskəs] N Damasco *m*
damask [ˈdæməsk] ADJ [*cloth*] adamascado; [*steel*] damasquinado
N (= *cloth*) damasco *m*; (= *steel*) acero *m* damasquinado
VT [+ *cloth*] adamascar; [+ *steel*] damasquinar
CPD ▸ **damask rose** rosa *f* de Damasco
dame [deɪm] N **1** • **Dame** (*Brit*) (= *title*) *título aristocrático para mujeres equivalente a "sir"*
2 (*esp Brit*†) dama *f*, señora *f*; (*Brit*) (*Theat*) *personaje de mujer anciana en las pantomimas británicas interpretado por un actor*; ▹ PANTOMIME
3 (*US*†*) (= *woman*) tía* *f*, gachí *f* (*Sp*‡)
damfool‡ [ˈdæmˈfuːl] ADJ = **damn-fool**
dammit‡ [ˈdæmɪt] EXCL ¡maldita sea!* • IDIOM: • **as near as ~** (*Brit*) casi, por un pelo
damn [dæm] VT **1** (*Rel*) (= *condemn*) condenar • **the effort was ~ed from the start** desde el principio el intento estaba condenado a fracasar • **the critics ~ed the book** los críticos pusieron *or* tiraron el libro por los suelos • **I'll see him ~ed first** antes lo veré colgado • IDIOM: • **to ~ sth/sb with faint praise** despachar algo/a algn con tímidos elogios
2 (= *swear at*) maldecir
3‡ (*in exclamations*) • **~ it!** ¡maldita sea!* • **~ him/you!** ¡maldito sea/seas!* • **~ this car!** ¡al diablo con este coche! • **well I'll be ~ed!** ¡caramba!*, ¡vaya!* • **I'll be ~ed if I will!** ¡ni en broma!, ¡ni pensarlo!, ¡ni de coña! (*Sp*‡)
EXCL ‡ ¡maldita sea!*, ¡caray!*, ¡me cago en la leche! (*Sp*‡), ¡carajo! (*LAm*‡)
N ‡ • **I don't give a ~** me importa un pito *or* bledo*, me importa un carajo‡ • **it's not worth a ~** no vale un pimiento*, no vale un carajo‡
ADJ ‡ maldito*, condenado*, fregado (*LAm**) • **~ Yankee** (*US*) sucio/a yanqui *mf*
ADV ‡ • **it's ~ hot/cold!** ¡vaya calor/frío que hace!, ¡hace un calor/frío del demonio!* • **he's ~ clever!** ¡mira que es listo!, ¡es más listo que el hambre!* • **he ~ near killed me** por poco me mata, casi me mata • **"did you tell him so?" — "~ right, I did!"** —¿eso le dijiste? —¡pues claro! *or* ¡ya lo creo! • **I should ~ well think so!** ¡hombre, eso espero!
damnable†* [ˈdæmnəbl] ADJ detestable
damnably†* [ˈdæmnəblɪ] ADV terriblemente
damn-all‡ [ˈdæmˈɔːl] ADJ • **it's damn-all use** no sirve para nada en absoluto
N • **he does damn-all** no da (ni) golpe* • **I know damn-all about it** (*Brit*) no tengo ni pajolera idea del tema*
damnation [dæmˈneɪʃən] N (*Rel*) perdición *f*
EXCL* ¡maldición!
damned [dæmd] ADJ **1** [*soul*] condenado, maldito
2‡ maldito*, condenado*, fregado (*LAm**) • **that ~ book** ese maldito libro • **it's a ~ shame** es una verdadera lástima *or* pena
ADV ‡ muy, extraordinariamente • **it's ~ awkward** es terriblemente difícil • **it's ~ hot!** ¡vaya calor/frío que hace!, ¡hace un calor del demonio!*
N • **the ~** las almas en pena
damnedest* [ˈdæmdɪst] N • **to do one's ~ to succeed** hacer lo imposible para tener éxito
damn-fool‡ [ˈdæmfuːl] ADJ estúpido, tonto • **some damn-fool driver** algún imbécil de conductor • **that's a damn-fool thing to say!** ¡qué estupidez *or* tontería!
damning [ˈdæmɪŋ] ADJ [*evidence*] irrefutable
Damocles [ˈdæməkliːz] N Damocles
damp [dæmp] ADJ (COMPAR: **damper**, SUPERL: **dampest**) [*house, air, skin, grass*] húmedo • **wipe with a ~ cloth** límpielo con un trapo húmedo • **~ conditions are the worst enemy of old manuscripts** la humedad es el peor enemigo de los manuscritos • **it smells ~ in here** aquí huele a humedad *or* a húmedo • **a ~ patch** una mancha de humedad • IDIOM: • **to be a ~ squib**: • **the concert was a bit of a ~ squib** el concierto fue decepcionante, nos llevamos un chasco con el concierto
N (*also* **dampness**) humedad *f*; ▹ **rising**
VT **1** (= *moisten*) humedecer
2 = **dampen**
3 (= *deaden*) [+ *sounds*] amortiguar; [+ *vibration*] mitigar
CPD ▸ **damp course** aislante *m* hidrófugo
▸ **damp down** VT + ADV [+ *fire*] sofocar
dampen [ˈdæmpən] VT **1** (= *moisten*) humedecer
2 (*fig*) [+ *hopes*] frustrar; [+ *enthusiasm, zeal*] enfriar • **his words ~ed her hopes** sus palabras frustraron sus esperanzas, sus palabras le hicieron perder las esperanzas • **I don't want to ~ your enthusiasm, but …** no quiero enfriar tu entusiasmo, pero …, no quiero hacer que pierdas tu entusiasmo, pero … • **to ~ sb's spirits** desanimar *or* desalentar a algn • **to ~ sb's ardour** apagar el ardor de algn
▸ **dampen down** VT + ADV [+ *demands, speculation*] contener; [+ *economy*] enfriar
dampener [ˈdæmpənəʳ] N • IDIOM: • **to put a ~ on** [*sad news*] [+ *celebration, party*] poner una nota de tristeza a • **to put a ~ on things*** aguar la fiesta
damper [ˈdæmpəʳ] N (*Mus*) sordina *f*, apagador *m*; [*of fire*] regulador *m* de tiro; (*Tech*) amortiguador *m* • IDIOM: • **to put a ~ on** [*sad news*] [+ *celebration, party*] poner una nota de tristeza a • **to put a ~ on things*** aguar la fiesta
dampish [ˈdæmpɪʃ] ADJ algo húmedo
damply [ˈdæmplɪ] ADV **1** (= *wetly*) • **his T-shirt clung ~ to him** la camiseta mojada se le ceñía al cuerpo • **her hair clung ~ to her cheeks** el pelo mojado se le pegaba a las mejillas
2 (*fig*) (= *unenthusiastically*) sin ganas, sin (mucho) entusiasmo
dampness [ˈdæmpnɪs] N humedad *f*
damp-proof [ˈdæmppruːf] ADJ hidrófugo, a prueba de humedad
VT aislar contra la humedad
CPD ▸ **damp-proof course** = **damp course**
damsel† [ˈdæmzəl] N damisela *f*, doncella *f* • **a ~ in distress** (*hum*) una dama en apuros
damselfly [ˈdæmzəl,flaɪ] N caballito *m* del diablo
damson [ˈdæmzən] N (= *fruit*) ciruela *f* damascena; (= *tree*) ciruelo *m* damasceno
CPD ▸ **damson jam** mermelada *f* de ciruela damascena
Dan [dæn] N *familiar form of* **Daniel**
dan [dæn] N (*Sport*) dan *m*
dance [dɑːns] N **1** (= *act*) baile *m*; (= *art of dancing*) danza *f*, baile *m* • **~ of death** danza *f* de la muerte • IDIOM: • **to lead sb a (merry) ~** (*Brit*) traer loco a algn
2 (= *event*) baile *m*
VT bailar • IDIOM: • **to ~ attendance on sb** desvivirse por algn
VI bailar; (*artistically*) bailar, danzar; (*fig*) (= *skip*) saltar, brincar • **shall we ~?** ¿quieres bailar? • **to ~ about** (*with pain, joy etc*) saltar • **to ~ for joy** saltar *or* brincar de alegría • IDIOM: • **to ~ to sb's tune** bailar al son que algn toca
CPD ▸ **dance band** orquesta *f* de baile ▸ **dance class** clase *f* de baile ▸ **dance company** compañía *f* de danza ▸ **dance floor** pista *f* de baile ▸ **dance hall** salón *m* de baile, sala *f* de fiestas ▸ **dance music** música *f* de baile ▸ **dance studio** academia *f* de baile
▸ **dance off** VI + ADV (= *move away*) marcharse bailando • **the samba players ~d off to Fort Park** los sambistas se marcharon a Fort Park bailando
dancer [ˈdɑːnsəʳ] N (*gen*) bailarín/ina *m/f*; (*flamenco*) bailaor(a) *m/f*
dancing [ˈdɑːnsɪŋ] N baile *m*
CPD ▸ **dancing class** clase *f* de baile ▸ **dancing girl** bailarina *f* ▸ **dancing partner** pareja *f* de baile ▸ **dancing shoes** (*gen*) zapatos *mpl* de baile; (*for ballet*) zapatillas *fpl* de ballet
D and C N ABBR = **dilation and curettage**
dandelion [ˈdændɪlaɪən] N diente *m* de león
dander [ˈdændəʳ] N • IDIOM: • **to get sb's ~ up**† sacar a algn de sus casillas
dandified [ˈdændɪfaɪd] ADJ guapo, acicalado
dandle [ˈdændl] VT hacer saltar sobre las rodillas
dandruff [ˈdændrəf] N caspa *f*
CPD ▸ **dandruff shampoo** champú *m* anticaspa
dandy [ˈdændɪ] N (*pej*) (= *man*) dandi *m*, petimetre *m*
ADJ (*esp US**) excelente, chachi (*Sp**), macanudo (*LAm**) • **fine and ~** perfecto
Dane [deɪn] N danés/esa *m/f*

d

dang* [dæŋ] EXCL (*euph*) = **damn**

danger [ˈdeɪndʒəʳ] N peligro *m* • **to be in ~** estar en peligro, correr peligro • **to be in ~ of falling** correr el peligro *or* riesgo de caer • **there is a ~ of** hay peligro *or* riesgo de • **there was no ~ that he would be discovered** no había peligro de que lo descubrieran • **(to be) out of ~** (*also Med*) (estar) fuera de peligro • **to be a ~ to sth/sb/o.s.** ser un peligro para algo/para algn/para sí mismo • **"danger men at work"** "¡atención obras!", "¡peligro obras!" • **"danger keep out"** "¡peligro de muerte! prohibido el acceso"
CPD ▸ **danger area** = **danger zone** ▸ **danger list** (*Med*) • **to be on the ~ list** estar grave ▸ **danger money** plus *m* de peligrosidad ▸ **danger point** punto *m* crítico ▸ **danger signal** señal *f* de peligro ▸ **danger zone** área *f or* zona *f* de peligro

dangerous [ˈdeɪndʒrəs] ADJ [*animal, disease, person, place*] peligroso; [*strategy, decision, operation*] peligroso, arriesgado; [*driver*] peligroso, temerario; [*substance, drug*] peligroso, nocivo • **he was jailed for ~ driving** lo metieron en la cárcel por conducir con imprudencia temeraria • **it is ~ to play on railway lines** es peligroso jugar en las vías del tren

dangerously [ˈdeɪndʒrəslɪ] ADV peligrosamente, de forma peligrosa • **he was driving ~ close to the car in front** conducía tan pegado al coche de delante que era peligroso • **I came ~ close to hitting him** faltó muy poco para que le pegara • **he didn't die, but he came ~ close to it** no murió, pero estuvo a punto *or* le faltó poco • **to drive ~** conducir de forma temeraria; (*Jur*) conducir con imprudencia temeraria • **~ high** peligrosamente alto • **to be ~ ill** estar gravemente enfermo • **to live ~** (= *take risks*) llevar una vida arriesgada, vivir al límite • **go on, live ~, have another glass of wine!** (*hum*) venga, un día es un día, ¡tómate otra copa de vino! • **~ low** peligrosamente bajo

dangle [ˈdæŋgl] VT **1** [+ *arm, leg*] colgar; [+ *object on string etc*] dejar colgado
2 (*fig*) [+ *tempting offer*] • **to ~ sth in front of** *or* **before sb** tentar a algn con algo
VI colgar, pender • **to keep sb dangling** (*fig*) tener a algn pendiente

Daniel [ˈdænjəl] N Daniel

Danish [ˈdeɪnɪʃ] N **1** (*Ling*) danés *m*
2 • **the ~** los daneses
3 (*esp US*) = **Danish pastry**
ADJ danés, dinamarqués
CPD ▸ **Danish blue (cheese)** queso *m* azul danés ▸ **Danish pastry** *bollo de masa de hojaldre con pasas, manzana o crema*

dank [dæŋk] ADJ (COMPAR: **danker**, SUPERL: **dankest**) húmedo y oscuro

Dante [ˈdæntɪ] N Dante

Danube [ˈdænjuːb] N Danubio *m*

Daphne [ˈdæfnɪ] N Dafne

dapper [ˈdæpəʳ] ADJ (= *smart*) [*man, appearance*] pulcro

dapple [ˈdæpl] VT motear a colores

dappled [ˈdæpld] ADJ moteado; [*horse*] rodado

DAR N ABBR (US) (= **Daughters of the American Revolution**) *una organización de mujeres descendientes de combatientes de la Guerra de la Independencia americana*

DAUGHTERS OF THE AMERICAN REVOLUTION

La organización **Daughters of the American Revolution** o **DAR**, fundada en 1890, está formada por mujeres que descienden de familias que lucharon para defender las colonias contra los británicos durante la Guerra de la Independencia americana (1775-1783). Sus miembros han trabajado mucho para fomentar el patriotismo y preservar los lugares históricos.

Políticamente, es una organización muy conservadora que incluso se ha opuesto a la existencia de las Naciones Unidas.

Darby and Joan [ˈdɑːbɪənˈdʒəʊn] NPL *el matrimonio ideal, de ancianos que siguen viviendo en la mayor felicidad*
CPD ▸ **Darby and Joan club** (*Brit*) club *m* para personas de la tercera edad

Dardanelles [ˌdɑːdəˈnelz] NPL Dardanelos *mpl*

dare [dɛəʳ] N (= *challenge*) reto *m*, desafío *m* • **I did it for a ~** me retaron, por eso lo hice
VT **1** (= *challenge*) desafiar, retar • **to ~ sb to do sth** desafiar *or* retar a algn a hacer algo • **I ~ you!** ¡a que no te atreves!
2 (= *be so bold*) atreverse • **to ~ (to) do sth** atreverse a hacer algo • **I ~n't** no me atrevo • **I ~n't tell him** no me atrevo a decírselo • **how ~ you!** ¡cómo te atreves!, ¡qué cara! • **don't** *or* **just you ~!*** ¡ni se te ocurra!
3 • **I ~ say** (= *in my opinion*) en mi opinión; (= *possibly*) puede ser, tal vez • **I ~ say that …** no me sorprendería que (+ *subjun*) • **I ~ say you're tired** supongo que estás cansado • **~ I say it** me atrevería a decir
4 (*liter*) [+ *sb's anger*] hacer frente a

daredevil [ˈdɛədevl] ADJ temerario
N temerario/a *m/f*, atrevido/a *m/f*

daren't [ˈdɛənt] = **dare not**

daresay, **dare say** [ˌdɛəˈseɪ] ▹ **dare**

Dar-es-Salaam [ˌdɑːressəˈlɑːm] N Dar-es-Salaam *m*

daring [ˈdɛərɪŋ] ADJ **1** (= *bold*) [*plan, escape*] arriesgado; [*person*] atrevido, audaz
2 (= *provocative*) [*film, clothes*] atrevido
N audacia *f*, atrevimiento *m*

daringly [ˈdɛərɪŋlɪ] ADV atrevidamente, osadamente

Darius [dəˈraɪəs] N Darío

dark [dɑːk] ADJ (COMPAR: **darker**, SUPERL: **darkest**) **1** (= *not illuminated*) oscuro • **a ~ night** una noche cerrada • **the room/house was ~** (= *poky*) era una habitación/casa oscura; (= *badly-lit*) la habitación/casa estaba oscura; (= *lights not on*) la habitación/casa estaba a oscuras • **it was already ~ outside** ya había oscurecido, ya era de noche • **to get ~** oscurecerse, ponerse oscuro; (*at night-time*) oscurecer, hacerse de noche • **it gets ~ early in winter** en invierno oscurece pronto, en invierno se hace de noche pronto • **the ~ side of the moon** la cara oculta de la luna
2 (*in colour*) [*colour, clothes*] oscuro; [*complexion, hair*] moreno, prieto (*Mex*); [*cloud*] gris • **~ blue/red** *etc* azul/rojo *etc* oscuro • **he is tall and ~** es alto y moreno, es alto y prieto (*Mex*)
3 (= *sad, gloomy*) [*day, period*] aciago; [*mood, thoughts*] sombrío • **these are ~ days for the steel industry** son días aciagos para la industria del acero
4 (= *obscure, mysterious*) oscuro • **the ~ recesses of the human mind** los oscuros recovecos de la mente humana • **~est Africa** lo más recóndito de África • **a ~ corner of the world** un rincón recóndito del mundo • **to keep sth ~*** no decir ni pío de algo* • **keep it ~!*** ¡de esto ni una palabra a nadie! • IDIOM: • **he's a ~ horse** es una incógnita, es un enigma
5 (= *sinister*) [*secret, plan, threat*] siniestro • **who performed the ~ deed?** ¿quién llevó a cabo el vil acto? • **I got some ~ looks from Janet** Janet me lanzaba miradas asesinas
N • **after ~** después del anochecer • **until ~** hasta el anochecer • **I want to leave before ~** quiero salir antes de que anochezca, quiero salir antes del anochecer • **the ~** la oscuridad • **he is afraid of the ~** le tiene miedo a la oscuridad • **why are you sitting in the ~?** ¿por qué estás sentado en lo oscuro? • IDIOMS: • **to be in the ~ about sth*** no saber nada sobre algo • **I'm still in the ~ (about it)*** aún no sé nada (de eso) • **to keep/leave sb in the ~ about sth*** mantener/dejar a algn desinformado de algo, ocultar algo a algn; ▹ **shot**
CPD ▸ **the Dark Ages** la Alta Edad Media • **we're still living in the ~ ages** (*fig*) todavía vivimos en la Edad Media ▸ **dark chocolate** chocolate *m* amargo, chocolate *m* negro ▸ **dark glasses** gafas *fpl* oscuras ▸ **dark matter** (*Astron*) materia *f* oscura

darken [ˈdɑːkən] VT [+ *sky*] oscurecer; [+ *colour*] hacer más oscuro • **a ~ed room** un cuarto oscuro • IDIOM: • **to ~ sb's door**: • **never ~ my door again!** ¡no vuelvas nunca por aquí!
VI [*room, landscape*] oscurecerse; [*sky*] (*at nightfall*) oscurecerse; (= *cloud over*) nublarse; [*colour*] ponerse más oscuro; (*fig*) [*face, future*] ensombrecerse

darkey†** [ˈdɑːkɪ] N = **darkie**

dark-eyed [ˌdɑːkˈaɪd] ADJ de ojos oscuros

dark-haired [ˌdɑːkˈhɛəd] ADJ moreno

darkie†** [ˈdɑːkɪ] N (*Brit*) (*pej*) negro/a *m/f*

darkish [ˈdɑːkɪʃ] ADJ [*colour*] algo oscuro, tirando a oscuro; [*hair, complexion*] algo moreno, tirando a moreno

darkly [ˈdɑːklɪ] ADV (= *mysteriously*) enigmáticamente; (= *threateningly*) de manera amenazante • **the newspapers hinted ~ at conspiracies** los periódicos hacían enigmáticas referencias a conspiraciones • **"we'll see," he said ~** —ya veremos —dijo en tono amenazante • **~ comic** lleno de humor negro • **the freckles stood out ~ against her pale skin** las pecas resaltaban oscuras en su blanca piel

darkness [ˈdɑːknɪs] N **1** (= *blackness*) [*of complexion, hair, sky*] oscuridad *f* • **in the ~ of the night** en la oscuridad *or* lo oscuro de la noche • **the house was in ~** la casa estaba a oscuras • **~ fell, and we returned home** cayó la noche y volvimos a casa
2 (= *evil*) el mal • **the forces of ~** las fuerzas del mal • **the powers of ~** los poderes del mal

darknet [ˈdɑːknet] N red *f* oscura, darknet *f*

darkroom [ˈdɑːkrʊm] N (*Phot*) cuarto *m* oscuro

dark-skinned [ˌdɑːkˈskɪnd] ADJ moreno, morocho (*LAm*)

darky** [ˈdɑːkɪ] N = **darkie**

darling [ˈdɑːlɪŋ] N **1** (*gen*) cariño *m*, querido/a *m/f* • **yes, ~** sí, cariño *or* querida • **come here, ~** (*to child*) ven aquí, cielo • **be a ~ and …*** sé bueno y … • **she's a little ~** (*child*) es un encanto
2 (= *favourite*) preferido/a *m/f* • **the ~ of the muses** el preferido de las musas
ADJ **1** (= *beloved*) querido
2* (= *lovely*) [*house, dress*] mono • **what a ~ dress/house!** ¡qué vestido más mono/casa más mona!, ¡qué monada de vestido/casa!

darn¹ [dɑːn] N (*Sew*) zurcido *m*, zurcidura *f*
VT [+ *socks, cloth*] zurcir

darn²* [dɑːn] (*esp US*) EXCL • **~ (it)!** ¡caray!*
ADJ = **darned**
ADV = **darned**

darned* [dɑ:nd] (*esp US*) (ADJ) condenado, maldito • **I'll be ~!** ¡mecachis!* (ADV) • **free to do as you ~ well please** libre de hacer lo que te dé la real gana* • **we start working pretty ~ early** empezamos a trabajar tela de pronto*

darning ['dɑ:nɪŋ] (N) (= *action*) zurcido *m*; (= *items to be darned*) cosas *f* por zurcir (CPD) ▸ **darning needle** aguja *f* de zurcir ▸ **darning wool** hilo *m* de zurcir

dart [dɑ:t] (N) **1** (= *movement*) movimiento *m* rápido • **to make a ~ for** precipitarse hacia **2** (*Sport*) dardo *m*, rehilete *m* • **~s** (= *game*) dardos *mpl* • **to play ~s** jugar a los dardos **3** (= *weapon*) dardo *m*, flecha *f* **4** (*Sew*) pinza *f* (VT) [+ *look*] lanzar (VI) • **to ~ in/out** entrar/salir como una flecha • **to ~ at** *or* **for sth** lanzarse *or* precipitarse hacia algo ▸ **dart across** (VI + PREP) (= *cross quickly*) cruzar disparado • **she ~ed across the street** cruzó disparada la calle ▸ **dart away, dart off** (VI + ADV) salir como una flecha

dartboard ['dɑ:tbɔ:d] (N) diana *f*

Darwinian [dɑ:'wɪnɪən] (ADJ) darwiniano (N) darwinista *mf*

Darwinism ['dɑ:wɪnɪzəm] (N) darwinismo *m*

Darwinist ['dɑ:wɪnɪst] (ADJ) darwinista (N) darwinista *mf*

dash [dæʃ] (N) **1** (= *small quantity*) [*of liquid*] gota *f*, chorrito *m*; [*of salt, pepper*] pizca *f*; [*of colour*] toque *m* • **with a ~ of soda** con una gota *or* un chorrito de sifón **2** (= *punctuation mark*) (*also Morse*) raya *f* **3** (= *rush*) carrera *f* • **there was a mad ~ for the exit** todos se precipitaron hacia la salida • **to make a ~ at** *or* **towards** precipitarse hacia • **we had to make a ~ for it** tuvimos que salir corriendo **4** (*US*) (*Sport*) • **the 100-meter ~** los 100 metros lisos **5** (= *flair, style*) brío *m* • IDIOM: • **to cut a ~** destacar **6** (*Aut*) = **dashboard** (VT) **1** (= *throw*) • **to ~ sth to the ground** tirar *or* arrojar algo al suelo • **to ~ sth to pieces** hacer añicos algo, estrellar algo • **to ~ one's head against sth** dar con la cabeza contra algo **2** (*fig*) [+ *hopes*] frustrar, defraudar • **to ~ sb's spirits** desanimar a algn (VI) **1** (= *smash*) estrellarse • **the waves are ~ing against the rock** las olas rompen contra la roca **2** (= *rush*) ir de prisa, precipitarse • **to ~ away/back** salir/volver corriendo • **to ~ in/out** entrar/salir disparado • **to ~ past** pasar como un rayo • **to ~ up** [*person*] llegar corriendo; [*car*] llegar a toda velocidad • **I must ~*** me voy corriendo (EXCL) • **~ it (all)!**†* ¡demontre!*, ¡porras!* ▸ **dash off** (VT + ADV) [+ *letter, drawing*] hacer a la carrera (VI + ADV) salir corriendo, marcharse apresuradamente

dashboard ['dæʃbɔ:d] (N) (*Aut*) salpicadero *m*

dashed†* [dæʃt] (ADJ) (*euph*) = **damned**

dashing ['dæʃɪŋ] (ADJ) gallardo, apuesto

dashingly ['dæʃɪŋlɪ] (ADV) [*behave*] gallardamente, arrojadamente; [*dress*] garbosamente

dastardly ['dæstədlɪ] (ADJ) ruin, vil

DAT (N ABBR) = **digital audio tape**

data ['deɪtə] (NPL) (*with sing or pl vb*) datos *mpl* (CPD) ▸ **data bank** banco *m* de datos ▸ **data capture** grabación *f* de datos ▸ **data collection** recogida *f* de datos, recopilación *f* de datos ▸ **data dictionary, data directory** guía *f* de datos ▸ **data entry** entrada *f* de datos ▸ **data file** archivo *m* de datos ▸ **data link** medio *m* de transmisión de datos ▸ **data management** gestión *f* de datos ▸ **data mining** minería *f* de datos ▸ **data preparation** preparación *f* de datos ▸ **data processing** (= *action*) procesamiento *m* de datos, proceso *m* de datos; (= *science*) informática *f* ▸ **data processor** procesador *m* de datos ▸ **data protection** protección *f* de datos ▸ **data protection act** ley *f* de protección de datos ▸ **data security** seguridad *f* de los datos ▸ **data transmission** transmisión *f* de datos, telemática *f*

database ['deɪtəbeɪs] (N) base *f* de datos (CPD) ▸ **database manager** (= *software*) gestor *m* de base de datos

datable ['deɪtəbl] (ADJ) datable, fechable (to en)

Datapost® ['deɪtəpəʊst] (N) (*Brit*) • **by ~** por correo urgente

date¹ [deɪt] (N) **1** (= *year, day of month*) fecha *f* • **what's the ~ today?** • **what ~ is it today?** ¿qué fecha es hoy? • **~ of birth** fecha *f* de nacimiento • **closing ~** fecha *f* tope • **at an early ~** (*in the future*) en fecha próxima, dentro de poco • **at some future ~** en alguna fecha futura • **~ of issue** fecha *f* de emisión • **at a later ~** en una fecha posterior • **opening ~** fecha *f* de apertura • **to ~** hasta la fecha; ▹ **out-of-date, up-to-date** **2** (= *appointment*) cita *f*, compromiso *m*; (*with girlfriend, boyfriend*) cita *f* • **to have a ~ with sb** tener una cita con algn • **have you got a ~ tonight?** ¿tienes algún compromiso para esta noche? • **to make a ~ with sb** citarse *or* quedar con algn • **they made a ~ for eight o'clock** se citaron para las ocho, quedaron a las ocho **3** (= *person one is dating*) pareja *f*, acompañante *mf* • **who's your ~ for tonight?** ¿con quién sales esta noche? **4** (= *concert etc*) actuación *f* (VT) **1** (= *put date on*) [+ *letter*] fechar, poner fecha a **2** (= *establish age of*) [+ *object*] fechar, datar **3** (= *show age of*) [+ *person*] • **you remember the Tremeloes? that really ~s you!** ¿recuerdas a los Tremeloes? ¡eso demuestra lo viejo que eres! **4** (= *go out with*) [+ *girl etc*] salir con, pololear con (*Chile*) (VI) **1** (= *show age*) pasar de moda **2** • **to ~ back to** [+ *time*] remontarse a • **to ~ from** datar de **3** (= *go out with sb*) • **is she dating?** ¿sale con chicos? • **they've been dating for three months** llevan saliendo juntos tres meses (CPD) ▸ **date book** (*US*) agenda *f* ▸ **date rape** violación *f* durante una cita amorosa ▸ **date stamp** (*on library book, fresh food*) sello *m* de fecha; (= *postmark*) matasellos *m inv*; ▹ **date-stamp**

date² [deɪt] (N) (*Bot*) (= *fruit*) dátil *m*; (*also* **date palm**) palmera *f* datilera

dated ['deɪtɪd] (ADJ) [*clothes, ideas*] pasado de moda, anticuado

dateline ['deɪtlaɪn] (N) **1** (*Geog*) línea *f* de cambio de fecha **2** (*in newspaper*) • **~ Beirut** fechado en Beirut

date-stamp ['deɪtstæmp] (VT) estampar la fecha en; ▹ **date**

dating ['deɪtɪŋ] (N) (*Archeol*) datación *f* (CPD) ▸ **dating agency** agencia *f* de contactos ▸ **dating service** servicio *m* de contactos

dative ['deɪtɪv] (ADJ) dativo (N) (*also* **dative case**) dativo *m*

datum ['deɪtəm] (N) (PL: **data**) dato *m*; ▹ **data**

daub [dɔ:b] (N) (= *smear*) mancha *f*; (= *bad painting*) pintarrajo *m* (VT) (= *smear*) embadurnar • **to ~ a wall with paint** • **~ paint onto a wall** embadurnar una pared de pintura (VI) pintarrajear

dauber ['dɔ:bəʳ], **daubster** ['dɔ:bstəʳ] (N) pintor(a) *m/f* de brocha gorda, mal(a) pintor(a) *m/f*

daughter ['dɔ:təʳ] (N) hija *f*; ▹ DAUGHTERS OF THE AMERICAN REVOLUTION

daughterboard ['dɔ:tə,bɔ:d] (N) (*Comput*) placa *f* hija

daughter-in-law ['dɔ:tərɪnlɔ:] (N) (PL: **daughters-in-law**) nuera *f*, hija *f* política

daunt [dɔ:nt] (VT) (= *inhibit*) intimidar, amedrentar; (= *dishearten*) desmoralizar, desalentar • **nothing ~ed** sin dejarse intimidar, sin dejarse amedrentar, sin inmutarse

daunted ['dɔ:ntɪd] (ADJ) intimidado • **to feel ~** sentirse intimidado

daunting ['dɔ:ntɪŋ] (ADJ) (= *inhibiting*) abrumador, amedrentador; (= *disheartening*) desalentador, desmoralizante • **a ~ task** una tarea abrumadora, una gigantesca tarea

dauntingly ['dɔ:ntɪŋlɪ] (ADV) • **the queues were ~ long** las colas asustaban de lo largas que eran • **she is ~ articulate** se expresa con una elocuencia que intimida

dauntless ['dɔ:ntlɪs] (ADJ) [*person*] intrépido; [*courage*] tenaz

dauntlessly ['dɔ:ntlɪslɪ] (ADV) • **to carry on ~** continuar sin amilanarse, continuar impávido

dauphin ['dɔ:fɪn] (N) (*Hist*) delfín *m*

Dave [deɪv] (N) *familiar form of* **David**

davenport ['dævnpɔ:t] (N) (*US*) sofá *m* cama; (*Brit*) (= *desk*) escritorio *m* pequeño

David ['deɪvɪd] (N) David

davit ['dævɪt] (N) pescante *m*

Davy Jones ['deɪvɪ'dʒəʊnz] (N) • **~' locker** (*Naut*) el fondo del mar (*tumba de los marineros ahogados*)

dawdle ['dɔ:dl] (VI) (*in walking*) andar muy despacio; (*over food, work*) entretenerse, demorarse (VT) • **to ~ away** malgastar

dawdler ['dɔ:dləʳ] (N) (= *idler*) holgazán/ana *m/f*, ocioso/a *m/f*; (= *slowcoach*) rezagado/a *m/f*

dawdling ['dɔ:dlɪŋ] (ADJ) (= *lagging behind*) rezagado (N) pérdida *f* de tiempo

dawn [dɔ:n] (N) **1** (= *daybreak*) amanecer *m* • **at ~** al amanecer • **to get up with the ~** levantarse al amanecer • **from ~ to dusk** de sol a sol **2** (*liter*) (= *beginning*) albores *mpl* • **the ~ of the radio age** los albores de la era de la radio (VI) [*day*] amanecer • **a new epoch has ~ed** ha nacido una época nueva (CPD) ▸ **dawn chorus** (*Brit*) canto *m* de los pájaros al amanecer ▸ **dawn raid** (*Police*) *redada efectuada en la madrugada*; (*Econ*) *compra inesperada de acciones de una empresa como paso previo a una OPA* ▸ **dawn on, dawn upon** (VI + PREP) • **it suddenly ~ed on him that ...** se dio cuenta *or* cayó en la cuenta de repente de que ...

dawning ['dɔ:nɪŋ] (ADJ) [*hope etc*] naciente (N) (= *beginning*) albores *mpl* • **the ~ of the space age** los albores de la era espacial • **the first ~ of hope** el primer atisbo *or* rayo de esperanza

day [deɪ] (N) **1** (= *24 hours*) día *m* • **what day is it today?** ¿qué día es hoy? • **he works eight hours a day** trabaja ocho horas al día • **twice a day** dos veces al día • **the day after** el día siguiente • **the day after tomorrow** pasado

mañana • **day after day** día tras día • **two days ago** hace dos días • **any day** un día cualquiera • **any day now** cualquier día de estos • **any old day*** el mejor día • **the day before** el día anterior • **the day before yesterday** anteayer • **the day before his birthday** la víspera de su cumpleaños • **two days before Christmas** dos días antes de Navidad • **day by day** de un día para otro, de día a día (*LAm*) • **every day** cada día, todos los días • **one fine day** el día menos pensado • **on the following day** al día siguiente • **for days on end** durante días • **from day to day** de día en día • **from one day to the next** de un día a otro • **to live from day to day** *or* **from one day to the next** vivir al día • **day in day out** un día sí y otro también • **you don't look a day older** no pasan por ti los días, no pareces un día más viejo • **on the day everything will be all right** para el día en cuestión todo estará en orden • **one day** un día • **the other day** el otro día • **every other day** un día sí y otro no • **some day** un día • **(on) that day** aquel día • **that day when we ...** aquel día en que nosotros ... • **one of these days** un día de estos • **this day next week** • **this day week** (*Brit*) (de) hoy en ocho días • **50 years ago to the day** (hoy) hace exactamente 50 años • IDIOMS: • **he's fifty if he's a day*** debe tener cincuenta años mínimo • **to carry** *or* **win the day** ganar la victoria • **to give sb his day in court** dar a algn la oportunidad de explicarse • **to make sb's day**: • **it made my day to see him smile** me hizo feliz verlo sonreír • **that'll be the day, when he offers to pay!*** ¡él nos invitará cuando las ranas críen pelo!; ▸ **black**
2 (= *daylight hours, working hours*) jornada *f* • **to work an eight-hour day** trabajar una jornada de ocho horas • **it's a fine day** hace buen tiempo hoy • **to work all day** trabajar todo el día • **a day at the seaside** un día de playa • **to travel by day** • **travel during the day** viajar de día • **paid by the day** pagado por día • **good day!** ¡buenos días! • **to work day and night** trabajar día y noche • **a day off** un día libre • **to take a day off** darse un día libre, no presentarse en el trabajo • **on a fine/wet day** un día bonito/lluvioso • **one summer's day** un día de verano • **day of reckoning** (*fig*) día *m* de ajustar cuentas • **to work days** trabajar de día • IDIOMS: • **it's all in a day's work** son gajes del oficio • **to call it a day*** (*for good*) darse por vencido, abandonar; (*for today*) dejarlo por hoy • **let's call it a day** terminemos ya
3 (= *period*) • **during the early/final days of the strike** durante los primeros/últimos días de la huelga • **it has seen better days** ya no vale lo que antes • **until my dying day** hasta la muerte • **it's early days yet** todavía es pronto • **the happiest days of your life** los mejores días de su vida • **in those days** en aquellos tiempos • **in days to come** en días venideros • **in this day and age** • **in the present day** hoy en día • **in my day** en mis tiempos • **in Queen Victoria's day** en la época de la reina Victoria • **he was famous in his day** fue famoso en sus tiempos • **in the good old days** en los viejos tiempos • **these days** hoy en día • **those were the days, when ...** esa fue la buena época, cuando ... • **to this day** hasta el día de hoy • **in his younger days** en su juventud • IDIOM: • **to have had one's day**: • **he's had his day** pasó de moda, está acabado; ▸ **dog, time**
CPD ▸ **day bed** (*US*) meridiana *f* ▸ **day boarder** (*Brit*) (*Scol*) alumno/a *m/f* de media pensión ▸ **day boy** (*Brit*) (*Scol*) externo *m* ▸ **day centre** (*Brit*) centro *m* de día ▸ **day girl** (*Brit*) (*Scol*) externa *f* ▸ **day job** trabajo *m* habitual, ocupación *f* habitual • IDIOM: • **don't give up the day job!** (*hum*) ¡sigue en lo tuyo! ▸ **Day of Judgement** día *m* del Juicio Final ▸ **day labourer, day laborer** (*US*) jornalero *m* ▸ **day nurse** enfermero/a *m/f* de día ▸ **day nursery** guardería *f* ▸ **day one** • **from day one** (= *from the beginning*) desde el principio *or* el primer día • **on day one** (= *at the beginning*) el primer día ▸ **day pass** (*for museum, train*) pase *m* de un día; (*at ski resort*) forfait *m* de un día ▸ **day pupil** (*Brit*) (*at boarding school*) alumno/a *m/f* externo/a ▸ **day rate** (= *daily rate*) tarifa *f* diaria; (*as opposed to night rate*) tarifa *f* diurna ▸ **day release** • **to be on day release** [*prisoner*] estar en régimen de prisión abierta ▸ **day release job** (*for prisoner*) trabajo *m* fuera de la cárcel ▸ **day release course** (*Brit*) (*Comm, Ind*) curso *m* de un día a la semana (para trabajadores) ▸ **day return (ticket)** (*Brit*) billete *m* de ida y vuelta en el día ▸ **day school** colegio *m* sin internado ▸ **day shift** (*in factory etc*) turno *m* de día ▸ **day surgery** cirugía *f* ambulatoria ▸ **day trader** (*Comm*) *operador que realiza operaciones de compraventa en el mismo día* ▸ **day trip** excursión *f* (de un día) • **to go on a day trip to London** ir un día de excursión *or* (*LAm*) de paseo a Londres ▸ **day tripper** excursionista *mf*

-day [-deɪ] SUFFIX • **two-day** (*adj*) de dos días

daybook ['deɪbʊk] N (*Brit*) diario *m* de entradas y salidas, libro *m* de entradas y salidas; (*US*) agenda *f*

daybreak ['deɪbreɪk] N amanecer *m* • **at ~** al amanecer

daycare ['deɪkɛə'] N (*for children*) servicio *m* de guardería; (*for adults*) servicio *m* asistencial durante el día
CPD ▸ **daycare centre, daycare center** (*US*) (*for children*) guardería *f*; (*for adults*) centro *m* (asistencial) de día ▸ **daycare services** (*Brit*) (*for children*) servicios *mpl* de guardería; (*for adults*) servicios *mpl* asistenciales durante el día ▸ **daycare worker** (*US*) (*for children*) empleado/a *m/f* de una guardería; (*for adults*) empleado/a *m/f* de un centro de día

daydream ['deɪdriːm] N ensueño *m*, ilusión *f*
VI soñar despierto

Day-glo® ['deɪgləʊ] ADJ [*colours etc*] fosforescente, fosforito*

daylight ['deɪlaɪt] N luz *f* (del día) • **at ~** (= *dawn*) al amanecer • **in the ~** • **by ~** de día • **in broad ~** a plena luz del día, en pleno día • IDIOMS: • **to see ~**: • **I am beginning to see ~** (= *understand*) empiezo a ver las cosas claras; (= *approach the end of a job*) ya vislumbro el final • **to beat** *or* **knock the (living) ~s out of sb*** dar una tremenda paliza a algn • **to scare the (living) ~s out of sb*** dar un susto de muerte a algn • **it's ~ robbery!** (*Brit*) ¡es un robo *or* una estafa!
CPD ▸ **daylight attack** ataque *m* diurno ▸ **daylight hours** horas *fpl* de luz

daylight-saving time [ˌdeɪlaɪt'seɪvɪŋˌtaɪm] N (*US*) horario *m* de verano

daylong ['deɪˌlɒŋ] ADJ que dura todo el día
ADV todo el día

day-old ['deɪ'əʊld] ADJ [*chick*] de un día

dayroom ['deɪrʊm] N (*in hospital etc*) *sala de estar para los internos*

daytime ['deɪtaɪm] N día *m* • **in the ~** de día
ADJ de día • **please give a ~ telephone number** por favor dé un teléfono de contacto durante el día
CPD ▸ **daytime TV** programación *f* de televisión matinal *or* matutina, televisión *f* matinal *or* matutina

day-to-day ['deɪtə'deɪ] ADJ cotidiano, diario • **the day-to-day running of the centre** la gestión cotidiana *or* diaria del centro • **on a day-to-day basis** día por día, de día a día (*LAm*)

daze [deɪz] N aturdimiento *m* • **to be in a ~** estar aturdido
VT **1** [*drug, blow*] atontar, aturdir; (= *confuse*) aturdir
2 (*fig*) [*news*] aturdir, atolondrar

dazed [deɪzd] ADJ (= *confused*) aturdido

dazzle ['dæzl] N deslumbramiento *m*
VT deslumbrar • **he was ~d by the bright light** lo deslumbró el resplandor de la luz • **she was ~d by his knowledge of the world** (se) quedó deslumbrada por su conocimiento del mundo

dazzling ['dæzlɪŋ] ADJ (*lit, fig*) deslumbrante

dazzlingly ['dæzlɪŋlɪ] ADV [*shine*] deslumbradoramente • **~ beautiful** de una belleza deslumbrante

DB ABBR = **database**

dB ABBR (= **decibel**) dB

DBMS N ABBR = **database management system**

DBS N ABBR **1** = **direct broadcasting by satellite**
2 = **direct broadcasting satellite**

DC N ABBR **1** (*Elec*) (= **direct current**) C.C.
2 (*US*) = **District of Columbia**

DC - DISTRICT OF COLUMBIA

District of Columbia es el distrito donde se encuentra el gobierno de Estados Unidos. No forma parte de ningún estado, sino que es un distrito autónomo que comprende únicamente la capital del país, Washington. Se halla en el este de los Estados Unidos y tiene un área de unos 180 kilómetros cuadrados, donados por los estados de Maryland y Virginia. Normalmente se hace referencia a este distrito mediante sus siglas, **DC**, y se usa después del nombre de la capital: **Washington DC**.

DCC® N ABBR = **digital compact cassette**

DCF N ABBR = **discounted cash-flow**

DCI N ABBR (*Brit*) = **Detective Chief Inspector**

DD N ABBR **1** (*Univ*) = **Doctor of Divinity**
2 (*Comm, Econ*) = **direct debit**
3 (*US*) (*Mil*) = **dishonorable discharge**

dd ABBR (*Comm*) **1** = **delivered**
2 = **dated**
3 = **demand draft**

D/D ABBR = **direct debit**

D-day ['diːdeɪ] N (*Hist*) el día D, el día de la invasión aliada de Normandía (*6 junio 1944*); (*fig*) día *m* D

DDS N ABBR (*US*) **1** (*Univ*) = **Doctor of Dental Science**
2 (*Univ*) = **Doctor of Dental Surgery**

DDT N ABBR (= **dichlorodiphenyltrichloroethane**) DDT *m*

DE ABBR (*US*) = **Delaware**
N ABBR (*Brit*) = **Department of Employment**

de... [diː] PREFIX de...

DEA N ABBR (*US*) (= **Drug Enforcement Administration**) *departamento para la lucha contra la droga*

deacon ['diːkən] N diácono *m*

deaconess ['diːkənes] N diaconisa *f*

deactivate [diː'æktɪveɪt] VT desactivar

dead [ded] ADJ **1** [*person, animal, plant*] muerto, difunto (*frm*); [*leaf*] marchito, seco • **~ man** muerto *m* • **the ~ king** el difunto rey • **to be ~** estar muerto • **he's been ~ for two years** hace dos años que murió • **~ or alive**

vivo o muerto • **to be ~ on arrival** (*in hospital*) ingresar cadáver • **~ and buried** (*lit, fig*) muerto y bien muerto • **to drop (down) ~** caer muerto • **drop ~!*** ¡vete al cuerno!* • **to fall down ~** caer muerto • IDIOMS: • **over my ~ body!*** ¡ni muerto!, ¡ni de chiste! • **as ~ as a dodo** *or* **a doornail** *or* **mutton** más muerto que mi abuela • **~ duck**: • **he's a ~ duck** está quemado • **that issue is a ~ duck** esa cuestión ya no tiene interés • **to be ~ on one's feet** estar hecho migas *or* polvo* • **~ from the neck up*** bruto, imbécil, zoquete* • **to flog a ~ horse** • **beat a ~ horse** (*US*) machacar en hierro frío • **you're ~ meat!*** ¡te vas a enterar!, ¡vas a ver lo que es bueno! • **I wouldn't be seen ~ there** ni muerto ni vivo me verán allí • **to be ~ in the water** [*economy, talks etc*] haberse ido al garete; [*politician, sportsperson etc*] estar acabado • **he/she was ~ to the world** (= *asleep*) estaba dormido/a como un tronco • PROVERB: • **~ men tell no tales** los muertos no hablan

2* (= *finished with*) • **is that glass/drink ~?** ¿ha terminado su vaso?, ¿puedo levantar su vaso?

3 (= *inactive*) [*volcano, fire*] apagado; [*cigarette, match*] gastado; [*battery*] agotado; [*telephone line*] cortado, desconectado; [*wire*] sin corriente; [*language, love, town, party*] muerto; [*custom*] anticuado; (*Sport*) [*ball*] parado, fuera de juego • **the line has gone ~** (*Telec*) la línea está cortada *or* muerta

4 (= *numb*) • **my fingers have gone ~** (*gen*) se me han dormido los dedos; (*with cold*) se me han entumecido los dedos • **he is ~ to all pity** es incapaz de sentir compasión

5 (= *complete*) [*silence, calm*] total, completo; (= *exact*) [*centre*] justo • **a ~ cert*** una cosa segura • **to fall into a ~ faint** desmayarse totalmente • **a ~ loss*** (= *person*) un inútil; (= *thing*) una birria • **a ~ ringer for*** el doble de, la viva imagen de • **to come to a ~ stop** pararse en seco

(ADV) **1** (= *completely, exactly*) • **he stopped ~** se paró en seco • **"dead slow"** (*Aut*) "reducir la marcha"; (*Naut*) "muy despacio" • **to be ~ against sth** estar totalmente opuesto a algo • **~ ahead** todo seguido, todo derecho • **~ between the eyes** justo entre los ojos • **~ level** completamente plano • **to be ~ set on doing sth** estar decidido a hacer algo • **to be ~ set against sth** estar totalmente opuesto a algo • **~ straight** todo seguido, todo derecho • **~ on target** justo en el blanco • **~ on time** a la hora exacta

2 (*Brit**) (= *very*) • **to be ~ beat** estar hecho polvo* • **~ broke** sin un duro • **~ certain** completamente seguro • **~ drunk** borracho perdido • **~ easy** facilón, chupado‡ • **~ tired** muerto (de cansancio)

3 • IDIOM: • **to cut sb ~*** hacer el vacío a algn

(N) **1** • **the ~** los muertos *mpl* • **to come back** *or* **rise from the ~** resucitar

2 • **at ~ of night** • **in the ~ of night** a altas horas de la noche • **in the ~ of winter** en pleno invierno

(CPD) ▸ **dead end** (*lit, fig*) callejón *m* sin salida • **to come to a ~ end** (*fig*) llegar a un punto muerto; ▹ **dead-end** ▸ **dead hand** (*fig*) [*of state, bureaucracy*] peso *m* muerto ▸ **dead heat** (*Sport*) empate *m*; ▹ **dead-heat** ▸ **dead letter** letra *f* muerta ▸ **dead march** marcha *f* fúnebre ▸ **dead matter** materia *f* inanimada ▸ **dead reckoning** estima *f* ▸ **Dead Sea** mar *m* Muerto • **the Dead Sea Scrolls** los manuscritos del mar Muerto ▸ **the dead season** (*Tourism*) la temporada baja ▸ **dead weight** peso *m* muerto; [*of vehicle*] tara *f*; (*fig*) lastre *m*, carga *f* inútil

dead-and-alive ['dedənə'laɪv] (ADJ) aburrido, monótono

deadbeat* ['dedbi:t] (N) (*US*) haragán/ana *m/f*

deadbolt ['dedbəʊlt] (N) cerrojo *m* de seguridad

deaden ['dedn] (VT) [+ *noise, shock*] amortiguar; [+ *feeling*] embotar; [+ *pain*] aliviar, calmar

dead-end ['ded'end] (ADJ) [*street*] sin salida; [*job*] sin porvenir • **dead-end kids** (*US*) chicos *mpl* de la calle; ▹ **dead**

deadening ['dednɪŋ] (ADJ) [*boredom*] de mala muerte

dead-head, deadhead ['dedhed] (VT) (*Brit*) [+ *plant*] cortar las flores marchitas a • **dead-head roses as the blooms fade** corta las rosas conforme se vayan marchitando

(N) (*US**) (= *idiot*) estúpido/a *m/f*

dead-heat ['ded'hi:t] (VI) (*Sport*) empatar (**with** con); ▹ **dead**

deadline ['dedlaɪn] (N) (*Press, Comm*) fecha *f* tope • **to meet a ~** respetar un plazo • **we cannot meet the government's ~** no podemos terminarlo *etc* en el plazo señalado por el gobierno

deadliness ['dedlɪnɪs] (N) **1** [*of poison*] letalidad *f*; [*of aim*] certeza *f*

2 (= *boredom*) tedio *m*

deadlock ['dedlɒk] (N) punto *m* muerto • **to reach ~** llegar a un punto muerto, quedar estancado • **the ~ is complete** no se ve salida alguna

(VT) • **to be ~ed** estar en un punto muerto

deadly ['dedlɪ] (ADJ) (COMPAR: **deadlier**, SUPERL: **deadliest**) **1** (= *lethal*) [*poison, disease, combination*] mortal; [*weapon, attack*] mortífero • **he has a ~ aim with a rifle** tiene una puntería infalible con el rifle • **to use ~ force (against sb)** (*Police, Mil*) abrir fuego (contra algn)

2 (= *devastating*) • **with ~ accuracy** (*Sport etc*) con precisión mortífera; (*Mil etc*) con precisión letal *or* mortal • **he was in ~ earnest** iba muy en serio • **to be ~ enemies** ser enemigos mortales, ser enemigos a muerte • **she argued with ~ logic** argumentaba con una lógica aplastante • **she levelled a ~ look at Nick** le lanzó una mirada asesina a Nick • **there was ~ silence** se hizo un silencio sepulcral

3* (= *very boring*) aburridísimo

(ADV) • **it was ~ cold** hacía un frío de muerte • **the trip was ~ dull** el viaje fue un aburrimiento de muerte, el viaje fue aburridísimo • **she was ~ pale** estaba pálida como un cadáver, tenía una palidez cadavérica (*liter*) • **she thought he was joking but he was ~ serious** ella pensaba que bromeaba, pero lo decía completamente en serio

(CPD) ▸ **deadly nightshade** belladona *f* ▸ **deadly sins** • **the seven ~ sins** los siete pecados capitales

deadness ['dednɪs] (N) inercia *f*, falta *f* de vida

dead-nettle ['ded,netl] (N) ortiga *f* muerta

deadpan ['ded,pæn] (ADJ) [*face, humour*] inexpresivo

deadstock [,ded'stɒk] (N) aperos *mpl*

deadwood ['ded,wʊd] (N) (= *person*) persona *f* inútil; (= *people*) gente *f* inútil; (= *things*) cosas *fpl* inútiles • **to get rid of the ~** (*in organization*) eliminar al personal inútil

deaf [def] (ADJ) (COMPAR: **deafer**, SUPERL: **deafest**) **1** (= *unable to hear*) sordo • **~ in one ear** sordo de un oído • IDIOM: • **to be as ~ as a (door)post** estar más sordo que una tapia

2 (= *unwilling to hear*) • **~ to all appeals** sordo a todos los ruegos • IDIOMS: • **to turn a ~ ear to sth** hacer oídos sordos *or* no prestar oídos a algo • **the plea fell on ~ ears** el ruego cayó en saco roto

(NPL) **the deaf** los sordos *mpl*

(CPD) ▸ **deaf aid** audífono *m*, sonotone® *m*

deaf-and-dumb‡ ['defən'dʌm] (ADJ) [*person, alphabet*] sordomudo

deafen ['defn] (VT) ensordecer

deafening ['defnɪŋ] (ADJ) ensordecedor

deaf-mute‡ ['def'mju:t] (N) sordomudo/a *m/f*

deafness ['defnɪs] (N) sordera *f*

deal¹ [di:l] (VB: PT, PP: **dealt**) (N) **1** (= *agreement*) acuerdo *m*, trato *m* • **a new ~ for the miners** un nuevo acuerdo salarial para los mineros • **we're looking for a better ~** buscamos un arreglo más equitativo • **it's a ~!*** ¡trato hecho! • **to do** *or* **make a ~ with sb** hacer un trato con algn, llegar a un acuerdo con algn • **the New Deal** (*US*) (*Pol*) *la nueva política económica de los EE.UU. aplicada por Roosevelt entre 1933 y 1940* • **pay ~** acuerdo *m* salarial • IDIOM: • **it's a done ~** (*esp US*) es cosa hecha *or* segura, está atado y bien atado

2 (= *transaction*) trato *m*, transacción *f* • **the company lost thousands of pounds on the ~** la empresa perdió miles de libras con ese trato *or* en esa transacción • **arms ~** venta *f* de armas • **big ~!** (*iro*) ¡vaya cosa! • **he only asked me out for a drink, what's the big ~?** solo me invitó a tomar algo por ahí, ¿qué tiene eso de raro? • **this sort of thing happens every day, it's no big ~** estas cosas pasan todos los días, no es nada del otro mundo • **business ~** (*between companies, countries*) acuerdo *m or* trato *m* comercial; (*by individual*) negocio *m* • **to make a big ~ (out) of sth*** dar mucha *or* demasiada importancia a algo • **I tried not to make a big ~ out of it but I was really annoyed** intenté no darle mucha *or* demasiada importancia pero estaba muy enfadado • **don't make such a big ~ out of it!** ¡no hagas una montaña de un grano de arena!

3 (= *treatment*) trato *m* • **a bad/fair/good ~** un trato malo/justo/bueno • **homeowners are getting a bad ~ from this government** los propietarios de viviendas están saliendo malparados con este gobierno • **working women are not getting a fair ~** las mujeres que trabajan no están recibiendo un trato justo; ▹ **raw, square**

4 (= *bargain*) ganga *f* • **they are offering good ~s on flights to Australia** tienen viajes a Australia a muy buen precio

5 (= *amount*) • **he had a ~ of work to do**† tenía mucho trabajo que hacer • **a good ~** • **a great ~** mucho • **a good** *or* **great ~ of money** una gran cantidad de dinero, mucho dinero • **it can save you a good ~ of time** te puede ahorrar mucho tiempo • **there's a good ~ of truth in what you say** hay mucho de verdad en lo que dices • **she's a good ~ cleverer than her brother** es mucho *or* bastante más inteligente que su hermano • **she knew a great ~ about him** sabía muchas cosas sobre él • **"does he get out much?" — "not a great ~"** —¿sale mucho? —no mucho *or* demasiado • **it means a great ~ to me** significa mucho para mí • **he thinks a great ~ of his father** admira mucho a su padre • **the new law will not make a great ~ of difference to the homeless** la nueva ley apenas va a afectar a la gente sin hogar

6 (*Cards*) (= *distribution*) reparto *m* • **whose ~ is it?** ¿a quién le toca dar *or* repartir?

(VT) **1** [+ *blow*] asestar, dar • **to ~ a blow to sth/sb** (*fig*) ser un golpe para algo/algn • **the news dealt a severe blow to their hopes/the economy** la noticia fue un duro golpe para sus esperanzas/la economía

2 (*Cards*) dar, repartir • **I was dealt a very bad**

d

hand (*at cards*) me dieron una mano malísima; (*fig*) (= *had bad luck*) tuve muy mala suerte
(VI) (*Cards*) dar, repartir
▸ **deal in** (VI + PREP) **1** (*Comm*) [+ *goods*] comerciar con, negociar con; [+ *antiques, used cars*] dedicarse a la compraventa de; [+ *drugs*] traficar con; (*Econ, St Ex*) [+ *stocks, shares, currency*] operar con • **he was suspected of ~ing in smuggled tobacco** se sospechaba que se dedicaba al contrabando de tabaco • **we're ~ing in facts here, not theories** aquí estamos tratando con hechos, nada de teoría
2 (*Cards*) [+ *person*] • **~ me in on the next hand** a mí me das (cartas) en la siguiente ronda
▸ **deal out** (VT + ADV) [+ *playing cards, plates*] repartir; [+ *punishment*] imponer • **you have to make the best of what life ~s out to you** tienes que sacar el máximo provecho de lo que te toca en la vida • **the injustice dealt out to her family** la injusticia que se había cometido con su familia
▸ **deal with** (VI + PREP) **1** (= *have dealings with*) tratar con • **you're ~ing with professionals here** ahora estás tratando con profesionales • **they ~ a lot with the Far East** hacen mucho negocio *or* comercian mucho con el Extremo Oriente • **we don't ~ with hostage takers** no negociamos con secuestradores
2 (= *handle, cope with*) [+ *problem, task*] ocuparse de, encargarse de; [+ *difficult person*] manejar, tratar; (= *attend to*) [+ *customer, order, application, complaint*] atender; [+ *person*] manejar, tratar • **he ~s with all the paperwork** él se ocupa *or* se encarga de todo el papeleo • **don't worry, I'm ~ing with it** no te preocupes, ya me ocupo *or* encargo de ello • **my boss will ~ with you from now on** a partir de ahora mi jefe será quien le atienda • **she knows how to ~ with difficult customers** sabe (cómo) manejar *or* tratar a los clientes difíciles • **she's not easy to ~ with** tiene un carácter difícil • **the way that banks ~ with complaints** la forma en que los bancos atienden las quejas • **I'll ~ with your questions afterwards** contestaré (a) sus preguntas después • **we teach people how to ~ with stress** enseñamos a la gente a lidiar con el estrés
3 (= *sort out, solve*) [+ *problem*] solucionar, resolver; [+ *emotion*] superar • **have you dealt with that paperwork yet?** ¿has resuelto todo el papeleo ya?, ¿has terminado ya todo el papeleo? • **don't worry, I've dealt with it** no te preocupes, ya lo he *or* tengo solucionado • **I'll see that the problem is dealt with** yo me ocuparé de que se solucione *or* se resuelva el problema • **he couldn't ~ with his jealousy** no podía superar los celos que sentía • **I'll ~ with you later!** (= *rebuke, punish*) ¡luego me encargaré de ti! • **anyone who disobeys will be severely dealt with** cualquiera que desobedezca será tratado con mucha severidad
4 (= *be about*) [*book, film*] tratar de

deal² [di:l] (N) **1** (= *wood*) (*pine*) madera *f* de pino; (*fir*) madera *f* de abeto
2 (= *plank*) tablón *m*; (= *beam*) viga *f*
(ADJ) • **a ~ table** una mesa de pino

deal-breaker ['di:lbreɪkəʳ] (N) motivo *m* de ruptura

dealer ['di:ləʳ] (N) **1** (*Comm*) comerciante *mf* (**in** de); (*in cattle, horses*) tratante *mf* (**in** de); (= *retailer*) (*gen*) distribuidor(a) *m/f*, proveedor(a) *m/f*; (*in cars*) concesionario/a *m/f* • **your local Honda ~** su concesionario Honda más próximo • **he's a ~ in stolen goods** es comerciante de mercancías robadas • **a major London currency ~** un importante agente de cambio londinense • **he's a property/second-hand car ~** se dedica a la compraventa de propiedades/coches de segunda mano; ▹ **antique, arm², drug, scrap**
2 (*Cards*) repartidor(a) *m/f* de cartas • **the ~ gave him a nine** el que repartía le dio un nueve

dealership ['di:ləʃɪp] (N) (*US*) representación *f*, concesión *f*

dealing ['di:lɪŋ] (N) **1** (*Comm*) • **we have a reputation for honest ~** tenemos fama de ser honrados en nuestros negocios
2 (*St Ex*) transacciones *fpl* (bursátiles) • **a computerized ~ system** un sistema informatizado de transacciones (bursátiles) • **~ was sluggish today** hoy ha habido muy poco movimiento *or* muy poca actividad (bursátil) • **when ~ started the price soared** cuando se abrió el mercado (bursátil) la cotización se disparó
3 (*in drugs, arms*) tráfico *m* (**in** de)
4 (*also* **dealing out**) (*gen, Cards*) reparto *m*
(CPD) ▸ **dealing room** (*Comm*) sala *f* de operaciones

dealings ['di:lɪŋz] (NPL) **1** (= *relationship*) trato *msing*, relaciones *fpl* • **our aim is to be honest in our ~ with our customers** nuestro objetivo es la honradez en nuestro trato con los clientes • **he was not very successful in his ~ with women** no le iba muy bien en sus relaciones con las mujeres • **have you had any ~ with them?** ¿ha tratado con ellos alguna vez?
2 (*Comm, Econ*) negocios *mpl* • **we have a lot of ~ with her company** hacemos mucho(s) negocio(s) con su empresa • **his business ~ suffered as a result of the restrictions** sus negocios se vieron afectados por las restricciones • **he was accused of illegal share ~** lo acusaron de operar ilegalmente en la Bolsa

dealt [delt] (PT), (PP) *of* **deal¹**

dean [di:n] (N) (*Rel*) deán *m*; (*Univ*) decano *m*
(CPD) ▸ **Dean's list** (*US*) (*Univ*) lista *f* de honor académica

> **DEAN'S LIST**
> Se llama **Dean's List** a la relación honorífica de alumnos que se hace en muchas universidades estadounidenses al final de cada año académico o al final de la carrera. En algunas universidades para figurar en ella se ha de haber obtenido A o B en todas las asignaturas, aunque normalmente la lista se basa en la nota media, conocida como **grade-point average**. Los estudiantes que han recibido la máxima puntuación, A, en todo, aparecen a veces en otra lista, llamada **scholars' list** o **president's list**. En algunas escuelas también publican listas similares, conocidas como **honor roll**.

deanery ['di:nərɪ] (N) (*Rel*) **1** (= *parishes*) jurisdicción *f* del deán
2 (= *house*) casa *f* del deán

dear [dɪəʳ] (ADJ) (COMPAR: **dearer**, SUPERL: **dearest**) **1** (= *loved*) querido • **she's a very ~ friend of mine** es una amiga mía muy querida • **my ~est friend** mi amigo más querido, mi amigo del alma
2 (= *lovable*) • **he's a ~ boy, but rather impetuous** es un chico muy majo, pero un poco impulsivo • **what a ~ little boy!** ¡este niño es un encanto! • **what a ~ little necklace that is!*** ¡qué bonita que es esa gargantilla!
3 (= *precious*) • **to hold sth ~** apreciar algo • **the values and beliefs which our society holds ~** los valores y las creencias que nuestra sociedad aprecia • **I had to leave everything I held most ~** tuve que dejar atrás todas las cosas que más quería • **his family life was very ~ to him** su familia era muy importante para él • **your country is very ~ to me** tengo su país en mucha estima • **it is a subject ~ to her heart** es uno de sus temas preferidos; ▹ **life**
4 (*in letter writing*) • **Dear Daddy** Querido papá • **Dear Peter** Estimado Peter; (*to closer friend*) Querido Peter • **Dear Mr/Mrs Smith** Estimado Sr./Estimada Sra. Smith; (*more formally*) Distinguido Sr./Distinguida Sra. Smith • **Dear Mr and Mrs Smith** Estimados señores (de) Smith • **Dear Madam** Estimada Señora, Muy señora mía, De mi/nuestra consideración (*esp LAm*) • **Dear Sir(s)** Estimado(s) Señor(es), Muy señor(es) mío(s), De mi/nuestra consideración (*esp LAm*) • **Dear Sir or Madam** Estimado Señor(a)
5 (*form of address*) querido • **my ~ fellow, I won't hear of it!** amigo mío *or* mi querido amigo, ni se le ocurra • **my ~ girl, nothing could be further from the truth** querida, estás muy equivocada
6 (= *expensive*) [*product, shop, price*] caro • **~ money** (*Econ*) dinero *m* caro
(EXCL) • **~, ~, have you hurt your knee?** ¡ay, mi niño! ¿te has hecho daño en la rodilla? • **~ me, it's nearly one o'clock!** ¡madre mía, es casi la una! • **oh ~, we're going to be late** vaya hombre *or* vaya por Dios, vamos a llegar tarde • **~, oh ~, look at the mess you're in!** ay, Dios mío *or* qué horror, ¡mira qué desastre vienes hecho!
(N)* (*as form of address*) cariño *m* • **come along, ~** ven, cariño • **would you be a ~ and pass me my book?** anda, sé bueno y pásame el libro • **(you) poor ~!** ¡pobrecito! • **he's such a ~** es un cielo, es un encanto
(ADV) [*sell, buy, pay*] caro

dearest ['dɪərɪst] (N) (= *darling*) queridísimo/a *m/f*
(ADJ) **1** (= *darling*) [*person*] queridísimo • **~ Paul** queridísimo Paul • **~ Maria** queridísima María
2 (= *most cherished*) [*hope, wish*] mayor • **my ~ hope** mi mayor esperanza • **my ~ wish** mi mayor deseo; ▹ **near**

dearie* ['dɪərɪ] (N) (*esp Brit*) (= *form of address*) cariño *m*; (*as excl*) • **~ me!** ¡madre mía!

dearly ['dɪəlɪ] (ADV) **1** (= *very much*) mucho, de verdad • **I loved him ~** lo quería mucho *or* de verdad • **I should ~ love to go** me encantaría ir • **his ~ beloved wife** su amada esposa • **~ beloved, we are gathered here today ...** queridos *or* amados hermanos, estamos aquí reunidos hoy ... • **the ~ departed** (*frm*) el queridísimo difunto/la queridísima difunta
2 (= *at great cost*) caro • **victory for the Russians was ~ bought** los rusos pagaron un precio muy alto por la victoria • **to cost sb ~** costar caro a algn • **it cost him ~** le costó caro • **to pay ~ for sth** pagar algo caro • **he paid ~ for his mistake** pagó caro su error

dearness ['dɪənɪs] (N) (= *expensiveness*) alto precio *m*, lo caro

dearth [dɜ:θ] (N) [*of food, resources, money*] escasez *f*; [*of ideas*] carencia *f*

death [deθ] (N) **1** muerte *f*, fallecimiento *m* • **to be in at the ~** (*Hunting*) ver el final de la caza • **it will be the ~ of him** (*lit*) será su perdición • **you'll be the ~ of me** (*fig*) vas a acabar conmigo • **till ~ us do part** hasta que la muerte nos separe • **this is ~ to our hopes** esto acaba con nuestras esperanzas • **it was ~ to the company** arruinó la empresa • **~ to traitors!** ¡muerte a los traidores! • **a fight to the ~** una lucha a muerte • **to fight to the ~**

luchar a muerte • IDIOMS: • **to catch one's ~ (of cold)** coger un catarro de muerte • **to be at ~'s door** estar a las puertas de la muerte • **to hold on like grim ~** estar firmemente agarrado; (*fig*) resistir con la mayor firmeza • **to look like ~ warmed up** *or* (*US*) **warmed over*** estar muy demacrado, estar hecho una pena

2 • **to ~: to be bored to ~*** estar muerto de aburrimiento • **it frightens me to ~** me da un miedo espantoso • **to put sb to ~** dar muerte a algn • **to sentence sb to ~** condenar a algn a muerte • **I'm sick to ~ of it*** estoy hasta la coronilla de ello • **he's working himself to ~** trabaja tanto que va a acabar con su vida • **he works his men to ~** a sus hombres los mata a trabajar • **it worries me to ~** me preocupa muchísimo

CPD ▸ **death benefit** (*Insurance*) indemnización *f* por fallecimiento ▸ **death blow** golpe *m* mortal ▸ **death by misadventure** (*Brit*) muerte *f* accidental ▸ **death camp** campo *m* de exterminio ▸ **death cell** celda *f* de los condenados a muerte ▸ **death certificate** partida *f* de defunción ▸ **death duties** (*Brit*) impuesto *m* de sucesiones ▸ **death house** (*US*) pabellón *m* de los condenados a muerte ▸ **death knell** toque *m* de difuntos, doble *m* • **it sounded the ~ knell of the empire** (*fig*) anunció el fin del imperio, presagió la caída del imperio ▸ **death march** marcha *f* fúnebre ▸ **death mask** mascarilla *f* ▸ **death penalty** pena *f* de muerte ▸ **death rate** tasa *f* de mortalidad, mortalidad *f* ▸ **death rattle** estertor *m* ▸ **death ray** rayo *m* mortal ▸ **death roll** número *m* de víctimas, lista *f* de víctimas ▸ **death row** (*US*) celdas *fpl* de los condenados a muerte, corredor *m* de la muerte ▸ **death sentence** pena *f* de muerte ▸ **death squad** escuadrón *m* de la muerte ▸ **death taxes** (*US*) impuesto *msing* de sucesiones ▸ **death threat** amenaza *f* de muerte ▸ **death throes** agonía *fsing* ▸ **death toll** número *m* de víctimas ▸ **death warrant** orden *f* de ejecución • IDIOM: • **to sign one's own ~ warrant** firmar su sentencia de muerte ▸ **death wish** ganas *fpl* de morir

deathbed [ˈdeθbed] N lecho *m* de muerte • **on one's ~** en su lecho de muerte

CPD ▸ **deathbed confession** confesión *f* en el lecho de muerte ▸ **deathbed conversion** conversión *f* in artículo mortis ▸ **deathbed repentance** arrepentimiento *m* de última hora

death-dealing [ˈdeθdiːlɪŋ] ADJ (*liter*) [*blow, missile*] mortífero, letal

deathless [ˈdeθlɪs] ADJ inmortal

deathlike [ˈdeθlaɪk] ADJ como de muerto, cadavérico

deathly [ˈdeθlɪ] ADJ (COMPAR: **deathlier**, SUPERL: **deathliest**) [*appearance, pallor*] cadavérico; [*silence*] sepulcral

ADV • **~ pale** pálido como un muerto

death's-head [ˈdeθshed] N calavera *f*

CPD ▸ **death's-head moth** mariposa *f* de la muerte

deathtrap [ˈdeθtræp] N (= *place*) lugar *m* peligroso; (= *vehicle*) vehículo *m* peligroso • **this car's a ~** este coche es un peligro *or* una trampa mortal

deathwatch [ˌdeθwɒtʃ] N (*also* **deathwatch beetle**) (escarabajo *m* del) reloj *m* de la muerte

deb* [deb] N = **debutante**

debacle, débâcle [deɪˈbɑːkl] N debacle *f*, desastre *m*; (*Mil*) derrota *f*

debag [ˈdiːˈbæg] VT (*Brit*) (*hum*) quitar (violentamente) los pantalones a

debar [dɪˈbɑːʳ] VT excluir, expulsar • **to ~ sb from sth** excluir a algn de algo • **to ~ sb from doing sth** prohibir a algn hacer algo

debark [dɪˈbɑːk] VI (*US*) desembarcar

debarkation [diːbɑːˈkeɪʃən] N (*US*) desembarco *m*

debarment [dɪˈbɑːmənt] N exclusión *f*, expulsión *f*

debase [dɪˈbeɪs] VT **1** (= *degrade*) [+ *language*] corromper; [+ *person, culture, tradition*] degradar • **to ~ o.s. (by doing sth)** degradarse (haciendo algo)

2 (= *devalue*) [+ *currency*] devaluar

debasement [dɪˈbeɪsmənt] N **1** [*of language*] corrupción *f*; [*of person, culture, tradition*] degradación *f*

2 [*of currency*] devaluación *f*

debatable [dɪˈbeɪtəbl] ADJ discutible

debate [dɪˈbeɪt] VT [+ *topic, question, idea*] debatir, discutir

VI discutir, debatir • **to ~ with sb (about** *or* **on** *or* **upon sth)** discutir con algn (sobre algo) • **to ~ with o.s. (about** *or* **on** *or* **upon sth)** vacilar (sobre algo) • **we ~d whether to go or not** dudamos *or* nos planteamos si ir o no

N debate *m*, discusión *f* • **after much ~** después de mucho discutir • **that is open to ~** ese es un tema discutido

debater [dɪˈbeɪtəʳ] N polemista *mf* • **he was a brilliant ~** brillaba en los debates

debating [dɪˈbeɪtɪŋ] N • **~ is a difficult skill to learn** el saber debatir es una habilidad difícil de adquirir

CPD ▸ **debating chamber** cámara *f* de debates ▸ **debating society** círculo *m* de debates

debauch [dɪˈbɔːtʃ] VT [+ *person, morals, taste*] depravar, corromper; [+ *woman*] seducir

debauched [dɪˈbɔːtʃt] ADJ depravado, libertino

debaucher [dɪˈbɔːtʃəʳ] N [*of person, taste, morals*] corruptor *m*; [*of woman*] seductor *m*

debauchery [dɪˈbɔːtʃərɪ] N libertinaje *m*, depravación *f*

debenture [dɪˈbentʃəʳ] N (*Econ*) bono *m*, obligación *f*

CPD ▸ **debenture bond** obligación *f* ▸ **debenture capital** capital *m* en obligaciones ▸ **debenture holder** obligacionista *mf* ▸ **debenture stock** obligaciones *fpl*

debilitate [dɪˈbɪlɪteɪt] VT debilitar

debilitated [dɪˈbɪlɪteɪtɪd] ADJ debilitado

debilitating [dɪˈbɪlɪteɪtɪŋ] ADJ debilitante, que debilita

debility [dɪˈbɪlɪtɪ] N debilidad *f*

debit [ˈdebɪt] N (*in the books of a business*) pasivo *m*; (*in a bank account*) debe *m*, débito *m*; (= *individual sum taken*) cargo *m*

VT • **to ~ an account with a sum** cargar una suma en cuenta • **to ~ sb with a sum** cargar una suma en la cuenta de algn • **to ~ an account directly** domiciliar una cuenta; ▷ **direct**

CPD ▸ **debit balance** saldo *m* deudor ▸ **debit card** tarjeta *f* de débito ▸ **debit entry** débito *m* ▸ **debit note** nota *f* de cargo ▸ **debit side** debe *m*; (*fig*) desventaja *f* • **on the ~ side** (*lit*) en el debe; (*fig*) entre las desventajas

deboard [dɪˈbɔːd] (*US*) VI (*from train, bus, plane, boat*) desembarcar

VT [+ *train, bus, plane, boat*] desembarcar de; [+ *passengers*] desembarcar

debonair [ˌdebəˈnɛəʳ] ADJ (= *elegant*) gallardo; (= *courteous*) cortés; (= *cheerful*) alegre

debone [diːˈbəʊn] VT [+ *meat*] deshuesar; [+ *fish*] quitar las espinas a

Deborah [ˈdebərə] N Débora

debouch [dɪˈbaʊtʃ] VI (*frm*) • **to ~ into** [*river*] desembocar en

Debrett [dəˈbret] N *libro de referencia de la aristocracia del Reino Unido*; (*loosely*) anuario *m* de la nobleza

debrief [ˌdiːˈbriːf] VT hacer dar parte

debriefing [ˌdiːˈbriːfɪŋ] N informe *m* sobre una operación *etc*

debris [ˈdebriː] N [*of building, construction*] escombros *mpl*; [*of aeroplane*] restos *mpl*; (*Geol*) rocalla *f*

debt [det] N **1** (= *money owed*) deuda *f* • **bad ~** deuda incobrable • **foreign ~** (*Pol*) deuda *f* externa *or* exterior • **a ~ of honour** una deuda de honor • **to be in ~ (to sb)** tener deudas *or* estar endeudado (con algn) • **I am five pounds in ~** debo cinco libras (**to a**) • **to get into ~** • **run into ~** • **run up ~s** contraer deudas • **to be out of ~** tener las deudas saldadas

2 (*fig*) • **a ~ of gratitude** una deuda de agradecimiento • **to be in sb's ~** estar en deuda con algn

CPD ▸ **debt burden** peso *m* de la deuda ▸ **debt collection** cobro *m* de morosos ▸ **debt collector** cobrador(a) *m/f* de morosos ▸ **debt forgiveness** perdón *m* de la deuda ▸ **debt ratio** tasa *f* de endeudamiento ▸ **debt relief** alivio *m* de deuda ▸ **debt repayment** (*by individual, country*) pago *m* de deudas ▸ **debt service, debt servicing** (*US*) amortización *f* de la deuda

debt-laden [ˈdetleɪdən] ADJ agobiado por las deudas

debtor [ˈdetəʳ] N deudor(a) *m/f*

CPD ▸ **debtor nation** nación *f* deudora

debt-ridden [ˈdetˌrɪdn] ADJ agobiado por las deudas

debug [ˌdiːˈbʌg] VT **1** (*Tech*) resolver los problemas de, suprimir las pegas de; (*Comput*) depurar, quitar los fallos a

2 (= *remove mikes from*) quitar los micrófonos ocultos de

debugger [ˌdiːˈbʌgəʳ] N (*Comput*) programa *m* de depuración

debugging [ˌdiːˈbʌgɪŋ] N (*Comput*) depuración *f*

debunk [ˈdiːˈbʌŋk] VT [+ *theory, claim, person, institution*] desacreditar

debut, début [ˈdeɪbuː] N (*Theat*) (= *first appearance*) debut *m*, presentación *f*; (*fig*) primer acto *m* • **to make one's ~** (*Theat*) debutar, hacer su presentación; (*in society*) presentarse en sociedad, ponerse de largo

VI [*artist, actor*] debutar; [*film, play*] estrenarse

CPD ▸ **debut album** (*Mus*) álbum *m* de debut, álbum *m* de presentación ▸ **debut appearance** [*of actor, player*] debut *m* ▸ **debut single** [*of singer, group*] primer single *m*

debutante, débutante [ˈdebjuːtɑ̃ːnt] N joven *f* que se presenta en sociedad, debutante *f*

Dec ABBR (= **December**) dic., dic.ᵉ, D.

dec. ABBR = **deceased**

decade [ˈdekeɪd] N década *f*, decenio *m*

decadence [ˈdekədəns] N decadencia *f*

decadent [ˈdekədənt] ADJ [*habits, person*] decadente

decaff*, decaf* [ˈdiːkæf] N (= *decaffeinated coffee*) descafeinado *m*

decaffeinated [ˌdiːˈkæfɪneɪtɪd] ADJ [*beverage, tea*] sin cafeína

CPD ▸ **decaffeinated coffee** café *m* descafeinado, descafeinado *m*

decagram, decagramme [ˈdekəgræm] N decagramo *m*

decal [dɪˈkæl] N (*US*) calcomanía *f*

decalcification [ˈdiːˌkælsɪfɪˈkeɪʃən] N descalcificación *f*

decalcify [ˌdiːˈkælsɪfaɪ] VT descalcificar

d

decalitre, **decaliter** (US) ['dekə,li:təʳ] N decalitro *m*
Decalogue ['dekəlɒg] N • **the ~** el Decálogo
decametre, **decameter** (US) ['dekə,mi:təʳ] N decámetro *m*
decamp [dɪ'kæmp] VI **1** (*Mil*) levantar el campamento
2* (= *make off*) escaparse; (= *move*) irse (**to** a)
decant [dɪ'kænt] VT [+ *wine etc*] decantar
decanter [dɪ'kæntəʳ] N licorera *f*
decapitate [dɪ'kæpɪteɪt] VT decapitar
decapitation [dɪ,kæpɪ'teɪʃən] N decapitación *f*, degollación *f*
decarbonization ['di:,kɑ:bənaɪ'zeɪʃən] N (*Aut*) descarburación *f*; [*of steel*] descarbonación *f*
decarbonize [di:'kɑ:bənaɪz] VT (*Aut*) descarburar
decasyllable ['dekəsɪləbl] N decasílabo *m*
decathlete [dɪ'kæθli:t] N decatlonista *mf*, decatleta *mf*
decathlon [dɪ'kæθlən] N decatlón *m*
decay [dɪ'keɪ] N **1** [*of vegetation, food*] putrefacción *f*, descomposición *f*; [*of teeth*] caries *f*; [*of building*] desmoronamiento *m*, ruina *f*
2 (*fig*) [*of civilization*] decadencia *f*; [*of faculties*] deterioro *m*
VI **1** (= *rot*) [*leaves, food*] pudrirse, descomponerse; [*teeth*] cariarse; [*building*] desmoronarse
2 (*fig*) [*civilization*] decaer, estar en decadencia; [*faculties*] deteriorarse
VT [+ *vegetation, food*] pudrir, descomponer; [+ *teeth*] cariar
decayed [dɪ'keɪd] ADJ **1** [*wood, food*] podrido; [*tooth*] cariado
2 (*fig*) [*family*] venido a menos
decaying [dɪ'keɪɪŋ] ADJ **1** [*food*] podrido, en estado de descomposición; [*vegetation*] podrido; [*flesh*] en estado de descomposición, en descomposición; [*tooth*] cariado; [*building*] muy deteriorado, ruinoso; [*stone*] que se descompone
2 (*fig*) [*civilization*] decadente, en decadencia
decease [dɪ'si:s] (*frm*) N fallecimiento *m*, defunción *f*
VI fallecer
deceased [dɪ'si:st] ADJ (*Jur, Police*) difunto
N • **the ~** el/la difunto/a
deceit [dɪ'si:t] N (= *misleading*) engaño *m*; (= *fraud*) fraude *m*; (= *deceitfulness*) falsedad *f* • **he was involved in a web of lies and ~** estaba metido en una maraña de mentiras y engaños • **they won the voters over by ~** conquistaron a los votantes engañándolos *or* mediante engaños
deceitful [dɪ'si:tfʊl] ADJ [*person*] falso; [*child*] mentiroso; [*statement, behaviour*] engañoso
deceitfully [dɪ'si:tfəlɪ] ADV engañosamente
deceitfulness [dɪ'si:tʃʊlnɪs] N falsedad *f*
deceive [dɪ'si:v] VT engañar • **she ~d me into thinking that …** me engañó, haciéndome pensar que … • **don't be ~d by appearances** no te dejes engañar por las apariencias • **let nobody be ~d by this** que nadie se llame a engaño por esto • **he thought his eyes were deceiving him** no creía lo que veían sus ojos • **if my memory does not ~ me** si mal no recuerdo • **to ~ o.s.** engañarse
deceiver [dɪ'si:vəʳ] N impostor(a) *m/f*, embustero/a *m/f*; [*of women*] seductor *m*
decelerate [di:'seləreɪt] VI (*Aut*) desacelerar, decelerar; (*fig*) frenarse, ralentizarse
deceleration ['di:,selə'reɪʃən] N desaceleración *f*, deceleración *f*, disminución *f* de velocidad
December [dɪ'sembəʳ] N diciembre *m*; ▹ **July**
decency ['di:sənsɪ] N **1** (= *propriety*) decencia *f*, decoro *m* • **to have a sense of ~** tener sentido del decoro • **offence against ~** atentado *m* contra el pudor
2 (= *politeness*) educación *f* • **it is no more than common ~ to let him know** hay que avisarle, aunque solo sea por una cuestión de educación
3 (= *kindness*) bondad *f*, amabilidad *f* • **he had the ~ to phone me** tuvo la amabilidad de llamarme
4 decencies buenas costumbres *fpl*
decent ['di:sənt] ADJ **1** (= *respectable*) [*person, house*] decente; (= *proper*) [*clothes, behaviour, language*] decoroso, decente • **are you ~?** (*hum*) ¿estás visible?
2 (= *kind*) amable • **he was very ~ to me** fue muy amable conmigo, se portó muy bien conmigo • **he's a ~ sort** es buena persona
3 (= *passable*) [*salary, meal*] adecuado, decente • **a ~ sum** una cantidad considerable
decenter [di:'sentəʳ] VT (US) = **decentre**
decently ['di:səntlɪ] ADV **1** (= *respectably*) decentemente, decorosamente
2 (= *kindly*) amablemente, con amabilidad • **he very ~ offered it to me** muy amablemente me lo ofreció
decentralization [di:,sentrəlaɪ'zeɪʃən] N descentralización *f*
decentralize [di:'sentrəlaɪz] VT descentralizar
decentralized [di:'sentrəlaɪzd] ADJ descentralizado
decentre, **decenter** (US) [di:'sentəʳ] VT descentrar
deception [dɪ'sepʃən] N engaño *m*
deceptive [dɪ'septɪv] ADJ engañoso
deceptively [dɪ'septɪvlɪ] ADV • **the village looks ~ near** el pueblo parece engañosamente cerca • **he was ~ obedient** no era tan sumiso como parecía
deceptiveness [dɪ'septɪvnɪs] N carácter *m* engañoso
decibel ['desɪbel] N decibelio *m*
decide [dɪ'saɪd] VT (*gen*) decidir • **to ~ where to go/what to do** decidir adónde ir/qué hacer • **to ~ to do sth** decidir hacer algo • **it was ~d that** se decidió que • **that ~d me** eso me convenció
VI decidir, decidirse • **to ~ against sth** decidirse en contra de algo • **to ~ against doing sth** decidirse en contra de hacer algo, decidir no hacer algo • **to ~ for** *or* **in favour of sb** decidirse por algn, decidir a favor de algn • **to ~ in favour of sth** decidirse por algo • **to ~ in favour of doing sth** determinar *or* resolver hacer algo • **the judge ~d in his favour** el juez decidió *or* resolvió a su favor
▸ **decide on** VI + PREP • **to ~ on sth** decidirse por algo • **to ~ on doing sth** decidir hacer algo
decided [dɪ'saɪdɪd] ADJ **1** (= *distinct*) [*difference, improvement*] indudable, marcado
2 (= *categorical*) [*person, tone, manner*] resuelto, decidido; [*opinion*] firme, categórico
decidedly [dɪ'saɪdɪdlɪ] ADV **1** (= *without doubt*) indudablemente, sin duda; (= *very, markedly*) decididamente • **it is ~ difficult** indudablemente es difícil
2 (= *resolutely*) con resolución, con decisión
decider [dɪ'saɪdəʳ] N (*Brit*) (*Sport*) (= *game*) partido *m* decisivo; (= *replay*) partido *m* de desempate, desempate *m*; (= *point, goal*) gol *m etc* decisivo
deciding [dɪ'saɪdɪŋ] ADJ decisivo, determinante • **the ~ factor** el factor decisivo *or* determinante • **the ~ goal/point** el gol/punto decisivo • **the ~ vote** el voto decisivo
deciduous [dɪ'sɪdjʊəs] ADJ [*tree*] de hoja caduca
decile ['desɪl] N decil *m*
decilitre, **deciliter** (US) ['desɪ,li:təʳ] N decilitro *m*
decimal ['desɪməl] ADJ decimal • **to three ~ places** con tres decimales
N decimal *m*
CPD ▸ **decimal currency** moneda *f* decimal ▸ **decimal fraction** fracción *f* decimal ▸ **decimal point** coma *f* decimal, coma *f* de decimales ▸ **decimal system** sistema *m* métrico decimal
decimalization [,desɪməlaɪ'zeɪʃən] N conversión *f* al sistema decimal, decimalización *f*
decimalize ['desɪməlaɪz] VT convertir al sistema decimal
decimate ['desɪmeɪt] VT (*lit, fig*) diezmar
decimation [,desɪ'meɪʃən] N (*lit, fig*) aniquilación *f*
decimetre, **decimeter** (US) ['desɪ,mi:təʳ] N decímetro *m*
decipher [dɪ'saɪfəʳ] VT (*lit, fig*) descifrar
decipherable [dɪ'saɪfərəbl] ADJ descifrable
decision [dɪ'sɪʒən] N **1** (*after consideration*) decisión *f*, determinación *f*; (*Jur*) fallo *m* • **to come to** *or* **reach a ~** llegar a una decisión • **to make** *or* **take a ~** tomar *or* adoptar una decisión
2 (= *resoluteness*) resolución *f*, decisión *f*
CPD ▸ **decision table** (*Comput*) tabla *f* de decisiones ▸ **decision time** hora *f* de tomar una decisión • **now it's ~ time** es hora de tomar una decisión
decision-maker [dɪ'sɪʒən,meɪkəʳ] N persona *f* que toma decisiones
decision-making [dɪ'sɪʒən,meɪkɪŋ] N toma *f* de decisiones • **he's good at decision-making** es bueno tomando decisiones
CPD ▸ **decision-making process** proceso *m* decisorio ▸ **decision-making unit** unidad *f* de adopción de decisiones
decisive [dɪ'saɪsɪv] ADJ **1** (= *conclusive*) [*victory, factor, influence*] decisivo, determinante
2 (= *resolute*) [*manner, reply*] decidido, tajante; [*person*] decidido, resuelto
decisively [dɪ'saɪsɪvlɪ] ADV **1** (= *conclusively*) • **to be ~ beaten** ser derrotado de modo decisivo
2 (= *resolutely*) con decisión, con resolución
decisiveness [dɪ'saɪsɪvnɪs] N [*of manner, reply*] carácter *m* tajante; [*of person*] firmeza *f*, decisión *f*
deck [dek] N **1** (*Naut*) cubierta *f* • **to go up on ~** subir a la cubierta • **below ~** bajo cubierta
2 (= *wooden flooring*) suelo *m* de madera
3 [*of bus*] piso *m* • **top** *or* **upper ~** piso *m* de arriba • **bottom** *or* **lower ~** piso *m* de abajo
4 (*esp US*) [*of cards*] baraja *f*
5 (*also* **record deck**) tocadiscos *m inv*; (*also* **cassette deck**) pletina *f*
6 (US) (*Drugs**) saquito *m* de heroína
7 • IDIOMS: • **to clear the ~s** despejar el terreno • **to hit the ~*** caer al suelo
VT **1** (*also* **deck out**) [+ *room*] adornar, engalanar (**with** con); [+ *person*] ataviar, engalanar (**with** con) • **all ~ed out** [*room*] adornado, todo engalanado; [*person*] de punta en blanco
2‡ (= *knock down*) derribar de un golpe
CPD ▸ **deck cabin** cabina *f* de cubierta ▸ **deck cargo** carga *f* de cubierta ▸ **deck shoe** marino *m* (*zapato*)
deckchair ['dek,tʃɛəʳ] N tumbona *f*, perezosa *f* (*LAm*)
-decker ['dekəʳ] N (*ending in compounds*)

• **single-decker** (= *bus*) autobús *m* de un piso • **three-decker** (*Naut*) barco *m* de tres cubiertas; ▸ **double-decker**

deckhand ['dekhænd] N marinero *m* de cubierta

deckhouse ['dekhaʊs] N (PL: **deckhouses** ['dek,haʊzɪz]) camareta *f* alta

decking ['dekɪŋ] N suelo *m* de madera

declaim [dɪ'kleɪm] VI declamar VT declamar

declamation [,deklə'meɪʃən] N declamación *f*

declamatory [dɪ'klæmətərɪ] ADJ declamatorio

declarable [dɪ'klɛərəbl] ADJ [*goods*] declarable

declaration [,deklə'reɪʃən] N (*written*) declaración *f* • **~ of war/love** declaración de guerra/amor

CPD ▸ **the Declaration of Independence** (*US*) (*Hist*) la Declaración de Independencia (*de Estados Unidos*)

declare [dɪ'klɛəʳ] VT **1** [+ *intentions, love*] declarar; [+ *dividend, result*] anunciar • **she ~d that she knew nothing about it** declaró *or* manifestó que no sabía nada al respecto • **to ~ war (on** *or* **against sb)** declarar la guerra (a algn) • **to ~ o.s.** declararse • **to ~ o.s. against/in favour of sth** pronunciarse *or* declararse en contra de/a favor de algo • **he ~d himself beaten** se dio por vencido • **to ~ o.s. surprised** confesar su sorpresa

2 (*Econ*) [+ *income*] declarar • **to ~ sth to the customs** declarar algo en la aduana • **have you anything to ~?** ¿tiene usted algo que declarar?

3 (*Bridge*) declarar

VI **1** (= *pronounce*) • **to ~ for • ~ in favour of** pronunciarse a favor de

2 (*in exclamation*) • **well, I ~!**† ¡vaya por Dios!

3 (*Bridge*) declarar

declared [dɪ'klɛəd] ADJ declarado, abierto

declaredly [dɪ'klɛərɪdlɪ] ADV declaradamente

declarer [dɪ'klɛərəʳ] N (*Bridge*) declarante *mf*

déclassé [deɪ'klæseɪ] ADJ desprestigiado, empobrecido

declassification [dɪ,klæsɪfɪ'keɪʃən] N [*of information*] desclasificación *f*

declassify [di:'klæsɪfaɪ] VT [+ *information*] levantar el secreto oficial que pesa sobre

declension [dɪ'klenʃən] N (*Ling*) declinación *f*

declinable [dɪ'klaɪnəbl] ADJ declinable

decline [dɪ'klaɪn] N **1** (= *decrease*) (*in numbers, sales*) descenso *m*, disminución *f* (**in** de); (*in support, interest*) disminución *f* • **to be on the ~** ir disminuyendo

2 (= *deterioration*) decadencia *f*, declive *m*, deterioro *m*; (*in standards*) descenso *m*, declive *m*; (*Med*) debilitamiento *m* • **the ~ of the Roman Empire** la decadencia del Imperio Romano • **to fall into ~** [*industry, town*] entrar en decadencia, entrar en declive • **to go into a ~** (*Med*) ir debilitándose

VT **1** (= *refuse*) rehusar, rechazar, declinar (*frm*) • **to ~ to do sth** rehusar hacer algo, declinar hacer algo (*frm*)

2 (*Ling*) declinar

VI **1** (= *decrease*) [*power, influence*] disminuir; (= *deteriorate*) decaer; (*in health*) debilitarse, decaer • **to ~ in importance** ir perdiendo importancia

2 (= *refuse*) negarse, rehusar

3 (*Ling*) declinarse

declining [dɪ'klaɪnɪŋ] ADJ [*industry*] en decadencia • **~ interest** pérdida *f* de interés • **in my ~ years** en mis últimos años

declivity [dɪ'klɪvɪtɪ] N declive *m*

declutch ['di:'klʌtʃ] VI desembragar • **to double ~** hacer un doble desembrague

decoction [dɪ'kɒkʃən] N decocción *f*

decode ['di:'kəʊd] VT descifrar; (*Ling, TV*) descodificar

decoder [di:'kəʊdəʳ] N (*Comput, TV*) descodificador *m*

decoding [di:'kəʊdɪŋ] N (*Comput*) descodificación *f*

decoke (*Brit*) (*Aut*) N ['di:kəʊk] descarburación *f*

VT [di:'kəʊk] descarburar

decollate [,di:kə'leɪt] VT separar, alzar

décolletage [deɪ'kɒlətɑ:ʒ] N escote *m*

décolleté, décolletée [deɪ'kɒlteɪ] ADJ [*dress*] escotado; [*woman*] en traje escotado

decolonization [di:,kɒlənaɪ'zeɪʃən] N descolonización *f*

decolonize [di:'kɒlənaɪz] VT descolonizar

decommission [,di:kə'mɪʃən] VT [+ *nuclear power station*] desmantelar; [+ *warship, aircraft, weapon*] desguazar, desmantelar

decommissioning [,di:kə'mɪʃənɪŋ] N [*of nuclear power station*] desmantelamiento *m*; [*of warship, aircraft, weapon*] desguace *m*, desmantelamiento *m*

decompartmentalization [,di:kɒmpɑ:t-,mentəlaɪ'zeɪʃən] N descompartimentación *f*

decompartmentalize [,di:kɒmpɑ:t-'mentəlaɪz] VT descompartimentar

decompose [,di:kəm'pəʊz] VT (= *rot*) descomponer, pudrir

VI descomponerse, pudrirse

decomposed [,di:kəm'pəʊzd] ADJ [*body*] descompuesto; [*plant*] podrido

decomposition [,di:kɒmpə'zɪʃən] N descomposición *f*, putrefacción *f*

decompress [,di:kəm'pres] VT descomprimir

decompression [,di:kəm'preʃən] N descompresión *f*

CPD ▸ **decompression chamber** cámara *f* de descompresión ▸ **decompression sickness** aeroembolismo *m*, embolia *f* gaseosa

decongestant [,di:kən'dʒestənt] N anticongestivo *m*, descongestionante *m*

decongestion [,di:kən'dʒestʃən] N descongestión *f*

deconsecrate [,di:'kɒnsɪkreɪt] VT secularizar

deconstruct [,di:kən'strʌkt] VT deconstruir

deconstruction [,di:kən'strʌkʃən] N deconstrucción *f*

decontaminate [,di:kən'tæmɪneɪt] VT descontaminar

decontamination ['di:kən,tæmɪ'neɪʃən] N descontaminación *f*

decontextualize [,di:kən'tekstjʊəlaɪz] VT descontextualizar

decontrol [,di:kən'trəʊl] N liberalización *f*

VT (*esp US*) [+ *prices, trade*] liberalizar

décor ['deɪkɔ:ʳ] N [*of house, room etc*] decoración *f*; (*Theat*) decorado *m*

decorate ['dekəreɪt] VT **1** (= *adorn*) decorar, adornar (**with** de)

2 (= *paint*) [+ *room, house*] pintar; (= *paper*) empapelar

3 (= *honour*) condecorar

decorating ['dekəreɪtɪŋ] N • **I got someone in to do the ~** traje a una persona para que pintara/empapelara la casa • **interior ~** decoración *f* de interiores, interiorismo *m*

decoration [,dekə'reɪʃən] N **1** (= *act*) decoración *f*

2 (= *ornament*) adorno *m*

3 (= *medal*) condecoración *f*

decorative ['dekərətɪv] ADJ (*in function*) de adorno, decorativo; (= *pleasant*) hermoso, elegante

CPD ▸ **decorative arts** artes *fpl* decorativas

decorator ['dekəreɪtəʳ] N (= *painter and decorator*) pintor *m* empapelador; (= *interior decorator*) interiorista *mf*, decorador(a) *m/f*

decorous ['dekərəs] ADJ [*behaviour, appearance*] decoroso

decorously ['dekərəslɪ] ADV decorosamente

decorum [dɪ'kɔ:rəm] N decoro *m*

decouple [di:'kʌpl] VT (*frm*) escindir (*frm*), desconectar

decoy N ['di:kɔɪ] (= *bird*) (*artificial*) señuelo *m*, reclamo *m*; (*live*) cimbel *m*, señuelo *m*, reclamo *m*; (*fig*) (= *bait*) cebo *m*, señuelo *m*

VT [dɪ'kɔɪ] atraer (con señuelo)

CPD ['di:kɔɪ] ▸ **decoy duck** pato *m* de reclamo

decrease N ['di:kri:s] (*gen*) disminución *f*, reducción *f*; (*in wages*) descenso *m*, bajada *f*; (*in prices*) bajada *f*, disminución *f* • **a ~ in speed/strength** una reducción de velocidad/fuerza • **a ~ of 50%** una reducción del 50% • **to be on the ~** ir disminuyendo

VT [di:'kri:s] [+ *quantity, pressure, dose, speed*] disminuir, reducir; [+ *wages*] bajar, reducir

VI [di:'kri:s] **1** [*power, strength, popularity, temperature, pressure*] disminuir; [*enthusiasm, interest*] disminuir, decaer • **to ~ by 10%** bajar *or* disminuir un 10%

2 (*Knitting*) menguar

decreasing [di:'kri:sɪŋ] ADJ decreciente

decreasingly [di:'kri:sɪŋlɪ] ADV decrecientemente

decree [dɪ'kri:] N decreto *m* • **to issue a ~** promulgar un decreto • **~ absolute/nisi** (= *divorce*) sentencia *f* definitiva/condicional de divorcio

VT (*gen*) decretar

decrepit [dɪ'krepɪt] ADJ [*person*] decrépito; [*building*] deteriorado, en mal estado

decrepitude [dɪ'krepɪtju:d] N [*of person*] decrepitud *f*; [*of building*] deterioro *m*, mal estado *m*

decriminalization [,di:'krɪmɪnəlaɪ'zeɪʃən] N despenalización *f*

decriminalize [di:'krɪmɪnəlaɪz] VT despenalizar

decry [dɪ'kraɪ] VT (= *strongly criticize*) criticar, censurar; (= *belittle*) menospreciar

decrypt [di:'krɪpt] VT (*Comput, Telec*) descodificar, descifrar

decryption [di:'krɪpʃən] N (*Comput, TV*) descodificación *f*, descifrado *m*

CPD ▸ **decryption software** software *m* de descodificación

dedicate ['dedɪkeɪt] VT **1** [+ *book*] dedicar (**to** a); [+ *church, monument*] dedicar, consagrar (**to** a) • **to ~ one's life to sth/to doing sth** dedicar *or* consagrar su vida a algo/a hacer algo • **to ~ o.s. to sth/to doing sth** dedicarse *or* consagrarse a algo/a hacer algo

2 (*US*) (= *inaugurate*) [+ *official building*] inaugurar oficialmente

dedicated ['dedɪkeɪtɪd] ADJ **1** [*person*] totalmente entregado • **a very ~ teacher** un maestro totalmente entregado a su trabajo • **~ followers of classical music** devotos seguidores de la música clásica

2 (*Comput*) especializado, dedicado

dedication [,dedɪ'keɪʃən] N **1** (= *act*) dedicación *f*, consagración *f*

2 (= *quality*) dedicación *f*, entrega *f*, devoción *f*

3 (*in book*) dedicatoria *f*

deduce [dɪ'dju:s] VT deducir • **to ~ sth from sth** deducir algo de algo • **what do you ~**

from that? ¿qué conclusión sacas de eso? • **to ~ (from sth) that …** deducir (de algo) que … • **as can be ~d from** según se deduce *or* se desprende de

deducible [dɪ'dju:sɪbl] ADJ deducible (**from** de)

deduct [dɪ'dʌkt] VT restar, descontar (**from** de); [*+ tax*] deducir (**from** de)

deductible [dɪ'dʌktəbl] ADJ deducible, descontable; (*for tax purposes*) desgravable, deducible

deduction [dɪ'dʌkʃən] N **1** (*= inference*) deducción *f*, conclusión *f* • **what are your ~s?** ¿cuáles son sus conclusiones?
2 (*= act of deducting*) deducción *f*; (*= amount deducted*) descuento *m* • **tax ~s** desgravaciones *fpl* fiscales, deducciones *fpl* fiscales

deductive [dɪ'dʌktɪv] ADJ deductivo

deed [di:d] N **1** (*= act*) acto *m*, acción *f*; (*= result*) hecho *m* • **brave ~** hazaña *f* • **good ~** buena acción *f*
2 (*Jur*) escritura *f* • **~ of covenant** *documento contractual mediante el que una persona se compromete a donar cantidades regulares de dinero a una entidad benéfica* • **~ of partnership** contrato *m* de sociedad • **~ of transfer** escritura *f* de traspaso
VT (*US*) (*Jur*) [*+ property*] transferir por acto notarial
CPD ▸ **deed poll** *escritura mediante la cual una persona se cambia el apellido oficialmente* • **to change one's name by ~ poll** cambiarse el apellido oficialmente

deejay* ['di:dʒeɪ] N pinchadiscos* *mf inv*

deem [di:m] VT (*frm*) juzgar, considerar • **she ~s it wise to …** considera prudente … • **he was ~ed to have consented** se juzgó que había dado su consentimiento

deep [di:p] ADJ (COMPAR: **deeper**, SUPERL: **deepest**) **1** (*= extending far down*) [*hole*] profundo, hondo; [*cut, wound, water*] profundo; [*pan, bowl, container*] hondo • **the water is two metres ~** el agua tiene una profundidad de dos metros • **they tramped through ~ snow** avanzaban con dificultad por una espesa capa de nieve • **the ~ end** (*of swimming pool*) lo hondo, la parte honda • **to be ~ in snow/water** estar hundido en la nieve/el agua • **he was waist-deep/thigh-deep in water** el agua le llegaba a la cintura/al muslo • **the van was axle-deep in mud** la furgoneta estaba metida en barro hasta el eje • **the snow lay ~** había una espesa capa de nieve • **a ~ or ~-pile carpet** una alfombra de pelo largo • IDIOMS: • **to go off (at) the ~ end*** enfadarse, ponerse de morros* • **I was thrown in (at) the ~ end*** me echaron *or* arrojaron a los leones* • **to be in ~ water** estar hasta el cuello (de problemas)
2 (*= extending far back*) [*shelf, cupboard*] hondo; [*border, hem*] ancho • **a cupboard a metre ~** un armario de un metro de fondo • **a plot 30 metres ~** un terreno de 30 metros de fondo • **the spectators were standing six ~** los espectadores estaban de pie de seis en fondo
3 (*= immersed*) • **to be ~ in debt** estar cargado de deudas • **to be ~ in thought/in a book** estar sumido *or* absorto en sus pensamientos/en la lectura
4 (*= low-pitched*) [*voice*] grave, profundo; [*note, sound*] grave
5 (*= intense*) [*emotion, relaxation, concern*] profundo; [*recession*] grave; [*sigh*] profundo, hondo • **to take a ~ breath** respirar profundamente *or* hondo *or* a pleno pulmón • **the play made a ~ impression on me** la obra me impresionó profundamente • **to be in ~ mourning** estar de luto riguroso • **she fell into a ~ sleep** se quedó profundamente dormida • **they expressed their ~ sorrow at her loss** le expresaron su profundo pesar por la pérdida que había sufrido • **to be in ~ trouble** estar en grandes apuros
6 [*colour*] intenso, subido; [*tan*] intenso
7 (*= profound*) • **it's too ~ for me** no lo entiendo, no alcanzo a entenderlo • **they're adventure stories, they're not intended to be ~** son historias de aventuras, sin intención de ir más allá
8 (*= unfathomable*) [*secret, mystery*] bien guardado • **he's a ~ one*** es un misterio
ADV **1** (*= far down*) • **don't go in too ~ if you can't swim** no te metas muy hondo si no sabes nadar • **he thrust his hand ~ into his pocket** metió la mano hasta el fondo del bolsillo • **the company is sliding even ~er into the red** la empresa está cada vez más cargada de deudas • **~ down he's a bit of a softie** en el fondo es un poco blandengue • **to go ~**: • **his anger clearly went ~** la ira le había calado muy hondo • **I was in far too ~ to pull out now** ahora estaba demasiado metido para echarme atrás • **to run ~**: • **the roots of racial prejudice run ~** los prejuicios raciales están profundamente arraigados; ▹ **dig, still**
2 (*= a long way inside*) • **~ in the forest** en lo hondo *or* profundo del bosque • **he gazed ~ into her eyes** la miró profundamente a los ojos • **~ in one's heart** en lo más profundo del corazón • **~ in the heart of the countryside** en medio del campo • **they worked ~ into the night** trabajaron hasta muy entrada la noche
N (*liter*) **1** (*= sea*) • **the ~** el piélago • **creatures of the ~** criaturas *fpl* de las profundidades
2 (*= depths*) • **in the ~ of winter** en pleno invierno
CPD ▸ **deep breathing** gimnasia *f* respiratoria, ejercicios *mpl* respiratorios ▸ **deep clean** limpieza *f* a fondo ▸ **deep freeze, deep freezer** (*domestic*) congelador *m*; ▹ **deep-freeze** ▸ **deep fryer** freidora *f* ▸ **the Deep South** (*US*) los estados del sureste de EE.UU. ▸ **deep space** espacio *m* interplanetario ▸ **deep structure** (*Ling*) estructura *f* profunda ▸ **deep vein thrombosis** trombosis *f* venosa profunda

deep-chested ['di:p'tʃestɪd] ADJ ancho de pecho

deepen ['di:pən] VT [*+ hole*] hacer más profundo; [*+ voice*] hacer más grave, ahuecar; [*+ colour*] intensificar; [*+ understanding*] aumentar; [*+ love, friendship*] hacer más profundo *or* intenso, ahondar; [*+ crisis*] agudizar, acentuar
VI [*water*] hacerse más profundo *or* hondo; [*voice*] hacerse más grave *or* profundo; [*frown*] acentuarse; [*colour, emotion*] intensificarse; [*night*] avanzar, cerrarse; [*darkness*] hacerse más profundo; [*mystery, suspicion*] aumentar; [*understanding, love, friendship*] hacerse más profundo *or* intenso; [*crisis*] agudizarse, acentuarse • **the colour in her face ~ed** se puso aún más colorada

deepening ['di:pənɪŋ] ADJ [*darkness, gloom, conflict, division*] cada vez más profundo; [*unease*] cada vez mayor; [*friendship*] cada vez más profundo *or* intenso; [*crisis*] que se agudiza, que se acentúa

deep-fat fryer [ˌdi:pfæt'fraɪə^r] N freidora *f*

deep-felt ['di:p'felt] ADJ profundo • **a deep-felt need** una profunda necesidad

deep-freeze ['di:p'fri:z] VT (*at home*) congelar; (*in factory*) ultracongelar; ▹ **deep**

deep-freezing [ˌdi:p'fri:zɪŋ] N (*at home*) congelación *f*; (*in factory*) ultracongelación *f*

deep-fried ['di:pfraɪd] ADJ frito sumergido en aceite

deep-frozen [ˌdi:p'frəʊzn] ADJ ultracongelado

deep-fry ['di:p'fraɪ] VT freír sumergiendo en aceite

deep-laid ['di:p'leɪd] ADJ [*plan*] bien preparado

deeply ['di:plɪ] ADV **1** [*dig*] en profundidad; [*drink*] a grandes tragos; [*breathe, sigh*] profundamente, hondo; [*sleep, regret*] profundamente; [*think*] a fondo • **to blush ~** enrojecer violentamente • **to go ~ into sth** entrar de lleno en algo • **a ~ held conviction** una convicción profunda • **they looked ~ into each other's eyes** se miraron profundamente a los ojos • **to love sb ~** querer profundamente a algn • **to regret sth ~** lamentar algo profundamente
2 (*= profoundly, intensely*) [*worrying, sceptical, disappointed, shocked*] sumamente; [*concerned, troubled, grateful, religious*] profundamente; [*offensive, unhappy, depressed*] terriblemente • **to be ~ in debt** estar lleno de deudas, estar cargado de deudas • **it remains a ~ divided nation** sigue siendo una nación muy dividida • **I was ~ embarrassed by his question** su pregunta me hizo sentirme muy violenta • **~ embedded dirt** suciedad profundamente incrustado • **I was ~ hurt by her remarks** sus comentarios me hirieron en lo más hondo *or* profundo, sus comentarios me dolieron mucho • **we are ~ indebted to you** le debemos muchísimo • **to be ~ in love** estar profundamente enamorado • **she appeared to be ~ moved** parecía estar muy *or* profundamente conmovida • **we were ~ saddened by his death** su muerte nos entristeció profundamente • **~ tanned** con un bronceado intenso

deepness ['di:pnɪs] N profundidad *f*

deep-pan pizza [ˌdi:ppæn'pi:tsə] N pizza *f* gruesa

deep-rooted ['di:p'ru:tɪd] ADJ (*Bot*) (*also fig*) profundamente arraigado

deep-sea ['di:p'si:] ADJ [*creature, plant*] abisal, de alta mar; [*fisherman*] de altura
CPD ▸ **deep-sea diver** buzo *m* ▸ **deep-sea diving** buceo *m* de altura ▸ **deep-sea fishing** pesca *f* de gran altura

deep-seated ['di:p'si:tɪd] ADJ profundamente arraigado

deep-set ['di:p'set] ADJ [*eyes*] hundido

deep-six* [ˌdi:p'sɪks] VT (*US*) (*= throw out*) tirar; (*= kill*) cargarse*

deer [dɪə^r] N (PL: **deer** *or* **deers**) ciervo *m*, venado *m* (*esp LAm*); (*= red deer*) ciervo *m* común; (*= roe deer*) corzo *m*; (*= fallow deer*) gamo *m*

deerhound ['dɪəhaʊnd] N galgo *m* (para cazar venados), galgo *m* escocés (de pelo lanoso)

deerskin ['dɪəskɪn] N piel *f* de ciervo, gamuza *f*

deerstalker ['dɪəˌstɔ:kə^r] N **1** (*= person*) cazador *m* de ciervos al acecho
2 (*= hat*) gorro *m* de cazador

deerstalking ['dɪəˌstɔ:kɪŋ] N caza *f* de venado

de-escalate [ˌdi:'eskəleɪt] VT [*+ tension*] reducir; [*+ crisis, conflict*] desacelerar, frenar la escalada de; [*+ war*] frenar la escalada de

de-escalation [di:ˌeskə'leɪʃən] N (*Mil, Pol*) freno *m* a la escalada

deface [dɪ'feɪs] VT [*+ wall, monument*] llenar de pintadas; [*+ work of art, poster, book*] pintarrajear

defaced [dɪ'feɪst] ADJ [*voucher, document*] pintarrajeado

de facto [deɪˈfæktəʊ] ADJ, ADV de facto, de hecho

defalcation [ˌdiːfælˈkeɪʃən] N desfalco *m*

defamation [ˌdefəˈmeɪʃən] N difamación *f*

defamatory [dɪˈfæmətərɪ] ADJ [*article, statement*] difamatorio

defame [dɪˈfeɪm] VT difamar, calumniar

default [dɪˈfɔːlt] N **1** (*on contract*) incumplimiento *m* (**on** de); (*on payment*) impago *m* (**on** de) • **to be in ~** estar en mora • **judgment by ~** juicio *m* en rebeldía • **he won by ~** ganó por incomparecencia de su adversario • **we must not let it go by ~** no debemos dejarlo escapar por descuido *or* sin hacer nada • **in ~ of** a falta de
2 (*Comput*) valor *m* por defecto
VI **1** (= *not pay*) no pagar, faltar al pago • **to ~ on one's payments** no pagar los plazos
2 (*Sport*) (= *not appear*) no presentarse, no comparecer
3 (*Comput*) • **it always ~s to the C drive** siempre va a la unidad de disco C por defecto
CPD ▸ **default option** (*Comput*) opción *f* por defecto

defaulter [dɪˈfɔːltəʳ] N **1** (*Comm, Econ*) (*on payments*) moroso/a *m/f*
2 (*Mil*) rebelde *mf*

defaulting [dɪˈfɔːltɪŋ] ADJ **1** (*St Ex*) moroso
2 (*Jur*) en rebeldía

defeat [dɪˈfiːt] N [*of army, team*] derrota *f*; [*of ambition, plan*] fracaso *m*; [*of bill, amendment*] rechazo *m* • **eventually he admitted ~** al final se dio por vencido
VT [+ *army, team, opponent*] vencer, derrotar; [+ *plan, ambition*] hacer fracasar, frustrar; [+ *hopes*] frustrar, defraudar; (*Pol*) [+ *party*] derrotar; [+ *bill, amendment*] rechazar; (*fig*) vencer • **this will ~ its own ends** esto será contraproducente • **the problem ~s me** el problema me supera • **it ~ed all our efforts** burló todos nuestros esfuerzos

defeated [dɪˈfiːtɪd] ADJ [*army, team, player*] derrotado • **he left the room a ~ man** cuando abandonó la sala era un hombre derrotado

defeatism [dɪˈfiːtɪzəm] N derrotismo *m*

defeatist [dɪˈfiːtɪst] ADJ derrotista
N derrotista *mf*

defecate [ˈdefəkeɪt] VI defecar

defecation [ˌdefəˈkeɪʃən] N defecación *f*

defect N [ˈdiːfekt] (*gen*) defecto *m*; (*mental*) deficiencia *f* • **moral ~** defecto *m* moral; ▸ **speech**
VI [dɪˈfekt] (*Pol*) desertar (**from** de, **to** a) • **he ~ed to the USA** desertó de su país para irse a los EE.UU.

defection [dɪˈfekʃən] N (*Pol*) (*to different country*) deserción *f*; (*to different party*) cambio *m* de filas, defección *f* (*frm*)

defective [dɪˈfektɪv] ADJ defectuoso • **~ verb** (*Ling*) verbo *m* defectivo • **to be ~ in sth** [*person*] ser deficiente en algo
N **1**‡ (= *person*) persona *f* anormal
2 (*Gram*) defectivo *m*

defector [dɪˈfektəʳ] N (*to different country*) desertor(a) *m/f*; (*to different party*) tránsfuga *mf*

defence, **defense** (*US*) [dɪˈfens] N (*all senses*) defensa *f* • **as a ~ against** como defensa contra • **the body's ~s against disease** las defensas del organismo contra la enfermedad • **the case for the ~** el argumento de la defensa • **counsel for the ~** abogado/a *m/f* defensor(a) • **Department of Defense** (*US*) = **Ministry of Defence** • **in his ~** en su defensa • **what have you to say in your own ~?** ¿qué tiene usted que decir *or* alegar en defensa propia? • **in ~ of sth** en defensa de algo • **to come out in ~ of** salir en defensa de • **Minister of Defence** (*Brit*) Ministro *m* de Defensa • **Ministry of Defence** (*Brit*) Ministerio *m* de Defensa • **Secretary (of State) for Defence** (*Brit*) • **Secretary of Defense** (*US*) Ministro *m* de Defensa • **witness for the ~** testigo *mf* de cargo, testigo *mf* de la defensa
CPD [*policy, strategy, costs*] de defensa ▸ **defence counsel** abogado/a *m/f* defensor(a) ▸ **defence forces** fuerzas *fpl* defensivas ▸ **defence mechanism** mecanismo *m* de defensa ▸ **defence spending** gastos *mpl* de defensa

defenceless, **defenseless** (*US*) [dɪˈfenslɪs] ADJ indefenso

defencelessness, **defenselessness** (*US*) [dɪˈfenslɪsnɪs] N indefensión *f*

defenceman [dɪˈfensmən] N (PL: **defencemen**) (*Ice hockey*) defensa *m*

defend [dɪˈfend] VT (*all senses*) defender (**against** contra, **from** de) • **to ~ o.s.** defenderse
VI (*Sport*) jugar de defensa

defendant [dɪˈfendənt] N (*Jur*) (*civil*) demandado/a *m/f*; (*criminal*) acusado/a *m/f*

defender [dɪˈfendəʳ] N (*gen*) defensor(a) *m/f*; (*Sport*) defensa *mf*

defending [dɪˈfendɪŋ] ADJ • **~ champion** (*Sport*) campeón *m* vigente • **~ counsel** (*Jur*) abogado/a *m/f* defensor(a)

defense [dɪˈfens] N (*US*) = **defence**

defenseless [dɪˈfenslɪs] ADJ (*US*) = **defenceless**

defenselessness [dɪˈfenslɪsnɪs] N (*US*) = **defencelessness**

defensible [dɪˈfensɪbl] ADJ defendible; [*action*] justificable

defensive [dɪˈfensɪv] ADJ [*attitude, measures, play*] defensivo
N defensiva *f* • **to be/go on the ~** estar/ponerse a la defensiva
CPD ▸ **defensive works** fortificaciones *fpl*

defensively [dɪˈfensɪvlɪ] ADV [*say*] en tono defensivo; (*Sport*) [*play*] de defensa

defensiveness [dɪˈfensɪvnɪs] N (= *tone*) tono *m* defensivo; (= *attitude*) actitud *f* defensiva

defer[1] [dɪˈfɜːʳ] VT **1** (= *postpone*) [+ *meeting, business*] posponer, diferir; [+ *payment*] aplazar, diferir, postergar (*LAm*)
2 (*Mil*) [+ *conscript*] dar una prórroga a • **his military service was ~red** le concedieron una prórroga militar

defer[2] [dɪˈfɜːʳ] VI (= *submit*) • **to ~ to sth** deferir a algo (*frm*) • **in this I ~ to you** a este respecto defiero a su opinión (*frm*), a este respecto me adhiero a su opinión • **to ~ to sb's (greater) knowledge** deferir a los (mayores) conocimientos de algn (*frm*)

deference [ˈdefərəns] N deferencia *f*, respeto *m* • **out of** *or* **in ~ to sb/sb's age** por deferencia *or* respeto a algn/la edad de algn

deferential [ˌdefəˈrenʃəl] ADJ deferente, respetuoso

deferentially [ˌdefəˈrenʃəlɪ] ADV deferentemente, respetuosamente

deferment [dɪˈfɜːmənt], **deferral** [dɪˈfɜːrəl] N (= *postponement*) aplazamiento *m*; (*Mil*) prórroga *f*

deferred [dɪˈfɜːd] CPD ▸ **deferred annuity** anualidad *f* diferida ▸ **deferred credit** crédito *m* diferido ▸ **deferred liabilities** pasivo *msing* diferido ▸ **deferred payment** pago *m* a plazos

defiance [dɪˈfaɪəns] N (= *attitude*) desafío *m*; (= *resistance*) resistencia *f* terca • **a gesture/an act of ~** un gesto/acto desafiante • **in ~ of the law** desafiando a la ley

defiant [dɪˈfaɪənt] ADJ (= *insolent*) [*person*] atrevido, insolente; (= *challenging*) [*tone, stare*] desafiante, retador

defiantly [dɪˈfaɪəntlɪ] ADV [*act*] atrevidamente, insolentemente; [*say, answer*] en tono desafiante *or* retador, en son de reto

defibrillator [dɪˈfɪbrɪˌleɪtəʳ] N desfibrilador *m*

deficiency [dɪˈfɪʃənsɪ] N **1** (*gen*) deficiencia *f*; (= *lack*) falta *f*; (*Med*) (= *weakness*) debilidad *f* • **vitamin ~** avitaminosis *f*, déficit *m* vitamínico
2 (*in system, plan, character etc*) defecto *m*
3 (*Econ*) déficit *m*
CPD ▸ **deficiency disease** mal *m* carencial

deficient [dɪˈfɪʃənt] ADJ (*gen*) deficiente; (*in quantity*) insuficiente; (= *incomplete*) incompleto; (= *defective*) defectuoso • **to be ~ in sth** estar falto de algo • **his diet is ~ in vitamin C** su dieta está falta de vitamina C • **mentally ~** deficiente mental

deficit [ˈdefɪsɪt] N (*esp Econ*) déficit *m* • **the balance of payments is in ~** la balanza de pagos es deficitaria
CPD ▸ **deficit financing** financiación *f* mediante déficit ▸ **deficit spending** gasto *m* deficitario

defile[1] [ˈdiːfaɪl] N desfiladero *m*

defile[2] [dɪˈfaɪl] VT [+ *honour*] manchar; [+ *flag*] ultrajar; [+ *sacred thing, memory*] profanar; [+ *language*] corromper; [+ *woman*] deshonrar

defilement [dɪˈfaɪlmənt] N [*of person, community*] corrupción *f*; [*of sacred thing, memory*] profanación *f*; [*of language*] corrupción *f*; [*of woman*] deshonra *f*

definable [dɪˈfaɪnəbl] ADJ definible

define [dɪˈfaɪn] VT **1** (= *give definition for*) definir; (= *characterize*) caracterizar; (= *delimit*) determinar, delimitar; (= *outline*) destacar • **she doesn't ~ herself as a feminist** no se define como feminista • **how would you ~ yourself politically?** ¿cómo se definiría políticamente?
2 (*Comput*) definir

definite [ˈdefɪnɪt] ADJ **1** (= *fixed*) [*time, offer, plan*] definitivo; [*decision, agreement*] final • **I don't have any ~ plans** no tengo ningún plan definitivo • **are you ready to make a ~ order?** ¿puede mandarnos ya un pedido en firme? • **it is ~ that he will retire** ya es seguro *or* definitivo que se jubilará • **14 September is ~ for the trip** el 14 de septiembre es la fecha definitiva para el viaje • **nothing ~** nada definitivo • **I don't intend to go, and that's ~** no pienso ir, y no voy a cambiar de idea • **is that ~?** ¿es seguro?
2 (= *clear*) [*improvement, advantage*] indudable; [*feeling, impression*] inequívoco; [*increase*] claro • **he had a ~ advantage** tuvo una ventaja indudable • **it's a ~ possibility** es una posibilidad clara • **there is a ~ possibility that we will get the contract** está claro que existe la posibilidad de que consigamos el contrato, es muy posible que consigamos el contrato
3 (= *sure*) • **are you ~ about that?** ¿estás seguro de eso? • **to know sth for ~** saber algo con seguridad • **I don't know** *or* **can't say for ~ yet** no lo sé seguro todavía, no puedo asegurarlo todavía
4 (= *emphatic*) [*manner, tone*] firme, terminante; [*views, opinions*] firme • **he was very ~ about it** lo dijo de forma categórica • **he was very ~ about wanting to resign** dijo categóricamente que quería dimitir
5 (*Ling*) • **~ article** artículo *m* definido • **past ~ (tense)** (tiempo *m*) pretérito *m*

definitely [ˈdefɪnɪtlɪ] ADV **1** (= *definitively*) [*agree, arrange, decide*] definitivamente • **I haven't ~ decided on law school** todavía

no he decidido hacer derecho definitivamente • **the date has not yet been ~ decided** aún no se ha decidido una fecha definitiva • **they have not said ~ whether they will attend** no han dicho de forma definitiva que vayan a asistir
2 (= *certainly*) • **something should ~ be done about that** decididamente, deberían hacer algo al respecto • **yes, we ~ do need a car** sí, está clarísimo que necesitamos un coche, sí, decididamente necesitamos un coche • **he is ~ leaving** es seguro que se va, definitivamente se va • **they are ~ not for sale** definitivamente no están a la venta • **I'll ~ go** seguro que iré • **she ~ said two o'clock** estoy seguro de que dijo a las dos en punto • **she said ~ two o'clock** dijo que seguro que a las dos en punto • **I will ~ get it finished by tomorrow** definitivamente lo termino para mañana, seguro que lo termino para mañana • **it's ~ better** es sin duda mejor • **"are you going to Greece this summer?" — "yes, ~"** —¿te vas a Grecia este verano? —sí, seguro • **"do you think she'll pass?" — "definitely"** —¿crees que aprobará? —seguro *or* sin duda • **"will you accept his offer?" — "~ not!"** —¿vas a aceptar su oferta? —¡de ninguna manera! • **"can I go on my own?" — "~ not!"** —¿puedo ir solo? —¡ni hablar!
3 (= *emphatically*) [*say, deny*] terminantemente, categóricamente; [*state*] firmemente

definiteness ['defɪnɪtnɪs] (N) carácter *m* definitivo

definition [ˌdefɪ'nɪʃən] (N) **1** [*of word, concept*] definición *f*; [*of powers, boundaries, duties*] delimitación *f* • **by ~** por definición
2 (*Phot*) nitidez *f*, definición *f*

definitive [dɪ'fɪnɪtɪv] (ADJ) definitivo • **it is the ~ work on Mahler** es la obra más autorizada sobre Mahler

definitively [dɪ'fɪnɪtɪvlɪ] (ADV) de manera definitiva, definitivamente

deflate [diː'fleɪt] (VT) **1** [+ *tyre*] desinflar, deshinchar; [+ *economy*] reducir la inflación de, deflactar
2 (= *humble*) [+ *pompous person*] bajar los humos a
3 (= *depress*) desanimar, desalentar • **at this news he felt very ~d** con esta noticia se desanimó por completo
(VI) [*tyre*] desinflarse, deshincharse; [*economy*] sufrir deflación

deflation [diː'fleɪʃən] (N) [*of tyre etc*] desinflamiento *m*; (*Econ*) deflación *f*

deflationary [diː'fleɪʃənərɪ] (ADJ) (*Econ*) deflacionario

deflationist [diː'fleɪʃənɪst] (ADJ) deflacionista

deflator [diː'fleɪtəʳ] (N) medida *f* deflacionista

deflect [dɪ'flekt] (VT) [+ *ball, bullet*] desviar; (*fig*) [+ *person*] desviar (**from** de)
(VI) [*ball, bullet*] desviarse

deflection [dɪ'flekʃən] (N) desvío *m*, desviación *f*

deflector [dɪ'flektəʳ] (N) deflector *m*

defloration [ˌdiːflɔː'reɪʃən] (N) desfloración *f*

deflower [diː'flaʊəʳ] (VT) desflorar

defog [diː'fɒg] (VT) desempañar

defogger [diː'fɒgəʳ] (N) (*US*) luneta *f* térmica, dispositivo *m* antivaho

defoliant [diː'fəʊlɪənt] (N) defoliante *m*

defoliate [diː'fəʊlɪeɪt] (VT) defoliar

defoliation [ˌdiːfəʊlɪ'eɪʃən] (N) defoliación *f*

deforest [diː'fɒrɪst] (VT) deforestar, despoblar de árboles

deforestation [diːˌfɒrə'steɪʃən] (N) deforestación *f*, despoblación *f* forestal

deform [dɪ'fɔːm] (VT) deformar

deformation [ˌdiːfɔː'meɪʃən] (N) deformación *f*

deformed [dɪ'fɔːmd] (ADJ) [*person, limb, body*] deforme; [*structure*] deformado

deformity [dɪ'fɔːmɪtɪ] (N) deformidad *f*

DEFRA ['defrə] (N ABBR) (*Brit*) (= **Department for Environment, Food and Rural Affairs**) ≈ Ministerio *m* de Agricultura

defrag ['diːˌfræg] (*Comput*) (VT) [+ *disk, file, PC*] desfragmentar
(VI) desfragmentar
(CPD) ▸ **defrag tool** herramienta *f* de desfragmentación

defragment [ˌdiːfræg'ment] (VT) (*Comput*) [+ *disk, file, PC*] desfragmentar

defragmentation [ˌdiːfrægmən'teɪʃən] (*Comput*) (N) desfragmentación *f*
(CPD) ▸ **defragmentation tool** herramienta *f* de desfragmentación

defraud [dɪ'frɔːd] (VT) (*frm*) [+ *person, authorities*] estafar, defraudar • **to ~ sb of sth** estafar algo a algn • **he ~ed the firm of £1,000** le estafó 1.000 libras a la compañía

defrauder [dɪ'frɔːdəʳ] (N) defraudador(a) *m/f*

defray [dɪ'freɪ] (VT) (*frm*) sufragar, costear • **to ~ sb's expenses** sufragar *or* costear los gastos de algn

defrayal [dɪ'freɪəl], **defrayment** [dɪ'freɪmənt] (N) pago *m*

defreeze [diː'friːz] (VT) descongelar

defriend [diː'frend] (VT) (*Internet*) quitar de amigo a

defrock [diː'frɒk] (VT) apartar del sacerdocio

defrost [diː'frɒst] (VT) [+ *refrigerator*] descongelar, deshelar; [+ *frozen food*] descongelar

defroster [diː'frɒstəʳ] (N) (*US*) descongelador *m*; (*Aut*) spray *m* antihielo

deft [deft] (ADJ) (COMPAR: **defter**, SUPERL: **deftest**) diestro, hábil

deftly ['deftlɪ] (ADV) diestramente, con destreza, hábilmente

deftness ['deftnɪs] (N) destreza *f*, habilidad *f*

defunct [dɪ'fʌŋkt] (ADJ) (*frm*) **1** [*company, organization*] desaparecido, extinto; [*idea*] caduco; [*scheme*] paralizado, suspendido
2 (= *deceased*) difunto

defuse [diː'fjuːz] (VT) [+ *bomb*] desactivar; (*fig*) [+ *tension*] calmar, apaciguar; [+ *situation*] reducir la tensión de

defy [dɪ'faɪ] (VT) **1** (= *challenge*) [+ *person*] desafiar, retar • **I ~ you to do it** te desafío a hacerlo
2 (= *refuse to obey*) [+ *person*] desobedecer, enfrentarse a; [+ *order*] contravenir
3 (= *fly in the face of*) • **it defies definition** se escapa a toda definición • **it defies description** resulta imposible describirlo, es indescriptible • **to ~ gravity** desafiar la ley de la gravedad • **people defied the bad weather to get away for Easter** a pesar del mal tiempo, la gente salió de vacaciones durante la Semana Santa • **to ~ death** (= *face without fear*) desafiar a la muerte; (= *narrowly escape*) escapar de una muerte segura

-defying [dɪ'faɪɪŋ] (SUFFIX) • **death-defying** que desafía a la muerte • **gravity-defying** que desafía a la gravedad

degeneracy [dɪ'dʒenərəsɪ] (N) degeneración *f*, depravación *f*

degenerate (ADJ) [dɪ'dʒenərɪt] degenerado
(N) [dɪ'dʒenərɪt] degenerado/a *m/f*
(VI) [dɪ'dʒenəreɪt] degenerar (**into** en) • **the debate ~d into a shouting match** el debate degeneró en una discusión a voz en grito

degeneration [dɪˌdʒenə'reɪʃən] (N) degeneración *f*

degenerative [dɪ'dʒenərətɪv] (ADJ) [*disease*] degenerativo

deglamorize [diː'glæməraɪz] (VT) quitar el atractivo de

degradable [dɪ'greɪdəbl] (ADJ) degradable

degradation [ˌdegrə'deɪʃən] (N) degradación *f*

degrade [dɪ'greɪd] (VT) **1** (*gen*) degradar • **to ~ o.s.** degradarse
2 (*Chem, Phys*) (= *break down*) degradar
3 (*Mil*) [+ *weaponry etc*] mermar, diezmar
(VI) **1** (*gen*) degradarse
2 (*Chem, Phys*) (= *break down*) degradarse

degrading [dɪ'greɪdɪŋ] (ADJ) degradante

degree [dɪ'griː] (N) **1** (*gen*) (*Geog, Math*) grado *m* • **ten ~s below freezing** diez grados bajo cero
2 (= *extent*) punto *m*, grado *m* • **to such a ~ that …** hasta tal punto que … • **a high ~ of uncertainty** un alto grado de incertidumbre • **with varying ~s of success** con mayor o menor éxito • **they have some** *or* **a certain ~ of freedom** tienen cierto grado de libertad • **to some** *or* **a certain ~** hasta cierto punto • **to the highest ~** en sumo grado • **he is superstitious to a ~** (*esp Brit*) es sumamente supersticioso
3 (= *stage in scale*) grado *m* • **by ~s** poco a poco, gradualmente, por etapas • **first/second/third ~ burns** quemaduras *fpl* de primer/segundo/tercer grado • **first ~ murder** • **murder in the first ~** homicidio *m* en primer grado • **second ~ murder** • **murder in the second ~** homicidio *m* en segundo grado • IDIOM: • **to give sb the third ~** interrogar a algn brutalmente, sacudir a algn*
4 (*Univ*) título *m* • **first ~** licenciatura *f*

DEGREE

Al título universitario equivalente a la licenciatura se le conoce como **Bachelor's degree**, que se obtiene generalmente tras tres años de estudios. Las titulaciones más frecuentes son las de Letras: **Bachelor of Arts** o **BA** y Ciencias: **Bachelor of Science** o **BSc** en el Reino Unido, **BS** en Estados Unidos.

En el Reino Unido, la mayoría de los estudiantes reciben un **honours degree**, cuyas calificaciones, en orden descendente son: **first** (1) la nota más alta, seguida de **upper second** (2-1), **lower second** (2-2) y **third** (3). En algunas ocasiones se puede obtener un **ordinary degree**, por ejemplo en el caso de que no se aprueben los exámenes para obtener el título pero los examinadores consideren que a lo largo de la carrera se han tenido unos resultados mínimos satisfactorios.

En Estados Unidos los estudiantes no reciben calificaciones en sus titulaciones de fin de carrera, pero sí existe la matrícula de honor (**honors**), que puede ser, de menor a mayor importancia: **cum laude**, **magna cum laude** y **summa cum laude**.

Master's degree es normalmente un título que se recibe tras estudios de postgrado, en los que se combinan horas lectivas o investigación con una tesina final, conocida como **dissertation**. Las titulaciones más frecuentes son las de **Master of Arts** o **MA**, **Master of Science** o **MSc** y **Master of Business Administration** o **MBA**. El título se concede con la única calificación de apto. En algunas universidades, como las escocesas, el título de **master's degree** no es de postgrado, sino que corresponde a la licenciatura.

El título universitario más alto es el de doctorado, **doctorate** o **doctor's degree**, abreviado normalmente como **PhD** o **DPhil**.

• **higher ~** doctorado *m* • **honorary ~** doctorado *m* "honoris causa" • **she's got a ~ in English** es licenciada en filología inglesa • **to get a ~** sacar un título • **to take a ~ in** (= *study*) hacer la carrera de; (= *graduate*) licenciarse en
5 (= *social standing*) rango *m*, condición *f* social
(CPD) ▸ **degree ceremony** (*Brit*) ceremonia *f* de graduación ▸ **degree course** (*Brit*) (*Univ*) licenciatura *f* • **to do a ~ course** hacer una licenciatura ▸ **degree day** (*at university*) día *m* de la graduación

dehumanization [di:ˌhju:mənaɪ'zeɪʃən] (N) deshumanización *f*

dehumanize [di:'hju:mənaɪz] (VT) deshumanizar

dehumanizing [di:'hju:mənaɪzɪŋ] (ADJ) deshumanizante

dehumidifier [ˌdi:hju:'mɪdɪfaɪəʳ] (N) deshumidificador *m*

dehumidify [ˌdi:hju:'mɪdɪfaɪ] (VT) (*US*) deshumedecer

dehydrate [di:'haɪdreɪt] (VT) deshidratar

dehydrated [ˌdi:haɪ'dreɪtɪd] (ADJ) (*Med, Tech*) deshidratado; [*vegetables*] seco; [*milk, eggs*] en polvo

dehydration [ˌdi:haɪ'dreɪʃən] (N) deshidratación *f*

de-ice [di:'aɪs] (VT) descongelar

de-icer ['di:'aɪsəʳ] (N) (*Aer*) descongelador *m*; (*Aut*) descongelante *m*

de-icing [di:'aɪsɪŋ] (N) descongelación *f*
(CPD) ▸ **de-icing fluid** anticongelante *m*

deictic ['daɪktɪk] (N) deíctico *m*

deification [ˌdi:ɪfɪ'keɪʃən] (N) deificación *f*

deify ['di:ɪfaɪ] (VT) deificar

deign [deɪn] (VT) • **to ~ to do sth** dignarse hacer algo

deism ['di:ɪzəm] (N) deísmo *m*

deist ['di:ɪst] (N) deísta *mf*

deity ['di:ɪtɪ] (N) deidad *f* • **the Deity** Dios *m*

deixis ['daɪksɪs] (N) deixis *f*

déjà vu [deɪʒɑ:'vu:] (N) déjà vu *m*

deject [dɪ'dʒekt] (VT) desanimar, abatir

dejected [dɪ'dʒektɪd] (ADJ) [*person, look*] desanimado, abatido

dejectedly [dɪ'dʒektɪdlɪ] (ADV) [*sit, gaze*] con desánimo, desalentado; [*say*] con tono de abatimiento

dejection [dɪ'dʒekʃən] (N) (= *emotion*) desánimo *m*, abatimiento *m*

de jure [ˌdeɪ'dʒʊərɪ] (ADJ), (ADV) de iure

dekko* ['dekəʊ] (N) (*Brit*) vistazo *m* • **let's have a ~*** déjame verlo

Del. (ABBR) (*US*) = **Delaware**

del. (ABBR) = **delete**

delay [dɪ'leɪ] (N) (= *hold-up*) retraso *m*, demora *f* (*esp LAm*); (= *act of delaying*) retraso *m*, dilación *f*; (*to traffic*) retención *f*, atasco *m*; (*to train*) retraso *m* • **the tests have caused some ~** las pruebas han ocasionado algún retraso • **there will be ~s to traffic** habrá retenciones *or* atascos en las carreteras • **"delays possible until Dec 2009"** "posibles retenciones hasta Diciembre de 2009" • **without ~** sin demora • **these measures should be implemented without further ~** estas medidas deben ponerse en práctica sin más demora
(VT) (= *hold up*) [+ *person*] retrasar, entretener; [+ *train*] retrasar; [+ *start, opening*] retrasar, demorar (*LAm*); (= *postpone*) aplazar, demorar (*LAm*); (= *obstruct*) impedir • **the train was ~ed for two hours** el tren se retrasó dos horas • **we decided to ~ our departure** decidimos retrasar la salida • **what ~ed you?** ¿por qué has tardado tanto? • **to ~ doing sth: we ~ed going out until Jane arrived** retrasamos la salida hasta que llegara Jane • **the illness could have been treated if you hadn't ~ed going to the doctor** se hubiera podido tratar la enfermedad si no hubieras tardado tanto en ir al médico • **~ed broadcast** (*US*) transmisión *f* en diferido • **~ed effect** efecto *m* retardado
(VI) tardar, demorarse (*LAm*) • **don't ~!** (*in doing sth*) ¡no pierdas tiempo!; (*on the way*) ¡no te entretengas!, ¡no tardes!, ¡no te demores! (*LAm*)

delayed-action [dɪ'leɪd'ækʃən] (ADJ) de acción retardada • **delayed-action bomb** bomba *f* de acción retardada

delayering [di:'leɪərɪŋ] (N) (*Admin*) reducción *f* de niveles jerárquicos

delaying [dɪ'leɪɪŋ] (ADJ) [*action*] dilatorio
(CPD) ▸ **delaying tactics** tácticas *fpl* dilatorias

delectable [dɪ'lektəbl] (ADJ) delicioso

delectation [ˌdi:lek'teɪʃən] (N) deleite *m*, delectación *f* (*frm*)

delegate (N) ['delɪgɪt] delegado/a *m/f* (**to** en)
(VT) ['delɪgeɪt] [+ *task, power*] delegar (**to** en); [+ *person*] delegar (**to do sth** para hacer algo) • **I was ~d to do it** me delegaron para hacerlo • **that task cannot be ~d** ese cometido no se puede delegar en otro

delegation [ˌdelɪ'geɪʃən] (N) (= *act, group*) delegación *f*

delete [dɪ'li:t] (VT) tachar, suprimir (**from** de); (*Comput*) borrar, suprimir • **"delete where inapplicable"** "táchese lo que no proceda"
(CPD) ▸ **delete key** tecla *f* de borrado, tecla *f* de supresión

deleterious [ˌdelɪ'tɪərɪəs] (ADJ) (*frm*) nocivo, perjudicial (**to** para)

deletion [dɪ'li:ʃən] (N) supresión *f*, tachadura *f*; (*Comput*) borrado *m*, supresión *f*

delft [delft] (N) porcelana *f* de Delft

Delhi ['delɪ] (N) Delhi *m*

deli* ['delɪ] (N) delicatessen *m*
(CPD) ▸ **deli counter** mostrador *m* de delicatessen

deliberate (ADJ) [dɪ'lɪbərɪt] **1** (= *intentional*) deliberado, premeditado
2 (= *cautious*) prudente
3 (= *unhurried*) pausado, lento
(VT) [dɪ'lɪbəreɪt] (= *think about*) [+ *issue, question*] reflexionar sobre, deliberar sobre; (= *discuss*) deliberar sobre, discutir • **I ~d what to do** estuve pensando qué debería hacer • **I ~d whether to do it** estuve pensando *or* deliberando si hacerlo o no
(VI) [dɪ'lɪbəreɪt] (= *think*) reflexionar, meditar (**on** sobre); (= *discuss*) deliberar (**on** sobre)

deliberately [dɪ'lɪbərɪtlɪ] (ADV)
1 (= *intentionally*) a propósito, deliberadamente; (*with adj*) [*rude, misleading*] deliberadamente
2 (= *cautiously*) prudentemente; (= *slowly*) lentamente, pausadamente

deliberation [dɪˌlɪbə'reɪʃən] (N)
1 (= *consideration*) deliberación *f*, reflexión *f*; (= *discussion*) (*usu pl*) deliberación *f*, discusión *f* • **after due ~** después de pensarlo bien
2 (= *slowness*) pausa *f*, lentitud *f*; (= *caution*) prudencia *f*

deliberative [dɪ'lɪbərətɪv] (ADJ) deliberativo

delicacy ['delɪkəsɪ] (N) **1** (= *fineness, subtlety*) [*of flavour, workmanship, instrument*] delicadeza *f*
2 (= *fragility*) [*of china, person, balance*] fragilidad *f*
3 (= *sensitivity, awkwardness*) [*of situation, problem*] lo delicado • **a matter of some ~** un asunto algo delicado
4 (= *tact*) [*of person, inquiry*] delicadeza *f*
5 (= *special food*) exquisitez *f*, manjar *m* exquisito

delicate ['delɪkɪt] (ADJ) **1** (= *fine, subtle*) [*features, fabric, workmanship, instrument*] delicado; [*flavour, fragrance, food*] exquisito; [*touch*] suave
2 (= *fragile*) [*china, balance, ecosystem*] frágil; [*person, health, skin, liver*] delicado • **I'm feeling rather ~ this morning** (*hum*) estoy un tanto delicado esta mañana (*hum*)
3 (= *sensitive, awkward*) [*situation, problem, task, negotiations*] delicado, difícil

delicately ['delɪkɪtlɪ] (ADV) **1** [*say, act*] con delicadeza, delicadamente • **~ worded** expresado con delicadeza • **... as you so ~ put it** (*iro*) ... como tú tan delicadamente *or* con tanta delicadeza has expresado
2 [*flavoured, scented, carved*] exquisitamente • **this may upset the ~ balanced ecosystem** esto puede alterar el frágil equilibrio del ecosistema

delicatessen [ˌdelɪkə'tesn] (N) (= *shop*) delicatessen *m*

delicious [dɪ'lɪʃəs] (ADJ) [*food, taste, smell*] delicioso, exquisito, riquísimo; [*sensation*] delicioso

deliciously [dɪ'lɪʃəslɪ] (ADV) deliciosamente, exquisitamente

delight [dɪ'laɪt] (N) **1** (= *feeling of joy*) deleite *m*, placer *m*; (= *jubilation*) regocijo *m* • **much to her ~, they lost** perdieron, con gran regocijo de su parte • **to take ~ in sth** disfrutar con algo, deleitarse con algo • **to take ~ in doing sth** disfrutar haciendo algo, deleitarse en hacer algo
2 (= *pleasurable thing*) encanto *m* • **one of the ~s of Majorca** uno de los encantos de Mallorca • **the book is sheer ~** el libro es una verdadera delicia *or* maravilla • **she is a ~ to teach** (*said of schoolgirl*) es un placer ser su maestra • **a ~ to the eye** un placer para la vista
(VT) [+ *person*] encantar, deleitar
(VI) • **to ~ in sth** disfrutar con algo, deleitarse con algo • **to ~ in doing sth** disfrutar haciendo algo, deleitarse en hacer algo

delighted [dɪ'laɪtɪd] (ADJ) • **delighted!** ¡encantado! • **I'd be ~** con (mucho) gusto • **to be ~ at** *or* **with sth** estar encantado con algo • **we are ~ with it** estamos encantados con ello • **(I'm) ~ to meet you** (estoy) encantado de conocerlo, mucho gusto de conocerlo • **I was ~ to hear the news** me alegró mucho recibir la noticia • **we shall be ~ to come** estaremos encantados de ir

delightedly [dɪ'laɪtɪdlɪ] (ADV) con alegría • **she smiled ~** sonrió encantada, sonrió contentísima

delightful [dɪ'laɪtfʊl] (ADJ) [*person*] encantador; [*outfit*] precioso; [*food, breeze*] delicioso

delightfully [dɪ'laɪtfəlɪ] (ADV) (*after vb*) [*play, dance etc*] maravillosamente • **the water was ~ cool** el agua estaba tan fresquita que daba gusto

Delilah [dɪ'laɪlə] (N) Dalila

delimit [di:'lɪmɪt] (VT) delimitar

delimitation [ˌdi:lɪmɪ'teɪʃən] (N) delimitación *f*

delimiter [di:'lɪmɪtəʳ] (N) (*Comput*) delimitador *m*

delineate [dɪ'lɪnɪeɪt] (VT) **1** (= *draw*) [+ *outline*] delinear, trazar
2 (= *describe*) [+ *character*] describir, pintar; [+ *plans*] trazar
3 (= *delimit*) definir

delineation [dɪˌlɪnɪ'eɪʃən] (N) delineación *f*

delinquency [dɪ'lɪŋkwənsɪ] (N)

d

delincuencia f; ▸ juvenile
delinquent [dɪˈlɪŋkwənt] ADJ delincuente
N delincuente mf; ▸ juvenile
deliria [dɪˈlɪrɪə] NPL of delirium
delirious [dɪˈlɪrɪəs] ADJ 1 (Med) delirante • to be ~ delirar, desvariar
2 (fig) (with happiness etc) loco • to be ~ with joy estar loco de alegría
deliriously [dɪˈlɪrɪəslɪ] ADV [rant, rave] con desvarío, como un loco • to be ~ happy estar loco de alegría • to be ~ in love estar locamente enamorado
delirium [dɪˈlɪrɪəm] N (PL: delirium or deliria [dɪˈlɪrɪə]) (Med) (also fig) delirio m
CPD ▸ delirium tremens delírium m tremens
delist [diːˈlɪst] VT (= remove from list) descatalogar; (St Ex) quitar de la lista de compañías o títulos admitidos a cotización oficial
VI (St Ex) dejar de formar parte de la lista de compañías que cotizan en Bolsa
deliver [dɪˈlɪvəʳ] VT 1 (= hand over) [+ goods] entregar (to a); [+ mail] repartir; [+ message] llevar, comunicar • he ~ed me home safely me acompañó hasta casa, me dejó en casa • he ~ed the goods* (fig) cumplió or hizo lo que se esperaba de él
2† (= save) librar (from de) • ~ us from evil líbranos del mal
3 (= give) [+ speech, verdict] pronunciar; [+ lecture] dar • to ~ an ultimatum dar un ultimátum
4 (= throw) [+ blow, punch] asestar, dar; [+ ball, missile] lanzar
5 (= surrender, hand over) (also deliver up, deliver over) entregar (to a) • to ~ a town (up or over) into the hands of the enemy entregar una ciudad al enemigo • to ~ o.s. up entregarse (to a)
6 (Med) [+ baby] asistir en el parto de • Doctor Hamilton ~ed the twins el Doctor Hamilton asistió en el parto de los gemelos • she was ~ed of a child† (frm) dio a luz (a) un niño
7 • to ~ o.s. of (frm) [+ speech] pronunciar; [+ opinion] expresar; [+ remark] hacer (con solemnidad)
VI 1 (Comm) • "we deliver" "(servicio de) entrega a domicilio"
2* cumplir lo prometido • the match promised great things but didn't ~ el partido prometía mucho, pero no estuvo a la altura de lo que se esperaba
deliverance [dɪˈlɪvərəns] N (poet) liberación f (from de)
deliverer [dɪˈlɪvərəʳ] N (= saviour) libertador(a) m/f, salvador(a) m/f
delivery [dɪˈlɪvərɪ] N 1 [of goods] entrega f; [of mail] reparto m • allow 28 days for ~ la entrega se realizará en un plazo de 28 días • the balance is payable on ~ el saldo pendiente se hará efectivo a la entrega • to take ~ of recibir • General Delivery (US) Lista f de Correos
2 [of speaker] presentación f oral, forma f de hablar en público
3 (Med) parto m, alumbramiento m (frm)
4 (= saving) liberación f (from de)
CPD [date, order, time] de entrega ▸ delivery boy recadero m, mensajero m ▸ delivery charge gastos mpl de envío ▸ delivery man repartidor m ▸ delivery note nota f de entrega, albarán m (de entrega) ▸ delivery room (Med) sala f de partos ▸ delivery service servicio m de entrega a domicilio ▸ delivery suite (in hospital) sala f de partos ▸ delivery truck (US), delivery van (Brit) furgoneta f de reparto, camioneta f de reparto
dell [del] N vallecito m
delouse [diːˈaʊs] VT despiojar, espulgar
Delphi [ˈdelfaɪ] N Delfos m
Delphic [ˈdelfɪk] ADJ délfico
delphinium [delˈfɪnɪəm] N (PL: delphiniums or delphinia [delˈfɪnɪə]) espuela f de caballero
delta [ˈdeltə] N 1 (Geog) delta m
2 (= letter) delta f
CPD ▸ Delta Force (US) Fuerza f Delta
delta-winged [ˈdeltəˈwɪŋgd] ADJ con alas en delta
deltoid [ˈdeltɔɪd] ADJ deltoideo
N deltoides m
delude [dɪˈluːd] VT engañar • to ~ sb into thinking (that) ... hacer creer a algn (que) ... • to ~ o.s. engañarse • to ~ o.s. into thinking (that) ... engañarse pensando (que) ...
deluded [dɪˈluːdɪd] ADJ iluso, engañado
deluge [ˈdeljuːdʒ] N [of rain] diluvio m; [of floodwater] inundación f • the Deluge (Rel) el Diluvio • a ~ of protests una avalancha de protestas
VT (fig) inundar (with de) • he was ~d with gifts se vio inundado de regalos, le llovieron los regalos • he was ~d with questions lo acribillaron a preguntas, le llovieron las preguntas • we are ~d with work tenemos trabajo hasta encima de las cabezas, estamos hasta las cejas de trabajo
delusion [dɪˈluːʒən] N (= false impression) engaño m, error m; (= hope) ilusión f; (Psych) delirio m • ~s of grandeur delirios mpl de grandeza • to labour under a ~ abrigar una falsa ilusión • she's labouring under the ~ that she's going to get the job abriga la falsa ilusión de que va a conseguir el puesto, se engaña pensando que va a conseguir el puesto
delusive [dɪˈluːsɪv], **delusory** [dɪˈluːsərɪ] ADJ engañoso, ilusorio
de luxe [dɪˈlʌks] ADJ de lujo
delve [delv] VI • to ~ into [+ pocket, cupboard] hurgar en, rebuscar en; [+ subject] profundizar en, ahondar en; [+ past] hurgar en • we must ~ deeper tenemos que profundizar or ahondar todavía más
Dem. (US) (Pol) N ABBR = Democrat
ADJ ABBR = Democratic
demagnetize [diːˈmægnɪtaɪz] VT desimantar
demagogic [ˌdeməˈgɒgɪk] ADJ demagógico
demagogue, **demagog** (US) [ˈdeməgɒg] N demagogo/a m/f
demagoguery [deməˈgɒgərɪ] N demagogia f
demagogy [ˈdeməgɒgɪ] N demagogia f
de-man [ˌdiːˈmæn] VT (Brit) (= reduce manpower in) reducir el personal en
demand [dɪˈmɑːnd] N 1 (= request) petición f, solicitud f (for de) • his ~ for compensation was rejected rechazaron su petición or solicitud de indemnización • on ~ a libre disposición de todos, a petición • abortion on ~ aborto m libre • by popular ~ a petición del público
2 (= urgent claim) exigencia f; (for payment) aviso m, reclamación f; (Pol, Ind) reivindicación f • the ~s of duty las exigencias del deber • final ~ (for payment of bill) último aviso m • there are many ~s on my time tengo muchas ocupaciones • it makes great ~s on our resources pone a prueba nuestros recursos • her children make great ~s on her time sus hijos absorben gran parte de su tiempo
3 (Comm) demanda f (for de) • ~ for coal is down ha bajado la demanda de carbón • there is a ~ for existe demanda de • to be in great ~ • be much in ~ tener mucha demanda; (fig) [person] estar muy solicitado, ser muy popular
VT 1 (= insist on) exigir; (= claim) reclamar • I ~ed to know why insistí en que me explicaran por qué • he ~ed to see my passport insistió en or exigió ver mi pasaporte • to ~ that insistir en que • "who are you?" he ~ed —¿quién es usted? —preguntó • to ~ sth (from or of sb) exigir algo (a algn) • I ~ an explanation exijo una explicación • I ~ my rights reclamo mis derechos
2 (= require) exigir, requerir • the job ~s care el trabajo exige or requiere cuidado
CPD ▸ demand bill letra f a la vista ▸ demand curve curva f de la demanda ▸ demand draft letra f a la vista ▸ demand management control m de la demanda ▸ demand note pagaré m a la vista
demanding [dɪˈmɑːndɪŋ] ADJ [person] exigente; [work] (= tiring) agotador; [part, role] difícil • it's a very ~ job es un trabajo que exige mucho • a ~ child un niño que requiere mucha atención
de-manning [ˌdiːˈmænɪŋ] N (Brit) (Ind) reducción f de personal, despidos mpl
demarcate [ˈdiːmɑːkeɪt] VT demarcar
demarcation [ˌdiːmɑːˈkeɪʃən] N demarcación f
CPD ▸ demarcation dispute conflicto m de competencias laborales ▸ demarcation line línea f de demarcación
démarche [ˈdeɪmɑːʃ] N gestión f, diligencia f
dematerialize [ˌdɪməˈtiːərɪəlaɪz] VI desmaterializarse
demean [dɪˈmiːn] VT degradar • to ~ o.s. rebajarse, degradarse
demeaning [dɪˈmiːnɪŋ] ADJ degradante
demeanour, **demeanor** (US) [dɪˈmiːnəʳ] N conducta f, comportamiento m; (= bearing) porte m
demented [dɪˈmentɪd] ADJ demente; (fig) loco
dementedly [dɪˈmentɪdlɪ] ADV (fig) como un loco
dementia [dɪˈmenʃɪə] N demencia f • senile ~ demencia f senil
demerara [ˌdeməˈreərə] N (also demerara sugar) azúcar m moreno
demerge [ˌdiːˈmɜːdʒ] VT (Brit) [+ company] dividir, fragmentar, separar
demerger [ˌdiːˈmɜːdʒəʳ] N (Brit) división f, fragmentación f, separación f
demerit [diːˈmerɪt] N (usu pl) demérito m, desmerecimiento m
demesne [dɪˈmeɪn] N (Jur) heredad f; [of manor, country house] tierras fpl solariegas
demi... [ˈdemɪ] PREFIX semi..., medio...
demigod [ˈdemɪgɒd] N semidiós m
demijohn [ˈdemɪdʒɒn] N damajuana f
demilitarization [ˈdiːˌmɪlɪtəraɪˈzeɪʃən] N desmilitarización f
demilitarize [ˈdiːˈmɪlɪtəraɪz] VT desmilitarizar • ~d zone zona f desmilitarizada
demimonde [ˌdemɪˈmɒnd] N mujeres fpl mundanas
de-mining [diːˈmaɪnɪŋ] N (= removing landmines) eliminación f de minas
demise [dɪˈmaɪz] N (frm) (= death) fallecimiento m; (fig) [of institution etc] desaparición f
demisemiquaver [ˈdemɪsemɪˌkweɪvəʳ] N (Brit) fusa f
demission [dɪˈmɪʃən] N dimisión f
demist [diːˈmɪst] VT (Aut) desempañar
demister [diːˈmɪstəʳ] N (Aut) luneta f térmica, dispositivo m antivaho
demisting [diːˈmɪstɪŋ] N eliminación f del vaho
demitasse [ˈdemɪtæs] N [of coffee] taza f

pequeña, tacita *f* (de café)
demi-vegetarian [ˌdemɪvedʒɪˈtɛərɪən] N semi-vegetariano/a *m/f*
demo* [ˈdeməʊ] (= **demonstration**) N
1 (*Brit*) (*Pol*) manifestación *f*, mani* *f*
2 (*Comm*) [*of machine, product*] demostración *f*
3 = **demo tape**
CPD ▸ **demo disk** (*Mus*) disco *m* de demostración; (*Comput*) disquete *m* de demostración ▸ **demo tape** (*Mus*) cinta *f* de demostración
demob* [ˈdiːˈmɒb] (*Brit*) N desmovilización *f*
VT desmovilizar
CPD ▸ **demob suit*** traje *m* de civil
demobbed* [diːˈmɒbd] (*Brit*) ADJ [*soldier*] desmovilizado
demobilization [ˈdiːˌməʊbɪlaɪˈzeɪʃən] N desmovilización *f*
demobilize [diːˈməʊbɪlaɪz] VT desmovilizar
democracy [dɪˈmɒkrəsɪ] N democracia *f*
Democrat [ˈdeməkræt] N (*US*) demócrata *mf* • **Christian ~** democratacristiano/a *m/f*, democristiano/a *m/f* • **Social ~** socialdemócrata *mf*
democrat [ˈdeməkræt] N demócrata *mf*
democratic [ˌdeməˈkrætɪk] ADJ **1** [*country, society, government, election*] democrático
2 (*US*) (*Pol*) • **Democratic** [*candidate, nomination, convention*] demócrata • **the Democratic Party** el Partido Demócrata • **the Democratic Congress** el congreso demócrata • **the Democratic Republic of ...** la República Democrática de ...; ▹ **liberal, social**
3 (= *egalitarian*) [*style, ethos, boss, atmosphere*] democrático
democratically [ˌdeməˈkrætɪklɪ] ADV democráticamente
democratization [dɪˌmɒkrətaɪˈzeɪʃən] N democratización *f*
democratize [dɪˈmɒkrətaɪz] VT democratizar
démodé [deɪˈmɒdeɪ] ADJ pasado de moda
demographer [dɪˈmɒgrəfəʳ] N demógrafo/a *m/f*
demographic [ˌdeməˈgræfɪk] ADJ demográfico
demographics [ˌdeməˈgræfɪks] NPL estadísticas *fpl* demográficas, perfil *msing* demográfico
demography [dɪˈmɒgrəfɪ] N demografía *f*
demolish [dɪˈmɒlɪʃ] VT [+ *building*] demoler, derribar, echar abajo; (*fig*) [+ *argument*] echar por tierra; [+ *opposition*] arrasar; (*hum*) [+ *cake*] zamparse*
demolisher [dɪˈmɒlɪʃəʳ] N (*lit, fig*) demoledor(a) *m/f*
demolition [ˌdeməˈlɪʃən] N demolición *f*, derribo *m*
CPD ▸ **demolition squad** equipo *m* de demolición ▸ **demolition zone** zona *f* de demolición
demon [ˈdiːmən] N demonio *m* • **he's a ~ for work*** es una fiera para el trabajo
ADJ **1** • **the ~ drink** el demonio de la bebida
2* • **he's a ~ squash-player** es un as del squash*, jugando al squash es fabuloso*
demonetization [diːˌmʌnɪtaɪˈzeɪʃən] N desmonetización *f*
demonetize [diːˈmʌnɪtaɪz] VT desmonetizar
demoniac [dɪˈməʊnɪæk] ADJ = **demoniacal**
N demoníaco/a *m/f*, demoniaco/a *m/f*
demoniacal [ˌdiːməˈnaɪəkəl] ADJ demoníaco, demoniaco, diabólico
demonic [dɪˈmɒnɪk] ADJ **1** (*lit*) [*forces, possession, influence*] demoníaco
2 (*fig*) = **demoniacal**

demonize [ˈdiːmənaɪz] VT demonizar
demonology [ˌdiːməˈnɒlədʒɪ] N demonología *f*
demonstrable [ˈdemənstrəbl] ADJ demostrable
demonstrably [ˈdemənstrəblɪ] ADV manifiestamente • **a ~ false statement** una afirmación manifiestamente falsa
demonstrate [ˈdemənstreɪt] VT **1** (= *prove*) [+ *theory*] demostrar, probar • **you have to ~ that you are reliable** tienes que demostrar que se puede confiar en ti
2 (= *explain*) [+ *method, product*] hacer una demostración de
3 (= *display*) [+ *emotions*] manifestar, expresar; [+ *talent, ability*] demostrar
VI (*Pol*) manifestarse (**against** en contra de, **in support of** en apoyo de, **in favour of** a favor de)
demonstration [ˌdemənˈstreɪʃən] N
1 (= *illustration*) demostración *f*
2 (= *manifestation*) muestra *f*, demostración *f*
3 (*Pol*) manifestación *f* • **to hold a ~** hacer una manifestación
CPD ▸ **demonstration model** modelo *m* de muestra
demonstrative [dɪˈmɒnstrətɪv] ADJ
1 [*person*] expresivo • **not very ~** más bien reservado
2 • **to be ~ of sth** (= *illustrative*) demostrar algo
3 (*Gram*) demostrativo
N demostrativo *m*
demonstratively [dɪˈmɒnstrətɪvlɪ] ADV efusivamente, calurosamente
demonstrator [ˈdemənstreɪtəʳ] N (*Pol*) manifestante *mf*; (*Univ etc*) ayudante *mf*, auxiliar *mf*; (*in shop*) demostrador(a) *m/f*
demoralization [dɪˌmɒrəlaɪˈzeɪʃən] N desmoralización *f*
demoralize [dɪˈmɒrəlaɪz] VT desmoralizar
demoralized [dɪˈmɒrəlaɪzd] ADJ desmoralizado
demoralizing [dɪˈmɒrəlaɪzɪŋ] ADJ desmoralizador
Demosthenes [dɪˈmɒsθəniːz] N Demóstenes
demote [dɪˈməʊt] VT (*gen*) rebajar de categoría; (*Mil*) degradar
demotic [dɪˈmɒtɪk] ADJ demótico
demotion [dɪˈməʊʃən] N (*gen*) descenso *m* de categoría; (*Mil*) degradación *f*
demotivate [ˌdiːˈməʊtɪveɪt] VT desmotivar
demotivation [ˌdiːməʊtɪˈveɪʃən] N desmotivación *f*
demotivational [ˌdiːməʊtɪˈveɪʃənəl] ADJ desmotivador
demount [diːˈmaʊnt] VT (= *take to pieces*) desmontar
demur [dɪˈmɜːʳ] VI (*frm*) objetar, poner reparos (**at** a)
N • **without ~** sin poner reparos, sin objeción
demure [dɪˈmjʊəʳ] ADJ [*person*] (= *modest*) recatado; (= *coy*) tímido y algo coqueto; [*clothing, appearance*] recatado • **in a ~ little voice** en tono dulce y algo coqueta
demurely [dɪˈmjʊəlɪ] ADV (= *modestly*) recatadamente; (= *coyly*) con coqueta timidez
demureness [dɪˈmjʊənɪs] N recato *m*
demurrage [dɪˈmʌrɪdʒ] N (*Naut*) estadía *f*; (*Comm*) sobrestadía *f*
demurrer [dɪˈmʌrəʳ] N (*Jur*) ≈ excepción *f* perentoria
demutualize [diːˈmjuːtjʊəlaɪz] VI (*Econ*) dejar de ser una mutualidad
demystification [diːˌmɪstɪfɪˈkeɪʃən] N desmitificación *f*
demystify [diːˈmɪstɪfaɪ] VT desmitificar
demythification [diːˌmɪθɪfɪˈkeɪʃən] N desmitificación *f*
demythify [diːˈmɪθɪˌfaɪ] VT desmitificar
demythologize [ˌdiːmɪˈθɒlədʒaɪz] VT desmitificar
den [den] N **1** (*wild animal's*) guarida *f*; [*of fox*] madriguera *f* • **a den of iniquity** *or* **vice** un antro de vicio y perversión • **a den of thieves** una guarida de ladrones
2 (*US*) (= *private room*) estudio *m*, gabinete *m*
denationalization [ˈdiːˌnæʃnəlaɪˈzeɪʃən] N desnacionalización *f*
denationalize [diːˈnæʃnəlaɪz] VT desnacionalizar
denatured [diːˈneɪtʃəd] ADJ [*food*] desnaturalizado
CPD ▸ **denatured alcohol** (*US*) alcohol *m* desnaturalizado
dendrite [ˈdendraɪt] N dendrita *f*
dendrochronology [ˌdendrəʊkrəˈnɒlədʒɪ] N dendrocronología *f*
dengue [ˈdeŋgɪ] N dengue *m*
CPD ▸ **dengue fever** dengue *m*
denial [dɪˈnaɪəl] N **1** [*of accusation, guilt*] negación *f* • **he shook his head in ~** negó con la cabeza • **he met the accusation with a flat ~** negó *or* desmintió rotundamente la acusación • **the government issued an official ~** el gobierno lo desmintió oficialmente, el gobierno emitió un desmentido oficial
2 (= *refusal*) [*of request*] denegación *f*; (= *rejection*) rechazo *m*; [*of report, statement*] desmentido *m*, mentís *m inv* • **a ~ of justice** una denegación de justicia
3 (= *self-denial*) abnegación *f* • **to be in ~ about sth** no querer reconocer algo
denier [ˈdenɪəʳ] N **1** (= *weight*) denier *m* • **20 ~ stockings** medias *fpl* de 20 denier
2 (= *coin*) denario *m*
denigrate [ˈdenɪgreɪt] VT denigrar
denigration [ˌdenɪˈgreɪʃən] N denigración *f*
denigratory [ˌdenɪˈgreɪtərɪ] ADJ denigratorio
denim [ˈdenɪm] N tela *f* vaquera; **denims** vaqueros *mpl*, bluyín *msing* (*esp LAm*)
CPD ▸ **denim jacket** chaqueta *f* vaquera, cazadora *f* vaquera, saco *m* de vaquero (*LAm*)
denizen [ˈdenɪzn] N (*liter*) morador(a) *m/f*, habitante *mf* • **the ~s of the deep** los moradores de las profundidades del mar (*liter*)
Denmark [ˈdenmɑːk] N Dinamarca *f*
denominate [dɪˈnɒmɪneɪt] VT denominar
denomination [dɪˌnɒmɪˈneɪʃən] N
1 (= *class*) clase *f*, categoría *f*
2 (*Rel*) confesión *f*
3 [*of coin*] valor *m*; [*of measure, weight*] unidad *f*
4 (= *name*) denominación *f*
denominational [dɪˌnɒmɪˈneɪʃənl] ADJ (*Rel*) confesional; (*US*) [*school*] confesional, religioso
denominator [dɪˈnɒmɪneɪtəʳ] N (*Math*) denominador *m*; ▹ **common**
denotation [ˌdiːnəʊˈteɪʃən] N **1** (*gen*) denotación *f* (*also Ling, Philos*); (= *meaning*) sentido *m*
2 (= *symbol*) símbolo *m*, señal *f*
denotative [dɪˈnəʊtətɪv] ADJ (*Ling*) denotativo
denote [dɪˈnəʊt] VT denotar, indicar; [*word*] significar; (*Ling, Philos*) denotar
denouement, dénouement [deɪˈnuːmɒn] N desenlace *m*
denounce [dɪˈnaʊns] VT (= *accuse publicly*) censurar, denunciar; (*to police etc*) denunciar; [+ *treaty*] denunciar, abrogar
denouncement [dɪˈnaʊnsmənt] N = **denunciation**
denouncer [dɪˈnaʊnsəʳ] N denunciante *mf*
dense [dens] ADJ (COMPAR: **denser**, SUPERL:

d

densest) 1 (= thick) [forest, vegetation, fog] denso, espeso; [crowd] nutrido; [population] denso
2 [Phys] [liquid, substance] denso
3* [person] corto de entendederas*, duro de mollera*
densely ['densli] (ADV) densamente
• ~ **packed pages** páginas repletas de información • ~ **populated** densamente poblado
denseness ['densnis] (N) 1 (= stupidity) estupidez f
2 = density
density ['densiti] (N) 1 (= thickness) [of forest, vegetation, fog] densidad f, lo espeso; [of population] densidad f
2 (Phys) [of material, substance] densidad f
• **single/double ~ disk** disco m de densidad sencilla/de doble densidad
dent [dent] (N) (in metal) abolladura f; (in wood) muesca f, marca f • **to make a ~ in sth** [+ metal] abollar algo; [+ wood] hacer una muesca or marca en algo • **it's made a ~ in my savings*** se ha comido una buena parte de mis ahorros*
(VT) 1 [+ car, hat etc] abollar
2 (fig) [+ enthusiasm, confidence] hacer mella en • **his reputation was somewhat ~ed** su reputación quedó un tanto en entredicho • **his pride was somewhat ~ed** su orgullo resultó un tanto herido
dental ['dentl] (ADJ) dental
(N) (Ling) dental f
(CPD) ▸ **dental appointment** cita f con el dentista ▸ **dental floss** seda f dental, hilo m dental ▸ **dental hygienist** higienista mf dental ▸ **dental nurse** auxiliar mf en odontología, enfermero/a m/f dental ▸ **dental records** ficha fsing dental ▸ **dental science** odontología f ▸ **dental surgeon** odontólogo/a m/f, dentista mf ▸ **dental surgery** (= procedures) cirugía f dental; (= place) clínica f dental ▸ **dental technician** protésico/a m/f dental
dented ['dentid] (ADJ) abollado, con abolladuras
dentifrice ['dentifris] (N) (frm) dentífrico m
dentine ['denti:n] (N) dentina f, esmalte m dental
dentist ['dentist] (N) dentista mf, odontólogo/a m/f • **at the ~'s** en el dentista • **~'s chair** silla f del dentista • **~'s surgery** • **~'s office** (US) clínica f dental, consultorio m dental
dentistry ['dentistri] (N) odontología f, dentistería f (CAm)
dentition [den'tiʃən] (N) dentición f
denture ['dentʃəʳ] (N) dentadura f; **dentures** dentadura f postiza
denuclearize [di:'nju:kliəraiz] (VT) desnuclearizar • **a ~d zone** una zona desnuclearizada
denude [di'nju:d] (VT) 1 (Geol, Geog) denudar
2 (= strip) despojar (of de)
denuded [di'nju:did] (ADJ) [terrain] denudado • ~ **of** despojado de
denunciation [di,nʌnsi'eiʃən] (N) (gen) denuncia f
denunciator [di'nʌnsieitəʳ] (N) denunciante mf
Denver boot [,denvə'bu:t], **Denver clamp** [,denvə'klæmp] (N) (US) cepo m
deny [di'nai] (VT) 1 [+ charge] negar, rechazar; [+ report] desmentir; [+ possibility, truth of statement] negar • **to ~ having done sth** negar haber hecho algo • **to ~ that ...** negar que ... • **he denies that he said it** • **he denies having said it** niega haberlo dicho • **I don't ~ it** no lo niego • **she denied everything** lo negó todo • **there's no ~ing it** no se puede negar, es innegable
2 (= refuse) [+ request] denegar • **to ~ sb sth** negar algo a algn, privar a algn de algo • **to ~ o.s. sth** privarse de algo • **he was not going to be denied his revenge** nada iba a impedir su venganza
3 (= renounce) [+ faith] renegar de
deodorant [di:'əudərənt] (N) desodorante m
deodorize [di:'əudəraiz] (VT) desodorizar
deontology [,di:ɒn'tɒlədʒi] (N) deontología f
deoxidize [di:'ɒksidaiz] (VT) desoxidar
deoxygenate [,di:'ɒksidʒəneit] (VT) deoxigenar
deoxyribonucleic acid [di:,ɒksi,raibəunju:-,kleiik'æsid] (N) ácido m desoxirribonucleico
dep. (ABBR) (= **departs, departure**) (on timetables) salida
depart [di'pɑ:t] (VI) [person] partir, irse, marcharse (**from** de); [train etc] salir (**at a, for** para, **from** de) • **to ~ from** [+ custom, truth etc] apartarse de, desviarse de • **the train is about to ~** el tren está a punto de salir
(VT) • **to ~ this life** or **this world** (liter or hum) dejar este mundo
departed [di'pɑ:tid] (ADJ) 1 (= bygone) [days etc] pasado
2 (liter) (euph) (= dead) difunto
(N) • **the ~** (sing) el difunto, la difunta; (pl) los difuntos, las difuntas
department [di'pɑ:tmənt] (N) 1 (gen) departamento m; (in shop) sección f; (Admin) sección f, oficina f • **the toy ~** la sección de juguetes • **the English ~** el departamento de inglés
2 [of government] ministerio m, secretaría f (Mex) • **Department of Employment** Ministerio m or (Mex) Secretaría f de Trabajo
3* [of activity] • **gardening is my wife's ~** del jardín se encarga mi mujer • **men? I don't have any problems in that ~** ¿los hombres? no tengo ningún problema en ese campo
(CPD) ▸ **Department for Education and Employment** (Brit) Ministerio m de Educación y Trabajo ▸ **Department of Health** ≈ Ministerio m de Sanidad ▸ **Department of Homeland Security** (US) Departamento m de Seguridad Nacional ▸ **Department of State** (US) Ministerio m or (Mex) Secretaría f de Asuntos Exteriores ▸ **department store** (grandes) almacenes mpl, tienda f por departamento (Carib)
departmental [,di:pɑ:t'mentl] (ADJ) departamental
(CPD) ▸ **departmental head** jefe m de departamento/sección ▸ **departmental manager** director(a) m/f de departamento ▸ **departmental meeting** reunión f de departamento, reunión f departamental ▸ **departmental policy** política f del departamento
departmentalization [,di:pɑ:t,mentəlai-'zeiʃən] (N) división f en departamentos, compartimentación f
departmentalize [,di:pɑ:t'mentəlaiz] (VT) dividir en departamentos, compartimentar
departmentally [,di:pɑ:t'mentəli] (ADV) por departamentos
departure [di'pɑ:tʃəʳ] (N) 1 [of person] partida f, marcha f (**from** de); [of train, plane] salida f (**from** de) • **the ~ of this flight has been delayed** se ha retrasado la salida de este vuelo • **his sudden ~ worried us** su marcha repentina nos dejó preocupados • **"Departures"** (Aer, Rail) "Salidas" • **point of ~** punto m de partida • **to take one's ~** (frm) marcharse
2 (fig) (from custom, principle) desviación f (**from** de) • **this is a ~ from the norm** esto se aparta de la norma • **this is a ~ from the truth** esto no representa la verdad
3 (= trend, course) • **a new ~** un rumbo nuevo, una novedad
(CPD) ▸ **departure board** (Aer, Rail) tablón m de salidas, panel m de salidas ▸ **departure gate** (Aer) puerta f de embarque ▸ **departure language** (Ling) lengua f de origen ▸ **departure lounge** (Aer) sala f de embarque ▸ **departure tax** (= airport tax) tasas fpl de aeropuerto ▸ **departure time** hora f de salida
depend [di'pend] (VI) 1 (= rely) • **to ~ (up)on** contar con • **you can ~ on me!** ¡cuenta conmigo! • **can we ~ on you to do it?** ¿podemos contar contigo para hacerlo?, ¿podemos confiar en que tú lo hagas? • **you can ~ on it!** ¡tenlo por seguro! • **you can ~ on him to be late** ten por seguro que llegará tarde
2 (= be dependent) • **to ~ (up)on** depender de • **he ~s on her for everything** depende de ella para todo • **he has to ~ on his pen** tiene que vivir de su pluma
3 (= be influenced by) • **to ~ on** depender de • **your success ~s on how hard you work** tu éxito depende del trabajo que hagas • **it (all) ~s on the weather** (todo) depende del tiempo • **it (all) ~s what you mean** depende de lo que quieras decir • **that ~s** eso depende • **~ing on the weather, we can go tomorrow** según el tiempo que haga, podemos ir mañana
dependability [di,pendə'biliti] (N) [of person] seriedad f, formalidad f; [of machine] fiabilidad f
dependable [di'pendəbl] (ADJ) [person] serio, formal, cumplidor; [machine] fiable
dependance [di'pendəns] (N) = **dependence**
dependant [di'pendənt] (N) persona a cargo de algn • **I have no ~s** no tengo cargas familiares • **how many ~s does he have?** ¿cuántas personas tiene a su cargo?
dependence [di'pendəns] (N) dependencia f (on de) • **she wants to be cured of her ~ on tranquillizers** quiere curarse de su dependencia de los tranquilizantes • **his ~ on her for financial support** su dependencia económica de ella • ~ **on drugs** • **drug ~** drogodependencia f (frm)
dependency [di'pendənsi] (N) 1 (Pol) (= territory) posesión f, dominio m
2 (= dependence) dependencia f • ~ **culture** cultura f de dependencia
dependent [di'pendənt] (ADJ) 1 (= reliant) • **he has no ~ relatives** no tiene cargas familiares, no tiene familiares a su cargo • **to be ~ on** or **upon sth/sb** depender de algo/algn • **to be financially ~ on sb** depender económicamente de algn • **to be ~ on drugs** ser drogodependiente (frm) • **to become ~ on** or **upon sth/sb** llegar a depender de algo/algn • **he had become ~ on her for affection** había llegado a depender de ella afectivamente
2 (Ling) [clause] subordinado
3 (= conditional) • **to be ~ on** or **upon sth** depender de algo • **tourism is ~ on (the) climate** el turismo depende del clima
(N) (esp US) = **dependant**
depersonalize [di:'pɜ:sənəlaiz] (VT) despersonalizar
depict [di'pikt] (VT) (in picture) representar, pintar; (in words) describir
depiction [di'pikʃən] (N) (in picture) representación f; (in writing) descripción f
depilatory [di'pilətəri] (ADJ) depilatorio
(N) (also **depilatory cream**) depilatorio m, crema f depilatoria
deplane [di:'plein] (VI) (US) bajar del avión, desembarcar

deplenish [dɪˈplenɪʃ] VT ▸ deplete

deplete [dɪˈpliːt] VT (*= reduce*) mermar; (*= exhaust totally*) agotar • **stocks have been ~d by overfishing** la fauna marina se ha visto mermada debido a una actividad pesquera desmesurada • **substances that ~ the ozone layer** sustancias que destruyen la capa de ozono • **Lee's exhausted and ~d army** el ejército cansado y diezmado de Lee • **that holiday rather ~d our savings** esas vacaciones mermaron *or* redujeron bastante nuestros ahorros

depleted uranium [dɪˈpliːtɪdjʊəˈreɪnɪəm] N uranio *m* empobrecido

depletion [dɪˈpliːʃən] N (*= reduction*) reducción *f*, merma *f*; (*= exhaustion*) agotamiento *m* • **the ~ of the ozone layer** la rarefacción *or* destrucción de la capa de ozono

deplorable [dɪˈplɔːrəbl] ADJ **1** (*= sad*) lamentable • **it would be ~ if** sería lamentable que (*+ subjun*)
2 (*= disgraceful*) deplorable • **it is ~ that** es deplorable que (*+ subjun*)

deplorably [dɪˈplɔːrəblɪ] ADV (*= sadly*) lamentablemente; (*= disgracefully*) deplorablemente • **in ~ bad taste** de un mal gusto lamentable

deplore [dɪˈplɔːʳ] VT (*= regret*) lamentar; (*= censure*) deplorar • **it is to be ~d** (*= unfortunate*) es lamentable; (*= disgraceful*) es deplorable

deploy [dɪˈplɔɪ] VT **1** (*Mil*) desplegar
2 (*fig*) [*+ resources*] utilizar
VI (*Mil*) desplegarse

deployment [dɪˈplɔɪmənt] N **1** (*Mil*) despliegue *m*
2 (*fig*) [*of resources*] utilización *f*

depolarization [diːˌpəʊləraɪˈzeɪʃən] N despolarización *f*

depolarize [diːˈpəʊləraɪz] VT despolarizar

depoliticize [ˌdiːpəˈlɪtɪsaɪz] VT despolitizar

deponent [dɪˈpəʊnənt] N **1** (*Ling*) deponente *m*
2 (*Jur*) declarante *mf*
ADJ • **a ~ verb** un verbo deponente

depopulate [diːˈpɒpjʊleɪt] VT despoblar

depopulated [diːˈpɒpjʊleɪtɪd] ADJ [*area*] despoblado

depopulation [ˈdiːˌpɒpjʊˈleɪʃən] N [*of region*] despoblación *f*

deport [dɪˈpɔːt] VT **1** (*= expel*) deportar
2 (*= behave*) • **to ~ o.s.**† comportarse

deportation [ˌdiːpɔːˈteɪʃən] N deportación *f*
CPD ▸ **deportation order** orden *f* de deportación

deportee [ˌdiːpɔːˈtiː] N deportado/a *m/f*

deportment [dɪˈpɔːtmənt] N (*= behaviour*) conducta *f*, comportamiento *m*; (*= carriage*) porte *m*

depose [dɪˈpəʊz] VT [*+ ruler*] deponer, destituir
VI (*Jur*) declarar, deponer

deposit [dɪˈpɒzɪt] N **1** (*in bank*) depósito *m* • **to have £50 on ~** tener 50 libras en cuenta de ahorros
2 (*Comm*) (*= part payment*) (*on hire purchase, car*) depósito *m*, enganche *m* (*Mex*); (*on house*) desembolso *m* inicial, entrada *f* (*Sp*); (*= returnable security*) señal *f*, fianza *f* • **to put down a ~ of £50** dejar un depósito de 50 libras • **he paid a £2,000 ~ on the house** hizo un desembolso inicial de 2.000 libras para la casa, dio una entrada de 2.000 libras para la casa (*Sp*) • **to lose one's ~** (*Brit*) (*Pol*) perder el depósito
3 (*Chem*) poso *m*, sedimento *m*
4 (*Geol*) [*of gas*] depósito *m*; [*of mineral*] yacimiento *m*
VT **1** (*= put down*) depositar; (*= leave*) [*+ luggage*] consignar, dejar (en consigna); [*+ eggs*] poner; [*+ object*] depositar (**with** en), dejar (**with** con)
2 (*in bank*) [*+ money*] depositar, ingresar (**in** en) • **I want to ~ £10 in my account** quiero ingresar 10 libras en mi cuenta • **to ~ £2,000 on a house** hacer un desembolso inicial *or* (*Sp*) dar una entrada de 2.000 libras para una casa
3 (*Geol, Chem*) depositar
CPD ▸ **deposit account** cuenta *f* de ahorros ▸ **deposit slip** hoja *f* de ingreso

depositary [dɪˈpɒzɪtərɪ] N **1** (*= person*) depositario/a *m/f*
2 = **depository**

deposition [ˌdiːpəˈzɪʃən] N **1** [*of ruler*] deposición *f*, destitución *f*
2 (*Jur*) declaración *f*, deposición *f*

depositor [dɪˈpɒzɪtəʳ] N (*Econ*) depositante *mf*, impositor(a) *m/f*

depository [dɪˈpɒzɪtərɪ] N (*= storage place*) almacén *m*; (*fig*) (*= person*) depositario/a *m/f*
CPD ▸ **depository library** (*US*) biblioteca *f* de depósito

depot [ˈdepəʊ] N (*= storehouse*) almacén *m*, depósito *m*; (*for vehicles*) parque *m*, cochera *f*; (*= bus station*) terminal *f*; (*US*) (*Rail*) estación *f*; (*Mil*) depósito *m*
CPD ▸ **depot ship** buque *m* nodriza

depravation [ˌdeprəˈveɪʃən] N = **depravity**

deprave [dɪˈpreɪv] VT depravar

depraved [dɪˈpreɪvd] ADJ depravado

depravity [dɪˈprævɪtɪ] N depravación *f*

deprecate [ˈdeprɪkeɪt] VT (*frm*) (*= censure*) desaprobar, lamentar; (*= disparage*) menospreciar

deprecating [ˈdeprɪkeɪtɪŋ] ADJ [*tone*] de desaprobación, de reprobación; [*smile*] de desprecio

deprecatingly [ˈdeprɪkeɪtɪŋlɪ] ADV (*= disapprovingly*) con desaprobación, con reprobación; (*= disparagingly*) con desprecio

deprecation [deprɪˈkeɪʃən] N desaprobación *f*, reprobación *f*

deprecatory [ˈdeprɪkətərɪ] ADJ [*attitude, gesture*] de desaprobación; [*smile*] de disculpa

depreciable [dɪˈpriːʃəbl] ADJ (*Econ*) depreciable

depreciate [dɪˈpriːʃɪeɪt] VI [*currency, shares*] depreciarse
VT **1** (*Econ*) [*+ value*] depreciar; [*+ assets*] depreciar, amortizar
2 (*= belittle*) menospreciar, desdeñar

depreciation [dɪˌpriːʃɪˈeɪʃən] N [*of value*] depreciación *f*; [*of assets*] depreciación *f*, amortización *f*
CPD ▸ **depreciation account** cuenta *f* de amortización ▸ **depreciation allowance** reservas *fpl* para depreciaciones

depredations [ˌdeprɪˈdeɪʃənz] NPL estragos *mpl*, expolios *mpl* • **the ~ of time** los estragos del tiempo

depress [dɪˈpres] VT **1** [*+ person*] (*= make miserable*) deprimir, abatir; (*= discourage*) desalentar; (*Psych*) tener un efecto depresivo sobre; (*Med*) [*+ immune system*] deprimir
2 (*Econ*) [*+ trade, price*] reducir
3 (*frm*) (*= press down*) [*+ button, accelerator*] apretar; [*+ lever*] bajar

depressant [dɪˈpresnt] ADJ (*Med*) depresivo
N (*Med*) depresivo *m*

depressed [dɪˈprest] ADJ **1** [*person*] deprimido, abatido • **to feel ~ (about sth)** estar deprimido *or* abatido (por algo) • **to get ~ (about sth)** deprimirse (por algo)
2 (*Econ*) [*market, economy, industry*] deprimido • **the government has tried to reduce unemployment in ~ areas** el gobierno ha intentado reducir el desempleo de las zonas deprimidas • **share prices were ~ following the announcement** los precios de las acciones habían caído tras el anuncio
3 (*Med*) [*bone*] hundido; [*immune system*] disminuido • **a ~ fracture** una fractura por aplastamiento

depressing [dɪˈpresɪŋ] ADJ deprimente • **what a ~ thought!** ¡qué idea tan deprimente!

depressingly [dɪˈpresɪŋlɪ] ADV [*say, reply*] tristemente • **Dad had become ~ weak** era deprimente ver lo débil que se había quedado papá • **it all sounded ~ familiar** me sonaba todo tanto que era deprimente • **it was a ~ familiar story** era una historia tan sabida *or* oída que resultaba deprimente

depression [dɪˈpreʃən] N **1** (*= dejection*) depresión *f*, abatimiento *m*
2 (*Met*) depresión *f*
3 (*Econ*) depresión *f*, crisis *f inv* (económica) • **the Depression** la Depresión
4 (*= hollow*) (*in surface*) depresión *f*; (*in ground, road*) bache *m*, hoyo *m*

depressive [dɪˈpresɪv] ADJ depresivo
N depresivo/a *m/f*

depressurization [dɪˌpreʃəraɪˈzeɪʃən] N despresurización *f*

depressurize [diːˈpreʃəraɪz] VT despresurizar

deprivation [ˌdeprɪˈveɪʃən] N (*Psych*) (*= act*) privación *f*; (*= state*) necesidad *f* • **he lived a life of ~** vivía en la necesidad, vivió una vida llena de privaciones • **the ~s of the past thirty years** las privaciones de los últimos treinta años • **sleep ~** falta *f* de sueño • **social ~** marginación *f* social

deprive [dɪˈpraɪv] VT • **to ~ sb of sth** privar a algn de algo • **to ~ o.s. of sth** privarse de algo • **they had been ~d of their freedom** les habían privado de su libertad • **they were ~d of affection as children** de niños no recibieron el suficiente afecto • **he was ~d of sleep/food for seven days** no le dejaron dormir/no le dieron de comer durante siete días • **the brain was ~d of oxygen** el cerebro no recibía su aporte de oxígeno • **"would you like some chocolate?" — "no thanks, I don't want to ~ you"** (*hum*) —¿quieres chocolate? —no, gracias, para ti

deprived [dɪˈpraɪvd] ADJ [*child, family*] necesitado, desventajado; [*area, district*] marginado • **she had a ~ childhood** tuvo una niñez llena de privaciones • **emotionally ~ children** niños con carencias afectivas • **to feel ~** sentirse en desventaja

deprogramme, deprogram (*US*) [diːˈprəʊgræm] VT desprogramar

Dept, dept. ABBR (= **department**) Dep., Dpto.

depth [depθ] N **1** [*of water, hole, shelf*] profundidad *f*; [*of room, building*] fondo *m*; [*of hem*] ancho *m*; [*of colour, feelings*] intensidad *f*; [*of voice*] gravedad *f*, profundidad *f* • **at a ~ of three metres** a tres metros de profundidad • **~ of field** (*Phot*) profundidad *f* de campo • **the trench was two metres in ~** la zanja tenía dos metros de profundidad • **to study a subject in ~** estudiar un tema a fondo *or* en profundidad • **it shows a great ~ of knowledge of the subject** muestra un conocimiento muy profundo de la materia • **to get out of one's ~** (*lit*) perder pie; (*fig*) meterse en honduras, salirse de su terreno • **to be out of one's ~** (*lit*) no tocar fondo, no hacer pie • **I'm out of my ~ with physics** (*fig*) no entiendo nada de física • **he felt out of his ~ with these people** se sentía perdido entre esta gente • **it is deplorable that anyone should sink to such ~s** es deplorable que uno pueda caer tan bajo

d

d

2 • **the ~s**: **in the ~s of the sea** en las profundidades del mar, en el fondo del mar • **to be in the ~s of despair** estar hundido en la desesperación • **in the ~s of winter** en lo más crudo del invierno; ▹ **plumb**
CPD ▸ **depth charge** carga *f* de profundidad
depthless ['depθlɪs] ADJ poco profundo
deputation [ˌdepjʊ'teɪʃən] N delegación *f*
depute [dɪ'pjuːt] VT [+ *job, authority*] delegar • **to ~ sth to sb** delegar algo en algn • **to ~ sb to do sth** delegar en algn para que haga algo
deputize ['depjʊtaɪz] VI • **to ~ for sb** desempeñar las funciones de algn, sustituir a algn
deputy ['depjʊtɪ] N suplente *mf*, sustituto/a *m/f*; (*Pol*) diputado/a *m/f*; (= *agent*) representante *mf*
CPD ▸ **deputy chairman** vicepresidente/a *m/f* ▸ **deputy director** director(a) *m/f* adjunto/a, subdirector(a) *m/f* ▸ **deputy head** (= *manager, teacher*) subdirector(a) *m/f* ▸ **deputy headmaster** subdirector *m* ▸ **deputy headmistress** subdirectora *f* ▸ **deputy leader** (*Brit*) [*of party*] vicepresidente/a *m/f* ▸ **deputy manager** subdirector(a) *m/f* ▸ **deputy mayor** teniente *mf* de alcalde ▸ **deputy minister** viceministro/a *m/f* ▸ **deputy president** vicepresidente/a *m/f* ▸ **deputy prime minister** viceprimer(a) ministro/a *m/f* ▸ **Deputy Secretary** (*US*) viceministro/a *m/f* ▸ **deputy sheriff** (*US*) ayudante *mf* del sheriff
derail [dɪ'reɪl] VT hacer descarrilar
VI descarrilar
derailment [dɪ'reɪlmənt] N descarrilamiento *m*
derange [dɪ'reɪndʒ] VT **1** (= *upset*) [+ *plans*] desarreglar, descomponer
2 (*mentally*) [+ *person*] volver loco, desquiciar
deranged [dɪ'reɪndʒd] ADJ [*person*] loco, desquiciado; [*mind*] perturbado • **to be (mentally) ~** estar desquiciado, ser un perturbado mental
derangement [dɪ'reɪndʒmənt] N
1 (= *disturbance*) desarreglo *m*
2 (*Med*) trastorno *m* mental
derby¹ ['dɑːbɪ], (*US*) ['dɜːbɪ] N **1** (*Sport*) • **local ~** derbi *m*
2 • **the Derby** (*Brit*) (*Horse racing*) el Derby (*importante carrera de caballos en Inglaterra*)
derby² ['dɜːbɪ] N (*US*) (*also* **derby hat**) sombrero *m* hongo, bombín *m*
Derbys ABBR (*Brit*) = **Derbyshire**
deregulate [diː'regjʊleɪt] VT desregular
deregulation [diːˌregjʊ'leɪʃən] N desregulación *f*
derelict ['derɪlɪkt] ADJ (= *abandoned*) abandonado; (= *ruined*) en ruinas
N (= *person*) indigente *mf*; (= *ship*) derrelicto *m*; (= *building*) edificio *m* abandonado
dereliction [ˌderɪ'lɪkʃən] N [*of property*] abandono *m* • **~ of duty** negligencia *f*
deride [dɪ'raɪd] VT ridiculizar, mofarse de
de rigueur [dərɪ'gɜːʳ] ADV de rigor
derision [dɪ'rɪʒən] N mofa *f*, burla *f*, irrisión *f* • **this was greeted with hoots of ~** esto fue recibido con gran mofa *or* sonoras burlas, esto provocó gran irrisión
derisive [dɪ'raɪsɪv] ADJ [*laughter*] burlón
derisively [dɪ'raɪsɪvlɪ] ADV burlonamente
de-risk [diː'rɪsk] VT (*Comm*) eliminar los riesgos de
derisory [dɪ'raɪsərɪ] ADJ **1** [*amount*] irrisorio
2 = **derisive**
derivable [dɪ'raɪvəbl] ADJ (*Ling, Philos, Chem*) derivable
derivation [ˌderɪ'veɪʃən] N [*of word*] derivación *f*
derivative [dɪ'rɪvətɪv] ADJ (*Chem, Ling*) derivado; (= *unoriginal*) [*literary work, style*] poco original
N (*Chem, Ling, Econ*) derivado *m*
derive [dɪ'raɪv] VT [+ *comfort, pleasure*] encontrar (**from** en); [+ *profit*] sacar, obtener (**from de**) • **it ~s its name** *or* **its name is ~d from the Latin word "linum"** su nombre viene *or* procede del latín "linum" • **~d demand** demanda *f* indirecta
VI • **to ~ from** [*word, name*] proceder de, venir de; [*view, notion*] basarse en; [*problem, power, fortune*] provenir de
dermatitis [ˌdɜːmə'taɪtɪs] N dermatitis *f inv*
dermatologist [ˌdɜːmə'tɒlədʒɪst] N dermatólogo/a *m/f*
dermatology [ˌdɜːmə'tɒlədʒɪ] N dermatología *f*
dermis ['dɜːmɪs] N dermis *f*
derogate ['derəgeɪt] VI • **to ~ from** (= *detract from*) quitar mérito *or* valor a; (= *reduce*) [+ *authority*] menoscabar; (= *deviate from*) desviarse de
derogation [ˌderə'geɪʃən] N [*of authority*] menoscabo *m* (**from** de); (= *deviation*) desviación *f*, descarrío *m* (*liter*) (**from** de)
derogatory [dɪ'rɒgətərɪ] ADJ despectivo • **he was very ~ about her singing** hizo comentarios muy despectivos de su forma de cantar
derrick ['derɪk] N (*in port*) grúa *f*; (*above oil well*) torre *f* de perforación, derrick *m*
derring-do ['derɪŋ'duː] N (*liter*) • **tales of derring-do** relatos *mpl* épicos • **deeds of derring-do** gestas *fpl*, hazañas *fpl*
derringer ['derɪndʒəʳ] N *pistola de cañón corto y calibre ancho*
derv [dɜːv] N (*Brit*) gasoil *m*
dervish ['dɜːvɪʃ] N derviche *mf*; (*fig*) salvaje *mf*
DES N ABBR (*Brit*) (*formerly*) = **Department of Education and Science**
desalinate [diː'sælɪneɪt] VT desalinizar
desalination [diːˌsælɪ'neɪʃən] N desalinización *f*
CPD ▸ **desalination plant** planta *f* desalinizadora
descale [diː'skeɪl] VT desincrustar • **descaling agent/product** agente *m*/producto *m* desincrustante
descant ['deskænt] N (*Mus*) contrapunto *m*
descend [dɪ'send] VT **1** (*frm*) (= *go down*) [+ *stairs*] descender, bajar
2 (= *originate*) • **to be ~ed from sb** descender de algn
VI **1** (*frm*) (= *go down*) descender, bajar (**from** de); ▹ **descending**
2 (= *invade, take over*) • **to ~ (up)on** [*fog, silence*] caer sobre; [*army, reporters*] invadir; (*hum*) [*visitors*] invadir • **we've got the whole family ~ing on us this weekend** nos va a invadir toda la familia este fin de semana
3 (= *sink*) • **I'd never ~ to that level** nunca me rebajaría a ese nivel • **to ~ to doing sth** rebajarse a hacer algo
4 (= *be inherited*) [*property, custom*] pasar (**to** a)
5 (= *originate*) • **to ~ from** [+ *ancestors*] descender de • **his family ~s from William the Conqueror** su familia desciende de Guillermo el Conquistador
descendant [dɪ'sendənt] N descendiente *mf* • **to leave no ~s** no dejar descendencia
descending [dɪ'sendɪŋ] ADJ descendente • **in ~ order of importance** por orden decreciente *or* descendente de importancia
descent [dɪ'sent] N **1** (= *going down*) descenso *m*, bajada *f*; (= *slope*) cuesta *f*, pendiente *f*; (= *fall*) descenso *m* (**in de**)
2 (= *raid*) ataque *m* (**on** sobre), incursión *f* (**on** en)
3 (= *ancestry*) ascendencia *f* (**from** de) • **of Italian ~** de ascendencia italiana • **line of ~** linaje *m* • **he claimed ~ from Peter the Great** afirmaba descender de Pedro el Grande
descramble ['diː'skræmbl] VT (*TV*) descodificar
descrambler ['diː'skræmbləʳ] N (*TV*) descodificador *m*
describe [dɪs'kraɪb] VT **1** [+ *scene, person*] describir • **~ him for us** descríbenoslo • **the feeling is impossible to ~** la sensación es indescriptible • **she ~s herself as an executive** se define como una ejecutiva • **I wouldn't ~ her as a feminist** no la calificaría de *or* describiría como feminista
2 (*Geom*) [+ *circle*] describir
description [dɪs'krɪpʃən] N **1** [*of person, scene, object*] descripción *f* • **do you know anyone of this ~?** ¿sabe de alguien que responda a esta descripción? • **beyond ~** indescriptible; ▹ **answer**
2 (= *sort*) • **he carried a gun of some ~** llevaba un arma de algún tipo • **of every ~** de toda clase
descriptive [dɪs'krɪptɪv] ADJ descriptivo
descriptivism [dɪs'krɪptɪvɪzəm] N descriptivismo *m*
descriptivist [dɪs'krɪptɪvɪst] N descriptivista *mf*
descry [dɪs'kraɪ] VT (*liter*) divisar
Desdemona [ˌdezdɪ'məʊnə] N Desdémona
desecrate ['desɪkreɪt] VT profanar
desecration [ˌdesɪ'kreɪʃən] N profanación *f*
desecrator ['desɪkreɪtəʳ] N profanador(a) *m/f*
deseed [ˌdiː'siːd] VT [+ *fruit*] despepitar
desegregate [diː'segrəgeɪt] VT abolir la segregación de
desegregation ['diːˌsegrə'geɪʃən] N abolición *f* de la segregación
deselect [ˌdiːsɪ'lekt] VT no renovar la candidatura de, no reelegir
deselection [diːsɪ'lekʃən] N no renovación *f* de la candidatura, rechazo *m* de la reelección
desensitize [diː'sensɪtaɪz] VT insensibilizar; (*Phot*) hacer insensible a la luz
desert¹ ['dezət] N desierto *m*
CPD [*climate, region*] desértico; [*tribe, people*] del desierto ▸ **desert boots** botines *mpl* de ante ▸ **desert island** isla *f* desierta ▸ **desert rat** (*Mil*) rata *f* del desierto
desert² [dɪ'zɜːt] VT (*Mil, Jur etc*) desertar de; [+ *person*] abandonar • **his courage ~ed him** su valor le abandonó *or* se esfumó
VI (*Mil*) desertar (**from** de, **to** a)
deserted [dɪ'zɜːtɪd] ADJ [*place, street*] desierto; [*husband, wife*] abandonado
deserter [dɪ'zɜːtəʳ] N (*Mil*) desertor(a) *m/f*; (*Pol*) tránsfuga *mf*
desertification [ˌdezɜːtɪfɪ'keɪʃən] N desertización *f*
desertify [de'zɜːtɪfaɪ] VT desertizar
desertion [dɪ'zɜːʃən] N (*Mil*) deserción *f*; [*of spouse*] abandono *m*
deserts [dɪ'zɜːts] NPL • IDIOMS: • **to get one's just ~** llevarse su merecido • **to give sb his/her just ~** dar a algn su merecido
deserve [dɪ'zɜːv] VT merecer • **to ~ to do sth** merecer hacer algo • **he ~s to win** merece ganar • **he got what he ~d** se llevó su merecido • **it's an area of France that ~s further exploration** es una región de Francia digna de ser explorada más a fondo
VI • **to ~ well of** merecer ser bien tratado por • **I thought I ~d better than that** opinaba que me tenían que haber tratado mejor
deservedly [dɪ'zɜːvɪdlɪ] ADV con razón, merecidamente • **and ~ so** y con razón

deserving [dɪ'zɜːvɪŋ] ADJ [*cause*] meritorio • **to be ~ of** merecer, ser digno de

deshabille [ˌdezə'biːl] N desabillé *m*

desiccant ['desɪkənt] N secante *m*

desiccate ['desɪkeɪt] VT desecar

desiccated ['desɪkeɪtɪd] ADJ **1** (= *dried*) seco
2 (*fig*) [*person*] marchito, mustio
CPD ▸ **desiccated coconut** coco rallado y seco

desiccation [ˌdesɪ'keɪʃən] N desecación *f*

desideratum [dɪˌzɪdə'rɑːtəm] N (PL: **desiderata** [dɪˌzɪdə'rɑːtə]) desiderátum *m*

design [dɪ'zaɪn] N **1** [*of building*] (= *plan, drawing*) proyecto *m*, diseño *m*; (= *ground plan*) distribución *f*; (= *preliminary sketch*) boceto *m*; (= *pattern*) motivo *m*; [*of cloth, wallpaper etc*] dibujo *m*; (= *style*) estilo *m*, líneas *fpl*; (= *art of design*) diseño *m* • **industrial ~** diseño *m* industrial
2 (= *intention*) intención *f*, propósito *m*; (= *plan*) plan *m*, proyecto *m* • **by ~** a propósito, adrede • **whether by accident or ~, he managed it** lo consiguió, ya sea por casualidad o a propósito • **grand ~** plan *m* general; (*Mil*) estrategia *f* general • **to have ~s on sth/sb** tener las miras puestas en algo/algn
VT **1** [+ *building etc*] diseñar, proyectar; [+ *dress, hat*] diseñar; [+ *course*] estructurar • **a well ~ed house** una casa bien diseñada • **a well ~ed programme** un programa bien concebido • **we will ~ an exercise plan specially for you** elaboraremos un programa de ejercicios especial para usted
2 (= *intend*) • **to be ~ed for sth/sb: a course ~ed for foreign students** un curso concebido *or* pensado para los estudiantes extranjeros • **a product ~ed for sensitive skin** un producto creado para pieles delicadas • **it was not ~ed for that** [*tool*] no fue diseñado para eso • **to be ~ed to do sth: clothes that are ~ed to appeal to young people** ropa que está diseñada para atraer a la juventud • **the strike was ~ed to cause maximum disruption** la huelga se planeó para causar el mayor trastorno posible
CPD ▸ **design and technology** (*Brit*) (*Scol*) ≈ dibujo *m* y tecnología ▸ **design brief** instrucciones *fpl* para el diseño ▸ **design department** departamento *m* de diseño, departamento *m* de proyectos ▸ **design engineer** ingeniero/a *m/f* diseñador(a) ▸ **design fault** fallo *m* de diseño ▸ **design feature** elemento *m* del diseño ▸ **design flaw** fallo *m* de diseño ▸ **design studio** estudio *m* de diseño

designate VT ['dezɪgneɪt] (= *name*) denominar; (= *appoint*) nombrar, designar; (= *indicate*) señalar, indicar • **to ~ sb to do sth** nombrar *or* designar a algn para hacer algo • **I was ~d as their representative** me nombraron *or* designaron representante de su grupo • **some of the rooms were ~d as offices** destinaron algunas de las habitaciones a oficinas • **the woodland has been ~d (as) a bird sanctuary** el bosque ha sido declarado reserva ornitológica
ADJ ['dezɪgnɪt] designado, nombrado

designated ['dezɪgneɪtɪd] ADJ (= *appointed*) designado, nombrado; (= *indicated*) señalado, indicado; (= *set aside*) [*area, place, room*] delimitado
CPD ▸ **designated area** área *f* delimitada ▸ **designated driver** conductor(a) *m/f* designado/a

designation [ˌdezɪg'neɪʃən] N (= *title*) denominación *f*; (= *appointment*) nombramiento *m*, designación *f*

designedly [dɪ'zaɪnɪdlɪ] ADV de propósito

designer [dɪ'zaɪnəʳ] N [*of machines etc*] diseñador(a) *m/f*; (= *fashion designer*) diseñador(a) *m/f* de moda, modisto/a *m/f*; (*in theatre*) escenógrafo/a *m/f*; (*TV*) diseñador(a) *m/f*
CPD ▸ **designer baby** bebé *m* de diseño ▸ **designer clothes** ropa *fsing* de diseño ▸ **designer drug** droga *f* de diseño, droga *f* de laboratorio ▸ **designer jeans** vaqueros *mpl* de marca ▸ **designer label** marca *f* de moda ▸ **designer stubble** barba *f* de tres días (*según la moda*)

designing [dɪ'zaɪnɪŋ] ADJ intrigante
N diseño *m*, el diseñar

desirability [dɪˌzaɪərə'bɪlɪtɪ] N [*of plan*] conveniencia *f*; [*of person*] atractivo *m* • **the ~ of the plan is not in question** nadie pone en duda la conveniencia del proyecto

desirable [dɪ'zaɪərəbl] ADJ [*woman*] deseable, atractiva; [*offer*] atrayente; [*property*] deseable; [*action*] conveniente, deseable • **"experience desirable but not essential"** "la experiencia se valorará pero no es imprescindible" • **I don't think it ~ to tell him** *or* **that we tell him** no creo que sea conveniente decírselo

desirably [dɪ'zaɪərəblɪ] ADV • **~ located** con una situación ideal

desire [dɪ'zaɪəʳ] N deseo *m* (**for** de, **to do sth** de hacer algo) • **I have no ~ to see him** no tengo el más mínimo deseo de verlo
VT **1** (= *want*) [+ *wealth, success*] desear • **to ~ to do sth** desear hacer algo • **it leaves much to be ~d** deja mucho que desear
2 (*sexually*) [+ *person*] desear
3 (= *request*) • **to ~ that …** rogar que … • **to ~ sb to do sth** rogar a algn que haga algo

desired [dɪ'zaɪəd] ADJ [*result, effect*] deseado

desirous [dɪ'zaɪərəs] ADJ (*frm*) deseoso (**of** de) • **to be ~ of** desear • **to be ~ that** desear que (+ *subjun*) • **to be ~ to do sth** desear hacer algo

desist [dɪ'zɪst] VI • **to ~ from sth** desistir de algo • **to ~ from doing sth** dejar *or* desistir de hacer algo • **we begged him to ~** le rogamos que desistiera *or* que lo dejara

desk [desk] N **1** (*in office, study etc*) escritorio *m*, mesa *f* de trabajo; (*Scol*) pupitre *m*; (= *bureau*) escritorio *m*
2 (= *section*) [*of ministry, newspaper*] sección *f*
3 (*Brit*) (*in airport, hospital*) mostrador *m*; (*in shop, restaurant*) (*for payment*) caja *f*; (*in hotel*) recepción *f*
CPD ▸ **desk clerk** (*US*) recepcionista *mf* ▸ **desk diary** agenda *f* de escritorio ▸ **desk job** trabajo *m* de oficina ▸ **desk lamp** lámpara *f* de escritorio ▸ **desk pad** bloc *m* de notas ▸ **desk study** estudio *m* sobre el papel

desk-bound ['deskbaʊnd] ADJ sedentario

deskill [diː'skɪl] VT [+ *job*] desprofesionalizar

desktop ['desktɒp] ADJ [*computer*] de sobremesa, de escritorio
CPD ▸ **desktop publishing** autoedición *f*

desolate ADJ ['desəlɪt] [*place*] desolado, desierto; [*outlook, future*] desolador; [*person*] (= *griefstricken*) desolado, afligido; (= *friendless*) solitario
VT ['desəleɪt] [+ *place*] asolar, arrasar; [+ *person*] desolar, afligir • **we were utterly ~d** quedamos profundamente desolados *or* afligidos

desolately ['desəlɪtlɪ] ADV [*say*] tristemente

desolation [ˌdesə'leɪʃən] N **1** (= *deserted state*) [*of landscape*] desolación *f*
2 (= *grief*) [*of person*] desolación *f*, desconsuelo *m*
3 (= *act*) asolamiento *m*, arrasamiento *m*

despair [dɪs'pɛəʳ] N **1** (= *emotion*) desesperación *f* • **to be in ~** estar desesperado
2 (= *person*) • **he is the ~ of his parents** trae locos a sus padres
VI perder la esperanza, desesperarse • **to ~ of sth** perder la esperanza de algo • **we ~ed of ever seeing her again** perdimos la esperanza de volver a verla • **don't ~!** ¡ánimo!, ¡anímate!

despairing [dɪs'pɛərɪŋ] ADJ [*look, sigh*] de desesperación; [*parent, sufferer*] desesperado

despairingly [dɪs'pɛərɪŋlɪ] ADV desesperadamente

despatch [dɪs'pætʃ] = **dispatch**

desperado [ˌdespə'rɑːdəʊ] N (PL: **desperados** *or* **desperadoes**) bandido *m*

desperate ['despərɪt] ADJ **1** [*person, act, attempt, situation*] desesperado • **to feel ~** estar desesperado • **to be ~ for sth** necesitar algo urgentemente • **I'm ~ (for the lavatory)!*** me muero de ganas de ir al lavabo • **to get** *or* **grow ~** desesperarse • **to resort to ~ measures** recurrir a medidas desesperadas, recurrir a fruto de la de desesperación • **you're going out with her? you must be ~!** (*hum*) ¿sales con esa? ¡muy desesperado debes estar! • **to be in ~ need of sth** necesitar algo urgentemente • **the company's ~ financial position** la crítica posición económica de la empresa • **to do something ~** cometer un acto desesperado, cometer una locura, hacer algo a la desesperada • **to be ~ to do sth: I was ~ to see her** estaba desesperada por verla, quería verla a toda costa, me moría por verla • **she was ~ to find a new job** estaba desesperada por encontrar otro trabajo • **both countries are ~ to avoid war** ambos países quieren evitar la guerra a toda costa
2* (= *very bad*) [*book, film, meal*] atroz, pésimo • **the play was pretty ~** la obra era atroz *or* pésima

desperately ['despərɪtlɪ] ADV **1** (= *urgently, frantically*) [*say, look*] desesperadamente, con desesperación; [*try, struggle, look for*] desesperadamente; [*fight*] encarnizadamente; [*need, require*] urgentemente, desesperadamente • **to hope ~ for sth** desear algo con todas sus fuerzas • **to be ~ in love** estar locamente *or* perdidamente enamorado • **to be ~ in need of sth** necesitar algo urgentemente • **I ~ wanted to become a film director** quería ser director de cine más que nada en el mundo *or* con todo el alma
2 (= *horribly*) [*lonely, thin, shy, poor*] terriblemente • **we're not ~ busy at the moment** no estamos lo que se dice terriblemente ocupados en este momento • **it's ~ cold** hace un frío terrible • **to try ~ hard to do sth** esforzarse mucho por hacer algo • **I'm ~ hungry** me muero de hambre • **~ ill** muy grave, gravemente enfermo • **I'm not ~ keen on the idea*** la idea no me vuelve loco • **to be ~ short of sth** andar escasísimo de algo • **he's ~ unhappy** es terriblemente desdichado • **my parents were ~ worried** mis padres estaban preocupadísimos
3* (= *very much, very*) • **"do you want to have children?" — "not ~"** —¿quieres tener hijos? —no estoy desesperado por tenerlos • **it's not ~ important/urgent** no es terriblemente importante/urgente • **I'm not ~ keen** no es que me entusiasme • **"hungry?" — "not ~"** —¿tienes hambre? —puedo aguantar

desperation [ˌdespə'reɪʃən] N desesperación *f* • **she drove him to ~** le llevó al borde de la desesperación, le hizo caer en la desesperación • **in (sheer) ~** • **out of (sheer) ~** a la desesperada, de pura desesperación

d

despicable [dɪs'pɪkəbl] ADJ vil, despreciable
despicably [dɪs'pɪkəblɪ] ADV despreciablemente; [*behave*] de manera despreciable
despise [dɪs'paɪz] VT despreciar
despite [dɪs'paɪt] PREP a pesar de, pese a
despoil [dɪs'pɔɪl] VT despojar (**of** de)
despondency [dɪs'pɒndənsɪ] N, **despondence** [dɪs'pɒndəns] N abatimiento *m*, desaliento *m*, pesimismo *m*
despondent [dɪs'pɒndənt] ADJ (= *dejected*) abatido, desanimado; (= *disheartened*) descorazonado; [*letter etc*] de tono triste, pesimista • **he was very ~ about our chances** habló en términos pesimistas de nuestras posibilidades • **he was too ~ to smile** le faltaron ánimos para sonreír
despondently [dɪs'pɒndəntlɪ] ADV • **he sighed ~** suspiró desanimado
despot ['despɒt] N déspota *mf*
despotic [des'pɒtɪk] ADJ déspota
despotically [des'pɒtɪkəlɪ] ADV despóticamente
despotism ['despətɪzəm] N despotismo *m*
des. res.* ['dez'rez] N = **desirable residence**
dessert [dɪ'zɜ:t] N postre *m* • **what's for ~?** ¿qué hay de postre?
CPD ▸ **dessert apple** manzana *f* para repostería ▸ **dessert chocolate** chocolate *m* para postres ▸ **dessert menu** carta *f* de postres, menú *m* de postres ▸ **dessert plate** plato *m* de postre ▸ **dessert wine** vino *m* dulce (*para el postre*)
dessertspoon [dɪ'zɜ:tspu:n] N cuchara *f* de postre
destabilization [di:,steɪbɪlaɪ'zeɪʃən] N desestabilización *f*
destabilize [di:'steɪbɪlaɪz] VT desestabilizar
destination [,destɪ'neɪʃən] N destino *m*
destine ['destɪn] VT destinar (**for, to** para)
destined ['destɪnd] ADJ **1** (= *intended*) • **~ for** destinado a
2 (= *fated*) • **to be ~ to do sth** estar destinado a hacer algo • **it was ~ to fail** estaba destinado *or* condenado a fracasar • **she was ~ for greater things** estaba destinada *or* predestinada a llegar lejos • **it was ~ to happen this way** tenía que ocurrir así • **we were ~ never to meet again** el destino no quiso que nos volviéramos a encontrar
3 (= *travelling*) • **~ for London** con destino a Londres
destiny ['destɪnɪ] N (= *fate*) destino *m*
destitute ['destɪtju:t] ADJ **1** (= *poverty-stricken*) indigente • **to be (utterly) ~** estar en la (más absoluta) miseria
2 (= *lacking*) • **~ of** desprovisto de
destitution [,destɪ'tju:ʃən] N indigencia *f*, miseria *f*
de-stress, destress [di:'stres] VI desestresarse
VT desestresar
destroy [dɪs'trɔɪ] VT (*gen*) destruir, destrozar; (= *kill*) matar; [+ *pet*] sacrificar; [+ *vermin*] exterminar; (*fig*) [+ *relationship, hopes etc*] destrozar, acabar con • **the factory was ~ed by a fire** la fábrica quedó destrozada *or* fue arrasada por un incendio
destroyer [dɪs'trɔɪəʳ] N (*Naut*) destructor *m*
destruct [dɪ'strʌkt] VT destruir
VI destruirse; ▹ **self-destruct**
CPD ▸ **destruct button** botón *m* de destrucción ▸ **destruct mechanism** mecanismo *m* de destrucción
destructible [dɪs'trʌktəbl] ADJ destructible
destruction [dɪs'trʌkʃən] N **1** (*gen*) destrucción *f*; (*fig*) [*of reputation*] destrucción *f*; [*of person*] ruina *f*, perdición *f* • **to test a machine to ~** someter una máquina a pruebas límite; ▹ **scene**
2 (= *ruins, damage*) destrozos *mpl*
destructive [dɪs'trʌktɪv] ADJ [*weapon, person, behaviour, influence, emotion*] destructivo; [*effect*] destructor; [*child*] destrozón; [*criticism, comment*] destructivo, negativo; [*relationship*] destructivo, dañino • **the ~ power of nuclear weapons** el poder destructivo *or* destructor de las armas nucleares • **to be ~ of** *or* **to sth: products that are ~ of** *or* **to the environment** productos que destruyen el medio ambiente
destructively [dɪs'trʌktɪvlɪ] ADV destructivamente, de modo destructivo • **the storm struck violently and ~** la tormenta se abatió violenta y destructiva
destructiveness [dɪs'trʌktɪvnɪs] N [*of fire, war, weapon*] capacidad *f* destructora; [*of child*] tendencia *f* destructiva; [*of criticism, attitude, behaviour*] carácter *m* destructivo
destructor [dɪs'trʌktəʳ] N (*Brit*) (*also* **refuse destructor**) incinerador *m* de basuras, quemador *m* de basuras
desuetude [dɪ'sjʊɪtju:d] N (*frm*) desuso *m* • **to fall into ~** caer en desuso
desulphurization [,di:sʌlfəraɪ'zeɪʃən] N desulfurización *f*
desultory ['desəltərɪ] (*frm*) ADJ [*way of working etc*] poco metódico; [*applause*] poco entusiasta; [*gunfire*] intermitente, esporádico • **they made ~ conversation** entablaron sin ganas una conversación
det. ABBR **1** = **detached**
2 = **detective**
detach [dɪ'tætʃ] VT (= *separate*) separar (**from** de); (= *unstick*) despegar; (*Mil*) destacar • **to ~ o.s. from a group** separarse de un grupo • **to ~ o.s. from a situation** distanciarse de una situación
detachable [dɪ'tætʃəbl] ADJ [*collar, lining*] postizo, separable; [*parts*] desmontable, extraíble
detached [dɪ'tætʃt] ADJ **1** (= *separate*) separado, suelto; (*from friends, family*) distanciado • **to become ~ (from)** [*part, fragment*] desprenderse (de) • **she had become ~ from reality** había perdido contacto con la realidad • **they live ~ from everything** viven desligados de todo
2 (= *impartial*) [*opinion*] objetivo, imparcial; (= *unemotional*) [*manner*] indiferente • **to take a ~ view of** considerar objetivamente
CPD ▸ **detached house** casa *f* independiente, chalet *m* individual ▸ **detached retina** desprendimiento *m* de la retina
detachment [dɪ'tætʃmənt] N
1 (= *separation*) separación *f*, desprendimiento *m*
2 (= *impartiality*) objetividad *f*, imparcialidad *f*; (= *indifference*) indiferencia *f* • **an air of ~** un aire de indiferencia
3 (*Mil*) destacamento *m*
detail ['di:teɪl] N **1** (*gen*) detalle *m* • **there are still one or two ~s to sort out** hay todavía un par de detalles *or* cosas que concretar • **to go into ~(s)** entrar en detalles, pormenorizar • **down to the last ~** hasta el más mínimo detalle • **for further ~s contact J. Sims** para más información póngase en contacto con J. Sims
2 (*taken collectively*) detalles *mpl* • **the wonderful ~ of the painting** la maravillosa minuciosidad del cuadro • **attention to ~** minuciosidad *f* • **in ~** en detalle, detalladamente
3 (*Mil*) destacamento *m*
VT **1** [+ *facts, story*] detallar
2 (*Mil*) destacar (**to do sth** para hacer algo)
detailed ['di:teɪld] ADJ [*information, report, description*] detallado, pormenorizado; [*plan, map, instructions, knowledge, picture*] detallado; [*examination, investigation*] minucioso, detenido; [*history*] pormenorizado
detain [dɪ'teɪn] VT **1** (= *arrest*) detener, arrestar
2 (= *keep waiting*) retener • **I was ~ed at the office** me entretuve *or* demoré en la oficina • **I was ~ed by fog** me retrasé por la niebla • **don't let me ~ you** no quiero entretenerla
detainee [,di:teɪ'ni:] N detenido/a *m/f*
detect [dɪ'tekt] VT (= *discover*) descubrir; (= *notice*) percibir, detectar; [+ *crime*] descubrir; [+ *criminal*] identificar; (*Tech*) (*by radar etc*) detectar
detectable [dɪ'tektəbl] ADJ perceptible, detectable
detection [dɪ'tekʃən] N (= *discovery*) descubrimiento *m*; (= *perception*) percepción *f*; (*by detective*) investigación *f*; (*Tech*) detección *f* • **to escape ~** [*criminal*] no ser descubierto; [*mistake*] pasar desapercibido
detective [dɪ'tektɪv] N detective *mf* • **private ~** detective *mf* privado/a
CPD ▸ **detective chief inspector** (*Brit*) ≈ comisario *m* ▸ **detective chief superintendent** (*Brit*) ≈ comisario/a *m/f* jefe ▸ **detective constable** (*Brit*) ≈ agente *mf* (de policía) ▸ **detective inspector** (*Brit*) ≈ inspector(a) *m/f* (de policía) ▸ **detective novel** novela *m* policíaca ▸ **detective sergeant** (*Brit*) ≈ oficial *mf* de policía ▸ **detective story** novela *f* policíaca ▸ **detective superintendent** (*Brit*) ≈ comisario/a *m/f* (de policía) ▸ **detective work** (*fig*) trabajo *m* detectivesco, trabajo *m* de investigación
detector [dɪ'tektəʳ] N (= *gadget*) detector *m*
CPD ▸ **detector van** (*Brit*) camioneta *f* de detección (*de televisores sin licencia*)
détente ['deɪtɑ̃:nt] N distensión *f*
detention [dɪ'tenʃən] N [*of criminal, spy*] detención *f*, arresto *m*; [*of schoolchild*] castigo *m* • **to get a ~** quedarse castigado después de clase
CPD ▸ **detention centre, detention center** (*US*) centro *m* de detención ▸ **detention home** (*US*) centro *m* de rehabilitación
deter [dɪ'tɜ:ʳ] VT (= *discourage*) desalentar; (= *dissuade*) disuadir; (= *prevent*) impedir • **to ~ sb from doing sth** (= *dissuade*) disuadir a algn de hacer algo; (= *prevent*) impedir a algn hacer algo, impedir a algn que haga algo • **I was ~red by the cost** el precio me hizo abandonar la idea • **a weapon which ~s nobody** un arma que no asusta a nadie, un arma sin poder disuasorio • **don't let the weather ~ you** no desistas por el mal tiempo
detergent [dɪ'tɜ:dʒənt] ADJ detergente
N detergente *m*
deteriorate [dɪ'tɪərɪəreɪt] VI [*work, situation, weather, condition*] empeorar; [*health*] empeorar, deteriorarse; [*materials, building, relationship*] deteriorarse • **he was worried about her deteriorating health** le preocupaba que cada vez estuviera peor de salud • **the meeting ~d into a free-for-all** la reunión degeneró en una pelea
deterioration [dɪ,tɪərɪə'reɪʃən] N [*of work, situation, condition*] empeoramiento *m* (**in, of** de); [*of health*] deterioro *m*, empeoramiento *m* (**in, of** de); [*of materials, building, relationship*] deterioro *m* (**in, of** de)
determent [dɪ'tɜ:mənt] N disuasión *f*
determinable [dɪ'tɜ:mɪnəbl] ADJ determinable

determinant [dɪ'tɜ:mɪnənt] ADJ determinante
N determinante *m*

determinate [dɪ'tɜ:mɪnɪt] ADJ (*frm*) (= *fixed*) determinado; (*Jur*) [*sentence*] definitivo

determination [dɪˌtɜ:mɪ'neɪʃən] N
1 (= *resolve*) determinación *f*, resolución *f*, decisión *f* • **he set off with great ~** partió muy resuelto • **in his ~ to do it** por su determinación *or* decisión a hacerlo
2 (= *ascertaining*) [*of cause, position*] determinación *f*

determinative [dɪ'tɜ:mɪnətɪv] ADJ determinativo
N determinativo *m*

determine [dɪ'tɜ:mɪn] VT **1** (= *ascertain, define*) [+ *cause, meaning*] determinar; [+ *price, date*] fijar, determinar; [+ *scope, limits, boundary*] definir, determinar • **to ~ what is to be done** determinar *or* decidir lo que hay que hacer • **to ~ whether sth is true** determinar si algo es verdad
2 (= *be the deciding factor in*) [+ *fate, character*] determinar • **demand ~s supply** la demanda determina la oferta • **to be ~d by** depender de
3 (= *make determined*) • **to ~ sb to do sth** hacer que algn se decida a hacer algo • **this ~d him to go** esto hizo que se decidiera a ir
4 (= *resolve*) • **to ~ to do sth** decidir hacer algo, determinar hacer algo
▸ **determine on** VI + PREP [+ *course of action*] optar por, decidirse por

determined [dɪ'tɜ:mɪnd] ADJ [*person*] decidido, resuelto; [*effort*] resuelto, enérgico • **he walked in with a ~ look on his face** entró con aire resuelto • **her refusal made me even more ~** su negativa solo sirvió para que me decidiese aún más • **to be ~ that ...** estar decidido a que (+ *subjun*) • **she is ~ that her children should go to college** está decidida a que sus hijos vayan a la universidad • **to be ~ to do sth** estar decidido *or* resuelto a hacer algo • **she's ~ to pass the exam** está decidida *or* resuelta a aprobar el examen • **his enemies are ~ to ruin him** sus enemigos se han empeñado en arruinarle, sus enemigos quieren arruinarle a toda costa • **to make a ~ attempt** *or* **effort to do sth** poner todo su empeño en hacer algo

determinedly [dɪ'tɜ:mɪndlɪ] ADV [*say*] resueltamente; [*persevere*] con determinación • **he walked in ~** entró con aire resuelto *or* decidido • **he was ~ optimistic** estaba resuelto a ver el lado bueno

determiner [dɪ'tɜ:mɪnəʳ] N determinante *m*

determining [dɪ'tɜ:mɪnɪŋ] ADJ • **~ factor** factor *m* determinante

determinism [dɪ'tɜ:mɪnɪzəm] N determinismo *m*

determinist [dɪ'tɜ:mɪnɪst] ADJ determinista
N determinista *mf*

deterministic [dɪˌtɜ:mɪ'nɪstɪk] ADJ determinista

deterrence [dɪ'terəns] N disuasión *f*

deterrent [dɪ'terənt] N (*also Mil*) elemento *m* disuasivo, elemento *m* disuasorio • **to act as a ~** servir de elemento disuasivo • **nuclear ~** fuerza *f* nuclear disuasiva • **these penalties are no ~ to criminals** estos castigos no disuaden a los criminales
ADJ disuasivo, disuasorio

detest [dɪ'test] VT detestar, aborrecer • **to ~ doing sth** detestar *or* odiar hacer algo

detestable [dɪ'testəbl] ADJ detestable, aborrecible

detestably [dɪ'testəblɪ] ADV de forma detestable

detestation [ˌdi:tes'teɪʃən] (*frm*) N detestación *f*, odio *m*, aborrecimiento *m* • **to hold in ~** detestar, odiar, aborrecer

dethrone [di:'θrəʊn] VT destronar

dethronement [di:'θrəʊnmənt] N destronamiento *m*

detonate ['detəneɪt] VT hacer detonar
VI detonar, estallar

detonation [ˌdetə'neɪʃən] N detonación *f*

detonator ['detəneɪtəʳ] N detonador *m*

detour ['di:tʊəʳ] N rodeo *m*, vuelta *f*; (*Aut*) desvío *m* • **to make a ~** desviarse, dar un rodeo
VT (*US*) desviar
VI (*US*) desviarse, dar un rodeo

detox* ['di:tɒks] N = **detoxication, detoxification**
VT = **detoxicate, detoxify**

detoxicate [di:'tɒksɪkeɪt] VT = **detoxify**

detoxication [di:ˌtɒksɪ'keɪʃən], **detoxification** [di:ˌtɒksɪfɪ'keɪʃən] N desintoxicación *f*
CPD ▸ **detoxification centre, detoxification center** (*US*) centro *m* de desintoxicación ▸ **detoxification programme, detoxification program** (*US*) programa *f* de desintoxicación

detoxify [di:'tɒksɪfaɪ] VT [+ *alcoholic*] desintoxicar; [+ *chemical*] eliminar la toxicidad de

detract [dɪ'trækt] VI • **to ~ from** [+ *value*] quitar mérito *or* valor a; [+ *reputation*] empañar

detraction [dɪ'trækʃən] N detracción *f*

detractor [dɪ'træktəʳ] N detractor(a) *m/f*

detrain [di:'treɪn] VI bajarse del tren

detriment ['detrɪmənt] N detrimento *m*, perjuicio *m* • **to the ~ of** en detrimento *or* perjuicio de • **without ~ to** sin (causar) detrimento *or* perjuicio a

detrimental [ˌdetrɪ'mentl] ADJ perjudicial (to para)

detritus [dɪ'traɪtəs] N (*frm*) detrito(s) *m(pl)*, detritus *m*

de trop [də'trəʊ] (*frm*) ADV • **to be ~** estar de más, sobrar

deuce¹ [dju:s] N (*Tennis*) cuarenta iguales *mpl*, deuce *m*

deuce²† [dju:s] N • **a ~ of a row** un tremendo jaleo • **a ~ of a mess** una terrible confusión • **the ~ it is!** ¡qué demonio! • **what/where the ~ ...?** ¿qué/dónde demonios ...? • **to play the ~ with** estropear, echar a perder

deuced [dju:st] ADJ maldito
ADV diabólicamente, terriblemente

deuterium [dju:'tɪərɪəm] N deuterio *m*
CPD ▸ **deuterium oxide** óxido *m* deutérico

Deuteronomy [ˌdju:tə'rɒnəmɪ] N Deuteronomio *m*

deutschmark ['dɔɪtʃmɑ:k] N marco *m* alemán

devaluate [di:'væljʊeɪt] VT = **devalue**

devaluation [ˌdɪvæljʊ'eɪʃən] N (*Econ*) devaluación *f*; [*of person*] subvaloración *f*

devalue ['di:'vælju:] VT (*Econ*) devaluar; [+ *person*] subvalorar, subestimar

devalued [ˌdi:'vælju:d] ADJ [*achievement, institution*] devaluado; [*person*] subvalorado, subestimado

devastate ['devəsteɪt] VT (= *destroy*) [+ *place*] devastar, asolar; (*fig*) [+ *opponent, opposition*] aplastar, arrollar; (= *overwhelm*) [+ *person*] dejar desolado, dejar destrozado • **we were simply ~d** estábamos verdaderamente desolados *or* destrozados

devastating ['devəsteɪtɪŋ] ADJ
1 (= *destructive*) [*flood, storm, consequence*] devastador; [*attack*] demoledor • **nuclear war would be ~ for Europe** una guerra nuclear tendría un efecto devastador sobre Europa
2 (= *crushing*) [*blow, loss*] tremendo; [*argument, opposition, logic, defeat*] aplastante; [*news*] terrible; [*criticism, report*] demoledor; [*wit*] apabullante • **the ~ news that she had cancer** la terrible noticia de que tenía cáncer • **the news is ~** la noticia es un golpe tremendo *or* durísimo • **a strike would be ~ to the economy** una huelga sería un golpe tremendo para la economía
3 (= *stunning*) [*beauty, woman, charm*] irresistible

devastatingly ['devəsteɪtɪŋlɪ] ADV [*beautiful*] irresistiblemente; [*effective, successful, funny*] tremendamente • **a ~ attractive woman** una mujer de un atractivo irresistible • **a ~ simple solution** una solución terriblemente simple • **these missiles are ~ accurate** estos misiles tienen una precisión devastadora • **she demolished his arguments briefly and ~** destruyó sus argumentos de forma lacónica y aplastante

devastation [ˌdevə'steɪʃən] N **1** (= *act*) devastación *f*
2 (= *state*) devastación *f*, destrozos *mpl*

develop [dɪ'veləp] VT **1** (= *make bigger, stronger etc*) [+ *mind, body*] desarrollar; (*fig*) [+ *argument, idea*] desarrollar • **I ~ed his original idea** yo desarrollé su idea original
2 (= *generate*) [+ *plan*] elaborar; [+ *process*] perfeccionar
3 (= *acquire*) [+ *interest, taste, habit*] adquirir; [+ *disease*] contraer; [+ *tendency*] coger, desarrollar; [+ *engine trouble*] empezar a tener • **she ~ed a liking for whisky** le cogió el gusto al whisky
4 (= *build on*) [+ *region*] desarrollar, fomentar; [+ *land*] urbanizar; [+ *site*] ampliar • **this land is to be ~ed** se va a construir en *or* urbanizar este terreno
5 (= *exploit*) [+ *resources, mine etc*] explotar
6 (*Phot*) revelar • **to get a film ~ed** revelar un carrete
VI **1** (= *change, mature*) desarrollarse • **girls ~ faster than boys** las chicas se desarrollan más rápido que los chicos • **to ~ into** convertirse *or* transformarse en • **the argument ~ed into a fight** la discusión se convirtió en una pelea
2 (= *progress*) [*country*] desarrollarse • **how is the book ~ing?** ¿qué tal va el libro?
3 (= *come into being*) aparecer; [*symptoms*] aparecer, mostrarse • **a crack was ~ing in the wall** se estaba abriendo una grieta en la pared
4 (= *come about*) [*idea, plan, problem*] surgir • **it later ~ed that ...** más tarde quedó claro que ...

developed [dɪ'veləpt] ADJ [*country, world*] desarrollado; [*sense of humour, justice etc*] profundo

developer [dɪ'veləpəʳ] N **1** (*also* **property developer**) promotor(a) *m/f* inmobiliario/a
2 (*Physiol*) • **I was a late ~** maduré tarde
3 (*Phot*) revelador *m*

developing [dɪ'veləpɪŋ] ADJ [*country*] en (vías de) desarrollo; [*crisis, storm*] que se avecina
N (*Phot*) revelado *m*
CPD ▸ **developing bath** baño *m* de revelado

development [dɪ'veləpmənt] N **1** (*gen*) desarrollo *m*; (= *unfolding*) evolución *f*
2 (= *change in situation*) novedad *f*, cambio *m*; (= *event*) acontecimiento *m* • **there are no new ~s to report** no se registra ninguna novedad *or* ningún cambio • **what is the latest ~?** ¿hay alguna novedad? • **awaiting ~s** en espera de novedades

d

3 [*of resources*] explotación *f*; [*of land*] urbanización *f*
4 (= *area of new housing*) urbanización *f*
CPD ▸ **development agency** agencia *f* de desarrollo ▸ **development area** ≈ zona *f* de urgente reindustrialización, ≈ polo *m* de desarrollo ▸ **development bank** banco *m* de desarrollo ▸ **development company** [*of property*] promotora *f* inmobiliaria; [*of resources*] compañía *f* de explotación ▸ **development corporation** [*of new town*] corporación *f* de desarrollo, corporación *f* de promoción ▸ **development officer** director(a) *m/f* de promoción ▸ **development plan** plan *m* de desarrollo

developmental [dɪˌveləp'mentl] ADJ [*process*] de desarrollo; [*abnormality*] del desarrollo
CPD ▸ **developmental psychologist** psicólogo/a *m/f* del desarrollo ▸ **developmental psychology** psicología *f* del desarrollo

deviance ['diːvɪəns], **deviancy** ['diːvɪənsɪ] N (*gen*) (*also Psych*) desviación *f*

deviant ['diːvɪənt] ADJ (*gen*) (*also Psych, Ling*) desviado
N *persona de conducta desviada*

deviate ['diːvɪeɪt] VI desviarse (**from** de)

deviation [ˌdiːvɪ'eɪʃən] N desviación *f* (**from** de)

deviationism [ˌdiːvɪ'eɪʃənɪzəm] N desviacionismo *m*

deviationist [ˌdiːvɪ'eɪʃənɪst] ADJ desviacionista
N desviacionista *mf*

device [dɪ'vaɪs] N 1 (= *gadget*) aparato *m*; (= *mechanism*) mecanismo *m*, dispositivo *m*; (= *explosive*) artefacto *m* • **nuclear ~** ingenio *m* nuclear
2 (= *scheme*) estratagema *f*, recurso *m* • **to leave sb to his own ~s** dejar a algn hacer lo que le dé la gana; (*to solve problem*) dejar que algn se las arregle solo
3 (= *emblem*) emblema *m*; (= *motto*) lema *m*

devil ['devl] N 1 (= *evil spirit*) demonio *m*, diablo *m* • **the Devil** el Diablo • **go to the ~!**‡ ¡vete al diablo!‡, ¡vete a la porra! (*Sp**) • **the ~ take it!**† ¡que se lo lleve el diablo! • **~s on horseback** *ciruelas pasas envueltas en beicon servidas sobre pan tostado* • IDIOMS: • **to be between the ~ and the deep blue sea** estar entre la espada y la pared • **(to) give the ~ his due** ser justo hasta con el diablo • **to play the ~ with** arruinar, estropear • **to play (the) ~'s advocate** hacer de abogado del diablo • **to raise the ~** armar la gorda • **speak** *or* **talk of the ~!*** hablando del rey de Roma (por la puerta asoma) • PROVERBS: • **better the ~ you know** vale más lo malo conocido que lo bueno por conocer • **the ~ finds work for idle hands** cuando el diablo no tiene que hacer con el rabo mata moscas; ▹ **luck**
2* (= *person*) demonio *m* • **poor ~** pobre diablo, pobrecito/a *m/f* • **go on, be a ~!** ¡anda, atrévete *or* lánzate! • **you little ~!** ¡qué diablillo *or* malo eres!
3* (*as intensifier*) • **the ~ it is!** ¡qué demonio! • **a ~ of a noise** un ruido de todos los demonios • **it was the ~ of a job to do!** ¡menudo trabajo que (me) costó! • **we had the ~ of a job** *or* **the ~'s own job to find it** nos costó horrores encontrarlo • **I'm in the ~ of a mess** estoy en un lío tremendo • **to work/run like the ~** trabajar/correr como un descosido • **how/what/why/who the ~ ...?** ¿cómo/qué/por qué/quién demonios ...? • **there will be the ~ to pay** esto va a costar caro
4 (*Jur*) aprendiz *m* (de abogado); (*Typ*) aprendiz *m* de imprenta
VT 1 [+ *meat*] asar con mucho picante
2 (*US**) fastidiar
VI • **to ~ for** (*Jur*) trabajar de aprendiz para
CPD ▸ **devil worship** satanismo *m* ▸ **devil's food cake** (*US*) *pastel de chocolate*

devilfish ['devlfɪʃ] N (PL: **devilfish** *or* **devilfishes**) raya *f*, manta *f*

devilish ['devlɪʃ] ADJ (= *wicked*) diabólico; (= *mischievous*) travieso
ADV† (= *devilishly*) la mar de, sumamente • **~ cunning** la mar de ingenioso

devilishly ['devlɪʃlɪ] ADV [*behave*] endemoniadamente • **~ clever** la mar de listo, sumamente listo

devil-may-care ['devlmeɪ'keəʳ] ADJ despreocupado; (= *rash*) temerario, arriesgado

devilment ['devlmənt] N = **devilry**

devilry ['devlrɪ] N (= *wickedness*) maldad *f*, crueldad *f*; (= *mischief*) diablura *f*, travesura *f*, pillería *f*

devious ['diːvɪəs] ADJ 1 (= *twisting, winding*) [*path*] tortuoso, sinuoso; [*argument*] intrincado, enrevesado
2 (= *crafty*) [*means*] dudoso, artero; [*person*] taimado

deviously ['diːvɪəslɪ] ADV [*act, behave*] taimadamente

deviousness ['diːvɪəsnɪs] N 1 (= *twistiness*) tortuosidad *f*
2 (= *craftiness*) [*of person*] artería *f*

devise [dɪ'vaɪz] VT (= *conceive*) [+ *strategy*] concebir, idear; [+ *gadget*] inventar; [+ *plan*] elaborar; [+ *solution*] encontrar • **to ~ a way to kill sb** tramar la muerte de algn

deviser [dɪ'vaɪzəʳ] N [*of scheme, plan*] inventor(a) *m/f*

devitalize [diː'vaɪtəlaɪz] VT privar de vitalidad

devoid [dɪ'vɔɪd] ADJ • **~ of** desprovisto de

devolution [ˌdiːvə'luːʃən] N delegación *f* (de poderes); (*Pol*) traspaso *m* de competencias; (*Brit*) (*Pol*) descentralización *f* • **most Welsh people wanted ~** la mayoría de los galeses querían la autonomía

devolve [dɪ'vɒlv] VT [+ *power*] delegar; [+ *government*] descentralizar
VI recaer (**on, upon** sobre) • **it ~d on me to tell him** me tocó a mí decírselo

devo max ['diːvəʊ'mæks] N ABBR (*Brit*) (= *devolution maximum*) autonomía *f* plena

Devonian [de'vəʊnɪən] ADJ (*Geol*) devónico

devote [dɪ'vəʊt] VT • **to ~ sth to sth** dedicar algo a algo • **he ~d three chapters to Japanese politics** dedicó tres capítulos a la política japonesa • **she ~d four years to studying history** dedicó cuatro años a estudiar historia • **she ~d her life to finding a cure for the disease** dedicó *or* consagró su vida a encontrar una cura para la enfermedad • **they do not ~ enough attention to their children** no dedican la suficiente atención a sus hijos • **we will ~ 30% of the money to research** asignaremos *or* destinaremos el 30% del dinero a la investigación • **to ~ o.s. to sth** dedicarse a algo

devoted [dɪ'vəʊtɪd] ADJ [*wife, husband, mother, son etc*] abnegado; [*couple, family*] unido; [*friend*] leal, fiel; [*follower, admirer*] ferviente • **a ~ Manchester United fan** una forofa del Manchester United • **a ~ Beatles fan** una devota fan de los Beatles • **years of ~ service** años de dedicación y servicio • **to be ~ to sb** adorar a algn, sentir devoción por algn • **they are ~ to one another** se adoran, sienten devoción el uno por el otro • **to be ~ to sth** estar dedicado a algo • **this chapter is ~ to politics** este capítulo está dedicado a la política • **organizations ~ to helping children** organizaciones de ayuda a la infancia • **the institute is ~ to discovering young artists** el instituto se dedica al descubrimiento de jóvenes artistas

devotedly [dɪ'vəʊtɪdlɪ] ADV [*care for, love, follow*] con devoción; [*loyal*] fervientemente

devotee [ˌdevəʊ'tiː] N 1 (*Rel*) devoto/a *m/f*
2 (= *enthusiast*) partidario/a *m/f* (**of** de)

devotion [dɪ'vəʊʃən] N 1 (*to spouse, relative, football team, pop star*) (*also Rel*) devoción *f* (**to** por); (*to friend*) lealtad *f* (**to** a); (*to studies, duty, work, cause*) dedicación *f* (**to** a)
2 **devotions** (*Rel*) oraciones *fpl* • **to be at one's ~s** estar rezando

devotional [dɪ'vəʊʃənl] ADJ piadoso, devoto

devour [dɪ'vaʊəʳ] VT [+ *food*] devorar • **to be ~ed with jealousy** morirse de envidia • **to be ~ed with curiosity** verse devorado *or* corroído por la curiosidad

devouring [dɪ'vaʊərɪŋ] ADJ (*fig*) [*passion*] devorador; [*curiosity*] acuciante

devout [dɪ'vaʊt] ADJ 1 (*Rel*) [*Christian, Muslim, Methodist etc*] devoto • **they're very ~** son muy devotos *or* piadosos • **she's a ~ Catholic** es muy católica
2 (= *fervent*) [*Communist*] convencido; [*supporter*] ferviente; [*thanks, prayer*] sincero • **it was his ~ wish that his son should become a lawyer** deseaba de todo corazón que su hijo se hiciese abogado

devoutly [dɪ'vaʊtlɪ] ADV [*pray*] con devoción; [*hope, wish*] de todo corazón; [*believe*] fervientemente • **~ religious** muy religioso

dew [djuː] N rocío *m*

dewdrop ['djuːdrɒp] N gota *f* de rocío

dewlap ['djuːlæp] N papada *f*

dewy ['djuːɪ] ADJ (COMPAR: **dewier**, SUPERL: **dewiest**) [*grass*] cubierto de rocío; [*eyes*] húmedo

dewy-eyed ['djuːɪ'aɪd] ADJ (= *innocent*) ingenuo

dexterity [deks'terɪtɪ] N (*physical, mental*) destreza *f*, habilidad *f*

dexterous ADJ, **dextrous** ['dekstrəs] ADJ diestro, hábil • **by the ~ use of** por el diestro uso de

dexterously, dextrously ['dekstrəslɪ] ADV [*pass, snatch etc*] con destreza; [*avoid*] diestramente, hábilmente

dextrose ['dekstrəʊs] N dextrosa *f*

DfEE N ABBR (*Brit*) = **Department for Education and Employment**

DG N ABBR (= **Director General**) D.G. *mf*
ABBR (= **Deo gratias**) a.D.g.

dg ABBR (= **decigram, decigrams**) dg

DH N ABBR (*Brit*) = **Department of Health**

dhal ['dɑːl] N (= *lentil dish*) *plato con lentillas típico de la comida hindú*

dhow [daʊ] N dhow *m*

DHSS N ABBR (*Brit*) (*formerly*) = **Department of Health and Social Security**

DI N ABBR 1 = **Donor Insemination**
2 (*Brit*) (*Police*) = **Detective Inspector**

Di [daɪ] N *familiar form of* **Diana**

di... [daɪ] PREFIX di...

diabesity [ˌdaɪə'biːsɪtɪ] N (*Med*) diabesidad *f*

diabetes [ˌdaɪə'biːtiːz] NSING diabetes *f inv*

diabetic [ˌdaɪə'betɪk] ADJ [*patient*] diabético; [*chocolate*] para diabéticos
N diabético/a *m/f*

diabolic [ˌdaɪə'bɒlɪk] ADJ 1 [*forces, powers*] diabólico
2 = **diabolical**

diabolical [ˌdaɪə'bɒlɪkəl] ADJ 1 (= *devilish*) [*laughter, plan, plot*] diabólico
2* (= *very bad*) horrendo • **it's a ~ liberty!** ¡es un descaro intolerable!

diabolically [ˌdaɪə'bɒlɪkəlɪ] ADV

1 (= *devilishly*) [*behave, laugh*] diabólicamente • **~ difficult** endemoniadamente difícil • **it was ~ hot** hacía un calor de infierno
2* (= *very badly*) [*play, sing etc*] pésimamente, fatal*

diachronic [ˌdaɪəˈkrɒnɪk] ADJ diacrónico

diacritic [ˌdaɪəˈkrɪtɪk] ADJ diacrítico
N signo *m* diacrítico

diacritical [ˌdaɪəˈkrɪtɪkəl] ADJ diacrítico

diadem [ˈdaɪədem] N diadema *f*

diaeresis, dieresis (US) [daɪˈerɪsɪs] N (PL: **diaereses** [daɪˈerɪsiːz]) diéresis *f inv*

diagnose [ˈdaɪəgnəʊz] VT (*Med*) (*also fig*) diagnosticar • **she was ~d with cancer** le diagnosticaron (un) cáncer

diagnosis [ˌdaɪəgˈnəʊsɪs] N (PL: **diagnoses** [ˌdaɪəgˈnəʊsiːz]) (= *opinion, conclusion*) diagnóstico *m* (*also Med*)

diagnostic [ˌdaɪəgˈnɒstɪk] ADJ diagnóstico

diagnostics [ˌdaɪəgˈnɒstɪks] NSING diagnóstica *f*, diagnosis *f*

diagonal [daɪˈægənl] ADJ diagonal
N diagonal *f*

diagonally [daɪˈægənəlɪ] ADV [*cut, fold*] diagonalmente, en diagonal • **to go ~ across** cruzar diagonalmente • **~ opposite** diagonalmente opuesto

diagram [ˈdaɪəgræm] N (= *plan*) esquema *m*; (= *chart*) gráfica *f*; (*Math*) diagrama *m*

diagrammatic [ˌdaɪəgrəˈmætɪk] ADJ esquemático

dial [ˈdaɪəl] N 1 [*of clock*] esfera *f*, carátula *f* (*Mex*); [*of instrument*] esfera *f*, cuadrante *m*; [*of radio*] dial *m*; (*Aut*) (*on dashboard*) cuadrante *m*; (= *tuner*) selector *m*; [*of telephone*] disco *m*
2* (= *face*) jeta* *f*, cara *f*
VT (*Telec*) marcar, discar (*LAm*) • **to ~ a wrong number** equivocarse de número (al marcar) • **can I ~ Bombay direct?** ¿puedo llamar a Bombay directamente?, ¿hay discado directo a Bombay? (*LAm*) • **to ~ 999** • **to ~ 911** (*US*) llamar al teléfono de emergencia
VI (*Telec*) marcar, discar (*LAm*)
CPD ▸ **dial code** (*US*) prefijo *m* ▸ **dial tone** (*US*) señal *f* de marcar, tono *m* de marcar

dial. ABBR = **dialect**

dialect [ˈdaɪəlekt] N dialecto *m*
CPD ▸ **dialect atlas** atlas *m inv* lingüístico ▸ **dialect survey** estudio *m* dialectológico ▸ **dialect word** dialectalismo *m*

dialectal [ˌdaɪəˈlektl] ADJ dialectal

dialectic [ˌdaɪəˈlektɪk] N dialéctica *f*
ADJ dialéctico

dialectical [ˌdaɪəˈlektɪkəl] ADJ dialéctico
CPD ▸ **dialectical materialism** materialismo *m* dialéctico

dialectics [ˌdaɪəˈlektɪks] N dialéctica *f*

dialectology [ˌdaɪəlekˈtɒlədʒɪ] N dialectología *f*

dialler, dialer (US) [ˈdaɪələʳ] N (*Telec, Internet*) dialer *m*, marcador *m*

dialling, dialing (US) [ˈdaɪəlɪŋ] N marcación *f*, discado *m* (*LAm*)
CPD ▸ **dialling code** (*Brit*) prefijo *m* ▸ **dialling tone** (*Brit*) señal *f* de marcar, tono *m* de marcar

dialogue, dialog (US) [ˈdaɪəlɒg] N diálogo *m*
VI dialogar
CPD ▸ **dialogue box, dialog box** (*US*) (*Comput*) cuadro *m* de diálogo

dial-up service [ˈdaɪəlˌʌpˈsɜːvɪs] N servicio *m* de enlace entre cuadrantes

dialysis [daɪˈælɪsɪs] N (PL: **dialyses** [daɪˈælɪsiːz]) (*Med*) diálisis *f inv*
CPD ▸ **dialysis machine** máquina *f* de diálisis, riñón *m* artificial

diamanté [diːəˈmɑːnteɪ] N strass *m*
CPD de strass

diameter [daɪˈæmɪtəʳ] N diámetro *m* • **it is one metre in ~** tiene un diámetro de un metro, tiene un metro de diámetro

diametric [ˌdaɪəˈmetrɪk] ADJ = **diametrical**

diametrical [ˌdaɪəˈmetrɪkəl] ADJ diametral

diametrically [ˌdaɪəˈmetrɪkəlɪ] ADV • **~ opposed** diametralmente opuesto (**to** a)

diamond [ˈdaɪəmənd] N 1 (= *mineral*) diamante *m*; (= *jewel*) brillante *m*, diamante *m* • IDIOM: • **~ cut ~** tal para cual
2 (= *shape*) rombo *m*
3 (*Cards*) (= *standard pack*) diamante *m*; (*Spanish cards*) oro *m*; **diamonds** (= *suit*) diamantes *mpl*; (*in Spanish pack*) oros *mpl* • **the Queen of ~s** la dama *or* reina de diamantes
4 (*Baseball*) campo *m* de béisbol
CPD ▸ **diamond jubilee** sexagésimo aniversario *m* ▸ **diamond merchant** comerciante *mf* en diamantes ▸ **diamond mine** mina *f* de diamantes ▸ **diamond necklace** collar *m* de diamantes ▸ **diamond ring** anillo *m* de diamantes, sortija *f* de diamantes ▸ **diamond wedding (anniversary)** bodas *fpl* de diamante

diamond-cutter [ˈdaɪəməndˌkʌtəʳ] N diamantista *mf*

diamond-shaped [ˈdaɪəməndʃeɪpt] ADJ de forma de rombo, en forma de rombo

diamorphine [ˌdaɪəˈmɔːfiːn] N diamorfina *f*

Diana [daɪˈænə] N Diana

dianthus [daɪˈænθəs] N (PL: **dianthuses**) (*Bot*) dianthus *m*

diapason [ˌdaɪəˈpeɪzən] N diapasón *m*

diaper [ˈdaɪəpəʳ] (*US*) N pañal *m*
CPD ▸ **diaper pin** imperdible *m*, seguro *m* (*LAm*) ▸ **diaper rash** irritación *f* • **to have ~ rash** estar escaldado

diaphanous [daɪˈæfənəs] ADJ diáfano

diaphragm [ˈdaɪəfræm] N 1 (*Anat*) diafragma *m*
2 (= *contraceptive*) diafragma *m*

diarist [ˈdaɪərɪst] N diarista *mf*

diarrhoea, diarrhea (US) [ˌdaɪəˈriːə] N diarrea *f*; ▹ **verbal**

diary [ˈdaɪərɪ] N (= *journal*) diario *m*; (*for engagements*) agenda *f* • **I keep a ~** estoy escribiendo un diario; ▹ **desk**

diaspora [daɪˈæspərə] N diáspora *f*

diastole [daɪˈæstəlɪ] N diástole *f*

diastolic [ˌdaɪəˈstɒlɪk] ADJ • **~ pressure** presión *f* diastólica

diatonic [ˌdaɪəˈtɒnɪk] ADJ diatónico
CPD ▸ **diatonic scale** escala *f* diatónica

diatribe [ˈdaɪətraɪb] N diatriba *f* (**against** contra)

dibber [ˈdɪbəʳ] N (*Brit*) plantador *m*

dibble [ˈdɪbl] N plantador *m*
VT (*also* **dibble in**) plantar con plantador

dibs [dɪbz] N 1 (*Brit*‡) (= *money*) parné‡ *m*; (= *game of jacks*) taba(s) *f(pl)*
2 (*US**) • **~ on the cookies!** ¡las galletas pa' mí! • **I want ~ on this one if we get him alive** si sigue vivo cuando lo cojamos pido ser el primero en darle una buena paliza

dice [daɪs] N dado *m*; (*as pl*) dados *mpl*; (= *shapes*) cubitos *mpl* • **no ~!** (*US**) ¡ni hablar!, ¡nada de eso!; ▹ **load**
VT [+ *vegetables*] cortar en cubitos • **~d vegetables** menestra *f* de verduras
VI jugar a los dados • **to ~ with death** jugar con la muerte

dicey* [ˈdaɪsɪ] ADJ (COMPAR: **dicier**, SUPERL: **diciest**) (*Brit*) (= *uncertain*) incierto, dudoso; (= *hazardous*) peligroso, arriesgado

dichotomy [dɪˈkɒtəmɪ] N dicotomía *f*

Dick [dɪk] N *familiar form of* **Richard**

dick [dɪk] N 1 (*US**) sabueso *mf*
2** polla *f* (*Sp***), verga** *f*

dickens [ˈdɪkɪnz] (*euph*) = **devil**

Dickensian [dɪˈkenzɪən] ADJ dickensiano

dicker [ˈdɪkəʳ] VI 1 vacilar, titubear
2 (*US*) (*Comm*) regatear, cambalachear

dickey* [ˈdɪkɪ] N 1 (= *shirt front*) pechera *f* postiza
2 (*Brit*) (*also* **dickey bow**) pajarita *f* (*Sp*), corbata *f* de moño (*LAm*)
3 (*Brit*) (*also* **dickey seat**) spider *m*
CPD ▸ **dickey bird** (*baby talk*) pajarito *m* • IDIOM: • **I won't say a ~ bird*** no diré ni pío*

dickhead** [ˈdɪkhed] N imbécil* *mf*, gilipollas** *mf inv*

dicky* [ˈdɪkɪ] ADJ (COMPAR: **dickier**, SUPERL: **dickiest**) 1 = **dickey**
2 • **to have a ~ heart** (*Brit*) tener el corazón fastidiado

dicta [ˈdɪktə] NPL *of* **dictum**

Dictaphone® [ˈdɪktəfəʊn] N dictáfono® *m*

dictate VT [dɪkˈteɪt] 1 (*to secretary*) [+ *letter*] dictar
2 (= *order*) mandar; [+ *terms, conditions*] imponer • **he decided to act as circumstances ~d** decidió actuar según (mandasen) las circunstancias
VI [dɪkˈteɪt] dictar • **to ~ to one's secretary** dictar a su secretaria
N [ˈdɪkteɪt] mandato *m*; **dictates** dictados *mpl* • **the ~s of conscience/reason** los dictados de la conciencia/razón
▸ **dictate to** VI + PREP [+ *person*] dar órdenes a • **I won't be ~d to** a mí nadie me da órdenes

dictation [dɪkˈteɪʃən] N (*to secretary, schoolchild etc*) dictado *m* • **to take (a) ~** escribir al dictado • **at ~ speed** a velocidad de dictado

dictator [dɪkˈteɪtəʳ] N dictador(a) *m/f*

dictatorial [ˌdɪktəˈtɔːrɪəl] ADJ [*manner etc*] dictatorial

dictatorially [dɪktəˈtɔːrɪəlɪ] ADV dictatorialmente

dictatorship [dɪkˈteɪtəʃɪp] N dictadura *f*

diction [ˈdɪkʃən] N (= *pronunciation*) dicción *f*; (*Literat*) lengua *f*, lenguaje *m*

dictionary [ˈdɪkʃənrɪ] N diccionario *m*
CPD ▸ **dictionary definition** definición *f* del diccionario

dictum [ˈdɪktəm] N (PL: **dictums, dicta** [ˈdɪktə]) sentencia *f*, aforismo *m*; (*Jur*) dictamen *m*

did [dɪd] PT *of* **do**

didactic [daɪˈdæktɪk] ADJ (= *educational*) didáctico; (= *moralistic*) [*tone*] moralizador

didactically [dɪˈdæktɪkəlɪ] ADV didácticamente

diddle* [ˈdɪdl] VT estafar, timar • **to ~ sb out of sth** estafar algo a algn

diddly-squat‡ [ˈdɪdlɪˈskwɒt] N nada de nada

didgeridoo [ˌdɪdʒərɪˈduː] N didgeridoo *m* (*instrumento musical australiano*)

didn't [ˈdɪdənt] = **did not**

Dido [ˈdaɪdəʊ] N Dido

die[1] [daɪ] (PRESENT PARTICIPLE: **dying**) VI
1 [*person, animal, plant*] morir (**of, from** de) • **her father was dying** su padre se moría *or* se estaba muriendo *or* estaba moribundo • **to die a natural death** morir de muerte natural • **to die a violent death** tener una muerte violenta • **he died a hero** murió convertido en un héroe • **to die for one's country** morir por la patria • **the secret died with her** se llevó el secreto a la tumba • **I nearly died!*** (*laughing*) ¡me moría de la risa!; (*with embarrassment*) ¡me moría de vergüenza!; (*with fear*) ¡casi me muero del susto! • IDIOMS: • **to die like flies** morir como chinches, caer como moscas • **a dress/house to die for*** un vestido/una casa para

caerse de espaldas*, un vestido/una casa de ensueño • PROVERBS: • **never say die*** no hay que darse por vencido • **old habits die hard** genio y figura hasta la sepultura
2 (*fig*) [*friendship, interest*] morir, desaparecer; [*light*] extinguirse; [*engine*] pararse, apagarse • **the day was dying fast** (*liter*) la luz del día iba apagándose rápidamente
3 • **to be dying to do sth** morirse de ganas de hacer algo • **I'm dying for a cigarette** me muero de ganas de fumar un cigarrillo
▸ **die away** (VI + ADV) [*voice, sound*] irse apagando
▸ **die back** (VI + ADV) (*Bot*) secarse
▸ **die down** (VI + ADV) [*fire*] apagarse; [*wind, storm*] remitir, amainar; [*battle*] hacerse menos violento; [*shelling*] disminuir; [*discontent, excitement, protests*] calmarse, apaciguarse
▸ **die off** (VI + ADV) [*plants, animals*] morirse, desaparecer
▸ **die out** (VI + ADV) [*custom*] desaparecer, caer en desuso; [*family, race, species*] extinguirse; [*fire*] apagarse, extinguirse; [*showers*] desaparecer

die[2] [daɪ] (N) **1** (PL: **dice** [daɪs]) dado *m* • IDIOM: • **the die is cast** la suerte está echada
2 (PL: **dies**) (= *stamp*) troquel *m*, cuño *m*; (= *mould*) matriz *f*, molde *m*; ▹ **straight**

die-casting [ˈdaɪˌkɑːstɪŋ] (N) fundición *f* a troquel

diectic [daɪˈektɪk] (N) diéctico *m*

diehard [ˈdaɪhɑːd] (ADJ) acérrimo
(N) intransigente *mf*

dieldrin [ˈdiːldrɪn] (N) dieldrina *f*

dielectric [ˌdaɪəˈlektrɪk] (ADJ) dieléctrico
(N) dieléctrico *m*

dieresis [daɪˈerɪsɪs] (N) (PL: **diereses** [daɪˈerɪsiːz]) (*US*) = **diaeresis**

diesel [ˈdiːzəl] (N) **1** (= *car, train*) vehículo *m* diesel
2 (= *fuel*) gasóleo *m*, gasoil *m*
(CPD) ▸ **diesel engine** motor *m* diesel
▸ **diesel fuel, diesel oil** gasóleo *m*, gasoil *m*
▸ **diesel train** tren *m* diesel

diesel-electric [ˈdiːzəlɪˈlektrɪk] (ADJ) dieseleléctrico

die-sinker [ˈdaɪˌsɪŋkəʳ] (N) grabador *m* de troqueles

die-stamp [ˈdaɪˌstæmp] (VT) grabar

diet[1] [ˈdaɪət] (N) **1** (= *customary food*) dieta *f*, alimentación *f*
2 (= *slimming diet*) régimen *m*, dieta *f* • **to be/go on a ~** estar/ponerse a régimen *or* dieta • **to put sb on a ~** poner a algn a régimen *or* dieta
(VI) estar a régimen
(CPD) [*soft drink*] light (*inv*) ▸ **diet pill** píldora *f* para adelgazar

diet[2] [ˈdaɪət] (N) (*Pol*) dieta *f*

dietary [ˈdaɪətərɪ] (ADJ) [*supplement*] dietético; [*needs, habits*] alimenticio
(CPD) ▸ **dietary fibre** fibra *f* dietética

dieter [ˈdaɪətəʳ] (N) persona *f* que está a régimen *or* dieta

dietetic [ˌdaɪəˈtetɪk] (ADJ) [*research*] dietético; (*US*) [*meal, food, drink*] de régimen

dietetics [ˌdaɪəˈtetɪks] (N) dietética *f*

dietician [ˌdaɪɪˈtɪʃən] (N) médico/a *m/f* especialista en dietética, dietista *mf*

differ [ˈdɪfəʳ] (VI) **1** (= *be unlike*) ser distinto, diferenciarse, diferir (*frm*) (**from** de)
2 (= *disagree*) [*people*] no estar de acuerdo, discrepar; [*texts, versions*] discrepar • **to ~ with sb (on** *or* **over** *or* **about sth)** no estar de acuerdo con algn (en algo), discrepar de algn (en algo) • **I beg to ~** siento tener que disentir *or* discrepar, lamento estar en desacuerdo *or* no estar de acuerdo; ▹ **agree**

difference [ˈdɪfrəns] (N) **1** (= *dissimilarity*) diferencia *f* (**between** entre) • **I see no ~ between them** no veo diferencia alguna entre ellos • **a car with a ~** un coche diferente *or* especial • **that makes all the ~** eso cambia totalmente la cosa • **it makes no ~** da igual, da lo mismo • **it makes no ~ to me** me da igual *or* lo mismo • **it will make no ~ to us** nos dará igual *or* lo mismo, no nos afectará en lo más mínimo • **what ~ does it make?** ¿qué más da? • **it makes a lot of ~** importa mucho; ▹ **split**
2 (*between numbers, amounts*) diferencia *f* • **I'll pay the ~** yo pagaré la diferencia
3 (= *change*) • **the ~ in her is amazing!** ¡cuánto ha cambiado!
4 (*euph*) (= *quarrel*) riña *f* • **a ~ of opinion** un desacuerdo; ▹ **put aside, settle**

different [ˈdɪfrənt] (ADJ) **1** (= *not alike*) diferente, distinto • **the two brothers couldn't be more ~ from each other** los dos hermanos no podían ser más diferentes *or* distintos el uno del otro • **that's ~ to** *or* **from what I was told** eso es diferente de *or* a lo que me contaron, eso es distinto de *or* a lo que me contaron • **that's quite a ~ matter** eso es harina de otro costal; ▹ **chalk**
2 (= *changed*) • **I feel a ~ person** me siento otro
3 (= *various*) varios, distintos • **~ people noticed it** varias *or* distintas personas lo vieron
4 (*iro*) (= *distinctive*) distinto, original • **"what do you think of my new hairstyle?" — "well ... it's certainly ~"** —¿qué te parece mi nuevo peinado? —pues ... desde luego es algo distinto *or* original

differential [ˌdɪfəˈrenʃəl] (ADJ) [*rate*] diferencial
(N) **1** (*esp Brit*) (*Econ*) diferencial *m*; ▹ **wage**
2 (*Math*) diferencial *f*
(CPD) ▸ **differential calculus** cálculo *m* diferencial ▸ **differential equation** ecuación *f* diferencial

differentiate [ˌdɪfəˈrenʃɪeɪt] (VT) **1** (*gen*) diferenciar, distinguir (**from** de) • **to ~ A from B** (= *tell the difference*) distinguir A de B; (= *make the difference*) diferenciar A de B
2 (*Math*) diferenciar
(VI) **1** (*gen*) distinguir (**between** entre)
2 (*Bio*) diferenciarse

differentiation [ˌdɪfərenʃɪˈeɪʃən] (N) diferenciación *f*

differently [ˈdɪfrəntlɪ] (ADV) de modo distinto • **she wanted to do things ~** quería hacer las cosas de otro modo *or* de modo distinto

difficult [ˈdɪfɪkəlt] (ADJ) **1** (= *hard*) [*task, book, question*] difícil; [*writer*] complicado, complejo • **there's nothing ~ about it** no es nada difícil • **it is ~ to describe the feeling** es difícil describir la sensación • **these dogs are ~ to control** estos perros son difíciles de controlar • **many youngsters find it ~ to get work** a muchos jóvenes les resulta difícil encontrar trabajo • **it was ~ for him to leave her** le resultó difícil dejarla • **she is determined to make life ~ for him** está decidida a hacerle la vida imposible • **to put sb in a ~ position** poner a algn en una posición comprometida • **she is determined to make things ~ for him** está decidida a hacerle la vida imposible • **this is a ~ time for us** son tiempos difíciles para nosotros; ▹ EASY, DIFFICULT, IMPOSSIBLE
2 (= *awkward*) [*person, child, character*] difícil • **why are you always trying to be ~?** ¿por qué siempre estás intentando crear problemas?

difficulty [ˈdɪfɪkəltɪ] (N) **1** (= *hardness*) dificultad *f* • **to have ~ (in) doing sth** tener dificultades para hacer algo, resultarle difícil a algn hacer algo • **he has ~ (in) walking** tiene dificultades para andar, le resulta difícil andar • **I had no ~ finding the house** no tuve problemas para encontrar la casa, no me resultó difícil encontrar la casa • **with ~** con dificultad • **with great ~** con gran dificultad • **with the greatest ~** a duras penas
2 (= *problem*) problema *m*, dificultad *f* • **to get into ~** *or* **difficulties** [*person*] (*gen*) meterse en problemas *or* apuros; (*while swimming*) empezar a tener problemas; [*ship*] empezar a peligrar • **to have difficulties with sth** tener problemas con algo • **to be in difficulties** *or* **~** estar teniendo problemas • **they are in financial difficulties** tienen problemas económicos, están pasando dificultades económicas • **to make difficulties for sb** crear problemas a algn; ▹ **learning, run into**

diffidence [ˈdɪfɪdəns] (N) inseguridad *f*, falta *f* de confianza en sí mismo

diffident [ˈdɪfɪdənt] (ADJ) inseguro, cohibido

diffidently [ˈdɪfɪdəntlɪ] (ADV) tímidamente, de forma insegura

diffract [dɪˈfrækt] (VT) difractar
(VI) difractarse

diffraction [dɪˈfrækʃən] (N) difracción *f*

diffuse (ADJ) [dɪˈfjuːs] (= *spread out*) [*light*] difuso; (= *long-winded*) [*style, writer*] difuso, prolijo
(VT) [dɪˈfjuːz] [+ *light*] difundir; [+ *heat*] difundir, esparcir; [+ *information, ideas*] difundir
(VI) [dɪˈfjuːz] [*heat, gas*] difundirse, esparcirse

diffused [dɪˈfjuːzd] (ADJ) difuso

diffuseness [dɪˈfjuːsnɪs] (N) [*of style, writer*] prolijidad *f*

diffuser [dɪˈfjuːzəʳ] (N) (*for light*) difusor *m*

diffusion [dɪˈfjuːʒən] (N) [*of light, heat, information, ideas*] difusión *f*

dig [dɪɡ] (VB: PT, PP: **dug**) (N) **1** (*Archeol*) excavación *f*
2 (= *prod*) (*gen*) empujón *m*; (*with elbow*) codazo *m*
3* (= *taunt*) indirecta *f*, pulla *f* • **to have a dig at sb** lanzar una indirecta *or* una pulla a algn
(VT) **1** [+ *hole*] [*person*] cavar, excavar; [*machine*] excavar; [*animal*] cavar, escarbar • IDIOM: • **to dig one's own grave** cavar su propia tumba
2 (= *break up*) [+ *ground*] remover
3 (= *cultivate*) [+ *garden*] cultivar, cavar en
4 (= *add*) [+ *fertilizer, compost*] meter (**into** en), añadir (**into** a)
5 (= *extract*) [+ *coal*] extraer, sacar
6 (= *thrust*) • **to dig sth into sth** clavar algo en algo, hundir algo en algo
7 (= *prod*) empujar; (*with elbow*) dar un codazo a • **to dig sb in the ribs** dar a algn un codazo en las costillas
8 (*esp US†**) (= *enjoy*) • **I don't dig jazz** no me gusta el jazz, el jazz no me dice nada • **I really dig that** eso me chifla* • **dig this!** ¡mira esto!
(VI) **1** [*person*] (*gen*) cavar; (*Archeol, Tech*) excavar; [*dog, pig*] escarbar • **to dig for gold** excavar en busca de oro
2 (= *search*) ahondar • **to dig deeper into a subject** ahondar *or* profundizar en un tema • **he dug into his pockets for a coin** hurgó en los bolsillos para buscar una moneda • IDIOM: • **to dig deep into one's pocket** rascarse el bolsillo
▸ **dig around** (VI + ADV) (*for information*) rebuscar • **to dig around in sb's past** rebuscar en el pasado de algn • **to dig around for sth** rebuscar algo

▸ **dig in** (VI + ADV) **1*** (= *eat*) meter mano a la comida • **dig in!** ¡a comer!
2 (*also* **dig o.s. in**) (*Mil*) atrincherarse; (*fig*) (*in negotiations, argument*) atrincherarse en su postura
(VT + ADV) **1** (= *add*) [+ *compost*] añadir al suelo
2 (= *thrust*) [+ *nails, claws, knife*] clavar, hundir
• IDIOM: • **to dig in one's heels** mantenerse en sus trece, empecinarse
3 (*Mil*) • **his troops are now well dug in** sus tropas se hallan ahora bien atrincheradas
▸ **dig into** (VI + PREP) **1** [+ *reserves*] consumir, usar • **I had to dig into my savings to pay for it** tuve que recurrir a *or* echar mano de mis ahorros para pagarlo
2 [+ *sb's past*] remover, hurgar en
3* [+ *food*] hincar el diente a, atacar • **to dig into a meal** hincar el diente a una comida
▸ **dig out** (VT + ADV) **1** [+ *buried object*] (*gen*) desenterrar, sacar; (*from rubble*) sacar (de entre los escombros)
2 (= *extract*) [+ *thorn in flesh*] extraer, quitar
3 (= *search out*) buscar
▸ **dig over** (VT + ADV) [+ *earth*] remover; [+ *garden*] remover la tierra de
▸ **dig up** (VT + ADV) **1** [+ *potatoes*] sacar; [+ *weeds*] arrancar; [+ *plant*] desarraigar; [+ *flowerbed*] cavar en, remover la tierra de; [+ *roadway*] levantar; [+ *grave*] abrir; [+ *treasure, body, artifacts*] desenterrar
2 [+ *information*] desenterrar, sacar a la luz;
▹ **dirt, past**

digest (VT) [daɪˈdʒest] **1** [+ *food*] digerir • **easy to ~** fácil de digerir
2 (= *assimilate*) [+ *news*] asimilar, digerir
3 (= *summarize*) resumir
(VI) [daɪˈdʒest] digerir
(N) [ˈdaɪdʒest] **1** (= *summary*) resumen *m*
2 (= *journal*) boletín *m*
3 (*Jur*) digesto *m*, recopilación *f* de leyes

digester [daɪˈdʒestəʳ] (N) digestor *m*, cuba *f* de digestión

digestibility [daɪˌdʒestɪˈbɪlɪtɪ] (N) [*of food*] digestibilidad *f*

digestible [dɪˈdʒestəbl] (ADJ) **1** [*food*] digerible • **easily ~** fácil de digerir
2 (= *understandable*) [*information*] asimilable, fácil de digerir • **he presents the information in an easily ~ form** presenta la información de un modo fácil de digerir *or* fácilmente asimilable

digestion [dɪˈdʒestʃən] (N) digestión *f*

digestive [dɪˈdʒestɪv] (ADJ) digestivo
(N) (*also* **digestive biscuit**) galleta *f* dulce integral, bizcocho *m* (*LAm*)
(CPD) ▸ **digestive juices** jugos *mpl* digestivos, jugos *mpl* gástricos ▸ **digestive system** aparato *m* digestivo ▸ **digestive tract** tubo *m* digestivo

digger [ˈdɪgəʳ] (N) **1** (= *machine*) excavadora *f*; (= *person*) (*Archeol*) excavador(a) *m/f*
2* (= *Australian*) australiano/a *m/f*

digging [ˈdɪgɪŋ] (N) **1** (*with spade, of hole*) • **Helen always did the ~** Helen era la que siempre cavaba
2 (*Min*) excavación *f*
3 diggings (*Min, Archeol*) excavaciones *fpl*

digicam [ˈdɪdʒɪkæm] (N) cámara *f* digital

digit [ˈdɪdʒɪt] (N) **1** (*Math*) dígito *m*, cifra *f*
2 (= *finger, toe*) dedo *m*

digital [ˈdɪdʒɪtəl] (ADJ) [*watch, display, recording*] digital
(CPD) ▸ **digital audio tape** cinta *f* digital de audio ▸ **digital camera** cámara *f* digital ▸ **digital compact cassette** cinta *f* digital ▸ **digital divide** brecha *f* digital ▸ **digital immigrant** inmigrante *mf* digital ▸ **digital native** nativo/a *m/f* digital ▸ **digital pen** lápiz *m* digital ▸ **digital radio** radio *f* digital ▸ **digital recording** (= *process, product*) grabación *f* digital ▸ **digital switchover** apagón *m* analógico ▸ **digital television** televisión *f* digital ▸ **digital wallet** cartera *f* digital

digitalis [ˌdɪdʒɪˈteɪlɪs] (N) digital *f*

digitalization [ˌdɪdʒɪtəlaɪˈzeɪʃən] (N) digitalización *f*

digitally [ˈdɪdʒɪtlɪ] (ADV) [*scan, record, store*] digitalmente • **~ remastered** [*sound recording*] reprocesado digitalmente

digitize [ˈdɪdʒɪtaɪz] (VT) digitalizar

digitizer [ˈdɪdʒɪtaɪzəʳ] (N) digitalizador *m*

diglossia [daɪˈglɒsɪə] (N) diglosia *f*

dignified [ˈdɪgnɪfaɪd] (ADJ) [*person*] de aspecto solemne, de aspecto digno; [*manner, air*] solemne, digno; [*bearing*] solemne, majestuoso; [*silence*] decoroso • **it's not ~ to do that** no es elegante hacer eso

dignify [ˈdɪgnɪfaɪ] (VT) **1** (= *exalt*) dignificar
2 (= *lend credence to*) (*gen*) honrar, otorgar reconocimiento a; (*with title*) dar un título altisonante a • **I see no point in ~ing this speculation with a comment** me parece que estas especulaciones no son siquiera dignas de comentario

dignitary [ˈdɪgnɪtərɪ] (N) dignatario/a *m/f*

dignity [ˈdɪgnɪtɪ] (N) **1** (= *self-esteem*) dignidad *f* • **that would be beneath my ~** no me rebajaría a eso • IDIOM: • **to stand on one's ~** ponerse en su lugar
2 (= *solemnity*) [*of occasion*] solemnidad *f*
3 (= *respectability*) [*of work, labour*] dignidad *f*, honorabilidad *f*

digress [daɪˈgres] (VI) hacer una digresión; (*pej*) divagar • **to ~ from the subject** apartarse del tema • **but I ~** (*esp hum*) pero me estoy apartando del tema

digression [daɪˈgreʃən] (N) digresión *f*

digressive [daɪˈgresɪv] (ADJ) que se aparta del tema principal

digs* [dɪgz] (NPL) (*Brit*) alojamiento *msing* • **to be in ~** estar alojado, vivir en una pensión, estar de patrona*†

dike [daɪk] (N) = **dyke**

diktat [dɪkˈtɑːt] (N) dictado *m*, imposición *f*

dilapidated [dɪˈlæpɪdeɪtɪd] (ADJ) [*building*] desmoronado, ruinoso; [*vehicle*] desvencijado

dilapidation [dɪˌlæpɪˈdeɪʃən] (N) [*of building*] estado *m* ruinoso

dilate [daɪˈleɪt] (VI) **1** [*veins, pupils, cervix*] dilatarse
2 (*frm*) (= *expatiate*) • **to ~ (up)on sth** explayarse sobre algo
(VT) dilatar • **her pupils were ~d** tenía las pupilas dilatadas

dilation [daɪˈleɪʃən] (N) dilatación *f* • **~ and curettage** (*Med*) raspado *m*, legrado *m*

dilatoriness [ˈdɪlətərɪnɪs] (N) (*frm*) tardanza *f*, demora *f*

dilatory [ˈdɪlətərɪ] (ADJ) (*frm*) [*person*] lento, tardo; [*tactics*] dilatorio • **to be ~ in replying** tardar mucho en contestar

dildo [ˈdɪldəʊ] (N) consolador *m*

dilemma [daɪˈlemə] (N) dilema *m* • **to be in a ~** estar en *or* tener un dilema; ▹ **horn**

dilettante [ˌdɪlɪˈtæntɪ] (N) (PL: **dilettantes** *or* **dilettanti** [ˌdɪlɪˈtæntɪ]) diletante *mf*

dilettantism [ˌdɪləˈtæntɪzəm] (N) diletantismo *m*

diligence [ˈdɪlɪdʒəns] (N) diligencia *f*

diligent [ˈdɪlɪdʒənt] (ADJ) [*person*] diligente; [*work, search*] concienzudo

diligently [ˈdɪlɪdʒəntlɪ] (ADV) diligentemente

dill [dɪl] (N) eneldo *m*
(CPD) ▸ **dill pickle** (*US*) pepinillos *mpl* en vinagre al eneldo

dilly* [ˈdɪlɪ] (N) (*US*) • **she's a ~** (= *girl*) está muy bien* • **it's a ~** (= *problem*) es un rompecabezas

dilly-dally* [ˈdɪlɪdælɪ] (VI) **1** (= *loiter*) entretenerse, demorarse
2 (= *hesitate*) andarse con titubeos

dilly-dallying [ˈdɪlɪdælɪɪŋ] (N) **1** (= *loitering*) pérdida *f* de tiempo
2 (= *hesitation*) vacilación *f*, titubeo *m*

dilute [daɪˈluːt] (VT) **1** [+ *fruit juice, flavour*] diluir • **"~ to taste"** (*in instructions*) "diluya a su gusto"
2 (*fig*) [+ *power*] debilitar; [+ *effect*] reducir
(ADJ) diluido

dilution [daɪˈluːʃən] (N) **1** [*of substance, flavour*] disolución *f*, dilución *f* (*frm*)
2 (*fig*) [*of power*] debilitamiento *m*; [*of effectiveness*] reducción *f*

diluvial [daɪˈluːvɪəl], **diluvian** [daɪˈluːvɪən] (ADJ) diluviano

dim [dɪm] (ADJ) (COMPAR: **dimmer**, SUPERL: **dimmest**) **1** (= *not bright*) [*light*] débil, tenue; [*room*] oscuro, poco iluminado • **she read the letter by the dim light of a torch** leyó la carta con la ayuda de la débil *or* tenue luz de una linterna • **even in the dim light the furniture looked dirty** incluso con la poca luz que había los muebles parecían sucios • **her eyes were dim with tears** sus ojos estaban nublados por las lágrimas • **to grow dim** [*light*] atenuarse, ir atenuándose; [*room*] oscurecer, ir oscureciendo • **his eyes had grown dim with age** (*liter*) su vista se había ido debilitando con la edad
2 (= *indistinct*) [*figure, shape, outline*] borroso; [*memory*] borroso, vago • **in the dim and distant past** en un pasado muy remoto
3 (= *gloomy*) [*prospects*] poco prometedor • **to take a dim view of sth*** ver algo con malos ojos
4* (= *unintelligent*) corto, lerdo* • **he's a bit dim** es un poco corto, no tiene muchas luces
(VT) **1** (= *make less bright*) [+ *light*] bajar, atenuar; [+ *room*] oscurecer; [+ *colours*] apagar; [+ *metals*] deslucir, deslustrar; [+ *eyesight*] debilitar • **to dim the lights** (*in room, theatre*) bajar *or* atenuar la luz • **to dim one's (head)lights** poner las luces cortas *or* de cruce, poner las luces bajas (*LAm*) • **she looked at him through eyes dimmed by tears** lo miró con los ojos nublados por las lágrimas
2 (= *dampen, diminish*) [+ *hopes*] hacer perder, empañar (*liter*); [+ *senses*] debilitar • **the passing years had not dimmed her beauty** el paso de los años no había marchitado su belleza • **to dim sb's spirits** desanimar a algn, desalentar a algn
3 (= *fade*) [+ *outline, memory*] borrar
(VI) **1** (= *become less bright*) [*light*] atenuarse, ir atenuándose; [*metal*] deslucirse, ir desluciéndose; [*colour*] apagarse, ir apagándose; [*eyesight*] debilitarse, ir debilitándose
2 (= *diminish*) [*hopes*] ir perdiéndose, ir empañándose (*liter*); [*beauty*] marchitarse, ir marchitándose
3 (= *fade*) [*outline, memory*] hacerse borroso

dime [daɪm] (*US*) (N) (*Canada, US*) *moneda de diez centavos* • **they're a ~ a dozen** son muy baratos; (*fig*) los hay a montones*
(CPD) ▸ **dime novel** novelucha *f* ▸ **dime store** ≈ todo a cien *m* (*Sp*) (*tienda que vende mercadería barata*)

dimension [dɪˈmenʃən] (N) **1** (*Phys, Math*) dimensión *f*
2 dimensions (= *size, scope*) dimensiones *fpl* • **they did not realize the ~s of the problem** no se daban cuenta de las dimensiones *or* de la envergadura *or* del alcance del problema
3 (= *aspect*) dimensión *f* • **the human ~ of the tragedy** la dimensión humana de la

tragedia
-dimensional [daɪˈmenʃənl] ADJ (*ending in compounds*) ▹ **three-dimensional, two-dimensional**
diminish [dɪˈmɪnɪʃ] VT (*gen*) disminuir; [*+ numbers, speed, strength*] disminuir, reducir
VI (*gen*) disminuir
diminishable [dɪˈmɪnɪʃəbl] ADJ disminuible
diminished [dɪˈmɪnɪʃt] ADJ [*value*] reducido; [*ability*] limitado; (*Mus*) [*interval*] disminuido • **a ~ staff** una plantilla reducida
CPD ▸ **diminished responsibility** (*Jur*) responsabilidad *f* disminuida
diminishing [dɪˈmɪnɪʃɪŋ] ADJ [*number*] decreciente, cada vez menor; [*value, resources, funds*] cada vez menor, cada vez más reducido; [*strength*] cada vez menor • **the law of ~ returns** la ley de rendimiento decreciente
diminuendo [dɪˌmɪnjʊˈendəʊ] N (*Mus*) diminuendo *m*
VI hacer un diminuendo
diminution [ˌdɪmɪˈnjuːʃən] N (*frm*) disminución *f*
diminutive [dɪˈmɪnjʊtɪv] ADJ **1** (= *very small*) diminuto
2 (*Ling*) diminutivo
N (*Ling*) diminutivo *m*
dimly [ˈdɪmlɪ] ADV **1** [*shine, glow*] débilmente, tenuemente • **~ lit** poco iluminado, iluminado con una luz tenue
2 (= *vaguely*) [*remember, recollect*] vagamente • **I ~ remember …** recuerdo vagamente … • **I was ~ aware that …** era vagamente consciente de que … • **you could ~ make out the shape** apenas se entreveía la forma
dimmer [ˈdɪməʳ] N **1** (*on light switch*) regulador *m* de intensidad de luz
2 (*US*) (*Aut*) interruptor *m* de las luces cortas *or* de cruce, interruptor *m* de las luces bajas (*LAm*)
CPD ▸ **dimmer switch** regulador *m* de intensidad de luz
dimming [ˈdɪmɪŋ] N [*of light*] oscurecimiento *m*; [*of reputation*] empañamiento *m*
dimness [ˈdɪmnɪs] N **1** [*of light*] lo tenue; [*of room*] penumbra *f*, la poca luz; [*of eyesight*] debilidad *f*
2 [*of figure, shape, outline*] lo borroso; [*of memory*] vaguedad *f*
3 [*of prospects*] lo poco prometedor
4* (= *stupidity*) cortedad *f*, torpeza *f*
dimple [ˈdɪmpl] N **1** (*in chin, cheek*) hoyuelo *m*
2 (= *small depression*) hoyito *m*
VT [*+ hand, arm, thigh*] hacer hoyitos en; [*+ water*] rizar
VI [*water*] rizarse • **her cheeks ~d, she had a lovely smile** le salían hoyuelos en las mejillas, tenía una sonrisa preciosa
dimpled [ˈdɪmpld] ADJ [*cheek, chin*] con hoyuelo; [*hand, arm, thigh*] con hoyitos
dimwit* [ˈdɪmwɪt] N lerdo/a* *m/f*
dim-witted* [ˈdɪmˈwɪtɪd] ADJ lerdo*, corto de alcances
DIN [dɪn] N ABBR = **Deutsche Industrie Normen**
din [dɪn] N [*of traffic, roadworks*] estruendo *m*, estrépito *m*; [*of voices, music*] alboroto *m*, bulla* *f*
VT • **to din sth into sb** inculcar algo a algn • **I had it dinned into me as a child** me lo inculcaron desde niño
VI • **his words still dinned in my head** el eco de sus palabras aún resonaba en mi cabeza
dinar [ˈdiːnɑːʳ] N dinar *m*
din-dins* [ˈdɪndɪns] NPL (*baby talk*) (= *mid-day meal*) comidita *f*; (= *evening meal*) cenita *f*

dine [daɪn] VI (*frm*) cenar • **to ~ on** *or* **off sth** cenar algo
VT ▹ **wine**
▸ **dine in** VI + ADV cenar en casa
▸ **dine out** VI + ADV cenar fuera • **this was a story he could ~ out for months on** (*fig*) a esta historia le podía sacar muchísimo partido
diner [ˈdaɪnəʳ] N **1** (= *person*) comensal *mf*
2 (*Rail*) coche *m* comedor, vagón *m* restaurante, buffet *m* (*Peru*)
3 (*US*) (= *eating place*) casa *f* de comidas, lonchería *f* (*LAm*); (= *transport café*) cafetería *f* de carretera
dinero* [dɪˈnɛərəʊ] N (*US*) guita* *f*, pasta *f* (*Sp**), plata *f* (*LAm**), lana *f* (*LAm**)
dinette [dɪˈnet] N pequeño comedorcito *m* • **kitchen-dinette** cocina-comedor *f*
CPD ▸ **dinette set** (*US*) vajilla *f* de diario
ding-a-ling [ˌdɪŋəˈlɪŋ] N **1** [*of bell, telephone*] tilín *m*
2 (*US‡*) bobo/a* *m/f*
dingbat‡ [ˈdɪŋbæt] N gilipollas‡ *m*
ding-dong* [ˈdɪŋˈdɒŋ] N **1** (= *sound*) • **ding-dong!** ¡din dan!, ¡din don!
2 (= *argument*) agarrada* *f*, bronca *f*
ADJ • **a ding-dong battle** una batalla campal
dinghy [ˈdɪŋgɪ] N (= *rubber dinghy*) lancha *f* neumática; (= *sailing dinghy*) bote *m*
dinginess [ˈdɪndʒɪnɪs] N (= *shabbiness*) [*of furniture, decor*] lo deslucido, falta *f* de lustre; (= *gloominess*) [*of town, house, room*] lo sombrío, lobreguez *f*; (= *dirtiness*) suciedad *f*
dingo [ˈdɪŋgəʊ] N (PL: **dingoes**) dingo *m*
dingy [ˈdɪndʒɪ] ADJ (COMPAR: **dingier**, SUPERL: **dingiest**) (= *shabby*) [*furniture, decor*] deslustrado, deslucido; (= *gloomy*) [*town, house, room*] sombrío, lóbrego; (= *dirty*) sucio
dining [ˈdaɪnɪŋ] CPD ▸ **dining area** (*in room*) comedor *m* • **the main ~ area** [*of restaurant*] el comedor principal ▸ **dining car** coche *m* comedor, vagón *m* restaurante ▸ **dining chair** silla *f* de comedor ▸ **dining hall** comedor *m*, refectorio *m* ▸ **dining kitchen** cocina *f* con office ▸ **dining room** comedor *m* ▸ **dining room suite** juego *m* de comedor ▸ **dining table** mesa *f* de comedor
dink‡ [dɪŋk] N (*US*) tontorrón/ona‡ *m/f*
dinkie* [ˈdɪŋkɪ] N ABBR (= **double** *or* **dual income no kids**) *pareja sin hijos con dos sueldos*
dinky* [ˈdɪŋkɪ] ADJ (COMPAR: **dinkier**, SUPERL: **dinkiest**) (*Brit*) (= *small*) pequeñito; (= *nice*) mono, precioso
dinner [ˈdɪnəʳ] N (= *evening meal*) cena *f*; (= *lunch*) almuerzo *m*, comida *f*, lonche *m* (*Mex*); (= *banquet*) cena *f* de gala • **to have ~** (*in the evening*) cenar; (*at midday*) almorzar, comer • **can you come to ~?** ¿puedes venir a cenar? • **we're having people to ~** tenemos invitados para *or* a cenar • **to go out to ~** salir a cenar (fuera) • **we sat down to ~ at 10.30** nos sentamos a cenar a las 10.30
CPD ▸ **dinner bell** campana *f* de la cena ▸ **dinner dance** cena *f* seguida de baile ▸ **dinner duty** (*Scol*) supervisión *f* de comedor ▸ **dinner hour** (= *lunch hour*) hora *f* del almuerzo ▸ **dinner jacket** esmoquin *m*, smoking *m* ▸ **dinner knife** cuchillo *m* grande ▸ **dinner lady** *empleada que da el servicio de comidas en las escuelas* ▸ **dinner money** (*Brit*) dinero *m* para la comida ▸ **dinner party** cena *f* (*con invitados*) ▸ **dinner plate** plato *m* llano ▸ **dinner roll** panecillo *m* ▸ **dinner service** vajilla *f* ▸ **dinner suit** traje *m* de etiqueta ▸ **dinner table** mesa *f* de comedor ▸ **dinner time** hora *f* de cenar/comer ▸ **dinner trolley, dinner wagon** carrito *m* de la comida; ▹ **school**
dinnerware [ˈdɪnəwɛəʳ] N (*esp US*) vajilla *f*
CPD ▸ **dinnerware set** (*US*) vajilla *f*
dinosaur [ˈdaɪnəsɔːʳ] N **1** (= *reptile*) dinosaurio *m*
2 (= *old-fashioned person*) carcamal* *mf*; (= *old-fashioned organization*) reliquia *f* del pasado
dint[1] [dɪnt] N • **by ~ of** a fuerza de
dint[2] [dɪnt] = **dent**
diocesan [daɪˈɒsɪsən] ADJ diocesano
diocese [ˈdaɪəsɪs] N diócesis *f inv*
diode [ˈdaɪəʊd] N diodo *m*
Dionysian [ˌdaɪəˈnɪzɪən] ADJ dionisiaco
Dionysius [ˌdaɪəˈnɪsɪəs] N Dionisio
diorama [daɪəˈrɑːmə] N diorama *m*
dioxide [daɪˈɒksaɪd] N dióxido *m*; ▹ **carbon, sulphur**
dioxin [daɪˈɒksɪn] N dioxina *f*
DIP [dɪp] N ABBR (*Comput*) = **Dual-In-Line Package**
dip [dɪp] N **1** (= *swim*) baño *m*, chapuzón *m*, zambullida *f* (*LAm*) • **to go for a dip** ir a darse un baño *or* un chapuzón
2 (= *slope*) declive *m*, pendiente *f*; (= *hollow*) hondonada *f*, depresión *f*
3 (*Geol*) [*of rock strata, fault*] inclinación *f* • **angle of dip** buzamiento *m*, angulo *m* de inclinación • **magnetic dip** inclinación *f* (magnética)
4 (*Culin*) salsa *f* (*para mojar*)
5 (*Agr*) (*for sheep, poultry*) baño *m* de desinfección; ▹ **lucky**
VT **1** (= *thrust*) (*into liquid*) sumergir, bañar (**in, into** en); [*+ pen*] mojar (**in, into** en); [*+ hand*] (*into bag*) meter (**in, into** en); [*+ ladle, scoop*] meter (**in, into** en); [*+ sheep*] bañar con desinfectante
2 (= *lower*) [*+ flag*] bajar, saludar con; (*Aer*) [*+ wings*] saludar con • **to dip one's (head)lights** (*Brit*) poner las luces cortas *or* de cruce, poner las luces bajas (*LAm*) • **dipped headlights** luces *fpl* cortas *or* de cruce, luces *fpl* bajas (*LAm*)
VI **1** (= *slope down*) [*road*] bajar en pendiente; [*land*] formar una hondonada
2 (= *move down*) [*bird, plane*] bajar en picado; [*temperature*] bajar; [*sun*] esconderse • **the sun dipped below the hill** el sol se escondió tras la colina
3 (= *draw on*) • **to dip into one's savings** (*fig*) echar mano de los ahorros
4 (= *read superficially*) • **to dip into a book** hojear un libro
CPD ▸ **dip switch** (*Aut*) interruptor *m* de las luces cortas *or* de cruce, interruptor *m* de las luces bajas (*LAm*)
Dip. ABBR = **Diploma**
Dip Ed [dɪpˈed] N ABBR (*Brit*) (*Univ*) (= **Diploma in Education**) *título de magisterio*
diphtheria [dɪfˈθɪərɪə] N difteria *f*
diphthong [ˈdɪfθɒŋ] N diptongo *m*
diphthongize [ˈdɪfθɒŋaɪz] VT diptongar
VI diptongarse
diploma [dɪˈpləʊmə] N diploma *m*
diplomacy [dɪˈpləʊməsɪ] N **1** (*Pol*) diplomacia *f*
2 (= *tact*) diplomacia *f*
diplomat [ˈdɪpləmæt] N diplomático/a *m/f*
diplomatic [ˌdɪpləˈmætɪk] ADJ **1** (*Pol*) diplomático
2 (= *tactful*) diplomático
CPD ▸ **diplomatic bag** valija *f* diplomática ▸ **diplomatic corps** cuerpo *m* diplomático ▸ **diplomatic immunity** inmunidad *f* diplomática ▸ **diplomatic pouch** (*US*) = **diplomatic bag** ▸ **diplomatic relations** • **to break off ~ relations** romper las relaciones diplomáticas ▸ **diplomatic service** servicio *m* diplomático
diplomatically [ˌdɪpləˈmætɪkəlɪ] ADV [*say, act*] diplomáticamente; [*isolated*] desde el punto de vista diplomático

diplomatist [dɪ'pləʊmətɪst] (N) diplomático/a *m/f*
dipole ['daɪ,pəʊl] (N) **1** (*Elec*) dipolo *m*
2 (*TV, Rad*) (*also* **dipole aerial**) antena *f* dipolar, dipolar *f*
dipper¹ ['dɪpəʳ] (N) (*Orn*) mirlo *m* acuático
dipper² ['dɪpəʳ] (N) • **big ~** (*at fair*) montaña *f* rusa • **the Big Dipper** (*US*) (*Astron*) la Osa Mayor
dipper³ ['dɪpəʳ] (N) (*Culin*) cazo *m*, cucharón *m*
dipping ['dɪpɪŋ] (N) (*Agr*) baño *m* de desinfección
dippy* ['dɪpɪ] (ADJ) chiflado*
dipso* ['dɪpsəʊ] (N) = **dipsomaniac**
dipsomania [,dɪpsəʊ'meɪnɪə] (N) dipsomanía *f*
dipsomaniac [,dɪpsəʊ'meɪnɪæk] (N) dipsomaníaco/a *m/f*, dipsómano/a *m/f*
dipstick ['dɪpstɪk] (N) **1** (*Aut*) varilla *f* del aceite, cala *f*
2** (= *fool*) capullo *m* (*Sp***), gilipollas *mf inv* (*Sp***)
diptych ['dɪptɪk] (N) díptico *m*
dir. (ABBR) (= **director**) Dir., Dtor(a.)
dire [daɪəʳ] (ADJ) (SUPERL: **direr**) **1** (= *terrible*) [*event, consequences, results*] nefasto, funesto; [*situation*] desesperado; [*warning, prediction*] alarmante; [*poverty*] extremo • **to be in ~ need of sth** necesitar algo desesperadamente • **to be in ~ straits** estar en un serio aprieto *or* apuro
2* (= *awful*) [*film, book*] pésimo, malísimo
direct [daɪ'rekt] (ADJ) **1** (= *without detour*) [*route, train, flight*] directo
2 (= *immediate*) [*cause, result*] directo; [*contact, control, responsibility, descendant*] directo • **"keep away from ~ heat"** "no exponer directamente al calor" • **to make a ~ hit** dar en el blanco • **he's the ~ opposite** es exactamente el contrario
3 (= *straightforward, not evasive*) [*answer, refusal*] claro, inequívoco; [*manner, character*] abierto, franco
(ADV) **1** (= *straight*) [*go, fly, pay*] directamente • **we fly ~ to Santiago** volamos directo *or* directamente a Santiago
2 (= *frankly*) con franqueza, sin rodeos
(VT) **1** (= *aim*) [+ *remark, gaze, attention*] dirigir (**at, to** a)
2 (= *give directions to*) • **can you ~ me to the station?** ¿me puede indicar cómo llegar a la estación?
3 (= *control*) [+ *traffic, play, film*] dirigir
4 (= *instruct*) • **to ~ sb to do sth** mandar a algn hacer algo • **to ~ that ...** mandar que ...
(CPD) ▸ **direct access** (*Comput*) acceso *m* directo ▸ **direct action** acción *f* directa ▸ **direct advertising** publicidad *f* directa ▸ **direct cost** costo *m* directo ▸ **direct current** (*Elec*) corriente *f* continua ▸ **direct debit** pago *m* a la orden ▸ **direct debiting** domiciliación *f* (de pagos) ▸ **direct dialling** servicio *m* (telefónico) automático, discado *m* directo (*LAm*) ▸ **direct discourse** (*esp US*) (*Gram*) estilo *m* directo ▸ **direct free kick** golpe *m* libre directo ▸ **direct grant school** (*Brit†*) escuela *f* subvencionada ▸ **direct hit** (*Mil*) impacto *m* directo ▸ **direct mail** publicidad *f* por correo, correspondencia *f* directa ▸ **direct mail shot** (*Brit*) campaña *f* publicitaria por correo, mailing *m* ▸ **direct marketing** márketing *m* directo ▸ **direct object** (*Gram*) complemento *m* directo ▸ **direct rule** gobierno *m* directo ▸ **direct selling** ventas *fpl* directas ▸ **direct speech** (*Ling*) estilo *m* directo ▸ **direct tax** impuesto *m* directo ▸ **direct taxation** tributación *f* directa
direction [dɪ'rekʃən] (N) **1** (= *course*) dirección *f* • **in the ~ of** hacia, en dirección a • **sense of ~** sentido *m* de la orientación • **in the opposite ~** en sentido contrario • **in all ~s** por todos lados • **they ran off in different ~s** salieron corriendo cada uno por su lado
2 (*fig*) (= *purpose*) orientación *f*; (= *control*) mando *m*; [*of play, film*] dirección *f*
3 directions (= *instructions*) (*for use*) instrucciones *fpl*; (*to a place*) señas *fpl* • **~s for use** modo *m* de empleo, instrucciones *fpl* de uso
(CPD) ▸ **direction finder** radiogoniómetro *m* ▸ **direction indicator** (*Aut*) intermitente *m*
directional [dɪ'rekʃənl] (ADJ) direccional • **~ aerial** antena *f* dirigida • **~ light** (*Aut*) intermitente *m*
directionless [dɪ'rekʃənlɪs] (ADJ) [*activity*] sin dirección, que no conduce a ninguna parte • **to be/feel ~** andar/sentirse sin rumbo ni dirección
directive [dɪ'rektɪv] (N) directiva *f*
directly [dɪ'rektlɪ] (ADV) **1** (= *exactly*) justo • **~ above/below sth/sb** justo encima de/debajo de algo/algn • **~ opposite sth/sb** justo enfrente de algo/algn • **the sun was ~ overhead** el sol caía de pleno
2 (= *straight*) [*go, fly, look, pay*] directamente • **my salary is paid ~ into my account** me ingresan el sueldo directamente en mi cuenta • **he was looking ~ at me when he said it** me estaba mirando directamente a la cara cuando lo dijo
3 (= *personally*) [*affect*] directamente • **this decision doesn't affect us ~** esta decisión no nos afecta directamente • **I hold you ~ responsible for this!** ¡te considero el responsable directo de esto!
4 (= *immediately*) inmediatamente • **~ after/before sth** inmediatamente después de/antes de algo • **the two murders are not ~ related** *or* **linked** los dos asesinatos no están directamente relacionados • **to be ~ descended from sb** descender directamente de algn, descender de algn por línea directa
5 (= *shortly*) enseguida, de inmediato • **she will be here ~** vendrá enseguida *or* de inmediato
6 (= *frankly*) [*speak, explain*] con franqueza
(CONJ) (*esp Brit*) (= *as soon as*) en cuanto • **~ he heard the door close he picked up the telephone** en cuanto oyó cerrarse la puerta cogió el teléfono • **~ you hear it, ...** en cuanto lo oigas, ...
directness [daɪ'rektnɪs] (N) [*of person, speech, reply*] franqueza *f*
director [dɪ'rektəʳ] (N) [*of company*] directivo/a *m/f*; (*on board of directors*) miembro *mf* del consejo de administración, consejero/a *m/f*; [*of institution, department*] (*also Theat, Cine, Rad, TV*) director(a) *m/f*; ▹ **board, executive, funeral, managing, music**
(CPD) ▸ **director general** director(a) *m/f* general ▸ **Director of Public Prosecutions** (*Brit*) ≈ Fiscal *mf* General del Estado ▸ **director of studies** jefe/a *m/f* de estudios ▸ **director's chair** silla *f* del director ▸ **director's cut** (*Cine*) versión *f* íntegra
directorate [daɪ'rektərɪt] (N) **1** (= *post*) dirección *f*, cargo *m* de director
2 (= *body*) junta *f* directiva, consejo *m* de administración
directorial [daɪrek'tɔːrɪəl] (ADJ) [*talent, experience*] como director; [*career, work*] de director • **to make one's ~ debut** debutar como director
directorship [dɪ'rektəʃɪp] (N) (= *post*) dirección *f*, cargo *m* de director; (= *term as director*) gerencia *f*, periodo *m* de gestión
directory [dɪ'rektərɪ] (N) (*also* **telephone directory**) guía *f* (telefónica); (= *street directory*) callejero *m*, guía *f* de calles; (= *trade directory*) directorio *m* de comercio; (*Comput*) directorio *m*
(CPD) ▸ **directory assistance** (*US*) información *f* (telefónica) ▸ **directory enquiries** (*Brit*) = **directory assistance**
dirge [dɜːdʒ] (N) canto *m* fúnebre, endecha *f*
dirigible ['dɪrɪdʒəbl] (ADJ) dirigible
(N) dirigible *m*
dirk [dɜːk] (N) (*Scot*) puñal *m*
dirndl ['dɜːndl] (N) falda *f* acampanada
dirt [dɜːt] (N) **1** (= *unclean matter*) suciedad *f*; (= *piece of dirt*) suciedad *f*, mugre *f* • **to treat sb like ~*** tratar a algn como si fuese basura, tratar a patadas a algn • IDIOM: • **to dig up ~ on sb** sacar los trapos sucios de algn
2 (= *earth*) tierra *f*; (= *mud*) barro *m*, lodo *m*
3* (= *obscenity*) porquerías *fpl*, cochinadas* *fpl* • **this book is nothing but ~** este libro está lleno de porquerías *or* cochinadas*
(CPD) ▸ **dirt bike** moto *f* todoterreno ▸ **dirt farmer*** (*US*) pequeño granjero *m* (sin obreros) ▸ **dirt road** (*US*) camino *m* de tierra ▸ **dirt track** (*Sport*) pista *f* de ceniza; (= *road*) camino *m* de tierra
dirt-cheap* ['dɜːt'tʃiːp] (ADJ) tirado de precio*, baratísimo, regalado
dirtily ['dɜːtɪlɪ] (ADV) **1** (= *not cleanly*) [*eat, drink*] sin modales • **they live ~** viven rodeados de suciedad
2 (= *indecently*) [*laugh, smile*] lascivamente
3 (= *unfairly*) [*act, behave*] de una forma traicionera • **to play ~** [*footballer*] jugar sucio • **to fight ~** [*boxer*] no luchar limpiamente
dirtiness ['dɜːtɪnɪs] (N) suciedad *f*
dirt-poor, dirt poor [,dɜːt'pʊəʳ] (ADJ) paupérrimo
dirty ['dɜːtɪ] (ADJ) (COMPAR: **dirtier**, SUPERL: **dirtiest**) **1** (= *unclean*) [*hands, clothes, dishes*] sucio • **your hands are ~** tienes las manos sucias • **to get (o.s.) ~** ensuciarse • **to get sth ~** ensuciar algo • **to get one's hands ~** ensuciarse *or* mancharse las manos • **his ~ habits get on my nerves** tiene unas costumbres asquerosas que me sacan de quicio • **cleaning the cooker is a ~ job** limpiar la cocina es un trabajo muy sucio • **there was a ~ mark on his shirt** tenía una mancha en la camisa • IDIOM: • **to wash one's ~ linen in public** sacar los trapos sucios a relucir; ▹ **nappy**
2 (= *dull*) [*grey, white*] sucio • **the sky was a ~ grey** el cielo tenía un color gris sucio
3 (= *nasty*) [*weather*] horrible, feo; [*night*] horrible
4 (= *indecent*) [*story, joke*] verde, colorado (*Mex*); [*book*] cochino*, de guarrerías (*Sp**); [*magazine, film*] porno*; [*laugh*] lascivo • **to have a ~ mind** tener una mente pervertida, tener una mente guarra (*Sp**) • **~ old man** viejo *m* verde • **~ weekend** (*Brit**) (*hum*) fin *m* de semana de lujuria (*hum*) • **to go on a ~ weekend (with sb)** ir a pasar un fin de semana de lujuria (con algn) • **~ word** palabrota *f*, lisura *f* (*And, S. Cone*) • **communism has become almost a ~ word** "comunismo" se ha convertido casi en una palabrota
5* (= *underhand*) sucio • **~ business** negocio *m* sucio • **~ money** dinero *m* sucio • **~ play** (*Sport*) juego *m* sucio • **there are some ~ players in the team** algunos de los miembros del equipo juegan sucio • **~ pool** (*US‡*) juego *m* sucio • **a ~ trick** una mala pasada, una jugarreta* • **to play a ~ trick on sb** jugar una mala pasada a algn, hacer una jugarreta a algn* • **~ tricks** chanchullos *mpl* • **~ tricks department** *sección de actividades secretas para desacreditar al contrario* • **~ war** guerra *f* sucia • **to do sb's ~ work**: • **he always gets other people to do his ~ work**

d

siempre consigue que los demás le hagan el trabajo sucio
6* (= *despicable*) asqueroso*, de mierda** • **you're a ~ liar‡** eres un cerdo mentiroso‡, eres un mentiroso de mierda** • **you ~ rat!‡** ¡canalla!‡, ¡cerdo!‡
7* (= *angry*) • **to give sb a ~ look** echar una mirada asesina a algn*
(ADV) **1** (*Sport*) (= *unfairly*) • **to fight ~** [*boxer*] no luchar limpiamente • **to play ~** [*footballer*] jugar sucio
2 (= *indecently*) • **to talk ~** decir cochinadas*, decir guarrerías (*Sp**)
3‡ • **~ great: a ~ great dog/lorry/hole** un perrazo/camionazo/agujerazo* • **his ~ great hands** sus manazas*, sus manotas*
(VT) ensuciar • **don't ~ your clothes** no te ensucies la ropa
(N) • **to do the ~ on sb** (*Brit**) jugar una mala pasada a algn, hacer una jugarreta a algn*
(CPD) ▸ **dirty bomb** bomba *f* sucia ▸ **dirty dog†*** tipo *m* asqueroso*, tío *m* guarro (*Sp**)

dirty-minded [ˌdɜːtɪˈmaɪndɪd] (ADJ) con la mente sucia

dis‡ [dɪs] (VT) = **diss**

disability [ˌdɪsəˈbɪlɪtɪ] (N) **1** (= *state*) invalidez *f*, discapacidad *f*, minusvalía *f*; (= *injury, illness, condition*) discapacidad *f*, minusvalía *f* • **people with a ~** los discapacitados, los minusválidos
2 (*fig*) desventaja *f*
(CPD) ▸ **disability allowance** (*permanent*) subsidio *m* por incapacidad laboral permanente; (*temporary*) subsidio *m* por incapacidad laboral transitoria ▸ **disability pension** pensión *f* de invalidez

disable [dɪsˈeɪbl] (VT) **1** (= *cripple*) [+ *person*] dejar inválido
2 (= *make unfit for use*) [+ *tank, gun, device*] inutilizar
3 (= *disqualify*) incapacitar, inhabilitar (**for** para)

disabled [dɪsˈeɪbld] (ADJ) [*person*] minusválido, discapacitado
(NPL) • **the ~** los discapacitados, los minusválidos

disablement [dɪsˈeɪblmənt] (N) **1** (= *state*) invalidez *f*, discapacidad *f*, minusvalía *f*
2 [*of tank, gun, device*] inutilización *f*

disabling [dɪsˈeɪblɪŋ] (ADJ) [*injury, condition*] discapacitante

disabuse [ˌdɪsəˈbjuːz] (VT) desengañar (**of** de) • **I was rapidly ~d of this notion** pronto me desengañé de esta idea, pronto salí del error

disaccord [ˌdɪsəˈkɔːd] (N) desacuerdo *m*
(VI) no estar de acuerdo

disadvantage [ˌdɪsədˈvɑːntɪdʒ] (N) desventaja *f*, inconveniente *m* • **to sb's ~** perjudicial para algn • **to the ~ of** en perjuicio *or* detrimento de • **to be at a ~** estar en desventaja, estar en una situación desventajosa • **this put him at a ~** esto lo dejó en situación desventajosa
(VT) perjudicar

disadvantaged [ˌdɪsədˈvɑːntɪdʒd] (ADJ) [*person*] perjudicado • **she comes from a ~ background** proviene de un entorno desfavorecido
(NPL) • **the ~** los desfavorecidos, los marginados

disadvantageous [ˌdɪsædvɑːnˈteɪdʒəs] (ADJ) (= *unfavourable*) [*circumstances*] desventajoso

disaffected [ˌdɪsəˈfektɪd] (ADJ) desafecto (**towards** hacia)

disaffection [ˌdɪsəˈfekʃən] (N) descontento *m*, desafección *f*

disaffiliate [ˌdɪsəˈfɪlɪeɪt] (VI) desafiliarse (**from** de)

disagree [ˌdɪsəˈgriː] (VI) **1** (= *have different opinion*) no estar de acuerdo, estar en desacuerdo • **to ~ with sb (on** *or* **about sth)** no estar de acuerdo *or* estar en desacuerdo con algn (sobre algo) • **I ~ with you** no estoy de acuerdo contigo, no comparto tu opinión
2 (= *not approve*) • **I ~ with bullfighting** yo no apruebo los toros, no me gustan los toros
3 (= *quarrel*) reñir, discutir (**with** con)
4 (= *not coincide*) [*accounts, versions*] diferir, no cuadrar (**with** con) • **their findings ~** sus conclusiones difieren
5 (= *make unwell*) • **to ~ with sb** [*climate, food*] sentar mal a algn • **onions ~ with me** las cebollas me sientan mal

disagreeable [ˌdɪsəˈgriːəbl] (ADJ) **1** (= *unpleasant*) [*experience, task*] desagradable • **she was very ~ to us** nos trató con bastante aspereza
2 (= *bad-tempered*) [*person*] desagradable, antipático; [*tone of voice*] malhumorado, áspero • **he's rather ~ in the mornings** por la mañana suele estar de bastante mal humor

disagreeableness [ˌdɪsəˈgriːəblnɪs] (N) [*of task, experience*] desagrado *m*; [*of person*] antipatía *f*

disagreeably [ˌdɪsəˈgriːəblɪ] (ADV) [*say*] con aspereza, de mala manera • **a ~ pungent taste** un sabor agrio de lo más desagradable

disagreement [ˌdɪsəˈgriːmənt] (N) **1** (*with opinion*) desacuerdo *m*, disconformidad *f* • **the talks ended in ~** no se alcanzó un acuerdo *or* no hubo acuerdo en las conversaciones
2 (= *quarrel*) riña *f*, discusión *f*
3 (*between accounts, versions*) discrepancia *f* (**with** con)

disallow [ˈdɪsəˈlaʊ] (VT) **1** [+ *claim*] rechazar
2 (*Ftbl*) [+ *goal*] anular
3 (*Jur*) [+ *evidence*] desestimar, rechazar; [+ *conviction*] anular, invalidar

disambiguate [ˌdɪsæmˈbɪgjʊeɪt] (VT) [+ *term, phrase*] desambiguar

disambiguation [ˌdɪsæmbɪgjʊˈeɪʃən] (N) desambiguación *f*

disappear [ˌdɪsəˈpɪəʳ] (VI) desaparecer • **he ~ed from sight** *or* **view** desapareció de la vista • **to make sth ~** hacer desaparecer algo
(VT)* hacer desaparecer

disappearance [ˌdɪsəˈpɪərəns] (N) desaparición *f*

disappeared [ˌdɪsəˈpɪəd] (NPL) (*Pol*) • **the ~** los desaparecidos

disappoint [ˌdɪsəˈpɔɪnt] (VT) [+ *person*] defraudar, decepcionar, desilusionar; [+ *hopes, ambitions*] defraudar • **her daughter ~ed her** su hija la defraudó *or* decepcionó • **the course ~ed her** el curso la defraudó *or* decepcionó *or* desilusionó • **she has been ~ed in love** el amor la ha defraudado *or* decepcionado
(VI) decepcionar

disappointed [ˌdɪsəˈpɔɪntɪd] (ADJ) [*person*] decepcionado, desilusionado; [*hopes*] frustrado • **she'll be terribly ~ when she hears the news** se llevará una gran decepción *or* una desilusión muy grande cuando se entere de la noticia • **she's ~ about** *or* **at having to give up her career** siente mucho tener que dejar su carrera • **to be ~ by sth** estar decepcionado por algo • **I'm ~ in you** me has defraudado, me has decepcionado • **she gave me a ~ look** me miró decepcionada, me dirigió una mirada de decepción • **I was ~ that my mother was not there** me sentí defraudada porque mi madre no estaba allí, me decepcionó (el) que mi madre no estuviera allí • **to be ~ to see/learn sth** quedar decepcionado *or* defraudado al ver/enterarse de algo • **we were ~ not to see her** sentimos mucho no verla • **to be ~ with sth** estar decepcionado con algo • **they are ~ with the result** están decepcionados con el resultado, el resultado los ha decepcionado • **if you see him on stage you won't be ~** si lo ves actuar no te defraudará *or* decepcionará

disappointing [ˌdɪsəˈpɔɪntɪŋ] (ADJ) decepcionante • **it's ~ that nobody wants to help** es decepcionante que nadie quiera ayudar • **the film/hotel was very ~** la película/el hotel fue una decepción • **how ~!** ¡qué decepción!, ¡qué desilusión!

disappointingly [ˌdɪsəˈpɔɪntɪŋlɪ] (ADV) [*react, lose*] de manera decepcionante • **the boat performed ~ in the race** el barco tuvo una actuación decepcionante en la regata • **progress is ~ slow** el progreso es tan lento que resulta decepcionante • **~, nothing happened** lamentablemente, no pasó nada, lo decepcionante fue que no pasó nada

disappointment [ˌdɪsəˈpɔɪntmənt] (N) **1** (= *feeling*) decepción *f*, desilusión *f* • **to our ~** para nuestra decepción, para nuestra gran desilusión • **reserve your place now to avoid ~** haga ahora su reserva para no llevarse una desilusión
2 (= *cause of regret*) • **he is a big ~ to us** nos ha decepcionado muchísimo • **the holiday was such a ~!** ¡las vacaciones fueron una decepción tan grande!, ¡las vacaciones fueron tan decepcionantes! • **~s in love** desengaños *mpl* amorosos

disapprobation [ˌdɪsæprəʊˈbeɪʃən] (N) desaprobación *f*

disapproval [ˌdɪsəˈpruːvəl] (N) desaprobación *f* • **she pursed her lips in ~** frunció los labios en un gesto de desaprobación

disapprove [ˌdɪsəˈpruːv] (VI) • **to ~ of sth** estar en contra de algo, desaprobar algo • **to ~ of sb** mirar mal a algn, no mirar con buenos ojos a algn • **her father ~d of me** su padre me miraba mal *or* no me miraba con buenos ojos • **I think he ~s of me** creo que no me mira con buenos ojos, creo que me tiene poca simpatía • **he ~s of gambling** está en contra del juego, desaprueba la práctica del juego • **I strongly ~** yo estoy firmemente en contra • **I wanted to go but father ~d** yo quería ir pero papá no quiso permitirlo • **your mother would ~** tu madre estaría en contra *or* lo desaprobaría

disapproving [ˌdɪsəˈpruːvɪŋ] (ADJ) [*look, glance*] de desaprobación

disapprovingly [ˌdɪsəˈpruːvɪŋlɪ] (ADV) [*look, frown*] con desaprobación • **he shook his head ~** hizo un gesto de desaprobación con la cabeza

disarm [dɪsˈɑːm] (VT) **1** (*Mil*) [+ *troops, attacker*] desarmar
2 (= *deactivate*) [+ *bomb*] desactivar
3 (= *conciliate*) [+ *opponent*] desarmar
4 (= *render ineffective*) [+ *criticism*] echar por tierra, desbaratar; [+ *opposition*] desbaratar
(VI) (*Mil*) desarmarse

disarmament [dɪsˈɑːməmənt] (N) desarme *m* • **nuclear ~** desarme *m* nuclear

disarmer [dɪsˈɑːməʳ] (N) partidario/a *m/f* del desarme

disarming [dɪsˈɑːmɪŋ] (ADJ) [*smile*] que desarma, encantador; [*modesty*] que desarma; [*frankness*] apabullante

disarmingly [dɪsˈɑːmɪŋlɪ] (ADV) [*smile*] encantadoramente; [*frank*] apabullantemente • **he was ~ modest** era tan modesto que (te) desarmaba

disarrange [ˌdɪsəˈreɪndʒ] (VT) desarreglar, descomponer

disarranged [ˌdɪsəˈreɪndʒd] (ADJ) [*bed*]

deshecho; [*hair*] despeinado; [*clothes*] desarreglado
disarray [ˌdɪsəˈreɪ] N (*frm*) [*of house, flat*] desorden *m*; [*of clothes*] desaliño *m*; [*of institution, economy, government*] desorganización *f* • **to be in ~** [*house, flat*] estar totalmente desordenado; [*clothes*] estar muy desarreglado *or* desaliñado; [*thoughts*] estar en desorden; [*institution, economy, government*] estar sumido en el caos, estar totalmente desorganizado • **the troops fled in ~** las tropas huyeron a la desbandada • **this threw our plans into ~** esto dio al traste con nuestros planes
disassemble [ˌdɪsəˈsembl] VT desmontar, desarmar
VI desmontarse, desarmarse
disassociate [ˌdɪsəˈsəʊʃɪeɪt] = **dissociate**
disaster [dɪˈzɑːstəʳ] N **1** (= *catastrophe*) desastre *m*; ▷ **court, strike**
2 (= *inept person*) desastre *m*
CPD ▸ **disaster area** zona *f* catastrófica • **he's a walking ~ area** (*hum*) es un puro desastre ▸ **disaster fund** fondo *m* de ayuda para casos de desastre ▸ **disaster movie** película *f* de catástrofes ▸ **disaster relief** (= *aid*) ayuda *f* a las víctimas de una catástrofe ▸ **disaster victim** víctima *f* de una catástrofe ▸ **disaster zone** zona *f* catastrófica
disastrous [dɪˈzɑːstrəs] ADJ **1** (= *catastrophic*) [*decision, reforms*] desastroso, catastrófico; [*earthquake, flood*] catastrófico • **that would be ~!** ¡eso sería una catástrofe! • **with ~ consequences** con consecuencias desastrosas *or* nefastas
2* (= *unsuccessful*) [*marriage, cake, novel*] desastroso • **his first movie was ~** su primera película fue desastrosa *or* un desastre
disastrously [dɪˈzɑːstrəslɪ] ADV
1 (= *catastrophically*) desastrosamente • **the race started ~ for Smith** la carrera tuvo un comienzo desastroso para Smith • **to go ~ wrong** salir terriblemente mal
2* (= *atrociously*) pésimamente • **we performed ~** actuamos pésimamente, tuvimos una actuación horrorosa
disavow [ˌdɪsəˈvaʊ] VT **1** (= *reject*) [+ *one's principles, religion*] abdicar de, abjurar de; [+ *one's past*] renegar de
2 (= *deny*) • **they ~ed any knowledge of his activities** negaban tener conocimiento de sus actividades
disavowal [ˌdɪsəˈvaʊəl] N **1** (= *rejection*) abdicación *f*
2 (= *denial*) desmentido *m*
disband [dɪsˈbænd] VT [+ *army*] licenciar; [+ *organization*] disolver
VI disolverse
disbar [dɪsˈbɑːʳ] VT [+ *barrister*] inhabilitar para el ejercicio de la abogacía, prohibir ejercer • **he was ~red** le prohibieron ejercer la abogacía
disbarment [dɪsˈbɑːmənt] N inhabilitación *f* (*para el ejercicio de la abogacía*)
disbelief [ˌdɪsbəˈliːf] N incredulidad *f* • **in ~** con incredulidad
disbelieve [ˌdɪsbəˈliːv] VT [+ *person*] no creer a; [+ *story*] no creer
VI (*esp Rel*) no creer (**in** en)
disbeliever [ˌdɪsbəˈliːvəʳ] N incrédulo/a *m/f*; (*Rel*) descreído/a *m/f*
disbelieving [ˌdɪsbɪˈliːvɪŋ] ADJ incrédulo
disburden [dɪsˈbɜːdn] (*frm*) VT descargar • **to ~ o.s. of** descargarse de
disburse [dɪsˈbɜːs] VT (*frm*) desembolsar
disbursement [dɪsˈbɜːsmənt] N (*frm*) desembolso *m*
disc, disk (*US*) [dɪsk] N (*also Anat*) disco *m*; (= *identity disc*) chapa *f*; (*Comput*) = **disk**
CPD ▸ **disc brakes** (*Aut*) frenos *mpl* de disco ▸ **disc drive** (*Brit*) (*Comput*) = **disk drive** ▸ **disc jockey** discjockey *mf*, pinchadiscos* *mf inv*
disc. ABBR (*Comm*) = **discount**
discard VT [dɪsˈkɑːd] [+ *unwanted thing*] deshacerse de; [+ *idea, plan*] desechar, descartar; [+ *clothing*] desembarazarse de; [+ *habit*] renunciar a; (*Cards*) descartarse de; [+ *person*] desembarazarse de
VI [dɪsˈkɑːd] (*Cards*) descartarse
N [ˈdɪskɑːd] (*Cards*) descarte *m*; (= *unwanted thing*) desecho *m*
discern [dɪˈsɜːn] VT **1** (= *see*) distinguir
2 (= *taste, smell*) distinguir, apreciar
3 (= *detect*) [+ *problem, mistake*] localizar; [+ *sb's intentions*] discernir • **two major trends may be ~ed** se pueden distinguir dos tendencias fundamentales
discernible [dɪˈsɜːnəbl] ADJ **1** (= *perceptible*) [*difference*] perceptible, apreciable; [*effect*] apreciable • **for no ~ reason** sin un motivo aparente
2 (= *visible*) distinguible
discernibly [dɪˈsɜːnəblɪ] ADV [*affected*] visiblemente; [*different*] sensiblemente, notablemente
discerning [dɪˈsɜːnɪŋ] ADJ [*person*] entendido; [*eye*] experto • **~ taste** muy buen gusto *m*
discernment [dɪˈsɜːnmənt] N (= *good judgment*) discernimiento *m*; (= *good taste*) buen gusto *m*
discharge N [ˈdɪstʃɑːdʒ] **1** [*of cargo*] descarga *f*; [*of gun*] descarga *f*, disparo *m*
2 (= *release*) [*of patient*] alta *f*; [*of prisoner*] liberación *f*, puesta *f* en libertad; [*of bankrupt*] rehabilitación *f* • **he got his ~** (*Mil*) lo licenciaron
3 (= *dismissal*) [*of worker*] despido *m*; (*Mil*) baja *f*
4 (= *emission*) (*Elec*) descarga *f*; [*of liquid, waste*] vertido *m*; [*of gas, chemicals*] emisión *f*; (*Med*) (*from wound*) secreción *f*, supuración *f*; (*from vagina*) flujo *m* vaginal
5 (= *completion*) [*of duty*] ejercicio *m*, cumplimiento *m*
VT [dɪsˈtʃɑːdʒ] **1** (= *unload*) [+ *ship, cargo*] descargar
2 (= *fire*) [+ *gun*] descargar, disparar; [+ *shot*] hacer; [+ *arrow*] disparar
3 (= *release*) [+ *patient*] dar de alta, dar el alta a; [+ *prisoner*] liberar, poner en libertad; [+ *bankrupt*] rehabilitar • **they ~d him from hospital on Monday** le dieron de *or* el alta el lunes
4 (= *dismiss*) [+ *employee*] despedir; [+ *soldier*] dar de baja del ejército
5 (= *emit*) [+ *liquid, waste*] verter; [+ *gas, chemicals*] emitir; (*Med*) [+ *pus*] segregar, supurar
6 (= *settle*) [+ *debt*] saldar
7 (= *complete*) [+ *task, duty*] cumplir
VI [dɪsˈtʃɑːdʒ] [*river*] desembocar (**into** en); [*battery*] decargarse; [*wound, sore*] supurar
discharged [dɪsˈtʃɑːdʒd] ADJ • **~ bankrupt** quebrado rehabilitado
disci [ˈdɪskaɪ] NPL *of* **discus**
disciple [dɪˈsaɪpl] N (*Rel*) discípulo/a *m/f*; (*fig*) discípulo/a *m/f*, seguidor(a) *m/f*
disciplinarian [ˌdɪsɪplɪˈnɛərɪən] N • **he was a strict ~** imponía una férrea disciplina (en el cumplimiento de las normas)
disciplinary [ˈdɪsɪplɪnərɪ] ADJ disciplinario • **~ action** *or* **measure** medida *f* disciplinaria • **~ procedures** procedimiento *m* disciplinario
CPD ▸ **disciplinary committee** (*gen*) comité *m* disciplinario; (*Sport*) comité *m* de competición ▸ **disciplinary hearing** audiencia *f* disciplinaria
discipline [ˈdɪsɪplɪn] N **1** (= *obedience*) disciplina *f*; (= *punishment*) castigo *m*; (= *self-control*) autodisciplina *f* • **to keep** *or* **maintain ~** mantener la disciplina
2 (= *field of study*) disciplina *f*
VT **1** (= *punish*) [+ *pupil, soldier*] castigar; [+ *employee*] sancionar
2 (= *control*) [+ *child*] disciplinar; [+ *one's mind*] adiestrar • **to ~ o.s. (to do sth)** disciplinarse (para hacer algo)
disciplined [ˈdɪsɪplɪnd] ADJ [*person, approach*] disciplinado
disclaim [dɪsˈkleɪm] VT [+ *statement*] desmentir, negar; [+ *responsibility*] negar; (*Jur*) renunciar a • **he ~ed all knowledge of it** dijo que no sabía nada en absoluto de ello
disclaimer [dɪsˈkleɪməʳ] N (*Jur*) [*of a right*] renuncia *f*; (= *denial*) (*to newspaper etc*) desmentido *m* • **to issue a ~** declarar descargo *or* limitación de responsabilidad
disclose [dɪsˈkləʊz] VT revelar
disclosure [dɪsˈkləʊʒəʳ] N revelación *f*
disco [ˈdɪskəʊ] ABBR (= **discotheque**) disco *f*, discoteca *f*
CPD ▸ **disco dancing** baile *m* de música disco ▸ **disco lights** luces *fpl* de discoteca ▸ **disco music** música *f* disco
discography [dɪsˈkɒɡrəfɪ] N discografía *f*
discolour, discolor (*US*) [dɪsˈkʌləʳ] VT (= *fade*) de(s)colorar; (= *stain*) manchar
VI (= *lose colour*) de(s)colorarse; (= *run*) desteñir
discolouration, discoloration (*US*) [dɪsˌkʌləˈreɪʃən] N (= *fading*) de(s)coloramiento *m*; (= *staining*) mancha *f*
discoloured, discolored (*US*) [dɪsˈkʌləd] ADJ (= *faded*) de(s)colorado; (= *stained*) manchado
discombobulate [ˌdɪskəmˈbɒbjʊleɪt] VT (*esp US*) [+ *person, plans*] dislocar
discomfit [dɪsˈkʌmfɪt] VT desconcertar
discomfited [dɪsˈkʌmfɪtɪd] ADJ (= *uncomfortable*) desconcertado
discomfiture [dɪsˈkʌmfɪtʃəʳ] N desconcierto *m*, turbación *f*
discomfort [dɪsˈkʌmfət] N (= *lack of comfort*) incomodidad *f*; (= *uneasiness*) incomodidad *f*, turbación *f*; (*physical*) molestia *f*, malestar *m* • **the injury gave him some ~** la herida le causaba molestia
discomposure [ˌdɪskəmˈpəʊʒəʳ] N (*frm*) desconcierto *m*, confusión *f*
disconcert [ˌdɪskənˈsɜːt] VT desconcertar
disconcerted [ˌdɪskənˈsɜːtɪd] ADJ desconcertado
disconcerting [ˌdɪskənˈsɜːtɪŋ] ADJ desconcertante
disconcertingly [ˌdɪskənˈsɜːtɪŋlɪ] ADV de modo desconcertante • **he spoke in a ~ frank way** desconcertó a todos hablando con tanta franqueza
disconnect [ˌdɪskəˈnekt] VT **1** (*gen*) desconectar
2 (*Telec*) • **I've been ~ed** (*for non-payment*) me han cortado el teléfono *or* la línea (por no pagar); (*in mid-conversation*) se ha cortado
disconnected [ˌdɪskəˈnektɪd] ADJ (*fig*) inconexo
disconnection [ˌdɪskəˈnekʃən] N desconexión *f*, corte *m* (*de línea/suministro*)
disconsolate [dɪsˈkɒnsəlɪt] ADJ desconsolado
disconsolately [dɪsˈkɒnsəlɪtlɪ] ADV desconsoladamente
discontent [ˌdɪskənˈtent] N descontento *m*, malestar *m*
discontented [ˌdɪskənˈtentɪd] ADJ descontento (**with, about** con)
discontentment [ˌdɪskənˈtentmənt] N descontento *m*
discontinuance [ˌdɪskɒnˈtɪnjʊəns] N

d

= discontinuation
discontinuation [ˌdɪskənˌtɪnjʊ'eɪʃən] (N) (*frm*) [*of practice*] abandono *m*; [*of production*] suspensión *f*, interrupción *f*
discontinue [ˌdɪskən'tɪnju:] (VT) [*+ production, payment*] suspender; [*+ practice*] abandonar; (*Comm*) [*+ product*] dejar de fabricar; (*Med*) [*+ treatment*] interrumpir, suspender • **"discontinued"** (*Comm*) "fin de serie"
discontinuity [ˌdɪskɒntɪ'nju:ɪtɪ] (N) (= *lack of continuity*) discontinuidad *f*; (= *interruption*) interrupción *f*
discontinuous [ˌdɪskən'tɪnjʊəs] (ADJ) (= *interrupted*) interrumpido; (*Math*) [*curve*] discontinuo
discord ['dɪskɔ:d] (N) **1** (= *quarrelling*) discordia *f* • **to sow ~ among** sembrar la discordia entre, sembrar cizaña entre
2 (*Mus*) disonancia *f*
discordance [dɪs'kɔ:dəns] (N) discordancia *f*
discordant [dɪs'kɔ:dənt] (ADJ) [*ideas, opinions*] discorde, opuesto; [*sound*] disonante
discotheque ['dɪskəʊtek] (N) discoteca *f*
discount (N) ['dɪskaʊnt] (*gen*) descuento *m*, rebaja *f* • **to give a 10% ~** dar un descuento del 10% • **to sell (sth) at a ~** vender (algo) con descuento *or* a precio reducido
(VT) [dɪs'kaʊnt] **1** (= *lower price of*) [*+ merchandise*] descontar, rebajar • **~ed cash flow** cashflow *m* actualizado
2 (= *disregard*) [*+ report, rumour*] descartar
(CPD) ['dɪskaʊnt] ▸ **discount card** tarjeta *f* de descuento ▸ **discount house** (*US*) tienda *f* de rebajas ▸ **discount price** • **they are available at ~ prices** se venden con descuento ▸ **discount rate** tasa *f* de descuento ▸ **discount store** (*US*) economato *m*
discounter ['dɪskaʊntəʳ] (N) (= *organization*) empresa *f* que vende con descuento
discourage [dɪs'kʌrɪdʒ] (VT) **1** (= *dishearten*) desanimar, desalentar • **to get** *or* **become ~d** desanimarse, desalentarse
2 (= *deter*) [*+ offer, advances*] rechazar; [*+ tendency, relationship*] oponerse a • **smoking is ~d** se recomienda no fumar
3 (= *dissuade*) • **to ~ sb from doing sth** disuadir a algn de hacer algo • **I don't want to ~ you, but …** no pretendo disuadirte *or* desanimarte, pero …
discouragement [dɪs'kʌrɪdʒmənt] (N) **1** (= *depression*) desánimo *m*, desaliento *m*
2 (= *dissuasion*) disuasión *f*
3 (= *deterrent*) impedimento *m* • **it's a real ~ to progress** es un verdadero impedimento para el progreso
discouraging [dɪs'kʌrɪdʒɪŋ] (ADJ) desalentador • **he was ~ about it** habló de ello en tono pesimista
discouragingly [dɪs'kʌrɪdʒɪŋlɪ] (ADV) desalentadoramente
discourse (N) ['dɪskɔ:s] **1** (= *talk*) conversación *f*, plática *f* (*LAm*)
2 (= *essay*) tratado *m*
3 (*Ling*) discurso *m*
(VI) [dɪs'kɔ:s] • **to ~ (up)on sth** disertar sobre algo
(CPD) ['dɪskɔ:s] ▸ **discourse analysis** análisis *m inv* del discurso
discourteous [dɪs'kɜ:tɪəs] (ADJ) descortés
discourteously [dɪs'kɜ:tɪəslɪ] (ADV) descortésmente
discourtesy [dɪs'kɜ:tɪsɪ] (N) descortesía *f*
discover [dɪs'kʌvəʳ] (VT) **1** [*+ new country, species, talent*] descubrir; [*+ object*] (*after search*) encontrar, hallar
2 (= *notice*) [*+ loss, mistake*] darse cuenta de • **I ~ed that I'd left it at home** me di cuenta de que lo había dejado en casa
discoverer [dɪs'kʌvərəʳ] (N) descubridor(a) *m/f*
discovery [dɪs'kʌvərɪ] (N) **1** (= *finding*) [*of new country, drug, talent*] descubrimiento *m*
2 (= *thing or person found*) descubrimiento *m*
discredit [dɪs'kredɪt] (N) (= *dishonour*) descrédito *m*, deshonor *m* • **it was to the general's ~ that …** fue un descrédito para el general que … • **to bring ~ (up)on sth/sb** desacreditar algo/a algn, suponer un descrédito para algo/algn
(VT) **1** (= *prove untrue*) [*+ theory*] rebatir, refutar • **that theory is now ~ed** esa teoría ya ha sido rebatida *or* refutada
2 (= *cast doubt upon*) poner en duda • **all his evidence is thus ~ed** por lo tanto se pone en duda todo su testimonio
3 (= *sully reputation of*) [*+ family*] deshonrar, desacreditar; [*+ organization, profession*] desacreditar
discreditable [dɪs'kredɪtəbl] (ADJ) deshonroso, vergonzoso
discreditably [dɪs'kredɪtəblɪ] (ADV) vergonzosamente
discreet [dɪs'kri:t] (ADJ) [*person, inquiry, decor, uniform*] discreto • **at a ~ distance** a una distancia prudencial
discreetly [dɪs'kri:tlɪ] (ADV) [*speak, behave, leave, dress*] discretamente, con discreción
discreetness [dɪ'skri:tnɪs] (N) (= *discretion*) discreción *f*; [*of jewellery, clothing, decoration*] sobriedad *f*
discrepancy [dɪs'krepənsɪ] (N) discrepancia *f* (**between** entre)
discrete [dɪs'kri:t] (ADJ) [*stages, phases, events*] específico, separado
discretion [dɪs'kreʃən] (N) **1** (= *tact*) discreción *f* • PROVERB: • **~ is the better part of valour** una retirada a tiempo es una victoria
2 (= *judgment*) criterio *m*, juicio *m* • **use your own ~** usa tu propio criterio *or* juicio • **I will leave it to your ~** te lo dejaré a tu criterio *or* juicio • **at the ~ of the judge** a discreción *or* a criterio del juez • **the age of ~** (la edad de) la madurez
discretionary [dɪs'kreʃənərɪ] (ADJ) discrecional
discriminate [dɪs'krɪmɪneɪt] (VI) **1** (= *distinguish*) distinguir (**between** entre)
2 (= *show prejudice*) • **to ~ against sb** discriminar a algn • **to ~ in favour of sb** hacer discriminaciones en favor de algn
3 (= *show good judgment*) tener buen criterio
(VT) distinguir (**from** de)
discriminating [dɪs'krɪmɪneɪtɪŋ] (ADJ) [*person*] entendido; [*taste*] refinado
discrimination [dɪsˌkrɪmɪ'neɪʃən] (N) **1** (= *prejudice*) discriminación *f* (**against** de, contra, **in favour of** a favor de) • **racial/sexual ~** discriminación *f* racial/sexual
2 (= *good judgment*) buen criterio *m*, discernimiento *m*
discriminatory [dɪs'krɪmɪnətərɪ] (ADJ) [*duty etc*] discriminatorio
discursive [dɪs'kɜ:sɪv] (ADJ) divagador, prolijo; (*Ling, Philos*) discursivo
discus ['dɪskəs] (N) (PL: **discuses** *or* **disci**) (*Sport*) **1** (= *object*) disco *m* • **to throw the ~** lanzar el disco
2 (= *event*) • **she won a gold medal in the ~** ganó la medalla de oro en la prueba de disco
discuss [dɪs'kʌs] (VT) **1** (= *talk about*) [*+ topic*] hablar de, discutir; [*+ person*] hablar de; [*+ problem, essay*] cambiar opiniones sobre, discutir
2 (*in exam question*) [*+ statement*] tratar, analizar
discussant [dɪs'kʌsənt] (N) (*US*) miembro *mf* de la mesa (de la sección de un congreso)
discussion [dɪs'kʌʃən] (N) discusión *f* • **we had a long ~ about it** hablamos largo y tendido de ello, tuvimos una larga discusión sobre ello • **to come up for ~** someterse a discusión • **it is under ~** se está discutiendo
(CPD) ▸ **discussion board** (*Internet*) foro *m* de discusión ▸ **discussion document** proposición *f* (para el debate) ▸ **discussion forum** (*Internet*) foro *m* de discusión ▸ **discussion group** coloquio *m* ▸ **discussion paper** = discussion document
disdain [dɪs'deɪn] (N) desdén *m*, desprecio *m*
(VT) • **to ~ sth** desdeñar *or* despreciar algo • **to ~ to do sth** no dignarse (a) hacer algo
disdainful [dɪs'deɪnfʊl] (ADJ) [*look, expression, attitude*] desdeñoso, de desdén • **to be ~ of sth** desdeñar *or* despreciar algo, mostrar desdén *or* desprecio hacia algo • **to be ~ towards** *or* **of sb** desdeñar *or* despreciar a algn, mostrar desdén *or* desprecio hacia algn
disdainfully [dɪs'deɪnfəlɪ] (ADV) desdeñosamente, con desdén
disease [dɪ'zi:z] (N) enfermedad *f*; (*fig*) mal *m*, enfermedad *f*
diseased [dɪ'zi:zd] (ADJ) [*person, animal, plant*] enfermo; [*tissue*] dañado, afectado; [*mind*] enfermo, morboso
disembark [ˌdɪsɪm'bɑ:k] (VT), (VI) desembarcar
disembarkation [ˌdɪsembɑ:'keɪʃən] (N) [*of goods*] desembarque *m*; [*of persons*] desembarco *m*
disembodied [ˌdɪsɪm'bɒdɪd] (ADJ) incorpóreo
disembowel [ˌdɪsɪm'baʊəl] (VT) desentrañar, destripar
disempower [ˌdɪsɪm'paʊəʳ] (VT) restar autoridad a, despojar de sus derechos a
disempowerment [ˌdɪsɪm'paʊəmənt] (N) pérdida *f* de libertades *o* de derechos
disenchant [ˌdɪsɪn'tʃɑ:nt] (VT) desencantar, desilusionar
disenchanted [ˌdɪsɪn'tʃɑ:ntɪd] (ADJ) desencantado, desilusionado • **to be ~ with sth/sb** estar desencantado *or* desilusionado con algo/algn • **to become ~ with sth/sb** quedar desencantado *or* desilusionado con algo/algn
disenchantment [ˌdɪsɪn'tʃɑ:ntmənt] (N) desencanto *m*, desilusión *f*
disenfranchise [ˌdɪsɪn'fræntʃaɪz] (VT) privar del derecho de voto
disengage [ˌdɪsɪn'geɪdʒ] (VT) **1** (= *free*) soltar • **she gently ~d her hand (from his)** soltó su mano (de la de él) con suavidad
2 (*Mil*) [*+ troops*] retirar
3 (*Mech*) desacoplar, desconectar • **to ~ the clutch** desembragar, soltar el embrague
(VI) **1** (*Mil*) retirarse
2 (*Fencing*) separarse
disengaged [ˌdɪsɪn'geɪdʒd] (ADJ) libre, desocupado
disengagement [ˌdɪsɪn'geɪdʒmənt] (N) **1** (*Mil*) retirada *f*
2 (*Mech*) desacoplamiento *m*, desconexión *f*
disentangle [ˌdɪsɪn'tæŋgl] (VT) **1** [*+ string, hair*] desenredar, desenmarañar (**from** de) • **to ~ o.s. from** (*fig*) desenredarse de
2 (*fig*) [*+ problem, mystery*] desentrañar, esclarecer
disequilibrium [ˌdɪsi:kwɪ'lɪbrɪəm] (N) desequilibrio *m*
disestablish [ˌdɪsɪs'tæblɪʃ] (VT) [*+ church*] separar del Estado
disestablishment [ˌdɪsɪs'tæblɪʃmənt] (N) [*of church*] separación *f* del Estado
disfavour, **disfavor** (*US*) [dɪs'feɪvəʳ] (N) **1** (= *disapproval*) desaprobación *f* • **to fall into**

~ [*custom, practice*] caer en desuso; [*person*] caer en desgracia • **to look with ~ on sth** ver algo con malos ojos, desaprobar algo
2 (= *disservice*) • **to do sb a ~** • **do a ~ to sb** hacer un flaco favor a algn, no hacer ningún favor a algn
disfigure [dɪsˈfɪgəʳ] VT [+ *face, body*] desfigurar; [+ *area*] afear
disfigured [dɪsˈfɪgəd] ADJ desfigurado
disfigurement [dɪsˈfɪgəmənt] N [*of face, body*] desfiguración *f*; [*of area*] afeamiento *m*
disfranchise [ˈdɪsˈfræntʃaɪz] VT = **disenfranchise**
disgorge [dɪsˈgɔːdʒ] VT **1** [+ *food*] [*person, animal*] vomitar, arrojar; [*bird*] desembuchar
2 [+ *contents, passengers*] • **the coaches were disgorging hordes of tourists** de los autocares manaban hordas de turistas • **the ship ~d its cargo of oil into the sea** el barco derramó su cargamento de petróleo en el mar
disgrace [dɪsˈgreɪs] N **1** (= *state of shame*) deshonra *f*, ignominia *f* • **there is no ~ in being poor** no es ninguna deshonra ser pobre • **to be in ~** [*adult*] estar totalmente desacreditado, haber caído en desgracia; [*pet, child*] estar castigado • **she was sent home in ~** la mandaron a casa castigada • **to bring ~ on** deshonrar
2 (= *shameful thing*) vergüenza *f* • **it's a ~** es una vergüenza • **you're a ~!** ¡lo tuyo es una vergüenza! • **to be a ~ to the school/family** ser una deshonra para la escuela/la familia
3 (= *downfall*) caída *f*
VT [+ *family, country*] deshonrar • **he ~d himself** se deshonró • **he was ~d and banished** lo destituyeron de su cargo y lo desterraron
disgraced [dɪsˈgreɪst] ADJ caído en desgracia
disgraceful [dɪsˈgreɪsfʊl] ADJ vergonzoso; [*behaviour*] escandaloso • **disgraceful!** ¡qué vergüenza!
disgracefully [dɪsˈgreɪsfəlɪ] ADV vergonzosamente; [*behave*] escandalosamente
disgruntled [dɪsˈgrʌntld] ADJ (= *unhappy*) [*employee, staff, customer*] descontento; (= *bad-tempered*) contrariado, malhumorado
disguise [dɪsˈgaɪz] N disfraz *m* • **to be in ~** estar disfrazado
VT [+ *person*] disfrazar (**as** de); [+ *voice*] simular, cambiar; [+ *feelings*] ocultar, disimular; [+ *bad points, error*] ocultar • **to ~ o.s. as** disfrazarse de • **she ~d herself as a man** se disfrazó de hombre
disguised [dɪsˈgaɪzd] ADJ **1** (= *in disguise*) [*person*] disfrazado • **to be heavily ~** estar irreconocible bajo su disfraz • **eagle-eyed viewers might spot a heavily ~ Sarah Stone** los telespectadores con vista de lince puede que identifiquen a una Sarah Stone irreconocible bajo su disfraz • **to be ~ as sb/sth** ir disfrazado de algn/algo • **he was ~ as a policeman** iba disfrazado de policía
2 [*criticism, contempt, anger*] disimulado • **~ as sth** disimulado como algo
disgust [dɪsˈgʌst] N **1** (= *revulsion*) repugnancia *f*, asco *m* • **it fills me with ~** me da asco
2 (= *anger*) indignación *f* • **she left in ~** se marchó indignada
VT dar asco a, repugnar • **the thought ~s me** la idea me repugna • **you ~ me** me das asco
disgusted [dɪsˈgʌstɪd] ADJ [*viewer, reader, customer*] indignado; [*tone, voice*] de indignación • **I am ~ at the way we were treated** estoy indignado por la manera en que nos trataron • **he was ~ by his failure** estaba muy enojado consigo mismo por su fracaso • **I am ~ with you** estoy indignado contigo
disgustedly [dɪsˈgʌstɪdlɪ] ADV (= *with revulsion*) con asco; (= *angrily*) con indignación • **... he said ~** ... dijo indignado
disgusting [dɪsˈgʌstɪŋ] ADJ **1** (= *revolting*) [*habit, taste, smell, food, place*] asqueroso, repugnante; [*person*] repugnante • **you're ~** me das asco, eres repugnante • **the kitchen is in a ~ mess** la cocina está que da asco, la cocina está asquerosa • **how ~!** ¡qué asco! • **it looks ~** tiene una pinta asquerosa • **it smells ~** tiene un olor asqueroso *or* repugnante, huele que da asco • **it tastes ~** tiene un sabor asqueroso *or* repugnante
2 (= *obscene*) [*book, film, photo*] repugnante, asqueroso; [*language*] indecente, cochino*
3 (= *disgraceful*) [*attitude, behaviour, manners*] vergonzoso • **she returned the book in a ~ condition** devolvió el libro en un estado vergonzoso
4* (= *terrible*) [*weather*] asqueroso, de perros*
disgustingly [dɪsˈgʌstɪŋlɪ] ADV asquerosamente • **it was ~ dirty** estaba asquerosamente sucio, estaba tan sucio que daba asco • **they are ~ rich** son tan ricos que da asco
dish [dɪʃ] N **1** (= *plate*) plato *m*; (= *serving dish*) fuente *f*; (= *food*) plato *m*, platillo *m* (*Mex*) • **to wash** *or* **do the ~es** fregar los platos • **a typical Spanish ~** un plato típico español
2 (*TV*) antena *f* parabólica; (*Astron*) reflector *m*
3* (= *girl, boy*) bombón* *m*
VT [+ *hopes, chances*] desbaratar
CPD ▸ **dish aerial** (*Brit*), **dish antenna** (*US*) antena *f* parabólica ▸ **dish soap** (*US*) lavavajillas *m inv*
▸ **dish out** VT + ADV [+ *food*] servir; [+ *money*] repartir; [+ *advice*] dar, impartir; [+ *punishment*] infligir, impartir; [+ *criticism*] hacer
▸ **dish up** VT + ADV **1** (= *serve*) [+ *food*] servir
2 (= *present*) ofrecer • **he ~ed up the same old arguments** repitió los argumentos de siempre
VI + ADV servir
dishabille [ˌdɪsæˈbiːl] N desnudez *f*
disharmony [ˈdɪsˈhɑːmənɪ] N discordia *f*; (*Mus*) disonancia *f*
dishcloth [ˈdɪʃklɒθ] N (PL: **dishcloths** [ˈdɪʃklɒðz]) (*for washing*) bayeta *f*; (*for drying*) paño *m* (de cocina), trapo *m*
dishearten [dɪsˈhɑːtn] VT desalentar, desanimar • **don't be ~ed!** ¡ánimo!, ¡no te desanimes!
disheartening [dɪsˈhɑːtnɪŋ] ADJ desalentador
dishevelled, disheveled (*US*) [dɪˈʃevəld] ADJ [*hair*] despeinado; [*clothes*] desarreglado, desaliñado
dishmop [ˈdɪʃmɒp] N fregona *f* para lavar los platos
dishonest [dɪsˈɒnɪst] ADJ [*person*] poco honrado, deshonesto; [*means, plan*] fraudulento, deshonesto
dishonestly [dɪsˈɒnɪstlɪ] ADV fraudulentamente, deshonestamente • **to act ~** obrar con poca honradez *or* de forma poco honrada
dishonesty [dɪsˈɒnɪstɪ] N [*of person*] falta *f* de honradez, deshonestidad *f*; [*of declaration*] falsedad *f*; [*of means*] carácter *m* fraudulento, fraudulencia *f*
dishonour, dishonor (*US*) [dɪsˈɒnəʳ] N deshonra *f*, deshonor *m* • **to bring** *or* **cast ~ on sth/sb** traer la deshonra a algo/a algn, deshonrar algo/a algn
VT [+ *country, family*] deshonrar; [+ *cheque*] devolver, rechazar; [+ *debt*] dejar sin pagar, incumplir el pago de; [+ *promise*] faltar a, no cumplir
dishonourable, dishonorable (*US*) [dɪsˈɒnərəbl] ADJ deshonroso • **~ discharge** (*US*) (*Mil*) baja *f* por conducta deshonrosa
dishonourably, dishonorably (*US*) [dɪsˈɒnərəblɪ] ADV deshonrosamente • **to be ~ discharged** ser dado de baja con deshonor *or* por conducta deshonrosa
dishpan [ˈdɪʃpæn] N (*US*) palangana *f*
dishrack [ˈdɪʃræk] N escurreplatos *m inv*, escurridor *m*
dishrag [ˈdɪʃræg] N trapo *m* para fregar los platos, bayeta *f*
dishtowel [ˈdɪʃtaʊəl] N (*US*) paño *m* de cocina, trapo *m*
dishware [ˈdɪʃweəʳ] N (*US*) loza *f*, vajilla *f*
dishwasher [ˈdɪʃˌwɒʃəʳ] N (= *machine*) lavaplatos *m inv*, lavavajillas *m inv*; (= *person*) (*in restaurant*) friegaplatos *mf inv*, lavaplatos *mf inv*
dishwashing liquid [ˈdɪʃwɒʃɪŋˌlɪkwɪd] N (*US*) lavavajillas *m inv*
dishwater [ˈdɪʃwɔːtəʳ] N agua *f* de lavar platos; (*fig*) agua *f* sucia
dishy* [ˈdɪʃɪ] ADJ (COMPAR: **dishier**, SUPERL: **dishiest**) (*Brit*) guapísimo • **he's/she's really ~** está buenísimo/buenísima
disillusion [ˌdɪsɪˈluːʒən] N desilusión *f*; (*more intense*) desencanto *m*
VT desilusionar; (*more intensely*) desencantar
disillusioned [ˌdɪsɪˈluːʒənd] ADJ desilusionado; (*more intense*) desencantado • **to be/become ~ with sth/sb** estar/quedar desilusionado con algo/algn; (*more intensely*) estar/quedar desencantado con algo/algn
disillusionment [ˌdɪsɪˈluːʒənmənt] N desilusión *f*; (*more intense*) desencanto *m*
disincentive [ˌdɪsɪnˈsentɪv] N factor *m* desmotivador (**to** para)
disinclination [ˌdɪsɪnklɪˈneɪʃən] N (*frm*) poca disposición *f* (**for a, to do sth** a hacer algo) • **one of his characteristics was an extreme ~ to part with money** una de sus características era su extremado apego al dinero • **they showed a marked ~ to compromise** se mostraron manifiestamente reacios a comprometerse
disinclined [ˈdɪsɪnˈklaɪnd] ADJ (*frm*) • **to be ~ to do sth** estar poco dispuesto a hacer algo, ser reacio a hacer algo • **I feel very ~ to go** no tengo ningunas ganas de ir
disinfect [ˌdɪsɪnˈfekt] VT desinfectar
disinfectant [ˌdɪsɪnˈfektənt] N desinfectante *m*
disinfection [ˌdɪsɪnˈfekʃən] N desinfección *f*
disinflation [ˌdɪsɪnˈfleɪʃən] N reducción *f* de la inflación
disinflationary [ˌdɪsɪnˈfleɪʃənərɪ] ADJ desinflacionista
disinformation [ˌdɪsɪnfəˈmeɪʃən] N desinformación *f*
disingenuous [ˌdɪsɪnˈdʒenjʊəs] ADJ falso, poco sincero
disingenuously [ˌdɪsɪnˈdʒenjʊəslɪ] ADV [*say, claim, remark*] con poca sinceridad
disingenuousness [ˌdɪsɪnˈdʒenjʊəsnɪs] N falsedad *f*, falta *f* de sinceridad
disinherit [ˈdɪsɪnˈherɪt] VT desheredar
disintegrate [dɪsˈɪntɪgreɪt] VI **1** (*lit*) [*rock*] desintegrarse; [*piece of machinery, furniture, toy*] destrozarse
2 (*fig*) [*country, family, organization*] desintegrarse
VT [+ *rock*] desintegrar
disintegration [dɪsˌɪntɪˈgreɪʃən] N desintegración *f*

disinter [ˈdɪsɪnˈtɜːʳ] VT [*+ corpse*] desenterrar, exhumar; [*+ idea, law*] desenterrar

disinterest [dɪsˈɪntrəst] N **1** (*= indifference*) desinterés *m*, apatía *f*
2 (*= impartiality*) imparcialidad *f*

disinterested [dɪsˈɪntrɪstɪd] ADJ
1 (*= impartial*) desinteresado, imparcial
2 (*= uninterested*) indiferente

disinterestedly [dɪsˈɪntrɪstɪdlɪ] ADV
1 (*= impartially*) de manera desinteresada, desinteresadamente
2 (*= uninterestedly*) con indiferencia

disinterestedness [dɪsˈɪntrɪstɪdnɪs] N
1 (*= impartiality*) imparcialidad *f*
2 (*= indifference*) desinterés *m*

disinterment [ˌdɪsɪnˈtɜːmənt] N exhumación *f*, desenterramiento *m*

disinvest [ˌdɪsɪnˈvest] VI desinvertir (**from** de)

disinvestment [ˌdɪsɪnˈvestmənt] N desinversión *f*

disjointed [dɪsˈdʒɔɪntɪd] ADJ [*words, sentences, arguments*] inconexo, deslavazado

disjointedly [dɪsˈdʒɔɪntɪdlɪ] ADV de forma incoherente, de forma inconexa

disjunctive [dɪsˈdʒʌŋktɪv] ADJ disyuntivo

disk [dɪsk] N **1** (*esp US*) = **disc**
2 (*Comput*) disco *m* • **single-/double-sided ~** disco *m* de una cara/dos caras
CPD ▸ **disk drive** unidad *f* de disco ▸ **disk operating system** sistema *m* operativo de disco ▸ **disk pack** unidad *f* de discos duros ▸ **disk space** espacio *m* en disco ▸ **disk storage** almacenamiento *m* en disco

diskette [dɪsˈket] N disquete *m*, diskette *m*

diskless [ˈdɪsklɪs] ADJ sin disco(s)

dislike [dɪsˈlaɪk] N **1** (*= antipathy*) aversión *f*, antipatía *f* (**of** a, hacia) • **to take a ~ to sb** coger *or* (*LAm*) tomar antipatía a algn
2 (*= thing disliked*) • **likes and ~s** aficiones *fpl* y fobias *or* manías, cosas *fpl* que gustan y cosas que no
VT [*+ person*] tener antipatía a; (*more intensely*) tener aversión a • **I ~ her intensely** le tengo mucha antipatía *or* auténtica aversión • **it's not that I ~ him** no es que me caiga mal, no es que yo le tenga antipatía • **I ~ pop music/flying** no me gusta la música pop/ir en avión

dislocate [ˈdɪsləʊkeɪt] VT **1** (*= put out of joint*) [*+ bone*] dislocarse • **he ~d his shoulder** se dislocó el hombro
2 (*= disrupt*) [*+ traffic*] trastornar; [*+ plans*] trastocar
3 (*= displace*) [*+ person*] desplazar

dislocation [ˌdɪsləʊˈkeɪʃən] N **1** (*Med*) dislocación *f*
2 (*= disruption*) [*of traffic*] trastorno *m*; [*of plans*] trastocamiento *m*
3 (*= displacement*) desplazamiento *m*

dislodge [dɪsˈlɒdʒ] VT **1** (*= remove*) [*+ stone, obstruction*] sacar; [*+ enemy*] desalojar (**from** de); [*+ party, ruler*] desbancar
2 (*= cause to fall*) hacer caer

disloyal [ˈdɪsˈlɔɪəl] ADJ desleal (**to** con)

disloyalty [ˈdɪsˈlɔɪəltɪ] N deslealtad *f* (**to** con)

dismal [ˈdɪzməl] ADJ **1** (*= gloomy, depressing*) [*weather*] deprimente; [*place*] sombrío, deprimente; [*day, tone, thought*] sombrío; [*person*] taciturno, de carácter sombrío • **to be in a ~ mood** estar *or* sentirse abatido
2 (*= poor*) [*performance, condition*] pésimo; [*future*] desalentador, poco prometedor • **my prospects of getting a job are ~/pretty ~** mis posibilidades de conseguir un trabajo son ínfimas/bastante escasas • **a ~ failure** un rotundo fracaso

dismally [ˈdɪzməlɪ] ADV **1** (*= sadly*) [*say, reply*] en tono sombrío
2 (*= poorly*) • **to perform ~** [*actor*] actuar pésimamente; [*athlete*] tener una actuación pésima • **to fail ~** fracasar estrepitosamente
3 (*as intensifier*) • **the play was ~ bad** la obra fue pésima

dismantle [dɪsˈmæntl] VT [*+ machine*] desmontar, desarmar; [*+ fort, ship*] desmantelar; [*+ system, organization*] desmantelar

dismast [dɪsˈmɑːst] VT desarbolar

dismay [dɪsˈmeɪ] N consternación *f* • **there was general ~** todos estaban consternados • **in ~** consternado • **(much) to my ~** para (gran) consternación mía • **to fill sb with ~** consternar a algn
VT consternar • **I am ~ed to hear that …** me da pena *or* me produce consternación enterarme de que … • **don't look so ~ed!** ¡no te aflijas!

dismember [dɪsˈmembəʳ] VT desmembrar

dismemberment [dɪsˈmembəmənt] N desmembramiento *m*, desmembración *f*

dismiss [dɪsˈmɪs] VT **1** (*from job*) [*+ worker*] despedir; [*+ official*] destituir • **to be ~ed from the service** (*Mil*) ser dado de baja, ser separado del servicio
2 (*= send away*) (*gen*) despachar; [*+ troops*] dar permiso (para irse) • **class ~ed!** (*Scol*) eso es todo por hoy
3 (*= reject, disregard*) [*+ thought*] rechazar, apartar de sí; [*+ request*] rechazar; [*+ possibility*] descartar, desechar; [*+ problem*] hacer caso omiso de • **with that he ~ed the matter** con eso dio por concluido el asunto
4 (*Jur*) [*+ court case*] anular; [*+ appeal*] desestimar, rechazar • **the case was ~ed** el tribunal absolvió al acusado
5 (*= beat*) [*+ opponent*] vencer
VI (*Mil*) romper filas • **dismiss!** ¡rompan filas!

dismissal [dɪsˈmɪsəl] N **1** (*from job*) [*of worker*] despido *m*; [*of official*] destitución *f*
2 [*of suggestion, idea*] rechazo *m*
3 (*Jur*) desestimación *f*

dismissive [dɪsˈmɪsɪv] ADJ (*= disdainful*) [*gesture, wave, attitude*] despectivo, desdeñoso • **he said in a ~ tone** dijo como quien no quería tomar la cosa en serio • **he was very ~ about it** parecía no tomar la cosa en serio • **he is very ~ of her capabilities** siempre está infravalorando *or* subestimando sus capacidades

dismissively [dɪsˈmɪsɪvlɪ] ADV
1 (*= disdainfully*) [*speak, wave*] despectivamente, con desdén
2 (*sending sb away*) • **"that's all," he said ~** —eso es todo —se limitó a decir él

dismount [dɪsˈmaʊnt] VI desmontar • **she ~ed from her horse** desmontó (del caballo), se apeó *or* se bajó del caballo
VT [*+ rider*] desmontar

Disneyland [ˈdɪznɪˌlænd] N Disneylandia *f*

disobedience [ˌdɪsəˈbiːdɪəns] N desobediencia *f*

disobedient [ˌdɪsəˈbiːdɪənt] ADJ desobediente

disobey [ˈdɪsəˈbeɪ] VT [*+ person, rule*] desobedecer
VI desobedecer

disobliging [ˈdɪsəˈblaɪdʒɪŋ] ADJ poco servicial

disorder [dɪsˈɔːdəʳ] N **1** (*= confusion, untidiness*) desorden *m* • **to be in ~** estar en desorden • **to retreat in ~** retirarse a la desbandada
2 (*Pol*) (*= rioting*) disturbios *mpl*
3 (*Med*) dolencia *f*, trastorno *m* • **mental ~** trastorno *m* mental
VT **1** (*= make untidy*) desordenar
2 (*Med*) [*+ mind*] trastornar

disordered [dɪsˈɔːdəd] ADJ **1** [*room, thoughts*] desordenado
2 (*Med*) [*mind*] trastornado

disorderly [dɪsˈɔːdəlɪ] ADJ **1** (*= untidy, disorganized*) [*room, queue*] desordenado; [*person, mind*] poco metódico • **the ~ flight of the refugees** la caótica huída de los refugiados
2 (*= unruly*) [*behaviour*] indisciplinado, turbulento; [*crowd*] indisciplinado, alborotado; [*hooligan*] desmandado; [*meeting*] turbulento • **to become ~** [*meeting, person*] alborotarse • **~ conduct** (*Jur*) alteración *f* del orden público • **~ house** (*euph*) (*= brothel*) burdel *m*, prostíbulo *m*; (*= gambling den*) casa *f* de juego • **to keep a ~ house** (*= brothel*) regentar un burdel *or* prostíbulo; (*= gambling den*) regentar una casa de juego; ▸ **drunk**

disorganization [dɪsˌɔːɡənaɪˈzeɪʃən] N desorganización *f*

disorganize [dɪsˈɔːɡənaɪz] VT (*gen*) desorganizar; [*+ communications*] interrumpir

disorganized [dɪsˈɔːɡənaɪzd] ADJ desorganizado

disorient [dɪsˈɔːrɪənt] VT = **disorientate**

disorientate [dɪsˈɔːrɪənteɪt] VT desorientar

disorientated [dɪsˈɔːrɪənteɪtɪd], **disoriented** [dɪsˈɔːrɪentɪd] ADJ desorientando • **to become ~** (*= confused*) sentirse desorientado; (*= lost*) desorientarse

disorientating [dɪsˈɔːrɪənteɪtɪŋ], **disorienting** [dɪsˈɔːrɪentɪŋ] ADJ [*experience, effect*] desconcertante

disorientation [dɪsˌɔːrɪənˈteɪʃən] N desorientación *f*

disown [dɪsˈəʊn] VT **1** (*= repudiate*) [*+ son, daughter, husband, wife*] desconocer, repudiar
2 (*= deny*) [*+ responsibility*] negar; [*+ belief*] renegar de

disparage [dɪsˈpærɪdʒ] VT [*+ person, achievements*] menospreciar, despreciar

disparagement [dɪsˈpærɪdʒmənt] N menosprecio *m*

disparaging [dɪsˈpærɪdʒɪŋ] ADJ [*remark*] despectivo • **to be ~ about sth/sb** menospreciar algo/a algn

disparagingly [dɪsˈpærɪdʒɪŋlɪ] ADV • **to speak ~ of** hablar en términos despreciativos de

disparate [ˈdɪspərɪt] ADJ dispar

disparity [dɪsˈpærɪtɪ] N (*= inequality, dissimilarity*) disparidad *f*

dispassion [dɪsˈpæʃən] N (*= impartiality*) imparcialidad *f*; (*= lack of passion*) falta *f* de pasión

dispassionate [dɪsˈpæʃnɪt] ADJ (*= unbiased*) [*appraisal, observer*] imparcial; (*= unemotional*) [*voice, tone*] desapasionado

dispassionately [dɪsˈpæʃnɪtlɪ] ADV de modo desapasionado, sin apasionamientos

dispatch [dɪsˈpætʃ] N **1** (*= sending*) [*of person*] envío *m*; [*of goods*] envío *m*, expedición *f*
2 (*= report*) (*in press*) reportaje *m*, informe *m*; (*= message*) despacho *m*; (*Mil*) parte *m*, comunicado *m* • **to be mentioned in ~es** (*Mil*) recibir menciones de elogio (*por su valor en combate*)
3 (*= promptness*) (*frm*) celeridad *f*, prontitud *f*
VT **1** (*= send*) [*+ letter, goods*] enviar, expedir; [*+ messenger, troops*] enviar
2 (*= deal with*) [*+ business*] despachar
3 (*= carry out*) [*+ duty*] ejercer, realizar
4 (*hum*) (*= eat*) [*+ food*] despachar
5 (*= kill*) despachar
CPD ▸ **dispatch box** (*Brit*) cartera *f* ▸ **dispatch case** portafolios *m inv* ▸ **dispatch department** departamento *m* de envíos

▸ **dispatch documents** documentos *mpl* de envío ▸ **dispatch note** nota *f* de envío, nota *f* de expedición ▸ **dispatch rider** (= *motorcyclist*) mensajero/a *m/f* (*con moto*); (= *horseman*) correo *m*; (*Mil*) correo *m*

dispatcher [dɪs'pætʃəʳ] N transportista *m*

dispel [dɪs'pel] VT [+ *fog, smell, doubts, fear, worry*] disipar

dispensable [dɪs'pensəbl] ADJ prescindible

dispensary [dɪs'pensərɪ] N (*gen*) dispensario *m*; (*in hospital*) farmacia *f*

dispensation [,dɪspen'seɪʃən] N
1 (= *exemption*) exención *f*
2 (= *distribution*) [*of drugs*] dispensación *f*
3 (= *implementation*) [*of justice*] administración *f*
4 (*Rel*) dispensa *f* • **~ of Providence** designio *m* divino
5 (= *ruling*) decreto *m*

dispense [dɪs'pens] VT 1 (= *distribute*) [+ *food, money*] repartir; [+ *advice*] ofrecer; [+ *drug, prescription*] despachar • **this machine ~s coffee** esta máquina expende café
2 (= *implement*) [+ *justice*] administrar
3 (= *exempt*) • **to ~ sb from sth** dispensar *or* eximir a algn de algo
▸ **dispense with** VI + PREP 1 (= *do without*) prescindir de
2 (= *get rid of*) deshacerse de

dispenser [dɪs'pensəʳ] N 1 (= *person*) farmacéutico/a *m/f*
2 (= *container*) (*for soap*) dosificador *m*; (= *machine*) distribuidor *m* automático, máquina *f* expendedora • **cash ~** (*Brit*) cajero *m* automático

dispensing chemist [dɪs'pensɪŋ'kemɪst] N (= *shop*) farmacia *f*; (= *person*) farmacéutico/a *m/f*

dispersal [dɪs'pɜːsəl] N (= *scattering*) [*of army, crowd*] dispersión *f*; [*of light*] descomposición *f*

dispersant [dɪs'pɜːsənt] N (*Chem*) dispersante *m*

disperse [dɪs'pɜːs] VT (= *scatter*) [+ *crowd*] dispersar; [+ *news*] propagar; [+ *light*] descomponer
VI [*crowd, army, troops*] dispersarse; [*mist*] disiparse

dispersed [dɪ'spɜːst] ADJ (= *scattered*) disperso

dispersion [dɪs'pɜːʃən] N = **dispersal**

dispirit [dɪs'pɪrɪt] VT desanimar, desalentar

dispirited [dɪs'pɪrɪtɪd] ADJ desanimado, desalentado

dispiritedly [dɪs'pɪrɪtɪdlɪ] ADV con desánimo, con desaliento

dispiriting [dɪs'pɪrɪtɪŋ] ADJ desalentador

displace [dɪs'pleɪs] VT 1 (*Phys*) [+ *liquid, mass*] desplazar
2 (= *replace*) reemplazar
3 (= *remove from office*) destituir
4 (= *force to leave home*) desplazar

displaced [dɪs'pleɪst] ADJ • **~ person** desplazado/a *m/f*

displacement [dɪs'pleɪsmənt] N 1 (*Phys*) [*of liquid, mass*] desplazamiento *m*
2 (= *replacement*) reemplazo *m*
3 (= *removal*) eliminación *f*; (= *dismissal*) destitución *f*
4 (= *forced relocation*) desplazamiento *m*
5 (*Psych*) [*of energy*] sublimación *f*

display [dɪs'pleɪ] N 1 (= *act of displaying*) [*of merchandise*] exposición *f*; (*in gallery, museum*) exposición *f*, exhibición *f*; [*of emotion, interest*] manifestación *f*, demostración *f*; [*of force*] despliegue *m* • **to be on ~** estar expuesto
2 (= *array*) [*of merchandise*] muestrario *m*, surtido *m*; (*in gallery, museum*) exposición *f* • **window ~** (*in shop*) escaparate *m*
3 (= *show*) (*Mil*) exhibición *f*, demostración *f* • **a firework(s) ~** fuegos *mpl* artificiales
4 (= *ostentation*) • **the party made a ~ of unity** el partido se esforzó en dar una imagen de unidad
5 (*Comput*) (= *act*) visualización *f*
VT 1 (= *put on view*) [+ *goods, painting, exhibit*] exponer, exhibir; [+ *notice, results*] exponer, hacer público
2 (= *show*) [+ *emotion, ignorance*] mostrar, manifestar; [+ *courage*] demostrar, hacer gala de
3 (= *show ostentatiously*) [+ *one's knowledge*] alardear de, hacer alarde de
4 (*Comput*) desplegar, visualizar
CPD ▸ **display advertising** (*Press*) pancartas *fpl* publicitarias, publicidad *f* gráfica ▸ **display cabinet** vitrina *f* ▸ **display case** vitrina *f* ▸ **display screen, display unit** (*Comput*) monitor *m* ▸ **display window** escaparate *m*

displease [dɪs'pliːz] VT (= *be disagreeable to*) desagradar; (= *annoy*) disgustar

displeased [dɪs'pliːzd] ADJ • **to be ~ at sth/sb** estar disgustado con algo/algn

displeasing [dɪs'pliːzɪŋ] ADJ desagradable

displeasure [dɪs'pleʒəʳ] N desagrado *m*, disgusto *m*

disport [dɪs'pɔːt] VT • **to ~ o.s.** divertirse

disposability [dɪs,pəʊzə'bɪlɪtɪ] N carácter *m* desechable

disposable [dɪs'pəʊzəbl] ADJ 1 (= *not reusable*) [*nappy*] desechable, de usar y tirar • **~ goods** productos *mpl* desechables *or* no reutilizables
2 (= *available*) disponible • **~ assets** activos *mpl* disponibles • **~ income** renta *f* disponible
N (= *nappy*) pañal *m* desechable, pañal *m* de usar y tirar

disposal [dɪs'pəʊzəl] N 1 (= *sale, transfer*) [*of goods*] venta *f*; [*of property*] traspaso *m*; [*of rights*] enajenación *f*
2 [*of waste*] • **refuse ~** eliminación *f* de basuras; ▹ **bomb**
3 (= *distribution*) [*of ornaments, furniture*] disposición *f*, colocación *f*; [*of troops*] despliegue *m*
4 (= *availability for use*) disposición *f* • **to put sth at sb's ~** poner algo a disposición de algn • **to have sth at one's ~** tener algo a su disposición, disponer de algo • **it's/I'm at your ~** está/estoy a tu disposición

dispose [dɪs'pəʊz] VT 1 (= *arrange*) [+ *furniture, ornaments*] disponer, colocar; [+ *troops*] desplegar
2 (*frm*) (= *incline*) predisponer • **her behaviour did not ~ me to help her** su comportamiento no me predisponía a ayudarla, su comportamiento no hacía que me sintiese inclinado a ayudarla
3 (= *decide*) disponer, decidir
▸ **dispose of** VI + PREP 1 (= *get rid of*) [+ *evidence, body*] deshacerse de; [+ *rubbish*] tirar, botar (*LAm*)
2 (= *sell, transfer*) [+ *goods*] vender; [+ *property*] traspasar; [+ *rights*] enajenar, ceder
3 (= *deal with*) [+ *matter, problem*] resolver; [+ *business*] despachar
4 (= *disprove*) [+ *argument*] echar por tierra
5 (= *have at one's command*) disponer de
6 (*hum*) (= *eat*) [+ *food*] comerse, despachar
7 (= *kill*) matar, despachar

disposed [dɪs'pəʊzd] ADJ (*frm*) • **to be ~ to do sth** estar dispuesto a hacer algo • **to be favourably ~ towards sth/sb** tener una disposición favorable hacia algo/algn; ▹ **ill-disposed, well-disposed**

disposition [,dɪspə'zɪʃən] N
1 (= *temperament*) carácter *m*, temperamento *m*
2 (= *placing*) [*of ornaments, furniture*] disposición *f*, colocación *f*; [*of troops*] despliegue *m*
3 (= *inclination*) predisposición *f* (**to** a) • **I have no ~ to help him** no estoy dispuesto a ayudarle
4 **dispositions** preparativos *mpl* • **to make one's ~s** hacer preparativos

dispossess ['dɪspə'zes] VT [+ *tenant*] desahuciar • **to ~ sb of** desposeer *or* despojar a algn de

dispossession [,dɪspə'zeʃən] N desposeimiento *m*

disproportion [,dɪsprə'pɔːʃən] N desproporción *f*

disproportionate [,dɪsprə'pɔːʃnɪt] ADJ desproporcionado (**to** en relación con)

disproportionately [,dɪsprə'pɔːʃnɪtlɪ] ADV desproporcionadamente

disprovable [dɪs'pruːvəbl] ADJ refutable

disprove [dɪs'pruːv] VT [+ *theory, argument*] refutar, rebatir; [+ *claim, allegation*] desmentir

disputable [dɪs'pjuːtəbl] ADJ discutible

disputation [,dɪspjuː'teɪʃən] N debate *m*

disputatious [,dɪspjuː'teɪʃəs] ADJ discutidor, disputador

dispute [dɪs'pjuːt] N (= *quarrel*) disputa *f*, discusión *f*; (= *debate*) discusión *f*; (= *controversy*) polémica *f*, controversia *f*; (= *industrial dispute*) conflicto *m*; (*Jur*) contencioso *m* • **it is beyond ~ that …** es indudable que … • **in** *or* **under ~** [*territory*] en litigio
VT 1 (= *gainsay*) [+ *statement, claim*] poner en duda • **I ~ that** lo dudo • **I do not ~ the fact that …** no niego *or* no discuto que …
2 (= *fight for*) • **to ~ possession of a house with sb** tener un contencioso con algn sobre la posesión de una casa • **the final will be ~d between Federer and Nadal** Federer y Nadal se disputarán la final
VI (= *argue*) discutir (**about, over** sobre)

disputed [dɪs'pjuːtɪd] ADJ [*decision*] discutido; [*territory*] en litigio • **a ~ matter** un asunto contencioso, un asunto en litigio

disqualification [dɪs,kwɒlɪfɪ'keɪʃən] N
1 (= *act, effect*) inhabilitación *f*; (*Sport*) descalificación *f*
2 (= *thing that disqualifies*) impedimento *m*

disqualify [dɪs'kwɒlɪfaɪ] VT • **to ~ sb (from)** (= *disable*) inhabilitar *or* incapacitar a algn (para); (*Sport*) descalificar a algn (para) • **to ~ sb from driving** retirar el permiso de conducir a algn

disquiet [dɪs'kwaɪət] N preocupación *f*, inquietud *f*
VT inquietar

disquieting [dɪs'kwaɪətɪŋ] ADJ inquietante

disquietude [dɪs'kwaɪɪtjuːd] N (*frm*) inquietud *f*, intranquilidad *f*

disquisition [,dɪskwɪ'zɪʃən] N disquisición *f*

disregard ['dɪsrɪ'gɑːd] N (= *indifference*) (*for feelings, money, danger*) indiferencia *f* (**for** por, hacia); (= *non-observance*) [*of law, rules*] desacato *m* (**of** a, de) • **with complete ~ for** sin atender en lo más mínimo a • **with complete ~ for his own safety** haciendo caso omiso de su propia seguridad
VT [+ *remark, feelings*] hacer caso omiso de; [+ *authority, duty*] desatender

disrepair ['dɪsrɪ'pɛəʳ] N • **in a state of ~** en mal estado • **to fall into ~** [*house*] desmoronarse; [*machinery etc*] deteriorarse

disreputable [dɪs'repjʊtəbl] ADJ [*person, place*] de mala fama; [*clothing*] desaliñado

disreputably [dɪs'repjʊtəblɪ] ADV

d

vergonzosamente
disrepute ['dɪsrɪ'pju:t] (N) • **to bring into ~** desprestigiar • **to fall into ~** desprestigiarse
disrespect ['dɪsrɪs'pekt] (N) falta *f* de respeto • **I meant no ~** no quería ofenderle
(VT) faltar el respeto a
disrespectful [ˌdɪsrɪs'pektfʊl] (ADJ) irrespetuoso • **to be ~ to** *or* **towards sb** faltar al respeto a algn
disrespectfully [ˌdɪsrɪs'pektfʊlɪ] (ADV) irrespetuosamente • **... he said ~** ... dijo de forma irrespetuosa
disrobe ['dɪs'rəʊb] (*frm*) (VT) desnudar, desvestir
(VI) desnudarse
disrupt [dɪs'rʌpt] (VT) [+ *meeting, communications etc*] interrumpir; [+ *plans*] alterar, trastocar
disruption [dɪs'rʌpʃən] (N) [*of meeting, communications*] interrupción *f*; [*of plans*] alteración *f*
disruptive [dɪs'rʌptɪv] (ADJ) perjudicial
diss‡, **dis**‡ [dɪs] (VT) • **to ~ sb** faltar al respeto a algn
dissatisfaction ['dɪsˌsætɪs'fækʃən] (N) insatisfacción *f* (**with** con)
dissatisfied ['dɪs'sætɪsfaɪd] (ADJ) descontento, insatisfecho (**with** con) • **everyone was ~ with the result** el resultado dejó descontento *or* insatisfecho a todo el mundo
dissect [dɪ'sekt] (VT) [+ *animal*] disecar; (*fig*) analizar minuciosamente
dissection [dɪ'sekʃən] (N) [*of animal*] disección *f*; (*fig*) análisis *m inv* minucioso
dissemble [dɪ'sembl] (VT) ocultar, disimular
(VI) disimular
disseminate [dɪ'semɪneɪt] (VT) [+ *information*] divulgar, difundir
dissemination [dɪˌsemɪ'neɪʃən] (N) diseminación *f*, difusión *f*
dissension [dɪ'senʃən] (N) disensión *f*, desacuerdo *m*
dissent [dɪ'sent] (N) disentimiento *m*, disconformidad *f*; (*Rel, Pol*) disidencia *f*
(VI) disentir (**from** de), estar disconforme (**from** con); (*Rel*) disidir
dissenter [dɪ'sentəʳ] (N) (*Pol, Rel*) disidente *mf*
dissentient [dɪ'senʃɪənt] (*frm*) (ADJ) = **dissenting**
(N) disidente *mf*
dissenting [dɪ'sentɪŋ] (ADJ) [*voice*] discrepante • **there was one ~ voice** hubo una voz discrepante *or* en contra • **a long ~ tradition** una larga tradición de disidencia
dissertation [ˌdɪsə'teɪʃən] (N) disertación *f*; (*US*) (*Univ*) tesis *f inv*; (*Brit*) (*Univ*) tesina *f*
disservice ['dɪs'sɜ:vɪs] (N) perjuicio *m* • **to do sb a ~** perjudicar a algn
dissidence ['dɪsɪdəns] (N) disidencia *f*
dissident ['dɪsɪdənt] (ADJ) disidente
(N) disidente *mf*
dissimilar ['dɪ'sɪmɪləʳ] (ADJ) distinto, diferente (**to** de)
dissimilarity [ˌdɪsɪmɪ'lærɪtɪ] (N) desemejanza *f* (**between** entre)
dissimulate [dɪ'sɪmjʊleɪt] (VT) disimular
dissimulation [dɪˌsɪmjʊ'leɪʃən] (N) disimulación *f*
dissipate ['dɪsɪpeɪt] (VT) **1** (= *dispel*) [+ *fear, doubt etc*] disipar
2 (= *waste*) [+ *efforts, fortune*] derrochar
(VI) disiparse
dissipated ['dɪsɪpeɪtɪd] (ADJ) [*person*] disipado, licencioso; [*behaviour, life*] disoluto
dissipation [ˌdɪsɪ'peɪʃən] (N) **1** (= *act of dispelling*) disipación *f*; (= *waste*) derroche *m*, desperdicio *m*
2 (= *debauchery*) disipación *f*, libertinaje *m*
dissociate [dɪ'səʊʃɪeɪt] (VT) disociar (**from** de) • **to ~ o.s. from sth/sb** disociarse *or* desligarse de algo/algn
dissociation [dɪˌsəʊsɪ'eɪʃən] (N) disociación *f*
dissoluble [dɪ'sɒljʊbl] (ADJ) disoluble
dissolute ['dɪsəlu:t] (ADJ) disoluto
dissolution [ˌdɪsə'lu:ʃən] (N) (*gen*) (*Pol*) disolución *f*
dissolvable [dɪ'zɒlvəbl] (ADJ) soluble
dissolve [dɪ'zɒlv] (VT) (*gen*) (*Comm*) disolver
(VI) (*gen*) disolverse • **it ~s in water** se disuelve en agua • **the crowd ~d** la muchedumbre se dispersó • **she ~d into tears** se deshizo en lágrimas
dissonance ['dɪsənəns] (N) disonancia *f*
dissonant ['dɪsənənt] (ADJ) disonante
dissuade [dɪ'sweɪd] (VT) disuadir (**from** de) • **to ~ sb from doing sth** disuadir a algn de hacer algo
dissuasion [dɪ'sweɪʒən] (N) disuasión *f*
dissuasive [dɪ'sweɪsɪv] (ADJ) (*gen*) [*voice, person*] disuasivo; [*powers*] disuasorio
dist. (ABBR) **1** (= **distance**) dist
2 (= **district**) dist
distaff ['dɪsta:f] (N) rueca *f*
(CPD) ▸ **the distaff side** la rama femenina • **on the ~ side** por parte de madre
distance ['dɪstəns] (N) **1** (*in space*) distancia *f* • **what ~ is it from here to London?** ¿qué distancia hay de aquí a Londres? • **we followed them at a ~** les seguimos a distancia • **at a ~ of two metres** a dos metros de distancia • **I can't see her face at this ~** a esta distancia no puedo ver su cara • **within easy ~ (of sth)** a poca distancia (de algo), no muy lejos (de algo) • **the hotel is a fair ~ from the airport** el hotel está bastante lejos del aeropuerto • **from a ~** desde lejos • **from a ~ you look like your mother** desde lejos te pareces a tu madre • **he had no choice but to admire her from a ~** no podía hacer otra cosa más que admirarla desde lejos • **to go the ~** (*Sport*) llegar hasta el final • **a lot of people start the course with enthusiasm but are unable to go the ~** muchos empiezan el curso con entusiasmo pero son incapaces de completarlo • **it's a good ~ (from here)** está muy *or* bastante lejos (de aquí) • **to be within hearing ~** estar al alcance de la voz • **in the ~** a lo lejos • **in the near ~** a poca distancia • **in the middle ~** en segundo término • **in the far ~** muy a lo lejos, en la lejanía • **to keep one's ~** (*lit*) mantenerse a distancia; (*fig*) guardar las distancias • **keep your ~!** ¡mantén la distancia! • **to keep sb at a ~** (*fig*) guardar las distancias con algn • **he can't walk long ~s yet** aún no puede andar largas distancias • **it's no ~** está cerquísima, está a nada de aquí • **it's only a short ~ away** está a poca distancia, está bastante cerca • **stopping ~** (*Aut*) distancia *f* de parada • **to be within striking ~ of sth** estar muy cerca de algo, estar a un paso *or* dos pasos de algo • **it is within walking ~** se puede ir andando;
▹ **long-distance**
2 (*in time*) • **at a ~ of 400 years** después de 400 años • **at this ~ in time** después de tanto tiempo
(VT) • **to ~ o.s.** (*from problems, situations etc*) distanciarse (**from sth** de algo)
(CPD) ▸ **distance learning** enseñanza *f* a distancia, enseñanza *f* por correspondencia
▸ **distance race** carrera *f* de larga distancia
▸ **distance runner** corredor(a) *m/f* de fondo
distant ['dɪstənt] (ADJ) **1** (*in space*) [*country, land*] distante, lejano; [*star, galaxy*] lejano, remoto; [*sound*] lejano • **the nearest hospital was 200km ~** el hospital más cercano se hallaba a 200km (de distancia) • **the school is 2km ~ from the church** la escuela está a 2km (de distancia) de la iglesia • **as Neptune is so ~ from the sun** como Neptuno está tan lejos del sol • **in a ~ part of the country** en una remota región del país • **we could hear ~ thunder** se oían truenos lejanos *or* en la distancia • **we had a ~ view of the sea** veíamos el mar a lo lejos
2 (*in time*) [*future, past, ancestor*] lejano • **in the ~ future** en un lejano futuro • **in the not too** *or* **very ~ future** en un futuro no demasiado *or* no muy lejano • **last summer's drought is a ~ memory** la sequía del verano pasado es ya un recuerdo lejano • **in the ~ past** en un lejano pasado, en un pasado remoto • **at some ~ point in the future** en algún momento del futuro lejano • **a ~ prospect** una remota posibilidad
3 (= *not closely related*) [*relative, cousin*] lejano; [*connection*] remoto
4 (= *aloof*) [*person, manner, voice*] distante • **he is courteous but ~** es cortés pero distante • **to become ~** volverse distante • **she became increasingly ~ towards him** se distanció cada vez más de él
5 (= *removed*) • **all this seems so ~ from the Spain of today** todo esto parece muy alejado de la realidad española de hoy, todo esto parece no tener nada que ver con la España de hoy • **Steve gradually became more ~ from reality** poco a poco, Steve se iba alejando cada vez más de la realidad • **he has become somewhat ~ from the day-to-day operations of the department** se ha distanciado un tanto de las operaciones diarias del departamento
6 (= *distracted*) [*person, look*] ausente • **there was a ~ look in her eyes** tenía la mirada ausente *or* ida
distantly ['dɪstəntlɪ] (ADV) **1** (= *not closely*) [*resemble*] ligeramente • **to be ~ related to sb** ser pariente lejano de algn • **we are ~ related** somos parientes lejanos
2 (= *far away*) • **Rose heard a buzzer sound ~** Rose oyó el sonido de un timbre a lo lejos *or* en la distancia • **he looked down at the pigeons flying ~ below** miró hacia abajo a las palomas que volaban muy por debajo de él
3 (= *in a detached manner*) [*greet, say*] con frialdad, fríamente
4 (= *distractedly*) [*smile, nod*] distraídamente
distaste ['dɪs'teɪst] (N) aversión *f* (**for** por, a) • **she looked at his grubby clothes with ~** miró su ropa mugrienta con expresión de repugnancia
distasteful [dɪs'teɪstfʊl] (ADJ) desagradable; [*task*] ingrato • **it is ~ to me to have to do this** no me resulta nada grato tener que hacer esto
distastefully [dɪs'teɪstfʊlɪ] (ADV) (= *unappealingly*) desagradablemente; (= *with distaste*) con desagrado
Dist. Atty. (ABBR) (*US*) = **District Attorney**
distemper[1] [dɪs'tempəʳ] (N) (= *paint*) temple *m*
(VT) pintar al temple
distemper[2] [dɪs'tempəʳ] (N) (*Vet*) moquillo *m*; (*fig*) mal *m*
distend [dɪs'tend] (VT) dilatar, hinchar
(VI) dilatarse, hincharse
distended [dɪs'tendɪd] (ADJ) [*stomach*] dilatado, hinchado
distension [dɪs'tenʃən] (N) distensión *f*, dilatación *f*, hinchazón *f*
distich ['dɪstɪk] (N) dístico *m*
distil, distill (*US*) [dɪs'tɪl] (VT) destilar • **~led water** agua *f* destilada
distillation [ˌdɪstɪ'leɪʃən] (N) destilación *f*

distilled [dɪs'tɪld] ADJ destilado
distiller [dɪs'tɪləʳ] N destilador *m*
distillery [dɪs'tɪlərɪ] N destilería *f*
distinct [dɪs'tɪŋkt] ADJ **1** (= *different*) [*types, species, groups*] diferente, distinto • **the book is divided into two ~ parts** el libro está dividido en dos partes bien diferenciadas • **~ from** diferente a, distinto a • **engineering and technology are disciplines quite ~ from one another** la ingeniería y la tecnología son disciplinas muy diferentes *or* distintas • **as ~ from** a diferencia de
2 (= *clear, definite*) [*shape, memory*] claro, definido; [*image, sound*] claro, nítido; [*increase, rise, fall*] marcado; [*advantage, disadvantage*] claro, obvio; [*possibility, improvement*] claro; [*lack*] evidente; [*flavour*] inconfundible • **we noticed a ~ change in her attitude** notamos un claro cambio en su actitud • **he had the ~ feeling that they were laughing at him** tuvo la clara sensación de que se estaban riendo de él • **I got the ~ impression that ...** tuve la clara impresión de que ... • **there is a ~ possibility that ...** existe una clara posibilidad de que ... (+ *subjun*) • **there are ~ signs of progress** existen señales evidentes *or* inconfundibles de progreso
distinction [dɪs'tɪŋkʃən] N **1** (= *difference*) distinción *f* • **to draw a ~ between** hacer una distinción entre
2 (= *eminence*) distinción *f* • **a man of ~** un hombre distinguido • **a writer of ~** un escritor destacado • **to gain** *or* **win ~** distinguirse (**as** como) • **you have the ~ of being the first** a usted le corresponde el honor de ser el primero
3 (*Univ, Scol*) sobresaliente *m* • **he got a ~ in English** le dieron un sobresaliente en inglés
distinctive [dɪs'tɪŋktɪv] ADJ [*sound, colour*] característico; [*flavour, smell, voice*] inconfundible, característico; [*plumage, fur*] distintivo, característico; [*style*] característico, particular; [*clothing, decor*] peculiar, particular • **one of the ~ features of Elizabethan architecture** uno de los rasgos característicos de la arquitectura isabelina • **stone walls are a ~ feature of the countryside** los muros de piedra son característicos del campo • **what was most ~ about him was his extreme nervousness** lo que más le caracterizaba era su extremo nerviosismo
distinctively [dɪs'tɪŋktɪvlɪ] ADV [*dressed*] de forma muy peculiar, de forma muy particular; [*furnished*] de una forma muy particular, de una forma muy personal • **the decor has a ~ masculine feel to it** la decoración tiene un aire claramente *or* ostensiblemente masculino • **~ patterned** con un diseño muy particular
distinctiveness [dɪs'tɪŋktɪvnɪs] N peculiaridad *f*
distinctly [dɪs'tɪŋktlɪ] ADV **1** (= *clearly*) [*see, hear, remember*] claramente, perfectamente; [*promise*] definitivamente; [*prefer*] claramente • **I ~ remember locking the door** recuerdo claramente *or* perfectamente haber cerrado la puerta • **he speaks very ~** habla con mucha claridad
2 (= *very*) [*odd*] verdaderamente; [*uncomfortable, nervous*] realmente; [*better*] marcadamente • **his was a ~ unhappy childhood** su infancia fue verdaderamente desdichada • **she was ~ unhappy about the new arrangements** estaba realmente *or* muy descontenta con los nuevos planes • **it was ~ cold outside** fuera hacía verdadero *or* mucho frío • **it is ~ awkward** es realmente difícil • **he is ~ lacking in imagination** carece totalmente de imaginación • **his work has a ~ modern flavour** su trabajo tiene un inconfundible sabor a moderno • **it is ~ possible that ...** bien podría ser que ... (+ *subjun*)
distinguish [dɪs'tɪŋgwɪʃ] VT
1 (= *differentiate*) distinguir • **they are so alike, it's hard to ~ them** son tan parecidos que es difícil distinguirlos • **he is unable to ~ brown from green** *or* **brown and green** no es capaz de distinguir el marrón del verde *or* el marrón y el verde
2 (= *make different*) distinguir (**from de**) • **it is his professionalism that ~es him from his rivals** su profesionalismo es lo que le distingue de sus rivales • **to ~ o.s.** destacarse (**as como**) • **he ~ed himself during his career in the army** se destacó durante su carrera en el ejército • **you've really ~ed yourself!** (*iro*) ¡te has lucido! (*iro*)
3 (= *characterize*) caracterizar • **her work is ~ed by its excellent presentation** su trabajo se caracteriza por una excelente presentación
4 (= *discern*) [+ *landmark*] distinguir, vislumbrar; [+ *voice*] distinguir; [+ *change*] distinguir, reconocer
VI distinguir (**between** entre) • **I can't ~ between the two of them** no puedo distinguir entre los dos
distinguishable [dɪs'tɪŋgwɪʃəbl] ADJ
1 (= *possible to differentiate*) distinguible • **the two types are easily ~** los dos tipos son fácilmente distinguibles, los dos tipos se distinguen fácilmente • **~ groups such as the disabled** grupos que se pueden diferenciar, como los minusválidos • **this vintage port is ~ by its deep red colour** este oporto añejo se caracteriza por su color rojo oscuro • **the copy is barely ~ from the original** la copia apenas puede distinguirse del original • **she is barely ~ from her younger sister** casi no se la puede distinguir de su hermana menor
2 (= *discernible*) • **to be clearly ~** [*landmark, shape*] distinguirse claramente *or* fácilmente • **no words were ~** no se distinguía ninguna palabra con claridad
distinguished [dɪs'tɪŋgwɪʃt] ADJ [*guest, appearance, career*] distinguido; [*professor, scholar, writer*] distinguido, eminente • **he retired after 25 years of ~ service** se retiró tras 25 años de distinguido servicio • **to look ~** tener un aspecto distinguido
CPD ▸ **distinguished service professor** (*US*) (*Univ*) *profesor de universidad americana que ocupa una cátedra de prestigio*
distinguishing [dɪs'tɪŋgwɪʃɪŋ] ADJ distintivo • **~ features** [*of landscape, sb's work*] rasgos *mpl* característicos, características *fpl*; [*of animal*] rasgos *mpl* distintivos • **~ mark** marca *f* distintiva
distort [dɪs'tɔːt] VT [+ *shape etc*] deformar; [+ *sound, image*] distorsionar; (*fig*) [+ *judgment*] distorsionar; [+ *truth*] tergiversar
distorted [dɪs'tɔːtɪd] ADJ (*lit, fig*) distorsionado • **he gave us a ~ version of the events** nos dio una versión distorsionada de los hechos • **a ~ impression** una impresión distorsionada
distortion [dɪs'tɔːʃən] N [*of shape*] deformación *f*; [*of sound, image*] distorsión *f*; (*fig*) distorsión *f*; [*of truth*] tergiversación *f*
distr. ABBR **1** = **distribution**
2 = **distributor**
distract [dɪs'trækt] VT [+ *person*] • **to ~ sb (from sth)** distraer a algn (de algo) • **to ~ sb's attention (from sth)** desviar la atención de algn (de algo) • **she is easily ~ed** se distrae fácilmente
distracted [dɪs'træktɪd] ADJ **1** (= *preoccupied*) distraído
2† (= *mad*) loco • **like one ~** como un loco • **to be ~ with anxiety** estar loco de inquietud
distractedly [dɪs'træktɪdlɪ] ADV
1 (= *absently*) [*speak, behave*] distraídamente
2 (= *madly*) locamente, como un loco
distracting [dɪs'træktɪŋ] ADJ que distrae la atención, molesto
distraction [dɪs'trækʃən] N **1** (= *interruption*) distracción *f*
2 (= *entertainment*) diversión *f*
3 (= *distress, anxiety*) aturdimiento *m* • **to drive sb to ~** volver loco a algn
distractor [dɪs'træktəʳ] N (*in multiple-choice question*) respuesta *f* trampa
distrain [dɪs'treɪn] VI (*Jur*) • **to ~ upon** secuestrar, embargar
distraint [dɪs'treɪnt] N (*Jur*) secuestro *m*, embargo *m*
distrait [dɪs'treɪ] ADJ (*liter*) distraído
distraught [dɪs'trɔːt] ADJ afligido, alterado (*LAm*) • **in a ~ voice** con una voz embargada por la emoción
distress [dɪs'tres] N **1** (= *pain*) dolor *m*; (= *mental anguish*) angustia *f*, aflicción *f*; (*Med*) (*after exertion*) agotamiento *m*, fatiga *f* • **to be in great ~** estar sufriendo mucho
2 (= *danger*) peligro *m* • **to be in ~** [*ship etc*] estar en peligro
3 (= *poverty*) miseria *f* • **to be in financial ~** pasar apuros económicos
VT (*physically*) doler; (*mentally*) angustiar, afligir; (*Med*) agotar, fatigar
CPD ▸ **distress call** llamada *f* de socorro ▸ **distress rocket** cohete *m* de señales ▸ **distress signal** señal *f* de socorro
distressed [dɪs'trest] ADJ **1** (= *upset*) afligido, angustiado • **I am very ~ at the news** estoy muy afligido por la noticia • **I am ~ to hear that ...** lamento profundamente enterarme de que ...
2† (= *poverty-stricken*) • **in ~ circumstances** en penuria económica, en dificultades económicas
distressful [dɪs'tresfʊl] ADJ = **distressing**
distressing [dɪs'tresɪŋ] ADJ [*situation, experience*] angustioso, doloroso; [*poverty, inadequacy*] acuciante
distressingly [dɪs'tresɪŋlɪ] ADV dolorosamente, penosamente • **a ~ bad picture** un cuadro tan malo que daba pena
distributable [dɪs'trɪbjuːtəbl] ADJ distribuible
distribute [dɪs'trɪbjuːt] VT (= *deal out, spread out*) repartir; (*Comm*) [+ *goods*] distribuir
distributed [dɪs'trɪbjuːtɪd] ADJ (= *spread*) distribuido, extendido
distribution [ˌdɪstrɪ'bjuːʃən] N [*of wealth, population etc*] distribución *f*; (= *handing out*) reparto *m*; (*Comm*) [*of goods*] distribución *f*; (*Ling*) distribución *f*
CPD ▸ **distribution cost** gastos *mpl* de distribución ▸ **distribution network** red *f* de distribución ▸ **distribution rights** derechos *mpl* de distribución
distributional [ˌdɪstrɪ'bjuːʃənəl] ADJ distribucional
distributive [dɪs'trɪbjʊtɪv] ADJ distributivo
N (*Ling*) adjetivo *m* distributivo
CPD ▸ **distributive trade** comercio *m* de distribución
distributor [dɪs'trɪbjʊtəʳ] N **1** (= *person handing out*) repartidor(a) *m/f*, distribuidor(a) *m/f*
2 (*Comm*) (= *firm*) compañía *f* distribuidora, distribuidora *f*; (*Cine*) distribuidora *f*
3 (*Elec, Mech*) distribuidor *m*; (*Aut*) distribuidor *m* (del encendido), delco® *m* (*Sp*)

distributorship [dɪs'trɪbjʊtəʃɪp] (N) (*Comm*) (= *company*) compañía *f* distribuidora, distribuidora *f*; (= *right to supply*) distribución *f*

district ['dɪstrɪkt] (N) [*of country*] región *f*, zona *f*; [*of town*] distrito *m*, barrio *m*; (= *administrative area*) (*gen*) (*Pol*) distrito *m* • **postal ~** distrito *m* postal
(CPD) ▸ **district attorney** (*US*) fiscal *mf* (de distrito) ▸ **district commissioner** (*Brit*) jefe/a *m/f* de policía de distrito ▸ **district council** (*Brit*) municipio *m* ▸ **district court** (*US*) tribunal *m* de distrito ▸ **district manager** representante *mf* regional ▸ **district nurse** (*Brit*) *enfermero/a de la Seguridad Social encargado/a de una zona determinada* ▸ **District of Columbia** (*US*) Distrito *m* de Columbia

distrust [dɪs'trʌst] (N) desconfianza *f* (**of** en), recelo *m* (**of** de)
(VT) desconfiar de, recelar de

distrustful [dɪs'trʌstfʊl] (ADJ) desconfiado, receloso

disturb [dɪs'tɜ:b] (VT) **1** (= *bother*) [+ *person, animal*] molestar • **"please do not disturb"** "se ruega no molestar" • **sorry to ~ you** perdona la molestia • **try not to ~ Joseph, he's asleep** intenta no despertar a Joseph, está durmiendo
2 (= *interrupt*) [+ *order, balance*] alterar; [+ *meeting, sleep*] interrumpir; [+ *silence*] romper • **a car alarm ~ed her sleep** una alarma de coche interrumpió su sueño *or* la despertó • **to ~ the peace** (*Jur*) alterar el orden público • **they ~ed a burglar breaking into their house** sorprendieron a un ladrón que estaba intentando entrar en su casa • **her constant questions ~ed his concentration** sus constantes preguntas le impedían concentrarse
3 (= *worry*) preocupar; (= *upset*) afectar • **the news ~ed him greatly** la noticia le preocupó enormemente • **the photos of the war victims ~ed her** las fotos de las víctimas de guerra la afectaron
4 (= *disarrange*) [+ *papers*] desordenar; [+ *water, sediment*] agitar • **somebody had been in her room and ~ed her things** alguien había estado en su cuarto y había revuelto sus cosas • **the police asked if anything had been ~ed** la policía preguntó si había algo fuera de su sitio

disturbance [dɪs'tɜ:bəns] (N) **1** (= *act, state*) perturbación *f* • **~ of the peace** (*Jur*) alteración *f* del orden público
2 (*social, political*) disturbio *m*; (*in house, street*) alboroto *m*; [*of mind*] trastorno *m*; (= *fight*) altercado *m*, bronca *f* (*LAm*) • **to cause a ~** armar alboroto • **there was a ~ in the crowd** hubo un altercado entre algunos de los espectadores • **the ~s in the north** los disturbios en el norte
3 (= *nuisance*) molestia *f*
4 (= *interruption*) interrupción *f* (**to** de)

disturbed [dɪs'tɜ:bd] (ADJ) **1** (= *worried*) preocupado, angustiado; (= *upset*) afectado • **I was ~ to hear that ...** me afectó mucho el enterarme de que ... • **he was ~ that ...** le preocupaba que ... (+ *subjun*), le inquietaba que ... (+ *subjun*)
2 (*Psych*) **a** (= *unhappy*) [*childhood, adolescence*] problemático • **children from ~ backgrounds** niños que proceden de hogares con problemas
b (= *unbalanced*) [*person, mind*] trastornado; [*behaviour*] desequilibrado • **she is very ~** está muy trastornada, tiene muchos problemas mentales • **to be emotionally/mentally ~** tener trastornos afectivos/mentales
3 (= *interrupted*) [*sleep*] interrumpido • **to have a ~ night** dormir mal

disturbing [dɪs'tɜ:bɪŋ] (ADJ) [*influence, thought*] perturbador; [*event*] inquietante, preocupante • **it is ~ that ...** es inquietante que ...

disturbingly [dɪs'tɜ:bɪŋlɪ] (ADV) de manera inquietante • **a ~ large number** un número tan grande que resulta inquietante • **the bomb fell ~ close** la bomba cayó tan cerca que causó inquietud

disunite [ˌdɪsjʊ'naɪt] (VT) desunir

disunited ['dɪsjʊ'naɪtɪd] (ADJ) desunido

disunity [ˌdɪs'ju:nɪtɪ] (N) desunión *f*

disuse ['dɪs'ju:s] (N) desuso *m* • **to fall into ~** caer en desuso

disused ['dɪs'ju:zd] (ADJ) abandonado

disyllabic [ˌdɪsɪ'læbɪk] (ADJ) disílabo

ditch [dɪtʃ] (N) (*gen*) zanja *f*; (*at roadside*) cuneta *f*; (= *irrigation channel*) acequia *f*; (*as defence*) foso *m*
(VT)* (= *get rid of*) [+ *car*] deshacerse de; [+ *person*] dejar plantado* • **to ~ a plane** hacer un amaraje forzoso

ditching ['dɪtʃɪŋ] (N) **1** (= *digging ditches*) abertura *f* de zanjas • **hedging and ~** mantenimiento *m* de setos y zanjas
2 (*Aer*) amaraje *m*

ditchwater ['dɪtʃˌwɔ:təʳ] (N) • IDIOM: • **to be as dull as ~*** ser muy soso, no tener gracia ninguna

dither ['dɪðəʳ] (N) • **to be in a ~** • **be all of a ~** (= *be nervous*) estar muy nervioso; (= *hesitate*) no saber qué hacer, vacilar
(VI) (= *be nervous*) estar nervioso; (= *hesitate*) no saber qué hacer, vacilar • **to ~ over a decision** vacilar al tomar una decisión

ditherer ['dɪðərəʳ] (N) (*esp Brit*) indeciso/a *m/f* • **don't be such a ~!** ¡no seas tan indeciso!

dithering ['dɪðərɪŋ] (N) **1** (= *hesitation*) vacilación *f*
2 (*Comput*) (*graphics mode*) tramado *m*

dithery ['dɪðərɪ] (ADJ) (= *nervous*) nervioso; (= *hesitant*) indeciso, vacilante; (*from old age*) chocho

ditto ['dɪtəʊ] (N) ídem, lo mismo • **"I'd like coffee" — "~ (for me)"** —yo quiero café —yo lo mismo *or* y yo • **"~," said Graham** —yo también —dijo Graham
(CPD) ▸ **ditto marks, ditto sign** comillas *fpl*

ditty ['dɪtɪ] (N) cancioncilla *f*

ditzy*, ditsy* ['dɪtsɪ] (ADJ) (= *dizzy*) atolondrado

diuretic [ˌdaɪjʊə'retɪk] (ADJ) diurético
(N) diurético *m*

diurnal [daɪ'ɜ:nl] (ADJ) diurno

diva ['di:və] (N) (PL: **divas** *or* **dive** ['di:vɪ]) diva *f*

Divali [dɪ'vɑ:lɪ] (N) = **Diwali**

divan [dɪ'væn] (N) diván *m*; (*Brit*) (*also* **divan bed**) cama *f* turca

dive [daɪv] (N) **1** (*into water*) salto *m* de cabeza (al agua), zambullida *f*, clavado *m* (*CAm, Mex*); (*by professional diver, of submarine*) inmersión *f*
2 (*Aer*) picado *m*, picada *f* (*LAm*)
3 (= *leap*) • **to make a ~ for sth** lanzarse *or* abalanzarse sobre algo
4 (*Ftbl*) estirada *f* • **to take a ~** (*Ftbl*) tirarse a la piscina (*dejarse caer deliberadamente con la intención de conseguir un tiro libre o un penalty*)
5 (*fig*) (= *fall*) • **his reputation has taken a ~*** su reputación ha caído en picado
6 (*pej**) (= *club etc*) garito *m*
(VI) **1** [*swimmer*] tirarse, zambullirse, dar un clavado (*CAm, Mex*), clavarse (*CAm, Mex*); (*artistically*) saltar; (*underwater*) bucear; [*submarine*] sumergirse • **the kids were diving for coins** los niños se tiraban al agua para recoger monedas • **to ~ for pearls** buscar perlas • **to ~ into the water** tirarse al agua, zambullirse
2 (*Aer*) bajar en picado
3 (= *leap*) • **the goalkeeper ~d for the ball** el portero se lanzó a parar el balón • **to ~ for cover** precipitarse en busca de cobijo • **he ~d for the exit** se precipitó hacia la salida • **he ~d into the crowd** se metió entre la muchedumbre • **to ~ into one's pocket** meter la mano en el bolsillo • **to ~ into a bar** entrar a toda prisa en un bar • **I ~d into the shop for a paper** pasé corriendo por la tienda a por un periódico, me metí corriendo a la tienda a por un periódico
4 (= *fall*) [*prices etc*] bajar de golpe, caer en picado *or* (*LAm*) picada

dive-bomb ['daɪvbɒm] (VT) [+ *town etc*] bombardear en picado

dive-bomber ['daɪvˌbɒməʳ] (N) bombardero *m* en picado

dive-bombing ['daɪvˌbɒmɪŋ] (N) bombardeo *m* en picado

diver ['daɪvəʳ] (N) **1** (= *swimmer*) saltador(a) *m/f*, clavadista *mf* (*LAm*); (= *deep-sea diver*) submarinista *mf*, buzo *m*; (*sub-aqua*) escafandrista *mf*
2 (*Orn*) colimbo *m*

diverge [daɪ'vɜ:dʒ] (VI) [*roads*] bifurcarse; (*fig*) [*opinions*] divergir (**from** de)

divergence [daɪ'vɜ:dʒəns] (N) divergencia *f*

divergent [daɪ'vɜ:dʒənt] (ADJ) divergente

divers ['daɪvɜ:z] (ADJ) (*liter*) diversos, varios

diverse [daɪ'vɜ:s] (ADJ) (= *varied*) diverso, variado

diversification [daɪˌvɜ:sɪfɪ'keɪʃən] (N) diversificación *f*

diversify [daɪ'vɜ:sɪfaɪ] (VT) (*gen*) (*also Comm*) diversificar
(VI) (*Comm*) diversificarse, ampliar el campo de acción

diversion [daɪ'vɜ:ʃən] (N) **1** (*Brit*) [*of traffic*] desviación *f*, desvío *m* • **"Diversion"** (*road sign*) "Desvío"
2 (= *distraction*) • **to create a ~** (*gen*) distraer; (*Mil*) producir una diversión
3 (= *pastime*) diversión *f*

diversionary [daɪ'vɜ:ʃnərɪ] (ADJ) de diversión

diversity [daɪ'vɜ:sɪtɪ] (N) [*of opinions etc*] diversidad *f*

divert [daɪ'vɜ:t] (VT) **1** [+ *traffic, train etc*] desviar; [+ *conversation*] cambiar
2 (= *amuse*) divertir, entretener

diverticular disease [ˌdaɪvɜ:'tɪkjʊlədɪˌzi:z] (N) enfermedad *f* diverticular

diverticulitis [ˌdaɪvɜ:tɪkjʊ'laɪtɪs] (N) diverticulitis *f*

diverticulosis [ˌdaɪvɜ:tɪkjʊ'ləʊsɪs] (N) diverticulosis *f*

diverting [daɪ'vɜ:tɪŋ] (ADJ) divertido

divest¹ [daɪ'vest] (VT) • **to ~ sb of sth** despojar a algn de algo • **to ~ o.s. of one's rights** renunciar a sus derechos • **he ~ed himself of his coat** (*frm*) se despojó de su abrigo (*frm*)

divest² [daɪ'vest] (VT), (VI) (*US*) (*Econ*) desinvertir

divestment [daɪ'vestmənt] (N) (*US*) (*Econ*) desinversión *f*

divide [dɪ'vaɪd] (VT) **1** (= *separate*) separar • **the Pyrenees ~ France from Spain** los Pirineos separan Francia de España
2 (*also* **divide up**) (= *split*) [+ *money, work, kingdom*] dividir, repartir (**among, between** entre); [+ *sweets*] repartir (**among, between** entre); [+ *apple, orange, cake*] partir, dividir (**among, between** entre, **into** en) • **they ~d it among themselves** se lo repartieron entre sí • **when he died his property was ~d between his daughters** cuando murió su propiedad se repartió *or* se dividió entre sus hijas • **she tried to ~ her time fairly between the children** intentaba repartir su tiempo de

forma equitativa entre los niños • **the house has been ~d into flats** la casa se ha dividido en apartamentos • **~ the dough into four pieces** dividir la masa en cuatro trozos
3 (*Math*) dividir • **48 ~d by 8 is 6** 48 dividido entre *or* por 8 es 6 • **~ 6 into 36** divide 36 entre *or* por 6 • **you can't ~ 7 into 50** 50 no es divisible entre *or* por 7
4 (= *cause disagreement among*) dividir
5 (*Pol*) (*Brit*) • **to ~ the House** hacer que la Cámara proceda a la votación
VI **1** (= *separate*) [*road, river*] bifurcarse
2 (*also* **divide up**) (= *split*) [*cells, people*] dividirse • **we ~d into groups for the first activity** nos dividimos en grupos para la primera actividad • **~ and rule** divide y vencerás
3 (*Math*) dividir
4 (*Brit*) (*Pol*) votar • **the House ~d** la Cámara procedió a la votación
N **1** (*US*) (*Geog*) línea *f* divisoria de aguas, divisoria *f* de aguas
2 (*fig*) (= *gap*) división *f* • **there is a clear ~ between the upper and lower classes** hay una clara división entre las clases superiores y las inferiores
▸ **divide off** VT + ADV dividir, separar
VI + ADV dividirse
▸ **divide out** VT + ADV [+ *sweets, biscuits*] repartir (**between, among** entre)
▸ **divide up** VT + ADV [+ *money, work, kingdom*] dividir, repartir (**between, among** entre); [+ *sweets*] repartir (**between, among** entre); [+ *apple, orange, cake*] partir, dividir (**between, among** entre, **into** en)
VI + ADV [*people*] dividirse • **we ~d up to look for the missing child** nos dividimos para buscar al niño que se había perdido • **~ up into pairs** dividíos en parejas

divided [dɪˈvaɪdɪd] ADJ **1** (= *disunited*) [*nation, government, society*] dividido • **public opinion was ~** la opinión pública estaba dividida • **to have ~ loyalties** sufrir un conflicto de lealtades • **to be ~ on** *or* **over sth** [*people*] tener opiniones divididas sobre algo • **opinions are ~ on** *or* **over that** las opiniones respecto a eso están muy divididas
2 (*Bot*) seccionado
CPD ▸ **divided highway** (*US*) autovía *f* ▸ **divided skirt** (*US*) falda *f* pantalón

dividend [ˈdɪvɪdend] N **1** (*Econ*) dividendo *m*
2 (*fig*) beneficio *m* • **this should pay handsome ~s** esto ha de proporcionar grandes beneficios
CPD ▸ **dividend cover** cobertura *f* de dividendo ▸ **dividend payment** pago *m* de dividendos ▸ **dividend warrant** cédula *f* de dividendo ▸ **dividend yield** rendimiento *m* del dividendo

divider [dɪˈvaɪdəʳ] N (*between areas of room, garden*) tabique *m*, mampara *f* • **a curtain acts as a ~ between this class and another** una cortina hace de separación entre esta clase y la otra

dividers [dɪˈvaɪdəz] NPL compás *msing* de puntas

dividing [dɪˈvaɪdɪŋ] ADJ [*wall, fence*] divisorio
CPD ▸ **dividing line** línea *f* divisoria

divination [ˌdɪvɪˈneɪʃən] N adivinación *f*

divine¹ [dɪˈvaɪn] ADJ (*Rel*) divino; (*fig*) (= *sublime*) sublime; (= *wonderful*) divino, maravilloso
N teólogo *m*
CPD ▸ **divine right** derecho *m* divino ▸ **divine service** culto *m*, oficio *m* divino

divine² [dɪˈvaɪn] VT adivinar

divinely [dɪˈvaɪnlɪ] ADV (*Rel*) divinamente; (*fig*) (= *sublimely*) sublimemente; (= *wonderfully*) divinamente, maravillosamente

diviner [dɪˈvaɪnəʳ] N adivinador(a) *m/f*; (= *water diviner*) zahorí *mf*

diving [ˈdaɪvɪŋ] N (*professional*) submarinismo *m*, buceo *m*; (*sporting*) salto *m* de trampolín, clavado *m* (*CAm, Mex*); (*from side of pool*) salto *m*, zambullida *f*
CPD ▸ **diving bell** campana *f* de buzo ▸ **diving board** trampolín *m* ▸ **diving suit** escafandra *f*, traje *m* de buceo

divining rod [dɪˈvaɪnɪŋrɒd] N varilla *f* de zahorí

divinity [dɪˈvɪnɪtɪ] N **1** (= *deity, quality*) divinidad *f*
2 (*as study*) teología *f*

divisible [dɪˈvɪzəbl] ADJ divisible

division [dɪˈvɪʒən] N **1** (*gen, Math*) división *f*; (= *sharing*) reparto *m*, distribución *f* • **~ of labour** división *f* del trabajo
2 (*Comm*) (= *department*) sección *f*
3 (*Mil, Brit Police*) división *f*
4 (= *partition*) separación *f*, división *f*; (= *line*) línea *f* divisoria; (*Ftbl etc*) división *f*
5 (= *conflict, discord*) discordia *f* • **there is a ~ of opinion about this** las opiniones respecto a esto están divididas
6 (*Brit*) (*Parl*) votación *f* • **to call a ~** exigir una votación • **approved without a ~** aprobado por unanimidad
CPD ▸ **division sign** signo *m* de división

divisional [dɪˈvɪʒənl] ADJ de división

divisive [dɪˈvaɪsɪv] ADJ divisivo, causante de divisiones

divisiveness [dɪˈvaɪsɪvnɪs] N • **the ~ of this decision** las disensiones causadas/que serán causadas por esta decisión

divisor [dɪˈvaɪzəʳ] N divisor *m*

divorce [dɪˈvɔːs] N **1** (*Jur*) divorcio *m* • **to get a ~** divorciarse (**from** de)
2 (*fig*) separación *f* (**from** de)
VT **1** (*Jur*) divorciarse de • **to get ~d** divorciarse
2 (*fig*) separar • **to ~ sth from sth** separar algo de algo
VI divorciarse
CPD ▸ **divorce court** tribunal *m* de pleitos matrimoniales ▸ **divorce proceedings** pleito *msing* de divorcio ▸ **divorce rate** tasa *f* de divorcio

divorcé [dɪˌvɔːˈsiː] N divorciado *m*

divorced [dɪˈvɔːst] ADJ divorciado

divorcee [dɪˌvɔːˈsiː] N divorciado/a *m/f*

divot [ˈdɪvɪt] N (= *piece of turf*) (*gen*) terrón *m*; (*Golf*) chuleta *f*

divulge [daɪˈvʌldʒ] VT divulgar, revelar

divvy¹* [ˈdɪvɪ] N, ABBR (*Brit*) = **dividend**
VT (*also* **divvy up**) repartir

divvy²*‡ [ˈdɪvɪ] N (*Brit*) (= *fool*) tontaina* *mf*

Diwali [dɪˈwɑːlɪ], **Divali** [dɪˈvɑːlɪ] N Diwali *m* (*fiesta religiosa hindú*)

Dixie [ˈdɪksɪ] N *el sur de los Estados Unidos*

dixie [ˈdɪksɪ] N (*Brit*) (*Mil*) (*also* **dixie can**) olla *f*, marmita *f*

DIY ABBR (= **do-it-yourself**) bricolaje *m*
CPD ▸ **DIY enthusiast** aficionado/a *m/f* al bricolaje

dizzily [ˈdɪzɪlɪ] ADV **1** (= *giddily*) [*walk, sway*] con una sensación de mareo • **her head began to spin ~** la cabeza empezó a darle vueltas y vueltas
2 (*fig*) [*rise, fall*] vertiginosamente
3* (= *in a scatterbrained way*) de manera atolondrada • **she has been behaving rather ~ lately** ha estado bastante atolondrada últimamente
4 (*in a silly way*) con aire alelado • **she smiled ~** sonrió alelada

dizziness [ˈdɪzɪnɪs] N (*gen*) mareo *m*; (*caused by height*) vértigo *m* • **to have an attack of ~** tener *or* sufrir un mareo

dizzy ADJ [ˈdɪzɪ] (COMPAR: **dizzier**, SUPERL: **dizziest**) **1** (= *giddy*) [*person*] mareado • **to feel ~** (*ill, drunk etc*) estar mareado, marearse • **if I look down I feel ~** si miro hacia abajo me da vértigo • **changes in altitude make you ~** los cambios de altitud causan mareo *or* hacen que te mareas • **you're making me ~** me estás mareando • **this drug may make you ~** este medicamento puede provocarle mareos • **it makes one ~ to think of it** marea solo de pensarlo • **she had a ~ spell** tuvo *or* le dio un mareo • **to be ~ with success** estar borracho de éxito
2 (*fig*) [*pace, speed*] vertiginoso • **she rose to the ~ heights of director's secretary** ascendió ni más ni menos que al puesto de secretaria del director
3* (= *scatterbrained*) atolondrado
VT (= *confuse*) aturdir • **they had been dizzied by the pace of technological change** el ritmo del cambio tecnológico les había aturdido

dizzying [ˈdɪzɪɪŋ] ADJ [*speed*] vertiginoso; [*heights, number*] mareante

DJ N ABBR (= **disc jockey**) pinchadiscos *mf*
ABBR (= **dinner jacket**) smoking *m*

Djakarta [dʒəˈkɑːtə] N Yakarta *f*

djellabah [ˈdʒeləbə] N chilaba *f*

DJIA N ABBR (*US*) (*St Ex*) = **Dow Jones Industrial Average**

Djibouti [dʒɪˈbuːtɪ] N Yibuti *m*

dl ABBR (= **decilitre(s)**) dl

DLit, DLitt [ˌdiːˈlɪt] N ABBR **1** = **Doctor of Letters**
2 = **Doctor of Literature**

DLO N ABBR (= **dead-letter office**) *oficina de Correos que se encarga de las cartas que no llegan a su destino*

D-lock [ˈdiːlɒk] N barra *f* antirrobo en forma de U

DLP ABBR = **digital light processing** • **DLP projector** proyector DLP

DM N ABBR **1** (= **Deutschmark**) DM
2 (= *direct message*) (mensaje *m*) directo *m*
VT ABBR (= *direct-message*) enviar un (mensaje) directo a

dm ABBR (= **decimetre(s)**) dm

D-mark [ˈdiːmɑːk] N ABBR (= **Deutschmark**) DM *m*

DMU N ABBR = **decision-making unit**

DMus ABBR = **Doctor of Music**

DMZ N ABBR = **demilitarized zone**

DNA N ABBR (= **deoxyribonucleic acid**) ADN *m*
CPD ▸ **DNA fingerprinting, DNA profiling** identificación *f* mediante el análisis del

DIXIE

Dixie o **Dixieland** es el sobrenombre con el que se conoce de forma global a los estados sureños de EE.UU., en especial a los once estados que formaron los Estados Confederados de América durante la Guerra Civil: Alabama, Arkansas, Georgia, Florida, Luisiana, Mississippi, Carolina del Norte, Carolina del Sur, Tennessee, Texas y Virginia. También se usa como un adjetivo para describir características de los estados sureños y de sus habitantes, así como el jazz que surgió en ellos. Se supone que el nombre **Dixie** proviene de Luisiana, donde los billetes de diez dólares llevaban impreso en el anverso la palabra francesa **dix**. Para otros la palabra proviene de la línea simbólica Mason-Dixon, que separa el norte del sur.

▸ **MASON-DIXON LINE**

ADN ▸ **DNA sequence** secuencia *f* del ADN ▸ **DNA test** prueba *f* del ADN ▸ **DNA testing** pruebas *fpl* del ADN

DNB (N ABBR) = **Dictionary of National Biography**

DNF (ABBR) (*Athletics*) = **did not finish**

DNS (ABBR) (*Athletics*) = **did not start**

d

do[1] [du:]

TRANSITIVE VERB
INTRANSITIVE VERB
AUXILIARY VERB
NOUN
PHRASAL VERBS

(3RD PERS SING PRESENT: **does**, PT: **did**, PP: **done**)

TRANSITIVE VERB

1 hacer • **what are you doing tonight?** ¿qué haces esta noche? • **I would never do a thing like that** yo nunca haría una cosa así • **what's this doing on my chair?** ¿qué hace esto en mi silla? • **I've got nothing to do** no tengo nada que hacer • **he does nothing but complain** no hace más que quejarse • **what's to be done?** ¿qué se puede hacer? • **what's the weather doing?** ¿qué tal tiempo hace? • **to do sth again** volver a hacer algo, hacer algo de nuevo • **it will have to be done again** habrá que volver a hacerlo, habrá que hacerlo de nuevo • **what's he ever done for me?** ¿qué ha hecho él por mí? • **what can I do for you?** ¿en qué puedo servirle?, ¿qué se le ofrece? (*LAm*) • **could you do something for me?** ¿me podrías hacer un favor? • **what are we going to do for money?** ¿de dónde vamos a sacar dinero? • **that dress doesn't do a lot for you*** este vestido no te queda muy bien • **the new measures will do a lot for small businesses** las nuevas medidas serán de gran ayuda para las pequeñas empresas • **after the accident she couldn't do much for herself** después del accidente casi no podía valerse por sí misma • **if you do anything to him I'll kill you** si le haces algo te mato • **what's he done to his hair?** ¿qué se ha hecho en el pelo? • **I could see what the stress was doing to him** era evidente cómo le estaba afectando el estrés • **what have you done with my slippers?** ¿dónde has puesto mis zapatillas? • **what am I going to do with you?** ¿qué voy a hacer contigo? • **what are you doing with yourself these days?** ¿qué haces ahora? • **what am I going to do with myself for the rest of the day?** ¿qué puedo hacer el resto del día? • **she didn't know what to do with herself once the children had left home** se encontró un poco perdida cuando sus hijos se fueron de casa; ▹ **living**

2 (*= carry out*) [+ *work, essay*] hacer • **the work is being done by a local builder** un albañil de la zona está haciendo el trabajo • **I've got a few jobs that need doing around the house** tengo algunas cosas que hacer en la casa • **she was doing the crossword** estaba haciendo el crucigrama • **to do the washing** hacer la colada

Some **do** *+ noun combinations require a more specific Spanish verb:*

• **Edmund does all the accounts** Edmund se encarga de *or* lleva la contabilidad • **to do the cooking** cocinar • **he did a drawing/portrait of her** la dibujó/retrató, hizo un dibujo/retrato de ella • **to do one's duty (by sb)** cumplir con su deber (con algn) • **to do the ironing** planchar • **we did a lot of talking** hablamos mucho

3 (*= clean*) • **to do the dishes** lavar los platos • **to do the silver** limpiar la plata • **to do one's teeth** lavarse los dientes

4 (*= arrange, prepare*) [+ *vegetables*] preparar; [+ *room*] hacer, arreglar • **this room needs doing** hay que hacer *or* arreglar esta habitación • **to do the flowers** arreglar las flores • **to do one's nails** hacerse *or* arreglarse las uñas; ▹ **hair**

5 (*= spend*) pasar • **he did six years (in jail)** pasó seis años en la cárcel • **he did two years as ambassador in Lagos** estuvo dos años como embajador en Lagos • **I did five years as a policeman** fui policía durante cinco años • **they have to do two years military service** tienen que hacer dos años de servicio militar

6 (*= finish*) • **I've only done three pages** solo he hecho tres páginas • **now you've (gone and) done it!*** ¡ahora sí que la has hecho buena!* • **that's done it!* we're stuck now** ¡la hemos fastidiado!* ahora no podemos salir de aquí • **that does it!* that's the last time I lend him my car** ¡es el colmo! *or* ¡hasta aquí hemos llegado!, es la última vez que le dejo el coche • **have you done moaning?*** ¿has acabado de quejarte?; ▹ **good**

7 (*= offer, make available*) • **they do a summer course in painting** dan un curso de verano de pintura • **we only do one make of gloves** solo tenemos una marca de guantes • **they do an estate version of this car** fabrican un modelo familiar de este coche • **we do evening meals if ordered in advance** servimos cenas si se encargan con antelación • **I can do you a discount on this model** le puedo hacer un descuento en este modelo

8 (*= study*) [+ *university course, option*] hacer, estudiar • **I want to do Physics at university** quiero hacer *or* estudiar física en la universidad • **to do Italian** hacer *or* estudiar italiano • **we're doing Orwell this term** estamos estudiando a Orwell este trimestre

9 (*Theat*) [+ *play*] representar, poner; [+ *part*] hacer • **he did King Lear in a BBC production** hizo (el papel) de King Lear en una producción de la BBC

10 (*= mimic*) [+ *person*] imitar • **he does his maths master to perfection** imita a su profesor de matemáticas a la perfección • **she was doing the worried mother bit*** hacía el numerito de la típica madre preocupada*

11 (*Aut, Rail etc*) (*= travel at*) [+ *speed*] ir a; (*= cover*) [+ *distance*] cubrir • **the car can do 100 miles per hour** el coche puede ir a 100 millas por hora • **the car was doing 100 miles per hour** el coche iba a 100 millas por hora • **we've done 200km already** ya hemos hecho 200km • **we did London to Edinburgh in 8 hours** fuimos de Londres a Edimburgo en 8 horas

12 (*= attend to*) • **the barber said he'd do me next** el barbero dijo que después me tocaría a mí • **they do you very well in this hotel** en este hotel te dan muy buen servicio; ▹ **proud**

13* (*= visit*) [+ *city, museum*] visitar, recorrer; [+ *country*] visitar, viajar por • **we did six countries in an 8-week tour** visitamos seis países durante un viaje de 8 semanas

14* (*= be suitable, sufficient for*) • **will a kilo do you?** ¿le va bien un kilo? • **that'll do me nicely** (*= be suitable*) eso me vendrá muy bien; (*= suffice*) con eso me basta

15* (*= cheat*) estafar, timar; (*= rob*) robar • **I've been done!** ¡me han estafado *or* timado!

16* (*= prosecute*) procesar; (*= fine*) multar • **she was done for shoplifting** la procesaron por robar en una tienda • **he was done for speeding** le multaron por exceso de velocidad

17* (*= beat up*) dar una paliza a • **I'll do you if I get hold of you!** ¡te voy a dar una paliza como te pille!

INTRANSITIVE VERB

1 (*= act*) hacer • **do as I do** haz como yo • **you would do better to accept** sería aconsejable que aceptaras • **he did right** hizo lo correcto • **do as you think best** haga lo que mejor le parezca • **do as you are told!** ¡haz lo que te digo! • **she was up and doing at 6 o'clock** a las 6 de la mañana ya estaba levantada y trajinando • **you would do well to take his advice** harías bien en seguir su consejo • **you could do a lot worse than marry her** casarte con ella no es lo peor que podrías hacer; ▹ **well**

2 (*= get on*) • **he did badly in the exam** le fue mal en el examen • **the team hasn't done badly this season** al equipo no le ha ido mal esta temporada • **you didn't do so badly** no lo has hecho del todo mal • **you can do better than that** (*essay, drawing*) puedes hacerlo mejor; (*iro*) (*= find better excuse*) ¡y qué más! • **how is your father doing?** ¿cómo está tu padre?, ¿cómo le va a tu padre? • **how are you doing?*** ¿qué tal?, ¿cómo te va? • **how did you do in the audition?** ¿qué tal *or* cómo te fue en la audición? • **he's doing well at school** le va bien en el colegio • **her son's doing well for himself** a su hijo le van muy bien las cosas • **his business is doing well** los negocios le van bien • **the patient is doing well** el paciente está respondiendo bien • **the roses are doing well this year** las rosas han florecido muy bien este año **how do you do?** (*greeting*) ¿cómo está usted?, gusto en conocerlo (*LAm*); (*as answer*) ¡mucho gusto!, ¡encantado!

3 (*= be suitable*) • **it doesn't do to upset her** cuidado con ofenderla • **will this one do?** ¿te parece bien este? • **this room will do** esta habitación ya me va bien • **will it do if I come back at eight?** ¿va bien si vuelvo a las ocho? • **will tomorrow do?** ¿iría bien mañana? • **it's not exactly what I wanted, but it will** *or* **it'll do** no es exactamente lo que quería pero servirá • **this coat will do as a blanket** este abrigo servirá de manta • **that will have to do** tendremos que conformarnos con eso • **that won't do, you'll have to do it again** así no está bien, tendrás que volver a hacerlo • **you can't go on your own, that would never do!** no podemos consentir que vayas sola, ¡eso no puede ser!; ▹ **make**

4 (*= be sufficient*) bastar • **three bottles of wine should do** bastará con tres botellas de vino • **will £20 do?** ¿bastarán 20 libras?, ¿tendrás bastante con 20 libras? • **that'll do** con eso basta • **that will do!** ¡basta ya! • **that will do for the moment** de momento ya está bien

5 (*= happen*) • **there's not much doing in this town** no hay mucha animación en esta ciudad • **"could you lend me £50?" — "nothing doing!"** —¿me podrías prestar 50 libras? —¡de ninguna manera! *or* —¡ni hablar!

6* (*= finish*) (*in past tenses only*) terminar, acabar • **have you done?** ¿ya has terminado *or* acabado? • **don't take it away, I've not done yet** no te lo lleves, ¡aún no he terminado *or* acabado! • **I haven't done telling you** ¡no he terminado de contarte! • **I've done with travelling** ya no voy a viajar más, he renunciado a los viajes • **I've done**

with all that nonsense ya no tengo nada que ver *or* ya he terminado con todas esas tonterías • **have you done with that book?** ¿has terminado con este libro?

7* (*= clean*) hacer la limpieza (en casa) • **I've got a lady who does for me** tengo una señora que me viene a hacer la limpieza en la casa

AUXILIARY VERB

There is no equivalent in Spanish to the use of **do** *in questions, negative statements and negative commands.*

1 (*in questions*) • **do you understand?** ¿comprendes?, ¿entiendes? • **where does he live?** ¿dónde vive? • **didn't you like it?** ¿no te gustó? • **why didn't you come?** ¿por qué no viniste?

2 (*negation*) • **I don't understand** no entiendo *or* comprendo • **don't let's argue** no discutamos • **don't worry!** ¡no te preocupes! • **don't you tell me what to do!** ¡no me digas lo que tengo que hacer! • **she did not go** no fue

3 (*for emphasis*) • **do tell me!** ¡dímelo, por favor! • **do sit down** siéntese, por favor, tome asiento, por favor (*frm*) • **she does look lovely in that dress** está preciosa con este vestido • **I do hope so** así lo espero • **I do wish I could come with you** ¡ojalá pudiera ir contigo! • **but I do like it!** ¡sí que me gusta!, ¡por supuesto que me gusta! • **so you do know him!** ¡así que sí lo conoces! • **but I did do it** pero sí que lo hice

4 (*with inversion*) • **rarely does it happen that …** rara vez ocurre que … • **not once did they offer to pay** no se ofrecieron a pagar ni una sola vez

5 (*verb substitute*) **a** • **you speak better than I do** tú hablas mejor que yo • **"did you fix the car?" — "I did"** —¿arreglaste el coche? —sí • **"I love it" — "so do I"** —me encanta —a mí también • **I don't like sport and neither does he** no me gusta el deporte ni a él tampoco • **you didn't see him but I did** tú no lo viste pero yo sí • **I told him he'd fail and he did** le dije que iba a suspender y suspendió • **he went for a walk as he often did** fue a dar un paseo como solía hacer • **she always says she'll come but she never does** siempre dice que vendrá pero nunca viene • **"he borrowed the car" — "oh he did, did he?"** —pidió el coche prestado —¿ah sí? ¡no me digas! • **I like this colour, don't you?** me gusta este color, ¿a ti no? • **"do you speak English?" — "yes, I do/no I don't"** —¿habla usted inglés? —sí, hablo inglés/no, no hablo inglés • **"may I come in?" — "(please) do!"** —¿se puede pasar? —¡pasa (por favor)! • **"who made this mess?" — "I did"** —¿quién lo ha desordenado todo? —fui yo • **"shall I ring her again?" — "no, don't!"** —¿la llamo otra vez? —¡no, no la llames!

b (*in question tags*) • **he lives here, doesn't he?** vive aquí, ¿verdad? *or* ¿no es cierto? *or* ¿no? • **I don't know him, do I?** no lo conozco, ¿verdad? • **it doesn't matter, does it?** no importa, ¿no? • **she said that, did she?** ¿eso es lo que dijo?

NOUN

1 (*Brit*)* (= *party*) fiesta *f*; (= *formal gathering*) reunión *f* • **they had a big do for their twenty-fifth anniversary** dieron una gran fiesta por su vigésimo quinto aniversario

2 (*in phrases*) • **the do's and don'ts of buying a house** lo que debe y lo que no debe hacerse al comprar una casa • **he gave us a series of dos and don'ts** nos explicó lo que podíamos y lo que no podíamos hacer • **fair dos!*** (= *be fair*) ¡hay que ser justo!, ¡seamos justos!; (= *fair shares*) ¡a partes iguales! • **it's a poor do when …** es una vergüenza cuando …

▸ **do away with** (VI + PREP) **1** (= *get rid of*) [+ *controls*] suprimir, eliminar; [+ *nuclear weapons*] eliminar, acabar con; [+ *injustice, exploitation, system*] acabar con; [+ *capital punishment*] abolir • **it does away with the need for a middleman** con esto ya no hace falta el intermediario, con esto uno se ahorra el intermediario

2* (= *kill*) matar, liquidar* • **to do away with o.s.** matarse, suicidarse

▸ **do by** (VI + PREP) • **to do well/badly by sb** portarse bien/mal con algn, tratar bien/mal a algn • **he did well by his mother** se portó bien con su madre • **employees felt hard done by** los empleados se sintieron injustamente tratados • PROVERB: • **do as you would be done by** trata como quieres ser tratado; ▹ **hard**

▸ **do down** (VT + ADV) (*Brit*) **1** (= *denigrate*) menospreciar • **to do o.s. down** subestimarse

2 (= *cheat*) timar, estafar; (= *play false*) hacer una mala pasada a

▸ **do for*** (VI + PREP) **1** (= *kill*) acabar con, matar • **smoking will do for him in the end** el tabaco acabará con él, el tabaco lo acabará matando • **I thought we were done for** pensaba que nos íbamos a matar • **one false move and he was done for** un movimiento en falso y era hombre muerto

2 (= *finish off*) • **as a politician he's done for** como político está acabado • **they've seen him, he's done for!** lo han visto, ¡está perdido! • **if I can't talk to my own wife about these things, I'm done for** si ni siquiera puedo hablar con mi mujer de estas cosas, estoy acabado* • **I'm done for** (= *exhausted*) estoy rendido *or* molido*

▸ **do in*** (VT + ADV) **1** (= *kill*) liquidar*, cargarse*

2 (= *exhaust*) reventar*, hacer polvo* • **he's absolutely done in** está totalmente reventado*, está hecho polvo*

3 (= *ruin*) [+ *back*] hacerse daño en, fastidiar (*Sp**); [+ *engine*] cargarse (*Sp**), arruinar (*LAm*) • **he'll do the engine in, driving the way he does** se cargará el motor conduciendo de esa manera (*Sp**)

▸ **do out** (VT + ADV) **1** (*Brit*) [+ *room*] (= *clean*) limpiar a fondo

2 [+ *room*] (= *paint*) pintar; (= *wallpaper*) empapelar; (= *furnish*) decorar • **a room done out in Mexican style** una habitación decorada al estilo mejicano

3 • **to do sb out of sth***: **he has done me out of thousands of pounds** me quedé sin miles de libras por su culpa • **he did her out of a job** le quitó el trabajo, se quedó sin el trabajo por su culpa • **they did me out of my big chance** me pisaron mi gran oportunidad*

▸ **do over** (VT + ADV) **1** (*US**) (= *repeat*) volver a hacer, hacer de nuevo

2 (= *redecorate*) volver a pintar/empapelar; (= *refurnish*) volver a decorar

3 (*Brit**) (= *beat up*) dar una paliza a*

▸ **do up** (VT + ADV) **1** (= *fasten*) [+ *shoes, shoelaces*] atar; [+ *dress*] (*gen*) abrochar; (*with zip*) cerrar *or* subir la cremallera de; [+ *buttons, coat, necklace*] abrochar; [+ *tie*] hacer el nudo de; [+ *zip*] cerrar, subir

2 (= *wrap up*) [+ *parcel*] envolver • **have you done up that parcel yet?** ¿has envuelto ya ese paquete?

3 (= *renovate*) [+ *house*] reformar, hacer reformas en

4 (= *dress up*) • **she was all done up in her best clothes** iba de punta en blanco* • **Mark was done up in a beret and cravat*** Mark iba luciendo una boina y un fular

▸ **do with** (VI + PREP) **1** (= *need*) • **I could do with some help/a beer** no me vendría mal un poco de ayuda/una cerveza • **we could have done with you there** nos hiciste mucha falta • **you could do with a bath** te vendría bien un baño

2 (= *have connection with*) • **it is to do with**: • **"what did you want to see her about?" — "it's to do with her application"** —¿de qué querías hablarle? —es respecto a su solicitud • **it's nothing to do with me** no tiene nada que ver conmigo • **to have to do with** tener que ver con • **that has nothing to do with you!** ¡eso no tiene nada que ver contigo! • **what has that got to do with it?** ¿eso qué tiene que ver? • **that has nothing to do with it!** ¡eso no tiene nada que ver! • **I won't have anything to do with it/him** no quiero tener nada que ver con este asunto/con él, no quiero saber nada de este asunto/de él

3* • **I can't be doing with pop music** tengo mejores cosas que hacer que escuchar música pop • **I can't be doing with his finicky eating habits** no soporto sus manías a la hora de comer

▸ **do without** (VI + PREP) • **I can't do without my computer** yo no puedo pasar sin el ordenador • **"I haven't brought my gym kit" — "you'll have to do without then!"** —no he traído mi equipo de gimnasia —pues vas a tener que apañártelas sin él • **you can't do without money** no se puede vivir sin dinero • **I can do without your advice** no necesito tus consejos • **I could do without them poking their noses in*** no necesito que vengan ellos metiendo las narices en lo que no les importa* • **this bus strike is something I could do without*** esta huelga de autobuses es lo último que me faltaba

do² [dəʊ] (N) (*Mus*) do *m*

do. (ABBR) (= **ditto**) lo mismo, ídem, íd.

DOA (ADJ ABBR) (= **dead on arrival**) ingresó cadáver

doable* ['du:əbəl] (ADJ) [*project*] factible • **do you think it is ~?** ¿te parece factible?

d.o.b. (N ABBR) = **date of birth**

Doberman ['dəʊbəmən] (N) (*also* **Doberman pinscher**) dóberman *m*

doc [dɒk] (N) (*esp US**) = **doctor**
(ABBR) (= **document**) doc.

docile ['dəʊsaɪl] (ADJ) dócil, sumiso

docilely ['dəʊsaɪllɪ] (ADV) [*behave*] dócilmente

docility [dəʊ'sɪlɪtɪ] (N) docilidad *f*

dock¹ [dɒk] (N) (*Bot*) acedera *f*, ramaza *f*

dock² [dɒk] (VT) **1** [+ *animal's tail*] cortar, cercenar (*frm*)

2 (*Brit*) • **to ~ sb's pay** descontar dinero del sueldo a algn • **I've been ~ed £1** me han descontado una libra

dock³ [dɒk] (N) **1** (*Naut*) dársena *f*, muelle *m*; (*with gates*) dique *m* • **to be in ~** (*Brit**) [*ship*] estar en puerto; [*car*] estar en el taller

2 docks muelles *mpl*, puerto *m*

(VT) [+ *ship*] atracar; [+ *spacecraft*] acoplar

(VI) **1** (*Naut*) atracar; (*loosely*) llegar • **the ship has ~ed** el barco ha atracado • **we ~ed at five** llegamos a las cinco, entramos en el puerto a las cinco • **when we ~ed at Vigo** cuando llegamos a Vigo

2 [*spacecraft*] acoplarse (**with** a)

(CPD) ▸ **dock dues** derechos *mpl* de atraque *or* de dársena ▸ **dock labourer, dock laborer** (*US*) = **dock worker** ▸ **dock walloper*** (*US*)

d

= dock worker ▸ **dock warrant** resguardo *m* de muelle, conocimiento *m* de almacén
▸ **dock worker** trabajador *m* portuario
dock⁴ [dɒk] (N) (*Brit*) (*in court*) banquillo *m* de los acusados
docker ['dɒkəʳ] (N) (*Brit*) estibador *m*
docket ['dɒkɪt] (N) **1** (= *label*) etiqueta *f*, marbete *m*; (*esp Brit*) (= *certificate*) resguardo *m*, certificado *m*; (= *bill*) factura *f*
2 (*US*) (*Jur*) lista *f* de casos pendientes
docking ['dɒkɪŋ] (N) [*of spacecraft*] atraque *m*, acoplamiento *m*
(CPD) ▸ **docking manoeuvre, docking maneuver** (*US*) maniobra *f* de atraque
dockland ['dɒklænd] (N), **docklands** ['dɒklændz] (NPL) (*Brit*) zona *f* del puerto, zona *f* portuaria
dockside ['dɒksaɪd] (N) (= *quayside*) zona *f* del muelle
(ADJ) [*area, complex*] del muelle; [*apartment*] en el muelle
dockyard ['dɒkjɑːd] (N) astillero *m*
doctor ['dɒktəʳ] (N) **1** (*Med*) médico/a *m/f* • **to go to the ~'s** ir al médico • **Doctor Brown** el doctor Brown • **to be under the ~*** estar bajo tratamiento médico • IDIOM: • **it was just what the ~ ordered*** fue mano de santo
2 (*Univ*) doctor(a) *m/f* (**of** en); ▷ DEGREE
(VT) **1** (= *tamper with*) [+ *food, drink*] adulterar; [+ *document*] manipular
2 (= *treat*) [+ *cold*] tratar, curar • **to ~ o.s.** automedicarse
3* (= *castrate*) [+ *cat, dog etc*] castrar
(CPD) ▸ **Doctor of Philosophy** (= *person*) doctor(a) *m/f*; (= *degree*) doctorado *m*
▸ **doctor's degree** doctorado *m* ▸ **doctor's excuse** (*US*), **doctor's line** (*Brit*), **doctor's note** (*Brit*) baja *f* (médica)
▸ **doctor up** (VT + ADV) [+ *machine etc*] remendar, arreglar de cualquier modo
doctoral ['dɒktərəl] (ADJ) doctoral
(CPD) ▸ **doctoral dissertation** (*US*) = doctoral thesis ▸ **doctoral thesis** (*Brit*) tesis *f inv* doctoral
doctorate ['dɒktərɪt] (N) doctorado *m*; ▷ DEGREE
doctoring ['dɒktərɪŋ] (N) (= *falsification*) [*of text, document, picture, figures*] falsificación *f*
doctrinaire [ˌdɒktrɪ'nɛəʳ] (ADJ) doctrinario
(N) doctrinario/a *m/f*
doctrinal [dɒk'traɪnl] (ADJ) doctrinal
doctrine ['dɒktrɪn] (N) doctrina *f*
docudrama ['dɒkjʊˌdrɑːmə] (N) docudrama *m*
document (N) ['dɒkjʊmənt] documento *m*
(VT) ['dɒkjʊment] documentar
(CPD) ['dɒkjʊmənt] ▸ **document case, document holder** portadocumentos *m inv*
▸ **document reader** (*Comput*) lector *m* de documentos
documentarian [ˌdɒkjʊmen'tɛərɪən] (N) documentarista *mf*
documentary [ˌdɒkjʊ'mentərɪ] (ADJ) documental; (*Comm, Econ*) documentario
(N) (*Cine, TV*) documental *m*
(CPD) ▸ **documentary bill of exchange** letra *f* de cambio documentaria
▸ **documentary evidence** pruebas *fpl* documentales ▸ **documentary film** documental *m* ▸ **documentary (letter of) credit** crédito *m* documentario
documentation [ˌdɒkjʊmen'teɪʃən] (N) documentación *f*
docu-soap ['dɒkjʊsəʊp] (N) (*TV*) *documental sobre la vida cotidiana de un grupo de personas*
DOD (N ABBR) (*US*) = **Department of Defense**
dodder ['dɒdəʳ] (VI) (*walking*) renquear; [*hand*] temblequear
dodderer ['dɒdərəʳ] (N) chocho *m*
doddering ['dɒdərɪŋ], **doddery** ['dɒdərɪ] (ADJ) renqueante, chocho (*pej*)
doddle* ['dɒdl] (N) • **it's a ~** (*Brit*) es pan comido*, está chupado
Dodecanese [ˌdəʊdɪkə'niːz] (NPL) • **the ~** el Dodecaneso
dodecaphonic [ˌdəʊdekə'fɒnɪk] (ADJ) dodecafónico
dodge [dɒdʒ] (N) **1** (= *movement*) regate *m*; (*Boxing etc*) finta *f*
2 (*Brit**) (= *trick*) truco *m*
(VT) (= *elude*) [+ *blow, ball*] esquivar; [+ *pursuer*] dar esquinazo a; [+ *acquaintance, problem*] evitar; [+ *tax*] evadir; [+ *responsibility, duty, job*] eludir • **to ~ the issue** eludir el tema
(VI) escabullirse; (*Boxing*) hacer una finta • **to ~ out of the way** echarse a un lado • **to ~ behind a tree** ocultarse tras un árbol • **to ~ round a corner** escabullirse detrás de una esquina
▸ **dodge about** (VI + ADV) ir de aquí para allá
dodgem ['dɒdʒəm] (N) (*Brit*) (*also* **dodgem car**) coche *m* de choque • **the ~s** los coches de choque
dodger ['dɒdʒəʳ] (N) (= *trickster*) tunante/a *m/f*, gandul *mf*
dodgy* ['dɒdʒɪ] (ADJ) (*Brit*) (COMPAR: **dodgier**, SUPERL: **dodgiest**) **1** (= *dishonest*) [*person*] de poco fiar, poco fiable; [*business, deal, district*] oscuro, chungo (*Sp‡*); [*practice*] dudoso • **there's something ~ about him** hay algo en él que me da mala espina* • **the whole business seemed a bit ~** todo el asunto parecía un poco oscuro
2 (= *unreliable, uncertain*) [*plan*] arriesgado; [*weather*] inestable • **the clutch is a bit ~** el embrague no anda muy bien, el embrague está un poco chungo (*Sp‡*) • **he's in a ~ situation financially** su situación económica es un poco peliaguda • **the sausages looked ~** las salchichas tenían una pinta sospechosa • **to have a ~ back** tener la espalda fastidiada, estar fastidiado de la espalda • **to have a ~ heart** estar fastidiado del corazón
dodo ['dəʊdəʊ] (N) (PL: **dodos** *or* **dodoes**)
1 (*Zool*) dodó *m*; ▷ dead
2 (*US**) (= *fool*) bobo/a *m/f*
DOE (N ABBR) **1** (*Brit*) = **Department of the Environment**
2 (*US*) = **Department of Energy**
doe [dəʊ] (N) (PL: **does** *or* **doe**) (= *deer*) cierva *f*, gama *f*; (= *rabbit*) coneja *f*; (= *hare*) liebre *f*
doer ['duːəʳ] (N) **1** (= *author of deed*) hacedor(a) *m/f*
2 (= *active person*) persona *f* enérgica, persona *f* dinámica
does [dʌz] (VB) *3rd pers sing of* **do**
doeskin ['dəʊskɪn] (N) ante *m*, piel *f* de ante
doesn't ['dʌznt] = **does not**
doff [dɒf] (VT) (*frm*) quitarse • **to ~ one's hat** quitarse el sombrero
dog [dɒg] (N) **1** (*Zool*) perro/a *m/f* • IDIOMS: • **dog eat dog**: • **it's dog eat dog in this place** aquí se despedazan unos a otros • **to go to the dogs*** [*person*] echarse a perder; [*nation, country*] ir a la ruina • **dog's breakfast*** revoltijo *m* • **to have a dog's chance**: • **he hasn't a dog's chance** no tiene la más remota posibilidad • **it's a dog's life** es una vida de perros • **to be dressed up like a dog's dinner*** ir hecho un adefesio • **to be a dog in the manger** [*person*] ser como el perro del hortelano • **to put on the dog** (*US**) vestirse de punta en blanco • **to be top dog** ser el gallo del lugar, triunfar • **the dog's bollocks** (*Brit**‡*) la hostia*‡ • PROVERBS: • **every dog has its day** a cada cerdo le llega su San Martín • **let sleeping dogs lie** más vale no meneallo
2 (= *male*) (*fox*) macho *m*
3* (*term of abuse*) canalla *m*, bribón *m* • **you dog!** ¡canalla!; (*hum*) ¡tunante!
4‡ (= *unattractive girl*) callo *m* (malayo)*
5* (= *person*) • **dirty dog** tío *m* guarro*, tipo *m* asqueroso* • **you lucky dog!** ¡qué suerte tienes! • **he's a lucky dog** es un tío suertudo • IDIOM: • **there's life in the old dog yet** (al abuelo) aún le queda cuerda para rato
6 • **the dogs** (*Brit**) (= *greyhounds*) las carreras de galgos; ▷ GREYHOUND RACING
7 (*Brit‡*) (= *telephone*) teléfono *m*
(VT) (= *follow closely*) seguir (de cerca) • **he dogs my footsteps** me sigue los pasos • **he was dogged by ill luck** le perseguía la mala suerte
(CPD) ▸ **dog basket** cesto *m* del perro ▸ **dog biscuit** galleta *f* de perro ▸ **dog breeder** criador(a) *m/f* de perros ▸ **dog collar** collar *m* de perro; (*Rel*) (*hum*) gola *f*, alzacuello(s) *m inv* ▸ **dog days** canícula *f* ▸ **dog fancier** (= *connoisseur*) entendido/a *m/f* en perros; (= *breeder*) criador(a) *m/f* de perros ▸ **dog food** comida *f* para perros ▸ **dog fox** zorro *m* macho ▸ **dog guard** (*Aut*) reja *f* separadora ▸ **dog handler** (*Police*) adiestrador(a) *m/f* de perros ▸ **dog kennel** (*Brit*) perrera *f* ▸ **dog Latin** latín *m* macarrónico ▸ **dog licence** permiso *m* para perros ▸ **dog paddle** braza *f* de perro (*forma de nadar*); ▷ dog-paddle ▸ **dog rose** escaramujo *m*, rosal *m* silvestre ▸ **dog show** exposición *f* canina ▸ **Dog Star** Sirio *m* ▸ **dog tag** (*US*) (*Mil*) placa *f* de identificación ▸ **dog track** (*Sport*) canódromo *m*
dogcart ['dɒgkɑːt] (N) dócar *m*
doge [dəʊdʒ] (N) dux *m*
dog-eared ['dɒgɪəd] (ADJ) sobado, muy manoseado
dog-end* ['dɒgend] (N) colilla *f*, toba* *f*
dogfight ['dɒgfaɪt] (N) (*Aer*) combate *m* aéreo (reñido y confuso); (= *squabble**) trifulca *f*, refriega *f*
dogfish ['dɒgfɪʃ] (N) (PL: **dogfish** *or* **dogfishes**) perro *m* marino, cazón *m*
dogged ['dɒgɪd] (ADJ) (= *obstinate*) porfiado, terco; (= *tenacious*) tenaz
doggedly ['dɒgɪdlɪ] (ADV) tenazmente
doggedness ['dɒgɪdnɪs] (N) tenacidad *f*
doggerel ['dɒgərəl] (N) coplas *fpl* de ciego, malos versos *mpl*
doggie ['dɒgɪ] (N) = **doggy**
doggo* ['dɒgəʊ] (ADV) (*Brit*) • **to lie ~** quedarse escondido
doggone* [ˌdɒg'gɒn] (*US*) (EXCL) ¡maldita sea!
(ADJ) condenado, maldito
doggy* ['dɒgɪ] (N) (*baby talk*) perrito *m* • **to have sex ~ fashion** hacer el amor al estilo perrito
(CPD) ▸ **doggy bag** bolsita *f* con los restos de la comida (*en restaurante*) ▸ **doggy paddle** braza *f* de perro; ▷ doggy-paddle
doggy-paddle ['dɒgɪˌpædl] (VI) nadar como los perros; ▷ doggy
doghouse ['dɒghaʊs] (N) (PL: **doghouses** ['dɒghaʊzɪz]) (*US*) caseta *f* del perro • IDIOM: • **to be in the ~*** [*person*] estar castigado
dogleg ['dɒgleg] (N) (*in road etc*) codo *m*, ángulo *m* abrupto
doglike ['dɒglaɪk] (ADJ) de perro
dogma ['dɒgmə] (N) (PL: **dogmas** *or* **dogmata** ['dɒgmətə]) dogma *m*
dogmatic [dɒg'mætɪk] (ADJ) dogmático
dogmatically [dɒg'mætɪkəlɪ] (ADV) dogmáticamente
dogmatism ['dɒgmətɪzəm] (N) dogmatismo *m*
dogmatist ['dɒgmətɪst] (N) dogmático/a *m/f*
dogmatize ['dɒgmətaɪz] (VI) dogmatizar
do-gooder* ['duː'gʊdəʳ] (N) (*pej*) hacedor(a)

m/f de buenas obras
dog-paddle ['dɒg,pædl] VI nadar como los perros; ▹ dog
dogsbody* ['dɒgzbɒdɪ] N (Brit) burro m de carga • **to be the general ~** ser el burro de carga de todo el mundo
dogsled ['dɒgsled] N trineo m tirado por perros
dog-tired* ['dɒg'taɪəd] ADJ rendido*, hecho polvo*
dogtooth ['dɒgtu:θ] N (*in architecture, fashion*) diente m de perro
ADJ de diente de perro
dogtrot ['dɒgtrɒt] N trote m lento
dogwatch ['dɒgwɒtʃ] N (*Naut*) guardia f de cuartillo
dogwood ['dɒgwʊd] N (= *tree, bush*) cornejo m
doh [dəʊ] N (*Mus*) do m EXCL* ¡jolines!
doily ['dɔɪlɪ] N (*under cake*) blonda f; (*under ornament*) pañito m de adorno
doing ['du:ɪŋ] N **1** • **this is your ~** esto es cosa tuya • **it was none of my ~** yo no he tenido nada que ver • **it will take a lot of** *or* **some ~** va a ser muy difícil hacerlo, costará mucho hacerlo • **that takes some ~!** ¡eso no es nada fácil!; ▹ **nothing**
2 doings (= *activities*) actividades fpl; (= *actions*) acciones fpl; (= *happenings*) sucesos mpl • **he recounted the day's ~s** hizo recuento de las actividades del día
doings‡ ['du:ɪŋz] NSING (Brit) (= *thing*) chisme m • **that ~ with two knobs** aquel chisme con dos botones
do-it-yourself ['du:ɪtjə'self] N bricolaje m
CPD ▸ **do-it-yourself enthusiast**, **do-it-yourself expert** aficionado/a m/f al bricolaje ▸ **do-it-yourself kit** modelo m para armar ▸ **do-it-yourself shop** tienda f de bricolaje
do-it-yourselfer* [,du:ɪtjə'selfəʳ] N aficionado/a m/f al bricolaje, bricolero/a m/f
doldrums ['dɒldrəmz] NPL (*Naut*) zona f de las calmas ecuatoriales • IDIOM: • **to be in the ~** [*person*] estar abatido; [*business*] estar estancado; (*St Ex*) estar en calma
dole* [dəʊl] (Brit) N subsidio m de desempleo, subsidio m de paro (*Sp*), paro m (*Sp*) • **to be on the ~** estar desempleado, estar parado (*Sp*), cobrar el paro (*Sp*)
CPD ▸ **dole money** (Brit) subsidio m de desempleo, subsidio m de paro (*Sp*) ▸ **dole office** (Brit) oficina f del paro ▸ **dole queue** cola f del paro
▸ **dole out** VT + ADV repartir, distribuir
doleful ['dəʊlfʊl] ADJ triste
dolefully ['dəʊlfəlɪ] ADV tristemente
doll [dɒl] N **1** (= *toy*) muñeca f
2 (*esp US**) (= *girl*) muñeca f, preciosidad f • **you're a ~ to help me** eres un ángel, gracias por ayudarme
CPD ▸ **doll's house** casa f de muñecas
▸ **doll up*** VT + ADV emperifollar, emperejilar • **to ~ o.s. up** emperifollarse, emperejilarse
dollar ['dɒləʳ] N dólar m • IDIOMS: • **you can bet your bottom ~ that ...** puedes apostarte lo que quieras a que ... • **it's ~s to doughnuts that ...** (*US**) es tan cierto como hay Dios que ...*
CPD ▸ **dollar area** zona f del dólar ▸ **dollar bill** billete m de un dólar ▸ **dollar cost averaging** costo m promedio en dólares ▸ **dollar diplomacy** (*US*) (*Pol*) diplomacia f a golpe de dólar ▸ **dollar rate** cambio m del dólar ▸ **dollar sign** signo m del dólar
dollop ['dɒləp] N [*of jam, ketchup etc*] pegote m
dolly ['dɒlɪ] N **1*** (*baby talk*) (= *doll*) muñequita f
2* (= *girl*) chica f, jovencita f
3 (*Cine, TV*) travelín m, plataforma f rodante
4 (*US*) carretilla f
CPD ▸ **dolly bird‡** (Brit) niña f mona*
dolomite ['dɒləmaɪt] N dolomía f, dolomita f
Dolomites ['dɒləmaɪts] NPL • **the ~** las Dolomitas, los Alpes Dolomíticos
dolphin ['dɒlfɪn] N delfín m
dolphinarium [,dɒlfɪ'nɛərɪəm] N delfinario m
dolt* [dəʊlt] N imbécil mf • **you ~!** ¡imbécil!
doltish* ['dəʊltɪʃ] ADJ estúpido
domain [dəʊ'meɪn] N **1** (= *lands etc*) dominio m, propiedad f
2 (*fig*) campo m, competencia f • **the matter is now in the public ~** el asunto es ya del dominio público
CPD ▸ **domain name** (*Internet*) nombre m de dominio
dome [dəʊm] N (*on building etc*) cúpula f; (*Geog*) colina f redonda
domed [dəʊmd] ADJ [*roof*] abovedado; [*forehead*] en forma de huevo
Domesday Book ['du:mzdeɪ,bʊk] N • **the ~** el Domesday Book (*libro del registro catastral realizado en Inglaterra en 1086*)
domestic [də'mestɪk] ADJ **1** (= *household*) [*activities, duty, life, animal*] doméstico; [*fuel*] de uso doméstico; [*harmony, quarrel*] familiar; [*violence*] en el hogar • **for ~ use** para uso doméstico • **she does ~ work for a living** trabaja como empleada del hogar *or* empleada doméstica • **a scene of ~ bliss** una escena de felicidad familiar *or* doméstica
2 (= *home-loving*) casero, hogareño
3 (*Econ, Pol*) (= *internal*) [*flight, industry, news, economy, politics*] nacional; [*market, consumption, policy*] nacional, interior; [*affairs, problems*] nacional, interno
N doméstico/a m/f, empleado/a m/f doméstico/a
CPD ▸ **domestic abuse** violencia f doméstica ▸ **domestic appliance** aparato m doméstico, aparato m de uso doméstico ▸ **domestic help** empleado/a m/f del hogar, empleado/a m/f doméstico/a ▸ **domestic science** (*esp Brit*) (*Scol*) economía f doméstica, hogar m (*Sp*) ▸ **domestic science teacher** (*esp Brit*) (*Scol*) profesor(a) m/f de economía doméstica, profesor(a) m/f de hogar (*Sp*) ▸ **domestic servant** sirviente/a m/f, doméstico/a m/f ▸ **domestic service** servicio m doméstico • **to be in ~ service** trabajar en el servicio doméstico ▸ **domestic staff** (*in hospital, institution*) personal m de servicio; (*in private household*) servicio m doméstico ▸ **domestic worker** empleado/a m/f doméstico/a
domestically [də'mestɪkəlɪ] ADV **1** (= *nationally*) nacionalmente • **~ and internationally** nacional e internacionalmente • **a ~ produced article** un artículo producido en el país • **~ produced goods** productos mpl nacionales
2 (= *in the home*) • **he's not very ~ inclined** (= *not homely*) no es lo que se dice una persona muy casera; (= *not keen on housework*) no le van mucho las tareas de la casa
domesticate [də'mestɪkeɪt] VT [+ *wild animal*] domesticar
domesticated [də'mestɪkeɪtɪd] ADJ [*animal*] domesticado; [*person*] casero, hogareño
domestication [də,mestɪ'keɪʃən] N domesticación f
domesticity [,dəʊmes'tɪsɪtɪ] N domesticidad f
domicile ['dɒmɪsaɪl] (*frm*) N (*also* **place of domicile**) domicilio m
VT • **to be ~d in** tener domicilio en
domiciliary [,dɒmɪ'sɪlɪərɪ] ADJ domiciliario
dominance ['dɒmɪnəns] N **1** (= *supremacy*) [*of person*] dominio m (**over** sobre); [*of class, nation*] dominio m, dominación f (**over** sobre)
2 (= *predominance*) predominio m
3 (*Bio, Ecol*) [*of gene, species, male*] dominancia f
dominant ['dɒmɪnənt] ADJ **1** (= *supremely powerful*) [*person, factor, role*] dominante • **Britain was once ~ in the world market** Gran Bretaña fue en su día una nación dominante en el mercado mundial
2 (= *predominant*) [*feature, theme*] predominante
3 (*Bio, Ecol*) [*gene, species, male*] dominante
4 (*Mus*) dominante • **~ seventh** séptima f dominante
N (*Mus*) dominante f
dominate ['dɒmɪneɪt] VT, VI dominar
dominating ['dɒmɪneɪtɪŋ] ADJ dominante, dominador
domination [,dɒmɪ'neɪʃən] N (= *act of dominating*) dominación f; (= *control*) dominio m
dominatrix [,dɒmɪ'neɪtrɪks] N (PL: **dominatrices** [,dɒmɪnə'traɪsi:z]) ama f (*prostituta especializada en servicios sadomasoquistas*)
domineer [,dɒmɪ'nɪəʳ] VI dominar, tiranizar (**over** a)
domineering [,dɒmɪ'nɪərɪŋ] ADJ dominante, autoritario
Dominic ['dɒmɪnɪk] N Domingo
Dominica [,dɒmɪ'ni:kə] N Dominica f
Dominican [də'mɪnɪkən] ADJ dominicano
N **1** (*Pol*) dominicano/a m/f
2 (*Rel*) dominico m, dominicano m
CPD ▸ **Dominican Republic** República f Dominicana
dominion [də'mɪnɪən] N **1** (= *control*) dominio m • **to hold** *or* **have ~ over sb** ejercer dominio sobre algn
2 (*Brit*) (*Pol*) dominio m
domino ['dɒmɪnəʊ] N (PL: **dominoes**)
1 (= *piece in game*) ficha f de dominó • **~es** (= *game*) dominó msing • **to play ~es** jugar al dominó, jugar dominó (*LAm*)
2 (= *dress*) dominó m
CPD ▸ **domino effect** (*Pol*) reacción f en cadena ▸ **domino theory** (*Pol*) teoría f de la reacción en cadena
Domitian [də'mɪʃɪən] N Domiciano
don¹ [dɒn] N **1** (*Brit*) (*Univ*) catedrático/a m/f
2 (*US*) • **a Mafia don** un capo de la Mafia
don² [dɒn] VT (*liter*) [+ *garment*] ponerse, ataviarse con
donate [dəʊ'neɪt] VT donar • **to ~ blood** donar sangre
donation [dəʊ'neɪʃən] N **1** (= *act*) donación f
2 (= *gift*) donativo m, donación f • **to make a ~ to a fund** hacer un donativo *or* una donación a un fondo
done [dʌn] PP *of* **do¹**
ADJ **1** (= *finished*) terminado, acabado • **the job's ~** el trabajo está terminado *or* acabado • **it's as good as ~** eso está hecho • **to get ~ with sth** terminar *or* acabar de hacer algo • **why don't you tell him and have ~ with it?** ¿por qué no se lo dices y acabas de una vez? • PROVERB: • **what's ~ cannot be undone** a lo hecho, pecho; ▹ **over, say**
2 (= *accepted*) • **it's just not ~!** ¡eso no se hace! • **it's not ~ to voice your opinions here** aquí está mal visto que uno exprese sus opiniones • **it's not ~ to put your elbows on the table** poner los codos en la mesa es de mala educación
3 (*in exclamations*) • **done!** (= *agreed*) ¡trato hecho! • **well ~!** ¡muy bien!, ¡bravo!

4 (*Culin*) • **the vegetables are ~** la verdura está cocida *or* hecha • **how do you like your steak ~?** ¿cómo te gusta el filete? • **I like my steak well ~** me gusta el filete muy hecho
5 (= *exhausted*) agotado, hecho polvo*; ▹ **do for, do in**

donee [dəʊ'ni:] (N) (*Jur*) donatario/a *m/f*

dong‡* [dɒŋ] (N) verga‡* *f*, polla *f* (*Sp*‡*)

dongle ['dɒŋgəl] (N) (*Comput*) llave *f* de hardware

Don Juan [dɒn'hwɑ:n] (N) (*fig*) Don Juan *m*

donkey ['dɒŋkɪ] (N) burro *m* • **female ~** burra *f* • IDIOM: • **for ~'s years** (*Brit**) durante un porrón de *or* muchísimos años • **I haven't seen him for ~'s years** (*Brit**) hace siglos que no lo veo; ▹ **hind**¹
(CPD) ▸ **donkey derby** (*Brit*) carrera *f* de burros ▸ **donkey jacket** (*Brit*) chaqueta *f* de lanilla de trabajo ▸ **donkey engine** pequeña máquina *f* de vapor, motor *m* auxiliar ▸ **donkey work*** (*Brit*) trabajo *m* pesado

donnish ['dɒnɪʃ] (ADJ) [*life, discussion etc*] de erudito, de profesor; (*in appearance*) de aspecto erudito; (*pej*) profesoril, pedantesco

donor ['dəʊnəʳ] (N) donante *mf*
(CPD) ▸ **donor card** carnet *m* de donante ▸ **donor organ** órgano *m* donado

Don Quixote [dɒn'kwɪksət] (N) Don Quijote

don't [dəʊnt] (VB) = **do not**
(N) ▹ **do**¹
(CPD) ▸ **the don't knows** los que no saben

donut ['dəʊnʌt] (N) (*esp US*) = **doughnut**

doobee‡ ['du:bi:] (N) (= *cannabis*) chocolate‡ *m*

doodah* ['du:dɑ:], **doodad*** (*US*) ['du:dæd] (N) (= *thing*) chisme *m*

doodle ['du:dl] (N) dibujito *m*, garabato *m*
(VI) hacer dibujitos, hacer garabatos

doodlebug ['du:dlbʌg] (N) (*Brit*) bomba *f* volante

doofer* ['du:fəʳ*] (N) (*Brit*) **1** = **doodah**
2 (= *remote control*) mando *m* a distancia, telemando *m*

doohickey* [,du:'hɪkɪ] (N) (*US*) trasto *m*

doolally‡ [,du:'lælɪ] (ADJ) tarumba*

doom [du:m] (N) (= *terrible fate*) destino *m* funesto; (= *death*) muerte *f*; (*Rel*) juicio *m* final • **a sense of ~** una sensación de desastre • **it's all ~ and gloom here** aquí reina el catastrofismo
(VT) (= *destine*) condenar (**to** a) • **~ed to failure** condenado al fracaso • **to be ~ed to die** estar condenado a morir • **the ~ed ship** el buque siniestrado

doom-laden ['du:m,leɪdn] (ADJ) [*warning, prophecy*] aciago

doomsday ['du:mzdeɪ] (N) día *m* del juicio final • **till ~** (*fig*) hasta el día del juicio final
(CPD) ▸ **doomsday cult** secta *f* apocalíptica ▸ **the doomsday scenario** la peor de las perspectivas, la perspectiva más catastrófica ▸ **Doomsday Clock** Reloj *m* del Apocalipsis

doomwatcher ['du:m,wɒtʃəʳ] (N) cataclismista *mf*, catastrofista *mf*

doomwatching ['du:m,wɒtʃɪŋ] (N) cataclismismo *m*, catastrofismo *m*

Doona® ['du:nə] (N) (*Australia*) edredón *m*

door [dɔ:ʳ] (N) **1** (= *hinged object*) [*of room, vehicle*] puerta *f* • **to answer the ~** (ir a) abrir la puerta • **she answered the ~ as soon as I knocked** llamé a la puerta y vino a abrir al momento • **"performance starts at 8pm, doors open at 7"** "la actuación empieza a las 8, pero las puertas se abrirán a las 7" • **to shut** *or* **slam the ~ in sb's face** cerrar la puerta a algn en las narices*, dar a algn con la puerta en las narices* • IDIOMS: • **to lay the blame for sth at sb's ~** echar la culpa de algo a algn • **the blame is always laid at the ~ of the government** siempre se le echa la culpa al gobierno • **I'm not sure his death can be laid at the doctor's ~** no estoy seguro de que se le pueda achacar su muerte al médico, no estoy seguro de que se pueda echar la culpa *or* culpar al médico de su muerte • **to close the ~ on sth** (= *make impossible*) cerrar la puerta a algo; (= *bring to an end*) poner punto final a algo • **behind closed ~s** a puerta cerrada • **to open the ~ to sth** abrir la(s) puerta(s) a algo • **meeting him opened the ~ to success for me** el encuentro con él me abrió la(s) puerta(s) al éxito • **this could open the ~ to a flood of claims for compensation** esto podría dar pie a una avalancha de reclamaciones de indemnización • PROVERB: • **as one ~ shuts, another opens** cuando una puerta se cierra, otra se abre; ▹ **darken, knock, sliding, slam**
2 (= *entrance*) puerta *f* • **he stopped at the ~ of his office** se detuvo a *or* en la puerta de su oficina • **to pay at the ~** (*Cine, Theat*) pagar a la entrada *or* al entrar • **to be on the ~** [*of nightclub*] hacer de portero, estar en la puerta; (*Theat*) hacer de acomodador(a) *m/f* • **"tickets £5 in advance, £6 on the door"** "la entrada cuesta 5 libras por adelantado, 6 en la puerta" • **to see** *or* **show sb to the ~** acompañar a algn a la puerta • **to show sb the ~** (*euph*) decir a algn dónde está la puerta
3 (= *building*) puerta *f* • **she lived a few ~s down from me** ella vivía unas cuantas puertas más abajo (de mí) • **three ~s down the street** tres puertas más abajo • **(from) ~ to ~** de puerta en puerta • **it took seven hours to get there, ~ to ~** de puerta a puerta tardamos siete horas • **next ~** (= *in the next house*) en la casa de al lado; (= *in the next room*) en la habitación de al lado • **out of ~s** al aire libre; ▹ **foot**
(CPD) ▸ **door chain** cadena *f* (de seguridad) de la puerta ▸ **door handle** (*gen*) picaporte *m*; [*of car*] manija *f* ▸ **door jamb** jamba *f* de la puerta ▸ **door key** llave *f* (de la puerta) ▸ **door knocker** aldaba *f*, llamador *m*

doorbell ['dɔ:bel] (N) timbre *m*

do-or-die ['du:ə'daɪ] (ADJ) [*effort*] extraordinario • **it's do-or-die** es todo o nada

doorframe ['dɔ:freɪm] (N) marco *m* de la puerta

doorkeeper ['dɔ:,ki:pəʳ] (N) portero/a *m/f*, conserje *mf*

doorknob ['dɔ:nɒb] (N) pomo *m* de la puerta, manilla *f* (*LAm*)

doorman ['dɔ:mən] (N) (PL: **doormen**) [*of hotel, block of flats*] portero/a *m/f*, conserje *mf*

doormat ['dɔ:mæt] (N) felpudo *m*, estera *f* • IDIOM: • **to treat sb like a ~**: • **he treats her like a ~** le trata como a un esclavo, la pisotea

doornail ['dɔ:neɪl] (N) ▹ **dead**

doorplate ['dɔ:pleɪt] (N) placa *f* de la casa

doorpost ['dɔ:pəʊst] (N) jamba *f* de puerta

doorstep ['dɔ:step] (N) (= *threshold*) umbral *m*; (= *step*) peldaño *m* de la puerta • **on our ~** en la puerta de casa • **we don't want an airport on our ~** no queremos un aeropuerto aquí tan cerca
(VT) (*Brit**) *ir los periodistas a la casa de una persona para hacerle fotos o una entrevista, a menudo en contra de su voluntad*

doorstop ['dɔ:stɒp] (N) tope *m*

door-to-door ['dɔ:tədɔ:ʳ] (ADJ) [*selling*] a domicilio
(CPD) ▸ **door-to-door salesman** vendedor *m* a domicilio

doorway ['dɔ:weɪ] (N) [*of house*] entrada *f*, puerta *f*; [*of block of flats, building*] portal *m*; (*fig*) puertas *fpl*, sendero *m*

dope [dəʊp] (N) **1*** (= *drugs*) drogas *fpl*; (= *cannabis*) chocolate* *m*, mota *f* (*LAm*); (*Sport*) estimulante *m* • **to do ~** (*esp US*) drogarse
2* (= *information*) información *f*, informes *mpl* • **to give sb the ~** informar a algn • **what's the ~ on him?** ¿qué es lo que se sabe de él?
3* (= *stupid person*) idiota *mf*, imbécil *mf* • **you ~!** ¡bobo!
4 (= *varnish*) barniz *m*
(VT) [+ *horse, person*] drogar; [+ *food, drink*] adulterar con drogas
(CPD) ▸ **dope fiend*** drogata* *mf* ▸ **dope peddler*** , **dope pusher*** camello* *m* ▸ **dope sheet*** (*US*) (*Horse racing*) periódico *m* de carreras de caballos ▸ **dope test** prueba *f* antidoping, control *m* antidoping
▸ **dope up*** (VT + ADV) • **to be ~d up on** *or* **with Valium** ir ciego a Valium*

dopehead* ['dəʊphed] (N) porrero/a* *m/f*

dopey* ['dəʊpɪ] (ADJ) (COMPAR: **dopier**, SUPERL: **dopiest**) (= *drugged*) drogado, colocado*; (= *fuddled*) atontado; (= *stupid*) corto*

doping ['dəʊpɪŋ] (N) (*Sport*) dopaje *m*, doping *m*

Doppler effect ['dɒplərɪ,fekt] (N) (*Astron*) efecto *m* Doppler

dopy ['dəʊpɪ] = **dopey**

Dordogne [dɔ:'dɔɪn] (N) (= *region*) Dordoña *f*; (= *river*) Dordoña *m*

Doric ['dɒrɪk] (ADJ) (*Archit*) dórico

dork‡ [dɔ:k] (N) (*esp US*) zumbado/a *m/f*

dorm* [dɔ:m] (N) = **dormitory**

dormancy ['dɔ:mənsɪ] (N) [*of volcano*] inactividad *f*; [*of virus*] estado *m* latente; [*of plant*] reposo *m* (vegetativo)

dormant ['dɔ:mənt] (ADJ) [*volcano*] inactivo; (*Bio, Bot*) durmiente; [*energy*] latente • **to lie ~** (*lit*) estar inactivo; (*fig*) quedar por realizarse

dormer ['dɔ:məʳ] (N) (*also* **dormer window**) buhardilla *f*, lucerna *f*

dormice ['dɔ:maɪs] (NPL) *of* **dormouse**

dormitory ['dɔ:mɪtrɪ] (N) **1** (= *bedroom*) dormitorio *m*
2 (*US*) (= *hall of residence*) residencia *f*
(CPD) ▸ **dormitory suburb** (*Brit*) barrio *m* dormitorio ▸ **dormitory town** (*Brit*) ciudad *f* dormitorio

Dormobile® ['dɔ:məbi:l] (N) (*Brit*) combi *f*

dormouse ['dɔ:maʊs] (N) (PL: **dormice**) lirón *m*

Dorothy ['dɒrəθɪ] (N) Dorotea

Dors (ABBR) (*Brit*) = **Dorset**

dorsal ['dɔ:sl] (ADJ) dorsal
(CPD) ▸ **dorsal fin** aleta *f* dorsal

dory¹ ['dɔ:rɪ] (N) (= *fish*) gallo *m*, pez *m* de San Pedro

dory² ['dɔ:rɪ] (N) (= *boat*) arenera *f*

DOS [dɒs] (N ABBR) = **disk operating system**

dosage ['dəʊsɪdʒ] (N) [*of medicine*] dosificación *f*; (*in instructions for use of medication*) posología *f*; (= *amount*) dosis *f inv*

dose [dəʊs] (N) **1** [*of medicine*] dosis *f inv* • IDIOM: • **like a ~ of salts***: • **it went through her like a ~ of salts*** le hizo hacer de vientre en menos que canta un gallo*
2 (*fig*) (= *amount*) dosis *f inv* • **in small ~s** en pequeñas dosis *or* cantidades
3* [*of flu*] ataque *m*
(VT) **1** (*also* **dose up**) medicar (**with con**) • **to ~ o.s. (up)** medicarse (**with con**)
2 [+ *wine*] adulterar

dosh‡ [dɒʃ] (N) (*Brit*) guita* *f*, pasta *f* (*Sp**), plata *f* (*LAm**), lana *f* (*LAm**)

doss* [dɒs] (*Brit*) (N) **1** (= *bed*) camastro *m*; (= *sleep*) sueño *m*
2 (= *easy task*) • **he thought the course would be a ~** pensó que el curso sería pan comido*
(VI) **1** (*also* **doss down**) (= *sleep*) echarse a dormir
2 (= *laze*) • **to ~ around** gandulear, no hacer nada

dosser* ['dɒsəʳ] (N) (*Brit*) vagabundo/a *m/f*, pobre *mf*

dosshouse* ['dɒshaʊs] (N) (PL: **dosshouses** ['dɒshaʊzɪz]) (*Brit*) pensión *f* de mala muerte

dossier ['dɒsɪeɪ] (N) (*gen*) informe *m*, dossier *m*; (*Admin*) expediente *m* (**on** sobre)

DOT (N ABBR) (*US*) = **Department of Transportation**

Dot [dɒt] (N) *familiar form of* **Dorothy**

dot [dɒt] (N) punto *m* • **dots and dashes** (*Morse*) puntos y rayas • **dot, dot, dot** (*Typ*) puntos suspensivos • **at seven o'clock on the dot** a las siete en punto • **to pay on the dot** pagar puntualmente • IDIOM: • **since the year dot** (*Brit*) desde los tiempos de Maricastaña
(VT) **1** [+ *letter*] poner el punto sobre • IDIOM: • **to dot the i's and cross the t's** poner los puntos sobre las íes; ▷ **dotted line**
2 (= *scatter*) esparcir, desparramar • **they are dotted about the country** están esparcidos por todo el país • **dotted with flowers** salpicado de flores
3 (= *speckle*) puntear, motear, salpicar de puntos
4* (= *hit*) • **to dot sb a blow** pegar *or* arrear* un golpe a algn • **he dotted him one** le pegó *or* arreó* (un porrazo)
(CPD) ▸ **dot command** (*Comput*) instrucción *f* (precedida) de punto ▸ **dot prompt** (*Comput*) indicación *f* de punto

dotage ['dəʊtɪdʒ] (N) chochez *f* • **to be in one's ~** chochear, estar chocho

dotcom, dot-com [dɒt'kɒm] (N) puntocom *f*
(CPD) ▸ **dotcom company, dot-com company** empresa *f* puntocom

dote [dəʊt] (VI) • **to ~ on** adorar, chochear por

doting ['dəʊtɪŋ] (ADJ) **1** (= *loving*) • **her ~ parents** sus padres, que la adoran
2 (= *senile*) chocho

dot-matrix printer [,dɒt,meɪtrɪks'prɪntəʳ] (N) impresora *f* matricial de agujas

dotted line [,dɒtɪd'laɪn] (N) línea *f* de puntos • **"tear along the ~"** "cortar por la línea de puntos" • IDIOM: • **to sign on the ~** firmar

dotty* ['dɒtɪ] (ADJ) (COMPAR: **dottier**, SUPERL: **dottiest**) (*Brit*) [*person*] chiflado*; [*idea, scheme*] estrafalario, disparatado • **you must be ~!** ¿estás loco o qué? • **it's driving me ~** esto me trae loco

double ['dʌbl] (ADJ) **1** (= *twice*) doble • **it is ~ what it was** es el doble de lo que era • **my income is ~ that of my neighbour** gano dos veces más que mi vecino, gano el doble que mi vecino • **he's ~ your age** te dobla la edad • **he's ~ the age of his sister** le dobla en edad a su hermana • **~ the size** el doble de grande • **~ the amount of money** el doble de dinero • **twins: ~ the trouble, and ~ the fun!** mellizos: el doble de problemas ¡y el doble de diversión!
2 (= *extra-big*) doble • **a ~ dose of cough mixture** una dosis doble de jarabe para la tos • **a ~ helping of ice cream** una porción doble de helado • **a ~ whisky** un whisky doble
3 (= *two, dual*) • **it is spelt with a ~ "m"** se escribe con dos emes • **~ five two six (5526)** (*Telec*) cinco, cinco, dos, seis, cincuenta y cinco, veintiséis • **a box with a ~ bottom** una caja con doble fondo • **to lead a ~ life** llevar una doble vida • **it serves a ~ purpose** sirve un doble propósito • **throw a ~ six to commence play** para empezar el juego tiene que sacar un seis doble al tirar los dados • **the egg had a ~ yolk** el huevo tenía dos yemas; ▷ **figure**
(ADV) **1** (= *twice as much*) [*cost, pay*] el doble • **he earns ~ what I earn** gana el doble que yo • **you should have bought ~ that amount** deberías haber comprado el doble • **if you land on a pink square it counts ~** si caes en una casilla rosa vale el doble *or* vale por dos • **to see ~** ver doble
2 (= *in half*) por la mitad • **the blanket had been folded ~** habían doblado la manta por la mitad • **to be bent ~** (*with age*) estar encorvado • **to be bent ~ with pain** retorcerse de dolor
(N) **1** (= *drink*) doble *m*
2 (= *double room*) habitación *f* doble
3 (*Cine*) (= *stand-in*) doble *mf*
4 (= *lookalike*) doble *mf*
5 (*in games*) doble *m* • **throw a ~ to start** para empezar tienes que sacar un doble • **~ or quits** • **~ or nothing** doble o nada
6 doubles (*Tennis, Badminton*) dobles *mpl* • **to play ~s** jugar dobles • **a game of mixed/ ladies' ~s** un partido de dobles mixtos/ femininos
7 (*Sport*) (= *double victory*) • **the ~** el doblete
8 • **at the ~*** (= *very quickly*) a la carrera, corriendo • **they ate their food at the ~** comieron a la carrera, comieron corriendo • **get into bed, at the ~!** ¡a la cama corriendo!
9 • **on the ~*** (= *immediately*) ya mismo • **we'd better go on the ~** mejor vamos ya mismo
(VT) **1** (= *increase twofold*) [+ *money, quantity, profits*] doblar, duplicar; [+ *price, salary*] doblar; [+ *efforts*] redoblar • **think of a number and ~ it** piensa en un número y multiplícalo por dos *or* duplícalo • **he ~d my offer** ofreció el doble que yo • **he has already ~d his birth weight** ya pesa el doble de lo que pesaba al nacer
2 (*also* **double over**) (= *fold*) [+ *paper, blanket*] doblar
3 (*Theat*) • **he ~s the parts of courtier and hangman** hace dos papeles, el de cortesano y el de verdugo • **he's doubling the part of Kennedy for Steve Newman** es el doble de Steve Newman en el papel de Kennedy
4 (*in card games*) doblar • **to ~ one's stake** doblar la apuesta • **I'll ~ you!** ¡te doblo la apuesta!
5 (= *circumnavigate*) [+ *headland*] doblar
(VI) **1** (= *become twice as great*) [*quantity*] doblarse, duplicarse • **these figures have ~d since last year** estas cifras se han duplicado desde el año pasado
2 (= *have two functions*) • **to ~ as sth** hacer las veces de algo • **the sofa ~s as a spare bed** el sofá hace las veces de cama para los invitados
3 (*Theat*) • **to ~ for sb** doblar a algn • **he ~d as Hamlet's father** también hizo el papel del padre de Hamlet
4 (= *change direction suddenly*) girar sobre sí mismo
5 (*Bridge*) doblar
(CPD) ▸ **double act** (= *pair of performers*) pareja *f*; (= *performance*) dúo *m* • **to do a ~ act** formar un dúo ▸ **double agent** doble agente *mf* ▸ **double bar** (*Mus*) barra *f* doble ▸ **double bass** contrabajo *m* ▸ **double bassoon** contrafagot *m* ▸ **double bed** cama *f* de matrimonio ▸ **double bedroom** habitación *f* doble ▸ **double bend** (*Aut*) curva *f* en S ▸ **double bill** (*Cine*) programa *m* doble ▸ **double bind** dilema *m* sin solución, callejón *m* sin salida* ▸ **double bluff** • **perhaps, he thought, it's a kind of ~ bluff** quizás, pensó, intenta hacerme creer que está mintiendo pero en realidad dice la verdad ▸ **double boiler** (*US*) cazos *mpl* para hervir al baño María ▸ **double booking** (= *booking for two*) reserva *f* para dos; (= *over-booking*) doble reserva *f* ▸ **double chin** papada *f* ▸ **double cream** (*Brit*) crema *f* doble, nata *f* (para montar) (*Sp*), doble crema *f* (*Mex*) ▸ **double dealer** traidor(a) *m/f* ▸ **double density disk** (*Comput*) disco *m* de doble densidad ▸ **double doors** puerta *fsing* de dos hojas ▸ **double Dutch*** (*Brit*) chino* *m* • **it's ~ Dutch to me** para mí es chino* • **to talk ~ Dutch*** hablar en chino* ▸ **double eagle** doble eagle *m* ▸ **double entry** partida *f* doble ▸ **double entry book-keeping** contabilidad *f* por partida doble ▸ **double exposure** (*Phot*) doble exposición *f* ▸ **double fault** (*Tennis*) falta *f* doble; ▷ **double-fault** ▸ **double feature** (*Cine*) sesión *f* doble, programa *m* doble ▸ **double figures** • **to be into ~ figures** rebasar la decena, pasar de diez • **only three batsmen reached ~ figures** solo tres bateadores marcaron más de diez tantos ▸ **double first** (*Univ*) *título universitario británico con nota de sobresaliente en dos especialidades* ▸ **double flat** (*Mus*) doble bemol *m* ▸ **double garage** garaje *m* doble ▸ **double glazing** doble acristalamiento *m*, doble ventana *f* ▸ **double helix** (*Chem*) hélice *f* doble ▸ **double indemnity** (*US*) (*Insurance*) doble indemnización *f* ▸ **double indemnity coverage** (*US*) seguro *m* de doble indemnización ▸ **double jeopardy** (*US*) (*Jur*) procesamiento *m* por segunda vez ▸ **double knitting** lana *f* de doble hebra ▸ **double knot** nudo *m* doble ▸ **double lock** cerradura *f* doble; ▷ **double-lock** ▸ **double marking** doble corrección *f* ▸ **double meaning** doble sentido *m* ▸ **double negative** (*Gram*) doble negación *f* (*construcción gramatical, incorrecta en inglés, en la que se utilizan dos formas negativas*) ▸ **double pay** paga *f* doble • **everybody gets ~ pay on Sundays** todo el mundo recibe paga doble los domingos ▸ **double pneumonia** pulmonía *f* doble ▸ **double room** habitación *f* doble ▸ **double saucepan** (*Brit*) cazos *mpl* para hervir al baño María ▸ **double sharp** (*Mus*) doble sostenido *m* ▸ **double spacing** • **in ~ spacing** a doble espacio ▸ **double standard** • **to have ~ standards** • **have a ~ standard** aplicar una regla para unos y otra para otros ▸ **double star** estrella *f* binaria ▸ **double stopping** doble cuerda *f* ▸ **double take** • **to do a ~ take** (= *look twice*) tener que mirar dos veces • **when I told him the news, he did a ~ take** cuando le di la noticia no daba crédito a sus oídos *or* no se lo creía ▸ **double talk** lenguaje *m* con doble sentido ▸ **double time** (*Ind, Comm*) tarifa *f* doble • **we earn ~ time on Sundays** los domingos nos pagan el doble; (*Mil*) • **in ~ time** a paso ligero ▸ **double track** vía *f* doble ▸ **double vision** doble visión *f*, diplopía *f* ▸ **double wedding** boda *f* doble ▸ **double whammy*** palo *m* doble* ▸ **double white lines** líneas *fpl* blancas continuas ▸ **double windows** ventanas *fpl* dobles ▸ **double yellow lines** (*Aut*) *línea doble amarilla de prohibido aparcar*, ≈ línea *fsing* amarilla continua

▸ **double back** (VI + ADV) [*person*] volver sobre sus pasos • **to ~ back on itself** [*road*] volver sobre sí mismo
(VT + ADV) [+ *blanket*] doblar

▸ **double over** (VT + ADV) doblar

▸ **double up** (VT + ADV) • **to be ~d up with laughter** troncharse de risa • **to be ~d up with pain** doblarse de dolor
(VI + ADV) **1** (= *bend over*) doblarse • **he ~d up with laughter** se partió de la risa
2 (= *share bedroom*) compartir (una habitación)

double-acting [,dʌbl'æktɪŋ] (ADJ) de doble acción

double-barrelled ['dʌbl,bærəld] ADJ **1** [*gun*] de dos cañones
2 (*Brit*) [*surname*] compuesto
double-blind ['dʌbl,blaɪnd] ADJ
• **double-blind experiment** *experimento en el que ni el analizador ni el sujeto conoce las características* • **double-blind method** *método según el cual ni el analizador ni el sujeto conoce las características del producto*
double-book [,dʌbl'bʊk] VT • **I was double-booked** (*in diary of engagements*) tenía dos compromisos para la misma hora • **we found the room had been double-booked** encontramos que habían reservado la habitación para dos parejas distintas
double-breasted ['dʌbl'brestɪd] ADJ cruzado, con botonadura doble
double-check ['dʌbl'tʃek] VT volver a comprobar, comprobar de nuevo • **to double-check that ...** volver a comprobar que ..., asegurarse bien de que ...
VI volver a comprobar, asegurarse bien • **to double-check with sb** confirmarlo con algn
N doble comprobación *f*, revisión *f*
double-click ['dʌbl,klɪk] (*Comput*) VI hacer doble click (**on** en)
VT hacer doble click en
double-cross* ['dʌbl'krɒs] N engaño *m*, trampa *f*, traición *f*
VT traicionar, engañar
double-date [,dʌbl'deɪt] VT engañar con otro/otra
VI salir dos parejas
double-dealing ['dʌbl'di:lɪŋ] N trato *m* doble, juego *m* doble, duplicidad *f*
double-decker ['dʌbl'dekə^r] N (*also* **double-decker bus**) autobús *m* de dos pisos
CPD ▸ **double-decker sandwich** sandwich *m* club
double-declutch [,dʌbldi:'klʌtʃ] VI (*Aut*) hacer un doble desembrague
double-digit [,dʌbl'dɪdʒɪt] ADJ de dos dígitos
double-edged ['dʌbl'edʒd] ADJ [*remark*] con segundas • IDIOM: • **it's a double-edged sword** es un arma de doble filo
double entendre ['du:blɑ̃:n'tɑ̃:ndr] N equívoco *m*, frase *f* ambigua
double-faced [,dʌbl'feɪst] ADJ [*material*] reversible; (*pej*) [*person*] de dos caras
double-fault [,dʌbl'fɔ:lt] VI (*Tennis*) cometer doble falta; ▹ **double fault**
double-figure [,dʌbl'fɪgə^r] ADJ = **double-digit**
double-glaze [,dʌbl'gleɪz] VT • **to double-glaze a window** termoaislar una ventana
double-glazed [,dʌbl'gleɪzd] ADJ con doble acristalamiento
double-header ['dʌbl,hedə^r] N (*esp US*) (*Sport*) *dos encuentros consecutivos entre los mismos o diferentes equipos*
double-jointed ['dʌbl'dʒɔɪntɪd] ADJ con articulaciones muy flexibles
double-lock [,dʌbl'lɒk] VT cerrar con dos vueltas; ▹ **double lock**
double-page spread [,dʌblpeɪdʒ'spred] N doble página *f*
double-park [,dʌbl'pɑ:k] VI (*Aut*) aparcar en doble fila, estacionar en doble fila
double-parking [,dʌbl'pɑ:kɪŋ] N (*Aut*) aparcamiento *m* en doble fila, estacionamiento *m* en doble fila
double-quick [,dʌbl'kwɪk] ADV rapidísimamente, en un santiamén; (*Mil*) a paso ligero
ADJ • **in double-quick time** rapidísimamente, en un santiamén
double-sided disk [,dʌbl,saɪdɪd'dɪsk] N disco *m* de dos caras
double-space [,dʌbl'speɪs] VT escribir a doble espacio
double-spaced ['dʌbl'speɪst] ADV a doble espacio
doublespeak ['dʌbl'spi:k] N (*pej*) doble lenguaje *m*
doublet ['dʌblɪt] N **1**†† (= *garment*) jubón *m*
2 (*Ling*) doblete *m*
doublethink ['dʌblθɪŋk] N razonamiento *m* contradictorio • **a piece of ~** una contradicción en sí misma
doubleton ['dʌbltən] N dubletón *m*
doubling ['dʌblɪŋ] N [*of number*] multiplicación *f* por dos; [*of letter*] duplicación *f*
doubly ['dʌblɪ] ADV **1** (= *twice as*) [*important, difficult, dangerous*] doblemente • **we are ~ determined to win this time** esta vez estamos doblemente *or* mucho más empeñados en ganar • **you'll have to be ~ careful from now on** a partir de ahora tienes que tener el doble de cuidado • **since then she has been ~ careful to lock the door** desde entonces se cuida todavía más de cerrar la puerta con llave • **he has to work ~ hard to make up for lost time** tiene que trabajar el doble para recuperar el tiempo perdido • **to make ~ sure** asegurarse muy bien
2 (= *in two ways*) por partida doble • **Fran was ~ mistaken** Fran estaba equivocada por partida doble • **it's a delicious dessert, ~ so when you use cream instead of milk** es un postre riquísimo, y el doble de rico si usas nata en vez de leche
doubt [daʊt] N (= *uncertainty, qualm*) duda *f* • **there is some ~ about it** sobre esto existen dudas • **beyond ~** fuera de duda • **beyond all reasonable ~** más allá de toda duda • **to cast ~ on** poner en duda • **to clear up sb's ~s** sacar a algn de dudas • **to have one's ~s about sth** tener sus dudas acerca de algo • **to be in ~** [*person*] tener dudas, dudar; [*sb's honesty etc*] ser dudoso • **she was in ~ whether to ...** dudaba si ... • **the matter is still in some ~** el caso sigue siendo dudoso • **if** *or* **when in ~** en caso de duda • **no ~!** ¡sin duda! • **no ~ he will come** seguro que viene • **there is no ~ of that** de eso no cabe duda • **there is no ~ that** es indudable que, no cabe duda de que • **I have no ~ that it is true** no me cabe duda de que es verdad • **let there be no ~ about it** que nadie dude de esto • **the marks left no ~ about how he died** las señales no dejaban lugar a dudas sobre cómo murió • **to throw ~ on** poner en duda • **without (a) ~** sin duda (alguna); ▹ **plant**
VT **1** [+ *truth of statement etc*] dudar • **I ~ it very much** lo dudo mucho • **I never ~ed you** nunca tuve dudas acerca de ti • **to ~ sb's loyalty** dudar de la lealtad de algn
2 (= *be uncertain*) • **to ~ whether** *or* **if** dudar si • **I don't ~ that he will come** no dudo que vaya a venir
VI dudar • **~ing Thomas** (*fig*) incrédulo/a *m/f*, escéptico/a *m/f*
doubter ['daʊtə^r] N escéptico/a *m/f*
doubtful ['daʊtfʊl] ADJ **1** (= *uncertain*) [*result, success, future*] incierto, dudoso
2 (= *unconvinced*) [*expression*] de duda • **"all right then," he said in a ~ tone** —bueno, vale —dijo con un tono de duda en la voz • **Jeremy nodded his head, but he still looked ~** Jeremy asintió pero no parecía aún convencido • **I'm a bit ~** no estoy convencido del todo • **to be ~ that** dudar que (+ *subjun*) • **he was ~ that he would be able to lift it** dudaba que pudiera levantarlo • **I am ~ whether we should accept the offer** dudo si deberíamos aceptar la oferta o no • **to be ~ about sth** tener dudas sobre algo
3 (= *unlikely*) dudoso • **a reconciliation between the two sides seems ~** una reconciliación entre las dos partes parece dudosa • **it is ~ that they will reach an agreement** es dudoso *or* poco probable que lleguen a un acuerdo • **it is ~ that there will be any survivors** se duda *or* es poco probable que haya sobrevivientes • **for a moment it seemed ~ that he would move at all** por un momento pareció que no se iba a mover en absoluto • **it is ~ whether** es poco probable que (+ *subjun*) • **~ starter** (*Sport*) participante *mf* dudoso
4 (= *questionable*) [*taste, reputation, quality, value*] dudoso • **in ~ taste** de dudoso gusto • **the weather looks a bit ~** el tiempo no parece muy estable
doubtfully ['daʊtfəlɪ] ADV **1** (= *unconvincedly*) sin estar convencido • **Ralph looked at him ~** Ralph lo miró muy poco convencido • **"I suppose not," he said ~** —supongo que no —dijo él poco convencido *or* sin demasiado convencimiento
2 (= *questionably*) dudosamente • **the painting is ~ ascribed to Picasso** el cuadro se ha atribuído dudosamente a Picasso
doubtfulness ['daʊtfʊlnɪs] N
1 (= *uncertainty*) incertidumbre *f*, dudas *fpl*; (= *hesitation*) vacilación *f*, duda *f* • **there is some ~ as to whether he did indeed live there** existe cierta incertidumbre *or* existen algunas dudas sobre si realmente vivió ahí
2 (= *questionable quality*) carácter *m* dudoso
doubtless ['daʊtlɪs] ADV sin duda, seguramente
douceur [du:'sɜ:^r] N (*frm*) (= *gift, tip etc*) gratificación *f*
douche [du:ʃ] N ducha *f*; (*Med*) jeringa *f*
VT duchar
VI ducharse
dough [dəʊ] N **1** (*Culin*) masa *f*, pasta *f*
2‡ (= *money*) guita* *f*, pasta *f* (*Sp**), plata *f* (*LAm**), lana *f* (*LAm**)
doughboy* ['dəʊbɔɪ] N (*US*) soldado *m* de infantería; (*Hist*) *soldado de la Primera Guerra Mundial*
doughnut ['dəʊnʌt] N donut® *m*, dona *f* (*LAm*)
doughty ['daʊtɪ] ADJ (COMPAR: **doughtier**, SUPERL: **doughtiest**) [*person*] valiente, esforzado; [*deed*] hazañoso
doughy ['dəʊɪ] ADJ pastoso
dour ['dʊə^r] ADJ (= *grim*) adusto, arisco • **a ~ Scot** un escocés adusto *or* arisco • **a ~ struggle** una batalla muy reñida
dourly [dʊəlɪ] ADV adustamente, ariscamente
Douro ['dʊərəʊ] N Duero *m*
douse [daʊs] VT (*with water*) mojar (**with** con); [+ *flames, light*] apagar
dove¹ [dʌv] N (*Orn*) paloma *f*; (*Pol*) (= *person opposed to war*) pacifista *mf*
dove² [dəʊv] (*US*) PT *of* **dive**
dovecote ['dʌvkɒt] N palomar *m*
dove-grey [,dʌv'greɪ] ADJ gris paloma
Dover ['dəʊvə^r] N Dover *m*
CPD ▸ **Dover sole** lenguado *m*
dovetail ['dʌvteɪl] N (*also* **dovetail joint**) cola *f* de milano
VT **1** (*Carpentry*) ensamblar a cola de milano
2 (*fig*) (= *fit*) encajar; (= *link*) enlazar
VI (*fig*) encajar, enlazar • **to ~ with** encajar perfectamente con
dovish ['dʌvɪʃ] ADJ (*Pol*) blando
dowager ['daʊədʒə^r] N viuda *f* de un noble
CPD ▸ **dowager duchess** duquesa *f* viuda

dowdiness ['daʊdɪnɪs] N falta *f* de elegancia
dowdy ['daʊdɪ] ADJ (COMPAR: **dowdier**, SUPERL: **dowdiest**) [*person*] anticuado, trasnochado; [*clothes*] trasnochado, pasado de moda
dowel ['daʊəl] N clavija *f*
Dow Jones average [ˌdaʊdʒəʊnz'ævərɪdʒ], **Dow Jones index** [ˌdaʊdʒəʊnz'ɪndeks] N (*US*) (*Econ*) índice *m* Dow-Jones
down[1] [daʊn]

*When **down** is an element in a phrasal verb, eg **back down, glance down, play down**, look up the verb.*

ADV **1** (*physical movement*) abajo, hacia abajo; (= *to the ground*) a tierra • **there was snow all the way ~ to London** estuvo nevando todo el camino hasta Londres • **to fall ~** caerse • **I ran all the way ~** bajé toda la distancia corriendo
2 (*static position*) abajo; (= *on the ground*) por tierra, en tierra • **to be ~** (*Aer*) haber aterrizado, estar en tierra; [*person*] haber caído, estar en tierra • **I'll be ~ in a minute** ahora bajo • **he isn't ~ yet** (*eg for breakfast*) todavía no ha bajado • **the blinds are ~** están bajadas las persianas • **the sun is ~** el sol se ha puesto • **~ below** allá abajo • **~ by the river** abajo en la ribera • **~ here** aquí (abajo) • **~ on the shore** abajo en la playa • **~ there** allí (abajo)
3 (*Geog*) • **he came ~ from Glasgow to London** ha bajado *or* venido de Glasgow a Londres • **to be ~ from college** haber terminado el curso universitario • **he lives ~ South** vive en el sur • **~ under** (*Brit**) (= *in Australia*) en Australia; (= *in New Zealand*) en Nueva Zelanda • **to go ~ under** (*Brit**) (= *to Australia*) ir a Australia; (= *to New Zealand*) ir a Nueva Zelanda
4 (*in writing*) • **write this ~** apunta esto • **you're ~ for the next race** estás inscrito para la próxima carrera • **you're ~ for Tuesday** te hemos apuntado para el martes
5 (*in volume, degree, status*) • **the tyres are ~** los neumáticos están desinflados • **his temperature is ~** le ha bajado la temperatura • **the price of meat is ~** ha bajado el precio de la carne • **England are two goals ~** Inglaterra está perdiendo por dos tantos • **I'm £20 ~** he perdido 20 libras • **I'm ~ to my last cigarette** me queda un cigarrillo nada más
6 (*indicating a series or succession*) • **from the year 1600 ~ to the present day** desde el año 1600 hasta el presente • **from the biggest ~ to the smallest** desde el más grande hasta el más pequeño
7 (= *ill*) • **I've been ~ with flu** he estado con gripe
8 • **~ to: it's ~ to him** (= *due to, up to*) le toca a él, le incumbe a él • **it's all ~ to us now** ahora nosotros somos los únicos responsables
9 (*as deposit*) • **to pay £50 ~** pagar un depósito de 50 libras, hacer un desembolso inicial de 50 libras
10 (*in exclamations*) • **down!** ¡abajo!; (*to dog*) ¡quieto! • **~ with traitors!** ¡abajo los traidores!
11 (= *completed etc*) • **one ~, five to go** uno en el bote y quedan cinco
12 (*esp US*) • **to be ~ on sb** tener manía *or* inquina a algn*
PREP **1** (*indicating movement*) • **he went ~ the hill** fue cuesta abajo • **to go ~ the road** ir calle abajo • **he's gone ~ the pub*** se ha ido al bar • **looking ~ this road, you can see ...** mirando carretera abajo, se ve ... • **he ran his finger ~ the list** pasó el dedo por la lista • **the rain was running ~ the trunk** la lluvia corría por el tronco
2 (= *at a lower point on*) • **he lives ~ the street (from us)** vive en esta calle, más abajo de nosotros • **~ the ages** a través de los siglos • **face ~** boca abajo • **~ river** río abajo (**from** de)
ADJ **1** (= *depressed*) deprimido
2 (= *not functioning*) • **the computer is ~** el ordenador no funciona • **the power lines are ~** los cables de alta tensión están cortados • **the telephone lines are ~** las líneas de teléfono están cortadas
3 (*Brit*) [*train, line*] de bajada
VT* **1** [+ *food*] devorar; [+ *drink*] beberse (de un trago), tragarse • **he ~ed a pint of beer** tragó una pinta de cerveza
2 [+ *opponent*] tirar al suelo, echar al suelo; [+ *plane*] derribar, abatir • IDIOM: • **to ~ tools** (*Brit*) declararse en huelga
N • **to have a ~ on sb** (*Brit**) tenerle manía *or* inquina a algn*
CPD ▸ **down bow** (*Mus*) descenso *m* de arco ▸ **down cycle** (*Econ*) ciclo *m* de caída ▸ **down payment** (*Econ*) (= *initial payment*) entrada *f*; (= *deposit*) desembolso *m* inicial
down[2] [daʊn] N (*on bird*) plumón *m*, flojel *m*; (*on face*) bozo *m*; (*on body*) vello *m*; (*on fruit*) pelusa *f*; (*Bot*) vilano *m*
down[3] [daʊn] N (*Geog*) colina *f* • **the Downs** (*Brit*) las Downs (*colinas del sur de Inglaterra*)
down-and-out ['daʊnən,aʊt] N (= *tramp*) indigente *mf*, vagabundo/a *m/f*
ADJ • **to be down-and-out** no tener donde caerse muerto, estar sin un cuarto
down-at-heel ['daʊnət'hiːl] ADJ [*person, appearance*] desastrado; [*bar, café*] de mala muerte; [*shoes*] gastado
downbeat ['daʊn,biːt] ADJ (= *gloomy*) pesimista, deprimido; (= *unemphatic*) [*tone, statement*] moderado
N (*Mus*) compás *m* acentuado
downcast ['daʊnkɑːst] ADJ (= *sad*) abatido; [*eyes*] bajo, alicaído
downer* ['daʊnə^r] N **1** (= *tranquilizer*) tranquilizante *m*
2 (= *depressing experience*) experiencia *f* deprimente
downfall ['daʊnfɔːl] N **1** (= *collapse*) caída *f*
2 (= *ruin*) perdición *f*, ruina *f* • **it will be his ~** será su perdición
downgrade ['daʊngreɪd] N • **to be on the ~** ir cuesta abajo, estar en plena decadencia
VT [daʊn'greɪd] [+ *job, hotel*] bajar de categoría • **he's been ~d to assistant manager** le han bajado a ayudante de dirección
downhearted ['daʊn'hɑːtɪd] ADJ descorazonado • **don't be ~** no te dejes desanimar
downhill ['daʊn'hɪl] ADV cuesta abajo • **to go ~** [*road*] bajar; [*car*] ir cuesta abajo; (*fig*) [*person*] ir cuesta abajo; [*industry*] estar en declive, estar de capa caída; [*company*] ir de mal en peor
ADJ en pendiente; [*skiing*] de descenso • **it was ~ all the way after that** (*fig*) (= *got easier*) a partir de entonces la cosa fue más fácil; (= *got worse*) a partir de entonces la cosa fue de mal en peor
CPD ▸ **downhill race** descenso *m*
down-home* [,daʊn'həʊm] ADJ (*US*) (= *from the South*) del sur; (= *narrow-minded*) cerrado de miras
Downing Street ['daʊnɪŋ,striːt] N Downing Street (*calle de Londres en que están las residencias oficiales del ministro de Hacienda y del primer ministro británicos*)

DOWNING STREET
Downing Street es la calle de Londres, cerrada al público, donde se encuentran las residencias oficiales del Primer Ministro (**Prime Minister**) y del Ministro de Economía y Hacienda (**Chancellor of the Exchequer**), normalmente en los números 10 y 11 respectivamente. Los términos **Downing Street**, **Number Ten**, o **Ten Downing Street** se usan a menudo en los medios de comunicación para referirse al Primer Ministro o al Gobierno.

down-in-the-mouth ['daʊnɪnðə'maʊθ] ADJ decaído, deprimido
download [ˌdaʊn'ləʊd] VT descargar
N descarga *f*
downloadable ['daʊn,ləʊdəbl] ADJ (*Comput*) descargable
downloading [ˌdaʊn'ləʊdɪŋ] N descarga *f*
downmarket [ˌdaʊn'mɑːkɪt] ADJ [*product*] para el sector popular del mercado
ADV • **to go ~** buscar clientela en el sector popular
downpipe ['daʊn,paɪp] N (*Brit*) canal *f* bajante, bajante *f or m*
downplay ['daʊn'pleɪ] VT quitar importancia a, restar importancia a
downpour ['daʊnpɔː^r] N aguacero *m*, chaparrón *m*, chubasco *m* (*LAm*)
downright ['daʊnraɪt] ADJ [*nonsense, lie*] patente, manifiesto; [*refusal*] categórico
ADV [*rude, angry*] realmente
downriver, down-river [ˌdaʊn'rɪvə^r] ADV río abajo • **to be ~ from** estar río abajo de • **to move ~** bajar por el río
ADJ (= *downstream*) [*city, building*] río abajo
downscale* VT ['daʊnskeɪl] reducir el tamaño de
VI ['daʊnskeɪl] (= *cut costs*) cortar gastos
ADJ [daʊn'skeɪl] popular
downshift ['daʊnʃɪft] VI **1** (*to simpler lifestyle*) reducir el ritmo
2 (*US*) (= *change gear*) reducir
downside ['daʊnsaɪd] N (*fig*) pega *f*, desventaja *f*, lo malo (**of** de)
downsize [ˌdaʊn'saɪz] VT hacer recortes de personal *or* (*Sp*) plantilla en
VI reducir (el) personal, reducir (la) plantilla (*Sp*)
downsizing ['daʊnsaɪzɪŋ] N [*of company, industry*] recorte *m* de personal, recorte *m* de plantillas (*Sp*), reajuste *m* de plantillas (*Sp*)
downspout ['daʊnspaʊt] N (*US*) tubo *m* de desagüe, cañería *f*
Down's Syndrome ['daʊnz,sɪndrəʊm] N síndrome *m* de Down
downstage [ˌdaʊn'steɪdʒ] ADV (= *towards the front of the stage*) hacia la parte delantera del escenario; (= *at the front of the stage*) en la parte delantera del escenario
downstairs ['daʊn'stɛəz] ADJ (= *on the ground floor*) de la planta baja; (= *on the floor underneath*) del piso de abajo • **a ~ window** una ventana de la planta baja
ADV en la planta baja, abajo • **to fall ~** caer por las escaleras • **to come/go ~** bajar la escalera
N • **the ~** [*of building*] la planta baja
downstate ['daʊn,steɪt] (*US*) N campo *m*, sur *m* del estado
ADJ del campo, del sur del estado
ADV [*be*] en el campo, en el sur; [*go*] al campo, hacia el sur
downstream ['daʊn'striːm] ADV río abajo (**from** de) • **to go ~** ir río abajo • **to swim ~** nadar con la corriente • **a town ~ from Soria** una ciudad pasando Soria río abajo • **about 5km ~ from Zamora** a unos 5km de Zamora

río abajo

downstroke ['daʊnstrəʊk] N **1** (*with pen*) pierna *f*; (*by child when learning*) palote *m*
2 (*Mech*) carrera *f* descendente

downswept ['daʊnswept] ADJ [*wings*] con caída posterior

downswing ['daʊnswɪŋ] N (*fig*) recesión *f*, caída *f*

downtime ['daʊn,taɪm] N tiempo *m* de inactividad, tiempo *m* muerto

down-to-earth ['daʊntʊ'ɜ:θ] ADJ (= *natural*) [*person*] natural, llano; (= *practical*) [*person, policy, outlook*] práctico, realista

downtown ['daʊn'taʊn] (*US*) ADV al centro
ADJ • **~ San Francisco** el centro de San Francisco

downtrend ['daʊn,trend] N (*Econ*) tendencia *f* a la baja • **in** *or* **on a ~** en baja

downtrodden ['daʊn,trɒdn] ADJ [*person*] oprimido, pisoteado

downturn ['daʊntɜ:n] N (*in economy*) deterioro *m*; (*in sales, production*) disminución *f*

downward ['daʊnwəd] ADJ [*curve, movement*] descendente; [*slope*] hacia abajo; [*tendency*] a la baja
ADV [*go, look*] hacia abajo • **from the President ~** todos, incluso el Presidente

downwards ['daʊnwədz] ADV (*esp Brit*) = **downward**

downwind ['daʊn,wɪnd] ADV a favor del viento

downy ['daʊnɪ] ADJ velloso; (= *and soft*) blando, suave

dowry ['daʊrɪ] N dote *f*

dowse [daʊz] VT = **douse**

dowser ['daʊzəʳ] N zahorí *mf*

doyen ['dɔɪən] N decano *m*

doyenne ['dɔɪen] N decana *f*

doz. ABBR (= **dozen**) doc.

doze [dəʊz] N sueñecito *m*, siestecita *f* • **to have a ~** (*after meal*) echar una siestecita
VI dormitar
▸ **doze off** VI + ADV dormirse

dozen ['dʌzn] N docena *f* • **80p a ~** 80 peniques la docena • **a ~ eggs** una docena de huevos • **they arrived in their ~s** *or* **by the ~** llegaban docenas de ellos • **~s of times/ people** cantidad *f* de veces/gente

dozily ['dəʊzɪlɪ] ADV amodorradamente

doziness ['dəʊzɪnɪs] N modorra *f*

dozy ['dəʊzɪ] ADJ (COMPAR: **dozier**, SUPERL: **doziest**) **1** (= *sleepy*) amodorrado, soñoliento
2 (*Brit**) (= *stupid*) corto*, lerdo*

DP N ABBR = **data processing**

DPh, DPhil [,di:'fɪl] N ABBR (= **Doctor of Philosophy**) ▹ DEGREE

d.p.i. ABBR (= **dots per inch**) p.p.p.

DPM N ABBR = **Diploma in Psychological Medicine**

DPP N ABBR (*Brit*) (*Jur*) = **Director of Public Prosecutions**

DPT N ABBR (= **diphtheria, pertussis, tetanus**) vacuna *f* trivalente

dpt ABBR (= **department**) dto

DPW N ABBR (*US*) = **Department of Public Works**

DQ ABBR (*Athletics*) = **Disqualified**

Dr ABBR **1** (*Med*) (= **Doctor**) Dr(a)
2 (*Econ*) = **debtor**
3 (= *street*) = **Drive**

dr ABBR **1** = **debtor**
2 = **dram**
3 = **drachma**

drab [dræb] ADJ (COMPAR: **drabber**, SUPERL: **drabbest**) [*colour*] apagado; [*life*] monótono, gris
N **1** (= *fabric*) *tela de color marrón o gris apagado*
2 ▹ **dribs**

drably ['dræblɪ] ADV [*dressed*] anodinamente; [*painted*] sin gracia

drabness ['dræbnɪs] N [*of life*] monotonía *f*; [*of clothes, colours*] lo soso

drachm [dræm] N **1** (*Pharm*) (= *measure*) dracma *f*
2 = **drachma**

drachma ['drækmə] N (PL: **drachmas** *or* **drachmae** ['drækmi:]) dracma *m or f*

draconian [drə'kəʊnɪən] ADJ draconiano, severo, riguroso

Dracula ['drækjʊlə] N Drácula *m*

draft [drɑ:ft] N **1** (= *outline*) (*in writing*) borrador *m*; (= *drawing*) boceto *m*
2 (*Mil*) (= *detachment*) destacamento *m*; (= *reinforcements*) refuerzos *mpl* • **the ~** (*US*) (*Mil*) (= *conscription*) la llamada a filas, el servicio militar
3 (*Comm*) (*also* **banker's draft**) letra *f* de cambio, giro *m*
4 (*Comput*) borrador *m*
5 (*US*) = **draught**
VT **1** (*also* **draft out**) [+ *document*] (= *write*) redactar; [+ *first attempt*] hacer un borrador de; [+ *scheme*] elaborar, trazar
2 (*Mil*) (*for specific duty*) destacar; (= *send*) mandar (**to** a); (*US*) (*Mil*) (= *conscript*) reclutar, llamar al servicio militar; (*fig*) forzar, obligar
CPD ▸ **draft agreement** proyecto *m* de (un) acuerdo ▸ **draft bill** anteproyecto *m* de ley ▸ **draft board** (*US*) (*Mil*) junta *f* de reclutamiento ▸ **draft card** (*US*) (*Mil*) cartilla *f* militar ▸ **draft dodger** (*US*) (*Mil*) prófugo *m* ▸ **draft excluder** (*US*) burlete *m* ▸ **draft law** = **draft bill** ▸ **draft horse** (*US*) caballo *m* de tiro ▸ **draft letter** borrador *m* de carta; (*more formal*) proyecto *m* de carta ▸ **draft version** versión *f* preliminar
▸ **draft in** VT + ADV arrastrar de un lado a otro

drafty ['drɑ:ftɪ] ADJ (*US*) = **draughty**

drag [dræg] VT arrastrar
VI (= *go very slowly*) [*time*] pasar lentamente
N **1** * (= *boring thing*) lata* *f*, rollo *m* (*Sp**)
2 (*women's clothes*) **a man in ~** un hombre vestido de mujer
CPD ▸ **drag and drop** (*Comput*) arrastrar y soltar *m*
▸ **drag along** VT + ADV [+ *person*] arrastrar
▸ **drag around** VT + ADV arrastrar de un lado a otro
▸ **drag away** VT + ADV **1** (*lit*) [+ *person*] llevar a la fuerza
2 (*fig*) • **I'm sorry to ~ you away from your meal** siento interrumpirte la comida, siento hacerte levantar de la mesa • **you can never ~ him away from the television** no hay forma de apartarlo del televisor, no hay forma de despegarlo del televisor*
▸ **drag down** VT + ADV • **you may have made a terrible mistake but you're not going to ~ me down with you** habrás cometido un grave error pero no voy a cargar con las consecuencias yo también • **he could ~ down the entire party in this election** podría hacer fracasar a todo el partido en estas elecciones
▸ **drag in** VT + ADV [+ *subject*] sacar a relucir; ▹ **cat**
▸ **drag on** VI + ADV [*meeting, conversation*] alargarse; [*film, play*] hacerse pesadísimo; [*speech*] hacerse interminable • **the case could ~ on for months** el caso podría alargarse durante meses
▸ **drag out** VT + ADV [+ *process*] alargar
▸ **drag up** VT + ADV **1** [+ *subject*] • **do you have to ~ that up again?** ¿otra vez tienes que sacar a relucir eso? • **this ~ged up painful memories for her** esto despertó en ella recuerdos dolorosos
2 (*Brit**) (= *bring up*) [+ *person*] • **where were you ~ged up?** ¿dónde te han enseñado eso?, ¿dónde has aprendido esos modales?

draglift ['dræglɪft] N (*Ski*) arrastre *m*, remonte *m*

dragnet ['drægnet] N **1** (= *net*) red *f* de arrastre, red *f* barredera
2 (*fig*) (*by police*) operación *f* policial de captura, emboscada *f*
3 (*US*) (*Pol*) dragadora *f*

dragon ['drægən] N **1** (*Myth*) dragón *m*
2* (= *woman*) bruja *f*

dragonfly ['drægənflaɪ] N libélula *f*, caballito *m* del diablo

dragoon [drə'gu:n] N (*Mil*) dragón *m*
VT • **to ~ sb into (doing) sth** obligar *or* forzar a algn a (hacer) algo

dragster ['drægstəʳ] N coche *m* trucado

drain [dreɪn] N **1** (= *outlet*) (*in house*) desagüe *m*; (*in street*) boca *f* de alcantarilla, sumidero *m*; (*Agr*) zanja *f* de drenaje • **the ~s** (= *sewage system*) el alcantarillado *msing*
• IDIOMS: • **to throw one's money down the ~*** tirar el dinero (por la ventana) • **to go down the ~*** perderse, echarse a perder; ▹ **laugh**
2 (*fig*) (= *source of loss*) • **to be a ~ on** [+ *energies, resources*] consumir, agotar • **they are a great ~ on our reserves** ellos se llevan gran parte de nuestras reservas • **it has been a great ~ on her** la ha agotado
VT **1** (*Agr*) [+ *land, marshes, lake*] drenar, desecar; [+ *vegetables, last drops*] escurrir; [+ *glass, radiator etc*] vaciar; (*Med*) [+ *wound etc*] drenar
2 (*fig*) agotar, consumir • **to feel ~ed (of energy)** sentirse agotado *or* sin fuerzas • **the country is being ~ed of wealth** al país lo están empobreciendo
VI [*washed dishes, vegetables*] escurrir; [*liquid*] desaguar; [*stream*] desembocar (**into** en)
CPD ▸ **drain rods** varas *fpl* de drenaje
▸ **drain away** VT + ADV [+ *liquid*] (*from vegetables etc*) escurrir; (*Med, Mech*) drenar
VI + ADV [*liquid*] irse; [*strength*] agotarse
▸ **drain off** VT + ADV [+ *liquid*] (*from vegetables etc*) escurrir; (*Med, Mech*) drenar
VI + ADV [*liquid*] irse

drainage ['dreɪnɪdʒ] N **1** [*of land*] (*naturally*) desagüe *m*; (*artificially*) drenaje *m*; [*of lake*] desecación *f*
2 (= *sewage system*) alcantarillado *m*
CPD ▸ **drainage area, drainage basin** (*Geol*) cuenca *f* hidrográfica ▸ **drainage channel** zanja *f* de drenaje ▸ **drainage ditch** acequia *f* de drenaje ▸ **drainage holes** (*in plant pot*) agujeros *mpl* de drenaje ▸ **drainage tube** (*Med*) tubo *m* de drenaje

drainboard ['dreɪnbɔ:d] N (*US*) = **draining board**

drainer ['dreɪnəʳ] N escurridor *m*

draining ['dreɪnɪŋ] ADJ (= *exhausting*) agotador • **emotionally ~** agotador

draining board ['dreɪnɪŋ,bɔ:d] N escurridero *m*

drainpipe ['dreɪnpaɪp] N tubo *m* de desagüe, cañería *f*
CPD ▸ **drainpipe trousers** (*Brit*) pantalones *mpl* de pitillo

Drake [dreɪk] N Draque

drake [dreɪk] N pato *m* (macho)

Dralon® ['dreɪlɒn] N Dralón® *m*

DRAM, D-RAM ['di:ræm] ABBR (*Comput*) = **dynamic random access memory**

dram [dræm] N (*Brit*) [*of drink*] trago *m*; (*Pharm*) dracma *f*

drama ['drɑ:mə] N **1** (= *dramatic art*) teatro *m*; (= *play*) obra *f* dramática, drama *m*
2 (*fig*) (= *event*) drama *m*; (= *excitement*) dramatismo *m*
CPD ▸ **drama critic** crítico/a *m/f* de teatro ▸ **drama queen*** (*pej*) peliculero/a *m/f*

• **you're such a ~ queen** eres demasiado peliculero ▸ **drama school** escuela *f* de arte dramático ▸ **drama student** estudiante *mf* de arte dramático

drama-doc* ['drɑːmədɒk], **drama-documentary** ['drɑːmə,dɒkjʊ'mentərɪ] N docudrama *m*

dramatic [drə'mætɪk] ADJ **1** (= *marked*) [*increase, rise, decline*] espectacular; [*change*] radical, drástico; [*improvement*] espectacular, impresionante; [*effect*] espectacular, dramático
2 (= *exciting*) [*entrance*] espectacular, teatral; [*escape*] espectacular; [*decor*] de gran efecto, efectista • **she lifted the lid with a ~ gesture** levantó la tapa con gesto teatral
3 (*Theat*) [*works, film*] dramático, teatral • **~ art** arte *m* dramático • **the ~ arts** las artes dramáticas
CPD ▸ **dramatic society** club *m* de teatro

dramatically [drə'mætɪkəlɪ] ADV
1 (= *markedly*) [*change*] radicalmente; [*increase, improve, rise, fall*] espectacularmente • **this plan is ~ different** este plan es radicalmente diferente • **the results were ~ better** los resultados fueron notablemente mejores
2 (= *theatrically*) [*pause, sigh*] de forma teatral, con mucho teatro
3 (*Theat*) desde el punto de vista dramático • **~, it was very effective** desde el punto de vista dramático funcionó muy bien

dramatics [drə'mætɪks] NSING (*Theat*) arte *m* dramático, teatro *m* • **amateur ~** teatro *m* amateur, teatro *m* de aficionados
NPL (= *histrionics*) dramatismo *msing* • **George's ~ were beginning to irritate me** el dramatismo de George me estaba empezando a irritar

dramatis personae ['dræmətɪspɜː'səʊnaɪ] N personajes *mpl* (*del drama etc*)

dramatist ['dræmətɪst] N dramaturgo/a *m/f*

dramatization [,dræmətaɪ'zeɪʃən] N dramatización *f*

dramatize ['dræmətaɪz] VT **1** [+ *events etc*] dramatizar; (*Cine, TV*) (= *adapt*) [+ *novel*] adaptar a la televisión/al cine
2 (= *exaggerate*) dramatizar, exagerar

Drambuie® [dræm'bjuːɪ] N Drambuie® *m*

drank [dræŋk] PT *of* **drink**

drape [dreɪp] VT [+ *object*] cubrir (**with** con, de) • **~ this round your shoulders** ponte esto sobre los hombros • **he ~d a towel about himself** se cubrió con una toalla • **he ~d an arm about my shoulders** me rodeó los hombros con el brazo
NPL **drapes** (*US*) cortinas *fpl*

draper ['dreɪpəʳ] N pañero/a *m/f*

draper's ['dreɪpəz] N pañería *f*, mercería *f*

drapery ['dreɪpərɪ] N **1** (= *draper's shop*) pañería *f*, mercería *f*
2 (= *cloth for hanging*) colgaduras *fpl*; (*as merchandise*) pañería *f*, mercería *f* (*LAm*)

drastic ['dræstɪk] ADJ [*measures, change, reduction*] drástico; [*effect*] notorio • **to take ~ action** tomar medidas drásticas

drastically ['dræstɪkəlɪ] ADV drásticamente • **to be ~ reduced** sufrir una reducción drástica • **he ~ revised his ideas** cambió radicalmente *or* drásticamente de ideas • **it/things went ~ wrong** salió/las cosas salieron muy mal

drat* [dræt] EXCL • **~!** • **~ it!** ¡maldita sea!*, ¡mecachis!*

dratted* ['drætɪd] ADJ maldito*

draught, **draft** (*US*) [drɑːft] N **1** [*of air*] corriente *f* de aire; (*for fire*) tiro *m* • **there's a ~ from the window** entra corriente por la ventana • IDIOM: • **to feel the ~** pasar apuros (económicos)
2 (= *drink*) trago *m* • **he took a long ~ of cider** se echó un buen trago de sidra • **at one ~** de un trago • **on ~** de barril
3 (*Med*) dosis *f inv*
4 (*Naut*) calado *m*
CPD ▸ **draught beer** cerveza *f* de barril ▸ **draught excluder** burlete *m* ▸ **draught horse** caballo *m* de tiro

draughtboard ['drɑːftbɔːd] N (*Brit*) tablero *m* de damas

draughtiness, **draftiness** (*US*) ['drɑːftɪnɪs] N corriente *f* de aire

draught-proof, **draft-proof** (*US*) ['drɑːftpruːf] ADJ a prueba de corrientes de aire

draught-proofing, **draft-proofing** (*US*) ['drɑːft,pruːfɪŋ] N burlete *m*

draughts [drɑːfts] N (*Brit*) juego *m* de damas • **to play ~** jugar a las damas

draughtsman, **draftsman** (*US*) ['drɑːftsmən] N (PL: **draughtsmen**) **1** (*in drawing office*) delineante *mf*, dibujante *mf*
2 (*Brit*) (*in game*) dama *f*, pieza *f*

draughtsmanship, **draftsmanship** (*US*) ['drɑːftsmənʃɪp] N (= *skill*) arte *m* del delineante; (= *quality*) habilidad *f* para el dibujo

draughtswoman, **draftswoman** (*US*) ['drɑːfts,wʊmən] N (PL: **draughtswomen**) dibujante *f*

draughty, **drafty** (*US*) ['drɑːftɪ] ADJ (COMPAR: **draughtier**, SUPERL: **draughtiest**) [*room*] con mucha corriente; [*street corner*] de mucho viento

draw [drɔː] (VB: PT: **drew**, PP: **drawn**) N
1 (= *lottery*) lotería *f*; (= *picking of ticket*) sorteo *m* • **the ~ takes place on Saturday** el sorteo es el sábado • **it's the luck of the ~** es la suerte
2 (= *equal score*) empate *m*; (*Chess*) tablas *fpl* • **the match ended in a ~** el partido terminó en empate
3 (= *attraction*) atracción *f*
4 • **to beat sb to the ~** (*lit*) desenfundar más rápido que algn; (*fig*) adelantarse a algn • **to be quick on the ~** (*lit*) ser rápido en sacar la pistola; (*fig*) ser muy avispado
5 [*of chimney*] tiro *m*
VT **1** (= *pull*) [+ *bolt, curtains*] (*to close*) correr; (*to open*) descorrer; [+ *caravan, trailer*] tirar, jalar (*LAm*) • **she drew him to one side** lo llevó a un lado • **she drew him towards her** lo atrajo hacia sí • **we drew him into the plan** le persuadimos para que participara en el proyecto • **to ~ a bow** tensar un arco • **he drew his finger along the table** pasó el dedo por la superficie de la mesa • **to ~ one's hand over one's eyes** pasarse la mano por los ojos • **he drew his hat over his eyes** se caló el sombrero hasta los ojos
2 (= *extract*) [+ *gun, sword, confession, tooth*] sacar; [+ *cheque*] girar; [+ *salary*] cobrar; [+ *number, prize*] sacarse; [+ *trumps*] arrastrar; (*Culin*) [+ *fowl*] destripar; (*Med*) [+ *boil*] hacer reventar • **to ~ a bath** preparar el baño • **to ~ blood** sacar sangre • **to ~ (a) breath** respirar • **to ~ a card** robar una carta • **to ~ comfort from sth** hallar consuelo en algo • **to ~ inspiration from sth** encontrar inspiración en algo • **to ~ lots** echar suertes • **to ~ a smile from sb** arrancar una sonrisa a algn; ▹ **breath**
3 (= *attract*) [+ *attention, crowd, customer*] atraer • **their shouts drew him to the place** llegó al lugar atraído por sus gritos • **to feel ~n to sb** simpatizar con algn • **he refuses to be ~n** se niega a hablar de ello, se guarda de hacer comentario alguno
4 (= *cause*) [+ *laughter*] causar, provocar; [+ *applause*] despertar, motivar; [+ *criticism*] provocar • **it drew no reply** no hubo contestación a esto
5 (= *sketch*) [+ *scene, person*] dibujar; [+ *plan, line, circle, map*] trazar; (*fig*) [+ *situation*] explicar; [+ *character*] trazar • **to ~ a picture** hacer un dibujo • **to ~ a picture of sb** hacer un retrato de algn • IDIOM: • **to ~ the line at sth:** • **I ~ the line at (doing) that** a (hacer) eso no llego
6 (= *formulate*) [+ *conclusion*] sacar (**from** de) • **to ~ a comparison between A and B** comparar A con B • **to ~ a distinction** distinguir (**between** entre)
7 (*Sport, Games*) • **to ~ a match/game** (*gen*) empatar un partido; (*Chess*) entablar
8 (*Naut*) • **the boat ~s two metres** el barco tiene un calado de dos metros
9 (*Tech*) [+ *wire*] estirar
VI **1** (= *move*) • **he drew ahead of the other runners** se adelantó a los demás corredores • **to ~ to an end** llegar a su fin • **the train drew into the station** el tren entró en la estación • **the two horses drew level** los dos caballos se igualaron • **to ~ near** acercarse • **the car drew over to the kerb** el coche se acercó a la acera • **he drew to one side** se apartó • **to ~ towards** acercarse a
2 (*Cards*) • **to ~ for trumps** echar triunfos
3 [*chimney etc*] tirar
4 (= *infuse*) [*tea*] reposar
5 (= *be equal*) [*two teams, players*] empatar; (*Chess*) entablar • **we drew two all** empatamos a dos • **the teams drew for second place** los equipos empataron en segundo lugar
6 (= *sketch*) dibujar

▸ **draw ahead** VI + ADV adelantarse (**of a**)

▸ **draw aside** VT + ADV [+ *covering*] apartar; [+ *curtain*] descorrer; [+ *person*] apartar, llevar a un lado
VI + ADV ir aparte, apartarse

▸ **draw away** VT + ADV apartar, llevar aparte
VI + ADV alejarse, apartarse; (*in race*) dejar atrás a los otros • **to ~ away from the kerb** apartarse *or* alejarse de la acera • **he drew away from her** se alejó *or* apartó de ella

▸ **draw back** VT + ADV [+ *object, hand*] retirar; [+ *curtains*] descorrer
VI + ADV (= *move back*) echarse atrás (**from** de) • **to ~ back from doing sth** no atreverse a hacer algo

▸ **draw down** VT + ADV **1** (= *pull down*) [+ *blind*] bajar
2 (*fig*) [+ *blame, ridicule*] atraer

▸ **draw forth** VT + ADV [+ *comment etc*] motivar, provocar, dar lugar a

▸ **draw in** VI + ADV **1** [*car*] (= *stop*) detenerse, pararse (*LAm*); [*train*] (= *enter station*) entrar en la estación
2 (*Brit*) • **the days are ~ing in** los días se van acortando, los días se van haciendo más cortos
VT + ADV **1** [+ *breath, air*] aspirar
2 (= *pull back in*) [+ *claws*] retraer
3 (= *attract*) [+ *crowds*] atraer

▸ **draw off** VT + ADV **1** [+ *gloves*] quitarse
2 [+ *liquid*] vaciar, trasegar
3 [+ *pursuers*] apartar, desviar

▸ **draw on** VI + ADV [*night*] acercarse
VI + PREP [+ *source*] inspirarse en; [+ *text*] poner a contribución; [+ *resources*] usar, hacer uso de, explotar; [+ *experience*] recurrir a, servirse de; [+ *bank account*] retirar dinero de • **he drew on his own experience to write the book** recurrió a *or* se sirvió de su propia experiencia para escribir el libro
VT + ADV **1** [+ *gloves*] ponerse
2 • **to ~ sb on** engatusar a algn

d

▸ **draw out** (VT + ADV) **1** (= *take out*) [+ *handkerchief, money from bank*] sacar • **to ~ sb out (of his shell)** (*fig*) hacer que algn salga de sí mismo
2 (= *prolong*) [+ *meeting etc*] alargar
3 (= *lengthen*) [+ *wire*] estirar
(VI + ADV) **1** [*train etc*] arrancar
2 [*days*] hacerse más largos
▸ **draw together** (VT + ADV) reunir, juntar
(VI + ADV) reunirse, juntarse; (*fig*) hacerse más unidos
▸ **draw up** (VT + ADV) **1** (= *formulate*) [+ *will, contract*] redactar; [+ *report etc*] redactar, preparar; [+ *plan*] elaborar, trazar
2 (= *move*) [+ *chair*] acercar; [+ *troops*] ordenar, disponer • **to ~ o.s. up (to one's full height)** enderezarse, erguirse
3 (= *raise*) levantar, alzar; (*from well*) [+ *water*] sacar
(VI + ADV) [*car etc*] detenerse, parar
▸ **draw upon** (VI + PREP) ▹ **draw on**

drawback ['drɔːbæk] (N) inconveniente *m*, desventaja *f*

drawbridge ['drɔːbrɪdʒ] (N) puente *m* levadizo

drawee [drɔː'iː] (N) girado/a *m/f*, librado/a *m/f*

drawer¹ [drɔːʳ] (N) (*in desk etc*) cajón *m*; ▹ **top**

drawer² ['drɔːəʳ] (N) (*Comm*) girador(a) *m/f*, librador(a) *m/f*

drawers† [drɔːz] (NPL) (*man's*) calzoncillos *mpl*; (*woman's*) bragas *fpl*

drawing ['drɔːɪŋ] (N) **1** (= *picture*) dibujo *m*
2 (= *activity*) • **I'm no good at ~** no sirvo para el dibujo, no se me da bien el dibujo
(CPD) ▸ **drawing account** cuenta *f* de anticipos, fondo *m* para gastos ▸ **drawing board** mesa *f* de dibujo • IDIOM: • **back to the ~ board!** ¡a comenzar de nuevo! ▸ **drawing office** oficina *f* de delineación ▸ **drawing paper** papel *m* de dibujo ▸ **drawing pen** tiralíneas *m inv* ▸ **drawing pin** chincheta *f* (*Sp*), chinche *m or f* (*LAm*) ▸ **drawing power** [*of speaker, entertainer*] poder *m* de convocatoria, tirón* *m* ▸ **drawing rights** derechos *mpl* de giro ▸ **drawing room** salón *m*, sala *f*

drawl [drɔːl] (N) voz *f* cansina • **a Southern ~** un acento del sur
(VT) decir alargando las palabras
(VI) hablar alargando las palabras

drawn [drɔːn] (PP) *of* **draw**
(ADJ) **1** (= *haggard*) (*with tiredness*) demacrado, ojeroso; (*with pain*) macilento
2 (= *with no winner*) [*game*] empatado
3 (= *prolonged*) • **long ~ out** larguísimo, prolongado
4 (= *unsheathed*) • **with ~ sword** con la espada en la mano
(CPD) ▸ **drawn butter** (*US*) mantequilla *f* derretida

drawstring ['drɔːstrɪŋ] (N) cordón *m*

dray [dreɪ] (N) carro *m* pesado

dread [dred] (N) terror *m*, pavor *m* • **to fill sb with ~** infundir terror a algn • **he lives in ~ of being caught** vive aterrorizado por la idea de que lo cojan *or* (*LAm*) agarren
(VT) tener pavor a • **I ~ going to the dentist** me da pavor ir al dentista • **I ~ what may happen when he comes** me horroriza lo que pueda pasar cuando venga • **I ~ to think of it*** ¡solo pensarlo me da horror!
(ADJ) espantoso

dreadful ['dredfʊl] (ADJ) [*crime, sight, suffering*] espantoso; [*news, accident, experience*] espantoso, terrible; [*disease, person, noise*] terrible; [*night, moment, place*] horrible; [*book, film*] pésimo; [*weather, conditions*] pésimo, fatal (*Sp**); [*situation, mistake*] horroroso, terrible • **how ~!** ¡qué horror! • **he is a ~ coward** es un cobarde asqueroso • **a ~ business** un asunto horroroso • **I feel ~!** (= *ill*) ¡me encuentro muy mal!, ¡me encuentro fatal! (*Sp**); (= *ashamed*) ¡qué vergüenza me da!, ¡qué pena me da! (*LAm*), me da muchísima vergüenza *or* (*LAm*) pena • **I feel ~ about forgetting his birthday** me siento fatal por haber olvidado su cumpleaños* • **to look ~** (= *ill*) tener mala cara*; (= *unattractive*) [*person*] estar horrible, tener una pinta horrorosa*; [*thing*] quedar horroroso • **I look ~ in this hat** estoy horrible con este sombrero, tengo una pinta horrorosa con este sombrero* • **that brown wallpaper looks ~** ese papel pintado marrón queda horroroso

dreadfully* ['dredfəlɪ] (ADV) **1** (= *very*) [*boring*] mortalmente; [*late, difficult*] increíblemente, muy • **I'm ~ sorry** lo siento muchísimo • **I felt something was ~ wrong** sentía que había pasado algo horrible
2 (= *very much*) [*suffer*] muchísimo, lo indecible; [*hurt*] a rabiar • **I miss Janet ~** echo muchísimo de menos a Janet
3 (= *badly*) [*behave, treat, sing*] muy mal, espantosamente, fatal (*Sp**)

dreadlocks ['dredlɒks] (NPL) *rizos de estilo rastafari*

dreadnought ['drednɔːt] (N) (*Hist*) acorazado *m*

dream [driːm] (VB: PT, PP: **dreamed, dreamt**)
(N) **1** (*while asleep*) sueño *m* • **a bad ~** una pesadilla • **I had a ~ that my father had died** soñé que mi padre se había muerto • **to have a ~ about sth/sb** soñar con algo/algn • **to see sth in a ~** ver algo en sueños • **sweet ~s!** ¡que sueñes con los angelitos!; ▹ **wet**
2 (= *daydream*) sueño *m*, ensueño *m* • **she goes about in a ~** siempre está en las nubes
3 (= *fantasy, ideal*) sueño *m* • **my (fondest) ~ is to ...** el sueño de mi vida es ..., mi mayor ilusión es ... • **the house/man/woman of my ~s** mi casa/hombre/mujer ideal, la casa/el hombre/la mujer de mis sueños • **the museum was an archaeologist's ~** para un arqueólogo, el museo era un sueño • **he thinks he's every girl's ~** se cree que es el tipo ideal para cualquier chica • **the American Dream** el sueño americano • **it was like a ~ come true** fue como un sueño hecho realidad • **a ~ holiday in Jamaica** unas vacaciones de ensueño en Jamaica • **in your ~s!*** ¡ni en sueños!* • **she succeeded beyond her wildest ~s** consiguió más éxito del que jamás había soñado • **never in my wildest ~s did I expect to win** ni en mis sueños más dorados hubiera podido imaginar que ganaría • **he lives in a ~ world** vive en un mundo de fantasía *or* de ensueño • **in a ~ world no one would be poor** en un mundo ideal, nadie sería pobre; ▹ **pipe**
4* (= *marvel*) • **"how was the holiday?" — "it was a ~!"** —¿qué tal las vacaciones? —¡de ensueño! • **it worked like a ~** funcionó de maravilla *or* a las mil maravillas • **that car goes like a ~** ese coche funciona de maravilla
(VT) **1** (*while asleep*) soñar • **I ~ed that I was being chased** soñé que me perseguían • **I ~ed a strange ~** tuve un sueño extraño
2 (= *imagine*) soñar, imaginarse • **you must have ~ed it** lo habrás soñado, te lo habrás imaginado • **I never ~ed that she would accept** jamás soñé con que aceptaría, jamás me imaginé que aceptaría
3 (*as ambition*) • **I ~ that my son will find a good job** mi sueño es que mi hijo encuentre un buen trabajo
(VI) **1** (*while asleep*) soñar (**of, about** con)
2 (= *daydream*) estar en las nubes • **I'm sorry, I was ~ing** disculpa, estaba en las nubes *or* pensando en las musarañas
3 (= *fantasize*) soñar • **she ~ed of having her own business** soñaba con llegar a tener su propio negocio • **they have a lifestyle most of us only ~ of** *or* **about** llevan un tren de vida que para la mayoría de nosotros no pasa de ser un sueño • **~ on!*** ¡ni en sueños!*
4 (= *imagine*) soñar, imaginarse; (*in neg context*) imaginarse • **there were more than I'd ever ~ed of** había más de lo que jamás hubiera podido soñar *or* imaginar • **who would ever ~ of a disaster like this?** ¿quién hubiera podido imaginarse una catástrofe así?
5 (= *consider*) • **"will you ask them?" — "I wouldn't ~ of it!"** —¿les preguntarás? —¡ni pensarlo! *or* ¡ni en sueños!* • **I wouldn't ~ of going!** ¿ir? ¡ni pensarlo! *or* ¡ni en sueños!* • **I wouldn't ~ of doing such a thing** jamás se me ocurriría hacer tal cosa
(CPD) ▸ **dream house** casa *f* de ensueño • **my ~ house** la casa de mis sueños ▸ **dream team** (= *ideal group*) equipo *m* de ensueño, dream team *m* ▸ **dream ticket** (*Pol*) candidatos *mpl* ideales
▸ **dream away** (VT + ADV) • **to ~ away the day** pasar el día soñando
▸ **dream up** (VT + ADV) [+ *plan*] trazar, idear • **only you could ~ up such a stupid idea** solo a ti se te podría ocurrir una idea tan tonta

dreamboat* ['driːmbəʊt] (N) bombón* *m*

dreamer ['driːməʳ] (N) (= *impractical person*) soñador(a) *m/f* • **he's a bit of a ~** (= *idealistic*) es un soñador; (= *absent-minded*) es un despistado

dreamily ['driːmɪlɪ] (ADV) como si estuviera soñando

dreaminess ['driːmɪnɪs] (N) carácter *m* onírico

dreamland ['driːmlænd] (N) reino *m* del ensueño, país *m* de los sueños; (= *utopia*) utopía *f*

dreamless ['driːmlɪs] (ADJ) sin sueños

dreamlike ['driːmlaɪk] (ADJ) de ensueño, como de sueño

dreamt [dremt] (PT), (PP) *of* **dream**

dreamy ['driːmɪ] (ADJ) (COMPAR: **dreamier**, SUPERL: **dreamiest**) [*character, person*] soñador; [*smile, tone*] distraído; [*music*] de ensueño, suave

drearily ['drɪərɪlɪ] (ADV) (= *depressingly*) • **a ~ familiar scenario** una situación tristemente familiar

dreariness ['drɪərɪnɪs] (N) [*of landscape, weather*] lo inhóspito; [*of routine, job*] monotonía *f*, lo aburrido

dreary ['drɪərɪ] (ADJ) (COMPAR: **drearier**, SUPERL: **dreariest**) [*landscape, weather*] gris, inhóspito; [*life, work*] monótono, aburrido; [*book, speech*] pesado

dredge¹ [dredʒ] (N) (*Mech*) draga *f*
(VT) [+ *river, canal*] dragar
▸ **dredge up** (VT + ADV) sacar con draga; (*fig*) [+ *unpleasant facts*] sacar a la luz

dredge² [dredʒ] (N) (*Culin*) espolvoreador *m*

dredger¹ ['dredʒəʳ] (N) (= *ship*) draga *f*

dredger² ['dredʒəʳ] (N) (*Culin*) espolvoreador *m*

dredging¹ ['dredʒɪŋ] (N) dragado *m*, obras *fpl* de dragado

dredging² ['dredʒɪŋ] (N) (*Culin*) espolvoreado *m*

dregs [dregz] (NPL) **1** [*of tea, coffee etc*] posos *mpl*, heces *fpl* • **to drain a glass to the ~** apurar un vaso (hasta las heces)
2 (*fig*) • **the ~ of society** la escoria de la sociedad

drench [drentʃ] (VT) empapar (**with de**) • **to get ~ed** empaparse • **he was ~ed to the skin**

estaba empapado *or* calado hasta los huesos
N (*Vet*) poción *f*

drenching ['drentʃɪŋ] ADJ [*rain*] torrencial
N • **to get a ~** empaparse

Dresden ['drezdən] N Dresde *m*
CPD ▸ **Dresden china** loza *f* de Dresde

dress [dres] N **1** (= *frock*) vestido *m*
2 (= *clothing*) ropa *f* • **he's usually smart in his ~** suele vestir con elegancia • **a Maori in Western ~** un maorí vestido a la forma occidental • **they were wearing traditional Nepalese ~** vestían el traje tradicional *or* típico de Nepal • **formal ~ will be required** el traje de etiqueta es de rigor; ▹ **evening**
VT **1** (= *put clothes on*) vestir • **she ~ed the baby in clean clothes** le puso ropita limpia al niño • **he hasn't learned how to ~ himself yet** todavía no ha aprendido a vestirse; ▹ **dressed**
2 (*Culin*) [+ *salad*] aliñar, aderezar; [+ *meat, fish*] preparar y condimentar
3 (= *decorate, arrange*) [+ *hair*] peinar, arreglar; [+ *shop window*] decorar; [+ *Christmas tree*] adornar, decorar
4 (*Med*) [+ *wound*] vendar
5 (*Agr*) [+ *land*] abonar
6 (*Mil*) [+ *troops*] alinear
7 [+ *stone, metal*] dar el acabado a; [+ *skins*] curtir
VI **1** (= *put on clothes*) vestirse • **he ~ed quickly and left** se vistió deprisa y se marchó
2 (= *wear specified clothes*) vestir • **she ~es very well** viste muy bien, va muy bien vestida • **she always used to ~ in jeans/black** solía ir siempre vestida con vaqueros/de negro • **to ~ to the left/right** colgar hacia la izquierda/derecha
3 (= *wear formal clothes*) • **to ~ for dinner** [*man*] ponerse smoking para cenar; [*woman*] ponerse traje de noche para cenar • **they always ~ for dinner** siempre (se) ponen elegantes para cenar
4 (*Mil*) alinearse • **right ~!** ¡vista a la derecha!
CPD ▸ **dress circle** anfiteatro *m*, (piso *m*) principal *m* ▸ **dress coat** frac *m* ▸ **dress code** *regulaciones en materia de indumentaria o uniforme* ▸ **dress designer** modisto/a *m/f* ▸ **dress length** (= *material*) corte *m* de vestido ▸ **dress parade** (*US*) (*Mil*) desfile *m* de gala ▸ **dress rehearsal** ensayo *m* general ▸ **dress sense** gusto *m* para vestir • **he has no ~ sense** no tiene gusto para vestir • **he has immaculate ~ sense** tiene un gusto impecable para vestir ▸ **dress shirt** camisa *f* de frac, camisa *f* de etiqueta ▸ **dress suit** traje *m* de etiqueta ▸ **dress uniform** (*Mil*) uniforme *m* de gala
▸ **dress down** VI + ADV vestirse informalmente
VT + ADV* (= *rebuke*) reprender
▸ **dress up** VI + ADV (*in smart clothes*) ponerse elegante; (*formally*) vestirse de etiqueta; (*in fancy dress*) disfrazarse
VT + ADV **1** (*in smart clothes*) poner elegante; (*in fancy dress*) disfrazar • **you're all ~ed up, are you going somewhere?** vas muy elegante, ¿es que vas a algún sitio? • **to ~ sb up as sth** disfrazar *or* vestir a algn de algo; ▹ **nine**
2 (= *improve appearance of*) [+ *facts, events*] disfrazar • **it was a pile of scrap metal ~ed up as art** era un montón de chatarra disfrazado de arte • **they ~ed the setback up as a triumph** hicieron creer que el revés había sido en realidad un triunfo

dressage ['dresɑːʒ] N *método de adiestramiento de caballos para que realicen movimientos controlados*

dressed [drest] ADJ vestido • **to be casually ~** ir (vestido) informal *or* de sport • **to be smartly ~** ir (vestido) elegante • **~ as a man/woman** vestido de hombre/mujer • **to be ~ for tennis/the country** ir vestido para jugar al tenis/para ir al campo • **fully ~** completamente vestido • **to get ~** vestirse • **~ in black** vestido de negro • **to be ~ in a skirt/trousers** llevar falda/pantalones
• IDIOM: • **to be ~ to kill*** ir despampanante*; ▹ **dress, dress up, well-dressed**
CPD ▸ **dressed crab** cangrejo *m* preparado

dresser ['dresəʳ] N **1** (= *furniture*) (*in kitchen*) aparador *m*; (= *dressing table*) tocador *m*
2 (*Theat*) ayudante *mf* de camerino
3 (= *person*) • **he's an elegant ~** se viste elegantemente

dressing ['dresɪŋ] N **1** (= *act*) • **allow time for ~** déjese tiempo suficiente para vestirse
2 (*Med*) (= *bandage*) vendaje *m*
3 (*Culin*) (= *salad dressing*) aliño *m*
4 (*Agr*) (= *fertilizer*) abono *m*, fertilizante *m*
CPD ▸ **dressing case** neceser *m* ▸ **dressing gown** bata *f* ▸ **dressing room** (*Theat*) camerino *m*; (*Sport*) vestuario *m* ▸ **dressing station** (*Mil*) puesto *m* de socorro ▸ **dressing table** tocador *m*

dressing-down* ['dresɪŋ'daʊn] N • **to give sb a dressing-down** echar un rapapolvo a algn*

dressmaker ['dresmeɪkəʳ] N modista *f*, costurera *f*

dressmaking ['dresmeɪkɪŋ] N costura *f*, corte *m* y confección

dressy* ['dresɪ] ADJ (COMPAR: **dressier**, SUPERL: **dressiest**) [*person*] de mucho vestir; [*clothing*] elegante

drew [druː] PT *of* **draw**

dribble ['drɪbl] N **1** [*of saliva*] babeo *m*; [*of water*] gotitas *fpl* • **the water came out in a ~** (*thin stream*) salía un hilillo de agua; (*dripping*) el agua goteaba • **a ~ of water** (= *thin stream*) un hilillo de agua; (= *drops*) gotas de agua
2 (*Ftbl*) control *m* del balón; (*past opponents*) regate *m*, dribling *m*
VT **1** [+ *liquid*] • **he ~d his milk all down his chin** le chorreaba la leche por la barbilla
2 (*Ftbl*) regatear, driblar
VI **1** [*baby*] babear; [*liquid*] gotear
2 (*Ftbl*) controlar el balón • **to ~ past sb** regatear *or* driblar a algn

dribbler ['drɪbləʳ] N (*Sport*) driblador *m*

driblet ['drɪblɪt] N adarme *m* • **in ~s** por adarmes

dribs [drɪbz] NPL • IDIOM: • **in ~ and drabs** poco a poco, con cuentagotas • **the money came in in ~ and drabs** el dinero fue llegando poco a poco *or* con cuentagotas • **the guests arrived in ~ and drabs** los invitados fueron llegando poco a poco

dried [draɪd] PT, PP *of* **dry**
ADJ [*flowers, mushrooms, lentils*] seco; [*milk*] en polvo
CPD ▸ **dried fruit(s)** frutas *fpl* pasas

dried-out [ˌdraɪd'aʊt] ADJ [*alcoholic*] seco

dried-up [ˌdraɪd'ʌp] ADJ [*river-bed, stream, oasis*] seco

drier ['draɪəʳ] N = **dryer**

drift [drɪft] N **1** (= *deviation from course*) deriva *f*; (= *movement*) movimiento *m*; (= *change of direction*) cambio *m* (de dirección) • **the ~ to the city** el movimiento migratorio hacia la ciudad • **the ~ from the land** el éxodo rural, la despoblación del campo • **the ~ of events** la marcha de los acontecimientos
2* (= *meaning*) [*of questions*] significado *m* • **to catch sb's ~** seguir *or* entender a algn • **I don't get your ~** no te entiendo
3 (= *mass*) [*of snow*] ventisquero *m*; [*of sand*] montón *m*; [*of clouds, leaves*] banco *m*; (*Geol*) morrena *f* • **continental ~** deriva *f* continental
VI **1** (*in wind, current*) dejarse llevar, ir a la deriva; (= *be off course*) [*boat*] ir a la deriva; [*person*] vagar, ir a la deriva • **to ~ downstream** dejarse llevar río abajo • **he ~ed into marriage** se casó sin pensárselo • **to let things ~** dejar las cosas como están • **to ~ from job to job** cambiar a menudo de trabajo sin propósito fijo
2 [*snow, sand*] amontonarse
VT (= *carry*) impeler, llevar; (= *pile up*) amontonar
CPD ▸ **drift ice** hielo *m* flotante ▸ **drift net** traína *f*
▸ **drift apart** VI + ADV irse separando poco a poco
▸ **drift away** VI + ADV dejarse llevar por la corriente
▸ **drift off** VI + ADV (= *doze off*) dormirse, quedarse dormido

drifter ['drɪftəʳ] N **1** (*Naut*) trainera *f*
2 (= *person*) vago/a *m/f*, vagabundo/a *m/f*

drifting ['drɪftɪŋ] N nieve *f* acumulada (*después de una tormenta*)

driftwood ['drɪftwʊd] N madera *f* de deriva

drill¹ [drɪl] N **1** (*for wood, metal*) taladradora *f*, taladro *m*; (= *bit*) broca *f*; (*Min*) (*for oil etc*) barrena *f*, perforadora *f*; (= *dentist's drill*) fresa *f*; (= *pneumatic drill*) martillo *m* neumático
2 (*Agr*) (= *furrow*) surco *m*; (= *machine*) sembradora *f*
VT [+ *wood, road*] taladrar, perforar; [+ *tooth*] agujerear; [+ *oil well*] perforar; (*Agr*) sembrar con sembradora • **he ~ed a hole in the wall** hizo *or* taladró un agujero en la pared
VI perforar (**for** en busca de)

drill² [drɪl] N (= *exercises*) (*Mil*) instrucción *f*; (*Scol*) ejercicios *mpl* • **fire ~** simulacro *m* de incendio • **you all know the ~*** todos sabéis lo que hay que hacer • **what's the ~?*** ¿qué es lo que tenemos que hacer?
VT [+ *soldiers*] ejercitar • **to ~ pupils in grammar** hacer ejercicios de gramática con los alumnos • **to ~ good manners into a child** enseñar buenos modales a un niño • **I had it ~ed into me as a boy** me lo inculcaron de niño
VI (*Mil*) hacer instrucción

drill³ [drɪl] N (= *fabric*) dril *m*

drilling¹ ['drɪlɪŋ] N (*for oil etc*) perforación *f*
CPD ▸ **drilling platform** plataforma *f* de perforación ▸ **drilling rig** torre *f* de perforación

drilling² ['drɪlɪŋ] N (*Mil*) instrucción *f*

drily ['draɪlɪ] ADV **1** (= *with dry humour*) • **... he said ~** ... dijo con un humor cargado de ironía
2 (= *unemotionally*) secamente, con sequedad
3 • **he coughed ~** emitió una tos seca

drink [drɪŋk] (VB: PT: **drank**, PP: **drunk**) N
1 (= *liquid to drink*) bebida *f* • **there's food and ~ in the kitchen** hay comida y bebidas en la cocina, hay cosas de comer y de beber en la cocina • **have you got ~s for the children?** ¿habéis traído algo para que beban los niños? • **I need a ~ of water** necesito un poco de agua • **cold ~s** (*non-alcoholic*) refrescos *mpl* • **to give sb a ~** darle algo de beber a algn • **can I have a ~?** ¿me podrías dar algo de beber *or* (*LAm*) tomar? • **hot ~s will be available** se servirá café y té • **I felt better after a hot ~** me sentía mejor después de beber algo caliente; ▹ **meat, soft**
2 (= *glass of alcohol*) copa *f*, trago *m* • **to go (out) for a ~** salir a tomar algo, salir a tomar una copa • **they've asked us round for ~s** nos

d

han invitado a su casa a tomar algo *or* a tomar unas copas • **to have a ~** tomar algo • **we had a ~ or two** tomamos unas copas *or* unos tragos; ▹ **drive**
3 (= *alcoholic liquor*) alcohol *m*, bebida *f* • **he's given up ~** ha dejado de beber, ha dejado el alcohol *or* la bebida • **he has a ~ problem** tiene problemas con el alcohol *or* la bebida • **to take to ~** darse a la bebida; ▹ **worse**
4 • **the ~*** (= *the water*) (*gen*) el agua; (= *sea*) el mar

d

(VT) beber, tomar (*esp LAm*) • **would you like something to ~?** ¿quieres tomar algo? • **in the end he drank himself to death** al final la bebida lo llevó a la tumba • **this coffee isn't fit to ~** este café no se puede beber • **to ~ sb's health** brindar por la salud de algn • **we drank ourselves into a stupor** bebimos hasta perder el sentido • **to ~ sb under the table*** darle cien vueltas a algn bebiendo • **to ~ a toast to sth/sb** brindar por algo/algn
(VI) **1** (= *imbibe liquid*) beber • **to ~ from the bottle** beber de la botella • **to ~ out of paper cups** beber en vasos de plástico
2 (= *imbibe alcohol*) beber, tomar (*LAm*) • **he doesn't ~** no bebe (alcohol), no toma (alcohol) (*esp LAm*) • **don't ~ and drive** si bebes, no conduzcas • **he ~s like a fish** bebe como una esponja • **to ~ to sth/sb** brindar por algo/algn
(CPD) ▸ **drink driver** (*Brit*) conductor(a) *m/f* en estado de embriaguez • **a campaign against ~ drivers** una campaña contra los que beben y conducen ▸ **drink problem** • **to have a ~ problem** tener un problema con la bebida ▸ **drinks cabinet** mueble *m* bar ▸ **drinks party** cóctel *m*
▸ **drink down** (VT + ADV) beber de un trago
▸ **drink in** (VT + ADV) **1** (*fig*) [+ *fresh air*] respirar; [+ *story, sight, atmosphere*] empaparse de; [+ *words*] estar pendiente de • **he stood, ~ing in the view** se quedó parado, empapándose de la vista • **she sat there ~ing in his words** estaba ahí sentada, pendiente de sus palabras • **the children were ~ing it all in** a los niños no les escapaba nada
2 [*plant, soil*] absorber
▸ **drink up** (VT + ADV) [+ *one's drink*] terminar de beber, terminar de tomar (*LAm*); [+ *all drink available*] beberse, tomarse (*LAm*)
(VI + ADV) • **~ up now, please!** ¡terminen sus bebidas!

drinkable ['drɪŋkəbl] (ADJ) (= *not poisonous*) potable; (= *palatable*) aceptable, que se deja beber • **quite ~** nada malo

drink-drive limit [ˌdrɪŋk'draɪvˌlɪmɪt] (N) (*Brit*) tasa *f* máxima de alcoholemia

drink-driving ['drɪŋk'draɪvɪŋ] (N) el conducir en estado de embriaguez, el manejar en estado de embriaguez (*LAm*) • **he was arrested for drink-driving** lo arrestaron por conducir en estado de embriaguez (*frm*), lo arrestaron por conducir borracho • **there are strict laws on drink-driving** hay leyes muy estrictas en lo que respecta a conducir en estado de embriaguez
(CPD) ▸ **drink-driving campaign** campaña *f* contra el alcohol en carretera ▸ **drink-driving offence** delito *m* de conducir en estado de embriaguez • **drink-driving offences must be severely dealt with** conducir en estado de embriaguez debe ser severamente castigado • **he was guilty of several drink-driving offences** le habían detenido varias veces por conducir en estado de embriaguez

drinker ['drɪŋkəʳ] (N) bebedor(a) *m/f* • **he was a heavy ~** era un bebedor empedernido

drinking ['drɪŋkɪŋ] (N) **1** [*of any liquid*] • **my sore throat made ~ painful** al tener la garganta irritada me dolía mucho al beber
2 [*of alcohol*] • **his ~ caused his marriage to break up** la bebida fue la causa de la ruptura de su matrimonio • **she had to put up with his ~** tuvo que aguantar sus borracheras • **heavy ~ can cause weight problems** beber mucho puede ocasionar problemas de peso • **I'm not a ~ person** no soy bebedor, no bebo mucho
(CPD) ▸ **drinking bout** juerga *f*, farra *f* (*LAm**) ▸ **drinking chocolate** chocolate *m* (*bebida*) ▸ **drinking companion** compañero/a *m/f* de copas ▸ **drinking culture** cultura *f* de la bebida ▸ **drinking fountain** fuente *f* (de agua potable) ▸ **drinking problem** • **to have a ~ problem** tener un problema con la bebida ▸ **drinking session** juerga *f*, farra *f* (*LAm**) ▸ **drinking song** canción *f* de taberna ▸ **drinking straw** pajita *f* ▸ **drinking trough** abrevadero *m*, camellón *m* ▸ **drinking water** agua *f* potable

drinking-up time [ˌdrɪŋkɪŋ'ʌpˌtaɪm] (N) *tiempo permitido para terminar las bebidas en el pub antes de cerrar*

drip [drɪp] (N) **1** (= *droplet*) gota *f*
2 (= *dripping sound*) goteo *m* • **the ~, ~, ~ of the tap was beginning to irritate her** el constante goteo del grifo estaba empezando a irritarla • **she could hear the constant ~ of the rain outside** oía el constante gotear de la lluvia fuera
3* (= *spineless person*) soso/a *m/f*
4 (*Med*) gotero *m*, gota a gota *m inv* • **she is on a ~** tiene puesto un gotero *or* gota a gota
(VT) • **the children came in ~ping water all over the floor** los niños entraron chorreando agua por todo el suelo • **try not to ~ sauce onto the tablecloth** procura que la salsa no gotee en el mantel • **you're ~ping paint all over the place** estás chorreando pintura por todas partes, lo estás poniendo todo perdido de pintura • **her knee was ~ping blood** su rodilla estaba chorreando sangre
(VI) [*tap, faucet*] gotear • **oil was ~ping from under the car** el coche perdía aceite • **the rain was ~ping down the wall** las gotas de lluvia se deslizaban por la pared • **sweat was ~ping from his brow** le caían gotas de sudor de la frente • **blood ~ped from her finger** le caían gotas de sangre del dedo • **I washed my jumper and left it to ~** lavé el jersey y lo dejé escurrir; ▹ **dripping**

drip-dry ['drɪp'draɪ] (ADJ) inarrugable

drip-feed ['drɪpˌfiːd] (N) alimentación *f* gota a gota, gota a gota *m inv* • **to be on a drip-feed** recibir alimentación gota a gota
(VT) (PT, PP: **drip-fed**) alimentar gota a gota

dripmat ['drɪpmæt] (N) posavasos *m inv*

dripping ['drɪpɪŋ] (N) (*Culin*) pringue *m or f*
(ADJ) **1** (= *soaking*) [*washing, coat*] que chorrea, que gotea; [*person, hair*] empapado • **to be ~ wet*** estar empapado *or* chorreando • **~ with blood** chorreando sangre • **to be ~ with sweat** estar sudando a chorros, estar chorreando de sudor • **his voice was ~ with sarcasm** su voz rezumaba sarcasmo • **women ~ with diamonds and furs** mujeres cargadas de diamantes y pieles
2 [*tap, gutter*] que gotea

drippy* ['drɪpɪ] (ADJ) [*person, idea, book*] ñoño

drivability [ˌdraɪvə'bɪlɪtɪ] (N) manejabilidad *f*, capacidad *f* de maniobras

drive [draɪv] (VB: PT: **drove**, PP: **driven**) (N)
1 (= *journey, outing*) • **it's a long ~** se tarda mucho en coche • **it's only a short ~ from here** desde aquí se tarda poco en coche • **one hour's ~ from London** a una hora en coche de Londres • **it's a 50 mile ~** está a una distancia de 50 millas • **to go for a ~** ir a dar una vuelta *or* un paseo en coche; ▹ **test**
2 (= *private road*) (*in front of garage*) entrada *f*; (*to large house*) camino *m* (de acceso), avenida *f* • **his car was parked in the ~** su coche estaba aparcado en la entrada
3 (*Tennis*) golpe *m* directo, drive *m*; (*Golf*) drive *m*
4 (= *energy, motivation*) empuje *m*, dinamismo *m* • **to have ~** tener empuje *or* dinamismo • **to lack ~** no tener empuje *or* dinamismo
5 (*Psych*) (= *impulse*) impulso *m*, instinto *m* • **sex ~** libido *f*, líbido *f*, apetito *m* sexual • **to have a high/low sex ~** tener la libido *or* líbido alta/baja, tener mucho/poco apetito sexual
6 (= *campaign, effort*) campaña *f* • **a recruitment ~** una campaña de reclutamiento • **a sales ~** una promoción de ventas • **the ~ towards industrialization** el camino hacia la industrialización
7 (*Tech*) (= *power transmission system*) transmisión *f*, propulsión *f*; (*Aut*) • **four-wheel ~** tracción *f* en las cuatro ruedas • **a four-wheel ~ jeep** un jeep con tracción en las cuatro ruedas • **front-wheel/rear-wheel ~** tracción *f* delantera/trasera • **a left-hand/right-hand ~ car** un coche con el volante a la izquierda/derecha
8 (= *gear position in automatic car*) marcha *f* • **to put the car in ~** poner el coche en marcha
9 (*Comput*) (*also* **disk drive**) unidad *f* de disco • **CD-ROM ~** unidad *f* de CD-ROM
10 (= *tournament*) • **whist ~** certamen *m* de whist
11 (*Mil*) (= *attack*) ofensiva *f*
(VT) **1** (= *operate*) [+ *car, bus, train*] conducir, manejar (*LAm*); [+ *racing car, speedboat*] pilotar • **he ~s a taxi** es taxista • **she ~s a Mercedes** tiene un Mercedes
2 (= *carry*) [+ *passenger*] llevar (en coche) • **I'll ~ you home** te llevo a tu casa • **he drove me to the station** me llevó a la estación
3 (= *power*) [+ *machine, vehicle*] hacer funcionar
4 (= *cause to move*) • **they ~ the cattle to new pastures** conducen el ganado a otros pastos • **the wind drove the rain into our eyes** el viento hacía que la lluvia nos azotara en los ojos • **a strong wind was driving the clouds across the sky** un viento fuerte arrastraba las nubes por el cielo • **the gale drove the ship off course** el temporal hizo que el barco perdiera su rumbo • **troops drove the demonstrators off the streets** las tropas obligaron a los manifestantes a abandonar las calles
5 (= *push, hammer*) [+ *nail, stake*] clavar (**into** en) • **to ~ a post into the ground** clavar *or* hincar un poste en el suelo • **she drove her fist straight into his face** le dio con el puño justo en la cara; ▹ **home**
6 (= *excavate*) [+ *tunnel*] abrir, construir; [+ *hole*] perforar; [+ *furrow*] hacer
7 (= *force*) • **I was ~n to it** me vi forzado a ello • **competition has ~n prices down** la competencia ha hecho que bajen los precios • **hunger eventually drove him out of the house** finalmente el hambre lo empujó a salir de la casa • **high prices are driving local people out of the area** el que los precios sean tan altos está haciendo que la gente se vaya a vivir a otras zonas • **the recession drove them into bankruptcy** la recesión los llevó a la bancarrota • **to ~ sb to despair** llevar a algn a la desesperación • **to ~ sb to drink** • **his worries drove him to drink** sus problemas le llevaron a la bebida • **it's enough to ~ you to drink** (*hum*) te crispa los nervios • **to ~ sb mad** volver loco a algn;

▹ **bargain, home**
8 (= *impel, motivate*) empujar, mover • **he was ~n by greed/ambition** lo empujaba *or* movía la avaricia/ambición • **to ~ sb to do sth** • **~ sb into doing sth** empujar *or* llevar a algn a hacer algo • **depression drove him to attempt suicide** la depresión le empujó *or* llevó a intentar suicidarse • **what drove you to write this book?** ¿qué le empujó *or* llevó a escribir este libro?
9 (= *overwork*) • **to ~ sb hard** hacer trabajar mucho a algn • **she is driving herself too hard** se está exigiendo demasiado
10 (*Sport*) [+ *ball*] mandar
VI **1** (= *operate vehicle*) conducir, manejar (*LAm*) • **can you ~?** ¿sabes conducir *or* (*LAm*) manejar? • **to ~ on the left** circular por la izquierda
2 (= *go*) • **he drove alone** hizo el viaje en coche solo • **we've ~n 50 miles in the last hour** hemos recorrido 80km (con el coche) en la última hora • **next time we'll ~ there** la próxima vez iremos en coche • **he ~s around in an expensive car** va por ahí en un coche de esos caros • **to ~ at 50km an hour** ir (en un coche) a 50km por hora • **we'll ~ down in the car this weekend** este fin de semana bajaremos en coche • **he drove into a wall** chocó con un muro • **to ~ to London** ir a Londres en coche
3 (= *handle*) conducirse, manejarse (*LAm*) • **the new Ford ~s really well** el nuevo Ford se conduce *or* (*LAm*) se maneja muy bien
4 (= *beat*) • **heavy rain drove against the window** la fuerte lluvia azotaba el cristal
CPD ▸ **drive shaft** (*Aut*) árbol *m* motor
▸ **drive along** VT + ADV [*wind, current*] empujar
VI + ADV [*vehicle*] circular; [*person*] conducir
▸ **drive at*** VI + PREP (*fig*) (= *intend, mean*) insinuar, dar a entender • **what are you driving at?** ¿qué (es lo que) estás insinuando *or* dando a entender?
▸ **drive away** VT + ADV **1** (= *chase away*) [+ *person*] ahuyentar; [+ *cares*] alejar, quitarse de encima • **the smoke drove the mosquitos away** el humo ahuyentó a los mosquitos • **in the end his jealousy drove her away** al final sus celos la ahuyentaron
2 (*in vehicle*) llevarse (en coche)
VI + ADV = **drive off**
▸ **drive back** VT + ADV **1** (= *force to retreat*) [+ *person, army*] hacer retroceder
2 (*in vehicle*) llevar de vuelta (en coche)
VI + ADV volver (en coche)
▸ **drive off** VT + ADV (= *force to retreat*) [+ *enemy*] ahuyentar; (= *force to leave*) expulsar, echar
VI + ADV irse, marcharse (en coche); [*vehicle*] partir
▸ **drive on** VI + ADV [*person, vehicle*] (*after accident*) no parar; (*after stopping*) seguir adelante • **~ on!** ¡siga!
VT + ADV (= *incite, encourage*) empujar, mover • **it was the desire to win that drove her on** era su deseo de ganar lo que la empujaba *or* movía (a seguir)
▸ **drive on to** VI + PREP [+ *ferry*] embarcar en
▸ **drive out** VT + ADV (= *force to leave*) • **invading tribes drove them out** las tribus invasoras los expulsaron de sus tierras • **the smell drove me out** el olor me obligó a salir • **it is said to ~ out evil spirits** se dice que ahuyenta a los espíritus malignos
▸ **drive over** VT + ADV (= *convey*) llevar en coche
VI + PREP (= *crush*) aplastar
VI + ADV (= *come*) venir en coche; (= *go*) ir en coche • **we drove over in two hours** vinimos en dos horas • **we drove over to see them** fuimos a verlos (en coche)
▸ **drive up** VT + ADV [+ *price*] hacer subir
VI + ADV [*person*] acercarse (en coche); [*vehicle*] pararse • **the car drove up in front of the police station** el coche se paró delante de la comisaría • **he drove up in a limousine** se acercó en una limusina
driveability [ˌdraɪvəˈbɪlɪtɪ] N = **drivability**
drive-by [ˈdraɪvbaɪ] N (*also* **drive-by shooting**) tiroteo *m* desde el coche
drive-in [ˈdraɪvɪn] (*esp US*) N (= *restaurant*) *restaurante donde se sirve al cliente en su automóvil*; (= *cinema*) autocine *m*
ADJ [*bank etc*] *dispuesto para el uso del automovilista en su coche* • **drive-in cinema** autocine *m* • **a drive-in movie** una película de autocine
CPD ▸ **drive-in window** (*US*) *ventanilla desde la que se atiende directamente a alguien en un coche*

DRIVE-IN
En Estados Unidos, sobre todo, el término **drive-in** hace referencia a todos aquellos establecimientos, como cines, restaurantes o bancos, especialmente construidos para que el cliente pueda hacer uso de sus servicios sin tener que abandonar el vehículo que conduce. El primero de estos establecimientos se abrió en 1933. El término también se usa como adjetivo, como por ejemplo en **a drive-in movie**. A veces se usa la forma **drive-through** o **drive-thru**, que se aplica especialmente a las hamburgueserías, bancos y otros establecimientos en los que las transacciones son muy breves y no hay necesidad de aparcar el vehículo.

drivel* [ˈdrɪvl] N (= *nonsense*) tonterías *fpl*, chorradas* *fpl*, babosadas *fpl* (*LAm**)
VI decir tonterías, decir chorradas*, decir babosadas (*LAm**)
driven [ˈdrɪvn] PP *of* **drive**
-driven [ˈdrɪvn] ADJ (*ending in compounds*) que funciona con, accionado por • **electricity-driven** que funciona con electricidad, accionado por electricidad • **steam-driven** impulsado por vapor, a vapor
driver [ˈdraɪvəʳ] N **1** [*of car, bus*] conductor(a) *m/f*, chofer *mf* (*LAm*); [*of taxi*] taxista *mf*; [*of lorry*] camionero/a *m/f*; [*of carriage*] cochero *m*; (*Brit*) [*of train*] maquinista *mf* • **he's a bus ~** es conductor de autobús • **she's an excellent ~** conduce muy bien
2 (*Golf*) driver *m*
CPD ▸ **driver's license** (*US*) permiso *m* de conducir *or* (*LAm*) manejar, carnet *m* de conducir *or* (*LAm*) manejar ▸ **driver's seat** = **driving seat**
drive-through, drive-thru [ˈdraɪvθruː] N (*US*) = **drive-in**
drive-up window [ˌdraɪvʌpˈwɪndəʊ] N (*US*) taquilla *f* para automovilistas
driveway [ˈdraɪvweɪ] N entrada *f*
drive-yourself service [ˌdraɪvjɔːˈself,sɜːvɪs] N servicio *m* de alquiler sin chófer
driving [ˈdraɪvɪŋ] N (*Aut*) • **his ~ was a bit erratic** su forma de conducir *or* (*LAm*) manejar era bastante imprevisible • **we share the ~** nos turnamos al volante • **why don't you let me do the ~?** ¿por qué no me dejas conducir *or* (*LAm*) manejar a mí?; ▹ **drunken, reckless**
ADJ [*force*] impulsor; [*rain*] torrencial; [*wind*] azotador • **she is the ~ force behind the organization** ella es la (fuerza) impulsora de la organización
CPD ▸ **driving belt** correa *f* de transmisión ▸ **driving instructor** profesor(a) *m/f* de autoescuela ▸ **driving lesson** clase *f* de conducir *or* (*LAm*) manejar ▸ **driving licence** (*Brit*) permiso *m* de conducir *or* (*LAm*) manejar, carnet *m* de conducir *or* (*LAm*) manejar • **provisional/full ~ license** permiso *m* de conducir provisional/ definitivo, carnet *m* de conducir provisional/definitivo ▸ **driving mirror** retrovisor *m*, espejo *m* retrovisor ▸ **driving range** *zona de un campo de golf para practicar tiros de salida* ▸ **driving school** autoescuela *f* ▸ **driving seat** asiento *m* del conductor • IDIOM: • **to be in the ~ seat** estar al mando • **he's in the ~ seat now** ahora él es quien manda ▸ **driving test** examen *m* de conducir *or* (*LAm*) manejar ▸ **driving wheel** (*Tech*) rueda *f* motriz

DRIVING LICENCE/DRIVER'S LICENSE
En el Reino Unido se puede obtener el permiso de conducir desde los 17 años. Antes, es necesario solicitar un permiso provisional (**provisional (driving) licence**), el cual permite llevar un coche siempre y cuando el conductor novato vaya acompañado por otra persona con al menos tres años de carnet. Este carnet provisional no lleva la fotografía del conductor y no es obligatorio llevarlo encima cuando se conduce, aunque la policía puede pedir que se presente el documento en comisaría. Una vez obtenido el carnet definitivo (**full driving licence**), no hace falta renovarlo hasta los setenta años.
La edad para obtener el permiso de conducir en Estados Unidos varía, según el estado, entre 15 y 21 años. Sin embargo, los jóvenes pueden obtener un permiso **junior**, para conducir en determinadas circunstancias, por ejemplo, para ir a clase. Este carnet se ha de llevar siempre encima y es un documento válido para acreditar la identidad o la edad, que tiene que renovarse a los 4 ó 6 años. Solo tiene validez estatal, por lo que si alguien se traslada a otro estado debe sacar otro carnet, para lo cual debe hacer otro examen escrito.
En el Reino Unido son los conductores que no han aprobado aún el examen de conducir quienes llevan la L, llamada **L-plate** (de **learner**).

drizzle [ˈdrɪzl] N llovizna *f*, garúa *f* (*LAm*)
VI lloviznar
drizzly [ˈdrɪzlɪ] ADJ lloviznoso
droid* [drɔɪd] N (*Science Fiction*) (= *android*) androide *m*
droll [drəʊl] ADJ gracioso, divertido
dromedary [ˈdrɒmɪdərɪ] N dromedario *m*
drone [drəʊn] N **1** (= *male bee*) zángano *m*
2 (= *noise*) [*of bees, engine*] zumbido *m*; [*of voice*] tono *m* monótono
3 (= *sponger*) parásito/a *m/f*
4 (= *unmanned aircraft*) dron *m*
VI [*bee, engine, aircraft*] zumbar; [*voice, person*] (*also* **drone on**) hablar monótonamente • **he ~d on and on** hablaba y hablaba en tono monótono
drool [druːl] VI (= *slobber*) babear • **she ~ed over the kittens/her grandchildren** (*fig*) se le caía la baba con los gatitos/sus nietos
droop [druːp] VI [*head*] inclinarse; [*shoulders*] encorvarse; [*flower*] marchitarse • **his spirits ~ed** quedó abatido *or* desanimado
VT inclinar, dejar caer (**over** por)
drooping [ˈdruːpɪŋ] ADJ [*flower*] marchito; [*ears, head*] gacho; [*movement*] lánguido, desmayado

d

droopy ['dru:pɪ] ADJ (COMPAR: **droopier**, SUPERL: **droopiest**) **1** [*moustache, tail, breasts*] colgón
2 (*hum*) (= *tired*) mustio

drop [drɒp] N **1** [*of liquid*] gota *f* • **"would you like some milk?" — "just a ~"** —¿quieres leche? —una gota nada más • **in three weeks we didn't have a ~ of rain** no cayó ni una gota en tres semanas • **would you like a ~ of soup?** ¿quieres un poco de sopa? • **there's just a ~ left** queda solo una gota • **he's had a ~ too much*** ha bebido más de la cuenta • **I haven't touched a ~** no he probado una sola gota • IDIOM: • **a ~ in the ocean** una gota de agua en el mar
2 drops (*Med*) gotas *fpl*
3 (= *sweet*) pastilla *f*
4 (= *fall*) (*in price*) bajada *f*, caída *f*; (*in demand*) disminución *f*, reducción *f* • **a ~ of 10%** una bajada del 10 por ciento • **to take a ~ in salary** aceptar un salario más bajo • **a ~ in temperature** una bajada de las temperaturas • IDIOM: • **at the ~ of a hat** con cualquier pretexto
5 (= *steep incline*) pendiente *f*; (= *fall*) caída *f* • **a ~ of ten metres** una caída de diez metros
6 (*by parachute*) [*of supplies, arms etc*] lanzamiento *m*
7 (*for secret mail*) escondrijo *m* (*para correo secreto*)
8 • IDIOM: • **to have the ~ on sb** (*US**) llevar la delantera a algn, tener ventaja sobre algn
9 (*Theat*) telón *m* de boca
VT **1** (= *let fall*) **a** (*deliberately*) [+ *object*] dejar caer; (= *release, let go of*) soltar; [+ *bomb, parachutist*] lanzar; [+ *anchor*] echar; [+ *liquid*] echar gota a gota • **the cat ~ped the mouse at my feet** el gato soltó al ratón junto a mis pies • **don't ~ your coat on the floor, hang it up** no sueltes el abrigo en el suelo, cuélgalo • **to ~ a letter in the postbox** echar una carta al buzón • **~ it!*** (*gun*) ¡suéltalo!
b (*accidentally*) • **I ~ped the glass** se me cayó el vaso • **I've ~ped a stitch** (*Knitting*) se me escapó un punto
2 (= *lower*) [+ *eyes, voice, price, hem*] bajar
3 (= *set down*) (*from car*) [+ *object, person*] dejar; (*from boat*) [+ *cargo, passengers*] descargar • **could you ~ me at the station?** ¿me puedes dejar en la estación?
4 (= *utter casually*) [+ *remark, name, clue*] soltar • **to ~ (sb) a hint about sth** echar (a algn) una indirecta sobre algo • **to ~ a word in sb's ear** decir algo a algn en confianza
5 (= *send casually*) [+ *postcard, note*] echar • **to ~ sb a line** mandar unas líneas a algn
6 (= *omit*) (*from text*) suprimir • **to ~ one's h's** *or* **aitches** no pronunciar las haches • **I've been ~ped from the team** me han sacado del equipo
7 (= *abandon*) [+ *conversation, correspondence*] dejar; [+ *candidate*] rechazar; [+ *boyfriend*] dejar, plantar; [+ *friend*] romper con; [+ *charges*] retirar; [+ *claim, plan*] renunciar a, abandonar • **we had to ~ what we were doing** tuvimos que dejar lo que estábamos haciendo • **they ~ped him like a hot brick** lo abandonaron como a perro sarnoso • **I'm going to ~ chemistry** no voy a dar más química • **to ~ everything** soltarlo todo • **~ it!*** (*subject*) ¡ya está bien! • **let's ~ the subject** cambiemos de tema
8 (= *lose*) [+ *game*] perder
9 (*Drugs*) • **to ~ acid‡** tomar ácido
VI **1** (= *fall*) [*object, person*] caer(se) • **to ~ with exhaustion** caer rendido • **~ dead!*** ¡vete al cuerno!* • **I'm fit to ~*** estoy que no me tengo • **he let it ~ that ...** reveló que ... • **so we let the matter ~** así que dejamos el asunto
2 (= *decrease*) [*wind*] calmarse, amainar; [*temperature, price, voice*] bajar; [*numbers, crowd, demand*] disminuir • **the temperature will ~ tonight** la temperatura bajará esta noche
CPD ▸ **drop goal** (*Rugby*) drop *m* ▸ **drop handlebars** manillar *msing* de (bicicleta de) carreras ▸ **drop kick** puntapié *m* de botepronto ▸ **drop shot** dejada *f* ▸ **drop zone** (*Aer*) zona *f* de salto
▸ **drop across*** VI + ADV • **we ~ped across to see him** nos dejamos caer por su casa* • **he ~ped across to see us** se dejó caer por casa*
▸ **drop away** VI + ADV [*attendance etc*] disminuir
▸ **drop back** VI + ADV quedarse atrás
▸ **drop behind** VI + ADV (*in race, competition*) quedarse atrás; (*in work etc*) rezagarse
▸ **drop by** VI + ADV = **drop in**
▸ **drop down** VI + ADV caerse; (= *crouch*) agacharse • **we ~ped down to the coast** bajamos hacia la costa
▸ **drop in*** VI + ADV (= *visit*) pasar por casa *etc*, dejarse caer por casa *etc* • **do ~ in any time** ven a vernos cuando quieras • **to ~ in on** pasar por casa de • **they ~ped in on us yesterday** pasaron por casa ayer, nos visitaron de improviso ayer
▸ **drop off** VI + ADV **1** (= *fall asleep*) dormirse
2 (= *decline*) [*sales, interest*] disminuir
3 [*part*] desprenderse, soltarse
VT + ADV (*from car*) [+ *person, thing*] dejar • **could you ~ me off at the station?** ¿me puedes dejar en la estación?
▸ **drop out** VI + ADV [*contents etc*] derramarse, salirse; (*fig*) (*from competition*) retirarse • **to ~ out of society/university** abandonar la sociedad/la universidad • **to ~ out of a team** salirse de un equipo • **to ~ out of a race** abandonar una carrera • **he ~ped out of my life** desapareció de mi vida
▸ **drop round** VT + ADV • **I'll ~ it round to you** pasaré por casa para dártelo
VI + ADV = **drop in**

drop-dead‡ ['drɒpded] ADJ • **a drop-dead cute boy** un chico que te mueres* *or* te cagas‡ • **a drop-dead gorgeous girl** una chica guapa hasta no poder más • **a drop-dead gorgeous song** una canción chulísima *or* que te mueres*

drop-in centre ['drɒpɪn,sentəʳ] N (*Brit*) centro *m* de acogida

drop-leaf table [,drɒpli:f'teɪbl] N mesa *f* de ala(s) abatible(s)

droplet ['drɒplɪt] N gotita *f*

drop-off ['drɒpɒf] N disminución *f*

dropout ['drɒpaʊt] N **1** (*from society*) marginado/a *m/f*; (*from university*) *estudiante que abandona la universidad antes de graduarse*
2 (*Rugby*) puntapié *m* de saque

drop-out rate ['drɒpaʊt,reɪt] N (*from college*) índice *m* de abandono educativo

dropper ['drɒpəʳ] N (*Med etc*) cuentagotas *m inv*

dropping-out [,drɒpɪŋ'aʊt] N automarginación *f*; (*Univ*) abandono *m* de los estudios

droppings ['drɒpɪŋz] NPL [*of bird, animal*] excrementos *mpl*, cacas* *fpl*

dropsical ['drɒpsɪkəl] ADJ hidrópico

dropsy ['drɒpsɪ] N hidropesía *f*

dross [drɒs] N (*fig*) escoria *f*

drought [draʊt] N sequía *f*

drove [drəʊv] PT *of* **drive**
N [*of cattle*] manada *f* • **~s of people** una multitud de gente • **they came in ~s** acudieron en tropel

drover ['drəʊvəʳ] N boyero *m*, pastor *m*

drown [draʊn] VT **1** [+ *people, animals*] ahogar; [+ *land*] inundar • **to ~ o.s.** ahogarse • **a boy was ~ed here yesterday** un chico se ahogó ayer aquí • IDIOM: • **like a ~ed rat** calado hasta los huesos
2 (*also* **drown out**) [+ *sound*] ahogar • **his cries were ~ed by the noise of the waves** sus gritos se perdieron en el estruendo de las olas; ▹ **sorrow**
VI ahogarse, perecer ahogado • **a boy ~ed here yesterday** un chico se ahogó *or* pereció ahogado ayer aquí
▸ **drown out** VT + ADV [+ *voice, sound, words*] ahogar

drowning ['draʊnɪŋ] N ahogo *m*

drowse [draʊz] VI dormitar • **to ~ off** adormilarse

drowsily ['draʊzɪlɪ] ADV • **"what?" she asked ~** —¿qué? —preguntó soñolienta *or* medio dormida

drowsiness ['draʊzɪnɪs] N (= *sleepiness*) somnolencia *f*; (= *sluggishness*) modorra *f*, sopor *m* • **these tablets may cause ~** estas pastillas pueden producir somnolencia

drowsy ['draʊzɪ] ADJ (COMPAR: **drowsier**, SUPERL: **drowsiest**) **1** (= *sleepy*) [*person*] adormilado, soñoliento, somnoliento (*frm*); [*smile, look, voice*] soñoliento, somnoliento (*frm*) • **"who?" he asked in a ~ voice** —¿quién? —preguntó con voz soñoliento *or* con voz de sueño • **to be** *or* **feel ~** [*person*] tener sueño *or* modorra, estar soñoliento *or* adormilado; (*because of medication*) tener somnolencia • **to become** *or* **grow ~** quedarse adormilado • **she grew ~ and was put to bed** se quedaba adormilada y la acostaron, se estaba quedando dormida y la acostaron • **I became pleasantly ~** me empezó a entrar un sueñecito agradable • **these tablets will make you ~** estas pastillas le producirán somnolencia
2 (= *soporific*) [*afternoon, atmosphere*] soporífero; [*countryside*] apacible

drub [drʌb] VT (= *thrash*) apalear, vapulear; (*fig*) (= *defeat*) dar una paliza a*, cascar*

drubbing ['drʌbɪŋ] N (= *thrashing*) paliza *f*; (*fig*) (= *defeat*) paliza* *f*

drudge [drʌdʒ] N (= *person*) esclavo/a *m/f*; (= *job*) trabajo *m* pesado
VI trabajar como un esclavo

drudgery ['drʌdʒərɪ] N trabajo *m* pesado • **to take the ~ out of work** hacer el trabajo menos pesado

drug [drʌg] N (*Med*) medicamento *m*, fármaco *m*; (= *addictive substance*) droga *f*; (= *illegal substance*) droga *f*, narcótico *m* • **to take ~s** drogarse • **he's on ~s** se droga • **hard/soft ~s** drogas *fpl* duras/blandas • IDIOM: • **to be a ~ on the market** ser invendible
VT [+ *person*] drogar; [+ *wine etc*] echar una droga en • **to be in a ~ged sleep** dormir bajo los efectos de una droga • **to ~ o.s.** drogarse
CPD ▸ **drug abuse** toxicomanía *f* ▸ **drug abuser** toxicómano/a *m/f* ▸ **drug addict** drogadicto/a *m/f* ▸ **drug addiction** drogadicción *f*, toxicomanía *f* ▸ **drug baron** capo *m* ▸ **drug check** prueba *f* de la droga, control *m* antidoping ▸ **drug company** compañía *f* farmacéutica ▸ **drug czar** jefe/a *m/f* de la lucha contra el narcotráfico ▸ **drug dealer** traficante *mf* de drogas ▸ **drug dependency** drogodependencia *f* ▸ **drug driver** persona *f* que conduce drogada ▸ **drug driving** conducción *f* bajo el efecto de las drogas ▸ **drug habit** adicción *f* (a las drogas) ▸ **drug offence** delito *m* en materia de drogas ▸ **drug peddler, drug pusher** traficante *mf* de drogas, camello* *mf* ▸ **drug raid** (*US*) redada *f* antidroga ▸ **drug ring** (*US*) red *f* de narcotráfico ▸ **drug runner, drug smuggler** narcotraficante *mf* ▸ **drug squad** brigada *f* antidrogas, brigada *f* de

estupefacientes ▸ **drugs raid** redada *f* antidroga ▸ **drugs ring** red *f* de narcotráfico ▸ **drugs test** = drug test ▸ **drug taker** = drug user ▸ **drug test** (*Sport*) control *m* antidoping; (*for employees, students etc*) prueba *f* de detección de drogas ▸ **drug traffic** narcotráfico *m*, tráfico *m* de drogas ▸ **drug trafficker** traficante *mf* de drogas, narcotraficante *mf* ▸ **drug trafficking** narcotráfico *m*, tráfico *m* de drogas ▸ **drug tsar** jefe/a *m/f* de la lucha contra el narcotráfico ▸ **drug user** consumidor(a) *m/f* de drogas, drogadicto/a *m/f*

druggist ['drʌgɪst] (N) (*US*) farmacéutico/a *m/f*

druggy* ['drʌgɪ] (N) drogata* *mf*, drogota* *mf*

drug-induced [ˌdrʌgɪn'djuːst] (ADJ) [*behaviour, hallucination*] (*caused by narcotics*) provocado por las drogas; (*caused by medicine*) provocado por los medicamentos

drug-related ['drʌgrɪˌleɪtɪd] (ADJ) relacionado con la droga • **drug-related crime** drogodelincuencia *f*

drugster* ['drʌgstəʳ] (N) = **druggy**

drugstore ['drʌgstɔːʳ] (N) (*US*) *tienda de comestibles, periódicos y medicamentos*

drug-taking ['drʌg,teɪkɪŋ] (N) consumo *m* de drogas

druid ['druːɪd] (N) druida *m*

drum [drʌm] (N) **1** (*Mus*) tambor *m* • **to play (the) ~s** tocar la batería • IDIOM: • **to beat** *or* **bang the ~ for sth/sb** dar bombo a algo/algn, anunciar algo/a algn a bombo y platillo
2 (= *container*) (*for oil*) bidón *m*; (*Tech*) (= *cylinder, machine part*) tambor *m*
3 (*Anat*) (*also* **eardrum**) tímpano *m*
(VT) • **to ~ one's fingers on the table** tamborilear con los dedos sobre la mesa • **to ~ sth into sb** (*fig*) meter algo a algn en la cabeza por la fuerza • **I had it ~med into me as a child** de niño me hicieron comprender eso a la fuerza *or* a fuerza de repetírmelo
(VI) (*Mus*) tocar el tambor *etc*; (= *tap*) (*with fingers*) tamborilear • **the noise was ~ming in my ears** el ruido me estaba taladrando los oídos • **his words ~med in my mind** el eco de sus palabras resonaba en mi cabeza
(CPD) ▸ **drum brake** (*Aut*) freno *m* de tambor ▸ **drum machine** caja *f* de ritmos ▸ **drum major** (*Brit*) tambor *m* mayor ▸ **drum majorette** (*esp US*) bastonera *f* ▸ **drum set** batería *f*
▸ **drum out** (VT + ADV) • **to ~ sb out** expulsar a algn
▸ **drum up** (VT + ADV) [+ *enthusiasm*] despertar; [+ *support*] movilizar; [+ *trade*] fomentar

drumbeat ['drʌm,biːt] (N) redoble *m*

drumfire ['drʌm,faɪəʳ] (N) (*Mil*) cañonazos *mpl* continuos

drumhead ['drʌmhed] (N) parche *m* de tambor
(CPD) ▸ **drumhead court-martial** consejo *m* de guerra sumarísimo

drumkit ['drʌmkɪt] (N) batería *f*

drummer ['drʌməʳ] (N) (*in military band etc*) tambor *m*; (*in jazz/pop group*) batería *mf*

drumming ['drʌmɪŋ] (N) tamborileo *m*

drumroll ['drʌm,rəʊl] (N) redoble *m*

drumstick ['drʌmstɪk] (N) **1** (*Mus*) baqueta *f*, palillo *m* de tambor
2 (= *chicken leg*) muslo *m*

drunk [drʌŋk] (PP) *of* **drink**
(ADJ) (COMPAR: **drunker**, SUPERL: **drunkest**)
1 borracho, tomado (*LAm*) • **~ and disorderly behaviour** (*Jur*) embriaguez *f* y alteración *f* del orden público • **he was arrested for being ~ and disorderly** lo detuvieron por embriaguez y alteración del orden público • **to get ~** emborracharse • **to get sb ~** emborrachar a algn • **to be ~ on whisky** estar borracho de whisky • **to get ~ on wine** emborracharse de vino • IDIOM: • **to be as ~ as a lord** *or* **a skunk*** estar borracho como una cuba*
2 (*fig*) ebrio • **to be ~ on** *or* **with success** estar ebrio de éxito
(N) borracho/a *m/f*
(CPD) ▸ **drunk driver** conductor(a) *m/f* en estado de embriaguez • **a campaign against ~ drivers** una campaña contra los que beben y conducen ▸ **drunk driving** (*esp US*) = **drink-driving**

drunkard ['drʌŋkəd] (N) borracho/a *m/f*

drunken ['drʌŋkən] (ADJ) **1** (= *intoxicated*) [*person*] borracho; [*brawl, orgy*] de borrachos; [*night, evening*] de borrachera; [*violence*] provocado por el alcohol; [*voice*] de borracho, de cazallero • **a ~ old man** un viejo borracho • **her ~ husband** el borracho de su marido • **~ driving** conducir *or* (*LAm*) manejar en estado de embriaguez • **a ~ party** una juerga • **in a ~ rage** en un ataque de furia provocado por el alcohol • **in a ~ state** borracho • **in a ~ stupor** flotando en los vapores del alcohol
2 (*fig*) (= *crooked*) • **at a ~ angle** torcido

drunkenly ['drʌŋkənlɪ] (ADV) [*walk*] tambaleándose (borracho), haciendo eses*; [*speak, say, sing*] con voz de borracho • **the two men were arguing ~** los dos hombres discutían borrachos • **he staggered ~ out of the pub** salió del bar tambaleándose borracho *or* haciendo eses*

drunkenness ['drʌŋkənnɪs] (N) (= *state*) borrachera *f*, embriaguez *f* (*more frm*); (= *habit, problem*) alcoholismo *m*

drunkometer [drʌŋ'kɒmɪtəʳ] (N) (*US*) alcoholímetro *m*

drupe [druːp] (N) drupa *f*

druthers* ['drʌðəz] (N) (*US*) • **if I had my ~*** si por mí fuera

dry [draɪ] (ADJ) (COMPAR: **drier**, SUPERL: **driest**) **1** (= *not moist*) [*clothes, paint, leaves, weather*] seco; [*climate*] árido, seco • **it was warm and dry yesterday afternoon** ayer hizo una tarde cálida y seca • **wait till the glue is dry** espere a que la cola se seque • **he rubbed himself dry with a towel** se secó frotándose con una toalla • **her throat/mouth was dry** • **she had a dry throat/mouth** tenía la garganta/boca seca • **his mouth was dry with fear** tenía la boca seca de miedo • **her eyes were dry** (= *without tears*) no había lágrimas en sus ojos • **there wasn't a dry eye in the house** no había nadie que no estuviera llorando • **for dry skin/hair** para piel seca/pelo seco • **"keep in a dry place"** "mantener en un lugar seco" • **dry bread** (*without butter*) pan *m* sin mantequilla; (*stale*) pan *m* seco • **a dry cough** una tos seca • **to get dry** secarse • **on dry land** en tierra firme • **to run dry** [*river, well*] secarse; [*inspiration*] agotarse • **to wipe sth dry** secar algo (con un trapo) • IDIOM: • **as dry as a bone** más seco que una pasa
2* (= *thirsty*) • **to be** *or* **feel dry** tener sed, estar seco*
3* (= *prohibiting alcohol*) [*country, state*] seco • **due to a storm, the island was dry for a week** a causa de una tormenta, durante una semana no hubo ni una gota de alcohol en la isla
4 (= *wry*) [*humour, wit*] mordaz; [*laugh*] sardónico • **he has a very dry sense of humour** tiene un sentido del humor muy mordaz *or* cargado de ironía
5 (= *harsh*) • **it broke with a dry snapping sound** se rompió con un ruido seco
6 (= *uninteresting*) [*lecture, subject, book*] árido; [*voice*] seco • IDIOM: • **as dry as dust** terriblemente árido
7 (= *not sweet*) [*wine, sherry, cider*] seco; [*champagne*] brut, seco • **a dry white wine** un vino blanco seco
8 (= *not producing milk*) • **the old cow went dry** la vaca vieja se quedó sin leche
(N) • **the dry** (*Brit*) lo seco • **such cars grip the road well, even in the dry** estos coches se agarran bien al firme, incluso en seco • **come on into the dry** métete aquí que no llueve
(VT) secar • **to dry one's hands/eyes** secarse las manos/las lágrimas • **to dry the dishes** secar los platos • **to dry o.s.** secarse
(VI) **1** (= *become dry*) secarse • **leave it to dry** déjalo que se seque • **would you rather wash or dry?** ¿prefieres lavar o secar?
2 (*esp Brit*) (*Theat*) quedarse en blanco
(CPD) ▸ **dry cell** pila *f* seca ▸ **dry cleaner's** tintorería *f*, tinte *m* (*Sp*) ▸ **dry cleaning** limpieza *f* en seco ▸ **dry dock** dique *m* seco ▸ **dry fly** (*Fishing*) mosca *f* seca ▸ **dry ginger** ginebra *f* seca ▸ **dry goods** (*US*) artículos *mpl* de confección ▸ **dry goods store** (*US*) mercería *f* ▸ **dry ice** nieve *f* carbónica ▸ **dry measure** medida *f* para áridos ▸ **dry rot** *putrefacción seca de la madera causada por un hongo* ▸ **dry run** (*fig*) ensayo *m* ▸ **the dry season** la estación seca ▸ **dry shampoo** champú *m* seco ▸ **dry shave** • **to have a dry shave** afeitarse en seco ▸ **dry ski slope** pista *f* artificial de esquí ▸ **dry stone wall** muro *m* seco
▸ **dry off** (VI + ADV) [*clothes etc*] secarse
(VT + ADV) secar
▸ **dry out** (VI + ADV) **1** (*lit*) (= *dry*) secarse
2* (*fig*) [*alcoholic*] seguir una cura de desintoxicación de alcohol
(VT + ADV) **1** (*lit*) (= *dry*) [+ *clothes, ground, food, skin*] secar
2* (*fig*) [+ *alcoholic*] curar del alcoholismo
▸ **dry up** (VI + ADV) **1** [*river, well*] secarse; [*moisture*] evaporarse, desaparecer; [*source of supply*] agotarse
2 (= *dry the dishes*) secar los platos
3* (= *fall silent*) [*speaker*] callarse • **dry up!** ¡cierra el pico!*

dry-as-dust ['draɪəz'dʌst] (ADJ) terriblemente árido

dry-clean ['draɪ'kliːn] (VT) limpiar en seco, lavar en seco • **"dry-clean only"** (*on label*) "limpiar *or* lavar en seco"

dryer ['draɪəʳ] (N) (*for hair*) secador *m*; (*for clothes*) (= *machine*) secadora *f*; (= *rack*) tendedero *m*

dry-eyed ['draɪ'aɪd] (ADJ) sin lágrimas

drying ['draɪɪŋ] (ADJ) [*wind*] seco
(CPD) ▸ **drying cupboard** armario *m* de tender ▸ **drying room** habitación *f* de tender

drying-up ['draɪɪŋ'ʌp] (N) [*of river, well*] desecación *f*; [*of skin*] deshidratación *f* • **to do the drying-up** secar los platos

dryly ['draɪlɪ] (ADV) = **drily**

dryness ['draɪnɪs] (N) **1** [*of hair, skin, climate*] sequedad *f*
2 [*of wit, humour*] mordacidad *f*
3 [*of wine, sherry, cider, champagne*] lo seco
4 [*of lecture, subject, book*] aridez *f*

dry-roasted ['draɪ,rəʊstɪd] (ADJ) [*peanuts*] tostado

dry-shod ['draɪ'ʃɒd] (ADV) a pie enjuto

drysuit, dry-suit ['draɪsuːt] (N) traje *m* de neopreno

DS (N ABBR) (*Brit*) (*Police*) = **Detective Sergeant**

D/s (ABBR) (= **days after sight**) a ... días vista

DSC (*Brit*) (N ABBR) (= **Distinguished Service Cross**) ≈ cruz *f* al mérito militar

DSc (N ABBR) (*Univ*) = **Doctor of Science**

DSL (ABBR) (*Comput, Internet*) (= **digital**

subscriber line) DSL *f*, línea *f* de abonado digital • **DSL connection/operator/service** conexión/operadora/servicio de DSL

DSM (*Brit*) (N ABBR) (= **Distinguished Service Medal**) = medalla *f* al mérito militar

DSO (*Brit*) (N ABBR) = **Distinguished Service Order**

DSS (N ABBR) (*Brit*) = **Department of Social Security**

DST (N ABBR) (*US*) = **Daylight Saving Time**

DT (N ABBR) (*Comput*) = **data transmission**

DTD (N ABBR) (= **Document Type Definition**) DTD *f*

DTI (N ABBR) (*Brit*) (*Admin*) = **Department of Trade and Industry**

DTP (N ABBR) = **desktop publishing**

DTs* (NPL ABBR) = **delirium tremens**

DU (N ABBR) = **depleted uranium**

dual ['djʊəl] (ADJ) doble
(CPD) ▸ **dual carriageway** (*Brit*) autovía *f*, carretera *f* de doble calzada ▸ **dual control** doble mando *m* ▸ **dual controls** controles *mpl* dobles ▸ **dual nationality** doble nacionalidad *f* ▸ **dual ownership** condominio *m* ▸ **dual personality** doble personalidad *f*

dualism ['djʊəlɪzəm] (N) dualismo *m*

dualist ['djʊəlɪst] (ADJ) dualista
(N) dualista *mf*

duality [djʊ'ælɪtɪ] (N) dualidad *f*

dual-purpose ['djʊəl'pɜːpəs] (ADJ) de doble uso

duathlon [djuː'æθlɒn] (N) (*Sport*) duatlón *m*

dub [dʌb] (VT) **1** (*Cine*) doblar • **the film was dubbed into Spanish** la película estaba doblada al español
2 (= *nickname*) apodar • **they dubbed him "Shorty"** lo apodaron "Shorty"
3 [+ *knight*] armar caballero a

Dubai [duː'baɪ] (N) Dubai *m*

dubbin ['dʌbɪn] (N) adobo *m* impermeable, cera *f*

dubbing ['dʌbɪŋ] (N) (*Cine*) doblaje *m*
(CPD) ▸ **dubbing mixer** mezclador(a) *m/f* de sonido

dubiety [djuː'baɪətɪ] (N) incertidumbre *f*

dubious ['djuːbɪəs] (ADJ) **1** (= *questionable*) [*reputation, claim, privilege, taste*] dudoso; [*person, character, motives*] sospechoso; [*company, offer*] poco fiable; [*business deal, practice*] sospechoso, turbio; [*idea, measure*] discutible; [*compliment*] equívoco • **to have the ~ honour/pleasure of doing sth** tener el dudoso honor/placer de hacer algo • **that pâté looks a bit ~*** ese paté tiene una pinta un poco sospechosa • **of ~ benefit** de beneficios dudosos • **of ~ origin** de origen dudoso • **of ~ quality** de dudosa calidad
2 (= *unsure*) [*look, smile*] indeciso • **to be ~** tener dudas *or* reservas • **I was ~ at first, but he convinced me** al principio tenía mis dudas *or* reservas, pero él me convenció • **I'm very ~ about it** tengo grandes dudas *or* reservas sobre ello • **I am ~ that** *or* **whether the new law will achieve anything** tengo mis dudas *or* reservas sobre si la nueva ley va a lograr algo • **he looked ~** parecía tener dudas *or* reservas, parecía dudar • **he sounded ~** parecía tener dudas *or* reservas, parecía dudar

dubiously ['djuːbɪəslɪ] (ADV) [*look at, smile*] con recelo, con desconfianza; [*say*] con desconfianza • **a concerto ~ attributed to Albinoni** un concierto atribuido sin verdadera fundamento a Albinoni

Dublin ['dʌblɪn] (N) Dublín *m*
(CPD) ▸ **Dublin Bay prawn** cigala *f*

Dubliner ['dʌblɪnəʳ] (N) dublinés/esa *m/f*

ducal ['djuːkəl] (ADJ) ducal

ducat ['dʌkɪt] (N) ducado *m* (*moneda*)

duchess ['dʌtʃɪs] (N) duquesa *f*

duchy ['dʌtʃɪ] (N) ducado *m* (*territorio*)

duck¹ [dʌk] (N) (PL: **ducks** *or* **duck**) **1** (*Orn*) pato *m*; (*female*) pata *f* • **wild ~** pato *m* salvaje • IDIOMS: • **to be a dead ~**: • **he's a dead ~** está quemado • **that issue is a dead ~** esa cuestión ya no tiene interés • **to play ~s and drakes** hacer saltar una piedra plana sobre el agua • **to play ~s and drakes with** despilfarrar • **to take to sth like a ~ to water** sentirse como pez en el agua en *or* con algo, encontrarse en seguida en su elemento con algo; ▹ **lame, water**
2 (*Cricket*) cero *m* • **to make a ~** • **be out for a ~** (*Brit*) ser eliminado a cero
3 (= *movement*) (*under water*) zambullida *f*; (*to escape, avoid*) agachada *f*; (*Boxing*) finta *f*, esquiva *f*
4* (*as form of address*) • **yes, ~(s)** (*Brit*) sí, cariño
(VT) **1** (= *plunge in water*) [+ *person, head*] zambullir
2 (= *lower*) • **to ~ one's head** agachar la cabeza
3 (= *avoid*) [+ *problem, question*] eludir, esquivar
(VI) (*also* **duck down**) agacharse, agachar la cabeza; (*in fight*) esquivar el golpe; (*under water*) sumergirse
(CPD) ▸ **duck soup*** (*US*) (*fig*) • **it's just ~ soup** es pan comido, es coser y cantar
▸ **duck out of*** (VI + PREP) escabullirse de

duck² [dʌk] (N) (*US*) dril *m*

duckbill ['dʌkbɪl], **duck-billed platypus** ['dʌkbɪld'plætɪpəs] (N) ornitorrinco *m*

duckboard ['dʌkbɔːd] (N) pasadera *f*

duckie* ['dʌkɪ] (N) (*Brit*) = **ducky**

ducking ['dʌkɪŋ] (N) zambullida *f* • **to give sb a ~** meter la cabeza en el agua a algn

ducking-and-diving* [ˌdʌkɪŋən'daɪvɪŋ] (N) • **he did a lot of ducking-and-diving in London's drug-world** estuvo metido en muchos trapicheos en el mundo de la droga de Londres* • **ducking-and-diving is all part of political life** los políticos saben siempre cómo escaquearse*

duckling ['dʌklɪŋ] (N) patito *m*

duckpond ['dʌkpɒnd] (N) estanque *m* de patos

duckweed ['dʌkwiːd] (N) lenteja *f* de agua

ducky* ['dʌkɪ] (N) • **~!** ¡cariño!
(ADJ) (*US*) muy mono

duct [dʌkt] (N) **1** (*for ventilation, liquid*) conducto *m*
2 (*Anat*) conducto *m*, canal *m*

ductile ['dʌktaɪl] (ADJ) (*Tech*) [*metal*] dúctil

ductless ['dʌktlɪs] (ADJ) endocrino
(CPD) ▸ **ductless gland** glándula *f* endocrina

dud* [dʌd] (ADJ) **1** (= *useless*) [*cheque*] sin fondos; [*merchandise*] invendible; (= *not working*) [*machine etc*] estropeado; [*shell, bomb*] que no estalla
2 (= *false*) [*coin, note*] falso
(N) (= *thing*) filfa *f*; (= *person*) desastre *m*, inútil *mf*; (= *coin*) moneda *f* falsa; (= *shell*) obús *m* que no estalla

dude* [djuːd] (*US*) (N) (= *guy*) tío* *m*, tipo* *m*; (= *dandy*) petimetre *m*
(CPD) ▸ **dude ranch** rancho *m* para turistas

dudgeon ['dʌdʒən] (N) • **in high ~** muy enojado, enfurecido

duds* [dʌdz] (NPL) (= *clothes*) prendas *fpl* de vestir, trapos* *mpl*

due [djuː] (ADJ) **1** (= *expected*) • **when is the plane due (in)?** ¿a qué hora llega el avión? • **the train is due (in)** *or* **due to arrive at eight** el tren llega a las ocho, el tren tiene su hora de llegada a las ocho • **the train was due (in) ten minutes ago** el tren tenía que haber llegado hace diez minutos • **the results are due (in) today** está previsto que los resultados salgan hoy • **the magazine/film/record is due out in December** la revista/la película/el disco sale en diciembre • **I'm due in Chicago tomorrow** mañana me esperan en Chicago • **he is due back tomorrow** estará de vuelta mañana, está previsto que vuelva mañana • **when is it due to happen?** ¿para cuándo se prevé? • **it is due to be demolished** tienen que demolerlo • **when is the baby due?** ¿cuándo se espera que nazca el niño?
2 (= *owing*) [*sum, money*] pagadero, pendiente • **it's due on the 30th** el plazo vence el día 30 • **he's due a salary raise** (*US*) le corresponde un aumento de sueldo • **I am due six days' leave** se me deben seis días de vacaciones • **when is the rent due?** ¿cuándo se paga el alquiler?, ¿cuándo hay que pagar el alquiler? • **I feel I'm about due a holiday!** ¡me parece que necesito unas vacaciones! • **to fall due** (*Econ*) vencer • **he is due for a rise/promotion** le corresponde un aumento de sueldo/un ascenso • **I have £50 due to me** me deben 50 libras • **our thanks are due to him** le estamos muy agradecidos • **they must be treated with the respect due to their rank/age** deben ser tratados con el respeto que su rango/edad merece
3 (= *appropriate*) [*care, attention*] debido • **to drive without due care and attention** (*Jur*) conducir *or* (*LAm*) manejar sin el cuidado y la atención debidos • **after due consideration** después de la debida consideración • **we'll let you know in due course** le avisaremos a su debido tiempo • **he has never received due credit for his achievements** nunca ha recibido el crédito que merece por sus logros • **due process (of law)** (*Jur*) (el buen hacer de) la justicia • **with (all) due respect (to Mrs Harrison)** con el debido respeto (hacia la señora Harrison)
4 • **due to** (= *caused by*) debido a • **due to repairs, the garage will be closed next Saturday** esta gasolinera estará cerrada por obras el próximo sábado • **his death was due to natural causes** su muerte se debió a causas naturales • **what's it due to?** ¿a qué se debe? • **it is due to you that he is alive today** gracias a ti está todavía vivo
(ADV) • **due west of** justo hacia el oeste de • **to face due north** [*person*] mirar justo hacia el norte; [*building*] estar orientado completamente hacia el norte • **to go due north** ir derecho hacia el norte
(N) **1** (= *due credit*) • **to give him his due, he did try hard** para ser justo, se esforzó mucho
2 dues (= *club, union fees*) cuota *fsing*; (= *taxes*) derechos *mpl* • **harbour/port dues** derechos *mpl* de puerto • IDIOM: • **to pay one's dues** cumplir con su deber
(CPD) ▸ **due date** (*Econ*) [*of loan, debt*] fecha *f* de vencimiento • **when is your due date?** (*for birth*) ¿cuándo cumples? • **she is five days**

DUDE RANCH

Se llama **dude ranch** a un rancho del oeste de Estados Unidos que se abre a los turistas para ofrecerles el sabor de la vida del oeste al aire libre. Puede ser un rancho que funciona como tal en la realidad o uno que recrea la atmósfera tradicional de los vaqueros. Los turistas pueden montar a caballo, ayudar en las tareas del rancho o probar la comida hecha en el carromato (**chuck-wagon**) alrededor de la hoguera. **Dude** es una palabra que pertenece al argot americano, usada para referirse a una persona de ciudad muy bien vestida o a alguien del este.

past her due date cumplió hace cinco días, salió de cuentas hace cinco días (*Sp*)
duel ['djʊəl] N duelo *m* • **to fight a ~** batirse en duelo
VI batirse en duelo
duellist, duelist (*US*) ['djʊəlɪst] N duelista *m*
duet [dju:'et] N (= *players, composition*) dúo *m* • **to sing/play a ~** cantar/tocar a dúo
duff[1]* [dʌf] (*Brit*) ADJ (= *useless*) inútil; (= *poor quality*) de tres al cuarto
duff[2]* [dʌf] VT • **to ~ sb up** dar una paliza a algn
duff[3] [dʌf] N (*Culin*) budín *m*, pudín *m*
duff[4]‡ [dʌf] N culo‡ *m* • **he just sits on his ~ all day** pasa el día sin hacer nada • **get off your ~!** ¡no te quedes ahí sentado y haz algo!
duffel-bag ['dʌfəlbæg] N bolsa *f* de lona; (*Mil*) talego *m* (*para efectos de uso personal*)
duffel-coat ['dʌfəlkəʊt] N trenca *f*
duffer* ['dʌfəʳ] N zoquete* *m*
duffle-bag ['dʌfəlbæg] N = **duffel-bag**
duffle-coat ['dʌfəlkəʊt] N = **duffel-coat**
dug[1] [dʌg] PT, PP *of* **dig**
dug[2] [dʌg] N (*Zool*) teta *f*, ubre *f*
dugout ['dʌgaʊt] N **1** (*Ftbl*) caseta *f*
2 (*Mil*) refugio *m* subterráneo
duh‡ [dɜ:] EXCL jo
DUI N ABBR (*US*) (= **driving under (the) influence (of alcohol)**) conducción *f* or (*LAm*) manejo *m* bajo los efectos del alcohol
dui [dju:i:] NPL *of* **duo**
duke [dju:k] N duque *m*
dukedom ['dju:kdəm] N ducado *m* (*título*)
dukes‡ [dju:ks] NPL puños *mpl*
dulcet ['dʌlsɪt] ADJ dulce, suave
dulcimer ['dʌlsɪməʳ] N dulcémele *m*
dull [dʌl] ADJ (COMPAR: **duller**, SUPERL: **dullest**) **1** (= *boring*) [*person, speech, book, evening, job*] aburrido, pesado; [*place*] aburrido, soso; [*style, food*] soso • **deadly ~** terriblemente aburrido, aburridísimo • **there's never a ~ moment here in the office** aquí en la oficina no nos aburrimos nunca • IDIOM: • **as ~ as ditchwater** terriblemente aburrido
2 (= *not bright*) [*colour, metal, glow*] apagado; [*eyes*] apagado, sin brillo; [*hair, skin, complexion*] sin brillo; [*weather*] nublado; [*sky, day*] gris • **his eyes were ~ and lifeless** sus ojos estaban apagados y sin vida • **~, lifeless hair** pelo sin brillo, sin vida • **it will be ~ at first** (*Met*) al principio estará nublado
3 (= *not sharp*) [*pain, feeling, sound*] sordo • **it fell with a ~ thud** *or* **thump** cayó con un golpe sordo
4 (= *lethargic, withdrawn*) [*person, mood*] deprimido, desanimado
5 (= *slow-witted*) [*person, mind*] torpe; [*pupil*] lento • **his senses** *or* **faculties are growing ~** está perdiendo facultades • **to be ~ of hearing** ser duro de oído
6 (= *blunt*) [*blade, knife*] romo
7 (*Comm*) [*trade, business, market*] flojo
VT [+ *senses, blade*] embotar; [+ *emotions*] enfriar; [+ *pain*] aliviar; [+ *sound*] amortiguar; [+ *mind, memory*] entorpecer; [+ *colour*] apagar; [+ *mirror, metal*] deslustrar, quitar el brillo de; [+ *sensitivity*] embrutecer; [+ *grief*] atenuar • **the explosion ~ed her hearing** la explosión la dejó dura de oído
VI [*light*] amortiguarse; [*colour*] apagarse, perder intensidad; [*metal*] deslustrarse, perder brillo; [*memory*] entorpecerse; [*senses*] embotarse • **his eyes ~ed** sus ojos perdieron brillo
dullard ['dʌləd] N zoquete* *m*
dullness ['dʌlnɪs] N **1** (= *lack of interest*) [*of book, lecture, person*] lo aburrido, pesadez *f*
2 (= *lack of brightness*) [*of colour, metal*] falta *f* de brillo, lo opaco; [*of landscape*] monotonía *f*; [*of room*] lo lúgubre; [*of sound, pain*] lo sordo
3 (= *slow-wittedness*) [*of person*] torpeza *f* • **~ of hearing** dureza *f* de oído
dullsville* ['dʌlzvɪl] N (*US*) • **it's ~ here*** esto es un muermo*
dully ['dʌllɪ] ADV **1** (= *boringly*) [*speak, write*] de manera aburrida
2 (= *dimly*) [*glow, gleam, shine*] pálidamente, débilmente
3 (= *without enthusiasm*) [*say, reply*] sin entusiasmo; [*think*] de forma confusa • **he looked ~ about the room** sus ojos recorrieron la habitación sin entusiasmo
4 (= *with a muffled sound*) sordamente, con ruido sordo
5 (= *with a dull pain*) • **his arm throbbed ~** tenía un dolor sordo en el brazo
duly ['dju:lɪ] ADV **1** (= *as expected*) [*arrive, land*] como estaba previsto • **he ~ arrived at three** llegó a las tres, como estaba previsto • **I was ~ grateful for his assistance** como cabe esperar, le agradecí su asistencia • **the visitors were ~ impressed** los visitantes quedaron muy impresionados, como era de esperar
2 (= *properly*) [*elect, sign*] debidamente • **the point was ~ noted in the minutes** se tomó debida nota de ese punto
dumb [dʌm] ADJ (COMPAR: **dumber**, SUPERL: **dumbest**) **1** (*Med*‡) mudo; (*with surprise etc*) sin habla • **a ~ person** un mudo • **to become ~** quedar mudo • **she's deaf and ~**‡ es sordomuda • **~ animals** animales *mpl* indefensos • **the ~ millions** los millones que no tienen voz • **to be struck ~** (*fig*) quedarse sin habla
2* (= *stupid*) tonto, bobo • **to act ~** hacerse el tonto • **don't be so ~!** ¡no seas tonto *or* bobo! • **that was a really ~ thing I did!** ¡lo que hice fue una verdadera tontería *or* bobada! • **he says some ~ things** ¡dice cada tontería *or* bobada! • **~ blonde** rubia *f* descerebrada *or* sin seso • IDIOM: • **as ~ as an ox** más bruto que un arado
▸ **dumb down** VT + ADV embrutecer, empobrecer intelectualmente
dumb-ass‡ ['dʌmæs] (*US*) ADJ, N burro/a *m/f*
dumbbell ['dʌmbel] N **1** (*in gymnastics*) pesa *f*
2* (= *fool*) bobo/a *m/f*
dumbcluck* ['dʌmklʌk] N borde* *mf*
dumbfound [dʌm'faʊnd] VT dejar mudo • **we were ~ed** nos quedamos mudos de asombro
dumbing down [ˌdʌmɪŋ'daʊn] N [*of culture, programmes*] embrutecimiento *m*, empobrecimiento *m* intelectual
dumbly ['dʌmlɪ] ADV (= *without speaking*) sin abrir la boca
dumbness ['dʌmnɪs] N **1** (*Med*) mudez *f*
2* (= *stupidity*) estupidez *f*
dumbo* ['dʌmbəʊ] N tonto/a *m/f*
dumbstruck ['dʌmstrʌk] ADJ • **we were ~** nos quedamos mudos de asombro
dumbwaiter ['dʌm,weɪtəʳ] N (= *lift*) montaplatos *m inv*; (*Brit*) (*at table*) bandeja *f* giratoria
dum-dum bullet [ˌdʌmdʌm'bʊlɪt] N bala *f* dum-dum
dummy ['dʌmɪ] ADJ (= *not real*) [*gun*] de juguete; [*ammunition*] de fogueo; [*container*] vacío
N **1** (*for clothes*) maniquí *m*
2 (*for baby*) chupete *m*
3 (*Comm*) (= *sham object*) envase *m* vacío
4 (*Ftbl*) finta *f*
5 (*Bridge*) muerto *m*
6* (= *idiot*) tonto/a *m/f*
CPD ▸ **dummy assault, dummy attack** simulacro *m* de ataque ▸ **dummy company** empresa *f* fantasma ▸ **dummy number** (*Press*) número *m* cero ▸ **dummy run** (*Brit*) ensayo *m*, prueba *f*
dump [dʌmp] N **1** (= *place for refuse*) vertedero *m*, basurero *m*, basural *m* (*LAm*), tiradero(s) *m(pl)* (*Mex*); (= *pile of rubbish*) montón *m* de basura • **a rubbish ~** un vertedero, un basurero
2 (*Mil*) depósito *m*
3* (*pej*) (= *town*) poblacho *m*; (= *hotel etc*) cuchitril *m* • **it's a real ~!** ¡es una auténtica pocilga!
4 (*Comput*) vuelco *m* de memoria, volcado *m* de memoria
5 • IDIOM: • **to be (down) in the ~s*** tener murria, estar deprimido
6 • **to have a ~** (*Brit*‡) (= *defecate*) jiñar‡, cagar*‡
VT **1** [+ *rubbish etc*] verter, descargar
2* (= *put down*) [+ *parcel*] dejar, soltar; [+ *passenger*] dejar, plantar*; [+ *sand, load*] descargar, verter • **to ~ sth down*** poner algo (con mucho ruido) • **can I ~ this here?*** ¿puedo dejar esto aquí?
3* (= *get rid of*) [+ *person*] deshacerse de, librarse de; [+ *girlfriend, boyfriend*] plantar*
4 (= *reject*) rechazar
5 (= *throw away*) [+ *thing*] tirar
6 (*Comm*) [+ *goods*] inundar el mercado de
7 (*Comput*) volcar
VI (*Brit*‡) (= *defecate*) jiñar‡, cagar*‡
dumper ['dʌmpəʳ] N (*also* **dumper truck**) volquete *m*
dumping ['dʌmpɪŋ] N **1** [*of rubbish, waste*] vertido *m* • **"no dumping"** "prohibido verter basuras"
2 (*Comm*) dúmping *m*
CPD ▸ **dumping ground** vertedero *m*
dumpling ['dʌmplɪŋ] N *bola de masa hervida para servir con guiso*
Dumpster® ['dʌmpstəʳ] N (*US*) contenedor *m* de escombros *or* deshechos
dumptruck ['dʌmptrʌk] N (*US*) volquete *m*
dumpy ['dʌmpɪ] ADJ (COMPAR: **dumpier**, SUPERL: **dumpiest**) regordete
dun[1] [dʌn] ADJ pardo
dun[2] [dʌn] VT • **to dun sb** apremiar a algn para que pague lo que debe; (*fig*) dar la lata a algn*
dunce [dʌns] N (*Scol*) zopenco/a *m/f*
dunderhead ['dʌndəhed] N zoquete* *m*
Dundonian [dʌn'dəʊnɪən] N habitante *mf* de Dundee, nativo/a *m/f* de Dundee
ADJ de Dundee
dune [dju:n] N duna *f*
CPD ▸ **dune buggy** buggy *m* (*vehículo para terrenos arenosos*)
dung [dʌŋ] N [*of horse, camel etc*] excrementos *mpl*; (*as manure*) estiércol *m*
CPD ▸ **dung beetle** escarabajo *m* pelotero
dungarees [ˌdʌŋgə'ri:z] NPL (*for work*) mono *msing*, overol *m* (*LAm*); (*casual wear*) pantalón *msing* de peto
dungeon ['dʌndʒən] N calabozo *m*, mazmorra *f*
dunghill ['dʌŋhɪl] N estercolero *m*
dunk [dʌŋk] VT **1** [+ *biscuit, cake etc*] mojar
2 (*Basketball*) machacar
Dunkirk [dʌn'kɜ:k] N Dunquerque *m*
dunno‡ [də'nəʊ] = **(I) don't know**; no sé, ni flores*
dunnock ['dʌnək] N acentor *m* (común)
dunny* ['dʌnɪ] N (*Australia*) retrete *m*, wáter *m*
duo ['dju:əʊ] N (PL: **duos** *or* **dui** ['dju:i:]) (*Mus, Theat*) dúo *m*
duodecimal [ˌdju:əʊ'desɪməl] ADJ duodecimal

d

duodenal [ˌdju:əʊ'di:nl] ADJ duodenal
CPD ▸ **duodenal ulcer** úlcera *f* de duodeno
duodenum [ˌdju:əʊ'di:nəm] N (PL: **duodenums** *or* **duodena** [ˌdju:əʊ'di:nə]) duodeno *m*
duopoly [djʊ'ɒpəlɪ] N duopolio *m*
dupe [dju:p] N inocentón/ona *m/f* • **to be the ~ of** ser víctima de
VT (= *trick*) engañar, embaucar; (= *swindle*) timar • **to ~ sb (into doing sth)** engañar *or* embaucar a algn (para que haga algo)
duple ['dju:pl] ADJ (= *double*) (*gen*) doble
CPD ▸ **duple time** (*Mus*) tiempo *m* doble
duplex ['dju:pleks] (*US*) N (*also* **duplex house**) *casa para dos familias formada por dos viviendas adosadas*; (*also* **duplex apartment**) dúplex *m inv*
duplicate VT ['dju:plɪkeɪt] **1** (= *copy*) [+ *document, letter*] duplicar; (*on machine*) copiar
2 (= *repeat*) [+ *action*] repetir
N ['dju:plɪkɪt] (= *copy of letter etc*) duplicado *m*, copia *f* • **in ~** por duplicado
ADJ ['dju:plɪkɪt] [*copy*] duplicado
CPD ['dju:plɪkɪt] ▸ **duplicate key** duplicado *m* de una llave
duplicating machine ['dju:plɪkeɪtɪŋmə'ʃi:n] N multicopista *f*
duplication [ˌdju:plɪ'keɪʃən] N (= *copying*) duplicación *f*; (= *repetition*) repetición *f* innecesaria
duplicator ['dju:plɪkeɪtəʳ] N multicopista *f*
duplicitous [dju:'plɪsɪtəs] ADJ (*frm*) tramposo
duplicity [dju:'plɪsɪtɪ] N (*frm*) doblez *f*, duplicidad *f*
Dur ABBR (*Brit*) = **Durham**
durability [ˌdjʊərə'bɪlɪtɪ] N durabilidad *f*, lo duradero
durable ['djʊərəbl] ADJ duradero • **~ goods** (*US*) bienes *mpl* (de consumo) duraderos *or* no perecederos
NPL **durables** bienes *mpl* (de consumo) duraderos *or* no perecederos; ▹ **consumer**
duration [djʊə'reɪʃən] N duración *f* • **courses are of two years' ~** los cursos tienen una duración de dos años • **for the ~ of the war** mientras dure la guerra
Dürer ['djʊərəʳ] N Durero
duress [djʊə'res] N • **under ~** bajo presión
Durex® ['djʊəreks] N preservativo *m*
during ['djʊərɪŋ] PREP **1** (= *throughout*) durante
2 (= *in the course of*) durante
durst†† [dɜ:st] PT of **dare**
durum ['djʊərəm] N (*also* **durum wheat**) trigo *m* duro
dusk [dʌsk] N **1** (= *nightfall*) anochecer *m*, atardecer *m* • **at ~** al anochecer *or* atardecer
2 (= *gloom*) oscuridad *f* • **in the gathering ~** en la creciente oscuridad
dusky ['dʌskɪ] ADJ [*pink, blue*] oscuro; [*complexion*] moreno
dust [dʌst] N **1** (*in house, on ground*) polvo *m* • **there was thick ~** • **the ~ lay thick** había una gruesa capa de polvo • **to raise a cloud of ~** levantar una nube de polvo • **to raise a lot of ~** (*lit*) levantar mucho polvo; (*fig*) (= *cause a scandal*) levantar una polvareda • IDIOMS: • **to kick up** *or* **raise a ~*** armar un escándalo • **if you ask for a volunteer, you won't see her for ~!*** ¡en cuanto pides un voluntario pone los pies en polvorosa! • **when the ~ has settled** cuando haya pasado la tempestad • **to throw ~ in sb's eyes** engañar a algn; ▹ **ash², bite, dry, gather**
2* (= *act of dusting*) • **to give sth a ~** quitar el polvo a algo • **she gave the ornaments a quick ~** le quitó un poco el polvo a los adornos
VT **1** [+ *furniture*] quitar el polvo a *or* de; [+ *room*] limpiar el polvo a *or* de • IDIOM: • **it's done and ~ed** (*Brit*) todo ha terminado • **the deal is done and ~ed** el trato está cerrado
2 (*with flour, icing sugar*) espolvorear • **to ~ o.s. with talc** ponerse talco; ▹ **dust down, dust off**
VI (= *clean up*) limpiar el polvo
CPD ▸ **dust bowl** (*Geog*) *terreno erosionado por el viento* ▸ **dust cloth** (*US*) trapo *m* del polvo ▸ **dust cover** [*of book*] sobrecubierta *f*; (*for furniture*) guardapolvo *m* ▸ **dust devil** remolino *m* de polvo ▸ **dust jacket** sobrecubierta *f* ▸ **dust sheet** (*Brit*) guardapolvo *m*, funda *f* ▸ **dust storm** vendaval *m* de polvo, tormenta *f* de polvo
▸ **dust down** VT + ADV **1** (*lit*) [+ *furniture, shelf*] quitar el polvo a *or* de, desempolvar • **he stood and ~ed down his suit** se levantó y se sacudió el polvo del traje
2 (*fig*) desempolvar • **they ~ed down a project that had been shelved years ago** desempolvaron un proyecto que había sido aparcado hacía años • **to ~ o.s. down** sobreponerse • **he ~ed himself down and started again** se sobrepuso y volvió a empezar
▸ **dust off** VT + ADV = **dust down**
▸ **dust out** VT + ADV [+ *box, cupboard*] quitar el polvo a *or* de
dustbag ['dʌstbæg] N bolsa *f* de aspiradora
dustbin ['dʌstbɪn] (*Brit*) N cubo *m* de la basura
CPD ▸ **dustbin liner** bolsa *f* de basura ▸ **dustbin man** (*Brit*) basurero *m*
dustcart ['dʌstkɑ:t] N camión *m* de la basura
dustcloud ['dʌstklaʊd] N polvareda *f*
duster ['dʌstəʳ] N **1** (= *cloth for dusting*) trapo *m*; (*for blackboard*) borrador *m* • **feather ~** plumero *m*
2 (*US*) (= *housecoat*) guardapolvo *m*
dustheap ['dʌsthi:p] N basurero *m*
dustiness ['dʌstɪnɪs] N cantidad *f* de polvo
dusting ['dʌstɪŋ] N **1** (= *cleaning*) limpieza *f*
2* (= *beating*) paliza *f*
3 (*Culin*) (= *sprinkling*) espolvoreado *m*
CPD ▸ **dusting powder** polvos *mpl* secantes
dustman ['dʌstmən] N (PL: **dustmen**) (*Brit*) basurero *m*
dustpan ['dʌstpæn] N cogedor *m*
dust-proof ['dʌstpru:f] ADJ a prueba de polvo
dustsheet ['dʌstʃi:t] N (*Brit*) funda *f* (*para proteger del polvo*)
dust-up* ['dʌstʌp] N (*Brit*) pelea *f*, bronca *f* • **to have a dust-up with** pelearse con, tener una bronca con
dusty ['dʌstɪ] ADJ (COMPAR: **dustier**, SUPERL: **dustiest**) **1** (= *covered in dust*) [*town, ground, track, atmosphere*] polvoriento; [*furniture, book, car*] cubierto de polvo • **to get ~** [*table, book*] cubrirse de polvo; [*room, house*] llenarse de polvo
2 (= *greyish*) grisáceo • **~ blue** azul *m* grisáceo • **~ pink** rosa *m* grisáceo, rosa *m* viejo
3 (*Brit**) • **a ~ answer** *or* **reply** una respuesta evasiva • **"how are you?" — "not so ~** *or* **not too ~, thanks"** —¿cómo estás? —no mal del todo, gracias
Dutch [dʌtʃ] ADJ holandés • **she's ~** es holandesa • IDIOMS: • **to be in ~ with sb** (*US**) estar en la lista negra de algn • **to talk to sb like a ~ uncle** decirle cuatro verdades a algn
N **1** (*Ling*) neerlandés *m*, holandés *m*
2 • **the ~** (= *people*) los holandeses
ADV • IDIOM: • **to go ~*** [*two people*] pagar a medias; [*more than two*] pagar a escote
CPD ▸ **Dutch auction** subasta *f* a la baja ▸ **Dutch barn** *granero abierto a los lados con el tejado curvo* ▸ **Dutch cap** diafragma *m* ▸ **Dutch courage** *envalentonamiento del que ha bebido* ▸ **Dutch elm disease** enfermedad *f* del olmo, grafiosis *f* ▸ **Dutch oven** olla *f* ▸ **Dutch school** (*Art*) escuela *f* holandesa ▸ **Dutch treat** *comida etc en la que cada uno paga lo suyo*
Dutchman ['dʌtʃmən] N (PL: **Dutchmen**) holandés *m* • **it's him or I'm a ~*** que me maten si no es él
Dutchwoman ['dʌtʃˌwʊmən] N (PL: **Dutchwomen**) holandesa *f*
dutiable ['dju:tɪəbl] ADJ sujeto a derechos de aduana
dutiful ['dju:tɪfʊl] ADJ [*child*] obediente; [*husband*] sumiso; [*employee*] cumplido
dutifully ['dju:tɪfəlɪ] ADV obedientemente, sumisamente
duty ['dju:tɪ] N **1** (*moral, legal*) deber *m*, obligación *f* • **it is my ~ to inform you that …** es mi deber *or* obligación informarles de que … • **I feel it to be my ~** creo que es mi deber • **it was his ~ to tell the police** su deber era decírselo a la policía • **I am ~ bound to say that …** es mi deber decir que … • **to do one's ~ (by sb)** cumplir con su deber (hacia algn, para con algn) • **to fail in one's ~** faltar a su deber • **to make it one's ~ to do sth** encargarse de hacer algo • **it is no part of my ~ to do this** no me corresponde a mí hacer esto • **out of a sense of ~** por sentido del deber
2 (= *task, responsibility*) función *f*, responsabilidad *f* • **my duties consist of …** mis funciones *or* responsabilidades son … • **to do ~ as** servir de • **to do ~ for** servir en lugar de • **to neglect one's duties** faltar a sus responsabilidades • **to be off ~** (*gen*) estar libre • **an off ~ policeman** un policía fuera de servicio • **to be on ~** (*Med*) [*doctor, nurse, sentry*] estar de guardia; [*policeman*] estar de servicio; (*Admin, Scol*) estar de turno • **to go on ~** entrar de servicio • **to take up one's duties** entrar en funciones
3 (*Econ*) (= *tax*) derechos *mpl* • **to pay ~ on sth** pagar derechos por algo
CPD ▸ **duty call** visita *f* de cumplido ▸ **duty chemist** farmacia *f* de guardia ▸ **duty officer** (*Mil*) oficial *mf* de servicio ▸ **duty roster, duty rota** lista *f* de turnos
duty-free ['dju:tɪ'fri:] ADJ [*goods, perfume*] libre de impuestos, exento de derechos de aduana
CPD ▸ **duty-free allowance** cantidad *f* de productos libres de impuestos ▸ **duty-free shop** tienda *f* "duty free" ▸ **duty-free shopping** compras *f* libres de impuestos
duty-frees* [ˌdju:ti'fri:z] NPL (*Brit*) productos *mpl* libres de impuestos
duty-paid [ˌdju:tɪ'peɪd] ADJ con aranceles pagados
duvet ['du:veɪ] (*Brit*) N edredón *m* (nórdico)
CPD ▸ **duvet cover** funda *f* de edredón (nórdico)
DV ADV ABBR (= **Deo volente**) (= *God willing*) D. m.
DVD N ABBR (= **digital versatile** *or* **video disc**) DVD *m*, disco *m* de vídeo digital, disco digital polivalente
CPD ▸ **DVD burner** grabadora *f* de DVDs ▸ **DVD player** lector *m* de DVDs ▸ **DVD-Rom** DVD-Rom *m* ▸ **DVD writer** grabadora *f* de DVDs
DVD-A N ABBR (= **digital versatile disc audio**) DVD-A *m*
DVLA N ABBR (*Brit*) (= **Driver and Vehicle Licensing Agency**) *organismo encargado de la expedición de permisos de conducir y matriculación de vehículos*, ≈ DGT *f* (*Sp*)
DVLC N ABBR (*Brit*) (= **Driver and Vehicle Licensing Centre**) *centro de donde se expiden los*

permisos de conducir y matriculación de vehículos, ≈ DGT *f* (*Sp*)
DVM (N ABBR) (*US*) (*Univ*) = **Doctor of Veterinary Medicine**
DVR (ABBR) = **digital video recorder**
DVT (N ABBR) (= **deep vein thrombosis**) TVP *f*, trombosis *f* venosa profunda
dwarf [dwɔːf] (ADJ) (*gen*) enano
(N) ‡ (PL: **dwarfs** *or* **dwarves** [dwɔːvz]) enano/a *m/f*
(VT) (= *dominate*) [+ *building, person*] empequeñecer, hacer que parezca pequeño; [+ *achievement*] eclipsar
(CPD) ▸ **dwarf bean** judía *f* enana, fríjol *m*
dweeb‡ [dwiːb] (N) (*esp US*) memo/a* *m/f*
dwell [dwel] (PT, PP: **dwelt**) (VI) (*poet*) morar, vivir
▸ **dwell on, dwell upon** (VI + PREP) **1** (= *think about*) dar vueltas a, pensar obsesivamente en; (= *talk about*) insistir en (hablar de) • **don't let's ~ upon it** no hay que insistir
2 (= *emphasize*) hacer hincapié en; (= *lengthen*) [+ *note, syllable*] alargar, poner énfasis en
dweller ['dweləʳ] (N) morador(a) *m/f*, habitante *mf*
dwelling ['dwelɪŋ] (N) (*frm, poet*) morada *f*, vivienda *f*
(CPD) ▸ **dwelling house** (*frm*) casa *f* particular
dwelt [dwelt] (PT), (PP) *of* **dwell**
DWEM [dwem] (N ABBR) (*esp US*) = **Dead White (European) Male**
dwindle ['dwɪndl] (VI) reducirse, menguar • **to ~ to** quedar reducido a • **to ~ away** [*money, sound*] disminuir, menguar • **his life was dwindling away** se consumía poco a poco
dwindling ['dwɪndlɪŋ] (ADJ) (*gen*) menguante
(N) disminución *f*
dye [daɪ] (N) tinte *m* • **hair dye** tinte *m* para el pelo
(VT) [+ *fabric, hair*] teñir • **to dye sth red** teñir algo de rojo • **to dye one's hair blond** teñirse el pelo de rubio
dyed-in-the-wool ['daɪdɪnðə'wʊl] (ADJ) (*fig*) testarudo
dyeing ['daɪɪŋ] (N) tinte *m*, tintura *f*
dyer ['daɪəʳ] (N) tintorero/a *m/f* • **~'s** tintorería *f*
dyestuff ['daɪstʌf] (N) tinte *m*, colorante *m*
dyeworks ['daɪwɜːks] (NPL) tintorería *fsing*
dying ['daɪɪŋ] (PP) *of* **die**
(ADJ) [*man*] moribundo, agonizante; [*moments*] final; [*custom, race*] en vías de extinción • **his ~ words were ...** sus últimas palabras fueron ...
(NPL) • **the ~** los moribundos
dyke [daɪk] (N) **1** (= *barrier*) dique *m*; (= *channel*) canal *m*, acequia *f*; (= *causeway*) calzada *f*; (= *embankment*) terraplén *m*
2** (*offensive*) (= *lesbian*) tortillera** *f*
dynamic [daɪ'næmɪk] (ADJ) (*Phys*) (*also fig*) dinámico
(N) dinámica *f*
dynamically [daɪ'næmɪkəlɪ] (ADV) dinámicamente
dynamics [daɪ'næmɪks] (NSING) dinámica *f*
dynamism ['daɪnəmɪzəm] (N) dinamismo *m*
dynamite ['daɪnəmaɪt] (N) **1** (= *explosive*) dinamita *f*
2 (*fig**) • **he's ~!** ¡es estupendo! • **the story is ~** (*Press*) la noticia es una bomba *or* pura dinamita
(VT) [+ *bridge etc*] dinamitar, volar con dinamita
dynamo ['daɪnəməʊ] (N) dínamo *f*, dinamo *f*, dínamo *m* (*LAm*), dinamo *m* (*LAm*)
dynastic [daɪ'næstɪk] (ADJ) dinástico
dynasty ['dɪnəstɪ] (N) dinastía *f*
d'you [djuː] (ABBR) = **do you**
dysentery ['dɪsntrɪ] (N) disentería *f*
dysfunction [dɪs'fʌŋkʃən] (N) disfunción *f*
dysfunctional [dɪs'fʌŋkʃənəl] (ADJ) disfuncional
dyslexia [dɪs'leksɪə] (N) dislexia *f*
dyslexic [dɪs'leksɪk] (ADJ) disléxico
(N) disléxico/a *m/f*
dysmenorrhoea, dysmenorrhea (*US*) [ˌdɪsmenə'rɪə] (N) dismenorrea *f*
dysmorphia [dɪs'mɔːfɪə] (N) dismorfia *f*
dyspepsia [dɪs'pepsɪə] (N) dispepsia *f*
dyspeptic [dɪs'peptɪk] (ADJ) dispéptico
dysphasia [dɪs'feɪzɪə] (N) disfasia *f*
dyspraxia [dɪs'præksɪə] (N) dispraxia *f*
dystrophy ['dɪstrəfɪ] (N) distrofia *f*
• **muscular ~** distrofia *f* muscular

Ee

e

E¹, e [iː] (N) **1** (= *letter*) E, e *f* • **E for Edward** E de Enrique
2 (*Mus*) • **E** mi *m* • **E major/minor** mi mayor/menor • **E sharp/flat** mi sostenido/bemol
3 (*Brit*) = **elbow** • **to give sb the big E*** [+ *lover*] dejar plantado *or* plantar a algn*; [+ *employee*] echar a algn a la calle*, despedir a algn
(CPD) ▸ **E number** número *m* E
E² (ABBR) **1** (= **east**) E
2 (*Drugs**) (= **ecstasy**) éxtasis *m*
E111 (N ABBR) (*Brit*) (*also* **form E111**) *impreso para la asistencia sanitaria en el extranjero*
e- [iː] (PREFIX) electrónico
EA (ABBR) (*US*) = **educational age**
ea (ABBR) (= **each**) c/u
each [iːtʃ] (ADJ) cada • **~ day** cada día • **~ house has its own garden** todas las casas tienen jardín • **~ one of them** cada uno (de ellos) • **~ and every one of them** todos y cada uno de ellos
(PRON) **1** cada uno • **~ of us** cada uno de nosotros, cada quien (*LAm*) • **he gave ~ of us £10** nos dio 10 libras a cada uno • **a little of ~** un poco de cada
2 • **~ other: they looked at ~ other** se miraron (uno a otro) • **they help ~ other** se ayudan mutuamente *or* entre ellos • **people must help ~ other** hay que ayudarse (uno a otro) • **they love ~ other** se quieren • **we write to ~ other** nos escribimos • **they don't know ~ other** no se conocen • **they were sorry for ~ other** se compadecían entre ellos • **their houses are next to ~ other** sus casas están una al lado de la otra *or* (*LAm*) juntas
(ADV) • **we gave them one apple ~** les dimos una manzana por persona • **they cost £5 ~** costaron 5 libras cada uno
eager [ˈiːgəʳ] (ADJ) **1** [*person*] (= *enthusiastic*) entusiasta, entusiasmado; (= *impatient*) impaciente, ansioso; (= *hopeful*) ilusionado • **don't be so ~!** ¡ten paciencia! • **to be ~ to do sth: we were ~ to leave** estábamos impacientes *or* ansiosos por marcharnos • **he is ~ to find a new job** está impaciente *or* ansioso por encontrar otro trabajo • **the children are ~ to go camping** los niños están deseando ir de acampada • **to be ~ to help** estar deseoso de ayudar • **to be ~ to learn** tener muchas ganas *or* muchos deseos de aprender • **to be ~ to please** desear complacer • **to be ~ to succeed** estar ansioso por triunfar • **to be ~ for** [+ *affection, knowledge, power*] tener ansias de; [+ *vengeance*] tener sed de • **to be ~ for change** ansiar *or* desear mucho un cambio • **to be ~ for sb to do sth** estar ansioso porque algn haga algo, estar deseando que algn haga algo • **he was ~ for me to meet his family** estaba ansioso porque conociera a su familia, estaba deseando que conociera a su familia • **to be ~ for sth to happen** ansiar que algo pase, desear ardientemente que algo pase • IDIOM: • **to be an ~ beaver*** ser muy diligente
2 [*desire*] vivo, ardiente
eagerly [ˈiːgəlɪ] (ADV) (= *enthusiastically*) [*say, accept*] con entusiasmo; (= *impatiently*) [*await, anticipate*] con impaciencia, ansiosamente; (= *hopefully*) con ilusión; (= *avidly*) [*read, listen*] con avidez
eagerness [ˈiːgənɪs] (N) (= *enthusiasm*) entusiasmo *m*; (= *impatience*) impaciencia *f*; (= *hopefulness*) ilusión *f* • **~ to do sth: ~ to succeed** ansias *fpl* de éxito • **~ to learn/leave** ganas *fpl* de aprender/marcharse, ansias *fpl* de aprender/marcharse • **~ to help/please** deseo *m* de ayudar/agradar • **in his ~ to get there first** en su ansia por llegar el primero
EAGGF (N ABBR) (= **European Agricultural Guidance and Guarantee Fund**) FEOGA *m*
eagle [ˈiːgl] (N) águila *f* • **with (an) ~ eye** con ojos de lince
(CPD) ▸ **Eagle Scout** (*US*) *boy scout con el máximo rango posible*
eagle-eyed [ˈiːglˈaɪd] (ADJ) [*person*] • **to be eagle-eyed** tener ojos de lince
eaglet [ˈiːglɪt] (N) aguilucho *m*
E & OE [ˌiːəndˈəʊiː] (ABBR) (= **errors and omissions excepted**) s.e.u.o.
ear¹ [ɪəʳ] (N) **1** (*Anat*) (= *outer part*) oreja *f*; (= *rest of organ*) oído *m* • **she has small ears** tiene las orejas pequeñas • **he could not believe his ears** no daba crédito a sus oídos • **he was grinning from ear to ear** la mueca le llegaba de oreja a oreja • **he whispered in her ear** le susurró al oído • **inner/middle/outer ear** oído *m* interno/medio/externo • **to prick up one's ears** [*person*] aguzar el oído; [*animal*] empinar las orejas • **he was looking for a sympathetic ear** buscaba a alguien que le escuchara • **a word in your ear** una palabra en confianza • IDIOMS: • **to be all ears** ser todo oídos • **to bend sb's ear*** machacar la cabeza a algn* • **I bet his ears were burning** apuesto a que le zumbaban *or* pitaban los oídos • **to close** *or* **shut one's ears to sth** hacer caso omiso de algo • **they closed** *or* **shut their ears to everything that was being said** hicieron caso omiso de todo lo que se dijo • **to fall** *or* **crash down around** *or* **about one's ears** venirse abajo • **the house is falling down around my ears** la casa se está viniendo abajo • **it brought their world crashing down around their ears** hizo que el mundo se les viniera abajo • **to fall on deaf ears** caer en oídos sordos • **it goes in one ear and out the other** por un oído le/me entra y por otro le/me sale • **to have/keep one's ear(s) to the ground** estar con la oreja pegada*, estar al tanto • **to have sb's ear** tener enchufe con algn* • **to lend an ear (to sth)** prestar atención (a algo) • **they're always willing to lend an ear and offer advice** siempre están dispuestos a escuchar y dar consejos • **to listen with half an ear** escuchar a medias • **to be out on one's ear*** verse en la calle (sin trabajo)* • **if you don't work harder, you'll be out on your ear** como no arrimes más el hombro te verás en la calle* • **to pin back one's ears*** escuchar bien • **to give sb a thick ear*** dar una torta *or* un tortazo a algn* • **to be up to one's ears (in sth)*** (*in work, papers*) estar hasta arriba (de algo); (*in difficulties, debt, scandal*) estar hasta el cuello (de algo) • **to have money/houses coming out of one's ears** tener dinero/casas para dar y tomar • **I had football/pizza coming out of my ears** el fútbol/la pizza me salía por las orejas, estaba harto de fútbol/pizza • **to be wet behind the ears*** estar verde*; ▹ **cauliflower, deaf, flea, pig, box²**
2 (= *sense of hearing*) oído *m* • **her voice was very pleasing to the ear** tenía una voz muy agradable al oído • **to play sth by ear** (*lit*) tocar algo de oído • **we don't know what to expect, we'll just have to play it by ear** (*fig*) no sabemos a qué atenernos, tendremos que improvisar sobre la marcha • **she has an ear for languages** tiene oído para los idiomas • **she has a good ear (for music)** tiene buen oído (para la música)
(CPD) ▸ **ear infection** infección *f* de oído ▸ **ear lobe** lóbulo *m* de la oreja ▸ **ear, nose and throat department** sección *f* de otorrinolaringología ▸ **ear, nose and throat specialist** otorrinolaringólogo/a *m/f* ▸ **ear trumpet** trompetilla *f* acústica ▸ **ear wax** cerumen *m*, cera *f* de los oídos
ear² [ɪəʳ] (N) [*of cereal*] espiga *f*
earache [ˈɪəreɪk] (N) dolor *m* de oídos • **to have ~** tener dolor de oídos
eardrops [ˈɪədrɒps] (NPL) (*Med*) gotas *fpl* para el oído
eardrum [ˈɪədrʌm] (N) tímpano *m*
earflap [ˈɪəflæp] (N) orejera *f*
earful* [ˈɪəfʊl] (N) **1** • **I got an ~ of Wagner** me llenaron los oídos de Wagner • **she gave me an ~ of her complaints** me soltó el rollo de sus quejas* • **get an ~ of this** (*Brit*) escucha esto
2 (= *telling-off*) • **to give sb an ~** echar la *or* una bronca a algn*, regañar a algn
earhole* [ˈɪəhəʊl] (N) agujero *m* de la oreja
earl [ɜːl] (N) conde *m*
earldom [ˈɜːldəm] (N) condado *m*
earlier [ˈɜːlɪəʳ] (ADJ COMPAR) **1** (= *previous*) [*meeting, edition, report, idea*] anterior • **at an ~ date** en una fecha anterior
2 (= *not so late*) [*time*] más temprano
(ADV) antes • **I can't come any ~** no puedo venir antes • **I saw him ~** le vi antes • **a month ~** un mes antes • **~ this year** antes en este mismo año • **~ than** antes que • **she left ~ than us** se marchó antes que nosotros
earliest [ˈɜːlɪɪst] (ADJ SUPERL) *of* **early**
(N) • **at the ~** como muy pronto • **it will happen in March at the ~** ocurrirá en marzo como muy pronto
early [ˈɜːlɪ] (COMPAR: **earlier**, SUPERL: **earliest**)

(ADJ) **1** (= *before appointed time*) • **to be ~** llegar temprano *or* pronto • **you're ~!** ¡llegas temprano *or* pronto! • **you're five minutes ~** llegas con cinco minutos de adelanto • **I was half an hour ~ for the meeting** llegué a la reunión con media hora de adelanto, llegué a la reunión media hora antes de que empezase
2 (= *before usual time*) [*death, menopause*] prematuro, temprano • **Easter is ~ this year** la Semana Santa cae pronto este año • **~ frosts** heladas *fpl* prematuras *or* tempranas • **to have an ~ lunch** almorzar temprano, comer temprano • **she was pressurized into an ~ marriage** la presionaron para que se casase muy joven • **to have an ~ night** acostarse temprano • **~ retirement** jubilación *f* anticipada • **it was an ~ summer** el verano se había adelantado, el verano había llegado pronto
3 (= *soon*) pronto • **it's too ~ to say** es demasiado pronto para saber • **at your earliest convenience** (*Comm*) con la mayor brevedad posible
4 (= *towards beginning*) **a** (*of morning*) • **we need two seats on an ~ flight** necesitamos dos plazas en un vuelo que salga por la mañana temprano *or* un vuelo a primera hora de la mañana • **to get up at an ~ hour** levantarse temprano, levantarse de madrugada • **to keep ~ hours** acostarse y levantarse temprano • **we arrived home in the ~ hours (of the morning)** llegamos a casa de madrugada • **we worked until the ~ hours of the morning** trabajamos hasta altas horas de la madrugada • **it was ~ in the morning** era muy de mañana, era muy temprano • **in the ~ morning** a primeras horas de la mañana • **we went for an ~ morning drive** nos fuimos a dar un paseo en coche por la mañana temprano • **to be an ~ riser** ser madrugador • **to get off to** *or* **make an ~ start** salir temprano
b [*period, process*] • **the ~ days/months/years of sth** los primeros días/meses/años de algo • **in the ~ 60s/70s** a principios de los 60/70 • **she's in her ~ forties/seventies** tiene poco más de cuarenta/setenta años, tiene cuarenta/setenta y pocos (años) • **she became famous in her ~ thirties** se hizo famosa a los treinta y pocos • **there were two ~ goals** se marcaron dos goles al inicio del partido • **in ~ January/March** a principios de enero/marzo • **it's still ~** (*in process*) es pronto todavía • **the ~ afternoon** a primera hora de la tarde • **at an ~ age** a una edad temprana • **from an ~ age** desde pequeño, desde una edad temprana (*frm*) • **his ~ career/childhood** los primeros años de su carrera/infancia • **an ~ diagnosis** un diagnóstico precoz • **it was ~ evening** era media tarde • **we'll arrive there in the ~ evening** llegaremos a media tarde • **her ~ life** los primeros años de su vida • **in the ~ spring** a principios de la primavera • **it flowers from ~ spring to ~ autumn** florece desde principios de la primavera a principios del otoño • **the disease is hard to detect in its ~ stages** es difícil detectar la enfermedad en sus fases iniciales • **at an earlier stage of the project** en una etapa anterior del proyecto • **he's in his ~ teens** tendrá unos trece o catorce años • **he began painting in his ~ teens** empezó a pintar a los trece o catorce años • **his ~ youth** su primera juventud • IDIOM: • **it's ~ days yet**: • **we may have to modify the plans, but it's ~ days yet** (*esp Brit*) quizás tengamos que modificar los planes, pero aún es pronto para saberlo
5 (= *first*) [*man, Church*] primitivo; [*settlers, pioneers, Christians*] primer • **the ~ Victorians** los primeros victorianos • **an ~ Victorian table** una mesa de principios de la era victoriana • **Shakespeare's ~ work** las primeras obras de Shakespeare
6 (*Hort*) [*fruit, vegetable, crop*] temprano
(ADV) **1** (= *ahead of time*) [*arrive, leave, get up, go to bed*] temprano, pronto • **he arrived ten minutes ~** llegó diez minutos de la hora, llegó con diez minutos de anticipación • **he took his summer holiday ~** se tomó las vacaciones de verano pronto • **to book ~** reservar con anticipación • **I don't want to get there too ~** no quiero llegar demasiado pronto • PROVERB: • **~ to bed, ~ to rise (makes a man healthy, wealthy and wise)** a quien madruga, Dios le ayuda; ▹ **bright**
2 (= *soon*) pronto • **the earliest I can do it is Tuesday** lo más pronto que lo podré hacer será el martes • **as ~ as possible** lo más pronto posible, cuanto antes • **as ~ as 1978** ya en 1978
3 (= *towards beginning of sth*) **a** (*in morning*) temprano • **you get up too ~** te levantas demasiado temprano, madrugas demasiado
b (*in period, process*) • **~ in sth**: • **~ in the afternoon** a primera hora de la tarde • **~ in the book** en las primeras páginas del libro • **~ in the war** a principios de la guerra • **~ in the week** a principios de semana • **~ in the year** a principios de año • **~ in 1915** a principios de 1915 • **~ in his life** en su juventud • **Red Ribbon fell ~ in the race** Red Ribbon tuvo una caída al principio de la carrera • **~ last century** a principios del siglo pasado • **~ next year** a principios del año que viene • **~ on in his career** en los primeros años de su carrera • **earlier on** anteriormente, antes • **~ this month** a principios de (este) mes • **~ today** a primera hora de hoy
(CPD) ▸ **early adopter** usuario/a *m/f* pionero/a ▸ **early bird*** madrugador(a) *m/f* • PROVERB: • **it's the ~ bird that catches the worm** al que madruga Dios le ayuda ▸ **early closing** (*also* **early-closing day**) (*Brit*) *día en que muchas tiendas solo abren por la mañana* • **~ closing is on Mondays** el lunes muchas tiendas solo abren por la mañana ▸ **the Early Middle Ages** la Alta Edad Media ▸ **early riser** madrugador(a) *m/f* ▸ **early warning radar system** sistema *m* de radar de alerta temprana ▸ **early warning system** sistema *m* de alarma temprana *or* precoz, sistema *m* de alerta temprana *or* precoz • **pain acts as the body's ~ warning system** el dolor actúa como un sistema de alarma *or* alerta precoz

early-stage ['ɜːlɪˌsteɪdʒ] (ADJ) [*disease*] en fase inicial

earmark ['ɪəmɑːk] (VT) destinar (**for** a)

earmuff ['ɪəmʌf] (N) orejera *f*

earn [ɜːn] (VT) [+ *money, wages etc*] ganar; (*Comm*) [+ *interest*] devengar; [+ *praise*] ganarse • **she ~s £5 an hour** gana 5 libras a la hora • **to ~ one's living** ganarse la vida • **~ed income** ingresos *mpl* devengados, renta *f* salarial *or* del trabajo • **it ~ed him the nickname of Crazy Harry** le valió el apodo de Crazy Harry • IDIOM: • **to ~ a** *or* **one's crust*** ganarse el pan, ganarse los garbanzos
(VI) • **to be ~ing** estar trabajando

earner ['ɜːnəʳ] (N) asalariado/a *m/f* • **there are three ~s in the family** en la familia hay tres personas asalariadas *or* que ganan un sueldo • **the shop is a nice little ~** (*Brit**) la tienda es rentable *or* una buena fuente de ingresos

earnest[1] ['ɜːnɪst] (ADJ) (= *serious*) [*person, character etc*] serio, formal; (= *sincere*) sincero; (= *eager*) [*wish, request*] vivo, ferviente • **it is my ~ wish that** deseo fervientemente que (+ *subjun*)
(N) • **in ~** en serio • **are you in ~?** ¿lo dices en serio?

earnest[2] ['ɜːnɪst] (N) prenda *f*, señal *f* • **~ money** fianza *f*

earnestly ['ɜːnɪstlɪ] (ADV) [*speak*] en serio; [*work*] afanosamente, con empeño; [*pray*] fervorosamente, fervientemente • **I ~ entreat you** (*frm or liter*) se lo suplico de todo corazón

earnestness ['ɜːnɪstnɪs] (N) (= *seriousness*) seriedad *f*, formalidad *f*; (= *sincerity*) sinceridad *f*

earning ['ɜːnɪŋ] (N) **earnings** (= *wages*) sueldo *msing*, salario *msing*; (= *income*) ingresos *mpl*; (= *profits*) ganancias *fpl*, beneficios *mpl* • **average ~s rose two percent last year** los ingresos medios aumentaron un dos por ciento el año pasado
(CPD) ▸ **earning potential** potencial *m* de rentabilidad ▸ **earning power** poder *m* adquisitivo ▸ **earnings related benefit** prestación *f* calculada según los ingresos

earphones ['ɪəfəʊnz] (NPL) (*Telec etc*) auriculares *mpl*

earpiece ['ɪəpiːs] (N) (*Telec*) auricular *m*

ear-piercing ['ɪəˌpɪəsɪŋ] (ADJ) penetrante, que taladra el oído

earplugs ['ɪəplʌgz] (NPL) tapones *mpl* para los oídos

earring ['ɪərɪŋ] (N) (= *long*) pendiente *m*, arete *m* (*LAm*); (= *round*) arete *m*, zarcillo *m*; (= *stud*) pendiente *m* (en forma de bolita)

earset ['ɪəset] (N) (*Telec*) auricular *m* con micrófono

earshot ['ɪəʃɒt] (N) • **to be within ~** estar al alcance del oído • **to be out of ~** estar fuera del alcance del oído

ear-splitting ['ɪəˌsplɪtɪŋ] (ADJ) que rompe el tímpano, que taladra el oído, ensordecedor

earth [ɜːθ] (N) **1** (= *the world*) • **(the) Earth** la Tierra • **here on ~** en este mundo • **she looks like nothing on ~*** está hecha un desastre • **it tasted like nothing on ~*** (= *good*) sabía de maravilla*; (= *bad*) sabía a rayos* • **nothing on ~ would make me do it** no lo haría por nada del mundo • **nothing on ~ will stop me now** no lo dejo ahora por nada del mundo • **what/where/who on ~ ...?*** ¿qué/dónde/quién demonios *or* diablos ...? • **what on ~ are you doing here?** ¿qué demonios *or* diablos haces aquí? • **why on ~ do it now?** ¿por qué demonios *or* diablos vamos a hacerlo ahora? • IDIOMS: • **to come down to ~** volver a la realidad • **it must have cost the ~!*** ¡te habrá costado un ojo de la cara! • **to promise the ~** prometer el oro y el moro; ▹ **planet**
2 (= *ground*) tierra *f*, suelo *m*; (= *soil*) tierra *f* • **to fall to ~** caer al suelo
3 [*of fox*] madriguera *f*, guarida *f* • **to go to ~** [*fox*] meterse en su madriguera; [*person*] esconderse, refugiarse • **to run to ~** [+ *animal*] cazar *or* atrapar en su guarida; [+ *person*] perseguir y encontrar
4 (*Elec*) toma *f* de tierra, tierra *f*
(VT) (*Elec*) [+ *apparatus*] conectar a tierra
(CPD) ▸ **earth cable, earth lead** cable *m* de toma de tierra ▸ **earth mother** (*Myth*) la madre tierra; (= *woman**) venus *f* ▸ **earth sciences** *ciencias concernientes a la Tierra*; (= *geology*) geología *f* ▸ **Earth Summit** Cumbre *f* de la Tierra ▸ **earth tremor** temblor *m* de tierra ▸ **earth wire** conductor *m* de tierra, cable *m* de tierra
▸ **earth up** (VT + ADV) (*Agr*) [+ *plant*] acollar

earthbound ['ɜːθbaʊnd] ADJ (= *moving towards earth*) en dirección a la Tierra; (= *stuck on earth*) terrestre; (= *unimaginative*) prosaico

earthed [ɜːθt] ADJ (*Elec, Electronics*) [*plug, appliance*] con toma de tierra

earthen ['ɜːθən] ADJ de tierra; [*pot*] de barro

earthenware ['ɜːθənwɛəʳ] N loza *f* (de barro)
CPD de barro

earthiness ['ɜːθɪnɪs] N [*of person*] sencillez *f*

earthling ['ɜːθlɪŋ] N terrícola *mf*

earthly ['ɜːθlɪ] ADJ **1** (= *terrestrial*) terrenal; (= *worldly*) mundano • **~ paradise** paraíso *m* terrenal
2* (= *possible*) • **there is no ~ reason to think ...** no existe razón alguna para pensar ... • **it's of no ~ use** no sirve para nada
N (*Brit**) • **he hasn't an ~** no tiene posibilidad alguna, no tiene ninguna esperanza

earthquake ['ɜːθkweɪk] N terremoto *m*

earthscape ['ɜːθskeɪp] N *vista de la tierra desde una nave espacial*

earth-shaking ['ɜːθˌʃeɪkɪŋ] ADJ, **earth-shattering** ['ɜːθˌʃætərɪŋ] ADJ trascendental

earthward ['ɜːθwəd], **earthwards** (*esp Brit*) ['ɜːθwədz] ADV hacia la tierra

earthwork ['ɜːθwɜːk] N terraplén *m*

earthworm ['ɜːθwɜːm] N lombriz *f*

earthy ['ɜːθɪ] ADJ **1** (= *like earth*) [*colour*] terroso • **an ~ taste** un sabor a tierra
2 (= *uncomplicated*) [*character*] sencillo
3 (= *vulgar*) [*humour*] grosero

earwig ['ɪəwɪg] N tijereta *f*

ease [iːz] N **1** (= *effortlessness*) facilidad *f* • **the ~ with which he found work** la facilidad con la que encontró trabajo • **for ~ of reference** para facilitar la referencia • **the camera's ~ of use** la facilidad de uso de la cámara • **with ~** con facilidad
2 (= *relaxed state*) • **his ~ with money** su soltura *or* ligereza con el dinero • **people immediately feel at ~ with her** la gente inmediatamente se siente a gusto *or* cómoda con ella • **he was completely at ~ with himself** se encontraba completamente a gusto consigo mismo • **I would feel more at ~ if I knew where she was** me sentiría más tranquilo si supiera dónde está • **to put sb at his/her ~** hacer que algn se relaje, tranquilizar a algn • **to put** *or* **set sb's mind at ~** tranquilizar a algn • **if it will put your mind at ~ I'll tell you** si te tranquiliza te lo digo • **his ~ of manner** su naturalidad • **to take one's ~** descansar; ▹ **ill**
3 (= *comfort*) comodidad *f* • **a life of ~** una vida cómoda *or* desahogada • **to live a life of ~** vivir cómodamente
4 (*Mil*) • **stand at ~!** • **stand easy!** (*Mil*) ¡descansen! • **at ~, Sergeant** descanse, Sargento
VT **1** (= *relieve, lessen*) [+ *pain, suffering*] aliviar; [+ *pressure, tension*] aliviar, relajar; [+ *burden*] aligerar; [+ *impact, effect*] mitigar, paliar; [+ *sanctions, restrictions*] relajar • **these measures will ~ the burden on small businesses** estas medidas aligerarán la carga de las pequeñas empresas • **she gave them money to ~ her conscience** les dio dinero para quedarse con la conciencia tranquila • **it will ~ her mind to know the baby's all right** le tranquilizará saber que el bebé está bien • **aid to help ~ the plight of refugees** ayuda para paliar la difícil situación de los refugiados • **attempts to ~ traffic congestion** intentos de descongestionar el tráfico • **this will help to ~ the workload** esto ayudará para hacer menos pesado el trabajo
2 (= *facilitate*) [+ *transition, task*] facilitar
3 (= *loosen*) aflojar
4 (= *move carefully*) • **he ~d the car into the parking space** aparcó el coche en el aparcamiento con cuidado • **she ~d her foot off the clutch** soltó el pie del embrague con cuidado • **he ~d himself into the chair** se sentó con cuidado en la silla
VI **1** (= *diminish*) [*pain*] ceder, disminuir; [*tension*] disminuir; [*wind, rain*] amainar; [*interest rates*] bajar
2 (= *improve*) [*situation*] calmarse

▸ **ease off** VI + ADV **1** (= *diminish*) [*pain*] ceder, disminuir; [*rain*] amainar; [*pressure*] disminuir • **the snow had ~d off** había dejado de nevar con tanta fuerza
2 (= *take things more easily*) tomarse las cosas con más tranquilidad
3 (= *work less hard*) aflojar el ritmo (de trabajo)
VT + ADV **1** (= *remove*) [+ *lid*] quitar; [+ *shoes, boots*] quitarse
2 (= *stop pressing on*) [+ *accelerator, clutch*] soltar

▸ **ease up** VI + ADV **1** (= *take things more easily*) tomarse las cosas con más tranquilidad • **if you don't ~ up, you'll make yourself ill** como no te tomes las cosas con más tranquilidad te vas a poner malo
2 (= *work less intensively*) bajar el ritmo (de trabajo) • **we can't afford to ~ up yet** no podemos relajarnos *or* bajar el ritmo todavía
3 (= *relax*) relajarse • **~ up a bit!** ¡relájate un poco!
4 (= *slow down*) [*runner*] aflojar el paso, aminorar la marcha; [*driver, car*] reducir *or* disminuir la velocidad, aminorar la marcha
5 • **to ~ up on** [+ *restrictions, sanctions*] relajar, aflojar • **you'd better ~ up on the chocolate** más vale que dejes de comer tanto chocolate • **~ up on him, he's only a child** no seas tan estricto con él, es solo un niño

easel ['iːzl] N caballete *m*

easily ['iːzɪlɪ] ADV **1** (= *without difficulty*) [*win, climb, break, tire, cry*] fácilmente, con facilidad • **he makes friends ~** hace amigos fácilmente *or* con facilidad • **he talked ~ about himself** habló sobre sí mismo de forma relajada • **don't give up so ~** no te rindas tan fácilmente • **she's ~ pleased/upset** es fácil complacerla/disgustarla, se contenta/disgusta fácilmente • **the park is ~ accessible by car** el parque tiene fácil acceso con coche • **don't worry, it's ~ done** (*replying to apology*) no te preocupes, le puede pasar a cualquiera • **there were ~ 500 at the meeting** había fácilmente 500 en la reunión • **it holds four litres ~** caben cuatro litros largos, caben cuatro litros fácilmente • **that will cost you £50 ~** eso te costará fácilmente *or* por lo menos 50 libras • **as ~ as (if)** con la misma facilidad que (si)
2 (= *very possibly*) perfectamente, fácilmente • **he may ~ change his mind** puede perfectamente *or* fácilmente cambiar de opinión, fácilmente cambia de opinión (*LAm*) • **it could very ~ happen again** podría perfectamente *or* fácilmente ocurrir de nuevo • **this could ~ be his last race** bien podría ser esta su última carrera
3 (= *by far*) con mucho • **he was ~ the best candidate** era con mucho el mejor candidato • **there was ~ enough to go round** había más que suficiente para todos

easiness ['iːzɪnɪs] N [*of task, exam question*] lo fácil; [*of laughter, voice, tone*] naturalidad *f*; [*of manner*] soltura *f*, naturalidad *f*

east [iːst] N este *m*, oriente *m* • **the East** (= *Orient*) el Oriente; (*Pol*) el Este • **in the ~ of the country** al este *or* en el este del país • **the wind is in the** *or* **from the ~** el viento viene del este • **to the ~ of** al este de
ADJ [*side*] este, del este, oriental • **an ~ wind** un viento del este • **the ~ coast** la costa este, la costa oriental
ADV (= *eastward*) hacia el este; (= *in the east*) al este, en el este • **we were travelling ~** viajábamos hacia el este • **~ of the border** al este de la frontera • **it's ~ of London** está al este de Londres
CPD ▸ **East Africa** África *f* Oriental ▸ **East Berlin** Berlín *m* Este ▸ **the East End** [*of London*] *zona del Este de Londres* ▸ **East Germany** Alemania *f* Oriental ▸ **the East Indies** las Indias Orientales ▸ **the East Side** [*of New York*] *zona del Este de Nueva York* ▸ **East Timor** Timor *m* Oriental; ▹ **East European, East German, East Timorese**

eastbound ['iːstbaʊnd] ADJ [*traffic*] en dirección este; [*carriageway*] de dirección este, en dirección este

Eastender [ˌiːst'endəʳ] N nativo/a *m/f or* habitante *mf* del este de Londres

Easter ['iːstəʳ] N Pascua *f* (de Resurrección), Semana *f* Santa • **at ~** por Pascua, en Semana Santa • **the ~ holidays** las vacaciones de Semana Santa
CPD ▸ **Easter bonnet** sombrero *m* de primavera ▸ **Easter Day** Domingo *m* de Resurrección ▸ **Easter egg** huevo *m* de Pascua ▸ **Easter Island** isla *f* de Pascua ▸ **Easter Monday** lunes *m inv* de Pascua de Resurrección ▸ **Easter parade** procesión *f* de Semana Santa ▸ **Easter Sunday** Domingo *m* de Resurrección ▸ **Easter week** Semana *f* Santa

easterly ['iːstəlɪ] ADJ [*wind*] del este • **we were headed in an ~ direction** íbamos hacia el este *or* rumbo al este *or* en dirección este • **the most ~ point in Wales** el punto más oriental *or* más al este de Gales
N viento *m* del este

eastern ['iːstən] ADJ del este, oriental • **the ~ part of the island** la parte oriental *or* la parte este de la isla • **the ~ coast** la costa este *or* oriental • **in ~ Spain** en el este *or* al este de España • **~ religions** religiones orientales
CPD ▸ **the Eastern bloc** (*Pol Hist*) el bloque del Este ▸ **Eastern Europe** Europa *f* del Este, Europa *f* Oriental

easterner ['iːstənəʳ] N (*esp US*) habitante *mf* del este

easternmost ['iːstənməʊst] ADJ más oriental, más al este • **the ~ point of Spain** el punto más oriental *or* más al este de España

Eastertide ['iːstətaɪd] N (*liter*) = **Easter**

East European ADJ de la Europa del Este, de la Europa Oriental
N europeo/a *m/f* del Este

east-facing ['iːstˌfeɪsɪŋ] ADJ con cara al este, orientado hacia el este • **east-facing slope** vertiente *f* este

East German [ˌiːst'dʒɜːmən] N (= *person*) alemán/ana *m/f* oriental
ADJ germanooriental

east-northeast [ˌiːstnɔːθ'iːst] N estenor(d)este *m*
ADJ estenor(d)este
ADV (= *toward east-northeast*) hacia el estenor(d)este; [*situated*] al estenor(d)este

east-southeast [ˌiːstsaʊθ'iːst] N estesudeste *m*, estesureste *m*
ADJ estesudeste, estesureste
ADV (= *toward east-southeast*) hacia el estesudeste *or* estesureste; (*situated*) al estesudeste *or* estesureste, en el estesudeste *or* estesureste

East Timorese N timorés/esa *m/f* oriental

(ADJ) de Timor Oriental, timorés/esa oriental

eastward [ˈiːstwəd] (ADJ) [*movement, migration*] hacia el este, en dirección este (ADV) hacia el este, en dirección este

eastwards [ˈiːstwədz] (ADV) (*esp Brit*) = **eastward**

easy [ˈiːzɪ] (ADJ) (COMPAR: **easier**, SUPERL: **easiest**) **1** (= *not difficult*) [*task, job, decision, victory*] fácil • **it is ~ to see that ...** es fácil ver que ... • **he's ~ to work with** es fácil trabajar con él • **he's ~ to get on with** es muy fácil llevarse bien con él • **fluorescent jackets are ~ to see at night** las chaquetas fluorescentes son fáciles de ver por la noche • **there are no ~ answers** no hay respuestas fáciles • **to be far from ~** no ser nada fácil • **he came in an ~ first** llegó el primero sin problemas • **that's ~ for you to say** para ti es fácil decirlo • **to have it ~** tenerlo fácil • **the ~ life** la vida fácil • **~ listening** (= *music*) música *f* fácil de escuchar • **they made it very ~ for us** nos lo pusieron muy fácil • **"Russian made ~"** "ruso sin esfuerzo" • **to be no ~ matter** no ser cosa fácil • **it's an ~ mistake to make** es un error que se comete fácilmente • **~ money** dinero *m* fácil • **to be none too ~** no ser nada fácil • **to be ~ on the eye/ear** ser *or* resultar agradable a la vista/al oído • **eat something that's ~ on the stomach** come algo que sea fácil de digerir • **to go for** *or* **take the ~ option** optar por lo más fácil • **that's the ~ part** eso es lo fácil • **~ pickings** botín *m* fácil • **~ prey** presa *f* fácil • **to be within ~ reach of sth** estar muy cerca de algo • **to make ~ reading** ser fácil de leer • **to have an ~ ride** (*fig*) tener las cosas fáciles • **that's easier said than done!** ¡eso se dice pronto!, es fácil decirlo, pero hacerlo ... • **I'd love to tell her to get lost but that's easier said than done** me encantaría mandarla al cuerno pero no es tan fácil de hacer • **in** *or* **by ~ stages** por etapas fáciles de superar • **to be no ~ task** no ser cosa fácil • **to buy sth on ~ terms** (*Comm*) comprar algo con facilidades de pago • **to have an ~ time** no tener problemas • **to take the ~ way out** (*fig*) optar por el camino más fácil • IDIOMS: • **it's as ~ as ABC** *or* **falling off a log** *or* **pie** es facilísimo • **to be on ~ street** estar forrado
2 (= *relaxed*) [*life*] cómodo, relajado; [*manners*] relajado, natural; [*disposition, conversation, conscience*] tranquilo; [*smile*] fácil; [*voice, tone, style*] natural; [*pace*] lento, pausado; [*movement*] suelto, relajado • **I'm ~*** (= *not particular*) me es igual *or* me da igual • **to feel ~ (in one's mind)** sentirse tranquilo • **I don't feel ~ about leaving the children with that woman** no me siento tranquilo dejando a los niños con esa mujer • **we relaxed into ~ laughter** nos relajamos y empezamos a reírnos con naturalidad • **he has** *or* **enjoys an ~ relationship with his stepchildren** tiene una relación muy buena *or* se lleva muy bien con los hijos de su mujer • **you can rest ~** puedes estar tranquilo • **to be on ~ terms with sb** estar en confianza con algn
3 (= *promiscuous*) [*woman*] fácil • **a woman of ~ virtue**† (*euph*) una mujer ligera de cascos
(ADV) • **we can all breathe ~ now** ahora todos podemos respirar tranquilos • **taking orders doesn't come ~ to him** no le resulta fácil obedecer órdenes • **~ come, ~ go** tal y como viene se va • **~ does it!** ¡despacio!, ¡cuidado!, ¡con calma! • **go ~ with the sugar** no te pases con el azúcar • **go ~ on him** no seas muy duro con él • **to take things ~** • **take it ~** (= *rest*) descansar; (= *go slowly*) tomárselo con calma • **take it ~!*** (= *don't worry*) ¡cálmete!, ¡no te pongas nervioso!; (= *don't rush*) ¡despacio!, ¡no corras!; ▹ **stand**
(CPD) ▸ **easy chair** butaca *f*, sillón *m* (*Sp*) ▸ **easy touch*** (= *person*) • **he's an ~ touch** es fácil de convencer

EASY, DIFFICULT, IMPOSSIBLE

▹ **Fácil, difícil** *and* **imposible** *are followed directly by the infinitive when they qualify the action itself:*

Solving the problem is easy
It's easy to solve the problem
Es fácil resolver el problema
It is sometimes difficult/impossible to control oneself
En ocasiones es difícil/imposible controlarse

▹ *When the adjective qualifies a noun or pronoun rather than the verb,* **de** *is inserted before the infinitive:*

The problem is easy to solve
El problema es fácil de resolver
That's difficult *or* **hard to believe**
Eso es difícil de creer
Semtex is impossible to detect
El Semtex es imposible de detectar

NOTE: Remember in this case to make the adjective agree with the noun or pronoun it describes:

Some of his works are difficult to classify
Algunas de sus obras son difíciles de encasillar

For further uses and examples, see main entry.

easy-care [ˈiːzɪkɛəʳ] (ADJ) (*Brit*) *que no necesita cuidados especiales*

easy-going [ˈiːzɪˈɡəʊɪŋ] (ADJ) [*person*] acomodadizo; [*attitude*] de trato fácil, relajado • **she's very easy-going and gets on well with everybody** es una persona de trato fácil y se lleva bien con todos

easy-peasy* [ˌiːzɪˈpiːzɪ] (ADJ) (*Brit*) (*child language*) tirado*, chupado‡

eat [iːt] (PT: **ate**, PP: **eaten**) (VT) comer • **there's nothing to eat** no hay nada de *or* que comer • **would you like something to eat?** ¿quieres comer algo? • **he won't eat you*** no te va a morder • **what's eating you?*** ¿qué mosca te ha picado? • **to eat one's fill** hartarse • **to eat one's lunch** comer, almorzar • **to eat one's way through the menu** pedir todos los platos de la carta • IDIOMS: • **he's eating us out of house and home*** come por ocho • **to eat one's words** tragarse las palabras
(VI) comer • **he eats like a horse** come más que una lima nueva • **he always eats well** siempre tiene buen apetito • IDIOM: • **I've got him eating out of my hand** lo tengo dominado

▸ **eat away** (VT + ADV) (= *wear away*) desgastar; (= *corrode*) corroer; [*mice etc*] roer

▸ **eat away at** (VI + PREP) **1** [*sea*] desgastar; [*acid, rust*] corroer; [*rot, damp*] comerse; [*mice etc*] roer; [*insect pest*] comerse, devorar
2 (*fig*) devorar

▸ **eat in** (VI + ADV) comer en casa

▸ **eat into** (VI + PREP) (= *wear away*) desgastar; [+ *metal*] [*acid*] corroer; [+ *savings*] mermar; [+ *leisure time*] reducir

▸ **eat out** (VI + ADV) comer fuera
(VT + ADV) • **to eat one's heart out** consumirse • **I've written a novel: Marcel Proust, eat your heart out!*** he escrito una novela: ¡chúpate esa, Marcel Proust!*

▸ **eat up** (VT + ADV) [+ *food*] comerse • **it eats up electricity** consume mucha electricidad • **to eat up the miles** tragar los kilómetros • **to be eaten up with envy** consumirse de envidia
(VI + ADV) • **eat up!** ¡venga, come!, ¡apúrate! (*LAm*)

eatable [ˈiːtəbl] (ADJ) (= *fit to eat*) comible, pasable; (= *edible*) comestible

eatables* [ˈiːtəblz] (NPL) comestibles *mpl*

eaten [ˈiːtn] (PP) *of* **eat**

eater [ˈiːtəʳ] (N) **1** (= *person*) • **to be a big ~** tener siempre buen apetito, ser comilón • **I'm not a big ~** yo como bastante poco
2 (= *apple*) manzana *f* de mesa

eatery* [ˈiːtərɪ] (N) (*US*) restaurante *m*

eating [ˈiːtɪŋ] (N) **1** (= *act*) el comer
2 • **to be good ~** ser sabroso
(CPD) ▸ **eating apple** manzana *f* de mesa ▸ **eating disorder** desorden *m* alimenticio ▸ **eating habits** hábitos *mpl* alimentarios, hábitos *mpl* alimenticios ▸ **eating olives** aceitunas *fpl* de boca

eating-house [ˈiːtɪŋhaʊs] (N) (PL: **eating-houses** [ˈiːtɪŋhaʊzɪz]) restaurante *m*

eats* [iːts] (NPL) comida *fsing*, comestibles *mpl* • **let's get some ~** vamos a comer algo

eau de Cologne [ˈəʊdəkəˈləʊn] (N) (agua *f* de) colonia *f*

eaves [iːvz] (NPL) alero *msing*

eavesdrop [ˈiːvzdrɒp] (VI) escuchar a escondidas • **to ~ on a conversation** escuchar una conversación a escondidas

eavesdropper [ˈiːvzˌdrɒpəʳ] (N) fisgón/ona *m/f* (*que escucha conversaciones a escondidas*)

e-banking [ˈiːbæŋkɪŋ] (N) banca *f* electrónica

ebb [eb] (N) [*of tide*] reflujo *m* • **the ebb and flow** [*of tide*] el flujo y reflujo; (*fig*) los altibajos • IDIOM: • **to be at a low ebb** [*person, spirits*] estar decaído; [*business*] estar de capa caída • **at a low ebb in his fortunes** en un bache de su vida
(VI) bajar, menguar; (*fig*) decaer • **to ebb and flow** [*tide*] fluir y refluir • **life is ebbing from him** le están abandonando sus últimas fuerzas
(CPD) ▸ **ebb tide** marea *f* baja, bajamar *f*

▸ **ebb away** (VI + ADV) menguar, disminuir

EBIT (ABBR) (*Econ, Comm*) (= **earnings before interest and taxes**) EBIT *m*, beneficios *mpl* antes de intereses e impuestos

EBITDA (ABBR) (*Econ, Comm*) (= **earnings before interest, depreciation and amortization**) EBIDTA *m*, beneficios *mpl* antes de intereses, impuestos, depreciación y amortización

Ebola [iːˈbəʊlə] (N) ébola *m* • **the ~ virus** el virus ébola

ebonite [ˈebənaɪt] (N) ebonita *f*

ebony [ˈebənɪ] (N) ébano *m*
(CPD) de ébano

e-book [ˈiːbʊk] (N) libro *m* electrónico

EBRD (N ABBR) (= **European Bank for Reconstruction and Development**) BERD *m*

EBT (ABBR) (= **earnings before taxes**) EBT *m*, beneficios *mpl* antes de impuestos

EBU (N ABBR) (= **European Broadcasting Union**) UER *f*

ebullience [ɪˈbʌlɪəns] (N) entusiasmo *m*, animación *f*

ebullient [ɪˈbʌlɪənt] (ADJ) entusiasta, animado

e-business [ˈiːˌbɪznɪs] (N) **1** (= *company*) negocio *m* electrónico
2 (= *commerce*) comercio *m* electrónico, comercio *m* E

EC (N ABBR) (= **European Community**) CE *f*
(CPD) [*directive, membership, states etc*] de la CE

e-card [ˈiːkɑːd] (N) tarjeta *f* electrónica

ECB (N ABBR) (= **European Central Bank**) BCE *m* (*Banco Central Europeo*)

eccentric [ɪk'sentrɪk] ADJ excéntrico
N excéntrico/a *m/f* • **she was a bit of an ~** era un poco excéntrica

eccentrically [ɪk'sentrɪkəlɪ] ADV [*behave, dress*] de manera excéntrica

eccentricity [,eksən'trɪsɪtɪ] N excentricidad *f*

Ecclesiastes [ɪ,kli:zɪ'æsti:z] N (*Bible*) • **the Book of ~** el Libro de Eclesiastés

ecclesiastic [ɪ,kli:zɪ'æstɪk] N eclesiástico *m*

ecclesiastical [ɪ,kli:zɪ'æstɪkəl] ADJ eclesiástico

ECG N ABBR (= **electrocardiogram, electrocardiograph**) ECG *m*

ECGD N ABBR (= **Export Credits Guarantee Department**) *servicio de garantía financiera a la exportación*

echelon ['eʃəlɒn] N (= *level*) nivel *m*; (= *degree*) grado *m*; (*Mil*) escalón *m* • **the upper ~s of the corporation** los cuadros directivos de la compañía

echo ['ekəʊ] N (PL: **echoes**) (*also fig*) eco *m*
VT [+ *sound*] repetir; [+ *opinion etc*] hacerse eco de
VI [*sound*] resonar, hacer eco; [*place*] resonar • **his footsteps ~ed in the street** se oía el eco de sus pasos *or* sus pasos resonaban en la calle • **the valley ~ed with shouts** resonaban los gritos por el valle
CPD ▸ **echo chamber** (*Rad, TV*) cámara *f* de resonancia ▸ **echo sounder** sonda *f* acústica

echolocation [,ekəʊləʊ'keɪʃən] N ecolocación *f*

e-cigarette ['e:sɪgə,ret] N cigarrillo *m* electrónico

ECJ N ABBR = **European Court of Justice**

ECLA N ABBR (= **Economic Commission for Latin America**) CEPAL *f*

éclair ['eɪkleəʳ] N *pastelito relleno de nata y cubierto de chocolate*

eclampsia [ɪ'klæmpsɪə] N eclampsia *f*

éclat ['eɪklɑ:] N brillo *m*; (= *success*) éxito *m* brillante • **with great ~** brillantemente

eclectic [ɪ'klektɪk] ADJ, N ecléctico/a *m/f*

eclecticism [ɪ'klektɪsɪzəm] N eclecticismo *m*

eclipse [ɪ'klɪps] N eclipse *m* • **partial/total ~** eclipse *m* parcial/total
VT (*lit, fig*) eclipsar

eclogue ['eklɒg] N égloga *f*

eclosion [ɪ'kləʊʒən] N eclosión *f*

ECM N ABBR **1** = **electronic counter-measure**
2 (*US*) (= **European Common Market**) MCE *m*

eco... ['i:kəʊ] PREFIX eco...

ecobalance ['i:kəʊ,bæləns] N equilibrio *m* ecológico

ecocide ['i:kə,saɪd] N ecocidio *m*

eco-city ['i:kəʊ,sɪtɪ] N ecociudad *f*

ecoclimatic [,i:kəʊklaɪ'mætɪk] ADJ ecoclimático

ecoconscious [,i:kəʊ'kɒnʃəs] ADJ con conciencia ecológica

eco-friendly ['i:kəʊ'frendlɪ] ADJ amigo de la ecología, ecológicamente puro

ecohome ['i:kəʊhəʊm] N ecovivienda *f*

eco-label ['i:kəʊleɪbl] N ecoetiqueta *f*

eco-labelled, eco-labeled (*US*) ['i:kəʊleɪbəld] ADJ ecoetiquetado

eco-labelling, eco-labeling (*US*) [,i:kəʊ'leɪbəlɪŋ] N ecoetiquetado *m*

E. coli [,i:'kəʊlaɪ] N (*Med*) E. coli *m*

ecological [,i:kəʊ'lɒdʒɪkəl] ADJ ecológico

ecologically [,i:kəʊ'lɒdʒɪkəlɪ] ADV ecológicamente • **an ~ sound scheme** un plan ecológicamente razonable, un plan razonable desde el punto de vista ecológico • **~, the new fishing regulations are a good move** desde el punto de vista ecológico, la nueva normativa sobre la pesca es una buena medida

ecologist [ɪ'kɒlədʒɪst] N (= *scientist*) ecólogo/a *m/f*; (= *conservationist*) ecologista *mf*

ecology [ɪ'kɒlədʒɪ] N ecología *f*
CPD ▸ **ecology movement** movimiento *m* ecologista

e-commerce ['i:,kɒmɜ:s] N comercio *m* electrónico, comercio *m* E

econometric [ɪ,kɒnə'metrɪk] ADJ econométrico

econometrician [ɪ,kɒnəmə'trɪʃən] N econometrista *mf*

econometrics [ɪ,kɒnə'metrɪks] NSING econometría *f*

econometrist [ɪ,kɒnə'metrɪst] N econometrista *mf*

economic [,i:kə'nɒmɪk] ADJ **1** (= *financial*) [*problems, development, geography*] económico
2 (= *profitable*) [*business, price*] rentable
CPD ▸ **economic aid** ayuda *f* económica ▸ **economic embargo** embargo *m* económico ▸ **economic forecast** previsiones *fpl* económicas ▸ **economic growth** crecimiento *m* económico ▸ **economic indicator** indicador *m* económico ▸ **economic migrant, economic refugee** emigrante *mf* por razones económicas • **the government divides asylum-seekers into ~ migrants and genuine refugees** el gobierno divide a los solicitantes de asilo en emigrantes por razones económicas y refugiados genuinos ▸ **economic sanctions** sanciones *fpl* económicas

economical [,i:kə'nɒmɪkəl] ADJ [*person, method, car*] económico • **it's more ~ to have a diesel-engined car** resulta más económico tener un coche de gasoil • **my car is very ~ to run** mi coche me sale muy económico • **to be ~ with the truth** no decir toda la verdad, no ser muy pródigo con la verdad

economically [,i:kə'nɒmɪkəlɪ] ADV
1 (= *financially*) económicamente
• **~ depressed areas** áreas *fpl* económicamente deprimidas • **an ~ powerful country** un país de gran poder económico • **~ speaking** respecto a la economía, económicamente hablando • **~, the plan makes good sense** desde el punto de vista económico, el plan tiene sentido
2 (= *cheaply*) [*use, live*] de manera económica • **this machine could be more ~ operated** esta máquina se podría operar a un costo más bajo • **to be ~ priced** tener un precio módico *or* muy económico
3 (= *concisely*) [*write, describe*] con economía de palabras

economics [,i:kə'nɒmɪks] NSING (= *science*) economía *f* • **he's doing ~ at university** estudia económicas en la universidad; ▹ **home**
NPL (= *financial aspects*) aspectos *mpl* económicos • **the ~ of the situation** los aspectos económicos de la situación • **the ~ of the third world countries** la economía de los países tercermundistas

economist [ɪ'kɒnəmɪst] N economista *mf*

economize [ɪ'kɒnəmaɪz] VI economizar • **to ~ on sth** economizar en algo
VT economizar, ahorrar

economy [ɪ'kɒnəmɪ] N **1** (= *thrift*) economía *f*; (= *a saving*) ahorro *m* • **~ of scale** economía *f* de escala • **to make economies** economizar, ahorrar
2 (= *system*) economía *f*
CPD ▸ **economy class** clase *f* económica *or* turista ▸ **economy class syndrome** síndrome *m* de la clase turista ▸ **economy drive** • **to have an ~ drive** economizar, ahorrar ▸ **economy measure** medida *f* económica ▸ **economy pack** (*Comm*) envase *m* familiar ▸ **economy size** tamaño *m* familiar

ecosensitive ['i:kəʊ'sensɪtɪv] ADJ ecosensible

ecosphere ['i:kəʊ,sfɪəʳ] N ecosfera *f*

ecosystem ['i:kəʊ,sɪstɪm] N ecosistema *m*

eco-tax ['i:kəʊtæks] N ecotasa *f*

eco-tourism ['i:kəʊ,tʊərɪzəm] N ecoturismo *m*, turismo *m* verde *or* ecológico

eco-tourist ['i:kəʊ,tʊərɪst] N ecoturista *mf*

eco-town ['i:kəʊ,taʊn] N ecociudad *f*

ecotype ['i:kəʊ,taɪp] N ecotipo *m*

eco-village ['i:kəʊ,vɪlɪdʒ] N ecoaldea *f*

eco-warrior* ['i:kəʊ,wɒrɪəʳ] N activista *mf* del ecologismo, ecologista *mf* militante

ecru ['eɪkru:] ADJ de color crudo
N color *m* crudo

ECS N ABBR (*Comput*) = **extended character set**

ECSC N ABBR (*formerly*) (= **European Coal and Steel Community**) CECA *f*

ecstasy ['ekstəsɪ] N **1** (*Rel*) (*also fig*) éxtasis *m inv* • **to go into ecstasies over sth** extasiarse ante algo • **to be in ~** estar en éxtasis • **to be in ecstasies** estar en éxtasis
2 (*Drugs**) éxtasis *m inv*

ecstatic [eks'tætɪk] ADJ (*Rel*) extático; (*fig*) contentísimo, eufórico

ecstatically [eks'tætɪkəlɪ] ADV (*Rel*) en estado de éxtasis; (*fig*) con gran euforia

ECT N ABBR = **electroconvulsive therapy**

ectomorph ['ektəʊ,mɔ:f] N ectomorfo *m*

ectopic pregnancy [ek,tɒpɪk'pregnənsɪ] N embarazo *m* ectópico

ectoplasm ['ektəʊplæzəm] N ectoplasma *m*

ECU ['eɪkju:] N ABBR (= **European Currency Unit**) ECU *m*, UCE *f*

Ecuador ['ekwədɔ:ʳ] N Ecuador *m*

Ecuadoran [,ekwə'dɔ:rən], **Ecuadorian** [,ekwə'dɔ:rɪən] ADJ ecuatoriano
N ecuatoriano/a *m/f*

ecumenical [,i:kjʊ'menɪkəl] ADJ ecuménico
CPD ▸ **ecumenical council** consejo *m* ecuménico ▸ **ecumenical movement** movimiento *m* ecuménico

ecumenicism [,i:kjʊ'menɪsɪzəm], **ecumenism** [i:'kju:mənɪzəm] N ecumenismo *m*

eczema ['eksɪmə] N eczema *m*, eccema *m* • **she's got ~** tiene eczema

ED ABBR = **emergency department**

Ed [ed] N *familiar form of* **Edward**

ed ABBR **1** (= **edition**) ed
2 (= **editor**) ed
3 (= **edited by**) en edición de

Edam ['i:dæm] N (*also* **Edam cheese**) queso *m* de Edam, queso *m* de bola

EDC N ABBR = **European Defence Community**

Eddie ['edɪ] N *familiar form of* **Edward**

eddy ['edɪ] N remolino *m*
VI [*water*] hacer remolinos, arremolinarse

edelweiss ['eɪdlvaɪs] N edelweiss *m*

edema [ɪ'di:mə] N (*esp US*) = **oedema**

Eden ['i:dn] N Edén *m*

edentate [ɪ'denteɪt] ADJ desdentado
N desdentado/a *m/f*

EDF N ABBR (= **European Development Fund**) FED *m*

edge [edʒ] N **1** (= *border, rim*) [*of cliff, wood, chair, bed*] borde *m*; [*of town*] afueras *fpl*; [*of lake, river*] orilla *f*; [*of cube, brick*] arista *f*; [*of paper*] borde *m*, margen *m*; [*of coin*] canto *m* • **the fabric was fraying at the ~s** la tela se estaba deshilachando por los bordes • **she was standing at the water's ~** estaba de pie en la orilla del agua • **the trees at the ~ of the road** los árboles que bordean la carretera • **he sat down on the ~ of the bed** se sentó al borde la cama • **a house on the ~**

of town una casa a las afueras de la ciudad • **someone pushed him over the ~ of the cliff** alguien lo empujó por el borde del precipicio • IDIOMS: • **to live close to the ~** vivir al límite • **to be on ~** tener los nervios de punta • **my nerves are on ~ today** hoy tengo los nervios de punta, hoy estoy de los nervios • **to set sb's teeth on ~** [*sound, voice*] dar dentera a algn; [*person*] poner los pelos de punta a algn • **to drive/push sb over the ~** llevar a algn al límite • **to be on the ~ of one's seat** estar en suspense *or* vilo *or* ascuas
2 (= *brink*) borde *m* • **he was on the ~ of a breakthrough** estaba al borde de un gran adelanto
3 (= *sharp side*) [*of blade*] filo *m* • **to put an ~ on sth** afilar algo • **army life will smooth the rough ~s off him** la vida militar le calmará; ▹ **cutting, leading**
4 (= *sharpness*) • **there was an ~ to her voice** había un tono de crispación en su voz • **his performance lacked ~** a su interpretación le faltaba mordacidad • **the wind had a sharp ~** hacía un viento cortante • **to take the ~ off sth**: • **talking to her took the ~ off my grief** hablar con ella mitigó mi dolor • **that took the ~ off my appetite** con eso maté el hambre *or* engañé el estómago
5 (= *advantage*) ventaja *f* • **their technology gave them the competitive ~** su tecnología les dio una posición de ventaja con respecto a la competencia • **to have the** *or* **an ~ on** *or* **over sb** llevar la delantera a algn, llevar ventaja a algn
(VT) **1** (= *provide border for*) [+ *garment*] ribetear; [+ *path*] bordear • **a top ~d with lace** un top ribeteado con encaje • **a mahogany tray ~d with brass** una bandeja de caoba con el borde de bronce • **narrow green leaves ~d with red** hojas verdes delgadas con los bordes rojos
2 (= *move carefully*) • **he ~d the car into the traffic** sacó el coche con cuidado y se unió al resto del tráfico • **she ~d her way through the crowd** se abrió paso poco a poco entre la multitud • **the song ~d its way up the charts** la canción fue poco a poco subiendo puestos en las listas de éxitos
3 (= *sharpen*) • **her voice was ~d with panic** había un tono de pánico en su voz
(VI) (= *move slowly*) • **she ~d away from him** poco a poco se alejó de él • **he ~d closer to the telephone** se acercó lentamente al teléfono • **to ~ forward** avanzar poco a poco • **Labour have ~d into the lead** el partido laborista ha conseguido tomar la delantera por muy poco • **to ~ past** pasar con dificultad
▸ **edge out** (VT + ADV) (= *defeat*) [+ *rival, opposing team*] derrotar por muy poco • **Germany and France have ~d out the British team** Alemania y Francia han derrotado a Gran Bretaña por muy poco • **they were ~d out of the number one slot** les arrebataron el primer puesto por muy poco
(VI + ADV) • **the car ~d out into the traffic** el coche salió con cuidado y se unió al resto del tráfico
▸ **edge up** (VI + ADV) **1** [*shares, currency, price*] subir poco a poco
2 • **to ~ up to sb** acercarse con cautela a algn
edgeways ['edʒweɪz], **edgewise** ['edʒwaɪz] (ADV) de lado, de canto • **I couldn't get a word in ~*** no pude meter baza*
edgily ['edʒɪlɪ] (ADV) [*say*] con tono crispado
edginess ['edʒɪnɪs] (N) crispación *f*
edging ['edʒɪŋ] (N) borde *m*; [*of ribbon, silk*] ribete *m*
edgy ['edʒɪ] (ADJ) (COMPAR: **edgier**, SUPERL: **edgiest**) **1** (= *tense*) crispado
2 (= *innovative*) [*comedy, thriller, comedian*] de vanguardia
edibility [,edɪ'bɪlɪtɪ] (N) comestibilidad *f*
edible ['edɪbl] (ADJ) comestible
edict ['iːdɪkt] (N) (*Hist*) edicto *m*; (*Jur*) decreto *m*, auto *m*; (*Pol*) decreto *m*; (*by mayor*) bando *m*, edicto *m*
edification [,edɪfɪ'keɪʃən] (N) enseñanza *f*
edifice ['edɪfɪs] (N) (*frm*) edificio *m* (imponente)
edify ['edɪfaɪ] (VT) edificar
edifying ['edɪfaɪɪŋ] (ADJ) edificante
Edinburgh ['edɪnbərə] (N) Edimburgo *m*

EDINBURGH FESTIVAL

El Festival de Edimburgo, el mayor festival de este tipo del mundo, se celebra cada año en agosto durante tres semanas, en las que el festival está presente en toda la ciudad. Además del programa oficial del festival, que ofrece actuaciones de artistas de categoría internacional, también hay una enorme cantidad de actividades artísticas de todo tipo, desde lo más tradicional hasta lo más extravagante, teatro, danza, música, artistas callejeros etc., a lo que se llama **Fringe Festival**, pues comenzó siendo un festival alternativo al oficial. Al mismo tiempo, se celebra un festival de jazz, otro de cine y una exhibición militar llamada **Military Tattoo**, que tiene lugar en el Castillo de Edimburgo.

edit ['edɪt] (VT) (= *be in charge of*) [+ *newspaper, magazine etc*] dirigir; (= *prepare for printing*) corregir, revisar; (= *cut*) cortar, reducir; (*Cine, TV*) montar; (*Rad*) editar; (*Comput*) editar • **~ed by** [*newspaper*] bajo la dirección de; [*text, book*] edición de, editado por
(N) corrección *f*
(CPD) ▸ **edit key** tecla *f* de edición
▸ **edit out** (VT + ADV) eliminar, suprimir
editable ['edɪtəbl] (ADJ) (*Comput*) [*file*] editable
editing ['edɪtɪŋ] (N) (= *management*) [*of magazine*] redacción *f*; [*of newspaper, dictionary*] dirección *f*; (= *preparation for printing*) [*of article, series of texts, tape*] edición *f*; [*of film*] montaje *m*, edición *f*; [*of video*] edición *f*; (*Comput*) edición *f*
(CPD) ▸ **editing room** (*Cine, TV*) sala *f* de montaje
edition [ɪ'dɪʃən] (N) (*gen*) edición *f*; (= *number printed*) tirada *f*, impresión *f*
editor ['edɪtəʳ] (N) [*of newspaper, magazine*] director(a) *m/f*; (= *publisher's editor*) redactor(a) *m/f*; (*Cine, TV*) montador(a) *m/f*, editor(a) *m/f*; (*Rad*) editor(a) *m/f* • **~'s note** nota *f* de la redacción • **the sports ~** el/la redactor(a) de la sección de deportes
editorial [,edɪ'tɔːrɪəl] (ADJ) [*decision, control, page, policy*] editorial; [*board, meeting, assistant*] de redacción • **~ experience** experiencia *f* en edición de textos • **~ staff** redacción *f*
(N) (= *article*) editorial *m*, artículo *m* de fondo
editorialist [,edɪ'tɔːrɪəlɪst] (N) (*US*) editorialista *mf*
editorialize [,edɪ'tɔːrɪəlaɪz] (VI) editorializar
editorially [,edɪ'tɔːrɪəlɪ] (ADV) desde el punto de vista editorial
editor-in-chief ['edɪtərɪn'tʃiːf] (N) jefe/a *m/f* de redacción
editorship ['edɪtəʃɪp] (N) dirección *f*
Edmund ['edmənd] (N) Edmundo
EDP (N ABBR) (= **electronic data processing**) PED *m*
EDT (N ABBR) (*US*) = **Eastern Daylight Time**
educability [,edjʊkə'bɪlɪtɪ] (N) educabilidad *f*
educable ['edjʊkəbl] (ADJ) educable
educate ['edjʊkeɪt] (VT) (= *teach*) enseñar; (= *train*) educar, formar; (= *provide instruction in*) instruir • **where were you ~d?** ¿dónde cursó sus estudios? • **he is being privately ~d** cursa estudios en un colegio privado
educated ['edjʊkeɪtɪd] (ADJ) [*person, voice*] culto • **an ~ guess** una suposición bien fundamentada
-educated ['edjʊkeɪtɪd] (SUFFIX) • **Oxford-educated** educado en Oxford • **American-educated** educado en los Estados Unidos • **ill-educated** inculto; ▹ **well-educated**
education [,edjʊ'keɪʃən] (N) educación *f*, formación *f*; (= *teaching*) enseñanza *f*; (= *knowledge, culture*) cultura *f*; (= *studies*) estudios *mpl*; (= *training*) formación *f*; (*Univ*) (= *subject*) pedagogía *f* • **Ministry of Education** Ministerio *m or* (*LAm*) Secretaría *f* de Educación • **primary/secondary ~** enseñanza *f* primaria/secundaria, primera/segunda enseñanza *f* • **higher ~** educación *f* superior, enseñanza *f* superior • **physical/political ~** educación *f* física/política • **literary/professional ~** formación *f* literaria/profesional • **there should be more investment in ~** debería invertirse más dinero en educación • **she works in ~** trabaja en la enseñanza • **I never had much ~** pasé poco tiempo en la escuela • **they paid for his ~** le pagaron los estudios
(CPD) ▸ **education authority** (*Brit*) ≈ delegación *f* de educación, ≈ consejería *f* de educación (*Sp*) ▸ **education department** (*Brit*) [*of local authority*] ≈ departamento *m* de educación; (= *ministry*) Ministerio *m* de Educación
educational [,edjʊ'keɪʃənl] (ADJ)
1 (= *instructive*) [*film, book, toy, visit*] educativo, instructivo; [*role*] docente; [*function*] docente, educativo; [*event, experience*] educativo
2 (= *relating to education*) [*system*] educativo, de enseñanza; [*needs, opportunities, supplies, material*] educativo; [*establishment, institution*] docente, de enseñanza; [*achievement, qualification*] académico; [*standards*] de educación; [*policy*] educacional, relativo a la educación; [*methods*] educativo, de educación; [*theory*] pedagógico • **falling ~ standards** estándares *mpl* de educación cada vez más bajos
(CPD) ▸ **educational adviser** (*Brit*) (*Scol, Admin*) consejero/a *m/f* de enseñanza ▸ **educational psychologist** psicopedagogo/a *m/f* ▸ **educational psychology** psicopedagogía *f* ▸ **educational technology** tecnología *f* educativa ▸ **educational television** televisión *f* educativa
educationalist [,edjʊ'keɪʃnəlɪst] (N) (*esp Brit*) pedagogo/a *m/f*
educationally [,edjʊ'keɪʃnəlɪ] (ADV) [*stimulate, encourage*] desde el punto de vista educativo • **~, the school is very good** desde el punto de vista educativo, el colegio es muy bueno • **~ backward adults** adultos *mpl* con carencias educativas • **~ deprived children** niños *mpl* privados de educación • **~ sound principles** principios *mpl* con una base pedagógica sólida • **~ subnormal** con dificultades de aprendizaje
educationist [,edjʊ'keɪʃnɪst] (N) (*esp Brit*) = **educationalist**
educative ['edjʊkətɪv] (ADJ) educativo
educator ['edjʊkeɪtəʳ] (N) educador(a) *m/f*
educe [ɪ'djuːs] (VT) educir, sacar
edutainment [,edjʊ'teɪnmənt] (N) (*esp US*) *juego de ordenador ameno y educativo al mismo tiempo*
Edward ['edwəd] (N) Eduardo • **~ the Confessor** Eduardo el Confesor

e

Edwardian [ed'wɔ:dɪən] (ADJ) eduardiano (N) eduardiano/a *m/f*
EE (ABBR) = **electrical engineer**
EEC (N ABBR) (= **European Economic Community**) CEE *f*
EEG (N ABBR) = **electroencephalogram**
eek [i:k] (EXCL) ¡aj!
eel [i:l] (N) anguila *f*
e'en [i:n] (*poet*) = **even**
EENT (ABBR) (*US*) (*Med*) = **eye, ear, nose and throat**
EEOC (N ABBR) (*US*) (= **Equal Employment Opportunity Commission**) *comisión que investiga la discriminación racial o sexual en el empleo*
e'er [ɛəʳ] (*poet*) = **ever**
eerie ['ɪərɪ] (ADJ) [*sound, experience*] sobrecogedor, espeluznante; [*silence*] estremecedor, inquietante, sobrecogedor
eerily ['ɪərɪlɪ] (ADV) [*deserted*] misteriosamente; [*similar, familiar*] sorprendentemente • **the whole town was ~ quiet** el pueblo entero estaba sumido en un silencio inquietante • **his footsteps echoed ~ along the High Street** sus pasos resonaron de manera sobrecogedora por la calle Mayor
EET (N ABBR) = **Eastern European Time**
eff‡ [ef] (VI) • **he was effing all over the place** soltaba palabrotas por todas partes • **he told her to eff off** la mandó a la mierda‡ • IDIOM: • **to eff and blind** soltar palabrotas*
efface [ɪ'feɪs] (VT) borrar • **to ~ o.s.** no hacerse notar, lograr pasar inadvertido
effect [ɪ'fekt] (N) **1** (*gen*) efecto *m*; (= *result*) resultado *m*, consecuencia *f* • **to feel the ~(s) of** sentir los efectos de • **to such good ~ that ...** con tan buenos resultados que ... • **to have an ~ on sb** hacer efecto a algn • **to have an ~ on sth** afectar (a) algo • **it will have the ~ of preventing ...** tendrá como consecuencia impedir ... • **to have the desired ~** producir el efecto deseado • **to have no ~** • **be of no ~** no surtir efecto • **in ~** (= *in fact*) en realidad; (= *practically*) de hecho • **to be in ~** (*Jur*) estar vigente, tener vigencia • **to come into ~** (*Jur*) entrar en vigor • **to put into ~** [+ *rule*] poner en vigor; [+ *plan*] poner en práctica • **to take ~** [*drug*] surtir efecto • **to no ~** inútilmente, sin resultado • **with ~ from April** (*esp Brit*) a partir de abril • **an increase with immediate ~** un aumento efectivo a partir de hoy
2 (= *sense*) [*of words etc*] sentido *m* • **a circular to this ~ will be issued next week** la próxima semana se hará pública una circular en este sentido • **an announcement to the ~ that ...** un aviso informando de que ... • **his letter is to the ~ that ...** en su carta manifiesta que ... • **to the same ~** en el mismo sentido • **or words to that ~** o algo por el estilo
3 (= *impression*) efecto *m*, impresión *f* • **a pleasing ~** una impresión agradable • **to create an ~** impresionar • **he said it for ~** lo dijo solo para impresionar • **special ~s** (*Cine, TV*) efectos *mpl* especiales
4 effects (= *property*) efectos *mpl* • **personal ~s** efectos *mpl* personales
(VT) (*frm*) (= *bring about*) [+ *sale, purchase, payment, reform, reduction*] efectuar; [+ *cure, improvement, transformation*] lograr • **to ~ change** lograr *or* efectuar un cambio • **to ~ a saving** hacer un ahorro
effective [ɪ'fektɪv] (ADJ) **1** (= *efficient, useful*) [*treatment, method, deterrent, system*] efectivo, eficaz; [*remark, argument*] eficaz • **the method is simple, but ~** el método es simple pero efectivo *or* eficaz • **to be ~ against sth** [*drug*] ser eficaz contra algo • **~ capacity** (*Tech*) capacidad *f* útil • **to be ~ in doing sth** ser eficaz para hacer algo • **~ life** (*Pharm*) vida *f* útil • **~ power** (*Tech*) potencia *f* real • **~ ways of reducing pollution** formas *fpl* efectivas *or* eficaces de reducir la polución
2 (= *striking*) [*display, outfit, decoration*] impresionante, logrado; [*combination*] logrado • **to look ~** causar efecto • **blinds can look very ~** las persianas pueden causar muy buen efecto *or* mucho efecto
3 (= *operative*) • **to become ~** entrar en vigor, hacerse efectivo (**from, on** a partir de) • **~ date** fecha *f* de vigencia, fecha *f* efectiva • **it will be ~ from 1 April** entrará en vigor *or* será efectivo a partir del 1 de abril
4 (= *actual*) [*aid, contribution, leader*] real; [*control, increase*] efectivo; [*income*] en efectivo
5 (*Econ*) [*demand, interest rate*] efectivo
(NPL) **effectives** (*Mil*) efectivos *mpl*
effectively [ɪ'fektɪvlɪ] (ADV) **1** (= *efficiently*) [*treat, teach, work*] eficazmente, de manera eficaz; [*function*] de manera eficaz • **it's very difficult to treat this disease ~** es muy difícil tratar esta enfermedad eficazmente *or* de manera eficaz
2 (= *strikingly*) [*displayed, decorated, combined*] de manera impresionante, con mucho efecto
3 (= *in effect*) realmente, de hecho • **the contest was ~ won in the first five minutes** realmente *or* de hecho, el concurso estaba ganado en los primeros cinco minutos
effectiveness [ɪ'fektɪvnɪs] (N) **1** (= *efficiency*) [*of method, system*] eficacia *f*, eficiencia *f*; [*of treatment, deterrent, argument*] eficacia *f*
2 (= *striking quality*) efecto *m*
effectual [ɪ'fektjʊəl] (ADJ) eficaz
effectually [ɪ'fektjʊəlɪ] (ADV) (*frm*) eficazmente, con eficacia
effectuate [ɪ'fektjʊeɪt] (VT) (*frm*) efectuar, lograr
effeminacy [ɪ'femɪnəsɪ] (N) afeminación *f*, afeminamiento *m*
effeminate [ɪ'femɪnɪt] (ADJ) afeminado
effervesce [ˌefə'ves] (VI) **1** (*lit*) [*liquid*] estar en efervescencia • **to begin to ~** entrar en efervescencia
2 (*fig*) [*person*] rebosar vitalidad
effervescence [ˌefə'vesns] (N) efervescencia *f*
effervescent [ˌefə'vesnt] (ADJ) **1** (*lit*) efervescente
2 (*fig*) [*person*] rebosante de vitalidad
effete [ɪ'fi:t] (ADJ) agotado, cansado
effeteness [ɪ'fi:tnɪs] (N) cansancio *m*
efficacious [ˌefɪ'keɪʃəs] (ADJ) (*frm*) [*remedy, method*] eficaz, efectivo (**against** contra) • **to be ~ in the treatment of sth** ser eficaz para *or* efectivo en el tratamiento de algo
efficacy ['efɪkəsɪ] (N) (*frm*) eficacia *f*
efficiency [ɪ'fɪʃənsɪ] (N) **1** [*of person, manager*] eficiencia *f*; [*of method, remedy, product, army*] eficacia *f*
2 (*Mech, Phys*) [*of machine*] rendimiento *m*
(CPD) ▸ **efficiency apartment** (*US*) estudio *m*
efficient [ɪ'fɪʃənt] (ADJ) **1** [*person, manager*] eficaz, eficiente; [*method, remedy, product, system*] eficaz; [*service, company, organization, army*] eficiente • **to be ~ at doing sth** ser eficiente a la hora de hacer algo
2 (*esp Mech, Phys*) [*machine*] de buen rendimiento
efficiently [ɪ'fɪʃəntlɪ] (ADV) **1** (= *competently, well*) eficientemente, de manera eficiente • **she works ~** trabaja eficientemente *or* de manera eficiente • **she dealt with my application very ~** tramitó mi solicitud de manera muy eficiente • **our muscles need oxygen to work ~** los músculos necesitan oxígeno para trabajar con eficacia • **the new machine works ~** la máquina nueva da un buen rendimiento
2 (= *effectively*) de manera eficaz • **use "Cleano" to banish stains ~** utilice "Cleano" para acabar con las manchas de manera eficaz
effigy ['efɪdʒɪ] (N) efigie *f*
effing‡ ['efɪŋ] (ADJ) (*Brit*) (*euph*) = **fucking**
effloresce [ˌeflə'res] (VI) (*Chem*) eflorescer
efflorescence [ˌeflə'resns] (N) **1** (*Chem, Med*) eflorescencia *f*; (*Bot*) floración *f*
2 (*fig*) (*liter*) florecimiento *m*, prosperidad *f*
efflorescent [ˌeflɔ:'resnt] (ADJ) eflorescente
effluent ['eflʊənt] (N) aguas *fpl* residuales
effluvium [e'flu:vɪəm] (N) (PL: **effluviums** *or* **effluvia** [e'flu:vɪə]) efluvio *m*, emanación *f*, tufo *m*
effort ['efət] (N) **1** (= *hard work*) esfuerzo *m* • **all his ~ was directed to ...** todos sus esfuerzos iban dirigidos a ... • **it was an ~ to get up** • **getting up was an ~** levantarse resultaba un esfuerzo • **put a bit of ~ into it!** ¡esfuérzate un poco!, ¡pon un poco más de esfuerzo! • **to spare no ~ to do sth** no regatear esfuerzos para hacer algo • **without ~** sin ningún esfuerzo • **it's not worth the ~** no merece la pena • **it's well worth the ~** merece la pena
2 (= *attempt*) intento *m*, tentativa *f* • **it's not bad for a first ~** no está mal para ser su primer intento *or* la primera vez que lo intenta • **a good ~** un feliz intento • **in an ~ to solve the problem/be polite** en un esfuerzo por resolver el problema/ser amable • **his latest ~** (*hum*) su último intento • **what did you think of his latest ~?** ¿qué te pareció su última obra? • **to make an ~ to do sth** esforzarse en hacer algo, hacer un esfuerzo por hacer algo • **he made no ~ to be polite** no hizo ningún esfuerzo por ser amable • **please make every ~ to come** haz un esfuerzo por venir • **thank you for making the ~ to be here** gracias por tomarse la molestia de venir • **it was a pretty poor ~** fue un intento bastante flojo • **the war ~** *los esfuerzos realizados por la población civil durante una guerra*
effortless ['efətlɪs] (ADJ) [*success, victory*] fácil; [*charm, superiority, grace*] natural • **she danced across the room with light, ~ movements** cruzó la habitación bailando con movimientos ligeros, hechos sin esfuerzo • **with ~ ease** sin ningún esfuerzo • **to make sth seem ~** hacer que algo parezca muy fácil • **an author renowned for his ~ style** un autor famoso por su estilo fluido
effortlessly ['efətlɪslɪ] (ADV) [*win, succeed*] fácilmente; [*move, lift*] sin ningún esfuerzo
effortlessness ['efətlɪsnɪs] (N) facilidad *f*
effrontery [ɪ'frʌntərɪ] (N) descaro *m* • **he had the ~ to say that ...** tuvo el descaro de decir que ...
effusion [ɪ'fju:ʒən] (N) efusión *f*
effusive [ɪ'fju:sɪv] (ADJ) [*person, welcome, letter*] efusivo • **we were embarrassed by his ~ apologies** la efusividad con la que se disculpó nos hizo sentirnos violentos
effusively [ɪ'fju:sɪvlɪ] (ADV) efusivamente, con efusión
effusiveness [ɪ'fju:sɪvnɪs] (N) efusividad *f*
E-fit ['i:fɪt] (N) fotorrobot *f* digital, retrato *m* robot digital
EFL (N ABBR) (= **English as a Foreign Language**) ▸ TEFL/EFL, TESL/ESL, ELT, TESOL/ESOL
EFT (N ABBR) = **electronic funds transfer**
eft [eft] (N) tritón *m*
EFTA ['eftə] (N ABBR) (= **European Free Trade Association**) AELC *f*
EFTPOS (N ABBR) = **electronic funds transfer at point of sale**
EFTS (N ABBR) = **electronic funds transfer system**

e.g. ADV, ABBR (= **exempli gratia**) (= *for example*) p.ej.

EGA N ABBR = **enhanced graphics adaptor**

egalitarian [ɪ,gælɪ'tεərɪən] ADJ igualitario

egalitarianism [ɪ,gælɪ'tεərɪənɪzəm] N igualitarismo *m*

egg [eg] N **1** huevo *m*, blanquillo *m* (*Mex*); (= *cell*) óvulo *m* • **fried/scrambled/ soft-boiled/hard-boiled egg** huevo *m* frito/ revuelto/pasado por agua/duro • **boiled egg** huevo *m* pasado por agua, huevo *m* a la copa (*And, S. Cone*) • IDIOMS: • **to have egg on one's face*** quedar en ridículo • **as sure as eggs are** *or* **is eggs** como que dos y dos son cuatro, sin ningún género de dudas • PROVERB: • **don't put all your eggs in one basket** no te lo juegues todo a una carta
2* (= *person*) • **bad egg** sinvergüenza *mf* • **she's a good egg** es una buena persona
CPD ▸ **egg beater** batidor *m* de huevos; (*US**) helicóptero *m* ▸ **egg cup** huevera *f* ▸ **egg custard** natillas *fpl* ▸ **egg flip** ponche *m* (de huevo) ▸ **egg roll** (= *sandwich*) panecito *m* de huevo duro; (= *paté*) *paté a base de huevo con carne de cerdo y legumbres* ▸ **egg timer** reloj *m* de arena (*para cocer huevos*) ▸ **egg whisk** batidor *m* de huevos ▸ **egg white** clara *f* de huevo ▸ **egg yolk** yema *f* de huevo
▸ **egg on** VT + ADV (= *urge*) incitar • **to egg sb on to do sth** incitar a algn a hacer algo

egg-and-spoon race [,egən'spu:n,reɪs] N juego *m* del huevo con la cuchara

egghead* ['eghed] N (*pej*) (= *intellectual*) lumbrera *f*, intelectual *mf*

eggnog ['eg'nɒg] N yema *f* mejida, ponche *m* de huevo

eggplant ['egplɑ:nt] N (*esp US*) berenjena *f*

egg-shaped ['egʃeɪpt] ADJ en forma de huevo

eggshell ['egʃel] N cáscara *f* de huevo
CPD ▸ **eggshell white** blanco *m* semimate

egis ['i:dʒəs] (*US*) = **aegis**

eglantine ['egləntaɪn] N eglantina *f*

EGM N ABBR = **extraordinary general meeting**

ego ['i:gəʊ] ['egəʊ] N **1** (*Psych*) • **the ego** el ego, el yo
2 (= *pride*) orgullo *m* • **to boost one's ego** alimentar el ego
CPD ▸ **ego boost** inyección *f* de moral para el ego • **then you've got the added ego boost of knowing your interest is reciprocated** y tienes la inyección de moral añadida de saber que tu interés es correspondido • **the thrill of being recognized, which is partly an ego boost** la emoción de ser reconocido, que en parte hace que se te alimente el ego ▸ **ego surfing** *actividad consistente en buscar apariciones de tu propio nombre en Internet* ▸ **ego trip*** • **to be on an ego trip** creerse el centro del universo *or* el ombligo del mundo

egocentric [,i:gəʊ'sentrɪk] [,egəʊ'sentrɪk] ADJ egocéntrico

egocentrical [,i:gəʊ'sentrɪkəl] [,egəʊ'sentrɪkəl] ADJ = **egocentric**

egoism ['i:gəʊɪsəm] ['egəʊɪzəm] N egoísmo *m*

egoist ['i:gəʊɪst] ['egəʊɪst] N egoísta *mf*

egoistic [,i:gəʊ'ɪstɪk] [,egəʊ'ɪstɪk] ADJ (= *egotistic*) egoísta

egoistical [,i:gəʊ'ɪstɪkəl] [,egəʊ'ɪstɪkəl] ADJ egoísta

egomania [,i:gəʊ'meɪnɪə] [,egəʊ'meɪnɪə] N egocentrismo *m* exagerado

egomaniac [,i:gəʊ'meɪnɪæk] [,egəʊ'meɪnɪæk] N ególatra *mf*

egosurf ['i:gəʊ,sɜ:f] VI buscarse en la Red

egotism ['i:gəʊtɪzəm] ['egəʊtɪzəm] N egolatría *f*, egocentrismo *m*

egotist [i:gəʊtɪst] ['egəʊtɪst] N ególatra *mf*, egocéntrico(a) *m/f*

egotistic [,i:gəʊ'tɪstɪk] [,egəʊ'tɪstɪk] ADJ egotista

egotistical [,i:gəʊ'tɪstɪkəl] [,egəʊ'tɪstɪkəl] ADJ = **egotistic**

egregious [ɪ'gri:dʒəs] ADJ atroz, enorme; [*liar etc*] notorio

egress ['i:gres] N (*frm*) salida *f*

egret ['i:gret] N garceta *f*

Egypt ['i:dʒɪpt] N Egipto *m*

Egyptian [ɪ'dʒɪpʃən] ADJ egipcio
N egipcio/a *m/f*

Egyptologist [,i:dʒɪp'tɒlədʒɪst] N egiptólogo/a *m/f*

Egyptology [,i:dʒɪp'tɒlədʒɪ] N egiptología *f*

eh [eɪ] EXCL (= *please repeat*) ¿cómo?, ¿qué?; (*inviting assent*) ¿no?, ¿verdad?, ¿no es así?

EHIC ABBR (= **European Health Insurance Card**) TSE *f*

EIB N ABBR (= **European Investment Bank**) BEI *m*

Eid ['i:d] N (*also* **Eid-al-Fitr**, **Eid-ul-Fitr**) Eid-al-Fitr *m* (*celebración que marca el final del Ramadán*)

eider ['aɪdəʳ] N = **eider duck**

eiderdown ['aɪdədaʊn] N edredón *m*

eider duck ['aɪdə'dʌk] N eider *m*, pato *m* de flojel

eidetic [aɪ'detɪk] ADJ [*memory, vision*] eidético

Eiffel Tower [,aɪfəl'taʊəʳ] N torre *f* Eiffel

eight [eɪt] ADJ, PRON ocho • **she's ~ (years old)** tiene ocho años • **there are ~ of us** somos ocho • **all ~ of them came** vinieron los ocho
N (= *numeral*) ocho *m* • IDIOM: • **he's had one over the ~*** lleva una copa de más; ▹ **five**

eighteen ['eɪ'ti:n] ADJ, PRON dieciocho • **she's ~ (years old)** tiene dieciocho años
N (= *numeral*) dieciocho *m*; ▹ **five**

eighteenth ['eɪ'ti:nθ] ADJ decimoctavo • **on her ~ birthday** cuando cumple/cumplió los dieciocho años
N decimoctavo/a *m/f*; (= *fraction*) decimoctava parte *f*, dieciochoavo *m*; ▹ **fifth**

eighth [eɪtθ] ADJ octavo • **the ~ floor** el octavo piso • **the ~ of August** el ocho de agosto • **~ note** (*US*) (*Mus*) corchea *f*
N octavo/a *m/f*; (= *fraction*) octava parte *f*, octavo *m*; ▹ **fifth**

eighth-grader [,eɪtθ'greɪdəʳ] N (*US*) alumno/a *m/f* de octavo curso (*de entre 13 y 14 años*)

eightieth ['eɪtɪɪθ] ADJ octogésimo • **the ~ anniversary** el ochenta aniversario
N octogésimo/a *m/f*; (= *fraction*) octogésima parte *f*, octogésimo *m*; ▹ **fifth**

eighty ['eɪtɪ] ADJ, PRON ochenta • **she's ~ (years old)** tiene ochenta años
N ochenta *m* • **the eighties** los años ochenta • **to be in one's eighties** tener más de ochenta años; ▹ **five**

Eire ['εərə] N Eire *m*, República *f* de Irlanda

EIS N ABBR (= **Educational Institute of Scotland**) *sindicato de profesores*

Eisteddfod [aɪs'teðvɒd] N *festival galés en el que se celebran concursos de música y poesía*

> **EISTEDDFOD**
> En Gales un **eisteddfod** es un concurso de poesía, canto, música y danza, en el que las canciones, los poemas y los relatos son mayormente en galés. Cada año tienen lugar muchos de estos **eisteddfodau** por todo Gales y el nivel de competición suele ser muy alto en los concursos más importantes. En Llangollen, al noreste de Gales, se celebra anualmente un concurso internacional en el que hay participantes de todo el mundo, pero el concurso principal, el **National Eisteddfod** se celebra en un lugar diferente cada año.

either ['aɪðəʳ] ADJ **1** (= *one or other*) (*positive*) cualquiera de los dos; (*negative*) ninguno de los dos • **~ day would suit me** cualquiera de los dos días me viene bien • **I don't like ~ book** no me gusta ninguno de los dos libros • **you can do it ~ way** puedes hacerlo de este modo o del otro
2 (= *each*) cada • **in ~ hand** en cada mano • **on ~ side of the road** a ambos lados de la carretera
PRON (*positive*) cualquiera de los dos; (*negative*) ninguno de los dos • **"which bus will you take?" — "either"** —¿qué autobús vas a coger? —cualquiera de los dos • **give it to ~ of them** dáselo a cualquiera de los dos • **~ of us** cualquiera de nosotros • **I don't want ~ of them** no quiero ninguno de los dos • **I don't like ~ of them** no me gusta ninguno de los dos
CONJ • **either ... or** o ... o • **~ come in or stay out** o entra o quédate fuera • **I have never been to ~ Paris or Rome** no he estado nunca ni en París ni en Roma • **you can have ~ ice cream or yoghurt** puedes tomar o helado o yogur
ADV tampoco • **he can't sing ~** tampoco sabe cantar • **no, I haven't ~** no, yo tampoco • **I don't like milk and I don't like eggs ~** no me gusta la leche y tampoco me gustan los huevos

ejaculate [ɪ'dʒækjʊleɪt] VT **1** (= *cry out*) exclamar
2 [+ *semen*] eyacular
VI (*Physiol*) eyacular

ejaculation [ɪ,dʒækjʊ'leɪʃən] N **1** (= *cry*) exclamación *f*
2 (*Physiol*) eyaculación *f*

ejaculatory [ɪ'dʒækjʊlətərɪ] ADJ (*Physiol*) eyaculador

eject [ɪ'dʒekt] VT (*Aer, Tech*) [+ *bomb, flames*] expulsar; [+ *cartridge*] expulsar, eyectar; [+ *troublemaker*] echar; [+ *tenant*] desahuciar
VI [*pilot*] eyectarse

ejection [ɪ'dʒekʃən] N expulsión *f*; [*of tenant*] desahucio *m*; [*of pilot*] eyección *f*

ejector [ɪ'dʒektəʳ] N (*Tech*) expulsor *m*
CPD ▸ **ejector seat** (*Aer*) asiento *m* eyectable

eke [i:k] VT • **to eke out** [+ *food, supplies*] escatimar; [+ *money, income*] hacer que alcance • **to eke out a living** ganarse la vida a duras penas

EKG N ABBR (*US*) = ECG

el* [el] N ABBR (*US*) = **elevated railroad**

elaborate ADJ [ɪ'læbərɪt] [*design, hairstyle, costume, ceremony*] muy elaborado; [*plan*] detallado, muy elaborado; [*architecture*] con mucha ornamentación; [*furniture*] con muchos adornos, muy recargado; [*equipment, network, preparations*] complicado; [*meal*] muy complicado de hacer; [*excuse*] rebuscado • **an ~ hoax** un elaborado engaño
VT [ɪ'læbəreɪt] **1** (= *develop*) [+ *plan, theory*] elaborar, desarrollar
2 (= *explain*) [+ *idea, point*] explicar en detalle, desarrollar
VI [ɪ'læbəreɪt] • **he refused to ~** se negó a dar más detalles • **would you care to ~?** ¿le importaría explicarlo de forma más detallada? • **he ~d on it** lo explicó con más detalles

elaborately [ɪ'læbərɪtlɪ] ADV **1** (= *ornately*) [*decorated, carved, dressed*] de forma muy elaborada; [*describe*] de forma muy detallada, de forma muy minuciosa; [*bow*] con mucha afectación
2 (= *carefully*) [*planned*] cuidadosamente, minuciosamente

elaboration [ɪ,læbə'reɪʃən] N elaboración *f*

élan [eɪ'lɑ:n, eɪ'læn] N (*liter*) elán *m*

elapse [ɪˈlæps] VI pasar, transcurrir

elastic [ɪˈlæstɪk] ADJ elástico; (*fig*) flexible
N (*in garment*) elástico *m*, jebe *m* (*S. Cone*)
CPD ▸ **elastic band** (*esp Brit*) gomita *f*, goma *f* elástica

elasticated [ɪˈlæstɪkeɪtɪd] ADJ (*Brit*) [*waist, waistband*] con elástico

elasticity [ˌiːlæsˈtɪsɪtɪ] N elasticidad *f*; (*fig*) flexibilidad *f*

elasticized [ɪˈlæstɪsaɪzd] ADJ (*US*) con elástico

Elastoplast® [ɪˈlæstəˌplɑːst] N esparadrapo *m*

elate [ɪˈleɪt] VT regocijar

elated [ɪˈleɪtɪd] ADJ (= *excited*) entusiasmado; (= *happy*) eufórico, alborozado

elation [ɪˈleɪʃən] N (= *excitement*) entusiasmo *m*; (= *happiness*) euforia *f*, alborozo *m*, júbilo *m*

Elba [ˈelbə] N Elba *f*

elbow [ˈelbəʊ] N (*Anat*) codo *m*; (*in road*) recodo *m* • **at one's ~** al alcance de la mano • **out at the ~(s)** raído, descosido • IDIOM: • **he doesn't know his arse** *or* **ass from his ~**** confunde el culo con las témporas‡
VT • **to ~ sb aside** apartar a algn a codazos • **to ~ one's way through the crowd** abrirse paso a codazos por la muchedumbre
CPD ▸ **elbow grease*** • **it's a matter of ~ grease** es una cuestión de esfuerzo • **use a bit of ~ grease!** ¡dale con más fuerza! • **it will take a bit of ~ grease to shift this** va a costar trabajo mover esto ▸ **elbow joint** articulación *f* del codo ▸ **elbow room** (= *space*) espacio *m* para moverse; (= *leeway*) margen *m* de maniobra

elbowing [ˈelbəʊɪŋ] N (*Ice hockey*) • **~ is a punishable offence** empujar con el codo está castigado con una falta

elbow-rest [ˈelbəʊˌrest] N [*of chair*] brazo *m*

elder[1] [ˈeldəʳ] ADJ [*brother etc*] mayor • **my ~ sister** mi hermana mayor • **~ statesman** viejo estadista *m*; (*fig*) persona *f* respetada • **Pliny the Elder** Plinio el Viejo
N (= *senior*) mayor *m*; [*of tribe*] anciano *m*; (*in certain Protestant churches*) *persona laica que ejerce funciones educativas, pastorales y/o administrativas* • **my ~s** mis mayores • **don't criticize your ~s and betters** no critiques a tus mayores; ▸ CHURCHES OF ENGLAND/SCOTLAND

elder[2] [ˈeldəʳ] N (*Bot*) saúco *m*

elderberry [ˈeldəˌberɪ] N baya *f* del saúco
CPD ▸ **elderberry wine** vino *m* de saúco

elderly [ˈeldəlɪ] ADJ mayor, de edad • **an ~ gentleman** un señor mayor, un caballero de edad avanzada • **an ~ man** un anciano • **to be getting ~** ir para viejo
NPL • **the ~** las personas mayores, los ancianos

eldest [ˈeldɪst] ADJ [*child*] mayor • **my ~ sister** mi hermana mayor • **he's the ~** él es el mayor • **the ~ of the four** el mayor de los cuatro

Eleanor [ˈelɪnəʳ] N Leonor

e-learning [ˈiːˌlɜːnɪŋ] N aprendizaje *m* en línea

elec ABBR **1** = **electric**
2 = **electricity**

elect [ɪˈlekt] VT **1** (*Pol etc*) elegir (**to** para) • **he was ~ed chairman** fue elegido presidente
2 (= *choose*) elegir • **he ~ed to remain** eligió quedarse
ADJ (*after noun*) electo • **the president ~** el/la presidente/a electo/a
N • **the ~** los elegidos, los predestinados

elected [ɪˈlektɪd] ADJ elegido • **~ government** gobierno *m* elegido

election [ɪˈlekʃən] N (*gen*) elección *f* • **general ~** elecciones *fpl or* comicios *mpl* generales • **to call/hold an ~** convocar elecciones
CPD ▸ **election agent** secretario/a *m/f* electoral ▸ **election campaign** campaña *f* electoral ▸ **election day** día *m* de las elecciones ▸ **election expenses** gastos *mpl* de la campaña electoral ▸ **the election machine** el aparato electoral ▸ **election night** noche *f* electoral

electioneer [ɪˌlekʃəˈnɪəʳ] VI hacer campaña (electoral); (*pej*) hacer electoralismo

electioneering [ɪˌlekʃəˈnɪərɪŋ] N campaña *f* electoral; (*pej*) electoralismo *m*

elective [ɪˈlektɪv] ADJ **1** (*Univ*) [*course*] optativo, opcional; [*assembly*] electivo
2 [*surgery*] optativo
N (*US*) (*Scol*) asignatura *f* optativa, optativa *f*

elector [ɪˈlektəʳ] N elector(a) *m/f*

electoral [ɪˈlektərəl] ADJ electoral
CPD ▸ **electoral college** colegio *m* electoral ▸ **electoral district, electoral division** circunscripción *f* electoral ▸ **electoral register, electoral roll** registro *m* electoral, censo *m* electoral (*Sp*) ▸ **electoral vote** (*US*) (*Pol*) voto *m* electoral

ELECTORAL COLLEGE
Los norteamericanos no votan directamente a su Presidente o a su vicepresidente, sino que votan a unos compromisarios (**electors**) que a su vez se comprometen a votar a determinados candidatos. Estos compromisarios conforman el **electoral college**, tal y como se contempla en la Constitución. El número de votos que tiene un estado para elegir al Presidente es igual al de senadores y diputados. Cada partido político elige a un grupo de compromisarios y en el día de las elecciones presidenciales el pueblo vota al grupo que apoya al candidato de su elección. Como el grupo que gana usa todos los votos del estado para votar a su candidato, podría ocurrir, en teoría, que un candidato ganara el voto popular pero no las elecciones, si le han apoyado colegios electorales con un número pequeño de votos.

electorally [ɪˈlektərəlɪ] ADV [*popular, damaging, disastrous*] desde el punto de vista electoral; [*compete, succeed*] (*gen*) electoralmente; (*in specific election*) en las elecciones

electorate [ɪˈlektərɪt] N electorado *m*

electric [ɪˈlektrɪk] ADJ [*appliance, current, motor*] eléctrico • **the atmosphere was ~** (*fig*) el ambiente era electrizante, el ambiente estaba cargado de electricidad
CPD [*blanket, cooker, fire, guitar, mixer, organ*] eléctrico ▸ **electric bill** (*US*) factura *f or* (*Sp*) recibo *m* de la electricidad ▸ **electric blue** azul *m* eléctrico ▸ **electric chair** silla *f* eléctrica • **to go to the ~ chair** acabar en la silla eléctrica ▸ **electric charge** carga *f* eléctrica ▸ **electric eel** anguila *f* eléctrica ▸ **electric eye** célula *f* fotoeléctrica ▸ **electric fence** valla *f* electrificada, cercado *m* electrificado ▸ **electric field** campo *m* eléctrico ▸ **electric kettle** hervidora *f* de agua eléctrica ▸ **electric light** luz *f* eléctrica ▸ **electric ray** (*Zool*) torpedo *m* ▸ **electric shock** (*from wire, socket*) descarga *f* eléctrica; (*from static electricity*) calambre *m* • **I got an ~ shock from the tap** el grifo me dio calambre ▸ **electric shock treatment** tratamiento *m* por electrochoque ▸ **electric storm** tormenta *f* eléctrica ▸ **electric window(s)** (*Aut*) elevalunas *m inv* eléctrico

electrical [ɪˈlektrɪkəl] ADJ [*equipment, appliance, component, system*] eléctrico • **an ~ fault** un fallo (en el sistema) eléctrico • **household ~ goods** electrodomésticos *mpl*
CPD ▸ **electrical engineer** (= *electrician*) técnico/a *m/f* electricista; (*with university degree*) ingeniero/a *m/f* electrotécnico/a ▸ **electrical engineering** electrotecnia *f*; (*at university*) ingeniería *f* eléctrica ▸ **electrical failure** fallo *m* eléctrico ▸ **electrical fitter** técnico/a *m/f* electricista ▸ **electrical fittings** accesorios *mpl* eléctricos ▸ **electrical storm** tormenta *f* eléctrica ▸ **electrical tape** cinta *f* aislante ▸ **electrical wiring** instalación *f* eléctrica

electrically [ɪˈlektrɪkəlɪ] ADV • **~ charged** cargado de electricidad • **to be ~ controlled** controlarse eléctricamente • **to be ~ driven/powered** funcionar eléctricamente • **to be ~ operated** manejarse eléctricamente *or* por medio de la electricidad, funcionar eléctricamente

electric-blue [ɪˌlektrɪkˈbluː] ADJ (de color) azul eléctrico

electrician [ɪlekˈtrɪʃən] N electricista *mf*

electricity [ɪlekˈtrɪsɪtɪ] N electricidad *f* • **to switch on/off the ~** encender/apagar la electricidad *or* la luz
CPD ▸ **electricity bill** (*Brit*) factura *f or* (*Sp*) recibo *m* de la electricidad ▸ **electricity board** (*Brit*) compañía *f* eléctrica, compañía *f* de luz (*LAm*) ▸ **electricity dispute** conflicto *m* del sector eléctrico ▸ **electricity meter** contador *m* de la electricidad

electrics* [ɪˈlektrɪks] NPL • **the ~** (*Brit*) [*of car, appliance*] el sistema eléctrico; [*of building*] la instalación eléctrica

electrification [ɪˌlektrɪfɪˈkeɪʃən] N electrificación *f*

electrify [ɪˈlektrɪfaɪ] VT **1** (= *charge with electricity*) [+ *railway system*] electrificar • **electrified fence** valla *f* electrificada, cercado *m* eléctrico
2 (*fig*) electrizar

electrifying [ɪˈlektrɪfaɪɪŋ] ADJ [*performance*] electrizante

electro... [ɪˌlektrəʊ] PREFIX electro...

electrocardiogram [ɪˌlektrəʊˈkɑːdɪəgræm] N electrocardiograma *m*

electrocardiograph [ɪˌlektrəʊˈkɑːdɪəgræf] N electrocardiógrafo *m*

electrochemical [ɪˌlektrəʊˈkemɪkəl] ADJ electroquímico

electrochemistry [ɪˌlektrəʊˈkemɪstrɪ] N electroquímica *f*

electroconvulsive therapy [ɪˌlektrəʊkənvʌlsɪvˈθerəpɪ] N electroterapia *f*; ▸ **ECT**

electrocute [ɪˈlektrəʊkjuːt] VT electrocutar

electrocution [ɪˌlektrəʊˈkjuːʃən] N electrocución *f*

electrode [ɪˈlektrəʊd] N electrodo *m*

electrodialysis [ɪˌlektrəʊdaɪˈæləsɪs] N electrodiálisis *f*

electrodynamic [ɪˌlektrəʊdaɪˈnæmɪk] ADJ electrodinámico

electrodynamics [ɪˈlektrəʊdaɪˈnæmɪks] NSING electrodinámica *f*

electroencephalogram [ɪˌlektrəʊ-ɪnˈsefələgræm] N electroencefalograma *m*

electroencephalograph [ɪˈlektrəʊ-ɪnˈsefələgrɑːf] N electroencefalógrafo *m*

electrolyse [ɪˈlektrəʊlaɪz] VT electrolizar

electrolysis [ɪlekˈtrɒlɪsɪs] N electrólisis *f inv*

electrolyte [ɪˈlektrəʊlaɪt] N electrolito *m*

electromagnet [ɪˈlektrəʊˈmægnɪt] N

electroimán *m*
electromagnetic [ɪˈlektrəʊmæɡˈnetɪk] (ADJ) electromagnético
(CPD) ▸ **electromagnetic field** campo *m* electromagnético
electromagnetism [ɪˌlektrəʊˈmæɡnɪtɪzəm] (N) electromagnetismo *m*
electromechanical [ɪˌlektrəʊmɪˈkænɪkəl] (ADJ) electromecánico
electromechanics [ɪˌlektrəʊmɪˈkænɪks] (NSING) electromecánica *f*
electrometallurgy [ɪˌlektrəʊmɪˈtælədʒɪ] (N) electrometalurgia *f*
electrometer [ɪlekˈtrɒmɪtəʳ] (N) electrómetro *m*
electromotive [ɪˌlektrəʊˈməʊtɪv] (ADJ) electromotor
electron [ɪˈlektrɒn] (N) electrón *m*
(CPD) ▸ **electron camera** cámara *f* electrónica ▸ **electron gun** cañón *m* de electrones ▸ **electron microscope** microscopio *m* electrónico
electronic [ɪlekˈtrɒnɪk] (ADJ) [*equipment, circuit, information, signal*] electrónico • **the ~ age** la edad de la electrónica
(CPD) ▸ **electronic banking** banca *f* electrónica ▸ **electronic book** libro *m* electrónico ▸ **electronic cigarette** cigarrillo *m* electrónico ▸ **electronic data processing** procesamiento *m* electrónico de datos ▸ **electronic engineer** ingeniero/a *m/f* electrónico/a ▸ **electronic engineering** ingeniería *f* electrónica ▸ **electronic funds transfer** transferencia *f* electrónica de fondos ▸ **electronic ink** tinta *f* electrónica ▸ **electronic mail** correo *m* electrónico ▸ **electronic mailbox** buzón *m* electrónico ▸ **electronic music** música *f* electrónica ▸ **electronic news gathering** recogida *f* electrónica de noticias ▸ **electronic point of sale** punto *m* de venta electrónico ▸ **electronic publishing** edición *f* electrónica ▸ **electronic shopping** compra *f* computerizada ▸ **electronic smog** radiación *f* electromagnética ▸ **electronic surveillance** vigilancia *f* electrónica ▸ **electronic tagging** (*of products*) etiquetado *m* electrónico; (*of prisoners*) control *m* telemático
electronically [ɪlekˈtrɒnɪklɪ] (ADV) electrónicamente
electronics [ɪlekˈtrɒnɪks] (NSING) (= *science*) electrónica *f*
(NPL) [*of machine*] componentes *mpl* electrónicos
(CPD) ▸ **electronics engineer** ingeniero/a *m/f* electrónico/a ▸ **electronics industry** industria *f* electrónica ▸ **electronics manufacturer** fabricante *mf* de productos electrónicos
electrophysiological [ɪˌlektrəʊˌfɪzɪəˈlɒdʒɪkəl] (ADJ) electrofisiológico
electrophysiology [ɪˌlektrəʊˌfɪzɪˈɒlədʒɪ] (N) electrofisiología *f*
electroplate [ɪˈlektrəʊpleɪt] (VT) galvanizar, electrochapar
electroplated [ɪˈlektrəʊpleɪtɪd] (ADJ) galvanizado, electrochapado
electroplating [ɪˈlektrəʊpleɪtɪŋ] (N) (= *process*) galvanoplastia *f*
electroshock therapy [ɪˌlektrəʊʃɒkˈθerəpɪ] (N) electroterapia *f*
electroshock treatment [ɪˌlektrəʊʃɒkˈtriːtmənt] (N) electrochoque *m*
electrostatic [ɪˌlektrəʊˈstætɪk] (ADJ) electrostático
electrostatics [ɪˌlektrəʊˈstætɪks] (NSING) electrostática *f*
electrosurgery [ɪˌlektrəʊˈsɜːdʒərɪ] (N) electrocirugía *f*
electrosurgical [ɪˌlektrəʊˈsɜːdʒɪkəl] (ADJ) electroquirúrgico
electrotechnological [ɪˌlektrəʊˌteknəˈlɒdʒɪkəl] (ADJ) electrotecnológico
electrotechnology [ɪˌlektrəʊtekˈnɒlədʒɪ] (N) electrotecnología *f*
electrotherapeutic [ɪˌlektrəʊˌθerəˈpjuːtɪk] (ADJ) electroterapéutico
electrotherapeutics [ɪˌlektrəʊˌθerəˈpjuːtɪks] (N) electroterapia *f*
electrotherapist [ɪˌlektrəʊˈθerəpɪst] (N) electroterapeuta *mf*
electrotherapy [ɪˌlektrəʊˈθerəpɪ] (N) electroterapia *f*
electrotype [ɪˈlektrəʊˌtaɪp] (N) electrotipo *m*
(VT) electrotipar
elegance [ˈelɪɡəns] (N) elegancia *f*
elegant [ˈelɪɡənt] (ADJ) [*person, clothes, writing*] elegante • **she looked very ~** estaba muy elegante
elegantly [ˈelɪɡəntlɪ] (ADV) **1** [*move, dance, dress, furnish*] con elegancia, elegantemente • **an ~ simple room** una habitación de una elegancia sencilla • **an ~ simple idea** una idea simple e inteligente
2 [*written, described*] con elegancia
elegiac [ˌelɪˈdʒaɪək] (ADJ) elegíaco
elegy [ˈelɪdʒɪ] (N) elegía *f*
element [ˈelɪmənt] (N) **1** (*gen*) (*Chem*) elemento *m*; (*Elec*) resistencia *f*; (= *factor*) factor *m* • **an ~ of surprise** un elemento de sorpresa • **an ~ of truth** una parte de verdad • **it's the personal ~ that counts** es el factor personal el que cuenta • IDIOMS: • **to be in one's ~** estar en su elemento, estar como pez en el agua • **to be out of one's ~** estar fuera de su elemento
2 elements: **a** (= *rudiments*) elementos *mpl*, nociones *fpl* básicas • **the ~s of mathematics** las nociones básicas de las matemáticas
b (= *weather*) • **open to the ~s** a la intemperie • **to brave the ~s** arrostrar la tempestad; (= *go out*) salir a la intemperie
elemental [ˌelɪˈmentl] (ADJ) elemental
elementary [ˌelɪˈmentərɪ] (ADJ) **1** (= *basic*) [*idea, precautions, rules*] elemental, básico • **~ politeness requires that ...** la cortesía más elemental requiere que ... • **~, my dear Watson!** ¡elemental, querido Watson!
2 (= *introductory*) [*maths, level, exercises*] elemental, básico
(CPD) ▸ **elementary education** (*US*) enseñanza *f* primaria ▸ **elementary particle** partícula *f* elemental ▸ **elementary school** (*US*) escuela *f* de enseñanza primaria ▸ **elementary student** (*US*) alumno/a *m/f* de (la escuela) primaria ▸ **elementary teacher** (*US*) maestro/a *m/f* de (enseñanza) primaria
elephant [ˈelɪfənt] (N) (PL: **elephants** *or* **elephant**) elefante *m*; ▹ **white**
(CPD) ▸ **elephant in the room** *asunto imposible de ignorar pero que todos evitan mencionar*
elephantiasis [ˌelɪfənˈtaɪəsɪs] (N) elefantiasis *f inv*
elephantine [ˌelɪˈfæntaɪn] (ADJ) (*fig*) elefantino
elevate [ˈelɪveɪt] (VT) **1** (*lit*) (= *raise*) elevar
2 (*in rank*) ascender (**to** a); (*Rel*) alzar; (*fig*) elevar
elevated [ˈelɪveɪtɪd] (ADJ) (*lit*) elevado; (*fig*) elevado, sublime
(CPD) ▸ **elevated railway** (*US*), **elevated railroad** (*US*) ferrocarril *m* urbano elevado
elevating [ˈelɪveɪtɪŋ] (ADJ) [*reading*] enriquecedor
elevation [ˌelɪˈveɪʃən] (N) **1** (*lit*) (= *act*) elevación *f*
2 (*in rank*) ascenso *m*; (*fig*) elevación *f*
3 [*of style*] sublimidad *f*
4 (= *hill*) elevación *f*; (= *height*) (*esp above sea level*) altitud *f*
5 (*Archit*) alzado *m*
elevator [ˈelɪveɪtəʳ] (N) **1** (*US*) (= *lift*) ascensor *m*, elevador *m* (*Mex*)
2 (= *hoist for goods*) montacargas *m inv*
3 (*Aer*) timón *m* de profundidad
4 (*Agr*) elevador *m* de granos
5 (*US*) (*also* **elevator shoe**) zapato *m* de tacón alto
(CPD) ▸ **elevator car** (*US*) caja *f* or cabina *f* de ascensor ▸ **elevator shaft** (*US*) hueco *m* del ascensor
eleven [ɪˈlevn] (ADJ), (PRON) once • **she's ~ (years old)** tiene once años
(N) (= *numeral*) once *m*; (*Sport*) once *m*, alineación *f* • **the ~ plus** (*Brit*) (*Scol*) (*formerly*) *examen selectivo realizado por niños mayores de 11 años*; ▹ **five**
elevenses* [ɪˈlevnzɪz] (NPL) (*Brit*) tentempié *m* de las once, onces *fpl* (*LAm*) • **to have ~** tomar un tentempié a las once, tomar las onces (*LAm*)
eleventh [ɪˈlevnθ] (ADJ) undécimo • IDIOM: • **at the ~ hour** a última hora
(N) undécimo/a *m/f*; (= *fraction*) undécima parte *f*, onceavo *m*; ▹ **fifth**
eleventh-grader [ɪˌlevənθˈɡreɪdəʳ] (N) (*US*) alumno/a *m/f* de penúltimo curso (*de entre 16 y 17 años*)
elf [elf] (N) (PL: **elves**) duende *m*, elfo *m*; (*Nordic Myth*) elfo *m*
elfin [ˈelfɪn] (ADJ) de los duendes; (*Nordic Myth*) de los elfos
elfish [ˈelfɪʃ] (ADJ) **1** (= *mischievous*) travieso
2 (= *fairy*) = **elfin**
Elgin Marbles [ˈelɡɪnˈmɑːblz] (NPL) • **the ~** los mármoles del Partenón
elicit [ɪˈlɪsɪt] (VT) [+ *interest*] suscitar; [+ *reaction*] provocar • **to ~ sth (from sb)** [+ *reply, support, information*] obtener algo (de algn) • **my comment ~ed no response from him** no respondió a mi comentario
elide [ɪˈlaɪd] (VT) [+ *vowel, syllable*] elidir
(VI) [*vowel, syllable*] elidirse
eligibility [ˌelɪdʒəˈbɪlɪtɪ] (N) elegibilidad *f*
eligible [ˈelɪdʒəbl] (ADJ) elegible; (= *desirable*) deseable, atractivo • **to be ~ for** (= *suitable*) cumplir los requisitos para; (= *entitled*) tener derecho a • **an ~ young man** un buen partido • **he's the most ~ bachelor in town** es el soltero más cotizado de la ciudad
Elijah [ɪˈlaɪdʒə] (N) Elías
eliminate [ɪˈlɪmɪneɪt] (VT) (*gen*) eliminar; [+ *suspect, possibility*] descartar; [+ *bad language, mistakes, details*] suprimir, eliminar
elimination [ɪˌlɪmɪˈneɪʃən] (N) (= *suppression*) supresión *f*, eliminación *f*; (= *being eliminated*) eliminación *f* • **by process of ~** por eliminación
(CPD) ▸ **elimination round** eliminatoria *f*
eliminator [ɪˈlɪmɪneɪtəʳ] (N) (*Boxing*) combate *m* eliminatorio
Elishah [ɪˈlaɪʃə] (N) Eliseo
elision [ɪˈlɪʒən] (N) elisión *f*
elite, élite [eɪˈliːt] (N) élite *f*
(CPD) [*group, unit, force*] de élite; [*school, university*] de élite, exclusivo
elitism [ɪˈliːtɪzəm] (N) elitismo *m*
elitist [ɪˈliːtɪst] (ADJ) elitista
(N) elitista *mf*
elixir [ɪˈlɪksəʳ] (N) elixir *m*
Elizabeth [ɪˈlɪzəbəθ] (N) Isabel
Elizabethan [ɪˌlɪzəˈbiːθən] (ADJ) isabelino
(N) isabelino/a *m/f*
elk [elk] (N) (PL: **elk** *or* **elks**) (*Zool*) alce *m*
ellipse [ɪˈlɪps] (N) elipse *f*
ellipsis [ɪˈlɪpsɪs] (N) (PL: **ellipses** [ɪˈlɪpsiːz]) (= *omission*) elipsis *f inv*; (= *dots*) puntos *mpl* suspensivos
elliptic [ɪˈlɪptɪk] (ADJ) = **elliptical**

elliptical [ɪ'lɪptɪkəl] ADJ elíptico

elliptically [ɪ'lɪptɪkəlɪ] ADV de manera elíptica

elm [elm] N (*also* **elm tree**) olmo *m*

elocution [ˌelə'kju:ʃən] N elocución *f*

elocutionist [ˌelə'kju:ʃənɪst] N profesor(a) *m/f* de elocución, recitador(a) *m/f*

elongate ['i:lɒŋgeɪt] VT [*+ material, object*] alargar, extender

elongated ['i:lɒŋgeɪtɪd] ADJ alargado

elongation [ˌi:lɒŋ'geɪʃən] N (= *act*) alargamiento *m*; (= *part elongated*) extensión *f*

elope [ɪ'ləʊp] VI [*two persons*] fugarse para casarse • **to ~ with sb** [*one person*] fugarse con algn

elopement [ɪ'ləʊpmənt] N fuga *f*

eloquence ['eləkwəns] N elocuencia *f*

eloquent ['eləkwənt] ADJ [*person, speech*] elocuente; [*gesture, look, silence*] revelador, elocuente • **his lawyer made an ~ plea for leniency** su abogado solicitó con elocuencia que el juez fuese indulgente • **to be ~ proof of sth** ser una prueba fehaciente de algo; ▹ **wax**²

eloquently ['eləkwəntlɪ] ADV [*speak, express*] con elocuencia, elocuentemente; [*write, demonstrate*] elocuentemente; [*nod, smile*] de manera elocuente

El Salvador [el'sælvədɔ:ʳ] N El Salvador

else [els] ADV **1** (*after pron*) • **all ~** todo lo demás • **anybody ~** cualquier otro • **anybody ~ would do it** cualquier otro lo haría • **I don't know anyone ~ here** aquí no conozco a nadie más • **anything ~**: • **anything ~ is impossible** cualquier otra cosa es imposible • **have you anything ~ to tell me?** ¿tienes algo más que decirme? • **anything ~, sir?** (*in shop*) ¿algo más, señor? • **anywhere ~** en cualquier otro sitio • **everyone ~** todos los demás • **everything ~** todo lo demás • **nobody ~** nadie más • **nobody ~ knows** no lo sabe nadie más • **nothing ~** nada más • **there was nothing ~ I could do** no había otro remedio • **nothing ~, thank you** (*in shop*) nada más, gracias, es todo, gracias • **nowhere ~** en ningún otro sitio • **somebody ~** otra persona • **somebody ~'s coat** el abrigo de otro • **there's somebody ~, isn't there?** hay alguien más, ¿verdad? • **something ~** otra cosa; (= *wonderful**) estupendo • **somewhere ~** en otro sitio, en otra parte
2 (*after interrog*) • **how ~?** ¿de qué otra manera? • **what ~ ...?** ¿qué más ...? • **where ~ ...?** ¿en qué otro sitio ...?, ¿dónde más ...? (*LAm*) • **where ~ can he have gone?** ¿a qué otro sitio habrá podido ir? • **who ~ ...?** ¿quién si no ...?, ¿quién más ...? • **who ~ could do it as well as you?** ¿quién si no *or* quién más podría hacerlo tan bien como usted?
3 (*adv of quantity*) • **there is little ~ to be done** poco se puede hacer aparte de eso • **he said that, and much ~** dijo eso y mucho más
4 (= *otherwise*) • **or ~** si no • **red or ~ black** rojo o bien negro • **or ~ I'll do it** si no, lo hago yo • **keep quiet or ~ go away** cállate o vete • **do as I say, or ~!*** (*expressing threat*) ¡haz lo que te digo o si no verás!
5 (*standing alone*) • **how could I have done it ~?** ¿de qué otro modo hubiera podido hacerlo?

elsewhere ['els'wɛəʳ] ADV [*be*] en otra parte, en otro sitio; [*go, send*] a otra parte, a otro sitio • **the document must be ~** el documento debe estar en otra parte *or* en otro sitio • **her thoughts were ~** tenía la cabeza en otra parte • **conditions are worse ~ in the country** las condiciones son peores en otros lugares *or* en otras partes del país • **we had to look ~ for entertainment** tuvimos que buscar diversión en otra parte

ELT N ABBR (= **English Language Teaching**) ▹ **English**, **TEFL/EFL**, **TESL/ESL**, **ELT**, **TESOL/ESOL**

elucidate [ɪ'lu:sɪdeɪt] VT aclarar, elucidar

elucidation [ɪˌlu:sɪ'deɪʃən] N aclaración *f*, elucidación *f*

elucidatory [ɪ'lu:sɪdeɪtərɪ] ADJ aclaratorio

elude [ɪ'lu:d] VT [*+ pursuer*] burlar; [*+ capture, arrest*] eludir, escapar a; [*+ grasp, blow*] esquivar, zafarse de; [*+ question*] eludir; [*+ obligation*] eludir, zafarse de • **the answer has so far ~d us** hasta ahora no hemos dado con la respuesta • **his name ~s me** ahora no recuerdo su nombre • **success has ~d him** el éxito le ha eludido *or* le ha sido esquivo

elusive [ɪ'lu:sɪv] ADJ [*prey, enemy*] esquivo, escurridizo; [*thoughts, word*] inaprensible; [*success*] esquivo, difícil de conseguir • **he is very ~** no es fácil encontrarlo

elusively [ɪ'lu:sɪvlɪ] ADV • **to behave ~** comportarse de manera esquiva • **... he said ~** ... dijo, esquivo, ... dijo, mostrándose esquivo

elusiveness [ɪ'lu:sɪvnɪs] N carácter *m* esquivo

elusory [ɪ'lu:sərɪ] = **elusive**

elver ['elvəʳ] N angula *f*

elves [elvz] NPL *of* **elf**

Elysium [ɪ'lɪzɪəm] N Elíseo *m*

EM N ABBR (*US*) **1** = **Engineer of Mines**
2 = **enlisted man**

emaciated [ɪ'meɪsɪeɪtɪd] ADJ demacrado • **to become ~** demacrarse

emaciation [ɪˌmeɪsɪ'eɪʃən] N demacración *f*

email, **e-mail** ['i:meɪl] N email *m*, correo *m* electrónico
VT • **to ~ sb** mandar un email *or* un correo electrónico a algn • **to ~ sth to sb** • **~ sb sth** mandar algo a algn por Internet, mandar algo a algn en un email *or* en un correo electrónico
CPD ▸ **email account** cuenta *f* de correo ▸ **email address** email *m*, dirección electrónica • **"my ~ address is jones at collins dot uk"** —mi email *or* mi dirección electrónica es jones arroba collins punto uk

emanate ['eməneɪt] VI • **to ~ from** [*idea, proposal*] surgir de; [*light, smell*] emanar de, proceder de

emanation [ˌemə'neɪʃən] N emanación *f*

emancipate [ɪ'mænsɪpeɪt] VT [*+ women, slaves*] emancipar; (*fig*) liberar

emancipated [ɪ'mænsɪpeɪtɪd] ADJ [*women, slaves*] emancipado; (*fig*) libre

emancipation [ɪˌmænsɪ'peɪʃən] N [*of women, slaves*] emancipación *f*; (*fig*) liberación *f*

emasculate [ɪ'mæskjʊleɪt] VT **1** (*genitally*) castrar, emascular
2 (*fig*) mutilar, estropear; (= *weaken*) debilitar

emasculated [ɪ'mæskjʊleɪtɪd] ADJ
1 (*genitally*) castrado, emasculado
2 (*fig*) [*text, film*] mutilado; [*style*] empobrecido; (= *weakened*) debilitado

emasculation [ɪˌmæskjʊ'leɪʃən] N
1 (*genital*) emasculación *f*
2 (= *weakening*) debilitamiento *m*

embalm [ɪm'bɑ:m] VT embalsamar

embalmer [ɪm'bɑ:məʳ] N embalsamador(a) *m/f*

embalming [ɪm'bɑ:mɪŋ] N embalsamamiento *m*
CPD ▸ **embalming fluid** líquido *m* embalsamador

embankment [ɪm'bæŋkmənt] N [*of path, railway*] terraplén *m*; [*of canal, river*] dique *m*

embargo [ɪm'bɑ:gəʊ] N (PL: **embargoes**) (*Comm, Naut*) embargo *m*; (= *prohibition*) prohibición *f* (**on** de) • **there is an ~ on arms** está prohibido comerciar con armas, hay un embargo del comercio de armas • **there is an ~ on that subject** está prohibido discutir ese asunto • **to lift an ~** levantar un embargo *or* una prohibición • **to put an ~ on sth** establecer un embargo sobre algo, embargar algo; (*fig*) (= *prohibit*) prohibir algo • **to be under (an) ~** estar embargado
VT prohibir; (*Jur*) embargar

embark [ɪm'bɑ:k] VT embarcar
VI (*Naut, Aer*) embarcarse (**for** con rumbo a, **on en**) • **to ~ on** [*+ journey*] emprender; [*+ business venture, explanation, discussion*] lanzarse a, embarcarse en

embarkation [ˌembɑ:'keɪʃən] N [*of goods*] embarque *m*; [*of people*] embarco *m*
CPD ▸ **embarkation card** tarjeta *f* de embarque

embarrass [ɪm'bærəs] VT hacer pasar vergüenza a, avergonzar, apenar (*LAm*) • **you seem to enjoy ~ing me** parece que disfrutas haciéndome pasar vergüenza *or* avergonzándome • **I was ~ed by the question** la pregunta me avergonzó, la pregunta hizo sentirme violenta • **his decision could ~ the government** su decisión podría poner al gobierno en una situación embarazosa *or* comprometida

embarrassed [ɪm'bærəst] ADJ [*silence*] violento, incómodo; [*laugh*] nervioso • **to be ~**: **I was so ~!** ¡me dio tanta vergüenza!, ¡me sentí tan violento! • **many people are ~ about discussing their age** a mucha gente le da vergüenza hablar de su edad • **it's nothing to be ~ about** no hay por qué avergonzarse • **I feel ~ when I have to speak in public** me da vergüenza cuando tengo que hablar en público, me da corte cuando tengo que hablar en público (*Sp**) • **to be financially ~** estar *or* andar mal de dinero, tener dificultades económicas • **he sang so badly I was** *or* **felt ~ for him** cantó tan mal que sentí vergüenza ajena • **she was ~ to be seen with him** le daba vergüenza que la vieran con él, le daba corte que la vieran con él (*Sp**)

embarrassing [ɪm'bærəsɪŋ] ADJ [*experience, situation*] embarazoso, violento; [*question, mistake*] embarazoso; [*performance*] penoso • **that was an ~ moment for me** pasé muchísima vergüenza, fue un momento muy embarazoso • **he finds it ~ to talk about himself** le da vergüenza hablar de sí mismo, le resulta violento hablar de sí mismo, le da corte hablar de sí mismo (*Sp**) • **he has put the government in an ~ position** (= *awkward*) ha puesto al gobierno en una situación embarazosa *or* comprometida • **he tries to dance like a teenager — it's ~ to watch** intenta bailar como un quinceañero — da vergüenza ajena verlo

embarrassingly [ɪm'bærəsɪŋlɪ] ADV [*fail, flop*] de manera vergonzosa, bochornosamente • **there were ~ few people** era vergonzoso la poca gente que había • **her acting was ~ bad** actuó de pena*

embarrassment [ɪm'bærəsmənt] N
1 (= *state*) vergüenza *f*, pena *f* (*LAm*) • **I am in a state of some ~** mi situación es algo delicada • **financial ~** dificultades *fpl* económicas • **to have an ~ of riches** tener mucho donde elegir
2 (= *cause*) molestia *f*, vergüenza *f* • **you are an ~ to us** eres un estorbo para nosotros

embassy ['embəsɪ] N embajada *f* • **the British Embassy in Rome** la embajada británica en Roma • **the Spanish Embassy** la embajada de España

embattled [ɪm'bætld] ADJ [*army*] en orden

de batalla; [*city*] sitiado

embed [ɪm'bed] VT [+ *weapon, teeth*] clavar, hincar (**in** en); [+ *jewel*] engastar, incrustar; (*Ling*) incrustar • **to ~ itself in** empotrarse en
VI [*journalist, reporter*] incrustar • **to ~ with a unit** incrustar en una unidad
N (= *embedded journalist*) periodista *mf* incrustado/a

embedded [ɪm'bedɪd] ADJ **1** [*object*] incrustado, clavado • **to be ~ in sth** [*thorn*] estar incrustado *or* clavado en algo; [*bullet*] estar alojado en algo
2 [*values, attitudes*] arraigado • **to be ~ in sth** [*value, attitude*] [+ *mind, psyche, culture, society*] estar arraigado en algo • **it is ~ in my memory** lo tengo clavado en la memoria
3 [*journalist, reporter*] incrustado

embedding [ɪm'bedɪŋ] N **1** (*also Ling*) incrustación *f*
2 [*of journalist, reporter*] incrustación *f*

embellish [ɪm'belɪʃ] VT (= *decorate*) embellecer (**with** con); (*fig*) [+ *story, truth*] adornar (**with** con)

embellishment [ɪm'belɪʃmənt] N embellecimiento *m*; (*fig*) adorno *m*

ember ['embəʳ] N brasa *f*, ascua *f* • **the dying ~s** el rescoldo

embezzle [ɪm'bezl] VT [+ *funds, money*] malversar, desfalcar

embezzlement [ɪm'bezlmənt] N malversación *f* (de fondos), desfalco *m*

embezzler [ɪm'bezləʳ] N malversador(a) *m/f*, desfalcador(a) *m/f*

embitter [ɪm'bɪtəʳ] VT [+ *person*] amargar; [+ *relationship, dispute*] envenenar

embittered [ɪm'bɪtəd] ADJ resentido, amargado • **to be very ~** estar muy amargado, estar muy resentido (**about** por, **against** contra)

embittering [ɪm'bɪtərɪŋ] ADJ [*experience*] amargo

embitterment [ɪm'bɪtəmənt] N amargura *f*

emblazon [ɪm'bleɪzən] VT engalanar *or* esmaltar con colores brillantes; (*fig*) escribir *or* adornar de modo llamativo

emblazoned [ɪm'bleɪzənd] ADJ • **to be ~ on sth** [*design, logo*] estar estampado en algo • **to be ~ with sth** [*flag*] estar engalanado con *or* de algo; [*shirt, cloth*] estar estampado con *or* de algo

emblem ['embləm] N emblema *m*

emblematic [,emblɪ'mætɪk] ADJ emblemático

embodiment [ɪm'bɒdɪmənt] N encarnación *f* • **to be the very ~ of virtue** ser la encarnación de la virtud, ser la virtud en persona

embody [ɪm'bɒdɪ] VT **1** [+ *spirit, quality*] encarnar; [+ *idea, thought, theory*] expresar, plasmar (**in** en)
2 (= *include*) incorporar (**in** en)

embolden [ɪm'bəʊldən] VT • **to ~ sb to do sth** animar a algn a hacer algo, envalentonar a algn para que haga algo

embolism ['embəlɪzəm] N (*Med*) embolia *f*

emboss [ɪm'bɒs] VT [+ *metal, leather*] repujar; [+ *paper*] gofrar, estampar (en relieve) • **~ed with the royal arms** con el escudo real en relieve

embossed [ɪm'bɒst] ADJ [*writing paper*] con membretes en relieve; [*metal, velvet, leather*] repujado, labrado; [*wallpaper*] labrado

embouchure [,ɒmbʊ'ʃʊəʳ] N (*Mus*) boquilla *f*

embrace [ɪm'breɪs] N abrazo *m*
VT **1** [+ *person*] abrazar
2 [+ *offer*] aceptar; [+ *opportunity*] aprovechar; [+ *course of action*] adoptar; [+ *doctrine, party*] adherirse a; [+ *religion*] abrazar; [+ *cause, profession*] dedicarse a
3 (= *include*) abarcar
VI abrazarse

embrasure [ɪm'breɪʒəʳ] N (*Archit*) alféizar *m*; (*Mil*) tronera *f*, aspillera *f*

embrocation [,embrəʊ'keɪʃən] N embrocación *f*, linimento *m*

embroider [ɪm'brɔɪdəʳ] VT **1** (= *sew*) bordar
2 (*fig*) (= *embellish*) [+ *truth, facts, story*] adornar
VI bordar

embroidered [ɪm'brɔɪdəd] ADJ **1** [*silk, linen, tablecloth*] bordado • **~ in silk** bordado en seda
2 (*fig*) [*story, version*] adornado

embroidery [ɪm'brɔɪdərɪ] N bordado *m* • **I do ~ in the afternoon** bordo por las tardes
CPD ▸ **embroidery frame** bastidor *m*, tambor *m* de bordar ▸ **embroidery silk** hilo *m* de bordar ▸ **embroidery thread** = **embroidery silk**

embroil [ɪm'brɔɪl] VT enredar • **to ~ sb in sth** enredar a algn en algo • **to ~ o.s. in sth** • **get ~ed in sth** enredarse en algo • **to ~ sb with** indisponer a algn con • **to ~ A with B** mezclar a A con B

embroilment [ɪm'brɔɪlmənt] N embrollo *m*

embryo ['embrɪəʊ] N embrión *m*; (*fig*) germen *m*, embrión *m* • **in ~** en embrión
CPD [*research*] embrionario

embryological [,embrɪə'lɒdʒɪkəl] ADJ embriológico

embryologist [,embrɪ'ɒlədʒɪst] N embriólogo/a *m/f*

embryology [,embrɪ'ɒlədʒɪ] N embriología *f*

embryonic [,embrɪ'ɒnɪk] ADJ embrionario

emcee ['em'siː] (*US*) N presentador(a) *m/f*
VT presentar • **to ~ a show** presentar un espectáculo

EMCF N ABBR (= **European Monetary Cooperation Fund**) FECOM *m*

em dash ['emdæʃ] N (*Typ*) raya *f*

emend [ɪ'mend] VT enmendar

emendation [,iːmen'deɪʃən] N enmienda *f*

emerald ['emərəld] N (= *stone*) esmeralda *f*; (= *colour*) verde *m* esmeralda
ADJ (*also* **emerald green**) verde esmeralda
CPD [*necklace, bracelet, ring*] de esmeraldas ▸ **the Emerald Isle** la verde Irlanda

emerge [ɪ'mɜːdʒ] VI salir (**from** de); [*truth*] saberse, resplandecer; [*facts, problems*] surgir, presentarse; [*theory, new nation*] surgir • **it ~s that** resulta que • **what has ~d from this inquiry?** ¿qué se saca de esta investigación?

emergence [ɪ'mɜːdʒəns] N aparición *f*

emergency [ɪ'mɜːdʒənsɪ] N **1** (*gen*) emergencia *f* • **quick! this is an ~!** ¡rápido! ¡es una emergencia! • **prepared for any ~** preparado para cualquier emergencia, prevenido contra toda eventualidad (*frm*) • **she is good in an ~** es buena en casos de emergencia • **in case of ~, please call ...** en caso de emergencia, por favor llamen al ... • **there is a national ~** existe una crisis nacional • **to declare a state of ~** declarar el estado de excepción
2 (*Med*) urgencia *f* • **she was admitted for ~ surgery** fue admitida para ser sometida a una operación de urgencia; ▹ **accident**
CPD [*meeting, measures, talks, airstrip*] de emergencia ▸ **emergency brake** (*esp US*) freno *m* de mano ▸ **emergency call** llamada *f* de urgencia ▸ **emergency case** caso *m* de emergencia ▸ **emergency centre** centro *m* de emergencia ▸ **emergency department** • **the ~ department** urgencias *fpl* ▸ **emergency exit** salida *f* de emergencia ▸ **emergency fund** fondos *mpl* de reserva ▸ **emergency landing** (*Aer*) aterrizaje *m* forzoso ▸ **emergency lane** (*US*) arcén *m* ▸ **emergency operation** (*Med*) operación *f* de urgencia ▸ **emergency powers** poderes *mpl* extraordinarios ▸ **emergency ration** ración *f* de reserva ▸ **emergency road service** (*US*) servicio *m* de asistencia en carretera ▸ **emergency room** (*US*) urgencias *fpl* ▸ **emergency services** (= *police, fire brigade, ambulance*) servicios *mpl* de urgencia, servicios *mpl* de emergencia ▸ **emergency stop** (*Aut*) parada *f* de emergencia ▸ **emergency supply** provisión *f* de reserva ▸ **emergency telephone** teléfono *f* de emergencia ▸ **emergency ward** sala *f* de urgencias ▸ **emergency worker** socorrista *mf*

emergent [ɪ'mɜːdʒənt] ADJ [*countries*] emergente

emerging [ɪ'mɜːdʒɪŋ] ADJ = **emergent**

emeritus [iː'merɪtəs] ADJ emérito

emery ['emərɪ] N esmeril *m*
CPD ▸ **emery board** lima *f* de uñas ▸ **emery cloth** tela *f* de esmeril ▸ **emery paper** papel *m* de esmeril

emetic [ɪ'metɪk] ADJ emético, vomitivo
N emético *m*, vomitivo *m*

emigrant ['emɪgrənt] ADJ emigrante
N emigrante *mf*

emigrate ['emɪgreɪt] VI emigrar

emigration [,emɪ'greɪʃən] N emigración *f*

émigré, émigrée ['emɪgreɪ] N emigrado/a *m/f*

Emily ['emɪlɪ] N Emilia

eminence ['emɪnəns] N **1** (= *fame*) prestigio *m*, renombre *m* • **to gain** *or* **win ~** alcanzar prestigio (**as** como)
2 (*frm*) (= *hill*) promontorio *m*, prominencia *f*
3 (*Rel*) (= *title of cardinal*) eminencia *f* • **His/Your Eminence** Su/Vuestra Eminencia

eminence grise ['emɪnəns'griːz] N eminencia *f* gris

eminent ['emɪnənt] ADJ **1** (= *distinguished*) [*doctor, scientist*] eminente, ilustre • **she is ~ in the field of avionics** es una eminencia en el campo de la aviónica
2 (*frm*) (= *great*) [*charm, fairness, good sense*] extraordinario • **she was chosen for her ~ suitability for the job** la eligieron por ser sumamente idónea para el puesto

eminently ['emɪnəntlɪ] ADV [*suitable, qualified, respectable*] sumamente • **his earliest work is ~ forgettable** sus primeras obras no tienen nada de memorables

emir [e'mɪəʳ] N emir *m*

emirate [e'mɪərɪt] N emirato *m*

emissary ['emɪsərɪ] N emisario/a *m/f*

emission [ɪ'mɪʃən] N **1** [*of light, smell*] emisión *f*; (*Anat*) [*of semen*] expulsión *f*
2 emissions (= *fumes*) emisiones *fpl*
CPD ▸ **emission controls** controles *mpl* de emisiones ▸ **emissions trading** comercio *m* de derechos de emisión de gases

emit [ɪ'mɪt] VT [+ *sparks*] echar; [+ *light, signals*] emitir; [+ *smoke, heat, smell*] despedir; [+ *cry*] dar; [+ *sound*] producir

emitter [ɪ'mɪtəʳ] N (*Electronics*) emisor *m*

Emmanuel [ɪ'mænjʊəl] N Manuel

Emmy ['emɪ] N (PL: **Emmys** *or* **Emmies**) (*US*) (*TV*) Emmy *m*

emoji [ɪ'məʊdʒɪ] N (*pl* **emojis**) emoji *m*

emollient [ɪ'mɒlɪənt] ADJ emoliente
N emoliente *m*

emolument [ɪ'mɒljʊmənt] N (*often pl*) (*frm*) (= *salary*) emolumentos *mpl*; (= *fees*) honorarios *mpl*

e-money ['iːmʌnɪ] N dinero *m* electrónico

emote* [ɪ'məʊt] VI actuar de una manera muy emocionada

emoticon [ɪ'məʊtɪkɒn] N emoticón *m*, emoticono *m*

emotion [ɪ'məʊʃən] N **1** (= *passion*)

emoción *f* • **her voice trembled with ~** su voz temblaba de emoción • **he never shows any ~** nunca deja ver ninguna emoción • **the split between reason and ~** la división entre la razón y los sentimientos, el conflicto entre los dictados de la mente y del corazón
2 (= *sensation*) (*eg happiness, love, fear, anger*) sentimiento *m* • **he struggled to control his ~s** luchaba para controlar sus sentimientos

emotional [ɪˈməʊʃənl] ADJ **1** (= *concerning the emotions*) [*well-being, problem, tension, development*] emocional; [*abuse, need, relationship*] afectivo; [*support, disorder*] emocional, afectivo • **on an ~ level** a nivel emocional • **to be on an ~ roller coaster** sufrir altibajos emocionales • **to be an ~ wreck** estar destrozado emocionalmente
2 (= *emotive, moving*) [*scene, farewell, welcome, subject*] emotivo; [*experience, situation, appeal, speech*] emotivo, conmovedor
3 (= *excitable*) [*outburst*] impulsivo; [*response*] emotivo • **Latins are very ~ people** los latinos son muy expresivos con sus sentimientos • **to become** *or* **get ~** reaccionar de una forma emocional • **there's no need to get all ~!** ¡no te pongas así!
4 (= *sentimental*) [*person, behaviour*] sentimental, emotivo; [*decision*] impulsivo • **I got very ~ when the time came to say goodbye** a la hora de despedirnos me puse muy sentimental • **to become** *or* **get ~** emocionarse • **he became** *or* **got very ~ at the farewell party** se emocionó mucho en la fiesta de despedida
CPD ▸ **emotional baggage** (*fig*) bagaje *m* emocional ▸ **emotional blackmail** chantaje *m* emocional

emotionalism [ɪˈməʊʃnəlɪzəm] N emoción *f*, emotividad *f*; (*pej*) sentimentalismo *m*

emotionally [ɪˈməʊʃnəlɪ] ADV **1** (= *mentally*) [*mature, unstable*] emocionalmente • **~ I was a wreck** emocionalmente *or* desde el punto de vista emocional estaba destrozado • **to remain ~ detached** no involucrarse emocionalmente • **to be ~ drained** estar agotado emocionalmente; ▹ **deprived**
2 (= *with emotion*) [*speak, appeal*] emotivamente, de forma conmovedora; [*respond*] emotivamente • **an ~ charged atmosphere** una atmósfera cargada de emotividad • **an ~ worded article** un artículo redactado con mucha emotividad
3 (= *sentimentally*) • **they became ~ involved** entablaron una relación sentimental

emotionless [ɪˈməʊʃənlɪs] ADJ sin emoción

emotive [ɪˈməʊtɪv] ADJ emotivo

empanel [ɪmˈpænl] VT [+ *jury*] seleccionar • **to ~ sb for a jury** inscribir a algn para jurado

empathetic [ˌempəˈθetɪk] ADJ = **empathic**

empathetically [ˌempəˈθetɪkəlɪ] ADV = **empathically**

empathic [ˌempəˈθetɪk] ADJ comprensivo, empático

empathically [ˌempəˈθetɪkəlɪ] ADV con comprensión, con empatía

empathize [ˈempəθaɪz] VI identificarse (**with** con)

empathy [ˈempəθɪ] N identificación *f*, empatía *f* • **to feel ~ with sb** identificarse con algn

emperor [ˈempərəʳ] N emperador *m*
CPD ▸ **emperor penguin** pingüino *m* emperador *or* real

emphasis [ˈemfəsɪs] N (PL: **emphases** [ˈemfəsiːz]) **1** (*in word*) acento *m*; (*in sentence*) énfasis *m inv* • **the ~ is on the first syllable** el acento (re)cae en la primera sílaba • **to put ~ on a word** enfatizar una palabra
2 (*fig*) énfasis *m inv* • **there has been a change of ~** ya no se hace hincapié en lo mismo • **he said it twice, for ~** lo dijo dos veces, para enfatizar *or* para recalcar • **the ~ is on sport** se da más énfasis al deporte • **this year the ~ is on femininity** este año se resalta la feminidad • **to place** *or* **put** *or* **lay ~ on sth** hacer hincapié en algo, poner énfasis en algo • **too much ~ is placed on research** se pone demasiado énfasis en la investigación, se hace demasiado hincapié en la investigación • **to put special ~ on sth** poner especial énfasis en algo • **to speak with ~** hablar con énfasis

emphasize [ˈemfəsaɪz] VT **1** [+ *word, syllable*] enfatizar; [+ *fact, point*] hacer hincapié en, enfatizar, subrayar, recalcar • **I must ~ that …** debo insistir en que …
2 (*Ling*) acentuar
3 [*garment*] (= *accentuate*) hacer resaltar

emphatic [ɪmˈfætɪk] ADJ **1** (= *forceful*) [*statement, declaration, response*] categórico, contundente; [*denial, refusal*] categórico, rotundo; [*tone, gesture*] enérgico, enfático; [*condemnation*] categórico, enérgico • **Wendy was ~, "you must do it," she said** Wendy fue categórica, —debes hacerlo, dijo • **she's ~ that business is improving** mantiene firmemente que el negocio está mejorando • **they were quite ~ that they were not going** dijeron categóricamente que no iban • **Pat was ~ about how valuable the course was** Pat hizo hincapié en lo valioso que era el curso • **they were ~ in denying their involvement** negaron categóricamente su participación • **an ~ no** un no rotundo • **an ~ yes** un sí contundente
2 (= *decisive*) [*victory, win*] rotundo; [*success*] arrollador; [*defeat*] aplastante; [*winner, result*] contundente

emphatically [ɪmˈfætɪkəlɪ] ADV **1** (= *forcefully*) [*say, reply, reject*] categóricamente, enérgicamente; [*deny, refuse*] rotundamente, categóricamente • **he shook his head ~** dijo que no con la cabeza de manera rotunda • **most ~** [*say, reply*] de la forma más contundente; [*deny, refuse*] de la forma más rotunda
2 (= *definitely*) decididamente, sin lugar a dudas

emphysema [emfɪˈsiːmə] N enfisema *m*

Empire [ˈempaɪəʳ] ADJ [*costume, furniture*] estilo Imperio

empire [ˈempaɪəʳ] N imperio *m*
CPD ▸ **the Empire State** (*US*) el estado de Nueva York

empire-builder [ˈempaɪəˌbɪldəʳ] N (*fig*) constructor(a) *m/f* de imperios

empire-building [ˈempaɪəˌbɪldɪŋ] N (*fig*) construcción *f* de imperios

empiric [emˈpɪrɪk] ADJ = **empirical**

empirical [emˈpɪrɪkəl] ADJ [*method*] empírico

empirically [emˈpɪrɪkəlɪ] ADV empíricamente

empiricism [emˈpɪrɪsɪzəm] N empirismo *m*

empiricist [emˈpɪrɪsɪst] N empírico/a *m/f*

emplacement [ɪmˈpleɪsmənt] N (*Mil*) emplazamiento *m*

emplane [ɪmˈpleɪn] VI (*US*) subir al avión, embarcar (en avión)

employ [ɪmˈplɔɪ] VT [+ *person*] emplear, dar empleo a; [+ *object, method*] emplear, usar; [+ *time*] ocupar • **the factory ~s 600 people** la fábrica da empleo a 600 trabajadores • **thousands of people are ~ed in tourism** miles de personas trabajan en el sector del turismo
N • **to be in the ~ of sb** (*frm*) (*as company employee*) ser empleado de algn; (*as servant*) estar al servicio de algn

employable [ɪmˈplɔɪəbl] ADJ [*person*] con capacidad para trabajar; [*skill*] útil, utilizable

employee [ˌemplɔɪˈiː] N empleado/a *m/f*
CPD ▸ **employee benefits** prestaciones *fpl* para los empleados ▸ **employee contribution, employee's contribution** (*to pension fund*) aportación *f* del trabajador ▸ **employee rights** derechos *mpl* de los trabajadores

employer [ɪmˈplɔɪəʳ] N (= *business person*) empresario/a *m/f*; (= *boss*) patrón/ona *m/f* • **the ~s' federation** • **the ~s' organization** la patronal • **the ~'s interests** los intereses empresariales • **my ~** mi jefe
CPD ▸ **employer contribution, employer's contribution** (*to pension fund*) aportación *f* de la empresa

employment [ɪmˈplɔɪmənt] N empleo *m*, trabajo *m* • **to be in ~** tener empleo *or* trabajo • **to find ~** encontrar empleo *or* trabajo • **to give ~ to** emplear a, dar trabajo a • **to look for ~** buscar empleo *or* trabajo • **conditions of ~** condiciones *fpl* de empleo • **full ~** pleno empleo *m* • **a high level of ~** un alto nivel de empleo • **her ~ prospects are poor** tiene pocas posibilidades de colocarse • **Secretary (of State) for** *or* **Minister of Employment** (*Brit*) • **Secretary for Employment** (*US*) Ministro *m* de Trabajo • **Department of Employment** (*Brit*) Ministerio *m* de Trabajo
CPD ▸ **employment agency** agencia *f* de colocación ▸ **employment exchange** (*Brit*) oficina *f* de empleo ▸ **employment law** derecho *m* laboral ▸ **employment office** (*US*) oficina *f* de empleo ▸ **Employment Service** (*US*) *organismo del gobierno encargado de ayudar a que los desempleados encuentren trabajo*, ≈ Instituto *m* Nacional de Empleo (*Sp*) ▸ **employment statistics** estadística *f* del empleo, cifras *fpl* del paro ▸ **employment tribunal** tribunal *m* de lo social

emporium [emˈpɔːrɪəm] N (PL: **emporiums** *or* **emporia** [emˈpɔːrɪə]) almacenes *mpl*, emporio *m* (*LAm*)

empower [ɪmˈpaʊəʳ] VT **1** (= *authorize*) • **to ~ sb to do sth** autorizar a algn para hacer algo
2 [+ *women, workers, minorities*] atribuir poderes a

empowerment [ɪmˈpaʊəmənt] N [*of women, workers, minorities*] atribución *f* de poder

empress [ˈemprɪs] N emperatriz *f*

emptiness [ˈemptɪnɪs] N **1** (= *bareness, barrenness*) desolación *f*, vacío *m* • **the ~ of the desert** la desolación *or* el vacío del desierto
2 (= *void*) vacío *m* • **the ~ he felt inside** el vacío que sentía en su interior • **the ~ of his life** el vacío *or* (*frm*) la vacuidad de su vida

empty [ˈemptɪ] ADJ (COMPAR: **emptier**, SUPERL: **emptiest**) **1** (= *containing nothing, nobody*) [*box, bottle, glass, street, room, hands*] vacío; [*seat, chair*] (*in bus, restaurant*) libre, desocupado; (*in living room*) vacío; [*place*] desierto; [*landscape*] desierto, desolado; [*gun*] descargado; [*post, job*] vacante • **the flat next door is ~** (= *unoccupied*) el piso de al lado está desocupado • **to be ~ of sth**: • **the parks are ~ of children** en los parques no hay niños • **his face was ~ of all expression** su rostro no expresaba ninguna emoción • **she was staring into ~ space** miraba al infinito • **there was an ~ space at the table** había un sitio vacío *or* sin ocupar en la mesa • **on an ~ stomach** en ayunas, con el estómago vacío • PROVERB: • **~ vessels make the most noise** mucho ruido y pocas nueces

2 (= *meaningless*) [*threat, promise, dream*] vano; [*words, rhetoric*] hueco, vacío; [*exercise*] inútil; [*life*] sin sentido, vacío • **it's an ~ gesture** es un gesto vacío • **she felt trapped in an ~ marriage** se sentía atrapada en una relación matrimonial vacía • **his promises were just so much ~ talk** sus promesas no eran más que palabras huecas *or* vanas • **my life is ~ without you** mi vida no tiene sentido sin ti
3 (= *numb*) [*person*] vacío; [*feeling*] de vacío • **when I heard the news I felt ~** cuando me enteré de la noticia me sentí vacío
(N) 1 (*usu pl*) (= *empty bottle*) envase *m* (vacío), casco *m* (vacío); (= *empty glass*) vaso *m* (vacío)
2 (*Aut*) • **the car was running on ~** el coche estaba con el depósito vacío • **I was running on ~** (*fig*) no me quedaba energía
(VT) [+ *container, tank, glass, plate*] vaciar • **television has emptied the cinemas** la televisión ha dejado los cines vacíos • **I emptied the dirty water down the drain** tiré el agua sucia por el sumidero • **she emptied the ashtray into the bin** vació el cenicero en el cubo de la basura • **we emptied the cupboards of junk** vaciamos los armarios de trastos • **he emptied the gun of bullets** descargó la pistola • **I tried to ~ my mind of distractions** intenté vaciar la mente de distracciones • **I emptied the contents of the bag onto the bed** vacié la bolsa en la cama • **to ~ out one's pockets** vaciarse los bolsillos • **he emptied the water out of his boots** se sacó el agua de las botas
(VI) 1 (= *become empty*) [*room, building, theatre, bath*] vaciarse; [*street*] quedarse desierto, vaciarse; [*train, coach, plane*] quedarse vacío, vaciarse • **the auditorium quickly emptied of students** los estudiantes desalojaron el auditorio rápidamente
2 (= *flow*) • **to ~ into sth** [*river*] desembocar en algo

empty-handed ['emptɪ'hændɪd] (ADJ) • **to arrive/leave/return empty-handed** llegar/marcharse/volver con las manos vacías

empty-headed ['emptɪ'hedɪd] (ADJ) casquivano

Empyrean [empɪ'ri:ən] (N) • **the ~** (*liter*) el empíreo

em rule ['emru:l] (N) (*Typ*) raya *f*

EMS (N ABBR) (= **European Monetary System**) SME *m*

EMT (N ABBR) = **emergency medical technician**

EMU (N ABBR) (= **economic and monetary union**) UME *f*, UEM *f*

emu ['i:mju:] (N) emú *m*

emulate ['emjʊleɪt] (VT) emular (*also Comput*)

emulation [,emjʊ'leɪʃən] (N) emulación *f* (*also Comput*)

emulator ['emjʊ,leɪtəʳ] (N) (*Comput*) emulador *m*

emulsifier [ɪ'mʌlsɪ,faɪəʳ] (N) agente *m* emulsionador, emulsionante *m*

emulsify [ɪ'mʌlsɪfaɪ] (VT) emulsionar

emulsion [ɪ'mʌlʃən] (N) (= *liquid*) emulsión *f*; (*also* **emulsion paint**) pintura *f* emulsión

EN (N ABBR) (*Brit*) (= **Enrolled Nurse**) ≈ ATS *mf*

enable [ɪ'neɪbl] (VT) 1 (= *make able*) • **to ~ sb to do sth** permitir a algn hacer algo
2 (= *make possible*) posibilitar • **the new system will ~ better communication between doctor and patient** el nuevo sistema posibilitará *or* hará posible una mejor comunicación entre el médico y el paciente

-enabled [ɪn'eɪbəld] (SUFFIX) (*Comput*) • **web-enabled** con conexión a la web • **Java-enabled** con Java

enabling [ɪn'eɪblɪŋ] (ADJ) 1 (*Jur*) [*legislation, act*] de autorización, de habilitación
2 (= *fostering personal development*) que fomenta el desarrollo personal • **an ~ school** un colegio que fomenta el desarrollo personal
(CPD) ▸ **enabling technology** • **the internet is an ~ technology** Internet es una tecnología que permite que las personas realicen cosas

enact [ɪ'nækt] (VT) 1 (*Jur*) decretar (**that** que); [+ *law*] promulgar
2 (= *perform*) [+ *play, scene, part*] representar

enactment [ɪ'næktmənt] (N) 1 [*of law*] promulgación *f*
2 [*of play, scene, part*] representación *f*

enamel [ɪ'næməl] (N) (*gen, of teeth*) esmalte *m*
(VT) esmaltar
(CPD) ▸ **enamel jewellery** alhajas *fpl* de esmalte ▸ **enamel paint** (pintura *f* al) esmalte *m* ▸ **enamel saucepan** cacerola *f* esmaltada

enamelled, enameled (*US*) [ɪ'næməld] (ADJ) esmaltado

enamelling, enameling (*US*) [ɪ'næməlɪŋ] (N) esmaltado *m*

enamelware [ɪ'næməlweəʳ] (N) utensilios *mpl* de hierro esmaltado

enamour, enamor (*US*) [ɪ'næməʳ] (VT) • **to be ~ed of** (*liter, hum*) [+ *person*] estar enamorado de; [+ *thing*] estar entusiasmado con

en bloc [,ɒn'blɒk] (ADV) [*act, resign, vote*] en bloque

enc. (ABBR) (*on letter*) 1 (= **enclosure**) material *m* adjunto
2 (= **enclosed**) adjunto

encamp [ɪn'kæmp] (VI) acamparse

encampment [ɪn'kæmpmənt] (N) campamento *m*

encapsulate [ɪn'kæpsjʊleɪt] (VT) 1 (= *enclose*) encerrar
2 (*fig*) (= *summarize*) resumir
3 (*Pharm*) encapsular

encapsulation [ɪn,kæpsjʊ'leɪʃən] (N) [*of mood, spirit, essence*] síntesis *f*

encase [ɪn'keɪs] (VT) encerrar; (*Tech*) revestir • **to be ~d in** estar revestido de

encash [ɪn'kæʃ] (VT) cobrar, hacer efectivo

encashment [ɪn'kæʃmənt] (N) cobro *m*

encephalic [ensɪ'fælɪk] (ADJ) encefálico

encephalitis [,ensefə'laɪtɪs] (N) encefalitis *f*

encephalogram [ɪn'sefələgræm] (N) encefalograma *m*

enchain [ɪn'tʃeɪn] (VT) (*frm*) encadenar

enchant [ɪn'tʃɑ:nt] (VT) (*often passive*) encantar; (= *use magic on*) encantar, hechizar • **we were ~ed with the place** el sitio nos encantó

enchanter [ɪn'tʃɑ:ntəʳ] (N) hechicero/a *m/f*

enchanting [ɪn'tʃɑ:ntɪŋ] (ADJ) encantador

enchantingly [ɪn'tʃɑ:ntɪŋlɪ] (ADV) de manera encantadora, deliciosamente

enchantment [ɪn'tʃɑ:ntmənt] (N) (= *act*) encantamiento *m*; (= *delight*) encanto *m*; (= *charm, spell*) encantamiento *m*, hechizo *m* • **it lent ~ to the scene** le daba encanto a la escena

enchantress [ɪn'tʃɑ:ntrɪs] (N) hechicera *f*

enchilada [,entʃɪ'lɑ:də] (N) enchilada *f* • **big ~** (*US**) peso *m* pesado

encipher [ɪn'saɪfəʳ] (VT) cifrar

encircle [ɪn'sɜ:kl] (VT) rodear (**with** de); (*Mil*) sitiar; [+ *waist, shoulders*] ceñir • **it is ~d by a wall** está rodeado de una tapia

encirclement [ɪn'sɜ:klmənt] (N) (*Mil*) envolvimiento *m*

encircling [ɪn'sɜ:klɪŋ] (ADJ) [*movement*] envolvente

encl, encl. (ABBR) (*on letter*) 1 (= **enclosure**) material *m* adjunto
2 (= **enclosed**) adjunto

enclave ['enkleɪv] (N) enclave *m*

enclitic [ɪn'klɪtɪk] (ADJ) enclítico

enclose [ɪn'kləʊz] (VT) 1 [+ *land, garden*] cercar, vallar • **to ~ with** cercar *or* vallar con
2 (= *put in a receptacle*) meter, encerrar
3 (= *include*) encerrar
4 (*with letter*) remitir adjunto, adjuntar • **I ~ a cheque** (remito) adjunto un cheque

enclosed [ɪn'kləʊzd] (ADJ) 1 (*with letter*) adjunto • **please find ~** le enviamos adjunto *or* anexo • **the ~ letter** la carta adjunta
2 [*garden, land*] cercado, vallado

enclosure [ɪn'kləʊʒəʳ] (N) 1 (= *act*) cercamiento *m*
2 (= *place*) recinto *m*; (*at racecourse*) reservado *m*
3 (*in letter*) anexo *m*

encode [ɪn'kəʊd] (VT) 1 (= *encrypt*) codificar, cifrar
2 (*Ling*) cifrar

encoder [ɪn'kəʊdəʳ] (N) (*Comput*) codificador *m*

encoding [ɪn'kəʊdɪŋ] (N) (*Comput, Ling*) codificación *f*

encomium [ɪn'kəʊmɪəm] (N) (PL: **encomiums** *or* **encomia** [ɪn'kəʊmɪə]) elogio *m*, encomio *m*

encompass [ɪn'kʌmpəs] (VT) 1 (= *surround*) cercar, rodear (**with** de)
2 (= *include*) abarcar
3 (= *bring about*) lograr, efectuar

encore [ɒŋ'kɔ:ʳ] (EXCL) ¡otra!
(N) bis *m* • **to call for an ~** pedir un bis • **to give an ~** hacer un bis, repetir a petición del público • **to sing a song as an ~** cantar como bis una canción
(VT) [+ *song*] pedir un bis de; [+ *person*] pedir un bis *or* otra a

encounter [ɪn'kaʊntəʳ] (N) (= *meeting, fight*) encuentro *m*
(VT) [+ *person*] encontrar, encontrarse con; [+ *difficulty, danger, enemy*] tropezar con
(CPD) ▸ **encounter group** grupo *m* de encuentro

encourage [ɪn'kʌrɪdʒ] (VT) [+ *person*] animar, alentar; [+ *industry, growth*] estimular, fomentar • **to ~ sb to do sth** animar a algn a hacer algo • **the discovery ~d him in his belief that she was still alive** el hallazgo reafirmó su creencia de que aún seguía viva

encouragement [ɪn'kʌrɪdʒmənt] (N) (= *act*) estímulo *m*; [*of industry*] fomento *m*; (= *support*) aliento *m*, ánimo(s) *m(pl)* • **to give ~ to** dar ánimos a, animar • **to give ~ to the enemy** dar aliento al enemigo

encouraging [ɪn'kʌrɪdʒɪŋ] (ADJ) [*smile*] alentador; [*news, prospect*] alentador, halagüeño; [*words*] de aliento • **it is not an ~ prospect** es una perspectiva poco halagüeña • **he was always very ~** siempre me daba ánimos

encouragingly [ɪn'kʌrɪdʒɪŋlɪ] (ADV) [*speak, say*] en tono alentador; [*smile, nod*] de modo alentador • **the theatre was ~ full** el teatro estaba lleno, lo cual resultaba alentador • **~, inflation is slowing down** resulta alentador que la inflación se vaya ralentizando

encroach [ɪn'krəʊtʃ] (VI) avanzar • **to ~ (up)on** [+ *time*] quitar; [+ *rights*] usurpar; [+ *land*] (*of neighbour*) invadir, traspasar los límites de; [+ *land*] (*by sea*) hurtar, invadir; [+ *someone's subject*] invadir

encroachment [ɪn'krəʊtʃmənt] (N) usurpación *f* (**on** de) • **this new ~ on our liberty** esta nueva usurpación de nuestra libertad

encrust [ɪn'krʌst] (VT) incrustar (**with** de)

encrustation [,ɪnkrʌs'teɪʃən] (N)

incrustación *f*

encrusted [ɪn'krʌstɪd] ADJ • **~ with** incrustado de

encrypt [ɪn'krɪpt] VT codificar, encriptar

encrypted [ɪn'krɪptɪd] ADJ [*data, message, signal*] codificado, encriptado

encryption [ɪn'krɪpʃən] N codificación *f*, encriptación *f*

encumber [ɪn'kʌmbəʳ] VT [*+ person, movement*] estorbar; (*with debts*) cargar; [*+ place*] llenar (**with** de) • **to be ~ed with** tener que cargar con; [*+ debts*] estar cargado de

encumbrance [ɪn'kʌmbrəns] N estorbo *m*; (*Econ, Jur*) carga *f*, gravamen *m* • **without ~** (*frm*) sin familia

encyclical [en'sɪklɪkəl] N encíclica *f*

encyclopaedia, **encyclopedia** [en,saɪkləʊ'pi:dɪə] N enciclopedia *f*

encyclopaedic, **encyclopedic** [en,saɪkləʊ'pi:dɪk] ADJ enciclopédico

encyclopaedist, **encyclopedist** [en,saɪkləʊ'pi:dɪst] N enciclopedista *mf*

end [end] N **1** [*of street*] final *m*; [*of line, table*] extremo *m*; [*of rope, stick*] punta *f*; [*of estate*] límite *m*; (*Sport*) lado *m*; [*of town*] parte *f*, zona *f* • **at the end of** [*+ street, corridor*] al final de; [*+ rope, cable*] en la punta de • **to change ends** (*Sport*) cambiar de lado • **the ends of the earth** (*fig*) el ultimo rincón del mundo • **to go to the ends of the earth** ir hasta el fin del mundo • **from one end to the other** de un extremo a otro • **the end of the line** (*fig*) el término, el acabóse • **to stand sth on end** poner algo de punta • **his hair stood on end** se le puso el pelo de punta • **the end of the road** (*fig*) el término, el acabóse • **from end to end** de punta a punta • **to place end to end** poner uno tras otro • **to read a book to the very end** leer un libro hasta el mismo final • **to start at the wrong end** empezar por el fin • IDIOMS: • **to keep one's end up*** (*in undertaking*) hacer su parte; (*in argument*) defenderse bien • **to tie up the loose ends** atar cabos • **to make ends meet** hacer llegar *or* alcanzar el dinero • **to get hold of the wrong end of the stick** tomar el rábano por las hojas • **to be at the end of one's tether** no poder más, no aguantar más; ▷ **deep, shallow**

2 [*of time, process, journey, resources*] fin *m*, final *m*; [*of story*] fin *m*, conclusión *f* • **the end of the empire** el fin del imperio • **at the end of three months** al cabo de tres meses • **at the end of the century** a fines del siglo • **towards the end of** [*+ book, film*] hacia el final de; [*+ century*] hacia fines de; [*+ month*] hacia fin de • **that was the end of him** así terminó él • **that's the end of the matter** asunto concluido • **that was the end of that!** ¡y se acabó! • **that was the end of our car*** así se acabó el coche • **we'll never hear the end of it*** esto va a ser cuento de nunca acabar • **there's no end to it*** esto no se acaba nunca • **we see no end to it** no entrevemos posibilidad alguna de que termine • **to be at an end** [*meeting, interview*] haber concluido • **to be at the end of** [*+ strength, patience*] estar al límite de • **we're at the end of our supplies** se nos están agotando las provisiones • **we are almost at the end of our holidays** se nos están acabando las vacaciones • **to be at the end of one's resources** haber agotado los recursos • **to come to a bad end** acabar mal • **to the bitter end** hasta el último suspiro • **to bring to an end** [*+ work, speech, relationship*] dar por terminado • **to come to an end** llegar a su fin, terminarse • **to draw to an end** llegar a su fin, terminarse • **I am getting to the end of my patience** estoy llegando al límite de mi paciencia • **in the end** al fin • **to make an end of** acabar con, poner fin a • **I enjoyed it no end*** me gustó muchísimo • **to think no end of sb** tener un muy alto concepto de algn • **no end of*** la mar de* • **it caused no end of trouble** causó la mar de problemas • **no end of an expert** sumamente experto, más experto que nadie • **three days on end** tres días seguidos • **for days on end** día tras día, durante una infinidad de días • **for hours on end** hora tras hora • **to put an end to** [*+ argument, relationship, sb's tricks*] poner fin a, acabar con • **that's the end!*** ¡eso es el colmo! • **he's the end!*** ¡es el colmo! • **that movie is the end!** (*US**) esa película es el no va más • **without end** interminable • **the end of the world** el fin del mundo • **it's not the end of the world*** el mundo no se va a acabar por eso • IDIOM: • **at the end of the day** al fin y al cabo, a fin de cuentas

3 (= *death*) (*liter or hum*) muerte *f* • **to meet one's end** encontrar la muerte

4 (= *remnant*) [*of loaf, candle, meat*] resto *m*, cabo *m* • **the end of a roll** [*of cloth, carpet*] el retal de un rollo; ▷ **cigarette**

5 (= *aim*) fin *m*, propósito *m* • **an end in itself** un fin en sí • **the end justifies the means** el fin justifica los medios • **to achieve one's end** alcanzar su objetivo • **to no end** en vano • **to the end that ...** a fin de que (*+ subjun*) • **to this end** • **with this end in view** con este propósito • **with what end?** ¿para qué?

VT [*+ argument*] terminar, poner fin a; [*+ book*] concluir; [*+ speech*] concluir, terminar; [*+ relationship*] terminar; [*+ abuse, speculation*] acabar con • **that was the meal to end all meals!*** ¡eso fue el no va más en comidas! • **to end one's days** vivir sus últimos días • **to end it all*** suicidarse • **to end one's life** suicidarse

VI [*lesson, work, war, meeting*] terminar, acabar, concluir (*more frm*); [*road*] terminar(se); [*period of time, programme, film, story*] terminar • **to end by saying** terminar diciendo • **to end in** terminar en • **to end with** terminar con

CPD ▸ **end date** [*of contract*] fecha *f* de terminación ▸ **end game** (*Chess*) fase *f* final ▸ **the end house** la última casa ▸ **end line** (*Basketball*) línea *f* de fondo ▸ **end note** nota *f* final ▸ **end product** (*Ind*) producto *m* final; (*fig*) consecuencia *f* ▸ **end result** resultado *m* ▸ **end table** (*US*) mesita *f* (*para poner revistas, bebidas*) ▸ **end user** usuario/a *m/f* final ▸ **end value** valor *m* final ▸ **end zone** (*American Ftbl*) zona *f* de marca

▸ **end off** VT + ADV poner fin a

▸ **end up** VI + ADV terminar (**in** en); [*road, path*] llevar, conducir (**in** a)

end-all ['endɔ:l] N ▷ **be-all**

endanger [ɪn'deɪndʒəʳ] VT [*+ life, health, position*] poner en peligro • **an ~ed species** [*of animal*] una especie en peligro de extinción

endangerment [ɪn'deɪndʒəmənt] N (*Jur*) imprudencia *f* temeraria

endear [ɪn'dɪəʳ] VT • **to ~ sb to** [*+ others*] ganar para algn la simpatía de • **this did not ~ him to the public** esto no le granjeó las simpatías de la gente • **to ~ o.s. to sb** ganarse la simpatía de algn

endearing [ɪn'dɪərɪŋ] ADJ [*person, smile*] entrañable, simpático; [*characteristic, quality*] atractivo, atrayente; [*personality, habit*] encantador • **she has a very ~ manner** tiene una manera de ser encantadora

endearingly [ɪn'dɪərɪŋlɪ] ADV [*say, smile*] de manera encantadora • **he is ~ shy/eccentric** es encantadoramente tímido/excéntrico

endearment [ɪn'dɪəmənt] N cariño *m* • **term of ~** palabra *f* de cariño

endeavour, **endeavor** (*US*) [ɪn'devəʳ] N (= *attempt*) intento *m*, tentativa *f*; (= *effort*) esfuerzo *m* • **in spite of my best ~s** a pesar de todos mis esfuerzos • **to make/use every ~ to do sth** procurar por todos los medios hacer algo

VI • **to ~ to do sth** procurar hacer algo, esforzarse por hacer algo

endemic [en'demɪk] ADJ endémico

ending ['endɪŋ] N **1** (= *end*) fin *m*, final *m*; [*of book, story, play*] final *m*, desenlace *m* • **the tale has a happy ~** el cuento tiene un final *or* desenlace feliz

2 (*Ling*) terminación *f*

endive ['endaɪv] N endibia *f*

endless ['endlɪs] ADJ **1** (= *interminable*) [*road, queue, summer, speech*] interminable; [*variety, patience, desert*] infinito; [*supply*] inacabable, inagotable • **the list is ~** la lista es interminable • **this job is ~** este trabajo no se acaba nunca • **an ~ round of meetings** una ronda interminable de reuniones

2 (= *countless*) continuo • **I'm tired of his ~ questions/complaining** estoy cansada de sus continuas preguntas/quejas • **he asked me ~ questions** me hizo un sinfín de preguntas • **the possibilities are ~** las posibilidades son infinitas

3 (*Tech*) [*screw, belt*] sin fin (*adj inv*)

endlessly ['endlɪslɪ] ADV [*repeat*] una y otra vez, hasta la saciedad; [*discuss*] hasta la saciedad; [*argue*] continuamente; [*talk*] sin parar; [*recycle*] una y otra vez • **she talks ~ about her job** no para de hablar de su trabajo • **the desert stretched ~ before her** el desierto se extendía interminable ante ella • **he could see his life stretching out ~ before him** veía su vida extendiéndose interminablemente ante sus ojos • **she is ~ patient** tiene una paciencia infinita

endocardium [endəʊ'kɑ:dɪəm] N (PL: **endocardia** [endəʊ'kɑ:dɪə]) endocardio *m*

endocarp ['endəkɑ:p] N endocarpio *m*

endocrine ['endəʊkraɪn] ADJ endocrino

N glándula *f* endocrina

CPD ▸ **endocrine gland** glándula *f* endocrina ▸ **endocrine system** sistema *m* endocrino

endocrinologist [,endəʊkrɪ'nɒlədʒɪst] N endocrinólogo/a *m/f*

endocrinology [,endəʊkrɪ'nɒlədʒɪ] N endocrinología *f*

endodontics [,endəʊ'dɒntɪks] NSING endodoncia *f*

endogenous [,en'dɒdʒɪnəs] ADJ endógeno

endometriosis [,endəʊ,mi:trɪ'əʊsɪs] N endometriosis *f*

endomorph ['endəʊmɔ:f] N endomorfo/a *m/f*

endorphin [,en'dɔ:fɪn] N endorfina *f*

endorse [ɪn'dɔ:s] VT **1** (= *sign*) [*+ cheque, document*] endosar

2 (= *approve*) [*+ opinion, claim, plan*] aprobar; (= *support*) [*+ decision*] respaldar

3 (*Brit*) (*Aut*) • **to ~ a licence** anotar los detalles de una sanción en el permiso de conducir

endorsee [ɪn,dɔ:'si:] N endosatario/a *m/f*

endorsement [ɪn'dɔ:smənt] N

1 (= *signature*) endoso *m*

2 (= *approval*) aprobación *f*; (= *support*) respaldo *m*

3 (*Brit*) (*Aut*) (*on licence*) nota *f* de sanción

endorser [ɪn'dɔ:səʳ] N endosante *mf*

endoscope ['endəʊ,skəʊp] N endoscopio *m*

endoscopy [,en'dɒskəpɪ] N endoscopia *f*

endow [ɪn'daʊ] VT **1** (= *found*) [*+ prize, professorship*] fundar, crear; (= *donate*) dotar, hacer una donación a

2 (*fig*) • **to be ~ed with** estar dotado de

endowment [ɪn'daʊmənt] N **1** (= *act*) dotación *f*; (= *creation*) fundación *f*, creación *f*; (= *amount*) donación *f*
2 (*fig*) dote *f*
CPD ▸ **endowment assurance** seguro *m* mixto, seguro *m* de vida-ahorro ▸ **endowment fund** fondo *m* de beneficiencia ▸ **endowment insurance** = **endowment assurance** ▸ **endowment mortgage** (*Brit*) hipoteca *f* avalada por una dote ▸ **endowment policy** (*Brit*) póliza *f* dotal

endpaper ['endpeɪpəʳ] N guarda *f*

endue [ɪn'dju:] VT dotar (**with** de)

endurable [ɪn'djʊərəbl] ADJ aguantable, soportable

endurance [ɪn'djʊərəns] N resistencia *f* • **to come to the end of one's ~** no poder más, llegar a sus límites • **past** *or* **beyond ~** inaguantable, insoportable • **to be tried beyond ~** ser puesto a prueba • **it tested his powers of ~** puso a prueba su resistencia
CPD ▸ **endurance race** carrera *f* de resistencia ▸ **endurance test** prueba *f* de resistencia

endure [ɪn'djʊəʳ] VT (= *suffer*) [+ *pain, heat*] resistir, aguantar; (= *tolerate*) aguantar, soportar • **she can't ~ being laughed at** no soporta que se rían de ella • **I can't ~ being corrected** no aguanto que me corrijan • **to ~ doing sth** aguantar hacer algo • **I can't ~ him** no lo puedo ver, no lo aguanto *or* soporto • **I can't ~ it a moment longer** no lo aguanto un momento más
VI (= *last*) durar; (= *not give in*) aguantar, resistir

enduring [ɪn'djʊərɪŋ] ADJ duradero, perdurable • **an ~ friendship** una amistad duradera • **an ~ affection/memory** un cariño/un recuerdo duradero

endways ['endweɪz] ADV (= *end to end*) de punta; (= *with end facing*) de lado, de canto

ENE ABBR (= **east-northeast**) ENE

ENEA N ABBR = **European Nuclear Energy Authority**

enema ['enɪmə] N (PL: **enemas** *or* **enemata** ['enɪmətə]) enema *m*

enemy ['enɪmɪ] N (= *person*) enemigo/a *m/f*; (*Mil*) enemigo *m* • **the ~ within** el enemigo en casa • **to go over to the ~** pasarse al enemigo • **to make an ~ of sb** enemistarse con algn • IDIOM: • **he is his own worst ~** su peor enemigo es él mismo
CPD [*territory, forces, aircraft*] enemigo ▸ **enemy alien** extranjero/a *m/f* enemigo/a

enemy-occupied [ˌenəmɪ'ɒkjʊpaɪd] ADJ [*territory*] ocupado por el enemigo

energetic [ˌenə'dʒetɪk] ADJ [*person*] activo, lleno de energía; [*activity, sport*] que requiere mucha energía, duro; [*walk*] duro; [*campaign*] activo; [*performance*] lleno de energía; [*protest, efforts*] vigoroso; [*denial, refusal*] enérgico • **I've had a very ~ day** he tenido un día muy activo • **to feel ~** sentirse lleno de energía • **I'm not feeling very ~ today** hoy no me siento con muchas energías

energetically [ˌenə'dʒetɪkəlɪ] ADV [*play, run*] con energía; [*work, deny*] enérgicamente; [*campaign*] activamente, vigorosamente

energize ['enədʒaɪz] VT activar, dar energía a

energizing ['enədʒaɪzɪŋ] ADJ [*food*] energético, que da energías

energy ['enədʒɪ] N (*gen*) energía *f*; (= *strength*) vigor *m* • **electrical/atomic/solar ~** energía *f* eléctrica/atómica/solar • **Secretary (of State) for Energy** Secretario/a *m/f* (de Estado) de Energía • **Minister of Energy** Ministro/a *m/f* de Energía
CPD ▸ **energy bar** (= *food*) barrita *f* energética ▸ **energy company** empresa *f* de energía ▸ **energy conservation** conservación *f* de la energía ▸ **energy consumption** consumo *m* de energía ▸ **energy crisis** crisis *f inv* energética ▸ **energy drink** bebida *f* energética ▸ **energy efficiency** eficacia *f* energética ▸ **energy food** comida *f* energética *or* que da energías ▸ **energy level** nivel *m* energético ▸ **energy needs** necesidades *fpl* energéticas ▸ **energy policy** política *f* de energía ▸ **energy resources** recursos *mpl* energéticos ▸ **energy saving** ahorro *m* de energía

energy-efficient [ˌenədʒɪə'fɪʃənt] ADJ [*light bulb, refrigerator*] de bajo consumo; [*building, system, industry*] energéticamente eficiente

energy-giving ['enədʒɪˌgɪvɪŋ] ADJ [*food etc*] energético, que da energías

energy-intensive [ˌenədʒɪɪn'tensɪv] ADJ [*industry*] consumidor de gran cantidad de energía

energy-saving ['enədʒɪˌseɪvɪŋ] ADJ [*device, system*] que ahorra energía; [*policy*] para ahorrar energía

enervate ['enəveɪt] VT enervar, debilitar

enervated ['enəveɪtɪd] ADJ (= *weak*) enervado

enervating ['enəveɪtɪŋ] ADJ enervador

e-newsletter ['i:ˌnju:zletəʳ] N boletín *m* electrónico

enfant terrible [ˌɒnfɒnte'ri:blə] N niño/a *m/f* terrible, enfant *mf* terrible

enfeeble [ɪn'fi:bl] VT debilitar

enfeebled [ɪn'fi:bld] ADJ debilitado

enfeeblement [ɪn'fi:blmənt] N debilitación *f*

enfilade [ˌenfɪ'leɪd] VT enfilar

enfold [ɪn'fəʊld] VT envolver • **to ~ sb in one's arms** abrazar a algn, estrechar a algn entre los brazos

enforce [ɪn'fɔ:s] VT **1** (= *make effective*) [+ *law*] hacer cumplir; [+ *argument*] imponer; [+ *claim*] hacer valer; [+ *rights*] hacer respetar; [+ *demand*] insistir en; [+ *sentence*] ejecutar
2 (= *compel*) [+ *obedience, attendance*] imponer (**on** a)

enforceable [ɪn'fɔ:səbl] ADJ [*law, rule*] ejecutable, que se puede hacer cumplir

enforced [ɪn'fɔ:st] ADJ [*idleness, exile, silence*] forzoso, forzado

enforcement [ɪn'fɔ:smənt] N [*of law*] aplicación *f*; [*of sentence*] ejecución *f* • **law ~ agency** organismo *m* de seguridad del Estado

enfranchise [ɪn'fræntʃaɪz] VT (*Pol*) conceder el derecho de voto a; (= *free*) emancipar; [+ *slave*] liberar

enfranchisement [ɪn'fræntʃɪzmənt] N emancipación *f* (**of** de); (*Pol*) concesión *f* del derecho de votar (**of** a)

ENG N ABBR = **electronic news gathering**

Eng ABBR **1** = **England**
2 = **English**

engage [ɪn'geɪdʒ] VT **1** (= *hire*) [+ *servant, lawyer, worker*] contratar
2 (= *attract*) [+ *attention*] llamar, captar
3 (= *occupy*) [+ *attention, interest*] ocupar • **to ~ sb in conversation** entablar conversación con algn • **to ~ the enemy in battle** entablar batalla *or* combate con el enemigo
4 (*Mech*) [+ *cog*] engranar con; [+ *coupling*] acoplar; [+ *gear*] meter • **to ~ the clutch** embragar
VI **1** • **to ~ in** [+ *discussion*] entablar; [+ *politics*] meterse en; [+ *sport*] tomar parte en
2 (= *initiate battle*) entablar batalla, entablar combate
3 (*Mech*) engranar (**with** con)

engagé [ɑ̃:ŋgæ'ʒeɪ] ADJ [*writer, artist*] comprometido

engaged [ɪn'geɪdʒd] ADJ **1** • **to be ~** (= *busy*) [*seat, person*] estar ocupado; (*Brit*) [*toilet*] estar ocupado • **to be ~ in** estar ocupado en, dedicarse a • **what are you ~ in?** ¿a qué se dedica Vd?
2 (*Brit*) (*Telec*) • **to be ~** estar comunicando *or* (*LAm*) ocupado
3 • **to be ~ (to be married)** estar prometido; [*2 persons*] estar prometidos, ser novios • **they've been ~ for two years** llevan dos años de relaciones formales • **to get ~** prometerse (**to** con) • **the ~ couple** los novios
CPD ▸ **engaged signal, engaged tone** señal *f* de comunicando *or* (*LAm*) ocupado

engagement [ɪn'geɪdʒmənt] N **1** (*to marry*) compromiso *m*; (= *period of engagement*) noviazgo *m* • **they announced their ~ yesterday** anunciaron su compromiso ayer • **the ~ lasted ten months** el noviazgo duró diez meses • **the ~ is announced of Miss A to Mr B** la Srta. A y el Sr. B han anunciado su compromiso (matrimonial)
2 (= *appointment*) compromiso *m*, cita *f* • **I have a previous ~** ya tengo un compromiso
3 (= *undertaking*) compromiso *m* • **to enter into an ~ to do sth** comprometerse a hacer algo
4 (*Mil*) (= *battle*) batalla *f*, combate *m*
5 (= *contract*) contrato *m* • **a long ~ at a theatre** un contrato largo con un teatro
CPD ▸ **engagement book** dietario *m*; (*at work*) agenda *f* de trabajo ▸ **engagement diary** = **engagement book** ▸ **engagement party** fiesta *f* de compromiso ▸ **engagement ring** anillo *m* de compromiso *or* de pedida

engaging [ɪn'geɪdʒɪŋ] ADJ atractivo; [*enthusiasm etc*] contagioso

engagingly [ɪn'geɪdʒɪŋlɪ] ADV [*smile, write*] de manera atractiva, con encanto • **he was ~ honest about the reasons for his action** se ganó nuestra simpatía con su honestidad al explicar los motivos de su acto

engender [ɪn'dʒendəʳ] VT engendrar; (*fig*) engendrar, suscitar

engine ['endʒɪn] N **1** (= *motor*) (*in car, ship, plane*) motor *m*
2 (*Rail*) locomotora *f*, máquina *f* • **facing the ~** de frente a la máquina • **with your back to the ~** de espaldas a la máquina
CPD ▸ **engine block** (*Aut*) bloque *m* del motor ▸ **engine driver** (*Brit*) [*of train*] maquinista *mf* ▸ **engine failure** avería *f* del motor ▸ **engine room** (*Naut*) sala *f* de máquinas ▸ **engine shed** (*Brit*) (*Rail*) cochera *f* de tren ▸ **engine trouble** = **engine failure**

-engined ['endʒɪnd] ADJ (*ending in compounds*) • **four-engined** de cuatro motores, cuatrimotor • **petrol-engined** con motor de gasolina

engineer [ˌendʒɪ'nɪəʳ] N ingeniero/a *m/f*; (*for repairs*) técnico/a *m/f*; (*US*) (*Rail*) maquinista *mf* • **ship's ~** ingeniero/a *m/f* naval • **electrical/TV ~** técnico/a *m/f* electricista/de televisión • **the Royal Engineers** (*Mil*) el Cuerpo de Ingenieros
VT (= *contrive*) [+ *plan*] maquinar; [+ *meeting*] organizar

engineering [ˌendʒɪ'nɪərɪŋ] N ingeniería *f*
CPD ▸ **engineering factory** fábrica *f* de maquinaria ▸ **engineering industry** industria *f* de ingeniería ▸ **engineering works** taller *m* de ingeniería

England ['ɪŋglənd] N Inglaterra *f*
CPD ▸ **England team** • **the ~ team** el equipo inglés

English ['ɪŋglɪʃ] ADJ inglés
N (*Ling*) inglés *m* • **Old ~** inglés *m* antiguo • **King's/Queen's ~** inglés *m* correcto • **in**

plain ~ en el habla corriente, ≈ en cristiano* • **~ as a Foreign Language** inglés para extranjeros • **~ as a Second Language** inglés como segunda lengua • **the ~** (= *people*) los ingleses
(CPD) ▸ **English breakfast** desayuno *m* inglés *or* a la inglesa ▸ **the English Channel** el Canal de la Mancha ▸ **English Heritage** ≈ Patrimonio *m* Histórico-Artístico ▸ **English Language Teaching** enseñanza *f* del inglés ▸ **English speaker** anglohablante *mf*

ENGLISH
En el Reino Unido, se llama **Received Pronunciation** o **RP** a un tipo de acento no asociado a ninguna región en concreto (si bien tuvo su origen en el inglés hablado en el sur de Inglaterra) que hoy en día usan especialmente las personas educadas en colegios privados, las clases dirigentes y los locutores en los informativos nacionales de la BBC. En los medios de comunicación se acepta ya el uso de acentos regionales siempre y cuando se use la norma lingüística, es decir, utilicen un inglés gramaticalmente correcto, el llamado **Standard English**. La pronunciación **RP** suele también tomarse como norma en la enseñanza del inglés británico como lengua extranjera. Todavía goza de cierto prestigio, aunque la gran mayoría de la población habla con el acento de su región, que puede ser más o menos marcado según su educación o clase social.
El inglés americano difiere del inglés británico principalmente en la pronunciación, aunque también hay diferencias ortográficas y léxicas. Tiene también una pronunciación estándar, conocida por el nombre de **Network Standard**, que es la que se usa en los medios de comunicación, así como diversas variedades regionales. A diferencia del Reino Unido, la asociación de acento y clase social no es muy evidente.

Englishman [ˈɪŋglɪʃmən] (N) (PL: **Englishmen**) inglés *m*
English-speaking [ˈɪŋglɪʃ,spiːkɪŋ] (ADJ) de habla inglesa, anglohablante
Englishwoman [ˈɪŋglɪʃ,wʊmən] (N) (PL: **Englishwomen**) inglesa *f*
Eng Lit [ˈɪŋˈlɪt] (N ABBR) = **English Literature**
engorged [ɪnˈgɔːdʒd] (ADJ) dilatado, hinchado • **to become ~** dilatarse, hincharse
engrave [ɪnˈgreɪv] (VT) (*Art, Typ*) grabar; (*fig*) grabar, imprimir
engraver [ɪnˈgreɪvəʳ] (N) (= *person*) grabador(a) *m/f*
engraving [ɪnˈgreɪvɪŋ] (N) (= *picture*) grabado *m*
engross [ɪnˈgrəʊs] (VT) **1** [+ *attention, person*] absorber
2 (*Jur*) copiar
engrossed [ɪnˈgrəʊst] (ADJ) absorto • **to be ~ in work/reading/one's thoughts** estar absorto en el trabajo/la lectura/los pensamientos • **to become ~ in** [+ *activity*] dedicarse por completo a
engrossing [ɪnˈgrəʊsɪŋ] (ADJ) absorbente
engulf [ɪnˈgʌlf] (VT) (= *swallow up*) tragar; (= *immerse*) sumergir, hundir • **to be ~ed by** (*lit*) quedar sumergido bajo • **she felt ~ed by her grief** se sentía abrumada *or* hundida por el desconsuelo
enhance [ɪnˈhɑːns] (VT) [+ *beauty, attraction*] realzar, dar realce a; [+ *position, reputation, chances*] mejorar; [+ *value, powers*] aumentar
enhancement [ɪnˈhɑːnsmənt] (N) [*of beauty, attraction*] realce *m*, intensificación *f*; [*of reputation*] mejora *f*; [*of value, powers*] aumento *m*, incremento *m*
enhancer [ɪnˈhɑːnsəʳ] (N) (*also* **flavour enhancer**) potenciador *m*
enigma [ɪˈnɪgmə] (N) enigma *m*
enigmatic [,enɪgˈmætɪk] (ADJ) enigmático
enigmatically [,enɪgˈmætɪkəlɪ] (ADV) enigmáticamente
enjambement [ɪnˈdʒæmmənt] (N) encabalgamiento *m*
enjoin [ɪnˈdʒɔɪn] (VT) (*frm*) [+ *obedience, silence, discretion*] imponer, exigir • **to ~ sth on sb** imponer algo a algn • **to ~ sb to sth/to do sth** exigir a algn algo/hacer algo • **to ~ sb from doing sth** (*US*) prohibir a algn hacer algo
enjoy [ɪnˈdʒɔɪ] (VT) **1** (= *take pleasure in*) [+ *meal, wine, occasion*] disfrutar de, disfrutar • **to ~ sth/doing sth: I ~ reading** me gusta leer • **did you ~ the game?** ¿te gustó el partido? • **I hope you ~ your holiday** que lo pases muy bien en las vacaciones • **to ~ life** disfrutar de la vida • **~ your meal!** ¡que aproveche! • **to ~ o.s.** pasarlo bien, divertirse • **we really ~ed ourselves** lo pasamos en grande, nos divertimos mucho • **he ~ed himself in London/on holiday** (se) lo pasó bien en Londres/las vacaciones • **~ yourself!** ¡que lo pases bien!, ¡que te diviertas!
2 (= *have benefit of*) [+ *good health, income, respect*] disfrutar de, gozar de; [+ *advantage*] poseer
enjoyable [ɪnˈdʒɔɪəbl] (ADJ) (= *pleasant*) agradable; (= *amusing*) divertido
enjoyably [ɪnˈdʒɔɪəblɪ] (ADV) agradablemente
enjoyment [ɪnˈdʒɔɪmənt] (N) **1** (= *pleasure*) placer *m* • **he listened with real ~** escuchó con verdadero placer • **to find ~ in sth/in doing sth** disfrutar *or* gozar de algo/haciendo algo
2 (= *possession*) [*of good health etc*] posesión *f*, disfrute *m*
enlarge [ɪnˈlɑːdʒ] (VT) (*Phot*) ampliar; (*Med*) dilatar; [+ *house, business, circle of friends*] ampliar, extender
(VI) **1** extenderse, aumentarse
2 • **to ~ (up)on** (= *explain*) entrar en detalles sobre
enlarged [ɪnˈlɑːdʒd] (ADJ) [*edition*] aumentado; (*Med*) [*organ, gland*] hipertrofiado
(CPD) ▸ **enlarged prostate** hipertrofia *f* de (la) próstata
enlargement [ɪnˈlɑːdʒmənt] (N) (= *act*) aumento *m*; (*Phot*) ampliación *f*
enlarger [ɪnˈlɑːdʒəʳ] (N) (*Phot*) ampliadora *f*
enlighten [ɪnˈlaɪtn] (VT) (= *inform*) informar, instruir; (*Rel*) (*frm*) iluminar • **can you ~ me?** ¿puedes explicármelo *or* aclarármelo? • **to ~ sb about** *or* **on sth** (= *inform*) poner a algn al corriente de algo; (= *clarify*) aclarar algo a algn
enlightened [ɪnˈlaɪtnd] (ADJ) [*person, society, policy, attitude*] progresista • **an ~ despot** un déspota ilustrado • **in this ~ age** *or* **in these ~ times** (*esp iro*) en esta época de tantos adelantos *or* progresos
enlightening [ɪnˈlaɪtnɪŋ] (ADJ) informativo; [*experience etc*] instructivo
enlightenment [ɪnˈlaɪtnmənt] (N)
1 (= *clarification*) • **we need some ~ on this point** necesitamos una aclaración sobre este punto
2 (= *tolerance*) progresismo *m* • **sexual ~** progresismo *m* sexual • **the (Age of) Enlightenment** el Siglo de las Luces
3 (*Rel*) iluminación *f* • **spiritual ~** iluminación *f* espiritual
enlist [ɪnˈlɪst] (VT) **1** (*Mil*) reclutar, alistar • **~ed man** (*US*) (*Mil*) soldado *m* raso
2 [+ *support etc*] conseguir
(VI) (*Mil*) alistarse (**in** en)
enlistment [ɪnˈlɪstmənt] (N) alistamiento *m*
enliven [ɪnˈlaɪvn] (VT) (= *stimulate*) animar; (= *make lively*) avivar, animar
en masse [ɑ̃ːŋˈmæs] (ADV) en masa, masivamente
enmesh [ɪnˈmeʃ] (VT) (*lit*) coger en una red • **to get ~ed in** enredarse en
enmity [ˈenmɪtɪ] (N) (= *hatred*) enemistad *f*
ennoble [ɪˈnəʊbl] (VT) ennoblecer
ennui [ɑ̃ːˈnwiː] (N) tedio *m*, hastío *m*
enology *etc* [iːˈnɒlədʒɪ] (N) (*US*) = **oenology** *etc*
enormity [ɪˈnɔːmɪtɪ] (N) [*of task*] enormidad *f*; [*of crime, action*] gravedad *f*
enormous [ɪˈnɔːməs] (ADJ) **1** (*in physical size*) [*building, object*] enorme, inmenso; [*person, animal*] enorme • **an ~ great thing*** una cosa grandísima
2 (*fig*) [*patience, relief*] enorme; [*effort, variety*] enorme, inmenso; [*problems, difficulties*] enorme, muy grande; [*profits, losses*] enorme, cuantioso; [*appetite*] voraz • **he was on our side, and that made an ~ difference** él estaba de nuestra parte y eso supuso una enorme diferencia • **an ~ amount/number of sth** una cantidad enorme de algo • **the country's industrial success has been bought at an ~ cost to the environment** el medio ambiente ha pagado un precio muy alto por el éxito industrial del país • **it gives me ~ pleasure to welcome Ed Lilly** es para mí un inmenso placer dar la bienvenida a Ed Lilly • **I get ~ pleasure from reading** la lectura es una enorme fuente de placer para mí
enormously [ɪˈnɔːməslɪ] (ADV) [*improve, vary, help*] enormemente; [*enjoy*] muchísimo, enormemente; [*like*] muchísimo; [*important, difficult, popular*] tremendamente; [*relieved*] inmensamente, enormemente • **it's ~ expensive** es tremendamente *or* enormemente caro, es carísimo • **he runs an ~ successful business** dirige un negocio muy próspero • **he launched an ~ successful stage career** inició una carrera teatral de enorme éxito
enough [ɪˈnʌf] (ADJ) suficiente, bastante • **we have ~ apples** tenemos suficientes *or* bastantes manzanas • **I've got ~ problems of my own** ya tengo suficientes *or* bastantes problemas con los míos • **I haven't ~ room** no tengo suficiente *or* bastante espacio, no tengo espacio suficiente • **did you get ~ sleep?** ¿has dormido bastante *or* lo suficiente? • **they didn't have ~ money to pay the rent** no tenían suficiente dinero (como) para pagar el alquiler • **more than ~ money/time** dinero/tiempo más que suficiente, dinero/tiempo de sobra • **to be proof ~ that …** (*frm*) ser prueba suficiente de que …, probar a las claras que …
(ADV) **1** (*with vb*) [*suffer, help, talk*] bastante, lo suficiente • **I can't thank you ~** no puedo agradecértelo bastante *or* lo suficiente • **he opened the door just ~ to see out** abrió la puerta lo suficiente *or* lo bastante *or* lo justo (como) para poder mirar fuera
2 (*with adj*) (lo) suficientemente, lo bastante • **it's not big ~** no es (lo) suficientemente grande, no es lo bastante grande • **he's old ~ to go alone** es (lo) suficientemente mayor *or* es lo bastante mayor (como) para ir solo • **that's a good ~ excuse** esa es una buena

excusa • **I'm sorry, that's not good ~** lo siento, pero eso no basta • **she seems happy ~** parece bien contenta • **she was fool ~** *or* **stupid ~ to listen to him** fue tan estúpida que le hizo caso • **he was kind ~ to lend me the money** tuvo la bondad *or* amabilidad de prestarme el dinero • **it's hard ~ to cope with two children, let alone with five** ya es difícil defenderse con dos niños, cuanto peor con cinco; ▹ **fair, sure**
3 (*with adv*) • **he can't do it fast ~** no lo puede hacer lo bastante *or* lo suficientemente rápido, no lo puede hacer con la suficiente rapidez • **when he saw her coming he couldn't get away fast ~** cuando la vio venir desapareció todo lo rápido que pudo • **he hadn't prepared the report carefully ~** no había preparado el informe con la debida atención • **curiously** *or* **oddly** *or* **strangely ~** por extraño *or* raro que parezca • **you know well ~ that ...** sabes muy bien *or* de sobra que ... • **they seem to be settling down well ~** parece que se están adaptando bastante bien • **he writes well ~, I suppose** no escribe mal, supongo; ▹ **funnily**
(PRON) bastante, suficiente • **there are ~ for everyone** hay bastantes *or* suficientes para todos • **will £15 be ~?** ¿habrá bastante *or* suficiente con 15 libras?, ¿bastarán 15 libras?, ¿serán suficientes 15 libras? • **that's ~, thanks** con eso basta *or* ya es suficiente, gracias • **that's ~!** ¡basta ya!, ¡ya está bien! • **as if that weren't ~** por si eso fuera poco • **have you had ~ to eat?** ¿has comido bastante *or* lo suficiente? • **you don't eat ~** no comes bastante *or* lo suficiente • **we don't get paid ~** no nos pagan bastante *or* lo suficiente • **I have ~ to do without taking on more work** tengo ya bastante que hacer (como) para aceptar más trabajo • **we earn ~ to live on** ganamos lo bastante *or* lo suficiente (como) para vivir • **it's ~ to drive you mad*** es (como) para volverse loco • **enough's enough** ¡basta ya!, ¡ya está bien! • **it is ~ for us to know that ...** nos basta con saber que ... • **we've got more than ~** tenemos más que suficiente(s) *or* más que de sobra • **he has had more than ~ to drink** ha bebido más de la cuenta • **I've had ~ of his silly behaviour** ya estoy harto de sus tonterías • **you can never have ~ of this scenery** nunca se cansa uno de este paisaje • **I think you have said ~** creo que ya has dicho bastante *or* suficiente • **PROVERB:** • **~ is as good as a feast** rogar a Dios por santos mas no por tantos

enquire *etc* [ɪnˈkwaɪəʳ] ▹ **inquire** *etc*
enquiring [ɪnˈkwaɪərɪŋ] (ADJ) = **inquiring**
enquiringly [ɪnˈkwaɪərɪŋlɪ] (ADV) = **inquiringly**
enrage [ɪnˈreɪdʒ] (VT) enfurecer, hacer rabiar
enrapture [ɪnˈræptʃəʳ] (VT) embelesar, extasiar
enraptured [ɪnˈræptʃəd] (ADJ) embelesado
enrich [ɪnˈrɪtʃ] (VT) **1** (= *improve*) **a** [+ *sb's life, society, language*] enriquecer • **it was an ~ing experience** fue una experiencia enriquecedora
b [+ *food*] enriquecer; [+ *soil*] fertilizar, abonar
c (*Phys*) [+ *uranium*] enriquecer
2 (= *make wealthy*) enriquecer
enriched [ɪnˈrɪtʃt] (ADJ) [*food, uranium*] enriquecido • **bread ~ with folic acid** pan *m* enriquecido con ácido fólico
-enriched [ɪnˈrɪtʃt] (SUFFIX) • **vitamin-enriched** enriquecido con vitaminas • **calcium-enriched** enriquecido con calcio • **oxygen-enriched** enriquecido con oxígeno
enrichment [ɪnˈrɪtʃmənt] (N) **1** (= *improvement*) **a** [*of sb's life, society, of language*] enriquecimiento *m*
b [*of soil*] fertilización *f*
c (*Phys*) [*of uranium*] enriquecimiento *m*
2 (*financial*) enriquecimiento *m*
enrol, enroll (US) [ɪnˈrəʊl] (VT) [+ *member*] inscribir; [+ *student*] matricular; (*Mil*) alistar
(VI) (*on a course*) matricularse, inscribirse; (*in a club*) inscribirse, hacerse socio
enrolment, enrollment (US) [ɪnˈrəʊlmənt] (N) **1** [*of member*] inscripción *f*; [*of student*] matrícula *f*, inscripción *f*
2 (= *numbers*) matrícula *f*
(CPD) ▸ **enrolment fee, enrollment fee** (US) (*for member*) tasa *f* de inscripción; (*for student*) matrícula *f*
en route [ɑ̃:nˈru:t] (ADV) • **to be ~ for** *or* **to** ir camino de *or* a • **to be ~ from** venir de camino de • **it was stolen ~** se lo robaron durante el viaje
ensconce [ɪnˈskɒns] (VT) • **to ~ o.s.** instalarse cómodamente, acomodarse • **to be ~d in** estar cómodamente instalado en
ensemble [ɑ̃:nsɑ̃:mbl] (N) **1** (= *whole*) conjunto *m*; (= *general effect*) impresión *f* de conjunto
2 (= *dress*) conjunto *m*
3 (*Mus*) conjunto *m* (musical)
enshrine [ɪnˈʃraɪn] (VT) (*fig*) encerrar, englobar • **to be ~d in law** ser consagrado por la ley
enshroud [ɪnˈʃraʊd] (VT) (*liter*) (*lit*) envolver, cubrir • **the case remains ~ed in mystery** el caso permanece envuelto en misterio
ensign [ˈensaɪn] (N) **1** (= *flag*) enseña *f*, pabellón *m*; ▹ **red, white**
2 (US) (*Naut*) (= *rank*) alférez *mf*
enslave [ɪnˈsleɪv] (VT) esclavizar
enslavement [ɪnˈsleɪvmənt] (N) esclavitud *f*; (= *action*) esclavización *f*
ensnare [ɪnˈsnɛəʳ] (VT) (*lit, fig*) atrapar, coger en una trampa
ensue [ɪnˈsju:] (VI) (= *follow*) seguir(se); (= *result*) resultar (**from** de)
ensuing [ɪnˈsju:ɪŋ] (ADJ) (= *subsequent*) subsiguiente; (= *resulting*) consiguiente
en suite [ɑ̃ˈswi:t] (ADJ) • **with bathroom ~** • **with an ~ bathroom** con baño adjunto
ensure [ɪnˈʃʊəʳ] (VT) asegurar (**that** que)
ENT (ABBR) (*Med*) = **ear, nose and throat**
entail [ɪnˈteɪl] (VT) **1** (= *necessitate*) suponer, implicar; [+ *hardship, suffering*] acarrear, traer consigo • **it ~s a lot of work** supone *or* implica mucho trabajo • **it ~ed buying a new car** supuso comprar un coche nuevo • **what does the job ~?** ¿en qué consiste el trabajo?
2 (*Jur*) vincular
(N) (*Jur*) vínculo *m*
entangle [ɪnˈtæŋgl] (VT) **1** [+ *thread etc*] enredar, enmarañar
2 (*fig*) • **to become ~d in sth** verse envuelto en algo, enredarse en algo • **to get ~d with sb** liarse con algn*
entanglement [ɪnˈtæŋglmənt] (N) **1** (= *being entangled*) enredo *m*; (*fig*) lío* *m*
2 (= *love affair*) lío *m* amoroso*
3 (*Mil*) alambrada *f*
entente [ɒnˈtɒnt] (N) (*Pol*) entente *f*
(CPD) ▸ **entente cordiale** entente *f* cordial
enter [ˈentəʳ] (VT) **1** (= *go into, come into*) [+ *room, country, tunnel*] entrar en; [+ *bus, train*] subir a • **the phrase has already ~ed the**

ENOUGH

Agreement

▹ *When used as an adjective or a pronoun,* **bastante,** *like* **suficiente,** *agrees with the noun it describes or refers to:*
Are there enough potatoes?
¿Hay bastantes patatas?
Eggs? Yes, there are enough
¿Huevos? Sí, hay bastantes

▹ *Don't add an "s" to the adverb* **bastante** *(i.e. when it modifies an adjective or verb other than* **ser, parecer** *etc):*
They're not poor enough to get money from the State
No son lo bastante pobres (como) para recibir dinero del Estado
We've studied these photographs enough
Ya hemos estudiado bastante estas fotografías

After verbs - adverbial use

▹ *When a purpose is implied or stated, translate using* **lo suficiente** *or, especially in affirmative phrases,* **lo bastante***:*
We know enough to be able to say that these techniques are safe
Sabemos lo suficiente *or* lo bastante (como) para afirmar que estas técnicas son seguras

▹ *When no purpose is implied or stated, translate using either* **bastante** *or* **lo suficiente:**
He says he hasn't had enough to eat
Dice que no ha comido bastante *or* no ha comido lo suficiente
We shall never be able to thank you enough
Nunca se lo podremos agradecer bastante *or* lo suficiente

After adjectives and adverbs

▹ *Translate using* **lo** + **bastante** + *adjective/adverb or* **(lo) suficientemente** *+ adjective/adverb:*
He isn't good enough to take part in the Olympics
No es lo bastante *or* (lo) suficientemente bueno (como) para participar en las Olimpiadas
She couldn't run fast enough to catch him
No pudo correr lo bastante *or* (lo) suficientemente rápido (como) para atraparlo
No pudo correr lo bastante *or* lo suficiente (como) para atraparlo

To be enough

▹ **To be enough** *can often be translated using* **bastar:**
That's enough!
¡Basta ya!
That's enough to feed an army!
Con eso basta para dar de comer a un regimiento

As **bastar** *is an impersonal verb, it often takes an indirect object:*
Promises are no longer enough for him
Ya no le bastan las promesas
That's enough for him
Con eso le basta

For further uses and examples, see main entry.

language la frase ya ha entrado en el idioma • **where the River Wyre ~s the Thames** donde el río Wyre confluye con el Támesis • **the ship ~ed harbour** el barco entró en el puerto • **the thought never ~ed my head** jamás se me ocurrió, jamás se me pasó por la cabeza • **to ~ hospital** (*frm*) ingresar en el hospital
2 (*= penetrate*) [*+ market*] introducirse en; (*sexually*) penetrar
3 (*= join*) [*+ army, navy*] alistarse en, enrolarse en; [*+ college, school*] entrar en; [*+ company, organization*] incorporarse a, entrar a formar parte de; [*+ profession*] ingresar en, entrar en; [*+ discussion, conversation*] unirse a, intervenir en; [*+ war*] entrar en • **he ~ed the church** se hizo sacerdote • **he decided to ~ a monastery** decidió hacerse monje • **he ~ed politics at a young age** se metió en la política cuando era joven
4 (*= go in for*) [*+ live competition, exam*] presentarse a; [*+ race, postal competition*] participar en, tomar parte en
5 (*= enrol*) [*+ pupil*] (*for school*) matricular, inscribir; (*for examination*) presentar • **how many students are you ~ing this year?** ¿a cuántos alumnos presentas este año? • **to ~ sth/sb for sth: he ~ed his son for Eton** matriculó *or* inscribió a su hijo en Eton • **to ~ a horse for a race** inscribir a un caballo para una carrera • **she had intended to ~ the piece of work for a competition** su intención había sido presentar el trabajo a un concurso
6 (*= write down*) [*+ name*] escribir, apuntar; [*+ claim, request*] presentar, formular; (*Econ*) [*+ amount, transaction*] registrar, anotar; (*Comm*) [*+ order*] registrar, anotar • **~ your answers in the boxes provided** escriba las respuestas en las casillas
7 (*= begin*) entrar en • **as the war ~s its second month** al entrar la guerra en su segundo mes • **the crisis is ~ing a new phase** la crisis está entrando en una nueva fase
8 (*Comput*) [*+ data*] introducir
9 (*Jur*) • **to ~ an appeal** presentar un recurso de apelación • **to ~ a plea of guilty/not guilty** declararse culpable/no culpable
(VI) **1** (*= come in, go in*) entrar • **~!** (*frm*) ¡adelante!, ¡pase!
2 (*Theat*) entrar en escena • **~, stage left** entra en escena por la izquierda del escenario • **~ Macbeth** entra en escena Macbeth
3 • **to ~ for** [*+ live competition*] (*= put name down for*) inscribirse en; (*= take part in*) presentarse a; [*+ race, postal competition*] (*= put name down for*) inscribirse en; (*= take part in*) participar en • **are you going to ~ for the exam?** ¿te vas a presentar al examen?
▸ **enter into** (VI + PREP) **1** (*= engage in*) [*+ agreement*] llegar a; [*+ contract*] firmar; [*+ relationship, argument*] iniciar; [*+ explanation, details*] entrar en; [*+ conversation, correspondence, negotiations*] entablar • **to ~ into the spirit of things** ambientarse; ▹ **partnership**
2 (*= affect*) [*+ plans, calculations*] influir en • **do their wishes ~ into your plans at all?** ¿sus deseos influyen para algo en tus planes? • **money doesn't ~ into it** el dinero no tiene nada que ver
▸ **enter on, enter upon** (VI + PREP) [*+ career*] emprender; [*+ period, term of office*] empezar; (*Comm, Econ*) [*+ transaction, investment*] realizar
▸ **enter up** (VT + ADV) [*+ facts, information*] escribir, anotar; [*+ diary, ledger*] poner al día
enteric [en'terɪk] (ADJ) entérico
(CPD) ▸ **enteric fever** fiebre *f* entérica

enteritis [ˌentə'raɪtɪs] (N) enteritis *f inv*
enterprise ['entəpraɪz] (N) **1** (*= firm, undertaking*) empresa *f*
2 (*= initiative*) iniciativa *f* • **free ~** la libre empresa • **private ~** la empresa privada
(CPD) ▸ **the enterprise culture** la cultura empresarial ▸ **enterprise zone** *zona declarada de especial interés para el fomento de actividades empresariales*
enterprising ['entəpraɪzɪŋ] (ADJ) [*person, spirit*] emprendedor; [*company, idea, scheme*] innovador • **that was ~ of her!** ¡qué emprendedora!
enterprisingly ['entəpraɪzɪŋlɪ] (ADV) con mucha iniciativa
entertain [ˌentə'teɪn] (VT) **1** (*= amuse*) [*+ audience*] divertir, entretener
2 (*= offer hospitality to*) [*+ guest*] recibir • **to ~ sb to dinner** (*frm*) invitar a algn a cenar
3 (*= consider*) [*+ idea, hope*] abrigar; [*+ proposal*] tomar en consideración; [*+ doubts*] albergar • **I wouldn't ~ it for a moment** jamás se me ocurriría tal cosa
(VI) **1** (*= amuse*) [*book, film, performer*] entretener
2 (*= have visitors*) recibir visitas • **they ~ a good deal** reciben muchos invitados
entertainer [ˌentə'teɪnəʳ] (N) artista *mf*
entertaining [ˌentə'teɪnɪŋ] (ADJ) [*person*] divertido; [*film, book, account, evening*] entretenido, ameno
(N) • **I like ~** me gusta tener invitados • **she does a lot of ~** invita a gente a menudo, recibe a menudo (*frm*)
entertainingly [ˌentə'teɪnɪŋlɪ] (ADV) [*say, talk*] de manera divertida, de modo ameno • **an ~ irreverent book** un libro irreverente y divertido
entertainment [ˌentə'teɪnmənt] (N)
1 (*= amusement*) [*of guests*] entretenimiento *m*; [*of audience*] diversión *f* • **for your ~** para divertiros
2 (*= show*) espectáculo *m*; (*= musical entertainment*) concierto *m* • **to put on an ~** organizar un espectáculo • **the world of ~** el mundo del espectáculo
(CPD) ▸ **entertainment allowance** gastos *mpl* de representación ▸ **entertainment expenses** = **entertainment allowance** ▸ **entertainment guide** guía *f* del ocio ▸ **entertainment tax** impuesto *m* de espectáculos ▸ **the entertainment world** el mundo del espectáculo
enthral, enthrall (*US*) [ɪn'θrɔːl] (VT) (*gen passive*) cautivar, embelesar • **we listened ~led** escuchamos embelesados
enthralling [ɪn'θrɔːlɪŋ] (ADJ) cautivador, embelesador
enthrone [ɪn'θrəʊn] (VT) (*lit*) entronizar; (*fig*) [*+ idea*] consagrar
enthronement [ɪn'θrəʊnmənt] (N) (*lit*) entronización *f*; (*fig*) consagración *f*
enthuse [ɪn'θuːz] (VI) • **to ~ over** *or* **about sth/sb** entusiasmarse con algo/algn
enthused [ɪn'θuːzd] (ADJ) (*= enthusiastic*) entusiasmado • **to be ~ about sth** estar entusiasmado con algo
enthusiasm [ɪn'θuːzɪæzəm] (N)
1 (*= excitement*) entusiasmo *m* (**for** por) • **without ~** sin entusiasmo • **the news aroused little ~ in the White House** la noticia despertó poco entusiasmo en la Casa Blanca • **the idea filled her with ~** la idea la entusiasmó • **to show ~ for sth** mostrarse entusiasmado por algo; ▹ **work up**
2 (*= interest, hobby*) interés *m* • **photography is one of her many ~s** la fotografía es uno de sus muchos intereses
enthusiast [ɪn'θuːzɪæst] (N) entusiasta *mf*

• **he is a jazz/bridge ~** es un entusiasta del jazz/bridge • **a Vivaldi ~** un enamorado *or* entusiasta de Vivaldi
enthusiastic [ɪnˌθuːzɪ'æstɪk] (ADJ) [*skier, supporter, crowd, applause*] entusiasta • **to be ~ about** [*+ photography, chess, art*] ser un entusiasta de; [*+ idea, suggestion*] estar entusiasmado con • **to be ~ about doing sth** estar entusiasmado por hacer algo • **to become ~ about sth** entusiasmarse con algo • **she was less than ~ about the idea** no le entusiasmaba nada la idea • **I tried to sound ~** intenté parecer entusiasmado
enthusiastically [ɪnˌθuːzɪ'æstɪkəlɪ] (ADV) [*greet, support, speak*] con entusiasmo • **he shouted ~** gritó entusiasmado
entice [ɪn'taɪs] (VT) (*= tempt*) atraer, tentar; (*= seduce*) seducir • **to ~ sb away from sb** convencer a algn de que deje a algn • **to ~ sb into a room** engatusar a algn para que entre en una habitación • **to ~ sb into doing sth** *or* **to do sth** tentar a algn a hacer algo • **to ~ sb with food/an offer** tentar a algn con comida/una oferta
enticement [ɪn'taɪsmənt] (N) **1** (*= attraction*) tentación *f*, atracción *f*
2 (*= seduction*) seducción *f*
3 (*= bait*) atractivo *m*
enticing [ɪn'taɪsɪŋ] (ADJ) tentador, atractivo
enticingly [ɪn'taɪsɪŋlɪ] (ADV) atractivamente, de manera atractiva
entire [ɪn'taɪəʳ] (ADJ) **1** (*= whole*) entero • **the ~ world** el mundo entero, todo el mundo • **she cleaned the ~ house** limpió toda la casa, limpió la casa entera • **he didn't speak throughout the ~ evening** no habló en toda la tarde • **his ~ earnings for a year** la totalidad de sus ingresos anuales • **he has my ~ confidence** tiene toda mi confianza
2 (*= complete*) completo • **an ~ dinner service** una vajilla completa
entirely [ɪn'taɪəlɪ] (ADV) **1** (*= completely*) [*satisfied, convinced*] completamente, enteramente; [*different*] totalmente, completamente; [*possible*] totalmente • **that's another matter ~** eso es otra cosa, eso es una cosa completamente distinta • **I don't ~ agree** no estoy totalmente de acuerdo • **that is not ~ true** eso no es del todo *or* no es enteramente cierto
2 (*= exclusively*) enteramente, exclusivamente • **it's ~ up to you** depende de ti exclusivamente, depende enteramente de ti • **it was his fault ~** fue totalmente *or* enteramente culpa suya • **the concert was devoted ~ to Mozart** el concierto estuvo enteramente *or* exclusivamente dedicado a Mozart, el concierto estuvo dedicado a Mozart en su totalidad • **to be made ~ of wood** estar hecho totalmente de madera
entirety [ɪn'taɪərətɪ] (N) • **in its ~** en su totalidad, íntegramente
entitle [ɪn'taɪtl] (VT) **1** [*+ book etc*] titular • **the book is ~d ...** el libro se titula ...
2 (*= give right*) dar derecho a • **to ~ sb to sth/to do sth** dar derecho a algn a algo/a hacer algo • **to be ~d to sth/to do sth** tener derecho a algo/a hacer algo • **you are quite ~d to do as you wish** tienes todo el derecho a hacer lo que quieras • **I think I am ~d to some respect** creo que se me debe cierto respeto
entitlement [ɪn'taɪtlmənt] (N) derecho *m* • **holiday ~** derecho *m* a vacaciones
entity ['entɪtɪ] (N) entidad *f* • **legal ~** persona *f* jurídica
entomb [ɪn'tuːm] (VT) (*liter*) sepultar
entombment [ɪn'tuːmmənt] (N) (*liter*) sepultura *f*
entomological [ˌentəmə'lɒdʒɪkəl] (ADJ)

entomológico

entomologist [ˌentəˈmɒlədʒɪst] N entomólogo/a *m/f*

entomology [ˌentəˈmɒlədʒɪ] N entomología *f*

entourage [ˌɒntʊˈrɑːʒ] N séquito *m*

entr'acte [ˈɒntrækt] N intermedio *m*, entreacto *m*

entrails [ˈentreɪlz] NPL entrañas *fpl*; (*US*) asadura *f*, menudos *mpl*

entrain [ɪnˈtreɪn] VI (*esp Mil*) tomar el tren (**for** a)

entrance¹ [ˈentrəns] N **1** (= *way in*) entrada *f* • **front/back ~** entrada *f* principal/trasera
2 (= *act*) entrada *f* (**into** en); (*into profession etc*) ingreso *m*; (*Theat*) entrada *f* en escena • **to make one's ~** hacer su entrada; (*Theat*) entrar en escena
3 (= *right to enter*) (derecho *m* de) entrada *f* • **to gain ~ to** [+ *a place*] conseguir entrar en *or* acceder a; [+ *a profession etc*] conseguir ingresar en
CPD ▸ **entrance card** pase *m* ▸ **entrance exam(ination)** (*to school*) examen *m* de ingreso ▸ **entrance fee** (*to a show*) (precio *m* de) entrada *f*; (*to a club, society etc*) cuota *f* de ingreso ▸ **entrance hall** vestíbulo *m*, antesala *f* ▸ **entrance qualifications** = **entrance requirements** ▸ **entrance ramp** (*US*) (*Aut*) rampa *f* de acceso ▸ **entrance requirements** requisitos *mpl* de ingreso

entrance² [ɪnˈtrɑːns] VT **1** (= *bewitch*) encantar, hechizar
2 (*gen passive*) (= *captivate*) • **we listened ~d** escuchamos extasiados *or* embelesados

entrancing [ɪnˈtrɑːnsɪŋ] ADJ [*film, music*] fascinante • **she looked ~** estaba cautivadora

entrancingly [ɪnˈtrɑːnsɪŋlɪ] ADV [*play, dance, sing*] maravillosamente • **she is ~ beautiful** tiene una belleza cautivadora • **it's ~ simple** es tan sencillo que resulta fascinante

entrant [ˈentrənt] N (*in race, competition*) participante *mf*, concurrente *mf*; (*in exam*) candidato/a *m/f*; (*to profession*) principiante *mf*

entrap [ɪnˈtræp] VT coger en una trampa; (*fig*) entrampar

entrapment [ɪnˈtræpmənt] N (*Jur*) *acción por la que agentes de la ley incitan a algn a cometer un delito para poder arrestarlo* • **he complained of ~** se quejó de que le habían hecho caer en una trampa

entreat [ɪnˈtriːt] VT rogar, suplicar • **to ~ sb to do sth** suplicar a algn que haga algo

entreating [ɪnˈtriːtɪŋ] ADJ suplicante
N súplicas *fpl*, imploraciones *fpl*

entreatingly [ɪnˈtriːtɪŋlɪ] ADV [*look, ask*] de modo suplicante

entreaty [ɪnˈtriːtɪ] N súplica *f*, ruego *m* • **they ignored our entreaties** hicieron caso omiso de nuestras súplicas *or* nuestros ruegos • **a look of ~** una mirada suplicante

entrée [ˈɒntreɪ] N **1** (= *entrance*) entrada *f*
2 (*Culin*) plato *m* fuerte *or* principal

entrench [ɪnˈtrentʃ] VT **1** (= *consolidate*) consolidar, afianzar • **to ~ o.s.** consolidarse, afianzarse • **to ~ o.s. in a position/an idea** atrincherarse en una posición/idea
2 (*Mil*) atrincherar • **to ~ o.s.** atrincherarse

entrenched [ɪnˈtrentʃt] ADJ **1** (*pej*) (= *established*) [*idea, belief, attitude*] arraigado; [*position, power*] afianzado • **deeply ~** [*idea, belief, attitude*] profundamente arraigado; [*position, power*] firmemente afianzado • **to be ~ in the belief/view that ...** mantener obcecadamente la creencia/opinión de que ... • **he's too ~ in the past** está demasiado anclado en el pasado
2 (*Mil*) atrincherado

entrenchment [ɪnˈtrentʃmənt] N **1** (*Mil*) trinchera *f*
2 (= *establishment*) [*of rights, standards*] afianzamiento *m*

entrepôt [ˈɒntrəpəʊ] N (= *town*) centro *m* comercial, centro *m* de distribución; (= *warehouse*) almacén *m*, depósito *m*

entrepreneur [ˌɒntrəprəˈnɜːʳ] N (*Comm*) empresario/a *m/f*; (*Econ*) capitalista *mf*

entrepreneurial [ˌɒntrəprəˈnɜːrɪəl] ADJ empresarial

entrepreneurship [ˌɒntrəprəˈnɜːʃɪp] N espíritu *m* empresarial *or* emprendedor • **to promote ~** promover la iniciativa empresarial

entropy [ˈentrəpɪ] N entropía *f*

entrust [ɪnˈtrʌst] VT • **to ~ sth to sb** • **~ sb with sth** confiar algo a algn

entry [ˈentrɪ] N **1** (= *entrance*) **a** (= *act of entering*) (*into organization*) entrada *f* (**into** en); (*into profession*) ingreso *m* (**into** en); (= *access*) acceso *m* (**into** a) • **Britain's ~ into the EC** la entrada de Gran Bretaña en la CE • **she was denied ~ into the country** le negaron acceso al país • **~ into the hall had been forbidden** se había prohibido el acceso a la sala • **"no entry"** "prohibida la entrada"; (*Aut*) "prohibido el paso" • **he gained ~ to the house by breaking a window** consiguió entrar en la casa rompiendo una ventana • **they opposed France's ~ into the war** se opusieron a que Francia entrara en la guerra • **to make one's ~** hacer su entrada • **point of ~** (*into country*) punto *m* de entrada • **port of ~** puerto *m* de entrada
b (= *doorway, hall*) entrada *f*
2 (= *sth recorded*) (*in diary*) anotación *f*, apunte *m*; (*in account*) entrada *f*, partida *f*, rubro *m* (*LAm*); (*in record, ship's log*) entrada *f*, apunte *m*; (*in reference book*) entrada *f*
3 (*in competition*) (= *total of competitors*) participantes *mpl*; (= *person*) participante *mf* • **the first correct ~ pulled from our postbag on January 24** la primera carta con la respuesta correcta que se saque de nuestra saca de correo el día 24 de enero • **entries must be submitted by 29 March** las cartas/los cuentos/los diseños *etc* deben llegar antes del 29 de marzo • **the winning ~ in a writing competition** la obra ganadora de un concurso de redacción
CPD ▸ **entry coupon** (*for competition*) cupón *m* de participación ▸ **entry fee** cuota *f* de inscripción ▸ **entry form** formulario *m* de inscripción, impreso *m* de inscripción ▸ **entry permit** permiso *m* de entrada ▸ **entry phone** portero *m* automático ▸ **entry qualifications, entry requirements** requisitos *mpl* de entrada ▸ **entry visa** visado *m* de entrada ▸ **entry word** (*US*) (*in reference book*) entrada *f*

entry-level [ˈentrɪlevl] ADJ **1** (= *starting*) [*salary, position*] inicial
2 (*Comput*) básico

entryway [ˈentrɪweɪ] N (*esp US*) (= *entrance*) entrada *f*

entwine [ɪnˈtwaɪn] VT (= *plait*) entrelazar; (= *twist around*) enroscar

E-number [ˈiːnʌmbəʳ] N (*Brit*) número *m* e, aditivo *m* alimentario

enumerate [ɪˈnjuːməreɪt] VT (= *list*) enumerar

enumeration [ɪˌnjuːməˈreɪʃən] N enumeración *f*

enunciate [ɪˈnʌnsɪeɪt] VT [+ *word, sound*] pronunciar, articular; [+ *theory, idea*] enunciar

enunciation [ɪˌnʌnsɪˈeɪʃən] N [*of word, sound*] pronunciación *f*, articulación *f*; [*of theory, idea*] enunciación *f*

enuresis [ˌenjʊəˈriːsɪs] N enuresis *f*

enuretic [ˌenjʊəˈretɪk] ADJ enurético

envelop [ɪnˈveləp] VT (*lit, fig*) envolver (**in** en)

envelope [ˈenvələʊp] N [*of letter*] sobre *m*; (*fig*) (= *wrapping*) funda *f* • IDIOM: • **to push the ~** romper moldes

enveloping [ɪnˈveləpɪŋ] ADJ [*movement*] envolvente

envelopment [ɪnˈveləpmənt] N envolvimiento *m*

envenom [ɪnˈvenəm] VT envenenar

enviable [ˈenvɪəbl] ADJ envidiable

envious [ˈenvɪəs] ADJ [*person*] envidioso; [*glance, look, tone*] de envidia • **to be ~ that** tener envidia de que (+ *subjun*), tener envidia porque • **she's ~ that you have what she doesn't** tiene envidia de que tú tengas *or* porque tú tienes lo que ella no tiene • **it makes me ~** me da envidia • **to be ~ of sth/sb** tener envidia de algo/algn, envidiar algo/a algn • **I am ~ of your good luck** envidio tu suerte

enviously [ˈenvɪəslɪ] ADV con envidia

environment [ɪnˈvaɪərənmənt] N
1 (= *surroundings*) (*gen*) entorno *m*, ambiente *m*; (*Zool, Bot*) entorno *m*, medio *m* • **a safe working ~** un entorno *or* un ambiente de trabajo seguro • **a working-class ~** un entorno *or* ambiente de clase trabajadora • **to observe animals in their natural ~** observar a los animales en su entorno *or* medio natural • **the ~** (*Ecol*) el medio ambiente • **measures to protect the ~** medidas *fpl* para proteger el medio ambiente • **Department of the Environment** (*Brit*) Ministerio *m* del Medio Ambiente
2 (*Comput*) entorno *m*

environmental [ɪnˌvaɪərənˈmentl] ADJ
1 (= *ecological*) [*pollution, policy, issues*] medioambiental; [*problems, disaster, damage*] ecológico, medioambiental; [*group, movement*] ecologista; [*impact*] ambiental • **it will have disastrous ~ effects** tendrá efectos desastrosos en el medio ambiente
2 (= *situational*) • **the ~ factors in mental illness** la influencia de los factores del medio ambiente en las enfermedades mentales
CPD ▸ **environmental health** salud *f* ambiental ▸ **Environmental Health Department** (*Brit*) Departamento *m* de Sanidad y Medio Ambiente ▸ **environmental health officer** (*Brit*) funcionario/a *m/f* del Departamento de Sanidad y Medio Ambiente ▸ **environmental health regulation** normativa *f* de sanidad y medio ambiente ▸ **Environmental Health Service** Servicio *m* de Sanidad y Medio Ambiente ▸ **environmental impact** [*of development, transport*] impacto *m* ambiental ▸ **environmental impact assessment** evaluación *f* de impacto ambiental ▸ **environmental impact report** informe *m* sobre el impacto ambiental ▸ **environmental impact study** estudio *m* del impacto ambiental ▸ **Environmental Protection Agency** (*US*) Organización *f* de Protección del Medio Ambiente ▸ **environmental studies** (= *subject*) ecología *fsing*; (= *research*) estudios *mpl* medioambientales

environmentalism [ɪnˌvaɪərənˈmentəlɪzəm] N ambientalismo *m*

environmentalist [ɪnˌvaɪərənˈmentəlɪst] ADJ ambiental, ecologista
N ecologista *mf*

environmentally [ɪnˌvaɪərənˈmentəlɪ]

ADV **1** (= *ecologically*) • **we're more ~ aware now** ahora somos más conscientes del medio ambiente • **their policies are ~ sound** las medidas que adoptan son correctos desde el punto de vista medioambiental • **their products are ~ friendly** sus productos son ecológicos, sus productos no dañan el medio ambiente • **~ sensitive areas** zonas *fpl* de riesgo medioambiental
2 (= *in the environment*) • **an ~ acquired** *or* **induced disease** una enfermedad que se adquiere a través del medio ambiente

environment-friendly [ɪnˈvaɪərənmənt-ˈfrendlɪ] ADJ ecológico, que no daña el medio ambiente

environs [ɪnˈvaɪərənz] N alrededores *mpl*, inmediaciones *fpl*

envisage [ɪnˈvɪzɪdʒ] VT **1** (= *expect*) prever • **it is ~d that ...** se prevé que ... • **an increase is ~d next year** está previsto un aumento para el año que viene
2 (= *imagine*) imaginarse • **it is hard to ~ such a situation** es difícil imaginarse tal situación

envision [ɪnˈvɪʒən] VT (*US*) = **envisage**

envoy [ˈenvɔɪ] N (= *messenger*) mensajero/a *m/f*; (= *diplomat*) enviado/a *m/f* • **special ~** enviado/a *m/f* especial

envy [ˈenvɪ] N envidia *f* • **a look of ~** una mirada de envidia • **filled with ~** lleno de envidia • **to do sth out of ~** hacer algo por envidia • **it was the ~ of everyone** era la envidia de todos • IDIOM: • **to be green with ~** morirse de envidia
VT envidiar, tener envidia de • **she envies her sister** envidia a su hermana, tiene envidia de su hermana, le tiene envidia a su hermana • **I don't ~ you!** ¡no te envidio!, ¡no te tengo ninguna envidia! • **to ~ sb sth** envidiar algo a algn • **she envied him his confidence** le envidiaba la seguridad que tenía en sí mismo

enzyme [ˈenzaɪm] N enzima *f*
CPD ▸ **enzyme deficiency** deficiencia *f* enzimática

EOC N ABBR (*Brit*) (= **Equal Opportunities Commission**) ≈ PIO *m* (*Sp*)

Eocene [ˈiːəʊsiːn] ADJ (*Geol*) eoceno

eolithic [ˌiːəʊˈlɪθɪk] ADJ eolítico

eon [ˈiːən, ˈiːɒn] N (*US*) = **aeon**

EP N ABBR (= **extended play**) maxi-single *m*

EPA N ABBR (*US*) = **Environmental Protection Agency**

e-pal [ˈiːpæl] N amigo/a *m/f* por correo electrónico

epaulette [ˈepɔːlet] N charretera *f*

epee, epée [ˈepeɪ] N espada *f* de esgrima

ephedrine [ˈefɪdrɪn] N efedrina *f*

ephemera [ɪˈfemərə] NPL (PL: **ephemeras** *or* **ephemerae** [ɪˈfeməriː]) (= *transitory items*) cosas *fpl* efímeras; (= *collectables*) objetos *mpl* coleccionables (*sin valor*)

ephemeral [ɪˈfemərəl] ADJ efímero

Ephesians [ɪˈfiːʒənz] NPL efesios *mpl*

epic [ˈepɪk] ADJ épico; (*fig**) excepcional, épico
N epopeya *f*; (= *film*) película *f* épica

epicene [ˈepɪsiːn] ADJ epiceno

epicentre, epicenter (*US*) [ˈepɪsentəʳ] N epicentro *m*

epicure [ˈepɪkjʊəʳ] N gastrónomo/a *m/f*

epicurean [ˌepɪkjʊˈriːən] ADJ epicúreo
N epicúreo *m*

epicureanism [ˌepɪkjʊəˈrɪənɪzəm] N epicureísmo *m*

epidemic [ˌepɪˈdemɪk] ADJ epidémico
N epidemia *f*; (*fig*) ola *f*

epidemiological [ˌepɪˌdiːmɪəˈlɒdʒɪkəl] ADJ epidemiológico

epidemiologist [ˌepɪdiːmɪˈɒlədʒɪst] N epidemiólogo/a *m/f*

epidemiology [ˌepɪˌdiːmɪˈɒlədʒɪ] N epidemiología *f*

epidermis [ˌepɪˈdɜːmɪs] N epidermis *f*

epidural [ˌepɪˈdjʊərəl] ADJ epidural
N (*also* **epidural anaesthetic**) (anestesia *f*) epidural *f*

epiglottis [ˌepɪˈglɒtɪs] N (PL: **epiglottises** *or* **epiglottides** [ˌepɪˈglɒtɪdiːz]) epiglotis *f inv*

epigram [ˈepɪgræm] N epigrama *m*

epigrammatic [ˌepɪgrəˈmætɪk] ADJ epigramático

epigrammatical [ˌepɪgrəˈmætɪkəl] ADJ = **epigrammatic**

epigraph [ˈepɪgrɑːf] N epígrafe *m*

epigraphy [ɪˈpɪgrəfɪ] N epigrafía *f*

epilepsy [ˈepɪlepsɪ] N epilepsia *f*

epileptic [ˌepɪˈleptɪk] ADJ epiléptico
N epiléptico/a *m/f*
CPD ▸ **epileptic fit** ataque *m* de epilepsia, acceso *m* epiléptico

epilogue, epilog (*US*) [ˈepɪlɒg] N epílogo *m*

Epiphany [ɪˈpɪfənɪ] N Epifanía *f*

episcopacy [ɪˈpɪskəpəsɪ] N episcopado *m*

episcopal [ɪˈpɪskəpəl] ADJ episcopal
CPD ▸ **Episcopal Church** • **the Episcopal Church** la Iglesia Episcopal

episcopalian [ɪˌpɪskəˈpeɪlɪən] ADJ episcopalista
N • **Episcopalian** episcopalista *mf*

episcopate [ɪˈpɪskəʊpɪt] N episcopado *m*

episiotomy [əˌpiːzɪˈɒtəmɪ] N episiotomía *f*

episode [ˈepɪsəʊd] N (= *event*) acontecimiento *m*; (*TV, Rad*) capítulo *m*, episodio *m*; (*Press*) entrega *f*; (*Med*) ataque *m*

episodic [ˌepɪˈsɒdɪk] ADJ episódico

epistemological [ɪˌpɪstɪməˈlɒdʒɪkəl] ADJ epistemológico

epistemology [ɪˌpɪstəˈmɒlədʒɪ] N epistemología *f*

epistle [ɪˈpɪsl] N (*hum*) (= *letter*) epístola *f* • **Epistle** (*Rel*) Epístola *f*

epistolary [ɪˈpɪstələrɪ] ADJ epistolar

epitaph [ˈepɪtɑːf] N epitafio *m*

epithet [ˈepɪθet] N epíteto *m*

epitome [ɪˈpɪtəmɪ] N representación *f*, paradigma *m* • **to be the ~ of virtue** ser la virtud en persona *or* personificada

epitomize [ɪˈpɪtəmaɪz] VT personificar, resumir • **he ~d resistance to the enemy** él era el paradigma de la resistencia al enemigo • **she ~s today's career woman** es el prototipo de la mujer de carrera moderna

EPNS N ABBR = **electroplated nickel silver**

epoch [ˈiːpɒk] N época *f* • **to mark an ~** hacer época, marcar un hito

epochal [ˈepəkəl] ADJ (*frm*) = **epoch-making**

epoch-making [ˈiːpɒkˌmeɪkɪŋ] ADJ que hace época

eponym [ˈepənɪm] N (*Ling*) epónimo *m*

eponymous [ɪˈpɒnɪməs] ADJ epónimo

EPOS [ˈiːpɒs] N ABBR (= **electronic point of sale**) *sistema computerizado en tiendas para registrar el precio de las compras*

epoxy resin [ɪˈpɒksɪˈrezɪn] N resina *f* epoxídica

EPROM [ˈiːprɒm] N ABBR (*Comput*) = **erasable programmable read only memory**

Epsom salts [ˈepsɒmˌsɔːlts] NPL epsomita *fsing*

EPU N ABBR (= **European Payments Union**) UEP *f*

EPW N ABBR (*US*) = **enemy prisoner of war**

equable [ˈekwəbl] ADJ [*climate etc*] estable; [*person*] ecuánime; [*tone*] tranquilo, afable

equably [ˈekwəblɪ] ADV sosegadamente, con ecuanimidad

equal [ˈiːkwəl] ADJ **1** (= *identical in size, value*) [*number, amount*] igual • **the cake was divided into twelve ~ parts** el pastel estaba dividida en doce partes iguales • **to be of ~ importance/value** tener igual importancia/el mismo valor • **with ~ ease/indifference** con igual *or* la misma facilidad/indiferencia • **to come ~ first/second** (*in competition*) compartir el primer/segundo puesto; (*in race*) llegar ambos en primer/segundo lugar • **to be ~ in sth**: • **they are ~ in strength** son igual de fuertes, tienen la misma fuerza • **they are ~ in size** son del mismo tamaño, son iguales de tamaño • **they are ~ in value** tienen el mismo valor, tienen igual valor • **on ~ terms** de igual a igual • **all** *or* **other things being ~** si no intervienen otros factores • **an amount ~ to half your salary** una cantidad equivalente a la mitad de tu sueldo • **to be ~ to sth** (= *equivalent*) equivaler a algo • **his silence was ~ to an admission of guilt** su silencio equivalía a una admisión de culpabilidad • **a metre is ~ to 39 inches** un metro equivale a 39 pulgadas • **she is ~ to her mother in intelligence** es tan inteligente como su madre, es igual de inteligente que su madre • PROVERB: • **we are all ~ before** *or* **in the eyes of God** todos somos iguales a los ojos de Dios; ▹ **footing**
2 (= *capable*) • **to be/feel ~ to sth**: • **I'm confident that he is ~ to the task** tengo la seguridad de que está capacitado para desempeñar la tarea • **she did not feel ~ to going out** no se sentía con fuerzas *or* ánimo para salir • **she was ~ to the situation** estaba a la altura de la situación
N **1** (= *person*) igual *mf* • **she is his ~** ella es su igual • **she has no ~** no hay nadie que se la iguale • **they are intellectual ~s** intelectualmente están a la par • **to treat sb as an ~** tratar a algn de igual a igual
2 (= *thing*) • **to have no ~** • **be without ~** no tener igual • **the film has no ~ in cinema history** la película no tiene igual en la historia del cine • **a talent without ~** un talento sin igual *or* sin par
VT **1** (*Math*) ser igual a • **let x ~ y** si x es igual a y, suponiendo que x sea igual a y • **two plus two ~s four** dos y dos son cuatro
2 [+ *record, rival, quality*] igualar • **there is nothing to ~ it** no hay nada que se le iguale, no hay nada que lo iguale • **prices not to be ~led** precios sin competencia
CPD ▸ **equal opportunities** igualdad *fsing* de oportunidades ▸ **Equal Opportunities Commission** (*Brit*) Comisión *f* para la Igualdad de Oportunidades ▸ **equal opportunities** *or* **opportunity employer** empresa *f* no discriminatoria ▸ **equal pay** igual salario *m* • **~ pay for ~ work** igual salario *or* el mismo salario para el mismo trabajo ▸ **equal rights** igualdad *fsing* de derechos ▸ **equals sign, equal sign** (*Math*) signo *m* de igual ▸ **equal time** (*US*) (*Rad, TV*) derecho *m* de respuesta

equality [ɪˈkwɒlɪtɪ] N igualdad *f* • **~ of opportunity** igualdad *f* de oportunidades

equalization [ˌiːkwəlaɪˈzeɪʃən] N igualización *f*; (*Econ*) compensación *f*
CPD ▸ **equalization account** cuenta *f* de compensación ▸ **equalization fund** fondo *m* de compensación

equalize [ˈiːkwəlaɪz] VT igualar
VI (*Brit*) (*Sport*) empatar

equalizer [ˈiːkwəlaɪzəʳ] N **1** (*Brit*) (*Sport*) tanto *m* del empate
2 (*US‡*) (= *pistol*) pipa‡ *f*, pistola *f*

equally [ˈiːkwəlɪ] ADV **1** (= *evenly*) [*divide, share*] equitativamente, por igual • **the fence posts should be ~ spaced** el espacio entre los postes de la valla debería ser igual
2 (= *in the same way*) por igual • **all foreigners**

should be treated ~ todos los extranjeros deberían ser tratados por igual *or* con igualdad • **this rule applies ~ to everyone** esta regla se aplica a todos por igual • **this applies ~ to men and to women** esto se aplica tanto a los hombres como a las mujeres
3 (*= just as*) [*important, difficult, responsible*] igualmente, igual de; [*well*] igual de • **her mother was ~ disappointed** su madre estaba igualmente decepcionada *or* igual de decepcionada • **she gave the task to her ~ capable assistant** le encargó la tarea a su asistente, que estaba igualmente capacitado *or* que estaba igual de capacitado • **his second novel was ~ successful** su segunda novela tuvo el mismo éxito • **she is ~ as intelligent as her sister** es igual de inteligente que su hermana, es tan inteligente como su hermana
4 (*= by the same token*) al mismo tiempo • **she cannot marry him, but ~ she cannot live alone** no se puede casar con él, pero, al mismo tiempo, no puede vivir sola • **~, you must remember ...** asimismo *or* al mismo tiempo, hay que recordar ...
equanimity [ˌekwəˈnɪmɪtɪ] (N) ecuanimidad *f*
equate [ɪˈkweɪt] (VT) **1** (*= compare*) equiparar (**to, with** con); (*= link*) identificar (**to, with** con)
2 (*Math*) poner en ecuación
(VI) • **to ~** to equivaler a
equation [ɪˈkweɪʒən] (N) **1** (*Math*) ecuación *f* • **to enter (into) the ~** (*fig*) entrar en juego • **fairness did not seem to enter into the ~** la justicia no parecía entrar en juego
2 (*= linking*) • **the ~ of sth with sth** la identificación de algo con algo
equator [ɪˈkweɪtə^r] (N) ecuador *m*
equatorial [ˌekwəˈtɔːrɪəl] (ADJ) ecuatorial
(CPD) ▸ **Equatorial Guinea** Guinea *f* Ecuatorial
equerry [ˈekwərɪ] (N) caballerizo *m* del rey
equestrian [ɪˈkwestrɪən] (ADJ) ecuestre
(N) caballista *mf*, jinete *mf*
equestrianism [ɪˈkwestrɪənɪzəm] (N) equitación *f*
equi... [ˈiːkwɪ] (PREFIX) equi...
equidistant [ˈiːkwɪˈdɪstənt] (ADJ) equidistante
equilateral [ˈiːkwɪˈlætərəl] (ADJ) equilátero
equilibrium [ˌiːkwɪˈlɪbrɪəm] (N) (PL: **equilibriums** *or* **equilibria** [ˌiːkwɪˈlɪbrɪə]) equilibrio *m* • **to maintain/lose one's ~** (*also fig*) mantener/perder el equilibrio
equine [ˈekwaɪn] (ADJ) equino
equinoctial [ˌiːkwɪˈnɒkʃəl] (ADJ) equinoccial
equinox [ˈiːkwɪnɒks] (N) equinoccio *m*
equip [ɪˈkwɪp] (VT) [*+ office, workshop*] equipar (**with** con); [*+ person*] proveer (**with** de) • **to be ~ped with** [*person*] estar provisto de; [*machine etc*] estar equipado con, estar dotado de • **he is well ~ped for the job** está bien preparado para el trabajo • **to be well ~ped to** (*+ infin*) estar bien preparado para (*+ infin*)
equipment [ɪˈkwɪpmənt] (N) (*gen*) equipo *m*; (*= tools, utensils etc*) herramientas *fpl*; (*mental*) aptitud *f*, dotes *fpl*
equipoise [ˈiːkwɪpɔɪz] (N) (*frm*) estabilidad *f*
equitable [ˈekwɪtəbl] (ADJ) (*frm*) equitativo
equitably [ˈekwɪtəblɪ] (ADV) (*frm*) equitativamente, de forma equitativa
equity [ˈekwɪtɪ] (N) **1** (*= fairness*) equidad *f*; (*Jur*) derecho *m* de equidad, derecho *m* natural
2 (*Econ*) [*of debtor*] valor *m* líquido; (*also* **equity capital**) neto *m* patrimonial, patrimonio *m* neto
3 equities (*St Ex*) acciones *fpl* ordinarias
4 • **Equity** (*Brit*) (*Theat*) *sindicato de actores*
equivalence [ɪˈkwɪvələns] (N) equivalencia *f*
equivalent [ɪˈkwɪvələnt] (ADJ) equivalente (**to a, in** en) • **to be ~ to** equivaler a
(N) equivalente *m*
equivocal [ɪˈkwɪvəkəl] (ADJ) [*statement, behaviour*] equívoco
equivocally [ɪˈkwɪvəklɪ] (ADV) de manera equívoca *or* ambigua
equivocate [ɪˈkwɪvəkeɪt] (VI) ser evasivo
equivocation [ɪˌkwɪvəˈkeɪʃən] (N) evasivas *fpl*
ER (ABBR) **1** (= **Elizabeth Regina**) *la reina Isabel*
2 (*US*) (*Med*) = **emergency room**
er* [3ː^r] (EXCL) (*in hesitation*) esto (*Sp*), este (*LAm*)
ERA (N ABBR) **1** (*US*) (*Pol*) = **Equal Rights Amendment**
2 (*Brit*) = **Education Reform Act**
era [ˈɪərə] (N) era *f* • **to mark an era** hacer época
eradicate [ɪˈrædɪkeɪt] (VT) [*+ disease, crime, superstition, injustice*] erradicar; [*+ poverty, discrimination*] acabar con, erradicar; [*+ weeds*] desarraigar, arrancar
eradication [ɪˌrædɪˈkeɪʃən] (N) erradicación *f*
erasable [ɪˈreɪzəbl] (ADJ) regrabable • **~ programmable read only memory** (*Comput*) memoria de solo lectura regrabable y programable
erase [ɪˈreɪz] (VT) **1** (*gen*) (*Comput*) borrar
2 (*US‡*) (*= kill*) liquidar*
eraser [ɪˈreɪzə^r] (N) (*esp US*) (*= rubber*) goma *f* de borrar
Erasmism [ɪˈræzmɪzəm] (N) erasmismo *m*
Erasmist [ɪˈræzmɪst] (ADJ) erasmista
(N) erasmista *mf*
Erasmus [ɪˈræzməs] (N) Erasmo
erasure [ɪˈreɪʒə^r] (N) borradura *f*, raspadura *f*; (*Comput*) borrado *m*
ERDF (N ABBR) (= **European Regional Development Fund**) FEDER *m*
ere [ɛə^r] (*poet*) (PREP) antes de • **ere long** dentro de poco
(CONJ) antes de que
e-reader [ˈiːriːdə^r] (N) lector *m* de libros electrónicos
erect [ɪˈrekt] (ADJ) [*person, head, posture*] erguido, derecho; [*plant, stem*] vertical, recto; [*tail, ears*] tieso, parado (*LAm*); [*penis*] erecto
(ADV) • **to walk ~** caminar derecho *or* erguido • **to hold o.s.** *or* **stand ~** mantenerse derecho *or* erguido
(VT) [*+ monument, statue, temple*] erigir (*frm*); [*+ mast, wall, building, barricade*] levantar; [*+ tent, scaffolding*] montar
erectile [ɪˈrektaɪl] (ADJ) eréctil
erection [ɪˈrekʃən] (N) **1** (*= act*) erección *f*, construcción *f*; (*= assembly*) montaje *m*
2 (*= building*) construcción *f*
3 (*Physiol*) [*of penis*] erección *f*
erectly [ɪˈrektlɪ] (ADV) erguidamente
erector set [ɪˈrektəset] (N) (*US*) juego *m* de construcciones
erg [3ːg] (N) ergio *m*, erg *m*
ergative [ˈ3ːgətɪv] (ADJ) (*Ling*) ergativo
ergo [ˈ3ːgəʊ] (CONJ) (*frm or hum*) ergo
ergonomic [ˌ3ːgəʊˈnɒmɪk] (ADJ) ergonómico
ergonomically [ˌ3ːgəʊˈnɒmɪklɪ] (ADV) atendiendo a principios ergonómicos
ergonomics [ˌ3ːgəʊˈnɒmɪks] (NSING) ergonomía *f*
ergonomist [3ːˈgɒnəmɪst] (N) ergonomista *mf*, ergónomo/a *m/f*
ergot [ˈ3ːgət] (N) cornezuelo *m* (del centeno)
ergotism [ˈ3ːgətɪzəm] (N) ergotismo *m*
Eric [ˈerɪk] (N) Erico
Erie [ˈɪərɪ] (N) • **Lake ~** el Lago Erie
Erin [ˈerɪn] (N) Erín *m* (*nombre antiguo y sentimental de Irlanda*)
ERISA [əˈrɪsə] (N ABBR) (*US*) (= **Employee Retirement Income Security Act**) *ley que regula pensiones de jubilados*
Eritrea [ˌerəˈtreɪə] (N) Eritrea *f*
Eritrean [erɪˈtreɪən] (ADJ) eritreo
(N) (*= person*) eritreo/a *m/f*
ERM (N ABBR) (= **Exchange Rate Mechanism**) mecanismo *m* de cambios
ermine [ˈ3ːmɪn] (N) (PL: **ermines** *or* **ermine**) armiño *m*
Ernest [ˈ3ːnɪst] (N) Ernesto
ERNIE [ˈ3ːnɪ] (N ABBR) (*Brit*) (= **Electronic Random Number Indicator Equipment**) *ordenador utilizado para sortear los bonos del Estado premiados*
erode [ɪˈrəʊd] (VT) **1** (*lit*) (*Geol*) erosionar; [*acid*] corroer
2 (*fig*) [*+ confidence, power, authority*] mermar; [*+ support, rights*] reducir • **inflation has ~d the value of their savings** la inflación ha mermado el valor de sus ahorros
(VI) **1** (*Geol*) erosionarse
2 (*fig*) [*confidence*] mermarse; [*support*] disminuir • **support for his party is eroding** el apoyo a su partido está disminuyendo
erogenous [ɪˈrɒdʒənəs] (ADJ) erógeno
(CPD) ▸ **erogenous zone** zona *f* erógena
Eros [ˈɪərɒs] (N) Eros
erosion [ɪˈrəʊʒən] (N) **1** (*Geol*) erosión *f*; [*of metal*] corrosión *f*
2 (*fig*) desgaste *m*
erosive [ɪˈrəʊzɪv] (ADJ) erosivo, erosionante
erotic [ɪˈrɒtɪk] (ADJ) erótico
erotica [ɪˈrɒtɪkə] (NPL) literatura *f* erótica
erotically [ɪˈrɒtɪklɪ] (ADV) eróticamente • **~ charged** con una gran carga erótica
eroticism [ɪˈrɒtɪsɪzəm] (N) erotismo *m*
eroticize [ɪˈrɒtɪsaɪz] (VT) erotizar
erotomania [ɪˌrɒtəʊˈmeɪnɪə] (N) erotomanía *f*
err [3ː^r] (VI) (*= be mistaken*) equivocarse; (*= sin*) pecar • **to err on the side of mercy/caution** *etc* pecar de piadoso/cauteloso *etc* • PROVERB: • **to err is human** errar es de humanos, quien tiene boca se equivoca
errand [ˈerənd] (N) recado *m*, mandado *m* (*esp LAm*) • **to run ~s** hacer recados • **~ of mercy** tentativa *f* de salvamento
(CPD) ▸ **errand boy** recadero *m*, mandadero *m* (*esp LAm*)
errant [ˈerənt] (ADJ) (*frm*) errante; ▹ **knight**
errata [eˈrɑːtə] (NPL) *of* **erratum**
erratic [ɪˈrætɪk] (ADJ) [*person*] (*by temperament*) imprevisible, voluble; (*in performance*) irregular; [*behaviour, mood*] imprevisible, variable; [*movement, pattern, pulse, breathing*] irregular; [*results, progress, performance*] desigual, poco uniforme • **police officers noticed his ~ driving** los policías notaron que conducía de modo irregular • **I work ~ hours** tengo un horario de trabajo irregular
erratically [ɪˈrætɪkəlɪ] (ADV) [*behave*] de forma imprevisible; [*work, drive, play*] de modo irregular; [*breathe*] de forma irregular, irregularmente • **his heart was beating ~** su corazón latía irregularmente *or* de forma irregular
erratum [eˈrɑːtəm] (N) (PL: **errata**) errata *f*
erroneous [ɪˈrəʊnɪəs] (ADJ) erróneo
erroneously [ɪˈrəʊnɪəslɪ] (ADV) erróneamente
error [ˈerə^r] (N) error *m*, equivocación *f* • **~s and omissions excepted** salvo error u omisión • **by ~** por error, por equivocación • **to be in ~** estar equivocado • **human ~** error *m* humano • **spelling ~** falta *f* de ortografía • **typing ~** error *m* de mecanografía • IDIOM: • **to see the ~ of one's**

ways reconocer su error
CPD ▸ **error message** (*Comput*) mensaje *m* de error ▸ **error of judgment** error *m* de juicio
ersatz ['ɛəzæts] ADJ sucedáneo
N sucedáneo *m*
erstwhile ['ɜ:stwaɪl] ADJ (*liter*) antiguo
eruct [ɪ'rʌkt], **eructate** [ɪ'rʌkteɪt] VI (*hum, frm*) eructar
eructation [,i:rʌk'teɪʃən] N (*hum*) eructo *m*
erudite ['erʊdaɪt] ADJ erudito
eruditely ['erʊdaɪtlɪ] ADV eruditamente
erudition [,erʊ'dɪʃən] N erudición *f*
erupt [ɪ'rʌpt] VI **1** [*volcano*] (= *begin to erupt*) entrar en erupción; (= *go on erupting*) estar en erupción
2 (*fig*) [*spots*] hacer erupción; [*war, fighting, anger*] estallar • **he ~ed into the room** irrumpió en el cuarto
eruption [ɪ'rʌpʃən] N **1** [*of volcano, spots*] erupción *f*
2 (*fig*) [*of war, fighting, anger*] estallido *m*
erysipelas [,erɪ'sɪpɪləs] N erisipela *f*
erythrocyte [ɪ'rɪθrəʊ,saɪt] N eritrocito *m*
ES N ABBR = **expert system**
ESA N ABBR (= **European Space Agency**) AEE *f*
Esau ['i:sɔ:] N Esaú
escalate ['eskəleɪt] VI **1** [*costs, prices*] subir vertiginosamente • **production costs have ~d** los costes de producción han subido vertiginosamente • **escalating costs** costes *mpl* que van en continuo aumento • **the cost of the project has ~d to £8.7 million** el coste del proyecto ha subido vertiginosamente a 8,7 millones de libras
2 [*violence, tension, conflict*] intensificarse • **the violence could ~ into a war** la violencia podría intensificarse hasta llegar a una guerra
VT [+ *conflict*] intensificar; [+ *demands*] aumentar
escalation [,eskə'leɪʃən] N [*of costs, prices*] aumento *m* (vertiginoso), escalada *f*; [*of tension, conflict*] intensificación *f*; [*of violence*] intensificación *f*, escalada *f* • **the threat of nuclear ~ remains** sigue en pie la amenaza de una intensificación del conflicto nuclear
escalator ['eskəleɪtə^r] N escalera *f* mecánica
CPD ▸ **escalator clause** (*Comm*) cláusula *f* de revisión *or* actualización
escalope ['eskəlɒp] N (*Brit*) escalope *m*, filete *m*
escapade [,eskə'peɪd] N (= *adventure*) aventura *f*; (= *misdeed*) travesura *f*
escape [ɪs'keɪp] N **1** (*from detention*) fuga *f*; (*from country*) huida *f* • **there is no ~ from this prison** no hay forma de escapar *or* fugarse de esta cárcel • **to make one's ~** escapar(se)
2 (*from injury, harm*) • **there was no ~ from the noise** no había forma de escapar al ruido • **she saw prostitution as her only means of ~ from poverty** vió la prostitución como el único medio de escapar a la pobreza • **to have a lucky** *or* **narrow ~** (*lit, fig*) salvarse por los pelos • **he had a lucky** *or* **narrow ~** (*from death*) tuvo suerte de escapar *or* salir con vida, se salvó por los pelos
3 (*from real world*) evasión *f* • **for me television is an ~** a mí la televisión me sirve de evasión
4 [*of water, gas*] fuga *f*, escape *m*
VT **1** (= *avoid*) [+ *pursuer*] escapar de, librarse de; [+ *punishment, death*] librarse de; [+ *consequences*] evitar • **they managed to ~ capture/detection** consiguieron evitar que les capturaran/detectaran • **they jumped out of the window to ~ the fire** saltaron por la ventana para escapar del fuego • **they were lucky to ~ injury** tuvieron mucha suerte de salir ilesos • **there was no way I could ~ meeting him** no había manera de poder evitar verme con él • **they left the country to ~ the press** se fueron del país para escapar de la prensa • **he just ~d being run over** por poco lo atropellan
2 (= *elude*) • **his name ~s me** no logro acordarme de su nombre • **nothing ~s her** no se le escapa nada • **it had ~d his notice** *or* **attention that …** se le había escapado que …
3 (*esp liter*) (= *issue from*) • **a cry ~d his lips** dejó escapar un grito
VI **1** (= *get away*) (*gen*) escaparse; [*prisoner*] fugarse, escapar(se) • **to ~ from** [+ *prison*] escapar(se) de, fugarse de; [+ *cage*] escaparse de; [+ *danger, harm*] huir de; [+ *reality*] evadirse de • **he kept me talking and I couldn't ~ from him** hacía que siguiera hablando y no podía escaparme de él • **he wanted to ~ from the world for a while** quería evadirse del mundo durante un tiempo • **in winter I think of escaping to the sun** en invierno pienso en escaparme a un sitio con sol • **he ~d to a neutral country** huyó a un país neutral • **she ~d unhurt** salió ilesa • **he ~d with a few bruises** solo sufrió algunas magulladuras • **he was lucky to ~ with his life** tuvo suerte de salir con vida
2 (= *leak*) [*liquid, gas*] salirse
3 (= *issue*) • **a moan ~d from her lips** dejó escapar un gemido • **tendrils of hair were escaping from under her hat** algunos mechones de pelo le salían por debajo del sombrero
CPD ▸ **escape artist** escapista *mf* ▸ **escape attempt** intento *m* de fuga ▸ **escape clause** (*in agreement*) cláusula *f* de excepción ▸ **escape hatch** (*in plane, space rocket*) escotilla *f* de salvamento ▸ **escape key** (*Comput*) tecla *f* de escape ▸ **escape pipe** tubo *m* de desagüe ▸ **escape plan** plan *m* de fuga ▸ **escape route** ruta *f* de escape ▸ **escape valve** válvula *f* de escape ▸ **escape velocity** (*Aer*) velocidad *f* de escape
escaped [ɪs'keɪpt] ADJ [*prisoner*] fugado; [*animal*] escapado
escapee [ɪskeɪ'pi:] N (*from prison*) fugitivo/a *m/f*, prófugo/a *m/f*
escapement [ɪs'keɪpmənt] N [*of watch*] escape *m*
escapism [ɪs'keɪpɪzəm] N escapismo *m*, evasión *f*
escapist [ɪs'keɪpɪst] ADJ escapista • **~ literature** literatura *f* de evasión
N escapista *mf*
escapologist [,eskə'pɒlədʒɪst] N escapista *mf*
escarpment [ɪs'kɑ:pmənt] N escarpa *f*
eschatological [,eskətə'lɒdʒɪkəl] ADJ (*Rel*) escatológico
eschatology [,eskə'tɒlədʒɪ] N (*Rel*) escatología *f*
eschew [ɪs'tʃu:] VT evitar, renunciar a
escort N ['eskɔ:t] **1** (= *group*) séquito *m*, acompañamiento *m*; (*lady's*) acompañante *m*
2 (= *girl from agency*) señorita *f* de compañía
3 (*Mil, Naut*) escolta *f* • **to travel under ~** viajar con escolta • **a police ~** una escolta policial
VT [ɪs'kɔ:t] **1** acompañar • **to ~ sb home** acompañar a algn a su casa • **to ~ sb in** acompañar a algn al entrar
2 (*Mil, Naut*) escoltar
CPD ['eskɔ:t] ▸ **escort agency** agencia *m* de servicios de compañía ▸ **escort duty** servicio *m* de escolta ▸ **escort vessel** buque *m* escolta
escrow ['eskrəʊ] N depósito *m* en fideicomiso • **in ~** en depósito
CPD ▸ **escrow account** (*Econ*) cuenta *f* de plica
escudo [es'ku:dəʊ] N (PL: **escudos**) escudo *m*
escutcheon [ɪs'kʌtʃən] N escudo *m* de armas, blasón *m*; (*fig*) honor *m*
ESE ABBR (= **east-southeast**) ESE
ESF N ABBR (= **European Social Fund**) FSE *m*
e-shop ['i:ʃɒp] N tienda *f* electrónica
e-shopping ['i:ʃɒpɪŋ] N compras *fpl* online
Eskimo ['eskɪməʊ] ADJ esquimal
N (PL: **Eskimos, Eskimo**) **1** (= *person*) esquimal *mf*
2 (*Ling*) esquimal *m*
ESL N ABBR (= **English as a Second Language**) ▹ **TEFL/EFL, TESL/ESL, ELT, TESOL/ESOL**
ESN ADJ ABBR = **educationally subnormal**
ESOL N ABBR (= **English for Speakers of Other Languages**) ▹ **TEFL/EFL, TESL/ESL, ELT, TESOL/ESOL**
esophagus [ɪ'sɒfəgəs] N (PL: **esophaguses** *or* **esophagi** [ɪ'sɒfədʒaɪ]) (*US*) = **oesophagus**
esoteric [,esəʊ'terɪk] ADJ esotérico
ESP N ABBR **1** (= **extrasensory perception**) percepción *f* extrasensorial
2 = **English for Special Purposes**
esp. ABBR = **especially**
espadrille [,espə'drɪl] N alpargata *f*
espalier [ɪ'spæljə^r] N espaldar *m*
esparto [e'spɑ:təʊ] N esparto *m*
especial [ɪs'peʃəl] ADJ (*frm*) especial, particular
especially [ɪs'peʃəlɪ] ADV **1** (= *particularly*) especialmente • **~ in summer/when it rains** especialmente *or* sobre todo en verano/ cuando llueve • **why me, ~?** ¿por qué yo precisamente?
2 (= *expressly*) especialmente • **I came ~ to see you** vine especialmente para verte • **to do sth ~ for sb/sth** hacer algo especialmente para algn/algo
3 (= *more than usually*) [*important, difficult, sensitive*] especialmente, particularmente • **she did ~ well in her French exam** el examen de francés le fue especialmente *or* particularmente bien • **"is she pretty?" — "not ~"** —¿es guapa? —no especialmente
Esperantist [,espə'ræntɪst] N esperantista *mf*
Esperanto [,espə'ræntəʊ] N esperanto *m*
espionage [,espɪə'nɑ:ʒ] N espionaje *m* • **industrial ~** espionaje *m* industrial
esplanade [,esplə'neɪd] N paseo *m* marítimo; (*Mil*) explanada *f*
espousal [ɪs'paʊzl] N (*frm*) adherencia *f* (**of** a), adopción *f* (**of de**)
espouse [ɪs'paʊz] VT (*frm*) [+ *cause*] adherirse a; [+ *plan*] adoptar
espresso [es'presəʊ] N café *m* exprés
CPD ▸ **espresso bar** café *m*, cafetería *f* (*donde se sirve café exprés*)
esprit de corps ['espri:də'kɔ:^r] N espíritu *m* de cuerpo
espy [ɪs'paɪ] VT (*liter*) divisar
Esq. ABBR (*Brit*) (*frm*) (= **esquire**) Don, D.
esquire [ɪs'kwaɪə^r] N (*Brit*) (*on envelope*) Señor don • **Colin Smith Esquire** Sr. D. Colin Smith
essay N ['eseɪ] (*Literat*) ensayo *m*; (*Scol, Univ*) trabajo *m*
VT [e'seɪ] (*frm*) probar, ensayar; [+ *task*] intentar • **to ~ to** (+ *infin*) intentar (+ *infin*)
CPD ['eseɪ] ▸ **essay question** pregunta *f* para desarrollar
essayist ['eseɪɪst] N (*Literat*) ensayista *mf*
essence ['esəns] N **1** esencia *f* • **the ~ of the matter is …** lo esencial del asunto es … • **in ~** en lo esencial • **time is of the ~** el tiempo es primordial

2 (= *extract*) esencia *f*, extracto *m*

essential [ɪ'senʃəl] ADJ **1** (= *necessary*) esencial, imprescindible • **it is ~ that** es esencial que, es imprescindible que • **it is ~ to** (+ *infin*) es esencial *or* imprescindible (+ *infin*) • **it is absolutely ~ to remain calm** es absolutamente esencial *or* es imprescindible mantener la calma • **in this job accuracy is ~** para este trabajo la exactitud es esencial *or* imprescindible *or* es un imperativo • **a list of ~ reading** una lista de lecturas esenciales • **~ services** servicios *mpl* básicos

2 (= *fundamental*) [*quality, fact, difference, element*] fundamental, esencial • **play is an ~ part of a child's development** el juego es una parte fundamental *or* esencial en el desarrollo del niño • **man's ~ goodness** la bondad esencial *or* fundamental del ser humano

N **1** (= *necessary thing*) • **in my job a car is an ~** en mi trabajo, un coche es una necesidad • **the ~s of everyday life** las necesidades básicas de la vida diaria • **we have all the ~s** tenemos todo lo necesario • **we picked up a few ~s for the trip** tomamos algunas cosas esenciales para el viaje • **accuracy is one of the ~s** la exactitud es uno de los elementos esenciales *or* fundamentales • **we can only take the bare ~s with us** solo podemos llevarnos lo imprescindible

2 essentials (= *fundamentals*) • **the ~s of German grammar** los rudimentos de la gramática alemana • **in all ~s** fundamentalmente

CPD ▸ **essential oil** aceite *m* esencial

essentially [ɪ'senʃəlɪ] ADV **1** (= *at bottom*) básicamente • **~, it is a story of ordinary people** básicamente, es una historia de gente normal • **she was ~ a generous person** era básicamente *or* en esencia una persona generosa

2 (= *on the whole*) en lo esencial, en lo fundamental • **~, we agree** estamos de acuerdo en lo esencial *or* fundamental • **his theory is ~ correct** su teoría es correcta en lo esencial, fundamentalmente *or* en lo fundamental su teoría es correcta

EST N ABBR **1** (*US*) = **Eastern Standard Time**

2 = **electric shock treatment**

est. ABBR **1** = **estimate(d)**

2 = **established** • **~ 1888** se fundó en 1888

establish [ɪs'tæblɪʃ] VT **1** (= *set up*) [+ *business, state, committee*] establecer, fundar; [+ *custom, rule, peace, order*] establecer; [+ *precedent*] establecer, sentar; [+ *relations*] establecer, entablar; [+ *power, authority*] afirmar; [+ *reputation*] ganarse • **to ~ sb in a business** poner un negocio a algn • **the book ~ed him as a writer** el libro lo consagró como escritor • **to ~ o.s.** establecerse, consolidarse

2 (= *prove*) [+ *fact, rights*] comprobar, demostrar; [+ *identity*] verificar; [+ *sb's innocence*] probar, demostrar • **we have ~ed that …** hemos comprobado que …

3 (= *find out, discover*) averiguar; [+ *date*] determinar

established [ɪs'tæblɪʃt] ADJ [*person, business*] establecido, consolidado; [*custom*] establecido, arraigado; [*fact*] probado; [*church*] oficial, del Estado; [*staff*] fijo, en plantilla • **a well-established business** un negocio establecido *or* consolidado

establishment [ɪs'tæblɪʃmənt] N

1 (= *setting-up*) establecimiento *m*; (= *creation*) creación *f*

2 (= *proof*) [*of innocence, guilt*] determinación *f*

3 (= *business, house*) establecimiento *m* • **a teaching/nursing ~** un centro de enseñanza/de reposo • **they have a smaller ~ nowadays** ahora mantienen una casa más modesta, tienen menos servicio ahora

4 (*Admin, Mil, Naut*) (= *personnel*) personal *m* • **to be on the ~** estar en plantilla

5 • **the Establishment** la clase dirigente • **the literary/musical Establishment** las altas esferas del mundo literario/musical; ▹ **anti-Establishment**

ESTABLISHMENT

En el Reino Unido el término **Establishment** hace referencia a la clase dirigente, es decir, al Gobierno, los altos cargos de la Administración pública, la Iglesia, las Fuerzas Armadas y a otras personas en puestos de influencia. Por lo general, se piensa que esta clase dirigente apoya el status quo tanto a nivel político como cultural o social.

En Estados Unidos, el **Establishment** se asocia sobre todo con Washington, donde se encuentra el gobierno federal, y en concreto con aquellos que estudiaron en universidades del noreste, especialmente **Yale** y **Harvard**.

▹ **IVY LEAGUE**

estate [ɪs'teɪt] N **1** (= *land*) finca *f*, hacienda *f*; (= *country estate*) finca *f*, hacienda *f* (*LAm*), estancia *f* (*S. Cone*); (= *housing estate*) urbanización *f*; (= *industrial estate*) polígono *m* industrial

2 (= *property*) propiedad *f*; (= *assets*) patrimonio *m*; [*of deceased*] herencia *f* • **she left a large ~** dejó una gran herencia • **personal ~** patrimonio *m* personal; ▹ **real**

3 (*Pol*) estado *m*; ▹ **fourth, third**

4 (*Brit*) = **estate car**

CPD ▸ **estate agency** (*esp Brit*) agencia *f* inmobiliaria ▸ **estate agent** (*esp Brit*) agente *mf* inmobiliario/a ▸ **estate agent's** (*Brit*) agencia *f* inmobiliaria ▸ **estate car** (*Brit*) ranchera *f*, coche *m* familiar, rural *f* (*S. Cone*), camioneta *f* (*LAm*) ▸ **estate duty** (*Brit*) impuesto *m* de sucesiones

esteem [ɪs'tiːm] VT (*frm*) **1** [+ *person*] estimar, apreciar • **my ~ed colleague** mi estimado colega

2 (= *consider*) considerar, estimar • **I would ~ it an honour** lo consideraría un honor

N estima *f*, aprecio *m* • **to hold sb in high ~** tener a algn en gran estima • **he lowered himself in my ~** bajó en mi estima • **he went up in my ~** ganó valor a mis ojos

ester ['estəʳ] N (*Chem*) éster *m*

Esther ['estəʳ] N Ester

esthete *etc* ['iːsθiːt] N (*US*) = **aesthete** *etc*

esthetics [iːs'θetɪks] N (*US*) = **aesthetics**

Esthonia [es'təʊnɪə] N = **Estonia**

Esthonian [es'təʊnɪən] ADJ, N = **Estonian**

estimable ['estɪməbl] ADJ estimable

estimate N ['estɪmɪt] **1** (= *judgment*) estimación *f*, cálculo *m*; (= *approximate assessment*) (*for work etc*) presupuesto *m* • **to form an ~ of sth/sb** formarse una opinión de algo/algn • **to give sb an ~ of** [+ *cost etc*] presentar a algn un presupuesto de • **rough ~** cálculo *m* aproximativo • **at a rough ~** aproximadamente

2 • **Estimates** (*Parl*) presupuestos *mpl* generales del Estado

VT ['estɪmeɪt] (= *judge*) calcular aproximadamente; (= *assess*) juzgar, estimar • **to ~ that** calcular que • **to ~ the cost at …** calcular el precio en …

VI ['estɪmeɪt] • **to ~ for** [+ *building work etc*] hacer un presupuesto de

estimated ['estɪmeɪtɪd] ADJ [*quantity, value*] estimado • **there are an ~ 90,000 gangsters in the country** se estima que hay 90.000 gángsters en el país

estimation [ˌestɪ'meɪʃən] N **1** (= *judgment*) juicio *m*, opinión *f* • **according to** *or* **in my ~** a mi juicio, en mi opinión • **what is your ~ of him?** ¿qué concepto tienes de él?

2 (= *esteem*) estima *f*, aprecio *m*

estimator ['estɪmeɪtəʳ] N tasador(a) *m/f*

Estonia [e'stəʊnɪə] N Estonia *f*

Estonian [e'stəʊnɪən] ADJ estonio

N **1** (= *person*) estonio/a *m/f*

2 (*Ling*) estonio *m*

e-store ['iːstɔːʳ] N tienda *f* electrónica

estrange [sɪ'treɪndʒ] VT enajenar, distanciar (**from** de)

estranged [ɪs'treɪndʒd] ADJ separado • **his ~ wife** su mujer que vive separada de él • **to become ~** separarse

estrangement [ɪs'treɪndʒmənt] N distanciamiento *m*

estrogen ['iːstrəʊdʒən] N (*US*) = **oestrogen**

estrous ['estrəs] N (*US*) = **oestrous**

estrus ['estrəs] N (*US*) = **oestrus**

estuary ['estjʊərɪ] N estuario *m*, ría *f*

CPD ▸ **Estuary English** (*Brit*) *variedad de inglés que se ha puesto de moda entre los jóvenes de zonas adyacentes al estuario del Támesis, en el SE de Inglaterra*

ET N ABBR (*US*) = **Eastern Time**

ETA N ABBR = **estimated time of arrival**

e-tail ['iːteɪl] N venta *f* via *or* por Internet

CPD ▸ **e-tail site** sitio *m* de venta via *or* por Internet

e-tailer ['iːteɪləʳ] N vendedor *m* en línea, vendedor *m* via *or* por Internet

e-tailing ['iːteɪlɪŋ] N venta *f* en línea, venta *f* via *or* por Internet

et al [et'æl] ABBR (= **et alii, and others**) y col., y otros

etc ABBR (= **et cetera**) etc.

etcetera [ɪt'setrə] ADV etcétera

NPL **etceteras** extras *mpl*, adornos *mpl*

etch [etʃ] VT grabar al aguafuerte; (*fig*) grabar • **it is ~ed on my memory forever** lo tengo grabado para siempre en mi memoria

etching ['etʃɪŋ] N (= *process*) grabado *m* al aguafuerte; (= *print made from plate*) aguafuerte *m or f* • **he invited her in to see his ~s** (*hum*) la invitó a entrar a ver su colección de sellos

ETD N ABBR = **estimated time of departure**

eternal [ɪ'tɜːnl] ADJ **1** (= *everlasting*) [*life, bliss*] eterno

2 (*pej*) (= *incessant*) constante • **in the background was that ~ hum** se oía aquel constante zumbido de fondo • **can't you stop this ~ quarrelling?** ¿no podéis dejar de pelearos constantemente?

CPD ▸ **the eternal triangle** el triángulo amoroso

eternally [ɪ'tɜːnəlɪ] ADV **1** (= *everlastingly*) [*exist, live*] eternamente; [*damned, joined*] para siempre, eternamente

2 (*fig*) (= *perpetually*) [*grateful, optimistic, young*] eternamente; [*quarrel, criticize*] constantemente • **why do you have to be ~ quarrelling?** ¿por qué os tenéis que estar constantemente *or* siempre peleando? • **he's ~ complaining** se pasa la vida quejándose

eternity [ɪ'tɜːnɪtɪ] N eternidad *f* • **it seemed like an ~** pareció una eternidad *or* un siglo

CPD ▸ **eternity ring** anillo *m* de brillantes

e-text ['iːtekst] N texto *m* electrónico

ETF N ABBR = **electronic transfer of funds**

ethane ['iːθeɪn] N etano *m*

ethanol ['eθənɒl] N etanol *m*

ether ['iːθəʳ] N (*Chem*) éter *m*

ethereal [ɪ'θɪərɪəl] ADJ (*fig*) etéreo

Ethernet® ['iːθənet] N Ethernet® *f*

ethic ['eθɪk] N ética *f*; ▹ work
ethical ['eθɪkəl] ADJ ético; (= *honourable*) honrado
ethically ['eθɪklɪ] ADV [*behave*] éticamente, con ética; [*sound, unacceptable*] desde el punto de vista ético
ethics ['eθɪks] NSING (= *subject*) ética *fsing* NPL (= *honourableness*) moralidad *f*
Ethiopia [ˌi:θɪ'əʊpɪə] N Etiopía *f*
Ethiopian [ˌi:θɪ'əʊpɪən] ADJ etíope N etíope *mf*
ethnic ['eθnɪk] ADJ **1** (= *racial*) [*origin, community*] étnico; [*conflict, tension*] racial
2 (= *non-Western*) [*music*] étnico; [*food, jewellery*] exótico
N (*esp US*) (= *person*) *miembro de una minoría étnica* • **white ~** *miembro de una minoría étnica de raza blanca*
CPD ▸ **ethnic cleansing** limpieza *f* étnica ▸ **ethnic group** etnia *f*, grupo *m* étnico ▸ **ethnic minority** minoría *f* étnica
ethnically ['eθnɪklɪ] ADV [*pure, homogeneous, distinct*] étnicamente • **it is one of the most ~ diverse areas of the world** es una de las zonas de más diversidad étnica del mundo • **an ~ mixed region** una región con una gran mezcla de razas *or* de etnias • **~ related violence** violencia *f* de origen racial • **~ cleansed areas** zonas *fpl* en las que ha tenido lugar una limpieza étnica • **~, it's not a stable country** desde el punto de vista étnico, no es un país estable
ethnicity [eθ'nɪsɪtɪ] N etnicidad *f*
ethnocentric [ˌeθnəʊ'sentrɪk] ADJ etnocéntrico
ethnocentrism [ˌeθnəʊ'sentrɪzəm] N etnocentrismo *m*
ethnographer [eθ'nɒgrəfəʳ] N etnógrafo/a *m/f*
ethnographic [ˌeθnəʊ'græfɪk] ADJ etnográfico
ethnography [eθ'nɒgrəfɪ] N etnografía *f*
ethnolinguistics [ˌeθnəʊlɪŋ'gwɪstɪks] N etnolingüística *f*
ethnological [ˌeθnəʊ'lɒdʒɪkl] ADJ etnológico
ethnologist [eθ'nɒlədʒɪst] N etnólogo/a *m/f*
ethnology [eθ'nɒlədʒɪ] N etnología *f*
ethnomusicology [ˌeθnəʊmju:zɪ'kɒlədʒɪ] N etnomusicología *f*
ethos ['i:θɒs] N [*of culture, group*] espíritu *m*, escala *f* de valores
ethyl ['i:θaɪl] N etilo *m*
CPD ▸ **ethyl alcohol** alcohol *m* etílico
ethylene ['eθɪli:n] N etileno *m*
e-ticket ['i:ˌtɪkɪt] N billete *m* electrónico (*Sp*), boleto *m* electrónico (*LAm*)
etiolated ['i:tɪəleɪtɪd] ADJ **1** (*Bot*) decolorado, reblanquecido
2 (*fig*) (*frm*) desmayado, lánguido
etiology [ˌi:tɪ'ɒlədʒɪ] N etiología *f*
etiquette ['etɪket] N etiqueta *f*, protocolo *m* • **court ~** (*royal*) ceremonial *m* de la corte; (*Jur*) protocolo *m* de la corte • **legal ~** ética *f* legal • **professional ~** ética *f* profesional • **~ demands that ...** la etiqueta *or* el protocolo exige que ... • **it is not good ~** no está bien visto
Eton crop ['i:tn'krɒp] N corte *m* a lo garçon
e-trading ['i:treɪdɪŋ] N comercio *m* electrónico
ADJ de comercio electrónico
Etruscan [ɪ'trʌskən] ADJ etrusco
N **1** (= *person*) etrusco/a *m/f*
2 (*Ling*) etrusco *m*
et seq. ABBR (= **et sequentia**) y sigs
ETU N ABBR (*Brit*) (= **Electrical Trades Union**) *sindicato de electricistas*
ETV N ABBR (*US*) = **Educational Television**
etyma ['etɪmə] NPL *of* **etymon**
etymological [ˌetɪmə'lɒdʒɪkəl] ADJ etimológico
etymologically [ˌetɪmə'lɒdʒɪkəlɪ] ADV etimológicamente
etymologist [ˌetɪ'mɒlədʒɪst] N etimólogo/a *m/f*, etimologista *mf*
etymology [ˌetɪ'mɒlədʒɪ] N etimología *f*
etymon ['etɪmɒn] N (PL: **etymons, etyma** ['etɪmə]) étimo *m*
EU N ABBR (= **European Union**) UE *f*
eucalyptus [ˌju:kə'lɪptəs] N (PL: **eucalyptuses** *or* **eucalypti** [ˌju:kə'lɪptaɪ]) (= *tree*) eucalipto *m*; (= *oil*) esencia *f* de eucalipto
Eucharist ['ju:kərɪst] N Eucaristía *f*
Eucharistic [ju:kə'rɪstɪk] ADJ de la Eucaristía, eucarístico
Euclid ['ju:klɪd] N Euclides
Euclidean [ju:'klɪdɪən] ADJ euclidiano
Eugene ['ju:dʒi:n] N Eugenio
eugenic [ju:'dʒenɪk] ADJ eugenésico
eugenics [ju:'dʒenɪks] NSING eugenesia *f*
eulogistic [ˌju:lə'dʒɪstɪk] ADJ elogioso, ensalzador
eulogize ['ju:lədʒaɪz] VT elogiar, encomiar
eulogy ['ju:lədʒɪ] N elogio *m*, encomio *m*
eunuch ['ju:nək] N eunuco *m*
euphemism ['ju:fɪmɪzəm] N eufemismo *m* • **a ~ for ...** un eufemismo de ...
euphemistic [ˌju:fɪ'mɪstɪk] ADJ eufemístico
euphemistically [ˌju:fɪ'mɪstɪklɪ] ADV [*call, describe*] eufemísticamente
euphonic [ju:'fɒnɪk] ADJ eufónico
euphonious [ju:'fəʊnɪəs] ADJ = **euphonic**
euphonium [ju:'fəʊnɪəm] N bombardino *m*
euphony ['ju:fənɪ] N eufonía *f*
euphoria [ju:'fɔ:rɪə] N euforia *f*
euphoric [ju:'fɒrɪk] ADJ [*person, atmosphere, laughter*] eufórico
Euphrates [ju:'freɪti:z] N Eufrates *m*
Eurailpass ['jʊəreɪlˌpɑ:s] N Eurailpass *m*
Eurasia [jʊə'reɪʃə] N Eurasia *f*
Eurasian [jʊə'reɪʃn] ADJ eurasiático
N eurasiático/a *m/f*
Euratom [jʊər'ætəm] N ABBR = **European Atomic Energy Commission**
eureka [jʊə'ri:kə] EXCL ¡eureka!
eurhythmics [ju:'rɪðmɪks] NSING euritmia *f*
Euripides [jʊ'rɪpɪdi:z] N Eurípides
euro ['jʊərəʊ] N euro *m*
Euro..., euro... ['jʊərəʊ] PREFIX euro...
Eurobonds ['jʊərəʊbɒndz] NPL eurobonos *mpl*
Eurocentric ['jʊərəʊˌsentrɪk] ADJ eurocentrista, centrado en Europa
Eurocentrism ['jʊərəʊˌsentrɪzəm] N eurocentrismo *m*
Eurocheque ['jʊərəʊtʃek] N eurocheque *m*
CPD ▸ **Eurocheque card** tarjeta *f* de eurocheque
Eurocommunism ['jʊərəʊˌkɒmjʊnɪzəm] N eurocomunismo *m*
Eurocommunist ['jʊərəʊˌkɒmjʊnɪst] ADJ eurocomunista
N eurocomunista *mf*
Eurocorps ['jʊərəʊˌkɔ:ʳ] N (*Mil*) Eurocuerpo *m*
Eurocrat ['jʊərəʊkræt] N (*hum, pej*) eurócrata *mf* (*burócrata de la UE*)
Eurocredit ['jʊərəʊˌkredɪt] N Eurocrédito *m*
eurocurrency ['jʊərəʊˌkʌrənsɪ] N eurodivisa *f*
Eurodollar ['jʊərəʊˌdɒləʳ] N eurodólar *m*
Euroland ['jʊərəʊlænd] N zona *f* (del) euro, territorio *m* (del) euro
Euromarket ['jʊərəʊˌmɑ:kɪt], **Euromart** ['jʊərəʊˌmɑ:t] N euromercado *m*, Mercado *m* Común
Euro-MP ['jʊərəʊˌemˌpi:] N ABBR (= **Member of the European Parliament**) eurodiputado/a *m/f*
Europe ['jʊərəp] N Europa *f* • **to go into** *or* **join ~** (*Brit*) (*Pol*) entrar en la Unión Europea
European [ˌjʊərə'pi:ən] ADJ europeo
N europeo/a *m/f*
CPD ▸ **European Commission** Comisión *f* Europea ▸ **European Court of Human Rights** Tribunal *m* Europeo de Derechos Humanos ▸ **European Court of Justice** Tribunal *m* de Justicia Europeo ▸ **European Currency Unit** Unidad *f* de Cuenta Europea, ECU *m* ▸ **European Economic Community** Comunidad *f* Económica Europea ▸ **European Health Insurance Card** tarjeta *f* sanitaria europea ▸ **European Monetary System** Sistema *m* Monetario Europeo ▸ **European Parliament** Parlamento *m* Europeo ▸ **European plan** (*US*) habitación *f* (de hotel) con servicios (pero sin comidas) ▸ **European Social Fund** Fondo *m* Social Europeo ▸ **European Union** Unión *f* Europea
europeanization [ˌjʊərəˌpɪənaɪ'zeɪʃən] N europeización *f*
europeanize [ˌjʊərə'pɪənaɪz] VT europeizar
Europhile ['jʊərəʊfaɪl] N europeísta *mf*
ADJ europeísta
Europhobe ['jʊərəʊfəʊb] N eurófobo/a *m/f*
Europhobia [ˌjʊərəʊ'fəʊbɪə] N eurofobia *f*
Europhobic [ˌjʊərəʊ'fəʊbɪk] N eurófobo/a *m/f*
ADJ eurófobo
Europol ['jʊərəʊpɒl] N Europol *f*
Euro-sceptic, Eurosceptic ['jʊərəʊˌskeptɪk] N euroescéptico/a *m/f*
Euro-size ['jʊərəʊˌsaɪz] N • **Euro-size 1** (*Comm*) talla *f* europea 1
Eurospeak ['jʊərəʊspi:k] N (*hum*) jerga *f* burocrática de la UE
Eurostar® ['jʊərəʊˌstɑ:ʳ] N Eurostar® *m*
Eurotunnel ['jʊərəʊˌtʌnl] N Eurotúnel *m*
Eurovision ['jʊərəvɪʒən] N Eurovisión *f*
CPD ▸ **Eurovision Song Contest** Festival *m* de Eurovisión
Eurozone ['jʊərəʊzəʊn] N eurozona *f*, zona *f* euro
Eurydice [jʊ'rɪdɪsi:] N Eurídice
Eustachian tube [ju:ˌsteɪʃən'tju:b] N trompa *f* de Eustaquio
euthanasia [ˌju:θə'neɪzɪə] N eutanasia *f*
evacuate [ɪ'vækjʊeɪt] VT **1** [+ *people*] evacuar • **he was ~d to a hospital in Haifa** lo evacuaron a un hospital de Haifa
2 [+ *building, area*] evacuar
3 (*frm*) [+ *bowels*] evacuar
VI **1** [*people, troops*] • **civilians were given the order to ~** les dieron órdenes a los civiles de que evacuaran la zona • **the British decided to ~** los británicos decidieron abandonar el lugar
2 (*frm*) [*bowels*] evacuar
evacuation [ɪˌvækjʊ'eɪʃən] N **1** [*of people*] evacuación *f*
2 [*of building, area*] evacuación *f*
3 (*frm*) [*of bowels*] evacuación *f*
evacuee [ɪˌvækjʊ'i:] N evacuado/a *m/f*
evade [ɪ'veɪd] VT [+ *capture, pursuers*] eludir; [+ *punishment, blow*] evitar; [+ *question, issue, responsibility*] eludir, evadir; [+ *military service*] eludir, zafarse de; [+ *taxation, customs duty*] evadir, sustraerse a; [+ *sb's gaze*] esquivar
evaluate [ɪ'væljʊeɪt] VT **1** (= *assess value of*) valorar, calcular el valor de
2 (= *judge*) evaluar • **to ~ evidence** evaluar las pruebas
evaluation [ɪˌvæljʊ'eɪʃən] N **1** [*of value*]

valoración *f*, cálculo *m*
2 [*of evidence etc*] evaluación *f*
evaluative [ɪˈvæljʊətɪv] (ADJ) evaluativo
evanescence [ˌiːvəˈnesəns] (N) (*liter*) evanescencia *f*
evanescent [ˌiːvəˈnesnt] (ADJ) (*liter*) evanescente, fugaz, efímero
evangelical [ˌiːvænˈdʒelɪkəl] (ADJ) (*Rel*) evangélico
(N) evangélico/a *m/f*
evangelism [ɪˈvændʒəˌlɪzəm] (N) evangelismo *m*
evangelist [ɪˈvændʒəlɪst] (N) 1 (= *writer*) (*also* **Evangelist**) Evangelista *m* • **St John the Evangelist** San Juan Evangelista
2 (= *preacher*) evangelizador(a) *m/f*
evangelize [ɪˈvændʒɪlaɪz] (VT) evangelizar
(VI) predicar el Evangelio
evaporate [ɪˈvæpəreɪt] (VT) evaporar
(VI) [*liquid*] evaporarse; (*fig*) [*hopes, fears, anger*] desvanecerse
evaporated milk [ɪˌvæpəreɪtɪdˈmɪlk] (N) leche *f* evaporada
evaporation [ɪˌvæpəˈreɪʃən] (N) evaporación *f*
evasion [ɪˈveɪʒən] (N) evasión *f*; (= *evasive answer etc*) evasiva *f*; ▹ **tax**
evasive [ɪˈveɪzɪv] (ADJ) [*answer, person*] evasivo • **to be ~ (about sth)** mostrarse evasivo (acerca de algo) • **to take ~ action** (*Mil*) adoptar tácticas evasivas
evasively [ɪˈveɪzɪvlɪ] (ADV) evasivamente • **"it was no problem," I said ~** —no hubo problema —dije evasivamente • **he answered ~** contestó con evasivas • **"I can't remember the exact details," she answered ~** —no recuerdo los detalles exactos —contestó evasivamente *or* de forma evasiva
evasiveness [ɪˈveɪzɪvnɪs] (N) esquivez *f* • **voters are fed up with the party's ~ on economic matters** los votantes están hartos de la esquivez del partido en cuestiones económicas
eve[1] [iːv] (N) víspera *f* • **on the eve of** (*lit*) en la víspera de; (*fig*) en vísperas de
eve[2] [iːv] (N) (*liter*) (= *evening*) tarde *f*
Eve [iːv] (N) Eva
even [ˈiːvən] (ADJ) 1 (= *smooth, flat*) [*surface, ground*] plano • **the floorboards are not very ~** las tablas del suelo no están muy niveladas • **to make sth ~** nivelar algo, allanar algo
2 (= *uniform*) [*speed, temperature, progress*] constante; [*breathing*] regular; [*distribution, colour, work*] uniforme • **he has ~ features** tiene facciones regulares; ▹ **keel**
3 (= *equal*) [*quantities, distances*] igual; [*distribution*] equitativo • **divide the dough into 12 ~ pieces** divida la masa en 12 piezas iguales • **a more ~ distribution of wealth** una distribución más equitativa de la riqueza • **to break ~** llegar a cubrir los gastos • **he has an ~ chance of winning the election** (*Brit*) tiene las mismas posibilidades de ganar las elecciones que de perderlas, tiene un cincuenta por ciento de posibilidades de ganar las elecciones • **to get ~ with sb** ajustar cuentas con algn • **I'll get ~ with you for that!** ¡me las pagarás por eso!* • **that makes us ~** (*in game*) así quedamos empatados; (*regarding money*) así quedamos en paz *or* (*LAm*) a mano • **they are an ~ match** (*in sports, games*) los dos son igual de buenos; (*fig*) no le tiene nada que envidiar el uno al otro • **I'll give you ~ money that Arsenal will win** (*Brit*) para mí que Arsenal tiene las mismas posibilidades de ganar que de perder • **the odds are about ~** (*Brit*) las posibilidades son más o menos iguales • **our score is ~** estamos igualados *or* empatados • **to be ~ with sb** (*in game*) estar igualado con algn; (*regarding money*) estar en paz *or* (*LAm*) a mano con algn • IDIOM: • **to give sb an ~ break** (*esp US*) dar a algn su *or* una oportunidad; ▹ **even-handed, even-stevens**
4 (= *calm*) • **he has an ~ temper** no se altera fácilmente • **to say sth with an ~ voice** decir algo sin alterar la voz • **to keep one's voice ~** no alterar la voz; ▹ **even-tempered**
5 (= *not odd*) [*number*] par
(ADV) 1 hasta, incluso • **I have ~ forgotten his name** hasta *or* incluso he olvidado su nombre • **~ on Sundays** hasta *or* incluso los domingos • **~ the priest was there** hasta *or* incluso el cura estaba allí • **pick them all, ~ the little ones** recógelos todos incluso los pequeños • **~ I know that!** ¡eso lo sé hasta yo! • **and he ~ sings** e incluso canta • **if you ~ tried a bit harder** si tan solo te esforzaras un poco más
2 (*with compar adj or adv*) aún, todavía • **~ faster** aún *or* todavía más rápido • **~ better** aún *or* todavía mejor • **~ more easily** aún *or* todavía más fácilmente • **~ less money** aún *or* todavía menos dinero
3 (*with negative*) • **not ~ …** ni siquiera … • **he can't ~ read** ni siquiera sabe leer • **he didn't ~ kiss me** ni me besó siquiera • **don't ~ think about it!** ¡ni lo pienses! • **without ~ reading it** sin leerlo siquiera
4 (*in phrases*) • **~ as**: • **~ as he spoke the door opened** en ese mismo momento se abrió la puerta • **~ as a child I used to drink cider** incluso de niño solía beber sidra • **~ as he had wished it** (*frm*) exactamente como él lo había deseado • **~ if** aunque (+ *subjun*), incluso si (+ *subjun*) • **~ if you tried** aunque lo intentaras, incluso si lo intentaras, así lo procuraras (*LAm*) • **not … ~ if** • **not ~ if**: • **he won't talk to you ~ if you do go there** no hablará contigo aunque vayas allí • **I wouldn't do it ~ if you paid me a fortune** no lo haría aunque me pagaras una fortuna • **I couldn't be prouder, not ~ if you were my own son** no me sentiría más orgulloso, aunque fuera mi propio hijo • **~ now** todavía • **~ now, you could still change your mind** todavía estás a tiempo de cambiar de idea • **~ so** aun así • **~ so he was disappointed** aun así, quedó decepcionado • **yes but ~ so …** sí, pero aun así … • **~ then** aun así • **and ~ then she wasn't happy** y aún así no estaba contenta • **~ though** aunque • **he didn't listen, ~ though he knew I was right** no me hizo caso, aunque sabía que tenía razón • **~ when** incluso cuando • **~ when I was young I never had any ambition** incluso cuando era joven no tenía ninguna ambición • **he never gets depressed, ~ when things go badly** nunca se deprime, incluso *or* ni siquiera cuando las cosas andan mal • **not ~ when** ni siquiera cuando • **we were never in love, not ~ when we got married** nunca estuvimos enamorados, ni siquiera cuando nos casamos
(VT) 1 (= *smooth, flatten*) [+ *surface, ground*] nivelar, allanar
2 (= *equalize*) igualar • **to ~ the score** (*lit*) igualar el marcador • **he was determined to ~ the score** (= *get revenge*) estaba decidido *or* empeñado a desquitarse
(NPL) **evens** (*esp Brit*) • **the bookmakers are offering ~s** los corredores de apuestas ofrecen el doble de la cantidad aportada
▸ **even out** (VT + ADV) 1 (= *smooth*) [+ *surface*] allanar, nivelar
2 (= *equalize*) [+ *number, score*] igualar • **to ~ things out** (= *bring greater equality*) nivelar la situación *or* las cosas
3 (= *regularize*) [+ *expenses, work, exports*] nivelar • **to ~ out the peaks and troughs** nivelar los altibajos
(VI + ADV) 1 (= *become equal*) nivelarse, quedar compensado
2 (= *become more regular*) • **the work will ~ out** el trabajo irá siendo más regular
▸ **even up** (VT + ADV) (*lit, fig*) igualar, poner parejos • **to ~ things up** nivelar la situación *or* las cosas
(VI + ADV) • **to ~ up with sb** ajustar cuentas con algn
even-handed [ˈiːvənˈhændɪd] (ADJ) [*person*] imparcial; [*distribution*] equitativo
even-handedly [ˈiːvənˈhændɪdlɪ] (ADV) [*behave*] imparcialmente; [*distribute*] equitativamente
even-handedness [ˌiːvənˈhændɪdnɪs] (N) imparcialidad *f*
evening [ˈiːvnɪŋ] (N) (*before dark*) tarde *f*; (*after dark*) noche *f* • **in the ~** por la tarde/noche • **this ~** esta tarde/noche • **tomorrow/yesterday ~** mañana/ayer por la tarde/noche • **on Sunday ~** el domingo por la tarde/noche • **~ was coming on** estaba atardeciendo/anocheciendo • **she spends her ~s knitting** pasa las tardes haciendo punto • **good ~!** (*early*) ¡buenas tardes!; (*after sunset*) ¡buenas noches!
(CPD) ▸ **evening class** clase *f* nocturna ▸ **evening dress** (*woman's*) traje *m* de noche; (*man's*) traje *m* de etiqueta • **in ~ dress** (*man, woman*) vestido/a de etiqueta ▸ **evening fixture** (*Sport*) partido *m* por la noche ▸ **evening institute** escuela *f* nocturna ▸ **evening match** = **evening fixture** ▸ **evening meal** cena *f* ▸ **evening paper** periódico *m* de la tarde, vespertino *m* ▸ **evening performance** (*Theat*) función *f* de noche ▸ **evening prayers** = **evening service** ▸ **evening primrose** onagra *f* ▸ **evening primrose oil** aceite *m* de onagra ▸ **evening reception** (*at wedding*) banquete *m* (*por la noche*) ▸ **evening service** (*Rel*) vísperas *fpl*, misa *f* vespertina ▸ **evening star** estrella *f* de Venus ▸ **evening wear** ropa *f* para la noche
evenly [ˈiːvənlɪ] (ADV) 1 (= *uniformly*) [*breathe, flow*] con regularidad, regularmente; [*mix*] uniformemente • **the cake should rise ~** el pastel debe subir de manera uniforme *or* todo por igual • **distribute the sugar ~ over the fruit** distribuye el azúcar por igual sobre la fruta • **the rise in unemployment was ~ spread across the country** el aumento del desempleo afectaba de forma regular a todo el país • **space the curtain rings ~** coloque los aros de las cortinas a la misma distancia unos de otros
2 (= *equally*) [*distribute, share*] por igual, equitativamente (*more frm*), parejo (*LAm*) • **the wealth is ~ distributed** la riqueza está dividida equitativamente *or* por igual • **to divide/split sth ~** dividir algo a partes iguales • **public opinion is fairly ~ divided** la opinión pública está dividida en partes bastante iguales • **they are ~ matched** están muy igualados
3 (= *calmly*) [*say, reply, ask*] sin alterarse, serenamente; [*look at*] serenamente
evenness [ˈiːvənnɪs] (N) 1 (= *smoothness*) [*of ground, surface*] lo liso, lo nivelado
2 (= *uniformity*) [*of speed, temperature, progress*] lo constante; [*of breathing, features*] regularidad *f*; [*of distribution, colours*] uniformidad *f*
3 (= *calmness*) • **~ of temper** serenidad *f*, ecuanimidad *f* • **the ~ of his voice did not betray the anger he felt inside** el tono sosegado de su voz no revelaba la ira que sentía dentro

e

evensong ['i:vənsɒŋ] N vísperas *fpl*, misa *f* vespertina

even-stevens* [,i:vən'sti:vənz] ADV • **to be even-stevens with sb** estar en paz con algn; (*in competition*) ir parejo con algn • **they're pretty well even-stevens** están más o menos igualados

event [ɪ'vent] N **1** (= *happening*) acontecimiento *m* • **this is quite an ~!** ¡esto es todo un acontecimiento! • **in** *or* **during the course of ~s** en el curso de los acontecimientos • **in the normal course of ~s** normalmente, por lo común • **current ~s** temas *mpl* de actualidad • **to be expecting a happy ~** estar en estado de buena esperanza • IDIOM: • **to be wise after the ~** mostrar sabiduría cuando ya no hay remedio
2 (= *case*) • **at all ~s** • **in any ~** pase lo que pase, en todo caso • **in either ~** en cualquiera de los dos casos • **in the ~ ...** (*Brit*) resultó que ... • **in the ~ of ...** en caso de ... • **in the ~ of his dying** en caso de que muriese • **in the ~ that ...** en caso de que (+ *subjun*) • **in that ~** en ese caso
3 (*in a programme*) número *m*; (= *ceremony*) acto *m* • **coming ~s** atracciones *fpl* venideras • **programme of ~s** (*civic*) programa *m* de actos; (= *shows*) programa *m* de atracciones
4 (*Sport*) prueba *f*; ▹ **field, track**

even-tempered ['i:vən'tempəd] ADJ ecuánime, apacible

eventer [ɪ'ventəʳ] N (*Horse riding*) *jinete participante en el concurso completo*

eventful [ɪ'ventfʊl] ADJ [*journey, match*] lleno de incidentes; [*life*] azaroso

eventide home ['i:vəntaɪd,həʊm] N hogar *m* de ancianos

eventing [ɪ'ventɪŋ] N concursos *mpl* hípicos (de tres días)

eventual [ɪ'ventʃʊəl] ADJ final

eventuality [ɪ,ventʃʊ'ælɪtɪ] N eventualidad *f* • **in that ~** ante esa eventualidad • **in the ~ of** ante la eventualidad de • **to be ready for any ~** estar preparado para cualquier eventualidad

eventually [ɪ'ventʃʊəlɪ] ADV **1** (= *finally*) finalmente, al final • **he ~ agreed that she was right** finalmente *or* al final admitió que ella tenía razón • **he ~ became Prime Minister** finalmente *or* con el tiempo llegó a ser primer ministro
2 (= *at some future time*) con el tiempo • **I'll get round to it ~** lo haré con el tiempo

eventuate [ɪ'ventjʊeɪt] VI • **to ~ in** (*US*) resultar en

ever ['evəʳ] ADV **1** (= *always*) siempre • **~ after** desde entonces • **they lived happily ~ after** vivieron felices • **as ~** como siempre; (*ending letter*) un abrazo ... • **for ~** (= *always*) siempre • **for ~ and ~** • **for ~ and a day** por siempre jamás; (= *until end of time*) para siempre • **~ ready** siempre dispuesto • **~ since** (*as adv*) desde entonces; (*as conj*) desde que • **yours ~** (*ending letter*) un abrazo ...
2 (= *at any time*) • **all she ~ does is make jam** se pasa la vida haciendo mermelada • **if you ~ go there** si vas allí alguna vez • **nothing ~ happens** nunca pasa nada • **we haven't ~ tried it** nunca lo hemos probado • **did you ~ find it?** ¿lo encontraste por fin? • **did you ~ meet him?** ¿llegaste a conocerlo? • **have you ~ been there?** ¿has estado allí alguna vez? • **better than ~** mejor que nunca • **hardly ~** casi nunca • **seldom, if ~** rara vez o nunca • **now, if ~, is the time** *or* **moment to ...** ahora o nunca es el momento de ... • **he's a liar if ~ there was one** él sí que es un mentiroso • **a nice man, if ~ I saw one** hombre simpático donde los haya *or* si los hay • **more than ~** más que nunca • **more beautiful than ~** más hermoso que nunca • IDIOM: • **did you ~?*** ¡habráse visto!
3 (*used as intensifier*) • **is it ~ big!** (*US**) ¡qué grande es!, ¡si vieras lo grande que es! • **as if I ~ would!** ¿me crees capaz de hacer algo semejante? • **as soon as ~ you can** lo antes *or* lo más pronto posible • **before ~ you were born** antes de que nacieras • **never ~** (nunca) jamás • **~ so** (*esp Brit**) muy • **it's ~ so cold** hace un frío terrible • **we're ~ so grateful** estamos muy agradecidos • **~ so many things** tantísimas cosas, la mar de cosas • **~ so much** mucho, muchísimo • **he's ~ so nice** es simpatiquísimo • **why ~ did you do it?** ¿por qué demonios lo hiciste? • **why ~ not?** ¿y por qué no?
4 (*after superl*) • **it's the best ~** jamás ha habido mejor • **the coldest night ~** la noche más fría que nunca hemos tenido

ever-changing [,evə'tʃeɪndʒɪŋ] ADJ siempre variable, infinitamente mudable

Everest ['evərɪst] N (*also* **Mount Everest**) (monte *m*) Everest *m*

Everglades ['evəgleɪdz] NPL • **the ~** (*US*) los Everglades, *región pantanosa subtropical de Florida, al sur del Lago Okeechobee*

evergreen ['evəgri:n] ADJ **1** [*tree, shrub*] de hoja perenne
2 [*memory*] imperecedero; [*song*] clásico, de toda la vida
N (= *tree*) árbol *m* de hoja perenne; (= *plant*) planta *f* de hoja perenne
CPD ▸ **evergreen oak** encina *f*

ever-growing [,evə'grəʊɪŋ] ADJ = **ever-increasing**

ever-increasing [,evərɪn'kri:sɪŋ] ADJ [*number, size*] cada vez mayor, creciente; [*population, threat, need*] creciente

everlasting [,evə'lɑ:stɪŋ] ADJ (= *eternal*) [*gratitude, shame, regret*] eterno; [*fame*] imperecedero • **~ life** la vida eterna • **to her ~ regret, she refused the offer** para su eterno arrepentimiento, rechazó la oferta

everlastingly [,evə'lɑ:stɪŋlɪ] ADV [*grateful*] eternamente; [*patient*] infinitamente

evermore ['evə'mɔ:ʳ] ADV eternamente • **for ~** por siempre jamás, para siempre jamás

every ['evrɪ] ADJ **1** (= *each*) cada (*inv*) • **~ day** cada día • **~ three days** • **~ third day** cada tres días • **~ few days** cada dos o tres días • **~ bit of the cake** la torta entera • **~ bit as clever as ...** tan *or* (*LAm*) igual de listo como ... • **I have to account for ~ last penny** tengo que dar cuentas de cada penique que gasto • **I enjoyed ~ minute of the party** disfruté cada minuto de la fiesta • **~ now and then** • **~ now and again** de vez en cuando • **~ other** *or* **second month** un mes sí y otro no, cada dos meses • **~ other person has a car** de cada dos personas una tiene coche • **he'd eaten ~ single chocolate** se había comido todos los bombones, se había comido hasta el último bombón • **~ single time** cada vez sin excepción • **~ so often** cada cierto tiempo, de vez en cuando • **he brings me a present ~ time he comes** cada vez que viene me trae un regalo • **this recipe gives you perfect results ~ time** esta receta siempre le dará resultados perfectos • IDIOMS: • **(it's) ~ man for himself** ¡sálvese quien pueda! • **~ man Jack of them voted against** todos y cada uno de ellos votaron en contra • PROVERB: • **~ little helps** un grano no hace granero pero ayuda al compañero, todo es ayuda
2 (= *all*) • **he was following my ~ move** me vigilaba constantemente • **not ~ child is as fortunate as you** no todos los niños son tan afortunados como tú • **~ one of them passed the exam** todos ellos aprobaron el examen • **he criticized her at ~ opportunity** no dejaba escapar oportunidad alguna para criticarla • **he spends ~ penny he earns** gasta hasta el último centavo que gana • **in ~ way** en todos los aspectos • **his ~ wish** todos sus deseos • **I mean ~ word I say** lo digo muy en serio
3 (= *any*) todo • **~ parent will have experienced this at one time or another** todo padre se habrá encontrado con esto en algún momento
4 (= *all possible*) • **I gave you ~ assistance** te ayudé en todo lo que podía • **she had ~ chance** se le dieron todas las posibilidades • **I have ~ confidence in him** tengo entera *or* plena confianza en él • **~ effort is being made to trace him** se está haciendo todo lo posible para localizarlo • **I have ~ reason to think that ...** tengo razones sobradas para pensar que ... • **we wish you ~ success** te deseamos todo el éxito posible

everybody ['evrɪbɒdɪ] PRON todos/as, todo el mundo • **~ else** todos los demás

everyday ['evrɪdeɪ] ADJ [*occurrence, experience*] cotidiano; [*expression*] corriente; [*use*] diario, cotidiano; [*shoes, clothes*] de uso diario • **for ~ (use)** de diario • **in ~ use** de uso corriente • **~ clothes** ropa *f* de diario

everyman ['evrɪmæn] N hombre *m* cualquiera, hombre *m* de la calle

everyone ['evrɪwʌn] PRON = **everybody**

everyplace ['evrɪpleɪs] ADV (*US*) = **everywhere**

everything ['evrɪθɪŋ] PRON todo • **~ is ready** todo está dispuesto • **~ nice had been sold** se había vendido todo lo bonito • **he sold ~** lo vendió todo • **~ you say is true** es verdad todo lo que dices • **time is ~** el tiempo lo es todo • **money isn't ~** el dinero no lo es todo • **he did ~ possible** hizo todo lo posible • **I've argued with him and ~, but he won't listen** he razonado y todo eso con él, pero no quiere escuchar

everywhere ['evrɪwɛəʳ] ADV [*go*] a todas partes; [*be*] en todas partes • **I looked ~** busqué en todas partes • **~ in Spain** en todas partes de España • **~ you go you'll find the same** en todas partes encontrarás lo mismo

everywoman ['evrɪ,wʊmən] N mujer *f* cualquiera

evict [ɪ'vɪkt] VT [+ *tenant*] desahuciar, desalojar

eviction [ɪ'vɪkʃən] N desahucio *m*, desalojo *m*
CPD ▸ **eviction notice** aviso *m* de desalojo
▸ **eviction order** orden *f* de desalojo

evidence ['evɪdəns] N **1** (= *proof*) pruebas *fpl* • **~ of/that ...** pruebas de/de que ... • **circumstantial ~** pruebas *fpl* circunstanciales • **there is no ~ against him** no hay pruebas contra él • **to hold sth in ~** esgrimir algo como prueba • **what ~ is there for this belief?** ¿qué pruebas corroboran esta creencia?
2 (= *sign*) indicio *m*, señal *f* • **to show ~ of** dar muestras de
3 (= *testimony*) testimonio *m* • **to call sb in ~** llamar a algn como testigo • **to give ~** prestar declaración, deponer (*more frm*) • **to turn King's** *or* **Queen's** *or* (*US*) **State's ~** delatar a un cómplice
4 • **to be in ~** (= *noticeable*) estar bien visible
VT **1** (= *make evident*) manifestar; [+ *emotion*] dar muestras de
2 (= *prove*) probar, demostrar • **as is ~d by the fact that ...** según lo demuestra el hecho de que ...

evident ['evɪdənt] ADJ evidente, manifiesto • **his distress was ~** era evidente *or* manifiesta su aflicción • **it is ~ from the way he talks ...** resulta evidente por su forma de hablar ... • **it is ~ from his speech that ...** su discurso deja patente que ... • **as is ~ from her novel** como queda bien claro en su novela • **to be ~ in** manifestarse en • **it is ~ that ...** queda patente *or* manifiesto que ... • **as is all too ~** como queda bien patente

evidently [ˈevɪdəntlɪ] ADV **1** (= *clearly*) evidentemente • **the two men ~ knew each other** evidentemente, los dos hombres se conocían, era evidente que los dos hombres se conocían • **he was ~ very angry** era evidente que estaba muy enfadado
2 (= *apparently*) aparentemente, por lo visto • **"was it suicide?" — "~ not"** —¿fue un suicidio? —por lo visto, no *or* —parece que no

evil [ˈiːvl] ADJ **1** (= *wicked*) [*person, deed, thought*] malvado; [*reputation*] de malvado; [*spirit*] maligno, maléfico; [*influence*] maléfico, funesto; [*place, plan*] diabólico; [*hour, times*] funesto; [*effect*] nocivo • **to put the ~ eye on sb** • **give sb the ~ eye** echar el mal de ojo a algn • **an ~ spell** un maleficio • **~ tongues may say that ...** las malas lenguas dirán que ... • **he had his ~ way with her** se aprovechó de ella, se la llevó al huerto (*hum*) • **the ~ weed** (= *tobacco*) el vicio (*hum*)
2 (= *nasty*) [*smell, taste*] horrible • **to put off the ~ day** posponer el día funesto • **to have an ~ temper** tener un genio endiablado
N **1** (= *wickedness*) mal *m* • **the conflict between good and ~** el conflicto entre el bien y el mal • **there wasn't a trace of ~ in her** no había ni un rastro del maldad en ella • **the forces of ~** las fuerzas del mal • **to speak ~ of sb** hablar mal de algn
2 (= *harmful thing*) mal *m* • **the lesser of two ~s** el menor de dos males • **a necessary ~** un mal necesario • **social ~s** males *mpl* sociales
CPD ▸ **evil spirit** espíritu *m* maligno

evildoer [ˈiːvlduːəʳ] N malhechor(a) *m/f*

evilly [ˈiːvɪlɪ] ADV [*behave, plot*] malvadamente; [*laugh, smile*] diabólicamente, malvadamente

evil-minded [ˈiːvlˈmaɪndɪd] ADJ (= *suspicious*) malpensado; (= *nasty*) malintencionado

evil-smelling [ˈiːvlˈsmelɪŋ] ADJ fétido, maloliente, hediondo

evil-tempered [ˈiːvlˈtempəd] ADJ de muy mal genio *or* carácter

evince [ɪˈvɪns] VT mostrar, dar señales de

eviscerate [ɪˈvɪsəreɪt] VT destripar

evocation [ˌevəˈkeɪʃən] N evocación *f*

evocative [ɪˈvɒkətɪv] ADJ evocador (**of** de)

evocatively [ɪˈvɒkətɪvlɪ] ADV de manera evocadora

evoke [ɪˈvəʊk] VT [+ *memories*] evocar; [+ *admiration*] suscitar, provocar

evolution [ˌiːvəˈluːʃən] N **1** (= *development*) desarrollo *m*
2 (*Bio*) evolución *f*

evolutionary [ˌiːvəˈluːʃnərɪ] ADJ evolutivo

evolutionism [ˌiːvəˈluːʃənɪzəm] N evolucionismo *m*

evolutionist [ˌiːvəˈluːʃənɪst] N evolucionista *mf*
ADJ evolucionista

evolve [ɪˈvɒlv] VT **1** [+ *system, theory, plan*] desarrollar
2 [+ *gas, heat*] desprender
VI **1** [*species*] evolucionar
2 [*system, plan, science*] desarrollarse

e-voting [ˈiːvəʊtɪŋ] N voto *m* electrónico

ewe [juː] N oveja *f*

ewer [ˈjuːəʳ] N aguamanil *m*

ex [eks] PREP (= *out of*) • **ex dividend** sin dividendo • **the price ex works** el precio de *or* en fábrica, el precio franco fábrica; ▹ **ex officio**
N* • **my ex** (= *husband*) mi ex (marido); (= *wife*) mi ex (mujer); (= *boyfriend, girlfriend*) mi ex (novio/a)

ex- [eks] PREFIX (= *former*) ex • **the ex-ambassador to Moscow** el ex embajador en Moscú • **the ex-leader of** el antiguo jefe de • **ex-minister** ex-ministro/a *m/f* • **ex-president** ex-presidente/a *m/f*; ▹ **ex-husband, ex-serviceman** *etc*

exacerbate [ɪgˈzæsəbeɪt] VT [+ *pain, disease*] exacerbar; [+ *relations, situation*] empeorar

exacerbation [ɪgˌzæsəˈbeɪʃən] N exacerbación *f*

exact [ɪgˈzækt] ADJ **1** (= *precise*) [*number, copy, translation*] exacto; [*meaning, instructions, time, amount, date, location*] exacto, preciso; [*cause, nature*] preciso • **his ~ words were ...** lo que dijo, textualmente, era ... • **to be ~, there were three of us** para ser exactos, éramos tres, en concreto, éramos tres • **can you be more ~?** precise, por favor • **to be an ~ likeness of sth/sb** ser exactamente igual a algo/algn • **until this ~ moment** hasta este preciso momento • **to be the ~ opposite (of)** ser exactamente *or* justo lo contrario (de) • **the ~ same place/house** (*US*) exactamente el mismo sitio/la misma casa
2 (= *meticulous*) [*description, analysis, scientist, work, study*] preciso, meticuloso; [*instrument*] preciso
VT [+ *money, payment, obedience, allegiance*] (= *demand*) exigir; (= *obtain*) obtener (**from** de); [+ *promise*] conseguir, arrancar; [+ *taxes*] recaudar • **to ~ revenge** vengarse
CPD ▸ **exact science** ciencia *f* exacta • **history is not an ~ science** la historia no es una ciencia exacta ▸ **the exact sciences** las ciencias exactas

exacting [ɪgˈzæktɪŋ] ADJ [*task, activity, profession*] duro; [*boss, person*] exigente; [*conditions*] severo, riguroso

exaction [ɪgˈzækʃən] N exacción *f*

exactitude [ɪgˈzæktɪtjuːd] N exactitud *f*

exactly [ɪgˈzæktlɪ] ADV [*know, resemble*] exactamente; [*calculate, measure, describe*] exactamente, con precisión • **at ~ five o'clock** a las cinco en punto • **what did you tell him ~?** • **what ~ did you tell him?** ¿qué le dijiste exactamente? • **that's ~ what I was thinking** eso es exactamente lo que yo estaba pensando • **he's ~ like his father** es exactamente igual que su padre, es clavado a su padre* • **nobody knows who ~ will be in charge** nadie sabe con exactitud quién será el encargado • **I wanted to get everything ~ right** quería hacerlo todo a la perfección • **"do you mean that we are stuck here?" — "exactly!"** —¿quieres decir que no nos podemos mover de aquí? —¡exacto! *or* —¡efectivamente! • **he wasn't ~ pleased** (*iro*) no estaba precisamente contento, no estaba muy contento, que digamos • **it's not ~ interesting** (*iro*) no es lo que se dice interesante • **"is she sick?" — "not ~"** —¿está enferma? —no exactamente

exactness [ɪgˈzæktnɪs] N [*of words, translation, copy*] exactitud *f*; [*of measurement, description, instructions*] precisión *f*

exaggerate [ɪgˈzædʒəreɪt] VT exagerar
VI exagerar

exaggerated [ɪgˈzædʒəreɪtɪd] ADJ exagerado

exaggeratedly [ɪgˈzædʒəreɪtɪdlɪ] ADV exageradamente

exaggeration [ɪgˌzædʒəˈreɪʃən] N exageración *f*

exalt [ɪgˈzɔːlt] VT (= *elevate*) exaltar, elevar; (= *praise*) ensalzar

exaltation [ˌegzɔːlˈteɪʃən] N exaltación *f*, elevación *f*; (= *praise*) ensalzamiento *m*

exalted [ɪgˈzɔːltɪd] ADJ (= *high*) [*position*] elevado; [*person*] eminente; (= *elated*) excitado

exam* [ɪgˈzæm] N, CPD = **examination**

examination [ɪgˌzæmɪˈneɪʃən] N **1** (*Scol, Univ*) (= *test*) examen *m* • **our chemistry ~** nuestro examen de química • **to take** *or* **sit an ~** presentarse a un examen • **to take an ~ in** examinarse de • **oral ~** examen *m* oral
2 (= *inspection*) [*of premises*] inspección *f*; [*of luggage*] registro *m*; [*of account*] revisión *f*, inspección *f*; [*of witness, suspect*] interrogatorio *m* • **on ~** al examinarlo/examinarlos *etc*
3 (= *inquiry*) investigación *f*, estudio *m* (**into** de) • **the matter is under ~** el asunto está siendo investigado *or* estudiado
4 (*Med*) reconocimiento *m*
CPD ▸ **examination board** (*Brit*) *una de las varias juntas que coordinan los exámenes a nivel nacional* ▸ **examination paper** examen *m* (*la hoja*) ▸ **examination results** resultados *mpl* de los exámenes ▸ **examination room** sala *f* del examen

examine [ɪgˈzæmɪn] VT **1** [+ *student, candidate*] examinar • **I was ~d in maths** me examinaron de matemáticas
2 (= *inspect*) [+ *premises*] inspeccionar; [+ *luggage*] registrar; [+ *witness, suspect, accused*] interrogar
3 (= *investigate*) estudiar, investigar • **we are examining the question** estamos estudiando *or* investigando la cuestión
4 (*Med*) [+ *patient*] examinar, hacer un reconocimiento médico a; [+ *part of body*] examinar

examinee [ɪgˌzæmɪˈniː] N examinando/a *m/f*

examiner [ɪgˈzæmɪnəʳ] N examinador(a) *m/f*

examining board [ɪgˈzæmɪnɪŋˌbɔːd] N (*Brit*) *una de las varias juntas que coordinan los exámenes a nivel nacional*

example [ɪgˈzɑːmpl] N (*gen*) ejemplo *m*; (= *copy, specimen*) ejemplar *m* • **for ~** por ejemplo • **to quote sth/sb as an ~** citar algo/a algn como ejemplo • **to follow sb's ~** seguir el ejemplo de algn • **to set a good/bad ~** dar buen/mal ejemplo • **to make an ~ of sb** • **to punish sb as an ~** dar a algn un castigo ejemplar

exasperate [ɪgˈzɑːspəreɪt] VT exasperar, sacar de quicio

exasperated [ɪgˈzɑːspəreɪtɪd] ADJ exasperado • **to be ~ at** *or* **with sth/sb** estar exasperado con algo/algn • **we were ~ with Joe/the situation** Joe/la situación nos tenía exasperados, estábamos exasperados con Joe/la situación • **to become** *or* **get** *or* **grow ~** exasperarse

exasperating [ɪgˈzɑːspəreɪtɪŋ] ADJ [*person, situation, problem*] exasperante • **you're so ~!** ¡sacas de quicio a cualquiera! • **it's so ~!** ¡es exasperante!, es para volverse loco*

exasperatingly [ɪgˈzɑːspəreɪtɪŋlɪ] ADV • **the train was ~ slow** el tren era tan lento que me/lo *etc* exasperaba • **she's ~ stupid** es tan estúpida que le saca a uno de quicio, es de una estupidez exasperante

exasperation [ɪgˌzɑːspəˈreɪʃən] N exasperación *f* • **"hurry!" he cried in ~** —¡date prisa! —gritó exasperado *or* con exasperación

ex cathedra [ekskəˈθiːdrə] ADJ, ADV ex cátedra

excavate [ˈekskəveɪt] VT excavar

excavation [ˌekskəˈveɪʃən] N excavación *f*

excavator [ˈekskəveɪtəʳ] N (= *machine*) excavadora *f*; (= *person*) excavador(a) *m/f*

exceed [ɪkˈsiːd] VT [+ *estimate*] exceder (**by**

en); [+ *number*] pasar de, exceder de; [+ *limit, bounds, speed limit*] sobrepasar, rebasar; [+ *rights*] ir más allá de, abusar de; [+ *powers, instructions*] excederse en; [+ *expectations, fears*] superar • **a fine not ~ing £50** una multa que no pase de 50 libras

exceedingly [ɪk'si:dɪŋlɪ] ADV sumamente, extremadamente

excel [ɪk'sel] VT superar • **to ~ o.s.** (*esp iro*) lucirse, pasarse (*LAm*)
VI • **to ~ at** *or* **in** sobresalir en, destacar en • **to ~ as** destacarse como

excellence ['eksələns] N excelencia *f*

Excellency ['eksələnsɪ] N Excelencia *f* • **His ~** su Excelencia *f* • **yes, Your ~** sí, Excelencia

excellent ['eksələnt] ADJ excelente

excellently ['eksələntlɪ] ADV excelentemente, muy bien • **to do sth ~** hacer algo muy bien

excelsior [ek'selsɪɔ:ʳ] N (*US*) virutas *fpl* de embalaje

except [ɪk'sept] PREP • **~ (for)** excepto, salvo, menos • **~ that/if/when/where** *etc* salvo que/si/cuando/donde *etc* • **there is nothing we can do ~ wait** no nos queda otra (cosa) que esperar
VT excluir, exceptuar (**from** de) • **present company ~ed** con excepción de los presentes

excepting [ɪk'septɪŋ] PREP excepto, salvo • **always ~ the possibility that ...** excluyendo la posibilidad de que ... • **not ~ ...** incluso ..., inclusive ...

exception [ɪk'sepʃən] N excepción *f* • **to make an ~** hacer una excepción • **to take ~ to sth** ofenderse por algo • **with the ~ of** a excepción de • **without ~** sin excepción • **the ~ proves the rule** la excepción confirma la regla

exceptionable [ɪk'sepʃənəbl] ADJ [*conduct*] censurable, objetable; [*proposal*] impugnable, refutable

exceptional [ɪk'sepʃənl] ADJ [*courage, ability, circumstances*] excepcional; [*achievement, performance*] extraordinario, excepcional • **your wife was a most ~ woman** su esposa era una mujer de lo más excepcional
CPD ▸ **exceptional child** (*US*) (*Scol*) (= *gifted*) niño/a *m/f* superdotado/a; (= *handicapped*) niño/a *m/f* que requiere una atención diferenciada

exceptionally [ɪk'sepʃənəlɪ] ADV [*difficult, valuable, intelligent, high*] excepcionalmente, extraordinariamente; [*good, large, easy, rare*] extraordinariamente • **an ~ talented player** un jugador de un talento excepcional *or* extraordinario • **~, in times of emergency we can ...** de forma excepcional, en casos de urgencia podemos ...

excerpt ['eksɜ:pt] N extracto *m*

excess [ɪk'ses] N **1** (= *surplus*) exceso *m* • **an ~ of** [+ *precautions, enthusiasm, details*] un exceso de • **a sum in ~ of £100,000** una cifra superior a las 100.000 libras • **the painting is expected to fetch in ~ of £100,000** se espera que el cuadro se venda por una cifra superior a las 100.000 libras • **I don't smoke or drink to ~** no fumo ni bebo en exceso • **to carry sth to ~** llevar algo al extremo
2 (= *overindulgence*) excesos *mpl* • **she was sick of her life of ~** estaba harta de su vida de excesos • **the ~es of the regime** los excesos del régimen; (*more serious*) las atrocidades del régimen
3 (*Brit*) (*Insurance*) franquicia *f*
ADJ **1** (= *surplus*) • **always remove ~ fat from pork** quítele siempre el exceso de grasa a la carne de cerdo • **she lost the ~ weight she had gained on holiday** perdió los kilos de más que había engordado durante las vacaciones • **she burns off ~ energy by cycling** quema el exceso de energía montando en bicicleta
2 (= *additional*) [*profit, charge*] extraordinario
CPD ▸ **excess baggage** exceso *m* de equipaje ▸ **excess demand** exceso *m* de demanda ▸ **excess fare** suplemento *m* ▸ **excess luggage** = **excess baggage** ▸ **excess postage** (*Brit*) insuficiencia *f* de franqueo ▸ **excess profits tax** impuesto *m* sobre los beneficios extraordinarios ▸ **excess supply** exceso *m* de oferta ▸ **excess weight** exceso *m* de peso

excessive [ɪk'sesɪv] ADJ [*amount, use, consumption, heat*] excesivo; [*demands, interest, ambition*] excesivo, desmesurado; [*price*] excesivo, abusivo • **the use of ~ force by the police** el uso excesivo de la fuerza por parte de la policía • **the accident was caused by the driver's ~ speed** el exceso de velocidad con que iba el conductor causó el accidente • **the dangers of ~ drinking** los peligros de beber en exceso • **£10? that's a bit ~** ¿10 libras? eso es un poco exagerado, ¿10 libras? eso es pasarse*

excessively [ɪk'sesɪvlɪ] ADV [*eat, smoke, worry, spend*] demasiado, en exceso; [*ambitious, optimistic, proud, cautious*] excesivamente • **prices are ~ high** los precios son excesivamente *or* demasiado altos

exchange [ɪks'tʃeɪndʒ] N **1** (= *act*) [*of prisoners, publications, stamps*] intercambio *m*, canje *m*; [*of ideas, information, contracts*] intercambio *m* • **in ~ for** a cambio de • **~ of gunfire** tiroteo *m* • **~ of views** cambio *m* de impresiones • **~ of words** diálogo *m*
2 (= *barter*) trueque *m*
3 (*Econ*) [*of currency*] cambio *m* • **foreign ~** (= *money*) divisas *fpl*, moneda *f* extranjera
4 (= *building*) (*for trade in corn, cotton*) lonja *f*; (= *stock exchange*) bolsa *f* • **(telephone) ~** (*public*) central *f* telefónica; (*private*) centralita *f*, conmutador *m* (*LAm*)
VT **1** (*gen*) cambiar (**for** por); [+ *prisoners, publications, stamps*] canjear (**for** por, **with** con); [+ *greetings, shots*] cambiar; [+ *courtesies*] hacerse; [+ *blows*] darse • **we ~d glances** nos miramos el uno al otro, cruzamos una mirada
2 (= *barter*) trocar
CPD ▸ **exchange control** control *m* de cambios ▸ **exchange programme, exchange program** (*US*) programa *m* de intercambio ▸ **exchange rate** tipo *m* de cambio ▸ **Exchange Rate Mechanism** mecanismo *m* de paridades *or* de cambio del Sistema Monetario Europeo ▸ **exchange restrictions** restricciones *fpl* monetarias ▸ **exchange student** estudiante *mf* de intercambio ▸ **exchange value** contravalor *m* ▸ **exchange visit** visita *f* de intercambio

exchangeable [ɪks'tʃeɪndʒəbl] ADJ cambiable; [*prisoners, publications, stamps*] canjeable

exchequer [ɪks'tʃekəʳ] N (= *government department*) hacienda *f*, tesoro *m*; (= *treasury funds*) fisco *m*, fondos *mpl* • **the Exchequer** (*Brit*) (*Pol*) la Hacienda, el Fisco

excisable [ek'saɪzəbl] ADJ tasable

excise[1] ['eksaɪz] N (*also* **excise duty**) impuestos *mpl* indirectos; (*Brit*) (= *department*) • **the Customs and Excise** la Aduana

excise[2] [ek'saɪz] VT **1** (*Med*) (= *remove*) extirpar
2 (= *delete*) suprimir, eliminar

excision [ek'sɪʒən] N (*Med*) extirpación *f*; (= *deletion*) supresión *f*, eliminación *f*

excitability [ɪk'saɪtə'bɪlɪtɪ] N [*of person*] excitabilidad *f*; [*of mood, temperament*] nerviosismo *m*

excitable [ɪk'saɪtəbl] ADJ [*person, creature*] excitable; [*mood, temperament*] nervioso

excite [ɪk'saɪt] VT **1** (= *make excited*) entusiasmar • **what ~s me about the idea is ...** lo que me entusiasma *or* me parece excitante de la idea es ... • **don't ~ yourself, Grandpa** no te excites *or* agites, abuelo
2 (= *arouse*) [+ *curiosity, admiration, envy*] provocar, suscitar; [+ *enthusiasm, interest*] despertar, suscitar; [+ *anger, passion*] provocar; [+ *imagination*] estimular; [+ *desire*] incitar, despertar
3 (*sexually*) excitar
4 (*Phys*) [+ *atom, particle*] excitar
5 (*Med*) [+ *nerve, heart*] excitar

excited [ɪk'saɪtɪd] ADJ **1** (= *exhilarated*) [*adult*] entusiasmado; [*child*] excitado, alborotado; [*voice, chatter*] excitado; [*cry, shout*] de excitación • **I'm very ~ about the new house** la nueva casa me hace mucha ilusión, estoy muy ilusionado *or* entusiasmado con la nueva casa • **to get ~ (about sth)** entusiasmarse (con algo) • **the children are getting ~ about the trip** los niños están cada vez más ilusionados *or* más entusiasmados con la idea del viaje • **don't get ~, I only said she might come** ¡tranquilízate!, solo dije que puede que venga • **it's nothing to get ~ about** no es para tanto
2 (= *agitated*) [*person, animal*] agitado, nervioso; [*crowd*] alborotado; [*state*] de agitación, de nerviosismo; [*voice*] nervioso, excitado • **to get ~** [*person*] excitarse, ponerse nervioso; [*crowd*] alborotarse; [*discussion*] acalorarse • **don't get ~! I'm not suggesting that ...** ¡no te excites! *or* ¡no te pongas nervioso! *or* ¡no te acalores! no estoy sugiriendo que ...
3 (*sexually*) excitado • **to get ~** excitarse
4 (*Phys*) [*atom, molecule*] excitado

excitedly [ɪk'saɪtɪdlɪ] ADV [*wave, shout*] con excitación • **they were talking ~** hablaban muy excitados

excitement [ɪk'saɪtmənt] N
1 (= *exhilaration*) emoción *f*, excitación *f* • **why all the ~?** • **what's all the ~ about?** ¿a qué se debe tanta excitación? • **she's looking for a bit of ~ in her life** está buscando algo de emoción en su vida • **in her ~, she forgot to close the door** con la emoción, se olvidó de cerrar la puerta • **the book has caused great ~ in literary circles** el libro ha causado mucha conmoción en círculos literarios
2 (= *agitation*) agitación *f*, alboroto *m*
3 (*sexual*) excitación *f*

exciting [ɪk'saɪtɪŋ] ADJ **1** (= *exhilarating*) [*experience, day, game*] emocionante; [*idea, possibility, discovery*] apasionante; [*person*] fascinante; [*book, play, film*] emocionante, apasionante • **it was not an ~ prospect** no era una perspectiva muy fascinante • **how ~!** ¡qué ilusión!
2 (*sexually*) excitante

excitingly [ɪk'saɪtɪŋlɪ] ADV [*describe, write*] de manera emocionante • **it was an ~ close finish** la llegada fue muy reñida y emocionante

excl., excl ABBR **1** = **excluding**
2 = **exclusive**

exclaim [ɪks'kleɪm] VT exclamar
VI • **to ~ at sth** exclamar ante algo

exclamation [ˌekskləˈmeɪʃən] N exclamación *f*
CPD ▸ **exclamation mark, exclamation point** (*US*) (*Ling*) signo *m* de admiración

exclamatory [eks'klæmətərɪ] ADJ exclamativo

exclude [ɪks'klu:d] VT **1** (= *keep out*) excluir

2 (= *discount*) [+ *mistakes*] exceptuar; [+ *possibility of error*] evitar
3 (*Scol*) [+ *pupil*] expulsar

excluding [ɪks'klu:dɪŋ] PREP excepto, menos • **everything ~ the piano** todo excepto *or* menos el piano

exclusion [ɪks'klu:ʒən] N exclusión *f* • **to the ~ of** con exclusión de
CPD ▸ **exclusion clause** cláusula *f* de exclusión ▸ **(total) exclusion zone** zona *f* de exclusión (total)

exclusionary [ɪks'klu:ʒənrɪ] ADJ (*frm*) exclusivista • **the club had ~ policies** el club practicaba una política exclusivista

exclusive [ɪks'klu:sɪv] ADJ **1** (= *for nobody else*) [*information, use, interview, pictures*] exclusivo • **an ~ report/story** (*Press*) un reportaje en exclusiva • **to have (the) ~ rights to sth** tener la exclusiva *or* los derechos exclusivos para algo • **many of their designs are ~ to our store** muchos de sus diseños son exclusivos nuestros
2 (= *select*) [*area, club, resort, restaurant*] selecto, exclusivo • **we attended an ~ gathering of theatre people** asistimos a una selecta reunión de gente del teatro
3 (= *undivided*) [*interest, attention*] exclusivo
4 (= *not inclusive*) • **from 1st to 15th ~** del 1 al 15 exclusive • **~ of sth** sin incluir algo, excluyendo algo • **~ of postage and packing** gastos *mpl* de envío y empaquetado exclusivos, sin incluir gastos de envío y empaquetado • **~ of taxes** impuestos *mpl* excluidos, excluyendo los impuestos; ▹ **mutually**
N (*Press*) (= *story*) exclusiva *f*, reportaje *m* en exclusiva

exclusively [ɪks'klu:sɪvlɪ] ADV exclusivamente • **this is not ~ the fault of the government** esto no es culpa del gobierno exclusivamente • **available ~ from ...** de venta exclusiva en ...

exclusiveness [ɪks'klu:sɪvnɪs] N exclusividad *f*

exclusivity [ɪksklu:'sɪvətɪ] N exclusividad *f*

excommunicate [ˌekskə'mju:nɪkeɪt] VT excomulgar

excommunication ['ekskəˌmju:nɪ'keɪʃən] N excomunión *f*

ex-con* [ˌeks'kɒn] N ex presidiario/a *m/f*

excoriate [ɪks'kɔ:rɪeɪt] VT (*frm*) [+ *person, organization, idea*] vilipendiar

excrement ['ekskrɪmənt] N excremento *m*

excrescence [ɪks'kresns] N excrecencia *f*

excreta [eks'kri:tə] NPL excremento *msing*

excrete [eks'kri:t] VT (*frm*) excretar

excretion [eks'kri:ʃən] N (= *act*) excreción *f*; (= *substance*) excremento *m*

excretory [eks'kri:tərɪ] ADJ excretorio

excruciating [ɪks'kru:ʃɪeɪtɪŋ] ADJ **1** [*pain, suffering, noise*] atroz, insoportable
2* (= *very bad*) [*film, speech, party*] horroroso

excruciatingly [ɪks'kru:ʃɪeɪtɪŋlɪ] ADV [*hurt, suffer*] terriblemente • **it was ~ funny** era para morirse de risa • **it was ~ painful** dolía terriblemente

exculpate ['ekskʌlpeɪt] VT exculpar

excursion [ɪks'kɜ:ʃən] N (= *journey*) excursión *f*; (*fig*) digresión *f*
CPD ▸ **excursion ticket** billete *m* de excursión ▸ **excursion train** tren *m* de recreo

excursionist [ɪk'skɜ:ʃənɪst] N excursionista *mf*

excursus [ek'skɜ:sɪz] N excursus *m inv*

excusable [ɪks'kju:zəbl] ADJ perdonable, disculpable

excuse N [ɪks'kju:s] (= *justification*) excusa *f*, disculpa *f*; (= *pretext*) pretexto *m* • **there's no ~ for this** esto no admite disculpa • **it's only an ~** es un pretexto nada más • **on the ~ that ...** con el pretexto de que ... • **to make ~s for sb** presentar disculpas por algn • **he's only making ~s** está buscando pretextos • **he made his ~s and left** presentó sus excusas y se marchó • **he gives poverty as his ~** alega su pobreza • **what's your ~ this time?** ¿qué excusa *or* disculpa me das esta vez?
VT [ɪks'kju:z] **1** (= *forgive*) disculpar, perdonar • **to ~ sb sth** perdonar algo a algn • **~ me!** (*asking a favour*) por favor, perdón; (*interrupting sb*) perdóneme; (*when passing*) perdón, con permiso; (= *sorry*) ¡perdón!; (*on leaving table*) ¡con permiso! • **~ me?** (*US*) ¿perdone?, ¿mande? (*Mex*) • **now, if you will ~ me ...** con permiso ... • **if you will ~ me I must go** con permiso de ustedes tengo que marcharme • **may I be ~d for a moment?** ¿puedo salir un momento?
2 (= *justify*) justificar • **that does not ~ his conduct** eso no justifica su conducta • **to ~ o.s. (for sth/for doing sth)** pedir disculpas (por algo/por haber hecho algo)
3 (= *exempt*) • **to ~ sb (from sth/from doing sth)** dispensar *or* eximir a algn (de algo/de hacer algo) • **to ~ o.s. (from sth/from doing sth)** dispensarse (de algo/de hacer algo) • **after ten minutes he ~d himself** después de diez minutos pidió permiso y se fue • **to ask to be ~d** pedir permiso • **I must ask to be ~d this time** esta vez les ruego que me dispensen *or* disculpen

ex-directory [ˌeksdɪ'rektərɪ] (*Brit*) ADJ • **the number is ex-directory** el número no figura en la guía • **they are ex-directory** su número no figura en la guía • **he had to go ex-directory** tuvo que pedir que su número no figurara en la guía

exec [ɪg'zek] N (= **executive**) ejecutivo/a *m/f*

execrable ['eksɪkrəbl] ADJ (*frm*) execrable (*frm*), abominable (*frm*)

execrably ['eksɪkrəblɪ] ADV (*frm*) execrablemente (*frm*)

execrate ['eksɪkreɪt] VT (*frm*) execrar (*frm*), abominar (de) (*frm*)

execration [ˌeksɪ'kreɪʃən] N (*frm*) execración *f* (*frm*), abominación *f* (*frm*)

executable ['eksɪkju:təbl] ADJ ejecutable
CPD ▸ **executable file** (*Comput*) fichero *m* ejecutable

executant [ɪg'zekjʊtənt] N ejecutante *mf*

execute ['eksɪkju:t] VT **1** (= *put to death*) (*gen*) ejecutar; (*by firing squad*) fusilar
2 (= *carry out, perform*) [+ *plan*] llevar a cabo, ejecutar; [+ *work of art*] realizar; [+ *order*] ejecutar, cumplir; [+ *scheme, task, duty*] desempeñar; [+ *will*] ejecutar; [+ *document*] otorgar; (*Comput*) ejecutar

execution [ˌeksɪ'kju:ʃən] N **1** (= *putting to death*) (*gen*) ejecución *f*; (*by firing squad*) fusilamiento *m*
2 (= *carrying out*) [*of plan*] ejecución *f*; [*of act, crime*] comisión *f* • **in the ~ of one's duty** en el cumplimiento de sus deberes

executioner [ˌeksɪ'kju:ʃnə^r] N verdugo *m*

executive [ɪg'zekjʊtɪv] ADJ **1** (= *managerial*) [*powers, role*] ejecutivo; [*position, duties, decision*] directivo, de nivel ejecutivo; [*pay, salaries*] de los ejecutivos; [*offices, suite*] (= *for executives*) para ejecutivos; (= *used by executives*) de los ejecutivos; [*car*] de ejecutivo
2 (*esp Brit**) (= *up-market*) [*briefcase, chair, toy*] de ejecutivo
N **1** (= *person*) ejecutivo/a *m/f* • **a sales ~** un(a) ejecutivo/a de ventas; ▹ **chief**
2 (= *group*) [*of company*] comité *m* ejecutivo; [*of trade union, party*] ejecutiva *f* • **to be on the ~** [*of company*] pertenecer al comité ejecutivo; [*of trade union, party*] pertenecer a la ejecutiva
3 (= *part of government*) poder *m* ejecutivo, ejecutivo *m*
CPD ▸ **executive board** (*Admin, Ind*) junta *f* directiva ▸ **executive chairman** presidente/a *m/f* ejecutivo/a ▸ **executive committee** (*Admin, Ind*) comité *m* ejecutivo ▸ **executive director** (*Brit*) director(a) *m/f* ejecutivo/a ▸ **executive job** puesto *m* de ejecutivo ▸ **executive lounge** (*in airport*) sala *f* ejecutiva ▸ **executive officer** (*US*) (*Mil, Naut*) segundo/a comandante *m/f* ▸ **executive pay** salario *m* de ejecutivo ▸ **executive president** presidente/a *m/f* ejecutivo/a ▸ **executive privilege** (*US*) (*Pol*) inmunidad *f* del poder ejecutivo ▸ **executive producer** (*Cine, Theat, TV*) productor(a) *m/f* ejecutivo/a ▸ **executive secretary** secretario/a *m/f* de dirección

EXECUTIVE PRIVILEGE
Se conoce como **executive privilege** el derecho que tiene el Presidente de Estados Unidos a no revelar cierta información al Congreso o a la judicatura en lo que se refiere a las actividades de su oficina. Suelen alegarse normalmente motivos de seguridad nacional o la necesidad de no desvelar ciertas conversaciones privadas del gobierno, pero no puede pedirse por razones personales. Varios presidentes han pedido durante su mandato que se les concediera este derecho de forma absoluta, pero los tribunales se lo han denegado. Durante el escándalo Watergate, el presidente Richard Nixon intentó acogerse a este derecho para no revelar ciertas grabaciones de conversaciones telefónicas de la Comisión de Investigación del Senado, pero le fue denegado por el Tribunal Supremo.

executor [ɪg'zekjʊtə^r] N [*of will*] albacea *mf*, testamentario/a *m/f*

executrix [ɪg'zekjʊtrɪks] N (PL: **executrixes** *or* **executrices** [ɪgˌzekjʊ'traɪsi:z]) albacea *f*, testamentaria *f*

exegesis [ˌeksɪ'dʒi:sɪs] N (PL: **exegeses** [ˌeksɪ'dʒi:si:z]) exégesis *f*

exemplar ['ɪgzemplɑ:] (*frm*) N **1** (= *example*) ejemplar *m*
2 (= *model*) ejemplo *m*

exemplary [ɪg'zemplərɪ] ADJ ejemplar

exemplification [ɪgˌzemplɪfɪ'keɪʃən] N ejemplificación *f*

exemplify [ɪg'zemplɪfaɪ] VT (= *illustrate*) ejemplificar, ilustrar; (= *be an example of*) demostrar • **as exemplified by his refusal to cooperate** según lo demuestra su negativa de cooperar

exempt [ɪg'zempt] ADJ exento (**from** de) • **to be ~ from paying** estar exento de pagar • **~ from tax** libre de impuestos
VT • **to ~ sth/sb (from sth/from doing sth)** eximir algo/a algn (de algo/de hacer algo), dispensar algo/a algn (de algo/de hacer algo)

exemption [ɪg'zempʃən] N exención *f* (**from** de) • **tax ~** exención *f* de impuestos, exención *f* tributaria
CPD ▸ **exemption certificate** certificado *m* de exención ▸ **exemption clause** (*in contract*) cláusula *f* de exención

exercise ['eksəsaɪz] N **1** (*physical*) (*also Scol*) ejercicio *m* • **to do (physical) ~s** hacer gimnasia • **to take ~** hacer ejercicio
2 (= *carrying out*) ejercicio *m* • **in the ~ of my duties** en el ejercicio de mi cargo
3 (*Mil*) (= *manoeuvres*) maniobras *fpl*
4 exercises (*Sport*) ejercicios *mpl*; (*US*) (= *ceremony*) ceremonia *fsing*
VT **1** (= *use*) [+ *authority, right, influence*] ejercer; [+ *patience, tact*] emplear, hacer uso

de • **to ~ care** tener cuidado, proceder con cautela • **to ~ restraint** contenerse, mostrarse comedido
2 (= *preoccupy*) [+ *mind*] preocupar
3 (*physically*) [+ *muscle, limb*] ejercitar; [+ *horse, team*] entrenar; [+ *dog*] sacar a pasear
VI hacer ejercicio
CPD ▸ **exercise bicycle** bicicleta *f* estática ▸ **exercise bike** = **exercise bicycle** ▸ **exercise book** cuaderno *m* de ejercicios ▸ **exercise class** (= *keep fit class*) clase *m* de gimnasia (*para mantenerse en forma*) ▸ **exercise equipment** aparatos *mpl* de ejercicios ▸ **exercise programme, exercise program** (US) programa *m* de ejercicios ▸ **exercise video** vídeo *m* de ejercicios, video *m* de ejercicios (*LAm*) ▸ **exercise yard** [*of prison*] patio *m*

exercycle [ˈeksəsaɪkl] = **exercise bicycle**

exert [ɪgˈzɜːt] VT [+ *strength, force*] emplear; [+ *influence, authority*] ejercer • **to ~ o.s.** (*physically*) esforzarse (**to do sth** por hacer algo); (= *overdo things*) esforzarse *or* trabajar demasiado • **don't ~ yourself!** (*iro*) ¡no te vayas a quebrar *or* herniar! (*iro*) • **he doesn't ~ himself at all** no hace el más mínimo esfuerzo

exertion [ɪgˈzɜːʃən] N esfuerzo *m*; (= *overdoing things*) esfuerzo *m* excesivo, trabajo *m* excesivo

exeunt [ˈeksɪʌnt] VI (*Theat*) salen, se van

exfoliant [eksˈfəʊlɪənt] N exfoliante *m*

exfoliate [eksˈfəʊlɪeɪt] VT exfoliar
VI exfoliarse

exfoliating cream [eksˈfəʊlɪeɪtɪŋˌkriːm] N crema *f* exfoliante

exfoliation [eksˌfəʊlɪˈeɪʃən] N exfoliación *f*

ex gratia [ˌeksˈgreɪʃə] ADJ [*payment*] ex-gratia, graciable

exhalation [ˌekshəˈleɪʃən] N exhalación *f*

exhale [eksˈheɪl] VT [+ *air, fumes*] despedir
VI espirar

exhaust [ɪgˈzɔːst] N (= *fumes*) gases *mpl* de escape; (*Aut*) escape *m*; (*also* **exhaust pipe**) tubo *m* de escape *m*
VT (*all senses*) agotar • **to be ~ed** estar agotado • **to ~ o.s.** agotarse
CPD ▸ **exhaust fumes, exhaust gases** gases *mpl* de escape ▸ **exhaust system** sistema *m* de escape

exhaustible [ɪgˈzɔːstəbl] ADJ [*resource*] que se puede agotar, limitado

exhausting [ɪgˈzɔːstɪŋ] ADJ agotador

exhaustion [ɪgˈzɔːstʃən] N (= *fatigue*) agotamiento *m*; (= *nervous exhaustion*) postración *f* nerviosa

exhaustive [ɪgˈzɔːstɪv] ADJ exhaustivo

exhaustively [ɪgˈzɔːstɪvlɪ] ADV de modo exhaustivo, exhaustivamente

exhaustiveness [ɪgˈzɔːstɪvnɪs] N exhaustividad *f*

exhibit [ɪgˈzɪbɪt] N (= *painting, object*) (*in museum, art gallery*) objeto *m* expuesto; (*Jur*) prueba *f* instrumental, documento *m* • **to be on ~** estar expuesto
VT [+ *painting, object*] exponer; [+ *film*] exhibir, presentar; [+ *signs of emotion*] mostrar, manifestar; [+ *courage, skill, ingenuity*] demostrar
VI [*painter, sculptor*] exponer (sus obras)

exhibition [ˌeksɪˈbɪʃən] N **1** (= *act, instance*) manifestación *f*; (= *public show*) exposición *f* • **to be on ~** estar expuesto • **to make an ~ of o.s.** quedar en ridículo • **an ~ of bad temper** una demostración de mal genio
2 (*Brit*) (*Univ*) beca *f*
CPD ▸ **exhibition centre** centro *m* de exposiciones ▸ **exhibition game** partido *m* de exhibición ▸ **exhibition match** = **exhibition game**

exhibitionism [ˌeksɪˈbɪʃənɪzəm] N exhibicionismo *m*

exhibitionist [ˌeksɪˈbɪʃənɪst] ADJ exhibicionista
N exhibicionista *mf*

exhibitor [ɪgˈzɪbɪtəʳ] N expositor(a) *m/f*

exhilarate [ɪgˈzɪləreɪt] VT alegrar, entusiasmar • **to feel ~d** sentirse muy entusiasmado *or* alegre

exhilarating [ɪgˈzɪləreɪtɪŋ] ADJ estimulante, vigorizador

exhilaration [ɪgˌzɪləˈreɪʃən] N (= *elation*) alegría *f*, regocijo *m*; (= *excitement*) excitación *f* • **the ~ of speed** lo emocionante de la velocidad

exhort [ɪgˈzɔːt] VT • **to ~ sb (to sth/to do sth)** exhortar a algn (a algo/a hacer algo)

exhortation [ˌegzɔːˈteɪʃən] N exhortación *f*

exhumation [ˌekshjuːˈmeɪʃən] N exhumación *f*

exhume [eksˈhjuːm] VT exhumar, desenterrar

ex-husband [ˌeksˈhʌzbənd] N ex marido *m*

exigence [ˈeksɪdʒəns] N = **exigency**

exigency [ɪgˈzɪdʒənsɪ] N (= *need*) exigencia *f*; (= *emergency*) caso *m* de urgencia

exigent [ˈeksɪdʒənt] ADJ exigente; (= *urgent*) urgente

exiguous [egˈzɪgjʊəs] ADJ exiguo

exile [ˈeksaɪl] N **1** (= *state*) exilio *m*, destierro *m* • **he spent many years in ~** vivió muchos años en el exilio, vivió muchos años exiliado • **government in ~** gobierno *m* en el exilio • **to send sb into ~** desterrar a algn, mandar a algn al exilio
2 (= *person*) exiliado/a *m/f*, desterrado/a *m/f*
VT desterrar, exiliar

exiled [ˈeksaɪld] ADJ exiliado

exist [ɪgˈzɪst] VI **1** (= *live*) vivir; (= *survive*) subsistir • **I just ~ed from one visit to the next** de una visita a la otra me limitaba a sobrevivir • **to ~ on very little money** vivir *or* subsistir con muy poco dinero • **you can't ~ on packet soup!** no puedes vivir solo a base de sopa de sobre
2 (= *occur, be in existence*) existir • **it only ~s in her imagination** solo existe en su imaginación • **there ~s a possibility that** *or* **the possibility ~s that she is still alive** existe la posibilidad de que siga con vida • **I want to live, not just ~** quiero vivir, no simplemente existir • **to cease to ~** dejar de existir • **to continue to ~** [*situation, conditions, doubt*] persistir; [*institution, person*] (*after death*) seguir existiendo

existence [ɪgˈzɪstəns] N existencia *f*; (= *way of life*) vida *f* • **to be in ~** existir • **to come into ~** nacer • **the only one in ~** el único existente

existent [ɪgˈzɪstənt] ADJ existente, actual

existential [ˌegzɪsˈtenʃəl] ADJ existencial

existentialism [ˌegzɪsˈtenʃəlɪzəm] N existencialismo *m*

existentialist [ˌegzɪsˈtenʃəlɪst] ADJ existencialista
N existencialista *mf*

existing [ɪgˈzɪstɪŋ] ADJ [*customers, products, facilities*] existente; [*law, arrangements, system*] actual, existente • **under ~ circumstances** en las circunstancias actuales *or* existentes

exit [ˈeksɪt] N (= *place, act*) salida *f*; (*esp Theat*) mutis *m inv* • **"no exit"** "prohibida la salida" • **to make one's ~** salir, marcharse
VI (*Theat*) hacer mutis; (*Comput*) salir • **~ Hamlet** vase Hamlet
VT (*Comput*) salir de • **if we have to ~ the plane** (US) si tenemos que abandonar el avión, si tenemos que salir del avión
CPD ▸ **exit interview** entrevista *f* de salida ▸ **exit permit** permiso *m* de salida ▸ **exit poll** (*Pol*) *encuesta de votantes a la salida del colegio electoral* ▸ **exit ramp** (US) vía *f* de acceso ▸ **exit route** (*lit, fig*) salida *f* ▸ **exit sign** (*in building*) señal *m* de salida ▸ **exit strategy** estrategia *f* de salida ▸ **exit visa** visa *f or* visado *m* de salida ▸ **exit wound** orificio *f* de salida

ex nihilo [ˌeksˈnɪhɪləʊ] ADV ex nihilo

exodus [ˈeksədəs] N (*also Rel*) éxodo *m* • **there was a general ~** hubo un éxodo general

ex officio [ˌeksəˈfɪʃɪəʊ] ADV [*act*] ex officio, oficialmente
ADJ [*member*] nato, ex officio

exonerate [ɪgˈzɒnəreɪt] VT • **to ~ sb (from)** [+ *obligations, blame*] exonerar a algn (de)

exoneration [ɪgˌzɒnəˈreɪʃən] N exculpación *f*

exorbitance [ɪgˈzɔːbɪtəns] N exorbitancia *f*

exorbitant [ɪgˈzɔːbɪtənt] ADJ [*rent, price, fee*] exorbitante, abusivo; [*demands*] desorbitado, desmesurado

exorbitantly [ɪgˈzɔːbɪtəntlɪ] ADV exorbitantemente • **it was ~ expensive** era exorbitantemente caro • **to pay sb/charge sb ~** pagar/cobrar a algn una cantidad exorbitante *or* abusiva • **some bosses are paid ~** a algunos jefes se les paga unos salarios exorbitantes • **~ priced shoes** zapatos *mpl* a precios exorbitantes *or* abusivos

exorcise [ˈeksɔːsaɪz] VT = **exorcize**

exorcism [ˈeksɔːsɪzəm] N exorcismo *m*

exorcist [ˈeksɔːsɪst] N exorcista *mf*

exorcize [ˈeksɔːsaɪz] VT **1** [+ *pain, memory*] conjurar
2 [+ *evil spirit*] exorcizar

exoskeleton [ˌeksəʊˈskelɪtən] N exoesqueleto *m*

exotic [ɪgˈzɒtɪk] ADJ [*flower, bird, fruit, food, place*] exótico; [*holiday*] en un lugar exótico
N (*Bot*) planta *f* exótica

exotica [ɪgˈzɒtɪkə] NPL objetos *mpl* exóticos

exotically [ɪgˈzɒtɪklɪ] ADV [*named, dressed, designed*] exóticamente, de forma exótica

exoticism [ɪgˈzɒtɪsɪzəm] N exotismo *m*

expand [ɪksˈpænd] VT **1** [+ *market, operations, business*] ampliar; [+ *metal*] dilatar; [+ *number*] aumentar; [+ *chest*] expandir; [+ *wings*] abrir, desplegar; [+ *influence, knowledge*] aumentar, ampliar
2 (= *develop*) [+ *statement, notes*] ampliar
3 (= *broaden*) [+ *experience, mind*] ampliar, extender; [+ *horizons*] ampliar, ensanchar
VI **1** [*gas, metal, lungs*] dilatarse; [*market, operations, business*] ampliarse • **to ~ (up)on** [+ *notes, story*] ampliar, desarrollar
2 [*person*] (= *relax*) distenderse

expandable [ɪkˈspændəbl] ADJ expandible

expanded [ɪksˈpændɪd] ADJ (*Metal, Tech*) dilatado
CPD ▸ **expanded polystyrene** poliestireno *m* dilatado

expander [ɪksˈpændəʳ] N = **chest expander**

expanding [ɪksˈpændɪŋ] ADJ [*metal*] dilatable; [*bracelet*] expandible; [*market, industry, profession*] en expansión • **the ~ universe** el universo en expansión • **~ file** carpeta *f* de acordeón • **a job with ~ opportunities** un empleo con perspectivas de futuro • **a rapidly ~ industry** una industria en rápida expansión

expanse [ɪksˈpæns] N extensión *f*; [*of wings*] envergadura *f*

expansion [ɪksˈpænʃən] N [*of metal*] dilatación *f*; [*of town, economy, territory*] desarrollo *m*; [*of subject, idea, trade, market*] ampliación *f*, desarrollo *m*; [*of production, knowledge*] aumento *m*, extensión *f*; [*of number*] aumento *m*; (*Math*) desarrollo *m*
CPD ▸ **expansion board** (*Comput*) placa *f* de expansión ▸ **expansion bottle** (*Aut*)

depósito *m* del agua ▸ **expansion bus** (*Comput*) bus *m* de expansión ▸ **expansion card** (*Comput*) tarjeta *f* de expansión ▸ **expansion slot** (*Comput*) ranura *f* para tarjetas de expansión ▸ **expansion tank** (*Aut*) depósito *m* del agua

expansionary [ɪks'pænʃənərɪ] ADJ expansionista, de expansión

expansionism [ɪks'pænʃənɪzəm] N expansionismo *m*

expansionist [ɪks'pænʃənɪst] ADJ expansionista

expansive [ɪks'pænsɪv] ADJ **1** (= *affable*) comunicativo, sociable, expansivo (*liter*) • **he was becoming more ~ as he relaxed** se volvía más comunicativo *or* sociable a medida que se relajaba • **he was in an ~ mood** estaba muy comunicativo *or* sociable
2 (= *broad*) [*area, room*] extenso; [*view*] extenso, amplio • **with an ~ gesture he indicated the wonderful view** abrió los brazos señalando la fantástica vista
3 (= *expanding*) [*economy, phase*] expansivo
4 (*Phys*) expansivo

expansively [ɪks'pænsɪvlɪ] ADV **1** (= *affably*) [*welcome, say, smile*] calurosamente
2 (= *in detail*) [*relate, write*] extensamente • **he talked ~ of his travels** habló extensamente sobre sus viajes, se explayó sobre sus viajes

expansiveness [ɪk'spænsɪvnɪs] N [*of person*] carácter *m* sociable

expat* [eks'pæt] N = **expatriate**

expatiate [eks'peɪʃɪeɪt] VI • **to ~ on sth** hablar extensamente sobre algo

expatriate [eks'pætrɪɪt] N expatriado/a *m/f*
ADJ expatriado
VT desterrar • **to ~ o.s.** expatriarse

expect [ɪks'pekt] VT **1** (= *anticipate, hope for, wait for*) esperar • **I did not know what to ~** yo no sabía qué esperar • **it's not what I ~ed** no es lo que yo esperaba • **you know what to ~** ya sabes a qué atenerte • **we'll ~ you for supper** te esperamos a cenar • **is he ~ing you?** ¿tiene usted cita con él? • **it's easier than I ~ed** es más fácil de lo que esperaba • **to ~ to do sth** esperar hacer algo • **they ~ to arrive tomorrow** esperan llegar mañana • **I ~ him to arrive soon** creo que llegará pronto • **it is ~ed that ...** se espera que (+*subjun*), se prevé que ... • **we ~ great things of him** tenemos depositadas grandes esperanzas en él • **I ~ed as much** • **just what I ~ed** ya me lo imaginaba *or* figuraba • **that was (only) to be ~ed** eso era de esperar • **as was to be ~ed** • **as might have been ~ed** • **as one might ~** como era de esperar • **when least ~ed** el día menos pensado • **~ me when you see me*** no cuentes conmigo
2 (= *suppose*) imaginarse, suponer • **I ~ so** supongo que sí, a lo mejor • **yes, I ~ it is** así tenía que ser • **I ~ it was John** me imagino que fue John • **I ~ she's there by now** me imagino que ya habrá llegado • **I ~ he'll be late** seguro que llega tarde
3 (= *require*) • **to ~ sth (of/from sb)** esperar algo (de algn) • **I think you're ~ing too much of me** creo que esperas demasiado de mí • **to ~ sb to do sth** esperar que algn haga algo • **I ~ you to be punctual** cuento con que serás puntual • **how can you ~ me to sympathize?** ¿y me pides compasión? • **you can't ~ too much from him** no debes esperar demasiado de él • **she can't be ~ed to know that** no se puede esperar *or* pretender que sepa eso • **what do you ~ me to do about it?** ¿qué pretendes que haga yo? • **it is hardly to be ~ed that ...** apenas cabe esperar que (+*subjun*)
VI • **she's ~ing** está encinta, está en estado

expectancy [ɪks'pektənsɪ] N (= *state*) expectación *f*; (= *hope, chance*) expectativa *f* (of de) • **there was a buzz of ~ in the air** había un clima de expectación en el ambiente • **life ~** esperanza *f* de vida

expectant [ɪks'pektənt] ADJ [*person, crowd*] expectante; [*look*] de esperanza • **~ mother** mujer *f* encinta, futura madre *f*

expectantly [ɪks'pektəntlɪ] ADV con expectación

expectation [,ekspek'teɪʃən] N **1** (= *state*) expectación *f* • **in ~ of** en espera de, previendo
2 (= *hope*) expectativa *f*, esperanza *f* • **against** *or* **contrary to all ~(s)** en contra de todos los pronósticos *or* todas las expectativas • **it didn't live up to our ~s** no estuvo a la altura de lo que esperábamos • **the holiday didn't come up to my ~s** las vacaciones no resultaron tan buenas como me esperaba • **the response exceeded all our ~s** la respuesta sobrepasó todas nuestras expectativas • **to fall below one's ~s** no llegar a lo que se esperaba

expected [ɪk'spektɪd] ADJ previsto • **the contract will provide an ~ 900 new jobs** se espera que el contrato cree 900 nuevos puestos de trabajo

expectorant [eks'pektərənt] N expectorante *m*
ADJ expectorante

expectorate [eks'pektəreɪt] VT expectorar

expedience [ɪks'pi:dɪəns], **expediency** [ɪks'pi:dɪənsɪ] N conveniencia *f*, oportunidad *f*; (*pej*) oportunismo *m*

expedient [ɪks'pi:dɪənt] ADJ (= *convenient, politic*) oportuno, conveniente
N recurso *m*

expedite ['ekspɪdaɪt] VT (= *speed up*) [+ *business, deal*] acelerar; [+ *official matter, legal matter*] dar curso a; [+ *process, preparations*] facilitar; [+ *task*] despachar (con prontitud) • **to ~ matters** acelerar las cosas

expedition [,ekspɪ'dɪʃən] N expedición *f* • **to go on a fishing/hunting ~** ir de pesca/caza, hacer una expedición de pesca/caza • **to go on a shopping ~** ir de compras *or* de tiendas

expeditionary [,ekspɪ'dɪʃənrɪ] ADJ expedicionario • **~ force** cuerpo *m* expedicionario

expeditious [,ekspɪ'dɪʃəs] ADJ rápido, pronto

expeditiously [,ekspɪ'dɪʃəslɪ] ADV con toda prontitud

expel [ɪks'pel] VT [+ *air*] (*from container*) arrojar, expeler; [+ *person*] expulsar • **to get ~led** (*from school*) ser expulsado

expend [ɪks'pend] VT [+ *money*] gastar; [+ *time, effort, energy*] dedicar (**on** a); [+ *resources*] consumir, agotar; [+ *ammunition*] usar

expendability [ɪks,pendə'bɪlətɪ] N prescindibilidad *f*

expendable [ɪks'pendəbl] ADJ [*equipment*] fungible; [*person, luxury*] prescindible
NPL **expendables** equipo *m or* material *m* fungible

expenditure [ɪks'pendɪtʃə^r] N [*of money*] gasto *m*, desembolso *m*; [*of time, effort*] gasto *m*, empleo *m*; (= *money spent*) gastos *mpl* • **I resent the ~ of time and effort on trivialities** me molesta el empleo de *or* me molesta emplear tiempo y esfuerzo en cosas triviales; ▹ **capital, public**

expense [ɪks'pens] N (= *cost*) gasto *m*, costo *m*; **expenses** gastos *mpl* • **travelling/repair ~s** gastos *mpl* de viaje/reparación • **with all ~s paid** con todos los gastos pagados • **at great ~** gastándose muchísimo dinero • **at my ~** a cuenta mía • **they thought they would have a joke at my ~** querían reírse a costa mía • **at the ~ of** (*fig*) a costa de • **you needn't go to the ~ of buying a new one** no es preciso que te gastes dinero en comprar uno nuevo • **they went to great ~ to send her to a private school** se metieron en muchos gastos para mandarla a un colegio privado • **to meet the ~ of** hacer frente a *or* correr con los gastos de • **he apologized for putting us to so much ~** se disculpó por habernos ocasionado tantos gastos • **regardless of ~** sin escatimar gastos • **to be a great ~ to sb** suponer a algn un gasto importante; ▹ **business**
CPD ▸ **expense account** cuenta *f* de gastos de representación

expensive [ɪks'pensɪv] ADJ [*goods, shop, hobby*] caro • **it is very ~ to live in London** resulta muy caro vivir en Londres • **learning to drive is an ~ business** aprender a conducir sale caro *or* resulta muy costoso • **he has ~ tastes** tiene gustos caros • **she has an ~ lifestyle** lleva un tren de vida caro • **it was an ~ mistake** el error nos ha salido caro

expensively [ɪks'pensɪvlɪ] ADV • **he loves to eat ~** le gusta la comida cara • **she was ~ dressed** vestía con ropa cara • **they had been ~ educated** habían recibido una educación cara • **we can do that fairly easily and not too ~** podemos hacer eso fácilmente y sin gastar mucho *or* y sin que nos cueste mucho • **the room was ~ furnished** la habitación estaba amueblada por todo lo alto

expensiveness [ɪks'pensɪvnɪs] N lo caro

experience [ɪks'pɪərɪəns] N **1** (= *knowledge*) experiencia *f* • **to learn by ~** aprender por la experiencia • **I know from bitter/personal ~** lo sé por mi amarga experiencia/por experiencia propia • **he has no ~ of grief/being out of work** no conoce la tristeza/el desempleo
2 (= *skill, practice*) práctica *f*, experiencia *f* • **he has plenty of ~** tiene mucha práctica • **have you any previous ~?** ¿tiene usted experiencia previa? • **practical ~** experiencia *f* práctica • **teaching ~** experiencia *f* docente • **a driver with ten years' ~** un conductor con diez años de experiencia; ▹ **work**
3 (= *event*) experiencia *f*, aventura *f* • **to have a pleasant/frightening ~** tener una experiencia agradable/aterradora • **it was quite an ~** fue toda una experiencia
VT (= *feel*) [+ *emotion, sensation*] experimentar; (= *suffer*) [+ *defeat, loss, hardship*] sufrir; [+ *difficulty*] tener, tropezar con • **he ~s some difficulty/pain in walking** tiene dificultades/dolor al andar • **he ~d a loss of hearing after the accident** después del accidente, sufrió una pérdida del oído

experienced [ɪks'pɪərɪənst] ADJ [*teacher, nurse*] con experiencia • **"experienced drivers required"** "se necesitan conductores con experiencia" • **we need someone more ~** necesitamos a alguien con más experiencia • **she is not ~ enough** no tiene la suficiente experiencia • **to be ~ (in sth/in doing sth)** tener experiencia (en algo/en hacer algo) • **to the ~ eye/ear** para el ojo/oído experto • **with an ~ eye** con ojo experto • **to be sexually ~** tener experiencia sexual

experiential [ɪks,pɪərɪ'enʃəl] ADJ (*Philos*) experiencial

experiment [ɪks'perɪmənt] N (*gen*) experimento *m* • **to perform** *or* **carry out an ~** realizar un experimento • **as an ~** • **by way of ~** como experimento
VI (*gen*) experimentar; (*scientifically*) experimentar, hacer experimentos • **he ~ed**

e

on fellow students experimentó *or* hizo experimentos con sus compañeros • **youngsters who ~ with drugs** jóvenes *mpl* que experimentan con drogas • **~ with different methods to find the best one for you** experimenta *or* prueba con distintos métodos para encontrar el que te va mejor

experimental [eks,perɪ'mentl] ADJ [*science, method, music*] experimental; [*theatre, novel*] vanguardista; [*cinema*] de arte y ensayo • **to be at** *or* **in the ~ stage** estar en la fase experimental • **he gave an ~ tug at the door handle** hizo el experimento de tirar del picaporte

experimentally [eks,perɪ'mentəlɪ] ADV [*study, test, introduce*] experimentalmente, de forma experimental; [*try out*] como experimento • **he lifted the cases ~ to see how heavy they were** hizo el experimento de levantar las maletas para ver lo que pesaban

experimentation [eks,perɪmen'teɪʃən] N experimentación *f*

experimenter [ɪks'perɪmentəʳ] N investigador(a) *m/f*

expert ['ekspɜːt] ADJ [*craftsman, surgeon*] experto, especialista; (*Jur*) [*evidence, witness*] pericial • **we'll need an ~ opinion** necesitaremos la opinión de un experto *or* especialista • **he ran an ~ eye over the photographs** echó un vistazo a las fotografías con ojo experto • **to be ~ at (doing) sth** ser experto en (hacer) algo • **~ system** (*Comput*) sistema *m* experto • **~ valuation** tasación *f* pericial
N experto/a *m/f* • **to be an ~ at (doing) sth** ser un experto en (hacer) algo • **he's an ~ on computers** es un experto en ordenadores • **I'm no ~ on the subject** no soy un experto en la materia • **he's a computer ~** es especialista en ordenadores • **to examine sth with the eye of an ~** examinar algo con ojo experto
CPD ▸ **expert advice** opinión *f* de un experto

expertise [,ekspə'tiːz] N (= *experience*) experiencia *f*; (= *knowledge*) conocimientos *mpl*; (= *skills*) pericia *f*

expertly ['ekspɜːtlɪ] ADV con habilidad, con pericia (*more frm*) • **she drove ~ through the traffic** condujo con habilidad *or* con pericia entre el tráfico • **he handled the controls ~** manejaba expertamente los mandos, manejaba los mandos con la habilidad de un experto

expertness ['ekspɜːtnɪs] N pericia *f*

expiate ['ekspɪeɪt] VT expiar

expiation [,ekspɪ'eɪʃən] N expiación *f*

expiatory ['ekspɪətərɪ] ADJ expiatorio

expiration [,ekspaɪə'reɪʃən] N **1** = **expiry**
2 [*of breath*] espiración *f*
CPD ▸ **expiration date** (= *expiry date*) [*of warranty, visa, contract*] fecha *f* de vencimiento; [*of medicine, food*] fecha *f* de caducidad

expire [ɪks'paɪəʳ] VI **1** (= *end*) [*time, period*] terminar, finalizar; [*ticket, passport*] caducar, vencer; [*lease, contract*] vencer, expirar • **my passport has ~d** mi pasaporte ha caducado *or* vencido
2 (*frm*) (= *die*) expirar
3 (= *breathe out*) espirar

expiry [ɪks'paɪərɪ] N [*of time, period*] terminación *f*, finalización *f*; [*of visa, passport*] vencimiento *m*, caducidad *f*; [*of lease, contract*] vencimiento *m*, expiración *f*
CPD ▸ **expiry date** [*of visa, contract*] fecha *f* de vencimiento; [*of medicine, food item*] fecha *f* de caducidad

explain [ɪks'pleɪn] VT (= *make clear*) [+ *meaning, problem*] explicar; [+ *plan*] explicar, exponer; [+ *mystery*] explicar, aclarar; (= *account for*) [+ *conduct*] explicar, justificar • **I ~ed it to him** se lo expliqué • **that ~s it** eso lo explica, con eso queda todo aclarado • **to ~ o.s.** (*clearly*) explicarse; (*morally*) justificarse, defenderse • **kindly ~ yourself!** ¡explíquese Vd!
VI • **will you call him and ~?** ¿le llamas tú y se lo explicas? • **I tried to ~, but ...** intenté explicárselo, pero ...
▸ **explain away** VT + ADV dar explicaciones (convincentes) de, justificar; (= *excuse*) disculpar • **try and ~ that away!** ¡a ver cómo justificas eso!

explainable [ɪks'pleɪnəbl] ADJ explicable

explanation [,eksplə'neɪʃən] N (= *act, statement*) explicación *f*; [*of plan*] explicación *f*, exposición *f*; [*of problem, mystery*] aclaración *f*; (= *excuse*) disculpa *f* • **what is the ~ of this?** ¿cómo se explica esto? • **there must be some ~** tiene que haber alguna explicación • **to offer** *or* **give an ~** dar explicaciones • **they gave no ~ for the delay** no dieron ninguna explicación por el retraso

explanatory [ɪks'plænətərɪ] ADJ explicativo; [*note*] aclaratorio

expletive [eks'pliːtɪv] N (*Gram*) palabra *f* expletiva; (= *oath*) palabrota *f*, improperio *m*
ADJ (*Gram*) expletivo

explicable [eks'plɪkəbl] ADJ explicable

explicate ['eksplɪkeɪt] VT (*frm*) explicar; [+ *poem, painting*] comentar

explication [,eksplɪ'keɪʃən] N (= *explanation*) explicación *f*

explicit [ɪks'plɪsɪt] ADJ [*instructions, reference, intention*] explícito, claro; [*description, picture*] gráfico; [*statement, denial*] categórico • **the ~ nature of the photographs** el carácter gráfico de las fotos • **to describe sth in ~ detail** describir algo gráficamente • **he was ~ about his intentions** fue explícito *or* claro acerca de sus intenciones • **he was ~ on this point** fue muy claro sobre esto • **sexually ~** con claro contenido sexual

explicitly [ɪks'plɪsɪtlɪ] ADV [*state, mention, acknowledge*] explícitamente, de forma explícita; [*forbid, reject, deny*] categóricamente; [*racist, political*] explícitamente, claramente • **~ sexual photographs** fotografías *fpl* con claro contenido sexual

explicitness [ɪk'splɪsɪtnɪs] N [*of instructions, reference*] carácter *m* explícito, lo explícito; [*of description, picture*] lo gráfico; [*of statement*] lo categórico

explode [ɪks'pləʊd] VI estallar, explotar, hacer explosión; (*fig*) reventar, estallar • **to ~ with laughter** estallar en carcajadas • **to ~ with anger** tener un arrebato de ira • **to ~ with jealousy** tener un ataque de celos
VT **1** hacer estallar, hacer explotar, explosionar
2 (= *refute*) [+ *rumour*] desmentir; [+ *myth, theory*] echar por tierra

exploit ['eksplɔɪt] N hazaña *f*, proeza *f*
VT [ɪks'plɔɪt] [+ *resources*] explotar, aprovechar; (*pej*) [+ *person, situation*] explotar

exploitable [eks'plɔɪtəbl] ADJ explotable

exploitation [,eksplɔɪ'teɪʃən] N explotación *f*

exploitative [eks'plɔɪtətɪv] ADJ explotador

exploiter [eks'plɔɪtəʳ] N explotador(a) *m/f*

exploration [,eksplɔː'reɪʃən] N (*also Med*) exploración *f*; [*of subject*] análisis *m inv*, estudio *m*

exploratory [eks'plɒrətərɪ] ADJ [*surgery, research, study*] exploratorio; [*discussions*] preliminares, de tanteo; [*drilling*] de sondeo

explore [ɪks'plɔːʳ] VT **1** [+ *country*] explorar; (*Med*) examinar
2 (*fig*) [+ *problems, subject*] investigar; [+ *opinion*] sondear • **to ~ every possibility** considerar todas las posibilidades • **to ~ every avenue** estudiar todas las vías posibles
VI explorar

explorer [ɪks'plɔːrəʳ] N explorador(a) *m/f*

explosion [ɪks'pləʊʒən] N **1** (*gen*) explosión *f*; (= *noise*) explosión *f*, estallido *m*
2 (*fig*) (= *outburst*) [*of anger*] arranque *m*, arrebato *m*; [*of laughter*] estallido *m*; [*of feeling, emotion*] arrebato *m* • **there has been an ~ of interest in her books** el interés por sus libros ha experimentado un auge repentino • **population ~** explosión *f* demográfica • **price ~** aumento *m* general de precios

explosive [ɪks'pləʊzɪv] ADJ **1** (*lit*) [*gas, mixture, force*] explosivo • **an ~ device** un artefacto explosivo
2 (*fig*) [*combination, growth*] explosivo; [*situation, issue*] explosivo, candente • **he has an ~ temper** tiene un temperamento explosivo
N explosivo *m*
CPD ▸ **explosive belt, explosives belt** cinturón *m* de explosivos ▸ **explosives expert** artificiero/a *m/f*

explosively [ɪks'pləʊzɪvlɪ] ADV **1** (*lit*) • **sodium reacts ~ with water** el sodio reacciona con el agua produciendo una explosión, el sodio explota en contacto con el agua
2 (*fig*) **a** (= *angrily*) • **"shut up!" — she said ~** —¡cállate! —explotó
b (= *by leaps and bounds*) • **the number of customers has grown ~** el número de clientes ha crecido vertiginosamente

explosiveness [ɪks'pləʊzɪvnɪs] N carácter *m* explosivo

expo ['ekspəʊ] N ABBR (= **exposition**) expo *f*

exponent [eks'pəʊnənt] N [*of idea*] exponente *mf*; [*of cause*] partidario/a *m/f*; (= *interpreter*) intérprete *mf*; (*Gram, Math*) exponente *m*

exponential [,ekspəʊ'nenʃəl] ADJ exponencial

exponentially [,ekspəʊ'nenʃəlɪ] ADV de manera exponencial

export ['ekspɔːt] N (= *act*) exportación *f*; (= *commodity*) artículo *m* de exportación; ▹ **invisible**
VT [eks'pɔːt] exportar
CPD ['ekspɔːt] [*market, goods, permit, licence*] de exportación ▸ **export credit** crédito *m* a la exportación ▸ **export drive** campaña *f* de exportación ▸ **export duty** derechos *mpl* de exportación ▸ **export earnings** ganancias *fpl* por exportación ▸ **export licence, export license** (*US*) permiso *m* de exportación, licencia *f* de exportación ▸ **export sales** ventas *fpl* de exportación ▸ **export trade** comercio *m* de exportación

exportable [eks'pɔːtəbl] ADJ exportable

exportation [,ekspɔː'teɪʃən] N exportación *f*

exporter [eks'pɔːtəʳ] N exportador(a) *m/f*

exporting [ek'spɔːtɪŋ] ADJ exportador
CPD ▸ **exporting company** empresa *f* exportadora ▸ **exporting country** país *m* exportador

expose [ɪks'pəʊz] VT (= *uncover*) dejar al descubierto; (= *leave unprotected*) exponer; (= *display*) exponer, presentar; (*Phot*) exponer; (*fig*) (= *reveal*) [+ *plot, crime*] poner al descubierto; [+ *criminal, imposter*] desenmascarar; [+ *weakness, one's ignorance*] revelar, poner en evidencia • **to be ~d to view** estar a la vista de todos • **to ~ one's**

head to the sun exponer la cabeza al sol • to ~ sb/o.s. to ridicule poner a algn/ponerse en ridículo • to ~ o.s. to [+ risk, danger] exponerse a • to ~ o.s. (sexually) hacer exhibicionismo
exposé [ek'spəʊzeɪ] (N) exposición f, revelación f
exposed [ɪks'pəʊzd] (ADJ) 1 (= unsheltered) [hillside, site, garden] desprotegido, expuesto • the house is in an ~ position la casa está en un lugar desprotegido or expuesto • ~ to the wind desprotegido del viento, expuesto al viento
2 (= vulnerable) desprotegido, expuesto • this leaves the party in an ~ position esto deja al partido en una posición desprotegida or expuesta • ~ to enemy fire expuesto al fuego enemigo
3 (= uncovered) [pipe, brickwork, skin] al descubierto; [nerve] al descubierto, expuesto; [wire] al aire • use on all ~ parts of the body aplíquese en las zonas del cuerpo que estén al descubierto
4 (Phot) [film] (in normal process) expuesto; (= ruined) velado
exposition [ˌekspə'zɪʃən] (N) 1 [of facts, theories] exposición f • to give an ~ of sth hacer una exposición de algo
2 (= exhibition) exposición f
expostulate [ɪks'pɒstjʊleɪt] (VI) protestar, reconvenir • to ~ with sb about sth discutir con algn por algo
(VT) protestar
expostulation [ɪksˌpɒstjʊ'leɪʃən] (N) protesta f
exposure [ɪks'pəʊʒəʳ] (N) 1 (= contact, laying open) (to weather, heat, cold, light) exposición f • this strategy reduces your ~ to risk (Econ) esta estrategia reduce el riesgo al que está expuesto • to die of ~ morir de frío, morir por estar a la intemperie
2 (= disclosure) [of plot] denuncia f; [of imposter, criminal] desenmascaramiento m • to threaten sb with ~ amenazar con desenmascarar or descubrir a algn
3 (= public exposure) publicidad f • he's getting a lot of ~ está recibiendo mucha publicidad; ▷ indecent
4 (= outlook) orientación f • a house with a southerly ~ una casa orientada hacia el sur
5 (Phot) (gen) exposición; (= aperture) abertura f de diafragma; (= speed) velocidad f de obturación; (= photo) foto f, fotografía f
(CPD) ▸ exposure meter (Phot) fotómetro m, exposímetro m
expound [ɪks'paʊnd] (VT) [+ theory, one's views] exponer, explicar
(VI) • to ~ on sth exponer algo en profundidad
ex-president [ˌeks'prezɪdənt] (N) ex presidente/a m/f
express [ɪks'pres] (VT) 1 (verbally, non-verbally) expresar • her eyes ~ed annoyance sus ojos expresaban irritación • they ~ed interest in ... expresaron su interés en ... • he ~ed his surprise at the result expresó su sorpresa ante el resultado • I'd like to ~ my thanks to everyone for ... quiero expresar mi agradecimiento a todos por ... • she had ~ed a wish to meet them había manifestado su deseo de conocerlos • to ~ o.s. expresarse • to ~ o.s. in or through [+ art, music etc] expresarse a través de
2 (= send) [+ letter, parcel] enviar por correo urgente or exprés
3 (Math) (= represent) expresar • here it is ~ed as a percentage aquí está expresado en forma de porcentaje
4 (frm) (= squeeze out) [+ juice] exprimir (from de); [+ milk] sacarse
(ADJ) 1 (frm) (= specific) [purpose, intention] expreso • to give sb ~ instructions to do sth dar instrucciones expresas a algn para que se haga algo • ~ warranty garantía f escrita
2 (= fast) [letter, delivery, mail] urgente, exprés; [laundry, photography service] rápido • to send sth by ~ delivery or mail enviar algo por correo urgente or exprés, enviar algo exprés
(ADV) • to send or post sth ~ enviar algo por correo urgente or exprés • to travel ~ viajar en un tren rápido or expreso
(N) (= train) expreso m, rápido m
(CPD) ▸ express delivery service servicio m de entrega urgente ▸ express train expreso m, rápido m
expression [ɪks'preʃən] (N) (gen, facial) expresión f; (= feeling) expresión f; (= token) señal f; (Ling) frase f, expresión f • she had a puzzled ~ on her face había una expresión de perplejidad en su rostro • as an ~ of gratitude en señal de agradecimiento or gratitud • if you'll pardon the ~ con perdón de la expresión
expressionism [eks'preʃənɪzəm] (N) expresionismo m
expressionist [eks'preʃənɪst] (ADJ) expresionista
(N) expresionista mf
expressionistic [eksˌpreʃə'nɪstɪk] (ADJ) expresionista
expressionless [ɪks'preʃənlɪs] (ADJ) sin expresión, inexpresivo
expressive [ɪks'presɪv] (ADJ) [person, face, language] expresivo; [ability] de expresión • to be ~ of sth (frm) expresar algo • his gesture was ~ of anger su gesto expresaba rabia
expressively [ɪks'presɪvlɪ] (ADV) de forma expresiva, expresivamente
expressiveness [ɪks'presɪvnɪs] (N) expresividad f
expressly [ɪks'preslɪ] (ADV) 1 (= explicitly) [state, inform, deny, forbid] explícitamente, claramente; [instruct] expresamente
2 (= specially) expresamente, especialmente
expresso [ɪk'spresəʊ] (N) = espresso
expressway [ɪks'presweɪ] (N) (US) autopista f
expropriate [eks'prəʊprɪeɪt] (VT) expropiar
expropriation [eksˌprəʊprɪ'eɪʃən] (N) expropiación f
expulsion [ɪks'pʌlʃən] (N) expulsión f • in doing this she was risking ~ (from school) haciendo esto se arriesgaba a que la expulsaran
(CPD) ▸ expulsion order orden f de expulsión
expunge [ɪks'pʌndʒ] (VT) suprimir
expurgate ['ekspəgeɪt] (VT) expurgar
expurgated ['ekspəgeɪtɪd] (ADJ) [version] expurgado
exquisite [eks'kwɪzɪt] (ADJ) 1 [craftsmanship, food, manners] exquisito; [object, ornament] (= beautiful) de una belleza exquisita; (= tasteful) de un gusto exquisito • a woman of ~ beauty una mujer de una belleza exquisita • he has ~ taste tiene un gusto exquisito • in ~ detail con una atención exquisita a los detalles
2 (= keen) [pleasure, irony] exquisito; [joy, pain] muy intenso
exquisitely [eks'kwɪzɪtlɪ] (ADV) 1 (= tastefully) [embroidered, decorated, dressed] con un gusto exquisito; (= skilfully) [made, carved] de forma exquisita • an ~ carved figure of an angel una figura de un ángel tallada de forma exquisita • her dress was ~ detailed su vestido tenía unos detalles exquisitos
2 (as intensifier) • ~ beautiful/delicate de una belleza/delicadeza exquisita • ~ painful sumamente doloroso
ex-service [ˌeks'sɜːvɪs] (ADJ) (Brit) (Mil) retirado del servicio activo
ex-serviceman [ˌeks'sɜːvɪsmən] (N) (PL: ex-servicemen) militar m retirado, ex militar m
ex-servicewoman [ˌeks'sɜːvɪsˌwʊmən] (N) (PL: ex-servicewomen) militar f retirada, ex militar f
ex-smoker [ˌeks'sməʊkəʳ] (N) (US) persona f que ha dejado de fumar
ext (ABBR) 1 (Telec) (= extension) Ext.
2 (= exterior) Ext.
extant [eks'tænt] (ADJ) existente
extemporaneous [ɪksˌtempə'reɪnɪəs], **extemporary** [ɪks'tempərərɪ] (ADJ) improvisado
extempore [eks'tempərɪ] (ADV) de improviso
(ADJ) improvisado
extemporize [ɪks'tempəraɪz] (VI) improvisar
extend [ɪks'tend] (VT) 1 (= stretch out) [+ hand, arm] extender; (to sb) tender, alargar
2 (= offer) [+ one's friendship, help, hospitality] ofrecer; [+ one's thanks, congratulations, condolences, welcome] dar; [+ invitation] enviar; [+ credit] extender, otorgar
3 (= prolong) [+ road, line, visit] prolongar
4 (= enlarge) [+ building] ampliar; [+ knowledge, research] ampliar, profundizar en; [+ powers, business] ampliar, aumentar; [+ frontiers] extender; [+ vocabulary] enriquecer, aumentar
5 (= push to the limit) [+ athlete] pedir el máximo esfuerzo a • that child is not sufficiently ~ed a ese niño no se le exige el rendimiento que es capaz de dar • the staff is fully ~ed el personal trabaja a pleno rendimiento • to ~ o.s. trabajar al máximum, esforzarse
(VI) 1 [land, wall] • to ~ to or as far as extenderse a or hasta, llegar hasta • the farm ~s over 40,000 hectares la finca abarca unas 40.000 hectáreas
2 (fig) • to ~ to abarcar, incluir • does that ~ to me? ¿eso me incluye a mí?
3 [meeting] • to ~ to or into prolongarse hasta • to ~ for prolongarse por espacio de, prolongarse durante
extendable [ɪks'tendɪbl] (ADJ) extensible
extended [ɪks'tendɪd] (ADJ) (= stretched out) extendido; (= prolonged) [stay] prolongado • to grant sb ~ credit conceder a algn un crédito ilimitado • he has been granted ~ leave se le ha concedido una prórroga del permiso
(CPD) ▸ extended family familia f extendida ▸ extended forecast (US) pronóstico m a largo plazo ▸ extended memory (Comput) memoria f extendida ▸ extended play EP m, maxi-single m
extended-play [ɪksˌtendɪd'pleɪ] (ADJ) [record] EP (inv), de duración ampliada • extended-play single maxi-single m
extendible [ɪks'tendəbl] = extendable
extensible [ɪks'tensɪbl] (ADJ) extensible
extension [ɪks'tenʃən] (N) (= act, part added) extensión f; [of powers] ampliación f; [of building] ampliación f; [of road, stay, visit] prolongación f; [of term, contract, credit] prórroga f; (Telec) extensión, interno m (S. Cone), anexo m (S. Cone) • ~ three one three seven, please con la extensión tres uno tres siete, por favor • by ~ por extensión
(CPD) ▸ extension cable, extension cord (US) alargador m, alargadera f ▸ extension courses cursos externos organizados por una universidad ▸ extension ladder escalera f extensible ▸ extension lead (Elec) alargador m, alargadera f ▸ extension number (número m de) extensión f or (Arg,

Uru) interno *m or* anexo (*Chile, Peru*) *m*

extensive [ɪks'tensɪv] ADJ **1** (= *covering large area*) [*grounds, estate, area*] extenso; [*network, tour*] extenso, amplio; [*surgery*] de envergadura; [*burns*] de consideración
2 (= *comprehensive*) [*collection, list*] extenso; [*range, reforms, interests*] amplio; [*enquiry, tests, research*] exhaustivo; [*knowledge*] vasto, amplio • **it got ~ coverage in the British papers** obtuvo una amplia cobertura en la prensa británica
3 (= *considerable*) [*damage, investments*] considerable, importante; [*experience*] amplio, vasto; [*repairs*] de consideración; [*powers*] amplio • **many buildings suffered ~ damage in the blast** la explosión causó daños considerables *or* importantes en muchos edificios • **to make ~ use of sth** usar *or* utilizar algo mucho • **the machine developed a fault after ~ use** la máquina falló después de usarse mucho

extensively [ɪks'tensɪvlɪ] ADV **1** (= *on a large scale*) [*work, travel*] mucho; [*write, speak*] ampliamente, mucho; [*damage*] considerablemente; [*restore, modify*] considerablemente, en gran parte • **he travelled ~ in Mexico** viajó mucho por México • **the story was covered ~ in the papers** la historia tuvo una amplia cobertura en la prensa • **these grapes are grown ~ in Bordeaux** estas uvas se cultivan extensamente en Burdeos
2 (= *in detail*) [*discuss, write*] mucho; [*study, research, revise*] exhaustivamente, a fondo • **I have quoted ~ from the article** he utilizado muchas citas del artículo

extent [ɪks'tent] N **1** (*in space*) [*of land, road*] extensión *f*
2 (= *scope*) [*of knowledge, damage, activities*] alcance *m*; [*of power*] límite *m* • **the ~ of the problem** el alcance *or* la envergadura del problema • **we did not know the ~ of his injuries until later** no tuvimos conocimiento del alcance de sus lesiones hasta más tarde
3 (= *degree*) [*of commitment, loss*] grado *m* • **to what ~?** ¿hasta qué punto? • **to a certain** *or* **to some ~** hasta cierto punto • **to a large ~** en gran parte *or* medida • **to a small ~** en menor grado • **to such an ~ that** hasta tal punto que • **to the ~ of** (= *as far as*) hasta el punto de; (*in money*) por la cantidad de • **to that ~, she is right** en ese sentido, ella tiene razón

extenuate [eks'tenjʊeɪt] VT atenuar, mitigar, disminuir (la gravedad de)

extenuating [eks'tenjʊeɪtɪŋ] ADJ • **~ circumstances** circunstancias *fpl* atenuantes

exterior [eks'tɪərɪəʳ] ADJ [*wall, door, surface*] exterior
N exterior *m*; (= *outward appearance*) apariencia *f*, aspecto *m* exterior • **on the ~** (*lit, fig*) por fuera

exteriorize [eks'tɪərɪəraɪz] VT exteriorizar

exterminate [eks'tɜːmɪneɪt] VT exterminar

extermination [eks,tɜːmɪ'neɪʃən] N [*of people*] exterminio *m*; [*of pests*] exterminación *f*

exterminator [eks'tɜːmɪneɪtəʳ] N (*US*) exterminador *m* de plagas

extern ['ekstɜːn] N (*US*) (*Med*) externo/a *m/f*

external [eks'tɜːnl] ADJ **1** (= *outer*) [*wall, surface*] externo, exterior; [*appearance, injury, gills, skeleton*] externo • **"for external use only"** (*Med*) "de uso tópico *or* externo"
2 (= *outside*) [*world, influences, factor*] externo
3 (= *foreign*) [*affairs, relations*] exterior
N **externals** las apariencias *fpl* • **to judge by ~s** juzgar por las apariencias
CPD ▸ **external account** cuenta *f* con el exterior ▸ **external audit** auditoría *f* externa ▸ **external debt** deuda *f* externa, deuda *f* exterior ▸ **external degree** (*Brit*) (*Univ*) licenciatura *f* por libre ▸ **external examination** examen *m* externo ▸ **external examiner** examinador(a) *m/f* externo/a ▸ **external student** (*Brit*) (*Univ*) alumno/a *m/f* externo/a, alumno/a *m/f* libre ▸ **external trade** comercio *m* exterior

externalize [ɪks'tɜːnəlaɪz] VT [+ *ideas, feelings*] exteriorizar

externally [eks'tɜːnəlɪ] ADV **1** (= *on the outside, outwardly*) por fuera, exteriormente • **~, it looks like a car** por fuera *or* exteriormente parece un coche • **~, he seemed calm** por fuera *or* exteriormente parecía tranquilo
2 (*Med*) [*apply, use*] tópicamente, externamente • **"to be used externally"** "de uso tópico *or* externo" • **to examine a patient ~** hacer un reconocimiento externo de un paciente
3 (*by outsiders*) • **the proofreading is done ~** la corrección de pruebas se hace con personal de fuera • **~ imposed conditions** condiciones impuestas desde el exterior

extinct [ɪks'tɪŋkt] ADJ [*volcano*] extinto, apagado; [*animal, race*] extinto, desaparecido • **to become ~** extinguirse, desaparecer • **dinosaurs are ~** los dinosaurios se extinguieron

extinction [ɪks'tɪŋkʃən] N extinción *f*

extinguish [ɪks'tɪŋgwɪʃ] VT [+ *fire*] extinguir, apagar; [+ *light, cigarette*] apagar; (*fig*) [+ *hope, faith*] destruir; (= *suppress*) [+ *title*] suprimir

extinguisher [ɪks'tɪŋgwɪʃəʳ] N **1** (*for fire*) extintor *m*, extinguidor *m* (*LAm*)
2 (*for candle*) apagador *m*, apagavelas *m inv*

extirpate ['ekstɜːpeɪt] VT extirpar

extirpation [,ekstə'peɪʃən] N extirpación *f*

extn ABBR (*Telec*) (= **extension**) Ext.

extol, extoll (*US*) [ɪks'tɒl] VT [+ *merits, virtues*] ensalzar, alabar; [+ *person*] alabar, elogiar

extort [ɪks'tɔːt] VT [+ *promise, confession*] obtener por la fuerza, arrancar • **to ~ money from sb** extorsionar a algn; (*less formal*) arrancar dinero a algn con amenazas

extortion [ɪks'tɔːʃən] N extorsión *f*, exacción *f*; (*by public figure*) concusión *f*

extortionate [ɪks'tɔːʃənɪt] ADJ [*price*] abusivo, exorbitante; [*demand*] excesivo, desmesurado

extortioner [ɪks'tɔːʃənəʳ], **extortionist** [ɪks'tɔːʃənɪst] N extorsionador(a) *m/f*; (= *official*) concusionario *m*

extra ['ekstrə] ADJ **1** (= *reserve*) de más, de sobra • **take an ~ pair of shoes** lleva un par de zapatos de más *or* de sobra • **take some ~ money just to be on the safe side** coge dinero de más *or* de sobra para más seguridad
2 (= *additional*) más (*inv*), adicional (*more frm*) • **he gave me an ~ blanket** me dio una manta más • **we need two ~ chairs** necesitamos dos sillas más • **they laid on some ~ trains** pusieron algunos trenes adicionales *or* más • **I've set an ~ place at the table** he puesto otro cubierto en la mesa, he puesto un cubierto más en la mesa • **to earn an ~ £20 a week** ganar 20 libras más a la semana • **to go to ~ expense** gastar de más • **to work ~ hours** trabajar horas extra • **the ~ money will come in handy** el dinero extra vendrá bien • **~ pay** sobresueldo *m* • **five tons ~ to requirements** un excedente de cinco toneladas
3 (= *special, added*) excepcional • **you must make an ~ effort** tienes que hacer un esfuerzo excepcional *or* extra • **for ~ whiteness** para una mayor blancura, para conseguir una blancura excepcional • **for ~ safety** para mayor seguridad • **take ~ care!** ¡ten muchísimo cuidado!
4 (= *over, spare*) de más, de sobra • **an ~ chromosome** un cromosoma de más *or* de sobra • **these copies are ~** estas copias sobran
5 (= *not included in price*) • **wine is ~** el vino es aparte *or* no está incluido • **postage and packing ~** los gastos de envío son aparte, gastos de envío no incluidos • **~ charge** recargo *m*, suplemento *m* • **they delivered it at no ~ charge** lo enviaron sin recargo
ADV **1** (= *more*) más • **it is better to pay a little ~ for better quality** es mejor pagar un poco más y ganar en calidad • **you have to pay ~ for a single room** hay que pagar más por una habitación individual, hay un recargo por habitación individual • **wine costs ~** el vino es aparte *or* no está incluido • **send 95p ~ for postage and packing** manda 95 peniques de más para los gastos de envío
2 (= *especially*) extraordinariamente, super* • **to sing ~ loud** cantar extraordinariamente fuerte, cantar super fuerte* • **he did ~ well in the written exam** el examen escrito le salió extraordinariamente bien, el examen escrito le salió super bien* • **he was ~ polite/nice to her** fue super educado/amable con ella*, fue re(te) educado/amable con ella (*esp LAm**) • **to be ~ careful** tener un cuidado excepcional • **~ fine** [*nib*] extrafino • **to work ~ hard** trabajar super duro* • **~ large** [*size*] muy grande • **~ special** muy especial, super especial* • **to take ~ special care over sth** tomar extremadas precauciones en algo • **~ strong** [*bag, glue, mint*] extra fuerte; [*coffee*] super cargado; [*nylon*] reforzado
N **1** (= *luxury, addition*) extra *m* • **(optional) ~s** (*Aut*) extras *mpl*
2 (= *charge*) extra *m* • **there are no hidden ~s** no hay extras escondidos
3 (*Cine*) extra *mf*
4 (*Press*) número *m* extraordinario • **"~, ~! read all about it!"** "¡extra, extra! ¡últimas noticias!"
5 (*US*) (= *gasoline*) súper *f*
6 (*US*) (= *spare part*) repuesto *m*
CPD ▸ **extra time** (*Ftbl*) prórroga *f*

extra... ['ekstrə] PREFIX extra...

extract N ['ekstrækt] (*from book, film*) extracto *m*, fragmento *m*; (*Pharm*) extracto *m*; (*Culin*) [*of beef, yeast*] extracto *m*, concentrado *m* • **~s from "Don Quijote"** (*as book*) selecciones *fpl* del "Quijote"
VT [ɪks'trækt] **1** (= *take out*) [+ *cork, tooth*] sacar; [+ *bullet*] (*from wound*) extraer; [+ *mineral*] extraer, obtener; [+ *juice*] exprimir
2 (= *obtain*) [+ *information, money*] obtener, sacar; [+ *confession*] sacar, arrancar
3 (= *select*) (*from book etc*) seleccionar
4 (*Math*) extraer

extraction [ɪks'trækʃən] N (*gen*) extracción *f* • **of Spanish ~** de extracción española

extractor [ɪks'træktəʳ] N extractor *m*
CPD ▸ **extractor fan** (*Brit*) extractor *m* de humos ▸ **extractor hood** (*Brit*) campana *f* extractora

extracurricular [,ekstrəkə'rɪkjʊləʳ] ADJ (*Scol*) [*activities*] extraescolar

extraditable ['ekstrədaɪtəbl] ADJ sujeto a extradición

extradite ['ekstrədaɪt] VT extraditar • **to ~ sb (from/to)** extraditar a algn (de/a)

extradition [,ekstrə'dɪʃən] N extradición *f*

CPD ▸ **extradition agreement** acuerdo *m* de extradición ▸ **extradition warrant** orden *f* de extradición

extramarital [ˌekstrəˈmærɪtəl] ADJ [*affair, sex*] extramarital, fuera del matrimonio

extramural [ˌekstrəˈmjʊərəl] ADJ [*course*] externo, de extensión; (*Univ*) [*activities*] extracurricular • **Department of Extramural Studies** (*Brit*) (*Univ*) Departamento *m* de Cursos de Extensión

extraneous [eksˈtreɪnɪəs] ADJ [*influence*] extraño, externo; [*issue*] irrelevante, superfluo • **~ to** ajeno a

extranet [ˈekstrənet] N extranet *f*

extraordinaire [eksˌtrɔːdɪˈnɛəʳ] ADJ (*after n*) sin igual • **he's a film-maker ~** es un cineasta como no hay otro igual

extraordinarily [ɪksˈtrɔːdnrɪlɪ] ADV
1 (= *exceptionally*) [*difficult, beautiful, kind*] extraordinariamente
2 (= *strangely*) • **~, nobody was killed in the explosion** lo increíble es que nadie muriese en la explosión

extraordinary [ɪksˈtrɔːdnrɪ] ADJ
1 (= *exceptional*) [*courage, career, skill, person*] extraordinario • **there's nothing ~ about that** eso no tiene nada de extraordinario *or* increíble
2 (= *strange*) [*tale, adventure, action*] increíble, insólito • **it's an ~ building** es un edificio increíble • **I find it ~ that he hasn't replied** me parece increíble que no haya contestado • **how ~!** (= *strange*) ¡qué raro!, ¡qué extraño!; (= *incredible*) ¡es increíble!
3 (*frm*) (= *additional, special*) [*meeting, measure, powers*] extraordinario • **~ general meeting** junta *f* general extraordinaria • **~ meeting of shareholders** junta *f* extraordinaria de accionistas • **~ reserve** (*Econ*) reserva *f* extraordinaria

extrapolate [ɪksˈtræpəleɪt] VT extrapolar • **to ~ sth from sth** extrapolar algo a partir de algo
VI hacer una extrapolación • **to ~ (from sth)** hacer una extrapolación (a partir de algo)

extrapolation [ɪksˌtræpəˈleɪʃən] N extrapolación *f*

extrasensory [ˈekstrəˈsensərɪ] ADJ extrasensorial
CPD ▸ **extrasensory perception** percepción *f* extrasensorial

extraterrestrial [ˌekstrətəˈrestrɪəl] ADJ extraterrestre

extraterritorial [ˈekstrəˌterɪˈtɔːrɪəl] ADJ extraterritorial

extravagance [ɪksˈtrævəgəns] N
1 (= *wastefulness*) derroche *m*, despilfarro *m*
2 (= *indulgence*) extravagancia *f* • **buying a yacht is just an ~** comprar un yate es una extravagancia • **I know it's an ~, but I love lobster** ya sé que es una extravagancia, pero me encanta la langosta • **caviare! I'm not used to such ~** ¡caviar! no estoy acostumbrada a estos lujos
3 (*fig*) [*of praise*] lo excesivo; [*of claim, opinion*] lo extraordinario; [*of behaviour, gesture*] lo extravagante

extravagant [ɪksˈtrævəgənt] ADJ
1 (= *wasteful, lavish*) [*person*] derrochador, despilfarrador; [*taste*] caro; [*lifestyle*] de muchos lujos; [*gift*] caro; [*price*] exorbitante, desorbitado • **I'd love to go but isn't it a bit ~?** me encantaría ir pero ¿no te parece un poco caro?, me encantaría ir pero ¿no te parece una extravagancia? • **it was very ~ of him to buy this ring** se ha pasado comprando este anillo • **to be ~ with electricity/one's money** derrochar electricidad/el dinero
2 (= *exaggerated*) [*praise*] excesivo; [*claim, opinion*] extraordinario; [*behaviour, person, design*] extravagante; [*gesture*] exagerado • **to be ~ in one's praise of sth/sb** excederse elogiando a algo/algn
3 (= *odd*) raro, extravagante • **you have the most ~ ideas** se te ocurren unas ideas de lo más extravagantes *or* raras

extravagantly [ɪksˈtrævəgəntlɪ] ADV
1 (= *wastefully, lavishly*) [*spend*] profusamente, con gran despilfarro; [*live, decorate*] por todo lo alto, con todo lujo • **to use sth ~** derrochar algo • **the room was ~ furnished** la habitación estaba amueblada por todo lo alto *or* con mucho lujo
2 (= *exaggeratedly*) [*praise, thank*] excesivamente, exageradamente; [*dress, behave*] de forma extravagante

extravaganza [eksˌtrævəˈgænzə] N (= *show*) gran espectáculo *m*; (= *film*) película *f* espectacular; (= *building*) espectáculo *m* arquitectónico

extravehicular [ˌekstrəvɪˈhɪkjʊləʳ] ADJ fuera de la nave

extravert [ˈekstrəvɜːt] ADJ, N = **extrovert**

extreme [ɪksˈtriːm] ADJ **1** (= *very great*) [*heat, danger, poverty, discomfort*] extremo; [*care, caution*] sumo, extremo; [*sorrow, anger*] profundo, enorme • **a matter of ~ importance** una cuestión de suma importancia • **in ~ old age** en *or* a una edad muy avanzada
2 (= *exceptional*) [*case, circumstances*] extremo
3 (= *radical*) [*views, opinion*] extremista; [*behaviour*] extremado; [*method, action, measure*] extremo • **the ~ left/right** (*Pol*) la extrema izquierda/derecha • **to be ~ in one's opinions** tener opiniones extremistas • **there's no need to be so ~** no es necesario llegar a esos extremos
4 (= *furthest*) [*point,*] extremo • **the ~ opposite** el extremo opuesto • **winds from the ~ north** vientos de la región más septentrional • **the room at the ~ end of the corridor** la habitación al final del todo del pasillo
N extremo *m* • **she's a woman of ~s** es una mujer de extremos • **to be driven to ~s** verse obligado a tomar medidas extremas • **to go to ~s** tomar medidas extremas • **to go to any ~** llegar a cualquier extremo • **to go from one ~ to the other** pasar de un extremo al otro • **to take** *or* **carry sth to ~s** llevar algo al extremo • **~s of temperature** las temperaturas extremas • **in the ~** (*frm*) en extremo, en sumo grado
CPD ▸ **extreme sports** deportes *mpl* de aventura, deportes *mpl* extremos ▸ **extreme unction** (*Rel*) extremaunción *f*

extremely [ɪksˈtriːmlɪ] ADV sumamente, extremadamente • **it is ~ difficult** es dificilísimo, es sumamente difícil, es extremadamente difícil • **he did ~ well in the exam** el examen le salió sumamente bien • **we are ~ glad** nos alegramos muchísimo • **it's ~ unlikely that you'll win** es muy poco probable que ganes

extremism [ɪksˈtriːmɪzəm] N extremismo *m*

extremist [ɪksˈtriːmɪst] ADJ extremista
N extremista *mf*

extremity [ɪksˈtremɪtɪ] N **1** (= *end*) (*usu pl*) extremo *m*, punta *f*
2 (*fig*) [*of despair etc*] extremo *m* • **in his ~, he went to her for help** ante la necesidad, acudió a ella en busca de ayuda
3 extremities (*Anat*) extremidades *fpl*

extricate [ˈekstrɪkeɪt] VT (= *disentangle*) desenredar; (= *free*) [+ *victim*] rescatar, sacar • **to ~ o.s. from** [+ *difficulty, situation*] lograr salir de • **he ~d himself from her grip** logró soltarse de la mano de ella

extrication [ˌekstrɪˈkeɪʃən] N (*frm*) (*lit*) [*of trapped person, object*] extracción *f*; (*fig*) (*from situation*) salida *f*

extrinsic [eksˈtrɪnsɪk] ADJ extrínseco

extroversion [ˌekstrəˈvɜːʃən] N extroversión *f*

extrovert [ˈekstrəʊvɜːt] ADJ extrovertido
N extrovertido/a *m/f*

extroverted [ˈekstrəʊvɜːtɪd] ADJ (*esp US*) = **extrovert**

extrude [eksˈtruːd] VT extrudir

extrusion [eksˈtruːʒən] N extrusión *f*

exuberance [ɪgˈzuːbərəns] N **1** [*of person*] (= *euphoria*) euforia *f*; (= *enthusiasm*) entusiasmo *m* • **youthful ~** el entusiasmo (excesivo) de la juventud
2 [*of style, painting*] exuberancia *f*; [*of film, music*] vitalidad *f*
3 (*Bot*) (= *vigour*) [*of growth, foliage*] exuberancia *f*

exuberant [ɪgˈzuːbərənt] ADJ **1** [*person*] (= *euphoric*) eufórico; (= *enthusiastic*) entusiasta • **he felt ~** estaba eufórico
2 [*style, colour, painting*] exuberante; [*film, music, show*] lleno de vitalidad
3 (*Bot*) (= *vigorous*) [*growth, foliage*] exuberante

exuberantly [ɪgˈzuːbərəntlɪ] ADV
1 (= *euphorically*) [*laugh, shout*] eufóricamente
2 (*Bot*) (= *vigorously*) [*grow*] de forma exuberante

exude [ɪgˈzjuːd] VT **1** [+ *liquid*] rezumar, exudar; [+ *odour*] desprender
2 (*fig*) [+ *optimism, confidence, enthusiasm*] rebosar; [+ *sympathy, hostility*] rezumar
VI rezumar, exudar

exult [ɪgˈzʌlt] VI • **to ~ in** *or* **at** *or* **over** regocijarse por

exultant [ɪgˈzʌltənt] ADJ [*person, shout, expression*] exultante, jubiloso

exultantly [ɪgˈzʌltəntlɪ] ADV jubilosamente

exultation [ˌegzʌlˈteɪʃən] N exultación *f*, júbilo *m*

ex-wife [ˌeksˈwaɪf] N (PL: **ex-wives**) ex mujer *f*

ex-works [ˌeksˈwɜːks] ADJ (*Brit*) [*price*] franco fábrica, de fábrica, en fábrica

eye [aɪ] N **1** (*gen*) ojo *m* • **to have good eyes** tener buena vista • **to rub one's eyes** restregarse los ojos • **I couldn't believe my (own) eyes** no daba crédito a lo que veían mis ojos • **black eye** ojo *m* morado *or* amoratado • **I gave him a black eye** le puse un ojo morado • **she had a black eye** tenía *or* llevaba un ojo morado • **to catch sb's eye** llamar la atención de algn • **he accidentally caught her eye and looked away** su mirada se cruzó por casualidad con la de ella y apartó la vista • **it was the biggest one I'd ever clapped eyes on** era el más grande que jamás me había echado a la cara • **to cry one's eyes out** llorar a moco tendido *or* a lágrima viva • **there wasn't a dry eye in the house** no había ojos sin lágrimas en todo el teatro • **to have an eye** *or* **a keen eye for a bargain** tener mucha vista *or* buen ojo para las gangas • **we need someone with an eye for detail** nos hace falta alguien que sea meticuloso • **he's got his eye on you** (= *monitoring*) no te quita ojo, no te pierde de vista; (= *attracted to*) te tiene echado el ojo • **I've got my eye on that sofa in the sale** le tengo echado el ojo a ese sofá que vimos en las rebajas • **she had eyes only for me** solo tenía ojos para mí, no tenía ojos más que para mí • **it hits you in the eye** salta a la vista • **in the eyes of** a los ojos de • **in the eyes of the law** a los ojos de la ley • **to keep an eye on sth/sb** (= *watch*) vigilar algo/a algn, echar una mirada a algo/algn; (= *look* *after*) cuidar algo/a algn • **keep your eyes on the road!** ¡no quites los ojos de la carretera! • **I'm keeping an eye on things while the boss is away** yo estoy al cargo del negocio mientras el jefe está fuera • **at eye level** a la altura de los ojos • **to look sb (straight) in the eye** mirar a algn (directamente) a los ojos • **with the naked eye** a simple vista • **he couldn't keep his eyes off the girl** se le fueron los ojos tras la chica • **to keep an eye out** *or* **one's eyes open for sth/sb** estar pendiente de algo/algn • **keep an eye out for the postman** estáte atento *or* pendiente a ver si ves al cartero • **keep an eye out for snakes** cuidado por si hay culebras • **keep your eyes open for bag-snatchers!** ¡mucho ojo, no te vayan a dar el tirón! • **I haven't seen any recently but I'll keep my eyes open** últimamente no he visto ninguno pero estaré al tanto • **I could hardly keep my eyes open** se me cerraban los ojos • **I saw it with my own eyes** lo vi con mis propios ojos • **to be in the public eye** estar a la luz pública • **eyes right/left/front!** ¡vista a la derecha/izquierda/al frente! • **to run one's eye over sth** (*from curiosity*) recorrer algo con la vista; (*checking*) echar un vistazo a algo • **as far as the eye can see** hasta donde alcanza la vista • **it's five years since I last set** *or* **laid eyes on him** hace cinco años que no lo veo • **the sun is in my eyes** me da el sol en los ojos • **he didn't take his eyes off her for one second** no le quitó los ojos de encima ni por un segundo • **with an eye to sth/to doing sth** con vistas *or* miras a algo/a hacer algo • **with an eye to the future** cara al futuro • **use your eyes!*** ¡abre los ojos! • **it happened before my very eyes** ocurrió delante de mis propios ojos • **the grass grows before your very eyes** crece la hierba a ojos vistas • **under the watchful eye of** bajo la atenta mirada de • **to look at sth with** *or* **through the eyes of an expert** ver algo con ojos de experto • IDIOMS: • **he was all eyes** era todo *or* (*LAm*) puros ojos • **to have eyes in the back of one's head** tener ojos en la nuca • **he must have eyes in the back of his head!** ¡no se le escapa una! • **I haven't got eyes in the back of my head** (*iro*) ¿te crees que tengo ojos en la nuca o qué? • **to give sb the (glad) eye*** tirar los tejos a algn con miraditas* • **there's more to this than meets the eye** esto tiene más enjundia de lo que parece, esto tiene su miga • **the decision was one in the eye for the president*** la decisión supuso un auténtico varapalo para el presidente • **to open sb's eyes to sth** abrir los ojos de algn a algo • **to keep one's eyes peeled** estar alerta • **to do sth with one's eyes (wide) open** hacer algo con los ojos abiertos • **to make (sheep's) eyes at sb*** lanzar miraditas insinuantes a algn, hacer ojitos a algn* • **to shut one's eyes to** [+ *truth, evidence, dangers*] cerrar los ojos a; [+ *sb's shortcomings*] hacer la vista gorda a • **I don't see eye to eye with him** no estoy de acuerdo con él • **in the twinkling of an eye** en un abrir y cerrar de ojos • **to be up to one's eyes** (*in work etc*) estar hasta aquí *or* agobiado de trabajo • PROVERB: • **an eye for an eye (and a tooth for a tooth)** ojo por ojo (y diente por diente); ▹ **blind, feast, mind, sight**

2 [*of potato*] yema *f*

3 [*of storm*] ojo *m*

4 (*Sew*) [*of needle*] ojo *m*; [*of hook and eye*] hembra *f* de corchete

(VT) mirar detenidamente, observar • **she eyed him sullenly/with suspicion** lo miró detenidamente con gesto hosco/con recelo • **she eyed the package curiously** observó (detenidamente) el paquete con curiosidad • **I didn't like the way they eyed me up and down** no me gustaba la forma que tenían de mirarme de arriba abajo • **an expensive leather jacket I had been eyeing for some time** una cazadora de cuero muy cara a la que hacía tiempo (que) le había echado el ojo

(CPD) ▸ **eye candy*** regalo *m* para la vista ▸ **eye clinic** clínica *f* oftalmológica ▸ **eye colour** color *m* de los ojos ▸ **eye contact** contacto *m* ocular ▸ **eye cream** crema *f* para los ojos ▸ **eye doctor** (*US*) oculista *mf* ▸ **eye dropper** cuentagotas *m inv* ▸ **eye drops** gotas *fpl* para los ojos ▸ **eye examination** examen *m* de la vista ▸ **eye patch** parche *m* ▸ **eye pencil** lápiz *m* de ojos ▸ **eye shadow** sombra *f* de ojos ▸ **eye socket** cuenca *f* del ojo ▸ **eye test** test *m* visual *or* de visión

▸ **eye up** (VT + ADV) • **he eyed up his fellow passengers** estudió detenidamente *or* pasó revista a sus compañeros de viaje • **he was eyeing the girl up** se comía a la joven con los ojos; ▹ **talent**

eyeball [ˈaɪbɔːl] (N) globo *m* ocular • **to be ~ to ~** (= *in confrontation*) enfrentarse cara a cara • IDIOM: • **to be up to one's ~s in debt** estar hasta arriba de deudas • **to be drugged up to the ~s: they've got him drugged up to the ~s*** lo tienen medicado a tope

(VT) (*US*) clavar la mirada en

eyeball-to-eyeball* [ˌaɪbɔːltəˈaɪbɔːl] (ADJ) • **an eyeball-to-eyeball encounter** un encuentro frente a frente

eyebath [ˈaɪbɑːθ] (N) **1** (= *small bowl*) lavaojos *m inv*

2 (= *action*) baño *m* ocular *or* de ojos

eyebrow [ˈaɪbraʊ] (N) ceja *f* • **to raise one's ~s** arquear las cejas • **he looked at her with raised ~s** la miró asombrado *or* sorprendido • **he never raised an ~ at it** no se sorprendió en lo más mínimo, ni se inmutó • **there were a lot of raised ~s when she was appointed** mucha gente se sorprendió cuando la nombraron a ella

(CPD) ▸ **eyebrow pencil** lápiz *m* de cejas ▸ **eyebrow tweezers** pinzas *fpl* para las cejas

eye-catcher [ˈaɪˌkætʃəʳ] (N) *cosa que llama la atención*

eye-catching [ˈaɪˌkætʃɪŋ] (ADJ) llamativo, vistoso

eyecup [ˈaɪˌkʌp] (N) = **eyebath**

-eyed [aɪd] (ADJ) (*ending in compounds*) de ojos • **green-eyed** de ojos verdes • **one-eyed** tuerto

eyeful [ˈaɪfʊl] (N) • **he got an ~ of mud** el lodo le dio de lleno en el ojo • **get an ~ of this!*** ¡echa un vistazo a esto!, ¡mira esto! • **she's quite an ~!*** ¡está buenísima!*

eyeglass [ˈaɪglɑːs] (N) lente *m or f*; (*worn in the eye*) monóculo *m*; **eyeglasses** (*esp US*) gafas *fpl* (*Sp*), lentes *mpl or fpl* (*LAm*)

eyehole [ˈaɪhəʊl] (N) mirilla *f*

eyelash [ˈaɪlæʃ] (N) pestaña *f*; ▹ **false**

eyelet [ˈaɪlɪt] (N) ojete *m*

eye-level [ˈaɪˌlevəl] (ADJ) [*grill, oven, locker*] en alto

eyelid [ˈaɪlɪd] (N) párpado *m*; ▹ **bat³**

eyeliner [ˈaɪˌlaɪnəʳ] (N) lápiz *m* de ojos, delineador *m* de ojos

eye-opener* [ˈaɪˌəʊpnəʳ] (N) **1** revelación *f*, sorpresa *f* grande • **it was a real eye-opener to** *or* **for me** fue una verdadera revelación para mí

2 (*US*) copa *f* para despertarse

eyepiece [ˈaɪpiːs] (N) ocular *m*

eyeshade [ˈaɪʃeɪd] (N) visera *f*

eyesight [ˈaɪsaɪt] (N) vista *f* • **to have good/poor ~** tener buena/mala vista

eyesore [ˈaɪsɔːʳ] (N) monstruosidad *f*

eyestrain [ˈaɪstreɪn] (N) vista *f* cansada, fatiga *f* visual • **inadequate lighting can cause ~** una iluminación insuficiente puede cansar la vista *or* producir fatiga visual

eyetooth [ˈaɪtuːθ] (N) (PL: **eyeteeth**) colmillo *m* • IDIOM: • **I'd give my eyeteeth for a car like that/to see it*** daría cualquier cosa por un coche como ese/por verlo

eyewash [ˈaɪwɒʃ] (N) (*Med*) colirio *m* • **it's a lot of ~!** ¡es puro cuento!

eyewear [ˈaɪwɛəʳ] (N) (*Comm*) (= *glasses*) gafas *fpl*

eyewitness [ˈaɪˌwɪtnɪs] (N) testigo *mf* presencial *or* ocular

(CPD) ▸ **eyewitness account** relato *m* de un testigo presencial

eyrie [ˈɪərɪ] (N) aguilera *f*

Ezekiel [ɪˈziːkɪəl] (N) Ezequiel

e-zine [ˈiːziːn] (N) (*Internet*) revista *f* electrónica, revista *f* digital

Ff

F[1], f[1] [ef] (N) **1** (= *letter*) F, f *f* • **F for Frederick** F de Francia
2 (*Mus*) • **F** fa *m* • **F major/minor** fa mayor/menor • **F sharp/flat** fa sostenido/bemol
F[2] (ABBR) **1** = **Fahrenheit**
2 (*Rel*) (= **Father**) P., P.e
f[2] (ABBR) **1** (*Math*) = **foot, feet**
2 (= **following**) sig., sgte.
3 (*Bio*) (= **female**) hembra *f*
FA (N ABBR) **1** (*Brit*) (*Sport*) (= **Football Association**) ≈ AFE *f* • **FA Cup** Copa *f* de la FA
2‡ = **Fanny Adams**
fa [fɑː] (N) (*Mus*) fa *m*
FAA (N ABBR) (*US*) = **Federal Aviation Administration**
fab* [fæb] (ADJ) (*Brit*) fabuloso, bárbaro*, macanudo (*S. Cone**), chévere (*Col, Ven**)
Fabian ['feɪbɪən] (ADJ) fabianista
(N) fabianista *mf*
(CPD) ▸ **Fabian Society** Sociedad *f* Fabiana
fable ['feɪbl] (N) fábula *f*
fabled ['feɪbld] (ADJ) legendario, fabuloso
fabric ['fæbrɪk] (N) **1** (= *cloth*) tela *f*, tejido *m*; (*gen*) (= *textiles*) tejidos *mpl*
2 (*Archit*) estructura *f* • **the upkeep of the ~** el mantenimiento (estructural) de los edificios
3 (*fig*) • **the ~ of society** el tejido social, la estructura de la sociedad • **the ~ of Church and State** los fundamentos de la Iglesia y del Estado
(CPD) ▸ **fabric conditioner, fabric softener** suavizante *m* ▸ **fabric ribbon** (*for typewriter*) cinta *f* de tela
fabricate ['fæbrɪkeɪt] (VT) **1** (= *manufacture*) [+ *goods etc*] fabricar
2 (*fig*) inventar; [+ *document, evidence*] falsificar
fabricated ['fæbrɪkeɪtɪd] (ADJ) (= *invented*) [*evidence*] falsificado; [*story*] inventado
fabrication [ˌfæbrɪ'keɪʃən] (N)
1 (= *manufacture*) fabricación *f*
2 (*fig*) invención *f*; [*of document, evidence*] falsificación *f* • **the whole thing is a ~** todo es pura invención *or* un cuento
fabulous ['fæbjʊləs] (ADJ) **1*** (= *incredible*) increíble; (= *wonderful*) fabuloso, estupendo
2 (*liter*) (= *mythical*) [*beast, monster*] fabuloso, de fábula
fabulously ['fæbjʊləslɪ] (ADV) fabulosamente • **~ rich** fabulosamente rico • **it was ~ successful** tuvo un éxito fabuloso
façade [fə'sɑːd] (N) (*Archit*) fachada *f*; (*fig*) apariencia *f*
face [feɪs] (N) **1** (= *part of body*) cara *f*, rostro *m* • **the wind was blowing in our ~s** el viento soplaba de cara • **the bomb blew up in his ~** la bomba estalló delante suyo • **it all blew up in his ~*** (*fig*) le salió el tiro por la culata* • **I could never look him in the ~ again** no tendría valor para mirarle a la cara de nuevo • **to say sth to sb's ~** decirle algo a la cara a algn • **I told him to his ~** se lo dije a la cara • **to bring sb face to face with sb** confrontar algn con algn • **to bring two people face to face** poner a dos personas cara a cara, confrontar a dos personas • **to come face to face with** [+ *person*] encontrarse cara a cara con; [+ *problem, danger*] enfrentarse con • **~ up** boca arriba • IDIOMS: • **to put a brave** *or* (*US*) **good ~ on it** poner al mal tiempo buena cara • **get out of my ~!‡** ¡déjame en paz!* • **to lose ~** quedar mal, desprestigiarse • **to be off one's ~** (*Brit‡*) estar como una cuba* • **to put one's ~ on*** maquillarse, pintarse • **to save ~** salvar las apariencias, quedar bien • **to set one's ~ against sth** oponerse resueltamente a algo • **to show one's ~** dejarse ver • **shut your ~!‡** ¡cállate la boca!*, ¡calla la boca!*; ▹ **blue, egg, laugh, plain, pretty, slap, stuff**
2 (= *expression*) cara *f*, expresión *f* • **a happy ~** una cara alegre *or* de Pascua • **his ~ fell** puso cara larga • **a long ~** una cara larga • **to make** *or* **pull ~s (at sb)** hacer muecas (a algn) • **to pull a (wry) ~** poner mala cara; ▹ **straight**
3 (= *person*) cara *f* • **there were plenty of familiar ~s at the party** había muchas caras conocidas en la fiesta • **we need some new** *or* **fresh ~s on the team** el equipo necesita sangre nueva
4 (= *surface*) superficie *f*; [*of dial, watch*] esfera *f*; [*of sundial*] cuadrante *m*; [*of mountain, cliff, coin, playing card*] cara *f*; [*of building*] fachada *f*, frente *m* • IDIOM: • **it's vanished off the ~ of the earth** ha desaparecido de la faz de la tierra
5 (= *aspect*) • **the unacceptable ~ of capitalism** los aspectos inadmisibles del capitalismo • **the changing ~ of modern politics** la cambiante fisonomía de la política actual
6 (= *effrontery*) descaro *m*, cara *f*, caradura *f* • **to have the ~ to do sth** tener el descaro de hacer algo
7 (= *typeface*) tipo *m* de imprenta
8 (*in set expressions*) • **~ down(wards)** [*person, card*] boca abajo • **in the ~ of** [+ *enemy*] frente a; [+ *threats, danger*] ante; [+ *difficulty*] en vista de, ante • **on the ~ of it** a primera vista, a juzgar por las apariencias • **~ up(ward)** [*person, card*] boca arriba • IDIOM: • **to fly in the ~ of reason** oponerse abiertamente a la razón
(VT) **1** (= *be facing*) [+ *person, object*] estar de cara a; (= *be opposite*) estar enfrente de • **~ the wall!** ¡ponte de cara a la pared! • **turn it to ~ the fire** gíralo para que esté de cara al fuego • **to sit facing the engine** estar sentado de frente a la locomotora • **they sat facing each other** se sentaron uno frente al *or* enfrente del otro • IDIOM: • **to ~ both ways** dar una de cal y otra de arena
2 [*room, building*] **a** (= *overlook*) dar a, tener vista a • **my room ~s the sea** mi cuarto da al mar
b (= *be opposite to*) [+ *building*] estar enfrente de • **the flat ~s the Town Hall** el piso está enfrente del Ayuntamiento
3 (= *confront*) [+ *enemy, danger, problem, situation*] enfrentarse a; [+ *consequences*] hacer frente a, afrontar • **many people are facing redundancy** muchas personas se ven enfrentadas al desempleo • **I can't ~ him** (*ashamed*) no podría mirarle a los ojos • **we are ~d with serious problems** se nos plantean graves problemas • **he ~s a fine of £200 if convicted** le espera una multa de £200 si lo declaran culpable • **he was ~d with a class who refused to cooperate** se encontraba ante una clase que se negaba a cooperar • **~d with the prospect of living on his own, he …** ante la perspectiva de vivir solo, … • **to ~ facts** aceptar los hechos *or* la realidad • **to ~ the fact that …** reconocer que … • **we will ~ him with the facts** le expondremos los hechos *or* la realidad • **let's ~ it!** ¡seamos realistas!, ¡reconozcámoslo! • IDIOM: • **to ~ the music** afrontar las consecuencias
4 (= *bear, stand*) • **I can't ~ breakfast this morning** hoy no podría desayunar nada • **I can't ~ this alone** no me veo capaz de enfrentar esto solo • **I can't ~ changing jobs again** no me veo capaz de volver a cambiar de trabajo
5 (= *clad*) revestir • **a wall ~d with concrete** una pared revestida de hormigón
6 (*Sew*) (*on inside*) forrar; (*on outside*) recubrir • **the hood is ~d with silk** la capucha está forrada de seda
(VI) **1** [*person, animal*] (= *look*) mirar hacia; (= *turn*) volverse hacia • **~ this way!** ¡vuélvete hacia aquí! • **right ~!** (*US*) (*Mil*) ¡derecha! • **about ~!** (*US*) (*Mil*) ¡media vuelta!
2 [*building*] • **which way does the house ~?** ¿en qué dirección está orientada la casa? • **it ~s east/towards the east** da al este/mira hacia el este
(CPD) ▸ **face card** (*US*) figura *f* ▸ **face cloth** = **face flannel** ▸ **face cream** crema *f* para la cara ▸ **face flannel** (*Brit*) toallita *f*; (= *glove*) manopla *f* (*para lavarse la cara*) ▸ **face mask** mascarilla *f*; (*Cosmetics*) = **face pack** ▸ **face pack** mascarilla *f* facial ▸ **face paint** *pintura ornamental para la cara* ▸ **face painting** (*for children*) pintura *f* facial ▸ **face powder** polvos *mpl* para la cara ▸ **face scrub** = **facial scrub** ▸ **face value** [*of coin, stamp*] valor *m* nominal • IDIOM: • **to take sb at ~ value** juzgar a algn por las apariencias • **I took his statement at (its) ~ value** tomé lo que dijo en sentido literal
▸ **face down** (VT + ADV) (*esp US*) amilanar
▸ **face on to** (VI + PREP) dar a, mirar hacia
▸ **face out** (VT + ADV) • **to ~ it out** afrontar las consecuencias • **to ~ out a crisis** hacer frente a una crisis
▸ **face up to** (VI + PREP) [+ *difficulty*] afrontar, hacer frente a • **to ~ up to the fact that …** reconocer *or* admitir (el hecho de) que … • **she ~d up to it bravely** hizo frente a la

f

situación con valentía

-faced [feɪst] (ADJ) (*ending in compounds*) de cara ... • **brown-faced** de cara morena • **long-faced** de cara larga

faceless ['feɪslɪs] (ADJ) sin rostro; (= *anonymous*) anónimo

facelift ['feɪslɪft] (N) **1** (*Med*) lifting *m*, estiramiento *m* (facial) • **to have a ~** hacerse un lifting
2 (*fig*) reforma *f* (superficial), modernización *f* (ligera) • **to give a ~ to** [+ *building*] remozar, mejorar de aspecto • **the building has had a ~** han remozado el edificio

face-off ['feɪsɒf] (N) confrontación *f*

facer* ['feɪsəʳ] (N) (*Brit*) problema *m* desconcertante • **that's a ~!** ¡vaya problemazo!*

face-saver ['feɪs,seɪvəʳ] (N) maniobra *f* para salvar las apariencias

face-saving ['feɪs,seɪvɪŋ] (ADJ) para salvar las apariencias
(N) • **face-saving is important** importa salvar las apariencias • **this is a piece of blatant face-saving** esto es una maniobra descarada para salvar las apariencias

facet ['fæsɪt] (N) (= *feature*) faceta *f*, aspecto *m*; [*of gem*] lado *m*, faceta *f*

facetious [fə'siːʃəs] (ADJ) [*person*] ocurrente, ingenioso; [*remark*] jocoso, gracioso • **don't be ~** deja de decir frivolidades

facetiously [fə'siːʃəslɪ] (ADV) chistosamente • **he said ~** dijo con mucha guasa

facetiousness [fə'siːʃəsnɪs] (N) guasa *f*, jocosidad *f*

face-to-face [,feɪstə'feɪs] (ADJ) • **a face-to-face argument** un enfrentamiento *or* una discusión cara a cara
(ADV) ▹ **face**

facia ['feɪʃɪə] = **fascia**

facial ['feɪʃəl] (ADJ) de la cara, facial
(N) tratamiento *m* facial
(CPD) ▸ **facial hair** vello *m* facial ▸ **facial scrub** exfoliante *m* facial

facially ['feɪʃəlɪ] (ADV) (= *from a facial point of view*) de cara; (= *with the face*) [*express*] con la expresión (de la cara) • **to be ~ disfigured** tener la cara desfigurada

facie ['feɪʃɪ] ▹ **prima facie**

facile ['fæsaɪl] (ADJ) [*remark, expression*] superficial; [*writer*] vulgar; [*victory*] fácil

facilitate [fə'sɪlɪteɪt] (VT) (= *make easier*) facilitar; (= *assist progress of*) favorecer

facilitator [fə'sɪlɪteɪtəʳ] (N) facilitador(a) *m/f*

facility [fə'sɪlɪtɪ] (N) **1** (= *equipment, place*) instalación *f* • **the hotel's facilities are open to non-residents** las instalaciones del hotel están abiertas a los no residentes • **the flat has no cooking facilities** el piso no está equipado para cocinar • **recreational facilities** instalaciones *fpl* recreativas • **sports facilities** instalaciones *fpl* deportivas
2 (= *service, provision*) servicio *m* • **the main ~ is the library** el servicio principal es la biblioteca • **the company offers day-care facilities for children** la empresa ofrece un servicio de guardería para los niños • **toilet facilities** servicios *mpl*, aseos *mpl* • **transport facilities** servicios *mpl* de transporte
3 (*Econ*) • **credit facilities** facilidades *fpl* (de pago), crédito *m* • **overdraft ~** crédito *m* al descubierto
4 (= *function*) función *f* • **the oven has an automatic timing ~** el horno dispone de una función de reloj automático • **the watch has a stopwatch ~** el reloj también posee la función de cronómetro • **there's a ~ for storing data** dispone de un servicio de almacenamiento de datos
5 (= *centre*) centro *m* • **a state ~ for women prisoners** un centro penitenciario estatal para mujeres • **a medical ~** un centro médico, un punto de asistencia médica • **a nuclear ~** un complejo nuclear
6 (= *talent, ease*) facilidad *f* • **he had a ~ for languages** tenía facilidad para los idiomas, se le daban bien los idiomas • **he writes with great ~** escribe con gran facilidad
7 (= *ability*) habilidad *f*, facultad *f*; (= *capacity*) capacidad *f* • **humans have lost the ~ to use their sense of smell** los humanos han perdido la habilidad *or* la facultad de utilizar el olfato • **the new model has the ~ to reproduce speech** el nuevo modelo tiene la capacidad de *or* es capaz de reproducir el habla

facing ['feɪsɪŋ] (PREP) de cara a, frente a
(ADJ) opuesto, de enfrente • **the houses ~** las casas de enfrente • **on the ~ page** en la página opuesta *or* de enfrente
(N) (*Archit*) paramento *m*, revestimiento *m*; (*Sew*) guarnición *f*; **facings** (*Sew*) vueltas *fpl*

-facing ['feɪsɪŋ] (ADJ) (*ending in compounds*) • **south-facing** con orientación sur, orientado hacia el sur

facsimile [fæk'sɪmɪlɪ] (ADJ) facsímil
(N) facsímile *m*, facsímil *m*
(CPD) ▸ **facsimile machine** máquina *f or* aparato *m* de fax ▸ **facsimile transmission** (transmisión *f* por) fax *m*

fact [fækt] (N) **1** (= *detail, circumstance*) hecho *m* • **the ~ that** ... el hecho de que ... • **the ~ that she knew is not the point** el hecho de que ella lo supiera no viene al caso • **he still loved her in spite of the ~ that she had left him** aunque le había dejado él aún la quería • **my family accepts the ~ that I'm a vegetarian** mi familia acepta que sea vegetariano • **their priority is to establish the ~s of the case** su prioridad es esclarecer los hechos *or* lo que ocurrió realmente • **hard ~s** hechos *mpl* innegables • **to stick to the ~s** atenerse a los hechos
2 (= *piece of information*) dato *m* • **~s and figures** datos *mpl* • **the ~s of life** los detalles de la reproducción • **get your ~s right before you start accusing people** infórmate bien antes de empezar a acusar a la gente • **he accused her of getting her ~s wrong** la acusó de no contar con la información correcta
3 (= *reality*) realidad *f* • **the ~ remains that** ... la realidad sigue siendo que ... • **the ~ (of the matter) is that** ... la verdad *or* el hecho es que ... • **I accept what he says as ~** acepto lo que dice como cierto • **a story founded on ~** una historia basada en hechos verídicos *or* reales • **it has no basis in ~** carece de base (real) • **it's a ~ that** ... es un hecho que ... • **to face (the) ~s** enfrentarse a la realidad *or* los hechos • **he can't tell ~ from fiction** no es capaz de distinguir la realidad de la ficción • **to know for a ~ that** ... saber a ciencia cierta que ... • **in ~** de hecho • **it sounds simple, but in ~ it's very difficult** parece sencillo, pero de hecho *or* en realidad es muy difícil • **I don't like it, as a matter of ~ I'm totally against it** no me gusta, de hecho estoy totalmente en contra • **"don't tell me you like it" — "as a matter of ~ I do"** —no me digas que te gusta —pues sí, la verdad es que sí • **they're very alike, in point of ~ you can't tell the difference** son muy parecidos, de hecho no puedes distinguirlos • **is that a ~!** (*iro*) ¡no me digas! • **he's a dull writer, and that's a ~** es un escritor aburrido, eso no hay quien lo discuta; ▹ **face**
4 (*Jur*) (= *event*) • **before/after the ~** antes/después de los hechos; ▹ **accessory**
(CPD) ▸ **fact sheet** hoja *f* informativa, informe *m*

fact-finding ['fækt,faɪndɪŋ] (ADJ) • **on a fact-finding tour/mission** en viaje/misión de reconocimiento • **a fact-finding committee** una comisión de investigación

faction ['fækʃən] (N) facción *f*

factional ['fækʃənl] (ADJ) [*fighting, violence*] entre distintas facciones

factionalism ['fækʃənəlɪzəm] (N) enfrentamientos *mpl* entre distintas facciones

factionalize ['fækʃənlaɪz] (VT) fragmentar, dividir en facciones
(VI) dividirse en facciones

factious ['fækʃəs] (ADJ) faccioso

factitious [fæk'tɪʃəs] (ADJ) facticio

factitive ['fæktɪtɪv] (ADJ) factitivo, causativo

factor ['fæktəʳ] (N) **1** (= *consideration*) factor *m* • **safety ~** factor *m* de seguridad • **the human ~** el factor humano
2 (*Math*) factor *m* • **highest common ~** máximo común divisor *m* • **to increase by a ~ of five** aumentar cinco veces, multiplicarse por cinco
3 (*Comm*) agente *mf* comisionado/a
(VI) (*Comm*) comprar deudas
▸ **factor in** (VT + ADV) • **to ~ sth in** incluir algo como factor a tener en cuenta
▸ **factor into** (VT + PREP) • **~ it into your decision-making** tenlo en cuenta a la hora de tomar una decisión

factorial [fæk'tɔːrɪəl] (ADJ) factorial
(N) factorial *m or f*

factoring ['fæktərɪŋ] (N) factorización *f*

factory ['fæktərɪ] (N) fábrica *f*
(CPD) ▸ **Factory Acts** (*Brit*) *leyes que regulaban las condiciones de trabajo en las fábricas en el siglo XIX* ▸ **factory farm** granja *f* de cría intensiva ▸ **factory farming** cría *f* intensiva ▸ **factory floor** fábrica *f* • **workers on the ~ floor** trabajadores *mpl* de fábrica • **~ floor opinion** opinión *f* de los obreros ▸ **factory inspector** inspector(a) *m/f* de trabajo ▸ **factory outlet** tienda *f* de fábrica ▸ **factory ship** buque *m* factoría ▸ **factory shop** tienda *f* de fábrica ▸ **factory work** trabajo *m* de fábrica ▸ **factory worker** obrero/a *m/f* industrial

factotum [fæk'təʊtəm] (N) factótum *mf*

factual ['fæktjʊəl] (ADJ) [*report, description*] objetivo, basado en datos objetivos; [*error*] de hecho

factually ['fæktjʊəlɪ] (ADV) objetivamente • **~ speaking, I would say** ... limitándome a los hechos, diría que ...

faculty ['fækəltɪ] (N) **1** (= *power of body, mind*) facultad *f* • **to have** *or* **be in possession of all one's faculties** estar en pleno uso de sus facultades
2 (= *ability*) aptitud *f*, facilidad *f* • **to have a ~ for sth/doing sth** tener aptitud *or* facilidad para algo/hacer algo
3 (*Univ*) facultad *f*; (*esp US*) (*Univ*) (= *teaching staff*) profesorado *m* (de facultad *or* universidad)

fad [fæd] (N) (= *fashion*) moda *f* • **a passing fad** una moda pasajera • **it's just a fad** es la novedad nada más, es una moda pasajera • **the fad for Italian clothes** la moda de la ropa italiana • **he has his fads** tiene sus caprichos

faddish ['fædɪʃ] (ADJ) pasajero, poco duradero

faddy ['fædɪ] (ADJ) (*Brit*) [*person*] que tiene sus manías, difícil de contentar; [*distaste, desire*] idiosincrático

fade [feɪd] (VI) **1** (= *lose colour, intensity*) [*fabric*] desteñirse, perder color; [*colour*] perder intensidad • **"guaranteed not to ~"** "no destiñe" • **the black had ~d to grey** el negro se había vuelto gris • **my tan soon ~d** el

moreno se me quitó pronto • **the light was fading rapidly** estaba oscureciendo rápidamente, la luz se iba rápidamente • **in the fading light he failed to see her** no la vio en la penumbra
2 (*= melt away*) [*sound*] desvanecerse; [*signal*] debilitarse; [*voice, music*] apagarse; (*Cine, TV*) [*image*] fundirse • **the sound of the engine ~d into the distance** el ruido del motor se desvanecía *or* se perdía en la distancia • **her voice ~d to a whisper** su voz se apagó hasta convertirse en un susurro • **the music ~d** la música se fue apagando • **the laughter ~s and we hear birds singing** las risas se apagan *or* se desvanecen y se oye el canto de unos pájaros • **the image ~d** la imagen se fundió, hubo un fundido • **~s to music, production credits** fundido a música y títulos de créditos
3 (*= deteriorate, decline*) [*flower, beauty*] marchitarse; [*organization, culture*] decaer; [*strength*] debilitarse; [*person*] consumirse • **he was unconscious and fading fast** estaba inconsciente y se consumía por momentos • **the team ~d in the second half** el equipo perdió fuerza en el segundo tiempo
4 (*= begin to disappear*) [*hopes, memories, smile*] desvanecerse; [*appeal*] pasarse; [*scar*] borrarse • **he saw his chances fading** veía como se iban agotando sus posibilidades • **once he became used to it the novelty began to ~** cuando se acostumbró a ello dejó pronto de ser una novedad • **he's the sort of person who always ~s into the background** es el tipo de persona que siempre se queda en un segundo plano • **to ~ from sight** *or* **view** perderse de vista
5 (*Aut*) [*engine*] perder potencia
6 (*Sport*) [*ball*] desviarse • **to ~ to the left/right** desviarse a la izquierda/derecha
VT **1** (*= discolour*) [*+ fabric*] desteñir, hacer perder el color a; [*+ colour*] desteñir; [*+ flower*] marchitar
2 (*Cine, TV*) fundir
N (*Cine*) fundido *m* • **~ to music, closing credits** fundido a música y títulos de créditos finales • **~ to black** fundido en negro
▸ **fade away** VI + ADV [*sound, music*] apagarse; [*emotion*] irse apagando; [*sick person*] consumirse • **her voice ~d away** su voz se fue apagando • **the applause ~d away** los aplausos se fueron apagando • **we'd watched her fading away in front of our eyes** la veíamos consumirse delante de nuestros propios ojos • **you'll ~ away if you don't eat more** te vas a quedar en los huesos como no comas más
▸ **fade in** (*Cine, TV*) VT + ADV [*+ image*] meter con un fundido; [*+ sound*] meter poco a poco
VI + ADV [*image*] entrar en fundido (**to** con); [*sound*] entrar (**over** sobre) • **a hymn ~s in over the voices** se oye un himno que entra sobre las voces • **we'll ~ in on a view of the island at dawn** entramos con un fundido de la isla al amanecer
▸ **fade out** VT + ADV (*Cine, TV*) [*+ image*] cerrar en fundido, fundir; [*+ sound*] apagar lentamente, bajar el volumen de
VI + ADV **1** (*Cine, TV*) [*image*] fundirse (**to** en); [*sound*] apagarse, dejar de oírse
2 (*fig*) • **he ~d out of public life when he became ill** al enfermar desapareció de la vida pública
▸ **fade up** VT + ADV = **fade in**

faded ['feɪdɪd] ADJ [*garment*] descolorido, desteñido; [*colour*] apagado, desvaído; [*photograph*] desvaído; [*plant, glory*] marchito

fade-in ['feɪdɪn] N (*Cine, TV*) (entrada *f* en) fundido *m*

fade-out ['feɪdaʊt] N (*Cine, TV*) fundido *m* (en negro), (cierre *m* en) fundido *m*

faecal, fecal (*US*) ['fi:kəl] ADJ fecal
CPD ▸ **faecal matter** materia *f* fecal

faeces, feces (*US*) ['fi:si:z] NPL (*frm*) excrementos *mpl*, heces *fpl* (*frm*)

Faeroes ['fɛərəʊz], **Faeroe Islands** ['fɛərəʊ,aɪləndz] = **Faroes**

faff* [fæf] VI (*Brit*) • **to ~ about** *or* **around** perder el tiempo, ocuparse en bagatelas • **stop ~ing about** *or* **around!** ¡déjate de tonterías!

fag [fæg] N **1** (*Brit**) (*= cigarette*) pitillo* *m*, cigarro *m*
2 (*esp US‡*) (*pej*) (*= homosexual*) marica* *m*
3 (*Brit†**) (*= effort, job*) lata* *f* • **what a fag!** ¡qué lata! • **it's just too much of a fag** la verdad, es mucho trabajo
4 (*Brit*) (*Scol*) *alumno joven que trabaja para otro mayor*
VT* (*also* **fag out**) (*= exhaust*) dejar rendido • **to be fagged (out)** estar rendido
VI • **to fag for sb** (*Brit*) (*Scol*) trabajar para algn
CPD ▸ **fag end*** [*of cigarette*] colilla *f*; (*fig*) (*= remainder*) final *m* ▸ **fag hag‡** *mujer a la que le gusta la compañía de hombres homosexuales*

faggot¹, fagot (*US*) ['fægət] N **1** (*for fire*) haz *m* de leña
2 (*Brit*) (*Culin*) albóndiga *f*

faggot² ** ['fægət] N (*esp US*) (*pej*) (*= homosexual*) marica* *m*

fah [fɑ:] N (*Mus*) fa *m*

Fahrenheit ['færənhaɪt] N Fahrenheit *m* (*termómetro, grados etc*)
CPD ▸ **Fahrenheit thermometer** termómetro *m* de (grados) Fahrenheit

FAI N ABBR = **Football Association of Ireland**

fail [feɪl] VI **1** (*= not succeed*) [*candidate in examination*] suspender; [*plan*] fracasar, no dar resultado; [*show, play*] fracasar; [*business*] quebrar; [*remedy*] fallar, no surtir efecto; [*hopes*] frustrarse, malograrse • **to ~ by five votes** perder por cinco votos • **to ~ in one's duty** faltar a su deber, no cumplir con su obligación
2 [*light*] irse, apagarse; [*crops*] perderse; [*health, sight, voice*] debilitarse; [*strength*] acabarse; [*engine, brakes, mechanism*] fallar, averiarse; [*water supply*] acabarse; [*power supply*] cortarse, fallar • **the light was ~ing** iba anocheciendo
VT **1** [*+ exam, subject*] suspender; [*+ candidate*] suspender (a) • **a ~ed painter** un pintor fracasado
2 (*= let down*) [*+ person*] fallar (a); [*memory, strength*] fallar • **don't ~ me!** ¡no me falles!, ¡no faltes! • **his strength ~ed him** le fallaron las fuerzas • **his heart ~ed him** se encontró sin ánimo • **his courage ~ed him** le faltó valor • **words ~ me!** ¡no encuentro palabras!
3 (*= not succeed*) • **to ~ to be elected** no lograr ser elegido • **to ~ to win a prize** no obtener un premio
4 (*= omit, neglect*) • **to ~ to do sth** no hacer algo, dejar de hacer algo • **don't ~ to visit her** no deje de visitarla
5 (*= be unable*) • **I ~ to see why/what** *etc* no veo *or* alcanzo a ver por qué/qué *etc*
N **1** • **without ~** sin falta
2 (*Univ*) suspenso *m* (**in** en)

failed [feɪld] ADJ [*attempt, coup*] fallido; [*marriage, relationship*] fracasado

failing ['feɪlɪŋ] PREP a falta de • **~ that, ...** de no ser posible, ...
N (*= flaw*) falta *f*, defecto *m* • **the plan has numerous ~s** el plan tiene muchos defectos • **it's his only ~** es su único punto débil
ADJ • **he was in ~ health** su salud era cada vez más débil • **I had to stop work because of ~ eyesight** tuve que dejar de trabajar porque me fallaba la vista • **we reached the top in ~ light** anochecía cuando llegamos a la cumbre • **a ~ marriage** un matrimonio que anda mal

fail-safe ['feɪlseɪf] ADJ [*device*] de seguridad, a prueba de fallos; [*method*] infalible

failure ['feɪljə^r] N **1** (*= lack of success*) fracaso *m*; (*in exam*) suspenso *m*; [*of crops*] pérdida *f*; [*of supplies*] corte *m*, interrupción *f*; [*of hopes*] frustración *f*, malogro *m* • **to end in ~** acabar mal, malograrse (*LAm*) • **it was a complete ~** fue un fracaso total • **the crop was a total ~** la cosecha se perdió por completo; ▹ **power**
2 (*Tech*) fallo *m*, avería *f*; (*Med*) crisis *f inv*, ataque *m*; (*Econ*) quiebra *f*; ▹ **heart**
3 (*= person*) fracasado/a *m/f*
4 (*= neglect*) falta *f* • **his ~ to come** su ausencia, el que no viniera • **~ to pay** incumplimiento *m* en el pago, impago *m*
CPD ▸ **failure rate** (*in exams*) porcentaje *m* de suspensos; [*of machine*] porcentaje *m* de averías

fain†† [feɪn] ADV (*used only with "would"*) de buena gana

faint [feɪnt] ADJ (COMPAR: **fainter**, SUPERL: **faintest**) **1** (*= light, weak*) [*breeze*] débil, ligero; [*outline*] borroso, indistinto; [*trace, mark, line*] tenue; [*colour*] pálido; [*light*] tenue; [*sound*] apagado, débil; [*smell*] tenue, casi imperceptible; [*taste, resemblance*] ligero; [*voice, breathing*] débil; [*hope*] remoto; [*smile*] leve; [*idea, memory*] vago; [*heart*] medroso • **I haven't the ~est idea*** no tengo ni la más remota idea
2 (*Med*) • **to feel ~** marearse, tener vahídos • **she was ~ with hunger** estaba que se desmayaba de hambre
N (*Med*) desmayo *m*, desvanecimiento *m* • **to be in a ~** estar desmayado *or* sin conocimiento • **to fall down in a ~** desmayarse
VI (*Med*) (*also* **faint away**) desmayarse, perder el conocimiento (**from** de) • **he was ~ing with tiredness** estaba que se caía de cansancio

fainthearted ['feɪnt'hɑ:tɪd] ADJ pusilánime, apocado, medroso • **this film is not for the ~** es una película muy fuerte

faintheartedness [,feɪnt'hɑ:tɪdnɪs] N pusilanimidad *f*

fainting fit ['feɪntɪŋ,fɪt] N, **fainting spell** ['feɪntɪŋ,spel] N síncope *m*, desvanecimiento *m*

faintly ['feɪntlɪ] ADV **1** (*= lightly, weakly*) [*call, say*] débilmente; [*breathe, shine*] débilmente, ligeramente; [*write, mark, scratch*] levemente, débilmente
2 (*= slightly*) [*disappointed*] ligeramente • **this is ~ reminiscent of ...** esto me recuerda vagamente a ...

faintness ['feɪntnɪs] N **1** (*= weakness*) [*of light*] tenuidad *f*; [*of outline*] lo indistinto; [*of voice, breathing*] debilidad *f*
2 (*Med*) desmayo *m*, desfallecimiento *m*

fair¹ [fɛə^r] ADJ (COMPAR: **fairer**, SUPERL: **fairest**) **1** (*= just*) [*person, treatment, wage, exchange*] justo; [*decision, report, hearing*] imparcial; [*comment*] razonable, válido; [*sample*] representativo; [*price*] justo, razonable; [*deal*] justo, equitativo; [*fight, election*] limpio; [*competition*] leal • **that's ~ comment** esa es una observación razonable *or* válida • **it's not ~!** ¡no es justo!, ¡no hay derecho! • **it's not ~ to expect you to wash up** no es justo pretender que friegues • **it's ~ to say that ...** es cierto que ..., lo cierto es que ... • **be ~, darling, it's not their fault** sé

justo *or* razonable, cariño, no es culpa suya • **to be ~ ...** (= *truth to tell*) a decir verdad ..., en honor a la verdad ...; (= *not to be unjust*) para ser justo ... • **~ enough!** ¡vale!, ¡muy bien! • **fair's fair, it's my turn now** vale ya *or* ya basta, ahora me toca a mí • **~ game** (*fig*) blanco *m* legítimo • **it's not ~ on the old** es injusto *or* no es justo para (con) los ancianos • **it's only ~ that ...** lo más justo sería que ... • **as is only ~** como es justo • **~ play** (*in game*) juego *m* limpio • **sense of ~ play** (*fig*) sentido *m* de la justicia • **she's had more than her ~ share of problems in life** ha pasado mucho *or* lo suyo en la vida • **they are not paying their ~ share** no están pagando la cantidad que les corresponde *or* que les toca • **to be ~ to sb** ser justo con algn • **that's not true, you're not being ~ to him** eso no es verdad, no estás siendo justo con él • **~ trade** comercio *m* justo • IDIOM: • **by ~ means or foul** por las buenas o por las malas • PROVERB: • **all's ~ in love and war** todo vale en el amor y la guerra
2 (= *reasonable, average*) [*work*] pasable, regular • **she has a ~ chance** tiene bastantes posibilidades • **you've got to give him a ~ chance** le tienes que dar una oportunidad con todas las de la ley • **I have a ~ idea of what to expect** sé más o menos qué esperar • **~ to middling** regular • **"how are you?" — "~ to middling"** —¿qué tal estás? —regular • **he's been given ~ warning** no puede decir que no se le ha avisado
3 (= *quite large*) [*sum, speed*] considerable • **a ~ amount of** bastante • **this happens in a ~ number of cases** esto sucede en bastantes casos • **we've still got a ~ way to go** aún nos queda un buen trecho que recorrer
4 (= *pale, light-coloured*) [*hair, person*] rubio, güero (*Mex*); [*complexion, skin*] blanco, güero (*Mex*)
5 (= *fine, good*) [*weather*] bueno • **if it's ~ tomorrow** si hace buen tiempo mañana • **~ copy** copia *f* en limpio • **to make a ~ copy of sth** hacer una copia en limpio de algo, pasar algo en limpio • **his legal career seemed set ~** su carrera como abogado parecía tener el éxito asegurado • IDIOM: • **in ~ weather or foul** (*referring to present, future*) haga bueno o malo; (*referring to past*) hiciera bueno o malo
6 (*liter*) (= *beautiful*) bello, hermoso • **this ~ city of ours** esta bella ciudad nuestra • **the ~ sex** el bello sexo
ADV **1** • **to play ~** jugar limpio • **to win ~ and square** ganar con todas las de la ley • **it hit the target ~ and square** dio justo en el centro del blanco
2†* (= *positively*) verdaderamente • **we were ~ terrified** estábamos verdaderamente asustados • **it ~ took my breath away** te/os juro que me dejó sin habla*

fair² [fɛəʳ] N **1** (= *market*) feria *f* • **antiques/craft ~** feria *f* de antigüedades/artesanía • **book ~** feria *f* del libro; ▷ **trade**
2 (*Brit*) (= *funfair*) parque *m* de atracciones

STATE FAIR
En todos los estados de EE.UU. se celebra una feria en otoño llamada **state fair** a la que acude gran cantidad de gente de todo el estado. Estas ferias son generalmente agrícolas y en ellas se celebran concursos de animales y productos del campo, de gastronomía y de artesanía. También se organizan juegos y se instalan stands en los que fabricantes y comerciantes hacen demostraciones de sus productos. La feria más grande de todo el país es la Feria de Texas, que se celebra cada octubre en Dallas.

fairground [ˈfɛəgraʊnd] N parque *m* de atracciones
CPD ▸ **fairground ride** atracción *f* (*en parque de atracciones*)

fair-haired [ˈfɛəˈhɛəd] ADJ, **fair-headed** [ˈfɛəˈhedɪd] ADJ [*person*] rubio, güero (*Mex*)

fairly [ˈfɛəlɪ] ADV **1** (= *justly*) justamente, con justicia; (= *impartially*) con imparcialidad; (= *equally*) equitativamente • **our workers are treated ~** tratamos justamente *or* con justicia a nuestros trabajadores • **he always enforced rules ~** siempre aplicó las reglas con imparcialidad • **the blame must be placed ~ and squarely on the shoulders of the government** todo el peso de la culpa debe recaer de lleno sobre el gobierno
2 (= *according to the rules*) [*play*] limpiamente, limpio
3 (= *quite*) bastante • **I'm ~ sure** estoy bastante *or* casi segura • **~ good** bastante bueno
4* (*as intensifier*) verdaderamente • **the literature ~ bulges with illustrations of this** el material publicado está verdaderamente repleto de ilustraciones de esto • **he ~ ran out of the room** poco menos que salió corriendo del cuarto

fairly-traded [ˌfɛəlɪˈtreɪdɪd] ADV [*product, coffee, chocolate*] de comercio justo

fair-minded [ˈfɛəˈmaɪndɪd] ADJ imparcial

fair-mindedness [ˌfɛəˈmaɪndɪdnɪs] N imparcialidad *f*

fairness [ˈfɛənɪs] N **1** (= *justice*) justicia *f*; (= *impartiality*) imparcialidad *f* • **in all ~** (= *truth to tell*) a decir verdad, en honor a la verdad; (= *to be fair*) para ser justo • **in all ~, he had to admit that she had a point** para ser justo con ella, tenía que reconocer que llevaba algo de razón • **in (all) ~ to him** para ser justo con él
2 (= *paleness*) [*of hair, person*] lo rubio; [*of complexion, skin*] blancura *f*
3 (*liter*) (= *beauty*) belleza *f*, hermosura *f*
CPD ▸ **Fairness Doctrine** (*US*) Doctrina *f* de la Imparcialidad

FAIRNESS DOCTRINE
La **Fairness Doctrine** (Doctrina de la Imparcialidad) es un principio llevado a la práctica en Estados Unidos por la **Federal Communications Commission** o **FCC** por el que, cuando se trata de noticias importantes de carácter local o nacional, la radio y la televisión deben ofrecer los distintos puntos de vista de forma equilibrada. Este principio, establecido por la **FCC** en 1949 con el apoyo del Congreso, no tiene carácter de ley y cuenta entre sus atribuciones con el control equitativo del tiempo en los espacios electorales dedicados a cada uno de los líderes políticos en campaña. También se utilizó en 1967 en la lucha antitabaco, cuando la **FCC** estableció que los fabricantes debían dejar claro en sus anuncios los peligros del tabaco, aunque hoy día la **Fairness Doctrine** ya ha dejado prácticamente de tener influencia en publicidad.
▷ **FCC**

fair-sized [ˈfɛəsaɪzd] ADJ bastante grande

fair-skinned [ˌfɛəˈskɪnd] ADJ de tez blanca

fairway [ˈfɛəweɪ] N **1** (*Golf*) calle *f*
2 (*Naut*) canalizo *m*

fair-weather friend [ˌfɛəweðəˈfrend] N amigo/a *m/f* en la prosperidad *or* del buen viento

fairy [ˈfɛərɪ] N **1** (= *creature*) hada *f*
2‡ (*pej*) (= *homosexual*) maricón‡ *m*, marica* *m*
CPD ▸ **fairy cycle** bicicleta *f* de niño ▸ **fairy footsteps** pasos *mpl* ligeros ▸ **fairy godmother** hada *f* madrina ▸ **fairy lights** bombillas *fpl* de colorines ▸ **fairy queen** reina *f* de las hadas ▸ **fairy story, fairy tale** cuento *m* de hadas; (*fig*) (= *lie*) cuento *m*, patraña *f*

fairyland [ˈfɛərɪlænd] N país *m* de las hadas; (*fig*) país *m* de ensueño • **he's living in ~*** vive en la luna

fairytale [ˈfɛərɪteɪl] ADJ [*castle, world*] fantástico, de ensueño
CPD ▸ **fairytale romance** (*fig*) amor *m* de cuento de hadas

fait accompli [ˌfeɪtəˈkɒmplɪ] N hecho *m* consumado

faith [feɪθ] N **1** (*Rel*) fe *f*; (= *doctrine*) creencia *f*, doctrina *f*; (= *sect, confession*) religión *f* • **what ~ does he belong to?** ¿qué religión tiene?
2 (= *trust*) fe *f*, confianza *f* • **to have ~ in sth/sb** tener fe *or* confianza en algo/algn, fiarse de algo/algn • **to put one's ~ in sth/sb** confiar en algo/algn • **to break ~** faltar a la palabra (**with** dada a) • **to keep ~** cumplir la palabra (**with** dada a) • **in (all) good ~** de buena fe • **in bad ~** de mala fe
CPD ▸ **faith healer** curandero/a *m/f* ▸ **faith healing** curación *f* por fe ▸ **faith school** escuela *f* confesional

faithful [ˈfeɪθfʊl] ADJ **1** (*also Rel*) fiel (**to** a); [*friend, servant, spouse*] leal
2 (= *trustworthy*) digno de confianza; [*account*] detallado; [*translation*] fiel
NPL • **the ~** (*Rel*) los fieles

faithfully [ˈfeɪθfəlɪ] ADV [*serve*] fielmente, lealmente; [*describe, translate*] fielmente, con exactitud • **Yours ~** (*Brit*) (*in letter*) le saluda atentamente

faithfulness [ˈfeɪθfʊlnɪs] N fidelidad *f*

faithless [ˈfeɪθlɪs] ADJ desleal, infiel

faithlessness [ˈfeɪθlɪsnɪs] N infidelidad *f*, deslealtad *f*, perfidia *f*

fake [feɪk] N (= *thing, picture*) falsificación *f*; (= *person*) impostor(a) *m/f*, embustero/a *m/f*; (*as term of abuse*) farsante *mf*
ADJ falso
VT **1** [+ *accounts*] falsificar • **to ~ an illness** fingirse enfermo
2 (*US*) (= *improvise*) improvisar
VI fingir, simular

fakir [ˈfɑːkɪəʳ] N faquir *m*

falcon [ˈfɔːlkən] N halcón *m*

falconer [ˈfɔːlkənəʳ] N halconero/a *m/f*

falconry [ˈfɔːlkənrɪ] N halconería *f*, cetrería *f*

Falklander [ˈfɔːlkləndəʳ], **Falkland Islander** [ˌfɔːlklənd'aɪləndəʳ] N habitante *mf* de las islas Malvinas, malvinense *mf*

Falkland Islands [ˈfɔːlklənd,aɪləndz], **Falklands** [ˈfɔːlkləndz] NPL (islas *fpl*) Malvinas *fpl*

fall [fɔːl] (VB: PT: **fell**, PP: **fallen**) N **1** (= *tumble*) caída *f* • **he had a bad ~** sufrió una mala caída • **the Fall** (*Rel*) la Caída • IDIOM: • **to be heading** *or* **riding for a ~** presumir demasiado
2 [*of building, bridge etc*] derrumbamiento *m*; [*of rocks*] desprendimiento *m*; [*of earth*] corrimiento *m* • **a ~ of snow** una nevada
3 (= *decrease*) disminución *f*; (*in prices, temperature, demand*) descenso *m* (**in** de); (*Econ*) baja *f*
4 (= *downfall*) caída *f*, ocaso *m*; (= *defeat*) derrota *f*; [*of city*] rendición *f*, caída *f*; (*from favour, power etc*) alejamiento *m*
5 (= *slope*) [*of ground*] declive *m*, desnivel *m*
6 falls (= *waterfall*) salto *msing* de agua, cascada *fsing*, catarata *fsing* • **Niagara Falls** las cataratas del Niágara
7 (*US*) (= *autumn*) otoño *m*
VI **1** (= *fall down*) [*person, object*] caerse • **to ~**

into the river caerse al río • **to ~ on one's feet** caer de pie; (*fig*) salir bien parado • **to ~ to** *or* **on one's knees** arrodillarse, caer de rodillas
• IDIOMS: • **to ~ on one's ass** (*US***) hacer el ridi* • **to ~ flat** [*joke*] no hacer gracia; [*party*] fracasar; ▹ **flat**
2 (= *drop*) [*leaves, bomb, rain, snow, night*] caer; [*rocks*] desprenderse • **he fell into bed exhausted** se desplomó en la cama, exhausto • **they left as darkness fell** partieron al caer la noche • **to let sth ~** dejar caer algo • **to let ~ that ...** soltar que ... • **night was ~ing** anochecía, se hacía de noche • **it all began to ~ into place** (*fig*) todo empezó a encajar • **to ~ short of sb's expectations** defraudar las esperanzas de algn • **to ~ short of perfection** no llegar a la perfección • **the arrow fell short of the target** la flecha no alcanzó la diana • **to ~ into temptation** sucumbir a la tentación • **to ~ among thieves** (*esp Bible*) ir a parar entre ladrones
3 [*person*] (*morally etc*) caer • **to ~ from grace** (*Rel*) perder la gracia; (*fig*) caer en desgracia
4 (= *slope*) [*ground*] descender, caer en declive
5 (= *hang*) [*hair, drapery*] caer
6 (= *decrease*) disminuir; [*price, level, temperature etc*] bajar, descender; [*wind*] amainar • **at a time of ~ing interest rates** en un período cuando bajan los tipos de interés • **he fell in my estimation** perdió mucho a mis ojos
7 (= *be defeated*) [*government*] caer, ser derrotado; [*city*] rendirse, ser tomado
8 (*liter*) (= *die*) [*soldier*] caer, morir
9 (= *become*) • **to ~ asleep** quedarse dormido, dormirse • **to ~ to bits** (*Brit*) hacerse pedazos+ • **to ~ due** vencer • **to ~ heir to sth** heredar algo • **to ~ ill** caer enfermo, enfermarse • **to ~ in love (with sth/sb)** enamorarse (de algo/algn) • **to ~ open** abrirse • **to ~ to pieces** hacerse pedazos • **to ~ silent** callarse
(CPD) ▸ **fall guy*** (= *easy victim*) víctima *f* (de un truco); (= *scapegoat*) cabeza *f* de turco
▸ **fall about*** (VI + ADV) (*Brit*) (*also* **fall about laughing**) morirse *or* partirse de risa
▸ **fall apart** (VI + ADV) [*object*] caerse a pedazos, deshacerse; [*empire*] desmoronarse; [*scheme, marriage*] fracasar
▸ **fall away** (VI + ADV) **1** (= *slope steeply*) [*ground*] descender abruptamente (**to** hacia)
2 (= *crumble*) [*plaster*] desconcharse; [*cliff*] desmoronarse; [*stage of rocket, part*] desprenderse
3 (= *diminish*) [*numbers etc*] bajar, disminuir; [*enthusiasm*] enfriarse; [*trade, interest*] decaer; (*in quality*) empeorar
▸ **fall back** (VI + ADV) **1** (= *retreat*) retroceder; (*Mil*) replegarse
2 • **it fell back into the sea** volvió a caer al mar
3 [*price etc*] bajar
4 (*fig*) • **to ~ back on sth** [+ *remedy etc*] recurrir a algo • **something to ~ back on** algo a lo que recurrir
▸ **fall backwards** (VI + ADV) caer hacia atrás
▸ **fall behind** (VI + ADV) (*in race etc*) quedarse atrás, rezagarse; (*fig*) (*with work, payments*) retrasarse
▸ **fall down** (VI + ADV) **1** [*person*] caerse (al suelo); [*building*] hundirse, derrumbarse • **to ~ down and worship sb** arrodillarse en adoración a algn
2 (*fig*) (= *fail*) fracasar, fallar • **that is where you fell down** ahí es donde fallaste • **to ~ down on the job** no estar a la altura del trabajo, hacerlo mal
(VI + PREP) • **to ~ down the stairs** caer rodando por la escalera
▸ **fall for*** (VI + PREP) **1** (= *feel attracted to*) [+ *person*] enamorarse de; [+ *object, place*] quedarse encantado con; [+ *idea*] interesarse por
2 (= *be deceived by*) [+ *trick*] dejarse engañar por, tragarse* • **he fell for it** picó*, se lo tragó*
▸ **fall in** (VI + ADV) **1** [*person*] caerse (dentro); [*roof, walls*] desplomarse
2 (*Mil*) formar filas • **~ in!** ¡en filas!
▸ **fall into** (VI + PREP) **1** (= *be divided*) • **it ~s into four parts** se divide en cuatro partes • **it ~s into this category** está incluido en esta categoría • **his poems ~ into three categories** sus poemas se dividen en tres categorías; ▹ **fall**
2 (*fig*) • **to ~ into error/bad habits/bad ways** incurrir en error/adquirir malos hábitos/ coger *or* tomar un mal camino • **to ~ into conversation with sb** entablar conversación con algn
▸ **fall in with** (VI + PREP) **1** (= *meet*) [+ *person*] encontrarse *or* juntarse con
2 (= *agree to*) [+ *plan, proposal etc*] aceptar, quedar de acuerdo con; [+ *opinion*] adherirse a
▸ **fall off** (VI + ADV) **1** (*gen*) caerse; [*part*] desprenderse
2 (= *diminish*) (*in amount, numbers*) disminuir; [*interest*] decaer; [*enthusiasm*] enfriarse; [*quality*] empeorar
(VI + PREP) (*gen*) caerse de; [*part*] desprenderse de
▸ **fall on, fall upon** (VI + PREP) **1** [*accent, stress*] recaer en
2 [*tax etc*] incidir en
3 (*Mil*) caer sobre
4 • **to ~ on one's food** lanzarse sobre la comida, lanzarse a comer • **people were ~ing on each other in delight** todos se abrazaban de puro contentos
5 [*birthday, Christmas etc*] caer en
6 (= *find*) tropezar con, dar con • **to ~ on a way of doing sth** dar por casualidad con la forma de hacer algo
7 (= *alight on*) • **my gaze fell on certain details** me fijé en ciertos detalles
8 (= *be one's duty*) = **fall to**
▸ **fall out** (VI + ADV) **1** [*person, object*] caerse (**of** de)
2 (*Mil*) romper filas
3 (*fig*) (= *quarrel*) • **to ~ out (with sb) (over sth)** enfadarse *or* (*LAm*) enojarse (con algn) (por algo)
4 (= *happen*) • **it fell out that** resultó que • **events fell out (just) as we had hoped** todo salió como habíamos deseado
▸ **fall over** (VI + ADV) [*person, object*] caer, caerse
(VI + PREP) **1** [+ *object*] tropezar con
2 (*fig**) • **he was ~ing over himself** *or* **over backwards to be polite** se desvivía en atenciones • **they were ~ing over each other to get it** se pegaban por conseguirlo
▸ **fall through** (VI + ADV) [*plans etc*] fracasar
▸ **fall to** (VI + PREP) **1** (= *begin*) • **to ~ to doing sth** empezar *or* ponerse a hacer algo • **he fell to wondering if/to thinking (about) ...** empezó a preguntarse si/a pensar (en) ...
2 (= *be one's duty*) corresponder a, tocar a • **it ~s to me to say ...** me corresponde a mí decir ... • **the responsibility ~s to you** la responsabilidad es tuya *or* recae en ti
(VI + ADV) (= *begin working*) ponerse a trabajar; (= *begin eating*) empezar a comer • **~ to!** ¡a ello!, ¡vamos!
▸ **fall upon** (VI + PREP) ▸ **fall on**
fallacious [fəˈleɪʃəs] (ADJ) (= *incorrect*) erróneo; (= *misleading*) engañoso, falaz
fallacy [ˈfæləsɪ] (N) (= *false belief*) falacia *f*; (= *false reasoning*) sofisma *m*, argucia *f*
fallback [ˈfɔːlbæk] (ADJ) • **~ position** segunda línea *f* de defensa; (*fig*) posición *f* de repliegue
fallen [ˈfɔːlən] (PP) *of* **fall**
(ADJ) **1** (*lit*) caído
2 (*morally*) [*woman*] perdido; [*angel*] caído
(NPL) • **the ~** (*Mil*) los caídos
fallibility [ˌfælɪˈbɪlɪtɪ] (N) falibilidad *f*
fallible [ˈfæləbl] (ADJ) falible
falling [ˈfɔːlɪŋ] (ADJ) que cae; (*Comm*) en baja
(CPD) ▸ **falling star** estrella *f* fugaz
falling-off [ˈfɔːlɪŋˈɒf] (N) (*in numbers etc*) disminución *f*; (*in standards*) empeoramiento *m*
falling-out* [ˈfɔːlɪŋˈaʊt] (N) (= *quarrel*) altercado *m*, pelea *f* • **to have a falling-out** pelear
Fallopian tube [fəˌləʊpɪənˈtjuːb] (N) trompa *f* de Falopio
fallout [ˈfɔːlaʊt] (N) **1** [*of radioactivity*] lluvia *f* radiactiva
2 (*fig*) consecuencias *fpl*, repercusiones *fpl*
(CPD) ▸ **fallout shelter** refugio *m* atómico *or* nuclear
fallow [ˈfæləʊ] (ADJ) (*Agr*) en barbecho; (*fig*) [*period*] improductivo • **to lie ~** (*Agr*) estar en barbecho; (*fig*) quedar sin utilizar, no ser utilizado
(N) (*Agr*) barbecho *m*
(CPD) ▸ **fallow deer** gamo *m*
false [fɔːls] (ADJ) **1** (= *untruthful*) [*statement, accusation*] falso; (= *mistaken*) [*idea, assumption, accusation*] equivocado • **to give a ~ impression** dar una impresión falsa • **~ move** movimiento *m* en falso • **one ~ move and you're dead** un movimiento en falso y te mato • **~ note** nota *f* falsa • **a ~ sense of security** una falsa sensación de seguridad • **~ step** paso *m* en falso; ▹ **lull, true**
2 (= *deceitful*) • **under ~ pretences** con engaños, con insidias • **to extort money under ~ pretences** obtener dinero con engaños *or* insidias • **you came here under ~ pretences** viniste aquí con engaños • **to bear ~ witness** (*esp Bible*) levantar falso testimonio
3 (= *inappropriate, insincere*) • **that was ~ economy** fue un mal ahorro • **to give sb ~ hope(s)** dar falsas esperanzas a algn • **to raise ~ hopes** crear falsas esperanzas • **~ modesty** falsa modestia *f* • **~ pride** falso orgullo *m* • **his words rang ~** sus palabras sonaban a falso • **~ smile** sonrisa *f* forzada
4 (= *artificial*) [*hair, eyelashes*] postizo • **a suitcase with a ~ bottom** una maleta con doble fondo • **he registered in** *or* **under a ~ name** se registró bajo un nombre falso
5† (= *disloyal*) [*friend*] desleal, pérfido; (= *unfaithful*) [*lover*] infiel
(CPD) ▸ **false alarm** falsa alarma *f* ▸ **false arrest** detención *f* ilegal ▸ **false ceiling** cielo *m* raso, falso techo *m* ▸ **false dawn** (*fig*) espejismo *m* ▸ **false friend** (*Ling*) falso amigo *m* ▸ **false imprisonment** (*by police*) detención *f* ilegal; (*by criminal*) retención *f* ilegal ▸ **false memory syndrome** síndrome *m* de (la) falsa memoria ▸ **false negative** (= *result*) falso negativo *m* ▸ **false positive** (= *result*) falso positivo *m* ▸ **false start** (*Sport*) salida *f* nula; (*fig*) comienzo *m* fallido ▸ **false teeth** dentadura *fsing* postiza, dientes *mpl* postizos ▸ **false tooth** diente *m* postizo
falsehood [ˈfɔːlshʊd] (N) (= *falsity*) falsedad *f*; (= *lie*) mentira *f*
falsely [ˈfɔːlslɪ] (ADV) **1** (= *untruthfully*) falsamente; (= *mistakenly*) equivocadamente • **she had ~ claimed that ...** había asegurado falsamente que ... • **he was ~ accused of**

stealing (= *untruthfully*) se le acusó falsamente de robo; (= *mistakenly*) se le acusó equivocadamente de robo • **they sometimes test ~ positive** algunas veces dan resultados positivos falsos • **she had been ~ diagnosed with cancer** se equivocaron cuando le diagnosticaron cáncer
2 (= *insincerely*) fingidamente • **he was being ~ enthusiastic about the idea** se mostró fingidamente entusiasmado con la idea • **she sounded ~ cheerful** parecía fingir la alegría, su alegría sonaba falsa
falseness ['fɔːlsnɪs] (N) **1** (= *incorrectness*) [*of argument, claim*] falsedad *f*; [*of assumption*] lo equivocado
2 (= *insincerity*) falsedad *f*
3† (= *disloyalty*) [*of friend*] deslealtad *f*, perfidia *f*; [*of lover*] infidelidad *f*
falsetto [fɔːl'setəʊ] (N) falsete *m*
(ADJ) [*voice*] con falsete
(ADV) [*sing*] con falsete
falsies* ['fɔːlsɪz] (NPL) rellenos *mpl*
falsification [ˌfɔːlsɪfɪ'keɪʃən] (N) falsificación *f*
falsify ['fɔːlsɪfaɪ] (VT) [+ *document*] falsificar; [+ *evidence*] falsificar, falsear; [+ *accounts, figures*] falsear
falsity ['fɔːlsɪtɪ] (N) falsedad *f*
falter ['fɔːltəʳ] (VI) (= *waver*) [*person*] vacilar, titubear; [*voice*] entrecortarse, quebrarse; [*steps*] vacilar; [*courage*] fallar, faltar • **without ~ing** sin vacilar
(VT) decir titubeando
faltering ['fɔːltərɪŋ] (ADJ) [*voice*] entrecortado, quebrado; [*step*] vacilante
falteringly ['fɔːltərɪŋlɪ] (ADV) [*say*] con voz entrecortada, con la voz quebrada
fame [feɪm] (N) fama *f* • **Margaret Mitchell, of "Gone with the Wind" ~** Margaret Mitchell, famosa por su novela "Lo que el viento se llevó" • **~ and fortune** fama *f* y fortuna *f*
famed [feɪmd] (ADJ) famoso, afamado
familial [fə'mɪlɪəl] (ADJ) (*frm*) (= *relating to families*) familiar; (= *typical of families*) de familia
familiar [fə'mɪlɪəʳ] (ADJ) **1** (= *well-known*) [*face, person, place*] conocido, familiar • **his voice sounds ~** me suena (familiar) su voz • **it doesn't sound ~** no me suena • **to be on ~ ground** (*fig*) estar en su elemento, dominar la materia
2 (= *common*) [*experience, complaint, event*] corriente, común • **it's a ~ feeling** es un sentimiento común
3 (= *well-acquainted*) • **to be ~ with** estar familiarizado con, conocer • **to make o.s. ~ with** familiarizarse con
4 (= *intimate*) [*tone of voice etc*] íntimo, de confianza; [*language etc*] familiar; (*pej*) (= *over-intimate*) fresco, que se toma demasiadas confianzas • **to be on ~ terms with sb** tener confianza con algn • **he got too ~** se tomó demasiadas confianzas
familiarity [fəˌmɪlɪ'ærɪtɪ] (N) **1** [*of sight, event etc*] familiaridad *f*
2 (= *knowledge, acquaintance*) conocimiento *m* (**with** de) • PROVERB: • **~ breeds contempt** donde hay confianza hay asco
3 (= *intimacy*) [*of tone etc*] familiaridad *f*, confianza *f*; (*pej*) frescura *f*, exceso *m* de familiaridad
4 familiarities familiaridades *fpl*, confianzas *fpl*
familiarization [fəˌmɪlɪəraɪ'zeɪʃən] (N) familiarización *f* • **a process of ~** un proceso de familiarización
familiarize [fə'mɪlɪəraɪz] (VT) familiarizar (**with** con) • **to ~ o.s. with** familiarizarse con
familiarly [fə'mɪlɪəlɪ] (ADV) con demasiada confianza
family ['fæmɪlɪ] (N) (= *close relatives, group of animals*) familia *f* • **she's one of the ~** es como de la familia • **do you have any ~?** (= *relatives*) ¿tiene usted parientes?; (= *children*) ¿tiene usted hijos? • **to run in the ~** ser cosa de familia • IDIOM: • **to be in the ~ way**†* estar en estado de buena esperanza • **to get** *or* **put a girl in the ~ way**†* dejar encinta a una joven
(CPD) [*jewels*] de la familia; [*dinner, resemblance*] de familia; [*Bible*] familiar
▸ **family album** (= *photo album*) álbum *m* de familia ▸ **family allowance** (*Brit*) (*formerly*) ≈ ayuda *f* familiar ▸ **family business** negocio *m* familiar ▸ **family butcher** carnicero *m* doméstico ▸ **family circle** círculo *m* familiar ▸ **family credit** (*Brit*) ≈ ayuda *f* familiar ▸ **Family Crisis Intervention Unit** (*US*) *unidad de intervención en crisis familiares* ▸ **Family Division** (*Brit*) (*Jur*) *sala del High Court que entiende de derecho de familia* ▸ **family doctor** médico/a *m/f* de cabecera ▸ **family friend** amigo/a *m/f* de la familia ▸ **family hotel** hotel *m* familiar ▸ **family income** ingresos *mpl* familiares ▸ **family life** vida *f* doméstica ▸ **family man** (= *having family*) padre *m* de familia; (= *home-loving*) hombre *m* casero *or* de su casa ▸ **family name** apellido *m* ▸ **family pet** animal *m* doméstico ▸ **family planning** planificación *f* familiar ▸ **family planning clinic** centro *m* de planificación familiar ▸ **family practice** (*US*) (*Med*) (= *work*) medicina *f* general; (= *place*) consulta *f* ▸ **family practitioner** (*esp US*) médico/a *m/f* de familia ▸ **family room** (*US*) (*in house*) sala *f* de estar; (*Brit*) (*in pub*) *sala donde se permite la entrada a menores*; (*in hotel*) habitación *f* familiar ▸ **family therapy** terapia *f* familiar ▸ **family tree** árbol *m* genealógico ▸ **family values** valores *mpl* familiares
family-minded [ˌfæmɪlɪ'maɪndɪd] (ADJ) • **to be family-minded** estar apegado a la familia
family-size ['fæmɪlɪsaɪz], **family-sized** ['fæmɪlɪsaɪzd] (ADJ) [*packet*] (tamaño) familiar
famine ['fæmɪn] (N) (= *hunger*) hambruna *f*; (= *shortage*) escasez *f*
(CPD) ▸ **famine relief** ayuda *f* contra el hambre
famished* ['fæmɪʃt] (ADJ) famélico; (*fig*) muerto de hambre
famous ['feɪməs] (ADJ) famoso, célebre (**for** por); (*hum*) dichoso • **~ last words!*** (*hum*) ¡para qué habré dicho nada!, ¡me hubiera callado mejor! (*LAm*)
famously ['feɪməslɪ] (ADV) **1** • **as Wilde ~ remarked** como bien señalara Wilde • **there have been hurricanes in England, most ~ in 1987** ha habido huracanes en Inglaterra, el más famoso ocurrido en 1987
2†* (= *very well*) • **to get on ~** llevarse a las mil maravillas
fan¹ [fæn] (N) abanico *m*; (*Agr*) aventador *m*; (= *machine*) ventilador *m* • **electric fan** ventilador *m* eléctrico • IDIOM: • **when the shit hits the fan**** cuando se arme la gorda*
(VT) [+ *face, person*] abanicar; (*mechanically*) ventilar; (*Agr*) aventar; [+ *flames*] atizar, avivar; (*fig*) avivar, excitar • **to fan o.s.** abanicarse, darse aire
(CPD) ▸ **fan belt** (*in motor*) correa *f* del ventilador ▸ **fan heater** (*Brit*) calentador *m* de aire, estufa *f* eléctrica (de aire caliente) ▸ **fan oven** horno *m* con ventilador ▸ **fan vaulting** (*Archit*) bóveda *f* de abanico
▸ **fan out** (VT + ADV) [+ *cards etc*] ordenar en abanico
(VI + ADV) (*Mil etc*) desplegarse en abanico, avanzar en abanico
fan² [fæn] (N) (*gen*) aficionado/a *m/f*; (*Sport*) hincha *mf*, forofo/a *m/f* (*Sp*), adicto/a *m/f* (*LAm*); [*of pop star etc*] fan *mf*, admirador(a) *m/f* • **the fans** la afición • **I am not one of his fans** no soy de sus admiradores, yo no soy de los que lo admiran
(CPD) ▸ **fan base** = fanbase ▸ **fan club** club *m* de admiradores; (*Mus*) club *m* de fans ▸ **fan mail** correspondencia *f* de los admiradores
fan-assisted oven ['fænəˌsɪstɪd'ʌvən] (N) horno *m* con ventilador
fanatic [fə'nætɪk] (ADJ) fanático
(N) fanático/a *m/f*
fanatical [fə'nætɪkəl] (ADJ) fanático
fanatically [fə'nætɪklɪ] (ADV) fanáticamente • **they were ~ loyal to their Emperor** su lealtad hacia el emperador llegaba al fanatismo
fanaticism [fə'nætɪsɪzəm] (N) fanatismo *m*
fanbase ['fænbeɪs] (N) [*of sports team*] afición *f*; [*of band, actor, singer*] fans *mfpl*
fanboy* ['fænbɔɪ] (N) fan *m*
fanciable* ['fænsɪəbl] (ADJ) (*Brit*) guapo, bueno*
fancied ['fænsɪd] (ADJ) **1** (= *imaginary*) imaginario, ficticio
2 (*Sport*) [*horse, runner*] favorito
fancier ['fænsɪəʳ] (N) ▸ **pigeon**
fanciful ['fænsɪfʊl] (ADJ) [*drawings*] fantástico; [*ideas, story, account*] descabalado, rocambolesco; [*person*] imaginativo, fantasioso; [*temperament*] caprichoso; [*imagination*] vivo, rico
fancy ['fænsɪ] (N) **1** (= *liking*) • **to catch** *or* **take sb's ~** atraer a algn • **they stole anything that took their ~** robaban cualquier cosa que les gustaba *or* atraía • **I eat whatever takes my ~** como lo que me apetece • **to take a ~ to** [+ *person*] (*amorously*) quedarse prendado de, prendarse de; [+ *thing*] encapricharse con • **he had taken a ~ to one of the secretaries** se había quedado prendado *or* se había prendado de una de las secretarias • **he seems to have taken a ~ to you** parece que le gustas
2 (= *whim*) capricho *m*, antojo *m* • **a passing ~** un capricho pasajero • **when the ~ takes him** cuando se le antoja • **as the ~ takes her** según su capricho; ▸ **tickle**
3 (= *imagination*) fantasía *f*, imaginación *f* • **in the realm of ~** en el mundo de la fantasía
4 (= *vague idea*) • **I have a ~ that he'll be late** tengo *or* me da la sensación de que llegará tarde
(ADJ) (COMPAR: **fancier**, SUPERL: **fanciest**)
1 (= *elaborate*) muy elaborado • **I like good, plain food, nothing ~** me gusta la buena comida, sencilla, nada muy elaborado *or* nada demasiado historiado • **she uses all these ~ words I don't understand** usa todas esas palabrejas que yo no entiendo • **~ footwork** (*in football, dancing*) filigranas *fpl*, florituras *fpl* (*con los pies*); (*fig*) gran habilidad *f*
2 (= *elegant*) [*restaurant*] de lujo, muy chic; [*house, car*] lujoso; [*clothes*] elegante, chic
3 (= *exaggerated*) [*price*] desorbitado; [*idea*] estrambótico
(VT) **1** (= *imagine*) imaginarse, figurarse • **~ that!*** ¡fíjate!, ¡imagínate! • **~ meeting you here!** ¡qué casualidad encontrarte aquí! • **~ him winning!** ¡qué raro que ganara él! • **~ letting him get away with it!** ¡mira que dejarle salirse con la suya!, ¡mira que dejar que se saliese con la suya! • **~ throwing that away, there's nothing wrong with it** ¡a quién se le ocurre tirar eso! está en perfectas condiciones • **he fancied he saw a glint of amusement in her face** le pareció

ver una chispa de diversión en su rostro • **I rather ~ he's gone out** me da la impresión *or* se me hace que ha salido, se me antoja que ha salido (*liter*) • **he fancies he knows it all** se cree un pozo de sabiduría
2 (= *like, want*) **a** (*at particular moment*) • **what do you ~?** ¿qué quieres tomar?, ¿qué te apetece? • **do you ~ an Indian meal?** ¿te apetece *or* (*LAm*) se te antoja un una comida india?
b (*in general*) • **I've always fancied living there** siempre me hubiese gustado vivir allí • **I don't ~ the idea** no me gusta la idea • **he fancies himself*** es un creído *or* un presumido • **he fancies himself as a bit of an actor*** se piensa que es un actor • **he fancies himself as a footballer*** se las da de futbolista • **he fancies himself as the next prime minister*** se cree que va a ser el próximo primer ministro
3 (*esp Brit**) (= *be attracted to*) • **I could tell he fancied me** notaba que le gustaba mucho, notaba que se sentía atraído por mí
4 (= *rate*) • **I don't ~ his chances of winning** no creo que tenga muchas posibilidades de ganar • **which horse do you ~ for the Grand National?** ¿qué caballo es tu favorito para el Grand National? • **I ~ England to win** yo creo que ganará Inglaterra
(CPD) ▸ **fancy dress** disfraz *m* • **are you going in ~ dress?** ¿vas a ir disfrazado *or* con disfraz? • **they were wearing ~ dress** iban disfrazados ▸ **fancy dress ball** baile *m* de disfraces ▸ **fancy dress party** fiesta *f* de disfraces ▸ **fancy goods** (*Comm*) artículos *mpl* de regalo ▸ **fancy man†*** (*pej*) • **her ~ man** su amante, su amiguito* ▸ **fancy woman†*** (*pej*) • **his ~ woman** su querida, su amiguita*

fancy-free ['fænsɪ'fri:] (ADJ) sin compromiso; ▹ **footloose**

fancywork ['fænsɪwɜ:k] (N) (= *embroidery*) bordado *m*

fandango [fæn'dæŋgəʊ] (N) (PL: **fandangos**) fandango *m*

fanfare ['fænfɛəʳ] (N) fanfarria *f*

fanfold paper ['fænfəʊld,peɪpəʳ] (N) papel *m* plegado en abanico *or* acordeón

fang [fæŋ] (N) colmillo *m*

fangirl* ['fæŋgɜ:l] (N) fan *f*

fanlight ['fænlaɪt] (N) montante *m* de abanico

Fanny ['fænɪ] (N) **1** *familiar form of* **Frances**
2 • **sweet ~ Adams** (*Brit‡*) nada de nada, na' de na'*

fanny ['fænɪ] (N) **1** (*Brit***) (= *vagina*) coño** *m*, concha *f* (*LAm***)
2 (*US**) (= *buttocks*) culo* *m*
(CPD) ▸ **fanny pack** (*US*) riñonera *f*

fan-shaped ['fænʃeɪpt] (ADJ) de *or* en abanico

fansite ['fænsaɪt] (N) (*on internet*) (página *f*) web *f* de fans • **a Harry Potter ~** una (página) web de fans de Harry Potter

fantabulous* [fæn'tæbjʊləs] (ADJ) superguay*

fantail ['fænteɪl] (N) (= *pigeon*) paloma *f* colipava

fantasia [fæn'teɪzɪə] (N) (*Literat, Mus*) fantasía *f*

fantasist ['fæntəzɪst] (N) fantaseador(a) *m/f*

fantasize ['fæntəsaɪz] (VI) fantasear, hacerse ilusiones

fantastic [fæn'tæstɪk] (ADJ) **1*** (= *fabulous, terrific*) [*person, achievement, opportunity, news*] fantástico, estupendo, regio (*LAm**), macanudo (*S. Cone**), chévere (*Col, Ven**) • **it's ~ to see you again!** ¡qué alegría verte de nuevo! • **you look ~!** (= *healthy*) ¡qué buen aspecto tienes!; (= *attractive*) ¡qué guapo estás!
2* (= *huge*) [*amount, profit, speed*] increíble
3 (= *exotic*) [*creature, world*] fantástico; [*shapes, images*] extraño
4 (= *improbable*) [*story, idea*] fantástico

fantastical [fæn'tæstɪkl] (ADJ) (*liter*) fabuloso, fantástico

fantastically [fæn'tæstɪkəlɪ] (ADV)
1 (= *extraordinarily*) [*expensive, complicated*] increíblemente • **~ learned** enormemente erudito
2 (= *imaginatively*) [*wrought, coloured*] maravillosamente

fantasy ['fæntəzɪ] (N) **1** (= *imagination*) fantasía *f* • **to live in a ~ world** *or* **in ~ land** vivir en un mundo de ensueño
2 (= *fanciful idea, wish*) fantasía *f*, sueño *m*
(CPD) ▸ **fantasy football** liga *f* fantástica, fútbol *m* manager

fanzine ['fænzi:n] (N) fanzine *m*

FAO (N ABBR) (= **Food and Agriculture Organization**) OAA *f*, FAO *f*

FAQ (ABBR) (*Comm*) = **free alongside quay**
(N ABBR) (*Comput*) = **Frequently Asked Question(s)** • **FAQ (file)** fichero *m* de preguntas frecuentes

faq (ABBR) = **of fair average quality**

far [fɑ:ʳ] (COMPAR: **farther, further**, SUPERL: **farthest, furthest**) (ADV) **1** (*distance*) (*lit, fig*) lejos, a lo lejos • **is it far (away)?** ¿está lejos? • **is it far to London?** ¿hay mucho hasta Londres? • **it's not far (from here)** no está lejos (de aquí) • **far away** *or* **off** lejos • **far away** *or* **off in the distance** a lo lejos • **not far away** *or* **off** no muy lejos • **far away from one's family** lejos de la familia • **far beyond** mucho más allá de • **how far is it to the river?** ¿qué distancia *or* cuánto hay de aquí al río? • **how far have you got with your work/plans?** ¿hasta dónde has llegado en tu trabajo/tus planes? • **to walk far into the hills** penetrar profundamente en los montes • **far into the night** hasta altas horas de la noche • **from far and near** de todas partes • **Christmas is not far off** la Navidad no está lejos • **he's not far off 70** tiene casi 70 años, frisa en los 70 años • **she was not far off tears** estaba al borde de las lágrimas • **far out at sea** en alta mar • **our calculations are far out** nuestros cálculos yerran *or* se equivocan por mucho • **so far** (*in distance*) tan lejos; (*in time*) hasta ahora • **so far this year** en lo que va del año • **so far so good** por *or* hasta ahora, bien • **in so far as …** en la medida en que …, en cuanto … • **so** *or* **thus far and no further** hasta aquí, pero ni un paso más • **a bridge too far** un puente de más • **the plans are too far advanced** los proyectos están demasiado adelantados • **far and wide** por todas partes • **he wasn't far wrong** *or* **off** *or* **out** casi acertaba, casi estaba en lo justo
2 • **as far as** hasta • **as far as the eye can see** hasta donde alcanza la vista • **to go as far as Milan** ir hasta Milán • **to come from as far away as Milan** venir de sitios tan lejanos como Milán • **she climbed as far as the rest of the team** escaló tanto como el resto del grupo • **as far back as I can remember** hasta donde me alcanza la memoria • **as far back as 1945** ya en 1945 • **as far as possible** en lo posible • **the theory is good as far as it goes** la teoría es buena dentro de sus límites • **I will help you as far as I can** te ayudaré en lo que pueda • **as** *or* **so far as I know** que yo sepa • **as** *or* **so far as I am concerned** por lo que a mí se refiere *or* respecta • **I would go as** *or* **so far as to say that …** me atrevería a decir que …
3 • **far from** [+ *place*] lejos de • **far from approving it, I …** lejos de aprobarlo, yo … • **far from it!** ¡todo lo contrario!, ¡ni mucho menos! • **he is far from well** no está nada bien • **far be it from me to interfere, but …** no quiero entrometerme, pero … • **far from easy** nada fácil
4 • **to go far**: • **how far are you going?** ¿hasta dónde vas? • **he'll go far** (*fig*) llegará lejos • **it doesn't go far enough** (*fig*) no va bastante lejos, no tiene todo el alcance que quisiéramos • **he's gone too far this time** (*fig*) esta vez se ha pasado • **he's gone too far to back out now** (*fig*) ha ido demasiado lejos para echarse atrás *or* retirarse ahora • **it won't go far** [*money, food*] no alcanzará mucho • **for a white wine you won't go far wrong with this** si buscas un vino blanco este ofrece bastante garantía • IDIOM: • **he was far gone*** (= *ill*) estaba muy acabado; (= *drunk*) estaba muy borracho
5 (= *very much*) mucho • **far better** mucho mejor • **it is far better not to go** más vale no ir • **it's far and away the best** • **it's by far the best** es con mucho el mejor • **she's the prettier by far** es con mucho la más guapa • **this car is far faster (than)** este coche es mucho más rápido (que) • **far superior to** muy superior a
(ADJ) • **the far east** *etc* **of the country** el extremo este *etc* del país • **the far left/right** (*Pol*) la extrema izquierda/derecha • **at the far end of** en el otro extremo de, al fondo de • **on the far side of** en el lado opuesto de • IDIOM: • **it's a far cry from** tiene poco que ver con
(CPD) ▸ **the Far East** el Extremo *or* Lejano Oriente ▸ **the Far North** el Polo Norte

farad ['færəd] (N) faradio *m*

faraway ['fɑ:rəweɪ] (ADJ) **1** [*place*] remoto, lejano
2 (*fig*) [*voice*] distraído; [*look*] ausente, perdido

farce [fɑ:s] (N) **1** (*Theat*) farsa *f*
2 (*fig*) absurdo *m* • **this is a ~** esto es absurdo • **what a ~ this is!** ¡qué follón! • **the trial was a ~** el proceso fue una farsa

farcical ['fɑ:sɪkəl] (ADJ) absurdo, ridículo

far-distant ['fɑ:'dɪstənt] (ADJ) lejano, remoto

fare [fɛəʳ] (N) **1** (= *cost*) precio *m*, tarifa *f*; (= *ticket*) billete *m*, boleto *m* (*LAm*); (*Naut*) pasaje *m* • **"~s please!"** (*on bus*) "¡billetes por favor!"
2 (= *passenger in taxi*) pasajero/a *m/f*
3 (*frm*) (= *food*) comida *f*; ▹ **bill¹**
(VI) • **they ~d badly/well** lo pasaron mal/bien, les fue mal/bien • **how did you ~?** ¿qué tal te fue? • **to ~ alike** correr la misma suerte
(CPD) ▸ **fare dodger** (*Brit*) *persona que pretende viajar en un medio de transporte público sin pagar* ▸ **fare stage, fare zone** (*US*) (*on bus*) zona *f* de tarifa fija

Far Eastern ['fɑ:r'i:stən] (ADJ) del Extremo Oriente

farewell [fɛə'wel] (N) adiós *m*; (= *ceremony*) despedida *f* • **to bid ~ (to sb)** despedirse (de algn) • **to say one's ~s** despedirse • **you can say ~ to your wallet** (*fig*) te puedes ir despidiendo de tu cartera
(EXCL) (*liter*) ¡adiós!
(CPD) ▸ **farewell dinner** cena *f* de despedida ▸ **farewell party** fiesta *f* de despedida

far-fetched ['fɑ:'fetʃt] (ADJ) [*story, explanation*] inverosímil, poco probable; [*idea, scheme*] descabellado

far-flung ['fɑ:flʌŋ] (ADJ) extenso

farinaceous [,færɪ'neɪʃəs] (ADJ) farináceo

farm [fɑ:m] (N) granja *f*, chacra *f* (*LAm*); (= *large*) hacienda *f*, finca *f*, estancia *f* (*LAm*),

f

rancho *m* (*Mex*); [*of mink, oysters etc*] criadero *m*; (= *buildings*) alquería *f*, casa *f* de labranza, quinta *f*, ranchería *f* (*Mex*); ▹ **dairy**
VT cultivar, labrar • **he ~s 300 acres** cultiva 300 acres
VI (*as profession*) ser granjero • **he ~s in Devon** tiene una granja en Devon
CPD agrícola ▸ **farm animal** animal *m* de granja ▸ **farm labourer, farm laborer** (*US*) jornalero/a *m/f* (del campo), obrero/a *m/f* agrícola ▸ **farm produce** productos *mpl* agrícolas ▸ **farm shop** tienda *f* rural (*donde se venden directamente los productos de una granja*) ▸ **farm tractor** tractor *m* ▸ **farm worker** = **farm labourer**
▸ **farm out*** VT + ADV [+ *work*] mandar hacer fuera (**to sb** a algn); (*hum*) [+ *children*] dejar (**on**) a *or* con
farmed ['fɑ:md] ADJ [*venison, turkey*] de granja; [*fish, salmon*] de criadero; ▹ **farm, intensively, organically**
farmer ['fɑ:məʳ] N agricultor(a) *m/f*, granjero/a *m/f*, chacarero/a *m/f* (*LAm*); [*of large farm*] hacendado/a *m/f*, estanciero/a *m/f* (*LAm*), ranchero/a *m/f* (*Mex*)
CPD ▸ **farmers' market, farmers market** mercadillo *m* agrícola
farmhand ['fɑ:mhænd] N obrero/a *m/f* agrícola, jornalero/a *m/f* (del campo)
farmhouse ['fɑ:mhaʊs] N (PL: **farmhouses** ['fɑ:mhaʊzɪz]) alquería *f*, casa *f* de labranza, caserío *m* (*Sp*), casa *f* grande (*LAm*), casa *f* de hacienda (*LAm*)
farming ['fɑ:mɪŋ] N (*gen*) agricultura *f*; [*of land*] cultivo *m*; [*of animals*] cría *f* • **good ~ practice** técnicas *fpl* agrícolas reconocidas
CPD agrícola ▸ **the farming community** los agricultores ▸ **farming methods** métodos *mpl* de cultivo
farmland ['fɑ:mlænd] N tierras *fpl* de labranza *or* cultivo
farmstead ['fɑ:msted] N alquería *f*, casa *f* de labranza
farmyard ['fɑ:mjɑ:d] N corral *m*
Faroe Islands ['fɛərəʊ,aɪləndz], **Faroes** ['fɛərəʊz] NPL islas *fpl* Feroe
far-off ['fɑ:r'ɒf] ADJ lejano, remoto
far-out* [,fɑ:r'aʊt] ADJ **1** (= *odd*) raro, extraño; (= *zany*) estrafalario
2 (= *modern*) muy moderno, de vanguardia
3 (= *superb*) guay*, fenomenal*
farrago [fə'rɑ:gəʊ] N (PL: **farragos** *or* **farragoes**) fárrago *m*
far-reaching ['fɑ:'ri:tʃɪŋ] ADJ [*effect*] transcendental, de gran alcance
farrier ['færɪəʳ] N (*esp Brit*) herrador(a) *m/f*
far-right [,fɑ:'raɪt] ADJ [*leader, group, party*] de extrema derecha
farrow ['færəʊ] N lechigada *f* de puercos
VT parir
VI parir (la cerda)
far-seeing ['fɑ:'si:ɪŋ] ADJ clarividente, previsor
Farsi ['fɑ:si:] N persa *m*
far-sighted ['fɑ:'saɪtɪd] ADJ **1** (*US*) (*Med*) hipermétrope
2 (*fig*) [*person*] clarividente; [*plan, decision, measure*] con visión de futuro
far-sightedly ['fɑ:'saɪtɪdlɪ] ADV de modo clarividente, con visión de futuro
far-sightedness ['fɑ:'saɪtɪdnɪs] N **1** (*US*) (*Med*) hipermetropía *f*, presbicia *f*
2 (*fig*) clarividencia *f*, visión *f* de futuro
fart‡ [fɑ:t] N **1** pedo‡ *m*
2 • **he's a boring old ~** es un tío pesadísimo*, es un pelmazo*
VI tirarse *or* echarse un pedo‡
▸ **fart about‡, fart around‡** VI + ADV ▹ **mess about**
farther ['fɑ:ðəʳ] ADV = **further**
ADJ (*compar of* **far**) • **she was sitting at the ~ end of the bar** estaba sentada al otro extremo de la barra • **on the ~ side of the lake** al otro lado del lago, en la otra orilla del lago
farthermost ['fɑ:ðəməʊst] ADJ = **furthermost**
farthest ['fɑ:ðɪst] ADJ = **furthest**
farthing ['fɑ:ðɪŋ] N cuarto *m* de penique
FAS ABBR = **free alongside ship**
fascia ['feɪʃə] (*Brit*) N **1** (*on building*) faja *f*
2 (*for mobile phone*) carcasa *f*
3 (*Brit*) (*Aut*) tablero *m*
fascicle ['fæsɪkl] N, **fascicule** ['fæsɪkju:l] N fascículo *m*
fascinate ['fæsɪneɪt] VT fascinar • **it ~s me how/why ...** me maravilla cómo/por qué ...
fascinated ['fæsɪneɪtɪd] ADJ fascinado • **to be ~ with sth** estar fascinado por algo
fascinating ['fæsɪneɪtɪŋ] ADJ fascinante
fascinatingly ['fæsɪneɪtɪŋlɪ] ADV [*talk, describe*] de forma fascinante; [*beautiful*] fascinantemente; (*introducing sentence*) es fascinante
fascination [,fæsɪ'neɪʃən] N fascinación *f* • **his ~ with the cinema** su fascinación por el cine
fascism ['fæʃɪzəm] N fascismo *m*
fascist ['fæʃɪst] ADJ fascista
N fascista *mf*
fashion ['fæʃən] N **1** (= *manner*) manera *f*, modo *m* • **after a ~** así así, más o menos • **I play after a ~** toco algo • **after the ~ of** a la manera de • **in his usual ~** a su manera *or* modo • **in one's own ~** a su propio modo • **in the Greek ~** a la griega, al estilo griego • **it is not my ~ to pretend** (*frm*) yo no acostumbro fingir
2 (= *vogue*) (*in clothing, speech etc*) moda *f* • **it's all the ~ now** ahora está muy de moda • **it's no longer the ~** ya no está de moda • **it's the ~ to say that ...** es un tópico decir que ... • **to be in/out of ~** estar de moda/pasado de moda • **to come into/go out of ~** ponerse de/pasar de moda • **to set a ~ for sth** imponer la moda de algo • **the latest ~** la última moda • **the new Spring ~s** la nueva moda de primavera • **women's/men's ~s** moda para la mujer/el hombre
3 (= *good taste*) buen gusto *m* • **what ~ demands** lo que impone el buen gusto • **a man of ~** un hombre elegante
VT (= *shape*) formar; (= *make*) fabricar; (= *mould*) moldear; (= *design*) diseñar
CPD ▸ **fashion design** estilismo *m* ▸ **fashion designer** modisto/a *m/f*, diseñador(a) *m/f* de modas ▸ **fashion editor** director(a) *m/f* de revista de modas ▸ **fashion house** casa *f* de modas ▸ **fashion magazine** revista *f* de modas ▸ **fashion model** modelo *mf* ▸ **fashion page** sección *f* de modas ▸ **fashion parade** desfile *m or* pase *m* de modelos ▸ **fashion plate** figurín *m* de moda ▸ **fashion shoot** sesión *f* de fotos de moda • **to do a ~ shoot** hacer una sesión de fotos de moda ▸ **fashion show** desfile *m or* pase *m* de modelos ▸ **fashion victim*** esclavo/a *m/f* de la moda
fashionable ['fæʃnəbl] ADJ **1** [*dress etc*] de moda, moderno, a la moda; [*place, restaurant*] de moda • **~ people** gente *f* elegante, gente *f* guapa* • **in ~ society** en la buena sociedad • **it is ~ to do ...** está de moda hacer ...
2 (= *popular*) [*writer, subject for discussion*] de moda, popular • **he is hardly a ~ painter now** es un pintor que no está ahora muy de moda
fashionably ['fæʃnəblɪ] ADV • **to be ~ dressed** ir vestido a la moda
fashion-conscious ['fæʃən,kɒnʃəs] ADJ pendiente de la moda
fashionista [,fæʃə'ni:stə] N fashionista *mf*, fashion *mf*
fast¹ [fɑ:st] ADJ (COMPAR: **faster**, SUPERL: **fastest**) **1** (= *speedy*) rápido; (*Phot*) [*film*] de alta sensibilidad • **he's a ~ worker** es un trabajador (muy) rápido • **he's a ~ talker*** es un pretencioso • **he was too ~ for me** corrió más que yo; (*fig*) se me adelantó • **~ and furious** vertiginoso • IDIOM: • **to pull a ~ one on sb*** jugar una mala pasada a algn
2 [*clock*] adelantado • **my watch is five minutes ~** mi reloj está *or* va cinco minutos adelantado
3 (*Sport*) [*pitch*] seco y firme; [*court*] rápido
4 (= *dissipated*) [*person*] lanzado, fresco; [*life*] disoluto, disipado
5 (= *firm*) fijo, firme • **to make sth ~** sujetar algo • **to make a rope ~** atar bien una cuerda • **to make a boat ~** amarrar una barca • **~ friends** íntimos amigos
6 [*colour, dye*] que no destiñe
ADV **1** (= *quickly*) rápidamente, deprisa • **as ~ as I can** lo más rápido posible • **he ran off as ~ as his legs would carry him** se fue corriendo a toda velocidad • **how ~ can you type?** ¿a qué velocidad escribes a máquina? • **don't speak so ~** habla más despacio • **~er!** ¡más (rápido)! • **not so ~!*** (*interrupting*) ¡un momento! • **he'll do it ~ enough if you offer him money** se dará más prisa si le ofreces dinero • **the rain was falling ~** llovía mucho • **as ~ as I finished them he wrapped them up** a medida que yo los terminaba él los envolvía • IDIOM: • **to play ~ and loose with** jugar con
2 (= *firmly*) firmemente • **~ asleep** profundamente dormido • **to hold ~** agarrarse bien; (*fig*) mantenerse firme • **to stand ~** mantenerse firme • **tie it ~** átalo bien • **it's stuck ~** está bien pegado; [*door*] está atrancado *or* atascado • **to be stuck ~ in the mud** quedar atascado en el lodo • **to be stuck ~ in a doorway** haberse quedado atascado en una puerta
CPD ▸ **fast bowler** (*Cricket*) lanzador(a) *m/f* rápido/a ▸ **fast food** comida *f* rápida, platos *mpl* preparados ▸ **fast lane** (*on road*) • **the ~ lane** (*in countries with right-hand drive*) ≈ el carril de la derecha; (*in countries with left-hand drive*) ≈ el carril de la izquierda ▸ **fast track** (*fig*) vía *f* rápida • **to be on the ~ track to sth** ir por la vía rápida hacia algo; ▹ **fast-track** ▸ **fast train** tren *m* rápido, ≈ Intercity *m* (*Sp*), ≈ Talgo *m* (*Sp*)
fast² [fɑ:st] N ayuno *m* • **to break one's ~** (*frm*) interrumpir el ayuno
VI ayunar
CPD ▸ **fast day** día *m* de ayuno
fast-breeder reactor [,fɑ:stbri:dəri:'æktəʳ] N reactor *m* reproductor rápido
fasten ['fɑ:sn] VT **1** (= *secure*) [+ *belt, dress, seat belt*] abrochar; [+ *door, box, window*] cerrar; (*with rope*) atar; (*with paste*) pegar; (*with bolt*) echar el cerrojo a • **to ~ two things together** pegar/sujetar dos cosas
2 (= *attach*) sujetar; (*fig*) atribuir • **to ~ the blame/responsibility (for sth) on sb** echar la culpa/atribuir la responsabilidad (de algo) a algn • **they're trying to ~ the crime on me** tratan de achacarme *or* atribuirme el crimen a mí
VI [*door, box*] cerrarse; [*dress*] abrocharse • **it ~s in front** se abrocha por delante
▸ **fasten down** VT + ADV [+ *envelope, blind etc*] cerrar
▸ **fasten on** VT + ADV (= *tie*) atar
VT + PREP ▹ **fasten upon**
VI + PREP ▹ **fasten upon**
▸ **fasten on to** VI + PREP agarrarse de,

pegarse a; (*fig*) fijarse en • **he ~ed on to me at once** se fijó en mí en seguida; (*as companion*) se me pegó en seguida • **to ~ on to a pretext** echar mano *or* valerse de un pretexto
▸ **fasten up** (VT + ADV) [+ *clothing*] abrochar (VI + ADV) • **it ~s up in front** se abrocha por delante
▸ **fasten upon**, **fasten on** (VT + PREP) [+ *gaze*] fijar en (VI + PREP) [+ *excuse*] valerse de • **to ~ (up)on the idea of doing sth** aferrarse a la idea de hacer algo

fastener [ˈfɑːsnəʳ] (N) [*of necklace, bag, box*] cierre *m*; (*on dress*) corchete *m*; (*for papers*) grapa *f*; (= *zip fastener*) cremallera *f*

fastening [ˈfɑːsnɪŋ] (N) = **fastener**

fast-flowing [ˌfɑːstˈfləʊɪŋ] (ADJ) [*water, stream*] de corriente rápida

fast-food chain [ˌfɑːstˈfuːdˌtʃeɪn] (N) cadena *f* de comida rápida

fast-food restaurant [ˌfɑːstˈfuːdˌrestərɒŋ] (N) establecimiento *m* de comida rápida, restaurante *m* de comida rápida; (*selling hamburgers*) hamburguesería *f*

fast forward [ˈfɑːstˈfɔːwəd] (N) (*also* **fast forward button**) botón *m* de avance rápido (VT) pasar para delante, adelantar (VI) avanzar rápidamente

fast-growing [ˌfɑːstˈgrəʊɪŋ] (ADJ) [*tree, plant*] de crecimiento rápido; [*sector, economy*] de desarrollo rápido • **to be fast-growing** [*tree, plant*] crecer rápidamente; [*sector, economy*] desarrollarse rápidamente

fastidious [fæsˈtɪdɪəs] (ADJ) [*person*] (*about cleanliness etc*) escrupuloso; (= *touchy*) quisquilloso; [*taste*] fino

fastidiously [fæsˈtɪdɪəslɪ] (ADV) [*examine, clean, check*] meticulosamente, quisquillosamente

fastidiousness [fæsˈtɪdɪəsnɪs] (N) meticulosidad *f*, exigencia *f*

fasting [ˈfɑːstɪŋ] (N) (= *going without food*) ayuno *m*

fast-moving [ˌfɑːstˈmuːvɪŋ] (ADJ) rápido, veloz; [*target*] que cambia rápidamente de posición; [*goods*] de venta rápida, que se venden rápidamente; [*plot*] muy movido, lleno de acciones, que se desarrolla rápidamente

fastness [ˈfɑːstnɪs] (N) (= *stronghold*) fortaleza *f*; [*of mountain etc*] lo más intrincado • **in their Cuban mountain ~** en las espesuras serranas de Cuba

fast-track [ˈfɑːsttræk] (ADJ) rápido, por la vía rápida

fat [fæt] (ADJ) (COMPAR: **fatter**, SUPERL: **fattest**) **1** (= *plump*) [*person*] gordo; [*face, cheeks, limbs*] relleno, gordo • **to get fat** engordar • **he grew fat on the proceeds** *or* **profits** (*fig*) se enriqueció con los beneficios • IDIOM: • **it's not over till the fat lady sings*** mientras hay vida, hay esperanza, hasta el rabo todo es toro*
2 (= *fatty*) [*meat, pork*] graso • **fat bacon** tocino *m* graso, tocino *m* con mucha grasa
3 (= *thick*) [*book*] grueso
4 (= *substantial*) [*profit*] grande, pingüe; [*salary*] muy elevado, muy alto • **a fat cheque** un cheque muy cuantioso • **the fat years** los años de las vacas gordas
5* (= *minimal*) • **fat chance!** ¡ni soñarlo! • **a fat lot he knows about it!** ¡qué sabrá él! • **a fat lot of good that is!** ¡eso no sirve de nada!, y eso ¿de qué sirve?
(N) (*on person, in food*) grasa *f*; (*for cooking*) manteca *f* • **he needs to get rid of that excess fat** necesita eliminar toda esa grasa que le sobra • **a short, middle-aged man, tending to fat** un hombre bajito, de mediana edad, más bien gordo • **animal/vegetable fats** grasas *fpl* animales/vegetales • **beef/chicken fat** grasa *f* de vaca *or* (*Sp*) ternera/de pollo • **fry in deep fat** freír en aceite abundante • **double cream is 48 per cent fat** la nata para montar tiene un 48 por ciento de materia grasa • IDIOMS: • **now the fat's in the fire** se va a armar la gorda* • **to live off the fat of the land** vivir a cuerpo de rey; ▹ **body**
(CPD) ▸ **fat cat*** pez *m* gordo*; ▹ **fat-cat** ▸ **fat content** contenido *m* de materia grasa • **it has a very high fat content** tiene un contenido muy alto de materia grasa ▸ **fat farm*** (*US*) clínica *f* de adelgazamiento

fatal [ˈfeɪtl] (ADJ) **1** (= *causing death*) [*accident, injury*] mortal
2 (= *disastrous*) [*mistake*] fatal; [*consequences*] funesto (**to** para) • **it's ~ to mention that** es peligrosísimo mencionar eso
3 (= *fateful*) fatídico
(CPD) ▸ **fatal accident enquiry** (*Scot*) *investigación sobre las causas de un accidente mortal*

fatalism [ˈfeɪtəlɪzəm] (N) fatalismo *m*

fatalist [ˈfeɪtəlɪst] (N) fatalista *mf*

fatalistic [ˌfeɪtəˈlɪstɪk] (ADJ) fatalista

fatality [fəˈtælɪtɪ] (N) **1** (= *death*) muerte *f*
2 (= *victim*) muerto/a *m/f*, víctima *f* • **luckily there were no fatalities** por fortuna no hubo víctimas

fatally [ˈfeɪtəlɪ] (ADV) mortalmente • **~ wounded** herido mortalmente *or* de muerte

fat-cat* [ˈfætkæt] (ADJ) • **a fat-cat industrialist** un opulento industrial

fate [feɪt] (N) **1** (= *destiny*) destino *m* • **what ~ has in store for us** lo que nos guarda *or* depara el destino • **~ decided otherwise** el destino no lo quiso así
2 (= *person's lot*) suerte *f* • **to leave sb to his ~** abandonar a algn a su suerte • **this sealed his ~** esto acabó de perderle • **to meet one's ~** (= *die*) encontrar la muerte • **Italy could suffer the same ~ as India** Italia podría correr la misma suerte que la India, a Italia le podría pasar lo mismo que a la India • **that's a ~ worse than death** no hay cosa peor
3 • **the Fates** (*Myth*) las Parcas

fated [ˈfeɪtɪd] (ADJ) (= *governed by fate*) [*person, project, friendship etc*] predestinado; (= *doomed*) condenado • **to be ~ to do sth** estar predestinado a hacer algo • **it was ~ that ...** era inevitable que ...

fateful [ˈfeɪtfʊl] (ADJ) [*day, event*] fatídico; [*words*] profético

fat-free [ˈfætfriː] (ADJ) [*diet, food*] sin grasa

fathead* [ˈfæthed] (N) imbécil *mf* • **you ~!** ¡imbécil!

fat-headed* [ˈfætˌhedɪd] (ADJ) imbécil

father [ˈfɑːðəʳ] (N) **1** (*gen*) padre *m* • **to talk to sb like a ~** hablar a algn en tono paternal • **to be passed on** *or* **handed down from ~ to son** pasar de padre a hijo • **my ~ and mother** mis padres • IDIOM: • **a ~ and mother of a row*** una bronca fenomenal* *or* de padre y muy señor mío* • PROVERB: • **like ~ like son** de tal palo, tal astilla
2 • **Our Father** (*Rel*) Padre Nuestro • **to say three Our Fathers** rezar tres padrenuestros
3 • **Father Brown** (*Rel*) (el) padre Brown
4 (*fig*) (= *founder*) padre *m* • **the ~ of English poetry** el padre de la poesía inglesa • **the Fathers of the Church** los Santos Padres de la Iglesia; ▹ **city**
(VT) [+ *child*] engendrar; (*fig*) inventar, producir
(CPD) ▸ **Father Christmas** (*Brit*) Papá *m* Noel ▸ **father confessor** (*Rel*) confesor *m*, padre *m* *or* director *m* espiritual ▸ **Father's Day** Día *m* del Padre ▸ **father figure** figura *f* paterna ▸ **(Old) Father Time** el Tiempo

fatherhood [ˈfɑːðəhʊd] (N) paternidad *f*

father-in-law [ˈfɑːðərɪnlɔː] (N) (PL: **fathers-in-law**) suegro *m*

fatherland [ˈfɑːðəlænd] (N) patria *f*

fatherless [ˈfɑːðəlɪs] (ADJ) huérfano de padre

fatherly [ˈfɑːðəlɪ] (ADJ) [*person*] paternal; [*advice, behaviour*] paterno

fathom [ˈfæðəm] (N) braza *f* • **water five ~s deep** agua de una profundidad de cinco brazas
(VT) **1** (*Naut*) sond(e)ar
2 (*fig*) (*also* **fathom out**) descifrar, llegar a entender; [+ *mystery*] desentrañar • **I can't ~ why** no me explico por qué • **I can't ~ him/it out at all** no le/lo entiendo en absoluto

fathomless [ˈfæðəmlɪs] (ADJ) insondable

fatigue [fəˈtiːg] (N) **1** (= *weariness*) cansancio *m*, fatiga *f*; ▹ **battle**
2 (*Tech*) fatiga *f*; ▹ **metal**
3 (*Mil*) faena *f*, fajina *f*; **fatigues** traje *msing* de faena
(VT) fatigar, cansar
(CPD) ▸ **fatigue dress** = **fatigues** ▸ **fatigue duty** (*Mil*) servicio *m* de fajina ▸ **fatigue party** (*Mil*) destacamento *m* de fajina

fatigued [fəˈtiːgd] (ADJ) fatigado

fatiguing [fəˈtiːgɪŋ] (ADJ) fatigoso

fatless [ˈfætlɪs] (ADJ) [*food*] sin grasa

fatness [ˈfætnɪs] (N) [*of person*] gordura *f*; [*of meat*] grasa *f*; [*of book*] grosor *m*

fatso‡ [ˈfætsəʊ] (N) (PL: **fatsos** *or* **fatsoes**) (*pej*) gordo/a *m/f*

fatstock [ˈfætstɒk] (N) (*Agr*) animales *mpl* de engorde

fatted [ˈfætɪd] (ADJ) • **to kill the ~ calf** tirar la casa por la ventana

fatten [ˈfætn] (VT) (*also* **fatten up**) [+ *animal*] cebar, engordar
(VI) engordar

fattening [ˈfætnɪŋ] (ADJ) [*food*] que hace engordar • **chocolate is ~** el chocolate engorda
(N) (*Agr*) engorde *m*

fatty [ˈfætɪ] (ADJ) (COMPAR: **fattier**, SUPERL: **fattiest**) **1** [*food*] graso
2 (*Anat*) [*tissue*] adiposo
(N)* (*pej*) gordo/a *m/f* • **~!** ¡gordo!
(CPD) ▸ **fatty acid** ácido *m* graso

fatuity [fəˈtjuːɪtɪ] (N) necedad *f*, fatuidad *f*

fatuous [ˈfætjʊəs] (ADJ) [*remark*] necio, fatuo; [*smile*] tonto

fatuously [ˈfætjʊəslɪ] (ADV) neciamente

fatuousness [ˈfætjʊəsnɪs] (N) necedad *f*, fatuidad *f*

fatwa [ˈfætwə] (N) fatwa *f*

faucet [ˈfɔːsɪt] (N) (*US*) (= *tap*) grifo *m*, llave *f*, canilla *f* (*LAm*)

fault [fɔːlt] (N) **1** (= *defect*) (*in character*) defecto *m*; (*in manufacture*) defecto *m*, falla *f* (*LAm*); (*in supply, machine*) avería *f* • **with all his ~s** con todos sus defectos • **her ~ is excessive shyness** peca de tímida • **generous to a ~** excesivamente generoso • **to find ~** poner reparos • **to find ~ with sth/sb** criticar algo/a algn
2 (= *blame, responsibility*) culpa *f* • **it's all your ~** tú tienes toda la culpa • **it's not my ~** no es culpa mía • **you were at ~ in not telling us** hiciste mal en no decírnoslo • **your memory is at ~** no te acuerdas bien • **you were not at ~** no por culpa suya • **through no ~ of his own** sin falta alguna de su parte • **whose ~ is it (if ...)?** ¿quién tiene la culpa (si ...)?
3 (*Tennis*) falta *f*
4 (*Geol*) falla *f*
(VT) criticar • **it cannot be ~ed** es intachable • **you cannot ~ him on spelling** su ortografía es impecable
(CPD) ▸ **fault line** (*Geol*) línea *f* de falla; (*in*

system, process) debilitamiento *m*
fault-finder ['fɔːltˌfaɪndəʳ] (N) criticón/ona *m/f*
fault-finding ['fɔːltˌfaɪndɪŋ] (ADJ) criticón, reparón
(N) manía *f* de criticar
faultless ['fɔːltlɪs] (ADJ) [*person, behaviour*] intachable, impecable; [*appearance, clothing, logic*] impecable; [*work, performance*] perfecto • **Hans's English was ~** Hans hablaba un inglés perfecto
faultlessly ['fɔːltlɪslɪ] (ADV) [*dress*] impecablemente; [*perform, recite*] perfectamente
faulty ['fɔːltɪ] (ADJ) (COMPAR: **faultier**, SUPERL: **faultiest**) **1** [*machine etc*] defectuoso
2 (= *imperfect*) [*reasoning, argument etc*] imperfecto
faun [fɔːn] (N) fauno *m*
fauna ['fɔːnə] (N) (PL: **faunas** *or* **faunae**) fauna *f*
Faust [faʊst] (N) Fausto
Faustian ['faʊstɪən] (ADJ) de Fausto
faux pas ['fəʊ'pɑː] (N) metedura *f or* (*LAm*) metida *f* de pata*
fava bean ['fɑːvəbiːn] (N) (*US*) haba *f*
fave* ['feɪv] (ADJ) (= *favourite*) preferido/a
(N) preferido/a *m/f*
favour, favor (*US*) ['feɪvəʳ] (N) **1** (= *kindness*) favor *m* • **I don't expect any ~s in return** no espero que me devuelvas/devuelvan *etc* el favor • **he did it as a ~ (to me)** (me) lo hizo como un favor • **to ask a ~ of sb** pedir un favor a algn • **to do sb a ~** hacer un favor a algn • **do me the ~ of closing the door** ¿me hace el favor de cerrar la puerta? • **do me a ~!*** (*iro*) ¡haz el favor! (*iro*) • **do me a ~ and clear off*** ¡haz el favor de largarte!* • **do yourself a ~ and get a haircut** si te cortas el pelo te harás un favor • **those suits you wear do you no ~s** esos trajes que te pones no te favorecen nada
2 (= *approval*) • **to curry ~ with sb** tratar de ganar el favor de algn • **to fall from ~** [*person*] caer en desgracia; [*product, style*] perder aceptación • **to find ~ with sb** [*person*] ganarse la aceptación de algn; [*suggestion, product, style*] tener buena acogida por parte de algn, ser bien acogido por algn • **to gain ~ with sb** ganarse la aceptación de algn • **to be in ~ with sb** [*person*] gozar del favor de algn; [*product, style*] gozar de la aceptación de algn • **to lose ~** perder aceptación • **he's currently out of ~ with the prime minister** actualmente no goza del favor del primer ministro • **British companies are clearly out of ~** se ve claramente que las compañías británicas no tienen aceptación • **to fall out of ~** [*person*] caer en desgracia; [*product, style*] perder aceptación • **to win sb's ~** ganarse la aceptación de algn • **his proposals were not looked upon with ~** sus propuestas no fueron consideradas favorablemente
3 (= *support, advantage*) favor *m* • **to be in ~ of (doing) sth** estar a favor de (hacer) algo, ser partidario de (hacer) algo • **he is in ~ of the death penalty** está a favor de *or* es partidario de la pena de muerte • **I am in ~ of selling the house** soy partidario de *or* estoy a favor de vender la casa • **the result of the vote was 111 in ~ and 25 against** el resultado de la votación fue 111 votos a favor y 25 en contra • **the traffic lights are in our ~** los semáforos están a favor nuestro • **it's in our ~ to act now** nos beneficia actuar ahora • **a cheque made out in ~ of** un cheque extendido a nombre de • **the court found in their ~** el tribunal falló a *or* en su favor • **"balance in your favour"** "saldo *m* a su favor" • **that's a point in his ~** es un punto a su favor
4 (= *favouritism*) favoritismo *m* • **to show ~ to sb** favorecer a algn, tratar a algn con favoritismo
5 • **your ~ of the 5th inst†** (*Comm*) su atenta del 5 del corriente
6 (*Hist*) (= *token*) prenda *f*, favor† *m*
7 favours (*euph*) (*sexual*) favores *mpl*
(VT) **1** (= *support*) [+ *idea, scheme, view*] estar a favor de, ser partidario de • **he ~s higher taxes** está a favor de *or* es partidario de impuestos más elevados
2 (= *be beneficial to*) favorecer • **the scholarship programme ~s boys** el programa de becas favorece a los chicos • **circumstances that ~ this scheme** circunstancias *fpl* que favorecen este plan, circunstancias *fpl* propicias para este plan
3 (= *prefer, like*) preferir • **they ~ British-made cars** prefieren los coches de fabricación británica
4 (= *treat with favouritism*) tratar con favoritismo
5 (*frm*) (= *honour*) • **to ~ sb with sth** honrar a algn con algo • **he eventually ~ed us with a visit** (*hum*) por fin nos honró con su visita, por fin se dignó a visitarnos
6 (= *resemble*) parecerse a, salir a • **he ~s his father** se parece a su padre, sale a su padre
7 (= *protect*) [+ *injured limb*] tener cuidado con
8 (*Sport*) • **he is ~ed to win** es el favorito para ganar
favourable, favorable (*US*) ['feɪvərəbl] (ADJ) [*report*] favorable (**to** para); [*conditions, weather*] propicio, favorable • **to show sb in a ~ light** dar una buena imagen de algn
favourably, favorably (*US*) ['feɪvərəblɪ] (ADV) favorablemente
favoured, favored (*US*) ['feɪvəd] (ADJ) [*person, object*] favorito, preferido • **Biarritz was their ~ resort** Biarritz era su lugar de vacaciones favorito *or* preferido • **the ~ method is ...** el método preferido es ... • **one of the ~ few** uno de los pocos afortunados • **most ~ nation treatment** trato *m* de nación más favorecida
favourite, favorite (*US*) ['feɪvərɪt] (ADJ) favorito, preferido
(N) **1** (= *object*) favorito/a *m/f*; (= *person*) preferido/a *m/f*, favorito/a *m/f*; (*spoilt*) consentido/a *m/f*; (*at court*) valido *m*, privado *m*; (= *mistress*) querida *f* • **he sang some old ~s** cantó algunas de las viejas y conocidas canciones
2 (*in race, contest, election*) favorito/a *m/f* • **Liverpool are ~s to win** el Liverpool es el gran favorito
(CPD) ▸ **favorite son** (*US*) (*Pol*) hijo *m* predilecto
favouritism, favoritism (*US*) ['feɪvərɪtɪzəm] (N) favoritismo *m*
fawn¹ [fɔːn] (N) **1** (*Zool*) cervato *m*
2 (= *colour*) pardo *m* claro
(ADJ) de color pardo claro
fawn² [fɔːn] (VI) • **to ~ (up)on sb** [*animal*] hacer carantoñas a algn; (*fig*) [*person*] adular *or* lisonjear a algn
fawning ['fɔːnɪŋ] (ADJ) adulador, servil
fax [fæks] (N) (= *document*) fax *m*; (= *machine*) fax *m*
(VT) mandar por fax
(CPD) ▸ **fax machine** (máquina *f or* aparato *m* de) fax *m* ▸ **fax message** fax *m* ▸ **fax number** número *m* de fax
fay [feɪ] (N) (*liter*) (= *fairy*) hada *f*
faze* [feɪz] (VT) (= *disturb*) perturbar, desconcertar
fazed* [feɪzd] (ADJ) pasmado, anonadado
FBA (N ABBR) = **Fellow of the British Academy**
FBI (N ABBR) (*US*) (= **Federal Bureau of Investigation**) ≈ BIC *f*
FC (N ABBR) (= **football club**) C. F. *m*
FCA (N ABBR) **1** = **Fellow of the Institute of Chartered Accountants**
2 (*US*) = **Farm Credit Administration**
FCC (N ABBR) (*US*) (= **Federal Communications Commission**) ▹ **FAIRNESS DOCTRINE**

> **FCC**
> La **Federal Communications Commission** o **FCC** es un organismo gubernamental independiente que regula y supervisa las transmisiones de radio, televisión y comunicación por cable y satélite en Estados Unidos. Entre las funciones más importantes de la **FCC** están la de conceder la licencia de emisión a las cadenas de radio y televisión privadas, así como la de asignarles sus frecuencias de transmisión. Además, tiene una gran influencia en la programación de las cadenas de televisión, entre las que ha introducido, por ejemplo, un espacio de dos horas para toda la familia por las noches, un límite a la cantidad de programas nacionales que pueden ser transmitidos por una cadena local y una **Fairness Doctrine** o doctrina de imparcialidad para los asuntos más polémicos. La comisión se compone de cinco miembros nombrados por el Presidente de EE.UU., y es responsable de sus actividades ante el Congreso.
> ▹ **FAIRNESS DOCTRINE**

FCO (N ABBR) (*Brit*) (= **Foreign and Commonwealth Office**) ≈ Min. de AA.EE.
FD (N ABBR) (*US*) = **Fire Department**
(ABBR) **1** (*Brit*) (= **Fidei Defensor**) Defensor *m* de la Fe
2 (*Comm*) = **free delivered at dock**
FDA (N ABBR) (*US*) (= **Food and Drug Administration**) *organismo que fija niveles de calidad de los productos alimentarios y farmacéuticos*

> **FDA**
> El **FDA** o **Food and Drug Administration** es el organismo de atención al consumidor más antiguo de Estados Unidos. Su función es la de analizar los alimentos, aditivos alimentarios, medicinas y cosméticos para asegurarse de que son aptos para el consumo. El **FDA** es muy conocido en el extranjero por su papel en el análisis de los nuevos productos, de su efectividad y de sus posibles efectos nocivos, así como en el control de su consumo una vez han sido puestos a la venta.

FDD (N ABBR) (*Comput*) = **floppy disk drive**
FDIC (N ABBR) (*US*) = **Federal Deposit Insurance Corporation**
FDR (ABBR) = **Franklin Delano Roosevelt**
FE (ABBR) = **Further Education**
fealty ['fiːəltɪ] (N) (*Hist*) lealtad *f* (feudal)
fear [fɪəʳ] (N) **1** (= *terror*) miedo *m* • **he has overcome his ~ of dogs** ha superado su miedo a los perros • **to be in ~ of** *or* **for one's life** temer por su propia vida • **workers at the plant frequently went in ~ of their lives** a menudo los trabajadores de la fábrica temían por su vida • **to live in ~ of sth/sb** vivir atemorizado por algo/algn • **she lives in ~ of being found out** vive atemorizada de que la descubran • **to have no ~** no tener ningún miedo • **have no ~!††** (= *don't be afraid*) ¡pierde cuidado! • **~ of heights** miedo *m* a las alturas • **~ of flying** miedo *m* a volar • **in ~ and trembling** temblando de miedo • **she was trembling with ~** estaba temblando de

miedo • **without ~ or favour** con imparcialidad, imparcialmente • IDIOM: • **to put the ~ of God into sb** meter el miedo en el cuerpo a algn
2 (= *worry*) temor *m* • **his worst ~s were confirmed** sus mayores temores se vieron confirmados • **there are ~s that ...** se teme que (+ *subjun*) • **there are ~s that he may be dead** se teme que esté muerto • **there were ~s that he would raise taxes** se temía que subiera los impuestos • **I didn't go in for ~ of disturbing them** no entré por temor *or* miedo a molestarles • **she never goes out for ~ that it will happen again** nunca sale por temor *or* miedo a que suceda de nuevo • **there are grave ~s for their safety** se teme enormemente por su seguridad • **have no ~!** (*freq hum*) (= *don't worry*) ¡no se preocupe! • **you need have no ~ on that score** no tenga miedo en ese sentido
3 (= *chance*) posibilidad *f*; (= *danger*) peligro *m* • **there's not much ~ of his coming** no hay muchas posibilidades de que venga • **there's no ~ of that!** ¡no hay peligro de eso! • **no ~!*** ¡ni hablar!
(VT) **1** (= *be afraid of*) temer, tener miedo a • **I do not ~ death** no temo a la muerte, no tengo miedo a la muerte • **he was ~ed and hated by his subjects** sus súbditos le temían y odiaban • **to ~ that** temer que (+ *subjun*) • **we ~ed that he would escape** temíamos que se escapara • **they began to ~ that he was dangerous** empezaron a temer que fuera peligroso • **two people are missing and ~ed dead** hay dos personas desaparecidas y se teme que hayan muerto • **to ~ the worst** temer(se) lo peor
2 (= *think regretfully*) temerse • **to ~ that** temerse que • **I ~ that he won't come** me temo que no vendrá • **I ~ that you are right** me temo que tiene razón • **I ~ you may be right** me temo que tenga razón • **I ~ so/not** me temo que sí/no
3 (= *respect*) [+ *God*] temer
(VI) temer • **to ~ for sth/sb** temer por algo/algn • **she ~ed for her life** temía por su vida • **I ~ for him** temo por él, tengo miedo por él • **never ~** no hay cuidado*

fearful ['fɪəfʊl] (ADJ) **1** (= *frightened*) temeroso (of de) • **to be ~ that** tener miedo de que (+ *subjun*)
2 (= *frightening*) espantoso
3†* (= *awful*) horrible

fearfully ['fɪəfəlɪ] (ADV) **1** (= *timidly*) [*cower etc*] con miedo; [*say*] tímidamente
2†* (= *very*) terriblemente

fearfulness ['fɪəfʊlnɪs] (N) (= *fear*) medrosidad *f*; (= *shyness*) timidez *f*

fearless ['fɪəlɪs] (ADJ) (= *courageous*) valiente; (= *daring*) audaz; (= *adventurous*) intrépido • **he was a ~ opponent of slavery** era un valiente opositor de la esclavitud • **a ~ warrior** un valiente *or* audaz *or* intrépido guerrero • **she is completely ~** no le tiene miedo a nada • **he entered, ~ of what he might find there** entró, sin temor a lo que podría encontrarse allí

fearlessly ['fɪəlɪslɪ] (ADV) (= *courageously*) valientemente; (= *adventurously*) intrépidamente • **he's ~ outspoken** no tiene miedo a la hora de expresar su opinión

fearlessness ['fɪəlɪsnɪs] (N) (= *courage*) valor *m*, valentía *f*; (= *daring*) audacia *f*; (= *spirit of adventure*) intrepidez *f*

fearsome ['fɪəsəm] (ADJ) [*opponent, reputation, weapon*] temible; [*sight*] espantoso; [*competition*] encarnizado • **he has a ~ serve** tiene un saque temible *or* tremendo

fearsomely ['fɪəsəmlɪ] (ADV) tremendamente

feasibility [ˌfiːzə'bɪlɪtɪ] (N) viabilidad *f* • **to doubt the ~ of a scheme** poner en duda la viabilidad de un proyecto, dudar si un proyecto es factible
(CPD) ▸ **feasibility analysis** análisis *m inv* de viabilidad ▸ **feasibility study** estudio *m* de viabilidad

feasible ['fiːzəbl] (ADJ) **1** (= *practicable*) [*plan, suggestion*] factible, viable • **to make sth ~** posibilitar algo
2 (= *likely*) [*story, theory*] posible, plausible

feasibly ['fiːzəblɪ] (ADV) de forma factible

feast [fiːst] (N) **1** (= *meal*) banquete *m*; (= *big meal**) comilona* *f*, tragadera *f* (*Mex**) • IDIOM: • **it's ~ or famine** cuando mucho, cuando nada
2 (*Rel*) fiesta *f*
3 (*fig*) (= *treat*) • **the film promises a ~ of special effects** la película promete ser un derroche de efectos especiales
(VT) (*liter*) [+ *guest*] agasajar • **to ~ one's eyes on sth/sb** regalarse la vista con algo/algn
(VI) darse un banquete • **to ~ on sth** darse un banquete con algo
(CPD) ▸ **feast day** (*Rel*) fiesta *f*, día *m* festivo

feasting ['fiːstɪŋ] (N) (= *eating*) • **the ~ and drinking continued for several days** el festín y la bebida duraron varios días

feat [fiːt] (N) hazaña *f*, proeza *f*

feather ['feðəʳ] (N) pluma *f* • IDIOMS: • **in fine ~**† de excelente humor • **that is a ~ in his cap** es un tanto que se apunta • **you could have knocked me down with a ~*** me quedé de piedra • **as light as a ~** (tan) ligero como una pluma; ▹ **white**
(VT) **1** emplumar • IDIOM: • **to ~ one's nest** hacer su agosto
2 (*Rowing*) [+ *oar*] volver horizontal
(CPD) [*mattress, pillow*] de plumas ▸ **feather bed** colchón *m* de pluma(s) ▸ **feather boa** boa *f* de plumas ▸ **feather duster** plumero *m*

featherbed ['feðə'bed] (VT), (VI) (*Ind*) *estar expuesto a o imponer "featherbedding"*

featherbedding ['feðəˌbedɪŋ] (N) (*Ind*) *la práctica de disminuir la producción, duplicar el trabajo o el número de trabajadores al objeto de evitar despidos o crear más puestos de trabajo*

featherbrain ['feðəbreɪn] (N) cabeza *f* de chorlito*

featherbrained ['feðəbreɪnd] (ADJ) [*idea*] disparatado, descabellado • **to be ~** [*person*] ser un/una cabeza de chorlito*

feathered ['feðəd] (ADJ) [*bird*] plumado, con plumas • **our ~ friends** (*hum*) nuestros amigos plumados, nuestros amigos las aves

feathering ['feðərɪŋ] (N) plumaje *m*

featherweight ['feðəweɪt] (N) (*Boxing*) peso *m* pluma
(CPD) ▸ **featherweight champion** campeón/ona *m/f* de peso pluma ▸ **featherweight title** título *m* de peso pluma

feathery ['feðərɪ] (ADJ) [*texture*] plumoso; (= *light*) ligero como pluma

feature ['fiːtʃəʳ] (N) **1** [*of face*] rasgo *m* • **~s** rasgos *mpl*, facciones *fpl*
2 [*of countryside, building*] característica *f*
3 (*Comm, Tech*) elemento *m*, rasgo *m*
4 (*Theat*) número *m*; (*Cine*) película *f*
5 (*Press*) artículo *m* de fondo • **a regular ~** una crónica regular
6 (*Ling*) (*also* **distinctive feature**) rasgo *m* distintivo
(VT) **1** [+ *actor, news*] presentar; [+ *event*] ocuparse de, enfocar; (*in paper etc*) presentar • **a film featuring Garbo as ...** una película que presenta a la Garbo en el papel de ...
2 (= *be equipped with*) [*machine*] estar provisto de, ofrecer
(VI) **1** (*gen*) • **it ~d prominently in ...** tuvo un papel destacado en ...
2 (*Cine*) figurar, aparecer (**in** en)
(CPD) ▸ **feature article** artículo *m* de fondo ▸ **feature film** (película *f* de) largometraje *m* ▸ **features editor** redactor(a) *m/f* (jefe) de reportajes ▸ **feature writer** articulista *mf*, cronista *mf*

feature-length ['fiːtʃəleŋθ] (ADJ) [*documentary, drama*] especial • **feature-length film** (película *f* de) largometraje *m*

featureless ['fiːtʃəlɪs] (ADJ) monótono, anodino

Feb (ABBR) (= **February**) feb.

febrile ['fiːbraɪl] (ADJ) febril

February ['febrʊərɪ] (N) febrero *m*; ▹ **July**

fecal ['fiːkəl] (US) (ADJ) = **faecal**
(CPD) ▸ **fecal matter** materia *f* fecal

feces ['fiːsiːz] (NPL) (US) = **faeces**

feckless ['feklɪs] (ADJ) (= *weak*) débil, incapaz; (= *irresponsible*) irresponsable

fecund ['fiːkənd] (ADJ) fecundo

fecundity [fɪ'kʌndɪtɪ] (N) fecundidad *f*

Fed [fed] (N ABBR) **1** (*US**) (= **federal officer**) federal* *mf*
2 (*US*) (*Banking*) = **Federal Reserve Board**
(ABBR) (*esp US*) = **federal, federated, federation**

fed [fed] (PT), (PP) *of* **feed**

Fedayeen [fedɑː'jiːn] (NPL) fedayín *mpl*

federal ['fedərəl] (ADJ) federal
(N) (*US*) (*Hist*) federal *mf*
(CPD) ▸ **Federal Aviation Administration** (*US*) Administración *f* Federal de Aviación ▸ **Federal Bureau** (*US*) Departamento *m* de Estado ▸ **Federal Bureau of Investigation** (*US*) FBI *m*, ≈ Brigada *f* de Investigación Criminal ▸ **Federal Court** (*US*) Tribunal *m* Federal ▸ **federal holiday** (*US*) fiesta *f* nacional ▸ **federal officer** (*US*) federal *mf* ▸ **Federal Republic of Germany** República *f* Federal de Alemania ▸ **Federal Reserve Bank** (*US*) banco *m* de la Reserva Federal ▸ **Federal Reserve Board** (*US*) junta *f* de gobierno de la Reserva Federal ▸ **Federal Reserve System** (*US*) Reserva *f* Federal (*banco central de los EE. UU.*) ▸ **federal tax** impuesto *m* federal; ▹ **FCC**

federalism ['fedərəlɪzəm] (N) federalismo *m*

federalist ['fedərəlɪst] (ADJ) federalista
(N) federalista *mf*

federalize ['fedərəlaɪz] (VT) federar, federalizar

federate ['fedəreɪt] (VT) federar
(VI) federarse

federated ['fedəreɪtɪd] (ADJ) [*state, society*] federado

federation [ˌfedə'reɪʃən] (N) (= *group, system*) federación *f*

fedora [fə'dɔːrə] (N) sombrero *m* flexible, sombrero *m* tirolés

fed up* [ˌfed'ʌp] (ADJ) harto • **to be ~ (with sth/sb)** estar harto (de algo/algn) • **to be ~ with doing sth** estar harto de hacer algo

fee [fiː] (N) (= *professional*) honorarios *mpl*, emolumentos *mpl*; (*Comm*) pago *m*; (*for doctor's visit*) precio *m* de visita • **admission fee** precio *m* de entrada • **entrance/membership fee** cuota *f* • **course/tuition/school fees** matrícula *fsing* • **what's your fee?** ¿cuánto cobra Vd? • **for a small fee** por una pequeña *or* módica cantidad; ▹ **transfer**

feeble ['fiːbl] (ADJ) (COMPAR: **feebler**, SUPERL: **feeblest**) **1** (= *weak*) [*person, cry, protest*] débil; [*smile, laugh*] lánguido, débil; [*light*] tenue
2 (= *ineffective*) [*effort, attempt, resistance*] débil; [*excuse, argument*] poco convincente, flojo; [*joke*] soso

feeble-minded ['fiːbl'maɪndɪd] (ADJ) [*person*] bobo, zonzo (*LAm*)

feeble-mindedness [ˌfiːbl'maɪndɪdnɪs] (N) (*Med*) debilidad *f* mental

f

feebleness ['fi:blnɪs] (N) **1** (= *weakness*) [*of person*] debilidad *f*
2 (= *ineffectiveness*) [*of argument*] lo poco convincente, lo flojo
feebly ['fi:blɪ] (ADV) **1** (= *weakly*) [*move, struggle*] débilmente; [*smile, laugh*] lánguidamente, débilmente; [*shine*] tenuemente
2 (= *ineffectually*) [*protest*] sin fuerzas
feed [fi:d] (VB: PT, PP: **fed**) (VT) **1** (*lit*) **a** (= *give meal to*) [+ *person, animal*] dar de comer a; [+ *baby*] (= *bottle-feed*) dar el biberón a; (= *breastfeed*) dar de mamar a, dar el pecho a; [+ *plant*] alimentar • **they fed us well at the hotel** nos dieron de comer bien en el hotel • **have you fed the horses?** ¿has dado de comer a los caballos? • **"(please) do not feed the animals"** "prohibido dar de comer a los animales" • **you've made enough food to ~ an army** has hecho comida para un regimiento • **he has just started ~ing himself** acaba de empezar a comer solo
b (= *provide food for*) dar de comer (a), alimentar • **now there was another mouth to ~** ahora había que dar de comer a una boca más, ahora había una boca más que alimentar • **~ing a family can be expensive** dar de comer a *or* alimentar a una familia puede resultar caro • **it is enough to ~ the population for several months** es suficiente para alimentar a la población durante varios meses
c • **to ~ sb sth** • **~ sth to sb** dar algo (de comer) a algn • **you shouldn't ~ him that** no deberías darle eso • **he fed her ice cream with a spoon** • **he fed ice cream to her with a spoon** le dio helado con una cuchara • **he was ~ing bread to the ducks** les estaba echando pan a los patos • **what do you ~ your dog on?** ¿qué le das (de comer) a tu perro? • **they have been fed a diet of cartoons and computer games** los han tenido a base de dibujos animados y juegos de ordenador
2 (= *supply*) suministrar • **gas fed through pipelines** gas suministrado a través de tuberías • **the blood vessels that ~ blood to the brain** los vasos sanguíneos que suministran sangre al cerebro • **two rivers ~ this reservoir** dos ríos vierten sus aguas en este embalse • **he stole money to ~ his drug habit** robaba dinero para costear su drogadicción • **to ~ the (parking) meter** echar *or* meter monedas en el parquímetro
3 (= *tell*) • **to ~ sb sth** • **~ sth to sb: they fed us details of troop movements in the area** nos facilitaron detalles de movimientos de tropas en la zona • **he was being fed false information** le estaban pasando información falsa • **he was surrounded by people who fed him lies** estaba rodeado de gente que le llenaba la cabeza de mentiras • IDIOM: • **to ~ sb a line*** contar *or* soltar una bola a algn*
4 (= *insert*) • **to ~ sth into sth** meter *or* introducir algo en algo • **I fed a sheet of paper into the typewriter** metí *or* puse una hoja de papel en la máquina de escribir • **to ~ data into a computer** meter *or* introducir datos en un ordenador
5 (= *fuel*) [+ *fire, emotion, feeling*] alimentar; [+ *imagination*] estimular • **these rumours fed his fears** estos rumores alimentaron sus miedos • **to ~ the flames** (*lit, fig*) echar leña al fuego
6 (*Sport*) [+ *ball*] pasar
(VI) **1** (= *take food*) (*gen*) comer; (*at breast*) mamar • **to ~ on sth** (*lit*) alimentarse de algo, comer algo; (*fig*) alimentarse de algo • **the press ~s on intrigue** la prensa se alimenta de las intrigas
2 (= *lead*) • **a river that ~s into the Baltic Sea** un río que desemboca en el mar Báltico • **this road ~s into the motorway** esta carretera va a parar a la autopista • **the money spent by consumers ~s back into industry** el dinero que gastan los consumidores revierte en la industria
(N) **1** (= *food*) (*for animal*) forraje *m*, pienso *m* • **the six o'clock ~** (*for baby*) (= *breast or bottle feed*) la toma de las seis; (= *baby food*) la papilla de las seis; (= *ordinary food*) la comida de las seis • **it's time for his ~** le toca comer • **to be off one's ~** no tener apetito, estar desganado; ▹ **chicken**
2* (= *meal*) • **a good ~** una buena comida
3 (*Tech, Comput*) alimentador *m*; (= *tube*) tubo *m* de alimentación
4 (*Theat**) (= *straight man*) *personaje serio en una pareja cómica*; (= *line*) material *m* (*de un sketch cómico*)
(CPD) ▸ **feed bag** morral *m* ▸ **feed merchant** vendedor(a) *m/f* de forraje *or* pienso ▸ **feed pipe** tubo *m* de alimentación
▸ **feed back** (VT + ADV) [+ *information, results*] proporcionar, facilitar
▸ **feed in** (VT + ADV) **1** (= *insert*) [+ *coins, paper*] meter, introducir
2 (*Comput*) [+ *data*] meter, introducir
▸ **feed up** (VT + ADV) [+ *person*] engordar; [+ *animal*] cebar, engordar
feedback ['fi:dbæk] (N) **1** (*from person*) reacción *f* • **we're not getting much ~** no nos tienen demasiado informados de cómo vamos
2 (*from loudspeaker*) realimentación *f*, feedback *m*
feeder ['fi:dəʳ] (N) **1** (*Mech*) alimentador *m*, tubo *m* de alimentación
2 (*Aut, Rail*) ramal *m*
3 (*Geog*) afluente *m*
4 (*Brit*) (= *bib*) babero *m*
5 (= *device*) (*for birds etc*) comedero *m*
(CPD) ▸ **feeder (primary) school** (*Brit*) *escuela primaria que envía alumnos a un determinado colegio de enseñanza secundaria* ▸ **feeder service** (*US*) servicio *m* secundario (de transportes)
feeding ['fi:dɪŋ] (N) (= *act*) alimentación *f*; (= *meals*) comida *f*
(CPD) ▸ **feeding bottle** (*esp Brit*) biberón *m* ▸ **feeding frenzy** • **the birds engage in a ~ frenzy** los pájaros inician un frenético festín • **she was caught in a media ~ frenzy** se vio convertida en el centro de una atención febril por parte de los medios de comunicación ▸ **feeding ground** (*lit*) fuente *f* de alimentación; (*fig*) mina *f* de oro • **the factory will soon be a ~ ground for lawyers** la fábrica será pronto una mina de oro para los abogados ▸ **feeding time** (*at zoo*) hora *f* de comer; (*baby's*) (= *time for breast feed*) hora *f* del pecho; (= *time for bottle feed*) hora *f* del biberón
feedstuffs ['fi:dstʌfs] (NPL) piensos *mpl*
feel [fi:l] (VB: PT, PP: **felt**) (VT) **1** (= *touch*) tocar, palpar; [+ *pulse*] tomar • **I'm still ~ing my way** (*fig*) todavía me estoy familiarizando con la situación/el trabajo *etc* • **to ~ one's way (towards)** (*lit*) ir a tientas (hacia) • **we're ~ing our way towards an agreement** estamos tanteando el terreno para llegar a un acuerdo
2 (= *be aware of*) [+ *blow, pain, heat*] sentir; [+ *responsibility*] ser consciente de • **she felt a hand on her shoulder** sintió una mano en el hombro • **I felt something move** sentí que algo se movía • **I felt it getting hot** sentí que se iba calentando • **I do ~ the importance of this** soy plenamente consciente de la importancia de ello
3 (= *experience*) [+ *pity, anger, grief*] sentir • **the consequences will be felt next year** las consecuencias se harán sentir el año próximo • **they are beginning to ~ the effects of the trade sanctions** están empezando a sentir *or* notar los efectos de las sanciones económicas • **I ~ no interest in it** no me interesa en absoluto, no siento ningún interés por ello • **I felt myself blush** noté que me estaba sonrojando • **I felt myself being swept up in the tide of excitement** noté que me estaba dejando llevar por la oleada de entusiasmo • **I felt a great sense of relief** sentí un gran alivio
4 (= *be affected by, suffer from*) ser sensible a • **he doesn't ~ the cold** no es sensible al frío • **don't you ~ the heat?** ¿no te molesta el calor? • **he ~s the loss of his father very deeply** está muy afectado por la muerte de su padre
5 (= *think, believe*) • **what do you ~ about it?** ¿qué te parece a ti? • **I ~ that you ought to do it** creo que deberías hacerlo • **I ~ strongly that we should accept their offer** me parece muy importante que aceptemos su oferta • **he felt it necessary to point out that ...** creyó *or* le pareció necesario señalar que ...
(VI) **1** (*physically*) sentirse, encontrarse • **how do you ~ now?** ¿qué tal *or* cómo te sientes *or* te encuentras ahora? • **I ~ much better** me siento *or* me encuentro mucho mejor • **you'll ~ all the better for a rest** te sentirás mucho mejor después de descansar • **to ~ cold/hungry/sleepy** tener frío/hambre/sueño • **I felt (as if I was going to) faint** sentí como si fuera a desmayarme • **she's not ~ing quite herself** no se encuentra del todo bien • **to ~ ill** sentirse mal • **to ~ old** sentirse viejo • **do you ~ sick?** ¿estás mareado? • **I ~ quite tired** me siento bastante cansado • **I don't ~ up to a walk just now*** ahora mismo no me encuentro con fuerzas para dar un paseo
2 (*mentally*) • **how does it ~ to go hungry?** ¿cómo se siente uno pasando hambre? • **how do you ~ about him/about the idea?** ¿qué te parece él/la idea? • **how do you ~ about going for a walk?** ¿te apetece *or* (*LAm*) se te antoja dar un paseo? • **I ~ as if there is nothing we can do** tengo la sensación de que no hay nada que hacer, me da la impresión de que no podemos hacer nada • **he ~s bad about leaving his wife alone** siente haber dejado sola a su mujer • **I ~ very cross** estoy muy enfadado *or* (*LAm*) enojado • **I ~ for you!** (= *sympathize*) ¡lo siento por ti!, ¡te compadezco! • **we ~ for you in your loss** le acompañamos en el sentimiento • **since you ~ so strongly about it ...** ya que te parece tan importante ... • **I ~ sure that** estoy seguro de que
3 • **to ~ like a** (= *resemble*) • **it ~s like silk** parece seda al tocarlo • **what does it ~ like to do that?** ¿qué se siente al hacer eso? • **it felt like being drunk** parecía como si estuviera uno borracho
b (= *give impression, have impression*) • **it ~s like (it might) rain** parece que va a llover • **I felt (like) a fool** me sentí (un) estúpido • **I felt like a new man/woman** me sentí como un hombre nuevo/una mujer nueva
c (= *want*) • **I ~ like an apple** me apetece una manzana • **do you ~ like a walk?** ¿quieres dar un paseo?, ¿te apetece dar un paseo? • **I go out whenever I ~ like it** salgo cuando me apetece *or* cuando quiero • **I don't ~ like it** no me apetece, no tengo ganas • **I don't ~ like going out now** no tengo ganas de salir ahora
4 (= *give impression*) • **it ~s colder out here** se siente más frío aquí fuera • **the house ~s**

damp la casa parece húmeda • to ~ hard/cold/damp etc (to the touch) ser duro/frío/húmedo etc al tacto
5 (also feel around) (= grope) tantear, ir a tientas • to ~ around in the dark ir a tientas or tantear en la oscuridad • he was ~ing around in the dark for the door iba tanteando en la oscuridad para encontrar la puerta • she felt in her pocket for her keys rebuscó en el bolsillo para encontrar las llaves
(N) 1 (= sensation) sensación f • the ~ of them against his palm la sensación que producían al tocarlas • she liked the ~ of the breeze on her face le gustaba sentir la brisa en la cara • I don't like the ~ of wool against my skin no me gusta el contacto de la lana contra la piel • the fabric has a papery ~ la tela tiene una textura como de papel • to know sth by the ~ of it reconocer algo por el tacto
2 (= sense of touch) tacto m • to be rough to the ~ ser áspero al tacto
3 (= act) • let me have a ~! ¡déjame que lo toque!
4 (fig) (= impression, atmosphere) ambiente m, aspecto m • the room has a cosy ~ la habitación tiene un ambiente acogedor • to get the ~ of (fig) [+ new job, place] ambientarse a, familiarizarse con; [+ new car, machine] familiarizarse con • repeat this a few times to get the ~ of it repítelo unas cuantas veces hasta que te acostumbres or te cojas el tino • to get a ~ for (= get impression) hacerse una idea de • to have a ~ for languages/music tener talento para los idiomas/la música
▸ **feel out*** (VT + ADV) (fig) [+ person] tantear
▸ **feel up**‡ (VT + ADV) • to ~ sb up meter mano a algn*

feeler ['fi:lər] (N) 1 (Zool) [of insect, snail] antena f
2 (fig) sondeo m • IDIOM: • to put out ~s hacer un sondeo

feelgood ['fi:lgʊd] (ADJ) • the ~ factor la sensación de bienestar • a ~ movie una película que te hace sentir bien

feeling ['fi:lɪŋ] (N) 1 (physical) sensación f • a cold ~ una sensación de frío • to have no ~ in one's arm • have lost all ~ in one's arm no sentir un brazo
2 (= emotion) sentimiento m • bad or ill ~ rencor m, hostilidad f • to speak/sing with ~ hablar/cantar con sentimiento • she showed no ~ for him se mostró totalmente indiferente con él
3 feelings sentimientos mpl • to appeal to sb's finer ~s apelar a los sentimientos nobles de algn • no hard ~s! ¡todo olvidado! • to have ~s for sb querer a algn • to hurt sb's ~s herir los sentimientos de algn, ofender a algn • you can imagine my ~s! ¡ya te puedes imaginar cómo me sentía! • ~s ran high about it causó mucha controversia • to relieve one's ~s desahogarse • to spare sb's ~s no herir los sentimientos de algn; ▹ fine
4 (= impression) impresión f, sensación f • a ~ of security/isolation una sensación de seguridad/aislamiento • I have a (funny) ~ that ... tengo la (extraña) sensación de que ... • I get the ~ that ... me da la impresión de que ...
5 (= opinion) opinión f • there was a general ~ that ... la opinión general era que ... • our ~s do not matter nuestras opiniones no valen para nada • what are your ~s about the matter? ¿qué opinas tú del asunto? • my ~ is that ... creo que ...
6 (= sensitivity) sensibilidad f • a man of ~ un hombre sensible
7 (= aptitude) • to have a ~ for music tener talento para la música • he has no ~ for music no sabe apreciar la música

feelingly ['fi:lɪŋlɪ] (ADV) con honda emoción

fee-paying ['fi:,peɪɪŋ] (ADJ) [pupil] que paga pensión
(CPD) ▸ fee-paying school colegio m de pago

feet [fi:t] (NPL) of foot

FEFC (N ABBR) (Brit) (= Further Education Funding Council) *organismo de financiación de la formación profesional*

feign [feɪn] (VT) [+ surprise, indifference] fingir • to ~ madness/sleep/death fingirse loco/dormido/muerto • to ~ not to know fingir no saber

feigned [feɪnd] (ADJ) fingido

feint [feɪnt] (N) (Boxing, Fencing) finta f
(VI) fintar

feisty* ['faɪstɪ] (ADJ) (COMPAR: feistier, SUPERL: feistiest) (esp US) (= lively) animado; (= quarrelsome) pendenciero

feldspar ['feldspɑ:r] (N) feldespato m

felicitate [fɪ'lɪsɪteɪt] (VT) (frm) felicitar, congratular

felicitations [fɪlɪsɪ'teɪʃənz] (NPL) (frm) felicitaciones fpl

felicitous [fɪ'lɪsɪtəs] (ADJ) (frm) feliz, oportuno

felicity [fɪ'lɪsɪtɪ] (N) (frm) felicidad f; (= aptness) [of words] acierto m

feline ['fi:laɪn] (ADJ) felino
(N) felino m

fell[1] [fel] (PT) of fall

fell[2] [fel] (VT) (with a blow) derribar; [+ tree] talar, cortar; [+ cattle] acogotar

fell[3] [fel] (ADJ) • with one ~ blow con un golpe feroz • at one ~ swoop de un solo golpe

fell[4] [fel] (N) (Brit) (= moorland) páramo m, brezal m; (= hill) (usu pl) colina f rocosa

fell[5] [fel] (N) (= hide, pelt) piel f

fella* ['felə] (N) tipo* m, tío m (Sp*)

fellate [fe'leɪt] (VT) (frm) hacer una felación a

fellatio [fɪ'leɪʃɪəʊ] (N), **fellation** [fɪ'leɪʃən] (N) felación f

feller* ['felər] (N) tipo* m, tío m (Sp*)

fellow ['feləʊ] (N) 1 (= chap) hombre m, tipo* m, tío* m • can't a ~ get any peace! ¡es mucho pedir que le dejen a uno en paz! • my dear ~! ¡hombre! • well, this journalist ~ bueno, el tal periodista • those journalist ~s los periodistas esos • nice ~ buen chico m, buena persona f • he's an odd ~ es un tipo raro • old ~ viejo m • look here, old ~ mira, amigo • poor ~! ¡pobrecito! • young ~ chico m
2 (= comrade) compañero m
3 [of association, society etc] socio/a m/f
4 (Brit) (Univ etc) *miembro de la junta de gobierno de un colegio universitario*
5 (frm) (= other half) pareja f; (= equal) igual mf • it has no ~ no tiene par
(CPD) ▸ fellow being = fellow creature ▸ fellow citizen conciudadano/a m/f ▸ fellow countryman/-woman compatriota mf • "my ~ countrymen, ..." (in speech) —queridos compatriotas, ... ▸ fellow creature prójimo m ▸ fellow feeling compañerismo m ▸ fellow inmate compañero/a m/f de cárcel ▸ fellow member consocio/a m/f ▸ fellow men prójimos mpl, semejantes mpl ▸ fellow passenger compañero/a m/f de viaje ▸ fellow student compañero/a m/f de clase or curso ▸ fellow sufferer *persona que tiene la misma enfermedad que algn*; (fig) compañero/a m/f en la desgracia ▸ fellow traveller, fellow traveler (US) (lit) = fellow passenger (Pol) (with communists) simpatizante mf ▸ fellow worker compañero/a m/f de trabajo, colega mf

fellowship ['feləʊʃɪp] (N) 1 (= companionship) compañerismo m
2 (= club, society) asociación f
3 (Brit) (Univ) (= paid research post) puesto m de becario (de investigación); (US) (Univ) (= grant) beca f de investigación

fell-walking ['fel,wɔ:kɪŋ] (N) (Brit) senderismo m

felon ['felən] (N) (Jur) criminal mf, delincuente mf (de mayor cuantía)

felonious [fɪ'ləʊnɪəs] (ADJ) (Jur) criminal, delincuente

felony ['felənɪ] (N) (Jur) crimen m, delito m grave

felspar ['felspɑ:r] (N) feldespato m

felt[1] [felt] (PT), (PP) of feel

felt[2] [felt] (N) fieltro m
(CPD) ▸ felt hat sombrero m de fieltro ▸ felt pen rotulador m

felt-tip ['felttɪp] (N) (also felt-tip pen) rotulador m

fem. (ABBR) 1 = female
2 = feminine

female ['fi:meɪl] (ADJ) 1 [animal, plant] hembra • the ~ hippopotamus el hipopótamo hembra
2 [population] femenino; [vote] de las mujeres; [slave, subject] del sexo femenino • a ~ friend una amiga • ~ labour trabajo m femenino or de mujeres • the ~ sex el sexo femenino • a ~ student una estudiante • ~ suffrage derecho m de las mujeres a votar • a ~ voice una voz de mujer
(N) 1 (= animal) hembra f
2 (pej) (= woman) chica f
(CPD) ▸ female condom condón m femenino ▸ female impersonator (Theat) *actor que representa a una mujer*

femicide ['femɪsaɪd] (N) (= act) feminicidio m

Femidom® ['femɪdɒm] (N) Femidón® m

feminine ['femɪnɪn] (ADJ) femenino • ~ form (Ling) forma f femenina
(N) (Ling) femenino m • in the ~ en femenino

femininity [,femɪ'nɪnɪtɪ] (N) feminidad f

feminism ['femɪnɪzəm] (N) feminismo m

feminist ['femɪnɪst] (ADJ) feminista
(N) feminista mf

feminize ['femɪnaɪz] (VT) (frm) feminizar

femme [fæm, fem] (N)‡ *la que hace de "chica" en una relación lesbiana*
(ADJ)‡ (in lesbian relationship) femenina
(CPD) ▸ femme fatale mujer f fatal

femoral ['femərəl] (ADJ) femoral

femur ['fi:mər] (N) (PL: femurs or femora ['femərə]) fémur m

fen [fen] (N) (Brit) (often pl) zona f pantanosa, pantano m; ▹ Fens

fence [fens] (N) 1 (gen) valla f, cerca f; (= wire fence) alambrada f; (Racing) valla f • IDIOMS: • to mend one's ~s (= restore relations) mejorar las relaciones; (= restore reputation) restablecer la reputación • to sit on the ~ no comprometerse, mirar los toros desde la barrera
2* (= receiver of stolen goods) perista mf
(VT) 1 [+ land] vallar, cercar • ~d area zona f cercada or vallada
2 [+ machinery etc] cubrir, proteger
(VI) 1 (Sport) practicar esgrima
2 (fig) defenderse con evasivas
(CPD) ▸ fence post poste m
▸ **fence in** (VT + ADV) [+ animals, fig] encerrar; [+ land] vallar, cercar
▸ **fence off** (VT + ADV) separar con una valla or cerca

fencer ['fensər] (N) (Sport) esgrimista mf, esgrimidor(a) m/f

fencing ['fensɪŋ] (N) 1 (Sport) esgrima f
2 (= material) vallado m, cercado m
(CPD) ▸ fencing master maestro m de esgrima
▸ fencing match encuentro m de esgrima

f

fend [fend] VI • **to ~ for o.s.** defenderse solo, arreglárselas por cuenta propia
▸ **fend off** VT + ADV [+ *attack*] repeler, rechazar; [+ *assailant*] repeler; [+ *blow*] desviar, esquivar; [+ *awkward question*] soslayar, eludir
fender ['fendəʳ] N (*round fire*) guardafuego *m*; (*US*) (*Aut*) guardabarros *m inv*, guardafango *m* (*LAm*), salpicadera *f* (*Mex*), tapabarro *m* (*Peru*); (*US*) (*Rail*) trompa *f*; (*Naut*) defensa *f*
fenestration [ˌfenɪs'treɪʃən] N (*Tech*) ventanaje *m*
feng shui [ˌfeŋ'ʃuːɪ] N feng shui *m*
fenland ['fenlənd] N (*Brit*) terreno *m* pantanoso, marisma *f*
fennel ['fenl] N hinojo *m*
Fens [fenz] NPL (*Brit*) • **the ~** *las tierras bajas de Norfolk (antes zona de marismas)*
FEPC N ABBR (*US*) = **Fair Employment Practices Committee**
feral ['fɪərəl] ADJ (*frm*) silvestre, salvaje
FERC N ABBR (*US*) = **Federal Energy Regulatory Commission**
Ferdinand ['fɜːdɪnænd] N Fernando
ferment N ['fɜːment] **1** (= *leaven*) fermento *m*; (= *process*) fermentación *f*
2 (*fig*) (= *excitement*) agitación *f*, conmoción *f* • **in a (state of) ~** en un estado de agitación, conmocionado
VT [fə'ment] (*lit*) hacer fermentar; (*fig*) fomentar
VI [fə'ment] (*lit*) fermentar
fermentation [ˌfɜːmen'teɪʃən] N fermentación *f*
fermium ['fɜːmɪəm] N fermio *m*
fern [fɜːn] N helecho *m*
ferocious [fə'rəʊʃəs] ADJ **1** (= *savage*) [*animal*] fiero, feroz; [*attack*] feroz
2 (= *intense*) [*storm, wind*] violento; [*fire*] voraz; [*battle*] feroz, encarnizado; [*energy*] tremendo; [*heat*] atroz
ferociously [fə'rəʊʃəslɪ] ADV [*bark, glare*] ferozmente, con ferocidad; [*fight, attack*] ferozmente • **the sun was ~ hot** hacía un calor atroz, el calor era implacable • **he worked ~ hard** trabajaba durísimo
ferociousness [fə'rəʊʃəsnɪs] N = **ferocity**
ferocity [fə'rɒsɪtɪ] N **1** (= *savagery*) [*of person, animal, attack, battle*] ferocidad *f*
2 (= *intensity*) [*of storm, wind, fire*] furia *f*; [*of feelings*] intensidad *f*; [*of criticism*] dureza *f*
ferret ['ferɪt] N hurón *m*
VI cazar con hurones
▸ **ferret about, ferret around** VI + ADV hurgar (**in** en)
▸ **ferret out** VT + ADV [+ *person*] dar con; [+ *secret, truth*] desentrañar
ferric ['ferɪk] ADJ férrico
Ferris wheel ['ferɪswiːl] N (*US*) noria *f*
ferrite ['feraɪt] N ferrito *m*, ferrita *f*
ferro- ['ferəʊ] PREFIX ferro-
ferro-alloy ['ferəʊ'ælɔɪ] N ferroaleación *f*
ferrous ['ferəs] ADJ ferroso
ferrule ['feruːl] N regatón *m*, contera *f*
ferry ['ferɪ] N (*also* **ferryboat**) barca *f* (de pasaje); (*large*) (*for cars etc*) transbordador *m*, ferry *m*
VT • **to ~ sth/sb across** *or* **over** llevar algo/a algn a la otra orilla • **to ~ people to and fro** (*fig*) (*in car etc*) llevar *or* transportar a la gente de un lado para otro
CPD ▸ **ferry company** compañía *f* de ferry ▸ **ferry crossing** travesía *f* en ferry ▸ **ferry operator** operador(a) *m/f* de ferries ▸ **ferry port** puerto *m* de ferries ▸ **ferry terminal** terminal *f* de ferry
ferryboat ['ferɪbəʊt] N = **ferry**
ferryman ['ferɪmən] N (PL: **ferrymen**) barquero *m*

fertile ['fɜːtaɪl] ADJ **1** (*Agr*) [*land, valley, soil*] fértil
2 (*Bio*) [*woman, animal, phase*] fértil; [*egg*] fértil, fecundo
3 (*fig*) (= *productive*) fértil; (= *creative*) [*imagination, mind*] fecundo, fértil • **this was her most ~ period of writing** como escritora, esta fue su época más fértil • **this situation provides a ~ breeding ground for racists** esta situación es un caldo de cultivo para el racismo
CPD ▸ **fertile period** [*of woman, animal*] periodo *m* fértil
fertility [fə'tɪlɪtɪ] N [*of land, woman, animal*] fertilidad *f*
CPD ▸ **fertility clinic** clínica *f* de fertilidad ▸ **fertility drug** medicamento *m* para el tratamiento de la infertilidad ▸ **fertility rite** rito *m* de fertilidad ▸ **fertility symbol** símbolo *m* de la fertilidad ▸ **fertility treatment** tratamiento *m* contra la esterilidad
fertilization [ˌfɜːtɪlaɪ'zeɪʃən] N fecundación *f*, fertilización *f*
fertilize ['fɜːtɪlaɪz] VT **1** [+ *egg*] fecundar
2 (*Agr*) [+ *land, soil*] abonar, fertilizar
fertilizer ['fɜːtɪlaɪzəʳ] N (*for soil, land*) abono *m* (artificial), fertilizante *m*
fervent ['fɜːvənt] ADJ [*prayer*] ferviente; [*desire*] ardiente; [*belief*] firme; [*supporter*] acérrimo, ferviente; [*denial*] enfático • **he is a ~ believer in neoliberalism** es un acérrimo *or* ferviente partidario del neoliberalismo • **it is my ~ hope that …** espero fervientemente que …
fervently ['fɜːvəntlɪ] ADV [*pray*] con fervor, fervientemente; [*believe*] firmemente; [*hope, desire*] fervientemente, ardientemente; [*deny*] enfáticamente, con vehemencia; [*support*] con fervor, fervorosamente • **he is ~ patriotic** es un patriota acérrimo *or* ferviente • **he was ~ opposed to the war** se oponía enérgicamente a la guerra
fervid ['fɜːvɪd] ADJ (*frm*) = **fervent**
fervour, fervor (*US*) ['fɜːvəʳ] N fervor *m*
fess up [ˌfes'ʌp] VI + ADV (*US**) desembuchar*
fest* [fest] N • **film ~** festival *m* de cine • **gore ~** orgía *f* de sangre
fester ['festəʳ] VI (*Med*) [*wound, sore*] enconarse; (*fig*) [*anger, resentment*] enconarse
festival ['festɪvəl] N (*Rel etc*) fiesta *f*; (*Mus etc*) festival *m*
festive ['festɪv] ADJ (*gen*) festivo; (= *happy*) alegre • **in (a) ~ mood** muy alegre • **the ~ season** las Navidades
festivity [fes'tɪvɪtɪ] N **1** (= *celebration*) fiesta *f*, festividad *f*; (= *joy*) regocijo *m*
2 festivities festejos *mpl*, fiestas *fpl*
festoon [fes'tuːn] N guirnalda *f*, festón *m*; (*Sew*) festón *m*
VT adornar, engalanar (**with** de) • **to be ~ed with** estar adornado *or* engalanado de
FET N ABBR (*US*) = **Federal Excise Tax**
feta ['fetə] N (*also* **feta cheese**) feta *m*
fetal ['fiːtl] ADJ (*US*) = **foetal**
fetch [fetʃ] VT **1** (= *go and get, bring*) [+ *object*] traer; [+ *person*] ir a buscar a • **can you ~ my coat?** ¿me trae el abrigo? • **I'll go and ~ it for you** te lo voy a buscar • **~ (it)!** (*to dog*) ¡busca! • **they're ~ing the doctor** han ido (a) por el médico • **please ~ the doctor** llama al médico • **they ~ed him all that way** le hicieron venir desde tan lejos • **to ~ sb back from Spain** hacer que algn vuelva de España
2 (= *sell for*) venderse por • **how much did it ~?** ¿por cuánto se vendió?
3 [+ *blow, sigh*] dar
VI • **to ~ and carry** ir de acá para allá, trajinar • **to ~ and carry for sb** ser el sirviente de algn

▸ **fetch in** VT + ADV [+ *object*] meter; [+ *person*] hacer entrar
▸ **fetch out** VT + ADV sacar
▸ **fetch up*** VI + ADV (= *reappear, end up*) [*person, object*] ir a parar (**in** a)
VT + ADV (*Brit*) (= *vomit*) vomitar, arrojar
fetching ['fetʃɪŋ] ADJ (= *attractive*) atractivo
fetchingly ['fetʃɪŋlɪ] ADV atractivamente
fête [feɪt] N **1** (= *party*) fiesta *f* • **to be en ~** estar de fiesta
2 (*for charity*) feria *f* benéfica
VT (= *honour*) ensalzar; (= *have a celebration for*) festejar
fetid ['fetɪd] ADJ fétido
fetish ['fetɪʃ] N (= *object of cult, sexual*) fetiche *m*; (*fig*) (= *obsession*) obsesión *f*
fetishism ['fetɪʃɪzəm] N fetichismo *m*
fetishist ['fetɪʃɪst] N fetichista *mf*
fetishistic [ˌfetɪ'ʃɪstɪk] ADJ fetichista
fetlock ['fetlɒk] N **1** (*Zool*) (= *joint*) espolón *m*
2 (= *hair*) cernejas *fpl*
fetter ['fetəʳ] VT [+ *person*] encadenar, poner grilletes a; [+ *horse*] trabar; (*fig*) poner trabas a
fetters ['fetəz] NPL grilletes *mpl*; (*fig*) trabas *fpl*
fettle ['fetl] N • **in fine ~** (= *condition*) en buenas condiciones; (= *mood*) de muy buen humor
fettuccine [ˌfetə'tʃiːnɪ] N fettuchini *mpl*
fetus ['fiːtəs] N (*US*) = **foetus**
feud [fjuːd] N enemistad *f* heredada • **a family ~** una disputa familiar
VI pelearse • **to ~ with sb** pelearse con algn
feudal ['fjuːdl] ADJ feudal
CPD ▸ **feudal system** feudalismo *m*
feudalism ['fjuːdəlɪzəm] N feudalismo *m*
fever ['fiːvəʳ] N **1** (= *disease, high temperature*) fiebre *f*, calentura *f* (*LAm*) • **he has a ~** tiene fiebre • **a bout of ~** un ataque de fiebre • **a slight/high ~** un poco de/mucha fiebre
2 (*fig*) • **the gambling ~** la fiebre del juego • **a ~ of excitement/impatience** una emoción/impaciencia febril • **she's in a ~ about the party** la fiesta la tiene muy alterada
CPD ▸ **fever blister** (*US*) (= *cold sore*) herpes *m inv* labial, pupa* *f* ▸ **fever pitch** • **it reached ~ pitch** se puso al rojo vivo
fevered ['fiːvəd] ADJ = **feverish**
feverish ['fiːvərɪʃ] ADJ **1** (*Med*) febril, calenturiento • **to be ~** tener fiebre
2 (*fig*) febril
feverishly ['fiːvərɪʃlɪ] ADV febrilmente
feverishness ['fiːvərɪʃnɪs] N (*Med*) (*also fig*) febrilidad *f*
few [fjuː] ADJ, PRON (COMPAR: **fewer**, SUPERL: **fewest**) **1** (= *not many*) pocos/as • **few books** pocos libros • **few of them** pocos (de ellos) • **only a few** solo unos pocos • **only a few of them came** solo vinieron unos pocos • **there are very few of us** • **we are very few** somos muy pocos • **few (people) managed to do it** muy pocos consiguieron hacerlo • **the few who …** los pocos que … • **she is one of the few (people) who …** ella es una de los pocos que … • **such men are few** hay pocos hombres así • **as few as three of them** nada más que tres • **every few weeks** cada dos o tres semanas • **with few exceptions** con pocas excepciones • **they are few and far between** son contados • **the lucky few** unos pocos *or* unos cuantos afortunados • **in** *or* **over the next few days** en *or* durante los próximos días, en estos días (*LAm*) • **in** *or* **over the past few days** en *or* durante los últimos días • **the last** *or* **remaining few minutes** el poco tiempo que queda/quedaba • **too few** demasiado pocos • **there were three too few** faltaban tres

2 (= *some, several*) • **a few** algunos • **a good few** • **quite a few** bastantes • **a good few** *or* **quite a few (people) came** vinieron bastantes, vino bastante gente • **he'd had a few (drinks)*** llevaba ya una copa de más • **a few more** algunos más • **(in) a few more days** dentro de unos pocos días • **a few of them** algunos de ellos

fewer ['fju:əʳ] (ADJ), (PRON) (*compar of* **few**) menos • ~ **than ten** menos de diez • **no ~ than ...** no menos de ... • **they have ~ than I** tienen menos que yo • **the ~ the better** cuantos menos mejor; ▷ LESS THAN, FEWER THAN

fewest ['fju:ɪst] (ADJ), (PRON) (*superl of* **few**) los/las menos

fewness ['fju:nɪs] (N) corto número *m*

fey [feɪ] (ADJ) vidente

fez [fez] (N) (PL: **fezzes**) fez *m*

ff (ABBR) (= **and the following**) sigs., sgtes.

FFA (N ABBR) = **Future Farmers of America**

FFV (ABBR) (= **First Families of Virginia**) *descendientes de los primeros colonos de Virginia*

FGM (N ABBR) (= *female genital mutilation*) MGF *f*, mutilación *f* genital femenina

FH (N ABBR) = **fire hydrant**

FHA (N ABBR) (US) = **Federal Housing Association**

FHSA (N ABBR) (Brit) = **Family Health Services Authority**

fiancé [fɪ'ɑ̃:nseɪ] (N) novio *m*, prometido *m*

fiancée [fɪ'ɑ̃:nseɪ] (N) novia *f*, prometida *f*

fiasco [fɪ'æskəʊ] (N) (PL: **fiascos, fiascoes**) fiasco *m*, desastre *m*

fiat ['faɪæt] (N) fíat *m*, autorización *f*

fib* [fɪb] (N) mentirijilla *f* • **to tell a fib** decir una mentirijilla
(VI) decir mentirijillas

fibber* ['fɪbəʳ] (N) mentirosillo/a *m/f*

fibre, fiber (US) ['faɪbəʳ] (N) **1** (= *thread*) fibra *f*, hilo *m*; (= *fabric*) fibra *f*
2 (*fig*) nervio *m*, carácter *m*
3 (*in diet*) fibra *f*
(CPD) ▸ **fibre optics, fiber optics** (US) transmisión *f* por fibra óptica

fibreboard, fiberboard (US) ['faɪbəbɔ:d] (N) fibra *f* vulcanizada

fibreglass, fiberglass (US) ['faɪbəglɑ:s] (N) fibra *f* de vidrio
(CPD) de fibra de vidrio

fibre-optic, fiber-optic (US) [,faɪbər'ɒptɪk] (ADJ) de fibra óptica
(CPD) ▸ **fibre-optic cable** cable *m* de fibra óptica

fibre-tip ['faɪbətɪp] (N) (*also* **fibre-tip pen**) (*Brit*) rotulador *m* de punta de fibra

fibroid ['faɪbrɔɪd] (N) fibroma *m*

fibrositis [,faɪbrə'saɪtɪs] (N) fibrositis *f inv*

fibrous ['faɪbrəs] (ADJ) fibroso

fibula ['fɪbjʊlə] (N) (PL: **fibulas** *or* **fibulae** ['fɪbjʊli:]) peroné *m*

FIC (N ABBR) (US) = **Federal Information Center**

FICA (N ABBR) (US) = **Federal Insurance Contributions Act**

fickle ['fɪkl] (ADJ) inconstante, veleidoso, voluble

fickleness ['fɪklnɪs] (N) inconstancia *f*, veleidad *f*, volubilidad *f*

fiction ['fɪkʃən] (N) **1** (*Literat*) literatura *f* de ficción, narrativa *f* • **a work of ~** una obra de ficción
2 (= *untruth*) ficción *f*, invención *f*

fictional ['fɪkʃənl] (ADJ) ficticio

fictionalize ['fɪkʃənəlaɪz] (VT) novelar

fictionalized ['fɪkʃənəlaɪzd] (ADJ) novelado

fictitious [fɪk'tɪʃəs] (ADJ) **1** = **fictional**
2 (= *false*) falso

Fid. Def. (ABBR) (= **Fidei Defensor**) (= *Defender of the Faith*) Defensor *m* de la Fe

fiddle ['fɪdl] (N) **1** (= *violin*) violín *m* • IDIOMS: • **to play second ~** desempeñar un papel secundario • **to play second ~ to sb** estar a la sombra de algn • **he's fed up with playing second ~ to his older brother** está harto de estar a la sombra de su hermano mayor
2 (*esp Brit**) (= *cheat*) trampa *f*, superchería *f* • **it's a ~** aquí hay trampa • **tax ~** evasión *f* fiscal • **to work a ~** hacer trampa • **to be on the ~** dedicarse a hacer chanchullos*
(VI) **1** (*Mus*) tocar el violín • IDIOM: • **to ~ while Rome burns** perder el tiempo con nimiedades e ignorar el verdadero problema
2 (= *fidget*) enredar • **do stop fiddling!** ¡deja ya de enredar! • **to ~ (about** *or* **around) with sth** enredar *or* juguetear con algo • **someone has been fiddling (about** *or* **around) with it** alguien lo ha estropeado, alguien ha estado enredando con él
3 (*esp Brit**) (= *cheat*) hacer trampas
(VT) (*esp Brit**) [+ *accounts, results, expenses claim etc*] manipular • **to ~ one's income tax** defraudar impuestos
▸ **fiddle about***, **fiddle around*** (VI + ADV) perder el tiempo

fiddler ['fɪdləʳ] (N) **1** (*Mus*) violinista *mf*
2 (*esp Brit**) (= *cheat*) tramposo/a *m/f*

fiddlesticks* ['fɪdlstɪks] (EXCL) ¡tonterías!

fiddliness ['fɪdlɪnɪs] (N) (*Brit*) complejidad *f*

fiddling ['fɪdlɪŋ] (ADJ) trivial, insignificante
(N)* (= *cheating*) chanchullos* *mpl*

fiddly ['fɪdlɪ] (ADJ) (COMPAR: **fiddlier**, SUPERL: **fiddliest**) [*job*] complicado, difícil; [*object*] difícil de manejar

FIDE (N ABBR) (= **Fédération Internationale des Échecs**) FIDE *f*

fidelity [fɪ'delɪtɪ] (N) (= *faithfulness*) fidelidad *f*; (= *closeness to original*) exactitud *f*, fidelidad *f*

fidget ['fɪdʒɪt] (N) **1** (= *person*) persona *f* inquieta, azogado/a *m/f*
2 • **to have the ~s** no parar quieto, ser un azogue
(VI) (*also* **fidget about, fidget around**) no parar de moverse • **to ~ with sth** juguetear con algo • **don't ~!** • **stop ~ing!** ¡estáte quieto!

fidgety ['fɪdʒɪtɪ] (ADJ) nervioso, inquieto • **to be ~** no parar quieto

fiduciary [fɪ'dju:ʃɪərɪ] (ADJ) fiduciario
(N) fiduciario/a *m/f*

fie†† [faɪ] (EXCL) • **fie on him!** ¡al diablo con él!

fief [fi:f] (N) feudo *m*

fiefdom ['fi:fdəm] (N) feudo *m*

field [fi:ld] (N) **1** (*Agr*) campo *m*; (= *meadow*) prado *m*; (*Geol*) yacimiento *m*
2 (*Sport*) campo *m*, terreno *m* de juego, cancha *f* (*LAm*); (= *participants*) participantes *mpl*; (*for post*) opositores *mpl*, candidatos *mpl* • **is there a strong ~?** ¿se ha presentado gente buena? • **to lead the ~** (*Sport, Comm*) llevar la delantera • **to take the ~** (*Sport*) salir al campo, saltar al terreno de juego • IDIOM: • **to play the ~*** alternar con cualquiera
3 (= *sphere of activity*) campo *m*, esfera *f* • **~ of activity** esfera *f* de actividades, campo *m* de acción • **my particular ~** mi especialidad • **it's not my ~** no es mi campo *or* especialidad, no es lo mío • **what's your ~?** ¿qué especialidad tiene Vd? • **in the ~ of painting** en el campo *or* mundo de la pintura • **to be the first in the ~** ser líder en su campo
4 (= *real environment*) • **a year's trial in the ~** un año de prueba en el mercado • **to study sth in the ~** estudiar algo sobre el terreno
5 (*Comput*) campo *m*
6 (*Mil*) campo *m* • **~ of battle** campo *m* de batalla • **to die in the ~** morir en combate
7 (*Elec etc*) campo *m* • **~ of vision** campo *m* visual
8 (*Heraldry*) campo *m*
(VI) (*Baseball, Cricket*) fildear
(VT) (*Sport*) [+ *team*] alinear; (*Baseball, Cricket*) [+ *ball*] recoger, fildear; (*fig*) [+ *question*] sortear
(CPD) ▸ **field day** (*Mil*) día *m* de maniobras • IDIOM: • **to have a ~ day** sacar el máximo provecho ▸ **field event** concurso *m* (atlético) de salto/lanzamiento ▸ **field glasses** (= *binoculars*) gemelos *mpl* ▸ **field goal** (*Basketball*) tiro *m* de campo; (US) (*Ftbl*) gol *m* de campo ▸ **field hockey** (US) hockey *m* (sobre hierba) ▸ **field gun** cañón *m* de campaña ▸ **field hand** (US) jornalero/a *m/f* ▸ **field hospital** hospital *m* de campaña ▸ **field kitchen** cocina *f* de campaña ▸ **field marshal** (*Brit*) mariscal *m* de campo, ≈ capitán *m* general del ejército ▸ **field officer** oficial *mf* superior ▸ **field sports** *la caza y la pesca* ▸ **field study** estudio *m* de campo ▸ **field test, field trial** (*Comm*) prueba *f* de mercado; ▷ **field-test** ▸ **field trip** viaje *m or* excursión *f* de estudios ▸ **field work** (*Sociol etc*) trabajo *m* de campo ▸ **field worker** investigador(a) *m/f* de campo

fielder ['fi:ldəʳ] (N) (*Baseball, Cricket*) fildeador(a) *m*; ▷ CRICKET, BASEBALL

fieldfare ['fi:ldfɛəʳ] (N) zorzal *m* real

fieldmouse ['fi:ldmaʊs] (N) (PL: **fieldmice**) ratón *m* de campo

fieldsman ['fi:ldzmən] (N) (PL: **fieldsmen**) = **fielder**

field-test (VT) ['fi:ld,test] (*Comm*) probar en el mercado

fiend [fi:nd] (N) **1** (= *devil*) demonio *m*, diablo *m*
2* (= *person*) malvado/a *m/f*
3* (= *addict*) • **drugs ~** drogadicto/a *m/f* • **sex ~** maníaco *m* sexual

fiendish ['fi:ndɪʃ] (ADJ) (= *fierce*) feroz; (= *mildly wicked*) muy travieso; (= *clever and wicked*) diabólico; (= *difficult**) dificilísimo

fiendishly ['fi:ndɪʃlɪ] (ADV) terriblemente • **~ difficult** terriblemente difícil • **~ expensive** carísimo

fierce [fɪəs] (ADJ) (COMPAR: **fiercer**, SUPERL: **fiercest**) **1** (= *ferocious*) [*animal*] feroz, fiero; [*gesture, expression*] feroz; [*temper*] temible • **the prime minister came under ~ attack from the opposition** la oposición atacó ferozmente al primer ministro • **she gave me a ~ look** me lanzó una mirada furibunda
2 (= *intense*) [*competition, argument*] encarnizado; [*storm, wind, opposition, resistance*] violento; [*opponent*] empedernido, acérrimo; [*pride, loyalty*] impasionado; [*heat*] intenso • **~ fighting broke out in the capital** se produjeron enfrentamientos encarnizados en la capital • **the fire was so ~ that it took several hours to put it out** el fuego era tan intenso que se tardaron varias horas en apagarlo

fiercely ['fɪəslɪ] (ADV) **1** (= *ferociously*) [*look, scowl*] ferozmente, con ferocidad; [*attack*] ferozmente
2 (= *intensely*) [*independent, competitive, loyal*] tremendamente; [*oppose, resist*] ferozmente; [*fight, compete*] encarnizadamente • **she is a ~ independent woman** es una mujer tremendamente independiente • **it was a ~ contested match** fue un partido extremadamente reñido • **they are ~ protective of their privacy** protegen su intimidad con uñas y dientes • **the building was burning ~** el edificio ardía en llamas • **the storm raged ~ outside** fuera, el temporal rugía con fuerza

fierceness ['fɪəsnɪs] (N) **1** (= *ferocity*) [*of animal, person*] ferocidad *f*

2 (= *intensity*) [*of heat, sun, passion*] intensidad *f*; [*of storm*] furia *f*

fieriness ['faɪərɪnɪs] (N) **1** [*of temperament, speech, performance*] fogosidad *f*
2 (= *spiciness*) [*of food*] lo picante

fiery ['faɪərɪ] (ADJ) (COMPAR: **fierier**, SUPERL: **fieriest**) **1** [*heat, sun*] abrasador
2 (*fig*) [*sky, sunset, red*] encendido; [*taste*] picante; [*temperament, speech, performance*] acalorado, fogoso; [*horse*] fogoso; [*liquor*] fuerte

fiesta [fɪ'estə] (N) fiesta *f*

FIFA ['fi:fə] (N ABBR) (= **Fédération Internationale de Football Association**) FIFA *f*

fife [faɪf] (N) pífano *m*

FIFO ['faɪfəʊ] (ABBR) (= **first in, first out**) primero en entrar, primero en salir

fifteen [fɪf'ti:n] (ADJ), (PRON) quince • **about ~ people** unas quince personas
(N) (= *numeral*) quince *m*; (*Rugby*) quince *m*, equipo *m*; ▹ **five**

fifteenth [fɪf'ti:nθ] (ADJ) decimoquinto
(N) (*in series*) decimoquinto/a *m/f*; (= *fraction*) quinceavo *m*, quinceava parte *f*; ▹ **fifth**

fifth [fɪfθ] (ADJ) quinto • **he came ~ in the competition** ocupó el quinto lugar *or* terminó quinto en la competición • **in the ~ century** (*in writing*) en el siglo V; (*speaking*) en el siglo quinto *or* cinco • **Henry the Fifth** (*in writing*) Enrique V; (*speaking*) Enrique Quinto • **the ~ of July** • **July the ~** el cinco de julio • **~ form** (*Brit*) (*Scol*) quinto *m*, quinto curso
(N) **1** (*in series*) quinto/a *m/f* • **I was the ~ to arrive** yo fui el quinto en llegar • **I wrote to him on the ~** le escribí el día cinco; ▹ **amendment**
2 (= *fraction*) quinto *m*, quinta parte *f*
3 (*Mus*) quinta *f*
(CPD) ▸ **fifth column** (*Pol*) quinta columna *f* ▸ **fifth columnist** (*Pol*) quintacolumnista *mf*

fifth-grader [ˌfɪfθ'greɪdəʳ] (N) (*US*) alumno/a *m/f* de quinto curso (*de entre 10 y 11 años*)

fiftieth ['fɪftɪɪθ] (ADJ) quincuagésimo • **the ~ anniversary** el cincuenta aniversario
(N) (*in series*) quincuagésimo/a *m/f*; (= *fraction*) quincuagésimo *m*, quincuagésima parte *f*

fifty ['fɪftɪ] (ADJ), (PRON) cincuenta • **about ~ people/cars** alrededor de cincuenta personas/coches • **he'll be ~ (years old) this year** cumple *or* va a cumplir cincuenta este año
(N) (= *numeral*) cincuenta *m* • **the fifties** (= *1950s*) los años cincuenta • **to be in one's fifties** andar por los cincuenta • **the temperature was in the fifties** hacía más de cincuenta grados • **to do ~ (miles per hour)** (*Aut*) ir a cincuenta (millas por hora)

fifty-fifty ['fɪftɪ'fɪftɪ] (ADJ) • **we have a fifty-fifty chance of success** tenemos un cincuenta por ciento de posibilidades de éxito • **it's a fifty-fifty deal** es un negocio a medias • **we'll do it on a fifty-fifty basis** lo haremos a medias
(ADV) • **to go fifty-fifty with sb** ir a medias con algn

fiftyish ['fɪftɪɪʃ] (ADJ) de unos cincuenta años

fig [fɪg] (N) **1** (*Bot*) higo *m*; (*early*) breva *f*; (*also* **fig tree**) higuera *f*
2 • **I don't give a fig for JB!**†* ¡me importa un comino JB!
(CPD) ▸ **fig leaf** hoja *f* de higuera; (*fig*) (*Art*) hoja *f* de parra

fig. (ABBR) = **figure**

fight [faɪt] (VB: PT, PP: **fought**) (N) **1** (*between individuals*) **a** (*physical, verbal*) pelea *f* (**over** por) • **to have a ~ with sb** pelearse con algn, tener una pelea con algn • **to look for a ~** (*physical*) buscar pelea; (*verbal*) querer pelearse • **I'm not looking for a ~ over this issue** no quiero pelearme por este asunto; ▹ **pick**
b (*Boxing*) combate *m*, pelea *f*
2 (*Mil*) (*between armies*) lucha *f*, contienda *f*
3 (= *struggle, campaign*) lucha *f* (**for** por, **against** contra) • **the ~ for justice/against inflation** la lucha por la justicia/contra la inflación • **he won't give up without a ~** no se rendirá sin luchar antes • **if he tries to sack me he'll have a ~ on his hands** si intenta despedirme le va a costar lo suyo
4 (= *fighting spirit*) ánimo *m* de lucha • **there was no ~ left in him** ya no le quedaba ánimo de lucha, ya no tenía ánimo para luchar • **we still had a lot of ~ in us** todavía nos quedaba mucho ánimo para luchar • **to show (some) ~** mostrarse dispuesto a pelear
5 (= *resistance*) • **police believe the victim put up a ~** la policía cree que la víctima opuso resistencia • **they beat us but we put up a good ~** nos vencieron pero nos defendimos bien
(VT) **1** (*Mil*) [+ *enemy*] luchar contra, combatir contra; (*Boxing*) [+ *opponent*] pelear contra, luchar contra • **to ~ a battle** (*Mil*) librar una batalla; (*fig*) luchar • **I've had to ~ quite a battle to get as far as this** he tenido que luchar mucho para llegar hasta aquí • **I don't ask you to ~ my battles for me** no te pido que libres mis batallas • **to ~ a duel** batirse en duelo • **to ~ sb for sth**: • **he fought the council for the right to build on his land** se enfrentó al ayuntamiento por el derecho a edificar en sus tierras • **I'd like to ~ him for the title** me gustaría luchar *or* pelear contra él por el título • **to ~ one's way through a crowd** abrirse paso a la fuerza entre una multitud
2 (= *combat*) [+ *fire*] combatir; [+ *poverty, inflation, crime*] combatir, luchar contra; [+ *proposal*] oponerse a • **I've made up my mind so don't try and ~ me on it** lo he decidido, así que no intentes oponerte • **I had to ~ the urge to giggle** tuve que esforzarme para no reír, tuve que contener las ganas de reír
3 (= *try to win*) [+ *campaign*] tomar parte en; [+ *election*] presentarse a • **he says he'll ~ the case all the way to the Supreme Court** dice que si es necesario llevará el caso hasta el Tribunal Supremo • **he fought his case in various courts for ten years** defendió su causa en varios tribunales durante diez años • **he's decided to ~ the seat for a third time** (*Pol*) ha decidido presentarse por tercera vez como candidato para el escaño
(VI) **1** (= *do battle*) [*troops, countries*] luchar, combatir (**against** contra); [*person, animal*] pelear; (*Boxing*) luchar, pelear • **did you ~ in the war?** ¿luchó usted en la guerra?, ¿tomó usted parte en la guerra? • **the boys were ~ing in the street** los chicos estaban peleándose en la calle • **they'll ~ to the death** lucharán a muerte • **I fought for my country** luché por mi país • **the dogs were ~ing over a bone** los perros estaban peleando por un hueso
2 (= *quarrel*) discutir, pelear(se) (**with** con) • **they usually ~ about** *or* **over who pays the bills** suelen discutir *or* pelear(se) por quién paga las facturas
3 (= *struggle*) luchar (**for** por, **against** contra) • **to ~ against disease/crime** luchar contra la enfermedad/el crimen • **she was ~ing against sleep** luchaba contra el sueño • **to ~ for sth/sb** luchar por algo/algn • **he was ~ing for his life** estaba luchando por su vida • **he was ~ing for breath** le faltaba la respiración, respiraba con enorme dificultad • IDIOMS: • **to go down ~ing** seguir luchando hasta el fin • **to ~ shy of** rehuir, evitar
▸ **fight back** (VI + ADV) (= *resist*) (*in fight, argument*) defenderse; (*Sport*) contraatacar • **they fought back from 2-0 down to win 3-2** contraatacaron, pasando de perder por 2-0 a ganar por 3-2
(VT + ADV) [+ *tears*] contener; [+ *anger, feeling*] contener, reprimir; [+ *despair*] dominar • **I fought back the urge to slap him** reprimí *or* contuve las ganas de darle una bofetada • **I fought back the urge to laugh** contuve las ganas de reír
▸ **fight down** (VT + ADV) [+ *anger, feeling*] contener, reprimir; [+ *anxiety*] dominar, reprimir • **she fought down the impulse to run** reprimió el impulso de correr
▸ **fight off** (VT + ADV) **1** (= *repel*) [+ *attack, attacker*] repeler, rechazar • **they successfully fought off a takeover bid** consiguieron defenderse contra una oferta de adquisición
2 (= *resist*) [+ *disease, infection*] combatir • **he was ~ing off sleep** se esforzaba para combatir el sueño • **I had to ~ off an impulse to scream** tuve que reprimir el impulso de gritar
▸ **fight on** (VI + ADV) seguir luchando
▸ **fight out** (VT + ADV) **1** (*with fists*) resolver a golpes • **they decided to ~ it out in the street** decidieron resolverlo a golpes en la calle
2 (*fig*) (= *resolve*) resolver • **we'll have to ~ it out in court** tendremos que resolverlo en los tribunales
3 (= *compete*) • **they'll be ~ing it out for the top prize** competirán por el primer premio

fightback ['faɪtbæk] (N) (*Brit*) contraataque *m*

fighter ['faɪtəʳ] (N) **1** combatiente *mf*; (*Boxing*) boxeador(a) *m/f*, púgil *m*; (= *warrior*) guerrero/a *m/f*, soldado *mf*; (*fig*) luchador(a) *m/f* • **a bonny ~** un valiente guerrero
2 (= *airplane*) avión *m* de combate, caza *m*
(CPD) ▸ **fighter bomber** cazabombardero *m* ▸ **fighter command** jefatura *f* de cazas ▸ **fighter jet** reactor *m* de combate ▸ **fighter pilot** piloto *mf* de caza ▸ **fighter plane** avión *m* de combate, caza *m*

fighting ['faɪtɪŋ] (N) (*between troops, armies*) enfrentamientos *mpl*; (*between individuals*) (*lit, fig*) peleas *fpl* • **he hates ~** odia las peleas; ▹ **street**
(ADJ) • **we still have a ~ chance of beating them** aún tenemos una buena posibilidad de vencerlos • **this treatment at least gives her a ~ chance** este tratamiento le da al menos una posibilidad
(ADV) • **to be ~ fit** estar en plena forma
(CPD) ▸ **fighting bull** toro *m* de lidia ▸ **fighting cock** gallo *m* de pelea ▸ **fighting dog** perro *m* de pelea ▸ **fighting force** fuerza *f* de combate ▸ **fighting line** frente *m* de combate ▸ **fighting man** guerrero *m*, soldado *m* ▸ **fighting spirit** espíritu *m* de lucha, combatividad *f* ▸ **fighting strength** número *m* de soldados (listos para el combate) ▸ **fighting talk** • **the Prime Minister's ~ talk at the Rome summit** las declaraciones de tono beligerante que hizo el Primer Ministro en la cumbre de Roma • **this is typical ~ talk from the defending champion** esta es una típica bravuconada del actual campeón

figment ['fɪgmənt] (N) • **a ~ of the imagination** un producto de la imaginación

figurative ['fɪgərətɪv] (ADJ) **1** [*meaning*] figurado; [*expression*] metafórico
2 (*Art*) figurativo

figuratively ['fɪgərətɪvlɪ] (ADV)

figuradamente, en sentido figurado • **he was speaking ~** hablaba en sentido figurado • **you should understand this ~** hay que entender esto en sentido figurado
figure ['fɪgəʳ] (N) **1** (= *shape, silhouette*) figura *f* • **a ~ in a blue dress** una figura vestida de azul
2 (= *bodily proportions*) tipo *m*, figura *f* • **she's got a nice ~** tiene buen tipo *or* una buena figura • **he's a fine ~ of a man** es un hombre con un tipo imponente • **clothes for the fuller ~** tallas *fpl* grandes • **to keep/lose one's ~** guardar/perder la línea *or* el tipo • **to watch one's ~** cuidar la línea *or* el tipo
3 (= *person*) figura *f* • **a key ~ in twentieth century music** una figura clave en la música del siglo veinte • **a ~ of authority** una figura de autoridad • **he cut a dashing ~ in his new uniform** se veía muy elegante con su nuevo uniforme • **today she cuts a lonely ~** hoy aparece como una figura solitaria • **father ~** figura *f* paterna • **these days he's become a ~ of fun** últimamente se ha convertido en el hazmerreír de todos • **mother ~** figura *f* materna • **public ~** personaje *m* público
4 (= *numeral*) cifra *f* • **how did you arrive at these ~s?** ¿cómo has llegado a estas cifras? • **he was the only player to reach double ~s** era el único jugador que marcó más de diez tantos • **we want inflation brought down to single ~s** queremos que la inflación baje a menos del diez por cien
5 figures (= *statistics*) estadísticas *fpl*, datos *mpl*; (= *calculations*) cálculos *mpl* • **the latest ~s show that ...** las últimas estadísticas *or* los últimos datos muestran que ... • **he's always been good at ~s** siempre se le han dado bien los números, siempre se le ha dado bien la aritmética
6 (= *amount*) [*of money*] cifra *f*, suma *f*; (= *number*) [*of items*] cifra *f*, número *m* • **what sort of ~ did you have in mind?** ¿qué cifra *or* suma tenías en mente? • **I wouldn't like to put a ~ on it** no quisiera dar una cifra • **some estimates put the ~ as high as 20,000 dead** algunos cálculos dan una cifra *or* un número de hasta 20.000 muertos
7 (= *diagram*) figura *f*
8 (*Art*) figura *f*
9 (*Geom, Dance, Skating*) figura *f* • **a ~ of eight** • **a ~ eight** (*US*) un ocho
10 (*Ling*) • **~ of speech** figura *f* retórica
(VI) **1** (= *appear*) figurar (**as** como, **among** entre) • **his name doesn't ~ on the list** su nombre no figura en la lista • **this issue ~d prominently in the talks** este tema ocupó un papel prominente en las negociaciones
2 (*esp US**) (= *make sense*) • **it doesn't ~** no tiene sentido, no encaja • **that ~s!** ¡lógico!, ¡obvio!
(VT) (*esp US*) (= *think*) imaginarse, figurarse; (= *estimate*) calcular • **I ~ they'll come** me imagino *or* me figuro que vendrán • **I ~d there'd be about 20** calculé que habría unos 20 • **she ~d that they had both learned from the experience** pensaba *or* creía que los dos habían aprendido de la experiencia
(CPD) ▸ **figure skater** patinador(a) *m/f* artístico/a ▸ **figure skating** patinaje *m* artístico
▸ **figure in*** (VT + ADV) (*US*) contar
▸ **figure on*** (VI + PREP) (*esp US*) contar con • **he hadn't ~d on the problems that would arise** no había contado con los problemas que surgirían • **the meeting was longer than I'd ~d on** la reunión fue más larga de lo que yo esperaba • **I wasn't figuring on going** no contaba con ir • **are you figuring on going?** ¿piensas ir?
▸ **figure out*** (VT + ADV) **1** (= *understand*) [+ *person*] entender; [+ *writing*] entender, descifrar • **I just can't ~ it out!** ¡no me lo explico!, ¡no lo entiendo!
2 (= *work out*) [+ *sum*] calcular; [+ *problem*] resolver • **can you ~ out how to do this?** ¿entiendes cómo se hace esto? • **I couldn't ~ out the answer** no pude encontrar la respuesta *or* solución • **they had it all ~d out** lo tenían todo calculado
▸ **figure up** (VT + ADV) (*US*) calcular
-figure ['fɪgəʳ] (ADJ) (*ending in compounds*) • **a four-figure sum** una suma superior a mil (libras *etc*) • **a seven-figure sum** un número de siete cifras
figure-conscious ['fɪgə,kɒnʃəs] (ADJ) • **to be figure-conscious** cuidar la línea *or* el tipo
figurehead ['fɪgəhed] (N) (*on ship*) mascarón *m* de proa; (*fig*) testaferro *m*
figure-hugging ['fɪgə,hʌgɪŋ] (ADJ) ajustado, ceñido al cuerpo
figure-skate ['fɪgə,skeɪt] (VI) hacer patinaje artístico (sobre hielo)
figurine [fɪgə'ri:n] (N) figurilla *f*, estatuilla *f*
Fiji ['fi:dʒi:] (N) (*also* **the Fiji Islands**) las islas Fiji
Fijian [fɪ'dʒi:ən] (ADJ) de (las islas) Fiji
(N) (= *person*) nativo/a *m/f* de (las islas) Fiji, habitante *mf* de (las islas) Fiji
filament ['fɪləmənt] (N) (*Elec*) filamento *m*
filbert ['fɪlbət] (N) avellana *f*
filch* [fɪltʃ] (VT) (= *steal*) birlar*, mangar*
file¹ [faɪl] (N) (= *tool*) lima *f*; (*for nails*) lima *f* (de uñas)
(VT) (*also* **file down, file away**) limar
file² [faɪl] (N) **1** (= *folder*) carpeta *f*; (= *dossier*) archivo *m*, carpeta *f*, expediente *m*; (*eg loose-leaf file*) archivador *m*, clasificador *m*; (= *bundle of papers*) legajo *m*; (= *filing system*) fichero *m* • **the ~s** los archivos • **the Lucan ~** el expediente Lucan • **police ~s** archivos policiales • **to close the ~ on sth** dar carpetazo a algo • **to have sth on ~** tener algo archivado • **to have a ~ on sb** tener fichado a algn
2 (*Comput*) fichero *m*, archivo *m* • **to open/close a ~** abrir/cerrar un fichero *or* archivo
(VT) **1** (*also* **file away**) [+ *notes, information, work*] archivar; (*under heading*) clasificar
2 (= *submit*) [+ *claim, application, complaint*] presentar • **to ~ a petition for divorce** entablar pleito de divorcio • **to ~ a suit against sb** (*Jur*) entablar pleito *or* presentar una demanda contra algn
(CPD) ▸ **file cabinet** (*US*) fichero *m*, archivador *m* ▸ **file clerk** (*US*) archivero/a *m/f* ▸ **file manager** (*Comput*) gestor *m* de archivos ▸ **file name** (*Comput*) nombre *m* de fichero, nombre *m* de archivo ▸ **file server** (*Jur*) portador(a) *m/f* de notificaciones judiciales
▸ **file for** (VI + PREP) (*Jur*) • **to ~ for divorce** entablar pleito de divorcio • **to ~ for bankruptcy** presentar una declaración de quiebra • **to ~ for custody (of the children)** reclamar la custodia (de los hijos)
file³ [faɪl] (N) (= *row*) fila *f*, hilera *f* • **in single ~** en fila india
(VI) • **to ~ in/out** entrar/salir en fila • **to ~ past** desfilar • **they ~d past the general** desfilaron ante el general
file-sharing ['faɪlʃeərɪŋ] (*Comput*) (N) intercambio *m* de archivos
(CPD) [*program, software, network, company*] de intercambio de archivos
filet [fɪ'leɪ] (N) (*US*) = **fillet**
filial ['fɪlɪəl] (ADJ) filial
filiation [,fɪlɪ'eɪʃən] (N) filiación *f*
filibuster ['fɪlɪbʌstəʳ] (*esp US*) (*Pol*) (N) (= *person*) (*also* **filibusterer**) obstruccionista *mf*; (= *act*) discurso *m* obstruccionista
(VI) dar un discurso obstruccionista
filibustering ['fɪlɪ,bʌstərɪŋ] (N) (*Pol*) maniobras *fpl* obstruccionistas, filibusterismo *m*
filigree ['fɪlɪgri:] (N) (*in metal*) filigrana *f*
(ADJ) de filigrana
filing ['faɪlɪŋ] (N) **1** [*of documents*] clasificación *f* • **to do the ~** archivar documentos
2 [*of claim etc*] formulación *f*, presentación *f*
(CPD) ▸ **filing cabinet** fichero *m*, archivador *m* ▸ **filing clerk** (*esp Brit*) archivero/a *m/f*
filings ['faɪlɪŋz] (NPL) limaduras *fpl*
Filipino [fɪlɪ'pi:nəʊ] (ADJ) filipino
(N) **1** (= *person*) filipino/a *m/f*
2 (*Ling*) tagalo *m*
fill [fɪl] (VT) **1** (= *make full*) [+ *container*] llenar (**with** de) • **~ a saucepan with water** llenar un cazo de agua • **I am ~ed with admiration for her achievements** sus logros me llenan de admiración • **he was ~ed with remorse** estaba lleno de remordimiento • **he was ~ed with despair** estaba desesperado • **the wind ~ed the sails** el viento henchía las velas
2 (= *occupy*) [+ *space*] llenar (**with** de); [+ *time*] ocupar • **his plays always ~ the theatres** sus obras siempre llenan los teatros • **airlines can always ~ seats in the summer** las compañías aéreas siempre logran ocupar las plazas en verano • **rooms ~ed with furniture** habitaciones *fpl* llenas de muebles • **shouts ~ed the air** resonaron unos gritos en el aire • **the house was ~ed with the smell of burning** el olor a quemado invadía la casa • **she needs a routine to ~ her day** le hace falta una rutina que le llene el día • **the text ~s 231 pages** el texto ocupa 231 páginas
3 (= *plug*) [+ *cavity, hole*] rellenar, tapar (**with** con), llenar (**with** de); [+ *tooth*] empastar, emplomar (*S. Cone*) (**with** con); (*fig*) [+ *gap, vacuum*] llenar • **she ~ed a gap in his life** ella llenó un hueco en su vida
4 (= *fulfill*) [+ *need*] cubrir, satisfacer; [+ *requirement*] llenar, satisfacer; [+ *role*] cumplir, desempeñar; ▹ **bill¹**
5 (= *supply*) [+ *order*] despachar
6 (= *appoint sb to*) [+ *vacancy*] cubrir; [+ *post*] ocupar • **the position is already ~ed** la vacante ya está cubierta • **she was chosen to ~ the post of Education Secretary** la eligieron para ocupar el puesto de Ministra de Educación
(VI) **1** llenarse (**with** de) • **the room ~ed with smoke** la habitación se llenó de humo • **her eyes ~ed with tears** los ojos se le llenaron de lágrimas
2 [*sails*] henchirse
(N) **1** (= *sufficiency*) • **to eat/drink one's ~ (of sth)** comer/beber (algo) hasta saciarse, hartarse de comer/beber (algo) • **to have had one's ~ of sth** (*fig*) haberse hartado de algo, estar harto de algo
2 (= *gravel, stones*) relleno *m*
▸ **fill in** (VT + ADV) **1** [+ *hole, gap, outline*] rellenar
2 (= *occupy*) [+ *time*] ocupar, pasar • **I had an hour to ~ in before my train** tenía que ocupar *or* pasar una hora de alguna forma hasta que llegase mi tren • **"what are you doing here?" — "just ~ing in time"** —¿qué haces aquí? —pasar el tiempo
3 (= *complete*) [+ *form*] rellenar, llenar; [+ *details*] completar; (= *write*) [+ *one's name*] escribir, poner • **~ in the blanks in the following sentences** rellenar los espacios vacíos en las siguientes frases
4 (= *inform*) • **to ~ sb in (on sth)** poner a algn al corriente (de algo) • **Jackie will ~ you in on the rest of the office procedures** Jackie te

pondrá al corriente de cómo funciona todo lo demás en la oficina
(VI + ADV) • to ~ in for sb suplir a algn, sustituir a algn • **can you find someone to ~ in at such short notice?** ¿puedes encontrar a alguien con tan poco tiempo que haga de suplente?
▸ **fill out** (VT + ADV) **1** (= *complete*) [+ *form, application*] rellenar, llenar; [+ *details*] completar; (= *write*) [+ *one's name*] escribir, poner
2 (= *occupy all of*) [+ *garment*] llenar
3 (= *make more substantial*) [+ *essay, information*] rellenar
(VI + ADV) [*person*] engordar; [*face*] rellenarse, redondearse; [*sail*] henchirse
▸ **fill up** (VI + ADV) **1** (= *become full*) [*room, hall*] llenarse
2 (*Aut*) (*with petrol*) echar gasolina; (*with diesel*) echar diesel
3 (= *eat*) • **he doesn't eat proper meals, he ~s up on snacks** no come como es debido, se llena el estómago picando
(VT + ADV) [+ *container, suitcase*] llenar (**with** de) • **~ it** *or* **her up!*** (*Aut*) ¡llena el tanque! • **I can't drink too much before a meal, it ~s me up** no puedo beber mucho antes de una comida, me llena • **to ~ o.s. up with sth** llenarse (el estómago) de algo • **I do it to ~ up the time** lo hago para pasar el tiempo
-filled [fɪld] (ADJ) • **flower-filled** repleto de flores • **smoke-filled** lleno de humo
filler [ˈfɪləʳ] (N) **1** (*for cracks in wood, plaster*) masilla *f*; (*in foodstuffs*) relleno *m*; (*Press*) relleno *m*
2 (= *device*) [*of bottle, tank*] rellenador *m*; (= *funnel*) embudo *m*
(CPD) ▸ **filler cap** tapa *f* del depósito de gasolina
fillet [ˈfɪlɪt] (N) [*of meat, fish*] filete *m*
(VT) [+ *meat, fish*] cortar en filetes
(CPD) ▸ **fillet steak** (*individual*) bistec *m*, solomillo *m* (*Sp*), bife *m* de lomo (*Arg, Uru*); (= *meat*) solomillo *m* (*Sp*), lomo *m* de res (*LAm*)
fill-in [ˈfɪlɪn] (N) sustituto *m*, suplente *mf*
filling [ˈfɪlɪŋ] (N) **1** [*of tooth*] empaste *m*, emplomadura *f* (*S. Cone*)
2 (*Culin*) relleno *m*
(ADJ) [*food, dish*] que llena mucho • **this dish is very ~** este plato llena mucho
(CPD) ▸ **filling station** = **petrol station**
fillip [ˈfɪlɪp] (N) estímulo *m* • **to give a ~ to** estimular
filly [ˈfɪlɪ] (N) potra *f*
film [fɪlm] (N) (= *thin skin*) película *f*; [*of dust*] capa *f*; [*of smoke etc*] velo *m*; (*Cine, Phot*) (= *negatives*) película *f*; (= *roll of film*) carrete *m*, rollo *m*; (*at cinema*) película *f*, film *m*, filme *m*; (*full-length*) largometraje *m*; (*short*) corto(metraje) *m* • **the ~s** el cine • **silent ~** película *f* muda • **to make a ~ of** [+ *book*] llevar al cine, hacer una película de; [+ *event*] filmar
(VT) [+ *book*] llevar al cine, hacer una película de; [+ *event*] filmar; [+ *scene*] rodar
(VI) rodar, filmar
(CPD) [*camera, festival*] cinematográfico, de cine ▸ **film buff** cinéfilo/a *m/f* ▸ **film censor** censor(a) *m/f* cinematográfico/a ▸ **film clip** clip *m* de película ▸ **film company** productora *f* (de cine) ▸ **film crew** equipo *m* cinematográfico ▸ **film critic** crítico/a *m/f* de cine ▸ **film fan** aficionado/a *m/f* al cine ▸ **film festival** festival *m* de cine ▸ **film library** cinemateca *f* ▸ **film noir** cine *m* negro • **it's the best ~ noir I've seen in a long time** es la mejor película de cine negro que he visto desde hace tiempo ▸ **film première** estreno *m* oficial, premier *f* ▸ **film producer** productor(a) *m/f* (cinematográfico) ▸ **film rating** (*Brit*) calificación *f* (de películas) ▸ **film rights** derechos *mpl* cinematográficos ▸ **film script** guión *m* ▸ **film set** plató *m* ▸ **film star** estrella *f* de cine ▸ **film strip** película *f* de diapositivas ▸ **film studio** estudio *m* de cine ▸ **film test** prueba *f* cinematográfica
▸ **film over** (VI + ADV) [*eyes*] empañarse
filmgoer [ˈfɪlmgəʊəʳ] (N) aficionado/a *m/f* al cine
filmic [ˈfɪlmɪk] (ADJ) fílmico
filming [ˈfɪlmɪŋ] (N) rodaje *m*, filmación *f*
film-maker [ˈfɪlmmeɪkəʳ] (N) cineasta *mf*
film-making [ˈfɪlmmeɪkɪŋ] (N) cinematografía *f*
filmography [fɪlˈmɒgrəfɪ] (N) filmografía *f*
filmsetting [ˈfɪlmsetɪŋ] (N) fotocomposición *f*
filmy [ˈfɪlmɪ] (ADJ) [*fabric, material*] vaporoso
filo [ˈfiːləʊ], **filo pastry** [ˈfiːləʊpeɪstrɪ] (N) masa *f* filo
Filofax® [ˈfaɪləʊˌfæks] (N) agenda *f* de anillas
filter [ˈfɪltəʳ] (N) **1** (*also Phot*) filtro *m*
2 (*Brit*) (*Aut*) semáforo *m* de flecha de desvío
(VT) [+ *liquid, air*] filtrar
(VI) [*liquid, light*] filtrarse • **to ~ to the left** (*Aut*) tomar el carril izquierdo
(CPD) ▸ **filter cigarette** cigarrillo *m* con filtro ▸ **filter coffee** (= *powder*) café *m* para filtrar; (= *cup of coffee*) café *m* hecho con cafetera de filtro ▸ **filter lane** (*Aut*) carril *m* de giro ▸ **filter light** semáforo *m* de flecha de desvío ▸ **filter paper** papel *m* de filtro ▸ **filter tip** (= *filter*) boquilla *f*; (= *cigarette*) cigarrillo *m* con filtro
▸ **filter back** (VI + ADV) [*news, rumour*] llegar; [*people*] volver poco a poco
▸ **filter in** (VI + ADV) [*light*] filtrarse; [*news, rumour*] llegar; [*people*] entrar (poco a poco)
▸ **filter out** (VT + ADV) [+ *impurities*] quitar filtrando
(VI + ADV) [*news*] trascender, llegar a saberse
▸ **filter through** (VI + ADV) = **filter in**
filter-tipped [ˈfɪltəˌtɪpt] (ADJ) [*cigarette*] con filtro *or* boquilla
filth [fɪlθ] (N) **1** (*lit*) (= *dirt*) suciedad *f*, mugre *f*; (= *excrement*) heces *fpl*
2 (*fig*) **a** (= *people*) basura *f* • **those people are nothing but ~** esa gente no es más que basura
b (= *bad language*) groserías *fpl*, obscenidades *fpl* • **I've never read such ~** jamás he leído groserías *or* obscenidades semejantes
3‡ (= *police*) • **the ~** la policía, la pasma (*Sp*‡), la bofia (*Sp*‡), la cana (*S. Cone*‡)
filthiness [ˈfɪlθɪnɪs] (N) **1** (*lit*) (= *dirtiness*) suciedad *f*, mugre *f*
2 (*fig*) [*of behaviour*] lo grosero, lo obsceno; (= *bad language*) groserías *fpl*, obscenidades *fpl*; (= *obscenity*) obscenidad *f*
filthy [ˈfɪlθɪ] (ADJ) (COMPAR: **filthier**, SUPERL: **filthiest**) **1** (*lit*) (= *dirty*) [*hands, room, house*] asqueroso; [*bathtub*] mugriento, mugroso (*LAm*); [*clothes*] muy sucio; [*water*] inmundo
2 (= *indecent*) [*language, behaviour*] grosero, obsceno; [*joke*] verde; [*sense of humour*] obsceno
3 (= *despicable*) asqueroso • **she called him a ~ murderer** lo llamó un asesino asqueroso
4* [*weather*] asqueroso*, de perros*; [*temper*] de perros*, de mil diablos* • **she was in a ~ temper** estaba con un humor de perros *or* de mil diablos*
(ADV) • **the children came home ~ dirty** los niños llegaron a casa sucísimos, los niños llegaron a casa hechos un asco* • **they're ~ rich*** están podridos de dinero*, son unos ricachos*
filtration [fɪlˈtreɪʃən] (N) filtración *f*
fin [fɪn] (N) (*all senses*) aleta *f*
fin. (ABBR) = **finance**
finagle* [fɪˈneɪgəl] (VT) conseguir • **to ~ sth out of sb** conseguir algo de algn • **to ~ one's way out of sth** conseguir salir de algo
final [ˈfaɪnl] (ADJ) **1** (= *last*) (*in series*) último; [*stage*] final, último; (*Univ*) [*exam*] de fin de carrera • **in the ~ stages of her illness** en la fase final *or* en la última fase de su enfermedad • **I'd like to say one ~ word ...** por último me gustaría añadir lo siguiente ... • **~ demand** último aviso *m* de pago • **~ dividend** dividendo *m* complementario • **~ edition** (*Journalism*) última edición *f*; ▹ **analysis**
2 (= *conclusive*) [*approval*] definitivo; [*result*] final • **the judge's decision is ~** la decisión del juez es inapelable • **and that's ~!** ¡y punto!, ¡y no se hable más!
3 (= *ultimate*) [*destination*] final
(N) **1** (*Sport*) final *f* • **she went on to reach the ~** siguió hasta llegar a la final
2 finals (*Univ*) exámenes *mpl* de fin de carrera
(CPD) ▸ **final curtain** • **the ~ curtain** el telón final ▸ **final demand** última notificación *f* de pago ▸ **final edition** última edición *f*
▸ **final instalment** (= *payment*) último plazo *m*; [*of TV series*] episodio *m* final; [*of serialized novel*] fascículo *m* final ▸ **final whistle** • **the ~ whistle** el pitido final
finale [fɪˈnɑːlɪ] (N) (*Mus*) final *m*; (*Theat*) escena *f* final • **the grand ~** el gran final, la gran escena final; (*fig*) el final apoteósico *or* triunfal
finalist [ˈfaɪnəlɪst] (N) (*Sport*) finalista *mf*
finality [faɪˈnælɪtɪ] (N) (= *conclusiveness*) [*of death*] lo irreversible; [*of decision*] carácter *m* definitivo • **he said with ~** dijo de modo terminante
finalization [ˌfaɪnəlaɪˈzeɪʃən] (N) ultimación *f*, conclusión *f*
finalize [ˈfaɪnəlaɪz] (VT) [+ *preparations, arrangements*] concluir; [+ *agreement, plans, contract*] ultimar; [+ *report, text*] completar; [+ *date*] fijar, acordar • **to ~ a decision** tomar una decisión final
finally [ˈfaɪnəlɪ] (ADV) **1** (= *lastly*) por último, finalmente • **~, I would like to say ...** por último *or* finalmente, me gustaría añadir ...
2 (= *eventually, at last*) por fin • **she ~ decided to accept** por fin decidió aceptar
3 (= *once and for all*) de manera definitiva • **they decided to separate, ~ and irrevocably** decidieron separarse de manera definitiva e irrevocable
finance [faɪˈnæns] (N) (*gen*) finanzas *fpl*, asuntos *mpl* financieros; (= *funds*) (*also* **finances**) fondos *mpl* • **(the state of) the country's ~s** la situación económica del país • **Minister of Finance** Ministro/a *m/f* de Economía y Hacienda
(VT) [+ *project*] financiar • **he stole to ~ his drug habit** robaba para costearse su adicción a las drogas
(CPD) [*company*] financiero; [*page, section*] de economía, de negocios ▸ **finance director** director(a) *m/f* financiero/a
financial [faɪˈnænʃəl] (ADJ) [*services, aid, backing, affairs, security*] financiero; [*policy, resources, problems*] económico; [*page, section*] de economía, de negocios
(CPD) ▸ **financial adviser** asesor(a) *m/f* financiero/a ▸ **financial institution** entidad *f* financiera ▸ **financial management** gestión *f* financiera
▸ **financial plan** plan *m* de financiación
▸ **financial services** servicios *mpl* financieros ▸ **financial statement** estado *m* financiero, balance *m* ▸ **Financial Times Index** índice *m* bursátil del Financial Times

▸ **financial year** [*of company*] ejercicio *m* (financiero); [*of government*] año *m* fiscal
financially [faɪˈnænʃəlɪ] (ADV) [*independent, sound*] económicamente • **the scheme was ~ successful** el plan tuvo éxito desde el punto de vista económico • **this is not ~ possible** esto no es posible por razones financieras • **~, he would be much better off** desde el punto de vista económico *or* económicamente, saldría ganando
financial-service [faɪˌnænʃəlˈsɜːvɪs] (CPD) [*firm, industry*] de servicios financieros; [*product*] financiero • **financial-service companies** empresas de servicios financieros
financier [faɪˈnænsɪəʳ] (N) financiero/a *m/f*
financing [faɪˈnænsɪŋ] (N) financiación *f*
finch [fɪntʃ] (N) pinzón *m*
find [faɪnd] (VB: PT, PP: **found**) (VT) **1** (*after losing*) encontrar • **did you ~ your purse?** ¿encontraste tu monedero? • **I looked but I couldn't ~ it** lo busqué pero no pude encontrarlo • **you distracted me, now I can't ~ my place again** me has distraído y ahora no sé por dónde iba; ▹ **foot, tongue**
2 (= *locate*) encontrar • **the plant is found all over Europe** la planta se encuentra *or* existe en toda Europa • **did you ~ the man?** ¿encontraste *or* localizaste al hombre? • **the book is nowhere to be found** el libro no se encuentra por ninguna parte • **to ~ one's way: can you ~ your (own) way to the station?** ¿sabes llegar a la estación sin ayuda?, ¿puedes encontrar la estación solo? • **this found its way into my drawer** esto vino a parar a mi cajón • **to ~ one's way around** orientarse • **to ~ one's way around a new city** orientarse en una ciudad nueva • **it took me a while to ~ my way around their kitchen** me llevó un rato familiarizarme con su cocina
3 (= *chance upon*) encontrar • **I found a pound coin in the street** me encontré una moneda de una libra en la calle
(N) hallazgo *m* • **your new assistant is a real ~** tu nueva ayudante es todo un hallazgo • **that was a lucky ~!** ¡qué buen hallazgo! • **archaeological ~s** hallazgos *mpl* arqueológicos • **to make a ~** realizar un descubrimiento
▸ **find out** (VT + ADV) **1** (= *check out*) averiguar • **~ out everything you can about him** averigua todo lo que puedas sobre él • **she phoned to ~ out when the bus left** llamó por teléfono para averiguar cuándo *or* enterarse de cuándo salía el autobús
2 (= *discover*) descubrir • **they never found out how he escaped** nunca descubrieron cómo se había escapado • **I found out what he was really like** descubrí su verdadera personalidad, me di cuenta de cómo era realmente • **~ out more by writing to ...** infórmese escribiendo a ... • **I found out that she had been lying** descubrí *or* me enteré que había estado mintiendo • **I found out from his teacher that he hadn't been to school** me enteré a través de su profesor de que había faltado al colegio
3 (= *expose*) • **to ~ sb out** descubrir a algn • PROVERB: • **(you can) be sure your sins will ~ you out** puedes estar seguro de que tarde o temprano tus mismas acciones te delatarán
4 (= *realize*) darse cuenta de, descubrir • **they'll be sorry when they ~ out their mistake** se van a arrepentir cuando se den cuenta de su error
(VI + ADV) **1** (= *become aware*) enterarse • **they'll soon ~ out** pronto se enterarán • **to ~ out about sth** enterarse de algo, descubrir algo • **she was afraid her husband would ~ out about their relationship** le daba miedo que su marido se enterase de *or* descubriese su relación
2 (= *enquire*) • **to ~ out about sth** informarse acerca de algo • **why don't you ~ out about training courses?** ¿por qué no te informas sobre cursos de capacitación?
finder [ˈfaɪndəʳ] (N) descubridor(a) *m/f* • IDIOM: • **~s keepers (losers weepers)** quien se lo encuentra se lo queda
finding [ˈfaɪndɪŋ] (N) **1** (= *discovery*) descubrimiento *m*
2 (= *conclusion*) resultado *m*
3 (*Jur*) fallo *m* • **to make a ~** fallar
4 findings (= *conclusions*) conclusiones *fpl*; (= *results*) resultados *mpl*
fine¹ [faɪn] (ADJ) (COMPAR: **finer**, SUPERL: **finest**) **1** (= *delicate, thin*) [*thread, hair*] fino, delgado; [*rain, point, nib*] fino; [*line*] delgado, tenue; (= *small*) [*particle*] minúsculo • **~-nibbed pen** bolígrafo *m* de punta fina; ▹ **print**
2 (= *good*) [*performance, example*] excelente; (= *imposing*) [*house, building*] magnífico; (= *beautiful*) [*object*] hermoso • **she's a very ~ musician** es una música verdaderamente excelente • **we use only the ~st ingredients** solo usamos ingredientes de primerísima calidad • **he's a ~-looking boy** es un muchacho bien parecido • IDIOM: • **he's got it down to a ~ art** lo hace a la perfección; ▹ **chance**
3 (= *subtle*) [*distinction*] sutil • **she has a ~ eye for a bargain** tiene mucho ojo *or* muy buen olfato para las gangas • **there's a ~ line between love and hate** la línea que separa el amor del odio es muy tenue, del amor al odio solo hay un paso • **not to put too ~ a point on it** hablando en plata • **the ~r points of the argument** los puntos más sutiles del argumento
4 (= *refined*) [*taste, manners*] refinado • **he has no ~r feelings whatsoever** no tiene nada de sensibilidad; ▹ **feeling**
5 (= *acceptable*) bien • **"is this ok?" — "yes, it's ~"** —¿vale así? —sí, está bien • **~! ¡de acuerdo!, ¡vale!, ¡cómo no!** (*esp LAm*) • **that's ~ by me** por mí bien, de acuerdo • **"would you like some more?" — "no, I'm ~, thanks"** —¿quieres un poco más? —no, gracias, con esto me basta • IDIOM: • **~ and dandy**: • **everything may look ~ and dandy to you** puede que tú todo lo veas de color de rosa
6 (= *quite well*) muy bien • **he's ~, thanks** está muy bien, gracias
7 [*weather*] bueno • **if the weather is ~** si hace buen tiempo • **it's a ~ day today** hoy hace buen tiempo • **the weather kept ~ for the match** duró el buen tiempo hasta el partido • **one ~ day, we were out walking** un día que hacia buen tiempo habíamos salido de paseo
8 (*iro*) menudo • **a ~ friend you are!** ¡valiente amigo estás hecho! (*iro*), ¡menudo amigo eres tú! (*iro*) • **you're a ~ one to talk!** ¡mira quién habla! • **a ~ thing!** ¡hasta dónde hemos llegado!
9 (= *pure*) [*metal*] puro, fino
(ADV) **1** (= *well*) bien • **"how did you get on at the dentist's?" — "~"** —¿qué tal te ha ido en el dentista? —bien • **you're doing ~** lo estás haciendo bien • **mother and baby are doing ~** la madre y el bebé están bien • **to feel ~** [*person*] encontrarse bien • **these shoes feel ~** estos zapatos son cómodos • **five o'clock suits me ~** a las cinco me viene bien
2 (= *finely*) • **to chop sth up ~** picar algo en trozos menudos, picar algo muy fino • IDIOM: • **to cut it ~** (*of time*) ir con el tiempo justo; (*of money*) calcular muy justo • **we'll be cutting it pretty ~ if we leave at ten** vamos a ir con el tiempo muy justo si salimos a las diez
(CPD) ▸ **fine art, the fine arts** las Bellas Artes ▸ **fine wines** vinos *mpl* selectos
fine² [faɪn] (N) multa *f* • **to get a ~ (for sth/doing sth)** ser multado (por algo/hacer algo) • **I got a ~ for ...** me pusieron una multa por ...
(VT) • **to ~ sb (for sth/doing sth)** multar a algn (por algo/hacer algo)
fine-drawn [ˈfaɪnˈdrɔːn] (ADJ) [*wire*] muy delgado; [*distinction*] sutil
fine-grained [ˈfaɪnˈgreɪnd] (ADJ) de grano fino
finely [ˈfaɪnlɪ] (ADV) **1** (= *splendidly, well*) [*dressed, written*] con elegancia
2 (= *delicately*) [*carved, woven*] delicadamente • **a ~ detailed embroidery** un bordado trabajado con mucho detalle • **this could upset the whole ~ balanced process** esto podría trastornar el precario equilibrio del proceso
3 (= *very small*) [*chopped*] en trozos muy menudos, muy fino; [*sliced*] en rodajas finas, en lonchas finas
4 (= *with precision*) [*tuned, judged*] con precisión
fineness [ˈfaɪnnɪs] (N) **1** (= *thinness*) [*of thread, hair*] lo fino, lo delgado
2 (= *excellent quality*) excelente calidad *f*
3 (= *delicacy*) exquisitez *f*, lo delicado • **observe the ~ of detail in the painting** observe la exquisitez de los detalles en el cuadro
4 (= *precision*) precisión *f*
5 (= *purity*) [*of metal*] pureza *f*
finery [ˈfaɪnərɪ] (N) galas *fpl* • **spring in all its ~** (*liter*) la primavera con todo su esplendor
fine-spun [ˈfaɪnspʌn] (ADJ) [*yarn*] fino; (*fig*) [*hair*] fino, sedoso
finesse [fɪˈnes] (N) **1** (*in judgement*) finura *f*, delicadeza *f*; (*in action*) diplomacia *f*, sutileza *f*; (= *cunning*) astucia *f*
2 (*Cards*) impasse *m*
(VT) hacer el impasse a
fine-tooth comb [ˌfaɪnˌtuːθˈkəʊm] (N) peine *m* de púas finas • IDIOM: • **to go over** *or* **through sth with a fine-tooth comb** revisar *or* examinar algo a fondo
fine-tune [ˌfaɪnˈtjuːn] (VT) **1** [+ *engine*] poner a punto
2 (*fig*) [+ *plans, strategy*] afinar, matizar; [+ *economy*] ajustar; [+ *text*] dar los últimos retoques a
fine-tuning [ˌfaɪnˈtjuːnɪŋ] (N) **1** [*of engine*] puesta *f* a punto
2 (*fig*) [*of plans, strategy*] matización *f*; [*of economy*] ajuste *m*; [*of text*] últimos retoques *mpl*
finger [ˈfɪŋgəʳ] (N) **1** (*Anat*) dedo *m* • **I can count on the ~s of one hand the number of times you've taken me out** con los dedos de la mano se pueden contar las veces que me has sacado • **to cross one's ~s** • **keep one's ~s crossed**: • **I'll keep my ~s crossed for you** cruzo los dedos (por ti), ojalá tengas suerte • **~s crossed!** (*for someone*) ¡(que tengas) suerte!, ¡buena suerte!; (*for o.s.*) ¡deséame suerte! • **index ~** (dedo *m*) índice *m* • **they never laid a ~ on her** no le pusieron la mano encima • **he didn't lift a ~ to help us** no movió un dedo para ayudarnos • **she never lifts a ~ around the house** nunca mueve un dedo para ayudar en la casa • **little ~** (dedo *m*) meñique *m* • **middle ~** (dedo *m*) corazón *m or* medio *m* • **ring ~** (dedo *m*) anular *m* • **to snap one's ~s** chasquear los dedos • **she only has to snap her ~s and he comes running** no tiene más que chasquear

los dedos y él viene corriendo • IDIOMS: • **to burn one's ~s** • **get one's ~s burnt** pillarse los dedos • **to get** *or* **pull one's ~ out*** espabilarse • **to have a ~ in every pie** estar metido en todo • **to point the ~ at sb** acusar a algn, señalar a algn • **evidence points the ~ of suspicion at his wife** las pruebas señalan a su mujer como sospechosa • **to put one's ~ on sth**: • **there's something wrong, but I can't put my ~ on it** hay algo que está mal, pero no sé exactamente qué • **there was nothing you could put your ~ on** no había nada concreto • **to slip through one's ~s** escapársele de las manos • **to be all ~s and thumbs** ser un/una manazas, ser muy desmañado/a • **he's got her twisted round his little ~** hace con ella lo que quiere • **to put two ~s up at sb** • **give sb the two ~s*** ≈ hacer un corte de mangas a algn* • **to work one's ~s to the bone** dejarse la piel trabajando*; ▹ **pulse, twist**
2 [*of glove*] dedo *m*
3 (= *shape*) franja *f* • **a ~ of smoke** una franja de humo • **a ~ of land projecting into the sea** una lengua de tierra adentrándose en el mar
4 (= *measure*) [*of drink*] dedo *m*
VT **1** (= *touch*) toquetear
2 (*Brit**) (= *betray, inform on*) delatar
3 (*Mus*) [+ *piano*] teclear; [+ *guitar*] rasguear; [+ *music score*] marcar la digitación de
CPD ▸ **finger bowl** lavafrutas *m inv* ▸ **finger buffet** buffet *m* de canapés ▸ **finger food** (*for babies*) *comida que los bebés pueden agarrar y comer con las manos*; (*US*) canapés *mpl* ▸ **finger paint** pintura *f* para pintar con los dedos ▸ **finger painting** pintura *f* de dedos

fingerboard ['fɪŋgəbɔːd] N (*on piano*) teclado *m*; (*on stringed instrument*) diapasón *m*

fingering ['fɪŋgərɪŋ] N (*Mus*) digitación *f*

fingermark ['fɪŋgəmɑːk] N huella *f*

fingernail ['fɪŋgəneɪl] N uña *f*

finger-paint ['fɪŋgəpeɪnt] VI pintar con los dedos

finger-pointing ['fɪŋgə,pɔɪntɪŋ] N acusaciones *fpl*

fingerprint ['fɪŋgəprɪnt] N huella *f* digital *or* dactilar
VT [+ *person*] tomar las huellas digitales *or* dactilares a; (*Med*) identificar genéticamente

fingerstall ['fɪŋgəstɔːl] N dedil *m*

fingertip ['fɪŋgətɪp] N punta *f or* yema *f* del dedo • **to have sth at one's ~s** tener algo a mano; (= *know sth*) saber(se) algo al dedillo
CPD ▸ **fingertip search** búsqueda *f* exhaustiva • **officers continued a ~ search of the area yesterday** los agentes continuaron ayer la búsqueda exhaustiva de la zona

finicky ['fɪnɪkɪ] ADJ **1** [*person*] melindroso (about con) • **she's a ~ eater** • **she is ~ about her food** es muy melindrosa con la comida
2 [*job*] complicado

finish ['fɪnɪʃ] N **1** (= *end*) final *m* • **to be in at the ~** presenciar el final • **a fight to the ~** una lucha a muerte • **to fight to the ~** luchar a muerte • **from start to ~** de principio a fin
2 (*Sport*) [*of race*] final *m* • **it's going to be a close ~** va a ser un final reñido • **the replays showed a close ~** la repetición mostraba que habían cruzado la meta casi a la vez
3 (= *appearance*) acabado *m* • **a table with an oak ~** una mesa con un acabado en roble • **gloss(y) ~** acabado *m* brillo • **matt ~** acabado *m* mate • **a surface with a rough/smooth ~** una superficie sin pulir/pulida
4 (= *refinement*) refinamiento *m* • **she's a beautiful model, but she lacks ~** es una modelo bella, pero le falta refinamiento
VT **1** (= *complete*) terminar, acabar • **I've nearly ~ed the ironing** casi he terminado *or* acabado de planchar • **what time do you ~ work?** ¿a qué hora terminas el trabajo? • **I'll be ~ing my course next year** termino *or* acabo el curso el año que viene • **to ~ doing sth** terminar *or* acabar de hacer algo • **as soon as he ~ed eating, he excused himself** en cuanto terminó *or* acabó de comer, se excusó
2 (= *use up, consume*) [+ *food, resources*] terminar, acabar • **~ your soup** termínate la sopa, acábate la sopa • **if you ~ the milk, let me know** si terminas (toda) la leche, dímelo
3 (= *round off*) rematar • **~ the dish with a sprinkling of parsley** remate el plato espolvoreándolo con perejil • **we ~ed the afternoon with tea at the Ritz** rematamos la tarde tomando té en el Ritz
4* (= *defeat, destroy*) acabar con • **that last kilometre nearly ~ed me** el kilómetro final casi acabó conmigo
5 (= *apply surface to*) • **~ the wood with wax or varnish** dele un acabado final a la madera con cera o barniz
VI **1** (= *come to an end*) terminar, acabar • **the party was ~ing** la fiesta se estaba terminando *or* acabando • **have you quite ~ed?** ¿has acabado ya?; (= *can I speak now?*) ¿puedo hablar ya? • **she ~ed by saying that …** terminó *or* acabó diciendo que … • **I've ~ed with the paper** he acabado el periódico, he terminado con el periódico • **come back, I haven't ~ed with you yet!** ¡vuelve, que todavía no he terminado *or* acabado contigo!
2 (*Sport*) (= *end race*) terminar, acabar • **she ~ed first/last** terminó *or* acabó en primer lugar/en último lugar
3 (= *end association*) romper, terminar (with con) • **she's ~ed with him** ha roto *or* terminado con él
4 (*Econ*) • **our shares ~ed at $70** al cierre de la Bolsa, nuestras acciones se cotizaban a 70 dólares
CPD ▸ **finish line** (*US*) = **finishing line**

▸ **finish off** VT + ADV **1** (= *conclude*) terminar
2 (= *use up, consume*) terminar(se), acabar(se) • **he ~ed off the bottle in one swallow** se terminó *or* se acabó la botella de un trago
3 (= *exhaust*) dejar destrozado, dejar hecho polvo*
4 (= *kill*) [+ *victim*] acabar con, liquidar*; [+ *wounded person/animal*] rematar; (= *defeat*) [+ *opponent*] derrotar, vencer
VI + ADV (= *end*) terminar, concluir (*frm*) • **I'd like to ~ off by proposing a toast** quisiera terminar *or* (*frm*) concluir proponiendo un brindis • **let's ~ off now** terminemos ahora

▸ **finish up** VT + ADV (= *use up, consume*) [+ *food, leftovers*] terminarse, acabarse • **~ up your drinks now please** termínense lo que estén bebiendo ahora, por favor
VI + ADV (= *end up*) terminar, acabar • **he ~ed up in Paris** terminó *or* acabó en París • **he'll probably ~ up in jail** probablemente termine *or* acabe en la cárcel

finished ['fɪnɪʃt] ADJ **1** (= *concluded*) terminado • **it's not ~ yet** aún no está terminado *or* acabado • **when will you be ~?** ¿(para) cuándo vas a terminar? • **a half-finished meal** una comida a medio terminar • **he sent off the ~ manuscript/version** envió el manuscrito terminado/la versión final • **he's ~ with politics** ha renunciado a la política • **I'm not ~ with you yet** aún no he terminado *or* acabado contigo
2 (= *completed*) acabado • **the ~ product** el producto acabado *or* final
3 (= *polished*) [*performance, production*] pulido
4* (= *tired*) rendido, hecho polvo*; (= *destroyed*) acabado • **their marriage is ~** su matrimonio está acabado • **as a film star she's ~** como estrella está acabada
5 (= *surfaced*) • **walnut-finished kitchen accessories** accesorios *mpl* de cocina con un acabado de nogal • **a building ~ in smoked glass** un edificio acabado con cristales ahumados

finisher ['fɪnɪʃəʳ] N (*esp Brit*) (*Ftbl*) rematador(a) *m/f*; (*Cycling, Running*) *persona que llega a la meta*

finishing ['fɪnɪʃɪŋ] N **1** [*of product*] acabado *m*
2 (*esp Brit*) (*Ftbl*) capacidad *f* de remate
CPD ▸ **finishing date** fecha *f* de finalización ▸ **finishing line** (*Sport*) línea *f* de meta, meta *f* ▸ **finishing school** *escuela privada para señoritas donde se les enseña a comportarse en la alta sociedad* ▸ **finishing touch** toque *m* final • **to put the ~ touches to sth** dar los últimos toques a algo

finite ['faɪnaɪt] ADJ **1** (= *limited*) (*of distance*) finito; [*resources*] limitado • **is the universe ~?** ¿el universo es finito? • **to make the best use of ~ resources** hacer el mejor uso posible de recursos limitados • **we have only a ~ amount of money to invest** solo disponemos de una cantidad limitada de dinero para invertir
2 (*Ling*) [*mood, verb*] conjugado
CPD ▸ **finite verb** verbo *m* conjugado

fink* [fɪŋk] N (*US*) (= *informer*) soplón/ona* *m/f*; (= *strikebreaker*) rompehuelgas *mf inv*, esquirol *m*

▸ **fink out*** VI + ADV (*US*) acobardarse

Finland ['fɪnlənd] N Finlandia *f*

Finn [fɪn] N finlandés/esa *m/f*

Finnish ['fɪnɪʃ] ADJ finlandés
N (*Ling*) finlandés *m*

Finno-Ugrian ['fɪnəʊ'uːgrɪən], **Finno-Ugric** ['fɪnəʊ'uːgrɪk] ADJ fino-húngaro
N (*Ling*) fino-húngaro *m*

fiord [fjɔːd] N = **fjord**

fir [fɜːʳ] N (*also* **fir tree**) abeto *m*
CPD ▸ **fir cone** piña *f*

fire [faɪəʳ] N **1** (= *flames*) fuego *m* • **much of the town was destroyed by ~** el fuego causó la destrucción de gran parte de la ciudad • **~ and brimstone** el fuego eterno • **a ~ and brimstone speech** un discurso lleno de referencias apocalípticas • **to catch ~** [*curtains, furniture*] prender fuego; [*house*] incendiarse; [*engine, car*] empezar a arder • **the aircraft caught ~ soon after take off** poco después de despegar se inició un incendio en el avión • **~ damaged goods** mercancías *fpl* dañadas por el fuego • **to be on ~** (*lit*) estar ardiendo; (*fig*) (*with passion, pain*) arder • **to set ~ to sth** • **set sth on ~** prender fuego a algo • **to set o.s. on ~** prenderse fuego • IDIOMS: • **to fight ~ with ~** pagar con la misma moneda • **to play with ~** jugar con fuego • **to set the world on ~** comerse el mundo • **to go** *or* **come through ~ and water (to do sth)** pasar lo indecible (por hacer algo); ▹ **smoke**
2 (*in grate*) fuego *m*, lumbre *f* • **to lay** *or* **make up a ~** preparar el fuego *or* la lumbre • **to light a ~** encender un fuego *or* una lumbre
3 (= *bonfire*) hoguera *f*, fogata *f* • **to make a ~** hacer una hoguera *or* una fogata
4 (= *fireplace*) lumbre *f*, chimenea *f* • **come and sit by the ~** ven y siéntate a la lumbre *or* a lado de la chimenea
5 (*accidental*) incendio *m* • **87 people died in the ~** 87 personas murieron en el incendio • **to be insured against ~** estar asegurado contra incendios • **bush ~** incendio *m* de monte • **forest ~** incendio *m* forestal
6 (= *heater*) estufa *f* • **electric/gas ~** estufa *f*

eléctrica/de gas
7 (*Mil*) fuego *m* • **to draw sb's ~** distraer a algn (*disparando a algo que no es el objetivo real*) • **to draw ~** (*fig*) provocar críticas • **the proposed tax has already drawn ~ from the opposition** el impuesto propuesto ya ha provocado las críticas de la oposición • **to exchange ~ (with sb)** tirotearse (con algn) • **an exchange of ~** un tiroteo • **to hold (one's) ~** (*lit*) no disparar; (*fig*) esperar • **hold your ~!** (*when already firing*) ¡alto al fuego! • **to open ~ (on sth/sb)** abrir fuego (sobre algo/algn) • **to return (sb's) ~** responder a los disparos (de algn); [*troops*] responder al fuego enemigo • **to be/come under ~** (*lit*) estar/caer bajo fuego enemigo; (*fig*) ser atacado • **the President's plan came under ~ from the opposition** el plan del presidente fue atacado por la oposición • IDIOM: • **to hang ~**: • **banks and building societies were hanging ~ on interest rates** los bancos y las sociedades de préstamos hipotecarios dejaron en suspenso los tipos de interés • **several projects were hanging ~ in his absence** varios proyectos quedaron interrumpidos en su ausencia; ▹ line
8 (= *passion*) ardor *m* • IDIOM: • **to have ~ in one's belly*** ser muy ardoroso *or* apasionado
VT 1 (= *shoot*) [+ *gun*] disparar; [+ *missile, arrow*] disparar, lanzar; [+ *rocket*] lanzar; [+ *shot*] efectuar • **to ~ a gun at sb** disparar contra algn • **he ~d a question at her** le lanzó una pregunta • **he continued to ~ (off) questions at her** continuó acosándola con preguntas • **to ~ a salute** tirar una salva
2 (= *operate*) • **gas/oil ~d central heating** calefacción *f* central a *or* de gas/de petróleo
3 (= *set fire to*) [+ *property, building*] incendiar, prender fuego a
4* (= *dismiss*) echar (a la calle), despedir • **you're ~d!** ¡queda usted despedido!
5 (*in kiln*) [+ *pottery*] cocer
6 (= *stimulate*) [+ *imagination*] estimular • **~d with enthusiasm/determination, the crowd ...** impulsados por el entusiasmo/por la determinación, la multitud ... • **she ~s others with energy** llena a los demás de energía
VI 1 (*Mil*) disparar (**at** a, contra, **on** sobre) • **riot police ~d on the crowd** la policía antidisturbios disparó sobre la multitud • **ready, aim, ~!** ¡atención, apunten, fuego!
2 (*Aut*) [*engine*] encenderse, prender (*LAm*)
3* (= *dismiss*) ▹ hire
CPD ▸ **fire alarm** alarma *f* contra *or* de incendios ▸ **fire blanket** manta *f* ignífuga ▸ **fire brigade, fire department** (*US*) cuerpo *m* de bomberos • **we called the ~ brigade** llamamos a los bomberos ▸ **fire chief** (*US*) jefe/a *m/f* de bomberos ▸ **fire crew** equipo *m* de bomberos ▸ **fire curtain** telón *m* contra incendios ▸ **fire damage** daños *mpl* del incendio • **the building showed evidence of ~ damage** el edificio mostraba signos de haber sufrido un incendio ▸ **fire department** (*US*) = fire brigade ▸ **fire dog** morillo *m* ▸ **fire door** puerta *f* contra incendios ▸ **fire drill** simulacro *m* de incendio ▸ **fire engine** coche *m* de bomberos ▸ **fire escape** escalera *f* de incendios ▸ **fire exit** salida *f* de incendios ▸ **fire extinguisher** extintor *m* ▸ **fire hazard** • **the spilt oil was a ~ hazard** el aceite derramado podía haber provocado un incendio ▸ **fire hose** manguera *f* contra incendios, manguera *f* de incendios ▸ **fire hydrant** boca *f* de incendios ▸ **fire insurance** seguro *m* contra incendios ▸ **fire irons** utensilios *mpl* para la chimenea ▸ **fire master** (*Scot*) jefe *m* de bomberos ▸ **fire practice** = fire drill ▸ **fire prevention** prevención *f* de incendios ▸ **fire regulations** normas *fpl* para la prevención de incendios ▸ **fire retardant** ignirretardante *m* ▸ **fire risk** = fire hazard ▸ **fire sale** venta *f* de liquidación por incendio ▸ **fire screen** pantalla *f* de chimenea ▸ **fire service** = fire brigade ▸ **fire station** estación *f or* (*Sp*) parque *m* de bomberos ▸ **fire tender** (*US*) coche *m* de bomberos ▸ **fire tower** (*US*) torre *f* de vigilancia contra incendios ▸ **fire trap** *edificio muy peligroso en caso de incendio* ▸ **fire truck** (*US*) coche de bomberos ▸ **fire warden** (*US*) *persona encargada de la lucha contra incendios*
▸ **fire away*** VI + ADV • **"may I ask you something?" — "sure, ~ away!"** —¿puedo preguntarle algo? —¡adelante! *or* (*LAm*) —¡siga nomás!
▸ **fire off** VT + ADV ▹ fire
▸ **fire up** VT + ADV (*fig*) enardecer • **to be/get ~d up about sth** estar enardecido/ enardecerse por algo

firearm ['faɪərɑːm] N arma *f* de fuego
CPD ▸ **firearms certificate** licencia *f* de armas
fireball ['faɪəbɔːl] N bola *f* de fuego
Firebird ['faɪəbɜːd] N • **the ~** (*Mus*) el Pájaro de fuego
firebomb ['faɪəbɒm] N bomba *f* incendiaria
VT colocar una bomba incendiaria en; (*Aer*) bombardear con bombas incendiarias
firebrand ['faɪəbrænd] N 1 tea *f*
2 (*fig*) agitador(a) *m/f*, revoltoso/a *m/f*
firebreak ['faɪəbreɪk] N cortafuego *m*
firebrick ['faɪəbrɪk] N ladrillo *m* refractario
firebug ['faɪəbʌg] N (*US*) incendiario/a *m/f*, pirómano/a *m/f*
fireclay ['faɪəkleɪ] N (*Brit*) arcilla *f* refractaria
firecracker ['faɪə,krækəʳ] N petardo *m*
firedamp ['faɪədæmp] N grisú *m*
fire-eater ['faɪər,iːtəʳ] N (*lit*) tragafuegos *mf inv*; (*fig*) pendenciero/a *m/f*
firefight ['faɪə,faɪt] N (*Mil*) (*journalese*) tiroteo *m*
firefighter ['faɪə,faɪtəʳ] N bombero/a *m/f*
firefighting ['faɪə,faɪtɪŋ] N lucha *f* por apagar incendios
CPD ▸ **firefighting equipment** equipo *m* contra incendios
firefly ['faɪəflaɪ] N luciérnaga *f*
fireguard ['faɪəgɑːd] N pantalla *f* de chimenea
firehouse ['faɪəhaʊs] N (PL: **firehouses** ['faɪəhaʊzɪz]) (*US*) estación *f or* (*Sp*) parque *m* de bomberos
firelight ['faɪəlaɪt] N luz *f* de la lumbre *or* del hogar • **by ~** a la luz de la lumbre *or* del hogar
firelighter ['faɪə,laɪtəʳ] N pastilla *f* enciendefuegos, *barra de material inflamable que se utiliza para encender fuego en una chimenea*
fireman ['faɪəmən] N (PL: **firemen**) [*of fire service*] bombero/a *m/f*; (*Rail*) fogonero/a *m/f* • **~'s lift** *manera de llevar a una persona sobre un solo hombro*
fireplace ['faɪəpleɪs] N chimenea *f*, hogar *m*
fireplug ['faɪəplʌg] N (*US*) = **fire hydrant**
firepower ['faɪə,paʊəʳ] N (*Mil*) potencia *f* de fuego
fireproof ['faɪəpruːf] ADJ [*material*] incombustible, ignífugo; [*suit, clothing*] ignífugo, a prueba de fuego; [*safe*] a prueba de fuego; [*dish*] refractario
VT cubrir con material ignífugo
CPD ▸ **fireproof dish** plato *m* refractario
fire-raiser ['faɪə,reɪzəʳ] N (*Brit*) incendiario/a *m/f*, pirómano/a *m/f*
fire-raising ['faɪə,reɪzɪŋ] N (*Brit*) (delito *m* de) incendiar *m*, piromanía *f*
fire-resistant ['faɪərɪ,zɪstənt] ADJ ignífugo
fire-retardant ['faɪərɪ,tɑːdənt] ADJ resistente al fuego
fireside ['faɪəsaɪd] N • **by the ~** junto a la chimenea, al amor de la lumbre
CPD hogareño, familiar ▸ **fireside chair** sillón *m* cerca de la lumbre ▸ **fireside chat** charla *f* íntima
firestorm ['faɪəstɔːm] N tormenta *f* ígnea
firewall ['faɪəwɔːl] N (*Internet*) cortafuegos *m inv*, firewall *m*
firewater* ['faɪə,wɔːtəʳ] N (*US*) aguardiente *m*
firewood ['faɪəwʊd] N leña *f*
firework ['faɪəwɜːk] N artilugio *m* pirotécnico (*frm*) • **a stray ~ fell onto the roof** un cohete perdido cayó en el techo; **fireworks** fuegos *mpl* artificiales • **there'll be ~s at the meeting*** (*fig*) en la reunión se va a armar la gorda*
CPD ▸ **firework display** fuegos *mpl* artificiales
firing ['faɪərɪŋ] N 1 (= *bullets*) disparos *mpl*; (= *exchange of fire*) tiroteo *m*
2 (*Aut*) encendido *m*
3 [*of bricks, pottery*] cocción *f*
4 (*esp US**) despido *m*
CPD ▸ **firing hammer** = firing pin ▸ **firing line** línea *f* de fuego • IDIOM: • **to be in the ~ line** (*Mil*) (*also fig*) estar en la línea de fuego ▸ **firing pin** martillo *m*, percutor *m* ▸ **firing squad** pelotón *m* (de fusilamiento)
firm¹ [fɜːm] ADJ (COMPAR: **firmer**, SUPERL: **firmest**) 1 (= *solid*) [*base*] firme, sólido; [*mattress, stomach, thighs*] duro; (= *secure*) [*hold*] firme, seguro • **these legends have a ~ basis in fact** estas leyendas están sólidamente basadas en hechos reales • **to be on ~ ground** (*fig*) pisar terreno firme • **as ~ as a rock** (tan) firme como una roca
2 (= *staunch*) [*belief, support*] firme; [*friends*] íntimo; [*friendship*] sólido • **she's a ~ believer in justice/discipline** cree firmemente en la justicia/la disciplina
3 (= *resolute, decisive*) [*decision, measures*] firme; [*voice*] seguro, firme; [*steps*] decidido, resuelto • **he was very ~ about it** se mostró muy firme *or* decidido • **we are taking a ~ stand on this issue** mantenemos una postura firme con respecto a esta cuestión
4 (= *severe*) estricto, firme • **to be ~ with sb** ser estricto *or* firme con algn • **a ~ hand: this horse needs a ~ hand** a este caballo hay que tratarlo con firmeza • **this child needs a ~ hand** este niño necesita mano dura • **he governed the country with a ~ hand** dirigió el país con mano dura
5 (= *definite*) [*offer, order*] en firme; [*evidence*] concluyente, contundente • **they won't go ahead without a ~ commitment from us** no van a seguir adelante hasta que no les demos una garantía en firme • **they are ~ favourites to win the trophy** son los grandes favoritos para llevarse el trofeo • **chocolate is a ~ favourite with children** el chocolate siempre tiene el éxito asegurado con los niños
6 (= *set*) firme • **beat the egg whites until ~** bata las claras a punto de nieve
7 (*Econ*) (= *not subject to change*) [*price*] estable
ADV • **to stand ~** mantenerse firme
▸ **firm up** VT + ADV 1 (= *reinforce*) [+ *structure*] fortalecer, reforzar; [+ *thighs, muscles*] endurecer
2 (= *make more specific*) [+ *proposal, deal*] concretar
3 (*Culin*) [+ *mixture*] dar consistencia a
4 (*Econ*) [+ *prices*] consolidar

f

(VI + ADV) (*Culin*) [*mixture*] hacerse consistente
firm² [fɜːm] (N) firma *f*, empresa *f* • **a ~ of accountants** una firma *or* empresa de contabilidad • **she joined a law ~** se incorporó a un bufete de abogados
firmament [ˈfɜːməmənt] (N) firmamento *m*
firmly [ˈfɜːmlɪ] (ADV) **1** (= *unwaveringly*) [*fixed, entrenched*] firmemente • **she had her eye ~ fixed on the dog** tenía la mirada fija en el perro
2 (= *staunchly*) [*believe*] firmemente, con firmeza • **the crowd was ~ behind him** tenía todo el apoyo del público, el público le apoyaba firmemente • **they remain ~ opposed/committed to the plan** se mantienen firmes en su oposición/entrega al proyecto
3 (= *decisively, severely*) [*speak, say*] con firmeza
firmness [ˈfɜːmnɪs] (N) **1** (= *hardness*) [*of mattress, muscles, thighs*] dureza *f*
2 (= *tightness*) [*of grip*] fuerza *f*
3 (= *determination*) firmeza *f* • **~ of character/purpose** firmeza *f* de carácter/propósito
4 (= *severity*) firmeza *f*, mano *f* dura
firmware [ˈfɜːmwɛəʳ] (N) (*Comput*) firmware *m*
first [fɜːst] (ADJ) primero; (*before m sing n*) primer • **I was ~!** ¡yo iba *or* estaba primero! • **during the ~ three months of pregnancy** durante los primeros tres meses de embarazo • **he felt a bit lonely for the ~ few days** los primeros días se sentía un poco solo • **the ~ three correct answers win a prize** las tres primeras respuestas correctas se llevan un premio • **at ~** al principio • **on the ~ floor** (*Brit*) en el primer piso; (*US*) en la planta baja • **from ~ to last** de principio a fin • **in the ~ place** en primer lugar • **to win ~ place** (*in competition*) conseguir el primer puesto, ganar • **to win ~ prize** ganar el primer premio • **~ strike weapon** arma *f* de primer golpe • **the ~ time** la primera vez; ▹ **instance, thing**
(ADV) **1** (*in place, priority*) primero • **~ one, then another** primero uno, después otro • **we arrived ~** fuimos los primeros en llegar, llegamos los primeros • **ladies ~** las señoras primero • **women and children ~!** ¡las mujeres y los niños primero! • **~ of all** ante todo, antes que nada • **to come ~** (*in race*) ganar, llegar el primero; (= *have priority*) estar primero, tener prioridad • **the customer/your homework must come ~** el cliente es lo primero/tus deberes son lo primero • **~ and foremost** ante todo, antes que nada • **to get in ~** (*in conversation, process*) adelantarse • **you go ~!** ¡tú primero!, ¡pasa tú! • **head ~** de cabeza • **you have to put your children's needs ~** primero están las necesidades de tus hijos • IDIOM: • **~ come, ~ served** el que llega primero tiene prioridad • **free tickets, on a ~-come-first-served basis** entradas gratis, por riguroso orden de llegada
2 (*in time*) (= *before anything else*) primero, antes de nada • **~, I need a drink** primero *or* antes de nada *or* antes que nada, necesito una copa • **~, I don't like it, second, I haven't got the money** lo primero: no me gusta, lo segundo: no dispongo del dinero • **~ and last** (= *above all*) por encima de todo • **~ off*** primero de todo, antes de nada
3 (= *for the first time*) por primera vez • **the word was ~ used in 1835** la palabra se usó por primera vez en 1835 • **I ~ met him in Paris** lo conocí en París
4 (= *rather*) primero, antes • **let him in this house? I'd kill him ~!** ¿dejarle pisar esta casa? ¡primero *or* antes lo mato! • **I'd die ~!** ¡antes me muero!
(PRON) • **the ~ of January** el primero de enero, el uno de enero • **it's the ~ I've heard of it** ahora me entero, no lo sabía • **Charles the First** Carlos Primero • **he came in an easy ~** llegó el primero con ventaja • **from the (very) ~** desde el principio • **to be the ~ to do sth** ser el primero en hacer algo • **they were the ~ to arrive** fueron los primeros en llegar, llegaron los primeros
(N) **1** (*Aut*) primera *f* • **in ~** en primera
2 (*Brit*) (*Univ*) ≈ sobresaliente *m* • **he got a ~ in French** ≈ se ha licenciado en francés con una media de sobresaliente; ▹ DEGREE
(CPD) ▸ **first aid** primeros auxilios *mpl*; ▹ **first-aid** ▸ **first aider** socorrista *mf* ▸ **first base** (*Baseball*) primera base *f* • IDIOM: • **not to get to ~ base** (*US**) quedar en agua de borrajas ▸ **first blood** • **to draw ~ blood** anotar el primer tanto • **~ blood to sb** primer tanto para algn ▸ **first cousin** primo/a *m/f* hermano/a ▸ **first degree** licenciatura *f* ▸ **first edition** primera edición *f*; [*of early or rare book*] edición *f* príncipe ▸ **first family** (*US*) [*of president*] • **the ~ family** la familia del presidente ▸ **first form** *or* **year** (*Scol*) *primer curso de secundaria* • **~-year student** (*Univ*) estudiante *mf* de primer año (*de carrera universitaria*) ▸ **first gear** (*Aut*) primera *f* ▸ **first grade** (*US*) primero *m* de primaria; ▹ **first-grade** ▸ **first hand** • **at ~ hand** directamente • IDIOM: • **to see sth at ~ hand** ver algo de primera mano ▸ **first lady** (*US*) primera dama *f* • **the ~ lady of jazz** la gran dama del jazz ▸ **first language** (= *mother tongue*) lengua *f* materna; [*of country*] lengua *f* principal ▸ **first lieutenant** (*US*) (*Aer*) teniente *mf*; (*Brit*) (*Naut*) teniente *mf* de navío ▸ **first light** amanecer *m*, alba *f* • **at ~ light** al amanecer, al alba ▸ **first mate** primer oficial *m*, primera oficial *f* ▸ **first minister** (*in Scotland*) primer(a) ministro/a *m/f* ▸ **first name** nombre *m* (de pila) • **to be on ~ name terms with sb** tutear a algn ▸ **first night** (*Theat*) estreno *m* ▸ **first offender** (*Jur*) delincuente *mf* sin antecedentes penales ▸ **first officer** primer oficial *m*, primera oficial *f* ▸ **first performance** (*Theat, Mus*) estreno *m* ▸ **first person** (*Ling*) primera persona *f* ▸ **first person plural** (*Gram*) • **the ~ person plural** la primera persona del plural ▸ **first school** (*Brit*) *escuela para niños entre cinco y nueve años* ▸ **first secretary, First Secretary** (*in Wales*) primer(a) ministro/a *m/f* de Gales ▸ **first violin** primer violín *m*, primera violín *f* ▸ **First World** • **the First World** el primer mundo ▸ **First World countries** los países del primer mundo ▸ **First World War** • **the First World War** la Primera Guerra Mundial ▸ **First World War battlefield** campo *m* de batalla de la Primera Guerra Mundial ▸ **first year** (*Scol*) = **first form**
first-aid [fɜːstˈeɪd] (CPD) ▸ **first-aid box** botiquín *m* de primeros auxilios ▸ **first-aid course** curso *m* de primeros auxilios ▸ **first-aid kit** botiquín *m* de primeros auxilios ▸ **first-aid post, first-aid station** (*US*) puesto *m* de socorro
first-born [ˈfɜːstbɔːn] (N) primogénito/a *m/f*
(ADJ) primogénito • **the first-born son** el hijo primogénito
first-class [ˈfɜːstklɑːs] (ADJ) **1** [*passenger, accommodation*] de primera clase; [*travel, compartment, train*] de primera (clase); [*stamp*] *referido a un sello de correos, que asegura mayor rapidez en la entrega*
2 (= *very good*) [*education, performance*] de primera (calidad)
(ADV) • **to travel first-class** viajar en primera • **to send a letter first-class** *enviar una carta por el sistema de correos que asegura una entrega rápida*
(CPD) ▸ **first-class compartment** (*Rail*) compartimento *m* de primera ▸ **first-class honours degree** (*Univ*) licenciatura *f* con matrícula de honor; ▹ **honour** ▸ **first-class mail, first-class post** *servicio de correos que asegura mayor rapidez en la entrega* ▸ **first-class ticket** (*Rail*) billete *m or* (*LAm*) boleto *m* de primera clase
first-day cover [ˌfɜːstdeɪˈkʌvəʳ] (N) (*Post*) sobre *m* de primer día
first-degree burns [ˌfɜːstdɪgriːˈbɜːnz] (NPL) quemaduras *fpl* de primer grado
first-degree murder [ˌfɜːstdɪgriːˈmɜːdəʳ] (N) (*US*) asesinato *m* premeditado
first-ever [ˈfɜːstˌevəʳ] (ADJ) primerísimo
first-floor [ˌfɜːstˈflɔːʳ] (CPD) **1** (*Brit*) (*above ground floor*) [*flat, sitting room, restaurant, balcony*] de la primera planta
2 (*US*) (= *ground-floor*) [*apartment*] de la planta baja
first-footing [ˌfɜːstˈfʊtɪŋ] (N) (*Scot*) • **to go first-footing** *ser el primero en visitar a amigos y familiares tras las doce en Nochevieja*; ▹ HOGMANAY
first-generation [ˈfɜːstˌdʒenəˈreɪʃən] (ADJ) de primera generación • **he's a first-generation American** es americano de primera generación
first-grade [ˌfɜːstˈgreɪd] (ADJ) (*US*) [*teacher, class, student*] de primero de primaria
first-grader [ˌfɜːstˈgreɪdəʳ] (N) (*US*) alumno/a *m/f* de primer curso (*de entre 6 y 7 años*)
first-hand [ˈfɜːstˈhænd] (ADJ) [*information, account*] de primera mano; [*experience, knowledge*] de primera mano
(ADV) directamente
firstly [ˈfɜːstlɪ] (ADV) **1** (= *before anything else*) antes que nada, en primer lugar, primero • **~, we must stop the bleeding** antes que nada *or* en primer lugar *or* primero tenemos que cortar la hemorragia
2 (= *on the first occasion*) primero • **we went there ~ as tourists, then bought a house there** fuimos allí primero como turistas, luego nos compramos una casa
3 (= *in the first place*) en primer lugar • **~, it's too small and secondly, it's too expensive** en primer lugar, es demasiado pequeño y en segundo lugar, es demasiado caro
first-named [ˌfɜːstˈneɪmd] (ADJ) • **the first-named** el primero, la primera
first-nighter [ˈfɜːstˈnaɪtəʳ] (N) estrenista *mf*
first-past-the-post system [ˌfɜːstpɑːstðəˈpəʊstˌsɪstəm] (N) sistema *m* mayoritario uninominal
first-person [ˌfɜːstˈpɜːsən] (CPD) [*account, narrative*] en primera persona
first-rate [ˈfɜːstˈreɪt] (ADJ) de primera categoría *or* clase • **she is first-rate at her work** su trabajo es de primera clase • **first-rate!** ¡magnífico!
first-time [ˈfɜːstˈtaɪm] (ADJ) • **first-time buyer** *persona que compra su primera vivienda*
first-timer [ˌfɜːstˈtaɪməʳ] (N) novato/a *m/f*, principiante *mf*
firth [fɜːθ] (N) (*Scot*) estuario *m*, ría *f*
FIS (N ABBR) (*Brit*) (= **Family Income Supplement**) *ayuda estatal familiar*
FISA (N ABBR) = **Fédération Internationale de l'Automobile**
fiscal [ˈfɪskəl] (ADJ) [*policy, system, incentive*] fiscal
(N) (*Scot*) (*Jur*) fiscal *mf*
(CPD) ▸ **fiscal year** año *m* fiscal
fish [fɪʃ] (N) (PL: **fish** *or* **fishes**) **1** (*alive*) pez *m*; (*as food*) pescado *m* • IDIOMS: • **neither ~ nor fowl** ni chicha ni limoná • **I've got other ~ to fry*** tengo cosas más importantes que hacer • **there are other ~ in the sea** hay otros peces en el mar • **to be like a ~ out of water**

estar como pez fuera del agua
2* (= *person*) tipo/a* *m/f*, tío/a *m/f* (*Sp**) • **odd ~** bicho *m* raro* • **big ~** pez *m* gordo • IDIOM: • **he's a (bit of a) cold ~*** es un tipo frío*
(VI) pescar; [*trawler*] faenar • **he goes ~ing at weekends** sale a pescar los fines de semana • **I'm going ~ing** voy de pesca • **to go salmon ~ing** ir a pescar salmón • **to ~ for** [+ *trout, salmon etc*] pescar; [+ *compliments, information*] andar a la caza de • **to ~ (around) in one's pocket for sth** buscarse algo en el bolsillo • IDIOM: • **to ~ in troubled waters** pescar en río revuelto
(VT) [+ *river, pond*] pescar en; [+ *trout, salmon etc*] pescar
(CPD) ▸ **fish and chips** pescado *m* frito con patatas fritas ▸ **fish and chip shop** *tienda de comida rápida principalmente de pescado frito y patatas fritas* ▸ **fish course** (plato *m* de) pescado *m* ▸ **fish factory** fábrica *f* de pescado ▸ **fish farm** piscifactoría *f*, criadero *m* de peces ▸ **fish farmer** piscicultor(a) *m/f* ▸ **fish farming** piscicultura *f*, cría *f* de peces ▸ **fish finger** (*Brit*) palito *m* de pescado empanado ▸ **fish glue** cola *f* de pescado ▸ **fish knife** cuchillo *m* de pescado ▸ **fish manure** abono *m* de pescado ▸ **fish market** lonja *f* de pescado (*Sp*) ▸ **fish meal** harina *f* de pescado ▸ **fish restaurant** restaurante *m* de pescado • **they had dinner in a nearby ~ restaurant** cenaron en un restaurante de pescado cercano ▸ **fish seller** (*US*) = **fishmonger** ▸ **fish shop** pescadería *f* ▸ **fish slice** pala *f* para el pescado ▸ **fish soup** sopa *f* de pescado ▸ **fish stick** (*US*) croqueta *f* de pescado ▸ **fish store** (*US*) pescadería *f* ▸ **fish tank** acuario *m*
▸ **fish out** (VT + ADV) (*from water, from box*) sacar • **they ~ed him out of the water** lo sacaron del agua • **she ~ed a handkerchief out of her handbag** sacó un pañuelo del bolso
▸ **fish up** (VT + ADV) sacar
fishbone [ˈfɪʃbəʊn] (N) espina *f*, raspa *f*
fishbowl [ˈfɪʃbəʊl] (N) pecera *f*
fishcake [ˈfɪʃkeɪk] (N) croqueta *f* de pescado
fisherman [ˈfɪʃəmən] (N) (PL: **fishermen**) pescador *m*
fishery [ˈfɪʃərɪ] (N) (= *area*) caladero *m*, pesquería *f*; (= *industry*) pesca *f*, industria *f* pesquera; ▹ **agriculture**
(CPD) ▸ **fishery policy** política *f* pesquera ▸ **fishery protection** protección *f* pesquera
fish-eye [ˈfɪʃaɪ] (N) (*in door*) mirilla *f*
(CPD) ▸ **fish-eye lens** (*Phot*) objetivo *m* de ojo de pez
fishhook [ˈfɪʃhʊk] (N) anzuelo *m*
fishing [ˈfɪʃɪŋ] (N) pesca *f* • **to go on a ~ expedition** ir de pesca
(CPD) ▸ **fishing boat** barco *m* pesquero *or* de pesca ▸ **fishing fleet** flota *f* pesquera ▸ **fishing grounds** caladeros *mpl*, pesquerías *fpl* ▸ **fishing industry** industria *f* pesquera ▸ **fishing licence** licencia *f* de pesca ▸ **fishing line** sedal *m* ▸ **fishing net** red *f* de pesca ▸ **fishing permit** licencia *f* de pesca ▸ **fishing port** puerto *m* pesquero ▸ **fishing rod** caña *f* de pescar ▸ **fishing tackle** equipo *m* de pesca ▸ **fishing village** pueblo *m* de pescadores
fishmonger [ˈfɪʃmʌŋgəʳ] (N) (*Brit*) pescadero/a *m/f* • **~'s (shop)** pescadería *f*
fishnet [ˈfɪʃnet] (N) 1 (*US, Canada*) red *f* de pesca
2 (= *material*) red *f*
(CPD) ▸ **fishnet stockings** medias *fpl* de red *or* malla ▸ **fishnet tights** leotardo *m* de red
fishpaste [ˈfɪʃpeɪst] (N) pasta *f* de pescado
fishplate [ˈfɪʃpleɪt] (N) (*Rail*) eclisa *f*
fishpond [ˈfɪʃpɒnd] (N) estanque *m* (de peces)
fishwife [ˈfɪʃwaɪf] (N) (PL: **fishwives** [ˈfɪʃwaɪvz]) pescadera *f*; (*pej*) verdulera *f*
fishy [ˈfɪʃɪ] (ADJ) (COMPAR: **fishier**, SUPERL: **fishiest**) 1 [*smell, taste*] a pescado
2* (= *suspect*) sospechoso • **there's something ~ about him** hay algo en él que resulta sospechoso • **it sounds ~ to me** me huele a chamusquina (*Sp**) • **there's something ~ going on here** aquí hay gato encerrado, me huele a chamusquina (*Sp**)
fissile [ˈfɪsaɪl] (ADJ) físil
fission [ˈfɪʃən] (N) (*Phys*) fisión *f*; (*Bio*) escisión *f* • **atomic/nuclear ~** fisión *f* atómica/nuclear
fissionable [ˈfɪʃnəbl] (ADJ) fisionable
fissure [ˈfɪʃəʳ] (N) hendidura *f*, grieta *f*; (*Anat, Geol, Metal*) fisura *f*
fissured [ˈfɪʃəd] (ADJ) agrietado
fist [fɪst] (N) puño *m* • **he banged his ~ on the table** dio un puñetazo en la mesa • **to shake one's ~ at sb** amenazar con el puño a algn • IDIOM: • **to make a poor ~ of sth** hacer algo mal; ▹ **clench**
(CPD) ▸ **fist fight** pelea *f* a puñetazos
fistful [ˈfɪstfʊl] (N) puñado *m*
fisticuffs [ˈfɪstɪkʌfs] (NPL) puñetazos *mpl*
fistula [ˈfɪstjʊlə] (N) (PL: **fistulas** *or* **fistulae** [ˈfɪstjʊliː]) fístula *f*
fit¹ [fɪt] (ADJ) (COMPAR: **fitter**, SUPERL: **fittest**)
1 (= *suitable*) adecuado • **he is not fit company for my daughter** no es compañía adecuada para mi hija • **fit for sth**: • **fit for human consumption/habitation** comestible/habitable • **he's not fit for the job** no sirve para el puesto, no es apto para el puesto • **a meal fit for a king** una comida digna de reyes • **fit for nothing** inútil • **to be fit to do sth**: • **he's not fit to teach** no sirve para profesor • **you're not fit to be seen** no estás presentable, no estás para que te vea la gente • **the meat was not fit to eat** *or* **to be eaten** (= *unhealthy*) la carne no estaba en buenas condiciones; (= *bad-tasting*) la carne era incomible, la carne no se podía comer • **you're not fit to drive** no estás en condiciones de conducir
2 (= *healthy*) (*Med*) sano; (*Sport*) en forma • **to be fit for duty** (*Mil*) ser apto para el servicio • **to be fit for work** (*after illness*) estar en condiciones de trabajar • **to get fit** (*Med*) reponerse; (*Sport*) ponerse en forma • **to keep fit** mantenerse en forma • **to pass sb fit** (*after illness, injury*) dar a algn el alta • **she's not yet fit to travel** todavía no está en condiciones de viajar • IDIOM: • **to be (as) fit as a fiddle** estar rebosante de salud
3* (= *ready*) • **I'm fit to drop** estoy que me caigo* • **he was laughing fit to bust** *or* **burst** se tronchaba *or* desternillaba de risa
4 (= *right*) • **to see/think fit to do sth**: • **you must do as you think fit** debes hacer lo que estimes conveniente *or* lo que creas apropiado • **she didn't see fit to mention it** no creyó apropiado mencionarlo
fit² [fɪt] (VT) 1 (= *be right size*) [*clothes*] quedar bien a; [*key*] entrar en, encajar en • **it fits me like a glove** me queda como un guante • **he can't find shirts to fit him** no encuentra camisas que le queden *or* vengan bien • **the key doesn't fit the lock** la llave no entra *or* encaja en la cerradura
2 (= *measure*) tomar las medidas a • **I went to get fitted for a suit** fui a que me tomaran las medidas para un traje • **to fit a dress (on sb)** probar un vestido (a algn)
3 (= *match*) [+ *facts*] corresponderse con; [+ *description*] encajar con; [+ *need*] adecuarse a • **your story doesn't fit the facts** tu historia no se corresponde con los hechos • **she doesn't fit the feminine stereotype** no encaja con el estereotipo femenino • **the punishment should fit the crime** el castigo debe adecuarse al delito; ▹ **bill**
4 (= *put*) • **he fitted the shelf to the wall** fijó el estante a la pared • **to fit sth into place** hacer encajar algo • **I finally began to fit the pieces together** (*fig*) finalmente empecé a encajar todas las piezas
5 (= *install*) [+ *windows*] instalar, poner; [+ *carpet*] poner; [+ *kitchen, bathroom, domestic appliance*] instalar • **they're having a new kitchen fitted** les van a instalar una cocina nueva
6 (= *supply*) equipar de • **to be fitted with sth** estar equipado con algo • **a car fitted with a catalytic converter** un coche equipado con un conversor catalítico • **all our coaches are fitted with seat belts** todos nuestros autobuses están equipados con cinturones de seguridad • **he has been fitted with a new hearing aid** le han puesto un audífono nuevo
7 (*frm*) (= *make suitable*) • **to fit sb for sth/to do sth** capacitar a algn para algo/para hacer algo • **her experience fits her for the job** su experiencia la capacita para el trabajo
(VI) 1 [*clothes, shoes*] • **the dress doesn't fit very well** el vestido no le queda muy bien; ▹ **cap**
2 (= *go in/on*) • **this key doesn't fit** esta llave no encaja *or* entra • **will the cupboard fit into the corner?** ¿cabrá el armario en el rincón? • **it fits in/on here** se encaja aquí • **the lid won't fit on this saucepan** la tapa no encaja en esta cazuela
3 (= *match*) [*facts, description*] concordar, corresponderse • **it doesn't fit with what he said to me** no concuerda *or* no se corresponde con lo que me dijo a mí • **it all fits now!** ¡todo encaja ahora!; ▹ **fit in**
4* (= *belong*) encajar • **his face doesn't fit** él no encaja aquí
(N) • **the lycra in the fabric ensures a good fit** la licra de la tela hace que se ajuste perfectamente • **that suit is not a very good fit** ese traje no te queda bien • **when it comes to shoes, a good fit is essential** en lo que se refiere a los zapatos, es esencial que se ajusten bien *or* que sean el número correcto • **it was a perfect fit** le quedaba perfectamente • **it's rather a tight fit** me está un poco justo *or* apretado • **she put the key into the lock — it was a tight fit** metió la llave en la cerradura — entraba muy justo
▸ **fit in** (VI + ADV) 1 (= *correspond*) [*fact, statement*] concordar, cuadrar (**with** con) • **that fits in with what he told me** eso concuerda *or* cuadra *or* se corresponde con lo que me dijo él
2 (= *adapt*) • **to fit in with sb's plans** amoldarse *or* adaptarse a los planes de algn • **I'll fit in with whatever dates you've agreed on** me amoldaré *or* me adaptaré a las fechas que hayáis acordado • **she was trying to arrange her work to fit in with her home life** intentaba organizar el trabajo de forma que se adaptara a su vida doméstica
3 (= *belong*) [*person*] • **he left because he didn't fit in** se marchó porque no congeniaba con los demás *or* no encajaba • **she was great with the children and fitted in beautifully** con los niños era genial, y se adaptó perfectamente
4 (= *go in*) (*into cupboard, car, corner*) caber; (*into jigsaw puzzle*) encajar • **will we all fit in?** ¿cabremos todos?
(VT + ADV) 1 (= *make room for*) • **can you fit another book/passenger in?** ¿te cabe otro libro/pasajero más? • **you could fit an illustration in here** aquí podrías poner una ilustración, aquí tienes sitio para poner

una ilustración
2 (= *make time for*) • **I could fit you in next Friday** podría hacerte un hueco el próximo viernes • **I fitted in a trip to Ávila** logré incluir una excursión a Ávila • **we could fit in a round of golf before lunch** nos da tiempo a hacer un recorrido de golf antes de comer • **we rushed around trying to fit everything in** corrimos como locos intentando abarcarlo todo
▸ **fit out** (VT + ADV) [+ *ship, expedition*] equipar; [+ *warship*] armar • **to fit sb out with sth** proveer a algn de algo, equipar a algn con algo • **we need to get you fitted out with a new wardrobe** tenemos que equiparte con un nuevo vestuario • **the tailor will fit you out with a new suit for the wedding** el sastre te hará un traje nuevo para la boda
▸ **fit up** (VT + ADV) **1** (= *install*) instalar
2 (*Brit*) (= *equip, supply*) equipar • **to fit sth/sb up with sth** proveer algo/a algn de algo, equipar algo/a algn con algo
3* (= *frame*) • **I've been fitted up!** ¡han hecho que aparezca como el culpable!

fit³ [fɪt] (N) **1** (*Med*) ataque *m* • **epileptic fit** ataque *m* epiléptico • **fainting fit** desmayo *m* • **she had a fit last night** anoche tuvo un ataque
2 (= *outburst*) • **a fit of anger** un arranque *or* un arrebato *or* (*frm*) un acceso de cólera • **a fit of coughing** un ataque *or* (*frm*) un acceso de tos • **a fit of enthusiasm** un arranque de entusiasmo • **I had a fit of (the) giggles** me dio un ataque de risa • **to have a fit*** ponerse histérico* • **he'd have a fit if he knew** le daría un síncope si se enterara*, se pondría histérico si se enterara* • **to be in fits*** partirse de risa* • **she was so funny, she used to have us all in fits** era tan graciosa, que nos tenía a todos muertos de risa* • **she had a laughing fit** le dio un ataque de risa • **she was in fits of laughter** se partía de risa* • **he shot her in a fit of jealous rage** disparó sobre ella en un arranque *or* arrebato de celos y furia • **by** *or* **in fits and starts** a tropezones, a trompicones* • **to throw a fit*** ponerse histérico* • **she'll throw a fit if she finds out** le dará un síncope si se entera*, se pondrá histérica si se entera* • **a fit of weeping** una llorera; ▹ **pique**

fitful ['fɪtfʊl] (ADJ) [*breeze, showers, gunfire*] intermitente; [*breathing, progress*] irregular • **she fell into a ~ sleep** se durmió pero no descansó bien • **I passed a ~ night** dormí muy mal

fitfully ['fɪtfəlɪ] (ADV) [*work*] de manera irregular; [*sleep*] muy mal • **he dozed ~** echó alguna que otra cabezada • **the candle burned ~** la llama de la vela parpadeaba

fitment ['fɪtmənt] (N) **1** (*Brit*) mueble *m*
2 (= *accessory*) [*of machine*] aparejo *m*
3 = fitting

fitness ['fɪtnɪs] (N) **1** (= *suitability*) (*gen, for post*) aptitud *f*, capacidad *f* (**for** para) • **she doubted his ~ to drive** dudaba que se encontrase en condiciones de conducir
2 (= *state of health*) estado *m* físico; (= *good health*) buena forma *f* • **to be at the peak of ~** estar en condiciones óptimas, estar en plena forma
(CPD) ▸ **fitness centre** centro *m* de fitness ▸ **fitness fanatic** fanático/a *m/f* del mantenimiento físico ▸ **fitness instructor** monitor(a) *m/f* de fitness ▸ **fitness programme, fitness program** (*US*) programa *m* de mantenimiento físico ▸ **fitness test** prueba *f* de estado físico ▸ **fitness trainer** [*of team*] entrenador(a) *m/f* de fitness; [*of individual*] preparador(a) *m/f* físico/a ▸ **fitness training** entrenamiento *m*

fitted ['fɪtɪd] (ADJ) **1** (= *made to measure*) [*jacket, shirt*] entallado; [*sheet*] de cuatro picos • **~ carpet** alfombra *f* de pared a pared, moqueta *f* (*Sp*)
2 (= *integral*) [*cupboards*] empotrado • **~ bathroom** cuarto *m* de baño con todos los elementos • **~ kitchen** cocina *f* con armarios empotrados, cocina *f* integral
3 (= *suited*) • **to be ~ to do sth** estar capacitado para hacer algo, reunir las cualidades necesarias para hacer algo • **he is well ~ to be king** reúne todas las cualidades necesarias para ser rey • **she wasn't ~ for the role of motherhood** no estaba capacitada para desempeñar la labor de madre

fitter ['fɪtəʳ] (N) **1** (*in garage*) mecánico/a *m/f*; ▹ **electrical, gas**
2 [*of garment*] probador(a) *m/f*

fitting ['fɪtɪŋ] (ADJ) **1** (= *appropriate*) [*end*] adecuado, apropiado; [*tribute*] digno • **it is ~ that ...** es apropiado que ... • **it seemed ~ to ...** (+ *infin*) parecía apropiado *or* oportuno ... (+ *infin*)
2 (= *worthy*) digno • **that's not ~ for an officer** eso no es digno de un oficial
(N) **1** (= *trying on*) [*of dress*] prueba *f*; (= *size*) [*of shoe*] número *m*, tamaño *m*
2 **fittings** [*of house*] accesorios *mpl*; [*of shop*] mobiliario *msing* • **bathroom ~s** accesorios *mpl* de baño • **electrical/gas ~s** instalaciones *fpl* eléctricas/de gas; ▹ **fixture, light**
(CPD) ▸ **fitting room** (*in shop*) probador *m*

-fitting [-'fɪtɪŋ] (ADJ) • **loose-fitting** amplio • **tight-fitting** [*lid, cap*] que ajusta bien; [*trousers, shirt, clothes*] ajustado • **glass bottles with tight-fitting caps** botes de cristal con tapas que ajustan bien

fittingly ['fɪtɪŋlɪ] (ADV) **1** (= *appropriately*) [*named*] apropiadamente; [*dressed*] convenientemente, adecuadamente • **the ~ named Dark Valley** el apropiadamente denominado Valle Oscuro • **her work is most ~ described as minimalist** la calificación más adecuada de su trabajo es la de minimalista • **the speech was ~ solemn** el discurso fue solemne, como correspondía
2 (= *worthily*) dignamente

five [faɪv] (ADJ), (PRON) cinco • **she is ~ (years old)** tiene cinco años (de edad) • **it costs ~ pounds** cuesta *or* vale cinco libras • **they live at number ~** viven en el número cinco • **there are ~ of us** somos cinco • **all ~ of them came** vinieron los cinco • **to divide sth into ~** dividir algo en cinco • **~ and a quarter/half** cinco y cuarto/medio • **~ times ten** diez por cinco • **~-day week** semana *f* inglesa
(N) (= *numeral*) cinco *m* • **it's ~ (o'clock)** son las cinco • **see you at ~!** ¡hasta las cinco! • **they are sold in ~s** se venden de cinco en cinco
(CPD) ▸ **five a day** cinco *fpl* al día (*consumo diario recomendado de cinco piezas de fruta o verdura*) ▸ **five spot*** (*US*) billete *m* de cinco dólares

five-and-ten-cent store [ˌfaɪvən'tensent-ˌstɔːʳ] (N), **five-and-dime** [ˌfaɪvən'daɪm] (N), **five-and-ten** [ˌfaɪvən'ten] (N) (*US*) almacén *m* de baratillo

five-a-side ['faɪvəˌsaɪd] (ADJ) [*team*] de futbito • **five-a-side football** (*outdoors*) futbito *m*; (*indoors*) fútbol *m* sala

five-door [ˌfaɪv'dɔːʳ] (N) (= *car*) cinco puertas *m inv*

five-fold ['faɪvˌfəʊld] (ADJ) quíntuplo
(ADV) cinco veces

five-o'-clock shadow ['faɪvəklɒk'ʃædəʊ] (N) barba *f* crecida

fiver* ['faɪvəʳ] (N) (= *banknote*) (*Brit*) billete *m* de cinco libras; (*US*) billete de cinco dólares; (= *amount*) (*Brit*) cinco libras *fpl*; (*US*) cinco dólares *mpl*

five-star ['faɪvstɑːʳ] (ADJ) [*hotel*] de cinco estrellas; [*restaurant*] de cinco tenedores

five-year ['faɪv'jɪəʳ] (ADJ) [*period, term of office*] de cinco años
(CPD) ▸ **five-year plan** plan *m* quinquenal

fix [fɪks] (VT) **1** (= *position*) fijar, asegurar • **to fix sth in place** fijar *or* asegurar algo en su sitio • **to fix a stake in the ground** clavar *or* fijar una estaca en el suelo
2 (= *attach*) **a** (*with nails*) clavar; (*with string*) atar, amarrar; (*with glue*) pegar • **to fix sth to sth: fix the mirror to the wall** fije el espejo a la pared • **I fixed the hose to the tap** ajusté la manguera al grifo • **the phone is fixed to the wall** el teléfono está colgado de la pared • **the chairs and desks are fixed to the floor** las sillas y mesas están sujetas *or* atornilladas al suelo • **they fixed the two pieces of bone together with a metal plate** unieron los dos trozos de hueso con una placa de metal
b [+ *bayonet*] calar • **with fixed bayonets** con bayonetas caladas
3 (*fig*) (= *set firmly*) • **to fix sth in one's memory/mind** grabar algo en la memoria/ la mente • **the image of her was now firmly fixed in his mind** su imagen estaba ahora firmemente grabada en su mente
4 (= *lay*) • **to fix the blame on sb** echar la culpa a algn
5 (= *arrange, settle*) [+ *date, time*] fijar; [+ *meeting*] fijar, convenir • **we must fix a date to have lunch** tenemos que fijar un día para quedar a comer • **nothing's been fixed yet** todavía no se ha decidido *or* acordado nada • **I've fixed it for you to meet her** lo he arreglado para que la conozcas • **how are you fixed for this evening?** ¿tienes planes para esta noche? • **how are we fixed for money?** ¿qué tal andamos de dinero? • **how are we fixed for time?** ¿cómo vamos de tiempo?
6 (= *set*) **a** (*honestly*) [+ *price, rate*] fijar
b (= *rig*) [+ *fight, race, election*] amañar; [+ *price*] fijar • **they're in a dispute over price fixing** tienen una disputa por la fijación de los precios
7 (= *rivet*) [+ *eyes, gaze*] fijar, clavar; [+ *attention*] fijar • **she fixed her eyes on him** le clavó los ojos, fijó la mirada en él • **he fixed his gaze on the horizon** miró fijamente al horizonte • **she fixed him with an angry glare** lo miró fijamente con indignación • **she had fixed all her hopes on passing the exam** tenía todas sus esperanzas puestas en aprobar el examen
8 (= *repair*) [+ *car, appliance*] arreglar, reparar • **to get** *or* **have sth fixed** arreglar *or* reparar algo • **I've got to get my car fixed this week** tengo que arreglar *or* reparar el coche esta semana, tengo que llevar el coche a arreglar *or* reparar esta semana • **I should have my teeth fixed** tendría que arreglarme los dientes
9 (= *solve*) [+ *problem*] solucionar
10* (= *deal with*) encargarse de*; (= *kill*) cargarse a* • **I'll soon fix him!** ¡ya me encargo yo de él!*, ¡ya le ajustaré las cuentas!*
11 (= *prepare*) [+ *meal, drink*] preparar • **I fixed myself a coffee** me preparé un café
12 (*esp US*) (= *tidy up*) [+ *hair, makeup*] arreglar • **to fix one's hair** arreglarse el pelo
13 (= *make permanent*) [+ *film, colour, dye*] fijar
14* (= *neuter*) [+ *animal*] operar
(VI) (*US*) **1** (= *intend*) tener intención de • **I'm fixing to go to graduate school** tengo intención de *or* tengo pensado hacer estudios de postgraduado

2 (= *arrange*) • **we had already fixed to go to the theatre** ya habíamos quedado para ir al teatro
(N) **1*** (= *predicament*) apuro *m*, aprieto *m* • **to be in/get into a fix** estar/meterse en un apuro *or* un aprieto
2* [*of drug*] (*gen*) dosis *f inv*; (*when injected*) pinchazo* *m*, chute *m* (*Sp*‡) • **to give o.s. a fix** pincharse*, chutarse (*Sp*‡) • **she needs her daily fix of publicity** necesita su dosis diaria de publicidad
3 (*Aer, Naut*) posición *f* • **to get a fix on sth** (*lit*) establecer la posición de algo, localizar algo • **it's been hard to get a fix on what's going on** (*fig*) ha sido difícil entender lo que pasa
4* (= *set-up*) tongo* *m* • **the fight/result was a fix** hubo tongo en la pelea/el resultado*
5* (= *solution*) arreglo *m*, apaño* *m* • **there is no quick-fix solution to this problem** no existe un arreglo *or* apaño* rápido para este problema
▸ **fix on** (VT + ADV) [+ *top, lid*] colocar
(VI + PREP) (= *decide on*) [+ *date, time*] fijar • **they haven't fixed on a name yet** no se han decidido por un nombre todavía
▸ **fix up** (VT + ADV) **1** (= *arrange*) [+ *date*] fijar; [+ *meeting*] fijar, convenir • **I fixed up an appointment to see her** concerté una cita para verla • **to fix sth up with sb** quedar con algn en algo, convenir algo con algn
2 (= *repair*) arreglar • **he buys properties to fix them up** compra casas para arreglarlas
3 (= *set up, install*) instalar, poner • **he fixed up the lighting in my flat** instaló la iluminación de mi piso, puso las luces de mi piso
4 (= *put in order*) arreglar • **I'll have to fix the place up a bit before they arrive** tendré que arreglar un poco la casa antes de que lleguen
5 (= *provide*) • **to fix sb up with sth: to fix sb up with a job** encontrar *or* conseguir un trabajo para algn • **I can fix you up with a place to stay** puedo conseguirte un sitio para alojarte
6* (= *find partner for*) • **they're always trying to fix me up with friends of theirs** siempre están intentando encontrarme un novio entre sus amigos
(VI + ADV) • **to fix up with sb** arreglarlo con algn • **to fix up with sb to** (+ *infin*) convenir con algn en (+ *infin*)
fixate [fɪk'seɪt] (VT) [+ *point*] fijar la atención en
(VI) • **to ~ on sth/sb** obsesionarse con algo/algn
fixated [fɪk'seɪtɪd] (ADJ) • **to be ~ on sth/sb** estar obsesionado con algo/algn, tener una fijación con algo/algn • **to become** *or* **get ~ on** *or* **with sth/sb** obsesionarse con algo/algn • **mother-fixated** con fijación materna *or* en la madre
fixation [fɪk'seɪʃən] (N) (*Psych*) (*also fig*) obsesión *f*, fijación *f* • **mother ~** fijación *f* materna *or* en la madre
fixative ['fɪksətɪv] (N) fijador *m*
fixed [fɪkst] (ADJ) **1** (= *permanent, invariable*) [*amount, number, rate*] fijo • **of no ~ abode** *or* **address** (*Jur*) sin domicilio fijo
2 (= *prearranged*) establecido • **at a ~ time** a una hora establecida • **there's no ~ agenda** no hay un orden del día fijo
3 (= *immovable*) [*smile*] inamovible; [*stare*] fijo • **she kept a ~ smile on her face** mantuvo una sonrisa inamovible • **to keep one's eyes ~ on sth** mantener la mirada fija en algo
4 (= *inflexible*) [*opinion*] firme, rígido • **he has very ~ ideas** es de ideas fijas
(CPD) ▸ **fixed assets** activo *msing* fijo ▸ **fixed charge** cargo *m* fijo ▸ **fixed costs** costos *mpl* fijos ▸ **fixed penalty (fine)** sanción *f* fija ▸ **fixed price** precio *m* fijo
fixed-interest ['fɪkst,ɪntrɪst] (ADJ) a interés fijo
fixedly ['fɪksɪdlɪ] (ADV) fijamente
fixed-price ['fɪkstpraɪs] (ADJ) [*contract*] a precio fijo
(CPD) ▸ **fixed-price menu** menú *m* del día
fixed-rate ['fɪkst,reɪt] (ADJ) (*Econ*) a tipo fijo
fixed-term contract [,fɪkstɜ:m'kɒntrækt] (N) contrato *m* de duración determinada
fixed-wing aircraft [,fɪkstwɪŋ'ɛəkrɑ:ft] (N) avión *m* de ala fija
fixer* ['fɪksəʳ] (N) (= *person*) apañador(a)* *m/f*, amañador(a) *m/f*; (*Phot*) fijador *m*
fixings ['fɪksɪŋz] (NPL) (*US*) (*Culin*) guarniciones *fpl*
Fixit* ['fɪksɪt] (N) • **Mr ~** Señor *m* Arreglalotodo*
fixity ['fɪksɪtɪ] (N) (= *fixedness*) fijeza *f* • **she believed in the ~ of the class system** creía en la continuidad del sistema de clases
fixture ['fɪkstʃəʳ] (N) **1** [*of house etc*] **fixtures** instalaciones *fpl* fijas • **the house was sold with ~s and fittings** la casa se vendió totalmente equipada
2 (*Sport*) encuentro *m*
3 (= *permanent feature*) elemento *m* fijo; (= *date*) fecha *f* fija • **he's become a permanent ~ in this house** (*hum*) es como si fuera parte del mobiliario de la casa
(CPD) ▸ **fixture list** lista *f* de encuentros
fizz [fɪz] (N) **1** (= *fizziness*) efervescencia *f*, gas *m*
2 (= *fizzing noise*) silbido *m*, ruido *m* sibilante
3* champán *m*; (*US*) (= *soft drink*) gaseosa *f*
4 (*fig*) chispa *f* • **the ~ had gone out of their relationship** a su relación no le quedaba chispa
(VI) [*drink*] burbujear; (= *make fizzing noise*) hacer un ruido sibilante, silbar
fizzle ['fɪzl] (VI) silbar, hacer un ruido sibilante
▸ **fizzle out** (VI + ADV) [*fire, firework*] apagarse; [*enthusiasm, interest*] morirse; [*plan*] quedar en agua de borrajas *or* en nada
fizzy ['fɪzɪ] (*esp Brit*) (ADJ) (COMPAR: **fizzier**, SUPERL: **fizziest**) [*drink*] gaseoso, con gas
fjord [fjɔ:d] (N) fiordo *m*
FL (ABBR) (*US*) = **Florida**
Fla. (ABBR) (*US*) = **Florida**
flab* [flæb] (N) gordura *f*
flabbergasted ['flæbəgɑ:stɪd] (ADJ) pasmado, atónito • **I was ~ by the news** la noticia me dejó pasmado *or* atónito
flabbergasting* ['flæbəgɑ:stɪŋ] (ADJ) impresionante, alucinante (*Sp**)
flabbiness ['flæbɪnɪs] (N) **1** (= *chubbiness*) gordura *f*
2 (*fig*) [*of speech, argument*] flojedad *f*, debilidad *f*
flabby ['flæbɪ] (ADJ) (COMPAR: **flabbier**, SUPERL: **flabbiest**) (= *soft*) fofo; (= *fat*) gordo; (*fig*) flojo, soso
flaccid ['flæksɪd] (ADJ) fláccido
flaccidity [flæk'sɪdɪtɪ] (N) flaccidez *f*
flag¹ [flæg] (N) [*of country*] bandera *f*; (*Naut*) pabellón *m*; (*for charity*) banderita *f*; (*small, as souvenir, also Sport*) banderín *m* • **~ of convenience** pabellón *m* de conveniencia • **~ of truce** bandera *f* blanca • **to raise/lower the ~** izar/arriar la bandera • IDIOMS: • **to keep the ~ flying** mantener alto el pabellón • **to show the ~** hacer acto de presencia • **to wrap o.s.** *or* **drape o.s. in the ~** (*esp US*) escudarse en el patriotismo
(VT) (= *mark*) [+ *path*] señalar con banderitas; [+ *item, reference*] señalar, marcar; (*also* **flag down**) [+ *taxi*] (hacer) parar
(CPD) ▸ **flag bearer** (*lit, fig*) abanderado/a *m/f* ▸ **flag day** *día de colecta de una organización benéfica* ▸ **Flag Day** (*US*) día *m* de la Bandera (*14 junio*) ▸ **flag officer** (*Naut*) oficial *mf* superior de la marina ▸ **flag stop** (*US*) parada *f* discrecional
▸ **flag down** (VT + ADV) [+ *taxi*] (hacer) parar • **to ~ sb down** hacer señales a algn para que se detenga
flag² [flæg] (VI) [*strength, person*] flaquear; [*enthusiasm*] enfriarse, decaer; [*conversation*] decaer
flag³ [flæg] (N) (*also* **flagstone**) losa *f*
flag⁴ [flæg] (N) (*Bot*) falso ácoro *m*, lirio *m*
flagellate ['flædʒəleɪt] (VT) flagelar
flagellation [,flædʒə'leɪʃən] (N) flagelación *f*
flageolet [,flædʒə'let] (N) flageolet *m*, *flauta dulce de seis u ocho agujeros*
flagged ['flægd] (ADJ) (= *paved*) pavimentado
flagging ['flægɪŋ] (ADJ) [*strength*] que flaquea; [*enthusiasm, interest*] que se enfría; [*popularity, conversation*] que decae • **he soon revived their ~ spirits** les levantó el ánimo rápidamente
flagon ['flægən] (N) (*approx*) jarro *m*; (*as measure*) *botella de unos dos litros*
flagpole ['flægpəʊl] (N) asta *f* de bandera
flagrant ['fleɪgrənt] (ADJ) [*violation, breach, injustice*] flagrante • **in ~ defiance of the rules** en un acto de flagrante rebeldía contra las normas • **with ~ disregard for safety/the law** con total desacato a las normas de seguridad/a la ley
flagrantly ['fleɪgrəntlɪ] (ADV) flagrantemente
flagship ['flægʃɪp] (N) **1** (*Naut*) buque *m* insignia, buque *m* almirante
2 (*fig*) punta *f* de lanza • **the newspaper is the ~ of his media empire** el periódico es la punta de lanza de su imperio mediático
flagstaff ['flægstɑ:f] (N) asta *f* de bandera
flagstone ['flægstəʊn] (N) losa *f*
flag-waving ['flæg,weɪvɪŋ] (N) (*fig*) patriotismo *m* de banderita
flail [fleɪl] (N) (*Agr*) mayal *m*
(VT) **1** (*Agr*) desgranar
2 (= *beat*) golpear, azotar
3 (= *agitate*) [+ *arms, legs*] agitar
(VI) • **to ~ (about)** [*arms, legs*] agitarse; [*person*] revolverse • **I tried to grab his ~ing arms** intenté agarrarle los brazos que no paraba de agitar
▸ **flail around** (VI + ADV) revolverse • **he started ~ing around and hitting Vincent in the chest** comenzó a revolverse y a golpear a Vincent en el pecho
flair [flɛəʳ] (N) (= *gift*) don *m*; (= *instinct*) instinto *m*; (= *style*) elegancia *f*, estilo *m* • **to have a ~ for languages** tener don de lenguas, tener facilidad para los idiomas • **she had a natural ~ for getting on with people** tenía mano izquierda con la gente *or* don de gentes
flak [flæk] (N) **1** fuego *m* antiaéreo
2* (= *criticism*) críticas *fpl* • **to get a lot of ~** ser muy criticado
(CPD) ▸ **flak jacket** chaleco *m* antibalas
flake [fleɪk] (N) [*of paint*] desconchón *m*; [*of skin, soap*] escama *f*; [*of snow*] copo *m*
(VI) (*also* **flake off, flake away**) [*paint*] descascarillarse, desconcharse; [*skin*] pelarse
(VT) [+ *cooked fish*] desmenuzar
▸ **flake out*** (VI + ADV) (*Brit*) (= *faint*) desplomarse; (= *fall asleep*) caer rendido • **I ~d out on the bed** caí rendido en la cama • **to be ~d out*** estar rendido
flaked almonds [,fleɪk'tɑ:məndz] (NPL) almendras *fpl* fileteadas
flaky ['fleɪkɪ] (ADJ) (COMPAR: **flakier**, SUPERL: **flakiest**) **1** [*paintwork*] desconchado; [*skin*]

f

escamoso
2* [*idea*] descabellado; [*person*] raro
CPD ▸ **flaky pastry** (*Culin*) hojaldre *m*
flambé ['flɑ:mbeɪ] ADJ flam(b)eado
VT flam(b)ear
flamboyance [flæm'bɔɪəns] N [*of person, behaviour*] extravagancia *f*; [*of clothes, colour*] vistosidad *f*, lo llamativo
flamboyant [flæm'bɔɪənt] ADJ [*person, behaviour, style*] extravagante; [*clothes, colour*] vistoso, llamativo • **he's a ~ dresser** viste con mucha extravagancia
flamboyantly [flæm'bɔɪəntlɪ] ADV extravagantemente, llamativamente
flame [fleɪm] N **1** llama *f* • **to be in ~s** arder *or* estar en llamas • **to burst into ~s** [*car, plane*] estallar en llamas • **to commit sth to the ~s** echar algo al fuego • **to fan the ~s** avivar el fuego • **he watched the house go up in ~s** miraba cómo la casa era pasto de las llamas
2* (= *lover*) • **old ~*** antiguo amor *m*
VI **1** (*also* **flame up**) [*fire*] llamear; [*passion*] encenderse; [*person*] acalorarse
2 [*eyes*] brillar; [*sky*] llamear, enrojecerse • **her cheeks ~d with embarrassment** se puso colorada de vergüenza
VT (*Internet*) insultar a través de la Red, abuchear en la Red
CPD ▸ **flame retardant** = **fire retardant**
flame-coloured, flame-colored (*US*) ['fleɪm,kʌləd] ADJ de un amarillo intenso
flamenco [flə'meŋkəʊ] N flamenco *m*
CPD [*music*] flamenco; [*dancer*] de flamenco
flameproof ['fleɪmpru:f] ADJ ignífugo, a prueba de fuego
flame-retardant ['fleɪmrɪ,tɑ:dənt] ADJ = **fire-retardant**
flamethrower ['fleɪm,θrəʊəʳ] N lanzallamas *m inv*
flaming ['fleɪmɪŋ] ADJ **1** [*torch*] llameante; [*vehicle*] en llamas
2 [*red, orange*] encendido • **she had ~ red hair** tenía el pelo de un rojo encendido
3 (*Brit**) (= *furious*) • **we had a ~ row** tuvimos una acalorada discusión
4‡ condenado*, maldito*
flamingo [flə'mɪŋgəʊ] N (PL: **flamingos** *or* **flamingoes**) flamenco *m*
flammable ['flæməbl] ADJ inflamable
flan [flæn] N tarta *f*
Flanders ['flɑ:ndəz] N Flandes *m*
flange [flændʒ] N (*Tech*) (*on wheel*) pestaña *f*; (*on pipe*) reborde *m*
flanged [flændʒd] ADJ [*wheel*] con pestaña; [*coupling*] rebordeado
flank [flæŋk] N [*of person*] costado *m*; [*of animal*] ijar *m*, ijada *f*; (*Mil*) flanco *m*; [*of hill*] ladera *f*, falda *f*
VT (= *stand at side of*) [+ *entrance, statue etc*] flanquear (*also Mil*) • **it is ~ed by hills** está flanqueado por colinas • **he was ~ed by two policemen** iba escoltado por dos policías
CPD ▸ **flank attack** ataque *m* de flanco
flannel ['flænl] N **1** (= *face flannel*) manopla *f*; (= *fabric*) franela *f*; **flannels** (= *trousers*) pantalones *mpl* de franela
2 (*Brit**) (= *waffle*) palabrería *f*, paja* *f*
ADJ de franela
VI (*Brit**) (= *waffle*) meter paja*
flannelette [,flænə'let] N franela *f* de algodón
flap [flæp] N **1** [*of pocket, envelope*] solapa *f*; [*of table*] hoja *f* (plegable); [*of counter*] trampa *f*; [*of skin*] colgajo *m*; (*Aer*) alerón *m*
2 (= *act*) [*of wing*] aletazo *m*; (= *sound*) (ruido *m* del) aleteo *m*
3 (*Brit**) (= *crisis*) crisis *f inv*; (= *row*) lío* *m* • **there's a big ~ on** se ha armado un buen lío* • **to get into a ~*** ponerse nervioso
VT [*bird*] [+ *wings*] batir; (= *shake*) [+ *sheets, newspaper*] sacudir; [+ *arms*] agitar
VI **1** [*wings*] aletear; [*sails*] agitarse; [*flag*] ondear, agitarse
2* (= *panic*) ponerse nervioso • **don't ~!** ¡con calma!
flapdoodle* ['flæp,du:dl] N chorrada* *f*
flapjack ['flæpdʒæk] N (*US*) (= *pancake*) torta *f*, panqueque *m* (*LAm*); (*Brit*) *torta de avena*
flapper* ['flæpəʳ] N (*Hist*) joven *f* a la moda (*de los 1920*)
flare [flɛəʳ] N **1** (= *blaze*) llamarada *f*; (= *signal*) bengala *f* (*also Mil*) (*for target*); (*on runway*) baliza *f* • **solar ~** erupción *f* solar
2 (*Sew*) vuelo *m*
3 **flares** (= *trousers*) pantalones *mpl* de campana
VI **1** [*match, torch*] llamear; [*light*] brillar
2 (= *widen*) [*skirt*] hacer vuelo; [*trousers, nostrils*] ensancharse
3 [*riots*] estallar
4 [*tempers*] caldearse, encenderse
▸ **flare up** VI + ADV **1** [*fire*] llamear
2 (*fig*) [*person*] estallar, ponerse furioso (**at** con); [*riots*] estallar; [*epidemic*] declararse
3 [*wound*] resentirse, volver a dar problemas; [*rash*] recrudecerse
flared [flɛəd] ADJ [*skirt*] de mucho vuelo, acampanado; [*trousers*] acampanado; [*nostrils*] ensanchado
flarepath ['flɛəpɑ:θ] N pista *f* iluminada con balizas
flare-up ['flɛər'ʌp] N [*of anger*] arranque *m*; (= *quarrel*) riña *f*; [*of violence*] estallido *m*; [*of illness, acne*] recrudecimiento *m*
flash [flæʃ] N **1** [*of light*] destello *m*; [*of gun*] fogonazo *m*; [*of jewel*] centelleo *m*, destellos *mpl* • **he saw a ~ of green vanishing round the next bend** vio un destello verde que desaparecía en la siguiente curva • **the ~ of expensive jewellery** el centelleo de alhajas costosas • **a ~ of lightning** un relámpago
2 (= *burst*) • **a ~ of anger** un arranque *or* un arrebato de cólera • **a ~ of inspiration** una ráfaga *or* un momento de inspiración • **a ~ of wit** un ramalazo de ingenio • IDIOM: • **a ~ in the pan** algo pasajero, flor de un día • **the affair was nothing more than a ~ in the pan** el asunto no fue más que algo pasajero *or* flor de un día • **their win was no ~ in the pan** su victoria no se debió a un golpe de suerte, no ganaron por chiripa*
3 (= *instant*) instante *m* • **in a ~** en un abrir y cerrar de ojos, en un instante • **it all happened in a ~** todo sucedió en un abrir y cerrar de ojos *or* en un instante • **it came to him in a ~** de repente lo vio todo claro • **I'll be back in a ~** vuelvo en un instante • **quick as a ~** como un relámpago *or* un rayo
4 (= *news flash*) noticia *f* de última hora
5 (*Phot*) flash *m*
6 (= *marking*) (*on animal*) mancha *f*
7 (*Brit*) (*Mil*) (= *insignia*) distintivo *m*
8 (*US*) (= *torch*) linterna *f*
VT **1** (= *direct*) [+ *look*] lanzar; [+ *smile*] dirigir • **he ~ed me a look of surprise** me lanzó una mirada de sorpresa • **she ~ed him a grateful smile** le dirigió una breve sonrisa de agradecimiento
2 (= *shine*) • **he ~ed his torch into the boat** enfocó el barco con la linterna • **she ~ed the light in my eyes** me enfocó con la luz en los ojos • **to ~ one's (head)lights** (*Aut*) hacer señales con las luces
3 (= *send quickly*) [+ *news, information*] transmitir rápidamente • **the pictures were ~ed around the world** las imágenes circularon rápidamente por todo el mundo
4 (= *display briefly*) mostrar • **the screen ~es a message** aparece brevemente un mensaje en la pantalla, la pantalla muestra brevemente un mensaje • **I ~ed my card at the security guard** le enseñé *or* mostré brevemente mi tarjeta al guardia de seguridad
5 (= *flaunt*) hacer alarde de, fardar de* • **they're rich but they don't ~ their money around** son ricos pero no van fardando de dinero por ahí*, son ricos pero no hacen alarde de su riqueza
VI **1** (= *shine*) [*light, eyes, teeth*] brillar; [*jewels*] brillar, lanzar destellos • **a light was ~ing on the horizon** brillaba una luz en el horizonte • **cameras ~ed as she stepped from the car** las cámaras disparaban los flashes cuando ella salía del coche • **a police car raced past, lights ~ing** pasó un coche de policía a toda velocidad, con las luces lanzando destellos • **his brake lights ~ed** las luces de freno se iluminaron de repente • **a ~ing neon sign** un anuncio de neón intermitente • **lightning was ~ing all around** relampagueaba por todas partes • **headaches accompanied by ~ing lights** dolores *mpl* de cabeza acompañados de destellos de luz en la visión • **her eyes ~ed with anger** se le encendieron los ojos
2 (*Aut*) • **I ~ed to let him out** le hice señales con las luces para que pasara
3 (= *move quickly*) • **a thought ~ed through my mind** una idea me cruzó la mente como un relámpago • **his whole life ~ed before his eyes** volvió a revivir toda su vida en unos instantes • **a message ~ed up on the screen** apareció brevemente un mensaje en la pantalla • **to ~ by** *or* **past** [*vehicle, person*] pasar a toda velocidad, pasar como un rayo; [*time*] pasar volando • **the landscape ~ed by in a blur** el paisaje iba pasando con velocidad, fundiéndose en una imagen borrosa
4 (*Cine*) • **to ~ back to** retroceder a • **to ~ forward to** adelantarse hasta
5* (= *expose o.s.*) exhibirse
ADJ* (= *showy*) [*car, clothes*] llamativo, fardón* • **a ~ restaurant** un restaurante ostentoso, un restaurante de esos impresionantes*
CPD ▸ **flash bulb** bombilla *f* de flash ▸ **flash card** tarjeta *f* ▸ **flash drive** memoria *f* flash, llave *f* de memoria ▸ **flash fire** fuego *m* repentino ▸ **flash flood** riada *f* ▸ **flash gun** (*Phot*) disparador *m* de flash ▸ **flash memory** memoria *f* flash ▸ **flash mob** movilización *f* relámpago convocada por internet ▸ **flash photography** fotografía *f* con flash
flashback ['flæʃbæk] N (*Cine*) escena *f* retrospectiva, flashback *m*
flashcube ['flæʃkju:b] N (*Phot*) cubo *m* de flash
flasher* ['flæʃəʳ] N **1** (= *man*) exhibicionista *m*
2 (*Brit*) (*Aut*) intermitente *m*
flash-freeze [flæʃ'fri:z] VT someter a un proceso de congelación muy rápido
flashily ['flæʃɪlɪ] ADV • **to dress ~** vestirse de manera llamativa
flashing ['flæʃɪŋ] N **1** (*on roof*) tapajuntas *m inv*
2* (= *exposing o.s.*) exhibicionismo *m*
flashlight ['flæʃlaɪt] N (*US*) (= *torch*) linterna *f*
flashpoint ['flæʃpɔɪnt] N **1** punto *m* de inflamación
2 (*fig*) punto *m* crítico • **it could prove the ~ for war** podría aún dar lugar al estallido de la guerra
flashy ['flæʃɪ] ADJ (COMPAR: **flashier**, SUPERL: **flashiest**) [*jewellery, clothes, car*] llamativo, ostentoso; [*colour*] chillón; [*person*] llamativo

flask [flɑːsk] N (for brandy) petaca f; (= vacuum flask) termo m; (Chem) matraz m, redoma f

flat¹ [flæt] ADJ (COMPAR: flatter, SUPERL: flattest) 1 (= level) [surface, roof] plano; [countryside] llano • he was lying ~ on the floor estaba tumbado en el suelo • he laid his hands ~ on the table puso las manos extendidas sobre la mesa • keep your feet ~ on the floor mantén los pies bien pegados al suelo • the sea was calm and ~ el mar estaba en calma y no había olas • lie ~ on your back túmbate de espaldas en el suelo • he was ~ on his back for a month after the accident tuvo que guardar cama durante un mes después del accidente • to fall ~ on one's face (lit) caer(se) de bruces • the government's campaign fell ~ on its face la campaña del gobierno resultó un fracaso • IDIOM: • ~ as a pancake* liso como la palma de la mano; ▹ spin
2 (= smooth, even) [road, surface] liso, llano • to smooth sth ~ [+ paper etc] alisar algo
3 (= shallow) [dish] llano; [box] plano
4 [foot, shoe] plano; [nose] chato • to have ~ feet tener los pies planos
5 (= deflated) [tyre, ball] pinchado, desinflado • we got a ~ tyre se nos pinchó una rueda, se nos ponchó una llanta (Mex) • I had a ~ tyre tenía una rueda pinchada or desinflada, tenía un pinchazo, tenía una ponchada (Mex)
6 (= dull, lifeless) [voice, colour] apagado; [taste, style] soso; [light] sin contraste; [drink] sin burbujas or gas; [battery] descargado • the atmosphere at the party was a bit ~ el ambiente de la fiesta estaba un poco apagado • I've got a ~ battery se me ha descargado la batería • I'm feeling rather ~ estoy un poco deprimido • she meant it as a joke, but it fell ~ lo dijo de broma, pero nadie le vio la gracia • the champagne has gone ~ al champán se le ha ido la fuerza or se le han ido las burbujas
7 (= inactive) [trade, business] flojo • sales have been ~ this summer las ventas han estado flojas este verano, no ha habido mucho movimiento de ventas este verano
8 (= outright) [refusal, denial] rotundo, terminante • his suggestion met with a ~ refusal su sugerencia recibió una negativa rotunda or terminante • he says he's not going and that's ~* dice que no va y sanseacabó
9 (Mus) a [voice, instrument] desafinado • she/her singing was ~ desafinaba cantando
b (of key) bemol • E ~ major mi bemol mayor
10 (= fixed) [rate, fee, charge] fijo
11 (Horse racing) • ~ jockey jinete mf de carreras sin obstáculos • the ~ season la temporada de carreras de caballos sin obstáculos
12 (= not shiny) (of painted surface) mate, sin brillo
ADV 1 (= absolutely) • to be ~ broke* estar pelado*, estar sin un duro (Sp*), estar sin un peso (LAm*)
2 (= outright) [refuse] rotundamente, terminantemente • I told her ~ that she couldn't have it le dije terminantemente que no se lo podía quedar • to turn sth down ~ rechazar algo rotundamente or de plano
3 (= exactly) • he did it in ten minutes ~ lo hizo en diez minutos justos or exactos
4 (esp Brit) • ~ out: ~ out, the car can do 140mph cuando pones el coche a toda máquina, llega a las 140 millas por hora • to go ~ out ir a toda máquina • to go ~ out for sth intentar conseguir algo por todos los medios • she went ~ out for the title intentó por todos los medios conseguir el título • to work ~ out (to do sth) trabajar a toda máquina (para hacer algo)
5 (Mus) • to play/sing ~ tocar/cantar demasiado bajo, desafinar
N 1 [of hand] palma f; [of sword] cara f de la hoja
2 (Mus) bemol m
3 (Aut) pinchazo m, ponchada f (Mex) • we got a ~ se nos pinchó una rueda, se nos ponchó una llanta (Mex) • I had a ~ tenía una rueda pinchada or desinflada, tenía un pinchazo, tenía una ponchada (Mex)
4 flats (Geog) (= marshland) marismas fpl; (= sand) bancos mpl de arena • mud ~s marismas fpl • salt ~s salinas fpl
5 (Theat) bastidor m
6 (Horse racing) • the ~ las carreras de caballos sin obstáculos
CPD ▸ flat cap gorra de lana con visera ▸ flat pack • it comes in a ~ pack viene en una caja plana para el automontaje; ▹ flat-pack ▸ flat racing carreras fpl de caballos sin obstáculos ▸ flat rate [of interest, tax] tanto m alzado; (Internet, Telec) tarifa f plana; ▹ flat-rate ▸ flat screen (TV, Comput) pantalla f plana; ▹ flat-screen

flat² [flæt] N (Brit) apartamento m, piso m (Sp), departamento m (LAm)

flatbed ['flætbed] N (= vehicle) camión m plataforma
CPD ▸ flatbed lorry (Brit) camión m plataforma ▸ flatbed scanner escáner m plano ▸ flatbed truck (esp US) camión m plataforma

flat-bottomed ['flæt'bɒtəmd] ADJ [boat] de fondo plano

flat-chested ['flæt'tʃestɪd] ADJ de pecho plano

flatfish ['flætfɪʃ] N (PL: flatfish or flatfishes) pez m plano; (Tech) (pez m) pleuronectiforme m (p.ej. platija, lenguado)

flat-footed ['flæt'fʊtɪd] ADJ 1 de pies planos • to be flat-footed tener los pies planos
2* (fig) (= clumsy) patoso (Sp*)

flatiron ['flæt,aɪən] N plancha f

flatlet ['flætlɪt] N (Brit) apartamento m or (Sp) piso m or (LAm) departamento m pequeño

flatly ['flætlɪ] ADV 1 (= without emotion) [read, recite] monótonamente; [say, reply] de manera inexpresiva
2 (= categorically, completely) [refuse, deny] terminantemente, rotundamente; [contradict] de plano • we are ~ opposed to it nos oponemos terminantemente or rotundamente a ello

flatmate ['flætmeɪt] N compañero/a m/f de apartamento, compañero/a m/f de piso (Sp), compañero/a m/f de departamento (LAm)

flatness ['flætnɪs] N 1 [of land] llanura f, lo llano; [of surface] lisura f
2 [of drink] lo poco gaseoso
3 (fig) [of atmosphere, relationship, voice] monotonía f • her voice had a weary ~ su voz tenía una monotonía cansina

flat-pack ['flætpæk] ADJ • flat-pack furniture muebles automontables embalados en cajas planas

flat-rate ['flætreɪt] ADJ [tax, charge] a tanto alzado

flat-screen ['flætskriːn] ADJ de pantalla plana

flatten ['flætn] VT 1 (= compress, squash) [+ road, grass] allanar, aplanar; [+ hair, paper] alisar • ~ the dough with a rolling pin aplanar or extender la masa con un rodillo • I ~ed myself against the wall me pegué a la pared
2 (= level out) [+ surface] nivelar
3 (= knock down) [+ building, city] arrasar; [+ person] tumbar • he could ~ me with one blow podría tumbarme de un solo golpe
4 (fig) (= defeat, subdue) desanimar, desalentar • she felt ~ed se sintió desalentada
VI 1 (= lie flat) • the dog's ears ~ed el perro bajó las orejas
2 (= become flat) [road, countryside] nivelarse, allanarse
▸ **flatten out** VI + ADV 1 (= become flat) [road, countryside] nivelarse, allanarse
2 (= increase less rapidly) • sales have ~ed out el ritmo de las ventas ha decrecido
VT + ADV [+ road] allanar, aplanar; [+ paper, map] extender, alisar

flatter ['flætəʳ] VT 1 (= praise, compliment) a (sincerely) halagar • you ~ me! ¡me halagas! • to say that she is tactless is to ~ her (iro) decir que no tiene tacto es como echarle un piropo
b (insincerely) adular, lisonjear • he only said it to ~ you te lo dijo solo para adularte
2 (= gratify) halagar • I was very ~ed to be asked me halagó que me lo pidieran • to feel ~ed sentirse halagado
3 (= show to advantage) favorecer • that colour ~s you ese color te favorece • it's a dress that will ~ any figure es un vestido que favorece a cualquiera
4 • to ~ o.s. a (= pride o.s.) • to ~ o.s. on sth/that enorgullecerse de algo/de que
b (= deceive o.s.) • don't ~ yourself, I didn't come all this way just to see you no te hagas ilusiones, no he venido hasta aquí solo para verte a ti • you ~ yourself! what makes you think he fancies you? ¡no seas engreída! ¿qué te hace pensar que le gustas?

flatterer ['flætərəʳ] N adulador(a) m/f

flattering ['flætərɪŋ] ADJ 1 (= complimentary) [remark, words] halagador • the play had very ~ reviews la obra recibió críticas muy halagadoras or halagüeñas • he was very ~ about you habló muy bien de ti • that's not very ~ to him! ¡vaya imagen que pintas de él! (iro)
2 (= gratifying) • it was ~ to be told how indispensable he was le halagó que le dijeran lo indispensable que era • he found the interest in him ~ se sentía halagado por la atención que le prestaban
3 (= fawning) adulador • she was surrounded by ~ admirers estaba rodeada de admiradores que la adulaban
4 [photo, clothes] favorecedor • that dress isn't ~ at all on you ese vestido no te favorece nada

flatteringly ['flætərɪŋlɪ] ADV [speak] de forma halagadora • he was ~ attentive era tan atento que resultaba halagador

flattery ['flætərɪ] N halagos mpl, lisonjas fpl • it wasn't just ~, I meant what I said no eran simplemente halagos or lisonjas, lo decía en serio • ~ will get you nowhere! (iro) ¡con halagos or lisonjas no vas a conseguir nada! • ~ will get you everywhere! (iro) ¡con halagos or lisonjas se consigue todo!; ▹ imitation

flattop* ['flættɒp] N (US) (= aircraft carrier) portaaviones m inv

flatulence ['flætjʊləns] N flatulencia f

flatulent ['flætjʊlənt] ADJ flatulento

flatware ['flætweəʳ] N (US) (= cutlery) cubertería f

flatworm ['flætwɜːm] N platelminto m

flaunt [flɔːnt] VT (pej) [+ wealth, knowledge] alardear de, hacer alarde de • to ~ o.s. pavonearse

flautist ['flɔ:tɪst] (N) (*esp Brit*) flautista *mf*
flavin ['fleɪvɪn] (N) flavina *f*
flavour, flavor (US) ['fleɪvəʳ] (N) (*gen*) sabor *m*, gusto *m* (**of** a); (= *flavouring*) condimento *m*; (*fig*) sabor *m*, aire *m* • **with a banana ~** con sabor *or* gusto a plátano • **steaming the vegetables retains the maximum ~** cocinando las verduras al vapor se conserva su sabor al máximo • **the decor has a Victorian ~** la decoración tiene un sabor *or* aire victoriano
(VT) (*Culin*) condimentar, sazonar (**with** con) • **the pudding is ~ed with liqueur** el postre tiene licor
(CPD) ▸ **flavour enhancer** potenciador *m* del sabor ▸ **flavour of the month** • **to be ~ of the month*** [*person*] ser el/la guapo/a de turno
flavoured, flavored (US) ['fleɪvəd] (ADJ) (= *seasoned*) condimentado • **highly ~** (= *spicy*) muy condimentado • **richly ~ aromatic meat** carne aromática y llena de sabor • **delicately ~ cheese** queso con un sabor delicado • **sponge cakes ~ with orange** bizcochos con sabor a naranja
-flavoured, -flavored (US) [-,fleɪvəd] (SUFFIX) • **fruit-flavoured sparkling water** agua con gas con sabor a frutas • **strawberry-flavoured** de fresa • **vanilla-flavoured** con aroma de vainilla
flavouring, flavoring (US) ['fleɪvərɪŋ] (N) condimento *m* • **artificial ~** aromatizante *m* artificial • **vanilla ~** esencia *f* de vainilla
flavourless, flavorless (US) ['fleɪvəlɪs] (ADJ) insípido, soso
flavoursome, flavorsome (US) ['fleɪvəsəm] (ADJ) (= *tasty*) sabroso
flaw [flɔ:] (N) (= *defect*) (*in character, system*) defecto *m*, fallo *m*; (*in material, beauty, diamond*) desperfecto *m*, tara *f*; (*in reasoning*) error *m*, fallo *m*; (= *crack*) grieta *f*
flawed [flɔ:d] (ADJ) [*system, goods*] defectuoso; [*theory*] erróneo • **the agreement is fatally ~** el acuerdo presenta fallos que lo condenan al fracaso
flawless ['flɔ:lɪs] (ADJ) [*diamond, skin*] perfecto, sin defectos; [*beauty*] inmaculado; [*plan*] perfecto; [*conduct*] intachable, impecable • **she spoke in ~ English** habló en un inglés perfecto
flawlessly ['flɔ:ləslɪ] (ADV) (= *perfectly*) perfectamente
flax [flæks] (N) (*Bot*) lino *m*
(CPD) ▸ **flax seed** linaza *f*
flaxen ['flæksən] (ADJ) (*poet*) [*hair*] muy rubio
flay [fleɪ] (VT) **1** (= *skin*) desollar • **he'll ~ me alive if I'm late*** si llego tarde, me despelleja vivo
2 (= *criticize*) [+ *person*] despellejar; [+ *book, film*] hacer trizas
3 (= *defeat*) dar una paliza a*
flea [fli:] (N) pulga *f* • IDIOM: • **to send sb away with a ~ in his ear*** despachar a algn con cajas destempladas
(CPD) ▸ **flea collar** collar *m* antipulgas *or* antiparasitario ▸ **flea market** mercadillo *m*, rastro *m* (*Sp*) ▸ **flea powder** polvo *m* antipulgas
fleabag‡ ['fli:bæg] (N) (*Brit*) (= *person*) guarro/a *m/f*; (US) (= *hotel*) hotelucho *m* de mala muerte*
fleabite ['fli:baɪt] (N) picadura *f* de pulga; (*fig*) nada *f*, nimiedad *f*
flea-bitten* ['fli:bɪtn] (ADJ) (*lit*) [*dog*] pulgoso; (*fig*) miserable
fleapit* ['fli:pɪt] (N) cine *m* de mala muerte
fleck [flek] (N) [*of mud, paint, dust*] mota *f*; [*of spit, foam*] salpicadura *f*; [*of colour*] mota *f* • **his eyes are green with ~s of gold** tiene los ojos verdes con motas doradas
(VT) salpicar (**with** de) • **black ~ed with white** negro moteado de blanco *or* con motas blancas
-flecked [flekt] (SUFFIX) • **mud-flecked** salpicado de barro • **green-flecked wallpaper** papel de pared moteado de verde
fled [fled] (PT), (PP) *of* **flee**
fledged [fledʒd] (ADJ) plumado
fledgling, fledgeling ['fledʒlɪŋ] (N) (= *young bird*) pajarito *m*; (*fig*) novato/a *m/f*
(CPD) [*democracy, writer*] en ciernes; [*company, industry*] joven
flee [fli:] (PT, PP: **fled**) (VT) huir de • **to ~ the country** huir del país
(VI) huir (**from** de), darse a la fuga • **they fled to the West/the mountains** huyeron hacia el oeste/las montañas
fleece [fli:s] (N) **1** (*on sheep*) lana *f*; (*shorn*) vellón *m*
2 (= *jacket*) forro *m* polar
(VT) [+ *sheep*] esquilar; (*fig**) (= *rob*) desplumar*
fleece-lined [,fli:s'laɪnd] (ADJ) forrado de corderito *or* vellón
fleecy ['fli:sɪ] (ADJ) (COMPAR: **fleecier**, SUPERL: **fleeciest**) **1** (= *woolly*) lanoso, lanudo
2 [*clouds*] aborregado
fleet[1] [fli:t] (N) **1** (*Aer, Naut*) flota *f* • **the British ~** la armada británica • **Fleet Air Arm** (*Brit*) Fuerzas *fpl* Aéreas de la Armada
2 [*of cars, coaches etc*] parque *m* (móvil)
fleet[2] [fli:t] (*poet*) (ADJ) (COMPAR: **fleeter**, SUPERL: **fleetest**) (*also* **fleet-footed, fleet of foot**) veloz
fleeting ['fli:tɪŋ] (ADJ) **1** (= *brief*) [*impression*] momentáneo; [*visit*] breve; [*moment*] breve, fugaz • **to have** *or* **catch a ~ glimpse of sth/sb** alcanzar a ver algo/a algn fugazmente • **a ~ glance** una breve mirada
2 (= *ephemeral*) [*joy, popularity*] fugaz, efímero; [*beauty*] pasajero
fleetingly ['fli:tɪŋlɪ] (ADV) [*smile, see, think, recall*] fugazmente • **he wondered ~ if she knew** se preguntó por un instante si ella lo sabía • **the joy they shared so ~** esa alegría tan efímera que compartieron
Fleet Street ['fli:t,stri:t] (N) (*Brit*) (= *street*) Fleet Street, *calle de Londres en la que muchos periódicos tenían sus oficinas*; (= *industry*) *la prensa británica*
Fleming ['flemɪŋ] (N) flamenco/a *m/f*
Flemish ['flemɪʃ] (ADJ) flamenco
(N) (*Ling*) flamenco *m*
flesh [fleʃ] (N) (*gen*) carne *f*; [*of fruit*] pulpa *f* • **in the ~** en carne y hueso, en persona • **my own ~ and blood** mi propia sangre • **to put on ~** echar carnes • **the sins of the ~** los pecados de la carne • **it's more than ~ and blood can stand** no hay quien lo aguante • IDIOMS: • **to make sb's ~ crawl** *or* **creep** poner carne de gallina a algn • **to go the way of all ~** pasar a mejor vida; ▹ **press**
(CPD) ▸ **flesh colour, flesh color** (US) (*also Art*) color *m* de la piel ▸ **flesh wound** herida *f* superficial
▸ **flesh out** (VT + ADV) desarrollar
flesh-coloured, flesh-colored (US) ['fleʃ,kʌləd] (ADJ) del color de la piel
flesh-eating ['fleʃi:tɪŋ] (ADJ) carnívoro
fleshly ['fleʃlɪ] (ADJ) (*frm*) [*lusts, desires*] carnal, de la carne
fleshpots ['fleʃpɒts] (NPL) (*fig*) antros *mpl* de libertinaje
fleshy ['fleʃɪ] (ADJ) (COMPAR: **fleshier**, SUPERL: **fleshiest**) (= *fat*) gordo; (*Bot*) [*fruit*] carnoso
flew [flu:] (PT) *of* **fly**[2]
flex [fleks] (N) (*Brit*) [*of lamp, telephone*] cable *m*, cordón *m*
(VT) [+ *arms, knees*] flexionar, doblar • **to ~ one's muscles** (*in exercises*) hacer ejercicios de calentamiento de músculos; (*to impress*) sacar los músculos • **the government is ~ing its muscles in Europe** el gobierno está haciendo alarde de su poder en Europa
(VI) doblarse, flexionarse
flex-fuel ['fleksfjʊəl] (ADJ) [*vehicle, engine*] de combustible flexible
flexibility [,fleksɪ'bɪlɪtɪ] (N) flexibilidad *f*
flexible ['fleksəbl] (ADJ) (*lit, fig*) flexible • **we have to be ~ about this** tenemos que ser flexibles en este asunto • **we have ~ (working) hours** tenemos un horario de trabajo flexible
flexibly ['fleksɪblɪ] (ADV) (*lit, fig*) con flexibilidad
flexion ['flekʃən] (N) flexión *f*
flexitime ['fleksɪtaɪm] (N) (*Brit*) horario *m* flexible
flexor ['fleksəʳ] (N) flexor *m*, músculo *m* flexor
(ADJ) flexor
flextime ['flekstaɪm] (N) (US) = **flexitime**
flibbertigibbet ['flɪbətɪ'dʒɪbɪt] (N) casquivana *f*
flick [flɪk] (N) **1** [*of tail*] coletazo *m*; [*of finger*] capirotazo *m*, papirotazo *m*; [*of duster*] pasada *f*; [*of whip*] latigazo *m* • **with a ~ of the whip** de un latigazo • **with a ~ of the wrist** con un movimiento rápido de la muñeca; ▹ **switch**
2 (*Brit**) película *f*, peli* *f* • **the ~s** el cine
(VT) (*with finger*) dar un capirotazo a • **she ~ed her hair out of her eyes** se apartó el pelo de los ojos • **to ~ sth away** quitar algo con un movimiento rápido
(VI) • **the snake's tongue ~ed in and out** la víbora metía y sacaba la lengua • **to ~ over the pages** hojear rápidamente las páginas
(CPD) ▸ **flick knife** (*Brit*) navaja *f* automática, navaja *f* de resorte (*Mex*)
▸ **flick off** (VT + ADV) [+ *dust, ash*] sacudir; [+ *light, TV*] apagar
▸ **flick on** (VT + ADV) [+ *light, TV*] encender
▸ **flick through** (VI + PREP) [+ *book, pages*] hojear rápidamente
flicker ['flɪkəʳ] (N) **1** [*of light, eyelid*] parpadeo *m*; [*of flame*] destello *m*
2 (= *hint*) • **a ~ of amusement crossed his face** por un momento se atisbó en su rostro una expresión divertida • **a ~ of surprise/dismay crossed his face** por un momento en su rostro pudo verse un atisbo de sorpresa/consternación • **she said it without a ~ of expression** lo dijo sin inmutarse • **without a ~ of regret** sin el menor signo de arrepentimiento • **they showed barely a ~ of interest** apenas dieron muestras de interés
(VI) [*light*] parpadear; [*flame*] vacilar; [*snake's tongue*] vibrar • **the candle ~ed and went out** la vela parpadeó y se apagó
flickering ['flɪkərɪŋ] (ADJ) [*flame, candle*] tembloroso; (*before going out*) vacilante; [*light*] parpadeante; [*needle*] oscilante
flier ['flaɪəʳ] (N) **1** aviador(a) *m/f*
2 (US) folleto *m*, volante *m* (*LAm*)
flight[1] [flaɪt] (N) **1** (*Aer*) [*of bird*] vuelo *m*; [*of bullet*] trayectoria *f* • **how long does the ~ take?** ¿cuánto dura el vuelo? • **in ~** en vuelo • **~s of fancy** (*fig*) ilusiones *fpl* • **to take ~** [*bird*] alzar el vuelo
2 (= *group*) [*of birds*] bandada *f*; [*of aircraft*] escuadrilla *f* • **in the top ~** (*fig*) de primera categoría
3 [*of stairs*] tramo *m* • **I walked up six ~s of stairs** subí seis tramos de escaleras • **he lives two ~s up** vive dos pisos más arriba
(CPD) ▸ **flight attendant** auxiliar *mf* de vuelo *or* de cabina, aeromozo/a *m/f* (*LAm*), sobrecargo *mf* (*Mex*), cabinero/a *m/f* (*Col*) ▸ **flight bag** bolso *m* de bandolera ▸ **flight crew** tripulación *f* ▸ **flight data recorder**

registrador *m* de datos de vuelo ▸ **flight deck** (*on aircraft carrier*) cubierta *f* de aterrizaje/despegue; [*of aeroplane*] cubierta *f* de vuelo ▸ **flight engineer** mecánico/a *m/f* de vuelo ▸ **flight lieutenant** teniente *mf* de aviación ▸ **flight log** diario *m* de vuelo ▸ **flight number** [*of plane*] número *m* de vuelo • **I don't know his ~ number** no sé su número de vuelo ▸ **flight path** trayectoria *f* de vuelo ▸ **flight plan** plan *m or* carta *f* de vuelo ▸ **flight recorder** registrador *m* de vuelo ▸ **flight sergeant** (*Brit*) sargento *mf* de aviación ▸ **flight simulator** simulador *m* de vuelo ▸ **flight socks** medias *fpl* de descanso (*para vuelos prolongados*) ▸ **flight supplement** cargo *m* adicional • **there is weekend ~ supplement of £12 per person** hay un cargo adicional de 12 libras por persona por volar en fin de semana ▸ **flight test** vuelo *m* de prueba; ▹ **flight-test**

flight² [flaɪt] (N) (= *act of fleeing*) fuga *f*, huida *f* • **to put to ~** ahuyentar; (*Mil*) poner en fuga • **to take ~** fugarse, huir • **a picture of a deer in full ~** una foto de un ciervo en plena huida • **the enemy were in full ~** el enemigo huía en desbandada • **the ~ of capital** la fuga de capitales

flightless ['flaɪtlɪs] (ADJ) [*bird*] no volador

flight-test ['flaɪttest] (VT) probar en vuelo

flighty ['flaɪtɪ] (ADJ) (COMPAR: **flightier**, SUPERL: **flightiest**) [*idea, remark*] frívolo, poco serio; [*girl*] caprichoso, voluble

flimflam* ['flɪmflæm] (N) (= *rubbish*) tonterías *fpl*; (= *lies*) cuentos *mpl* chinos

flimsily ['flɪmzɪlɪ] (ADV) [*constructed*] con poca solidez; [*dressed*] muy ligeramente

flimsiness ['flɪmzɪnɪs] (N) [*of dress, material*] ligereza *f*; [*of structure*] lo endeble, la poca solidez; [*of excuse*] lo pobre; [*of argument, evidence*] lo poco sólido, inconsistencia *f*

flimsy ['flɪmzɪ] (ADJ) (COMPAR: **flimsier**, SUPERL: **flimsiest**) **1** (= *thin*) [*dress*] muy ligero; [*material*] muy ligero, muy delgado; [*paper*] muy fino
2 (= *weak, insubstantial*) [*structure*] poco sólido, endeble; [*excuse, pretext*] pobre; [*argument, evidence*] poco sólido, inconsistente
(N) (*Brit*) (= *thin paper*) papel *m* de copiar; (= *copy*) copia *f*

flinch [flɪntʃ] (VI) **1** (= *shrink back*) estremecerse • **he ~ed at the pain** se estremeció del dolor • **I ~ed when he touched me** cuando me tocó, me estremecí • **he struck her hard but she did not ~** la golpeó con fuerza, pero ni se inmutó • **without ~ing** sin inmutarse
2 (= *shirk*) • **he did not ~ from his responsibilities** no se retrajo de sus obligaciones

fling [flɪŋ] (VB: PT, PP: **flung**) (N) **1** • **to have one's last ~** echar la última cana al aire • **to have one's ~** • **go on a ~** echar una canita al aire • **to have a ~ at doing sth** intentar algo
2* aventura *f* amorosa
3 (*also* **Highland fling**) ▹ **highland**
(VT) [+ *stone*] arrojar, lanzar • **to ~ one's arms round sb** echar los brazos al cuello a algn • **the door was flung open** la puerta se abrió de golpe • **she was flung to the ground by her horse** el caballo la lanzó *or* tiró *or* arrojó al suelo • **to ~ sb into jail** meter a algn en la cárcel • **to ~ o.s. over a cliff** despeñarse por un precipicio • **she flung herself at him** se arrojó *or* lanzó *or* tiró sobre él • **to ~ o.s. into a chair** dejarse caer de golpe en una silla • **to ~ o.s. into a job** lanzarse a hacer un trabajo • **to ~ off/on one's clothes** quitarse/ponerse la ropa de prisa

▸ **fling away** (VT + ADV) (*fig*) (= *waste*) [+ *money, chance*] desperdiciar

▸ **fling out** (VT + ADV) [+ *rubbish*] tirar, botar (*LAm*); [+ *remark*] lanzar; [+ *person*] echar

flint [flɪnt] (N) (*Geol*) (= *material*) sílex *m*; (= *one piece*) pedernal *m*; [*of lighter*] piedra *f*
(CPD) ▸ **flint axe** hacha *f* de sílex

flintlock ['flɪntlɒk] (N) (= *gun*) fusil *m* de chispa

flinty ['flɪntɪ] (ADJ) **1** [*material*] de sílex; [*soil*] silíceo
2 (*fig*) [*eyes, gaze, stare*] duro; [*heart*] de piedra

flip¹ [flɪp] (N) capirotazo *m*; (*Aer**) vuelo *m*
(VT) (*gen*) tirar • **to ~ a coin** lanzar una moneda al aire, echar cara o cruz • **he ~ped the book open** abrió el libro de golpe
• IDIOM: • **to ~ one's lid*** perder los estribos
(VI)* perder la chaveta*
(CPD) ▸ **flip chart** flip chart *m*, *bloc de papel de grandes dimensiones que se monta sobre un armazón y sirve para ilustrar conferencias, charlas, demostraciones etc* ▸ **flip side** cara *f* B

▸ **flip out** (VI + ADV) perder la chaveta*

▸ **flip over** (VI + ADV) (*Aut etc*) capotar, dar una vuelta de campana
(VT + ADV) [+ *cassette*] dar la vuelta a

▸ **flip through** (VI + PREP) [+ *book*] hojear; [+ *records, index cards*] repasar • **I ~ped through the pages/my notes** hojeé las páginas/mis notas

flip²* [flɪp] (EXCL) ¡porras!*

flip³* [flɪp] (ADJ) = **flippant**

flip-flop ['flɪpflɒp] (N) **1 flip-flops** (= *sandals*) chancletas *fpl*
2 (*Comput*) circuito *m* basculante *or* biestable, flip-flop *m*
3 (*fig*) (*US**) cambio *m* radical, golpe *m* de timón
(VI) (*fig*) (*US**) cambiar radicalmente, dar un golpe de timón

flippancy ['flɪpənsɪ] (N) ligereza *f*, frivolidad *f*, falta *f* de seriedad • **she was irritated by his ~** estaba molesta por su frivolidad *or* falta de seriedad • **there was a note of ~ in her voice** había un dejo de ligereza *or* frivolidad en su voz

flippant ['flɪpənt] (ADJ) [*remark, reply*] ligero, frívolo • **sorry, I didn't mean to sound ~** perdona, no era mi intención parecer frívolo • **don't be ~** deja de decir ligerezas *or* frivolidades

flippantly ['flɪpəntlɪ] (ADV) [*answer, talk*] con poca seriedad • **such words should not be used ~** esas palabras no deberían usarse con ligereza *or* ligeramente

flipper ['flɪpəʳ] (N) aleta *f*

flipping* ['flɪpɪŋ] (ADJ) (*Brit*) condenado*

flip-top ['flɪptɒp] (ADJ) [*bin, pack*] con tapa abatible

flirt [flɜːt] (N) coqueto/a *m/f* • **he's/she's a great ~** es terriblemente coqueto/a, le gusta muchísimo flirtear
(VI) coquetear, flirtear (**with** con) • **to ~ with death** jugar con la muerte • **to ~ with an idea** acariciar una idea

flirtation [flɜː'teɪʃən] (N) flirteo *m*, coqueteo *m*

flirtatious [flɜː'teɪʃəs] (ADJ) [*man*] mariposón; [*woman*] coqueta; [*glance etc*] coqueta

flirty ['flɜːtɪ] (ADJ) [*person, dress, smile*] coqueto

flit [flɪt] (VI) [*bat, butterfly*] revolotear • **to ~ in/out** [*person*] entrar/salir precipitadamente • **she ~s from one job to another** salta de un trabajo a otro
(N) • IDIOM: • **to do a (moonlight) ~** (*Brit*) marcharse de una casa a la francesa

flitch [flɪtʃ] (N) • **~ of bacon** hoja *f* de tocino

flitting ['flɪtɪŋ] (N) (*N Engl, Scot*) mudanza *f*

Flo [fləʊ] (N) *familiar form of* **Florence**

float [fləʊt] (N) [*of raft, seaplane*] flotador *m*; (*for fishing line*) corcho *m*; (= *swimming aid*) flotador *m*; (*in procession*) carroza *f*; (= *sum of money*) reserva *f*; (*in shop*) fondo *m* de caja, *dinero en caja antes de empezar las ventas del día (para cambios etc)*
(VT) **1** [+ *boat, logs*] hacer flotar • IDIOM: • **it doesn't ~ my boat*** no me da ni frío ni calor*, no me llama la atención
2 (= *render seaworthy*) poner a flote
3 (= *launch*) [+ *company*] fundar, constituir
4 (*Econ*) [+ *currency*] hacer fluctuar, hacer flotar; [+ *shares*] emitir, lanzar al mercado; [+ *loan*] emitir
5 • **to ~ an idea** sugerir una idea
(VI) (*gen*) flotar; [*bather*] hacer la plancha; (= *move in wind*) flotar, ondear • **it ~ed to the surface** salió a la superficie • **to ~ downriver** ir río abajo • **we shall let the pound ~** dejaremos que la libra esterlina flote *or* fluctúe
(CPD) ▸ **float plane** (*US*) (= *seaplane*) hidroavión *m*

▸ **float around** (VI + ADV) [*rumour*] circular, correr

▸ **float away, float off** (VI + ADV) (*in water*) ir a la deriva; (*in air*) irse volando

floating ['fləʊtɪŋ] (ADJ) [*object, assets, currency, debt, dock*] flotante; (*Brit*) [*voter*] indeciso • **the ~ vote** el voto de los indecisos

flock¹ [flɒk] (N) [*of sheep, goats*] rebaño *m*; [*of birds*] bandada *f*; [*of people*] tropel *m*, multitud *f*; (*Rel*) grey *f*, rebaño *m* • **they came in ~s** acudieron en tropel
(VI) (= *move in numbers*) ir en tropel • **they ~ed to the station** fueron en tropel hacia la estación • **to ~ around sb** apiñarse en torno a algn • **to ~ together** congregarse, reunirse

flock² [flɒk] (N) (= *wool*) borra *f*

floe [fləʊ] (N) (= *ice floe*) témpano *m* de hielo

flog [flɒg] (VT) **1** (= *whip*) azotar; (= *beat*) dar una paliza a • IDIOM: • **to ~ a dead horse*** predicar en el desierto, machacar en hierro frío
2 (*Brit**) (= *sell*) vender

flogger ['flɒgəʳ] (N) partidario/a *m/f* del restablecimiento de la pena de azotes

flogging ['flɒgɪŋ] (N) azotes *mpl*, flagelación *f* • **to give sb a ~** azotar *or* flagelar a algn

flood [flʌd] (N) [*of water*] inundación *f*; (*in river*) avenida *f*; [*of words, tears*] torrente *m*; (= *flood tide*) pleamar *f* • **the Flood** (*Rel*) el Diluvio • **the river is in ~** el río está crecido • **a ~ of letters** una avalancha de cartas • **she was in ~s of tears** lloraba a lágrima viva
(VT) (*Aut*) (*gen*) inundar • **to ~ the market with sth** inundar *or* saturar el mercado de algo • **we have been ~ed with applications** nos han llovido las solicitudes, nos han inundado de solicitudes • **the room was ~ed with light** el cuarto se inundó de luz
(VI) [*river*] desbordarse • **the people ~ed into the streets** la gente inundó la calle
(CPD) ▸ **flood control** medidas *fpl* para controlar las inundaciones ▸ **flood damage** daños *mpl* causados por las inundaciones ▸ **flood defences** (*Brit*) protecciones *fpl* contra las inundaciones ▸ **flood tide** pleamar *f*, marea *f* creciente

▸ **flood in** (VI + ADV) [*people*] entrar a raudales

▸ **flood out** (VT + ADV) [+ *house*] inundar completamente • **they were ~ed out** tuvieron que abandonar su casa debido a la inundación

floodgate ['flʌdgeɪt] (N) compuerta *f*, esclusa *f* • **to open the ~s to sth** (= *open the way to*) abrirle las puertas a algo

flooding ['flʌdɪŋ] (N) inundación *f*

floodlight ['flʌdlaɪt] (VB: PT, PP: **floodlit**) (N) foco *m*
(VT) iluminar con focos

floodlighting ['flʌdlaɪtɪŋ] (N) iluminación *f* con focos

floodlit ['flʌdlɪt] (PT), (PP) *of* **floodlight** (ADJ) iluminado

floodplain ['flʌdpleɪn] (N) llanura *f* sujeta a inundaciones de un río

floodwater ['flʌdwɔːtəʳ] (N) crecida *f*, riada *f*

floor [flɔːʳ] (N) **1** (*gen*) suelo *m*; [*of room*] suelo *m*, piso *m* (*LAm*); [*of sea*] fondo *m*; (= *dance floor*) pista *f* • **a tiled ~** un suelo embaldosado • **the Floor** (*St Ex*) el parqué • **to cross the ~ (of the House)** cambiar de adscripción política • **to have the ~** [*speaker*] tener la palabra • **to hold the ~** hacer uso de la palabra • **to take the ~** [*dancer*] salir a bailar • IDIOM: • **to wipe the ~ with sb*** dar un buen repaso a algn*, hacer picadillo a algn*
2 (= *storey*) **a** (*Brit*) piso *m* • **the first ~** el primer piso • **the ground ~** la planta baja • **the second ~** el segundo piso • **the top ~** el último piso
b (*US*) piso *m* • **the first ~** la planta baja • **the second ~** el primer piso • **the top ~** el último piso
(VT) **1** [+ *room*] solar (**with** de)
2* (= *knock down*) [+ *opponent*] derribar
3* (= *baffle, silence*) dejar sin respuesta
4 (*US*) (*Aut*) [+ *accelerator*] pisar
(CPD) ▸ **floor area** superficie *f* total ▸ **floor cloth** bayeta *f* ▸ **floor covering** tapiz *m* para el suelo ▸ **floor cushion** cojín *m* de suelo ▸ **floor exercise** (*Gymnastics*) ejercicio *m* de suelo ▸ **floor lamp** lámpara *f* de pie ▸ **floor manager** (*in department store*) jefe/a *m/f* de sección; (*Cine, TV*) jefe/a *m/f* de plató ▸ **floor plan** plano *m*, planta *f* ▸ **floor polish** cera *f* para suelos ▸ **floor polisher** enceradora *f* ▸ **floor show** cabaret *m* ▸ **floor space** espacio *m*

floorboard ['flɔːbɔːd] (N) tabla *f* del suelo

-floored [flɔːd] (SUFFIX) • **marble-floored** con suelo de mármol • **tile-floored** con suelo alicatado

flooring ['flɔːrɪŋ] (N) suelo *m*; (= *material*) solería *f*

floorwalker† ['flɔːˌwɔːkəʳ] (N) (*US*) jefe/a *m/f* de sección

floosie*, **floozie***, **floozy*** ['fluːzɪ] (N) putilla* *f*

flop [flɒp] (N)* (= *failure*) fracaso *m* • **the film was a ~** la película fue un fracaso
(VI) **1** (= *fall*) [*person*] dejarse caer (**into, on** en)
2* (= *fail*) [*play, book*] fracasar

flophouse* ['flɒphaʊs] (N) (PL: **flophouses** ['flɒphaʊzɪz]) (*US*) pensión *f* de mala muerte*, fonducha* *f*

floppy ['flɒpɪ] (ADJ) (COMPAR: **floppier**, SUPERL: **floppiest**) [*hat*] flexible; [*doll*] de trapo • **a dog with ~ ears** un perro con las orejas caídas
(N) = **floppy disc**
(CPD) ▸ **floppy disc** *or* **disk** (*Comput*) disquete *m*, disco *m* flexible

flora ['flɔːrə] (N) (PL: **floras** *or* **florae** ['flɔːriː]) flora *f*

floral ['flɔːrəl] (ADJ) [*display*] de flores, floral; [*fabric, dress*] de flores, floreado; [*fragrance, design, wallpaper, curtains*] de flores
(CPD) ▸ **floral arrangement** arreglo *m* floral ▸ **floral print** estampado *m* de flores *or* floreado ▸ **floral tribute** ofrenda *f* floral; (*at funeral*) corona *f* de flores

Florence ['flɒrəns] (N) Florencia *f*

Florentine ['flɒrəntaɪn] (ADJ) florentino
(N) florentino/a *m/f*

florescence [flə'resns] (N) florescencia *f*

floret ['flɒrət] (N) [*of flower*] flósculo *m*; [*of cauliflower, broccoli*] grumo *m*, cabezuela *f*

florid ['flɒrɪd] (ADJ) [*complexion*] colorado, rubicundo; [*style*] florido

Florida ['flɒrɪdə] (N) Florida *f*

florin ['flɒrɪn] (N) florín *m*; (*Brit*) (*formerly*) florín *m*, *moneda de dos chelines*

florist ['flɒrɪst] (N) florista *mf* • **~'s (shop)** floristería *f*, tienda *f* de flores

floss [flɒs] (N) **1** (*also* **floss silk**) cadarzo *m*
2 (*for embroidery*) seda *f* floja
3 (*also* **dental floss**) hilo *m or* seda *f* dental
(VT) (*Dentistry*) • **to ~ one's teeth** limpiarse los dientes con hilo *or* seda dental
(VI) (*Dentistry*) limpiarse los dientes con hilo *or* seda dental

Flossie ['flɒsɪ] (N) *familiar form of* **Florence**

flossy ['flɒsɪ] (ADJ) **1** [*cloud, hair*] vaporoso, ahuecado
2 (*US**) (= *showy*) llamativo, espectacular, ostentoso

flotation [fləʊ'teɪʃən] (N) **1** (*lit*) [*of boat etc*] flotación *f*
2 (*Econ*) [*of shares, loan etc*] emisión *f*; [*of company*] lanzamiento *m*, salida *f* a bolsa
(CPD) ▸ **flotation tank** tanque *m* de flotación

flotilla [flə'tɪlə] (N) flotilla *f*

flotsam ['flɒtsəm] (N) • **~ and jetsam** restos *mpl* (de naufragio); (*Tech*) (*frm*) pecios *mpl*

flounce[1] [flaʊns] (N) (= *frill*) volante *m*

flounce[2] [flaʊns] (VI) • **to ~ in/out** entrar/salir haciendo aspavientos
▸ **flounce off** (VI + ADV) (= *leave in a huff*) salir haciendo aspavientos • **she will ~ off and argue when asked to leave the room** sale haciendo aspavientos y discutiendo cuando le pidan que abandone la sala

flounced [flaʊnst] (ADJ) [*dress*] guarnecido con volantes

flounder[1] ['flaʊndəʳ] (N) (PL: **flounder** *or* **flounders**) (= *fish*) platija *f*

flounder[2] ['flaʊndəʳ] (VI) **1** (*also* **flounder about**) (*in water, mud etc*) (= *flap arms*) debatirse; (= *splash*) revolcarse
2 (*in speech etc*) perder el hilo

flour ['flaʊəʳ] (N) harina *f*
(CPD) ▸ **flour bin** harinero *m* ▸ **flour mill** molino *m* de harina

flourish ['flʌrɪʃ] (N) (= *movement*) floritura *f*, ademán *m* ostentoso; (*under signature*) rúbrica *f*; (*Mus*) floreo *m*; (= *fanfare*) toque *m* de trompeta • **to do sth with a ~** hacer algo con una floritura *or* con gesto triunfal
(VT) [+ *weapon, stick etc*] blandir
(VI) [*plant etc*] crecer; [*person, business, civilization*] florecer, prosperar

flourishing ['flʌrɪʃɪŋ] (ADJ) [*plant*] lozano; [*person, business*] floreciente, próspero

floury ['flaʊərɪ] (ADJ) harinoso

flout [flaʊt] (VT) (= *ignore*) no prestar atención a, ignorar; (= *mock*) burlarse de; [+ *law*] incumplir

flow [fləʊ] (N) [*of river, tide, Elec*] corriente *f*, flujo *m*; (= *direction*) curso *m*; [*of blood*] (*from wound*) flujo; [*of words etc*] torrente *m* • **the ~ of traffic** la circulación (del tráfico) • **to maintain a steady ~** [*of people, vehicles*] mantener un movimiento constante • IDIOM: • **to go with the ~** dejarse llevar
(VI) [*river*] fluir, discurrir; [*tide*] subir, crecer; [*blood*] (*from wound*) manar; (*through body*) circular; [*tears*] correr; [*hair*] caer suavemente *or* con soltura; [*words*] fluir • **tears ~ed down her cheeks** le corrían las lágrimas por las mejillas • **the river ~s through the valley** el río fluye *or* discurre por el valle • **the river ~ed over its banks** el río se desbordó • **the river ~s into the sea** el río desemboca en el mar • **water was ~ing from the pipe** el agua brotaba de la tubería • **traffic is now ~ing normally** el tráfico ya circula *or* fluye *or* discurre con normalidad • **money ~ed in** el dinero entraba a raudales • **people are ~ing in** entra la gente a raudales • **to keep the conversation ~ing** mantener viva la conversación • **the town ~ed with wine and food** el pueblo abundaba en vino y comida; ▹ **ebb**
(CPD) ▸ **flow chart, flow diagram** organigrama *m* ▸ **flow sheet** (*Comput*) diagrama *m* de flujo, ordinograma *m*; (*Admin*) organigrama *m*

flower ['flaʊəʳ] (N) **1** (*Bot*) flor *f* • **in ~** en flor
2 (= *best*) • **the ~ of the army** la flor y nata del ejército • **she was in the ~ of her youth** estaba en la flor de la vida
(VI) florecer
(CPD) ▸ **flower arrangement** (= *exhibit*) (*on table*) arreglo *m* floral; (*in park*) adorno *m* floral; (= *art*) = **flower arranging** ▸ **flower arranging** arte *m* floral ▸ **flower child** (= *hippy*) hippy *mf*, hippie *mf* ▸ **flower garden** jardín *m* (de flores) ▸ **flower head** cabezuela *f* ▸ **flower people** hippies *mpl* ▸ **flower power** filosofía *f* hippy ▸ **flower seller** florista *mf*, vendedor(a) *m/f* de flores ▸ **flower shop** floristería *f*, tienda *f* de flores ▸ **flower show** exposición *f* de flores ▸ **flower stall** puesto *m* de flores

flowerbed ['flaʊəbed] (N) arriate *m*, parterre *m*, cantero *m* (*S. Cone*)

flowered ['flaʊəd] (ADJ) [*cloth, shirt*] floreado, de flores

flowering ['flaʊərɪŋ] (ADJ) floreciente, en flor
(N) floración *f*

flowerpot ['flaʊəpɒt] (N) maceta *f*, tiesto *m*

flowery ['flaʊərɪ] (ADJ) [*meadow, field*] florido; [*fragrance, perfume*] de flores; [*fabric, dress, wallpaper*] de flores, floreado; [*language*] florido

flowing ['fləʊɪŋ] (ADJ) [*movement*] fluido; [*stream*] corriente; [*hair, clothing*] suelto; [*style*] fluido

flown [fləʊn] (PP) *of* **fly**[2]

fl. oz. (ABBR) = **fluid ounce**

F/Lt (ABBR) = **Flight Lieutenant**

flu [fluː] (N) gripe *f*, gripa *f* (*Col, Mex*) • **I've got flu** tengo gripe • **to get** *or* **catch flu** agarrar la gripe, agriparse (*LAm*)
(CPD) ▸ **flu bug** virus *m inv* de la gripe • **a nasty flu bug has been going around the office** ha estado rondando un desagradable virus de la gripe por la oficina ▸ **flu jab*** vacuna *f* contra la gripe ▸ **flu vaccine** vacuna *f* antigripal

flub* [flʌb] (*US*) (VT) meter la pata en*
(VI) meter la pata*
(N) metedura *f* de pata*

fluctuate ['flʌktjʊeɪt] (VI) [*cost*] oscilar; [*prices, temperature*] fluctuar, oscilar • **to ~ between** [*person*] vacilar entre

fluctuation [ˌflʌktjʊ'eɪʃən] (N) [*of prices, temperature*] fluctuación *f*, oscilación *f*

flue [fluː] (N) humero *m*

fluency ['fluːənsɪ] (N) **1** (*in foreign language*) fluidez *f*, soltura *f* • **she speaks French with great ~** habla francés con mucha fluidez *or* soltura, domina bien el francés • **you need ~ in at least one foreign language** necesita dominar al menos una lengua • **I was impressed by his ~ in English** me impresionó su dominio del inglés
2 (*in speaking, reading, writing*) fluidez *f*, soltura *f*
3 [*of movement*] soltura *f*

fluent ['fluːənt] (ADJ) **1** (*in foreign language*) • **he is a ~ Japanese speaker** *or* **speaker of Japanese** habla japonés con fluidez *or* soltura, domina bien el japonés • **to speak ~ French** • **be ~ in French** hablar francés con

fluidez *or* soltura, dominar bien el francés • **to become ~ in French** llegar a hablar francés con fluidez *or* soltura, llegar a tener un buen dominio del francés
2 (= *not hesitant*) [*written style, speech, sentence*] fluido; [*speaker, debater, writer*] desenvuelto • **a ~ reader** una persona que lee con fluidez *or* soltura • **she speaks in ~ sentences** habla con frases fluidas • **rage was making him ~** la ira le hacía hablar sin trabarse
3 (= *graceful*) [*movement, dancing*] fluido

fluently [ˈfluːəntlɪ] ADV **1** (= *like a native*) • **he speaks Russian ~** habla ruso con fluidez *or* soltura, domina bien el ruso
2 (= *without hesitation*) [*speak, write, read*] con fluidez, con soltura
3 (= *gracefully*) [*dance, move*] con soltura, con fluidez

fluey* [ˈfluːiː] ADJ (*Brit*) griposo • **to feel ~** estar griposo

fluff [flʌf] N (*from blankets etc*) pelusa *f*, lanilla *f*; [*of chicks*] plumón *m*; [*of kittens*] pelo *m*, pelusa *f*
VT **1** (*also* **fluff out**) [+ *feathers*] ahuecar • **to ~ up the pillows** mullir las almohadas
2 (*Theat**) [+ *lines*] hacerse un lío con

fluffy [ˈflʌfɪ] ADJ (COMPAR: **fluffier**, SUPERL: **fluffiest**) [*toy*] de peluche; [*material*] mullido; [*bird*] plumoso; [*surface*] lleno de pelusa

fluid [ˈfluːɪd] ADJ [*substance, movement*] fluido; [*plan, arrangements*] flexible; [*opinions*] variable
N (*Phys*) fluido *m*; (*Physiol*) fluido *m*, líquido *m* • **drink plenty of ~s** tome mucho líquido, beba mucho
CPD ▸ **fluid ounce** onza *f* líquida

fluidity [fluːˈɪdɪtɪ] N [*of substance, movement*] fluidez *f*; [*of situation*] inestabilidad *f*

fluke¹ [fluːk] N chiripa *f*, golpe *m* de suerte • **to win by a ~** ganar de *or* por chiripa

fluke² [fluːk] N (*Zool*) trematodo *m*; (*Fishing*) *especie de platija*

fluky* [ˈfluːkɪ] ADJ afortunado

flume [fluːm] N **1** (= *ravine*) barranco *m*
2 (= *channel*) canal *m*
3 (*in swimming pool*) tubo *m*

flummox [ˈflʌməks] VT (= *disconcert*) desconcertar, confundir; (= *startle*) asombrar • **I was completely ~ed** me quedé totalmente desconcertado

flung [flʌŋ] PT, PP *of* **fling**

flunk* [flʌŋk] (*esp US*) VT [+ *student, course, exam*] suspender, catear (*Sp**), reprobar (*LAm*) • **I ~ed Maths** suspendí las matemáticas
VI suspender, catear (*Sp**) • **I ~ed** suspendí, cateé (*Sp**), me reprobaron (*LAm*)
▸ **flunk out*** VI + ADV (*US*) salirse del colegio *etc* sin recibir un título

flunkey, flunky [ˈflʌŋkɪ] N (*pej*) (= *servant*) lacayo *m*; (= *servile person*) adulador(a) *m/f*, lacayo *m*

fluorescence [flʊəˈresns] N fluorescencia *f*

fluorescent [flʊəˈresnt] ADJ [*lighting, tube, lamp*] fluorescente

fluoridate [ˈflʊərɪdeɪt] VT fluorizar

fluoridation [ˌflʊərɪˈdeɪʃən] N fluoración *f*, fluorización *f*

fluoride [ˈflʊəraɪd] N fluoruro *m*
CPD ▸ **fluoride toothpaste** pasta *f* de dientes con flúor

fluorine [ˈflʊəriːn] N flúor *m*

flurry [ˈflʌrɪ] N [*of wind, snow*] racha *f*, ráfaga *f*; [*of rain*] chaparrón *m*; (*fig*) [*of excitement*] frenesí *m* • **to be in a ~** estar nervioso • **a ~ of activity** un frenesí de actividad

flush¹ [flʌʃ] N **1** (= *blush*) • **there was a slight ~ on his cheeks** tenía las mejillas un poco coloradas • **she felt a faint ~ of colour rising in her face** notó que se le dibujaba cierto rubor en el rostro • **the pink ~ of dawn spread across the sky** (*liter*) el arrebol del alba se extendía por el cielo (*liter*)
2 (= *glow*) [*of beauty, health*] resplandor *m*
3 (= *surge*) [*of anger, excitement*] arrebato *m* • **she felt a ~ of excitement on hearing this** al oír esto sintió un arrebato de emoción • **in the first ~ of youth** en la flor de la juventud • **in the (first) ~ of victory** con la euforia del triunfo
4 • **to have hot ~es** (*Med*) tener sofocos
VI [*person, face*] ponerse colorado, sonrojarse, ruborizarse (*liter*) (**with** de)

flush² [flʌʃ] N [*of toilet*] (= *device*) cisterna *f*; (= *sound*) sonido *m* de la cisterna; (= *action*) descarga *f* de agua
VT (*also* **flush out**) [+ *sink, yard*] limpiar con agua, baldear • **to ~ the toilet** *or* **lavatory** tirar de la cadena
▸ **flush away** VT + ADV (*down sink*) echar al fregadero; (*down lavatory*) echar al váter

flush³ [flʌʃ] ADJ **1** (= *level*) a ras (**with** de), al mismo nivel (**with** que); (*DIY*) empotrado (**with** con) • **a door ~ with the wall** una puerta al mismo nivel que la pared • **to make two things ~** nivelar dos cosas
2* • **to be ~ (with money)** estar forrado*, andar muy bien de dinero

flush⁴ [flʌʃ] VT (*also* **flush out**) [+ *game, birds*] levantar; (*fig*) [+ *criminal*] sacar de su escondrijo a

flush⁵ [flʌʃ] N (*Cards*) color *m*, flux *m inv*

flushed [flʌʃt] ADJ **1** (= *red*) [*face, cheeks*] colorado, rojo • **she arrived looking ~** llegó colorada • **to be ~ from alcohol/sleep** estar colorado por el alcohol/de haber dormido • **to be ~ with anger** estar rojo de ira • **to be ~ with embarrassment** estar rojo de vergüenza, estar sonrojado
2 (= *excited*) • **to be ~ with success** estar eufórico por el éxito • **to be ~ with excitement** estar arrebatado de entusiasmo • **to be ~ with victory** estar eufórico por el triunfo
3 (= *tinged*) • **white flowers ~ with pink** flores *fpl* blancas teñidas de rosa

Flushing [ˈflʌʃɪŋ] N Flesinga *m*

fluster [ˈflʌstəʳ] N aturdimiento *m*, confusión *f* • **to be in a ~** estar aturdido *or* confuso
VT (= *confuse, upset*) aturdir, poner nervioso • **to get ~ed** ponerse nervioso, aturdirse

flute [fluːt] N flauta *f*; (*in Andes, S. Cone*) (= *bamboo*) quena *f*

fluted [ˈfluːtɪd] ADJ (*Archit*) estriado, acanalado

fluting [ˈfluːtɪŋ] ADJ [*voice*] aflautado • **a ~ and melodic Scottish accent** un aflautado y melódico acento escocés

flutist [ˈfluːtɪst] N (*US*) flautista *mf*

flutter [ˈflʌtəʳ] N **1** (= *movement*) [*of wings*] aleteo *m*; [*of eyelashes*] pestañeo *m*
2 (= *tremor*) • **to be in a ~** (*fig*) estar nervioso • **to cause a ~** causar revuelo • **to feel a ~ of excitement** estremecerse de la emoción • **there was a ~ of fear in her voice** la voz le temblaba por el miedo
3* (= *bet*) • **to have a ~** echar una apuesta • **to have a ~ on a race** apostar a un caballo
VT [+ *wings*] batir • **the sparrow was ~ing its wings** el gorrión batía las alas, el gorrión aleteaba • **to ~ one's eyelashes at sb** hacer ojitos a algn
VI [*bird*] revolotear; [*butterfly*] mover las alas; [*flag*] ondear; [*heart*] palpitar • **a leaf came ~ing down** una hoja cayó balanceándose • **the bird ~ed about the room** el pájaro revoloteaba por la habitación • **a butterfly ~ed away** una mariposa pasó revoloteando

fluty [ˈfluːtɪ] ADJ [*tone*] aflautado

fluvial [ˈfluːvɪəl] ADJ fluvial

flux [flʌks] N • **to be in a state of ~** estar inestable, estar cambiando continuamente

fly¹ [flaɪ] N **1** (= *insect*) mosca *f* • IDIOMS: • **people were dropping like flies** la gente caía como moscas • **he wouldn't hurt a fly** sería incapaz de matar una mosca • **there are no flies on him** no tiene un pelo de tonto • **the fly in the ointment** la única pega, el único inconveniente • **I wish I were a fly on the wall** me gustaría estar allí para ver qué pasa
2 (*on trousers*) (*also* **flies**) bragueta *f*
3 **flies** (*Theat*) peine *msing*, telar *msing*
4 (= *carriage*) calesa *f*
5 • IDIOM: • **to do sth on the fly** hacer algo por la vía rápida, hacer algo a la carrera
CPD ▸ **fly button** botón *m* de la bragueta
▸ **fly spray** (espray) *m* matamoscas *m inv*

fly² [flaɪ] (PT: **flew**, PP: **flown**) VI **1** (= *be airborne*) [*plane, bird, insect*] volar; [*air passengers*] ir en avión • **"how did you get here?" — "I flew"** —¿cómo llegaste aquí? —en avión • **do you fly often?** ¿viajas mucho en avión? • **she's flying home tomorrow** sale en avión para casa mañana • **I'm flying back to New York tonight** esta noche tomo un vuelo de regreso a Nueva York • **we were flying at 5,000ft** volábamos a 5.000 pies de altura • **we fly (with) Iberia** volamos con Iberia • **to fly into Gatwick airport** llegar (en avión) al aeropuerto de Gatwick • **the plane flew over London** el avión sobrevoló Londres • IDIOM: • **to be flying high**: • **we were flying high after our success in the championship** estábamos como locos tras el éxito en el campeonato • **the company is flying high** la empresa va viento en popa; ▹ **bird**
2 (= *fly a plane*) pilotar un avión, volar • **to learn to fly** aprender a pilotar un avión *or* a volar • **to fly blind** (*lit*) volar a ciegas *or* guiándose solo por los instrumentos; (*fig*) ir a ciegas
3 (= *flutter, wave*) [*flag*] ondear • **her hair was flying in the wind** su pelo ondeaba al viento; ▹ **flag**
4 (= *move quickly*) • **the dust flew in our eyes** se nos metió el polvo en los ojos • **my hat flew into the air** se me voló el sombrero, el sombrero salió volando • **her hand flew to her mouth** se llevó la mano a la boca • **the train was flying along** el tren iba como una exhalación • **rumours are flying around the office that ...** por la oficina corre el rumor de que ... • **to go flying**: • **the vase went flying** el jarrón salió por los aires *or* salió volando • **to let fly** (*fig*) (*verbally*) empezar a despotricar; (*physically*) empezar a repartir golpes *or* tortazos; (*Ftbl*) (= *shoot*) disparar • **he let fly with a shot from 20 metres** lanzó un disparo desde unos 20 metros • **to let fly at sb** (*verbally*) empezar a despotricar contra algn, arremeter contra algn; (*physically*) arremeter contra algn, empezar a dar golpes *or* tortazos a algn • **the door flew open** la puerta se abrió de golpe • **he/the ball came flying past me** él/la pelota pasó volando junto a mí • **to fly into a rage** montar en cólera • **the blow sent him flying** el golpe hizo que saliera despedido • **she kicked off her shoes and sent them flying across the room** de una patada se quitó los zapatos y los mandó volando al otro lado de la habitación; ▹ **spark**
5 (= *rush*) ir volando, ir corriendo • **I must fly!** ¡me voy volando *or* corriendo!, ¡me tengo que ir volando *or* corriendo! • **she flew upstairs to look for it** subió volando *or* a toda

prisa a buscarlo • **to fly to sb's aid** *or* **assistance** ir volando a socorrer a algn • **to fly to sb's side** volar al lado de algn • **to fly at sb** (*physically*) lanzarse sobre algn, arremeter contra algn; (*fig*) ponerse furioso con algn • **the dog flew at him and bit him** el perro se lanzó *or* se abalanzó sobre él y le mordió • IDIOM: • **to fly in the face of sth** ir en contra de algo, desafiar algo • **ideas that fly in the face of common sense** ideas que desafían el sentido común • **she has a reputation for flying in the face of authority** tiene fama de ir en contra de la autoridad; ▹ **handle**
6 (= *pass quickly*) [*time*] pasar *or* irse volando • **the years flew by** los años pasaron volando
7† (= *flee*) huir, escaparse (**from** de)
(VT) **1** [+ *aircraft*] pilotar, pilotear (*esp LAm*); [+ *passenger*] llevar en avión; [+ *goods*] transportar en avión; [+ *distance*] recorrer (en avión); [+ *flag*] enarbolar • **to fly the Atlantic** atravesar el Atlántico en avión • **which routes does the airline fly?** ¿qué rutas cubre la aerolínea? • **to fly a kite** hacer volar una cometa
2 (= *flee*) [+ *country*] abandonar, huir de • IDIOMS: • **to fly the nest** echar a volar, dejar *or* abandonar el nido • **to fly the coop** tomar las de Villadiego, agarrar *or* tomar el portante (y marcharse)
▸ **fly away** (VI + ADV) [*bird*] salir volando, emprender el vuelo
▸ **fly in** (VI + ADV) [*plane*] llegar; [*person*] llegar en avión • **he flew in from Rome** llegó en avión desde Roma • **a bee flew in through the window** una abeja entró volando por la ventana
(VT + ADV) [+ *supplies, troops*] (= *take*) llevar en avión; (= *bring*) traer en avión • **the seafood was flown in from Hawaii** el marisco venía en avión desde Hawai
▸ **fly off** (VI + ADV) **1** [*bird, plane*] alejarse volando; [*person in plane*] marcharse (en avión) (**to a**) • **I'd love to fly off to a Caribbean island** me encantaría marcharme a una isla del Caribe
2 (= *come off*) [*hat*] salir volando; [*lid, handle, wheel*] saltar, salir disparado • **sparks flew off in all directions** saltaban chispas por todos lados
▸ **fly out** (VI + ADV) [*person in plane*] salir en avión, irse en avión; [*plane*] salir • **... and we're flying out two weeks later** y nosotros salimos *or* nos vamos en avión para allá dos semanas después • **I had to fly out to California to pick him up** tuve que ir en avión a California a recogerlo
(VT + ADV) **1** (= *take out*) • **we shall fly supplies out to them** les enviaremos provisiones por avión
2 (= *bring out*) • **the hostages have been flown out** han sacado a los rehenes en avión
fly³ [flaɪ] (ADJ) (*esp Brit*) avispado, espabilado
flyaway ['flaɪəweɪ] (ADJ) **1** [*hair*] suelto, lacio
2 (= *frivolous*) frívolo
fly-blown ['flaɪbləʊn] (ADJ) (*lit*) lleno de cresas; (*fig*) viejo, gastado
flyby ['flaɪ,baɪ] (N) (PL: **flybys**) (*esp US*) desfile *m* aéreo
fly-by-night ['flaɪbaɪnaɪt] (ADJ) informal, poco fiable
(N) casquivano/a *m/f*
flycatcher ['flaɪ,kætʃəʳ] (N) (*Orn*) papamoscas *m inv*
fly-drive holiday [,flaɪdraɪv'hɒlɪdɪ] (N) vacaciones *fpl* con vuelo y coche (de alquiler)
flyer ['flaɪəʳ] = **flier**
fly-fishing ['flaɪ,fɪʃɪŋ] (N) pesca *f* a *or* con mosca
fly-half ['flaɪ,hɑːf] (N) medio apertura *m*
flying ['flaɪɪŋ] (ADJ) [*glass, debris*] que vuela por los aires • **he took a ~ leap at the man** dio un salto *or* saltó sobre el hombre • **he launched himself in a ~ tackle and brought the intruder to the ground** se lanzó por el aire *or* se lanzó en plancha y derribó al intruso • **to make a ~ visit** hacer una visita relámpago • IDIOMS: • **to come through (sth) with ~ colours** salir airoso (de algo) • **he passed all his exams with ~ colours** aprobó todos sus exámenes con éxito • **to get off to a ~ start** empezar con muy buen pie
(N) (*gen*) vuelo *m*; (= *aviation*) aviación *f* • **I had done 60 hours of ~** había realizado 60 horas de vuelo • **I don't like ~** no me gusta ir en avión *or* volar • **to have a fear of ~** tener miedo al avión
(CPD) ▸ **flying ambulance** (= *plane*) ambulancia *f* aérea; (= *helicopter*) helicóptero *m* sanitario ▸ **flying boat** hidroavión *m* ▸ **flying bomb** bomba *f* volante ▸ **flying buttress** arbotante *m* ▸ **flying doctor** médico/a *m/f* rural (que se traslada en avión) ▸ **flying fish** pez *m* volador ▸ **flying fortress** fortaleza *f* volante ▸ **flying fox** panique *m* ▸ **flying lesson** clase *f* *or* lección *f* de vuelo ▸ **flying machine** máquina *f* de volar ▸ **flying officer** teniente *mf* de aviación ▸ **flying picket** piquete *m* volante *or* móvil ▸ **flying saucer** platillo *m* volante ▸ **flying squad** (*Brit*) brigada *f* móvil ▸ **flying suit** traje *m* de vuelo ▸ **flying time** (= *length of journey*) duración *f* del vuelo; (= *hours flown*) horas *fpl* de vuelo ▸ **flying trapeze** trapecio *m* volador
flyleaf ['flaɪliːf] (N) (PL: **flyleaves**) guarda *f*
fly-on-the-wall documentary ['flaɪənðəwɔːl,dɒkjʊ'mentərɪ] (N) docu-reality *m* • **a fly-on-the-wall documentary about the Queen's life** un docu-reality sobre la vida de la reina; ▹ **fly¹**
flyover ['flaɪ,əʊvəʳ] (N) (*Brit*) (*Aut*) paso *m* elevado, paso *m* a desnivel (*LAm*); (*US*) (= *flypast*) desfile *m* aéreo
flypaper ['flaɪ,peɪpəʳ] (N) papel *m* matamoscas
flypast ['flaɪpɑːst] (N) desfile *m* aéreo
fly-posting ['flaɪ,pəʊstɪŋ] (N) pegada *f* (ilegal) de carteles
flysheet ['flaɪʃiːt] (N) (*for tent*) doble techo *m*
fly-swat ['flaɪswɒt], **fly-swatter** ['flaɪswɒtəʳ] (N) matamoscas *m inv*
fly-tipping ['flaɪ,tɪpɪŋ] (N) descarga *f* (ilegal) de basura *etc*
flyweight ['flaɪweɪt] (N) peso *m* mosca
(CPD) ▸ **flyweight contest** combate *m* de pesos mosca
flywheel ['flaɪwiːl] (N) (*Tech*) volante *m*
FM (ABBR) **1** (*Brit*) (*Mil*) = **Field Marshal**
2 (*Rad*) (= **frequency modulation**) FM *f*, M. F. *f*
3 = **foreign minister**
FMB (N ABBR) (*US*) = **Federal Maritime Board**
FMCG, fmcg (ABBR) = **fast-moving consumer goods**
FMCS (N ABBR) (*US*) (= **Federal Mediation and Conciliation Services**) ≈ IMAC *m*
FO (N ABBR) (*Brit*) (*Pol*) (= **Foreign Office**) Min. de AA.EE.
(ABBR) (*Aer*) = **Flying Officer**
fo. (ABBR) (= **folio**) f.°, fol.
foal [fəʊl] (N) potro *m*
(VI) [*mare*] parir
foam [fəʊm] (N) (*gen*) espuma *f*
(VI) [*sea*] hacer espuma • **to ~ at the mouth** echar espumarajos; (*fig*) subirse por las paredes
(CPD) ▸ **foam bath** baño *m* de espuma ▸ **foam extinguisher** lanzaespumas *m inv*, extintor *m* de espuma ▸ **foam rubber** gomaespuma *f*
foamy ['fəʊmɪ] (ADJ) espumoso
FOB, f.o.b. (ABBR) (= **free on board**) f.a.b.
fob [fɒb] (VT) • **to fob sb off (with sth): I've asked her about it but she fobs me off** se lo he preguntado, pero me da largas • **she wants an answer, she won't be fobbed off** quiere una respuesta, no aceptará más evasivas • **don't be fobbed off with excuses** no te dejes engatusar con excusas
(N)† **1** (= *watch pocket*) faltriquera *f* de reloj
2 (= *watch chain*) leontina *f*
(CPD) ▸ **fob watch** reloj *m* de cadena *or* de bolsillo
FOC (ABBR) = **free of charge**
focal ['fəʊkəl] (ADJ) (*Tech*) focal
(CPD) ▸ **focal distance** distancia *f* focal ▸ **focal plane** plano *m* focal ▸ **focal point** punto *m* focal; (*fig*) centro *m* de atención
focus ['fəʊkəs] (N) (PL: **focuses** *or* **foci** ['fəʊsaɪ]) (*gen*) foco *m*; [*of attention*] centro *m*, foco *m* • **he was the ~ of attention** era el centro *or* foco de atención • **to be in ~** (*Phot*) estar enfocado • **to be out of ~** (*Phot*) estar desenfocado
(VT) [+ *camera, instrument*] enfocar (**on** a); [+ *attention*] centrar, concentrar (**on** en) • **to ~ one's eyes on sth/sb** fijar la mirada en algo/algn • **all eyes were ~sed on her** todos la miraban fijamente
(VI) • **to ~ (on)** [*light*] converger (en); [*heat rays*] concentrarse (en); [*eyes*] fijarse (en) • **to ~ on sth** (*Phot*) enfocar algo
(CPD) ▸ **focus group** grupo *m* de discusión
focused, focussed ['fəʊkəst] (ADJ)
1 (= *purposeful*) [*person*] centrado • **I spent the next year just wandering, I wasn't ~** me pasé el siguiente año distraído, no estaba centrado
2 (= *targeted*) centrado • **the voting is now more ~** el voto está ahora más centrado • **they promised a new, more ~ approach** prometieron un nuevo enfoque más centrado
fodder ['fɒdəʳ] (N) pienso *m*, forraje *m*; ▹ **cannon**
(CPD) ▸ **fodder grain** cereales *mpl* forrajeros
FOE¹, FoE (N ABBR) (*Brit*) (= **Friends of the Earth**) *organización ecologista*
FOE² (N ABBR) (*US*) (= **Fraternal Order of Eagles**) *sociedad benéfica*
foe [fəʊ] (N) (*poet*) enemigo *m*
foetal, fetal (*US*) ['fiːtl] (ADJ) fetal
foetid ['fetɪd] (ADJ) = **fetid**
foetus, fetus (*US*) ['fiːtəs] (N) feto *m*
fog [fɒg] (N) **1** (*Met*) niebla *f*
2 (*fig*) confusión *f* • **to be in a fog** estar confundido *or* desconcertado
(VT) **1** (*Phot*) velar
2 (= *confuse*) [+ *matter*] enredar, complicar; [+ *person*] confundir, ofuscar • **to fog the issue** complicar el asunto
3 (*also* **fog up**) [+ *spectacles, window*] empañar
(VI) (*also* **fog up**) empañarse
(CPD) ▸ **fog bank** banco *m* de niebla ▸ **fog lamp, fog light** (*Aut*) faro *m* antiniebla ▸ **fog signal** aviso *m* de niebla
fogbound ['fɒgbaʊnd] (ADJ) inmovilizado por la niebla
fogey ['fəʊgɪ] (N) • **old ~*** carroza* *mf*, persona *f* chapada a la antigua
foggy ['fɒgɪ] (ADJ) (COMPAR: **foggier**, SUPERL: **foggiest**) **1** (*Met*) [*weather*] brumoso; [*day*] de niebla, brumoso • **it's ~** hay niebla • **I haven't the foggiest (idea)*** no tengo la más remota idea
2 (*Phot*) velado
foghorn ['fɒghɔːn] (N) sirena *f* de niebla • **to have a voice like a ~** tener un vozarrón*
FOIA (N ABBR) (*US*) (= **Freedom of Information Act**) ▹ FREEDOM OF

INFORMATION ACT

foible ['fɔɪbl] N manía *f*

foie gras [ˌfwɑː'grɑː] N foie gras *m inv*

foil¹ [fɔɪl] N **1** (*also* **tinfoil**) papel *m* de aluminio, papel *m* de plata
2 (*fig*) • **to act as a ~ to sth/sb** servir de contraste con algo/algn

foil² [fɔɪl] N (*Fencing*) florete *m*

foil³ [fɔɪl] VT (= *thwart*) [+ *person*] desbaratar los planes de; [+ *attempt*] frustrar

foist [fɔɪst] VT • **to ~ sth on sb** endosar algo a algn • **the job was ~ed on me** me endosaron el trabajo • **to ~ o.s. on sb** pegarse a algn, insistir en acompañar a *or* ir con algn

fol. ABBR (= **folio**) f.º, fol.

fold¹ [fəʊld] N (*Agr*) redil *m* • **to return to the ~** (*Rel*) volver al redil

fold² [fəʊld] N (*in paper etc*) pliegue *m*, doblez *m*; (*Geol*) pliegue *m*
VT [+ *paper, map, sheet, blanket*] doblar; (*esp several times*) plegar; [+ *wings*] recoger • **she ~ed the newspaper in two** dobló en dos el periódico • **to ~ a piece of paper in half** doblar un trozo de papel por la mitad • **to ~ one's arms** cruzar los brazos • **to ~ sb in one's arms** abrazar a algn tiernamente, estrechar a algn contra el pecho
VI **1** (*lit*) [*chair, table*] plegarse, doblarse
2* (= *fail*) [*business venture*] fracasar, quebrar; [*play*] fracasar
▸ **fold away** VI + ADV [*table, bed*] plegarse
VT + ADV [+ *clothes, newspaper*] doblar (*para guardar*); [+ *bed*] plegar
▸ **fold back** VT + ADV doblar hacia abajo, plegar
▸ **fold down** VT + ADV = **fold back**
VI + ADV • **it ~s down at night** de noche se dobla hacia abajo
▸ **fold in** VT + ADV (*Culin*) [+ *flour, sugar*] mezclar
▸ **fold over** VT + ADV [+ *paper*] plegar; [+ *blanket*] hacer el embozo con
▸ **fold up** VI + ADV **1** (*lit*) doblarse, plegarse • **to ~ up (with laughter)*** troncharse de risa*
2* (= *fail*) [*business venture*] quebrar, fracasar
VT + ADV [+ *paper, map, sheet, blanket*] doblar; [+ *chair*] plegar • **she ~ed the chair up and walked off** plegó la silla y se marchó

-fold [fəʊld] ADJ, ADV (*ending in compounds*) • **thirty-fold** (*as adj*) de treinta veces; (*as adv*) treinta veces

foldaway ['fəʊldəweɪ] ADJ plegable, plegadizo

folded ['fəʊldɪd] ADJ **1** [*paper, clothes, blanket, leaf*] doblado • **~ into a rectangle** doblado en forma de rectángulo
2 (= *crossed*) [*hands, arms*] cruzado • **to stand with one's arms ~** estar de pie con los brazos cruzados

folder ['fəʊldəʳ] N (= *file*) carpeta *f*; (= *binder*) carpeta *f* de anillas

folding ['fəʊldɪŋ] ADJ [*seat, table, ruler*] plegable
CPD ▸ **folding chair** silla *f* plegable *or* de tijera ▸ **folding doors** puertas *fpl* de fuelle *or* plegadizas ▸ **folding ruler** regla *f* plegable

foldout ['fəʊldaʊt] ADJ [*section of book etc*] desplegable

fold-up ['fəʊldʌp] ADJ plegable, plegadizo

foliage ['fəʊlɪɪdʒ] N follaje *m*, hojas *fpl*

foliation [ˌfəʊlɪ'eɪʃən] N foliación *f*

folic acid [ˌfəʊlɪk'æsɪd] N ácido *m* fólico

folio ['fəʊlɪəʊ] N (= *sheet*) folio *m*; (= *book*) infolio *m*, libro *m* en folio

folk [fəʊk] N **1** (= *people*) gente *f* • **country/city ~** la gente de campo/ciudad • **ordinary ~** la gente llana • **they're strange ~ here** aquí la gente es algo rara • **the common ~** el pueblo • **my ~s*** (= *parents*) mis viejos* *mpl*; (= *family*) mi familia • **the old ~s** los viejos • **hello ~s!** ¡hola, amigos!
2 = **folk music**
CPD ▸ **folk art** artesanía *f* popular *or* tradicional ▸ **folk dance** baile *m* popular ▸ **folk dancing** danza *f* folklórica ▸ **folk medicine** medicina *f* tradicional ▸ **folk music** (*traditional*) música *f* tradicional *or* folklórica; (*contemporary*) música *f* folk ▸ **folk rock** folk rock *m* ▸ **folk singer** cantante *mf* de música folk ▸ **folk song** canción *f* tradicional ▸ **folk tale** cuento *m* popular ▸ **folk wisdom** saber *m* popular

folklore ['fəʊklɔːʳ] N folklore *m*

folkloric ['fəʊkˌlɔːrɪk] ADJ folklórico, folclórico

folksy* ['fəʊksɪ] ADJ **1** (= *rustic*) [*furniture*] rústico; [*music*] folklórico; [*clothes*] de campesino • **they sold ~ country furniture** vendían muebles rústicos típicos del campo
2 (*pej*) (= *affected*) de una rusticidad fingida
3 (*US*) (= *affable*) [*person, manner*] campechano; [*speech, comment*] de estilo campechano

foll. ABBR (= **following**) sig., sigs., sgte., sgtes.

follicle ['fɒlɪkl] N folículo *m*

follow ['fɒləʊ] VT **1** (= *come, go after*) seguir • **~ that car!** ¡siga a ese coche! • **~ me** sígame • **she arrived first, ~ed by the ambassador** ella llegó primero, seguida del embajador • **to ~ sb about** *or* **around** seguir a algn a todas partes • **he ~ed me into the room** entró en la habitación detrás de mí • **I ~ed her out into the garden** salí al jardín detrás de ella • **we ~ed her up the steps** la seguimos escaleras arriba, subimos (las escaleras) detrás de ella • IDIOM: • **to ~ one's nose** (= *go straight on*) ir todo seguido; (= *use one's instinct*) dejarse guiar por el instinto
2 (= *succeed*) • **the days ~ing her death** los días que siguieron a su muerte • **the dinner will be ~ed by a concert** después de la cena habrá un concierto • **he ~ed his father into the business** siguió los pasos de su padre en el negocio • **they ~ed this with threats** tras esto empezaron a amenazarnos • **the bombing ~s a series of recent attacks** los bombardeos se han producido tras una serie de ataques recientes • **~ing our meeting I spoke to the director** tras nuestra reunión hablé con el director • IDIOM: • **as sure(ly) as night ~s day** como dos y dos son cuatro; ▹ **act**
3 (= *pursue*) seguir • **we're being ~ed** nos están siguiendo, nos vienen siguiendo • **she could feel his eyes ~ing her** sentía que la seguía con la mirada • **to have sb ~ed** mandar seguir a algn • **to ~ a lead** seguir una pista
4 (= *keep to*) [*road, river*] seguir, ir por • **the road ~s the coast** la carretera sigue la costa *or* va por la costa
5 (= *observe*) [+ *instructions, advice, example, fashion*] seguir; [+ *rules*] obedecer, cumplir • **I wouldn't advise you to ~ that course of action** no le aconsejo que tome ese camino *or* esas medidas; ▹ **pattern, suit**
6 (= *engage in*) [+ *career*] emprender; [+ *profession*] ejercer; [+ *trade*] dedicarse a; [+ *religion*] profesar, ser seguidor de
7 (= *be interested in*) [+ *news*] seguir, mantenerse al corriente de; [+ *TV serial*] seguir; [+ *sb's progress*] seguir • **do you ~ football?** ¿eres aficionado al fútbol? • **which team do you ~?** ¿de qué equipo eres?
8 (= *understand*) [+ *person, argument*] seguir, entender • **do you ~ me?** ¿me sigue?, ¿me entiende? • **I don't quite ~ you** no te acabo de entender • **it was a difficult plot to ~** era una trama difícil de seguir
VI **1** (= *come after*) • **they led her in and I ~ed** la llevaron dentro y yo entré detrás • **to ~, there was roast lamb** de segundo había cordero asado • **roast chicken, with apple pie to ~** pollo asado y después de postre un pastel de manzana • **what ~s is an eye-witness account** lo que viene a continuación es la versión de un testigo presencial • **further price rises are sure to ~** no cabe duda de que tras esto los precios subirán aún más • **as ~s:** • **the text reads as ~s** el texto dice lo siguiente, el texto dice así • **the winners are as ~s** los ganadores son los siguientes; ▹ **heel, footstep**
2 (= *result, ensue*) deducirse • **that doesn't ~** eso no cuadra, de ahí no se puede deducir eso • **it ~s that ...** (de lo cual) se deduce que ..., se deduce pues que ... • **it doesn't ~ that ...** no significa que ...
3 (= *understand*) entender • **I don't quite ~** no lo sigo del todo, no lo acabo de entender
▸ **follow on** VI + ADV **1** (= *come after*) • **we'll ~ on behind** nosotros seguiremos, vendremos después
2 (= *result*) • **it ~s on from what I said** es la consecuencia lógica de lo que dije
▸ **follow out** VT + ADV [+ *idea, plan*] llevar a cabo; [+ *order*] ejecutar, cumplir; [+ *instructions*] seguir
▸ **follow through** VT + ADV **1** (= *continue to the end*) • **~ it through, it might be the only lead we've got** síguela *or* investígala, puede que sea la única pista que tengamos • **that's all you need to make a start and ~ it through** eso es todo lo que hace falta para empezar y seguir adelante • **I was trained as an actress but I didn't ~ it through** estudié arte dramático pero luego no seguí con ello
2 (*Sport*) [+ *shot*] acompañar
VI + ADV **1** (= *take further action*) continuar, seguir • **he decided to ~ through with his original plan** decidió continuar *or* seguir con lo que tenía pensado en un principio • **to ~ through on** (*US*) [+ *commitment*] cumplir con; [+ *promise*] cumplir; [+ *plan, initiative*] continuar con, seguir con; [+ *threat*] cumplir, llevar a cabo
2 (*Ftbl*) rematar; (*Golf, Tennis*) acompañar el golpe
▸ **follow up** VT + ADV **1** (= *investigate*) [+ *case*] investigar • **to ~ up a lead** seguir *or* investigar una pista
2 (= *take further action on*) [+ *offer*] reiterar; [+ *job application*] hacer un seguimiento de; [+ *suggestion*] investigar
3 (= *reinforce*) [+ *victory, advantage, success*] consolidar • **they imposed trade sanctions and ~ed that up with an oil embargo** impusieron sanciones comerciales y las consolidaron con un embargo de petróleo • **they ~ed the visit up with a series of talks** consolidaron la visita con una serie de conferencias
VI + ADV (*Ftbl*) rematar

follower ['fɒləʊəʳ] N (= *disciple*) discípulo/a *m/f*, seguidor(a) *m/f*; [*of team*] aficionado/a *m/f*; (*Pol etc*) partidario/a *m/f* • **the ~s of fashion** los que siguen la moda

following ['fɒləʊɪŋ] ADJ **1** (= *next*) siguiente • **the ~ day** el día siguiente • **the ~ day dawned bright and sunny** el día siguiente *or* al día siguiente amaneció con un sol radiante • **we saw him again the ~ day** lo volvimos a ver al día siguiente
2 (= *favourable*) [*wind*] en popa • IDIOM: • **with a ~ wind** con un poco de suerte • **with a ~ wind you could win the competition** con un poco de suerte podrías ganar el torneo
N **1** (= *supporters*) [*of party, movement, person*]

f

seguidores *mpl*, partidarios *mpl*; [*of product, company*] clientes *mpl*; [*of TV programme*] audiencia *f*, seguidores *mpl*; [*of sport*] afición *f*, aficionados *mpl* • **he has a large ~ in the local community** cuenta con numerosos seguidores *or* partidarios entre la población local • **the programme has a huge ~ in the US** el programa tiene una enorme audiencia *or* muchos seguidores en EE.UU. • **football has no ~ here** aquí no hay afición por el fútbol
2 • **the ~: he said the ~** dijo lo siguiente • **do you use any of the ~?** ¿utiliza alguna de estas cosas? • **as for hardier plants, the ~ are all well worth trying** por lo que respecta a plantas más resistentes, se puede probar con cualquiera de las siguientes

follow-my-leader [ˌfɒləʊmə'liːdəʳ] N *juego en el que los participantes hacen lo que alguien manda* • **to play follow-my-leader** jugar a lo que haga el rey

follow-on [ˌfɒləʊ'ɒn] N continuación *f* • **a follow-on to sth** una continuación de algo • **this course for bridge players with some experience is intended as a follow-on to the beginners' course** este curso de bridge para jugadores con algo de experiencia es una continuación del curso para principiantes

follow-the-leader [ˌfɒləʊðə'liːdəʳ] N (*US*) = **follow-my-leader**

follow-through ['fɒləʊ'θruː] N (= *continuation*) continuación *f*; (= *further action*) seguimiento *m*; (*Golf, Tennis*) acompañamiento *m* • **there was no follow-through to the training programme we went on** el programa de formación al que asistimos no tuvo continuación • **how can we make sure that there is follow-through on this agreement?** ¿cómo podemos asegurarnos de que se realizará un seguimiento del acuerdo?

follow-up ['fɒləʊ'ʌp] N (= *further action*) seguimiento *m* (**to** de); (= *continuation*) continuación *f* (**to** de) • **subsequent follow-up is an essential part of the program** un seguimiento posterior es parte fundamental del programa • **this is a follow-up to the meeting held last Sunday** esto es la continuación de la reunión celebrada el domingo
CPD ▸ **follow-up appointment** (*with doctor, dentist, vet*) revisión *f* ▸ **follow-up (phone) call** (*Telec*) llamada *f* de reiteración ▸ **follow-up care** (*postoperative*) atención *f* pos(t)operatoria; (*following initial treatment*) seguimiento *m* clínico ▸ **follow-up interview** entrevista *f* complementaria ▸ **follow-up letter** carta *f* recordatoria ▸ **follow-up study** estudio *m* de seguimiento ▸ **follow-up survey** investigación *f* complementaria ▸ **follow-up treatment** (*postoperative*) tratamiento *m* pos(t)operatorio; (*following initial treatment*) tratamiento *m* complementario ▸ **follow-up visit** (= *inspection*) visita *f* de inspección *or* comprobación; (*Med*) revisión *f*

folly ['fɒlɪ] N **1** (= *foolishness, act of folly*) locura *f* • **it would be ~ to do it** sería una locura hacerlo
2 (*Archit*) disparate *m*

foment [fəʊ'ment] VT (*frm*) (*also Med*) fomentar; [+ *revolt, violence*] provocar, instigar a

fomentation [ˌfəʊmen'teɪʃən] N (*frm*) instigación *f*

fond [fɒnd] ADJ (COMPAR: **fonder**, SUPERL: **fondest**) **1** • **to be ~ of sb** tener cariño a algn, querer mucho a algn • **I am very ~ of Inga** a Inga le tengo mucho cariño *or* la quiero mucho • **they were very ~ of each other** se tenían mucho cariño, se querían mucho • **I've become** *or* **grown ~ of him** me he encariñado con él, le he cogido cariño
2 • **to be ~ of sth: she is very ~ of marmalade/shopping** le gusta mucho la mermelada/ir de compras • **she is very ~ of animals** le gustan mucho los animales • **he's very ~ of his old Mini** le tiene mucho cariño a su viejo Mini • **he is very ~ of handing out advice** (*pej*) es demasiado aficionado a dar consejos • **he became** *or* **grew very ~ of gardening** le cogió gusto a la jardinería
3 (= *affectionate*) [*wife, parent, relative*] cariñoso, afectuoso • **she gave him a ~ smile** le sonrió cariñosa • **they exchanged ~ looks** intercambiaron miradas cariñosas • **to bid sb a ~ farewell** • **bid a ~ farewell to sb** despedirse de algn cariñosamente; ▹ **absence**
4 (= *pleasant*) • **to have ~ memories of sth** tener muy buenos recuerdos de algo
5 (= *foolish*) [*belief, hope*] ingenuo, vano • **in the ~ belief that** con la ingenua *or* vana creencia de que
6 (= *fervent*) [*wish*] ferviente

fondant ['fɒndənt] N pasta *f* de azúcar, glaseado *m*
CPD ▸ **fondant icing** glaseado *m* fondant

fondle ['fɒndl] VT acariciar

fondly ['fɒndlɪ] ADV **1** (= *affectionately*) [*say, smile*] cariñosamente, con cariño; [*remember*] con cariño
2 (= *foolishly*) [*imagine, believe, hope*] ingenuamente

fondness ['fɒndnɪs] N (*for person*) cariño *m* (**for** por); (*for thing*) afición *f* (**for** a) • **his ~ for cooking** su afición a la cocina • **there were rumours about her ~ for alcohol** corrían rumores sobre su afición al alcohol • **he has a ~ for all things Italian** le gusta mucho todo lo italiano, tiene inclinación por todo lo italiano • **I remember my childhood with ~** recuerdo mi infancia con cariño

fondue [fɒn'duː] N fondue *f*
CPD ▸ **fondue set** fondue *f*

font [fɒnt] N **1** (*Typ*) fundición *f*; (*Comput*) fuente *f*, tipo *m* de letra
2 (*in church*) pila *f*

fontanelle, fontanel [ˌfɒntə'nel] N fontanela *f*

food [fuːd] N (= *things to eat*) comida *f*; (= *food item*) alimento *m*; (*for plants*) abono *m* • **I've no ~ left in the house** no me queda comida en casa • **we need to buy some ~** hay que comprar cosas de comer • **she gave him ~** le dio de comer • **the ~ was terrible** la comida era fatal • **the ~ is good here** aquí se come bien • **he likes plain ~** le gustan las comidas sencillas • **the cost of ~** el coste de la alimentación • **to send ~ and clothing** enviar alimentos y ropa • **to be off one's ~*** estar desganado • IDIOM: • **to give ~ for thought** ser motivo de reflexión; ▹ **cat, dog**
CPD ▸ **food additive** aditivo *m* alimenticio ▸ **food aid** ayuda *f* alimenticia ▸ **food allergy** alergia *f* alimentaria ▸ **food bank** banco *m* de alimentos ▸ **food chain** cadena *f* alimenticia ▸ **food colouring** colorante *m* alimentario ▸ **food counter** mostrador *m* de alimentos ▸ **food crop** cosecha *f* de alimentos ▸ **food fascist** intolerante *mf* con la dieta • **the ~ fascists tell us we shouldn't eat fried ~** los intolerantes con la dieta afirman que no se debe comer comida frita ▸ **food group** grupo *m* de alimentos, grupo *m* de comida ▸ **food industry** industria *f* alimentaria ▸ **food labelling** el etiquetado de los alimentos ▸ **food miles** *distancia que recorre un alimento desde el lugar en el que es producido hasta el lugar en el que es consumido* ▸ **food mixer** batidora *f* ▸ **food parcel** paquete *m* de alimentos ▸ **food poisoning** intoxicación *f* alimenticia ▸ **food prices** precios *mpl* de los alimentos ▸ **food processing** preparación *f* de alimentos ▸ **food processor** robot *m* de cocina ▸ **food product** producto *m* alimenticio, comestible *m* ▸ **food rationing** racionamiento *m* de víveres ▸ **food science** ciencia *f* de la alimentación ▸ **food security** seguridad *f* alimentaria ▸ **food shop** tienda *f* de comestibles ▸ **food shopping** compra *f* de la comida • **to do ~ shopping** hacer la compra de la comida • **I do a lot of ~ shopping at my local supermarket** hago mucho la compra de la comida en el supermercado de mi barrio ▸ **food stamp** (*US*) *cupón para canjear por comida que reciben las personas de pocos recursos* ▸ **Food Standards Agency** (*Brit*) *agencia británica de normas alimentarias*, ≈ AESA *f* (*Sp*) ▸ **food store** = **food shop** ▸ **food subsidy** subvención *f* alimenticia ▸ **food supplement** suplemento *m* alimenticio ▸ **food supplies** víveres *mpl* ▸ **food supply** suministro *m* de alimentos ▸ **food technology** tecnología *f* de la alimentación ▸ **food value** valor *m* nutritivo; ▹ **FDA**

foodie* ['fuːdɪ] N *persona que se interesa con entusiasmo en la preparación y consumo de los alimentos*

foodstuffs ['fuːdstʌfs] NPL comestibles *mpl*, productos *mpl* alimenticios

fool¹ [fuːl] N **1** (= *idiot*) tonto/a *m/f*, zonzo/a *m/f* (*LAm*) • **don't be a ~!** ¡no seas tonto! • **I was a ~ not to go!** ¡qué tonto fui en no ir! • **to act the ~** hacer el tonto • **to be ~ enough to do sth** ser lo bastante tonto como para hacer algo • **to send sb on a ~'s errand** enviar a algn a una misión inútil • **to make a ~ of sb** poner *or* dejar a algn en ridículo • **to make a ~ of o.s.** quedar en ridículo • **I'm nobody's ~** yo no me chupo el dedo, yo no tengo un pelo de tonto • **to play the ~** hacer el tonto • **some ~ of a civil servant** algún funcionario imbécil • **you ~!** ¡idiota!, ¡imbécil! • IDIOM: • **to live in a ~'s paradise** vivir de ilusiones • PROVERBS: • **there's no ~ like an old ~** la cabeza blanca y el seso por venir • **a ~ and his money are soon parted** a los tontos no les dura el dinero • **~s rush in (where angels fear to tread)** la ignorancia es osada
2 (= *jester*) bufón *m*
ADJ (*US*) tonto, zonzo (*LAm*)
VT (= *deceive*) engañar • **you can't ~ me** a mí no me engañas • **"my husband has always been faithful to me" — "you could have ~ed me!"** (*iro*) —mi marido siempre me ha sido fiel —¡qué fiel ni qué ocho cuartos!* • **you had me ~ed there** casi lo creí, por poco me lo trago* • **that ~ed him!** ¡aquello coló!*, ¡se lo tragó!* • **that ~ed nobody** aquello no engañó a nadie, nadie se tragó aquello*
VI hacer el tonto • **no ~ing** en serio • **I was only ~ing** solo era una broma • **quit ~ing!** ¡déjate de tonterías!
CPD ▸ **fool's gold** (= *iron pyrites*) pirita *f* de hierro • IDIOM: • **a quest for ~'s gold** una búsqueda insensata

▸ **fool about, fool around** VI + ADV
1 (= *waste time*) perder el tiempo
2 (= *act the fool*) hacer el tonto • **to ~ about with sth** (= *play with*) jugar con algo; (*and damage*) estropear algo; (= *mess with*) [+ *drugs, drink, electricity*] jugar con
3 (= *have an affair*) • **to ~ around with sb** tontear con algn

▸ **fool with** VI + PREP • **to ~ with sb** jugar con algn, hacer el tonto con algn

fool² [fu:l] (N) (*Brit*) (*Culin*) (*also* **fruit fool**) *puré de frutas con nata o natillas*
foolery ['fu:lərɪ] (N) bufonadas *fpl*; (= *nonsense*) tonterías *fpl*
foolhardiness ['fu:l,hɑ:dɪnɪs] (N) temeridad *f*
foolhardy ['fu:l,hɑ:dɪ] (ADJ) (= *rash*) temerario
foolish ['fu:lɪʃ] (ADJ) **1** (= *unwise, foolhardy*) [*person*] insensato; [*mistake*] estúpido, tonto; [*decision*] imprudente • **he will be remembered as a ~ man** se le recordará como un insensato • **don't be ~** no seas tonto • **I was ~ but I won't resign** hice una tontería pero no voy a dimitir • **it would be ~ to believe him** sería una tontería *or* una estupidez creerle • **don't do anything ~** no hagas ninguna tontería *or* insensatez • **it was ~ of him to do that** fue una tontería por su parte hacer eso • **it would be ~ of him to resign** sería una tontería que dimitiese • **to do something ~** hacer una tontería *or* insensatez • **what a ~ thing to do!** ¡hacer eso fue una tontería!
2 (= *ridiculous, laughable*) [*person, question*] estúpido, tonto • **to feel ~** sentirse ridículo, sentirse idiota • **to look ~** hacer el ridículo, quedar como un idiota* • **to make sb look ~** dejar a algn en ridículo
foolishly ['fu:lɪʃlɪ] (ADV) tontamente, como un tonto • **he saw me standing there, grinning ~ at him** me vio allí de pie, sonriéndole tontamente *or* como un tonto • **to act ~** hacer el tonto • **to behave ~** portarse como un tonto
foolishness ['fu:lɪʃnɪs] (N) insensatez *f*, estupidez *f*
foolproof ['fu:lpru:f] (ADJ) [*mechanism, scheme etc*] infalible
foolscap ['fu:lskæp] (N) papel *m* de tamaño folio
(CPD) ▸ **foolscap envelope** ≈ sobre *m* tamaño folio ▸ **foolscap sheet** ≈ folio *m*
foosball ['fu:sbɔ:l] (N) (*US*) futbolín *m*
foot [fʊt] (N) (PL: **feet**) **1** (*Anat*) pie *m*; [*of animal, chair*] pata *f* • **my feet are aching** me duelen los pies • **to get to one's feet** ponerse de pie, levantarse, pararse (*LAm*) • **lady, my ~!*** ¡dama, ni hablar! • **on ~** a pie, andando, caminando (*LAm*) • **to be on one's feet** estar de pie, estar parado (*LAm*) • **he's on his feet all day long** está trajinando todo el santo día, no descansa en todo el día • **he's on his feet again** ya está recuperado *or* repuesto • **to rise to one's feet** ponerse de pie, levantarse, pararse (*LAm*) • **I've never set ~ there** nunca he estado allí • **to set ~ inside sb's door** poner los pies en la casa de algn, pasar el umbral de algn • **to set ~ on dry land** poner el pie en tierra firme • **it's wet under ~** el suelo está mojado • **to trample sth under ~** pisotear algo • **the children are always under my feet** siempre tengo los niños pegados • **to put one's feet up*** descansar • IDIOMS: • **to put one's best ~ forward** animarse a continuar • **to get cold feet** entrarle miedo a algn • **to get one's ~ in the door** meter el pie en la puerta • **to put one's ~ down** (= *say no*) plantarse; (*Aut*) acelerar • **to drag one's feet** dar largas al asunto, hacerse el roncero • **to fall on one's feet** tener suerte, caer de pie • **to find one's feet** ponerse al corriente • **to have one ~ in the grave** estar con un pie en la sepultura • **to have one's feet on the ground** ser realista • **to put one's ~ in it*** meter la pata* • **to start off on the right ~** entrar con buen pie • **to shoot o.s. in the ~** pegarse un tiro en el pie • **to sit at sb's feet** ser discípulo de algn • **to stand on one's own two feet** volar con sus propias alas • **to sweep a girl off her feet** enamorar perdidamente a una chica • **she never put a ~ wrong** no cometió ningún error • **it all started off on the wrong ~** todo empezó mal
2 [*of mountain, page, stairs, bed*] pie *m* • **at the ~ of the hill** al pie de la colina
3 (= *measure*) pie *m* • **he's six ~** *or* **feet tall** mide seis pies, mide un metro ochenta;
▷ IMPERIAL SYSTEM
(VT) **1** (= *pay*) • IDIOM: • **to ~ the bill (for sth)** pagar (algo), correr con los gastos (de algo)
2 • **to ~ it** (= *walk*) ir andando *or* (*LAm*) caminando; (= *dance*) bailar
(CPD) ▸ **foot brake** (*Aut*) freno *m* de pie ▸ **foot fault** (*Tennis*) falta *f* de saque ▸ **foot passenger** pasajero/a *m/f* de a pie ▸ **foot patrol** patrulla *f* a pie • **to be on ~ patrol** estar patrullando a pie ▸ **foot pump** bomba *f* de pie ▸ **foot rot** uñero *m* ▸ **foot soldier** soldado *mf* de infantería
footage ['fʊtɪdʒ] (N) (*Cine*) metraje *m*; (= *pictures*) imágenes *fpl*, secuencias *fpl*
foot-and-mouth ['fʊtən'maʊθ], **foot-and-mouth disease** (N) fiebre *f* aftosa, glosopeda *f*
football ['fʊtbɔ:l] (N) (*Sport*) fútbol *m*; (= *ball*) balón *m* de fútbol • **to play ~** jugar al fútbol
(CPD) ▸ **football coupon** (*Brit*) boleto *m* de quinielas ▸ **football ground** campo *m* or (*LAm*) cancha *f* de fútbol ▸ **football hooligan** (*Brit*) hooligan *mf* ▸ **football hooliganism** (*Brit*) hooliganismo *m*, violencia *f* en las gradas ▸ **football league** liga *f* de fútbol ▸ **football match** partido *m* de fútbol ▸ **football pitch** (*Brit*) campo *m* de fútbol ▸ **football player** jugador(a) *m/f* de fútbol, futbolista *mf* ▸ **football pools** quinielas *fpl* ▸ **football season** temporada *f* de fútbol ▸ **football supporter** hincha *mf* ▸ **football team** equipo *m* de fútbol
footballer ['fʊtbɔ:ləʳ] (N) (*Brit*) futbolista *mf*
footballing ['fʊtbɔ:lɪŋ] (ADJ) [*career, skills*] futbolístico • **~ countries** países *mpl* en los que se juega al fútbol
footboard ['fʊtbɔ:d] (N) estribo *m*
footbridge ['fʊtbrɪdʒ] (N) puente *m* peatonal
foot-dragging ['fʊtdrægɪŋ] (N) tácticas *f* dilatorias • **foot-dragging over sth** tácticas dilatorias con respecto a algo • **to accuse sb of foot-dragging** acusar a algn de emplear tácticas dilatorias
-footed ['fʊtɪd] (ADJ) (*ending in compounds*) • **four-footed** cuadrúpedo • **light-footed** rápido, veloz
footer ['fʊtəʳ] (N) **1** (*Brit**) fútbol *m*
2 (*Typ, Comput*) pie *m* de página
-footer ['fʊtəʳ] (N) (*ending in compounds*) • **he's a six-footer** mide seis pies, mide un metro ochenta
footfall ['fʊtfɔ:l] (N) paso *m*, pisada *f*
footgear ['fʊtgɪəʳ] (N) calzado *m*
foothills ['fʊthɪlz] (NPL) estribaciones *fpl*
foothold ['fʊthəʊld] (N) asidero *m*, punto *m* de apoyo (*para el pie*) • **to gain a ~** (*fig*) lograr establecerse
footie*, **footy*** ['fʊtɪ] (*Brit*) (N) fútbol *m*
(CPD) [*season, fan, player*] de fútbol
footing ['fʊtɪŋ] (N) **1** (= *foothold*) asidero *m* • **to lose one's ~** perder pie
2 (*fig*) (= *basis*) • **on an equal ~** en pie de igualdad • **to be on a friendly ~ with sb** tener amistad con algn • **to gain a ~** lograr establecerse • **to put a company on a sound financial ~** enderezar la situación económica de una empresa • **on a war ~** en pie de guerra
footle ['fu:tl] (VT) • **to ~ away** malgastar
(VI) (= *waste time*) perder el tiempo; (= *act the fool*) hacer el tonto
footlights ['fʊtlaɪts] (NPL) (*in theatre*) candilejas *fpl*
footling ['fu:tlɪŋ] (ADJ) trivial, insignificante
footlocker ['fʊtlɒkəʳ] (N) (*US*) baúl *m*
footloose ['fʊtlu:s] (ADJ) • **~ and fancy free** libre como el aire
footman ['fʊtmən] (N) (PL: **footmen**) lacayo *m*
footmark ['fʊtmɑ:k] (N) huella *f*, pisada *f*
footnote ['fʊtnəʊt] (N) nota *f* a pie de página
footpath ['fʊtpɑ:θ] (N) (= *track*) sendero *m*, vereda *f*; (= *pavement*) acera *f*, vereda *f* (*And, S. Cone*), andén *m* (*CAm, Col*), banqueta *f* (*Mex*)
footplate ['fʊtpleɪt] (N) (*esp Brit*) plataforma *f* del maquinista
footprint ['fʊtprɪnt] (N) huella *f*, pisada *f*
footrest ['fʊtrest] (N) [*of wheelchair*] reposapiés *m inv*; [*of motorbike*] estribo *m*
Footsie* ['fʊtsɪ] (N) = **Financial Times Stock Exchange Index**
footsie* ['fʊtsɪ] (N) • IDIOM: • **to play ~ with** acariciar con el pie a
footslog* ['fʊtslɒg] (VI) andar, marchar
footslogger* ['fʊtslɒgəʳ] (N) peatón(a) *m/f*; (*Mil*) soldado *mf* de infantería
footsore ['fʊtsɔ:ʳ] (ADJ) • **to be ~** tener los pies cansados y doloridos
footstep ['fʊtstep] (N) paso *m*, pisada *f* • **I can hear ~s on the stairs** oigo pasos *or* pisadas en la escalera • IDIOM: • **to follow in sb's ~s** seguir los pasos de algn
footstool ['fʊtstu:l] (N) escabel *m*
footway ['fʊt,weɪ] (N) acera *f*
footwear ['fʊtweəʳ] (N) calzado *m*
footwork ['fʊtwɜ:k] (N) (*Sport*) juego *m* de piernas; ▷ fancy
footy* ['fʊtɪ] (N) = footie
foozball ['fu:zbɔ:l] (N) (*US*) futbolín *m*
fop [fɒp] (N) petimetre *m*, currutaco *m*
foppish ['fɒpɪʃ] (ADJ) petimetre, litri*
FOR (ABBR) (= **free on rail**) franco en ferrocarril

for [fɔ:ʳ]

PREPOSITION
CONJUNCTION

When **for** *is part of a phrasal verb, eg* **look for**, **make for**, **stand for**, *look up the verb. When it is part of a set combination, eg* **as for**, **a gift for**, **for sale**, **eager for**, *look up the other word.*

PREPOSITION
1 (= *going to*) para • **the train for London** el tren para *or* de Londres • **he left for Rome** salió para Roma • **the ship left for Vigo** el buque partió (con) rumbo a Vigo • **he swam for the shore** fue nadando hacia la playa
2 (= *intended for*) para • **a table for two** una mesa para dos • **a cupboard for toys** un armario para los juguetes • **a cloth for polishing silver** un paño para sacarle brillo a la plata • **it's not for cutting wood** no sirve para cortar madera • **there's a letter for you** hay una carta para ti • **is this for me?** ¿es para mí esto? • **I have news for you** tengo que darte una noticia • **hats for women** sombreros de señora • **clothes for children** ropa infantil • **I decided that it was the job for me** decidí que era el puesto que me convenía • **she decided that hang-gliding was not for her*** decidió que el vuelo con ala delta no era lo suyo
3 (*to express purpose*) para • **he went there for a rest** fue allí para descansar • **we went to**

Tossa for our holidays fuimos a pasar las vacaciones a Tossa, fuimos a Tossa para las vacaciones • **what for?** ¿para qué? • **what's it for?** ¿para qué es *or* sirve? • **what do you want it for?** ¿para qué lo quieres? • **what did you do that for?** ¿por qué hiciste eso?
4 (employment) para • **he works for the government** trabaja para el gobierno • **to write for the papers** escribir para los periódicos
5 (= on behalf of) • **I'll ask him for you** se lo preguntaré de tu parte • **I'll go for you** iré yo en tu lugar • **"I can't iron this shirt" — "don't worry, I'll iron it for you"** —no puedo planchar esta camisa —no te preocupes, yo te la plancho • **"I still haven't booked the ticket" — "I'll do it for you"** —no he reservado el billete todavía —ya lo haré yo • **who is the representative for your group?** ¿quién es el representante de vuestro grupo?
6 (= as in) de • **G for George** G de Gerona
7 (= in exchange for) por • **I'll give you this book for that one** te cambio este libro por ese • **he'll do it for £25** lo hará por 25 libras • **for every one who voted yes, 50 voted no** por cada persona que votó a favor, 50 votaron en contra • **to pay 50 pence for a ticket** pagar 50 peniques por una entrada • **pound for pound, it's cheaper** es más económico de libra en libra • **the government will match each donation pound for pound** el gobierno igualará cada donativo, libra a libra • **I sold it for £5** lo vendí por *or* en 5 libras
8 (= to the value of) • **a cheque for £500** un cheque *or* talón por valor de 500 libras • **how much is the cheque for?** ¿por cuánto es el cheque?
9 (after adjective) **a** (*making comparisons*) para • **he's tall/mature for his age** es alto/maduro para su edad *or* para la edad que tiene • **he's nice for a policeman** para policía es muy simpático • **it's cold for July** para ser julio hace frío • **it's quite good for a six-year-old** está bastante bien para un niño de seis años
b (*specifying*) • **it was too difficult for her** era demasiado difícil para ella, le era demasiado difícil • **it was difficult for him to leave her** le resultó difícil dejarla • **that's easy for you to say** para ti es fácil decirlo, a ti te es fácil decirlo • **they made it very easy for us** nos lo pusieron muy fácil
10 (= in favour of) a favor de • **I'm for the government** yo estoy a favor del gobierno • **I'm for helping him** yo estoy a favor de ayudarle • **anyone for a game of cards?** ¿alguien se apunta a una partida de cartas? • **are you for or against the idea?** ¿estás a favor o en contra de la idea? • **are you for or against us?** ¿estás con nosotros o en contra? • **I'm all for it** estoy completamente a favor • **the campaign for human rights** la campaña pro derechos humanos, la campaña en pro de los derechos humanos • **a collection for the poor** una colecta a beneficio de los pobres
11 (= as, by way of) • **what's for dinner?** ¿qué hay para cenar? • **I had a sandwich for lunch** para almorzar me comí un bocadillo
12 (= because of) por • **it's famous for its cathedral** es famosa por su catedral • **if it weren't for you** si no fuera por ti • **he was sent to prison for fraud** lo mandaron a la cárcel por fraude • **she felt better for losing a bit of weight** se sentía mejor por haber adelgazado un poco • **I couldn't see her for pot plants** no la veía por taparla las plantas • **we chose it for its climate** lo escogimos por el clima • **for fear of being criticized** por miedo a la crítica, por temor a ser criticado • **to shout for joy** gritar de alegría
13 (= in spite of) a pesar de • **for all his wealth** a pesar de su riqueza • **for all that** a pesar de todo • **for all he promised to come, he didn't** a pesar de habérmelo prometido, no vino
14 (in expressions of time) **a** (*future/past duration*)

*When translating **for** and a period of time, it is often unnecessary to translate **for**, as in the examples below where **durante** is optional:*

• **she will be away for a month** estará fuera un mes • **he worked in Spain for two years** trabajó dos años en España • **I'm going for three weeks** me voy tres semanas, estaré allí tres semanas

*Alternatively, translate **for** using **durante**, or, especially when talking about very short periods, **por**. Use **por** also with the verb **ir**, although again it is often optional in this case:*

• **they waited for over two hours** estuvieron esperando durante más de dos horas • **for a moment, he didn't know what to say** por un momento, no supo qué decir • **I'm going to the country for a while** me voy al campo (por) una temporada • **I'm going away for a few days** me voy (por) unos cuantos días • **he won't be back for a couple of hours/days** no regresará hasta dentro de un par de horas/días, tardará un par de horas/días en regresar • **we went to the seaside for the day** fuimos a pasar el día en la playa
b (*with English perfect tenses*)

*Use **hace ... que** and the present to describe actions and states that started in the past and are still going on. Alternatively use the present and **desde hace**. Another option is sometimes **llevar** and the gerund. Don't use the present perfect in Spanish to translate phrases like these, unless they are in the negative.*

• **he has been learning French for two years** hace dos años que estudia francés, estudia francés desde hace dos años, lleva dos años estudiando francés • **it has not rained for 3 weeks** hace 3 semanas que no llueve, no llueve *or* no ha llovido desde hace 3 semanas, lleva 3 semanas sin llover • **I have known her for years** hace años que la conozco, la conozco desde hace años • **I haven't seen her for two years** hace dos años que no la veo, no la he visto desde hace dos años, no la veo desde hace dos años, llevo dos años sin verla

*Notice how the tenses change when talking about something that **had** happened or **had been** happening **for** a time:*

• **he had been learning French for two years** hacía dos años que estudiaba francés, estudiaba francés desde hacía dos años, llevaba dos años estudiando francés • **I hadn't seen her for two years** hacía dos años que no la veía, no la había visto desde hacía dos años, no la veía desde hacía dos años, llevaba dos años sin verla
15 (= by, before) para • **can you do it for tomorrow?** ¿lo puedes hacer para mañana? • **when does he want it for?** ¿para cuándo lo quiere?
16 (= on the occasion of) para • **I'll be home for Christmas** estaré en casa para las Navidades • **he asked his daughter what she would like for her birthday** le preguntó a su hija qué le gustaría para su cumpleaños
17 (= for a distance of) • **there were roadworks for five miles** había obras a lo largo de cinco millas • **we walked for two kilometres** caminamos dos kilómetros • **you can see for miles from the top of the hill** desde lo alto de la colina se puede ver hasta muy lejos
18 (with infinitive clauses) • **for this to be possible ...** para que esto sea posible ... • **it's not for me to tell him what to do** yo no soy quien para decirle *or* no me corresponde a mí decirle lo que tiene que hacer • **it's not for you to blame him** tú no eres quien para culparle • **he brought it for us to see** lo trajo para que lo viéramos • **their one hope is for him to return** su única esperanza es que regrese • **it's bad for you to smoke so much** te perjudica fumar tanto • **it's best for you to go** es mejor que te vayas • **there is still time for you to do it** todavía tienes tiempo para hacerlo
19 (in other expressions) • **what's the German for "hill"?** ¿cómo se dice "colina" en alemán? • **oh for a cup of tea!** ¡lo que daría por una taza de té! • IDIOMS: • **you're for it!*** ¡las vas a pagar!* • **I'll be for it if he catches me here!*** ¡me la voy a cargar si me pilla aquí!* • **there's nothing for it but to jump** no hay más remedio que tirarse; ▸ **example**
CONJUNCTION
(*liter*) pues, puesto que • **she avoided him, for he was rude and uncouth** lo eludía puesto que *or* pues era grosero y ordinario

fora [ˈfɔːrə] (NPL) *of* **forum**
forage [ˈfɒrɪdʒ] (N) (*for cattle*) forraje *m*
(VI) • **they ~d for food in the jungle** se adentraron en la selva en busca de alimento
(CPD) ▸ **forage cap** gorra *f* de campaña
foray [ˈfɒreɪ] (N) (*esp Mil*) incursión *f* (**into** en)
forbad, forbade [fəˈbæd] (PT) *of* **forbid**
forbear [fɔːˈbɛəʳ] (PT: **forbore**, PP: **forborne**)
(VI) contenerse • **to ~ to do sth** abstenerse de hacer algo
forbearance [fɔːˈbɛərəns] (N) paciencia *f*
forbearing [fɔːˈbɛərɪŋ] (ADJ) paciente
forbears [ˈfɔːbɛəz] (NPL) = **forebears**
forbid [fəˈbɪd] (PT: **forbad(e)**, PP: **forbidden**)
(VT) **1** (= *not allow*) prohibir • **such actions are ~den by international law** el derecho internacional prohíbe este tipo de acciones • **to ~ sb alcohol** prohibir el alcohol a algn • **to ~ sb to do sth** • **~ sb from doing sth** prohibir a algn hacer algo, prohibir a algn que haga algo • **I forbade her to see him** le prohibí verlo *or* que lo viera • **I ~ you to go** te prohíbo que vayas • **she was ~den to leave** *or* **from leaving the country** se le prohibió salir del país, le estaba prohibido salir del país • **I ~ you to!** ¡te lo prohíbo!
2 (= *prevent*) impedir • **his pride ~s him from asking for help** • **his pride ~s his asking for help** su orgullo le impide pedir ayuda • **custom ~s any modernization** la tradición impide *or* hace imposible cualquier modernización • **God** *or* **Heaven ~!*** ¡Dios nos libre!, ¡Dios no lo quiera! • **God** *or* **Heaven ~ (that) I should do anything illegal** Dios me libre de hacer nada ilegal • **God** *or* **Heaven ~ that he should come here!** ¡quiera Dios *or* Dios quiera que no venga por aquí!
forbidden [fəˈbɪdn] (PT) *of* **forbid**
(ADJ) **1** (= *not allowed*) [*book, food, love*] prohibido • **to be ~** estar prohibido • **smoking is ~** está prohibido fumar • **abortion is ~ in this country** el aborto es ilegal *or* está prohibido en este país • **to be strictly ~** estar terminantemente prohibido

• **it is ~ to** (*+ infin*) está prohibido (*+ infin*) • **preaching was ~ to women** predicar estaba prohibido para las mujeres, predicar les estaba prohibido a las mujeres
2 (*= out of bounds*) [*area, zone*] prohibido, vedado; [*city*] prohibido • **some cities are ~ to foreigners** a los extranjeros se les prohíbe *or* les está prohibido entrar en algunas ciudades • IDIOM: • **that's ~ territory** eso es tabú
3 (*= taboo*) [*word, feeling*] tabú • **a ~ subject** un (tema) tabú
CPD ▸ **the forbidden city** la ciudad prohibida ▸ **forbidden fruit** fruto *m* prohibido • IDIOM: • **~ fruits are always the sweetest** el fruto prohibido es siempre el más dulce

forbidding [fəˈbɪdɪŋ] ADJ [*person, manner*] severo, intimidante; [*place, building, room*] imponente, intimidante; [*landscape*] inhóspito; [*task*] ingente, arduo

forbore [fɔːˈbɔːʳ] PT *of* **forbear**

forborne [fɔːˈbɔːn] PP *of* **forbear**

force [fɔːs] N **1** (*= strength*) fuerza *f* • **the building took the full ~ of the blast** el edificio recibió toda la fuerza *or* todo el impacto de la explosión • **to do sth by ~** hacer algo por la fuerza • **they removed him from the bar by ~** lo sacaron del bar a la fuerza *or* por la fuerza • **by ~ of arms** por la fuerza de las armas • **by ~ of circumstance(s)** debido a las circunstancias • **by sheer ~** (*physical*) solo a base de fuerza • **by (sheer) ~ of numbers** por pura superioridad numérica • **she tried to convert people by ~ of argument** intentaba convencer a la gente a fuerza de *or* a base de argumentos • **by** *or* **through sheer ~ of personality** a fuerza de *or* a base de puro carácter • **from ~ of habit** por la fuerza de la costumbre • **the ~ of gravity** la fuerza de la gravedad • **the police were out in ~** la policía había salido en masa, había un enorme despliegue policial • **to resort to ~** recurrir a la fuerza • **to use ~** hacer uso de la fuerza; ▹ **brute**
2 (*Met*) • **a ~ five wind** un viento de fuerza cinco
3 (*= influence*) fuerza *f* • **the social and economic ~s that influence our decisions** las fuerzas sociales y económicas que influyen en nuestras decisiones • **he is a powerful ~ in the trade union movement** es una persona con mucho peso dentro del movimiento sindicalista • **the ~s of evil** las fuerzas del mal • **the ~s of nature** las fuerzas de la naturaleza • **Janet is obviously a ~ to be reckoned with** Janet es sin lugar a dudas una persona a (la que hay que) tener en cuenta; ▹ **driving, join, life, market**
4 (*= legitimacy*) fuerza *f* • **the guidelines do not have the ~ of law** las directrices no tienen fuerza de ley • **to be in ~** [*law, tax*] estar vigente *or* en vigor • **a curfew is in ~** se ha impuesto un toque de queda • **to come into ~** entrar en vigor, hacerse vigente
5 (*= body of people*) (*Mil*) fuerza *f* • **allied ~s** fuerzas *fpl* aliadas, ejércitos *mpl* aliados • **sales ~** (*Comm*) personal *m* de ventas • **the ~** (*= police force*) la policía, el cuerpo (de policía) • **the ~s** (*Brit*) (*Mil*) las fuerzas armadas
VT **1** (*= compel*) [*+ person*] obligar, forzar • **she was ~d to the conclusion that ...** se vio obligada *or* forzada a concluir que ... • **to ~ sb to do sth** obligar *or* forzar a algn a hacer algo • **I am ~d to admit that ...** me veo obligado *or* forzado a admitir que ... • **I had to ~ myself to pick it up** tuve que obligarme *or* forzarme a recogerlo del suelo • **I had to ~ myself to stay calm** tuve que obligarme *or* forzarme a permanecer sereno • **to ~ sb into doing sth** obligar *or* forzar a algn a hacer algo • **they ~d me into signing the agreement** me obligaron *or* forzaron a firmar el acuerdo • **to ~ sb into a corner** (*fig*) arrinconar a algn • IDIOM: • **to ~ sb's hand** (*intentionally*) apretar las tuercas *or* las clavijas a algn; (*by circumstances*) no dejar a algn más remedio que actuar
2 (*= impose*) • **to ~ sth on sb** imponer algo a algn • **he ~d his views on them** les impuso su punto de vista • **the decision was ~d on him** la decisión le fue *or* le vino impuesta • **to ~ o.s. on sb: I don't want to ~ myself on you, but ...** no quisiera importunarte (con mi presencia), pero ... • **he ~d himself on one of the girls** (*sexually*) forzó a una de las chicas
3 (*= push, squeeze*) • **he ~d the clothes into the suitcase** metió la ropa en la maleta a la fuerza, embutió la ropa en la maleta • **they ~d their way into the flat** se metieron en el piso a *or* por la fuerza • **the lorry ~d the car off the road** el camión obligó *or* forzó al coche a salirse de la carretera, el camión hizo que el coche se saliera de la carretera • **he was ~d out of office** lo obligaron *or* forzaron a dimitir del cargo • **she ~d her way through the crowd** se abrió paso entre la muchedumbre a *or* por la fuerza • **to ~ a bill through Parliament** hacer que se apruebe un proyecto de ley en el Parlamento
4 (*= break open*) [*+ lock, door*] forzar • **to ~ sth open** [*+ drawer, door, window*] forzar algo
5 (*= exert, strain*) [*+ voice*] forzar • **to ~ the pace** (*lit*) forzar el ritmo *or* la marcha; (*fig*) forzar la marcha de los acontecimientos • **don't ~ the situation** no fuerces la situación
6 (*= produce with effort*) [*+ answer*] forzar • **to ~ a smile** forzar una sonrisa, sonreír de manera forzada
7 (*Hort, Agr*) [*+ vegetable, fruit*] acelerar el crecimiento de
8 (*= obtain by force*) conseguir a *or* por la fuerza • **to ~ a confession from** *or* **out of sb** obtener una confesión de algn a *or* por la fuerza • **we ~d the secret out of him** le sacamos el secreto a *or* por la fuerza • **to ~ a vote on sth** forzar una votación sobre algo
CPD ▸ **force majeure** fuerza *f* mayor

▸ **force back** VT + ADV **1** [*+ crowd, enemy*] obligar a retroceder, hacer retroceder (a la fuerza)
2 [*+ laughter, tears*] contener • **she ~d back her desire to laugh** contuvo las ganas de reírse • **to ~ back one's tears** contener las lágrimas

▸ **force down** VT + ADV **1** [*+ food*] tragarse a la fuerza • **can you ~ a bit more down?** (*hum*) ¿te cabe un poco más?
2 [*+ aeroplane*] obligar a aterrizar
3 [*+ prices*] hacer bajar, hacer que bajen

▸ **force out** VT + ADV **1** [*+ person*] (*from office*) obligar a dejar el cargo
2 [*+ words*] conseguir pronunciar • **he ~d out an apology** con un esfuerzo enorme, pidió perdón

▸ **force up** VT + ADV [*+ prices*] hacer subir, hacer que suban

forced [fɔːst] ADJ **1** (*= obligatory*) [*march*] forzado; [*repatriation*] forzoso; [*marriage*] forzado, por la fuerza
2 (*= from necessity*) [*landing*] forzoso
3 (*= contrived, strained*) [*smile*] forzado • **to sound ~** parecer forzado
4 (*Hort, Agr*) [*vegetable, fruit*] de crecimiento acelerado • **~ lettuces** lechugas *fpl* de crecimiento acelerado
CPD ▸ **forced entry** (*Jur*) allanamiento *m* de morada • **there was no sign of ~ entry** no había señales de que hubieran forzado la entrada ▸ **forced labour** trabajos *mpl* forzados

force-feed [ˈfɔːsfiːd] (PT, PP: **force-fed**) VT alimentar a la fuerza

force-feeding [ˈfɔːs,fiːdɪŋ] N alimentación *f* a la fuerza

forceful [ˈfɔːsfʊl] ADJ [*personality*] enérgico, fuerte; [*argument*] contundente, convincente

forcefully [ˈfɔːsfʊlɪ] ADV [*say, express*] enérgicamente; [*argue*] de forma convincente; [*push, shove*] violentamente • **he condemned the president for not acting more ~** condenó al presidente por no actuar de forma más enérgica *or* contundente • **it ~ struck him that ...** le llamó poderosamente la atención que ...

forcefulness [ˈfɔːsfʊlnɪs] N [*of person*] fortaleza *f*; [*of argument*] contundencia *f*

forcemeat [ˈfɔːsmiːt] N (*Culin*) relleno *m* de carne picada

forceps [ˈfɔːseps] NPL fórceps *m inv*
CPD ▸ **forceps delivery** parto *m* con fórceps

forcible [ˈfɔːsəbl] ADJ **1** (*= done by force*) [*repatriation, deportation*] forzoso
2 (*= effective*) [*argument, style*] contundente • **a ~ reminder of sth** un vivo recordatorio de algo

forcibly [ˈfɔːsəblɪ] ADV **1** (*= by force*) [*remove, restrain, separate*] a la fuerza, por la fuerza
2 (*= effectively*) [*express, argue*] de forma contundente, convincentemente

forcing-house [ˈfɔːsɪŋ,haʊs] N (PL: **forcing-houses** [ˈfɔːsɪŋ,haʊzɪz]) (*Agr etc*) maduradero *m*; (*fig*) *instituto etc donde se llevan a cabo cursos intensivos*

ford [fɔːd] N vado *m*
VT vadear

fordable [ˈfɔːdəbl] ADJ vadeable

fore [fɔːʳ] ADV (*Naut*) • **~ and aft** de proa a popa
ADJ anterior, delantero; (*Naut*) de proa
N • **to come to the ~** empezar a destacar • **to be at the ~** ir delante
EXCL (*Golf*) ¡atención!

forearm [ˈfɔːrɑːm] N (*Anat*) antebrazo *m*

forearmed [fɔːrˈɑːmd] ADJ • IDIOM: • **forewarned is ~** hombre prevenido vale por dos, hombre precavido vale por dos

forebears [ˈfɔːbeəz] NPL antepasados *mpl*

forebode [fɔːˈbəʊd] VT presagiar, anunciar

foreboding [fɔːˈbəʊdɪŋ] N presentimiento *m* • **to have a ~ that ...** presentir que ... • **to have ~s** tener un presentimiento *or* una corazonada

forecast [ˈfɔːkɑːst] (VB: PT, PP: **forecast**) N
1 (*for weather*) pronóstico *m* • **the weather ~** el pronóstico meteorológico *or* del tiempo • **what is the ~ for the weather?** ¿qué tiempo va a hacer?
2 (*= prediction*) previsión *f* • **according to all the ~s** según todas las previsiones
VT (*gen*) pronosticar

forecaster [ˈfɔːkɑːstəʳ] N (*Econ, Pol, Sport*) pronosticador(a) *m/f*; (*Met*) meteorólogo/a *m/f*

forecastle [ˈfəʊksl] N camarote *m* de la tripulación; (*Hist*) castillo *m* de proa

foreclose [fɔːˈkləʊz] (*Jur*) VT [*+ mortgage*] extinguir el derecho de redimir
VI extinguir el derecho de redimir una/la hipoteca

foreclosure [fɔːˈkləʊʒəʳ] N apertura *f* de un juicio hipotecario

forecourt [ˈfɔːkɔːt] (*esp Brit*) N (*gen*) entrada *f*; [*of hotel*] patio *m* (delantero), terraza *f*; [*of petrol station*] patio *m* (delantero)

foredeck [ˈfɔːdek] N [*of ship*] cubierta *f* de proa

foredoomed [fɔːˈduːmd] ADJ (*liter*) • **to be ~ to do sth** estar condenado de antemano a hacer algo

forefathers [ˈfɔː,fɑːðəz] NPL antepasados *mpl*

forefinger [ˈfɔːˌfɪŋgəʳ] N dedo *m* índice, índice *m*

forefoot [ˈfɔːfʊt] N (PL: **forefeet** [ˈfɔːfiːt]) pie *m* delantero, pata *f* delantera

forefront [ˈfɔːfrʌnt] N • **to be in the ~ of** estar en la vanguardia de

foregather [fɔːˈgæðəʳ] VI (*liter*) reunirse

forego [fɔːˈgəʊ] (PT: **forewent**, PP: **foregone**) VT **1** (= *give up*) renunciar a; (= *do without*) pasar sin, privarse de
2 (= *precede*) preceder

foregoing [ˈfɔːgəʊɪŋ] ADJ anterior, precedente

foregone [ˈfɔːgɒn] PP *of* forego
ADJ • **it was a ~ conclusion** era un resultado inevitable

foreground [ˈfɔːgraʊnd] N primer plano *m*, primer término *m* • **in the ~** (*fig*) en primer plano *or* término
VT [+ *object in photo, picture*] traer al primer plano; (*fig*) [+ *issue, problem*] destacar, subrayar
CPD ▸ **foreground processing** tratamiento *m* prioritario

forehand [ˈfɔːhænd] N (*Tennis*) drive *m*

forehead [ˈfɒrɪd] N frente *f*

foreign [ˈfɒrɪn] ADJ **1** (*gen*) [*person, country, language*] extranjero; [*import*] del extranjero; [*debt*] exterior • **this was her first ~ holiday** estas eran sus primeras vacaciones en el extranjero • **her job involves a lot of ~ travel** su trabajo supone que tiene que viajar a menudo por el extranjero • **~ news** noticias *fpl* internacionales
2 (*Pol*) [*minister, ministry*] de asuntos exteriores; [*policy, relations*] exterior
3 (*frm*) (= *extraneous*) [*object, substance*] extraño
4 • **~ to a** (= *uncharacteristic of*) ajeno a, impropio de • **such behaviour was ~ to his nature** este comportamiento era ajeno a *or* impropio de su carácter
b (= *unfamiliar to*) ajeno a • **it's an idea which is completely ~ to them** es una idea que les resulta totalmente ajena
CPD ▸ **foreign affairs** asuntos *mpl* exteriores • **Secretary of State for Foreign Affairs** Secretario/a *m/f* de Estado para Asuntos Exteriores ▸ **foreign affairs correspondent** corresponsal *mf* de asuntos exteriores ▸ **foreign agent** agente *mf* extranjero/a ▸ **foreign aid** (= *aid to other countries*) ayuda *f* al extranjero, ayuda *f* internacional; (= *aid from abroad*) ayuda *f* internacional ▸ **foreign body** (*frm*) cuerpo *m* extraño (*frm*) ▸ **foreign correspondent** corresponsal *mf* en el extranjero ▸ **foreign currency** moneda *f* extranjera ▸ **foreign currency income** ingresos *mpl* de moneda extranjera • **tourism is a major source of our ~ currency income** el turismo es una importante fuente de ingresos de moneda extranjera para nuestro país ▸ **foreign debt** deuda *f* externa *or* exterior ▸ **foreign exchange** (= *currency*) divisas *fpl*; (= *reserves*) reservas *fpl* de divisas; (= *market*) mercado *m* de divisas; (= *system*) cambio *m* de divisas • **tourism is Thailand's biggest earner of ~ exchange** el turismo es la principal fuente de divisas para Tailandia • **on the ~ exchanges** en los mercados de divisas ▸ **foreign exchange dealer** agente *mf* de cambio, operador(a) *m/f* cambiario/a *or* de cambio ▸ **foreign exchange market** mercado *m* de divisas ▸ **foreign exchange rate** tipo *m* de cambio de divisas ▸ **foreign exchange reserves** reservas *fpl* de divisas ▸ **foreign exchange trader** = foreign exchange dealer ▸ **foreign exchange trading** operaciones *fpl* de cambio (de divisas) ▸ **foreign investment** (*from abroad*) inversión *f* extranjera; (*in other countries*) inversión *f* en el extranjero ▸ **the Foreign Legion** la legión extranjera ▸ **Foreign Minister** Ministro/a *m/f* de Asuntos Exteriores ▸ **Foreign Ministry** Ministerio *m* de Asuntos Exteriores ▸ **foreign national** ciudadano/a *m/f* extranjero/a ▸ **the Foreign Office** (*Brit*) el Ministerio de Asuntos Exteriores ▸ **foreign policy** política *f* exterior ▸ **Foreign Secretary** (*Brit*) Ministro/a *m/f* de Asuntos Exteriores ▸ **foreign service** (*US*) servicio *m* exterior ▸ **foreign trade** comercio *m* exterior

foreigner [ˈfɒrɪnəʳ] N extranjero/a *m/f*

foreknowledge [fɔːˈnɒlɪdʒ] N presciencia *f*, conocimiento *m* previo • **to have ~ of sth** saber algo de antemano

foreland [ˈfɔːlənd] N cabo *m*, promontorio *m*

foreleg [ˈfɔːleg] N pata *f* delantera

forelock [ˈfɔːlɒk] N guedeja *f* • IDIOMS: • **to take time by the ~** tomar la ocasión por los pelos • **to tug one's ~ to sb** (*Brit*) (*fig*) doblegarse ante algn

foreman [ˈfɔːmən] N (PL: **foremen**) [*of workers*] capataz *m*; (*Constr*) maestro *m* de obras; (*Jur*) [*of jury*] presidente/a *m/f* del jurado

foremast [ˈfɔːmɑːst] N palo *m* trinquete, trinquete *m*

foremost [ˈfɔːməʊst] ADJ (= *outstanding*) más destacado; (= *main, first*) primero, principal; ▹ **first**

forename [ˈfɔːneɪm] N nombre *m*, nombre *m* de pila

forenoon [ˈfɔːnuːn] N (*esp Scot*) mañana *f*

forensic [fəˈrensɪk] ADJ forense; [*medicine*] legal, forense
CPD ▸ **forensic evidence** pruebas *fpl* forenses • **to be convicted on ~ evidence** ser condenado en base a pruebas forenses ▸ **forensic scientist** científico/a *m/f* forense

forepaw [ˈfɔːpɔː] N [*of cat, lion*] zarpa *f*; [*of dog, wolf*] uña *f*

foreplay [ˈfɔːpleɪ] N caricias *fpl* estimulantes

forequarters [ˈfɔːˌkwɔːtəz] NPL cuartos *mpl* delanteros

forerunner [ˈfɔːˌrʌnəʳ] N precursor(a) *m/f*

foresaid [ˈfɔːsed] ADJ = aforesaid

foresail [ˈfɔːseɪl] N trinquete *m*

foresee [fɔːˈsiː] (PT: **foresaw**, PP: **foreseen**) VT prever

foreseeable [fɔːˈsiːəbl] ADJ [*opportunity*] previsible • **in the ~ future** en un futuro previsible

foreseeably [fɔːˈsiːəblɪ] ADV previsiblemente

foreshadow [fɔːˈʃædəʊ] VT anunciar, presagiar

foreshore [ˈfɔːʃɔːʳ] N playa *f* (*entre pleamar y bajamar*)

foreshorten [fɔːˈʃɔːtn] VT escorzar

foreshortening [fɔːˈʃɔːtnɪŋ] N escorzo *m*

foresight [ˈfɔːsaɪt] N previsión *f* • **to have** *or* **show ~** ser previsor *or* precavido • **he had the ~ to ...** tuvo la precaución de ... • **lack of ~** imprevisión *f*, falta *f* de previsión

foreskin [ˈfɔːskɪn] N (*Anat*) prepucio *m*

forest [ˈfɒrɪst] N (*temperate*) bosque *m*; (*tropical*) selva *f*; ▹ **tree**
CPD ▸ **Forest Enterprise** (*Brit*) *agencia del gobierno británico antiguamente responsable de cuidar de los bosques del país* ▸ **forest fire** incendio *m* forestal ▸ **forest floor** suelo *m* forestal ▸ **forest ranger** guardabosques *mf inv* ▸ **forest track, forest trail** camino *m* forestal

forestall [fɔːˈstɔːl] VT (= *anticipate*) [+ *event, accident*] prevenir; [+ *rival, competitor*] adelantarse a; (*Comm*) acaparar

forestation [ˌfɒrɪˈsteɪʃən] N = afforestation

forested [ˈfɒrɪstɪd] ADJ arbolado, de bosques • **densely** *or* **heavily ~** cubierto de bosques • **only eight per cent of Britain is ~** las áreas forestales de Gran Bretaña se reducen al ocho por ciento del territorio

forester [ˈfɒrɪstəʳ] N (= *expert*) ingeniero/a *m/f* de montes; (= *keeper*) guardabosques *mf inv*

forestry [ˈfɒrɪstrɪ] N silvicultura *f*; (*Univ*) ingeniería *f* forestal
CPD ▸ **Forestry Commission** (*Brit*) ≈ Comisión *f* del Patrimonio Forestal

foretaste [ˈfɔːteɪst] N anticipo *m*, muestra *f*

foretell [fɔːˈtel] (PT, PP: **foretold**) VT (= *predict*) predecir, pronosticar; (= *forebode*) presagiar

forethought [ˈfɔːθɔːt] N previsión *f*

foretold [fɔːˈtəʊld] PT, PP *of* foretell

forever [fərˈevəʳ] ADV **1** (= *eternally*) para siempre • **he's gone ~** se ha ido para siempre
2* (= *incessantly, repeatedly*) constantemente • **she's ~ complaining** se queja constantemente, siempre se está quejando; ▹ **ever**

forewarn [fɔːˈwɔːn] VT avisar, advertir • **to be ~ed** estar prevenido • PROVERB: • **~ed is forearmed** hombre prevenido *or* precavido vale por dos

forewent [fɔːˈwent] PT *of* forego

forewoman [ˈfɔːˌwʊmən] N (PL: **forewomen**) (*Jur*) presidenta *f* del jurado; [*of workers*] capataz *f*, capataza *f*

foreword [ˈfɔːwɜːd] N prefacio *m*, prólogo *m*

forex [ˈfɒreks] N (*Econ*) divisas *fpl*
CPD ▸ **forex market** mercado *m* de divisas

forfeit [ˈfɔːfɪt] N (*in game*) prenda *f*; (= *fine*) multa *f*
VT [+ *one's rights etc*] perder; (*Jur*) decomisar

forfeiture [ˈfɔːfɪtʃəʳ] N pérdida *f*

forgather [fɔːˈgæðəʳ] VI = **foregather**

forgave [fəˈgeɪv] PT *of* forgive

forge [fɔːdʒ] N (= *furnace*) fragua *f*, forja *f*; [*of blacksmith*] herrería *f*; (= *factory*) fundición *f*
VT **1** (*lit, fig*) fraguar, forjar
2 (= *falsify*) [+ *document, painting etc*] falsificar • **she ~d his signature** falsificó su firma • **~d money** moneda *f* falsa
VI • **to ~ ahead** avanzar a grandes pasos • **to ~ ahead of sb** adelantarse a algn

forger [ˈfɔːdʒəʳ] N falsificador(a) *m/f*

forgery [ˈfɔːdʒərɪ] N (= *act, thing*) falsificación *f* • **it's a ~** es falso

forget [fəˈget] (PT: **forgot**, PP: **forgotten**) VT olvidar, olvidarse de • **to ~ to do sth** olvidarse de hacer algo • **I forgot to close the window** me olvidé de *or* se me olvidó cerrar la ventana • **I forgot to tell you why** se me olvidó decirte por qué • **we shouldn't ~ that ...** no debemos olvidar que ... • **never to be forgotten** inolvidable • **~ it!*** (= *don't worry*) ¡no te preocupes!, ¡no importa!; (= *you're welcome*) de nada, no hay de qué; (= *no way*) ¡ni hablar!, ¡ni se te ocurra! • **and don't you ~ it!** ¡y que no se te olvide esto! • **to ~ o.s.** (= *lose self-control*) pasarse, propasarse
VI (*gen*) olvidar; (= *have a bad memory*) tener mala memoria • **I ~** no recuerdo, me he olvidado • **but I forgot** pero se me olvidó • **I'm sorry, I'd completely forgotten!** ¡lo siento, se me había olvidado por completo! • **I forgot all about it** se me olvidó por completo • **if there's no money, you can ~ (all) about the new car** si no hay dinero, puedes olvidarte del nuevo coche • **let's ~**

about it! (*in annoyance*) ¡olvidémoslo!, ¡basta!; (*in forgiveness*) más vale olvidarlo

> **FORGET**
>
> *You can use* **olvidar** *in 3 ways when translating* **to forget**: **olvidar**, **olvidarse de** *or the impersonal* **olvidársele algo a alguien**.
>
> µ *When* **forgetting** *is accidental, the impersonal construction with* **se me, se le** *etc is the commonest option – it emphasizes the involuntary aspect. Here, the object of* **forget** *becomes the subject of* **olvidar**:
>
> **I forgot**
> Se me olvidó
> **I've forgotten what you said this morning**
> Se me ha olvidado lo que dijiste esta mañana
> **He forgot his briefcase**
> Se le olvidó el maletín
>
> **Olvidarse de** *and* **olvidar** *would be more formal alternatives.*
>
> µ *In other contexts, use either* **olvidarse de** *or* **olvidar**:
>
> **Have you forgotten what you promised me?**
> ¿Te has olvidado de *or* Has olvidado lo que me prometiste?
> **In the end he managed to forget her**
> Al final consiguió olvidarse de ella *or* consiguió olvidarla
> **Don't forget me**
> No te olvides de mí, No me olvides
>
> *For further uses and examples, see main entry.*

forgetful [fəˈgetfʊl] ADJ (= *lacking memory*) olvidadizo; (= *absent-minded*) despistado; (= *neglectful*) (*of one's duties etc*) descuidado • **he's terribly ~** es tremendamente despistado, tiene una memoria pésima • **~ of all else** olvidando todo lo demás, sin hacer caso de todo lo demás

forgetfulness [fəˈgetfʊlnɪs] N olvido *m*, falta *f* de memoria; (= *absentmindedness*) despiste *m*; (= *neglect*) descuido *m*

forget-me-not [fəˈgetmɪnɒt] N nomeolvides *m inv*

forgettable [fəˈgetəbl] ADJ poco memorable

forgivable [fəˈgɪvəbl] ADJ perdonable

forgivably [fəˈgɪvəblɪ] ADV comprensiblemente • **he was ~ tense** estaba comprensiblemente tenso • **~, she walked out without answering** es comprensible que se marchara sin responder

forgive [fəˈgɪv] (PT: **forgave**, PP: **forgiven**) VT [+ *person, fault*] perdonar, disculpar (*esp LAm*) • **I ~ you** te perdono • **to ~ sb for doing sth** perdonar a algn por haber hecho algo • **~ me** (= *excuse me*) perdone, con permiso (*LAm*)
VI perdonar • **why don't you just ~ and forget?** intenta perdonar y olvidarte

forgiven [fəˈgɪvn] PP *of* **forgive**

forgiveness [fəˈgɪvnɪs] N (= *pardon*) perdón *m*; (= *willingness to forgive*) compasión *f*

forgiving [fəˈgɪvɪŋ] ADJ [*person, smile*] compasivo • **to feel ~** estar dispuesto a perdonar

forgo [fɔːˈgəʊ] (PT: **forwent**, PP: **forgone** [ˈfɔːgɒn]) VT = **forego**

forgot [fəˈgɒt] PT *of* **forget**

forgotten [fəˈgɒtn] PP *of* **forget**

fork [fɔːk] N (*at table*) tenedor *m*; (*Agr*) horca *f*, horquilla *f*; (*in road*) bifurcación *f*; (*in river*) horcajo *m*; [*of tree*] horcadura *f*
VT (*Agr*) (*also* **fork over**) cargar con la horca
VI [*road*] bifurcarse • **~ right for Oxford** tuerza a la derecha para ir a Oxford
▸ **fork out*** VT + ADV [+ *money, cash*] aflojar*
VI + ADV pagar
▸ **fork over** VT + ADV = **fork**
▸ **fork up** VT + ADV **1** [+ *soil*] remover con la horquilla
2* = **fork out**

forked [fɔːkt] ADJ [*tail*] hendido; [*branch*] bifurcado; [*lightning*] en zigzag; [*tongue*] bífido

forkful [ˈfɔːkfʊl] N pinchada *f* (con el tenedor) • **I put a ~ of steak in my mouth** pinché un trozo de filete y me lo metí en la boca

fork-lift truck [ˈfɔːklɪftˌtrʌk] N carretilla *f* elevadora

forlorn [fəˈlɔːn] ADJ [*person*] triste, melancólico; (= *deserted*) [*cottage*] abandonado; (= *desperate*) [*attempt*] desesperado • **to look ~** tener aspecto triste • **why so ~?** ¿por qué tan triste? • **a ~ hope** una vana esperanza

forlornly [fəˈlɔːnlɪ] ADV tristemente

form [fɔːm] N **1** (= *shape*) forma *f*; (= *figure, shadow*) bulto *m*, silueta *f* • **the same thing in a different ~** lo mismo pero con otra forma • **~ and content** forma *f* y contenido • **in the ~ of** en forma de • **I'm against hunting in any ~** estoy en contra de cualquier forma de caza • **to take ~** concretarse, tomar *or* cobrar forma • **it took the ~ of a cash prize** consistió en un premio en metálico • **what ~ will the ceremony take?** ¿en qué consistirá la ceremonia?
2 (= *kind, type*) clase *f*, tipo *m* • **a new ~ of government** un nuevo sistema de gobierno • **as a ~ of apology** como disculpa
3 (= *way, means*) forma *f* • **in due ~** en la debida forma • **~ of payment** modo *m* de pago • **what's the ~?** ¿qué es lo que hemos de hacer? • **that is common ~** eso es muy corriente
4 (*Sport*) (*also fig*) forma *f* • **to be in good ~** estar en buena forma • **he was in great ~ last night** estaba en plena forma anoche • **to be on ~** estar en forma • **to be out of ~** estar desentrenado • **in top ~** en plena forma • **true to ~** como de costumbre
5 (= *document*) (*gen*) formulario *m*, impreso *m* • **application ~** solicitud *f* • **to fill in** *or* **out a ~** rellenar un formulario *or* un impreso
6 (*Brit*) (*frm*) (= *etiquette*) apariencias *fpl* • **for ~'s sake** por pura fórmula, para guardar las apariencias • **it's bad ~** está mal visto • **it's a matter of ~** es una formalidad
7 (= *bench*) banco *m*
8 (*Brit*) (*Scol*) curso *m*, clase *f* • **she's in the first ~** está haciendo primer curso de secundaria *or* primero de secundaria
9 (*Brit*) (*Racing*) • **to study the ~** estudiar resultados anteriores
VT (= *shape, make*) formar; [+ *clay etc*] modelar, moldear; [+ *company*] formar, fundar; [+ *plan*] elaborar, formular; [+ *sentence*] construir; [+ *queue*] hacer; [+ *idea*] concebir, formular; [+ *opinion*] hacerse, formarse; [+ *habit*] crear • **he ~ed it out of clay** lo modeló *or* moldeó en arcilla • **to ~ a government** formar gobierno • **to ~ a group** formar un grupo • **to ~ part of sth** formar parte de algo
VI tomar forma, formarse • **an idea ~ed in his mind** una idea tomó forma en su mente • **how do ideas ~?** ¿cómo se forman las ideas?
CPD ▸ **form feed** (*Comput*) salto *m* de página ▸ **form letter** (*US*) carta *f* tipo ▸ **form of words** (= *formulation*) formulación *f*
▸ **form up** VT + ADV [+ *troops*] formar
VI + ADV alinearse; (*Mil*) formar

formal [ˈfɔːməl] ADJ [*person*] (= *correct*) correcto; (= *reliable, stiff*) formal; (= *solemn*) [*greeting, language, occasion, announcement*] solemne; [*dress*] de etiqueta; [*visit*] de cumplido; (*Pol*) [*visit*] oficial; [*function*] protocolario; [*garden*] simétrico; (= *official*) [*evidence*] documental; [*acceptance*] por escrito • **in English, "residence" is a ~ term** en inglés, "residence" es un término formal • **don't be so ~!** ¡no te andes con tantos cumplidos! • **there was no ~ agreement** no había un acuerdo en firme • **~ clothes** ropa *f* formal, ropa *f* de etiqueta • **a ~ dinner** una cena de gala • **he has no ~ education** no tiene formación académica • **~ training** formación *f* profesional
CPD ▸ **formal dress** (= *smart clothes*) ropa *f* formal, ropa *f* de etiqueta; (= *evening dress*) traje *m* de noche • **29% of companies now require employees to wear ~ dress at all times** el 29% de las empresas exigen que sus empleados lleven ropa formal en todo momento

formaldehyde [fɔːˈmældɪhaɪd] N formaldehido *m*

formalin, formaline [ˈfɔːməlɪn] N formalina *f*

formalism [ˈfɔːməlɪzəm] N formalismo *m*

formalist [ˈfɔːməlɪst] ADJ formalista
N formalista *mf*

formalistic [fɔːməˈlɪstɪk] ADJ formalista

formality [fɔːˈmælɪtɪ] N **1** [*of occasion*] lo ceremonioso; [*of person*] (= *stiffness*) formalidad *f*; (= *correctness*) corrección *f* • **with all due ~** en la debida forma
2 (= *matter of form*) • **it's a mere ~** no es más que una formalidad • **let's dispense with the formalities** prescindamos de las formalidades
3 formalities (*bureaucratic*) trámites *mpl*, gestiones *fpl* • **first there are certain formalities** primero hay ciertos requisitos

formalization [ˌfɔːməlaɪˈzeɪʃən] N formalización *f*

formalize [ˈfɔːməlaɪz] VT [+ *plan, agreement*] formalizar

formally [ˈfɔːməlɪ] ADV (*gen*) formalmente; (= *officially*) oficialmente; (= *ceremoniously*) con mucha ceremonia; [*dress etc*] de etiqueta; (= *stiffly*) con formalidad

format [ˈfɔːmæt] N formato *m*
VT (*Comput*) formatear
CPD ▸ **format line** (*Comput*) línea *f* de formato

formation [fɔːˈmeɪʃən] N (*gen*) formación *f* • **in battle ~** en formación de combate
CPD ▸ **formation flying** vuelo *m* en formación

formative [ˈfɔːmətɪv] ADJ **1** [*influence etc*] formativo; [*years*] de formación
2 (*Gram*) formativo
N (*Gram*) formativo *m*

formatting [ˈfɔːmætɪŋ] N formateado *m*, formateo *m*

former [ˈfɔːmə^r] ADJ **1** (= *earlier, previous*) antiguo; [*chairman, wife etc*] ex • **a ~ pupil** un antiguo alumno • **in ~ days** antiguamente • **the ~ president** el ex-presidente; ▷ **OLD**
2 (*of two*) primero • **your ~ idea was better** tu primera idea fue mejor
PRON • **night and day, the ~ dark, the latter light** la noche y el día, aquella oscura y este lleno de luz

formerly [ˈfɔːməlɪ] ADV antiguamente

Formica® [fɔːˈmaɪkə] N formica® *f*

formic acid [ˌfɔːmɪkˈæsɪd] N ácido *m* fórmico

formidable [ˈfɔːmɪdəbl] ADJ [*person*]

formidable; [*opponent*] temible; [*task, challenge, obstacle*] tremendo, impresionante; [*reputation, team, combination, talents*] formidable, extraordinario • **he has a ~ temper** tiene un genio tremendo • **she was a ~ woman** era una mujer formidable *or* que imponía
formidably ['fɔːmɪdəblɪ] ADV tremendamente, enormemente
formless ['fɔːmlɪs] ADJ informe
formula ['fɔːmjʊlə] N (PL: **formulas** *or* **formulae** ['fɔːmjʊliː]) **1** (*gen*) (*Math, Chem etc*) fórmula *f* • **winning ~** fórmula *f* del éxito • **peace ~** fórmula *f* de paz
2 (= *baby milk*) leche *f* en polvo (para bebés), leche *f* maternizada
3 (*Motor racing*) fórmula *f* • **Formula One** Fórmula *f* uno • **a ~-one car** un coche de Fórmula uno
formulaic [,fɔːmjʊ'leɪɪk] ADJ formulaico, formulario
formulate ['fɔːmjʊleɪt] VT [+ *theory, policy*] formular
formulation [,fɔːmjʊ'leɪʃən] N (= *act*) [*of idea, theory, policy*] formulación *f*; (= *medicine*) fórmula *f*; (= *form of words*) formulación *f*
fornicate ['fɔːnɪkeɪt] VI (*frm*) fornicar
fornication [,fɔːnɪ'keɪʃən] N (*frm*) fornicación *f*
fornicator ['fɔːnɪkeɪtəʳ] N fornicador(a) *m/f*
forsake [fə'seɪk] (PT: **forsook**, PP: **forsaken**) VT (= *abandon*) abandonar; (= *give up*) [+ *plan*] renunciar a; [+ *belief*] renegar de
forsaken [fə'seɪkən] PP *of* **forsake**
forsook [fə'sʊk] PT *of* **forsake**
forsooth†† [fə'suːθ] ADV en verdad
EXCL • **~!** ¡caramba!
forswear [fɔː'swɛəʳ] (PT: **forswore**, PP: **forsworn**) VT (*frm*) abjurar de, renunciar a • **to ~ o.s.** (= *perjure o.s.*) perjurarse
forsythia [fɔː'saɪθɪə] N forsitia *f*
fort [fɔːt] N (*Mil*) fortaleza *f*, fuerte *m*
• IDIOM: • **to hold the ~** quedarse a cargo • **hold the ~ till I get back** hazte cargo hasta que yo regrese
CPD ▸ **Fort Knox** *lugar donde se guardan las reservas de oro de EE.UU.* • **they've turned their house into Fort Knox** (*fig*) han convertido su casa en un búnker
forte ['fɔːtɪ], (*US*) [fɔːt] N (= *strong point*) fuerte *m*; (*Mus*) forte *m*
forth [fɔːθ]

*When **forth** is an element in a phrasal verb, eg **pour forth, venture forth**, look up the verb.*

ADV **1**† (= *onward*) adelante • **to go ~** marcharse • **from this day ~** de hoy en adelante; ▹ **back**
2 • **and so ~** etcétera, y así sucesivamente
forthcoming [fɔːθ'kʌmɪŋ] ADJ **1** (= *future*) [*event, election*] próximo; [*weeks, months*] venidero; [*book*] de próxima publicación; [*film*] de próximo estreno; [*album*] de próxima aparición • **their ~ marriage** su próximo enlace • **"~ titles"** "libros *mpl* en preparación"
2 (= *available*) • **no explanation was ~** no dieron ninguna explicación • **he shot her a desperate look but no help was ~** le lanzó una mirada de desesperación pero no obtuvo ninguna ayuda • **no answer was ~** no hubo respuesta • **if funds are ~** si nos facilitan fondos
3 (= *open*) [*person*] comunicativo • **he's not ~ with strangers** no es muy comunicativo *or* abierto con los desconocidos • **you could have been more ~ with information** podrías haber sido más generoso con la información • **to be ~ about** *or* **on sth** mostrarse comunicativo con respecto a algo • **he wasn't very ~ about it** dijo poco sobre el asunto, se mostró poco comunicativo al respecto
forthright ['fɔːθraɪt] ADJ [*person, answer etc*] franco, directo
forthwith ['fɔːθ'wɪθ] ADV (*frm*) en el acto, de inmediato
fortieth ['fɔːtɪɪθ] ADJ cuadragésimo • **the ~ anniversary** el cuarenta aniversario
N **1** (*in series*) cuadragésimo/a *m/f*
2 (= *fraction*) cuarentavo *m*, cuadragésima parte *f*; ▹ **fifth**
fortification [,fɔːtɪfɪ'keɪʃən] N (= *act, means of defence*) fortificación *f*
fortify ['fɔːtɪfaɪ] VT **1** (*Mil*) fortificar; (= *strengthen*) fortalecer
2 (*fig*) [+ *person*] fortalecer • **to ~ sb in a belief** confirmar la opinión que tiene algn • **to ~ o.s.** fortalecerse
3 (= *enrich*) [+ *food*] enriquecer; [+ *wine*] encabezar • **fortified wine** vino *m* encabezado
fortissimo [fɔː'tɪsɪməʊ] (*Mus*) ADV fortissimo
ADJ fortissimo
fortitude ['fɔːtɪtjuːd] N fortaleza *f*, valor *m*
fortnight ['fɔːtnaɪt] N (*Brit*) quince días *mpl*, quincena *f* • **a ~ (from) today** de hoy en quince días
fortnightly ['fɔːtnaɪtlɪ] (*Brit*) ADJ quincenal
ADV quincenalmente, cada quince días
FORTRAN ['fɔːtræn] N ABBR (*Comput*) (= **formula translator**) FORTRAN *m*
fortress ['fɔːtrɪs] N fortaleza *f*, plaza *f* fuerte
fortuitous [fɔː'tjuːɪtəs] ADJ fortuito, casual
fortuitously [fɔː'tjuːɪtəslɪ] ADV fortuitamente, por casualidad
fortuitousness [fɔː'tjuːɪtəsnɪs], **fortuity** [fɔː'tjuːɪtɪ] N carácter *m* fortuito
fortunate ['fɔːtʃənɪt] ADJ [*person, occurrence*] afortunado; [*coincidence*] feliz • **those less ~ than ourselves** los menos afortunados • **he is ~ in having no dependents to worry about** tiene suerte de no tener personas a su cargo por las que preocuparse • **I was ~ enough to escape** yo tuve la suerte de poder escaparme • **that was ~ for you** en eso tuviste suerte • **how ~!** ¡qué suerte! • **it was ~ that no one was injured** fue una suerte que nadie resultara herido
fortunately ['fɔːtʃənɪtlɪ] ADV afortunadamente, por suerte
fortune ['fɔːtʃən] N **1** (= *luck*) fortuna *f*, suerte *f* • **by good ~** por fortuna • **we had the good ~ to find him** tuvimos la suerte de encontrarlo • **the ~s of war** las vicisitudes *or* las peripecias de la guerra • **he restored the company's ~s** restableció la prosperidad de la empresa, devolvió el éxito a la compañía • **to seek one's ~ elsewhere** buscar fortuna en otro lugar • **to try one's ~** probar fortuna
2 (= *fate*) suerte *f*, destino *m* • **to tell sb's ~** decir a algn la buenaventura
3 (= *property, wealth*) fortuna *f* • **to come into a ~** heredar una fortuna • **to marry a ~** casarse con un hombre/una mujer acaudalado/a
4 (= *huge amount of money*) dineral *m*, platal *m* (*LAm**) • **to cost a ~** costar un ojo de la cara*, valer un dineral • **to make a ~** enriquecerse, ganar un dineral • **a small ~** un montón de dinero, un dineral
CPD ▸ **fortune cookie** (*esp US*) *galleta china con un mensaje sobre la suerte* ▸ **fortune hunter** cazafortunas *mf inv*
fortune-teller ['fɔːtʃən,teləʳ] N adivino/a *m/f*
fortune-telling ['fɔːtʃən,telɪŋ] N adivinación *f*
forty ['fɔːtɪ] ADJ, PRON cuarenta • IDIOM: • **to have ~ winks*** echar un sueñecito
N (= *numeral*) cuarenta *m* • **the forties** (= 1940s) los años cuarenta • **to be in one's forties** tener más de cuarenta años, ser cuarentón; ▹ **fifty**
fortyish ['fɔːtɪɪʃ] ADJ de unos cuarenta años
forum ['fɔːrəm] N (PL: **forums** *or* **fora** ['fɔːrə]) foro *m*; (*fig*) tribunal *m*, foro *m*
forward ['fɔːwəd]

*When **forward** is an element in a phrasal verb, eg **bring forward, come forward, step forward**, look up the verb.*

ADJ **1** (*in position*) delantero; (*in movement*) hacia adelante; (*in time*) adelantado, avanzado; [*position*] (*Mil etc*) avanzado; (*Naut*) de proa
2 (= *advanced*) [*child*] precoz; [*season, crop*] adelantado
3 (= *presumptuous*) [*person, remark*] atrevido
ADV (*gen*) adelante, hacia adelante; (*Naut*) hacia la proa • **~!** ¡adelante! • **~ march!** (*Mil*) de frente ¡mar! • **the lever is placed well ~** la palanca está colocada bastante hacia adelante • **from that day ~** desde ese día en adelante, a partir de entonces • **from this time ~** de aquí en adelante • **to come ~** hacerse conocer • **to go ~** ir hacia adelante, avanzar; (*fig*) progresar, hacer progresos; ▹ **look forward**
N (*Sport*) delantero/a *m/f*
VT **1** (= *dispatch*) [+ *goods*] expedir, enviar; (= *send on*) [+ *letter*] remitir • **"please ~"** "remítase al destinatario"
2 (= *advance*) [+ *career, cause, interests*] promover
CPD ▸ **forward buying** (*Comm*) compra *f* a término ▸ **forward contract** (*Comm*) contrato *m* a término ▸ **forward delivery** (*Comm*) entrega *f* en fecha futura ▸ **forward exchange** (*Comm*) cambio *m* a término ▸ **forward gear** (*Aut*) marcha *f* de avance ▸ **forward line** (*Sport*) delantera *f*; (*Mil*) primera línea *f* de fuego ▸ **forward market** (*Comm*) mercado *m* de futuros ▸ **forward pass** (*Rugby*) pase *m* adelantado ▸ **forward planning** planificación *f* por anticipado ▸ **forward rate** (*Comm*) tipo *m* a término ▸ **forward sales** (*Comm*) ventas *fpl* a término ▸ **forward slash** barra *f* oblicua
forwarding ['fɔːwədɪŋ] N [*of letter, luggage*] envío *m*
CPD ▸ **forwarding address** destinatario *m* • **she left no ~ address** no dejó dirección (a la que mandarle el correo) ▸ **forwarding agent** agente *mf* de tránsito
forward-looking ['fɔːwəd,lʊkɪŋ] ADJ [*plan, policy*] con miras al futuro; [*person*] previsor; (*Pol*) progresista
forwardness ['fɔːwədnɪs] N **1** (= *boldness*) atrevimiento *m*, frescura *f*, descaro *m*
2 [*of crop etc*] precocidad *f*
forwards ['fɔːwədz] ADV (*esp Brit*) = **forward**
forward-thinking ['fɔːwəd,θɪŋkɪŋ] ADJ de criterio avanzado; (*Pol*) progresista
forwent [fɔː'went] PT *of* **forgo**
Fosbury flop [,fɒzbərɪ'flɒp] N (*Sport*) fosbury-flop *m*
fossil ['fɒsl] N fósil *m*
CPD fósil ▸ **fossil energy** energía *f* fósil ▸ **fossil fuel** hidrocarburo *m*
fossilization [,fɒsɪlaɪ'zeɪʃən] N fosilización *f*
fossilized ['fɒsɪlaɪzd] ADJ fosilizado
foster ['fɒstəʳ] VT **1** [+ *child*] acoger
2 (= *encourage*) fomentar, promover; (= *aid*) favorecer; [+ *hope*] alentar

(CPD) [*parent, child*] de acogida ▸ **foster brother** hermano *m* de leche ▸ **foster home** casa *f* de acogida ▸ **foster mother** madre *f* de acogida; (= *wet nurse*) ama *f* de leche

fosterage ['fɒstərɪdʒ] (N) = **fostering**

fostering ['fɒstərɪŋ] (N) acogimiento *m* familiar

fought [fɔːt] (PT), (PP) *of* **fight**

foul [faʊl] (ADJ) (COMPAR: **fouler**, SUPERL: **foulest**) **1** (= *disgusting*) [*place*] asqueroso; [*smell*] pestilente, fétido; [*taste*] repugnante, asqueroso
2 (= *bad*) [*water*] sucio, contaminado; [*air*] viciado; [*breath*] fétido
3* (= *nasty*) [*weather*] de perros*, malísimo • **it's a ~ day** hace un día de perros*, hace un día malísimo • **I've had a ~ day** he tenido un día malísimo, he tenido un día de perros* • **he was in a ~ mood** estaba de un humor de perros* • **you were ~ to me yesterday** ayer te portaste fatal conmigo* • **she has a ~ temper** tiene muy malas pulgas*, tiene un genio de mil demonios*
4 (= *obscene*) ordinario, grosero • **to use ~ language** decir groserías • IDIOM: • **to have a ~ mouth*** ser mal hablado
5 (= *base, immoral*) [*lie, calumny, crime*] vil, terrible
6 (*Sport*) [*shot, ball*] nulo; [*blow, tackle*] sucio; [*kick*] antirreglamentario
7 (*in phrases*) • **someone is sure to cry ~** es seguro que alguien dice que no hemos jugado limpio • **to fall ~ of sb** ponerse a malas con algn • **to fall ~ of the law** enfrentarse con la justicia, vérselas con la ley*
(N) (*Sport*) falta *f* (**on** contra)
(VT) **1** (= *pollute*) [+ *air*] viciar, contaminar; [+ *water*] contaminar; (= *dirty*) ensuciar • **the dog ~ed the pavement** el perro ensució la acera
2 (*Sport*) [+ *opponent*] cometer una falta contra
3 (= *entangle*) [+ *fishing line, net, rope*] enredar • **something had ~ed the propellers** algo se había enredado en las hélices • **the boat had ~ed her anchor** el ancla del barco se había atascado
4 (= *block*) [+ *pipe*] atascar, obstruir
5 (*Naut*) (= *hit*) chocar contra
(VI) **1** (*Sport*) cometer faltas
2 (= *become entangled*) [*fishing line, rope, nets*] enredarse
(CPD) ▸ **foul play** (*Sport*) jugada *f* antirreglamentaria, juego *m* sucio • **the police suspect ~ play** (*Jur*) la policía sospecha que se trata de un crimen
▸ **foul up*** (VT + ADV) **1** (= *spoil*) [+ *activity, event, plans*] dar al traste con, echar a perder • **it's the little things that can ~ up your plans** los detalles son los que pueden dar al traste con *or* echar a perder los planes de uno
2 (= *make a mess of*) • **he has ~ed up his exams** los exámenes le han ido mal, ha metido la pata en los exámenes*
(VI + ADV) meter la pata*

foulmouthed ['faʊl'maʊðd] (ADJ) malhablado

foul-smelling ['faʊl'smelɪŋ] (ADJ) pestilente, fétido

foul-tasting ['faʊl'teɪstɪŋ] (ADJ) repugnante, desagradable (*al paladar*)

foul-tempered ['faʊl'tempəd] (ADJ) • **to be foul-tempered** (*habitually*) tener un genio de mil demonios*; (*on one occasion*) estar de mal humor, estar de un humor de perros*

foul-up* ['faʊlʌp] (N) desastre *m*

foul-weather gear [ˌfaʊlweðə'gɪəʳ] (N) impermeables *mpl*

found¹ [faʊnd] (PT), (PP) *of* **find**

found² [faʊnd] (VT) [+ *town, school etc*] fundar; [+ *opinion, belief*] fundamentar, basar (on en) • **a statement ~ed on fact** una declaración basada en los hechos

found³ [faʊnd] (VT) (*Tech*) fundir

foundation [faʊn'deɪʃən] (N) **1** (= *act*) fundación *f*, establecimiento *m*
2 (*fig*) (= *basis*) fundamento *m*, base *f* • **the story is without ~** la historia carece de fundamento
3 foundations (*Archit*) cimientos *mpl* • **to lay the ~s** (*also fig*) echar los cimientos (**of** de)
4 (= *organization*) fundación *f*
5 (= *make-up*) maquillaje *m* de fondo, base *f*
(CPD) ▸ **foundation course** curso *m* preparatorio ▸ **foundation cream** crema *f* de base ▸ **foundation garment** corsé *m* ▸ **foundation stone** (*Brit*) primera piedra *f*; (*fig*) piedra *f* angular

founder¹ ['faʊndəʳ] (N) (= *originator*) fundador(a) *m/f*
(CPD) ▸ **founder member** (*Brit*) miembro *mf* fundador(a)

founder² ['faʊndəʳ] (VI) (*Naut*) hundirse, irse a pique; (*fig*) fracasar (**on** debido a)

founding ['faʊndɪŋ] (N) fundación *f*
(CPD) ▸ **founding fathers** fundadores *mpl*, próceres *mpl* (*LAm*) ▸ **Founding Fathers** (*US*) (*Hist*) Padres *mpl* Fundadores

foundling ['faʊndlɪŋ] (N) niño/a *m/f* expósito/a, inclusero/a *m/f*
(CPD) ▸ **foundling hospital** inclusa *f*

foundry ['faʊndrɪ] (N) fundición *f*, fundidora *f* (*LAm*)

fount [faʊnt] (N) **1** (*poet*) (= *source*) fuente *f*, manantial *m* • **~ of knowledge/wisdom** fuente *f* de sabiduría
2 (*Brit*) (*Typ*) fundición *f*

fountain ['faʊntɪn] (N) (*natural*) (*also fig*) fuente *f*, manantial *m*; (*artificial*) fuente *f*, surtidor *m*; (= *jet*) chorro *m* • **drinking ~** fuente *f* (de agua potable)
(CPD) ▸ **fountain pen** estilográfica *f*, plumafuente *f* (*LAm*)

fountainhead ['faʊntɪnhed] (N) fuente *f*, origen *m* • **to go to the ~** acudir a la propia fuente

four [fɔːʳ] (ADJ), (PRON) cuatro; ▹ **corner**
(N) **1** (= *numeral*) cuatro *m* • **to form ~s** formar a cuatro, dividirse en grupos de cuatro • **to make up a ~ for bridge** completar los cuatro para jugar al bridge
2 • **on all ~s** a gatas • **to go on all ~s** ir a gatas; ▹ **five**

four-colour, four-color (*US*) [fɔːˌkʌləʳ] (ADJ) a cuatro colores
(CPD) ▸ **four-colour (printing) process** cuatricromía *f*

four-cycle ['fɔːˌsaɪkl] (ADJ) (*US*) = **four-stroke**

four-door ['fɔː'dɔːʳ] (ADJ) [*car*] de cuatro puertas

four-engined ['fɔːr'endʒɪnd] (ADJ) cuatrimotor, tetramotor
(CPD) ▸ **four-engined plane** cuatrimotor *m*

four-eyes‡ ['fɔːraɪz] (N) cuatrojos* *mf inv*

four-figure [ˌfɔː'fɪgəʳ] (ADJ) [*number*] de cuatro cifras • **four-figure sum** cantidad *f* de 1000 libras o más

fourflusher* ['fɔː'flʌʃəʳ] (N) (*US*) embustero/a *m/f*

fourfold ['fɔːfəʊld] (ADJ) cuádruple
(ADV) cuatro veces

four-footed ['fɔː'fʊtɪd] (ADJ) cuadrúpedo

four-four time [ˌfɔːfɔː'taɪm] (N) (*Mus*) compás *m* de cuatro por cuatro

four-handed [ˌfɔː'hændɪd] (ADJ) (*Cards*) de cuatro jugadores

four-leaf clover [fɔːliːf'kləʊvəʳ] (N) trébol *m* de cuatro hojas

four-legged [ˌfɔː'legɪd] (ADJ) [*animal*] cuadrúpedo • **our four-legged friends** (*hum*) nuestros amigos cuadrúpedos (*hum*)

four-letter word [ˌfɔːletə'wɜːd] (N) palabrota *f*, taco *m*, grosería *f*

four-minute [ˌfɔː'mɪnɪt] (ADJ) • **a four-minute egg** un huevo pasado cuatro minutos • **he was the first to run a four-minute mile** fue el primero en correr una milla en cuatro minutos

four-part ['fɔːpɑːt] (ADJ) [*song*] para cuatro voces • **to sing in four-part harmony** cantar a cuatro voces

four-ply ['fɔːplaɪ] (ADJ) [*wood*] de cuatro capas; [*wool*] de cuatro hebras

four-poster ['fɔːˌpəʊstəʳ] (N) (*also* **four-poster bed**) cama *f* de columnas

fourscore† ['fɔː'skɔː'] (ADJ) ochenta

four-seater [ˌfɔː'siːtəʳ] (N) coche *m* con cuatro asientos

foursome ['fɔːsəm] (N) grupo *m* de cuatro

foursquare ['fɔːskweəʳ] (ADJ) (= *firm*) firme; (= *forthright*) franco, sincero
(ADV) • **to stand ~ behind sb** respaldar completamente a algn

four-star ['fɔːstɑːʳ] (ADJ) [*hotel*] de cuatro estrellas
(CPD) ▸ **four-star petrol** (*Brit*) ≈ gasolina *f* súper

four-stroke ['fɔːstrəʊk] (ADJ) (*Aut*) de cuatro tiempos

fourteen ['fɔː'tiːn] (ADJ), (PRON) catorce
(N) (= *numeral*) catorce *m*; ▹ **five**

fourteenth ['fɔː'tiːnθ] (ADJ) decimocuarto
(N) **1** (*in series*) decimocuarto/a *m/f*
2 (= *fraction*) catorceavo *m*, catorceava parte *f*; ▹ **fifth**

fourth [fɔːθ] (ADJ) cuarto
(N) **1** (*in series*) cuarto/a *m/f* • **the Fourth of July** (*US*) el cuatro de julio
2 (*US*) (= *fraction*) cuarto *m*, cuarta parte *f*
3 (*Aut*) (*also* **fourth gear**) cuarta *f* (velocidad)
4 (*Mus*) cuarta *f*; ▹ **fifth**
(CPD) ▸ **fourth dimension** cuarta dimensión *f* ▸ **the fourth estate** (*hum*) el cuarto poder, la prensa ▸ **fourth form** (*Brit*) cuarto *m* (curso) ▸ **fourth note** (*US*) (*Mus*) cuarta *f* ▸ **Fourth of July** • **the Fourth of July** (= *US Independence Day holiday*) el cuatro de julio ▸ **Fourth of July holiday** • **the Fourth of July holiday** (*in USA*) la fiesta del cuatro de julio ▸ **Fourth of July picnic** (*in USA*) un picnic por el cuatro de julio

FOURTH OF JULY

El 4 de julio, Día de la Independencia (**Independence Day**), es la fiesta nacional más importante de Estados Unidos y se celebra para conmemorar el aniversario de la Declaración de Independencia en 1776. Como una auténtica fiesta de cumpleaños del país, las celebraciones presentan un marcado carácter patriótico y la bandera nacional ondea en las casas de muchos norteamericanos, a la vez que tienen lugar acontecimientos públicos por todo el país, con fuegos artificiales, desfiles y comidas en el campo.

fourth-grader [ˌfɔːθ'greɪdəʳ] (N) (*US*) alumno/a *m/f* de cuarto curso (*de entre 9 y 10 años*)

fourthly ['fɔːθlɪ] (ADV) en cuarto lugar

fourth-rate ['fɔːθ'reɪt] (ADJ) de cuarta categoría

four-wheel drive [ˌfɔːwiːl'draɪv] (N) (= *system*) tracción *f* de cuatro por cuatro, tracción *f* a las cuatro ruedas; (= *car*) todoterreno *m inv*

fowl [faʊl] (N) **1** (= *hens etc*) (*collective n*) aves *fpl* de corral; (= *one bird*) ave *f* de corral; (*served*

as food) ave *f*
2†† *(= bird in general)* ave *f* • **the ~s of the air** las aves
CPD ▸ **fowl pest** peste *f* aviar
fowling-piece ['faʊlɪŋ,pi:s] N escopeta *f*
fox [fɒks] N **1** *(= dog fox)* zorro *m*; *(= female fox)* zorra *f*
2 *(fig) (= cunning person)* zorro *m* • **he's an old fox** es un viejo zorro
VT *(esp Brit) (= deceive)* engañar; *(= puzzle)* dejar perplejo a • **this will fox them** esto les despistará • **you had me completely foxed there** eso me tuvo completamente despistado
CPD ▸ **fox cub** cachorro *m* (de zorro) ▸ **fox fur** piel *f* de zorro ▸ **fox terrier** foxterrier *m*, perro *m* raposero *or* zorrero
foxed [fɒkst] ADJ *[book]* manchado
foxglove ['fɒksglʌv] N dedalera *f*
foxhole ['fɒkshəʊl] N madriguera *f* de zorro; *(Mil)* hoyo *m* de protección
foxhound ['fɒkshaʊnd] N perro *m* raposero
foxhunt ['fɒkshʌnt] N cacería *f* de zorro
foxhunting ['fɒks,hʌntɪŋ] N caza *f* del zorro • **to go ~** ir a cazar zorros
foxtrot ['fɒkstrɒt] N fox *m inv*, foxtrot *m*
foxy ['fɒksɪ] ADJ **1** *(= crafty)* astuto
2 *(esp US*) [woman]* sexy
foyer ['fɔɪeɪ] N vestíbulo *m*
FP ABBR **1** *(US)* (= **fireplug**) boca *f* de incendio
2 *(Brit)* = **former pupil**
FPA N ABBR *(Brit)* = **Family Planning Association**
Fr ABBR *(Rel)* **1** (= **Father**) P., P^{e}.
2 (= **Friar**) Fr.
fr. ABBR (= **franc(s)**) fr(s).
fracas ['frækɑ:] N gresca *f*, reyerta *f*
fracking ['frækɪŋ] N fracking *m*, fractura *f* hidráulica
fractal ['fræktəl] *(Geom)* ADJ fractal
N fractal *m*
CPD ▸ **fractal geometry** geometría *f* fractal
fraction ['frækʃən] N **1** *(Math)* fracción *f*, quebrado *m*
2 *(fig)* pequeña porción *f*, parte *f* muy pequeña • **move it just a ~** muévelo un poquito • **for a ~ of a second** por un instante
fractional ['frækʃənl] ADJ fraccionario; *(fig)* muy pequeño
fractionally ['frækʃnəlɪ] ADV mínimamente
fractious ['frækʃəs] ADJ *(= irritable)* irritable; *(= unruly)* díscolo
fractiousness ['frækʃəsnɪs] N *(= irritability)* irritabilidad *f*; *(= naughtiness)* carácter *m* travieso
fracture ['fræktʃə^{r}] N *(Med) (gen)* fractura *f*
VT fracturar • **to ~ one's arm** fracturarse el brazo
VI fracturarse
fractured ['fræktʃəd] ADJ **1** *[bone]* fracturado • **he suffered a ~ skull** sufrió una fractura de cráneo
2 *[organization, society]* fragmentado
fragile ['frædʒaɪl] ADJ **1** *(= easily broken) [glass, china, object]* frágil • **"fragile, handle with care"** "cuidado, frágil"
2 *(= delicate, fine) [plant, beauty, person]* delicado
3 *(= frail) [person]* débil; *[health]* delicado, precario • **I'm feeling rather ~ this morning** *(esp hum)* me siento un poco pachucho esta mañana*
4 *(= unstable) [peace, democracy, relationship]* precario, frágil • **the ~ state of the economy** el precario *or* frágil estado de la economía
fragility [frə'dʒɪlɪtɪ] N **1** *(= breakable nature) [of object]* fragilidad *f*
2 *(= delicacy, fineness) [of plant, beauty, person]* delicadeza *f*
3 *(= frailty) [of person]* debilidad *f*; *[of health]* precariedad *f*
4 *(= instability) [of relationship]* fragilidad *f*, precariedad *f*
fragment N ['frægmənt] fragmento *m*
VT [fræg'ment] fragmentar
VI [fræg'ment] *[alliance, group]* fragmentarse; *[glass, china]* hacerse añicos
fragmentary [fræg'mentərɪ] ADJ *[evidence, account]* fragmentario
fragmentation [,frægmen'teɪʃən] N fragmentación *f*
CPD ▸ **fragmentation grenade** granada *f* de fragmentación
fragmented [fræg'mentɪd] ADJ fragmentado
fragrance ['freɪgrəns] N *(= smell)* fragancia *f*; *(= perfume)* perfume *m*
fragrant ['freɪgrənt] ADJ fragante, oloroso; *(fig) [memory]* dulce
frail [freɪl] ADJ (COMPAR: **frailer**, SUPERL: **frailest**) *[person]* débil; *[health]* delicado, frágil; *[chair etc]* frágil; *(fig) [hope]* leve; *[relationship]* frágil
frailty ['freɪltɪ] N *[of person]* debilidad *f*; *[of health]* lo delicado, fragilidad *f*; *[of happiness]* lo efímero; *[of character]* flaqueza *f*
frame [freɪm] N **1** *(= framework) [of ship, building etc]* armazón *m or f*, estructura *f*; *[of furniture etc]* armadura *f*; *[of spectacles]* montura *f*; *[of bicycle]* cuadro *m*
2 *(= border) [of picture, window, door]* marco *m*; *(Sew)* tambor *m*, bastidor *m* para bordar
3 *(TV, Video)* cuadro *m*; *(Cine)* fotograma *m*
4 *(= body)* cuerpo *m* • **his large ~** su cuerpo fornido • **her whole ~ was shaken by sobs** todo su cuerpo se estremecía por los sollozos
5 *(fig)* • **~ of mind** estado *m* de ánimo • **when you're in a better ~ of mind** cuando estés de mejor humor • **~ of reference** marco *m* de referencia
VT **1** *[+ photo]* enmarcar, poner un marco a
2 *(= enclose)* enmarcar; *(Phot) [+ subject]* encuadrar • **he appeared ~d in the doorway** apareció en el marco de la puerta • **she was ~d against the sunset** el ocaso le servía de marco, tenía la puesta de sol de fondo
3 *(= formulate) [+ plan etc]* formular, elaborar; *[+ question]* formular; *[+ sentence]* construir
4* *[+ innocent person]* • **to ~ sb** tender una trampa a algn para incriminarlo • **I've been ~d!** ¡me han tendido una trampa!
CPD ▸ **frame house** *(US)* casa *f* de madera ▸ **frame rucksack** mochila *f* con armazón
frameless ['freɪmlɪs] ADJ *[spectacles]* sin montura
framer ['freɪmə^{r}] N *(also* **picture framer***)* fabricante *mf* de marcos
frame-up* ['freɪmʌp] N trampa *f*, montaje *m* (para incriminar a algn) • **it's a frame-up** aquí hay trampa, esto es un montaje
framework ['freɪmwɜ:k] N **1** *(lit)* armazón *m or f*, estructura *f*
2 *(fig) [of essay, society]* marco *m* • **within the ~ of** dentro del marco de
CPD ▸ **framework agreement** *(Ind, Pol)* acuerdo *m* marco
framing ['freɪmɪŋ] N **1** *(also* **picture framing***)* enmarcado *m*
2 *(Art, Phot)* encuadrado *m*
Fran [fræn] N *familiar form of* **Frances**
franc [fræŋk] N franco *m*
France [frɑ:ns] N Francia *f*
Frances ['frɑ:nsɪs] N Francisca
franchise ['fræntʃaɪz] N **1** *(Pol)* sufragio *m*
2 *(Comm)* concesión *f*, franquicia *f*
VT otorgar la concesión de, franquiciar
CPD ▸ **franchise holder** franquiciado/a *m/f*, concesionario/a *m/f*
franchisee [,fræntʃaɪ'zi:] N franquiciado/a *m/f*, concesionario/a *m/f*
franchising ['fræntʃaɪzɪŋ] N franquiciamiento *m*
franchisor [,fræntʃaɪ'zɔ:^{r}] N franquiciador(a) *m/f*, (compañía *f*) concesionaria *f*
Francis ['frɑ:nsɪs] N Francisco
Franciscan [fræn'sɪskən] ADJ franciscano
N franciscano/a *m/f*
francium ['frænsɪəm] N francio *m*
Franco- ['fræŋkəʊ] PREFIX franco- • **Franco-British** franco-británico
franco invoice [,fræŋkəʊ'ɪnvɔɪs] N *(Comm)* factura *f* franca
francophile ['fræŋkəʊfaɪl] N francófilo/a *m/f*
francophobe ['fræŋkəʊfəʊb] N francófobo/a *m/f*
Francophone ['fræŋkəʊfəʊn] N francófono/a *m/f*
frangipane ['frændʒɪpeɪn] N, **frangipani** [,frændʒɪ'pɑ:nɪ] N (PL: **frangipanis, frangipani**) *(= perfume, pastry)* frangipani *m*; *(= shrub)* flor *f* de cebo, frangipani *m* blanco, jazmín *m* de las Antillas
franglais ['frɒŋgleɪ] N *(hum)* franglés *m*
Frank[1] [fræŋk] N *(Hist)* franco/a *m/f*
Frank[2] [fræŋk] N *familiar form of* **Francis**
frank[1] [fræŋk] ADJ (COMPAR: **franker**, SUPERL: **frankest**) franco • **to be ~ (with you)** para serte franco, sinceramente
frank[2] [fræŋk] VT *[+ letter]* franquear
frank[3]* *(US)* [fræŋk] = **frankfurter**
Frankfurt ['fræŋkfɜ:t] N Fráncfort *m*, Frankfurt *m*
frankfurter ['fræŋk,fɜ:tə^{r}] N salchicha *f* de Frankfurt
frankincense ['fræŋkɪnsens] N incienso *m*
franking machine ['fræŋkɪŋmə'ʃi:n] N (máquina *f*) franqueadora *f*
Frankish ['fræŋkɪʃ] ADJ *(Hist)* fráncico
N *(Ling)* fráncico *m*
frankly ['fræŋklɪ] ADV francamente
frankness ['fræŋknɪs] N franqueza *f*, sinceridad *f*
frantic ['fræntɪk] ADJ *[activity, pace]* frenético; *(= desperate) [need, desire, person]* desesperado • **she was ~ with worry** estaba loca de inquietud • **to drive sb ~** sacar a algn de quicio
frantically ['fræntɪkəlɪ] ADV frenéticamente, con frenesí
frape‡ ['freɪp] VT • **to frape sb** *(on social media)* cambiar detalles del perfil personal de alguien sin su permiso
frappé ['fræpeɪ] N frappé *m*
frat* [fræt] N *(US) (Univ)* = **fraternity**
▷ SORORITY/FRATERNITY
fraternal [frə'tɜ:nl] ADJ fraterno
fraternity [frə'tɜ:nɪtɪ] N **1** *(= comradeship)* fraternidad *f*
2 *(US) (Univ)* círculo *m* estudiantil;
▷ SORORITY/FRATERNITY
3 *(= organization)* hermandad *f* • **the criminal ~** el mundo del hampa • **the yachting ~** los aficionados a la vela
fraternization [,frætənaɪ'zeɪʃən] N fraternización *f*
fraternize ['frætənaɪz] VI *(esp Mil)* confraternizar **(with** con)
fratricidal [,frætrɪ'saɪdəl] ADJ *[war, conflict]* fratricida
fratricide ['frætrɪsaɪd] N **1** *(= act)* fratricidio *m*
2 *(= person)* fratricida *mf*
fraud [frɔ:d] N **1** *(Jur)* fraude *m*

2 (= *trickery*) estafa *f*; (= *trick, con*) engaño *m*, timo *m*
3 (= *person*) impostor(a) *m/f*, farsante *mf*
CPD ▸ **fraud squad** brigada *f* de delitos económicos, brigada *f* anticorrupción

fraudster* ['frɔːdstəʳ] N defraudador(a) *m/f*

fraudulence ['frɔːdjʊləns] N fraudulencia *f*, fraude *m*

fraudulent ['frɔːdjʊlənt] ADJ fraudulento
CPD ▸ **fraudulent conversion** (*Jur*) apropiación *f* ilícita

fraudulently ['frɔːdjʊləntlɪ] ADV 1 (= *by deceitful means*) [*obtain*] fraudulentamente
2 (= *falsely*) [*claim, act*] fraudulentamente

fraught [frɔːt] ADJ 1 (= *tense*) tenso • **things got a bit ~** la situación se puso difícil
2 • **to be ~ with** [+ *tension*] estar cargado de; [+ *problems*] estar lleno de • **to be ~ with danger** ser peligrosísimo

fray¹ [freɪ] N (= *fight*) combate *m*, lucha *f* • **to be ready for the ~** (*lit, fig*) estar dispuesto a pelear • **to enter the ~** (*fig*) entrar en acción *or* en liza

fray² [freɪ] VI 1 [*cloth, garment, cuff*] deshilacharse; [*rope*] desgastarse
2 (*fig*) • **tempers ~ed in the discussion that followed** los ánimos se caldearon en la discusión que siguió
VT 1 [+ *cloth, garment, cuff*] deshilachar, raer; [+ *rope*] desgastar
2 [+ *nerves*] crispar • **the constant tapping was beginning to ~ my nerves** el constante repiqueteo me estaba empezando a crispar los nervios

frayed [freɪd] ADJ 1 [*cloth, garment, cuff*] deshilachado, raído; [*rope*] desgastado
2 [*nerves*] crispado • **tempers were getting ~** los ánimos se estaban caldeando, la gente estaba perdiendo la paciencia
3 [*person*] (= *strained*) tenso • **he's beginning to look a bit ~ around the edges** (*fig*) ya se le empiezan a notar los años

frazzle* ['fræzl] N • **it was burned to a ~** quedó carbonizado • **to beat sb to a ~** (*Sport*) dar una soberana paliza a algn* • **to be worn to a ~** estar hecho un trapo *or* migas*
VT (*US*) agotar, rendir

FRB N ABBR (*US*) = **Federal Reserve Bank**

FRCM N ABBR (*Brit*) = **Fellow of the Royal College of Music**

FRCO N ABBR (*Brit*) = **Fellow of the Royal College of Organists**

FRCP N ABBR (*Brit*) = **Fellow of the Royal College of Physicians**

FRCS N ABBR (*Brit*) = **Fellow of the Royal College of Surgeons**

freak [friːk] N 1 (= *person*) monstruo *m*, fenómeno *m*; (= *plant, animal*) monstruo *m*; (= *event*) anomalía *f* • **a ~ of nature** un fenómeno de la naturaleza • **the result was a ~** el resultado fue totalmente anómalo
2* (= *enthusiast*) fanático/a *m/f*, adicto/a *m/f* • **health ~** maniático/a *m/f* en cuestión de salud • **peace ~** fanático/a *m/f* de la paz; ▹ **Jesus**
ADJ (= *abnormal*) [*storm, conditions*] anómalo, anormal; [*victory*] inesperado
VI ‡ = **freak out**
VT ‡ = **freak out**
CPD ▸ **freak show** (*at circus etc*) espectáculo *m* de fenómenos de feria; (*fig*) espectáculo *m* de bichos raros*
▸ **freak out‡** VI + ADV (= *get excited*) flipar‡, alucinar‡; (*on drugs*) viajar‡, flipar‡
VT + ADV (= *frighten*) dejar helado*; ▹ **freak-out**

freaking* ['friːkɪŋ] ADJ (*US*) (*euph*) (= *frigging*) dichoso*

freakish ['friːkɪʃ] ADJ 1 [*appearance*] extravagante; [*result*] inesperado
2 (= *changeable*) [*moods, weather*] variable, caprichoso

freak-out‡ ['friːkaʊt] N desmadre *m*; (= *party*) fiesta *f* loca*; (*on drug*) viaje‡ *m*

freaky* ['friːkɪ] ADJ raro, estrafalario

freckle ['frekl] N peca *f*

freckled ['frekld] ADJ, **freckly** ['freklɪ] ADJ pecoso, lleno de pecas

Fred [fred], **Freddie**, **Freddy** ['fredɪ] N *familiar forms of* **Frederick**

Frederick ['fredrɪk] N Federico

free [friː] ADJ (COMPAR: **freer**, SUPERL: **freest**)
1 (= *at liberty*) libre; (= *untied*) libre, desatado • **to break ~** escaparse • **to get ~** escaparse • **to let sb go ~** dejar a algn en libertad • **to pull sth/sb ~** (*from wreckage*) sacar algo/a algn; (*from tangle*) sacar *or* desenredar algo/a algn • **to set ~** [+ *prisoner*] liberar; [+ *slave*] emancipar, liberar; [+ *animal*] soltar • **the screw had worked itself ~** el tornillo se había aflojado
2 (= *unrestricted*) libre; [*choice, translation*] libre • **the fishing is ~** la pesca está autorizada • **she opened the door with her ~ hand** abrió la puerta con la mano que tenía libre • **to have one's hands ~** (*lit*) tener las manos libres • **~ and easy** (= *carefree*) desenfadado • **"can I borrow your pen?" — "feel ~!"** —¿te puedo coger el bolígrafo? —¡por supuesto! *or* —¡claro que sí! • **feel ~ to ask questions** haced las preguntas que queráis • **feel ~ to help yourself** sírvete con toda libertad • **to be ~ to do sth** ser libre de hacer algo, tener libertad para hacer algo • **he is not ~ to choose** no tiene libertad de elección
• IDIOMS: • **to give ~ rein to** dar rienda suelta a • **to give sb a ~ hand** dar a algn carta blanca • **to have a ~ hand to do sth** tener carta blanca para hacer algo • **as ~ as a bird** *or* **the air** libre como el viento
3 (= *clear, devoid*) • **~ from** *or* **of sth**: • **a world ~ of nuclear weapons** un mundo sin armas nucleares • **the area is ~ of malaria** ya no hay paludismo en la región • **to be ~ from pain** no sufrir *or* padecer dolor • **we are ~ of him at last** por fin nos hemos librado de él • **~ of duty** libre de derechos de aduana
4 (*Pol*) (= *autonomous, independent*) [*country, state*] libre • **~ elections** elecciones *fpl* libres • **the right of a ~ press** la libertad de prensa • **it's a ~ country!*** ¡es una democracia!
5 (= *costing nothing*) [*ticket, delivery*] gratuito, gratis; [*sample, offer, transport, health care*] gratuito • **catalogue ~ on request** solicite nuestro catálogo gratuito • **"admission ~"** "entrada *f* libre" • **~ on board** (*Comm*) franco a bordo • **~ of charge** gratis, gratuito • **to get sth for ~** obtener algo gratis • IDIOMS: • **there's no such thing as a ~ lunch** no te regalan nada • **to get a ~ ride*** aprovecharse de la situación; ▹ **tax-free**
6 (= *not occupied*) [*seat, room, person, moment*] libre; [*post*] vacante; [*premises*] desocupado • **is this seat ~?** ¿está libre este asiento?, ¿está ocupado este asiento? • **are you ~ tomorrow?** ¿estás libre mañana?
7 (= *generous, open*) generoso (**with** con) • **to make ~ with sth** usar algo como si fuera cosa propia • **to be ~ with one's money** no reparar en gastos, ser manirroto* • **he's too ~ with his remarks** tiene una lengua muy suelta
ADV 1 (= *without charge*) • **I got in (for) ~** entré gratis *or* sin pagar • **they'll send it ~ on request** si lo solicita se lo mandarán gratis
2 (= *without restraint*) • **animals run ~ in the park** los animales campan a sus anchas por el parque • **he allowed his imagination to run ~** dio rienda suelta a su imaginación
VT 1 (= *release*) [+ *prisoner, people*] liberar, poner en libertad; (*from wreckage etc*) rescatar; (= *untie*) [+ *person, animal*] desatar, soltar • **to ~ one's hand/arm** soltarse la mano/el brazo • **she ~d herself from his embrace** se desligó de sus brazos
2 (= *make available*) [+ *funds, resources*] hacer disponible, liberar • **this will ~ him to pursue other projects** esto lo dejará libre para dedicarse a otros proyectos, esto le permitirá dedicarse a otros proyectos
3 (= *rid, relieve*) • **to ~ sb from sth** liberar a algn de algo • **to ~ sb from pain** quitar *or* aliviar a algn el dolor • **their aim is to ~ the country of disease** se han propuesto acabar con la enfermedad en el país • **to ~ o.s. from** *or* **of sth** librarse de algo
N • **the land of the ~** el país de la libertad (*Estados Unidos*)
CPD ▸ **free agent** persona *f* independiente • **he's a ~ agent** tiene libertad de acción, es libre de hacer lo que quiere ▸ **free association** (*Psych*) asociación *f* libre *or* de ideas ▸ **Free Church** (*Brit*) Iglesia *f* no conformista ▸ **free clinic** (*US*) (*Med*) dispensario *m* ▸ **free collective bargaining** ≈ negociación *f* colectiva ▸ **free enterprise** libre empresa *f*; ▹ **free-enterprise** ▸ **free fall** caída *f* libre • **to be in ~ fall** [*currency, share prices*] caer en picado *or* (*LAm*) picada • **to go into ~ fall** empezar a caer en picado *or* (*LAm*) picada; ▹ **freefall** ▸ **free flight** vuelo *m* sin motor ▸ **free gift** obsequio *m*, regalo *m* ▸ **free house** (*Brit*) *pub que es libre de vender cualquier marca de cerveza por no estar vinculado a ninguna cervecería en particular* ▸ **free kick** (*Ftbl*) tiro *m* libre ▸ **free labour** trabajadores *mpl* no sindicados ▸ **free love** amor *m* libre ▸ **free market** (*Econ*) mercado *m* libre (**in** de); ▹ **free-market** ▸ **free marketeer** partidario/a *m/f* del libre mercado ▸ **free pass** pase *m* gratuito ▸ **free period** (*Scol*) hora *f* libre ▸ **free port** puerto *m* franco ▸ **free radical** (*Chem*) radical *m* libre ▸ **free running** parkour *m* ▸ **free school** escuela *f* especial libre ▸ **free speech** libertad *f* de expresión ▸ **free spirit** persona *f* libre de convencionalismos ▸ **free trade** libre cambio *m*; ▹ **free-trade** ▸ **free trader** librecambista *mf* ▸ **free verse** verso *m* libre ▸ **free vote** (*Brit*) (*Parl*) voto *m* de confianza (independiente de la línea del partido) ▸ **free will** libre albedrío *m* • **he did it of his own ~ will** lo hizo por voluntad propia ▸ **the free world** el mundo libre, los países libres
▸ **free up** VT + ADV [+ *funds, resources*] hacer disponible, liberar; [+ *staff*] dejar libre

-free [friː] ADJ (*ending in compounds*) • **problem-free** fácil, sin problemas • **lead-free** sin plomo • **a meat-free diet** una dieta alimenticia exenta de carne • **stress-free** sin estrés *or* tensiones

freebase* ['friːbeɪs] (*Drugs*) N crack‡ *m*
VT • **to ~ cocaine** fumar crack
VI fumar crack

freebie* ['friːbɪ] ADJ gratuito
N comida *f*/bebida *f* etc gratuita • **it's a ~** es gratis

freeboard ['friːbɔːd] N (*Naut*) obra *f* muerta

freebooter ['friːbuːtəʳ] N filibustero *m*

free-diving [ˌfriː'daɪvɪŋ] N buceo *m* libre

freedom ['friːdəm] N 1 (*gen*) libertad *f* • **~ of action** libertad *f* de acción • **~ of association** libertad *f* de asociación • **~ of choice** libertad *f* de elección • **~ of information** libertad *f* de información • **Freedom of Information Act** ley *f* del derecho a la información • **~ of the press** libertad *f* de prensa • **~ of speech** libertad *f* de expresión • **~ of worship** libertad *f* de culto • **to give sb the ~ of a city** hacer a algn ciudadano

f

honorífico *or* hijo predilecto de la ciudad
2 *(from care, responsibility etc)* • **they want ~ from government control** no quieren estar sometidos al control del gobierno, quieren estar libres del control del gobierno • **she found her sudden ~ from responsibility exhilarating** viéndose de repente liberada de sus responsabilidades, se sentía eufórica
3 (= *liberation*) liberación *f*
CPD ▸ **freedom fighter** guerrillero/a *m/f* ▸ **freedom of expression** libertad *f* de expresión

FREEDOM OF INFORMATION ACT
El **Freedom of Information Act** o **FOIA** es la ley estadounidense del derecho a la información, que obliga a los organismos federales a proporcionar información sobre sus actividades a cualquiera que lo solicite, lo que resulta muy útil, sobre todo a los periodistas. Esta información debe ser facilitada por el Estado en un plazo de diez días laborables y, en caso de que no se acceda a la solicitud, esta decisión tiene que ser debidamente justificada. Los motivos para retener la información pueden ser varios, entre ellos el que se ponga en peligro la seguridad nacional, se revelen secretos comerciales o que la información afecte a la vida privada de los ciudadanos. Entre otras noticias, el **FOIA** ha hecho posible la publicación de información anteriormente catalogada como secreta sobre asuntos de extrema importancia, como la guerra de Vietnam y las actividades de espionaje ilegal del **FBI**.
El Reino Unido tiene un **freedom of information act** similar.

free-enterprise [,fri:'entəpraɪz] ADJ • **free-enterprise economy** economía *f* de libre empresa
freefall ['fri:fɔ:l] ADJ • **~ parachuting** paracaidismo *m* en caída libre
free-fire zone [,fri:'faɪəzəʊn] N *(Mil) zona militar sin restricciones para el uso de armas de fuego, explosivos etc*
free-floating [,fri:'fləʊtɪŋ] ADJ libre, que flota libremente
Freefone® ['fri:fəʊn] N = **Freephone**
free-for-all* ['fri:fər'ɔ:l] N (= *brawl*) pelea *f*, bronca *f*; (= *argument*) discusión *f* general
free-form ['fri:fɔ:m] ADJ de estilo libre
freegan ['fri:gən] N frigano/a *m/f*
freehand ['fri:hænd] ADJ hecho a pulso
freehold ['fri:həʊld] *(Brit)* ADJ *[property, land]* de pleno dominio
N pleno dominio *m*, propiedad *f* absoluta
freeholder ['fri:,həʊldəʳ] N *(Brit)* titular *mf* del pleno dominio *or* de la propiedad absoluta
freeing ['fri:ɪŋ] N puesta *f* en libertad
freelance ['fri:lɑ:ns] ADJ independiente, por cuenta propia
VI trabajar por cuenta propia
N = **freelancer**
freelancer ['fri:lɑ:nsəʳ] N trabajador(a) *m/f* por cuenta propia
freeload* ['fri:ləʊd] VI gorronear* (**off de**)
freeloader* ['fri:ləʊdəʳ] N gorrón/ona* *m/f*
freely ['fri:lɪ] ADV **1** (= *unrestrictedly*) libremente, con libertad • **they cannot move ~ about the country** no pueden viajar libremente *or* con libertad por el país • **you may come and go ~** puedes ir y venir libremente *or* con toda libertad • **you use that word a little too ~** usas esa palabra con demasiada libertad • **the hens are allowed to roam ~** las gallinas pueden deambular sueltas *or* en libertad • **to be ~ available** ser fácil de conseguir, conseguirse con facilidad
2 (= *openly*) *[speak]* con toda libertad, francamente
3 (= *willingly*) de buen grado • **the contract was ~ entered into** el contrato se firmó de buen grado • **I ~ admit I was wrong** soy el primero en admitir que estaba equivocado
4 (= *generously*) *[give]* generosamente, con liberalidad; *[flow]* copiosamente • **he spent his money ~** gastaba el dinero con liberalidad *or* a manos llenas • **the wine flowed ~** el vino fluía copiosamente
5 (= *loosely*) *[translate]* libremente • **he has ~ adapted the original** ha hecho una adaptación libre del original
freeman ['fri:mən] N (PL: **freemen**) *(Hist)* hombre *m* libre; *[of city]* ciudadano *m* de honor
free-market [,fri:'mɑ:kɪt] ADJ • **free-market economy** economía *f* de libre mercado
freemason ['fri:,meɪsn] N (franc)masón *m*
freemasonry ['fri:,meɪsnrɪ] N masonería *f*, francmasonería *f*; *(fig)* compañerismo *m*, camaradería *f*
Freephone® ['fri:fəʊn] N *(Brit)* *(Telec)* teléfono *m* gratuito
freepost ['fri:,pəʊst] N franqueo *m* pagado
free-range ['fri:reɪndʒ] ADJ *[hen, eggs]* de corral, de granja
CPD ▸ **free-range chicken** pollo *m* de corral, pollo *m* de granja
free-ranging ['fri:'reɪndʒɪŋ] ADJ *[discussion]* sobre temas muy diversos; *[role]* libre, amplio
freesia ['fri:zɪə] N fresia *f*
free-spirited [,fri:'spɪrɪtɪd] ADJ libre de convencionalismos
free-standing ['fri:'stændɪŋ] ADJ independiente
freestyle ['fri:staɪl] N • **100 metres ~** *(Swimming)* 100 metros libres
CPD ▸ **freestyle race** carrera *f* de estilo libre ▸ **freestyle wrestling** lucha *f* libre
freethinker ['fri:'θɪŋkəʳ] N librepensador(a) *m/f*
freethinking ['fri:'θɪŋkɪŋ] ADJ librepensador
N librepensamiento *m*
free-to-air [,fri:tə'ɛəʳ] ADJ *[programme, channel]* en abierto
ADV *[televise]* en abierto
free-trade [,fri:'treɪd] ADJ • **free-trade zone** zona *f* franca
freeware ['fri:wɛəʳ] N *(Comput)* programas *mpl* de dominio público, software *m* gratuito
freeway ['fri:weɪ] N *(US)* autopista *f*
freewheel ['fri:'wi:l] VI (= *coast*) *(on bicycle)* ir (en bicicleta) sin pedalear; *(in car)* ir en punto muerto
N *[of bicycle]* rueda *f* libre
freewheeling ['fri:,wi:lɪŋ] ADJ *[discussion]* desenvuelto; (= *free*) libre, espontáneo; (= *careless*) irresponsable
freezable ['fri:zəbl] ADJ congelable
freeze [fri:z] (PT: **froze**, PP: **frozen**) VT **1** *(lit)* *[+ water]* helar; *[+ food]* congelar
2 *(fig)* *[+ prices, wages, assets]* congelar
VI **1** *(gen)* helarse, congelarse • **it will ~ tonight** esta noche va a caer una helada • **to ~ to death** morirse de frío
2 (= *be motionless*) quedarse inmóvil • **~!** ¡no te muevas! • **the smile froze on his lips** se le heló la sonrisa en los labios
N **1** *(Met)* helada *f*
2 *[of prices, wages etc]* congelación *f*
▸ **freeze out** VT + ADV marginar, excluir
▸ **freeze over** VI + ADV *[lake, river]* helarse; *[windows, windscreen]* cubrirse de escarcha • **the lake has frozen over** el lago está helado
▸ **freeze up** VI + ADV *[handle, pipes]* helarse, congelarse; *[windows]* cubrirse de escarcha
VT + ADV • **we're frozen up at home** en casa se han helado las cañerías
freeze-dried [,fri:z'draɪd] ADJ liofilizado, deshidratado por congelación
freeze-dry [,fri:z'draɪ] VT liofilizar, deshidratar por congelación
freeze-frame ['fri:z,freɪm] N (= *picture*) imagen *f* congelada • **to watch sth in freeze-frame** ver algo imagen por imagen
CPD ▸ **freeze-frame button** botón *m* de congelación de imagen
freezer ['fri:zəʳ] N congelador *m*
CPD ▸ **freezer bag** bolsa *f* de congelación ▸ **freezer compartment** congelador *m* ▸ **freezer container** contenedor *m* para congelación
freeze-up ['fri:zʌp] N helada *f*, ola *f* de frío
freezing ['fri:zɪŋ] ADJ glacial, helado • **I'm ~** estoy helado • **it's ~ in here** aquí se congela uno, aquí hace un frío que pela*
ADV • **it's ~ cold** hace un frío horrible *or* que pela*
N **1** (*also* **freezing point**) punto *m* de congelación • **five degrees below ~** cinco grados bajo cero
2 (= *deep freezing*) (ultra)congelación *f*
3 *(fig)* *[of prices, wages, assets]* congelación *f*
CPD ▸ **freezing fog** niebla *f* helada
freight [freɪt] N (= *goods transported*) flete *m*; (= *load*) carga *f*; (= *goods*) mercancías *fpl*; (= *charge*) flete *m*, gastos *mpl or* costos *mpl* de transporte • **to send sth (by) ~** enviar algo por flete • **~ forward** • **~ collect** *(US)* *(Comm)* flete *m or* porte *m* debido • **~ free** *(Comm)* franco de porte • **~ inward** *(Comm)* flete *m* sobre compras • **~ paid** *(Comm)* porte *m* pagado
VT (= *transport*) *[+ goods]* fletar, transportar
CPD ▸ **freight car** *(US)* vagón *m* de mercancías ▸ **freight charges** gastos *mpl or* costos *mpl* de transporte ▸ **freight forwarder** (agente *mf*) transitario/a *m/f*, agente *mf* expedidor(a) ▸ **freight plane** avión *m* de transporte de mercancías ▸ **freight terminal** terminal *f* de mercancías; *(Aer)* terminal *f* de carga ▸ **freight train** *(US)* tren *m* de mercancías ▸ **freight yard** área *f* de carga
freightage ['freɪtɪdʒ] N flete *m*
freighter ['freɪtəʳ] N **1** *(Naut)* buque *m* de carga, nave *f* de mercancías
2 (= *person: carrier*) transportista *m*; (= *agent*) fletador *m*
freightliner ['freɪt,laɪnəʳ] N tren *m* de mercancías de contenedores
French [frentʃ] ADJ francés; *[ambassador]* de Francia
N **1** *(Ling)* francés *m* • IDIOM: • **pardon my ~*** *(euph)* con perdón (de la expresión)
2 • **the ~** (= *people*) los franceses
CPD ▸ **French bean** *(Brit)* judía *f* verde, ejote *m* *(Mex)*, poroto *m* verde *(Chile)* ▸ **French bread** pan *m* francés ▸ **French chalk** jaboncillo *m*, jabón *m* de sastre ▸ **French doors** *(US)* puertaventana *fsing* ▸ **French dressing** *(Culin)* vinagreta *f* ▸ **French fried potatoes, French fries** patatas *fpl* fritas, papas *fpl* fritas *(LAm)* ▸ **French Guiana** la Guayana Francesa ▸ **French horn** trompa *f* de llaves ▸ **French kiss** beso *m* en la boca (con la lengua); ▹ **French-kiss** ▸ **French leave** despedida *f* a la francesa ▸ **French letter*** condón *m* ▸ **French loaf** barra *f* de pan francés ▸ **French mustard** mostaza *f* francesa ▸ **French pastry** pastelito *m* relleno de nata *or* frutas ▸ **French polish** *(Brit)* laca *f*; ▹ **French-polish** ▸ **the French Riviera** la Riviera francesa ▸ **French stick** = **French**

loaf ▸ **French toast** (*Brit*) (= *toast*) tostada *f*; (= *fried bread in egg*) torrija *f* ▸ **French windows** puertaventana *fsing*

French-Canadian ['frentʃkə'neɪdɪən] ADJ francocanadiense
N **1** (= *person*) francocanadiense *mf*
2 (*Ling*) francés *m* canadiense

Frenchified* ['frentʃɪfaɪd] ADJ afrancesado

French-kiss [ˌfrentʃ'kɪs] VI besarse en la boca (con la lengua)
VT besar en la boca (con la lengua)

Frenchman ['frentʃmən] N (PL: **Frenchmen**) francés *m*

French-polish [ˌfrentʃ'pɒlɪʃ] VT (*Brit*) lacar

French-speaking ['frentʃˌspiːkɪŋ] ADJ francófono, francohablante, de habla francesa

Frenchwoman ['frentʃˌwʊmən] N (PL: **Frenchwomen**) francesa *f*

Frenchy* ['frentʃɪ] N (*pej*) gabacho/a *m/f*, franchute *mf*

frenetic [frɪ'netɪk] ADJ frenético

frenetically [frɪ'netɪkəlɪ] ADV frenéticamente

frenzied ['frenzɪd] ADJ [*effort etc*] frenético; [*crowd etc*] enloquecido

frenzy ['frenzɪ] N frenesí *m*, delirio *m* • **in a ~ of anxiety** enloquecido por la preocupación; ▹ **feeding**

frequency ['friːkwənsɪ] N (*also Elec*) frecuencia *f* • **this is happening with increasing ~** esto está ocurriendo con cada vez mayor frecuencia • **high/low ~** alta/baja frecuencia
CPD ▸ **frequency band** banda *f* de frecuencia ▸ **frequency distribution** (*Statistics*) distribución *f* de frecuencia ▸ **frequency modulation** frecuencia *f* modulada

frequent ADJ ['friːkwənt] frecuente • **his ~ absences from home** sus frecuentes ausencias del hogar • **it's a ~ cause of headaches** es una causa frecuente de los dolores de cabeza • **his demands for money became increasingly ~** pedía dinero con cada vez mayor frecuencia • **they stopped at ~ intervals to rest** paraban con frecuencia para descansar • **Fiona was a ~ visitor there** Fiona solía ir allí con frecuencia
VT [frɪ'kwent] frecuentar
CPD ['friːkwənt] ▸ **frequent flyer** • **to be a ~ flyer** ser un(a) pasajero/a frecuente (*de una compañía aérea*) ▸ **frequent wash shampoo** champú *m* de uso frecuente

frequentative [frɪ'kwentətɪv] (*Gram*) ADJ frecuentativo
N frecuentativo *m*

frequenter [frɪ'kwentəʳ] N frecuentador(a) *m/f* (**of** de)

frequent-flyer programme N programa *m* de fidelización

frequently ['friːkwəntlɪ] ADV con frecuencia, frecuentemente • **all too ~** con demasiada frecuencia
CPD ▸ **frequently asked questions** preguntas *fpl* frecuentes

fresco ['freskəʊ] N (PL: **frescoes** *or* **frescos**) fresco *m*

fresh [freʃ] ADJ (COMPAR: **fresher**, SUPERL: **freshest**) **1** (= *not stale, not preserved*) [*fruit, milk etc*] fresco; [*bread*] recién hecho; [*smell, taste*] a fresco • **I need some ~ air** necesito un poco de aire fresco, necesito salir a respirar aire fresco • **to get some ~ air** tomar el fresco • **to let in some ~ air** dejar que entre un poco de aire • **in the ~ air** al aire libre • IDIOM: • **as ~ as a daisy** fresco como una rosa
2 (= *not salt*) [*water*] dulce
3 (= *cool*) [*breeze*] fresco; [*wind*] fuerte • **it's quite ~ out** hace bastante fresco fuera
4 (= *healthy*) [*face, complexion*] lozano, saludable
5 (= *rested*) [*person*] descansado • **it's better done in the morning when you're ~** se hace mejor por la mañana, cuando estás descansado
6 (= *clean and new*) [*sheet of paper*] en blanco; [*shirt, sheets*] limpio • **to give sth a ~ coat of paint** dar otra mano de pintura a algo • **"~ paint"** (*esp US*) "recién pintado" • **we need some ~ faces** necesitamos ver caras nuevas • **to make a ~ start** volver a empezar, empezar de nuevo
7 (= *further*) [*outbreak, supplies*] nuevo • **he has had a ~ attack** ha sufrido un nuevo ataque
8 (= *recent*) [*footprints, tracks*] reciente • **while it is still ~ in our minds** mientras lo tenemos fresco en la memoria • **I've just made a ~ pot of coffee** acabo de hacer una cafetera de café • **~ from the oven** recién salido del horno • **the vegetables are ~ from the garden** la verdura está recién traída del huerto • **a teacher ~ from college** un profesor recién salido de la universidad • **milk ~ from the cow** leche *f* recién ordeñada
9* (= *cheeky*) [*person*] impertinente, descarado • **to get ~ with sb** (= *be cheeky with*) ponerse impertinente con algn, ponerse chulo con algn*; (= *take liberties with*) propasarse con algn • **don't get ~ with me!** ¡no te pongas impertinente conmigo!, ¡no te pongas chulo conmigo!* • **he got a bit ~ with her** se propasó un poco con ella
ADV • **~ ground black pepper** pimienta *f* negra recién molida • **I picked the beans ~ this morning** acabo de recoger *or* coger las judías esta mañana • **to be ~ out of sth: we're ~ out of pan scrubs** [*shopkeeper*] acabamos de vender los últimos estropajos; se nos han acabado los estropajos; [*householder*] se nos han acabado los estropajos • **this government is ~ out of ideas** a este gobierno se le han agotado las ideas

fresh- [freʃ-] PREFIX • **fresh-cut** recién cortado • **fresh-mown** recién cortado

fresh-air fiend* [ˌfreʃ'ɛəˌfiːnd] N • **he's a fresh-air fiend** siempre quiere estar al aire libre

freshen ['freʃn] VT **1** [+ *air, breath*] refrescar
2 • **let me ~ your drink** déjame que te llene la copa
VI [*wind*] arreciar
▸ **freshen up** VT + ADV (= *wash*) lavar • **to ~ o.s. up** refrescarse, lavarse
VI + ADV (= *wash o.s.*) refrescarse, lavarse

freshener ['freʃnəʳ] N ▹ **air, skin**

fresher* ['freʃəʳ] (*Brit*) (*Univ*) N ▹ **freshman**
CPD ▸ **freshers' week** semana *f* de bienvenida para nuevos universitarios

fresh-faced ['freʃfeɪst] ADJ **1** (= *youthful-looking*) lozano, saludable
2 (= *inexperienced*) sin experiencia, nuevo

freshly ['freʃlɪ] ADV recién • **~ squeezed orange juice** zumo *m* de naranja recién exprimido • **~ painted** recién pintado • **~ baked** recién salido del horno

freshman ['freʃmən] N (PL: **freshmen**) **1** (*Univ*) estudiante *mf* de primer año
2 (*Scol*) (= *beginner*) novato/a *mf*; ▹ GRADE

freshness ['freʃnɪs] N **1** [*of food*] frescura *f*
2 [*of air*] frescor *m*
3 [*of face, complexion*] frescura *f*, lozanía *f*
4 (= *originality, spontaneity*) [*of style*] originalidad *f*, frescura *f*

freshwater ['freʃˌwɔːtəʳ] ADJ de agua dulce
CPD ▸ **freshwater fish** pez *m* de agua dulce

fret¹ [fret] VI (= *worry*) preocuparse, apurarse • **don't ~** no te preocupes, no te apures • **the baby is ~ting for its mother** el niño echa de menos a su madre
VT **1** (= *worry*) preocupar • **to ~ the hours away** pasar las horas consumiéndose de inquietud
2 (= *wear away*) corroer, raer, desgastar
N • **to be in a ~** estar muy inquieto • **to get into a ~** apurarse

fret² [fret] N (*Mus*) traste *m*

fretful ['fretfʊl] ADJ [*child*] inquieto

fretfully ['fretfəlɪ] ADV (*gen*) inquietamente; [*complain*] fastidiosamente

fretfulness ['fretfʊlnɪs] N inquietud *f*

fretsaw ['fretsɔː] N sierra *f* de calar *or* de marquetería

fretwork ['fretwɜːk] N calado *m*

Freudian ['frɔɪdɪən] ADJ freudiano
N freudiano /a *m/f*
CPD ▸ **Freudian slip** lapsus *m inv* linguae

FRG N ABBR (*Hist*) (= **Federal Republic of Germany**) RFA *f*

Fri. ABBR (= **Friday**) vier.

friable ['fraɪəbl] ADJ friable, desmenuzable

friar ['fraɪəʳ] N fraile *m*; (*before name*) fray *m* • **black ~** dominico *m* • **grey ~** franciscano *m* • **white ~** carmelita *m*

friary ['fraɪərɪ] N monasterio *m*

fricassee ['frɪkəsiː] N (*Culin*) estofado *m*

fricative ['frɪkətɪv] ADJ fricativo
N fricativa *f*

friction ['frɪkʃən] N **1** (*Tech*) fricción *f*; (*Med etc*) frote *m*, frotamiento *m*
2 (*fig*) roces *mpl*, fricción *f* (**about, over** por)
CPD ▸ **friction feed** (*on printer*) avance *m* por fricción

Friday ['fraɪdɪ] N viernes *m inv*; ▹ **Tuesday, good**
CPD ▸ **Friday 13th** ≈ martes *m* y trece ▸ **Friday prayers** (*Muslim*) oración *fsing* del viernes

fridge [frɪdʒ] (*esp Brit*) N frigorífico *m*, nevera *f*, refrigerador *m*, refrigeradora *f* (*LAm*), heladera *f* (*S. Cone*)
CPD ▸ **fridge freezer** frigorífico-congelador *m*, combi *m* ▸ **fridge magnet** imán *m* de nevera

fried [fraɪd] ADJ (*Culin*) frito
CPD ▸ **fried egg** huevo *m* frito ▸ **fried fish** pescado *m* frito

friend [frend] N amigo/a *m/f*; (*at school, work etc*) compañero/a *m/f* • **~!** (*Mil*) ¡gente de paz! • **a ~ of mine** un amigo mío • **he's no ~ of mine** no es mi amigo, no es amigo mío • **a ~ of the family** un amigo de la familia • **let's be ~s** hagamos las paces • **to be ~s with sb** ser amigo de algn • **we're the best of ~s** somos muy amigos • **we're just good ~s** somos solo amigos, somos amigos nada más • **a ~ with benefits*** un(a) amigovio/a* • **to make ~s with sb** hacerse amigo de algn, trabar amistad con algn • **he makes ~s easily** hace amigos con facilidad • **he is no ~ to violence** no es partidario de la violencia • **to have a ~ at court** (*fig*) tener enchufe • **the Society of Friends** (*Rel*) los cuáqueros • **Friends of the Earth** Amigos *mpl* de la Tierra • **Friends of the National Theatre** Asociación *f* de Amigos del Teatro Nacional • PROVERB: • **a ~ in need is a ~ indeed** en las malas es cuando se conoce a los amigos
VT (*Internet*) añadir como amigo a

friendless ['frendlɪs] ADJ sin amigos

friendliness ['frendlɪnɪs] N **1** (= *warmth*) cordialidad *f*, simpatía *f*
2 (= *friendship*) cordialidad *f*, amistad *f*

friendly ['frendlɪ] ADJ (COMPAR: **friendlier**, SUPERL: **friendliest**) **1** [*person, dog, cat*] simpático; [*atmosphere, place*] agradable; [*smile, gesture*] simpático, cordial; [*relationship, greeting, tone*] amistoso, cordial

f

• **it was an attempt to establish ~ relations** fue un intento de establecer relaciones amistosas *or* cordiales • **I'm giving you a ~ warning** te estoy advirtiendo como amigo, te estoy dando una advertencia de amigo • **let me give you a piece of ~ advice** déjame que te dé un consejo de amigo • **to become ~ with sb** hacerse amigo de algn, trabar amistad con algn • **we became ~** nos hicimos amigos • **it's nice to see a ~ face** es agradable ver una cara conocida • **to get ~ with sb** hacerse amigo de algn • **we remained on ~ terms after we split up** después de cortar, seguimos siendo amigos • **it's important to keep on ~ terms with them** es importante seguir manteniendo una relación amistosa con ellos • **that wasn't a very ~ thing to do** eso no se hace con los amigos • **to be ~ to sb**: • **they are not very ~ to strangers** no se muestran muy amables con los extraños • **she wasn't very ~ to me** no estuvo demasiado amable conmigo, no se mostró muy amable conmigo • **Yul and Steve were ~ with one another** Yul y Steve eran amigos; ▹ **environmentally**
2 (= *not competitive*) [*match, rivalry, argument*] amistoso
3 (= *not enemy*) [*nation, forces*] amigo
(N) (*also* **friendly match**) (*Ftbl*) partido *m* amistoso
(CPD) ▸ **friendly fire** (*Mil*) fuego *m* amigo
▸ **friendly society** ≈ mutualidad *f*, ≈ mutua *f*, ≈ mutual *f* (*LAm*)

-friendly ['frendlɪ] (ADJ) (*ending in compounds*) • **child-friendly facilities in pubs** instalaciones *fpl* para los niños en los pubs • **dolphin-friendly tuna** *atún pescado sin causar daño a los delfines*; ▹ **environment-friendly, user-friendly** *etc*

friendship ['frendʃɪp] (N) amistad *f*; (*at school, work etc*) compañerismo *m*

frier ['fraɪəʳ] (N) = **fryer**

fries [fraɪz] (NPL) (*esp US*) patatas *fpl* fritas, papas *fpl* fritas (*LAm*)

Friesian ['fri:ʒən] = **Frisian**

Friesland ['fri:zlənd] (N) Frisia *f*

frieze [fri:z] (N) (*Archit*) friso *m*; (= *painting*) fresco *m*

frig** [frɪg] (VI) • **to ~ about** *or* **around** hacer gilipolleces‡, joder**

frigate ['frɪgɪt] (N) (*Naut*) fragata *f*

frigging** ['frɪgɪŋ] (ADJ) • **do I need to do every ~ thing myself!** ¿por qué porras tengo que hacerlo yo todo?* • **it's a ~ nuisance!** ¡es un coñazo!‡
(ADV) • **she's so ~ lazy!** ¡es una vaga de la hostia!‡

fright [fraɪt] (N) **1** (= *sudden fear*) susto *m*, sobresalto *m*; (= *state of alarm*) miedo *m* • **to get a ~** asustarse • **what a ~ you gave me!** ¡qué susto me diste *or* has dado! • **to take ~ (at)** asustarse (de)
2* (= *person*) espantajo *m* • **she looked a ~** iba hecha un espantajo

frighten ['fraɪtn] (VT) asustar • **to be ~ed** tener miedo **(of a)** • **don't be ~ed!** ¡no te asustes! • **she is easily ~ed** se asusta con facilidad, es asustadiza • **to ~ sb into doing sth** convencer a algn con amenazas de que haga algo • **I was ~ed out of my wits** *or* **to death** estaba aterrorizado
▸ **frighten away, frighten off** (VT + ADV) espantar, ahuyentar

frighteners‡ ['fraɪtnəz] (NPL) • **to put the ~ on sb** meter a algn miedo en el cuerpo, ponérselos de corbata a algn*

frightening ['fraɪtnɪŋ] (ADJ) espantoso, aterrador

frighteningly ['fraɪtnɪŋlɪ] (ADV) [*thin*] alarmantemente; [*ugly*] espantosamente; [*expensive, uncertain*] terriblemente

frightful ['fraɪtfʊl] (ADJ) (= *terrible*) [*tragedy, experience, shame*] horroroso; (= *awful*) [*noise, weather*] espantoso

frightfully†* ['fraɪtfəlɪ] (ADV) (*Brit*) terriblemente, tremendamente • **it's ~ hard** es terriblemente difícil • **it's ~ good** es la mar de bueno • **I'm ~ sorry** lo siento muchísimo, lo siento en el alma

frightfulness ['fraɪtfʊlnɪs] (N) horror *m*

frigid ['frɪdʒɪd] (ADJ) **1** (*sexually*) frígido
2 (= *unfriendly*) [*atmosphere, look etc*] frío, glacial

frigidity [frɪ'dʒɪdɪtɪ] (N) **1** (*sexual*) frigidez *f*
2 (= *unfriendliness*) frialdad *f*

frill [frɪl] (N) **1** (*on dress etc*) volante *m*
2 frills (*fig*) adornos *mpl* • **a package holiday without ~s** unas vacaciones organizadas de lo más sencillo *or* sin grandes lujos • **~s and furbelows** encajes *mpl* y puntillas *fpl*

frilly ['frɪlɪ] (ADJ) (COMPAR: **frillier**, SUPERL: **frilliest**) con volantes, con adornos

Fringe [frɪndʒ] (N) (*Brit*) (*Theat*) (*also* **Fringe Festival, Festival Fringe**) *festival alternativo de Edimburgo*; ▹ **EDINBURGH FESTIVAL**

fringe [frɪndʒ] (N) **1** [*of shawl, rug*] (ribete *m* de) flecos *mpl*
2 (*Brit*) [*of hair*] flequillo *m*
3 (*also* **fringes**) [*of forest*] linde *m or f*, lindero *m*; [*of city*] periferia *f* • **on the ~s of the lake** en los bordes del lago • **to live on the ~ of society** vivir al margen de la sociedad
4 (= *group of people*) elementos *mpl* marginales
(CPD) ▸ **fringe benefits** suplementos *mpl*, ventajas *fpl* adicionales ▸ **fringe group** grupo *m* marginal ▸ **fringe meeting** reunión *f* paralela ▸ **fringe organization** organización *f* marginal *or* no oficial
▸ **fringe theatre** (*Brit*) teatro *m* experimental

fringed ['frɪndʒd] (ADJ) [*clothes, curtains, lampshade*] con flecos • **~ with** [+ *trees, plants etc*] bordeado con • **her eyes were large and brown and ~ with incredibly long lashes** sus ojos eran grandes y marrones con unas pestañas increíblemente largas

frippery ['frɪpərɪ] (N) (*esp Brit*) perifollos *mpl*, perejiles *mpl*

Frisbee® ['frɪzbɪ] (N) disco *m* volador

Frisian ['frɪʒən] (ADJ) frisio
(N) **1** (= *person*) frisio/a *m/f*
2 (*Ling*) frisio *m*
(CPD) ▸ **the Frisian Islands** las islas Frisias

frisk [frɪsk] (VT)* (= *search*) cachear, registrar
(VI) (= *frolic*) brincar; [*people*] juguetear; [*animals*] retozar

friskiness ['frɪskɪnɪs] (N) vivacidad *f*

frisky ['frɪskɪ] (ADJ) (COMPAR: **friskier**, SUPERL: **friskiest**) [*person, horse*] juguetón • **he's pretty ~ still** sigue bastante activo

frisson ['fri:sɒn] (N) [*of horror, fear*] repelús *m*; [*of excitement*] escalofrío *m*

fritter¹ ['frɪtəʳ] (N) (*Culin*) buñuelo *m* • **corn ~** arepa *f* (*Col, Ven*)

fritter² ['frɪtəʳ] (VT) (*also* **fritter away**) malgastar, desperdiciar

frivolity [frɪ'vɒlɪtɪ] (N) (*gen*) frivolidad *f*

frivolous ['frɪvələs] (ADJ) frívolo

frivolously ['frɪvələslɪ] (ADV) frívolamente

frizz [frɪz] (N) rizos *mpl* pequeños y muy apretados
(VT) [+ *hair*] rizar con rizos pequeños y muy apretados

frizzle [frɪzl] (N), (VT) = **frizz**

frizzy ['frɪzɪ] (ADJ) (COMPAR: **frizzier**, SUPERL: **frizziest**) [*hair*] ensortijado, crespo • **to go ~** ensortijarse, encresparse

fro [frəʊ] (ADV) • **to and fro** de un lado para otro, de aquí para allá

frock [frɒk] (N) (*woman's*) vestido *m*; [*of monk*] hábito *m*
(CPD) ▸ **frock coat** levita *f*

Frog‡ [frɒg], **Froggy**‡ ['frɒgɪ] (N) (*pej*) gabacho/a *m/f*, franchute *mf*

frog [frɒg] (N) rana *f* • IDIOM: • **to have a ~ in one's throat** tener carraspera
(CPD) ▸ **frogs' legs** (*Culin*) ancas *fpl* de rana

frogging ['frɒgɪŋ] (N) alamares *mpl*

frogman ['frɒgmən] (N) (PL: **frogmen**) hombre rana *m*

frog-march ['frɒgmɑ:tʃ] (VT) • **to frog-march sb in/out** meter/sacar a algn por la fuerza

frogspawn ['frɒgspɔ:n] (N) huevas *fpl* de rana

frolic ['frɒlɪk] (PT, PP: **frolicked**) (N) (= *prank*) travesura *f*; (= *merrymaking*) fiesta *f*, jolgorio *m*
(VI) juguetear, brincar

frolicsome ['frɒlɪksəm] (ADJ) retozón, juguetón; (= *mischievous*) travieso

from [frɒm] (PREP) **1** (*indicating starting place*) de, desde • **where are you ~?** ¿de dónde eres? • **where has he come ~?** ¿de dónde ha venido? • **he comes ~ Segovia** es de Segovia • **he had gone ~ home** se había ido de su casa • **the train ~ Madrid** el tren de Madrid, el tren procedente de Madrid • **~ London to Glasgow** de Londres a Glasgow • **~ house to house** de casa en casa • **~ A to Z** de A a Z, desde A hasta Z
2 (*indicating time*) de, desde • **~ now on** de aquí en adelante • **~ that time** desde aquel momento • **~ one o'clock to** *or* **until two** desde la una hasta las dos • **(as) ~ Friday** a partir del viernes • **~ a child** • **~ childhood** desde niño • **~ time to time** de vez en cuando
3 (*indicating distance*) de, desde • **the hotel is 1km ~ the beach** el hotel está a 1km de la playa • **a long way ~ home** muy lejos de casa • **to be far ~ the truth** estar lejos de la verdad
4 (*indicating sender etc*) de • **a letter ~ my sister** una carta de mi hermana • **a telephone call ~ Mr Smith** una llamada de parte del Sr. Smith • **a message ~ him** un mensaje de parte de él • **tell him ~ me** dile de mi parte
5 (*indicating source*) de • **to drink ~ a stream/~ the bottle** beber de un arroyo/de la botella • **we learned it ~ him** lo aprendimos de él • **we learned it ~ a book** lo aprendimos en un libro • **a quotation ~ Shakespeare** una cita de Shakespeare • **to steal sth ~ sb** robar algo a algn • **to pick sb ~ the crowd** escoger a algn de la multitud • **I'll buy it ~ you** te lo compraré • **where did you get that ~?** ¿de dónde has sacado *or* sacaste eso? • **take the gun ~ him!** ¡quítale el revólver! • **one of the best performances we have seen ~ him** uno de los mejores papeles que le hayamos visto • **painted ~ life** pintado del natural
6 (*indicating price, number etc*) desde, a partir de • **we have shirts ~ £8 (upwards)** tenemos camisas desde *or* a partir de 8 libras • **prices range ~ £10 to £50** los precios varían entre 10 y 50 libras • **there were ~ 10 to 15 people there** había allí entre 10 y 15 personas
7 (*indicating change*) • **things went ~ bad to worse** las cosas fueron de mal en peor • **the interest rate increased ~ 6% to 10%** la tasa de interés ha subido del 6 al 10 por ciento • **he went ~ office boy to director in five years** pasó de ser recadero a director en cinco años
8 (*indicating difference*) • **to be different ~ sb** ser distinto de algn • **he can't tell red ~ green** no distingue entre rojo y verde • **to know good ~ bad** saber distinguir entre el

bien y el mal, saber distinguir el bien del mal
9 (= *because of, on the basis of*) por • **to act ~ conviction** obrar por convicción • **~ sheer necessity** por pura necesidad • **weak ~ hunger** debilitado por el hambre • **~ what I can see** por lo que veo • **~ what he says** por lo que dice, según lo que dice • **~ experience** por experiencia • **to die ~ exposure** morir de frío
10 (= *away from*) • **to shelter ~ the rain** protegerse de la lluvia • **to escape ~ sth/sb** escapar de algo/algn • **to prevent sb ~ doing sth** impedir a algn hacer algo
11 (*with prep, adv*) • **~ above** desde arriba • **~ afar** desde lejos • **~ among the crowd** de entre la multitud • **~ beneath** *or* **underneath** desde abajo • **~ inside/outside the house** desde dentro/fuera de la casa

fromage frais [ˈfrɒmɑːʒˈfreɪ] (N) *queso fresco descremado*

frond [frɒnd] (N) fronda *f*

front [frʌnt] (N) **1** (= *exterior*) [*of house, building*] fachada *f*; [*of shirt, dress*] pechera *f*; [*of book*] (= *cover*) portada *f* • **it fastens at the ~** se abrocha por delante • **back to ~** al revés • **her dress had ripped down the ~** el vestido se le había roto por delante • **you've spilled food all down your ~** te has derramado comida por toda la pechera
2 (= *forepart*) [*of stage, desk, building*] parte *f* de delante, parte *f* delantera; [*of train, bus*] parte *f* delantera; [*of queue*] principio *m* • **there's a dedication at the ~ of the book** hay una dedicatoria al principio del libro • **there are still some seats left at the ~** todavía quedan asientos delante • **he sat at the ~ of the train** se sentó en la parte delantera del tren • **he sat at the ~ of the class** se sentó en la primera fila de la clase • **at the ~ of the line** *or* **queue** al principio de la cola • **I want to sit in the ~** quiero sentarme delante • **he laid the baby on its ~** puso al bebé boca abajo • **the car's out ~** (*US*) el coche está delante *or* enfrente de la casa
3 • **in ~** delante • **to send sb on in ~** enviar a algn por delante • **the car in ~** el coche de delante • **to be in ~** (*gen*) ir primero, ir delante; (*in race*) ir a la cabeza, llevar la delantera; (*in scoring*) llevar (la) ventaja • **in ~ of** delante de • **don't argue in ~ of the children** no discutas delante de los niños • **a car was parked in ~ of the house** había un coche aparcado delante de la casa • **she sat down in ~ of her mirror** se sentó delante del espejo, se sentó frente al espejo
4 (*Met*) frente *m* • **cold/warm ~** (*Met*) frente *m* frío/cálido
5 (*Mil, Pol*) frente *m* • **he fought at the ~ during the War** luchó en el frente durante la guerra • **we must present a united ~** debemos parecer un frente unido
6 (*Brit*) (= *promenade*) paseo *m* marítimo; (= *beach*) playa *f*
7 (= *area of activity*) materia *f* • **is there any news on the wages ~?** ¿se sabe algo nuevo en materia de salarios? • **we have made progress on a variety of ~s** hemos avanzado en varios campos *or* varias esferas • **on all ~s** en todos los frentes • **the government's failings on the home** *or* **domestic ~** las deficiencias del gobierno a nivel nacional
8 (= *show*) • **it's all just a ~ with him** lo suyo no es más que una fachada *or* no son más que apariencias • **he kept up a brave ~ to the world** delante de todos ponía buena cara
9* (= *cover-up*) fachada *f*, tapadera *f* • **to be a ~ for sth** servir de fachada *or* tapadera para algo
(ADJ) **1** (= *foremost*) [*wheel, leg*] delantero, de delante, de adelante (*LAm*) • **I was in the ~ seat** yo estaba en el asiento delantero *or* de delante *or* (*LAm*) de adelante • **if we run, we can get a ~ seat** si corremos, podemos pillar un asiento en la parte delantera *or* la parte de delante *or* (*LAm*) la parte de adelante • **he's in the ~ garden** está en el jardín de delante de la casa
2 (*Phon*) [*vowel*] frontal
(VI) **1** • **to ~ onto sth** [*house, window*] dar a algo
2 • **to ~ for sth** servir de fachada *or* tapadera para algo
(VT) **1** (= *head*) [+ *organization*] estar al frente de, liderar
2 [+ *TV show*] presentar
3 [+ *band, group*] estar al frente de, ser el cantante de
4 (*frm*) (= *face*) dar a • **the house ~s the river** la casa da al río
(CPD) ▸ **front benches** (*Brit*) • **the ~ benches** (= *seats*) *la primera fila de escaños de cada lado del parlamento ocupada por miembros del gobierno y de la oposición*; (= *people*) *miembros del gobierno o de la oposición* ▸ **front crawl** (*Swimming*) crol *m* ▸ **front desk** (*US*) recepción *f* (*de un hotel*) ▸ **front door** puerta *f* principal ▸ **front end** [*of vehicle*] parte *f* delantera ▸ **front line** (*Mil*) primera línea *f* ▸ **front man** (*for activity*) testaferro *m*; [*of band, group*] líder *m*; (*TV*) presentador *m* ▸ **front organization** organización *f* fachada ▸ **front page** (*Press*) primera plana *f* ▸ **front room** (*Brit*) (= *living room*) salón *m* ▸ **front row** primera fila *f* ▸ **front runner** (*in race*) corredor(a) *m/f* que va en cabeza; (*in election*) favorito/a *m/f* ▸ **front tooth** incisivo *m*, paleta* *f* ▸ **front view** • **the ~ view of the hotel is very impressive** el frente del hotel *or* la parte de delante del hotel es impresionante

> **FRONT BENCH**
> El término genérico **front bench** se usa para referirse a los escaños situados en primera fila a ambos lados del Presidente (**Speaker**) de la Cámara de los Comunes del Parlamento británico. Dichos escaños son ocupados por los parlamentarios que son miembros del gobierno a un lado y por los del gobierno en la sombra (**shadow cabinet**) al otro y, por esta razón, se les conoce como **frontbenchers**.
> ▷ **BACKBENCHER**

frontage [ˈfrʌntɪdʒ] (N) [*of building*] fachada *f*

frontal [ˈfrʌntl] (ADJ) (*Anat*) frontal; [*attack*] de frente, frontal

frontbencher [ˌfrʌntˈbentʃəʳ] (N) (*Brit*) (*Parl*) *diputado con cargo oficial en el gobierno o la oposición*; ▷ **FRONT BENCH**

front-end [ˈfrʌntend] (ADJ) • **front-end costs** gastos *mpl* iniciales • **front-end processor** procesador *m* frontal

front-fastening bra [ˈfrʌntˌfɑːsnɪŋˈbrɑː] (N) sujetador *m* con cierre delantero

frontier [ˈfrʌntɪəʳ] (N) (= *border, also fig*) frontera *f*; (= *dividing line*) línea *f* divisoria • **to push back the ~s of knowledge** ensanchar *or* ampliar los límites del conocimiento
(CPD) fronterizo ▸ **frontier dispute** conflicto *m* fronterizo ▸ **frontier post** puesto *m* fronterizo; ▷ **post** ▸ **frontier technology** tecnología *f* de vanguardia

frontiersman [frʌnˈtɪəzmən] (N) (PL: **frontiersmen**) hombre *m* de la frontera

frontispiece [ˈfrʌntɪspiːs] (N) [*of book*] frontispicio *m*

front-line [ˈfrʌntlaɪn] (ADJ) [*troops, news*] de primera línea; [*countries, areas*] fronterizo a una zona en guerra

front-loader [ˌfrʌntˈləʊdəʳ] (N) (*also* **front-loading washing machine**) lavadora *f* de carga frontal

front-loading [ˌfrʌntˈləʊdɪŋ] (ADJ) de carga frontal
(CPD) ▸ **front-loading washing machine** lavadora *f* de carga frontal

front-page [ˌfrʌntˈpeɪdʒ] (ADJ) de primera página, de primera plana
(CPD) ▸ **front-page news** noticias *fpl* de primera plana

frontward [ˈfrʌntwəd] (ADV) de frente, con la parte delantera primero

frontwards [ˈfrʌntwədz] (ADV) (*esp Brit*) = **frontward**

front-wheel drive [ˌfrʌntwiːlˈdraɪv] (N) tracción *f* delantera

frosh* [frɒʃ] (N) (*US*) (*Univ*) estudiante *mf* de primer año; (*Scol*) novato/a *m/f*

frost [frɒst] (N) (= *substance*) escarcha *f*; (= *weather*) helada *f* • **four degrees of ~** (*Brit*) cuatro grados bajo cero
(VT) **1** • **the grass was ~ed over** el césped apareció cubierto de escarcha
2 (*esp US*) (*Culin*) escarchar
(VI) • **to ~ over** *or* **up** cubrirse de escarcha, escarcharse

frostbelt [frɒstbelt] (N) (*US*) (*Geog*) *estados del norte de Estados Unidos caracterizados por su clima frío*; ▷ **SUNBELT**

frostbite [ˈfrɒstbaɪt] (N) congelación *f*

frostbitten [ˈfrɒstˌbɪtn] (ADJ) congelado

frostbound [ˈfrɒstbaʊnd] (ADJ) [*field, land*] helado; [*road*] bloqueado por la helada; [*village*] aislado por la helada

frosted [ˈfrɒstɪd] (ADJ) (*esp US*) [*cake*] escarchado
(CPD) ▸ **frosted glass** vidrio *m* *or* cristal *m* esmerilado

frostily [ˈfrɒstɪlɪ] (ADV) (*fig*) glacialmente

frostiness [ˈfrɒstɪnɪs] (N) [*of smile, manner*] frialdad *f* • **there was a certain ~ in his smile** había una cierta frialdad en su sonrisa

frosting [ˈfrɒstɪŋ] (N) (*esp US*) (= *icing*) escarcha *f*

frosty [ˈfrɒstɪ] (ADJ) (COMPAR: **frostier**, SUPERL: **frostiest**) **1** [*weather*] de helada; [*surface*] escarchado • **on a ~ morning** una mañana de helada • **it was ~ last night** anoche cayó una helada *or* heló
2 (*fig*) [*smile*] glacial

froth [frɒθ] (N) **1** (= *foam*) espuma *f*
2 (*fig*) (= *frivolous talk*) naderías *fpl*, banalidades *fpl*
(VI) hacer espuma; (*at the mouth*) echar espumarajos

frothy [ˈfrɒθɪ] (ADJ) (COMPAR: **frothier**, SUPERL: **frothiest**) **1** (= *foamy*) espumoso
2 (*fig*) banal, superficial

frown [fraʊn] (N) ceño *m* • **he said with a ~** dijo frunciendo el ceño *or* entrecejo
(VI) fruncir el ceño, fruncir el entrecejo • **to ~ at** mirar con el ceño fruncido
▸ **frown on, frown upon** (VI + PREP) (*fig*) desaprobar

frowning [ˈfraʊnɪŋ] (ADJ) (*fig*) ceñudo, amenazador, severo

frowsy, frowzy [ˈfraʊzɪ] (ADJ) (= *dirty*) sucio; (= *untidy*) desaliñado; (= *smelly*) fétido, maloliente; (= *neglected*) descuidado

froze [frəʊz] (PT) *of* **freeze**

frozen [ˈfrəʊzn] (PP) *of* **freeze**
(ADJ) **1** [*food*] congelado
2 • **we're simply ~** estamos totalmente helados • **I'm ~ stiff** estoy helado, estoy muerto de frío
(CPD) ▸ **frozen assets** (*Econ*) activo *msing* congelado ▸ **frozen food compartment** compartimento *m* de congelación

FRS (N ABBR) **1** (*Brit*) = **Fellow of the Royal Society**

2 (US) (= **Federal Reserve System**) *banco central de los EE.UU.*

Frs (ABBR) (*Rel*) (= **Fathers**) PP

fructify ['frʌktɪfaɪ] (VI) (*frm*) fructificar

fructose ['frʊktəʊs] (N) fructosa *f*

frugal ['fru:gəl] (ADJ) frugal

frugality [fru:'gælɪtɪ] (N) frugalidad *f*

frugally ['fru:gəlɪ] (ADV) [*give out*] en pequeñas cantidades; [*live*] económicamente, sencillamente

fruit [fru:t] (N) **1** (*also Bot*) fruto *m*; (= *piece of fruit*) fruta *f* • **would you like some ~?** ¿quieres fruta? • **to be in ~** [*tree, bush*] haber dado *or* echado fruto, tener fruta • **the ~s of the sea** los productos del mar • **to bear ~** (*lit, fig*) dar fruto

2 fruits (*fig*) (= *benefits*) • **the ~s of one's labour** los frutos del trabajo • **to enjoy the ~s of one's success** disfrutar de los frutos del éxito

3 (US‡) (*pej*) (= *male homosexual*) maricón* *m*

4†* (*as term of address*) • **hello, old ~!** ¡hola, compadre!*

(VI) dar fruto

(CPD) ▸ **fruit basket** frutero *m*, canasto *m* de la fruta ▸ **fruit bowl** frutero *m* ▸ **fruit cocktail** macedonia *f* de frutas ▸ **fruit cup** ≈ sangría *f* ▸ **fruit dish** frutero *m* ▸ **fruit drink** bebida *f* de frutas ▸ **fruit drop** bombón *m* de fruta ▸ **fruit farm** granja *f* frutícola *or* hortofrutícola ▸ **fruit farmer** fruticultor(a) *m/f*, granjero/a *m/f* frutícola *or* hortofrutícola ▸ **fruit farming** fruticultura *f* ▸ **fruit fly** mosca *f* de la fruta ▸ **fruit grower** fruticultor(a) *m/f*, granjero/a *m/f* frutícola *or* hortofrutícola ▸ **fruit growing** fruticultura *f* ▸ **fruit gum** (*Brit*) gominola *f* ▸ **fruit juice** zumo *m or* jugo *m* de frutas ▸ **fruit knife** cuchillo *m* de la fruta ▸ **fruit machine** (*Brit*) máquina *f* tragaperras ▸ **fruit salad** macedonia *f* de frutas ▸ **fruit salts** sal *f* de fruta(s) ▸ **fruit shop** frutería *f* ▸ **fruit stall** puesto *m* de frutas ▸ **fruit tree** árbol *m* frutal

fruitcake ['fru:tkeɪk] (N) **1** (*Culin*) tarta *f* de frutas

2‡ (= *eccentric person*) chiflado/a* *m/f* • IDIOM: • **he's as nutty as a ~** está más loco que una cabra*, está loco de atar*

fruiterer ['fru:tərəʳ] (N) (*Brit*) frutero/a *m/f* • **~'s (shop)** frutería *f*

fruitful ['fru:tfʊl] (ADJ) **1** (*gen*) fructífero; [*land*] fértil

2 (*fig*) productivo, provechoso

fruitfully ['fru:tfəlɪ] (ADV) (*fig*) provechosamente, fructíferamente

fruitfulness ['fru:tfʊlnɪs] (N) **1** [*of soil*] fertilidad *f*, productividad *f*; [*of plant*] fertilidad *f*, fecundidad *f*

2 (*fig*) [*of discussion etc*] utilidad *f*

fruition [fru:'ɪʃən] (N) [*of plan etc*] cumplimiento *m* • **to bring to ~** realizar • **to come to ~** [*hope*] cumplirse; [*plan*] realizarse, dar resultado

fruitless ['fru:tlɪs] (ADJ) (*fig*) infructuoso, inútil

fruitlessly ['fru:tlɪslɪ] (ADV) infructuosamente, sin resultado

fruity ['fru:tɪ] (ADJ) (COMPAR: **fruitier**, SUPERL: **fruitiest**) **1** [*taste*] a fruta; [*wine*] afrutado

2 [*voice*] pastoso

3 (*Brit**) (= *lewd*) [*joke*] verde; [*style*] picante

frump [frʌmp] (N) espantajo *m*, birria *f*

frumpish ['frʌmpɪʃ] (ADJ) desaliñado

frumpy ['frʌmpɪ] (ADJ) (COMPAR: **frumpier**, SUPERL: **frumpiest**) = **frumpish**

frustrate [frʌs'treɪt] (VT) [+ *plan, effort, person*] frustrar; [+ *hope*] defraudar • **to feel ~d** sentirse frustrado • **he's a ~d artist** es un artista frustrado

frustrating [frʌs'treɪtɪŋ] (ADJ) frustrante • **how ~!** ¡qué frustrante!

frustratingly [frʌs'treɪtɪŋlɪ] (ADV) [*slow, complex*] frustrantemente

frustration [frʌs'treɪʃən] (N) (*gen*) frustración *f*; (= *disappointment*) decepción *f*; (= *annoyance*) molestia *f*

fry¹ [fraɪ] (VT) (*Culin*) freír

(VI) freírse

(N) fritada *f*

fry² [fraɪ] (N) (*Fishing*) pececillos *mpl*; ▹ **small**

fryer ['fraɪəʳ] (N) **1** (= *pan*) sartén *f* (*m in LAm*) • **deep-fat ~** freidora *f*

2 (= *person*) empleado/a *m/f* de una freiduría

frying ['fraɪɪŋ] (N) • **there was a smell of ~** olía a frito

(CPD) ▸ **frying pan** sartén *f* (*m in LAm*) • IDIOM: • **to jump out of the ~ pan into the fire** salir de Guatemala para entrar en Guatepeor

frypan ['fraɪpæn] (N) (US) sartén *f* (*m in LAm*)

fry-up ['fraɪʌp] (N) (*Brit*) fritura *f*

FSA (N ABBR) (*Brit*) (*Econ*) (= **Financial Services Authority**) *organismo de control financiero en el Reino Unido*

FSLIC (N ABBR) (US) = **Federal Savings and Loan Insurance Corporation**

FT (N ABBR) (*Brit*) = **Financial Times**

ft (ABBR) = **foot, feet**

F/T (ABBR) (US) = **full-time**

FTC (N ABBR) (US) = **Federal Trade Commission**

FTP, ftp (N ABBR) (*Comput*) = **file transfer protocol** • **anonymous ftp** ftp anónimo

FTSE 100 Index [,fʊtsɪwʌn,hʌndred'ɪndeks] (N ABBR) (*Brit*) (*St Ex*) = **Financial Times Stock Exchange 100 Index**

fuchsia ['fju:ʃə] (N) fucsia *f*

fuck** [fʌk] (N) **1** • **to have a ~** echar un polvo**, joder** • **she's a good ~!** tiene un buen polvo**

2 (US) (= *stupid person*) • **you dumb ~!** ¡tonto de los cojones!**

3 • **like ~ he will!** ¡y un huevo!**, ¡por los cojones!** • **~ knows!** ¡qué coño sé yo!**

(VT) **1** (*lit*) joder**, tirarse**, follarse (*Sp***), coger (*LAm***)

2 • **~ (it)!** ¡joder!**, ¡carajo! (*LAm***), ¡chinga tu madre! (*Mex***) • **~ you!** ¡que te den por culo!**, ¡jódete!**, ¡tu madre! (*LAm***) • **~ this car!** ¡este jodido coche!**, ¡este coche del carajo! (*LAm***), ¡fregado coche! (*LAm***), ¡chingado coche! (*Mex***)

(VI) joder**, follar (*Sp***), coger (*LAm***)

▸ **fuck about****, **fuck around**** (VI + ADV) joder** • **to ~ about** or **around with** joder**, manosear, estropear

▸ **fuck off**** (VI + ADV) irse a la mierda** • **~ off!** ¡vete a tomar por el culo!**, ¡vete al carajo! (*LAm***), ¡vete a la chingada! (*Mex***)

▸ **fuck up**** (VT + ADV) joder**

(VI + ADV) cagarla‡

fuck-all** [,fʌk'ɔ:l] (*Brit*) (ADJ) • **it's fuck-all use** no sirve para maldita la cosa*

(N) • **I know fuck-all about it** no tengo ni puta idea** • **he's done fuck-all today** hoy no ha hecho más que tocarse los huevos *or* cojones**, hoy no ha pegado ni golpe*

fucker** ['fʌkəʳ] (N) hijo/a *m/f* de puta**, cabronazo** *m*

fucking** ['fʌkɪŋ] (ADJ) de los cojones (*LAm***), fregado (*Mex***), chingado (*Mex***) • **~ hell!** ¡joder!**, ¡coño!**

(ADV) • **it was ~ awful** fue de puta pena** • **it's ~ cold!** ¡hace un frío del carajo!** • **that's no ~ good** no vale una puta mierda** • **I don't ~ know!** ¡no lo sé, coño!**

(N) joder** *m*, jodienda** *f*

fuck-up** ['fʌkʌp] (N) cagada** *f*

fuckwit** ['fʌkwɪt] (N) (*Brit*) cabronazo/a *m/f* de mierda**

fuddled ['fʌdld] (ADJ) **1** (= *muddled*) confuso, aturdido

2* (= *tipsy*) borracho • **to get ~** emborracharse

fuddy-duddy* ['fʌdɪ,dʌdɪ] (ADJ) (= *old*) viejo; (= *old-fashioned*) chapado a la antigua

(N) carroza* *mf*

fudge [fʌdʒ] (N) (*Culin*) dulce *m* de azúcar

(VT) [+ *issue, problem*] esquivar, eludir

(VI) eludir la cuestión

fuel [fjʊəl] (N) **1** (*gen*) combustible *m*; (*for engine*) carburante *m*; (*specifically coal*) carbón *m*; (= *wood*) leña *f*

2 (*fig*) pábulo *m* • IDIOM: • **to add ~ to the flames** echar leña al fuego

(VT) **1** [+ *furnace etc*] alimentar; [+ *aircraft, ship etc*] repostar

2 (*fig*) [+ *speculation etc*] estimular, provocar; [+ *dispute*] avivar, acalorar

(VI) [*aircraft, ship*] repostar

(CPD) ▸ **fuel cap** (*Aut*) tapa *f* del depósito de gasolina ▸ **fuel cell** célula *f* de combustible ▸ **fuel crisis** crisis *f inv* energética ▸ **fuel efficiency** rendimiento *m* de combustible ▸ **fuel gauge** [*of car*] indicador *m* de combustible ▸ **fuel injection (engine)** motor *m* de inyección ▸ **fuel needs** necesidades *fpl* energéticas ▸ **fuel oil** fuel oil *m*, mazut *m* ▸ **fuel policy** política *f* energética ▸ **fuel pump** (*Aut*) surtidor *m* de gasolina ▸ **fuel tank** depósito *m* (de combustible)

-fueled [fjʊəld] (ADJ) (US) = **-fuelled**

fuel-efficient [,fjʊəlɪ'fɪʃənt] (ADJ) [*car, engine, boiler, stove*] que ahorra combustible • **diesel engines are more fuel-efficient than petrol** *or* (US) **gasoline ones** los motores diésel ahorran más combustible que los de gasolina

-fuelled, fueled (US) [fjʊəld] (ADJ) • **adrenaline-fuelled** cargado de adrenalina • **testosterone-fuelled** cargado de testosterona • **drug-fuelled crime(s)** delitos motivados por el consumo de drogas

fuel-saving ['fjʊəl,seɪvɪŋ] (ADJ) que ahorra combustible

fug [fʌg] (N) (*esp Brit*) aire *m* viciado • **what a fug!** ¡qué olor! • **there's a fug in here** aquí huele a cerrado

fuggy ['fʌgɪ] (ADJ) (*esp Brit*) [*air*] viciado, cargado; [*room*] que huele a cerrado

fugitive ['fju:dʒɪtɪv] (ADJ) **1** fugitivo

2 (*liter*) (= *fleeting*) efímero, pasajero

(N) fugitivo/a *m/f*; (= *refugee*) refugiado/a *m/f* • **~ from justice** prófugo/a *m/f* (de la justicia)

fugue [fju:g] (N) fuga *f*

> **FULBRIGHT**
> Las becas **Fulbright** son concedidas por el gobierno de Estados Unidos a los licenciados con el fin de facilitar la ampliación de estudios, así como el acceso a la investigación o la enseñanza en el extranjero. Miles de personas se han beneficiado de estas becas desde que se introdujo el programa **Fulbright** en 1946, como parte de la legislación establecida por el senador J. William Fulbright, un hombre de estado demócrata con gran experiencia en política exterior.

fulcrum ['fʌlkrəm] (N) (PL: **fulcrums** *or* **fulcra** ['fʌlkrə]) fulcro *m*; (*fig*) piedra *f* angular, punto *m* de apoyo

fulfil, fulfill (US) [fʊl'fɪl] (VT) **1** (= *carry out*) [+ *duty, promise*] cumplir con; [+ *role*] desempeñar; [+ *order*] cumplir; [+ *plan, task*] llevar a cabo, realizar

2 (= *meet*) [+ *condition, requirement*] satisfacer, cumplir; [+ *need*] satisfacer; [+ *hopes*] hacer realidad

3 (= *attain*) [+ *ambition*] realizar; [+ *potential*] alcanzar
4 (= *satisfy*) [+ *person*] satisfacer, llenar • **to ~ o.s.** realizarse (plenamente)
fulfilled [fʊl'fɪld] ADJ [*person*] realizado
fulfilling [fʊl'fɪlɪŋ] ADJ • **he has a ~ job** tiene un trabajo que le satisface *or* llena
fulfilment, fulfillment (US) [fʊl'fɪlmənt] N 1 [*of duty, promise, order*] cumplimiento *m*
2 [*of condition, requirement, need*] satisfacción *f*
3 [*of ambition, potential*] realización *f*
4 (= *satisfied feeling*) realización *f*, satisfacción *f*
full [fʊl] ADJ (COMPAR: **fuller**, SUPERL: **fullest**) 1 (= *filled*) [*room, hall, theatre*] lleno; [*vehicle*] completo; [*hotel*] lleno, completo • **"house full"** (*Theat*) "no hay localidades", "completo" • **~ to the brim** hasta el tope • **~ to bursting** lleno de bote en bote • **~ to overflowing** lleno hasta los bordes • **we are ~ up for July** estamos completos para julio • **his heart was ~** (*liter*) tenía el corazón apenado
2 • **to be ~ of ...** estar lleno de ... • **the papers were ~ of the murders** los periódicos no traían más que noticias de los asesinatos • **~ of cares** lleno de cuidados • **a look ~ of hate** una mirada cargada de odio • **~ of hope** lleno de esperanza, ilusionado • **he's ~ of good ideas** tiene muchísimas ideas buenas • **to be ~ of o.s.** *or* **one's own importance** ser muy engreído *or* creído • **to be ~ of life** estar lleno de vida • IDIOMS: • **to be ~ of it*** (= *excited*) estar animadísimo • **to be ~ of shit**** no tener puñetera idea‡
3 (= *complete*) completo, entero; [*account*] detallado, extenso; [*meal*] completo; [*power*] pleno; [*price, pay*] íntegro, sin descuento; [*speed, strength*] máximo; [*text*] íntegro; [*uniform*] de gala • **a ~ three miles** tres millas largas • **I waited a ~ hour** esperé una hora entera • **to take ~ advantage of the situation** aprovecharse al máximo de la situación • **to put one's headlights on ~ beam** poner las luces largas *or* de carretera • **in ~ bloom** en plena flor • **in ~ colour** a todo color • **in ~ daylight** en pleno día • **to pay ~ fare** pagar la tarifa íntegra • **to fall ~ length** caer cuán largo se es • **he was lying ~ length** estaba tumbado todo lo largo que era • **he's had a ~ life** ha llevado una vida muy completa • **the ~ particulars** todos los detalles • **he was suspended on ~ pay** se le suspendió sin reducción de sueldo • **to pay ~ price for sth** (*for goods, tickets*) pagar el precio íntegro de algo • **in the ~est sense of the word** en el sentido más amplio de la palabra • **at ~ speed** a toda velocidad • **~ speed** *or* **steam ahead!** (*Naut*) ¡avance a toda marcha! • **at ~ strength** [*team, battalion*] completo • IDIOMS: • **in ~ cry** a toda carrera • **to go ~ steam ahead** ponerse en marcha a todo vapor • **in ~ swing** en pleno apogeo
4 (= *ample*) [*face*] redondo; [*figure*] llenito; [*lips*] grueso; [*skirt, sleeves*] amplio • **clothes for the ~er figure** tallas *fpl* grandes
5 (= *busy*) [*day, timetable*] muy ocupado • **I've had a ~ day** he estado ocupado todo el día
6 (*Pol etc*) [*session*] pleno, plenario; [*member*] de pleno derecho
7 (*after eating*) • **I'm ~ (up)*** no puedo más, estoy harto *or* ahíto • **you'll work better on a ~ stomach** trabajarás mejor con el estómago lleno *or* después de haber comido
8 (*in titles*) • **~ colonel** coronel(a) *m/f* • **~ general** general *mf* • **~ professor** (US) profesor(a) *m/f* titular
ADV • **it hit him ~ in the face** le pegó en plena cara • **to turn the sound/volume up ~** subir el volumen a tope • **to go ~ out to do sth*** ir a por todas para hacer algo* • **~ well** muy bien, perfectamente • **to know ~ well that** saber perfectamente que • **he understands ~ well that** se da cuenta cabal de que
N • **in ~**: • **name in ~** nombre *m* y apellidos • **text in ~** texto *m* íntegro • **to pay in ~** pagar la deuda entera • **to write sth in ~** escribir algo por extenso • **to the ~** al máximo
CPD ▸ **full board** (*esp Brit*) pensión *f* completa ▸ **full brother** hermano *m* carnal ▸ **full cost** coste *m* total ▸ **full dress** traje *m* de etiqueta *or* de gala • **in ~ dress** vestido de etiqueta *or* de gala ▸ **full employment** pleno empleo *m* ▸ **full English breakfast, full English** desayuno *m* inglés completo, *desayuno que consiste principalmente en huevos fritos con bacon, tostadas, salchicha, morcilla y champiñones* ▸ **full fare** tarifa *f* completa; ▹ **full-fare** ▸ **full house** (*Cards*) full *m*; (*Bingo*) cartón *m*; (*Theat*) lleno *m* ▸ **full marks** puntuación *fsing* máxima • **~ marks for persistence!** (*fig*) ¡te mereces un premio a la perseverancia! ▸ **full measure** medida *f* or cantidad *f* completa ▸ **full moon** luna *f* llena ▸ **full name** nombre *m* y apellidos ▸ **full sister** hermana *f* carnal ▸ **full stop** (*Brit*) (*Gram*) punto *m* (y seguido) • **I'm not going, ~ stop!** ¡no voy, y punto *or* y se acabó! • IDIOM: • **to come to a ~ stop** pararse, paralizarse, quedar detenido en un punto muerto ▸ **full time** (*Brit*) (*Sport*) final *m* del partido; ▹ **full-time**
fullback ['fʊlbæk] N (*Ftbl*) defensa *mf*; (*Rugby*) zaguero *m*
full-beam ['fʊl'bi:m] ADJ • **full-beam headlights** luces *fpl* largas *or* de carretera
full-blast ['fʊl'blɑ:st] ADV [*work*] a pleno rendimiento; [*travel*] a toda velocidad; [*play music etc*] a todo volumen
full-blooded ['fʊl'blʌdɪd] ADJ 1 (= *vigorous*) [*attack*] vigoroso; [*character*] viril, vigoroso
2 (= *thoroughbred*) (de) pura sangre
full-blown ['fʊl'bləʊn] ADJ [*doctor etc*] hecho y derecho; [*attack, invasion etc*] a gran escala • **he has full-blown AIDS** tiene el SIDA en su estado más avanzado
full-bodied ['fʊl'bɒdɪd] ADJ [*cry*] fuerte; [*wine*] de mucho cuerpo
full-cream milk [ˌfʊlkri:m'mɪlk] N leche *f* (con toda la nata)
full-dress [ˌfʊl'dres] ADJ [*function*] de etiqueta, de gala
fuller's earth [ˌfʊləz'ɜ:θ] N tierra *f* de batán
full-face [ˌfʊl'feɪs] ADJ [*portrait*] de rostro entero
full-fare [ˌfʊl'fɛəʳ] CPD [*ticket, passenger, seat*] de tarifa completa
full-fledged [ˌfʊl'fledʒd] ADJ (US) = **fully-fledged**
full-frontal [ˌfʊl'frʌntl] ADJ (= *unrestrained*) desenfrenado
CPD ▸ **full-frontal nude** desnudo *m* visto de frente ▸ **full-frontal nudity** desnudo *m* integral
full-grown [ˌfʊl'grəʊn] ADJ maduro
full-length [ˌfʊl'leŋθ] ADJ [*portrait, dress*] de cuerpo entero; [*novel, study*] extenso; [*swimming pool etc*] de tamaño normal • **a full-length film** un largometraje
ADV • **he was lying full-length** estaba tumbado todo lo largo que era
fullness ['fʊlnɪs] N 1 [*of detail*] abundancia *f*
2 [*of figure*] plenitud *f*; [*of dress*] amplitud *f*
3 • **in the ~ of time** (*liter*) (= *eventually*) con el correr del tiempo; (= *at predestined time*) a su debido tiempo
full-on* [fʊl'ɒn] ADJ total, en toda regla
full-page [ˌfʊl'peɪdʒ] ADJ [*advert etc*] a toda plana
full-scale [ˌfʊl'skeɪl] ADJ [*plan, model*] de tamaño natural; [*search, retreat*] a gran escala; [*study*] amplio, extenso; [*investigation*] de gran alcance
full-size [ˌfʊl'saɪz] ADJ [*model, picture*] de tamaño natural
full-sized [ˌfʊl'saɪzd] ADJ de tamaño normal
full-throated [ˌfʊl'θrəʊtɪd] ADJ [*cry etc*] fuerte, a pleno pulmón
full-time [ˌfʊl'taɪm] ADJ [*employment*] a tiempo completo; [*employee*] que trabaja una jornada completa, que trabaja a tiempo completo • **he's a full-time musician** (= *professional*) es músico profesional • **a full-time job** un puesto de trabajo a tiempo completo • **a full-time course** un curso de dedicación plena
ADV • **to work full-time** trabajar a tiempo completo
full-timer [ˌfʊl'taɪməʳ] N (= *worker*) trabajador(a) *m/f* a tiempo completo • **the company employs six full-timers and one part-time worker** la empresa tiene empleados a seis trabajadores a tiempo completo y a uno a tiempo parcial
full up [ˌfʊl'ʌp] ADJ 1 [*place, institution*] lleno
2* (= *unable to eat any more*) • **I'm ~** no puedo más
fully ['fʊlɪ] ADV 1 (= *completely*) • **I was not ~ awake** no estaba completamente despierto, no estaba despierto del todo • **he was ~ aware of the problem** se daba perfecta cuenta del problema • **~ booked** todo reservado, completo • **~ dressed** completamente vestido • **I ~ expected to see you there** esperaba verte allí • **a ~ grown tiger** un tigre adulto • **I ~ intended to let you know** tenía la firme intención de decírtelo • **she is a ~ qualified swimming instructor** es profesora de natación diplomada • **when he has ~ recovered** cuando se haya recuperado completamente *or* del todo • **I don't ~ understand** no lo acabo de comprender, no lo entiendo del todo
2 (= *at least*) por lo menos • **he earns ~ as much as I do** gana por lo menos lo mismo que yo • **it is ~ three miles** son por lo menos tres millas
3 (= *in detail*) [*describe, explain*] con todo detalle; [*discuss*] a fondo
4 (= *in full*) [*reimburse*] enteramente
fully-fashioned [ˌfʊlɪ'fæʃnd] ADJ [*stocking*] menguado, de costura francesa
fully-featured [ˌfʊlɪ'fi:tʃəd] ADJ [*electronic product*] con todas las prestaciones
fully-fitted kitchen [ˌfʊlɪfɪtɪd'kɪtʃɪn] N cocina *f* totalmente equipada
fully-fledged [ˌfʊlɪ'fledʒd], **full-fledged** (US) [ˌfʊl'fledʒd] ADJ (*Brit*) [*bird*] adulto, en edad capaz de volar; (*fig*) hecho y derecho
fully-paid share [ˌfʊlɪpeɪd'ʃɛəʳ] N acción *f* liberada
fulminate ['fʌlmɪneɪt] VI (*frm*) • **to ~ against** tronar contra
fulmination [ˌfʌlmɪ'neɪʃən] N (*frm*) invectiva *f*, filípica *f* (**against** contra)
fulsome ['fʊlsəm] ADJ (*pej*) [*praise*] excesivo, exagerado; [*manner*] obsequioso
fumble ['fʌmbl] VT (= *drop*) dejar caer; (= *handle badly*) manosear, coger *or* (*LAm*) agarrar con torpeza • **to ~ one's way along** ir a tientas
VI (*also* **fumble about**) hurgar • **to ~ in one's pockets** hurgar en los bolsillos • **to ~ for sth** buscar algo con las manos • **to ~ for a word** titubear buscando una palabra • **to ~ with sth** manejar algo torpemente • **to ~ with a door** forcejear para abrir una puerta

fumbling ['fʌmblɪŋ] ADJ torpe

fume [fju:m] VI **1** [*chemicals etc*] humear, echar humo
2 (= *be furious*) estar furioso, echar humo • **to be fuming at** *or* **with sb** echar pestes de algn
NPL **fumes** (*gen*) humo *msing*, vapores *mpl*; (= *gas*) gases *mpl*

fumigate ['fju:mɪgeɪt] VT fumigar

fumigation [ˌfju:mɪ'geɪʃən] N fumigación *f*

fun [fʌn] N (= *enjoyment*) diversión *f*; (= *merriment*) alegría *f* • **it's great fun** es muy divertido • **he's great fun** es una persona muy divertida • **it's not much fun for us** para nosotros no es nada divertido • **it's only his fun** está bromeando, te está tomando el pelo • **for** *or* **in fun** en broma • **to do sth for the fun of it** hacer algo por divertirse • **fun and games** (= *lively behaviour*) travesuras *fpl*; (*fig*) (= *trouble*) jaleo *m*, bronca *f* • **she's been having fun and games with the washing machine** ha tenido muchos problemas con la lavadora • **to have fun** divertirse • **have fun!** ¡que os divirtáis!, ¡que lo paséis bien! • **what fun we had!** ¡qué bien lo pasamos!, ¡cómo nos divertimos! • **we had fun with the passports** (*iro*) nos armamos un lío con los pasaportes • **to make fun of sb** burlarse de algn, tomar el pelo a algn* • **to poke fun at** burlarse de • **to spoil the fun** aguar la fiesta
ADJ* • **it's a fun thing** es para divertirse • **she's a fun person** es una persona divertida
CPD ▸ **fun run** maratón *m* corto (*de ciudad para los no atletas*)

function ['fʌŋkʃən] N **1** (= *purpose*) [*of machine, person*] función *f* • **it's not part of my ~ to** (+ *infin*) no me corresponde a mí (+ *infin*)
2 (= *reception*) recepción *f*; (= *official ceremony*) acto *m*
3 (*Math*) función *f*
VI (= *operate*) funcionar, marchar • **to ~ as** hacer (las veces) de
CPD ▸ **function key** tecla *f* de función ▸ **function room** salón *m* (*para reuniones, fiestas etc*) ▸ **function word** palabra *f* funcional

functional ['fʌŋkʃnəl] ADJ [*design, clothes*] funcional
CPD ▸ **functional analysis** análisis *m inv* funcional

functionalism ['fʌŋkʃnəlɪzəm] N funcionalismo *m*

functionalist ['fʌŋkʃnəlɪst] (*frm*) ADJ funcionalista
N funcionalista *mf*

functionality [ˌfʌŋkʃə'nælɪtɪ] N [*of computer*] funcionalidad *f*

functionally ['fʌŋkʃnəlɪ] ADV [*designed, efficient*] funcionalmente • **~, they are identical** son idénticos funcionalmente • **he is ~ illiterate** es un analfabeto funcional

functionary ['fʌŋkʃənərɪ] N funcionario/a *m/f*

fund [fʌnd] N (*gen*) fondo *m*; (= *reserve*) reserva *f*; **funds** fondos *mpl*, recursos *mpl* • **to raise ~s** recaudar fondos • **to be in ~s** estar en fondos • **to be a ~ of information** ser una buena fuente de información • **to have a ~ of stories** saber un montón de historias
VT [+ *project*] financiar; [+ *debt*] consolidar

fundamental [ˌfʌndə'mentl] ADJ **1** (= *basic*) [*question, problem, principle*] fundamental • **they are being denied their ~ human rights** se les está privando de los derechos humanos fundamentales
2 (= *profound, great*) [*change, difference*] fundamental • **it is a ~ mistake to think that ...** es un error fundamental pensar que ...
3 (= *essential*) fundamental, esencial • **to be ~ to sth** ser fundamental *or* esencial para algo • **it is ~ to our understanding of the problem** es fundamental *or* esencial para que entendamos el problema
4 (= *intrinsic*) [*honesty, good sense*] intrínseco
NPL • **the ~s** los fundamentos, lo básico

fundamentalism [ˌfʌndə'mentəlɪzəm] N fundamentalismo *m*

fundamentalist [ˌfʌndə'mentəlɪst] ADJ fundamentalista, integrista
N fundamentalista *mf*, integrista *mf*

fundamentally [ˌfʌndə'mentəlɪ] ADV
1 (= *basically*) básicamente, en lo fundamental • **the situation remains ~ the same** básicamente *or* en lo fundamental, la situación no cambia • **~, your children are your responsibility** básicamente, sus hijos son responsabilidad suya • **he is still ~ optimistic about the situation** básicamente sigue sintiéndose optimista en cuanto a la situación
2 (= *profoundly*) fundamentalmente • **their lifestyle is ~ different to ours** su forma de vida es fundamentalmente distinta a la nuestra • **there is something ~ wrong in what he says** hay un error fundamental en lo que dice • **it is ~ important that this project continues** es de vital importancia *or* es fundamental que el proyecto siga adelante
3 (= *intrinsically*) intrínsecamente

fund-holding GP [ˌfʌndhəʊldɪŋˌdʒi:'pi:] N *médico de cabecera con responsabilidad sobre la gestión de fondos presupuestados para su zona*

funding ['fʌndɪŋ] N **1** (= *funds*) fondos *mpl*, finanzas *fpl*; (= *act of funding*) financiación *f*
2 [*of debt*] consolidación *f*

fund-raiser ['fʌndˌreɪzəʳ] N recaudador(a) *m/f* de fondos

fund-raising ['fʌndˌreɪzɪŋ] N recaudación *f* de fondos

funeral ['fju:nərəl] N (= *burial*) funeral *m*, entierro *m*; (= *wake*) velatorio *m*; (= *service*) exequias *fpl* • **state ~** entierro *m or* funeral *m* con honores de estado • **that's your ~!*** ¡con tu pan te lo comas!
CPD ▸ **funeral cortège** cortejo *m* fúnebre ▸ **funeral director** director(a) *m/f* de funeraria ▸ **funeral home** (*US*) = **funeral parlour** ▸ **funeral march** marcha *f* fúnebre ▸ **funeral oration** oración *f* fúnebre ▸ **funeral parlour** funeraria *f* ▸ **funeral procession** cortejo *m* fúnebre ▸ **funeral pyre** pira *f* funeraria ▸ **funeral service** exequias *fpl*

funerary ['fju:nərərɪ] ADJ (*frm*) [*monument*] funerario; [*ceremony*] fúnebre

funereal [fju:'nɪərɪəl] ADJ fúnebre, funéreo

funfair ['fʌnfɛəʳ] N (*Brit*) parque *m* de atracciones

fungal ['fʌŋgl] ADJ [*infection, disease*] micótico, de hongos

fungi ['fʌŋgaɪ] NPL *of* **fungus**

fungicide ['fʌŋgɪsaɪd] N fungicida *m*

fungoid ['fʌŋgɔɪd] ADJ parecido a un hongo, como un hongo; (*Med*) fungoide

fungous ['fʌŋgəs] ADJ fungoso

fungus ['fʌŋgəs] N (PL: **fungi**) hongo *m*

funicular [fju:'nɪkjʊləʳ], **funicular railway** [fju:ˌnɪkjʊlə'reɪlweɪ] N funicular *m*

funk [fʌŋk] N **1*** (= *fear*) • **to be in a (blue) ~** estar muerto de miedo
2 (*Mus*) funk *m*
VT • **to ~ it** rajarse • **to ~ doing something** dejar de hacer algo por miedo

funky* ['fʌŋkɪ] ADJ (COMPAR: **funkier**, SUPERL: **funkiest**) [*music*] vibrante, marchoso

fun-loving ['fʌnˌlʌvɪŋ] ADJ amigo de diversiones

funnel ['fʌnl] N (*for pouring*) embudo *m*; [*of ship, steam engine etc*] chimenea *f*
VT [+ *traffic etc*] canalizar (**through** por); [+ *aid, finance*] encauzar, canalizar (**through** a través de)

funnily ['fʌnɪlɪ] ADV **1** (= *amusingly*) con gracia
2 (= *oddly*) de forma extraña, de forma rara • **he was behaving rather ~ that day** ese día se estaba comportando de forma extraña *or* rara • **~ enough ...** aunque parezca extraño ... • **~ enough, it doesn't bother her at all** aunque parezca extraño, no le molesta en absoluto

funny ['fʌnɪ] ADJ (COMPAR: **funnier**, SUPERL: **funniest**) **1** (= *amusing*) [*person, joke, film, story*] gracioso • **you look so ~ in that costume** tienes una pinta graciosísima con ese disfraz • **it was so ~, I just couldn't stop laughing** era tan gracioso que no podía dejar de reírme • **he's trying to be ~** quiere hacerse el gracioso • **that's not ~** eso no tiene gracia
2 (= *odd*) raro • **~! I thought he'd left** ¡qué raro! creía que ya se había marchado • **it strikes me as ~** *or* **I find it ~ that ...** me extraña que (+ *subjun*), me parece raro que (+ *subjun*) • **(it's) ~ you should say that** qué curioso que digas eso • **there's something ~ going on here** aquí hay gato encerrado • **he's ~ that way** tiene esa manía • **I feel ~** (= *unwell*) no me encuentro muy bien • **it felt ~ going there on my own** se me hizo extraño ir allí solo • **I have the ~ feeling I'm going to regret this** tengo la extraña sensación de que me voy a arrepentir de esto • **I've got a ~ feeling in my stomach** tengo una sensación rara en el estómago • **he must be ~ in the head** tiene que estar ido *or* tocado de la cabeza • **children get some very ~ ideas sometimes!** ¡a los niños se les ocurre a veces cada idea! • **this smells/tastes ~** esto huele/sabe raro • **the ~ thing about it is that ...** lo curioso *or* extraño del caso es que ... • IDIOM: • **~ peculiar or ~ ha-ha?*** ¿extraño o divertido?
N • **the funnies** (*US*) las tiras cómicas
CPD ▸ **funny bone** hueso *m* del codo • **the show seems to have tickled everyone's ~bone** (*fig*) el programa parece haberle hecho gracia a todo el mundo ▸ **funny business** tejemanejes* *mpl* • **don't try any ~ business** nada de tejemanejes* ▸ **funny farm*** (*hum*) loquero* *m* ▸ **funny man** cómico *m* ▸ **funny money*** (= *large sum*) una millonada; (= *counterfeit money*) dinero *m* falso; (= *ill-gotten money*) dinero *m* mal habido

funnyman ['fʌnɪmæn] N (PL: **funnymen**) (= *comedian*) cómico *m*

fur [fɜ:ʳ] N **1** [*of animal*] pelo *m*, pelaje *m*; (= *single skin*) piel *f*; (= *coat*) abrigo *m* de pieles
2 (*in kettle*) sarro *m*
3 (*on tongue*) saburra *f*
VI [*kettle etc*] (*also* **fur up**) cubrirse de sarro, formar sarro
CPD ▸ **fur coat** abrigo *m* de pieles

furbish ['fɜ:bɪʃ] VT • **to ~ up** renovar, restaurar

furious ['fjʊərɪəs] ADJ **1** (= *angry*) [*person, reaction*] furioso • **to be ~ (with sb)** estar furioso (con algn) • **she'll be ~ if she finds out** se va a poner furiosa si se entera • **to get ~** ponerse furioso
2 (= *violent, unrestrained*) [*argument, struggle*] violento; [*activity*] frenético; [*pace, speed*] vertiginoso; [*storm, sea*] furioso; ▹ **fast¹**

furiously ['fjʊərɪəslɪ] ADV **1** (= *angrily*) con furia, furiosamente
2 (= *violently, energetically*) [*work, write*] frenéticamente • **he was silent, his mind**

working ~ estaba callado, su cerebro trabajando frenéticamente

furl [fɜːl] (VT) (*Naut*) aferrar; [+ *wings*] recoger

furlong [ˈfɜːlɒŋ] (N) estadio *m* (*octava parte de una milla*)

furlough [ˈfɜːləʊ] (N) (*US*) permiso *m*

furnace [ˈfɜːnɪs] (N) horno *m* • **the room was like a ~** la habitación era un horno

furnish [ˈfɜːnɪʃ] (VT) **1** [+ *room, house*] amueblar (**with** con) • **~ing fabric** tela *f* para revestir muebles • **~ed flat** piso *m* amueblado, departamento *m* amoblado (*LAm*)
2 (= *provide*) [+ *excuse, information*] proporcionar, facilitar; [+ *proof*] aducir • **to ~ sb with sth** [+ *supplies*] proveer a algn de algo; [+ *opportunity*] dar *or* proporcionar algo a algn

furnishings [ˈfɜːnɪʃɪŋz] (NPL) muebles *mpl*, mobiliario *msing*

furniture [ˈfɜːnɪtʃəʳ] (N) muebles *mpl*, mobiliario *m* • **a piece of ~** un mueble • **part of the ~*** (*fig*) parte *f* de la casa *or* del mobiliario
(CPD) ▸ **furniture mover** (*US*) = **furniture remover** ▸ **furniture polish** cera *f* para muebles ▸ **furniture remover** compañía *f* de mudanzas ▸ **furniture shop** tienda *f* de muebles ▸ **furniture van** camión *m* de mudanzas

furore [fjʊəˈrɔːrɪ], **furor** (*US*) [ˈfjʊərɔːʳ] (N) (= *protests*) ola *f* de protestas, escándalo *m*; (= *excitement*) ola *f* de entusiasmo

furred [fɜːd] (ADJ) [*tongue*] lleno de sarro

furrier [ˈfʌrɪəʳ] (N) peletero/a *m/f* • **~'s (shop)** peletería *f*

furrow [ˈfʌrəʊ] (N) (*Agr*) surco *m*; (*on forehead*) arruga *f* • IDIOM: • **to plough a lonely ~** ser el único en estudiar algo
(VT) [+ *forehead*] arrugar
(VI) arrugarse • **his brow ~ed** frunció el ceño

furrowed [ˈfʌrəʊd] (ADJ) • **with ~ brow** con ceño fruncido

furry [ˈfɜːrɪ] (ADJ) [*animal*] peludo; [*teddy bear*] de peluche
(CPD) ▸ **furry dice** (*Brit*) dados *mpl* afelpados (*tipo de colgante para el coche*) ▸ **furry toy** (juguete *m* de) peluche *m*

further [ˈfɜːðəʳ] (ADV) (*compar of* **far**) **1** (*in distance*) • **how much ~ is it?** ¿cuánto camino nos queda? • **have you much ~ to go?** ¿le queda mucho camino por hacer? • **let's go ~ north/south** vayamos más al norte/sur • **his car was parked ~ along** su coche estaba aparcado un poco más arriba/abajo • **a crowd was gathering ~ along the street** se estaba congregando una multitud de gente calle arriba/abajo • **we were too tired to go any ~ that day** estábamos demasiado cansados para continuar ese día • **move it ~ away** apártalo un poco más • **we live ~ away from the city centre** vivimos más lejos del centro de la ciudad • **~ back** más atrás • **I think it's ~ down the road** creo que está bajando un poco más la calle • **I was visiting a friend ~ down the street** estaba visitando a un amigo que vive bajando un poco la calle • **I don't think we want to go any ~ down that road** (*fig*) no creo que sea prudente seguir por ese camino (*fig*) • **I need to be a bit ~ forward** tengo que ponerme un poco más para delante • **nothing was ~ from my thoughts** nada más lejos de mi intención • **I sank even ~ in** me hundí aún más • **~ on** más adelante • **the track ended a mile ~ on** el camino terminaba una milla más adelante • **the boat drifted ~ out to sea** la barca iba siendo arrastrada mar adentro • **~ to the south** más al sur • **we decided to go ~ up the track** decidimos seguir avanzando por el camino
2 (*in time*) • **let's look a little ~ ahead** miremos un poco más adelante • **I never plan anything ~ than a week ahead** nunca planeo nada con más de una semana de antelación • **there is evidence of this even ~ back in history** incluso más antiguamente se ven evidencias de esto • **records go no ~ back than 1960** los archivos solo se remontan a 1960
3 (= *in progress*) • **you'll get ~ with her if you're polite** conseguirás más si se lo pides educadamente • **I got no ~ with him** (*in questioning*) no pude sacarle nada más • **we need to go ~ and address the issues** tenemos que ir más allá y proponer soluciones a los problemas • **he went ~, claiming the man had attacked him** no se quedó ahí, sino que aseguró que el hombre lo había atacado • **this mustn't go any ~** [*confidential matter*] esto que no pase de aquí • **to go ~ into a matter** estudiar una cosa más a fondo • **~ on in this chapter** más adelante en este capítulo • **I think we should take this matter ~** creo que deberíamos proseguir con este asunto
4 (= *more*) más • **they questioned us ~** nos hicieron más preguntas • **this will ~ damage the country's image** esto va a perjudicar más la imagen del país • **I heard nothing ~ from them** no supe más de ellos • **don't trouble yourself any ~** no se moleste más
5 (= *in addition*) además • **and I ~ believe that …** y creo además que …
6 (*Comm*) (*in correspondence*) • **~ to your letter of the 7th** con *or* en relación a su carta del 7
(ADJ) (*compar of* **far**) (= *additional*) más • **I have no ~ comment to make** no tengo nada más que añadir • **after ~ consideration** tras considerarlo más detenidamente • **without ~ delay** sin más demora • **please send me ~ details of your products** le ruego me envíen más información con respecto a sus productos • **we have no ~ need of your services** ya no necesitamos sus servicios • **until ~ notice** hasta nuevo aviso • **he was detained for ~ questioning** lo retuvieron para someterle a un nuevo interrogatorio • **recommendations for ~ reading** sugerencias de lecturas complementarias *or* adicionales
(VT) (= *promote*) [+ *cause, aim, understanding, career*] promover, fomentar • **she was accused of ~ing her own interests** la acusaron de actuar en beneficio de sus propios intereses
(CPD) ▸ **further education** (*Brit*) (*vocational, non-academic etc*) formación *f* continua, educación *f* postescolar ▸ **further education college** (*Brit*) ≈ centro *m* de formación continua

furtherance [ˈfɜːðərəns] (N) promoción *f*, fomento *m*

furthermore [ˈfɜːðɜːˈmɔːʳ] (ADV) además

furthermost [ˈfɜːðəməʊst] (ADJ) más lejano

furthest [ˈfɜːðɪst] (ADV) (*superl of* **far**) **1** (*in distance*) más lejos • **who has the ~ to go home?** ¿quién es el que vive más lejos? • **that's the ~ that anyone has gone** ese es el punto más lejano al que se ha llegado
2 (*in progress*) • **that was the ~ the club had ever gone** eso era lo máximo a lo que el club había llegado • **Poland has taken these ideas ~** Polonia ha sido el país que más ha desarrollado estas ideas
3 (= *most*) más • **prices have fallen ~ in the south of England** donde más han bajado los precios ha sido en el sur de Inglaterra
(ADJ) más lejano • **the ~ point** el punto más lejano • **the seat ~ from the window** el asiento que más lejos está de la ventana • **the ~ recesses of the mind** los recovecos más olvidados de la mente

furtive [ˈfɜːtɪv] (ADJ) [*glance, action*] furtivo; [*person*] sospechoso

furtively [ˈfɜːtɪvlɪ] (ADV) furtivamente

fury [ˈfjʊərɪ] (N) [*of person*] furia *f*, furor *m*; [*of storm etc*] furia *f* • **to be in a ~** estar furioso • **she flew into a ~** se puso furiosa • **she worked herself up into a ~** montó en cólera • **like ~*** con encono • **the Furies** las Furias

furze [fɜːz] (N) aulaga *f*, tojo *m*

fuse, fuze (*US*) [fjuːz] (N) **1** (*Elec*) plomo *m*, fusible *m* • **to blow a ~** [*equipment*] fundirse un fusible; [*person*] salirse de sus casillas • **there's been a ~ somewhere** • **a ~ has blown somewhere** un fusible se ha fundido en algún sitio
2 [*of bomb*] (= *cord*) mecha *f*; (= *detonating device*) espoleta *f* • IDIOM: • **he has a very short ~*** tiene un genio muy vivo
(VT) **1** [+ *lights, television etc*] fundir
2 [+ *metals*] fundir
(VI) **1** (*Elec*) • **the lights have ~d** se han fundido los plomos
2 [*metals*] fundirse
(CPD) ▸ **fuse box** caja *f* de fusibles ▸ **fuse wire** hilo *m* fusible
▸ **fuse together** (VT + ADV) [+ *bones*] unir
(VI + ADV) [*atoms*] fusionarse; [*bones*] unirse

fused [fjuːzd] (ADJ) (*Elec*) con fusible
(CPD) ▸ **fused plug** enchufe *m* con fusible

fuselage [ˈfjuːzəlɑːʒ] (N) fuselaje *m*

fusilier [ˌfjuːzɪˈlɪəʳ] (N) (*Brit*) fusilero *m*

fusillade [ˌfjuːzɪˈleɪd] (N) (*lit*) descarga *f* cerrada; (*fig*) lluvia *f*

fusion [ˈfjuːʒən] (N) [*of metals, fig*] fusión *f*

fuss [fʌs] (N) **1** (= *complaints, arguments*) escándalo *m*, alboroto *m* • **to make** *or* **kick up a ~ about sth** armar un escándalo por algo, armar un lío *or* un follón por algo* • **he's always making a ~ about nothing** siempre monta el número por cualquier tontería* • **I think you were quite right to make a ~** creo que hiciste bien en protestar • **there's no need to make such a ~** no hay por qué ponerse así, no es para tanto
2 (= *anxious preparations etc*) conmoción *f*, bulla *f* • **a lot of ~ about nothing** mucho ruido y pocas nueces • **such a ~ to get a passport!** ¡tanta lata para conseguir un pasaporte!* • **what's all the ~ about?** ¿a qué viene tanto jaleo?
3 • **to make a ~ of sb** (*Brit*) (= *spoil*) mimar *or* consentir a algn
(VI) preocuparse por pequeñeces
(VT) [+ *person*] molestar, fastidiar • **don't ~ me!** ¡deja ya de fastidiarme!
▸ **fuss about, fuss around** (VI + ADV) (= *busy o.s.*) andar de acá para allá; (= *worry unnecessarily*) preocuparse por pequeñeces
▸ **fuss over** (VI + PREP) [+ *person*] consentir a

fussbudget* [ˈfʌsˌbʌdʒɪt] (N) (*US*) = **fusspot**

fussed* [fʌst] (ADJ) (*Brit*) • **I'm not ~** me da igual, me da lo mismo • **I'm not ~ about going to the party** me da igual *or* lo mismo ir a la fiesta que no

fussily [ˈfʌsɪlɪ] (ADV) **1** (= *demandingly*) (*pej*) quisquillosamente; (= *scrupulously*) meticulosamente, escrupulosamente
2 (= *elaborately*) [*designed, dressed*] de manera recargada
3 (= *nervously*) nerviosamente

fussiness [ˈfʌsɪnɪs] (N) **1** (= *exacting nature*) **a** (*pej*) • **his ~ about food is driving me mad** sus manías para la comida me están volviendo loco
b (= *scrupulousness*) meticulosidad *f*, escrupulosidad *f* • **~ about details is an asset**

in this job la meticulosidad *or* escrupulosidad en los detalles es un punto a favor para este puesto
2 (= *elaborateness*) [*of design, clothes*] lo recargado

fusspot* ['fʌspɒt] (N) quisquilloso/a *m/f*

fussy ['fʌsɪ] (ADJ) (COMPAR: **fussier**, SUPERL: **fussiest**) **1** (= *exacting*) [*person*] **a** (*pej*) quisquilloso • **they'll think you're ~ if you ring them** van a creer que eres quisquilloso *or* difícil si les llamas • **children are often ~ eaters** los niños son a menudo quisquillosos *or* especiales para la comida
b (= *scrupulous*) • **he's very ~ about detail** es muy escrupuloso *or* meticuloso con los detalles
c (= *selective*) selectivo • **I'm very ~ about the parts I take on** soy muy selectivo a la hora de elegir papeles, no elijo cualquier papel • **I'm very ~ about what I wear** soy muy especial a la hora de vestir • **I'm not ~*** me da igual, me da lo mismo
2 (= *elaborate*) [*design, clothes*] recargado, con muchos ringorrangos*
3 (= *nervous*) [*manner*] nervioso

fusty ['fʌstɪ] (ADJ) (COMPAR: **fustier**, SUPERL: **fustiest**) rancio; [*air*] viciado; [*room*] que huele a cerrado

futile ['fju:taɪl] (ADJ) [*attempt*] vano; [*suggestion*] fútil

futility [fju:'tɪlɪtɪ] (N) inutilidad *f*, lo inútil

futon ['fu:tɒn] (N) futón *m*

future ['fju:tʃəʳ] (ADJ) **1** [*husband, generations*] futuro; [*plans*] para el futuro • **at some ~ date** *or* **time** en un futuro • **his ~ prospects are bleak** sus perspectivas de futuro no son nada halagüeñas • **in ~ years** en los años venideros; ▸ **reference**
2 (*Gram*) • **the ~ perfect** el futuro perfecto • **the ~ tense** el futuro
(N) **1** futuro *m* • **who knows what the ~ holds?** ¿quién sabe lo que nos depara el futuro? • **they see schoolchildren as their customers of the ~** ven a los niños en edad escolar como sus clientes del futuro • **we must look to the ~** tenemos que mirar al futuro • **in ~** de ahora en adelante • **in the ~** en el futuro • **in the near ~** en un futuro próximo *or* cercano • **in the not too distant ~** en un futuro no muy lejano
2 (= *prospects*) futuro *m*, porvenir *m* • **her ~ is assured** tiene el futuro *or* el porvenir asegurado • **he believes his ~ lies in comedy** piensa que su futuro *or* su porvenir está en la comedia • **there's no ~ in it** no tiene futuro
3 (*Gram*) futuro *m* • **in the ~** en futuro
4 futures (*Econ*) futuros *mpl*
(CPD) ▸ **the futures market** (*Econ*) el mercado de futuros

future-proof ['fju:tʃəpru:f] (ADJ) que funcionará en el futuro, listo para el futuro
(VT) [+ *equipment, software etc*] garantizar la funcionalidad futura de • **they want to know that their investment will be future-proofed** quieren saber que su inversión estará garantizada en el futuro

futurism ['fju:tʃərɪzəm] (N) futurismo *m*

futurist ['fju:tʃərɪst] (N) **1** (*esp US*) (= *futurologist*) futurólogo/a *m/f*
2 (*Art*) futurista *mf*

futuristic [,fju:tʃə'rɪstɪk] (ADJ) [*painting, design*] futurista

futurologist [,fju:tʃər'ɒlədʒɪst] (N) futurólogo/a *m/f*

futurology [,fju:tʃər'ɒlədʒɪ] (N) futurología *f*

fuze [fju:z] (N) (*US*) = **fuse**

fuzz [fʌz] (N) **1** (*on chin*) vello *m*; (= *fluff*) pelusa *f*
2 • **the ~‡** la poli*, la pasma (*Sp‡*), los tiras (*Chile‡*)

fuzzily ['fʌzɪlɪ] (ADV) **1** (= *hazily*) borrosamente
2 (= *confusedly*) confusamente

fuzzy [fʌzɪ] (ADJ) (COMPAR: **fuzzier**, SUPERL: **fuzziest**) **1** [*hair*] rizado; [*material*] velloso
2 (= *blurred*) [*photo, memory*] borroso; [*ideas, thinking*] confuso
(CPD) ▸ **fuzzy logic** (*Comput*) lógica *f* difusa, lógica *f* borrosa

fwd (ABBR) (*esp Comm*) = **forward**

f-word ['ef,wɜ:d] (N) • **to say the f-word** (*euph*) [*of "fuck"*] decir "jo...roba"

fwy (ABBR) (*US*) = **freeway**

FX* (NPL ABBR) (*Cine*) = **special effects**

FY (ABBR) = **fiscal year**

FYI (ABBR) = **for your information**

Gg

G, g[1] [dʒiː] N **1** (= *letter*) G, g *f* • **G for George** G de Gerona
2 (*Mus*) • **G** sol *m* • **G major/minor** sol mayor/menor • **G sharp/flat** sol sostenido/bemol
ABBR **1** (*Scol*) (= *mark*) (= **Good**) N
2 (*US*) (*Cine*) (= **general audience**) todos los públicos
3‡ (= **grand**) (*Brit*) mil libras *fpl*; (*US*) mil dólares *mpl*
g[2] ABBR (= **gram(s), gramme(s)**) g, gr
N ABBR (= **gravity**) g • **G-force** fuerza *f* de la gravedad
GA ABBR (*US*) = **Georgia**
g.a. ABBR = **general average**
GAB N ABBR = **General Arrangements to Borrow**
gab* [gæb] N • IDIOM: • **to have the gift of the gab** tener mucha labia, tener un pico de oro
VI (= *chatter*) parlotear, cotorrear
gabardine [ˌgæbəˈdiːn] N = **gaberdine**
gabble [ˈgæbl] N torrente *m* de palabras ininteligibles
VT farfullar
VI hablar atropelladamente • **they were gabbling away in French** parloteaban en francés
gabby‡ [ˈgæbɪ] ADJ hablador, locuaz
gaberdine [ˌgæbəˈdiːn] N (= *cloth, raincoat*) gabardina *f*
gable [ˈgeɪbl] N aguilón *m*, gablete *m*
CPD ▸ **gable end** hastial *m* ▸ **gable roof** tejado *m* de dos aguas
gabled [ˈgeɪbld] ADJ [*houses, roofs*] (con tejado) a dos aguas
Gabon [gəˈbɒn] N Gabón *m*
Gabriel [ˈgeɪbrɪəl] N Gabriel
gad[1] [gæd] VI • **to gad about** callejear, salir de picos pardos
gad[2]†* [gæd] EXCL (*also* **by gad**) ¡cáspita!
gadabout [ˈgædəbaʊt] N azotacalles *mf inv*, pindonga* *f*
gadfly [ˈgædflaɪ] N tábano *m*
gadget [ˈgædʒɪt] N (= *little thing*) artilugio *m*, chisme *m*; (= *device*) aparato *m*
gadgetry [ˈgædʒɪtrɪ] N chismes *mpl*, aparatos *mpl*
gadolinium [ˌgædəˈlɪnɪəm] N gadolinio *m*
gadwall [ˈgædwɔːl] N ánade *m* friso
Gael [geɪl] N gaélico/a *m/f*
Gaelic [ˈgeɪlɪk] ADJ gaélico
N (*Ling*) gaélico *m*
CPD ▸ **Gaelic coffee** café *m* irlandés
gaff[1] [gæf] N (*Fishing*) (= *harpoon*) arpón *m*, garfio *m*
VT arponear, enganchar
gaff[2]‡ [gæf] N (*Brit*) (= *home*) casa *f*
gaff[3] [gæf] N • IDIOM: • **to blow the ~*** irse de la lengua, descubrir el pastel
gaffe [gæf] N plancha *f* (*Sp*), metedura *f or* (*LAm*) metida *f* de pata • **to make a ~** meter la pata, tirarse una plancha (*Sp*)
gaffer [ˈgæfəʳ] N **1** (= *old man*) vejete* *m*
2 (*Brit*) (= *foreman*) capataz *m*; (= *boss*) jefe *m*
3 (*Cine, TV*) iluminista *mf*
CPD ▸ **gaffer tape** cinta *f* aislante
gag [gæg] N **1** (*over mouth*) mordaza *f*; (*Parl*) clausura *f* • **the new law will effectively put a gag on the free press** en efecto la nueva ley va a poner una mordaza a la prensa libre
2 (= *joke*) chiste *m*; (= *hoax*) broma *f*; (= *gimmick*) truco *m* publicitario • **it's a gag to raise funds** es un truco para recaudar fondos
VT [+ *prisoner*] amordazar; (*fig*) amordazar, hacer callar; (*Parl*) clausurar
VI (= *retch*) tener arcadas • **to gag on** [+ *food*] atragantarse con • IDIOM: • **to be gagging for it**‡ estar calentón *or* cachondo‡
CPD ▸ **gag rule*** (*US*) *regla que prohíbe la discusión de un asunto específico en el parlamento*
gaga* [ˈgɑːˈgɑː] ADJ gagá, lelo, chocho • **to go ~** • **to be going ~** (= *senile*) chochear; (= *ecstatic*) caérsele a algn la baba
gage [geɪdʒ] N, VT (*US*) = **gauge**
gagging order [ˈgægɪŋˌɔːdəʳ] N (*preventing media discussion*) orden *f* de amordazamiento
gaggle [ˈgægl] N [*of geese*] manada *f*; (*hum*) [*of people*] pandilla *f*, grupo *m*
gaiety [ˈgeɪɪtɪ] N **1** [*of occasion, person*] alegría *f*
2 [*of dress, costumes*] colorido *m*, vistosidad *f*
gaily [ˈgeɪlɪ] ADV **1** (= *brightly*) [*dressed, decorated*] vistosamente, alegremente • **~ coloured cushions** cojines de vistosos *or* alegres colores • **~ painted barges** barcazas pintadas con alegres colores
2 (= *cheerfully*) [*chatter, sing*] alegremente
3 (= *thoughtlessly*) alegremente, como si tal cosa • **people who ~ fritter away their time** gente que malgasta alegremente el tiempo *or* que malgasta el tiempo como si tal cosa • **she ~ admitted that she had lied** admitió alegremente que había mentido, admitió que había mentido como si tal cosa
gain [geɪn] VT **1** (= *obtain, win*) [+ *respect*] ganarse; [+ *approval, support, supporters*] conseguir; [+ *experience*] adquirir, obtener; [+ *freedom*] obtener, conseguir; [+ *popularity, time*] ganar; [+ *friends*] hacerse; [+ *qualification*] obtener • **what do you hope to ~ by it?** ¿qué provecho esperas sacar con esto?, ¿qué esperas ganar *or* conseguir con esto? • **there is nothing to be ~ed by feeling bitter** no se gana *or* consigue nada guardando rencores • **he had nothing to ~ by lying to me** no iba a ganar *or* conseguir nada mintiéndome • **Serbia's newly ~ed territories** los territorios recientemente adquiridos por Serbia • **to ~ an advantage over sb** sacar ventaja a algn • **to ~ confidence** adquirir confianza • **to ~ sb's confidence** • **to ~ the confidence of sb** ganar(se) la confianza de algn • **to ~ control of sth** hacerse con el control de algo • **Kenya ~ed independence from Great Britain in 1963** Kenia obtuvo *or* consiguió la independencia de Gran Bretaña en 1963 • **my daughter has just ~ed a place at university** mi hija acaba de obtener una plaza en la universidad • **Jones ~ed possession of the ball** Jones se hizo con el balón • **Labour has ~ed three seats from the Conservatives** los laboristas les han arrebatado tres escaños a los conservadores; ▹ **access, entry, ground, hand**
2 (= *increase*) • **the shares have ~ed four points** las acciones han aumentado *or* subido cuatro enteros • **my watch has ~ed five minutes** mi reloj se ha adelantado cinco minutos • **to ~ speed** ganar *or* cobrar velocidad • **to ~ strength** (*physically*) cobrar fuerzas; (*mentally*) hacerse más fuerte • **to ~ weight** engordar, aumentar de peso • **I've ~ed three kilos** he engordado tres kilos
3 (= *arrive at*) llegar a • **the steamer ~ed port** el vapor llegó a puerto
VI **1** (= *profit*) • **to ~ by/from sth** beneficiarse de algo • **who would ~ by** *or* **from his death?** ¿quién iba a beneficiarse de su muerte? • **no one ~s by putting others down** nadie sale beneficiando humillando a los demás • **I ~ed immensely from the experience** me beneficié mucho de la experiencia, saqué mucho provecho de la experiencia; ▹ **stand**
2 (= *advance*) [*watch*] adelantarse; [*runner*] ganar terreno
3 (= *increase, improve*) [*shares*] aumentar de valor, subir • **to ~ in sth**: • **to ~ in popularity** adquirir mayor popularidad • **to ~ in prestige** ganar prestigio • **his reputation ~ed in stature** su reputación aumentó *or* creció
N **1** (= *increase*) aumento *m* • **a ~ in weight** un aumento de peso • **Labour made ~s in the South** los laboristas ganaron terreno en el sur • **the effect of a modest ~ in the pound** el efecto de una pequeña subida en la libra • **a ~ of eight per cent** un aumento *or* una subida del ocho por ciento • **their shares showed a three-point ~** sus acciones experimentaron una subida de tres enteros • **productivity ~s** aumentos *mpl* en la productividad; ▹ **weight**
2 (= *benefit, advantage*) beneficio *m* • **they are using the situation for personal/political ~** están utilizando la situación en beneficio propio/para ganar terreno político • IDIOM: • **their loss is our ~** ellos pierden y nosotros ganamos
3 (*Econ*) (= *profit*) ganancia *f*, beneficio *m* • **the company reported pre-tax ~s of £759 million** la compañía anunció haber obtenido unos beneficios *or* unas ganancias brutas de 759 millones de libras; ▹ **capital**
▸ **gain on, gain upon** VI + PREP • **to ~ on sb** (*in polls*) ganar terreno a algn; (*in race*) alcanzar a algn • **the police car was ~ing on us fast** el coche de la policía nos estaba alcanzando rápidamente

gainer ['geɪnəʳ] (N) • **to be the ~** salir ganando
gainful ['geɪnfʊl] (ADJ) [*employment*] remunerado, retribuido
gainfully ['geɪnfʊlɪ] (ADV) • **to be ~ employed** tener un trabajo retribuido *or* remunerado • **there was nothing that could ~ be said** no podía decirse nada que pudiera ser de utilidad
gainsay [,geɪn'seɪ] (PT, PP: **gainsaid**) (VT) (*liter*) contradecir, negar • **it cannot be gainsaid** es innegable
gait [geɪt] (N) paso *m*, modo *m* de andar
gaiter ['geɪtəʳ] (N) polaina *f*
gal* [gæl] (N) = **girl**
gal. (ABBR) (PL: **gal.** *or* **gals.**) = **gallon(s)**
gala ['gɑːlə] (N) (= *festival*) fiesta *f*; (*Sport*) festival *m* • **swimming ~** festival *m* de natación
(CPD) ▸ **gala day** día *m* de gala ▸ **gala performance** función *f* de gala
galactic [gə'læktɪk] (ADJ) (*Astron*) galáctico; (*Med*) lácteo
Galapagos Islands [gə'læpəgəs,aɪləndz] (NPL) islas *fpl* (de los) Galápagos
Galatians [gə'leɪʃənz] (NPL) Galateos *mpl*
galaxy ['gæləksɪ] (N) (*Astron*) galaxia *f*; (*fig*) constelación *f*, pléyade *f*
gale [geɪl] (N) (= *strong wind*) vendaval *m*, viento *m* fuerte; (= *storm*) (*on land*) temporal *m*; (*at sea*) temporal *m*, tempestad *f* • **~ force ten** vientos *mpl* de fuerza diez • **it was blowing a ~ that night** aquella noche había vendaval, aquella noche soplaban vientos fuertes; ▹ **gale-force**
(CPD) ▸ **gale warning** aviso *m* de temporal
gale-force ['geɪlfɔːs] (ADJ) • **gale-force winds** vientos *mpl* huracanados; ▹ **gale**
Galen ['geɪlən] (N) Galeno
Galicia [gə'lɪʃɪə] (N) **1** (*Spain*) Galicia *f*
2 (*Central Europe*) Galitzia *f*
Galician [gə'lɪʃɪən] (ADJ) gallego
(N) **1** (= *person*) gallego/a *m/f*
2 (*Ling*) gallego *m*
Galilean [,gælɪ'liːən] (ADJ) (*Bible, Geog*) galileo; (*Astron*) galileico
(N) galileo/a *m/f* • **the ~** (*Bible*) el Galileo
Galilee ['gælɪliː] (N) Galilea *f*
gall [gɔːl] (N) **1** (*Anat*) bilis *f*, hiel *f*
2 (*Bot*) agalla *f*; (*on animal*) matadura *f*
3 (*fig*) (= *bitterness*) hiel *f*; (= *cheek**) descaro *m* • **she had the ~ to say that** tuvo el descaro de decir eso
(VT) molestar, dar rabia a
(CPD) ▸ **gall bladder** vesícula *f* biliar
gall. (ABBR) (PL: **gall.** *or* **galls.**) = **gallon(s)**
gallant† (ADJ) ['gælənt] **1** (= *brave*) [*warrior, officer*] gallardo; [*effort*] valiente, noble
2 (= *courteous*) galante, cortés
(N) [gə'lænt] galán *m*
gallantly ['gæləntlɪ] (ADV) **1** (= *bravely*) valientemente, valerosamente
2 (= *courteously*) galantemente, cortésmente
gallantry† ['gæləntrɪ] (N) **1** (= *bravery*) valor *m*, valentía *f*
2 (= *courtesy*) galantería *f*, cortesía *f* • **gallantries** galanterías *fpl*
galleon ['gælɪən] (N) galeón *m*
gallery ['gælərɪ] (N) (*gen*) galería *f* (*also Min, Theat*); (*for spectators*) tribuna *f*; (= *art gallery*) (*state owned*) museo *m* de arte; (*private*) galería *f* de arte • IDIOM: • **to play to the ~** actuar para la galería
galley ['gælɪ] (N) **1** (= *ship*) galera *f*
2 (= *ship's kitchen*) cocina *f*, fogón *m*
3 (*Typ*) galerada *f*, galera *f*
(CPD) ▸ **galley proof** (*Typ*) galerada *f* ▸ **galley slave** galeote *m*
Gallic ['gælɪk] (ADJ) (= *of Gaul*) galo; (= *French*) francés
gallicism ['gælɪsɪzəm] (N) galicismo *m*
galling ['gɔːlɪŋ] (ADJ) mortificante
gallium ['gælɪəm] (N) galio *m*
gallivant [,gælɪ'vænt] (VI) = **gad**¹
gallon ['gælən] (N) galón *m* (*Brit = 4,546 litros; US = 3,785 litros*); ▹ IMPERIAL SYSTEM
gallop ['gæləp] (N) (= *pace*) galope *m*; (= *distance covered*) galopada *f* • **at a ~** al galope • **at full ~** a galope tendido • **to break into a ~** ponerse a galopar
(VI) [*horse*] galopar • **to ~ up/off** llegar/alejarse al galope • **to ~ past** pasar al galope; (*in procession*) desfilar al galope • **he ~ed through his homework** terminó sus deberes a la carrera
(VT) hacer galopar
galloping ['gæləpɪŋ] (ADJ) • **~ consumption** (*Med*) tisis *f* galopante • **~ inflation** inflación *f* galopante
gallows ['gæləʊz] (NSING) horca *f*
(CPD) ▸ **gallows humour** (*fig*) humor *m* negro *or* macabro
gallstone ['gɔːlstəʊn] (N) cálculo *m* biliar
Gallup poll ['gæləp,pəʊl] (N) sondeo *m or* encuesta *f* Gallup
galoot‡ [gə'luːt] (N) (*esp US*) zoquete* *mf*
galore [gə'lɔːʳ] (ADV) en cantidad, a porrillo* • **bargains ~** gangas *fpl* a porrillo* *or* en cantidad
galosh [gə'lɒʃ] (N) chanclo *m* (de goma)
galumph* [gə'lʌmf] (VI) (*hum*) brincar alegre pero torpemente, brincar como un elefante contento
galvanic [gæl'vænɪk] (ADJ) galvánico
galvanism ['gælvənɪzəm] (N) galvanismo *m*
galvanize ['gælvənaɪz] (VT) **1** [+ *metal*] galvanizar
2 (*fig*) • **to ~ sb into action** mover a algn para que actúe • **to ~ sb into life** sacar a algn de su abstracción
galvanized ['gælvənaɪzd] (ADJ) galvanizado
galvanizing ['gælvənaɪzɪŋ] (ADJ) [*influence, force*] galvanizante; [*performance*] electrizante
galvanometer [,gælvə'nɒmɪtəʳ] (N) galvanómetro *m*
Gambia ['gæmbɪə] (N) • **(the) ~** Gambia *f*
Gambian ['gæmbɪən] (ADJ) gambiano
(N) gambiano/a *m/f*
gambit ['gæmbɪt] (N) (*Chess*) gambito *m*; (*fig*) táctica *f* • **opening ~** (*fig*) estrategia *f* inicial
gamble ['gæmbl] (N) (= *risk*) riesgo *m*; (= *bet*) apuesta *f* • **life's a ~** la vida es una lotería • **the ~ came off** la jugada salió bien • **to have a ~ on** [+ *horse*] jugar dinero a, apostar a; [+ *Stock Exchange*] jugar a • **to take a ~** arriesgarse
(VT) [+ *money*] jugar, apostar; [+ *one's life*] arriesgar • **to ~ everything/one's future (on sth)** jugarse todo/el porvenir (a algo)
(VI) (= *bet money*) jugar, apostar; (= *take a chance*) jugársela • **to ~ on sth** confiar en algo, contar con algo • **he ~d on my being there** confiaba en que yo estuviera allí, contaba con que yo estuviera allí • **to ~ on the Stock Exchange** jugar a la Bolsa • **to ~ with others' money** especular con el dinero ajeno
▸ **gamble away** (VT + ADV) perder en el juego
gambler ['gæmbləʳ] (N) jugador(a) *m/f*
gambling ['gæmblɪŋ] (N) juego *m* • **~ on the Stock Exchange** especulación *f* en la Bolsa
(CPD) ▸ **gambling debts** deudas *fpl* de juego ▸ **gambling den** garito *m*, casa *f* de juego ▸ **gambling losses** pérdidas *fpl* de juego ▸ **gambling man** • **I'm not a ~ man** yo no juego
gambol ['gæmbəl] (VI) brincar, retozar
game¹ [geɪm] (N) **1** (*lit*) **a** (= *entertainment*) juego *m* • **it's only a ~** no es más que un juego • **a ~ of chance/skill** un juego de azar/de habilidad • IDIOM: • **to play the ~** jugar limpio; ▹ **video**
b (= *match*) [*of football, rugby, cricket, tennis*] partido *m*; (*within tennis set*) juego *m*; [*of cards, chess, snooker*] partida *f* • **to have** *or* **play a ~ of football** jugar un partido de fútbol • **he plays a good ~ of football** juega bien al fútbol • **to have** *or* **play a ~ of chess** echar *or* jugar una partida de ajedrez • **they were (one) ~ all** (*Tennis*) iban iguales *or* empatados a un juego • **~, set and match** juego, set y partido • **~ to Johnston** juego a Johnston; ▹ **ball**¹, **board**, **card**¹
c (= *type of sport*) deporte *m* • **football is not my ~** el fútbol no se me da bien
2 games (= *contest*) juegos *mpl*; (*Brit*) (*Scol*) deportes *mpl* • **the Olympic Games** los Juegos Olímpicos, las Olimpiadas • **I was no good at ~s** no se me daban bien los deportes • **we have ~s on Thursdays** los jueves tenemos deportes
3 (= *play style*) • **my ~ picked up in the second set** empecé a mejorar el juego en el segundo set • **to be off one's ~** no estar en forma • **to put sb off his/her ~** afectar la forma de jugar de algn, hacer jugar mal a algn
4 (*Hunting*) (= *large animals*) caza *f* mayor; (= *birds, small animals*) caza *f* menor; ▹ **big**, **fair**¹
5 (*fig*) **a** (= *scheme*) juego *m* • **I'll play his ~ for a while** voy a seguirle el juego un rato • **we know his little ~** le conocemos el jueguecillo* • **what's your ~?** ¿qué estás tramando? • IDIOMS: • **to beat sb at his/her own ~** ganar a algn con sus propias armas • **to give the ~ away** descubrir el pastel* • **the faces of the two conspirators gave the ~ away** la expresión de su rostro delató a los dos conspiradores, la expresión del rostro de los dos conspiradores hizo que se descubriera el pastel* • **two can play at that ~** donde las dan las toman • **the ~ is up** se acabó el juego* • **the ~ is not worth the candle** la cosa no vale la pena • **the only ~ in town** la mejor alternativa; ▹ **waiting**
b (= *joke*) juego *m* • **this isn't a ~** esto no es ningún juego • **don't play ~s with me!** ¡no juegues conmigo! • **he's just playing silly ~s** no está más que jugando; ▹ **fun**
c* (= *business*) negocio *m* • **how long have you been in this ~?** ¿cuánto tiempo llevas metido en este negocio?, ¿cuánto tiempo hace que trabajas en esto? • **she's new to this ~** esto es nuevo para ella • IDIOM: • **to be ahead of the ~** llevar ventaja, llevar la delantera
d* (= *prostitution*) • **to be on the ~** hacer la calle*
e* (= *trouble*) lata* *f* • **it was a ~ getting here!** ¡menuda lata para llegar aquí!*
(ADJ) (= *willing*) • **are you ~?** ¿te animas?, ¿te apuntas? • **I'm ~ if you are** si tú te animas, yo también • **to be ~ to do sth** estar dispuesto a hacer algo • **to be ~ for anything** apuntarse a cualquier cosa *or* a todo
(VI) (= *gamble*) jugar (*por dinero*)
(CPD) ▸ **game bird** ave *f* de caza ▸ **game changer** cambio *m* en las reglas del juego • **this technology is a real ~ changer** esta tecnología cambia las reglas del juego ▸ **game fish** *pez de agua dulce pescado como deporte* ▸ **game fishing** *pesca deportiva de peces de agua dulce* ▸ **game laws** leyes *fpl* relativas a la caza ▸ **game park** parque *m* natural, reserva *f* natural ▸ **game pie** *empanada elaborada con una pieza de caza mayor o menor* ▸ **game plan** (*Sport*) plan *m* de juego; (*fig*) estrategia *f* ▸ **game preserve, game reserve** coto *m* de caza ▸ **game show** programa *m* concurso ▸ **game show host** (*on radio, TV*) presentador(a) *m/f* de concursos ▸ **games**

console consola *f* de videojuegos ▸ **games master** profesor *m* de deportes ▸ **games mistress** profesora *f* de deportes ▸ **game theory** teoría *f* de juegos ▸ **game warden** guarda *mf* de coto *or* de caza

game² [geɪm] ADJ (*= lame*) • **to have a ~ leg** tener una pierna coja

gamebag ['geɪmbæg] N morral *m*

Gameboy® ['geɪmbɔɪ] N Gameboy® *m*

game-changing ['geɪm,tʃeɪndʒɪŋ] ADJ que cambia las reglas del juego

gamecock ['geɪmkɒk] N gallo *m* de pelea

gamekeeper ['geɪm,kiːpəʳ] N guardabosques *mf inv*, guardabosque *mf*

gamely ['geɪmlɪ] ADV **1** (*= bravely*) valientemente, con el mejor de los ánimos
2 (*= sportingly*) animosamente

gamepad ['geɪmpæd] N gamepad *m*

gameplay ['geɪmpleɪ] N interactividad *f*, *experiencia total del jugador al interactuar con el videojuego*

gamer ['geɪməʳ] N (*playing video games*) jugador(a) *m/f* de videojuegos

gamesman ['geɪmzmən] N (PL: **gamesmen**) jugador *m* astuto

gamesmanship ['geɪmzmənʃɪp] N astucia *f* en el juego • **piece of ~** truco *m* para ganar

gamester ['geɪmstəʳ] N jugador(a) *m/f*, tahúr *mf*

gamete ['gæmiːt] N gameto *m*

gamey ['geɪmɪ] ADJ = **gamy**

gamin ['gæmɛ̃] N golfillo *m*

gamine [gæ'miːn] N *muchacha delgada y con aspecto de chico*
CPD ▸ **gamine haircut** corte *m* a la garçon

gaming ['geɪmɪŋ] N juego *m*
CPD ▸ **gaming house** casa *f* de juego ▸ **gaming laws** leyes *fpl* reguladoras del juego ▸ **gaming licence** licencia *f* de juego ▸ **gaming table** mesa *f* de juego

gamma ['gæmə] N gamma *f*
CPD ▸ **gamma radiation** radiación *f* gamma ▸ **gamma ray** rayo *m* gamma

gammon ['gæmən] N (*Brit*) jamón *m*
CPD ▸ **gammon steak** filete *m* de jamón

gammy* ['gæmɪ] ADJ (*Brit*) cojo

gamp†* [gæmp] N (*Brit*) paraguas *m inv*

gamut ['gæmət] N gama *f* • **to run the (whole) ~ of** (*fig*) recorrer toda la gama de

gamy ['geɪmɪ] ADJ [*meat*] *con olor a animal de caza*

gander ['gændəʳ] N **1** (*Zool*) ganso *m* (macho)
2* • **to have** *or* **take a ~** echar un vistazo (at a)

G & T, G and T [,dʒiːən'tiː] N ABBR gin-tonic *m inv*

gang [gæŋ] N [*of thieves*] banda *f*, pandilla *f*; [*of friends, youths*] grupo *m*; (*pej*) pandilla *f*; [*of workmen*] cuadrilla *f*, brigada *f* • **the Gang Of Four** (*Pol, Hist*) la Banda de los Cuatro • **he's one of the ~ now** ya es uno de los nuestros
CPD ▸ **gang rape** violación *f* en grupo ▸ **gang warfare** guerra *f* de pandillas
▸ **gang together** VI + ADV formar un grupo *or* una pandilla, agruparse
▸ **gang up** VI + ADV unirse (**with** a) • **to ~ up on** *or* **against sb** unirse en contra de algn • **I feel everybody's ~ing up on me** tengo la sensación de que todos se han unido en mi contra

gangbang‡ ['gæŋbæŋ] N violación *f* múltiple *or* colectiva
VT violar colectivamente

gangbanger* ['gæŋbæŋəʳ] N (*US*) (*= gang member*) pandillero *m*

gangbusters ['gæŋbʌstəz] NPL (*US*) • **to be going ~** ir viento en popa • **to do sth like ~** hacer algo con paso firme

ganger ['gæŋəʳ] N (*Brit*) capataz *m*

Ganges ['gændʒiːz] N • **the ~** el Ganges

gangland ['gæŋlænd] N mundo *m* del crimen
CPD ▸ **gangland boss** cabecilla *mf* del mundo del crimen ▸ **gangland murder** asesinato *m* en el mundo del crimen, asesinato *m* por ajuste de cuentas entre criminales

gangling ['gæŋglɪŋ] ADJ [*youth*] larguirucho, desgarbado; [*legs*] larguirucho, desproporcionado

ganglion ['gæŋglɪən] N (PL: **ganglions** *or* **ganglia** ['gæŋglɪə]) ganglio *m*

gangly ['gæŋglɪ] ADJ = **gangling**

gangmaster ['gæŋmɑːstəʳ] N contratista *mf* de mano de obra (*especialmente para la agricultura*)

gangplank ['gæŋplæŋk] N (*Naut*) plancha *f*

gangrene ['gæŋgriːn] N gangrena *f*

gangrenous ['gæŋgrɪnəs] ADJ gangrenoso

gangsta rap, gangster rap [,gæŋstə'ræp] N gangsta rap *m*, *género de rap centrado en la violencia y las drogas*

gangster ['gæŋstəʳ] N gán(g)ster *mf*
CPD ▸ **gangster rap** = **gangsta rap**

gangsterism ['gæŋstərɪzəm] N gan(g)sterismo *m*

gangway ['gæŋweɪ] N **1** (*Brit*) (*in theatre, aircraft*) pasillo *m*, pasadizo *m*
2 (*Naut*) (*on ship*) escalerilla *f*, pasarela *f*; (*from ship to shore*) pasarela *f* • **gangway!** ¡abran paso!

ganja‡ ['gændʒə] N maría *f* (*Sp**), marihuana *f*

gannet ['gænɪt] N **1** (*= bird*) alcatraz *m*
2* (*= glutton*) (*fig*) comilón/ona *m/f*

gantlet ['gæntlɪt] N (*US*) (*Rail*) vía *f* traslapada, vía *f* de garganta

gantry ['gæntrɪ] N (*gen*) caballete *m*; (*for crane, railway signal*) pórtico *m*; (*for rocket*) torre *f* de lanzamiento

GAO N ABBR (*US*) (*=* **General Accounting Office**) *oficina general de contabilidad gubernamental*

gaol [dʒeɪl] N (*Brit*) = **jail**

gaoler ['dʒeɪləʳ] N (*Brit*) = **jailer**

gap [gæp] N (*gen*) (*fig*) hueco *m*, vacío *m*; (*in wall etc*) boquete *m*, brecha *f*; (*= mountain pass*) quebrada *f*, desfiladero *m*; (*in traffic, vegetation*) claro *m*; (*between teeth, floorboards*) hueco *m*; (*between bars*) distancia *f*, separación *f*; (*= crack*) hendedura *f*, resquicio *m*; (*in text*) espacio *m* (en blanco); (*fig*) (*in knowledge*) laguna *f*; (*in conversation*) silencio *m*; [*of time*] intervalo *m* • **there's a gap in the hedge** hay un hueco en el seto • **there is a gap in the balance of payments** hay un desequilibrio en la balanza de pagos • **to close the gap** cerrar la brecha • **we discerned a gap in the market** vimos que había un hueco en el mercado • **leave a gap for the name** deje un espacio para poner el nombre • **to stop up** *or* **fill a gap** (*lit*) tapar un hueco • **to fill a gap** (*fig*) llenar un vacío *or* un hueco; (*in knowledge*) llenar una laguna • **he left a gap that will be hard to fill** dejó un hueco difícil de llenar
CPD ▸ **gap year** (*Brit*) año *m* sabático

gape [geɪp] VI **1** [*mouth*] estar abierto; [*hole*] estar muy abierto • **the chasm ~d before him** delante de él se abría la sima • **her blouse ~d at the neck** llevaba una blusa muy abierta por el cuello
2 [*person*] • **tourists go there to ~** los turistas van allí y se quedan boquiabiertos • **to ~ (at)** mirar boquiabierto (a) • **he ~d at me in amazement** se me quedó mirando boquiabierto

gap-fill ['gæpfɪl] N (*also* **gap-fill(ing) exercise**) ejercicio *m* de llenar los huecos en blanco

gaping ['geɪpɪŋ] ADJ **1** [*wound, mouth*] abierto; [*hole*] muy abierto, grande
2 [*person*] boquiabierto, embobado

gappy* ['gæpɪ] ADJ [*teeth*] separado

gap-toothed ['gæp'tuːθt] ADJ (*= with gaps between teeth*) con los dientes separados; (*= with teeth missing*) desdentado, con la dentadura llena de huecos, al/a la que le faltan varios dientes

garage ['gærɑːʒ] N [*of house*] garaje *m*; (*for car repairs*) taller *m*; (*= petrol station*) estación *f* de servicio, gasolinera *f*, grifo *m* (*Peru*), bencinera *f* (*Chile*); (*= bus depot*) cochera *f*
VT dejar en garaje
CPD ▸ **garage band** (*Mus*) grupo *m* de rock aficionado ▸ **garage mechanic** mecánico/a *m/f* ▸ **garage proprietor** propietario/a *m/f* de un taller de reparaciones ▸ **garage sale** venta *f* de objetos usados (*en el garaje de una casa particular*)

garageman ['gærɑːʒ,mæn] N (PL: **garagemen**) garajista *m*

garaging ['gærɑːʒɪŋ] N plazas *fpl* de párking *or* garaje • **there was ~ for 15 cars** había 15 plazas de párking *or* garaje

garb [gɑːb] N (*liter*) (*= clothes*) atuendo *m*
VT vestir (**in** de)

garbage ['gɑːbɪdʒ] (*esp US*) N (*= refuse*) basura *f*; (*= waste*) desperdicios *mpl*; (*fig*) (*= goods, film etc*) birria *f*, porquería *f*; (*spoken, written*) bobadas *fpl*, tonterías *fpl*, disparates *mpl* • **he talks a lot of ~** dice muchas bobadas *or* tonterías • **the book is ~** la novela es una basura *or* birria *or* porquería • **~ in, ~ out** (*Comput*) basura entra, basura sale
CPD ▸ **garbage bag** bolsa *f* de la basura ▸ **garbage can** cubo *m* de la basura ▸ **garbage chute** colector *m* de basura ▸ **garbage collector** basurero/a *m/f* ▸ **garbage disposal unit** triturador *m* de basura ▸ **garbage dump** vertedero *m* ▸ **garbage man** = **garbage collector** ▸ **garbage shute** colector *m* de basura ▸ **garbage truck** camión *m* de la basura

garble ['gɑːbl] VT **1** [+ *message, report*] confundir
2 [+ *text*] mutilar, falsear (*por selección*)

garbled ['gɑːbld] ADJ [*message, version, account, explanation*] confuso, incoherente

Garda ['gɑːdə] N (PL: **Gardaí** ['gɑːdiː]) policía *f* irlandesa

garden ['gɑːdn] N jardín *m*; (*= vegetable garden*) huerto *m* • **the Garden of Eden** el Edén • **(public) ~s** parque *msing*, jardines *mpl* • IDIOM: • **everything in the ~ is lovely** todo va a las mil maravillas
VI trabajar en el jardín *or* el huerto
CPD ▸ **garden apartment** (*US*) apartamento *m or* (*Sp*) piso *m or* (*LAm*) departamento *m* con jardín en planta baja ▸ **garden centre** centro *m* de jardinería, vivero *m* ▸ **garden city** (*Brit*) ciudad *f* jardín ▸ **garden flat** apartamento *m or* (*Sp*) piso *m or* (*LAm*) departamento *m* con jardín en planta baja ▸ **garden furniture** muebles *mpl* de jardín ▸ **garden gnome** gnomo *m* de jardín ▸ **garden hose** manguera *f* de jardín ▸ **garden of remembrance** *jardín en un cementerio en memoria de los difuntos* ▸ **garden party** recepción *f* al aire libre ▸ **garden path** sendero *m* • IDIOM: • **to lead sb up the ~ path** embaucar a algn ▸ **garden produce** productos *mpl* de la huerta ▸ **garden rubbish** basura *f* del jardín ▸ **garden seat** banco *m* de jardín ▸ **garden shears** tijeras *fpl* de jardín ▸ **garden suburb** *barrio residencial con muchas zonas verdes* ▸ **garden tools** útiles *mpl* de jardinería; ▹ **refuse²**

gardener ['gɑːdnəʳ] N (*gen*) jardinero/a *m/f*

g

gardenia [gɑːˈdiːnɪə] N gardenia *f*

gardening [ˈgɑːdnɪŋ] N (*gen*) jardinería *f*; (= *market gardening*) horticultura *f* • **who does the ~?** ¿quién es el jardinero?, ¿quién se encarga del jardín?

garden-variety [ˈgɑːdnvəˌraɪətɪ] ADJ (*US*) (= *ordinary*) común y corriente

garfish [ˈgɑːˌfɪʃ] N (PL: **garfish** *or* **garfishes**) aguja *f*

gargantuan [gɑːˈgæntjʊən] ADJ colosal, gigantesco

gargle [ˈgɑːgl] N (= *sound*) gárgaras *fpl*; (= *liquid*) gargarismo *m*
VI hacer gárgaras, gargarear (*LAm*)

gargoyle [ˈgɑːgɔɪl] N gárgola *f*

garish [ˈgɛərɪʃ] ADJ [*colour*] chillón, estridente; [*clothing*] chillón, llamativo, charro (*LAm**)

garishly [ˈgɛərɪʃlɪ] ADV • **~ coloured** con colores chillones *or* estridentes • **~ decorated/painted/dressed** decorado/pintado/vestido con colores chillones *or* con gusto chabacano *or* (*LAm**) de manera charra • **~ lit** estridentemente iluminado

garishness [ˈgɛərɪʃnɪs] N [*of clothes, décor*] chabacanería *f*, ordinariez *f*, lo charro (*LAm**); [*of colours, light*] estridencia *f*

garland [ˈgɑːlənd] N guirnalda *f*
VT engalanar (**with** con)

garlic [ˈgɑːlɪk] N ajo *m*
CPD ▸ **garlic bread** pan *m* de ajo ▸ **garlic mayonnaise** alioli *m* ▸ **garlic prawns** gambas *fpl* al ajillo ▸ **garlic press** triturador *m* de ajo ▸ **garlic salt** sal *f* de ajo ▸ **garlic sausage** salchichón *m* al ajo

garlicky [ˈgɑːlɪkɪ] ADJ [*taste*] a ajo; [*food*] con ajo; [*breath*] con olor a ajo

garment [ˈgɑːmənt] N prenda *f* (de vestir); **garments** ropa *fsing*, indumentaria *fsing*

garner [ˈgɑːnəʳ] N (*liter*†) (= *granary*) granero *m*
VT (*also* **garner in, garner up**) [+ *grain*] almacenar, entrojar; (*fig*) [+ *support*] conseguir, obtener; [+ *attention, publicity*] conseguir

garnet [ˈgɑːnɪt] N granate *m*

garnish [ˈgɑːnɪʃ] N (*Culin*) aderezo *m*, adorno *m*
VT aderezar, adornar (**with** con)

garnishing [ˈgɑːnɪʃɪŋ] N (*Culin*) aderezo *m*, adorno *m*

Garonne [gəˈrɒn] N Garona *m*

garotte [gəˈrɒt] N, VT = **garrotte**

garret [ˈgærɪt] N (= *attic room*) desván *m*, altillo *m* (*LAm*)

garrison [ˈgærɪsən] N guarnición *f*
VT guarnecer
CPD ▸ **garrison town** plaza *f* fuerte ▸ **garrison troops** tropas *fpl* de guarnición

garrotte [gəˈrɒt] N garrote *m*
VT agarrotar

garrulity [gəˈruːlɪtɪ] N garrulidad *f*

garrulous [ˈgærʊləs] ADJ [*person, manner*] gárrulo, parlanchín

garrulously [ˈgærʊləslɪ] ADV con garrulería *or* verborrea

garrulousness [ˈgærʊləsnɪs] N garrulidad *f*

garter [ˈgɑːtəʳ] N (*for stocking, sock*) liga *f*; (*US*) (= *suspender*) liguero *m*, portaligas *m inv* • **Order of the Garter** Orden *f* de la Jarretera • **Knight of the Garter** Caballero *m* de la Orden de la Jarretera
CPD ▸ **garter belt** (*US*) liguero *m*, portaligas *m inv*

gas [gæs] N (PL: **gas(s)es**) **1** (*gen*) gas *m*; (*as anaesthetic*) gas *m* anestésico; (*in mine*) grisú *m*
2 (*US*) (= *petrol*) gasolina *f*, nafta *f* (*S. Cone*), bencina *f* (*Chile*) • **to step on the gas*** acelerar, pisar el acelerador
3†* (= *gab*) • **to have a gas** charlar, parlotear*
4‡ (= *fun*) • **what a gas!** ¡qué divertido! • **he's a gas!** ¡es un tío divertidísimo!*
5 (*esp US*) (*Med**) (= *wind*) gases *mpl*, flatulencia *f*
VT [+ *person*] asfixiar con gas; (*Mil*) gasear • **to gas o.s.** suicidarse con gas
VI* (= *gab*) charlar, parlotear*
CPD [*industry, pipe*] de gas ▸ **gas bracket** brazo *m* de lámpara de gas ▸ **gas burner** mechero *m* de gas ▸ **gas can** (*US*) bidón *m* de gasolina ▸ **gas canister** = **gas cylinder** ▸ **gas central heating** calefacción *f* central a gas ▸ **gas chamber** cámara *f* de gas ▸ **gas cooker** cocina *f* de *or* a gas ▸ **gas cylinder** bombona *f* de gas ▸ **gas fire** estufa *f* de gas ▸ **gas fitter** fontanero *m* (*especializado en lo relacionado con el gas*) ▸ **gas fittings** instalación *fsing* de gas ▸ **gas guzzler*** chupagasolina* *m inv*, *vehículo que consume mucha gasolina* ▸ **gas heater** = **gas fire** ▸ **gas jet** llama *f* de mechero de gas ▸ **gas lamp** lámpara *f* de gas ▸ **gas leak** escape *m* de gas ▸ **gas lighter** encendedor *m* de gas ▸ **gas lighting** alumbrado *m* de gas ▸ **gas main** cañería *f* maestra de gas ▸ **gas mantle** manguito *m* incandescente ▸ **gas mask** careta *f* antigás ▸ **gas meter** contador *m* de gas, medidor *m* de gas (*LAm*) ▸ **gas mileage** (*US*) rendimiento *f* de la gasolina, *consumo de gasolina por distancia recorrida* ▸ **gas oil** gasóleo *m* ▸ **gas oven** cocina *f* de *or* a gas ▸ **gas pedal** (*esp US*) acelerador *m* ▸ **gas pipe** tubo *m* de gas ▸ **gas pipeline** gasoducto *m* ▸ **gas pump** (*US*) (*in car*) bomba *f* de gasolina; (*in gas station*) surtidor *m* de gasolina ▸ **gas ring** fuego *m* de gas ▸ **gas station** (*US*) gasolinera *f*, estación *f* de servicio, bencinera *f* (*Chile*), grifo *m* (*Peru*) ▸ **gas stove** cocina *f* de *or* a gas ▸ **gas tank** (*US*) (*Aut*) tanque *m* *or* depósito *m* (de gasolina) ▸ **gas tap** llave *f* del gas ▸ **gas turbine** turbina *f* de gas ▸ **gas worker** trabajador(a) *m/f* de la compañía de gas

gasbag [ˈgæsbæg] N **1** (*Aer*) bolsa *f* de gas
2‡ (= *talkative person*) charlatán/ana *m/f*

Gascon [ˈgæskən] ADJ gascón
N **1** gascón/ona *m/f*
2 (*Ling*) gascón *m*

Gascony [ˈgæskənɪ] N Gascuña *f*

gas-cooled reactor [ˌgæskuːldriːˈæktəʳ] N reactor *m* enfriado por gas

gaseous [ˈgæsɪəs] ADJ gaseoso

gas-fired [ˌgæsˈfaɪəd] ADJ de gas
CPD ▸ **gas-fired central heating** calefacción *f* central a gas ▸ **gas-fired power station** central *f* (térmica) de gas

gash¹ [gæʃ] N (*in flesh*) tajo *m*; (*from knife*) cuchillada *f*; (*in material*) raja *f*, hendidura *f*
VT [+ *arm, head*] hacer un tajo en; (*with knife*) acuchillar; [+ *seat etc*] rajar

gash²‡ [gæʃ] ADJ (*Brit*) (= *spare*) de sobra; (= *free*) gratuito

gasholder [ˈgæsˌhəʊldəʳ] N = **gasometer**

gasification [ˌgæsɪfɪˈkeɪʃən] N gasificación *f*

gasket [ˈgæskɪt] N (*Tech*) junta *f*

gaslight [ˈgæslaɪt] N luz *f* de gas, alumbrado *m* de gas

gaslit [ˈgæslɪt] ADJ con alumbrado de gas

gasman [ˈgæsmæn] N (PL: **gasmen**) (*gen*) empleado *m* del gas; (= *gas fitter*) fontanero *m* (*especializado en lo relacionado con el gas*)

gasohol [ˈgæsəʊhɒl] N (*US*) gasohol *m*

gasoline [ˈgæsəliːn] N (*US*) gasolina *f*, nafta *f* (*S. Cone*), bencina *f* (*Chile*)

gasometer [gæˈsɒmɪtəʳ] N (*Brit*) gasómetro *m*

gasp [gɑːsp] N (*for breath*) boqueada *f*; (= *panting*) jadeo *m*; [*of surprise*] grito *m* ahogado • **she gave a ~ of surprise** dio un grito ahogado de asombro • **to be at one's last ~** (= *dying*) estar agonizando, estar dando las últimas boqueadas
VI (*for air*) respirar con dificultad; (= *pant*) jadear; (*in surprise*) gritar • **he was ~ing for air** *or* **breath** le costaba respirar, le faltaba el aliento • **I was ~ing for a smoke** tenía unas ganas tremendas de fumar
VT (*also* **gasp out**) decir con voz entrecortada

gasper‡ [ˈgɑːspəʳ] N (*Brit*) pito* *m*, pitillo* *m*

gassed‡ [gæst] ADJ (= *drunk*) bebido

gassy [ˈgæsɪ] ADJ (COMPAR: **gassier**, SUPERL: **gassiest**) gaseoso

gastric [ˈgæstrɪk] ADJ gástrico
CPD ▸ **gastric band** (*Med*) banda *f* gástrica ▸ **gastric flu** gastroenteritis *f inv* ▸ **gastric juice** jugo *m* gástrico ▸ **gastric ulcer** úlcera *f* gástrica

gastritis [gæsˈtraɪtɪs] N gastritis *f inv*

gastro... [ˈgæstrəʊ] PREFIX gastro...

gastroenteritis [ˌgæstrəʊˌentəˈraɪtɪs] N gastroenteritis *f*

gastroenterologist [ˌgæstrəʊˌentəˈrɒlədʒɪst] N gastroenterólogo/a *m/f*

gastroenterology [ˌgæstrəʊˌentəˈrɒlədʒɪ] N gastroenterología *f*

gastrointestinal [ˌgæstrəʊɪnˈtestɪnəl] ADJ [*problems, system*] gastrointestinal

gastronome [ˈgæstrənəʊm], **gastronomist** [gæsˈtrɒnəmɪst] N gastrónomo/a *m/f*

gastronomic [ˌgæstrəˈnɒmɪk] ADJ gastronómico

gastronomy [gæsˈtrɒnəmɪ] N gastronomía *f*

gastropod [ˈgæstrəpɒd] N gastrópodo *m*

gastro-pub [ˈgæstrəʊpʌb] N bar *m* y restaurante (*que sirve comida de calidad*)

gastroscopy [gæsˈtrɒskəpɪ] N (*Med*) gastroscopia *f*

gasworks [ˈgæswɜːks] NSING, NPL fábrica *f* de gas

gat†‡ [gæt] N (*US*) (= *gun*) revólver *m*, quitapenas‡ *m*

gate [geɪt] N **1** [*of wood*] puerta *f* (*also of town, castle*); [*of metal*] verja *f*; (= *sluice*) compuerta *f*; [*of field, in station*] barrera *f*; (*Sport*) entrada *f* • **please go to ~ seven** diríjanse a la puerta siete
2 (*Sport*) (= *attendance*) público *m*, concurrencia *f*; (= *entrance money*) taquilla *f*, recaudación *f*
VT (*Brit**) [+ *pupil*] prohibir la salida fuera del recinto escolar (*como castigo*)
CPD ▸ **gate money** taquilla *f*, recaudación *f*

gâteau [ˈgætəʊ] N (PL: **gâteaux** [ˈgætəʊz]) torta *f*, pastel *m*, tarta *f* (*Sp*)

gatecrash* [ˈgeɪtkræʃ] VT [+ *party*] colarse en
VI colarse (de gorra)

gatecrasher* [ˈgeɪtˌkræʃəʳ] N colado/a *m/f*

gated community [ˈgeɪtɪdkəˌmjuːnɪtɪ] N unidad *f* residencial cerrada

gatehouse [ˈgeɪthaʊs] N (PL: **gatehouses** [ˈgeɪthaʊzɪz]) casa *f* del guarda *or* del portero

gatekeeper [ˈgeɪtˌkiːpəʳ] N portero/a *m/f*

gate-leg table [ˌgeɪtlegˈteɪbl], **gate-legged table** [ˌgeɪtlegdˈteɪbl] N mesa *f* de alas abatibles

gatepost [ˈgeɪtpəʊst] N poste *m* (de una puerta) • IDIOM: • **between you, me, and the ~** en confianza, entre nosotros

gateway [ˈgeɪtweɪ] N (*gen*) puerta *f* (de acceso) • **New York, the ~ to America** Nueva York, la puerta a América • **the ~ to success** la puerta al éxito
CPD ▸ **gateway drug** droga *f* de iniciación • **it is thought that cannabis is a ~ drug to**

harder substances se cree que el hachís es una droga de iniciación que da paso a otras más duras

gather ['gæðəʳ] (VT) **1** (*also* **gather together**) [*+ people, objects*] reunir, juntar; (*also* **gather up**) [*+ pins, sticks etc*] recoger; [*+ harvest, crop*] recoger, recolectar; [*+ flowers*] coger, recoger (*LAm*); [*+ information*] reunir, recopilar; [*+ hair*] recoger; (*Sew*) fruncir; [*+ taxes*] recaudar • **we ~ed enough firewood to last the night** reunimos leña suficiente para toda la noche • **to ~ dust** acumular polvo • **to ~ one's thoughts (together)** ordenar sus pensamientos • **she ~ed her coat around her** se envolvió en su abrigo
2 (= *gain*) • **to ~ speed** ir ganando *or* adquiriendo velocidad • **to ~ strength** cobrar fuerzas
3 • **to ~ that** (= *understand*) tener entendido que; (= *discover*) enterarse de que • **as you will have ~ed ...** se habrá dado cuenta de que ... • **as far as I could ~** hasta donde pude enterarme • **I ~ from him that ...** según lo que me dice ... • **what are we to ~ from this?** ¿qué consecuencia sacamos de esto?
(VI) **1** [*people*] (*also* **gather together**) reunirse, juntarse, congregarse; (= *crowd together*) amontonarse; [*dust*] acumularse; [*clouds*] acumularse, cerrarse • **they ~ed in the doorway** se apiñaron en la entrada
2 (*Med*) formar pus
(N) (*Sew*) frunce *m*
▸ **gather in** (VT + ADV) [*+ harvest, crops*] recoger, recolectar; [*+ taxes*] recaudar • **to ~ in the harvest/crops** recoger la cosecha, cosechar
▸ **gather round** (VI + ADV), (VI + PREP) • **to ~ round (sb)** agruparse alrededor (de algn) • **~ round!** ¡acercaos!
▸ **gather together** (VT + ADV) reunir, juntar (VI + ADV) reunirse, juntarse, congregarse
▸ **gather up** (VT + ADV) recoger

gathered ['gæðəd] (ADJ) (*Sew*) fruncido

gatherer ['gæðərəʳ] (N) [*of wood, flowers*] recolector(a) *m/f* • **intelligence ~** recopilador(a) *m/f* de información; ▹ **hunter**

gathering ['gæðərɪŋ] (N) **1** (= *assembly*) reunión *f*; (= *persons present*) concurrencia *f*
2 (*Med*) absceso *m*
3 (*Typ*) alzado *m*
(ADJ) [*force, speed*] creciente, en aumento • **the ~ storm** la tormenta que se aproxima

gator*, **'gator*** ['geɪtəʳ] (*US*) = **alligator**

GATT [gæt] (N ABBR) (= **General Agreement on Tariffs and Trade**) GATT *m*

gauche [gəʊʃ] (ADJ) [*person, behaviour*] torpe, desmañado; (*socially*) cohibido, falto de soltura

gaucheness [gəʊʃnɪs] (N) cohibición *f*, falta *f* de soltura

gaucherie [ˌgəʊʃə'riː] (N) **1** = **gaucheness**
2 (= *act, remark*) torpeza *f*

gaucho ['gaʊtʃəʊ] (ADJ) gauchesco
(N) gaucho *m*

gaudily ['gɔːdɪlɪ] (ADV) • **~ coloured** con colores chillones *or* llamativos • **~ decorated/painted/dressed** decorado/pintado/vestido con colores chillones *or* llamativos

gaudiness ['gɔːdɪnɪs] (N) [*of colours*] lo chillón, lo llamativo; [*of clothes, paint*] vulgaridad *f*; [*of place*] lo chabacano

gaudy ['gɔːdɪ] (ADJ) (COMPAR: **gaudier**, SUPERL: **gaudiest**) [*colour, clothes*] chillón, llamativo; [*shop, display*] ordinario, chabacano; [*place*] chabacano

gauge, **gage** (*US*) [geɪdʒ] (N) (= *standard measure*) [*of wire, bullet, gun*] calibre *m*; [*of railway track*] ancho *m*, entrevía *f*, trocha *f* (*LAm*); (= *instrument*) indicador *m*; (*fig*) indicación *f*, muestra *f* • **petrol** *or* (*US*) **gas ~** indicador *m* del nivel de gasolina • **oil ~** indicador *m* de(l) aceite • **pressure ~** manómetro *m*; ▹ **narrow**
(VT) [*+ temperature, pressure*] medir; (*fig*) [*+ sb's capabilities, character*] estimar, juzgar • **to ~ the distance with one's eye** medir la distancia al ojo • **he knows how to ~ the feeling of the crowd** sabe reconocer los deseos de la multitud • **to ~ the right moment** elegir el momento oportuno

Gaul [gɔːl] (N) **1** Galia *f*
2 (= *person*) galo/a *m/f*

Gaullist ['gəʊlɪst] (ADJ) gaulista, golista
(N) gaulista *mf*, golista *mf*

gaunt [gɔːnt] (ADJ) **1** [*face*] (= *drawn*) chupado; (= *unhealthy*) demacrado; [*person*] flaco y adusto
2 (*fig*) (= *grim*) [*building*] sobrio, adusto

gauntlet ['gɔːntlɪt] (N) [*of knight*] guantelete *m*, manopla *f*; [*of motorcyclist etc*] guante *m* • IDIOMS: • **to run the ~** (*Mil, Hist*) correr baquetas • **he had to run a ~ of abuse as he arrived for the meeting** tuvo que aguantar una sarta de improperios a su llegada a la reunión • **to throw down/take up the ~** arrojar/recoger el guante

gauze [gɔːz] (N) (*gen*) gasa *f*

gauzy ['gɔːzɪ] (ADJ) (= *semi-transparent*) vaporoso

gave [geɪv] (PT) *of* **give**

gavel ['gævl] (N) martillo *m* (*de presidente de reunión o subastador*)

gavotte [gə'vɒt] (N) gavota *f*

Gawd* [gɔːd] (EXCL) (*Brit*) = **god**; ¡Dios mío!

gawk* [gɔːk] (N) papamoscas *mf inv*
(VI) mirar boquiabierto • **to ~ at** mirar boquiabierto • **he stood there ~ing at her** quedó boquiabierto mirándola

gawkily ['gɔːkɪlɪ] (ADV) [*move, walk*] desgarbadamente, torpemente

gawky* ['gɔːkɪ] (ADJ) (COMPAR: **gawkier**, SUPERL: **gawkiest**) desgarbado, torpe

gawp* [gɔːp] (VI) (*Brit*) = **gawk**

gay [geɪ] (ADJ) **1** (= *homosexual*) [*man, community, movement*] gay (*adj inv*), homosexual; [*woman*] homosexual, lesbiano; [*bar*] gay (*adj inv*), de gays • **a centre for lesbians and gay men** un centro para lesbianas y gays • **gay men and women** hombres y mujeres homosexuales, gays y lesbianas • **gay sex** relaciones *fpl* homosexuales • **the gay scene** el ambiente gay *or* homosexual
2† (COMPAR: **gayer**, SUPERL: **gayest**) (= *cheerful*) [*person, colour, costume*] alegre; [*atmosphere, music, laughter*] alegre, festivo
3 (= *carefree*) • **with gay abandon** despreocupadamente, alegremente • **she's living the gay life in Paris** se da la gran vida en París, se pega la vida padre en París*
(N) (= *man*) gay *m*, homosexual *m*; (= *woman*) lesbiana *f*, homosexual *f*
(CPD) ▸ **the gay liberation movement, gay lib*** el movimiento de liberación homosexual ▸ **gay marriage** matrimonio *m* gay, matrimonio *m* homosexual ▸ **gay rights** derechos *mpl* de los homosexuales

gaydar* ['geɪdɑːʳ] (N) gaydar *m*, *capacidad intuitiva para reconocer a homosexuales*

gayness ['geɪnɪs] (N) homosexualidad *f*

Gaza Strip ['gɑːzə'strɪp] (N) franja *f* de Gaza

gaze [geɪz] (N) mirada *f* (fija) • **his ~ met mine** se cruzaron nuestras miradas
(VI) • **to ~ at** mirar fijamente • **to ~ at o.s. in the mirror** mirarse (fijamente) en el espejo • **they ~d into each other's eyes** se miraron fijamente a los ojos • **to ~ into space** mirar distraídamente al vacío

gazebo [gə'ziːbəʊ] (PL: **gazebos**) (N) cenador *m*

gazelle [gə'zel] (N) (PL: **gazelles** *or* **gazelle**) gacela *f*

gazette [gə'zet] (N) (= *newspaper*) gaceta *f*; (= *official publication*) boletín *m* oficial

gazetteer [ˌgæzɪ'tɪəʳ] (N) diccionario *m* geográfico

gazpacho [gæz'pætʃəʊ] (N) gazpacho *m*

gazump* [gə'zʌmp] (*Brit*) (VT) [*buyer*] ofrecer un precio más alto que; [*seller*] *rehusar la venta de una propiedad a la persona con quien se había acordado aceptando una oferta más alta* • **we were ~ed** ofrecieron más que nosotros
(VI) [*buyer*] ofrecer un precio más alto; [*seller*] *faltar al compromiso de vender una casa aceptando una oferta más alta*

gazumping* [gə'zʌmpɪŋ] (N) (*Brit*) *subida del precio de una casa tras haber sido apalabrado*

gazunder* [gə'zʌndəʳ] (*Brit*) (VT) [*+ person*] ofrecer un precio más bajo de lo antes convenido a • **we were ~ed** nos ofrecieron menos de lo antes convenido
(VI) ofrecer un precio más bajo de lo antes convenido
(N) *bajada del precio de una casa tras haber sido apalabrado*

GB (N ABBR) (= **Great Britain**) Gran Bretaña *f*

GBH (N ABBR) (*Brit*) (*Jur*) (= **grievous bodily harm**) graves daños *mpl* corporales

GBP, **gbp** (ABBR) = **Great British Pounds**

GBS (ABBR) (*Brit*) = **George Bernard Shaw**

GC (N ABBR) (*Brit*) (= **George Cross**) *medalla del valor civil*

GCA (N ABBR) = **ground-controlled approach**

GCE (N ABBR) (*Brit*) = **General Certificate of Education**

GCH (N ABBR) = **gas(-fired) central heating**

GCHQ (N ABBR) (*Brit*) (= **Government Communications Headquarters**) *entidad gubernamental que recoge datos mediante escuchas electrónicas*

GCSE (N ABBR) (*Brit*) = **General Certificate of Secondary Education**

> **GCSE**
> El **GCSE** o **General Certificate of Secondary Education** es el certificado académico que se expide en el Reino Unido (con la excepción de Escocia, cuyo equivalente son las **National Qualifications** or **NQs**) para cada una de las asignaturas de la Educación Secundaria Obligatoria. Los exámenes tienen lugar cuando el alumno tiene dieciséis años y las calificaciones van de la A a la G, (A es la máxima, G la mínima), y son el resultado de la combinación de una evaluación continua y de la nota de los exámenes finales, que son corregidos por un tribunal ajeno al centro escolar.
> ▹ **A LEVELS**

GDI (ABBR) = **gross domestic income**

gdn (ABBR) = **garden**

Gdns (ABBR) = **Gardens**

GDP (N ABBR) (= **gross domestic product**) PIB *m*, PGB *m* (*Chile*), PTB *m* (*And*)

GDR (N ABBR) (*Hist*) (= **German Democratic Republic**) RDA *f*

gear [gɪəʳ] (N) **1** (*Aut*) marcha *f*, velocidad *f* • **first/second ~** primera *f*/segunda *f* (velocidad) • **top** *or* (*US*) **high ~** (= *fifth*) quinta velocidad, superdirecta *f*; (= *fourth*) cuarta velocidad, directa *f* • **to change ~** (*Brit*) cambiar de marcha • **the election campaign moved into high ~ this week** la campaña electoral se intensificó esta semana • **in ~** embragado • **to put a car in ~** meter una marcha • **he left the car in ~** dejó el coche con una marcha metida • **he helped her get her life back into ~ after the divorce** la ayudó a poner su vida de nuevo en marcha tras el divorcio • **to get one's brain into ~** hacer

g

trabajar el cerebro • **out of ~** desembragado • **that threw all his plans out of ~** eso le desbarató todos los planes • **to shift ~** (*US*) cambiar de marcha • IDIOM: • **to get one's arse** *or* (*US*) **ass in ~**** mover el culo*
2* (= *equipment*) equipo *m*; (= *tools*) herramientas *fpl*; (*for fishing*) aparejo *m*; (= *belongings*) cosas *fpl*, bártulos *mpl*; (= *clothing*) ropa *f*
3 (*Mech*) engranaje *m*; (= *machinery*) mecanismo *m*, aparato *m*; ▹ **landing**
VT (*fig*) (= *adapt*) • **the book is ~ed to adult students** el libro está dirigido a estudiantes adultos • **we both ~ed our lives to the children** los dos orientamos nuestras vidas hacia los niños • **the factory was not ~ed to cope with an increase in production** la fábrica no estaba preparada para hacer frente a un aumento de la producción • **the service is ~ed to meet the needs of the disabled** el servicio está pensado para satisfacer las necesidades de los minusválidos
CPD ▸ **gear change** (= *act*) cambio *m* de marcha; (*US*) (= *control*) = **gear lever** ▸ **gear lever, gear stick** palanca *f* de cambios ▸ **gear ratio** [*of cycle*] proporción *f* entre plato y piñón
▸ **gear down** VI + ADV (*Aut*) reducir la marcha
▸ **gear up** VT + ADV (*fig*) • **to ~ o.s. up to do sth** prepararse (psicológicamente) para hacer algo • **we're ~ed up to do it** estamos preparados para hacerlo
VI + ADV prepararse, hacer preparativos • **they are ~ing up to fight** se están preparando para luchar • **the shops were ~ing up for Christmas** las tiendas se estaban preparando para las Navidades

gearbox ['gɪəbɒks] N (*Aut*) caja *f* de cambios *or* velocidades; (*Mech*) caja *f* de engranajes

gearshift ['gɪəʃɪft] (*US*) = **gear lever**

gearwheel ['gɪəwi:l] N rueda *f* dentada

gecko ['gekəʊ] N (PL: **geckos** *or* **geckoes**) geco *m*

GED N ABBR (*US*) (*Educ*) = **general equivalency diploma**

geddit‡ ['gedɪt] EXCL • **~?** ¿entiendes?, ¿lo pillas? (*Sp**), ¿lo coges? (*Sp**)

gee¹* [dʒi:] EXCL (*esp US*) ¡caramba! • **gee whiz!** ¡córcholis! • **gee up!** ¡arre!

gee²* [dʒi:] = **gee-gee**

gee-gee* ['dʒi:dʒi:] N (*child language*) caballito *m*, jaca *f*

geek* [gi:k] N (*esp US*) cretino/a *m/f*

geeky* ['gi:kɪ] ADJ (*esp US*) cretino

geese [gi:s] NPL *of* **goose**

geezer* ['gi:zəʳ] N (*Brit*) (= *fellow*) tío* *m*, colega‡ *m* • **(old) ~** viejo* *m*, tío *m* viejo*

Geiger counter ['gaɪgə,kaʊntəʳ] N contador *m* Geiger

geisha ['geɪʃə] N (PL: **geisha** *or* **geishas**) geisha *f*

gel [dʒel] N gel *m* • **hair gel** fijador *m*
VI **1** (*lit*) gelificarse
2 (*fig*) [*ideas, plans*] encajar (**with** en)

gelatin, gelatine ['dʒeləti:n] N gelatina *f*

gelatinous [dʒɪ'lætɪnəs] ADJ gelatinoso

geld [geld] VT castrar, capar

gelding ['geldɪŋ] N caballo *m* castrado

gelignite ['dʒelɪgnaɪt] N gelignita *f*

gelt‡ [gelt] N (*US*) pasta* *f*

gem [dʒem] N (= *jewel*) joya *f*, alhaja *f*; (= *stone*) piedra *f* preciosa *or* semipreciosa, gema *f* • **I must read you this gem*** tengo que leerte esto porque hace época • **my cleaner is a gem** la señora que me hace la limpieza es una joya

Gemini ['dʒemɪnaɪ] N **1** (= *sign, constellation*) Géminis *m*
2 (= *person*) géminis *mf* • **I'm (a) ~** soy géminis

Geminian ['dʒemɪnaɪən] N géminis *mf* • **to be (a) ~** ser géminis

gemstone ['dʒem,stəʊn] N piedra *f* preciosa *or* semipreciosa, gema *f*

Gen ABBR (*Mil*) (= **General**) Gen., Gral.

gen¹ ABBR **1** = **general, generally**
2 (= **gender**) gen.
3 (= **genitive**) gen.

gen²* [dʒen] N (*Brit*) información *f* • **to give sb the gen on sth** poner a algn al corriente de algo
▸ **gen up*** (*Brit*) VT + ADV • **to gen sb up (on sth)** poner a algn al corriente (de algo) • **I'm thoroughly genned up now** ahora estoy bien enterado, ahora estoy completamente al tanto
VI + ADV • **to gen up on sth** informarse acerca de algo

gendarme ['ʒɑ:ndɑ:m] N gendarme *mf*

gender ['dʒendəʳ] N (*Ling*) género *m*; (= *sex*) sexo *m*
CPD ▸ **gender gap** brecha *f* entre los sexos ▸ **gender selection** (= *choosing sex of a baby*) elección *f* del sexo ▸ **gender stereotype** estereotipo *m* sexual

gender-bender* ['dʒendəbendəʳ] N persona *f* de sexualidad ambigua

gene [dʒi:n] N (*Bio*) gene *m*, gen *m*
CPD ▸ **gene mapping** cartografía *f* genética ▸ **gene pool** acervo *m* genético ▸ **gene sequence** secuencia *f* genética ▸ **gene sequencing** secuenciamiento *m* genético ▸ **gene splicing** acoplamiento *m* de genes ▸ **gene technology** tecnología *f* genética ▸ **gene therapy** terapia *f* génica, terapia *f* de genes

genealogical [,dʒi:nɪə'lɒdʒɪkəl] ADJ genealógico

genealogist [,dʒi:nɪ'ælədʒɪst] N genealogista *mf*

genealogy [,dʒi:nɪ'ælədʒɪ] N genealogía *f*

genera ['dʒenərə] NPL *of* **genus**

general ['dʒenərəl] ADJ **1** (= *overall*) [*appearance, decline, attitude*] general • **the ~ standard of education is very high** el nivel general de educación es muy alto
2 (= *widespread*) [*view, interest*] general • **there was ~ agreement on this question** hubo un consenso general con respecto a esta cuestión • **contrary to ~ belief** contrariamente a *or* en contra de lo que comúnmente se cree • **there was ~ opposition to the proposal** la oposición a la propuesta fue general *or* generalizada • **for ~ use** para el uso general • **in ~ use** de uso general
3 (= *vague, non-specific*) general • **beware of making statements which are too ~** ten cuidado de hacer afirmaciones que sean demasiado generales • **the report was too ~** el informe era poco específico • **try to be more ~** intenta no entrar tanto en detalles • **we drove in the ~ direction of Aberdeen** fuimos conduciendo en dirección aproximada a Aberdeen • **please direct any ~ enquiries you may have to my secretary** le ruego solicite a mi secretaria cualquier información de carácter general • **I've got the ~ idea** tengo más o menos una idea • **I'm beginning to get the ~ picture** estoy empezando a hacerme una idea • **a ~ term** un término genérico • **in ~ terms** en líneas *or* términos generales
4 (= *usual*) • **as a ~ rule** por regla general
5 (= *not specialized*) [*reader, public*] no especializado • **we employ two ~ labourers** empleamos a dos obreros no especializados • **an introduction to psychology for the ~ reader** una introducción a la psicología para el lector no especializado
6 (*at end of title*) general • **secretary ~** secretario/a *m/f* general
N **1** • **in ~** en general • **we discussed work in ~** hablamos sobre el trabajo en general • **in ~ this kind of situation can be controlled** (= *normally*) en general *or* por lo general este tipo de situaciones pueden controlarse
2 • **the particular and the ~** lo particular y lo general
3 (*Mil*) (= *officer*) general *mf* • **General Croft arrived late** el general Croft llegó tarde • **good morning, General Croft** buenos días, General Croft
CPD ▸ **general anaesthesia** anestesia *f* general ▸ **general anaesthetic, general anesthetic** (*US*) anestesia *f* general ▸ **general assembly** asamblea *f* general ▸ **general audit** auditoría *f* general ▸ **general cargo** cargamento *m* mixto ▸ **General Certificate of Secondary Education** (*Brit*) (*Educ*) ▹ **GCSE** ▸ **the General Confession** (*Church of England*) la oración de confesión colectiva ▸ **general costs** gastos *mpl* generales ▸ **general dealer** (*US*) tienda *f*, almacén *m* (*S. Cone*) ▸ **general delivery** (*US, Canada*) lista *f* de correos ▸ **general election** elecciones *fpl or* comicios *mpl* generales ▸ **general expenses** gastos *mpl* generales ▸ **general headquarters** (*Mil*) cuartel *msing* general ▸ **general holiday** día *m* festivo ▸ **general hospital** hospital *m* ▸ **general knowledge** cultura *f* general ▸ **general manager** director(a) *m/f* general ▸ **general medicine** medicina *f* general ▸ **general meeting** asamblea *f* general ▸ **General Officer Commanding** (*Mil*) Comandante *mf* en Jefe ▸ **general partnership** (*Jur*) sociedad *f* regular colectiva ▸ **General Post Office** (*Brit*) (*Govt*) (*formerly*) Correos *m*; (= *main post office*) oficina *f* de correos ▸ **general practice** (*Brit*) (*Med*) (= *work*) medicina *f* general; (= *group*) consultorio *m* médico • **I am currently working in ~ practice** actualmente estoy trabajando como médico de medicina general • **to go into ~ practice** entrar a trabajar en medicina general ▸ **general practitioner** médico/a *m/f* de medicina general (*frm*), médico/a *m/f* de cabecera ▸ **the general public** el público en general, el gran público ▸ **general science** (*Scol*) Ciencias *fpl* ▸ **general science teacher** profesor(a) *m/f* de Ciencias ▸ **General Secretary** Secretario(a) *m/f* General ▸ **general staff** estado *m* mayor (general) ▸ **general store** (*US*) tienda *f*, almacén *m* (*S. Cone*) ▸ **general strike** huelga *f* general ▸ **General Studies** (*Brit*) estudios *m* generales

generalissimo [,dʒenərə'lɪsɪməʊ] N generalísimo *m*

generality [,dʒenə'rælɪtɪ] N [*of rule, belief*] generalidad *f* • **to talk in generalities** hablar en términos generales

generalization [,dʒenərəlaɪ'zeɪʃən] N generalización *f*

generalize ['dʒenərəlaɪz] VI generalizar • **to ~ about** generalizar sobre • **to ~ from** generalizar en base a

generalized ['dʒenərəlaɪzd] ADJ (= *general*) [*discussion, problem*] general; [*feeling*] generalizado, general
CPD ▸ **generalized anxiety disorder** trastorno *m* de ansiedad generalizada

generally ['dʒenərəlɪ] ADV **1** (= *on the whole*) en general, en líneas generales • **~, the course is okay** en general *or* en líneas generales el curso está bien • **his account was ~ accurate** su relato fue en general *or* en líneas generales exacto • **they broke the**

toys, fought, and ~ misbehaved rompieron los juguetes, se pelearon y en general se portaron mal
2 (= *usually*) generalmente, por lo general • **we ~ meet on Tuesdays** generalmente *or* por lo general nos reunimos los martes
3 (= *widely*) generalmente • **a ~ accepted definition** una definición generalmente aceptada, una definición aceptada por casi todo el mundo • **it is ~ believed that ...** la mayoría de la gente cree que ..., generalmente, se cree que ... • **it's not yet ~ available** (*on sale*) no está todavía a la venta *or* en el mercado
4 • **~ speaking** por lo general, en términos generales

general-purpose [ˌdʒenərəlˈpɜːpəs] ADJ [*tool, dictionary*] de uso general

generalship [ˈdʒenərəlʃɪp] N (= *period in office*) generalato *m*; (= *leadership*) dirección *f*, don *m* de mando

generate [ˈdʒenəreɪt] VT [+ *electricity, heat*] generar; [+ *employment, income, wealth, publicity*] generar; [+ *interest*] suscitar, generar

generating [ˈdʒenəreɪtɪŋ] CPD ▸ **generating set** grupo *m* electrógeno ▸ **generating station** central *f* generadora

generation [ˌdʒenəˈreɪʃən] N 1 (= *act*) generación *f*
2 (= *group of people*) generación *f* • **the younger ~** la nueva generación • **the older ~** los mayores • **first/second/third/fourth ~** (*Comput*) de primera/segunda/tercera/cuarta generación
CPD ▸ **the generation gap** la brecha entre las generaciones

generational [ˌdʒenəˈreɪʃənl] ADJ generacional

generative [ˈdʒenərətɪv] ADJ generativo
CPD ▸ **generative grammar** gramática *f* generativa

generator [ˈdʒenəreɪtəʳ] N generador *m*, grupo *m* electrógeno

generic [dʒɪˈnerɪk] ADJ genérico
CPD ▸ **generic drug** droga *f* genérica

generically [dʒɪˈnerɪklɪ] ADV genéricamente, de manera genérica

generosity [ˌdʒenəˈrɒsɪtɪ] N generosidad *f*

generous [ˈdʒenərəs] ADJ 1 (= *not mean*) [*person, mood*] generoso • **she must have been feeling ~** debía sentirse generosa *or* dadivosa • **she was ~ in her praise of him** se deshizo en elogios para con él • **she was ~ in her praise of what he'd done** hizo grandes elogios de lo que había realizado • **that's very ~ of you** eso es muy generoso de tu parte • **he was rather too ~ with the chilli sauce** se pasó un poco con la salsa picante, se le fue un poco la mano con la salsa picante • **to be ~ with one's money** ser generoso *or* desprendido con el dinero • **be ~ with the cream** no escatimes la nata • **he wasn't exactly ~ with the whisky** no fue muy espléndido que digamos con el whisky
2 (= *lavish, sizeable*) [*gift*] espléndido; [*donation*] cuantioso, generoso; [*rise*] importante, generoso; [*pay, offer*] generoso; [*portion*] grande, generoso; [*bosom, figure*] opulento • **very ~ credit terms** unas condiciones de crédito muy favorables • **a ~ amount of sth** una buena cantidad de algo • **a ~ helping of sth** una ración generosa de algo, una buena ración de algo
3 (= *kind*) [*person, gesture*] amable • **it was very ~ of Nigel to say what he did** fue muy amable por parte de Nigel decir lo que dijo • **thank you for your ~ remarks** gracias por sus amables observaciones

generously [ˈdʒenərəslɪ] ADV 1 (= *not meanly*) [*give, donate, reward*] generosamente • **please give ~ to this worthy cause** por favor, contribuyan generosamente a esta noble causa
2 (= *liberally*) • **season ~ with salt** condimentar con abundante sal • **~ cut shirts** camisas de corte amplio • **a ~ illustrated book** un libro ampliamente ilustrado • **she was a ~ proportioned woman** era una mujer de opulentas formas
3 (= *kindly*) [*offer, provide*] generosamente • **he ~ offered to cancel the debt** se ofreció generosamente a cancelar la deuda, en un gesto desinteresado, se ofreció a cancelar la deuda • **they very ~ offered to help us move house** se ofrecieron generosamente a ayudarnos a mudarnos de casa

genesis [ˈdʒenɪsɪs] N (PL: **geneses** [ˈdʒenɪsiːz]) 1 génesis *f inv*
2 • **Genesis** (*Bible*) Génesis *m*

genet [ˈdʒenɪt] N jineta *f*, gineta *f*

genetic [dʒɪˈnetɪk] ADJ genético
CPD ▸ **genetic algorithm** algoritmo *m* genético ▸ **genetic code** código *m* genético ▸ **genetic engineering** ingeniería *f* genética ▸ **genetic fingerprint** huella *f* genética ▸ **genetic fingerprinting** identificación *f* genética ▸ **genetic manipulation** manipulación *f* genética ▸ **genetic material** material *m* genético ▸ **genetic modification** modificación *f* genética ▸ **genetic pollution** contaminación *f* genética

genetically [dʒɪˈnetɪkəlɪ] ADV (*gen*) genéticamente • **~ engineered** manipulado genéticamente • **~ modified** [*plant, animal, organism, cell*] modificado genéticamente, transgénico • **~-modified foods** alimentos *mpl* transgénicos

geneticist [dʒɪˈnetɪsɪst] N (*Med*) genetista *mf*

genetics [dʒɪˈnetɪks] NSING genética *f*

Geneva [dʒɪˈniːvə] N Ginebra • **the ~ Convention** la convención de Ginebra

genial [ˈdʒiːnɪəl] ADJ [*manner, welcome*] cordial; [*person*] simpático, afable

geniality [ˌdʒiːnɪˈælɪtɪ] N simpatía *f*, afabilidad *f*

genially [ˈdʒiːnɪəlɪ] ADV afablemente

genie [ˈdʒiːnɪ] N (PL: **genii**) genio *m* • IDIOM: • **the ~ is out of the bottle** lo hecho, hecho está, es imposible dar marcha atrás

genital [ˈdʒenɪtl] ADJ genital
N **genitals** (órganos *mpl*) genitales *mpl*
CPD ▸ **genital herpes** herpes *m* genital

genitalia [ˌdʒenɪˈteɪlɪə] NPL genitales *mpl*

genitive [ˈdʒenɪtɪv] (*Ling*) N genitivo *m*
CPD ▸ **genitive case** caso *m* genitivo • **in the ~ case** en el genitivo

genius [ˈdʒiːnɪəs] N (PL: **geniuses**) (= *person*) genio *m*; (= *cleverness*) genialidad *f*; (= *talent*) don *m* • **he's a ~** es un genio, es genial • **you're a ~!** (*iro*) ¡eres un hacha! • **a man of ~** un hombre genial • **she's a mathematical ~** es un genio para las matemáticas • **to have a ~ for (doing) sth** tener un don especial para (hacer) algo • **you have a ~ for forgetting things** tienes un don especial para olvidar las cosas

genned up [ˈdʒendˈʌp] ADJ ▹ **gen up**

Genoa [ˈdʒenəʊə] N Génova *f*

genocidal [ˌdʒenəʊˈsaɪdl] ADJ genocida

genocide [ˈdʒenəʊsaɪd] N genocidio *m*

Genoese [ˌdʒenəʊˈiːz] ADJ genovés
N genovés/esa *m/f*

genome [ˈdʒiːnəʊm] N genoma *m*

genomic [dʒɪˈnɒmɪk] ADJ genómico
• **~ research** investigación *f* genómica

genomics [dʒɪˈnɒmɪks] NSING genómica *f*

genotype [ˈdʒenəʊtaɪp] N genotipo *m*

genre [ʒɑ̃ːnr] N género *m*

gent [dʒent] N ABBR 1 (= **gentleman**) caballero *m* • **what will you have, ~s?** (*hum*) ¿qué van a tomar los caballeros?
2 • **the ~s*** (= *lavatory*) el servicio (de caballeros), el baño (de señores) (*LAm*) • **can you tell me where the ~s is, please?** ¿el servicio de caballeros, por favor? • **"gents"** "caballeros"

genteel [dʒenˈtiːl] ADJ 1 (= *middle-class*) [*person*] elegante, refinado; [*manners*] refinado, fino; [*atmosphere*] elegante • **a ~ resort on the south coast** un elegante centro turístico de la costa del sur • **to live in ~ poverty** vivir modestamente pero con dignidad
2 (*pej*) (= *affected*) afectado

gentian [ˈdʒenʃɪən] N genciana *f*
CPD ▸ **gentian violet** violeta *f* de genciana

Gentile [ˈdʒentaɪl] ADJ no judío; (= *pagan*) gentil
N no judío/a *m/f*; (= *pagan*) gentil *mf*

gentility [dʒenˈtɪlɪtɪ] N [*of person, family*] refinamiento *m*, elegancia *f*; [*of place*] elegancia *f*

gentle [ˈdʒentl] ADJ (COMPAR: **gentler**, SUPERL: **gentlest**) 1 (= *kind, good-natured*) [*person*] de carácter dulce; [*manner, voice*] dulce, delicado; [*eyes, smile*] dulce, tierno; [*hint, reminder, rebuke*] discreto; [*animal*] manso, dócil • **to be ~ with sb/sth** (= *careful*) tener cuidado con algn/algo • **be ~ with him, he's had a terrible shock** ten consideración con él, ha sufrido un golpe muy duro • **to poke ~ fun at sb** burlarse sin malicia de algn, burlarse cariñosamente de algn • **the policy of ~ persuasion had failed** la política de la sutil persuasión había fracasado • **try a little ~ persuasion, he might say yes** intenta persuadirlo un poco, puede que diga que sí • **he needs a ~ push** necesita un pequeño empuje • **the ~ or ~r sex†** el bello sexo • IDIOM: • **as ~ as a lamb** más bueno que el pan, más manso que un cordero
2 (= *mild*) [*shampoo, soap, detergent*] suave • **it is ~ on the skin** no irrita la piel
3 (= *light*) [*touch, pressure, push, breeze*] suave, ligero • **there was a ~ tap at the door** se oyeron unos golpecitos a la puerta
4 (= *moderate*) [*exercise*] moderado • **cook for 30 minutes over a ~ heat** cocinar durante 30 minutos a fuego lento • **we jogged along at a ~ pace** hicimos footing a un ritmo suave • **it was too hot even for a ~ stroll** hacía demasiado calor incluso para pasear lentamente
5 (= *not steep*) [*slope*] suave, poco pronunciado; [*curve*] no muy cerrado • **~ rolling hills** colinas suaves y onduladas
6† (= *noble*) • **of ~ birth** de noble cuna • **~ reader** estimado *or* querido lector

gentleman [ˈdʒentlmən] N (PL: **gentlemen**) (= *man*) señor *m*; (*having gentlemanly qualities*) caballero *m*; (*at court††*) gentilhombre *m* • **there's a ~ waiting to see you** hay un señor esperando para verle • **young ~** señorito *m* • **to be a perfect ~** ser un perfecto caballero • **he's no ~** poco caballero es él • **"gentlemen"** (= *lavatory*) "caballeros"
CPD ▸ **gentleman's agreement** acuerdo *m* entre caballeros ▸ **gentleman farmer** terrateniente *m* ▸ **gentleman's gentleman** ayuda *m* de cámara

gentlemanly [ˈdʒentlmənlɪ] ADJ caballeroso

gentleness [ˈdʒentlnɪs] N 1 (= *gentle nature*) [*of person*] dulzura *f* (de carácter); [*of manner, voice*] dulzura *f*, delicadeza *f*; [*of smile*] dulzura *f*, ternura *f*; [*of hint, reminder, rebuke*] lo discreto; [*of animal*] mansedumbre *f*,

docilidad *f*
2 (= *care*) (*in handling sth/sb*) cuidado *m*; (= *consideration*) consideración *f*
3 (= *mildness*) [*of shampoo, soap etc*] suavidad *f*
4 (= *lightness*) [*of movement, touch, breeze*] suavidad *f*, ligereza *f*
5 (= *not steepness*) [*of slope*] suavidad *f*

gentlewoman†† ['dʒentl,wʊmən] N (PL: **gentlewomen**) (*by birth*) dama *f*, señora *f* de buena familia

gently ['dʒentlɪ] ADV **1** (= *softly, kindly*) [*say*] dulcemente, suavemente; [*smile*] dulcemente, con dulzura; [*hint, remind*] con delicadeza
2 (= *carefully*) [*handle*] con cuidado • **~ clean the wound with salt water** limpiar la herida con cuidado usando agua salada • **a lotion that ~ cleanses your skin** una loción que limpia la piel sin irritar • **~ does it!** ¡con cuidado!, ¡despacito!*
3 (= *lightly*) [*blow, touch, push, tap*] ligeramente, suavemente • **I shook her ~ and she opened her eyes** la sacudí ligeramente *or* suavemente y abrió los ojos
4 (= *slowly*) [*pick up speed*] poco a poco; [*simmer, cook*] a fuego lento • **simmer ~ until the sugar dissolves** hervir a fuego lento hasta que el azúcar se disuelva
5 (= *not steeply*) [*slope*] suavemente

gentrification [,dʒentrɪfɪ'keɪʃən] N aburguesamiento *m*

gentrified ['dʒentrɪ,faɪd] ADJ aburguesado

gentrify ['dʒentrɪfaɪ] VT aburguesar

gentry ['dʒentrɪ] N (*Brit*) alta burguesía *f*, pequeña aristocracia *f*; (*pej*) familias *fpl* bien, gente *f* bien; (= *set of people*) gente *f*

genuflect ['dʒenjʊflekt] VI (*frm*) hacer una genuflexión

genuflection, genuflexion (*US*) [dʒenjʊ'flekʃən] N genuflexión *f*

genuine ['dʒenjʊɪn] ADJ **1** (= *authentic*) [*picture, antique*] auténtico; [*claim, refugee*] verdadero • **it is a ~ Renoir** es un Renoir auténtico • **a ~ leather sofa** un sofá de cuero legítimo *or* auténtico • **this is no cheap imitation, it's the ~ article** esto no es una imitación barata, es genuino *or* auténtico • **this dancer is the ~ article** esta es una bailarina de verdad
2 (= *sincere*) [*concern, disbelief, interest, enthusiasm*] verdadero, sincero; [*love*] verdadero, de verdad; [*commitment, difficulty*] verdadero, auténtico; [*offer, buyer*] serio • **it was a ~ mistake** fue realmente un error • **if this offer is ~ I will gladly accept it** si esta oferta va en serio *or* es seria la aceptaré con mucho gusto • **she is very ~ and caring** es noble y bondadosa

genuinely ['dʒenjʊɪnlɪ] ADV
1 (= *authentically*) [*funny*] realmente, verdaderamente • **he claims, probably quite ~, to be ...** asegura, y probablemente sea cierto, ser ...
2 (= *sincerely*) [*believe*] sinceramente, realmente; [*want*] realmente, de verdad; [*interested, worried, upset*] verdaderamente, realmente • **he ~ wants to change** realmente *or* de verdad quiere cambiar • **they were ~ pleased to see me** se alegraban de verdad de verme • **I'm ~ sorry that Peter has gone** siento de verdad que Peter se haya ido, lamento sinceramente que Peter se haya ido

genuineness ['dʒenjʊɪnnɪs] N
1 (= *authenticity*) [*of painting, antique*] autenticidad *f*; [*of claim*] veracidad *f*
2 (= *sincerity*) [*of concern, feelings*] sinceridad *f*, autenticidad *f*
3 (= *honesty*) [*of person*] nobleza *f*

genus ['dʒenəs] N (PL: **genera** *or* **genuses**) (*Bio*) género *m*

geo... ['dʒi:əʊ] PREFIX geo...

geochemical [,dʒi:əʊ'kemɪkəl] ADJ geoquímico

geochemist [,dʒi:əʊ'kemɪst] N geoquímico/a *m/f*

geochemistry [,dʒi:əʊ'kemɪstrɪ] N geoquímica *f*

geodesic [,dʒi:əʊ'desɪk] ADJ geodésico

geodesy [dʒi:'ɒdɪsɪ] N geodesia *f*

geodetic [,dʒi:əʊ'detɪk] ADJ = **geodesic**

geoengineering [,dʒi:əʊendʒɪ'nɪərɪŋ] N geoingeniería *f*
CPD ▸ **geoengineering company** empresa *f* de geoingeniería ▸ **geoengineering solution** solución *f* de geoingeniería ▸ **geoengineering technology** tecnología *f* de geoingeniería

Geoffrey ['dʒefrɪ] N Geofredo, Godofredo

geographer [dʒɪ'ɒgrəfəʳ] N geógrafo/a *m/f*

geographic [dʒɪə'græfɪk] ADJ = **geographical**

geographical [dʒɪə'græfɪkəl] ADJ geográfico

geographically [dʒɪə'græfɪkəlɪ] ADV geográficamente • **~ speaking** desde el punto de vista geográfico

geography [dʒɪ'ɒgrəfɪ] N geografía *f* • **policemen who knew the local ~** policías que conocían bien el lugar

geolocate [,dʒi:əʊləʊ'keɪt] VT geolocalizar

geolocation [,dʒi:əʊləʊ'keɪʃən] N geolocalización *f*

geological [dʒɪəʊ'lɒdʒɪkəl] ADJ geológico

geologically [dʒɪə'lɒdʒɪkəlɪ] ADV geológicamente • **~ speaking** desde el punto de vista geológico

geologist [dʒɪ'ɒlədʒɪst] N geólogo/a *m/f*

geology [dʒɪ'ɒlədʒɪ] N geología *f*

geomagnetic [,dʒi:əʊmæg'netɪk] ADJ geomagnético

geomagnetism [,dʒi:əʊ'mægnɪ,tɪzəm] N geomagnetismo *m*

geometric [dʒɪə'metrɪk] ADJ geométrico

geometrical [dʒɪə'metrɪkəl] ADJ = **geometric**

geometrically [dʒɪə'metrɪkəlɪ] ADV geométricamente

geometrician [,dʒi:əmɪ'trɪʃən] N geómetra *mf*

geometry [dʒɪ'ɒmɪtrɪ] N geometría *f*

geomorphic [,dʒi:əʊ'mɔ:fɪk] ADJ geomórfico

geomorphologic [,dʒi:əʊ'mɔ:fə'lɒdʒɪk] ADJ = **geomorphological**

geomorphological [,dʒi:əʊ'mɔ:fə'lɒdʒɪkəl] ADJ geomorfológico

geomorphology [,dʒi:əʊmɔ:'fɒlədʒɪ] N geomorfología *f*

geophysical [,dʒi:əʊ'fɪzɪkəl] ADJ geofísico

geophysicist [,dʒi:əʊ'fɪzɪsɪst] N geofísico/a *m/f*

geophysics [dʒɪəʊ'fɪzɪks] NSING geofísica *f*

geopolitical [,dʒi:əʊpə'lɪtɪkəl] ADJ geopolítico

geopolitics ['dʒi:əʊ'pɒlɪtɪks] NSING geopolítica *f*

Geordie* ['dʒɔ:dɪ] N (*Brit*) *nativo/habitante de Tyneside en el NE de Inglaterra*

George [dʒɔ:dʒ] N Jorge

georgette [dʒɔ:'dʒet] N crêpe *f* georgette

Georgia ['dʒɔ:dʒɪə] N (*US, Asia*) Georgia *f*

Georgian ['dʒɔ:dʒɪən] ADJ (*Brit*) georgiano

geoscience [,dʒi:əʊ'saɪəns] N geociencia *f*

geoscientist [,dʒi:əʊ'saɪəntɪst] N geocientífico/a *m/f*

geostationary [,dʒi:əʊ'steɪʃənərɪ] ADJ geoestacionario

geostrategic [,dʒi:əʊstrə'ti:dʒɪk] ADJ geoestratégico

geostrategy [,dʒi:əʊstrə'ti:dʒɪ] N geoestrategia *f*

geotechnical [,dʒi:əʊ'teknɪkəl] ADJ geotécnico

geothermal [,dʒi:əʊ'θɜ:məl] ADJ geotérmico

geranium [dʒɪ'reɪnɪəm] N geranio *m*

gerbil ['dʒɜ:bɪl] N gerbo *m*, jerbo *m*

geriatric [,dʒerɪ'ætrɪk] ADJ **1** geriátrico • **~ home** residencia *f* geriátrica, centro *m* geriátrico • **~ medicine** geriatría *f*
2* (*pej*) • **~ judges** jueces que son unos vejestorios
N **1** (*Med*) persona *f* mayor
2* (*pej*) vejestorio* *m*

geriatrician [,dʒerɪə'trɪʃən] N geriatra *mf*

geriatrics [,dʒerɪ'ætrɪks] NSING geriatría *f*

germ [dʒɜ:m] N (*Bio*) (*also fig*) germen *m*; (*Med*) microbio *m*, germen *m* • **the ~ of an idea** el germen de una idea
CPD ▸ **germ carrier** portador(a) *m/f* de microbios *or* gérmenes ▸ **germ cell** célula *f* germinal ▸ **germ plasm** germen *m* plasma ▸ **germ warfare** guerra *f* bacteriológica

German ['dʒɜ:mən] ADJ alemán
N **1** (= *person*) alemán/ana *m/f*
2 (*Ling*) alemán *m*
CPD ▸ **German Democratic Republic** (*Hist*) República *f* Democrática Alemana ▸ **German measles** rubeola *f*, rubéola *f* ▸ **German shepherd (dog)** pastor *m* alemán, perro *m* lobo ▸ **German speaker** germanoparlante *mf*

germane [dʒɜ:'meɪn] ADJ (*frm*) (= *relevant*) • **that's not ~ to the discussion** eso no atañe a la discusión • **the remark is not ~** el comentario no viene al caso

Germanic [dʒɜ:'mænɪk] ADJ germánico

germanium [dʒɜ:'meɪnɪəm] N germanio *m*

germanophile [dʒɜ:'mænəfaɪl] N germanófilo/a *m/f*

germanophobe [dʒɜ:'mænəfəʊb] N germanófobo/a *m/f*

German-speaking ['dʒɜ:mən,spi:kɪŋ] ADJ de habla alemana

Germany ['dʒɜ:mənɪ] N Alemania *f* • **East ~** Alemania *f* Oriental • **West ~** Alemania *f* Occidental

germ-free [,dʒɜ:m'fri:] ADJ estéril; (= *sterilized*) esterilizado

germicidal [,dʒɜ:mɪ'saɪdl] ADJ germicida, microbicida

germicide ['dʒɜ:mɪsaɪd] N germicida *m*

germinate ['dʒɜ:mɪneɪt] VI germinar

germination [,dʒɜ:mɪ'neɪʃən] N germinación *f*

germ-killer ['dʒɜ:m,kɪləʳ] N germicida *m*

germproof ['dʒɜ:mpru:f] ADJ a prueba de microbios *or* gérmenes

gerontocracy [,dʒerɒn'tɒkrəsɪ] N gerontocracia *f*

gerontologist [,dʒerɒn'tɒlədʒɪst] N gerontólogo/a *m/f*

gerontology [,dʒerɒn'tɒlədʒɪ] N gerontología *f*

Gerry ['dʒerɪ] N *familiar form of* **Gerald, Gerard**

gerrymander ['dʒerɪmændəʳ] VT [+ *voting area*] *dividir de manera favorable a un partido*; (= *manipulate*) manipular
VI *dividir una zona electoral de manera favorable a un partido*

gerrymandering ['dʒerɪmændərɪŋ] N manipulaciones *fpl*

gerund ['dʒerənd] N (*Latin*) gerundio *m*; (*English*) sustantivo *m* verbal

gerundive [dʒə'rʌndɪv] ADJ gerundivo
N gerundio *m*

gestalt [gə'ʃtɑ:lt] N gestalt *m*
CPD ▸ **gestalt psychology** psicología *f*

gestalt ▸ **gestalt therapy** terapéutica *f* gestáltica

Gestapo [ges'tɑːpəʊ] (N) Gestapo *f*

gestate [dʒes'teɪt] (VT) **1** (*Bio*) gestar
2 (*fig*) [+ *idea, project*] gestar
(VI) [*idea, project*] gestarse

gestation [dʒes'teɪʃən] (N) (*Bio*) gestación *f* (*also fig*)

gesticulate [dʒes'tɪkjʊleɪt] (VI) gesticular

gesticulation [dʒes,tɪkjʊ'leɪʃən] (N) gesticulación *f*, manoteo *m*

gestural ['dʒestʃərəl] (ADJ) [*language*] gestual

gesture ['dʒestʃəʳ] (N) **1** (*lit*) ademán *m*, gesto *m*
2 (*fig*) demostración *f*; (= *small token*) muestra *f*, detalle *m* • **what a nice ~!** ¡qué gesto *or* detalle más agradable! • **as a ~ of friendship** en señal de amistad • **as a ~ of support** para demostrar nuestro apoyo • **empty ~** pura formalidad *f*
(VI) hacer gestos • **he ~d towards the door** señaló *or* apuntó hacia la puerta • **to ~ to sb to do sth** indicar a algn con la mano que haga algo
(VT) expresar con un ademán

get [get]

TRANSITIVE VERB
INTRANSITIVE VERB
PHRASAL VERBS

(PT, PP: **got**, (*US*) PP: **gotten**)

When **get** *is part of a set combination, eg* **get the sack, get hold of, get sth right**, *look up the other word.*

TRANSITIVE VERB

1 (= *obtain*) [+ *information, money, visa, divorce*] conseguir; [+ *benefit*] sacar, obtener • **I'll get the money somehow** conseguiré el dinero de alguna forma • **he had trouble getting a hotel room** tuvo dificultades para conseguir una habitación de hotel • **that's what got him the rise** eso fue lo que le consiguió el aumento • **he got it for me** él me lo consiguió • **you need to get permission off** *or* **from the owner** tienes que conseguir el permiso del dueño • **I got the idea off*** *or* **from a TV programme** saqué la idea de un programa de televisión • **he gets all his clothes off*** *or* **from his elder brother** hereda toda la ropa de su hermano mayor • **where did you get that idea from?** ¿de dónde sacaste esa idea? • **we shan't get anything out of him** no lograremos sacarle nada • **you won't get any money out of me** no vas a sacarme dinero • **what are you going to get out of it?** ¿qué vas a sacar de *or* ganar con ello? • **a good coach knows how to get the best out of his players** un buen entrenador sabe cómo sacar lo mejor de sus jugadores • **she gets a lot of pleasure out of gardening** disfruta mucho con la jardinería • **you may get some fun out of it** puede que te resulte divertido

2 (= *have*) tener • **I go whenever I get the chance** voy siempre que tengo ocasión • **to get something to eat** comer algo

3 (= *receive*) **a** [+ *letter, phone call*] recibir; [+ *wage*] ganar, cobrar; [+ *TV station, radio station*] coger, captar • **she gets a good salary** gana *or* cobra un buen sueldo • **not everyone gets a pension** no todo el mundo cobra una pensión • **I got lots of presents** me hicieron muchos regalos • **I think he got the wrong impression** creo que se ha llevado una impresión equivocada • **how much did you get for it?** ¿cuánto te dieron por él? • **he got 15 years for murder** le condenaron a 15 años por asesinato • **he gets his red hair from his mother** el pelo rojizo lo ha heredado de su madre • **I didn't get much from the film** la película no me dijo gran cosa • **I don't get much from his lectures** saco poco provecho de sus clases; ▸ **neck**

b

Some **get** *+ noun combinations are translated using a more specific Spanish verb. If in doubt, look up the noun.*

• **I never got an answer** no me contestaron, no recibí nunca una respuesta • **they get lunch at school** les dan de comer en el colegio • **this area doesn't get much rain** en esta área no llueve mucho • **I got a shock/surprise** me llevé un susto/una sorpresa • **this room gets a lot of sun** a esta habitación le da mucho el sol; ▸ **fine²**, **sentence**

4 (= *buy*) comprar • **I went out to get some milk** salí a comprar leche • **where did you get those shoes?** ¿dónde te has comprado esos zapatos? • **I got it cheap in a sale** lo conseguí barato en unas rebajas

5 (= *fetch*) [+ *glasses, book*] ir a buscar, traer; [+ *person*] ir a buscar, ir a por; (= *pick up*) [+ *goods, person*] recoger • **would you mind getting my glasses?** ¿te importaría ir a buscarme *or* traerme las gafas? • **can you get my coat from the cleaner's?** ¿puedes recogerme el abrigo de la tintorería? • **I'll get some lettuce from the garden** voy a coger un poco de lechuga del jardín • **quick, get help!** ¡rápido, ve a buscar ayuda! • **to get sth for sb** • **to get sb sth** ir a buscar algo a algn, traer algo a algn • **could you get me the scissors please?** ¿puedes ir a buscarme *or* me puedes traer las tijeras, por favor? • **can I get you a drink?** ¿te apetece beber *or* tomar algo?, ¿quieres beber *or* tomar algo? • **to go/come and get sth/sb:** • **I'll go and get it for you** voy a buscártelo, voy a traértelo • **go and get Jane will you?** vete a buscar a Jane, ve a por Jane • **phone me when you arrive and I'll come and get you** cuando llegues llama por teléfono y te iré a buscar *or* recoger

6 (= *call*) [+ *doctor, plumber*] llamar • **please get the doctor** por favor llame al médico

7 (= *answer*) [+ *phone*] contestar • **can you get the phone?** ¿puedes contestar el teléfono? • **I'll get it!** (*telephone*) ¡yo contesto!; (*door*) ¡ya voy yo!

8 (= *gain, win*) [+ *prize*] ganar, llevarse, conseguir; [+ *goal*] marcar; [+ *reputation*] ganarse • **she got first prize** ganó *or* se llevó *or* consiguió el primer premio • **correct, you get 5 points** correcto, gana *or* consigue 5 puntos • **he's in it for what he can get** lo único que quiere es sacarle provecho • **Jackie got good exam results** Jackie sacó buenas notas en los exámenes • **he got a pass/an A in French** sacó un aprobado/un sobresaliente en francés • **I have to get my degree first** antes tengo que acabar la carrera *or* conseguir mi diplomatura

9 (= *find*) [+ *job, flat*] encontrar, conseguir • **he got me a job** me encontró *or* consiguió un trabajo • **you get all sorts in this job** te encuentras con todo tipo de gente en este trabajo • **you don't get bears in this country** en este país no hay osos

10 (= *catch*) [+ *ball, disease, person*] coger, agarrar (*LAm*); [+ *thief*] coger, atrapar (*LAm*); [+ *bus*] coger, tomar (*LAm*); [+ *fish*] pescar • **I'm getting the bus into town** voy a coger el autobús al centro • **got you!*** ¡te pillé!*, ¡te cacé!*, ¡te agarré! (*LAm*) • **got you at last!** ¡por fin te he pillado *or* cazado!* • **I've been trying to get him alone** he estado intentando verle a solas • **to get sb by the throat/arm** agarrar *or* coger a algn de la garganta/del brazo • **I didn't get the details** no oí los detalles • **sorry, I didn't get your name** perdone, ¿cómo dice que se llama?, perdone, no me he enterado de su nombre • **did you get his (registration) number?** ¿viste el número de matrícula? • **you've got me there!*** ahí sí que me has pillado*
• IDIOM: • **to get it from sb:** • **he really got it from the teacher*** el profesor le echó un rapapolvo*; ▸ **bad, religion**

11 (= *reach, put through to*) • **get me Mr Jones, please** (*Telec*) póngame *or* (*esp LAm*) comuníqueme con el Sr. Jones, por favor • **you'll get him at home if you phone this evening** si le llamas esta tarde lo pillarás* *or* encontrarás en casa • **you can get me on this number** puedes contactar conmigo en este número • **I've been trying to get you all week** he estado intentando hablar contigo toda la semana

12* (= *attack, take revenge on*) • **I feel like everyone is out to get me** siento que todo el mundo va contra mí • **I'll get you for that!** ¡esto me lo vas a pagar! • **they're out to get him** van a cargárselo*

13 (= *hit*) [+ *target*] dar en • **the bullet got him in the leg** la bala le dio en la pierna • **it got him on the head** le dio en la cabeza

14 (= *finish*) • **the drink will get him in the end** la bebida acabará con él al final

15 (= *take, bring*) • **how can we get it home?** (*speaker not at home*) ¿cómo podemos llevarlo a casa?; (*speaker at home*) ¿cómo podemos traerlo a casa? • **I tried to get the blood off my shirt** intenté quitar la sangre de mi camisa • **get the knife off him!** ¡quítale ese cuchillo! • **I couldn't get the stain out of the tablecloth** no podía limpiar la mancha del mantel • **to get sth past customs** conseguir pasar algo por la aduana • **we'll get you there somehow** le llevaremos de una u otra manera • **we can't get it through the door** no lo podemos pasar por la puerta • **to get sth to sb** hacer llegar algo a algn • **to get the children to bed** meter a los niños en la cama • **where will that get us?** ¿de qué nos sirve eso? • IDIOMS: • **that will get you/him nowhere** • **that won't get you/him anywhere** eso no te/le va a llevar a ningún sitio

16 (= *prepare*) [+ *meal*] preparar, hacer • **to get breakfast** preparar *or* hacer el desayuno

17 (*with adjective*)

This construction is often translated using a specific Spanish verb. Look up the relevant adjective.

• **he got his leg broken** se rompió la pierna • **to get one's hands dirty** ensuciarse las manos • **to get sb drunk** emborrachar a algn • **to get one's feet wet** mojarse los pies • **you're getting me worried** estás haciendo que me preocupe

18 (*with infinitive/present participle*) • **to get sb to do sth** (= *persuade*) conseguir que algn haga algo, persuadir a algn a hacer algo; (= *tell*) decir a algn que haga algo • **we eventually got her to change her mind** por fin conseguimos que cambiase de idea, por fin le persuadimos a cambiar de idea • **I'll get him to ring you** le diré que te llame • **can you get someone to photocopy these**

g

puedes decirle *or* mandarle a alguien que me haga una fotocopia de estos • **I can't get the door to open** no puedo abrir la puerta, no logro que se abra la puerta • **I couldn't get the washing machine to work** no pude *or* no logré poner la lavadora en marcha • **I couldn't get the car going** *or* **to go** no pude poner el coche en marcha, no pude arrancar el coche • **to get a fire going** conseguir encender un fuego • **to get a conversation going** conseguir iniciar una conversación

19 (*"get sth done" construction*) **a** (= *do oneself*) • **you'll get yourself arrested looking like that** vas a acabar en la cárcel con esas pintas • **to get the washing/dishes done** lavar la ropa/fregar los platos • **we got no work done that day** no hicimos nada de trabajo ese día • **when do you think you'll get it finished?** ¿cuándo crees que lo vas a acabar? • **you'll get yourself killed driving like that** te vas a matar si conduces de esa forma

b (= *get someone to do*) • **to get one's hair cut** cortarse el pelo, hacerse cortar el pelo • **he knows how to get things done** sabe organizar muy bien a la gente • **to get sth fixed** arreglar *or* reparar algo • **I've got to get my car fixed this week** tengo que arreglar *or* reparar el coche esta semana, tengo que llevar el coche a arreglar *or* reparar esta semana • **I should get my teeth fixed** tendría que arreglarme los dientes • **we're going to get central heating put in** vamos a poner *or* instalar calefacción central • **I must get my car serviced** tengo que llevar el coche a una revisión

20* (*= understand*) entender • **I don't get you** no te entiendo • **(do you) get it?** ¿entiendes?; [+ *joke*] ¿lo coges?, ¿ya caes?* • **I've got it!** [+ *joke*] ¡ya caigo!, ¡ya lo entiendo!; [+ *solution*] ¡ya tengo la solución!, ¡ya he dado con la solución!, ¡ya lo tengo!; ▹ **point, wrong**

21* (*= annoy*) molestar, fastidiar • **what gets me is the way he always assumes he's right** lo que me molesta *or* fastidia es que siempre da por hecho que tiene razón • **what really gets me is his total indifference** lo que me molesta *or* fastidia es su total indiferencia

22* (*= thrill*) chiflar* • **this tune really gets me** esta melodía me chifla*, esta melodía me apasiona

23 • **to have got sth** (*Brit*) (= *have*) tener algo • **what have you got there?** ¿qué tienes ahí? • **I've got toothache** tengo dolor de muelas

INTRANSITIVE VERB

1 (*= reach, go*) llegar • **how do you get there?** ¿como se llega? • **he got there late** llegó tarde • **how did you get here?** ¿cómo viniste *or* llegaste? • **how did that box get here?** ¿cómo ha venido a parar esta caja aquí? • **I've got as far as page 10** he llegado hasta la página 10 • **he won't get far** no llegará lejos • **to get from A to B** ir de A a B, trasladarse de A a B • **to get home** llegar a casa • **to get to** llegar a • **how do you get to the cinema?** ¿cómo se llega al cine? • **I'll make sure it gets to you by tomorrow** me aseguraré de que te llegue mañana • **where did you get to?** (= *where were you?*) ¿dónde estabas?, ¿dónde te habías metido? • **where can he have got to?** ¿dónde se puede haber metido? • **it's a place that's difficult to get to** es un lugar de difícil acceso • **IDIOMS:** • **not to get anywhere:** • **you won't get anywhere with him** no conseguirás nada con él • **you won't get anywhere if you behave like that** no vas a conseguir nada comportándote así • **to get nowhere:** • **we're getting absolutely nowhere** • **we're getting nowhere fast** no estamos llegando a ningún sitio • **to get somewhere:** • **now we're getting somewhere** ahora empezamos a hacer progresos • **to get there:** • **"how's your thesis going?" — "I'm getting there"** —¿qué tal va tu tesis? —va avanzando • **to get to sb*** (= *affect*) afectar a algn; (= *annoy*) molestar a algn • **don't let it get to you*** (= *affect*) no dejes que te afecte; (= *annoy*) no te molestes por eso • **the whisky has got to him*** el whisky le ha afectado; ▹ **lane**

2 (*= become, be*) ponerse, volverse, hacerse

*As expressions with **get** + adjective, such as **get old, get drunk** etc, are often translated by a specific verb, look up the adjective.*

• **it's getting late** se está haciendo tarde • **how did it get like that?** ¿cómo se ha puesto así? • **how do people get like that?** ¿cómo puede la gente volverse así? • **this is getting ridiculous** esto roza los límites de lo ridículo • **how stupid can you get?** ¿hasta qué punto llega tu estupidez?, ¿cómo puedes ser tan estúpido? • **to get used to sth** acostumbrarse a algo • **IDIOM:** • **to get with it*** espabilarse • **you'd better get with it or we'll lose this contract*** espabílate o perderemos este contrato; ▹ **BECOME, GO, GET**

3 (*with past participle*) **a** (= *be*) • **he often gets asked for his autograph** a menudo le piden autógrafos • **we got beaten 3-2** perdimos 3 a 2 • **several windows got broken** se rompieron varias ventanas • **to get killed** morir, matarse • **I saw her the night she got killed** (*accidentally*) la vi la noche que murió *or* se mató; (= *murdered*) la vi la noche que la asesinaron • **do you want to get killed!** ¡¿es que quieres matarte?! • **to get paid** cobrar • **he got run over as he was coming out of his house** lo atropellaron al salir de casa

b (*reflexive action*) • **to get shaved** afeitarse • **to get washed** lavarse

4 (*= begin*) (*with gerund*) empezar a (+ *infin*), ponerse a (+ *infin*) • **let's get going** vamos a ponernos en marcha • **get going!** ¡muévete!, ¡a menearse! • **once she gets going on that subject she never stops** una vez que empieza con ese tema no para • **after midnight the party really got going** después de medianoche la fiesta empezó a animarse • **let's get moving** vamos a ponernos en marcha • **we got talking** empezamos a hablar *or* charlar • **I got to thinking that ...*** me di cuenta de que ..., empecé a pensar que ...

5 (*= come*) (*with infinitive*) • **to get to do sth** llegar a hacer algo • **he eventually got to be prime minister** al final llegó a ser primer ministro • **I got to be quite good at it** llegué a hacerlo bastante bien • **when do we get to eat?** ¿cuándo comemos? • **to get to know sb** llegar a conocer a algn • **he got to like her despite her faults** le llegó a gustar a pesar de sus defectos • **so when do I get to meet this friend of yours?** ¿cuándo me vas a presentar a este amigo tuyo? • **I never get to drive the car** nunca tengo oportunidad de conducir el coche • **to get to see sth/sb** lograr ver algo/a algn

6* (*= go*) • **get!** ¡lárgate!*

7 • **to have got to do sth** (*expressing obligation*) tener que hacer algo • **you've got to tell the police** tienes que denunciarlo a la policía • **why have I got to?** ¿por qué tengo que hacerlo?

▸ **get about** (VI + ADV) **1** [*invalid*] (= *walk*) caminar; (= *move around*) moverse • **he gets about with a stick/on crutches** camina con un bastón/con muletas • **she's quite frail and can't get about very much** está muy delicada y no puede moverse mucho

2 (= *travel*) viajar • **the sort of work I do means I get about a fair bit** el tipo de trabajo que hago significa que viajo *or* me desplazo bastante

3 (= *go out*) (*socially*) salir

4 (= *circulate*) [*rumour*] correr; [*story*] saberse, divulgarse • **it soon got about that they were getting divorced** al poco tiempo corrió el rumor de que se iban a divorciar *or* se divorciaban • **I don't want it to get about** no quiero que se sepa *or* divulgue

▸ **get above** (VI + PREP) • **to get above o.s.** volverse un engreído

▸ **get across** (VI + PREP) [+ *road*] cruzar; [+ *river, sea, desert*] cruzar, atravesar

(VI + ADV) **1** (= *cross road, river etc*) cruzar

2 (= *be understood*) [*meaning*] ser comprendido; [*person*] hacerse entender • **the message seems to be getting across** parece que está empezando a captar el mensaje • **to get across to sb** lograr comunicar con algn, hacerse entender por algn

(VT + ADV) **1** (= *communicate*) [+ *meaning, message*] comunicar, hacer entender • **she was anxious to get her point across** le preocupaba que se entendiese bien lo que quería decir

2 (= *transport across*) [+ *people, objects*] cruzar • **we can use one of the big patrol boats to get you across** podemos usar uno de esos barcos patrulleros grandes para cruzaros

▸ **get after** (VI + PREP) **1** (= *pursue*) perseguir; (= *hunt down*) dar caza a • **get after him! he's forgotten his wallet** ¡ve y lo alcanzas! ¡que se le ha olvidado la cartera!

2* (= *criticize, nag*) dar la vara a* • **she gets after me about the way I dress** siempre me está dando la vara por la forma en que visto*

▸ **get ahead** (VI + ADV) **1** (*in race*) tomar la delantera • **having got ahead of the other runners, he relaxed** tras tomar la delantera se relajó

2 (= *succeed*) (*by doing better than others*) ir por delante; (= *make progress*) progresar, avanzar • **to get ahead of sb** adelantar a algn

3 (*with work*) adelantar (**with** con)

▸ **get along** (VI + ADV) **1** (= *leave*) marcharse, irse • **it's time we were getting along** ya es hora de que nos marchemos *or* nos vayamos • **get along with you!** (= *go*) ¡vete ya!, ¡lárgate!; (*expressing disbelief**) ¡venga ya!, ¡anda ya!; (*joking*) ¡no digas bobadas!

2 (= *manage*) arreglárselas*, apañárselas* • **to get along without sth/sb** arreglárselas sin algo*, apañárselas sin algo* • **we get along (somehow)** vamos tirando

3 (= *progress*) • **how is he getting along?** ¿qué tal está?, ¿cómo le va? (*LAm*) • **try it and see how you get along** prueba a ver cómo te va • **we were getting along fine until he arrived** la cosa iba perfectamente hasta que llegó él

4 (= *be on good terms*) llevarse bien • **to get along well with sb** llevarse bien con algn

(VT + ADV) • **we'll try to get him along** trataremos de hacerle venir

▸ **get around** (VI + ADV) **1** = **get about**

2 = **get round**

▸ **get at** (VI + PREP) **1** (= *gain access to*) [+ *object*] alcanzar; [+ *place*] llegar a *or* hasta • **put the sweets somewhere he can't get at them** pon los caramelos en un sitio donde él no pueda alcanzarlos • **it was working fine until he got at it** funcionaba perfectamente hasta que cayó en sus manos • **the dog got at the meat** el perro pilló la carne • **as soon as he gets at the drink ...** en cuanto se pone

a beber … • **just let me get at him!** ¡deja que le ponga la mano encima!
2 (= *ascertain*) [+ *facts, truth*] establecer
3 (*Brit**) **a** (= *criticize*) meterse con* • **she's always getting at her brother** siempre se está metiendo con su hermano* • **I'm not getting at you, I just think that …** no te estoy echando la bronca, simplemente creo que …*
b (= *nag*) dar la lata a* • **she's always getting at me to have my hair cut** siempre me está dando la lata para que me corte el pelo*
4* (= *imply*) querer decir; (*negatively*) insinuar • **I couldn't see what he was getting at** no entendía qué quería decir
5 (= *influence unduly*) (*using bribery*) sobornar; (*using pressure*) presionar • **I feel I'm being got at** tengo la impresión de que están intentando influenciarme

▸ **get away** (VI + ADV) **1** (= *depart*) salir (**from** de); (*at start of race*) escapar; (= *go away*) irse • **I couldn't get away any sooner** (*from work*) no pude salir antes • **I didn't get away till seven thirty** no conseguí marcharme hasta las siete y media • **I can't get away before the 15th** no puedo escaparme *or* irme antes del 15 • **it would be lovely to get away somewhere** sería maravilloso irse a algún sitio • **get away!** (= *go away*) ¡vete ya!, ¡lárgate! • **to get away from** [+ *place, person*] escaparse de • **it's time we got away from this idea** es hora de que abandonemos esta idea • IDIOM: • **get away (with you)!*** (*expressing disbelief*) ¡venga ya!, ¡anda ya!; (*joking*) ¡no digas bobadas!
2 (= *move away*) apartarse (**from** de) • **I yelled at him to get away from the edge** le chillé que se apartase del borde
3 (= *escape*) escaparse (**from** de) • **you let them get away!** ¡dejaste que se escapasen! • **he let a golden opportunity get away** dejó escapar una oportunidad única • **to get away from it all** escapar de todo • **there's no getting away from it*** es algo que no podemos más que aceptar, no se lo puede negar; ▹ **get away with**
(VT + ADV) (= *remove*) • **to get sth away from sb** (= *remove*) quitar algo a algn • **get that snake away from me!** ¡quítame esa serpiente de delante! • **to get sb away from sth: I can't get him away from that computer** no puedo despegarlo del ordenador • **we managed to get her away from the party** conseguimos sacarla de la fiesta con grandes esfuerzos • **you must get her away to the country** tienes que llevártela al campo

▸ **get away with** (VI + PREP) **1** (= *steal*) llevarse
2 (= *go unpunished*) • **he got away with an official warning** solo se llevó una amonestación • **we can get away with just repainting it** bastará con volver a pintarlo • **do you think I'd be able to get away with a trouser suit?** ¿crees que iré bien con un traje pantalón?, ¿crees que pasará algo si llevo un traje pantalón? • **we mustn't let them get away with it** no debemos dejar que salgan impunes • **he broke the law and got away with it** infringió la ley y no le pillaron • **you won't get away with it!** (*with past action*) ¡esto no va a quedar así!; (*with possible action*) esto no te lo van a consentir • **he'll never get away with it** nunca se va a salir con la suya; ▹ **murder**
3 ▹ **get away**

▸ **get back** (VT + ADV) **1** (= *recover*) [+ *possessions, money, spouse*] recuperar; [+ *strength*] recobrar • **he never got the use of his arm back** nunca recuperó el uso de su brazo • **he resigned but we want to try and get him back** dimitió, pero queremos intentar que vuelva
2 (= *return*) [+ *object, person*] devolver • **I'll get him back to you by 7 pm** te lo devolveré antes de las 7; ▹ **own**
(VI + ADV) **1** (= *return*) volver • **to get back (home)** volver a casa • **get back into bed/the car** vuelve a la cama/al coche • **things are getting back to normal** las cosas están volviendo a la normalidad • **to get back to the point** volver al tema • **get back to what you were doing** sigue con lo que estabas haciendo • **let's get back to why you didn't come yesterday** volvamos a la cuestión de por qué no viniste ayer • **to get back to work** volver al trabajo
2 (= *talk*) • **I'll get back to you on that** te daré una respuesta • **can you get back to Harry about the flat?** ¿puedes volver a llamar a Harry para lo del piso?
3 (= *move back*) • **get back!** ¡atrás!

▸ **get back at*** (VI + PREP) • **to get back at sb (for sth)** vengarse de algn (por algo), desquitarse con algn (por algo)

▸ **get behind** (VI + ADV) **1** (*with work, payments*) retrasarse (**with** en)
2 (*in race*) quedarse atrás
(VI + PREP) **1** (= *move behind, sit behind*) ponerse detrás de • **she got behind the wheel and drove off** se puso al volante y se fue
2 (= *support*) [+ *team, government*] apoyar
(VT + PREP) (= *secure support of*) • **we must get the government behind us** tenemos que conseguir el apoyo del gobierno

▸ **get by** (VI + ADV) **1** (= *pass*) pasar
2* (= *manage*) arreglárselas*, apañárselas*; (*in language*) defenderse • **we'll get by** nos las arreglaremos*, nos las apañaremos* • **she manages to get by on what her son gives her** se las arregla *or* apaña para vivir con lo que le da su hijo* • **my pension is not enough to get by on** mi pensión no me da para vivir • **we'll have to get by without him** tendremos que arreglárnoslas sin él*, tendremos que apañárnoslas sin él*
3 (= *be acceptable*) pasar • **his work is not brilliant but it'll get by** su trabajo no es excepcional, pero pasará • **he gets by because of his charm rather than his ability** se salva por su encanto no por su habilidad

▸ **get down** (VT + ADV) **1** (= *take down*) [+ *book, jug*] bajar (**from** de); [+ *hanging object, light*] descolgar (**from** de) • **can you get that jar down for me?** ¿puedes bajarme esa jarra? • **I want to get that picture down from the wall** quiero quitar ese cuadro de la pared
2 (= *swallow*) tragarse, tragar
3 (= *note down*) escribir • **to get sth down in writing** *or* **on paper** poner algo por escrito
4 (= *reduce*) [+ *prices*] bajar • **I need to get my weight down a bit** tengo que bajar de peso un poco
5* (= *depress*) deprimir • **don't let it get you down** no dejes que eso te deprima • **this weather's getting me down** este invierno me está deprimiendo
6* (= *annoy*) molestar • **what gets me down is the way they take him for granted** lo que me molesta es que no sepan valorarlo
(VI + ADV) **1** (= *descend*) bajar (**from, off** de) • **get down from there!** ¡baja de ahí!
2 (= *reduce*) bajar • **I've got down to 62 kilos** he bajado a 62 kilos; ▹ **get down to**
3 (= *crouch*) agacharse • **quick, get down! they'll see you!** ¡rápido, agáchate, te van a ver! • **to get down on one's knees** ponerse de rodillas
4* (= *leave table*) levantarse de la mesa • **may I get down?** ¿puedo levantarme de la mesa?
5 (= *go*) bajar • **I'll try and get down this weekend** intentaré bajar este fin de semana

▸ **get down to** (VI + PREP) • **to get down to doing sth** ponerse a hacer algo • **let's get down to business** (= *start work*) pongámonos manos a la obra; (= *get to the point*) vayamos al grano • **when you get down to it there's not much difference between them** cuando lo miras bien, no se diferencian mucho • **to get down to work** ponerse a trabajar (en serio); ▹ **brass, get down, nitty-gritty**

▸ **get in** (VT + ADV) **1** (= *bring in*) [+ *person, animal*] hacer entrar; [+ *harvest*] recoger; [+ *supplies*] traer • **I'll get some beer in for the weekend** compraré cerveza para el fin de semana
2 (= *hand over*) entregar; (= *post in*) mandar • **did you get your essay in on time?** ¿entregaste tu trabajo a tiempo? • **you must get your entries in by 5 May** deben mandar sus inscripciones antes del 5 de mayo
3 (= *plant*) [+ *bulbs etc*] plantar
4 (= *summon*) [+ *expert etc*] llamar a
5 (= *insert*) [+ *object, comment*] meter; [+ *blow*] lograr dar • **I can't get any more in** no cabe nada más • **he got in a reference to his new book** logró mencionar su nuevo libro • **he managed to get in a game of golf** consiguió meter un partido de golf • **it was hard to get a word in** era muy difícil meter baza • **when I could get a word in I asked how they had found out** cuando pude meter palabra les pregunté cómo se habían enterado
6 (= *sneak in*) [+ *arms, drugs*] meter, pasar; [+ *visitor*] colar* • **I can get you in as a visitor** puedo colarte como visitante*
(VI + ADV) **1** (= *enter*) entrar, meterse • **how did that dog get in here?** ¿cómo ha entrado *or* se ha metido ese perro aquí? • **the rain gets in through the roof** la lluvia entra *or* se mete por el tejado
2 (= *arrive*) [*train, bus, plane*] llegar; (= *reach home*) [*person*] llegar (a casa) • **what time did you get in last night?** ¿a qué hora llegaste (a casa) anoche? • **I got in from Miami at 6 am** llegué de Miami a las 6 de la mañana
3 (= *be admitted*) (*to club*) ser admitido; (*Pol*) (= *be elected*) ser elegido
4 (= *intervene*) • **you'll have to get in there quick or you'll miss your chance** no se retrase o perderá su oportunidad • **he tried to say something but I got in first** intentó decir algo pero yo me adelanté

▸ **get in on** (VI + PREP) (= *become involved*) • **it's a big market and everyone wants to get in on it** es un mercado grande y todos quieren entrar en él • **how can we get in on the deal?** ¿cómo podemos entrar a formar parte del trato?; ▹ **act**

▸ **get into** (VI + PREP) **1** (= *enter*) [+ *house*] entrar en; [+ *vehicle*] subir a; [+ *bed, bath*] meterse en • **earth had got into the wound** se le había metido tierra en la herida • **to get into politics** meterse en la política • IDIOM: • **what's got into him?** ¿qué mosca le ha picado?, ¿pero qué le pasa? • **I don't know what's got into you!** ¡no sé qué mosca te ha picado!, ¡no sé qué demonios te pasa!
2 (= *reach*) [+ *office, school*] llegar a • **if this document gets into the wrong hands …** si este documento cae en manos de quien no debe …
3 (= *become member of*) [+ *club*] entrar en
4 (= *put on*) [+ *clothes*] ponerse
5 (= *become involved in*) [+ *situation, trouble, argument, fight*] meterse en • **I wish I'd never got into this** ojalá no me hubiera metido nunca en esto • **the yacht got into difficulties in a heavy sea** el yate empezó a tener problemas en el mar encrespado • **he**

got into trouble with the police se metió en problemas con la policía
6 (= *acquire*) • **to get into the habit of doing sth** coger *or* (*LAm*) agarrar la costumbre de hacer algo; ▹ **shape**
VT + PREP **1** (= *cause to enter*) meter en • **it took two of us to get him into the car** nos llevó a dos personas meterle en el coche • **we got the boat into the water** metimos la barca en el agua • **we need to get him into hospital** tenemos que llevarlo al hospital; ▹ **head, tooth**
2 (= *involve in*) • **to get sb into sth** meter a algn en algo • **you got me into this** tú me has metido en esto • **he's the one who got me into music** él es quien me aficionó a la música
▸ **get in with** VI + PREP (= *gain favour with*) congraciarse con • **he tried to get in with the headmaster** intentó congraciarse con el director • **he got in with a bad crowd** empezó a andar con malas compañías
▸ **get off** VT + ADV **1** (= *remove*) [+ *stain, top, lid*] quitar • **to get one's clothes off** quitarse la ropa
2 (= *send off*) [+ *letter, telegram*] mandar (**to** a) • **to get sb off to school** despachar a algn al colegio • **she got the baby off to sleep** logró dormir al niño
3 (= *save from punishment*) • **his lawyer managed to get him off** su abogado logró que se librase del castigo
4 (= *have as leave*) [+ *day, time*] tener libre • **we get a day off on the Queen's birthday** nos dan un día libre en el cumpleaños de la reina
5 (= *learn*) aprender • **to get sth off by heart** aprender algo de memoria
6 (= *rescue*) rescatar
VT + PREP **1** (= *cause to give up*) • **to get sb off** [+ *drugs, alcohol, addiction*] hacer que algn deje; ▹ **get**
2 (= *remove*) • **get your dog off me!** ¡quítame al perro de encima!
VI + PREP **1** (= *descend from*) [+ *bus, train, bike, horse*] bajarse de, apearse de (*frm*) • IDIOM: • **to get off sb's back**: • **I wish he would get off my back!*** ¡ojalá me dejara en paz!; ▹ **high**
2 (= *leave*) salir de • **get off my land!** ¡sal de mis tierras! • **get off my foot!** ¡deja de pisarme el pie! • **I couldn't get off the phone** no podía colgar el teléfono • **what time do you get off work/school?** ¿a qué hora sales del trabajo/del colegio?
3 (= *move away from*) • **let's get off this subject** cambiemos de tema, dejemos el tema • **we've rather got off the subject** nos hemos alejado bastante del tema
4* (= *escape*) [+ *chore etc*] escaquearse de* • **she got off the washing-up** se escaqueó de lavar los platos
5 (= *get up from*) levantarse de • **why don't you get off your backside and do some work?‡** ¿por qué no mueves el trasero y te pones a hacer algo de trabajo?‡
6 (= *give up*) [+ *drugs, alcohol, addiction*] dejar
VI + ADV **1** (*from bus, train, bike, horse*) bajarse, apearse (*frm*) • **get off!** (= *let go*) ¡suelta! • IDIOM: • **to tell sb where to get off*** cantar a algn las cuarenta*
2 (= *leave*) partir • **we got off at 6am** partimos a las 6 de la mañana • **can you get off early tomorrow?** (*from work*) ¿puedes salir del trabajo temprano mañana?
3 (= *escape injury, punishment*) librarse • **he got off** se libró (del castigo) • **you're not going to get off that lightly!** ¡no se va a librar con tan poco! • **he got off lightly, he could have been killed** tuvo suerte, podría haberse matado • **they got off lightly, we should have killed them** no se llevaron lo que se merecían, deberíamos haberlos matado • **he got off with a fine** se libró con una multa
4 • **to get off (to sleep)** dormirse
▸ **get off on‡** VT + PREP pirrarse por* • **he loves making fun of people, he really gets off on it** le encanta reírse de la gente, le chifla *or* se pirra*
▸ **get off with*** VI + PREP (*Brit*) (= *start relationship with*) enrollarse con*, liarse con*
▸ **get on** VI + ADV **1** (= *mount*) subir
2 (= *proceed*) seguir • **we must be getting on, Sue's waiting for us** tenemos que seguir, Sue nos está esperando • **get on, man!** ¡sigue!, ¡adelante! • **to get on with sth** seguir con algo • **now we can get on with our lives again** ahora podemos seguir con nuestras vidas • **get on with it!** ¡venga!, ¡apúrese! (*LAm*) • **get on with your work, please** seguid trabajando, por favor • **this will do to be getting on with** esto basta por ahora; ▹ **get on to**
3 (= *manage*) • **I was getting on fine till he came along** me iba bien hasta que llegó él • **how did you get on?** (*in exam, interview*) ¿qué tal te fue?, ¿cómo te fue? • **how are you getting on with him/the new computer?** ¿qué tal *or* cómo te va con él/el ordenador nuevo? • **she's getting on very well with Russian** está haciendo muchos progresos con el ruso
4 (= *progress*) progresar; (= *succeed*) tener éxito • **he's keen to get on** quiere progresar • **if you want to get on in life, you must ...** si quieres tener éxito en la vida, debes ...
5 • **to be getting on: it's getting on for nine** son casi las nueve • **he's getting on for 70** está rondando los 70, anda cerca de los 70 • **there were getting on for 50 people** había casi 50 personas • **her parents are getting on a bit** sus padres ya están un poco viejos • **time is getting on** se está haciendo tarde
6 (= *be on good terms*) llevarse bien • **I'm afraid we just don't get on** me temo que no nos llevamos *or* entendemos bien • **to get on (well) with sb** llevarse bien con algn • **I can't get on with computers** no me aclaro con los ordenadores, los ordenadores y yo no hacemos migas
VI + PREP **1** (= *mount*) [+ *vehicle*] subir(se) a; [+ *horse, bicycle*] subir(se) a, montar a
2 (= *be appointed/elected to*) [+ *committee*] entrar en
VT + ADV (= *put on*) [+ *clothes*] ponerse; [+ *lid, cover, dinner*] poner • **it's time I got the vegetables on** es hora de poner la verdura
▸ **get on at*** VI + PREP = **get at**
▸ **get on to, get onto** VI + PREP **1** (= *climb on to*) [+ *bike, horse*] montarse en, subir(se) a; [+ *bus, train*] subir(se) a
2 (= *enter*) • **we got on to the motorway at junction 15** entramos en la autopista en el acceso número 15
3 (= *enrol on*) [+ *course*] matricularse en
4 (= *be elected to*) [+ *committee*] ser elegido como miembro de
5 (= *start talking of*) [+ *subject*] empezar a hablar de; (= *move on to*) pasar a; (= *reach*) llegar a • **we got on to the subject of money** empezamos a hablar de dinero • **let's get on to the question of complaints** pasemos al tema de las reclamaciones • **don't let's get on to that again** no empecemos con eso otra vez • **by the time they got on to my question there was no time left** cuando llegaron a mi pregunta ya no había tiempo
6 (*Brit*) (= *contact*) ponerse en contacto con; (= *phone*) llamar; (= *talk to*) hablar con
7 (= *deal with*) ocuparse de • **I'll get on to it right away** ahora mismo lo hago
8 (= *get wise to*) • **how did the Russians get on to us?** ¿cómo nos descubrieron los rusos? • **how did the press get on to this?** ¿cómo se ha enterado la prensa de esto? • **the police got on to him at once** la policía se puso en seguida sobre su pista
9 = **get at**
VT + PREP **1** (= *make deal with*) poner a trabajar en • **I'll get my men on to it right away** pondré a mis hombres a trabajar en esto enseguida; (= *send*) ahora mismo mando a mis hombres • **I'm going to get my dad on to you!*** le voy a decir a mi papá que te arregle las cuentas
2 (= *cause to talk about*) • **we got him on to the subject of drugs** logramos que hablase de las drogas • **don't get him on to the subject of golf** no le des pie para que se ponga a hablar de golf
3 (= *make a member of*) • **we need to get some new people on to the committee** necesitamos conseguir gente nueva para el comité, necesitamos meter gente nueva en el comité
▸ **get out** VI + ADV **1** (*of room*) salir; (*of country*) marcharse; (*of vehicle*) bajarse, apearse (*frm*) • **get out!** ¡fuera de aquí! • **get out of the way!** ¡apártate!, ¡ponte de un lado! • **to get out of bed/one's chair** levantarse de la cama/de la silla • **she wanted to get out of teaching** quería dejar la enseñanza • **the company decided to get out of England** la compañía decidió dejar Inglaterra
2 (= *escape*) [*animal*] escaparse; [*prisoner*] escaparse, fugarse • **the lion got out of its cage** el león se escapó de la jaula • **you'll never get out of this one!** ¡de esta sí que no te escapas!
3 (= *be released*) [*prisoner*] salir
4 (= *go out*) salir • **you ought to get out a bit more** tendrías que salir un poco más
5 [*secret*] llegarse a saber; [*news*] (= *become public*) hacerse público; (= *leak*) filtrarse • **if this ever gets out we're done for** si esto se llega a saber alguna vez estamos perdidos
VT + ADV **1** (= *remove, bring out*) [+ *object, person, library book, money from bank*] sacar; [+ *tooth*] arrancar; [+ *stain*] quitar • **get that dog out of here!** ¡saque a ese perro de aquí! • **I can never get him out of bed in the morning** por las mañanas no puedo sacarlo de la cama • **get the cards out and we'll have a game** saca las cartas y echemos una partida • **he got his diary out of his pocket** se sacó la agenda del bolsillo • **I can't get it out of my mind** no me lo puedo quitar de la mente *or* de la cabeza • **it gets me out of the house** me hace salir de casa
2 (= *send for*) [+ *doctor, plumber, electrician*] llamar
3 (= *send out*) [+ *message*] mandar
4 (= *pronounce*) • **I couldn't get the words out** no me salían las palabras • **I'd hardly got the words out of my mouth before she silenced me** apenas había empezado a hablar cuando me hizo callar
5 (*Cricket*) [+ *batsman*] eliminar
▸ **get out of** VI + PREP **1** (= *escape*) [+ *duty, punishment*] librarse de; [+ *difficulty*] salir de • **some people will do anything to get out of paying taxes** algunas personas hacen lo imposible para librarse de pagar impuestos • **there's no getting out of it** no hay más remedio • **how are you going to get out of this one?** ¿cómo vas a salir de esta?
2 (= *lose*) • **to get out of the habit of doing sth** perder la costumbre de hacer algo; ▹ **get**
VT + PREP ▹ **get out**
▸ **get over** VI + PREP **1** (= *cross*) [+ *stream, road*]

cruzar, atravesar; [+ *wall, fence*] (= *go over*) pasar por encima de; (= *jump over*) saltar por encima de
2 (= *overcome, recover from*) [+ *problem, serious illness, disappointment*] superar; [+ *cold, virus*] reponerse de; [+ *shock, fright, grief*] sobreponerse a; [+ *surprise*] recuperarse de; [+ *resentment*] olvidar; [+ *shyness*] vencer, dominar • **she got over cancer 5 years ago** superó un cáncer hace 5 años • **she refused! I can't get over it!** ¡dijo que no! ¡no me cabe en la cabeza *or* no puedo creerlo! • **I can't get over how much he's changed** no puedo creer lo mucho que ha cambiado • **she never really got over him** nunca llegó realmente a olvidarlo
(VI + ADV) **1** (= *cross sth*) (*stream, road*) cruzar; (*wall, fence*) (= *go over*) pasar por encima; (= *climb over*) saltar por encima
2 (= *come*) venir; (= *go*) ir • **I'll see if I can get over later on** veré si puedo ir más tarde
(VT + ADV) **1** (= *transport across*) [+ *people, objects*] cruzar; (= *lift over*) hacer pasar por encima • **they made a rope bridge to get the guns/men over** construyeron un puente de cuerda para pasar las armas/a los hombres al otro lado
2 (= *send*) • **I'll get the documents over to you tomorrow** te haré llegar los documentos mañana • **get yourself over here as soon as you can** vente para acá tan pronto como puedas
3 (= *have done with*) acabar de una vez • **let's get it over (with)** acabemos de una vez • **I just want to get this interview over (with)** lo único que quiero es sacarme de encima esta entrevista
4 (= *communicate*) [+ *idea*] transmitir • **the film gets its message over very convincingly** la película transmite el mensaje de forma muy convincente • **I was trying to get it over to him that it was impossible** estaba intentando hacerle comprender que era imposible
(VT + PREP) **1** (= *transport across*) • **to get troops/supplies over a river** pasar tropas/suministros al otro lado del río
2 (= *lift over*) hacer pasar por encima de • **they got him over the gate** le pasaron al otro lado de la verja
▸ **get round** (VI + PREP) **1** (= *negotiate*) [+ *corner*] dar la vuelta a
2 (= *overcome*) [+ *problem*] superar
3 (= *avoid*) [+ *regulation*] sortear
4 (= *persuade*) • **to get round sb** engatusar a algn • **you're not going to get round me** no me vas a engatusar
5 (= *congregate at*) • **12 of us can't get round that table** no podemos sentarnos 12 personas alrededor de esa mesa • **we need to get round the table and discuss this** (*fig*) tenemos que juntarnos y discutir esto
6 (= *complete*) [+ *course, circuit*] completar
(VI + ADV) **1** (= *come*) venir; (= *go*) ir • **how can we get round to the back of the house?** ¿cómo podemos ir a la parte de atrás de la casa? • **I got round there as soon as I could** fui tan pronto como pude
2 • **to get round to (doing) sth: I shan't get round to that before next week** no lo podré hacer antes de la semana próxima • **we never seem to get round to it** parece que nunca tenemos tiempo para eso • **we never got round to exchanging addresses** al final no llegamos a intercambiarnos las señas
(VT + ADV) **1** (= *cause to come, go*) • **we'll get a car round to you for 9am** le mandaremos un coche para las 9 de la mañana • **we got all the neighbours round for a meeting** juntamos a todos los vecinos en casa para una reunión
2 (= *persuade*) convencer • **we soon got him round to our way of thinking** pronto logramos que pensase como nosotros
▸ **get through** (VI + PREP) **1** (= *pass through*) [+ *window, door, gap*] pasar por; [+ *crowd*] abrirse paso entre
2 (= *finish*) [+ *book, meal*] terminar • **we've got a lot of work to get through** tenemos mucho trabajo para hacer • **she can get through a whole box of chocolates at one go** es capaz de terminarse una caja entera de bombones de una vez
3 (= *survive*) aguantar • **how are they going to get through the winter?** ¿cómo van a aguantar el invierno?
4 (= *use up*) [+ *money*] gastar • **she gets through £300 a month on clothes** gasta 300 libras al mes en ropa • **he's got through two pairs of trousers already this term** ya ha gastado dos pares de pantalones este trimestre • **they get through three loaves of bread a day** comen tres panes al día
5 (= *pass*) [+ *exam*] aprobar, pasar; (*Sport*) [+ *qualifying round*] superar
(VT + PREP) • **we can't get it through the door** no lo podemos pasar por la puerta • **I'll never get the car through here** no voy a poder hacer que el coche pase por aquí • **coffee is the only thing that gets me through the day** el café es lo único que me ayuda a pasar el día • **I got 15 students through this exam** conseguí que 15 de mis alumnos aprobasen este examen • **to get a bill through parliament** conseguir que una ley se apruebe en el parlamento • **we have three children to get through university** tenemos tres hijos a los que tenemos que pagarles la carrera
(VT + ADV) **1** (= *cause to succeed*) [+ *student*] conseguir que apruebe • **it was his faith in God that got him through** su creencia en Dios fue lo que le ayudó a salir adelante *or* superar la crisis
2 (= *succeed in sending*) [+ *supplies*] conseguir entregar
3 (= *cause to be understood*) • **I can't get it through to him that ...** no puedo hacerle entender que ...
4 (*Pol*) [+ *bill*] conseguir que se apruebe, conseguir que sea aprobado
(VI + ADV) **1** (= *pass through*) abrirse paso; (= *arrive*) [*news, supplies etc*] llegar (a su destino)
2 (*Telec*) (lograr) comunicar (**to** con) • **I've been trying to get through to Buenos Aires** he estado intentando comunicar con Buenos Aires • IDIOM: • **to get through to sb** hacerse entender por algn • **I can't seem to get through to him any more** parece que ya no me entiende • **I think the message is getting through to him** creo que está empezando a captar el mensaje
3 (= *pass, succeed*) [*student*] aprobar; (*Sport*) [*team*] pasar; [*bill*] ser aprobado; [*candidate*] ser aceptado
4 (*esp US*) (= *finish*) acabar • **to get through with sth** terminar algo
▸ **get together** (VT + ADV) [+ *people, money, team*] reunir; [+ *objects*] reunir, juntar; [+ *show, concert*] preparar; [+ *proposal*] elaborar; [+ *thoughts, ideas*] poner en orden • **we couldn't get the down payment together** no pudimos reunir el dinero para la entrada • **it won't take me long to get my stuff together** no tardaré mucho en recoger mis cosas • **get yourself together and make sure you're there on time** organízate y asegúrate que estás allí a la hora; ▸ **act**
(VI + ADV) [*friends, group, club*] reunirse • **could we get together this evening?** ¿podemos reunirnos esta tarde? • **to get together about sth** reunirse para discutir algo • **you'd better get together with him before you decide** te conviene hablar con él antes de decidirte
▸ **get under** (VI + ADV) (= *pass underneath*) pasar por debajo
(VI + PREP) • **to get under a fence/rope** pasar por debajo de una cerca/cuerda • **to get under the covers** meterse debajo de las mantas
(VT + ADV) hacer pasar por debajo
(VT + PREP) hacer pasar por debajo de • **we couldn't get it under the bed** no podíamos meterlo debajo de la cama; ▸ **skin**
▸ **get up** (VI + ADV) **1** (= *stand*) levantarse, ponerse de pie; (*from bed*) levantarse • **get up!** ¡levántate!; (*to horse*) ¡arre!
2 (= *climb up*) subir
3 [*wind*] (= *start to blow*) levantarse; (= *become fiercer*) empezar a soplar recio; [*sea*] embravecerse; [*fire*] avivarse
(VT + ADV) **1** (= *raise*) [+ *person*] (*from chair, floor, bed*) levantar
2 (= *gather*) [+ *courage*] reunir • **I couldn't get up the nerve to ask the question** no conseguí reunir el valor necesario para hacer la pregunta • **we couldn't get up much enthusiasm for the idea** no conseguimos suscitar *or* despertar mucho entusiasmo entre la gente hacia la idea • **I want to get my strength up for this race** quiero ponerme en plena forma (física) para esta carrera, quiero cobrar fuerzas para esta carrera • **to get up speed** cobrar velocidad, ganar velocidad
3* (= *organize*) [+ *celebration*] organizar, preparar; [+ *petition*] organizar
4* (= *dress up*) [+ *person*] ataviar (**in** con) • **she'd got herself up in all her finery** se había ataviado con sus mejores galas • **beautifully got up** muy bien vestido • **to get o.s. up as** disfrazarse de, vestir de
▸ **get up to** (VI + PREP) **1** (= *reach*) llegar a • **I've got up to chapter four** he llegado al capítulo cuatro
2 (= *do*) • **to get up to mischief** hacer travesuras • **I don't want you getting up to any mischief** no quiero que hagas ninguna travesura • **what have you been getting up to lately?** ¿qué has estado haciendo últimamente? • **you never know what he'll get up to next** nunca se sabe qué locura va a hacer luego

---

get-at-able [getˈætəbl] (ADJ) accesible
getaway [ˈgetəweɪ] (N) escape *m*, huida *f*, fuga *f* • **to make one's ~** escaparse
(CPD) ▸ **getaway car** • **the thieves' ~ car** el coche en que huyeron los ladrones
get-rich-quick* [ˌgetˌrɪtʃˈkwɪk] (ADJ) • **get-rich-quick scheme** plan *m* para hacerse rico pronto, plan *m* para hacer una rápida fortuna
get-together* [ˈgettəˌgeðəʳ] (N) (= *meeting*) reunión *f*; (= *regular social gathering*) tertulia *f*; (= *party*) fiesta *f* • **we're having a little get-together on Friday, can you come?** vamos a reunirnos unos amigos el viernes, ¿puedes venir? • **a family get-together** una reunión familiar
getup* [ˈgetʌp] (N) atuendo *m*, traje *m*, atavío *m*
get-up-and-go* [ˌgetʌpəndˈgəʊ] (N) • **he's got lots of get-up-and-go** tiene mucho empuje
get-well card [ˌgetˈwel ˌkɑːd] (N) *tarjeta para*

g

un enfermo deseándole que se mejore

gewgaw† [ˈgjuːgɔː] N baratija *f*

geyser [ˈgiːzəʳ], (*US*) [ˈgaɪzəʳ] N (*Geog*) géiser *m*; (= *water heater*) calentador *m* de agua

G-Force [ˈdʒiːfɔːs] N ABBR = **force of gravity**

Ghana [ˈgɑːnə] N Ghana *f*

Ghanaian [gɑːˈneɪən] ADJ ghanés N ghanés/esa *m/f*

ghastliness [ˈgɑːstlɪnɪs] N **1** (= *awfulness*) [*of situation, experience, war*] horror *m*; [*of dress, wallpaper, décor*] lo espantoso
2 (= *pallor*) palidez *f*

ghastly [ˈgɑːstlɪ] ADJ (COMPAR: **ghastlier**, SUPERL: **ghastliest**) **1** (= *awful*) [*person*] inaguantable, horroroso; [*dress, wallpaper*] horrible, horroroso; [*situation, experience*] espantoso, horrendo, horroroso; [*mistake*] funesto • **how ~!** ¡qué horror! • **it must be ~ for her** debe ser horrible para ella
2 (= *pale*) pálido, cadavérico

ghee [giː] N mantequilla *f* clarificada

Ghent [gent] N Gante *m*

gherkin [ˈgɜːkɪn] N pepinillo *m*

ghetto [ˈgetəʊ] N (PL: **ghettos** *or* **ghettoes**) gueto *m*; (*Hist*) judería *f*

ghetto-blaster [ˈgetəʊˌblɑːstəʳ] N radiocasete *m* portátil (*muy grande*)

ghettoization [ˌgetəʊaɪˈzeɪʃən] N (*fig*) marginación *f*

ghettoize [ˈgetəʊˌaɪz] VT (*fig*) marginar

ghillie [ˈgɪlɪ] N = **gillie**

ghost [gəʊst] N fantasma *m*, espectro *m*; (*TV*) imagen *f* fantasma • **Holy Ghost** (*Rel*) Espíritu *m* Santo • **he hasn't the ~ of a chance** no tiene la más remota posibilidad • **she managed the ~ of a smile** consiguió esbozar un amago de sonrisa • IDIOM: • **to give up the ~** (= *die*) entregar el alma; (*hum*) [*car, washing machine etc*] pasar a mejor vida
VT [+ *book*] escribir por otro • **an autobiography ~ed by Peters** una autobiografía escrita por el negro Peters
CPD ▸ **ghost image** (*Cine, TV*) imagen *f* fantasma ▸ **ghost story** cuento *m* de fantasmas ▸ **ghost town** pueblo *m* fantasma ▸ **ghost train** tren *m* fantasma

ghosting [ˈgəʊstɪŋ] N (*TV*) fantasma *m*

ghostly [ˈgəʊstlɪ] ADJ fantasmal, espectral

ghost-write [ˈgəʊstˌraɪt] (PT: **ghost-wrote**, PP: **ghost-written**) VT = **ghost** ▹ VT

ghostwriter [ˈgəʊstˌraɪtəʳ] N negro/a *m/f*

ghoul [guːl] N (= *malevolent spirit*) demonio *m* necrófago; (= *person*) morboso/a *m/f*

ghoulish [ˈguːlɪʃ] ADJ [*practice, activity*] macabro; [*person, curiosity*] morboso

ghoulishly [ˈguːlɪʃlɪ] ADV macabramente

GHQ N ABBR (= **General Headquarters**) cuartel *m* general

GI* N ABBR (*US*) (= **Government Issue**) propiedad *f* del Estado; (*also* **GI Joe**) soldado *m* (raso) americano
ADJ • **GI bride** novia *f* or esposa *f* de un soldado americano

giant [ˈdʒaɪənt] N **1** (*physically*) gigante/a *m/f*
2 (*fig*) (*in importance, power*) gigante *m* • **Sol, the computer ~** Sol, líder en ordenadores • **he was a ~ among actors** como actor fue un coloso
ADJ [*tree, star*] gigantesco; [*animal, insect, bird, plant*] gigante; [*portion*] gigantesco, enorme; [*packet*] gigante, familiar; [*strides*] de gigante
CPD ▸ **giant panda** panda *mf* gigante ▸ **giant slalom** slalom *m* gigante

giantess [ˈdʒaɪənˈtes] N giganta *f*

giant-killer [ˈdʒaɪəntˌkɪləʳ] N (*Sport*) matagigantes *m inv*, *equipo que vence a otro muy superior*

giant-killing [ˈdʒaɪəntˌkɪlɪŋ] ADJ (*Sport*) • **Scarborough's giant-killing act against Chelsea** la hazaña de Scarborough de ser el David que venció al Goliat Chelsea • **Spain's giant-killing French Open champion** el matagigantes español, campeón en el Open francés

giant-size [ˈdʒaɪəntsaɪz], **giant-sized** [ˈdʒaɪəntsaɪzd] ADJ [*packet*] (de tamaño) gigante

Gib* [dʒɪb] N = **Gibraltar**

gibber [ˈdʒɪbəʳ] VI [*person*] farfullar, hablar atropelladamente; [*monkey*] chillar • **to ~ with rage/fear** farfullar a causa de la ira/del miedo

gibbering [ˈdʒɪbərɪŋ] ADJ • **I must have sounded like a ~ idiot** debí de sonar como un tonto balbuceando

gibberish [ˈdʒɪbərɪʃ] N galimatías *m inv*, guirigay *m*

gibbet [ˈdʒɪbɪt] N horca *f*

gibbon [ˈgɪbən] N gibón *m*

gibe [dʒaɪb] N mofa *f*, burla *f*
VI mofarse, burlarse (**at** de)

giblets [ˈdʒɪblɪts] NPL menudillos *mpl*, menudencias *fpl* (*And, Chile*)

Gibraltar [dʒɪˈbrɔːltəʳ] N Gibraltar *m*

Gibraltarian [ˌdʒɪbrɔːlˈteərɪən] ADJ gibraltareño
N gibraltareño/a *m/f*

giddily [ˈgɪdɪlɪ] ADV **1** (= *dizzily*) [*spin, twirl*] vertiginosamente • **she struggled ~ to her feet** se esforzó para ponerse en pie, con la cabeza dándole vueltas
2 (= *light-heartedly*) frívolamente

giddiness [ˈgɪdɪnɪs] N vértigo *m*

giddy[1] [ˈgɪdɪ] ADJ (COMPAR: **giddier**, SUPERL: **giddiest**) (= *dizzy*) mareado; (= *causing dizziness*) [*height, speed*] vertiginoso; (*of character*) atolondrado, ligero de cascos • **to feel ~** sentirse mareado • **it makes me ~** me marea, me da vértigo

giddy[2] [ˈgɪdɪ] EXCL • **~ up!** (*to horse*) ¡arre!

GIFT [gɪft] N ABBR = **Gamete Intrafallopian Transfer**

gift [gɪft] N **1** (= *present*) regalo *m*, obsequio *m* (*frm*); (*Comm*) (*also* **free gift**) obsequio *m*; (*Jur*) donación *f* • **it's a ~!*** (= *very cheap*) ¡es una ganga!; (= *very easy*) es pan comido, ¡está tirado!* • PROVERB: • **don't look a ~ horse in the mouth** a caballo regalado no le mires el dentado
2 (= *talent*) don *m*, talento *m* • **the ~ of tongues** el don de las lenguas • **he has a ~ for administration** tiene talento para la administración • **to have a ~ for languages** tener mucha facilidad para los idiomas • **he has artistic ~s** tiene dotes artísticas; ▹ **gab**
3 (= *power to give*) • **the office is in the ~ of …** el cometido está en manos de …
VT dar, donar; (*Sport*) [+ *goal*] regalar
CPD ▸ **gift certificate** (*US*) = **gift token** ▸ **gift coupon** cupón *m* de regalo ▸ **gift shop**, **gift store** (*US*) tienda *f* de regalos • **"gift shop"** "artículos *mpl* de regalo" ▸ **gift tax** impuesto *m* sobre donaciones ▸ **gift token**, **gift voucher** vale-obsequio *m*

gifted [ˈgɪftɪd] ADJ talentoso, de talento • **she is a very ~ writer** es una escritora de mucho talento • **the ~ child** el niño superdotado

giftwrap [ˈgɪftˌræp], **giftwrapping** [ˈgɪftˌræpɪŋ] N papel *m* de regalo

gift-wrap [ˈgɪftˌræp] VT envolver en papel de regalo

giftwrapped [ˈgɪftˌræpt] ADJ envuelto para regalo

gig [gɪg] N **1** (= *carriage*) calesa *f*
2 (*Naut*) lancha *f*, canoa *f*
3 (*Mus**) actuación *f*, concierto *m*
4 (*US*) (= *job*) trabajo *m* temporal

gigabyte [ˈgɪgəˌbaɪt] N gigabyte *m*

gigahertz [ˈgɪgəhɜːts] N gigahercio *m*

gigantic [dʒaɪˈgæntɪk] ADJ gigantesco

gigawatt [ˈgɪgəˌwɒt] N gigavatio *m*

giggle [ˈgɪgl] N risita *f* • **she got the ~s** le dio la risa tonta • **they did it for a ~** (*Brit*) lo hicieron para reírse
VI reírse tontamente

giggly [ˈgɪglɪ] ADJ dado a la risa tonta

GIGO [ˈgaɪgəʊ] N ABBR (*Comput*) (= **garbage in, garbage out**) BEBS

gigolo [ˈʒɪgələʊ] N gigoló *m*

gigot [ˈʒiːgəʊ, ˈdʒɪgət] N (*Culin*) gigot *m*

gild [gɪld] (PT: **gilded**, PP: **gilded**, **gilt**) VT [+ *metal, frame*] dorar • IDIOM: • **to ~ the lily** embellecer lo perfecto

gilded [ˈgɪldɪd] ADJ dorado
CPD ▸ **gilded cage** jaula *f* dorada

gilding [ˈgɪldɪŋ] N doradura *f*, dorado *m*

Giles [dʒaɪlz] N Gil

gill[1] [gɪl] N [*of fish*] branquia *f*, agalla *f* • IDIOM: • **to look green about the ~s** tener mala cara

gill[2] [dʒɪl] N (= *measure*) cuarta parte *f* de una pinta (= *0,142 litro*)

gillie [ˈgɪlɪ] N (*Scot*) **1** (*Hunting*) ayudante *mf* de cazador *or* pescador
2† (= *attendant*) criado *m*

gilt [gɪlt] PP *of* **gild**
N **1** dorado *m*
2 gilts (*Econ*) papel *msing* del Estado, valores *mpl* de máxima confianza
ADJ dorado

gilt-edged [ˈgɪltˈedʒd] ADJ **1** [*book*] con cantos dorados
2 (= *excellent*) [*chance, opportunity*] de oro
CPD ▸ **gilt-edged stock, gilt-edged securities** (*government-issued*) papel *m* del Estado

gimbal [ˈdʒɪmbəl], **gimbals** [ˈdʒɪmbəlz] N (*Aut, Naut*) cardán *m*

gimcrack [ˈdʒɪmkræk] ADJ [*furniture*] de pacotilla

gimlet [ˈgɪmlɪt] N (*for wood*) barrena *f* de mano • **he had ~ eyes** tenía una mirada muy penetrante

gimme‡ [ˈgɪmɪ] = **give me**

gimmick [ˈgɪmɪk] N truco *m* publicitario; (= *gadget*) artilugio *m* • **it's just a sales ~** es un truco para vender más

gimmickry [ˈgɪmɪkrɪ] N trucos *mpl*

gimmicky [ˈgɪmɪkɪ] ADJ efectista

gimp‡ [gɪmp] N (*US*) cojo/a *m/f*

gimpy* [ˈgɪmpɪ] (*US*) ADJ (= *limping*) cojo
N cojo/a *m/f*

gin[1] [dʒɪn] N (= *drink*) ginebra *f* • **gin and it** (*Brit*) vermú *m* con ginebra • **gin and tonic** gin-tonic *m*

gin[2] [dʒɪn] N **1** (*Brit*) (*also* **gin trap**) trampa *f*
2 (*Tech*) desmotadera *f* de algodón
CPD ▸ **gin rummy** gin rummy *m*

ginger [ˈdʒɪndʒəʳ] N (= *spice*) jengibre *m*; (*as nickname*) pelirrojo *m*
ADJ [*hair*] rojo; [*cat*] de color melado • **to have ~ hair** ser pelirrojo
CPD ▸ **ginger ale, ginger beer** gaseosa *f* de jengibre ▸ **ginger cake** torta *f* de jengibre ▸ **ginger group** (*Brit*) grupo *m* de activistas, grupo *m* de presión ▸ **ginger nut, ginger snap** galleta *f* de jengibre
▸ **ginger up** VT + ADV (*Brit*) espabilar, animar

gingerbread [ˈdʒɪndʒəbred] N pan *m* de jengibre

ginger-haired [ˌdʒɪndʒəˈhɛəd] ADJ pelirrojo

gingerly [ˈdʒɪndʒəlɪ] ADJ cauteloso
ADV con cautela

gingery [ˈdʒɪndʒərɪ] ADJ [*hair*] rojizo

gingham [ˈgɪŋəm] N (= *material*) guingán *m*

gingivitis [ˌdʒɪndʒɪˈvaɪtɪs] N gingivitis *f*

ginkgo ['gɪŋkgəʊ], **gingko** ['gɪŋkəʊ] (N) (*also* **ginkgo biloba**) ginkgo *m*

Ginny ['dʒɪnɪ] (N) *familiar form of* **Virginia**

ginormous* [dʒaɪ'nɔːməs] (ADJ) (*hum*) enorme de grande

ginseng ['dʒɪnseŋ] (N) ginseng *m*
(CPD) [*tea, tablets*] de ginseng

gippo‡ ['dʒɪpəʊ] (N) (*pej*) gitano/a *m/f*, calé *mf*

gipsy ['dʒɪpsɪ] (ADJ), (N) = **gypsy**

giraffe [dʒɪ'rɑːf] (N) (PL: **giraffes** *or* **giraffe**) jirafa *f*

gird [gɜːd] (PT, PP: **girded, girt**) (VT) (*liter*) ceñir, rodear (**with** de) • IDIOMS: • **to ~ o.s. for the fight** *or* **fray** aprestarse para la lucha • **to ~ (up) one's loins** aprestarse para la lucha; ▷ **loin**
▸ **gird on** (VT + ADV) • **to ~ on one's sword** ceñirse la espada

girder ['gɜːdəʳ] (N) viga *f*

girdle ['gɜːdl] (N) (= *corset*) faja *f*; (= *belt*) cinturón *m* (*also fig*)
(VT) ceñir, rodear (*also fig*) (**with** con)

girl [gɜːl] (N) chica *f*, muchacha *f*; (= *small*) niña *f*; (= *young woman*) chica *f*, joven *f*; (= *servant*) criada *f*, chica *f*; (= *girlfriend**) novia *f*, polola *f* (*Chile*) • **factory ~** obrera *f* • **shop ~** dependienta *f* • **old ~** (*Brit*) [*of school*] ex-alumna *f*, antigua alumna *f*; (= *elderly woman*†*) señora *f*, abuelita* *f* • **the old ~** (*Brit**) (= *wife*) la parienta*; (= *mother*) la vieja • **now listen to me, my ~!** ¡escúchame, guapa!
(CPD) ▸ **girl band** banda *f* femenina ▸ **girl Friday** empleada *f* de confianza ▸ **girl guide, girl scout** (*US*) exploradora *f*, guía *f* ▸ **girl power** poder *m* femenino

girlfriend ['gɜːlfrend] (N) [*of girl*] amiga *f*; [*of boy*] novia *f*, compañera *f*, polola *f* (*Chile*)

girlhood ['gɜːlhʊd] (N) juventud *f*, mocedad *f*

girlie* ['gɜːlɪ] (N) (*US*) nena *f*, chiquilla *f*
(CPD) ▸ **girlie magazine** revista *f* de desnudos

girlish ['gɜːlɪʃ] (ADJ) de niña; (*pej*) [*man, boy*] afeminado

girlishly ['gɜːlɪʃlɪ] (ADV) jovialmente • **she laughed ~** se rió con la jovialidad de una jovencita

giro ['dʒaɪrəʊ] (*Brit*) (N) giro *m* • **bank ~** transferencia *f* bancaria • **post-office ~** giro *m* postal • **National Giro** giro *m* postal
(CPD) ▸ **giro cheque** cheque *m* de giro ▸ **bank giro system** sistema *m* de giro bancario ▸ **giro transfer** • **by ~ transfer** mediante giro

Gironde [dʒɪ'rɒnd] (N) Gironda *m*

girt [gɜːt] (PT), (PP) *of* **gird**

girth [gɜːθ] (N) **1** (*for saddle*) cincha *f*
2 (= *measure*) [*of tree*] circunferencia *f*; [*of person's waist*] contorno *m* • **because of its great ~** por su gran tamaño, por lo abultado

gismo* ['gɪzməʊ] (N) = **gizmo**

gist [dʒɪst] (N) [*of speech, conversation*] lo esencial • **to get the ~ of sth** captar lo esencial de algo

git‡ [gɪt] (N) (*Brit*) cretino/a* *m/f*

give [gɪv]

TRANSITIVE VERB
INTRANSITIVE VERB
NOUN
PHRASAL VERBS

(PT: **gave**, PP: **given**)

TRANSITIVE VERB

When **give** *is part of a set combination, eg* **give evidence, give a lecture, give a party, give a yawn**, *look up the other word.*

1 (*+ possession, object*) dar; (*for special occasion*) regalar, obsequiar (*frm*); [+ *title, honour, award, prize*] dar, otorgar (*frm*); [+ *organ, blood*] dar, donar; (*Scol*) [+ *mark*] poner • **he was ~n a gold watch when he retired** le regalaron *or* (*frm*) obsequiaron un reloj de oro cuando se jubiló • **he gave her a dictionary for her birthday** le regaló un diccionario por su cumpleaños • **he was ~n an award for bravery** le dieron *or* otorgaron un galardón por su valentía • **to ~ sb a penalty** (*Sport*) conceder un penalti *or* penalty a algn • **to ~ o.s. to sb** entregarse a algn

2 (*= pass on*) [+ *message*] dar; [+ *goods, document*] dar, entregar (*more frm*); [+ *illness*] contagiar, pegar* • **~ them my regards** *or* **best wishes** dales saludos de mi parte • **can you ~ Mary the keys when you see her?** ¿puedes darle las llaves a Mary cuando la veas? • **to ~ sb a cold** contagiar el resfriado a algn, pegar el resfriado a algn* • **to ~ sth into sb's hands** (*liter*) entregar *or* confiar algo a algn

3 (*= offer*) [+ *party, dinner*] dar • **to ~ a party for sb** dar *or* ofrecer una fiesta en honor de algn • **why don't you ~ them melon to start with?** ¿por qué no les das melón para empezar? • **she gave us a wonderful meal** nos hizo una comida buenísima • **we can ~ them cava to drink** podemos darles cava para *or* de beber • **what can I ~ him to eat/for dinner?** ¿qué puedo hacerle para comer/cenar?

4 (*= provide*) [+ *money, information, idea*] dar; [+ *task*] dar, confiar • **can you ~ him something to do?** ¿puedes darle algo para hacer? • **I'll never be able to ~ you a child** nunca podré darte un hijo • **they gave us a lot of help** nos ayudaron mucho • **it gave us a good laugh*** nos hizo reír mucho • IDIOM: • **~ or take ...**: • **12 o'clock, ~ or take a few minutes** más o menos las doce • **in A.D. 500 ~ or take a few years** aproximadamente en el año 500 después de J.C.

5 (*= cause*) [+ *shock, surprise*] dar, causar; [+ *pain*] causar, provocar • **it ~s me great pleasure to welcome you all** es un gran placer para mí darles la bienvenida a todos • **to ~ sb a kick/push** dar una patada/un empujón a algn • **to ~ sb to believe that ...** hacer creer a algn que ... • **I was ~n to believe that ...** me hicieron creer que ... • **to ~ sb to understand that ...** dar a entender a algn que ...

6 (*= grant, allow*) **a** [+ *permission*] dar, conceder; [+ *chance, time*] dar • **let's ~ him one last chance** vamos a darle una última oportunidad • **can't you ~ me another week?** ¿no me puedes dar otra semana? • **I can ~ you 10 minutes** le puedo conceder 10 minutos • **~ yourself an hour to get there** necesitas una hora para llegar • **I gave myself 10 minutes to do it** me permití 10 minutos para hacerlo • **to ~ sb a choice** dar a elegir a algn • **he's honest, I ~ you that** es honrado, lo reconozco
b* (*predicting future*) • **how long would you ~ that marriage?** ¿cuánto tiempo crees que durará ese matrimonio? • **the doctors gave him two years to live** los médicos le dieron dos años de vida

7 (*= dedicate*) [+ *life, time*] dedicar • **he gave his life to helping the needy** dedicó su vida a ayudar a los necesitados • **I've ~n you the best years of my life** te he dado los mejores años de mi vida • **he gave it everything he'd got** dio lo mejor de sí

8 (*= sacrifice*) [+ *life*] dar • **he gave his life for his country** dio la vida por su país

9 (*= pay*) dar • **what will you ~ me for it?** ¿qué me das por ello? • **how much did you ~ for it?** ¿cuánto diste *or* pagaste por él? • IDIOMS: • **I'd ~ a lot** *or* **the world** *or* **anything to know ...** daría cualquier cosa por saber ... • **I don't** *or* **I wouldn't ~ much for his chances** no le doy muchas posibilidades

10 (*= put through to*) poner con • **could you ~ me Mr Smith/extension 3443?** ¿me podría poner con el Sr. Smith/con la extensión 3443?

11 (*= punish with*) • **the teacher gave him 100 lines** el profesor le castigó a copiar 100 líneas • **the judge gave him five years** el juez le dio cinco años • **to ~ it to sb*** (= *beat*) dar una paliza a algn; (*verbally*) poner a algn como un trapo*

12 (*= present*) presentar a • **ladies and gentlemen, I ~ you our guest speaker this evening, ...** damas y caballeros, les presento a nuestro conferenciante de esta noche, ...

13 (*in toast*) • **I ~ you the Queen** brindemos por la Reina

14 (*= produce, supply*) [+ *milk, fruit*] dar, producir; [+ *light, heat*] dar; [+ *result*] arrojar; [+ *help, advice*] dar, proporcionar • **it ~s a total of 80** arroja un total de 80 • **it ~s 6% a year** rinde un 6% al año • **it gave no sign of life** no daba señales de vida

15 (*= state*) [+ *name, age, address*] dar; (*on form*) poner • **to ~ the right/wrong answer** dar la respuesta correcta/equivocada • **if I may ~ an example** si se me permite dar *or* poner un ejemplo • **he gave the cause of death as asphyxia** señaló la asfixia como causa de la muerte

16 (*= care*) • **I don't ~ a damn*** me importa un comino *or* un bledo*

17 (*= make*) [+ *speech*] dar, pronunciar (*frm*); [+ *lecture, concert*] dar

18 • **to ~ way a** (= *collapse*) [*bridge, beam, floor, ceiling*] ceder, hundirse; [*cable, rope*] romperse; [*legs*] flaquear • **the ground gave way beneath him** la tierra se hundió bajo sus pies • **the chair gave way under his weight** la silla no soportó su peso, la silla cedió bajo su peso • **after months of stress his health gave way** después de meses de tensión su salud se vió afectada • **his strength gave way** le flaquearon las fuerzas
b (= *break*) [*rope*] romperse
c • **to ~ way (to sth)** (= *be replaced*) ser reemplazado (por algo); (*to demands*) ceder (a algo); (*to traffic*) ceder el paso (a algo) • **you gave way too easily** cediste con demasiada facilidad • **to ~ way to an impulse** dejarse llevar por un impulso • **she gave way to tears** se deshizo en lágrimas • **he never ~s way to despair** nunca se abandona a la desesperación • **"give way"** (*Brit*) (*Aut*) "ceda el paso" • **to ~ way to the left** ceder el paso a la izquierda

19 (*in idiomatic expressions*) • **don't ~ me that!*** ¡no me vengas con esas!* • **I'll ~ you something to cry about!*** ¡ya te daré yo razones para llorar! • **holidays? I'll ~ you holidays!*** ¿vacaciones? ya te voy a dar yo a ti vacaciones*, ¿vacaciones? ¡ni vacaciones ni narices!* • **he wants £100? I'll ~ him £100!*** ¿que quiere 100 libras? ¡ni cien libras ni nada! • **I'll ~ him what for!*** ¡se va a enterar!* • **~ me the old songs!** ¡para mí las canciones viejas! • **~ me a gas cooker every time!*** ¡prefiero mil veces una cocina de gas! • **children? ~ me dogs any time!** ¿niños? ¡prefiero mucho antes un perro! • **I wouldn't want it if you gave it to me** eso no lo quiero ni regalado • **he can ~ you 5 years** él tiene la ventaja de ser 5 años más joven que tú

INTRANSITIVE VERB

1 dar • **giving is better than receiving** dar es mejor que recibir • **please ~ generously** por favor, sean generosos • **to ~ to charity** hacer donativos a organizaciones benéficas, dar dinero a organizaciones benéficas • **to ~ and**

take hacer concesiones mutuas • IDIOM: • **to ~ as good as one gets** pagar con la misma moneda, devolver golpe por golpe

2 (= *give way*) **a** (= *collapse*) [*bridge, beam, floor, ceiling*] ceder, hundirse; [*knees*] flaquear • **the chair gave under his weight** la silla cedió bajo su peso, la silla no soportó su peso
b (= *break*) [*rope*] romperse
c (= *yield*) [*door*] ceder • **the floor gave slightly under his feet** el suelo cedió ligeramente bajo sus pies • IDIOM: • **something's got to ~!*** ¡por algún lado tiene que salir!

3 US* • **what ~s?** ¿qué pasa?, ¿qué se cuece por ahí?*

NOUN
(= *flexibility*) [*of material*] elasticidad *f* • **there's a lot of ~ in this chair/bed** esta silla/cama es muy mullida • **there's a lot of ~ in this rope** esta cuerda da mucho de sí • **there isn't a lot of ~ in these proposals** estas propuestas no son muy negociables • **how much ~ has there been on their side?** ¿cuánto han cedido ellos? • **~ and take**: • **you won't achieve an agreement without a bit of ~ and take** no vais a conseguir un acuerdo sin hacer concesiones mutuas • **a bit of ~ and take** un poco de toma y daca*

▸ **give away** VT + ADV **1** (*as gift*) [+ *money, goods*] regalar, obsequiar (*frm*); [+ *prizes*] entregar; [+ *bride*] llevar al altar; (*Sport*) (*also fig*) regalar • **we've got 200 CDs to ~ away** tenemos 200 CDs para regalar • **we gave away a silly goal** les regalamos un gol de la forma más tonta • **at this price I'm giving it away** a este precio lo estoy regalando
2 (= *reveal*) [+ *secret*] revelar • **he's been accused of giving away company secrets** lo han acusado de revelar secretos de la compañía • **he gave away his secret when he produced the wrong passport** se descubrió a sí mismo al mostrar el pasaporte que no debía • **his face gave nothing away** su rostro no delataba nada • **your taste in colours ~s away a lot about you** tus preferencias en los colores revelan mucho sobre tu personalidad • IDIOM: • **to ~ the game away*** descubrir el pastel*
3 (= *betray*) [+ *person*] (*lit*) (*fig*) delatar • **we mustn't ~ him away** no debemos delatarlo *or* traicionarlo • **the treads on his shoes gave him away** el dibujo de los suelos de los zapatos lo delataron • **to ~ o.s. away** delatarse, descubrirse

▸ **give back** VT + ADV (= *return*) [+ *sb's property, freedom*] devolver (**to** a) • **Peter's ~n her back her confidence** Peter le ha devuelto la confianza en sí misma • **he wants to ~ something back to society** quiere ofrecer algo a *or* hacer algo por la sociedad en compensación

▸ **give in** VT + ADV (= *hand in*) [+ *form, essay*] entregar • **to ~ in one's name** dar su nombre
VI + ADV (= *surrender*) rendirse; (= *yield*) ceder; (= *agree*) consentir • **I ~ in!** (*in guessing game*) ¡me rindo!, ¡me doy por vencido! • **I went on at my parents until they gave in** les insistí a mis padres hasta que cedieron • **to ~ in to** [+ *threats, pressure*] ceder *or* sucumbir ante • **she always ~s in to him** ella hace siempre lo que él quiere

▸ **give off** VT + ADV [+ *smell, smoke*] despedir; [+ *heat, radiation*] emitir

▸ **give onto** VI + PREP [*window, door, house*] dar a

▸ **give out** VT + ADV **1** (= *distribute*) repartir, distribuir
2 (= *make known*) [+ *news*] anunciar; (= *reveal*) revelar, divulgar • **it was ~n out that ...** (= *announced*) anunciaron que ...; (*falsely*) hicieron creer que ...
3 (= *give off*) [+ *smoke*] despedir
4 (*Rad*) [+ *signal*] emitir
5 (= *let out*) [+ *scream, cry*] dar • **he gave out a scream of pain** dio un grito de dolor
VI + ADV [*supplies*] agotarse; [*strength, patience*] agotarse, acabarse; [*engine*] pararse; [*heart*] fallar • **his legs gave out** le fallaron las piernas

▸ **give over** VI + ADV (*Brit**) (= *stop*) • **~ over!** ¡basta ya! • **~ over arguing!** ¡deja de discutir!

▸ **give over to** VT + PREP **1** (= *devote to*) dedicar • **mornings were ~n over to physical training** las mañanas estaban dedicadas al ejercicio físico • **most of the land had been ~n over to wheat-growing** la mayor parte de la tierra estaba destinada a la cultura del trigo • **the front page was ~n over to a report on ...** la primera página estaba dedicada a un informe sobre ... • **to ~ o.s. over to** [+ *activity, pleasure, children, family*] dedicarse a, entregarse a
2 (= *transfer*) [+ *property*] traspasar
3 (= *entrust to*) encomendar, entregar

▸ **give up** VT + ADV **1** (= *yield up*) [+ *seat, place*] ceder; [+ *authority*] ceder, traspasar • **to ~ o.s. up to the police** entregarse a la policía • **to ~ o.s. up to** [+ *vice*] entregarse a, darse a • **to ~ a child up for adoption** entregar a un hijo para que sea adoptado
2 (= *hand over*) [+ *ticket*] entregar
3 (= *renounce*) [+ *habit*] dejar; [+ *job, post*] renunciar a, dejar; [+ *friend*] dejar de ver; [+ *boyfriend*] dejar, romper con; [+ *beliefs, idea*] abandonar • **to ~ up smoking** dejar de fumar • **I've ~n up trying to persuade her** he dejado de intentar persuadirla *or* convencerla • **eventually he gave up trying** al final dejó de intentarlo • **I gave it up as a bad job*** me di por vencido
4 (= *devote*) [+ *one's life, time*] dedicar (**to** a) • **to ~ up one's life to music** dedicar su vida a la música
5 (= *sacrifice*) [+ *one's life*] entregar (**for** por); [+ *career*] renunciar a (**for** por) • **they gave up their lives for their country** entregaron *or* sacrificaron sus vidas por la patria • **she gave up her career for her family** renunció a su carrera profesional por su familia
6 (= *abandon hope for*) [+ *patient*] desahuciar • **the doctors had ~n him up** los médicos lo habían desahuciado • **we'd ~n you up** creíamos que ya no venías • **they gave him up for dead** lo dieron por muerto • **to ~ sb up for lost** dar por perdido a algn
VI + ADV (= *stop trying*) rendirse • **I ~ up!** (*trying to guess*) ¡me rindo!, ¡me doy por vencido! • **don't ~ up yet!** ¡no te rindas todavía!

▸ **give up on** VI + PREP **1** (= *renounce*) [+ *idea*] renunciar a • **I've ~n up on the idea** he renunciado a la idea
2 (= *stop expecting*) [+ *visitor*] • **I'd ~n up on you** creía que ya no venías • **I've ~n up on him, he's so unreliable** (= *lost faith in*) no quiero perder más tiempo con él, es muy informal
3 (= *fail*) • **the car gave up on us** nos falló el coche

give-and-take* [ˈgɪvənˈteɪk] N toma y daca *m*, concesiones *fpl* mutuas

giveaway [ˈgɪvəweɪ] N **1** (= *revelation*) revelación *f* involuntaria • **it's a dead ~** (= *obvious*) (eso) lo dice todo
2 (= *gift*) regalo *m* • **the exam was a ~!** ¡el examen estaba tirado!*
CPD ▸ **giveaway prices** precios *mpl* de regalo

given [ˈgɪvn] PP *of* give
ADJ **1** (= *fixed*) [*time, amount*] determinado • **on a ~ day** en un día determinado • **at any ~ time** en cualquier momento dado
2 • **to be ~ to doing sth** ser dado a hacer algo
CONJ • **~ (that) ...** dado que ... • **~ the circumstances ...** dadas las circunstancias ... • **~ time, it would be possible** con el tiempo, sería posible
N hecho *m* reconocido, dato *m* conocido
CPD ▸ **given name** (*esp US*) nombre *m* de pila

giver [ˈgɪvəʳ] N donante *mf*, donador(a) *m/f*

gizmo* [ˈgɪzməʊ] N artilugio *m*, chisme *m*, coso *m* (*LAm*)

gizzard [ˈgɪzəd] N molleja *f* • **it sticks in my ~** (*fig*) no lo puedo tragar

Gk ABBR (= **Greek**) griego

glacé [ˈglæseɪ] ADJ [*fruit*] escarchado
CPD ▸ **glacé icing** azúcar *m* glaseado

glacial [ˈgleɪsɪəl] ADJ **1** (*Geol*) [*erosion*] glaciar; [*period*] glacial; (= *cold*) [*weather, wind*] glacial
2 [*person, stare, atmosphere*] glacial

glaciation [ˌgleɪsɪˈeɪʃən] N glaciación *f*

glacier [ˈglæsɪəʳ] N glaciar *m*

glaciology [ˌglæsɪˈɒlədʒɪ] N glaciología *f*

glad [glæd] ADJ (COMPAR: **gladder**, SUPERL: **gladdest**) **1** (= *pleased*) • **to be ~** alegrarse • **"I had a great time" — "I'm (so) ~"** — me lo pasé fenomenal — me alegro (mucho) • **to be ~ that** alegrarse de que (+ *subjun*) • **I'm ~ that you could come** me alegro de que hayas podido venir • **I'm ~ that I relented in the end** me alegro de haber transigido al final • **to be ~ to do sth** (= *pleased*) alegrarse de hacer algo; (= *willing*) estar encantado de hacer algo • **I was ~ to see him** me alegré de verlo • **I am ~ to hear it** me alegra saberlo • **I'll be ~ to answer any questions** estaré encantado de responder a cualquier pregunta • **our receptionists will be ~ to help you make any theatre reservations** nuestros recepcionistas le ayudarán con el mayor agrado a reservar entradas para el teatro • **I would be only too ~ to take a job like that** me encantaría aceptar un trabajo como ese • **he assured her that he would be only too ~ to help** le aseguró que sería un verdadero placer ayudarla • **to be ~ about sth** alegrarse de algo • **Ralph was ~ of a chance to change the subject** Ralph se alegró de tener la oportunidad de cambiar de tema • **I was ~ of his help** me alegré de que me ayudase • **I'd be very ~ of your advice** le agradeceré mucho que me aconseje
2 (*before noun*) (*liter*) (= *joyful*) [*occasion*] feliz • **~ rags†*** trajes *mpl* de fiesta • **~ tidings** (*hum or liter*) buenas nuevas *fpl* • IDIOM: • **to give sb the ~ eye*** echar a algn una mirada insinuante; ▸ glad-hand

gladden [ˈglædn] (*liter*) VT alegrar, llenar de alegría • **she was ~ed by the news** la noticia la llenó de alegría • **to ~ sb's heart** llenar de alegría el corazón de algn, alegrar el corazón a algn • **it ~ed his heart to see the children play** ver jugar a los niños le llenaba el corazón de alegría *or* le alegraba el corazón

glade [gleɪd] N claro *m*

glad-hand* [ˈglædhænd] VT (*hum*) estrechar (con entusiasmo fingido) la mano de

gladiator [ˈglædɪeɪtəʳ] N gladiador *m*

gladiatorial [ˌglædɪəˈtɔːrɪəl] ADJ de gladiadores

gladiolus [glædɪˈəʊləs] N (PL: **gladiolus** *or* **gladioluses** *or* **gladioli** [ˌglædɪˈəʊlaɪ]) gladiolo *m*

gladly [ˈglædlɪ] ADV con mucho gusto, de buena gana • **he ~ accepted their invitation** aceptó con mucho gusto *or* de buena gana su invitación • **I'd ~ help her if I could** la ayudaría con mucho gusto *or* de buena gana si pudiera • **"will you help us?" — "gladly"** —¿nos ayudará? —con mucho gusto; ▹ suffer

gladness ['glædnɪs] (N) alegría *f*, gozo *m* (*liter*)

glam‡ [glæm] (VT) • **to ~ up** [*+ person*] acicalar; [*+ building, area*] mejorar el aspecto de
(ADJ) = **glamorous**
(N) = **glamour**
(CPD) ▸ **glam rock*** glam rock *m*

glamor ['glæməʳ] (N) (*US*) = **glamour**

glamorize ['glæməraɪz] (VT) hacer parecer más atractivo • **this programme ~s crime** este programa presenta el crimen bajo una luz favorable

glamorous ['glæmərəs] (ADJ) [*person, dress*] atractivo y sofisticado, glamo(u)roso; [*job*] con mucho glamour, rodeado de gloria *or* grandeza; [*life*] sofisticado; [*place, gathering*] elegante, sofisticado

glamorously ['glæmərəslɪ] (ADV) con mucho glamour

glamour, glamor (*US*) ['glæməʳ] (N) [*of person, job, place*] glamour *m*
(CPD) ▸ **glamour boy** niño *m* bonito ▸ **glamour girl** belleza *f* ▸ **glamour sport** deporte *m* rodeado de glamour

glance [glɑːns] (N) (*at person*) mirada *f*; (*at object*) vistazo *m*, ojeada *f* (**at** a) • **at a ~** de un vistazo • **without a backward ~** sin volver la vista atrás • **we exchanged a ~** intercambiamos una mirada • **at first ~** a primera vista • **to steal/take a ~ at sth/sb** echar un vistazo a algo/algn
(VI) (= *look*) mirar • **she ~d in my direction** miró hacia donde yo estaba • **to ~ at** [*+ person*] lanzar una mirada a; [*+ object*] echar un vistazo a, ojear • **to ~ over** *or* **through a report** hojear un informe
▸ **glance away** (VI + ADV) apartar los ojos
▸ **glance back** (VI + ADV) (*turning head*) volverse rápidamente a mirar • **to ~ back at sth/sb** (= *turn to look at*) volverse a mirar algo/a algn • **to ~ back at sth** (= *look at again*) volver a mirar algo
▸ **glance down** (VI + ADV) echar un vistazo (hacia abajo)
▸ **glance off** (VI + PREP) • **to ~ off sth** rebotar de algo
▸ **glance round** (VI + ADV) (*round about*) echar un vistazo alrededor; (*behind*) echar un vistazo atrás
(VI + PREP) • **he ~d round the room** echó un vistazo por la habitación
▸ **glance up** (VI + ADV) (= *raise eyes*) levantar la vista; (= *look upwards*) mirar hacia arriba

glancing ['glɑːnsɪŋ] (ADJ) [*blow*] oblicuo

gland [glænd] (N) (*Anat*) glándula *f*; ▹ lymph

glandes ['glændiːz] (NPL) *of* **glans**

glandular ['glændjʊləʳ] (ADJ) glandular
(CPD) ▸ **glandular fever** mononucleosis *f* infecciosa

glans [glænz] (N) (PL: **glandes**) • **~ (penis)** glande *m*

glare [glɛəʳ] (N) **1** [*of light, sun*] luz *f* deslumbradora; (= *dazzle*) deslumbramiento *m* • **because of the ~ of the light in Spain** debido a lo resplandeciente que es la luz en España • **in the full ~ of publicity** bajo los focos de la publicidad
2 (= *look*) mirada *f* feroz
(VI) **1** [*light*] deslumbrar
2 (= *look*) • **to ~ at sb** lanzar una mirada de odio a algn

glaring ['glɛərɪŋ] (ADJ) **1** (= *dazzling*) [*sun, light*] deslumbrante, resplandeciente; [*colour*] chillón
2 (= *obvious*) [*mistake*] patente, manifiesto

glaringly ['glɛərɪŋlɪ] (ADV) • **to be ~ obvious** estar totalmente claro, saltar a la vista

glasnost ['glæznɒst] (N) glasnost *f*

glass [glɑːs] (N) **1** (= *material*) vidrio *m*, cristal *m* • **under ~** [*exhibit*] bajo vidrio, en una vitrina; [*plant*] en invernadero
2 (= *glassware*) cristalería *f*, artículos *mpl* de cristal
3 (= *tumbler, schooner etc*) (= *drinking vessel for water*) vaso *m*; (*for wine, sherry, champagne*) copa *f*; (*for beer*) caña *f*; (*for liqueur, brandy*) copita *f*
4 (= *glassful*) [*of beer, water, wine*] vaso *m*; [*of liqueur, brandy*] copa *f*
5 (= *barometer*) barómetro *m*
6 (= *mirror*) espejo *m* • **to look at o.s. in the ~** mirarse en el espejo
7 (= *spyglass*) catalejo *m*
8 glasses (= *spectacles*) gafas *fpl*, lentes *mpl*, anteojos *mpl* (*esp LAm*); (= *binoculars*) gemelos *mpl*
(CPD) [*bottle, ornament, eye*] de vidrio *or* cristal; [*slipper*] de cristal ▸ **glass case** vitrina *f* ▸ **glass ceiling** tope *m or* barrera *f* invisible (*que impide ascender profesionalmente a las mujeres o miembros de minorías étnicas*) ▸ **glass door** puerta *f* vidriera *or* de cristales ▸ **glass eye** ojo *m* de cristal ▸ **glass fibre, glass fiber** (*US*) fibra *f* de vidrio; (*as modifier*) de fibra de vidrio • **a ~ fibre boat** una embarcación de fibra de vidrio ▸ **glass house** • PROVERB: • **people who live in ~ houses shouldn't throw stones** siempre habla el que más tiene que callar, mira quién fue a hablar ▸ **glass industry** industria *f* vidriera ▸ **glass slipper** zapatilla *f* de cristal ▸ **glass wool** lana *f* de vidrio

glassblower ['glɑːsˌbləʊəʳ] (N) soplador *m* de vidrio

glassblowing ['glɑːsˌbləʊɪŋ] (N) soplado *m* de vidrio

glasscutter ['glɑːsˌkʌtəʳ] (N) (= *tool*) cortavidrios *m inv*; (= *person*) cortador(a) *m/f* de vidrio

glassed-in [ˌglɑːst'ɪn] (ADJ) [*room, building*] de vidrio

glassful ['glɑːsfʊl] (N) vaso *m*; [*of wine, sherry, champagne*] copa *f*

glasshouse ['glɑːshaʊs] (N) (PL: **glasshouses** ['glɑːshaʊzɪz]) (*for plants*) invernadero *m*; (*Brit*) (*Mil*‡) cárcel *f* (militar); ▹ glass

glasspaper ['glɑːsˌpeɪpəʳ] (N) (*Brit*) papel *m* de vidrio

glassware ['glɑːswɛəʳ] (N) cristalería *f*, objetos *mpl* de cristal

glassworks ['glɑːswɜːks] (N) fábrica *f* de vidrio

glassy ['glɑːsɪ] (ADJ) (COMPAR: **glassier**, SUPERL: **glassiest**) [*substance*] vítreo; [*surface*] liso; [*water*] espejado; [*eye, look*] vidrioso

glassy-eyed [ˌglɑːsɪ'aɪd] (ADJ) de mirada vidriosa; (*from drugs, drink*) de mirada perdida; (*from displeasure*) de mirada glacial

> **GLASTONBURY**
> **Glastonbury** es una ciudad situada al suroeste de Inglaterra donde, desde 1969, se ha venido celebrando casi todos los veranos un festival de música pop de tres días de duración. El festival es lugar de encuentro para miles de visitantes que acuden a la ciudad para oír a los mejores nombres del pop, y que aprovechan para visitar los lugares que se asocian con la mítica tumba del rey Arturo y con el lugar donde José de Arimatea llevó el Santo Grial.

Glaswegian [glæz'wiːdʒən] (ADJ) de Glasgow
(N) nativo/a *m/f or* habitante *mf* de Glasgow

glaucoma [glɔː'kəʊmə] (N) glaucoma *m*

glaze [gleɪz] (N) **1** (*on pottery*) vidriado *m*
2 (*Culin*) (*on cake*) glaseado *m*
(VT) **1** [*+ window*] poner vidrios *or* cristales a
2 [*+ pottery*] vidriar
3 (*Culin*) glasear
(VI) • **to ~ over** [*eyes*] ponerse vidrioso

glazed [gleɪzd] (ADJ) **1** [*surface*] vidriado; [*paper*] satinado; [*eye*] vidrioso
2 (*Brit*) [*door, window etc*] con vidrio *or* cristal
3 (*Culin*) glaseado
4 (*US**) (= *tipsy*) achispado*

glazier ['gleɪzɪəʳ] (N) vidriero/a *m/f*

glazing ['gleɪzɪŋ] (N) **1** (= *act*) acristalamiento *m*; (= *glass*) cristales *mpl*; (= *trade*) cristaleros *mpl*
2 = **glaze** ▹ N

GLC (N ABBR) (*Brit*) (*formerly*) (= **Greater London Council**) *antigua corporación metropolitana de Londres*

gleam [gliːm] (N) **1** [*of light*] rayo *m*, destello *m*; [*of metal, water*] espejeo *m* • **with a ~ in one's eye** con ojos chispeantes
2 (*fig*) • **a ~ of hope** un rayo de esperanza
(VI) [*light*] brillar, lanzar destellos; [*metal, water*] espejear, relucir; [*eyes*] brillar (**with** de)

gleaming ['gliːmɪŋ] (ADJ) reluciente

glean [gliːn] (VT) **1** (*Agr*) espigar
2 (*fig*) [*+ information*] recoger • **from what I have been able to ~** por lo que yo he conseguido averiguar
(VI) espigar

gleaner ['gliːnəʳ] (N) espigador(a) *m/f*

gleanings ['gliːnɪŋz] (NPL) (*fig*) fragmentos *mpl* recogidos

glebe [gliːb] (N) terreno *m* beneficial

glee [gliː] (N) (= *joy*) regocijo *m*, alegría *f*, júbilo *m*
(CPD) ▸ **glee club** (*Mus*) orfeón *m*, sociedad *f* coral

gleeful ['gliːfʊl] (ADJ) [*smile, laugh*] jubiloso, alegre; (= *malicious*) malicioso

gleefully ['gliːfəlɪ] (ADV) con júbilo, con regocijo; (= *maliciously*) maliciosamente

glen [glen] (N) cañada *f*

glib [glɪb] (ADJ) [*person*] de mucha labia, poco sincero; [*explanation, excuse*] fácil; [*speech*] elocuente pero insincero

glibly ['glɪblɪ] (ADV) [*speak*] (elocuentemente pero) con poca sinceridad; [*explain*] con una facilidad sospechosa

glibness ['glɪbnɪs] (N) [*of person*] labia *f*, falta *f* de sinceridad; [*of explanation, excuse*] facilidad *f*

glide [glaɪd] (N) [*of dancer etc*] deslizamiento *m*; (*Aer*) planeo *m*, vuelo *m* sin motor; (*Mus*) ligadura *f*
(VI) **1** (= *move smoothly*) deslizarse • **she ~s to the door** se desliza hacia la puerta • **to ~ away** • **to ~ off** escurrirse *or* deslizarse sigilosamente
2 (*Aer*) planear

glider ['glaɪdəʳ] (N) **1** (*Aer*) planeador *m*; (*towed*) avión *m* remolcado
2 (*US*) (= *swing*) columpio *m*

gliding ['glaɪdɪŋ] (N) (*Aer*) vuelo *m* sin motor, planeo *m*

glimmer ['glɪməʳ] (N) **1** [*of light*] luz *f* trémula; [*of water*] espejeo *m*
2 (*fig*) • **without a ~ of understanding** sin dar el menor indicio de haber comprendido • **there is a ~ of hope** hay un rayo de esperanza
(VI) [*light*] brillar con luz trémula; [*water*] espejear

glimmering ['glɪmərɪŋ] (N) (= *faint sign*) asomo *m*

glimpse [glɪmps] (N) vislumbre *f*, destello *m* • **a ~ into the future** un destello de cómo va a ser el futuro • **to catch a ~ of** vislumbrar • **I only had a fleeting ~ of him** solo alcancé a verlo fugazmente
(VT) vislumbrar

glint [glɪnt] (N) [*of metal etc*] destello *m*, centelleo *m* • **he had a ~ in his eye** le chispeaban los ojos
(VI) lanzar destellos, centellear

glissade [glɪ'sɑ:d] (N) (*in dancing*) deslizamiento *m*

glissando [glɪ'sændəʊ] (N) glisando *m*
(ADV) glisando

glisten ['glɪsn] (VI) [*wet surface*] relucir; [*water*] espejear; [*eyes*] brillar • **her eyes ~ed with tears** le brillaban los ojos de las lágrimas

glitch* [glɪtʃ] (N) fallo *m* técnico

glitter ['glɪtəʳ] (N) [*of gold etc*] brillo *m*
(VI) [*gold etc*] relucir, brillar • PROVERB: • **all that ~s is not gold** no es oro todo lo que reluce

glitterati* [ˌglɪtə'rɑ:ti:] (NPL) (*hum*) celebridades *fpl* del mundillo literario y artístico

glittering ['glɪtərɪŋ], **glittery** ['glɪtərɪ] (ADJ) reluciente, brillante (*also fig*) • **~ prize** premio *m* rutilante

glitz* [glɪts] (N) ostentación *f*

glitzy* ['glɪtsɪ] (ADJ) (COMPAR: **glitzier**, SUPERL: **glitziest**) ostentoso

gloaming ['gləʊmɪŋ] (N) (*liter*) crepúsculo *m* • **in the ~** al anochecer

gloat [gləʊt] (VI) relamerse • **to ~ over** [+ *money*] recrearse contemplando; [+ *victory, good news*] recrearse en; [+ *enemy's misfortune*] saborear, regocijarse con

gloating ['gləʊtɪŋ] (ADJ) • **with a ~ smile** sonriendo satisfecho, con una sonrisa satisfecha

glob* [glɒb] (N) (*US*) pegote *m*

global ['gləʊbl] (ADJ) **1** (= *world-wide*) mundial • **on a ~ scale** a escala mundial • **this has ~ implications** esto tiene consecuencias a nivel global
2 (= *comprehensive*) [*sum, reform, change*] global • **a ~ view** una visión global
(CPD) ▸ **global positioning system** sistema *m* de posicionamiento global, sistema *m* de posición global ▸ **global reach** [*of company, industry*] alcance *m* global ▸ **the global village** la aldea global ▸ **global warming** calentamiento *m* global, calentamiento *m* del planeta

globalization [ˌgləʊbəlaɪ'zeɪʃən] (N) globalización *f*

globalize ['gləʊbəlaɪz] (VI) globalizarse
(VT) globalizar

globally ['gləʊbəlɪ] (ADV) (= *worldwide*) mundialmente; (= *comprehensively*) globalmente

globe [gləʊb] (N) (= *sphere*) globo *m*, esfera *f*; (= *the world*) mundo *m*; (= *spherical map*) esfera *f* terrestre, globo *m* terráqueo
(CPD) ▸ **globe artichoke** alcachofa *f*

globefish ['gləʊbfɪʃ] (N) pez *m* globo

globeflower ['gləʊbˌflaʊəʳ] (N) (*Bot*) trollius *m*

globe-trot, **globetrot** ['gləʊbtrɒt] (VI) viajar por el mundo

globe-trotter, **globetrotter** ['gləʊbˌtrɒtəʳ] (N) trotamundos *mf inv*

globe-trotting, **globetrotting** ['gləʊbˌtrɒtɪŋ] (N) viajar *m* por todo el mundo
(ADJ) trotamundos (*inv*)

globular ['glɒbjʊləʳ] (ADJ) globular

globule ['glɒbju:l] (N) [*of oil, water*] glóbulo *m*

glockenspiel ['glɒkənspi:l] (N) carillón *m*

gloom [glu:m] (N) **1** (= *darkness*) penumbra *f*, oscuridad *f*
2 (= *sadness, despondency*) melancolía *f*, tristeza *f* • **it's not all ~ and doom here** aquí no todo son pronósticos de desastre • **she's always full of ~ and doom** siempre lo ve todo negro

gloomily ['glu:mɪlɪ] (ADV) [*say, look*] con tristeza; [*predict*] con pesimismo

gloomy ['glu:mɪ] (ADJ) (COMPAR: **gloomier**, SUPERL: **gloomiest**) **1** (= *dark*) [*place*] sombrío, lúgubre; [*day, weather*] triste, sombrío
2 (= *sad*) [*atmosphere*] triste, lúgubre • **he's a bit of a ~ character** es un tipo un poco sombrío • **to feel ~** (= *sad*) estar bajo de moral, sentirse deprimido
3 (= *pessimistic*) [*person*] pesimista; [*forecast, assessment*] pesimista, nada prometedor • **to be ~ about sth** ser pesimista acerca de algo • **no wonder shopkeepers are feeling ~** no es de extrañar que los comerciantes se sientan pesimistas • **things are looking ~ for the England team** la cosa no se presenta muy halagüeña para el equipo inglés • **the outlook for next year is ~** las perspectivas para el próximo año no son nada prometedoras • **he paints a very ~ picture** pinta la cosa muy negra • **he takes a ~ view of everything** tiene una visión muy negativa de todo

gloop* [glu:p] (N) (= *goo*) sustancia *f* espesa y pegajosa

glorification [ˌglɔ:rɪfɪ'keɪʃən] (N) glorificación *f*

glorify ['glɔ:rɪfaɪ] (VT) (= *exalt*) [+ *God*] alabar; [+ *person*] glorificar; (*pej*) [+ *war, deeds*] embellecer • **it's just a glorified boarding house** es una simple pensión, aunque con pretensiones

glorious ['glɔ:rɪəs] (ADJ) [*career, victory*] glorioso; [*weather, view*] magnífico • **it was a ~ muddle** (*iro*) la confusión era mayúscula

gloriously ['glɔ:rɪəslɪ] (ADV) **1** (= *with glory*) [*win*] gloriosamente
2 (= *wonderfully*) magníficamente • **it was ~ sunny** hacía un sol magnífico • **we were ~ happy** estábamos contentísimos

glory ['glɔ:rɪ] (N) **1** (= *honour, fame*) (*also Rel*) gloria *f* • **~ be!** ¡gracias a Dios! • **she was in her ~** estaba toda ufana • **Rome at the height of its ~** Roma en la cima de su gloria • **she led her team to Olympic ~** condujo a su equipo a la victoria olímpica • IDIOM: • **to go to ~**† subir a los cielos; ▹ **reflect**
2 (= *splendour*) gloria *f*, esplendor *m*
(VI) • **to ~ in** [+ *one's success etc*] enorgullecerse *or* jactarse de; [+ *another's misfortune*] disfrutar maliciosamente de • **the café glories in the name of El Dorado** el café tiene el magnífico nombre de El Dorado
(CPD) ▸ **glory hole*** cuarto *m or* cajón *m etc* en desorden, leonera* *f* • **his room is something of a ~ hole** su habitación parece un trastero

Glos (ABBR) = **Gloucestershire**

gloss¹ [glɒs] (N) (= *note*) glosa *f*
(VT) glosar, comentar
▸ **gloss over** (VI + PREP) **1** (= *excuse*) disculpar
2 (= *play down*) paliar, restar importancia a
3 (= *cover up*) [+ *mistake etc*] encubrir

gloss² [glɒs] (N) **1** (= *shine*) brillo *m*, lustre *m*
2 (*also* **gloss paint**) pintura *f* de esmalte
(VT) lustrar, pulir
(CPD) ▸ **gloss finish** (= *paint*) acabado *m* brillante; (*on photo*) brillo *m* satinado ▸ **gloss paper** papel *m* satinado

glossary ['glɒsərɪ] (N) glosario *m*

glossily ['glɒsɪlɪ] (ADV) brillantemente • **~ illustrated** elegantemente ilustrado, ilustrado con lujo

glossy ['glɒsɪ] (ADJ) (COMPAR: **glossier**, SUPERL: **glossiest**) [*surface*] brillante, lustroso; [*hair*] brillante; [*cloth, paper*] satinado • **~ magazine** revista *f* de moda
(N) • **the glossies** (*Brit**) las revistas de moda

glottal ['glɒtl] (ADJ) glotal
(CPD) ▸ **glottal stop** (*Ling*) oclusión *f* glotal

glottis ['glɒtɪs] (N) (PL: **glottises** *or* **glottides** ['glɒtɪˌdi:z]) glotis *f inv*

Gloucs. (ABBR) = **Gloucestershire**

glove [glʌv] (N) guante *m* • IDIOM: • **to fit sb like a ~** sentar a algn como anillo al dedo
(CPD) ▸ **glove box**, **glove compartment** (*Aut*) guantera *f* ▸ **glove maker** guantero/a *m/f* ▸ **glove puppet** títere *m* (de guante)

gloved [glʌvd] (ADJ) [*hand*] enguantado

glover ['glʌvəʳ] (N) guantero/a *m/f*

glow [gləʊ] (N) **1** [*of lamp, sunset, fire, bright colour*] brillo *m*, resplandor *m*; [*of cheeks*] rubor *m*; (*in sky*) luz *f* difusa
2 (*fig*) (= *warm feeling*) sensación *f* de bienestar • **a ~ of satisfaction** una aureola de satisfacción
(VI) **1** [*lamp, colour, sunset, fire*] brillar, resplandecer
2 (*fig*) • **to ~ with pleasure** estar radiante de felicidad • **to ~ with health** rebosar de salud
(CPD) ▸ **glow worm** luciérnaga *f*

glower ['glaʊəʳ] (VI) mirar con el ceño fruncido (**at sb** a algn)

glowering ['glaʊərɪŋ] (ADJ) [*person*] ceñudo; [*sky*] encapotado

glowing ['gləʊɪŋ] (ADJ) **1** [*light etc*] brillante; [*fire, colour*] vivo; [*complexion, cheeks etc*] encendido
2 [*person*] (*with health, pleasure*) rebosante
3 (*fig*) [*report, description etc*] entusiasta

glowingly ['gləʊɪŋlɪ] (ADV) [*speak, describe*] elogiosamente • **to speak ~ about sb/sth** hablar elogiosamente de algn/algo

gloxinia [glɒk'sɪnɪə] (N) gloxínea *f*

glucose ['glu:kəʊs] (N) glucosa *f*

glue [glu:] (N) cola *f*, pegamento *m*; (*as drug*) pegamento *m*
(VT) **1** (*lit*) pegar (**to a**) • **to ~ two things together** pegar dos cosas (con goma *etc*)
2* (*fig*) • **her face was ~d to the window** tenía la cara pegada a la ventana • **she was ~d to the television** estaba pegada al televisor • **to be ~d to the spot** quedarse clavado
(CPD) ▸ **glue sniffer** esnifador(a) *m/f* de pegamento, persona *f* que inhala *or* esnifa pegamento ▸ **glue sniffing** inhalación *f* de pegamento

gluey ['glu:ɪ] (ADJ) pegajoso, viscoso

glum [glʌm] (ADJ) (COMPAR: **glummer**, SUPERL: **glummest**) [*person*] melancólico; [*mood, expression*] triste; [*tone*] melancólico, sombrío

glumly ['glʌmlɪ] (ADV) [*walk, shake one's head*] sombríamente; [*answer*] tristemente, sombríamente; [*look, inspect*] taciturnamente, tristemente

glut [glʌt] (N) superabundancia *f*, exceso *m* • **to be a ~ on the market** inundar el mercado
(VT) **1** (*Comm*) [+ *market*] inundar
2 [+ *person*] hartar, saciar • **to ~ o.s.** atracarse (**with** de) • **to be ~ted with fruit** haberse atracado de fruta

glutamate ['glu:təmeɪt] = **monosodium glutamate**

glutamic acid [glu:ˌtæmɪk'æsɪd] (N) ácido *m* glutámico

glute* ['glu:t] (N) (*usu pl*) (= *gluteus muscle*) glúteo *m*

gluteal [glʊ'ti:əl] (ADJ) glúteo

gluten ['glu:tən] (N) gluten *m*

gluten-free [ˌglu:tən'fri:] (ADJ) sin gluten, libre de gluten

glutenous ['glu:tənəs] (ADJ) glutenoso
gluteus [glu:'ti:əs] (N) (PL: **glutei** [glu:'ti:aɪ]) glúteo *m*
glutinous ['glu:tɪnəs] (ADJ) glutinoso
glutton ['glʌtn] (N) glotón/ona *m/f*, comilón/ona* *m/f* • ~ **for work** trabajador(a) *m/f* incansable • ~ **for punishment** masoquista *mf*
gluttonous ['glʌtənəs] (ADJ) glotón, goloso
gluttony ['glʌtənɪ] (N) glotonería *f*, gula *f*
glycerin, glycerine [ˌglɪsə'ri:n] (N) glicerina *f*
glycerol ['glɪsərɒl] (N) glicerol *m*
glycin, glycine ['glaɪsi:n] (N) glicina *f*
glycogen ['glaɪkəʊdʒen] (N) glicógeno *m*
glycol ['glaɪkɒl] (N) glicol *m*
GM (N ABBR) **1** (= **general manager**) director(a) *m/f* general
2 (Brit) (= **George Medal**) *medalla del valor civil*
3 (US) = **General Motors**
(CPD) ▸ **GM crop** (= *genetically-modified crop*) cultivo *m* transgénico, cultivo *m* modificado genéticamente ▸ **GM foods** (= *genetically-modified foods*) alimentos *mpl* transgénicos, alimentos *mpl* modificados genéticamente
gm (ABBR) (= **gram(me)**) g, gr
G-man ['dʒi:mæn] (N) (PL: **G-men**) (US) agente *m* del FBI
GMAT (N ABBR) (US) = **Graduate Management Admissions Test**
GMB (N ABBR) (Brit) (= **General, Municipal and Boilermakers**) *sindicato*
GMC (ABBR) (Brit) = **General Medical Council**
GM-free [ˌdʒi:em'fri:] (ADJ) [*food*] sin ingredientes transgénicos; [*plant, crop*] no transgénico
GMO (= **genetically modified organism**) (N ABBR) OMG *m* (*organismo modificado genéticamente*)
(ADJ ABBR) [*food, crop*] modificado genéticamente, transgénico
gms (ABBR) (= **grams, grammes**) g, gr
GMT (N ABBR) (= **Greenwich Mean Time**) hora *f* media de Greenwich
GMWU (N ABBR) (Brit) (= **General and Municipal Workers' Union**) *sindicato de trabajadores autónomos y municipales*
gnarled [nɑ:ld] (ADJ) [*wood, hands*] nudoso
gnash [næʃ] (VT) • **to ~ one's teeth** rechinar los dientes
gnashing ['næʃɪŋ] (N) • ~ **of teeth** rechinamiento *m* de dientes
(ADJ) rechinante
gnat [næt] (N) mosquito *m*, jején *m* (*LAm*)
gnaw [nɔ:] (VT) (= *chew, also fig*) roer, carcomer • **~ed by doubts/hunger** atormentado por las dudas/el hambre
(VI) roer • **to ~ through** roer *or* carcomer haciendo un agujero en • **to ~ at** (*lit, fig*) roer
▸ **gnaw away** (VI + ADV) • **to ~ away at sb** [*fear, feeling*] carcomer *or* corroer a algn
▸ **gnaw off** (VT + ADV) roer
gnawing ['nɔ:ɪŋ] (ADJ) **1** [*sound*] persistente
2 (*fig*) [*remorse, anxiety etc*] corrosivo; [*hunger*] con retortijones; [*pain*] punzante • **I had a ~ feeling that something had been forgotten** me atormentaba la idea de que se había olvidado algo
gneiss [naɪs] (N) gneis *m*
gnocchi ['nɒkɪ] (NPL) ñoquis *mpl*
gnome [nəʊm] (N) gnomo *m* • **the Gnomes of Zurich** (*hum*) los banqueros suizos
gnomic ['nəʊmɪk] (ADJ) gnómico
gnostic ['nɒstɪk] (ADJ) gnóstico
(N) gnóstico/a *m/f*
gnosticism ['nɒstɪˌsɪzəm] (N) gnosticismo *m*
GNP (N ABBR) (= **gross national product**) PNB *m*
gnu [nu:] (N) (PL: **gnus** *or* **gnu**) ñu *m*
GNVQ (N ABBR) (Brit) (Scol) (= **General National Vocational Qualification**) *diploma nacional de formación profesional*

go [gəʊ]

INTRANSITIVE VERB
TRANSITIVE VERB
MODAL VERB
NOUN
ADJECTIVE
PHRASAL VERBS

(VB: PT: **went**, PP: **gone**; N: PL: **goes**)

When **go** *is part of a set combination such as* **go cheap, go far, go down the tube**, *look up the other word.*

INTRANSITIVE VERB

1 (= *move, travel*) ir • **she was going too fast** iba demasiado rápido • **to go and do sth** ir a hacer algo • **I'll go and see** voy a ver • **I'll go and fetch it for you** te lo voy a buscar • **he went and shut the door** cerró la puerta • **now you've gone and done it!*** ¡ahora sí que la has hecho buena! • **to go and see sb** • **go to see sb** ir a ver a algn • **to go along a corridor** ir por un pasillo • **we can talk as we go** podemos hablar por el camino • **add the sugar, stirring as you go** añada el azúcar, removiendo al mismo tiempo, añada el azúcar, sin dejar de remover • **to go at 30 mph** ir a 30 millas por hora • **to go by car/bicycle** ir en coche/bicicleta • **the train goes from London to Glasgow** el tren va de Londres a Glasgow • **to go home** irse a casa • **to go on a journey** ir de viaje • **there he goes!** ¡ahí va! • **to go to a party** ir a una fiesta • **to go to the doctor('s)** ir al médico • **she's gone to the optician('s) for a sight test** ha ido al oculista a graduarse la vista • **she went to the headmaster** fue a ver al director • **the child went to his mother** el niño fue a *or* hacia su madre • **to go to sb for advice** consultar a algn • **where do we go from here?** (*fig*) ¿qué hacemos ahora? • **halt, who goes there?** alto, ¿quién va *or* vive?

2 (= *depart*) [*person*] irse, marcharse; [*train, coach*] salir • **I'm going now** me voy ya, me marcho ya • **"where's Judy?" — "she's gone"** —¿dónde está Judy? —se ha ido *or* se ha marchado • **"food to go"** (US) "comida para llevar"

3 (*euph*) (= *die*) irse • **after I've gone** cuando yo me haya ido

4 (= *disappear*) [*object*] desaparecer; [*money*] gastarse; [*time*] pasar • **the cake is all gone** se ha acabado todo el pastel • **gone are the days when …** ya pasaron los días cuando … • **that sideboard will have to go** tendremos que deshacernos de ese aparador • **military service must go!** ¡fuera con el servicio militar! • **there goes my chance of promotion!** ¡adiós a mi ascenso! • **only two days to go** solo faltan dos días • **eight down and two to go** ocho hechos y dos por hacer; ▹ **missing**

5 (= *be sold*) venderse (for por, en) • **it went for £100** se vendió por *or* en 100 libras • **it's going cheap** se vende barato • **going, going, gone!** (*at auction*) ¡a la una, a las dos, a las tres!

6 (= *extend*) extenderse, llegar • **the garden goes down to the lake** el jardín se extiende *or* llega hasta el lago • **a huge sweater that goes down to my knees** un jersey enorme que me llega hasta las rodillas • **money doesn't go far nowadays** hoy día el dinero apenas da para nada • **he went up to £1,000** (*at auction*) llegó a las 1.000 libras

7 (= *function*) [*machine*] funcionar • **it's a magnificent car but it doesn't go** es un coche magnífico, pero no funciona • **I couldn't get the car to go at all** no podía arrancar el coche • **the washing machine was going so I didn't hear the phone** la lavadora estaba en marcha, así es que no oí el teléfono • **to make sth go** • **to get sth going** poner algo en marcha

8 (= *endure*) aguantar • **I don't know how much longer we can go without food** no sé cuánto tiempo más podremos aguantar sin comida • **to go hungry/thirsty** pasar hambre/sed

9 (*with activities, hobbies*) • **to go fishing/riding/swimming** ir a pescar/montar a caballo/nadar • **to go for a walk** dar un paseo • **to go for a swim** ir a nadar *or* a bañarse

10 (= *progress*) ir • **the meeting went well** la reunión fue bien • **how did the exam go?** ¿cómo te fue en el examen? • **how's it going?*** • **how goes it?*** • **what goes?** (US*) ¿qué tal?*, ¿qué tal va?*, ¡qué hubo! (*Mex, Chile**) • **we'll see how things go*** veremos cómo van las cosas • **to make a party go (with a swing)** dar ambiente a una fiesta • **the day went slowly** el día pasó lentamente • **all went well for him until …** todo le fue bien hasta que …

11 (= *match, combine with*) [*colours, clothes*] hacer juego, pegar* (**with** con) • **mustard and lamb don't go** • **mustard doesn't go with lamb** la mostaza no va bien con el cordero, la mostaza no pega con el cordero* • **cava goes well with anything** el cava va bien *or* combina con todo

12 (= *become*)

For phrases with **go** *and an adjective, such as* **to go bad, go soft, go pale**, *you should look under the adjective.*

• **it's just gone seven** acaban de dar las siete • **to go red/green** ponerse rojo/verde • **you're not going to go all sentimental/shy/religious on me!** ¡no te me pongas sentimental/tímido/religioso!*, ¡no te hagas el sentimental/tímido/religioso conmigo! • **to go communist** [*constituency, person*] volverse comunista • **to go mad** (*lit, fig*) volverse loco • **to go to sleep** dormirse; ▹ BECOME, GO, GET

13 (= *fit*) caber • **it won't go in the case** no cabe en la maleta • **4 into 3 won't go** 3 entre 4 no cabe • **4 into 12 goes 3 times** 12 entre cuatro son tres, 12 dividido entre cuatro son tres

14 (= *be accepted*) valer • **anything goes*** todo vale • **that goes for me too** (= *applies to me*) eso va también por mí; (= *I agree*) yo también estoy de acuerdo; ▹ **say**

15 (= *fail*) [*material*] desgastarse; [*chair, branch*] romperse; [*elastic*] ceder; [*fuse, light bulb*] fundirse; [*sight, strength*] fallar • **this jumper has gone at the elbows** este jersey se ha desgastado por los codos • **his health is going** su salud se está resintiendo • **his hearing/mind is going** está perdiendo el oído/la cabeza • **his nerve was beginning to go** estaba empezando a perder la sangre fría • **her sight is going** le está empezando a fallar la vista • **my voice has gone** me he quedado afónico

16 (= *be kept*) ir • **where does this book go?** ¿dónde va este libro?

17 (= *be available*) • **there are several jobs going** se ofrecen varios puestos • **there's a flat going here** aquí hay un piso libre • **is there any tea going?** (= *is there any left?*) ¿queda té?; (= *will you get me one?*) ¿me haces un té? • **I'll**

take whatever is going acepto lo que sea
18 *= get underway* • **whose turn is it to go?** (*in game*) ¿a quién le toca?, ¿quién va ahora? • **go!** (*Sport*) ¡ya! • **all systems go** (*Space*) (*also fig*) todo listo • IDIOMS: • **from the word go*** desde el principio • **there you go again!*** ¡otra vez con lo mismo!*
19 *= be destined* [*inheritance*] pasar; [*fund*] destinarse • **all his money goes on drink** se le va todo el dinero en alcohol • **the inheritance went to his nephew** la herencia pasó a su sobrino • **the money goes to charity** el dinero se destina a obras benéficas • **the prize went to Fiona Lilly** el premio fue para Fiona Lilly • **the qualities which go to make him a great writer** las cualidades que le hacen un gran escritor • **the money will go towards the holiday** el dinero será para las vacaciones
20 *= sound* [*doorbell, phone*] sonar
21 *= run* • **how does that song go?** [*tune*] ¿cómo va esa canción?; [*words*] ¿cómo es la letra de esa canción? • **the tune goes like this** la melodía va así • **the story goes that ...** según dicen ...
22 *= do* hacer • **go like that (with your right hand)** haz así (con la mano derecha)
23* *= go to the toilet* ir al baño • **I need to go** tengo que ir al baño
24 *in set expressions* • **it's a fairly good garage as garages go** es un garaje bastante bueno, para como son normalmente los garajes • **he's not bad, as estate agents go** no es un mal agente inmobiliario, dentro de lo que cabe • **let's get going!** (*= be on our way*) ¡vamos!, ¡vámonos!, ¡ándale! (*Mex*); (*= start sth*) ¡manos a la obra!, ¡adelante! • **to get going on** *or* **with sth** ponerse con algo • **I've got to get going on** *or* **with my tax** tengo que ponerme con los impuestos • **once he gets going ...** una vez que se pone ..., una vez que empieza ... • **to keep going** (*= moving forward*) seguir; (*= enduring*) resistir, aguantar; (*= functioning*) seguir funcionando • **to keep sb going: this medicine kept him going** esta medicina le daba fuerzas para seguir • **a cup of coffee is enough to keep him going all morning** una taza de café le basta para funcionar toda la mañana • **enough money to keep them going for a week or two** suficiente dinero para que pudiesen tirar* *or* funcionar una o dos semanas • **to keep sth going**: • **the workers are trying to keep the factory going** los trabajadores están intentando mantener la fábrica en funcionamiento *or* en marcha • **to let sb go** (*= release*) soltar a algn; (*euph*) (*= make redundant*) despedir a algn • **let (me) go!** ¡suéltame! • **we'll let it go at that** por esta vez pase • **you're wrong, but we'll let it go** no llevas razón, pero vamos a dejarlo así • **to let o.s. go** (*physically*) dejarse, descuidarse; (*= have fun*) soltarse el pelo* • **to let go of sth/sb** soltar algo/a algn; ▹ **far**

TRANSITIVE VERB

1 *= travel* [*+ route*] hacer • **which route does the number 29 go?** ¿qué itinerario hace el 29? • **which way are you going?** ¿por dónde vais a ir?, ¿qué camino vais a tomar? • **he went his way** siguió su camino • **we had only gone a few kilometres when ...** solo llevábamos unos kilómetros cuando ... • IDIOM: • **to go it**: • **the car was really going it*** el coche iba a una buena marcha*; ▹ **distance**
2 *= make* hacer • **the car went "bang!"** el coche hizo "bang"
3* *= say* soltar* • **"shut up!" he goes** —¡cállate! —suelta • **he goes to me, "what do you want?"** va y me dice *or* me suelta: —¿qué quieres?*
4 *Gambling* (*= bet*) apostar • **he went £50 on the red** apostó 50 libras al rojo • **I can only go £15** solo puedo llegar a 15 libras
5* • IDIOMS: • **to go one better** ganar el remate • **to go it alone** obrar por su cuenta

MODAL VERB

ir • **I'm going/I was going to do it** voy/iba a hacerlo • **it's going to rain** va a llover • **there's going to be trouble** se va a armar un lío*, va a haber follón* **to go doing sth** • **don't go getting upset*** venga, no te enfades • **to go looking for sth/sb** ir a buscar algo/a algn

NOUN

1 *= turn* • **whose go is it?** ¿a quién le toca? • **it's your go** te toca a ti
2 *= attempt* intento *m* • **to have a go (at doing sth)** probar (a hacer algo) • **shall I have a go?** ¿pruebo yo?, ¿lo intento yo? • **to have another go** probar otra vez, intentarlo otra vez • **at** *or* **in one go** de un (solo) golpe
3* *= bout* • **he's had a bad go of flu** ha pasado una gripe muy mala • **they've had a rough go of it** lo han pasado mal, han pasado una mala racha
4* *= energy* empuje *m*, energía *f* • **to be full of go** estar lleno de empuje *or* energía • **there's no go about him** no tiene empuje *or* energía
5* *= success* • **to make a go of sth** tener éxito en algo
6 • IDIOMS: • **it's all go** aquí no se para nunca • **it's all the go** hace furor • **to have a go at sb*** (*physically*) atacar a algn; (*verbally*) tomarla con algn* • **it's no go** es inútil • **on the go**: • **he's always on the go** nunca para • **to keep sb on the go** tener a algn siempre en danza • **I've got two projects on the go** tengo dos proyectos en marcha

ADJECTIVE

(*Space*) • **you are go for moon-landing** estás listo para alunizar • **all systems are go** (*lit, fig*) todo listo; ▹ COME, GO

▸ **go about** VI + PREP 1 (*= move around*) • **he goes about the house with no clothes on** anda *or* va por la casa desnudo
2 (*= set to work on*) [*+ task*] emprender; [*+ problem*] abordar • **how does one go about joining?** ¿qué hay que hacer para hacerse socio? • **he knows how to go about it** sabe lo que hay que hacer, sabe cómo hacerlo
3 (*= busy o.s. with*) • **to go about one's business** ocuparse de sus cosas
VI + ADV 1 (*= circulate*) [*news, rumour*] correr, circular; [*virus*] rodar • **there's a rumour going about that they're getting married** corre *or* circula el rumor de que se van a casar • **there's a bug going about** hay un virus por ahí rondando • **he goes about in a Rolls** se pasea por ahí en un Rolls • **to go about barefoot/in torn jeans** ir descalzo/con unos vaqueros rotos • **you shouldn't go about bullying people like that?** no deberías ir por ahí intimidando a la gente de esa manera
2 (*Naut*) (*= change direction*) virar

▸ **go across** VI + PREP [*+ river, road*] cruzar, atravesar
VI + ADV (*= cross*) cruzar • **she's gone across to Mrs Kelly's** ha ido enfrente *or* ha cruzado a casa de la señora Kelly

▸ **go after** VI + PREP (*= follow*) seguir; [*+ criminal*] perseguir; [*+ job, record*] andar tras; [*+ girl*] andar tras, perseguir* (*hum*) • **we're not going after civilian targets** no vamos a por objetivos civiles

▸ **go against** VI + PREP 1 (*= be unfavourable to*) [*result, events, evidence*] ir en contra de • **the decision went against him** la decisión iba en contra de él
2 (*= be contrary to*) [*+ principles, conscience*] ser contrario a
3 (*= act against*) [*+ sb's wishes*] actuar en contra de

▸ **go ahead** VI + ADV (*= carry on*) seguir adelante (**with** con) • **the exhibition will go ahead as planned** la exposición seguirá adelante tal y como estaba planeado • **go (right) ahead!** ¡adelante!

▸ **go along** VI + ADV 1 (*= proceed*) seguir • **I'll tell you as we go along** te lo diré de camino • **Cordy's having a party, shall we go along?** Cordy da una fiesta, ¿vamos? • **why don't you go along and see your doctor?*** ¿por qué no vas al médico? • **check as you go along** ve corrigiendo sobre la marcha • **I'm learning as I go along** voy aprendiendo poco a poco • **things are going along nicely*** las cosas marchan bien
2 • **to go along with** (*= accompany*) acompañar; (*= agree with*) [*+ person, idea*] estar de acuerdo con • **we don't go along with that** no estamos de acuerdo con eso

▸ **go around** VI + ADV 1 = **go round**
2 • PROVERB: • **what goes around comes around** a todos los cerdos les llega su sanmartín
VI + PREP = **go round**

▸ **go at*** VI + PREP 1 (*= attack*) atacar, arremeter contra
2 (*= tackle*) [*+ job etc*] empecinarse en (hacer)

▸ **go away** VI + ADV 1 [*person*] (*= depart*) irse, marcharse; (*on holiday*) irse de vacaciones • **he's gone away with my keys** se ha ido *or* marchado con mis llaves, se ha llevado mis llaves • **go away!** ¡vete!, ¡lárgate!* • **I think we need to go away and think about this** creo que ahora debemos pensárnoslo un poco • **don't go away with the idea that ...** no te vayas con la idea de que ...
2 [*pain, problem*] desaparecer

▸ **go back** VI + ADV 1 (*= return*) volver, regresar (**to** a) • **to go back home** volver *or* regresar a casa • **when do the schools go back?** ¿cuándo empieza el colegio? • **the strikers have voted to go back to work** los huelguistas han votado en favor de volver al trabajo • **he's gone back to his wife** ha vuelto con su mujer • **this dress will have to go back (to the shop)** habrá que devolver este vestido • **going back to the point you raised earlier, ...** volviendo al tema que planteaste antes, ... • **to go back to the beginning** volver al principio; ▹ **go back to**
2 (*= retreat*) volverse atrás • **there's no going back now** ya no podemos volvernos atrás
3 (*= extend*) extenderse • **the path goes back to the river** el camino llega *or* se extiende hasta el río • **the cave goes back 300 metres** la cueva tiene 300 metros de fondo, la cueva tiene una extensión de 300 metros
4 (*= date back*) remontarse • **we go back a long way** nos conocemos desde hace mucho • **my memories don't go back so far** mis recuerdos no se remontan tan lejos • **it goes back to Elizabeth I** se remonta a Isabel I • **the controversy goes back to 1929** la controversia se remonta a 1929
5 (*= change*) • **when do the clocks go back?** ¿cuándo hay que atrasar los relojes? • **the clocks go back on Sunday** los relojes se atrasan el domingo

▸ **go back on** VI + PREP [*+ decision*] volverse atrás en; [*+ promise*] incumplir • **to go back on one's word** faltar a su palabra

▸ **go back to** VI + PREP (*= revert to*) volver a • **I sold the car and went back to a bicycle** vendí el coche y volví a la bicicleta • **he went back to his former habits** volvió a sus antiguas costumbres • **go back to sleep!** ¡vuelve a dormir!; ▹ **go back**

▸ **go before** (VI + ADV) (= *precede*) preceder • **all that has gone before** todo lo que ha pasado antes • **those who are** *or* **have gone before** (*euph*) (= *die*) aquellos que ya pasaron a mejor vida
(VI + PREP) • **the matter has gone before a grand jury** el asunto se ha sometido a un gran jurado

▸ **go below** (VI + ADV) (*Naut*) bajar

▸ **go beyond** (VI + PREP) ir más allá de • **in this series I have tried to go beyond the basics** en este serie he intentado ir más allá de lo básico *or* esencial • **his interests went beyond political economy** sus intereses iban más allá de la economía política

▸ **go by** (VI + PREP) **1** (= *drop by*) pasarse por • **can we go by Sally's house?** ¿podemos pasarnos por casa de Sally? • **did you remember to go by the ironmonger's?** ¿te has acordado de pasarte por la ferretería?
2 (= *be guided by*) [+ *watch, compass*] guiarse por • **to go by appearances** guiarse por las apariencias • **you can't go by that** no hay que dejarse guiar por eso • **you can't go by what he says** no puedes fiarte de lo que dice
3 • **to go by the name of** llamarse
(VI + ADV) (= *pass by*) [*opportunity*] pasar; [*time*] pasar, transcurrir; [*person, car*] pasar (cerca); (= *overtake*) adelantar, rebasar (*Mex*) • **in days gone by** en tiempos pasados, antaño • **as time goes by** con el tiempo, con el transcurso del tiempo

▸ **go down** (VI + PREP) bajar, descender • **to go down a slope** bajar (por) una pendiente • **to go down a mine** bajar a una mina
(VI + ADV) **1** (= *descend*) [*sun*] ponerse; [*person*] (= *go downstairs*) bajar • **to go down to the coast** bajar a la costa • **go down to the bottom of the page** mira a pie de página
2 (= *fall*) [*person, horse*] caerse
3 (= *crash*) [*plane*] estrellarse, caer
4 (= *sink*) [*ship, person*] hundirse
5 (= *decrease, decline*) [*price, temperature*] bajar, descender; [*tide, flood, water level*] bajar • **he has gone down in my estimation** ha bajado en mi estima • **the house has gone down in value** la casa ha perdido valor *or* se ha devaluado • **this neighbourhood has really gone down** este barrio ha perdido mucho, este barrio ya no es lo que era • **she's really gone down since I last saw her** [*sick person*] ha dado un buen bajón* *or* ha empeorado mucho desde la última vez que la vi; [*elderly person*] ha perdido muchas facultades desde la última vez que la vi
6 (= *deflate*) [*balloon, airbed*] desinflarse, deshincharse (*Sp*) • **the swelling in my leg has gone down** me ha bajado la hinchazón de la pierna
7 (= *be defeated*) perder • **Italy went down against Brazil in the semi-final** Italia perdió ante Brasil en la semifinal
8 (*Comput*) (= *break down*) bloquearse, dejar de funcionar
9 (= *be remembered*) • **to go down in history/to posterity** pasar a la historia/a la posteridad; ▹ **go down as**
10 (*Brit*) (*Univ*) (*at end of term*) marcharse; (*at end of degree*) terminar la carrera, dejar la universidad
11 (= *be swallowed*) • **that omelette went down a treat*** esa tortilla estaba riquísima • **it went down the wrong way** se me atragantó
12 (= *be accepted, approved*) • **to go down well/badly** ser bien/mal recibido • **his speech didn't go down at all well** su discurso fue muy mal recibido • **that should go down well (with him)*** eso le va a gustar • **I wonder how that will go down with her parents** me pregunto cómo les sentará eso a sus padres
13 (*Theat*) [*curtain*] bajar; [*lights*] apagarse

▸ **go down as** (VI + PREP) (= *be regarded as*) considerarse; (= *be remembered as*) pasar a la historia como • **it has to go down as the worst performance of my career** se considerará la peor actuación de mi carrera, pasará a la historia como la peor actuación de mi carrera • **he will go down in history as ...** pasará a la historia como ...

▸ **go down on**‡ (VI + PREP) • **to go down on sb** chupárselo *or* chupársela a algn*‡

▸ **go down with*** (VI + PREP) [+ *illness, virus, food poisoning*] pillar*, coger, agarrar (*LAm*)

▸ **go for** (VI + PREP) **1** (= *attack*) (*physically, verbally*) atacar • **suddenly the dog went for me** de pronto el perro me atacó *or* fue a por mí • **go for him!** (*to dog*) ¡a él!
2* (= *like, fancy*) • **I don't go for his films very much** no me gustan mucho sus películas • **I don't go for that sort of talk** no me va esa clase de conversación • **I could really go for him!** ¡me gusta muchísimo!, ¡me mola cantidad! (*Sp**) • **I go for quiet, unassuming types** me gustan *or* me van más los tipos callados y sin pretensiones
3 (= *strive for*) dedicarse a obtener • **go for it!*** ¡a por ello!, ¡adelante! • **I decided to go for it*** decidí intentarlo
4 (= *choose*) escoger, optar por • **I'll go for the cream caramel** para mí flan
5 • IDIOM: • **to have a lot going for one**: • **he has a lot going for him** tiene mucho a su favor • **the theory has a lot going for it** la teoría cuenta con muchas ventajas

▸ **go forward** (VI + ADV) **1** (= *move ahead*) [*person, vehicle*] avanzar
2 (= *change*) [*clocks*] • **when do the clocks go forward?** ¿cuándo se adelantan los relojes?
3 (*fig*) **a** (= *proceed*) (*with sth*) seguir adelante (**with** con) • **if we go forward with these radical proposals ...** si seguimos adelante con estas propuestas radicales ... • **if our present plans go forward, we'll have to take on more staff** si nuestros planes actuales progresan *or* siguen adelante, tendremos que emplear a más personal
b (= *be put forward*) [*suggestion*] presentarse

▸ **go in** (VI + ADV) **1** (= *enter*) entrar • **please do go in** pase, por favor • **they went in by the back door** entraron por la puerta trasera
2 (= *attack*) atacar • **the troops are going in tomorrow** las tropas atacarán mañana • **British troops will not go in alone** las tropas británicas no serán las únicas en entrar en combate
3 (= *fit*) caber
4 [*sun*] ocultarse (**behind** tras, detrás de)
5 (*Cricket*) entrar a batear

▸ **go in for** (VI + PREP) **1** (= *enter for*) [+ *race, competition*] presentarse a; [+ *examination*] presentarse a
2 (= *take as career*) dedicarse a
3 (= *be interested in*) [+ *hobby, sport*] interesarse por • **we don't go in for such things here** (*activities*) aquí esas cosas no se hacen
4 (= *use*) utilizar

▸ **go into** (VI + PREP) **1** (= *enter*) (*lit*) entrar en • **she went into the kitchen** entró en la cocina • **to go into politics** entrar en la política, dedicarse a la política • **he doesn't want to go into industry** no quiere dedicarse a la industria • **he's thinking about going into the police force** está pensando entrar en el cuerpo de policía; ▹ **hiding**
2 (= *go to*) • **Ed has had to go into work** Ed ha tenido que ir a trabajar • **he's had to go into hospital** ha tenido que ingresar en el hospital
3 (= *embark on*) [+ *explanation, details*] meterse en; (= *investigate, examine*) examinar a fondo • **let's not go into all that now** dejemos todo eso por ahora
4 (= *fall into*) [+ *trance, coma*] entrar en • **he went into fits of laughter** le entró *or* le dio un ataque de risa
5 (= *be spent on*) [*money, resources*] dedicarse a • **a lot of money went into the research** se dedicó mucho dinero a la investigación
6 (*Aut*) • **to go into first gear** meter primera velocidad • **they went into the back of a lorry in the ice** resbalaron sobre el hielo y chocaron contra la parte trasera de un camión

▸ **go in with** (VI + PREP) asociarse con, unirse con • **we're going in with an American company** nos vamos a unir a una empresa americana • **she went in with her sister to buy the present** entre ella y su hermana compraron el regalo

▸ **go off** (VI + ADV) **1** (= *leave*) marcharse, irse • **he went off with the au pair** se largó* *or* se marchó con la chica au pair
2 (= *stop*) [*TV, light, heating*] apagarse; [*pain*] irse, pasarse
3 (= *be activated*) [*bomb*] estallar; [*gun*] dispararse; [*alarm clock*] sonar
4 (= *go bad*) [*food*] echarse a perder; [*milk*] pasarse, echarse a perder
5 (= *pass off*) salir • **the party went off well** la fiesta salió bien
6* (*to sleep*) quedarse dormido • **I must have gone off for a few moments** debo haberme quedado dormido unos instantes • **he goes off to sleep the moment his head touches the pillow** en cuanto pone la cabeza en la almohada se queda dormido
(VI + PREP) (= *no longer like*) [+ *thing*] perder el gusto por; [+ *person*] dejar de querer a • **I've gone off the idea** ya no me gusta la idea

▸ **go on** (VI + PREP) **1** (= *be guided by*) [+ *evidence*] basarse en • **there isn't much evidence to go on** no hay muchos indicios en los que basarse, no hay muchas pruebas en las que basarse • **there's nothing to go on** no hay nada en que basarse • **what are you going on?** ¿en qué te basas? • **the police had no clues to go on** la policía no tenía pistas que le sirvieran de guía
2 (= *like*) • **I don't go much on that** eso no me gusta
3 (= *continue*) • **to go on doing sth** seguir haciendo algo, continuar haciendo algo
4* (= *approach*) • **she's going on 50** anda cerca de la cincuentena, va para los cincuenta • **Ann's 25 going on 50** Ann tiene 25 años pero parece que tuviera 50
5 (= *be spent on*) • **most of their money goes on drink** la mayor parte del dinero se les va en bebida
6 (= *start taking*) [+ *drug*] empezar a tomar • **she's to go on the pill** tiene que empezar a tomar la píldora
(VI + ADV) **1** (= *fit*) • **the lid won't go on** la tapa no le va • **these shoes won't go on** no me entran estos zapatos
2 (= *continue*) [*war, talks*] seguir, continuar; [*person*] (*on journey*) seguir el camino • **I went on up the road and met Philippa** seguí carretera arriba y me encontré con Philippa • **everything is going on normally** todo sigue con normalidad • **"so," he went on ...** —así es que —continuó • **go on!** (= *continue*) sigue, continúa; (*giving encouragement*) ¡venga!; (*showing incredulity*) ¡no digas bobadas!*, ¡anda ya!*, ¡venga ya!* • **to go on doing sth** seguir *or* continuar haciendo algo • **go on,**

g

tell me what the problem is! ¡venga, dime cuál es el problema! • **go on with your work** sigue con tu trabajo • **that'll do to be going on with*** con eso basta por ahora • **I've got enough to be going on with** tengo suficiente por el momento • IDIOM: • **go on with you!*** (*showing incredulity*) ¡no digas bobadas!*, ¡anda ya!*, ¡venga ya!*
3 (= *last*) durar • **the concert went on until 11 o'clock at night** el concierto duró hasta las 11 de la noche • **how long will this go on for?** ¿cuánto tiempo durará esto?
4 (= *proceed*) • **to go on to do sth** pasar a hacer algo • **after having taught herself Italian, she went on to learn Arabic** después de haber aprendido italiano por su cuenta, empezó a estudiar árabe • **he went on to say that ...** añadió que ...
5* (= *talk*) • **he does go on so** habla más que siete*, no para de hablar • **to go on about sth** no parar de hablar de algo, dar la tabarra *or* la matraca con algo* • **she's always going on about it** nunca para de hablar de eso, siempre está con la misma cantinela* • **he's always going on about the government** (= *criticize*) siempre está echando pestes contra el gobierno* • **don't go on about it!** ¡déjalo ya!, ¡deja ya de dar la tabarra *or* la matraca con el tema!*
6* (= *nag*) • **to go on at sb** dar la lata a algn* (**about con**)
7 (= *happen*) pasar, ocurrir • **it had been going on in her absence** había pasado no estando ella • **there's something odd going on** aquí hay gato encerrado • **what's going on here?** ¿qué pasa *or* ocurre aquí?
8 (= *pass, go by*) [*time, years*] pasar, transcurrir
9 (= *come on*) [*lights, machine*] encenderse, prenderse (*LAm*)
10 (*Theat*) salir (a escena)
11 (*Sport*) • **to go on as a substitute** entrar como suplente
12* (= *behave*) • **what a way to go on!** (*pej*) ¡qué manera de comportarse!

▸ **go on for** VI + PREP (*with numbers*) • **he's going on for 60** anda por los 60 • **it's going on for two o'clock** son casi las dos, van a ser las dos • **it's going on for 100km to Vilafranca** Vilafranca está a unos 100km de aquí

▸ **go out** VI + ADV **1** (= *be extinguished, switch off*) [*fire, light*] apagarse • IDIOM: • **to go out like a light** dormirse al instante, quedarse frito*
2 (= *exit*) salir • **to go out of a room** salir de un cuarto • **to go out shopping** salir de compras *or* de tiendas • **to go out for a meal** salir a comer/cenar (fuera) • **she goes out to work** trabaja (fuera) • **to go out (of fashion)** pasar de moda • **the mail has gone out** ha salido el correo • **there's a lot of money going out on household bills** se gasta mucho dinero en facturas domésticas • **you must go out and get a job** tienes que ponerte a encontrar trabajo • **TV violence incites people to go out and cause trouble** la violencia en la televisión incita a la gente a salir a la calle y causar problemas
3 (*romantically*) • **to go out with sb** salir con algn • **how long have you been going out together?** ¿cuánto tiempo hace que salís juntos?
4 (= *ebb*) [*tide*] bajar, menguar
5 (= *travel*) viajar (**to a**) • **she went out to Bangkok to join her husband** viajó a Bangkok para reunirse con su esposo
6 (= *be issued*) [*pamphlet, circular*] salir, publicarse; [*invitation*] mandarse; (= *be broadcast*) [*radio programme, TV programme*] emitirse • **an appeal has gone out for people to give blood** se ha hecho un llamamiento a la población para que done sangre • **the programme goes out on Friday evenings** el programa se emite los viernes por la noche
7 (*Sport*) (= *be eliminated*) quedar eliminado • **our team went out to a second division side** nuestro equipo fue eliminado por uno de segunda división
8 (*commiserating*) • **my heart went out to him** le compadecí mucho, sentí mucha pena por él • **all our sympathy goes out to you** te damos nuestro más sentido pésame, te acompañamos en el sentimiento

▸ **go out of** VI + PREP (= *desert*) • **all the vitality has gone out of her** se ha quedado sin vitalidad • **the vigour has gone out of the debate** el debate no tiene ya fuerza *or* vigor

▸ **go over** VI + PREP **1** (= *examine, check*) [+ *report, figures*] examinar, revisar
2 (= *rehearse, review*) [+ *speech, lesson*] repasar, revisar • **to go over sth in one's mind** repasar algo mentalmente • **let's go over the facts again** repasemos los hechos otra vez
3 (= *touch up*) retocar
4 (= *pass over*) [+ *wall*] pasar por encima de • **to go over the same ground: we went over the same ground time and again, trying to sort out the facts** volvimos a lo mismo una y otra vez, intentando esclarecer los hechos
VI + ADV **1** • **to go over to a** (= *cross over to*) cruzar a; (*fig*) (*changing habit, sides etc*) pasarse a • **to go over to America** ir a América • **shall we go over to Inga's?** ¿vamos a casa de Inga? • **to go over to the enemy** pasarse al enemigo
b (= *approach*) acercarse a, dirigirse a
2 (= *be received*) recibirse • **how did it go over?** ¿qué tal fue recibido *or* se recibió? • **his speech went over well** su discurso tuvo buena acogida

▸ **go round** VI + ADV **1** (= *revolve*) girar, dar vueltas • **the wheel was going round very fast** la rueda giraba *or* daba vueltas muy de prisa • **the idea was going round in my head** la idea me daba vueltas en la cabeza • **my head is going round** la cabeza me da vueltas
2 (= *circulate*) • **he goes round in a Rolls** se pasea por ahí en un Rolls • **to go round barefoot/in torn jeans** andar descalzo/con unos vaqueros rotos • **people who go round spreading rumours** la gente que va por ahí esparciendo rumores • **there's a bug going round** hay un virus por ahí rondando • **there's a rumour going round that they're getting married** corre *or* circula el rumor de que se van a casar • **he often goes round with Jimmy** se le ve a menudo con Jimmy
3 (= *suffice*) alcanzar, bastar • **is there enough food to go round?** ¿hay comida suficiente para todos?
4 (= *visit*) • **let's go round to John's place** vamos a casa de John
5 (= *make a detour*) dar la vuelta
VI + PREP **1** (= *spin round*) girar alrededor de • **the Earth goes round the sun** la Tierra gira alrededor del sol
2 (= *visit*) visitar • **we want to go round the museum** queremos visitar el museo • **I love going round the shops** me encanta ir de tiendas • **to go round the world** dar la vuelta al mundo
3 (= *patrol*) [+ *grounds*] patrullar (por), recorrer
4 (= *make a detour round*) [+ *obstacle*] dar la vuelta a

▸ **go through** VI + PREP **1** (= *pass through*) pasar por; (= *cross*) atravesar • **I've never liked going through tunnels** nunca me ha gustado pasar por túneles • **we went through London to get to Brighton** pasamos por *or* atravesamos Londres para llegar a Brighton • **you have to go through the sitting-room to go to the kitchen** para ir a la cocina tienes que pasar por la sala de estar
2 (= *suffer*) pasar por; (= *bear*) aguantar • **I know what you're going through** sé por lo que estás pasando
3 (= *examine*) [+ *list, book*] repasar; (= *search through*) [+ *pile, possessions, pockets*] registrar
4 (= *use up*) [+ *money*] gastar; [+ *food*] comerse; [+ *drink*] beberse; (= *wear out*) [+ *garment*] gastar • **the book went through 8 editions** el libro tuvo 8 ediciones
5 (= *perform*) [+ *formalities*] cumplimentar; [+ *ceremony*] realizar • **we'll go through some warm-up exercises first** primero haremos algunos ejercicios de calentamiento
VI + ADV **1** (*lit*) pasar • **let's go through to the other room** vamos a pasar a la otra sala • **the bullet went right through** la bala pasó de parte a parte
2 [*proposal, bill, motion*] ser aprobado, aprobarse; [*deal*] concluirse, hacerse • **it all went through all right** todo se llevó a cabo sin problemas
3 [*clothing*] romperse *or* agujerearse con el uso • **it has gone through at the elbows** con el uso se ha roto *or* agujereado por los codos

▸ **go through with** VI + PREP [+ *plan, crime*] llevar a cabo • **I can't go through with it!** ¡no puedo seguir con esto!

▸ **go to** VI + PREP **1** • IDIOM: • **go to it!** ¡adelante!, ¡empieza!; ▹ **go**
2 (= *take*) • **you needn't go to the expense of buying a new one** no es preciso que te gastes dinero para comprar uno nuevo • **they went to great expense to send her to a private school** se metieron *or* (*frm*) incurrieron en muchos gastos para mandarla a un colegio privado • **to go to (all) the trouble of doing sth** tomarse la molestia de hacer algo • **I went to a lot of trouble to get it for her** me tomé muchas molestias para conseguírselo

▸ **go together** VI + ADV **1** (= *harmonize*) [*colours*] hacer juego; [*ideas*] complementarse • **green and mauve go well together** el verde y el malva hacen juego
2 (= *coincide*) [*events, conditions*] ir de la mano • **poor living conditions and tuberculosis go together** la pobreza y la tuberculosis van siempre de la mano
3* [*couple*] salir juntos • **Ann and Peter are going together** Ann y Peter salen juntos

▸ **go toward, go towards** VI + PREP (= *contribute to*) • **the extra money will go toward a holiday** el dinero extra será para unas vacaciones

▸ **go under** VI + PREP • **he now goes under the name of Curtis** ahora se conoce por Curtis
VI + ADV **1** (= *sink*) [*ship, person*] hundirse
2 (= *fail*) [*business, firm*] quebrar

▸ **go up** VI + ADV **1** (= *rise*) [*temperature, price*] subir • **the total goes up to ...** el total asciende a ... • **Hartlepool should go up this season** (*Sport*) el Hartlepool debería ascender esta temporada
2 (= *travel*) • **to go up to London** ir a Londres
3 (= *approach*) • **to go up to sb** acercarse a algn, abordar a algn
4 (= *go upstairs*) subir (*a la planta de arriba*)
5 (= *be built*) [*tower block, building*] levantarse
6 (= *explode*) estallar • **to go up in flames** arder en llamas, ser pasto de las llamas
7 (= *be heard*) • **a gasp went up from the crowd** la multitud dio un grito entrecortado
8 (*Brit*) (*Univ*) • **to go up to university** (*to begin studies*) entrar en la universidad; (*after vacation*) volver a la universidad

9 (*Theat*) [*curtain*] subir, abrirse, levantarse; [*lights*] encenderse
▸ **go with** VI + PREP **1** (= *accompany*) ir con, acompañar a • **the house goes with the job** la casa va con el trabajo
2* (= *go steady with*) salir con
3 (*sexually*) acostarse con
4* (= *agree with*) • **I'll go with you there** en eso estoy (de acuerdo) contigo, en eso te doy la razón • **yes, I'd go with that** sí, en eso estoy de acuerdo
5* (= *choose*) escoger, optar por
6 (= *match*) ▸ **go**
▸ **go without** VI + PREP pasar sin, prescindir de
VI + ADV arreglárselas, pasar • **you'll have to go without** tendrás que arreglártelas *or* pasar sin ello

goad [gəʊd] VT **1** (*lit*) aguijonear, picar
2 (*fig*) incitar, provocar; (= *anger*) irritar; (= *taunt*) provocar con insultos • **to ~ sb into fury** provocar a algn poniéndole furioso • **to ~ sb into doing sth/to do sth** incitar a algn a hacer algo
N **1** (*Agr*) aguijón *m*, puya *f*
2 (*fig*) estímulo *m*
▸ **goad on** VT + ADV pinchar, provocar • **to ~ sb on to doing sth** provocar a algn para que haga algo
go-ahead ['gəʊəhed] ADJ (*esp Brit*) emprendedor
N • **to give sth/sb the go-ahead** autorizar algo/a algn
goal [gəʊl] N **1** (*Sport*) (= *score*) gol *m*; (= *net etc*) portería *f*, meta *f*, arco *m* (*LAm*) • **to keep ~** • **to play in ~** ser portero *or* (*LAm*) arquero • **goal!** ¡gol! • **to score a ~** marcar un gol • **they won by two ~s to one** ganaron por dos goles *or* tantos a uno
2 (= *aim*) (*in life*) meta *f*, objetivo *m*; (*in journey*) fin *m* • **to reach one's ~** llegar a la meta, realizar una ambición
CPD ▸ **goal area** área *f* de portería, área *f* de meta ▸ **goal average** promedio *m* de goles, golaverage *m* ▸ **goal difference** gol *m* average, diferencia *f* de goles ▸ **goal kick** saque *m* de puerta ▸ **goal line** línea *f* de portería
goalie* ['gəʊlɪ] N = **goalkeeper**
goalkeeper ['gəʊl,kiːpəʳ] N portero/a *m/f*, guardameta *mf*, arquero *m* (*LAm*)
goalkeeping ['gəʊl,kiːpɪŋ] N actuación *f* como portero, actuación *f* del portero
goalless ['gəʊllɪs] ADJ sin goles, con empate a cero • **a ~ draw** un empate a cero (goles)
goalmouth ['gəʊlmaʊθ] N portería *f*
goalpost ['gəʊlpəʊst] N poste *m* (de la portería) • IDIOM: • **to move the ~s** cambiar las reglas del juego
goalscorer ['gəʊl,skɔːrəʳ] N goleador(a) *m/f*
goat [gəʊt] N (*gen*) cabra *f*; (*male*) chivo *m*, macho cabrío *m* • IDIOM: • **to get sb's ~*** fastidiar *or* molestar a algn
CPD ▸ **goat cheese, goat's cheese** queso *m* de cabra
goatee [gəʊ'tiː] N (*short*) perilla *f*; (*long*) barba *f* de chivo
goatfish ['gəʊtfɪʃ] N (*US*) salmonete *m*
goatherd ['gəʊthɜːd] N cabrero *m*
goatskin ['gəʊtskɪn] N piel *f* de cabra
gob‡ [gɒb] N **1** (= *spit*) salivazo *m*
2 (*Brit*) (= *mouth*) bocaza* *f*
VT (*Brit*) escupir
VI (*Brit*) escupir
go-bag ['gəʊbæg] N (*of emergency essentials*) bolsa *f* con artículos de primera necesidad
gobbet* ['gɒbɪt] N [*of food etc*] trocito *m*, pequeña porción *f* • **~s of information** pequeños elementos *mpl* de información
gobble ['gɒbl] N gluglú *m*
VT (*also* **gobble down, gobble up**) engullir, tragar
VI [*turkey*] gluglutear
gobbledegook*, gobbledygook* ['gɒbldɪguːk] N jerigonza *f*, galimatías *m inv*
gobbler ['gɒbləʳ] N (= *turkey*) pavo *m*
go-between ['gəʊbɪ,twiːn] N intermediario/a *m/f*; (= *pimp*) alcahuete/a *m/f*
Gobi Desert ['gəʊbɪ'dezət] N desierto *m* del Gobi
goblet ['gɒblɪt] N copa *f*
goblin ['gɒblɪn] N duende *m*, trasgo *m*
gobshite**‡ ['gɒbʃaɪt] N (= *idiot*) chulo/a *m/f* de mierda**‡
gobsmacked‡ ['gɒbsmækt] ADJ (*Brit*) • **I was ~** me quedé alucinado*
gobstopper* ['gɒb,stɒpəʳ] N (*Brit*) *caramelo grande y redondo*
go-by* ['gəʊbaɪ] N • **to give sth the go-by** pasar algo por alto, omitir algo • **to give a place the go-by** dejar de visitar un sitio • **to give sb the go-by** desairar a algn (*no haciendo caso de él/ella*), no hacer caso de algn
goby ['gəʊbɪ] N (= *fish*) gobio *m*
GOC N ABBR = **General Officer Commanding**
go-cart ['gəʊkɑːt] N cochecito *m* de niño
god [gɒd] N **1** dios *m* • **God** Dios *m* • **(my) God!** • **good God!*** ¡Dios mío!, ¡santo Dios! • **God forbid** ¡Dios me libre! • **he thinks he's God's gift to women*** se cree que lo creó Dios para ser la felicidad de las mujeres • **God help them if that's what they think** que Dios les ayude si piensan así • **I hope to God she'll be happy** Dios quiera que sea feliz • **God (only) knows** solo Dios sabe, sabe Dios • **what in God's name is he doing?** ¿qué demonios está haciendo? • **please God!** ¡quiera Dios! • **for God's sake!** ¡por Dios! • **thank God!** ¡gracias a Dios! • **God willing** si Dios quiere, Dios mediante • PROVERB: • **God helps those who help themselves** a quien madruga Dios le ayuda; ▸ **forbid**
2 • **the gods** (*Theat*) el gallinero, el paraíso
god-awful‡ ['gɒd'ɔːfʊl] ADJ horrible, fatal*
god-botherer* ['gɒd,bɒðərəʳ] N (*pej*) pesado/a *m/f* de la religión
godchild ['gɒdtʃaɪld] N (PL: **godchildren**) ahijado/a *m/f*
goddam, goddamn‡ ['gɒd'dæm] (*US*) ADJ (*also* **goddamn(ed)**) maldito, puñetero*
EXCL (*also* **goddammit**) ¡maldición!
N • **I don't give a good ~(n)!** ¡me importa un pito!*, ¡me importa un carajo!‡
goddaughter ['gɒd,dɔːtəʳ] N ahijada *f*
goddess ['gɒdɪs] N diosa *f*
godfather ['gɒd,fɑːðəʳ] N padrino *m* (**to** de)
god-fearing ['gɒd,fɪərɪŋ] ADJ temeroso de Dios
godforsaken* ['gɒdfə,seɪkn] ADJ [*place*] olvidado de Dios; [*person*] dejado de la mano de Dios
Godfrey ['gɒdfrɪ] N Godofredo
godhead ['gɒdhed] N divinidad *f*
godless ['gɒdlɪs] ADJ **1** (= *wicked*) [*life*] pecaminoso
2 (= *unbelieving*) ateo
godlike ['gɒdlaɪk] ADJ divino
godliness ['gɒdlɪnɪs] N piedad *f*; ▸ **cleanliness**
godly ['gɒdlɪ] ADJ (COMPAR: **godlier**, SUPERL: **godliest**) devoto
godmother ['gɒd,mʌðəʳ] N madrina *f* (**to** de)
godparents ['gɒd,peərənts] NPL padrinos *mpl*
godsend ['gɒdsend] N don *m* del cielo • **it was a ~ to us** nos llegó en buena hora
godson ['gɒdsʌn] N ahijado *m*
Godspeed†† [,gɒd'spiːd] EXCL • **~!** ¡buena suerte!, ¡ande usted con Dios!
-goer ['gəʊəʳ] N (*ending in compounds*) • **cinema-goer** asiduo/a *m/f* del cine; ▸ **opera-goer, theatre-goer**
goes [gəʊz] VB *3rd pers sing present of* **go**
go-faster stripes* [gəʊ,fɑːstə'straɪps] NPL (*Aut*) bandas *fpl* laterales decorativas
gofer ['gəʊfəʳ] N recadero/a *m/f*
go-getter* ['gəʊgetəʳ] N ambicioso/a *m/f*
go-getting* ['gəʊgetɪŋ] ADJ dispuesto, resuelto
goggle ['gɒgl] VI • **to ~ at** mirar con ojos desorbitados, mirar sin comprender
CPD ▸ **goggle box*** (*Brit*) (*TV*) caja *f* tonta*
goggle-eyed* ['gɒgl,aɪd] ADJ con ojos desorbitados
goggles ['gɒglz] NPL **1** (*Aut etc*) anteojos *mpl*; [*of diver*] gafas *fpl* de submarinismo
2* (= *glasses*) gafas *fpl*
go-go ['gəʊgəʊ] ADJ **1** [*dancer, dancing*] gogó
2 (*US*) [*market, stocks*] especulativo
3 (*US**) [*team etc*] dinámico
going ['gəʊɪŋ] N **1** (= *departure*) salida *f*, partida *f*; ▸ **coming**
2 (= *progress*) • **it was slow ~** se avanzaba a paso lento • **good ~!** ¡bien hecho! • **that was good ~** eso fue muy rápido • **the climb was hard ~** la subida fue muy dura • **the meeting was hard ~** en la reunión se complicaron bastante las cosas • **the book was heavy ~** la lectura del libro resultó pesada • **it's heavy ~ talking to her** es pesado hablar con ella
3 (= *state of surface etc*) estado *m* del camino; (*Horse racing etc*) estado *m* de la pista • **let's cross while the ~ is good** aprovechemos para cruzar • **we made money while the ~ was good** mientras las condiciones eran favorables ganábamos dinero
ADJ **1** (= *thriving*) [*business, concern*] establecido
2 (= *current*) [*price, rate*] corriente
3* (= *available*) • **the best one ~** el mejor que hay
going-over ['gəʊɪŋ'əʊvəʳ] N (PL: **goings-over**) **1** (= *check*) inspección *f* • **we gave the car a thorough going-over** revisamos el coche de arriba a abajo • **we gave the house a thorough going-over** (= *search*) registramos la casa de arriba abajo
2* (*fig*) (= *beating*) paliza *f* • **they gave him a going-over** le dieron una paliza
goings-on* ['gəʊɪŋz'ɒn] NPL tejemanejes *mpl*
goitre, goiter (*US*) ['gɔɪtəʳ] N bocio *m*
go-kart ['gəʊkɑːt] N kart *m*
go-karting ['gəʊ,kɑːtɪŋ] N karting *m*
Golan Heights ['gəʊlæn'haɪts] NPL • **the ~** los Altos del Golán
gold [gəʊld] N **1** (= *metal, commodity, currency*) oro *m* • **he paid for it in ~** lo pagó en oro • **to invest in ~** invertir en oro • **she only wears ~** solo lleva (joyas de) oro • **they stole 12 million pounds worth of ~** robaron oro por valor de 12 millones de libras • **24-carat ~** oro *m* de 24 quilates • **to be made of ~** ser de oro • **pure ~** (*lit*) oro *m* puro • **she's pure ~** (*fig*) es una joya, vale su peso en oro • **solid ~** oro *m* macizo; ▸ **glitter, good, heart, strike, weight**
2 (= *colour*) dorado *m* • **autumnal browns and ~s** los marrones y dorados del otoño
3 (= *gold medal*) medalla *f* de oro • **he won (the) ~ in Barcelona** ganó la medalla de oro en Barcelona • **to go for ~** intentar ganar la medalla de oro
ADJ **1** (= *made of gold*) [*jewellery, coins, tooth*]

de oro; ▸ **lamé**
2 (*= gold-coloured*) [*paint, lettering, frame*] dorado; [*fabric, dress, shirt*] color oro (*inv*), dorado • **the sign was written in ~ letters** el cartel estaba escrito con letras doradas • **she decided to paint it ~** decidió pintarlo color oro *or* dorado • **a green and ~ flag** una bandera verde y oro
(CPD) ▸ **gold bar** barra *f* de oro ▸ **gold braid** galón *m* de oro ▸ **gold card** tarjeta *f* oro ▸ **the Gold Coast** (*Hist*) la Costa de Oro ▸ **gold digger** (*lit*) buscador(a) *m/f* de oro; (*fig*) cazafortunas *mf inv* ▸ **gold disc** (*Mus*) disco *m* de oro ▸ **gold dust** oro *m* en polvo • **IDIOM:** • **biros are like ~ dust in this office** (*Brit*) (*fig*) en esta oficina no encuentras un bolígrafo ni por casualidad ▸ **gold fever** fiebre *f* del oro ▸ **gold filling** empaste *m* de oro ▸ **gold foil** papel *m* de oro ▸ **gold leaf** oro *m* en hojas, pan *m* de oro ▸ **gold market** mercado *m* del oro ▸ **gold medal** (*Sport*) medalla *f* de oro ▸ **gold medallist** medallero/a *m/f* de oro ▸ **gold mine** (*lit, fig*) mina *f* de oro ▸ **gold miner** minero *m* de oro ▸ **gold mining** minería *f* de oro ▸ **gold plate** (*= tableware*) vajilla *f* de oro; (*= covering*) baño *m* de oro • **it isn't solid ~ just ~ plate** no es oro puro sino un baño de oro • **doors covered with ~ plate** puertas revestidas de un baño de oro ▸ **gold record** disco *m* de oro ▸ **gold reserves** reservas *fpl* de oro ▸ **gold rush** fiebre *f* del oro ▸ **gold standard** patrón *m* oro • **to come off** *or* **leave the ~ standard** abandonar el patrón de oro

goldbrick* ['gəʊld'brɪk] (*US*) (N) **1** (*= worthless thing*) timo* *m*
2 (*Mil*) (*= shirker*) gandul *m*
(VI) escurrir el bulto

goldbricker* ['gəʊldbrɪkəʳ] (N) (*US*) = **goldbrick**

goldcrest ['gəʊldkrest] (N) reyezuelo *m* (sencillo)

golden ['gəʊldən] (ADJ) **1** (*in colour*) dorado • **a beautiful girl with bright ~ hair** una chica preciosa con un pelo dorado y brillante • **it gives your face an instant ~ tan** da un tono dorado instantáneo al rostro • **the wine is ~ in colour** el vino es de un color dorado • **fry the chicken pieces until ~** dorar los trozos de pollo
2 (*= made of gold*) de oro
3 (*fig*) (*= outstanding*) [*years, era*] dorado; [*future*] excelente • **this is a ~ opportunity for peace** esta es una oportunidad de oro para la paz, esta es una excelente oportunidad para la paz • **the ~ days of …** la época dorada de …
(CPD) ▸ **golden age** edad *f* de oro ▸ **the Golden Age** (*in Spanish Literature*) el Siglo de Oro ▸ **golden boy*** niño *m* bonito* ▸ **the golden calf** el becerro de oro ▸ **Golden Delicious (apple)** manzana *f* golden ▸ **golden eagle** águila *f* real ▸ **the Golden Fleece** el vellocino de oro ▸ **the Golden Gate** el Golden Gate ▸ **golden girl*** niña *f* bonita* ▸ **golden goal** (*Ftbl*) gol *m* de oro ▸ **golden goodbye** (*Comm, Ind*) *dinero que una compañía ofrece a un empleado como gratificación al jubilarlo o al despedirlo* ▸ **golden handcuffs** (*Comm, Ind*) *dinero que una compañía paga a un empleado para inducirle a continuar en la empresa* ▸ **golden handshake** (*Comm, Ind*) *dinero que una compañía ofrece a un empleado como gratificación al jubilarlo o al despedirlo* ▸ **golden hello** (*Comm, Ind*) *dinero que una compañía paga a alguien para inducirle a que trabaje para esa compañía* ▸ **golden jubilee** cincuentenario *m*, cincuenta aniversario *m* ▸ **the golden mean** el punto medio ▸ **golden oldie*** (*= song*) viejo éxito *m*; (*= footballer, singer etc*) vieja gloria *f* ▸ **golden opportunity** oportunidad *f* de oro • **a ~ opportunity to do sth** una oportunidad de oro para hacer algo • **a ~ opportunity for peace** una oportunidad de oro para la paz ▸ **golden parachute** (*Comm, Ind*) *cláusula del contrato de un alto ejecutivo por el que se le otorgan beneficios especiales en caso de que resulte cesante debido a la adquisición de la empresa por otra* ▸ **golden retriever** golden retriever *m* ▸ **golden rule** regla *f* de oro ▸ **golden share** participación *f* mayoritaria ▸ **golden syrup** (*Brit*) miel *f* de caña, melaza *f* de caña ▸ **the Golden Triangle** el Triángulo Dorado *or* de Oro ▸ **golden wedding (anniversary)** bodas *fpl* de oro

goldenrod ['gəʊldən,rɒd] (N) vara *f* de oro

goldfield ['gəʊldfiːld] (N) campo *m* aurífero

gold-filled ['gəʊld,fɪld] (ADJ) lleno de oro; (*Tech*) revestido de oro, enchapado en oro; [*tooth*] empastado de oro

goldfinch ['gəʊldfɪntʃ] (N) jilguero *m*

goldfish ['gəʊldfɪʃ] (N) (PL: **goldfish** *or* **goldfishes**) pez *m* de colores
(CPD) ▸ **goldfish bowl** pecera *f* • **IDIOM:** • **to live in a ~ bowl** vivir como en una vitrina

Goldilocks ['gəʊldɪlɒks] (N) Rubiales

gold-plated [,gəʊld'pleɪtɪd] (ADJ) chapado en oro; (*fig*) [*deal, contract*] de oro

gold-rimmed [,gəʊld'rɪmd] (ADJ) [*spectacles*] con montura de oro

goldsmith ['gəʊldsmɪθ] (N) orfebre *mf* • **~'s (shop)** taller *m* de orfebrería

golf [gɒlf] (N) golf *m*
(VI) jugar al golf
(CPD) ▸ **golf ball** pelota *f* de golf; (*Typ*) cabeza *f* de escritura ▸ **golf buggy** cochecito *m* de golf ▸ **golf club** (*= society*) club *m* de golf; (*= stick*) palo *m* de golf ▸ **golf course** campo *m or* (*LAm*) cancha *f* de golf ▸ **golf links** campo *m* de golf (*junto al mar*); ▹ **professional**

golfer ['gɒlfəʳ] (N) golfista *mf*

golfing ['gɒlfɪŋ] (N) golf *m*
(ADJ) [*equipment, trousers*] de golf; [*holiday*] golfístico

Golgotha ['gɒlgəθə] (N) Gólgota *m*

Goliath [gə'laɪəθ] (N) Goliat

golliwog ['gɒlɪwɒg] (N) (*Brit*) muñeco *m* negrito

golly¹* ['gɒlɪ] (N) (*Brit*) = **golliwog**

golly²†* ['gɒlɪ] (EXCL) (*Brit*) (*also* **by golly**) ¡caramba! • **and by ~, he's done it too!** ¡vaya si lo ha hecho!, ¡anda que lo ha hecho!

golosh [gə'lɒʃ] (N) chanclo *m*, galocha *f*

Gomorrah [gə'mɒrə] (N) Gomorra *f*

gonad ['gɒnæd] (N) gónada *f*

gondola ['gɒndələ] (N) **1** (*= boat*) góndola *f*
2 [*of hot-air balloon*] barquilla *f*
(CPD) ▸ **gondola car** (*US*) (*Rail*) vagón *m* descubierto, batea *f*

gondolier [,gɒndə'lɪəʳ] (N) gondolero *m*

gone [gɒn] (PP) *of* **go**

goner‡ ['gɒnəʳ] (N) • **he's a ~** está en las últimas, se nos va

gong [gɒŋ] (N) **1** gong *m*
2 (*Brit**) (*= medal*) medalla *f*, condecoración *f*; (*in civil service*) cinta *f*, cintajo* *m*

gonna* ['gɒnə] (*esp US*) = **going to**

gonorrhoea, gonorrhea (*US*) [,gɒnə'rɪə] (N) gonorrea *f*

goo* [guː] (N) **1** (*= substance*) • **why do you put all that goo on your face?** ¿por qué te pones tanto mejunje en la cara? • **the rice had turned into a heap of goo** el arroz quedó hecho un mazacote
2 (*fig*) (*= sentimentality*) lenguaje *m* sentimental, sentimentalismo *m*

goober* ['guːbəʳ] (N) (*US*) **1** (*= peanut*) cacahuete *m* (*Sp*), maní *m* (*LAm*), cacahuate *m* (*Mex*)
2 (*= idiot*) bobo/a* *m/f*

good [gʊd]

ADJECTIVE
ADVERB
NOUN
COMPOUNDS

ADJECTIVE
(COMPAR: **better**, SUPERL: **best**)

*When **good** is part of a set combination, eg **in a good temper, a good deal of, good heavens**, look up the noun.*

*The commonest translation of **good** is **bueno**, which must be shortened to **buen** before a masculine singular noun.*

1 (*= satisfactory*) **a** bueno • **a ~ book** un buen libro • **at the end of the day, it's a ~ investment** a fin de cuentas es una buena inversión

*Note that **bueno/buena** etc precede the noun in general comments where there is no attempt to compare or rank the person or thing involved:*

• **if he set his mind to it, he could be a very ~ painter** si se lo propusiera podría ser muy buen pintor • **she was a ~ wife and mother** era una buena esposa y madre • **she has a ~ figure** tiene buen tipo

***Bueno/buena** etc follow the noun when there is implied or explicit comparison:*

• **we could make a list of ~ teachers** podríamos hacer una lista de profesores buenos • **I'm not saying it's a ~ thing or a bad thing** no digo que sea una cosa buena, ni mala

*Use **ser** rather than **estar** with **bueno** when translating **to be good**, unless describing food:*

• **the idea is a ~ one** la idea es buena • **it's ~ to be aware of the views of intelligent people** es bueno conocer los puntos de vista de la gente inteligente • **the paella was very ~** la paella estaba muy buena

*Use **estar** with the adverb **bien** to give a general comment on a situation:*

• **you've written a book, which is ~** has escrito un libro, lo que está bien • **his hearing is ~** del oído está bien, el oído lo tiene bien
b • **she's ~ at maths** se le dan bien las matemáticas, es buena en matemáticas • **she's ~ at singing** canta bien • **she's ~ at putting people at their ease** tiene la capacidad de hacer que la gente se sienta relajada • **that's ~ enough for me** eso me basta • **it's just not ~ enough!** ¡esto no se puede consentir! • **40% of candidates are not ~ enough to pass** el 40% de los candidatos no dan el nivel *or* la talla para aprobar • **to feel ~** sentirse bien • **I started to feel ~ about myself again** empecé a recuperar mi autoestima *or* la moral • **I don't feel very ~ about that*** (*= I'm rather ashamed*) me da bastante vergüenza • **we've never had it so ~!*** ¡nunca nos ha ido tan bien!, ¡jamás lo hemos tenido tan fácil! • **how ~ is her eyesight?** ¿qué tal está de la vista? • **you're looking ~** ¡qué guapa estás! • **things are looking ~** las cosas van bien, la

cosa tiene buena pinta* • **you look ~ in that** eso te sienta *or* te va bien • **you can have too much of a ~ thing** lo mucho cansa (y lo poco agrada) • **it's too ~ to be true** no puede ser, es demasiado bueno para ser cierto • **he sounds too ~ to be true!** ¡algún defecto tiene que tener! • **she's ~ with cats** entiende bien a los gatos, sabe manejarse bien con los gatos; ▹ **good, manner, mood², time**

2 (*= of high quality*) • **always use ~ ingredients** utilice siempre ingredientes de calidad *or* los mejores ingredientes • **it's made of ~ leather** está hecho con cuero del bueno

3 (*= pleasant*) [*holiday, day*] bueno, agradable; [*weather, news*] bueno • **it was as ~ as a holiday** aquello fue como unas vacaciones • **have a ~ journey!** ¡buen viaje! • **how ~ it is to know that ...!** ¡cuánto me alegro de saber que ...! • **it's ~ to see you** me alegro de verte, gusto en verte (*LAm*) • **it's ~ to be here** da gusto estar aquí • **have a ~ trip!** ¡buen viaje!; ▹ **alive, life**

4 (*= beneficial, wholesome*) [*food*] bueno, sano; [*air*] puro, sano • **it's ~ for burns** es bueno para las quemaduras • **it's ~ for you** *or* **your health** te hace bien • **spirits are not ~ for me** los licores no me sientan bien • **he eats more than is ~ for him** come más de lo que le conviene • **all this excitement isn't ~ for me!** ¡a mí todas estas emociones no me vienen *or* sientan nada bien! • **it's ~ for the soul!** (*hum*) ¡ennoblece el espíritu!, ¡te enriquece (como persona)! • **if you know what's ~ for you you'll say yes** por la cuenta que te tiene dirás que sí • **some children know more than is ~ for them** algunos niños son demasiado listos *or* saben demasiado

5 (*= favourable*) [*moment, chance*] bueno • **it's a ~ chance to sort things out** es una buena oportunidad de *or* para arreglar las cosas • **I tried to find something ~ to say about him** traté de encontrar algo bueno que decir de él • **it would be a ~ thing** *or* **idea to ask him** no estaría mal *or* no sería mala idea preguntárselo • **this is as ~ a time as any to do it** es tan buen momento como cualquier otro para hacerlo

6 (*= useful*) • **the only ~ chair** la única silla que está bien, la única silla servible *or* sana • **to be ~ for (doing) sth** servir para (hacer) algo • **it'll be ~ for some years** durará todavía algunos años • **he's ~ for ten years yet** tiene todavía por delante diez años de vida • **John's ~ for a few hundred pounds*** John seguramente puede prestarnos unos cientos de libras • **I'm ~ for another mile** todavía puedo aguantar otra milla más • **the ticket is ~ for three months** el billete es válido *or* valedero para tres meses • **he's ~ for nothing** es un inútil, es completamente inútil

7 (*= sound, valid*) [*excuse*] bueno • **unless you have a ~ excuse** a menos que tengas una buena excusa • **for no ~ reason** sin motivo alguno • **he is a ~ risk** (*financially*) concederle crédito es un riesgo asumible, se le puede prestar dinero; ▹ **word**

8 (*= kind*) • **that's very ~ of you** es usted muy amable, ¡qué amable (de su parte)! • **he was so ~ as to come with me** tuvo la amabilidad de acompañarme • **please would you be so ~ as to help me down with my case?** ¿me hace el favor de bajarme la maleta?, ¿tendría la bondad de bajarme la maleta? (*more frm*) • **would you be so ~ as to sign here?** ¿me hace el favor de firmar aquí? • **he's a ~ sort** es buena persona *or* gente • **he was ~ to me** fue muy bueno *or* amable conmigo, se portó bien conmigo; ▹ **nature**

9 (*= well-behaved*) [*child*] bueno • **be ~!** (*morally*) ¡sé bueno!; (*in behaviour*) ¡pórtate bien!; (*at this moment*) ¡estáte formal! • IDIOM: • **to be as ~ as gold*** portarse como un ángel *or* santo

10 (*= upright, virtuous*) bueno • **he's a ~ man** es una buena persona, es un buen hombre • **I think I'm as ~ as him** yo me considero tan buena persona como él • **the twelve ~ men and true** los doce hombres justos • **yes, my ~ man** sí, mi querido amigo • **send us a photo of your ~ self** (*frm*) tenga a bien enviarnos una foto suya • **she's too ~ for him** ella es más de lo que él se merece; ▹ **lady**

11 (*= close*) bueno • **he's a ~ friend of mine** es un buen amigo mío • **my ~ friend Fernando** mi buen *or* querido amigo Fernando

12 (*= middle-class, respectable*) • **to live at a ~ address** vivir en una buena zona *or* en un buen barrio • **he's got no money but he's of ~ family** no tiene dinero pero es *or* viene de buena familia

13 (*= creditable*) • **he came in a ~ third** llegó en un meritorio tercer puesto

14 (*= considerable*) [*supply, number*] bueno • **we were kept waiting for a ~ hour/thirty minutes** nos tuvieron esperando una hora/media hora larga, nos tuvieron esperando por lo menos una hora/media hora • **a ~ three hours** tres horas largas • **a ~ 10km** 10kms largos • **a ~ £10** lo menos 10 libras • **a ~ many** *or* **few people** bastante gente

15 (*= thorough*) [*scolding*] bueno • **to have a ~ cry** llorar a lágrima viva, llorar a moco tendido* • **to have a ~ laugh** reírse mucho • **to take a ~ look (at sth)** mirar bien (algo) • **to have a ~ wash** lavarse bien

16 • **the ~ ship Domino** el (buque) Domino

17 (*in greetings*) • **~ morning** buenos días • **~ afternoon/evening** buenas tardes • **~ day†** (*= hello*) ¡buenos días!; (*= goodbye*) ¡hasta mañana! • **~ night** buenas noches • **with every ~ wish** • **with all ~ wishes** (*in letter*) saludos, un fuerte abrazo • **Robert sends (his) ~ wishes** Robert manda recuerdos

18 (*in exclamations*) • **good!** ¡muy bien! • **(that's) ~!** ¡qué bien!, ¡qué bueno! (*LAm*) • **very ~, sir** sí, señor • **~ for you!** ¡bien hecho!; (*= congratulations*) ¡enhorabuena! • **~ one!** (*= well done, well said*) ¡muy bien!, ¡sí señor!; ▹ **old**

19 (*in other set expressions*) **as good as** • **it's as ~ as new** está como nuevo • **I'll soon be as ~ as new** pronto estaré como nuevo • **the job is as ~ as done** el trabajo puede darse por acabado • **it's as ~ as lost** puede darse por perdido • **they're as ~ as beaten** pueden darse por vencidos • **as ~ as saying ...** tanto como decir ... • **she as ~ as told me so** poco menos que me lo dijo • **he as ~ as called me a liar** me llamó poco menos que mentiroso

to come good • **things will come ~ eventually*** todo se arreglará al final

good and ... • **~ and hot*** bien calentito* • **~ and strong*** bien fuerte • **I'll do it when I'm ~ and ready*** lo haré cuando a mí me parezca

to hold good valer (**for** para) • **the same advice holds ~ for us** el mismo consejo vale para nosotros

it's a good job • **(it's a) ~ job he came!*** ¡menos mal que ha venido!; ▹ **make, riddance, thing**

ADVERB

1 (*as intensifier*) bien • **a ~ strong stick** un palo bien fuerte • **a ~ long walk** un paseo bien largo, un buen paseo • IDIOM: • **to give as ~ as one gets** pagar con la misma moneda, devolver golpe por golpe

good and proper • **they were beaten ~ and proper*** les dieron una buena paliza* • **they were cheated ~ and proper*** les timaron bien timados*, les timaron con todas las de la ley*

2 (*esp US*)* (*= well*) bien • **you did ~** hiciste bien • **"how are you?" — "thanks, I'm ~"** —¿cómo estás? —muy bien, gracias

NOUN

1 (*= virtuousness*) el bien • **to do ~** hacer (el) bien • **~ and evil** el bien y el mal • **he is a power for ~** su influencia es muy buena *or* beneficiosa, hace mucho bien • **for ~ or ill** para bien o para mal • **there's some ~ in him** tiene algo bueno • **to be up to no ~*** estar tramando algo

2 (*= advantage, benefit*) bien *m* • **the common ~** el bien común • **if it's any ~ to you** si te sirve de algo • **a rest will do you some ~** un descanso te sentará bien • **the sea air does you ~** el aire del mar le hace *or* sienta a uno bien • **a (fat) lot of ~ that will do you!*** (*iro*) ¡menudo provecho te va a traer! • **much ~ may it do you!** ¡no creo que te sirva de mucho!, ¡para lo que te va a servir! • **it does my heart ~ to see him** verlo me alegra la existencia • **for your own ~** por tu propio bien • **for the ~ of the country** por el bien del país • **to be in ~ with sb** estar a bien con algn • **that's all to the ~!** ¡menos mal! • **what ~ will that do you?** ¿y eso de qué te va a servir? • **what's the ~ of worrying?** ¿de qué sirve *or* para qué preocuparse?

3 (*= people of virtue*) **the good** los buenos

4 (*in set expressions*) **any good** • **is he any ~?** [*worker, singer etc*] ¿qué tal lo hace?, ¿lo hace bien? • **is this any ~?** ¿sirve esto? • **is she any ~ at cooking?** ¿qué tal cocina?, ¿cocina bien?

for good (and all) (*= for ever*) para siempre • **he's gone for ~** se ha ido para siempre *or* para no volver

no good • **it's no ~** (*= no use*) no sirve • **it's no ~, I'll never get it finished in time** así no hay manera, nunca lo terminaré a tiempo • **it's no ~ saying that** de nada sirve *or* vale decir eso • **it's no ~ worrying** de nada sirve *or* vale preocuparse, no se saca nada preocupándose • **that's no ~** eso no vale *or* sirve • **I'm no ~ at maths** las matemáticas no se me dan nada bien • **that's no ~ to me** eso no me sirve para nada • **to come to no ~** acabar mal

COMPOUNDS

▸ **the Good Book** (*Rel*) la Biblia ▸ **good deeds** = good works ▸ **good faith** buena fe *f* • **in ~ faith** de buena fe ▸ **Good Friday** (*Rel*) Viernes *m* Santo ▸ **good guy** (*Cine*) bueno *m* ▸ **good looks** atractivo *msing* físico ▸ **good name** buen nombre *m* • **to protect sb's ~ name** proteger el buen nombre de algn • **he wanted to protect his friend's ~ name** quería proteger el buen nombre de su amigo ▸ **good works** buenas obras *fpl*

goodbye [ˈgʊdˈbaɪ] (EXCL) ¡adiós!, ¡hasta luego!
(N) despedida *f* • **to say ~ to** (*lit*) [*+ person*] despedirse de; (*fig*) [*+ thing*] despedirse de, dar por perdido • **you can say ~ to your wallet** ya puedes despedirte de tu cartera, ya no volverás a ver la cartera

good-for-nothing [ˈgʊdfəˌnʌθɪŋ] (ADJ) inútil
(N) inútil *mf*, gandul(a) *m/f*

good-hearted [ˌgʊdˈhɑːtɪd] (ADJ) de buen corazón

good-humoured, good-humored (US) [ˈgʊdˈhjuːməd] (ADJ) [*person*] amable, de buen humor; [*remark, joke*] jovial; [*discussion*] de tono amistoso

good-humouredly, good-humoredly (US) [ˌgʊdˈhjuːmədlɪ] (ADV) [*say*] de buen humor; [*tease*] amistosamente

goodies* ['gʊdɪ] NPL (= *food*) golosinas *fpl*; (= *little luxuries*) regalos *mpl* • **a little bag of ~** una bolsa de golosinas

good-looker* [ˌgʊd'lʊkəʳ] N (= *man*) tío *m* bueno*; (= *woman*) tía *f* buena*; (= *horse etc*) caballo *m etc* de buena estampa

good-looking ['gʊd'lʊkɪŋ] ADJ guapo, bien parecido

goodly ['gʊdlɪ] (*frm*) ADJ **1** (= *fine*) agradable, excelente; (= *handsome*) bien parecido
2 [*sum etc*] importante; [*number*] crecido

good-natured ['gʊd'neɪtʃəd] ADJ [*person*] amable, simpático; [*discussion*] de tono amistoso

good-naturedly [ˌgʊd'neɪtʃədlɪ] ADV [*complain, joke*] con cordialidad

goodness ['gʊdnɪs] N **1** (= *virtue*) bondad *f*
2 (= *kindness*) amabilidad *f* • **out of the ~ of his heart** de lo bondadoso que es
3 (= *good quality*) calidad *f*
4 (= *essence*) sustancia *f*, lo mejor
5* (*in phrases*) • **(my) ~!** • **~ gracious!** ¡Dios mío! • **thank ~!** ¡menos mal! • **for ~' sake!** ¡por Dios! • **I wish to ~ I'd never met him** ojalá nunca lo hubiera conocido

goodnight, good night [ˌgʊd'naɪt] EXCL ¡buenas noches! • **to say ~ to sb** dar las buenas noches a algn • **to kiss sb ~** dar un beso de buenas noches a algn
CPD ▸ **goodnight kiss** beso *m* de buenas noches

goods [gʊdz] NPL (= *possessions*) bienes *mpl*; (= *products*) productos *mpl*; (*Comm etc*) géneros *mpl*, mercancías *fpl*; (= *objects*) artículos *mpl* • **leather ~** géneros *mpl* de cuero • **canned ~** conservas *fpl* en lata • **consumer ~** bienes *mpl* de consumo • **~ and chattels** bienes *mpl* • IDIOM: • **to deliver the ~** cumplir con lo prometido
CPD ▸ **goods siding** apartadero *m* de mercancías ▸ **goods station** estación *f* de mercancías ▸ **goods train** tren *m* de mercancías ▸ **goods vehicle** vehículo *m* de transporte, camión *m* ▸ **goods wagon** vagón *m* de mercancías ▸ **goods yard** estación *f* de mercancías

good-tempered ['gʊd'tempəd] ADJ [*person*] amable, de buen humor; [*tone*] afable, amistoso; [*discussion*] sereno, sin pasión

good-time girl* [ˌgu:dtaɪm'gɜ:l] N chica *f* alegre

goodwill ['gʊd'wɪl] N **1** buena voluntad *f* • **as a gesture of ~** como muestra de buena voluntad
2 (*Comm*) clientela *f* y renombre *m* comercial
CPD ▸ **goodwill ambassador** embajador(a) *m/f* de buena voluntad ▸ **goodwill mission** misión *f* de buena voluntad

goody* ['gʊdɪ] ADJ (*US*) beatuco*, santurrón
EXCL (*also* **goody goody**) ¡qué bien!, ¡qué estupendo!*
N **1** (*Culin*) golosina *f*
2 (*Cine*) bueno/a *m/f* • **the goodies** los buenos
CPD ▸ **goody bag*** bolsa *f* de regalos

goody-goody* (*pej*) [ˌgʊdɪ'gʊdɪ] ADJ beatuco*, santurrón
N (PL: **goody-goodies**) santurrón/ona *m/f*

gooey* ['gu:ɪ] ADJ (COMPAR: **gooier**, SUPERL: **gooiest**) pegajoso, viscoso; (= *sweet*) empalagoso

goof* [gu:f] N bobo/a *m/f*
VI **1** (= *err*) tirarse una plancha*
2 (*US*) (*also* **goof off**) gandulear
▸ **goof around*** VI + ADV (*US*) hacer el tonto

goofball* ['gu:fbɔ:l] N (*esp US*) memo/a* *m/f*

goofy* ['gu:fɪ] ADJ (COMPAR: **goofier**, SUPERL: **goofiest**) **1** (*esp US*) (= *silly*) bobo
2 [*teeth*] salido, de conejo*

Google® ['gu:gl] N Google® *m*

google® ['gu:gl] VI buscar *or* hacer búsquedas en Google®, buscar *or* hacer búsquedas en Internet, googlear
VT (= *do search on*) [+ *person*] buscar información *or* hacer una búsqueda en Google® sobre, buscar informacion en Internet sobre, googlear

Googleable ['gu:gləbl] ADJ que se puede buscar en Google®

googler ['gu:gləʳ] N usuario/a *m/f* de Google®

gook‡ [gu:k] N (*US*) (*pej*) asiático/a *m/f*

goolies‡ ['gu:lɪz] N pelotas‡ *fpl*, cataplines *mpl* (*Sp*‡)

goon [gu:n] N **1** (= *fool*) imbécil *mf*
2 (*US*) (= *thug*) gorila *m*, matón/ona *m/f*; (*Hist*) *gorila contratado para sembrar el terror entre los obreros*

goose [gu:s] (PL: **geese**) N (*domestic*) ganso/a *m/f*, oca *f*; (*wild*) ánsar *m* • IDIOMS: • **to cook sb's ~** hacer la santísima a algn • **to kill the ~ that lays the golden eggs** matar la gallina de los huevos de oro
VT* (= *prod*) meter mano a
CPD ▸ **goose bumps** = gooseflesh ▸ **goose pimples** = gooseflesh

gooseberry ['gʊzbərɪ] N **1** (*Bot*) grosella *f* espinosa
2 (*Brit*) • IDIOM: • **to play ~** hacer de carabina
CPD ▸ **gooseberry bush** grosellero *m* espinoso

gooseflesh ['gu:sfleʃ] N carne *f* de gallina

goose-step ['gu:sstep] N paso *m* de ganso, paso *m* de la oca
VI marchar a paso de ganso *or* de la oca

GOP N ABBR (*US*) (*Pol*) (= **Grand Old Party**) Partido *m* Republicano

gopher ['gəʊfəʳ] N **1** (*Zool*) ardillón *m*
2 (*Comput*) gopher *m*
3 = gofer

gorblimey‡ [ˌgɔ:'blaɪmɪ] EXCL (*Brit*) ¡puñetas!‡

Gordian ['gɔ:dɪən] ADJ • IDIOM: • **to cut the ~ knot** cortar el nudo gordiano

gore[1] [gɔ:ʳ] N (= *blood*) sangre *f* derramada

gore[2] [gɔ:ʳ] VT (= *injure*) cornear

gorge [gɔ:dʒ] N **1** (*Geog*) cañón *m*, barranco *m*
2 (*Anat*) garganta *f* • **my ~ rises at it** me da asco
VT • **to ~ o.s.** atracarse (**with, on** de)
VI atracarse (**on** de)

gorgeous ['gɔ:dʒəs] ADJ **1** (= *lovely*) [*object, scenery, colour, music*] precioso; [*food, wine*] delicioso, riquísimo; [*weather*] espléndido, magnífico • **she wears the most ~ clothes** lleva una ropa preciosa • **~ silks and jewels** sedas y joyas preciosas *or* espléndidas • **oh! it's absolutely ~!** ¡oh! ¡es una preciosidad! • **the garden looks absolutely ~** el jardín está precioso • **it smells ~** huele delicioso • **this tastes ~** está riquísimo • **the weather was ~** hacía un tiempo espléndido *or* magnífico • **what a ~ day!** ¡hace un día precioso *or* espléndido!
2* (= *beautiful*) [*woman*] guapísimo, precioso; [*man*] guapísimo; [*child, baby*] riquísimo*, monísimo*; [*eyes, hair*] precioso • **he/she's ~!** ¡es guapísimo/guapísima! • **hello, ~!*** (*to woman*) ¡hola, preciosa!*; (*to man*) ¡hola, guapo!* • **what a ~ hunk!**‡ ¡qué tío más bueno!‡; ▹ **drop-dead**

gorgeously ['gɔ:dʒəslɪ] ADV [*dressed*] magníficamente, divinamente; [*decorated*] espléndidamente, magníficamente • **it is a ~ decadent work** es una obra fastuosamente decadente

gorgeousness ['gɔ:dʒəsnɪs] N (= *loveliness*) preciosidad *f*; (= *splendour*) magnificencia *f*; (= *beauty*) belleza *f*

gorgon ['gɔ:gən] N **1** • **Gorgon** (*Myth*) Gorgona *f*
2 (*fig*) (= *woman*) pécora *f*

Gorgonzola [ˌgɔ:gən'zəʊlə] N gorgonzola *m*

gorilla [gə'rɪlə] N **1** (*Zool*) gorila *m*
2* (= *thug*) gorila *m*

gormandize ['gɔ:məndaɪz] VI (*frm*) glotonear

gormless* ['gɔ:mlɪs] ADJ (*Brit*) corto (de entendimiento)*

gorse [gɔ:s] N aulaga *f*, tojo *m*
CPD ▸ **gorse bush** mata *f* de tojo

gory ['gɔ:rɪ] ADJ (COMPAR: **gorier**, SUPERL: **goriest**) [*battle, death*] sangriento • **he told me all the ~ details** (*hum*) me contó todo con pelos y señales

gosh* [gɒʃ] EXCL ¡cielos! • **~ darn!** (*US*) ¡caramba!

goshawk ['gɒshɔ:k] N azor *m*

gosling ['gɒzlɪŋ] N ansarino *m*

go-slow ['gəʊ'sləʊ] N (*Brit*) (*Ind*) huelga *f* de brazos caídos
VI hacer huelga de celo; (*strictly*) trabajar con arreglo a las bases

gospel ['gɒspəl] N (*Rel*) evangelio *m* • **the Gospel according to St John** el Evangelio según San Juan • IDIOM: • **to take sth as ~*** aceptar algo como si estuviera escrito en el evangelio
CPD ▸ **gospel music** música *f* espiritual negra ▸ **gospel song** canción *f* espiritual negra ▸ **gospel truth** • **as though it were ~ truth** como si estuviera escrito en el evangelio

goss* [gɒs] N (*Brit*) (= *gossip*) cotilleo* *m* • **have you heard the latest ~?** ¿has oído el último cotilleo?

gossamer ['gɒsəməʳ] N (= *web*) telaraña *f*; (= *fabric*) gasa *f* • **~-thin** muy delgado

gossip ['gɒsɪp] N **1** (= *scandal, malicious stories*) cotilleo *m*, chismorreo *m*
2 (= *chatter*) charla *f* • **we had a good old ~** charlamos un buen rato
3 (= *person*) cotilla *mf*, chismoso/a *m/f*
VI **1** (= *scandalmonger*) cotillear, chismorrear
2 (= *chatter*) charlar
CPD ▸ **gossip column** ecos *mpl* de sociedad ▸ **gossip columnist, gossip writer** cronista *mf* de sociedad

gossiping ['gɒsɪpɪŋ] ADJ cotilla, chismoso
N cotilleo *m*, chismorreo *m*

gossipmonger ['gɒsɪpˌmʌŋgəʳ] N cotilla *mf*

gossipmongering ['gɒsɪpˌmʌŋgərɪŋ] N cotilleo *m*

gossipy ['gɒsɪpɪ] ADJ de cotilleo, chismoso; [*style*] familiar, anecdótico

got [gɒt] PT, PP *of* **get**

gotcha* ['gɒtʃə] EXCL **1** (= *I see*) entiendo
2 (*when catching sb*) ¡te pillé!

Goth [gɒθ] N (*Hist*) godo/a *m/f*

Gothic ['gɒθɪk] ADJ [*race*] godo; (*Archit, Typ*) gótico; [*novel etc*] gótico
N (*Archit, Ling etc*) gótico *m*

gotta* ['gɒtə] (*esp US*) = **got to**

gotten ['gɒtn] (*US*) PP *of* **get**

gouache [gʊ'ɑ:ʃ] N guache *m*, gouache *m*

gouge [gaʊdʒ] N gubia *f*
VT [+ *hole etc*] excavar
▸ **gouge out** VT + ADV [+ *hole etc*] excavar • **to ~ sb's eyes out** sacar los ojos a algn

goulash ['gu:læʃ] N *especie de guisado húngaro*

gourd [gʊəd] N calabaza *f*

gourmand ['gʊəmənd] N glotón/ona *m/f*

gourmet ['gʊəmeɪ] N gastrónomo/a *m/f*
ADJ [*food, dinner*] de gastronomía • **~ cooking** la gastronomía

gout [gaʊt] N (*Med*) gota *f*

gouty ['gaʊtɪ] ADJ gotoso

gov‡ [gʌv] N ABBR (*Brit*) (= **governor**) jefe *m*,

patrón *m* • **yes gov!** ¡sí, jefe!
Gov. ABBR = **Governor**
govern ['gʌvən] VT **1** (= *rule*) [+ *country*] gobernar
2 (= *control*) [+ *city, business*] dirigir; [+ *choice, decision*] guiar; [+ *emotions*] dominar
3 (*Ling*) regir
VI (*Pol*) gobernar
governance ['gʌvənəns] N (*frm*) forma *f* de gobierno
governess ['gʌvənɪs] N institutriz *f*, gobernanta *f*
governing ['gʌvənɪŋ] ADJ (*Pol*) [*party*] gobernante, en el gobierno
CPD ▸ **governing board** (*Brit*) (*Scol*) consejo *m* directivo de escuela ▸ **governing body** consejo *m* de administración ▸ **governing principle** principio *m* rector
government ['gʌvnmənt] N **1** (*Pol*) gobierno *m* • **the Labour Government** el gobierno *or* la administración laborista; ▹ **local**
2 (*Gram etc*) régimen *m*
CPD [*intervention, support, loan*] estatal, del estado; [*responsibility, decision*] gubernamental, del gobierno
▸ **government body** ente *m* gubernamental *or* oficial ▸ **government bonds** bonos *mpl* del Estado ▸ **government department** ministerio *m*, departamento *m* gubernamental, secretaría *f* (*Mex*) ▸ **government expenditure** = **government spending** ▸ **government grant** subvención *f* estatal ▸ **government health warning** ≈ advertencia *f* del Ministerio de Sanidad ▸ **Government House** (*Brit*) palacio *m* del gobernador/de la gobernadora ▸ **government housing** (*US*) vivienda *f* social ▸ **government issue** propiedad *f* del Estado ▸ **government policy** política *f* gubernamental *or* del gobierno ▸ **government securities** bonos *mpl* del Estado ▸ **government spending** el gasto público ▸ **government stock** reservas *fpl* del Estado ▸ **government subsidy** subvención *f* estatal, subvención *f* del gobierno
governmental [ˌgʌvən'mentl] ADJ gubernamental, gubernativo
government-owned [ˌgʌvənmənt'əʊnd] ADJ [*company, industry*] del Estado, estatal; [*land*] del Estado
governor ['gʌvənəʳ] N **1** [*of colony, state etc*] gobernador(a) *m/f*
2 (*esp Brit*) [*of prison*] director(a) *m/f*
3 (*Brit*) [*of school*] miembro *mf* del consejo
4 (*Brit‡*) (= *boss*) jefe *m*, patrón *m*; (= *father*) viejo* *m* • **thanks, ~!** ¡gracias, jefe!
5 (*Mech*) regulador *m*
CPD ▸ **governor general** (*Brit*) gobernador(a) *m/f* general
governorship ['gʌvənəʃɪp] N gobierno *m*, cargo *m* de gobernador(a)
Govt., govt. ABBR (= **government**) gob.^no^
gown [gaʊn] N (= *dress*) vestido *m* largo; (*Jur, Univ*) toga *f*
GP N ABBR (= **general practitioner**) médico/a *m/f* de cabecera
GPA N ABBR (*US*) = **grade-point average**
GPMU N ABBR (*Brit*) (= **Graphical, Paper and Media Union**) *sindicato de trabajadores del sector editorial*
GPO N ABBR **1** (*Brit*) (*formerly*) = **General Post Office**
2 (*US*) = **Government Printing Office**
GPS N ABBR (= **global positioning system**) GPS *m*
gr. ABBR **1** (= **gross**) (= *12 dozen*) gruesa *f*
2 (*Comm*) (= **gross**) bto
grab [græb] N **1** (= *snatch*) • **to make a ~ at** *or* **for sth** intentar agarrar algo • **it's all up for ~s*** está a disposición de cualquiera
2 (*esp Brit*) (*Tech*) cuchara *f*
VT **1** (= *seize*) coger, agarrar (*LAm*); (*greedily*) echar mano a • **to ~ sth from sb** arrebatarle algo a algn • **to ~ hold of sth/sb** agarrar algo/a algn
2 (*fig*) [+ *chance etc*] aprovechar • **I'll just ~ a quick shower** me voy a dar una ducha rápida • **we can ~ a sandwich on the way** comeremos un bocadillo por el camino • **I managed to ~ him before he left** conseguí pillarle antes de que se marchara
3* (= *attract, appeal to*) • **how does that ~ you?** ¿qué te parece? • **that really ~bed me** aquello me entusiasmó de verdad • **it doesn't ~ me** no me va
VI • **to ~ at** (= *snatch*) tratar de coger *or* (*LAm*) agarrar; (*in falling*) tratar de asir
CPD ▸ **grab bag*** (*US*) (= *lucky dip*) pesca *f* milagrosa ▸ **grab bar, grab rail** barra *f* de apoyo
grace [greɪs] N **1** (= *elegance*) [*of form, movement etc*] gracia *f*, elegancia *f*; [*of style*] elegancia *f*, amenidad *f*
2 (*Rel*) gracia *f*, gracia *f* divina • **by the ~ of God** por la gracia de Dios • **there but for the ~ of God go I** le podría ocurrir a cualquiera • **to fall from ~** (*Rel*) perder la gracia divina; (*fig*) caer en desgracia
3 (= *graciousness*) cortesía *f*, gracia *f* • **he had the ~ to apologize** tuvo la cortesía de pedir perdón • **with (a) good ~** de buen talante • **with (a) bad ~** a regañadientes; ▹ **saving**
4 • **to get into sb's good ~s** congraciarse con algn
5 (= *respite*) demora *f* • **days of ~** (*Brit*) (*Jur*) días *mpl* de gracia • **three days' ~** un plazo de tres días
6 (= *prayer*) bendición *f* de la mesa • **to say ~** bendecir la mesa
7 (*in titles*) **a** (= *duke*) • **His Grace the Duke** su Excelencia el duque • **yes, Your Grace** sí, Excelencia
b (*Rel*) • **His Grace Archbishop Roberts** su Ilustrísima, Arzobispo Roberts • **yes, your Grace** sí, Ilustrísima
VT **1** (= *adorn*) adornar, embellecer
2 (= *honour*) [+ *occasion, event*] honrar • **he ~d the meeting with his presence** honró a los asistentes con su presencia; ▹ **presence**
CPD ▸ **grace note** (*Mus*) apoyadura *f* ▸ **grace period** (*Jur, Econ*) período *m* de gracia
graceful ['greɪsfʊl] ADJ **1** (= *elegant*) [*person, animal, building*] elegante
2 (= *flowing*) [*movement*] elegante, airoso; [*lines*] grácil
3 (= *dignified*) digno • **he was never a ~ loser** nunca supo perder con dignidad
gracefully ['greɪsfəlɪ] ADV **1** (= *elegantly*) [*move*] elegantemente
2 (= *in a dignified manner*) con dignidad • **to grow old ~** envejecer con dignidad • **he never could lose ~** nunca supo perder con dignidad • **she apologized, none too ~** pidió perdón a regañadientes
gracefulness ['greɪsfʊlnɪs] N [*of movement*] gracia *f*, elegancia *f*; [*of building, handwriting, bow, manner*] elegancia *f*
graceless ['greɪslɪs] ADJ **1** (= *inelegant, clumsy*) desgarbado, torpe
2 (= *impolite*) descortés, grosero
gracelessly ['greɪsləslɪ] ADV **1** (= *clumsily*) torpemente
2 (= *impolitely*) con descortesía
gracious ['greɪʃəs] ADJ **1** (= *refined, courteous*) [*person, gesture, smile, letter*] gentil, cortés; [*era*] refinado • **by (the) ~ consent of** (*frm*) por la gracia de • **to be ~ enough to do sth** tener la cortesía de hacer algo • **he was ~ in defeat/victory** era correcto a la hora de la derrota/del triunfo • **he has always been a ~ loser** siempre ha sabido perder con dignidad • **by ~ permission of Her Majesty the Queen** (*frm*) por la gracia de Su Majestad la Reina • **to be ~ to sb** ser gentil *or* cortés con algn
2 (= *merciful*) [*God*] misericordioso
3 (= *elegant, comfortable*) [*place, building*] elegante, refinado • **she loved fine clothes and ~ living** le encantaba la ropa elegante y la vida refinada
EXCL • **~!** • **good ~ (me)!** ¡Santo cielo!, ¡Dios mío! • **"you know Jack, don't you?" — "good ~, yes!"** —conoces a Jack, ¿no? —¡por supuesto que sí! • **good ~, what does that matter!** ¡por amor de Dios! ¿qué importancia tiene eso?; ▹ **goodness**
graciously ['greɪʃəslɪ] ADV [*wave, smile*] gentilmente, cortésmente; [*accept*] gentilmente; [*live*] con refinamiento • **she has ~ consented to be my wife** (*frm*) ha tenido la gentileza de aceptar mi propuesta de matrimonio • **His Royal Highness has ~ consented to our proposal** (*frm*) Su Alteza se ha dignado aceptar nuestra propuesta
graciousness ['greɪʃəsnɪs] N **1** (= *refinement, courtesy*) [*of person*] gentileza *f*, cortesía *f*; [*of gesture*] gentileza *f*, gracia *f* • **~ in defeat/victory** la corrección a la hora de la derrota/del triunfo
2 [*of God*] misericordia *f*
3 (= *elegance, comfort*) [*of house, room*] elegancia *f*, refinamiento *m*
grad* [græd] (*US*) N = **graduate**
gradate [grə'deɪt] VT degradar
VI degradarse
gradation [grə'deɪʃən] N gradación *f*
grade [greɪd] N **1** (= *level, standard*) (*on scale*) clase *f*, categoría *f*; (*in job*) grado *m*, categoría *f* • **to be promoted to a higher ~** ser ascendido a un grado *or* una categoría superior • IDIOM: • **to make the ~** llegar, alcanzar el nivel
2 (*Mil*) (= *rank*) graduación *f*, grado *m*
3 (= *quality*) clase *f*, calidad *f* • **high-/low-grade material** material *m* de alta/baja calidad
4 (*Scol*) (= *mark*) nota *f*
5 (*US*) (= *school class*) • **he's in fifth ~** está en quinto (curso); ▹ HIGH SCHOOL
6 (*US*) (= *gradient*) pendiente *f*, cuesta *f*
7 (*US*) (= *ground level*) • **at ~** al nivel del suelo
VT **1** [+ *goods, eggs*] clasificar, graduar; [+ *colours*] degradar
2 (*Scol*) (= *mark*) calificar
CPD ▸ **grade book** (*US*) libreta *f* de calificaciones ▸ **grade crossing** (*US*) (*Rail*) paso *m* a nivel ▸ **grade point average** (*US*) nota *f* promedio ▸ **grade school** (*US*) escuela *f* primaria ▸ **grade sheet** (*US*) hoja *f* de calificaciones
▸ **grade down** VT + ADV bajar de categoría
▸ **grade up** VT + ADV subir de categoría

GRADE
En Estados Unidos y Canadá, los cursos escolares se denominan **grades**, desde el primer año de primaria **first grade** hasta el último curso de la enseñanza secundaria **12th grade**. A los alumnos de los últimos cursos se les suele conocer por un nombre distinto según el curso en el que estén: **freshmen** si están en el **9th grade**, **sophomores** si están en el **10th grade**, **juniors** en el **11th grade** y **seniors** en el **12th grade**.
▹ HIGH SCHOOL

graded ['greɪdɪd] ADJ graduado
grader ['greɪdəʳ] N (*US*) (*Scol*)

examinador(a) *m/f*

-grader ['greɪdəʳ] SUFFIX (*US*) ▸ **first-grader, second-grader, third-grader** *etc*

gradient ['greɪdɪənt] N (*esp Brit*) pendiente *f*, cuesta *f* • **a ~ of one in seven** una pendiente del uno por siete

grading ['greɪdɪŋ] N (*gen*) graduación *f*; (*by size*) gradación *f*; (*Scol etc*) calificación *f*

gradual ['grædjʊəl] ADJ **1** (= *slow*) [*change, improvement, decline*] gradual, paulatino
2 (= *not steep*) [*slope, incline*] suave

gradualism ['grædjʊəlɪzəm] N gradualismo *m*

gradually ['grædjʊəlɪ] ADV **1** (= *slowly*) gradualmente, paulatinamente • **the situation was ~ improving** la situación iba mejorando gradualmente *or* paulatinamente
2 (= *not steeply*) suavemente • **the ground rises ~ to the north** el terreno se va elevando suavemente hacia el norte

graduate N ['grædjʊɪt] **1** (*Univ*) licenciado/a *m/f*, graduado/a *m/f*, egresado/a *m/f* (*LAm*)
2 (*US*) (*Scol*) bachiller *mf*
VT ['grædjʊeɪt] **1** [+ *thermometer etc*] graduar
2 (*US*) (*Scol, Univ*) otorgar el título a
VI ['grædjʊeɪt] **1** (*Univ*) graduarse *or* licenciarse (**from** en), recibirse (*LAm*) (**as** de)
2 (*US*) (*Scol*) acabar el bachiller
3 (= *progress*) • **to ~ from sth to sth** pasar de algo a algo
CPD ['grædjʊɪt] ▸ **graduate course** curso *m* para graduados ▸ **graduate school** (*US*) departamento *m* de graduados ▸ **graduate student** (*US*) estudiante *mf* de posgrado; ▷ COLLEGE

graduated ['grædjʊeɪtɪd] ADJ [*tube, flask, tax etc*] graduado • **in ~ stages** en pasos escalonados
CPD ▸ **graduated pension** (*Brit*) pensión *f* escalonada

graduation [,grædjʊ'eɪʃən] N (*Univ, Scol*) graduación *f*
CPD ▸ **graduation ceremony** ceremonia *f* de graduación, graduación *f* ▸ **graduation day** día *m* de la graduación

graffiti [grə'fiːtɪ] NPL graffiti *msing or mpl*, pintadas *fpl*
CPD ▸ **graffiti artist** artista *mf* de graffiti

graffito [græ'fiːtəʊ] NSING *of* **graffiti**

graft¹ [grɑːft] (*Bot, Med*) N injerto *m*
VT injertar (**in, into, on to en**)

graft² [grɑːft] N **1** (*US*) (= *corruption*) soborno *m*, coima *f* (*And, S. Cone*), mordida *f* (*CAm, Mex*)
2 (*Brit**) • **hard ~** trabajo *m* muy duro
VI **1** (*Brit**) (= *work*) currar*
2 (= *swindle*) trampear

grafter ['grɑːftəʳ] N **1** (= *swindler etc*) timador(a) *m/f*, estafador(a) *m/f*
2 (*Brit**) (= *hard worker*) persona *f* que trabaja mucho

graham flour ['greɪəm,flaʊəʳ] N (*US*) harina *f* de trigo sin cerner

Grail [greɪl] N • **the (Holy) ~** el (Santo) Grial

grain [greɪn] N **1** (= *single particle of wheat, sand etc*) grano *m*
2 (*no pl*) (= *cereals*) cereales *mpl*; (*US*) (= *corn*) trigo *m*
3 (*fig*) [*of sense, truth*] pizca *f* • **there's not a ~ of truth in it** en eso no hay ni pizca de verdad • IDIOM: • **with a ~ of salt** con reservas
4 [*of wood*] fibra *f*, hebra *f*; [*of stone*] veta *f*, vena *f*; [*of leather*] flor *f*; [*of cloth*] granilla *f*; (*Phot*) grano *m* • **against the ~** a contrapelo • **to saw with the ~** aserrar a hebra • IDIOM: • **it goes against the ~** no me pasa, no me entra
5 (*Pharm*) grano *m*

grainy ['greɪnɪ] ADJ (COMPAR: **grainier**, SUPERL: **grainiest**) (*Phot*) granulado, con grano; [*substance*] granulado

gram [græm] N gramo *m*

grammar ['græməʳ] N **1** gramática *f* • **that's bad ~** eso es gramaticalmente incorrecto
2 (*also* **grammar book**) libro *m* de gramática
CPD ▸ **grammar school** (*Brit*) instituto *m* de segunda enseñanza (*al que se accede a través de pruebas selectivas*)

> **GRAMMAR SCHOOL**
> En el Reino Unido, una **grammar school** es un centro estatal de educación secundaria selectiva que proporciona formación especialmente dirigida a los alumnos que vayan a continuar hasta una formación universitaria. Normalmente no son centros mixtos y para entrar en ellos se exige un examen escrito. Debido a la introducción en los años sesenta y setenta de las **comprehensive schools** para las que no hace falta una prueba de acceso, hoy día quedan pocas **grammar schools**, aunque sí que continúa el debate sobre si la calidad de la educación en estos centros es mejor o si solo sirven para favorecer el elitismo en la enseñanza.
> ▷ COMPREHENSIVE SCHOOLS

grammarian [grə'mɛərɪən] N gramático/a *m/f*

grammatical [grə'mætɪkəl] ADJ **1** [*rule, structure, error*] gramatical
2 (= *correct*) • **in ~ English** en inglés correcto • **that's not ~** eso es gramaticalmente incorrecto

grammaticality [grə,mætɪ'kælətɪ] N gramaticalidad *f*

grammatically [grə'mætɪkəlɪ] ADV [*write*] bien, correctamente • **~ correct** correcto gramaticalmente • **it's ~ correct to say ...** desde el punto de vista gramático, es correcto decir ...

grammaticalness [grə'mætɪkəlnɪs] N gramaticalidad *f*

gramme [græm] N (*Brit*) gramo *m*

Grammy ['græmɪ] N (PL: **Grammys** *or* **Grammies**) (*US*) ≈ Premio *m* Grammy

gramophone† ['græməfəʊn] (*Brit*) N gramófono *m*
CPD ▸ **gramophone needle** aguja *f* de gramófono ▸ **gramophone record** disco *m* de gramófono

Grampian ['græmpɪən] N • **the ~ Mountains** • **the ~s** los Montes Grampianos

gramps* [græmps] N (*US*) abuelo *m*, yayo* *m*

grampus ['græmpəs] N (PL: **grampuses**) orca *f*

gran* [græn] N (*Brit*) abuelita *f*

Granada [grə'nɑːdə] N Granada *f*

granary ['grænərɪ] N granero *m*
CPD ▸ **granary bread** (*Brit*) pan *m* de cereales ▸ **granary loaf** (*Brit*) pan *m* de cereales

grand [grænd] (COMPAR: **grander**, SUPERL: **grandest**) ADJ **1** (= *impressive*) [*building, architecture*] imponente, grandioso; [*clothes*] elegante; [*person*] distinguido • **the job isn't as ~ as it sounds** el trabajo no es de tanta categoría como parece • **I went to a rather ~ dinner** fui a una cena bastante lujosa *or* solemne • **to make a ~ entrance** hacer una entrada solemne • **~ finale** broche *m* de oro • **for the ~ finale ...** como broche de oro ... • **last night diplomats were preparing for the summit's ~ finale** anoche los diplomáticos se preparaban para la apoteosis de la conferencia cumbre • **a ~ gesture** (*magnanimous*) un gesto magnánimo; (*ostentatious*) un gesto grandilocuente • **in the ~ manner** por todo lo alto • **it was a very ~ occasion** fue una ocasión muy espléndida • **the ~ old man of English politics** el patriarca de la política inglesa • **~ opening** apertura *f* solemne • **on a ~ scale** a gran escala • **to do sth in ~ style** hacer algo a lo grande *or* por todo lo alto
2 (= *ambitious*) [*scheme, plan, design, strategy*] ambicioso
3†* (= *great*) [*adventure, experience*] maravilloso, fabuloso; [*weather, day, person*] estupendo • **what ~ weather we've been having!** ¡qué tiempo más estupendo nos ha estado haciendo!, ¡qué tiempo tan estupendo hemos tenido! • **we've had some ~ times together, haven't we?** nos lo hemos pasado estupendamente juntos, ¿verdad? • **that's ~!** ¡fabuloso!
4 (*in hotel names*) gran
N **1‡** (= *thousand*) • **ten ~** (*Brit*) diez mil libras; (*US*) diez mil dólares • **we still need another couple of ~** aún necesitamos otras dos mil
2 (*also* **grand piano**) piano *m* de cola; ▷ **baby**
CPD ▸ **the Grand Canyon** (*US*) el Gran Cañón del Colorado ▸ **grand duchess** gran duquesa *f* ▸ **grand duchy** gran ducado *m* ▸ **grand duke** gran duque *m* ▸ **grand jury** (*esp US*) (*Jur*) jurado *m* de acusación (*que decide si hay suficiente causa para llevar a algn a juicio*) ▸ **grand larceny** (*US*) (*Jur*) hurto *m* de mayor cuantía ▸ **grand mal** (*Med*) grand mal *m* ▸ **grand master** (*Chess*) gran maestro *m* (de ajedrez) ▸ **the Grand National** (*Brit*) (*Horse racing*) el Grand National ▸ **the Grand Old Party** (*US*) *mote que tiene el partido republicano de Estados Unidos desde 1880* ▸ **grand opera** gran ópera *f* ▸ **grand piano** piano *m* de cola ▸ **Grand Prix** Grand Prix *m*, Gran Premio *m* ▸ **grand slam** (*Sport*) gran slam *m* • **to win the ~ slam** ganar el gran slam ▸ **grand total** total *m* • **a ~ total of £50** un total de 50 libras ▸ **grand tour** (*hum*) (= *trip*) recorrido *m* de rigor (*hum*) • **we'll give you a ~ tour of the house** te haremos el recorrido de rigor por la casa ▸ **the Grand Tour** (*Hist*) la gran gira europea ▸ **grand vizier** (*Hist*) gran visir *m*

> **GRAND JURY**
> En el sistema legal estadounidense, un **grand jury** es un jurado de consulta que decide si debe acusarse a una persona de un delito y llevarla a juicio. Este jurado está compuesto por un número de miembros que oscila entre doce y veintitrés, y normalmente llevan a cabo sus reuniones en secreto. El **grand jury** tiene autoridad para citar a testigos a prestar declaración.
> Además del **grand jury**, existe en la legislación americana otro jurado llamado **trial jury** (jurado de juicio) o **petit jury**, compuesto de doce miembros, cuya función es la de determinar la inocencia o culpabilidad del acusado ante el tribunal.

grandad, granddad* ['grændæd] N abuelo *m* • **yes, grand(d)ad** sí, abuelo

grandaddy, granddaddy* ['grændædɪ] N (*US*) abuelito *m*

grandchild ['grænt∫aɪld] N (PL: **grandchildren**) nieto/a *m/f*

granddaughter ['græn,dɔːtəʳ] N nieta *f*

grandee [,græn'diː] N grande *m* (*de España*)

grandeur ['grændjəʳ] N [*of occasion, scenery, house etc*] lo imponente; [*of style*] lo elevado

grandfather ['grænd,fɑːðəʳ] N abuelo *m*

CPD ▸ **grandfather clock** reloj *m* de pie, reloj *m* de caja

grandiloquence [græn'dɪləkwəns] N altisonancia *f*, grandilocuencia *f*

grandiloquent [græn'dɪləkwənt] ADJ altisonante, grandilocuente

grandiloquently [græn'dɪləkwəntlɪ] ADV con grandilocuencia, con altisonancia

grandiose ['grændɪəʊz] ADJ **1** (= *imposing*) [*style, building etc*] imponente, grandioso
2 (*pej*) [*building etc*] ostentoso, hecho para impresionar; [*scheme, plan*] vasto, ambicioso; [*style*] exagerado, pomposo

grandly ['grændlɪ] ADV **1** (= *impressively*) • **to live ~** vivir por todo lo alto • **~ decorated** suntuosamente decorado
2 (= *importantly*) [*announce, proclaim*] (= *solemnly*) solemnemente, con solemnidad; (= *pompously*) pomposamente, en tono pomposo; [*stand, walk*] majestuosamente • **"my daughter's a PhD," he said ~** —mi hija tiene un doctorado —dijo pomposamente *or* en tono pomposo • **what was ~ named "the Palace"** lo que grandiosamente *or* pomposamente llamaban "el Palacio"

grandma* ['grænmɑː], **grandmama** ['grænməˌmɑː] N abuela *f* • **yes, ~** sí, abuela

grandmother ['grænˌmʌðəʳ] N abuela *f*
• IDIOM: • **stop trying to teach your ~ to suck eggs** (*Brit*) ¿qué me vas a enseñar tú a mí?

grandness ['grændnɪs] N **1** (= *impressiveness*) [*of building, architecture*] lo espléndido, grandiosidad *f*; [*of clothes*] suntuosidad *f*; [*of occasion, spectacle*] solemnidad *f*; [*of person*] distinción *f*
2 (= *pompousness*) [*of manner, behaviour*] pomposidad *f*

grandpa* ['grænpɑː], **grandpapa** ['grænpəˌpɑː] N abuelo *m* • **yes, ~** sí, abuelo

grandparents ['grænˌpɛərənts] NPL abuelos *mpl*

grandson ['grænsʌn] N nieto *m*

grandstand ['grændstænd] N (*Sport*) tribuna *f*
VI* (*fig*) fanfarronear
CPD ▸ **grandstand view** • **to have a ~ view of** tener una vista magnífica de

grandstanding ['grændstændɪŋ] N (*pej*) (= *playing to the gallery*) demagogia *f*

grange [greɪndʒ] N (*US*) (*Agr*) cortijo *m*, alquería *f*; (*Brit*) casa *f* solariega, casa *f* de señor

granite ['grænɪt] N granito *m*

granny, grannie ['grænɪ] N* abuela *f* • **yes, ~** sí, abuela
CPD ▸ **granny flat*** (*Brit*) pisito *m or* (*LAm*) departamentito *m* para la abuela ▸ **granny knot** nudo *m* corredizo

grant [grɑːnt] N **1** (= *act*) otorgamiento *m*, concesión *f*; (= *thing granted*) concesión *f*; (*Jur*) cesión *f*; (= *gift*) donación *f*
2 (*Brit*) (= *scholarship*) beca *f*; (= *subsidy*) subvención *f*
VT **1** (= *allow*) [+ *request, favour*] conceder; (= *provide, give*) [+ *prize*] otorgar; (*Jur*) ceder
2 (= *admit*) reconocer • **~ed, he's rather old** de acuerdo, es bastante viejo • **~ed** *or* **~ing that …** en el supuesto de que … • **I ~ him that** le concedo eso
3 • **to take sth for ~ed** dar algo por supuesto *or* sentado • **we may take that for ~ed** eso es indudable • **he takes her for ~ed** no sabe valorarla

grant-aided [ˌgrɑːnt'eɪdɪd] ADJ (*Brit*) subvencionado

grantee [grɑːn'tiː] N cesionario/a *m/f*

grant-in-aid [ˌgrɑːntɪn'eɪd] N (PL: **grants-in-aid**) subvención *f*

grant-maintained [ˌgrɑːntmeɪn'teɪnd] ADJ (*Brit*) [*school*] *que recibe dinero del gobierno central, y no de la administración local*

> **GRANT-MAINTAINED SCHOOL**
> Una **grant-maintained school** es un colegio público británico financiado por el gobierno central. Este sistema de organización escolar fue establecido para dotar a los colegios de una mayor autonomía y para reducir a la vez el poder de intervención que los ayuntamientos tenían anteriormente en la educación. Aunque muchos centros han preferido seguir adscritos a la autoridad local, los que han optado por el sistema de **grant-maintained school** son controlados directamente por un equipo directivo con una representación importante del personal del colegio y de los padres de los alumnos. Este comité se encarga de tomar decisiones tales como la contratación de nuevo personal, el reparto del presupuesto, o el mantenimiento del edificio, asuntos de los que antes se ocupaba la autoridad educativa local.

grantor [grɑːn'tɔːʳ, 'grɑːntəʳ] N cedente *mf*

granular ['grænjʊləʳ] ADJ granular

granulate ['grænjʊleɪt] VT [+ *salt, sugar, soil, metal*] granular; [+ *surface*] hacer granuloso

granulated ['grænjʊleɪtɪd] ADJ [*paper*] granulado; [*surface*] rugoso
CPD ▸ **granulated sugar** azúcar *m or f* granulado *or* granulada

granule ['grænjuːl] N [*of sugar etc*] gránulo *m*

grape [greɪp] N uva *f* • IDIOMS: • **sour ~s!** ¡están verdes de envidia!, ¡pura envidia! • **it's just sour ~s with him** es un envidioso, lo que pasa es que tiene envidia
CPD ▸ **grape harvest** vendimia *f* ▸ **grape hyacinth** jacinto *m* de penacho ▸ **grape jelly** (*US*) gelatina *f* de uva ▸ **grape juice** (*for making wine*) mosto *m*; (= *drink*) zumo *m or* (*LAm*) jugo *m* de uva ▸ **grape variety** (*used to make wine*) cepa *f*

grapefruit ['greɪpfruːt] N (PL: **grapefruit** *or* **grapefruits**) pomelo *m*, toronja *f* (*esp LAm*)
CPD ▸ **grapefruit juice** jugo *m* de pomelo, jugo *m* de toronja (*esp LAm*)

grapeshot ['greɪpʃɒt] N metralla *f*

grapevine ['greɪpvaɪn] N **1** (*lit*) vid *f*, parra *f*
2* (*fig*) teléfono *m* árabe, radio *f* macuto (*Sp**) • **I heard it on** *or* **through the ~** me contó un pajarito, me enteré en radio macuto (*Sp**)

graph [grɑːf] N gráfica *f*, gráfico *m*
CPD ▸ **graph paper** papel *m* cuadriculado

grapheme ['græfiːm] N grafema *m*

graphic ['græfɪk] ADJ **1** (= *vivid*) [*description, picture*] muy gráfico • **to describe sth in ~ detail** describir algo con todo lujo de detalles
2 (*Art, Math*) gráfico
CPD ▸ **graphic artist** grafista *mf* ▸ **graphic arts** artes *fpl* gráficas ▸ **graphic design** diseño *m* gráfico ▸ **graphic design department** departamento *m* de diseño gráfico ▸ **graphic designer** grafista *mf* ▸ **graphic equalizer** ecualizador *m* gráfico

graphical ['græfɪkəl] ADJ (*gen*) (*also Math*) gráfico
CPD ▸ **graphical display unit** (*Comput*) unidad *f* de demostración gráfica ▸ **graphical user interface** (*Comput*) interfaz *m* gráfico de usuario, interfaz *f* gráfica de usuario

graphically ['græfɪkəlɪ] ADV **1** (= *vividly*) gráficamente • **their suffering is ~ described** su sufrimiento se describe gráficamente *or* en términos gráficos
2 (= *with graphics*) gráficamente

graphics ['græfɪks] N **1** (= *art of drawing*) artes *fpl* gráficas
2 (= *graphs*) gráficas *fpl*
3 (*Comput*) gráficos *mpl*
4 (= *pictures*) dibujos *mpl*
CPD ▸ **graphics card** tarjeta *f* gráfica ▸ **graphics environment** (*Comput*) entorno *m* gráfico ▸ **graphics pad** (*Comput*) tablero *m* de gráficos ▸ **graphics tablet** tableta *f* gráfica

graphite ['græfaɪt] N grafito *m*

graphologist [græ'fɒlədʒɪst] N grafólogo/a *m/f*

graphology [græ'fɒlədʒɪ] N grafología *f*

grapnel ['græpnəl] N rezón *m*, arpeo *m*

grapple ['græpl] VI [*wrestlers etc*] luchar cuerpo a cuerpo (**with** con) • **to ~ with a problem** (*fig*) confrontar un problema
VT asir, agarrar; (*Naut*) aferrar

grappling iron ['græplɪŋˌaɪən] N (*Naut*) rezón *m*

grasp [grɑːsp] N **1** (= *handclasp*) apretón *m* • **to be within sb's ~** estar al alcance de la mano de algn • **he has a strong ~** agarra muy fuerte • **to lose one's ~ on sth** desasirse de algo
2 (*fig*) (= *power*) garras *fpl*, control *m*; (= *range*) alcance *m*; (= *understanding*) comprensión *f* • **it's within everyone's ~** está al alcance de todos • **it is beyond my ~** está fuera de mi alcance • **to have a good ~ of sth** dominar algo
VT **1** (= *take hold of*) agarrar, asir; (= *hold firmly*) sujetar; [+ *hand*] estrechar, apretar; [+ *weapon etc*] empuñar
2 (*fig*) [+ *chance, opportunity*] aprovechar; [+ *power, territory*] apoderarse de
3 (= *understand*) comprender, entender

▸ **grasp at** VI + PREP **1** (*lit*) [+ *rope etc*] tratar de asir
2 (*fig*) [+ *hope*] aferrarse a; [+ *opportunity*] aprovechar

grasping ['grɑːspɪŋ] ADJ (*fig*) avaro, codicioso

grass [grɑːs] N **1** (*Bot*) hierba *f*, yerba *f*; (= *lawn*) césped *m*, pasto *m* (*LAm*), grama *f* (*LAm*); (= *pasture*) pasto *m* • **"keep off the grass"** "prohibido pisar la hierba" • **to put a horse out to ~** echar un caballo al pasto
• IDIOM: • **not to let the ~ grow under one's feet** no dormirse • PROVERB: • **the ~ is always greener on the other side (of the fence)** nadie está contento con su suerte
2‡ (= *marijuana*) marihuana *f*, mota *f* (*LAm**)
3 (*Brit‡*) (= *person*) soplón/ona *m/f*
VI (*Brit‡*) soplar*, dar el chivatazo* • **to ~ on** delatar a
VT (*also* **grass over**) cubrir de hierba
CPD ▸ **grass court** (*Tennis*) pista *f* de hierba ▸ **grass cutter** cortacésped *m* ▸ **grass roots** (*fig*) base *f*; ▹ **grass-roots** ▸ **grass snake** culebra *f* ▸ **grass widow** (*esp US*) (*divorced, separated*) mujer *f* separada o divorciada; (*Brit*) (*hum*) mujer *f* cuyo marido está ausente ▸ **grass widower** (*esp US*) (*divorced, separated*) hombre *m* separado o divorciado; (*Brit*) (*hum*) marido *m* cuya mujer está ausente

grass-green ['grɑːsˌgriːn] ADJ verde hierba

grasshopper ['grɑːsˌhɒpəʳ] N saltamontes *m inv*, chapulín *m* (*Mex, CAm*)

grassland ['grɑːslænd] N pradera *f*, pampa *f* (*LAm*)

grass-roots ['grɑːs'ruːts] ADJ [*movement*] de base; [*support, opinion*] de las bases • **grass-roots politics** política *f* donde se trata de los problemas corrientes de la gente; ▹ grass

grassy ['grɑːsɪ] ADJ (COMPAR: **grassier**, SUPERL: **grassiest**) herboso, pastoso (*LAm*)

grate¹ [greɪt] N (= *grid*) parrilla *f*; (= *fireplace*) chimenea *f*

g

grate[2] [greɪt] VT **1** [*+ cheese etc*] rallar • **~d cheese** queso *m* rallado
2 (*= scrape*) [*+ metallic object, chalk etc*] hacer chirriar • **to ~ one's teeth** hacer rechinar los dientes
VI **1** [*chalk, hinge etc*] chirriar (**on, against** al desplazarse por)
2 (*fig*) • **it really ~s (on me)** me pone los pelos de punta • **to ~ on the ear** hacer daño a los oídos • **it ~s on my nerves** me pone los nervios de punta, me destroza los nervios

grateful [ˈgreɪtfʊl] ADJ (*= thankful*) agradecido; [*smile*] de agradecimiento • **a ~ client** un cliente agradecido • **to be ~ for sth** agradecer algo • **I am ~ for any help I can get** agradezco cualquier ayuda que pueda recibir • **I would be ~ if you would send me …** le agradecería que me mandase … • **I should like to extend my ~ thanks to …** me gustaría extender mi más sincero agradecimiento a … • **with ~ thanks** con mi más sincero agradecimiento • **to be ~ to sb** estar agradecido a algn • **I am very** *or* **most ~ to you for talking to me** le estoy muy agradecido por hablar conmigo • **I am ~ to Dr Jones for the loan of the book** le estoy agradecido al Dr Jones por prestarme el libro, le agradezco al Dr Jones que me prestase el libro • **she was just ~ to have been released** se sentía agradecida de que la hubiesen liberado • **he was ~ that he was still alive** daba gracias por estar todavía vivo

gratefully [ˈgreɪtfəlɪ] ADV [*accept, say, smile*] con gratitud • **she shook my hand ~** me apretó la mano agradecida *or* con gratitud • **~, I accepted** acepté agradecido • **the contribution of various individuals is ~ acknowledged** agradecemos la colaboración de varias personas • **all contributions/donations will be ~ received** agradecemos todo tipo de colaboración/cualquier donativo

grater [ˈgreɪtəʳ] N (*Culin*) rallador *m*

gratification [ˌgrætɪfɪˈkeɪʃən] N
1 (*= satisfaction*) satisfacción *f* • **to my great ~** con gran satisfacción mía
2 (*= reward*) gratificación *f*, recompensa *f*

gratified [ˈgrætɪfaɪd] ADJ contento, satisfecho

gratify [ˈgrætɪfaɪ] VT [*+ person*] complacer; [*+ desire, whim etc*] satisfacer • **I am gratified to know** me complace saberlo • **he was much gratified** se puso muy contento

gratifying [ˈgrætɪfaɪɪŋ] ADJ grato • **it is ~ to know that …** me es grato saber que … • **with ~ speed** con loable prontitud

gratin [ˈgrætæn] N gratinado *m*

grating[1] [ˈgreɪtɪŋ] N (*in wall, pavement*) reja *f*, enrejado *m*

grating[2] [ˈgreɪtɪŋ] ADJ [*tone etc*] áspero

gratis [ˈgrɑːtɪs] ADV gratis
ADJ gratuito

gratitude [ˈgrætɪtjuːd] N gratitud *f*, agradecimiento *m* • **he expressed his ~ for Britain's support** expresó su gratitud *or* agradecimiento por el apoyo de Gran Bretaña • **he felt a sense of ~ towards her** se sentía agradecido hacia ella • **there's** *or* **that's ~ for you!** (*iro*) ¡así me/te *etc* lo agradecen!

gratuitous [grəˈtjuːɪtəs] ADJ (*= free*) gratuito; (*= needless*) [*violence, sex*] gratuito

gratuitously [grəˈtjuːɪtəslɪ] ADV gratuitamente, de manera gratuita

gratuity [grəˈtjuːɪtɪ] N **1** (*frm*) (*= tip*) propina *f*
2 (*Brit*) (*Mil*) gratificación *f*

gravamen [grəˈveɪmen] N (PL: **gravamina** [grəˈvæmɪnə]) (*Jur*) *fundamento principal de una acusación*

grave[1] [greɪv] ADJ (COMPAR: **graver**, SUPERL: **gravest**) **1** (*= serious*) [*danger, problem, mistake*] grave; [*threat, suspicion*] serio • **he expressed ~ concern about the matter** expresó su seria preocupación por el problema • **the situation is very ~** la situación es muy grave • **you do him a ~ injustice** estás cometiendo una grave injusticia con él
2 (*= solemn*) [*face, expression*] grave, serio; [*person*] serio • **his face was ~** su rostro era grave *or* serio

grave[2] [greɪv] N tumba *f*, sepultura *f*; (*with monument*) sepulcro *m*, tumba *f* • **common ~** fosa *f* común • **from beyond the ~** (*fig*) desde ultratumba • IDIOM: • **he sent her to an early ~** él fue la causa de que muriera tan joven; ▹ **dig, turn**

grave[3] [grɑːv] ADJ (*Ling*) • **~ accent** acento *m* grave

gravedigger [ˈgreɪvˌdɪgəʳ] N sepulturero/a *m/f*

gravel [ˈgrævəl] N grava *f*, gravilla *f*
CPD ▸ **gravel bed** gravera *f* ▸ **gravel path** camino *m* de grava ▸ **gravel pit** gravera *f*

gravelled, graveled (US) [ˈgrævəld] ADJ de grava, de gravilla

gravelly [ˈgrævəlɪ] ADJ **1** (*lit*) con grava, con gravilla
2 [*voice*] áspero

gravely [ˈgreɪvlɪ] ADV **1** (*= seriously*) [*ill, wounded, injured*] gravemente • **five soldiers were ~ wounded** cinco soldados resultaron gravemente heridos *or* heridos de gravedad • **we are ~ concerned about** *or* **by his decision** estamos muy *or* seriamente preocupados por su decisión
2 (*= solemnly*) [*say, speak*] con gravedad, con seriedad • **he nodded ~** asintió con gravedad

graven [ˈgreɪvən] ADJ (*liter*) • **~ image** ídolo *m* • **it is ~ on my memory** lo tengo grabado en la memoria

graveness [ˈgreɪvnɪs] N gravedad *f*

graveside [ˈgreɪvsaɪd] N • **at the ~** junto a la tumba

gravestone [ˈgreɪvstəʊn] N lápida *f* (sepulcral)

graveyard [ˈgreɪvjɑːd] N cementerio *m*, camposanto *m*
CPD ▸ **graveyard shift** (*esp US*) turno *m* de noche, turno *m* nocturno

graving dock [ˈgreɪvɪŋdɒk] N (*Naut*) dique *m* de carena

gravitas [ˈgrævɪtæs] N (*frm*) gravitas *f*, seriedad *f* • **a certain air of ~** cierto aire de seriedad

gravitate [ˈgrævɪteɪt] VI gravitar • **to ~ towards** (*fig*) (*= be drawn to*) tender hacia; (*= move*) dirigirse hacia

gravitation [ˌgrævɪˈteɪʃən] N (*Phys*) gravitación *f*; (*fig*) tendencia *f* (**towards** a)

gravitational [ˌgrævɪˈteɪʃənl] ADJ gravitatorio, gravitacional

gravity [ˈgrævɪtɪ] N **1** (*Phys*) gravedad *f* • **the law of ~** la ley de la gravedad
2 (*= seriousness*) [*of situation, event*] gravedad *f* • **this is a situation of the utmost ~** esta es una situación de la mayor gravedad
3 (*= solemnity*) [*of tone, manner*] gravedad *f*
CPD ▸ **gravity feed** alimentación *f* por gravedad

gravlax [ˈgrævlæks] N gravlax *m*

gravy [ˈgreɪvɪ] N **1** (*Culin*) salsa *f* de carne, gravy *m*
2 (*US*‡) (*= easy money*) dinero *m* fácil
CPD ▸ **gravy boat** salsera *f* ▸ **gravy train*** (*fig*) dinero *m* fácil • IDIOM: • **to get on the ~ train** pillar un chollo‡

gray *etc* [greɪ] ADJ (*US*) = **grey** *etc*

graze[1] [greɪz] (*Agr*) VI pacer, pastar
VT [*+ grass, field*] usar como pasto; [*+ cattle*] apacentar, pastar

graze[2] [greɪz] N (*= injury*) roce *m*
VT **1** (*= touch lightly*) rozar
2 (*= scrape*) [*+ skin*] raspar • **to ~ one's knees** rasparse las rodillas

grazed [ˈgreɪzd] ADJ [*arm, knee*] raspado

grazier [ˈgreɪzɪəʳ] N (*esp Brit*) pastor *m*

grazing [ˈgreɪzɪŋ] N **1** (*= land*) pasto *m*
2 (*= act*) pastoreo *m*

GRE N ABBR (*US*) (*Univ*) (= **Graduate Record Examination**) *examen de acceso a estudios de posgrado*

grease [griːs] N (*= oil, fat etc*) grasa *f*; [*of candle*] sebo *m*; (*= dirt*) mugre *f*; (*= lubricant*) lubricante *m*
VT [*+ baking tin*] engrasar; (*Aut etc*) engrasar, lubricar • IDIOMS: • **like ~d lightning*** como un relámpago • **to ~ sb's palm** untar la mano a algn
CPD ▸ **grease gun** pistola *f* engrasadora, engrasadora *f* a presión ▸ **grease monkey*** (*US*) mecánico/a *m/f*, maquinista *mf* ▸ **grease nipple** (*Aut*) engrasador *m* ▸ **grease remover** quitagrasas *m inv*

greaseboard [ˈgriːsbɔːd] N (*US*) pizarra *f* blanca

greasepaint [ˈgriːspeɪnt] N maquillaje *m*

greaseproof [ˈgriːspruːf] ADJ (*Brit*) a prueba de grasa, impermeable a la grasa
CPD ▸ **greaseproof paper** papel *m* encerado

greaser‡ [ˈgriːsəʳ] N **1** (*= mechanic*) mecánico/a *m/f*
2† (*= motorcyclist*) motociclista *mf*
3 (*pej*) (*= ingratiating person*) pelota* *mf*, lameculos* *mf*
4 (*US*) (*pej*) (*= Latin American*) sudaca* *mf*

greasiness [ˈgriːsɪnɪs] N [*of substance, hands, clothes*] lo grasiento, lo grasoso (*esp LAm*); [*of hair, skin*] lo graso, lo grasoso (*esp LAm*); [*of food*] lo grasiento; [*of road*] lo resbaladizo

greasy [ˈgriːsɪ] ADJ (COMPAR: **greasier**, SUPERL: **greasiest**) **1** (*= oily*) [*substance, hands*] grasiento, grasoso (*esp LAm*); [*clothes*] lleno de grasa, mugriento; [*hair, skin*] graso, grasoso (*esp LAm*); [*food*] grasiento; [*road*] resbaladizo
2* (*= ingratiating*) [*person*] adulón, zalamero
CPD ▸ **greasy spoon*** (*= café*) figón *m*

great [greɪt] ADJ (COMPAR: **greater**, SUPERL: **greatest**) **1** (*= huge*) (*in size*) [*house, room, object*] enorme, inmenso; (*in amount, number*) [*effort, variety*] grande; [*shock, surprise*] verdadero, enorme • **she lived to a ~ age** vivió hasta una edad muy avanzada • **I'll take ~ care of it** lo cuidaré mucho • **he didn't say a ~ deal** no dijo mucho • **a ~ deal of time/money/effort** mucho tiempo/dinero/esfuerzo • **a ~ deal of suffering** mucho sufrimiento • **with ~ difficulty** con gran *or* mucha dificultad • **we had ~ difficulty convincing them** hemos tenido muchas dificultades para convencerlos • **he had ~ difficulty staying awake** le costaba mucho mantenerse despierto • **to a ~ extent** en gran parte • **to an even ~er extent** incluso en mayor parte • **we had ~ fun** lo pasamos fenomenal • **~ heavens!**† ¡Cielo Santo!†, ¡Válgame el cielo! • **to be a ~ help** ser de gran ayuda • **well, you've been a ~ help!** (*iro*) ¡vaya ayuda la tuya!, ¡pues sí que has sido una ayuda! • **I'm in no ~ hurry** • **I'm not in any ~ hurry** no tengo mucha prisa • **you ~ idiot!*** ¡pedazo de idiota!* • **a ~ many people believe he was right** mucha gente cree que tenía razón • **a ~ many of us are uneasy about these developments** a muchos de nosotros estos sucesos nos tienen intranquilos • **it was a ~ pity you didn't come** fue una verdadera pena que no vinieses • **with ~**

pleasure con gran placer • **it's my ~ pleasure to introduce …** es un gran placer para mí presentar a … • **~ progress has been made** se han hecho grandes progresos • **~ Scott!**† ¡Cielo Santo!†, ¡Válgame el cielo! • **the concert was a ~ success** el concierto fue un enorme éxito; ▹ **guns**
2 (= *important*) [*achievement, occasion, event*] grande • **the ~ cultural achievements of the past** los grandes logros culturales del pasado • **one of the ~ issues of the day** uno de los temas más importantes del día • **everyone said she was destined for ~ things** todos decían que llegaría lejos • **~ work** (= *masterpiece*) obra *f* maestra
3 (= *outstanding*) [*person, nation, skill*] grande • **one of the ~est engineers of this century** uno de los más grandes ingenieros de este siglo • **a player of ~ ability** un jugador de gran habilidad • **she has a ~ eye for detail** tiene muy buen ojo para los detalles
4 (*with names*) • **Frederick/Peter the Great** Federico/Pedro el Grande • **Alexander the Great** Alejandro Magno • **the ~ George Padmore** el gran George Padmore
5 (= *real*) (*as intensifier*) grande • **I am a ~ admirer of his work** soy un gran admirador de su obra • **they are ~ friends** son grandes amigos • **I'm a ~ chocolate-lover** me encanta el chocolate • **he was a ~ womanizer** era un gran mujeriego • **she is a ~ believer in hard work** es una gran partidaria del trabajo duro • **I'm a ~ believer in being frank** soy muy partidario de la franqueza • **she's a ~ one for antique shops** le encantan las tiendas de antigüedades, es una fanática de las tiendas de antigüedades • **he's a ~ one for criticizing others** es único para criticar a los demás, se las pinta solo para criticar a los demás*
6* (= *excellent*) [*person, thing, idea*] estupendo, genial* • **they're a ~ bunch of guys** son un grupo de tíos estupendos *or* geniales* • **you were ~!** ¡estuviste genial!* • **I think she's ~** creo que es genial* • **it's a ~ idea** es una idea estupenda, es una idea genial* • **"how was the movie?" — "it was ~!"** —¿que tal fue la película? —¡genial!* • **(that's) ~!** ¡eso es estupendo! • **I heard a ~ piece of music on the radio** oí en la radio una pieza de música genial* • **wouldn't it be ~ to do that?** ¿no sería fabuloso *or* genial hacer eso? • **camping holidays are ~ for kids** las vacaciones en un camping son estupendas para los críos, las vacaciones en un camping son geniales para los críos* • **she was just ~ about it** se lo tomó muy bien • **he's ~ at football** juega estupendamente al fútbol • **she's ~ at maths** se le dan genial las matemáticas* • **to feel ~** sentirse fenómeno *or* fenomenal* • **you look ~!** (= *attractive*) ¡estás guapísimo!; (= *healthy*) ¡tienes un aspecto estupendo! • **she's ~ on jazz** sabe un montón de jazz* • **the ~ thing is that you don't have to iron it** lo mejor de todo es que no tienes que plancharlo
7 (*Bot, Zool*) grande
(EXCL) **1*** (= *excellent*) • **(oh) ~!** ¡fenómeno!*, ¡fenomenal!, ¡qué bien!
2 (*iro*) • **(oh) ~! that's all I need!** ¡maravilloso! ¡eso es lo que me faltaba! • **if that's what you want to believe, ~!** si es eso lo que quieres creer, allá tú
(ADV) • **~ big*** grandísimo
(N) (= *person*) grande *mf* • **the golfing ~s** los grandes del golf • **one of the all-time ~s** uno de los grandes de todos los tiempos • **the ~** los grandes • **history remembers only the ~** la historia recuerda solo a los grandes • **the ~ and the good** (*hum*) los abonados a las buenas causas
(CPD) ▸ **great ape** antropoide *mf* ▸ **the Great Australian Bight** el Gran Golfo Australiano ▸ **the Great Barrier Reef** la Gran Barrera de Coral, el Gran Arrecife Coralino ▸ **the Great Bear** (*Astron*) la Osa Mayor ▸ **Great Britain** Gran Bretaña *f* ▸ **Great Dane** gran danés *m* ▸ **the Great Dividing Range** la Gran Cordillera Divisoria ▸ **the Great Lakes** los Grandes Lagos ▸ **the Great Plains** las Grandes Llanuras ▸ **the great powers** las grandes potencias ▸ **great tit** paro *m* grande, herrerillo *m* grande ▸ **the Great Wall of China** la (Gran) Muralla China ▸ **the Great War** la Primera Guerra Mundial

GREAT, BIG, LARGE

"Grande" shortened to "gran"

▹ **Grande** *must be shortened to* **gran** *before a singular noun of either gender:*
Great Britain
(La) Gran Bretaña

Position of "grande"

▹ *Put* **gran/grandes** *before the noun in the sense of "great":*
It's a great step forward in the search for peace
Es un gran paso en la búsqueda de la paz
He is a (very) great actor
Es un gran actor

▹ *In the sense of* **big** *or* **large**, *the adjective will precede the noun in the context of a general, subjective comment. However, when there is implicit or explicit comparison with other things or people that are physically bigger or smaller, it will follow the noun:*
It's a big problem
Es un gran problema
… the difference in price between big flats and small ones …
… la diferencia de precio entre los pisos grandes y pequeños …
… a certain type of large passenger plane …
… cierto tipo de avión grande para el transporte de pasajeros …

▹ *Compare the following examples:*
… a great man …
… un gran hombre …
… a big man …
… un hombre grande …

For further uses and examples, see **great, big, large**

great-aunt ['greɪt'ɑ:nt] (N) tía *f* abuela
greatcoat ['greɪtkəʊt] (N) gabán *m*; (*Mil etc*) sobretodo *m*
greater ['greɪtəʳ] (ADJ) (*compar of* **great**) (*also Bot, Zool*) mayor • **Greater London** el gran Londres (*incluyendo los barrios de la periferia*)
(CPD) ▸ **Greater Manchester** área *f* metropolitana de Manchester
greatest ['greɪtɪst] (ADJ) (*superl of* **great**) el mayor, la mayor • **Ireland's ~ living poet** el mayor poeta vivo de Irlanda • **with the ~ difficulty** con suma dificultad • **he's the ~!*** ¡es el mejor!
great-grandchild ['greɪt'græntʃaɪld] (N) (PL: **great-grandchildren**) bisnieto/a *m/f*
great-granddaughter [ˌgreɪt'grændˌdɔ:təʳ] (N) bisnieta *f*
great-grandfather ['greɪt'grænˌfɑ:ðəʳ] (N) bisabuelo *m*
great-grandmother ['greɪt'grænˌmʌðəʳ] (N) bisabuela *f*
great-grandparents ['greɪt'grænˌpeərənts] (NPL) bisabuelos *mpl*
great-grandson ['greɪt'grændsʌn] (N) bisnieto *m*
great-great-grandfather ['greɪt'greɪt-'grænˌfɑ:ðəʳ] (N) tatarabuelo *m*
great-great-grandparents ['greɪt'greɪt-'grænˌpeərənts] (NPL) tatarabuelos *mpl*
great-great-grandson ['greɪt'greɪt-'grænsʌn] (N) tataranieto *m*
great-hearted ['greɪt'hɑ:tɪd] (ADJ) valiente
greatly ['greɪtlɪ] (ADV) **1** (*with adj or pp used as adj*) muy • **~ superior** muy superior • **she found him ~ changed** ella lo encontró muy *or* enormemente cambiado • **he was ~ influenced by Debussy** estuvo muy *or* enormemente influenciado por Debussy
2 (*with verb*) [*contribute, improve, vary, admire, regret*] enormemente, mucho • **I ~ regret having told her about it** me arrepiento mucho *or* enormemente de habérselo dicho • **it is ~ to be regretted** (*frm*) es muy de lamentar
great-nephew ['greɪtˌnefju:] (N) sobrinonieto *m*
greatness ['greɪtnɪs] (N) grandeza *f* • **he was destined for ~** su destino era grande
great-niece ['greɪtˌni:s] (N) sobrinanieta *f*
great-uncle ['greɪtˌʌŋkl] (N) tío *m* abuelo
grebe [gri:b] (N) zampullín *m*, somormujo *m*
Grecian ['gri:ʃən] (ADJ) griego
Greece [gri:s] (N) Grecia *f*
greed [gri:d] (N) avaricia *f*, codicia *f*; (*for food*) gula *f*, glotonería *f*
greedily ['gri:dɪlɪ] (ADV) con avidez; [*eat*] con voracidad
greediness ['gri:dɪnɪs] (N) = **greed**
greedy ['gri:dɪ] (ADJ) (COMPAR: **greedier**, SUPERL: **greediest**) codicioso (**for** de); (*for food*) goloso • **don't be so ~!** ¡no seas glotón!
greedy-guts* ['gri:dɪˌgʌts] (N) (*Brit*) (*hum*) comilón/ona* *m/f*
Greek [gri:k] (ADJ) griego
(N) **1** (= *person*) griego/a *m/f*
2 (*Ling*) griego *m* • **ancient ~** griego *m* antiguo • IDIOM: • **it's all ~ to me*** para mí es chino, no entiendo ni palabra
(CPD) ▸ **Greek Orthodox Church** Iglesia *f* Ortodoxa griega
Greek-Cypriot ['gri:k'sɪprɪət] (ADJ) grecochipriota
(N) grecochipriota *mf*
green [gri:n] (ADJ) (COMPAR: **greener**, SUPERL: **greenest**) **1** (*in colour*) verde • **dark ~** verde oscuro (*adj inv*) • **light ~** verde claro (*adj inv*) • **she was wearing a light ~ blouse** llevaba una blusa verde claro • **blue ~** verde azulado (*adj inv*) • **it's a very ~ city** es una ciudad con muchas zonas verdes • **to turn** *or* **go ~** [*tree*] verdear • **she went ~ at the thought** (= *nauseous*) se puso blanca solo de pensarlo • IDIOMS: • **to be ~ with envy** morirse de envidia • **to make sb ~ with envy** ponerle a algn los dientes largos • **the ~ shoots of recovery** los primeros indicios de la recuperación; ▹ **gill**¹
2 (= *unripe*) [*banana, tomato, wood*] verde
3 (*fig*) (= *inexperienced*) novato; (= *naive*) inocente • **I'm not as ~ as I look!** ¡no soy tan inocente como parezco! • IDIOM: • **he's as ~ as grass** es más inocente que un niño
4 (= *ecological*) [*movement, vote, person*] verde, ecologista; [*issues, policy, product*] ecologista
(N) **1** (= *colour*) verde *m*
2 (= *grassy area*) **a** (= *lawn*) césped *m*; (= *field*) prado *m*; (*also* **village green**) césped *m* comunal
b (*Sport*) (*in Golf*) green *m*; (*for bowls*) pista *f*; ▹ **bowling, putting**

g

3 greens (*Culin*) verdura *fsing* • **eat up your ~s!** ¡cómete la verdura!
4 (*Pol*) • **the Greens** los verdes
ADV (*Pol*) • **to vote ~** votar por el partido ecologista, votar a los verdes* • **to think ~** pensar en el medio ambiente
VT (*ecologically*) hacer más verde
CPD ▸ **green algae** algas *fpl* verdes ▸ **green bacon** tocino *m* sin ahumar, beicon *m* sin ahumar (*Sp*), panceta *f* (*S. Cone*) ▸ **green bean** judía *f* verde, ejote *m* (*Mex*), poroto *m* verde (*And, S. Cone*), chaucha *f* (*Arg*) ▸ **green belt** (*Brit*) zona *f* verde ▸ **Green Beret** (*Brit, US*) (= *person*) boina *mf* verde ▸ **green card** (*in EC*) (*Aut*) carta *f* verde; (*in US*) *permiso de residencia y trabajo en los EE.UU.* ▸ **green channel** (*at customs*) canal *m* verde (*en aduana*) ▸ **the Green Cross Code** (*Brit*) código *m* de seguridad vial ▸ **green fingers** (*Brit*) • IDIOM: • **to have ~ fingers**: • **he has ~ fingers** se le dan muy bien las plantas ▸ **green goddess*** (*Brit*) *coche de bomberos del ejército* ▸ **green light** luz *f* verde • IDIOM: • **to give sb/sth the ~ light** dar luz verde a algn/algo ▸ **green onion** (*US*) cebolleta *f*, cebollino *m* ▸ **green paper** (*Brit*) (*Pol*) libro *m* verde ▸ **the Green Party** (*Pol*) el partido ecologista, los verdes* ▸ **green peas** guisantes *mpl* ▸ **green pepper** (= *vegetable*) pimiento *m* verde, pimentón *m* verde (*LAm*) ▸ **green pound** (*ethical shopping*) *dinero de los que tienen una sensibilidad medioambiental* ▸ **green revolution, Green Revolution** revolución *f* verde ▸ **green room** (*Theat*) camerino *m* ▸ **green salad** ensalada *f* (*de lechuga, pepino, pimiento verde etc*) ▸ **green tax** ecotasa *f* ▸ **green thumb** (*US*) • IDIOM: • **to have a ~ thumb**: • **he has a ~ thumb** se le dan muy bien las plantas ▸ **green vegetables** verduras *fpl* de hoja verde

greenback* ['gri:nbæk] N (*US*) billete *m* (de banco)

green-collar ['gri:nkɒləʳ] CPD ▸ **green-collar economy** sector *m* de las tecnologías alternativas ▸ **green-collar job** trabajo *m* en el sector de las tecnologías alternativas ▸ **green-collar worker** trabajador(a) *m/f* del sector de las tecnologías alternativas

greenery ['gri:nərɪ] N follaje *m*

green-eyed ['gri:naɪd] ADJ de ojos verdes • IDIOM: • **the green-eyed monster** (*hum*) la envidia

greenfield ['gri:n,fi:ld] N (*also* **greenfield site**) solar *m or* terreno *m* sin edificar

greenfinch ['gri:nfɪntʃ] N verderón *m*

greenfly ['gri:nflaɪ] N (PL: **greenfly** *or* **greenflies**) pulgón *m*

greengage ['gri:ngeɪdʒ] N claudia *f*

greengrocer ['gri:n,grəʊsəʳ] N (*Brit*) verdulero/a *m/f* • **~'s (shop)** verdulería *f*

greenhorn ['gri:nhɔ:n] N bisoño *m*, novato *m*

greenhouse ['gri:nhaʊs] N (PL: **greenhouses** ['gri:nhaʊzɪz]) invernadero *m*
CPD ▸ **greenhouse effect** efecto *m* invernadero ▸ **greenhouse gas** gas *m* invernadero ▸ **greenhouse gas emissions** emisión *fsing* de gases de *or* con efecto invernadero ▸ **greenhouse warming** calentamiento *m* por efecto invernadero

greening ['gri:nɪŋ] N (= *increase in environmental awareness*) [*of person, organization*] concientización *f* ecológica

greenish ['gri:nɪʃ] ADJ verdoso

Greenland ['gri:nlənd] N Groenlandia *f*

Greenlander ['gri:nləndəʳ] N groenlandés/esa *m/f*

Greenlandic [,gri:n'lændɪk] ADJ groenlandés
N (*Ling*) groenlandés *m*

greenness ['gri:nnɪs] N **1** (= *colour*) verdor *m*, lo verde *m*
2 (= *unripeness*) lo verde
3 (*fig*) (= *inexperience*) inexperiencia *f*; (= *naivety*) inocencia *f*

Greenpeace ['gri:npi:s] N Greenpeace *m*

greenstuff ['gri:nstʌf] N verduras *fpl*, legumbres *fpl*

greensward ['gri:nswɔ:d] N (*poet*) césped *m*

green-wellie brigade [,gri:n'welɪbrɪ,geɪd] N señoritos *m* del campo

> **GREEN-WELLIE BRIGADE**
> En el Reino Unido las botas altas de goma verdes **green wellingtons** se suelen asociar con las clases acomodadas, ya que son las botas que se utilizan normalmente para ir de caza o de pesca, deportes que han sido tradicionalmente asociados a la clase alta. Por este motivo, el término **green-wellie brigade** (que podría traducirse al español por el de **señoritos del campo**), se utiliza a veces despectivamente para referirse a ciertos aspectos negativos del comportamiento de dicha clase social.

Greenwich mean time [,grenɪtʃ'mi:ntaɪm] N hora *f* media de Greenwich

greet [gri:t] VT (*gen*) saludar; (= *welcome*) recibir; [*sight, smell etc*] [+ *sb, sb's eyes*] presentarse a • **the statement was ~ed with laughter** la declaración fue recibida entre risas • **this was ~ed with relief by everybody** todos recibieron la noticia con gran alivio

greeting ['gri:tɪŋ] N **1** (*with words etc*) saludo *m*; (= *welcome*) bienvenida *f*, acogida *f*
2 greetings saludos *mpl*, recuerdos *mpl* • **~s!** ¡bienvenido!
CPD ▸ **greetings card, greeting card** (*US*) tarjeta *f* de felicitación

Greg [greg] N *familiar form of* **Gregory**

gregarious [grɪ'gɛərɪəs] ADJ [*animal*] gregario; [*person*] sociable

Gregorian [grɪ'gɔ:rɪən] ADJ gregoriano
CPD ▸ **Gregorian chant** canto *m* gregoriano

Gregory ['gregərɪ] N Gregorio

gremlin* ['gremlɪn] N duendecillo *m*, diablillo *m*

Grenada [gre'neɪdə] N Granada *f*

grenade [grɪ'neɪd] N (*also* **hand grenade**) granada *f*
CPD ▸ **grenade launcher** lanzagranadas *m inv*

Grenadian [gre'neɪdɪən] ADJ granadino
N granadino/a *m/f*

grenadier [,grenə'dɪəʳ] N granadero *m*

grenadine ['grenədi:n] N granadina *f*

grew [gru:] PT *of* **grow**

grey, gray (*US*) [greɪ] ADJ (COMPAR: **greyer**, SUPERL: **greyest**) **1** (*in colour*) gris; [*face, complexion*] ceniciento; [*hair, beard*] gris, canoso, cano (*liter*); [*horse*] rucio • **the sky was ~** el cielo estaba gris • **dark ~** gris oscuro (*adj inv*) • **light ~** gris claro (*adj inv*) • **a light ~ shirt** una camisa gris claro • **he's very ~ for his age** tiene el pelo muy gris *or* canoso para su edad • **to have ~ hair** tener el pelo gris *or* canoso • **to go ~** [*hair*] volverse gris *or* canoso • **she's going ~** le están saliendo canas • **to turn ~** [*person, face*] palidecer
2 (= *bleak*) [*place, day*] gris • **the future looked ~** el futuro se presentaba sombrío
3 (= *boring*) [*person*] gris • **people are fed up with stereotype politicians, the men in ~ suits** la gente está cansada de los políticos estereotipados, los personajes incoloros
4* [*pound, vote*] de la tercera edad
N **1** (= *colour*) gris *m* • **dressed in ~** vestido de gris
2 (= *horse*) rucio *m*
VI [*hair*] encanecer • **he was ~ing at the temples** se le estaban encaneciendo las sienes
CPD ▸ **grey area** (= *unclear area*) área *f* poco definida, área *f* gris; (= *intermediate area*) área *f* intermedia • **it's rather a ~ area** es un área poco definida *or* bastante gris ▸ **grey friar** ▹ **friar** ▸ **grey matter** (*Anat, hum*) materia *f* gris ▸ **grey mullet** mújol *m* ▸ **grey seal** foca *f* gris ▸ **grey squirrel** ardilla *f* gris ▸ **grey vote** voto *m* de la tercera edad ▸ **grey water** aguas *fpl* grises ▸ **grey wolf** lobo *m* gris

greybeard, graybeard (*US*) ['greɪbɪəd] N (*liter*) anciano *m*, viejo *m*

grey-haired, gray-haired (*US*) ['greɪ'hɛəd] ADJ canoso

Greyhound ['greɪhaʊnd] N (*US*) (*also* **Greyhound bus**) autobús *m* de largo recorrido

greyhound, grayhound (*US*) ['greɪhaʊnd] N galgo/a *m/f*
CPD ▸ **greyhound racing** carreras *fpl* de galgos ▸ **greyhound track** canódromo *m*

> **GREYHOUND RACING**
> Las carreras de galgos son un deporte muy popular en el Reino Unido, sobre todo entre aquellos a quienes les gusta apostar. Los corredores de apuestas (**bookmakers**) tienen mucha clientela con las carreras que llaman **the dogs**. El canódromo puede ser ovalado o redondo y los galgos persiguen una liebre mecánica que corre sobre un carril.

greying, graying (*US*) ['greɪɪŋ] ADJ [*hair*] grisáceo, canoso

greyish, grayish (*US*) ['greɪɪʃ] ADJ grisáceo; [*hair*] entrecano

greyness, grayness (*US*) ['greɪnɪs] N
1 (= *grey colour*) [*of sky, clouds*] lo gris; [*of hair*] lo canoso
2 (= *bleakness*) [*of situation*] lo deprimente; [*of future*] lo poco prometedor • **the ~ of his suits exactly matched the ~ of his mind** el gris de sus trajes reflejaba lo gris de su mentalidad • **in a world full of ~ this was her only hope** en un mundo tan sombrío esta era su única esperanza

grid [grɪd] N **1** (= *grating*) (*in wall, pavement*) rejilla *f*
2 (*Brit*) (*Elec, Gas*) (= *network*) red *f* • **the (national) ~** la red nacional
3 (*on map*) cuadrícula *f*
4 (*US*) (*Sport*) = **gridiron**
CPD ▸ **grid map** mapa *m* cuadriculado ▸ **grid reference** coordenadas *fpl*

griddle ['grɪdl] N plancha *f*
VT asar a la plancha

gridiron ['grɪd,aɪən] N **1** (*Culin*) parrilla *f*
2 (*US*) (*Sport*) campo *m* de fútbol (americano)

gridlock ['grɪdlɒk] N **1** (*Aut*) embotellamiento *m*
2 (*fig*) punto *m* muerto

gridlocked ['grɪdlɒkt] ADJ **1** [*road*] paralizado • **traffic is ~ in the cities** el tráfico está paralizado en las ciudades
2 (*fig*) [*negotiations*] en un punto muerto

grief [gri:f] N **1** (= *sorrow*) pena *f*, dolor *m* • IDIOM: • **to come to ~** fracasar, ir al traste
2 (= *cause of sorrow*) tristeza *f*
3 (*Brit**) (= *trouble*) • **to give sb ~** dar problemas a algn, dar la vara a algn*
4 (*as exclamation*) • **good ~!** ¡demonio!

grief-stricken ['gri:f,strɪkən] ADJ apesadumbrado

grievance ['gri:vəns] N (= *complaint*) queja *f*; (= *cause for complaint*) motivo *m* de queja; [*of workers*] reivindicación *f* • **to have a ~**

against sb tener queja de algn
CPD ▸ **grievance procedure** sistema *m* de trámite de quejas

grieve [griːv] VT dar pena a, causar tristeza a, afligir • **it ~s me to see** … me da pena ver …
VI afligirse, acongojarse (**about, at** por) • **to ~ for sb** llorar la pérdida de algn

grieved [griːvd] ADJ [*tone etc*] lastimoso, apenado

grieving ['griːvɪŋ] ADJ [*family, relatives*] afligido • **the ~ process** el duelo

grievous ['griːvəs] ADJ [*loss etc*] doloroso, penoso; [*blow*] severo; [*pain*] fuerte; [*crime, offence, error*] grave; [*task*] penoso
CPD ▸ **grievous bodily harm** (*Jur*) daños *mpl* físicos graves, lesiones *fpl* corporales graves

grievously ['griːvəslɪ] ADV [*hurt, offend*] gravemente; [*err, be mistaken*] lamentablemente • **~ wounded** gravemente herido

griffin ['grɪfɪn] N grifo *m*

griffon ['grɪfən] N (= *dog*) grifón *m*

grifter‡ ['grɪftəʳ] N (*US*) estafador(a) *m/f*, timador(a) *m/f*

grill [grɪl] N **1** (*Brit*) (*on cooker, also restaurant*) parrilla *f*
2 (= *food*) parrillada *f* • **a mixed ~** una parrillada mixta
3 = grille
VT **1** (*Culin*) asar a la parrilla
2* (= *interrogate*) interrogar
CPD ▸ **grill room** parrilla *f*, grill *m*

grille [grɪl] N rejilla *f*; [*of window*] reja *f*; (= *screen*) verja *f*

grilled [grɪld] ADJ (*Culin*) (asado) a la parrilla

grilling* ['grɪlɪŋ] N (*fig*) interrogatorio *m* intenso • **to give sb a ~** interrogar a algn intensamente

grilse [grɪls] N salmón *m* joven (*que solo ha estado una vez en el mar*)

grim [grɪm] (COMPAR: **grimmer**, SUPERL: **grimmest**) ADJ **1** (= *gloomy*) [*news, situation, prospect*] desalentador; [*reminder*] duro, crudo; [*building, place, town*] sombrío, lúgubre • **where she made the ~ discovery of a body** donde hizo el macabro descubrimiento de un cadáver • **the situation looked ~** la situación se presentaba muy negra • **to paint a ~ picture of sth** pintar un cuadro muy negro de algo • **the ~ reality** la dura *or* cruda realidad • **the ~ truth** la cruda verdad • **he gave a ~ warning to the British people** hizo una advertencia nada alentadora al pueblo británico • **the weather has been ~** el tiempo ha estado deprimente
2 (= *stern*) [*person*] adusto; [*face, expression*] serio, adusto; [*smile*] forzado • **she hung** *or* **held on to the rope like ~ death** se agarró *or* aferró a la cuerda como si la vida le fuera en ello • **she walked on with ~ determination** siguió caminando con absoluta determinación • **he looked ~** tenía una expresión seria *or* adusta • **his voice was ~** su voz tenía un tono severo *or* adusto
3 (= *macabre*) [*humour, joke, story*] macabro
4* (= *awful*) [*experience, effect*] espantoso*, penoso* • **it was pretty ~** fue bastante espantoso *or* penoso* • **to feel ~** estar *or* encontrarse fatal*
CPD ▸ **the Grim Reaper** (*liter*) la Parca, la muerte

grimace [grɪ'meɪs] N mueca *f*
VI hacer muecas

grime [graɪm] N mugre *f*, suciedad *f*

grimly ['grɪmlɪ] ADV (= *gravely*) gravemente; (= *determinedly*) denodadamente • **"he's badly hurt," she said ~** —está muy malherido —dijo gravemente *or* en tono grave, —está gravemente herido —dijo con seriedad • **"this isn't good enough," he said ~** —esto no vale —dijo con seriedad • **he fought ~ to keep afloat** luchó con todas sus fuerzas *or* denodadamente para mantenerse a flote • **his face was ~ determined** tenía una expresión de total determinación • **"I'll be careful," he smiled ~** —tendré cuidado —dijo con una sonrisa forzada

grimness ['grɪmnɪs] N **1** (= *gloominess*) [*of situation, outlook*] lo desalentador, lo funesto; [*of building, place, town*] lo sombrío, lo lúgubre
2 (= *sternness*) [*of expression, face*] seriedad *f*, gravedad *f* • **there was a ~ in his voice** su voz tenía un tono de seriedad *or* gravedad
3 (= *sinister quality*) [*of humour, joke, story*] lo macabro

grimy ['graɪmɪ] ADJ (COMPAR: **grimier**, SUPERL: **grimiest**) mugriento, sucio

grin [grɪn] N (= *smile*) sonrisa *f*; (*sardonic*) sonrisa *f* burlona; (= *grimace*) mueca *f*
VI sonreír abiertamente (**at a**) • IDIOM: • **to ~ and bear it** poner al mal tiempo buena cara

grind [graɪnd] (PT, PP: **ground**) VT **1** [+ *coffee*] moler; [+ *corn, flour*] moler, machacar; [+ *stone*] pulverizar; (*US*) (*Culin*) [+ *meat*] picar • **to ~ sth into** *or* **to a powder** reducir algo a polvo, pulverizar algo • **to ~ sth into the earth** clavar algo en el suelo • **to ~ one's teeth** rechinar los dientes
2 (= *sharpen*) [+ *knife*] amolar, afilar
3 (= *polish*) [+ *gem, lens*] esmerilar
VI [*machine etc*] funcionar con dificultad • **to ~ against** ludir ruidosamente con • **to ~ to a halt** *or* **standstill** pararse en seco
N* (= *dull hard work*) trabajo *m* pesado • **the work was such a ~** el trabajo era tan pesado • **the daily ~** la rutina diaria
▸ **grind away*** VI + ADV (= *work hard*) trabajar como un esclavo; (*Mus*) tocar laboriosamente • **to ~ away at grammar** empollar *or* machacar la gramática*
▸ **grind down** VT + ADV **1** (*lit*) pulverizar • **to ~ sth down to (a) powder** reducir algo a polvo, pulverizar algo
2 (= *wear away*) desgastar
3 (= *oppress*) agobiar, oprimir • **to ~ down the opposition** destruir lentamente a la oposición
▸ **grind on** VI + ADV • **the case went ~ing on for months** el pleito se desarrolló penosamente durante varios meses
▸ **grind out** VT + ADV [+ *tune*] tocar mecánicamente; [+ *essay, novel etc*] producir (*a costa de mucho esfuerzo*)
▸ **grind up** VT + ADV pulverizar

grinder ['graɪndəʳ] N **1** (= *machine*) (*for coffee*) molinillo *m*; (*US*) (*for meat*) picadora *f* de carne
2 (*for sharpening*) afiladora *f*
3 (= *person*) molendero/a *m/f*; (*Tech*) amolador *m*; ▹ organ-grinder
4 grinders (= *teeth*) muelas *fpl*

grinding ['graɪndɪŋ] ADJ **1** • **~ sound** rechinamiento *m* • **to come to a ~ halt** [*vehicle, traffic*] detenerse en seco; [*work, progress*] llegar a un punto muerto, estancarse
2 • **~ poverty** miseria *f* (absoluta)
N [*of coffee*] molienda *f*; [*of stone*] pulverización *f*; [*of knife*] afilado *m*

grindingly ['graɪndɪŋlɪ] ADV • **a ~ familiar routine** una rutina tremendamente monótona • **~ poor** pobrísimo

grindstone ['graɪndstəʊn] N muela *f* • IDIOM: • **to keep one's nose to the ~** batir el yunque

gringo*‡ ['grɪŋgəʊ] N (*US*) (*pej*) gringo/a *m/f*

grip [grɪp] N **1** (= *handclasp*) apretón *m* (de manos) • **he lost his ~ on the branch** se le escapó la rama de las manos, la rama se le fue de las manos
2 (*fig*) • **in the ~ of winter** paralizado por el invierno • **in the ~ of a strike** paralizado por una huelga • **to come to ~s with** luchar a brazo partido con • **to get to ~s with sth/sb** enfrentarse con algo/algn • **he lost his ~ of the situation** la situación se le fue de las manos • **to have a good ~ of a subject** entender algo a fondo • **get a ~ (on yourself)!*** ¡cálmate!, ¡contrólate!
3 (= *handle*) asidero *m*, asa *f*; [*of weapon*] empuñadura *f*
4 (= *bag*) maletín *m*, bolsa *f*
VT **1** (= *hold*) agarrar, asir; [+ *weapon*] empuñar; [+ *hands*] apretar, estrechar • **the wheels ~ the road** las ruedas se agarran a la carretera
2 (*fig*) (= *enthrall*) fascinar; [*fear*] apoderarse de • **~ped by fear** presa del pánico
VI [*wheel*] agarrarse

gripe [graɪp] N **1*** (= *complaint*) queja *f*
2 (*Med*) (*also* **gripes**) retortijón *m* de tripas
VI* (= *complain*) quejarse (**about** de)
VT* (= *anger*) dar rabia a

griping ['graɪpɪŋ] ADJ [*pain*] retortijante
N* quejadumbre *f*

gripping ['grɪpɪŋ] ADJ [*story, novel*] absorbente, muy emocionante

grisly ['grɪzlɪ] ADJ (COMPAR: **grislier**, SUPERL: **grisliest**) (= *horrible*) horroroso; (= *horrifying*) horripilante

grist [grɪst] N • IDIOM: • **it's all ~ to the mill** de todo hay que sacar provecho

gristle ['grɪsl] N cartílago *m*, ternilla *f*

gristly ['grɪslɪ] ADJ cartilaginoso, ternilloso

grit [grɪt] N **1** (= *gravel*) grava *f*; (*for caged birds, poultry*) arenilla *f* silícea, arena *f*; (= *dust*) polvo *m*
2 (*fig*) (= *courage*) valor *m*, ánimo *m*; (= *firmness of character*) firmeza *f*; (= *endurance*) aguante *m*
3 grits (*US*) (*Culin*) sémola *fsing*
VT **1** [+ *road*] echar grava a
2 • **to ~ one's teeth** apretar los dientes

gritter ['grɪtəʳ] N (= *vehicle*) *vehículo que suelta grava o arena en las carreteras en tiempo de heladas*

gritty ['grɪtɪ] ADJ (COMPAR: **grittier**, SUPERL: **grittiest**) **1** (= *grainy*) [*soil, powder, texture*] arenoso; [*surface, floor*] arenoso, granuloso • **the sheets felt ~** las sábanas parecían tener arena
2 (= *courageous*) [*person, display, performance*] enérgico, resuelto • **~ determination** obstinada determinación
3 (= *true to life*) [*drama, story, portrayal*] crudo

grizzle ['grɪzl] VI (*Brit*) (= *whine*) quejumbrar

grizzled ['grɪzld] ADJ [*hair*] entrecano

grizzly ['grɪzlɪ] ADJ **1** (= *grey*) gris, canoso
2* (= *whining*) quejumbroso
N (*also* **grizzly bear**) oso *m* pardo

groan [grəʊn] N [*of pain, dismay etc*] gemido *m*, quejido *m*; (= *mumble*) gruñido *m*
VI **1** gemir, quejarse; (= *mumble*) gruñir, refunfuñar
2 (= *creak*) [*tree, gate etc*] crujir • **borrowers are ~ing under the burden of high interest rates** los prestatarios están agobiados por la carga de los altos tipos de interés • **the table ~ed under the weight of all the food** la mesa crujía bajo el peso de toda esa comida
VT • **"yes," he ~ed** —sí —gimió

groats [grəʊts] NPL avena *fsing* a medio moler

grocer ['grəʊsəʳ] N (*esp Brit*) tendero/a *m/f*, almacenero/a *m/f* (*S. Cone*), abarrotero/a *m/f* (*And, Mex, CAm*), bodeguero/a *m/f* (*And, Carib, CAm*) • **~'s (shop)** tienda *f* de comestibles,

g

almacén *m* (*S. Cone*), tienda *f* de abarrotes (*And, Mex, CAm*), bodega *f* (*And, Carib, CAm*)

groceries ['grəʊsərɪz] NPL comestibles *mpl*, abarrotes *mpl* (*LAm*)

grocery ['grəʊsərɪ] N (*US*) (*also* **grocery store**) tienda *f* de comestibles, tienda de abarrotes (*And, Mex, CAm*), almacén *m* (*S. Cone*), bodega *f* (*And, Carib, CAm*)

grog [grɒg] N grog *m*

groggily ['grɒgɪlɪ] ADV como atontado, como grogui *or* zombi

groggy ['grɒgɪ] ADJ (COMPAR: **groggier**, SUPERL: **groggiest**) (*from blow*) atontado; (*from alcohol*) tambaleante; (*Boxing*) groggy, grogui • **I feel a bit ~** estoy un poco mareado

groin [grɔɪn] N (*Anat*) ingle *f*
CPD ▸ **groin injury, groin strain** lesión *f* inguinal, lesión *f* en la ingle

grommet ['grɒmɪt] N (*Brit*) (*Med*) tubo *m* de drenaje

groom [gru:m] N **1** (*in stable*) mozo *m* de cuadra
2 (= *bridegroom*) novio *m*
VT **1** [+ *horse*] almohazar, cuidar • **to ~ o.s.** acicalarse • **the cat was ~ing itself** el gato se lamía • **well ~ed** [*person*] muy acicalado
2 (= *prepare*) [+ *person*] • **to ~ sb as/to be** preparar a algn para/para ser • **to ~ sb for a post** preparar a algn para un puesto
3 [*paedophile*] [+ *child*] ganarse la confianza de

groomed ['gru:md] ADJ arreglado

grooming ['gru:mɪŋ] N **1** (*gen, also well-groomedness*) acicalamiento *m*
2 [*of horse*] almohazamiento *m*; [*of dog*] cepillado *m*

groove [gru:v] N **1** (*in wood, metal etc*) ranura *f*, estría *f*; [*of record*] surco *m* • IDIOM: • **to be (stuck) in a ~** estar metido en una rutina
2 • **to be in the ~*** estar en forma
3 (*Mus**) (= *rhythm*) ritmo *m*
VT (= *put groove in*) estriar, acanalar
VI* (= *dance*) bailar

grooved [gru:vd] ADJ estriado, acanalado

groovy* ['gru:vɪ] ADJ (COMPAR: **groovier**, SUPERL: **grooviest**) (= *marvellous*) estupendo*, total*, guay (*Sp**)

grope [grəʊp] VI (*also* **grope around, grope about**) andar a tientas, tantear • **to ~ for sth** (*lit, fig*) buscar algo a tientas
VT **1** • **to ~ one's way (through/towards)** avanzar a tientas (por/hacia)
2* • **to ~ sb** (*sexually*) toquetear a algn
N* (*sexual*) • **they had a ~** se estuvieron toqueteando, se estuvieron metiendo mano*

grosgrain ['grəʊgreɪn] N grogrén *m*, cordellate *m*

gross [grəʊs] (COMPAR: **grosser**, SUPERL: **grossest**) ADJ **1** (= *unacceptable*) [*injustice, inequality, mismanagement*] flagrante; [*exaggeration, simplification*] burdo • **a ~ injustice has been done to him** se ha cometido una flagrante injusticia con él • **~ ignorance** ignorancia *f* supina, crasa ignorancia *f* • **~ incompetence** incompetencia *f* absoluta • **~ violations of human rights** flagrantes violaciones de los derechos humanos • **that is a ~ understatement** eso es quedarse muy corto
2 (= *revolting*) [*person, remark, joke*] ordinario, basto • **he's totally ~*** es de lo más basto • **(how) ~!*** ¡qué asco!*
3 (= *tasteless*) ordinario, de muy mal gusto • **she was wearing really ~ earrings** llevaba unos pendientes de lo más ordinario *or* de un gusto pésimo
4 (= *obese*) gordísimo, cebón* • **after eating so much chocolate she felt really ~*** después de comer tanto chocolate se sentía como una bola *or* foca*
5 (= *total*) [*income, profit, weight*] bruto • **their ~ income is £205 a week** sus ingresos brutos son de 205 libras a la semana • **its ~ weight is 100 grams** su peso bruto es de 100 gramos
ADV (= *in total*) [*earn, pay, weigh*] en bruto • **she earns £30,000 ~ per annum** gana 30.000 libras al año brutas *or* en bruto • **it weighs 12kg ~** pesa 12 kilos brutos *or* en bruto • **how much do you earn ~?** ¿cuánto ganas bruto *or* en bruto?
VT (*Comm*) (*gen*) obtener unos ingresos brutos de; (*from savings, bonds*) obtener unos beneficios brutos de • **the company ~ed $100,000 last year** el año pasado la compañía obtuvo unos beneficios brutos de 100.000 dólares
N **1** (PL: **grosses**) (= *total income*) ingresos *mpl* brutos
2 (PL: **gross**) (= *twelve dozen*) doce docenas *fpl* • **he bought them by the ~** los compró en cantidades de doce docenas
CPD ▸ **gross domestic product** (*Econ*) producto *m* interno bruto ▸ **gross indecency** (*Jur*) ultraje *m* contra la moral pública ▸ **gross margin** margen *m* bruto ▸ **gross misconduct** falta *f* grave ▸ **gross national product** (*Econ*) producto *m* nacional bruto ▸ **gross negligence** (*Jur*) culpa *f* grave ▸ **gross output** (*Ind*) producción *f* bruta

▸ **gross out*** VT + ADV (*US*) asquear, dar asco a

▸ **gross up** VT + ADV (*US*) [+ *salary etc*] recaudar en bruto

grossly ['grəʊslɪ] ADV **1** (= *extremely*) [*unfair, inadequate*] sumamente; [*inaccurate, negligent, inefficient*] sumamente, extremadamente; [*misleading, incompetent, irresponsible, exaggerated*] sumamente, tremendamente; [*mislead*] de forma escandalosa • **he is ~ overweight** está obeso, está gordísimo* • **the police were ~ negligent** la policía incurrió en graves negligencias • **many employees are ~ underpaid** muchos empleados perciben unos sueldos extremadamente bajos
2 (= *crassly*) burdamente • **he didn't put it as ~ as that** no lo puso en términos tan crudos

grossness ['grəʊsnɪs] N **1** (= *fatness*) obesidad *f*, gordura *f*
2 (= *seriousness*) [*of crime, abuse*] crudeza *f*
3 (= *tastelessness*) [*of joke, language, behaviour*] ordinariez *f*

grot* [grɒt] N (= *dirt*) porquería *f*

grotesque [grəʊ'tesk] ADJ **1** (= *hideous*) [*appearance, idea, sight, spectacle*] grotesco; [*allegation, proposal*] absurdo
2 (*Art*) grotesco
N grotesco *m*

grotesquely [grəʊ'tesklɪ] ADV grotescamente; [*exaggerated*] bestialmente; [*insensitive*] brutalmente • **it was ~ unfair** fue tremendamente injusto

grotto ['grɒtəʊ] N (PL: **grottos** *or* **grottoes**) gruta *f*

grotty* ['grɒtɪ] ADJ (COMPAR: **grottier**, SUPERL: **grottiest**) (*Brit*) asqueroso • **I feel ~** me siento fatal*

grouch* [graʊtʃ] VI refunfuñar, quejarse
N **1** (= *person*) refunfuñón/ona *m/f*, cascarrabias *mf inv*
2 (= *complaint*) queja *f*

grouchiness* ['graʊtʃɪnɪs] N humos *mpl*, malas pulgas *fpl*

grouchy* ['graʊtʃɪ] ADJ (COMPAR: **grouchier**, SUPERL: **grouchiest**) malhumorado

ground[1] [graʊnd] N **1** (= *soil*) tierra *f*, suelo *m*
2 (= *terrain*) terreno *m* • **high/hilly ~** terreno *m* alto/montañoso • **to break new ~** hacer algo nuevo • **common ~** terreno *m* común • **to cover a lot of ~** (*lit*) recorrer una gran distancia • **he covered a lot of ~ in his lecture** abarcó mucho en la clase • **to be on dangerous ~** entrar en territorio peligroso • **to be on firm ~** hablar con conocimiento de causa • **to gain ~** ganar terreno • **to go to ~** [*fox*] meterse en su madriguera; [*person*] esconderse, refugiarse • **to hold one's ~** (*lit*) no ceder terreno; (*fig*) mantenerse firme • **to be on (one's) home ~** tratar materia que uno conoce a fondo • **to lose ~** perder terreno • **to run sb to ~** localizar (por fin) a algn, averiguar el paradero de algn • **to shift one's ~** cambiar de postura • **to stand one's ~** (*lit*) no ceder terreno; (*fig*) mantenerse firme • **to be on sure ~** hablar con conocimiento de causa • IDIOMS: • **to cut the ~ from under sb's feet** quitarle terreno a algn • **it suits me down to the ~** me conviene perfectamente, me viene de perilla; ▹ **prepare**
3 (= *surface*) suelo *m*, tierra *f* • **above ~** sobre la tierra • **below ~** debajo de la tierra • **to fall to the ~** (*lit*) caerse al suelo; (*fig*) fracasar • **to get off the ~** [*aircraft*] despegar; [*plans etc*] ponerse en marcha • **on the ~** en el suelo; ▹ **raze**
4 (= *pitch*) terreno *m*, campo *m* • **they won on their own ~** ganaron en su propio terreno; ▹ **parade, recreation**
5 (= *estate, property*) tierras *fpl*
6 grounds (= *gardens*) jardines *mpl*, parque *msing*
7 (*Art etc*) (= *background*) fondo *m*, trasfondo *m* • **on a blue ~** sobre un fondo azul
8 (*US*) (*Elec*) tierra *f*
9 (= *reason*) (*usu pl*) razón *f*, motivo *m*; (= *basis*) fundamento *m* • **~s for complaint** motivos *mpl* de queja • **what ~(s) do you have for saying so?** ¿en qué se basa para decir eso? • **on the ~(s) of …** con motivo de …, por causa de …, debido a … • **on the ~(s) that …** a causa de que …, por motivo de que … • **on good ~s** con razón • **on medical ~s** por razones de salud
VT **1** [+ *ship*] varar, hacer encallar
2 [+ *plane, pilot*] obligar a permanecer en tierra • **he ordered the planes to be ~ed** ordenó que permaneciesen los aviones en tierra • **to be ~ed by bad weather** no poder despegar por el mal tiempo
3 (*US*) (*Elec*) conectar con tierra
4 (= *teach*) • **to ~ sb in maths** enseñar a algn los rudimentos de las matemáticas • **to be well ~ed in** tener un buen conocimiento de, estar versado en
5 (*esp US*) [+ *student*] encerrar, no dejar salir
VI (*Naut*) encallar, varar; (*lightly*) tocar (**on** en)
CPD ▸ **ground attack** ataque *m* de tierra; (*Aer*) ataque *m* a superficie ▸ **ground bass** bajo *m* rítmico ▸ **ground cloth** = **groundcloth** ▸ **ground colour** fondo *m*, primera capa *f* ▸ **ground control** (*Aer*) control *m* desde tierra ▸ **ground crew** (*Aer*) personal *m* de tierra ▸ **ground floor** (*Brit*) planta *f* baja • **~-floor flat** (*Brit*) piso *m or* (*LAm*) departamento *m* de planta baja • IDIOM: • **he got in on the ~ floor** empezó por abajo ▸ **ground forces** (*Mil*) fuerzas *fpl* de tierra ▸ **ground frost** escarcha *f* ▸ **ground ivy** hiedra *f* terrestre ▸ **ground level** nivel *m* del suelo ▸ **ground plan** plano *m*, planta *f* ▸ **ground pollution** contaminación *f* del suelo ▸ **ground rent** (*esp Brit*) alquiler *m* del terreno ▸ **ground rules** reglas *fpl* básicas • **we can't change the ~ rules at this stage** a estas alturas no podemos cambiar las reglas ▸ **ground staff** = **ground crew** ▸ **ground troops** tropas *fpl* de tierra

▸ **ground wire** *(US)* cable *m* de toma de tierra ▸ **Ground Zero** *(in New York)* zona *f* cero

ground² [graʊnd] (PT), (PP) *of* **grind**
(ADJ) *[coffee etc]* molido; *[glass]* deslustrado; *(US) [meat]* picado
(N) **grounds** *[of coffee]* poso *msing*, sedimento *msing*
(CPD) ▸ **ground almonds** almendras *fpl* molidas ▸ **ground beef** *(US)* picadillo *m*

groundbait ['graʊnd,beɪt] (N) cebo *m* de fondo

groundbreaking ['graʊnd,breɪkɪŋ] (ADJ) *[research, work, book]* revolucionario

groundcloth ['graʊndklɒθ] (N) *(US)* = groundsheet

grounder ['graʊndəʳ] (N) *(US) (Sport)* bola *f* a ras de suelo

groundhog ['graʊndhɒg] (N) *(US)* marmota *f* de América

GROUNDHOG DAY
Groundhog Day (el día de la marmota) es una simpática tradición estadounidense según la cual se puede predecir supuestamente la duración del invierno. La marmota (en inglés **groundhog**, o **ground squirrel**, o **woodchuck**) despierta de su hibernación el dos de febrero (**Groundhog Day**). Si hace sol, el animal se asusta al ver su propia sombra y vuelve a su madriguera durante otras seis semanas, lo cual indica que el invierno será más largo. El acontecimiento tiene tal importancia que es televisado a todo el país desde la madriguera más famosa de Punxsutawney, en Pensilvania.

grounding ['graʊndɪŋ] (N) **1** *(Naut)* varada *f*
2 *(in education)* conocimientos *mpl* básicos • **to give sb a ~ in** enseñar a algn los rudimentos de

groundkeeper ['graʊnd,kiːpəʳ], **groundskeeper** *(US)* (N) encargado *m (del mantenimiento de una pista de deporte)*

groundless ['graʊndlɪs] (ADJ) sin fundamento

groundnut ['graʊndnʌt] (N) *(Brit)* cacahuete *m (Sp)*, maní *m (LAm)*, cacahuate *m (Mex)*
(CPD) ▸ **groundnut oil** aceite *m* de cacahuete

groundsel ['graʊnsl] (N) hierba *f* cana

groundsheet ['graʊndʃiːt] (N) *(in tent)* aislante *m* (de tienda de campaña), suelo *m* (de tienda de campaña)

groundskeeper ['graʊndz,kiːpəʳ] (N) *(US)* = groundkeeper

groundsman ['graʊndzmən] (N) (PL: **groundsmen**) *(Brit) (Sport)* encargado *m (del mantenimiento de una pista de deporte)*

groundspeed ['graʊnd,spiːd] (N) *(Aer)* velocidad *f* respecto a la tierra

groundswell ['graʊndswel] (N) mar *m* de fondo; *(fig)* marejada *f*

ground-to-air ['graʊndtʊ'ɛəʳ] (ADJ) tierra-aire • **ground-to-air missile** misil *m* tierra-aire

ground-to-ground ['graʊndtə'graʊnd] (ADJ) tierra-tierra • **ground-to-ground missile** misil *m* tierra-tierra

groundwater ['graʊndwɔːtəʳ] (N) agua *f* subterránea, aguas *fpl* superficiales

groundwork ['graʊndwɜːk] (N) trabajo *m* preliminar *or* preparatorio • **to do the ~ for sth** poner las bases de algo

group [gruːp] (N) **1** *[of people, objects]* grupo *m*; *(for specific purpose)* agrupación *f*, asociación *f*; *(= gang)* pandilla *f*, banda *f*; *(Mus)* conjunto *m*, grupo *m*; *[of languages]* familia *f* • **they stood in a ~** estaban en grupo • **ethnic ~** grupo *m* étnico • **family ~** familia *f*, grupo *m* familiar • **a human rights ~** una agrupación *or* asociación pro derechos humanos; ▹ **interest, support**
2 *(Comm) [of companies]* grupo *m*
(VT) *(also* **group together***)* agrupar • **we ~ the children by ability** agrupamos a los niños según sus habilidades • **we ~ed ourselves around the piano** nos agrupamos alrededor del piano • **the report's conclusions are ~ed together under one heading** las conclusiones del informe están agrupadas bajo un mismo encabezamiento
(VI) agruparse • **the children ~ed around her** los niños se agruparon alrededor de ella
(CPD) ▸ **group booking** reserva *f* hecha para un grupo ▸ **group captain** *(Brit) (Aer)* jefe *m* de escuadrilla ▸ **group discussion** debate *m* en grupo ▸ **group dynamics** dinámica *fsing* de grupo ▸ **group photo** foto *f* de conjunto ▸ **group practice** *(Med)* consultorio *m* (de médicos) ▸ **group sex** sexo *m* en grupo ▸ **group therapy** terapia *f* de grupo

GROUP

Agreement

▹ *When* **grupo** *is followed by* **de** *+ plural noun, following verbs can be in the plural or, less commonly, in the singular:*
A group of youths came up to him
Un grupo de jóvenes se le acercaron *or* se le acercó

▹ *Otherwise, use the singular form of the verb:*
The group is *or* **are well-known for being aggressive**
El grupo es conocido por su agresividad

For further uses and examples, see main entry.

grouper ['gruːpəʳ] (N) *(= fish)* mero *m*

groupie* ['gruːpɪ] (N) grupi* *mf, fan de un grupo pop*

grouping ['gruːpɪŋ] (N) agrupamiento *m*

groupware ['gruːpwɛəʳ] (N) *(Comput)* groupware *m*

grouse¹ [graʊs] (N) (PL: **grouse** *or* **grouses**) *(Orn)* urogallo *m* • **black ~** gallo *m* lira • **red ~** lagópodo *m* escocés

grouse²* [graʊs] (N) *(= complaint)* queja *f*
(VI) quejarse (**about** de)

grout [graʊt] (N) lechada *f*
(VT) enlechar

grouting ['graʊtɪŋ] (N) lechada *f*

grove [grəʊv] (N) arboleda *f*, bosquecillo *m* • **~ of pines** pineda *f* • **~ of poplars** alameda *f*

grovel ['grɒvl] (VI) *(lit, fig)* arrastrarse (**to** ante)

grovelling, groveling *(US)* ['grɒvlɪŋ] (ADJ) rastrero, servil

grow [grəʊ] (PT: **grew**, PP: **grown**) (VI) **1** *[plant, hair, person, animal]* crecer • **how you've ~n!** ¡cómo has crecido! • **he has ~n five centimetres** ha crecido cinco centímetros • **she's letting her hair ~** se está dejando crecer el pelo, se está dejando el pelo largo • **the hair will ~ back eventually** con el tiempo le volverá a crecer el pelo • **that plant does not ~ in England** esa planta no crece *or* no se da en Inglaterra • **will it ~ here?** ¿se puede cultivar aquí? • **to ~ to** *or* **into manhood** llegar a la edad adulta • **these sharks can ~ to six metres** estos tiburones pueden llegar a medir hasta seis metros
2 *(= increase) (in number, amount)* aumentar • **the number of unemployed has ~n by more than 10,000** el número de parados ha aumentado en más de 10.000 • **the economy continues to ~** la economía sigue en su fase de crecimiento • **opposition grew and the government agreed to negotiate** la oposición cobró más fuerza y el gobierno decidió entrar en negociaciones • **the winds grew to gale force** la intensidad del viento aumentó hasta alcanzar velocidades de temporal • **to ~ in popularity** ganar popularidad • **she has ~n in my esteem** se ha ganado mi estima
3 *(= develop) [friendship, love]* desarrollarse; *[person]* madurar • **I feel I have ~n immensely as a result of the experience** siento que he madurado muchísimo como consecuencia de la experiencia • **to ~ spiritually** madurar espiritualmente
4 *(with adjective) (= become)* volverse, ponerse, hacerse *(but often translated by vi or reflexive)* • **our eyes gradually grew accustomed to the light** los ojos se nos fueron acostumbrando a la luz • **to ~ angry** enfadarse • **the light grew brighter** la luz se hizo más intensa • **to ~ cold**: • **the coffee had ~n cold** el café se había enfriado • **we grew colder as the night wore on** a medida que pasaba la noche nos fue entrando cada vez más frío • **it's ~n a lot colder, hasn't it?** ha enfriado mucho ¿verdad? • **to ~ dark** *(gen)* oscurecer; *(at dusk)* oscurecer, anochecer • **to ~ fat** engordar • **her eyes grew heavy** se le cerraban los ojos • **she has ~n quite knowledgeable on the subject** ha aprendido mucho sobre el tema • **the noise grew louder** el ruido aumentó de volumen • **to ~ old** envejecer(se) • **you will realize this as you ~ older** te darás cuenta de esto a medida que te hagas mayor • **he grew tired of waiting** se cansó de esperar • **to ~ used to sth** acostumbrarse a algo • **she grew weaker with each passing day** se fue debilitando día tras día • **to ~ worse**: • **the housing shortage is ~ing worse** la escasez de viviendas es cada vez mayor • **she grew worse that day and died during the night** ese día se puso peor *or* su condición empeoró y murió durante la noche
5 • **to ~ to like sb** llegar a querer a algn, encariñarse con algn • **he grew to love his work** llegó a tomarle gusto a su trabajo • **in time he grew to accept it** con el tiempo llegó a aceptarlo
(VT) **1** *[+ plant, crop]* cultivar • **I ~ my own vegetables** tengo mi propio huerto, cultivo mis verduras
2 *[+ hair, beard, moustache, nails]* dejarse crecer • **she has ~n her hair long** se ha dejado el pelo largo, se ha dejado crecer el pelo • **the lizard grew a new tail** al lagarto le salió una cola nueva

▸ **grow apart** (VI + ADV) *[friends]* distanciarse; *[couple]* • **he and his wife grew apart** la relación entre él y su mujer se entibió *or* se debilitó • **couples often ~ apart as they get older** a menudo las parejas se van distanciando con la edad

▸ **grow away from** (VI + PREP) distanciarse de • **we have ~n away from each other** nos hemos distanciado el uno del otro

▸ **grow from** (VI + PREP) *[friendship, theory, idea]* surgir de, nacer de • **I started out with just two clients and the business grew from that** empecé con solo dos clientes y el negocio surgió *or* nació de ahí

▸ **grow in** (VI + ADV) *[nail]* crecer hacia adentro

▸ **grow into** (VI + PREP) **1** *[+ clothes]* • **the trousers are a bit big but he'll ~ into them** los pantalones son un poco grandes pero ya crecerá y le sentarán bien
2 *(= get used to)* • **to ~ into a job** acostumbrarse a un trabajo

g

3 (= *become*) convertirse en • **he's ~n into quite a handsome boy** se ha convertido en un chico muy apuesto • **to ~ into a man** hacerse un hombre

▸ **grow on** (VI + PREP) • **the tune ~s on you after a while** la melodía te empieza a gustar con el tiempo • **the idea had ~n on her all morning** a medida que avanzó la mañana le fue gustando más la idea

▸ **grow out** (VI + ADV) • **she let her perm ~ out** se dejó crecer el pelo para cortarse la permanente
(VT + ADV) [+ *hair*] dejar crecer

▸ **grow out of** (VI + PREP) **1** (= *get too big for*) [+ *clothes*] • **you've ~n out of your shoes again** se te han vuelto a quedar pequeños los zapatos
2 (= *stop*) [+ *habit*] • **isn't it time you grew out of fighting with your sister?** ¿no te estás haciendo un poco mayor para seguir peleándote con tu hermana? • **most children who stammer ~ out of it** a casi todos los niños el tartamudeo se les quita con la edad • **she grew out of the habit of waiting up for the children** con el tiempo perdió la costumbre de esperar a los niños despierta
3 (= *arise from*) surgir de

▸ **grow together** (VI + ADV) • **couples who have ~n together over the years** parejas que han ido uniéndose más con el paso de los años • **there are many ways in which Europe can ~ together** hay muchas formas en las que los países europeos pueden reforzar sus vínculos

▸ **grow up** (VI + ADV) **1** (= *become adult*) hacerse mayor • **I watched Tim ~ up** vi a Tim hacerse mayor, vi como Tim se hacía mayor • **when I ~ up I'm going to be a doctor** cuando sea mayor voy a ser médico • **she grew up into a beautiful woman** con el tiempo se convirtió en una mujer hermosa • **~ up!*** ¡no seas niño!
2 (= *spend young life*) crecer • **we grew up together** crecimos juntos • **she grew up in the country/during the depression** creció *or* se crió en el campo/en los años de la depresión
3 (= *develop*) [*friendship*] desarrollarse; [*hatred*] crecer; [*town, industry*] desarrollarse, crecer; [*custom*] arraigar, imponerse • **a close friendship had ~n up between us** entre nosotros se había desarrollado una íntima amistad • **a barrier had ~n up between them** se había levantado una barrera entre ellos • **new industries grew up alongside the port** nuevas industrias se desarrollaron alrededor del puerto

growbag ['grəʊbæg] (N) bolsa *f* de cultivo

grower ['grəʊəʳ] (N) cultivador(a) *m/f*

growing ['grəʊɪŋ] (ADJ) **1** (= *developing*) **a** (*Bot, Agr*) [*crop, plant*] que está creciendo
b [*child*] en edad de crecimiento
2 (= *expanding, increasing*) [*business*] en fase de desarrollo; [*friendship*] creciente; [*population, family*] creciente • **there is ~ concern that he won't be found alive** cada vez es mayor la preocupación de no encontrarlo con vida • **there is a ~ demand for this service** está aumentando la demanda de este servicio • **with ~ horror we realized that ...** cada vez más horrorizados, nos dimos cuenta de que ... • **a ~ number of refugees** un número creciente *or* cada vez mayor de refugiados • **I felt a ~ sense of unease** me sentía cada vez más nervioso
(CPD) ▸ **growing pains** (*lit*) dolores *mpl* de crecimiento; (*fig*) problemas *mpl* iniciales ▸ **growing season** [*of crop*] época *f* de cultivo; [*of plant*] época *f* de crecimiento

growl [graʊl] (N) gruñido *m*
(VI) [*animal*] gruñir; [*person*] refunfuñar; [*thunder*] reverberar
(VT) • **"yes," he ~ed** —sí —refunfuñó

grown [grəʊn] (PP) *of* **grow**
(ADJ) (*also* **fully grown**) adulto, maduro

grown-up ['grəʊn'ʌp] (ADJ) adulto
(N) adulto/a *m/f*, persona *f* mayor

growth [grəʊθ] (N) **1** (= *development*) [*of person, animal, plant*] crecimiento *m* • **spiritual ~** desarrollo *m* espiritual
2 (= *expansion*) [*of city*] crecimiento *m*; (*Econ*) crecimiento *m*, desarrollo *m* • **the ~ of national industries** el desarrollo *or* el crecimiento de las industrias nacionales; ▹ **capital**
3 (= *increase*) (*in productivity, profits, demand*) aumento *m* • **population ~** crecimiento *m* demográfico
4 (*Bot*) (= *vegetation*) vegetación *f*; (= *buds, leaves*) brotes *mpl* • **the pine tree was putting out new ~** el pino estaba echando brotes nuevos
5 (= *beard*) • **with three days' ~ on his face** con barba de tres días
6 (*Med*) tumor *m*
(CPD) ▸ **growth area** (*Econ*) [*of country*] polo *m* de desarrollo; [*of industry*] sector *m* en crecimiento *or* expansión ▸ **growth hormone** hormona *f* del crecimiento ▸ **growth industry** industria *f* en crecimiento *or* expansión ▸ **growth point** punto *m* de desarrollo ▸ **growth potential** potencial *m* de crecimiento ▸ **growth rate** (*Econ*) tasa *f* de crecimiento ▸ **growth shares** (*US*) = **growth stock** ▸ **growth stock** acciones *fpl* con perspectivas de valorización ▸ **growth town** ciudad *f* en vías de desarrollo

groyne [grɔɪn] (N) espolón *m*

GRSM (N ABBR) (*Brit*) = **Graduate of the Royal Schools of Music**

GRT (N ABBR) (= **gross register tons**) TRB *fpl*

grub [grʌb] (N) **1** (= *larva*) larva *f*, gusano *m*
2‡ (= *food*) comida *f* • **~('s) up!** ¡la comida está servida!
(VI) • **to ~ about in the earth for sth** remover la tierra buscando algo
(CPD) ▸ **Grub Street*†** (*Brit*) *el mundillo de los escritores desconocidos*

▸ **grub up** (VT + ADV) arrancar, desarraigar; (= *discover*) desenterrar

grubbiness ['grʌbɪnɪs] (N) suciedad *f*

grubby ['grʌbɪ] (ADJ) (COMPAR: **grubbier**, SUPERL: **grubbiest**) (= *dirty*) mugriento, sucio, mugroso (*LAm*)

grudge [grʌdʒ] (N) resentimiento *m*, rencor *m* (**against** a) • **to bear sb a ~** • **to have a ~ against sb** guardar rencor a algn
(VT) **1** (= *give unwillingly*) dar de mala gana • **to ~ sb sth** dar algo a algn a regañadientes
2 (= *envy*) envidiar • **I don't ~ you your success** no te envidio el éxito • **he ~s us our pleasures** mira con malos ojos nuestros placeres
3 (= *resent*) • **to ~ doing sth** hacer algo de mala gana
(CPD) ▸ **grudge match*** (*Sport*) enfrentamiento *m* entre antagonistas, enfrentamiento *m* entre rivales inconciliables; (*fig*) enfrentamiento *m* personal

grudging ['grʌdʒɪŋ] (ADJ) [*attitude, praise*] reticente • **he earned the ~ admiration/respect of his rivals** se ganó, aunque con reticencias, el respeto/la admiración de sus rivales • **she gave us a ~ apology** se disculpó de mala gana *or* a regañadientes

grudgingly ['grʌdʒɪŋlɪ] (ADV) de mala gana, a regañadientes

gruel [grʊəl] (N) gachas *fpl*

gruelling, grueling (*US*) ['grʊəlɪŋ] (ADJ) [*task*] penoso, duro; [*match, race*] agotador

gruesome ['gru:səm] (ADJ) espantoso, horrible

gruesomely ['gru:səmlɪ] (ADV) (= *horribly*) espantosamente

gruff [grʌf] (ADJ) (COMPAR: **gruffer**, SUPERL: **gruffest**) [*voice*] ronco; [*manner*] brusco

gruffly ['grʌflɪ] (ADV) bruscamente

gruffness ['grʌfnɪs] (N) [*of voice*] ronquera *f*; [*of person, manner*] brusquedad *f*

grumble ['grʌmbl] (N) **1** (= *complaint*) queja *f*
2 (= *noise*) retumbo *m*
(VI) **1** (= *complain*) quejarse (**about** de)
2 [*thunder*] retumbar (a lo lejos)

grumbler ['grʌmbləʳ] (N) quejica *mf*

grumbling ['grʌmblɪŋ] (N) • **I couldn't stand his constant ~** no podía soportar que estuviera gruñendo todo el rato
(ADJ) [*person, tone*] gruñón • **~ sound** gruñido *m* • **a ~ appendix** síntomas *mpl* de apendicitis

grump* [grʌmp] (N) **1** (= *person*) • **to be a ~** ser un gruñón
2 (= *bad mood*) • **to be in a ~** • **to have the ~s** estar de mal humor

grumpily* ['grʌmpɪlɪ] (ADV) gruñonamente, malhumoradamente

grumpiness* ['grʌmpɪnɪs] (N) mal humor *m*

grumpy* ['grʌmpɪ] (ADJ) (COMPAR: **grumpier**, SUPERL: **grumpiest**) [*person*] malhumorado, gruñón; [*voice*] de gruñón

grunge ['grʌndʒ] (N) (= *musical style*) grunge *m*

grungy* ['grʌndʒɪ] (ADJ) (COMPAR: **grungier**, SUPERL: **grungiest**) (= *dirty*) cutre (*Sp*), roñoso; (*Mus*) de grunge

grunt [grʌnt] (N) [*of animal, person*] gruñido *m*
(VI) [*animal, person*] gruñir
(VT) • **"yes," he ~ed** —sí —gruñó

gruppetto [gru:'petəʊ] (N) (PL: **gruppetti** [gru:'peti:]) grupeto *m*

gr. wt. (ABBR) = **gross weight**

gryphon ['grɪfən] (N) = **griffin**

GS (N ABBR) (= **General Staff**) E.M.

GSA (N ABBR) (*US*) = **General Services Administration**

GSM (N ABBR) (= **Global System for Mobile Communications**) GSM *m*

GSOH* (N ABBR) (= **good sense of humour**) (buen) sentido *m* del humor

G-string ['dʒi:strɪŋ] (N) (*Mus*) cuerda *f* de sol; (= *clothing*) tanga *f*, taparrabo *m*

GSUSA (N ABBR) (*US*) = **Girl Scouts of the United States of America**

GT (N ABBR) (= **gran turismo**) GT

Gt (ABBR) = **Great**

GTi (N ABBR) (= **Gran Turismo injection**) GTi *m*

GU (ABBR) (*US*) = **Guam**

guacamole [,gwɑ:kə'məʊlɪ] (N) guacamole *m*

Guadeloupe [,gwɑ:də'lu:p] (N) Guadalupe *f*

Guam [gwɑ:m] (N) Guam *f*

guano ['gwɑ:nəʊ] (N) guano *m*

guarantee [,gærən'ti:] (N) **1** (*gen*) (*Comm*) garantía *f*; (= *surety*) caución *f* • **it is under ~** está bajo garantía • **there is no ~ that** no hay seguridad de que (+ *subjun*) • **I give you my ~** se lo aseguro
2 (= *guarantor*) fiador(a) *m/f*
(VT) (*Comm*) [+ *goods*] garantizar (**against** contra); (= *ensure*) [+ *service, delivery*] asegurar; (= *make o.s. responsible for*) [+ *debt*] ser fiador de • **~d for three months** garantizado durante tres meses • **I ~ that ...** les garantizo que ... • **I can't ~ good weather** no respondo del tiempo • **he can't ~ that he'll come** no está seguro de poder venir

guaranteed [,gærən'ti:d] (ADJ) [*goods, price,*

service, delivery] garantizado
CPD ▸ **guaranteed bonus** bonificación *f* garantizada ▸ **guaranteed loan** préstamo *m* garantizado

guarantor [ˌgærən'tɔːʳ] N (*Jur*) garante *mf*, fiador(a) *m/f* • **to act** *or* **stand as ~ for sb** avalar a algn

guaranty ['gærəntɪ] N (*Econ*) garantía *f*, caución *f*; (= *agreement*) garantía *f*

guard [gɑːd] N **1** (= *soldier*) guardia *mf*; (= *sentry*) centinela *mf*; (= *squad of soldiers*) guardia *f*; (= *escort*) escolta *f* • **to change (the) ~** relevar la guardia • **he's one of the old ~** pertenece a la vieja guardia; ▹ **advance**
2 (*Mil*) (*also* **guard duty**) (= *watch*) guardia *f*; (*fig*) (= *watchfulness*) vigilancia *f* • **to drop one's ~** bajar la guardia, descuidarse • **to keep ~** vigilar • **to keep ~ over sth/sb** (*Mil*) (*also fig*) vigilar algo/a algn • **to lower one's ~** bajar la guardia, descuidarse • **to mount ~** montar guardia • **to be off one's ~** estar desprevenido • **to catch sb off his ~** coger *or* agarrar a algn desprevenido *or* (*LAm*) de imprevisto • **to be on ~** estar de guardia • **to be on one's ~** (*fig*) estar en guardia (**against** contra) • **to put sb on his ~** poner a algn en guardia, prevenir a algn (**against** contra) • **to stand ~ over sth** montar guardia sobre algo • **to be under ~** estar vigilado • **to keep sb under ~** vigilar a algn
3 (= *security guard*) guardia *mf* de seguridad
4 (*esp US*) (= *prison guard*) carcelero/a *m/f*
5 (*Brit*) (*Rail*) jefe *m* de tren
6 (*Sport*) defensa *mf*
7 (*Fencing*) guardia *f* • **on ~!** ¡en guardia!
8 (= *safety device*) (*on machine*) salvaguardia *f*, resguardo *m*; [*of sword*] guarda *f*, guarnición *f*; (*also* **fireguard**) guardafuego *m*; (= *protection*) protección *f* • **he wears goggles as a ~ against accidents** lleva unas gafas especiales como protección contra accidentes
VT [+ *prisoner, treasure*] vigilar, custodiar; (*while travelling*) escoltar; [+ *secret*] guardar; (= *protect*) [+ *place*] guardar, proteger (**against, from** de); [+ *person*] proteger (**against, from** de) • **a closely ~ed secret** un secreto muy bien guardado
CPD ▸ **guard dog** perro *m* guardián *or* de guarda ▸ **guard duty** turno *m* de guardia • **to be on ~ duty** estar de guardia, hacer el turno de guardia ▸ **guard of honour** (*Brit*) guardia *f* de honor ▸ **guard's van** (*Brit*) (*Rail*) furgón *m*
▸ **guard against** VI + PREP [+ *illness*] guardarse de; [+ *suspicion, accidents*] evitar • **in order to ~ against this** para evitar esto • **to ~ against doing sth** evitar hacer algo

guarded ['gɑːdɪd] ADJ [*person*] cauto, comedido; [*reply, tone*] cauteloso; [*optimism*] comedido, moderado • **she was ~ about committing herself** fue cautelosa *or* cauta a la hora de comprometerse

guardedly ['gɑːdɪdlɪ] ADV [*say, reply*] cautelosamente, con cautela • **I feel ~ optimistic** me siento comedidamente *or* moderadamente optimista

guardedness ['gɑːdɪdnɪs] N cautela *f*, circunspección *f* (*frm*)

guardhouse ['gɑːdhaʊs] N (PL: **guardhouses** ['gɑːdˌhaʊzɪz]) (*for guards*) cuartel *m* de la guardia; (*for prisoners*) cárcel *f* militar

guardian ['gɑːdɪən] N **1** protector(a) *m/f*, guardián/ana *m/f*
2 (*Jur*) [*of child*] tutor(a) *m/f*
CPD ▸ **guardian angel** ángel *m* custodio, ángel *m* de la guarda

guardianship ['gɑːdɪənʃɪp] N tutela *f*, custodia *f* • **she was placed under her mother's ~** quedó sometida a la tutela de su madre

guardrail ['gɑːdreɪl] N pretil *m*, baranda *f*

guardroom ['gɑːdrʊm] N cuarto *m* de guardia

guardsman ['gɑːdzmən] N (PL: **guardsmen**) (*Brit*) soldado *m* de la guardia real; (*US*) soldado *m* de la guardia (nacional)

Guatemala [ˌgwɑːtɪ'mɑːlə] N Guatemala *f*

Guatemalan [ˌgwɑːtɪ'mɑːlən] ADJ guatemalteco
N guatemalteco/a *m/f*

guava ['gwɑːvə] N guayaba *f*

Guayana [gaɪ'ɑːnə] N Guayana *f*

gubbins* ['gʌbɪnz] N (*Brit*) **1** (= *thing*) chisme *m*, cacharro* *m*
2 (= *silly person*) bobo/a *m/f*

gubernatorial [ˌguːbənə'tɔːrɪəl] ADJ (*esp US*) de(l) gobernador/de (la) gobernadora • **~ election** elección *f* de gobernador/gobernadora

gudgeon[1] ['gʌdʒən] N (= *fish*) gobio *m*

gudgeon[2] ['gʌdʒən] N (*Tech*) gorrón *m*

Guernsey ['gɜːnzɪ] N Guernesey *m*

guerrilla [gə'rɪlə] N guerrillero/a *m/f* • **urban ~** guerrillero/a *m/f* urbano/a
CPD ▸ **guerrilla band** guerrilla *f* ▸ **guerrilla group** grupo *m* guerrillero ▸ **guerrilla leader** líder *mf* guerrillero/a ▸ **guerrilla war** guerra *f* de guerrillas ▸ **guerrilla warfare** guerra *f* de guerrillas

guess [ges] N (= *conjecture*) conjetura *f*, suposición *f*; (= *estimate*) estimación *f* aproximada • **to make/have a ~** adivinar • **have a ~** • **I'll give you three ~es** a ver si lo adivinas • **at a (rough) ~** a ojo • **my ~ is that ...** yo creo que ... • **it's anybody's ~** ¿quién sabe? • **your ~ is as good as mine!** ¡vete a saber!
VT **1** [+ *answer, meaning*] acertar; [+ *height, weight, number*] adivinar • **~ what!** ¡a que no lo adivinas! • **~ who!** ¡a ver si adivinas quién soy! • **I ~ed as much** me lo suponía • **you've ~ed it!** ¡has acertado! • **I never ~ed it was so big** nunca supuse que fuera tan grande • **I ~ed him to be about 20** le eché unos 20 años
2 (*esp US*) (= *suppose*) creer, suponer • **I ~ you're right** supongo que tienes razón • **I ~ we'll buy it** me imagino que lo compraremos
VI **1** (= *make a guess*) adivinar; (= *guess correctly*) acertar • **you'll never ~** no lo adivinarás nunca • **he's just ~ing** no hace más que especular • **to keep sb ~ing** mantener a algn a la expectativa • **to ~ at sth** intentar adivinar algo • **all that time we never ~ed** en todo ese tiempo no lo sospechábamos
2 (*esp US*) (= *suppose*) suponer, creer • **I ~ so** creo que sí • **he's happy, I ~** supongo que está contento

guessable ['gesəbl] ADJ [*answer, number*] que se puede adivinar

guessing game ['gesɪŋˌgeɪm] N acertijo *m*, adivinanza *f*

guesstimate* ['gestɪmɪt] N estimación *f* aproximada

guesswork ['geswɜːk] N conjeturas *fpl* • **it's all ~** son meras conjeturas

guest [gest] N (*at home*) invitado/a *m/f*; (*at hotel, guesthouse*) huésped *mf* • **they had ~s that weekend** tenían invitados *or* visita(s) ese fin de semana • **~ of honour** invitado/a *m/f* de honor • **"do you mind if I sit here?" — "be my ~"*** —¿le importa si me siento aquí? —por supuesto que no • **we were their ~s last summer** nos invitaron a su casa el verano pasado
VI (*US*) aparecer como invitado • **he's ~ing on tonight's show** aparecerá como invitado en el show de esta noche
CPD ▸ **guest appearance** aparición *f* especial • **to make a ~ appearance on sb's show** aparecer en el show de algn ▸ **guest artist** = **guest star** ▸ **guest book** libro *m* de los huéspedes ▸ **guest list** lista *f* de invitados ▸ **guest of honour** (*Brit*), **guest of honor** (*US*) invitado/a *m/f* de honor ▸ **guest room** cuarto *m* de huéspedes ▸ **guest speaker** orador(a) *m/f* invitado/a ▸ **guest star** estrella *f* invitada ▸ **guest worker** trabajador(a) *m/f* invitado/a

guesthouse ['gesthaʊs] (PL: **guesthouses** ['gesthaʊzɪz]) N **1** (*Brit*) (= *hotel*) pensión *f*, casa *f* de huéspedes
2 (*US*) (*in grounds of large house*) casa *f* de invitados

guff* [gʌf] N chorradas* *fpl*

guffaw [gʌ'fɔː] N carcajada *f*
VI reírse a carcajadas

GUI ['guːɪ] N ABBR (*Comput*) = **graphical user interface**

Guiana [gaɪ'ɑːnə] N Guayana *f*

guidance ['gaɪdəns] N **1** (= *counselling*) consejo *m*; (= *leadership*) dirección *f* • **marriage/vocational ~** orientación *f* matrimonial/profesional • **under the ~ of** bajo la dirección de • **I tell you this for your ~** te lo digo para que puedas orientarte
2 [*of missile*] dirección *f*
CPD ▸ **guidance system** (*for missile, rocket*) sistema *m* de guía

guide [gaɪd] N **1** (= *person*) guía *mf*; (= *girl guide*) exploradora *f*, guía *f*; (= *book*) guía *f* turística
2 (= *fig*) guía *f* • **let conscience be your ~** haz lo que te dicte tu conciencia
VT (*round town, building*) guiar; (*in choice, decision*) orientar; (= *govern*) dirigir, gobernar • **to be ~d by sth/sb** dejarse guiar por algo/algn
CPD ▸ **guide dog** perro *m* guía
▸ **guide through** VT + PREP • **to ~ sb through sth** [+ *process, complexities*] guiar a algn en algo

guidebook ['gaɪdbʊk] N guía *f* turística

guided ['gaɪdɪd] CPD ▸ **guided missile** misil *m* teledirigido ▸ **guided tour** visita *f* guiada ▸ **guided writing** escritura *f* guiada

guideline ['gaɪdlaɪn] N (línea *f*) directriz *f*; (*for writing*) falsilla *f*

guidelines ['gaɪdlaɪnz] NPL directriz *f* • **new ~** nuevas directrices • **to issue ~ on sth** [*government*] establecer directrices sobre algo • **to set ~ for doing sth** establecer directrices para hacer algo

guidepost ['gaɪdpəʊst] N poste *m* indicador

Guides [gaɪdz] NPL • **the ~** las exploradoras, las guías

guiding ['gaɪdɪŋ] ADJ • **~ principle** principio *m* director • **~ star** estrella *f* de guía

guild [gɪld] N gremio *m*

guilder ['gɪldəʳ] N (PL: **guilders** *or* **guilder**) florín *m* (holandés)

guildhall ['gɪldˌhɔːl] N (= *town hall*) ayuntamiento *m*

guile [gaɪl] N astucia *f*

guileful ['gaɪlfəl] ADJ astuto, mañoso

guileless ['gaɪllɪs] ADJ inocente, candoroso

guillemot ['gɪlɪmɒt] N arao *m*

guillotine [ˌgɪlə'tiːn] N guillotina *f*
VT guillotinar

guilt [gɪlt] N (*gen*) culpa *f*, culpabilidad *f*; (*Jur*) culpabilidad *f* • **feelings of ~** sentimientos *mpl* de culpa *or* de culpabilidad • **to admit one's ~** confesarse culpable • **she was racked with ~** la atormentaba el remordimiento
CPD ▸ **guilt complex** complejo *m* de

g

culpabilidad *or* de culpa ▸ **guilt trip*** • **there's no point in having a ~ trip about it** no merece la pena empezar con sentimientos de culpabilidad, no merece la pena sentirse culpable

guiltily ['gɪltɪlɪ] ADV (= *feeling guilty*) sintiéndose culpable, con sentimiento de culpabilidad; (= *looking guilty*) con aire de culpabilidad

guiltless ['gɪltlɪs] ADJ inocente, libre de culpa • **she was considered ~ of his death** la consideraron inocente de su muerte

guilty ['gɪltɪ] ADJ (COMPAR: **guiltier**, SUPERL: **guiltiest**) culpable • **their parents were ~ of gross neglect** sus padres eran culpables de grave negligencia • **he had a ~ look on his face** su rostro reflejaba culpabilidad • **she wondered why the children were looking so ~** se preguntaba por qué los niños tenían esa cara de culpa, sentirse culpable • **to feel ~ (about sth)** sentirse culpable (por algo) • **to find sb ~/not ~** declarar a algn culpable/inocente • **to be ~ of sth** ser culpable de algo • **the ~ party** el/la culpable • **"how do you plead? — ~ or not ~?"** —¿cómo se declara? —¿culpable o inocente? • **he has a ~ secret** tiene un secreto que le remuerde la conciencia *or* que le hace sentirse culpable • **a ~ smile** una sonrisa de culpabilidad • **a verdict of ~** una sentencia de culpabilidad • **a verdict of not ~** una declaración de inocencia; ▹ **plea, plead**
CPD ▸ **guilty conscience** • **to have a ~ conscience** tener remordimientos de conciencia • **a man with a ~ conscience** un hombre con remordimientos de conciencia

Guinea ['gɪnɪ] N Guinea *f*
CPD ▸ **guinea fowl** gallina *f* de Guinea, pintada *f* ▸ **guinea pig** cobayo *m*, cobaya *f*, conejillo *m* de Indias, cuy *m* (*And, S. Cone*); (*fig*) conejillo *m* de Indias

guinea ['gɪnɪ] N (*Brit*) (*formerly*) guinea *f* (= 21 *chelines*)

Guinea-Bissau ['gɪnɪbɪ'saʊ] N Guinea-Bissau *f*

Guinean ['gɪnɪən] ADJ guineano
N guineano/a *m/f*

Guinevere ['gwɪnɪvɪəʳ] N Ginebra

guise [gaɪz] N • **in that ~** de esa manera • **under the ~ of** (= *disguised as*) bajo el disfraz de; (*fig*) con el pretexto de

guitar [gɪ'tɑːʳ] N guitarra *f*; (= *electric guitarist*) guitarra *mf*

guitarist [gɪ'tɑːrɪst] N guitarrista *mf*

Gujarati, Gujerati [ˌgʊdʒə'rɑːtɪ] ADJ gujarati
N **1** (= *person*) Gujarati *mf*
2 (*Ling*) gujarati *m*

gulch [gʌlʃ] N (*US*) barranco *m*

gulf [gʌlf] N (= *bay*) golfo *m*; (= *chasm*) (*also fig*) abismo *m* • **the (Persian) Gulf** el golfo (Pérsico) • **the Gulf of Mexico** el golfo de México • **the Gulf of Suez** el golfo de Suez
CPD ▸ **the Gulf crisis** la crisis del Golfo ▸ **the Gulf States** los países del Golfo ▸ **the Gulf Stream** la corriente del Golfo ▸ **Gulf War** guerra *f* del Golfo

gull [gʌl] N (= *bird*) gaviota *f*
VT estafar, timar

gullet ['gʌlɪt] N esófago *m*, garganta *f*

gulley ['gʌlɪ] = **gully**

gullibility [ˌgʌlɪ'bɪlɪtɪ] N credulidad *f*, simpleza *f*

gullible ['gʌlɪbl] ADJ crédulo, simplón

gully ['gʌlɪ] N (= *ravine*) barranco *m*; (= *channel*) hondonada *f*

gulp [gʌlp] N trago *m* • **in** *or* **at one ~** de un trago • **"yes," he said with a ~** —sí —dijo tragando saliva
VT (*also* **gulp down**) tragarse, engullir
VI (*while drinking*) tragar; (*through fear*) tener un nudo en la garganta; (= *swallow saliva*) tragar saliva

gum¹ [gʌm] N (*Anat*) encía *f*
CPD ▸ **gum disease** enfermedad *f* de las encías

gum² [gʌm] N (*gen*) goma *f*; (= *glue*) goma *f*, pegamento *m*, cemento *m* (*LAm*); (*also* **chewing gum**) chicle *m*; (= *sweet*) pastilla *f* de caramelo
VT (= *stick together*) pegar con goma; (*also* **gum down**) [+ *label, envelope*] pegar
CPD ▸ **gum arabic** goma *f* arábiga
▸ **gum up** VT + ADV (*fig*) estropear, paralizar • IDIOM: • **to gum up the works*** meter un palo en la rueda

gum³ [gʌm] EXCL • **by gum!** ¡caramba!

gumball ['gʌmbɔːl] N (*esp US*) bola *f* de chicle

gumbo ['gʌmbəʊ] N (*US*) (*Culin*) *sopa o estofado espesado con quingombó*

gumboil ['gʌmbɔɪl] N flemón *m*

gumboots ['gʌmbuːts] NPL botas *fpl* altas de goma

gumdrop ['gʌmdrɒp] N pastilla *f* de goma

gummed [gʌmd] ADJ [*envelope, label*] engomado

gummy ['gʌmɪ] ADJ gomoso

gump* [gʌmp] N **1** (= *sense*) sentido *m* común
2 (= *fool*) tonto/a *m/f*, imbécil *mf*

gumption* ['gʌmpʃən] N (= *initiative*) iniciativa *f*; (*Brit*) (= *common sense*) seso *m*, sentido *m* común

gumshield ['gʌmʃiːld] N (*Sport*) protector *m* de dientes

gumshoe ['gʌmʃuː] N (*US*) **1** (= *overshoe*) zapato *m* de goma
2* (= *detective*) detective *mf*

gumtree ['gʌmtriː] N (*gen*) árbol *m* gomero; (= *eucalyptus*) eucalipto *m* • IDIOM: • **to be up a ~** (*Brit**) estar en un aprieto

gun [gʌn] N **1** (= *pistol*) pistola *f*, revólver *m*; (= *rifle*) fusil *m*; (= *shotgun*) escopeta *f*; (= *cannon*) cañón *m* • **a 21-gun salute** una salva de 21 cañonazos • **the guns** (*Mil*) la artillería • **big gun*** pez *m* gordo, espadón *m* • **to draw a gun on sb** apuntar a algn con un arma • **to jump the gun** salir antes de tiempo; (*fig*) obrar con demasiada anticipación • IDIOMS: • **to be going great guns** hacer grandes progresos, ir a las mil maravillas • **to stick to one's guns** mantenerse firme, mantenerse en sus trece
2 (*Brit*) (= *person*) pistolero/a *m/f*
VT disparar sobre
CPD ▸ **gun barrel** cañón *m* ▸ **gun battle** tiroteo *m* ▸ **gun carriage** cureña *f*; (*at funeral*) armón *m* de artillería ▸ **gun control** control *m* de armas de fuego ▸ **gun control laws** legislación *fsing* sobre el control de armas de fuego ▸ **gun crew** dotación *f* de un cañón ▸ **gun crime(s)** delitos *mpl* con arma de fuego ▸ **gun culture** cultura *m* de las armas ▸ **gun dog** perro *m* de caza ▸ **gun law** (= *rule by the gun*) ley *f* del terror, pistolerismo *m*; (*Jur*) ley *f* que rige la tenencia y uso de armas de fuego ▸ **gun licence** licencia *f* de armas ▸ **gun lobby** grupo *m* de presión a favor de las armas de fuego, lobby *m* de las armas ▸ **gun maker** armero/a *m/f* ▸ **gun room** (*in house*) sala *f* de armas; (*Brit*) (*Naut*) sala *f* de suboficiales ▸ **gun turret** torreta *f*
▸ **gun down** VT + ADV abatir a tiros, abalear (*LAm*)
▸ **gun for** VI + PREP (*fig*) ir a por • **it's really the boss they're gunning for** en realidad van a por el jefe

gunboat ['gʌnbəʊt] N (*seagoing*) cañonero *m*; (*small*) lancha *f* cañonera
CPD ▸ **gunboat diplomacy** diplomacia *f* cañonera

guncotton ['gʌnˌkɒtn] N algodón *m* pólvora

gunfight ['gʌnfaɪt] N tiroteo *m*

gunfighter ['gʌnfaɪtəʳ] N pistolero *m*

gunfire ['gʌnfaɪəʳ] N disparos *mpl*; (*from artillery*) cañoneo *m*, fuego *m* de cañón

gunge* [gʌndʒ] N mugre *f*
VT • **to ~ up** atascar, obstruir

gung-ho ['gʌŋ'həʊ] ADJ **1** (= *over-enthusiastic*) (tontamente) optimista, (locamente) entusiasta
2 (= *jingoistic*) patriotero (en exceso), jingoísta

gungy* ['gʌndʒɪ] ADJ asqueroso

gunk* [gʌŋk] N = **gunge**

gunman ['gʌnmən] N (PL: **gunmen**) pistolero *m*, gatillero *m* (*LAm*)

gunmetal ['gʌnˌmetl] N bronce *m* de cañón

gunnel ['gʌnəl] N = **gunwale**

gunner ['gʌnəʳ] N artillero/a *m/f*

gunnery ['gʌnərɪ] N **1** (= *art, skill*) puntería *f*; (= *science*) tiro *m*
2 (= *guns*) artillería *f*
CPD ▸ **gunnery officer** oficial *mf* de artillería ▸ **gunnery range** campo *m* de artillería

gunny ['gʌnɪ] N arpillera *f*; (*also* **gunny bag, gunny sack**) saco *m* de yute

gunpoint ['gʌnpɔɪnt] N • **at ~** a punta de pistola • **to hold sb at ~** tener a algn a punta de pistola

gunpowder ['gʌnˌpaʊdəʳ] N pólvora *f*
CPD ▸ **Gunpowder Plot** (*Brit*) Conspiración *f* de la Pólvora; ▹ GUY FAWKES NIGHT

gunrunner ['gʌnˌrʌnəʳ] N contrabandista *mf* or traficante *mf* de armas

gunrunning ['gʌnˌrʌnɪŋ] N contrabando *m* or tráfico *m* de armas

gunship ['gʌnʃɪp] N helicóptero *m* artillado *or* de combate

gunshot ['gʌnʃɒt] N (= *noise*) disparo *m*; (*from artillery*) cañonazo *m*; (*from shotgun*) escopetazo *m* • **within ~** a tiro de fusil
CPD ▸ **gunshot wound** escopetazo *m*

gun-shy ['gʌnʃaɪ] ADJ (*lit*) que se asusta con los disparos; (*fig*) acobardado

gunslinger* ['gʌnslɪŋəʳ] N pistolero/a *m/f*

gunsmith ['gʌnsmɪθ] N armero/a *m/f*

gun-toting ['gʌntəʊtɪŋ] ADJ armado

gunwale ['gʌnl] N borda *f*, regala *f*

guppy ['gʌpɪ] N guppy *m*

gurgle ['gɜːgl] N [*of liquid*] borboteo *m*, gluglú *m*; [*of baby*] gorjeo *m*
VI [*liquid*] borbotear; [*baby*] gorjear

Gurkha ['gɜːkə] N gurkha *mf*, gurja *mf*

gurney ['gɜːnɪ] N (*US*) camilla *f*

guru ['gʊruː] N gurú *mf*

Gus [gʌs] N *familiar form of* **Angus, Augustus**

gush [gʌʃ] N **1** [*of liquid*] chorro *m*; [*of words*] torrente *m*; [*of feeling*] efusión *f*
2 (= *sentimentalism*) sentimentalismo *m*
VT [+ *blood*] chorrear, derramar a borbotones; [+ *water*] chorrear, derramar
VI **1** (*also* **gush out**) [*water, blood*] chorrear (**from** de)
2* (= *enthuse*) hablar con entusiasmo (**about, over** de)

gusher ['gʌʃəʳ] N **1** (= *oilwell*) pozo *m* surtido
2 • **to be a ~** [*person*] ser muy efusivo

gushing ['gʌʃɪŋ] ADJ efusivo

gusset ['gʌsɪt] N escudete *m*

gust [gʌst] N [*of wind*] ráfaga *f*, racha *f*
VI soplar racheado • **the wind ~ed up to 120km/h** el viento soplaba en rachas de hasta 120km/h

gustatory ['gʌstətɔːrɪ] ADJ (*frm*) [*sense*] gustativo; [*delights, pleasures*] gastronómico, del paladar
gusto ['gʌstəʊ] N • **with ~** con entusiasmo
gusty ['gʌstɪ] ADJ (COMPAR: **gustier**, SUPERL: **gustiest**) [*weather*] borrascoso; [*wind*] racheado
gut [gʌt] N **1** (= *alimentary canal*) intestino *m*; (*for violin, racket*) cuerda *f* de tripa • IDIOM: • **to bust a gut**‡ echar los bofes, echar el hígado
2 guts* (= *innards*) tripas *fpl*; (= *courage*) agallas* *fpl*, coraje *m*; (= *staying power*) aguante *m*, resistencia *f*; (= *moral strength*) carácter *m*; (= *content*) meollo *m*, sustancia *f* • **to have guts** tener agallas* • **I hate his guts*** no lo puedo ver ni en pintura • **to spill one's guts**‡ contar la propia vida y milagros • **to work one's guts out** echar los bofes, echar el hígado • IDIOM: • **I'll have his guts for garters!*** ¡le hago trizas!
3 (*Naut*) estrecho *m*
VT **1** [+ *poultry, fish*] destripar
2 [+ *building*] no dejar más que las paredes de
CPD ▸ **gut feeling** instinto *m* visceral ▸ **gut instinct** instinto *m* ▸ **gut reaction** reacción *f* instintiva
gutless* ['gʌtlɪs] ADJ cobarde, sin agallas*
gutsy* ['gʌtsɪ] ADJ (COMPAR: **gutsier**, SUPERL: **gutsiest**) valiente, con agallas*
gutta-percha ['gʌtə'pɜːtʃə] N gutapercha *f*
gutted* ['gʌtɪd] ADJ (*Brit*) (= *disappointed*) • **I was ~** me quedé hecho polvo*
gutter¹ ['gʌtəʳ] N (*in street*) arroyo *m*, cuneta *f*, desagüe *m* (*CAm*); (*on roof*) canal *m*, canalón *m* • **the ~** (*fig*) los barrios bajos; (= *underworld*) el hampa • **he rose from the ~** (*fig*) salió de la nada
CPD ▸ **the gutter press** (*pej*) la prensa amarilla; ▹ BROADSHEETS AND TABLOIDS
gutter² ['gʌtəʳ] VI [*candle*] irse consumiendo
guttering ['gʌtərɪŋ] N canales *mpl*, canalones *mpl*
guttersnipe ['gʌtəsnaɪp] N golfillo *m*
guttural ['gʌtərəl] ADJ [*accent, sound*] gutural
guv [gʌv] N = **governor** • **thanks, guv!** ¡gracias, jefe!
guv'nor* ['gʌvnəʳ] N = **governor**
guy¹* [gaɪ] N (= *man*) tío* *m*, tipo* *m*, cuate *m* (*Mex*); (= *effigy*) efigie *f* • **he's a nice guy** es un buen tío *or* tipo • **hey, (you) guys!** ¡eh, amigos! • **are you guys ready to go?** ¿están todos listos para salir?; ▹ **wise**
VT (= *make fun of*) ridiculizar; (*Theat*) parodiar
guy² [gaɪ] N (*also* **guy rope**) (*for tent*) viento *m*, cuerda *f*
Guy [gaɪ] N Guido • **Guy Fawkes Day** • **Guy Fawkes Night** (*Brit*) *cinco de noviembre, aniversario de la Conspiración de la Pólvora*

GUY FAWKES NIGHT
La noche del cinco de noviembre, **Guy Fawkes Night** se celebra en el Reino Unido el fracaso de la conspiración de la pólvora **Gunpowder Plot**, un intento fallido de volar el Parlamento de Jaime I en 1605. Esa noche se lanzan fuegos artificiales y se hacen hogueras en las que se queman unos muñecos de trapo que representan a **Guy Fawkes**, uno de los cabecillas de la revuelta. Días antes, los niños tienen por costumbre pedir a los transeúntes **a penny for the guy**, dinero que emplean en comprar cohetes.

Guyana [gaɪ'ænə] N Guayana *f*
Guyanese [,gaɪə'niːz] ADJ guyanés
N guyanés/esa *m/f*
guzzle ['gʌzl] VT **1** [+ *food*] engullirse, tragarse; [+ *drink*] soplarse, tragarse (*LAm*)
2* (*hum*) [*car*] [+ *petrol*] tragar mucho
VI (= *eat*) engullir, tragar; (= *drink*) soplar, tragar (*LAm*)
guzzler ['gʌzləʳ] N tragon/ona *m/f*, comilón/ona *m/f*; ▹ **gas**
-guzzling ['gʌzlɪŋ] SUFFIX • **gas-guzzling** tragapetróleo (*inv*) • **energy-guzzling** tragaenergía (*inv*)
gym* [dʒɪm] N (= *gymnasium*) gimnasio *m*; (= *gymnastics*) gimnasia *f*
CPD ▸ **gym class** clase *f* de gimnasia ▸ **gym shoes** zapatillas *fpl* de gimnasia
gymkhana [dʒɪm'kɑːnə] N gincana *f*
gymnasium [dʒɪm'neɪzɪəm] N (PL: **gymnasiums** *or* **gymnasia** [dʒɪm'neɪzɪə]) gimnasio *m*
gymnast ['dʒɪmnæst] N gimnasta *mf*
gymnastic [dʒɪm'næstɪk] ADJ gimnástico
gymnastics [dʒɪm'næstɪks] N gimnasia *f*
gymslip ['dʒɪmslɪp] N (*Brit*) túnica *f* de gimnasia
gynaecological, **gynecological** (*US*) [,gaɪnɪkə'lɒdʒɪkəl] ADJ ginecológico
gynaecologist, **gynecologist** (*US*) [,gaɪnɪ'kɒlədʒɪst] N ginecólogo/a *m/f*
gynaecology, **gynecology** (*US*) [,gaɪnɪ'kɒlədʒɪ] N ginecología *f*
gyp¹* [dʒɪp] (*US*) N **1** (= *swindle*) estafa *f*, timo *m*
2 (= *swindler*) estafador(a) *m/f*, timador(a) *m/f*
VT estafar, timar
gyp²* [dʒɪp] N (*Brit*) • IDIOM: • **to give sb gyp** (= *scold*) echar un rapapolvo de aúpa a algn • **it's giving me gyp** (= *hurting*) me duele una barbaridad
gypsum ['dʒɪpsəm] N yeso *m*
gypsy ['dʒɪpsɪ] N gitano/a *m/f*
CPD [*life, caravan, music*] gitano ▸ **gypsy moth** lagarta *f*
gyrate [dʒaɪ'reɪt] VI (= *spin*) girar; (= *dance*) bailar enérgicamente
gyration [,dʒaɪ'reɪʃən] N giro *m*, vuelta *f*
gyratory [,dʒaɪ'reɪtərɪ] ADJ giratorio
gyro... ['dʒaɪrəʊ] PREFIX giro...
gyrocompass ['dʒaɪrəʊ'kʌmpəs] N girocompás *m*
gyroscope ['dʒaɪrəskəʊp] N giroscopio *m*, giróscopo *m*

g

Hh

h

H, h [eɪtʃ] N (= *letter*) H, h *f* • **H for Harry** H de Historia
h. ABBR (= **hour(s)**) h, hs
ha [hɑ:] EXCL ¡ah!
ha. ABBR (= **hectare**) Ha.
habeas corpus ['heɪbɪəs'kɔ:pəs] N (*Jur*) hábeas corpus *m*
haberdasher ['hæbədæʃəʳ] N mercero/a *m/f*; (*US*) camisero/a *m/f* • **~'s (shop)** mercería *f*; (*US*) camisería *f*
haberdashery [,hæbə'dæʃərɪ] N (= *shop*) mercería *f*; (*US*) camisería *f*; (= *goods*) mercería *f*; (*US*) artículos *mpl* de moda para caballeros
habit ['hæbɪt] N **1** (= *customary behaviour*) costumbre *f* • **a bad ~** un vicio, una mala costumbre • **to get into the ~ of doing sth** acostumbrarse a hacer algo • **to get out of the ~ of doing sth** perder la costumbre de hacer algo • **to have a ~*** (= *drugs*) drogarse habitualmente • **to be in the ~ of doing sth** tener la costumbre de hacer algo, acostumbrar *or* soler hacer algo • **to make a ~ of doing sth** acostumbrarse a hacer algo • **we mustn't make a ~ of arriving late** no debemos acostumbrarnos a llegar tarde • **you can phone me at work as long as you don't make a ~ of it** puedes llamarme al trabajo mientras no lo tomes por costumbre • **let's hope he doesn't make a ~ of it** esperamos que no siga haciéndolo • **I always make a ~ of arriving early** tengo por norma *or* por costumbre llegar siempre pronto • **out of ~** por costumbre • **out of sheer ~** por pura costumbre
2 (= *dress*) [*of monk*] hábito *m*; (= *riding habit*) traje *m* de montar
habitability [,hæbɪtə'bɪlɪtɪ] N [*of building, area*] habitabilidad *f*
habitable ['hæbɪtəbl] ADJ habitable
habitat ['hæbɪtæt] N hábitat *m*
habitation [,hæbɪ'teɪʃən] N **1** (= *act*) habitación *f* • **to be fit/unfit for (human) ~** estar/no estar en condiciones de habitabilidad • **there was no sign of (human) ~** no había señales de que estuviera habitado
2 (= *dwelling*) residencia *f*, morada *f*; (= *house*) domicilio *m*
habit-forming ['hæbɪt,fɔ:mɪŋ] ADJ que crea hábito
habitual [hə'bɪtjʊəl] ADJ habitual, acostumbrado; [*drunkard, liar etc*] inveterado, empedernido
habitually [hə'bɪtjʊəlɪ] ADV (= *usually*) por costumbre; (= *constantly*) constantemente
habituate [hə'bɪtjʊeɪt] VT acostumbrar, habituar (**to** a)
habitué, habituée [hə'bɪtjʊeɪ] N asiduo/a *m/f*, parroquiano/a *m/f*
hacienda [,hæsɪ'endə] N (*US*) hacienda *f*
hack¹ [hæk] N (= *cut*) corte *m*, tajo *m*; (= *blow*) (*with axe*) hachazo *m*; (*with machete*) machetazo *m*
VT **1** (= *cut*) cortar • **to ~ one's way through sth** abrirse paso por algo a machetazos *etc* • **to ~ sth to pieces** hacer algo pedazos (a hachazos)
2 • **I can't ~ it** (*US**) no puedo hacerlo
VI **1** (= *cut*) dar tajos (**at a**) • **he was ~ing at a loaf of bread** estaba dándole tajos a una hogaza de pan
2 (*Comput*) • **to ~ into a system** piratear un sistema, conseguir entrar en un sistema
▸ **hack around*** VI + ADV (*US*) gandulear, vaguear
▸ **hack down** VT + ADV [+ *tree etc*] derribar a hachazos
hack² [hæk] N **1** (= *old horse*) jamelgo *m*, rocín *m*; (= *hired horse*) caballo *m* de alquiler
2 (= *writer*) escritorzuelo/a *m/f*, plumífero/a *m/f*; (= *journalist*) gacetillero/a *m/f*
3 (*US**) (= *taxi*) taxi *m*
VI • **to go ~ing** montar a caballo
CPD ▸ **hack reporter** reportero/a *m/f* de poca monta ▸ **hack writer** = **hack²**
hackberry ['hækberɪ] N almez *m*
hacked off* [,hækt'ɒf] ADJ (= *annoyed*) cabreado* • **to be ~ with sb** estar cabreado con algn*, estar harto de algn* • **I'm really ~ with you people!** ¡estoy harto de vosotros!*
hacker ['hækəʳ] N (*Comput*) pirata *mf* informático/a
hackery* ['hækərɪ] N **1** = **hackwork**
2 = **hacking²**
hackette* [hæ'ket] N periodista *f*
hackie* ['hækɪ] N (*US*) taxista *mf*
hacking¹ ['hækɪŋ] ADJ [*cough*] seco
hacking² ['hækɪŋ] N (*Comput*) piratería *f* informática
hacking jacket ['hækɪŋ,dʒækɪt] N chaqueta *f* de montar, saco *m* de montar (*LAm*)
hackles ['hæklz] NPL (*lit*) [*of dog*] (*on back of neck*) pelo *m* del pescuezo; (*on back*) pelo *m* del lomo • **with his ~ up** [*dog*] con el pelo erizado; [*person*] hecho una furia, furioso • IDIOM: • **to make sb's ~ rise** poner hecho una furia a algn, enfurecer a algn
hackney cab ['hæknɪ'kæb] N, **hackney carriage** ['hæknɪ'kærɪdʒ] N (*frm*) coche *m* de alquiler; (= *taxi*) taxi *m*
hackneyed ['hæknɪd] ADJ [*saying, expression*] trillado, gastado
hacksaw ['hæksɔ:] N sierra *f* para metales
hacktivist* ['hæktɪvɪst] N hacker *mf* activista
hackwork ['hækwɜ:k] N trabajo *m* de rutina; (*iro*) periodismo *m*
had [hæd] PT, PP *of* **have**
haddock ['hædək] N (PL: **haddock** *or* **haddocks**) eglefino *m*
Hades ['heɪdi:z] N el Hades
hadn't ['hædnt] = **had not**
Hadrian ['heɪdrɪən] N Adriano • **~'s Wall** la Muralla de Adriano
haematological, hematological (*US*) [,hi:mətə'lɒdʒɪkəl] ADJ hematológico
haematologist, hematologist (*US*) [,hi:mə'tɒlədʒɪst] N hematólogo/a *m/f*
haematology, hematology (*US*) [,hi:mə'tɒlədʒɪ] N hematología *f*
haematoma, hematoma (*US*) [,hi:mə'təʊmə] N (PL: **haematomas** *or* **haematomata** [,hi:mə'təʊmətə]) hematoma *m*
haemoglobin, hemoglobin (*US*) [,hi:məʊ'gləʊbɪn] N hemoglobina *f*
haemophilia, hemophilia (*US*) [,hi:məʊ'fɪlɪə] N hemofilia *f*
haemophiliac, hemophiliac (*US*) [,hi:məʊ'fɪlɪæk] ADJ hemofílico
N hemofílico/a *m/f*
haemorrhage, hemorrhage (*US*) ['hemərɪdʒ] N hemorragia(s) *f(pl)*
VI sangrar profusamente
haemorrhaging, hemorrhaging (*US*) ['hemərɪdʒɪŋ] N hemorragia(s) *f(pl)*
haemorrhoids, hemorrhoids (*US*) ['hemərɔɪdz] NPL hemorroides *fpl*
hafnium ['hæfnɪəm] N hafnio *m*
haft [hɑ:ft] N mango *m*, puño *m*
hag [hæg] N (= *ugly old woman*) vieja *f* fea, bruja *f*; (= *witch*) bruja *f*
haggard ['hægəd] ADJ (*from tiredness*) ojeroso; (= *unwell*) demacrado, macilento
haggis ['hægɪs] N (*Scot*) *asaduras de cordero, avena y especias, cocidas en las tripas del animal*
haggish ['hægɪʃ] ADJ como de bruja, brujeril
haggle ['hægl] VI **1** (= *bargain*) regatear • **to ~ over the price** regatear, regatear el precio
2 (= *argue*) discutir
▸ **haggle down** VT + ADV [+ *price*] rebajar • **I managed to ~ the price down to 200 rupees** conseguí rebajar el precio a 200 rupías • **eventually she ~d him down to £150** acabó consiguiendo que le dejara el precio en £150
haggling ['hæglɪŋ] N **1** (*over price*) regateo *m*
2 (= *discussion*) discusión *f*
hagiographer [,hægɪ'ɒgrəfəʳ] N hagiógrafo/a *m/f*
hagiography [,hægɪ'ɒgrəfɪ] N hagiografía *f*
hag-ridden ['hægrɪdn] ADJ (= *tormented*) atormentado (*por una pesadilla*); (*hum**) (= *hen-pecked*) dominado por una mujer
Hague [heɪg] N • **The ~** La Haya
hah [hɑ:] = **ha**
ha-ha ['hɑ:'hɑ:] EXCL ¡ja, ja!
hail¹ [heɪl] N **1** (*Met*) granizo *m*, pedrisco *m*
2 (*fig*) [*of bullets*] lluvia *f*; [*of abuse, insults*] sarta *f*, torrente *m*
VI granizar
▸ **hail down** VI + ADV (*fig*) llover
hail² [heɪl] N (= *call*) grito *m*; (= *greeting*) saludo *m* • **within ~** al alcance de la voz
EXCL †† • **~ Caesar!** ¡ave *or* salve, César! • **the Hail Mary** el Ave *f* María
VT **1** (= *acclaim*) aclamar (**as** como) • **to ~ sb as king** aclamar a algn (como) rey
2 (= *greet*) saludar

3 (= *call to*) llamar, gritar a
4 (= *signal*) [+ *taxi*] llamar, hacer señas a
VI • **to ~ from** [*person*] ser natural de, ser de • **he ~s from Scotland** es (natural) de Escocia • **where does that ship ~ from?** ¿de dónde es ese barco?

hail-fellow-well-met ['heɪl,feləʊ'wel'met] ADJ (demasiado) efusivo, campechano

hailstone ['heɪlstəʊn] N granizo *m*, piedra *f* (de granizo)

hailstorm ['heɪlstɔːm] N granizada *f*

hair [hɛəʳ] N **1** (= *head of hair*) pelo *m*, cabello *m*; (*on legs etc*) vello *m*; [*of animal*] pelo *m*, piel *f*; (= *fluff*) pelusa *f* • **to comb one's ~** peinarse • **to get/have one's ~ cut** cortarse el pelo • **to do one's ~** • **to have one's ~ done** arreglarse el pelo • **grey ~** canas *fpl* • **a fine head of ~** una hermosa cabellera • **he still has a full head of ~** aún conserva todo su pelo • **she's got long ~** tiene el pelo largo • **to part one's ~** hacerse la raya • **to remove unwanted ~** depilarse • **to put one's ~ up** recogerse el pelo • **to wash one's ~** lavarse la cabeza *or* el pelo • **white ~** canas *fpl* • IDIOMS: • **to get in sb's ~** sacar de quicio a algn • **to get sb out of one's ~** quitarse de encima a algn • **keep your ~ on!** (*Brit**) ¡cálmate! • **to let one's ~ down** echar una cana al aire, soltarse la melena, relajarse (*esp LAm*) • **to make sb's ~ stand on end** poner los pelos de punta a algn • **it was enough to make your ~ stand on end** te ponía los pelos de punta, era espeluznante • **to tear one's ~ out** ponerse frenético
2 (= *single hair*) pelo *m* • **by a ~'s breadth** por un pelo *or* los pelos • **to be within a ~'s breadth of** estar a dos dedos de • IDIOMS: • **the ~ of the dog (that bit you)*** una copita para que se pase la resaca • **what you need is a ~ of the dog that bit you** lo que te hace falta es tomarte otra para que se te pase la resaca • **to put ~s on one's chest**: • **this will put ~s on your chest!*** ¡esto te hará la mar de bien!* • **to split ~s** buscarle tres pies al gato, hilar muy fino • **to turn a ~**: • **he didn't turn a ~** ni se inmutó, ni siquiera pestañeó
CPD [*follicle, implant, transplant*] capilar; [*lacquer*] para el pelo; [*mattress*] de cerda
▸ **hair appointment** • **to have/make a ~ appointment** tener/pedir hora en la peluquería ▸ **hair care** cuidado *m* del cabello ▸ **hair clippers** maquinilla *f* para cortar el pelo ▸ **hair colour** (= *dye*) tinte *m* de pelo ▸ **hair conditioner** suavizante *m or* (*LAm*) enjuague *m* para el cabello ▸ **hair curler** rulo *m*, bigudí *m* ▸ **hair extension** postizo *m*; (= *false plait*) trenza *f* postiza ▸ **hair follicle** folículo *m* capilar ▸ **hair gel** fijador *m* ▸ **hair implant** implante *m* capilar ▸ **hair loss** pérdida *f* de cabello, caída *f* de pelo • **total ~ loss** pérdida *f* total del cabello, caída *f* total del pelo ▸ **hair oil** brillantina *f* ▸ **hair removal** depilación *f* ▸ **hair remover** depilatorio *m* ▸ **hair restorer** loción *f* capilar ▸ **hair salon** salón *m* de peluquería ▸ **hair shirt** cilicio *m* ▸ **hair slide** (*Brit*) pasador *m*, hebilla *f* (*S. Cone*) ▸ **hair specialist** especialista *mf* capilar ▸ **hair straighteners** alisador *msing* de pelo ▸ **hair style** peinado *m* ▸ **hair stylist** peluquero/a *m/f* estilista ▸ **hair transplant** trasplante *m* capilar ▸ **hair trigger** *gatillo que se dispara con un ligero toque*; ▹ **hair-trigger** ▸ **hair wash** (= *act*) lavado *m* de pelo; (= *substance*) champú *m*

hairball ['hɛəbɔːl] N (*in cats, calves etc*) bola *f* de pelo

hairband ['hɛəbænd] N cinta *f*

hairbrush ['hɛəbrʌʃ] N cepillo *m* (para el pelo)

hair-clip ['hɛəklɪp] N horquilla *f*, clipe *m*

haircream ['hɛəkriːm] N brillantina *f*; (*for setting*) fijador *m*, laca *f*

haircut ['hɛəkʌt] N corte *m* de pelo, corte *m* • **to have** *or* **get a ~** cortarse el pelo

hairdo* ['hɛəduː] N peinado *m*

hairdresser ['hɛə,dresəʳ] N peluquero/a *m/f* • **~'s** (= *salon*) peluquería *f*

hairdressing ['hɛədresɪŋ] N peluquería *f*
CPD ▸ **hairdressing salon** salón *m* de peluquería

hairdrier, hairdryer ['hɛədraɪəʳ] N secador *m* de pelo

-haired [hɛəd] ADJ (*ending in compounds*) • **fair-haired** rubio, güero (*CAm, Mex*), catire/a (*Carib, Col*) • **dark-haired** moreno • **long-haired** de pelo largo

hair-grip ['hɛəgrɪp] N (*Brit*) horquilla *f*, clipe *m*

hairiness ['hɛərɪnɪs] N vellosidad *f* • **is ~ a sign of virility?** ¿la vellosidad es un signo de virilidad?

hairless ['hɛəlɪs] ADJ sin pelo, calvo; (= *beardless*) lampiño

hairline ['hɛəlaɪn] N **1** (*on head*) nacimiento *m* del pelo • **to have a receding ~** tener entradas
2 (*Tech*) estría *f* muy delgada
CPD ▸ **hairline crack** grieta *f* fina ▸ **hairline fracture** fractura *f* fina

hairnet ['hɛənet] N redecilla *f*

hairpiece ['hɛəpiːs] N postizo *m*, tupé *m*; (= *false plait*) trenza *f* postiza

hairpin ['hɛəpɪn] N horquilla *f*
CPD ▸ **hairpin bend, hairpin curve** (*US*) revuelta *f*, curva *f* muy cerrada

hair-raising ['hɛə,reɪzɪŋ] ADJ [*story, adventure*] espeluznante

hair-splitting ['hɛə,splɪtɪŋ] ADJ nimio; [*discussion*] sobre detalles nimios
N sofismas *mpl*, sofistería *f*

hairspray ['hɛəspreɪ] N laca *f* (para el pelo)

hairspring ['hɛəsprɪŋ] N muelle *m* espiral muy fino (de un reloj)

hair-trigger ['hɛə,trɪgəʳ] ADJ (*fig*) [*temper, reaction*] explosivo; ▹ **hair**

hairwash ['hɛəwɒʃ] N ▹ **hair wash**

hairy ['hɛərɪ] ADJ (COMPAR: **hairier**, SUPERL: **hairiest**) **1** [*chest, legs, arms*] peludo, velludo; (= *long-haired*) melenudo • **he's got ~ legs** tiene las piernas peludas *or* velludas, tiene mucho pelo *or* vello en las piernas • **a ~ spider** una araña peluda
2* (= *frightening*) [*experience*] horripilante, espeluznante

Haiti ['heɪtɪ] N Haití *m*

Haitian ['heɪʃɪən] ADJ haitiano
N haitiano/a *m/f*

hake [heɪk] N (PL: **hake** *or* **hakes**) merluza *f*

halal [hə'lɑːl] ADJ *de animales sacrificados conforme a los preceptos musulmanes*

halberd ['hælbəd] N alabarda *f*

halcyon ['hælsɪən] ADJ • **~ days** días *mpl* felices

hale [heɪl] ADJ sano, robusto • **~ and hearty** robusto, sano y fuerte

half [hɑːf] N (PL: **halves**) **1** (*gen*) mitad *f* • **give me ~** dame la mitad • **~ of my friends** la mitad de mis amigos • **~ man ~ beast** mitad hombre mitad animal • **~ a cup** media taza *f* • **~ a day** medio día *m* • **a pound and a ~** • **one and a ~ pounds** libra *f* y media • **three and a ~ hours** tres horas y media • **we have a problem and a ~*** tenemos un problema mayúsculo, vaya problemazo que tenemos • **one's better ~*** (*hum*) su media naranja* • **by ~**: • **better by ~** con mucho el mejor • **it has increased by ~** ha aumentado en la mitad • **he's too clever by ~*** se pasa de listo • **he doesn't do things by halves** no hace las cosas a medias • **~ a dollar** (= *value*) medio dólar *m* • **~ a dozen** media docena *f* • **to go halves (with sb) (on sth)** ir a medias (con algn) (en algo) • **~ an hour** media hora *f* • **to cut/break sth in ~** cortar/partir algo por la mitad • **~ a moment!*** • **~ a second!*** ¡un momento! • **one's other ~*** (*hum*) su media naranja* • **they don't know the ~ of it*** no saben de la misa la media • **she's asleep ~ the time** (*iro*) se pasa la mitad del tiempo dormida; ▹ AVERAGE, HALF
2 (*Sport*) [*of match*] tiempo *m*; (= *player*) medio *m* • **first/second ~** primer/segundo tiempo *m*
3 (*Brit*) [*of beer*] media pinta *f*
4 (= *child's ticket*) billete *m* de niño • **one and two halves, please** un billete normal y dos para niños, por favor
ADJ [*bottle, quantity*] medio • **a ~-point cut in interest rates** una reducción de medio punto en los tipos de interés • **I have a ~ share in the flat** la mitad del piso es mío *or* de mi propiedad; ▹ **halfback, half-brother, half-sister**
ADV **1** (*gen*) medio, a medias • **I was ~ afraid that …** medio temía que … • **~ as**: • **~ as much** la mitad • **~ as big** la mitad de grande • **they paid ~ as much again** pagaron la mitad más • **their garden is ~ as big again** su jardín es la mitad más grande (que este) • **there were only ~ as many people as before** había solamente la mitad de los que había antes • **it wasn't ~ as bad as I had thought*** [*interview, trip to the dentist*] no lo pasé ni con mucho *or* ni de lejos tan mal como había imaginado • **~ asleep** medio dormido • **~ done** a medio hacer • **he ~ got up** se levantó a medias • **~ laughing, ~ crying** medio riendo, medio llorando • **I only ~ read it** lo leí solo a medias • **I was only ~ serious when I said that** aquello solo lo dije medio en broma; ▹ **half-baked**
2 (*time*) • **~ past four** las cuatro y media • **come at ~ three*** ven a las tres y media
3 (*with neg*) (*Brit**) • **not ~!** ¡y cómo!, ¡ya lo creo! • **he didn't ~ run** corrió muchísimo, corrió como un bólido • **it didn't ~ rain!** ¡había que ver cómo llovía! • **it wasn't ~ dear** nos costó un riñón, fue carísimo • **it isn't ~ hot** hace un calor de miedo
CPD ▸ **half fare** medio pasaje *m*; (*as adv*) • **to travel ~ fare** viajar pagando medio pasaje ▸ **half note** (*US*) (*Mus*) blanca *f* ▸ **half term** (*Brit*) (*Scol*) vacaciones *fpl* de mediados del trimestre

half-a-crown [,hɑːfə'kraʊn] N = **half-crown**

half-and-half [,hɑːfənd'hɑːf] ADJ [*mixture, solution*] a partes iguales, mitad y mitad
ADV a partes iguales, mitad y mitad • **mix the mayonnaise half-and-half with yogurt** mezcle la mayonesa a partes iguales *or* mitad y mitad con el yogur • **to split sth half-and-half** dividir algo en dos mitades (a partes iguales)

half-assed‡ ['hɑːfæst] ADJ (*US*) [*person*] que tiene pocas luces; [*idea*] muy poco brillante

halfback ['hɑːfbæk] N (*Ftbl*) medio/a *m/f*

half-baked ['hɑːf'beɪkt] ADJ (*fig*) [*plan, idea*] mal concebido, sin perfilar; [*person*] soso

half board [,hɑːf'bɔːd] N (*Brit*) (*in hotel*) media pensión *f*

half-bred ['hɑːfbred] ADJ mestizo

half-breed ['hɑːfbriːd] N (= *animal*) híbrido *m*; (= *person*) (*** pej*) mestizo/a *m/f*

half-brother ['hɑːf,brʌðəʳ] N medio hermano *m*, hermanastro *m*

half-caste** ['hɑːfkɑːst] ADJ mestizo
N mestizo/a *m/f*

half-century [hɑːf'sentjʊrɪ] N (*Cricket*)

h

cincuenta tantos *mpl*

half-circle ['hɑːfsɜːkl] N semicírculo *m*

half-closed [ˌhɑːf'kləʊzd] ADJ entreabierto

half-cock ['hɑːfkɒk] N posición *f* de medio amartillado (*de la escopeta etc*) • IDIOM: • **to go off at half-cock** [*person*] hacer las cosas antes de tiempo; [*plan*] irse al garete (por falta de preparación)*

half-cocked [ˌhɑːf'kɒkt] ADJ [*gun*] con el seguro echado; [*plan, scheme*] mal concebido

half-crown ['hɑːf'kraʊn] N (*formerly*) media corona *f* • **a half-crown** media corona

half-cup ['hɑːfˌkʌp] ADJ [*bra*] de media copa

half-day [ˌhɑːf'deɪ] N medio día *m*, media jornada *f*

CPD ▸ **half-day closing** • **half-day closing is on Mondays** los lunes se cierra por la tarde ▸ **half-day holiday** fiesta *f* de media jornada

half-dead ['hɑːf'ded] ADJ medio muerto, más muerto que vivo

half-dozen ['hɑːf'dʌzn] N media docena *f*

half-dressed [ˌhɑːf'drest] ADJ a medio vestir

half-educated [ˌhɑːf'edjʊkeɪtɪd] ADJ con poca cultura • **he is half-educated** tiene poca cultura

half-empty ['hɑːf'emptɪ] ADJ [*bottle, box, room, train*] medio vacío; [*hall etc*] semidesierto

half-forgotten [ˌhɑːffə'gɒtn] ADJ medio olvidado

half-frozen [ˌhɑːf'frəʊzən] ADJ medio congelado • **he was half-frozen when they found him** estaba medio congelado cuando lo encontraron, lo encontraron en estado de semicongelación

half-full ['hɑːf'fʊl] ADJ medio lleno, mediado

half-grown [ˌhɑːf'grəʊn] ADJ pequeño, no del todo crecido

half-hearted ['hɑːf'hɑːtɪd] ADJ [*effort*] tibio; [*applause*] tímido, poco entusiasta; [*smile*] de conejo, de dientes afuera (*LAm*) • **I made a half-hearted effort to dissuade him** intenté disuadirle sin demasiado entusiasmo, hice un tibio intento de disuadirle

half-heartedly ['hɑːf'hɑːtɪdlɪ] ADV con poco entusiasmo

half-heartedness [ˌhɑːf'hɑːtɪdnɪs] N falta *f* de entusiasmo

half-holiday ['hɑːf'hɒlɪdɪ] N (*Brit*) (*Scol*) fiesta *f* de media jornada; (*in shop*) descanso *m*

half-hour ['hɑːf'aʊəʳ] N media hora *f* • **the clock struck the half-hour** el reloj dio y media *or* dio la media • **on the half-hour** a y media

CPD [*meeting, session, drive*] de media hora

half-hourly [ˌhɑːf'aʊəlɪ] ADV cada media hora

ADJ • **at half-hourly intervals** cada media hora

half-inch [ˌhɑːf'ɪntʃ] N media pulgada *f*

ADJ • **cut into half-inch lengths** córtese en trozos de media pulgada de largo, córtese en trozos de algo más de un centímetro de largo

half-length ['hɑːfleŋθ] ADJ de medio cuerpo

half-life ['hɑːflaɪf] N (PL: **half-lives**) (*Phys*) media vida *f*

half-light ['hɑːflaɪt] N penumbra *f*

half-marathon ['hɑːf'mærəθən] N medio maratón *m*, media maratón *f*

half-mast ['hɑːf'mɑːst] N • **at half-mast** [*flag*] a media asta; [*trousers*] (= *very short*) muy cortos; (= *halfway down the legs*) medio bajados

half-measures ['hɑːf'meʒəz] NPL paños *mpl* calientes, medias tintas *fpl* • **we don't want any half-measures** no queremos andarnos con medias tintas *or* paños calientes

half-monthly [ˌhɑːf'mʌnθlɪ] ADJ quincenal

ADV cada quince días

half-moon ['hɑːf'muːn] N media luna *f*

half-naked ['hɑːf'neɪkɪd] ADJ semidesnudo

half-open [ˌhɑːf'əʊpən] ADJ entreabierto, medio abierto

half-panelled, half-paneled (*US*) [ˌhɑːf'pænəld] ADJ chapado hasta media altura

half-pay ['hɑːf'peɪ] N media paga *f* • **to retire on half-pay** jubilarse con media paga

CPD ▸ **half-pay officer** militar *m* retirado

halfpenny ['heɪpnɪ] N (PL: **halfpennies** *or* **halfpence** ['heɪpəns]) (*Hist*) medio penique *m* • IDIOM: • **not to have a ~ or two halfpennies to rub together** no tener un céntimo, estar sin blanca

half-pint [ˌhɑːf'paɪnt] N **1** (= *measure*) media pinta *f*

2* (= *small person*) enano/a *m/f*

half-price ['hɑːf'praɪs] ADV a mitad de precio

ADJ [*ticket etc*] a mitad de precio

half-seas over ['hɑːfsiːz'əʊvəʳ] ADV • IDIOM: • **to be half-seas over** estar entre dos velas

half-serious [ˌhɑːf'sɪərɪəs] ADJ entre serio y en broma

half-sister ['hɑːfˌsɪstəʳ] N media hermana *f*, hermanastra *f*

half-size ['hɑːfˌsaɪz] N (*in shoes*) medio número *m*

ADJ [*musical instrument, chair*] de la mitad de tamaño

half-sized [ˌhɑːf'saɪzd] ADJ = **half-size**

half-timbered [ˌhɑːf'tɪmbəd] ADJ con entramado de madera

half-time ['hɑːf'taɪm] N (*Sport*) descanso *m* • **at half-time** en el descanso

ADV • **to work half-time** trabajar media jornada

CPD ▸ **half-time score** marcador *m* en el descanso • **the half-time score was 1-0** el marcador en el descanso era 1-0 ▸ **half-time work** trabajo *m* de media jornada

half-tone ['hɑːftəʊn] ADJ • **half-tone illustration** fotograbado *m* a media tinta

N **1** (*Art*) fotograbado *m* a media tinta

2 (*US*) (*Mus*) semitono *m*

half-track ['hɑːftræk] N camión *m* semi-oruga

half-truth ['hɑːftruːθ] N (PL: **half-truths** ['hɑːftruːðz]) verdad *f* a medias

half-volley ['hɑːf'vɒlɪ] N media volea *f*

halfway ['hɑːf'weɪ] ADV **1** (*lit*) a medio camino • **Reading is ~ between Oxford and London** Reading está a medio camino entre Oxford y Londres • **we're ~ there** estamos a mitad de camino *or* a medio camino • **~ up/down the hill** a media cuesta • **her hair reaches ~ down her back** el pelo le llega hasta la mitad de la espalda • **they've travelled ~ around the world** han recorrido medio mundo • **~ through the film** hacia la mitad de la película, a (la) mitad de la película • **the decision only goes ~ toward giving the strikers what they want** la decisión solo satisface a medias las demandas de los huelguistas • IDIOM: • **to meet sb ~** llegar a un compromiso con algn

2* (*fig*) (= *at all, the least bit*) • **anything ~ decent will be incredibly expensive** cualquier cosa mínimamente decente va a ser carísima

ADJ [*mark*] a *or* de medio camino; [*stage*] intermedio; (*fig*) (= *incomplete*) a medias

CPD ▸ **halfway house** (*for rehabilitation*) centro *m* de reinserción; (*fig*) punto *m* medio, término *m* medio • **it's a ~ house between dance and drama** está a medio camino entre la danza y el teatro ▸ **halfway line** (*Rugby*) línea *f* media

halfwit ['hɑːfwɪt] N imbécil *mf*, tonto/a *m/f*

half-witted ['hɑːf'wɪtɪd] ADJ imbécil, tonto

half-year [ˌhɑːf'jɪəʳ] N medio año *m*, semestre *m*

CPD ▸ **half-year results** resultados *mpl* semestrales

half-yearly ['hɑːf'jɪəlɪ] ADV semestralmente

ADJ semestral

halibut ['hælɪbət] N (PL: **halibut** *or* **halibuts**) halibut *m*, hipogloso *m*

halitosis [ˌhælɪ'təʊsɪs] N halitosis *f*

hall [hɔːl] N **1** (= *entrance hall*) hall *m*, entrada *f*; (= *foyer*) vestíbulo *m*; (*US*) (= *passage*) pasillo *m*

2 (= *large room, building*) sala *f* • **concert ~** sala *f* de conciertos • **dance ~** salón *m* de baile • **church ~** sala *f* parroquial; ▹ **village**

3 (= *mansion*) casa *f* solariega

4 (*Brit*) (*Univ*) (= *central hall*) paraninfo *m*; (*also* **hall of residence**) residencia *f*, colegio *m* mayor

CPD ▸ **Hall of Fame** (= *people*) estrellas *fpl*; (*US*) (= *museum*) museo *m* • **the rock'n'roll ~ of fame** las estrellas del rock and roll ▸ **hall porter** (*Brit*) portero/a *m/f*, conserje *mf* ▸ **hall stand** perchero *m*

hallelujah [ˌhælɪ'luːjə] N, EXCL aleluya *f*

hallmark ['hɔːlmɑːk] N (*on gold, silver*) contraste *m*; (*fig*) sello *m* • **the attack bears all the ~s of the CLF** el atentado lleva el auténtico sello del CLF

hallo [hʌ'ləʊ] EXCL = **hello**

halloo [hə'luː] EXCL ¡sus!, ¡hala!

N grito *m*

VI gritar

hallow ['hæləʊ] VT santificar

hallowed ['hæləʊd] ADJ [*ground etc*] sagrado, santificado

Hallowe'en ['hæləʊ'iːn] N víspera *f* de Todos los Santos

HALLOWE'EN

La festividad de **Hallowe'en** se celebra, tanto en el Reino Unido como en EE.UU., la noche del 31 de octubre. Aunque antes la fiesta se asociaba con la creencia de que las almas de los difuntos regresaban a sus hogares en esa fecha, actualmente **Hallowe'en** no es más que un pretexto para la diversión. Los niños se disfrazan de fantasmas y brujas y hacen farolillos con calabazas vacías en cuyo interior colocan una vela. Así vestidos, van de casa en casa por todo el barrio pidiendo caramelos y dinero, una costumbre que se conoce sobre todo en Estados Unidos como **trick or treat** porque los niños amenazan con gastarle una broma al dueño de la casa si no reciben los caramelos. También suelen celebrarse en **Hallowe'en** fiestas de disfraces para niños y para adultos.

hallucinate [hə'luːsɪneɪt] VI alucinar, tener alucinaciones

hallucination [həˌluːsɪ'neɪʃən] N alucinación *f*

hallucinatory [hə'luːsɪnətərɪ] ADJ alucinante

hallucinogen [hə'luːsɪnəˌdʒen] N alucinógeno *m*

hallucinogenic [həˌluːsɪnəʊ'dʒenɪk] ADJ alucinógeno

(N) alucinógeno *m*
hallucinosis [hə,lu:sɪ'nəʊsɪs] (N) alucinosis *f*
hallway ['hɔ:lweɪ] (N) = hall
halo ['heɪləʊ] (N) (PL: **halo(e)s**) halo *m*, aureola *f*
halogen ['heɪləʊdʒɪn] (N) halógeno *m*
(CPD) ▸ **halogen lamp** lámpara *f* **halógena**
halogenous [hə'lɒdʒɪnəs] (ADJ) halógeno
halt [hɔ:lt] (N) **1** (= *stop, standstill*) alto *m*, parada *f* • **to bring sth to a ~** [+ *car*] parar *or* detener algo; [+ *event, process*] interrumpir algo • **to come to a ~** [*car*] pararse, detenerse; [*train*] hacer alto, detenerse; [*negotiations*] interrumpirse • **to call a ~ (to sth)** (*fig*) poner fin (a algo)
2 (*Brit*) (= *train stop*) apeadero *m*
(VT) [+ *vehicle, production*] parar, detener
(VI) (*gen*) pararse, detenerse; [*train*] hacer alto, detenerse; [*process*] interrumpirse • **~!** (*Mil*) ¡alto!
(CPD) ▸ **halt sign** señal *f* de stop
halter ['hɔ:ltə^r] (N) (*for horse*) cabestro *m*, ronzal *m*; (= *noose*) dogal *m*
halter-neck ['hɔ:ltə,nek] (N) *top sin espalda ni mangas*
(ADJ) [*dress, top*] sin espalda ni mangas
halting ['hɔ:ltɪŋ] (ADJ) (= *hesitant*) [*speech, movement*] titubeante, vacilante
haltingly ['hɔ:ltɪŋlɪ] (ADV) [*speak*] titubeando, vacilantemente
halve [hɑ:v] (VT) (= *divide*) partir por la mitad, partir en dos; (= *reduce by half*) reducir a la mitad
(VI) reducirse a la mitad
halves [hɑ:vz] (NPL) *of* **half**
halyard ['hæljəd] (N) driza *f*
ham [hæm] (N) **1** (*Culin*) jamón *m*
2 hams (*Anat*) nalgas *fpl*
3 (*Theat*) (*also* **ham actor**) comicastro *m*, actor *m* histriónico; (*also* **ham actress**) actriz *f* histriónica
4 (= *radio ham*) radioaficionado/a *m/f*
(VI) (*Theat**) actuar de una manera exagerada *or* melodramática
(CPD) ▸ **ham acting** histrionismo *m*
▸ **ham up*** (VT + ADV) • **to ham it up*** actuar de manera exagerada *or* melodramática
Hamburg ['hæmbɜ:g] (N) Hamburgo *m*
hamburger ['hæm,bɜ:gə^r] (N) hamburguesa *f*; (*US*) (*also* **hamburger meat**) carne *f* picada
ham-fisted [,hæm'fɪstɪd], **ham-handed** [,hæm'hændɪd] (ADJ) torpe, desmañado
Hamitic [hæ'mɪtɪk] (ADJ) camítico
hamlet ['hæmlɪt] (N) aldea *f*, caserío *m*
hammer ['hæmə^r] (N) (= *tool*) martillo *m*; (*Mus*) macillo *m*; [*of firearm*] percusor *m* • **the ~ and sickle** el martillo y la hoz • **to come under the ~** ser subastado • IDIOM: • **to go at it ~ and tongs*** (= *argue*) discutir acaloradamente; (= *fight*) luchar a brazo partido; (= *work*) darle duro*
(VT) **1** [+ *nail*] clavar; [+ *metal*] martillar, batir • **to ~ a post into the ground** hincar un poste en el suelo a martillazos • **to ~ sth into shape** [+ *metal*] forjar algo a martillazos; (*fig*) [+ *team etc*] forjar algo a golpes • **to ~ a point home** remachar un punto • **to ~ sth into sb** (*fig*) meter algo en la cabeza de algn
2* (= *defeat, thrash*) dar una paliza a*, machacar*
(VI) • **to ~ on** *or* **at a door** dar golpes en *or* golpear una puerta • **to ~ away at** [+ *subject*] insistir con ahínco en, machacar en; [+ *work*] trabajar asiduamente en • **to ~ away on the piano** aporrear el piano
(CPD) ▸ **hammer blow** (*fig*) duro golpe *m* • **to deliver a ~ blow to sth** asestar un duro golpe a algo ▸ **hammer throw** lanzamiento *m* de martillo ▸ **hammer thrower** lanzador(a) *m/f* de martillo
▸ **hammer down** (VT + ADV) [+ *lid etc*] asegurar con clavos; [+ *nail*] meter a martillazos
▸ **hammer in** (VT + ADV) meter a martillazos
▸ **hammer out** (VT + ADV) [+ *nail*] sacar; [+ *dent*] alisar a martillazos; (*fig*) [+ *solution, agreement*] negociar no sin esfuerzo
▸ **hammer together** (VT + ADV) [+ *pieces of wood etc*] clavar
hammered* ['hæməd] (ADJ) (*Brit*) (= *drunk*) mamado*
hammerhead ['hæməhed] (N) (= *shark*) pez *m* martillo
hammering ['hæmərɪŋ] (N) **1** (*lit*) martilleo *m*
2* paliza* *f* • **to give sb a ~** dar una paliza a algn* • **to get** *or* **take a ~** recibir una paliza*
hammertoe ['hæmətəʊ] (N) dedo *m* (en) martillo
hammock ['hæmək] (N) hamaca *f*; (*Naut*) coy *m*
hammy* ['hæmɪ] (ADJ) [*actor*] exagerado, melodramático
hamper¹ ['hæmpə^r] (N) cesto *m*, canasta *f*
hamper² ['hæmpə^r] (VT) (= *hinder*) [+ *efforts, work*] dificultar, entorpecer; [+ *movement*] obstaculizar, impedir • **the investigation was ~ed by their lack of cooperation** la investigación se vio entorpecida por su falta de colaboración
hamster ['hæmstə^r] (N) hámster *m*
hamstring ['hæmstrɪŋ] (VB: PT, PP: **hamstrung**) (N) [*of person*] tendón *m* de la corva; [*of animal*] tendón *m* del jarrete
(VT) (*lit*) desjarretar; (*fig*) paralizar
(CPD) ▸ **hamstring injury** lesión *f* del tendón de la corva
hand [hænd] (N) **1** (= *part of body*) mano *f* • **to have sth in one's ~** tener algo en la mano • **to be clever** *or* **good with one's ~s** ser hábil con las manos, ser un manitas • **a piece for four ~s** (*Mus*) una pieza para (piano a) cuatro manos • **to hold ~s** [*children*] ir cogidos de la mano, ir tomados de la mano (*LAm*); [*lovers*] hacer manitas • **on (one's) ~s and knees** a gatas • **~s off!*** ¡fuera las manos!, ¡no se toca! • **~s off those chocolates!** ¡los bombones ni tocarlos! • **~s off pensions!** ¡no a la reforma de las pensiones!, ¡dejad las pensiones en paz! • **to keep one's ~s off sth** no tocar algo • **~s up!** (*to criminal*) ¡arriba las manos!; (*to pupils*) ¡que levanten la mano! • IDIOMS: • **~ over fist**: • **to be making money ~ over fist** ganar dinero a espuertas • **to be losing money ~ over fist** hacerle agua el dinero • **to be ~ in glove with sb** (= *very close*) ser uña y carne con algn; (= *in cahoots*) estar conchabado con algn • **to work ~ in glove with sb** trabajar en estrecha colaboración con algn • **to live from ~ to mouth** vivir al día • **my ~s are tied** tengo las manos atadas, no puedo hacer nada • **I could do it with one ~ tied behind my back** lo podría hacer con una mano atada a la espalda • **he never does a ~'s turn** no da golpe • PROVERB: • **many ~s make light work** muchas manos facilitan el trabajo; ▹ **shake**
2 (= *needle*) [*of instrument*] aguja *f*; [*of clock*] manecilla *f*, aguja *f* • **the big ~** la manecilla grande, el minutero • **the little ~** la manecilla pequeña, el horario
3 (= *agency, influence*) mano *f*, influencia *f* • **his ~ was everywhere** se notaba su influencia por todas partes, su mano se notaba en todo • **to have a ~ in** tomar parte en, intervenir en • **he had no ~ in it** no tuvo arte ni parte en ello
4 (= *worker*) (*in factory*) obrero/a *m/f*; (= *farm hand*) peón *m*; (= *deck hand*) marinero *m* (de cubierta) • **all ~s on deck!** (*Naut*) ¡todos a cubierta! • **to be lost with all ~s** hundirse con toda la tripulación • IDIOM: • **to be an old ~ (at sth)** ser perro viejo (en algo)
5 (= *help*) mano *f* • **would you like a ~ with moving that?** ¿te echo una mano a mover eso? • **to give** *or* **lend sb a ~** echar una mano a algn • **can you give** *or* **lend me a ~?** ¿me echas una mano?
6 (= *handwriting*) letra *f*, escritura *f* • **he writes a good ~** tiene buena letra • **in one's own ~** de su (propio) puño y letra
7 (*Cards*) (= *round*) mano *f*, partida *f*; (= *cards held*) mano *f* • **a ~ of bridge/poker** una mano *or* una partida de bridge/póker
8 (= *measurement*) [*of horse*] palmo *m* • **he's 15 ~s high** mide 15 palmos de alto
9* (= *round of applause*) • **they gave him a big ~** le aplaudieron calurosamente • **let's have a big ~ for ...!** ¡muchos aplausos para ...!
10 (*phrases with verb*) • **to ask for sb's ~ (in marriage)** pedir la mano de algn • **to change ~s** cambiar de mano *or* de dueño • **just wait till I get my ~s on him!** ¡espera (a) que le ponga la mano encima! • **to lay ~s on** (= *get*) conseguir; (*Rel*) imponer las manos a • **I don't know where to lay my ~s on ...** no sé dónde conseguir ... • **she read everything she could lay her ~s on** leía todo lo que caía en sus manos • **to put** *or* **set one's ~ to sth** emprender algo • **to raise one's** *or* **a ~ to** *or* **against sb** poner a algn la mano encima • **to take a ~ in sth** tomar parte *or* participar en algo • **to try one's ~ at sth** probar algo • IDIOMS: • **to get one's ~ in** adquirir práctica, irse acostumbrando • **to give with one ~ and take away with the other** quitar con una mano lo que se da con la otra • **to keep one's ~ in** conservar *or* no perder la práctica **(at de)** • **to sit on one's ~s** (*US**) [*audience*] aplaudir con desgana; [*committee etc*] no hacer nada • **to turn one's ~ to sth** dedicarse a algo • **he can turn his ~ to anything** vale tanto para un barrido como para un fregado • **to wait on sb ~ and foot** desvivirse por algn, ponérselo todo en bandeja a algn; ▹ **eat, force, join, show, throw up, wash, win**
11 (*phrases with adjective*) • **to rule with a firm ~** gobernar con firmeza • **to have a free ~** tener carta blanca • **to give sb a free ~** dar carta blanca a algn • **to have one's ~s full (with sth/sb)** no parar un momento (con algo/algn), estar muy ocupado (con algo/algn) • **I've got my ~s full with the kids** con los niños no paro un momento • **I've got my ~s full running the firm while the boss is away** estoy muy ocupado llevando la empresa mientras el jefe está fuera • **don't worry, she's in good ~s** no te preocupes, está en buenas manos • **with a heavy ~** con mano dura • **to give sb a helping ~** echar una mano a algn • **with a high ~** despóticamente • **if this should get into the wrong ~s ...** si esto cayera en manos de quien no debiera ... • IDIOMS: • **to get** *or* **gain the upper ~** empezar a dominar • **to have the upper ~** tener *or* llevar la ventaja
12 (= *after preposition*) • **don't worry, help is at ~** no te preocupes, disponemos de *or* contamos con ayuda • **winter was at ~** se acercaba el invierno • **keep the book close at ~** ten el libro a mano • **we're close at ~ in case she needs help** nos tiene a mano *or* muy cerca si necesita ayuda • **at first ~** de primera mano • **I heard it only at second ~** lo supe solo de modo indirecto • **at the ~s of** a manos de • **they suffered a series of defeats at the ~s of the French** sufrieron una serie

de derrotas a manos de los franceses • **made by ~** hecho a mano • **to raise an animal by ~** criar un animal uno mismo • **to send a letter by ~** enviar una carta en mano • **delivered by ~** entregado en mano • **"by hand"** (*on envelope*) "en su mano" • **to take sb by the ~** coger *or* tomar a algn de la mano • **they were going along ~ in ~** iban cogidos de la mano • **it goes ~ in ~ with** está estrechamente relacionado con • **these plans should go ~ in ~** estos proyectos deben realizarse al mismo ritmo • **gun in ~** el revólver en la mano, empuñando el revólver • **to be in sb's ~s** estar en manos de algn • **it's in his ~s now** depende de él ahora • **I put myself in your ~s** me pongo en tus manos • **to have £50 in ~** tener 50 libras en el haber • **I like to have sth in ~** me gusta tener algo en reserva • **money in ~** dinero *m* disponible • **the cases I have in ~ at the moment** los casos que tengo entre manos en este momento • **the situation is in ~** tenemos la situación controlada *or* bajo control • **he has them well in ~** sabe manejarlos perfectamente • **let's concentrate on the job in ~** centrémonos en el trabajo que tenemos entre manos • **to take sth in ~** tomar algo a cuestas • **to take sb in ~** (= *take charge of*) hacerse cargo de algn; (= *discipline*) imponer disciplina a algn • **to play into sb's ~s** hacer el juego a algn • **to fall into the ~s of the enemy** caer en manos del enemigo • **to put sth into a lawyer's ~s** poner un asunto en manos de un abogado • **to take justice into one's own ~s** tomar la justicia por su propia mano • **to get sth off one's ~s** (= *get rid of*) deshacerse de algo; (= *finish doing*) terminar de hacer algo • **to take sth off sb's ~s** desembarazar a algn de algo • **the children are off our ~s now** nuestros hijos ya han volado del nido • **on the right/left ~** a derecha/izquierda, a mano derecha/ izquierda • **on the one ~ ... on the other ~** por una parte ... por otra parte, por un lado ... por otro lado • **on the other ~, she did agree to do it** pero el caso es que ella (sí) había accedido a hacerlo • **on every ~** • **on all ~s** por todas partes • **there are experts on ~ to give you advice** hay expertos a su disposición para ofrecerle asesoramiento • **I've got him on my ~s all day** está conmigo todo el día • **we've got a difficult job on our ~s** tenemos entre manos una difícil tarea • **he's got time on his ~s** tiene todo el tiempo del mundo • **to have sth left on one's ~s** tener que quedarse con algo • **he was left with the goods on his ~s** tuvo que quedarse con todo el género, el género resultó ser invendible • **to dismiss sth out of ~** descartar algo sin más • **the situation was getting out of ~** la situación se estaba escapando de las manos • **the children were getting out of ~** los niños se estaban desmandando • **to have sth to ~** tener algo a mano • **I don't have the information to ~ just now** ahora mismo no tengo a mano la información • **I hit him with the first thing that came to ~** le golpeé con lo primero que tenía a mano *or* que pillé • **your letter of the 23rd is to ~** (*frm*) he recibido su carta del día 23; ▹ **cap**

VT (= *pass*) • **to ~ sb sth** • **~ sth to sb** pasar algo a algn • **he ~ed me the book** me pasó el libro • IDIOM: • **you've got to ~ it to him*** hay que reconocérselo

CPD [*lotion, cream*] para las manos ▸ **hand baggage** (US) = **hand luggage** ▸ **hand controls** controles *mpl* manuales ▸ **hand drier, hand dryer** secamanos *m inv* automático ▸ **hand gel** gel *m* (limpiador) de manos ▸ **hand grenade** granada *f* (de mano) ▸ **hand lotion** loción *f* para las manos ▸ **hand luggage** equipaje *m* de mano ▸ **hand print** manotada *f* ▸ **hand puppet** títere *m* ▸ **hand signal** (*Aut*) señal *f* con el brazo • **with both indicators broken, he had to rely on ~ signals** con los intermitentes rotos tenía que hacer señales con el brazo *or* la mano • **they had to communicate in ~ signals** tuvieron que comunicarse por señas ▸ **hand towel** toalla *f* de manos; ▹ **hand-wash**

▸ **hand around** VT + ADV = **hand round**

▸ **hand back** VT + ADV devolver

▸ **hand down** VT + ADV [+ *suitcase etc*] bajar, pasar; [+ *heirloom*] pasar, dejar en herencia; [+ *tradition*] transmitir; (US) [+ *judgement*] dictar, imponer; [+ *person*] ayudar a bajar

▸ **hand in** VT + ADV [+ *form, homework*] entregar; [+ *resignation*] presentar

▸ **hand off** VT + ADV (*Rugby*) rechazar

▸ **hand on** VT + ADV [+ *tradition*] transmitir; [+ *news*] comunicar; [+ *object*] pasar

▸ **hand out** VT + ADV [+ *leaflets*] repartir, distribuir; [+ *advice*] dar

▸ **hand over** VT + ADV **1** (= *pass over*) pasar • **can you ~ me over the hammer please?** ¿me pasas el martillo, por favor?
2 (= *hand in*) [+ *driving licence, passport*] entregar; (= *surrender*) [+ *property, business*] traspasar, ceder; [+ *power, government*] ceder
VI + ADV (*to successor*) ceder su puesto a • **I'm now ~ing over to the studio** (*Rad, TV*) ahora devolvemos la conexión al estudio

▸ **hand round** VT + ADV [+ *information, bottle*] pasar (de mano en mano); [+ *chocolates, biscuits etc*] ofrecer; [+ *photocopies, leaflets, books*] repartir

▸ **hand up** VT + ADV [+ *person*] subir

hand- ['hænd-] PREFIX • **hand-crafted** hecho a mano • **artefacts and textiles hand-crafted in Rajasthan** artefactos y textiles hechos a mano en Rajasthan • **hand-built** construido a mano • **hand-sewn** cosido a mano • **hand-carved** tallado a mano • **a beautifully hand-carved garden seat** una silla de jardín preciosamente tallada a mano

handbag ['hændbæg] N bolso *m* (de mano), bolsa *f* (de mano), cartera *f* (*LAm*)
VT* poner fuera de combate a golpe de bolso, eliminar a bolsazos

handball ['hændbɔːl] N **1** (= *game*) balonmano *m*
2 (*Ftbl*) (= *offence*) mano *f*

handbasin ['hænd,beɪsn] N lavabo *m*

handbell ['hændbel] N campanilla *f*

handbill ['hændbɪl] N folleto *m*, octavilla *f*

handbook ['hændbʊk] N (= *manual*) manual *m*; (= *guide*) guía *f*

handbrake ['hændbreɪk] N (*Brit*) freno *m* de mano

h. & c. ABBR (= **hot and cold (water)**) con agua caliente y fría

handcart ['hændkɑːt] N carretilla *f*, carretón *m*

handclap ['hændklæp] N palmada *f* • **to give a player the slow ~** batir palmas a ritmo lento (*para que un jugador se esfuerce más o se dé prisa*)

handclasp ['hændklɑːsp] N = **handshake**

handcraft ['hændkrɑːft] VT (US) hacer a mano • **~ed products** productos *mpl* artesanales

handcream ['hændkriːm] N crema *f* para las manos

handcuff ['hændkʌf] VT poner las esposas a, esposar

handcuffs ['hændkʌfs] NPL esposas *fpl*

hand-delivered [,hænddɪ'lɪvəd] ADJ [*letter, parcel*] entregado a mano

-handed ['hændɪd] ADJ (*ending in compounds*) • **two-handed backhand** (*Tennis*) revés *m* a dos manos • **he drove one-handed** conducía con una sola mano • **four-handed game** juego *m* para cuatro personas; ▹ **empty-handed, heavy-handed** *etc*

-hander ['hændəʳ] N (*ending in compounds*) (*esp Brit*) • **two/three-hander** (*TV, Cine*) película *f* con dos/tres personajes; (*Theat*) obra *f* con dos/tres personajes; ▹ **left-hander, right-hander**

handfeed ['hændfiːd] VT (PT, PP: **handfed**) [+ *animal*] alimentar con la mano

handful ['hændfʊl] N (= *quantity*) manojo *m*, puñado *m*; (= *small number*) puñado *m* • **a ~ of people** un puñado de gente • **that child's a real ~*** ese niño es muy travieso

handgrip ['hændgrɪp] N = **handle, grip**

handgun ['hændgʌn] N (*esp US*) revólver *m*, pistola *f*

hand-held ['hændheld] ADJ de mano; (= *portable*) portátil

handhold ['hændhəʊld] N asidero *m*

handicap ['hændɪkæp] N **1** (= *disadvantage*) desventaja *f*; (= *impediment*) obstáculo *m*, estorbo *m*
2 (*Sport, Golf*) hándicap *m*; (= *horse race*) hándicap *m*
3 (*Med*) minusvalía *f*, discapacidad *f*
VT (= *prejudice*) perjudicar; (*Sport*) establecer un hándicap para • **he has always been ~ped by his accent** su acento siempre le ha perjudicado *or* le ha supuesto una desventaja

handicapped ['hændɪkæpt] ADJ • **mentally ~** mentalmente discapacitado, psíquicamente disminuido • **physically ~** minusválido, (físicamente) discapacitado • **to be mentally/physically ~** tener una discapacidad mental/física, ser (un) discapacitado mental/físico
N • **the ~** los minusválidos, los discapacitados • **the mentally ~** los discapacitados mentales, los disminuidos psíquicos

handicraft ['hændɪkrɑːft] N (= *art, product*) artesanía *f*; (= *skill*) destreza *f* manual
CPD ▸ **handicraft teacher** profesor(a) *m/f* de trabajos manuales

handily ['hændɪlɪ] ADV **1** (= *conveniently*) [*positioned, situated*] convenientemente, cómodamente
2 (= *dexterously*) con habilidad, con destreza
3 (US) (= *easily*) [*win*] fácilmente

handiness ['hændɪnɪs] N **1** (= *closeness*) proximidad *f* • **the advantage of this house is its ~ for the school** la ventaja de esta casa es su proximidad a la escuela *or* lo cerca que queda de la escuela • **because of the ~ of the library** debido a que la biblioteca está tan a mano *or* queda tan cerca, porque resulta tan cómodo ir a la biblioteca
2 [*of tool, gadget*] utilidad *f*
3 (= *skill*) habilidad *f*, destreza *f*

handiwork ['hændɪwɜːk] N **1** (= *craft*) trabajo *m*
2 (= *action*) obra *f* • **this looks like his ~** (*pej*) parece que es obra de él

handjob** ['hænddʒɒb] N • **to give sb a ~** hacerle una paja a algn**

handkerchief ['hæŋkətʃɪf] N pañuelo *m*; ▹ **pocket**

hand-knitted [,hænd'nɪtɪd] ADJ tricotado a mano, tejido a mano (*LAm*)

handle ['hændl] N **1** [*of knife, brush, spade, saucepan*] mango *m*; [*of broom*] palo *m*; [*of basket, bucket, jug*] asa *f*; [*of drawer*] tirador *m*, manija *f*; [*of door*] (= *round knob*) pomo *m*; (= *lever*) picaporte *m*, manilla *f* (*LAm*); [*of stretcher, wheelbarrow*] brazo *m*; [*of pump*]

palanca *f*; (*for winding*) manivela *f* • IDIOM: • **to fly off the ~** perder los estribos, salirse de sus casillas
2 (*fig*) (= *pretext*) excusa *f*, pretexto *m*; (= *opportunity*) oportunidad *f* • **to get a ~ on sth*** llegar a saber cómo lidiar con algo • **to have a ~ on sth*** tener algo controlado
3* (= *title*) título *m*; (= *name*) nombre *m*; (*on social network*) nombre *m* de usuario • **to have a ~ to one's name** (*aristocratic*) tener un título nobiliario
VT **1** (= *touch with hands*) tocar • **"please do not handle the fruit"** "se ruega no tocar la fruta" • **to ~ the ball** (*Ftbl*) tocar la pelota con la mano
2 (= *manipulate, move with hands*) [+ *food*] manipular • **her hands are black from handling newsprint** tiene las manos negras de andar con *or* andar manipulando periódicos • **flowers need to be ~d gently** las flores necesitan que se las trate con cuidado • **"handle with care"** "manéjese *or* trátese con cuidado" • **the police ~d him roughly** la policía lo maltrató • IDIOM: • **to ~ sb with kid gloves** tratar a algn con guantes de seda; ▷ **hot**
3 (= *use*) [+ *gun, machine*] manejar • **he knows how to ~ a gun** sabe cómo manejar una pistola • **"not to be taken before handling machinery"** "no ingerir en caso de ir a manejar maquinaria"
4 (= *drive, steer*) [+ *car*] conducir, manejar (*LAm*); [+ *ship*] gobernar; [+ *horse*] manejar
5 (= *tackle*) [+ *situation*] manejar; [+ *people*] tratar • **he ~d the situation very well** manejó *or* llevó muy bien la situación • **I could have ~d it better than I did** podría haberlo manejado mejor de lo que lo hice
6 (= *manage effectively*) [+ *people*] manejar bien; [+ *emotions*] controlar • **she can certainly ~ children** no cabe duda de que maneja bien a *or* sabe manejarse con los niños • **she can't ~ pressure** no puede con la presión • **I don't know if I can ~ the job** no sé si puedo sacar adelante el trabajo
7 (= *be responsible for*) [+ *case, investigation*] llevar, encargarse de • **the solicitor handling your case** el abogado que lleva *or* se encarga de tu caso • **we don't ~ criminal cases** nosotros no nos encargamos *or* ocupamos de las causas penales • **the treasurer ~s large sums of money** el tesorero maneja grandes cantidades de dinero • **I'll ~ this** yo me encargo (de esto)
8 (= *deal in*) [+ *goods*] comerciar con • **we don't ~ that type of product** no comerciamos con ese tipo de productos • **we don't ~ that type of business** no hacemos ese tipo de trabajos • **to ~ stolen goods** comerciar con objetos robados
9 (= *process*) • **a computer can store and ~ large amounts of information** un ordenador puede almacenar y trabajar con *or* procesar muchísima información • **can the port ~ big ships?** ¿tiene capacidad el puerto para buques grandes? • **the present system of handling refuse** el actual sistema de recogida y tratamiento de residuos • **there is an extra fee for handling and packing your order** hay un recargo por tramitación y embalaje de su pedido • **we ~ ten per cent of their total sales** movemos *or* trabajamos un diez por ciento del total de sus ventas • **we ~ 2,000 travellers a day** por aquí pasan 2.000 viajeros cada día
VI [*car, plane, horse*] comportarse; [*ship*] gobernarse • **this car ~s like a dream** este coche va *or* se comporta de maravilla

handlebar ['hændlbɑːʳ] N manillar *m*, manubrio *m*; **handlebars** manillar *msing*, manubrio *msing*
CPD ▸ **handlebar moustache** (*hum*) bigote *m* Dalí *or* daliniano

-handled ['hændld] ADJ (*ending in compounds*) • **a wooden-handled spade** una pala con mango de madera • **a long-handled spoon** una cuchara de mango largo • **a two-handled urn** una urna de dos asas

handler ['hændləʳ] N **1** (*Comm*) [*of stock*] tratante *mf*, comerciante *mf*
2 (*also* **dog handler**) adiestrador(a) *m/f*; ▷ **baggage**

handling ['hændlɪŋ] N **1** (*lit*) (= *treatment*) trato *m*; (= *manipulation*) manejo *m*; (= *exposure to hands*) manoseo *m* • **the care and ~ of antique textiles** el cuidado y el trato de tejidos antiguos • **the problem of safe ~ of radioactive waste** el problema del manejo seguro de los residuos radiactivos • **all that ~ has not improved the book's condition** tanto manoseo no ha favorecido para nada el estado de conservación del libro • **rough ~** mal trato *m*
2 (= *management*) [*of situation, animal, money*] manejo *m*; [*of person*] trato *m* • **the minister was criticized for his ~ of the economy** el ministro fue criticado por su forma de manejar *or* llevar la economía
3 (*Comm*) porte *m*
4 (*Aut*) [*of car*] conducción *f*, manejo *m* (*LAm*)
CPD ▸ **handling charges** gastos *mpl* de tramitación

handmade ['hænd'meɪd] ADJ hecho a mano
CPD ▸ **handmade paper** papel *m* de tina *or* de mano

handmaid ['hændmeɪd], **handmaiden** ['hændmeɪdən] N (*Hist*) criada *f*; (= *queen's servant*) azafata *f*

hand-me-down* ['hændmɪdaʊn] N prenda *f* usada

handout ['hændaʊt] N **1** (= *leaflet*) octavilla *f*, panfleto *m*; (= *pamphlet*) folleto *m*; (= *press handout*) nota *f* de prensa; (*at lecture*) hoja *f*
2* (= *money*) limosna *f*
3 (= *distribution*) distribución *f*, repartimiento *m*

handover ['hændəʊvəʳ] N (*Pol*) [*of government, power*] entrega *f*, transferencia *f*

hand-painted [ˌhænd'peɪntɪd] ADJ pintado a mano

hand-picked ['hænd'pɪkt] ADJ [*people, staff*] cuidadosamente seleccionado, muy escogido; [*fruit*] cosechado *or* (*LAm*) recogido a mano

handrail ['hændreɪl] N (*on staircase etc*) pasamanos *m inv*, barandilla *f*; (*on ship*) barandilla *f*

hand-rear [ˌhænd'rɪəʳ] VT (*with bottle*) criar a biberones, criar con biberón; (*less specific*) criar a mano

hand-reared [ˌhænd'rɪəd] ADJ criado con biberón

handrub ['hændrʌb] N (= *substance*) desinfectante *m* para manos

handsaw ['hændsɔː] N serrucho *m*

handset ['hændset] N (*Telec*) aparato *m*, auricular *m*

hands-free [ˌhændz'friː] ADJ [*telephone*] manos libres (*inv*)
CPD ▸ **hands-free kit, hands-free set** manos libres *m inv*

handshake ['hændʃeɪk] N apretón *m* de manos; (*Comput*) coloquio *m*; (*as data signal*) "acuse de recibo" • **she had a firm *or* strong ~** estrechaba la mano con fuerza • **she had a weak ~** estrechaba la mano muy débilmente

hands-off [hændz'ɒf] ADJ [*policy, approach*] de no intervención

handsome ['hænsəm] ADJ (COMPAR: **handsomer**, SUPERL: **handsomest**)
1 (= *attractive*) [*man*] guapo, bien parecido; [*building, house, furniture*] bello, espléndido • **a tall boy with a ~ face** un chico alto y guapo de cara • **a ~ woman** una mujer *or* señora de bandera, una buena moza (*LAm*) • **a ~ animal** un magnífico animal
2 (= *considerable*) [*fortune, profit*] cuantioso; [*salary, sum*] generoso, espléndido; [*increase, rise*] importante • **to make a ~ profit (on sth)** conseguir cuantiosos beneficios (de algo)
3 (= *convincing*) [*win, victory*] amplio, holgado

handsomely ['hænsəmlɪ] ADV
1 (= *attractively*) [*illustrated, dressed*] espléndidamente
2 (= *generously*) [*pay, reward*] generosamente, espléndidamente
3 (= *convincingly*) [*win, beat*] fácilmente, por un amplio margen • **this strategy has paid off ~** esta estrategia bien ha merecido la pena

hands-on [ˌhændz'ɒn] ADJ [*experience*] práctico; [*knowledge*] personal • **the museum has lots of hands-on exhibits** se permite manipular un gran número de los objetos expuestos en el museo

handspring ['hændsprɪŋ] N voltereta *f* sobre las manos, salto *m* de paloma

handstand ['hændstænd] N • **to do a ~** hacer el pino

hand-stitched [ˌhænd'stɪtʃt] ADJ cosido a mano

hand-to-hand ['hændtə'hænd] ADV, ADJ cuerpo a cuerpo

hand-to-mouth ['hændtə'maʊθ] ADJ [*existence*] precario
ADV • **to live hand-to-mouth** vivir precariamente

hand-wash ['hænd'wɒʃ] VT lavar a mano

handwash ['hænd'wɒʃ] N (= *liquid soap*) jabón *m* líquido para las manos

handwork ['hændwɜːk] N trabajo *m* a mano

hand-woven [ˌhænd'wəʊvən] ADJ tejido a mano

handwriting ['hændˌraɪtɪŋ] N letra *f*, escritura *f*

handwritten ['hænd'rɪtn] ADJ escrito a mano

handy ['hændɪ] ADJ (COMPAR: **handier**, SUPERL: **handiest**) **1** (= *at hand*) [*scissors, book*] a mano; (= *conveniently close*) [*shops, station*] cerca, a mano • **have you got a pen ~?** ¿tienes un bolígrafo a mano? • **our house is ~ for the shops** nuestra casa está *or* queda cerca de las tiendas • **to keep sth ~** tener algo a mano
2 (= *useful*) [*tool, gadget, hint*] práctico, útil • **credit cards can be ~** las tarjetas de crédito pueden resultar muy prácticas *or* útiles • **it turned out rather ~ that the trip was cancelled** nos vino bastante bien que cancelasen el viaje • **to come in ~** venir muy bien, ser muy útil • **the cheque came in very ~** el cheque nos vino muy bien
3 (= *skilful*) [*carpenter, mechanic*] hábil, diestro • **he's ~ around the home** es un manitas en la casa • **to be ~ with sth: she's ~ with a paint brush/needle** es muy mañosa para la pintura/costura, se le da muy bien la pintura/costura • **to be ~ with a gun** saber manejar una pistola • **to be ~ with one's fists** saber pelear, saber defenderse con los puños

handyman ['hændɪmən] N (PL: **handymen**) manitas *mf* (*Sp, Mex*) (*hombre que tiene dotes prácticas para hacer trabajos de carpintería etc en casa*)

hang [hæŋ]

TRANSITIVE VERB
INTRANSITIVE VERB
NOUN
PHRASAL VERBS

(PT, PP: **hung**)

TRANSITIVE VERB

1 (= *suspend*) [+ *coat, curtains*] colgar; [+ *picture*] (*on wall*) colgar; (*as exhibit*) exponer; [+ *washing*] tender; [+ *wallpaper*] pegar; [+ *door*] colocar; (*Culin*) [+ *game*] manir • **he hung the rope over the side of the boat** colgó la cuerda de la borda del barco • **are you any good at ~ing wallpaper?** ¿se te da bien empapelar? • IDIOM: • **to ~ one's head** bajar *or* agachar la cabeza • **he hung his head in shame** bajó *or* agachó la cabeza avergonzado; ▹ **peg, hung over**

2 (= *decorate*) adornar • **the walls were hung with tapestries** las paredes estaban adornadas con tapices • **trees hung with lights** árboles adornados con luces

3 (PT, PP: **hanged**) **a** [+ *criminal*] ahorcar • **he was ~ed, drawn and quartered** lo ahorcaron, destriparon y descuartizaron • **to ~ o.s.** ahorcarse • IDIOM: • **I might as well be ~ed for a sheep as a lamb** si me van a castigar que sea por algo gordo, de perdidos al río

b†* (= *damn*) • **~ the expense!** ¡al diablo (con) los gastos! • **~ it (all)!** ¡qué demonios! • **I'll be ~ed if I know!** ¡que me aspen *or* maten si lo sé!

4 (US) (= *turn*) • **~ a right here** gira *or* dobla *or* tuerce a la derecha aquí

5 (= *hold*) ▹ **fire**

INTRANSITIVE VERB

1 (= *be suspended*) colgar • **a light-bulb was ~ing from the ceiling** una bombilla colgaba del techo • **I was ~ing from the ledge by my fingertips** estaba colgado de la cornisa sujeto por la punta de los dedos • **his portrait ~s in the National Gallery** su retrato está expuesto en la National Gallery • **let your arms ~ loose at your sides** deje los brazos sueltos *or* caídos • **~ loose!** (*US**) (*fig*) ¡tranqui!*, ¡relájate! • **your coat is ~ing on the hook** tu abrigo está colgado en el perchero • **a picture ~ing on the wall** un cuadro colgado en la pared • IDIOM: • **and thereby ~s a tale** pero eso es harina de otro costal; ▹ **thread**

2 (= *be positioned*) • **to ~ open: the door hung open** (= *not closed*) la puerta estaba abierta; (= *partly off hinges*) la puerta estaba encajada • **her mouth hung open in surprise** se quedó boquiabierta • **to ~ out of the window** [*person*] asomarse por la ventana; [*thing*] colgar de la ventana • **I can't work with you ~ing over me like that** no puedo trabajar contigo pendiente de todo lo que hago

3 (= *flow*) [*rope, garment, hair*] caer • **her hair ~s down her back** el pelo le cae por la espalda • **it's a fabric that ~s well** es una tela que tiene muy buena caída

4 (PT, PP: **hanged**) (= *be hanged*) [*criminal*] morir en la horca • **he'll ~ for it** lo ahorcarán por esto

5 (= *hover*) [*fog*] flotar • **his breath hung in the icy air** su aliento flotaba en el aire helado • **the hawk hung motionless in the sky** el halcón se cernía inmóvil en el cielo • **the threat ~ing over us** la amenaza que se cierne sobre nosotros • **a question mark ~s over many of their futures** se cierne un *or* una interrogante sobre el porvenir de muchos de ellos

6 • IDIOMS: • **to go ~*** pudrirse* • **he can go ~ as far as I'm concerned** por mí que se pudra • **to ~ tough (on/for sth)** (*US*) mantenerse firme (en algo/para conseguir algo) • **she hung tough despite the pressure** pese a las presiones no dio su brazo a torcer

NOUN

1 (*of garment*) caída *f*

2 • IDIOMS: • **to get the ~ of sth*** coger el tranquillo a algo* • **I'll never get the ~ of this oven** nunca aprenderé a usar este horno, nunca le cogeré el tranquillo a este horno • **I don't give** *or* **care a ~*** me importa un comino*

▸ **hang about** (VI + ADV) **1** = hang around
2 (= *wait*) esperar • **~ about, you told me she'd agreed to it** (espera) un momento, me dijiste que ella estaba de acuerdo

▸ **hang around** (VI + ADV) **1** (= *spend time*) • **they always ~ around together** siempre van *or* andan juntos • **to ~ around with sb** juntarse *or* andar con algn
2 (= *loiter*) holgazanear • **they were just ~ing around, with nothing to do** estaban holgazaneando, sin nada que hacer
3 (= *wait*) quedarse a esperar • **I'm not ~ing around to find out** no voy a quedarme (a esperar) para ver qué pasa • **he got sick of ~ing around waiting for me** se hartó de andar de un lado para otro esperándome • **to keep sb ~ing around** hacer esperar a algn, tener a algn esperando
(VI + PREP) • **the usual crowd who hung around the café** el grupo de siempre que frecuentaba el café • **schoolboys who ~ around the streets after school** colegiales que rondan por las calles después de clase

▸ **hang back** (VI + ADV) **1** (= *hesitate*) no decidirse • **even his closest advisers believe he should ~ back no longer** incluso sus consejeros más allegados creen que debería decidirse ya *or* que no debería pensárselo más • **she hung back from offering** no tenía claro si debía ofrecerse
2 (= *stay behind*) quedarse atrás • **he hung back shyly in the doorway** se quedó atrás tímidamente en la puerta

▸ **hang in*** (VI + ADV) • **~ in there!** ¡aguanta! • **I didn't ~ in there long enough to find out for sure** no aguanté *or* seguí allí lo suficiente como para cerciorarme

▸ **hang on** (VI + PREP) **1** • **she hung on his arm** iba agarrada de su brazo • IDIOMS: • **to ~ on sb's every word** • **~ on sb's words** estar pendiente de todo lo que dice algn, no perder detalle de lo que dice algn
2 (= *depend on*) depender de • **everything ~s on his decision** todo depende de su decisión • **everything ~s on whether he saw her or not** todo depende de si la vio o no
(VI + ADV) **1** (= *grip, hold*) • **to ~ on (to sth)** agarrarse (a *or* de algo) • **~ on to the branch** agárrate a *or* de la rama • **~ on tight** agárrate fuerte • IDIOM: • **to ~ on (to sth) for dear life** agarrarse (a algo) como si fuera la vida en ello
2* (= *wait*) esperar • **~ on a minute!** ¡espera (un momento)! • **could you ~ on, please?** (*Telec*) no cuelgue, por favor • **to keep sb ~ing on** hacer esperar a algn, tener a algn esperando
3 (= *hold out*) aguantar • **he managed to ~ on till help came** consiguió aguantar hasta que llegó ayuda • **United hung on to take the cup** el United aguantó el tipo y ganó la copa • **~ on in there!*** ¡aguanta!

▸ **hang on to***, **hang onto*** (VI + PREP) (= *keep*) [+ *object*] quedarse (con), guardar; [+ *principle*] aferrarse a • **~ on to it till I see you** quédatelo *or* guárdalo hasta que nos veamos • **the president is trying to ~ on to power** el presidente está intentando aferrarse al poder • **he was unable to ~ on to his lead** no pudo mantener su ventaja

▸ **hang out** (VT + ADV) [+ *washing*] tender; [+ *flags, banner*] poner, colgar
(VI + ADV) **1** [*tongue, shirt tails*] • **the dog lay there panting, with his tongue ~ing out** el perro estaba ahí echado, jadeando con la lengua fuera *or* con la lengua colgando • **your shirt is ~ing out** llevas la camisa colgando, tienes la camisa fuera
2* (= *live*) vivir; (= *spend time*) pasar el rato • **he hung out in Paris for several years** pasó *or* vivió varios años en París • **on Saturdays we ~ out in the park** los sábados pasamos el rato en el parque • **I used to ~ out in supermarkets** solía frecuentar los supermercados • **she ~s out with some strange people** anda *or* se junta con gente rara
3* (= *hold out*) • **they're ~ing out for more money** siguen exigiendo más dinero, insisten en pedir más dinero
4 • IDIOM: • **to let it all ~ out** (*US**) soltarse el pelo *or* la melena

▸ **hang round** (VI + ADV), (VI + PREP) = **hang around**

▸ **hang together*** (VI + ADV) **1** (= *stay united*) [*people*] mantenerse unidos
2 (*logically*) (= *back one another up*) sostenerse; (= *follow internal logic*) tener coherencia • **his arguments just don't ~ together** sus argumentos no se sostienen • **it all ~s together** todo tiene coherencia • **it doesn't ~ together with what we know** no cuadra *or* no encaja con lo que sabemos

▸ **hang up** (VT + ADV) **1** [+ *coat*] colgar • IDIOM: • **to ~ up one's boots** colgar las botas • **he announced he was ~ing up his boots for good** anunció que colgaba las botas para siempre
2* • **to be hung up on sth** estar obsesionado por algo • **I've never been hung up on material things** nunca me han obsesionado las cosas materiales • **to be hung up on sb** estar colado por algn
3 (*Telec*) [+ *receiver*] colgar
(VI + ADV) **1** (= *be suspended*) estar colgado • **his hat was ~ing up in the hall** su sombrero estaba colgado en la entrada
2 (*Telec*) colgar • **don't ~ up!** ¡no cuelgues! • **to ~ up on sb** colgar a algn

hangar ['hæŋəʳ] (N) hangar *m*

hangdog ['hæŋdɒg] (ADJ) (= *guilty*) [*look, expression*] avergonzado; (= *depressed*) abatido

hanger ['hæŋəʳ] (N) (*for clothes*) percha *f*, gancho *m* (*LAm*)

hanger-on* ['hæŋər'ɒn] (N) (PL: **hangers-on**) parásito/a *m/f*, pegote *mf* (*Sp**)

hang-glide ['hæŋ,glaɪd] (VI) volar con ala delta

hang-glider ['hæŋ,glaɪdəʳ] (N) **1** (= *device*) ala *f* delta
2 (= *person*) piloto *mf* de ala delta

hang-gliding ['hæŋ,glaɪdɪŋ] (N) vuelo *m* con ala delta

hanging ['hæŋɪŋ] (N) **1** (*Jur*) **a** (= *death penalty*) (ejecución *f* en) la horca, ahorcamiento *m* • **~ would be too good for them** (la ejecución en) la horca *or* el ahorcamiento sería algo demasiado bueno para ellos
b (= *individual execution*) ejecución *f* en la horca, ahorcamiento *m* • **the last ~ in Britain** la última ejecución en la horca en Gran

Bretaña • **~s were commonplace then** entonces los ahorcamientos eran moneda corriente
2 (= *curtain*) colgadura *f* • **wall ~** tapiz *m*
ADJ [*bridge, plant, garden*] colgante; [*lamp*] de techo; [*cupboard*] para colgar • **~ space** espacio *m* para colgar ropa
CPD ▸ **hanging basket** macetero *m* colgante ▸ **hanging committee** junta *f* seleccionadora (*de una exposición*) ▸ **hanging judge** juez(a) *m/f* muy severo/a ▸ **hanging matter** (*fig*) • **it's not a ~ matter** no es cosa de vida o muerte ▸ **hanging offence, hanging offense** (US) (*lit*) delito *m* que se castiga con la horca • **prostitution is a ~ offence there** la prostitución allí es un delito que se castiga con la horca • **it's not a ~ offence** (*fig*) no es cosa de vida o muerte
hangman ['hæŋmən] N (PL: **hangmen**) verdugo *m*
hangnail ['hæŋneɪl] N padrastro *m*
hang-out* ['hæŋaʊt] N (*gen*) lugar *m*; (= *bar*) bar *m* habitual; [*of thieves etc*] guarida *f*
hangover ['hæŋˌəʊvəʳ] N **1** (*after drinking*) resaca *f*, cruda *f* (*LAm*)
2 (= *sth left over*) vestigio *m*, reliquia *f* • **it's a ~ from pre-war days** es un vestigio *or* una reliquia de la época de preguerra
hang-up* ['hæŋʌp] N **1** (= *problem*) problema *m*, lío* *m*
2 (= *complex*) complejo *m* (**about** con)
hank [hæŋk] N [*of wool*] madeja *f*; [*of hair*] mechón *m*
hanker ['hæŋkəʳ] VI • **to ~ after** *or* **for sth** añorar *or* anhelar algo
hankering ['hæŋkərɪŋ] N añoranza *f* (**for** de), anhelo *m* (**for** por) • **to have a ~ for sth** añorar *or* anhelar algo
hankie*, **hanky*** ['hæŋkɪ] N pañuelo *m*
hanky-panky* ['hæŋkɪ'pæŋkɪ] N **1** (US) (= *trickery*) • **there's some hanky-panky going on here** aquí hay trampa, esto huele a camelo*
2 (*Brit*) (*sexual*) relaciones *fpl* sospechosas • **we want no hanky-panky with the girls** nada de meterse mano con las chicas*
Hannibal ['hænɪbəl] N Aníbal
Hanover ['hænəvəʳ] N Hanovre *m*
Hanoverian [ˌhænəʊ'vɪərɪən] ADJ hanoveriano
N hanoveriano/a *m/f*
Hansard ['hænsɑːd] N *Actas oficiales de los debates del parlamento británico*
Hanseatic [ˌhænzɪ'ætɪk] ADJ • **the ~ League** La Liga Hanseática
hansom ['hænsəm] N cabriolé *m* (*con pescante trasero*)
Hants [hænts] N ABBR = **Hampshire**
Hanukkah ['hɑːnəkə] N Janucá *f*
ha'penny* ['heɪpnɪ] N = **halfpenny**
haphazard ['hæp'hæzəd] ADJ **1** (= *random*) [*selection*] al azar; [*manner, method*] poco sistemático • **the town has developed in a ~ way** la ciudad ha crecido sin planificación alguna *or* muy desordenadamente • **their approach to the problem has been rather ~** han abordado el problema de forma poco sistemática
2 (= *careless*) [*person*] descuidado
haphazardly [ˌhæp'hæzədlɪ] ADV [*arrange*] de cualquier modo; [*select*] al azar
hapless ['hæplɪs] ADJ desventurado
happen ['hæpən] VI **1** (= *occur*) pasar, ocurrir, suceder • **what's ~ing?** ¿qué pasa *or* ocurre *or* sucede? • **how did it ~?** ¿cómo pasó *or* ocurrió *or* sucedió?, ¿cómo fue? • **these things ~** estas cosas pasan, son cosas que pasan • **when did the accident ~?** ¿cuándo ocurrió *or* sucedió el accidente? • **whatever ~s** pase lo que pase • **don't let it ~ again** que no vuelva a ocurrir • **as if nothing had ~ed** como si nada, como si tal cosa • **how does it ~ that ...?** ¿cómo es posible que ...? (+ *subjun*) • **what has ~ed to him?** (= *befall*) ¿qué le ha pasado?; (= *become of*) ¿qué ha sido de él? • **it's the best thing that ever ~ed to me** es lo mejor que me ha pasado en la vida • **if anything should ~ to him ...** si le pasara algo ... • IDIOM: • **it's all ~ing here*** aquí es donde está la movida *or* marcha*; ▹ **accident**
2 (= *chance*) • **it ~ed that I was out that day** dio la casualidad de que *or* resulta que aquel día estuve fuera • **it might ~ that no one turns up** puede ocurrir que no venga nadie • **if you ~ to see John, let him know** si acaso vieras a John *or* si da la casualidad de que ves a John, díselo • **I ~ to know that ...** da la casualidad de que sé que ... • **he just ~s to be here now** da la casualidad de que está aquí ahora • **if anyone should ~ to see you** si acaso alguien te viera • **would you ~ to have a pen?** ¿no tendrá un bolígrafo por casualidad? • **it ~s to be true** da la casualidad de que es verdad • **as it ~s ..., • it (just) so ~s that ...** da la casualidad de que ... • **I do know him, as it ~s** pues da la casualidad de que sí le conozco
▸ **happen along** VI + ADV aparecer • **who should ~ along but Sheila** quién dirías que apareció, pues Sheila
▸ **happen on, happen upon** VI + PREP [+ *thing*] dar con, encontrar; [+ *person*] tropezar con, encontrarse con • **we ~ed (up)on this gem of a hotel in Ireland** dimos con *or* encontramos un hotel magnífico en Irlanda • **to ~ (up)on the solution** dar con *or* encontrar la solución
happening ['hæpnɪŋ] N (= *event*) suceso *m*, acontecimiento *m*; (*Theat*) happening *m*
ADJ* que es lo último*, de lo último
happenstance ['hæpənstæns] N (US) casualidad *f* • **by ~** por casualidad
happily ['hæpɪlɪ] ADV **1** (= *contentedly*) [*smile, say, play*] alegremente, felizmente • **it all ended ~** todo acabó felizmente, todo tuvo un final feliz • **they lived ~ together for many years** vivieron los dos felices durante muchos años • **I'm a ~ married man** soy un hombre feliz en mi matrimonio • **he said he would ~ lend us the money** dijo que nos dejaría el dinero con mucho gusto, dijo que gustosamente nos dejaría el dinero
2 (= *without difficulty*) sin ningún problema • **Muslims and Catholics live ~ together here** musulmanes y católicos conviven aquí sin ningún problema • **blackberries will grow ~ in any good soil** las moras crecen bien en cualquier tipo de tierra • **she'll ~ spend £100 on a dress** se puede gastar 100 libras en un vestido tan tranquilamente
3 (= *fortunately*) afortunadamente, por fortuna • **~, no one was hurt** afortunadamente *or* por fortuna, nadie resultó herido
happiness ['hæpɪnɪs] N (= *contentment*) felicidad *f*; (= *cheerfulness*) alegría *f* • **we wish you every ~** te deseamos toda la felicidad del mundo • **if you want to know real ~** si quieres ser verdaderamente feliz
happy ['hæpɪ] ADJ (COMPAR: **happier**, SUPERL: **happiest**) **1** (= *contented*) feliz • **we've been very ~ here** aquí hemos sido muy felices • **I don't think they're very ~ together** no creo que sean muy felices juntos • **to make sb ~** hacer feliz a algn • **you've just made me a very ~ man!** ¡me acabas de hacer el hombre más feliz del mundo! • IDIOM: • **to be as ~ as Larry** *or* **a lark** *or* **a sandboy** estar como unas pascuas
2 (= *cheerful*) alegre • **she has always been a ~ little girl** siempre ha sido una niña muy alegre • **he has a ~ temperament** tiene un temperamento alegre
3 (= *satisfied, pleased*) contento • **the boss is waiting for you and he isn't very ~** te está esperando el jefe y no parece muy contento • **to be ~ to do sth: I'm just ~ to be back running** solo estoy contento de poder volver a correr • **I am ~ to tell you that ...** tengo mucho gusto en comunicarle que ... • **we'll be ~ to help** estaremos encantados de ayudar • **I'd be ~ to check it for you** no me importa nada comprobártelo, con mucho gusto se lo comprobaré (*more frm*) • **yes, I'd be ~ to** sí, con mucho gusto • **he seems quite ~ to let things go on as they are** parece no importarle dejar que las cosas sigan como están • **we are not ~ about the plan** no estamos contentos con el proyecto • **we're very ~ for you** nos alegramos mucho por ti • **to keep sb ~** tener a algn contento • **she wasn't ~ with his work** no estaba contenta con su trabajo
4 (= *at ease, unworried*) tranquilo • **don't worry about keeping him waiting, he seems quite ~** no te preocupes por hacerle esperar, él parece muy tranquilo • **I'm quite ~ to wait** no me importa esperar
5 (= *pleasant, joyful*) [*childhood, life, marriage, home*] feliz; [*place, atmosphere*] alegre • **it was the happiest day of my life** fue el día más feliz de mi vida • **they were having such a ~ time splashing around** se lo estaban pasando tan bien chapoteando en el agua • **we spent many ~ hours playing on the beach** pasamos muchas horas maravillosas jugando en la playa • **~ birthday!** ¡feliz cumpleaños! • **~ Christmas!** ¡feliz Navidad!, ¡felices Navidades! • **a ~ ending** un final feliz • **a ~ event** un feliz acontecimiento • **~ New Year!** ¡feliz Año Nuevo!; ▹ **return**
6 (= *felicitous*) [*phrase*] afortunado, oportuno; [*position, chance*] afortunado; [*coincidence, idea*] feliz • **to strike a ~ medium** encontrar un término medio
7* (= *tipsy*) contentillo*, alegre*
CPD ▸ **happy couple** • **the ~ couple** la feliz pareja ▸ **happy families** (*Cards*) juego *m* de las familias ▸ **happy hour** happy hour *m* (*hora durante la cual se paga menos por la bebida en los bares*) ▸ **happy slapping*** (*Brit*) *agresión grabada con un móvil*
happy-go-lucky ['hæpɪgəʊ'lʌkɪ] ADJ despreocupado
Hapsburg ['hæpsbɜːg] N Habsburgo
haptic ['hæptɪk] ADJ táctil
hara-kiri ['hærə'kɪrɪ] N haraquiri *m*
harangue [hə'ræŋ] N arenga *f*
VT arengar
harass ['hærəs] VT acosar, hostigar; (*Mil*) hostilizar, hostigar
harassed ['hærəst] ADJ (= *exhausted*) agobiado; (= *under pressure*) presionado • **to look ~** parecer agobiado
harassment ['hærəsmənt] N acoso *m*; (*Mil*) hostigamiento *m* • **sexual ~** acoso *m* sexual
harbinger ['hɑːbɪndʒəʳ] N (= *person*) heraldo *m*, precursor *m*; (= *sign*) presagio *m*, precursor *m* • **~ of doom** presagio *m* del desastre • **the swallow is a ~ of spring** la golondrina anuncia la venida de la primavera
harbour, harbor (US) ['hɑːbəʳ] N puerto *m*
VT (= *retain*) [+ *fear, hope*] abrigar; (= *shelter*) [+ *criminal, spy*] dar abrigo *or* refugio a; (= *conceal*) esconder • **that corner ~s the dust** en ese rincón se amontona el polvo • **to ~ a grudge** guardar rencor
CPD ▸ **harbour dues** derechos *mpl* portuarios ▸ **harbour master** capitán *m* de puerto

h

hard [hɑːd] ADJ (COMPAR: **harder**, SUPERL: **hardest**) **1** (= *not soft*) [*object, substance, cheese, skin*] duro; [*ground, snow*] duro, compacto • **baked ~** endurecido (*al sol o en el horno*) • **to become** *or* **go ~** ponerse duro, endurecerse • **the water is very ~ here** aquí el agua es muy dura *or* tiene mucha cal • IDIOMS: • **to be as ~ as nails** [*person*] (*physically*) ser duro como una roca • **(as) ~ as a rock** [*object*] (tan) duro como una piedra; ▷ **nut**
2 (= *harsh, severe*) [*climate, winter, person*] duro, severo; [*frost*] fuerte; [*words, tone*] duro, áspero; [*expression, eyes, voice*] serio, duro; [*drink, liquor*] fuerte; [*drugs*] duro; [*fact*] concreto; [*evidence*] irrefutable • **a ~ blow** (*fig*) un duro golpe • **to take a long ~ look at sth** examinar algo detenidamente • **to be ~ on sb** ser muy duro con algn, darle duro a algn (*LAm*) • **don't be so ~ on him, it's not his fault** no seas tan duro con él, no es culpa suya • **aren't you being a bit ~ on yourself?** ¿no estás siendo un poco duro contigo mismo? • **to be ~ on one's clothes** destrozar la ropa • **the light was ~ on the eyes** la luz hacía daño a los ojos • IDIOM: • **to be as ~ as nails** (*in temperament*) ser muy duro, tener el corazón muy duro; ▷ **feeling**
3 (= *strenuous, tough*) [*work, day*] duro; [*fight, match*] muy reñido • **gardening is ~ work** arreglar el jardín es un trabajo duro • **phew, that was ~ work!** ¡uf!, ¡ha costado lo suyo! • **he's not afraid of ~ work** el trabajo duro no le asusta • **coping with three babies is very ~ work** tres bebés dan mucha tarea *or* mucho trabajo, arreglárselas con tres bebés es una dura *or* ardua tarea • **it's ~ work getting her to talk about herself** cuesta mucho *or* resulta muy trabajoso hacerla hablar sobre sí misma • **to be a ~ worker** ser muy trabajador(a)
4 (= *difficult*) [*exam, decision, choice*] difícil • **to be ~ to do: it's ~ to study on your own** es difícil estudiar por tu cuenta • **he found it ~ to make friends** le resultaba difícil hacer amigos • **I find it ~ to believe that …** me cuesta (trabajo) creer que … • **bloodstains are ~ to remove** las manchas de sangre son difíciles de quitar • **to be ~ to come by** ser difícil de conseguir • **that is a very ~ question to answer** esa es una pregunta muy difícil de responder • **to be ~ to deal with** ser de trato difícil • **to be ~ to please** ser muy exigente *or* quisquilloso • **to be ~ of hearing** ser duro de oído • **he's learning the ~ way** está aprendiendo a base de cometer errores • **we shall have to do it the ~ way** tendremos que hacerlo a pulso; ▷ **bargain, play**
5 (= *tough, unpleasant*) [*life, times*] duro • **it's a ~ life!** ¡qué vida más dura! • **those were ~ times to live in** aquellos eran tiempos duros, la vida era dura en aquellos tiempos • **her family had fallen on ~ times** su familia estaba pasando por dificultades económicas • **to have a ~ time** pasarlo mal • **to have a ~ time doing sth** tener problemas para hacer algo • **to give sb a ~ time** hacérselo pasar mal a algn • IDIOMS: • **to take a ~ line against/over sth** adoptar una postura intransigente contra algo/respecto a algo • **~ lines** (*Brit**) mala suerte *f* • **~ lines!** ¡qué mala suerte!, ¡qué mala pata!*; ▷ **going, hard-line, hard-liner**
6 (= *forceful*) [*push, tug, kick*] fuerte
7 (*Phon, Ling*) [*sound*] fuerte; [*consonant*] oclusivo
ADV (COMPAR: **harder**, SUPERL: **hardest**)
1 (= *with a lot of effort*) [*work*] duro, mucho; [*study*] mucho • **he had worked ~ all his life** había trabajado duro *or* mucho toda su vida • **he works very ~** trabaja muy duro, trabaja mucho • **she works ~ at keeping herself fit** se esfuerza mucho por mantenerse en forma • **he was ~ at work in the garden** estaba trabajando afanosamente *or* con ahínco en el jardín • **he was breathing ~** respiraba con dificultad • **we're saving ~ for our holidays** estamos ahorrando todo lo que podemos para las vacaciones, estamos ahorrando al máximo para las vacaciones • **to try ~**: • **she always tries ~** siempre se esfuerza mucho • **I can't do it, no matter how ~ I try** no puedo hacerlo, por mucho que lo intente • **to try one's ~est to do sth** esforzarse al máximo por hacer algo • **maybe you're trying too ~** a lo mejor tienes que tomártelo con más calma • IDIOM: • **to be ~ at it**: • **Bill was ~ at it in the garden*** Bill se estaba empleando a fondo en el jardín, Bill estaba dándole duro al jardín*
2 (= *with force*) [*hit*] fuerte, duro; [*pull, push, blow*] con fuerza; [*snow, rain*] fuerte, mucho • **she pushed the wardrobe as ~ as she could** empujó el armario con todas sus fuerzas • **the government decided to clamp down ~ on terrorism** el gobierno decidió tomar medidas duras contra el terrorismo • **she was feeling ~ done by** pensaba que la habían tratado injustamente • **~ hit** seriamente afectado • **to hit sb ~** (*fig*) ser un duro golpe para algn • **California has been (particularly) ~ hit by the crisis** California (en particular) se ha visto seriamente afectada por la crisis • **I would be ~ pushed** *or* **put to think of another plan** me resultaría difícil pensar en otro plan • **we'll be ~ pushed** *or* **put to finish this tonight!** ¡nos va a ser difícil terminar esto esta noche! • **to take sth ~** tomarse algo muy mal* • **he took it pretty ~** se lo tomó muy mal, fue un duro golpe para él, le golpeó mucho (*LAm*) • **to be ~ up*** estar pelado*, no tener un duro (*Sp**) • **to be ~ up for sth** estar falto *or* escaso de algo; ▷ **hard-pressed**
3 (= *solid*) • **to freeze ~** quedarse congelado • **to set ~** [*cement etc*] fraguar, endurecerse
4 (= *intently*) [*listen*] atentamente; [*concentrate*] al máximo • **to look ~ (at sth)** fijarse mucho (en algo) • **think ~ before you make a decision** piénsalo muy bien antes de tomar una decisión • **I thought ~ but I couldn't remember his name** por más que pensé *or* por más vueltas que le di no pude recordar su nombre
5 (= *sharply*) • **~ a-port/a-starboard** (*Naut*) todo a babor/estribor • **to turn ~ left/right** girar todo a la izquierda/derecha
6 (= *closely*) • **~ behind sth** justo detrás de algo • **I hurried upstairs with my sister ~ behind me** subí las escaleras corriendo con mi hermana que venía justo detrás • **~ upon sth** (= *just after*) justo después de algo • **the launch of the book followed ~ upon the success of the film** el lanzamiento del libro se produjo justo después del éxito de la película; ▷ **heel**
CPD ▸ **hard cash** dinero *m* contante y sonante, (dinero *m* en) efectivo *m* ▸ **hard centre, hard center** (*US*) relleno *m* duro ▸ **hard cider** (*US*) sidra *f* ▸ **hard copy** copia *f* impresa ▸ **the hard core** (= *intransigents*) los incondicionales, el núcleo duro; ▷ **hard-core** ▸ **hard court** (*Tennis*) cancha *f* (de tenis) de cemento, pista *f* (de tenis) de cemento ▸ **hard currency** moneda *f* fuerte, divisa *f* fuerte ▸ **hard disk** (*Comput*) disco *m* duro ▸ **hard drive** (*Comput*) unidad *f* de disco duro ▸ **hard goods** productos *mpl* no perecederos ▸ **hard hat** (= *riding hat*) gorra *f* de montar; [*of construction worker*] casco *m*; (= *construction worker*) albañil *mf* ▸ **hard labour, hard labor** (*US*) trabajos *mpl* forzados ▸ **hard landing** aterrizaje *m* duro ▸ **the hard left** (*esp Brit*) la extrema izquierda, la izquierda radical ▸ **hard luck** mala suerte *f* • **we had a bit of ~ luck this season** hemos tenido un poco de mala suerte esta temporada • **to be ~ luck on sb**: • **it was ~ luck on him** tuvo mala suerte • **~ luck!** ¡(qué) mala suerte! ▸ **hard news** noticias *fpl* fidedignas ▸ **hard palate** paladar *m* ▸ **hard porn*** porno *m* duro ▸ **the hard right** (*esp Brit*) la extrema derecha, la derecha radical ▸ **hard rock** (*Mus*) rock *m* duro ▸ **hard sell** venta *f* agresiva • **~ sell tactics** táctica *fsing* de venta agresiva • **~ sell techniques** técnicas *fpl* de venta agresiva ▸ **hard shoulder** (*Brit*) (*Aut*) arcén *m*, hombrillo *m* ▸ **hard stuff*** (= *alcohol*) alcohol *m* duro, bebidas *fpl* fuertes; (= *drugs*) droga *f* dura • **he fancied a drop of the ~ stuff** le apetecía una copita de algo fuerte ▸ **hard top** (= *car*) coche *m* no descapotable; (= *car roof*) techo *m* rígido ▸ **hard water** agua *f* dura, agua *f* con mucha cal

hard-and-fast [ˈhɑːdənˈfɑːst] ADJ [*rule*] rígido; [*decision*] definitivo, irrevocable

hardback [ˈhɑːdbæk] N (= *book*) libro *m* encuadernado, libro *m* de tapa dura
ADJ [*edition, book*] de tapa dura

hardball [ˈhɑːdbɔːl] N (= *Baseball*) béisbol *m* • IDIOM: • **to play ~** (= *get tough*) mostrarse implacable • **she is playing ~ in a world dominated by men 20 years her senior** se muestra implacable en un mundo dominado por hombres que le llevan 20 años de experiencia

hard-bitten [ˈhɑːdˈbɪtn] ADJ endurecido, amargado

hardboard [ˈhɑːdbɔːd] N aglomerado *m* (*de madera*)

hard-boiled [ˈhɑːdˈbɔɪld] ADJ **1** (= *hard*) [*egg*] duro
2 (= *tough, cynical*) duro de carácter, amargado

hardboot [ˈhɑːdbuːt] N (*Sport*) fanático/a *m/f* por las carreras de caballos

hard-core [ˈhɑːdkɔːʳ] ADJ [*pornography*] duro; [*supporter, militant, activist*] acérrimo; [*conservative, communist*] acérrimo, empedernido; ▷ **hard**

hard-cover [ˈhɑːdˌkʌvəʳ] ADJ [*book*] encuadernado, de tapa dura

hard-drinking [ˈhɑːdˈdrɪŋkɪŋ] ADJ bebedor

hard-earned [ˈhɑːdˈɜːnd] ADJ ganado con el sudor de la frente

hard-edged [ˈhɑːdˈedʒd] ADJ (*fig*) [*style, story*] contundente, duro

harden [ˈhɑːdn] VT **1** (= *make hard*) [+ *substance*] endurecer; [+ *steel*] templar; [+ *skin*] curtir, endurecer
2 (= *make tough, harsh*) endurecer • **the experience had ~ed her** la experiencia la había endurecido • **to ~ sb to adversity** acostumbrar a algn a hacerse fuerte ante la adversidad • IDIOM: • **to ~ one's heart**: • **years of putting up with his violent outbursts had ~ed her heart** después de años de sufrir sus arranques de violencia se le había endurecido el corazón • **she ~ed her heart and refused to have him back** hizo de tripas corazón *or* se hizo fuerte y se negó a aceptarlo de nuevo
3 (= *make determined*) • **these experiences ~ed her resolve** estas experiencias la afianzaron en su propósito • **the workers' behaviour only served to ~ the attitude of the managers** el comportamiento de los obreros solo contribuyó a reforzar la actitud de la dirección

4 (Comm) (= stabilize) estabilizar, consolidar
VI 1 (= become hard) [clay, arteries, icing] endurecerse; [cement] fraguar
2 (= become harsh, severe) [person, expression, eyes] endurecerse • **his voice ~ed** el tono de su voz se endureció, adoptó un tono más áspero • **my heart ~ed against her** mi corazón se volvió contra ella • **what happened only caused him to ~ in his determination to continue** lo que sucedió solo le afianzó más en su propósito de seguir
3 (Comm) (= stabilize) [prices, economy] estabilizarse, consolidarse

hardened ['hɑːdnd] ADJ 1 [drinker] empedernido; [criminal] reincidente • **to be ~ to sth** estar acostumbrado a algo • **we are becoming ~ to violence** nos hemos ido acostumbrando a la violencia
2 (Tech) [steel] templado

hardening ['hɑːdnɪŋ] N 1 (lit) endurecimiento m • **~ of the arteries** endurecimiento m de las arterias, arteriosclerosis f
2 (fig) [of attitude] radicalización f
3 (Comm) [of prices, economy] estabilización f, consolidación f

hard-faced ['hɑːdfeɪst] ADJ severo, inflexible

hard-fought ['hɑːd'fɔːt] ADJ muy reñido

hard-headed ['hɑːd'hedɪd] ADJ (= shrewd) realista, práctico; (= stubborn) terco

hard-hearted ['hɑːd'hɑːtɪd] ADJ duro de corazón • **to be hard-hearted** tener un corazón de piedra

hard-heartedness [ˌhɑːd'hɑːtɪdnɪs] N dureza f de corazón

hard-hit ['hɑːd'hɪt] ADJ muy afectado, muy perjudicado • **small businesses have been particularly hard-hit by these measures** los pequeños negocios se han visto especialmente afectados *or* perjudicados por estas medidas

hard-hitting ['hɑːdˌhɪtɪŋ] ADJ [speech etc] contundente

hardiness ['hɑːdɪnɪs] N resistencia f

hard-line ['hɑːd'laɪn] ADJ [communist, conservative] de línea dura, extremista; [approach, policy] radical

hard-liner [ˌhɑːd'laɪnəʳ] N duro/a m/f; (Pol) (= supporter) partidario/a m/f de línea dura; (= politician) político/a m/f de línea dura • **the hard-liners of the party** el ala dura del partido

hard-luck story [ˌhɑːdlʌk'stɔːrɪ] N • **he pitched me a hard-luck story** me contó sus infortunios *or* su historia tan trágica

hardly ['hɑːdlɪ] ADV apenas • **I ~ know him** apenas lo conozco, casi no lo conozco • **I can ~ believe it** apenas puedo creerlo, casi no puedo creerlo • **I could ~ understand a word** apenas entendí palabra, no pude entender casi nada • **she had ~ any money** apenas tenía dinero, no tenía casi dinero • **~ a day goes by when we don't argue** apenas pasa un día sin que discutamos • **we could ~ refuse** ¿cómo podíamos negarnos? • **she's ~ what you'd call a cordon bleu chef** (iro) no es precisamente *or* no es lo que se dice un cocinero de primera • **that can ~ be true** eso difícilmente puede ser verdad • **that is ~ likely** eso es poco probable • **it's ~ surprising!** ¡no me extraña *or* sorprende! • **"do you think he'll pass?" — "~!"** —¿crees que aprobará? —¡qué va! *or* ¡ni hablar! • **~ anyone** casi nadie • **~ anything** casi nada • **there was ~ anywhere to go** no había casi ningún sitio donde ir • **~ ever** casi nunca

hardness ['hɑːdnɪs] N 1 (= not softness) [of object, substance, water] dureza f
2 (= not easiness) [of exam, problem] dificultad f • **~ of hearing** dureza f de oído
3 (= harshness) [of person, measures] dureza f, severidad f; [of winter, frost] rigor m • **~ of heart** dureza f de corazón, insensibilidad f

hard-nosed [ˌhɑːd'nəʊzd] ADJ (fig) duro

hard-on** ['hɑːdɒn] N empalme m (Sp**), erección f • **he had a hard-on** se le puso dura, se empalmó (Sp**), se le empinó (Sp**)

hard-pressed ['hɑːdprest] ADJ • **to be hard-pressed** estar en apuros • **our hard-pressed economy** nuestra agobiada economía • **you'd be hard-pressed to find a better deal than that** le va a ser difícil encontrar una oferta mejor

hardship ['hɑːdʃɪp] N (= deprivation) privación f; (financial) apuro m; (= condition of life) miseria f • **to suffer ~(s)** pasar apuros • **it's no ~ to him (to give up the car)** no le cuesta nada (dejar de usar el coche)
CPD ▸ **hardship clause** (Jur) cláusula f de salvaguarda

hardtack ['hɑːdtæk] N (Naut) galleta f

hardware ['hɑːdweəʳ] N (for domestic use) ferretería f, quincalla f; (Mil) armas fpl, armamento m; (Comput) hardware m, soporte m físico
CPD ▸ **hardware dealer** ferretero/a m/f ▸ **hardware shop, hardware store** ferretería f ▸ **hardware specialist** (Comput) especialista mf en hardware

hard-wearing ['hɑːd'weərɪŋ] ADJ resistente, duradero

hard-wired, hardwired [ˌhɑːd'waɪəd] ADJ
1 (Comput) integrado
2 (into the brain) programado • **musicality seems to be hard-wired into our brains** parece que la musicalidad está programada en nuestro cerebro

hard-won ['hɑːd'wʌn] ADJ ganado a duras penas

hardwood ['hɑːdwʊd] N madera f noble *or* dura
CPD ▸ **hardwood tree** árbol m de hojas caducas

hard-working ['hɑːd'wɜːkɪŋ] ADJ trabajador

hardy ['hɑːdɪ] ADJ (COMPAR: **hardier**, SUPERL: **hardiest**) fuerte, robusto; (Bot) resistente

hare [heəʳ] N (PL: **hares** *or* **hare**) liebre f • PROVERB: • **first catch your ~** no hay que empezar por el tejado
VI* ir a todo correr*, ir a toda pastilla* • **to ~ away** *or* **off** irse a todo correr *or* a toda pastilla*, salir disparado* • **to ~ in/out/through** (Brit) entrar/salir/pasar a todo correr *or* a toda pastilla* • **he went haring past** pasó como un rayo

harebell ['heəbel] N campánula f

harebrained ['heəbreɪnd] ADJ [idea, scheme] disparatado, descabellado; [person] casquivano

harelip ['heə'lɪp] N labio m leporino

harelipped [ˌheə'lɪpt] ADJ de labio leporino, labihendido

harem [hɑː'riːm] N harén m

haricot ['hærɪkəʊ] N (also **haricot bean**) frijol m, judía f blanca (Sp)

hark [hɑːk] VI • **~!** (poet) ¡escucha! • **~ at him!*** ¡qué cosas dice!, ¡quién fue a hablar! • **~ at him singing!** ¡cómo canta! • **to ~ to** escuchar
▸ **hark back to** VI + PREP (= return to) volver a; (= recall) recordar • **he's always ~ing back to that** siempre está con la misma canción

harken ['hɑːkən] = **hearken**

Harlequin ['hɑːlɪkwɪn] N Arlequín

Harley Street ['hɑːlɪstriːt] N (Brit) *calle de Londres donde tienen su consulta muchos médicos especialistas prestigiosos*

harlot ['hɑːlət] N ramera f

harm [hɑːm] N daño m, mal m, perjuicio m • **to do sb ~** hacer daño a algn; (fig) perjudicar a algn • **it does more ~ than good** es peor el remedio que la enfermedad • **the ~ is done now** el daño *or* mal ya está hecho • **don't worry, no ~ done** no te preocupes, no ha sido nada • **there's no ~ in trying** nada se pierde con probar • **I see no ~ in that** no veo nada en contra de eso • **he means no ~** no tiene malas intenciones • **out of ~'s way** a salvo, fuera de peligro • **to keep out of ~'s way** evitar el peligro • **we moved the car out of ~'s way** quitamos el coche de en medio, movimos el coche a un lugar seguro
VT [+ person] hacer daño a, hacer mal a; [+ health, reputation, interests] perjudicar; [+ crops] dañar, estropear
VI sufrir daños • **will it ~ in the rain?** ¿lo estropeará la lluvia? • **it won't ~ for that** eso no le hará daño

harmful ['hɑːmfʊl] ADJ [substance, chemical] dañino, nocivo; [effects, consequences] perjudicial, pernicioso; (to reputation) perjudicial (**to** para) • **tobacco is ~ to the health** el tabaco perjudica seriamente la salud • **the chemical is not ~ to plants** el producto químico no es nocivo para *or* no daña las plantas

harmless ['hɑːmlɪs] ADJ [person, animal] inofensivo; [substance, chemical] inocuo; (= innocent) inocente

harmlessly ['hɑːmlɪslɪ] ADV [remark] inocuamente, inofensivamente; [explode, fall] sin causar daños

harmlessness ['hɑːmlɪsnɪs] N (lit, fig) carácter m inofensivo

harmonic [hɑː'mɒnɪk] ADJ armónico

harmonica [hɑː'mɒnɪkə] N armónica f

harmonically [hɑː'mɒnɪklɪ] ADV armónicamente

harmonics [hɑː'mɒnɪks] N armonía f

harmonious [hɑː'məʊnɪəs] ADJ 1 (Mus) [sound, chord] armonioso
2 (fig) [colour scheme, architecture, relationship] armonioso; [atmosphere] de armonía

harmoniously [hɑː'məʊnɪəslɪ] ADV
1 (= musically) armoniosamente
2 (= amicably) [live, work] en armonía; (= tastefully) [blend] armoniosamente

harmonium [hɑː'məʊnɪəm] N armonio m

harmonization [ˌhɑːmənaɪ'zeɪʃən] N armonización f

harmonize ['hɑːmənaɪz] VT, VI armonizar (**with** con)

harmony ['hɑːmənɪ] N armonía f • **to sing/live in ~ with sb** cantar/vivir en armonía con algn

harness ['hɑːnɪs] N (for horse) arreos mpl, jaeces mpl; (= safety harness) (for walking a child) andadores mpl, correas fpl; (on high chair, baby seat) correas fpl de sujeción *or* seguridad; (for mountaineer etc) arnés m • **to work in ~ (with)** trabajar conjuntamente (con) • IDIOMS: • **to die in ~** morir con las botas puestas • **to get back in ~** volver al trabajo
VT 1 (lit) [+ horse] enjaezar, poner los arreos a; (to carriage) enganchar • **to ~ a horse to a cart** enganchar un caballo a un carro
2 (fig) [+ resources, energy] utilizar, aprovechar
CPD ▸ **harness race** carrera f de trotones

harp [hɑːp] N arpa f
▸ **harp on*** VI + ADV • **to ~ on (about)** estar siempre con la misma historia (de), machacar (sobre)* • **stop ~ing on!** ¡no machaques!*, ¡corta el rollo!*

harpist ['hɑːpɪst] N arpista mf

harpoon [hɑː'puːn] N arpón m
VT arponear

harpsichord ['hɑ:psɪkɔ:d] N clavicémbalo *m*, clavecín *m*

harpsichordist ['hɑ:psɪkɔ:dɪst] N clavicembalista *mf*

harpy ['hɑ:pɪ] N arpía *f*

harquebus ['hɑ:kwɪbəs] N (*Hist*) arcabuz *m*

harridan ['hærɪdən] N bruja *f*

harried ['hærɪd] ADJ [*expression etc*] agobiado, preocupado

harrier ['hærɪəʳ] N **1** (= *dog*) lebrel *m* (*inglés*)
2 harriers (= *cross-country runners*) corredores *mpl* de cross
3 (*Orn*) aguilucho *m*

Harris Tweed® [,hærɪs'twi:d] N tweed® *m* producido en la isla de Harris

harrow ['hærəʊ] (*Agr*) N grada *f*, rastra *f*
VT **1** (*Agr*) gradar
2 (*fig*) torturar, destrozar

harrowed ['hærəʊd] ADJ [*look*] torturado

harrowing ['hærəʊɪŋ] ADJ (= *distressing*) angustioso; (= *awful*) espeluznante, terrible; (= *moving*) conmovedor

Harry ['hærɪ] N (*familiar form of* **Harold**, **Henry**) • IDIOM: • **to play old ~ with*** endiablar, estropear

harry ['hærɪ] VT (*Mil*) hostilizar, hostigar; [+ *person*] acosar, hostigar

harsh [hɑ:ʃ] ADJ (COMPAR: **harsher**, SUPERL: **harshest**) **1** (= *severe*) [*winter, weather, punishment*] duro, riguroso; [*words*] duro, áspero; [*remarks, criticism, conditions*] duro; [*person, sentence*] duro, severo • **to be ~ on sb** ser duro *or* severo con algn
2 (= *too bright*) [*light*] fuerte; [*colour*] chillón, estridente
3 (= *rough*) [*fabric, material*] áspero
4 (= *rough-sounding*) [*voice, sound*] áspero
5 (= *strong*) [*detergent*] fuerte; [*contrast*] violento

harshly ['hɑ:ʃlɪ] ADV [*treat, judge, speak*] con dureza; [*criticize*] duramente; [*say*] con voz áspera; [*laugh*] ásperamente • **a ~ worded attack** un ataque verbal muy duro • **the room was ~ illuminated** la habitación tenía una iluminación desagradable

harshness ['hɑ:ʃnɪs] N [*of climate*] rigor *m*, dureza *f*; [*of conditions, words*] dureza *f*; [*of punishment*] dureza *f*, severidad *f*; [*of light*] crudeza *f*; [*of colour*] estridencia *f*; [*of sound, fabric*] aspereza *f*

hart [hɑ:t] N (PL: **harts** *or* **hart**) ciervo *m*

harum-scarum ['hɛərəm'skɛərəm] ADJ atolondrado
ADV a tontas y a locas
N (= *person*) tarambana *mf*

harvest ['hɑ:vɪst] N **1** (= *act*) [*of cereals*] siega *f*; [*of fruit, vegetables*] cosecha *f*, recolección *f*; [*of grapes*] vendimia *f*
2 (= *product*) cosecha *f*
3 (*fig*) cosecha *f*
VT **1** (*Agr*) [+ *cereals*] cosechar; [+ *fruit, vegetables*] cosechar, recolectar; [+ *grapes*] vendimiar
2 (*fig*) cosechar
VI cosechar, segar
CPD ▸ **harvest festival** fiesta *f* de la cosecha ▸ **harvest home** (= *festival*) ≈ fiesta *f* de la cosecha; (= *season*) cosecha *f* ▸ **harvest moon** luna *f* llena ▸ **harvest time** cosecha *f*, siega *f*

harvester ['hɑ:vɪstəʳ] N **1** (= *person*) [*of cereals*] segador(a) *m/f*; [*of fruit, vegetables*] recolector(a) *m/f*; [*of grapes*] vendimiador(a) *m/f*
2 (= *machine*) cosechadora *f*; (= *combine harvester*) segadora-trilladora *f*

harvesting ['hɑ:vɪstɪŋ] N = **harvest**

has [hæz] VB *3rd person sing present of* **have**

has-been* ['hæzbi:n] N vieja gloria *f*

hash¹ [hæʃ] N **1** (*Culin*) picadillo *m*
2* lío* *m*, embrollo *m* • **to make a ~ of sth** hacer algo muy mal • **he made a complete ~ of the interview** la entrevista le fue fatal • IDIOM: • **to settle sb's ~** cargarse a algn*
CPD ▸ **hash browns** *croquetas de patata hervida y cebolla*

hash²* [hæʃ] N (= *hashish*) hachís *m*, chocolate‡ *m* (*Sp*), mota *f* (*CAm**)

hash³ [hæʃ] N (*Typ*) almohadilla *f*
CPD ▸ **hash key** tecla *f* almohadilla

hashish ['hæʃɪʃ] N hachís *m*

hashtag ['hæʃtæg] N (*on Twitter*) etiqueta *f*, hashtag *m*

hasn't ['hæznt] = **has not**

hasp [hɑ:sp] N (*for padlock*) hembrilla *f*; (*on window*) falleba *f*; (*on box, book*) cierre *m*

Hassidic [hə'sɪdɪk] ADJ hasídico

hassle ['hæsl] N* (= *problem, difficulty*) lío *m*, problema *m* • **no ~!** ¡no hay problema! • **it's not worth the ~** no vale la pena
VT molestar, fastidiar

hassle-free [,hæsl'fri:] ADJ [*experience, holiday, journey*] sin complicaciones • **the internet provides a hassle-free way of booking plane tickets** la Internet proporciona un medio sin complicaciones para la compra de billetes de avión

hassock ['hæsək] N (*Rel*) cojín *m*

hast†† [hæst] ▹ **have**

haste [heɪst] N prisa *f*, apuro *m* (*LAm*) • **to do sth in ~** hacer algo precipitadamente *or* de prisa • **to make ~** darse prisa, apurarse (*LAm*) • **to make ~ to do sth** apresurarse a hacer algo • PROVERBS: • **more ~ less speed** • **make ~ slowly** vísteme despacio que tengo prisa

hasten ['heɪsn] VT [+ *process*] acelerar; [+ *sb's end, downfall*] precipitar • **to ~ sb's departure** acelerar la partida *or* marcha de algn • **to ~ one's steps** apretar el paso • **to ~ death** precipitar *or* adelantar la muerte
VI apresurarse, darse prisa • **to ~ to do sth** apresurarse a hacer algo • **I ~ to add that …** me apresuro a añadir que … • **she ~ed to assure me that nothing was wrong** se apresuró a asegurarme que no pasaba nada
▸ **hasten away** VI + ADV marcharse precipitadamente (**from** de)
▸ **hasten back** VI + ADV volver con toda prisa
▸ **hasten on** VI + ADV seguir adelante con toda prisa

hastily ['heɪstɪlɪ] ADV **1** (= *hurriedly*) de prisa, apresuradamente • **I ~ suggested that …** me apresuré a sugerir que …
2 (= *rashly*) [*speak*] precipitadamente; [*judge*] a la ligera

hasty ['heɪstɪ] ADJ (COMPAR: **hastier**, SUPERL: **hastiest**) **1** (= *hurried*) apresurado, precipitado
2 (= *rash*) precipitado • **don't be so ~** no te precipites

hat [hæt] N sombrero *m* • **to raise one's hat** (*in greeting*) descubrirse • **to take off one's hat** quitarse el sombrero • IDIOMS: • **to eat one's hat**: • **I'll eat my hat if …** que me maten si … • **to hang one's hat up** jubilarse • **my hat!** ¡caramba! • **that's old hat** eso no es nada nuevo • **to pass the hat round** pasar el platillo • **to take one's hat off to sb** quitarse el sombrero *or* descubrirse ante algn • **I take my hat off to him** me descubro ante él • **to talk through one's hat*** decir disparates *or* tonterías • **to keep sth under one's hat** no decir palabra sobre algo • **keep it under your hat** de esto no digas ni pío* • **to wear two hats** ejercer un doble papel • **now wearing my other hat as …** hablando ahora en mi otra calidad de …; ▹ **ring¹**
CPD ▸ **hat rack** perchero *m* ▸ **hat shop** sombrerería *f* ▸ **hat stand**, **hat tree** (*US*) perchero *m* ▸ **hat trick** (*Ftbl, Rugby etc*) (= *three goals etc*) tres tantos *mpl or* goles *mpl* en un partido; (= *three consecutive wins*) serie *f* de tres victorias, tres triunfos *mpl* seguidos • **to get** *or* **score a hat trick** marcar tres tantos *or* goles en un partido

hatband ['hætbænd] N cinta *f* de sombrero

hatbox ['hætbɒks] N sombrerera *f*

hatch¹ [hætʃ] N **1** (*Naut*) escotilla *f*
2 (*Brit*) (= *serving hatch*) ventanilla *f*; ▹ **batten**

hatch² [hætʃ] VT **1** (*lit*) [+ *chick*] empollar; [+ *egg*] incubar
2 (*fig*) [+ *scheme*] idear; [+ *plot*] tramar
VI [*chick*] salir del huevo; [*insect, larva*] eclosionar (*frm*) • **the egg ~ed** el pollo rompió el cascarón y salió • **those eggs never ~ed** esos huevos resultaron ser hueros

hatch³ [hætʃ] VT (*Art*) sombrear

hatchback ['hætʃbæk] N **1** (= *car*) • **a ~** un tres/cinco puertas, un coche con puerta trasera
2 (= *door*) puerta *f* trasera, portón *m*

hat-check girl ['hættʃek,gɜ:l] N (*US*) encargada *f* del guardarropa

hatchery ['hætʃərɪ] N criadero *m*, vivero *m*

hatchet ['hætʃɪt] N hacha *f* (pequeña); ▹ **bury**
CPD ▸ **hatchet job*** crítica *f* vitriólica • **to do a ~ job on sb** poner por los suelos a algn, poner a algn a caer de un burro *or* a parir* ▸ **hatchet man*** (*US*) *ejecutor de faenas desagradables por cuenta de otro*; (= *assassin*) sicario *m*, asesino *m* a sueldo

hatchet-faced ['hætʃɪt,feɪst] ADJ de cara de cuchillo

hatching¹ ['hætʃɪŋ] N [*of egg*] incubación *f*; [*of chick*] salida *f* del huevo; [*of insect, larva*] eclosión *f* (*frm*); (*fig*) [*of scheme*] ideación *f*; [*of plot*] maquinación *f*

hatching² ['hætʃɪŋ] N (*Art*) sombreado *m*

hatchway ['hætʃweɪ] N ▹ **hatch¹**

hate [heɪt] N odio *m*; ▹ **pet**
VT odiar, detestar • **to ~ sb like poison** odiar a algn a muerte • **I ~ having to commute every day** no soporto tener que tomar el tren todos los días para ir a trabajar • **he ~s to be** *or* **he ~s being corrected** no soporta que se le corrija *or* que le corrijan • **I ~ to see him unhappy** me duele mucho *or* no soporto verlo triste • **I ~ to say it, but …** lamento tener que decirlo, pero … • **I ~ to trouble you, but …** siento muchísimo molestarle, pero …
CPD ▸ **hate campaign** campaña *f or* operación *f* de acoso (y derribo) • **to mount/wage a ~ campaign against sb** montar/realizar una campaña *or* operación de acoso y derribo contra algn ▸ **hate crime** *crimen motivado por el odio racial, xenófobo, religioso u homofóbico* • **they are calling for action on homophobic ~ crimes** piden que se tome acción contra los crímenes motivados por la homofobia ▸ **hate mail** cartas *fpl* amenazantes

hated ['heɪtɪd] ADJ (= *detested*) odiado, detestado

hateful ['heɪtfʊl] ADJ odioso

hater ['heɪtəʳ] N • **to be a ~ of sth** odiar algo, detestar algo; ▹ **woman-hater**

hath†† [hæθ] ▹ **have**

hatless ['hætlɪs] ADJ sin sombrero, descubierto

hatpin ['hætpɪn] N alfiler *m* de sombrero

hatred ['heɪtrɪd] N odio *m* (**for a**)

hatter ['hætəʳ] N sombrerero/a *m/f*; ▹ **mad**

haughtily ['hɔ:tɪlɪ] ADV altaneramente, altivamente

haughtiness ['hɔ:tɪnɪs] N altanería *f*, altivez *f*

haughty ['hɔːtɪ] (ADJ) (COMPAR: **haughtier**, SUPERL: **haughtiest**) altanero, altivo

haul [hɔːl] (N) **1** (= *act of pulling*) tirón *m*, jalón *m* (*LAm*) (**on** de)
2 (= *distance*) recorrido *m*, trayecto *m* • **it's a long ~** hay mucho trecho, hay una buena tirada* • **revitalizing the economy will be a long ~** hay por delante un largo trecho hasta conseguir revitalizar la economía • **over the long ~** a largo plazo
3 (= *amount taken*) [*of fish*] redada *f*; (*financial*) ganancia *f*; (*from robbery etc*) botín *m*; (= *arms haul, drugs haul*) alijo *m* • **the thieves made a good ~** los ladrones obtuvieron un cuantioso botín
(VT) **1** (= *drag*) [+ *heavy object*] arrastrar, jalar (*LAm*) • **he ~ed himself to his feet** se puso en pie con gran esfuerzo • **they ~ed me out of bed at five o'clock in the morning** me sacaron de la cama a las cinco de la mañana • **he was ~ed before the manager** tuvo que presentarse al gerente; ▷ **coal**
2 (= *transport*) transportar, acarrear
▸ **haul down** (VT + ADV) [+ *flag, sail*] arriar
▸ **haul in** (VT + ADV) [+ *fishing net*] ir recogiendo
▸ **haul up** (VT + ADV) **1** (*lit*) ir levantando
2 (*fig*) • **he was ~ed up in court** fue llevado ante el tribunal

haulage ['hɔːlɪdʒ] (N) (= *road transport*) transporte *m*, acarreo *m*; (= *cost*) gastos *mpl* de transporte
(CPD) ▸ **haulage company** compañía *f* de transportes (por carretera) ▸ **haulage contractor** transportista *mf*

hauler ['hɔːlər] (*US*) = **haulier**

haulier ['hɔːlɪər] (N) transportista *mf*

haunch [hɔːntʃ] (N) [*of animal*] anca *f*; [*of person*] cadera *f*; [*of meat*] pierna *f* • **to sit on one's ~es** sentarse en cuclillas

haunt [hɔːnt] (N) [*of animal, criminals*] guarida *f*; [*of person*] lugar *m* predilecto • **I know his usual/favourite ~s** sé dónde suele ir/cuáles son sus lugares predilectos • **it's a ~ of artists** es lugar de encuentro de artistas
(VT) **1** [*ghost*] [+ *castle etc*] aparecerse en, rondar • **the house is ~ed** en la casa hay fantasmas, la casa está encantada *or* embrujada
2 [*person*] [+ *place*] (= *frequent*) frecuentar, rondar
3 [*idea, fear*] [+ *person*] obsesionar • **he is ~ed by the thought that …** le obsesiona el pensamiento de que … • **he is ~ed by memories** le persiguen los recuerdos

haunted ['hɔːntɪd] (ADJ) [*look*] de angustia, obsesionado • **~ house** casa encantada *or* embrujada

haunting ['hɔːntɪŋ] (ADJ) [*sight, music*] evocador; [*melody*] inolvidable

hauntingly ['hɔːntɪŋlɪ] (ADV) • **a ~ lovely scene** una escena de una belleza inolvidable

haute couture [otkutyr] (N) alta costura *f*

haute cuisine [ˌəʊtkwɪ'ziːn] (N) alta cocina *f*

hauteur [əʊ'tɜː] (N) (*frm*) = **haughtiness**

Havana [hə'vænə] (N) La Habana

have [hæv]

TRANSITIVE VERB
AUXILIARY VERB
MODAL VERB
PHRASAL VERBS

(3RD PERS SING PRESENT: **has**, PT, PP: **had**)

*When **have** is part of a set combination, eg **have a look, have a good time, have breakfast, had better**, look up the other word. For **have** + adverb/preposition combinations, see also the phrasal verb section of this entry.*

TRANSITIVE VERB

1 (= *possess*) tener • **he's got** *or* **he has blue eyes** tiene los ojos azules • **~ you got** *or* **do you ~ 10p?** ¿tienes diez peniques? • **~ you got** *or* **do you ~ any brothers or sisters?** ¿tienes hermanos? • **she had her eyes closed** tenía los ojos cerrados • **he hasn't got** *or* **he doesn't ~ any friends** no tiene amigos • **I've got** *or* **I ~ a friend staying next week** tengo a un amigo en casa la semana que viene • **I've got** *or* **I ~ an idea** tengo una idea

*Don't translate the **a** in sentences like **has he got a girlfriend?, I haven't got a washing-machine** if the number of such items is not significant since people normally only have one at a time:*

• **has he got a girlfriend?** ¿tiene novia? • **I ~n't got a washing-machine** no tengo lavadora

*Do translate the **a** if the person or thing is qualified:*

• **he has a Spanish girlfriend** tiene una novia española • **all** *or* **everything I ~ is yours** todo lo que tengo es tuyo • **you must give it all** *or* **everything you ~** tienes que emplearte a fondo • **you must put all** *or* **everything you ~ into it** tienes que emplearte a fondo • **can I ~ a pencil please?** ¿me puedes dar un lápiz, por favor? • **the book has no name on it** el libro no lleva *or* tiene el nombre del dueño • **I've got** *or* **I ~ no Spanish** no sé español • **to ~ something to do** tener algo que hacer • **I've got some letters to write** tengo algunas cartas que escribir • **I've got** *or* **I ~ nothing to do** no tengo nada que hacer • **~n't you got anything to do?** ¿no tienes nada que hacer? • **hello, what ~ we here?** vaya, vaya, ¿qué tenemos aquí?; ▷ **handy, ready**

2 (= *eat, drink*) tomar • **what are we having for lunch?** ¿que vamos a comer? • **we had ice-cream for dessert** tomamos helado de postre • **to ~ something to eat/drink** comer/beber algo, tomar algo • **what will you ~?** ¿qué quieres tomar?, ¿qué vas a tomar? • **I'll ~ a coffee** tomaré un café • **will you ~ some more?** ¿te sirvo más?

3 (= *receive*) recibir • **thank you for having me** gracias por su hospitalidad • **you can ~ my ticket** puedes quedarte con mi billete • **we had some help from the government** recibimos ayuda del gobierno • **I had a letter from John** tuve carta de Juan, recibí una carta de Juan • **I must ~ them by this afternoon** necesito tenerlos para esta tarde • **to ~ no news** no tener noticias • **they had a lot of wedding presents** recibieron *or* les hicieron muchos regalos de boda • **we had a lot of visitors** (*at home*) tuvimos muchas visitas; (*at exhibition etc*) tuvimos muchos visitantes

4 (= *obtain*) • **they can be had for as little as £10 each** pueden conseguirse por tan solo 10 libras • **it's not to be had anywhere** no se consigue en ninguna parte • **there was no bread to be had** no quedaba pan en ningún sitio, no podía conseguirse pan en ningún sitio

5 (= *take*) • **I'll ~ a dozen eggs, please** ¿me pones una docena de huevos, por favor? • **which one will you ~?** ¿cuál quiere? • **can I ~ your name please?** ¿me da su nombre, por favor? • **you can ~ it** *or* **I'll let you ~ it for £10** te lo dejo en 10 libras, te lo puedes llevar por 10 libras, te lo vendo por 10 libras

6 (= *give birth to*) [+ *baby, kittens*] tener • **what did she ~?** ¿qué ha tenido? • **she had a boy** ha tenido un niño

7 (= *hold, catch*) tener • **I ~ him in my power** lo tengo en mi poder • **he had him by the throat** lo tenía agarrado por la garganta • **I ~ it on good authority that …** me consta que …, sé a ciencia cierta que …, sé de buena tinta que …* • **I've got it!** ¡ya! • **you ~ me there** • **there you ~ me** ahí sí que me has pillado*

8 (= *allow*) consentir, tolerar • **we can't ~ that** eso no se puede consentir • **I won't ~ this nonsense** no voy a consentir *or* tolerar estas tonterías • **I won't ~ it!** no lo voy a consentir *or* tolerar • **she won't ~ it said that …** no consiente *or* tolera que digan que … • **I won't ~ him risking his neck on that motorbike** no voy a consentir que se juegue el cuello en esa moto

9 (= *spend*) pasar • **to ~ a pleasant afternoon/evening** pasar una tarde agradable • **~ a nice day!** ¡que pases un buen día! • **I had a horrible day at school today** he tenido un día horrible en el colegio • **what sort of day ~ you had?** ¿qué tal día has tenido?

10 (*on telephone*) • **can I ~ Personnel please?** ¿me puede poner con Personal, por favor?

11* (= *have sex with*) acostarse con

12 (= *make*) • **I'll soon ~ it nice and shiny** enseguida lo dejo bien brillante • **he had us confused** nos tenía confundidos

13 (*in set structures*) **to have sth done** hacer que se haga algo, mandar hacer algo • **we had our luggage brought up** mandamos subir el equipaje • **I've had the brakes checked** he mandado revisar los frenos • **to ~ a suit made** (mandar) hacerse un traje • **to ~ one's hair cut** cortarse el pelo • **they had him killed** lo mataron
to have sb do sth mandar a algn hacer algo • **he had me do it again** me hizo hacerlo otra vez, me hizo que lo hiciese otra vez • **I had him clean the car** le hice limpiar el coche • **what would you ~ me do?**† ¿qué quiere que haga? • **I'll ~ you know that …** quiero que sepas que …
to have sth happen • **she had her bag stolen** le robaron el bolso • **he had his arm broken** le rompieron el brazo
to have sb doing sth • **she soon had them all reading and writing** (= *organized them*) enseguida los puso a leer y a escribir; (= *taught them*) enseguida les habían enseñado a leer y a escribir

14 (*in set expressions*) **to have sth against sb/sth** tener algo en contra de algn/algo
to have had it • **you've had it now! he knows all about it*** ¡ahora sí que te la has cargado! se ha enterado de todo • **this sofa has had it*** este sofá ya no da para más* • **I've had it up to here with his nonsense*** estoy hasta la coronilla *or* hasta el moño de sus tonterías*
to have it that • **he will ~ it that he is right** insiste en que tiene razón • **rumour has it that …** corre la voz de que …
to be had • **you've been had!*** ¡te han engañado!
to have to do with tener que ver con • **that's got** *or* **that has nothing to do with it!** ¡eso no tiene nada que ver! • **you'd better not ~ anything to do with him** más te vale no tener tratos con él
to let sb have sth (= *give*) dar algo a algn;

h

(= *lend*) dejar algo a algn, prestar algo a algn • **I'll let you ~ my reply tomorrow** les daré mi respuesta mañana • **let me ~ your address** dame tus señas • **let me ~ your pen for a moment** déjame el boli un momento • **let him ~ it!*** ¡dale!
what have you • **... and what ~ you ...** y qué sé yo qué más
would have it • **as ill-luck** *or* **fate would ~ it** desgraciadamente; ▹ **luck**
AUXILIARY VERB
1 haber • **I've already seen that film** ya he visto esa película • **he's been very kind** ha sido muy amable • **has he gone?** ¿se ha ido? • **hasn't he told you?** ¿no te lo ha dicho? • **she said she had spoken to them** dijo que había hablado con ellos • **had you phoned me** (*frm*) *or* **if you had phoned me I would ~ come round** si me hubieras llamado habría venido • **never having seen it before, I ...** como no lo había visto antes, ... • **having finished** *or* **when he had finished, he left** cuando terminó *or* cuando hubo terminado, se fue; ▹ **just, SINCE**
2 (*verb substitute*) **a** • **you've got more than I ~** tienes más que yo • **they've done more than we ~** ellos han hecho más que nosotros • **he hasn't worked as hard as you ~** él no ha trabajado tanto como tú • **"he's already eaten"** — **"so ~ I"** —él ya ha comido —yo también • **"we ~n't had any news yet"** — **"neither ~ we"** —no hemos tenido noticias todavía —nosotros tampoco • **"you've made a mistake"** — **"no I ~n't!"** —has cometido un error —no es verdad *or* cierto • **"we ~n't paid"** — **"yes we ~!"** —no hemos pagado —¡qué sí! • **"he's got a new job"** — **"oh has he?"** —tiene un trabajo nuevo —¿ah, sí? • **"you've written it twice"** — **"so I ~!"** —lo has escrito dos veces —es verdad *or* cierto • **"~ you read the book?"** — **"yes, I ~"** —¿has leído el libro? —sí • **"has he told you?"** — **"no, he hasn't"** —¿te lo ha dicho? —no
b (*in question tags*) • **he hasn't done it, has he?** no lo ha hecho, ¿verdad? • **you've done it, ~n't you?** lo has hecho, ¿verdad? *or* ¿no?
3 (*avoiding repetition of verb*) • **you've all been there before, but I ~n't** vosotros habéis estado allí antes, pero yo no • **he has never met her, but I ~** él no la ha llegado a conocer, pero yo sí • **~ you ever been there? if you ~ ...** ¿has estado alguna vez allí? si es así ... • **~ you tried it? if you ~n't ...** ¿lo has probado? (porque) si no ...; ▹ **so, nor**
MODAL VERB
(= *be obliged*) • **to ~ (got) to do sth** tener que hacer algo • **I've got to** *or* **I ~ to finish this work** tengo que terminar este trabajo • **~ we got to** *or* **do we ~ to leave early?** ¿tenemos que salir temprano? • **I ~n't got to** *or* **I don't ~ to wear glasses** no necesito (usar) gafas • **I shall ~ to go and see her** tendré que ir a verla • **it will just ~ to wait till tomorrow** tendrá que esperar hasta mañana • **he had to pay all the money back** tuvo que devolver todo el dinero • **she was having to get up at six each morning** tenía que levantarse a las seis cada mañana • **this has to be a mistake** esto tiene que ser un error • **do you ~ to make such a noise?** ¿tienes que hacer tanto ruido? • **you didn't ~ to tell her!** ¡no tenías por qué decírselo! • **it's nice not to ~ to work on Saturdays** es un gusto no tener que trabajar los sábados • **it has to be done this way** tiene que hacerse de este modo • **does it ~ to be ironed?** ¿hay que plancharlo?
▸ **have around** VT + ADV **1** (= *have available*) tener cerca; (= *to count on*) contar con • **Sarah was a joy to ~ around** era una delicia tener a Sarah cerca • **a great guy to ~ around** un tipo estupendo para tenerlo a tu lado • **the sort of player I'd like to ~ around** el tipo de jugador con el que me gustaría contar
2 (= *invite*) • **we're having Mary around tomorrow** hemos invitado a Mary para que venga mañana • **we're having some people around** tenemos invitados
▸ **have away‡** VT + ADV (*Brit*) = **have off**
▸ **have back** VT + ADV **1** (= *repossess*) • **please can I ~ my book back?** ¿me puedes devolver el libro, por favor?
2 (= *return invitation to*) devolver la invitación a • **we must ~ the Corks back soon** habrá que devolverles la invitación a los Cork dentro de poco • **they never ~ anyone back** nunca devuelven la invitación a nadie
3 (= *take back*) [+ *lover, partner*] volver a estar con; [+ *employee*] readmitir
▸ **have down** VT + ADV **1** (*for visit*) invitar a quedarse en casa • **we are having the Smiths down for a few days** los Smith vienen a pasar unos días con nosotros *or* en casa
2 (= *dismantle*) [+ *building, wall*] tirar, echar abajo; [+ *tent*] quitar, desmontar
3 (= *move*) [+ *picture*] quitar, descolgar
▸ **have in** VT + ADV **1** [+ *doctor*] llamar • **to ~ the plumber in** llamar al fontanero • **to ~ visitors in** tener invitados • **let's ~ the next one in** que pase el siguiente
2 • IDIOM: • **to ~ it in for sb*** tenerla tomada con algn*
▸ **have off** VT + ADV **1** (= *have as holiday*) • **I'm having a fortnight off in July** me voy a tomar dos semanas de vacaciones *or* permiso en julio • **the children ~ got a week off for half term** los niños tienen una semana de vacaciones a mitad del trimestre
2 (= *dislodge*) quitar • **he had the panelling off in no time** quitó las mamparas en un santiamén • **be careful or you'll ~ the pans off!** ¡ten cuidado, no vayas a tirar las cacerolas!
3 (*Brit*) • **to ~ it off‡** echar un polvo** • **to ~ it off with sb** tirarse a algn**
▸ **have on** VT + ADV **1** (= *wear*) [+ *dress, hat*] llevar • **she had on a beautiful black evening dress** llevaba (puesto) un precioso vestido de noche negro; ▹ **nothing**
2 (= *be busy with*) • **I've got so much on this week** tengo mucho que hacer esta semana • **~ you anything on tomorrow?** ¿tienes algo que hacer mañana?, ¿tienes compromiso para mañana?
3 (= *put on*) [+ *wallpaper, roof*] poner • **we'll ~ the paint on in no time** lo tendremos pintado en un santiamén
4 (*Brit**) (= *tease*) • **to ~ sb on** tomar el pelo a algn* • **he's having you on!** te está tomando el pelo*
▸ **have out** VT + ADV **1** (= *have removed*) • **to ~ a tooth out** sacarse una muela • **to ~ one's tonsils out** operarse de las amígdalas • **we had to ~ the old boiler out** tuvimos que quitar la caldera vieja • **we'll ~ the piano out in a trice** enseguida sacamos el piano
2 • **to ~ it out with sb** ajustar cuentas con algn
▸ **have over** VT + ADV **1** (= *invite*) • **we're having Mary over tomorrow** hemos invitado a Mary para que venga mañana • **we're having some people over** tenemos invitados • **we had them over to dinner last week** vinieron a cenar la semana pasada
2 (= *overturn*) volcar, tirar • **watch out, you'll ~ the coffee over!** ¡cuidado, que vas a volcar *or* tirar el café!
▸ **have round** VT + ADV = **have around**
▸ **have up** VT + ADV **1** (*Brit**) • **to be had up** (= *be prosecuted*) ser llevado a juicio • **he was had up for assault** le llevaron a juicio por asalto
2 [+ *guest*] invitar • **why don't we ~ George up for the weekend?** ¿por qué no invitamos a George el fin de semana?

have-a-go hero [ˌhævəˈgəʊˌhɪərəʊ] N héroe *m* anónimo, héroe *m* por un día
haven [ˈheɪvn] N refugio *m*; (= *port*) puerto *m*
have-nots [ˈhævnɒts] NPL ▹ **haves**
haven't [ˈhævnt] = **have not**
haversack [ˈhævəsæk] N mochila *f*, macuto *m* (*LAm*)
haves* [hævz] NPL • **the ~ and the have-nots** los ricos y los pobres
havoc [ˈhævək] N estragos *mpl* • **to cause** *or* **create ~** hacer estragos • **this latest decision will cause ~ in the tourist industry** esta última decisión hará estragos *or* provocará grandes trastornos en el sector turístico • **to play ~ with:** • **the recession is playing ~ with the government's balance sheets** la recesión está dando al traste con *or* haciendo estragos en los balances de ejercicio del gobierno • **the food in the hotel played ~ with my digestion** la comida del hotel me destrozó el estómago • **the weather played ~ with sporting fixtures this weekend** el mal tiempo arruinó los acontecimientos deportivos del fin de semana • **to wreak ~** hacer estragos • **the slugs are wreaking ~ in the garden** las babosas están arruinando *or* estropeando el jardín • **stress can wreak ~ on the immune system** el estrés puede causar serios trastornos en el sistema inmunológico
haw¹ [hɔː] N baya *f* del espino
haw² [hɔː] VI • **to hem and haw** • **to hum and haw** (= *be indecisive*) vacilar; (= *express reservations*) poner reparos
Hawaii [həˈwaɪiː] N (islas *fpl*) Hawai *m*
Hawaiian [həˈwaɪjən] ADJ hawaiano
N hawaiano/a *m/f*
hawfinch [ˈhɔːfɪntʃ] N picogordo *m*
hawk¹ [hɔːk] N (*Orn, Pol*) halcón *m* • **he was watching me like a ~** me vigilaba estrechamente, no me quitaba ojo
hawk² [hɔːk] VT [+ *goods for sale*] pregonar
hawk³ [hɔːk] VI (*also* **hawk up**) (= *clear one's throat*) carraspear
hawker [ˈhɔːkəʳ] N vendedor(a) *m/f* ambulante
hawk-eyed [ˌhɔːkˈaɪd] ADJ con ojos de lince
hawkish [ˈhɔːkɪʃ] ADJ (*Pol*) de línea dura
hawser [ˈhɔːzəʳ] N guindaleza *f*, calabrote *m*
hawthorn [ˈhɔːθɔːn] N espino *m*
hay [heɪ] N heno *m* • IDIOMS: • **that ain't hay** (*US**) eso no es moco de pavo* • **to hit the hay*** acostarse • **to make hay while the sun shines** aprovecharse la ocasión
CPD ▸ **hay fever** fiebre *f* del heno, alergia *f* al polen
haycock [ˈheɪkɒk] N montón *m* de heno
hayfork [ˈheɪfɔːk] N bieldo *m*
hayloft [ˈheɪlɒft] N henil *m*, henal *m*
haymaker [ˈheɪmeɪkəʳ] N heneador(a) *m/f*, labrador(a) *m/f* que trabaja en la siega *or* la recolección del heno
haymaking [ˈheɪmeɪkɪŋ] N siega *f* del heno, recolección *f* del heno
hayseed* [ˈheɪsiːd] N (*US*) palurdo/a *m/f*, paleto/a *m/f* (*Sp**)
haystack [ˈheɪstæk] N almiar *m* • IDIOM: • **to be like looking for a needle in a ~** ser como buscar una aguja en un pajar
haywire* [ˈheɪwaɪəʳ] ADJ • IDIOM: • **to go ~**

[*person*] volverse loco, perder la chaveta*; [*machine*] averiarse, malograrse (*LAm*); [*scheme etc*] irse a pique • **the switchboard went ~** se colapsó la centralita

hazard ['hæzəd] N peligro *m*; (*less serious*) riesgo *m* • **this heater is a fire ~** esta estufa puede provocar un incendio; ▹ **health**
VT **1** (= *venture*) [+ *answer, remark*] aventurar • **would you like to ~ a guess?** ¿quieres intentar adivinarlo?
2 (= *risk*) [+ *one's life*] poner en peligro, arriesgar
CPD ▸ **hazard lights, hazard warning lights** (*Aut*) luces *fpl* de emergencia ▸ **hazard pay** (*US*) prima *f* de riesgo

hazardous ['hæzədəs] ADJ [*waste, chemicals, weather conditions*] peligroso; [*occupation, journey, enterprise*] arriesgado, peligroso • **~ pay** (*US*) prima *f* or plus *m* de peligrosidad • **~ to health** peligroso para la salud

haze¹ [heɪz] N **1** (= *mist*) bruma *f*, neblina *f*; (*in hot weather*) calina *f*, calima *f* • **a ~ of tobacco smoke filled the room** el cuarto estaba lleno de humo de tabaco
2 (*fig*) • **she spent most of her life in a ~ of alcohol** pasaba la mayor parte de su vida embotada por el alcohol • **to be in a ~** (*fig*) andar atontado or aturdido

haze² [heɪz] VT (*US*) gastar novatadas a

hazel ['heɪzl] N (*tree*) avellano *m*
ADJ [*eyes*] color de avellana (*adj inv*)

hazelnut ['heɪzlnʌt] N avellana *f*

hazelwood ['heɪzl,wʊd] N madera *f* de avellano

hazily ['heɪzɪlɪ] ADV [*remember*] vagamente; [*think*] de manera confusa

haziness ['heɪzɪnɪs] N **1** [*of view, horizon, sky*] nebulosidad *f* • **the ~ of the morning gave the landscape a mysterious air** (*due to mist*) la bruma or neblina de la mañana daba al paisaje un aire de misterio; (*due to heat*) la calina de la mañana daba al paisaje un aire de misterio
2 (*fig*) (= *vagueness*) confusión *f*, vaguedad *f*

hazing ['heɪzɪŋ] N (*US*) novatadas *fpl*; ▹ **SORORITY/FRATERNITY**

hazy ['heɪzɪ] ADJ (COMPAR: **hazier**, SUPERL: **haziest**) **1** (= *not clear*) [*sunshine, morning, view, horizon, sky*] (*due to mist*) brumoso, neblinoso; (*due to heat*) calinoso • **it's a bit ~ today** (*due to mist*) hoy hay un poco de neblina or bruma; (*due to heat*) hoy hay un poco de calima
2 (= *confused, uncertain*) [*notion, details*] confuso; [*memory*] vago, confuso; [*ideas*] poco claro, confuso • **I'm a bit ~ about maths** tengo las matemáticas poco claras or un poco confusas • **I'm ~ about what happened** tengo solamente una vaga idea de lo que ocurrió, no recuerdo muy bien lo que ocurrió
3 (= *blurred*) [*outline, vision*] borroso; [*photograph*] nublado

HB ADJ (*on pencil*) HB

H-bomb ['eɪtʃbɒm] N bomba *f* H

HC ABBR (= **hot and cold (water)**) con agua caliente y fría

HCF N ABBR (= **highest common factor**) MCD *m*

HDD N ABBR (*Comput*) = **hard disk drive**

HD-DVD N ABBR (= **High Definition DVD**) HD-DVD *m*

HDTV N ABBR (= **high definition television**) televisión *f* de alta definición

HE ABBR **1** = **high explosive**
2 (= **His** or **Her Excellency**) S.E.
3 (= **His Eminence**) S.Em.ª

he [hiː] PERS PRON **1** (*emphatic, to avoid ambiguity*) él • **we went to the cinema but he didn't** nosotros fuimos al cine pero él no • **it is he who …** es él quien … • **you've got more money than he has** tienes más dinero que él

Don't translate the subject pronoun when not emphasizing or clarifying:

• **he's very tall** es muy alto • **there he is** allí está
2 (*frm*) • **he who wishes to …** el que desee …, quien desee …
N • **it's a he*** (= *animal*) es macho; (= *baby*) es un niño, es varón (*LAm*)
CPD macho ▸ **he-goat** cabra *f* macho

head [hed] N **1** (= *part of body*) cabeza *f* • **my ~ aches** me duele la cabeza • **the horse won by a (short) ~** el caballo ganó por una cabeza (escasa) • **he went ~ first into the ditch/wall** se cayó de cabeza en la zanja/se dio de cabeza contra la pared • **the government is ploughing ~ first into another crisis** el gobierno avanza irremediablemente hacia otra crisis • **from ~ to foot** de pies a cabeza • **to give a horse its ~** soltar las riendas a un caballo • **to give sb his/her ~** dar rienda suelta a algn • **wine goes to my ~** el vino se me sube a la cabeza • **success has gone to his ~** el éxito se le ha subido a la cabeza • **~ of hair** cabellera *f* • **to go ~ over heels** caer de cabeza • **to fall ~ over heels in love with sb** enamorarse perdidamente de algn • **to keep one's ~ down** (*lit*) no levantar la cabeza; (= *work hard*) trabajar de lo lindo; (= *avoid being noticed*) intentar pasar desapercibido • **to nod one's ~** decir que sí or asentir con la cabeza • **to shake one's ~** decir que no or negar con la cabeza • **he stands ~ and shoulders above the rest** (*lit*) les saca más de una cabeza a los demás; (*fig*) los demás no le llegan a la suela del zapato • **to stand on one's ~** hacer el pino • **I could do it standing on my ~*** lo podría hacer con los ojos cerrados • **she is a ~ taller than her sister** le saca una cabeza a su hermana • **from ~ to toe** de pies a cabeza • **I ought to bang** or **knock your ~s together** os voy a dar un coscorrón a los dos* • **he turned his ~ and looked back at her** volvió la cabeza y la miró • **IDIOMS**: • **I can't get my ~ around that*** no consigo entenderlo, para mí eso es un misterio • **to have one's ~ up one's arse** or (*US*) **ass*‡** (= *be pig-headed*) ser cabezón; (= *be self-obsessed*) mirarse al ombligón • **to bite sb's ~ off** echar un rapapolvo a algn • **to put** or **lay one's ~ on the block** jugársela, arriesgarse • **to get one's ~ down** (*to work*) poner manos a la obra; (*to sleep*) acostarse, echarse • **to go over sb's ~**: • **they went over my ~ to the manager** pasaron por encima de mí y fueron directamente al gerente • **to hold one's ~ up (high)** ir con la frente bien alta or erguida • **with ~ held high** con la frente bien alta or erguida • **to laugh one's ~ off** desternillarse de risa* • **to stand** or **turn sth on its ~** dar la vuelta a algo • **on your own ~ be it!** ¡allá tú!, tú sabrás lo que haces • **to want sb's ~ on a plate** querer la cabeza de algn • **to turn one's ~ the other way** hacer la vista gorda • **~s will roll** van a rodar cabezas • **to bury** or **hide** or **stick one's ~ in the sand** seguir la táctica del avestruz • **to scream/shout one's ~ off** desgañitarse • **I can't make ~ nor** or **or tail of it** no le encuentro ni pies ni cabeza • **I can't make ~ nor** or **or tail of what he's saying** no entiendo nada de lo que dice • **to turn ~s** llamar la atención • **she had the kind of looks that turn ~s** tenía ese tipo de belleza que llama la atención • **to keep one's ~ above water** (*fig*) ir tirando; ▹ **acid, cloud, hang, knock, price, rear, swell, top**
2 (= *intellect, mind*) cabeza *f* • **use your ~!** ¡usa la cabeza! • **you never know what's going on in his ~** nunca sabes lo que le está pasando por la cabeza • **it's gone right out of my ~** se me ha ido de la cabeza, se me ha olvidado • **it was the first thing that came into my ~** fue lo primero que me vino a la cabeza • **it was above their ~s** no lo entendían • **it's better to come to it with a clear ~ in the morning** es mejor hacerlo por la mañana con la cabeza despejada • **it never entered my ~** ni se me pasó por la cabeza siquiera • **you need your ~ examining** or **examined** tú estás mal de la cabeza • **to have a ~ for business/figures** ser bueno para los negocios/con los números • **I have no ~ for heights** tengo vértigo • **to do a sum in one's ~** hacer un cálculo mental • **he added it all up in his ~** lo sumó todo mentalmente • **he has got it into his ~ that …** se le ha metido en la cabeza que … • **I wish he would get it into his thick ~ that …** ya me gustaría que le entrara en ese cabezón que tiene que … • **who put that (idea) into your ~?** ¿quién te ha metido eso en la cabeza? • **don't put ideas into his ~** no le metas ideas en la cabeza • **I can't get that tune out of my ~** no puedo quitarme esa música de la cabeza • **it was over their ~s** no lo entendían • **it went way over my ~** no entendí nada • **I'm sure if we put our ~s together we can work something out** estoy seguro de que si intercambiamos ideas encontraremos una solución • **to take it into one's ~ to do sth**: • **he took it into his ~ to go to Australia** se le metió en la cabeza ir a Australia • **don't worry your ~ about it** no te preocupes, no le des muchas vueltas • **IDIOMS**: • **to keep one's ~** mantener la calma • **to lose one's ~** perder la cabeza or los estribos • **to be/go off one's ~*** estar/volverse majara* • **you must be off your ~!** ¡estás como una cabra! • **to be out of one's ~*** (= *mad*) haber perdido el juicio, estar mal de la cabeza; (= *drunk*) estar borracho como una cuba*; (= *on drugs*) estar colocadísimo‡, estar como una moto* • **he's got his ~ screwed on (the right way)** tiene la cabeza sobre los hombros • **to be soft** or **weak in the ~** estar mal de la cabeza • **to go soft in the ~** perder la cabeza • **all that flattery will turn his ~** todos esos halagos se le subirán a la cabeza • **PROVERB**: • **two ~s are better than one** cuatro ojos ven más que dos
3 (= *leader*) [*of firm*] director(a) *m/f*; (*esp Brit*) [*of school*] director(a) *m/f* • **~ of department** (*in school, firm*) jefe/a *m/f* de departamento • **~ of French** el jefe/la jefa del departamento de francés • **~ of (the) household** cabeza *mf* de familia • **~ of state** (*Pol*) jefe/a *m/f* de Estado
4 (= *top part*) [*of hammer, pin, spot*] cabeza *f*; [*of arrow, spear*] punta *f*; [*of stick, cane*] puño *m*; [*of bed, page*] cabecera *f*; [*of stairs*] parte *f* alta; (*on beer*) espuma *f*; [*of river*] cabecera *f*, nacimiento *m*; [*of valley*] final *m*; [*of mountain pass*] cima *f* • **at the ~ of** [+ *organization*] a la cabeza de; [+ *train*] en la parte delantera de • **to be at the ~ of the class** ser el mejor de la clase • **to be at the ~ of the league** ir a la cabeza de la liga • **to be at the ~ of the list** encabezar la lista • **to be at the ~ of the queue** ser el primero en la cola • **to sit at the ~ of the table** sentarse en la cabecera de la mesa, presidir la mesa
5 (*Bot*) [*of flower*] cabeza *f*, flor *f*; [*of corn*] mazorca *f* • **a ~ of celery/garlic** una cabeza de apio/ajo • **a ~ of lettuce** una lechuga
6 (*Tech*) (*on tape-recorder*) cabezal *m*, cabeza *f* magnética; [*of cylinder*] culata *f*; (*Comput*) cabeza *f* • **reading/writing ~** cabeza *f* de lectura/grabación

7 (*= culmination*) • **this will bring matters to a ~** esto llevará las cosas a un punto crítico • **to come to a ~** [*situation*] alcanzar un punto crítico
8 **heads** (*on coin*) cara *f* • **it came down ~s** salió cara • **~s or tails?** ¿cara o cruz?, ¿águila o sol? (*Mex*) • **to toss ~s or tails** echar a cara o cruz • IDIOM: • **~s I win, tails you lose** cara yo gano, cruz tú pierdes
9 (*no pl*) (*= unit*) • **20 ~ of cattle** 20 cabezas de ganado (vacuno) • **£15 a** *or* **per ~** 15 libras por cabeza *or* persona
10 (*Naut*) proa *f* • **~ to wind** con la proa a barlovento *or* de cara al viento
11 (*Geog*) cabo *m*
12 (*= pressure*) • **~ of steam** presión *f* de vapor • **~ of water** presión *f* de agua
13 (*= height*) [*of water*] • **there has to be a ~ of six feet between the tank and the bath** el tanque tiene que estar a una altura de dos metros con respecto al baño
14 (*= title*) titular *m*; (*= subject heading*) encabezamiento *m* • **this comes under the ~ of ...** esto viene en el apartado de ...
(VT) 1 (*= be at front of*) [*+ procession, league, poll*] encabezar, ir a la cabeza de; [*+ list*] encabezar
2 (*= be in charge of*) [*+ organization*] dirigir; (*Sport*) [*+ team*] capitanear
3 (*= steer*) [*+ ship, car, plane*] dirigir
4 (*Ftbl*) [*+ goal*] cabecear • **to ~ the ball** cabecear (el balón)
5 [*+ chapter*] encabezar
(VI) • **where are you ~ing** *or* **~ed?** ¿hacia dónde vas?, ¿para dónde vas? • **he hitched a ride on a truck ~ing** *or* **~ed west** hizo autostop y lo recogió un camión que iba hacia el oeste • **he ~ed up the hill** se dirigió hacia la cima de la colina • **they were ~ing home/back to town** volvían a casa/a la ciudad
(CPD) ▸ **head boy** (*Brit*) (*Scol*) ≈ delegado *m* de la escuela (*alumno*) ▸ **head buyer** jefe/a *m/f* de compras ▸ **head case*** (*Brit*) majara* *mf*, chiflado/a* *m/f* ▸ **head cheese** (*US*) queso *m* de cerdo, cabeza *f* de jabalí (*Sp*), carne *f* en gelatina ▸ **head chef** chef *mf*, jefe/a *m/f* de cocina ▸ **head clerk** encargado/a *m/f* ▸ **head coach** (*Sport*) primer(a) entrenador(a) *m/f* ▸ **head cold** resfriado *m* (de cabeza) ▸ **head count** recuento *m* de personas • **to take a ~ count** hacer un recuento de personas ▸ **head gardener** jefe/a *m/f* de jardineros ▸ **head girl** (*Brit*) (*Scol*) ≈ delegada *f* de la escuela (*alumna*) ▸ **head height** altura *f* de la cabeza • **at ~ height** a la altura de la cabeza ▸ **head injury** herida *f* en la cabeza ▸ **head lice** piojos *mpl* ▸ **head massage** masaje *m* en la cabeza • **to give sb a ~ massage** masajearle la cabeza a algn, darle un masaje en la cabeza a algn ▸ **head nurse** enfermero/a *m/f* jefe ▸ **head office** sede *f* central ▸ **head prefect** (*Brit*) (*Scol*) ≈ delegado/a *m/f* de la escuela (*alumno/alumna*) ▸ **head restraint** (*Aut*) apoyacabezas *m inv*, reposacabezas *m inv* ▸ **head start** ventaja *f* • **a good education gives your child a ~ start in life** una buena educación sitúa a su hijo en una posición aventajada en la vida • **to have a ~ start (over** *or* **on sb)** (*Sport, fig*) tener ventaja (sobre algn) • **he has a ~ start over other candidates** tiene ventaja sobre *or* les lleva ventaja a otros candidatos • **even if he had a ~ start he couldn't possibly win** ni empezando con ventaja podría ganar ▸ **head teacher** director(a) *m/f* ▸ **head waiter** maître *m* ▸ **head wound** herida *f* en la cabeza
▸ **head back** (VI + ADV) (*= set off back*) regresar • **he ~ed back to Europe to finalize the attack plan** regresó a Europa para finalizar el plan de ataque
▸ **head down** (VT + ADV) [*+ ball*] pasar de cabeza • **he ~ed the ball down to Perry, who scored** pasó el balón de cabeza a Perry, que marcó un gol
▸ **head for** (VI + PREP) 1 [*+ place*] • **where are you ~ing for?** ¿hacia dónde vas?, ¿para dónde vas? • **it's time we were ~ing for home** ya es hora de que nos vayamos para casa • **he picked up his coat and ~ed for the door** tomó el abrigo y se dirigió hacia la puerta • **when he comes home he ~s straight for the TV** nada más llegar a casa se va derechito para la televisión • **the car was ~ing straight for us** el coche venía derecho hacia nosotros • **the vessel was ~ing for the port of Cádiz** el navío iba rumbo al *or* se dirigía al puerto de Cádiz
2 (*fig*) • **to be ~ing for: you're ~ing for trouble** vas por mal camino • **he's ~ing for a disappointment** se va a llevar una decepción • **he's ~ing for a fall** va camino del fracaso
▸ **head off** (VI + ADV) (*= set out*) marcharse (**for** para, hacia, **toward(s)** hacia) • **I watched them ~ off into the sunset** les vi marcharse por donde se ponía el sol
(VT + ADV) 1 (*= intercept*) [*+ person*] atajar, interceptar
2 (*= ward off*) [*+ questions, criticism, trouble*] atajar; [*+ person*] distraer (**from** de) • **if she asks where we're going, try and ~ her off** si pregunta dónde vamos, intenta distraerla
▸ **head out** (VI + ADV) (*= go out*) [*person*] salir • **a fishing boat ~ing out to sea** un barco de pesca haciéndose a la mar
▸ **head up** (VT + ADV) [*+ group, team*] estar a la cabeza de, dirigir

headache ['hedeɪk] (N) 1 (*= pain*) dolor *m* de cabeza; (*= sick headache*) jaqueca *f*
2 (*= problem*) quebradero *m* de cabeza, dolor *m* de cabeza • **that's his ~** allá él

headachy* ['hed,eɪkɪ] (ADJ) • **to be ~** tener dolor de cabeza • **she felt ~** sentía dolor de cabeza • **a ~ mix** una mezcla que da dolor de cabeza

headband ['hedbænd] (N) cinta *f* (para la cabeza), vincha *f* (*And, S. Cone*), huincha *f* (*And, S. Cone*)

headboard ['hed,bɔːd] (N) cabecera *f*

headcount ['hedkaʊnt] (N) 1 (*Ind*) (*= workforce*) plantilla *f*, personal *m*
2 (*= count*) recuento *m* de personas • **to take a ~** hacer un recuento de personas

headdress ['heddres] (N) tocado *m*

headed ['hedɪd] (ADJ) [*notepaper*] membretado, con membrete

-headed ['hedɪd] (ADJ) (*ending in compounds*) de cabeza ... • **small-headed** de cabeza pequeña • **red-headed** pelirrojo

header ['hedəʳ] (N) 1 (*Ftbl*) cabezazo *m*, remate *m* de cabeza
2* (*= fall*) caída *f* de cabeza; (*= dive*) salto *m* de cabeza
3 (*Typ, Comput*) encabezamiento *m*

header-block ['hedə,blɒk] (N) bloque *m* de encabezamiento, encabezamiento *m*

headfirst ['hed'fɜːst] (ADV) (*lit, fig*) de cabeza

headgear ['hedgɪəʳ] (N) (*gen*) tocado *m*; (*= hat*) sombrero *m*; (*= cap*) gorra *f*; (*= helmet*) casco *m* • **workers must wear protective ~** los trabajadores deben llevar casco

headguard ['hedgɑːd] (N) casco *m* protector; (*on face*) protector *m* facial

headhunt ['hed,hʌnt] (VI) buscar talentos
(VT) • **he was ~ed by a bank** un banco lo escogió para su plantilla

headhunter ['hed,hʌntəʳ] (N) (*lit*) cazador *m* de cabezas; (*fig*) cazatalentos *mf inv*

headhunting ['hed,hʌntɪŋ] (N) (*lit*) caza *f* de cabezas; (*fig*) caza *f* de talentos
(CPD) ▸ **headhunting agency** agencia *f* de caza de talentos

headiness ['hedɪnɪs] (N) [*of scent*] aroma *m* embriagador; [*of atmosphere*] excitación *f* • **a wine that is characterized by its ~** un vino que se caracteriza por lo fácilmente que se sube a la cabeza

heading ['hedɪŋ] (N) (*= title*) encabezamiento *m*, título *m*; (*= letterhead*) membrete *m*; (*= section*) sección *f*, apartado *m* • **under various ~s** en varios apartados • **to come under the ~ of** estar incluido en

headlamp ['hedlæmp] (N) (*Aut*) faro *m*

headland ['hedlənd] (N) cabo *m*, punta *f*

headless ['hedlɪs] (ADJ) (*lit*) [*body*] sin cabeza; (*= leaderless*) acéfalo • IDIOM: • **to run around like a ~ chicken** (*Brit*) ir dando palos de ciego, ir de acá para allá sin saber qué hacer

headlight ['hedlaɪt] (N) = **headlamp**

headline ['hedlaɪn] (N) (*in newspaper*) titular *m*, cabecera *f* • **the (news) ~s** (*TV, Rad*) el resumen de las noticias • **to hit** *or* **make the ~s** salir en primera plana
(VT) anunciar con titulares
(CPD) ▸ **headline news** noticia *f* de cabecera • **to be ~ news** ser noticia de cabecera • **to make ~ news** salir en primera plana ▸ **headline rate** • **the ~ rate of inflation** la tasa de inflación (*calculada con variables como el tipo de interés hipotecario*)

headline-grabbing ['hedlaɪn,græbɪŋ] (ADJ) que salta a los titulares

headliner ['hedlaɪnəʳ] (N) estrella *f*

headlock ['hedlɒk] (N) llave *f* de cabeza • **to get/have sb in a ~** hacer a algn una llave de cabeza

headlong ['hedlɒŋ] (ADJ) [*fall*] de cabeza • **he made a ~ dive for the ball** se lanzó en plancha a por la pelota • **the ~ rush to the beaches every summer** la salida precipitada hacia las playas todos los veranos
(ADV) 1 (*= head first*) [*person*] de cabeza • **the lorry ploughed ~ into a wall** el camión se estrelló de frente contra una pared
2 (*= swiftly*) precipitadamente • **I dashed ~ up the stairs** subí precipitadamente por las escaleras

headman ['hedmæn] (N) (PL: **headmen** ['hedmen]) cacique *m*; (*hum*) jefe *m*

headmaster ['hed'mɑːstəʳ] (N) director *m* (de colegio)

headmistress ['hed'mɪstrɪs] (N) directora *f* (de colegio)

head-on ['hed'ɒn] (ADJ) [*collision*] de frente, frontal • **a head-on confrontation** un enfrentamiento directo *or* frontal
(ADV) [*collide*] de frente, frontalmente; [*clash*] frontalmente; [*meet*] cara a cara • **the two cars collided head-on** los dos coches colisionaron de frente *or* frontalmente • **to tackle sth head-on** (*fig*) enfrentarse de lleno con algo

headphones ['hedfəʊnz] (NPL) auriculares *mpl*, audífono(s) *m(pl)*

headquarter ['hedkwɔːtəʳ] (VT) (*US*) • **the company is ~ed in Reno** la compañía tiene su sede en Reno

headquarters ['hed'kwɔːtəz] (NPL) (*Mil*) cuartel *msing* general; (*police etc*) jefatura *fsing* de policía; [*of party, organization*] sede *fsing*; (*Comm*) oficina *fsing* central, central *fsing*
(CPD) ▸ **headquarters staff** plantilla *fsing* de la oficina central

headrest ['hedrest] (N) (*Aut*) apoyacabezas *m inv*, reposacabezas *m inv*; (*on chair*) cabezal *m*

headroom ['hedrʊm] (N) espacio *m* para

estar (derecho) de pie; (*under bridge etc*) altura *f* libre • **"2m headroom"** "2m de altura libre"

headscarf ['hedskɑːf] (N) (PL: **headscarfs** *or* **headscarves** ['hedskɑːvz]) pañuelo *m*

headset ['hedset] (N) = **headphones**

headship ['hedʃɪp] (N) (*gen*) dirección *f*; [*of school*] puesto *m* de director(a)

head-shrinker* ['hedʃrɪŋkəʳ] (N) psiquíatra *mf*, psiquiatra *mf*

headsman† ['hedzmən] (N) (PL: **headsmen**) verdugo *m*

headsquare ['hedskwɛəʳ] (N) pañuelo *m* de cabeza

headstand ['hedstænd] (N) posición *f* de cabeza • **to do a ~** hacer el pino

headstone ['hedstəʊn] (N) (*on grave*) lápida *f* (mortuoria)

headstrong ['hedstrɒŋ] (ADJ) (= *stubborn*) testarudo; (= *determined*) [*action*] decidido

heads-up* ['hedzʌp] (N) (*esp US*) información *f* (anticipada), dato *m* • **to give sb a ~** avisar a algn de algo

head-to-head [ˌhedtə'hed] (N) mano a mano *m inv*
(ADJ) mano a mano (*inv*)
(ADV) mano a mano • **to go head to head with** enfrentarse mano a mano con

headwaters ['hedˌwɔːtəz] (NPL) cabecera *fsing* (*de un río*)

headway ['hedweɪ] (N) • **to make ~** (*Naut*) avanzar; (*fig*) hacer progresos • **we could make no ~ against the current** no lográbamos avanzar contra la corriente, la corriente nos impedía avanzar • **I didn't make much ~ with him** no conseguí hacer carrera con él

headwind ['hedwɪnd] (N) viento *m* contrario; (*Naut*) viento *m* de proa

headword ['hedwɜːd] (N) lema *m*, cabeza *f* de artículo

heady ['hedɪ] (ADJ) (COMPAR: **headier**, SUPERL: **headiest**) **1** (= *intoxicating*) [*wine*] que se sube a la cabeza, cabezón*; [*scent*] embriagador • **a ~ brew** (*fig*) una mezcla embriagadora
2 (= *exhilarating*) [*days, experience*] excitante, emocionante; [*atmosphere*] excitante, embriagador • **to feel ~** sentirse emocionado • **the ~ heights of sth** las vertiginosas alturas de algo

heal [hiːl] (VT) [+ *wound*] curar; [+ *person*] sanar, curar (**of** de); (*fig*) [+ *differences*] reconciliar • **he tried to ~ the rift with his father** intentó salvar el distanciamiento con su padre
(VI) (*also* **heal up**) cicatrizar

healer ['hiːləʳ] (N) curandero(a) *m/f*

healing ['hiːlɪŋ] (ADJ) curativo, sanativo
(N) curación *f*
(CPD) ▸ **healing powers** [*of herb, stone*] virtudes *fpl* curativas; [*of body*] poder *m* de recuperación; [*of healer*] poderes *mpl* de curación

health [helθ] (N) salud *f* • **to be in good/bad ~** estar bien/mal de salud • **he was granted early retirement on grounds of ill ~** le concedieron la jubilación anticipada por razones de salud • **good ~!** ¡(a tu) salud! • **to drink (to) sb's ~** beber a la salud de algn, brindar por algn • **Minister of Health** Ministro/a *m/f* de Sanidad • **Ministry of Health** Ministerio *m* de Sanidad • **Department of Health and Human Services** (*US*) Ministerio *m* de Sanidad y Seguridad Social
(CPD) ▸ **health and safety** seguridad *f* e higiene ▸ **health and safety regulations** normas *fpl* de seguridad e higiene ▸ **health authority** administración *f* sanitaria ▸ **health benefit** (*US*) subsidio *m* de enfermedad ▸ **health care** asistencia *f* sanitaria, atención *f* sanitaria ▸ **health care worker** empleado/a *m/f* de los servicios de asistencia sanitaria • **the code says that ~ care workers should promote breast-feeding** el código dice que el personal de los servicios de asistencia sanitaria debería promover la lactancia materna ▸ **health centre, health center** (*US*) centro *m* de salud, centro *m* médico ▸ **health check** (= *examination*) visita *f* médica; (*more thorough*) chequeo *m* ▸ **health club** gimnasio *m* ▸ **health drink** bebida *f* saludable ▸ **health education** educación *f* sanitaria ▸ **health farm** centro *m* de adelgazamiento ▸ **health food(s)** alimentos *mpl* dietéticos, alimentos *mpl* naturales ▸ **health food shop** tienda *f* de alimentos dietéticos, herbolario *m* ▸ **health hazard** peligro *m* para la salud, riesgo *m* para la salud • **it's a ~ hazard** presenta un peligro *or* un riesgo para la salud ▸ **health inspector** inspector(a) *m/f* de higiene ▸ **health insurance** seguro *m* de enfermedad, seguro *m* médico ▸ **health minister** ministro/a *m/f* de salud ▸ **health officer** funcionario/a *m/f* de salud ▸ **health problem** (*personal*) problema *m* de salud; (*public*) problema *m* sanitario ▸ **health resort** (= *spa*) balneario *m*; (*in mountains*) sanatorio *m* ▸ **health risk** riesgo *m* para la salud ▸ **health scare** alerta *f* sanitaria ▸ **Health Service** (*Brit*) Servicio *m* de Sanidad, Servicio *m* de Salud Pública; ▹ **national** ▸ **Health Service doctor** médico *m* de la Seguridad Social ▸ **health spa** balneario *m* ▸ **health visitor** auxiliar *mf* sanitario/a (*en asistencia domiciliaria*) ▸ **health warning** (*on cigarette packet*) etiqueta de advertencia sobre el tabaco; ▹ **professional**

health-conscious ['helθkɒnʃəs] (ADJ) preocupado por la salud • **we're all becoming increasingly health-conscious these days** últimamente nos estamos preocupando cada vez más por la salud

healthful ['helθfʊl], **health-giving** ['helθˌgɪvɪŋ] (ADJ) sano, saludable

healthily ['helθɪlɪ] (ADV) [*live, eat*] de forma sana, sanamente

healthiness ['helθɪnɪs] (N) (*lit, fig*) salud *f*

healthy ['helθɪ] (ADJ) (COMPAR: **healthier**, SUPERL: **healthiest**) **1** (= *normal*) [*person, plant, cell, mind*] sano; [*skin, hair*] sano, saludable; [*society*] que goza de buena salud • **to be ~** [*person*] tener buena salud, estar sano • **to look ~** tener un aspecto saludable • **to have a ~ appetite** tener buen apetito
2 (= *beneficial*) [*diet, lifestyle, air, place*] sano, saludable
3 (= *thriving*) [*economy, company*] próspero
4 (= *substantial*) [*profit*] pingüe; [*bank account*] sustancioso
5 (= *sensible*) [*attitude, scepticism*] razonable • **to have a ~ interest in sth** tener un sano interés en algo • **to have a ~ respect for sb/sth** tenerle un respeto sano a algn/algo

heap [hiːp] (N) **1** (= *pile*) montón *m*, pila *f* • **her clothes lay in a ~ on the floor** su ropa estaba amontonada en el suelo
2 (*fig**) montón* *m* • **a whole ~ of trouble** un montón de disgustos* • **a whole ~ of people** un montón de gente*, muchísima gente; ▸ **heaps**
3* (= *old car*) cacharro* *m*
(VT) (*also* **heap up**) [+ *stones etc*] amontonar, apilar; [+ *bricks, coal*] amontonar (**onto** sobre) • **to ~ sth together** juntar algo en un montón • **to ~ a plate with food** colmar un plato de comida • **to ~ favours/praise on sb** colmar a algn de favores/elogios • **~ed tablespoonful** (*Culin*) cucharada *f* colmada
▸ **heap up** (VT + ADV) [+ *stones etc*] amontonar, apilar; [+ *wealth*] acumular

heaps* [hiːps] (NPL) (= *lots*) • **~ of** montones de, un montón de • **you've had ~ of opportunities** has tenido montones *or* un montón de oportunidades • **~ of times** muchísimas veces • **we have ~ of time** tenemos tiempo de sobra
(ADV) muchísimo • **~ better** muchísimo mejor

hear [hɪəʳ] (PT, PP: **heard**) (VT) **1** (= *perceive*) [+ *voice, sound*] oír • **can you ~ me?** ¿me oyes? • **I can't ~ you** no te oigo • **I can't ~ a thing** no oigo nada • **I ~d someone come in** he oído entrar a alguien • **I ~d you talking to her** te oí hablar con ella • **I never ~d such rubbish!** ¡en mi vida he oído tantos disparates! • **did you ~ what he said?** ¿has oído lo que ha dicho? • **let's ~ it for ...** un aplauso para ... • **I could hardly make myself ~d** apenas pude lograr que se me oyera • **I have ~d it said that ...** • **I've ~d tell that ...** he oído decir que ... • **I can't ~ myself think** el ruido no me deja pensar *or* concentrarme; ▹ **pin**
2 (= *discover, be told*) oír • **have you ~d the news?** ¿has oído la noticia?, ¿te has enterado de la noticia? • **what's this I ~ about you getting married?** ¿qué es eso que he oído de que te vas a casar? • **from what I ~, she hasn't long to live** por lo que he oído parece que le queda poco tiempo de vida • **I waited to ~ the result** me quedé esperando para enterarme del resultado • **I ~ bad reports of him** no me hablan bien de él • **I'm glad to ~ it** me alegro • **I'm sorry to ~ it** lo siento • **where did you ~ that?** ¿quién te ha dicho eso? • **to ~ that ...** enterarse de que ... • **I ~d you're going away** me he enterado de que te vas • **I ~ you've been ill** me he enterado de que *or* he oído decir que has estado enfermo • **I haven't ~d yet whether I've passed** aún no sé si he aprobado • **have you ~d anything of** *or* **from him since he left?** ¿has sabido algo *or* has tenido noticias de él desde que se fue? • **the first I ~d of it was when ...** lo primero que supe al respecto fue cuando ... • **that's the first I've ~d of it** no tenía ni idea, es la primera noticia que tengo • **you haven't ~d the last of this!** ¡aquí no se acaba esto! • **have you ~d the one about ...?** ¿te sabes el de ...?
3 (= *listen to*) [+ *radio programme, story*] escuchar, oír; [+ *lecture*] escuchar • **to ~ him (talk) you'd think he was an expert** por la forma en que habla, cualquiera creería *or* diría que es un experto • **I've ~d it all before** ya conozco la historia • **Lord, ~ our prayers** Señor, escucha nuestras plegarias *or* súplicas • **to ~ sb speak** (*in public*) escuchar a algn • **he likes to ~ himself talk** le gusta escucharse a sí mismo
4 (*Jur*) [+ *case*] ver
5 (*Rel*) • **to ~ mass** oír misa
(VI) **1** (= *perceive*) oír • **I can't ~** no oigo • **if you don't get out I'll call the police, (do) you ~?** si no te vas llamaré a la policía, ¿me oyes? • **he doesn't** *or* **can't ~ very well** no oye muy bien
2 • **to ~ about sth/sb**: • **I ~d about it from Maria** me enteré por María, lo supe a través de María • **did you ~ about Liz?** ¿te enteraste de lo de Liz? • **I don't want to ~ about it** no quiero oír hablar del tema • **to ~ from sb** saber de algn, tener noticias de algn • **have you ~d from him lately?** ¿has sabido algo de él últimamente?, ¿has tenido noticias de él últimamente? • **I ~ from my daughter every week** tengo noticias de mi hija todas las semanas • **hoping to ~ from you** (*in letter*) esperando recibir noticias tuyas • **you will be ~ing from my solicitor** mi abogado se

h

pondrá en contacto con usted • **the police are anxious to ~ from anyone who may know her** la policía pide a todos los que la conozcan que se pongan en contacto con ellos • **what are you ~ing from people there?** ¿qué opina *or* dice allí la gente? • **to ~ of sth** (= *come across*) oír hablar de algo; (= *become aware of*) saber de algo • **many people haven't ~d of reflexology** muchas personas no han oído hablar de la reflexología • **I've never ~d of such a thing!** ¡en mi vida he oído cosa igual! • **I ~d of this school through Leslie** supe de esta escuela por *or* a través de Leslie • **I won't ~ of it!** (= *allow*) ¡ni hablar! • **I offered to pay but she wouldn't ~ of it** me ofrecí a pagar pero dijo que ni hablar • **I always wanted to be an actor but Dad wouldn't ~ of it** siempre quise ser actor pero papá no me dejó • **to ~ of sb** (= *come across*) oír hablar de algn; (= *have news of*) saber de algn, tener noticias de algn • **everyone has ~d of her** todo el mundo ha oído hablar de ella *or* sabe quién es • **he wasn't ~d of for a long time** no se supo nada de él *or* no se tuvieron noticias de él durante mucho tiempo • **he was never ~d of again** nunca se supo más de él

3 • **hear! hear!** (= *bravo*) ¡sí señor!, ¡eso, eso!

▸ **hear out** VT + ADV [+ *story*] escuchar • **she ~d out their ideas then gave her recommendation** escuchó sus ideas y luego les dio su recomendación • **to ~ sb out** dejar que algn termine de hablar • **let's ~ him out** vamos a dejarle que termine de hablar

heard [hɜ:d] PT, PP *of* **hear**

hearer ['hɪərəʳ] N oyente *mf*

hearing ['hɪərɪŋ] N **1** (= *sense of hearing*) oído *m* • **to have good/poor ~** oír bien/poco • **in my ~** estando yo delante, en mi presencia • **if you must talk about it, do it out of my ~** si tienes que hablar de ello, hazlo sin que yo esté *or* sin que yo me entere • **within/out of ~ (distance)** al alcance/fuera del alcance del oído

2 (= *chance to speak*) oportunidad *f* de hablar; (*Jur*) vista *f*, audiencia *f* • **he never got a fair ~** en ningún momento se le permitió explicar su punto de vista; (*Jur*) no tuvo un juicio justo • **to give sb a ~** dar a algn la oportunidad de hablar

CPD ▸ **hearing aid** audífono *m* ▸ **hearing dog** perro *m* guía (para sordos) ▸ **hearing loss** pérdida *f* auditiva • **noise reduces performance and can cause permanent ~ loss** el ruido reduce el rendimiento y puede causar pérdida auditiva permanente ▸ **hearing problem** problema *m* de oído • **he has ~ problems** tiene problemas de oído

hearing-assisted ['hɪərɪŋə'sɪstɪd] CPD ▸ **hearing-assisted telephone** (*US*) teléfono *m* con sonido aumentado

hearing-impaired ['hɪərɪŋɪm,pɛəd] ADJ con problemas de audición
NPL • **the hearing-impaired** las personas con problemas de audición

hearken†† ['hɑ:kən] VI • **to ~ to** escuchar

hearsay ['hɪəseɪ] N rumores *mpl* • **it's just ~** son rumores nada más • **by ~** de oídas
CPD ▸ **hearsay evidence** testimonio *m* de oídas

hearse [hɜ:s] N coche *m or* (*LAm*) carro *m* fúnebre

heart [hɑ:t] N **1** (= *organ, symbol of love*) corazón *m* • **she waited with beating ~** le palpitaba el corazón mientras esperaba, esperaba con el corazón palpitante • **to clasp sb to one's ~** abrazar a algn estrechamente • **to have a weak ~** padecer *or* sufrir del corazón

2 (= *seat of emotions*) corazón *m* • **with all one's ~** de todo corazón, con toda su alma • **at ~** en el fondo • **to have sb's interests at ~** tener presente el interés de algn • **this is an issue which is close to his ~** este es un asunto que le toca muy de cerca • **to one's ~'s content** a gusto • **this is an issue which is dear to his ~** este es un asunto que le toca muy de cerca • **his words came from the ~** sus palabras salieron del corazón • **it would have done your ~ good** te habría alegrado el corazón • **he knew in his ~ that it was a waste of time** él en el fondo sabía que era una pérdida de tiempo • **you will always have a place in my ~** siempre te llevaré dentro (de mi corazón)

• **IDIOMS**: • **he's a man after my own ~** es un hombre de los que me gustan • **from the bottom of one's ~** con toda sinceridad, de corazón • **to break sb's ~** (*in love*) partir el corazón a algn; (*by behaviour etc*) matar a algn a disgustos • **to break one's ~ over** partirse el corazón por • **to die of a broken ~** morir de pena • **to cut sb to the ~** herir a algn en lo vivo • **to give one's ~ to** enamorarse de • **he has a ~ of gold** tiene un corazón de oro • **have a ~!*** ¡ten un poco de compasión *or* corazón! • **to have no ~** no tener corazón *or* entrañas • **with a heavy ~** apesadumbrado, compungido • **with heavy ~s, we turned our steps homeward** apesadumbrados *or* compungidos, encaminamos nuestros pasos de regreso a casa • **his ~ was not in it** lo hacía sin ganas, no tenía fe en lo que estaba haciendo • **in his ~ of ~s** en lo más íntimo de su corazón • **to lose one's ~ to** enamorarse de • **to open one's ~ to sb** abrir el corazón a algn • **to cry one's ~ out** llorar a lágrima viva • **to sing one's ~ out** cantar a voz en grito • **his ~ is in the right place** tiene buen corazón • **to let one's ~ rule one's head** dejar que el corazón guíe a la cabeza • **to set one's ~ on sth**: • **I've set my ~ on that coat I saw yesterday** quiero a toda costa (comprarme) ese abrigo que vi ayer • **she's set her ~ on winning the championship** ha puesto todo su empeño en ganar el campeonato • **she is the ~ and soul of the organization** ella es el alma de la organización • **to throw o.s. into sth ~ and soul** entregarse en cuerpo y alma a algo, meterse de lleno en algo • **to take sth to ~** tomarse algo a pecho • **to wear one's ~ on one's sleeve** llevar el corazón en la mano • **to win sb's ~** enamorar a algn • **she won the ~s of the people** se ganó el corazón *or* el afecto de la gente; ▹ **eat out, sick**

3 (= *courage*) • **I did not have the ~** *or* **I could not find it in my ~ to tell her** no tuve valor para decírselo • **IDIOMS**: • **to be in good ~** [*person*] estar de buen ánimo • **to lose ~** descorazonarse • **to have one's ~ in one's mouth** tener el alma en un hilo, tener el corazón en un puño • **to put new ~ into sb** infundir nuevos bríos a algn • **my ~ sank** me descorazoné, se me cayó el alma a los pies • **to take ~** cobrar ánimos, animarse • **we may take ~ from the fact that ...** que nos aliente el hecho de que ...

4 (= *centre*) [*of lettuce, celery*] cogollo *m*; [*of place, earth etc*] corazón *m*, seno *m*, centro *m* • **in the ~ of the country** en pleno campo • **the ~ of the matter** lo esencial *or* el meollo *or* el quid del asunto • **in the ~ of winter** en pleno invierno • **in the ~ of the wood** en el centro del bosque

5 (= *memory*) • **to learn/know/recite sth by ~** aprender/saber/recitar algo de memoria

6 hearts (*Cards*) corazones *mpl*; (*in Spanish pack*) copas *fpl*

CPD ▸ **heart attack** (*Med*) ataque *m* al corazón, infarto *m* (de miocardio) ▸ **heart complaint** enfermedad *f* cardíaca ▸ **heart condition** condición *f* cardíaca ▸ **heart disease** enfermedad *f* cardíaca ▸ **heart failure** (= *attack*) fallo *m* del corazón, paro *m* cardíaco; (*chronic*) insuficiencia *f* cardíaca ▸ **heart monitor** monitor *m* cardíaco ▸ **heart murmur** soplo *m* en el corazón ▸ **heart operation** operación *f* cardíaca ▸ **heart rate** ritmo *m* del corazón ▸ **heart surgeon** cirujano/a *m/f* cardiólogo/a ▸ **heart surgery** cirugía *f* cardíaca ▸ **heart transplant** trasplante *m* del corazón ▸ **heart trouble** problemas *mpl* de corazón, afecciones *fpl* cardíacas • **to have ~ trouble** padecer *or* sufrir del corazón

heartache ['hɑ:teɪk] N pena *f*, dolor *m*

heartbeat ['hɑ:tbi:t] N (*gen*) latido *m* del corazón

heartbreak ['hɑ:tbreɪk] N congoja *f*, sufrimiento *m*

heartbreaker ['hɑ:t,breɪkəʳ] N rompecorazones *mf*

heartbreaking ['hɑ:t,breɪkɪŋ] ADJ desgarrador, que parte el corazón

heartbroken ['hɑ:t,brəʊkən] ADJ acongojado, desconsolado • **she was ~ about it** estaba desconsolada

heartburn ['hɑ:tbɜ:n] N (*Med*) acidez *f*, ardor *m*

-hearted ['hɑ:tɪd] ADJ (*ending in compounds*) • **hard-hearted** duro/a de corazón • **warm-hearted** cariñoso/a; ▹ **broken-hearted, open-hearted**

hearten ['hɑ:tn] VT animar, alentar

heartened ['hɑ:tnd] ADJ animado, alentado • **to be ~ that ...** sentirse animado *or* alentado por el hecho de que ... • **I feel ~ by her progress** me siento alentado por su progreso

heartening ['hɑ:tnɪŋ] ADJ alentador

heartfelt ['hɑ:tfelt] ADJ [*sympathy*] sentido; [*thanks, apology*] sincero • **my ~ apologies** mis sinceras disculpas

hearth [hɑ:θ] N (*also fig*) hogar *m*; (= *fireplace*) chimenea *f*
CPD ▸ **hearth rug** alfombrilla *f*, tapete *m*

heartily ['hɑ:tɪlɪ] ADV **1** (= *enthusiastically*) [*laugh*] a carcajadas, de buena gana; [*eat*] con ganas, con apetito; [*say*] efusivamente; [*thank, welcome*] cordialmente, calurosamente

2 (= *thoroughly*) [*recommend*] encarecidamente; [*agree*] completamente, totalmente • **to be ~ sick of sth** estar completamente *or* realmente harto de algo • **to be ~ glad** alegrarse sinceramente • **he ~ dislikes cabbage** detesta el repollo

heartiness ['hɑ:tɪnɪs] N entusiasmo *m* • **he spoke with a ~ he did not feel** habló con un entusiasmo que no sentía • **he shook my hand with exaggerated ~** me estrechó la mano con una efusividad exagerada

heartland ['hɑ:tlænd] N **1** (*Geog*) zona *f* central, zona *f* interior • **the ~ of Tibet** el corazón del Tibet

2 (*fig*) • **the conservative ~ in south-east England** el feudo conservador del sudeste de Inglaterra

heartless ['hɑ:tlɪs] ADJ despiadado, cruel

heartlessly ['hɑ:tlɪslɪ] ADV despiadadamente, cruelmente

heartlessness ['hɑ:tlɪsnɪs] N crueldad *f*, inhumanidad *f*

heart-lung machine [,hɑ:t'lʌŋməʃi:n] N máquina *f* de circulación extracorpórea

heartrending ['hɑ:t,rendɪŋ] ADJ desgarrador, que parte el corazón • **it was ~ to see them** se me partía el corazón de verlos

heart-searching ['hɑ:t,sɜ:tʃɪŋ] N examen *m* de conciencia

heart-shaped ['hɑːtʃeɪpt] (ADJ) en forma de corazón

heartsick ['hɑːtsɪk] (ADJ) (*liter*) • **to be ~** estar abatido

heartstrings ['hɑːtstrɪŋz] (NPL) • IDIOM: • **to pull at** *or* **touch sb's ~** tocar la fibra sensible de algn

heartthrob* ['hɑːtθrɒb] (N) • **he's the ~ of the teenagers** es el ídolo de las quinceañeras • **Newman was my mother's ~** mi madre idolatraba a Newman • **we met her latest ~** conocimos a su amiguito del momento

heart-to-heart ['hɑːttə'hɑːt] (ADJ) íntimo, franco • **to have a heart-to-heart talk with sb** tener una conversación íntima con algn
(N) conversación *f* íntima • **to have a heart-to-heart with sb** tener una conversación íntima con algn

heart-warming ['hɑːt,wɔːmɪŋ] (ADJ) (= *pleasing*) grato, reconfortante; (= *moving*) conmovedor, emocionante

hearty ['hɑːtɪ] (COMPAR: **heartier**, SUPERL: **heartiest**) (ADJ) **1** (= *enthusiastic and friendly*) [*voice, greeting, welcome, thanks*] cordial, caluroso; [*laugh*] efusivo, campechano; [*person*] campechano, sanote • **please accept my ~ congratulations** por favor, acepte mi más cordial felicitación *or* mis más sinceras felicitaciones
2 (= *hard*) [*slap, kick*] fuerte
3 (= *substantial*) [*meal*] copioso; [*appetite*] bueno; [*soup*] sustancioso • **the men ate a ~ breakfast** los hombres tomaron un copioso desayuno; ▹ **hale**
(N)* tipo *m* campechano*

heat [hiːt] (N) **1** (= *warmth*) calor *m*; (*also* **heating**) calefacción *f* • **in the ~ of the day** en las horas de más calor • **on** *or* **over a low ~** (*Culin*) a fuego lento
2 (*fig*) (= *excitement*) calor *m*; (= *vehemence*) vehemencia *f*; (= *pressure*) presión *f* • **in the ~ of the moment/battle** en el calor del momento/de la batalla • **he replied with some ~** contestó bastante indignado *or* con bastante acaloramiento • **when the ~ is on** cuando hay presión • **it'll take the ~ off us** esto nos dará un respiro • **to take the ~ out of a situation** reducir la tensión de una situación • IDIOMS: • **to turn on the ~** empezar a ejercer presión; (*Pol*) crear un ambiente de crisis • **the ~ is on** ha llegado la hora de la verdad • **we played well when the ~ was on** a la hora de la verdad supimos jugar bien
3 (*Sport*) prueba *f* (eliminatoria) • **dead ~** empate *m*
4 (*Zool*) [*of dogs, cats*] celo *m* • **to be in** *or* **on ~** (*Brit*) estar en celo
5 • **the ~** (*US‡*) (= *police*) la poli*, la pasma (*Sp‡*), la cana (*S. Cone‡*)
6 (*US*) (= *criticism*) • **he took a lot of ~ for that mistake** se llevó muchos palos por ese error
(VT) (= *warm*) calentar • **they ~ their house with coal** su casa tiene calefacción de carbón
(VI) calentarse
(CPD) ▸ **heat exhaustion** agotamiento *m* por el calor ▸ **heat haze** calina *f*, calima *f* ▸ **heat loss** pérdida *f* de calor ▸ **heat rash** sarpullido *m* ▸ **heat shield** escudo *m* contra el calor ▸ **heat source** fuente *f* de calor ▸ **heat treatment** tratamiento *m* de calor
▸ **heat up** (VI + ADV) (*lit*) calentarse; (*fig*) [*discussion, debate*] acalorarse
(VT + ADV) (*gen*) calentar; [+ *food*] calentar, recalentar

heated ['hiːtɪd] (ADJ) **1** (*lit*) [*swimming pool*] climatizado; [*rollers*] caliente
2 (*fig*) [*discussion*] acalorado • **to grow** *or* **become ~** [*discussion, debate*] acalorarse
(CPD) ▸ **heated (swimming) pool** piscina *f* climatizada ▸ **heated rear window** luneta *f* térmica

heatedly ['hiːtɪdlɪ] (ADV) [*argue, debate*] acaloradamente, con acaloramiento; [*reply, say*] con vehemencia • **"not me!" he replied ~** —¡yo no! —contestó indignado *or* con vehemencia

heater ['hiːtəʳ] (N) calentador *m*, estufa *f*

heath [hiːθ] (N) (*esp Brit*) (= *moor etc*) brezal *m*, páramo *m* (*esp LAm*); (*also* **heather**) brezo *m*

heathen ['hiːðən] (ADJ) (= *pagan*) pagano; (*fig*) (= *uncivilised*) bárbaro, salvaje
(N) (PL: **heathens** *or* **heathen**) pagano/a *m/f*; (*fig*) bárbaro/a *m/f*, salvaje *mf*

heathenish ['hiːðənɪʃ] (ADJ) pagano

heathenism ['hiːðənɪzəm] (N) paganismo *m*

heather ['heðəʳ] (N) (= *plant*) brezo *m*

Heath Robinson [hiːθ'rɒbɪnsən] (ADJ) [*device etc*] aparatoso

heating ['hiːtɪŋ] (N) calefacción *f* • **central ~** calefacción central
(CPD) ▸ **heating bill** factura *f* de la calefacción ▸ **heating engineer** técnico/a *m/f* en calefacciones ▸ **heating plant** instalación *m* de calefacción ▸ **heating power** poder *m* calorífico ▸ **heating system** sistema *m* de calefacción

heatproof ['hiːtpruːf], **heat-resistant** ['hiːtrɪ,zɪstənt] (ADJ) termorresistente, a prueba de calor; [*ovenware*] refractario

heat-seeking ['hiːt,siːkɪŋ] (ADJ) [*missile*] termodirigido

heat-sensitive ['hiːt'sensɪtɪv] (ADJ) sensible al calor

heatstroke ['hiːtstrəʊk] (N) (*Med*) insolación *f*

heatwave ['hiːtweɪv] (N) ola *f* de calor

heave [hiːv] (N) (= *lift*) gran esfuerzo *m* (para levantar *etc*); (= *pull*) tirón *m*, jalón *m* (*LAm*) (**on** de); (= *push*) empujón *m*; (= *throw*) echada *f*, tirada *f*; (= *movement*) [*of waves, sea*] sube y baja *m* • **with a ~ of his shoulders** con un fuerte movimiento de hombros
(VT) (= *pull*) tirar, jalar (*LAm*); (= *drag*) arrastrar; (= *carry*) llevar; (= *lift*) levantar (con dificultad); (= *push*) empujar; (= *throw*) lanzar, tirar • **they ~d the body off the cliff** lanzaron *or* tiraron el cuerpo por el acantilado • **he ~d himself to a sitting position** se incorporó con gran esfuerzo • **to ~ a sigh** dar *or* echar un suspiro, suspirar • **to ~ a sigh of relief** suspirar aliviado
(VI) **1** (= *rise and fall*) [*water etc*] subir y bajar; [*chest, bosom*] palpitar
2 (= *pull*) tirar, jalar (*LAm*) (**at, on** de)
3 (= *retch*) hacer arcadas • **her stomach was heaving** le daban arcadas, se le revolvía el estómago • **it makes me ~** me da asco
4 (*Naut*) (PT, PP: **hove**) (= *move*) virar; (= *pitch*) cabecear; (= *roll*) balancearse • **to ~ in(to) sight** aparecer
▸ **heave to** (VI + ADV) ponerse al pairo
▸ **heave up** (VT + ADV) [*vomit*] devolver, arrojar

heave-ho ['hiːv'həʊ] (EXCL) ¡ahora!; (*Naut*) ¡iza! • IDIOM: • **to give sb the heave-ho*** dar el pasaporte a algn*

heaven ['hevn] (N) **1** (*Rel*) (*gen*) cielo *m* • **to go to ~** ir al cielo • **(good) ~s!** ¡cielos! • **an injustice that cries out to ~** una injusticia que clama al cielo • **~ forbid!** ¡no lo quiera Dios! • **~ forbid that we end up in the same hotel!** ¡ojalá no *or* quiera Dios que no terminemos en el mismo hotel! • **~ help them if they do** que Dios les ayude si lo hacen • **~ knows why** Dios sabe por qué • **~ knows I tried** no será porque no lo intenté • **what in ~'s name does that mean?** ¿qué demonios significa eso? • **the ~s opened** se abrieron los cielos, las nubes descargaron con fuerza • **for ~'s sake!** ¡por Dios! • **thank ~!** ¡gracias a Dios!, ¡menos mal! • IDIOMS: • **to move ~ and earth to do sth** remover cielo y tierra *or* Roma con Santiago para hacer algo • **to stink to high ~** heder a perro muerto • **to be in seventh ~** estar en el séptimo cielo
2 (*fig*) paraíso *m* • **this place is just ~** este lugar es el paraíso • **the trip was ~** el viaje fue una maravilla • **isn't he ~?** ¡qué maravilla de hombre!

heavenly ['hevnlɪ] (ADJ) **1** (*Rel*) celestial • **Heavenly Father** Padre *m* celestial
2* (= *lovely*) divino
(CPD) ▸ **heavenly body** (*Astron*) cuerpo *m* celeste

heaven-sent ['hevn'sent] (ADJ) milagroso, (como) llovido del cielo

heavenward ['hevnwəd] (ADV) hacia el cielo

heavenwards ['hevnwədz] (ADV) (*esp Brit*) = **heavenward**

heavily ['hevɪlɪ] (ADV) **1** (= *very much*) [*rain, bleed, sweat*] mucho; [*drink, smoke*] mucho, en exceso; [*criticize*] duramente; [*depend, rely*] en gran medida; [*biased, laden*] muy • **the dangers of drinking or smoking ~** los peligros de beber o fumar mucho *or* en exceso • **she drinks ~/more ~ when she's depressed** bebe mucho/mucho más cuando está deprimida • **he spoke in ~ accented English** hablaba inglés con un acento muy fuerte • **he had to borrow ~** tuvo que pedir grandes cantidades de *or* mucho dinero prestado • **to be ~ in debt** tener muchísimas deudas, estar muy endeudado • **to be ~ defeated** (*in election, war*) sufrir una derrota aplastante • **the book draws ~ on Marxism** el libro se inspira en gran medida en las teorías marxistas • **he was fined ~ by the Football Association** la Asociación de Fútbol le puso una multa muy severa • **to be ~ influenced by sb/sth** estar muy influido por algn/algo • **he's ~ into jazz/football*** le ha dado fuerte por el jazz/el fútbol • **he's ~ into drugs*** está muy metido en las drogas • **he invested ~ in commodities** invirtió grandes cantidades de dinero *or* invirtió mucho en materias primas • **to be ~ involved in** *or* **with sth** estar muy metido en algo* • **to lose ~** (*gambling*) perder grandes cantidades de dinero, perder muchísimo dinero; (*in election, vote, match*) sufrir una derrota aplastante • **she was ~ made up** llevaba muchísimo maquillaje • **a ~ populated area** una zona densamente poblada • **she was ~ pregnant** le quedaba poco para dar a luz, se encontraba en avanzado estado de gestación (*frm*) • **~ scented** con un fuerte olor • **~ spiced** con muchas especias, muy condimentado • **each word was ~ underlined** cada palabra estaba subrayada con trazo grueso • **to be ~ weighted against sb/in sb's favour** desfavorecer/favorecer en gran medida a algn
2 (= *well, strongly*) [*armed*] fuertemente; [*guarded, fortified*] muy bien
3 (= *deeply*) [*sleep*] profundamente • **to breathe ~** (*from exertion*) resoplar, jadear • **he breathed ~ as he slept** respiraba muy fuerte mientras dormía • **his face was ~ lined** su cara estaba muy marcada de arrugas • **Bernard sighed ~** Bernard exhaló un profundo suspiro
4 (= *weightily*) [*tread*] con paso pesado; [*move, walk*] pesadamente; [*say*] con gran pesar • **he sat down ~ in his chair** se desplomó en la silla • **he fell ~ and twisted his arm** tuvo una

mala caída y se torció el brazo • **~ built** corpulento, fornido • **it weighs ~ on him** (*fig*) le pesa mucho

heaviness ['hevɪnɪs] N [*of object*] lo pesado, peso *m*; [*of subject matter*] lo denso • **always test the ~ of a load** comprueba siempre lo pesada que es una carga *or* el peso de una carga • **I felt a ~ in my legs** sentía pesadez en las piernas • **~ of heart** pesadumbre *f* (*liter*)

heavy ['hevɪ] ADJ (COMPAR: **heavier**, SUPERL: **heaviest**) **1** (= *weighty*) pesado • **you mustn't lift ~ weights** no debes levantar cargas pesadas • **to be ~** pesar mucho • **is it ~?** ¿pesa mucho? • **how ~ are you?** ¿cuánto pesas? • **he has his father's ~ build** tiene la misma corpulencia de su padre • **his eyes were ~ (with sleep)** los párpados le pesaban de sueño • **my arms felt so ~** me pesaban tanto los brazos • **the mayor's ~ mob*** los gorilas del alcalde • **the trees were ~ with fruit** los árboles estaban cargados de fruta
2 (= *considerable*) [*traffic*] denso; [*rain, shower*] fuerte; [*crop*] abundante; [*loss*] considerable, cuantioso; [*fine*] fuerte; [*defeat*] aplastante; [*irony, symbolism*] enorme; [*fighting, fire*] intenso • **there had been a ~ fall of snow** había caído una fuerte nevada • **the news came as a ~ blow** la noticia fue un duro golpe • **a ~ concentration of troops** una gran concentración de tropas • **~ demand has depleted supplies** una intensa *or* enorme demanda ha reducido las existencias • **to be a ~ drinker** beber mucho • **the school places ~ emphasis on languages** la escuela da mucha importancia a los idiomas • **to be ~ on sth: the car is ~ on petrol** el coche consume mucha gasolina • **you've been a bit ~ on the butter** se te ha ido un poco la mano con la mantequilla • **he is under ~ pressure to resign** le están presionando enormemente para que dimita • **the ~ scent of honeysuckle** el intenso *or* fuerte olor a madreselva • **to be a ~ smoker** fumar mucho; ▹ **casualty, price**
3 (= *thick, solid*) [*cloth, coat, line*] grueso; [*features*] tosco; [*meal, food*] fuerte, pesado; [*soil*] arcilloso; [*fog, mist*] espeso, denso • **the going was ~ because of the rain** el terreno estaba muy blando debido a la lluvia • **~ crude (oil)** crudo *m* denso *or* pesado
4 (= *oppressive, gloomy*) [*atmosphere*] cargado; [*sky*] encapotado; [*burden, responsibility*] pesado • **I found this talk of marriage a bit ~** esa conversación sobre el matrimonio me resultaba algo pesada • **with a ~ heart** apesadumbrado, acongojado • **the air was ~ with scent** el aire estaba cargado de perfume
5 (= *deep*) [*sigh, sleep, silence*] profundo • **~ breather** (*on telephone*) maníaco *m* telefónico • **~ breathing** (*from exertion*) jadeos *mpl*, resoplidos *mpl* • **his ~ breathing kept me awake** respiraba tan fuerte que no me dejaba dormir, sus jadeos no me dejaban dormir • **to be a ~ sleeper** tener el sueño profundo
6 (= *arduous*) [*task, work*] pesado; [*schedule*] apretado • **I've had a ~ day** he tenido un día muy liado *or* ajetreado; ▹ **weather**
7 (= *boring, laboured*) [*book, film, humour*] denso, pesado • **to be ~ going** [*book, film*] ser muy denso • **the conversation was ~ going** era difícil encontrar temas de conversación • **his new album/book is pretty ~ stuff** su nuevo álbum es bastante fuerte
8 (= *bad*) • **to have a ~ cold** estar muy resfriado *or* acatarrado • **he had had a ~ fall** había tenido una mala caída • **to get ~**: • **things got a bit ~** (= *nasty*) la cosa se puso fea
9 (= *rough*) [*sea*] grueso
N **1*** (= *thug*) matón* *m*, gorila* *m*
2* (= *eminent person*) peso *m* pesado
3* (= *newspaper*) periódico *m* serio
4 (*Scot*) (*beer*) cerveza *f* tostada
ADV • **time hung ~ (on our hands)** las horas/los días *etc* se nos hacían interminables • **the shadow of war hung ~ over the city** la sombra de la guerra pesaba sobre la ciudad • **his son's troubles weighed ~ on his mind** los problemas de su hijo le preocupaban mucho
CPD ▸ **heavy artillery** artillería *f* pesada ▸ **heavy cream** (*US*) nata *f* para montar (*Sp*), nata *f* enriquecida ▸ **heavy goods** artículos *mpl* pesados ▸ **heavy goods vehicle** vehículo *m* pesado ▸ **heavy guns** = **heavy artillery** ▸ **heavy industry** industria *f* pesada ▸ **heavy metal** (*Chem, Ind*) metal *m* pesado; (*Mus*) heavy *m* (metal) ▸ **heavy type** negrita *f* ▸ **heavy water** (*Phys*) agua *f* pesada

heavy-duty [ˌhevɪ'dju:tɪ] ADJ fuerte, resistente

heavy-handed [ˌhevɪ'hændɪd] ADJ
1 (= *clumsy, tactless*) torpe, patoso
2 (= *harsh*) severo

heavy-hearted [ˌhevɪ'hɑ:tɪd] ADJ apesadumbrado, acongojado

heavy-laden [ˌhevɪ'leɪdn] ADJ lastrado

heavy-set ['hevɪ'set] ADJ (*esp US*) corpulento, fornido

heavyweight ['hevɪweɪt] ADJ pesado, de mucho peso
N (*Boxing*) (*also fig*) peso *m* pesado

Hebe‡ ['hi:bɪ] N (*US*) (*pej*) judío/a *m/f*

he-bear ['hi:bɛəʳ] N oso *m* macho

Hebraic [hɪ'breɪɪk] ADJ hebraico

Hebraist ['hi:breɪɪst] N hebraísta *mf*

Hebrew ['hi:bru:] ADJ hebreo
N **1** (= *person*) hebreo/a *m/f*
2 (*Ling*) hebreo *m*

Hebrides ['hebrɪdi:z] NPL Hébridas *fpl*; ▹ **outer**

heck* [hek] EXCL ¡jo! (*Sp**), ¡la pucha! (*LAm**)
N • **a ~ of a lot** un montón* • **I'm in one ~ of a mess** estoy metido en un lío de narices* • **what the ~ is he doing?** ¿qué narices está haciendo?* • **what the ~ did he mean?** ¿qué narices quiso decir?* • **what the ~!** ¡qué narices!*

heckle ['hekl] VT interrumpir, molestar con preguntas
VI interrumpir, molestar con preguntas

heckler ['hekləʳ] N *persona que interrumpe or molesta a un orador*

heckling ['heklɪŋ] N interrupciones *fpl*, protestas *fpl*

hectare ['hektɑ:ʳ] N hectárea *f*

hectic ['hektɪk] ADJ (*fig*) agitado • **he has a ~ life** lleva una vida muy agitada • **the ~ pace of modern life** el ritmo agitado de la vida moderna • **we had three ~ days** tuvimos tres días llenos de frenética actividad • **things are pretty ~ here** vamos como locos • **the journey was pretty ~** el viaje era para volverse loco

hectogram ['hektəʊgræm] N hectogramo *m*

hectogramme ['hektəʊgræm] N = **hectogram**

hectolitre, hectoliter (*US*) ['hektəʊˌli:təʳ] N hectolitro *m*

Hector ['hektəʳ] N Héctor

hector ['hektəʳ] VT intimidar con bravatas
VI echar bravatas

hectoring ['hektərɪŋ] ADJ [*person*] lleno de bravatas; [*tone, remark*] amedrentador

he'd [hi:d] = **he had, he would**

hedge [hedʒ] N **1** (*Hort, Agr*) seto *m* (vivo)
2 (*fig*) protección *f*; (*Econ*) cobertura *f* • **as a ~ against inflation** como protección contra la inflación
VT **1** (*Agr*) cercar con un seto
2 (*fig*) • **to be ~d with** estar erizado de • **to ~ one's bets** hacer apuestas compensatorias
VI **1** (= *be evasive*) contestar con evasivas • **stop hedging!** ¡dilo sin sofismas!
2 (*Econ*) • **to ~ against inflation** cubrirse contra la inflación
CPD ▸ **hedge clippers** tijeras *fpl* de podar ▸ **hedge fund** fondo *m* especulativo ▸ **hedge fund manager** gerente *mf* de fondos especulativos ▸ **hedge sparrow** acentor *m* (común)

▸ **hedge about** VT + ADV • **to be ~d about with** estar erizado de

▸ **hedge around** VT + ADV = **hedge about**

▸ **hedge in** VT + ADV (*with hedge*) cercar con un seto

▸ **hedge off** VT + ADV separar con un seto

hedgehog ['hedʒhɒg] N erizo *m*

hedgehop ['hedʒhɒp] VI volar a ras de tierra

hedgerow ['hedʒrəʊ] N seto *m* vivo

hedging ['hedʒɪŋ] N **1** (*Bot*) seto *m* vivo
2 (*fig*) (= *evasions*) evasivas *fpl*
3 (*Econ*) cobertura *f*
CPD ▸ **hedging plant** planta *f* para seto vivo

hedonism ['hi:dənɪzəm] N hedonismo *m*

hedonist ['hi:dənɪst] N hedonista *mf*

hedonistic [ˌhi:də'nɪstɪk] ADJ hedonista

heebie-jeebies* [ˌhi:bɪ'dʒi:bɪz] NPL • **to have the heebie-jeebies** (= *shaking*) tener un tembleque*; (= *fright, nerves*) estar hecho un flan* • **it gives me the heebie-jeebies** (= *revulsion*) me da asco; (= *fright, apprehension*) me pone los pelos de punta*, me da escalofríos

heed [hi:d] N • **to pay (no) ~ to sb** (no) hacer caso a algn • **to take (no) ~ of sth** (no) tener en cuenta algo • **to take ~ to** (+ *infin*) poner atención en (+ *infin*) • **take ~!** ¡ten cuidado!
VT [+ *person*] hacer caso a; [+ *warning*] tomar en cuenta

heedful ['hi:dfʊl] ADJ • **to be ~ of sb's warning/advice** hacer caso al aviso/consejo de algn • **it is small wonder that sailors are ~ of hurricane warnings** no es de extrañar que los marineros hagan caso de las alertas de huracán • **~ of the crisis gripping the country ...** consciente de la crisis de la que era presa el país ...

heedless ['hi:dlɪs] ADJ (= *careless*) descuidado, despreocupado • **to be ~ of ...** no hacer caso a ...

heedlessly ['hi:dlɪslɪ] ADV sin hacer caso

heehaw ['hi:hɔ:] N rebuzno *m*
VI rebuznar

heel¹ [hi:l] N **1** (*Anat*) talón *m* • **to turn on one's ~** dar media vuelta • **to keep to ~** [+ *dog*] seguir de cerca al dueño • IDIOMS: • **to be at** *or* **on sb's ~s** pisar los talones a algn • **to bring sb to ~** sobreponerse a algn, meter a algn en cintura • **to cool one's ~s*** estar plantado *or* de plantón • **I decided to leave him to cool his ~s** decidí hacerle esperar un rato, decidí dejarlo plantado *or* de plantón un rato* • **to dig in one's ~s*** empecinarse • **to drag one's ~s** arrastrar los pies • **to follow hard on sb's ~s** seguir a algn muy de cerca • **to follow hard on the ~s of sth** venir a renglón seguido de algo • **to be hot on sb's ~s** pisar los talones a algn • **to kick one's ~s*** estar plantado *or* de plantón • **to show sb a clean pair of ~s** hacer tragar polvo a algn • **to take to one's ~s*** echar a correr, poner pies en polvorosa* • **to be under the ~ of** estar bajo los talones de

2 [*of sock*] talón *m*; [*of shoe*] tacón *m* • **IDIOM**: • **to be down at ~** ir desharrapado; ▸ **down-at-heel**
3†* (= *person*) sinvergüenza *mf*, canalla *mf*
(VT) **1** [+ *shoe*] poner tapas a; ▸ **well-heeled**
2 [+ *ball*] taconear, dar de tacón a
(VI) • **~!** ¡ven aquí!
(CPD) ▸ **heel bar** rápido *m*, tienda *f* de reparación de calzado en el acto
heel[2] [hi:l] (VI) (*also* **heel over**) (*Naut*) zozobrar, escorar
heft* [heft] (*US*) (N) peso *m*; (*fig*) influencia *f* • **the ~ of** la mayor parte de
(VT) **1** (= *lift*) levantar
2 (= *assess weight of*) sopesar
hefty ['heftɪ] (ADJ) (COMPAR: **heftier**, SUPERL: **heftiest**) **1** (= *large*) [*person*] corpulento, fornido; [*object*] enorme, imponente*; [*increase*] considerable; [*profit, payment*] cuantioso; [*price, salary, fees*] alto; [*bill, debt*] enorme; [*meal*] abundante; [*dose*] grande, mayúsculo* • **a ~ fine** una multa muy cuantiosa, una buena multa* • **a ~ book** un mamotreto*
2 (= *powerful*) [*kick, punch*] fuerte
3 (= *heavy*) pesado
hegemony [hɪ'gemənɪ] (N) hegemonía *f*
hegira [he'dʒaɪərə] (N) hégira *f*
he-goat ['hi:gəʊt] (N) macho *m* cabrío
heid* ['hi:d] (N) (*Scot*) = **head**
heifer ['hefəʳ] (N) novilla *f*, vaquilla *f*
heigh [heɪ] (EXCL) ¡oye!, ¡eh!
heigh-ho ['heɪ'həʊ] (EXCL) ¡ay!
height [haɪt] (N) **1** (= *measurement*) [*of object*] altura *f*; [*of person*] estatura *f* • **to be 20 metres in ~** medir *or* tener 20 metros de alto, tener una altura de 20 metros • **we are the same ~** tenemos la misma estatura, somos igual de altos • **he was of medium** *or* **average ~ and build** era de estatura y constitución media • **he drew himself up to his full ~** se irguió todo lo alto que era • **she's about my ~** tiene mi altura *or* es de mi estatura más o menos • **he sometimes found his ~ a disadvantage** su altura le resultaba a veces una desventaja
2 (= *altitude*) altura *f* • **~ above sea level** altura *f or* altitud *f* sobre el nivel del mar • **at a ~ of 2,000 m** a una altura *or* altitud de 2.000 m • **to gain/lose ~** ganar/perder altura • **hold your arms out at shoulder ~** levanta los brazos a la altura de los hombros
3 (= *high place*) cumbre *f* • **to be afraid of ~s** tener miedo a las alturas, tener vértigo • **the ~s** las alturas; ▸ **head**
4 (= *peak, zenith*) cumbre *f*, cima *f* • **at the ~ of her career** en la cumbre *or* la cima de su carrera • **at its ~, the movement had millions of supporters** en su punto más álgido, el movimiento tenía millones de seguidores • **at the ~ of the battle** en los momentos más críticos de la batalla • **the ~ of fashion** la última moda • **at the ~ of summer** en pleno verano • **the dollar has soared to new ~s** el dólar ha escalado a nuevas cotas; ▸ **dizzy**
5 (= *utmost degree*) colmo *m* • **it is the ~ of arrogance/stupidity** es el colmo de la arrogancia/la estupidez
heighten ['haɪtn] (VT) **1** (= *increase*) aumentar, acrecentar
2 (= *enhance*) realzar, hacer destacar
(VI) (*fig*) aumentarse
heinous ['heɪnəs] (ADJ) atroz, nefasto
heir [ɛəʳ] (N) heredero/a *m/f* • **~ apparent** heredero/a *m/f* forzoso/a • **~ at law** (*Jur*) heredero/a *m/f* forzoso/a • **~ to the throne** heredero/a *m/f* al trono • **to be ~ to** (*fig*) ser heredero/a a
heiress ['ɛəres] (N) (= *wealthy woman*) soltera *f* adinerada; (= *heir*) heredera *f*
heirloom ['ɛəlu:m] (N) reliquia *f* de familia
heist* [haɪst] (N) (= *hold-up*) atraco *m* a mano armada
(VT) robar a mano armada
held [held] (PT), (PP) *of* **hold**
Helen ['helɪn] (N) Elena, Helena
helical ['helɪkəl] (ADJ) helicoidal
helices ['helɪsi:z] (NPL) *of* **helix**
helicopter ['helɪkɒptəʳ] (N) helicóptero *m*
(VT) • **to ~ troops in** transportar tropas por helicóptero, helitransportar tropas
(CPD) ▸ **helicopter gunship** helicóptero *m* de combate ▸ **helicopter pad** = **helipad**
▸ **helicopter ride** paseo *m* en helicóptero
▸ **helicopter station** = **heliport**
heliograph ['hi:lɪəʊgrɑ:f] (N) heliógrafo *m*
heliostat ['hi:lɪəʊstæt] (N) heliostato *m*
heliotrope ['hi:lɪətrəʊp] (N) heliotropo *m*
helipad ['helɪpæd] (N) plataforma *f* de helicóptero, pista *f* de helicóptero
heliport ['helɪpɔ:t] (N) helipuerto *m*
helium ['hi:lɪəm] (N) helio *m*
(CPD) ▸ **helium balloon** globo *m* de helio
helix ['hi:lɪks] (N) (PL: **helixes** *or* **helices** ['helɪ,si:z]) hélice *f*
hell [hel] (N) **1** (= *underworld, fig*) infierno *m* • **life became ~** la vida se convirtió en un infierno • **IDIOMS**: • **to be ~ on earth** ser un infierno • **till ~ freezes over** hasta que las ranas críen pelo • **to give sb ~**: • **she gave me ~ when she found out** (= *scold*) me puso de vuelta y media cuando se enteró, me puso como un trapo cuando se enteró* • **my back's giving me ~** esta espalda me está haciendo la vida imposible • **to go through ~** pasar las de Caín • **I've been going through ~, wondering where you were** he estado preocupadísimo, preguntándome dónde estarías • **come ~ or high water** pase lo que pase • **I'm going to finish this come ~ or high water** voy a terminar esto aunque me cueste la vida *or* pase lo que pase • **he's determined to support them come ~ or high water** está decidido a apoyarlos contra viento y marea *or* pase lo que pase • **~ for leather** como un(os) endemoniado(s) • **he drove ~ for leather to the airport** condujo hasta el aeropuerto como un endemoniado • **all ~ broke loose** *or* **was let loose** se armó el gran follón *or* la grande • **to play (merry) ~ with sth*** hacer estragos en algo, trastornar algo • **to raise ~ (about sth)*** (= *protest*) armarla (por algo)*, liar un taco (por algo)* • **I'll see you/her** *etc* **in ~ first** antes prefiero morir • **he doesn't stand a snowball** *or* **snowflake in ~'s chance** (*Brit*) no tiene ni la menor posibilidad, lo tiene muy difícil *or* muy crudo* • **PROVERBS**: • **~ hath no fury like a woman scorned** no hay mayor peligro que el de una mujer despechada • **the road** *or* **path** *or* **way to ~ is paved with good intentions** el camino del infierno está lleno de buenas intenciones
2* (*as intensifier*) • **(as) ... as ~**: • **it was as hot as ~** hacía un calor infernal • **I'm mad as ~** estoy como una cabra* *or* una chota* • **I sure as ~ won't be going back there** pierde cuidado que no volveré a ese sitio • **they did it just for the ~ of it** lo hicieron por puro capricho *or* porque sí • **like ~**: • **"I'll go myself" — "like ~ you will!"** —iré yo mismo —¡ni lo sueñes! *or* ¡ni hablar! • **"I swam 100 lengths" — "like ~ you did"** —nadé cien largos —¡eso no te lo crees ni tú! • **to run like ~** correr como un demonio *or* un diablo • **it hurts like ~** duele una barbaridad • **a ~ of a**: • **there were a ~ of a lot of people there** había un montañazo de gente • **that's one ~ of a lot of money** eso sí que es un verdadero dineral • **a ~ of a noise** un ruido de todos los demonios, un ruido tremendo • **we had a ~ of a time** (= *good*) lo pasamos en grande *or* (*LAm*) regio; (= *bad*) lo pasamos fatal • **the ~**: • **to beat the ~ out of sb** dar una paliza de padre y muy señor mío a algn* • **to scare the ~ out of sb** darle un susto de muerte a algn • **to ~**: • **I hope to ~ you're right** Dios quiera que tengas razón • **I wish to ~ he'd go** ojalá se fuera de una vez por todas • **what the ~, I've got nothing to lose** ¡qué narices! *or* ¡qué más da! no tengo nada que perder • **what the ~ do you want?** ¿qué demonios *or* diablos quieres? • **who the ~ are you?** ¿quién demonios *or* diablos eres tú?
3‡ (*as interjection*) • **(oh) ~!** ¡caray!*, ¡mierda!‡ • **~'s bells!**† ¡válgame Dios!* • **get the ~ out of here!** ¡vete al diablo!‡ • **let's get the ~ out of here!** ¡larguémonos de aquí!* • **go to ~!** ¡vete al diablo!‡ • **~, no!** ¡ni lo sueñes!, ¡ni hablar! • **~'s teeth!**† ¡válgame Dios!* • **to ~ with it!** ¡a hacer puñetas!‡ • **to ~ with him!** ¡que se vaya a hacer puñetas!‡; ▸ **bloody**
(CPD) ▸ **hell's angel** ángel *m* del infierno
he'll [hi:l] = **he will, he shall**
hellacious* [he'leɪʃəs] (ADJ) (*US*) infernal
hellbent ['hel'bent] (ADJ) • **to be ~ on doing sth** *or* (*US*) **to do sth** estar totalmente resuelto a hacer algo
hellcat ['helkæt] (N) harpía *f*, bruja *f*
hellebore ['helɪbɔ:ʳ] (N) eléboro *m*
Hellene ['heli:n] (N) heleno/a *m/f*
Hellenic [he'li:nɪk] (ADJ) helénico
Hellespont ['helɪspɒnt] (N) Helesponto *m*
hellfire ['hel'faɪəʳ] (N) llamas *fpl* del infierno
hellhole ['helhəʊl] (N) infierno *m*
hellish* ['helɪʃ] (ADJ) infernal, de muerte
(ADV) muy, terriblemente
hellishly* ['helɪʃlɪ] (ADV) muy, terriblemente
hello [hʌ'ləʊ] (EXCL) **1** (= *greeting*) ¡hola!, ¿qué tal?, ¿qué hubo? (*Mex, Chile*)
2 (*Telec*) (= *answering*) ¡diga!, ¡hola!, ¡bueno! (*Mex*), ¡aló! (*S. Cone*); (= *calling*) ¡oiga!, ¡escuche!
3 (= *surprise*) ¡vaya!, ¡ándale! (*LAm*) • **~, what's all this!** ¡vaya *or* hombre!, ¿qué tenemos aquí?
4 (= *attention*) ¡oiga!, ¡escuche!
hell-raiser* ['helreɪzəʳ] (N) • **he has a reputation as a hell-raiser** tiene fama de montar siempre la bronca • **he is a real hell-raiser** siempre monta la bronca*, es un broncas*
helluva‡ ['heləvə] = **hell of a** ▸ **hell**
helm [helm] (N) (*Naut*) timón *m* • **to be at the ~** (*lit, fig*) estar al timón
helmet ['helmɪt] (N) (*gen*) casco *m*; (*Hist*) yelmo *m*
helmeted ['helmɪtɪd] (ADJ) con casco
helmsman ['helmzmən] (N) (PL: **helmsmen**) timonel *m*
helmswoman ['helmz,wʊmən] (N) (PL: **helmswomen**) timonel *f*
help [help] (N) **1** (= *assistance*) ayuda *f* • **thanks for your ~** gracias por ayudarme, gracias por tu ayuda • **the books were not much ~** los libros no me sirvieron de mucho • **to ask (sb) for ~** pedir ayuda (a algn) • **he is beyond ~** ya no se puede hacer nada por él • **to call for ~** (= *ask for help*) pedir ayuda *or* auxilio; (= *shout for help*) pedir ayuda *or* auxilio a gritos • **to come to sb's ~** acudir en ayuda *or* auxilio de algn • **financial ~** ayuda *f* económica • **to get ~**: • **he rushed off to get ~** salió corriendo en busca de ayuda • **you'll get no ~ from me** yo no te pienso ayudar • **to go to sb's ~** acudir en ayuda *or* auxilio de algn • **you've been a great ~ to me** me has ayudado muchísimo • **you're a great ~!** (*iro*) ¡valiente ayuda! • **medical ~** asistencia *f*

médica • **it's no ~ (to say that)** no sirve de nada (decir eso) • **there's no ~ for it but to ...** no hay más remedio que (+*subjun*) • **to be of ~ to sb** ayudar a algn • **can I be of ~?** ¿puedo ayudar? • **I was glad to be of ~** me alegré de poder ayudar • **you should seek professional ~** deberías consultar a un profesional, deberías pedir asesoramiento • **to shout for ~** pedir ayuda *or* auxilio a gritos • **I could use some ~** una ayudita no me vendría mal • **with the ~ of** con la ayuda de • **with his brother's ~** con la ayuda de su hermano • **with the ~ of a knife** con un cuchillo, ayudándose con un cuchillo
2 (= *helpers*) • **we're short of ~ in the shop** nos falta personal en la tienda • **she has no ~ in the house** no tiene a nadie que le ayude en la casa
3 (= *cleaner*) asistenta *f*; ▷ **home, mother**
(VT) **1** (= *aid, assist*) ayudar • **he got his brother to ~ him** consiguió que su hermano lo ayudara • **that won't ~ you** eso no te va a servir de nada, eso no te va a ayudar • **can I ~ you?** (*in shop*) ¿qué deseaba?, ¿en qué le puedo servir? • **to ~ (to) do sth** ayudar a hacer algo • **to ~ sb (to) do sth** ayudar a algn a hacer algo • **to ~ each other/one another** ayudarse el uno al otro • **to ~ sb across the road** ayudar a algn a cruzar la calle • **to ~ sb to their feet** ayudar a algn a levantarse • **to ~ sb on/off with his coat** ayudar a algn a ponerse/quitarse el abrigo • **I couldn't stand so he ~ed me up** no me podía poner de pie así que él me ayudó • **let me ~ you with that suitcase** deja que te ayude *or* que te eche una mano con esa maleta • IDIOM: • **so ~ me God** (*as part of oath*) y que Dios me ayude • **so ~ me, I'll kill him!*** ¡te lo juro que lo mato!*
2 (*at table*) • **to ~ sb to soup/vegetables** servir sopa/verdura a algn
3 (= *avoid*) evitar • **"why are you laughing?" — "I can't ~ it"** —¿por qué te ríes? —no lo puedo evitar • **I can't ~ it, I just don't like him** es superior a mí, me cae mal • **"it's rather late now" — "I can't ~ that, you should have come earlier"** —ahora es bastante tarde —no es mi culpa, tenías que haber llegado antes • **it can't be ~ed** no hay más remedio, ¿qué se le va a hacer? • **he won't if I can ~ it** si de mí depende, no lo hará • **can I ~ it if it rains?** ¿es mi culpa si llueve? • **don't spend more than you can ~** no gastes más de lo necesario • **you can't ~ feeling sorry for him** no puede uno (por) menos de sentir lástima por él
4 • **to ~ o.s. a** (= *assist o.s.*) ayudarse a sí mismo • **don't think about ~ing others, think about ~ing yourself** no pienses en ayudar a los demás, piensa en ayudarte a ti mismo • **you won't ~ yourself by keeping silent** no te vas a hacer ningún favor guardando el silencio • PROVERB: • **God ~s those who ~ themselves** a Dios rogando y con el mazo dando
b (= *serve o.s.*) servirse • **~ yourself!** ¡sírvete! • **she ~ed herself to vegetables** se sirvió verdura
c (= *take sth*) • **"can I borrow your pen?" — "~ yourself"** —¿me prestas el bolígrafo? —cógelo
d* (= *steal*) • **he's ~ed himself to my pencil** me ha mangado el lápiz*
e (= *prevent o.s.*) • **I screamed with pain, I couldn't ~ myself** grité del dolor, no lo pude evitar
(VI) ayudar • **I was only trying to ~** solo intentaba ayudar • **that doesn't ~ much** eso no sirve de mucho • **it ~s if you plan ahead** resulta más fácil si haces los planes por adelantado • **every little ~s** todo ayuda
(EXCL) • **~!** ¡socorro!, ¡auxilio!
(CPD) ▸ **help desk** servicio *m* de asistencia ▸ **help menu** (*Comput*) menú *m* de ayuda
▸ **help along** (VT + ADV) • **she has done much to ~ these negotiations along** ha contribuido considerablemente a que las negociaciones sigan adelante
▸ **help out** (VI + ADV) ayudar, echar una mano • **Dad ~ed out with £200** papá ayudó *or* echó una mano con 200 libras
(VT + ADV) • **to ~ sb out** ayudar a algn, echar una mano a algn • **his parents ~ him out financially** sus padres le ayudan *or* le echan una mano económicamente

helper [ˈhelpəʳ] (N) (*gen*) ayudante *mf*; (= *co-worker*) colaborador(a) *m/f*

helpful [ˈhelpfʊl] (ADJ) [*person*] atento, servicial; [*suggestion, book, explanation*] útil; [*advice, tip*] útil, práctico; [*medicine, treatment*] eficaz; [*attitude, remark*] positivo • **this cream is ~ in the treatment of allergies** esta pomada es eficaz para tratar alergias • **it would be ~ if you could come** sería de gran ayuda que vinieses • **you have been most ~** ha sido muy amable • **he was very ~ during my illness** me ayudó mucho durante mi enfermedad • **to be ~ to sb** ayudar a algn

helpfully [ˈhelpfəlɪ] (ADV) [*say, suggest, offer*] amablemente • **they had ~ sent us a map** amablemente, nos habían mandado un mapa • **"it might be here," she said ~** —puede que esté aquí —dijo para ayudar • **the chairs were not very ~ arranged** las sillas no estaban colocadas de una forma muy conveniente

helpfulness [ˈhelpfʊlnɪs] (N) (= *kindness*) amabilidad *f*; (= *usefulness*) utilidad *f*

helping [ˈhelpɪŋ] (ADJ) • **to give** *or* **lend sb a ~ hand** echarle una mano a algn
(N) porción *f*, ración *f* • **he came back for second ~s** vino a servirse más

helpless [ˈhelplɪs] (ADJ) **1** (= *powerless*) [*victim*] indefenso, inerme (*more frm*); [*feeling*] impotente; [*gesture*] de impotencia; (= *incapacitated*) incapacitado • **he is ~ without his crutches** sin las muletas no puede hacer nada • **we were ~ to prevent it** no pudimos hacer nada para impedirlo • **to feel ~** sentirse impotente • **she is a ~ invalid** está inválida y no puede valerse por sí misma • **to be ~ with laughter** estar muerto de (la) risa • **he lay ~ on the ground** yacía indefenso *or* inerme en el suelo
2 (= *vulnerable*) indefenso • **as ~ as a baby** tan indefenso como un bebé

helplessly [ˈhelplɪslɪ] (ADV) **1** (= *powerlessly*) [*watch, stand by*] sin poder hacer nada; [*struggle*] en vano; [*shrug*] en un gesto de impotencia • **"I can't," he said ~** —no puedo —dijo con una expresión de impotencia
2 (= *uncontrollably*) [*laugh, sob, sneeze*] sin poder contenerse

helplessness [ˈhelplɪsnɪs] (N) (= *powerlessness*) impotencia *f* • **he threw up his hands in a gesture of ~** alzó las manos en un gesto de impotencia • **the ~ of the situation made her ill with worry** era una situación de impotencia tal que enfermó de preocupación • **our ~ against enemy aircraft** nuestra indefensión ante los aviones enemigos

helpline [ˈhelplaɪn] (N) (*esp Brit*) línea *f* de socorro

helpmate [ˈhelpmeɪt] (N) (= *companion*) buen(a) compañero/a *m/f*; (= *spouse*) esposo/a *m/f*

Helsinki [ˈhelsɪŋkɪ] (N) Helsinki *m*

helter-skelter [ˈheltəˈskeltəʳ] (ADV) (= *in a rush*) atropelladamente; (= *in confusion*) a la desbandada
(N) **1** (*Brit*) (*at fair*) tobogán *m*
2 (= *rush*) desbandada *f* general

hem [hem] (N) dobladillo *m*, bastilla *f*
(VT) (*Sew*) hacer el dobladillo de, coser el dobladillo de
▸ **hem in** (VT + ADV) (*lit*) (= *surround*) cercar; (= *corner*) arrinconar • **our forces were hemmed in to both east and west** nuestras fuerzas estaban cercadas por el este y el oeste • **I feel hemmed in** me siento constreñido *or* limitado

he-man [ˈhiːmæn] (N) (PL: **he-men**) macho *m*

hematological [ˌhiːmətəˈlɒdʒɪkəl] (ADJ) (US) = **haematological**

hematologist [ˌhiːməˈtɒlədʒɪst] (N) (US) = **haematologist**

hematology [ˌhiːməˈtɒlədʒɪ] (N) (US) = **haematology**

hematoma [ˌhiːməˈtəʊmə] (N) (US) = **haematoma**

hemicycle [ˈhemɪsaɪkl] (N) hemiciclo *m*

hemiplegia [hemɪˈpliːdʒɪə] (N) hemiplejía *f*

hemiplegic [ˌhemɪˈpliːdʒɪk] (ADJ) hemipléjico
(N) hemipléjico/a *m/f*

hemisphere [ˈhemɪsfɪəʳ] (N) (*Geog*) hemisferio *m*

hemispheric [ˈhemɪsferɪk] (ADJ) hemisférico

hemistich [ˈhemɪstɪk] (N) hemistiquio *m*

hemline [ˈhemlaɪn] (N) (*Sew*) bajo *m* (del vestido)

hemlock [ˈhemlɒk] (N) (= *plant, poison*) cicuta *f*

hemo... *etc* [ˈhiːməʊ] (US) = **haemo...** *etc*

hemp [hemp] (N) **1** (= *plant, fibre*) cáñamo *m*
2 (= *drug*) hachís *m*

hemstitch [ˈhemstɪtʃ] (N) vainica *f*

hen [hen] (N) (= *fowl*) gallina *f*; (= *female bird*) hembra *f*
(ADJ) • **the hen bird** el pájaro hembra
(CPD) ▸ **hen coop** gallinero *m* ▸ **hen night** (*esp Brit**) (= *girls' night*) reunión *f* de mujeres; (*before marriage*) despedida *f* de soltera ▸ **hen party** = **hen night**

henbane [ˈhenbeɪn] (N) beleño *m*

hence [hens] (ADV) **1** (= *therefore*) por lo tanto, de ahí • **~ my letter** de allí que le escribiera • **~ the fact that ...** de ahí que ...
2 (*frm*) (*time*) • **five years ~** de aquí a cinco años
3† (*place*) de *or* desde aquí • **~!** (*poet*) ¡fuera de aquí!

henceforth [ˈhensˈfɔːθ] (ADV) (*frm*) (= *from now on*) de hoy en adelante, a partir de hoy; (= *from then on*) en lo sucesivo

henceforward [ˈhensˈfɔːwəd] (ADV) = **henceforth**

henceforwards [ˈhensˈfɔːwədz] (ADV) (*esp Brit*) = **henceforth**

henchman [ˈhentʃmən] (N) (PL: **henchmen**) (*esp Pol*) (= *follower*) secuaz *m*; (= *guard*) guardaespaldas *m inv*

hendecasyllabic [ˈhendekəsɪˈlæbɪk] (ADJ) endecasílabo

hendecasyllable [ˈhendekəˌsɪləbl] (N) endecasílabo *m*

henhouse [ˈhenhaʊs] (N) (PL: **henhouses** [ˈhenhaʊzɪz]) gallinero *m*

henna [ˈhenə] (N) alheña *f*

hennaed [ˈhenəd] (ADJ) [*hair*] alheñado

henpecked [ˈhenpekt] (ADJ) dominado por su mujer • **a ~ husband*** un marido dominado por su mujer, un calzonazos (*Sp*)

Henry [ˈhenrɪ] (N) Enrique

hepatitis [ˌhepəˈtaɪtɪs] (N) hepatitis *f*

hepatologist [ˌhepəˈtɒlədʒɪst] (N) hepatólogo/a *m/f*

hepatology [ˌhepəˈtɒlədʒɪ] (N) hepatología *f*

h

heptagon ['heptəgən] N heptágono *m*

heptagonal [hep'tægənəl] ADJ heptagonal

heptameter [hep'tæmɪtəʳ] N heptámetro *m*

heptathlon [hep'tæθlən] N heptatlón *m*

her [hɜːʳ] PRON **1** (= *direct object*) la • **I can see her** la veo • **look at her!** ¡mírala! • **I have never seen her** a ella no la he visto nunca
2 (= *indirect object*) le; (*combined with direct object pron*) se • **you must tell her the truth** tienes que decirle la verdad • **yes of course I gave her the book** sí, claro que le di el libro • **yes of course I gave them to her** sí, claro que se los di • **I gave the book to her not Peter** le di el libro a ella, no a Peter • **I'm speaking to her not you** le estoy hablando a ella, no a ti • **give it to her when you go to Liverpool** dáselo cuando vayas a Liverpool • **I gave it to her not Peter** se lo di a ella, no a Peter
3 (*after prep, in comparisons, with verb "to be"*) ella • **he thought of her** pensó en ella • **without her** sin ella • **I'm going with her** voy con ella • **she was carrying it on her** lo llevaba consigo • **if I were her** yo que ella • **younger than her** más joven *or* menor que ella • **it's her** es ella
POSS ADJ (*with singular noun*) su; (*with plural noun*) sus • **her book/table** su libro/mesa • **her friends** sus amigos

Heracles ['herəˌkliːz] N Heracles

Heraclitus [ˌherə'klaɪtəs] N Heráclito

herald ['herəld] N (= *messenger*) heraldo *m*; (*fig*) precursor(a) *m/f*
VT (*fig*) anunciar

heraldic [he'rældɪk] ADJ heráldico

heraldry ['herəldrɪ] N heráldica *f*

herb [hɜːb], (*US*) [ɜːb] N hierba *f*
CPD ▸ **herb garden** jardín *m* de hierbas finas ▸ **herb tea** infusión *f* de hierbas

herbaceous [hɜː'beɪʃəs] ADJ herbáceo
CPD ▸ **herbaceous border** (*Brit*) parterre *m* de plantas herbáceas

herbage ['hɜːbɪdʒ] N herbaje *m*, vegetación *f*

herbal ['hɜːbəl] ADJ de hierbas, herbario
CPD ▸ **herbal remedy** remedio *m* a base de hierbas ▸ **herbal tea** infusión *f* de hierbas

herbalism ['hɜːbəlɪzəm] N fitoterapia *f* (*uso de plantas medicinales*)

herbalist ['hɜːbəlɪst] N herbolario/a *m/f*

herbarium [hɜː'bɛərɪəm] N (PL: **herbariums** *or* **herbaria** [hɜː'bɛərɪə]) herbario *m*

herbert†* ['hɜːbət] N (*Brit*) tipo* *m*, tío* *m* • **some ~** ... algún tío ...*

herbicide ['hɜːbɪsaɪd] N herbicida *m*

herbivore ['hɜːbɪˌvɔːʳ] N herbívoro *m*

herbivorous [hɜː'bɪvərəs] ADJ herbívoro

herculean [ˌhɜːkju'liːən], **Herculean** ADJ hercúleo • **~ task** obra *f* de romanos

Hercules ['hɜːkjuliːz] N Hércules

herd [hɜːd] N [*of cattle*] rebaño *m*, manada *f*; [*of goats*] rebaño *m*; [*of elephants*] manada *f*; [*of pigs*] piara *f*; [*of people*] multitud *f*, tropel *m* • **the common ~** el vulgo, las masas
VT (= *drive, gather*) [+ *animals*] llevar en manada; [+ *people*] reunir
CPD ▸ **herd instinct** instinto *m* gregario
▸ **herd together** VI + ADV apiñarse, agruparse
VT + ADV agrupar, reunir

herd-book ['hɜːdbʊk] N libro *m* genealógico

herdsman ['hɜːdzmən] N (PL: **herdsmen**) [*of cattle*] vaquero *m*; [*of sheep*] pastor *m*

here [hɪəʳ] ADV **1** (= *in this place*) aquí • **I live ~** vivo aquí • **she's not ~ at the moment** no está (aquí) en este momento • **I'm not ~ to listen to your complaints** no estoy aquí para escuchar tus quejas • **~!** (*at roll call*) ¡presente! • **winter is ~** ha llegado el invierno, ya está aquí el invierno • **my friend ~ will do it** este amigo mío lo hará • **he's well known around ~** es muy conocido por aquí • **in ~, please** aquí (dentro), por favor; ▹ **same, today**
2 (= *to this place*) aquí, acá (*esp LAm*) • **come ~!** ¡ven aquí *or* (*esp LAm*) acá!; ▹ **look**
3 (*stating or offering sth*) • **~ are the books** aquí están los libros • **~ he comes** ya viene • **~'s what I think** esto es lo que pienso • **~ we are, I've found it** aquí está, lo encontré • **~ it is, under the cushion** aquí está, debajo del cojín • **did you want the corkscrew? ~ it is** ¿querías el sacacorchos? aquí lo tienes • **~ you are, you can have my seat** toma, puedes sentarte en mi sitio • **~ you are, I've fixed it** toma *or* aquí lo tienes, lo he arreglado
4 (= *at this time*) • **and ~ he laughed** y entonces se rió • **~ I should remind you that** ... ahora os debería recordar que ... • **it's my job that's at risk ~** lo que me estoy jugando es el trabajo • **what we're talking about ~ is** ... de lo que esto se trata es ...
5 (= *on this point*) en este punto • **I disagree with you ~** no estoy de acuerdo contigo en este punto
6 (*in phrases*) • **~ we go again!** ¡ya estamos otra vez! • **~ goes!** ¡ahí va! • **~ lies** ... aquí yacen los restos de ... • **whether or not he realized was neither ~ nor there** el que se hubiera dado cuenta o no no venía al caso • **the difference of £5 was neither ~ nor there** las 5 libras de diferencia no iban a ninguna parte • **~ and now** ahora mismo • **I must warn you ~ and now that** ... te tengo que advertir ahora mismo que ... • **I'm out of ~*** me largo* • **~ and there** • **I do a bit of teaching ~ and there** suelo dar alguna que otra clase • **he could only understand a word ~ and there** solo entendía palabras sueltas • **~, there and everywhere** en todas partes • **~'s to** ...: • **~'s to the happy couple!** ¡a la salud de los novios! • **~'s to your new job!** ¡por tu nuevo trabajo!
EXCL • **~, you try and open it!** ¡toma, intenta abrirlo tú! • **~, that's my dinner you're eating!** ¡oye tú, que esa es mi cena!
N • **the ~ and now** el presente

hereabouts ['hɪərəˌbaʊts] ADV por aquí (cerca)

hereafter [hɪər'ɑːftəʳ] ADV (*frm*) a continuación; (= *from now on*) de aquí en adelante, a partir de ahora
N • **the ~** el más allá

hereby ['hɪə'baɪ] ADV (*frm*) por este medio; (*in letter, document*) por la presente

hereditable [hɪ'redɪtəbəl] ADJ hereditario

hereditaments [ˌherɪ'dɪtəmənts] NPL herencia *f*, bienes *mpl* por heredar

hereditary [hɪ'redɪtərɪ] ADJ hereditario • **~ disease** enfermedad *f* hereditaria

heredity [hɪ'redɪtɪ] N herencia *f*

herein [ˌhɪər'ɪn] ADV (*frm*) (= *in this matter*) en esto; (= *in this writing*) en esta

hereinafter [ˌhɪərɪn'ɑːftəʳ] ADV (*Jur*) más adelante, más abajo, a continuación

hereof [ˌhɪər'ɒv] ADV (*frm*) de esto

heresiarch [he'riːzɪɑːk] N heresiarca *mf*

heresy ['herəsɪ] N herejía *f*

heretic ['herətɪk] N hereje *mf*

heretical [hɪ'retɪkəl] ADJ herético

hereto [ˌhɪə'tuː] ADV (*Jur*) a esto • **the parties ~** las partes abajofirmantes

heretofore [ˌhɪətʊ'fɔːʳ] ADV (*frm*) (= *up to specified point*) hasta aquí; (= *up to now*) hasta ahora, hasta este momento; (= *previously*) con anterioridad

hereunto [ˌhɪərʌn'tuː] ADV (*frm*) = **hereto**

hereupon ['hɪərə'pɒn] ADV (*frm*) en ese momento, en esto

herewith ['hɪə'wɪð] ADV (*frm*) (*Comm*) • **I enclose ~ a letter** le adjunto (con la presente) una carta

heritable ['herɪtəbl] ADJ [*objects, property*] heredable, hereditable; [*person*] que puede heredar

heritage ['herɪtɪdʒ] N herencia *f*; (*fig*) (*also* **national heritage**) patrimonio *m* (nacional)
CPD ▸ **heritage centre** (*Brit*) museo *m* (*local, de artesanía etc*) ▸ **heritage industry** • **the ~ industry** la industria del turismo cultural *or* patrimonial

hermaphrodite [hɜː'mæfrədaɪt] ADJ hermafrodita
N hermafrodita *mf*

hermetic [hɜː'metɪk] ADJ hermético

hermetically [hɜː'metɪkəlɪ] ADV herméticamente • **~ sealed** cerrado herméticamente

hermeticism [hɜː'metɪsɪzəm] N hermetismo *m*

hermit ['hɜːmɪt] N ermitaño/a *m/f*
CPD ▸ **hermit crab** ermitaño *m*

hermitage ['hɜːmɪtɪdʒ] N ermita *f*

hernia ['hɜːnɪə] N (PL: **hernias** *or* **herniae** ['hɜːnɪiː]) (*Med*) hernia *f*

hero ['hɪərəʊ] N (PL: **heroes**) héroe *m*; [*of film, book*] protagonista *mf*, personaje *m* principal
CPD ▸ **hero worship** adulación *f*

Herod ['herəd] N Herodes

heroic [hɪ'rəʊɪk] ADJ heroico • **he made a ~ effort to get up** hizo un heroico esfuerzo por levantarse • **a stadium of ~ proportions** un estadio de dimensiones colosales; ▹ **heroics**

heroically [hɪ'rəʊɪkəlɪ] ADV heroicamente

heroics [hɪ'rəʊɪks] NSING (*pej*) (= *deeds*) acciones *fpl* heroicas, actos *mpl* de heroicidad; (= '*behaviour*) comportamiento *m* atrevido; (= *language*) lenguaje *m* altisonante • **we don't want any ~** no queremos actos heroicos *or* ninguna heroicidad

heroin ['herəʊɪn] N heroína *f* (*droga*)
CPD ▸ **heroin addict** heroinómano/a *m/f* ▸ **heroin addiction** adicción *f* a la heroína, dependencia *f* de la heroína, heroinomanía *f* ▸ **heroin user** heroinómano/a *m/f*

heroine ['herəʊɪn] N heroína *f*; [*of film, book*] protagonista *f*, personaje *m* principal

heroism ['herəʊɪzəm] N heroísmo *m*

heron ['herən] N garza *f* real

herpes ['hɜːpiːz] N herpes *m*

herring ['herɪŋ] N (PL: **herrings** *or* **herring**) arenque *m* • **red ~** (*fig*) pista *f* falsa, despiste *m*
CPD ▸ **herring gull** gaviota *f* argéntea ▸ **the herring pond** (*hum*) el charco • IDIOM: • **to cross the ~ pond** cruzar el charco

herringbone ['herɪŋbəʊn] ADJ • **~ pattern** (*on material*) diseño *m* en espiga; (*of floor*) espinapez *m* • **~ stitch** punto *m* de escapulario

hers [hɜːz] POSS PRON (*referring to singular possession*) (el/la) suyo/a; (*referring to plural possession*) (los/las) suyos/as • **this car is ~** este coche es suyo *or* de ella • **is that car ~?** ¿es suyo *or* de ella ese coche? • **"whose is this?" — "it's ~"** —¿de quién es esto? —es de ella • **a friend of ~** un amigo suyo • **my car is much bigger than ~** mi coche es mucho más grande que el suyo *or* el de ella • **"is this her coat?" — "no, ~ is black"** —¿es este su abrigo? —no, el suyo *or* el de ella es negro • **"is this her scarf?" — "no, ~ is red"** —¿es esta su bufanda? —no la suya *or* la de ella es roja • **my parents and ~** mis padres y los

h

suyos *or* los de ella
herself [hɜːˈself] PRON **1** (*reflexive*) se • **she washed ~** se lavó
2 (*emphatic*) ella misma; (*after prep*) sí (misma) • **she did it ~** lo hizo ella misma • **she went ~** fue ella misma *or* en persona • **she talked mainly about ~** habló principalmente de sí misma • **she said to ~** dijo entre *or* para sí
3 (*phrases*) • **she came by ~** vino sola • **she did it by ~** lo hizo ella sola • **she's not ~** no se encuentra nada bien
Herts [hɑːts] N ABBR = **Hertfordshire**
hertz [hɜːts] N hercio *m*, hertzio *m*, hertz *m*
he's [hiːz] = **he is, he has**
hesitancy [ˈhezɪtənsɪ] N = **hesitation**
hesitant [ˈhezɪtənt] ADJ (*gen*) vacilante; [*character*] indeciso • **to be ~ about doing sth** no decidirse a hacer algo
hesitantly [ˈhezɪtəntlɪ] ADV indecisamente; [*speak, suggest*] con vacilación
hesitate [ˈhezɪteɪt] VI (*gen*) vacilar; (*in speech*) vacilar, titubear • **to ~ to do sth** dudar en hacer algo, vacilar en hacer algo • **I will not ~ to take unpopular decisions** no dudaré *or* vacilaré en tomar decisiones poco populares • **I ~ to call this art** no me atrevo a llamar arte a esto • **don't ~ to ask (me)** no vaciles en pedírmelo, no dejes de pedírmelo • **I ~ to condemn him outright** no me decido a condenarlo del todo • **to ~ before doing sth** dudar antes de hacer algo • **to ~ about** *or* **over doing sth** vacilar en hacer algo • **he ~s at nothing** no vacila ante nada
hesitation [ˌhezɪˈteɪʃən] N vacilación *f*, indecisión *f* • **I have no ~ in saying ...** no vacilo en decir ... • **without the slightest ~** sin vacilar siquiera, sin pensarlo dos veces
hessian [ˈhesɪən] (*esp Brit*) N arpillera *f*
ADJ de arpillera
het* [het] ADJ ▸ **het up**
hetero* [ˈhetərəʊ] ADJ, N = **heterosexual**
heterodox [ˈhetərədɒks] ADJ heterodoxo
heterodoxy [ˈhetərədɒksɪ] N heterodoxia *f*
heterogeneity [ˈhetərəʊdʒəˈniːətɪ] N heterogeneidad *f*
heterogeneous [ˈhetərəʊˈdʒiːnɪəs] ADJ heterogéneo
heterosexism [ˈhetərəʊˈseksɪzm] N *ideología que discrimina contra la homosexualidad*
heterosexual [ˈhetərəʊˈseksjʊəl] ADJ heterosexual
N heterosexual *mf*
heterosexuality [ˈhetərəʊˌseksjʊˈælɪtɪ] N heterosexualidad *f*
het up* [ˌhetˈʌp] ADJ • **to get ~** acalorarse, emocionarse (**about, over** por) • **don't get so ~!** ¡tranquilízate!, ¡no te sulfures!
heuristic [hjʊəˈrɪstɪk] ADJ heurístico • **~ search** investigación *f* heurística
HEW N ABBR (*US*) = **Department of Health, Education and Welfare**
hew [hjuː] (PT: **hewed**, PP: **hewed, hewn**) VT (= *cut*) cortar; [+ *trees*] talar; (= *shape, work*) labrar, tallar
▸ **hew down** VT + ADV talar
▸ **hew out** VT + ADV excavar • **a figure hewn out of the rock** una figura tallada en la roca • **to hew out a career** hacerse una carrera
hewn [hjuːn] PP *of* **hew**
hex[1]* [heks] (*US*) N **1** (= *spell*) maleficio *m*, mal *m* de ojo
2 (= *witch*) bruja *f*
VT embrujar
hex[2] [heks] ADJ (*Comput*) hexadecimal • **hex code** código *m* hexadecimal
hexadecimal [ˌheksəˈdesɪməl] ADJ hexadecimal • **~ notation** notación *f* hexadecimal

hexagon [ˈheksəgən] N hexágono *m*
hexagonal [hekˈsægənəl] ADJ hexagonal
hexagram [ˈheksəˌgræm] N hexagrama *m*
hexameter [hekˈsæmɪtə^{r}] N hexámetro *m*
hey [heɪ] EXCL ¡oye!, ¡oiga!
heyday [ˈheɪdeɪ] N auge *m* • **in the ~ of the theatre** cuando el teatro estaba en su apogeo • **in his ~** en sus buenos tiempos
Hezbollah [ˌhezbəˈlɑː] N Hezbolá *m*, Hizbulá *m*
HF N ABBR = **high frequency**
hg N ABBR (= **hectogram(s)**) hg
HGH N ABBR (= **human growth hormone**) HCH *f*
HGV N ABBR (= **heavy goods vehicle**) vehículo *m* pesado
HH ABBR **1** (= **His** *or* **Her Highness**) S.A.
2 (*Rel*) (= **His Holiness**) S.S.
HHS N ABBR (*US*) = **Health and Human Services**
HI ABBR (*US*) = **Hawaii**
hi [haɪ] EXCL ¡oye!; (*greeting*) ¡hola!, ¡qué hubo! (*Mex, Chile*)
hiatus [haɪˈeɪtəs] N (PL: **hiatuses** *or* **hiatus**) (*Gram*) hiato *m*; (*fig*) vacío *m*, interrupción *f*
hibernate [ˈhaɪbəneɪt] VI hibernar, invernar
hibernation [ˌhaɪbəˈneɪʃən] N hibernación *f*, invernación *f*
Hibernia [haɪˈbɜːnɪə] N Hibernia *f*
hibiscus [hɪˈbɪskəs] N (PL: **hibiscuses**) hibisco *m*
hic [hɪk] EXCL ¡hip!
hiccough, hiccup [ˈhɪkʌp] N **1** hipo *m* • **it gives me ~s** me da hipo, me hace hipar • **to have ~s** tener hipo
2 • **a slight ~ in the proceedings** (*fig*) una pequeña dificultad *or* interrupción en los actos
VT decir hipando • **"yes," he ~ed** —sí —dijo hipando
VI hipar
hick* [hɪk] (*US*) (*pej*) ADJ rústico, de aldea
N pueblerino/a *m/f*, paleto/a *m/f* (*Sp**)
CPD ▸ **hick town*** (*US*) ciudad *f* de provincias
hickey* [ˈhɪkɪ] N (*US*) (= *pimple*) grano *m*; (= *love-bite*) mordisco *m* amoroso, chupón* *m*
hickory [ˈhɪkərɪ] N nuez *f* dura, nogal *m* americano
hid [hɪd] PT *of* **hide**
hidden [ˈhɪdn] PP *of* **hide[1]**
ADJ escondido; (*fig*) [*meaning, truth*] oculto, secreto • **~ assets** activo *msing* oculto • **~ reserves** reservas *fpl* ocultas
CPD ▸ **hidden agenda** motivos *mpl* ocultos • **to have a ~ agenda** tener motivos ocultos • **he accused foreign nations of having a ~ agenda to harm his country's influence** acusó a las naciones extranjeras de tener motivos ocultos para minar la influencia de su país
hide[1] [haɪd] (PT: **hid**, PP: **hidden**) VT (*gen*) esconder (**from** de); [+ *grief*] ocultar, disimular • **to ~ sth from sb** esconder algo de algn • **to ~ one's face in one's hands** taparse la cara con las manos • **to ~ the truth** encubrir la verdad • **I have nothing to ~** no tengo nada que ocultar
VI esconderse, ocultarse (**from de**) • **he's hiding behind his illness** se ampara en su enfermedad • **he's hiding behind his boss** está buscando la protección de su jefe
▸ **hide away** VI + ADV esconderse
VT + ADV esconder, ocultar
▸ **hide out, hide up** VI + ADV esconderse
hide[2] [haɪd] N (= *skin*) piel *f*, pellejo *m*; (*tanned*) cuero *m* • IDIOMS: • **to save one's ~** salvar el pellejo • **I haven't seen ~ nor hair of him** no le he visto el pelo* • **to tan sb's ~** darle una paliza a algn
hide[3] [haɪd] N (*Hunting*) paranza *f*, trepa *f*; (*Orn*) observatorio *m*
hide-and-seek [ˈhaɪdənˈsiːk], **hide-and-go-seek** [ˌhaɪdəngəʊˈsiːk] (*US*) N escondite *m* • **to play hide-and-seek** jugar al escondite
hideaway [ˈhaɪdəweɪ] N escondite *m*, escondrijo *m*
hidebound [ˈhaɪdbaʊnd] ADJ rígido, aferrado a la tradición
hideous [ˈhɪdɪəs] ADJ (*gen*) espantoso, horroroso; (= *repugnant*) repugnante, asqueroso • **a ~ mistake** un error terrible
hideously [ˈhɪdɪəslɪ] ADV horriblemente • **~ ugly** feísimo
hideousness [ˈhɪdɪəsnəs] N • **the building's general ~** lo horroroso que es el edificio en general • **the ~ of her purple scar** la horrorosa cicatriz morada
hideout [ˈhaɪdaʊt] N guarida *f*, escondrijo *m*
hidey-hole* [ˈhaɪdɪhəʊl] N escondite *m*, escondrijo *m*
hiding[1] [ˈhaɪdɪŋ] N • **to be in ~** estar escondido • **to go into ~** esconderse; (*Pol*) pasar a la clandestinidad
CPD ▸ **hiding place** escondite *m*, escondrijo *m*
hiding[2] [ˈhaɪdɪŋ] N (= *beating*) paliza *f* • **to give sb a ~** dar una paliza a algn • IDIOM: • **to be on a ~ to nothing** llevar todas las de perder
hie†† [haɪ] VT apresurar • **to hie o.s. home** apresurarse a volver a casa
VI ir volando, correr
hierarchic [ˌhaɪəˈrɑːkɪk] ADJ = **hierarchical**
hierarchical [ˌhaɪəˈrɑːkɪkəl] ADJ jerárquico
hierarchically [ˌhaɪəˈrɑːkɪklɪ] ADV jerárquicamente
hierarchy [ˈhaɪərɑːkɪ] N jerarquía *f*
hieratic [haɪəˈrætɪk] ADJ (*frm*) hierático
hieroglyph [ˈhaɪərəglɪf] N jeroglífico *m*
hieroglyphic [ˌhaɪərəˈglɪfɪk] ADJ jeroglífico
N jeroglífico *m*; **hieroglyphics** jeroglíficos *mpl*; (*fig**) garabatos *mpl*
hifalutin'* [ˌhaɪfəˈluːtɪn] = **highfalutin(g)**
hi-fi [ˈhaɪfaɪ] ABBR *of* **high fidelity**
N estéreo *m*
ADJ de alta fidelidad • **hi-fi equipment** equipo *m* de alta fidelidad • **hi-fi system** sistema *m* de alta fidelidad
higgledy-piggledy* [ˈhɪgldɪˈpɪgldɪ] ADV [*be*] en desorden; [*do*] de cualquier modo, a la buena de Dios
ADJ revuelto, desordenado
high [haɪ] ADJ (COMPAR: **higher**, SUPERL: **highest**) **1** (= *tall, elevated*) [*building, mountain*] alto; [*plateau*] elevado; [*altitude*] grande • **a building 60 metres ~** un edificio de 60 metros de alto *or* de altura • **it's 20 metres ~** tiene 20 metros de alto *or* de altura • **at ~ altitudes** a grandes altitudes • **the ceilings are very ~** los techos son muy altos • **~ cheekbones** pómulos *mpl* salientes • **he has a ~ forehead** tiene la frente muy ancha • **how ~ is Ben Nevis/that tree?** ¿qué altura tiene el Ben Nevis/ese árbol? • **economic reform is ~ on the agenda** la reforma económica figura entre los asuntos más importantes a tratar • **the river is ~** el río está crecido • **I've known her since she was so ~*** la conozco desde que era así (de pequeña) • **the sun was ~ in the sky** el sol daba de pleno • IDIOMS: • **~ and dry** [*boat*] varado • **the boats lay at the river's edge, ~ and dry** los botes estaban en la orilla del río, varados • **to leave sb ~ and dry** (= *in a difficult situation*) dejar a algn en la estacada
2 (= *considerable, great*) [*level, risk, rent, salary,*

principles] alto; [*price, tax, number*] alto, elevado; [*speed*] alto, gran; [*quality*] alto, bueno; [*colour*] subido; [*complexion*] (*characteristically*) rojizo; (*temporarily*) enrojecido; [*wind*] fuerte • **they offered me a ~er salary** me ofrecieron un sueldo más alto • **temperatures were in the ~ 80s** las temperaturas alcanzaron los ochenta y muchos, las temperaturas rondaron los 90 grados • **interest rates are ~** los intereses están muy altos • **we offer education of the ~est quality** ofrecemos una educación de la más alta *or* de la mejor calidad • **to have ~ blood pressure** tener la tensión alta, ser hipertenso • **his team was of the ~est calibre** su equipo era del más alto nivel • **to have ~ hopes of sth**: • **I had ~ hopes of being elected** tenía muchas esperanzas de que me eligieran • **parsley is ~ in calcium** el perejil es rico en calcio • **to have a ~ opinion of sb** (= *think highly of*) tener muy buena opinión *or* concepto de algn; (= *be fond of*) tener a algn en alta estima • **to pay a ~ price for sth** (*lit*) pagar mucho dinero por algo; (*fig*) pagar algo muy caro • **to have a ~ temperature** tener mucha fiebre, tener una fiebre muy alta • IDIOMS: • **to have a ~ old time*** pasarlo en grande* • **it's ~ time ...***: • **it's ~ time you were in bed*** ya deberías estar acostado desde hace un buen rato • **it's ~ time we were on our way*** ya deberíamos haber salido hace rato; ▷ **gear, priority, profile, spirit, stake, high**

3 (= *important, superior*) [*rank, position, office*] alto • **~ and mighty**: • **she's too ~ and mighty** es demasiado engreída • **you needn't act so ~ and mighty with me** no tienes por qué ponerte tan engreído conmigo • **she moves in the circles of the ~ and mighty** se mueve en círculos de los poderosos, se mueve en círculos de gente de mucho fuste (*pej*) • **~ official** alto funcionario/a *m/f* • IDIOMS: • **to get (up) on one's ~ horse** subirse a la parra • **there's no need to get (up) on your ~ horse!** ¡no hace falta que te subas a la parra! • **to come down off** *or* **get off one's ~ horse** bajar los humos • **in ~ places**: • **to have friends in ~ places** tener amigos importantes *or* con influencias • **people in ~ places** gente influyente *or* importante

4 (= *high-pitched*) [*sound, note*] alto; [*voice*] agudo • **he played another ~er note** tocó otra nota más alta • **she can still hit those ~ notes** todavía llega bien a los agudos • **in a ~ voice** con voz aguda • IDIOM: • **on a ~ note**: • **he ended his career on a ~ note** terminó su carrera con un gran éxito

5* (= *intoxicated*) • **to be ~ (on)** [+ *drink, drugs*] estar colocado (de)* • **to get ~ (on)** [+ *drink, drugs*] colocarse (de)* • **she was ~ on her latest success** estaba encantada *or* entusiasmada con su último éxito • IDIOM: • **to be (as) ~ as a kite** (*on drugs, drink*) estar totalmente colocado*; (= *confident*) estar que no se cabe en sí

6 (*Culin*) (= *mature*) [*game, cheese*] que huele fuerte; (= *rotten*) [*meat*] pasado

(ADV) (COMPAR: **higher**, SUPERL: **highest**) **1** (*in height*) [*fly, rise*] a gran altura • **it rose ~ in the air** se elevó a gran altura • **it sailed ~ over the house** volaba a gran altura por encima de la casa • **~ above**: • **an eagle circled ~ above** un águila circulaba en las alturas • **the town is perched ~ above the river** el pueblo está en un alto, sobre el río • **~ above my head** muy por encima de mi cabeza • **to run ~** [*sea*] estar embravecido; [*river*] estar crecido • **feelings were running ~** los ánimos estaban exaltados • **~ up**: • **his farm was ~ up in the mountains** su granja estaba en lo alto de las montañas • **we saw three birds circling very ~ up** vimos tres pájaros circulando en las alturas • **she had put it too ~ up for me to reach** lo había puesto demasiado alto y no llegaba • **his cousin is someone ~ up in the navy** su primo tiene un cargo importante en la marina • IDIOMS: • **to hold one's head (up) ~** mantener la cabeza bien alta • **to live ~ on the hog** (*US**) vivir como un rajá • **to hunt** *or* **search ~ and low (for sth/sb)** remover el cielo y la tierra (en busca de algo/algn); ▷ **aim, fly, head, stand**

2 (*in degree, number, strength*) • **the bidding went as ~ as £500** las ofertas llegaron hasta 500 libras

(N) **1** • **on ~** (= *in heaven*) en el cielo, en las alturas • **there's been a new directive from on ~** (*fig*) ha habido una nueva directriz de arriba

2 (= *peak*) • **sales have reached an all-time ~** las ventas han alcanzado cifras récord • IDIOM: • **to be on a ~*** estar a las mil maravillas

3 (*Econ*) máximo *m* • **the Dow Jones index reached a ~ of 2503** el índice de Dow Jones alcanzó un máximo de 2.503

4 (*Met*) zona *f* de altas presiones; (*esp US*) temperatura *f* máxima

5 (*US*) (*Aut*) (= *top gear*) directa *f* • **to be in ~** ir en directa

(CPD) ▸ **high altar** altar *m* mayor ▸ **high beam** (*US*) (*Aut*) • **he had his lights on ~ beam** llevaba las luces largas *or* de cruce ▸ **high camp** (*Theat*) amaneramiento *m* ▸ **high chair** silla *f* alta (para niño), trona *f* (*Sp*) ▸ **High Church** *sector de la Iglesia Anglicana muy cercano a la liturgia y ritos católicos* ▸ **high comedy** (*Theat*) comedia *f* de costumbres • **it was ~ comedy** (*fig*) era de lo más cómico ▸ **high command** (*Mil*) alto mando *m* ▸ **high commission** (= *international body*) alto comisionado *m*; (= *embassy*) embajada *f* (*que representa a uno de los países de la Commonwealth en otro*) ▸ **high commissioner** [*of international body*] alto comisario/a *m/f*; (= *ambassador*) embajador(a) *m/f* (*de un país de la Commonwealth en otro*) ▸ **High Court** (*Jur*) Tribunal *m* Supremo • **a ~ court judge** un juez del Tribunal Supremo ▸ **high definition** alta definición *f*; ▷ **high-definition** ▸ **high dependency unit** (*Med*) unidad *f* de alta dependencia ▸ **high diving** saltos *mpl* de trampolín de gran altura ▸ **high explosive** explosivo *m* de gran potencia; ▷ **high-explosive** ▸ **high fashion** alta costura *f* ▸ **high fidelity** alta fidelidad *f*; ▷ **high-fidelity** ▸ **high finance** altas finanzas *fpl* ▸ **high five, high-five** choque *m* de cinco • **to give sb a ~ five** chocar los cinco con algn ▸ **high flier** • **he's a ~ flier** es ambicioso, tiene talento y promete ▸ **High German** alto alemán *m* ▸ **high ground** (*fig*) • **they believe they have** *or* **occupy the moral ~ ground in this conflict** creen que tienen moralmente la razón de su parte en este conflicto ▸ **high hat** sombrero *m* de copa, cilindro* *m*; ▷ **high-hat** ▸ **high heels** (= *heels*) tacones *mpl* altos; (= *shoes*) zapatos *mpl* de tacón ▸ **high jinks**†* jolgorio *msing*, jarana *f* • **there were ~ jinks last night** hubo jolgorio *or* jarana anoche • **to get up to ~ jinks** meterse en jarana ▸ **high jump** (*Sport*) salto *m* de altura • IDIOMS: • **he's for the ~ jump** (*Brit**) (= *he'll be in trouble*) se la va a cargar, le va a caer una buena; (= *he'll be sacked*) le van a largar ▸ **high jumper** (*Sport*) saltador(a) *m/f* de altura ▸ **the high life** (*gen*) la buena vida; (*in high society*) la vida de la buena sociedad ▸ **high living** la buena vida ▸ **High Mass** misa *f* mayor ▸ **high noon** (= *midday*) mediodía *m*; (*fig*) (= *peak*) apogeo *m*; (= *critical point*) momento *m* crucial ▸ **high point** [*of show, evening*] punto *m* culminante, clímax *m inv*; [*of visit, holiday*] lo más destacado; [*of career*] punto *m* culminante, cenit *m* ▸ **high priest** sumo sacerdote *m* ▸ **high priestess** suma sacerdotisa *f* ▸ **high relief** alto relieve *m* • **to throw** *or* **bring sth into ~ relief** (*fig*) poner algo de relieve ▸ **high road** (*esp Brit*) carretera *f* • **the ~ road to success/disaster** el camino directo al éxito/desastre ▸ **high roller** (*US*) (*gen*) derrochón/ona *m/f*; (*gambling*) jugador(a) *m/f* empedernido* ▸ **high school** (*US, Brit*) instituto *m* de enseñanza secundaria, ≈ liceo *m* (*LAm*) • **junior ~ (school)** (*US*) *instituto donde se imparten los dos primeros años de bachillerato* ▸ **high school diploma** (*US*) ≈ bachillerato *m* ▸ **high school graduate** (*US*) ≈ bachiller *mf* ▸ **the high seas** alta mar *fsing* • **on the ~ seas** en alta mar ▸ **high season** temporada *f* alta • **~ season prices/rates** precios *mpl*/tarifas *fpl* de temporada alta ▸ **high sign** seña *f* (*acordada*) • **to give sb a ~ sign** hacer la seña a algn ▸ **high society** la alta sociedad ▸ **high spot** [*of show, evening*] punto *m* culminante, clímax *m inv*; [*of visit, holiday*] lo más destacado; [*of career*] punto *m* culminante, cenit *m* ▸ **high stakes** • **to play for ~ stakes** apostar fuerte, tener mucho en juego ▸ **high street** calle *f* mayor, calle *f* principal • **~ street banks** bancos *mpl* principales • **~ street shops** tiendas *fpl* de la calle principal ▸ **high summer** pleno verano *m*, pleno estío *m* ▸ **high table** (*gen*) mesa *f* principal, mesa *f* presidencial; (*Univ, Scol*) mesa *f* de los profesores ▸ **high tea** (*Brit*) merienda-cena *f* (*que se toma acompañada de té*) ▸ **high technology** alta tecnología *f* ▸ **high tide** pleamar *f*, marea *f* alta • **at ~ tide** en la pleamar, en marea alta ▸ **high treason** alta traición *f* ▸ **high water** pleamar *f*, marea *f* alta; ▷ **high-water mark** ▸ **high wire** cuerda *f* floja ▸ **high wire act** número *m* en la cuerda floja, número *m* de funambulismo

HIGH SCHOOL

En Estados Unidos las **high schools** son los institutos donde los adolescentes de 15 a 18 años realizan la educación secundaria, que dura tres o cuatro cursos **(grades)**, desde el noveno hasta el duodécimo año de la enseñanza; al final del último curso se realiza un libro conmemorativo con fotos de los alumnos y profesores de ese año (el **Yearbook**) y los alumnos reciben el diploma de **high school** en una ceremonia formal de graduación. Estos centros suelen ser un tema frecuente en las películas y programas de televisión estadounidenses en los que se resalta mucho el aspecto deportivo - sobre todo el fútbol americano y el baloncesto - además de algunos acontecimientos sociales como el baile de fin de curso, conocido como **Senior Prom**.

▷ **PROM, YEARBOOK**

highball ['haɪbɔːl] (N) (*US*) (= *drink*) jaibol *m*, whisky soda *m*

highboard ['haɪbɔːd] (N) (*for diving*) trampolín *m*

highborn ['haɪbɔːn] (ADJ) linajudo, de ilustre cuna

highboy ['haɪbɔɪ] (N) (*US*) cómoda *f* alta

highbrow ['haɪbraʊ] (N) intelectual *mf*, persona *f* culta; (*pej*) intelectualoide *mf* (ADJ) [*book, play, film*] para intelectuales

high-calibre, high-caliber (*US*) [ˌhaɪ'kælɪbəʳ] (ADJ) **1** [*person, staff*] de alto nivel

2 [*weapon, rifle*] de gran calibre
high-class [ˌhaɪˈklɑːs] ADJ (= *of good quality*) de (alta) categoría
high-definition [ˌhaɪdefɪˈnɪʃən] ADJ [*television, video*] de alta definición; ▹ **high**
high-density [ˌhaɪˈdensɪtɪ] ADJ • **high-density housing** alta densidad *f* de inquilinos
CPD ▸ **high-density disk** (*Comput*) disco *m* de alta densidad
high-end [ˈhaɪˌend] ADJ [*product*] de gama alta, de nivel superior
high-energy [ˌhaɪˈenədʒɪ] ADJ • **high-energy particle** partícula *f* de alta energía • **high-energy physics** física *f* de altas energías
higher [ˈhaɪəʳ] ADJ (*compar of* **high**) más alto; [*form of life, court*] superior; [*price*] más elevado; [*number, speed*] mayor • **any number ~ than six** cualquier número superior a *or* mayor de seis • **~ interest rates are a possibility** existe la posibilidad de una subida de los tipos de interés • **~ rate tax** impuesto *m* en la banda superior
ADV (*compar of* **high**) **1** (*lit*) más alto • **I can jump ~ than you** puedo saltar más alto que tú • **to fly ~ than the clouds** volar encima de las nubes • **to fly ~ still** volar a mayor altura todavía • **~ and ~** más y más (alto) • **the balloon climbed ~ and ~** el globo se elevaba más y más (alto) • **try hanging the picture a bit ~ up** prueba a poner el cuadro un poquito más alto *or* más arriba • **~ up the hill** más arriba en la colina
2 (*fig*) • **the dollar closed ~ today** la cotización del dólar ha cerrado más alta hoy • **unemployment is expected to rise even ~** se espera que el desempleo aumente aún más • **prices are rising ~ and ~** los precios están subiendo más y más, los precios son cada vez más altos
N (*Scot*) (*Scol*) = **Higher Grade**
CPD ▸ **higher education** educación *f* superior, enseñanza *f* superior ▸ **Higher Grade** (*Scot*) (*Scol*) *examen de estado que se realiza a la edad de 16 años* ▸ **Higher National Certificate** (*Brit*) (*Scol*) Certificado *m* Nacional de Estudios Superiores ▸ **Higher National Diploma** (*Brit*) (*Scol*) Diploma *m* Nacional de Estudios Superiores; ▹ **A LEVELS**
higher-up* [ˌhaɪərˈʌp] N (*US*) (= *powerful person*) pez *m* gordo*
highest [ˈhaɪɪst] ADJ (*superl of* **high**) el/la más alto/a • **he was a man of the ~ principles** era un hombre de los más altos principios • **the ~ common factor** (*Math*) el máximo común denominador
ADV (*superl of* **high**) • **the ~ scoring player** el máximo anotador • **Britain's ~ paid company director** el director de empresa mejor pagado de Gran Bretaña
high-explosive [ˈhaɪɪksˈpləʊsɪv] ADJ • **high-explosive shell** obús *m* de alto explosivo; ▹ **high**
highfalutin, highfaluting [ˈhaɪfəˈluːtɪn] ADJ presuntuoso, pomposo
high-fashion [ˌhaɪˈfæʃən] ADJ [*clothes, label*] de alta costura
high-fibre, high-fiber (*US*) [ˈhaɪˈfaɪbəʳ] ADJ • **a high-fibre diet** una dieta rica en fibra
high-fidelity [ˌhaɪfɪˈdelɪtɪ] ADJ de alta fidelidad; ▹ **high**
high-flown [ˈhaɪfləʊn] ADJ exagerado, altisonante
high-flying [ˈhaɪˈflaɪɪŋ] ADJ **1** [*aircraft*] de gran altura
2 (*fig*) [*aim, ambition*] de altos vuelos; [*executive, businessperson*] (= *promising*) prometedor; (= *in high-calibre job*) bien situado, de prestigio; [*career, student*] prometedor
high-frequency [ˌhaɪˈfriːkwənsɪ] ADJ de alta frecuencia
high-grade [ˈhaɪˈgreɪd] ADJ de calidad superior
high-handed [ˈhaɪˈhændɪd] ADJ arbitrario, despótico
high-handedly [ˌhaɪˈhændɪdlɪ] ADV arbitrariamente, despóticamente
high-hat* [ˈhaɪˈhæt] ADJ encopetado, esnob*; ▹ **high**
high-heeled [ˈhaɪhiːld] ADJ [*shoes*] de tacón (alto)
high-impact [ˌhaɪˈɪmpækt] ADJ [*material*] de gran resistencia; [*sport*] de alto impacto
high-income [ˌhaɪˈɪnkəm] ADJ [*earner, taxpayer, family*] de altos ingresos; [*fund, bond*] de alto rendimiento
high-intensity [ˌhaɪɪnˈtensɪtɪ] ADJ • **high-intensity lights** (*Aut*) faros *mpl* halógenos
high-interest [ˌhaɪˈɪntrəst] ADJ [*loan, mortgage*] a alto interés; [*account*] de alto rendimiento • **a high-interest bank account** una cuenta bancaria de alto rendimiento
highjack [ˈhaɪdʒæk] = **hijack**
highjacker [ˈhaɪdʒækəʳ] N = **hijacker**
highland [ˈhaɪlənd] ADJ montañés, de montaña; [*region*] montañoso • **Highland dress** *traje tradicional de las Tierras Altas de Escocia* • **Highland fling** *baile escocés* • **Highland Games** juegos *mpl* escoceses; ▹ **highlands**

HIGHLAND GAMES
Los **Highland Games** se celebran anualmente en distintos lugares de Escocia y en ellos se realizan competiciones de deportes tradicionales celtas, junto con bailes típicos y concursos de gaitas. Probablemente, de todos los juegos, el más famoso es el que tiene lugar en Braemar, cerca de Balmoral, en el noreste de Escocia. Entre las competiciones normalmente asociadas con estos juegos están el lanzamiento de troncos **(tossing the caber)** y el lanzamiento de martillo.

highlander [ˈhaɪləndəʳ] N montañés/esa *m/f* • **Highlander** (*Brit*) *habitante de las tierras altas de Escocia*
highlands [ˈhaɪləndz] NPL tierras *fpl* altas, sierra *fsing* (*LAm*) • **the Highlands** (*Brit*) las Tierras Altas de Escocia
high-level [ˈhaɪˈlevl] ADJ [*talks*] (*also Comput*) de alto nivel • **high-level nuclear waste** desechos *mpl* nucleares de alta radiactividad • **high-level language** lenguaje *m* de alto nivel
highlight [ˈhaɪlaɪt] N **1** (*Art*) toque *m* de luz
2 (*fig*) punto *m* culminante • **the ~ of the evening** el punto culminante de la velada • **they showed the ~s of the game on television** mostraron los momentos más interesantes del partido por televisión; (*Ftbl*) mostraron las jugadas más interesantes del partido por televisión
3 highlights (*in hair*) reflejos *mpl*
VT poner de relieve, destacar; [+ *hair*] poner reflejos en
highlighter [ˈhaɪlaɪtəʳ] N (= *pen*) rotulador *m* (*Sp*)
highly [ˈhaɪlɪ] ADV **1** (*with adj, pp used as adj*) [*effective, sensitive, controversial*] muy, sumamente; [*qualified, developed, sophisticated*] sumamente, altamente; [*significant*] sumamente, tremendamente • **~ acclaimed** sumamente elogiado • **~ charged** [*atmosphere, occasion, debate*] muy tenso • **~ coloured** [*clothes, picture*] de colores chillones; [*description, account*] muy exagerado • **~ educated** muy culto • **~ intelligent** sumamente inteligente, inteligentísimo • **it is ~ likely that he will win the competition** es muy *or* sumamente probable que gane la competición • **~ paid** [*person, job*] muy bien pagado • **a ~ placed official** un funcionario importante, un alto cargo • **he is ~ placed in the company** está muy bien situado en la compañía • **~ polished** [*shoes, furniture, tiles*] muy brillantes; [*book, film, description*] muy bueno, muy pulido • **~ qualified** muy preparado, muy cualificado • **this book is ~ recommended** este libro está muy recomendado • **she came to the job ~ recommended** vino muy bien recomendada • **a ~ regarded writer** un escritor de mucha reputación • **~ sexed** muy sensual, con mucho apetito sexual • **~ spiced** con muchas especias, muy condimentado • **~ strung** muy nervioso, muy excitable • **a ~ successful businessman** un hombre de negocios de muchísimo éxito • **~ trained soldiers** soldados sumamente adiestrados • **the staff are ~ trained** el personal está altamente capacitado • **it is ~ unlikely that she will see you** es muy poco probable que te reciba
2 (*with verb*) • **to praise sb ~** alabar *or* elogiar mucho a algn • **I can't praise him ~ enough** todo elogio que haga de él es poco • **I don't rate him very ~** no tengo muy buena opinión de él • **his chances of survival are not rated very ~** no se cree que tenga muchas posibilidades de sobrevivir • **he is ~ regarded by all his staff** está muy bien considerado por todo su personal • **these children score very ~ in intelligence tests** estos niños consiguen unas puntuaciones muy altas en los tests de inteligencia • **to speak ~ of sb/sth** hablar muy bien de algn/algo • **to think ~ of sb/sth** tener muy buena opinión de algn/algo • **to value sth ~** apreciar mucho algo
highly-charged [ˌhaɪlɪˈtʃɑːdʒd] ADJ [*atmosphere, debate*] muy tenso, muy crispado
high-minded [ˈhaɪˈmaɪndɪd] ADJ [*person*] de nobles pensamientos, magnánimo; [*act*] noble, altruista
high-mindedness [ˌhaɪˈmaɪndɪdnɪs] N nobleza *f* de pensamientos, magnanimidad *f*; (= *altruism*) altruismo *m*
high-necked [ˌhaɪˈnekt] ADJ de cuello alto
highness [ˈhaɪnɪs] N altura *f* • **Highness** (*as title*) Alteza *f* • **His/Her/Your Royal Highness** Su Alteza Real • **Your Royal Highnesses** Sus Altezas Reales
high-octane [ˈhaɪˌɒkteɪn] ADJ
1 • **high-octane petrol** gasolina *f* de alto octanaje, supercarburante *m*
2 (*fig*) [*film, book*] dinámico y con carácter; [*campaign*] dinámico e intenso; [*party scene*] lleno de energía y dinamismo; [*prose*] vigoroso
high-performance [ˌhaɪpəˈfɔːməns] ADJ de gran rendimiento
high-pitched [ˈhaɪˈpɪtʃt] ADJ [*sound, voice*] agudo; [*instrument*] de tono agudo, de tono alto
high-powered [ˈhaɪˈpaʊəd] ADJ **1** [*engine*] de gran potencia
2 (*fig*) (= *dynamic*) [*person*] enérgico, dinámico; (= *important*) importante
high-pressure [ˈhaɪˈpreʃəʳ] ADJ de alta presión; (*fig*) enérgico, dinámico • **high-pressure salesman** vendedor *m* agresivo • **high-pressure selling** venta *f* agresiva
high-priced [ˌhaɪˈpraɪst] ADJ muy caro
high-principled [ˌhaɪˈprɪnsəpld] ADJ

[*person*] de principios; [*manner*] íntegro
high-profile [ˌhaɪ'prəʊfaɪl] (ADJ) • **high-profile activity** actividad *f* prominente
high-protein [ˌhaɪ'prəʊtiːn] (ADJ) rico en proteínas
high-quality ['haɪ'kwɒlɪtɪ] (ADJ) de gran calidad, de calidad superior
high-ranking [ˌhaɪ'ræŋkɪŋ] (ADJ) de categoría; [*official*] de alto rango, de alto grado; (*Mil*) de alta graduación
high-resolution [ˌhaɪrezə'luːʃən] (ADJ) [*image, screen*] de alta resolución
high-rise ['haɪraɪz] (ADJ) • **high-rise block** (*residential*) torre *fsing* de pisos • **high-rise office block** edificio *m* de oficinas (de muchas plantas) • **there are too many high-rise buildings here** hay demasiados edificios altos aquí
(N) torre *fsing* de pisos
high-risk [ˌhaɪ'rɪsk] (ADJ) [*investment, policy*] de alto riesgo
highroad ['haɪrəʊd] (N) = **high road**
high-sided vehicle (N) vehículo *m* alto
high-sounding [ˌhaɪ'saʊndɪŋ] (ADJ) altisonante
high-speed [ˌhaɪ'spiːd] (ADJ) [*vehicle*] de alta velocidad; [*test*] rápido • **high-speed train** tren *m* de alta velocidad
high-spending [ˌhaɪ'spendɪŋ] (ADJ) que gasta mucho; (*pej*) derrochador, pródigo
high-spirited [ˌhaɪ'spɪrɪtɪd] (ADJ) [*person*] animado; [*horse*] fogoso
high-strung [ˌhaɪ'strʌŋ] (ADJ) (*US*) muy nervioso, muy excitable
hightail* ['haɪteɪl] (VT) • **to ~ it** (*esp US*) darse el piro‡, salir pitando*
high-tech* [ˌhaɪ'tek] (ADJ) al-tec*, de alta tecnología
high-tension [ˌhaɪ'tenʃən] (ADJ) de alta tensión
high-test [ˌhaɪ'test] (ADJ) • **high-test fuel** supercarburante *m*
high-up* ['haɪ'ʌp] (ADJ) de categoría, importante
(N) pez *mf* gordo*, mandamás* *mf inv*
high-visibility [ˌhaɪvɪzɪ'bɪlɪtɪ] (CPD) de alta visibilidad ▸ **high-visibility clothing** ropa *f* de alta visibilidad ▸ **high-visibility vest** chaleco *m* reflectante, chaleco *m* de alta visibilidad
high-water mark [ˌhaɪ'wɔːtəmɑːk] (N) **1** (*lit*) línea *f* de la pleamar
2 (*fig*) punto *m* culminante
highway ['haɪweɪ] (N) (= *main road*) carretera *f*; (= *motorway*) autopista *f* • **~s department** administración *f* de carreteras
(CPD) ▸ **Highway Code** Código *m* de la Circulación ▸ **highway robbery** salteamiento *m*, atraco *m* (en el camino)
highwayman ['haɪweɪmən] (N) (PL: **highwaymen**) salteador *m* de caminos
HIH (ABBR) (= **His** *or* **Her Imperial Highness**) S.A.I.
hijab [hɪ'dʒæb] (N) hiyab *m*
hijack ['haɪdʒæk] (VT) secuestrar; (*fig*) apropiarse de
(N) secuestro *m*; (*fig*) apropiación *f*
hijacker ['haɪdʒækəʳ] (N) secuestrador(a) *m/f*
hijacking ['haɪdʒækɪŋ] (N) secuestro *m*; (*fig*) apropiación *f*
hike[1] [haɪk] (VI) ir de excursión a pie, dar una caminata
(VT) • **to ~ it** ir a pie
(N) excursión *f* a pie, caminata *f* • **to go on a ~** hacer una excursión (a pie), dar una caminata • IDIOM: • **take a ~!*** ¡lárgate!*
hike[2]* [haɪk] (N) (= *increase*) aumento *m*
(VT) [+ *prices, rates*] aumentar, subir
▸ **hike up** (VT + ADV) **1** [+ *skirt, socks*] subirse
2 [+ *prices, amounts*] aumentar, subir
hiker ['haɪkəʳ] (N) excursionista *mf*
hiking ['haɪkɪŋ] (N) excursionismo *m* (a pie) • **to go ~** ir de excursión a pie
(CPD) ▸ **hiking boots** botas *fpl* de montaña ▸ **hiking trail** senda *f* de excursionismo
hilarious [hɪ'lɛərɪəs] (ADJ) (= *very funny*) divertidísimo, graciosísimo; (= *merry*) alegre
hilariously [hɪ'lɛərɪəslɪ] (ADV) [*speak, describe*] con mucha gracia • **it was ~ funny** fue para morirse de risa
hilarity [hɪ'lærɪtɪ] (N) hilaridad *f*
hill [hɪl] (N) (*gen*) colina *f*, cerro *m*, loma *f* (*esp LAm*); (*high*) montaña *f*; (= *slope*) cuesta *f* • **a house at the top of a ~** una casa en lo alto de una colina • **I climbed the ~ up to the office** subí la cuesta hasta la oficina; **the hills** la montaña *fsing*, la sierra *fsing* • IDIOMS: • **to be over the ~*** ir cuesta abajo • **to chase sb up ~ and down dale** perseguir a algn por todas partes • **to take to the ~s** echarse al monte • **as old as the ~s** más viejo que Matusalén
(CPD) ▸ **hill climb** (*Sport*) ascensión *f* de montaña ▸ **hill farm** granja *f* de montaña ▸ **hill farmer** agricultor(a) *m/f* de montaña ▸ **hill farming** agricultura *f* de montaña ▸ **hill start** (*in vehicle*) arranque *m* en cuesta • **to do a ~ start** arrancar (un coche) en cuesta ▸ **hill walker** montañero/a *m/f*, senderista *mf* ▸ **hill walking** montañismo *m*, senderismo *m* • **to go ~-walking** hacer montañismo, hacer senderismo
hillbilly* ['hɪl'bɪlɪ] (*US*) (N) rústico/a *m/f* montañés/esa; (*pej*) palurdo/a *m/f*
(CPD) ▸ **hillbilly music** música *f* country
hillfort ['hɪlfɔːt] (N) castro *m*
hilliness ['hɪlɪnɪs] (N) lo montañoso
hillock ['hɪlək] (N) montículo *m*, altozano *m*
hillside ['hɪlsaɪd] (N) ladera *f*, falda *f*
hilltop ['hɪltɒp] (N) cumbre *f*
hilly ['hɪlɪ] (ADJ) (COMPAR: **hillier**, SUPERL: **hilliest**) [*terrain*] montañoso, accidentado; [*road*] con fuertes pendientes
hilt [hɪlt] (N) puño *m*, empuñadura *f* • **(up) to the ~** hasta el cuello* • **he's in debt (right) up to the ~** está agobiado *or* hasta el cuello* de deudas • **to back sb up to the ~** apoyar a algn incondicionalmente • **to prove sth up to the ~** demostrar algo hasta la saciedad
him [hɪm] (PRON) **1** (= *direct object*) lo, le (*Sp*) • **I saw him** lo vi • **look at him!** ¡míralo! • **I have never seen him** a él no lo *or* (*also Sp*) le he visto nunca
2 (= *indirect object*) le; (*combined with direct object pron*) se • **you must tell him the truth** tienes que decirle la verdad • **yes of course I gave him the book** sí, claro que le di el libro • **yes of course I gave them to him** sí, claro que se los di • **I gave the book to him not his sister** le di el libro a él no a su hermana • **I'm speaking to him not you** le estoy hablando a él, no a ti • **give it to him when you go to Liverpool** dáselo cuando vayas a Liverpool • **I gave it to him not Charlotte** se lo di a él no a Charlotte
3 (*after prep, in comparisons, with verb "to be"*) él • **she thought of him** pensó en él • **without him** sin él • **I'm going with him** voy con él • **he was carrying it on him** lo llevaba consigo • **if I were him** yo que él • **younger than him** más joven *or* menor que él • **it's him** es él
Himalayan [ˌhɪmə'leɪən] (ADJ) del Himalaya, himalayo
Himalayas [ˌhɪmə'leɪəz] (NPL) • **the ~** los montes Himalaya, el Himalaya
himself [hɪm'self] (PRON) **1** (*reflexive*) se • **he washed ~** se lavó
2 (*emphatic*) él mismo; (*after prep*) sí (mismo) • **he did it ~** lo hizo él mismo • **he went ~** fue él mismo, fue en persona • **he talked mainly about ~** habló principalmente de sí mismo • **he said to ~** dijo entre *or* para sí
3 (*phrases*) • **he came by ~** vino solo • **he did it by ~** lo hizo él solo • **he's not ~** no se encuentra nada bien
hind[1] [haɪnd] (ADJ) [*leg, foot*] trasero, posterior • IDIOM: • **he could talk the ~ leg(s) off a donkey** (*Brit**) habla hasta por los codos*
hind[2] [haɪnd] (N) (PL: **hinds** *or* **hind**) cierva *f*
hinder[1] ['hɪndəʳ] (VT) (= *disturb, make difficult*) estorbar, dificultar; (= *prevent*) impedir; (= *obstruct*) obstaculizar, poner dificultades a; (= *slow down*) entorpecer • **to ~ sb from doing sth** impedir a algn hacer algo
hinder[2] ['haɪndəʳ] (ADJ) [*part*] trasero, posterior
Hindi ['hɪndiː] (N) (*Ling*) hindi *m*
hindmost ['haɪndməʊst] (ADJ) postrero, último
hindquarters ['haɪndˌkwɔːtəz] (NPL) cuartos *mpl* traseros
hindrance ['hɪndrəns] (N) (= *obstacle*) obstáculo *m* (**to** para); (= *disturbance*) estorbo *m*; (= *problem*) impedimento *m* • **to be a ~ to sb/sth** ser un estorbo para algn/algo
hindsight ['haɪndsaɪt] (N) • **with the benefit of ~** en retrospectiva
Hindu ['hɪn'duː] (ADJ) hindú
(N) hindú *mf*
Hinduism ['hɪnduːɪzəm] (N) (*Rel*) hinduismo *m*
Hindustan [ˌhɪndʊ'stɑːn] (N) Indostán *m*
Hindustani ['hɪndʊ'stɑːnɪ] (ADJ) indostaní, indostánico, indostanés
(N) (*Ling*) indostaní *m*
hinge [hɪndʒ] (N) [*of door, window*] bisagra *f*, gozne *m*; [*of shell*] charnela *f* (*also Zool*); (*for stamps*) fijasellos *m inv*; (*fig*) eje *m*
(VI) moverse sobre goznes • **to ~ on** moverse sobre, girar sobre; (*fig*) depender de
(VT) engoznar
hinged [hɪndʒd] (ADJ) de bisagra, con goznes
hint [hɪnt] (N) **1** (= *suggestion*) indirecta *f*, insinuación *f*; (= *advice*) consejo *m* • **~s for purchasers** consejos *mpl* a los compradores • **~s on maintenance** instrucciones *fpl* para la manutención • **broad ~** indicación *f* inconfundible • **to drop a ~** soltar *or* tirar una indirecta • **to drop a ~ that …** insinuar que … • **give me a ~** dame una idea • **to take a ~** captar una indirecta • **take a ~ from me** permite que te dé un consejo • **to take the ~** (*unspoken*) tomar algo a corazón; (*spoken*) darse por aludido
2 (= *trace*) señal *f*, indicio *m* • **without the least ~ of** sin la menor señal de • **with just a ~ of garlic** con un ligerísimo sabor a ajo • **with a ~ of irony** con un dejo de ironía
(VT) dar a entender, insinuar • **he ~ed that I had a good chance of getting the job** insinuó que tenía muchas posibilidades de conseguir el trabajo
(VI) soltar indirectas
▸ **hint at** (VI + PREP) referirse indirectamente a, hacer alusión a • **what are you ~ing at?** ¿qué estás insinuando?
hinterland ['hɪntəlænd] (N) hinterland *m*, interior *m*, traspaís *m*
hip[1] [hɪp] (N) (*Anat*) cadera *f* • **to shoot from the hip** (= *lit*) disparar sin apuntar; (*fig*) (= *act without thinking*) actuar sin pensar; (= *speak without thinking*) hablar sin pensar
(CPD) ▸ **hip bath** baño *m* de asiento, polibán *m* ▸ **hip flask** petaca *f* ▸ **hip joint** articulación *f* de la cadera ▸ **hip pocket** bolsillo *m* de atrás, bolsillo *m* trasero ▸ **hip replacement (operation)** operación *f* de trasplante de cadera ▸ **hip size** talla *f* de cadera

h

hip² [hɪp] (N) (*Bot*) escaramujo *m*
hip³ [hɪp] (EXCL) • **hip hip hurray!** ¡viva!
hip⁴* [hɪp] (ADJ) • **to be hip** (= *up-to-date*) estar al día; (= *well-informed*) estar al tanto (de lo que pasa), estar enterado
hipbone ['hɪpbəʊn] (N) hueso *m* de la cadera
hip-hop ['hɪphɒp] (N) hip hop *m*
hip-hugging ['hɪphʌgɪŋ] (ADJ) [*trousers*] de tiro bajo, de tiro corto
hipped¹ [hɪpt] (ADJ) (*Archit*) a cuatro aguas
hipped²* [hɪpt] (*US*) (ADJ) **1** (= *annoyed*) enojado, resentido
2 (= *interested*) • **to be ~ on sth** estar obsesionado por algo
3 (= *depressed*) • **to be ~** estar con la depre*
-hipped [-hɪpt] (SUFFIX) • **narrow-hipped** estrecho de caderas • **he is broad-chested and narrow-hipped** es ancho de hombros y estrecho de caderas
hippie* ['hɪpɪ] = **hippy**
hippo* ['hɪpəʊ] (N) hipopótamo/a *m/f*
Hippocrates [hɪ'pɒkrəti:z] (N) Hipócrates
Hippocratic [,hɪpəʊ'krætɪk] (ADJ) • **~ oath** juramento *m* hipocrático
hippodrome ['hɪpədrəʊm] (N) (*Hist*) hipódromo *m*
Hippolytus [hɪ'pɒlɪtəs] (N) Hipólito
hippopotamus [,hɪpə'pɒtəməs] (N) (PL: **hippopotamuses** or **hippopotami** [,hɪpə'pɒtəmaɪ]) hipopótamo/a *m/f*
hippy* ['hɪpɪ] (N) hippy* *mf*, hippie* *mf*
(ADJ) hippy*, hippie*
hipster ['hɪpstəʳ] (N) **1 hipsters** (*Brit*) *pantalón que se lleva a la altura de la cadera*
2 (*US**) entusiasta *mf* del jazz
(CPD) ▸ **hipster skirt** (*Brit*) falda *f* abrochada en la cadera
hire ['haɪəʳ] (VT) [+ *car, house*] alquilar, arrendar (*LAm*); [+ *employee*] contratar • **they ~d a lawyer** contrataron a un abogado • **~d hand** jornalero/a *m/f*, enganchado/a *m/f* • **~d assassin** or **killer** asesino/a *m/f* a sueldo • **~d car** coche *m* de alquiler
(VI) • **she's in charge of hiring and firing at the company** es la encargada de contratar y despedir al personal en la empresa
(N) [*of car*] alquiler *m*, arriendo *m* (*LAm*); [*of person*] salario *m*, jornal *m* • **for ~** se alquila or (*LAm*) arrienda; (*on taxi*) libre • **to be on ~** estar de alquiler • **we've got it on ~ for a week** lo tenemos alquilado para una semana
(CPD) ▸ **hire car** (*Brit*) coche *m* de alquiler ▸ **hire charges** tarifa *fsing* de alquiler ▸ **hire purchase** (*Brit*) compra *f* a plazos • **to buy sth on ~ purchase** comprar algo a plazos ▸ **hire purchase agreement** acuerdo *m* de compra a plazos ▸ **hire purchase finance company** compañía *f* de crédito comercial
▸ **hire out** (VT + ADV) alquilar, arrendar (*LAm*)
hireling ['haɪəlɪŋ] (N) mercenario *m*
hirsute ['hɜ:sju:t] (ADJ) hirsuto
his [hɪz] (POSS ADJ) (*with singular noun*) su; (*with plural noun*) sus • **his book/table** su libro/mesa • **his friends** sus amigos • **he took off his coat** se quitó el abrigo • **he's washing his hair** se está lavando el pelo • **someone stole his car** alguien le robó el coche
(POSS PRON) (*referring to singular possession*) (el/la) suyo/a; (*referring to plural possession*) (los/las) suyos/as • **this book is his** este libro es suyo or de él • **is that car his?** ¿es suyo or de él ese coche? • **"whose is this?" — "it's his"** —¿de quién es esto? —es de él • **a friend of his** un amigo suyo • **my car is much bigger than his** mi coche es mucho más grande que el suyo or el de él • **"is this his coat?" — "no, his is black"** —¿es este su abrigo? —no, el suyo or el de él es negro • **"is this his scarf?" — "no, his is red"** —¿es esta su bufanda? —no la suya or la de él es roja • **my parents and his** mis padres y los suyos or los de él
Hispanic [hɪs'pænɪk] (ADJ) hispánico; (*within US*) hispano
(N) (*within US*) hispano/a *m/f*
hispanicism [hɪs'pænɪsɪzəm] (N) hispanismo *m*
hispanicist [hɪs'pænɪst] (N) = **hispanist**
hispanicize [hɪs'pænɪsaɪz] (VT) españolizar, hispanizar
Hispanism ['hɪspənɪzəm] (N) hispanismo *m*
hispanist ['hɪspənɪst] (N) hispanista *mf*
Hispano... [hɪ'spænəʊ] (PREFIX) hispano...
hispanophile [hɪs'pænəʊfaɪl] (N) hispanófilo/a *m/f*
hispanophobe [hɪs'pænəʊfəʊb] (N) hispanófobo/a *m/f*
hiss [hɪs] (N) siseo *m*, silbido *m*; [*of protest*] silbido *m*, chiflido *m*; (*Elec*) silbido *m*
(VI) sisear; (*in protest*) silbar, chiflar
(VT) abuchear, silbar • **to ~ an actor off the stage** abuchear a un actor (hasta que abandone la escena)
hissy fit* [,hɪsɪ'fɪt] (N) (= *tantrum*) pataleta* *f* • **to throw a ~** patalear
histamine ['hɪstə,mi:n] (N) (*Med*) histamina *f*
histogram ['hɪstəgræm] (N) histograma *m*
histologist [hɪs'tɒlədʒɪst] (N) histólogo/a *m/f*
histology [hɪs'tɒlədʒɪ] (N) histología *f*
historian [hɪs'tɔ:rɪən] (N) historiador(a) *m/f*
historic [hɪs'tɒrɪk] (ADJ) histórico
historical [hɪs'tɒrɪkəl] (ADJ) histórico
historically [hɪs'tɒrɪkəlɪ] (ADV) históricamente
historicism [hɪ'stɒrɪsɪzəm] (N) historicismo *m*
historicist [hɪ'stɒrɪsɪst] (ADJ) historicista
historicity [,hɪstə'rɪsɪtɪ] (N) historicidad *f*
historiographer [,hɪstɒrɪ'ɒgrəfəʳ] (N) historiógrafo/a *m/f*
historiography [,hɪstɒrɪ'ɒgrəfɪ] (N) historiografía *f*
history ['hɪstərɪ] (N) historia *f* • **to go down in ~** pasar a la historia (**as** como) • **to make ~** hacer época, marcar un hito • **to know the inner ~ of an affair** conocer el secreto de un asunto • **he has a ~ of psychiatric disorder** tiene antecedentes de problemas psiquiátricos • **the highest salary in television ~** el sueldo más alto de la historia de la televisión • **a piece of ~** un trozo or fragmento de la historia • IDIOMS: • **that's ancient ~** esa es cosa vieja • **the rest is ~** el resto ya lo sabéis, el resto ya es historia
histrionic [,hɪstrɪ'ɒnɪk] (ADJ) histriónico
histrionics [,hɪstrɪ'ɒnɪks] (NPL) histrionismo *msing* • **I'm tired of his ~** estoy harto de sus payasadas
hit [hɪt] (VB: PT, PP: **hit**) (N) **1** (= *blow*) golpe *m*; (*Sport*) (= *shot*) tiro *m*; (*on target*) tiro *m* certero, acierto *m*; (*Baseball*) jit *m*; [*of bomb*] impacto *m* directo; (= *good guess*) acierto *m* • **we made three hits on the target** dimos tres veces en el blanco • **that was a hit at me** lo dijo por mí • **he made a hit at the government** hizo un ataque contra el gobierno
2 (*Mus, Theat*) éxito *m* • **to be a hit** tener éxito, ser un éxito • **the film was a massive hit** la película fue un éxito enorme • **she's a hit with everyone*** les cae bien a todos • **to make a hit with sb** caerle bien a algn
3 (*Internet*) (= *match on search engine*) correspondencia *f*; (= *visit to website*) visita *f*
(VT) (VB: PT, PP: **hit**) **1** (= *strike*) [+ *person*] pegar, golpear; (= *come into contact with*) dar con, dar contra; (*violently*) chocar con, chocar contra; [+ *ball*] pegar; [+ *target*] dar en • **to hit sb a blow** dar un golpe a algn • **to hit one's head against a wall** dar con la cabeza contra una pared • **the president was hit by three bullets** el presidente fue alcanzado por tres balas • **the house was hit by a bomb** la casa sufrió un directo • **I realized my plane had been hit** me di cuenta de que mi avión había sido tocado • **he was hit by a stone** le alcanzó una piedra • **the car hit a road sign** el coche chocó con una señal de tráfico • **he was hit by a car** le pilló un coche • **his father used to hit him** su padre le pegaba • **a lot of what he said hit home** gran parte de lo que dijo dio en el blanco or hizo mella • IDIOMS: • **then it hit me*** (*realization*) entonces caí en la cuenta • **to hit sb when he's down** rematar a algn • **to hit the mark** dar en el blanco, acertar • **to hit one's head against a wall** dar golpes al viento • **to hit the ground running** dar el do de pecho desde el principio
2 (= *affect adversely*) dañar; [+ *person*] afectar, golpear • **the news hit him hard** la noticia le afectó mucho • **the crops were hit by the rain** las lluvias dañaron los cultivos • **the company has been hard hit** la compañía se ha visto muy afectada
3 (= *find, reach*) [+ *road*] dar con; [+ *speed*] alcanzar; [+ *difficulty*] tropezar con; (= *achieve, reach*) [+ *note*] alcanzar; (*fig*) (= *guess*) atinar, acertar • **when we hit the main road** cuando lleguemos a la carretera • IDIOMS: • **to hit the bottle*** beber mucho • **to hit the ceiling*** perder los estribos, enloquecer • **to hit the jackpot** sacar el premio gordo • **to hit the hay** or **the sack*** tumbarse • **to hit somewhere**: • **we hit London at nightfall*** llegamos a Londres al anochecer • **to hit the road** or **the trail*** ponerse en camino or en marcha
4 (*Press*) • IDIOMS: • **to hit the front page** or **the headlines*** salir en primera plana • **to hit the papers*** salir en el periódico
5 • IDIOM: • **he hit me for ten bucks** (*US**) me dio un sablazo de diez dólares* • **how much can we hit them for?** ¿qué cantidad podremos sacarles?
(VI) golpear; (= *collide*) chocar • **to hit against** chocar con, dar contra • **to hit at** asestar un golpe a • **to hit and run** atacar y retirarse
(CPD) ▸ **hit list** (= *death list*) lista *f* de personas a las que se planea eliminar; (= *target list*) lista *f* negra ▸ **hit parade** lista *f* de éxitos ▸ **hit song** canción *f* éxito ▸ **hit squad** escuadrón *m* de la muerte
▸ **hit back** (VI + ADV) (*lit, fig*) devolver el golpe
(VT + ADV) devolver el golpe a
▸ **hit off** (VT + ADV) **1** (= *imitate*) imitar
2 • **to hit it off with sb** hacer buenas migas con algn • **they don't hit it off** no se llevan bien
▸ **hit on** (VI + PREP) **1** (= *stumble on*) dar con • **I hit on the idea of ...** se me ocurrió la idea de ...
2 (*esp US‡*) (= *make advances to*) intentar ligar con
▸ **hit out** (VI + ADV) asestar un golpe; (*wildly*) repartir golpes (**at a**) • **to hit out at sb** asestar un golpe a algn; (*fig*) atacar a algn
▸ **hit upon** = hit on
hit-and-miss [,hɪtən'mɪs] (ADJ) = **hit-or-miss**
hit-and-run ['hɪtən'rʌn] (ADJ) • **hit-and-run accident** *accidente de carretera en el que el conductor se da a la fuga* • **hit-and-run driver** *conductor(a) que atropella a alguien y huye* • **hit-and-run raid** ataque *m* relámpago
(N) *accidente en el que el culpable se da a la fuga*
hitch [hɪtʃ] (N) **1** (= *impediment, obstacle*) obstáculo *m*, impedimento *m* • **without a ~**

sin ningún problema • **there's been a slight ~** ha habido un pequeño contratiempo
2 (= *tug*) tirón *m*, jalón *m* (*LAm*)
3 (= *knot*) vuelta *f* de cabo
VT **1** • **to ~ a lift** hacer autoestop, hacer dedo*, pedir aventón (*Mex*) • **they ~ed a lift to Rome** llegaron a Roma haciendo autoestop
2 (= *fasten*) atar, amarrar (**to** a) • **to ~ a horse to a wagon** enganchar un caballo a un carro
3 • **to get ~ed‡** casarse
4 (= *shift*) mover de un tirón • **he ~ed a chair over** acercó una silla a tirones
VI* (*also* **hitchhike**) hacer autoestop, ir a dedo, hacer dedo*, pedir aventón (*Mex*)
▸ **hitch up** VT + ADV [+ *trousers, sleeves*] remangarse, subirse
hitcher* [ˈhɪtʃəʳ] N (*esp Brit*) autoestopista *mf*
hitchhike [ˈhɪtʃhaɪk] VI hacer autoestop, hacer dedo*, pedir aventón (*Mex*)
hitchhiker [ˈhɪtʃhaɪkəʳ] N autoestopista *mf*
hitchhiking [ˈhɪtʃhaɪkɪŋ] N autoestop *m*, autoestopismo *m*
hi-tech* [ˈhaɪˈtek] ADJ al-tec*, de alta tecnología
hither†† [ˈhɪðəʳ] ADV acá • **~ and thither** acá y acullá
hitherto [ˈhɪðəˈtuː] ADV hasta ahora
Hitlerian [hɪtˈlɪərɪən] ADJ hitleriano
hitman [ˈhɪtmæn] N (PL: **hitmen** [ˈhɪtmen]) sicario *m*, asesino *m* a sueldo
hit-or-miss [ˈhɪtɔːˈmɪs] ADJ al azar • **to have a hit-or-miss way of doing things** hacer las cosas al azar *or* sin ton ni son • **the way she painted the room was rather hit-or-miss** pintó la habitación a la buena de Dios *or* como Dios le dio a entender • **it's all rather hit-or-miss** es todo un poco a la buena de Dios
hitter [ˈhɪtəʳ] N **1** (*Baseball*) bateador(a) *m/f* • **one of the game's big ~s** (*Tennis*) uno de los tenistas con mejor saque
2 • IDIOMS: • **a big ~** • **a heavy ~** un pez gordo*
Hittite [ˈhɪtaɪt] ADJ heteo, hitita
N **1** (= *person*) heteo/a *m/f*, hitita *mf*
2 (*Ling*) hitita *m*
hitwoman [ˈhɪtˌwʊmən] N (PL: **hitwomen**) asesina *f* a sueldo
HIV N ABBR (= **human immunodeficiency virus**) VIH *m* • **HIV positive/negative** VIH positivo/negativo
CPD ▸ **HIV virus** virus *m* VIH
hive [haɪv] N colmena *f* • **a ~ of activity** (*fig*) un hervidero de actividad • **a ~ of industry** un lugar donde se trabaja muchísimo
▸ **hive off*** VT + ADV **1** (*Econ*) (= *sell off*) vender (por separado)
2 (= *privatize*) privatizar
VI + ADV (= *split from*) desligarse
hives [haɪvz] NPL (*Med*) urticaria *fsing*
hiya* [ˈhaɪjə] EXCL ¡hola!
Hizbollah, Hizbullah [ˌhɪzbəˈlɑː] N = **Hezbollah**
HK ABBR = **Hong Kong**
hl ABBR (= **hectolitre(s)**) hl
HM ABBR (= **Her** *or* **His Majesty**) S.M.
hm ABBR (= **hectometre(s)**) hm
h'm, hm [ˈhmmm] EXCL ¡mmm!
HMG N ABBR (*Brit*) = **Her** *or* **His Majesty's Government**
HMI N ABBR (*Brit*) = **Her** *or* **His Majesty's Inspector**
HMO N ABBR (*US*) (= **health maintenance organization**) *seguro médico global*
HMS N ABBR (*Brit*) (= **Her** *or* **His Majesty's Ship**) *buque de guerra*
HMSO N ABBR (*Brit*) (= **Her** *or* **His Majesty's Stationery Office**) *imprenta del gobierno*
HNC N ABBR (*Brit*) (*Scol*) (= **Higher National Certificate**) *título académico*
HND N ABBR (*Brit*) (*Scol*) (= **Higher National Diploma**) *título académico*, ≈ Diploma *m* Nacional de Estudios Superiores
HO ABBR **1** (*Comm etc*) = **head office**
2 (*Brit*) (*Pol*) = **Home Office**
hoard [hɔːd] N (= *treasure*) tesoro *m*; (= *stockpile*) provisión *f* • **~s of money*** montones *mpl* de dinero
VT **1** (*also* **hoard up**) (= *accumulate*) amontonar, acumular; [+ *money*] atesorar
2 (= *keep*) guardar
hoarder [ˈhɔːdəʳ] N • **to be a ~** ser un acaparador
hoarding¹ [ˈhɔːdɪŋ] N (= *fence*) valla *f*; (*for advertisements*) valla *f* publicitaria
hoarding² [ˈhɔːdɪŋ] N (= *act*) acumulación *f*, retención *f*
hoarfrost [ˈhɔːˈfrɒst] N escarcha *f*
hoarse [hɔːs] ADJ (COMPAR: **hoarser**, SUPERL: **hoarsest**) ronco • **to be ~** tener la voz ronca • **in a ~ voice** con voz ronca • **to shout o.s. ~** enronquecer a fuerza de gritar
hoarsely [ˈhɔːslɪ] ADV en voz ronca
hoarseness [ˈhɔːsnɪs] N (*Med*) ronquera *f*; (= *hoarse quality*) ronquedad *f*
hoary [ˈhɔːrɪ] ADJ (COMPAR: **hoarier**, SUPERL: **hoariest**) **1** (= *grey-haired*) cano
2 (= *old*) [*myth*] manido; [*joke*] muy viejo
hoax [həʊks] N engaño *m*
VT engañar
CPD ▸ **hoax call** *llamada efectuada a la policía, los bomberos etc. para dar un falso aviso de bomba, incendio etc*
hoaxer [ˈhəʊksəʳ] N (*esp Brit*) bromista *mf*
hob [hɒb] N (*Brit*) quemador *m*
hobble [ˈhɒbl] N **1** (= *lameness*) cojera *f* • **to walk with a ~** cojear
2 (= *rope*) maniota *f*
VT [+ *horse*] manear
VI (*also* **hobble along**) cojear, andar cojeando • **to ~ to the door** ir cojeando a la puerta
hobbledehoy†† [ˈhɒbldɪˈhɒɪ] N gamberro *m*
hobby [ˈhɒbɪ] N (= *leisure activity*) hobby *m*, pasatiempo *m* favorito • **it's just a ~** es solo un pasatiempo • **he began to paint as a ~** empezó a pintar como hobby
hobbyhorse [ˈhɒbɪhɔːs] N **1** (= *toy*) caballito *m* (de niño), caballo *m* mecedor
2 (*fig*) (= *preoccupation*) caballo *m* de batalla, tema *m* preferido • **he's on his ~ again** ya está otra vez con lo mismo
hobbyist [ˈhɒbɪɪst] N *persona que practica un hobby*
hobgoblin [ˈhɒbˌgɒblɪn] N duende *m*, trasgo *m*
hobnail [ˈhɒbneɪl] N clavo *m* (de botas)
hobnailed [ˈhɒbneɪld] ADJ [*boots*] con clavos
hobnob* [ˈhɒbnɒb] VI • **to ~ with** codearse con, alternar con
hobo [ˈhəʊbəʊ] N (PL: **hobo(e)s**) (*US*) vagabundo/a *m/f*
Hobson's choice [ˈhɒbsənzˈtʃɔɪs] N (*Brit*) opción *f* única • **it's ~** o lo tomas o lo dejas
hock¹ [hɒk] N [*of animal*] corvejón *m*
hock² [hɒk] N (= *wine*) vino *m* blanco del Rin
hock³* [hɒk] VT (= *pawn*) empeñar
N • **in ~** [*object*] empeñado; [*person*] endeudado
hockey [ˈhɒkɪ] N hockey *m*; (*also* **field hockey**) hockey *m* sobre hierba; (*also* **ice hockey**) hockey *m* sobre hielo
CPD ▸ **hockey player** jugador(a) *m/f* de hockey ▸ **hockey stick** palo *m* de hockey
hocus-pocus [ˈhəʊkəsˈpəʊkəs] N (= *trickery*) juego *m* de manos; (= *words*) jerigonza *f*
EXCL abracadabra
hod [hɒd] N capacho *m*
hodgepodge [ˈhɒdʒpɒdʒ] N (*esp US*) = **hotchpotch**
hoe [həʊ] N azada *f*, azadón *m*
VT [+ *earth*] azadonar, trabajar con la azada; [+ *crop*] sachar
hoedown [ˈhəʊdaʊn] N (*US*) contradanza *f*
hog [hɒg] N **1** (*esp US*) (= *pig*) cerdo *m*, puerco *m*, chancho *m* (*LAm*)
2 (*Brit*) (= *castrated pig*) cerdo *m* castrado • **he's a greedy hog*** es un cerdo* • IDIOM: • **to go the whole hog*** jugarse el todo por el todo
VT* acaparar • **to hog the limelight** acaparar toda la atención
Hogmanay [ˈhɒgmənеɪ] N (*Scot*) Nochevieja *f*

> **HOGMANAY**
> **Hogmanay** es el nombre que recibe el día de Nochevieja en Escocia. La gente suele organizar fiestas y, cuando suenan las doce campanadas, cantan **Auld Lang Syne**, una canción típica escocesa, y brindan por el nuevo año. Después es costumbre salir a visitar a los amigos para dar juntos la bienvenida al año que comienza. La costumbre de ser los primeros en hacerlo se denomina **first-footing**. Según la tradición es señal de prosperidad y buena suerte en el nuevo año si la primera persona que llega a la casa después de las doce de la noche es un hombre moreno que lleve algo de comida, bebida y un trozo de carbón.
> ▷ **AULD LANG SYNE**

hogshead [ˈhɒgzhed] N *medida de capacidad esp del vino (= 52,5 galones, aprox. 225 litros)*, pipa *f*
hogtie [ˈhɒgtaɪ] VT (*US*) (*lit, fig*) atar de pies y manos a • **we're ~d** estamos atados de pies y manos
hogwash [ˈhɒgwɒʃ] N tonterías *fpl*
ho ho [ˌhəʊˈhəʊ], **ho ho ho** [ˌhəʊˌhəʊˈhəʊ] EXCL (*laughter*) ja, ja, ja
ho hum [ˈhəʊˈhʌm] EXCL (*hum*) pues, vaya
hoi polloi [ˌhɔɪpəˈlɔɪ] N • **the ~** (*hum, iro*) la plebe, el vulgo
hoist [hɔɪst] VT (*also* **hoist up**) levantar, alzar; [+ *flag, sail*] izar • **to ~ onto** subir a
N (= *lift*) montacargas *m inv*; (= *crane*) grúa *f* • **to give sb a ~ (up)** ayudar a algn a subir
hoity-toity* [ˈhɔɪtɪˈtɔɪtɪ] ADJ presumido, engreído
EXCL ¡tate!
hokey-cokey [ˈhəʊkɪˈkəʊkɪ] N *canto y baile en grupo*
hokum* [ˈhəʊkəm] N (*esp US*) tonterías *fpl*
hold [həʊld] (VB: PT, PP: **held**) N **1** (= *grasp*) agarro *m*, asimiento *m* • **to catch ~ of** coger, agarrar (*LAm*) • **catch ~!** ¡toma! • **to get ~ of** coger, agarrar (*LAm*); (*fig*) (= *take over*) adquirir, apoderarse de; (= *obtain*) procurarse, conseguir • **where can I get ~ of some red paint?** ¿dónde puedo conseguir pintura roja? • **where did you get ~ of that?** ¿dónde has adquirido eso? • **where did you get ~ of that idea?** ¿de dónde te salió esa idea? • **you get ~ of some odd ideas** te formas unas ideas muy raras • **to get ~ of sb** (*fig*) (= *contact*) localizar a algn • **we're trying to get ~ of him** tratamos de ponernos en contacto con él • **to get (a) ~ of o.s.** (*fig*) dominarse • **to have ~ of** estar agarrado a • **to keep ~ of** seguir agarrado a; (*fig*) guardar para sí • **to lay ~ of** coger, agarrar (*LAm*) • **on ~**: • **to be on ~** (*Telec*) estar en espera • **to put sb on ~** (*Telec*) poner a algn en espera • **to put a plan on ~** suspender temporalmente la ejecución de un plan • **to relax one's ~** desasirse (**on** de) • **to seize ~ of** apoderarse

de • **to take ~ of** coger, agarrar (*LAm*)
2 (*Mountaineering*) asidero *m*
3 (*Wrestling*) presa *f*, llave *f* • **with no ~s barred** (*fig*) sin restricción, permitiéndose todo
4 (*fig*) (= *control, influence*) (*exerted by person*) influencia *f*, dominio *m* (**on, over** sobre); (*exerted by habit*) arraigo *m* (**on, over** en) • **her powerful ~ on her son** su poderosa influencia sobre su hijo • **this broke the dictator's ~** esto acabó con el dominio del dictador • **to gain a firm ~ over sb** llegar a dominar a algn • **to have a ~ on** *or* **over sb** dominar a algn, tener dominado a algn • **drink has a ~ on him** la bebida está muy arraigada en él, está atrapado por la bebida
5 (*Aer, Naut*) bodega *f*, compartimento *m* de carga
VT 1 (= *grasp*) tener; (= *grasp firmly*) sujetar; (= *take hold of*) coger, agarrar (*LAm*); (= *embrace*) abrazar • **he was ~ing a little mouse in his hand** tenía un ratoncillo en la mano • **she came in ~ing a baby/bunch of flowers** entró con un niño en brazos/con un ramo de flores en las manos • **he was ~ing her in his arms** (*romantically*) la tenía entre sus brazos • **he held my arm** me tuvo por el brazo • **~ the ladder** sujeta la escalera • **~ this for a moment** coge esto un momento • **~ him or he'll fall** sostenle que va a caer • **to ~ sb close** abrazar a algn estrechamente • **to ~ sth in place** sujetar algo en un lugar • **to ~ sth tight** agarrar algo fuertemente • **to ~ sb tight** abrazar a algn estrechamente; ▷ **nose**
2 (= *maintain, keep*) [+ *attention, interest*] mantener; [+ *belief, opinion*] tener, sostener; [+ *note*] sostener • **can he ~ an audience?** ¿sabe mantener el interés de un público? • **to ~ one's head high** mantenerse firme • **to ~ the line** (*Telec*) no colgar • **to ~ one's own** defenderse • **to ~ sb to his promise** hacer que algn cumpla su promesa • **this car ~s the road well** este coche se agarra muy bien • **he held us spellbound** nos tuvo embelesados • **to ~ o.s. upright** mantenerse recto
3 (= *keep back*) retener, guardar • **I will ~ the money for you** guardaré el dinero para ti • **"~ for arrival"** (*US*) (*on letters*) "no reexpedir", "reténgase" • **we are ~ing it pending inquiries** lo guardamos mientras se hagan indagaciones
4 (= *check, restrain*) [+ *enemy, breath*] contener • **~ it!** ¡para!, ¡espera! • **~ everything!** ¡que se pare todo! • **the police held him for three days** lo detuvo la policía durante tres días • **there was no ~ing him** no había manera de detenerle • **to ~ sb prisoner** tener preso a algn • **to ~ one's tongue** morderse la lengua, callarse la boca
5 (= *possess*) [+ *post, town, lands*] ocupar; [+ *passport, ticket, shares, title*] tener; (*Econ*) [+ *reserves*] tener en reserva, tener guardado; [+ *record*] ostentar; (*Mil*) [+ *position*] mantenerse en • **to ~ the fort** (*fig*) quedarse a cargo • **he ~s the key to the mystery** él tiene la clave del misterio • **to ~ office** (*Pol*) ocupar un cargo • **to ~ the stage** (*fig*) dominar la escena
6 (= *contain*) contener, tener capacidad *or* cabida para • **this stadium ~s 10,000 people** este estadio tiene capacidad *or* cabida para 10.000 personas • **this ~s the money** esto contiene el dinero • **this bag won't ~ them all** en este saco no caben todos • **a car that ~s six** un coche de seis plazas • **what the future ~s for us** lo que el futuro guarda para nosotros • **what does the future ~?** ¿qué nos reserva el futuro?
7 (= *carry on*) [+ *conversation*] mantener; [+ *interview, meeting, election*] celebrar; [+ *event*] realizar; (*formally*) celebrar • **the maths exam is being held today** hoy tiene lugar el examen de matemáticas • **the meeting will be held on Monday** se celebrará la reunión el lunes, la reunión tendrá lugar el lunes • **to ~ a mass** (*Rel*) celebrar una misa
8 (= *consider, believe*) creer, sostener • **to ~ that ...** creer que ..., sostener que ... • **I ~ that ...** yo creo *or* sostengo que ... • **it is held by some that ...** hay quien cree que ... • **to ~ sth dear** apreciar mucho algo • **to ~ sb dear** querer *or* apreciar mucho a algn • **to ~ sb in high esteem** tener a algn en gran *or* alta estima • **to ~ sb guilty** juzgar a algn culpable • **to ~ sb in respect** tener respeto a algn • **to ~ sb responsible for sth** echar la culpa a algn de algo, hacer a algn responsable de algo • **to ~ sth to be true** creer que algo es verdad; ▷ **peace**
9 (= *bear weight of*) soportar
VI 1 (= *stick*) pegarse; (= *not give way*) mantenerse firme, resistir; [*weather*] continuar, seguir bueno • **the ceasefire seems to be ~ing** el cese de fuego parece que se mantiene • **to ~ firm** *or* **fast** mantenerse firme
2 (= *be valid*) valer, ser valedero • **the objection does not ~** la objeción no vale
3 (*Telec*) • **please ~** no cuelgue, por favor
▸ **hold against** VT + PREP tener contra • **they held his origins against him** creían que sus orígenes eran deshonrosos para él • **you won't ~ this against me, will you?** ¿verdad que no vas a pensar mal de mí por esto?
▸ **hold back** VT + ADV (= *keep*) guardar, retener; (= *stop*) [+ *river, flood*] retener; [+ *progress*] refrenar; [+ *information*] ocultar, no revelar; [+ *names*] no comunicar; [+ *emotion, tears*] reprimir, contener • **are you ~ing sth back from me?** ¿me estás ocultando algo? • **to ~ o.s. back from doing sth** refrenarse de hacer algo
VI + ADV refrenarse; (*in doubt*) vacilar • **to ~ back from** refrenarse de • **to ~ back from doing sth** refrenarse de hacer algo
▸ **hold down** VT + ADV 1 [+ *object*] sujetar
2 [+ *prices*] mantener bajo
3 (= *oppress*) oprimir, subyugar
4 • **to ~ down a job** (= *retain*) mantenerse en su puesto; (= *be equal to*) estar a la altura de su cargo • **he can't ~ down a job** pierde todos los trabajos
▸ **hold forth** VI + ADV hablar largo y tendido (**about, on** de), perorar
▸ **hold in** VT + ADV 1 (= *squeeze in*) [+ *stomach*] contener
2 (= *suppress*) [+ *emotion*] contener
3 • **to ~ o.s. in** (*fig*) controlarse, aguantarse
▸ **hold off** VT + ADV 1 (= *resist*) [+ *attack, enemy*] rechazar; [+ *threat*] apartar; [+ *person*] defenderse contra; [+ *visitor*] (*fig*) hacer esperar
2 (= *postpone*) aplazar
VI + ADV 1 (= *stand back*) mantenerse a distancia, no tomar parte; [*person*] (= *wait*) esperar
2 • **if the rain ~s off** si no llueve
▸ **hold on** VI + ADV 1 (= *grip, cling*) agarrarse
2 (= *persevere*) aguantar, resistir • **~ on!** ¡ánimo! • **can you ~ on?** ¿te animas a continuar?
3 (= *wait*) esperar, seguir esperando • **~ on!** ¡espera!; (*Telec*) ¡no cuelgue! • **~ on, I'm coming!** ¡espera que ya voy!
VT + ADV sujetar
▸ **hold on to** VI + PREP 1 (= *grasp*) agarrarse a, agarrarse de
2 (= *keep*) guardar, quedarse con; (*fig*) (= *retain*) aferrarse a; [+ *post*] retener
▸ **hold out** VT + ADV [+ *object*] ofrecer, alargar; [+ *hand*] tender, alargar; [+ *arm*] extender; [+ *possibility*] ofrecer; [+ *hope*] dar • **to ~ out sth to sb** ofrecerle algo a algn
VI + ADV 1 (= *resist*) resistir (**against** a), aguantar • **to ~ out for sth** insistir hasta conseguir algo • **he held out for £10** insistió en 10 libras
2 (= *last*) [*supplies*] durar; [*weather*] seguir bueno
▸ **hold out on*** VI + PREP • **you've been ~ing out on me!** ¡no me habías dicho nada!
▸ **hold over** VT + ADV [+ *meeting*] aplazar, posponer
▸ **hold to** VT + PREP atenerse a
▸ **hold together** VT + ADV [+ *persons*] mantener unidos; [+ *company, group*] mantener la unidad de
VI + ADV 1 [*persons*] mantenerse unidos
2 [*argument*] ser sólido, ser lógico; [*deal*] mantenerse
▸ **hold up** VT + ADV 1 (= *support*) sujetar, sostener
2 (= *raise*) [+ *hand*] levantar, alzar; [+ *head*] mantener erguido • **~ up your hand** levanta la mano • **to ~ sth up to the light** poner algo a contraluz
3 (= *display*) mostrar, enseñar • **to ~ sth up as a model** presentar algo como modelo • **to ~ sb up to ridicule** poner en ridículo a algn
4 (= *delay*) [+ *person, traffic*] retrasar; (= *stop*) detener, parar; [+ *work*] interrumpir; [+ *delivery, payment*] suspender • **we were held up by the traffic** nos retrasamos por culpa del tráfico • **I was held up at the office** me entretuvieron en la oficina • **we were held up for three hours** no nos pudimos mover durante tres horas • **the train was held up** el tren sufrió un retraso • **the train was held up by fog** el tren venía con retraso debido a la niebla • **we are being held up by a shortage of bricks** la escasez de ladrillos nos está retrasando, la escasez de ladrillos está entorpeciendo el trabajo
5 (= *rob*) atracar, asaltar • **to ~ up a bank** atracar un banco
VI + ADV 1 [*weather*] seguir bueno
2 (= *survive, last*) resistir • **to ~ up under the strain** soportar bien la presión
3 (= *remain strong*) mantenerse bien
▸ **hold with** VI + PREP estar de acuerdo con, aprobar

holdall ['həʊldɔːl] N (*Brit*) bolsa *f* de viaje

holder ['həʊldəʳ] N 1 (= *tenant*) inquilino/a *m/f*
2 (= *bearer*) [*of letter*] portador(a) *m/f*; [*of bonds*] tenedor(a) *m/f*; [*of title, office*] titular *mf*; [*of record*] poseedor(a) *m/f*
3 (= *object*) • **pen ~** portaplumas *m inv* • **cigarette ~** boquilla *f* • **lamp ~** portalámparas *m inv*

holding ['həʊldɪŋ] N 1 (= *land*) pequeña propiedad *f*, parcela *f*, chacra *f* (*S. Cone*); **holdings** terrenos *mpl*
2 (*Comm*) valores *mpl* en cartera
3 (= *act*) tenencia *f*
CPD ▸ **holding company** (*Comm*) holding *m* ▸ **holding operation** operación *f* de contención

holdout ['həʊldaʊt] N (*US*) • **Britain has been the ~ in trying to negotiate** Gran Bretaña es el único que se resiste a negociar

holdup ['həʊldʌp] N 1 (= *robbery*) atraco *m* (a mano armada), asalto *m* (a mano armada) • **a bank clerk was injured in the ~** un empleado del banco resultó herido en el atraco *or* asalto
2 (= *stoppage, delay*) demora *f*, retraso *m* • **no-one explained the reason for the ~** nadie explicó el motivo de la demora *or* del retraso
3 (= *traffic jam*) embotellamiento *m*, atasco *m*

• **a ~ on the motorway** un embotellamiento *or* atasco en la autopista
CPD ▸ **holdup man** atracador *m*

hole [həʊl] N **1** (*gen*) agujero *m*, hoyo *m*; (*in road*) bache *m*; (= *gap, opening*) boquete *m*; (*in wall, defences, dam*) brecha *f*; (= *burrow*) madriguera *f*; (*Golf*) hoyo *m* • **through a ~ in the clouds** a través de un claro entre las nubes • **to dig a ~** cavar un hoyo • **these socks are full of ~s** estos calcetines están llenos de agujeros • **his argument is full of ~s** sus argumentos están llenos de fallas • **~ in the heart** soplo *m* cardíaco • **his injury leaves a ~ in the team** su lesión deja un vacío en el equipo • **to make a ~ in sth** hacer un agujero en algo • **buying the car made a ~ in his savings** la compra del coche le costó una buena parte de sus ahorros • **to pick ~s in sth** (*fig*) encontrar defectos en algo • **to wear a ~ in sth** agujerear algo; ▹ **hole-in-the-wall**
2* (*fig*) (= *difficulty*) aprieto *m*, apuro *m* • **to be in a ~*** estar en un apuro *or* aprieto • **he got me out of a ~*** me sacó de un aprieto *or* apuro
3* (= *dwelling, room*) cuchitril *m*, tugurio *m* (*esp LAm*); (= *town*) poblacho *m*, pueblo *m* de mala muerte*
VT **1** (= *make hole in*) (*gen*) agujerear; [+ *ship*] abrir una brecha en
2 [+ *ball*] (*Golf*) meter en el hoyo; (*Snooker*) meter en la tronera
VI (*Golf*) • **to ~ in one** hacer un hoyo de un golpe
▸ **hole up** VI + ADV esconderse

hole-and-corner [ˈhəʊlənˈkɔːnəʳ] ADJ furtivo • **to do sth in a hole-and-corner way** hacer algo de tapadillo

hole-in-the-wall* [ˈhəʊlɪnðəˈwɔːl] N (*Brit*) cajero *m* automático

holey* [ˈhəʊlɪ] ADJ [*shirt, sweater*] lleno de agujeros, lleno de rotos; [*socks*] con muchos tomates*

holiday [ˈhɒlədɪ] N (*esp Brit*) (= *period*) vacaciones *fpl*; (= *public*) fiesta *f*; (= *day*) día *m* de fiesta, día *m* feriado, feriado *m* (*LAm*) • **to be/go on ~** (*Brit*) estar/ir de vacaciones • **to take a ~** tomarse unas vacaciones • **~s with pay** vacaciones *fpl* retribuidas • **tomorrow is a ~** mañana es fiesta • **to declare a day a ~** declarar un día festivo • **it was no ~, I can tell you*** no fue ningún lecho de rosas, te lo aseguro
VI (*Brit*) pasar las vacaciones
CPD ▸ **holiday camp** (*Brit*) (*at beach*) colonia *f* de veraneo, colonia *f* de vacaciones ▸ **holiday clothes** (*Brit*) ropa *fsing* de veraneo ▸ **holiday cottage** casa *f* rural, casita *f* de campo ▸ **holiday entitlement** (= *number of days*) días *mpl* de vacaciones • **to take one's full ~ entitlement** tomarse todos los días de vacaciones que le corresponden a uno ▸ **holiday home** (*esp Brit*) casa *f or* piso *m etc* para ocupar durante las vacaciones ▸ **holiday job** (*Brit*) trabajo *m* para las vacaciones ▸ **holiday mood** (*Brit*) • **to be in the ~ mood** tener un espíritu festivo ▸ **holiday pay** (*esp Brit*) paga *f* de las vacaciones ▸ **holiday rep** (*Brit*) (= *travel rep, tour rep*) representante *mf* de la agencia de viajes ▸ **holiday resort** (*Brit*) lugar *m* de veraneo ▸ **holiday season** (*Brit*) época *f* de vacaciones; (*US*) Navidades *fpl* ▸ **the holiday spirit** el espíritu festivo ▸ **holiday traffic** tráfico *m* de las vacaciones ▸ **holiday village** pueblo *m* de veraneo

holiday-maker [ˈhɒlədɪˌmeɪkəʳ] N (*Brit*) (*gen*) turista *mf*; (*in summer*) veraneante *mf*

holier-than-thou [ˈhəʊlɪəðənˈðaʊ] ADJ (*pej*) [*attitude, tone of voice*] de superioridad moral • **she's always so holier-than-thou about everything** siempre está dando lecciones de moralidad sobre todo

holiness [ˈhəʊlɪnɪs] N [*of place, person*] santidad *f*; [*of day*] lo sagrado • **His Holiness (the Pope)** Su Santidad (el Papa)

holism [ˈhəʊlɪzəm] N holismo *m*

holistic [həʊˈlɪstɪk] ADJ holístico

Holland [ˈhɒlənd] N Holanda *f*

hollandaise [ˌhɒlənˈdeɪz] ADJ • **~ sauce** salsa *f* holandesa

holler* [ˈhɒləʳ] (*esp US*) VT gritar
VI gritar

hollow [ˈhɒləʊ] ADJ **1** [*tree, object*] hueco; [*cheeks, eyes*] hundido • **it's ~ (inside)** está hueco (por dentro) • **his eyes were ~** tenía los ojos hundidos • **she had a ~ feeling in her stomach** tenía una sensación de vacío en el estómago • **he felt ~ inside** se sentía vacío por dentro • **look how much you've eaten, you must have ~ legs!** ¡qué barbaridad, lo que has comido! ¡debes de tener la solitaria!
2 [*gesture, laugh*] falso; [*threat, promise*] vano, falso; [*words*] hueco, vacío; [*person, victory, success*] vacío • **their marriage was a ~ sham** su matrimonio era una pura farsa *or* pantomima • **to ring** *or* **sound ~** sonar (a) falso • **his denial has a ~ ring (to it)** su negativa suena a falso
3 [*sound, noise*] hueco • **a deep, ~ voice whispered his name** una voz profunda y cavernosa susurró su nombre • **her voice sounded tired and ~** su voz sonaba cansada y apagada
N **1** (= *hole*) hueco *m*
2 (= *depression*) (*in ground, surface*) hoyo *m* • **the ~ of one's hand** el cuenco *or* (*Mex*) la cuenca de la mano
ADV • **to beat sb ~*** dar una paliza a algn*
▸ **hollow out** VT + ADV ahuecar

hollow-cheeked [ˌhɒləʊˈtʃiːkt] ADJ de mejillas hundidas

hollow-eyed [ˈhɒləʊˈaɪd] ADJ de ojos hundidos; (*with fatigue*) ojeroso

hollowly [ˈhɒləʊlɪ] ADV • **she laughed ~** soltó una risa que sonaba a falsa

hollowness [ˈhɒləʊnɪs] N **1** [*of words, promise*] falsedad *f*; [*of gesture, threat, victory*] vacuidad *f*; [*of laugh*] lo falso
2 [*of object, surface*] el hecho de ser hueco; [*of cheeks, eyes*] lo hundido • **its ~ means it can float** el hecho de que es hueco significa que puede flotar, al ser hueco puede flotar • **the ~ of her voice** lo apagado de su voz

holly [ˈhɒlɪ] N acebo *m*
CPD ▸ **holly berry** baya *f* de acebo ▸ **holly tree** acebo *m*

hollyhock [ˈhɒlɪhɒk] N malva *f* loca

Hollywood [ˈhɒlɪˌwʊd] N Hollywood *m*

holmium [ˈhɒlmɪəm] N holmio *m*

holm oak [ˈhəʊmˈəʊk] N encina *f*

holocaust [ˈhɒləkɔːst] N (*fig*) holocausto *m*

hologram [ˈhɒləgræm] N holograma *m*

holograph [ˈhɒləgrɑːf] ADJ ológrafo
N ológrafo *m*

holography [hɒˈlɒgrəfɪ] N holografía *f*

hols* [hɒlz] NPL = **holidays**

holster [ˈhəʊlstəʳ] N funda *f* de pistola

holy [ˈhəʊlɪ] (COMPAR: **holier**, SUPERL: **holiest**) ADJ [*place, book*] sagrado, santo; [*church, shrine*] sagrado; [*person*] santo; [*day*] de precepto • **the holiest day in the Jewish calendar** el principal día de precepto *or* la principal fiesta de guardar del calendario judío • IDIOMS: • **~ cow** *or* **mackerel** *or* **smoke!*** ¡(por) Dios bendito!* • **~ shit!‡** ¡mierda!‡ • **to be a ~ terror** [*child*] ser (más malo que) un demonio
CPD ▸ **the Holy Bible** la Santa Biblia ▸ **the Holy City** la Ciudad Santa ▸ **Holy Communion** Sagrada Comunión *f* ▸ **the Holy Father** el Santo Padre ▸ **the Holy Ghost** el Espíritu Santo ▸ **the Holy Grail** el Santo Grial ▸ **the Holy Land** la Tierra Santa ▸ **holy man** santón *m* ▸ **holy matrimony** santo matrimonio *m* ▸ **holy of holies** (*lit, fig*) sanctasanctórum *m* ▸ **holy oil** santos óleos *mpl* ▸ **holy orders** órdenes *fpl* sagradas • **to be in ~ orders** ser sacerdote • **to take ~ orders** ordenarse sacerdote ▸ **the Holy Roman Empire** el Sacro Imperio Romano Germánico ▸ **Holy Saturday** Sábado *m* Santo ▸ **the Holy See** la Santa Sede ▸ **the Holy Sepulchre** el Santo Sepulcro ▸ **the Holy Spirit** el Espíritu Santo ▸ **the Holy Trinity** la Santísima Trinidad ▸ **holy war** guerra *f* santa ▸ **holy water** agua *f* bendita ▸ **Holy Week** Semana *f* Santa ▸ **Holy Writ**† Sagradas Escrituras *fpl*; ▹ **Scripture**

Holyrood [ˈhɒlɪruːd] N *el parlamento escocés*

homage [ˈhɒmɪdʒ] N homenaje *m* • **to pay ~ to** rendir homenaje a

homburg [ˈhɒmbɜːg] N sombrero *m* de fieltro

home [həʊm] N **1** (= *house*) casa *f*; (= *residence*) domicilio *m* • **there's no place like ~** como su casa no hay dos • **this tool has no ~** esta herramienta no tiene lugar propio • **at ~** en casa • **to feel at ~** sentirse como en casa • **make yourself at ~** estás en tu casa • **is Mr Lyons at ~?** ¿está el señor Lyons? • **to make sb feel at ~** hacer que algn se sienta en casa • **the duchess is at ~ on Fridays** la duquesa recibe los viernes • **Lady Rebecca is not at ~ to anyone** Lady Rebecca no recibe a nadie • **at ~ and abroad** dentro y fuera del país • **he is at ~ with the topic** domina bien la materia • **I'm not at ~ in Japanese** apenas me defiendo en japonés, sé muy poco de japonés • **~ from ~** (*Brit*) • **~ away from ~** (*US*) segunda casa • **for us this is a ~ from ~** aquí estamos como en casa, esta es como una segunda casa para nosotros • **to give sb/sth a ~** dar casa a algn/algo; (= *position, niche*) encontrar sitio para algn/algo • **he comes from a good ~** es de buena familia • **"good home wanted for puppy"** "búscase buen hogar para perrito" • **the puppy went to a good ~** el perrito fue a vivir con una buena familia • **to have a ~ of one's own** tener casa propia • **~ sweet ~** hogar, dulce hogar • PROVERB: • **an Englishman's ~ is his castle** para el inglés su casa es como su castillo
2 (= *refuge*) hogar *m*; (= *hospital, hostel*) asilo *m* • **~ for the aged** residencia *f* de ancianos, asilo *m* de ancianos • **children's ~** centro *m* de acogida de menores • **old people's ~** residencia *f* de ancianos, asilo *m* de ancianos
3 (= *country*) patria *f*; (= *town*) ciudad *f* natal; (= *origin*) cuna *f* • **we live in Madrid but my ~ is in Jaén** vivimos en Madrid pero nací en Jaén • **Scotland is the ~ of the haggis** Escocia es la patria del haggis • **he made his ~ in Italy** se estableció en Italia • **for some years he made his ~ in France** durante algunos años vivió en Francia
4 (*Bio*) hábitat *m*
5 (*Sport*) (= *target area*) meta *f*; (= *home ground*) • **to play at ~** jugar en casa • **Villasanta are at ~ to Castroforte** Villasanta recibe en casa a Castroforte • **they lost nine games at ~** perdieron nueve partidos en casa
6 (*Comput*) punto *m* inicial, punto *m* de partida
ADV **1** (*lit*) (= *at home*) en casa; (= *to home*) a casa • **to be ~** estar en casa; (= *upon return*) estar de vuelta en casa • **I'll be ~ at five o'clock** (*upon return*) estaré en casa a las cinco • **it's a long journey ~** hay mucho camino hasta llegar a casa • **as we say back**

~ como decimos en mi tierra • **back ~ in Australia** en mi tierra, (en) Australia • **to come ~** volver a casa • **to be ~ and dry** respirar tranquilo/a • **to get ~** llegar a casa • **to go ~** volver a casa; (*from abroad*) volver a la patria • **he leaves ~ at eight** sale de casa a las ocho • **she left ~ at the age of 17** se marchó de casa cuando tenía 17 años • **that remark came near ~** esa observación le hirió en lo vivo • **to see sb ~** acompañar a algn a su casa • **to send sb ~** mandar a algn a casa • **to stay ~** quedarse en casa • **it's nothing to write ~ about*** no tiene nada de particular
2 (*fig*) • **to bring sth ~ to sb** hacerle ver algo a algn • **it came ~ to me** me di cuenta de ello • **to drive sth ~**: • **to drive a point ~** subrayar un punto • **to drive a nail ~** hacer que un clavo entre a fondo • **to strike ~** (= *hit target*) [*shell, bullet*] dar en el blanco; (= *go right in*) [*hammer, nail*] remachar; ▹ **press**
VI [*pigeons*] volver a casa
CPD ▸ **home address** (*on form*) domicilio *m* • **my ~ address** mi dirección particular, las señas de mi casa ▸ **home assembly** montaje *m* propio • **for ~ assembly** para montaje propio; ▹ **home-assembly** ▸ **home automation** domótica *f* ▸ **home banking** banco *m* en casa ▸ **home base** [*of person*] lugar *m* de residencia; [*of guerrillas*] base *f* de operaciones; [*of company*] sede *f* ▸ **home birth** parto *m* a domicilio ▸ **home brew** (= *beer*) cerveza *f* casera; (= *wine*) vino *m* casero ▸ **home buying** compra *f* de vivienda ▸ **home comforts** comodidades *fpl* domésticas ▸ **home computer** ordenador *m* doméstico ▸ **home computing** informática *f* doméstica ▸ **home cooking** cocina *f* casera ▸ **the Home Counties** (*Brit*) *los condados alrededor de Londres* ▸ **home country** patria *f*, país *m* de origen ▸ **home delivery** [*of food*] entrega *f* a domicilio; [*of baby*] parto *m* a domicilio ▸ **home economics** (*Scol*) ciencia *f* del hogar ▸ **home field** (*US*) (*Sport*) casa *f* • **to play on one's ~ field** jugar en casa ▸ **home fries** (*US*) *carne picada frita con patatas y col* ▸ **home front** frente *m* interno ▸ **home ground** (*Sport*) • **to play at one's ~ ground** jugar en casa • **to be on ~ ground** (*fig*) estar en su terreno *or* lugar ▸ **Home Guard** (*Brit*) *cuerpo de voluntarios para la defensa nacional durante la segunda guerra mundial* ▸ **home help** (= *act*) atención *f* domiciliaria, ayuda *f* a domicilio; (*Brit*) (= *person*) asistente/a *m/f* (*especialmente los que, a cargo de la seguridad social, ayudan en las tareas domésticas a personas necesitadas*) ▸ **home helper** (*US*) asistente/a *m/f* ▸ **home improvements** reformas *fpl* en casa ▸ **home industries** (*Comm*) industrias *fpl* nacionales ▸ **home journey** viaje *m* a casa, viaje *m* de vuelta ▸ **home leave** permiso *m* para irse a casa ▸ **home life** vida *f* de familia, vida *f* doméstica ▸ **home loan** préstamo *m* para la vivienda ▸ **home market** (*Comm*) mercado *m* nacional, mercado *m* interior ▸ **home match** (*Sport*) partido *m* en casa ▸ **home movie** película *f* hecha por un aficionado ▸ **home nations** (*Brit*) • **the ~ nations** las cuatro naciones británicas ▸ **home news** (*gen*) noticias *fpl* de casa; (*Pol*) información *f* nacional ▸ **Home Office** (*Brit*) Ministerio *m* del Interior, Gobernación *f* (*Mex*) ▸ **home owner** propietario/a *m/f* de una casa • **~ owners** propietarios *mpl* de viviendas ▸ **home ownership** propiedad *f* de viviendas ▸ **home page** (*Internet*) (= *personal page*) página *f* personal; (= *webpage*) página *f* web; (= *start page*) página *f* de inicio ▸ **home port** puerto *m* de origen ▸ **home product** (*Comm*) producto *m* nacional ▸ **home rule** autonomía *f* ▸ **home run** (*Baseball*) jonrón *m*; (= *return journey*) [*of ship, truck*] viaje *m* de vuelta ▸ **home sales** ventas *fpl* nacionales ▸ **Home Secretary** (*Brit*) Ministro *m* del Interior ▸ **home shopping** venta *f* por correo; (*TV, Telec*) televenta *f* ▸ **the home side** (*Sport*) el equipo de casa, el equipo local ▸ **home straight** (*Sport*) recta *f* final • **to be in the ~ straight** (*fig*) estar en la última recta ▸ **home stretch** = **home straight** ▸ **the home team** (*Sport*) el equipo de casa, el equipo local ▸ **home town** ciudad *f* natal ▸ **home trade** (*Comm*) comercio *m* interior ▸ **home truths** • **to tell sb a few ~ truths** decir cuatro verdades a algn ▸ **home victory** (*Sport*) victoria *f* en casa ▸ **home video** vídeo *m* amateur, video *m* amateur (*LAm*) ▸ **home visit** visita *f* a domicilio ▸ **home waters** aguas *fpl* territoriales ▸ **home win** (*Sport*) victoria *f* en casa

▸ **home in on, home on to** VI + PREP
1 [*missiles*] dirigirse hacia • **to ~ in on the target** buscar el blanco
2 (*fig*) concentrarse en

> **HOME COUNTIES**
> Los **Home Counties** son los condados que se encuentran en los alrededores de Londres: Berkshire, Buckinghamshire, Essex, Hertfordshire, Kent, Surrey, Middlesex y Sussex, un alto porcentaje de cuya población se encuentra en buena posición económica. De ahí que el término **Home Counties** haya adquirido dimensiones culturales y a la gente que vive en ellos se les considere en general personas adineradas de clase media-alta que, además, tienen al hablar un acento muy particular, conocido como **RP**.
> ▹ **ENGLISH**

home-assembly [ˌhəʊmə'semblɪ] ADJ para montaje propio
home-baked ['həʊm'beɪkt] ADJ [*bread, cake*] casero
homebody ['həʊmbədɪ] N (PL: **homebodies**) (*US*) persona *f* hogareña, persona *f* casera
homebound ['həʊmbaʊnd] ADJ • **the ~ traveller** el viajero que vuelve a *or* se dirige a casa
homeboy* ['həʊmbɔɪ] N (*US*) chico *m* del barrio
homebred ['həʊmbred] ADJ (= *indigenous*) nativo, local
home-brewed ['həʊm'bruːd] ADJ hecho en casa, casero
homecoming ['həʊmkʌmɪŋ] N regreso *m* al hogar
CPD ▸ **Homecoming Queen** (*US*) *reina de la fiesta de antiguos alumnos*; ▹ **YEARBOOK**
homegirl* ['həʊmgɜːl] N (*US*) chica *f* del barrio
home-grown ['həʊm'grəʊn] ADJ de cosecha propia; (= *not imported*) del país
homeland ['həʊmlænd] N **1** (= *home country*) patria *f*, tierra *f* natal
2 (*South Africa*) territorio *m* nativo
homeless ['həʊmlɪs] ADJ sin hogar, sin vivienda • **the storm left a hundred ~** la tormenta dejó a cien personas sin hogar *or* vivienda • **to be made ~** quedarse sin hogar • **to make ~** (*gen*) dejar sin hogar; [+ *tenant*] desahuciar
NPL • **the ~** las personas sin hogar
homelessness ['həʊmlɪsnɪs] N el estar sin hogar • **the increase in ~** el aumento de la cifra de los que no tienen hogar
homeliness ['həʊmlɪnɪs] N llaneza *f*, sencillez *f*
home-lover ['həʊmˌlʌvəʳ] N persona *f* hogareña, persona *f* casera
home-loving ['həʊmˌlʌvɪŋ] ADJ hogareño, casero
homely ['həʊmlɪ] ADJ (COMPAR: **homelier**, SUPERL: **homeliest**) **1** (= *like home*) [*food*] casero; [*atmosphere*] familiar; [*advice*] prosaico • **it's very ~ here** aquí se está como en casa
2 (*Brit*) [*woman*] sencillo
3 (*US*) (= *unattractive*) poco atractivo
home-made ['həʊm'meɪd] ADJ hecho en casa
home-maker ['həʊmˌmeɪkəʳ] N (*US*) ama *f* de casa
homeopath *etc* ['həʊmɪəʊpæθ] N (*US*) = **homoeopath** *etc*
homepage ['həʊmpeɪdʒ] N = **home page**
Homer ['həʊməʳ] N Homero
homer* ['həʊməʳ] N (*Brit*) trabajo *m* fuera de hora, chollo‡ *m*
Homeric [həʊ'merɪk] ADJ homérico
homeroom ['həʊmrʊm] (*US*) N clase *f*
CPD ▸ **homeroom teacher** ≈ tutor(a) *m/f*
homesick ['həʊmsɪk] ADJ • **to be ~** tener morriña • **I feel ~** echo de menos mi casa
homesickness ['həʊmsɪknɪs] N nostalgia *f*, morriña *f*
homespun ['həʊmspʌn] ADJ tejido en casa, hecho en casa; (*fig*) llano
homestead ['həʊmsted] N (*esp US*) casa *f*, caserío *m*; (= *farm*) granja *f*
homeward ['həʊmwəd] ADJ de regreso
ADV (*also* **homewards**) hacia casa • **~ bound** camino a la casa; (*Naut*) con rumbo al puerto de origen
homewards ['həʊmwədz] ADV (*esp Brit*) = **homeward**
homework ['həʊmwɜːk] N deberes *mpl*, tarea *f* • **my geography ~** mis deberes de geografía, mi tarea de geografía • **to do one's ~** (= *schoolwork*) hacer los deberes *or* la tarea; (*fig*) documentarse, hacer el trabajo preparatorio • **have you done your ~?** ¿has hecho los deberes?
CPD ▸ **homework club** *club escolar para hacer los deberes*
homeworker ['həʊmwɜːkəʳ] N asalariado/a *m/f* que trabaja desde casa
homeworking ['həʊmwɜːkɪŋ] N trabajo *m* desde casa
homey* ['həʊmɪ] ADJ (COMPAR: **homier**, SUPERL: **homiest**) (*US*) íntimo, cómodo
homicidal [ˌhɒmɪ'saɪdl] ADJ homicida • **~ maniac** maniaco/a *m/f* con tendencias homicidas • **to feel ~** (*fig*) sentirse capaz de matar a alguien, tener ganas de matar a alguien
homicide ['hɒmɪsaɪd] N **1** (= *act*) homicidio *m*
2 (= *person*) homicida *mf*
homily ['hɒmɪlɪ] N (PL: **homilies**) homilía *f*; (*fig*) sermón *m*
homing ['həʊmɪŋ] ADJ [*missile*] buscador, cazador
CPD ▸ **homing device** dispositivo *m* buscador de blancos ▸ **homing instinct** instinto *m* de volver al hogar ▸ **homing pigeon** paloma *f* mensajera
hominid ['hɒmɪnɪd] N homínido *m*
hominy ['hɒmɪnɪ] N (*US*) maíz *m* molido
homo†‡ ['həʊməʊ] N (*abbr*) (= **homosexual**) (*pej*) marica‡ *m*
homoeopath, homeopath (*US*) ['həʊmɪəʊpæθ] N homeópata *mf*
homoeopathic, homeopathic (*US*) [ˌhəʊmɪəʊ'pæθɪk] ADJ homeopático
homoeopathy, homeopathy (*US*) [ˌhəʊmɪ'ɒpəθɪ] N homeopatía *f*
homoerotic [ˌhəʊməʊɪ'rɒtɪk] ADJ homoerótico
homoeroticism [ˌhəʊməʊɪ'rɒtɪsɪzəm] N homoerotismo *m*

homogeneity ['hɒməʊdʒə'niːɪtɪ] (N) homogeneidad *f*
homogeneous [ˌhɒmə'dʒiːnɪəs] (ADJ) homogéneo
homogenization [həˌmɒdʒənaɪ'zeɪʃən] (N) **1** [*of group, population, society*] uniformización *f* • **the ~ of culture** la uniformización de la cultura
2 [*of substance*] homogeneización *f*
homogenize [hə'mɒdʒənaɪz] (VT) homogeneizar
homogenized [hə'mɒdʒənaɪzd] (ADJ) [*group, population, society*] uniformizado
(CPD) ▸ **homogenized milk** leche *f* homogeneizada
homogenous [hə'mɒdʒɪnəs] (ADJ) = **homogeneous**
homograph ['hɒməʊgrɑːf] (N) homógrafo *m*
homonym ['hɒmənɪm] (N) homónimo *m*
homonymous [hə'mɒnɪməs] (ADJ) homónimo
homophobe [ˌhəʊməʊ'fəʊb] (N) homófobo/a *m/f*
homophobia ['hɒməʊ'fəʊbɪə] (N) homofobia *f*
homophobic ['hɒməʊ'fəʊbɪk] (ADJ) homofóbico
homophone ['hɒməfəʊn] (N) homófono *m*
homophonic [ˌhɒmə'fɒnɪk] (ADJ) homófono
homo sapiens [ˌhəʊməʊ'sæpɪenz] (N) homo sapiens *m*
homosexual ['hɒməʊ'seksjʊəl] (ADJ) homosexual
(N) homosexual *mf*
homosexuality ['hɒməʊseksju'ælɪtɪ] (N) homosexualidad *f*
hon* [hʌn] (N) (*US*) (= **honey**) cariño • **hi, hon!** ¡hola, cariño!
Hon. (ABBR) (*in titles*) = **Honorary** *or* **Honourable**
honcho* ['hɒntʃəʊ] (N) jefazo/a* *m/f* • **head ~** mandamás* *mf*
Honduran [hɒn'djuərən] (ADJ) hondureño
(N) hondureño/a *m/f*
Honduras [hɒn'djuərəs] (N) Honduras *f*
hone [həʊn] (VT) afilar
(N) piedra *f* de afilar
honest ['ɒnɪst] (ADJ) **1** (= *frank*) sincero • **to be (perfectly) ~ ...** para ser (totalmente) sincero *or* franco ... • **to be ~ about sth** ser sincero *or* franco con respecto a algo • **I'd like your ~ opinion** me gustaría que me dieras tu sincera opinión • **that's the ~ truth** eso es la pura verdad • **to be (perfectly) ~ with you** para serle sincero *or* franco, si quiere que le diga la verdad • **I'll be ~ with you** voy a serte sincero • **you haven't been ~ with us** no has sido sincero con nosotros • **be ~ with yourself** sé sincero contigo mismo • IDIOM: • **to make an ~ woman of sb**: • **he finally made an ~ woman of her** (*hum*) al final hizo lo que Dios manda y se casó con ella
2 (= *trustworthy, law-abiding*) [*person*] honrado, honesto • **he's very ~ in money matters** es muy honrado *or* honesto en lo que respecta al dinero • **he hasn't done an ~ day's work in his life** no ha trabajado honradamente en su vida • **to make an ~ living** ganarse la vida honradamente • **by ~ means** de forma honrada • **it was an ~ mistake** no fue un error deliberado • IDIOM: • **to earn an ~ penny** *or* **crust** ganarse el pan honradamente
3 (= *genuine*) sencillo • **good, ~ country cooking** cocina rústica buena y sencilla
(ADV)* de verdad • **I didn't know about it, ~** no lo sabía, de verdad, de verdad que no lo sabía • **~ to God** *or* **goodness** palabra (de honor), te lo juro • **~ injun†*** palabra, ¡por estas!
(CPD) ▸ **honest broker** (*Brit*) (*esp Pol*) mediador(a) *m/f*
honestly ['ɒnɪstlɪ] (ADV) **1** (= *truly*) sinceramente, francamente • **I ~ believe this is the right decision** creo sinceramente *or* francamente que esta es la decisión correcta • **he cannot ~ call this a good law** no puede, en honor a la verdad, llamar a esto una buena ley • **no, ~, I'm fine** no, de verdad *or* de veras *or* en serio, estoy bien • **I didn't do it, ~** de verdad que no lo hice • **do you ~ expect me to believe that?** ¿de verdad *or* de veras esperas que me lo crea? • **I can ~ say that it doesn't bother me** puedo decir con toda sinceridad *or* franqueza que no me importa • **I can't ~ say I ever knew him well** la verdad es que no puedo decir que lo conociese bien • **can you ~ say you've ever thought about it?** ¿puedes decir sin mentir que has pensado alguna vez en ello? • **I ~ thought you'd be pleased** de verdad *or* de veras pensé que te gustaría
2 (= *truthfully*) [*speak, answer*] sinceramente, con sinceridad
3 (= *legally*) honradamente • **if he couldn't get money ~, he stole** si no podía conseguir dinero honradamente, robaba
4 (*showing exasperation*) vamos, por favor • **"honestly," said Barbara, "that woman ..."** —vamos *or* por favor —dijo Barbara —esa mujer ... • **oh, ~!** ¡por favor!, ¡anda, anda!
honest-to-God ['ɒnɪstə'gɒd] (ADJ) cien por cien
honest-to-goodness ['ɒnɪstə'gʊdnɪs] (ADJ) = **honest-to-God**
honesty ['ɒnɪstɪ] (N) **1** (= *sincerity*) sinceridad *f* • **I admire his ~** admiro su sinceridad • **in all ~ ...** para ser sincero *or* franco ... • IDIOM: • **~ is the best policy** lo mejor es ir con la sinceridad por delante
2 (= *trustworthiness*) honradez *f*, honestidad *f*
(CPD) ▸ **honesty box** *caja donde se deposita el dinero para pagar algo cuando no hay nadie para recogerlo en persona*
honey ['hʌnɪ] (N) **1** (*from bees*) miel *f*
2 (*US**) (= *form of address*) cariño *m* • **hi, ~!** ¡hola, cariño! • **is everything ok, ~?** ¿todo bien, cariño *or* mi vida?* • **she's a ~** es un encanto
(CPD) ▸ **honey blonde** rubia *f* miel; ▹ **honey-blonde**
honeybee ['hʌnibiː] (N) abeja *f*
honey-blonde [ˌhʌnɪ'blɒnd] (ADJ) rubio miel; ▹ **honey**
honeybun* ['hʌnɪbʌn], **honeybunch*** ['hʌnɪbʌntʃ] (N) (*esp US*) cielito *m*
honey-coloured ['hʌnɪˌkʌləd] (ADJ) [*stone, hair*] (de) color miel • **the honey-coloured buildings of Salamanca** los edificios de color miel de Salamanca
honeycomb ['hʌnɪkəʊm] (N) panal *m*; (*fig*) laberinto *m*
(VT) (*fig*) • **the hill is ~ed with tunnels** el cerro está lleno de cuevas • **the building is ~ed with passages** hay un laberinto de pasillos en el edificio
honeydew melon ['hʌnɪdjuː'melən] (N) melón *m* dulce
honeyed ['hʌnɪd] (ADJ) meloso, melifluo
honeyfuggle* ['hʌnɪˌfʌgəl] (VT) (*US*) obtener mediante un truco
honeymoon ['hʌnɪmuːn] (N) (*lit, fig*) luna *f* de miel • **to go on ~** irse de luna de miel
(VI) pasar la luna de miel
(CPD) ▸ **the honeymoon couple** la pareja de recién casados ▸ **honeymoon period** (*Pol*) período *m* de gracia, cien días *mpl*
honeymooner ['hʌnɪˌmuːnəʳ] (N) *persona que está en su luna de miel*
honeypot ['hʌnɪpɒt] (N) mielera *f*
honeysuckle ['hʌnɪˌsʌkl] (N) madreselva *f*
honeytrap ['hʌnɪtræp] (N) trampa *f* (*por la que se seduce sexualmente a la víctima para obtener información*)
Hong Kong [ˌhɒŋ'kɒŋ] (N) Hong Kong *m*
honk [hɒŋk] (VI) [*driver*] tocar la bocina, tocar el claxon (*LAm*); [*goose*] graznar
(N) [*of goose*] graznido *m*; [*of horn*] bocinazo *m*
honkie*, **honky*** ['hɒŋkɪ] (N) (PL: **honkies**) (*US*) (*pej*) blanco/a *m/f*, blancucho/a* *m/f*
honky-tonk* ['hɒŋkɪˌtɒŋk] (N) **1** (*US*) (= *club*) garito *m*
2 (*Mus*) honky-tonk* *m*
Honolulu [ˌhɒnə'luːluː] (N) Honolulú *m*
honor ['ɒnəʳ] (N) (*US*) = **honour**
(CPD) ▸ **honor society** (*US*) club *m* de alumnos distinguidos
honorable ['ɒnərəbl] (ADJ) (*US*) = **honourable**
honorably ['ɒnərəblɪ] (ADV) (*US*) = **honourably**
honorarium [ˌɒnə'rɛərɪəm] (N) (PL: **honorariums** *or* **honoraria** [ˌɒnə'rɛərɪə]) honorarios *mpl*
honorary ['ɒnərərɪ] (ADJ) [*member, president*] de honor, honorario; [*title*] honorífico; [*secretary*] (= *unpaid*) no remunerado • **an ~ degree** un doctorado "honoris causa"
honorific [ɒnə'rɪfɪk] (ADJ) honorífico
(N) título *m* honorífico
honour, **honor** (*US*) ['ɒnəʳ] (N) **1** (= *integrity, good name*) honor *m* • **a man of ~** un hombre de honor • **to be/feel (in) ~ bound to do sth** estar/sentirse moralmente obligado a hacer algo • **it's a matter of ~** es una cuestión de honor • **on my ~!** ¡palabra de honor! • **remember, you are on your ~ to report any irregularities** recuerde, es su deber moral informar de cualquier irregularidad • **to put sb on his/her ~ to do sth** hacer prometer a algn que va a hacer algo • **to have a sense of ~** tener pundonor • **to be an ~ to one's profession** ser un orgullo para su profesión • PROVERB: • **(there is) ~ among thieves** entre bueyes no hay cornadas; ▹ **debt, word**
2 (= *distinction, privilege*) honor *m* • **it's a great ~ for him** es un gran honor para él • **I had the ~ of meeting him** tuve el honor de conocerlo • **may I have the ~ (of this dance)?** ¿me concede este baile? • **would you do me the ~ of having lunch with me?** ¿me haría el honor de almorzar conmigo? • **you do me great ~ by accepting** me concede usted un gran honor al aceptar • **to bury sb with full military ~s** sepultar a algn con todos los honores militares • IDIOM: • **to do the ~s** (*introducing people, serving drinks or food*) hacer los honores; ▹ **guard, guest, lap², maid, roll**
3 (= *award*) (*by the state*) condecoración *f*; (*in contest*) galardón *m*
4 (= *homage*) honor *m* • **to do ~ to sb** • **to do sb ~** rendir honores a algn • **in ~ of sth/sb** en honor a algo/algn • **he will attend a dinner in his ~** asistirá a una cena en su honor
5 (*as title*) • **His Honour Judge Brodrick** el señor Juez Brodrick • **Your Honour** (*to judge*) su Señoría, señor Juez; (*US*) (*to mayor*) Excelentísimo Señor, su Señoría
6† (= *chastity, virginity*) honra *f*
7 honours (*Brit*) (*Univ*) • **she got first/second class ~s in French** ≈ terminó la carrera de francés con matrícula de honor/con notable • **to take ~s in chemistry** ≈ licenciarse en químicas • **to graduate with ~s** ≈ licenciarse (*con nota*)
8 (*Bridge*) **honours** honores *mpl*
(VT) **1** (= *compliment*) honrar • **I am ~ed by your confidence in me** su confianza en mí me honra • **I am deeply ~ed to be asked** me siento muy honrado de que me lo pidan

• **I should be ~ed if …** sería un honor para mí si … • **~ed guest** invitado/a *m/f* de honor • **to ~ sb with one's presence** (*liter or hum*) honrar a algn con su presencia
2 (= *respect*) honrar • **thou shalt ~ thy father and thy mother** honrarás a tu padre y a tu madre
3 (= *pay homage to*) rendir homenaje a
4 (= *decorate*) [*the state, authorities*] condecorar; (*in contest*) galardonar
5 (= *fulfil*) [+ *agreement, contract, promise*] cumplir, cumplir con
6 (= *pay*) [+ *cheque*] aceptar, pagar; [+ *debt*] liquidar, pagar
CPD ▸ **honour guard** (*US*) guardia *f* de honor ▸ **honor roll** (*US*) cuadro *m* de honor ▸ **honours degree** (*Brit*) (*Univ*) ≈ licenciatura *f* • **she has an ~s degree in French** es licenciada en filología francesa ▸ **Honours List** (*Brit*) lista *f* de condecoraciones • **Birthday Honours List** *lista de condecoraciones que otorga el monarca el día de su cumpleaños* • **New Year Honours List** *lista de condecoraciones que otorga el monarca el día de Año Nuevo*; ▷ DEAN'S LIST, DEGREE

HONOURS LIST

La **Honours List** es una lista de personas a las que se considera merecedoras de un reconocimiento especial por su labor, tanto en la vida pública como por servicios prestados a la zona en la que viven. Esta lista es elaborada por el Primer Ministro británico con la aprobación del monarca y se publica dos veces al año, la primera en Año Nuevo - la **New Year's Honours List** - y la segunda en junio, el día del cumpleaños de la reina - la **Queen's Birthday Honours List**. En la mayoría de los casos a estas personas se les reconoce su mérito con la concesión del título de miembro de la Orden del Imperio Británico, **Member of the Order of the British Empire** o **MBE**, u oficial de la Orden del Imperio Británico **Officer of the Order of the British Empire** u **OBE**.

honourable, honorable (*US*) [ˈɒnərəbl] ADJ (= *upright*) honrado; [*title*] honorable • **~ mention** mención *f* honorífica • **the ~ member for Woodford** (*Brit*) (*Parl*) el señor diputado de Woodford
honourably, honorably (*US*) [ˈɒnərəblɪ] ADV honradamente
honour-bound, honor-bound (*US*) [ˌɒnəˈbaʊnd] ADJ • **to be honour-bound to do sth** estar moralmente obligado a hacer algo
Hons. (*Univ*) ABBR = **Honours**
Hons. ABBR (*Univ*) = **honours degree**
Hon. Sec. ABBR = **Honorary Secretary**
hooch* [huːtʃ] N licor *m* (*esp ilícito*)
hood [hʊd] N **1** [*of cloak, raincoat*] capucha *f*; (*Univ*) muceta *f*
2 (*Brit*) (*Aut*) capota *f*; (*US*) capó *m*
3 (= *cover*) (*on pram*) capota; (*on cooker*) tapa *f*; (*on chimney pot*) campana *f*
4 (*esp US**) (= *hoodlum*) matón/ona *m/f*, gorila* *m*
hooded [ˈhʊdɪd] ADJ encapuchado
hoodie* [ˈhʊdɪ] N **1** (= *top*) jersey *m* con capucha
2 (= *person*) joven *mf* con capucha
hoodlum* [ˈhuːdləm] N matón/ona *m/f*, gorila* *m*
hoodoo [ˈhuːduː] N (= *voodoo*) vudú *m*; (= *jinx*) gafe *m*, mala suerte *f* • **there's a ~ on it** tiene gafe
hoodwink [ˈhʊdwɪŋk] VT engañar
hooey* [ˈhuːɪ] N música *f* celestial*
hoof [huːf] N (PL: **hoofs** *or* **hooves**) **1** [*of horse*] casco *m*; [*of other animals*] pezuña *f* • **cloven ~** pata *f* hendida • **cattle on the ~** ganado *m* en pie • **~ and mouth disease** (*US*) fiebre *f* aftosa, glosopeda *f*
2* [*of person*] (= *foot*) pezuña* *f*, pata* *f*
VT* • **to ~ it** (= *walk*) ir a pata*; (= *depart*) liar el petate*
hoofed [huːft] ADJ ungulado
hoofer† [ˈhuːfəʳ] N (*esp US*) (= *dancer*) bailarín/ina *m/f*
hoo-ha* [ˈhuːˌhɑː] N **1** (= *fuss*) lío* *m*, marimorena* *f*, follón *m* (*Sp**) • **there was a great hoo-ha about it** se armó la marimorena*
2 (= *noise*) estrépito *m*
3 (*pej*) (= *publicity*) bombo* *m*
hook [hʊk] N **1** (*gen*) gancho *m*; (*for painting*) alcayata *f*; (= *meat hook*) garfio *m*; (*Fishing*) anzuelo *m* • **the jacket hung from a ~** la chaqueta estaba colgada de un gancho • **he hung the painting on the ~** colgó el cuadro de la alcayata • IDIOMS: • **by ~ or by crook** por las buenas o por las malas, a como dé lugar (*LAm*) • **~, line and sinker**: • **he fell for it ~, line and sinker** se tragó el anzuelo • **to get sb off the ~** sacar a algn de un apuro • **to let sb off the ~** dejar escapar a algn • **to sling one's ~‡** (= *leave*) largarse*
2 (*Telec*) • **to take the phone off the ~** descolgar el teléfono • **to leave the phone off the ~** dejar el teléfono descolgado • IDIOM: • **the phone was ringing off the ~** (*esp US**) el teléfono echaba humo, el teléfono no paraba de sonar
3 (= *hanger*) percha *f*, colgadero *m*
4 (*Sew*) • **~s and eyes** corchetes *mpl*, macho y hembra *msing*
5 (*Boxing*) gancho *m*, crochet *m*
6 (*Golf*) golpe *m* con efecto a la izquierda
7 hooks‡ manos *fpl*
VT **1** (= *fasten*) enganchar; (*Fishing*) pescar • **to ~ sth to a rope** enganchar algo a una cuerda • **to ~ one's arms/feet around sth** envolver algo con los brazos/los pies • **to ~ a rope round a nail** atar una cuerda a un clavo
2* (= *catch*) • **she finally ~ed him** por fin lo enganchó
3 • IDIOM: • **to ~ it*** largarse*
VI **1** (= *fasten*) [*dress*] abrocharse; (= *connect*) engancharse
2 (*US‡*) trabajar como prostituta, hacer la calle*
▸ **hook on** VI + ADV engancharse (**to a**)
VT + ADV enganchar (**to a**)
▸ **hook up** VI + ADV **1** [*dress*] abrocharse
2 (*Rad, TV*) transmitir en cadena
VT + ADV **1** [+ *dress*] abrochar
2 (*Rad, TV*) conectar
hookah [ˈhʊkɑː] N narguile *m*
hooked [hʊkt] ADJ **1** (= *having a hook*) ganchudo
2* (= *addicted*) • **to be ~ on sth** estar enganchado a algo*, ser adicto a algo • **to be ~ on drugs** estar enganchado a las drogas*, ser adicto a las drogas • **to get ~ on sth** volverse adicto a algo
hooker [ˈhʊkəʳ] N **1‡** (*US*) (= *prostitute*) puta *f*
2 (*Sport*) talonador *m*
hookey*, hooky* [ˈhʊkɪ] N (*esp US*) • **to play ~** hacer novillos, hacer pirola
hook-nosed [ˌhʊkˈnəʊzd] ADJ de nariz ganchuda
hook-up [ˈhʊkʌp] N (*Rad, TV*) transmisión *f* en cadena; (*Elec*) acoplamiento *m* • **a hook-up with Eurovision** una conexión con Eurovisión
hookworm [ˈhʊkwɜːm] N anquilostoma *m*
hooky* [ˈhʊkɪ] N = **hookey**
hooligan [ˈhuːlɪgən] N gamberro/a *m/f*
hooliganism [ˈhuːlɪgənɪzəm] N gamberrismo *m*
hoop [huːp] N (*gen*) aro *m*, argolla *f*; [*of barrel*] fleje *m*; (= *croquet hoop*) argolla *f* • IDIOM: • **to put sb through the ~** hacer pasar penas a algn
hoopla [ˈhuːplɑː] N *juego consistente en lanzar aros y engancharlos*
hoopoe [ˈhuːpuː] N abubilla *f*
hooray [hʊˈreɪ] EXCL = **hurrah**
CPD ▸ **Hooray Henry** (*Brit*) (*pej*) señorito *m*
hoot [huːt] N **1** (= *sound*) [*of owl*] ululato *m*; (*esp Brit*) [*of car*] bocinazo *m*; [*of train*] silbato *m*; [*of siren*] toque *m* de sirena • **I don't care a ~*** (no) me importa un comino*
2 (= *laugh*) risotada *f* • **it was a ~*** ¡era para morirse de (la) risa!
VT **1** [+ *person*] abuchear • **to ~ sb off the stage** echar a algn de la escena a chiflidos
2 (*esp Brit*) [+ *horn*] tocar • **he ~ed his horn** tocó la bocina *or* (*esp LAm*) el claxon
VI **1** (= *make sound*) [*owl*] ulular; [*person*] (*in scorn*) abuchear; [*ship, train, factory hooter*] silbar • **to ~ with laughter** carcajear
2 (*esp Brit*) (*Aut*) tocar la bocina, tocar el claxon (*esp LAm*)
hooter [ˈhuːtəʳ] (*Brit*) N **1** [*of ship, factory*] sirena *f*; (*Aut†*) bocina *f*, claxon *m* (*esp LAm*)
2* (= *nose*) napia* *f*
hoover® [ˈhuːvəʳ] N aspiradora *f*
VT pasar la aspiradora por
VI pasar la aspiradora
hoovering [ˈhuːvərɪŋ] N • **to do the ~** pasar la aspiradora • **I've finished off the ~ upstairs** he terminado de pasar la aspiradora arriba
hooves [huːvz] NPL *of* **hoof**
hop¹ [hɒp] N **1** (= *jump*) salto *m*, brinco *m* • **hop, skip and jump** (*Sport*) triple salto *m* • **in one hop** de un salto • IDIOM: • **to catch sb on the hop** (*Brit**) pillar *or* (*LAm*) agarrar a algn desprevenido • **the uncertainty should keep them on the hop** (*Brit**) la incertidumbre los mantendrá en estado de alerta
2†* (= *dance*) baile *m*
3 (*Aer*) vuelo *m* corto • **in one hop** sin hacer escala
VI [*person, bird, animal*] dar saltos, brincar (*LAm*) • IDIOM: • **to be hopping mad*** echar chispas*
VT • **to hop it** (*Brit**) largarse* • **hop it!** ¡lárgate!*
▸ **hop along** VI + ADV avanzar a saltos
▸ **hop off** VI + PREP (= *get down from*) bajar de
VI + ADV **1** (= *get down*) bajar
2* largarse* • **hop off!** ¡lárgate!*
▸ **hop on** VI + PREP subir a
VI + ADV subir • **hop on!** ¡sube!
▸ **hop out** VI + ADV salir de un salto • **to hop out of bed** saltar de la cama
▸ **hop over to** VI + PREP darse una vuelta por
hop² [hɒp] N (*Bot*) (*also* **hops**) lúpulo *m*
CPD ▸ **hop field** campo *m* de lúpulo ▸ **hop picking** recolección *f* del lúpulo
hope [həʊp] N **1** (= *expectation*) esperanza *f* • **where there's life there's ~** mientras hay vida, hay esperanza • **my ~ is that he'll see reason** espero que entre en razón • **to be beyond (all) ~** [*damaged article*] no tener posibilidad de reparación; [*person*] no tener remedio • **to build one's ~s up (about** *or* **over sth)** hacerse ilusiones (con algo) • **to be full of ~** estar lleno de esperanzas *or* ilusión • **to get one's ~s up (about** *or* **over sth)** hacerse ilusiones (con algo) • **don't get your ~s up** no te hagas ilusiones • **to give up ~ (of doing sth)** perder las esperanzas (de hacer algo) • **to have ~s of doing sth** tener esperanzas de hacer algo • **I haven't much ~ of succeeding** no tengo muchas esperanzas de conseguirlo • **I had great ~s of** *or* **for him**

tenía muchas esperanzas puestas en él • **he set out with high ~s** empezó lleno de esperanzas *or* ilusión, empezó con muchas esperanzas • **I ignored him in the ~ that he would go away** no le hice caso con la esperanza de que se fuera • **I don't think there's much chance but we live in ~** no creo que haya muchas posibilidades pero la esperanza es lo último que se pierde • **she lives in (the) ~ of seeing her son again** vive con la esperanza de volver a ver a su hijo • **to lose ~ (of doing sth)** perder las esperanzas (de hacer algo) • **to be past ~** [*damaged article*] no tener posibilidad de reparación; [*person*] no tener remedio • **to place one's ~(s) in/on sth** depositar las esperanzas en algo • **to raise sb's ~s** dar esperanzas a algn • **don't raise her ~s too much** no le des demasiadas esperanzas • **don't raise your ~s** no te hagas ilusiones; ▸ **false, forlorn, pin**
2 (= *chance*) posibilidad *f* • **he hasn't much ~ of winning** no tiene muchas posibilidades de ganar • **there is little ~ of reaching an agreement** hay pocas posibilidades *or* esperanzas de llegar a un acuerdo • **you haven't got a ~ in hell*** no tienes la más remota posibilidad • **there's no ~ of that** no hay posibilidad de eso • **not a ~!*** ¡ni en sueños! • **your only ~ is to ...** tu única esperanza es ... • **some ~(s)!*** • **"have you got the day off tomorrow?" — "some ~(s)!"** —¿libras mañana? —¡qué va! *or* ¡ya quisiera yo! • **"maybe she'll change her mind" — "some ~(s)!"** —tal vez cambie de idea —¡no caerá esa breva!
3 (= *person*) esperanza *f* • **he's the bright ~ of the team** es la gran esperanza del equipo • **you are my last/only ~** tú eres mi última/única esperanza
(VT) esperar • **your mother is well, I ~?** espero que su madre esté bien • **to ~ that ...** esperar que ... (+ *subjun*) • **I ~ he comes soon** espero que venga pronto, ojalá venga pronto • **I was hoping you'd stay** esperaba que te quedaras • **I ~ you don't think I'm going to do it!** ¡no pensarás que lo voy a hacer yo! • **I ~ to God** *or* **hell she remembers*** quiera el cielo que se acuerde • **to ~ to do sth** esperar hacer algo • **what do you ~ to gain from that?** ¿qué esperas ganar *or* conseguir con eso? • **hoping to hear from you** en espera *or* a la espera de recibir noticias tuyas • **let's ~ it doesn't rain** esperemos que no llueva • **I ~ not** espero que no • **I ~ so** espero que sí • **I should ~ so (too)!** ¡eso espero! • **"I washed my hands first" — "I should ~ so too!"** —me he lavado las manos antes —¡eso espero! • **"but I apologized" — "I should ~ so too!"** —pero me disculpé —¡faltaría más!
(VI) esperar • **to ~ against ~** esperar en vano • **to ~ for sth** esperar algo • **it's the best we can ~ for** no podemos esperar nada mejor • **we're hoping for a boy this time** esta vez esperamos que sea niño • **I shouldn't ~ for too much from this meeting** no depositaría muchas esperanzas en esta reunión • **I always knew it was too much to ~ for** siempre supe que era mucho pedir • **we'll just have to ~ for the best** esperemos que todo salga bien • **I'm just going to enter the competition and ~ for the best** voy a presentarme al concurso y que sea lo que Dios quiera • **to ~ in God** confiar en Dios
(CPD) ▸ **hope chest** (*US*) ajuar *m* (de novia)

hoped-for ['həʊpt,fɔːʳ] (ADJ) esperado • **their action had the hoped-for effect** su acción produjo el efecto esperado • **the hoped-for economic recovery** la tan esperada reactivación económica

hopeful ['həʊpfʊl] (ADJ) **1** (= *optimistic*) [*person*] esperanzado, optimista; [*face*] esperanzado, lleno de esperanza • **groups of beggars made ~ sorties towards the tourists** grupos de mendigos se dirigían esperanzados hacia los turistas • **he gave the engine a ~ kick** le dio al motor una patada con la esperanza de que eso lo hiciese funcionar • **I'll ask her, but I'm not too ~** le preguntaré, pero no me hago demasiadas ilusiones *or* no tengo muchas esperanzas • **to be ~ that** tener esperanzas de que, esperar que (+ *subjun*) • **to be ~ about sth** tener esperanzas con respecto a algo • **in the ~ anticipation that ...** con la esperanza de que ... • **ever ~, he never gave up the fight** con las esperanzas intactas, nunca abandonó la lucha • **to feel ~** sentirse optimista • **I am ~ of a positive outcome** tengo esperanzas de que las cosas salgan bien • **to be ~ of doing sth** tener esperanzas de hacer algo, esperar poder hacer algo
2 (= *promising*) [*sign, future, news*] esperanzador(a), prometedor(a)
(N) aspirante *mf* • **presidential ~s** aspirantes *mpl* a la presidencia • **he enjoys his job as football coach to young ~s** disfruta entrenando a jóvenes promesas del fútbol

hopefully ['həʊpfʊlɪ] (ADV) **1** (= *with feeling of hope*) • **"is he coming with us?" I asked ~** —¿viene con nosotros? —pregunté esperanzado • **I looked ~ around the room for a glimpse of my luggage** miré por la habitación con esperanzas de ver mi equipaje • **she smiled at me ~** me dirigió una sonrisa esperanzada
2* (= *one hopes*) • **~ we'll be able to sort something out** con un poco de suerte podremos arreglar algo • **the new legislation, ~, will lead to some improvements** es de esperar que la nueva legislación traiga consigo algunas mejoras • **~, it won't rain** esperemos que no llueva

hopefulness ['həʊpfʊlnɪs] (N) esperanza *f*

hopeless ['həʊplɪs] (ADJ) **1** (= *impossible*) [*task*] imposible; [*attempt*] vano; [*cause*] perdido; [*situation, position*] desesperado; [*love*] imposible • **his attempt to swim the river was ~ from the beginning** su tentativa de cruzar el río a nado estaba condenada al fracaso desde el principio • **it's ~!** ¡es inútil! • **a ~ case** (= *person*) un caso perdido • **he's a ~ case!** es un caso perdido, no tiene remedio • **the doctor says it is a ~ case** el médico dice que no tiene salvación, el médico lo ha desahuciado • **a ~ drunk** un borracho empedernido • **to be (in) a ~ mess** *or* **muddle** [*room*] estar hecho un desastre; [*plans*] estar muy embrollado; [*person*] estar hecho un lío • **a ~ romantic** un romántico incorregible
2 (= *despairing*) [*cry*] de desesperación; [*grief*] desesperado • **to feel ~** sentirse desesperanzado • **she gave a ~ sigh** suspiró desesperada
3* (= *not competent*) • **he's completely ~** es un inútil* • **she's a ~ manager** como jefa es una nulidad *or* es penosa* • **the buses round here are ~** los autobuses de por aquí son un desastre • **to be ~ at (doing) sth: he's ~ at football** es un desastre jugando al fútbol, es una nulidad para el fútbol* • **I was ~ at school** era un negado *or* una nulidad para los estudios* • **I'm ~ at maths/cooking** soy un negado para las matemáticas/la cocina • **I'd be ~ at working for somebody else** yo no serviría para trabajar para otros

hopelessly ['həʊplɪslɪ] (ADV) **1** (= *despairingly*) [*look, speak, continue*] sin esperanza
2 (*as intensifier*) [*inadequate, confused, lost*] totalmente, completamente • **he is ~ in debt** está totalmente *or* completamente endeudado • **to be ~ in love** estar perdidamente enamorado

hopelessness ['həʊplɪsnɪs] (N) **1** [*of situation*] lo desesperado
2 (= *despair*) desesperanza *f*
3 (= *incompetence*) inutilidad *f*

hophead* ['hɒphed] (N) (*US*) (*pej*) drogata* *mf*

hopper ['hɒpəʳ] (N) (= *chute*) tolva *f*

hopscotch ['hɒpskɒtʃ] (N) infernáculo *m*, rayuela *f* (*LAm*)

Horace ['hɒrɪs] (N) Horacio

Horatian [hɒ'reɪʃən] (ADJ) horaciano

horde [hɔːd] (N) (= *large number, crowd*) multitud *f*; (*Hist*) horda *f*

horizon [hə'raɪzn] (N) horizonte *m*; (*fig*) horizonte *m*, perspectiva *f* • **a boat on the ~** una barca en el horizonte • **there are new schemes on the ~** hay nuevos planes en perspectiva • **that's over the ~ now** eso queda ya a la espalda

horizontal [,hɒrɪ'zɒntl] (ADJ) horizontal • **~ integration** integración *f* horizontal
(N) horizontal *f*

horizontally [,hɒrɪ'zɒntəlɪ] (ADV) horizontalmente

hormonal [hɔː'məʊnəl] (ADJ) hormonal

hormone ['hɔːməʊn] (N) (*Med*) hormona *f*
(CPD) ▸ **hormone replacement therapy** terapia *f* hormonal sustitutiva ▸ **hormone treatment** tratamiento *m* de hormonas

horn [hɔːn] (N) **1** [*of bull*] cuerno *m*, cacho *m* (*LAm*); [*of deer*] asta *f*, cacho *m* (*LAm*); [*of snail*] cuerno *m*; (= *material*) cuerno *m*, carey *m* • **the Horn of Africa** el Cuerno de África • **~ of plenty** cuerno *m* de la abundancia, cornucopia *f* • **to be on the ~s of a dilemma** estar entre la espada y la pared • **to draw in one's ~s** (*fig*) (= *back down*) volverse atrás; (*with money*) hacer economías
2 (*Mus*) trompa *f*, cuerno *m* • **to play the ~** tocar la trompa *or* el cuerno
3 (*Aut*) bocina *f*, claxon *m* (*esp LAm*) • **to blow** *or* **sound one's ~** tocar la bocina *or* el claxon
4 (= *shoe horn*) calzador *m*
5 (*US‡*) teléfono *m* • **to get on the ~ to sb** llamar a algn (por teléfono)
▸ **horn in*** (VI + ADV) (*esp US*) entrometerse (on en)

hornbeam ['hɔːnbiːm] (N) carpe *m*

hornbill ['hɔːnbɪl] (N) búcero *m*

horned [hɔːnd] (ADJ) con cuernos, enastado

-horned [hɔːnd] (ADJ) (*in compounds*) de cuernos ...

hornet ['hɔːnɪt] (N) avispón *m* • **to stir up a ~'s nest** armar mucho revuelo

hornless ['hɔːnlɪs] (ADJ) sin cuernos, mocho

hornpipe ['hɔːnpaɪp] (N) **1** (*Mus*) chirimía *f*
2 (*Naut*) *cierto baile de marineros*

horn-rimmed ['hɔːnrɪmd] (ADJ) [*spectacles*] de concha, de carey

horny ['hɔːnɪ] (ADJ) (COMPAR: **hornier**, SUPERL: **horniest**) **1** (= *hard*) [*material*] córneo; [*hands*] calloso
2‡ (= *randy*) caliente*, cachondo (*Sp, Mex**)

horology [hɒ'rɒlədʒɪ] (N) horología *f*

horoscope ['hɒrəskəʊp] (N) horóscopo *m* • **to cast a ~** sacar un horóscopo

horrendous [hɒ'rendəs] (ADJ) **1** (= *horrific*) [*injury, attack, accident*] horrible, horrendo
2* (= *dreadful*) [*weather, traffic*] horroroso*, espantoso*; [*cost, price*] tremendo • **the company suffered ~ losses** la compañía sufrió enormes pérdidas

horrendously [hɒ'rendəslɪ] (ADV) [*difficult, expensive*] tremendamente, terriblemente

horrible ['hɒrɪbl] (ADJ) **1*** (= *unpleasant*) [*food, colour, smell, thought*] horroroso*, horrible* • **aren't those dresses ~?** ¿a que esos vestidos

h

son horrorosos?, ¿a que son feísimos esos vestidos? • **he was the most ~ person I've ever met** era la persona más mala que he conocido • **you're ~!** ¡qué malo eres! • **I've got a ~ feeling that ...** tengo la horrible sensación de que ... • **that jumper looks ~ on you** ese jersey te queda horroroso *or* espantoso • **it's all a ~ mess** es un lío horroroso • **we thought something ~ had happened** pensamos que algo horrible había pasado • **the press write some ~ things about him** la prensa cuenta cosas espantosas *or* horribles de él • **what a ~ thought!** ¡qué idea tan horrible! • **to be ~ to sb** tratar fatal a algn* • **she's ~ to her sister** trata fatal a su hermana • **don't be ~ to your brother** no seas malo con tu hermano
2 (= *horrific*) [*crime, scream, accident*] horrible, espantoso • **he died a ~ death** tuvo una muerte horrible

horribly [ˈhɒrɪblɪ] ADV 1* (= *dreadfully*) [*difficult, rich, embarrassed, expensive*] terriblemente, tremendamente • **I was ~ drunk** tenía una borrachera terrible*, estaba borrachísimo • **I felt ~ embarrassed by the whole thing** me sentía terriblemente *or* tremendamente abochornado por todo aquello* • **it's all gone ~ wrong** todo ha salido terriblemente mal
2 (= *horrifically*) [*die, injure, scream*] de una forma horrible; [*mutilated, disfigured*] horriblemente, espantosamente • **they died ~** murieron de una forma horrible, tuvieron una muerte horrible • **men with ~ scarred faces** hombres con unas cicatrices horribles en la cara

horrid [ˈhɒrɪd] ADJ (= *disagreeable, unpleasant*) horrible; (= *horrifying*) horroroso; (= *unkind*) antipático • **to be ~ to sb** tratar a algn muy mal, portarse muy mal con algn • **don't be ~!** ¡no seas antipático! • **you ~ thing!** ¡qué malo!, ¡qué antipático!

horridly [ˈhɒrɪdlɪ] ADV [*behave*] tremendamente mal, fatal

horrific [hɒˈrɪfɪk] ADJ [*injury, attack, accident*] horrible, horrendo

horrifically [hɒˈrɪfɪklɪ] ADV espantosamente, terriblemente • **~ injured** con heridas espantosas

horrify [ˈhɒrɪfaɪ] VT 1 (= *fill with horror*) horrorizar • **I was horrified to discover that ...** me horrorizó descubrir que ...
2 (= *shock*) escandalizar • **they were all horrified** se escandalizaron todos

horrifying [ˈhɒrɪfaɪɪŋ] ADJ horroroso, horripilante

horrifyingly [ˈhɒrɪˌfaɪɪŋlɪ] ADV horrorosamente, de manera horripilante

horror [ˈhɒrəʳ] N 1 (= *terror, dread*) horror *m*, pavor *m*; (= *loathing, hatred*) horror *m* • **to have a ~ of** tener horror a • **to my ~ I discovered I was locked out** descubrí con horror que me había dejado las llaves dentro • **then, to my ~, it moved!** luego ¡qué susto!, se movió • **the ~s of war** los horrores de la guerra • **that gives me the ~s*** eso me pone los pelos de punta* • **~s!** ¡qué horror!
2* diablo *m* • **that child is a little ~** ese niño es un diablillo • **you ~!** ¡bestia!
CPD ▸ **horror film** película *f* de terror ▸ **horror story** historia *f* de terror ▸ **horror writer** autor(a) *m/f* de historias de terror

horror-stricken [ˈhɒrəˌstrɪkən] ADJ horrorizado

horror-struck [ˈhɒrəˌstrʌk] ADJ = **horror-stricken**

hors de combat [ɔ:dəkɔ̃ba] ADJ fuera de combate

hors d'oeuvres [ɔ:ˈdɜ:vr] NPL entremeses *mpl*

horse [hɔ:s] N 1 (*Zool*) caballo *m* • IDIOMS: • **dark ~** incógnita *f* • **it's a case of ~s for courses** (*Brit*) en cada caso es distinto, a cada cual lo suyo • **to change ~s in midstream** cambiar de política (*or* personal *etc*) a mitad de camino • **a ~ of a different colour** harina *f* de otro costal • **to eat like a ~** comer como una vaca* • **to flog a dead ~** machacar en hierro frío • **to get on one's high ~** ponerse a pontificar • **don't look a gift ~ in the mouth** a caballo regalado, no le mires el diente • **hold your ~s!** ¡para el carro!, ¡despacito! • **to be straight from the ~'s mouth** ser de buena tinta
2 (*in gymnastics*) potro *m*
3 (*carpenter's*) caballete *m*
4 (= *cavalry*) caballería *f*
5‡ (= *heroin*) caballo‡ *m*, heroína *f*
CPD ▸ **horse artillery** artillería *f* montada ▸ **horse brass** jaez *m* ▸ **horse breaker** domador(a) *m/f* de caballos ▸ **horse breeder** criador(a) *m/f* de caballos ▸ **horse chestnut** (*Bot*) (= *tree*) castaño *m* de Indias; (= *fruit*) castaña *f* de Indias ▸ **horse collar** collera *f* ▸ **horse dealer** chalán *m* ▸ **horse doctor** veterinario/a *m/f* ▸ **Horse Guards** (*Brit*) Guardia *fsing* Montada ▸ **horse laugh** risotada *f*, carcajada *f* ▸ **horse mackerel** jurel *m* ▸ **horse manure** abono *m* de caballo ▸ **horse meat** (*Culin*) carne *f* de caballo ▸ **horse opera** (*US*) película *f* del Oeste ▸ **horse race** carrera *f* de caballos ▸ **horse racing** (*gen*) carreras *fpl* de caballos; (*as sport*) hípica *f* ▸ **horse rider** jinete *mf* ▸ **horse riding** (*Brit*) equitación *f* ▸ **horse sense** sentido *m* común ▸ **horse show** concurso *m* hípico ▸ **horse trader** (*Pol*) chalán/ana *m/f* ▸ **horse trading** (*Pol*) toma y daca *m*, chalaneo *m* ▸ **horse trailer** (*US*) remolque *m* para caballerías ▸ **horse trials** concurso *m* hípico
▸ **horse about***, **horse around*** VI + ADV hacer el tonto

horseback [ˈhɔ:sbæk] N • **on ~** a caballo
CPD ▸ **horseback riding** (*US*) equitación *f*

horsebox [ˈhɔ:sbɒks] N (*Brit*) remolque *m* para caballerías; (*Rail*) vagón *m* para caballerías

horse-drawn [ˈhɔ:sdrɔ:n] ADJ de tracción animal, tirado por caballos

horseflesh [ˈhɔ:sfleʃ] N 1 (= *horses*) caballos *mpl*
2 (*Culin*) carne *f* de caballo

horsefly [ˈhɔ:sflaɪ] N (PL: **horseflies**) tábano *m*

horsehair [ˈhɔ:sheəʳ] N crin *f*

horsehide [ˈhɔ:shaɪd] N cuero *m* de caballo

horseman [ˈhɔ:smən] N (PL: **horsemen**) (= *rider*) jinete *m*; (*skilful*) caballista *m*, charro *m* (*Mex*)

horsemanship [ˈhɔ:smənʃɪp] N (= *activity*) equitación *f*; (= *skill*) manejo *m* del caballo

horseplay [ˈhɔ:spleɪ] N payasadas *fpl*

horsepower [ˈhɔ:sˌpauəʳ] N caballo *m* de vapor • **a 20 ~ engine** un motor de 20 caballos

horseradish [ˈhɔ:sˌrædɪʃ] N (= *plant*) rábano *m* picante; (= *sauce*) salsa *f* de rábano

horseshit** [ˈhɔ:sʃɪt] N (*lit*) caca** *f* de caballo; (*fig*) gilipollada‡ *f*

horseshoe [ˈhɔ:sʃu:] N herradura *f*
CPD ▸ **horseshoe arch** arco *m* de herradura

horsewhip [ˈhɔ:swɪp] VT azotar
N fusta *f*

horsewoman [ˈhɔ:sˌwʊmən] N (PL: **horsewomen**) jinete *f*, amazona *f*, charra *f* (*Mex*)

horsey*, **horsy*** [ˈhɔ:sɪ] ADJ (COMPAR: **horsier**, SUPERL: **horsiest**) [*person*] aficionado a los caballos; [*appearance*] caballuno

horticultural [ˌhɔ:tɪˈkʌltʃərəl] ADJ hortícola • **~ show** exposición *f* de horticultura

horticulturalist [ˌhɔ:tɪˈkʌltʃərəlɪst] N horticultor(a) *m/f*

horticulture [ˈhɔ:tɪkʌltʃəʳ] N horticultura *f*

horticulturist [ˌhɔ:tɪˈkʌltʃərɪst] N horticultor(a) *m/f*

hose [həʊz] N 1 (*also* **hosepipe**) manga *f*, manguera *f*
2 (= *stockings*) medias *fpl*; (= *socks*) calcetines *mpl*; (*Hist*) calzas *fpl*
▸ **hose down** VT + ADV regar con manguera
▸ **hose out** VT + ADV regar con manguera

hosepipe [ˈhəʊzpaɪp] N manga *f*, manguera *f*
CPD ▸ **hosepipe ban** (*Brit*) *prohibición de usar mangueras por escasez de agua*

hosier [ˈhəʊʒɪəʳ] N calcetero/a *m/f*

hosiery [ˈhəʊʒɪərɪ] N calcetería *f*

hosp ABBR (= **hospital**) Hosp *m*

hospice [ˈhɒspɪs] N hospicio *m*

hospitable [hɒsˈpɪtəbl] ADJ acogedor, hospitalario

hospitably [hɒsˈpɪtəblɪ] ADV con hospitalidad

hospital [ˈhɒspɪtl] N hospital *m* • **maternity ~** casa *f* de maternidad • **mental ~** hospital *m* psiquiátrico, manicomio *m* • **to go into ~** ingresar en el hospital
CPD ▸ **hospital administration** administración *f* de hospital ▸ **hospital administrator** (*Brit*) administrador(a) *m/f* de hospital; (*US*) director(a) *m/f* de hospital ▸ **hospital bed** cama *f* de hospital ▸ **hospital bill** gastos *mpl* de hospitalización ▸ **hospital care** cuidados *mpl* hospitalarios • **many people who have the AIDS virus require ~ care** mucha gente que tiene el virus del SIDA requiere cuidados hospitalarios ▸ **hospital case** caso *m* clínico • **90% of ~ cases are released within three weeks** el 90% de los casos clínicos son dados de alta en tres semanas ▸ **hospital doctor** interno/a *m/f* ▸ **hospital drama** (*on TV*) serial *m* hospitalario ▸ **hospital facilities** instalaciones *fpl* hospitalarias ▸ **hospital management** (= *act*) gestión *f* hospitalaria; (= *persons*) dirección *f* del hospital ▸ **hospital nurse** enfermera *f* de hospital ▸ **hospital ship** buque *m* hospital

hospitality [ˌhɒspɪˈtælɪtɪ] N hospitalidad *f* • **corporate ~** hospitalidad *f* corporativa
CPD ▸ **hospitality area** zona *f* de recepción para invitados importantes ▸ **hospitality industry** industria *f* hotelera, hostelería *f* ▸ **hospitality tent** carpa *f* de recepción para invitados importantes

hospitalization [ˌhɒspɪtəlaɪˈzeɪʃən] N hospitalización *f*

hospitalize [ˈhɒspɪtəlaɪz] VT hospitalizar

host[1] [həʊst] N 1 (*to guest*) anfitrión/ona *m/f*; (*TV, Rad*) presentador(a) *m/f*; [*of inn*] hostelero *m*, mesonero *m* • **I thanked my ~s** di las gracias a los anfitriones *or* a los que me habían invitado • **we were ~s for a week to a Spanish boy** recibimos en casa durante una semana a un joven español
2 (*Bot, Zool*) huésped *m*
3 (*Comput*) (*also* **host computer**) servidor *m*
VT [+ *TV programme, games*] presentar; [+ *conference*] ser anfitrión de
CPD ▸ **host country** país *m* anfitrión ▸ **host family** [*of foreign student*] familia *f* de acogida

host[2] [həʊst] N 1 (= *crowd*) multitud *f* • **for a whole ~ of reasons** por un sinfín de razones • **I have a ~ of problems** tengo un sinfín *or* un montón de problemas • **they came in ~s** acudieron a millares

2†† (= *army*) hueste *f*, ejército *m*
host³ [həʊst] (N) (*Rel*) hostia *f*
hostage ['hɒstɪdʒ] (N) rehén *mf* • **to take sb ~** tomar *or* (*LAm*) agarrar a algn como rehén
hostage-taker ['hɒstɪdʒ,teɪkəʳ] (N) persona *f* que captura rehenes
hostel ['hɒstəl] (N) residencia *f*; (= *youth hostel*) albergue *m* juvenil; (*Univ*) residencia *f* de estudiantes
hosteller, hosteler (US) ['hɒstələʳ] (N) *persona que va de albergues para jóvenes*
hostelling, hosteling (US) ['hɒstəlɪŋ] (N) • **to go (youth) ~** viajar de alberguista
hostelry ['hɒstəlrɪ] (N) (PL: **hostelries**) (*esp Brit*) mesón *m*
hostess ['həʊstes] (N) huéspeda *f*, anfitriona *f*; (*in night club*) azafata *f*; (*Aer*) azafata *f*
(CPD) ▸ **hostess trolley** (*Brit*) mesa *f* rodante; (*with keep-warm facility*) carro *m* caliente
hostile ['hɒstaɪl], (US) ['hɒstəl] (ADJ) 1 (= *antagonistic*) [*person, question, atmosphere*] hostil • **to get a ~ reception** tener una recepción hostil • **to be ~ to** *or* **towards sth/sb** ser hostil a algo/con algn • **~ witness** (*Jur*) testigo *m* hostil *or* desfavorable
2 (*Mil*) [*force, aircraft, territory*] hostil
3 (= *unfavourable*) [*conditions, weather, environment*] adverso, desfavorable
4 (*Econ*) hostil • **a ~ takeover bid** una OPA hostil
hostility [hɒs'tɪlɪtɪ] (N) 1 (= *animosity*) hostilidad *f*
2 **hostilities** (*Mil*) hostilidades *fpl* • **to cease/resume hostilities** cesar/reanudar las hostilidades
hostler ['ɒsləʳ] (N) mozo *m* de cuadra
hot [hɒt] (ADJ) (COMPAR: **hotter**, SUPERL: **hottest**) 1 (*gen*) caliente; [*climate*] cálido; [*day, summer*] caluroso, de calor; [*sun*] abrasador • **with running hot and cold water** con agua corriente caliente y fría • **it was a very hot day** fue un día de mucho calor • **it was a hot and tiring walk** fue una caminata que nos hizo sudar y nos cansó mucho • **a nice hot bath** un buen baño caliente • **to be hot** [*thing*] estar caliente; [*weather*] hacer calor; [*person*] tener calor • **this room is hot** hace calor en esta habitación • **to be very hot** [*thing*] estar muy caliente; [*weather*] hacer mucho calor; [*person*] tener mucho calor • **I'm too hot** tengo demasiado calor • **it made me go hot and cold** me dio escalofríos • **to get hot** [*thing*] calentarse; [*weather*] empezar a hacer calor; [*person*] • **I'm getting hot** me está entrando calor • **to get (all) hot and bothered** sofocarse • **you're getting hot** (*fig*) (*when guessing*) caliente, caliente
2 (= *spicy, peppery*) [*taste, food*] picante • **this food is very hot** esta comida es muy picante • **Mexican food's too hot** la comida mejicana es demasiado picante
3 (*fig*) [*contest*] muy reñido; [*temper*] malo; [*dispute*] acalorado • **hot favourite** gran favorito *m* • **to make it hot for sb** hacerle la vida imposible a algn • **to make a place too hot for sb** hacer que algn se vaya de un lugar haciéndole la vida imposible • **hot money** dinero *m* caliente • **hot news** noticias *fpl* de última hora • **he's a pretty hot player** es un jugador experto • **he has a hot temper** tiene mal genio *or* carácter • **a hot tip** información *f* de buenas tintas *or* de fuente fidedigna • IDIOMS: • **to be in/get into hot water** estar/meterse en problemas • **to be hot under the collar*** estar acalorado • **to get hot under the collar*** acalorarse • **to be too hot to handle**: • **he's/it's too hot to handle** es demasiado • **that's a hot button** *or* **a hot-button issue** (*US*) ese es un asunto polémico, ese es un tema candente • **these accusations have hit a hot button in the black community** estas acusaciones han levantado ampollas entre la población negra; ▹ **pursuit**
(ADV) • **to be hot on sb's trail** *or* **heels** pisar los talones a algn • **news hot from the press** una noticia que acaba de publicarse en la prensa • IDIOM: • **to blow hot and cold** ser veleta, mudar a todos los vientos
(N) • **he's got the hots for her*** ella le pone cachondo
(CPD) ▸ **hot air** (*fig*) palabras *fpl* al aire ▸ **hot cross bun** *bollo a base de especias y pasas marcado con una cruz y que se come en Viernes Santo* ▸ **hot dog** (*Culin*) perrito *m* caliente, hot dog *m*, pancho *m* (*S. Cone*) ▸ **hot flash** (*US*) = **hot flush** ▸ **hot flush** (*Brit*) sofoco *m* de calor ▸ **hot goods** artículos *mpl* robados ▸ **hot key** tecla *f* de acceso directo ▸ **hot line** teléfono *m* rojo ▸ **hot link** hiperenlace *m* ▸ **hot potato*** cuestión *f* muy discutida ▸ **hot seat*** • **to be in the hot seat** estar expuesto ▸ **hot spot*** (*Pol*) lugar *m* de peligro; (*for amusement*) lugar *m* de diversión; (= *night club*) sala *f* de fiestas; (*for wireless access*) punto *m* caliente, hotspot *m* ▸ **hot springs** aguas *fpl* termales ▸ **hot stuff** • **to be hot stuff** (= *expert*) ser un hacha*; (= *sexy*) estar como un tren* • **he's pretty hot stuff at maths*** es un hacha *or* un as para las matemáticas ▸ **hot tub** jacuzzi® *m*
▸ **hot up*** (*esp Brit*) (VI + ADV) [*party*] animarse; [*competition, battle*] empezar a animarse; [*dispute*] acalorarse
(VT + ADV) [+ *food*] calentar; [+ *pace*] acelerar, forzar
hot-air balloon [,hɒt'ɛəbə'lu:n] (N) globo *m* de aire caliente
hotbed ['hɒtbed] (N) (*fig*) semillero *m*
hot-blooded ['hɒt'blʌdɪd] (ADJ) apasionado
hotcake ['hɒtkeɪk] (N) (*US*) = **pancake**
hotchpotch ['hɒtʃpɒtʃ] (N) (*Brit*) mezcolanza *f*
hot-desk [,hɒt'desk] (VI) • **some ministers will have to hot-desk until more accommodation can be found** algunos ministros tendrán que usar las mesas que estén disponibles en cada momento hasta que se consiga más espacio
hot-desking [,hɒt'deskɪŋ] (N) *práctica consistente en la asignación variable de mesas en una oficina, de tal forma que nadie ocupa permanentemente la misma*
hotel [həʊ'tel] (N) hotel *m*
(CPD) ▸ **hotel accommodation** alojamiento *m* en hotel • **travel to Holland is by ferry and minicoach with 3-star ~ accommodation** el viaje a Holanda es en ferry y mini-bus, con estancia en hotel de 3 estrellas ▸ **hotel chain** cadena *f* hotelera ▸ **the hotel industry** el sector hotelero ▸ **hotel manager** director(a) *m/f* de hotel ▸ **hotel receptionist** recepcionista *mf* de hotel ▸ **hotel room** habitación *f* de hotel ▸ **hotel staff** plantilla *f* de hotel ▸ **hotel work** trabajo *m* de hostelería ▸ **hotel workers** trabajadores/oras *mpl/fpl* de hostelería
hotelier [həʊ'telɪəʳ], **hotelkeeper** [həʊ'tel,ki:pəʳ] (N) hotelero/a *m/f*
hotfoot ['hɒt'fʊt] (ADV) a toda prisa
(VT) • **to ~ it*** ir volando
hothead ['hɒthed] (N) exaltado/a *m/f*
hot-headed ['hɒt'hedɪd] (ADJ) impulsivo, impetuoso
hothouse ['hɒthaʊs] (N) (PL: **hothouses** ['hɒthaʊzɪz]) invernadero *m*
hotly ['hɒtlɪ] (ADV) con pasión, con vehemencia • **he was ~ pursued by the policeman** el policía le seguía muy de cerca
hotpants ['hɒtpænts] (NPL) shorts *mpl*
hotplate ['hɒtpleɪt] (N) (*on stove*) hornillo *m*; (*for keeping food warm*) calientaplatos *m inv*
hotpot ['hɒtpɒt] (N) (*Brit*) (*Culin*) estofado *m*
hotrod* ['hɒtrɒd] (N) (*US*) (*Aut*) bólido *m*
hotshot* ['hɒtʃɒt] (ADJ) de primera, de aúpa*
(N) personaje *m*, pez *m* gordo*
hot-tempered [,hɒt'tempəd] (ADJ) de mal genio, de mal carácter
Hottentot ['hɒtəntɒt] (ADJ) hotentote
(N) 1 (= *person*) hotentote *mf*
2 (*Ling*) hotentote *m*
hottie ['hɒtɪ] (N) 1 (*Australia**) bolsa *f* de agua caliente
2 (*US‡*) (= *sexy person*) bombón *m*
hot-water bottle [hɒt'wɔ:tə,bɒtl] (N) bolsa *f* de agua caliente
hot-wire* ['hɒtwaɪəʳ] (VT) hacerle el puente a
hound [haʊnd] (N) perro *m* de caza • **the ~s** la jauría
(VT) (*fig*) perseguir, acosar • **they ~ed him for the money** le persiguieron *or* acosaron para conseguir el dinero • **I will not be ~ed into a decision** no permitiré que me presionen para tomar una decisión
▸ **hound down** (VT + ADV) perseguir sin descanso
▸ **hound on** (VT + ADV) • **to ~ sb on (to do sth)** incitar a algn (a hacer algo)
▸ **hound out** (VT + ADV) sacar a la fuerza
hour [aʊəʳ] (N) hora *f* • **after ~s** fuera de horario • **at all ~s (of the day and night)** a cualquier hora • **she's out till all ~s** no regresa hasta muy tarde, vuelve a casa a las tantas • **at 30 miles an ~** a 30 millas por hora • **~s and ~s** horas y horas, horas enteras • **to pay sb by the ~** pagar a algn por horas • **~ by ~** hora tras hora • **he thought his (last) ~ had come** (*fig*) pensó que había llegado su hora • **in the ~ of danger** en el momento de peligro • **in the early ~s** en la *or* de madrugada • **at the eleventh ~** a última hora • **I've been waiting for ~s** llevo horas esperando • **we waited ~s** esperamos horas y horas • **half an ~** media hora • **two and a half ~s** dos horas y media • **to keep late ~s** trasnochar, acostarse a altas horas de la noche • **to work long ~s** trabajar muchas horas • **lunch ~** hora *f* del almuerzo *or* de comer • **on the ~** a la hora en punto • **out of ~s** fuera de horario • **a quarter of an ~** un cuarto de hora • **to keep regular ~s** llevar una vida ordenada • **in the small ~s** en la *or* de madrugada • **to strike the ~** dar la hora • **he took ~s to do it** tardó horas en hacerlo • **she always takes ~s to get ready** siempre se tira horas para arreglarse • **visiting ~s** horas de visita
(CPD) ▸ **hour hand** horario *m*
hourglass ['aʊəglɑ:s] (N) reloj *m* de arena
(CPD) ▸ **hourglass figure** • **to have an ~ figure** tener figura de ánfora *or* de guitarra
hourly ['aʊəlɪ] (ADJ) [*rate, pay, earnings*] por hora; [*bus, train, service*] cada hora; [*news*] de cada hora • **they come at ~ intervals** llegan cada hora • **there are ~ buses** hay autobuses cada hora • **~ rate** *or* **wage** paga *f* por hora
(ADV) 1 (= *every hour*) cada hora • **trains from Madrid arrive ~** los trenes de Madrid llegan cada hora
2 (= *by the hour*) • **she's paid ~** le pagan por horas
3 (= *at any moment*) • **we expected him ~** le esperábamos de un momento a otro
(CPD) ▸ **hourly worker** trabajador(a) *m/f* pagado/a por horas
hourly-paid [,aʊəlɪ'peɪd] (ADJ) pagado por hora

house (N) [haʊs] (PL: **houses** [ˈhaʊzɪz])
1 (= *building*) casa *f* • **the party's at my/John's ~** la fiesta es en mi casa/en casa de John • **let's go to your ~** vamos a tu casa • **are you handy around the ~?** ¿eres un manitas para la casa? • **~ of cards** castillo *m* de naipes • **the ~ of God** la casa del Señor • **to move ~** mudarse (de casa) • **to keep open ~** tener la puerta siempre abierta, recibir a todo el mundo • IDIOM: • **to get on like a ~ on fire*** (= *progress*) ir sobre ruedas*; [*people*] llevarse de maravilla*; ▷ **coffee, eat, public, safe, steak**
2 (= *household*) casa *f* • **the noise woke the whole ~** el ruido despertó a toda la casa • **to keep ~ (for sb)** llevar la casa (a algn) • **the children were playing (at) ~** los niños estaban jugando a las casitas • **to set up ~** poner casa • IDIOM: • **to put** *or* **set** *or* **get one's ~ in order** poner sus asuntos en orden • **the government must put its economic ~ in order** el gobierno debe poner en orden la economía
3 (*Pol*) cámara *f* • **the House** (= *House of Commons*) la Cámara de los Comunes; (*US*) la Cámara de Representantes • **the upper/lower ~** la cámara alta/baja • **the House of Commons/Lords** (*Brit*) (= *building, members*) la Cámara de los Comunes/Lores • **the Houses of Parliament** (*Brit*) el Parlamento • **the House of Representatives** (*US*) la Cámara de Representantes; ▷ SPEAKER
4 (*in debate*) asamblea *f* • **this ~ believes that ...** esta asamblea cree que ...
5 (*Brit*) (*Scol*) *subdivisión de alumnos que se crea en algunos colegios para promover la competición entre ellos*
6 (*Theat*) (= *auditorium*) sala *f*; (= *audience*) público *m* • **full ~** (teatro *m*) lleno *m* • **"house full"** "no hay localidades" • **they played to packed ~s** llenaban las salas • **the second ~** la segunda función • IDIOM: • **to bring the ~ down** [*act, scene*] hacer que se venga abajo la sala *or* el teatro; [*joke*] hacer morirse de risa a todos
7 (*Comm*) casa *f* • **banking ~** entidad *f* bancaria • **fashion ~** casa *f* de modas • **finance ~** entidad *f* financiera • **we do our printing in ~** hacemos nuestra propia impresión, hacemos la impresión en la empresa • **it's on the ~** invita la casa • **TV programmes made out of ~** programas de televisión realizados por productoras externas • **publishing ~** (casa *f*) editorial *f*; ▷ **in-house**
8 (= *family, line*) casa *f*, familia *f* • **the House of Windsor** la casa de los Windsor
9 (*Cards*) • **full ~** full *m*
10 (*Astrol*) casa *f* (celeste)
(VT) [haʊz] **1** (= *provide accommodation for*) [+ *person, family*] alojar, dar alojamiento a
2 (= *have space for, contain*) albergar • **the building will not ~ them all** el edificio no podrá albergarlos a todos, no cabrán todos en el edificio
3 (= *store*) guardar, almacenar
4 (*Mech*) encajar
(CPD) [haʊs] ▸ **house agent** (*Brit*) agente *mf* inmobiliario/a ▸ **house arrest** arresto *m* domiciliario • **to be under ~ arrest** estar bajo arresto domiciliario ▸ **house call** consulta *f* a domicilio ▸ **house contents insurance** seguro *m* del contenido de una casa ▸ **house doctor** = house physician ▸ **house guest** invitado/a *m/f* ▸ **house hunter** persona *f* en busca de vivienda ▸ **house lights** (*Theat*) luces *fpl* de sala ▸ **house manager** (*Theat*) encargado/a *m/f* del teatro ▸ **house martin** avión *m* común ▸ **house number** número *m* de calle ▸ **house officer** interno/a *m/f* ▸ **house owner** propietario/a *m/f* de una casa ▸ **house painter** pintor(a) *m/f* (de brocha gorda) ▸ **house party** (*event*) *fiesta de varios días en una casa de campo*; (*people*) grupo *m* de invitados (*que pasan varios días en una casa de campo*) ▸ **house physician** (*Brit*) médico/a *m/f* interno/a ▸ **house plant** planta *f* de interior ▸ **house prices** el precio de la vivienda ▸ **house red** tinto *m* de la casa ▸ **house rule** (*in family*) regla *f* de la casa • **no drugs is a ~ rule** (*in institution*) aquí están prohibidas las drogas ▸ **house sale** venta *f* inmobiliaria ▸ **house sparrow** gorrión *m* común ▸ **house style** estilo *m* de la casa ▸ **house surgeon** (*Brit*) cirujano/a *m/f* interno/a ▸ **house wine** vino *m* de la casa

houseboat [ˈhaʊsbəʊt] (N) casa *f* flotante

housebound [ˈhaʊsbaʊnd] (ADJ) confinado en casa

houseboy† [ˈhaʊsbɔɪ] (N) sirviente *m*; (*in former colonies*) mucamo *m*

housebreaker [ˈhaʊsˌbreɪkəʳ] (N) ladrón/ona *m/f*

housebreaking [ˈhaʊsˌbreɪkɪŋ] (N) allanamiento *m* de morada, invasión *f* de morada

housebroken [ˈhaʊsˌbrəʊkən] (ADJ) (*US*) enseñado

house-clean [ˈhaʊskliːn] (VI) (*US*) hacer la limpieza (de la casa)

housecleaning, house-cleaning [ˈhaʊsˈkliːnɪŋ] (N) limpieza *f* de la casa

housecoat [ˈhaʊskəʊt] (N) bata *f*

housedress [ˈhaʊsdres] (N) vestido *m* de casa, vestido *m* sencillo

housefather [ˈhaʊsˌfɑːðəʳ] (N) *hombre encargado de una residencia de niños*

housefly [ˈhaʊsflaɪ] (N) (PL: **houseflies**) mosca *f*

houseful [ˈhaʊsfʊl] (N) • **there was a ~ of people** la casa estaba llena de gente

houseguest [ˈhaʊsgest] (N) huésped(a) *m/f*, invitado/a *m/f*

household [ˈhaʊshəʊld] (N) (= *home*) casa *f*; (= *family*) familia *f*
(CPD) ▸ **household accounts** cuentas *fpl* de la casa ▸ **household appliance** electrodoméstico *m* ▸ **Household Cavalry** (*Mil*) Guardia *f* Real ▸ **household chores** quehaceres *mpl* domésticos, tareas *fpl* de la casa ▸ **household expenses** gastos *mpl* de la casa ▸ **household gods** penates *mpl* ▸ **household goods** enseres *mpl* domésticos ▸ **household insurance** seguro *m* de hogar ▸ **household linen** ropa *f* blanca ▸ **household name** • **he's a ~ name** es una persona conocidísima ▸ **household refuse** basura *f* doméstica, residuos *mpl* domésticos ▸ **household rubbish** basura *f* doméstica ▸ **household soap** jabón *m* familiar ▸ **household troops** (*Brit*) guardia *fsing* real ▸ **household word** • **it's a ~ word** (*fig*) es el pan de cada día

householder [ˈhaʊsˌhəʊldəʳ] (N) (= *owner*) propietario/a *m/f*; (= *tenant*) inquilino/a *m/f*; (= *head of house*) cabeza *f* de familia

house-hunt [ˈhaʊshʌnt] (VI) (*Brit*) buscar casa

house-hunting [ˈhaʊsˌhʌntɪŋ] (N) • **to go househunting** ir buscando casa

house-husband [ˈhaʊsˌhʌzbənd] (N) *marido que se ocupa de las tareas de la casa*

housekeeper [ˈhaʊsˌkiːpəʳ] (N) ama *f* de llaves; (*in hotel*) gobernanta *f*

housekeeping [ˈhaʊsˌkiːpɪŋ] (N) (= *administration*) gobierno *m* de la casa; (= *housework*) quehaceres *mpl* domésticos, tareas *fpl* de la casa; (*Comput*) gestión *f* interna; (*esp Brit*) (*also* **housekeeping money**) dinero *m* para gastos domésticos

housemaid [ˈhaʊsmeɪd] (N) criada *f*

houseman [ˈhaʊsmən] (N) (PL: **housemen**) (*Brit*) (*in hospital*) interno/a *m/f*

housemaster [ˈhaʊsˌmɑːstəʳ] (N) (*Brit*) (*Scol*) *profesor a cargo de la subdivisión de un colegio de internado*

housemate [ˈhaʊsmeɪt] (N) compañero/a *m/f* de piso

housemistress [ˈhaʊsˌmɪstrɪs] (N) (*Brit*) (*Scol*) *profesora a cargo de la subdivisión de un colegio de internado*

housemother [ˈhaʊsˌmʌðəʳ] (N) *mujer encargada de una residencia de niños*

house-proud [ˈhaʊspraʊd] (ADJ) (*esp Brit*) • **she's very house-proud** le gusta tener la casa impecable

houseroom [ˈhaʊsrʊm] (N) • **to give sth ~** guardar algo en su casa • **I wouldn't give it ~*** no lo tendría en casa

house-sit [ˈhaʊssɪt] (VI) (PT, PP: **house-sat**) • **I'm house-sitting for the Sinclairs** vivo en la casa de los Sinclair para vigilarla en ausencia de los dueños

house-to-house [ˈhaʊstəˈhaʊs] (ADJ) de casa en casa • **to conduct house-to-house enquiries** hacer investigaciones de casa en casa

housetop [ˈhaʊstɒp] (N) tejado *m* • IDIOM: • **to shout sth from the ~s** pregonar algo a los cuatro vientos

house-train [ˈhaʊstreɪn] (VT) (*Brit*) educar, enseñar

house-trained [ˈhaʊstreɪnd] (ADJ) (*Brit*) enseñado

housewares [ˈhaʊswɛəz] (NPL) (*esp US*) artículos *mpl* de uso doméstico, utensilios *mpl* domésticos

house-warming [ˈhaʊsˌwɔːmɪŋ] (N) (*also* **house-warming party**) fiesta *f* de estreno de una casa

housewife [ˈhaʊswaɪf] (N) (PL: **housewives**) ama *f* de casa

housewifely [ˈhaʊswaɪflɪ] (ADJ) doméstico

housewifery [ˈhaʊswɪfərɪ] (N) (= *administration*) gobierno *m* de la casa; (= *housework*) quehaceres *mpl* domésticos, tareas *fpl* de la casa

housewives [ˈhaʊswaɪvz] (NPL) *of* **housewife**

housework [ˈhaʊswɜːk] (N) quehaceres *mpl* domésticos, tareas *fpl* de la casa

housing [ˈhaʊzɪŋ] (N) **1** (= *houses*) casas *fpl*, viviendas *fpl* • **there's a lot of new ~** hay muchas casas *or* viviendas nuevas
2 (*gen*) vivienda *f* • **the ~ problem** el problema de la vivienda
3 (*Mech*) caja *f*, cubierta *f*
(CPD) ▸ **housing association** asociación *f* de la vivienda ▸ **housing benefit** (*Brit*) subsidio *m* de vivienda ▸ **housing conditions** condiciones *fpl* de vivienda ▸ **housing cooperative** cooperativa *f* de la vivienda ▸ **housing development** (*US*) = **housing estate** ▸ **housing estate** (*Brit*) urbanización *f*, fraccionamiento *m* (*Mex*), reparto *m* (*Mex*); (= *council estate*) urbanización *f or* barrio *m* de viviendas protegidas ▸ **housing list** (*Brit*) *lista de espera para conseguir una vivienda de protección oficial* ▸ **housing market** mercado *m* de la vivienda ▸ **housing policy** política *f* de la vivienda ▸ **housing project** (*US*) urbanización *f or* barrio *m* de viviendas protegidas ▸ **housing scheme** (*Scot*) urbanización *f or* barrio *m* de viviendas protegidas ▸ **housing shortage** crisis *f inv* de la vivienda ▸ **housing stock** total *m* de viviendas ▸ **housing subsidy** subsidio *m* por vivienda

hove [həʊv] (PT), (PP) *of* **heave**

hovel ['hɒvəl] (N) casucha *f*, cuchitril *m*, tugurio *m* (*esp LAm*)
hover ['hɒvəʳ] (VI) **1** [*bird*] planear, cernerse
2 (*fig*) [*person*] rondar • **a couple of waiters were ~ing near our table** un par de camareros rondaban cerca de nuestra mesa • **she was ~ing in the doorway** andaba rondando por la entrada • **he was ~ing between life and death** se debatía entre la vida y la muerte
(CPD) ▸ **hover fly** mosca *f* de las flores
▸ **hover about** (VI + ADV), (VI + PREP) = **hover around**
▸ **hover around** (VI + ADV) rondar
(VI + PREP) • **to ~ around sb** rondar a algn, girar en torno a algn
hovercraft ['hɒvəkrɑːft] (N) aerodeslizador *m*
hoverport ['hɒvə,pɔːt] (N) puerto *m* de aerodeslizadores

---

how [haʊ]

ADVERB
CONJUNCTION
NOUN

ADVERB

1 (*in direct and indirect questions, reported speech*) **a** (*with verb*)

> *You can usually use* **cómo** *to translate* **how** *in questions as well as after report verbs and verbs of (un)certainty and doubt (e.g.* **no sé***):*

cómo • **how did you do it?** ¿cómo lo hiciste? • **how can that be?** ¿cómo puede ser eso? • **how are you?** ¿cómo estás?, ¿cómo *or* qué tal te va? (*LAm**), ¿qué tal (estás)? (*Sp**) • **how was the film?** ¿qué tal la película? • **please tell me how to do it** por favor, dígame cómo hacerlo • **I wasn't sure how to make soup** no sabía muy bien cómo hacer *or* preparar una sopa • **I explained to her how to make a paella** le expliqué cómo se hacía una paella • **I know how you did it** ya sé cómo lo hiciste • **to know how to do sth** saber hacer algo • **to learn how to do sth** aprender a hacer algo, aprender cómo se hace algo • **how do you like your steak?** ¿cómo le gusta el filete? • **how do you like the book?** ¿qué te parece el libro? • **how's that for cheek?** ¿no te parece de una cara dura increíble? • **I can't understand how it happened** no entiendo cómo ocurrió
b (= *to what degree*)

> **how** *+ adjective in questions can often be translated using* **cómo es/era de** *+ adjective (agreeing with the noun), but other constructions might be more usual depending on the context:*

• **how big is it?** ¿cómo es de grande? • **how difficult was the exam?** ¿cómo fue de difícil el examen? • **how old are you?** ¿cuántos años tienes? • **how wide is this bed?** ¿qué anchura tiene esta cama?, ¿cuánto mide de ancho esta cama?

> *With adverbs various translations are possible depending on the context. A very common construction is preposition +* **qué** *+ noun:*

• **how far away is it?** ¿a qué distancia queda?, ¿qué tan lejos queda? (*LAm*) • **how far is it (from here) to Edinburgh?** ¿qué distancia hay de aquí a Edimburgo? • **how fast can it go?** ¿a qué velocidad puede ir? • **how soon can you be ready?** ¿cuánto tardas en prepararte? • **how soon can you come?** ¿cuándo puedes venir?

> *To translate* **how** *+ adjective/adverb in reported speech,* **lo** *+ adjective/adverb is used. Note that the adjective agrees with the noun.*

• **you don't know how difficult it is** no sabes lo difícil que es • **I didn't know how expensive the tickets were** no sabía lo caras que eran las entradas • **they've been telling me how well you did in your exams** ya me han hablado de lo bien que hiciste los exámenes
and how! ¡y cómo!, ¡y tanto!
how about • **how about tomorrow?** ¿qué te parece mañana? • **how about a cup of tea?** ¿te apetece una taza de té? • **I like it, but how about you?** a mí me gusta, pero ¿y a ti? • **how about going to the cinema?** ¿qué tal si vamos al cine?, ¿y si vamos al cine?
how long • **how long is this bed?** ¿qué longitud tiene esta cama?, ¿cuánto mide de largo esta cama? • **how long will you be?** ¿cuánto vas a tardar? • **how long have you been here?** ¿cuánto tiempo llevas aquí?
how many • **how many are there?** ¿cuántos hay? • **how many cartons of milk did you buy?** ¿cuántos cartones de leche has comprado?
how much • **how much sugar do you want?** ¿cuánto azúcar quieres? • **how much is it?** ¿cuánto vale?, ¿cuánto es?
how often • **how often do you go?** ¿con qué frecuencia vas?; ▹ **else**
2 (*in other statements*)

> *Translate* **how** *with verbs other than report ones or verbs of (un)certainty and doubt using* **como** *without an accent:*

como • **this is how you do it** así es como se hace • **that was how I came to meet him** así es como lo conocí • **I'll do it how I like** lo haré como me parezca
3 (*in exclamations*)

> *You can often translate* **how** *+ adjective/adverb using* **qué** *+ adjective/adverb:*

qué • **how beautiful!** ¡qué bonito! • **how strange!** ¡qué raro! • **how quickly the time passed!** ¡qué de prisa pasó el tiempo! • **how glad I am to see you!** ¡cuánto me alegro de verte! • **how they talk!** ¡cuánto hablan! • **how sorry I am!** ¡cuánto lo siento! • **how she's changed!** ¡cuánto ha cambiado! • **how kind of you!** es usted muy amable

CONJUNCTION

(= *that**) que • **she told me how she'd seen him last night** me dijo que lo había visto anoche

NOUN

• **I want to know the how and the why of all this** quiero saber el cómo y el porqué de todo esto

---

howdah ['haʊdə] (N) howdah *f* (*silla para montar elefantes*)
howdy* ['haʊdɪ] (EXCL) (*US*) ¡hola!
how-d'ye-do ['haʊdjə'duː] (N) lío *m* • **this is a fine how-d'ye-do!** ¡en buen lío *or* berenjenal nos hemos metido!, ¡vaya lío!
however [haʊ'evəʳ] (ADV) **1** (= *nevertheless*) sin embargo, no obstante • **most men, ~, prefer black** la mayoría de los hombres, sin embargo *or* no obstante, prefieren el negro
2 (= *no matter how*) • **~ cold it is, we still manage to have fun** por mucho frío que haga, nos las arreglamos para pasarlo bien • **he'll never catch us ~ fast he runs** por muy rápido que vaya *or* por mucho que corra no nos alcanzará • **~ hard she tried, she couldn't remember his name** por mucho *or* más que lo intentaba, no lograba acordarse de su nombre • **wait 10 to 15 minutes, or ~ long it takes** espera 10 ó 15 minutos, o los que sean necesarios • **the 5,000 spectators, or ~ many were there** los 5.000 espectadores, o los que fuesen • **take about a metre of fabric, or ~ much you need** toma un metro de tela o lo que necesites
3 (*in questions*) (= *how*) cómo • **~ did you manage to do that?** ¿cómo te las arreglaste para hacer eso?
(CONJ) • **~ it's done, it has to look right** se haga como se haga, tiene que quedar bien • **~ we add it up, it doesn't come to 83** lo sumemos como lo sumemos, no da 83, hagamos la suma como la hagamos, no da 83 • **~ you want** *or* **like** como quieras • **you can do it ~ you want** puedes hacerlo como quieras

> **HOWEVER**
>
> *Unlike* **however, sin embargo** *and* **no obstante** *can never end a sentence; they must always go at the beginning of it or between the clauses:*
>
> **He has one problem, however**
> Sin embargo, tiene un problema
> **He does not expect to come out of the meeting with anything concrete, however**
> No obstante, no espera salir de la reunión con nada concreto

howitzer ['haʊɪtsəʳ] (N) obús *m*
howl [haʊl] (N) [*of animal*] aullido *m*; [*of wind*] rugido *m*; (*fig*) [*of protest*] clamor *m*, grito *m* • **a ~ of pain** un alarido de dolor • **~s of laughter** (*fig*) carcajadas *fpl* • **with a ~ of rage** dando un alarido de furia
(VI) [*animal*] aullar; [*person*] dar alaridos; [*wind*] rugir, bramar; [*child*] (= *weep*) berrear • **the dog ~ed all night** el perro estuvo aullando toda la noche • **he ~ed with pain** aullaba de dolor, daba alaridos de dolor • **to ~ with laughter** (*fig*) reír a carcajadas • **to ~ with rage** bramar de furia, bramar furioso
(VT) (= *shout*) gritar
▸ **howl down** (VT + ADV) hacer callar a gritos
howler ['haʊləʳ] (N) falta *f* garrafal
howling ['haʊlɪŋ] (ADJ) [*success*] clamoroso
howsoever [haʊsəʊ'evəʳ] (ADV) comoquiera que
hoy [hɔɪ] (EXCL) ¡eh!, ¡hola!
hoyden† ['hɔɪdn] (N) marimacho *m*
HP (N ABBR) **1** (*Brit**) = **hire purchase**
2 (= **horsepower**) C.V. *mpl*
h.p. (N ABBR) (= **horsepower**) C.V. *mpl*
HQ (N ABBR) (= **headquarters**) E.M.
HR (N ABBR) **1** = **Human Resources**
2 (*US*) = **House of Representatives**
hr (ABBR) (= **hour**) h
HRH (N ABBR) (= **Her** *or* **His Royal Highness**) S.A.R.
hrs (ABBR) (= **hours**) hs
HRT (N ABBR) = **hormone replacement therapy**
HS (ABBR) (*US*) = **high school**
HSS (N ABBR) (*US*) = **Health and Social Services**
HST (N ABBR) **1** (*Brit*) = **high speed train**
2 (*US*) = **Hawaiian Standard Time**
HT (N ABBR) = **high tension**

h

ht ABBR (= **height**) alt.
HTML N ABBR (= **hypertext markup language**) HTML *m*
http N ABBR (= **hypertext transfer protocol**) http *m*
HUAC N ABBR (*US*) (*Hist*) = **House Un-American Activities Committee**
hub [hʌb] N cubo *m*; (*fig*) eje *m*; (*Comput*) hub *m*, concentrador *m* • **wireless hub** hub *m* *or* concentrador *m* inalámbrico
CPD ▸ **hub airport** (*US*) aeropuerto *m* principal
hubbub [ˈhʌbʌb] N algarabía *f*, barahúnda *f* • **a ~ of voices** un barullo de voces
hubby* [ˈhʌbɪ] N marido *m*, maridito* *m*
hubcap [ˈhʌbkæp] N (*Aut*) tapacubos *m inv*
hubris [ˈhju:brɪs] N orgullo *m* desmesurado
huckster [ˈhʌkstəʳ] N (*US*) vendedor *m* ambulante, buhonero *m*
HUD N ABBR (*US*) = **Department of Housing and Urban Development**
huddle [ˈhʌdl] N [*of people*] tropel *m*; [*of things*] montón *m* • **to go into a ~*** hacer un corrillo para discutir algo en secreto
VI acurrucarse • **we ~d round the fire** nos arrimamos al fuego • **the chairs were ~d in a corner** las sillas estaban amontonadas en un rincón
▸ **huddle down** VI + ADV (= *snuggle*) acurrucarse; (= *crouch*) agacharse
▸ **huddle together** VI + ADV apiñarse • **they were huddling together for warmth** estaban apiñados *or* acurrucados para darse calor
▸ **huddle up** VI + ADV apretarse (**against** contra)
hue¹ [hju:] N (= *colour*) color *m*; (= *shade*) matiz *m* • **people of every political hue** gente de todos los matices políticos
hue² [hju:] N • **hue and cry** [*of protest*] griterío *m*, clamor *m* • **to raise a hue and cry** levantar protestas • **there was a hue and cry after him** se le persiguió enérgicamente
huff* [hʌf] N • **in a ~** enojado • **to go off in a ~** irse ofendido, picarse • **to take the ~** ofenderse
VI • **to ~ and puff** (*out of breath*) jadear, resollar • **he ~ed and puffed a lot and then said yes** (*fig*) resopló mucho y luego dijo que bueno
huffed* [hʌft] ADJ enojado
huffily [ˈhʌfɪlɪ] ADV malhumoradamente • **he said ~** dijo malhumorado
huffiness [ˈhʌfɪnɪs] N mal humor *m*
huffy [ˈhʌfɪ] ADJ (COMPAR: **huffier**, SUPERL: **huffiest**) (*of character*) enojadizo; (*in mood*) malhumorado, ofendido • **he was a bit ~ about it** se ofendió un tanto por ello
hug [hʌg] N abrazo *m* • **to give sb a hug** dar un abrazo a algn • **give me a hug** dame un abrazo
VT **1** (*lovingly*) abrazar; (= *squeeze*) [*bear*] ahogar, apretar • **they hugged each other** se abrazaron • **to hug o.s. to keep warm** acurrucarse para darse calor
2 (= *keep close to*) arrimarse a
huge [hju:dʒ] (COMPAR: **huger**, SUPERL: **hugest**) ADJ [*person, building, thing*] enorme, inmenso; [*bill, sum of money, investment*] enorme, astronómico*; [*increase, problem, difference*] enorme, tremendo • **~ amounts of** enormes cantidades de • **~ numbers of** gran número de • **they are making a ~ profit** están sacando enormes beneficios *or* beneficios astronómicos • **the result was human suffering on a ~ scale** el resultado fue sufrimiento humano en proporciones gigantescas • **to be a ~ success** tener un éxito enorme, ser todo un éxito
hugely [ˈhju:dʒlɪ] ADV **1** (*with adj*) [*expensive, popular, entertaining, important*] tremendamente, enormemente • **a ~ enjoyable book** un libro que se disfruta muchísimo • **a ~ successful film** una película de enorme éxito • **he is a ~ talented songwriter** es un compositor con un talento enorme
2 (*with verb*) [*vary, increase*] enormemente • **she seemed to be enjoying herself ~** parecía que se lo estaba pasando en grande
hugeness [ˈhju:dʒnɪs] N inmensidad *f*
hugger-mugger [ˈhʌgəˌmʌgəʳ] N confusión *f* • **a hugger-mugger of books** un montón de libros en desorden
ADV desordenadamente
-hugging [ˈhʌgɪŋ] ADJ (*ending in compounds*) • **figure-hugging** ajustado, ceñido al cuerpo
Hugh [hju:] N Hugo, Ugo
Huguenot [ˈhju:gənəʊ] ADJ hugonote
N hugonote/a *m/f*
huh [hʌ] EXCL ¡eh!
Hula Hoop® [ˈhu:ləˌhu:p] N Hula Hoop *m*
hulk [hʌlk] N **1** (*Naut*) (= *abandoned ship*) casco *m*; (*pej*) (= *clumsy ship*) carraca *f*
2 (= *large, ungainly building*) armatoste *m* • **a great ~ of a man*** un gigantón
hulking* [ˈhʌlkɪŋ] ADJ pesado • **a ~ great brute** un hombracho
hull [hʌl] N (*Naut*) casco *m*
VT [+ *fruit*] descascarar
hullabaloo* [ˌhʌləbəˈlu:] N (= *noise*) algarabía *f*; (= *fuss*) jaleo *m*, revuelo *m* • **a great ~ broke out** se armó un revuelo tremendo • **that ~ about the money** ese jaleo *or* revuelo que se armó por el dinero*
hullo [hʌˈləʊ] EXCL = **hello**
hum [hʌm] N (*gen*) (*Elec*) zumbido *m*; [*of voices*] murmullo *m*
VT [+ *tune*] canturrear, tararear
VI **1** [*insect, wire*] zumbar; [*person*] canturrear, tararear una canción
2 (*fig**) (= *be busy*) bullir, hervir • **the market place was humming** el mercado era un hervidero (de actividad), el mercado bullía *or* hervía de actividad • **to make things hum** hacer que la cosa marche* • **to hum with activity** bullir de actividad
3* (= *smell*) oler mal
4 • **to hum and haw** vacilar
human [ˈhju:mən] ADJ humano • **the ~ voice** la voz humana • **~ feet are made for weight bearing** los pies del ser humano *or* del hombre están hechos para soportar peso • **we bank managers are ~ too** los directores de banco también somos humanos • IDIOM: • **I'm/he's** *etc* **only ~** todos somos humanos
N ser *m* humano
CPD ▸ **human being** ser *m* humano ▸ **human chain** • **to form a ~ chain** formar una cadena humana ▸ **human consumption** • **to be fit for ~ consumption** ser apto para el consumo humano ▸ **human error** error *m* humano • **it was a case of ~ error** fue un (caso de) error humano ▸ **human genome** genoma *m* humano ▸ **human growth hormone** hormona *f* de crecimiento humano ▸ **human interest** interés *m* humano ▸ **human interest story** historia *f* de interés humano ▸ **human nature** naturaleza *f* humana • **it's ~ nature to do that** hacer eso es humano ▸ **the human race** la raza humana, el género humano ▸ **human resources** recursos *mpl* humanos ▸ **human resource manager** director(a) *m/f* de recursos humanos ▸ **human rights** derechos *mpl* humanos ▸ **human rights abuses** violaciones *fpl* de los derechos humanos ▸ **human rights activist** militante *mf* de la causa de los derechos humanos ▸ **human rights campaigner** defensor(a) *m/f* de los derechos humanos ▸ **human rights group** asociación *f* de defensa de los derechos humanos, asociación *f* pro derechos humanos ▸ **human rights organization** organización *f* de defensa de los derechos humanos, organización *f* pro derechos humanos ▸ **human rights record** historial *m* en materia de derechos humanos ▸ **human shield** • **to use sb as a ~ shield** usar a algn como escudo (humano)
humane [hju:ˈmeɪn] ADJ humano, humanitario
CPD ▸ **Humane Society** (*US*) • **the Humane Society** *la sociedad para la protección de animales* ▸ **humane studies** ciencias *fpl* humanas, humanidades *fpl*
humanely [hju:ˈmeɪnlɪ] ADV humanamente
humaneness [hju:ˈmeɪnnɪs] N humanidad *f*
humanism [ˈhju:mənɪzəm] N humanismo *m*
humanist [ˈhju:mənɪst] N humanista *mf*
humanistic [ˌhju:məˈnɪstɪk] ADJ humanístico
humanitarian [hju:ˌmænɪˈtɛərɪən] ADJ humanitario
N humanitario/a *m/f*
humanitarianism [hju:ˌmænɪˈtɛərɪənɪzəm] N humanitarismo *m*
humanity [hju:ˈmænɪtɪ] N **1** (*gen*) humanidad *f* • **crimes against ~** crímenes *mpl* contra la humanidad *or* de lesa humanidad
2 (*Literat, Art*) • **the humanities** las humanidades
3 (*Scol*) **humanities** letras *fpl*, humanidades *fpl*
humanization [ˌhju:mənaɪˈzeɪʃən] N humanización *f*
humanize [ˈhju:mənaɪz] VT humanizar
humankind [ˈhju:mənˈkaɪnd] N el género humano
humanly [ˈhju:mənlɪ] ADV humanamente • **to do everything ~ possible** hacer todo lo humanamente posible • **as quickly/well as is ~ possible** tan deprisa/bien como sea humanamente posible • **as far as is ~ possible** dentro de lo humanamente posible
humanoid [ˈhju:mənɔɪd] ADJ humanoide
N humanoide *mf*
humble [ˈhʌmbl] ADJ (COMPAR: **humbler**, SUPERL: **humblest**) **1** (= *unassuming*) [*person*] humilde, modesto; [*apology*] humilde • **she was very ~ about her achievements** era muy modesta respecto a sus éxitos • **my ~ apologies for keeping you waiting** (*frm*) mis más humildes disculpas por tenerle esperando • **in my ~ opinion** en mi humilde *or* modesta opinión • **I am** *or* **remain your ~ servant** (*frm*) (*in letters*) su humilde *or* seguro/a servidor(a)
2 (= *lowly*) [*person, origins, background*] humilde; [*house, home*] humilde, modesto • **the ~ maggot** el humilde gusano • **welcome to our ~ abode** (*hum*) bienvenido a nuestra humilde morada
VT **1** (= *make humble*) dar una lección de humildad a • **Ted's words ~d me** Ted me dio una lección de humildad con sus palabras • **it was a humbling experience** fue una lección de humildad • **to ~ o.s. before God** acercarse a Dios con humildad
2 (= *defeat*) humillar
CPD ▸ **humble pie** • IDIOM: • **to eat ~ pie** morder el polvo
humblebee [ˈhʌmblbi:] N abejorro *m*
humbled [ˈhʌmbld] ADJ lleno de humildad

• **I felt deeply honoured, yet very ~, by this awesome prospect** me sentí muy honrado, y a la vez lleno de humildad, ante esta imponente perspectiva

humbleness ['hʌmblnɪs] N humildad *f*

humbly ['hʌmblɪ] ADV **1** (= *meekly*) [*say, act*] humildemente
2 (*frm*) (= *respectfully*) [*ask*] humildemente; [*suggest, propose*] humildemente, modestamente • **to ~ apologise for sth** disculparse humildemente por algo • **I most ~ beg your pardon/thank you** le pido perdón/le doy las gracias con toda humildad
3 (= *modestly*) humildemente • **~ born** de origen humilde

humbug* ['hʌmbʌg] N **1** (= *person*) charlatán/ana *m/f* • **he's an old ~** es un farsante
2 (= *nonsense*) tonterías *fpl* • **~!** ¡bobadas!*
3 (*Brit*) (= *sweet*) caramelo *m* de menta

humdinger ['hʌmdɪŋəʳ] N • **it's a ~!*** ¡es una auténtica maravilla! • **a real ~ of a car** una maravilla de coche

humdrum ['hʌmdrʌm] ADJ monótono, rutinario

humerus ['hju:mərəs] N (PL: **humeri** ['hju:məraɪ]) húmero *m*

humid ['hju:mɪd] ADJ húmedo

humidifier [hju:'mɪdɪfaɪəʳ] N humedecedor *m*

humidify [hju:'mɪdɪfaɪ] VT [+ *room, air*] humidificar

humidity [hju:'mɪdɪtɪ] N humedad *f*

humidor ['hju:mɪ,dɔ:ʳ] N humidificador *m*

humiliate [hju:'mɪlɪeɪt] VT humillar

humiliated [hju:'mɪlɪeɪtɪd] ADJ humillado • **to feel ~** sentirse humillado • **I have never felt so ~ in my life** en mi vida me he sentido tan humillado

humiliating [hju:'mɪlɪeɪtɪŋ] ADJ humillante, vergonzoso

humiliatingly [hju:'mɪlɪeɪtɪŋlɪ] ADV de manera humillante, vergonzosamente • **we were ~ defeated** sufrimos una derrota vergonzosa

humiliation [hju:mɪlɪ'eɪʃən] N humillación *f*

humility [hju:'mɪlɪtɪ] N humildad *f*

humming ['hʌmɪŋ] N [*of insect*] zumbido *m*; [*of person*] tarareo *m*, canturreo *m*
CPD ▸ **humming top** trompa *f*

hummingbird ['hʌmɪŋbɜ:d] N colibrí *m*, picaflor *m*

hummock ['hʌmək] N montecillo *m*, morón *m*

hummus, hummous ['hʊməs] N *paté de garbanzos originario del Oriente Medio*

humongous* [hju'mɒŋgəs] ADJ • **she is such a ~ star** es una superestrella • **we had a ~ row** tuvimos una pelea de órdago*

humor ['hju:məʳ] N, VT (*US*) = **humour**

-humored ['hju:məd] ADJ (*ending in compounds*) (*US*) = **-humoured**

humorist ['hju:mərɪst] N humorista *mf*

humorless ['hju:məlɪs] ADJ (*US*) = **humourless**

humorous ['hju:mərəs] ADJ [*person*] gracioso, divertido; [*book, story*] divertido; [*situation, idea, tone*] cómico, gracioso

humorously ['hju:mərəslɪ] ADV con gracia

humour, humor (*US*) ['hju:məʳ] N
1 (= *amusingness*) (*gen*) humor *m*; [*of book, situation*] gracia *f* • **sense of ~** sentido *m* del humor • **to have a sense of ~** tener sentido del humor • **I see no ~ in that** no le veo la gracia a eso
2 (= *mood*) humor *m* • **to be in a good/bad ~** estar de buen/mal humor • **they were in no ~ for fighting** no estaban de humor para pelear • **to be out of ~** estar de mal humor
3 (*Med*) humor *m*
VT complacer, consentir

-humoured, -humored (*US*) ['hju:məd] ADJ (*ending in compounds*) de humor ...

humourless, humorless (*US*) ['hju:məlɪs] ADJ [*person*] arisco; [*joke*] sin gracia

humourlessly, humorlessly (*US*) ['hju:məlɪslɪ] ADV [*laugh, smile*] forzadamente

hump [hʌmp] N **1** (*Anat*) joroba *f*
2 [*of camel*] giba *f*
3 (*in ground*) montecillo *m* • **we're over the ~** (*fig*) ya pasamos lo peor
4 (*Brit**) (= *bad mood*) • **it gives me the ~** me fastidia, me molesta • **to have the ~** estar de mal humor
VT **1** (= *arch*) encorvar • **to ~ one's back** encorvarse
2* (= *carry*) llevar
3** (= *have sex with*) joder (*Sp***), coger (*LAm***)
VI** (= *have sex*) joder**, follar**

humpback ['hʌmpbæk] N **1** (= *person*) jorobado/a *m/f* • **to have a ~** ser jorobado
2 (= *whale*) (*also* **humpback whale**) rorcual *m*

humpbacked ['hʌmpbækt] ADJ [*person*] jorobado • **~ bridge** puente *m* encorvado

humph [mm] EXCL ¡bah!

humpy ['hʌmpɪ] ADJ (COMPAR: **humpier**, SUPERL: **humpiest**) desigual

humungous* [hju'mʌŋgəs] ADJ = **humongous**

humus ['hju:məs] N (*Bio*) humus *m*

humvee ['hʌmvi:] N humvee *m* (*vehículo militar*)

Hun [hʌn] N **1** (*Hist*) huno *m*
2 (*pej*) (= *German*) tudesco *m*, alemán *m*

hunch [hʌntʃ] N **1*** (= *idea*) corazonada *f*, presentimiento *m* • **it's only a ~** no es más que una corazonada *or* un presentimiento que tengo • **I had a ~** tuve una corazonada *or* un presentimiento • **the detective had one of his ~es** el detective tuvo una de sus corazonadas
2 (*Anat*) = **hump**
VT (*also* **hunch up**) encorvar • **to ~ one's back** encorvarse
VI encorvarse • **to be ~ed up** ser jorobado • **to sit ~ed up** estar sentado con el cuerpo doblado

hunchback ['hʌntʃbæk] N jorobado/a *m/f*

hunchbacked ['hʌntʃbækt] ADJ jorobado

hunched ['hʌntʃt] ADJ [*figure, person, shoulders, back*] encorvado • **he sat ~ in a corner** estaba sentado en un rincón, encorvado • **to sit ~ over sth** sentarse con la espalda encorvada sobre algo

hundred ['hʌndrɪd] N **1** • **a** *or* **one ~** (*before noun, or used alone*) cien; (*before numbers up to 99*) ciento • **a** *or* **one ~ people** cien personas • **to count up to a** *or* **one ~** contar hasta cien • **a ~ and one/two** ciento uno/dos • **a** *or* **one ~ and ten** ciento diez • **a** *or* **one ~ thousand** cien mil • **two ~** doscientos • **three ~** trescientos • **five ~ people** quinientas personas • **five ~ and one** quinientos uno • **seven ~ euros** setecientos euros • **nine ~ pounds** novecientas libras • **a ~ per cent** cien por cien • **to live to be a ~** llegar a los cien años • **the ~ and first** el centésimo primero
2 (= *figure*) ciento *m*
3 (= *large number*) • **in ~s** • **by the ~** a centenares • **for ~s of thousands of years** durante centenares de miles de años • **~s of people** centenares de personas • **I've got ~s of letters to write** tengo que escribir cientos de cartas • **I've told you ~s of times** te lo he dicho cientos *or* centenares de veces • **I've got a ~ and one things to do** tengo la mar de cosas que hacer
CPD ▸ **the Hundred Years' War** la Guerra de los Cien Años

> **HUNDRED**
>
> **"Ciento" or "cien"?**
>
> ▹ *Use* **cien** *before a noun (even when it follows* **mil**):
> **... a** *or* **one hundred soldiers ...**
> ... cien soldados ...
> **... eleven hundred metres ...**
> ... mil cien metros ...
>
> *NOTE: Don't translate numbers like* **eleven hundred** *literally. Translate their equivalent in thousands and hundreds instead.*
>
> ▹ *Use* **cien** *before* **mil** *and* **millón**:
> **... a** *or* **one hundred thousand dollars ...**
> ... cien mil dólares ...
> **... a** *or* **one hundred million euros ...**
> ... cien millones de euros ...
>
> ▹ *But use* **ciento** *before another number:*
> **... a** *or* **one hundred and sixteen stamps ...**
> ... ciento dieciséis sellos ...
>
> ▹ *When* **hundred** *follows another number, use the compound forms* (**doscientos, -as, trescientos, -as** *etc) which must agree with the noun:*
> **... two hundred and fifty women ...**
> ... doscientas cincuenta mujeres ...
>
> *For further uses and examples, see main entry.*

hundredfold ['hʌndrɪdfəʊld] ADJ céntuplo
ADV cien veces

hundredth ['hʌndrɪdθ] ADJ centésimo
N centésimo *m*, centésima parte *f*

hundredweight ['hʌndrɪdweɪt] N (*Brit*) = *112 libras = 50.8 kilogramos*; (*approx*) quintal *m*; (*US*) = *100 libras = 45.4 kilogramos*

hung [hʌŋ] PT, PP *of* **hang**
CPD ▸ **hung jury** *jurado cuyos miembros no se pueden poner de acuerdo* ▸ **hung parliament** *parlamento en el que ningún partido alcanza mayoría absoluta*

Hungarian [hʌŋ'gɛərɪən] ADJ húngaro
N **1** (= *person*) húngaro/a *m/f*
2 (*Ling*) húngaro *m*

Hungary ['hʌŋgərɪ] N Hungría *f*

hunger ['hʌŋgəʳ] N **1** (*for food*) hambre *f*
2 (*fig*) sed *f* • **to have a ~ for** [+ *adventure, knowledge*] tener hambre *or* sed de, estar hambriento *or* sediento de • **he had a ~ for love** estaba ávido de amor
VI estar hambriento, tener hambre
CPD ▸ **the hunger marches** (*Brit*) (*Hist*) *marchas protagonizadas por los obreros británicos y sus familias durante la Gran Depresión para protestar por sus condiciones de pobreza* ▸ **hunger strike** huelga *f* de hambre • **to be on ~ strike** estar haciendo huelga de hambre • **to go on ~ strike** ponerse en huelga de hambre ▸ **hunger striker** huelguista *mf* de hambre
▸ **hunger for, hunger after** VI + PREP (*fig*) [+ *adventure, knowledge*] tener hambre *or* sed de, estar hambriento *or* sediento de

hung over* [hʌŋ'əʊvəʳ] ADJ • **to be ~** tener resaca

hungrily ['hʌŋgrɪlɪ] ADV **1** [*eat*] ávidamente, con ansia; [*look*] con anhelo
2 (*fig*) (= *eagerly*) ansiosamente • **American businesses are ~ eyeing the British market**

las compañías americanas están observando ansiosamente el mercado británico

hungry ['hʌŋgrɪ] ADJ (COMPAR: **hungrier**, SUPERL: **hungriest**) **1** (*gen*) [*person, animal*] hambriento • **pictures of ~ children** imágenes de niños hambrientos • **he looked at the cake with ~ eyes** miró el pastel con anhelo • **digging up the road is ~ work** cavar la calle es un trabajo que da hambre *or* abre el apetito • **to be ~** tener hambre • **to feel ~** tener hambre • **to go ~** pasar hambre • **we were late for tea so we had to go ~** llegamos tarde para la cena y tuvimos que quedarnos sin comer • **all this work is making me ~** todo este trabajo me está dando hambre • **talking about food is making me ~** hablando de comida se me está abriendo el apetito
2 (*fig*) (= *eager*) • **to be ~ for** [+ *adventure, knowledge*] tener hambre *or* sed de, estar hambriento *or* sediento de • **to be ~ for power** tener sed *or* estar sediento de poder

-hungry ['hʌŋgrɪ] SUFFIX • **power-hungry** con ansias de poder • **money-hungry** avaricioso • **publicity-hungry** con ansias de publicidad

hung up* ADJ (= *obsessed*) • **to be ~ about sth** estar obsesionado por algo

hunk [hʌŋk] N **1** [*of bread, cheese, cake*] (buen) trozo *m*, pedazo *m* (grande)
2* (= *man*) monumento* *m*, cachas *m inv* (*Sp**)

hunker down [ˌhʌŋkə'daʊn] VI + ADV (US)
1 (= *squat*) agacharse
2 (= *lie low*) tratar de no llamar la atención, tratar de pasar desapercibido

hunky* ['hʌŋkɪ] ADJ (COMPAR: **hunkier**, SUPERL: **hunkiest**) **1** (= *strong*) fuerte, macizo
2 (= *attractive*) bueno*

hunky-dory* [ˌhʌŋkɪ'dɔːrɪ] ADJ (*esp US*) guay* • **it's all hunky-dory** es guay del Paraguay*

hunt [hʌnt] N **1** (*for animals*) caza *f*, cacería *f* (**for** de); (= *huntsmen*) partida *f* de caza, (grupo *m* de) cazadores *mpl*
2 (= *search*) busca *f*, búsqueda *f* (**for** de); (= *pursuit*) persecución *f* • **the ~ for the murderer** la busca *or* búsqueda del asesino • **to be on the ~ for** estar *or* andar a la caza de • **the ~ is on** ha comenzado la búsqueda • **we joined in the ~ for the missing key** ayudamos a buscar la llave perdida
VT **1** [+ *animal*] cazar; [+ *hounds*] emplear en la caza; [+ *area of country*] recorrer de caza, cazar en
2 (= *search for*) buscar; (= *pursue*) perseguir
VI **1** (*Sport*) cazar, ir de cacería • **to go ~ing** ir de caza
2 (= *search*) buscar por todas partes • **to ~ for** buscar • **he ~ed for it in his pocket** lo buscó en el bolsillo • **to ~ about** *or* **around for** buscar por todas partes
CPD ▸ **hunt ball** *baile organizado tras una cacería* ▸ **hunt saboteur** militante *mf* que ejecuta acciones directas contra la caza
▸ **hunt down** VT + ADV [+ *person*] dar caza a; [+ *thing*] buscar (hasta encontrar)
▸ **hunt out** VT + ADV buscar (hasta encontrar)
▸ **hunt up** VT + ADV buscar

hunter ['hʌntəʳ] N **1** (= *person*) cazador(a) *m/f*
2 (= *horse*) caballo *m* de caza
CPD ▸ **hunter gatherer** cazador-recolector *m*

hunting ['hʌntɪŋ] N (*Sport*) caza *f*, cacería *f*
CPD ▸ **hunting box** pabellón *m* de caza ▸ **the hunting fraternity** los aficionados a la caza ▸ **hunting ground** cazadero *m* • **a happy ~ ground for** (*fig*) un terreno fértil para ▸ **hunting horn** cuerno *m* de caza ▸ **hunting lodge** pabellón *m* de caza ▸ **hunting pink** chaqueta *f* de caza roja ▸ **hunting season** época *f* de caza

huntress ['hʌntrɪs] N cazadora *f*

Hunts [hʌnts] N ABBR = **Huntingdonshire**

huntsman ['hʌntsmən] N (PL: **huntsmen**) (= *hunter*) cazador *m*

hurdle ['hɜːdl] N (*Sport*) valla *f*; (*fig*) obstáculo *m*, barrera *f* • **the 100m ~s** (= *race*) los 100 metros vallas • **the high ~s** las vallas altas • IDIOM: • **to fall at the first ~** fracasar a las primeras de cambio, no superar el primer escollo
CPD ▸ **hurdle race** carrera *f* de vallas

hurdler ['hɜːdləʳ] N vallista *mf*, corredor(a) *m/f* de vallas

hurdling ['hɜːdlɪŋ] N salto *m* de vallas

hurdy-gurdy ['hɜːdɪ,gɜːdɪ] N organillo *m*

hurl [hɜːl] VT (= *throw*) arrojar • **to ~ abuse** *or* **insults at sb** lanzar *or* soltar una sarta de insultos a algn • **to ~ o.s. at sth/sb** abalanzarse sobre algo/algn • **to ~ o.s. into the fray** lanzarse a la batalla • **to ~ o.s. over a cliff** arrojarse por un precipicio
▸ **hurl back** VT + ADV [+ *enemy*] rechazar

hurley ['hɜːlɪ] N = **hurling**

hurling ['hɜːlɪŋ] N *juego irlandés parecido al hockey*

hurly-burly ['hɜːlɪ'bɜːlɪ] N alboroto *m*, tumulto *m* • **the hurly-burly of politics** la vida tumultuosa de la política

hurrah [hʊ'rɑː], **hurray** [hʊ'reɪ] EXCL ¡hurra! • **~ for Mr Brown!** ¡viva el señor Brown!
N vítor *m*

hurricane ['hʌrɪkən] N (*Met*) huracán *m*
CPD ▸ **hurricane lamp** lámpara *f* a prueba de viento ▸ **hurricane season** temporada *f* de los huracanes ▸ **hurricane warning** alerta *f* de huracán

hurricane-force wind N vientos *mpl* huracanados • **hurricane-force winds and giant waves ripped holes in the bottom of the tanker** vientos huracanados y olas gigantes abrieron agujeros en la base del buque cisterna

hurried ['hʌrɪd] ADJ [*footsteps*] apresurado; [*visit, meeting*] rápido, cortísimo; [*phone call, conversation*] rápido • **to eat** *or* **have a ~ meal** comer a toda prisa, comer deprisa y corriendo

hurriedly ['hʌrɪdlɪ] ADV [*go, dress*] apresuradamente, a toda prisa; [*study, look at, read*] por encima, rápidamente; [*write*] apresuradamente, a vuela pluma • **Tim ~ made his excuses and left** Tim se excusó atropelladamente y se marchó • **he rose and ~ left** se levantó y se marchó precipitadamente • **"it doesn't matter," she said ~** —no importa —se apresuró a decir ella

hurry ['hʌrɪ] N prisa *f*, apuro *m* (*LAm*) • **to be in a ~ (to do sth)** tener prisa *or* (*LAm*) apuro (por hacer algo) • **I'm in no ~** • **I'm not in any ~** no tengo prisa • **they were in no ~ to pay us** no se dieron prisa por pagarnos • **are you in a ~ for this?** ¿le corre prisa (esto)? • **in our ~ to leave we left the keys behind** con las prisas de *or* por marcharnos nos dejamos olvidadas las llaves • **to do sth in a ~** hacer algo de prisa • **he won't do that again in a ~*** eso no lo vuelve a hacer • **I shan't come back here in a ~** aquí no pongo los pies nunca más • **is there any ~?** ¿corre prisa? • **there's no (great) ~** no hay *or* corre prisa • **what's the ~?** ¿a qué viene tanta prisa?
VT [+ *person*] meter prisa a, apresurar, apurar (*LAm*); [+ *work, job*] hacer apresuradamente, hacer deprisa y corriendo • **this is a job that cannot be hurried** este es un trabajo que no admite prisas • **he won't be hurried** no le gusta que le metan prisa • **don't let yourself be hurried into making a decision** no te obligues a tomar una decisión precipitada • **they hurried him to a doctor** lo llevaron a toda prisa a un médico • **troops were hurried to the spot** se enviaron tropas con urgencia al lugar
VI darse prisa, apurarse (*LAm*) • **~!** ¡date prisa!, ¡apúrate! (*LAm*) • **don't ~!** ¡no hay prisa *or* (*LAm*) apuro! • **to ~ to do sth** darse prisa *or* (*LAm*) apurarse en hacer algo, apresurarse a hacer algo • **to ~ after sb** correr detrás de algn • **to ~ back** volver de prisa • **she hurried home** se dio prisa para llegar a casa • **to ~ in** entrar corriendo • **I must ~** tengo que correr *or* darme prisa • **to ~ out** salir corriendo • **he hurried over to us** vino a toda prisa *or* corriendo hasta nosotros
▸ **hurry along** VI + ADV apresurarse, correr • **~ along now!** ¡vamos, rápido!
VT + ADV [+ *person*] meter prisa a, apresurar, apurar (*LAm*); [+ *work, job*] apurar, acelerar
▸ **hurry away, hurry off** VI + ADV irse corriendo
VT + ADV [+ *object*] llevar a la carrera • **to ~ sb away** *or* **off** llevarse a algn apresuradamente *or* a la carrera • **I wanted to look but the teacher quickly hurried us away** yo quería mirar pero el profesor se apresuró a alejarnos • **the policeman hurried him away** el policía se lo llevó apresuradamente
▸ **hurry off** VI + ADV, VT + ADV = **hurry away**
▸ **hurry on** VI + ADV (= *move*) pasar rápidamente; (= *speak*) continuar apresuradamente
VT + ADV = **hurry along**
▸ **hurry up** VI + ADV darse prisa, apurarse (*LAm*) • **~ up!** ¡date prisa!, ¡apúrate! (*LAm*)
VT + ADV [+ *person*] meter prisa a, apresurar, apurar (*LAm*); [+ *work, job*] apurar, acelerar

hurt [hɜːt] (PT, PP: **hurt**) VT **1** (= *do physical damage to*) hacer daño a, lastimar (*LAm*) • **how did you ~ your finger/leg?** ¿cómo te has hecho daño en el dedo/la pierna?, ¿cómo te has lastimado el dedo/la pierna? (*LAm*) • **ten people were ~ in the accident** diez personas resultaron heridas en el accidente • **to ~ o.s.** hacerse daño, lastimarse (*LAm*) • **did you ~ yourself?** ¿te has hecho daño?, ¿te has lastimado? (*LAm*) • **mind you don't ~ yourself** cuidado no te hagas daño • **he's not badly ~** no está herido de gravedad • **to get ~** resultar herido • **someone is bound to get ~** seguro que alguien resulta herido • IDIOM: • **to ~ a fly**: • **he wouldn't ~ a fly** sería incapaz de matar una mosca
2 (= *cause physical pain to*) • **did I ~ you?** ¿te he hecho daño?, ¿te he lastimado? (*LAm*) • **stop it! you're ~ing me!** ¡para! ¡me estás haciendo daño!, ¡para! ¡me estás lastimando! (*LAm*) • **my leg is ~ing me** me duele la pierna • **my feet are ~ing me** me duelen los pies
3 (= *have bad effect on*) **a** [+ *person*] • **it wouldn't ~ you to try** no pierdes nada intentándolo • **it wouldn't ~ her to try and save some money** no le vendría mal intentar ahorrar algo de dinero • **one little glass of wine won't ~ him** un vasito de vino no le va a hacer daño • **a little hard work never ~ anyone** nadie se ha muerto nunca por trabajar un poco duro, trabajar duro nunca le ha hecho daño a nadie
b [+ *prospects, chances, reputation*] perjudicar • **high interest rates are ~ing small businesses** los tipos de interés altos están perjudicando a las pequeñas empresas

4 (*= cause emotional pain to*) hacer daño a • **I was deeply ~ by his attitude** su actitud me hizo mucho daño • **I didn't mean to ~ you** no era mi intención hacerte sufrir *or* hacerte daño • **this is going to ~ me much more than it's going to ~ you** esto me va a doler mucho más a mí que a ti • **to be easily ~** ser muy susceptible • **you've ~ her feelings** la has ofendido • **his feelings were ~ by what you said** lo que dijiste lo ofendió *or* hirió sus sentimientos • **she was bound to get ~** estaba claro que iba a terminar sufriendo
(VI) **1** (*= physically*) [*arm, leg, foot etc*] doler • **my arm ~s** me duele el brazo • **my feet ~** me duelen los pies • **ow, that ~s!** ¡ay! ¡duele! • **it doesn't ~ much** no duele mucho • **it only ~s a little bit** solo duele un poquito • **it ~s when I walk** me duele cuando ando *or* al andar • **does it ~?** ¿te duele? • **where does it ~?** ¿dónde te duele? • **I ~ all over** me duele todo el cuerpo • **my shoes are ~ing** me hacen daño los zapatos • IDIOM: • **to kick/hit sb where it ~s**: • **kick him where it ~s!** ¡dale una buena patada donde más les duele (a los hombres)! • **she hit him where it ~s - in his wallet** le dio donde más le duele - en la cartera
2 (*emotionally*) doler • **it ~s to admit it but ...** duele *or* cuesta admitirlo pero ... • **the truth ~s** la verdad duele
3 (*= do harm*) • **it doesn't ~ to ask** por preguntar no se pierde nada • **it wouldn't ~ to let your mum know you'll be late** no te costaría nada avisarle a tu madre que vas a llegar tarde
4 (*esp US**) (*= feel pain*) sufrir
(ADJ) **1** (*= injured*) [*part of body*] lastimado • **James, are you ~?** James, ¿te has hecho daño?, James, ¿te has lastimado? (*esp LAm*)
2 (*= upset*) [*person, tone*] dolido • **he gave me a slightly ~ look** me miró un poco dolido • **to be/feel ~** estar/sentirse dolido
(N) (*= emotional pain*) dolor *m*, pena *f*

hurtful ['hɜ:tfʊl] (ADJ) [*remark*] hiriente; [*act, behaviour*] ofensivo; [*experience*] doloroso

hurtfully ['hɜ:tfʊlɪ] (ADV) de manera hiriente

hurtle ['hɜ:tl] (VI) precipitarse • **to ~ along** ir como un rayo *or* a toda velocidad • **the car ~d past** el coche pasó como un rayo *or* a toda velocidad
(VT) arrojar (violentamente)

husband ['hʌzbənd] (N) marido *m*, esposo *m*
(VT) [*+ resources*] administrar bien, gestionar bien • **you must ~ your strength** debes dosificar tus fuerzas

husbandry ['hʌzbəndrɪ] (N) **1** (*Agr*) agricultura *f* • **animal ~** cría *f* de animales
2 (*= administration*) (*also* **good husbandry**) buena administración *f*, buena gestión *f*

hush [hʌʃ] (N) silencio *m* • **a ~ fell** se hizo un silencio
(VI) callarse • **~!** ¡cállate!, ¡chitón!
(VT) [*+ person*] hacer callar
(CPD) ▸ **hush money*** soborno *m*, coima *f* (*And, S. Cone*), mordida *f* (*Mex*)
▸ **hush up** (VT + ADV) [*+ affair*] encubrir, echar tierra a; [*+ person*] tapar la boca a
(VI + ADV) (*US*) callarse

hushed [hʌʃt] (ADJ) [*silence*] profundo; [*tone*] callado, muy bajo • **the room was ~** la sala estaba en silencio • **the atmosphere was ~** el ambiente era silencioso

hush-hush* ['hʌʃ'hʌʃ] (ADJ) muy secreto

husk [hʌsk] (N) (*gen*) cascarilla *f*, cáscara *f*, cascabillo *m* (*Agr*)
(VT) quitar la cascarilla a, descascarillar

huskily ['hʌskɪlɪ] (ADV) con voz ronca

huskiness ['hʌskɪnɪs] (N) ronquedad *f*

husky[1] ['hʌskɪ] (ADJ) (COMPAR: **huskier**, SUPERL: **huskiest**) **1** [*voice, person*] ronco
2 (*= tough*) [*person*] fornido, fuerte

husky[2] ['hʌskɪ] (N) perro *m* esquimal

hussar [hə'zɑ:^{r}] (N) húsar *m*

hussy ['hʌsɪ] (N) fresca* *f* • **she's a little ~** es una fresca

hustings ['hʌstɪŋz] (NPL) (*esp Brit*) (*Pol*) campaña *fsing* electoral

hustle ['hʌsl] (N) **1** (*= activity*) bullicio *m* • **~ and bustle** ajetreo *m*, vaivén *m*
2 (*US**) (*= trick*) timo *m*, chanchullo* *m*
(VT) **1** (*= jostle*) empujar, codear; (*= hurry up*) [*+ person*] dar prisa a • **they ~d him in/out** le hicieron entrar/salir a empujones *or* sin ceremonia • **he was ~d into a car** lo metieron en un coche a empujones *or* sin ceremonia
2 (*fig*) • **to ~ things along** llevar las cosas a buen paso • **to ~ sb into making a decision** meter prisa a algn para que tome una decisión • **I won't be ~d into anything** no voy a dejar que me empujen a nada
3 (*US**) • **they were paid to ~ drinks out of the customers** les pagaban para sacarles bebidas a los clientes • **they were hustling him for payment of the debt** le apretaban las clavijas para que saldara la deuda
(VI) **1*** (*= hurry*) darse prisa, apresurarse, apurarse (*LAm*)
2* (*= work hard*) trabajar duro, currar (*Sp**)
3‡ [*prostitute*] hacer la calle*

hustler* ['hʌslə^r] (N) **1** (*= go-getter*) persona *f* dinámica
2 (*= swindler*) estafador(a) *m/f*, timador(a) *m/f*
3 (*= prostitute*) puto(a) *m/f*

hut [hʌt] (N) (*= shed*) cobertizo *m*; (*= small house*) cabaña *f*; (*= hovel*) barraca *f*, choza *f*; (*Mil*) barracón *m*, barraca *f* • **mountain hut** albergue *m* de montaña

hutch [hʌtʃ] (N) conejera *f*

HV, h.v. (N ABBR) = **high voltage**

HVT (N ABBR) (= **high-velocity train**) TAV *m*

HWM (ABBR) = **high-water mark**

hyacinth ['haɪəsɪnθ] (N) (*Bot*) jacinto *m*

hyaena [haɪ'i:nə] (N) = **hyena**

hybrid ['haɪbrɪd] (N) **1** (*Bio*) híbrido *m*
2 (*= word*) palabra *f* híbrida
(ADJ) híbrido

hybridism ['haɪbrɪdɪzəm] (N) hibridismo *m*

hybridization [ˌhaɪbrɪdaɪ'zeɪʃən] (N) hibridación *f*

hybridize ['haɪbrɪdaɪz] (VT) hibridar
(VI) hibridar

hydra ['haɪdrə] (N) (PL: **hydras** *or* **hydrae** ['haɪdri:]) hidra *f* • **Hydra** (*Myth*) Hidra *f*

hydrangea [haɪ'dreɪndʒə] (N) (*Bot*) hortensia *f*

hydrant ['haɪdrənt] (N) boca *f* de riego • **fire ~** boca *f* de incendios

hydrate ['haɪdreɪt] (N) hidrato *m*
(VT) hidratar

hydraulic [haɪ'drɒlɪk] (ADJ) hidráulico
(CPD) ▸ **hydraulic brakes** frenos *mpl* hidráulicos ▸ **hydraulic fracturing** fracturación *f* hidráulica ▸ **hydraulic press** prensa *f* hidráulica ▸ **hydraulic suspension** suspensión *f* hidráulica

hydraulics [haɪ'drɒlɪks] (NSING) hidráulica *f*

hydro ['haɪdrəʊ] (N) (*Brit*) balneario *m*

hydro... ['haɪdrəʊ] (PREFIX) hidro...

hydrocarbon [ˌhaɪdrəʊ'kɑ:bən] (N) hidrocarburo *m*

hydrocephalus [ˌhaɪdrəʊ'sefələs] (N) hidrocefalia *f*

hydrochloric [ˌhaɪdrə'klɒrɪk] (ADJ) • **~ acid** ácido *m* clorhídrico

hydrocyanic [ˌhaɪdrəsaɪ'ænɪk] (ADJ) • **~ acid** ácido *m* cianhídrico

hydrodynamics [ˌhaɪdrəʊdaɪ'næmɪks] (NSING) hidrodinámica *f*

hydroelectric [ˌhaɪdrəʊɪ'lektrɪk] (ADJ) [*power*] hidroeléctrico • **~ power station** central *f* hidroeléctrica

hydroelectricity [ˌhaɪdrəʊɪlek'trɪsɪtɪ] (N) hidroelectricidad *f*

hydrofoil ['haɪdrəʊfɔɪl] (N) hidroala *m*, aliscafo *m*

hydrogen ['haɪdrɪdʒən] (N) hidrógeno *m*
(CPD) ▸ **hydrogen bomb** bomba *f* de hidrógeno ▸ **hydrogen chloride** cloruro *m* de hidrógeno ▸ **hydrogen peroxide** agua *f* oxigenada ▸ **hydrogen sulphide** ácido *m* sulfhídrico

hydrography [haɪ'drɒgrəfɪ] (N) hidrografía *f*

hydrolysis [haɪ'drɒlɪsɪs] (N) hidrólisis *f*

hydrolyze ['haɪdrəlaɪz] (VT) hidrolizar
(VI) hidrolizarse

hydromassage [ˌhaɪdrəʊ'mæsɑ:ʒ] (N) hidromasaje *m*

hydrometer [haɪ'drɒmɪtə^r] (N) areómetro *m*, hidrómetro *m*

hydrophobia [ˌhaɪdrə'fəʊbɪə] (N) hidrofobia *f*

hydrophobic [ˌhaɪdrə'fəʊbɪk] (ADJ) hidrofóbico

hydroplane ['haɪdrəʊpleɪn] (N) hidroavión *m*

hydroponic [ˌhaɪdrəʊ'pɒnɪk] (ADJ) hidropónico

hydroponics [ˌhaɪdrəʊ'pɒnɪks] (NSING) hidroponia *f*

hydropower ['haɪdrəʊˌpaʊə^r] (N) hidrofuerza *f*

hydrotherapy [ˌhaɪdrəʊ'θerəpɪ] (N) hidroterapia *f*
(CPD) ▸ **hydrotherapy pool** balsa *f* de hidroterapia

hydroxide [haɪ'drɒksaɪd] (N) hidróxido *m*

hyena [haɪ'i:nə] (N) hiena *f* • **to laugh like a ~** reírse como una hiena

hygiene ['haɪdʒi:n] (N) higiene *f*

hygienic [haɪ'dʒi:nɪk] (ADJ) higiénico

hygienically [haɪ'dʒi:nɪklɪ] (ADV) higiénicamente

hygienist [haɪ'dʒi:nɪst] (N) higienista *mf*

hymen ['haɪmen] (N) himen *m*

hymn [hɪm] (N) himno *m*
(CPD) ▸ **hymn book** himnario *m*

hymnal ['hɪmnəl] (N) himnario *m*

hype* [haɪp] (N) exageraciones *fpl*; (*Comm*) bombo *m* publicitario* • **it's just media ~** no es más que una campaña orquestada por los medios de comunicación
(VT) (*Comm*) dar bombo publicitario a* • **the much-hyped movie: Batman** la tan cacareada película: Batman*
▸ **hype up‡** (VT + ADV) [*+ product*] dar bombo a*; [*+ claim*] exagerar; [*+ person*] excitar
(VI + ADV) pincharse*, picarse*

hyped-up* [ˌhaɪpt'ʌp] (ADJ) (*= very excited*) sobreexcitado; (*= very anxious*) estresado

hyper* ['haɪpə^r] (ADJ) hiperactivo • **to go ~** desmadrarse*, ponerse hiperactivo

hyper... ['haɪpə^r] (PREFIX) hiper...

hyperacidity ['haɪpərə'sɪdɪtɪ] (N) hiperacidez *f*

hyperactive [ˌhaɪpər'æktɪv] (ADJ) hiperactivo

hyperactivity [ˌhaɪpəræk'tɪvɪtɪ] (N) hiperactividad *f*

hyperbola [haɪ'pɜ:bələ] (N) (PL: **hyperbolas** *or* **hyperbole** [haɪ'pɜ:bəli:]) hipérbola *f*

hyperbole [haɪ'pɜ:bəlɪ] (N) hipérbole *f*

hyperbolic [ˌhaɪpə'bɒlɪk] (ADJ) hiperbólico

hyperbolical [ˌhaɪpə'bɒlɪkəl] (ADJ) = **hyperbolic**

hyperconnectivity [ˌhaɪpəkɒnek'tɪvəti] (N) hiperconectividad *f*

hypercorrection [ˌhaɪpəkə'rekʃən] (N) hipercorrección *f*, ultracorrección *f*

h

hypercritical [ˈhaɪpəˈkrɪtɪkəl] (ADJ) hipercrítico, ultracrítico
hyperglycaemia [ˌhaɪpəglaɪˈsiːmɪə], **hyperglycemia** (US) (N) hiperglucemia *f*
hyperinflation [ˈhaɪpəɪnˈfleɪʃən] (N) hiperinflación *f*
hyperlink [ˈhaɪpəlɪŋk] (N) hipervínculo *m*
hypermarket [ˈhaɪpəˌmɑːkɪt] (N) hipermercado *m*
hypermetropia [ˌhaɪpəmɪˈtrəʊpɪə] (N) hipermetropía *f*
hypermetropy [ˌhaɪpəˈmetrəpɪ] (N) = **hypermetropia**
hyperopia [ˈhaɪpərˈəʊpɪə] (N) hipermetropía *f*
hypersensitive [ˈhaɪpəˈsensɪtɪv] (ADJ) hipersensible
hypertension [ˈhaɪpəˈtenʃən] (N) (*Med*) hipertensión *f*
hypertext [ˈhaɪpəˌtekst] (N) (*Comput*) hipertexto *m*
hyperthyroidism [ˌhaɪpəˈθaɪrɔɪˌdɪzəm] (N) hipertiroidismo *m*
hypertrophy [haɪˈpɜːtrəfɪ] (N) hipertrofía *f* (VI) hipertrofiarse
hyperventilate [ˌhaɪpəˈventɪleɪt] (VI) respirar aceleradamente
hyperventilation [ˌhaɪpəventɪˈleɪʃən] (N) hiperventilación *f*
hyphen [ˈhaɪfən] (N) guión *m*
hyphenate [ˈhaɪfəneɪt] (VT) escribir con guión, unir con guión
hyphenated [ˈhaɪfəneɪtɪd] (ADJ) [*word*] con guión
hyphenation [ˌhaɪfəˈneɪʃən] (N) partición *f* silábica • **~ program** (*Comput*) programa de partición silábica
hypnosis [hɪpˈnəʊsɪs] (N) (PL: **hypnoses** [hɪpˈnəʊsiːz]) hipnosis *f* • **she revealed under ~ that ...** bajo los efectos de la hipnosis reveló que ...
hypnotherapist [ˌhɪpnəʊˈθerəpɪst] (N) hipnoterapeuta *mf*
hypnotherapy [ˌhɪpnəʊˈθerəpɪ] (N) hipnoterapia *f*
hypnotic [hɪpˈnɒtɪk] (ADJ) [*state*] hipnótico; [*eyes, rhythm, sound*] hipnótico, hipnotizador (N) hipnótico *m*
hypnotism [ˈhɪpnətɪzəm] (N) hipnotismo *m*
hypnotist [ˈhɪpnətɪst] (N) hipnotista *mf*
hypnotize [ˈhɪpnətaɪz] (VT) hipnotizar
hypo [ˈhaɪpəʊ] (N) (*Phot*) hiposulfito *m* sódico
hypoallergenic [ˌhaɪpəʊˌæləˈdʒenɪk] (ADJ) hipoalérgeno
hypochondria [ˌhaɪpəʊˈkɒndrɪə] (N) hipocondría *f*
hypochondriac [ˌhaɪpəʊˈkɒndrɪæk] (ADJ) hipocondríaco (N) hipocondríaco/a *m/f*
hypocrisy [hɪˈpɒkrɪsɪ] (N) hipocresía *f*
hypocrite [ˈhɪpəkrɪt] (N) hipócrita *mf*
hypocritical [ˌhɪpəˈkrɪtɪkəl] (ADJ) hipócrita
hypocritically [ˌhɪpəˈkrɪtɪkəlɪ] (ADV) hipócritamente
hypodermic [ˌhaɪpəˈdɜːmɪk] (ADJ) hipodérmico (N) (*also* **hypodermic needle**) aguja *f* hipodérmica
hypoglycaemia, **hypoglycemia** (US) [ˌhaɪpəʊglaɪˈsiːmɪə] (N) hipoglucemia *f*
hypoglycaemic, **hypoglycemic** (US) [ˌhaɪpəʊglaɪˈsiːmɪk] (ADJ) hipoglucémico
hyponym [ˈhaɪpənɪm] (N) hipónimo *m*
hyponymy [haɪˈpɒnɪmɪ] (N) hiponimia *f*
hypostasis [haɪˈpɒstəsɪs] (N) (PL: **hypostases** [haɪˈpɒstəsiːz]) (*Rel*) hipóstasis *f*
hypostatic [ˌhaɪpəʊˈstætɪk] (ADJ) (*Rel*) hipostático
hypotenuse [haɪˈpɒtɪnjuːz] (N) (*Math*) hipotenusa *f*
hypothalamus [ˌhaɪpəˈθæləməs] (N) (PL: **hypothalami** [ˌhaɪpəˈθæləmaɪ]) hipotálamo *m*
hypothermia [ˌhaɪpəʊˈθɜːmɪə] (N) hipotermia *f*
hypothesis [haɪˈpɒθɪsɪs] (N) (PL: **hypotheses** [haɪˈpɒθɪsiːz]) hipótesis *f inv*
hypothesize [haɪˈpɒθɪsaɪz] (VI) realizar hipótesis, hacer hipótesis • **to ~ about** *or* **(up)on sth** realizar *or* hacer hipótesis sobre algo (VT) plantear la hipótesis de
hypothetic [ˌhaɪpəʊˈθetɪk] (ADJ) = **hypothetical**
hypothetical [ˌhaɪpəʊˈθetɪkəl] (ADJ) hipotético
hypothetically [ˌhaɪpəʊˈθetɪkəlɪ] (ADV) hipotéticamente
hyssop [ˈhɪsəp] (N) (*Bot*) hisopo *m*
hysterectomy [ˌhɪstəˈrektəmɪ] (N) histerectomía *f* • **she had to have a ~** le tuvieron que hacer una histerectomía
hysteria [hɪsˈtɪərɪə] (N) histeria *f*, histerismo *m* • **mass ~** histeria *f* colectiva
hysterical [hɪsˈterɪkəl] (ADJ) **1** (*Psych*) histérico
2 (= *out of control*) histérico • **you're being ~** te estás comportando como un histérico • **to get ~** ponerse histérico
3 (= *very funny*) [*situation*] para morirse de (la) risa; [*person*] graciosísimo, desternillante
hysterically [hɪsˈterɪkəlɪ] (ADV) histéricamente • **to weep/laugh ~** llorar/reír histéricamente • **it was ~ funny** fue para morirse de (la) risa, fue graciosísimo • **"come here!" — she shouted ~** —¡ven acá! —gritó, histérica
hysterics [hɪsˈterɪks] (NPL) **1** (= *tears, shouts*) histeria *f*, histerismo *m* • **she was in ~** tenía un ataque de histeria, estaba histérica • **to go into** *or* **have ~** ponerse histérico
2* (= *laughter*) ataque *m* de risa • **we were in ~ about it** estábamos muertos de risa
Hz (ABBR) (*Rad etc*) (= **hertz**) Hz

Ii

I, i¹ [aɪ] N (= *letter*) I, i *f* • **I for Isabel** I de Isabel • IDIOM: • **to dot the i's and cross the t's** poner los puntos sobre las íes

I² [aɪ] PERS PRON (*emphatic, to avoid ambiguity*) yo • **I'm not one to exaggerate** yo no soy de los que exageran • **it is I who …** soy yo quien … • **he was frightened but I wasn't** él estaba asustado pero yo no • **if I were you** yo que tú • **Ann and I** Ann y yo • **he is taller than I am** es más alto que yo

Don't translate the subject pronoun when not emphasizing or clarifying:

• **I've got an idea** tengo una idea • **I'll go and see** voy a ver

I. ABBR (*Geog*) (= **Island, Isle**) isla *f*

i. ABBR (*Econ*) = **interest**

IA, Ia. ABBR (*US*) = **Iowa**

IAAF N ABBR = **International Amateur Athletic Federation**

IAEA N ABBR (= **International Atomic Energy Agency**) OIEA *f or m*

iambic [aɪ'æmbɪk] ADJ yámbico
N yambo *m*, verso *m* yámbico
CPD ▸ **iambic pentameter** pentámetro *m* yámbico

IATA [aɪ'ɑːtə] N ABBR (= **International Air Transport Association**) AITA *f*

IBA N ABBR (*Brit*) (= **Independent Broadcasting Authority**) *entidad que controla los medios privados de televisión y radio*

Iberia [aɪ'bɪərɪə] N Iberia *f*

Iberian [aɪ'bɪərɪən] ADJ ibero, ibérico
N ibero/a *m/f*
CPD ▸ **the Iberian Peninsula** la Península Ibérica

IBEW N ABBR (*US*) = **International Brotherhood of Electrical Workers**

ibex ['aɪbeks] N (PL: **ibexes** *or* **ibex** *or* **ibices** ['aɪbɪˌsiːz]) cabra *f* montés, íbice *m*

ibid ['ɪbɪd] ADV ABBR (= **ibidem**) ibíd., ib.

ibis ['aɪbɪs] N (PL: **ibises** *or* **ibis**) ibis *f inv*

IBM N ABBR = **International Business Machines**

IBRD N ABBR (= **International Bank for Reconstruction and Development**) BIRD *m*

IBS N ABBR = **irritable bowel syndrome**

i/c ABBR (= **in charge (of)**) encargado (de)

ICA N ABBR **1** (*Brit*) = **Institute of Contemporary Arts**
2 (*Brit*) = **Institute of Chartered Accountants**
3 = **International Cooperation Administration**

ICAO N ABBR (= **International Civil Aviation Organization**) OACI *f*

ICBM N ABBR = **intercontinental ballistic missile**

ICC N ABBR **1** (= **International Chamber of Commerce**) CCI *f*
2 (*US*) = **Interstate Commerce Commission**

ice [aɪs] N **1** (= *frozen water*) hielo *m* • **as cold as ice** (tan) frío como el hielo • **my feet are like ice** tengo los pies helados • IDIOMS: • **to break the ice** romper el hielo • **to cut no ice**: • **arguments like that cut no ice with him** ese tipo de argumentos lo dejan frío • **to keep/put sth on ice**: • **we put the champagne on ice** pusimos el champán a enfriar • **she put her career on ice for ten years while she had children** dejó su carrera aparcada durante diez años para tener hijos • **to keep money on ice** tener dinero en reserva • **to put a project on ice** posponer un proyecto • **to skate on thin ice** pisar terreno peligroso
2 (= *ice cream*) helado *m*
VT **1** helar; [+ *drink*] enfriar, echar cubos de hielo a
2 [+ *cake*] glasear, escarchar
CPD ▸ **the Ice Age** la edad de hielo, el periodo glacial • **an ice-age rock/fossil** una roca/un fósil del periodo glacial ▸ **ice axe, ice ax** (*US*) piqueta *f* (de alpinista), piolet *m* ▸ **ice bucket** cubo *m* del hielo, hielera *f* (*LAm*) ▸ **ice cream** helado *m*; ▹ **ice-cream** ▸ **ice cube** cubito *m* de hielo ▸ **ice dance** baile *m* sobre hielo ▸ **ice field** campo *m* de hielo, banquisa *f* ▸ **ice floe** témpano *m* de hielo ▸ **ice hockey** hockey *m* sobre hielo ▸ **ice house** (*for storing ice*) nave *f* frigorífica (*edificio*); [*of Eskimo*] iglú *m* ▸ **ice lolly** (*Brit*) polo *m* (*Sp*), paleta *f* (*LAm*) ▸ **ice maiden*** mujer *f* de hielo ▸ **ice pack** compresa *f* de hielo ▸ **ice pick** (*Culin*) punzón *m* para el hielo ▸ **ice rink** pista *f* de patinaje sobre hielo, pista *f* de hielo ▸ **ice skate** patín *m* de hielo, patín *m* de cuchilla; ▹ **ice-skate** ▸ **ice skater** patinador(a) *m/f* (artístico/a), patinador(a) *m/f* sobre hielo ▸ **ice skating** patinaje *m* sobre hielo • **to go ice skating** ir a patinar sobre hielo ▸ **ice tray** cubitera *f*, hielera *f* (*LAm*), cubeta *f* (*Arg, Uru*) ▸ **ice water, iced water** agua *f* helada, agua *f* fría (*de la nevera*)
▸ **ice over, ice up** VI + ADV helarse, congelarse

iceberg ['aɪsbɜːg] N iceberg *m* • IDIOM: • **that's just the tip of the ~!** no es más que la punta del iceberg
CPD ▸ **iceberg lettuce** lechuga *f* repollo

ice-blue [ˌaɪs'bluː] ADJ azul claro, azul pálido

icebound ['aɪsbaʊnd] ADJ [*road, ship*] bloqueado por el hielo

icebox ['aɪsbɒks] N (*Brit*) (= *part of refrigerator*) congelador *m* • **this room is like an ~** este cuarto es como un congelador; (*US*†) (= *refrigerator*) nevera *f*, refrigeradora *f*, heladera *f* (*S. Cone*)

icebreaker ['aɪsˌbreɪkəʳ] N rompehielos *m inv* • **we used the video as an ~** el vídeo nos sirvió para romper el hielo

icecap ['aɪskæp] N casquete *m* glaciar, casquete *m* de hielo

ice-cold ['aɪs'kəʊld] ADJ [*hands, drink*] helado

ice-cool ['aɪs'kuːl] ADJ (= *very calm*) [*person*] aplomado, que no se inmuta por nada

ice-cream [ˌaɪs'kriːm] CPD ▸ **ice-cream cone** cucurucho *m* (de helado) ▸ **ice-cream maker** máquina *f* de helados ▸ **ice-cream parlour** heladería *f* ▸ **ice-cream soda** soda *f* mezclada con helado ▸ **ice-cream van** furgoneta *f* de los helados; ▹ **ice**

iced [aɪst] ADJ [*water*] helado, frío (*de la nevera*); [*drink*] con hielo; [*cake*] glaseado, escarchado

Iceland ['aɪslənd] N Islandia *f*
CPD ▸ **Iceland spar** espato *m* de Islandia

Icelander ['aɪsləndəʳ] N islandés/esa *m/f*

Icelandic [aɪs'lændɪk] ADJ islandés
N (*Ling*) islandés *m*

iceman ['aɪsmæn] N (PL: **icemen**) **1** (*US*) vendedor *m or* repartidor *m* de hielo
2 (*Archeol*) hombre *m* de hielo

ice-skate ['aɪsskeɪt] VI patinar sobre hielo

ichthyology [ˌɪkθɪ'ɒlədʒɪ] N ictiología *f*

icicle ['aɪsɪkl] N carámbano *m*

icily ['aɪsɪlɪ] ADV **1** (*lit*) glacialmente
2 (*fig*) [*say, stare*] glacialmente, con mucha frialdad • **he looked at me ~** me dirigió una mirada glacial

iciness ['aɪsɪnɪs] N **1** (*lit*) • **problems caused by the ~ of the roads** problemas causados por el hielo en las carreteras • **the ~ of the weather conditions** las condiciones glaciales (del tiempo)
2 (*fig*) • **the ~ of his look** su mirada glacial

icing ['aɪsɪŋ] N (*on plane, car, road, railway*) formación *f* de hielo; (*on cake*) glaseado *m* • IDIOM: • **this is the ~ on the cake** esto es la guinda que corona la torta; ▹ **butter, glacé**
CPD ▸ **icing sugar** azúcar *m* glasé, azúcar *m* en polvo, azúcar *m* flor (*S. Cone*)

ICJ N ABBR (= **International Court of Justice**) CIJ *f*

icky‡ ['ɪkɪ] ADJ (= *sticky*) todo pegajoso; (*fig*) (= *horrible*) asqueroso

icon ['aɪkɒn] N (*also Comput*) icono *m*

iconic [aɪ'kɒnɪk] ADJ [*image*] simbólico; (*Comput, Math*) icónico

iconoclasm [aɪ'kɒnəˌklæzəm] N iconoclastia *f*

iconoclast [aɪ'kɒnəklæst] N iconoclasta *mf*

iconoclastic [aɪˌkɒnə'klæstɪk] ADJ iconoclasta

iconographer [ˌaɪkɒ'nɒgrəfəʳ] N iconógrafo/a *m/f*

iconographic [aɪˌkɒnə'græfɪk] ADJ iconográfico

iconography [ˌaɪkɒ'nɒgrəfɪ] N iconografía *f*

ICR N ABBR (*US*) = **Institute for Cancer Research**

ICRC N ABBR (= **International Committee of the Red Cross**) CICR *m*

ICT N ABBR (= **information and communications technology**) informática *f*, tecnología *f* de la información

ICU N ABBR (= **intensive care unit**) UVI *f*, UCI *f*, UMI *f*

icy ['aɪsɪ] ADJ (COMPAR: **icier**, SUPERL: **iciest**)
1 (= *covered with ice*) [*road, ground*] helado, cubierto de hielo • **the icy conditions caused accidents** las heladas provocaron accidentes • **I don't like driving when it's icy** no me gusta conducir cuando hiela
2 (= *freezing*) [*air, wind, weather*] glacial; [*hand, water*] helado • **the water was icy cold** el agua estaba helada • **it's icy cold out here** aquí fuera hace un frío glacial
3 (*fig*) (= *cold*) [*stare, silence, tone, reception*] glacial

ID ABBR (*US*) = **Idaho**
N ABBR = **identification, identity**
CPD [*bracelet, tag, number*] de identidad ▸ **ID badge** chapa *f* de identificación ▸ **ID card** carnet *m* de identidad, ≈ DNI *m* (*Sp*), ≈ cédula *f* (de identidad) (*LAm*), C.I. *f* (*LAm*) ▸ **ID parade** (*Brit*) rueda *f* de reconocimiento, rueda *f* de identificación ▸ **ID theft** robo *m* de identidad ▸ **ID thief** ladrón/ona *m/f* de identidades

I'd [aɪd] = **I would, I had**

id [ɪd] N (*Psych*) id *m*

IDA N ABBR (= **International Development Association**) AIF *f*

Ida. ABBR (*US*) = **Idaho**

IDB N ABBR (= **International Development Bank**) BID *m*

IDD N ABBR (*Brit*) (*Telec*) (= **international direct dialling**) servicio *m* internacional automático

idea [aɪ'dɪə] N **1** (= *thought, plan*) idea *f* • **it wasn't my ~** no fue idea mía • **that's the ~** así es • **the ~ is to sell it** la idea *or* el plan es venderlo • **let's forget the whole ~** olvidémonos de todo el asunto • **I can't bear the ~ (of it)** solo de pensarlo me pongo mala • **it wouldn't be a bad ~ to paint it** no le vendría mal pintarlo • **it might not be a bad ~ to wait a few days** puede que no sea mala idea esperar unos cuantos días • **whose bright ~ was it to come this way?** (*iro*) ¿quién ha tenido la bonita *or* feliz idea de venir por aquí?* • **you'll have to buck up your ~s** tendrás que menearte • **the ~ never entered my head** ni se me pasó esa idea por la cabeza • **to get an ~ for a novel** encontrar una idea para una novela • **don't go getting ~s** (= *build up one's hopes*) no te hagas ilusiones; (= *be presumptuous*) no se te ocurra • **he got the ~ into his head that they didn't like him** se le metió en la cabeza (la idea de) que no les caía bien • **once she gets an ~ into her head there's no stopping her** como se le meta una idea en la cabeza no hay quien se la quite • **to get used to the ~ of sth** hacerse a la idea de algo • **to give sb ~s** meter ideas en la cabeza a algn • **whatever gave you that ~?** ¿cómo se te ha ocurrido semejante cosa? • **good ~!** ¡buena idea! • **what a good ~!** ¡qué idea más buena! • **to have an ~** tener una idea • **I suddenly had the ~ of going to see her** de repente se me ocurrió ir a verla, de repente tuve la idea de ir a verla • **he hit on the ~ of painting it red** se le ocurrió pintarlo de rojo • **to put ~s into sb's head** meter ideas en la cabeza a algn • **the very ~!** • **what an ~!** ¡qué ocurrencias!
2 (= *understanding*) idea *f* • **have you any ~ how ridiculous you look?** ¿tienes idea de lo ridículo que estás? • **I haven't the foggiest ~** no tengo ni la menor *or* más remota *or* más mínima idea • **what(ever) gave you that ~?** ¿de dónde sacaste eso? • **to get an ~ of sth** hacerse una idea de algo • **you're getting the ~** (= *understanding*) estás empezando a comprender; (= *getting the knack*) estás cogiendo el tino *or* truco • **I've got the general ~** he comprendido la idea general • **where did you get that ~?** ¿de dónde sacaste eso? • **don't get the wrong ~** no malinterpretes la situación • **many people have got the wrong ~ about him** mucha gente tiene un concepto equivocado de él • **I haven't the least ~** no tengo ni la menor *or* más remota *or* más mínima idea • **I've no ~!** ¡ni idea! • **it was awful, you've no ~** no te puedes hacer una idea de lo horrible que fue • **I had no ~ that ...** no tenía ni idea *or* la menor idea de que ... • **I haven't the slightest ~** no tengo ni la menor *or* más remota *or* más mínima idea • **he has some ~ of French** tiene algo de idea de francés
3 (= *conception, notion*) idea *f* • **there may be some truth in the ~ that ...** puede que haya algo de cierto en la idea de que ... • **she has some odd ~s about how to bring up children** tiene unas ideas muy raras *or* una opinión muy rara de cómo criar a los niños • **it wasn't my ~ of a holiday** no era la idea que yo tengo de unas vacaciones • **if that's your ~ of fun** si eso es lo que tú entiendes por diversión
4 (= *vague idea*) impresión *f* • **to have an ~ that ...** tener la impresión de que ... • **I have an ~ that she was going to Paris** tengo la impresión de que se iba a París
5 (= *purpose*) intención *f*, idea *f* • **the whole ~ of this trip was to relax** la única intención *or* idea del viaje era relajarse • **we went with the ~ of meeting new people** fuimos con la intención *or* idea de conocer a gente nueva • **what's the big ~?*** ¿a qué viene eso?*
6 (= *estimate*) idea *f* • **can you give me a rough ~ of how many you want?** ¿puede darme una idea aproximada de cuántos quiere?

ideal [aɪ'dɪəl] ADJ [*opportunity, weight, conditions, solution*] ideal • **we do not live in an ~ world** no vivimos en un mundo ideal • **he is the ~ person for the job** es la persona ideal para el puesto • **an ~ place to live** un sitio ideal para vivir
N ideal *m*

idealism [aɪ'dɪəlɪzəm] N idealismo *m*

idealist [aɪ'dɪəlɪst] N idealista *mf*

idealistic [aɪˌdɪə'lɪstɪk] ADJ idealista

idealization [ˌaɪdɪəlaɪ'zeɪʃən] N idealización *f*

idealize [aɪ'dɪəlaɪz] VT idealizar

idealized [aɪ'dɪəlaɪzd] ADJ [*image, person*] idealizado

ideally [aɪ'dɪəlɪ] ADV • **they're ~ suited** hacen una pareja ideal • **the hotel is ~ situated** el hotel tiene una situación ideal • **~, I'd like a garden** de ser posible, me gustaría tener jardín • **~, it will last forever** en el mejor de los casos, durará siempre • **~, all the children should live together** lo ideal *or* lo mejor sería que todos los hijos vivieran juntos

idée fixe ['iːdeɪ'fiːks] N idea *f* fija

idem ['aɪdem] PRON, ADJ ídem

ident* ['aɪdent] N (*also* **station ident**) (*TV, Rad*) identificativo *m*

identical [aɪ'dentɪkəl] ADJ idéntico • **their status is ~ to** *or* **with that of all other citizens** su condición es idéntica a *or* exactamente igual que la de cualquier otro ciudadano
CPD ▸ **identical twins** gemelos *mpl* idénticos

identically [aɪ'dentɪkəlɪ] ADV idénticamente • **~ sized** de tamaño idéntico, exactamente del mismo tamaño • **they always dress ~** siempre se visten igual

identifiable [aɪˌdentɪ'faɪəbl] ADJ identificable

identification [aɪˌdentɪfɪ'keɪʃən] N identificación *f* • **the state of the body made ~ difficult** el estado del cadáver dificultaba su identificación • **we have a positive ~ of the victim** disponemos ya de la identidad de la víctima • **the ~ of democracy with liberty** la identificación de la democracia con la libertad
CPD ▸ **identification badge** chapa *f* de identificación ▸ **identification card** = **identity card** ▸ **identification documents, identification papers** documentos *mpl* de identidad, documentación *f* ▸ **identification mark** señal *f* de identificación ▸ **identification parade** (*Brit*) rueda *f* de reconocimiento, rueda *f* de identificación ▸ **identification tag** (*US*) chapa *f* de identificación

identifier [aɪ'dentɪfaɪəʳ] N identificador *m*

identify [aɪ'dentɪfaɪ] VT [+ *person, problem*] identificar • **to ~ o.s.** identificarse • **to ~ o.s. with** identificarse con
VI • **to ~ with** identificarse con

Identikit picture [aɪˌdentɪkɪt'pɪktʃəʳ] N retrato-robot *m*

identity [aɪ'dentɪtɪ] N (*all senses*) identidad *f* • **a case of mistaken ~** un caso de identificación errónea • **to withhold sb's ~** silenciar la identidad de algn
CPD ▸ **identity badge** chapa *f* de identificación ▸ **identity bracelet** pulsera *f* identificativa, brazalete *m* identificativo ▸ **identity card** carnet *m* de identidad, cédula *f* (de identidad) (*LAm*) ▸ **identity crisis** crisis *f inv* de identidad ▸ **identity disc** chapa *f* de identidad ▸ **identity papers** documentos *mpl* de identidad, documentación *f* ▸ **identity parade** = **identification parade** ▸ **identity theft** robo *m* de identidad ▸ **identity thief** ladrón/ona *m/f* de identidades

ideogram ['ɪdɪəgræm] N ideograma *m*

ideographic [ˌɪdɪə'græfɪk] ADJ ideográfico

ideological [ˌaɪdɪə'lɒdʒɪkəl] ADJ ideológico

ideologically [ˌaɪdɪə'lɒdʒɪkəlɪ] ADV ideológicamente

ideologist [ˌaɪdɪ'ɒlədʒɪst] N ideólogo/a *m/f*

ideologue ['ɪdɪəlɒg] N ideólogo/a *m/f*

ideology [ˌaɪdɪ'ɒlədʒɪ] N ideología *f*

ides [aɪdz] NPL idus *mpl*

idiocy ['ɪdɪəsɪ] N idiotez *f*, imbecilidad *f*

idiolect ['ɪdɪəʊlekt] N idiolecto *m*

idiom ['ɪdɪəm] N **1** (= *phrase*) modismo *m*, giro *m*
2 (= *style of expression*) lenguaje *m*

idiomatic [ˌɪdɪə'mætɪk] ADJ idiomático

idiomatically [ˌɪdɪə'mætɪkəlɪ] ADV con modismos, usando giros idiomáticos

idiomaticity [ˌɪdɪəʊmə'tɪsɪtɪ] N idiomaticidad *f* • **his language lacked ~** a su lenguaje le faltaba idiomaticidad

idiosyncrasy [ˌɪdɪə'sɪŋkrəsɪ] N idiosincrasia *f* • **Victorian ~** la idiosincrasia victoriana • **it's one of her idiosyncrasies** es una de sus peculiaridades

idiosyncratic [ˌɪdɪəsɪŋ'krætɪk] ADJ idiosincrásico

idiot ['ɪdɪət] N (= *fool*) tonto/a *m/f*; (= *imbecile*) idiota *mf*, imbécil *mf* • **you (stupid) ~!** ¡imbécil! • **her ~ son** el idiota *or* imbécil de su hijo
CPD ▸ **idiot board*** (*TV*) chuleta* *f*, autocue *m*

idiotic [ˌɪdɪ'ɒtɪk] ADJ [*person*] idiota,

imbécil; [*behaviour, laughter, idea*] estúpido, idiota; [*price*] desorbitado • **that was an ~ thing to do!** ¡eso que hiciste fue una idiotez *or* estupidez!
idiotically [ˌɪdɪˈɒtɪkəlɪ] ADV tontamente, estúpidamente • **to laugh ~** reírse como un tonto
idiot-proof* [ˈɪdɪətpruːf] ADJ para torpes*, de fácil manejo
idle [ˈaɪdl] ADJ (COMPAR: **idler**, SUPERL: **idlest**) **1** (= *lazy*) perezoso, holgazán, flojo (*LAm*); (= *work-shy*) vago; (= *without work*) parado, desocupado; (= *inactive*) [*machine, factory*] parado; [*moment*] de ocio, libre • **the machine is never ~** la máquina no está nunca parada • **the reduction in orders made 100 workers ~** la caída en el número de pedidos dejó a 100 obreros sin trabajo • **to stand ~** - [*factory, machine*] estar parado
2 [*fear, speculation*] infundado; [*threat*] vano • **he is not one to indulge in ~ boasting/ speculation** no es de los que se da a fanfarronear/especular porque sí • **we sat making ~ conversation** pasamos el rato sentados charlando • **I asked out of ~ curiosity** lo pregunté por pura curiosidad • **it's just ~ gossip** no es más que cotilleo • **this is no ~ threat** no es esta una amenaza hecha a la ligera
VI **1** haraganear, gandulear • **we spent a few days idling in Paris** pasamos unos días ociosos en París • **we ~d over our meal** comimos con calma
2 (*Tech*) [*engine*] marchar en vacío • **idling speed** velocidad *f* de marcha en vacío
CPD ▸ **idle capacity** capacidad *f* sin utilizar ▸ **idle money** capital *m* improductivo ▸ **idle time** tiempo *m* de paro
▸ **idle away** VT + ADV [+ *time*] desperdiciar, echar a perder • **he ~s away his days in the garden** se pasa las horas muertas en el jardín
idleness [ˈaɪdlnɪs] N **1** (= *leisure*) ocio *m*, ociosidad *f*; (= *having nothing to do*) inactividad *f*, desocupación *f*; (= *laziness*) holgazanería *f*, pereza *f*, flojera *f* (*LAm*); (= *unemployment*) paro *m*, desempleo *m* (*LAm*) • **to live a life of ~** llevar una vida ociosa • **she was frustrated by her enforced ~** la desesperaba su forzada inactividad
2 (= *emptiness*) [*of threat, promise*] lo vano; [*of gossip, talk*] banalidad *f*, insustancialidad *f*
idler [ˈaɪdləʳ] N ocioso/a *m/f*, holgazán/ana *m/f*, vago/a *m/f*
idly [ˈaɪdlɪ] ADV (= *in a leisurely way*) ociosamente; (= *without doing anything*) sin hacer nada; (= *absentmindedly*) distraídamente; (= *to pass the time*) [*chat*] para pasar el rato; (= *uselessly*) vanamente, inútilmente • **she found it impossible to sit ~ at home** le resultaba imposible sentarse en casa sin hacer nada • **he glanced ~ out of the window** miró distraído por la ventana • **I wondered ~ if he had meant what he said** me preguntaba inadvertidamente si lo que había dicho iba en serio • **to stand** *or* **sit ~ by** estarse de brazos cruzados
idol [ˈaɪdl] N ídolo *m*
idolater [aɪˈdɒlətəʳ] N idólatra *mf*
idolatrous [aɪˈdɒlətrəs] ADJ idólatra, idolátrico
idolatry [aɪˈdɒlətrɪ] N idolatría *f*
idolize [ˈaɪdəlaɪz] VT idolatrar
IDP N ABBR (= **integrated data processing**) PID *m*
I'd've [ˈaɪdəv] = **I would have**
idyll [ˈɪdɪl] N idilio *m*
idyllic [ɪˈdɪlɪk] ADJ idílico
i.e. ABBR (= **id est**) (= *that is*) esto es, es decir, i.e.

IED N ABBR (= **improvised explosive device**) artefacto *m* explosivo improvisado
if [ɪf] CONJ **1** (*conditional*) si • **I'll go if you come with me** yo iré si tú me acompañas • **if you studied harder you would pass your exams** si estudiaras más aprobarías los exámenes • **if they are to be believed** si hacemos caso de lo que dicen • **if you ask me** en lo que a mí se refiere • **if you had come earlier, you would have seen him** si hubieras venido antes, le habrías visto • **if I had known I would have told you** de haberlo sabido te lo habría dicho, si lo sé te lo digo* • **if it hadn't been for you we would have all died** de no ser *or* de no haber sido por ti hubiéramos muerto todos • **you can go if you like** puedes ir si quieres • **if necessary** si es necesario, si hace falta • **if I were you I would go to Spain** yo que tú iría a España, yo en tu lugar iría a España • **if you were to say that you'd be wrong** si dijeras eso te equivocarías • **if it weren't for him, we wouldn't be in this mess!** ¡si estamos metidos en este lío, es por él!*, ¡no estaríamos metidos en este lío de no ser por él!* • **if and when she comes** si (en efecto) viene, en el caso de que venga
2 (= *whenever*) si, cuando • **if she wants any help she asks me** si *or* cuando necesita ayuda me la pide • **if it was fine we went out for a walk** si *or* cuando hacía buen tiempo dábamos un paseo
3 (= *although*) aunque, si bien • **it's a nice film if rather long** es una buena película, aunque *or* si bien algo larga • **I will do it, even if it is difficult** lo haré, aunque me resulte difícil • **I'll finish it if** *or* **even if it takes me all day** lo terminaré aunque me lleve todo el día • **even if he tells me himself I won't believe it** ni aunque me lo diga él mismo me lo creo • **I couldn't eat it if I tried** aunque me lo propusiera no lo podría comer
4 (= *whether*) si • **he asked me if I had eaten** me preguntó si había comido • **I don't know if he's here** no sé si está aquí • **I wonder if it's true** me pregunto si es *or* será verdad
5 (*in phrases*) • **if anything this one is better** hasta creo que este es mejor, este es mejor si cabe • **it's no bigger than our last house, if anything, it's even smaller** no es más grande que nuestra última casa si acaso, es incluso más pequeña • **I think you should paint it blue, if anything** en todo caso *or* si acaso, yo la pintaría de azul • **as if** como si • **she acts as if she were the boss** se comporta como si fuera la jefa • **as if by chance** como por casualidad • **it isn't as if we were rich** no es que seamos precisamente ricos, no es que seamos ricos que digamos • **if at all**: • **they aren't paid enough, if (they are paid) at all** les pagan poco, eso cuando les pagan • **change it to red, if at all** en todo caso *or* si acaso, cámbialo a rojo • **if it isn't old Garfield!** ¡pero si es el bueno de Garfield!, ¡hombre, Garfield, tú por aquí! • **if not** si no • **are you coming? if not, I'll go with Mark** ¿vienes? si no, iré con Mark • **if only I had known!** ¡de haberlo sabido! • **if only I could!** ¡ojalá pudiera! • **if only we had a car!** ¡ojalá tuviéramos coche!, ¡quién tuviera coche! • **I'll come, if only to see him** voy, aunque solo sea para verlo • **I'll try to be there, if only for a few minutes** trataré de estar allí, aunque solo sea unos minutos • **if so** si es así, de ser así • **are you coming? if so, I'll wait** ¿vienes? si es así *or* de ser así te espero; ▹ **as, even**
N • **that's** *or* **it's a big if** es un gran pero • **there are a lot of ifs and buts** hay muchas dudas sin resolver

IF

Indicative/Subjunctive after "si"

***Si** can be followed by both the indicative and the subjunctive. The indicative describes facts and likely situations; the subjunctive describes remote or hypothetical situations.*

Indicative

▹ *Use **si** + present indicative to translate **if** + present in English:*

If you go on overeating, you'll get fat
Si sigues comiendo tanto, vas a engordar
Don't do it if you don't want to
No lo hagas si no quieres

NOTE: *Don't use **si** with the present subjunctive.*

Subjunctive

▹ *Use **si** + imperfect subjunctive to translate **if** + past for remote or uncertain possibilities and hypotheses:*

If we won the lottery, we would never have to work again
Si nos tocase *or* tocara la lotería, no tendríamos que trabajar nunca más
What would you do if I weren't here?
¿Qué harías si yo no estuviese *or* estuviera aquí?

▹ *Use **si** + pluperfect subjunctive (= **hubiera** or **hubiese** + past participle) to translate **if** + **had** + past participle:*

If Paula hadn't lost her ticket, she would have left today
Si Paula no hubiera *or* hubiese perdido el billete, habría salido hoy

*Alternatively, instead of a clause with **si**, you can often use **de (no) haber** + past participle:*

If Paula hadn't lost her ticket, she would have left today
De no haber perdido Paula el billete, habría salido hoy

For further uses and examples, see main entry.

IFAD N ABBR (= **International Fund for Agricultural Development**) FIDA *m*
IFC N ABBR = **International Finance Corporation**
iffy* [ˈɪfɪ] ADJ dudoso, incierto
IFTO N ABBR = **International Federation of Tour Operators**
IG N ABBR (*US*) = **Inspector General**
igloo [ˈɪgluː] N iglú *m*
Ignatius [ɪgˈneɪʃəs] N Ignacio, Íñigo
igneous [ˈɪgnɪəs] ADJ ígneo
ignite [ɪgˈnaɪt] VT encender, prender fuego a (*LAm*)
VI encenderse, prender (*LAm*)
ignition [ɪgˈnɪʃən] N (= *igniting*) ignición *f*; (*Aut*) encendido *m*, arranque *m* • **to switch** *or* **turn on the ~** arrancar el motor, dar al contacto • **to switch** *or* **turn off the ~** apagar el motor, quitar el contacto • **I left the key in the ~** (*intentionally*) dejé la llave de contacto puesta; (*unintentionally*) me dejé la llave de contacto puesta
CPD ▸ **ignition coil** (*Aut*) bobina *f* de encendido ▸ **ignition key** llave *f* de contacto ▸ **ignition switch** interruptor *m* de encendido, interruptor *m* de arranque
ignoble [ɪgˈnəʊbl] ADJ (*frm*) innoble, vil

ignominious [ˌɪgnəˈmɪnɪəs] ADJ [*act, behaviour*] ignominioso, oprobioso; [*defeat*] vergonzoso

ignominiously [ˌɪgnəˈmɪnɪəslɪ] ADV ignominiosamente • **to be ~ defeated** sufrir una derrota vergonzosa

ignominy [ˈɪgnəmɪnɪ] N ignominia *f*, oprobio *m*, vergüenza *f*

ignoramus [ˌɪgnəˈreɪməs] N ignorante *mf*, inculto/a *m/f*

ignorance [ˈɪgnərəns] N ignorancia *f* (of de) • **to be in ~ of** ignorar, desconocer • **to keep sb in ~ of sth** ocultar algo a algn • **to show one's ~** demostrar su ignorancia

ignorant [ˈɪgnərənt] ADJ ignorante • **to be ~ of** ignorar, desconocer • **he can't be ~ of what's going on** seguro que no ignora *or* seguro que sabe lo que está pasando • **they are surprisingly ~ about their own culture** es sorprendente lo poco que saben de su propia cultura, es sorprendente lo poco que conocen su propia cultura • **he's an ~ fool** es un necio ignorante, es un inepto

ignorantly [ˈɪgnərəntlɪ] ADV ignorantemente • **we ~ went to the next house** al no saber, fuimos a la casa de al lado

ignore [ɪgˈnɔːʳ] VT [+ *person*] (= *disregard*) no hacer caso a; (= *spurn*) ignorar; [+ *remark, danger*] hacer caso omiso de, no hacer caso de; [+ *behaviour, rudeness*] pasar por alto; [+ *awkward fact*] cerrar los ojos ante • **I told him what he should do but he completely ~d me** le dije qué debía hacer pero no me hizo el menor caso • **I smiled but she ~d me** le sonreí pero me ignoró *or* hizo como si no me viera • **just ~ him** no le hagas caso • **we can safely ~ that** eso lo podemos dejar a un lado

iguana [ɪˈgwɑːnə] N iguana *f*

IHS ABBR (= **Jesus**) IHS, JHS

ikon [ˈaɪkɒn] N = **icon**

IL ABBR (*US*) = **Illinois**

ILA N ABBR (*US*) (= **International Longshoremen's Association**) *sindicato*

ILEA [ˈɪlɪə] N ABBR (*Brit*) (*Educ*) (*formerly*) (= **Inner London Education Authority**) *organismo que controlaba la enseñanza en la ciudad de Londres*

ileum [ˈɪlɪəm] N (*Anat*) íleon *m*

ilex [ˈaɪleks] N encina *f*

ILGWU N ABBR (*US*) = **International Ladies' Garment Workers Union**

Iliad [ˈɪlɪæd] N Ilíada *f*

ilk [ɪlk] N índole *f*, clase *f* • **and others of that ilk** y otros así *or* de esa clase, y otros de ese jaez

I'll [aɪl] = **I will, I shall**

ill [ɪl] ADJ (COMPAR: **worse**, SUPERL: **worst**)
1 (*Med*) enfermo • **to be ill** estar enfermo • **to be seriously ill** estar gravemente enfermo • **he's ill with cancer** tiene cáncer, está enfermo de cáncer • **to fall ill** caer *or* ponerse enfermo, enfermarse (*LAm*) • **to feel ill** encontrarse mal, sentirse mal • **to look ill** tener mal aspecto *or* mala cara • **to make sb ill** [*food, wine*] sentarle mal a algn; [*lifestyle, diet*] afectar a la salud de algn • **the soup made me ill** la sopa me sentó mal • **all the worry was making me ill** la preocupación estaba afectando a mi salud • **to make o.s. ill** ponerse enfermo, ponerse malo* • **to be taken ill** caer *or* ponerse enfermo, enfermarse (*LAm*); ▸ **mentally**
2 (= *bad*) [*fortune, luck*] malo • **ill at ease** a disgusto • **ill effects** efectos *mpl* adversos • **with no ill effects** sin mayores daños • **ill feeling** (= *hostility*) hostilidad *f*; (= *spite*) rencor *m* • **there are no ill feelings** no quedan rencores • **I have no ill feelings toward them** no les guardo rencor • **ill health** mala salud *f* • **to be in ill health** no estar bien (de salud), estar enfermo • **he retired because of ill health** se retiró por problemas de salud • **ill humour** mal humor *m* • **ill repute** (*liter or hum*) mala reputación *f* • **a house/lady of ill repute** una casa/mujer de mala reputación • **ill temper** mal genio *m* • **ill will** (= *hostility*) hostilidad *f*; (= *spite*) rencor *m* • **I bear you no ill will for that** no le guardo rencor por eso; ▸ **wind¹**
ADV mal • **to speak/think ill of sb** hablar/pensar mal de algn • **we can ill afford to lose him** mal podemos dejar que se vaya • **we can ill afford to buy it** no podemos permitirnos el lujo de comprarlo • **it ill becomes you to criticize** no te sienta bien criticar
N (*fig*) **1 ills** (*frm*) (= *problems*) males *mpl* • **the ills of the economy** los males de la economía • **the inevitable ills of old age** los inevitables males *or* achaques de la vejez
2† (= *evil*) • **no ill had befallen the child** el niño no había sufrido ningún mal • **to bode** *or* **augur ill** no augurar nada bueno
CPD ▸ **ill luck** mala suerte *f*

Ill. ABBR (*US*) = **Illinois**

ill-advised [ˈɪlədˈvaɪzd] ADJ [*remark*] inoportuno; [*plan*] desacertado; [*attempt*] imprudente • **you would be ill-advised to go** harías mejor en no ir, sería poco aconsejable que fueras

ill-assorted [ˈɪləˈsɔːtɪd] ADJ mal avenido

ill-at-ease [ˈɪlətˈiːz] ADJ (= *awkward*) molesto, incómodo; (= *uneasy*) inquieto, intranquilo

ill-bred [ˈɪlˈbred] ADJ mal educado, malcriado

ill-breeding [ˌɪlˈbriːdɪŋ] N mala educación *f*

ill-conceived [ˌɪlkənˈsiːvd] ADJ mal concebido

ill-considered [ˈɪlkənˈsɪdəd] ADJ [*plan, remark*] poco pensado, poco meditado; [*act, decision*] apresurado, irreflexivo

ill-defined [ˌɪldɪˈfaɪnd] ADJ mal definido

ill-disposed [ˌɪldɪsˈpəʊzd] ADJ • **to be ill-disposed toward sb** estar predispuesto en contra de algn • **he is ill-disposed toward the idea** no le gusta la idea • **they are ill-disposed to wait any longer** no están muy dispuestos a seguir esperando

illegal [ɪˈliːgəl] ADJ **1** (*Jur*) ilegal • **~ possession of sth** posesión *f* ilegal de algo • **it is ~ to do that** hacer eso es ilegal • **it is ~ for children to buy alcohol** está prohibido que los niños compren alcohol • **to make it ~ to do sth** prohibir hacer algo, prohibir que se haga algo
2 (*Sport*) [*tackle*] antirreglamentario
3 (*Comput*) • **to perform an ~ operation** realizar una operación ilegal *or* no válida
CPD ▸ **illegal alien** (= *illegal immigrant*) inmigrante *mf* ilegal ▸ **illegal immigrant** inmigrante *mf* ilegal ▸ **illegal substance** sustancia *f* ilegal

illegality [ˌɪliːˈgælɪtɪ] N ilegalidad *f*

illegally [ɪˈliːgəlɪ] ADV **1** (*Jur*) [*act, occupy, fish*] ilegalmente • **they were convicted of ~ using a handgun** se los declaró culpables de la utilización ilegal de un revólver
2 (*Sport*) [*tackle*] antirreglamentariamente

illegibility [ɪˌledʒɪˈbɪlɪtɪ] N ilegibilidad *f*

illegible [ɪˈledʒəbl] ADJ ilegible

illegibly [ɪˈledʒəblɪ] ADV de modo ilegible

illegitimacy [ˌɪlɪˈdʒɪtɪməsɪ] N ilegitimidad *f*

illegitimate [ˌɪlɪˈdʒɪtɪmɪt] ADJ ilegítimo

illegitimately [ˌɪlɪˈdʒɪtɪmɪtlɪ] ADV ilegítimamente

ill-equipped [ˈɪlɪˈkwɪpt] ADJ [*expedition etc*] mal equipado • **he was ill-equipped for the task** no estaba preparado para esa tarea • **the prisons are ill-equipped to cope with such large numbers** las cárceles carecen del equipamiento necesario para acoger a tanta población reclusa

ill-fated [ˈɪlˈfeɪtɪd] ADJ [*day*] funesto, nefasto; [*expedition, journey, attempt*] desafortunado, malhadado (*liter*)

ill-favoured, ill-favored (*US*) [ˈɪlˈfeɪvəd] ADJ (*liter*) (= *ugly*) mal parecido

ill-fitting [ˌɪlˈfɪtɪŋ] ADJ • **ill-fitting shoes** zapatos que quedan mal • **he wore an ill-fitting green corduroy suit** llevaba un traje de pana que le quedaba mal

ill-formed [ˌɪlˈfɔːmd] ADJ mal formado

ill-founded [ˈɪlˈfaʊndɪd] ADJ [*claim, fear*] infundado, sin fundamento

ill-gotten [ˈɪlˈgɒtn] ADJ • **ill-gotten gains** (*liter or hum*) ganancias *fpl* ilícitas

ill-humoured, ill-humored (*US*) [ˈɪlˈhjuːməd] ADJ malhumorado

illiberal [ɪˈlɪbərəl] ADJ (= *bigoted*) intolerante; (= *mean*) avaro, mezquino

illicit [ɪˈlɪsɪt] ADJ ilícito

illicitly [ɪˈlɪsɪtlɪ] ADV ilícitamente

illimitable [ɪˈlɪmɪtəbl] ADJ ilimitado, sin límites

ill-informed [ˈɪlɪnˈfɔːmd] ADJ [*judgment, criticism*] desinformado, inexacto; [*person*] mal informado

illiquid [ɪˈlɪkwɪd] ADJ falto de liquidez
CPD ▸ **illiquid assets** activos *mpl* no realizables (a corto plazo)

illiteracy [ɪˈlɪtərəsɪ] N analfabetismo *m*

illiterate [ɪˈlɪtərɪt] ADJ [*person*] (= *unable to read or write*) analfabeto; (= *ignorant*) ignorante, inculto; [*letter, handwriting*] plagado de faltas • **to be functionally ~** ser un analfabeto funcional • **he's sexually ~** en materia sexual está en mantillas
N analfabeto/a *m/f*

ill-judged [ˈɪlˈdʒʌdʒd] ADJ imprudente

ill-kempt [ˈɪlˈkempt] ADJ desaliñado, desaseado

ill-mannered [ˈɪlˈmænəd] ADJ mal educado, sin educación

ill-natured [ˈɪlˈneɪtʃəd] ADJ desabrido, malhumorado

illness [ˈɪlnɪs] N enfermedad *f*, dolencia *f* (*more frm*) • **~ prevented her going** una enfermedad le impidió asistir; ▸ **mental**

ill-nourished [ˌɪlˈnʌrɪʃt] ADJ malnutrido

illogic [ɪˈlɒdʒɪk] N falta *f* de lógica

illogical [ɪˈlɒdʒɪkəl] ADJ ilógico, falto de lógica

illogicality [ɪˌlɒdʒɪˈkælɪtɪ] N falta *f* de lógica

illogically [ɪˈlɒdʒɪkəlɪ] ADV ilógicamente

ill-omened [ˈɪlˈəʊmənd] ADJ [*day, event, occurrence*] nefasto, funesto

ill-prepared [ˌɪlprɪˈpeəd] ADJ mal preparado

ill-starred [ˈɪlˈstɑːd] ADJ malhadado, malogrado

ill-suited [ˈɪlˈsuːtɪd] ADJ • **as a couple they are ill-suited** como pareja no son compatibles, no hacen buena pareja • **he is ill-suited to the job** no es la persona indicada para el trabajo

ill-tempered [ˈɪlˈtempəd] ADJ [*person*] de mal genio; [*remark, tone etc*] malhumorado

ill-timed [ˈɪlˈtaɪmd] ADJ inoportuno, intempestivo

ill-treat [ˈɪlˈtriːt] VT [+ *person, animal*] maltratar, tratar mal

ill-treatment [ˈɪlˈtriːtmənt] N maltrato *m*, malos tratos *mpl*

illuminate [ɪˈluːmɪneɪt] VT **1** (= *light up*) [+ *room, building*] iluminar; [+ *street*]

iluminar, alumbrar • **the castle is ~d in summer** en verano el castillo está iluminado • **~d sign** letrero *m* luminoso
2 (= *clarify*) [+ *problem, question*] aclarar, echar luz sobre
3 (= *enlighten*) [+ *person*] iluminar
4 (*Art*) • **~d manuscript** manuscrito *m* iluminado

illuminating [ɪ'lu:mɪneɪtɪŋ] ADJ [*remark, observation*] esclarecedor; [*lecture, experience*] instructivo

illumination [ɪ,lu:mɪ'neɪʃən] N (*gen*) iluminación *f*; (*Art*) iluminación *f*; (*fig*) aclaración *f*; **illuminations** (*Brit*) (= *decorative lights*) luces *fpl*, iluminaciones *fpl*

illuminator [ɪ'lu:mɪneɪtəʳ] N iluminador(a) *m/f*

illumine [ɪ'lu:mɪn] VT = **illuminate**

illus. ABBR 1 (= **illustrated**) ilustrado
2 (= **illustration**) ilustración *f*

ill-use ['ɪl'ju:z] VT maltratar, tratar mal

illusion [ɪ'lu:ʒən] N 1 (= *deceptive appearance*) ilusión *f* • **optical ~** ilusión *f* óptica • **it gives an ~ of space** crea una ilusión *or* impresión de espacio
2 (= *misapprehension*) ilusión *f* • **to be under an ~** hacerse falsas ilusiones, estar en un error • **I am under no ~s on that score** sobre ese punto no me hago (falsas) ilusiones • **to be under the ~ that …** creerse que … • **he was under the ~ that he would win** se creía que iba a ganar • **he cherishes the ~ that …** abriga la esperanza de que … (+ *subjun*)

illusionary [ɪ'lu:ʒənərɪ] ADJ engañoso

illusionist [ɪ'lu:ʒənɪst] N prestidigitador(a) *m/f*, ilusionista *mf*

illusive [ɪ'lu:sɪv], **illusory** [ɪ'lu:sərɪ] ADJ ilusorio

illustrate ['ɪləstreɪt] VT 1 [+ *book*] ilustrar • **a book ~d by Ann Miles** un libro ilustrado por Ann Miles, un libro con ilustraciones de Ann Miles
2 (= *exemplify*) [+ *subject*] ilustrar; [+ *point*] demostrar • **I can best ~ this in the following way** esto puede ilustrarse del modo siguiente

illustrated ['ɪləstreɪtɪd] ADJ [*book, catalogue*] ilustrado
CPD ▸ **illustrated (news)paper** (*Hist*) revista *f* gráfica

illustration [,ɪləs'treɪʃən] N (*in book, paper*) ilustración *f*; (= *example*) ejemplo *m*, ilustración *f*; (= *explanation*) explicación *f* • **by way of ~** a modo de ejemplo, a título ilustrativo

illustrative ['ɪləstrətɪv] ADJ [*drawing*] ilustrativo; [*example*] ilustrativo • **to be ~ of sth** ejemplificar *or* demostrar algo

illustrator ['ɪləstreɪtəʳ] N ilustrador(a) *m/f*

illustrious [ɪ'lʌstrɪəs] ADJ ilustre

illustriously [ɪ'lʌstrɪəslɪ] ADJ ilustremente

ILO N ABBR (= **International Labour Organization**) OIT *f*

ILS N ABBR (*Aer*) = **Instrument Landing System**

ILWU N ABBR (*US*) = **International Longshoremen's and Warehousemen's Union**

IM, i.m. ABBR = **intramuscular(ly)**

I'm [aɪm] = **I am**

image ['ɪmɪdʒ] N 1 (*also Literat, Rel*) (= *representation, symbol*) imagen *f* • **the ~ I had of him was completely different** tenía una imagen de él totalmente distinta • **to make sb in one's own ~** hacer a algn a su imagen • IDIOM: • **to be the very** *or* **the spitting ~ of sb** ser el vivo retrato *or* la viva imagen de algn
2 (= *reflection*) reflejo *m* • **mirror ~** reflejo *m* exacto
3 (= *public image*) imagen *f* • **to have a good/bad ~** [*company, person*] tener buena/mala imagen • **we must improve our ~** tenemos que mejorar nuestra imagen • **the company has changed its ~** la empresa ha cambiado de imagen
CPD ▸ **image intensifier** intensificador *m* de imagen ▸ **image processing** proceso *m* de imágenes

image-conscious ['ɪmɪdʒ,kɒnʃəs] ADJ preocupado por la imagen, consciente de la imagen • **he is very image-conscious** le preocupa mucho la imagen, es muy consciente de la imagen

imager ['ɪmɪdʒəʳ] N • **thermal ~** cámara *f* térmica • **magnetic resonance ~** aparato *m* de resonancia magnética

imagery ['ɪmɪdʒərɪ] N imágenes *fpl*, imaginería *f*

imaginable [ɪ'mædʒɪnəbl] ADJ imaginable • **the biggest party ~** la fiesta más grande que se pueda imaginar

imaginary [ɪ'mædʒɪnərɪ] ADJ imaginario

imagination [ɪ,mædʒɪ'neɪʃən] N (= *mental ability*) imaginación *f*; (= *inventiveness*) imaginación *f*, inventiva *f* • **it's all in your ~** te lo estás imaginando, son imaginaciones tuyas • **was it my ~ or did I see you there?** ¿me lo he imaginado o te vi allí de verdad? • **to have a vivid ~** tener una imaginación muy viva *or* despierta • **she let her ~ run away with her** se dejó llevar por la imaginación • **her story caught the popular ~** su historia atrapó el interés popular • **it doesn't take much ~ to realize what happened** no hace falta tener mucha imaginación para darse cuenta de lo que ocurrió • **use your ~** usa la imaginación

imaginative [ɪ'mædʒɪnətɪv] ADJ [*person*] imaginativo, lleno de imaginación; [*drawing, story*] imaginativo

imaginatively [ɪ'mædʒɪnətɪvlɪ] ADV con imaginación

imaginativeness [ɪ'mædʒɪnətɪvnɪs] N imaginativa *f*

imagine [ɪ'mædʒɪn] VT 1 (= *visualize*) imaginarse, figurarse • **~ my surprise** imagínate *or* figúrate mi sorpresa • **you can ~ how I felt!** ¡imagínate *or* figúrate cómo me sentí! • **(just) ~!** ¡imagínate!, ¡figúrate! • **"is he angry?" — "I ~ so!"** —¿está enfadado? —¡me imagino que sí! • **I can't ~ a better end to the evening** la noche no podría acabar mejor • **I (just) can't ~** no me lo puedo imaginar • **what he's done with it I (just) can't ~** no tengo ni idea de qué puede haber hecho con ello • **you can't begin to ~ what it was like** no puedes hacerte (ni) idea de lo que fue aquello • **~ yourself on a Caribbean island** imagínate (que estás) en una isla del Caribe
2 (= *falsely believe*) • **you're just imagining things** te lo estás imaginando, son imaginaciones tuyas • **he ~d himself to be the Messiah** se creía *or* se imaginaba que era el Mesías
3 (= *suppose, think*) suponer, creer • **don't ~ that you're going to get it free** no te vayas a pensar *or* no te creas que te va a salir gratis • **she fondly ~s that …** se hace la ilusión de que …

imaging ['ɪmɪdʒɪŋ] N • **thermal ~** representación *f* óptica por cámara térmica • **magnetic resonance ~** representación *f* óptica por resonancia magnética

imaginings [ɪ'mædʒɪnɪŋz] NPL (*liter*) imaginaciones *fpl*, figuraciones *fpl*

imam [ɪ'mɑ:m] N imán *m*

imbalance [ɪm'bæləns] N desequilibrio *m*, falta *f* de equilibrio

imbalanced [ɪm'bælənst] ADJ [*distribution, structure*] desequilibrado

imbecile ['ɪmbəsi:l] N imbécil *mf* • **you ~!** ¡imbécil!
ADJ imbécil

imbecility [,ɪmbɪ'sɪlɪtɪ] N imbecilidad *f*

imbibe [ɪm'baɪb] VT (*frm*) (= *drink*) beber; (*fig*) [+ *atmosphere*] empaparse de; [+ *information*] imbuirse de (*frm*), empaparse de
VI † (*also hum*) beber

imbroglio [ɪm'brəʊlɪəʊ] N embrollo *m*, enredo *m*

imbue [ɪm'bju:] VT • **to ~ sth with** imbuir algo de *or* en (*frm*), empapar algo de • **to ~ sb with sth** [+ *quality, virtue*] infundir *or* conferir algo a algn, imbuir a algn de algo (*frm*) • **to be ~d with** estar imbuido (*frm*) *or* empapado de

IMF N ABBR (= **International Monetary Fund**) FMI *m*

IMHO ABBR = **In My Honest Opinion**

imitable ['ɪmɪtəbl] ADJ imitable

imitate ['ɪmɪteɪt] VT [+ *person, action, accent*] imitar; (*pej*) remedar; [+ *signature, writing*] reproducir, copiar

imitation [,ɪmɪ'teɪʃən] N (= *act*) imitación *f*; (*pej*) remedo *m*; (= *copy*) reproducción *f*, copia *f* • **in ~ of** a imitación de • **beware of ~s** desconfíe de las imitaciones • PROVERB: • **~ is the sincerest form of flattery** no hay mejor halago *or* lisonja que el que te imiten
CPD de imitación ▸ **imitation fur** piel *f* sintética ▸ **imitation gold** oro *m* de imitación ▸ **imitation jewellery, imitation jewels** bisutería *f*, joyas *fpl* de imitación ▸ **imitation leather** imitación *f* a piel ▸ **imitation marble** mármol *m* artificial

imitative ['ɪmɪtətɪv] ADJ imitativo • **a style ~ of Joyce's** un estilo que imita el de Joyce

imitator ['ɪmɪteɪtəʳ] N imitador(a) *m/f*

immaculate [ɪmækjʊlɪt] ADJ [*house, clothes*] impecable, inmaculado; [*hair, make-up, performance, taste*] impecable; [*conduct, behaviour*] impecable, intachable • **a hotel where the service is ~** un hotel donde el servicio es impecable • **to be in ~ condition** estar en perfectas condiciones • **to look ~** estar impecable • **the Immaculate Conception** (*Rel*) la Inmaculada Concepción

immaculately [ɪ'mækjʊlɪtlɪ] ADV [*behave*] impecablemente, intachablemente; [*dress*] impecablemente • **~ clean** impecablemente limpio, de un limpio inmaculado • **he was ~ dressed** iba impecablemente vestido, iba vestido de punta en blanco*

immanent ['ɪmənənt] ADJ inmanente

Immanuel [ɪ'mænjʊəl] N Emanuel

immaterial [,ɪmə'tɪərɪəl] ADJ 1 (= *irrelevant*) irrelevante • **that is quite ~** eso no tiene ninguna importancia, eso es irrelevante • **the difference between them is ~ to me** la diferencia entre ellos me es indiferente • **it is ~ whether …** no importa si …
2 (= *incorporeal*) inmaterial, incorpóreo

immature [,ɪmə'tjʊəʳ] ADJ 1 (= *childish*) [*person, attitude*] inmaduro
2 (= *half-grown*) [*tree, plant*] joven; [*fruit*] verde, inmaduro

immaturely [,ɪmə'tjʊəlɪ] ADV [*react, behave*] de forma inmadura

immaturity [,ɪmə'tjʊərɪtɪ] N inmadurez *f*, falta *f* de madurez; [*of tree, plant*] inmadurez *f*

immeasurable [ɪ'meʒərəbl] ADJ (= *not measurable*) inconmensurable, imposible de medir; (= *enormous*) [*benefit, value*] inconmensurable, incalculable

immeasurably [ɪ'meʒərəblɪ] ADV enormemente

immediacy [ɪ'mi:dɪəsɪ] N [*of text, image,*

style] inmediatez *f*; (= *urgency*) [*of task*] urgencia *f*

immediate [ɪ'mi:dɪət] ADJ **1** (= *instant*) [*decision, answer, reaction*] inmediato • **~ access** (*Comput*) entrada *f* inmediata • **to take ~ action** actuar inmediatamente *or* de inmediato • **for ~ delivery** para entrega inmediata • **these changes will take place with ~ effect** estos cambios tendrán lugar con un efecto inmediato
2 (= *urgent*) [*needs, problem*] urgente, apremiante; [*danger, threat, crisis, task*] inmediato • **my ~ concern was for Max** Max era mi primera preocupación • **the ~ needs of the refugees** las necesidades urgentes *or* apremiantes de los refugiados • **what are your ~ plans?** ¿cuáles son tus planes más inmediatos?
3 (= *near*) [*future, cause*] inmediato; [*predecessor, successor*] más inmediato • **my ~ family** mi familia más cercana • **in the ~ future** en el futuro inmediato • **my ~ neighbours** mis vecinos de al lado • **to the ~ north/south** directamente al norte/sur • **in the ~ vicinity** en las inmediaciones, en los alrededores

immediately [ɪ'mi:dɪətlɪ] ADV **1** (= *at once*) [*reply, come, agree*] inmediatamente, de inmediato • **do it ~!** ¡hazlo inmediatamente!, ¡hazlo de inmediato! • **the cause of the accident was not ~ apparent** la causa del accidente no se apreciaba a simple vista • **there was no one ~ available** no había nadie disponible en ese momento
2 (= *directly*) [*affect, concern*] directamente • **he is not ~ involved in the project** no está directamente involucrado en el proyecto • **~ above sth** justo *or* justamente encima de algo • **~ after/before sth** inmediatamente después de/antes de algo • **~ behind/below sth** justo *or* justamente detrás de/debajo de algo • **he is ~ below the managing director** (*in rank*) trabaja a las órdenes directas del director general, el director general es su superior más inmediato
CONJ • **~ he put the phone down, he remembered** nada más colgar el teléfono se acordó, en cuanto *or* (*LAm*) no más colgó el teléfono se acordó • **let me know ~ he arrives** avíseme en cuanto llegue, avíseme en el momento en que llegue

immemorial [,ɪmɪ'mɔ:rɪəl] ADJ inmemorial, inmemorable • **from time ~** desde tiempo(s) inmemorial(es)

immense [ɪ'mens] ADJ [*distance, difficulty, effort*] inmenso, enorme • **to his ~ relief/satisfaction** para gran alivio suyo/satisfacción suya • **it has been of ~ benefit to her** le ha resultado enormemente beneficioso

immensely [ɪ'menslɪ] ADV [*like, enjoy*] muchísimo; [*differ*] enormemente; [*difficult*] sumamente, enormemente; [*powerful*] inmensamente, enormemente • **I was ~ grateful/relieved** me sentía enormemente agradecido/aliviado

immensity [ɪ'mensɪtɪ] N [*of size*] inmensidad *f*; [*of difference, problem etc*] enormidad *f*, inmensidad *f*

immerse [ɪ'mɜ:s] VT (*lit*) • **to ~ sth in water** sumergir algo en el agua • **to be ~d in sth** (*fig*) estar metido de lleno *or* inmerso en algo • **he was totally ~d in his work** estaba metido de lleno *or* inmerso en su trabajo • **she was ~d in the newspaper** estaba absorta *or* inmersa en la lectura del periódico • **to ~ o.s. in sth** (*fig*) sumergirse en algo • **she ~d herself in the history and culture of the place** se metió de lleno *or* se sumergió en la historia y la cultura del lugar

immerser* [ɪ'mɜ:sə^r] N calentador *m* de inmersión

immersion [ɪ'mɜ:ʃən] N (*lit*) (*in liquid*) inmersión *f*, sumersión *f*; (*fig*) (*in work, thoughts*) absorción *f*
CPD ▸ **immersion course** curso *m* de inmersión ▸ **immersion heater** calentador *m* de inmersión

immigrant ['ɪmɪgrənt] ADJ inmigrante
N inmigrante *mf*
CPD ▸ **immigrant community** comunidad *f* de inmigrantes ▸ **immigrant worker** trabajador(a) *m/f* inmigrante

immigrate ['ɪmɪgreɪt] VI inmigrar

immigration [,ɪmɪ'greɪʃən] N inmigración *f*
CPD ▸ **immigration authorities** agencia *f* de inmigración ▸ **immigration control** control *m* de inmigración ▸ **immigration laws** leyes *fpl* inmigratorias ▸ **immigration officer** agente *mf* de inmigración ▸ **immigration quota** cuota *f* de inmigración

imminence ['ɪmɪnəns] N inminencia *f*

imminent ['ɪmɪnənt] ADJ (= *impending*) inminente

immobile [ɪ'məʊbaɪl] ADJ inmóvil

immobiliser [ɪ'məʊbɪlaɪzə^r] N (*Aut*) inmovilizador *m*

immobility [,ɪməʊ'bɪlɪtɪ] N inmovilidad *f*

immobilize [ɪ'məʊbɪlaɪz] VT [+ *person, troops, engine*] inmovilizar

immobilizer [ɪ'məʊbɪlaɪzə^r] N (*for car*) inmovilizador *m*

immoderate [ɪ'mɒdərɪt] ADJ [*opinion, reaction*] desmesurado; [*demand*] excesivo, inmoderado; [*person*] extremista, radical • **with ~ haste** (*frm*) con excesiva *or* desmesurada celeridad (*frm*)

immoderately [ɪ'mɒdərɪtlɪ] ADV [*hasty, eager*] excesivamente; [*laugh*] exageradamente; [*use*] en exceso • **to drink ~** beber en exceso

immodest [ɪ'mɒdɪst] ADJ (= *indecent*) [*behaviour*] indecoroso, impúdico; [*dress*] poco recatado; [*claim, statement*] poco modesto, presuntuoso

immodestly [ɪ'mɒdɪstlɪ] ADV [*behave*] indecorosamente, impúdicamente; [*dress*] sin recato; [*say, claim*] con presunción

immodesty [ɪ'mɒdɪstɪ] N (= *indecency*) [*of behaviour*] falta *f* de decoro, impudicia *f*; [*of dress*] falta *f* de recato; (= *boastfulness*) falta *f* de modestia, presunción *f*

immolate ['ɪməʊleɪt] VT inmolar

immoral [ɪ'mɒrəl] ADJ [*person, behaviour, practice*] inmoral • **to live off ~ earnings** vivir del proxenetismo, vivir del lenocinio (*frm*)

immorality [,ɪmə'rælɪtɪ] N inmoralidad *f*

immorally [ɪ'mɒrəlɪ] ADV inmoralmente, de modo inmoral

immortal [ɪ'mɔ:tl] ADJ [*person, god*] inmortal; [*memory, fame*] imperecedero
N inmortal *mf*

immortality [,ɪmɔ:'tælɪtɪ] N inmortalidad *f*

immortalize [ɪ'mɔ:təlaɪz] VT inmortalizar

immovable [ɪ'mu:vəbl] ADJ [*object*] imposible de mover, inamovible; [*person*] inconmovible; [*feast, post*] inamovible • **he was quite ~** estuvo inflexible
NPL **immovables** inmuebles *mpl*

immune [ɪ'mju:n] ADJ (*to disease*) inmune (*to* a); (*from tax, regulations*) exento (**from** de) • **to be ~ to sth** (*Med*) ser inmune a algo • **she is ~ to measles** es inmune al sarampión; (*fig*) • **they seemed ~ to the cold** parecían inmunes al frío • **he is ~ to criticism** es inmune *or* insensible a las críticas, no le afectan las críticas • **no one is ~ from this problem** nadie queda al margen de este problema, nadie es inmune a este problema
CPD ▸ **immune deficiency** inmunodeficiencia *f* ▸ **immune response** respuesta *f* inmunitaria, respuesta *f* inmunológica ▸ **immune system** sistema *m* inmunológico

immunity [ɪ'mju:nɪtɪ] N (*Med*) (*also fig*) inmunidad *f*; (*from tax, regulations*) exención *f* (**from** de) • **diplomatic ~** inmunidad *f* diplomática • **parliamentary ~** inmunidad *f* parlamentaria

immunization [,ɪmjʊnaɪ'zeɪʃən] N (*Med*) inmunización *f*

immunize ['ɪmjʊnaɪz] VT (*Med*) inmunizar

immunocompromised [ɪ,mjʊnəʊ'kɒmprə,maɪzd] ADJ (*Med*) inmunocomprometido

immunodeficiency [ɪ,mjʊnəʊdɪ'fɪʃənsɪ] N inmunodeficiencia *f*

immunodeficient [ɪ,mjʊnəʊdɪ'fɪʃənt] ADJ inmunodeficiente

immunodepressant [ɪ,mjʊnəʊdɪ'presnt] ADJ inmunodepresor
N inmunodepresor *m*

immunoglobulin [,ɪmjʊnəʊ'glɒbjʊlɪn] N inmunoglobulina *f*

immunological [ɪ,mju:nə'lɒdʒɪkəl] ADJ inmunológico
CPD ▸ **immunological defences** defensas *fpl* inmunológicas

immunologist [ɪmjʊ'nɒlədʒɪst] N inmunólogo/a *m/f*

immunology [,ɪmjʊ'nɒlədʒɪ] N inmunología *f*

immunosuppressant [ɪ'mju:nəʊ-sə'presənt] ADJ inmunosupresor, inmunosupresivo
N inmunosupresor *m*, inmunosupresivo *m*

immunosuppression [ɪ'mju:nəʊsə'preʃən] N inmunosupresión *f*

immunosuppressive [ɪ'mju:nəʊsə'presɪv] ADJ inmunosupresor, inmunosupresivo

immunotherapy [,ɪmjʊnəʊ'θerəpɪ] N inmunoterapia *f*

immure [ɪ'mjʊə^r] VT enclaustrar, encerrar; (*fig*) encerrar • **to be ~d in** estar encerrado en

immutability [ɪ,mju:tə'bɪlɪtɪ] N inmutabilidad *f*, inalterabilidad *f*

immutable [ɪ'mju:təbl] ADJ inmutable

immutably [ɪ'mju:təblɪ] ADV inmutablemente, inalterablemente

IMO ABBR = **In My Opinion**
N ABBR **1** = **International Miners' Organization**
2 (= **International Maritime Organization**) OMI *f*

imp [ɪmp] N diablillo *m*; (*fig*) diablillo *m*, pillín/ina *m/f*

imp. ABBR = **imperial**

impact ['ɪmpækt] N **1** (= *force, effect*) impacto *m* • **the book had a great ~ on me** el libro me impactó mucho *or* me causó gran impacto • **the speech made no ~** el discurso no hizo mella • **he wants to make an ~ in the company** pretende causar una buena impresión en la empresa • **the measure would have considerable ~ on consumers** la medida afectaría considerablemente a los consumidores
2 (= *crash*) choque *m* • **on ~** al chocar
VT (*US*) (= *affect*) afectar, tener impacto en
VI **1** (= *make contact*) impactar, hacer impacto
2 (= *have impact*) • **to ~ on sth** afectar a algo, tener impacto en algo
CPD ▸ **impact printer** impresora *f* de impacto

impacted [ɪm'pæktɪd] ADJ [*tooth*] incrustado

impair [ɪm'pɛəʳ] VT [+ *health, relations*] perjudicar, afectar; [+ *sight, hearing*] afectar, dañar; [+ *ability*] mermar; [+ *judgement*] afectar; [+ *visibility*] reducir • **~ed hearing** problemas *mpl* de audición

impaired [ɪm'pɛəd] ADJ [*heart, liver function*] dañado • **people with ~ vision** personas con problemas de la vista • **his memory is ~** tiene problemas de memoria • **to be mentally ~** ser discapacitado psíquico • **to be physically ~** ser discapacitado físico

impairment [ɪm'pɛəmənt] N (*physical, mental*) discapacidad *f*; (= *deterioration*) deterioro *m*

impala [ɪm'pɑːlə] N (PL: **impalas** *or* **impala**) impala *m*

impale [ɪm'peɪl] VT (*as punishment*) empalar; (*on sword, spike*) ensartar, atravesar • **to ~ o.s. on** atravesarse con • **the heads of their victims were ~d on spikes** las cabezas de sus víctimas eran ensartadas en postes • **he fell, impaling himself on the dagger** se cayó y se atravesó con la daga

impalpable [ɪm'pælpəbl] ADJ impalpable; (*fig*) intangible, inaprensible

imparity [ɪm'pærɪtɪ] N disparidad *f*

impart [ɪm'pɑːt] VT **1** (= *make known*) [+ *knowledge*] impartir, transmitir; [+ *information*] transmitir; [+ *ideas, values*] transmitir
2 (= *bestow*) [+ *wisdom*] otorgar; [+ *quality, sense*] conferir; [+ *flavour, taste*] dar

impartial [ɪm'pɑːʃəl] ADJ imparcial

impartiality [ɪm,pɑːʃɪ'ælɪtɪ] N imparcialidad *f*

impartially [ɪm'pɑːʃəlɪ] ADV imparcialmente, con imparcialidad

impassable [ɪm'pɑːsəbl] ADJ [*road*] intransitable; [*barrier, river*] infranqueable

impasse [æm'pɑːs] N punto *m* muerto, impasse *m or f* • **negotiations have reached an ~** las negociaciones han llegado a un punto muerto *or* impasse • **the government is in an ~** el gobierno se halla en un impasse

impassioned [ɪm'pæʃnd] ADJ [*speech, plea*] apasionado; [*person*] exaltado

impassive [ɪm'pæsɪv] ADJ impasible, imperturbable

impassively [ɪm'pæsɪvlɪ] ADV impasiblemente, sin inmutarse • **he listened ~** escuchó impasible *or* sin inmutarse

impassiveness [ɪm'pæsɪvnəs], **impassivity** [ɪmpæ'sɪvɪtɪ] N impasibilidad *f*

impatience [ɪm'peɪʃəns] N impaciencia *f*

impatiens [ɪm'peɪʃɪ,enz] N impatiens *f*

impatient [ɪm'peɪʃənt] ADJ **1** (= *irascible*) [*person*] impaciente, sin paciencia; [*gesture*] de impaciencia • **to get ~ (with sth/sb)** perder la paciencia *or* impacientarse (con algo/algn) • **to make sb ~** impacientar a algn
2 (= *eager*) impaciente • **to be ~ to do sth** estar impaciente por hacer algo

impatiently [ɪm'peɪʃəntlɪ] ADV con impaciencia, impacientemente

impeach [ɪm'piːtʃ] VT **1** (= *doubt*) [+ *character, motive*] poner en tela de juicio; [+ *witness*] recusar
2 [+ *public official*] (= *accuse*) acusar de prevaricación; (= *try*) procesar por prevaricación; [+ *president*] someter a un proceso de destitución

impeachable [ɪm'piːtʃəbl] ADJ [*act*] susceptible de acusación por prevaricación; [*witness*] recusable

impeachment [ɪm'piːtʃmənt] N (= *accusation*) acusación *f* de prevaricación; (= *trial*) proceso *m* por prevaricación; [*of president*] proceso *m* de destitución
CPD ▸ **impeachment hearing** juicio *m* por destitución ▸ **impeachment proceedings** proceso *m* de destitución

impeccable [ɪm'pekəbl] ADJ [*appearance, uniform, performance, manners*] impecable; [*behaviour, conduct, service*] impecable, intachable • **she has ~ taste in clothes** tiene un gusto impecable para la ropa • **she speaks ~ English** habla un inglés impecable

impeccably [ɪm'pekəblɪ] ADV impecablemente • **he behaved ~** se comportó impecablemente *or* de manera intachable • **~ clean** impecablemente limpio • **he was ~ dressed** iba impecablemente vestido, iba vestido de punta en blanco*

impecunious [,ɪmpɪ'kjuːnɪəs] ADJ (*frm or hum*) falto de dinero

impedance [ɪm'piːdəns] N (*Elec*) impedancia *f*

impede [ɪm'piːd] VT [+ *progress, movement, growth, development*] dificultar, obstaculizar

impediment [ɪm'pedɪmənt] N **1** (= *obstacle*) obstáculo *m*, impedimento *m* (**to** para); (*Jur*) impedimento *m* (**to** para)
2 (*Med*) defecto *m* • **speech ~** defecto *m* del habla

impedimenta [ɪm,pedɪ'mentə] NPL impedimenta *f*

impel [ɪm'pel] VT **1** (= *force, compel*) obligar • **I feel ~led to say ...** me veo obligado a decir ...
2 (= *drive*) impulsar, impeler (*frm*) • **hunger ~led him to do it** el hambre lo impulsó a hacerlo

impend [ɪm'pend] VI amenazar, ser inminente, cernerse

impending [ɪm'pendɪŋ] ADJ (*gen*) inminente • **his ~ retirement** su inminente jubilación • **a sign of ~ disaster** una señal de que se avecina un desastre

impenetrability [ɪm,penɪtrə'bɪlɪtɪ] N impenetrabilidad *f*

impenetrable [ɪm'penɪtrəbl] ADJ **1** (= *impassable*) [*jungle, barrier, fortress*] impenetrable
2 (= *difficult to understand*) [*writing, idea, accent*] incomprensible; [*mystery*] insondable, inescrutable; [*expression*] inescrutable

impenetrably [ɪm'penɪtrəblɪ] ADV • **winter brought the fogs, ~ thick** el invierno trajo las nieblas espesas, impenetrables

impenitence [ɪm'penɪtəns] N impenitencia *f*

impenitent [ɪm'penɪtənt] ADJ impenitente

impenitently [ɪm'penɪtəntlɪ] ADV impenitentemente, incorregiblemente

imperative [ɪm'perətɪv] ADJ **1** (= *essential*) imprescindible, fundamental • **it is ~ that he comes** es imprescindible *or* fundamental que venga • **it was ~ to destroy the bridge** era fundamental destruir el puente • **an ~ need** una necesidad imperiosa
2 (= *authoritative*) [*manner, command*] imperativo, imperioso
3 (*Ling*) imperativo
N **1** (*frm*) (= *need, drive*) imperativo *m* • **any animal's first ~ is to survive** el primer imperativo de cualquier animal es sobrevivir
2 (*Ling*) imperativo *m* • **a verb in the ~** un verbo en (el) imperativo
CPD ▸ **imperative mood** (*Ling*) modo *m* imperativo

imperatively [ɪm'perətɪvlɪ] ADV imperiosamente

imperceptible [,ɪmpə'septəbl] ADJ (*gen*) imperceptible

imperceptibly [,ɪmpə'septəblɪ] ADV imperceptiblemente

imperfect [ɪm'pɜːfɪkt] ADJ **1** (= *faulty*) [*machine, product*] defectuoso; [*hearing, vision*] deficiente; [*understanding, world, method*] imperfecto; [*knowledge*] incompleto, limitado; [*reasoning*] deficiente, incorrecto
2 (*Ling*) [*tense*] imperfecto
N (*Ling*) imperfecto *m* • **a verb in the ~** un verbo en imperfecto

imperfection [,ɪmpə'fekʃən] N **1** (= *state of being imperfect*) imperfección *f*
2 (= *fault*) defecto *m*

imperfectly [ɪm'pɜːfɪktlɪ] ADV [*design, create*] de manera defectuosa • **this process is still ~ understood by scientists** los científicos aún no entienden completamente este proceso, los científicos tienen aún un conocimiento limitado de este proceso • **she spoke English, though ~** hablaba inglés, aunque no perfectamente

imperial [ɪm'pɪərɪəl] ADJ **1** (= *of empire, emperor*) imperial
2 (= *imperious*) señorial
3 (*Brit*) [*weights, measures*] británico
CPD ▸ **imperial gallon** (*Brit*) galón *m* inglés ▸ **imperial system** sistema *m* británico de pesos y medidas

> **IMPERIAL SYSTEM**
> Aunque el sistema métrico decimal se implantó oficialmente en 1971 en el Reino Unido para medidas y pesos y es el que se enseña en los colegios, en el lenguaje cotidiano aún se sigue usando en muchos casos el llamado **imperial system**. Por ejemplo, en las tiendas se ve el peso en kilos y en libras (**pounds**) y la gente suele decir su peso en **stones** y **pounds**. La cerveza se mide en pintas (**pints**), las distancias en millas (**miles**) y la longitud, la altura o la profundidad en pies (**feet**) y pulgadas (**inches**).
> En Estados Unidos el sistema imperial también se usa para todas las medidas y pesos, aunque la capacidad de la onza (**ounce**), del galón (**gallon**) y de la pinta (**pint**) es ligeramente inferior a la del Reino Unido. Por otro lado, en EE.UU. la gente mide su peso solo en libras (**pounds**) y no en **stones**.

imperialism [ɪm'pɪərɪəlɪzəm] N imperialismo *m*

imperialist [ɪm'pɪərɪəlɪst] ADJ imperialista
N imperialista *mf*

imperialistic [ɪm,pɪərɪə'lɪstɪk] ADJ imperialista

imperil [ɪm'perɪl] VT (*frm*) arriesgar, poner en peligro

imperious [ɪm'pɪərɪəs] ADJ [*tone, manner*] imperioso; (= *urgent*) apremiante

imperiously [ɪm'pɪərɪəslɪ] ADV imperiosamente

imperishable [ɪm'perɪʃəbl] ADJ [*goods*] imperecedero, no perecedero; [*memory*] imperecedero

impermanence [ɪm'pɜːmənəns] N impermanencia *f*

impermanent [ɪm'pɜːmənənt] ADJ impermanente

impermeable [ɪm'pɜːmɪəbl] ADJ impermeable (**to** a)

impers. ABBR = **impersonal**

impersonal [ɪm'pɜːsnl] ADJ impersonal

impersonality [ɪm,pɜːsə'nælɪtɪ] N impersonalidad *f*

impersonally [ɪm'pɜːsnəlɪ] ADV impersonalmente, de manera impersonal

impersonate [ɪm'pɜːsəneɪt] VT hacerse

i

pasar por; (*Theat*) imitar

impersonation [ɪm,pɜːsəˈneɪʃən] N (*to commit crime*) suplantación *f*; (*Theat*) imitación *f* • **he does ~s** hace imitaciones

impersonator [ɪmˈpɜːsəneɪtəʳ] N imitador(a) *m/f*

impertinence [ɪmˈpɜːtɪnəns] N (= *cheek*) impertinencia *f*, insolencia *f* • **what ~!** • **the ~ of it!** ¡qué impertinencia!, ¡habráse visto qué insolencia! • **an ~** una impertinencia • **it would be an ~ to ask** preguntar sería una impertinencia

impertinent [ɪmˈpɜːtɪnənt] ADJ [*person, child, behaviour, manner*] impertinente, insolente • **to be ~ to sb** ser impertinente *or* insolente con algn • **don't be ~!** ¡no seas impertinente!

impertinently [ɪmˈpɜːtɪnəntlɪ] ADV impertinentemente

imperturbable [,ɪmpəˈtɜːbəbl] ADJ [*person, manner*] imperturbable, impasible

impervious [ɪmˈpɜːvɪəs] ADJ **1** (*lit*) (*to water*) impermeable (**to** a)
2 (*fig*) (*to remarks, threats*) inmune, insensible (**to** a) • **he is ~ to criticism** es inmune *or* insensible a las críticas, no le afectan las críticas

impetigo [,ɪmpɪˈtaɪgəʊ] N impétigo *m*

impetuosity [ɪm,petjʊˈɒsɪtɪ] N [*of person, behaviour*] impulsividad *f*

impetuous [ɪmˈpetjʊəs] ADJ [*person*] impetuoso, impulsivo; [*behaviour*] precipitado, impulsivo

impetuously [ɪmˈpetjʊəslɪ] ADV [*say*] impetuosamente, de forma impetuosa, impulsivamente; [*behave*] precipitadamente, impulsivamente

impetuousness [ɪmˈpetjʊəsnɪs] N impulsividad *f*

impetus [ˈɪmpɪtəs] N (*lit*) (= *force*) ímpetu *m*; (*fig*) impulso *m* • **to give an ~ to sales** impulsar *or* incentivar las ventas

impiety [ɪmˈpaɪətɪ] N impiedad *f*

impinge [ɪmˈpɪndʒ] VI • **to ~ on sth/sb** incidir en algo/algn, afectar a algo/algn • **to ~ on sb's freedom/rights** vulnerar la libertad/los derechos de algn

impingement [ɪmˈpɪndʒmənt] N intromisión *f*

impious [ˈɪmpɪəs] ADJ impío

impiously [ˈɪmpɪəslɪ] ADV impíamente

impish [ˈɪmpɪʃ] ADJ [*expression, smile*] pícaro, travieso

impishly [ˈɪmpɪʃlɪ] ADV [*say, smile*] pícaramente, socarronamente

impishness [ˈɪmpɪʃnɪs] N picardía *f*

implacable [ɪmˈplækəbl] ADJ [*enemy, hatred*] implacable

implacably [ɪmˈplækəblɪ] ADV implacablemente

implant N [ˈɪmplɑːnt] implante *m*
VT [ɪmˈplɑːnt] (*Med*) [+ *organ, tissue*] injertar, implantar; (*fig*) [+ *idea, principle*] inculcar

implantation [,ɪmplɑːnˈteɪʃən] N [*of embryo, egg*] implantación *f*

implausibility [ɪm,plɔːzəˈbɪlɪtɪ] N inverosimilitud *f*

implausible [ɪmˈplɔːzəbl] ADJ inverosímil, poco convincente

implausibly [ɪmˈplɔːzəblɪ] ADV inverosímilmente, poco convincentemente

implement N [ˈɪmplɪmənt] herramienta *f*, instrumento *m*
VT [ˈɪmplɪment] [+ *plan, decision, idea*] llevar a cabo, poner en práctica; [+ *measure*] aplicar, poner en práctica; [+ *law*] aplicar

implementation [,ɪmplɪmenˈteɪʃən] N [*of plan, decision*] ejecución *f*, puesta *f* en práctica; [*of idea*] puesta *f* en práctica; [*of law, measure*] aplicación *f*

implicate [ˈɪmplɪkeɪt] VT • **to ~ sb in sth** implicar *or* involucrar a algn en algo • **are you ~d in this?** ¿estás implicado en esto? • **he ~d three others** implicó a otros tres

implication [,ɪmplɪˈkeɪʃən] N
1 (= *consequence*) implicación *f*, consecuencia *f* • **we shall have to study all the ~s** tendremos que estudiar las posibles consecuencias *or* repercusiones • **the proposal has major ~s for schools** la propuesta tiene grandes implicaciones *or* acarrea importantes consecuencias para los colegios
2 (= *inference*) • **his ~ was that she was lying** estaba insinuando que ella mentía • **the ~ of this is that …** esto significa que … • **he did not realize the full ~s of his words** no se dio cuenta de la trascendencia de sus palabras • **by ~ then …** de ahí (se deduce) que …
3 (*in crime*) implicación *f*

implicit [ɪmˈplɪsɪt] ADJ **1** (= *implied*) [*threat, agreement*] implícito • **it is ~ in what you say** se sobreentiende por lo que dices
2 (= *unquestioning*) [*faith, belief*] incondicional, absoluto

implicitly [ɪmˈplɪsɪtlɪ] ADV **1** (= *by implication*) implícitamente
2 (= *unquestioningly*) [*trust*] sin reservas, incondicionalmente

implied [ɪmˈplaɪd] ADJ implícito, tácito • **it is not stated but it is ~** no se declara abiertamente pero se sobreentiende
CPD ▸ **implied warranty** garantía *f* implícita

implode [ɪmˈpləʊd] VT **1** implosionar
2 (*Phon*) pronunciar implosivamente
VI implosionar

implore [ɪmˈplɔːʳ] VT [+ *person*] suplicar, rogar; [+ *forgiveness*] implorar • **to ~ sb to do sth** suplicar a algn que haga algo • **I ~ you!** ¡se lo suplico!

imploring [ɪmˈplɔːrɪŋ] ADJ [*glance, gesture*] suplicante, de súplica

imploringly [ɪmˈplɔːrɪŋlɪ] ADV de modo suplicante

implosion [ɪmˈpləʊʒən] N implosión *f* (*also Phon*)

imply [ɪmˈplaɪ] VT (= *hint, suggest*) insinuar; (= *involve*) suponer, implicar • **are you ~ing that …?** ¿quieres decir que …?, ¿insinúas que …? • **what are you ~ing?** ¿qué insinúas? • **he implied he would do it** dio a entender que lo haría • **it implies a lot of work** supone *or* implica mucho trabajo

impolite [,ɪmpəˈlaɪt] ADJ [*person*] mal educado, descortés; [*behaviour*] descortés

impolitely [,ɪmpəˈlaɪtlɪ] ADV con descortesía

impoliteness [,ɪmpəˈlaɪtnɪs] N [*of person*] falta *f* de educación; [*of remark*] descortesía *f*

impolitic [ɪmˈpɒlɪtɪk] ADJ impolítico

imponderable [ɪmˈpɒndərəbl] ADJ imponderable
NPL **imponderables** (elementos *mpl*) imponderables *mpl*

import N [ˈɪmpɔːt] **1** (*Comm*) (= *article*) artículo *m* importado, artículo *m* de importación; (= *importing*) importación *f* • **luxury ~s** artículos *mpl* de lujo importados *or* de importación • **oil is their biggest ~** lo que más importan es petróleo • **the idea is an American ~** (*fig*) es una idea importada de América
2 (*frm*) (= *importance*) trascendencia *f*, importancia *f*; (= *meaning*) significado *m* • **to be of great ~** tener mucha trascendencia *or* importancia • **it is of no great ~** no tiene mayor trascendencia *or* importancia • **they were slow to realise the ~ of his speech** tardaron en darse cuenta de la trascendencia de su discurso
VT [ɪmˈpɔːt] **1** importar (**from** de, **into** en); ▹ **imported**
2 (*frm*) (= *mean, imply*) significar, querer decir
CPD [ˈɪmpɔːt] [*licence, quota*] de importación ▸ **import duty** derechos *mpl* de importación ▸ **import tax** derecho *m* de importación ▸ **import trade** comercio *m* importador

importable [ɪmˈpɔːtəbl] ADJ que se puede importar

importance [ɪmˈpɔːtəns] N importancia *f* • **to be of great/little ~** ser de gran/escasa importancia, tener mucha/poca importancia • **to attach great ~ to sth** conceder *or* dar mucha importancia a algo • **to be of no ~** carecer de importancia, no tener importancia • **to be full of one's own ~** darse ínfulas, creerse muy importante • **to be of some ~** ser de cierta importancia, tener cierta importancia

important [ɪmˈpɔːtənt] ADJ importante • **it is ~ that** es importante que • **it sounds/looks ~** parece importante • **to try to look ~** (*pej*) darse tono *or* importancia • **he told Henry to touch nothing, and more ~, to say nothing** le dijo a Henry que no tocase nada y, lo que era más importante, que no dijese nada • **to become ~** cobrar importancia • **your opinion is equally ~** tu opinión es igualmente importante *or* es de igual importancia • **to make sb feel ~** hacer que algn se sienta importante • **it is ~ for everyone to be here on time** es importante que todo el mundo esté aquí a la hora • **the ~ thing is …** lo importante es … • **the most ~ thing in life** lo más importante en la vida • **it was ~ to me to know** para mí era importante saberlo

importantly [ɪmˈpɔːtəntlɪ] ADV
1 (= *significantly*) • **these weapons figured ~ in the war** estas armas tuvieron un importante papel en la guerra • **this document differs ~ from the original** este documento presenta importantes diferencias respecto al original • **more ~, …** aún más importante, … • **I was hungry, and, more ~, my children were hungry** yo tenía hambre y, lo que era aún más importante, mis hijos tenían hambre
2 (= *arrogantly*) [*enter, walk, talk*] con un aire de importancia • **"I'll go," he said ~** —yo voy —dijo con un aire de importancia *or* dándose importancia

importation [,ɪmpɔːˈteɪʃən] N importación *f*

imported [ɪmˈpɔːtɪd] ADJ [*goods*] de importación • **~ beers** cervezas *fpl* de importación

importer [ɪmˈpɔːtəʳ] N (*Comm*) importador(a) *m/f*

import-export trade [,ɪmpɔːtˈekspɔːt,treɪd] N comercio *m* de importación y exportación

importing [ɪmˈpɔːtɪŋ] ADJ • **~ company** empresa *f* de importación • **~ country** país *m* importador

importunate [ɪmˈpɔːtjʊnɪt] ADJ [*demand*] importuno; [*person*] pertinaz

importune [,ɪmpɔːˈtjuːn] VT (*frm*) importunar, perseguir; (*Jur*) [*prostitute*] abordar con fines inmorales

importunity [,ɪmpɔːˈtjuːnɪtɪ] N (*frm*) importunidad *f*

impose [ɪmˈpəʊz] VT [+ *condition, fine, tax*] imponer (**on** a); (*Jur*) [+ *sentence*] imponer • **troops were brought in to ~ order** se movilizaron tropas para imponer el orden • **he tries to ~ his views on everyone else** intenta imponer sus puntos de vista a los

demás • **to ~ o.s. on sb** abusar de la amabilidad de algn • **I couldn't possibly ~ myself on you for dinner** estaría abusando de su amabilidad si me quedara a cenar
(VI) • **to ~ (up)on** (= *take advantage of*) [+ *kindness, hospitality*] abusar de • **I don't wish to ~ (upon you)** no quiero abusar, no quiero molestar(le)
imposing [ɪm'pəʊzɪŋ] (ADJ) imponente, impresionante
imposition [ˌɪmpə'zɪʃən] (N) (= *act*) imposición *f*; (= *burden*) molestia *f*; (= *liberty*) abuso *m*; (= *tax*) impuesto *m* • **it's a bit of an ~** me parece un abuso • **I'm afraid it's rather an ~ for you** me temo que le vaya a resultar molesto
impossibility [ɪmˌpɒsə'bɪlɪtɪ] (N) imposibilidad *f* • **the ~ of doing sth** la imposibilidad de hacer algo • **it's a physical ~** es físicamente imposible
impossible [ɪm'pɒsəbl] (ADJ) **1** (= *not possible*) [*task, dream*] imposible • **impossible!** ¡imposible!, ¡no es posible! • **it's almost ~ to read her writing** leer su letra es casi imposible, es casi imposible leer su letra • **this cooker is ~ to clean!** ¡esta cocina es imposible de limpiar!, ¡limpiar esta cocina es imposible! • **the fog made it ~ to see very far** la niebla impedía ver a mucha distancia • **it is ~ for me to leave now** me es imposible salir ahora • **it's not ~ that ...** existe la posibilidad de que ... • **to be physically ~** ser físicamente imposible; ▷ EASY, DIFFICULT, IMPOSSIBLE
2 (= *not tolerable*) [*person*] insufrible, insoportable; [*situation*] insostenible • **to be in an ~ position** hallarse en una situación insostenible • **you're ~!*** ¡eres insufrible *or* insoportable!
(N) • **the ~** lo imposible • **to ask for/do the ~** pedir/hacer lo imposible
impossibly [ɪm'pɒsəblɪ] (ADV) **1** (= *extremely*) [*late, expensive, small*] increíblemente, tremendamente • **~ difficult** tan difícil que resulta imposible, increíblemente *or* tremendamente difícil
2 (= *intolerably*) • **she was ~ rude to Ann** era grosera con Ann hasta un punto intolerable • **George behaved ~ at the wedding reception** George estuvo insoportable durante el banquete de bodas
impost ['ɪmpəʊst] (N) impuesto *m*
imposter, impostor [ɪm'pɒstəʳ] (N) impostor(a) *m/f*
imposture [ɪm'pɒstʃəʳ] (N) impostura *f*, engaño *m*
impotence ['ɪmpətəns] (N) (*gen*) impotencia *f*
impotent ['ɪmpətənt] (ADJ) (*gen*) impotente
impound [ɪm'paʊnd] (VT) [+ *vehicle*] retener, retirar de la vía pública; [+ *goods*] confiscar, incautar; [+ *dog*] llevar a la perrera municipal; (*Jur*) [+ *evidence*] recoger
impoundment [ɪm'paʊndmənt] (N) (*US*) (*Econ*) embargo *m*
impoverish [ɪm'pɒvərɪʃ] (VT) empobrecer; [+ *land*] agotar
impoverished [ɪm'pɒvərɪʃt] (ADJ) [*person*] empobrecido; [*land*] agotado, pobre
impoverishment [ɪm'pɒvərɪʃmənt] (N) empobrecimiento *m*; [*of land*] agotamiento *m*
impracticability [ɪmˌpræktɪkə'bɪlɪtɪ] (N) impracticabilidad *f*
impracticable [ɪm'præktɪkəbl] (ADJ) (= *unrealizable*) impracticable, no factible
impractical [ɪm'præktɪkəl] (ADJ) [*person*] poco práctico, falto de sentido práctico; [*plan*] poco factible • **he's so ~** no es nada práctico
impracticality [ɪmˌpræktɪ'kælɪtɪ] (N) [*of person*] falta *f* de sentido práctico; [*of plan*] lo poco práctico
imprecation [ˌɪmprɪ'keɪʃən] (N) imprecación *f*
imprecise [ˌɪmprɪ'saɪs] (ADJ) [*information, definition*] impreciso
imprecision [ˌɪmprɪ'sɪʒən] (N) [*of information, definition*] imprecisión *f*
impregnable [ɪm'pregnəbl] (ADJ) [*castle*] inexpugnable; (*lit, fig*) [*position*] invulnerable
impregnate ['ɪmpregneɪt] (VT) (= *permeate*) impregnar, empapar (**with** de); (= *fertilise*) [+ *person, animal, egg*] fecundar • **to become ~d with** impregnarse de
impregnation [ˌɪmpreg'neɪʃən] (N) (= *permeation*) impregnación *f*; (*Bio*) fecundación *f*
impresario [ˌɪmpre'sɑːrɪəʊ] (N) empresario/a *m/f*
impress (VT) [ɪm'pres] **1** (= *make good impression on*) impresionar • **he does it just to ~ people** lo hace sólo para impresionar a la gente • **he is not easily ~ed** no se deja impresionar fácilmente • **how did she ~ you?** ¿qué impresión te hizo *or* causó? • **he ~ed me quite favourably** me hizo muy buena impresión • **I'm very ~ed!** ¡estoy admirado! • **I was not ~ed** no me hizo buena impresión
2 (= *mark*) (*lit*) imprimir, estampar; (*fig*) (*in the mind*) grabar • **to ~ sth (up)on sb** (*fig*) convencer a algn de la importancia de algo • **I tried to ~ the importance of the job on him** traté de convencerle de la importancia del trabajo, traté de recalcar lo importante que era el trabajo • **I must ~ upon you that ...** tengo que subrayar que ... • **it ~ed itself upon my mind** se me quedó grabado en la mente
(VI) [ɪm'pres] causar buena impresión
(N) ['ɪmpres] impresión *f*; (*fig*) marca *f*, huella *f*
impression [ɪm'preʃən] (N) **1** (= *effect*) impresión *f* • **to make an ~ (on sb)** impresionar (a algn) • **she's out to make an ~** quiere impresionar • **to make a good/bad ~ (on sb)** causar buena/mala impresión (a algn) • **to make no ~ (on sth)** no tener el menor efecto (sobre algo) • **all our arguments seemed to make no ~ on him** nuestros argumentos no parecieron tener efecto alguno en él • **we had been digging for an hour but weren't making any ~** llevábamos una hora cavando pero sin ningún éxito
2 (= *vague idea, illusion*) impresión *f* • **to be under *or* have the ~ that ...** tener la impresión de que ... • **he gives the ~ of knowing a lot** da la impresión de saber mucho • **my ~s of Paris** mis impresiones de París • **I don't want you to get the wrong ~** no quiero que te lleves una falsa impresión • **they used cotton wool to give the ~ of snow** utilizaban algodón para simular la nieve
3 (= *mark*) impresión *f*; (*fig*) marca *f*, huella *f*
4 (*esp Brit*) (*Typ*) (*for first time*) impresión *f*, tirada *f*; (*thereafter*) reimpresión *f*
5 (*Theat*) imitación *f* • **to do ~s** hacer imitaciones
impressionable [ɪm'preʃnəbl] (ADJ) [*person*] impresionable, influenciable • **to be at an ~ age** estar en una edad en la que se es muy impresionable *or* influenciable
impressionism [ɪm'preʃənɪzəm] (N) (*Art*) impresionismo *m*
impressionist [ɪm'preʃənɪst] (ADJ) impresionista
(N) **1** (*Art*) impresionista *mf*
2 (*Theat*) imitador(a) *m/f*
impressionistic [ɪmˌpreʃə'nɪstɪk] (ADJ) impresionista
impressive [ɪm'presɪv] (ADJ) [*achievement, victory, display*] impresionante • **it was an ~ performance** (*Sport, Mus*) fue una actuación impresionante *or* soberbia • **the company has an ~ record in terms of profits** la empresa posee un impresionante *or* excelente historial de beneficios
impressively [ɪm'presɪvlɪ] (ADV) [*play, perform*] admirablemente, extraordinariamente • **he won both tournaments ~** ganó ambos torneos con una actuación impresionante • **she has an ~ long list of awards to her name** su nombre va unido a una lista impresionante de galardones • **she was ~ brave** tuvo un valor admirable *or* extraordinario
imprest system ['ɪmprestˌsɪstəm] (N) sistema *m* de fondo fijo
imprimatur [ɪmprɪ'meɪtəʳ] (N) (*Publishing*) (*also fig*) imprimátur *m*
imprint (VT) [ɪm'prɪnt] **1** (= *mark*) [+ *paper*] imprimir • **to ~ sth on sth** imprimir *or* estampar algo en algo
2 (*fig*) grabar • **it was ~ed on his mind** lo tenía grabado en la mente
3 (*Bio, Psych*) imprimir (**on a**)
(N) ['ɪmprɪnt] impresión *f*, huella *f*; (*Typ*) pie *m* de imprenta • **under the HarperCollins ~** publicado por HarperCollins
imprinting [ɪm'prɪntɪŋ] (N) (*Bio, Psych*) impresión *f*
imprison [ɪm'prɪzn] (VT) [+ *criminal*] (= *put in jail*) encarcelar, meter en la cárcel • **he was ~ed for debt/for ten years** lo encarcelaron *or* lo metieron en la cárcel por deudas/durante diez años
imprisonable [ɪm'prɪzənəbl] (ADJ) [*offence*] castigado con cárcel
imprisonment [ɪm'prɪznmənt] (N) (= *act*) encarcelamiento *m*; (= *term of imprisonment*) cárcel *f*, prisión *f* • **he was sentenced to ten years ~** fue condenado a diez años de prisión • **~ without trial** detención *f* sin procesamiento • **life ~** cadena *f* perpetua
improbability [ɪmˌprɒbə'bɪlɪtɪ] (N) (= *unlikelihood*) improbabilidad *f*; (= *implausibility*) inverosimilitud *f*
improbable [ɪm'prɒbəbl] (ADJ) [*event*] improbable; [*excuse, story*] inverosímil • **it is ~ that it will happen** es improbable *or* poco probable que ocurra
improbably [ɪm'prɒbəblɪ] (ADV) **1** (= *surprisingly*) sorprendentemente • **this area is, ~, one of the best in town** en contra de lo que cabría esperar, este barrio es uno de los mejores de la ciudad
2 (= *implausibly*) increíblemente • **an ~ blue sky** un cielo increíblemente azul
impromptu [ɪm'prɒmptjuː] (ADJ) (= *improvised*) [*performance, speech*] improvisado; (= *unexpected*) [*remark*] espontáneo, impremeditado
(ADV) (= *ad lib*) de improviso, sin preparación; (= *unexpectedly*) [*say*] espontáneamente
(N) improvisación *f*
improper [ɪm'prɒpəʳ] (ADJ) **1** (= *unseemly*) [*behaviour, laughter*] indecoroso, impropio
2 (= *indecent*) [*remark*] indecoroso; [*suggestion*] deshonesto
3 (= *incorrect*) [*use*] indebido
4 (= *illicit*) [*dealings*] deshonesto
improperly [ɪm'prɒpəlɪ] (ADV) [*behave, act*] (= *in unseemly way*) incorrectamente, indecorosamente, impropiamente; (= *indecently*) indecentemente; [*use*] indebidamente; (= *illicitly*) deshonestamente • **they threw me out for being ~ dressed** me echaron por ir vestido incorrectamente

impropriety [ˌɪmprəˈpraɪətɪ] (N) [*of person, behaviour*] (= *unseemliness*) incorrección *f*, falta *f* de decoro; (= *indecency*) indecencia *f*; [*of language*] impropiedad *f*; (= *illicit nature*) deshonestidad *f*

improv* [ˈɪmprɒv] (N) impro *f*

improve [ɪmˈpruːv] (VT) **1** (= *make better*) [+ *work*] mejorar; [+ *property*] hacer mejoras en • **to ~ o.s.** *or* **one's mind** cultivarse, instruirse • **to ~ o.s.** (*in wealth*) mejorar su situación **2** (= *favour*) [+ *appearance*] favorecer **3** (= *perfect*) [+ *skill*] perfeccionar; (= *add value to*) aumentar el valor de • **to ~ one's Spanish** perfeccionar sus conocimientos del español **4** (= *increase*) [+ *production, yield*] aumentar • **to ~ one's chances of success** aumentar *or* mejorar las posibilidades de éxito • **the management has refused to ~ its offer of 3%** la dirección se ha negado a mejorar su oferta del 3%
(VI) [*person*] (*in skill etc*) hacer progresos; (*after illness*) mejorar(se); [*health, weather, work, quality*] mejorar; [*production, yield*] aumentar; [*business*] mejorar, prosperar • **to ~ in sth** hacer progresos en algo • **to ~ with age/use** mejorar con el tiempo/el uso
▸ **improve on, improve upon** (VI + PREP) (*gen*) mejorar • **it cannot be ~d (up)on** es inmejorable • **to ~ (up)on sb's offer** ofrecer más que algn, mejorar la oferta de algn

improvement [ɪmˈpruːvmənt] (N) (*in quality*) mejora *f*, mejoramiento *m* (**in** de); (= *increase*) aumento *m* (**in** de); (= *progress*) progresos *mpl* (**in** en); [*of the mind*] cultivo *m*; (*Med*) mejoría *f* • **it's an ~ on the old one** supone una mejora con respecto al antiguo • **there is room for ~** podría mejorarse • **there has been some ~ in the patient's condition** el paciente ha mejorado algo • **they made ~s in safety procedures** mejoraron los mecanismos de seguridad • **to make ~s to** [+ *property*] hacer mejoras en
(CPD) ▸ **improvement grant** subvención *f* para modernizar (una casa *etc*)

improvidence [ɪmˈprɒvɪdəns] (N) imprevisión *f*

improvident [ɪmˈprɒvɪdənt] (ADJ) [*person*] imprevisor; [*action*] carente de previsión

improvidently [ɪmˈprɒvɪdəntlɪ] (ADV) imprevidamente

improving [ɪmˈpruːvɪŋ] (ADJ) [*book, programme*] edificante, instructivo

improvisation [ˌɪmprəvaɪˈzeɪʃən] (N) (= *act*) improvisación *f*; (= *improvised speech, music*) improvisación *f*

improvise [ˈɪmprəvaɪz] (VI), (VT) improvisar

imprudence [ɪmˈpruːdəns] (N) imprudencia *f*

imprudent [ɪmˈpruːdənt] (ADJ) imprudente

imprudently [ɪmˈpruːdəntlɪ] (ADV) imprudentemente

impudence [ˈɪmpjʊdəns] (N) [*of person*] insolencia *f*, descaro *m*; [*of behaviour*] insolencia *f* • **he had the ~ to say that ...** tuvo la insolencia *or* el descaro de decir que ... • **what ~!** ¡qué insolencia *or* descaro!

impudent [ˈɪmpjʊdənt] (ADJ) [*person*] insolente, descarado; [*behaviour*] insolente

impudently [ˈɪmpjʊdəntlɪ] (ADV) descaradamente, insolentemente

impugn [ɪmˈpjuːn] (VT) [+ *integrity, honesty, motives*] poner en duda; [+ *theory*] cuestionar; [+ *testimony*] impugnar

impulse [ˈɪmpʌls] (N) (*Tech*) (*also fig*) impulso *m* • **my first ~ was to hit him** mi primer impulso fue de golpearlo • **on ~** llevado por un impulso, impulsivamente • **to act on ~** obrar llevado por un impulso, obrar impulsivamente • **I bought it on ~** lo compré impulsivamente • **to yield to a sudden ~** dejarse llevar por un impulso
(CPD) ▸ **impulse buy** compra *f* impulsiva
▸ **impulse buying** compras *fpl* impulsivas
▸ **impulse sales** ventas *fpl* impulsivas

impulsion [ɪmˈpʌlʃən] (N) impulsión *f*

impulsive [ɪmˈpʌlsɪv] (ADJ) [*person, temperament*] impulsivo; [*act, remark*] irreflexivo

impulsively [ɪmˈpʌlsɪvlɪ] (ADV) [*act*] impulsivamente, llevado por un impulso; [*say*] sin pensar, sin reflexión • **~ she patted him on the arm** le dio palmaditas en el brazo impulsivamente

impulsiveness [ɪmˈpʌlsɪvnɪs], **impulsivity** [ɪmpʌlˈsɪvɪtɪ] (US) (N) impulsividad *f*, carácter *m* impulsivo

impunity [ɪmˈpjuːnɪtɪ] (N) impunidad *f* • **with ~** con impunidad, impunemente

impure [ɪmˈpjʊəʳ] (ADJ) (*Chem*) [*substance, drug*] impuro, con impurezas; [*water*] con impurezas, contaminado; (*morally*) [*person, thought*] impuro

impurity [ɪmˈpjʊərɪtɪ] (N) impureza *f*

imputation [ˌɪmpjʊˈteɪʃən] (N) (= *attribution*) imputación *f*; (= *accusation*) imputación *f*, acusación *f*

impute [ɪmˈpjuːt] (VT) • **to ~ sth to sb** imputar *or* atribuir algo a algn

IN (ABBR) (US) = **Indiana**

in [ɪn]

PREPOSITION
ADVERB
ADJECTIVE
NOUN

PREPOSITION

When **in** *is the second element in a phrasal verb, eg* **ask in, fill in, look in**, *etc, look up the verb. When it is part of a set combination, eg* **in the country, in ink, in danger, covered in**, *look up the other word.*

1 (*in expressions of place*) en; (= *inside*) dentro de • **it's in London/Scotland/Galicia** está en Londres/Escocia/Galicia • **in the garden** en el jardín • **in the house** en casa; (= *inside*) dentro de la casa • **our bags were stolen, and our passports were in them** nos robaron los bolsos, y nuestros pasaportes iban dentro

When phrases like **in Madrid, in Germany** *are used to identify a particular group,* **de** *is the usual translation:*

• **our colleagues in Madrid** nuestros colegas de Madrid • **the chairs in the room** las sillas de la habitación, las sillas que hay en la habitación *or* dentro de la habitación • **in here/there** aquí/allí dentro • **it's hot in here** aquí dentro hace calor

2 (*in expressions of time*) **a** (= *during*) en • **in 1986** en 1986 • **in May/spring** en mayo/primavera • **in the eighties/the 20th century** en los años ochenta/el siglo 20 • **in the morning(s)/evening(s)** por la mañana/la tarde • **at four o'clock in the morning/afternoon** a las cuatro de la mañana/la tarde
b (= *for*) • **she hasn't been here in years** hace años que no viene
c (= *in the space of*) en • **I did it in 3 hours/days** lo hice en 3 horas/días • **it was built in a week** fue construido en una semana
d (= *within*) dentro de • **I'll see you in three weeks' time** *or* **in three weeks** te veré dentro de tres semanas • **he'll be back in a moment/a month** volverá dentro de un momento/un mes

3 (*indicating manner, medium*) en • **in a loud/soft voice** en voz alta/baja • **in Spanish/English** en español/inglés • **to pay in dollars** pagar en dólares • **it was underlined in red** estaba subrayado en rojo • **a magnificent sculpture in marble and copper** una magnífica escultura de *or* en mármol y cobre

4 (= *clothed in*) • **she opened the door in her dressing gown** abrió la puerta en bata • **they were all in shorts** todos iban en *or* llevaban pantalón corto • **he went out in his new raincoat** salió con el impermeable nuevo • **you look nice in that dress** ese vestido te sienta bien

When phrases like **in the blue dress, in the glasses** *are used to identify a particular person,* **de** *is the usual translation:*

• **the man in the hat** el hombre del sombrero • **the boy in the checked trousers** el chico de los pantalones de cuadros • **the girl in green** la chica vestida de verde; ▹ **dressed**

5 (*giving ratio, number*) • **one person in ten** una persona de cada diez • **one in five pupils** uno de cada cinco alumnos • **he had only a one in fifty chance of survival** solo tenía una posibilidad entre cincuenta de sobrevivir • **what happened was a chance in a million** había una posibilidad entre un millón de que pasara lo que pasó • **20 pence in the pound** veinte peniques por (cada) libra • **once in a hundred years** una vez cada cien años • **in twos** de dos en dos • **these jugs are produced in their millions** estas jarras se fabrican por millones, se fabrican millones de estas jarras • **people came in their hundreds** acudieron cientos de personas, la gente acudió a centenares

6 (= *among*) entre • **this is common in children/cats** es cosa común entre los niños/los gatos • **you find this instinct in animals** este instinto se encuentra en *or* entre los animales, los animales poseen este instinto • **in (the works of) Shakespeare** en las obras de Shakespeare

7 (*talking about people*) • **she has it in her to succeed** tiene la capacidad de triunfar • **it's not in him to do that** no es capaz de hacer eso • **I couldn't find it in me to forgive him** no salía de mí perdonarle • **they have a good leader in him** él es buen líder para ellos, en él tienen un buen líder • **a condition rare in a child of that age** una dolencia extraña en *or* para un niño de esa edad • **it's something I admire in her** es algo que admiro de *or* en ella • **he had all the qualities I was looking for in a partner** tenía todas las cualidades que yo buscaba en un compañero

8 (*in profession etc*) • **to be in teaching** dedicarse a la enseñanza • **to be in publishing** trabajar el en mundo editorial • **he's in the motor trade** es vendedor de coches • **he's in the tyre business** se dedica al comercio de neumáticos; ▹ **army**

9 (*after superlative*) de • **the biggest/smallest in Europe** el más grande/pequeño de Europa

10 (*with verb*) • **in saying this** al decir esto • **in making a fortune he lost his wife** mientras hacía fortuna, perdió su mujer

11 (*in set expressions*)
in all en total
in itself de por sí
in that (= *since*) puesto que, ya que • **the new treatment is preferable in that ...** es preferible el nuevo tratamiento puesto *or* ya que ... • **in that, he resembles his father** en eso se parece a su padre

what's in it for me • I want to know what's in it for me quiero saber qué gano yo con eso; ▹ far

ADVERB

1 to be in (= *be at home*) estar (en casa); (= *be at work*) estar; (= *be gathered in*) [*crops, harvest*] estar recogido; (= *be at destination*) [*train, ship, plane*] haber llegado; (= *be alight*) estar encendido, arder; (*Sport*) [*ball, shuttlecock*] entrar • he wasn't in no estaba (en casa) • there's nobody in no hay nadie • is Mr Eccles in? ¿está el Sr. Eccles? • the boss isn't in yet el jefe no ha llegado aún • he's in for tests (*in hospital*) está ingresado para unas pruebas • he's in for larceny (*in prison*) está encerrado por ladrón • he's in for 5 years cumple una condena de 5 años • what's he in for? ¿de qué delito se le acusa? • when the Tories were in* (*in power*) cuando los conservadores estaban en el poder • the screw was not in properly el tornillo no estaba bien metido • the essays have to be in by Friday hay que entregar los trabajos para el viernes • strawberries are in es la temporada de las fresas, las fresas están en sazón • the fire is still in el fuego sigue encendido *or* aún arde • IDIOM: • my luck is in estoy de suerte

to be in and out • to be in and out of work no tener trabajo fijo • don't worry, you'll be in and out in no time no te preocupes, saldrás enseguida

to be in for sth • he's in for a surprise* le espera una sorpresa • we're in for a hard time vamos a pasar un mal rato • we may be in for some snow puede que nieve • you don't know what you're in for! ¡no sabes lo que te espera! • he's in for it lo va a pagar • to be in for a competition (= *be entered*) haberse inscrito en un concurso • to be in for an exam presentarse a un examen

to be in on sth (= *be aware, involved*) • to be in on the plan/secret* estar al tanto del plan/del secreto • are you in on it? ¿estás tú metido en ello?

to be well in with sb (= *be friendly*) • to be well in with sb* llevarse muy bien con algn

2 (*with other verbs*) • she opened the door and they all rushed in abrió la puerta y todos entraron *or* se metieron corriendo • she opened her bag and put the ticket in abrió el bolso y metió el billete

3 (*with time words*) • day in, day out día tras día • week in, week out semana tras semana

4 (*Sport*) • in! ¡entró!

ADJECTIVE*

1 (= *fashionable*) de moda • to be in estar de moda, llevarse • short skirts were in la falda corta estaba de moda, se llevaban las faldas cortas • it's the in thing es lo que se lleva • it's the in place to eat es el restaurante que está de moda • she wore a very in dress llevaba un vestido muy a la moda *or* de lo más moderno

2 (= *exclusive*) • it's an in joke es un chiste privado, es un chiste que tienen entre ellos/tenemos entre nosotros • if you're not in with the in crowd ... si no estás entre los elegidos ...

NOUN

1 • the ins and outs of: the ins and outs of the problem los pormenores del problema • the ins and outs of high finance los entresijos de las altas finanzas • dietary experts can advise on the ins and outs of dieting los expertos en alimentación pueden dar información pormenorizada sobre las dietas

2 (US) (*Pol*) • the ins* el partido del gobierno

in... [ɪn] PREFIX in...

in. ABBR = inch

inability [ˌɪnəˈbɪlɪtɪ] N incapacidad *f* • ~ to do sth incapacidad para hacer algo • his ~ to express himself su incapacidad para expresarse

in absentia [ˈɪnæbˈsentɪə] ADV in absentia

inaccessibility [ˈɪnækˌsesəˈbɪlɪtɪ] N inaccesibilidad *f*

inaccessible [ˌɪnækˈsesəbl] ADJ inaccesible • to be ~ by road/land ser inaccesible por carretera/tierra • to be ~ to cars resultar inaccesible en coche • to be ~ to sb ser inaccesible para algn • goods which are ~ to the average citizen bienes que son inaccesibles para el ciudadano medio

inaccuracy [ɪnˈækjʊrəsɪ] N 1 (= *imprecision*) [*of figures, information, statement*] inexactitud *f*; [*of shot, aim, instrument, method*] falta *f* de precisión, imprecisión *f*
2 (*usu pl*) (= *mistake*) error *m* • the report contained many inaccuracies el informe contenía muchos errores

inaccurate [ɪnˈækjʊrɪt] ADJ [*figures, information, reporting, statement*] inexacto, erróneo; [*shot, aim, instrument, method*] impreciso, poco preciso • the report gave a very ~ picture of the situation el informe daba una visión muy inexacta *or* errónea de la situación • the figures are wildly ~ las cifras son totalmente erróneas *or* del todo inexactas • his estimate was wildly ~ su cálculo era completamente errado

inaccurately [ɪnˈækjʊrɪtlɪ] ADV • he measured the room ~ no midió la habitación correctamente • a device which measures distance ~ un dispositivo que no mide las distancias con precisión • he described the event ~ su descripción del suceso fue inexacta

inaction [ɪnˈækʃən] N inacción *f*, inactividad *f*

inactive [ɪnˈæktɪv] ADJ [*person, animal, volcano, life, substance*] inactivo

inactivity [ˌɪnækˈtɪvɪtɪ] N inactividad *f*

inadequacy [ɪnˈædɪkwəsɪ] N
1 (= *insufficiency*) [*of funding, resources, measures, training*] insuficiencia *f*; [*of housing, diet*] lo inadecuado
2 (= *weakness*) [*of person*] incompetencia *f*, ineptitud *f*; [*of system*] deficiencia *f*

inadequate [ɪnˈædɪkwɪt] ADJ
1 (= *insufficient*) [*supply, funding, measures, training*] insuficiente; [*housing, diet*] inadecuado • the facilities are ~ las instalaciones dejan mucho que desear • the company had ~ resources to survive the recession la empresa no tenía recursos suficientes *or* no tenía los recursos adecuados para sobrevivir a la recesión
2 (= *weak*) incompetente, inepto • he makes me feel totally ~ hace que me sienta totalmente incompetente *or* un verdadero inepto

inadequately [ɪnˈædɪkwɪtlɪ] ADV • the projects were ~ funded los proyectos adolecían de insuficiencia de fondos • the police were ~ trained la policía no estaba lo suficientemente entrenada, la policía no había recibido el entrenamiento adecuado • I felt ~ prepared me sentía mal preparada *or* poco preparada

inadmissibility [ˈɪnədˌmɪsəˈbɪlɪtɪ] N inadmisibilidad *f*

inadmissible [ˌɪnədˈmɪsəbl] ADJ inadmisible

inadvertence [ˌɪnədˈvɜːtəns] N inadvertencia *f* • by ~ por inadvertencia, por descuido

inadvertent [ˌɪnədˈvɜːtənt] ADJ (= *unintentional*) [*error, oversight*] involuntario • this had the ~ effect of ... esto tuvo el efecto no buscado de ... • they were trying to trap him into an ~ admission estaban tratando de tenderle una trampa para que lo admitiera sin darse cuenta

inadvertently [ˌɪnədˈvɜːtəntlɪ] ADV sin darse cuenta, sin querer

inadvisability [ˈɪnədˌvaɪzəˈbɪlɪtɪ] N lo poco aconsejable, lo desaconsejable

inadvisable [ˌɪnədˈvaɪzəbl] ADJ poco aconsejable, desaconsejable

inalienable [ɪnˈeɪlɪənəbl] ADJ inalienable

inamorata [ɪnˌæməˈrɑːtə] N amada *f*, querida *f*

inane [ɪˈneɪn] ADJ [*remark*] necio, fatuo, sonso (*LAm*); [*laugh, task, activity*] tonto; [*expression*] (*on face*) estúpido

inanely [ɪˈneɪnlɪ] ADV [*talk*] a lo tonto* • they chatted on ~ about the weather siguieron charlando a lo tonto sobre el tiempo* • he went through the bar grinning ~ pasó por el bar riéndose como un tonto

inanimate [ɪnˈænɪmɪt] ADJ [*object*] inanimado

inanition [ˌɪnəˈnɪʃən] N inanición *f*

inanity [ɪˈnænɪtɪ] N (= *quality*) necedad *f*, fatuidad *f*; **inanities** (= *inane remarks*) estupideces *fpl*, sandeces *fpl*

inapplicable [ɪnˈæplɪkəbl] ADJ inaplicable

inapposite [ɪnˈæpəzɪt] ADJ inapropiado, fuera de lugar

inappropriate [ˌɪnəˈprəʊprɪɪt] ADJ [*action, punishment, treatment*] inadecuado, poco apropiado; [*word, phrase*] inoportuno; [*behaviour*] impropio

inappropriately [ˌɪnəˈprəʊprɪɪtlɪ] ADV [*act*] de manera impropia; [*dressed*] de manera poco adecuada *or* apropiada

inappropriateness [ˌɪnəˈprəʊprɪɪtnɪs] N [*of behaviour*] lo impropio; [*of remark*] lo inoportuno; [*of dress*] lo poco adecuado *or* apropiado

inapt [ɪnˈæpt] ADJ (= *unsuitable*) poco idóneo; (= *inapposite*) no pertinente

inaptitude [ɪnˈæptɪtjuːd] N (= *unsuitability*) falta *f* de idoneidad; (= *inappositeness*) falta *f* de pertinencia

inarticulate [ˌɪnɑːˈtɪkjʊlɪt] ADJ [*person*] con dificultad para expresarse; [*speech*] mal pronunciado; [*noise, sound*] inarticulado • he was ~ with rage de lo furioso que estaba no podía pronunciar palabra

inarticulately [ˌɪnɑːˈtɪkjʊlɪtlɪ] ADV • he speaks ~ tiene dificultad para expresarse • he was mumbling ~ hablaba entre dientes y apenas se le entendía

inartistic [ˌɪnɑːˈtɪstɪk] ADJ [*work*] poco artístico, antiestético; [*person*] falto de talento artístico

inasmuch [ɪnəzˈmʌtʃ] ADV • ~ as (= *seeing that*) puesto que, ya que, en vista de que; (= *to the extent that*) ▹ insofar

inattention [ˌɪnəˈtenʃən] N (= *inattentiveness*) falta *f* de atención; (= *neglect*) falta *f* de interés, desinterés *m*

inattentive [ˌɪnəˈtentɪv] ADJ (= *distracted*) desatento, distraído; (= *neglectful*) poco atento • she accused him of being ~ to her and the children lo acusó de no prestarles suficiente atención a ella y a los niños

inattentively [ˌɪnəˈtentɪvlɪ] ADV distraídamente

inattentiveness [ˌɪnəˈtentɪvnɪs] N falta *f* de atención

inaudible [ɪnˈɔːdəbl] ADJ inaudible • he was almost ~ apenas se le podía oír

inaudibly [ɪnˈɔːdəblɪ] ADV de forma *or* modo inaudible • he spoke almost ~ habló tan bajo que apenas se le podía oír

inaugural [ɪ'nɔːgjʊrəl] ADJ [*lecture, debate*] inaugural; [*speech*] de apertura • **the president's ~ address** el discurso de investidura *or* de toma de posesión del presidente

inaugurate [ɪ'nɔːgjʊreɪt] VT **1** [+ *policy, new era, building*] inaugurar
2 (= *swear in*) [+ *president, official*] investir

inauguration [ɪ,nɔːgjʊ'reɪʃən] N (= *start*) inauguración *f*; (= *opening*) ceremonia *f* de apertura; (= *swearing in*) [*of president*] investidura *f*, toma *f* de posesión
CPD ▸ **inauguration ceremony** [*of building*] ceremonia *f* de inauguración; [*of president*] ceremonia *f* de investidura *or* de toma de posesión ▸ **Inauguration Day** (*US*) día *m* de la investidura del nuevo presidente
▸ **inauguration speech** [*of president*] discurso *m* de investidura *or* de toma de posesión

inauspicious [,ɪnɔːs'pɪʃəs] ADJ [*occasion*] poco propicio; [*circumstances*] desfavorable; [*moment*] inoportuno, poco propicio • **the campaign got off to an ~ start** la campaña empezó de manera poco propicia

inauspiciously [,ɪnɔːs'pɪʃəslɪ] ADV de modo poco propicio, en condiciones desfavorables

in-between ['ɪnbɪ'twiːn] ADJ (*gen*) intermedio • **he's rather in-between** no es ni una cosa ni la otra

inboard ['ɪnbɔːd] ADJ [*engine*] dentro de borda, interior
CPD ▸ **inboard motor** motor *m* dentro de borda, motor *m* interior

inborn ['ɪnbɔːn] ADJ [*ability, talent*] innato

inbound ['ɪnbaʊnd] ADJ [*flight*] de llegada; [*passenger*] que llega/llegaba

inbox ['ɪnbɒks] N (*for email*) buzón *m* de entrada

inbred ['ɪnbred] ADJ (= *innate*) innato; (= *result of in-breeding*) engendrado por endogamia • **we're too ~ in this company** en esta empresa estamos demasiado cerrados al exterior

inbreeding ['ɪn,briːdɪŋ] N endogamia *f*

inbuilt ['ɪnbɪlt] ADJ **1** (= *innate*) [*feeling*] innato; [*prejudice*] inherente
2 (= *integral*) incorporado • **an answering machine with ~ fax and printer** un contestador automático con fax e impresora incorporados

Inc., Inc ABBR (*US*) (*Comm*) (= **Incorporated**) S.A.

inc. ABBR (= **included, including, inclusive (of)**) inc.

Inca ['ɪŋkə] ADJ incaico, incásico
N (PL: **Inca** *or* **Incas**) inca *mf*

incalculable [ɪn'kælkjʊləbl] ADJ incalculable

Incan ['ɪŋkən] ADJ inca, incaico

incandescence [,ɪnkæn'desns] N incandescencia *f*

incandescent [,ɪnkæn'desnt] ADJ incandescente • **she was ~ (with rage)** estaba que trinaba (de rabia)*

incantation [,ɪnkæn'teɪʃən] N conjuro *m*, ensalmo *m*

incapability [ɪn,keɪpə'bɪlɪtɪ] N incapacidad *f*

incapable [ɪn'keɪpəbl] ADJ **1** (= *unable*) • **to be ~ of doing sth** ser incapaz de hacer algo • **she is ~ of harming anyone** es incapaz de hacer daño a alguien • **to be ~ of speech/movement** quedarse sin habla/sin poder moverse, no poder hablar/moverse • **a problem ~ of solution** un problema insoluble • **he is ~ of shame** no tiene vergüenza
2 (= *incompetent*) [*worker*] incompetente
3 (= *helpless*) inútil • **he was drunk and ~** estaba totalmente borracho

incapacitate [,ɪnkə'pæsɪteɪt] VT [+ *person*] incapacitar; (*Jur*) inhabilitar, incapacitar • **he was ~d by arthritis** estaba incapacitado por la artritis • **he was ~d by alcohol** estaba en un estado de embriaguez • **physically ~d** incapacitado físicamente

incapacitating [,ɪnkə'pæsɪteɪtɪŋ] ADJ [*illness*] que incapacita • **the pain is a nuisance but not ~** el dolor es molesto, pero no me incapacita

incapacity [,ɪnkə'pæsɪtɪ] N incapacidad *f*

in-car ['ɪn,kaːr] ADJ • **in-car entertainment system/stereo** aparato *m* de música de coche

incarcerate [ɪn'kaːsəreɪt] VT encarcelar

incarceration [ɪn,kaːsə'reɪʃən] N encarcelamiento *m*, encarcelación *f*

incarnate ADJ [ɪn'kaːnɪt] (*Rel*) encarnado • **the word ~** el verbo encarnado • **the devil ~** el diablo personificado, el mismo diablo
VT ['ɪnkaːneɪt] encarnar

incarnation [,ɪnkaː'neɪʃən] N (*Rel*) encarnación *f* • **he is the ~ of evil** es la encarnación del mal

incautious [ɪn'kɔːʃəs] ADJ incauto, imprudente

incautiously [ɪn'kɔːʃəslɪ] ADV incautamente, imprudentemente

incendiary [ɪn'sendɪərɪ] ADJ [*bomb, device, speech*] incendiario
N **1** (= *bomb*) bomba *f* incendiaria
2 (= *arsonist*) incendiario/a *m/f*, pirómano/a *m/f*

incense¹ ['ɪnsens] N incienso *m*
CPD ▸ **incense burner** incensario *m*
▸ **incense stick** barrita *f* de incienso

incense² [ɪn'sens] VT indignar, encolerizar • **their behaviour so ~d him that ...** su comportamiento lo indignó hasta tal punto que ...

incensed [ɪn'senst] ADJ [*person*] furioso, furibundo

incentive [ɪn'sentɪv] N incentivo *m*, estímulo *m* • **an ~ to work harder** un incentivo *or* estímulo para trabajar más • **as an added ~, they paid her airfare** como incentivo adicional, le pagaron el billete de avión • **they have no ~ to get a job** no tienen ningún incentivo para encontrar trabajo • **production ~** incentivo *m* a la producción
CPD ▸ **incentive bonus** prima *f* de incentivación ▸ **incentive payment** incentivo *m* económico ▸ **incentive scheme** plan *m* de incentivos

inception [ɪn'sepʃən] N comienzo *m*, principio *m* • **from its ~** desde el comienzo, desde el principio, desde los comienzos

incertitude [ɪn'sɜːtɪtjuːd] N incertidumbre *f*

incessant [ɪn'sesnt] ADJ [*rain, demands, complaints, fighting*] incesante, constante

incessantly [ɪn'sesntlɪ] ADV sin cesar, incesantemente

incest ['ɪnsest] N incesto *m*

incestuous [ɪn'sestjʊəs] ADJ incestuoso

inch [ɪntʃ] N pulgada *f* (= 2.54 *cm*); **inches** (= *height*) [*of person*] estatura *f* • **not an ~ of territory** ni un palmo de territorio • **the car missed me by ~es** faltó poco para que me atropellara el coche • **~ by ~** palmo a palmo • **we searched every ~ of the room** registramos todos los rincones del cuarto • **every ~ of it was used** se aprovechó hasta el último centímetro • **he's every ~ a soldier** es todo un soldado • **he didn't give an ~** no hizo la menor concesión • **to lose a few ~es*** adelgazar un poco • **to be within an ~ of death/disaster** estar a dos dedos de la muerte/del desastre • IDIOM: • **give him an ~ and he'll take a mile** dale un dedo y se toma hasta el codo; ▷ IMPERIAL SYSTEM
CPD ▸ **inch tape** cinta *f* en pulgadas (para medir)
▸ **inch forward** VI + ADV • **to ~ forward** [*person, vehicle*] avanzar muy lentamente
VT + ADV [+ *vehicle*] hacer avanzar muy lentamente
▸ **inch out** VT + ADV [+ *opponent*] derrotar por muy poco
VI + ADV [*vehicle*] avanzar muy despacio
▸ **inch up** VI + ADV [*prices*] subir poco a poco

inchoate ['ɪnkəʊeɪt] ADJ [*idea*] que no ha tomado forma definitiva; [*anger*] inexpresado

inchoative [ɪn'kəʊətɪv] ADJ [*aspect, verb*] incoativo

incidence ['ɪnsɪdəns] N (= *extent*) [*of crime*] incidencia *f*, índice *m*; [*of disease*] incidencia *f*, frecuencia *f* • **the angle of ~** (*Phys*) el ángulo de incidencia

incident ['ɪnsɪdənt] N (= *event*) incidente *m*, suceso *m*; (*in book, play etc*) episodio *m*, incidente *m*; (= *confrontation*) incidente *m* • **a life full of ~** una vida azarosa *or* llena de acontecimientos • **the Agadir ~** el episodio de Agadir • **to provoke a diplomatic ~** provocar un incidente diplomático • **the police were called to the scene of the ~** llamaron a la policía para que acudiera al lugar del suceso • **without ~** sin incidentes
CPD ▸ **incident room** centro *m* de coordinación

incidental [,ɪnsɪ'dentl] ADJ **1** (= *related*) [*benefit*] adicional; [*effect*] secundario • **the troubles ~ to any journey** las dificultades que conlleva cualquier viaje • **~ expenses** gastos *mpl* imprevistos • **~ music** música *f* de acompañamiento
2 (= *secondary, minor*) [*details*] incidental, secundario • **but that is ~ to my purpose** (*frm*) pero eso queda al margen de mi propósito
3 (= *accidental, fortuitous*) fortuito
NPL **incidentals** (= *expenses*) (gastos *mpl*) imprevistos *mpl*

incidentally [,ɪnsɪ'dentəlɪ] ADV **1** (= *by the way*) a propósito, por cierto • **he spoke no English ~** por cierto *or* a propósito, no hablaba inglés
2 (= *in a minor way*) incidentalmente
3 (= *accidentally, fortuitously*) por casualidad, de forma casual

incinerate [ɪn'sɪnəreɪt] VT [+ *body*] incinerar; [+ *rubbish*] quemar

incineration [ɪn,sɪnə'reɪʃən] N incineración *f*

incinerator [ɪn'sɪnəreɪtəʳ] N incinerador *m*

incipient [ɪn'sɪpɪənt] ADJ [*infection, illness, democracy, inflation, recession*] incipiente; [*romance, friendship*] incipiente, naciente

incise [ɪn'saɪz] VT cortar; (*Art*) grabar, tallar; (*Med*) hacer una incisión en

incision [ɪn'sɪʒən] N incisión *f*

incisive [ɪn'saɪsɪv] ADJ [*mind*] penetrante; [*remark, criticism*] incisivo, mordaz; [*tone*] mordaz; [*wit*] incisivo

incisively [ɪn'saɪsɪvlɪ] ADV [*say, criticize*] de forma incisiva, mordazmente; [*express*] de forma incisiva

incisiveness [ɪn'saɪsɪvnɪs] N [*of remark, criticism*] lo incisivo, lo mordaz

incisor [ɪn'saɪzəʳ] N incisivo *m*

incite [ɪn'saɪt] VT [+ *violence, riots, hatred*] incitar, instigar • **to ~ sb to do sth** incitar *or* instigar a algn a hacer algo • **to ~ sb to violence** incitar *or* instigar a algn a la violencia

incitement [ɪn'saɪtmənt] N incitación *f*,

instigación *f* (to a)

incivility [ˌɪnsɪˈvɪlɪtɪ] N descortesía *f*

incl ABBR (= **included, including, inclusive (of)**) inc.

inclemency [ɪnˈklemənsɪ] N inclemencia *f*

inclement [ɪnˈklemənt] ADJ [*weather*] inclemente

inclination [ˌɪnklɪˈneɪʃən] N **1** (= *tendency*) tendencia *f*, inclinación *f* • **his natural ~s** su tendencia *or* inclinación natural • **she has musical ~s** tiene inclinación por *or* hacia la música • **to have an ~ to meanness** tener tendencia a ser tacaño
2 (= *desire*) • **I have no ~ to go** no tengo ganas de ir • **I have neither the time nor the ~ to get involved** no tengo ni tiempo ni ganas de meterme en el asunto • **her ~ was to ignore him** prefería no hacerle caso • **I decided to follow my own ~ and stay at home** decidí hacer lo que más me apetecía y quedarme en casa • **I went to the meeting, against my ~** fui a la reunión, aunque no sentía ningún deseo de hacerlo
3 (= *slope, bow*) inclinación *f*

incline N [ˈɪnklaɪn] pendiente *f*, cuesta *f*
VT [ɪnˈklaɪn] **1** (= *bend*) [+ *head*] bajar, inclinar
2 (= *slope*) inclinar
3 (*frm*) (= *dispose*) • **to ~ sb to do sth** predisponer a algn a hacer algo • **the factors which ~ us towards particular beliefs** los factores que nos predisponen a tener ciertas creencias
VI [ɪnˈklaɪn] **1** (= *slope*) inclinarse
2 (= *tend*) • **I ~ to** *or* **towards the belief/opinion that ...** me inclino a pensar que ...

inclined [ɪnˈklaɪnd] ADJ **1** (= *tilted*) inclinado
2 (= *apt*) • **to be ~ to do sth** tener tendencia a hacer algo, tender a hacer algo • **he was ~ to be moody** tenía tendencia *or* tendía a sufrir cambios de humor, era propenso a los cambios de humor • **it is ~ to break** tiene tendencia a romperse
3 (= *disposed*) • **to be ~ to do sth: I'm ~ to believe you** estoy dispuesto a creerte • **I'm ~ to agree** yo me inclino a pensar lo mismo • **I'm ~ to think that ...** me inclino a pensar que ... • **to be academically ~** estar dotado para los estudios • **to be artistically ~** tener inclinaciones artísticas • **I didn't feel at all ~ to go out** no me apetecía nada salir, no tenía ninguna gana de salir • **if you feel so ~** si te apetece; (*more formal*) si así lo deseas • **to be musically ~** tener inclinación por *or* hacia la música • **Florence is full of art galleries, if you are that way ~** Florencia está llena de museos, si eso es lo que te interesa • **I'm ~ toward the latter explanation** me inclino por la última explicación • **to be favourably ~ toward sth/sb** ver algo/a algn con buenos ojos

inclose [ɪnˈkləʊz] VT = **enclose**

include [ɪnˈkluːd] VT incluir; (*with letter*) adjuntar, incluir • **facilities ~ a gym, swimming pool and sauna** las instalaciones disponen de gimnasio, piscina y sauna • **your name is not ~d in the list** su nombre no figura en la lista • **does that remark ~ me?** ¿va ese comentario también por mí? • **he sold everything, books ~d** vendió todo, incluso los libros • **service is/is not ~d** el servicio está/no está *or* (*LAm*) va/no va incluido • **all the team members, myself ~d** todos los miembros del equipo, incluido yo
▸ **include out*** VT + ADV (*hum*) excluir, dejar fuera • **~ me out!** ¡no contéis conmigo!

including [ɪnˈkluːdɪŋ] PREP • **terms £80, not ~ service** precio 80 libras, servicio no incluido • **$20, ~ post and packing** $20 incluidos gastos de envío • **seven ~ this one** siete con este • **everyone, ~ the President** todos, incluido el Presidente • **that applies to everyone, ~ you** eso va por todos, tú incluido • **up to and ~ chapter seven** hasta el capítulo siete inclusive

inclusion [ɪnˈkluːʒən] N inclusión *f*

inclusive [ɪnˈkluːsɪv] ADJ [*sum, price*] global • **an ~ price of £32.90** un precio global de 32,90 libras, un precio de 32,90 libras (con) todo incluido • **£5,000 fully ~** 5.000 libras con todo incluido • **~ of tax/postage and packing** incluidos los impuestos/los gastos de envío • **to be ~ of sth** incluir algo • **all prices are ~ of VAT** todos los precios incluyen el IVA
ADV • **from the 10th to the 15th ~** del 10 al 15, ambos inclusive *or* ambos incluidos

inclusively [ɪnˈkluːsɪvlɪ] ADV = **inclusive**

inclusiveness [ɪnˈkluːsɪvnɪs] N inclusividad *f*

incognito [ɪnˈkɒɡnɪtəʊ] ADV [*travel*] de incógnito
ADJ • **to remain ~** permanecer en el anonimato
N incógnito *m*

incoherence [ˌɪnkəʊˈhɪərəns] N [*of ideas, policies*] incoherencia *f*, falta *f* de coherencia • **his attempts to explain degenerated into ~** en su intento por dar una explicación cayó en la más absoluta incoherencia

incoherent [ˌɪnkəʊˈhɪərənt] ADJ [*person, words, letter*] incoherente; [*argument*] falto de coherencia, incoherente; [*conversation*] sin sentido, incoherente • **to become ~** volverse incoherente • **he was ~ with rage** estaba tan furioso que casi no podía hablar, balbuceaba de rabia

incoherently [ˌɪnkəʊˈhɪərəntlɪ] ADV [*mumble, ramble, argue, write*] de forma incoherente; [*speak*] con incoherencia, incoherentemente; [*expressed*] de manera incoherente • **he collapsed on the floor, mumbling ~** se desplomó en el suelo, murmurando de forma incoherente *or* murmurando incoherencias

incohesive [ˌɪnkəʊˈhiːsɪv] ADJ sin cohesión

incombustible [ˌɪnkəmˈbʌstəbl] ADJ incombustible

income [ˈɪnkʌm] N (*gen*) ingresos *mpl*; (*from property*) renta *f*; (= *salary*) salario *m*, sueldo *m*; (= *takings*) entradas *fpl*; (= *interest*) réditos *mpl*; (= *profit*) ganancias *fpl* • **gross/net ~** ingresos *mpl* brutos/netos • **private ~** rentas *fpl* • **national ~** renta *f* nacional • **I can't live on my ~** no puedo vivir con lo que gano • **to live beyond one's ~** gastar más de lo que se gana • **to live within one's ~** vivir de acuerdo a los ingresos
CPD ▸ **income and expenditure account** cuenta *f* de gastos e ingresos ▸ **income bracket, income group** categoría *f* económica • **the lower ~ groups** los sectores de ingresos más bajos ▸ **income category** categoría *f* económica ▸ **income inequality** desigualdad *f* de ingresos ▸ **income source** fuente *f* de ingresos ▸ **incomes policy** política *f* salarial *or* de salarios ▸ **income stream** flujo *m* de ingresos ▸ **income support** (*Brit*) ≈ ayuda *f* compensatoria ▸ **income tax** impuesto *m* sobre la renta ▸ **income tax inspector** inspector(a) *m/f* de Hacienda, inspector(a) *m/f* de la Dirección General Impositiva (*Arg, Uru*) ▸ **income tax return** declaración *f* de impuestos

incomer [ˈɪnˌkʌməʳ] (*Brit*) N recién llegado/a *m/f*; (*to society, group*) persona *f* nueva; (= *immigrant*) inmigrante *mf*

incoming [ˈɪnˌkʌmɪŋ] ADJ [*passenger, flight*] que llega/llegaba; [*president*] entrante; [*tide*] que sube/subía • **all ~ calls are monitored** todas las llamadas que se reciben están sujetas a control • **~ mail** correo *m* de entrada, correspondencia *f* que se recibe
NPL **incomings** ingresos *mpl*

incommensurable [ˌɪnkəˈmenʃərəbl] ADJ (*frm*) inconmensurable

incommensurate [ˌɪnkəˈmenʃərɪt] ADJ (*frm*) desproporcionado • **to be ~ with** no guardar relación con

incommode [ˌɪnkəˈməʊd] VT (*frm*) incomodar, molestar

incommodious [ˌɪnkəˈməʊdɪəs] ADJ (*frm*) (= *cramped*) estrecho, nada espacioso; (= *inconvenient*) poco conveniente

incommunicado [ˌɪnkəmjʊnɪˈkɑːdəʊ] ADJ incomunicado • **to hold sb ~** mantener incomunicado a algn

in-company [ˈɪnkʌmpənɪ] ADJ • **in-company training** formación *f* en la empresa

incomparable [ɪnˈkɒmpərəbl] ADJ **1** (= *matchless*) [*beauty, skill*] incomparable, sin par; [*achievement*] inigualable, sin par
2 (= *not comparable*) • **to be ~ with sth** no poderse comparar con algo

incomparably [ɪnˈkɒmpərəblɪ] ADV incomparablemente • **this product is ~ better** este producto es incomparablemente mejor

incompatibility [ˈɪnkəmˌpætəˈbɪlɪtɪ] N incompatibilidad *f*

incompatible [ˌɪnkəmˈpætəbl] ADJ (*all senses*) incompatible (**with** con)

incompetence [ɪnˈkɒmpɪtəns] N **1** incompetencia *f* • **he was fired for ~** lo despidieron por incompetente; ▹ **gross**
2 (*Jur*) incapacidad *f*

incompetent [ɪnˈkɒmpɪtənt] ADJ **1** (= *inept*) [*person*] incompetente; [*attempt*] torpe; [*work*] deficiente • **he's ~** es un incompetente, es incompetente • **he is ~ at his job** es incompetente en su trabajo
2 (= *unqualified*) • **Lennox was declared ~** (*Jur*) a Lennox lo declararon incapacitado • **he is ~ to lead the party** no está capacitado para dirigir el partido, es incapaz de dirigir el partido

incompetently [ɪnˈkɒmpɪtəntlɪ] ADV de modo incompetente, de forma incompetente

incomplete [ˌɪnkəmˈpliːt] ADJ (= *partial*) incompleto; (= *unfinished*) inacabado, sin terminar • **the gathering would be ~ without him** sin él la reunión no estaría completa

incompletely [ˌɪnkəmˈpliːtlɪ] ADV de manera *or* forma incompleta • **an ~ formed foetus** un feto no completamente formado

incompleteness [ˌɪnkəmˈpliːtnɪs] N lo incompleto • **because of the ~ of the reforms** a causa de lo incompleto de las reformas

incomprehensible [ɪnˌkɒmprɪˈhensəbl] ADJ incomprensible • **it is ~ to me** me resulta incomprensible

incomprehensibly [ɪnˌkɒmprɪˈhensəblɪ] ADV de modo incomprensible, incomprensiblemente

incomprehension [ˌɪnkɒmprɪˈhenʃən] N incomprensión *f*

inconceivable [ˌɪnkənˈsiːvəbl] ADJ inconcebible

inconceivably [ˌɪnkənˈsiːvəblɪ] ADJ inconcebiblemente

inconclusive [ˌɪnkənˈkluːsɪv] ADJ (= *not decisive*) [*result*] no concluyente; (= *not convincing*) [*argument*] no convincente; [*evidence*] no concluyente • **the investigation was ~** la investigación no dio resultados concluyentes

i

inconclusively [ˌɪnkənˈklu:sɪvlɪ] ADV de forma no concluyente • **the talks ended ~** las conversaciones finalizaron sin resultados concluyentes

inconclusiveness [ˌɪnkənˈklu:sɪvnɪs] N [*of evidence, verdict, trial*] lo no concluyente; [*of talks*] falta *f* de resultados concluyentes

incongruity [ˌɪnkɒŋˈgru:ɪtɪ] N incongruencia *f*

incongruous [ɪnˈkɒŋgrʊəs] ADJ [*pair, alliance, image, sound*] incongruente • **it seems ~ that …** parece extraño que …

incongruously [ɪnˈkɒŋgrʊəslɪ] ADV (*gen*) de manera incongruente; [*dressed*] inapropiadamente • **he wore old jeans, with ~ smart shoes** llevaba unos vaqueros viejos con unos zapatos muy elegantes, lo que resultaba inapropiado

inconsequent [ɪnˈkɒnsɪkwənt] ADJ = **inconsequential**

inconsequential [ɪnˌkɒnsɪˈkwenʃəl] ADJ [*conversation*] sin trascendencia; (= *illogical*) ilógico

inconsequentially [ˌɪnkɒnsɪˈkwenʃəlɪ] ADV [*talk, say*] sin propósito serio

inconsiderable [ˌɪnkənˈsɪdərəbl] ADJ • **a not ~ sum** una cifra nada desdeñable *or* despreciable, una suma considerable

inconsiderate [ˌɪnkənˈsɪdərɪt] ADJ [*behaviour, person*] desconsiderado • **how ~ of him!** ¡qué falta de consideración de su parte! • **to be ~ to sb** no tener consideración con algn

inconsiderately [ˌɪnkənˈsɪdərɪtlɪ] ADV desconsideradamente

inconsistency [ˌɪnkənˈsɪstənsɪ] N **1** (= *inconsistent nature*) [*of behaviour*] carácter *m* contradictorio *or* incongruente; [*of statement, account, evidence, policy*] falta *f* de coherencia • **his worst fault is his ~** su peor defecto es que es un inconsecuente **2** (= *contradiction*) contradicción *f*

inconsistent [ˌɪnkənˈsɪstənt] ADJ **1** (= *erratic*) [*person*] inconsecuente, voluble; [*quality, work, performance*] irregular, desigual; [*behaviour, policies*] contradictorio, incongruente **2** (= *contradictory*) [*actions*] inconsecuente; [*statement, account, evidence*] contradictorio • **to be ~ with sth** (= *contradict*) contradecir algo, no concordar con algo; (= *not correspond with*) no encajar con algo, no concordar con algo

inconsistently [ˌɪnkənˈsɪstəntlɪ] ADV **1** (= *erratically*) [*behave*] de forma contradictoria *or* incongruente *or* desigual; [*work, perform*] de forma irregular **2** (= *contradictorily*) [*argue, reason*] sin congruencia, contradictoriamente

inconsolable [ˌɪnkənˈsəʊləbl] ADJ inconsolable

inconsolably [ˌɪnkənˈsəʊləblɪ] ADV inconsolablemente

inconspicuous [ˌɪnkənˈspɪkjʊəs] ADJ [*person*] que no llama la atención; [*colour*] poco llamativo, que no llama la atención; [*place*] que pasa desapercibido • **she tried to make herself ~** trató de no llamar la atención *or* de pasar desapercibida

inconspicuously [ˌɪnkənˈspɪkjʊəslɪ] ADV [*sit, move*] sin llamar la atención, discretamente • **~ placed** colocado donde no llama la atención, discretamente colocado

inconstancy [ɪnˈkɒnstənsɪ] N inconstancia *f*, veleidad *f*

inconstant [ɪnˈkɒnstənt] ADJ inconstante, veleidoso

incontestable [ˌɪnkənˈtestəbl] ADJ incontestable, incuestionable

incontestably [ɪnkənˈtestəblɪ] ADV incontestablemente, incuestionablemente

incontinence [ɪnˈkɒntɪnəns] N incontinencia *f*

incontinent [ɪnˈkɒntɪnənt] ADJ incontinente • **to be/become ~** tener incontinencia

incontrovertible [ɪnˌkɒntrəˈvɜ:təbl] ADJ [*fact, evidence*] incontrovertible

incontrovertibly [ɪnˌkɒntrəˈvɜ:tɪblɪ] ADV de manera incontrovertible • **this is ~ true** esta es una verdad incontrovertible

inconvenience [ˌɪnkənˈvi:nɪəns] N **1** (= *awkwardness*) [*of time, location*] inconveniencia *f*; [*of arrangements, house*] incomodidad *f* **2** (= *drawback*) inconveniente *m* • **living so far from the station is a great ~** vivir tan lejos de la estación es un gran inconveniente **3** (= *trouble*) molestias *fpl*, inconvenientes *mpl* • **you caused a lot of ~** causaste muchas molestias *or* muchos inconvenientes • **it makes up for the ~ of having to move** compensa las molestias *or* los inconvenientes de tener que mudarse • **to put sb to great ~** causar muchas molestias *or* muchos inconvenientes a algn VT (= *cause problems to*) causar molestias a; (= *disturb*) molestar • **I hope you haven't been ~d by the delay** espero que el retraso no le haya causado molestias • **I'm sorry to ~ you, but …** perdone que lo moleste, pero … • **don't ~ yourself** no se moleste

inconvenient [ˌɪnkənˈvi:nɪənt] ADJ [*time, appointment*] inoportuno; [*location, design*] poco práctico, incómodo • **it's an ~ place to get to** es un sitio mal comunicado, no es un sitio al que sea fácil llegar • **how ~!** ¡qué trastorno!, ¡vaya trastorno! • **to be ~** venir mal; (*more formal*) resultar inconveniente • **to be ~ for sb** venirle mal a algn; (*more formal*) resultarle inconveniente a algn

inconveniently [ˌɪnkənˈvi:nɪəntlɪ] ADV [*arranged, planned*] de modo poco práctico; [*arrive, turn up*] en mal momento, en un momento inoportuno • **to come ~ early** venir demasiado temprano • **the hotel is rather ~ situated** el hotel está mal situado

inconvertibility [ˈɪnkənˌvɜ:tɪˈbɪlɪtɪ] N inconvertibilidad *f*

inconvertible [ˌɪnkənˈvɜ:təbl] ADJ inconvertible

incorporate [ɪnˈkɔ:pəreɪt] VT (= *include*) incluir, comprender; (= *integrate*) incorporar (**in, into** a) • **a product incorporating vitamin Q** un producto que contiene vitamina Q • **to ~ a company** constituir una compañía en sociedad (anónima)

incorporated [ɪnˈkɔ:pəreɪtɪd] ADJ (*US*) (*Comm*) • **Jones & Lloyd Incorporated** Jones y Lloyd Sociedad Anónima

CPD ▸ **incorporated company** (*US*) sociedad *f* anónima

incorporation [ɪnˌkɔ:pəˈreɪʃən] N (= *inclusion*) inclusión *f*, incorporación *f*; (= *integration*) incorporación *f*; (*Comm*) constitución *f* en sociedad (anónima)

incorporeal [ˌɪnkɔ:ˈpɔ:rɪəl] ADJ (*liter*) incorpóreo

incorrect [ˌɪnkəˈrekt] ADJ **1** (= *wrong*) [*answer, spelling*] incorrecto; [*information, statement, assumption*] erróneo • **it is ~ to say that …** es erróneo decir que … • **that is ~, you are wrong** no es cierto, usted se equivoca **2** (= *bad*) [*posture, diet*] incorrecto, inadecuado **3** (= *improper*) [*behaviour*] incorrecto, impropio; [*dress*] inapropiado

incorrectly [ˌɪnkəˈrektlɪ] ADV **1** (= *wrongly*) [*spell, answer*] mal; (*more formal*) incorrectamente; [*state, conclude, assume, believe*] erróneamente; [*inform*] mal, erróneamente • **an ~ addressed letter** una carta con las señas mal puestas **2** (= *badly*) mal; (*more frm*) incorrectamente • **the doors had been fitted ~** habían puesto las puertas mal **3** (= *improperly*) [*behave*] incorrectamente; [*dress*] de manera inapropiada, de modo inapropiado

incorrigible [ɪnˈkɒrɪdʒəbl] ADJ [*womaniser, optimist*] incorregible, sin remedio • **you're ~!** ¡eres incorregible!, ¡no tienes remedio!

incorrigibly [ɪnˈkɒrɪdʒəblɪ] ADV incorregiblemente

incorruptible [ˌɪnkəˈrʌptəbl] ADJ incorruptible; (= *not open to bribery*) insobornable

increase VI [ɪnˈkri:s] [*number, size, speed, pain*] aumentar; [*prices, temperature, pressure*] subir, aumentar; [*wages, salaries, productivity, popularity*] aumentar • **to ~ in number** aumentar • **to ~ in weight/volume/size/value** aumentar de peso/volumen/tamaño/valor • **to ~ by 100** aumentar en 100 • **to ~ from 8% to 10%** aumentar de 8 a 10 por ciento

VT [ɪnˈkri:s] [+ *number, size, speed, pain*] aumentar; [+ *prices, temperature, pressure*] subir, aumentar; [+ *wages, salaries, taxes, interest rates, productivity*] aumentar • **to ~ one's efforts** redoblar sus esfuerzos • **there has been an ~d interest in his work** ha aumentado el interés por su trabajo • **profits were the result of ~d efficiency** los beneficios eran el resultado de una mayor eficiencia

N [ˈɪnkri:s] (*gen*) aumento *m*, incremento *m*; [*of prices*] subida *f*, aumento *m* • **an ~ in size/volume** un aumento de tamaño/volumen • **an ~ of £5/10%** un aumento de 5 libras/del 10 por ciento • **to be on the ~** estar *or* ir en aumento

increasing [ɪnˈkri:sɪŋ] ADJ [*number, amount*] creciente, cada vez mayor • **an ~ number of women are going out to work** un creciente número de mujeres va a trabajar, el número de mujeres que trabajan va en aumento *or* es cada vez mayor • **the president is under ~ pressure to resign** el presidente recibe cada vez más presiones para presentar la dimisión

increasingly [ɪnˈkri:sɪŋlɪ] ADV cada vez más • **he was finding it ~ difficult to make decisions** le resultaba cada vez más difícil tomar decisiones • **Spanish food is becoming ~ popular** la comida española se está volviendo cada vez más popular *or* está alcanzando una popularidad cada vez mayor • **it is becoming ~ obvious that …** está cada vez más claro que … • **they are relying ~ on foreign imports** cada vez dependen más de las importaciones extranjeras

incredible [ɪnˈkredəbl] ADJ increíble • **they found it ~ that I was still alive** les pareció increíble que todavía estuviera viva • **~ though it may seem** por increíble que parezca, aunque parezca mentira • **an ~ number of people** una cantidad de gente increíble

incredibly [ɪnˈkredəblɪ] ADV **1** (= *extremely*) [*ugly, rich, intelligent*] increíblemente • **it all happened ~ fast** todo sucedió con una rapidez increíble **2** (= *amazingly*) • **~, they did not come** por increíble que parezca, no vinieron, aunque parezca mentira, no llegaron

incredulity [ˌɪnkrɪˈdju:lɪtɪ] N incredulidad *f*

incredulous [ɪnˈkredjʊləs] ADJ [*expression*] de incredulidad • **I was ~** no lo creí

incredulously [ɪnˈkredjʊləslɪ] ADV con

incredulidad
increment ['ɪnkrɪmənt] (N) aumento *m*, incremento *m* (in de)
incremental [ɪnkrɪ'mentəl] (ADJ) [*change, process*] gradual; [*costs*] incremental
(CPD) ▸ **incremental compiler** compilador *m* incremental
incriminate [ɪn'krɪmɪneɪt] (VT) incriminar
incriminating [ɪn'krɪmɪneɪtɪŋ] (ADJ) [*evidence, document*] incriminatorio
incrimination [ɪn,krɪmɪ'neɪʃən] (N) incriminación *f*
incriminatory [ɪn'krɪmɪnətərɪ] (ADJ) = **incriminating**
incrust [ɪn'krʌst] (VT) = **encrust**
incrustation [,ɪnkrʌs'teɪʃən] (N) = **encrustation**
incubate ['ɪnkjʊbeɪt] (VT) (*gen*) incubar (VI) [*egg*] incubarse; [*hen*] empollar; (*fig*) [*idea*] incubarse
incubation [,ɪnkjʊ'beɪʃən] (N) [*of egg, disease*] incubación *f*
(CPD) ▸ **incubation period** período *m* de incubación
incubator ['ɪnkjʊbeɪtə^r] (N) (*for eggs, bacteria, baby*) incubadora *f*
incubus ['ɪŋkjʊbəs] (N) (PL: **incubuses** *or* **incubi** ['ɪŋkjʊ,baɪ]) íncubo *m*
inculcate ['ɪnkʌlkeɪt] (VT) • **to ~ sth in sb** inculcar algo a algn
inculcation [,ɪnkʌl'keɪʃən] (N) inculcación *f*
incumbency [ɪn'kʌmbənsɪ] (N) (*frm*)
1 (= *being in office*) ocupación *f* del cargo • **the benefits of ~** los beneficios de ocupar el cargo
2 (*Rel*) beneficio *m*
incumbent [ɪn'kʌmbənt] (ADJ) (*frm*) • **to be ~ on sb to do sth** incumbir a algn hacer algo • **I felt it ~ upon me to go** sentí que debía ir
(N) titular *mf*, poseedor(a) *m/f* (*de un cargo o dignidad*); (*Rel*) beneficiado *m*
incunabula [,ɪnkjʊ'næbjʊlə] (NPL) incunables *mpl*
incur [ɪn'kɜː^r] (VT) [+ *debt, obligation*] contraer; [+ *expense, charges*] incurrir en; [+ *loss*] sufrir; [+ *anger*] provocar • **I wouldn't wish to ~ his wrath** no me gustaría provocar su ira • **I did not wish to ~ his disapproval** no deseaba hacer que se pusiera en desacuerdo
incurable [ɪn'kjʊərəbl] (ADJ) **1** (*Med*) incurable
2 (*fig*) [*optimist, romantic*] incorregible
(N) incurable *mf*
incurably [ɪn'kjʊərəblɪ] (ADV) • **to be ~ ill** tener una enfermedad incurable • **to be ~ romantic/optimistic** ser un romántico/optimista incurable *or* incorregible
incurious [ɪn'kjʊərɪəs] (ADJ) indiferente • **to be ~ about sth** ser indiferente a algo
incuriously [ɪn'kjʊərɪəslɪ] (ADV) [*look*] con indiferencia
incursion [ɪn'kɜːʃən] (N) incursión *f*
Ind. (ABBR) (US) = **Indiana**
indebted [ɪn'detɪd] (ADJ) **1** (= *owing money*) endeudado • **to be (heavily) ~ (to sb)** estar (muy) endeudado (con algn)
2 (= *grateful*) • **I am ~ to you for your help** estoy muy agradecido por su ayuda • **we are greatly ~ to Shakespeare for his contribution to English literature** le debemos mucho a Shakespeare por su contribución a la literatura inglesa
indebtedness [ɪn'detɪdnɪs] (N) **1** (*Econ*) endeudamiento *m*, deuda *f* (to con)
2 (*fig*) deuda *f* (to con)
indecency [ɪn'diːsnsɪ] (N) indecencia *f*; ▹ **gross**
indecent [ɪn'diːsnt] (ADJ) **1** (= *obscene*) [*photograph, language, film, gesture, clothes*] indecente • **to make an ~ suggestion** sugerir algo indecente
2 (= *shocking*) escandaloso • **with ~ haste** con una prisa nada decorosa
(CPD) ▸ **indecent assault** (*Jur*) abusos *mpl* deshonestos ▸ **indecent behaviour** (*Brit*) (*Jur*) atentado *m* al pudor ▸ **indecent exposure** (*Jur*) exhibicionismo *m*
indecently [ɪn'diːsntlɪ] (ADV) **1** (= *obscenely*) indecentemente, de una forma indecente • **~ short skirts** faldas indecentemente cortas • **to ~ assault sb** realizar abusos deshonestos de algn • **to ~ expose o.s.** cometer un acto de exhibicionismo
2 (= *shockingly*) escandalosamente • **she is ~ rich** es asquerosamente rica
indecipherable [,ɪndɪ'saɪfərəbl] (ADJ) indescifrable
indecision [,ɪndɪ'sɪʒən] (N) indecisión *f*, falta *f* de decisión, irresolución *f* (*frm*)
indecisive [,ɪndɪ'saɪsɪv] (ADJ) **1** (= *hesitant*) [*person*] indeciso, irresoluto (*frm*)
2 (= *inconclusive*) [*result, vote*] no concluyente, no decisivo; [*battle*] no decisivo
indecisively [,ɪndɪ'saɪsɪvlɪ] (ADV)
1 (= *hesitantly*) con indecisión, con irresolución (*frm*) • **we waited as she stood there ~** esperamos mientras ella estaba ahí parada sin decidirse
2 (= *inconclusively*) [*end, conclude*] sin resultados definitivos, sin resultados decisivos
indecisiveness [,ɪndɪ'saɪsɪvnɪs] (N)
1 (= *hesitancy*) indecisión *f*, falta *f* de decisión, irresolución *f* (*frm*)
2 (= *inconclusiveness*) falta *f* de conclusión
indeclinable [,ɪndɪ'klaɪnəbl] (ADJ) indeclinable
indecorous [ɪn'dekərəs] (ADJ) indecoroso
indecorously [ɪn'dekərəslɪ] (ADV) indecorosamente
indecorum [,ɪndɪ'kɔːrəm] (N) indecoro *m*, falta *f* de decoro
indeed [ɪn'diːd] (ADV) **1** (= *in fact*) de hecho • **I feel, ~ I know, he is wrong** creo, de hecho sé *or* en realidad sé, que está equivocado • **we have nothing against diversity, ~, we want more of it** no tenemos nada en contra de la diversidad, de hecho queremos que haya más • **if ~ he is wrong** si es que realmente se equivoca, si efectivamente se equivoca • **the document was ~ missing** efectivamente el documento había desaparecido • **it is ~ true that ...** es en efecto verdad que ...
2 (*as intensifier*) • **that is praise ~** eso es todo un elogio, eso sí es una alabanza • **very ... ~: to be very good/small/intelligent ~** ser verdaderamente *or* realmente bueno/pequeño/inteligente • **you're doing very well ~** vas realmente bien • **we are taking the matter very seriously ~** nos estamos tomando la cuestión sumamente en serio *or* pero que muy en serio • **thank you very much ~** muchísimas gracias • **I'm very glad ~** me alegro muchísimo
3 (*in answer to a question*) • **"isn't it a beautiful day?" — "yes, ~!"** —¿a que es un día precioso? —¡desde luego! *or* —¡y que lo digas! *or* —¡ya lo creo! • **"did you know him?" — "I did ~"** —¿lo conocías? —sí que lo conocía *or* —claro que sí • **"are you Professor Ratburn?" — "~ I am"** *or* **"I am ~"** —¿es usted el profesor Ratburn? —sí, señor *or* —el mismo • **"may I go?" — "~ you may not!"** —¿puedo ir? —¡claro que no! *or* —¡por supuesto que no!
4 (*expressing interest*) • **indeed?** • **is it ~?** • **did you ~?** ¿de veras?, ¿de verdad?, ¿ah, sí?
5 (*expressing disbelief, surprise, scorn*) • **"I did the best I could" — "indeed!"** —lo hice lo mejor que pude —¡por supuesto! *or* —¡claro, claro! (*iro*) • **"he said he would do it" — "did he ~?"** —dijo que lo haría —¿eso dijo? *or* —¿no me digas? • **"he said I was too short" — "too short ~!"** —dijo que era demasiado bajo —¡sí, hombre, bajísimo! (*iro*)
indefatigable [,ɪndɪ'fætɪgəbl] (ADJ) incansable, infatigable
indefatigably [,ɪndɪ'fætɪgəblɪ] (ADV) incansablemente, infatigablemente
indefensible [,ɪndɪ'fensəbl] (ADJ)
1 (= *unjustifiable*) [*conduct, action*] injustificable, inexcusable; [*idea, policy*] indefendible, insostenible
2 (= *vulnerable*) [*town, country*] indefendible
indefensibly [,ɪndɪ'fensəblɪ] (ADV) [*behave, act*] de una forma injustificable
indefinable [,ɪndɪ'faɪnəbl] (ADJ) indefinible
indefinably [,ɪndɪ'faɪnəblɪ] (ADV) indefiniblemente
indefinite [ɪn'defɪnɪt] (ADJ) **1** (= *vague*) [*answer*] impreciso • **he was very ~ about it all** no fue muy preciso al respecto • **our plans are somewhat ~ as yet** nuestros planes están todavía por concretar
2 (= *not fixed*) [*time*] indefinido, indeterminado • **it will be closed for an ~ period** estará cerrado por tiempo indefinido • **to be on ~ leave** estar de permiso por tiempo indefinido
3 (*Ling*) indefinido
(CPD) ▸ **indefinite article** artículo *m* indefinido ▸ **indefinite pronoun** pronombre *m* indefinido
indefinitely [ɪn'defɪnɪtlɪ] (ADV) (*gen*) por tiempo indefinido • **it will keep ~** se conserva por tiempo indefinido • **we can carry on ~** podemos continuar hasta cuando sea *or* por tiempo indefinido
indeliberate [,ɪndɪ'lɪbərɪt] (ADJ) (*frm*) (= *unintentional*) inintencionado
indelible [ɪn'deləbl] (ADJ) **1** (= *not washable*) [*ink, stain*] indeleble • **~ pen** bolígrafo *m* de tinta indeleble
2 (= *unforgettable*) [*memory, image*] indeleble, imborrable • **it made an ~ impression on me** se me quedó grabado en la memoria
indelibly [ɪn'deləblɪ] (ADV) indeleblemente • **the horrors he experienced are imprinted ~ in his brain** los horrores que sufrió quedaron grabados de forma indeleble en su mente
indelicacy [ɪn'delɪkəsɪ] (N) indecoro *m*, falta *f* de decoro
indelicate [ɪn'delɪkɪt] (ADJ) (= *tactless*) indiscreto, falto de tacto; (= *crude*) indelicado
indelicately [ɪn'delɪkətlɪ] (ADV) (= *tactlessly*) de forma indelicada; (= *rudely*) groseramente; (= *crudely*) toscamente
indemnification [ɪn,demnɪfɪ'keɪʃən] (N) indemnización *f*
indemnify [ɪn'demnɪfaɪ] (VT)
1 (= *compensate*) • **to ~ sb for sth** indemnizar a algn por algo
2 (= *safeguard*) • **to ~ sb against sth** asegurar a algn contra algo
indemnity [ɪn'demnɪtɪ] (N) (= *compensation*) indemnización *f*, reparación *f*; (= *insurance*) indemnidad *f* • **double ~** doble indemnización *f*
indent [ɪn'dent] (VT) (*Typ*) [+ *word, line*] sangrar; (= *cut into*) dejar marcas en
(VI) • **to ~ for sth** (*Comm*) hacer un pedido de algo, encargar algo; (*Mil*) requisar algo
(N) (*Brit*) (*Comm*) pedido *m*; (*Mil*) requisición *f*
indentation [,ɪnden'teɪʃən] (N) (*in cloth*) muesca *f*; (*in coastline*) entrante *m*; (= *dent*) (*in wood, metal*) hendidura *f*; (*in metal*) abolladura *f*; (*Typ*) sangría *f*
indented [ɪn'dentɪd] (ADJ) [*type*] sangrado; [*surface*] abollado • **a deeply ~ coastline** una

costa muy accidentada
indenture [ɪn'dentʃəʳ] (N) **1** (*Comm*) escritura *f*
2 indentures contrato *m* de aprendizaje
indentured [ɪn'dentʃəd] (ADJ) [*servant, labourer*] *obligado a trabajar para alguien durante un periodo de tiempo determinado*
independence [ˌɪndɪ'pendəns] (N) independencia *f* • **war of ~** guerra *f* de independencia • **Zaire gained** *or* **won ~ in 1960** Zaire obtuvo la independencia *or* se independizó en 1960
(CPD) ▸ **Independence Day** Día *m* de la Independencia; ▷ **FOURTH OF JULY**
independent [ˌɪndɪ'pendənt] (ADJ)
1 (= *self-supporting*) [*person, country*] independiente; [*income*] propio • **to be ~** ser independiente • **to be ~ of sth/sb** no depender de algo/algn, ser independiente de algo/algn • **to become ~** [*country*] independizarse • **a person of ~ means** una persona con rentas propias *or* con independencia económica
2 (= *unconnected*) [*events*] independiente, no relacionado; (= *impartial*) [*inquiry, investigation*] independiente; [*witness*] imparcial • **you are advised to seek an ~ opinion** le aconsejamos que se haga asesorar por un tercero
3 (= *self-reliant*) [*person, child*] independiente • **he was incapable of ~ thought** era incapaz de pensar por su cuenta • **she has always been very ~ of her parents** siempre ha dependido muy poco de sus padres
4 (= *private*) [*school, sector*] privado; [*broadcasting company, radio station*] privado, independiente
(N) **1** (= *politician*) independiente *mf*, candidato/a *m/f* independiente
2 (= *company*) compañía *f* independiente
(CPD) ▸ **independent clause** (*Gram*) oración *f* independiente ▸ **independent school** (*Brit*) escuela *f* privada, colegio *m* privado
▸ **independent suspension** (*Aut*) suspensión *f* independiente
independently [ˌɪndɪ'pendəntlɪ] (ADV)
1 (= *self-reliantly*) [*live*] independientemente; [*act*] por su cuenta • **each child will work ~** cada niño trabajará de forma independiente *or* por su cuenta *or* solo • **for a child of six, he behaves very ~** para ser un niño de seis años es muy independiente
• **~ of sth/sb** independientemente de algo/algn • **~ of what he may decide** independientemente de lo que él decida
2 (= *separately*) por separado • **we both ~ came up with the same answer** los dos dimos con la misma respuesta por separado
3 (= *by an independent party*) • **you ought to get it valued ~** deberías hacer que un tercero te lo tasase
in-depth ['ɪnˌdepθ] (ADJ) [*study*] a fondo, exhaustivo • **in-depth investigation** investigación *f* a fondo *or* en profundidad
indescribable [ˌɪndɪs'kraɪbəbl] (ADJ) [*terror, horror*] indescriptible, increíble; [*beauty, joy*] indescriptible
indescribably [ˌɪndɪs'kraɪbəblɪ] (ADV) indescriptiblemente; (*pej*) indeciblemente • **~ bad** indescriptiblemente malo
indestructibility [ˌɪndɪstrʌktə'bɪlɪtɪ] (N) indestructibilidad *f*
indestructible [ˌɪndɪs'trʌktəbl] (ADJ) indestructible
indeterminable [ˌɪndɪ'tɜːmɪnəbl] (ADJ) indeterminable
indeterminacy [ˌɪndɪ'tɜːmɪnəsɪ] (N) carácter *m* indeterminado
indeterminate [ˌɪndɪ'tɜːmɪnɪt] (ADJ) indeterminado • **of ~ age** de edad indeterminada
(CPD) ▸ **indeterminate sentence** (*US*) (*Jur*) condena *f* indeterminada
indeterminately [ˌɪndɪ'tɜːmɪnɪtlɪ] (ADV) de modo indeterminado
index ['ɪndeks] (N) **1** (PL: **indexes**) (*in book*) índice *m*
2 (PL: **indices, indexes**) (= *pointer*) índice *m*, señal *m* (**to** de); (*Econ*) índice *m* • **cost of living ~** índice *m* del costo de la vida • **the Index** (*Rel*) el índice expurgatorio; ▷ **retail**
3 (*Math*) (PL: **indices**) exponente *m*
(VT) (= *put index in*) [+ *book*] poner índice a; (= *make index headings for*) [+ *book*] (*in catalogue*) catalogar; [+ *entry, item, subject*] poner en el índice • **it is ~ed under Smith** está clasificado bajo Smith
(CPD) ▸ **index card** ficha *f* ▸ **index finger** dedo *m* índice ▸ **index number** índice *m*
indexation [ˌɪndek'seɪʃən], **indexing** ['ɪndeksɪŋ] (N) indexación *f*, indización *f*, indiciación *f*
indexed ['ɪndekst] (ADJ) = **index-linked**
index-linked [ˌɪndeks'lɪŋkt] (ADJ) indexado, indiciado
index-linking [ˌɪndeks'lɪŋkɪŋ] (N) indexación *f*, indiciación *f*
index-tracking fund [ˌɪndeks'trækɪŋfʌnd], **index-tracker** [ˌɪndeks'trækəʳ], **index-tracker fund** (N) (*Econ*) fondo *m* (de inversión) indexado, fondo *m* (de inversión) en índices
India ['ɪndɪə] (N) India *f*
(CPD) ▸ **India paper** papel *m* de China, papel *m* biblia ▸ **India rubber** caucho *m*
Indian ['ɪndɪən] (ADJ) (= *from India*) [*culture, languages, customs*] indio, hindú; (= *American Indian*) indígena, indio
(N) (*from India*) indio/a *m/f*, hindú *mf*; (= *American Indian*) indígena *mf*, indio/a *m/f*
(CPD) ▸ **Indian corn** = **maize** ▸ **Indian elephant** elefante *m* asiático ▸ **Indian file** fila *f* india ▸ **Indian hemp** cáñamo *m* índico ▸ **Indian ink** tinta *f* china ▸ **the Indian Ocean** el Océano Índico ▸ **Indian restaurant** restaurante *m* indio, restaurante *m* hindú ▸ **Indian summer** (*in northern hemisphere*) veranillo *m* de San Martín; (*in southern hemisphere*) veranillo *m* de San Juan • **the publication of that book gave her career an ~ summer** la publicación de ese libro dio lugar a un éxito tardío en su carrera
▸ **Indian wrestling** (*US*) (= *arm wrestling*) pulso *m*, pulseada *f* (*Arg, Uru*)
indicate ['ɪndɪkeɪt] (VT) **1** (= *point out*) [+ *place*] indicar, señalar; (= *register*) [+ *temperature, speed*] marcar
2 (= *show, suggest*) [+ *change*] ser indicio de • **the gathering clouds ~d a change in the weather** las nubes que se iban acumulando eran indicio de un cambio de tiempo • **the coroner's report ~d drowning as the cause of death** el informe del juez de instrucción indicaba *or* señalaba que murió ahogado
3 (= *gesture*) indicar • **he ~d that I was to sit down** me indicó que me sentara
4 (= *recommend, require*) (*usu passive*) • **in this particular case, surgery is not ~d** en este caso en particular no es aconsejable operar • **I think a speedy departure is ~d** (*hum*) creo que habría que poner pies en polvorosa*
(VI) indicar, señalizar; (*esp Brit*) • **to ~ left/right** indicar *or* señalizar a la izquierda/derecha
indication [ˌɪndɪ'keɪʃən] (N) **1** (= *sign*) indicio *m* • **there is every ~ that ...** todo hace suponer que ... • **there is no ~ that ...** no hay indicios de que ... • **this is some ~ of ...** esto da una idea de ...
2 (= *mark*) señal *f*; (*on gauge*) marca *f*
3 (*Med*) (*often pl*) indicación *f*
indicative [ɪn'dɪkətɪv] (ADJ) **1** • **to be ~ of sth** ser indicio de algo
2 (*Ling*) [*mood*] indicativo
(N) (*Ling*) indicativo *m*
indicator ['ɪndɪkeɪtəʳ] (N) **1** (*gen*) (*also Chem, Econ*) indicador *m*
2 indicators (*Aut*) intermitentes *mpl*, direccionales *mpl* (*LAm*)
(CPD) ▸ **indicator light** [*of car*] intermitente *m*, direccional *f* (*LAm*)
indices ['ɪndɪsiːz] (NPL) *of* **index**
indict [ɪn'daɪt] (VT) **1** (*esp US*) (= *charge*) acusar • **to ~ sb for murder** acusar a algn de homicidio
2 (*fig*) condenar, criticar duramente
indictable [ɪn'daɪtəbl] (ADJ) • **~ offence** delito *m* procesable
indictment [ɪn'daɪtmənt] (N) **1** (= *charge, document*) acusación *f*; (= *act*) procesamiento *m* • **to bring an ~ against sb** formular cargos contra algn
2 (*fig*) condenación *f*, crítica *f* • **the report is an ~ of our system** (*fig*) el informe critica duramente nuestro sistema
indie* ['ɪndɪ] (ADJ) (*Brit*) (*Mus*) [*music, band*] independiente
(CPD) ▸ **indie label** (*Mus*) sello *m* independiente, sello *m* indie
Indies ['ɪndɪz] (NPL) ▷ **east, west**
indifference [ɪn'dɪfrəns] (N) indiferencia *f* (**to** ante) • **it is a matter of total ~ to me** no me importa en lo más mínimo, me es totalmente indiferente
indifferent [ɪn'dɪfrənt] (ADJ) **1** (= *uninterested*) indiferente • **she seemed ~ to what was happening** parecía que lo que ocurría le resultaba indiferente
2 (= *unsympathetic*) indiferente • **I could not remain ~ to their suffering** no podía permanecer indiferente a su sufrimiento
3 (*pej*) (= *mediocre*) mediocre, regular • **a glass of ~ wine** un vaso de un vino mediocre *or* regular • **the book has had ~ reviews** las críticas del libro lo dejan regular
4 (= *of no importance*) • **it is ~ to me** me es igual *or* indiferente
indifferently [ɪn'dɪfrəntlɪ] (ADV)
1 (= *uninterestedly*) con indiferencia
2 (= *unsympathetically*) con indiferencia • **to treat sb ~** tratar a algn con indiferencia
3 (= *in a mediocre way*) regularmente • **she performed ~** su actuación fue regular nada más
4 (= *without preference*) indistintamente
indigence ['ɪndɪdʒəns] (N) indigencia *f*
indigenous [ɪn'dɪdʒɪnəs] (ADJ) [*people, population*] indígena, autóctono • **the elephant is ~ to India** el elefante es autóctono de India
indigent ['ɪndɪdʒənt] (ADJ) indigente
indigestible [ˌɪndɪ'dʒestəbl] (ADJ) **1** (= *difficult to digest*) indigesto; (= *impossible to digest*) no digerible
2 (*fig*) [*book*] árido, difícil de leer; [*information, style, writing*] difícil de digerir
indigestion [ˌɪndɪ'dʒestʃən] (N) indigestión *f* • **it's nothing serious, just ~** no es nada serio, solo indigestión • **lentils give me ~** las lentejas me resultan indigestas
(CPD) ▸ **indigestion tablet** pastilla *f* para la indigestión
indignant [ɪn'dɪgnənt] (ADJ) [*person, mood, tone*] indignado • **she wrote an ~ letter to the local newspaper** escribió una carta en tono indignado al periódico local, escribió una carta al periódico local expresando su indignación • **to be ~ at/about sth** estar indignado ante/por algo • **he is ~ at the suggestion that ...** está indignado ante la sugerencia de que ... • **to become** *or* **get** *or*

grow ~ indignarse • **why is he looking so ~?** ¿por qué tiene esa cara de indignación?

indignantly [ɪn'dɪgnəntlɪ] ADV [*say, deny*] con indignación • **"that is not true," she said ~** —eso no es verdad —dijo indignada *or* con indignación

indignation [ˌɪndɪg'neɪʃən] N indignación *f* • **we expressed our ~ at the demands** expresamos *or* mostramos nuestra indignación ante las demandas

indignity [ɪn'dɪgnɪtɪ] N indignidad *f*, humillación *f* • **to suffer the ~ of losing** sufrir la indignidad *or* humillación de perder

indigo ['ɪndɪgəʊ] N (PL: **indigos** *or* **indigoes**) (= *colour*) añil *m*, índigo *m*
ADJ añil (*inv*), índigo (*inv*)
CPD ▸ **indigo blue** azul *m* añil *or* índigo

indirect [ˌɪndɪ'rekt] ADJ [*route, criticism, result, costs*] indirecto • **in an ~ way** de una forma indirecta
CPD ▸ **indirect discourse** (*US*) estilo *m* indirecto ▸ **indirect lighting** iluminación *f* indirecta ▸ **indirect object** (*Gram*) objeto *m or* complemento *m* indirecto ▸ **indirect question** (*Gram*) oración *f* interrogativa indirecta ▸ **indirect speech** (*Gram*) estilo *m* indirecto ▸ **indirect tax, indirect taxation** impuesto *m* indirecto

indirectly [ˌɪndɪ'rektlɪ] ADV [*cause, refer to*] indirectamente; [*answer*] con evasivas, evasivamente • **to be ~ responsible for sth** ser el responsable indirecto de algo

indirectness [ˌɪndɪ'rektnɪs] N carácter *m* indirecto • **the ~ of his reply made it difficult to ...** su respuesta era tan evasiva *or* velada que era difícil ...

indiscernible [ˌɪndɪ'sɜːnəbl] ADJ imperceptible

indiscipline [ɪn'dɪsɪplɪn] N indisciplina *f*

indiscreet [ˌɪndɪs'kriːt] ADJ [*person, remark, behaviour*] indiscreto • **to be ~ about sth** ser indiscreto respecto a algo • **it was ~ of her to mention it** fue muy indiscreta *or* cometió una indiscreción mencionándolo

indiscreetly [ˌɪndɪs'kriːtlɪ] ADV indiscretamente

indiscreetness [ˌɪndɪs'kriːtnɪs] N indiscreción *f*, falta *f* de discreción

indiscrete [ˌɪndɪ'skriːt] ADJ indiferenciado

indiscretion [ˌɪndɪs'kreʃən] N **1** (= *lack of discretion*) indiscreción *f*, falta *f* de discreción
2 (= *indiscreet act, remark*) indiscreción *f*

indiscriminate [ˌɪndɪs'krɪmɪnɪt] ADJ
1 (= *random*) [*bombing, killing, violence*] indiscriminado
2 (= *undiscerning*) [*person*] falto de discernimiento; [*admirer*] ciego • **~ use of pesticides** el uso indiscriminado de pesticidas

indiscriminately [ˌɪndɪs'krɪmɪnɪtlɪ] ADV
1 (= *randomly*) [*distribute, vary*] indistintamente, sin distinción; [*bomb, fire, kill*] indiscriminadamente
2 (= *without discernment*) [*use, view, read*] sin discernimiento, de forma indiscriminada; [*admire*] ciegamente

indispensable [ˌɪndɪs'pensəbl] ADJ imprescindible, indispensable • **to be ~ for sth** ser imprescindible *or* indispensable para algo • **to be ~ to sth/sb** ser indispensable para algo/algn

indisposed [ˌɪndɪs'pəʊzd] ADJ (= *ill*) indispuesto; (= *disinclined*) poco dispuesto (**to do sth** a hacer algo)

indisposition [ˌɪndɪspə'zɪʃən] N indisposición *f*

indisputable [ˌɪndɪs'pjuːtəbl] ADJ [*evidence*] irrefutable; [*fact*] incuestionable; [*winner*] indiscutible

indisputably [ˌɪndɪs'pjuːtəblɪ] ADV indiscutiblemente • **it is ~ the best** es el mejor indiscutiblemente *or* sin ningún género de dudas • **oh, ~** claro que sí

indissoluble [ˌɪndɪ'sɒljʊbl] ADJ indisoluble

indissolubly [ˌɪndɪ'sɒljʊblɪ] ADV indisolublemente • **to be ~ linked (with sth)** estar indisolublemente ligado (a algo)

indistinct [ˌɪndɪs'tɪŋkt] ADJ **1** (= *muted*) [*voice, noise*] indistinto • **her words were ~** no se le entendían las palabras
2 (= *blurred*) [*figure, shape, outline*] poco definido, borroso • **the boundaries between the work of the two departments were becoming increasingly ~** los límites entre ambos departamentos estaba cada vez menos definidos *or* más borrosos

indistinctly [ˌɪndɪs'tɪŋktlɪ] ADV (= *without distinction*) indistintamente, sin distinción; [*hear*] con poca claridad; [*see*] con poca claridad, borrosamente

indistinguishable [ˌɪndɪs'tɪŋgwɪʃəbl] ADJ
1 (= *impossible to differentiate*) indistinguible (**from de**) • **the two drawings are ~** los dos dibujos son indistinguibles *or* imposibles de distinguir, es imposible distinguir un dibujo del otro
2 (= *indiscernible*) [*sound*] indistinguible • **his accent is ~** no se le nota nada de acento

indistinguishably [ˌɪndɪs'tɪŋgwɪʃəblɪ] ADV sin distinción posible

indite [ɪn'daɪt] VT (*liter*) [+ *letter*] endilgar

individual [ˌɪndɪ'vɪdjʊəl] ADJ **1** (= *separate*) individual • **we are not able to comment on ~ cases** no podemos hacer comentarios sobre casos individuales • **we look after the welfare of ~ members** nos cuidamos del bienestar de cada miembro individualmente
2 (= *for one*) particular, propio • **each room has its ~ telephone** cada cuarto tiene su teléfono propio
3 (= *personal*) [*tastes*] personal • **the constitution respects ~ rights** la constitución respeta los derechos del individuo • **the programme is tailored to your ~ needs** el programa se adapta a sus necesidades particulares
4 (= *distinctive*) • **he has a very ~ style** tiene un estilo muy personal *or* original
N individuo *m* • **how could a single ~ have achieved all this?** ¿cómo podía haber conseguido todo esto un individuo por sí solo? • **he's a thoroughly nasty ~*** es un individuo sumamente desagradable

individualism [ˌɪndɪ'vɪdjʊəlɪzəm] N individualismo *m*

individualist [ˌɪndɪ'vɪdjʊəlɪst] N individualista *mf*

individualistic ['ɪndɪˌvɪdjʊə'lɪstɪk] ADJ individualista

individuality [ˌɪndɪˌvɪdjʊ'ælɪtɪ] N (= *personality*) individualidad *f*; (= *separateness*) particularidad *f*

individualize [ˌɪndɪ'vɪdjʊəlaɪz] VT individuar, individualizar

individualized [ˌɪndɪ'vɪdjʊəlaɪzd] ADJ [*system, approach, treatment*] individualizado

individually [ˌɪndɪ'vɪdjʊəlɪ] ADV
1 (= *separately*) por separado • **they're all right ~, but not together** (*of people*) por separado son simpáticos, pero no cuando están juntos • **we do not sell the volumes ~** no vendemos los tomos sueltos *or* por separado
2 (= *for each individual*) • **meals are ~ prepared** las comidas se preparan especialmente para cada individuo • **an ~ designed exercise programme** un programa de ejercicios diseñado según las necesidades de cada individuo

indivisibility [ˌɪndɪˌvɪzə'bɪlətɪ] N indivisibilidad *f*

indivisible [ˌɪndɪ'vɪzəbl] ADJ [*number*] indivisible

indivisibly [ˌɪndɪ'vɪzəblɪ] ADV indivisiblemente • **to be ~ linked to sth** estar indisolublemente ligado a algo

Indo- ['ɪndəʊ] PREFIX indo-

Indo-China ['ɪndəʊ'tʃaɪnə] N Indochina *f*

indoctrinate [ɪn'dɒktrɪneɪt] VT adoctrinar (**with, in** en) • **they have been totally ~d by this cult** están totalmente adoctrinados por esta secta

indoctrination [ɪnˌdɒktrɪ'neɪʃən] N adoctrinamiento *m*

Indo-European ['ɪndəʊˌjʊərə'piːən] ADJ indoeuropeo
N **1** indoeuropeo/a *m/f*
2 (*Ling*) indoeuropeo *m*

indolence ['ɪndələns] N indolencia *f*

indolent ['ɪndələnt] ADJ indolente

indolently ['ɪndələntlɪ] ADV indolentemente

indomitable [ɪn'dɒmɪtəbl] ADJ indómito, indomable

indomitably [ɪn'dɒmɪtəblɪ] ADV indómitamente, indomablemente

Indonesia [ˌɪndəʊ'niːzɪə] N Indonesia *f*

Indonesian [ˌɪndəʊ'niːzɪən] ADJ indonesio
N **1** indonesio/a *m/f*
2 (*Ling*) indonesio *m*

indoor ['ɪndɔːʳ] ADJ [*shoes*] para estar por casa; [*plant*] de interior; [*stadium, pool*] cubierto; [*photography*] de interiores • **the house had no electric light or ~ plumbing** la casa no tenía luz eléctrica ni instalación de agua en el interior
CPD ▸ **indoor aerial** antena *f* interior ▸ **indoor athletics** atletismo *m* en sala *or* en pista cubierta ▸ **indoor football** fútbol *m* (en) sala ▸ **indoor games** juegos *mpl* de salón

indoors [ɪn'dɔːz] ADV [*be*] dentro • **I like the outside but what's it like ~?** me gusta por fuera, pero ¿cómo es por dentro? • **to go ~** (= *home*) entrar (en la casa) • **we had to stay ~ because of the rain** tuvimos que quedarnos dentro a causa de la lluvia • **Her Indoors*** (*hum*) mi media naranja*, la parienta (*Sp**)

indrawn [ˌɪn'drɔːn] ADJ • **we watched with ~ breath** mirábamos casi sin respirar

indubitable [ɪn'djuːbɪtəbl] ADJ (*frm*) indudable

indubitably [ɪn'djuːbɪtəblɪ] ADV (*frm*) indudablemente, sin duda

induce [ɪn'djuːs] VT **1** (= *persuade*) inducir, persuadir • **to ~ sb to do sth** inducir *or* persuadir a algn a hacer algo • **nothing would ~ me to go** nada me induciría a ir, nada podría hacerme ir • **what on earth ~d him to do it?** ¿qué diablos lo indujo *or* lo llevó a hacerlo?
2 (= *cause*) [+ *sleep*] producir, inducir
3 (*Med*) [+ *birth*] inducir • **I was ~d** me tuvieron que provocar el parto
4 (*Elec*) inducir

-induced [-ɪnˌdjuːst] SUFFIX ▸ **drug-induced**

inducement [ɪn'djuːsmənt] N **1** (= *incentive*) incentivo *m*, aliciente *m* • **to hold out sth to sb as an ~** ofrecer algo a algn como aliciente • **it's no ~ to work harder** no supone ningún incentivo *or* aliciente para trabajar más
2 (*Med*) [*of birth*] inducción *f*

induct [ɪn'dʌkt] VT (*Rel*) instalar; [+ *new member*] iniciar (**into** en); (*US*) (*Mil*) reclutar, quintar (*Sp*)

induction [ɪn'dʌkʃən] N (*Rel*) instalación *f*; [*of new member, worker*] iniciación *f* (**into** en); (*US*) (*Mil*) reclutamiento *m*, quinta *f* (*Sp*); (*Med, Philos*) inducción *f*
CPD ▸ **induction coil** carrete *m* de

inducción ▸ **induction course** curso *m* or cursillo *m* introductorio ▸ **induction programme, induction program** (US) programa *m* introductorio

inductive [ɪnˈdʌktɪv] ADJ [*reasoning*] inductivo

indulge [ɪnˈdʌldʒ] VT (= *give in to*) [+ *desire, appetite*] satisfacer; [+ *whim*] consentir; [+ *person*] complacer; (= *spoil*) [+ *child*] mimar, consentir • **to ~ o.s.** darse un gusto • **go on, ~ yourself!** venga, ¡date ese gustazo *or* capricho!*
VI • **to ~ in** permitirse • **everyone ~s in fattening foods once in a while** todo el mundo se permite comer cosas que engordan de vez en cuando • **he is indulging in fantasy/speculation** se está dejando llevar por la fantasía/especulación

indulgence [ɪnˈdʌldʒəns] N **1** (= *gratification*) [*of desire, appetite*] satisfacción *f*
2 (= *spoiling*) complacencia *f*; ▸ **self-indulgence**
3 (= *tolerance*) indulgencia *f* • **she was treated with great ~ as a child** cuando era niña la trataban con mucha indulgencia *or* estaba muy consentida
4 (= *luxury item*) lujo *m* • **I do allow myself the occasional ~** me permito un lujo de vez en cuando
5 (= *bad habit*) vicio *m*
6 (*Rel*) indulgencia *f*

indulgent [ɪnˈdʌldʒənt] ADJ indulgente • **he took an ~ attitude toward their pranks** adoptó una actitud indulgente para con sus travesuras • **to be ~ to** *or* **toward** *or* **with sb** consentir a algn, ser indulgente con algn

indulgently [ɪnˈdʌldʒəntlɪ] ADV indulgentemente

Indus [ˈɪndəs] N • **the ~** el Indo

industrial [ɪnˈdʌstrɪəl] ADJ industrial
CPD ▸ **industrial accident** accidente *m* laboral *or* de trabajo ▸ **industrial action** (*Brit*) medidas *fpl* de presión *or* protesta laboral • **to take ~ action** tomar medidas de presión *or* protesta laboral ▸ **industrial alcohol** alcohol *m* de uso industrial ▸ **industrial archaeology** arqueología *f* industrial ▸ **industrial design** diseño *m* industrial ▸ **industrial diamond** diamante *m* natural *or* industrial ▸ **industrial disease** enfermedad *f* laboral ▸ **industrial dispute** (*Brit*) conflicto *m* laboral ▸ **industrial engineering** ingeniería *f* industrial ▸ **industrial espionage** espionaje *m* industrial ▸ **industrial estate** (*Brit*) zona *f or* (*Sp*) polígono *m* industrial ▸ **industrial goods** bienes *mpl* de producción ▸ **industrial injury** lesión *f* por accidente laboral ▸ **industrial park** (*US*) zona *f or* (*Sp*) polígono *m* industrial ▸ **industrial relations** relaciones *fpl* laborales • **~ relations legislation** legislación *f* laboral ▸ **Industrial Revolution** Revolución *f* Industrial ▸ **industrial tribunal** magistratura *f* de trabajo, tribunal *m* laboral ▸ **industrial unrest** agitación *f* obrera, conflictos *mpl* laborales ▸ **industrial waste** residuos *mpl* industriales

industrialism [ɪnˈdʌstrɪəlɪzəm] N industrialismo *m*

industrialist [ɪnˈdʌstrɪəlɪst] N industrial *mf*

industrialization [ɪnˌdʌstrɪəlaɪˈzeɪʃən] N industrialización *f*

industrialize [ɪnˈdʌstrɪəlaɪz] VT [+ *area, region*] industrializar
VI industrializarse

industrialized [ɪnˈdʌstrɪəlaɪzd] ADJ [*area, place, country*] industrializado

industrially [ɪnˈdʌstrɪəlɪ] ADV industrialmente • **the parts are produced ~** las piezas se producen industrialmente, las piezas se fabrican mediante un procedimiento industrial • **~, the country has advanced enormously** en el aspecto industrial *or* en el terreno industrial *or* desde el punto de vista industrial, el país ha avanzado enormemente

industrial-strength [ɪnˈdʌstrɪəlˈstreŋθ] ADJ **1** [*product*] muy resistente
2* (*hum*) (= *strong*) [*wine*] peleón*

industrious [ɪnˈdʌstrɪəs] ADJ (= *hardworking*) trabajador, laborioso; (= *studious*) aplicado, diligente

industriously [ɪnˈdʌstrɪəslɪ] ADV [*work*] laboriosamente; [*study*] con aplicación

industriousness [ɪnˈdʌstrɪəsnɪs] N [*of worker*] laboriosidad *f*; [*of student*] aplicación *f*, diligencia *f*

industry [ˈɪndəstrɪ] N **1** industria *f* • **the steel/coal/textile ~** la industria siderúrgica/minera/textil • **the banking/insurance/hotel ~** el sector bancario/de seguros/hotelero • **the tourist ~** el turismo • **a career in ~** una carrera en el sector empresarial; ▸ **heavy**
2 (= *industriousness*) laboriosidad *f*, aplicación *f*

inebriate (*frm*) N [ɪˈniːbrɪɪt] borracho/a *m/f*
VT [ɪˈniːbrɪeɪt] embriagar, emborrachar
ADJ [ɪˈniːbrɪɪt] = **inebriated**

inebriated [ɪˈniːbrɪeɪtɪd] ADJ (*frm*) ebrio

inebriation [ɪˌniːbrɪˈeɪʃən] N (*frm*) embriaguez *f*

inedible [ɪnˈedɪbl] ADJ (= *unpleasant*) incomible; (= *poisonous*) no comestible

ineducable [ɪnˈedjʊkəbl] ADJ ineducable

ineffable [ɪnˈefəbl] ADJ (*liter*) inefable

ineffably [ɪnˈefəblɪ] ADV (*liter*) • **her face was ~ well-bred** su cara era de una distinción indescriptible *or* (*liter*) inefable

ineffaceable [ˌɪnɪˈfeɪsəbl] ADJ imborrable

ineffective [ˌɪnɪˈfektɪv] ADJ [*measure, policy, drug*] ineficaz; [*person, committee*] incompetente, ineficaz; [*effort, attempt*] infructuoso • **the plan proved wholly ~** el proyecto no surtió ningún efecto *or* no dio ningún resultado • **to be ~ in doing sth** [*law, measure, drug*] ser *or* resultar ineficaz a la hora de hacer algo; [*person, committee*] ser incompetente *or* carecer de eficacia a la hora de hacer algo

ineffectively [ˌɪnɪˈfektɪvlɪ] ADV
1 (= *ineffectually*) infructuosamente, inútilmente
2 (= *badly*) [*govern, rule*] ineficazmente, de modo incompetente

ineffectiveness [ˌɪnɪˈfektɪvnɪs] N [*of measure, policy, drug*] ineficacia *f*; [*of person, committee*] incompetencia *f*, ineficacia *f*; [*of effort, attempt*] infructuosidad *f*

ineffectual [ˌɪnɪˈfektjʊəl] ADJ inútil

ineffectually [ˌɪnɪˈfektjʊəlɪ] ADV inútilmente • **"I couldn't help it," she said ~** —no lo pude evitar —dijo inútilmente

inefficacious [ˌɪnefɪˈkeɪʃəs] ADJ (*frm*) ineficaz

inefficacy [ɪnˈefɪkəsɪ] N (*frm*) ineficacia *f*

inefficiency [ˌɪnɪˈfɪʃənsɪ] N [*of method*] ineficiencia *f*; [*of person*] incompetencia *f*

inefficient [ˌɪnɪˈfɪʃənt] ADJ [*method*] ineficiente; [*person*] incompetente; [*factory, mine, industry*] poco productivo

inefficiently [ˌɪnɪˈfɪʃəntlɪ] ADV de forma ineficaz • **the company is ~ run** la compañía está llevada de forma ineficaz

inelastic [ˌɪnɪˈlæstɪk] ADJ [*demand, supply*] inelástico; (*fig*) rígido, poco flexible

inelasticity [ˌɪnɪlæsˈtɪsɪtɪ] N (*lit, fig*) falta *f* de elasticidad

inelegance [ɪnˈelɪgəns] N falta *f* de elegancia

inelegant [ɪnˈelɪgənt] ADJ poco elegante, inelegante

inelegantly [ɪnˈelɪgəntlɪ] ADV de manera poco elegante

ineligible [ɪnˈelɪdʒəbl] ADJ inelegible; (*for military service*) no apto • **to be ~ for sth** (*for candidacy, competition*) ser inelegible para algo; (*for benefit*) no tener derecho a algo • **I was ~ for unemployment benefit** no tenía derecho a cobrar el paro • **to be ~ to vote** no tener derecho al voto

ineloquent [ɪnˈeləkwənt] ADJ poco elocuente

ineluctable [ˌɪnɪˈlʌktəbl] ADJ (*frm*) ineluctable, ineludible

inept [ɪˈnept] ADJ **1** (= *unskilful*) [*person*] inepto, incapaz; [*performance*] malo • **their ~ handling of the case** la forma inepta en que llevaron el caso
2 (= *unsuitable*) [*policy*] inadecuado

ineptitude [ɪˈneptɪtjuːd], **ineptness** [ɪˈneptnɪs] N [*of person*] ineptitud *f*, incapacidad *f*; [*of policies*] lo inadecuado

inequality [ˌɪnɪˈkwɒlɪtɪ] N desigualdad *f* • **~ of wealth/between nations** la desigualdad en el reparto de la riqueza/entre naciones

inequitable [ɪnˈekwɪtəbl] ADJ no equitativo

inequity [ɪnˈekwɪtɪ] N injusticia *f*

ineradicable [ˌɪnɪˈrædɪkəbl] ADJ [*prejudice, hatred*] imposible de erradicar; [*differences*] insalvables

inert [ɪˈnɜːt] ADJ (= *inanimate*) [*substance, gas*] inerte; (= *motionless*) inerte, inmóvil • **he lay ~ on the floor** estaba inerte *or* inmóvil en el suelo

inertia [ɪˈnɜːʃə] N **1** [*of person*] inercia *f*, apatía *f*
2 (*Chem, Phys*) inercia *f*; ▸ **moment**

inertia-reel [ɪˈnɜːʃəˌriːl] ADJ • **inertia-reel seat-belt** cinturón *m* de seguridad retráctil

inescapable [ˌɪnɪsˈkeɪpəbl] ADJ [*duty*] ineludible; [*result*] inevitable; [*fact, reality*] que no se puede ignorar • **I have come to the ~ conclusion that ...** he llegado a la inevitable conclusión de que ...

inescapably [ˌɪnɪsˈkeɪpəblɪ] ADV ineludiblemente, incuestionablemente

inessential [ˈɪnɪˈsenʃəl] ADJ no esencial
N cosa *f* no esencial

inestimable [ɪnˈestɪməbl] ADJ [*value, benefit*] inapreciable, inestimable; [*harm*] incalculable

inevitability [ɪnˌevɪtəˈbɪlɪtɪ] N inevitabilidad *f*

inevitable [ɪnˈevɪtəbl] ADJ inevitable • **it was ~ that he would refuse** era inevitable que se negara • **this raised the ~ question of money** esto suscitó la inevitable cuestión del dinero
N • **the ~** lo inevitable

inevitably [ɪnˈevɪtəblɪ] ADV inevitablemente, forzosamente • **as ~ happens ...** como siempre ocurre ...

inexact [ˌɪnɪgˈzækt] ADJ inexacto

inexactitude [ˌɪnɪgˈzæktɪtjuːd] N inexactitud *f*

inexactly [ˌɪnɪgˈzæktlɪ] ADV de modo inexacto

inexcusable [ˌɪnɪksˈkjuːzəbl] ADJ [*behaviour, conduct*] imperdonable, inexcusable

inexcusably [ˌɪnɪksˈkjuːzəblɪ] ADV [*behave*] de modo inexcusable, de modo imperdonable • **she had been ~ careless** había cometido un descuido inexcusable *or* imperdonable

inexhaustible [ˌɪnɪgˈzɔːstəbl] ADJ [*supply*] inagotable • **she has ~ energy** tiene una energía inagotable

inexorable [ɪn'eksərəbl] ADJ inexorable, implacable
inexorably [ɪn'eksərəblɪ] ADV inexorablemente, implacablemente
inexpedient [,ɪnɪks'pi:dɪənt] ADJ inoportuno, inconveniente, imprudente
inexpensive [,ɪnɪks'pensɪv] ADJ económico
inexpensively [,ɪnɪks'pensɪvlɪ] ADV económicamente • **they are ~ priced** tienen un precio razonable
inexperience [,ɪnɪks'pɪərɪəns] N inexperiencia *f*, falta *f* de experiencia
inexperienced [,ɪnɪks'pɪərɪənst] ADJ [*player, team*] inexperto; [*staff*] sin experiencia; [*pilot, driver*] sin experiencia, inexperto • **to be ~ in** *or* **at sth/doing sth** no tener experiencia en algo/hacer algo
inexpert [ɪn'ekspɜ:t] ADJ inexperto, poco hábil
inexpertly [ɪn'ekspɜ:tlɪ] ADV con poca habilidad *or* pericia
inexpertness [ɪn'ekspɜ:tnɪs] N falta *f* de habilidad
inexplicable [,ɪnɪks'plɪkəbl] ADJ [*behaviour, event, delay*] inexplicable
inexplicably [,ɪnɪks'plɪkəblɪ] ADV inexplicablemente • **I was ~ moved** inexplicablemente, estaba conmovido
inexplicit [,ɪnɪk'splɪsɪt] ADJ no explícito
inexpressible [,ɪnɪks'presəbl] ADJ [*feelings, thoughts*] inexpresable; [*joy, beauty, sorrow*] inefable, indescriptible
inexpressive [,ɪnɪks'presɪv] ADJ [*style, person, look, face*] inexpresivo
inextinguishable [,ɪnɪks'tɪŋgwɪʃəbl] ADJ inextinguible, inapagable
in extremis [ɪnɪks'tri:mɪs] ADV (*frm*) in extremis
inextricable [,ɪnɪks'trɪkəbl] ADJ inextricable, inseparable
inextricably [,ɪnɪks'trɪkəblɪ] ADV inextricablemente • **our future is now ~ linked with Europe** nuestro futuro está ahora inextricablemente vinculado a Europa
infallibility [ɪn,fælə'bɪlɪtɪ] N infalibilidad *f* • **Papal ~** la infalibilidad del Papa
infallible [ɪn'fæləbl] ADJ (= *unfailing*) [*remedy, method, punctuality*] infalible • **she has the ~ knack of saying the wrong thing at the wrong time** no falla, siempre mete la pata en el momento más inoportuno*
infallibly [ɪn'fæləblɪ] ADV (= *unfailingly*) infaliblemente; (= *predictably*) indefectiblemente
infamous ['ɪnfəməs] ADJ [*person*] infame, de mala fama; [*conduct, crime, speech*] infame • **to be ~ for sth** ser infame por algo
infamy ['ɪnfəmɪ] N infamia *f*
infancy ['ɪnfənsɪ] N **1** (= *childhood*) infancia *f*, niñez *f*; (*Jur*) minoría *f* de edad • **from ~** desde niño, desde muy pequeño
2 (*fig*) (= *early stage*) infancia *f* • **the project is still in its ~** el proyecto está todavía en mantillas
infant ['ɪnfənt] N niño/a *m/f*; (*Jur*) menor *mf* de edad • **the ~ Jesus** el niño Jesús
CPD ▸ **infant carrier** portabebés *m inv* ▸ **infant class** clase *f* de párvulos ▸ **infant mortality** mortandad *f or* mortalidad *f* infantil ▸ **infant school** (*Brit*) *centro de educación primaria (primer ciclo)* ▸ **infant son** hijo *m* bebé
infanta [ɪn'fæntə] N infanta *f*
infante [ɪn'fæntɪ] N infante *m*
infanticide [ɪn'fæntɪsaɪd] N **1** (= *act*) infanticidio *m*
2 (= *person*) infanticida *mf*
infantile ['ɪnfəntaɪl] ADJ infantil (*also Med*) • **don't be so ~!** ¡no seas niño!
CPD ▸ **infantile paralysis** parálisis *f inv* infantil
infantilism [ɪn'fæntɪ,lɪzəm] N infantilismo *m*
infantilize [ɪn'fæntɪlaɪz] VT infantilizar
infantry ['ɪnfəntrɪ] N infantería *f*
CPD ▸ **infantry division** (*in army*) división *f* de infantería
infantryman ['ɪnfəntrɪmən] N (PL: **infantrymen**) soldado *m* de infantería; (*Hist*) infante *m*
infarct [ɪn'fɑ:kt] N (*Med*) infarto *m*
infarction [ɪn'fɑ:kʃən] N (*Med*) infarto *m*
infatuated [ɪn'fætjʊeɪtɪd] ADJ • **to be ~ with sb** estar encaprichado con *or* de algn, estar chiflado por algn* • **to become ~ with sb** encapricharse con *or* de algn • **he was ~ with the idea that ...** se había encaprichado con la idea de ...
infatuation [ɪn,fætjʊ'eɪʃən] N encaprichamiento *m*
infect [ɪn'fekt] VT [+ *wound, foot*] infectar; [+ *person*] contagiar; [+ *food*] contaminar • **to ~ sb with sth** contagiar algo a algn • **don't ~ us all with your cold!** ¡no nos contagies tu resfriado a todos!, ¡no nos pegues tu resfriado a todos!* • **he's ~ed everybody with his enthusiasm** contagió su entusiasmo a todos • **scientists ~ed mice with the disease** los científicos inocularon la enfermedad a *or* en ratones
infected [ɪn'fektɪd] ADJ [*wound, foot, blood, needle*] infectado; [*person*] contagiado, infectado • **to be ~** estar infectado • **to become** *or* **get ~** [*wound, eye*] infectarse
infection [ɪn'fekʃən] N **1** (= *illness*) infección *f* • **she has a slight ~** tiene una pequeña infección
2 (= *process*) contagio *m* • **the risk of ~** el riesgo de contagio
CPD ▸ **infection rate** [*of disease*] tasa *f* de infección
infectious [ɪn'fekʃəs] ADJ **1** (*Med*) [*disease*] infeccioso, contagioso • **he is no longer ~** ya le ha pasado el periodo del contagio
2 (*fig*) [*person, laugh, enthusiasm, rhythm*] contagioso
CPD ▸ **infectious hepatitis** hepatitis *f* infecciosa
infectiousness [ɪn'fekʃəsnɪs] N **1** (*Med*) lo contagioso, contagiosidad *f*
2 (*fig*) [*of enthusiasm*] lo contagioso
infective [ɪn'fektɪv] ADJ [*disease, agent*] infeccioso
infelicitous [,ɪnfɪ'lɪsɪtəs] ADJ (*frm*) poco feliz, inoportuno
infelicity [,ɪnfɪ'lɪsɪtɪ] N (*frm*) inoportunidad *f*
infer [ɪn'fɜ:ʳ] VT **1** (= *deduce*) inferir, deducir (**from** de)
2* (= *imply*) insinuar • **what are you ~ring?** ¿qué estás insinuando?
inference ['ɪnfərəns] N deducción *f*, inferencia *f* • **by ~** por deducción • **to draw ~s** sacar conclusiones • **to draw an ~ from sth** hacer una deducción de algo
inferential [,ɪnfə'renʃəl] ADJ ilativo, deductivo
inferentially [,ɪnfə'renʃəlɪ] ADV por inferencia, por deducción
inferior [ɪn'fɪərɪəʳ] ADJ **1** (*in quality, rank*) [*person, status, position*] inferior; [*product, work, service*] de calidad inferior • **to feel ~** sentirse inferior • **of ~ quality** de calidad inferior • **to be ~ to sth/sb** ser inferior a algo/algn
2 (*Anat, Bot*) (= *lower*) inferior
N **1** (= *inferior person*) inferior *mf*
2 (= *person lower in rank*) inferior *mf*, subalterno/a *m/f*
inferiority [ɪn,fɪərɪ'ɒrɪtɪ] N inferioridad *f* • **~ to sth/sb** inferioridad *f* frente a *or* con respecto a algo/algn
CPD ▸ **inferiority complex** (*Psych*) complejo *m* de inferioridad
infernal [ɪn'fɜ:nl] ADJ infernal; (*fig*) infernal, del demonio* • **stop that ~ racket!** ¡deja de hacer ese ruido infernal!, ¡deja de hacer ese ruido del demonio!*
infernally [ɪn'fɜ:nəlɪ] ADV • **it's ~ awkward** es terriblemente difícil
inferno [ɪn'fɜ:nəʊ] N (= *hell*) infierno *m*; (= *fire*) hoguera *f* • **in a few minutes the house was a blazing ~** en pocos minutos la casa era una hoguera • **it's like an ~ in there** allí dentro hace un calor insoportable
infertile [ɪn'fɜ:taɪl] ADJ [*land, soil*] yermo, infecundo; [*person, animal*] estéril
infertility [,ɪnfɜ:'tɪlɪtɪ] N [*of land, soil*] infecundidad *f*; [*of person, animal*] esterilidad *f*
CPD ▸ **infertility clinic** clínica *f* para el tratamiento de la infertilidad ▸ **infertility treatment** tratamiento *m* de la esterilidad
infest [ɪn'fest] VT infestar • **to be ~ed with sth** estar infestado *or* plagado de algo
infestation [,ɪnfes'teɪʃən] N infestación *f*, plaga *f*
infidel ['ɪnfɪdəl] ADJ infiel, descreído
N infiel *mf*, descreído/a *m/f* • **the Infidel** los descreídos, la gente descreída
infidelity [,ɪnfɪ'delɪtɪ] N (*to partner*) infidelidad *f* (**to** a); (*to principle, cause*) deslealtad *f* (**to** para con)
infighting* ['ɪnfaɪtɪŋ] N (*in organization*) lucha *f* interna; (*Boxing*) lucha *f* cuerpo a cuerpo • **political ~** peleas *fpl* políticas
infill ['ɪnfɪl] N (*Constr, Geol*) relleno *m*
infiltrate ['ɪnfɪltreɪt] VT [+ *organization*] infiltrarse en, infiltrar • **to ~ sb into sth** infiltrar a algn en algo
VI infiltrarse
infiltration [,ɪnfɪl'treɪʃən] N (*gen*) infiltración *f*
infiltrator ['ɪnfɪltreɪtəʳ] N infiltrado/a *m/f*
infinite ['ɪnfɪnɪt] ADJ infinito • **he took ~ pains over it** lo hizo con el mayor esmero • **an ~ amount of time/money** una infinidad de tiempo/dinero • **in their ~ wisdom they decided to demolish the building** en su infinita sabiduría, decidieron demoler el edificio
N • **the ~** el infinito
infinitely ['ɪnfɪnɪtlɪ] ADV infinitamente • **this is ~ harder** esto es muchísimo más difícil, esto es mil veces más difícil
infiniteness ['ɪnfɪnɪtnɪs] N infinidad *f*
infinitesimal [,ɪnfɪnɪ'tesɪməl] ADJ infinitesimal
infinitesimally [,ɪnfɪnɪ'tesɪməlɪ] ADV • **~ small** infinitésimamente pequeño
infinitive [ɪn'fɪnɪtɪv] ADJ (*Ling*) infinitivo
N infinitivo *m*
infinitude [ɪn'fɪnɪtju:d] N infinitud *f*
infinitum [,ɪnfɪ'naɪtəm] ▸ **ad infinitum**
infinity [ɪn'fɪnɪtɪ] N (*gen*) infinidad *f*; (*Math*) infinito *m* • **an ~ of** una infinidad de, un sinfín de
infirm [ɪn'fɜ:m] ADJ [*person*] (= *weak*) débil, endeble; (= *sickly*) enfermizo; (= *ill*) enfermo • **the old and ~** los ancianos y enfermos • **~ of purpose** irresoluto
infirmary [ɪn'fɜ:mərɪ] N (= *hospital*) hospital *m*, clínica *f*; (*in school, prison, barracks*) enfermería *f*
infirmity [ɪn'fɜ:mɪtɪ] N (= *state*) debilidad *f*; (= *illness*) enfermedad *f*, achaque *m*, dolencia *f*; (= *moral*) flaqueza *f* • **mental/physical ~** enfermedad *f* mental/física • **the infirmities of (old) age** los achaques de la vejez

infix [ˈɪnfɪks] (N) infijo *m*
in flagrante delicto [ɪnfləˈgræntɪdɪˈlɪktəʊ] (ADV) en flagrante
inflame [ɪnˈfleɪm] (VT) **1** (*Med*) [+ *wound*] inflamar • **to become ~d** inflamarse
2 (*fig*) [+ *person, feelings*] encender, inflamar; [+ *situation*] exacerbar; [+ *conflict*] avivar, exacerbar • **to be ~d with passion/anger/ jealousy** estar inflamado de pasión/ira/ celos
inflammable [ɪnˈflæməbl] (ADJ) **1** [*liquid, substance, fabric*] inflamable • **"highly inflammable"** "muy inflamable"
2 (*fig*) [*situation*] explosivo
inflammation [ˌɪnfləˈmeɪʃən] (N) (*Med*) [*of wound*] inflamación *f*
inflammatory [ɪnˈflæmətərɪ] (ADJ) (*Med*) inflamatorio; [*speech*] incendiario
inflatable [ɪnˈfleɪtəbl] (ADJ) [*boat*] inflable, hinchable (*Sp*)
inflate [ɪnˈfleɪt] (VT) **1** [+ *tyre, balloon*] inflar, hinchar (*Sp*) (**with de**)
2 (*fig*) [+ *prices*] inflar; [+ *currency*] provocar la inflación de; [+ *report*] exagerar • **don't ~ his ego** no le alimentes el ego
(VI) [*balloon, tyre*] inflarse, hincharse (*Sp*)
inflated [ɪnˈfleɪtɪd] (ADJ) **1** [*tyre, balloon*] inflado, hinchado (*Sp*) • **~ with pride** (*fig*) henchido de orgullo, envanecido
2 (= *exaggerated*) [*price, salary*] inflado; [*report*] exagerado; [*language*] altisonante, rimbombante • **he has an ~ ego** se cree muy importante
inflation [ɪnˈfleɪʃən] (N) (*Econ*) inflación *f*
(CPD) ▸ **inflation accounting** contabilidad *f* de inflación
inflationary [ɪnˈfleɪʃnərɪ] (ADJ) inflacionario, inflacionista
inflationism [ɪnˈfleɪʃənɪzəm] (N) inflacionismo *m*
inflationist [ɪnˈfleɪʃənɪst] (ADJ) inflacionario, inflacionista
(N) partidario/a *m/f* de la inflación
inflation-proof [ɪnˈfleɪʃənˌpruːf] (ADJ) resistente a la inflación
inflect [ɪnˈflekt] (VT) **1** [+ *voice*] modular
2 (*Gram*) [+ *noun*] declinar; [+ *verb*] conjugar
inflected [ɪnˈflektɪd] (ADJ) [*language*] flexivo
inflection [ɪnˈflekʃən] (N) inflexión *f*
inflectional [ɪnˈflekʃənl] (ADJ) con inflexión
inflexibility [ɪnˌfleksɪˈbɪlɪtɪ] (N) [*of substance, object*] rigidez *f*; (*fig*) [*of person, opinions, rules*] inflexibilidad *f*
inflexible [ɪnˈfleksəbl] (ADJ) [*substance, object*] rígido; (*fig*) [*person, opinions, rules*] inflexible
inflexion [ɪnˈflekʃən] (N) inflexión *f*
inflict [ɪnˈflɪkt] (VT) • **to ~ (on)** [+ *wound*] causar (a), inferir (a); [+ *blow*] asestar *or* dar (a); [+ *penalty, tax, punishment*] imponer (a); [+ *pain, suffering, damage*] causar (a), infligir (a) • **they ~ed a serious defeat on the enemy** infligieron una grave derrota al enemigo • **I don't wish to ~ my own wishes on anyone else** no quiero imponer mis deseos a nadie • **to ~ o.s. on sb** imponer su presencia a algn
infliction [ɪnˈflɪkʃən] (N) (= *act*) imposición *f*; (= *penalty etc*) pena *f*, castigo *m*
in-flight [ˈɪnflaɪt] (ADJ) • **in-flight entertainment** amenidades *fpl* ofrecidas durante el vuelo • **in-flight meal** comida *f* servida durante el vuelo • **in-flight movie** película *f* proyectada durante el vuelo • **in-flight services** servicios *mpl* de a bordo
inflow [ˈɪnfləʊ] (N) [*of capital, migrants*] afluencia *f*; [*of water*] entrada *f*
(CPD) ▸ **inflow pipe** tubo *m* de entrada
influence [ˈɪnflʊəns] (N) influencia *f* (**on** sobre) • **a man of ~** un hombre influyente • **to have an ~ on sth** [*person*] tener influencia en *or* sobre algo, influir en *or* sobre algo • **to be a good/bad ~ on sb** ejercer buena/mala influencia sobre algn • **to bring every ~ to bear on sb** ejercer todas las presiones posibles sobre algn • **to have ~ with sb** tener influencias con algn, tener enchufe con algn* • **to have ~ over sb** tener influencia *or* ascendiente sobre algn • **to be under the ~ of drink/drugs** estar ebrio/ drogado • **under the ~** (*hum*) borracho
(VT) [+ *person*] influenciar, influir en; [+ *action, decision*] influir en *or* sobre • **what factors ~d your decision?** ¿qué factores influyeron en tu decisión? • **don't let him ~ you** no te dejes influenciar por él • **the novelist has been ~d by Torrente** el novelista ha sufrido la influencia de *or* está influido por Torrente • **to be easily ~d** ser muy influenciable
influential [ˌɪnflʊˈenʃəl] (ADJ) [*person, ideas*] influyente; [*organization*] prestigioso • **he was ~ in securing the loan** influyó para que se consiguiera el préstamo • **he was ~ in government circles** tenía influencia en círculos gubernamentales
influenza [ˌɪnflʊˈenzə] (N) gripe *f*
influx [ˈɪnflʌks] (N) [*of people*] afluencia *f*; [*of objects, ideas*] flujo *m*; (*Mech*) aflujo *m*, entrada *f*
info* [ˈɪnfəʊ] (N) = **information**
infobahn [ˈɪnfəʊbɑːn] (N) = **information superhighway**
infomercial [ˈɪnfəʊmɜːʃl] (N) publirreportaje *m*
inform [ɪnˈfɔːm] (VT) (= *give information*) informar, avisar; (= *bring up to date*) poner al corriente • **to ~ sb about** *or* **of sth** informar a algn sobre *or* de algo • **I am pleased to ~ you that …** tengo el gusto de comunicarle que … • **keep me ~ed** téngame *or* manténgame al corriente • **why was I not ~ed?** ¿por qué no me informaron *or* avisaron? • **to ~ o.s. about sth** informarse sobre algo; ▸ **well-informed**
(VI) soplar • **to ~ on** *or* **against sb** delatar *or* denunciar a algn
informal [ɪnˈfɔːməl] (ADJ) **1** (= *unceremonious*) [*meal, clothes, atmosphere, manner*] informal; [*occasion*] informal, sin etiqueta; [*expression*] coloquial, familiar; [*person*] informal, poco ceremonioso • **dress is ~** vista ropa informal, no es necesaria etiqueta
2 (= *unofficial*) [*meeting, visit*] informal
informality [ˌɪnfɔːˈmælɪtɪ] (N) informalidad *f*, falta *f* de ceremonia
informally [ɪnˈfɔːməlɪ] (ADV) **1** (= *without ceremony*) [*speak, greet, welcome*] de manera informal, sin ceremonias; [*dress*] de manera informal; [*write*] con un lenguaje informal, con un estilo familiar
2 (= *unofficially*) [*meet, discuss, agree*] informalmente • **I have been ~ told that …** me han dicho de manera informal *or* extraoficial que …
informant [ɪnˈfɔːmənt] (N) informante *mf* • **my ~** el que me lo dijo • **who was your ~?** ¿quién se lo dijo?
informatics [ˌɪnfɔːmætɪks] (N) informática *f*
information [ˌɪnfəˈmeɪʃən] (N) información *f*; (= *knowledge*) conocimientos *mpl* • **a piece of ~** un dato • **"information"** "información" • **to ask for ~** pedir información • **to gather ~ about** *or* **on sth** reunir información sobre algo, informarse sobre algo • **to give sb ~ about** *or* **on sth/sb** proporcionar información a algn sobre algo/algn • **who gave you this ~?** ¿quién le dio esta información? • **we weren't given enough ~ about the risks involved** no nos informaron suficientemente sobre los riesgos que entrañaba • **we have no ~ on that point** no tenemos información sobre ese particular • **for your ~** para su información • **for your ~, I asked him to come!** para que te enteres, ¡le pedí que viniera!
(CPD) ▸ **information architecture** arquitectura *f* de la información ▸ **information bureau** oficina *f* de información ▸ **information centre** centro *m* de información ▸ **information desk** información *f* ▸ **information gathering** recabado *m* de información ▸ **information highway** • **the ~ highway** la autopista *or* (*LAm*) la carretera de la información ▸ **information office** = **information bureau** ▸ **information overload** sobrecarga *f* de información ▸ **information pack** (*Brit*) material *m* informativo ▸ **information processing** procesamiento *m* de la información ▸ **information retrieval** recuperación *f* de la información ▸ **information science** informática *f*, gestión *f* de la información ▸ **information service** servicio *m* de información ▸ **information superhighway** superautopista *f* de la información ▸ **information technology** informática *f* ▸ **information theory** teoría *f* de la información
informational [ˌɪnfəˈmeɪʃənl] (ADJ) [*needs, requirements*] de información; [*television, video*] informativo, didáctico
informative [ɪnˈfɔːmətɪv] (ADJ) informativo • **talking to him was very ~** la conversación que tuve con él resultó muy informativa • **his school report was not very ~** su boletín de calificaciones no era muy revelador
informativity [ɪnˌfɔːməˈtɪvɪtɪ] (N) informatividad *f*
informed [ɪnˈfɔːmd] (ADJ) [*person*] bien informado; [*debate*] llevado a cabo con conocimiento de causa • **to give (one's) ~ consent (to sth)** (*Med*) dar el consentimiento (para algo) con total conocimiento de causa • **an ~ guess** una conjetura bien fundamentada • **~ opinion is that …** la opinión de los que saben del tema es que …
informer [ɪnˈfɔːməʳ] (N) informante *mf*; (*pej*) delator(a) *m/f*, soplón/ona* *m/f* • **police ~** informante *mf* de la policía • **to turn ~** convertirse en delator
infotainment [ˌɪnfəʊˈteɪnmənt] (N) (*Brit*) (*TV*) • **~ programme** magazine *m* informativo
infotech* [ˈɪnfəʊˌtek] (N) informática *f*
(CPD) ▸ **infotech industry*** sector *m* informático
infra… [ˈɪnfrə] (PREFIX) infra …
infraction [ɪnˈfrækʃən] (N) infracción *f*, contravención *f*
infra dig†* [ˈɪnfrəˈdɪg] (ADJ ABBR) denigrante
infrared [ˈɪnfrəˈred] (ADJ) [*rays, light*] infrarrojo
infrasonic [ˈɪnfrəˌsɒnɪk] (ADJ) infrasónico
infrasound [ˈɪnfrəˌsaʊnd] (N) infrasonido *m*
infrastructure [ˈɪnfrəˌstrʌktʃəʳ] (N) infraestructura *f*
infrequency [ɪnˈfriːkwənsɪ] (N) infrecuencia *f*, poca frecuencia *f*
infrequent [ɪnˈfriːkwənt] (ADJ) [*visit, occurrence*] poco frecuente, infrecuente
infrequently [ɪnˈfriːkwəntlɪ] (ADV) rara vez, pocas veces • **not ~** no raramente, no pocas veces
infringe [ɪnˈfrɪndʒ] (VT) [+ *law, rights, copyright*] infringir, violar
(VI) • **to ~ (up)on** [+ *sb's rights, interests,*

privacy] violar

infringement [ɪnˈfrɪndʒmənt] N [*of law, rule*] infracción *f*, violación *f*; [*of rights*] violación *f*; (*Sport*) falta *f* • **they sued him for ~ of copyright** lo demandaron por no respetar los derechos de autor

infuriate [ɪnˈfjʊərɪeɪt] VT enfurecer, poner furioso • **to be/get ~d** estar/ponerse furioso • **this kind of thing ~s me** estas cosas me ponen furioso • **at times you ~ me** hay veces que me sacas de quicio

infuriating [ɪnˈfjʊərɪeɪtɪŋ] ADJ (*gen*) exasperante • **it's simply ~** es exasperante, es para volverse loco • **I find his habit ~** esa costumbre suya me saca de quicio

infuriatingly [ɪnˈfjʊərɪeɪtɪŋlɪ] ADV • **~, I was cut off** se cortó la línea, vamos, como para volverse loco • **his answer was ~ vague** su respuesta fue de una vaguedad exasperante

infuse [ɪnˈfjuːz] VT **1** [+ *courage, enthusiasm*] infundir (**into a**) • **to ~ courage into sb** infundir ánimo a algn • **they were ~d with a new hope** se les infundió nuevas esperanzas
2 (*Culin*) [+ *herbs, tea*] hacer una infusión de
VI • **to let sth ~** dejar algo en infusión

infusion [ɪnˈfjuːʒən] N [*of new talent, money, capital*] inyección *f*; (*Culin*) (= *tea etc*) infusión *f*

ingenious [ɪnˈdʒiːnɪəs] ADJ (*gen*) ingenioso; [*idea, scheme*] ingenioso, genial

ingeniously [ɪnˈdʒiːnɪəslɪ] ADV ingeniosamente, con inventiva

ingeniousness [ɪnˈdʒiːnɪəsnɪs] N = **ingenuity**

ingénue [ˈænʒənjuː] N ingenua *f*

ingenuity [ˌɪndʒɪˈnjuːɪtɪ] N [*of person*] ingenio *m*, inventiva *f*; [*of idea, scheme*] lo ingenioso

ingenuous [ɪnˈdʒenjʊəs] ADJ (= *naive*) ingenuo; (= *candid*) cándido

ingenuously [ɪnˈdʒenjʊəslɪ] ADV (= *naively*) ingenuamente; (= *candidly*) cándidamente

ingenuousness [ɪnˈdʒenjʊəsnɪs] N (= *naivety*) ingenuidad *f*; (= *candidness*) candidez *f*

ingest [ɪnˈdʒest] VT ingerir

ingestion [ɪnˈdʒestʃən] N ingestión *f*

inglenook [ˈɪŋglnʊk] N rincón *m* de la chimenea

inglorious [ɪnˈglɔːrɪəs] ADJ ignominioso, vergonzoso

ingloriously [ɪnˈglɔːrɪəslɪ] ADV ignominiosamente, vergonzosamente

in-going [ˈɪngəʊɪŋ] ADJ entrante

ingot [ˈɪŋgət] N lingote *m*
CPD ▸ **ingot steel** acero *m* en lingotes

ingrained [ˈɪnˈgreɪnd] ADJ **1** [*dirt, blood, stain*] incrustado
2 (*fig*) (= *deep-seated*) [*attitude, ideas, habit, tradition*] arraigado • **to be deeply ~ in sb** estar profundamente arraigado en algn

ingrate†† [ˈɪngreɪt] N ingrato/a *m/f*

ingratiate [ɪnˈgreɪʃɪeɪt] VT • **to ~ o.s. with sb** congraciarse con algn

ingratiating [ɪnˈgreɪʃɪeɪtɪŋ] ADJ [*smile, speech*] obsequioso; [*person*] halagador, congraciador, zalamero

ingratiatingly [ɪnˈgreɪʃɪeɪtɪŋlɪ] ADV de forma obsequiosa

ingratitude [ɪnˈgrætɪtjuːd] N ingratitud *f*

ingredient [ɪnˈgriːdɪənt] N (*Culin*) ingrediente *m*; [*of beauty product, medicine*] componente *m*; (*fig*) elemento *m*, factor *m* • **it is used as an ~ in sunscreen** se utiliza como componente de cremas solares con filtro • **this is the key ~ of her success** este es el factor clave de su éxito

ingress [ˈɪngres] N (*frm*) acceso *m*

in-group [ˈɪnˌgruːp] N grupo *m* exclusivista *or* excluyente, camarilla *f*

ingrowing [ˈɪnˌgrəʊɪŋ], **ingrown** (*US*) [ˈɪnˌgrəʊn] ADJ • **~ (toe)nail** uña *f* encarnada

inguinal [ˈɪŋgwɪnl] ADJ (*Tech*) inguinal

inhabit [ɪnˈhæbɪt] VT [+ *house*] ocupar; [+ *town, country*] vivir en, habitar (*frm*); [*animal*] habitar • **a place ~ed by ghosts** un lugar habitado por fantasmas

inhabitable [ɪnˈhæbɪtəbl] ADJ (*gen*) habitable

inhabitant [ɪnˈhæbɪtənt] N habitante *mf*

inhabited [ɪnˈhæbɪtɪd] ADJ habitado

inhalant [ɪnˈheɪlənt] N inhalante *m*

inhalation [ˌɪnhəˈleɪʃən] N aspiración *f*; (*Med*) inhalación *f*

inhalator [ˈɪnhəleɪtəʳ] N inhalador *m*

inhale [ɪnˈheɪl] VT (*Med*) [+ *gas*] inhalar, aspirar; [+ *smoke, vomit*] tragar
VI [*smoker*] tragar el humo; (*Med*) aspirar

inhaler [ɪnˈheɪləʳ] N inhalador *m*

inharmonious [ˌɪnhɑːˈməʊnɪəs] ADJ [*sounds*] inarmónico, disonante; (*fig*) discorde, falto de armonía

inhere [ɪnˈhɪəʳ] VI (*frm*) ser inherente (**in** a)

inherent [ɪnˈhɪərənt] ADJ inherente, intrínseco • **to be ~ in** *or* **to sth** ser inherente a algo • **with all the ~ difficulties** con todas las dificultades que conlleva

inherently [ɪnˈhɪərəntlɪ] ADV intrínsecamente

inherit [ɪnˈherɪt] VT (*gen*) heredar (**from** de) • **we ~ed these problems from the last government** estos problemas son un legado del gobierno anterior

inheritable [ɪnˈherɪtəbl] ADJ heredable

inheritance [ɪnˈherɪtəns] N herencia *f*; (*fig*) patrimonio *m* • **she received a small ~ from her aunt** su tía le dejó una pequeña herencia
CPD ▸ **inheritance law** ley *f* sucesoria
▸ **inheritance tax** impuesto *m* sobre sucesiones

inheritor [ɪnˈherɪtəʳ] N heredero/a *m/f*

inhibit [ɪnˈhɪbɪt] VT (= *check*) inhibir, reprimir; (= *prevent*) impedir • **to ~ sb from doing sth** impedir a algn hacer algo • **don't let my presence ~ the discussion** no quiero que mi presencia detenga la discusión • **we cannot ~ progress** no podemos reprimir el progreso

inhibited [ɪnˈhɪbɪtɪd] ADJ [*person*] cohibido, inhibido

inhibiting [ɪnˈhɪbɪtɪŋ] ADJ [*effect, factor, influence*] inhibidor

inhibition [ˌɪnhɪˈbɪʃən] N inhibición *f* • **to have/have no ~s** tener/no tener inhibiciones • **to lose one's ~s** perder las inhibiciones

inhibitory [ɪnˈhɪbɪtərɪ] ADJ inhibitorio

inhospitable [ˌɪnhɒsˈpɪtəbl] ADJ [*person*] inhospitalario, poco hospitalario; [*reception, behaviour*] poco hospitalario; [*place, country, terrain, climate*] inhóspito

inhospitably [ˌɪnhɒsˈpɪtəblɪ] ADV de modo poco hospitalario

inhospitality [ˈɪnˌhɒspɪˈtælɪtɪ] N falta *f* de hospitalidad, inhospitalidad *f*

in-house [ˈɪnˈhaʊs] ADV dentro de la empresa
ADJ [*staff*] interno
CPD ▸ **in-house training** formación *f* en la empresa

inhuman [ɪnˈhjuːmən] ADJ inhumano

inhumane [ˌɪnhjʊ(ː)ˈmeɪn] ADJ [*behaviour, treatment*] inhumano; [*person*] cruel

inhumanity [ˌɪnhjuːˈmænɪtɪ] N inhumanidad *f*, crueldad *f* • **man's ~ to man** la crueldad del hombre para con sus semejantes

inhumation [ˌɪnhjuːˈmeɪʃən] N inhumación *f*

inimical [ɪˈnɪmɪkəl] ADJ [*attitude*] hostil; [*influence*] adverso • **to be ~ to sth** ser adverso a algo

inimitable [ɪˈnɪmɪtəbl] ADJ inimitable

inimitably [ɪˈnɪmɪtəblɪ] ADV inimitablemente

iniquitous [ɪˈnɪkwɪtəs] ADJ inicuo, injusto

iniquitously [ɪˈnɪkwɪtəslɪ] ADV inicuamente, injustamente

iniquity [ɪˈnɪkwɪtɪ] N iniquidad *f*, injusticia *f*; **iniquities** [*of system*] injusticias *fpl*, iniquidades *fpl*; [*of person*] excesos *mpl*, desmanes *mpl*

initial [ɪˈnɪʃəl] ADJ [*shock, success, cost, report*] inicial • **my ~ reaction was to …** mi primera reacción fue … • **in the ~ stages** al principio, en la etapa inicial, en la primera etapa
N (= *letter*) inicial *f* • **to sign sth with one's ~s** firmar algo con las iniciales
VT [+ *letter, document*] firmar con las iniciales
CPD ▸ **initial expenses** gastos *mpl* iniciales
▸ **initial letter** inicial *f*

initialization [ɪˌnɪʃəlaɪˈzeɪʃən] N (*Comput*) inicialización *f*

initialize [ɪˈnɪʃəlaɪz] VT (*Comput*) inicializar

initially [ɪˈnɪʃəlɪ] ADV al principio, en un principio, inicialmente (*frm*)

initiate VT [ɪˈnɪʃɪeɪt] **1** (= *begin*) iniciar, dar comienzo a; [+ *talks*] entablar; [+ *reform*] poner en marcha; [+ *fashion*] introducir • **to ~ proceedings against sb** (*Jur*) entablar una demanda contra algn
2 • **to ~ sb into a society** admitir a algn en una asociación • **to ~ sb into a secret** iniciar a algn en un secreto
N [ɪˈnɪʃɪɪt] iniciado/a *m/f*

initiation [ɪˌnɪʃɪˈeɪʃən] N (= *beginning*) inicio *m*, comienzo *m*; (= *admission*) (*into society, organization*) admisión *f* (**into** en)
CPD ▸ **initiation ceremony, initiation rite** ceremonia *f* de iniciación

initiative [ɪˈnɪʃətɪv] N iniciativa *f* • **to use one's ~** obrar por propia iniciativa • **on one's own ~** por iniciativa propia, motu propio • **to take the ~** tomar la iniciativa

initiator [ɪˈnɪʃɪeɪtəʳ] N iniciador(a) *m/f*

initiatory [ɪˈnɪʃɪətərɪ] ADJ (= *introductory*) introductorio

inject [ɪnˈdʒekt] VT **1** (*Med*) [+ *medicine*] inyectar (**into** en); [+ *person*] poner una inyección a • **to ~ sb with sth** inyectar algo a algn • **he ~ed her with poison** le inyectó veneno
2 (*fig*) • **to ~ into** [+ *enthusiasm*] infundir a; [+ *money, capital*] inyectar en • **they've ~ed new life into the club** han infundido un espíritu nuevo al club • **she did her best to ~ some enthusiasm into her voice** hizo lo que pudo para que su voz sonara entusiasta

injection [ɪnˈdʒekʃən] N (*gen*) (*Med*) inyección *f* • **to give sb an ~** poner *or* dar una inyección a algn • **to have an ~** ponerse una inyección • **will I have to have an ~?** ¿me tendrán que poner *or* dar una inyección?

injudicious [ˌɪndʒʊˈdɪʃəs] ADJ imprudente, indiscreto

injudiciously [ˌɪndʒʊˈdɪʃəslɪ] ADV imprudentemente, indiscretamente

injunction [ɪnˈdʒʌŋkʃən] N (*Jur*) mandamiento *m* judicial • **to seek an ~ (against sth/sb) (to do sth)** obtener un mandamiento judicial (contra algo/algn) (para hacer algo)

injure [ˈɪndʒəʳ] VT **1** (*physically*) herir; (*esp Sport*) lesionar • **he was ~d in the accident** resultó herido en el accidente • **two players**

were ~d dos jugadores resultaron lesionados • **he was badly/slightly ~d** resultó gravemente/levemente herido • **he ~d his arm** resultó herido en el brazo; (*Sport*) se lesionó el brazo • **to ~ o.s.** (*in an accident*) resultar herido; (*deliberately*) causarse heridas, autolesionarse; (*in a match, race etc*) lesionarse
2 (*fig*) [*+ feelings, pride*] herir; [*+ reputation*] dañar; [*+ trade, chances*] perjudicar
injured ['ɪndʒəd] ADJ **1** (*physically*) [*person, animal, limb*] herido, lesionado; [*player*] lesionado
2 (*fig*) [*tone, look*] dolido; [*feelings*] herido • **to give sb an ~ look** mirar a algn con expresión dolida • **to say sth in an ~ tone** decir algo con tono dolido • **~ pride** orgullo *m* herido
3 (*Jur*) • **the ~ party** la parte perjudicada
NPL • **there were four ~** hubo cuatro heridos • **the ~** los heridos
injurious [ɪn'dʒʊərɪəs] ADJ (*frm*) perjudicial (**to** para) • **~ to health** perjudicial para la salud
injury ['ɪndʒərɪ] N **1** (*physical*) herida *f*; (*esp Sport*) lesión *f* • **he sustained minor injuries to the hands and face** sufrió heridas leves en las manos y la cara • **he was taken to hospital with serious injuries** lo llevaron al hospital herido de gravedad • **to do o.s. an ~*** hacerse daño • **to do sb an ~** hacer daño a algn
2 (*fig*) (*to reputation*) daño *m*, perjuicio *m*; (*to feelings*) agravio *m*; ▹ **insult**
CPD ▸ **injury list** (*Sport*) lista *f* de lesionados ▸ **injury time** (*Brit*) (*Sport*) tiempo *m* de descuento
injury-prone ['ɪndʒərɪˌprəʊn] ADJ propenso a las lesiones
injustice [ɪn'dʒʌstɪs] N injusticia *f* • **you do me an ~** está siendo injusto conmigo
ink [ɪŋk] N tinta *f*; (*= printing ink*) tinta *f* de imprenta • **in ink** con tinta
VT (*Typ*) entintar
CPD ▸ **ink blot** borrón *m* de tinta ▸ **ink pad** almohadilla *f*, tampón *m* (de entintar)
▸ **ink in** VT + ADV [*+ name*] (*= write*) escribir con tinta; (*on top of pencil*) repasar a tinta; [*+ line*] trazar con tinta; [*+ blank area*] entintar
▸ **ink out** VT + ADV tachar con tinta
▸ **ink over** VT + ADV repasar con tinta
inkblot ['ɪŋkblɒt] N mancha *f* de tinta
CPD ▸ **inkblot test** (*Psych*) test *m* de Rorschach
ink-jet printer ['ɪŋkdʒet'prɪntə^r] N impresora *f* de chorro de tinta
inkling ['ɪŋklɪŋ] N (*= vague idea*) idea *f* • **I had no ~ that …** no tenía ni la menor idea de que … • **we had some ~ of it** teníamos una vaga idea • **there was no ~ of the disaster to come** nadie podía imaginarse el desastre que iba a sobrevenir • **to give sb an ~ that …** insinuar a algn que …
inkpad ['ɪŋkpæd] N almohadilla *f*, tampón *m* (de entintar)
inkpot ['ɪŋkpɒt] N tintero *m*
inkstain ['ɪŋksteɪn] N mancha *f* de tinta
inkstained ['ɪŋkˌsteɪnd] ADJ manchado de tinta
inkstand ['ɪŋkstænd] N escribanía *f*
inkwell ['ɪŋkwel] N tintero *m*
inky ['ɪŋkɪ] ADJ (*lit*) [*page, fingers*] manchado de tinta; (*fig*) [*darkness*] profundo
INLA ['ɪnlə] N ABBR (*Brit*) = **Irish National Liberation Army**
inlaid ['ɪn'leɪd] ADJ (*with wood, tiles*) taraceado (**with** de); (*with jewels*) incrustado (**with** de)
CPD [*table, box*] de marquetería; [*floor*] con incrustaciones ▸ **inlaid work** taracea *f*
inland ['ɪnlənd] ADJ [*town*] del interior; [*trade*] interior
ADV (*in*) tierra adentro; (*towards*) hacia el interior
CPD ▸ **Inland Revenue** (*Brit*), **Inland Revenue Service** (*US*) ≈ Hacienda *f* ▸ **inland sea** mar *m* interior ▸ **inland waterways** canales *mpl* y ríos *mpl*
in-laws* ['ɪnˌlɔːz] NPL (*= partner's family*) parientes *mpl* políticos; (*= partner's parents*) suegros *mpl*
inlay N ['ɪnleɪ] [*of wood, tiles*] taracea *f*; [*of jewels*] incrustación *f*
VT [ɪn'leɪ] (PT, PP: **inlaid**) (*with wood*) taracear, embutir; (*with jewels*) incrustar • **a sword inlaid with jewels** una espada incrustada de joyas
inlet ['ɪnlet] N **1** (*Geog*) ensenada *f*, entrante *m*
2 (*Tech*) admisión *f*, entrada *f*
CPD ▸ **inlet pipe** tubo *m* de entrada ▸ **inlet valve** válvula *f* de admisión *or* entrada
inline skating ['ɪnlaɪn'skeɪtɪŋ] N patinar *m* con patines en línea
inmate ['ɪnmeɪt] N [*of hospital*] enfermo/a *m/f*; [*of prison*] preso/a *m/f*, presidiario/a *m/f*; [*of asylum*] internado/a *m/f*
inmost ['ɪnməʊst] ADJ [*place, chamber*] más recóndito; [*thoughts, feelings*] más íntimo, más secreto
inn [ɪn] N (*= pub*) taberna *f*; (*= hotel*) hostería *f*; (*= tavern††*) posada *f*, mesón *m*
CPD ▸ **inn sign** letrero *m* de mesón ▸ **the Inns of Court** (*Brit*) (*Jur*) el Colegio de Abogados (*en Londres*)
innards* ['ɪnədz] NPL tripas* *fpl*
innate [ɪ'neɪt] ADJ innato
innately [ɪ'neɪtlɪ] ADV de manera innata • **it is not ~ evil** no es malo de por sí
inner ['ɪnə^r] ADJ **1** [*room, wall, door, part*] interior • **~ circle** círculo *m* de personas más allegadas • **the White House's ~ circle** el círculo de personas más allegadas al presidente • **the ~ city** *barrios céntricos pobres de la ciudad que presentan problemas sociales* • **the ~ sanctum** el sanctasanctórum; ▹ **inner-city**
2 [*thoughts, emotions*] íntimo; [*voice, calm, conflict*] interior • **the ~ life** la vida interior • **the ~ man** (*= soul*) el alma; (*hum*) (*= stomach*) el estómago • **one's ~ self** el fuero interno de uno
N (*Archery*) blanco *m*
CPD ▸ **inner child** niño *m* interior ▸ **inner ear** oído *m* interno ▸ **Inner London** el centro de Londres ▸ **Inner Mongolia** Mongolia *f* Interior ▸ **inner sole** (*in shoe*) plantilla *f* ▸ **inner spring mattress** (*US*) colchón *m* de muelles interiores ▸ **inner tube** (*in tyre*) cámara *f*, llanta *f* (*LAm*)
inner-city [ˌɪnə'sɪtɪ] ADJ [*schools, problems*] de las zonas céntricas pobres, de los barrios céntricos pobres • **an inner-city area** un área pobre del centro
innermost ['ɪnəməʊst] ADJ [*thoughts, feelings*] más íntimo, más secreto; [*place, chamber*] más recóndito
inning ['ɪnɪŋ] N (*US*) (*Baseball*) inning *m*, entrada *f*; **innings** (*pl inv*) (*Cricket*) turno *m*, entrada *f*; (*fig*) turno *m*, oportunidad *f*
• IDIOM: • **he's had a good ~s** ha disfrutado de una larga vida, ha vivido sus buenos años
innit‡ ['ɪnɪt] EXCL (*Brit*) • **~?** ¿no?
innkeeper ['ɪnkiːpə^r] N [*of pub*] tabernero/a *m/f*; [*of inn††*] posadero/a *m/f*, mesonero/a *m/f*
innocence ['ɪnəsns] N inocencia *f* • **in all ~** con toda inocencia, de la forma más inocente
Innocent ['ɪnəsnt] N (*= pope*) Inocencio
innocent ['ɪnəsnt] ADJ **1** (*= not guilty*) inocente • **to find sb ~** declarar inocente a algn • **to be ~ of a crime** ser inocente de un crimen • **he was found ~ of murder** lo declararon inocente de asesinato
2 (*= innocuous*) [*question, remark*] inocente, sin malicia; [*fun*] sin malicia; [*mistake*] inocente
3 (*= naive*) inocente, ingenuo • **they seemed so young and ~** parecían tan jóvenes e inocentes *or* ingenuos • **she stood facing him with that ~ air she had** estaba frente a él, con ese aire inocente que tenía; ▹ **bystander**
4 (*liter*) (*= devoid*) • **to be ~ of sth: he was ~ of any desire to harm her** no tenía ningún deseo de hacerle daño • **a face ~ of any trace of make-up** una cara sin ningún rastro de maquillaje
N inocente *mf* • **he's an ~ when it comes to women** cuando se trata de mujeres es un inocente *or* inocentón • **I'm not a total ~** no soy tan inocente • **the Massacre of the Holy Innocents** la masacre de los Santos Inocentes
innocently ['ɪnəsntlɪ] ADV [*ask, smile*] inocentemente, con inocencia • **she looked at her father ~** dirigió a su padre una mirada llena de inocencia • **the joke had begun ~ enough** la broma había empezado de una forma muy inocente
innocuous [ɪ'nɒkjʊəs] ADJ [*substance*] inocuo; [*person, remark*] inofensivo
innovate ['ɪnəʊveɪt] VI innovar
innovation [ˌɪnəʊ'veɪʃən] N (*= act*) innovación *f*; (*= thing*) innovación *f*, novedad *f*
innovative ['ɪnəʊˌveɪtɪv] ADJ innovador
innovator ['ɪnəʊveɪtə^r] N innovador(a) *m/f*
innovatory ['ɪnəʊˌveɪtərɪ] ADJ (*Brit*) innovador
innuendo [ˌɪnjʊ'endəʊ] N (PL: **innuendos** *or* **innuendoes**) indirecta *f*, insinuación *f* • **his comments were full of sexual ~** sus comentarios estaban llenos de alusiones *or* connotaciones sexuales
Innuit ['ɪnjuːɪt] = **Inuit**
innumerable [ɪ'njuːmərəbl] ADJ innumerable • **she drank ~ cups of tea** se bebió innumerables tazas de té • **there are ~ reasons** hay infinidad de razones • **he helped us in ~ ways** nos ayudó de muy diversas maneras
innumeracy [ɪ'njuːmərəsɪ] N *incompetencia en matemáticas or en el cálculo*
innumerate [ɪ'njuːmərɪt] ADJ incompetente en el cálculo aritmético
inoculant [ɪ'nɒkjʊlənt] N (*Med*) inoculante *m*
inoculate [ɪ'nɒkjʊleɪt] VT [*+ person, animal*] vacunar • **to ~ sb against sth** vacunar a algn contra algo • **to ~ sb with sth** inocular algo a algn
inoculation [ɪˌnɒkjʊ'leɪʃən] N inoculación *f*
inodorous [ɪn'əʊdərəs] ADJ inodoro
inoffensive [ˌɪnə'fensɪv] ADJ inofensivo
inoperable [ɪn'ɒpərəbl] ADJ inoperable
inoperative [ɪn'ɒpərətɪv] ADJ inoperante
inopportune [ɪn'ɒpətjuːn] ADJ inoportuno
inopportunely [ɪn'ɒpətjuːnlɪ] ADV inoportunamente, a destiempo
inordinate [ɪ'nɔːdɪnɪt] ADJ (*= excessive*) excesivo; (*= unrestrained*) desmesurado, desmedido • **he spent an ~ amount of time/money on it** empleó en ello una cantidad excesiva de tiempo/dinero
inordinately [ɪ'nɔːdɪnɪtlɪ] ADV desmesuradamente, excesivamente
inorganic [ˌɪnɔː'gænɪk] ADJ (*Chem*) inorgánico
CPD ▸ **inorganic chemistry** química *f* inorgánica

inpatient ['ɪn,peɪʃənt] (N) paciente *mf* hospitalizado/a
input ['ɪnpʊt] (N) (*Elec*) entrada *f*; (*Comput*) entrada *f*, input *m*; (= *contribution*) contribución *f*, aportación *f*, aporte *m* (*LAm*); (= *effort, time*) inversión *f*; (*Econ*) dinero *m* invertido, inversión *f* • **we want more ~ from the local community** queremos mayor aportación por parte de la comunidad local
(VT) (*Comput*) [+ *data*] entrar
(CPD) ▸ **input device** (*Comput*) dispositivo *m* de entrada
input-output device [,ɪnpʊt'aʊtpʊtdɪ'vaɪs] (N) dispositivo *m* de entrada y salida
inquest ['ɪnkwest] (N) **1** (*Jur*) investigación *f*, pesquisa *f* judicial; (*by coroner*) *investigación llevada a cabo para averiguar las causas de una muerte violente o sospechosa*
2 (*fig*) • **they held an ~ into** *or* **on their election defeat** realizaron un análisis en profundidad de su derrota electoral • **he likes to hold an ~ on every game** le gusta discutir cada partido hasta la saciedad
inquietude [ɪn'kwaɪətju:d] (N) (*frm*) inquietud *f*
inquire [ɪn'kwaɪə^r] (VT) preguntar • **to ~ sth of sb** preguntar algo a algn • **to ~ when/whether ...** preguntar cuándo/si ... • **he ~d the price** preguntó cuánto costaba
(VI) preguntar • **to ~ about sth** preguntar por algo, informarse de algo • **I am inquiring about your advertisement in today's paper** (*by phone*) llamo para preguntar acerca de su anuncio en el periódico de hoy • **to ~ after** *or* **for** *or* **about sb** preguntar por algn • **she ~d after your health** preguntó por tu salud, preguntó qué tal andabas de salud • **to ~ into sth** investigar *or* indagar algo • **I shouldn't ~ too closely if I were you** yo que tú no haría demasiadas preguntas • **"inquire within"** "infórmese en el interior" • **"inquire at No. 14"** "razón: en el nº 14"
inquirer [ɪn'kwaɪərə^r] (N) (= *asker*) el/la que pregunta; (= *researcher*) investigador(a) *m/f* (into de)
inquiring [ɪn'kwaɪərɪŋ] (ADJ) [*mind*] inquieto, inquisitivo; [*look*] inquisitivo • **she looked at me with ~ eyes** me miró con expresión inquisitiva *or* de interrogante
inquiringly [ɪn'kwaɪərɪŋlɪ] (ADV) [*look etc*] inquisitivamente
inquiry [ɪn'kwaɪərɪ] (N) **1** (= *question*) interrogante *m or f*, pregunta *f* • **"Inquiries"** "Información *f*" • **"all inquiries to the secretary"** "para cualquier información diríjanse al secretario" • **on ~** al preguntar • **to make inquiries (about sth)** pedir información *or* informarse (sobre algo) • **I'll make some inquiries about flights** me informaré de los vuelos • **I went to make inquiries of his teacher** fui a preguntarle a su profesor • **a look of ~** una mirada inquisitiva
2 (= *investigation*) investigación *f*, pesquisa *f*; (= *commission*) comisión *f* investigadora, comisión *f* de investigación • **there will have to be an ~** tendrá que llevarse a cabo una investigación • **to hold an ~ into sth** llevar a cabo una investigación sobre algo, investigar algo • **they set up an ~ into the disaster** nombraron a una comisión para investigar el desastre • **the police are making inquiries** la policía está investigando el caso • **the ~ found that ...** la investigación concluyó que ...
3 (*Comput*) interrogación *f*
(CPD) ▸ **inquiry agent**† investigador(a) *m/f* privado/a ▸ **inquiry desk** mesa *f* de información ▸ **inquiry office** oficina *f* de información

inquisition [,ɪnkwɪ'zɪʃən] (N) inquisición *f*, investigación *f* • **the Spanish Inquisition** la Inquisición, el Santo Oficio
inquisitive [ɪn'kwɪzɪtɪv] (ADJ) (= *interested*) curioso; (= *prying*) entrometido, curioso; [*mind*] inquisitivo
inquisitively [ɪn'kwɪzɪtɪvlɪ] (ADV) con curiosidad
inquisitiveness [ɪn'kwɪzɪtɪvnɪs] (N) curiosidad *f*
inquisitor [ɪn'kwɪzɪtə^r] (N) inquisidor *m*
inquisitorial [ɪn,kwɪzɪ'tɔ:rɪəl] (ADJ) inquisitorial • **an ~ system of justice** un sistema judicial inquisitorial
inroads ['ɪnrəʊdz] (NPL) • **the ~ of mass tourism** los efectos del turismo de masas • **she had to make ~ into her savings** tuvo que recurrir a sus ahorros, tuvo que echar mano de sus ahorros* • **they made significant ~ into Chinese territory** realizaron grandes avances dentro del territorio chino • **they are making ~ into the European market** se están adentrando en el mercado europeo • **I can see you've made ~ into that cake** (*hum*) ya veo que le has metido mano a la tarta* • **to make ~ into sb's time** robar el tiempo a algn
inrush ['ɪnrʌʃ] (N) [*of mud, water*] tromba *f*; [*of tourists*] afluencia *f*; [*of foreign imports*] avalancha *f*
INS (N ABBR) (*US*) = **Immigration and Naturalization Service**
ins. (ABBR) **1** = **insurance**
2 = **inches**
insalubrious [,ɪnsə'lu:brɪəs] (ADJ) (*frm*) [*conditions*] insalubre, malsano; [*part of town*] deprimido
insane [ɪn'seɪn] (ADJ) **1** (= *mad*) loco • **he is quite ~** está completamente loco, es un demente • **the jury decided King was ~ at the time** el jurado decidió que King estaba loco *or* no estaba en su sano juicio en aquel momento • **she had killed him while temporarily ~** lo había matado mientras sufría demencia temporal • **to drive sb ~** enloquecer *or* volver loco a algn • **to go ~** volverse loco • **~ jealousy** celos *mpl* enfermizos
2* (*fig*) (= *crazy*) [*suggestion, idea*] descabellado; [*act*] insensato • **if I told them that, they'd think I was ~** si les dijese eso, pensarían que estoy completamente loca *or* que no estoy en mi sano juicio • **this idea is totally ~** esta idea es una verdadera locura *or* es totalmente descabellada • **to drive sb ~** sacar a algn de quicio • **it would be ~ to let him go by himself** sería una locura dejarle ir solo
(NPL) • **the ~** los enfermos mentales; ▹ **criminally**
(CPD) ▸ **insane asylum** (*US*) manicomio *m*, psiquiátrico *m*
insanely [ɪn'seɪnlɪ] (ADV) • **to laugh ~** reírse como un loco • **to be ~ jealous** (*by nature*) ser terriblemente celoso; (*at particular moment*) estar loco de celos
insanitary [ɪn'sænɪtərɪ] (ADJ) insalubre, malsano
insanity [ɪn'sænɪtɪ] (N) **1** (*Med*) demencia *f* • **to drive sb to ~** volver loco a algn
2 (= *foolishness*) locura *f*, insensatez *f* • **what he did was sheer ~** lo que hizo fue una verdadera locura *or* insensatez
insatiable [ɪn'seɪʃəbl] (ADJ) insaciable
insatiably [ɪn'seɪʃəblɪ] (ADV) [*eat*] con un hambre insaciable; [*kiss*] con una pasión insaciable • **to be ~ hungry/curious/greedy** tener un hambre/una curiosidad/una avaricia insaciable
inscribe [ɪn'skraɪb] (VT) (= *engrave*) grabar; (= *write*) inscribir; (= *dedicate*) [+ *book*] dedicar • **to ~ sth on sth** grabar algo en algo • **a set of pens ~d with his initials** un juego de plumas con sus iniciales grabadas
inscription [ɪn'skrɪpʃən] (N) (*on stone*) inscripción *f*; (*in book*) dedicatoria *f*
inscrutability [ɪn,skru:tə'bɪlɪtɪ] (N) inescrutabilidad *f*
inscrutable [ɪn'skru:təbl] (ADJ) inescrutable
inseam ['ɪnsi:m] (ADJ) (*US*) • **~ measurement** medida *f* de pernera
insect ['ɪnsekt] (N) insecto *m*; (*fig*) bicho *m*
(CPD) ▸ **insect bite** picadura *f* de insecto ▸ **insect pest control** desinsectación *f* ▸ **insect powder** insecticida *m* en polvo ▸ **insect repellent** repelente *m* contra insectos ▸ **insect spray** insecticida *m* en aerosol
insecticide [ɪn'sektɪsaɪd] (N) insecticida *m*
insectivorous [,ɪnsek'tɪvərəs] (ADJ) insectívoro
insecure [,ɪnsɪ'kjʊə^r] (ADJ) **1** (= *not confident*) inseguro • **to feel ~** sentirse inseguro • **he feels ~ about their relationship** se siente inseguro acerca de su relación • **she feels ~ about sharing her flat with somebody else** le preocupa la idea de compartir el piso con otra persona • **she is ~ about her performance as a mother** duda de su habilidad como madre
2 (= *not secure*) [*job, position*] poco seguro • **the hospital faces an ~ future** el hospital se enfrenta a un futuro incierto *or* poco seguro • **their lives are ~** hay mucha inseguridad en sus vidas
3 (= *not safe*) [*country, area, building*] poco seguro; [*situation*] inestable
4 (= *not firm*) [*door, ladder, load*] poco seguro
insecurely [,ɪnsɪ'kjʊəlɪ] (ADV) de manera poco segura
insecurity [,ɪnsɪ'kjʊərɪtɪ] (N) inseguridad *f*
inseminate [ɪn'semɪneɪt] (VT) inseminar
insemination [ɪn,semɪ'neɪʃən] (N) inseminación *f*
insensate [ɪn'senseɪt] (ADJ) **1** (= *lacking sensation*) insensato
2 (= *pointless*) [*violence, aggression*] absurdo
insensibility [ɪn,sensə'bɪlɪtɪ] (N) **1** insensibilidad *f* (to a)
2 (= *unconsciousness*) inconsciencia *f*
insensible [ɪn'sensəbl] (ADJ) (*frm*)
1 (= *unconscious*) inconsciente, sin conocimiento • **he drank himself ~** bebió hasta perder el conocimiento • **the blow knocked him ~** el golpe le hizo perder el conocimiento
2 (= *insensitive*) • **to be ~ to sth** ser insensible a algo • **~ to heat/cold** insensible al calor/al frío • **he seemed ~ to shame** no parecía saber lo que es tener vergüenza
3 (= *unaware*) • **to be ~ of sth** no ser consciente de algo, no darse cuenta de algo • **she seemed wholly ~ of the honour done to her** parecía que no era consciente en absoluto del honor que se le hacía, parecía no darse cuenta en absoluto del honor que se le hacía • **to be ~ of danger** no ser consciente del peligro
insensibly [ɪn'sensɪblɪ] (ADV) (*frm*) [*change, improve, rise*] imperceptiblemente, insensiblemente
insensitive [ɪn'sensɪtɪv] (ADJ) [*person*] insensible; [*behaviour, remark*] falto de sensibilidad • **to be ~** [*person*] no tener sensibilidad • **to be ~ to sth** ser insensible a algo • **to be ~ to heat/cold/pain** ser insensible al calor/frío/dolor • **she is ~ to other people's feelings** es insensible a los sentimientos de los demás • **he had become ~ to seeing people suffer** se había vuelto

i

insensible al sufrimiento de los demás
insensitively [ɪn'sensɪtɪvlɪ] ADV con falta de sensibilidad
insensitivity [ɪn,sensɪ'tɪvɪtɪ] N *(physical)* insensibilidad *f*; *(emotional)* falta *f* de sensibilidad • **~ to sth** [+ *cold, pain*] insensibilidad *f* a algo; [+ *people's feelings, problems*] falta *f* de sensibilidad ante algo
inseparable [ɪn'sepərəbl] ADJ inseparable • **the two brothers were ~** los dos hermanos eran inseparables • **the two questions are ~** los dos temas son inseparables • **pain is ~ from love** el dolor es inseparable del amor
inseparably [ɪn'sepərəblɪ] ADV inseparablemente, indisolublemente
insert N ['ɪnsɜːt] *(in book, magazine)* encarte *m*; *(Sew)* entredós *m*
VT [ɪn'sɜːt] (= *put in*) [+ *coin, finger, needle*] introducir, meter; (= *add*) [+ *word, paragraph*] intercalar, insertar; [+ *advertisement*] insertar, poner; *(Comput)* insertar
insertion [ɪn'sɜːʃən] N *(gen)* inserción *f*, introducción *f*; [*of advertisement*] publicación *f*, inserción *f*; (= *advertisement*) anuncio *m*
in-service ['ɪn'sɜːvɪs] CPD ▸ **in-service course** curso *m* de formación continua ▸ **in-service education** (US), **in-service training** formación *f* continua
inset ['ɪnset] N *(Typ)* recuadro *m*, *grabado o mapa o dibujo etc que se imprime en un ángulo de otro mayor*; (= *page(s)*) encarte *m*
VT (PT, PP: **inset**) *(Typ)* [+ *diagram, map*] insertar, imprimir como recuadro; [+ *page(s)*] imprimir como encarte; (= *indent*) sangrar
inshore ['ɪn'ʃɔːʳ] ADV [*be, fish*] cerca de la costa; [*sail, blow*] hacia la costa
ADJ costero
CPD ▸ **inshore fishing** pesca *f* de bajura
inside ['ɪn'saɪd] N **1** (= *inner part*) interior *m*, parte *f* de dentro • **he wiped the ~ of the glass** limpió el interior *or* la parte de dentro del vaso • **the ~ of the foot** la parte de dentro del pie • **I have a pain in my ~*** me duele el estómago • **from the ~**: • **the doors were locked from the ~** las puertas estaban cerradas (con llave) por dentro • **to know sth from the ~** saber algo por experiencia propia • **crisp on the outside and soft on the ~** crujiente por fuera y tierno por dentro • **~ out**: • **your jumper's ~ out** llevas el jersey al *or* del revés • **she turned the sock ~ out** le dio la vuelta al calcetín, volvió el calcetín del revés • **they turned the whole place ~ out** lo revolvieron todo, lo registraron todo de arriba abajo • **to know a subject ~ out** conocer un tema de cabo a rabo • **he knows the district ~ out** se conoce el distrito como la palma de la mano
2 (= *lining*) parte *f* de dentro • **the ~ of the jacket is sheepskin** la parte de dentro de la chaqueta es de piel de borrego
3 [*of road*] *(Brit)* lado *m* izquierdo; *(other countries)* lado *m* derecho • **to overtake** *or* **pass (sb) on the ~** *(Brit)* adelantar (a algn) por la izquierda; *(other countries)* adelantar (a algn) por la derecha • **walk on the ~ of the pavement** camina por la parte de dentro de la acera
4 insides [*of person, animal, fruit*] tripas *fpl*
ADV **1** (= *in*) dentro, adentro *(LAm)* • **once ~, he was trapped** una vez dentro estaba atrapado • **it gives me a lovely warm feeling ~** me produce una sensación muy agradable por dentro • **deep ~ he is worried** en el fondo está preocupado
2 (= *towards the inside*) adentro, dentro • **he opened the car door and shoved her ~** abrió la puerta del coche y la empujó adentro *or* dentro
3 (= *indoors*) dentro, adentro *(LAm)* • **wait for me ~** espérame dentro *or* *(LAm)* adentro • **please step ~** pase (usted) • **to come/go ~** entrar
4* (= *in prison*) • **to be ~** estar en chirona*, estar a la sombra*
PREP *(also* **inside of**) *(esp US)* **1** (*of place*) dentro de, en el interior de *(frm)* • **~ the envelope** dentro del sobre, en el interior del sobre *(frm)* • **he went ~ the house** entró en la casa • **75% of chief executives come from ~ the company** un 75% de los altos cargos directivos proceden de la propia empresa
2 (*of time*) en menos de • **~ four hours** en menos de cuatro horas • **her time was five seconds ~ the record** superó el récord por cinco segundos
ADJ **1** (= *internal*) interior • **the ~ pages of a newspaper** las páginas interiores de un periódico
2 (= *confidential, from inside*) • **an ~ job*** *un crimen cometido en una empresa, organización, etc por alguien que pertenece a la misma* • **it must be an ~ job*** tiene que haber sido alguien de dentro • **the ~ story** la historia (hasta ahora) secreta • **the KGB: the ~ story** la KGB: la historia secreta
CPD ▸ **inside forward** delantero/a *m/f* interior, interior *mf* ▸ **inside information** información *f* confidencial ▸ **the inside lane** *(Aut)* *(Brit)* el carril de la izquierda; *(most countries)* el carril de la derecha; *(Athletics)* la calle interior ▸ **inside left** interior *mf* izquierdo/a ▸ **inside leg (measurement)** medida *f* de la entrepierna ▸ **inside pocket** bolsillo *m* interior ▸ **inside right** *(Sport)* interior *mf* derecho/a ▸ **inside track** [*of sports track*] pista *f* interior • IDIOM: • **to get the ~ track on sth** (= *information*) obtener información de primera mano sobre algo
insider [ɪn'saɪdəʳ] N [*of firm*] empleado/a *m/f* de la empresa
CPD ▸ **insider dealing, insider trading** abuso *m* de información privilegiada
insidious [ɪn'sɪdɪəs] ADJ insidioso
insidiously [ɪn'sɪdɪəslɪ] ADV insidiosamente
insight ['ɪnsaɪt] N **1** (= *understanding*) perspicacia *f* • **a person of ~** una persona perspicaz
2 (= *new perception*) nueva percepción *f* • **to gain** *or* **get an ~ into sth** comprender algo mejor, adquirir una nueva percepción de algo • **the visit gave us an ~ into their way of life** la visita nos ofreció la oportunidad de comprender mejor su manera de vivir
insightful ['ɪn,saɪtfʊl] ADJ (US) penetrante, perspicaz
insignia [ɪn'sɪgnɪə] NPL (PL: **insignias** *or* **insignia**) insignias *fpl*
insignificance [,ɪnsɪg'nɪfɪkəns] N insignificancia *f*; ▹ **pale**
insignificant [,ɪnsɪg'nɪfɪkənt] ADJ [*person, number, amount*] insignificante; [*detail*] insignificante, sin importancia • **who left it here is ~, the important thing is ...** no tiene importancia quién lo dejó aquí, lo importante es ...
insincere [,ɪnsɪn'sɪəʳ] ADJ insincero, poco sincero
insincerely [,ɪnsɪn'sɪəlɪ] ADV de forma poco sincera
insincerity [,ɪnsɪn'serɪtɪ] N falta *f* de sinceridad, insinceridad *f*
insinuate [ɪn'sɪnjʊeɪt] VT **1** [+ *object*] introducir **(into en)** • **to ~ o.s. into sth** introducirse en algo • **to ~ o.s. into sb's favour** ganarse el favor de algn
2 (= *hint*) insinuar • **to ~ that** insinuar que, dar a entender que • **what are you insinuating?** ¿qué insinúas?
insinuating [ɪn'sɪnjʊeɪtɪŋ] ADJ [*remark*] malintencionado, con segunda intención
insinuation [ɪn,sɪnjʊ'eɪʃən] N **1** (= *hint*) insinuación *f* • **he made certain ~s** hizo algunas insinuaciones
2 (= *act*) introducción *f*
insipid [ɪn'sɪpɪd] ADJ insípido, soso
insipidity [,ɪnsɪ'pɪdɪtɪ] N insipidez *f*, sosería *f*, insulsez *f*
insist [ɪn'sɪst] VI insistir • **if you ~** si insistes • **to ~ on sth** (= *repeat*) insistir en algo; (= *demand*) exigir algo; (= *emphasize*) [+ *point, aspect, benefit*] hacer hincapié en algo • **she always ~s on the best** siempre exige lo mejor • **he ~s on his version of events** se reafirma en su versión de los hechos • **to ~ on doing sth** insistir en hacer algo • **he ~s on provoking me** insiste *or* se empeña en provocarme
VT • **to ~ that** insistir en que • **he ~ed that it was so** insistió en que era así • **I ~ed that it be done** insistí en que se hiciera
insistence [ɪn'sɪstəns] N insistencia *f* • **~ that** insistencia en que, empeño en que • **his ~ that we should have a drink** su insistencia *or* su empeño en que tomásemos una copa • **his ~ that he had switched the light off** su insistencia *or* su empeño en que había apagado la luz • **at his/her ~** ante su insistencia • **~ on sth** insistencia en algo • **his ~ on punctuality** su insistencia en la puntualidad • **her great ~ on this point** su enorme insistencia *or* su enorme empeño en este punto
insistent [ɪn'sɪstənt] ADJ [*person, demands, questions*] insistente • **to be ~ that** insistir en que • **he was ~ that we should have a drink** insistió en que tomásemos una copa • **he was ~ that he had switched the light off** insistía en que había apagado la luz • **to be ~ about sth** insistir en algo • **she was ~ about leaving at seven** insistió en salir a las siete • **to be ~ on sth** insistir en algo • **she is most ~ on this point** insiste mucho en este punto • **we could hear the ~ ringing of a telephone in another room** podríamos oír el insistente sonido de un teléfono en otra habitación • **in an ~ tone** con un tono apremiante
insistently [ɪn'sɪstəntlɪ] ADV [*ask, say, knock, ring*] insistentemente, con insistencia • **he was tugging ~ at his mother's sleeve** tiraba insistentemente *or* con insistencia de la manga de su madre • **he tried very ~ to sell us some toys** intentó con mucha insistencia vendernos unos juguetes
in situ [ɪn'sɪtjuː] ADV in situ
insofar [ɪnsə'fɑːʳ] • **~ as ...** CONJ en la medida en que ... • **~ as can be ascertained ...** en la medida en que se puede establecer ...
insole ['ɪnsəʊl] N plantilla *f*
insolence ['ɪnsələns] N insolencia *f*
insolent ['ɪnsələnt] ADJ insolente
insolently ['ɪnsələntlɪ] ADV insolentemente
insolubility [ɪn,sɒljʊ'bɪlətɪ] N insolubilidad *f*
insoluble [ɪn'sɒljʊbl] ADJ [*substance*] insoluble; [*problem*] sin solución, insoluble
insolvable [ɪn'sɒlvəbl] ADJ insoluble
insolvency [ɪn'sɒlvənsɪ] N [*of company*] insolvencia *f*
insolvent [ɪn'sɒlvənt] ADJ insolvente • **the company was declared ~** la empresa fue declarada insolvente
insomnia [ɪn'sɒmnɪə] N insomnio *m*
insomniac [ɪn'sɒmnɪæk] N insomne *mf*

ADJ insomne

insomuch [ˌɪnsəʊˈmʌtʃ] • **~ as** CONJ puesto que, ya que, por cuanto que • **~ that** hasta tal punto que

insouciance [ɪnˈsuːsɪəns] N despreocupación *f*

insouciant [ɪnˈsuːsɪənt] ADJ despreocupado

insourcing [ˈɪnsɔːsɪŋ] N utilización *f* de recursos de la propia empresa

Insp., insp. ABBR = **inspector**

inspect [ɪnˈspekt] VT **1** (= *examine*) [+ *goods, luggage*] inspeccionar, examinar; (*officially*) [+ *premises, building, school*] inspeccionar; [+ *machinery, vehicle*] inspeccionar, revisar; [+ *ticket, document*] revisar • **to ~ a product for flaws** examinar un producto para detectar defectos
2 (*Mil*) [+ *troops*] pasar revista a

inspection [ɪnˈspekʃən] N **1** [*of goods, premises, school*] inspección *f*; [*of ticket, document*] revisión *f* • **on closer ~ it turned out to be a fake** tras un examen más minucioso resultó ser falso
2 (*Mil*) [*of troops*] revista *f*
CPD ▸ **inspection pit** (*Aut*) foso *m* de reconocimiento

inspector [ɪnˈspektəʳ] N (= *official*) inspector(a) *m/f*; (*on bus, train*) revisor(a) *m/f*, controlador(a) *m/f* (*LAm*); (*in police, of school*) inspector(a) *m/f* • **~ of schools** (*Brit*) inspector(a) *m/f* de enseñanza • **~ of taxes** ≈ Inspector(a) *m/f* de Hacienda

inspectorate [ɪnˈspektərɪt] N (*esp Brit*) cuerpo *m* de inspectores, inspección *f*

inspiration [ˌɪnspəˈreɪʃən] N **1** (= *motivation*) inspiración *f* • **the war has provided the ~ for many novels** la guerra ha sido fuente de inspiración para muchas novelas • **to find ~ in** inspirarse en • **she has been an ~ to us all** ha sido un gran estímulo para todos nosotros
2 (= *inspired idea*) idea *f* genial • **she had a sudden ~** de pronto tuvo una idea genial

inspirational [ˌɪnspɪˈreɪʃənl] ADJ inspirador

inspire [ɪnˈspaɪəʳ] VT inspirar • **she has the sort of face that ~s terror/respect** tiene un rostro que inspira terror/respeto • **to ~ sb to do sth** mover a algn a hacer algo • **her achievements have ~d me to make more effort** sus logros me han movido a esforzarme más • **whatever ~d him to do that?** ¿qué lo impulsó *or* movió a hacer eso? • **this painting was ~d by Greek mythology** este cuadro está inspirado en la mitología griega • **he was ~d by her beauty to write the song** su belleza lo llevó *or* movió a escribir la canción • **the painting was divinely ~d** el cuadro fue pintado por inspiración divina • **to ~ confidence in sb** • **~ sb with confidence** infundir *or* inspirar confianza a algn

inspired [ɪnˈspaɪəd] ADJ [*musician, poet, artist, sportsman*] genial; [*performance*] inspirado; [*idea*] genial, excelente • **he gave an ~ performance** su actuación estuvo inspirada • **the pianist was playing like a man ~** el pianista tocaba como si los dioses guiasen sus manos • **it was an ~ choice** fue todo un acierto • **to feel ~** sentirse inspirado • **to make an ~ guess** tener una inspiración • **in an ~ moment** en un momento de inspiración

inspiring [ɪnˈspaɪərɪŋ] ADJ • **he was a brilliant and ~ speaker** fue un magnífico orador que conseguía inspirar a la gente • **as a teacher he is capable, but not ~** es un profesor competente pero que no consigue estimular a sus alumnos • **it is ~ to work with people like them** es estimulante trabajar con gente como ellos • **it was not an ~ spot** no era un sitio que inspirase

Inst. ABBR = **Institute**

inst. ABBR (= **instant**) (= *of the present month*) cte., corrte.

instability [ˌɪnstəˈbɪlɪtɪ] N inestabilidad *f*

instal, install (*US*) [ɪnˈstɔːl] VT **1** [+ *central heating, lighting, equipment*] instalar
2 (= *invest*) • **to be ~led in office** tomar posesión de su cargo
3 (*Comput*) [+ *program*] instalar

installation [ˌɪnstəˈleɪʃən] N **1** (*Tech*) (*gen*) instalación *f* • **military ~s** instalaciones *f* militares
2 [*of mayor, official*] toma *f* de posesión, investidura *f*

instalment, installment (*US*) [ɪnˈstɔːlmənt] N **1** (*Comm*) (= *part payment*) plazo *m*, cuota *f* (*LAm*) • **to pay in ~s** pagar a plazos • **monthly ~** plazo *m* mensual, cuota *f* mensual (*LAm*)
2 [*of serial, in magazine*] fascículo *m*; (*on radio, TV*) episodio *m*
CPD ▸ **installment plan** (*US*) plan *m* de financiación • **to buy sth/pay for sth on an ~ plan** comprar/pagar algo a plazos

instance [ˈɪnstəns] N **1** (= *example*) ejemplo *m* • **for ~** por ejemplo
2 (= *case*) caso *m* • **in that ~** en ese caso • **in many ~s** en muchos casos • **in the present ~** en el caso presente • **in the first ~** en primer lugar
3 (*Jur*) • **at the ~ of** a instancia *or* petición de
VT (= *exemplify*) citar como ejemplo • **this is perhaps best ~d by ...** quizás esto queda mejor ilustrado por ...

instant [ˈɪnstənt] ADJ **1** (= *immediate*) [*reply, reaction, success*] instantáneo, inmediato • **~ access to sth** acceso *m* instantáneo *or* inmediato a algo • **he took an ~ dislike to Derek** Derek le cayó mal desde el primer momento • **sweets give ~ energy** los dulces son una fuente instantánea de energía • **his book was an ~ hit** *or* **success** su libro fue un éxito instantáneo *or* inmediato
2 (*Culin*) [*coffee, soup*] instantáneo • **~ mash** puré *m* de patatas instantáneo
3 (*Brit*) (*Comm*) (*frm*) • **on the 1st ~** el primero del corriente; ▹ **inst.**
4 (*Jur*) • **in the ~ case** en el presente caso
N instante *m*, momento *m* • **the ~ I heard it** en el instante *or* momento en que lo supe • **an ~ later she was gone** un instante *or* momento después se había ido • **Jed hesitated for an ~** Jed dudó un instante *or* un momento • **in an ~** en un instante *or* momento • **the next ~** un momento después • **put it down this ~!** ¡deja eso ahora mismo! • **at that very ~ the phone rang** en ese mismo instante *or* momento sonó el teléfono
CPD ▸ **instant access account** cuenta *f* de acceso instantáneo *or* inmediato ▸ **instant death** muerte *f* instantánea *or* en el acto ▸ **instant gratification** satisfacción *f* inmediata ▸ **instant message** mensaje *m* instantáneo ▸ **instant messaging** mensajería *f* instantánea ▸ **instant replay** (*Sport*) repetición *f* de la jugada

instantaneous [ˌɪnstənˈteɪnɪəs] ADJ instantáneo

instantaneously [ˌɪnstənˈteɪnɪəslɪ] ADV instantáneamente

instantly [ˈɪnstəntlɪ] ADV [*recognise, know*] inmediatamente, al instante; [*die*] en el acto, instantáneamente • **the songs are ~ recognisable** las canciones se reconocen inmediatamente *or* al instante • **information will be ~ available to customers** los clientes podrán acceder a la información de forma instantánea

instead [ɪnˈsted] ADV • **I was tempted to spend the money, but I put it in the bank ~** tuve la tentación de gastar el dinero, pero en lugar de ello *or* en vez de eso, lo metí en el banco • **she wanted to run away, but ~ she carried on walking** quería echar a correr, pero sin embargo siguió andando • **she's allergic to soap, so she uses cleanser ~** es alérgica al jabón, así es que usa una crema limpiadora en su lugar • **he was busy, so I went ~** él estaba ocupado, así es que fui yo en su lugar • **we had expected to make £2,000, ~, we barely made £200** esperábamos sacar unas 2.000 libras y en cambio apenas sacamos 200
PREP • **~ of** en vez de, en lugar de • **I used margarine ~ of butter** usé margarina en vez de *or* en lugar de mantequilla • **we decided to walk ~ of taking the bus** decidimos andar en vez de *or* en lugar de tomar el autobús • **he went ~ of me** fue en mi lugar • **this is ~ of a Christmas present** esto hace las veces de regalo de Navidad

instep [ˈɪnstep] N empeine *m*

instigate [ˈɪnstɪgeɪt] VT [+ *rebellion, strike, crime*] instigar a; [+ *new ideas*] fomentar; [+ *change*] promover

instigation [ˌɪnstɪˈgeɪʃən] N instigación *f* • **at Brown's ~** • **at the ~ of Brown** a instancias de Brown • **at her ~, I went to see him** fui a verlo a instancias suyas

instigator [ˈɪnstɪgeɪtəʳ] N instigador(a) *m/f*

instil, instill (*US*) [ɪnˈstɪl] VT • **to ~ sth into sb** [+ *fear, confidence, pride*] inspirar *or* infundir algo a algn; [+ *awareness, moral values, responsibility*] inculcar algo a algn

instinct N [ˈɪnstɪŋkt] instinto *m* • **the ~ for self-preservation** el instinto de conservación *or* supervivencia • **by ~** por instinto • **she had an ~ for attracting the wrong type of man** se las pintaba sola para atraer al tipo de hombre que no le convenía*
ADJ [ɪnˈstɪŋkt] (*liter*) • **~ with** lleno de, imbuido de

instinctive [ɪnˈstɪŋktɪv] ADJ instintivo

instinctively [ɪnˈstɪŋktɪvlɪ] ADV instintivamente, por instinto

instinctual [ɪnˈstɪŋktjʊəl] ADJ instintivo

institute [ˈɪnstɪtjuːt] N (= *research centre*) instituto *m*; (= *professional body*) colegio *m*, asociación *f*; (*for professional training*) escuela *f*; (*US*) (= *course*) curso *m*, cursillo *m*
VT (= *begin*) [+ *inquiry*] iniciar, empezar; (= *found*) fundar, instituir; (*Jur*) [+ *proceedings*] entablar

institution [ˌɪnstɪˈtjuːʃən] N **1** (= *act*) (= *founding*) fundación *f*, institución *f*; (= *initiation*) iniciación *f*; (*Jur*) [*of proceedings*] entablación *f*
2 (= *organization*) institución *f*
3 (= *workhouse*) asilo *m*; (= *madhouse*) manicomio *m*; (= *hospital*) hospital *m*
4 (= *custom*) institución *f* • **tea is a British ~** el té es una institución en Gran Bretaña • **it is too much of an ~ to abolish** es una costumbre demasiado arraigada para poder abolirla
5 (= *person*) • **he became an ~ at the Daily Star** se convirtió en toda una institución en el Daily Star

institutional [ˌɪnstɪˈtjuːʃənl] ADJ [*structure, resources*] institucional, de las instituciones; [*change, inefficiency*] institucional
CPD ▸ **the institutional church** la iglesia institucional ▸ **institutional investor** inversor(a) *m/f* institucional

i

institutionalize [ˌɪnstɪˈtjuːʃnəlaɪz] VT
1 (*= put into institution*) [*+ patient*] internar en una institución
2 (*= establish officially*) [*+ practices, values*] institucionalizar

institutionalized [ˌɪnstɪˈtjuːʃənəˌlaɪzd] ADJ
1 (*= living in an institution*) • **~ elderly people** personas *fpl* mayores internadas en residencias • **~ children** niños *mpl* que están bajo la custodia • **~ mental patients** enfermos *mpl* mentales ingresados en una institución
2 (*= affected by living in an institution*) • **to become ~** (*Psych*) *habituarse al régimen de vida de un hospital, una cárcel u otra institución de forma que se convierte en un modo de vida*
3 (*= established*) [*custom, practice, value*] institucionalizado • **to become ~** institucionalizarse • **homelessness is becoming ~** el hecho de que exista gente sin hogar se está institucionalizando

institutionally [ˌɪnstɪˈtjuːʃənəlɪ] ADV [*racist, sexist, corrupt*] institucionalmente

in-store [ˈɪnˌstɔːʳ] ADJ en el establecimiento

instruct [ɪnˈstrʌkt] VT **1** (*= teach*) • **to ~ sb in sth** enseñar algo a algn, instruir a algn en algo
2 (*= order*) • **to ~ sb to do sth** mandar *or* ordenar a algn que haga algo • **we were ~ed to stay where we were** se nos ordenó que permaneciéramos donde estábamos
3 (*Brit*) [*+ solicitor, barrister*] dar instrucciones a, instruir

instruction [ɪnˈstrʌkʃən] N **1** (*= teaching*) instrucción *f*, enseñanza *f* • **to give sb ~ in mathematics/fencing** dar clases de matemáticas/esgrima a algn, enseñar matemáticas/esgrima a algn
2 (*= order*) orden *f* • **to give sb ~s to do sth** dar órdenes *or* instrucciones a algn de que haga algo • **I gave him strict ~s not to touch it** le di órdenes estrictas de que no lo tocara • **we have given ~s for the transfer of funds** hemos cursado órdenes para la transferencia de fondos • **~s for use** modo *msing* de empleo • **on the ~s of** por orden de
3 (*Comput*) instrucción *f*
CPD ▸ **instruction book, instruction booklet, instruction manual** manual *m* de instrucciones

instructional [ɪnˈstrʌkʃənəl] ADJ [*film, book, video*] instructivo, educativo

instructive [ɪnˈstrʌktɪv] ADJ [*experience*] instructivo

instructor [ɪnˈstrʌktəʳ] N instructor(a) *m/f*; (*US*) (*Univ*) profesor(a) *m/f* auxiliar; (*also* **ski instructor**) monitor(a) *m/f* • **dance ~** profesor(a) *m/f* de baile • **flying ~** monitor(a) *m/f* de vuelo; ▹ **driving**

instructress [ɪnˈstrʌktrɪs] N instructora *f* • **dance ~** profesora *f* de baile

instrument [ˈɪnstrʊmənt] N **1** (*Mus*) (*gen*) instrumento *m* • **surgical ~s** instrumental *m* quirúrgico • **set of ~s** instrumental *m* • **to fly on ~s** volar por instrumentos
2 (*fig*) instrumento *m* • **he was nothing more than her ~** él no era más que su instrumento
3 (*Jur*) instrumento *m*
CPD ▸ **instrument board, instrument panel** (*Aer*) tablero *m* de instrumentos, cuadro *m* de instrumentos; (*US*) (*Aut*) tablero *m* de mandos, salpicadero *m* (*Sp*)

instrumental [ˌɪnstrʊˈmentl] ADJ **1** • **to be ~ in** contribuir decisivamente a • **she had been ~ in getting him the job** ella contribuyó decisivamente a que consiguiera el empleo • **I was ~ in bringing Lisa and Danny together** yo hice que Liza y Danny se conocieran
2 [*music, piece*] instrumental

instrumentalist [ˌɪnstrʊˈmentəlɪst] N instrumentista *mf*

instrumentality [ˌɪnstrʊmenˈtælɪtɪ] N mediación *f*, agencia *f* • **by** *or* **through the ~ of** por medio de, gracias a

instrumentation [ˌɪnstrʊmenˈteɪʃən] N instrumentación *f*

insubordinate [ˌɪnsəˈbɔːdənɪt] ADJ [*person, behaviour*] insubordinado

insubordination [ˈɪnsəˌbɔːdɪˈneɪʃən] N insubordinación *f*

insubstantial [ˌɪnsəbˈstænʃəl] ADJ (*gen*) insustancial; [*meal*] poco sustancioso

insufferable [ɪnˈsʌfərəbl] ADJ [*impertinence, arrogance, smugness*] insufrible, insoportable; [*heat*] insoportable, inaguantable • **he's ~!** ¡es insufrible!, ¡no hay quien lo aguante!

insufferably [ɪnˈsʌfərəblɪ] ADV • **it was ~ hot** hacía un calor insoportable *or* inaguantable • **it was ~ boring** fue de un aburrido insoportable • **he was ~ rude/arrogant** fue de lo más grosero/arrogante

insufficiency [ˌɪnsəˈfɪʃənsɪ] N insuficiencia *f*

insufficient [ˌɪnsəˈfɪʃənt] ADJ insuficiente

insufficiently [ˌɪnsəˈfɪʃəntlɪ] ADV insuficientemente • **his troops were ~ equipped** sus tropas iban insuficientemente pertrechadas • **the office is ~ staffed** la oficina no tiene el personal suficiente

insulant [ˈɪnsjʊlənt] N aislante *m*

insular [ˈɪnsjələʳ] ADJ **1** (*Geog*) [*climate, location*] insular
2 (*fig*) [*person, attitude*] estrecho de miras

insularity [ˌɪnsjʊˈlærɪtɪ] N insularidad *f*; (*fig*) estrechez *f* de miras

insulate [ˈɪnsjʊleɪt] VT (*gen*) aislar (**from** de)

insulating material [ˈɪnsjʊleɪtɪŋməˌtɪərɪəl] N material *m* aislante

insulating tape [ˈɪnsjʊleɪtɪŋˌteɪp] N cinta *f* aislante

insulation [ˌɪnsjʊˈleɪʃən] N (*gen*) aislamiento *m*; (*from cold*) aislamiento *m* térmico
CPD ▸ **insulation material** material *m* aislante

insulator [ˈɪnsjʊleɪtəʳ] N (*= material*) aislante *m*; (*= appliance*) aislador *m*

insulin [ˈɪnsjʊlɪn] N insulina *f*

insult [ˈɪnsʌlt] N insulto *m*, injuria *f* (*frm*) • **they are an ~ to the profession** son un insulto para la profesión • IDIOM: • **and to add ~ to injury** y para colmo de males, y por si esto fuera poco
VT [ɪnˈsʌlt] [*+ person*] insultar, ofender • **he felt ~ed by this offer** tomó esta oferta como un insulto *or* una ofensa • **now don't feel ~ed** no te ofendas

insulting [ɪnˈsʌltɪŋ] ADJ insultante, ofensivo

insultingly [ɪnˈsʌltɪŋlɪ] ADV [*behave, talk*] ofensivamente, de modo insultante • **she was ~ dismissive** su desdén era insultante • **these adverts are ~ sexist** el sexismo de estos anuncios resulta todo un insulto

insuperable [ɪnˈsuːpərəbl] ADJ [*difficulty*] insuperable

insuperably [ɪnˈsuːpərəblɪ] ADV • **~ difficult** dificilísimo

insupportable [ˌɪnsəˈpɔːtəbl] ADJ insoportable

insurable [ɪnˈʃʊərəbl] ADJ asegurable

insurance [ɪnˈʃʊərəns] N (*Comm*) seguro *m* • **~ against theft/fire/damage** seguro *m* contra robo/incendio/daños • **comprehensive/third party ~** seguro *m* a todo riesgo/contra terceros • **to take out ~** hacerse un seguro
CPD ▸ **insurance adjuster** (*US*) liquidador(a) *m/f* de seguros ▸ **insurance agent** agente *mf* de seguros ▸ **insurance broker** corredor(a) *m/f* de seguros, agente *mf* de seguros ▸ **insurance certificate** certificado *m* de seguro ▸ **insurance claim** demanda *f* de seguro ▸ **insurance company** compañía *f* de seguros ▸ **insurance policy** póliza *f* de seguros ▸ **insurance premium** prima *f* del seguro

insure [ɪnˈʃʊəʳ] VT [*+ house, property*] asegurar • **to ~ sb** *or* **sb's life** hacer un seguro de vida a algn • **to ~ o.s.** *or* **one's life** hacerse un seguro de vida • **to ~ sth against fire/theft** asegurar algo contra incendios/robo • **to ~ one's life for £500,000** hacerse un seguro de vida por valor de 500.000 libras • **to be ~d to do sth** tener un seguro que permite hacer algo • **I'm ~d to drive any car** tengo un seguro que me permite conducir cualquier coche • **I'm ~d to drive my husband's car** estoy en el seguro del coche de mi marido

insured [ɪnˈʃʊəd] ADJ [*person, building, vehicle*] asegurado • **are you ~?** ¿estás asegurado?, ¿tienes seguro? • **what is the sum ~?** ¿qué suma cubre el seguro? • **to be ~ against fire/theft** estar asegurado contra incendios/robo • **it's ~ for £5,000** está asegurado en 5.000 libras
N • **the ~** el/la asegurado/a

insurer [ɪnˈʃʊərəʳ] N asegurador(a) *m/f*

insurgency [ɪnˈsɜːdʒənsɪ] N insurrección *f*

insurgent [ɪnˈsɜːdʒənt] N insurgente *mf*, insurrecto/a *m/f*
ADJ insurgente, insurrecto

insurmountable [ˌɪnsəˈmaʊntəbl] ADJ insuperable

insurrection [ˌɪnsəˈrekʃən] N insurrección *f*

insurrectionary [ˌɪnsəˈrekʃnərɪ] ADJ rebelde, insurreccional

insurrectionist [ˌɪnsəˈrekʃənɪst] N insurgente *mf*, insurrecto/a *m/f*

insusceptible [ˌɪnsəˈseptəbl] ADJ inmune • **~ to pain** inmune al dolor

Int. ABBR = **International**

int. ABBR (*Econ*) = **interest**

intact [ɪnˈtækt] ADJ intacto • **not a window was left ~** no quedó cristal sano *or* sin romper • **I managed to keep my sense of humour ~** conseguí mantener intacto *or* no perder mi sentido del humor

intake [ˈɪnteɪk] N **1** (*Tech*) [*of air, gas etc*] entrada *f*; [*of water*] toma *f*
2 (*= quantity*) [*of food*] consumo *m* • **what is your student ~?** ¿cuántos alumnos se matriculan (cada año)?
CPD ▸ **intake valve** válvula *f* de admisión, válvula *f* de entrada

intangible [ɪnˈtændʒəbl] ADJ (*gen*) intangible
CPD ▸ **intangible assets** activo *msing* intangible

integer [ˈɪntɪdʒəʳ] N entero *m*, número *m* entero

integral [ˈɪntɪgrəl] ADJ (*= essential*) [*part*] integrante, esencial • **it is an ~ part of the plan** es parte integrante *or* esencial del proyecto
N (*Math*) integral *f*
CPD ▸ **integral calculus** (*Math*) cálculo *m* integral

integrate [ˈɪntɪgreɪt] VT integrar (*also Math*) • **to ~ aid with long-term development** integrar la ayuda con el desarrollo a largo plazo • **to ~ a new pupil into the class** integrar a un nuevo alumno en la clase
VI integrarse (**into** en)

integrated [ˈɪntɪgreɪtɪd] ADJ [*plan*]

integrado, de conjunto; [*personality*] equilibrado; [*population, school*] integrado, sin separación racial • **to become ~ (into)** integrarse (en)
CPD ▸ **integrated circuit** (*Comput*) circuito *m* integrado

integration [ˌɪntɪˈgreɪʃən] N integración *f* (**in, into** en)

integrator [ˈɪntɪgreɪtəʳ] N integrador *m*

integrity [ɪnˈtegrɪtɪ] N [*of person*] integridad *f*, honradez *f*; (*Comput*) integridad *f*

integument [ɪnˈtegjʊmənt] N (*frm*) integumento *m*

intellect [ˈɪntɪlekt] N **1** (= *reasoning power*) intelecto *m*, inteligencia *f*
2 (= *person*) cerebro *m*

intellectual [ˌɪntɪˈlektjʊəl] ADJ intelectual *mf*
N intelectual *mf*
CPD ▸ **intellectual property** propiedad *f* intelectual

intellectualize [ˌɪntɪˈlektjʊəlaɪz] VT intelectualizar, racionalizar
VI dar razones

intellectually [ˌɪntɪˈlektjʊəlɪ] ADV [*stimulating, demanding, inferior*] intelectualmente; (= *from an intellectual point of view*) intelectualmente, desde el punto de vista del intelecto

intelligence [ɪnˈtelɪdʒəns] N **1** (= *cleverness*) inteligencia *f*
2 (= *information*) información *f*, inteligencia *f* • **according to our latest ~** según las últimas noticias
CPD ▸ **intelligence agency** agencia *f* de inteligencia ▸ **intelligence agent** agente *mf* de inteligencia, agente *mf* secreto ▸ **Intelligence Corps** (*Brit*) (*Mil*) Cuerpo *m* de Informaciones ▸ **intelligence gathering** recogida *f* de información ▸ **intelligence gathering agency** agencia *f* de inteligencia ▸ **intelligence gathering operation** operación *f* de recogida de información ▸ **intelligence officer** oficial *mf* de informaciones ▸ **intelligence quotient (IQ)** cociente *m* intelectual *or* de inteligencia ▸ **intelligence service** servicio *m* de información *or* inteligencia ▸ **intelligence test** test *m* de inteligencia ▸ **intelligence work** trabajo *m* de inteligencia

intelligent [ɪnˈtelɪdʒənt] ADJ inteligente
CPD ▸ **intelligent design** diseño *m* inteligente

intelligently [ɪnˈtelɪdʒəntlɪ] ADV inteligentemente

intelligentsia [ɪnˌtelɪˈdʒentsɪə] N intelectualidad *f*

intelligibility [ɪnˌtelɪdʒəˈbɪlɪtɪ] N inteligibilidad *f*

intelligible [ɪnˈtelɪdʒəbl] ADJ inteligible, comprensible • **his prose is so laboured it is scarcely ~** su prosa es tan elaborada que resulta apenas inteligible

intelligibly [ɪnˈtelɪdʒəblɪ] ADV inteligiblemente, de modo inteligible

INTELSAT [ˈɪntelˌsæt] N ABBR = **International Telecommunications Satellite Organization**

intemperance [ɪnˈtempərəns] N (= *lack of self-restraint*) intemperancia *f*, inmoderación *f*; (= *drunkenness*) exceso *m* en la bebida

intemperate [ɪnˈtempərɪt] ADJ [*person*] (= *immoderate*) desmedido, destemplado; (= *drunken*) dado a la bebida, que bebe con exceso; [*climate*] inclemente

intend [ɪnˈtend] VT **1** (*with noun*) • **it's ~ed for John** está destinado a Juan, es para Juan • **no offence was ~ed • he ~ed no offence** no tenía intención de ofender a nadie, no fue su intención ofender a nadie • **I ~ no disrespect** no es mi intención faltarle al respeto a nadie • **that remark was ~ed for you** esa observación iba dirigida a ti • **it was ~ed as a compliment** se dijo como un cumplido • **I ~ed no harm** lo hice sin mala intención • **is that what you ~ed?** ¿fue eso lo que se proponía?
2 (*with verb*) • **to ~ to do sth** • **~ doing sth** pensar hacer algo • **what do you ~ to do about it?** ¿qué piensas hacer al respecto? • **I ~ him to come too** quiero que venga él también • **this scheme is ~ed to help** este proyecto tiene la finalidad de ayudar • **I ~ that he should see it** quiero que él lo vea • **I fully ~ to punish him** tengo la firme intención de castigarlo

intendant [ɪnˈtendənt] N supervisor(a) *m/f*

intended [ɪnˈtendɪd] ADJ [*effect*] deseado
N† (*also hum*) prometido/a *m/f*

intense [ɪnˈtens] ADJ **1** (= *extreme*) [*heat, cold, pain*] intenso; [*interest, enthusiasm, happiness*] enorme; [*emotion, fear, anger, hatred*] intenso, profundo; [*gratitude*] profundo; [*colour*] intenso, vivo; [*light*] intenso, fuerte • **this sparked ~ speculation** esto dio pie a mucha especulación
2 (= *concentrated*) [*activity, fighting, negotiations*] intenso • **she wore an expression of ~ concentration** su expresión era de intensa concentración
3 (= *impassioned*) [*person, face, expression*] apasionado, vehemente; [*relationship*] intenso; [*eyes*] penetrante; [*gaze*] intenso, penetrante • **she's very ~** se lo toma todo como si le fuera la vida en ello • **an ~ debate** un intenso debate

intensely [ɪnˈtenslɪ] ADV **1** (= *extremely*) [*interesting, boring, competitive*] sumamente; [*irritated*] sumamente, tremendamente; [*grateful, moving*] profundamente, sumamente • **difficulties of an ~ personal nature** dificultades de carácter sumamente personal • **to be ~ angry** estar terriblemente enfadado *or* (*LAm*) enojado, estar enfadadísimo *or* (*LAm*) enojadísimo
2 (= *concentratedly*) [*work, fight, concentrate*] intensamente
3 (= *with passion*) [*look, love*] intensamente; [*discuss*] apasionadamente; [*say*] con pasión • **I dislike it ~** me desagrada profundamente • **why do you dislike her so ~?** ¿por qué te resulta tan antipática? • **he was staring ~ at me** me miraba fija e intensamente • **they argued the point ~** lo discutieron acaloradamente

intenseness [ɪnˈtensnɪs] N = **intensity**

intensification [ɪnˌtensɪfɪˈkeɪʃən] N intensificación *f*

intensifier [ɪnˈtensɪˌfaɪəʳ] N intensificador *m*

intensify [ɪnˈtensɪfaɪ] VI [*desire, frustration, dislike*] intensificarse; [*pain*] agudizarse; [*odour*] hacerse más intenso; [*rain*] arreciar; [*fighting*] recrudecerse, intensificarse
VT [+ *fear*] intensificar, incrementar; [+ *pain*] agudizar; [+ *attack*] recrudecer, intensificar

intensity [ɪnˈtensɪtɪ] N **1** (= *strength*) [*of heat, cold, emotion, pain, light*] intensidad *f*
2 (= *passion*) [*of expression, relationship, debate, fighting*] intensidad *f*; [*of person*] vehemencia *f* • **she looked at me with such ~ that ...** me miró con tal intensidad que ..., me miró de una forma tan intensa que ...

intensive [ɪnˈtensɪv] ADJ [*course*] intensivo; [*negotiations, bombardment*] intenso; [*study*] profundo, detenido; (*esp for exam*) intensivo
CPD ▸ **intensive care** cuidados *mpl* intensivos • **to be in ~ care** estar en cuidados intensivos ▸ **intensive care unit** unidad *f* de cuidados intensivos, unidad *f* de terapia intensiva (*S. Cone, Mex*) ▸ **intensive farming** agricultura *f* intensiva ▸ **intensive therapy unit, intensive treatment unit** unidad *f* de cuidados intensivos, unidad *f* de terapia intensiva (*S. Cone, Mex*)

-intensive [-ɪnˌtensɪv] SUFFIX
• **energy-intensive** de uso intensivo de energía • **energy-intensive industries** industrias de uso intensivo de energía • **resource-intensive** de uso intensivo de recursos; ▹ **labour-intensive**

intensively [ɪnˈtensɪvlɪ] ADV [*bombard*] intensamente; [*study*] profundamente, detenidamente; (*esp for exam*) intensivamente

intent [ɪnˈtent] ADJ **1** (= *determined*) • **to be ~ on doing sth** estar resuelto *or* decidido a hacer algo
2 (= *absorbed*) absorto • **to be ~ on sth** estar absorto en algo
N propósito *m*, intención *f* • **with ~ to** (+ *infin*) con el propósito de (+ *infin*) • **with ~ to kill** con intentos homicidas • **to all ~s and purposes** prácticamente, en efecto

intention [ɪnˈtenʃən] N intención *f*, propósito *m* • **I have no ~ of going** no tengo la menor intención de ir • **I have every ~ of going** tengo plena intención de ir • **with the best of ~s** con la mejor intención • **what are your ~s?** ¿qué piensas hacer?, ¿qué proyectos tienes? • **his ~s toward the girl were strictly honourable** pensaba casarse con la joven

intentional [ɪnˈtenʃənl] ADJ [*lie, insult*] deliberado; [*omission, injury, infliction of pain*] intencionado, deliberado • **if I offended you it wasn't ~** si te ofendí fue sin querer *or* no fue a propósito

intentionally [ɪnˈtenʃnəlɪ] ADV [*do, hurt, discriminate*] a propósito, adrede; [*mislead*] intencionadamente • **he believed he had been ~ misled** creía que había sido engañado intencionadamente *or* de forma intencionada • **the figures are ~ misleading** las cifras están presentadas de manera equívoca a propósito • **~ homeless** [*person*] *que se queda sin hogar intencionalmente* • **they claim that he became ~ homeless** aseguran que se quedó sin hogar intencionalmente

intently [ɪnˈtentlɪ] ADV atentamente, fijamente

intentness [ɪnˈtentnɪs] N (= *concentration*) atención *f*; [*of gaze*] intensidad *f* • **~ of purpose** resolución *f*

inter [ɪnˈtɜːʳ] VT enterrar, sepultar

inter... [ˈɪntəʳ] PREFIX inter..., entre...

interact [ˌɪntərˈækt] VI influirse mutuamente, interactuar • **to ~ with sb** relacionarse con algn

interaction [ˌɪntərˈækʃən] N interacción *f*, interrelación *f*

interactive [ˌɪntərˈæktɪv] ADJ (*also Comput*) interactivo

interactively [ˌɪntərˈæktɪvlɪ] ADV (*also Comput*) interactivamente

interactivity [ˌɪntərækˈtɪvɪtɪ] N interactividad *f*

inter alia [ˌɪntərˈælɪə] ADV entre otros

inter-bank [ˈɪntəˌbæŋk] ADJ interbancario
CPD ▸ **inter-bank loan** préstamo *m* entre bancos ▸ **inter-bank rate** tasa *f* de descuento entre bancos

interbreed [ˈɪntəˈbriːd] (PT, PP: **interbred** [ˈɪntəˈbred]) VT cruzar
VI cruzarse

intercalate [ɪnˈtɜːkəleɪt] VT intercalar

intercalation [ɪnˌtɜːkəˈleɪʃən] N intercalación *f*

intercede [ˌɪntəˈsiːd] VI interceder (**for** por, **with** con) • **to ~ on sb's behalf** interceder por algn

intercept [ˌɪntəˈsept] VT (= *interfere with*) [+ *message, missile*] interceptar; (= *stop*) detener; (= *cut off*) atajar, cortar; (*Sport*) [+ *pass*] cortar, interceptar; (*Math*) cortar

interception [ˌɪntəˈsepʃən] N [*of message, missile*] intercepción *f*; (*Sport*) corte *m*, intercepción *f*

interceptor [ˌɪntəˈseptəʳ] N interceptor *m*

intercession [ˌɪntəˈseʃən] N intercesión *f*, mediación *f*

interchange VT [ˌɪntəˈtʃeɪndʒ] **1** (= *exchange*) [+ *views, ideas*] intercambiar, cambiar; [+ *prisoners, publications*] canjear
2 (= *alternate*) alternar
N [ˈɪntətʃeɪndʒ] **1** [*of views, ideas*] intercambio *m*, cambio *m*; [*of prisoners, publications*] canje *m*
2 (*on motorway etc*) nudo *m* de carreteras, paso *m* elevado, paso *m* a desnivel (*LAm*)

interchangeable [ˌɪntəˈtʃeɪndʒəbl] ADJ intercambiable

interchangeably [ˌɪntəˈtʃeɪndʒəblɪ] ADV de manera intercambiable, intercambiando los dos *etc*

intercity [ˈɪntəˈsɪtɪ] N (*Brit*) (*Rail*) (*also* **intercity train**) tren *m* interurbano, tren *m* intercity (*Sp*)
ADJ interurbano, intercity (*Sp*)

intercollegiate [ˈɪntəkəˈliːdʒɪɪt] ADJ interuniversitario

intercom* [ˈɪntəkɒm] N intercomunicador *m*, interfono *m*

intercommunicate [ˌɪntəkəˈmjuːnɪkeɪt] VI [*people, rooms*] comunicarse

intercommunication [ˈɪntəkəˌmjuːnɪˈkeɪʃən] N intercomunicación *f*

intercommunion [ˌɪntəkəˈmjuːnɪən] N intercomunión *f*

inter-company [ˌɪntəˈkʌmpənɪ] ADJ • **inter-company relations** relaciones *fpl* entre compañías

interconnect [ˌɪntəkəˈnekt] VT (*Elec, Comput*) interconectar • **all these problems are ~ed** todos estos problemas están interrelacionados
VI [*concepts*] interrelacionarse; [*trains*] enlazar

interconnecting [ˌɪntəkəˈnektɪŋ] ADJ [*rooms*] comunicados; [*door, tunnel*] de comunicación; [*trains*] con correspondencia

interconnection [ˌɪntəkəˈnekʃən] N interconexión *f*

intercontinental [ˈɪntəˌkɒntɪˈnentl] ADJ intercontinental
CPD ▸ **intercontinental ballistic missile** misil *m* balístico intercontinental

intercostal [ˌɪntəˈkɒstl] ADJ intercostal

intercourse [ˈɪntəkɔːs] N **1** (*frm*) relaciones *fpl*, trato *m*; (*Comm*) comercio *m*
2 (*also* **sexual intercourse**) acto *m* sexual, coito *m* • **to have (sexual) ~ with sb** tener relaciones sexuales con algn

intercross [ˌɪntəˈkrɒs] (*Bio*) VT [+ *animals, plants*] cruzar
VI cruzarse
N cruce *m*

intercultural [ˌɪntəˈkʌltʃərəl] ADJ intercultural

intercut [ˌɪntəˈkʌt] VT alternar • **to be ~ with** (*Cine*) alternarse con

interdenominational [ˈɪntədɪˌnɒmɪˈneɪʃənl] ADJ interconfesional

interdepartmental [ˈɪntəˌdiːpɑːtˈmentl] ADJ interdepartamental

interdependence [ˌɪntədɪˈpendəns] N interdependencia *f*

interdependent [ˌɪntədɪˈpendənt] ADJ interdependiente

interdict [ˈɪntədɪkt] N entredicho *m*, interdicto *m*
VT (= *stop*) [+ *enemy shipping, aircraft, communications*] interceptar; (= *prohibit*) prohibir

interdiction [ˌɪntəˈdɪkʃən] N (*Rel*) interdicción *f*; (*Mil*) intercepción *f*

interdisciplinary [ˌɪntəˈdɪsɪplɪnərɪ] ADJ interdisciplinario

interest [ˈɪntrɪst] N **1** (= *curiosity*) interés *m* • **to arouse sb's ~** despertar el interés de algn • **to have an ~ in sth** estar interesado en algo • **I have no further ~ in talking to them** ya no estoy interesado en hablar con ellos • **to lose ~ (in sth)** perder el interés (por *or* en algo) • **of ~**: • **the guidebook describes all the places of ~** la guía describe todos los lugares de interés • **it is of no ~ to us** no nos interesa • **is this of any ~ to you?** ¿te interesa esto? • **I'm doing it just out of ~** lo hago simplemente porque me interesa • **just out of ~, how much did it cost?** por simple curiosidad, ¿cuánto costó? • **to show (an) ~ (in sth/sb)** mostrar interés (por *or* en algo/por algn) • **to take an ~ in sth/sb** interesarse por *or* en algo/por algn • **he took no ~ in his children** no se interesaba por sus hijos
2 (= *hobby*) interés *m* • **my main ~ is reading** mi interés principal *or* mi pasatiempo favorito es la lectura • **what are your ~s?** ¿qué cosas te interesan? • **special ~ holidays** vacaciones *fpl* de grupos con un interés común
3 (= *profit, advantage*) interés *m* • **a conflict of ~s** un conflicto de intereses • **in sb's ~(s)**: • **it is in your own ~ to confess** te conviene confesar • **it is not in his ~ to sell the house** no le conviene vender la casa • **they acted in the best ~s of their members** obraron en el mejor interés de sus miembros • **in the ~s of hygiene** por razones de higiene • **in the ~s of national unity** con el fin de preservar la unidad nacional; ▹ **heart, public, vested**
4 (= *share, stake*) (*gen*) interés *m*; (*in company*) participación *f* • **he has sold his ~ in the company** ha vendido su participación en la empresa • **British ~s in the Middle East** los intereses británicos en el Medio Oriente • **he has business ~s abroad** tiene negocios en el extranjero • **to have a controlling/financial ~ in a company** tener una participación mayoritaria/tener acciones en una compañía • **to have an ~ in sth** (*gen*) tener interés *or* estar interesado en algo; (*in company*) tener participación en algo • **the West has an ~ in promoting democracy there** Occidente tiene interés *or* está interesado en promover allí la democracia
5 (*Econ*) (*on loan, shares, savings*) interés *m* • **to bear ~** devengar *or* dar intereses • **it bears ~ at 5%** devenga *or* da un interés del 5% • **compound ~** interés *m* compuesto • **to earn ~** cobrar intereses • **the ~ on an investment** los intereses de una inversión • **simple ~** interés *m* simple • **shares that yield a high ~** acciones *fpl* que rinden bien • IDIOM: • **to repay sth/sb with ~**: • **I repaid his bad manners with ~!** ¡le devolví los malos modales con creces!
VT **1** (= *arouse interest*) interesar • **it may ~ you to know that ...** puede que te interese saber que ... • **can I ~ you in a new car?** ¿estaría interesado en comprar un coche nuevo?
2 (= *concern*) interesar • **the struggle against inflation ~s us all** la lucha contra la inflación nos interesa a todos
CPD ▸ **interest charges** intereses *mpl* ▸ **interest group** grupo *m* de gente con un mismo interés ▸ **interest payments** pago *m* de intereses ▸ **interest rate** tipo *m* *or* tasa *f* de interés

interest-bearing [ˈɪntrɪstˌbeərɪŋ] ADJ con interés

interested [ˈɪntrɪstɪd] ADJ interesado • **she seems very ~** parece muy interesada • **anyone ~ should apply in writing to ...** cualquier persona interesada debe dirigirse por escrito a ... • **I've got some books to sell, are you ~?** tengo unos libros que quiero vender, ¿te interesan? • **I'm going to the canteen, if anybody is ~** voy a la cafetería, si alguien se quiere apuntar • **to be ~ in sth**: • **he's ~ in buying a car** está interesado en comprar un coche • **I'm not ~ in football** no me interesa el fútbol • **would you be ~ in my old wardrobe?** ¿te interesaría quedarte con mi armario viejo? • **to become** *or* **grow** *or* **get ~ in sth/sb** interesarse por algn/algo • **to get sb ~ in sth** hacer que algn se interese por algo • **I tried to get him ~ in opera** intenté hacer que se interesase por la ópera • **I soon got her ~ in my idea** pronto conseguí tenerla interesada en mi idea, pronto conseguí que se interesase por mi idea • **the ~ party** la parte interesada • **she was ~ to see what he would do** tenía curiosidad por ver qué es lo que haría • **I'd be ~ to know the outcome** me interesaría saber el resultado

interest-free [ˌɪntrɪstˈfriː] ADJ sin interés

interesting [ˈɪntrɪstɪŋ] ADJ interesante • **it is ~ that** es interesante el hecho de que • **it was ~ for me** me pareció interesante • **that's an ~ point** ese es un punto interesante • **it will be ~ to see what happens** será interesante ver lo que ocurre

interestingly [ˈɪntrɪstɪŋlɪ] ADV [*speak, write*] de manera interesante • **~ enough, I've been there before** curiosamente, ya he estado allí

interface [ˈɪntəfeɪs] N (*Comput*) interfaz *m* *or f*, interface *m* *or f*
VI • **to ~ with** conectar con; (*Comput*) comunicarse mediante interfaz con

interfacing [ˈɪntəfeɪsɪŋ] N (= *interconnection*) interconexión *f*; (*Sew*) entretela *f*

interfaith [ˌɪntəˈfeɪθ] ADJ [*relations, dialogue*] interreligioso

interfere [ˌɪntəˈfɪəʳ] VI **1** (= *pry, intrude*) entrometerse, meterse (**in** en) • **he's always interfering** se mete en todo • **who told you to ~?** ¿quién te mete a ti en esto? • **stop interfering!** ¡deja de entrometerte!
2 (= *meddle*) • **to ~ with sth** manosear *or* tocar algo • **who has been interfering with the TV?** ¿quién ha estado tocando la televisión?
3 (= *hinder*) • **to ~ with sth** afectar a algo • **it mustn't ~ with my work** no debe afectar a mi trabajo • **I don't want to ~ with your plans** no quiero interferir con tus planes
4 (*Rad, TV*) • **to ~ with sth** interferir con algo

interference [ˌɪntəˈfɪərəns] N **1** (= *intrusion*) intromisión *f*
2 (*Rad, TV*) interferencia *f*

interfering [ˌɪntəˈfɪərɪŋ] ADJ [*neighbour*] entrometido

interferon [ˌɪntəˈfɪərɒn] N interferón *m*

intergalactic [ˌɪntəgəˈlæktɪk] ADJ intergaláctico

intergovernmental [ˌɪntəˌgʌvnˈmentl] ADJ intergubernamental

interim [ˈɪntərɪm] N • **in the ~** en el ínterin *or* interín
ADJ [*president*] interino, provisional;

[*measure, government, report, result*] provisional
CPD ▸ **interim dividend** dividendo *m* a cuenta ▸ **interim payment** pago *m* a cuenta ▸ **the interim period** el ínterin *or* interín ▸ **interim profits** (*Econ, Comm*) beneficios *mpl* trimestrales

interior [ɪn'tɪərɪəʳ] ADJ **1** (= *inside*) [*door, wall, decor*] interior
2 (*Geog*) (= *central*) interior
3 (*Pol*) (= *domestic*) [*affairs*] interno; [*minister, department*] del interior
4 (*frm*) (= *inner*) [*life, world*] interior; [*thoughts*] íntimo
N **1** (= *inside*) [*of building, container, car*] interior *m*
2 (*Geog*) (= *centre*) • **the ~** el interior (**of** de)
3 (*Pol*) (*in titles*) • **Minister of the Interior** Ministro/a *m/f* del Interior • **Ministry of the Interior** Ministerio *m* del Interior, Secretaría *f* de Gobernación (*Mex*)
CPD ▸ **interior angle** (*Math*) ángulo *m* interno ▸ **interior decoration** interiorismo *m* ▸ **interior decorator** interiorista *mf* ▸ **interior design** interiorismo *m*, decoración *f* de interiores ▸ **interior designer** interiorista *mf* ▸ **interior light** (*in car*) luz *f* de dentro ▸ **interior sprung mattress** colchón *m* de muelles

interject [ˌɪntə'dʒekt] VT [+ *question, remark*] interponer • **"that's not true," he ~ed** —eso no es cierto— interpuso él

interjection [ˌɪntə'dʒekʃən] N (= *exclamation*) exclamación *f*; (*Ling*) interjección *f*; (= *insertion*) interposición *f*

interlace [ˌɪntə'leɪs] VT entrelazar
VI entrelazarse

interlard [ˌɪntə'lɑːd] VT • **to ~ with** salpicar de, entreverar de

interleaf ['ɪntəˌliːf] N hoja *f* interfoliada

interleave [ˌɪntə'liːv] VT interfoliar, intercalar; (*Comput*) intercalar

interleaving [ˌɪntə'liːvɪŋ] N interfoliación *f*, intercalación *f*; (*Comput*) intercalación *f*

inter-library [ˌɪntə'laɪbrərɪ] ADJ • **inter-library loan** préstamo *m* interbibliotecario

interline [ˌɪntə'laɪn] VT **1** (*Typ*) interlinear, intercalar entre líneas
2 (*Sew*) entretelar

interlinear [ˌɪntə'lɪnɪəʳ] ADJ interlineal

interlink [ˌɪntə'lɪŋk] VT [+ *issues, interests*] interrelacionar, vincular • **the two issues are ~ed** las dos cuestiones están interrelacionadas, las dos cuestiones están vinculadas (entre sí)
VI interrelacionarse

interlock [ˌɪntə'lɒk] VT trabar, entrelazar; [+ *wheels*] endentar, engranar
VI trabarse, entrelazarse; [*wheels*] endentarse, engranar • **the parts of the plan ~** las partes del plan tienen una fuerte trabazón
N **1** (*Mech*) enclavamiento *m*
2 [*of fabric*] • **cotton ~ underwear** ropa *f* interior de algodón de punto

interlocutor [ˌɪntə'lɒkjʊtəʳ] N (*frm*) interlocutor(a) *m/f*

interloper ['ɪntələʊpəʳ] N intruso/a *m/f*

interlude ['ɪntəluːd] N intervalo *m*, intermedio *m*; (*in theatre*) intermedio *m*; (= *musical interlude*) interludio *m*

intermarriage [ˌɪntə'mærɪdʒ] N (*between races*) matrimonio *m* mixto; (*between relatives*) matrimonio *m* entre parientes

intermarry ['ɪntə'mærɪ] VI (*gen*) casarse entre sí; (*within family*) casarse entre parientes

intermediary [ˌɪntə'miːdɪərɪ] N intermediario/a *m/f*
ADJ intermediario

intermediate [ˌɪntə'miːdɪət] ADJ [*stage*] intermedio • **the course is available on three levels: beginner, ~ and advanced** el curso consta de tres niveles: elemental, medio *or* intermedio y avanzado
N intermediario/a *m/f*
CPD ▸ **intermediate range ballistic missile** misil *m* balístico de alcance intermedio ▸ **intermediate range weapon** arma *f* de alcance medio ▸ **intermediate stop** escala *f* ▸ **intermediate technology** tecnología *f* media

interment [ɪn'tɜːmənt] N entierro *m*, sepelio *m*

intermezzo [ˌɪntə'metsəʊ] N (PL: **intermezzos** *or* **intermezzi** [ˌɪntə'metsiː]) intermezzo *m*

interminable [ɪn'tɜːmɪnəbl] ADJ [*speech, rain, journey etc*] interminable

interminably [ɪn'tɜːmɪnəblɪ] ADV interminablemente

intermingle [ˌɪntə'mɪŋgl] VT entremezclar
VI entremezclarse

intermission [ˌɪntə'mɪʃən] N (= *pause*) interrupción *f*, intermisión *f*; (*between events*) intervalo *m*; (*Theat*) intermedio *m* • **it went on without ~** continuó sin interrupción

intermittent [ˌɪntə'mɪtənt] ADJ intermitente

intermittently [ˌɪntə'mɪtəntlɪ] ADV a ratos, a intervalos • **it rained ~** llovía a ratos *or* a intervalos • **they worked/met ~** trabajaban/se veían de cuando en cuando

intern VT [ɪn'tɜːn] internar, recluir
N ['ɪntɜːn] (*US*) (= *doctor*) interno/a *m/f*; (= *student on placement*) alumno/a *m/f* en prácticas

internal [ɪn'tɜːnl] ADJ **1** [*wall*] interior; [*affairs, conflict, divisions*] interno
2 (*Med*) [*bleeding, examination, organ, injury*] interno
CPD ▸ **internal audit** auditoría *f* interna ▸ **internal combustion engine** motor *m* de combustión interna *or* de explosión ▸ **internal market** mercado *m* interno *or* interior ▸ **Internal Revenue Service** (*US*) ≈ Hacienda *f*

internalization [ɪnˌtɜːnəlaɪ'zeɪʃən] N interiorización *f*

internalize [ɪn'tɜːnəlaɪz] VT interiorizar

internally [ɪn'tɜːnəlɪ] ADV **1** (= *within organization, country*) internamente
2 (= *within o.s.*) por dentro, internamente
3 (*Med*) [*bleed*] internamente • **"not to be taken internally"** "solo para uso externo"

international [ˌɪntə'næʃnəl] ADJ (*gen*) internacional
N (*Brit*) (*Sport*) (= *match*) partido *m* internacional; (= *player*) internacional *mf*
CPD ▸ **International Atomic Energy Agency** Organización *f* Internacional de Energía Atómica ▸ **the International Brigade** las Brigadas Internacionales ▸ **International Court of Justice** Corte *f* Internacional de Justicia ▸ **international date line** línea *f* de cambio de fecha ▸ **International Labour Organization** Organización *f* Internacional del Trabajo ▸ **international law** derecho *m* internacional ▸ **International Monetary Fund** Fondo *m* Monetario Internacional ▸ **international money order** giro *m* postal internacional ▸ **international relations** relaciones *fpl* internacionales ▸ **international reply coupon** cupón *m* de respuesta internacional ▸ **International Standards Organization** Organización *f* Internacional de Normalización

Internationale [ˌɪntəˌnæʃə'nɑːl] N • **the ~** la Internacional

internationalism [ˌɪntə'næʃnəlɪzəm] N internacionalismo *m*

internationalist [ˌɪntə'næʃnəlɪst] ADJ internacionalista
N internacionalista *mf*

internationalization [ˌɪntənæʃnəlaɪ'zeɪʃən] N [*of issue, business*] internacionalización *f* • **the increasing ~ of business** la creciente internacionalización de los negocios

internationalize [ˌɪntə'næʃnəlaɪz] VT internacionalizar

internationally [ˌɪntə'næʃnəlɪ] ADV [*function, compete*] internacionalmente; [*known, recognized*] mundialmente

internecine [ˌɪntə'niːsaɪn] ADJ [*strife, feud, warfare*] intestina
CPD ▸ **internecine war** guerra *f* de aniquilación mutua

internee [ˌɪntɜː'niː] N prisionero/a *m/f* de guerra (*civil*)

internet ['ɪntənet] N • **the ~** (el *or* la) Internet • **on the ~** [*shop, read, meet*] en Internet • **over the ~** [*book, distribute, send, sell*] por Internet • **via the ~** por Internet
CPD ▸ **internet access** acceso *m* a Internet ▸ **internet bank** banca *f* por Internet, banca *f* en Internet ▸ **internet café** cibercafé *m* ▸ **internet connection** conexión *f* a Internet ▸ **internet phone** teléfono *m* por Internet ▸ **internet phone call** llamada *f* telefónica por Internet ▸ **internet phone service** servicio *m* de teléfono por Internet ▸ **internet service provider** servidor *m*, proveedor *m* de servicios de Internet ▸ **internet site** sitio *m* en Internet ▸ **internet surfer, internet user** internauta *mf*, cibernauta *mf*

internist ['ɪntɜːnɪst] N (*US*) internista *mf*

internment [ɪn'tɜːnmənt] N internamiento *m*
CPD ▸ **internment camp** campo *m* de internamiento

internship ['ɪntɜːnʃɪp] N (*US*) **1** (*Med*) ≈ internado *m*
2 (*in company, organization*) periodo *m* de prácticas

interoperability [ˌɪntərɒpərə'bɪlɪtɪ] N (*Comput*) interoperabilidad *f*

interparty ['ɪntə'pɑːtɪ] ADJ interpartidario

interpersonal [ˌɪntə'pɜːsənl] ADJ interpersonal
CPD ▸ **interpersonal skills** habilidades *fpl* interpersonales

interphone ['ɪntəˌfəʊn] N interfono *m*

interplanetary [ˌɪntə'plænɪtərɪ] ADJ interplanetario

interplay ['ɪntəpleɪ] N interacción *f*

Interpol ['ɪntəˌpɒl] N ABBR (= **International Criminal Police Organization**) Interpol *f*

interpolate [ɪn'tɜːpəleɪt] VT interpolar

interpolation [ɪnˌtɜːpə'leɪʃən] N interpolación *f*

interpose [ˌɪntə'pəʊz] VT **1** (= *insert*) interponer • **she tried to ~ herself between them** trató de interponerse entre ellos
2 [+ *remark*] interponer • **"never!" ~d John** —¡jamás! —interpuso John

interpret [ɪn'tɜːprɪt] VT **1** (= *translate orally*) traducir, interpretar
2 (= *explain, understand*) interpretar • **how are we to ~ that remark?** ¿cómo hemos de interpretar ese comentario? • **that is not how I ~ it** yo no lo entiendo así, yo lo entiendo de otro modo
VI (= *translate*) traducir; (= *work as interpreter*) trabajar de intérprete

interpretation [ɪnˌtɜːprɪ'teɪʃən] N (*gen*) interpretación *f*; (*Ling*) interpretación *f*, traducción *f* • **what ~ am I to place on your**

conduct? ¿cómo he de interpretar tu conducta? • **the words bear another ~** las palabras pueden interpretarse de otro modo
interpretative [ɪnˈtɜːprɪtətɪv] ADJ = interpretive
interpreter [ɪnˈtɜːprɪtəʳ] N intérprete *mf*
interpreting [ɪnˈtɜːprɪtɪŋ] N interpretación *f*
interpretive [ɪnˈtɜːprɪtɪv] ADJ [*skills, process*] interpretativo
interracial [ˌɪntəˈreɪʃəl] ADJ (= *between races*) interracial; (= *multiracial*) multirracial
interregnum [ˌɪntəˈregnəm] N (PL: **interregnums** *or* **interregna** [ˌɪntəˈregnə]) interregno *m*
interrelate [ˌɪntərɪˈleɪt] VT interrelacionar VI interrelacionarse
interrelated [ɪntərɪˈleɪtɪd] ADJ interrelacionado
interrelation [ˌɪntərɪˈleɪʃən] N interrelación *f*
interrelationship [ˌɪntərɪˈleɪʃənʃɪp] N interrelación *f*
interrogate [ɪnˈterəgeɪt] VT [+ *person*] interrogar, someter a un interrogatorio; (*Comput*) interrogar
interrogation [ɪnˌterəˈgeɪʃən] N interrogatorio *m*; (*Comput*) interrogación *f*
CPD ▸ **interrogation mark, interrogation point** (*US*) signo *m* de interrogación, punto *m* de interrogación ▸ **interrogation room** sala *f* de interrogatorios
interrogative [ˌɪntəˈrɒgətɪv] ADJ [*look, tone*] interrogador; (*Ling*) [*pronoun*] interrogativo
N (*Ling*) interrogativo *m* • **in the ~** en (forma) interrogativa
interrogatively [ˌɪntəˌrɒgətɪvlɪ] ADV • **he looked up/looked at me ~** levantó la mirada/me miró con gesto interrogante
interrogator [ɪnˈterəgeɪtəʳ] N interrogador(a) *m/f*
interrogatory [ˌɪntəˈrɒgətərɪ] ADJ interrogante
interrupt [ˌɪntəˈrʌpt] VT interrumpir
VI interrumpir • **sorry to ~, but …** perdonen que les interrumpa, pero …, siento interrumpir, pero …
interrupter [ˌɪntəˈrʌptəʳ] N (*Elec*) interruptor *m*
interruption [ɪntəˈrʌpʃən] N interrupción *f* • **I need to be able to work without ~** necesito poder trabajar sin interrupciones *or* sin que nadie me interrumpa
intersect [ˌɪntəˈsekt] VT (*Math*) cortar
VI (*Math*) cortarse, intersecarse; [*roads*] cruzarse
intersection [ˌɪntəˈsekʃən] N (= *crossing*) intersección *f*, cruce *m*; (*Math*) intersección *f*
intersperse [ˌɪntəˈspɜːs] VT • **a border of begonias ~d with geraniums** un arriate de begonias entremezcladas *or* intercaladas con geranios • **a speech ~d with jokes** un discurso salpicado de chistes • **sunny periods ~d with showers** periodos *mpl* de sol con intervalos de chubascos irregulares
interstate [ˌɪntəˈsteɪt] ADJ [*relations, commerce*] interestatal, entre estados; (*US*) [*highway*] interestatal
interstellar [ˌɪntəˈsteləʳ] ADJ interestelar
interstice [ɪnˈtɜːstɪs] N intersticio *m*
intertextuality [ˌɪntətekstjʊˈælɪtɪ] N intertextualidad *f*
intertwine [ˌɪntəˈtwaɪn] VI [*limbs, fingers, plants*] entrelazarse; [*fates, destinies*] cruzarse, entrecruzarse
VT [+ *limbs, fingers, plants*] entrelazar; [+ *fates, destinies*] cruzar, entrecruzar; [+ *interests*] interrelacionar
interurban [ˌɪntɜːˈɜːbən] ADJ interurbano

interval [ˈɪntəvəl] N **1** (*in time, space*) intervalo *m*; (*Theat*) intermedio *m*; (*more formally*) entreacto *m*; (*Sport*) (= *half time*) descanso *m* • **at ~s** (*in time*) a intervalos; (*in space*) a intervalos, cada cierta distancia • **at regular ~s** (*in time, space*) a intervalos regulares • **baste the meat at ~s of 15 minutes** *or* **at 15-minute ~s** rocíe la carne con su jugo cada 15 minutos • **sunny ~s** claros *mpl* • **there was an ~ for meditation** se hizo una pausa para la meditación
2 (*Mus*) intervalo *m*
intervene [ˌɪntəˈviːn] VI **1** (= *take part*) [*person*] intervenir, tomar parte (**in** en); [*government*] intervenir (**in** en)
2 (= *step in*) [*person*] interponerse; [*fate*] cruzarse, interponerse • **we were to marry but the war ~d** íbamos a casarnos pero se interpuso la guerra • **to ~ (with sb) on sb's behalf** interceder por algn (ante algn)
3 (= *crop up*) surgir, sobrevenir • **if nothing ~s to prevent it** si no surge nada que lo impida
intervening [ˌɪntəˈviːnɪŋ] ADJ intermedio • **in the ~ period** en el ínterin *or* interín • **in the ~ years** en el transcurso de esos años
intervention [ˌɪntəˈvenʃən] N (*gen*) intervención *f*
CPD ▸ **intervention price** precio *m* de intervención
interventionism [ˌɪntəˈvenʃənɪzəm] N intervencionismo *m*
interventionist [ˌɪntəˈvenʃənɪst] ADJ intervencionista
N intervencionista *mf*
interview [ˈɪntəvjuː] N entrevista *f*; (*for press, TV*) entrevista *f*, interviú *f or m* • **to have an ~ with sb** entrevistarse con algn
VT [+ *person*] entrevistar; (*for press, TV*) hacer una entrevista *or* interviú a • **3% of those ~ed did not know that …** un 3 por cien de los entrevistados ignoraba que …
VI • **they are ~ing for this post tomorrow** mañana realizarán las entrevistas para este puesto • **I don't ~ very well** no se me dan muy bien las entrevistas
interviewee [ˈɪntəˌvjuːˈiː] N entrevistado/a *m/f*
interviewer [ˈɪntəvjuːəʳ] N (*on radio, for job*) entrevistador(a) *m/f*
inter vivos [ˈɪntəˈviːvɒs] ADJ (*Jur*) • **~ gift** donación *f* inter vivos
inter-war [ˌɪntəˈwɔːʳ] ADJ • **the inter-war years** el período de entreguerras
interweave [ˌɪntəˈwiːv] (PT: **interwove**, PP: **interwoven**) VT entretejer
intestate [ɪnˈtestɪt] ADJ • **to die ~** morir intestado
intestinal [ˌɪntesˈtaɪnl] ADJ [*tract, complaint*] intestinal
intestine [ɪnˈtestɪn] N intestino *m* • **small/large ~** intestino *m* delgado/grueso
intifada [ˌɪntɪˈfɑːdə] N intifada *f*
intimacy [ˈɪntɪməsɪ] N **1** (= *closeness*) intimidad *f* • **I read the letter in the ~ of my bedroom** leí la carta en la intimidad de mi habitación • **there had never been any sexual ~ between them** nunca habían mantenido relaciones íntimas • **the ~ of his knowledge on the subject** su profundo conocimiento de la materia
2 intimacies (*spoken*) intimidades *fpl*; (*sexual*) intimidad *f* (física), proximidad *f* (física)
intimate ADJ [ˈɪntɪmɪt] [*relationship, contact, conversation, meal*] íntimo; [*friend*] íntimo, de confianza; [*friendship, connection*] íntimo, estrecho; [*details*] íntimo, personal • **it's an ~ little restaurant** es un pequeño restaurante de ambiente íntimo • **an ~ atmosphere** un ambiente íntimo • **to be/become ~ with sb** (*friendly*) intimar con algn; (*sexually*) tener relaciones (íntimas) con algn • **~ hygiene** (*euph*) higiene *f* íntima • **to have an ~ knowledge of a subject** tener un profundo conocimiento de una materia, conocer una materia a fondo • **he had an ~ knowledge of the city** conocía muy bien la ciudad • **to be on ~ terms with sb** ser íntimo de algn
VT [ˈɪntɪmeɪt] insinuar, dar a entender • **he ~d his approval** insinuó *or* dio a entender que lo aprobaba • **she ~d that she was ready for a change** insinuó *or* dio a entender que estaba lista para un cambio • **he ~d to the president that …** le insinuó *or* le dio a entender al presidente que …
N [ˈɪntɪmɪt] amigo/a *m/f* de confianza; (*pej*) compinche *mf*
intimately [ˈɪntɪmɪtlɪ] ADV íntimamente • **to be ~ acquainted with sb** (*in a friendly way*) conocer a algn íntimamente • **to be ~ acquainted with a subject** tener un profundo conocimiento de una materia, conocer una materia a fondo • **to be ~ involved in sth** estar muy involucrado en algo • **Inspector Green was ~ involved in the case** el Inspector Green estaba muy involucrado en el caso *or* estaba metido a fondo en el caso • **to know sb ~** (*as friends*) conocer a algn íntimamente; (*sexually*) tener relaciones íntimas con algn • **musicians whose work she knew ~** músicos *mpl* cuyo trabajo conocía a fondo *or* en profundidad • **to talk ~** tener una conversación íntima
intimation [ˌɪntɪˈmeɪʃən] N **1** (= *suggestion*) indicación *f* • **it was the first ~ we had had of it** fue la primera indicación que tuvimos de ello • **did you have any ~ that this would happen?** ¿hubo algo que te hiciera pensar que esto sucedería?
2 (= *hint*) insinuación *f* • **her ~ that there would be redundancies worried me** su insinuación de que habría despidos me preocupó
intimidate [ɪnˈtɪmɪdeɪt] VT intimidar
intimidated [ɪnˈtɪmɪdeɪtɪd] ADJ intimidado • **to feel ~** sentirse intimidado • **women can come in here and not feel ~** las mujeres pueden venir aquí sin sentirse intimidadas
intimidating [ˌɪnˈtɪmɪdeɪtɪŋ] ADJ amedrentador, intimidante
intimidation [ɪnˌtɪmɪˈdeɪʃən] N intimidación *f*
intimidatory [ɪnˌtɪmɪˈdeɪtərɪ] ADJ intimidatorio
into [ˈɪntʊ] PREP

> *When* **into** *is an element in a phrasal verb, eg* **break into, enter into, look into, walk into,** *look up the verb*

1 (*of place*) en, dentro de • **put it ~ the car/bag/cupboard** mételo en el *or* dentro del coche/bolso/armario • **to get ~ bed** meterse a la cama • **to get ~ a car** subir(se) a un coche • **he helped his mother ~ the car** ayudó a su madre a subir al coche • **to go ~ the country** ir al campo • **I poured the milk ~ a cup** vertí la leche en una taza • **he went off ~ the desert** partió hacia el interior del desierto *or* adentrándose en el desierto • **he went further ~ the forest** siguió adentrándose en el bosque • **it fell ~ the lake** se cayó al lago • **they got ~ the plane** subieron al avión • **to come/go ~ a room** entrar en una habitación • **to go ~ town** ir al centro de la ciudad • **to go ~ the wood** adentrarse *or* penetrar en el bosque; ▹ **go into**
2 (*of time*) • **it continued well** *or* **far ~ 1996** siguió hasta bien entrado 1996 • **we talked**

far ~ the night charlamos hasta bien entrada la noche • **he's well ~ his fifties** tiene cincuenta y tantos largos
3 (*change in condition etc*) • **to change ~ a monster** volverse un *or* convertirse en un monstruo • **to change pounds ~ dollars** cambiar libras por dólares • **the rain changed ~ snow** la lluvia se convirtió en nieve • **they divided ~ two groups** se dividieron en dos grupos • **to translate sth ~ Spanish** traducir algo al español • **it turned ~ a pleasant day** resultó *or* se hizo un día muy agradable; ▸ **burst into, change, divide, grow, translate, turn**
4 (*Math*) • **to divide 3 ~ 12** dividir doce entre tres • **2 ~ 6 goes 3** seis entre dos son tres
5 • **to be ~ sth***: **he is really ~ jazz** es un gran aficionado al *or* del jazz • **to be ~ drugs** meterse drogas, andar metido en drogas • **she's ~ health food** le va mucho lo de la comida sana • **what are you ~ now?** ¿a qué te dedicas ahora? • **the children/puppies are ~ everything!** ¡los críos/perritos andan revolviéndolo todo!

intolerable [ɪnˈtɒlərəbl] ADJ intolerable • **this is ~!** ¡esto es intolerable! • **it is ~ that** es intolerable que (+ *subjun*), no se puede consentir que (+ *subjun*)

intolerably [ɪnˈtɒlərəblɪ] ADV [*ache*] insoportablemente • **he is ~ vain** es tremendamente vanidoso • **it was ~ hot** hacía un calor insoportable

intolerance [ɪnˈtɒlərəns] N (*gen*) intolerancia *f*; (= *bigotry*) intransigencia *f*; (*Med*) intolerancia *f* (**to, of** a) • **food ~** intolerancia *f* a los alimentos

intolerant [ɪnˈtɒlərənt] ADJ (*gen*) intolerante (**of**) con *or* para con; (= *bigoted*) intransigente (**of** con) • **to be ~ of sth** (*gen*) no tolerar algo; (*Med*) • **he is ~ of certain drugs/foods** tiene intolerancia a ciertos medicamentos/alimentos, su cuerpo no tolera ciertos medicamentos/alimentos

intonate [ˈɪntəʊneɪt] VT (*Ling*) entonar

intonation [ˌɪntəʊˈneɪʃən] N entonación *f*

intone [ɪnˈtəʊn] VT entonar; (*Rel*) salmodiar

in toto [ɪnˈtəʊtəʊ] ADV en total, en conjunto

intoxicant [ɪnˈtɒksɪkənt] ADJ embriagador
N (= *drink*) bebida *f* alcohólica; (= *drug*) estupefaciente *m*

intoxicate [ɪnˈtɒksɪkeɪt] VT **1** (*lit*) (*frm*) [*alcohol*] embriagar; [*poison*] intoxicar
2 (*fig*) (*liter*) [*victory, success, beauty*] embriagar (*liter*)

intoxicated [ɪnˈtɒksɪkeɪtɪd] ADJ **1** (*lit*) (*frm*) (= *drunk*) ebrio, en estado de embriaguez • **to become ~** alcanzar un estado de embriaguez
2 (*fig*) (*liter*) embriagado (*liter*), ebrio • **to be ~ by sth** (*by victory, success*) estar embriagado *or* ebrio a causa de algo • **to be ~ with sth** estar embriagado *or* ebrio de algo • **to feel ~** sentirse embriagado

intoxicating [ɪnˈtɒksɪkeɪtɪŋ] ADJ **1** (*frm*) (*lit*) [*substance*] narcótico, estupefaciente • **an ~ mixture of gin and vodka** una mezcla de ginebra y vodka con un efecto narcótico • **~ drink** *or* **liquor** bebida *f* alcohólica
2 (*fig*) (*liter*) [*success, perfume, atmosphere*] embriagador

intoxication [ɪnˌtɒksɪˈkeɪʃən] N **1** (*by alcohol*) embriaguez *f*, intoxicación *f* etílica (*frm or hum*); (*Med*) (*by toxic substance*) intoxicación *f*
2 (*fig*) (*liter*) embriaguez *f*

intra... [ˈɪntrə] PREFIX intra...

intractability [ɪnˌtræktəˈbɪlətɪ] N [*of person*] intratabilidad *f*; [*of situation*] dificultad *f*; [*of problem*] insolubilidad *f*; (*Med*) [*of illness*] incurabilidad *f*

intractable [ɪnˈtræktəbl] ADJ [*person*] intratable; (= *unruly*) indisciplinado; [*problem*] insoluble, espinoso; [*illness*] incurable

intraday [ˈɪntrədeɪ] ADJ (*St Ex*) intradía (*inv*), de intradía

intramural [ˌɪntrəˈmjʊərəl] ADJ (*US*) (*Univ*) dentro de la universidad; (= *within organization, country*) interno

intramuscular [ˌɪntrəˈmʌskjʊləʳ] ADJ intramuscular

intranet [ˈɪntrənet] N (*Comput*) intranet *f*

intransigence [ɪnˈtrænsɪdʒəns] N intransigencia *f*

intransigent [ɪnˈtrænsɪdʒənt] ADJ intransigente

intransitive [ɪnˈtrænsɪtɪv] ADJ (*Ling*) intransitivo
CPD ▸ **intransitive verb** verbo *m* intransitivo

intransitivity [ɪnˌtrænsɪˈtɪvɪtɪ] N intransitividad *f*

intrauterine [ˌɪntrəˈjuːtəraɪn] ADJ intrauterino
CPD ▸ **intrauterine device** dispositivo *m* intrauterino; (*coil-shaped*) espiral *f*

intravenous [ˌɪntrəˈviːnəs] ADJ intravenoso
CPD ▸ **intravenous drip** suero *f* intravenoso, gota *m inv* a gota intravenoso ▸ **intravenous drug use** consumo *m* de drogas por vía intravenosa • **a history of ~ drug use** antecedentes de consumo de drogas por vía intravenosa ▸ **intravenous drug user** drogadicto/a *m/f* que se inyecta por vía intravenosa

intravenously [ˌɪntrəˈviːnəslɪ] ADV por vía intravenosa

in-tray [ˈɪnˌtreɪ] N bandeja *f* de entrada

intrepid [ɪnˈtrepɪd] ADJ intrépido

intrepidity [ˌɪntrɪˈpɪdɪtɪ] N (*frm*) intrepidez *f*

intrepidly [ɪnˈtrepɪdlɪ] ADV intrépidamente

intricacy [ˈɪntrɪkəsɪ] N [*of pattern, design, machinery*] lo intrincado, complejidad *f*; [*of plot, problem*] complejidad *f* • **the intricacies of the law** los entresijos de la ley

intricate [ˈɪntrɪkɪt] ADJ [*pattern, design, machinery*] intrincado; [*plot, problem*] complejo

intricately [ˈɪntrɪkɪtlɪ] ADV intrincadamente, de modo intrincado

intrigue [ɪnˈtriːg] N (= *plot*) intriga *f*; (*amorous*) aventura *f* (sentimental), amorío *m* • **a web of ~** una maraña de intriga
VT fascinar • **I am ~d to know whether ...** me intriga saber si ..., estoy intrigado por saber si ... • **we were ~d by a sign outside a shop** nos llamó la atención el letrero de una tienda
VI intrigar (**against** contra)

intriguer [ɪnˈtriːgəʳ] N intrigante *mf*

intriguing [ɪnˈtriːgɪŋ] ADJ (= *fascinating*) [*question, problem*] intrigante; [*prospect, possibility*] fascinante; [*personality*] misterioso, enigmático • **a most ~ problem** un problema de lo más intrigante • **an ~ little gadget** un chisme curiosísimo *or* de lo más curioso • **how very ~!** ¡qué raro!, ¡muy interesante!
N intriga *f*

intriguingly [ɪnˈtriːgɪŋlɪ] ADV • **~, this was never confirmed** curiosamente, esto nunca fue confirmado • **~ different** intrigantemente diferente • **~ original** de una originalidad fascinante

intrinsic [ɪnˈtrɪnsɪk] ADJ intrínseco • **~ value** valor *m* intrínseco • **stress is ~ to the job** el estrés es algo inherente al trabajo • **the harp and fiddle are ~ to Irish music** el arpa y el violín son intrínsecos a *or* característicos de la música irlandesa

intrinsically [ɪnˈtrɪnsɪklɪ] ADV intrínsecamente

intro* [ˈɪntrəʊ] N (*Mus*) (= **introduction**) entrada *f*

intro... [ˈɪntrəʊ] PREFIX intro...

introduce [ˌɪntrəˈdjuːs] VT **1** (= *present, make acquainted*) presentar • **to ~ sb to sb** presentar a algn a algn • **may I ~ ...?** permítame presentarle a ..., le presento a ... • **I don't think we've been ~d** creo que no nos han presentado • **to ~ sb to sth** hacer conocer algo a algn, iniciar a algn en algo • **I was ~d to chess at eight** empecé a jugar al ajedrez a los ocho años • **I was ~d to Milton too young** me hicieron leer a Milton demasiado temprano
2 (= *bring in*) [+ *reform*] introducir; (*Pol*) [+ *bill*] presentar; (*TV, Rad*) [+ *programme*] presentar; [+ *product, new fashion*] lanzar; [+ *subject into conversation, idea*] introducir • **be careful how you ~ the subject** ten cuidado a la hora de abordar el tema • **it was you who ~d the subject, not me** fuiste tú el que sacaste el tema, no yo
3 (= *insert*) introducir • **the tube is ~d into the throat** el tubo se introduce por la garganta • **I was ~d into a dark room** me hicieron entrar en un cuarto oscuro
4 (= *write introduction for*) [+ *book*] prologar

introduction [ˌɪntrəˈdʌkʃən] N **1** [*of person*] presentación *f* • **to give sb an ~ to sb** dar a algn una carta de recomendación para algn • **a letter of ~** una carta de recomendación • **will you do** *or* **make the ~s?** ¿quieres hacer las presentaciones?
2 (= *initiation*) introducción *f* • **this book is a good ~ to his teachings** este libro es una buena introducción a sus enseñanzas • **my ~ to life in Cadiz** mi primera experiencia de la vida en Cádiz • **my ~ to maths** mi iniciación en las matemáticas
3 (*in book*) prólogo *m*, introducción *f*
4 (= *bringing in*) [*of legislation*] introducción *f*; (*Pol*) [*of bill*] presentación *f*
5 (= *insertion*) introducción *f*, inserción *f*

introductory [ˌɪntrəˈdʌktərɪ] ADJ [*remarks*] preliminar; [*lecture, talk*] introductorio, de introducción; [*course*] introductorio, de iniciación
CPD ▸ **introductory offer** oferta *f* de lanzamiento

introit [ˈɪntrɔɪt] N introito *m*

introspection [ˌɪntrəʊˈspekʃən] N introspección *f*

introspective [ˌɪntrəʊˈspektɪv] ADJ introspectivo

introspectiveness [ˌɪntrəʊˈspektɪvnɪs] N introspección *f*

introversion [ˌɪntrəʊˈvɜːʃən] N introversión *f*

introvert [ˈɪntrəʊvɜːt] ADJ introvertido
N introvertido/a *m/f*

introverted [ˌɪntrəʊˈvɜːtɪd] ADJ introvertido

intrude [ɪnˈtruːd] VI **1** (= *intervene*) entrometerse, inmiscuirse (**on, upon** en); (= *disturb*) molestar • **am I intruding?** ¿les molesto? • **to ~ on** *or* **upon sb** molestar a algn • **to ~ on sb's privacy** meterse en la vida privada de algn • **we mustn't ~ on their grief** debemos respetar la intimidad de su dolor
2 (= *encroach*) • **sometimes sentimentality ~s** a veces se asoma el sentimentalismo • **it kept intruding into my thoughts** siguió

interfiriendo en mis pensamientos
(VT) [+ *views, opinions*] imponer (**on, upon** a); [+ *subject*] introducir (sin derecho) • **I haven't come to ~ myself upon you** no he venido para molestarles con mi presencia

intruder [ɪn'tru:dəʳ] (N) intruso/a *m/f*
(CPD) ▸ **intruder alarm** alarma *f* contra intrusos

intrusion [ɪn'tru:ʒən] (N) intrusión *f*; (*on sb's privacy*) intromisión *f*, invasión *f* • **pardon the ~** siento tener que importunarla • **the ~ of sentimentality** la intrusión del sentimentalismo

intrusive [ɪn'tru:sɪv] (ADJ) [*reporter*] entrometido, indiscreto; [*question*] indiscreto; [*noise, presence*] molesto

intubate ['ɪntjʊbeɪt] (VT) (*Med*) intubar

intubation [,ɪntjʊ'beɪʃən] (N) (*Med*) intubación *f*

intuit [ɪn'tjʊɪt] (VT) (*esp US*) intuir

intuition [,ɪntju:'ɪʃən] (N) intuición *f*

intuitive [ɪn'tju:ɪtɪv] (ADJ) [*knowledge*] intuitivo; [*powers*] de intuición • **she had an ~ grasp of what was needed** intuía qué era lo que hacía falta

intuitively [ɪn'tju:ɪtɪvlɪ] (ADV) intuitivamente, por intuición

Inuit ['ɪnjʊɪt] (PL: **Inuit, Inuits**) (ADJ) Inuit (*inv*)
(N) Inuit *mf*, esquimal *mf* • **the ~s** los Inuit

inundate ['ɪnʌndeɪt] (VT) inundar • **we have been ~d with replies** nos hemos visto inundados *or* desbordados por las respuestas

inundation [,ɪnʌn'deɪʃən] (N) inundación *f*

inure [ɪn'jʊəʳ] (VT) (= *accustom*) acostumbrar, habituar (**to a**) • **to be ~d to sth** estar acostumbrado *or* habituado a algo • **to become ~d to sth** acostumbrarse *or* habituarse a algo

inv. (ABBR) (= **invoice**) f.ª

invade [ɪn'veɪd] (VT) (*Mil*) invadir; [+ *privacy*] invadir; [+ *sb's rights*] usurpar

invader [ɪn'veɪdəʳ] (N) invasor(a) *m/f*

invading [ɪn'veɪdɪŋ] (ADJ) invasor

invalid¹ ['ɪnvəlɪd] (N) inválido/a *m/f*, minusválido/a *m/f*
(ADJ) inválido, minusválido
(CPD) ▸ **invalid car, invalid carriage** coche *m* de minusválido, coche *m* de inválido
▸ **invalid chair** (*Brit*) silla *m* para minusválidos
▸ **invalid out** (VT + ADV) • **to ~ sb out of the army** (*esp Brit*) (*Mil*) licenciar a algn por invalidez

invalid² [ɪn'vælɪd] (ADJ) [*contract*] inválido, nulo; [*ticket, request*] inválido; [*theory, results, conclusions*] sin validez • **to become ~** caducar

invalidate [ɪn'vælɪdeɪt] (VT) [+ *document, argument, theory*] invalidar; [+ *contract*] anular, invalidar

invalidity [,ɪnvə'lɪdɪtɪ] (N) **1** [*of document, contract*] invalidez *f*, nulidad *f*
2 (= *illness, disablement*) invalidez *f*
(CPD) ▸ **invalidity benefit** (*Brit*) prestación *f* por invalidez ▸ **invalidity pension** pensión *f* de invalidez

invaluable [ɪn'væljʊəbl] (ADJ) inapreciable, inestimable

invariable [ɪn'veərɪəbl] (ADJ) invariable

invariably [ɪn'veərɪəblɪ] (ADV) invariablemente, siempre • **it ~ happens that ...** ocurre siempre que ... • **he is ~ late** siempre llega tarde, llega tarde invariablemente

invasion [ɪn'veɪʒən] (N) invasión *f* • **~ force** fuerza *f* invasora • **it would be an ~ of privacy to ...** sería una invasión de la intimidad ...

invasive [ɪn'veɪsɪv] (ADJ) [*surgery, cancer*] invasivo

invective [ɪn'vektɪv] (N) (= *accusation*) invectiva *f*; (= *abuse*) improperios *mpl*, palabras *fpl* fuertes

inveigh [ɪn'veɪ] (VI) • **to ~ against** vituperar, lanzar invectivas contra

inveigle [ɪn'vi:gl] (VT) • **she ~d him up to her room** lo indujo mañosamente a subir a su habitación • **to ~ sb into doing sth** inducir a algn mediante engaño a que haga algo • **he let himself be ~d into it** se dejó inducir a ello • **he was ~d into the duke's service** fue inducido hábilmente a entrar a servir al duque

invent [ɪn'vent] (VT) inventar

invention [ɪn'venʃən] (N) **1** (= *act*) invención *f*; (= *machine*) invento *m*, invención *f*
2 (= *inventiveness*) inventiva *f*
3 (= *falsehood*) mentira *f*, invención *f* • **it's pure ~** es pura invención • **it's ~ from start to finish** es mentira desde el principio hasta el fin

inventive [ɪn'ventɪv] (ADJ) (= *creative*) ingenioso, lleno de inventiva • **to have an ~ mind** tener ingenio *or* inventiva • **he's an ~ cook** es un cocinero con mucha inventiva *or* muy imaginativo • **~ powers** capacidad *f* inventiva, inventiva *f*

inventively [ɪn'ventɪvlɪ] (ADV) con inventiva *or* imaginación

inventiveness [ɪn'ventɪvnɪs] (N) inventiva *f*, ingenio *m*

inventor [ɪn'ventəʳ] (N) inventor(a) *m/f*

inventory ['ɪnvəntrɪ] (N) inventario *m* • **to draw up an ~ of sth** hacer un inventario de algo
(VT) inventariar
(CPD) ▸ **inventory control** control *m* de existencias *or* de inventario

inverse ['ɪn'vɜ:s] (ADJ) inverso
(N) • **the ~** lo inverso, lo contrario

inversely [ɪn'vɜ:slɪ] (ADV) a la inversa • **A is ~ proportional to B** A es inversamente proporcional a B • **interest rates and prices are ~ related** las tasas de interés y los precios guardan una relación inversamente proporcional

inversion [ɪn'vɜ:ʃən] (N) inversión *f*

invert [ɪn'vɜ:t] (VT) invertir, poner al revés

invertebrate [ɪn'vɜ:tɪbrɪt] (ADJ) invertebrado
(N) invertebrado/a *m/f*

inverted [ɪn'vɜ:tɪd] (ADJ) • **~ commas** (*Brit*) comillas *fpl* • **in ~ commas** entre comillas • **~ snob** *persona que desprecia las actitudes propias de la clase social a la que pertenece, intentando identificarse con gente de una clase supuestamente inferior* • **~ snobbery** esnobismo *m* regresivo

invert sugar ['ɪnvɜ:t'ʃʊgəʳ] (N) azúcar *m* invertido

invest [ɪn'vest] (VT) **1** [+ *money, capital, funds*] invertir (**in** en); [+ *person*] (*in office*) investir; (*fig*) [+ *time, effort*] dedicar • **~ed capital** capital *m* invertido
2 • **to ~ sb with sth** investir a algn de *or* con algo • **he was ~ed with a dignity** lo invistieron con una dignidad • **he ~ed it with a certain mystery** lo revistió de cierto misterio • **he seems to ~ it with some importance** parece que lo reviste de cierta importancia
3 (*Mil*†) sitiar, cercar
(VI) • **to ~ in** [+ *company, project*] invertir dinero en; (*hum*) (= *buy*) comprarse • **I've ~ed in a new pair of rubber gloves** me he comprado un nuevo par de guantes de goma • **to ~ with** [+ *bank, building society*] invertir dinero en

investigate [ɪn'vestɪgeɪt] (VT) **1** (= *inquire into*) [+ *crime, case*] investigar; [+ *person*] hacer indagaciones sobre; [+ *claim, possibility*] examinar, estudiar; [+ *complaint*] estudiar • **police are investigating two possibilities** la policía está investigando dos posibles pistas
2 (= *inspect*) examinar
3 (= *research*) investigar, llevar a cabo una investigación sobre
(VI) investigar • **I heard a noise downstairs, I'd better go and ~** he oído un ruido abajo, mejor que vaya a investigar

investigation [ɪn,vestɪ'geɪʃən] (N)
1 (= *inquiry*) (*by police, authorities, scientist*) investigación *f* • **the ~ into the causes of the accident** la investigación sobre las causas del accidente • **these allegations need further ~** estas acusaciones se tienen que investigar más a fondo
2 (= *inspection, search*) [*of place, site*] inspección *f*; [*of document*] examen *m*; (*Med*) exploración *f* • **doctors carried out a simple ~ under local anaesthetic** los médicos realizaron una simple exploración utilizando anestesia local
3 (= *in-depth study*) estudio *m* (**of, into** de)

investigative [ɪn'vestɪ,geɪtɪv] (ADJ) investigador
(CPD) ▸ **investigative journalism** periodismo *m* de investigación

investigator [ɪn'vestɪgeɪtəʳ] (N) investigador(a) *m/f*

investigatory [ɪn'vestɪ,geɪtərɪ] (ADJ) [*committee, panel*] investigador

investiture [ɪn'vestɪtʃəʳ] (N) investidura *f*

investment [ɪn'vestmənt] (N) **1** (*Comm*) inversión *f*
2 (*Mil*†) sitio *m*, cerco *m*
3 (= *investiture*) investidura *f*
(CPD) ▸ **investment analyst** analista *mf* financiero/a ▸ **investment bank** banco *m* de inversión ▸ **investment banker** banquero/a *m/f* de inversión ▸ **investment company** compañía *f* de inversiones ▸ **investment grant** subvención *f* para la inversión
▸ **investment income** renta *f* de inversiones
▸ **investment portfolio** cartera *f* de valores
▸ **investment trust** sociedad *f* de inversiones

investor [ɪn'vestəʳ] (N) inversionista *mf*

inveterate [ɪn'vetərɪt] (ADJ) [*gambler*] empedernido; [*laziness, selfishness*] inveterado

invidious [ɪn'vɪdɪəs] (ADJ) [*job, task*] odioso, ingrato; [*comparison*] injusto • **I find myself in an ~ position** me encuentro en una situación ingrata • **it would be ~ to mention names** sería inapropiado mencionar nombres

invigilate [ɪn'vɪdʒɪleɪt] (*Brit*) (VT) [+ *examination*] vigilar
(VI) vigilar (durante los exámenes)

invigilation [ɪn,vɪdʒɪ'leɪʃən] (N) (*Brit*) vigilancia *f* • **to do (the) ~** vigilar (durante los exámenes)

invigilator [ɪn'vɪdʒɪleɪtəʳ] (N) (*Brit*) celador(a) *m/f* (*en un examen*)

invigorate [ɪn'vɪgəreɪt] (VT) [+ *person*] vigorizar; [+ *campaign*] dar nuevo ímpetu a; [+ *economy*] estimular • **I felt refreshed, ~d and ready to tackle anything** me sentía descansado, lleno de energía y dispuesto a abordar cualquier tarea

invigorating [ɪn'vɪgəreɪtɪŋ] (ADJ) [*walk, shower, air*] vigorizante, tonificante • **how ~ she was to talk to!** ¡qué estimulante resultaba su conversación!

invincibility [ɪn,vɪnsɪ'bɪlɪtɪ] (N) invencibilidad *f*

invincible [ɪn'vɪnsəbl] ADJ [*army, team*] invencible; [*faith, belief*] inquebrantable • **he has an ~ lead over the other runners** les lleva una ventaja insuperable al resto de los corredores

invincibly [ɪn'vɪnsəblɪ] ADV • **the army marched ~ across Europe** el ejército cruzó Europa invencible

inviolability [ɪn,vaɪələ'bɪlɪtɪ] N inviolabilidad *f*

inviolable [ɪn'vaɪələbl] ADJ inviolable

inviolably [ɪn'vaɪələblɪ] ADV inviolablemente

inviolate [ɪn'vaɪəlɪt] ADJ [*land, possessions*] intacto; (*liter*) [*woman*] intacto, sin mancillar (*liter*)

invisibility [ɪn,vɪzə'bɪlɪtɪ] N invisibilidad *f*

invisible [ɪn'vɪzəbl] ADJ (*gen*) (*Comm*) invisible
NPL **invisibles** (*Comm*) ingresos *mpl* invisibles
CPD ▸ **invisible assets** activo *msing* invisible ▸ **invisible earnings** ingresos *mpl* invisibles ▸ **invisible exports** exportaciones *fpl* invisibles ▸ **invisible imports** importaciones *fpl* invisibles ▸ **invisible ink** tinta *f* simpática ▸ **invisible mending** zurcido *m* invisible

invisibly [ɪn'vɪzɪblɪ] ADV de manera invisible

invitation [,ɪnvɪ'teɪʃən] N invitación *f* • **an ~ to dinner** • **a dinner ~** una invitación para cenar • **I am here at the ~ of the director** he venido por invitación del director • **the house is an ~ to robbers** la casa es toda una atracción para los ladrones
CPD ▸ **invitation card** tarjeta *f* de invitación

invitational [,ɪnvɪ'teɪʃənl] ADJ (*Sport*) [*event, tournament*] invitacional (*en el que solo participan deportistas invitados*)

invite VT [ɪn'vaɪt] **1** [+ *person*] invitar; (*esp to important celebration*) convidar • **to ~ sb to do sth** invitar a algn a hacer algo • **to ~ sb to dinner/lunch** invitar a algn a cenar/almorzar • **to ~ sb to have a drink** invitar a algn a tomar algo • **to ~ sb in/up** invitar a algn a pasar/subir • **to ~ sb out** invitar a algn a salir • **they ~d me out to dinner** me invitaron a cenar (a un restaurante) • **I've ~d them over for drinks** los he invitado a tomar unas copas en casa
2 (= *request*) [+ *opinions*] pedir; (*more frm*) solicitar • **they are inviting applications for the post of ...** han abierto el plazo para recibir solicitudes para el puesto de ...
3 (= *provoke*) [+ *discussion, ridicule*] provocar • **to ~ trouble** buscarse problemas • **to do so would be to ~ defeat** hacer eso sería provocar la propia derrota • **A ~s comparison with B** A nos induce a compararlo con B • **she seems to ~ stares** parece que provoca las miradas de la gente
N* ['ɪnvaɪt] invitación *f*

inviting [ɪn'vaɪtɪŋ] ADJ **1** (= *appealing*) [*atmosphere, place, room*] acogedor; [*prospect*] atractivo; [*appearance*] (*of person*) atrayente; (*of food*) tentador; [*food*] apetitoso, apetecible; [*smell*] apetitoso; [*book*] que incita a la lectura, que invita a la lectura • **the water looked warm and ~** el agua aparecía cálida y tentadora • **she offered him the plate with an ~ smile** le ofreció el plato animándole a comer con una sonrisa • **with an ~ gesture, she showed him to his room** le hizo un gesto invitándole a seguirla y le enseñó su habitación
2 (= *seductive*) [*smile, look, gesture*] incitante, sugerente

invitingly [ɪn'vaɪtɪŋlɪ] ADV **1** (= *appealingly, welcomingly*) • **the food was displayed ~** la comida estaba dispuesta de forma atrayente • **"are you hungry?" she said ~** —¿tienes hambre? —dijo en un tono que invitaba a decir que sí • **"come in," he said ~** —entrad —dijo invitándoles a pasar • **the soup steamed ~** la sopa echaba un vaporcito que invitaba a comerla • **the water was ~ clear** el agua cristalina invitaba a bañarse • **the packet lay ~ open** el paquete estaba abierto de forma tentadora
2 (= *seductively*) [*smile, gesture*] de forma sugerente, de forma incitante; [*say, whisper*] en tono sugerente

in vitro [ɪn'vi:trəʊ] ADJ, ADV in vitro
CPD ▸ **in vitro fertilization** fecundación *f* in vitro

invocation [,ɪnvəʊ'keɪʃən] N invocación *f*

invoice ['ɪnvɔɪs] N factura *f* • **as per ~** según factura • **to send an ~** pasar *or* presentar factura
VT [+ *goods*] facturar • **to ~ sb for sth** pasar a algn factura por algo • **you will be ~d once the goods have been delivered** le pasaremos factura *or* le mandaremos la factura una vez le haya sido entregada la mercancía
CPD ▸ **invoice clerk** facturador(a) *m/f* ▸ **invoice value** valor *m* total de factura

invoicing ['ɪnvɔɪsɪŋ] N facturación *f*

invoke [ɪn'vəʊk] VT [+ *law*] recurrir *or* acogerse a, invocar; [+ *principle*] recurrir a, invocar; [+ *aid, protection, god, spirit*] invocar

involuntarily [ɪn'vɒləntərɪlɪ] ADV involuntariamente • **he had ~ hurt her feelings** la había ofendido sin querer

involuntary [ɪn'vɒləntərɪ] ADJ involuntario

involuted [,ɪnvə'lu:tɪd] ADJ [*design, system*] intrincado

involve [ɪn'vɒlv] VT **1** (= *implicate, associate*) implicar, involucrar • **a dispute involving a friend of mine** una disputa en la que estaba implicado *or* involucrado un amigo mío • **a crash involving three vehicles** una colisión en la que se vieron envueltos tres vehículos • **to ~ sb (in sth)** involucrar a algn (en algo) • **we would prefer not to ~ the children** preferiríamos no meter *or* involucrar a los niños • **they are trying to ~ him in the theft** están intentando implicarlo *or* involucrarlo en el robo • **try to ~ him in your leisure activities** intenta hacer que participe contigo en tus actividades de tiempo libre • **it may ~ you in extra cost** puede acarrearle costos adicionales • **the persons ~d** (*gen*) los interesados; (= *culprits*) los implicados • **to be ~d (in sth)**: • **how did he come to be ~d?** ¿cómo llegó a meterse en esto? • **he was ~d in a fight** se vio envuelto en una pelea • **he/his car was ~d in an accident** él/su coche se vio involucrado en un accidente • **she was only ~d in the final stages of the project** solo tomó parte en las fases finales del proyecto • **I was so ~d in my book that ...** estaba tan absorto en el libro que ... • **to become** *or* **get ~d (in sth)**: • **the police became ~d** la policía tomó cartas en el asunto • **I don't want to get ~d** no quiero meterme • **to get ~d in a fight** verse envuelto en una pelea • **to be/become/get ~d with sth/sb**: • **she's so ~d with the project she doesn't have time for me** está tan liada* con el proyecto que no tiene tiempo para mí, el proyecto la absorbe tanto que no tiene tiempo para mí • **she became ~d with the resistance movement** se involucró en el movimiento de resistencia • **she got ~d with some really weird people** se mezcló con una gente muy rara • **she likes him but she doesn't want to get ~d** él le gusta, pero no quiere comprometerse
2 (= *entail, imply*) suponer • **it ~d a lot of expense** supuso *or* acarreó muchos gastos • **there's a good deal of work ~d** supone *or* implica bastante trabajo • **the job ~s moving to London** el trabajo requiere que se traslade a Londres • **what does your job ~?** ¿en qué consiste su trabajo? • **how much money is ~d?** ¿cuánto dinero hay en juego? • **a question of principle is ~d** aquí hay principios en juego

involved [ɪn'vɒlvd] ADJ (= *complicated*) complicado, enrevesado

involvement [ɪn'vɒlvmənt] N **1** (= *implication, association*) • **we don't know the extent of his ~** no sabemos hasta qué punto está implicado • **a demonstration against US ~ in Vietnam** una manifestación contra la intervención estadounidense en Vietnam • **student ~ in campus affairs** la participación de los estudiantes en los asuntos universitarios • **I knew of his past ~ with drugs** sabía que en el pasado había estado metido en drogas
2 (= *relationship*) relación *f* • **she didn't know about my ~ with Corinne** no sabía de mi relación con Corinne

invulnerability [ɪn,vʌlnərə'bɪlɪtɪ] N invulnerabilidad *f* (**to** a)

invulnerable [ɪn'vʌlnərəbl] ADJ invulnerable (**to** a)

inward ['ɪnwəd] ADJ **1** (= *inner*) [*peace, happiness*] interior • **she gave an ~ sigh** suspiró para sus adentros • **Bridget watched him with an ~ smile** Bridget lo observó sonriendo para sus adentros • **I sighed with ~ relief** suspiré sintiendo gran alivio por dentro
2 (= *incoming*) [*flow, movement*] hacia el interior
ADV = **inwards**
CPD ▸ **inward investment** inversiones *fpl* extranjeras ▸ **inward investor** inversor(a) *m/f* extranjero/a

inward-looking ['ɪnwəd,lʊkɪŋ] ADJ [*person*] introvertido • **the country/company is too inward-looking** el país está muy encerrado en sí mismo/la compañía está muy encerrada en sí misma

inwardly ['ɪnwədlɪ] ADV [*think, sigh, groan, smile*] para sus adentros; [*know, struggle*] en su interior; [*feel*] por dentro • **she was ~ furious** por dentro estaba furiosa • **she felt ~ relieved** se sintió aliviada por dentro • **the house was outwardly clean but ~ filthy** la casa estaba limpia por fuera pero asquerosa por dentro

inwards ['ɪnwədz] ADV (*Brit*) hacia dentro • **the soil had subsided, pushing the walls ~** el suelo se había hundido, haciendo que los muros se fueran hacia dentro • **his frustration and anger turned ~** su frustración y su rabia se volvieron hacia su interior • **the door swung ~** la puerta se abrió hacia dentro
NPL* ['ɪnədz] = **innards**

in-your-face‡, **in-yer-face**‡ [,ɪnjə'feɪs] ADJ [*attitude, music, theatre*] agresivo y descarado

I/O ABBR (*Comput*) (= **input/output**) E/S
CPD ▸ **I/O error** error *m* de E/S

IOC N ABBR (= **International Olympic Committee**) COI *m*

iodide ['aɪədaɪd] N yoduro *m*

iodine ['aɪədi:n] N yodo *m*

iodoform [aɪ'ɒdəfɔ:m] N yodoformo *m*

IOM ABBR (*Brit*) = **Isle of Man**

ion ['aɪən] N ion *m*

Ionian [aɪ'əʊnɪən] ADJ jonio, jónico
CPD ▸ **Ionian Sea** Mar *m* Jónico

Ionic [aɪ'ɒnɪk] ADJ jónico

ionic [aɪ'ɒnɪk] ADJ (*Chem*) iónico

ioniser ['aɪənaɪzəʳ] = ionizer

ionization [,aɪənaɪ'zeɪʃən] N ionización *f*

ionize ['aɪənaɪz] VT ionizar

ionizer ['aɪənaɪzəʳ] N ionizador *m*

ionosphere [aɪ'ɒnəsfɪəʳ] N ionosfera *f*

iota [aɪ'əʊtə] N (= *letter*) iota *f*; (*fig*) pizca *f*, ápice *m* • **there's not one ~ of truth in it** eso no tiene ni pizca de verdad • **if he had an ~ of sense** si tuviera un pizca de inteligencia

IOU N ABBR (= **I owe you**) pagaré *m*, vale *m* (*LAm*)

IOW ABBR (*Brit*) = **Isle of Wight**

IPA N ABBR = **International Phonetic Alphabet**

IP address [aɪ'piːə,dres] N (*Comput*) (= **internet protocol address**) dirección *f* IP

ipecacuanha [,ɪpɪkækjʊ'ænə] N ipecacuana *f*

IPO N ABBR (*St Ex*) (= **initial public offering**) OPI *f* (*oferta pública inicial*)

iPod® ['aɪpɒd] N iPod® *m*

IP phone [aɪ'piːfəʊn] N (= **internet protocol phone**) teléfono *m* IP

ipso facto [,ɪpsəʊ'fæktəʊ] ADV ipso facto

IPTV N ABBR (= **internet protocol television**) IPTV *f*

IQ N ABBR (= **intelligence quotient**) C.I. *m*

IR N ABBR (*Brit*) = **Inland Revenue**

IRA N ABBR **1** (= **Irish Republican Army**) IRA *m*
2 (*US*) = **individual retirement account**

Irak [ɪ'rɑːk] = **Iraq**

Iraki [ɪ'rɑːkɪ] = **Iraqi**

Iran [ɪ'rɑːn] N Irán *m*

Iranian [ɪ'reɪnɪən] ADJ iraní
N (*ancient*) iranio/a *m/f*; (*modern*) iraní *mf*

Iraq [ɪ'rɑːk] N Irak *m*, Iraq *m*

Iraqi [ɪ'rɑːkɪ] ADJ iraquí
N iraquí *mf*

irascibility [ɪ,ræsɪ'bɪlɪtɪ] N irascibilidad *f*

irascible [ɪ'ræsɪbl] ADJ irascible, colérico

irascibly [ɪ'ræsɪblɪ] ADV • **he said ~** dijo colérico

irate [aɪ'reɪt] ADJ indignado, furioso • **he got very ~** se indignó mucho, se puso furioso

IRBM N ABBR = **intermediate range ballistic missile**

IRC N ABBR (= **Internet Relay Chat**) *sistema de mensajería instantánea que permite chatear en grupo o entre dos personas*

ire [aɪəʳ] N (*liter*) ira *f*, cólera *f* • **to rouse sb's ire** provocar la ira de algn

Ireland ['aɪələnd] N Irlanda *f* • **Northern ~** Irlanda *f* del Norte • **Republic of ~** República *f* de Irlanda

iridescence [,ɪrɪ'desns] N irisación *f*

iridescent [,ɪrɪ'desnt] ADJ iridiscente, irisado, tornasolado

iridium [ɪ'rɪdɪəm] N iridio *m*

iris ['aɪərɪs] N (PL: **irises**) **1** (*Anat*) iris *m inv*
2 (*Bot*) lirio *m*

Irish ['aɪərɪʃ] ADJ irlandés
N **1** • **the ~** (= *people*) los irlandeses
2 (*Ling*) irlandés *m*
CPD ▸ **Irish coffee** café *m* irlandés ▸ **Irish stew** estofado *m* irlandés ▸ **the Irish Free State** el Estado Libre de Irlanda ▸ **the Irish Sea** el Mar de Irlanda ▸ **Irish setter** setter *m* irlandés

Irishman ['aɪərɪʃmən] N (PL: **Irishmen**) irlandés *m*

Irishwoman ['aɪərɪʃ,wʊmən] N (PL: **Irishwomen**) irlandesa *f*

irk [ɜːk] VT fastidiar, molestar

irksome ['ɜːksəm] ADJ [*child, chore*] fastidioso, pesado

IRN N ABBR (*Brit*) (= **Independent Radio News**) *servicio de noticias en las cadenas de radio privadas*

IRO N ABBR **1** (*Brit*) = **Inland Revenue Office**
2 (*US*) (= **International Refugee Organization**) OIR *f*

iron ['aɪən] N **1** (= *metal*) hierro *m*, fierro *m* (*LAm*) • **cast ~** hierro *m* colado • **corrugated ~** chapa *f* ondulada • **old ~** chatarra *f*, hierro *m* viejo • **to have an ~ constitution** tener una constitución de hierro • **with an ~ hand** *or* **fist** con mano de hierro • **a man of ~** un hombre de hierro • **a will of ~** una voluntad férrea *or* de hierro • IDIOMS: • **to have a lot of/too many ~s in the fire** tener muchos/demasiados asuntos entre manos • **the ~ fist in the velvet glove** la mano de hierro en guante de terciopelo • **to strike while the ~ is hot** a hierro candente batir de repente
2 irons (= *fetters*) grilletes *mpl*, grillos *mpl* • **to put** *or* **clap sb in ~s** poner grilletes *or* grillos a algn, aherrojar a algn
3 (*Golf*) hierro *m*
4 (*for ironing clothes*) plancha *f*
5 (*for branding*) hierro *m* candente
6* (= *gun*) pistola *f*
VT [+ *clothes*] planchar
VI [*person*] planchar • **this blouse ~s really well** esta blusa es muy fácil de planchar
CPD [*bridge, bar, tool*] de hierro, de fierro (*LAm*); (*fig*) [*will, determination*] férreo ▸ **the Iron Age** la Edad de hierro ▸ **the iron and steel industry** la industria siderúrgica ▸ **Iron Cross** cruz *f* de hierro ▸ **the Iron Curtain** (*Hist, Pol*) el telón de acero, la cortina de hierro (*LAm*) • **the Iron Curtain Countries** los países más allá del telón de acero ▸ **the Iron Duke** el Duque de Wellington ▸ **iron foundry** fundición *f*, fundidora *f* (*LAm*) ▸ **the Iron Lady** (*Brit*) (*Pol*) la Dama de Hierro ▸ **iron lung** (*Med*) pulmón *m* de acero ▸ **iron ore** mineral *m* de hierro ▸ **iron oxide** óxido *m* de hierro ▸ **iron pyrites** pirita *f* ferruginosa ▸ **iron rations** ración *f* or víveres *mpl* de reserva
▸ **iron out** VT + ADV [+ *unevenness*] allanar; [+ *crease*] quitar, planchar; [+ *difficulties*] allanar, suprimir; [+ *problems*] resolver • **they managed to ~ out their differences** consiguieron resolver sus diferencias

ironclad ['aɪənklæd] ADJ acorazado; (*fig*) [*proof*] irrefutable, incontrovertible; [*alibi*] incontrovertible, incuestionable
N acorazado *m*

ironic [aɪ'rɒnɪk] ADJ irónico

ironical [aɪ'rɒnɪkəl] ADJ = ironic

ironically [aɪ'rɒnɪkəlɪ] ADV irónicamente; [*say etc*] con ironía • **~ enough** paradójicamente, como quiso la suerte

ironing ['aɪənɪŋ] N (= *act*) planchado *m*; (= *clothes*) (*awaiting ironing*) ropa *f* por planchar; (*ironed*) ropa *f* planchada • **to do the ~** planchar • **to give a dress an ~** planchar un vestido
CPD ▸ **ironing board** tabla *f* de planchar

ironist ['aɪərənɪst] N ironista *mf* • **the master ~** el maestro de la ironía

ironmonger ['aɪən,mʌŋgəʳ] N (*Brit*) ferretero/a *m/f*, quincallero/a *m/f* • **~'s (shop)** ferretería *f*, quincallería *f*

ironmongery ['aɪən,mʌŋgərɪ] N (*Brit*) (= *ironware*) quincalla *f*, ferretería *f* (*also fig*)

ironstone ['aɪən,stəʊn] N (= *china*) porcelana *f* resistente

ironwork ['aɪənwɜːk] N (*on piece of furniture*) herraje *m*; (*on building*) obra *f* de hierro

ironworks ['aɪənwɜːks] N (*sing and pl*) fundición *f*

irony ['aɪərənɪ] N ironía *f* • **the ~ of fate** las ironías del destino • **life's little ironies** las (pequeñas) ironías de la vida • **the ~ of it is that ...** lo irónico es que ...

Iroquois ['ɪrəkwɔɪ] ADJ iroqués
N **1** iroqués/esa *m/f*
2 (*Ling*) iroqués *m*

irradiate [ɪ'reɪdɪeɪt] VT irradiar

irradiation [ɪ,reɪdɪ'eɪʃən] N irradiación *f*

irrational [ɪ'ræʃənl] ADJ [*behaviour, person, belief*] irracional

irrationality [ɪ,ræʃə'nælɪtɪ] N irracionalidad *f*

irrationally [ɪ'ræʃnəlɪ] ADV irracionalmente

irreconcilable [ɪ,rekən'saɪləbl] ADJ [*enemies*] irreconciliable; [*ideas*] incompatible
CPD ▸ **irreconcilable differences** diferencias *fpl* irreconciliables

irrecoverable [,ɪrɪ'kʌvərəbl] ADJ irrecuperable; [*debt*] irrecuperable, incobrable

irredeemable [,ɪrɪ'diːməbl] ADJ irredimible; (*Econ*) perpetuo, no amortizable

irredeemably [,ɪrɪ'diːməblɪ] ADV irremediablemente • **~ lost/ruined** irremediablemente perdido/destruido

irredentism [,ɪrɪ'dentɪzəm] N (*fig*) irredentismo *m*

irredentist [,ɪrɪ'dentɪst] ADJ, N (*fig*) irredentista *mf*

irreducible [,ɪrɪ'djuːsəbl] ADJ irreducible

irrefutable [,ɪrɪ'fjuːtəbl] ADJ [*evidence, argument*] irrefutable

irrefutably [,ɪrɪ'fjuːtəblɪ] ADV irrefutablemente, de forma irrefutable

irregardless [ɪrɪ'gɑːdlɪs] ADV (*US*) (*incorrect usage*) de cualquier modo • **~ of what he says** a pesar de lo que él diga

irregular [ɪ'regjʊləʳ] ADJ **1** (= *uneven*) [*shape, surface, pattern*] irregular • **John had sharp, ~ features** las facciones de John eran duras, irregulares • **an ~ pentagon** (*Geom*) (= *asymmetrical*) un pentágono irregular
2 (= *spasmodic*) [*attendance, meals, breathing, heartbeat*] irregular • **he is very ~ in his attendance** no asiste de forma regular • **he leads a very ~ life** lleva una vida muy irregular • **I am not usually ~** (*euph*) normalmente voy como un reloj • **to keep ~ hours** tener un horario irregular • **at ~ intervals** a intervalos irregulares
3 (= *unorthodox*) [*practice*] poco ortodoxo, irregular; [*treatment*] poco ortodoxo; [*action*] poco ortodoxo, contrario a la práctica; [*payment*] irregular • **her behaviour was ~, to say the least** su comportamiento era un tanto irregular, por no decir algo peor • **~ business practices** negocios *mpl* poco ortodoxos • **all this is very ~** todo esto es muy poco ortodoxo • **this is most ~!** ¡esto es totalmente inadmisible! • **it was highly ~ of Blake to do it alone** era totalmente contrario a la práctica que Blake lo hiciese solo
4 (*Ling*) [*verb, adjective, noun*] irregular
5 (*Mil*) [*soldiers, forces, troops*] irregular
N soldado *mf* irregular

irregularity [ɪ,regjʊ'lærɪtɪ] N
1 (= *unevenness*) [*of shape, surface, features*] irregularidad *f*
2 (= *spasmodic nature*) [*of attendance, meals, pulse*] irregularidad *f*
3 (= *unorthodox nature*) [*of behaviour*] irregularidad *f* • **the ~ of his actions surprised us all** lo poco ortodoxo de su forma de actuar nos sorprendió a todos • **a number of irregularities were observed** se observaron una serie de irregularidades

irregularly [ɪ'regjʊləlɪ] ADV **1** (= *unevenly*) [*distribute, arrange, spread*] irregularmente, de manera irregular • **~ shaped** de forma irregular

2 (= *spasmodically*) [*eat, occur*] con irregularidad; [*attend*] de forma poco regular • **her heart was beating ~** su corazón latía con irregularidad • **I see her only ~** solo la veo ocasionalmente
3 (= *in an unorthodox manner*) de forma poco ortodoxa • **payments had been made ~** se habían realizado pagos, de forma poco ortodoxa • **he had behaved most ~ in signing the paper himself** el que hubiese firmado el papel él mismo era totalmente contrario a la práctica

irrelevance [ɪ'reləvəns] (N) irrelevancia *f*, intrascendencia *f* • **it highlighted the ~ of the project to the local community** puso de relieve lo intrascendente del proyecto para la comunidad local • **they dismiss religion as an ~** rechazan la religión como algo irrelevante *or* intrascendente

irrelevant [ɪ'reləvənt] (ADJ) [*details, information*] irrelevante, intrascendente • **what you are saying is ~** lo que dices no viene al caso, lo que dices es irrelevante • **those remarks are ~ to the present discussion** esas observaciones no tienen relación con lo que se está discutiendo • **the proposals are ~ to most of our customers** las propuestas les son indiferentes a la mayoría de nuestros clientes • **he was ~, merely to be disposed of** era una persona superflua de la que se podía prescindir

irrelevantly [ɪ'reləvəntlɪ] (ADV) [*say, think*] (*with past tense*) sin que viniera al caso

irreligious [,ɪrɪ'lɪdʒəs] (ADJ) [*people, behaviour, play*] irreligioso

irremediable [,ɪrɪ'mi:dɪəbl] (ADJ) irremediable

irremediably [,ɪrɪ'mi:dɪəblɪ] (ADV) irremediablemente

irremovable [,ɪrɪ'mu:vəbl] (ADJ) inamovible

irreparable [ɪ'repərəbl] (ADJ) irreparable

irreparably [ɪ'repərəblɪ] (ADV) irreparablemente

irreplaceable [,ɪrɪ'pleɪsəbl] (ADJ) irre(e)mplazable, insustituible

irrepressible [,ɪrɪ'presəbl] (ADJ) [*person*] irrefrenable; [*high spirits, laughter, urge*] incontenible, irreprimible

irrepressibly [,ɪrɪ'presəblɪ] (ADV) [*laugh*] incontenïblemente, irreprimiblemente • **~ cheerful/enthusiastic** con una alegría/un entusiasmo incontenible *or* irreprimible

irreproachable [,ɪrɪ'prəʊtʃəbl] (ADJ) [*conduct*] irreprochable, intachable

irreproachably [,ɪrɪ'prəʊtʃəblɪ] (ADV) irreprochablemente

irresistible [,ɪrɪ'zɪstəbl] (ADJ) irresistible • **she had an ~ urge to yawn** le entraron unas ganas irresistibles de bostezar • **she looked ~ in her new dress** estaba irresistible en su vestido nuevo • **he is ~ to women** las mujeres lo encuentran irresistible • **an ~ political force** una fuerza política a la que es imposible resistirse

irresistibly [,ɪrɪ'zɪstəblɪ] (ADV) irresistiblemente • **she was drawn ~ to him** se sentía irresistiblemente atraída hacia él • **he found her ~ beautiful** la encontraba de una belleza irresistible

irresolute [ɪ'rezəlu:t] (ADJ) [*person, character*] indeciso, irresoluto

irresolutely [ɪ'rezəlu:tlɪ] (ADV) irresolutamente, indecisamente

irresoluteness [ɪ'rezəlu:tnɪs] (N) irresolución *f*, indecisión *f*

irrespective [,ɪrɪ'spektɪv] (ADJ) • **~ of** sin tomar en consideración *or* en cuenta • **the same treatment for all, ~ of age or gender** el mismo trato para todos, sin distinción de edad o sexo

irresponsibility ['ɪrɪs,pɒnsə'bɪlɪtɪ] (N) irresponsabilidad *f*, falta *f* de responsabilidad

irresponsible [,ɪrɪs'pɒnsəbl] (ADJ) [*person, behaviour*] irresponsable

irresponsibly [,ɪrɪs'pɒnsəblɪ] (ADV) irresponsablemente, de modo irresponsable

irretrievable [,ɪrɪ'tri:vəbl] (ADJ) [*object*] irrecuperable; [*loss, damage, error*] irreparable

irretrievably [,ɪrɪ'tri:vəblɪ] (ADV) irreparablemente • **~ lost** irreparablemente perdido, totalmente perdido

irreverence [ɪ'revərəns] (N) irreverencia *f*, falta *f* de respeto

irreverent [ɪ'revərənt] (ADJ) [*person, action*] irreverente, irrespetuoso

irreverently [ɪ'revərəntlɪ] (ADV) de modo irreverente, irrespetuosamente

irreversible [,ɪrɪ'vɜ:səbl] (ADJ) [*process*] irreversible; [*decision*] irrevocable

irreversibly [,ɪrɪ'vɜ:səblɪ] (ADV) [*change, affect*] irreversiblemente; [*damage, harm*] irreparablemente

irrevocable [ɪ'revəkəbl] (ADJ) [*decision*] irrevocable

irrevocably [ɪ'revəkəblɪ] (ADV) irrevocablemente

irrigable ['ɪrɪgəbl] (ADJ) regable

irrigate ['ɪrɪgeɪt] (VT) (*Agr*) [+ *land, crops*] regar; (*Med*) irrigar • **~d land** tierras *fpl* de regadío

irrigation [,ɪrɪ'geɪʃən] (N) (*Agr*) irrigación *f*, riego *m*; (*Med*) irrigación *f*
(CPD) ▸ **irrigation channel** acequia *f*, canal *m* de riego ▸ **irrigation ditch** acequia *f* ▸ **irrigation system** sistema *m* de irrigación

irrigator ['ɪrɪgeɪtə^r] (N) (*Agr, Med*) irrigador *m*

irritability [,ɪrɪtə'bɪlɪtɪ] (N) irritabilidad *f*

irritable ['ɪrɪtəbl] (ADJ) **1** (= *easily annoyed*) [*person*] irritable; [*temperament*] irascible, colérico • **to get** *or* **become ~** irritarse • **to be in an ~ mood** estar irritable
2 (= *sensitive*) [*skin*] sensible
(CPD) ▸ **irritable bowel syndrome** síndrome *m* de colon irritable

irritably ['ɪrɪtəblɪ] (ADV) • **he said ~** dijo malhumorado

irritant ['ɪrɪtənt] (N) (*Med*) agente *m* irritante; (*fig*) molestia *f*

irritate ['ɪrɪteɪt] (VT) **1** (= *annoy*) irritar, fastidiar • **to get ~d** irritarse, enfadarse
2 (*Med*) irritar

irritating ['ɪrɪteɪtɪŋ] (ADJ) **1** (= *annoying*) [*person, habit*] irritante • **it's really most ~** es de lo más irritante
2 (*to skin, eyes*) [*substance*] irritante

irritatingly ['ɪrɪteɪtɪŋlɪ] (ADV) • **the answer proved ~ elusive** la respuesta fue esquiva hasta el punto de resultar irritante • **a stone was ~ lodged in his shoe** se le había metido una piedra en el zapato y le molestaba • **~, I was none the wiser after reading his book** para mi fastidio, la lectura de su libro no me había aclarado nada

irritation [,ɪrɪ'teɪʃən] (N) **1** (= *state*) irritación *f*, enfado *m* • **she could not conceal her ~** no podía disimular su irritación *or* enfado
2 (= *irritant*) molestia *f*
3 (*Med*) irritación *f* • **a minor skin ~** una irritación cutánea de poca importancia

irruption [ɪ'rʌpʃən] (N) irrupción *f*

IRS (N ABBR) (*US*) = **Internal Revenue Service**

is [ɪz] ▹ **be**

Is. (ABBR) = **Isle(s), Island(s)**

ISA ['aɪsə] (N ABBR) (*Brit*) (*Econ*) (= **Individual Savings Account**) *plan de ahorro personal para pequeños inversores con fiscalidad cero*

Isaac ['aɪzək] (N) Isaac

Isabel ['ɪzəbel] (N) Isabel

Isaiah [aɪ'zaɪə] (N) Isaías

ISBN (N ABBR) (= **International Standard Book Number**) ISBN *f*

ISDN (N ABBR) (= **Integrated Services Digital Network**) RDSI *f*

...ish [ɪʃ] (SUFFIX) **1** • **blackish** negruzco • **dearish** algo caro • **smallish** más bien pequeño • **coldish** un poco frío
2 • **at fourish** a eso de las cuatro • **she must be fortyish** tendrá alrededor de 40 años

isinglass ['aɪzɪŋglɑ:s] (N) cola *f* de pescado

Islam ['ɪzlɑ:m] (N) Islam *m*

Islamic [ɪz'læmɪk] (ADJ) islámico
(CPD) ▸ **Islamic fundamentalists** fundamentalistas *mpl* islámicos

Islamicist [ɪz'læmɪsɪst] (N) islamista *mf*

Islamism ['ɪzləmɪzəm] (N) islamismo *m*

Islamist ['ɪzləmɪst] (N) = **Islamicist**

Islamophobia [ɪz,lɑ:məʊ'fəʊbɪə] (N) islamofobia *f*

island ['aɪlənd] (N) isla *f*; (*in street*) refugio *m*, isla *f* (peatonal); ▹ **desert¹**
(CPD) isleño ▸ **island nation** nación *f* insular

islander ['aɪləndə^r] (N) isleño/a *m/f*

island-hopping* ['aɪləndhɒpɪŋ] (N) • **to go island-hopping** viajar de isla en isla

isle [aɪl] (N) (= *poet*) isla *f*
(CPD) ▸ **Isle of Man** • **the Isle of Man** la isla de Man ▸ **Isle of Wight** • **the Isle of Wight** la isla de Wight

islet ['aɪlɪt] (N) isleta *f*, islote *m*

ism ['ɪzəm] (N) (*pej*) ismo *m*

isn't ['ɪznt] = **is not**

ISO (N ABBR) (= **International Standards Organization**) OIN *f*

iso- ['aɪsəʊ] (PREFIX) iso-

isobar ['aɪsəʊbɑ:^r] (N) isobara *f*

isolate ['aɪsəʊleɪt] (VT) **1** (= *cut off*) aislar (**from** de) • **this policy could ~ China from the rest of the world** esta política podría aislar a China del resto del mundo • **it is difficult to ~ religion from politics** es difícil separar la religión de la política • **to ~ o.s.** aislarse
2 (= *pinpoint*) [+ *cause, source*] identificar; [+ *problem, virus, gene*] aislar
3 (*Med*) (= *quarantine*) [+ *person, animal*] aislar (**from** de)

isolated ['aɪsəʊleɪtɪd] (ADJ) **1** (= *remote, cut off*) [*house, village, community*] aislado, apartado; [*person*] aislado • **the islanders were very ~** los habitantes de la isla estaban muy aislados • **she lived a strange, ~ life** vivía una vida extraña y solitaria • **to feel ~** sentirse aislado • **to be ~ from one's family** estar aislado de su familia • **to keep sth/sb ~ from sth/sb** mantener algo/a algn aislado de algo/algn
2 (= *individual*) [*incident, case, example*] aislado

isolation [,aɪsəʊ'leɪʃən] (N) aislamiento *m* • **the ~ he endured while in captivity** el aislamiento que tuvo que soportar durante su cautividad • **we cannot discuss this in ~** no podemos discutir esto aisladamente • **things like this don't happen in ~** estas cosas no ocurren aisladas • **she's being kept in ~** (*Med*) la mantienen aislada • **we cannot consider this crime in ~ from the others he has committed** no podemos considerar este crimen aislado de los otros que ha cometido; ▹ **splendid**
(CPD) ▸ **isolation hospital** hospital *m* de infecciosos ▸ **isolation ward** pabellón *m* de infecciosos

isolationism [,aɪsəʊ'leɪʃənɪzəm] (N) aislacionismo *m*

isolationist [aɪsəʊ'leɪʃənɪst] (ADJ) aislacionista
(N) aislacionista *mf*

Isolde [ɪ'zɒldə] (N) Iseo, Isolda

i

isomer ['aɪsəmə^r] (N) isómero *m*
isometric [,aɪsəʊ'metrɪk] (ADJ) isométrico
• **~ exercises** ejercicios *mpl* isométricos
isometrics [,aɪsəʊ'metrɪks] (NSING) isométrica *fsing*
isomorphic [,aɪsəʊ'mɔ:fɪk] (ADJ) isomorfo
isosceles [aɪ'sɒsɪli:z] (ADJ) • **~ triangle** triángulo *m* isósceles
isotherm ['aɪsəʊθɜ:m] (N) isoterma *f*
isothermal [,aɪsəʊ'θɜ:məl] (ADJ) isotérmico
isotonic [,aɪsəʊ'tɒnɪk] (ADJ) isotónico
isotope ['aɪsəʊtəʊp] (N) isótopo *m*
ISP (N ABBR) = **Internet Service Provider**
I-spy ['aɪ'spaɪ] (N) (*Brit*) veo-veo *m*
Israel ['ɪzreɪl] (N) Israel *m*
Israeli [ɪz'reɪlɪ] (ADJ) israelí
(N) (PL: **Israelis** *or* **Israeli**) israelí *mf*
Israelite ['ɪzrɪəlaɪt] (ADJ) israelita
(N) israelita *mf*
ISS (N ABBR) (= **International Social Service**) SSI *m*
iss. (ABBR) = **issue**
ISSN (ABBR) (= **International Standard Serial Number**) ISSN *m*
issue ['ɪʃu:] (N) **1** (= *matter, question*) asunto *m*, cuestión *f* • **until the ~ is decided** hasta que se decida algo sobre el asunto *or* la cuestión *or* el tema • **I was earning a lot of money but that was not the ~** ganaba mucho dinero, pero esa no era la cuestión • **we need to address this ~** tenemos que tratar este asunto *or* esta cuestión *or* este tema • **the point at ~** el punto en cuestión • **his integrity is not at ~** no se está cuestionando su integridad • **they were at ~ over ...** estuvieron discutiendo (sobre) ... • **to avoid the ~** eludir *or* (*frm*) soslayar el problema • **to cloud** *or* **confuse the ~** crear confusión • **to face the ~** hacer frente a la cuestión *or* al problema, afrontar la situación • **to force the ~** forzar una decisión • **to join ~ with sb** enfrentarse a *or* con algn • **to make an ~ of sth**: • **I think we should make an ~ of this** creo que deberíamos insistir en este punto • **do you want to make an ~ of it?** ¿quieres hacer un problema de esto? • **he makes an ~ of every tiny detail** a todo le da mucha más importancia de la que tiene • **the main** *or* **real ~ is ...** lo fundamental es ... • **it's not a political ~** no es una cuestión política • **to take ~ with sth/sb** discrepar de algo/de *or* con algn • **I feel I must take ~ with you on** *or* **over that** permítame que discrepe de usted en *or* sobre eso; ▸ **side**
2 [*of shares, stamps, banknotes*] emisión *f*; [*of library book*] préstamo *m*; [*of document*] expedición *f*; [*of rations*] distribución *f*, reparto *m* • **an army ~ blanket** una manta del ejército • **a standard ~ army rifle** un rifle del ejército de fabricación estándar
3 (= *copy*) [*of magazine*] ejemplar *m*, número *m* • **the March ~** el ejemplar *or* número de marzo • **back ~** ejemplar *m* or número *m* atrasado
4 (*frm*) (= *outcome*) resultado *m*, consecuencia *f*
5 (*Jur*) (= *offspring*) descendencia *f* • **to die without ~** morir sin (dejar) descendencia
6 (*Med*) flujo *m*
(VT) [+ *library book*] prestar; [+ *tickets*] emitir; [+ *shares, stamps*] poner en circulación, emitir; [+ *rations*] distribuir, repartir; [+ *order*] dar; [+ *statement, proclamation*] hacer público; [+ *decree*] promulgar; [+ *passport, certificate*] expedir; [+ *licence*] facilitar; [+ *writ, summons*] extender • **a warrant has been ~d for his arrest** se ha ordenado su detención • **to ~ sth to sb** • **~ sb with sth** dar algo a algn • **we were ~d with ten rounds each** nos dieron diez cartuchos a cada uno • **staff will be ~d with new uniforms** se proveerá de uniformes nuevos al personal
(VI) **1** (= *come forth*) • **to ~ from sth** [*blood, water*] brotar *or* salir de algo; [*sound*] salir de algo; [*report, account*] provenir de algo • **reports issuing from opposition sources say that ...** informes provenientes de fuentes de la oposición afirman que ...
2 (= *derive*) derivar (**from** de)
3 (*frm*) (= *have as result*) • **to ~ in sth** resultar en algo, dar algo como resultado
(CPD) ▸ **issue price** precio *m* de emisión
issued ['ɪʃu:d] (ADJ) • **~ capital** capital *m* emitido
issuer ['ɪʃu:ə^r] (N) (*Econ, St Ex*) emisor *m*, sociedad *f* emisora
issuing ['ɪʃu:ɪŋ] (ADJ) [*company, office*] (*for shares*) emisor; (*for passport, official document*) expedidor
Istanbul ['ɪstæn'bu:l] (N) Estambul *m*
isthmus ['ɪsməs] (N) (PL: **isthmuses** *or* **isthmi**) istmo *m*
IT (N ABBR) **1** (*Comput*) (= **information technology**) informática *f*
2 (*Econ*) = **income tax**
it¹ [ɪt] (PRON) **1** (*specific*)

It as subject or following a preposition is often not translated.

(*direct object*) lo, la; (*indirect object*) le; (*after prep*) (*if translated*) él *m*, ella *f*; (*neuter*) ello • **it's on the table** está en la mesa • **where is it?** ¿dónde está? • **"here's the book" — "give it to me"** —aquí está el libro —dámelo • **if you have the list, give it to him** si tienes la lista, dásela • **it's a good film, have you seen it?** es una buena película, ¿la has visto? • **give it a kick** dale una patada • **I have no money for it** no tengo dinero para comprarlo • **I doubt it** lo dudo • **there's a wall in front of/behind it** hay una pared delante/detrás (de ello) • **she put a plate on top of it** le puso un plato encima, lo tapó con un plato • **it's a she** [*dog, cat etc*] es hembra • **it's a boy** [*baby*] es niño
2 (*indefinite*)

The indefinite subject is not translated.

• **it's raining** está lloviendo • **it's Friday tomorrow** mañana es viernes • **it's 10 October** *or* **the 10th of October** es el diez de octubre • **it's six o'clock** son las seis • **how far is it?** ¿a qué distancia está? • **it's ten miles to London** son diez millas de aquí a Londres • **I like it here, it's quiet** me gusta aquí, es tranquilo • **it was kind of you** fue muy amable de su parte • **it's easy to talk** hablar no cuesta nada • **it is not in him to do it** no es capaz de hacer eso • **it's me** soy yo • **don't worry, it's only me** soy yo, no te emociones • **it's no use worrying** no vale la pena inquietarse • **it is said that ...** se dice que ... • **I have heard it said that ...** he oído decir que ... • **it was Peter who phoned** fue Peter quien llamó • **what is it?** (= *what's the matter?*) ¿qué pasa? • **who is it?** ¿quién es?
3 (*special uses with "to be"*) • **how is it that ...?** ¿cómo es que ...?, ¿cómo resulta que ...? • **that's it for today** eso es todo por hoy • **that's it! just there is fine** ¡eso es! ahí mismo está bien • **that's it! I've had enough of this waiting!** ¡ya está bien! ¡estoy harto de esperar! • **that's it then! we leave on Sunday** ¡muy bien! *or* ¡solucionado! salimos el domingo • **that's just it!** ¡ahí está el problema! • **this is it** (= *it's time*) ya llegó la hora; (= *train, bus etc*) ahí viene
4 (*referring to situation*) • **he won't agree to it** no lo aceptará • **I spoke to him about it** lo hablé con él • **I'm against it** estoy en contra • **I'm (all) for it*** estoy (muy) a favor • **the worst of it is that ...** lo peor del caso es que ... • IDIOM: • **he's dropped us in it*** nos la ha hecho buena*; ▸ **at, get**
5 (*in games*) • **you're it!** ¡te tocó!
6* (= *sexual attraction*) • **you've either got it or you haven't** ese algo, o se tiene o no, no hay vuelta de hoja
7* (= *something special*) • **she thinks she's just it!*** se las da de maravillosa*
(CPD) ▸ **It Girl*** (*esp Brit*) *mujer muy moderna, famosa, que inicia modas*
it²* [ɪt] (N) vermú *m* or vermut *m* italiano
ITA (N ABBR) (*Brit*) (= **Initial Teaching Alphabet**) *alfabeto parcialmente fonético para enseñar lectura*
Italian [ɪ'tæljən] (ADJ) italiano
(N) **1** (= *person*) italiano/a *m/f*
2 (*Ling*) italiano *m*
Italianate [ɪ'tæljənɪt] (ADJ) de estilo italiano
italic [ɪ'tælɪk] (ADJ) (*Typ*) en cursiva *or* bastardilla
italicize [ɪ'tælɪsaɪz] (VT) poner en cursiva *or* bastardilla
italics [ɪ'tælɪks] (NPL) cursiva *f*, (letra *f*) bastardilla *f* • **in ~** en cursiva, en bastardilla • **my ~** • **the ~ are mine** lo subrayado es mío
Italy ['ɪtəlɪ] (N) Italia *f*
ITC (N ABBR) (*Brit*) = **Independent Television Commission**
itch [ɪtʃ] (N) picor *m*; (*less frequent*) picazón *f*, comezón *f* • **to have an ~** tener un picor; (*less frequent*) tener una picazón *or* una comezón • **I've got an ~ here, can you scratch it for me?** me pica aquí *or* tengo un picor aquí, ¿me puedes rascar? • **to have an ~ to do sth** (*fig*) rabiar por hacer algo; ▸ **seven**
(VI) **1** (= *be itchy*) • **my leg ~es** me pica la pierna; (*said by older people*) tengo picazón *or* comezón en la pierna • **I was ~ing all over** me picaba todo • **to be ~ing for sth*** (*fig*) estar deseando algo • **he was ~ing for a chance to play against the champion** estaba deseando tener la oportunidad de jugar contra el campeón • **he's ~ing for a fight** tiene ganas de pelea • **to be ~ing to do sth*** (*fig*) rabiar por hacer algo
2 (= *cause itchiness*) [*sweater, wool*] picar
itchiness ['ɪtʃɪnɪs] (N) picor *m*; (*less frequent*) picazón *f*, comezón *f*
itching ['ɪtʃɪŋ] (N) picor *m*; (*less frequent*) picazón *f*, comezón *f*
(CPD) ▸ **itching powder** polvos *mpl* de pica-pica
itchy ['ɪtʃɪ] (ADJ) (COMPAR: **itchier**, SUPERL: **itchiest**) **1** (= *irritated*) [*eyes, skin, scalp*] irritado; [*rash*] que produce picor • **~ eyes caused by hay fever** ojos *mpl* irritados a causa de la fiebre del heno • **my head is ~** me pica la cabeza; (*less frequent*) tengo picazón *or* comezón en la cabeza • **I've got an ~ nose** me pica la nariz • **she felt all ~** • **she felt ~ all over** le picaba todo • IDIOMS: • **to have ~ feet** estar muy inquieto • **to have ~ fingers**: • **I was getting ~ fingers, watching the two of them play chess** viéndolos a los dos jugar al ajedrez me estaban entrando ganas a mí • **to have an ~ palm**: • **the chief of police had an ~ palm and allowed himself to be bribed** al jefe de policía le podía su amor por el dinero y se dejaba sobornar
2 (= *irritating*) [*sweater, material*] que pica • **that jumper is too ~** ese jersey pica mucho
it'd ['ɪtd] = **it would, it had**
item ['aɪtəm] (N) (*in list, bill, catalogue*) artículo *m*; (*on agenda*) asunto *m* (a tratar), punto *m* (a tratar); (*in programme*) número *m*; (*in newspaper*) artículo *m*; (*TV, Rad*) noticia *f* • **~ of clothing** prenda *f* (de vestir) • **what's the**

next ~? (*in meeting*) ¿cuál es el siguiente punto *or* asunto a tratar? • **this books is a collector's ~** este libro es una pieza de colección • **basic/luxury food ~s** productos *mpl* alimenticios básicos/suntuarios • **they sell a selection of gift ~s** venden una selección de artículos de regalo • **a news ~** una noticia • **they're something of an ~*** son pareja

itemize ['aɪtəmaɪz] (VT) detallar • **~d bill** (*of customer*) cuenta *f* detallada; (*Comm*) factura *f* detallada

iterative ['ɪtərətɪv] (ADJ) iterativo
(CPD) ▸ **iterative statement** (*Comput*) sentencia *f* iterativa

itinerant [ɪ'tɪnərənt] (ADJ) [*preacher, lecturer, worker*] itinerante; [*salesperson*] ambulante

itinerary [aɪ'tɪnərərɪ] (N) (= *route*) itinerario *m*; (= *map*) ruta *f*

it'll ['ɪtl] = **it will, it shall**

ITN (N ABBR) (*Brit*) (= **Independent Television News**) *servicio de noticias en las cadenas privadas de televisión*

ITO (N ABBR) (= **International Trade Organization**) OIC *f*

it's [ɪts] = **it is, it has**

its [ɪts] (POSS ADJ) (*with singular noun*) su; (*with plural noun*) sus • **everything in its place** cada cosa en su sitio • **it has its advantages** tiene sus ventajas • **the dog is losing its hair** el perro está perdiendo el pelo • **the bird was in its cage** el pájaro estaba en su jaula
(POSS PRON) (el/la) suyo/a, (los/las) suyos/as

itself [ɪt'self] (PRON) **1** (*reflexive*) se, sí • **skin renews ~ every 28 days** la piel se renueva cada 28 días
2 (*emphatic*) • **Christmas ~ was an anticlimax** las Navidades mismas fueron una decepción • **he is always politeness ~** siempre es la cortesía personificada • **the door closed by ~** la puerta se cerró sola • **I loved him more than life ~** lo quería más que a mi propia vida • **that was an achievement in ~** eso fue un triunfo de por sí

itsy-bitsy* [,ɪtsɪ'bɪtsɪ], **itty-bitty*** [,ɪtɪ'bɪtɪ] (*US*) (ADJ) pequeñito*

ITU (N ABBR) (= **International Telecommunications Union**) UIT *f*

ITV (N ABBR) (= **Independent Television**) *cadena privada de televisión*

IUCD (N ABBR) (= **intrauterine contraceptive device**) = IUD

IUD (N ABBR) (= **intrauterine device**) DIU *m*

IV (N ABBR) (= **intravenous**) (*also* **IV drip**) gota a gota *m*
(ADJ ABBR) = **intravenous**

i.v. (ABBR) = **invoice value**

I've [aɪv] = **I have**

IVF (N ABBR) (= **in vitro fertilization**) FIV *f*

ivory ['aɪvərɪ] (N) marfil *m*; **ivories*** (= *teeth*) dientes *mpl*; (*Mus*) teclas *fpl*; (*Billiards*) bolas *fpl* • IDIOM: • **to tickle the ivories*** tocar el piano
(ADJ) [*cane, box*] de marfil; [*skin*] de color marfil
(CPD) ▸ **Ivory Coast** Costa *f* de Marfil ▸ **ivory hunter** cazador(a) *m/f* de marfil ▸ **ivory tower** (*fig*) torre *f* de marfil

ivy ['aɪvɪ] (N) (*Bot*) hiedra *f*, yedra *f*
(CPD) ▸ **the Ivy League** (*US*) *grupo de ocho universidades privadas muy prestigiosas de Nueva Inglaterra*

IVY LEAGUE

En el noreste de Estados Unidos, la **Ivy League** está formada por ocho universidades de gran prestigio tanto académico como social. El término procede de la época en la que estas ocho universidades, **Harvard**, **Yale**, **Pennsylvania**, **Princeton**, **Columbia**, **Brown**, **Dartmouth** y **Cornell** formaron una liga para impulsar las competiciones deportivas entre ellas y tiene su origen en la hiedra (**ivy**) que cubre los muros de las facultades y colegios universitarios. A los estudiantes de estas universidades se les denomina **Ivy Leaguers**.

Jj

J, j [dʒeɪ] (N) (= *letter*) J, j *f* • **J for Jack** J de José
JA (N ABBR) = **judge advocate**
J/A (ABBR) = **joint account**
jab [dʒæb] (N) **1** (= *poke*) (*gen*) pinchazo *m*; (*with elbow*) codazo *m*
2 (= *blow*) (*gen*) golpe *m*; (*Boxing*) golpe *m* rápido
3 (= *prick*) pinchazo *m*
4 (*Brit*) (*Med**) inyección *f*
5‡ [*of drug*] chute‡ *m*
(VT) • **to jab sth into sth** clavar algo en algo, hundir algo en algo • **he jabbed the knife into the table** clavó el cuchillo en la mesa • **to jab sb with one's elbow** dar un codazo a algn • **to jab a finger at sth** señalar algo con el dedo • **he jabbed a gun in my back** me puso un revólver en los riñones • **I jabbed the knife in my arm** me pinché el brazo con el cuchillo • **he jabbed me with his stick** me golpeó con la punta de su bastón
(VI) • **to jab at** [+ *person*] intentar golpear a; [+ *fire*] atizar • **to jab at sb with a knife** tratar de acuchillar a algn • **he jabbed at the map with a finger** dio con el dedo en el mapa
jabber [ˈdʒæbəʳ] (N) [*of person*] (= *fast talk*) chapurreo *m*, farfulla *f*; (= *chatter*) cotorreo *m*; (= *noise*) algarabía *f*; [*of monkeys*] chillidos *mpl* • **a ~ of French** un torrente de francés • **a ~ of voices** un jaleo de voces
(VT) farfullar
(VI) (= *talk fast*) farfullar; (= *chatter*) charlotear, parlotear; [*monkeys*] chillar • **they were ~ing away in Russian** charloteaban *or* parloteaban en ruso
jabbering [ˈdʒæbərɪŋ] (N) = **jabber**
jacaranda [ˌdʒækəˈrændə] (N) jacarandá *m*
Jack [dʒæk] (N) (*familiar form of* **John**) Juanito • **IDIOM:** • **I'm all right, ~!** ¡y a mí qué!
(CPD) ▸ **Jack Frost** *personificación del hielo* ▸ **Jack Ketch** *el verdugo* ▸ **Jack Robinson** • **before you can say ~ Robinson** en un santiamén, en un decir Jesús ▸ **Jack Tar** *el marinero*
jack [dʒæk] (N) **1** (*Aut, Tech*) gato *m*, gata *f* (*LAm*)
2 (*Elec*) toma *f* de corriente, enchufe *m* hembra
3 (*Bowls*) boliche *m*
4 (*Cards*) (*in ordinary pack of cards*) jota *f*; (*in Spanish pack*) sota *f*
5 (*also* **bootjack**) sacabotas *m inv*
6 (*Naut*) marinero *m*
7 (= *fish*) lucio *m* joven
8 jacks (= *game*) cantillos *mpl*
(CPD) ▸ **jack plane** garlopa *f* ▸ **jack plug** enchufe *m* de clavija ▸ **jack rabbit** (*US*) liebre *f* americana
▸ **jack in*** (VT + ADV) (*Brit*) dejar, abandonar
▸ **jack off**** (VI + ADV) (*US*) hacerse una paja**
▸ **jack up** (VT + ADV) **1** (*Tech*) levantar con el gato
2 (= *increase*) [+ *price, production*] aumentar
jackal [ˈdʒækɔːl] (N) chacal *m*
jackanapes [ˈdʒækəneɪps] (N) mequetrefe *m*
jackass [ˈdʒækæs] (N) (= *donkey*) asno *m*, burro *m*; (*fig*) (= *person*) burro *m*
jackboot [ˈdʒækbuːt] (N) bota *f* de montar, bota *f* militar • **under the Nazi ~** bajo el azote *or* la férula del nazismo
jackdaw [ˈdʒækdɔː] (N) grajilla *f*
jacket [ˈdʒækɪt] (N) **1** (= *garment*) chaqueta *f*, americana *f*, saco *m* (*LAm*)
2 (= *cover*) [*of boiler*] camisa *f*, envoltura *f*; [*of book*] sobrecubierta *f*; (*US*) [*of record*] funda *f*
3 [*of potato*] • **potatoes baked in their ~s** (*Brit*) patatas *fpl* asadas con piel, papas *fpl* asadas con cáscara (*LAm*)
(CPD) ▸ **jacket potatoes** (*Brit*) patatas *fpl* asadas con piel, papas *fpl* asadas con cáscara (*LAm*)
jackhammer [ˈdʒækˌhæməʳ] (N) (*esp US*) taladradora *f*, martillo *m* neumático
jack-in-the-box [ˈdʒækɪnðəbɒks] (N) caja *f* sorpresa, caja *f* de resorte
jackknife [ˈdʒæknaɪf] (N) (PL: **jackknives**) navaja *f*, chaveta *f* (*LAm*)
(VI) [*lorry*] colear
(CPD) ▸ **jackknife dive** salto *m* de la carpa, carpa *f*
jack-of-all-trades [ˈdʒækəvˈɔːltreɪdz] (N) (PL: **jacks of all trades**) factótum *mf* • **he's a jack-of-all-trades and master of none** es de los que mucho abarca y poco aprieta, sabe un poco de todo pero no es experto en nada
jack-o'-lantern [ˈdʒækəʊˈlæntən] (N) **1** (= *will-o'-the-wisp*) fuego *m* fatuo
2 (*US*) (= *Hallowe'en lantern*) *linterna hecha con una calabaza vaciada*
jackpot [ˈdʒækpɒt] (N) premio *m* gordo • **to hit the ~** sacar el premio gordo; (*fig*) ser todo un éxito *or* un exitazo
jackstraw [ˈdʒækstrɔː] (N) (*US*) pajita *f*
Jacob [ˈdʒeɪkəb] (N) Jacob
Jacobean [ˌdʒækəˈbiːən] (ADJ) de la época de Jacobo I (de Inglaterra)
Jacobin [ˈdʒækəbɪn] (ADJ) jacobino
(N) jacobino/a *m/f*
Jacobite [ˈdʒækəbaɪt] (ADJ) jacobita
(N) jacobita *mf*
Jacuzzi® [dʒəˈkuːzɪ] (N) jacuzzi® *m*, baño *m* de burbujas
jade¹ [dʒeɪd] (N) (= *stone*) jade *m*
(ADJ) (*also* **jade-green**) verde jade (*inv*)
(CPD) [*statue, carving, necklace*] de jade
jade² [dʒeɪd] (N) **1** (= *horse*) rocín *m*
2† (= *woman*) mujerzuela *f*
jaded [ˈdʒeɪdɪd] (ADJ) hastiado, harto • **to feel ~** estar hastiado *or* harto • **to get ~** hastiarse, hartarse
jade-green [ˈdʒeɪdˈgriːn] (ADJ) verde jade (*inv*)
JAG (N ABBR) = **Judge Advocate General**
Jag* [dʒæg] (N) (= *car*) Jaguar *m*
jag¹ [dʒæg] (N) **1** (= *jagged point*) punta *f*, púa *f*
2 (*Scot**) (= *jab*) inyección *f*
jag² [dʒæg] (N) (= *binge*) • **to go on a jag*** ir de juerga
jagged [ˈdʒægɪd] (ADJ) dentado
jaguar [ˈdʒægjʊəʳ] (N) jaguar *m*, tigre *m* (*LAm*)
jail [dʒeɪl] (N) cárcel *f*, prisión *f* • **to go to ~** ir a la cárcel • **sentenced to ten years in ~** condenado a diez años de cárcel *or* prisión
(VT) (*for crime*) encarcelar (**for** por); (*for length of time*) • **to ~ sb for two months** condenar a algn a dos meses de cárcel *or* de cárcel
(CPD) ▸ **jail cell** celda *f* de prisión ▸ **jail sentence** pena *f* de prisión *or* de cárcel • **to serve a ~ sentence** cumplir una pena de prisión *or* de cárcel • **to be given a ~ sentence** ser condenado a pena de prisión *or* de cárcel ▸ **jail term** condena *f* de cárcel
jailbait* [ˈdʒeɪlbeɪt] (N) *menor con la que el mantener relaciones sexuales está penado*
jailbird [ˈdʒeɪlbɜːd] (N) presidiario/a *m/f* reincidente, preso/a *m/f* reincidente
jailbreak [ˈdʒeɪlbreɪk] (N) fuga *f*, evasión *f* (*de la cárcel*)
jailbreaker [ˈdʒeɪlˌbreɪkəʳ] (N) evadido/a *m/f*, fugado/a *m/f* (*de la cárcel*)
jailer [ˈdʒeɪləʳ] (N) carcelero/a *m/f*
jailhouse [ˈdʒeɪlhaʊs] (N) (PL: **jailhouses**) cárcel *f*, prisión *f*
Jain [ˈdʒaɪn] (N) jain *mf*
(ADJ) jain (*inv*)
Jainism [ˈdʒaɪnɪzəm] (N) jainismo *m*
Jakarta [dʒəˈkɑːtə] (N) Yakarta *f*
jakes†‡ [dʒeɪks] (N) meadero‡ *m*
jalapeño [ˌhæləˈpeɪnjəʊ], **jalapeno** [ˌdʒæləˈpiːnəʊ] (N) (= *chilli pepper*) (chile) *m* jalapeño *m*
jaloppy* [dʒəˈlɒpɪ] (N) = **jalopy**
jalopy* [dʒəˈlɒpɪ] (N) cacharro *m*, armatoste *m*
jalousie [ˈʒælʊ(ː)ziː] (N) celosía *f*
jam¹ [dʒæm] (*Brit*) (N) **1** (= *food*) mermelada *f* • **strawberry jam** mermelada *f* de fresas • **you want jam on it!*** (*fig*) ¡y un jamón! • **IDIOM:** • **the jam is spread very thin*** hay cosas buenas pero apenas se notan
2* (= *luck*) chorra* *f* • **look at that for jam!** ¡qué chorra tiene el tío!*
(VT) hacer mermelada de
(CPD) ▸ **jam jar** (*Brit*) tarro *m* de mermelada, pote *m* de mermelada ▸ **jam pot** (*Brit*) = **jam jar** ▸ **jam roll** (*Brit*) brazo *m* de gitano con mermelada ▸ **jam tart** tarta *f* de mermelada
jam² [dʒæm] (N) **1** [*of people*] aglomeración *f* • **you never saw such a jam!** ¡había que ver cómo se agolpaba la gente! • **there was a jam in the doorway** había una aglomeración de gente en la puerta, se había agolpado la gente en la puerta
2 (= *traffic jam*) embotellamiento *m*, atasco *m* • **a 5km jam of cars** una caravana *or* un atasco de coches de 5km • **there are always jams here** aquí siempre se atasca el tráfico, aquí siempre hay atascos
3 (= *obstruction*) atasco *m* • **there's a jam in the pipe** se ha atascado *or* está atascada la cañería
4 (*fig**) (= *difficulty*) apuro *m*, aprieto *m* • **to be**

j

in a jam estar en un aprieto, estar en apuros • **to get into a jam** meterse en un aprieto, meterse en apuros • **to get sb out of a jam** sacar a algn del apuro
VT **1** (= *block*) [+ *mechanism, drawer, pipe*] atascar; [+ *wheel*] trabar; [+ *exit, road*] cerrar, obstruir • **it's got jammed** se ha atascado, no se puede mover/quitar/retirar *etc*
2 (= *cram*) [+ *passage, exit*] atestar, abarrotar; [+ *container*] atestar, llenar • **people jammed the exits** la gente se agolpaba en las salidas • **I jammed my finger in the door** me pillé el dedo con la puerta • **to jam sth into a box** meter algo a la fuerza en una caja • **we were all jammed together** estábamos todos apiñados • **the room was jammed with people** el cuarto estaba atestado de gente • **streets jammed with cars** calles atestadas de coches
3 (*Telec, Rad*) interferir
VI **1** [*mechanism, drawer, pipe*] atascarse, atorarse (*LAm*); [*nut, part, wheel*] atascarse, atrancarse; [*gun*] encasquillarse • **this part has jammed** esta pieza se ha atascado, no se puede mover esta pieza • **the drawer had jammed (shut/open)** el cajón no se podía abrir/cerrar
2 (*Mus**) improvisar
CPD ▸ **jam session** jam session *f* (*actuación improvisada de jazz, rock etc*)
▸ **jam in** VT + ADV • **if we can jam two more books in** si podemos introducir a la fuerza dos libros más • **there were 15 people jammed in one room** había 15 personas apretadas unas contra otras en un cuarto
▸ **jam on** VT + ADV **1** • **to jam one's brakes on** frenar en seco, dar un frenazo
2 • **he jammed his hat on his head** se encasquetó el sombrero • **with his hat jammed on his head** con el sombrero encasquetado en la cabeza
Jamaica [dʒəˈmeɪkə] N Jamaica *f*
Jamaican [dʒəˈmeɪkən] ADJ jamaicano
N jamaicano/a *m/f*
jamb [dʒæm] N jamba *f*
jamboree [ˌdʒæmbəˈriː] N **1** [*of Scouts*] congreso *m* de exploradores
2* francachela *f*, juerga *f*
James [dʒeɪmz] N Jaime, Diego; (*British kings*) Jacobo • **Saint ~** Santiago
jam-full [ˈdʒæmˈfʊl] ADJ (*of people*) abarrotado, atestado; (*of things*) atestado, repleto
jammed [ˈdʒæmd] ADJ **1** (= *stuck*) [*window, mechanism*] atascado; [*gun*] encasquillado
2 [*road*] colapsado • **to be ~ with** [+ *people, cars*] estar atestado de
3 [*switchboard*] saturado, colapsado • **the telephone lines are ~** las líneas de teléfono están saturadas *or* colapsadas
jamming [ˈdʒæmɪŋ] N (*Rad*) interferencia *f*
jammy* [ˈdʒæmɪ] ADJ (*Brit*) (COMPAR: **jammier**, SUPERL: **jammiest**) suertudo*, potrudo*
jam-packed [ˈdʒæmˈpækt] ADJ (*with people*) abarrotado, atestado; (*with things*) atestado, repleto
JAN N ABBR (*US*) = **Joint Army-Navy**
Jan ABBR (= **January**) ene., en.
Jane [dʒeɪn] N Juana
jangle [ˈdʒæŋgl] N tintineo *m*
VT [+ *coins, bracelets*] hacer tintinear
VI tintinear
jangling [ˈdʒæŋglɪŋ] ADJ tintineante
N cencerreo *m*
janitor [ˈdʒænɪtəʳ] N (= *doorkeeper*) portero/a *m/f*; (= *caretaker*) conserje *mf*
Jansenism [ˈdʒænsəˌnɪzəm] N jansenismo *m*
Jansenist [ˈdʒænsənɪst] ADJ jansenista
N jansenista *mf*
January [ˈdʒænjʊərɪ] N enero *m*; ▸ **July**
CPD ▸ **the January sales** las rebajas de enero
Janus [ˈdʒeɪnəs] N Jano
Jap** [dʒæp] (*offensive*) = **Japanese**
Japan [dʒəˈpæn] N el Japón
japan [dʒəˈpæn] N laca *f* japonesa
VT charolar con laca japonesa
Japanese [ˌdʒæpəˈniːz] ADJ japonés
N (PL: **Japanese**) **1** (= *person*) japonés/esa *m/f* • **the ~** (= *people*) los japoneses
2 (*Ling*) japonés *m*
jape [dʒeɪp] N burla *f*
japonica [dʒəˈpɒnɪkə] N rosal *m* de China, rosal *m* japonés
jar[1] [dʒɑːʳ] N (= *container*) tarro *m*, bote *m*; (= *jug*) (*gen*) jarra *f*; (*large*) tinaja *f* • **to have a jar*** tomar un trago *or* una copa
jar[2] [dʒɑːʳ] N **1** (= *jolt*) sacudida *f*, choque *m*
2 (*fig*) (= *shock*) conmoción *f*, sorpresa *f* desagradable • **it gave me a jar** me dejó de piedra
VT **1** (= *jog*) tocar • **he must have jarred the camera** ha debido de mover la cámara • **somebody jarred my elbow** alguien me dio en el codo
2 (= *shake*) sacudir, hacer vibrar • **I've jarred my back** me he lastimado la espalda
3 (*fig*) afectar, impresionar
VI (= *clash*) [*colours, sounds*] desentonar; [*opinions*] chocar (**with** con) • **to jar on sb's nerves** poner a algn los nervios de punta • **to jar on sb's ears** lastimar a algn el oído
jar[3] [dʒɑːʳ] N • **on the jar** = **ajar**
jargon [ˈdʒɑːgən] N jerga *f*
jarring [ˈdʒɑːrɪŋ] ADJ [*sound*] discordante, desafinado; [*opinions*] discordante; [*colour*] discordante, que desentona • **to strike a ~ note** (*fig*) ser la nota discordante, desentonar
Jas. ABBR = **James**
jasmine [ˈdʒæzmɪn] N jazmín *m*
CPD ▸ **jasmine tea** té *m* de jazmín
jasper [ˈdʒæspəʳ] N jaspe *m*
jaundice [ˈdʒɔːndɪs] N ictericia *f*
jaundiced [ˈdʒɔːndɪst] ADJ **1** (*Med*) con ictericia, que tiene ictericia
2 (*fig*) (= *embittered*) [*person*] amargado, resentido; [*attitude*] negativo, pesimista
3 (*fig*) (= *disillusioned*) desilusionado
jaunt [dʒɔːnt] N excursión *f*
jauntily [ˈdʒɔːntɪlɪ] ADV [*walk*] garbosamente, airosamente; [*dress*] de manera alegre, de manera desenfadada • **he replied ~** contestó alegremente *or* con desenfado
jauntiness [ˈdʒɔːntɪnɪs] N [*of tone*] desenfado *m*; [*of clothes*] vistosidad *f*; [*of step*] garbo *m*
jaunting car [ˈdʒɔːntɪŋˌkɑːʳ] N tílburi *m* (irlandés)
jaunty [ˈdʒɔːntɪ] ADJ (COMPAR: **jauntier**, SUPERL: **jauntiest**) (= *relaxed*) [*air, tone*] desenvuelto, desenfadado; (= *cheerful*) [*clothes, hat*] alegre; [*step*] garboso, airoso
Java[1] [ˈdʒɑːvə] N (= *island*) Java *f*
Java[2]® [ˈdʒɑːvə] N (*Comput*) Java® *m*
Javanese [ˌdʒɑːvəˈniːz] ADJ javanés
N (PL: **Javanese**) javanés/esa *m/f*
javelin [ˈdʒævlɪn] N **1** (= *object*) jabalina *f* • **to throw the ~** lanzar la jabalina
2 (= *event*) • **she won a gold medal in the ~** ganó la medalla de oro en lanzamiento de jabalina
CPD ▸ **javelin thrower** lanzador(a) *m/f* de jabalina ▸ **javelin throwing** lanzamiento *m* de jabalina
jaw [dʒɔː] N **1** (*Anat*) [*of person*] mandíbula *f*; [*of animal*] quijada *f*
2 jaws [*of animal*] fauces *fpl*; (*Tech*) [*of vice*] mordaza *fsing*; [*of channel*] boca *fsing*, embocadura *fsing* • **the jaws of death** (*fig*) las garras de la muerte
3* (= *chat*) cháchara *f* • **we had a good old jaw** charlamos largo y tendido • **it's just a lot of jaw** mucho ruido y pocas nueces • **hold your jaw!** ¡cállate la boca!
VT ‡ soltar el rollo a*
VI * charlar
jawbone [ˈdʒɔːbəʊn] N [*of person*] mandíbula *f*; [*of animal*] quijada *f*
VT (*US**) presionar, ejercer presión sobre
jawbreaker* [ˈdʒɔːˌbreɪkəʳ] N (*US*) trabalenguas *m inv*, palabra *f* kilométrica
jaw-dropping* [ˈdʒɔːˌdrɒpɪŋ] ADJ (*esp Brit*) (= *amazing*) alucinante* • **the new striker scored a jaw-dropping goal** el nuevo delantero marcó un gol alucinante*
jaw-droppingly* [ˈdʒɔːˌdrɒpɪŋlɪ] ADV (*esp Brit*) (= *amazingly*) alucinantemente*
jawline [ˈdʒɔːlaɪn] N mandíbula *f*
jay [dʒeɪ] N arrendajo *m*
jaywalk [ˈdʒeɪwɔːk] VI cruzar la calle imprudentemente
jaywalker [ˈdʒeɪˌwɔːkəʳ] N peatón/ona *m/f* imprudente
jaywalking [ˈdʒeɪˌwɔːkɪŋ] N imprudencia *f* al cruzar la calle
jazz [dʒæz] N **1** (*Mus*) jazz *m*
2* (= *talk*) palabrería *f* • **and all that ~*** y otras cosas por el estilo • **don't give me that ~!** ¡no me vengas con cuentos!
CPD ▸ **jazz ballet** jazz-ballet *m* ▸ **jazz band** orquesta *f* de jazz ▸ **jazz club** club *m* de jazz ▸ **jazz mag‡** (*Brit*) (*pornographic*) revista *f* porno
▸ **jazz up** VT + ADV **1** (*Mus*) sincopar
2 (*fig*) [+ *party*] animar; [+ *room*] alegrar
jazzman [ˈdʒæzmæn] N (PL: **jazzmen**) jazzista *m*
jazzy [ˈdʒæzɪ] ADJ (COMPAR: **jazzier**, SUPERL: **jazziest**) **1** (*Mus*) sincopado
2* (= *showy*) [*dress etc*] de colores llamativos, de colores chillones
JC N ABBR (= **Jesus Christ**) JC *m*
JCB ® N ABBR *excavadora para la construcción con pala hidráulica*
JCC N ABBR (*US*) = **Junior Chamber of Commerce**
JCR N ABBR (*Brit*) (*Univ*) = **Junior Common Room**
JCS N ABBR (*US*) = **Joint Chiefs of Staff**
jct., jctn ABBR (*Rail*) = **junction**
JD N ABBR (*US*) **1** (*Univ*) = **Doctor of Laws**
2 = **Justice Department**
jealous [ˈdʒeləs] ADJ **1** [*husband, wife, lover*] celoso • **to be ~ of sb** tener celos de algn • **to make sb ~** dar celos a algn
2 (= *envious*) (*of possessions, qualities*) envidioso • **to be ~ of sth** envidiar algo
jealously [ˈdʒeləslɪ] ADV **1** (= *enviously*) con envidia • **he was ~ watching the skaters** observaba a los patinadores con envidia
2 (= *protectively*) celosamente • **she ~ guards her family's privacy** guarda celosamente la intimidad de su familia • **she's ~ possessive of him** es celosa y posesiva con él
jealousy [ˈdʒeləsɪ] N **1** [*of husband, wife, lover*] celos *mpl*
2 (= *envy*) [*of possessions, qualities*] envidia *f*
jeans [dʒiːnz] NPL vaqueros *mpl*, bluejeans *m* (*esp LAm*)
Jeep®, jeep [dʒiːp] N jeep® *m*, yip *m*
jeer [dʒɪəʳ] N **1** (*from crowd*) abucheo *m*; (*from individual*) grito *m* de protesta
2 (= *insult*) insulto *m*
VI **1** (= *mock*) burlarse (**at** de)
2 (= *boo*) abuchear (**at** a)
VT **1** (= *mock*) burlarse de

2 (= *boo*) abuchear

jeering ['dʒɪərɪŋ] ADJ [*remark, laughter*] burlón, sarcástico • **he was led through a ~ crowd** le hicieron pasar por una multitud que le llenó de insultos, le hicieron pasar entre una multitud que lo colmó de insultos
N **1** (= *protests*) protestas *fpl*
2 (= *mockery*) burlas *fpl*
3 (= *insults*) insultos *mpl*
4 (= *booing*) abucheo *m*

Jeez* [dʒi:z] EXCL ¡Santo Dios!

jehad [dʒɪ'hæd] N = **jihad**

Jehovah [dʒɪ'həʊvə] N Jehová *m* • **~'s Witness** Testigo *m* de Jehová

jejune [dʒɪ'dʒu:n] ADJ **1** (= *naïve*) cándido
2 (= *dull*) [*subject*] árido; [*evening*] aburrido
3 (= *insipid*) insípido, sin sustancia

jell [dʒel] VI = **gel**

jellabah ['dʒeləbə] N chilaba *f*

jellied ['dʒelɪd] ADJ [*eels, meat*] en gelatina

jello®, **Jell-O**® ['dʒeləʊ] N (*US*) = **jelly¹**

jelly¹ ['dʒelɪ] N **1** (*Brit*) (= *dessert*) jalea *f*, gelatina *f* • **my legs turned to ~** me temblaban las piernas
2 (*US*) (= *jam*) mermelada *f*
3 (= *substance*) gelatina *f*
CPD ▸ **jelly baby** caramelo *m* de goma (*en forma de niño*) ▸ **jelly jar** (*US*) tarro *m* de mermelada ▸ **jelly roll** (*US*) brazo *m* de gitano

jelly²‡ ['dʒelɪ] N = **gelignite**

jellybean ['dʒelɪbi:n] N gominola *f*

jellyfish ['dʒelɪfɪʃ] N (PL: **jellyfish** *or* **jellyfishes**) medusa *f*, aguamala *f* (*Mex*), aguaviva *f* (*S. Cone*)

jemmy ['dʒemɪ] N (*Brit*) palanqueta *f*

Jennie, Jenny ['dʒenɪ] N *familiar form of* Jennifer

jeopardize ['dʒepədaɪz] VT (= *endanger*) arriesgar, poner en peligro; (= *compromise*) comprometer

jeopardy ['dʒepədɪ] N riesgo *m*, peligro *m* • **to be in ~** estar en peligro • **to put sth in ~** poner algo en peligro

jeremiad [,dʒerɪ'maɪəd] N jeremiada *f*

Jeremiah [,dʒerɪ'maɪə] N Jeremías

Jeremy ['dʒerɪmɪ] N Jeremías

Jericho ['dʒerɪkəʊ] N Jericó *m*

jerk [dʒɜ:k] N **1** (= *shake*) sacudida *f*; (= *pull*) tirón *m*, jalón *m* (*LAm*); (*Med*) espasmo *m* muscular • **physical ~s** (*Brit**) gimnasia *f*, ejercicios *mpl* (físicos) • **by ~s** a sacudidas • **he sat up with a ~** se incorporó de golpe • **to put a ~ in it*** menearse
2 (*US**) imbécil *mf*, gilipollas*‡ *mf inv*, pendejo *m* (*LAm*‡), huevón/ona *m/f* (*And, S. Cone*‡) • **what a ~!** ¡menudo imbécil!
VT **1** (= *pull*) dar un tirón a, tirar bruscamente de, jalar bruscamente de (*LAm*); (= *shake*) sacudir, dar una sacudida a; (= *throw*) arrojar con un movimiento rápido • **to ~ sth along** arrastrar algo a tirones • **to ~ o.s. along** moverse a sacudidas, avanzar a tirones • **he ~ed it away from me** me lo quitó de un tirón *or* (*LAm*) jalón • **to ~ o.s. free** soltarse de un tirón *or* (*LAm*) jalón
2 (*US*) [+ *meat*] atasajar
VI dar una sacudida • **to ~ along** moverse a sacudidas • **the bus ~ed to a halt** el autobús dio unas sacudidas y se paró
▸ **jerk off**‡ VI + ADV hacerse una paja‡
▸ **jerk out** VT + ADV [+ *words*] decir con voz entrecortada

jerkily ['dʒɜ:kɪlɪ] ADV [*move*] a tirones, a sacudidas; [*play, write*] de modo desigual, nerviosamente

jerkin ['dʒɜ:kɪn] N chaleco *m*

jerkiness ['dʒɜ:kɪnɪs] N [*of movement*] brusquedad *f*; [*of speech*] lo entrecortado

jerkwater* ['dʒɜ:k,wɔ:tə^r] ADJ (*US*) de poca monta • **a ~ town** un pueblucho*

jerky ['dʒɜ:kɪ] ADJ (COMPAR: **jerkier**, SUPERL: **jerkiest**) [*movement, motion*] brusco; [*speech*] entrecortado, vacilante

Jeroboam [,dʒerə'bəʊəm] N Jeroboam

Jerome [dʒə'rəʊm] N Jerónimo

Jerry¹ ['dʒerɪ] N *familiar form of* **Gerald, Gerard**

Jerry²* ['dʒerɪ] N (*Brit*) (*Mil*) • **a ~** un alemán • **~** los alemanes

jerry ['dʒerɪ] N (*Brit**) orinal *m*
CPD ▸ **jerry can** bidón *m*

jerry-builder ['dʒerɪ,bɪldə^r] N mal constructor *m*, tapagujeros *m inv*

jerry-building ['dʒerɪ,bɪldɪŋ] N mala construcción *f*, construcción *f* defectuosa

jerry-built ['dʒerɪbɪlt] ADJ mal construido, hecho con malos materiales

Jersey ['dʒɜ:zɪ] N **1** (*Geog*) isla *f* de Jersey, Jersey *m*
2 (= *cow*) vaca *f* de Jersey
CPD ▸ **Jersey cow** vaca *f* de Jersey

jersey ['dʒɜ:zɪ] N (= *garment*) jersey *m*, suéter *m*; (= *fabric*) tejido *m* de punto

Jerusalem [dʒə'ru:sələm] N Jerusalén *f*
CPD ▸ **Jerusalem artichoke** aguaturma *f*, pataca *f*

jessamine ['dʒesəmɪn] N jazmín *m*

jest [dʒest] N guasa *f*, broma *f* • **in ~** en broma, de guasa
VI bromear, estar de guasa • **he was only ~ing** lo dijo en broma nada más, solo estaba de guasa

jester ['dʒestə^r] N bufón *m*

jesting ['dʒestɪŋ] ADJ [*person*] chistoso, guasón; [*tone*] guasón; [*reference*] burlón, en broma
N chanzas *fpl*, bromas *fpl*

Jesuit ['dʒezjʊɪt] ADJ jesuita
N jesuita *m*

Jesuitical [,dʒezjʊ'ɪtɪkəl] ADJ jesuítico

Jesus ['dʒi:zəs] N Jesús *m* • **~ Christ** Jesucristo *m* • **~ Christ!*** ¡Santo Dios!
CPD ▸ **Jesus freak*** (*pej*) *cristiano ferviente evangélico* ▸ **Jesus sandals** sandalias *fpl* nazarenas

jet¹ [dʒet] N (= *stone*) azabache *m*
CPD ▸ **jet black** negro *m* azabache; ▹ **jet-black**
▸ **jet off*** VI + ADV salir de viaje (*en avión*)

jet² [dʒet] N **1** [*of liquid, steam*] chorro *m*; [*of flame*] llamarada *f*
2 (= *nozzle*) [*of gas burner*] mechero *m*
3 (*Aer*) (= *plane*) avión *m* a reacción, reactor *m*
VT lanzar en chorro, echar en chorro
VI chorrear, salir a chorro
CPD ▸ **the jet age** la época de los jet ▸ **jet aircraft** avión *m* a reacción, reactor *m* ▸ **jet engine** [*of plane*] motor *m* a reacción, reactor *m* ▸ **jet fighter** caza *m* a reacción ▸ **jet fuel** carburorreactor *m* ▸ **jet lag** jet lag *m* (*desfase debido a un largo viaje en avión*) • **to be suffering from jet lag** tener jet lag ▸ **jet plane** avión *m* a reacción, reactor *m* ▸ **jet propulsion** propulsión *f* por reacción, propulsión *f* a chorro ▸ **the jet set** la jet set (*Sp*), el jet set (*LAm*), la alta sociedad ▸ **jet ski** moto *f* acuática; ▹ **jet-ski** ▸ **jet stream** corriente *f* en chorro

jet-black ['dʒet'blæk] ADJ negro azabache (*inv*)

jetlagged ['dʒet,lægd] ADJ • **to be ~** tener jet lag, estar desfasado por el viaje en avión

jetliner ['dʒet,laɪnə^r] N (*US*) avión *m* de pasajeros

jet-powered ['dʒet'paʊəd] ADJ = **jet-propelled**

jet-propelled ['dʒetprə'peld] ADJ a reacción, a chorro

jetsam ['dʒetsəm] N echazón *f*, cosas *fpl* desechadas

jet-setter ['dʒet,setə^r] N miembro *mf* de la jet set (*Sp*), miembro *mf* del jet set (*LAm*)

jet-setting ['dʒetsetɪŋ] ADJ de la jet set (*Sp*), del jet set (*LAm*)

jet-ski ['dʒetski:] VI practicar el motociclismo acuático • **they were jet-skiing** iban en moto acuática

jettison ['dʒetɪsn] VT (*Naut*) echar al mar, echar por la borda; (*Aer*) vaciar; (*fig*) deshacerse de • **we can safely ~ that** bien podemos prescindir de eso

jetty ['dʒetɪ] N (= *breakwater*) malecón *m*; (= *pier*) muelle *m*, embarcadero *m*

Jew [dʒu:] N judío/a *m/f*
CPD ▸ **Jew's harp** birimbao *m*

jewel ['dʒu:əl] N (= *precious stone*) piedra *f* preciosa; (= *ornament*) joya *f*, alhaja *f*; (= *stone in watch*) rubí *m*; (*fig*) (= *person, thing*) joya *f*
CPD ▸ **jewel case** joyero *m*

jewelled, jeweled (*US*) ['dʒu:əld] ADJ adornado con piedras preciosas; [*watch*] con rubíes

jeweller, jeweler (*US*) ['dʒu:ələ^r] N joyero/a *m/f* • **~'s (shop)** joyería *f*

jewellery, jewelry (*US*) ['dʒu:əlrɪ] N joyas *fpl*, alhajas *fpl* • **a piece of ~** una joya
CPD ▸ **jewellery box** joyero *m* ▸ **jewelry store** (*US*) joyería *f*

Jewess† ['dʒu:ɪs] N (*gen pej*) (*offensive*) judía *f*

Jewish ['dʒu:ɪʃ] ADJ judío

Jewishness ['dʒu:ɪʃnɪs] N carácter *m* judaico

Jewry ['dʒʊərɪ] N judería *f*, los judíos

Jezebel ['dʒezəbel] N Jezabel

JFK N ABBR (*US*) = **John Fitzgerald Kennedy International Airport**

jib¹ [dʒɪb] N (*Naut*) foque *m*; [*of crane*] aguilón *m*, brazo *m*
CPD ▸ **jib boom** botalón *m* de foque

jib² [dʒɪb] VI [*horse*] plantarse; [*person*] rehusar, negarse • **to jib at (doing) sth** resistirse a (hacer) algo • **he jibbed at it** se negó a aprobarlo

jibe [dʒaɪb] N, VI = **gibe**

jiffy* ['dʒɪfɪ] N momento *m*, segundo *m* • **in a ~** en un santiamén, en un momento, en un segundito (*LAm*) • **to do sth in a ~** hacer algo en un santiamén *or* momento • **wait a ~** espera un momentito, momentito (*LAm*), ahorita voy (*Mex*)
CPD ▸ **Jiffy bag**® sobre *m* acolchado

jig [dʒɪg] N **1** (= *dance, tune*) giga *f*
2 (*Mech*) plantilla *f*; (*Min*) criba *f*; (*Rail*) gálibo *m*
VI (= *dance*) bailar dando brincos • **to jig along** • **jig up and down** [*person*] moverse a saltitos • **to keep jigging up and down** no poder estarse quieto
▸ **jig about** VI + ADV brincar

jigger¹* ['dʒɪgə^r] N **1** (= *whisky measure*) medida *f* (de whisky *etc*)
2 (*esp US*) (= *thingummy*) chisme *m*

jigger² ['dʒɪgə^r] N (*Min*) criba *f*; (*Mech*) aparato *m* vibratorio

jiggered ['dʒɪgəd] ADJ • **well I'm ~!** (*Brit**) ¡caramba! • **I'm ~ if I will** que me cuelguen si lo hago

jiggery-pokery* ['dʒɪgərɪ'pəʊkərɪ] N (*Brit*) trampas *fpl*, embustes *mpl* • **there's some jiggery-pokery going on** hay gato encerrado

jiggle ['dʒɪgl] N zangoloteo *m*
VT zangolotear
VI zangolotearse
▸ **jiggle around, jiggle about** VI + ADV [*person, objects*] sacudirse

jigsaw ['dʒɪgsɔ:] N **1** (*also* **jigsaw puzzle**) rompecabezas *m inv*, puzzle *m*
2 (= *tool*) sierra *f* de vaivén

jihad [dʒɪˈhæd] N (*Rel*) jihad *f* (*guerra santa musulmana*)
jihadism [dʒɪˈhædɪzəm] N Yihad *f*
jihadist [dʒɪˈhædɪst] N combatiente *mf* de la Yihad
jilbab [dʒɪlˈbɑːb] N hiyab *m*
jilt [dʒɪlt] VT [+ *fiancé*] dejar plantado a; [+ *fiancée*] dejar plantada a • **her ~ed lover** su amante rechazado
Jim [dʒɪm] N *familiar form of* **James**
jimdandy†* [ˈdʒɪmˈdændɪ] ADJ (*US*) estupendo*, fenomenal*
jimjams¹‡ [ˈdʒɪmdʒæmz] NPL delírium *m* tremens • **it gives me the ~** me horripila, me da grima
jimjams²* [ˈdʒɪmdʒæmz] NPL (*baby talk*) pijama *msing*, piyama *msing* (*LAm*)
Jimmy [ˈdʒɪmɪ] N **1** *familiar form of* **James**
2 • **to have a ~ (Riddle)*** (*hum*) mear*, cambiar *or* mudar el agua al canario*
jimmy [ˈdʒɪmɪ] N (*US*) = **jemmy**
jingle [ˈdʒɪŋgl] N **1** (= *sound*) tintineo *m*, retintín *m*
2 (*Literat*) poemita *m* popular, rima *f* infantil; (= *advertising jingle*) cancioncilla *f*, musiquilla *f* (de anuncio)
VT [+ *coins, jewellery*] hacer tintinear
VI [*bells*] tintinear
jingo [ˈdʒɪŋgəʊ] N (PL: **jingoes**) (*pej*) patriotero/a *m/f* • **by ~!** ¡caramba!
jingoism [ˈdʒɪŋgəʊɪzəm] N (*pej*) patriotería *f*
jingoistic [ˌdʒɪŋgəʊˈɪstɪk] ADJ (*pej*) patriotero
jink* [dʒɪŋk] VI (*Brit*) (= *zigzag*) dar un bandazo • **he ~ed out of the way** se salió del camino dando un bandazo
jinks [dʒɪŋks] NPL • **high ~**†* jolgorio *msing*, jarana *f* • **we had high ~ last night** anoche nos lo pasamos pipa
jinx [dʒɪŋks] N (= *person*) cenizo/a *m/f*, gafe *mf*; (= *spell*) gafe *m*, maleficio *m* • **there's a ~ on it** está gafado, tiene la negra • **to put a ~ on sth** echar mal de ojo a algo
VT traer mala suerte a, gafar (*Sp**) • **to be ~ed** [*person, project*] tener gafe
jitney* [ˈdʒɪtniː] N (*US*) **1** (= *bus*) autobús *m* pequeño, colectivo *m* (*LAm*)
2 (= *coin*) *moneda de cinco centavos*
jitterbug [ˈdʒɪtəbʌg] N (= *dance*) baile *acrobático al ritmo de jazz o bugui-bugui*; (= *person*) *persona aficionada a bailar ritmos de jazz o el bugui-bugui*
VI *bailar ritmos de jazz o el bugui-bugui*
jitters* [ˈdʒɪtəz] NPL • **the ~** el canguelo*, los nervios • **to get the ~** ponerse nervioso • **to give sb the ~** poner nervioso a algn • **to have the ~** tener el canguelo*, estar nervioso
jittery* [ˈdʒɪtərɪ] ADJ muy inquieto, nervioso • **to get ~** inquietarse, ponerse nervioso
jiujitsu [dʒuːˈdʒɪtsuː] N = **jujitsu**
jive [dʒaɪv] N **1** (= *music, dancing*) swing *m*
2 (*US**) (= *big talk*) alardes *mpl*, palabrería *f*; (= *nonsense*) chorradas* *fpl*; (= *slang used by Black people*) (*also* **jive talk**) jerga *f* (*de la población negra norteamericana, en especial de los músicos de jazz*) • **don't give me all that ~** deja de decir chorradas*
VI **1** (= *dance*) bailar el swing
2* (= *be kidding*) bromear
Jnr ABBR (= **junior**) jr
Jo [dʒəʊ] N **1** *familiar form of* **Josephine**
2 *familiar form of* **Joanne**
Joan [dʒəʊn] N Juana • **~ of Arc** Juana de Arco
Job [dʒəʊb] N Job • **Job's comforter** *el que queriendo animar a otro le desconsuela todavía más*
job [dʒɒb] N **1** (= *employment*) trabajo *m*, empleo *m* • **what would the job involve?** ¿en qué consistiría el trabajo *or* empleo? • **what's her job?** ¿de qué trabaja? • **we shall create 1,000 new jobs** vamos a crear 1.000 puestos de trabajo más • **he got a job as a clerk** consiguió un trabajo *or* empleo de oficinista • **I think he's the best man for the job** creo que es el más apropiado para el puesto • **to be in a job** tener trabajo • **to look for a job** buscar (un) trabajo *or* empleo • **to lose one's job** (*gen*) perder el trabajo *or* empleo; (= *be sacked*) ser despedido • **to be out of a job** estar sin trabajo *or* empleo • **if they go bankrupt we'll all be out of a job** si se arruinan nos quedaremos todos sin trabajo *or* empleo • **to put sb out of a job** quitar el trabajo *or* empleo a algn • IDIOM: • **jobs for the boys** (*Brit**) (*pej*) amiguismo *m*, enchufes* *mpl*; ▹ **day**
2 (= *piece of work*) trabajo *m* • **I have a job for you** tengo un trabajo para ti • **I'm afraid this is a job for a specialist** me parece que para esto hace falta un especialista • **it was a big job** dio mucho trabajo, era mucho trabajo • **it's a difficult job** es (un trabajo) muy difícil • **I'm paid by the job** me pagan a destajo • **I've got a few jobs to do** tengo algunas cosillas que hacer • **to do a job for sb** hacer un encargo para algn, hacer un recado a algn • **can you do a job for me?** ¿te puedo hacer un encargo?, ¿te puedo encargar algo? • **she's doing a good job** trabaja bien • **he has done a good job with the book** el libro le ha salido bien • **we could do a far better job of it** podríamos hacer un trabajo muchísimo mejor • **it's not ideal but it'll do the job** no es lo ideal pero valdrá • **let's get on with the job in hand** vamos a concentrarnos en el trabajo que tenemos entre manos • **to know one's job** conocer el oficio • **he really knows his job** es un experto en lo suyo • **you've made a good job of painting the doors** has pintado muy bien las puertas • **he's out on a job at the moment** en este momento ha salido a hacer un trabajo • **on the job: he fell asleep on the job** se quedó dormido trabajando • **there was no formal training — they learned on the job** no se ofrecía formación específica — aprendían trabajando *or* sobre la marcha • **he quit after five years on the job** se fue tras haber estado en el trabajo cinco años • **to be on the job*** (= *having sex*) estar haciéndolo* • IDIOM: • **to fall down on the job** demostrar no tener capacidad • PROVERB: • **if a job's worth doing, it's worth doing well** las cosas bien hechas bien parecen; ▹ **hatchet, nose, odd, repair**
3 (*Comput*) trabajo *m*
4 (= *duty, responsibility*) • **my job is to sell them** yo estoy encargado de venderlos • **that's not my job** eso no me incumbe a mí, eso no me toca a mí • **he's only doing his job** está cumpliendo con su deber, nada más • **I had the job of telling him** a mí me tocó decírselo
5* (= *undertaking*) • **it's quite a job, bringing up five children** es una tarea bastante dura, criar a cinco hijos
6* (= *difficulty*) • **to have a (hard) job doing/to do sth: we're having a hard job keeping up with the demand** nos está costando trabajo satisfacer la demanda • **we had quite a job getting here!** ¡vaya que nos costó (trabajo) llegar! • **we'll have a (hard) job to finish it in time** nos va a costar mucho trabajo terminarlo a tiempo
7* (= *state of affairs*) • **it's a bad job** es una situación difícil • **it's a good job he didn't see us** menos mal que no nos vio • **(and a) good job too!** ¡menos mal!* • IDIOMS: • **to make the best of a bad job** poner al mal tiempo buena cara • **we'll just have to make the best of a bad job** habrá que poner al mal tiempo buena cara • **to give sth up as a bad job** dejar algo por imposible • **she gave him up as a bad job** por imposible rompió con él
8* (= *crime*) golpe* *m* • **he was planning a bank job** planeaba un golpe en un banco • **he was caught doing a bank job** lo cogieron *or* (*LAm*) agarraron asaltando un banco • **that warehouse job** ese robo en el almacén; ▹ **put-up**
9 (*Brit**) (= *thing*) • **this machine is just the job** esta máquina nos viene que ni pintada*, esta máquina nos viene al pelo* • **a holiday in Majorca would be just the job** unas vacaciones en Mallorca nos vendrían de perlas *or* de maravilla
10 (*Brit**) (*child language*) • **to do a job** hacer caca*
VI **1** (= *do casual work*) hacer trabajos temporales
2 (= *work as middleman*) • **to job in sth** trabajar de intermediario en la compraventa de algo
CPD ▸ **job action** (*US*) movilización *f* (de trabajadores) ▸ **job advertisement** oferta *f* de trabajo *or* empleo, anuncio *m* de trabajo *or* empleo ▸ **job analysis** (*Ind*) análisis *m* del trabajo, análisis *m* ocupacional ▸ **job applicant** solicitante *mf* de empleo *or* trabajo, aspirante *mf* (a un puesto) ▸ **job application** solicitud *f* de trabajo *or* empleo ▸ **Job Centre** = Jobcentre ▸ **job club** grupo *m* de asesoramiento para desempleados ▸ **job control language** lenguaje *m* de control de trabajo ▸ **job creation** creación *f* de empleo, creación *f* de puestos de trabajo ▸ **job creation scheme** plan *m* de creación de puestos de trabajo, plan *m* de creación de nuevos empleos ▸ **job description** descripción *f* del trabajo ▸ **job evaluation, job grading** evaluación *f* de empleos ▸ **job holder** empleado/a *m/f* ▸ **job hunt** búsqueda *f* de trabajo *or* empleo ▸ **job hunting** búsqueda *f* de trabajo, búsqueda *f* de empleo • **to go job hunting** salir a buscar trabajo *or* empleo ▸ **job interview** entrevista *f* de trabajo ▸ **job losses** pérdida *fsing* de puestos de trabajo • **500 job losses** una pérdida de 500 puestos de trabajo ▸ **job lot** lote *m* • **to buy/sell sth as a job lot** comprar/vender algo en un lote ▸ **job market** mercado *m* laboral • **he soon found himself back on the job market** pronto se vio de nuevo buscando trabajo ▸ **job number** número *m* del trabajo ▸ **job offer** oferta *f* de trabajo *or* empleo ▸ **job opportunity** oportunidad *f* de trabajo ▸ **job queue** (*Comput*) cola *f* de trabajos ▸ **job requirement** requisito *m* para el puesto • **communication skills are a job requirement in public relations** la capacidad de comunicación es un requisito para el puesto de relaciones públicas ▸ **job satisfaction** satisfacción *f* en el trabajo, satisfacción *f* profesional ▸ **job search** búsqueda *f* de trabajo *or* empleo ▸ **job security** seguridad *f* en el trabajo ▸ **job seeker** demandante *mf* de empleo, persona *f* que busca trabajo ▸ **job seeker's allowance** (*Brit*) prestación *f* por desempleo ▸ **job sharing** • **job sharing is encouraged here** intentamos fomentar el empleo compartido • **I'm interested in the possibility of job sharing** me interesaría poder compartir el empleo con otra persona ▸ **job specification** (*for post*) requisitos *mpl* para el puesto ▸ **job title** (nombre *m* del) puesto *m* ▸ **job vacancy** puesto *m* vacante
jobber [ˈdʒɒbəʳ] N (*Brit*) (*St Ex*) corredor(a) *m/f* de Bolsa

jobbery ['dʒɒbərɪ] (N) (*Brit*) intrigas *fpl*, chanchullos *mpl* • **piece of ~** intriga *f*, chanchullo *m* • **by a piece of ~** por enchufe
jobbing ['dʒɒbɪŋ] (ADJ) (*Brit*) [*gardener, carpenter*] que trabaja a destajo, destajista • **~ printer** impresor *m* de circulares, folletos *etc*
(N) (*St Ex*) agiotaje *m*
Jobcentre ['dʒɒbsentəʳ] (N) (*Brit*) oficina *f* de empleo
jobless ['dʒɒblɪs] (ADJ) sin trabajo, desempleado, parado (*Sp*), cesante (*LAm*)
(NPL) • **the ~** los desempleados, los parados (*Sp*), los cesantes (*LAm*)
(CPD) ▸ **the jobless figures** las cifras del desempleo, las cifras de desempleados
joblessness ['dʒɒblɪsnɪs] (N) carencia *f* de trabajo
job-share ['dʒɒbʃɛəʳ] (ADJ) • **we operate a job-share scheme** tenemos en marcha un plan de empleo compartido
jobsworth* ['dʒɒbzwɜ:θ] (N) (*Brit*) *empleado excesivamente legalista con respecto a las normativas que rigen su trabajo*
Jock* [dʒɒk] (N) (*pej*) *el escocés típico* • **the ~s** los escoceses
jock [dʒɒk] (N) **1** = **jockstrap**
2 (*US*) deportista *m*
jockey ['dʒɒkɪ] (N) jockey *m*
(VT) • **to ~ sb into doing sth** convencer a algn para hacer algo • **to ~ sb out of sth** quitar algo a algn con artimañas • **to ~ sb out of a post** lograr con artimañas que algn renuncie a un puesto • **to ~ sb out of doing sth** disuadir a algn de hacer algo
(VI) • **to ~ for position** (*fig*) maniobrar para conseguir una posición
(CPD) ▸ **jockey box** (*US*) (= *glove box*) guantera *f*; (= *dispenser*) nevera *f* portátil con dispensador de bebidas ▸ **Jockey Shorts®** calzoncillos *mpl* de jockey
jockstrap ['dʒɒkstræp] (N) suspensorio *m*
jocose [dʒə'kəʊs] (ADJ) = **jocular**
jocular ['dʒɒkjʊləʳ] (ADJ) [*person*] gracioso; (= *merry*) alegre; [*manner*] bromista, chistoso; [*remark, reply*] jocoso, divertido
jocularity [ˌdʒɒkjʊ'lærətɪ] (N) jocosidad *f*
jocularly ['dʒɒkjʊləlɪ] (ADV) jocosamente
jocund ['dʒɒkənd] (ADJ) jocundo
jodhpurs ['dʒɒdpɜ:z] (NPL) pantalones *mpl* de montar
Joe* [dʒəʊ] (N) **1** (*familiar form of* **Joseph**) Pepe
2 (*US*) tipo* *m*, tío* *m* • **the average Joe** el hombre de la calle • **a good Joe** un buen chico
(CPD) ▸ **Joe Bloggs*** (*Brit*) *ciudadano de a pie británico* ▸ **Joe College*** (*US*) *típico estudiante norteamericano* ▸ **Joe Public*** = **Joe Bloggs** ▸ **Joe Soap*** fulano *m*
joey* ['dʒəʊɪ] (N) (*Australia*) (= *kangaroo*) cangurito *m*
jog [dʒɒg] (N) **1** (= *push*) (*gen*) empujoncito *m*; (*with elbow*) codazo *m*
2 (= *encouragement*) estímulo *m* • **to give sb's memory a jog** refrescar la memoria a algn
3 (= *pace*) (*also* **jog trot**) trote *m* corto • **to go at a steady jog** andar a trote corto
4 (= *run*) carrera *f* a trote corto • **to go for a jog** ir a hacer footing *or* jogging
(VT) **1** (= *push*) empujar (ligeramente) • **he jogged my arm** me dio ligeramente con el codo
2 (= *encourage*) estimular • **to jog sb's memory** refrescar la memoria a algn • **to jog sb into action** motivar a algn
(VI) **1** (*also* **jog along**) (*gen*) andar a trote corto; (*fig*) hacer algunos progresos, avanzar pero sin prisa
2 (*Sport*) (*also* **go jogging**) hacer footing, hacer jogging
(CPD) ▸ **jog trot** • **at a jog trot** a trote corto
▸ **jog along** (VI + ADV) [*vehicle*] avanzar despacio, ir sin prisa; (*fig*) • **we're jogging along** vamos tirando • **the work is jogging along nicely** el trabajo marcha bien
jogger ['dʒɒgəʳ] (N) corredor(a) *m/f* (de footing)
jogging ['dʒɒgɪŋ] (N) footing *m*, jogging *m*
(CPD) ▸ **jogging shoes** zapatillas *fpl* de deporte ▸ **jogging suit** chandal *m*
joggle* ['dʒɒgl] (N) sacudida *f* • **I gave his arm a ~** le sacudí el brazo, le di una sacudida en el brazo
(VT) sacudir
(VI) dar sacudidas
john¹‡ [dʒɒn] (N) (*esp US*) (= *lavatory*) • **the ~** el váter*, el retrete, el baño (*LAm*)
john²‡ [dʒɒn] (N) (*US*) (= *prostitute's customer*) putero* *m*, cliente *m* de prostituta
John [dʒɒn] (N) Juan • **Pope ~ Paul II** el Papa Juan Pablo II
(CPD) ▸ **John Bull** *personificación del pueblo inglés* ▸ **John Doe** (*US*) fulano *m* ▸ **John Dory** gallo *m* (*pez*) ▸ **John Hancock*** firma *f*, rúbrica *f* ▸ **John Henry** firma *f* ▸ **John of the Cross** (*also* **Saint John of the Cross**) San Juan de la Cruz ▸ **John Q Public*** (*US*) el hombre de la calle ▸ **John the Baptist** (*also* **St John the Baptist**) San Juan Bautista ▸ **John the Evangelist** (*also* **Saint John the Evangelist**) San Juan Evangelista
Johnny ['dʒɒnɪ] (N) Juanito
johnny* ['dʒɒnɪ] (N) tío* *m*, sujeto *m*
joie de vivre [ʒwɑ:də'vi:vr] (N) alegría *f* de vivir
join [dʒɔɪn] (VT) **1** (= *put together, link*) [+ *ends, pieces, parts*] unir, juntar; [+ *tables*] juntar • **to ~ (together) two ends of a chain** unir *or* juntar dos extremos de una cadena • **the island is ~ed to the mainland by a bridge** un puente une *or* conecta la isla a tierra firme • **to ~ A to B** • **to ~ A and B** unir *or* juntar A con B • **~ the dots to form a picture** una los puntos para formar un dibujo • **to ~ hands** cogerse *or* (*LAm*) tomarse de la mano
2 (= *merge with*) [+ *river*] desembocar en, confluir con; [+ *sea*] desembocar en; [+ *road*] empalmar con • **where does the River Wye ~ the Severn?** ¿a qué altura desemboca el Wye en el Severn?, ¿dónde confluye el Wye con el Severn? • **where the river ~s the sea** en la desembocadura del río en el mar • **where the track ~s the road** donde el camino empalma con la carretera
3 (= *enter, become part of*) [+ *university, firm, religious order*] ingresar en, entrar en; [+ *club, society*] hacerse socio de; [+ *political party*] afiliarse a, hacerse miembro de; [+ *army, navy*] alistarse en, ingresar en; [+ *queue*] meterse en; [+ *procession, strike, movement*] sumarse a, unirse a • **~ the club!*** ¡bienvenido al club! • **to ~ forces (with sb to do sth)** (*gen*) juntarse (con algn para hacer algo); (*Mil*) aliarse (con algn para hacer algo); (*Comm*) asociarse (con algn para hacer algo) • **we ~ed the motorway at junction 15** nos metimos en la autopista por la entrada 15 • **to ~ one's regiment** incorporarse a su regimiento • **to ~ one's ship** (= *return to*) volver a su buque; (= *go on board*) embarcar; ▹ **battle, rank¹**
4 (= *be with, meet*) [+ *person*] acompañar a • **may I ~ you?** (*at table*) ¿les importa que les acompañe? • **will you ~ us for dinner?** ¿nos acompañas a cenar?, ¿cenas con nosotros? • **if you're going for a walk, do you mind if I ~ you?** si vais a dar un paseo, ¿os importa que os acompañe? • **will you ~ me in** *or* **for a drink?** ¿se toma una copa conmigo? • **I'll ~ you later if I can** yo iré luego si puedo • **~ us at the same time next week for ...** (*Rad, TV*) la próxima semana tiene una cita con nosotros a la misma hora en ... • **Paul ~s me in wishing you ...** al igual que yo, Paul te desea ... • **they should ~ us in exposing government corruption** deberían unirse *or* sumarse a nosotros para sacar a la luz la corrupción del gobierno
(VI) **1** (= *connect*) [*ends, pieces, parts*] unirse, juntarse
2 (= *merge*) [*roads*] empalmar, juntarse; [*rivers*] confluir, juntarse; [*lines*] juntarse
3 • **to ~ together (to do sth)** (= *meet*) [*people*] reunirse (para hacer algo); (= *unite*) [*groups, organizations*] unirse (para hacer algo); (= *pool resources*) asociarse (para hacer algo) • **to ~ with sb in doing sth** unirse a algn para hacer algo • **Moscow and Washington have ~ed in condemning these actions** Moscú y Washington se han unido para protestar por estas acciones • **we ~ with you in hoping that ...** compartimos su esperanza de que ... (+ *subjun*), al igual que ustedes esperamos que ... (+ *subjun*)
4 (= *become a member*) (*of club*) hacerse socio; (*of political party*) afiliarse, hacerse miembro
(N) (*in wood, crockery*) juntura *f*, unión *f*; (*Tech*) junta *f* • **you could hardly see the ~** apenas se notaba la juntura *or* la unión
▸ **join in** (VI + PREP) [+ *game, celebration, conversation*] tomar parte en, participar en; [+ *protest*] sumarse a, unirse a • **they all ~ed in the game** todos tomaron parte *or* participaron en el juego • **can anyone ~ in this discussion?** ¿puede participar cualquiera en esta discusión? • **they all ~ed in the last song** todos cantaron la última canción
(VI + ADV) (*in game, celebration, conversation*) participar • **he doesn't ~ in much** apenas participa • **a couple began to dance and then we all ~ed in** una pareja salió a bailar y detrás fuimos todos • **she started singing, and the audience ~ed in** empezó a cantar, y el público se unió a ella • **~ in everyone!** (*in chorus*) ¡todo el mundo!, ¡todos!
▸ **join on** (VT + ADV) **1** (= *attach*) unir • **how do I ~ on the sleeves?** ¿cómo uno las mangas?
2 (= *add*) [+ *extra piece, building*] añadir
(VI + ADV) [*part*] unirse, juntarse • **where the muscles ~ on to the bone** donde los músculos se unen a *or* juntan con el hueso
▸ **join up** (VI + ADV) **1** (*Mil*) alistarse
2 (= *meet*) [*people*] reunirse, juntarse • **we ~ed up with him in Málaga** nos reunimos *or* nos juntamos con él en Málaga
3 (= *merge*) [*roads*] empalmar, juntarse; [*rivers*] confluir, juntarse
4 [*organizations, groups*] (= *unite, team up*) unirse, asociarse; (= *merge*) fusionarse
(VT + ADV) [+ *ends, pieces, parts*] unir, juntar • **~ up the dots to form a picture** una los puntos para formar un dibujo • **~ed up writing** escritura *f* cursiva, escritura *f* corrida
joiner ['dʒɔɪnəʳ] (N) (= *carpenter*) carpintero/a *m/f*
joinery ['dʒɔɪnərɪ] (N) carpintería *f*
joining fee ['dʒɔɪnɪŋˌfi:] (N) cuota *f* de ingreso
joint [dʒɔɪnt] (ADJ) [*work, declaration, consultation*] (*between two parties*) conjunto; (*more than two*) colectivo; [*agreement*] mutuo; [*decision*] de común acuerdo; [*responsibility*] compartido; [*committee*] mixto
(N) **1** (*Tech*) (*in metal*) juntura *f*, junta *f*; (*in wood*) ensambladura *f*; (= *hinge*) bisagra *f*
2 [*of meat*] cuarto *m* • **we had a ~ of lamb for lunch** comimos asado de cordero
3 (*Anat*) articulación *f*, coyuntura *f* • **to be out of ~** [*bone*] estar descoyuntado, estar dislocado; (*fig*) estar fuera de quicio • **to put**

a bone out of ~ dislocar un hueso • to put sb's nose out of ~* (fig) bajar los humos a algn • to throw sb's plans out of ~ estropear los planes a algn
4* (= place) garito m
5* (= cigarette containing cannabis) porro m, canuto m
6 (Bot) nudo m
VT 1 (Culin) despiezar, cortar en trozos
2 (= join) [+ parts] juntar, unir; [+ wood, pipes] ensamblar
CPD ▸ joint account cuenta f conjunta ▸ joint author coautor(a) m/f ▸ joint communiqué comunicado m conjunto ▸ joint consultations consultas fpl bilaterales ▸ joint heir coheredero/a m/f ▸ joint honours (Brit) carrera f de doble titulación • she graduated last year with ~ honours in anthropology and geography el año pasado se licenció en antropología y geografía ▸ joint interest (Comm) coparticipación f ▸ joint liability (Comm) responsabilidad f solidaria ▸ joint owners copropietarios mpl ▸ joint ownership copropiedad f ▸ joint partner copartícipe mf ▸ joint stock fondo m social ▸ joint stock bank banco m comercial ▸ joint stock company sociedad f anónima ▸ joint venture empresa f conjunta

jointed [ˈdʒɔɪntɪd] ADJ [doll] articulado; [fishing rod, tent pole] plegable

jointly [ˈdʒɔɪntlɪ] ADV en común, conjuntamente

jointure [ˈdʒɔɪntʃəʳ] N (Jur) bienes fpl gananciales de la esposa

joist [dʒɔɪst] N viga f, vigueta f

jojoba [həʊˈhəʊbə] N jojoba f
CPD [shampoo, conditioner, oil] de jojoba

joke [dʒəʊk] N (= witticism, story) chiste m; (= practical joke) broma f; (= hoax) broma f; (= person) hazmerreír m • what sort of a ~ is this? ¿qué clase de broma es esta? • the ~ is that ... lo gracioso es que ... • to take sth as a ~ tomar algo a broma • to treat sth as a ~ tomar algo a broma • it's (gone) beyond a ~ (Brit) esto no tiene nada de gracioso • to crack a ~ hacer un chiste • to crack ~s with sb contarse chistes con algn • they spent an evening cracking ~s together pasaron una tarde contándose chistes • for a ~ en broma • one can have a ~ with her tiene mucho sentido del humor • is that your idea of a ~? ¿es que eso tiene gracia? • he will have his little ~ siempre está con sus bromas • to make a ~ hacer un chiste (about sth sobre algo) • he made a ~ of the disaster se tomó el desastre a risa • it's no ~ no tiene nada de divertido • it's no ~ having to go out in this weather no tiene nada de divertido salir con este tiempo • the ~ is on you la broma la pagas tú • to play a ~ on sb gastar una broma a algn • I don't see the ~ no le veo la gracia • he's a standing ~ es un pobre hombre • it's a standing ~ here aquí eso siempre provoca risa • I can take a ~ tengo mucha correa or mucho aguante • he can't take a ~ no le gusta que le tomen el pelo • to tell a ~ contar un chiste (about sth sobre algo) • why do you have to turn everything into a ~? ¿eres incapaz de tomar nada en serio? • what a ~! (iro) ¡qué gracia! (iro)
VI (= make jokes) contar chistes, hacer chistes; (= be frivolous) bromear • to ~ about sth (= make jokes about) contar chistes sobre algo; (= make light of) tomarse algo a risa • I was only joking lo dije en broma, no iba en serio • I'm not joking hablo en serio • you're joking! • you must be joking! ¡no lo dices en serio!
CPD ▸ joke book libro m de chistes

joker [ˈdʒəʊkəʳ] N 1 (= wit) chistoso/a m/f, guasón/ona m/f; (= practical joker) bromista mf
2* (= idiot) payaso/a m/f; (stronger) idiota mf • some ~ will always start singing siempre hay algún payaso que se pone a cantar
3 (Cards) comodín m • he's the ~ in the pack (fig) es el gran desconocido, el la gran incógnita

jokester [ˈdʒəʊkstəʳ] N bromista mf

jokey [ˈdʒəʊkɪ] ADJ [person] chistoso, guasón; [reference] humorístico; [mood, tone] guasón

jokily [ˈdʒəʊkɪlɪ] ADV [say] en tono de broma; [do] en broma

joking [ˈdʒəʊkɪŋ] ADJ [tone] burlón; [reference] humorístico • I'm not in a ~ mood no estoy para bromas
N (= jokes) (practical) bromas fpl; (verbal) chistes mpl, cuentos mpl (LAm) • ~ apart or aside ... fuera de bromas ..., hablando en serio ...

jokingly [ˈdʒəʊkɪŋlɪ] ADV (= laughingly) en broma; (= mockingly) en son de burla • he said ~ dijo en broma, dijo guasón

jollification [ˌdʒɒlɪfɪˈkeɪʃən] N
1 (= merriment) regocijo m, festividades fpl
2 (= party) fiesta f, guateque m

jolliness [ˈdʒɒlɪnɪs] N jovialidad f

jollity [ˈdʒɒlɪtɪ] N alegría f, regocijo m

jolly [ˈdʒɒlɪ] ADJ (COMPAR: **jollier**, SUPERL: **jolliest**) [person] (= cheerful) alegre; (= amusing) divertido; [laugh] gracioso • it was all very ~ todo fue muy agradable • it wasn't very ~ for the rest of us los demás no nos divertimos tanto • we had a ~ time lo pasamos muy bien, nos divertimos mucho • to get ~* achisparse*
ADV (Brit*) muy, la mar de, bastante (LAm) • we were ~ glad estábamos la mar de contentos, nos alegramos muchísimo • it's ~ hard es terriblemente difícil • you did ~ well lo hiciste la mar de bien* • you've ~ well got to no tienes otro remedio, no te queda otra (LAm) • ~ good! ¡estupendo!, ¡macanudo! (Peru, S. Cone)
VT • to ~ sb along dar ánimos a algn, animar a algn • to ~ sb into doing sth engatusar a algn para que haga algo
CPD ▸ jolly boat esquife m ▸ Jolly Roger bandera f pirata

jolt [dʒəʊlt] N (= jerk) sacudida f; (= sudden bump) choque m; (fig) susto m • to give sb a ~ (fig) dar un susto a algn • it gave me a bit of a ~ me dio un buen susto
VT [vehicle] sacudir; [+ person, elbow] empujar (ligeramente), sacudir (levemente); (fig) afectar mucho • to ~ sb into (doing) sth mover a algn a hacer algo • to ~ sb out of his complacency hacer que algn se dé cuenta de la necesidad de hacer algo
VI [vehicle] traquetear, dar tumbos

jolting [ˈdʒəʊltɪŋ] N [of vehicle] traqueteo m

jolty [ˈdʒəʊltɪ] ADJ [vehicle] que traquetea, que da saltos

Jonah [ˈdʒəʊnə] N Jonás

Jonathan [ˈdʒɒnəθən] N Jonatás

jonquil [ˈdʒɒŋkwɪl] N junquillo m

Jordan [ˈdʒɔːdn] N 1 (= country) Jordania f
2 (= river) Jordán m

Jordanian [dʒɔːˈdeɪnɪən] ADJ jordano
N jordano/a m/f

Joseph [ˈdʒəʊzɪf] N José

Josephine [ˈdʒəʊzɪfiːn] N Josefina

josh* [dʒɒʃ] (esp US) VT tomar el pelo a
VI hacer bromas

Joshua [ˈdʒɒʃwə] N Josué

josser‡ [ˈdʒɒsəʳ] N (Brit) tío m, individuo m

joss stick [ˈdʒɒsstɪk] N pebete m

jostle [ˈdʒɒsl] VT empujar
VI empujar, dar empujones • to ~ against sb dar empujones a algn • to ~ for a place abrirse paso a empujones
N empujón m

jot [dʒɒt] N pizca f • there's not a jot of truth in it no tiene ni pizca de verdad; ▸ care
VT • to jot down apuntar, anotar

jotter [ˈdʒɒtəʳ] N (= notebook, pad) bloc m (de notas)

jottings [ˈdʒɒtɪŋz] NPL apuntes mpl, anotaciones fpl

joule [dʒuːl] N julio m, joule m

journal [ˈdʒɜːnl] N 1 (= diary) diario m; (Naut) diario m de navegación
2 (= periodical) periódico m; (= magazine) revista f
3 (Mech) gorrón m, muñón m
CPD ▸ journal bearing cojinete m

journalese [ˌdʒɜːnəˈliːz] N (pej) jerga f periodística

journalism [ˈdʒɜːnəlɪzəm] N periodismo m

journalist [ˈdʒɜːnəlɪst] N periodista mf, reportero/a m/f (LAm)

journalistic [ˌdʒɜːnəˈlɪstɪk] ADJ periodístico

journey [ˈdʒɜːnɪ] N (= trip) viaje m; (= distance) trayecto m, tramo m (LAm) • Scott's ~ to the Pole la expedición de Scott al Polo • the capsule's ~ through space el trayecto de la cápsula por el espacio • have you much ~ left? ¿le queda mucho camino? • to break one's ~ hacer una parada • to reach one's ~'s end llegar al final de su viaje, llegar a su destino • at ~'s end al fin del viaje • to be on a ~ estar de viaje • to go on a ~ hacer un viaje • to send sb on a ~ enviar a algn de viaje • the outward ~ el viaje de ida • pleasant ~! ¡buen viaje! • the return ~ el viaje de vuelta
VI viajar
CPD ▸ journey time duración f del trayecto or viaje • this added an extra half-hour to our ~ time esto supuso media hora más de viaje

journeyman [ˈdʒɜːnɪmən] N (PL: **journeymen**) oficial m

journo* [ˈdʒɜːnəʊ] N (Brit) periodista mf

joust [dʒaʊst] N justa f, torneo m
VI justar

jousting [ˈdʒaʊstɪŋ] N (Hist) justas fpl; (fig) competición f

Jove [dʒəʊv] N Júpiter • by ~! ¡caramba!, ¡por Dios!

jovial [ˈdʒəʊvɪəl] ADJ jovial

joviality [ˌdʒəʊvɪˈælɪtɪ] N jovialidad f

jovially [ˈdʒəʊvɪəlɪ] ADV jovialmente

jowl [dʒaʊl] N (gen pl) (= jaw) quijada f; (= cheek) carrillo m; (= chin) barbilla f; (Zool) papada f • a man with heavy ~s un hombre mofletudo

-jowled [ˈdʒaʊld] ADJ (ending in compounds) • square-jowled de mandíbulas cuadradas

jowly [ˈdʒaʊlɪ] ADJ de mejillas caídas

joy [dʒɔɪ] N (= happiness) alegría f; (= delight) júbilo m, regocijo m; (= source of delight) deleite m, alegría f • to be a joy to the eye ser un gozo para los ojos • it's a joy to hear him es un gusto oírlo, da gusto oírlo • the joys of opera los encantos de la ópera • the joys of camping (lit) (also hum) los placeres del camping • to be beside o.s. with joy no caber en sí de gozo • did you have any joy in finding it? ¿tuviste éxito en encontrarlo? • to jump or leap for joy saltar de alegría • no joy!* ¡sin resultado!, ¡sin éxito! • we got no joy out of it no logramos nada, no nos sirvió de nada • to our great joy ... para nuestra gran alegría ... • I wish you joy of it! (iro) ¡que lo disfrutes!, ¡enhorabuena!

joyful [ˈdʒɔɪfʊl] ADJ (gen) feliz; [event, occasion] festivo • to be ~ about sth alegrarse

J

de algo

joyfully ['dʒɔɪfəlɪ] ADV [*sing, play*] alegremente; [*greet, announce*] con júbilo

joyfulness ['dʒɔɪfʊlnɪs] N [*of atmosphere*] alegría *f*; [*of event, occasion*] festividad *f*; (*on hearing news*) júbilo *m*

joyless ['dʒɔɪlɪs] ADJ sin alegría, triste

joyous ['dʒɔɪəs] ADJ (*liter*) = **joyful**

joyously ['dʒɔɪəslɪ] ADV (*liter*) = **joyfully**

joypad ['dʒɔɪpæd] N gamepad *m*

joyride* ['dʒɔɪraɪd] N **1** (= *irresponsible action*) escapada *f*
2 (*in stolen car*) • **to go for a ~** dar una vuelta en un coche robado
VI dar una vuelta en un coche robado

joyrider ['dʒɔɪraɪdə^r] N *persona que se da una vuelta en un coche robado*

joyriding ['dʒɔɪraɪdɪŋ] N *delito de robar un coche para dar una vuelta en él*

joystick ['dʒɔɪstɪk] N (*Aer*) palanca *f* de mando; (*Comput*) palanca *f* de control, joystick *m*

JP N ABBR (*Brit*) = **Justice of the Peace**

JPEG, Jpeg ['dʒeɪpeg] N (= *format, image*) JPEG *m*, jpeg *m*
ADJ • **~ image** imagen *f* en formato JPEG

Jr ABBR (*US*) (= **junior**) jr.

JSA N ABBR (*Brit*) (*Admin*) = **job seeker's allowance**

JTPA N ABBR (*US*) (= **Job Training Partnership Act**) *programa gubernamental de formación profesional*

jubilant ['dʒu:bɪlənt] ADJ [*crowd*] jubiloso, exultante; [*cry, shout*] de júbilo, alborozado

jubilation [,dʒu:bɪ'leɪʃən] N júbilo *m*

jubilee ['dʒu:bɪli:] N (= *celebration*) jubileo *m*; (= *anniversary*) aniversario *m* • **silver ~** vigésimo quinto aniversario *m*

Judaea [dʒu:'dɪə] N Judea *f*

Judaeo-Christian, Judeo-Christian (*US*) [dʒu:,deɪəʊ'krɪstɪən] ADJ judeo-cristiano

Judah ['dʒu:də] N Judá *m*

Judaic [dʒu:'deɪɪk] ADJ judaico

Judaism ['dʒu:deɪɪzəm] N judaísmo *m*

Judaize ['dʒu:deraɪz] VI judaizar

Judaizer ['dʒu:deɪ,aɪzə^r] N judaizante *mf*

Judas ['dʒu:dəs] N (= *name*) Judas; (= *traitor*) judas *m*

judder ['dʒʌdə^r] (*Brit*) N vibración *f*
VI vibrar

Judeo-Spanish ['dʒu:deɪəʊ'spænɪʃ] ADJ judeoespañol, sefardí
N (*Ling*) judeoespañol *m*, ladino *m*

judge [dʒʌdʒ] N **1** (*Jur*) juez *mf*, juez(a) *m/f* • **(the Book of) Judges** el Libro de los Jueces • **~ of appeal** juez *mf* de alzadas, juez *mf* de apelaciones • **the ~'s rules** (*Brit*) los derechos del detenido
2 [*of contest*] juez *mf*, miembro *mf* del jurado; (*Sport*) árbitro *m*; (*in races*) juez *mf*
3 (= *knowledgeable person*) conocedor(a) *m/f* (**of** de), entendido/a *m/f* (**of** en); (= *expert*) perito/a *m/f* (**of** en) • **he's a fine ~ of horses** es un excelente conocedor de *or* entendido en caballos • **to be a good/bad ~ of character** ser buen/mal psicólogo, tener/no tener psicología para conocer a la gente • **I'm no ~ of wines** no entiendo de vinos • **I'll be the ~ of that** yo decidiré eso, lo juzgaré yo mismo
VT **1** [+ *person, case, contest*] juzgar; [+ *matter*] decidir, resolver • **who can ~ this question?** ¿quién puede resolver esta cuestión? • **he ~d the moment well** escogió el momento oportuno, atinó
2 (*Sport*) arbitrar
3 (= *estimate*) [+ *weight, size, distance*] calcular • **we ~d the distance right/wrong** calculamos bien/mal la distancia
4 (= *consider*) considerar • **I ~ him a fool** considero que es tonto • **I ~d it to be right** lo consideré acertado, me pareció correcto • **they thought that they were going to win easily, but they ~d wrong** creían que iban a ganar con facilidad, pero erraron en el juicio • **she suspected that his intentions were dishonest, and she ~d right** dudaba que sus intenciones fueran honestas, y acertó en el juicio • **as far as can be ~d** a mi modo de ver, según mi juicio • PROVERB: • **you can't ~ a book by its cover** no hay que fiarse de las apariencias, las apariencias engañan
VI (= *act as judge*) juzgar, ser juez • **judging from** *or* **to ~ by his expression** a juzgar por su expresión • **to ~ for o.s.** juzgar por sí mismo • **to ~ of** juzgar de, opinar sobre • **who am I to ~?** ¿es que yo soy capaz de juzgar? • **as far as I can ~** por lo que puedo entender, a mi entender • **only an expert can ~** solo lo puede decidir un experto
CPD ▸ **judge advocate** (*Mil*) auditor *m* de guerra

judgement ['dʒʌdʒmənt] N = **judgment**

judgemental [dʒʌdʒ'mentl] ADJ = **judgmental**

judging ['dʒʌdʒɪŋ] N (*at competition, show*) evaluación *f* • **the ~ was difficult as always** como siempre la evaluación resultó difícil

judgment ['dʒʌdʒmənt] N **1** (*Jur*) (= *decision*) sentencia *f*, fallo *m*; (= *act*) juicio *m* • **it's a ~ on you** es un castigo • **to pass** *or* **pronounce ~ (on sb/sth)** (*Jur*) pronunciar *or* dictar sentencia (sobre algn/en algo), emitir un fallo (sobre algn/algo); (*fig*) emitir un juicio crítico (sobre algn/algo), dictaminar (sobre algn/algo) • **to sit in ~ on sb** decidir sobre la culpabilidad de algn • **to sit in ~ on sth** juzgar algo • **Last Judgment** Juicio *m* Final
2 (= *opinion*) opinión *f*, parecer *m* • **a critical ~ of Auden** un juicio crítico de Auden
3 (= *understanding*) juicio *m*, criterio *m* • **in my ~** a mi juicio • **to the best of my ~** según mi leal saber y entender • **against my better ~** a pesar mío • **to have good** *or* **sound ~** tener buen juicio, tener buen criterio • **she showed excellent ~ in choosing the colour scheme** demostró tener buen gusto al escoger la combinación de colores; ▹ **colour**
CPD ▸ **judgment call** (*esp US*) *decisión que depende de la conciencia de cada uno* ▸ **Judgment Day** Día *m* del Juicio Final ▸ **judgment seat** tribunal *m*

judgmental [dʒʌdʒ'mentl] ADJ crítico

judicature ['dʒu:dɪkətʃə^r] N judicatura *f*

judicial [dʒu:'dɪʃəl] ADJ **1** [*decision, proceedings*] judicial; [*separation*] legal
2 [*mind, faculty*] crítico
CPD ▸ **judicial inquiry** investigación *f* judicial ▸ **judicial review** (*Brit*) control *m* jurisdiccional de la legalidad; (*US*) revisión *f* judicial

judicially [dʒu:'dɪʃəlɪ] ADV [*decide*] judicialmente; [*separate*] legalmente

judiciary [dʒu:'dɪʃɪərɪ] ADJ judicial
N (= *judges*) judicatura *f*; (= *court system*) poder *m* judicial

judicious [dʒu:'dɪʃəs] ADJ (*frm*) sensato, juicioso

judiciously [dʒu:'dɪʃəslɪ] ADV (*frm*) juiciosamente

Judith ['dʒu:dɪθ] N Judit

judo ['dʒu:dəʊ] N judo *m*, yudo *m*

judoka ['dʒu:dəʊ,kɑ:] N judoka *mf*

Judy ['dʒu:dɪ] N *familiar form of* **Judith**

jug [dʒʌg] N **1** (= *container*) jarro *m*, jarra *f*
2‡ (= *prison*) chirona *f*, chirola *f* (*LAm*)
3 jugs (*US‡*) (= *breasts*) tetas* *fpl*
VT **1** • **jugged hare** *estofado de liebre condimentado y regado con vino*
2‡ (= *imprison*) meter a la sombra‡

juggernaut ['dʒʌgənɔ:t] N **1** (*Brit*) (= *lorry*) camión *m* de gran tonelaje
2 (*fig*) (= *large and powerful entity*) monstruo *m* • **the group became a sales ~** el grupo se convirtió en un monstruo en ventas • **the ~ of tradition/religion** la fuerza irresistible de la tradición/religión

juggins‡ ['dʒʌgɪnz] N bobo/a *m/f*

juggle ['dʒʌgl] VI hacer juegos malabares (**with** con); (*fig*) darle vueltas (**with** a)
VT [+ *balls, plates*] hacer juegos malabares con; (*fig*) (*pej*) [+ *facts, figures*] amañar, falsear • **to ~ a career and a family** compaginar las responsabilidades profesionales con las familiares

juggler ['dʒʌglə^r] N malabarista *mf*

jugglery ['dʒʌglərɪ] N = **juggling**

juggling ['dʒʌglɪŋ] N juegos *mpl* malabares, malabarismo *m*; (*fig*) (*pej*) trampas *fpl*, fraude *m*
CPD ▸ **juggling act** (*fig*) malabarismos *mpl* • **balancing the budget is a complex ~ act** hay que hacer malabarismos para nivelar el presupuesto

Jugoslav ['ju:gəʊ'slɑ:v] ADJ yugoslavo
N yugoslavo/a *m/f*

Jugoslavia ['ju:gəʊ'slɑ:vɪə] N Yugoslavia *f*

jugular ['dʒʌgjʊlə^r] ADJ • **~ vein** yugular *f*, vena *f* yugular
N yugular *f*, vena *f* yugular

juice [dʒu:s] N **1** [*of fruit, vegetable*] jugo *m*, zumo *m* (*Sp*); [*of meat*] jugo *m*
2* (= *petrol*) gasolina *f*
3* (= *electricity*) corriente *f*
4 (*Anat*) • **digestive ~s** jugos *mpl* digestivos, jugos *mpl* gástricos
CPD ▸ **juice extractor** (*Brit*) exprimidor *m* eléctrico

juicer ['dʒu:sə^r] N (*US*) exprimidor *m* eléctrico

juiciness ['dʒu:sɪnɪs] N **1** [*of fruit, meat*] jugosidad *f*
2* [*of story*] lo sabroso, lo picante

juicy ['dʒu:sɪ] ADJ (COMPAR: **juicier**, SUPERL: **juiciest**) **1** [*fruit, meat*] jugoso
2 (*fig*) [*story*] sabroso, picante; [*contract*] sustancioso, jugoso

jujitsu [dʒu:'dʒɪtsʊ] N jiu-jitsu *m*

jujube ['dʒu:dʒu:b] N pastilla *f*

jujutsu [dʒu:'dʒɪtsʊ] N jiu-jitsu *m*

jukebox ['dʒu:kbɒks] N máquina *f* de discos, gramola® *f*, rocanola *f* (*LAm*)

Jul ABBR (= **July**) jul.

julep ['dʒu:lep] N julepe *m*

Julian ['dʒu:lɪən] N Juliano, Julián

Juliet ['dʒu:lɪet] N Julieta

Julius ['dʒu:lɪəs] N Julio • **~ Caesar** Julio César

July [dʒu:'laɪ] N julio *m* • **~ was wet this year** este año llovió mucho en julio • **at the beginning of ~** a principios de julio • **during (the month of) ~** durante el mes de julio • **each ~** cada mes de julio, todos los meses de julio • **at the end of ~** a finales de julio • **every ~** todos los meses de julio • **in (the month of) ~** en (el mes de) julio • **in ~ of next year** en julio del año que viene • **there are 31 days in ~** julio tiene treinta y un días • **in the middle of ~** a mediados de julio • **on the first/eleventh of ~** el primero/once de julio
CPD ▸ **July sales** • **the ~ sales** las rebajas de julio

jumble ['dʒʌmbl] N **1** [*of objects*] revoltijo *m*, batiburrillo *m*; (*fig*) confusión *f*, embrollo *m* • **a ~ of furniture** un batiburrillo de muebles, un montón de muebles revueltos • **a ~ of sounds** unos ruidos confusos
2 (*Brit*) (*at jumble sale*) (= *old clothes*) ropa *f* usada; (= *bric-à-brac*) objetos *mpl* usados
VT (*also* **jumble together, jumble up**)

mezclar, amontonar • **papers ~d up together** papeles revueltos • **they were just ~d together anyhow** estaban mezclados *or* amontonados de cualquier manera

CPD ▸ **jumble sale** (*Brit*) mercadillo *m* benéfico (*venta de objetos usados con fines benéficos*)

jumbo ['dʒʌmbəʊ] N **1** (= *elephant*) elefante/a *m/f*

2 = **jumbo jet**

ADJ* (*also* **jumbo sized**) gigante, de tamaño extra

CPD ▸ **jumbo jet** jumbo *m* ▸ **jumbo pack** (= *packet*) paquete *m* gigante; [*of bottles, cans*] pack *m* gigante

jump [dʒʌmp] N **1** (*Sport, Parachuting*) salto *m*; (= *leap*) salto *m*, brinco *m* • **what a great ~!** ¡qué gran salto! • **it was a three metre ~ to the other side** había que saltar tres metros para pasar al otro lado • **high ~** salto *m* de altura • **long ~** salto *m* de longitud • **in** *or* **at one ~** de un salto, de un brinco; ▹ **running**

2 (= *start*) • **she gave an involuntary ~** se sobresaltó sin querer • **my heart gave a ~** me dio un vuelco el corazón

3 (= *fence, obstacle*) obstáculo *m*

4 (*fig*) (= *step*) salto *m* • **in one ~ he went from novice to master** de un salto *or* golpe pasó de novicio a maestro • **Taiwan made the ~ from poverty to wealth in a single generation** Taiwán pasó de golpe *or* dio el salto de la pobreza a la riqueza en una sola generación • IDIOMS: • **to be one ~ ahead (of sb)** llevar ventaja *or* la delantera (a algn) • **try to keep one ~ ahead of the competition** intenta llevarle ventaja *or* la delantera a la competencia • **to keep one ~ ahead of the pack** mantenerse a la cabeza del pelotón • **to get a** *or* **the ~ on sb*** adelantarse a algn

5 (= *increase*) aumento *m*, subida *f* • **there has been a ~ in prices/unemployment** se ha producido un aumento *or* una subida de precios/del número de parados

VI **1** (= *leap*) (*gen*) saltar; (*from aeroplane*) lanzarse, tirarse • **how far can you ~?** ¿hasta qué distancia puedes saltar? • **how high can you ~?** ¿hasta qué altura puedes saltar? • **did he ~ or was he pushed?** (*lit*) ¿saltó o lo empujaron?, ¿se tiró o lo empujaron?; (*fig*) ¿se fue o lo echaron? • **to ~ across a stream** cruzar un arroyo de un salto, saltar por encima de un arroyo • **he ~ed back in horror** de un salto retrocedió horrorizado • **she ~ed into the river** se tiró al río • **to ~ into bed** meterse en la cama de un salto • **there were plenty of men ready to ~ into bed with me** (*fig*) había muchos hombres dispuestos a acostarse conmigo • **to ~ for joy** saltar de alegría • **to ~ off a bus/train** bajar de un autobús/tren de un salto • **to ~ on a bus/train** subir a un autobús/tren de un salto • **he ~ed out of a third floor window** saltó *or* se tiró desde una ventana del tercer piso • **to ~ out of bed** saltar de la cama • **he ~ed over the fence** saltó (por encima de) la valla • **he ~ed to his feet** se puso de pie de un salto • **~ to it!*** ¡venga, muévete!, ¡rápido!, ¡apúrate! (*LAm*) • **to ~ up** ponerse de pie de un salto • **I ~ed up and down to keep warm** me puse a dar saltos para que no me entrara frío

2 (= *start*) sobresaltarse • **he ~ed at the sound of her voice** se sobresaltó al oír su voz • **to make sb ~** dar un susto a algn, sobresaltar a algn • **you made me ~!** ¡qué susto me diste!; ▹ **skin**

3 (*fig*) (*with prep, adv*) • **to ~ at sth** no dejar escapar algo • **they offered me a really good salary and thought I'd ~ at it** me ofrecieron un sueldo buenísimo y creyeron que no lo dejaría escapar • **he'd ~ at the chance to get out of the office** si tuviera la oportunidad de irse de la oficina no la dejaría escapar • **then the film ~s forward 20 years** luego la película da un salto adelante de 20 años • **to ~ from one subject to another** saltar de un tema a otro • **he ~s on everything I say** le pone faltas a todo lo que digo; ▹ **bandwagon, conclusion, throat**

4 (= *increase*) [*sales, profits*] subir, aumentar; [*shares*] subir

VT **1** (*lit*) (*also* **jump over**) [+ *ditch, fence*] saltar (por encima de); (*in draughts, chess*) comerse

2 [+ *horse*] (= *cause to jump*) hacer saltar; (= *enter in competition*) presentar; (= *ride*) montar • **she ~ed her horse over the fence** hizo saltar la valla a su caballo

3 (*fig*) (= *skip*) saltarse • **the film ~ed the first ten years of his life** la película se saltó los diez primeros años de su vida • **you've ~ed a page** te has saltado una página • **to ~ the lights** (*Aut**) saltarse el semáforo (en rojo) • **to ~ the queue** (*Brit*) colarse

4 (= *leave, escape*) • **to ~ bail** (*Jur*) fugarse estando bajo fianza • **to ~ the rails** [*train*] descarrilar, salirse de la vía • **to ~ ship** (*lit*) desertar (de un buque); (*fig*) (= *leave*) marcharse; (= *join rival organization*) irse con la competencia • **my salary was lousy so I ~ed ship** tenía un sueldo mísero así que me marché • **to ~ town** (*US‡*) abandonar la ciudad

5 (= *anticipate*) • IDIOM: • **to ~ the gun*** precipitarse

6 (= *board*) • **to ~ a train** subirse a un tren sin billete

7* (= *attack*) echarse encima de • **one of them ~ed him from behind** uno de ellos se le echó encima por detrás

CPD ▸ **jump jet** avión *m* de despegue vertical ▸ **jump jockey** jockey *m* de carreras (*de obstáculos*) ▸ **jump leads** (*Brit*) (*Aut*) cables *mpl* de arranque (de batería) ▸ **jump rope** (*US*) comba *f*, cuerda *f* de saltar ▸ **jump seat** (*Aut, Aer*) asiento *m* plegable

▸ **jump about, jump around** VI + ADV **1** (*lit*) dar saltos, brincar

2 (*fig*) dar saltos • **the story ~s about a bit** la historia da muchos saltos

▸ **jump down** VI + ADV bajar de un salto

▸ **jump in** VI + ADV **1** (*into car*) subirse corriendo; (*into water*) tirarse • **~ in!** ¡sube!, ¡vamos!

2 (*fig*) (*in situation, conversation*) intervenir • **the government had to ~ in and buy millions of dollars worth of supplies** el gobierno tuvo que intervenir y comprar suministros por valor de millones de dólares

▸ **jump off** VI + ADV (*Showjumping*) desempatar

▸ **jump out** VI + ADV (= *appear suddenly*) salir de un salto; (*from vehicle*) bajar de un salto • **he ~ed out from behind a tree** salió de un salto de detrás de un árbol • **it ~s out at you** (*fig*) salta a la vista

jumped-up* ['dʒʌmpt'ʌp] ADJ (*Brit*) (*pej*) presumido

jumper ['dʒʌmpəʳ] N **1** (*Sport*) saltador(a) *m/f*

2 (*Brit*) (= *sweater*) jersey *m*, suéter *m*

3 (*US*) (= *pinafore dress*) falda *f* tipo mono, pichi *m*

CPD ▸ **jumper cables** (*US*) = **jump leads**

jumpiness ['dʒʌmpɪnɪs] N nerviosismo *m*

jumping ['dʒʌmpɪŋ] N (*Sport*) pruebas *fpl* de salto

CPD ▸ **jumping bean** judía *f* saltadora, fríjol *m* saltador ▸ **jumping jack** (= *firework*) buscapiés *m inv*; (= *puppet*) *muñeco que se acciona tirando de un hilo* ▸ **jumping rope** (*US*) comba *f*, cuerda *f* de saltar

jumping-off place [,dʒʌmpɪŋ'ɒf,pleɪs], **jumping-off point** [,dʒʌmpɪŋ'ɒf,pɔɪnt] N punto *m* de partida

jump-off ['dʒʌmpɒf] N (*Showjumping*) prueba *f* de desempate, saltos *mpl* de desempate

jump-start ['dʒʌmpstɑːt] N (*Aut*) (*pushing*) arranque *m* en frío (*empujando el automóvil*); (*using jump leads*) arranque *m* con puente • **he gave me a jump-start** (*pushing*) me ayudó a arrancar el coche empujándolo; (*using jump leads*) me ayudó a arrancar el coche haciendo un puente

VT [+ *car*] (*by pushing*) arrancar empujando; (*using jump leads*) arrancar haciendo un puente

jumpsuit ['dʒʌmpsuːt] N (*US*) mono *m*

jumpy ['dʒʌmpɪ] ADJ (COMPAR: **jumpier**, SUPERL: **jumpiest**) nervioso; (= *easily startled*) asustadizo

Jun ABBR **1** (= **June**) jun.

2 (= **junior**) jr

junction ['dʒʌŋkʃən] N **1** (= *joining*) [*of bones, pipes*] juntura *f*, unión *f*

2 (*Brit*) (= *meeting place*) [*of roads*] cruce *m*, crucero *m* (*LAm*); [*of railway lines*] empalme *m*; [*of rivers*] confluencia *f*

CPD ▸ **junction box** (*Elec*) caja *f* de empalmes

juncture ['dʒʌŋktʃəʳ] N (*fig*) (= *point*) coyuntura *f* • **at this ~** en este momento, a estas alturas

June [dʒuːn] N junio *m*; ▹ **July**

Jungian [jʊŋɪən] ADJ jungiano

N jungiano/a *m/f*

jungle ['dʒʌŋgl] N **1** selva *f*, jungla *f*; (*fig*) maraña *f*, selva *f* • **the law of the ~** (*fig*) la ley de la selva

2 (*Mus*) jungle *m*, *género de música de baile de ritmo acelerado*

CPD [*animal, bird*] de la selva, selvático; [*law, life, sounds*] de la selva ▸ **jungle bunny** (*US***) negrito/a* *m/f* ▸ **jungle gym** *armazón de barras para juegos infantiles* ▸ **jungle warfare** guerra *f* en la selva

junior ['dʒuːnɪəʳ] ADJ [*employee, executive, manager*] (*in age*) más joven; (*in length of service*) de menor antigüedad; (*in position, rank*) subalterno, auxiliar; [*partner*] segundo; [*section*] (*in competition*) juvenil • **Roy Smith, Junior** Roy Smith, hijo

N **1** (= *younger person*) menor *mf*, joven *mf*; (*US**) (= *son*) hijo *m*, niño *m* • **he is my ~ by three years** • **he is three years my ~** tiene tres años menos que yo, le llevo tres años

2 (*Brit*) (*Scol*) alumno/a *m/f* (*de 7 a 11 años*); (*US*) (*Univ*) estudiante *mf* de penúltimo año; ▹ GRADE

3 (*in rank*) subalterno/a *m/f*, auxiliar *mf*; (= *office junior*) recadero *m*

CPD ▸ **junior clerk** (*Jur*) secretario/a *m/f* judicial ▸ **junior college** (*US*) *centro universitario donde se imparten cursos de dos años* ▸ **junior doctor** médico/a *m/f* residente ▸ **junior executive** ejecutivo/a *m/f* joven ▸ **junior high school** (*US*) ≈ centro de enseñanza secundaria ▸ **junior minister** (*Pol*) ≈ secretario/a *m/f* de Estado, ≈ subsecretario/a *m/f* ▸ **junior partner** (*in firm*) socio/a *m/f* adjunto/a ▸ **junior school** (*Brit*) escuela *f* primaria ▸ **junior size** talla *f* infantil

juniper ['dʒuːnɪpəʳ] N enebro *m*

CPD ▸ **juniper berries** bayas *fpl* de enebro

junk¹ [dʒʌŋk] N **1** (= *worthless things*) trastos *mpl* viejos, cacharros* *mpl*; (= *bric-à-brac*) cachivaches *mpl*; (= *cheap goods*) baratijas *fpl*;

(= *things thrown away*) desperdicios *mpl*, desechos *mpl*; (= *iron*) chatarra *f*
2* (= *rubbish*) porquería *f* • **the play is a lot of ~** la obra es una chapuza *or* porquería • **this umbrella is a piece of ~** este paraguas es una porquería • **he eats nothing but ~** no come más que porquerías • **he talks a lot of ~** no dice más que tonterías
(VT)* [+ *object*] tirar, tirar a la basura; [+ *idea, theory etc*] desechar
(CPD) ▸ **junk bond** bono *m* basura ▸ **junk dealer** vendedor(a) *m/f* de objetos usados ▸ **junk food** comida *f* basura ▸ **junk heap** • **to end up on the ~ heap** terminar en el cubo de la basura ▸ **junk mail** propaganda *f* por correo ▸ **junk room** trastero *m* ▸ **junk shop** tienda *f* de objetos usados

junk[2] [dʒʌŋk] (N) (= *Chinese boat*) junco *m*

junket ['dʒʌŋkɪt] (N) **1** (*Culin*) dulce *m* de leche cuajada, cajeta *f* (*LAm*)
2* (= *party*) fiesta *f*
3 (*US*) (= *excursion at public expense*) *viaje de placer realizado por un funcionario público o miembro de un comité a expensas del contribuyente*
(VI) ir de juerga*, estar de fiesta

junketing ['dʒʌŋkɪtɪŋ] (N) (*also* **junketings**) festividades *fpl*, fiestas *fpl*

junkie* ['dʒʌŋkɪ] (N) (= *drug addict*) yonqui* *mf*; (= *esp of heroin*) heroinómano/a *m/f* • **chocolate ~** adicto/a *m/f* al chocolate

junkman ['dʒʌŋkmæn] (N) (PL: **junkmen**) chatarrero *m*

junkyard ['dʒʌŋkjɑ:d] (N) depósito *m* de chatarra, chatarrería *f*

Juno ['dʒu:nəʊ] (N) Juno

Junoesque [,dʒu:nəʊ'esk] (ADJ) [*figure*] imponente, majestuoso; [*woman*] de belleza majestuosa

Junr. (ABBR) (= **junior**) jr

junta ['dʒʌntə] (N) junta *f* militar

Jupiter ['dʒu:pɪtə[r]] (N) Júpiter *m*

Jurassic [dʒʊ'ræsɪk] (ADJ) jurásico

juridical [dʒʊə'rɪdɪkəl] (ADJ) jurídico

jurisdiction [,dʒʊərɪs'dɪkʃən] (N) jurisdicción *f* • **it falls** *or* **comes within our ~** entra dentro de nuestra jurisdicción, es de nuestra competencia • **it falls** *or* **comes outside our ~** se sale de nuestra jurisdicción, no es de nuestra competencia

jurisdictional [,dʒʊərɪs'dɪkʃənl] (ADJ) (*US*) [*dispute, rights*] jurisdiccional

jurisprudence [,dʒʊərɪs'pru:dəns] (N) jurisprudencia *f* • **medical ~** medicina *f* legal

jurist ['dʒʊərɪst] (N) jurista *mf*

juror ['dʒʊərə[r]] (N) (*Jur*) jurado *m*; (*for contest*) juez *m* • **a woman ~** una miembro del jurado

jury ['dʒʊərɪ] (N) jurado *m* • **trial by ~** proceso con jurado • **to serve** *or* **be on a ~** ser miembro de un jurado • IDIOM: • **the ~ is still out on that one** eso está por ver, no hay una opinión clara sobre eso; ▸ GRAND JURY
(CPD) ▸ **jury box** tribuna *f* del jurado ▸ **jury duty** • **to do ~ duty** actuar como jurado ▸ **jury foreman** (*in court of law*) portavoz *mf* del jurado (popular) ▸ **jury rigging** amaño *m* de un jurado ▸ **jury service** (*Brit*) • **to do ~ service** ser miembro de un jurado ▸ **jury system** (*Jur*) sistema *m* del jurado (popular)

juryman ['dʒʊərɪmən] (N) (PL: **jurymen**) miembro *m* del jurado

jurywoman ['dʒu:rɪwʊmən] (N) (PL: **jurywomen**) miembro *f* (femenino) del jurado

just[1] [dʒʌst] (ADJ) **1** (= *fair*) [*person, system*] justo • **as is only ~** como es justo, como es de razón
2 (= *deserved*) [*praise, reward*] merecido; [*punishment*] apropiado, justo
3 (= *justified*) [*complaint, criticism*] justificado; [*opinion*] lógico; ▸ **deserts**
4 (= *accurate*) [*account*] correcto; [*assessment*] correcto, exacto
(NPL) • **the ~** los justos

just[2] [dʒʌst]

ADVERB

1 (*relating to time*) **a** (= *at this moment*) ahora mismo • **we're ~ off** nos vamos ahora mismo • **I'm ~ coming!** ¡ya voy! • **"have some tea!" — "actually, I was ~ going"** —tómate un té —en realidad ya me iba
b (= *at that moment*) justo • **he was ~ leaving when the phone rang** estaba justo saliendo cuando sonó el teléfono
c (= *recently, a moment ago*) • **we were ~ talking about that** precisamente *or* ahora mismo estábamos hablando de eso • **~ cooked** recién hecho • **it's ~ gone 10 o'clock** acaban de dar las diez • **to have ~ done sth** acabar de hacer algo • **he has ~ left** acaba de irse • **he had ~ left** acababa de irse • **~ married** recién casados • **the book is ~ out** el libro acaba de salir • **it's ~ past 10 o'clock** acaban de dar las diez
d (*in expressions specifying "when"*) • **~ after I arrived** poco después de mi llegada • **~ after Christmas** justo después de Navidad • **it's ~ after 9 o'clock** son las nueve un poco pasadas • **~ as I arrived** justo cuando yo llegaba • **~ as it started to rain** justo cuando empezó a llover, en el momento en que empezó a llover • **~ before I arrived** poco antes de mi llegada • **~ before Christmas** justo antes de Navidad • **I saw him ~ this minute** lo he visto hace un momento • **I've ~ this minute finished it** acabo de terminarlo en este momento • **~ at that moment** en ese mismo momento *or* instante • **~ this morning** esta misma mañana • **~ when it was going well** ... precisamente *or* justamente cuando iba bien ... • **~ yesterday** ayer mismo • **"are you leaving?" — "not ~ yet"** —¿te vas? —aún *or* todavía no; ▸ **now, recently, then**

2 (= *barely*) por poco • **we (only) ~ missed it** lo perdimos por muy poco • **I (only) ~ caught it** lo alcancé por un pelo, por poco lo pierdo • **we had ~ enough money** teníamos el dinero justo • **he missed the train, but only ~** perdió el tren, pero por poco • **he passed, but only ~** aprobó pero por los pelos • **we arrived ~ in time** por poco no llegamos, llegamos justo a tiempo

3 (= *slightly*) • **~ over/under two kilos** un poco más de/menos de dos kilos • **it's ~ over/under two kilos** pasa de/no llega a los dos kilos • **~ to the left/right** un poco más a la izquierda/derecha • **~ to one side** a un lado

4 (= *exactly*) justo, exactamente • **it's ~ my size** es justo *or* exactamente mi talla • **it's ~ the same** es justo *or* exactamente igual • **~ here/there** aquí/ahí mismo • **~ behind/in front of/next to** *etc* justo detrás/delante de/al lado de *etc* • **it's ~ (on) 10 (o'clock)** son las diez en punto • **it cost ~ (on) £20** me costó veinte libras justas • **~ how many we don't know** no sabemos exactamente cuántos • **that's ~ it!** ¡ahí está!*, ¡esa es la cuestión! • **he's ~ like his father** (*physically, in behaviour*) es idéntico a su padre • **that's ~ like him, always late** es típico (de él), siempre llega tarde • **they are ~ like brothers** son como hermanos • **they have their problems ~ like the rest of us** tienen sus problemas, exactamente igual que el resto de nosotros • **I can't find £1,000 ~ like that** no puedo conseguir mil libras así sin más • **that's ~ the point!** ¡ahí está!*, ¡esa es la cuestión! • **he likes everything ~ so*** le gusta que todo esté perfecto • **it's ~ what I wanted** es justo *or* precisamente lo que quería • **that's ~ what I thought** eso es justo *or* precisamente lo que pensé • **~ what did he say?** ¿qué dijo exactamente? • **~ what are you implying?** ¿qué es exactamente lo que estás insinuando?; ▸ **luck, right**

5 (= *only*) solo, sólo, nomás (*LAm*)

In the past the standard spelling for **solo** *as an adverb was with an accent* (**sólo**)*. Nowadays the* **Real Academia Española** *advises that the accented form is only required where there might otherwise be confusion with the adjective* **solo***.*

• **they were ~ 15 when they got married** tenían solo *or* nada más 15 años cuando se casaron • **he's ~ a lad** no es más que un chaval, es solo un chaval • **it's ~ a mouse** es solo un ratón • **don't take any notice of her, she's ~ jealous** no le hagas ni caso, lo que está es celosa *or* lo que pasa es que está celosa • **it's ~ around the corner** está a la vuelta de la esquina • **I ~ asked!** (*hum*) ¡preguntaba nada más! • **~ a few** solo unos pocos, unos pocos nada más • **~ a little** solo un poco, un poco nada más • **~ once** una vez nada más, solamente *or* solo una vez • **it's ~ over there** está ahí mismo • **it's ~ a suggestion** es solo una sugerencia • **he's ~ teasing** solo está bromeando, está bromeando, nada más • **~ this once** solo esta vez • **we went ~ to see the museum** fuimos solo para ver el museo • **~ the two of us** los dos solos, solo nosotros dos • **I ~ wanted to say that** ... solo quería decir que ...; ▸ **friend, note**

6 (= *simply*) sencillamente • **I ~ told him to go away** le dije sencillamente que se fuera • **~ ask the way** simplemente pregunta por dónde se va • **I'm ~ phoning to remind you that** ... solo llamo para recordarte que ... • **let's ~ wait and see** es mejor esperar a ver (qué pasa) • **you should ~ send it back** deberías devolverlo sin más • **he couldn't ~ wait to see them** tenía unas ganas enormes de verlos • **it's ~ one of those things*** son cosas que pasan • **it's ~ that I don't like it** lo que pasa es que no me gusta • **I ~ thought that you would like it** yo pensé que te gustaría; ▸ **because, imagine, wonder**

7 (= *specially*) solo, sólo • **I did it ~ for you** lo hice solo por ti

8 (= *conceivably*) • **it may ~ be possible** puede que sea posible • **it's an old trick, but it could ~ work** es un viejo truco, pero puede que funcione

9 (*in comparisons*) • **~ as** tan • **it's ~ as good as yours** es tan bueno como el tuyo • **you sing ~ as well as he does** cantas tan bien como él • **the new one is ~ as big** el nuevo es igual de grande • **this model goes ~ as fast** este modelo va igual de rápido

10 (*in imperatives*) • **~ let me get my hands on him!*** ¡cómo lo coja!, ¡con que lo agarre! (*LAm*) • **~ listen to that rain!** ¡escucha *or* fíjate cómo llueve! • **~ listen a minute, will you?** ¡escúchame un momento!, ¿quieres? • **~ look at this mess!** ¡fíjate qué desorden! • **~ wait a minute!** ¡espera un momento! • **~ you wait, he'll come sure enough** (*reassuringly*) espera hombre, ya verás cómo viene • **~ (you) wait until I tell your father** (*threateningly*) ya verás cuando se lo cuente a tu padre, espera (nomás (*LAm*)) a que se lo cuente a tu padre • **~ you do!*** • **~ you try it!*** • **~ you dare!*** ¡inténtalo si te atreves!

11 (*emphatic*) • **she's ~ amazing!** es una mujer increíble • **"that dress is awful" — "isn't it ~?"*** —ese vestido es francamente horrible —¡y tanto! • **we're managing ~ fine** nos apañamos perfectamente • **it's ~ perfect!** ¡es absolutamente perfecto!; ▹ **plain**

12 (*imagining something*) • **I can ~ hear the roars of laughter** me puedo imaginar muy bien *or* perfectamente las carcajadas • **I can ~ imagine her reaction** me imagino muy bien *or* perfectamente su reacción • **I can ~ see her face if I told her** me puedo imaginar muy bien *or* perfectamente la cara que pondría si se lo dijese

13 (*in set expressions*) • **~ about:** • **I've ~ about finished this work** estoy a punto de terminar este trabajo • **it's ~ about finished** está casi terminado • **I think that it was ~ about here that I saw him** creo que yo estaba más o menos aquí cuando lo vi • **I've ~ about had enough of this noise!*** ¡estoy ya más que harto de este ruido! • **to be ~ about to do sth** estar a punto de hacer algo • **I was ~ about to phone** estaba a punto de llamar • **come ~ as you are** ven tal como estás • **leave it ~ as it is** déjalo tal como está • **~ as you wish** como usted quiera • **~ as I thought!** ¡ya me lo figuraba *or* imaginaba!, ¡lo que yo me figuraba *or* imaginaba! • **~ in case** por si acaso • **~ in case it rains** por si acaso llueve, por si llueve • **I've prepared some extra food, ~ in case** he preparado comida de más, por si las moscas* *or* por si acaso • **~ a minute!** • **~ one moment!** (= *coming*) ¡un momento, por favor!, ¡voy! • **~ a minute, I don't know if I agree with that ...** un momento, no sé si estoy de acuerdo con eso ... • **~ the same, I'd rather ...** de todas formas, prefiero ... • **that's ~ too bad!** (*iro*) ¡qué lástima!, ¡qué mala pata!* • **it's ~ as well** menos mal • **it's ~ as well it's insured** menos mal que está asegurado • **I wasn't expecting much, which was ~ as well** no esperaba mucho, y menos mal • **it would be ~ as well if we checked the prices** más valdría que comprobásemos los precios; ▹ **happen, soon**

---

justice [ˈdʒʌstɪs] N **1** (*Jur*) justicia *f* • **to bring sb to ~** llevar a algn ante los tribunales
2 (= *fairness*) justicia *f* • **to do o.s. ~** quedar bien • **to do sb ~** hacer justicia a algn • **this doesn't do him ~** [*photo etc*] no le favorece • **it doesn't do ~ to his skills** no está a la altura de sus capacidades • **to do ~ to a meal** hacer los honores a una comida
3 (= *person*) juez *mf* • **Justice of the Peace** (*Brit*) juez *mf* de paz • **(Lord) Chief Justice** Presidente *m* del Tribunal Supremo
CPD ▸ **Justice Department** (*in US*) Ministerio *m* de Justicia

justifiable [ˈdʒʌstɪfaɪəbl] ADJ **1** [*anger, pride, concern*] justificado • **that sort of behaviour is not ~** ese tipo de comportamiento no puede justificarse
2 (*Jur*) • **~ homicide** homicidio *m* justificado

justifiably [ˈdʒʌstɪfaɪəblɪ] ADV justificadamente, con razón • **he was ~ proud/angry** estaba orgulloso/enfadado y con razón, su orgullo/enfado era justificado • **he insisted, quite ~, that ...** insistía, justificadamente *or* con toda razón, en que ...

justification [ˌdʒʌstɪfɪˈkeɪʃən] N justificación *f* • **there's no ~ for it** esto no tiene justificación posible • **in ~ of** *or* **for sth** como justificación de algo

justified [ˈdʒʌstɪfaɪd] ADJ **1** (*gen*) justificado • **to be ~ in doing sth** tener motivos para hacer algo, tener razón al hacer algo • **am I ~ in thinking that ...?** ¿hay motivo para creer que ...?
2 (*Jur*) • **~ homicide** homicidio *m* justificado
3 (*Typ*) justificado • **right ~** justificado a la derecha

justify [ˈdʒʌstɪfaɪ] VT **1** (*gen*) justificar • **he tried to ~ his decision** trató de justificar su decisión • **the future does not ~ the slightest optimism** el futuro no da lugar al más leve optimismo
2 (*Typ, Comput*) alinear, justificar

justly [ˈdʒʌstlɪ] ADV (= *fairly*) justamente, con justicia; (= *rightly*) con razón • **it has been ~ said that ...** con razón se ha dicho que ...

justness [ˈdʒʌstnɪs] N justicia *f*

jut [dʒʌt] VI (*also* **jut out**) sobresalir

Jute [dʒu:t] N juto/a *m/f*

jute [dʒu:t] N yute *m*

juvenile [ˈdʒu:vənaɪl] ADJ [*books, sports etc*] juvenil; (*pej*) infantil; (*Jur*) [*court*] de menores • **~ delinquent** delincuente *mf* juvenil • **~ delinquency** delincuencia *f* juvenil
N joven *mf*, menor *mf*

juvenilia [ˌdʒu:vɪˈnɪlɪə] NPL obras *fpl* de juventud

juxtapose [ˈdʒʌkstəpəʊz] VT yuxtaponer

juxtaposition [ˌdʒʌkstəpəˈzɪʃən] N yuxtaposición *f*

j

Kk

K[1], **k** [keɪ] (N) (= *letter*) K, k *f* • **K for Kilo** K de Kilo

K[2] (ABBR) **1** (= **kilo-**) kilo-
2 (= *thousand*) • **he earns 30K** gana 30.000 libras
3 (*Brit*) (= **Knight**) *caballero de una orden*
4 (*Comput*) (= **kilobyte**) K *m*

K* [keɪ] (N ABBR) (= **ketamine**) ketamina *f*

Kabala [kə'bɑːlə] (N) Cábala *f*, Kábala *f*

Kaffir ['kæfəʳ] (N) (PL: **Kaffirs** *or* **Kaffir**) (*offensive*) cafre *mf*

Kafkaesque [ˌkæfkə'esk] (ADJ) kafkiano

kaftan ['kæftæn] (N) caftán *m*

Kaiser ['kaɪzəʳ] (N) káiser *m*

Kalahari Desert [ˌkælə'hɑːrɪ'dezət] (N) desierto *m* de Kalahari

Kalashnikov [kə'læʃnɪkɒf] (N) Kalashnikov *m*

kale [keɪl] (N) (*Bot*) col *f* rizada

kaleidoscope [kə'laɪdəskəʊp] (N) calidoscopio *m*, caleidoscopio *m*

kaleidoscopic [kəˌlaɪdə'skɒpɪk] (ADJ) calidoscópico

Kamasutra [ˌkɑːmə'suːtrə] (N) Kamasutra *m*

kamikaze [ˌkæmɪ'kɑːzɪ] (N) kamikaze *m*

Kampala [kæm'pɑːlə] (N) Kampala *f*

Kampuchea [ˌkæmpʊ'tʃɪə] (N) Kampuchea *f*

Kampuchean [ˌkæmpʊ'tʃɪən] (ADJ) kampucheano
(N) kampucheano/a *m/f*

Kan. (ABBR) (*US*) = **Kansas**

kanga ['kæŋgə] (N) *tela con unos diseños muy alegres usada como prenda por las mujeres del este de África*

kangaroo [ˌkæŋgə'ruː] (N) canguro/a *m/f*
(CPD) ▸ **kangaroo court** tribunal *m* desautorizado

Kans. (ABBR) (*US*) = **Kansas**

Kantian ['kæntɪən] (ADJ) kantiano
(N) kantiano/a *m/f*

kaolin ['keɪəlɪn] (N) caolín *m*

kapok ['keɪpɒk] (N) capoc *m*

kaput* [kə'pʊt] (ADJ) **1** [*object*] kaput • **to be ~** estar kaput
2 [*organization*] • **now he's dead the whole company is ~** ahora que ha fallecido, la empresa se ha ido al traste*

karaoke [kɑːrə'əʊkɪ] (N) karaoke *m*
(CPD) ▸ **karaoke machine** karaoke *m*

karat ['kærət] (N) (*US*) = **carat**

karate [kə'rɑːtɪ] (N) karate *m*

karma ['kɑːmə] (N) (*Rel*) karma *m*

kart [kɑːt] (N) kart *m*
(VI) hacer kárting • **to go ~ing** ir a hacer kárting

karting ['kɑːtɪŋ] (N) (*Sport*) kárting *m*

kasbah ['kæzbɑː] (N) casba(h) *f*

Kashmir [kæʃ'mɪəʳ] (N) Cachemira *f*

Kate [keɪt] (N) *familiar form of* **Catherine** *etc*

Katharine, Katherine ['kæθərɪn], **Kathleen** ['kæθliːn] (N) Catalina

katydid ['keɪtɪdɪd] (N) (*Zool*) chicharra *f*

kayak ['kaɪæk] (N) kayac *m*, kayak *m*

Kazak, Kazakh [kə'zɑːk] (ADJ) kazajo
(N) kazajo/a *m/f*

Kazakhstan [ˌkæzəks'tɑːn] (N) Kazajstán *m*

kazoo [kə'zuː] (N) kazoo *m*, chiflato *m*

KB (ABBR) (= **kilobyte**) K *m*

KBE (N ABBR) (= **Knight of the British Empire**) *título ceremonial*

KC (N ABBR) (*Brit*) (= **King's Counsel**) *abogado de categoría superior*
(ABBR) (*US*) = **Kansas City**

kc (ABBR) (= **kilocycle(s)**) k/c

kcal ['keɪkæl] (ABBR) = **kilocalorie**

KCB (N ABBR) (*Brit*) (= **Knight Commander of the Bath**) *un título ceremonial*

KD, kd (ABBR) (*US*) (= **knocked down**) desmontado

kebab [kə'bæb] (N) kebab *m*, pincho *m* moruno, anticucho *m* (*Peru, Bol, Chile*)

kedge [kedʒ] (N) anclote *m*

kedgeree [ˌkedʒə'riː] (N) (*Brit*) *plato de pescado desmenuzado, huevos y arroz*

keel [kiːl] (N) (*Naut*) quilla *f* • **on an even ~** (*Naut*) en iguales calados; (*fig*) en equilibrio, estable • IDIOM: • **to keep sth on an even ~** [+ *economy, company*] estabilizar algo • **they managed to get their marriage back on an even ~** consiguieron volver a estabilizar su matrimonio
▸ **keel over** (VI + ADV) (*Naut*) volcar(se), zozobrar; [*building, structure*] derrumbarse, venirse abajo; [*person*] desplomarse

keelhaul ['kiːlhɔːl] (VT) pasar por debajo de la quilla (*como castigo*)

keen [kiːn] (ADJ) (COMPAR: **keener**, SUPERL: **keenest**) **1** (= *enthusiastic*) [*supporter*] entusiasta; [*student*] aplicado • **she's a ~ photographer/gardener** es muy aficionada a la fotografía/la jardinería • **he's a ~ footballer** es muy aficionado a jugar al fútbol • **he's a ~ cook** le gusta mucho *or* le encanta cocinar • **she's just started and she's still very ~** acaba de empezar y tiene aún mucho entusiasmo • **try not to seem too ~** procura no parecer muy interesado • **to be ~ to do sth** tener interés por hacer algo • **I was ~ to get started** tenía muchas ganas de empezar • **the government is ~ to dismiss these rumours** al gobierno le interesa descartar estos rumores • **he was ~ to point out the financial benefits** tenía sumo interés por hacer resaltar las ventajas económicas, hizo mucho hincapié en las ventajas económicas • **to be ~ on sth** (*Brit*): • **I'm not all that ~ on grapes** no me gustan mucho las uvas • **he's ~ on fishing** es muy aficionado a la pesca, le gusta mucho la pesca • **I'm not ~ on the idea** no me entusiasma *or* no me hace mucha gracia la idea • **both companies were ~ on a merger** ambas compañías querían la fusión *or* tenían interés en la fusión • **I'm not very ~ on him** no es santo de mi devoción, no me cae demasiado bien • **to be ~ on doing sth**: **I'm very ~ on horse riding** (*Brit*) me gusta muchísimo montar a caballo, me encanta montar a caballo; (*as a hobby*) soy muy aficionada a montar a caballo • **I'm not ~ on going** no me apetece mucho ir • IDIOM: • **to be as ~ as mustard** ser extraordinariamente entusiasta
2 (= *intense*) [*desire*] fuerte, vivo; [*delight*] intenso; [*interest*] vivo, grande; [*competition, match, struggle*] reñido • **his ~ sense of loyalty** su gran sentido de la lealtad
3 (= *sharp*) [*edge, blade*] afilado; [*wind, air*] cortante; [*mind, intelligence*] agudo, penetrante; [*intellect, wit, sense of humour*] agudo; [*eyesight*] agudo, muy bueno; [*hearing*] fino • **to have a ~ appetite** tener buen apetito • **to have a ~ eye for detail** tener buen ojo para los detalles • **to have a ~ nose for sth** tener buen olfato para algo • **to have a ~ sense of smell** tener buen olfato
4 (= *competitive*) [*price, rate*] competitivo
5 (*US**) (= *good*) • **he plays a ~ game of squash** juega genial *or* fenomenal al squash*
(N) (*Irl*) (*Mus*) *lamento fúnebre por la muerte de una persona*
(VI) lamentar

keenly ['kiːnlɪ] (ADV) **1** (= *intensely*) [*discuss, debate*] vivamente, intensamente; [*feel*] profundamente; [*look*] fijamente; [*listen*] con interés • **his loss was ~ felt by all who knew him** todos los que lo conocían sintieron profundamente su muerte • **they're ~ aware that …** son muy conscientes de que … • **it was a ~ contested game** fue un partido muy reñido
2 (= *enthusiastically*) con entusiasmo

keenness ['kiːnnɪs] (N) **1** (= *sharpness*) [*of mind, sense of humour, eyesight*] agudeza *f*; [*of blade*] lo afilado; [*of wind*] lo cortante
2 (= *intensity*) intensidad *f*
3 (= *enthusiasm*) entusiasmo *m*

keep [kiːp]

TRANSITIVE VERB
INTRANSITIVE VERB
NOUN
PHRASAL VERBS

(VB: PT, PP: **kept**)

TRANSITIVE VERB

When **keep** *is part of a set combination, eg* **to keep an appointment**, **to keep a promise**, **to keep one's seat**, *look up the noun.*

1 (= *retain*) [+ *change, copy*] quedarse con; [+ *receipt*] guardar; [+ *business, customer, colour*] conservar • **you must ~ the receipt** debe guardar el recibo • **you can ~ the change** quédese con la vuelta *or* (*LAm*) el vuelto • **is this jacket worth ~ing?** ¿merece la pena guardar esta chaqueta? • **he is to ~ his job in spite of the incident** va a mantener *or* conservar el trabajo a pesar del incidente • **this material will ~ its colour/softness** este material conservará su color/suavidad • **to ~ sth for o.s.** quedarse con algo • IDIOM: • **if this is fashion, you can ~ it!**‡ ¡si esto es moda no la quiero ni regalada!

2 (*= save, put aside*) guardar, reservar • **I'm ~ing this wine in case we have visitors** voy a guardar *or* reservar este vino por si tenemos visitas • **ask the shop to ~ you one** pide en la tienda que te reserven uno • **I was ~ing it for you** lo guardaba para ti

3 (*= have ready*) • **I always ~ a torch in the car** siempre tengo una linterna en el coche • **~ this by you in case of emergencies** guárdate eso para un caso de emergencia

4 (*= store, put*) (*gen*) guardar; (*in museum*) conservar • **where do you ~ the sugar?** ¿dónde guardas el azúcar? • **~ it somewhere safe** guárdalo en un sitio seguro • **you must ~ it in a cold place** debes conservarlo en un sitio fresco

5 (*= house*) • **the puppies were kept in cramped conditions** tenían a los cachorros hacinados • **the tarantulas were kept in cages** las tarántulas estaban metidas en jaulas • **the prisoners were kept in a dark room** los prisioneros estaban encerrados en una habitación oscura • **he ~s his wives in separate houses** tiene a sus mujeres alojadas en casas separadas

6 (*= detain*) tener • **~ him in bed for a couple of days** tenlo en cama un par de días • **to ~ sb in prison** tener a algn preso • **he was kept in hospital over night** lo tuvieron una noche en el hospital, le hicieron pasar la noche en el hospital • **illness kept her at home** la enfermedad no le permitió salir de casa • **to ~ sb doing sth** tener a algn haciendo algo

7 (*= delay*) entretener • **I mustn't ~ you** no quiero entretenerte • **don't let me ~ you** no le entretengo más • **what kept you?** ¿por qué te has retrasado? • **am I ~ing you from your work?** quizá tienes trabajo y yo te estoy entreteniendo

8 (*= have*) [*+ shop, hotel, house, servant*] tener; [*+ pigs, bees, chickens*] criar • **he ~s a good cellar** tiene una buena bodega

9 (*= stock*) tener • **we don't ~ that model any more** ya no tenemos ese modelo

10 (*= support*) [*+ family, mistress*] mantener • **to ~ o.s.** mantenerse • **the extra money ~s me in beer and cigarettes** el dinero extra me da para (comprar) cerveza y cigarrillos • **our garden ~s us in vegetables all summer** el huerto nos da suficientes verduras para todo el verano

11 (*= fulfil, observe*) [*+ promise, agreement, obligation*] cumplir; [*+ law, rule*] observar; [*+ appointment*] acudir a, ir a; [*+ feast day*] observar • **to ~ the Sabbath** observar el sábado judío

12 (*= not divulge*) • **to ~ sth from sb** ocultar algo a algn • **~ it quiet** de esto no digas ni una palabra • **~ it to yourself*** no se lo digas a nadie • **but he kept the news to himself** pero se guardó la noticia, pero no comunicó la noticia a nadie

13 (*= maintain*) **a** [*+ accounts*] llevar; [*+ diary*] escribir • **to ~ a record of sth** llevar nota de algo

b (*with adjective*) mantener; (*less formal*) tener • **"keep Britain tidy"** "mantenga limpia Gran Bretaña" • **to ~ sth clean** conservar *or* mantener algo limpio; (*less formal*) tener algo limpio • **she always ~s the house very clean** tiene la casa siempre muy limpia • **to ~ o.s. clean** no ensuciarse, mantenerse limpio • **cats ~ themselves clean** los gatos son muy limpios • **exercise ~s you fit** haciendo ejercicio te mantienes en forma • **~ the sauce hot** (*in recipe book*) mantener la salsa caliente • **I'll ~ your supper hot** te guardaré la comida caliente • **to ~ inflation as low as possible** mantener la inflación tan baja como sea posible • **to ~ sth safe** guardar algo bien, guardar algo en un lugar seguro • **try to ~ your head still** intenta no mover la cabeza • **to ~ sth warm** mantener algo caliente • **the garden is well kept** el jardín está muy bien cuidado; ▸ **fixed, happy, post**

c (*+ -ing*) • **to ~ the engine running** dejar el motor en marcha • **to ~ sb talking** entretener a algn hablando • **~ him talking while I ...** entretenlo hablando mientras yo ... • **to ~ sb waiting** hacer esperar a algn • **he kept them working all night** los tuvo trabajando toda la noche; ▸ **go**

14 (*= hold*) • **to ~ sb at it** obligar a algn a seguir trabajando • **I'll ~ you to your promise** haré que cumplas tu promesa; ▸ **counsel**

15 (*= prevent*) • **to ~ sb from doing sth** impedir que algn haga algo • **what can we do to ~ it from happening again** ¿qué podemos hacer para evitar que se repita? • **to ~ o.s. from doing sth** contener las ganas de hacer algo, aguantarse de hacer algo*

16 (*= guard, protect*†) guardar • **God ~ you!** ¡Dios te guarde!

17 • **to ~ o.s. to o.s.** guardar las distancias

INTRANSITIVE VERB

1 (*= remain*) **a** (*with adjective*) • **try to ~ calm** intenta mantener la calma • **to ~ fit** mantenerse en forma • **it will ~ fresh for weeks** se conservará fresco durante semanas • **to ~ healthy** mantenerse sano • **~ very quiet** no hagas nada de ruido • **you must ~ still** tienes que estarte *or* quedarte muy quieto • **to ~ together** no separarse • **he was jumping up and down to ~ warm** estaba dando saltos para mantener el calor

b (*with preposition/adverb*) • **~ in the left lane** sigue por el carril de la izquierda • **she kept inside for three days** no salió en tres días

2 • **to ~ doing sth a** (*= continue*) seguir haciendo algo • **he kept walking** siguió caminando • **I ~ hoping she'll come back** sigo esperando que vuelva • **you must ~ moving** no pares • **~ smiling!*** ¡no te desanimes! • **~ going!** ¡no pares!

b (*= do repeatedly*) no hacer más que hacer algo • **he ~s mentioning his uncle** no hace más que mencionar a su tío • **I ~ thinking I'll wake up in a minute** no hago más que pensar que es todo un sueño • **she ~s bursting into tears** está todo el tiempo echándose a llorar • **he kept interrupting us** no paraba de interrumpirnos • **I ~ forgetting to pay the gas bill** siempre se me olvida pagar la factura del gas • **you mustn't ~ looking at your watch** no debes estar todo el tiempo mirando al reloj

3 (*in directions*) (*= continue*) seguir • **to ~ straight on** seguir todo recto *or* derecho • **~ due north until you come to ...** siga en dirección norte hasta que llegue a ... • **"keep left"** "circule por la izquierda"

4 (*= not go off*) [*food*] conservarse fresco, conservarse bien • **fish doesn't ~ very well** el pescado no se conserva muy bien • **an apple that ~s** una manzana que se conserva bien

5* (*= wait*) esperar • **the news will ~ till I see you** la noticia puede esperar hasta que nos veamos • **it can ~** puede esperar

6* (*talking about health*) • **how are you ~ing?** ¿qué tal (estás)? (*Sp**), ¿cómo *or* qué tal te va?*, ¿cómo sigues? (*LAm**), ¿qué hubo? (*Mex, Chile**) • **he's not ~ing very well** no está muy bien de salud • **she's ~ing better** está mejor, se encuentra mejor

7 (*= avoid*) • **to ~ from doing sth** evitar hacer algo; (*= abstain from*) abstenerse de hacer algo

NOUN

1 (*= livelihood, food*) • **I got £30 a week and my ~** me daban 30 libras a la semana y comida y cama • **I pay £50 a week for my ~** la pensión me cuesta 50 libras a la semana • **to earn one's ~** ganarse el sustento; (*fig*) justificar el gasto • **in a poem every word must earn its ~** en un poema cada palabra debe estar justificada

2 (*Archit*) torreón *m*, torre *f* del homenaje

3 (*= permanently*) • **for ~s*** para siempre

▸ **keep ahead** (VI + ADV) (*in market*) mantenerse al frente; (*in race*) mantenerse en cabeza • **to ~ ahead of sb** (*in market, race*) mantenerse por delante de algn

▸ **keep at** (VI + PREP) **1** • **to ~ at sth*** (*= persevere with*) perseverar en algo • **despite his problems he kept at his studies** a pesar de sus problemas siguió perseverando en los estudios • **~ at it!*** ¡ánimo!, ¡no te aflojes! (*LAm*)

2 • **to ~ at sb: she kept at him until she got an interview*** (*= pester*) no paró hasta que le concedió una entrevista • **I kept at them until they paid** seguí insistiendo hasta que me pagaron

(VT + PREP) • **he wanted to rest but I kept him at it until he had run an extra 100 metres** quería parar a descansar pero seguí animándole y corrió otros 100 metros

▸ **keep away** (VT + ADV) mantener alejado, mantener a distancia • **the police kept the crowds away** la policía mantuvo a la multitud alejada *or* a distancia • **~ him away!** ¡que no se acerque! • **vitamin C helps ~ colds away** la vitamina C ayuda a no pillar resfriados • **to ~ sb away from sb/sth** mantener a algn alejado de algn/algo • **they kept him away from school** (*= stopped him going*) no le dejaron ir al colegio; (*because ill*) no lo llevaron al colegio, lo tuvieron en casa • **~ medicines away from children** mantener los medicamentos fuera del alcance de los niños

(VI + ADV) no acercarse • **~ away!** ¡no te acerques! • **~ away from the fire** no te acerques al fuego • **he promised to ~ away from drink** prometió no tocar la bebida • **he seems to be ~ing away from me** parece que me evita • **you ~ away from my daughter!** ¡no te vuelvas a acercar a mi hija! • **he can't ~ away from the subject** siempre vuelve al mismo tema

▸ **keep back** (VT + ADV) **1** (*= contain*) [*+ crowds*] contener; [*+ enemy*] no dejar avanzar, tener a raya

2 (*= withhold*) [*+ part of sth given*] guardar, quedarse con • **~ back some of the parsley to garnish** guárdate parte del perejil para adornar

3 (*= restrain*) [*+ tears*] contener, reprimir

4 (*= conceal*) [*+ names of victims*] no comunicar • **to ~ sth back from sb** ocultar algo a algn • **I'm sure he's ~ing sth back** estoy segura de que oculta algo

5 (*= delay*) [*+ person*] retrasar • **I don't want to ~ you back** no quiero retrasarte • **he had been kept back after school** le habían hecho quedarse después del colegio

(VI + ADV) • **~ back, please!** ¡no se acerquen, por favor! • **~ well back from the bonfire** no te acerques a la fogata • **I kept well back** me mantuve bien alejado

▸ **keep down** (VT + ADV) **1** (*= not raise*) • **she kept her eyes down** no levantó los ojos • **~ your head down or you'll get shot** no

levantes la cabeza o te dispararán • **you'll have to ~ your head down for 48 hours** (*fig*) tendrás que mantener al margen durante 48 horas; ▹ **head**
2 (= *control*) [+ *anger, rebellion*] contener, reprimir; [+ *weeds*] no dejar crecer; [+ *dog*] sujetar
3 (= *limit*) [+ *prices, spending, temperature*] mantener bajo; [+ *costs, inflation*] mantener al mismo nivel • **could you ~ the noise down?** ¿puedes hacer menos ruido? • **you must try to ~ your weight down** tienes que intentar no subir de peso
4 (= *hold back*) **a** oprimir • **it's just a way to ~ women down** es solo una forma de oprimir a las mujeres • PROVERB: • **you can't ~ a good man down** los buenos siempre vuelven
b (*Scol*) • **he was kept down another year** tuvo que repetir (año)
5 (= *oppress*) [+ *spirits*] oprimir
6 (= *retain*) [+ *food*] • **he can't ~ anything down** lo devuelve *or* vomita todo
VI + ADV seguir agachado, no levantar la cabeza

▸ **keep in** VT + ADV **1** (= *prevent from going out*) impedir que salga, no dejar salir • **to ~ a child in after school** dejar a un niño castigado después de las clases
2 (= *hold in*) [+ *stomach*] meter; [+ *elbows*] pegar al cuerpo; [+ *anger*] contener • **~ your tummy in!** ¡mete estómago!
3 (= *keep alight*) [+ *fire*] mantener encendido; ▹ **hand**
VI + ADV **1** [*fire*] mantenerse encendido
2 • **to ~ in with sb*** mantener buenas relaciones con algn

▸ **keep off** VT + ADV (= *keep distant, repel*) • **put a cloth over it to ~ the flies off** pon un trapo encima para que no se posen las moscas • **he kept his hat off** no se puso el sombrero • **~ your hands off!*** ¡no toques!
VT + PREP **1** (= *keep away from*) • **~ your dog off my lawn** no deje que el perro me pise el césped • **~ your feet off the grass** no pises la hierba • **~ your hands off my daughter** no toques a mi hija • **they want to ~ young people off the streets** quieren evitar que los jóvenes pierdan el tiempo vagabundeando por las calles • **measures to ~ people off the unemployment register** medidas para que la gente no entre en las listas del paro • **he couldn't ~ his eyes off her*** no podía apartar los ojos de ella
2 (= *prevent from consuming*) • **I've been told to ~ him off processed foods** me han dicho que no le de alimentos procesados • **~ her off cheese for the next 10 days** que no tome queso durante los próximos 10 días
3 (= *steer away from*) • **to ~ sb off a subject** evitar que algn toque un tema • **try to ~ him off the subject of budgets** intenta que no toque el tema de los presupuestos
VI + PREP **1** (= *stay away from*) • **~ off my land!** ¡fuera de mi propiedad! • **"keep off the grass"** "prohibido pisar el césped"
2 (*fig*) [+ *food, subject*] evitar • **~ off politics!** ¡no hables de política!
VI + ADV • **if the rain ~s off** si no llueve

▸ **keep on** VT + ADV **1** (= *not take off*) [+ *hat, coat, gloves*] no quitarse
2 (= *not turn off*) [+ *light*] dejar encendido, dejar prendido (*LAm*)
3 (= *retain*) [+ *house*] conservar
4 (= *continue employing*) • **they kept him on for years** siguieron empleándole durante muchos años; ▹ **hair**
VT + PREP (= *restrict to*) • **~ him on light foods for the next few days** que solo tome alimentos ligeros en los próximos días • **he was kept on bread and water for three days** durante tres días solo le dieron pan y agua, le tuvieron a pan y agua durante tres días
VI + ADV **1** (= *continue*) seguir, continuar • **to ~ on doing sth** (*ceaselessly*) seguir *or* continuar haciendo algo; (*repeatedly*) no dejar de hacer algo • **he ~s on hoping** no pierde la esperanza, sigue teniendo esperanzas • **~ on along this road until ...** siga por esta carretera hasta ... • **he ~s on ringing me up** no deja de llamarme por teléfono • **she ~s on having migraines** tiene contínuos ataques de migraña
2* (= *talk*) • **she does ~ on** no para de hablar • **she ~s on about how much money they've got** no hace mas que hablar *or* siempre está hablando de todo el dinero que tienen • **he ~s on about her being stupid** no hace más que decir que es una estúpida
3* (= *nag*) • **she does ~ on** es muy machacona* • **he kept on about me being selfish** siguió dale que te pego con que soy egoísta* • **she ~s on at me about my cheap clothes** siempre me está dando la lata con que llevo ropa barata* • **I kept on at him about the leaking tap** le dije una y otra vez lo del grifo que perdía agua • **she ~s on at him to look for a job** le está siempre insistiendo que busque un trabajo

▸ **keep out** VT + ADV (= *exclude*) [+ *person, dog*] no dejar entrar • **we were kept out of the room** no nos dejaron entrar en la habitación • **to ~ sb out of trouble** evitar que algn se meta en líos • **to ~ sb out of the way** sacar a algn de en medio • **this coat should ~ out the cold** este abrigo tiene que proteger del frío • **have some brandy to ~ out the cold** tómate un coñac para entrar en calor • **let's ~ my mother's behaviour out of this!** no metamos lo del comportamiento de mi madre en esto • **let's try to ~ lawyers out of this** no nos metamos con abogados
VI + ADV (= *not enter*) no entrar, quedarse fuera • **please ~ out of the hall until further notice** por favor no entren en el hall hasta nuevo aviso • **"keep out"** "prohibida la entrada" • **to ~ out of trouble** no meterse en líos • **to ~ out of sb's way** (= *avoid*) evitar encontrarse con algn; (= *try not to annoy*) procurar no molestar a algn • **you ~ out of this!** ¡no te metas en esto!

▸ **keep to** VI + PREP [+ *promise*] cumplir con; [+ *subject, schedule, text*] ceñirse a • **to ~ to the left/right** circular por la izquierda/derecha, mantenerse por la izquierda/derecha • **to ~ to the main roads** no salir de las carreteras principales • **to ~ to one's room** no salir de su habitación • **to ~ to one's bed** guardar cama • **to ~ to one's diet** no salirse de la dieta • **they ~ to themselves** guardan las distancias
VT + PREP ▹ **keep**

▸ **keep together** VT + ADV [+ *team*] mantener unido; [+ *papers, photographs*] mantener juntos • **it has been hard to ~ the team together** ha sido difícil mantener al equipo unido, ha sido difícil hacer que el equipo siguiese junto • **we try to ~ families together** intentamos mantener a las familias unidas
VI + ADV no separarse • **~ together, children** no os separéis, niños

▸ **keep under** VT + ADV **1** (= *oppress*) [+ *people, race*] mantener sometido
2 (= *keep anaesthetized*) [+ *patient*] tener anestesiado

▸ **keep up** VT + ADV **1** (= *hold up*) [+ *shelf*] sostener, sujetar; [+ *stocking, trousers*] sujetar • **to ~ one's spirits** *or* **morale up** mantener la moral alta
2 (= *continue*) [+ *tradition*] mantener; [+ *correspondence, subscription, standards, pressure*] mantener; [+ *payments*] no retrasarse en • **~ up the good work!** ¡bien hecho!, ¡sigue así!, ¡síguele dando! (*LAm*) • **~ it up!** ¡sigue así!, ¡ánimo! • **he'll never ~ it up!** ¡no va a poder seguir así!, ¡no aguanta! (*LAm*) • **it's difficult to ~ up a relationship when you're far apart** es difícil mantener una relación cuando se está alejado uno del otro
3 (= *maintain*) [+ *property*] cuidar, mantener (en buenas condiciones); [+ *payments*] no retrasarse en • **you must try to ~ up your German** deberías intentar seguir con el alemán
4 (= *keep out of bed*) tener despierto hasta muy tarde, tener en vela, tener desvelado (*LAm*) • **I don't want to ~ you up** no quiero entretenerte más
VI + ADV **1** (= *continue*) [*weather*] seguir, mantenerse
2 (= *maintain level*) (*in race etc*) mantener el ritmo, no quedarse atrás; (*in comprehension*) seguir (el hilo) • **share prices have kept up well** los precios de las acciones se han mantenido bien • **to ~ up with sb** (*in race*) seguirle el ritmo a algn; (*in comprehension*) seguirle el hilo a algn • **to ~ up with the class** (*Scol, Univ*) mantenerse al nivel del resto de la clase • **it's important to ~ up with your languages** es importante que mantengas el nivel de los idiomas • **to ~ up with the times** ir con los tiempos, mantenerse al día • **I try to ~ up with the news/with current affairs** intento estar al día de las noticias/los temas de actualidad • **to ~ up with demand** responder a la demanda • **wage increases have kept up with inflation** las subidas salariales se han mantenido al nivel de la inflación • IDIOM: • **to ~ up with the Joneses** no ser menos que el vecino

keeper ['kiːpəʳ] N (*in park, zoo etc*) guarda *mf*, guardián/ana *m/f*; (= *gamekeeper*) guardabosque *mf*, guardabosques *mf inv*; (*in museum, art gallery*) conservador(a) *m/f*; (= *goalkeeper*) portero/a *m/f*, arquero/a *m/f* (*LAm*) • **am I my brother's ~?** (*Bible*) ¿acaso soy el guarda de mi hermano?

keep-fit [ˌkiːp'fɪt] (*Brit*) N gimnasia *f* (para mantenerse en forma)
CPD ▸ **keep-fit classes** clases *fpl* de gimnasia (para mantenerse en forma) ▸ **keep-fit exercises** ejercicios *mpl* para mantenerse en forma

keeping ['kiːpɪŋ] N **1** (= *harmony*) • **to be in ~ with** estar de acuerdo con, estar en armonía con • **to be out of ~ with** estar en desacuerdo con • **her clothes were totally out of ~ with the elegant setting** la ropa que llevaba desentonaba totalmente con el elegante entorno
2 (= *care, custody*) • **to be in the ~ of X** estar en manos de X • **to be in safe ~** estar en un lugar seguro, estar en buenas manos • **to give sth to sb for safe ~** poner algo al cuidado de algn

keepsake ['kiːpseɪk] N recuerdo *m*

keester* ['kiːstəʳ] N (*US*) trasero* *m*

keg [keg] N barrilete *m*
CPD ▸ **keg beer** cerveza *f* de barril

keister* ['kiːstəʳ] N (*US*) = **keester**

keks‡ [keks] NPL (*Brit*) pantalones *mpl*

kelp [kelp] N (*Bot*) quelpo *m* (de Patagonia)

Kelper* ['kelpəʳ] N nativo/a *m/f* de las Malvinas, habitante *mf* de las Malvinas

Ken [ken] N *familiar form of* **Kenneth**
ken [ken] N • **to be beyond sb's ken** ser incomprensible para algn
VT (*Scot*) [+ *person*] conocer; [+ *fact*] saber; (= *recognize*) reconocer
Ken. ABBR (*US*) = **Kentucky**
kennel ['kenl] N (= *doghouse*) caseta *f* de perro; **kennels** (= *dogs' home*) residencia *f* canina; (*for breeding*) criadero *m* de perros • **to put a dog in ~s** poner a un perro en una residencia canina *or* en una perrera
CPD ▸ **kennel maid** chica *f* que trabaja en una residencia canina
Kenya ['kenjə] N Kenia *f*
Kenyan ['kenjən] ADJ, N keniano/a *m/f*
kepi ['keɪpɪ] N quepis *m inv*
kept [kept] PT, PP *of* **keep**
ADJ • **~ woman** mantenida *f*
kerb [kɜːb] N (*Brit*) bordillo *m*, cordón *m* (*S. Cone*), cuneta *f* (*Chile*)
CPD ▸ **kerb crawler** *conductor que busca prostitutas desde su coche* ▸ **kerb crawling** *busca de prostitutas desde el coche* ▸ **kerb drill** prácticas *fpl* de cruce ▸ **kerb market** mercado *m* no oficial (*que funciona después del cierre de la Bolsa*)
kerbside ['kɜːbsaɪd] N borde *m* de la acera
kerbstone ['kɜːbstəʊn] N (*Brit*) piedra *f* del bordillo *etc*
kerchief ['kɜːtʃɪf] N pañuelo *m*, pañoleta *f*
kerfuffle* [kə'fʌfl] N (*Brit*) jaleo* *m*, follón *m* (*Sp**)
kernel ['kɜːnl] N [*of nut*] almendra *f*; (= *seed*) [*of fruit*] pepita *f*, pepa *f* (*LAm*); [*of grain*] grano *m*; (*fig*) [*of matter, question*] meollo *m*, núcleo *m* • **a ~ of truth** un grano de verdad
kerosene ['kerəsiːn] N keroseno *m*, queroseno *m*, querosén *m* (*LAm*)
CPD ▸ **kerosene lamp** lámpara *f* de petróleo
kestrel ['kestrəl] N cernícalo *m* (vulgar)
ketamine ['ketəmiːn] N ketamina *f*
ketch [ketʃ] N queche *m*
ketchup ['ketʃəp] N salsa *f* de tomate, catsup *m*
kettle ['ketl] N hervidor *m*, caldera *f* (*Bol, Uru*), pava *f* (*S. Cone*) • **I'll put the ~ on** voy a poner a hervir el agua (*para hacer café/té*) • IDIOM: • **that's a different ~ of fish** eso es harina de otro costal
kettledrum ['ketldrʌm] N timbal *m*
key [kiː] N **1** (*to door, safe, car etc*) llave *f*; (= *can-opener*) abridor *m*, abrelatas *m inv*
2 [*of typewriter, piano*] tecla *f*; [*of wind instrument*] llave *f*, pistón *m*
3 (*to code*) clave *f* • **the key to success** (*fig*) la clave del éxito
4 (*to map, diagram*) explicación *f* de los signos convencionales
5 (*Mus*) clave *f* • **what key is it in?** ¿en qué clave está? • **in the key of C** en clave de do • **to change key** cambiar de tonalidad • **to sing/play off key** cantar/tocar desafinado • **major/minor key** tono *m* mayor/menor
ADJ (= *crucial*) [*issue, job, role, witness*] clave (*adj inv*) • **he is a key figure in the negotiations** es una figura clave en las negociaciones • **all the key positions in the company are held by men** todos los puestos clave de la compañía están ocupados por hombres
VT (*Comput, Typ*) (*also* **key in, key up**) teclear
CPD ▸ **key card** (*for hotel room*) tarjeta *f* de acceso ▸ **key drive** (*Comput*) llave *f* de memoria ▸ **key money** entrada *f* ▸ **key pal** amigo/a *m/f* por correo electrónico ▸ **key player** (= *important person*) actor(a) *m/f* clave • **to be a key player in sth** ser un actor clave en algo ▸ **key ring** llavero *m* ▸ **key stage** (*Brit*) (*Scol*) *en Inglaterra, el País de Gales e Irlanda del Norte, una de las cuatro categorías de edad (5-7, 7-11, 11-14, 14-16) que corresponden a los niveles establecidos para el National Curriculum*
▸ **key in** VT + ADV (*Comput, Typ*) teclear
▸ **key up** VT + ADV **1** • **to be all keyed up** (= *tense*) estar nervioso; (= *excited*) estar entusiasmado • **the children were too keyed up to go to bed** los niños estaban demasiado entusiasmados para acostarse • **they are all keyed up to make a good impression when she arrives** están nerviosos porque quieren causarle una buena impresión cuando llegue
2 (*Comput, Typ*) teclear
keyboard ['kiːbɔːd] N teclado *m*; **keyboards** (*Mus*) teclados *mpl*
VT (*Comput*) [+ *text*] teclear
CPD ▸ **keyboard instrument** instrumento *m* de teclado ▸ **keyboard operator** = **keyboarder** ▸ **keyboard player** teclista *mf* ▸ **keyboard skills** habilidad *fsing* para teclear, habilidad *fsing* con el teclado • **~ skills are essential in most jobs these days** hoy en día, la habilidad para teclear *or* la habilidad con el teclado es esencial en la mayoría de los empleos
keyboarder ['kiːˌbɔːdə^{r}] N teclista *mf*
keyboarding ['kiːˌbɔːdɪŋ] N manejo *m* del teclado, tecleo *m*
keyboardist ['kiːˌbɔːdɪst] N teclista *mf*
keyhole ['kiːhəʊl] N ojo *m* de la cerradura
CPD ▸ **keyhole surgery** cirugía *f* mínimamente invasiva
keying ['kiːɪŋ] N (*Comput*) tecleado *m*
keyless ['kiːlɪs] ADJ • **~ access** acceso sin llave
keylogger ['kiːˌlɒgə^{r}] N keylogger *m*
Keynesian ['kiːnzɪən] ADJ, N keynesiano/a *m/f*
keynote ['kiːnəʊt] N (*Mus*) tónica *f*; (*fig*) (= *main emphasis*) tónica *f*, piedra *f* clave
CPD ▸ **keynote speech** discurso *m* de apertura, *discurso en que se sientan las bases de una política or programa*
keypad ['kiːpæd] N teclado *m* numérico
key-puncher ['kiːˌpʌntʃə^{r}] N teclista *mf*
keystone ['kiːstəʊn] N (*Archit*) dovela *f*; (*fig*) piedra *f* angular
keystroke ['kiːstrəʊk] N pulsación *f* (*de la tecla*)
keyword ['kiːwɜːd] N palabra *f* clave
Kg, kg ABBR (= **kilogram(s), kilogramme(s)**) kg
KGB N (*in former USSR*) KGB *f*
khaki ['kɑːkɪ] N (= *cloth, colour*) caqui *m*; **khakis** (= *military uniform*) uniforme *m* caqui
ADJ caqui (*inv*)
kharja ['xɑːʒə] N jarcha *f*
Khartoum [kɑː'tuːm] N Jartum *m*
Khmer [kmeə^{r}] N jemer *mf* • **the ~ Rouge** los jemeres rojos
ADJ jemer
Khyber Pass [ˌkaɪbə'pɑːs] N pasaje *m* de Kyber
kHz ABBR (= **kilohertz**) kHz, KHz
kibbutz [kɪ'bʊts] N (PL: **kibbutzim** [kɪ'bʊtsɪm]) kibutz *m*
kibitzer ['kɪbɪtsə^{r}] N (*US*) mirón/ona *m/f*
kibosh ['kaɪbɒʃ] N • IDIOM: • **to put the ~ on sth*** dar al traste con algo*
kick [kɪk] N **1** (*gen*) patada *f*, puntapié *m*; (*Sport*) puntapié *m*, tiro *m*; (*by animal*) coz *f* • **what he needs is a good ~ up the backside*** lo que necesita es una buena patada en el trasero* • **to give sth/sb a ~** dar una patada a algo/algn • **I gave him a ~ in the pants*** le di una patada en el trasero* • **he got** *or* **took a ~ on the leg** le dieron una patada en la pierna • **to take a ~ at goal** tirar a puerta • **it was a ~ in the teeth for him*** (*fig*) le sentó como una patada (en la barriga)*
2 [*of firearm*] culatazo *m*
3* [*of drink*] fuerza *f* • **a drink with a ~ to it** una bebida que pega fuerte*
4* (= *thrill*) • **I get a ~ out of seeing her happy** me encanta verla feliz • **he gets a ~ out of teasing her** se refocila tomándole el pelo • **to do something for ~s** hacer algo solo para divertirse *or* por pura diversión
5* (= *craze*) • **he's on a fishing ~ now** ahora le ha dado por la pesca*
VT **1** [+ *ball etc*] dar una patada *or* un puntapié a; [+ *goal*] marcar; [+ *person*] dar una patada a; [*animal*] dar una coz a • **he ~ed the stone away** apartó la piedra de una patada • **to ~ sb downstairs** echar a algn escaleras abajo de una patada • **to ~ one's legs in the air** agitar las piernas • **I could have ~ed myself*** ¡me hubiera dado de tortas!* • **to ~ sth out of the way** quitar algo de en medio de una patada • **she ~ed the door shut** cerró la puerta de una patada • IDIOMS: • **to ~ the bucket*** estirar la pata* • **to ~ ass** *or* **butt** (*esp US***) joder al personal** • **to ~ a man when he's down** dar a moro muerto gran lanzada; ▹ **heel**
2 (*fig**) (= *give up*) • **to ~ a habit** dejar un hábito • **I've ~ed smoking** ya no fumo
VI **1** [*person*] dar patadas *or* puntapiés; [*baby*] patalear; [*animal*] dar coces, cocear • **to ~ at** dar patadas a • **she dragged the child off ~ing and screaming** se llevó al niño a rastras
2 (*gun*) dar un culetazo, recular
CPD ▸ **kick boxing** kick boxing *m* ▸ **kick turn** (*Ski*) cambio *m* brusco de marcha
▸ **kick about, kick around** VT + ADV (*gen*) dar patadas a; [+ *idea*] darle vueltas a • **to ~ a ball about** divertirse dándole puntapiés a un balón de un lado para otro • **to ~ sb around** (*fig*) tratar a algn a patadas* • **he's been ~ed about a lot** le han maltratado mucho
VI + ADV* • **it's ~ing about here somewhere** anda por aquí en algún sitio • **I ~ed about in London for two years** anduve por Londres durante dos años
▸ **kick against** VI + PREP rebelarse contra • IDIOM: • **to ~ against the pricks** (*lit*) dar coces contra el aguijón; (*fig*) tener una actitud rebelde
▸ **kick back** VI + ADV (*gun*) dar culatazo, recular
VT + ADV [+ *ball*] devolver
▸ **kick down** VT + ADV derribar *or* echar abajo a patadas
▸ **kick in** VT + ADV **1** [+ *door*] derribar *or* echar abajo a patadas; (= *break*) romper a patadas • **to ~ sb's teeth in*** romper la cara a algn*
2 (*US**) (= *contribute*) contribuir, apoquinar (*Sp**)
VI + ADV (*US**) **1** (= *take effect*) surtir efecto
2 (= *contribute*) contribuir, apoquinar (*Sp**)
▸ **kick off** VI + ADV (*Ftbl*) hacer el saque inicial; (*fig**) [*meeting etc*] empezar
▸ **kick out** VI + ADV [*person*] dar patadas (**at** a); [*animal*] dar coces (**at** a) • **to ~ out against** ▹ **kick against**
VT + ADV* echar a patadas*; (*fig*) (*from job, home*) echar, poner de patitas en la calle*
▸ **kick up*** VT + ADV • **to ~ up a row** *or* **a din** (*lit*) armar un jaleo* • **to ~ up a fuss** *or* **stink about** *or* **over sth** armar un escándalo por algo
kickabout ['kɪkəbaʊt] N (*Ftbl*) • **to have a ~** pelotear
kickback ['kɪkbæk] N **1*** soborno *m*, coima *f* (*S. Cone**), mordida *f* (*Mex**)
2 (*fig*) reacción *f*, resaca *f*, contragolpe *m*
kicker ['kɪkə^{r}] N (*Rugby*) pateador *m*

k

kickoff ['kɪkɒf] (N) (*Ftbl*) saque *m* (inicial); (*fig*) comienzo *m* • **I'm not going there, for a ~*** para empezar, no pienso ir

kick-stand ['kɪkstænd] (N) [*of motorcycle*] pata *f* de apoyo

kick-start ['kɪk'stɑːt] (N) (*also* **kick-starter**) pedal *m* de arranque
(VT) [+ *engine*] arrancar con el pedal; [+ *economy, market*] activar

kid [kɪd] (N) **1** (*Zool*) (= *goat*) cabrito *m*, chivo *m*; (= *skin*) cabritilla *f*
2* (= *child*) chiquillo/a *m/f*, crío/a *m/f*, chaval/a *m/f* (*Sp*), cabro/a *m/f* (*Chile*), chamaco/a *m/f* (*CAm, Mex*), escuincle/a *m/f* (*Mex**), pibe/a *m/f* (*S. Cone**) • **when I was a kid** cuando yo era un crío, cuando yo era pequeño *or* (*LAm*) chico • **that's kid's stuff** (= *childish*) eso es de *or* para niños; (= *easy*) eso es un juego de niños
(VT)* **1** (= *deceive*) engañar • **who do you think you're kidding?** ¿a quién te crees que estás engañando? • **don't kid yourself** no te engañes • **I kid you not** (*hum*) no te engaño
2 (= *tease*) • **to kid sb about sth** tomar el pelo a algn por algo
3 (= *pretend to*) • **to kid sb that** hacer creer a algn que
(VI)* bromear • **I'm only kidding** lo digo en broma • **"they're mother and daughter" — "no kidding?"** —son madre e hija —¿en serio? *or* —¡no me digas! • **really! no kidding!** ¡en serio!, ¡de verdad!
(CPD) ▸ **kid brother*** hermano *m* menor *or* pequeño *or* (*LAm*) chico ▸ **kid gloves** guantes *mpl* de cabritilla • IDIOM: • **to handle sth/sb with kid gloves** tratar algo/a algn con guante blanco ▸ **kid sister*** hermana *f* menor *or* pequeña *or* (*LAm*) chica
▸ **kid along*** = kid on
▸ **kid on*** (VT + ADV) • **he's kidding you on** te está tomando el pelo*

kiddo* ['kɪdəʊ] (N) (*esp US*) muchacho(a) *m/f*

kiddy* ['kɪdɪ] (N) chiquillo/a *m/f*

kidnap ['kɪdnæp] (VT) secuestrar, raptar, plagiar (*Mex*)

kidnapper, kidnaper (*US*) ['kɪdnæpəʳ] (N) secuestrador(a) *m/f*, raptor(a) *m/f*, plagiador(a) *m/f* (*Mex*)

kidnapping, kidnaping (*US*) ['kɪdnæpɪŋ] (N) secuestro *m*, rapto *m*, plagio *m* (*Mex*)

kidney ['kɪdnɪ] (N) (*Anat, Culin*) riñón *m*; (*fig*) índole *f*, especie *f*
(CPD) ▸ **kidney bean** (*Culin*) frijol *m*, judía *f* (*Sp*), poroto *m* (*S. Cone*) ▸ **kidney disease** enfermedad *f* renal ▸ **kidney dish** batea *f* ▸ **kidney donor** donante *mf* de riñón ▸ **kidney failure** insuficiencia *m* renal ▸ **kidney machine** riñón *m* artificial ▸ **kidney stone** cálculo *m* renal ▸ **kidney transplant** trasplante *m* renal *or* de riñón

kidney-shaped ['kɪdnɪ,ʃeɪpt] (ADJ) ariñonado, con forma de riñon

kidology* [kɪ'dɒlədʒɪ] (N) (*Brit*) guasa* *f*

kike** [kaɪk] (N) (*US*) (*offensive*) judío/a *m/f*

Kilimanjaro [kɪlɪmænd'ʒɑːrəʊ] (N) Kilimanjaro *m*

kill [kɪl] (VT) **1** (*gen*) matar, dar muerte a (*frm*); (= *murder*) asesinar, matar; [+ *animal*] matar, sacrificar • **he was ~ed in the explosion** murió en la explosión • **he was ~ed by an enemy agent** lo mató un agente enemigo • **I'll ~ you for this!** ¡te voy a matar! • **to be ~ed in action** *or* **battle** morir en combate, morir luchando • **I'll do it if it ~s me** lo haré aunque me vaya en ello la vida • **the pace is ~ing him** el ritmo de trabajo lo está matando • **this heat is ~ing me*** este calor acabará conmigo* • **my feet are ~ing me*** los pies me están matando* • **to ~ o.s.** matarse; (= *commit suicide*) suicidarse • **he certainly doesn't ~ himself (with work)!** (*fig*) (*hum*) ¡desde luego ese a trabajar no se mata! • **he was ~ing himself laughing*** se moría de (la) risa • IDIOM: • **to ~ two birds with one stone** matar dos pájaros de un tiro
2 (*fig*) [+ *story*] suprimir; [+ *rumour*] acabar con; [+ *proposal, bill*] echar abajo; [+ *feeling, hope*] destruir; [+ *pain*] calmar; [+ *flavour, taste*] matar; [+ *sound*] amortiguar; [+ *engine*] parar, apagar; [+ *lights*] apagar • **to ~ time** matar el rato
3* hacer morir de risa* • **this will ~ you** te vas a morir de (la) risa*
(VI) • **thou shalt not ~** (*Bible*) no matarás • IDIOM: • **to be dressed to ~** ir despampanante
(N) (*Hunting, Bullfighting*) muerte *f*; (= *animal killed*) pieza *f*; (= *number of animals killed*) caza *f* • **to go in for the ~** (*lit*) entrar a matar • **to be in at the ~** (*lit*) asistir a la matanza
▸ **kill off** (VT + ADV) **1** (*lit*) exterminar, acabar con • **what ~ed off the dinosaurs?** ¿qué exterminó los dinosaurios?, ¿qué acabó con los dinosaurios? • **the recession is ~ing off many small firms** la recesión está acabando con muchas pequeñas empresas • **his character is ~ed off in the first episode** matan *or* eliminan a su personaje en el primer episodio
2 (*fig*) [+ *rumour*] acabar con; [+ *proposal*] echar abajo; [+ *hopes*] destruir

killer ['kɪləʳ] (N) **1** (= *murderer*) asesino/a *m/f* • **diphtheria used to be a ~** antiguamente la difteria era una enfermedad mortal
2* (*fig*) • **it's a ~** (= *joke*) es para morirse de risa*; (= *task*) es agotador; (= *question*) es muy difícil, es mortal*
(CPD) ▸ **killer application, killer app*** aplicación *f* rompedora, aplicación *f* de excelente rendimiento ▸ **killer bee** abeja *f* asesina ▸ **killer disease** enfermedad *f* mortal ▸ **killer instinct** (*also fig*) instinto *m* asesino ▸ **killer punch** puñetazo *m* mortal ▸ **killer shark** tiburón *m* asesino ▸ **killer whale** orca *f*

killing ['kɪlɪŋ] (ADJ) **1** [*blow, disease*] mortal
2* (= *exhausting*) [*work, journey*] agotador, durísimo
3* (= *funny*) divertidísimo, para morirse de (la) risa*
(N) (= *murder*) asesinato *m*; (*large scale, also of animals*) matanza *f* • IDIOM: • **to make a ~*** hacer su agosto
(CPD) ▸ **killing fields** campos *mpl* de la muerte

killingly ['kɪlɪŋlɪ] (ADV) • **~ funny** divertidísimo • **it was ~ funny** fue para morirse de (la) risa*

killjoy ['kɪldʒɔɪ] (N) aguafiestas *mf inv*

kiln [kɪln] (N) horno *m*

kilo ['kiːləʊ] (N) kilo *m*

kilobyte ['kɪləʊ,baɪt] (N) kilobyte *m*, kiloocteto *m*

kilocalorie ['kɪləʊ,kælərɪ] (N) kilocaloría *f*

kilocycle ['kɪləʊ,saɪkl] (N) kilociclo *m*

kilogram, kilogramme ['kɪləʊgræm] (N) kilo(gramo) *m*

kilohertz ['kɪləʊ,hɜːts] (N) kilohercio *m*

kilolitre, kiloliter (*US*) ['kɪləʊ,liːtəʳ] (N) kilolitro *m*

kilometre, kilometer (*US*) ['kɪləʊmiːtəʳ] (N) kilómetro *m*

kilometric [,kɪləʊ'metrɪk] (ADJ) kilométrico

kiloton ['kɪləʊ,tʌn] (N) kilotón *m*

kilovolt ['kɪləʊ,vəʊlt] (N) kilovoltio *m*

kilowatt ['kɪləʊwɒt] (N) kilovatio *m*

kilowatt-hour ['kɪləʊwɒt,aʊə] (N) kilovatio-hora *m* • **200 kilowatt-hours** 200 kilovatios-hora

kilt [kɪlt] (N) falda *f* escocesa

kilted ['kɪltɪd] (ADJ) [*man*] vestido con falda escocesa • **~ skirt** falda *f* escocesa

kilter ['kɪltəʳ] (N) • **to be out of ~** [*mechanism*] estar descentrado • **business is bad and everything's out of ~** el negocio va mal y todo anda desbaratado

kimono [kɪ'məʊnəʊ] (N) (PL: **kimonos**) kimono *m*, quimono *m*

kin [kɪn] (N) familiares *mpl*, parientes *mpl* • **next of kin** familiar(es) *m(pl)* *or* pariente(s) *m(pl)* más cercano(s)

kind [kaɪnd] (ADJ) (COMPAR: **kinder**, SUPERL: **kindest**) [*person*] amable, atento; [*act, word, offer*] amable; [*treatment*] bueno, cariñoso; [*voice*] tierno, cariñoso • **thank you for your ~ offer of help** gracias por ofrecerte amablemente a ayudarnos; (*more frm*) gracias por su amable oferta de ayuda • **the ~est thing that can be said about the play is that …** lo menos malo que se puede decir de la obra es que … • **he was ~ enough to help** tuvo la amabilidad de ayudar • **would you be ~ enough to** *or* **would you be so ~ as to close the door?** (*frm*) ¿haría el favor de cerrar la puerta, por favor?, ¿tendría la bondad de cerrar la puerta, por favor? (*frm*) • **to have a ~ heart** tener buen corazón • **that's very ~ of you** es usted muy amable; (*more frm*) es muy amable de su parte • **it was very ~ of you to pick us up** fuiste muy amable viniéndonos a recoger; (*more frm*) fue muy amable de su parte el venir a recogernos • **she was very ~ to me** fue muy amable conmigo, se portó muy bien conmigo • **life has been ~ to me** la vida me ha tratado bien • **you must be ~ to animals** hay que tratar bien a los animales • **a washing-up liquid that is ~ to your hands** un lavavajillas que no daña sus manos, un lavavajillas que es suave con sus manos
(N) **1** (= *type*) clase *f*, tipo *m* • **which ~ do you prefer?** ¿qué tipo prefieres? • **I prefer the ~ with handles** prefiero los que tienen asas • **she hated Lewis and his ~** odiaba a Lewis y a la gente como él • **many ~s of books/cars** muchos tipos de libros/coches • **people of all ~s** gente *f* de todas clases, gente *f* de todo tipo • **all ~s of things** toda clase de cosas • **it can fail for all ~s of reasons** puede fallar por todo tipo de razones • **a ~ of lizard** un tipo de lagarto • **she's the ~ (of person) that …** ella es de las que … • **what ~ of person do you take me for?** ¿por quién me tomas? • **what ~ of an answer is that?** • **what ~ of an answer do you call that?** ¿qué clase de respuesta es esa? • **I had a ~ of feeling that would happen** tuve el presentimiento de que ocurriría así • **you know the ~ of thing I mean** ya sabes a lo que me refiero • **it's not his ~ of film/thing** no es el tipo de película/cosa que (a él) le gusta • **he's not her ~ of man** no es su tipo de hombre • **it was tea of a ~** (*pej*) se supone que era té (*pej*) • **three/four of a ~** (*in card games*) tres/cuatro del mismo palo • **they're two of a ~** son tal para cual • **she's a very unusual woman, one of a ~** es una mujer muy poco corriente, única • **it's the only one of its ~** es único (en su género) • **the castle is the largest of its ~** el castillo es el más grande de los de su estilo • **something of the ~** algo por el estilo • **nothing of the ~!** ¡nada de eso!, ¡ni hablar! • **she never said anything of the ~** nunca dijo nada parecido
2 • **in ~:** • **payment in ~** pago *m* en especie • **to repay sth in ~** [+ *cruelty, ingratitude etc*] pagar algo con la misma moneda • **we repaid her generosity in ~** respondimos con nuestra generosidad a la suya
3 • **~ of*** (= *rather*) algo • **we're ~ of busy right now** ahora mismo estamos algo ocupados • **I ~ of felt it might happen** tenía el presentimiento de que iba a suceder • **it's ~**

of awkward at the moment ahora mismo me va mal, ahora no es el mejor momento • **it was ~ of sad, really** era un poco triste, la verdad • **she was ~ of cute** tenía cierto atractivo

kinda* ['kaɪndə] = **kind of** ▹ **kind**

kindergarten ['kɪndə,gɑ:tn] (N) jardín *m* de infancia, kindergarten *m*, kinder *m* (*LAm**)

kind-hearted ['kaɪnd'hɑ:tɪd] (ADJ) [*person, action*] bondadoso, de buen corazón • **to be kind-hearted** ser bondadoso, tener buen corazón

kind-heartedness ['kaɪnd'hɑ:tɪdnɪs] (N) bondad *f*

kindle ['kɪndl] (VT) [*+ wood*] prender fuego a; [*+ fire*] encender; (*fig*) [*+ emotion, interest*] despertar, suscitar
(VI) [*wood, fire*] prender, encenderse; (*fig*) (*with emotion*) despertarse

kindliness ['kaɪndlɪnɪs] (N) bondad *f*

kindling ['kɪndlɪŋ] (N) leña *f* (menuda), astillas *fpl*

kindly ['kaɪndlɪ] (ADJ) (COMPAR: **kindlier**, SUPERL: **kindliest**) [*person*] bondadoso; [*tone of voice*] tierno, cariñoso; [*face, eyes, smile*] afable, dulce; [*remark*] cariñoso • **a ~ soul** un alma caritativa *or* bondadosa
(ADV) **1** (= *thoughtfully*) amablemente • **"you seem tired this morning, Jenny," she said ~** —pareces cansada esta mañana, Jenny —dijo cariñosamente • **he very ~ helped** tuvo la amabilidad de ayudar • **to look ~ on sth** ver algo con buenos ojos • **to look ~ on sb** ser benévolo con algn • **to take ~ to sth:** • **he didn't take very ~ to her suggestion** no acogió muy bien su sugerencia • **the villagers do not take ~ to newcomers** a la gente del pueblo no les gustan mucho los recién llegados • **he doesn't take ~ to being kept waiting** no le hace ninguna gracia que le hagan esperar • **to think ~ of sb** tener un buen concepto de algn
2 (= *please*) (*frm*) • **~ wait a moment** haga el favor de esperar un momento, tenga la amabilidad de esperar un momento • **~ mind your own business** haz el favor de no meterte en lo que no te importa

kindness ['kaɪndnɪs] (N) **1** (= *thoughtfulness*) amabilidad *f* • **he was ~ itself** era la bondad personificada • **they treated him with every ~** lo trataron con todo género de atenciones • **out of the ~ of her heart** por pura amabilidad • **we were touched by her ~ to** *or* **towards us** su amabilidad para con nosotros nos enterneció *or* nos emocionó
2 (= *favour*) favor *m* • **it would be a ~ to tell him** decírselo sería un favor • **to do sb a ~** hacer un favor a algn

kindred ['kɪndrɪd] (ADJ) (= *related by blood or group*) emparentado; [*language*] de un tronco común; (*fig*) afín, semejante • **~ spirits** almas *fpl* gemelas • **to have a ~ feeling for sb** sentirse hermano de algn
(N) (= *relations*) familia *f*, parientes *mpl*

kinescope ['kɪnəskəʊp] (N) (*US*) tubo *m* de rayos catódicos, cinescopio *m*

kinesiology [kɪ,ni:sɪ'ɒlədʒɪ] (N) kinesiología *f*

kinetic [kɪ'netɪk] (ADJ) cinético
(CPD) ▸ **kinetic energy** energía *f* cinética

kinetics [kɪ'netɪks] (NSING) cinética *f*

kinfolk ['kɪnfəʊk] (NPL) = **kinsfolk**

king [kɪŋ] (N) **1** (*lit, fig*) rey *m* • **the ~ and queen** los reyes • **the Three Kings** los Reyes Magos • **an oil ~** un magnate del petróleo • **I'm the ~ of the castle!** (*child language*) ¡soy el rey!, ¡soy el amo y señor! • **to turn King's evidence** delatar a los cómplices • IDIOMS: • **they paid a ~'s ransom for it** les costó mucho dinero, les costó un dineral* • **to live like a ~** vivir a cuerpo de rey
2 (*Chess, Cards*) rey *m*; (*Draughts*) dama *f*
(CPD) ▸ **king cobra** cobra *f* real ▸ **king penguin** pingüino *m* real ▸ **King's Bench** (*Brit*) (*Jur*) departamento *m* del Tribunal Supremo ▸ **King's Counsel** (*Brit*) (*Jur*) abogado *mf* (*de categoría superior*); ▹ QC/KC

kingcup ['kɪŋkʌp] (N) botón *m* de oro

kingdom ['kɪŋdəm] (N) reino *m* • **animal/plant ~** reino *m* animal/vegetal • **the Kingdom of Heaven** el reino de los cielos • **till ~ come*** hasta el día del juicio final

kingfisher ['kɪŋfɪʃəʳ] (N) martín *m* pescador

kingly ['kɪŋlɪ] (ADJ) [*manner, presence, splendour*] regio; [*gift*] digno de un rey

kingmaker ['kɪŋ,meɪkəʳ] (N) persona *f* muy influyente

kingpin ['kɪŋpɪn] (N) (*Tech*) perno *m* real *or* pinzote; (*fig*) (= *person, object*) piedra *f* angular

kingship ['kɪŋʃɪp] (N) dignidad *f* real, monarquía *f* • **they offered him the ~** le ofrecieron el trono *or* la corona

king-size ['kɪŋsaɪz], **king-sized** ['kɪŋsaɪzd] (ADJ) (*gen*) tamaño gigante *or* familiar; [*cigarette*] extra largo
(CPD) ▸ **king-size(d) bed** cama *f* de matrimonio extragrande

kink [kɪŋk] (N) (*in rope etc*) retorcedura *f*, vuelta *f*; (*in hair*) onda *f*; (*in paper*) arruga *f*, pliegue *m*; (*fig*) (*emotional, psychological*) manía *f*, trauma *m*; (*sexual*) perversión *f*
(VI) enroscarse; [*hair*] ondularse

kinky ['kɪŋkɪ] (ADJ) (COMPAR: **kinkier**, SUPERL: **kinkiest**) **1*** (*sexually*) pervertido
2* (= *eccentric*) [*dress etc*] estrafalario; (*pej*) [*person*] raro, estrafalario
3 (= *curly*) [*hair*] ondulado

kinsfolk ['kɪnzfəʊk] (NPL) familiares *mpl*, parientes *mpl*

kinship ['kɪnʃɪp] (N) [*of family*] parentesco *m*; (*fig*) afinidad *f*

kinsman ['kɪnzmən] (N) (PL: **kinsmen**) familiar *m*, pariente *m*

kinswoman ['kɪnz,wʊmən] (N) (PL: **kinswomen**) familiar *f*

kiosk ['ki:ɒsk] (N) quiosco *m* • **telephone ~** (*Brit*) cabina *f* telefónica

kip* [kɪp] (*Brit*) (N) (= *sleep*) siestecita* *f*, sueño* *m*; (= *lodging*) alojamiento *m*; (= *bed*) pulguero* *m* • **to have a kip** echar un sueño*
(VI) dormir • **to kip down** echarse a dormir

kipper ['kɪpəʳ] (N) arenque *m* ahumado

kir [kɪəʳ] (N) *aperitivo preparado con vino blanco o champán y casis*

Kirbigrip®, **kirbygrip** ['kɜ:bɪ,grɪp] (N) horquilla *f* para el pelo

Kirghizia, **Kirgizia** [,kɜ:'gɪzɪə] (N) Kirguizia *f*

kirk [kɜ:k] (N) (*Scot*) iglesia *f* • **the Kirk** la Iglesia (Presbiteriana) de Escocia

kirsch [kɪəʃ] (N) kirsch *m*

kiss [kɪs] (N) beso *m*; (= *light touch*) roce *m* • **to blow sb a ~** tirar un beso a algn, dar un beso volado a algn • **the ~ of death** (*fig*) el golpe de gracia • **to give sb a ~** dar un beso a algn • **the ~ of life** (*Brit*) (= *artificial respiration*) respiración *f* boca a boca; (*fig*) nueva vida *f*, nuevas fuerzas *fpl*
(VT) besar • **to ~ sb's cheek/hand** besar a algn en la mejilla/besar la mano a algn • **to ~ sb goodbye/goodnight** dar un beso de despedida/de buenas noches a algn • **to ~ away sb's tears** enjugar las lágrimas a algn con besos • IDIOM: • **to ~ ass** (*esp US***) lamer culos** • **to ~ sb's ass** (*esp US***) lamer el culo a algn**, hacer la pelota a algn* • **~ my ass!** (*esp US***) ¡vete a la mierda!**, ¡vete al carajo! (*esp LAm***)
(VI) besarse • **they ~ed** se besaron, se dieron un beso • **to ~ and make up** hacer las paces
(CPD) ▸ **kiss curl** (*Brit*) caracol *m*

kissable ['kɪsəbl] (ADJ) [*mouth*] deliciosa • **a ~ girl** una chica a la que dan ganas de darle un beso

kissagram ['kɪsə,græm] (N) besograma *m*

kiss-and-tell [,kɪsən'tel] (ADJ) • **she is about to reveal all in her kiss-and-tell autobiography** está a punto de desvelarlo todo sobre su romance con una celebridad en su autobiografía

kisser‡ ['kɪsəʳ] (N) (= *face*) jeta‡ *f*; (= *mouth*) morrera‡ *f*

kiss-off* ['kɪsɒf] (*US*) (N) • **to give sth the kiss-off** tirar algo, despedirse de algo • **to give sb the kiss-off** (= *employee*) poner a algn de patitas en la calle*, despedir a algn; (= *boyfriend*) plantar a algn*, dejar a algn

kissogram ['kɪsə,græm] (N) = **kissagram**

kissproof ['kɪspru:f] (ADJ) indeleble

Kit [kɪt] (N) (*familiar form of* **Catherine, Christopher**)

kit [kɪt] (N) **1** (= *equipment, gear*) avíos *mpl*; (= *instruments, tools*) útiles *mpl*, herramientas *fpl*; (*Mil*) pertrechos *mpl*, petate *m*
2* (= *belongings*) bártulos* *mpl*; (= *clothes*) ropa *f*; (*for sports*) equipo *m*, indumentaria *f*; (= *luggage*) bultos* *mpl*, equipaje *m* • **to get one's kit off** (*Brit**) ponerse en cueros*, ponerse en pelotas‡, despelotarse*
3 (= *set of items*) equipo *m*, kit *m*; (= *first-aid kit*) botiquín *m* • **sewing kit** costurero *m*, neceser *m* de costura
4 (= *parts for assembly*) (= *toy, model*) maqueta *f*; (= *assembly kit*) kit *m*, juego *m* por piezas para armar • **a computer in kit form** un ordenador que se vende como kit *or* por piezas (y lo monta uno mismo); ▹ **caboodle**
(CPD) ▸ **kit car** *coche que se vende por piezas y lo arma uno mismo*
▸ **kit out, kit up** (VT + ADV) (*Brit*) (*often passive*) equipar (**with** de) • **to be kitted out in** [*+ clothing*] llevar puesto

kitbag ['kɪtbæg] (N) (*esp Brit*) saco *m* de viaje, macuto *m*; (*Mil*) mochila *f*

kitchen ['kɪtʃɪn] (N) cocina *f*
(CPD) [*cupboard, knife, equipment*] de cocina; [*window*] de la cocina ▸ **kitchen cabinet** armario *m* de cocina; (*Pol*) grupo *m* de asesores personales; ▹ CABINET ▸ **kitchen foil** papel *m* de aluminio ▸ **kitchen garden** huerto *m* ▸ **kitchen maid** ayudanta *f* de cocina ▸ **kitchen paper** toallitas *fpl* de papel ▸ **kitchen range** cocina *f* económica ▸ **kitchen roll** = kitchen paper ▸ **kitchen salt** sal *f* de cocina ▸ **kitchen sink** fregadero *m*, pila *f* • IDIOM: • **they took everything but the ~ sink*** (*hum*) se llevaron la casa a cuestas* ▸ **kitchen sink drama** obra *f* ultrarrealista ▸ **kitchen unit** módulo *m* de cocina

kitchenette [,kɪtʃɪ'net] (N) cocina *f* pequeña

kitchenware ['kɪtʃɪnweəʳ] (N) artículos *mpl* de cocina

kite [kaɪt] (N) **1** (= *toy*) cometa *f* • **to fly a ~** (*fig*) lanzar una idea (para sondear la opinión) • **go fly a ~!** (*US**) ¡vete al cuerno!*; ▹ **high**
2 (*Orn*) milano *m* real
3 (*US*) (*Econ‡*) cheque *m* sin valor
(VI)‡ presentar papeles falsos para conseguir dinero
(VT) (*US*) • **to ~ a cheque** presentar un cheque sin fondos
(CPD) ▸ **kite mark** (*Brit*) señal *f* de aprobación (de la BSI)

kith [kɪθ] (N) • **~ and kin** parientes *mpl* y amigos

kitsch [kɪtʃ] (ADJ) kitsch, cursi
(N) kitsch *m*, cursilería *f*

kitschy ['kɪtʃɪ] (ADJ) kitsch

kitten ['kɪtn] (N) gatito/a *m/f* • IDIOM: • **to**

k

have ~s*: • I nearly had ~s when I saw it casi me da un ataque (de nervios) cuando lo vi

kittenish ['kɪtənɪʃ] ADJ (fig) picaruelo, coquetón, retozón

kittiwake ['kɪtɪweɪk] N gaviota f tridáctila, gavina f

Kitty ['kɪtɪ] N familiar form of Catherine etc

kitty ['kɪtɪ] N 1 (= funds) fondo m común; (Cards) bote m, puesta f • how much have we got in the ~? ¿cuánto tenemos en el bote?
2* (= name for cat) minino* m
CPD ▸ Kitty Litter® (US) bandeja f higiénica para gatos, arena f higiénica para gatos

kiwi ['ki:wi:] N 1 (Orn) kiwi m
2* (= New Zealander) neozelandés/esa m/f
CPD ▸ kiwi fruit kiwi m

KKK N ABBR (US) = Ku Klux Klan

Klansman ['klænzmən] N (PL: Klansmen) miembro m del Ku Klux Klan

klaxon ['klæksn] N claxon m

Kleenex® ['kli:neks] N (PL: Kleenex or Kleenexes) Kleenex® m

kleptomania [ˌkleptəʊ'meɪnɪə] N cleptomanía f

kleptomaniac [ˌkleptəʊ'meɪnɪæk] N cleptómano/a m/f

klutz‡ [klʌts] N (US) patoso/a* m/f, torpe mf

km ABBR (= kilometre(s)) km

kmh, km/h ABBR (= kilometre(s) per hour) km/h, k.p.h.

knack [næk] N • it's just a ~ es un truco que se aprende • to get or learn the ~ of (doing) sth agarrar el truco or (Sp) el tranquillo a (hacer) algo* • she has the ~ of making people feel at home tiene el don de hacer que la gente se sienta cómoda a su alrededor • you have the ~ for drawing animals tienes mucha habilidad para dibujar animales • he seems to have the ~ of rubbing people up the wrong way no sé cómo se las arregla pero siempre acaba cayéndole mal a la gente

knacker ['nækəʳ] (Brit) N (for horses) matarife mf de caballos; (for ships) desguazador(a) m/f
VT* agotar, reventar* • I'm ~ed estoy reventado or hecho polvo*
CPD ▸ knacker's yard (for horses) matadero m; (for ships) desguace m

knapsack ['næpsæk] N (= small rucksack) mochila f

knave [neɪv] N (Hist) bellaco m, bribón m; (Cards) valet m; (in Spanish pack) sota f

knavery ['neɪvərɪ] N bellaquería f

knavish ['neɪvɪʃ] ADJ bellaco, bribón, vil

knead [ni:d] VT [+ dough] amasar, sobar; [+ clay] amasar, trabajar; [+ muscle] masajear, dar masaje a

knee [ni:] N (Anat) rodilla f; [of garment] rodilla f • on one's ~s, on bended ~ de rodillas • to bow the ~ to humillarse ante, someterse a • a sharp pain nearly brought me to my ~s un dolor agudo hizo que casi me cayera de rodillas • the embargo has brought the country to its ~s el embargo ha llevado al país al borde del desastre • to fall on one's ~s caer de rodillas • to go or get down on one's ~s arrodillarse, ponerse de rodillas • to go or get down on one's ~s to sb arrodillarse ante algn • to go to sb on (one's) bended ~s (fig) suplicar a algn de rodillas • his ~s were knocking le temblaban las rodillas; ▸ weak
VT dar un rodillazo a
CPD ▸ knee bend flexión f de piernas ▸ knee breeches calzón m corto ▸ knee jerk reflejo m rotular ▸ knee joint articulación f de la rodilla ▸ knee sock calcetín m alto

kneecap ['ni:kæp] N (Anat) rótula f
VT • to ~ sb disparar a las rodillas a algn

kneecapping ['ni:ˌkæpɪŋ] N disparo m a las rodillas

knee-deep ['ni:'di:p] ADJ • the water was knee-deep el agua cubría hasta las rodillas • to be knee-deep in estar metido hasta las rodillas en; (fig) estar metido hasta el cuello en • the place was knee-deep in paper había montones de papeles por todos lados
ADV • to go into the water knee-deep avanzar hasta que el agua llegue a las rodillas

knee-high ['ni:'haɪ] ADJ [grass] hasta las rodillas; [boots] de caña alta; [socks] largo • IDIOM: • he's been riding since he was knee-high to a grasshopper* lleva montando a caballo desde que era un renacuajo*

knee-jerk ['ni:dʒɜ:k] ADJ [reaction] instintivo, automático • he's a knee-jerk conservative es de derecha or (Sp) de derechas hasta la médula

kneel [ni:l] (PT, PP: knelt or kneeled) VI (also kneel down) (= act) arrodillarse, ponerse de rodillas; (= state) estar de rodillas • to ~ to (fig) hincar la rodilla ante

knee-length ['ni:leŋθ] ADJ [boots] de caña alta; [socks] largo; [coat, skirt] hasta la rodilla

kneeler ['ni:ləʳ] N (= cushion) cojín m; (= stool) banqueta f

knee-level ['ni:ˌlevl] N altura f de la rodilla

kneeling ['ni:lɪŋ] ADJ [figure] arrodillado, de rodillas

kneepad ['ni:pæd] N (for sport, work) rodillera f

kneeroom ['ni:rʊm] N espacio m para las piernas

knees-up* ['ni:zʌp] N (PL: knees-ups) (Brit) (hum) baile m, fiesta f

knell [nel] N toque m de difuntos, doble m; ▸ death

knelt [nelt] PT, PP of kneel

Knesset ['knesɪt] N • the ~ el Knéset

knew [nju:] PT of know

knickerbocker glory [ˌnɪkəbɒkə'glɔ:rɪ] N (Brit) especial m de helado (servido en copa alta)

knickerbockers ['nɪkəbɒkəz] NPL pantalones mpl cortos; (US) pantalones mpl de golf, pantalones mpl holgados

knickers ['nɪkəz] NPL 1 (Brit) bragas fpl, calzones mpl (LAm) • ~ to you!‡ ¡vete a al porra!*, ¡vete a tomar por saco! (Sp‡) • IDIOM: • to get one's ~ in a twist* ponerse nervioso
2†† = knickerbockers

knick-knack ['nɪknæk] N chuchería f, chisme m

knife [naɪf] N (PL: knives) (= table knife) cuchillo m; (= pocket knife) navaja f, cortaplumas m inv; (= dagger) puñal m; (= flick knife) navaja f, chaveta f (LAm); (= blade) cuchilla f • does he use a ~ and fork yet? ¿ha aprendido ya a usar los cubiertos? • I'll get the knives and forks out voy a sacar los cubiertos • IDIOMS: • to get one's ~ into sb tener inquina a algn • before you could say ~ en un decir Jesús • to turn the ~ in the wound hurgar en la herida • to put or stick the ~ in ensañarse, tirar con bala • like a (hot) ~ through butter sin problemas, con la gorra*
VT (= stab) acuchillar, apuñalar • to ~ sb to death matar a algn a navajazos or a puñaladas
CPD ▸ knife crime(s) delitos mpl con arma blanca ▸ knife edge filo m (de cuchillo) • IDIOM: • to be (balanced) on a ~ edge [person] estar con el alma pendiente de un hilo; [result] estar pendiente de un hilo ▸ knife grinder (= person) afilador(a) m/f ▸ knife sharpener (= tool) afilador m de cuchillos

knifebox ['naɪfbɒks] N portacubiertos m inv

knife-point ['naɪfpɔɪnt] N • at knife-point a punta de navaja

knifing ['naɪfɪŋ] N ataque m con cuchillo or navaja • the motiveless ~ of a young girl el apuñalamiento sin motivo de una chica joven

knight [naɪt] N (Hist) caballero m; (Chess) caballo m; (modern) (Brit) Sir m, caballero de una orden • ~ in shining armour príncipe m azul • Knight (of the Order) of the Garter (Brit) caballero m de la orden de la Jarretera
VT (Hist) armar caballero; (modern) (Brit) otorgar el título de Sir a
CPD ▸ knight errant caballero m andante ▸ Knight Templar caballero m templario, templario m

knight-errantry ['naɪt'erəntrɪ] N caballería f andante

knighthood ['naɪthʊd] N 1 (= order) caballería f
2 (= title) título m de caballero; (modern) (Brit) título m de Sir • he was given a ~ le otorgaron el título de Sir; (Hist) fue armado caballero

knightly ['naɪtlɪ] ADJ caballeroso, caballeresco

knit [nɪt] VT [+ garment] hacer (a punto de aguja), tricotar (Sp), tejer (LAm) • she can ~ up a sweater in a couple of days puede hacer un jersey en un par de días • to ~ one's brows fruncir el ceño • his task is to ~ the nation back together su tarea es la de volver a unir a la gente del país; ▸ close-knit
VI (also knit together, knit up) hacer punto or calceta, tricotar (Sp), tejer (LAm); [bones] soldarse; [wound] cerrarse, curarse
CPD ▸ knit stitch punto m de media
▸ **knit together** VI + ADV = knit
VT + ADV (fig) juntar, unir
▸ **knit up** VT + ADV montar
VI + ADV = knit

knitted ['nɪtɪd] ADJ tejido • ~ goods géneros mpl de punto

knitter ['nɪtəʳ] N persona f que tricota • she's a great ~ tricota muy bien

knitting ['nɪtɪŋ] N (= activity) labor f de punto; (= product) prenda f de punto; (= piece being worked on) labor f • I think I'll do some ~ creo que voy a ponerme a hacer punto or (LAm) tejer • she put her ~ down on the chair dejó la labor sobre la silla
CPD ▸ knitting machine tricotosa f (Sp), máquina f de tejer (LAm) ▸ knitting needle, knitting pin aguja f de hacer punto or (LAm) de tejer ▸ knitting pattern patrón m, instrucciones fpl para hacer punto, instrucciones fpl de tejido (LAm) ▸ knitting wool lana f para labores or (LAm) para tejer

knitwear ['nɪtweəʳ] N géneros mpl de punto

knives [naɪvz] NPL of knife

knob [nɒb] N 1 (= protuberance) protuberancia f, bulto m; (on treetrunk) nudo m
2 (= control) [of radio etc] botón m, mando m
3 (= handle) [of door] pomo m, tirador m; [of drawer] tirador m; [of stick] puño m
4 (= piece) • a ~ of butter (Brit) un pedazo de mantequilla
5 (Brit**) (= penis) verga** f, polla f (Sp**)

knobbly ['nɒblɪ], **knobby** ['nɒbɪ] ADJ (COMPAR: knobb(l)ier, SUPERL: knobb(l)iest) [stick] nudoso; [knees] huesudo

knock [nɒk] N 1 (gen) golpe m; (in collision) choque m; (on door) llamada f • a ~ on the head un golpe en la cabeza • there was a ~ at the door llamaron a la puerta • his pride took a ~ su orgullo sufrió un golpe • the

team took a hard ~ yesterday ayer el equipo recibió un rudo golpe • **he has had plenty of hard ~s** ha recibido muchos y duros golpes en la vida
2 (*in engine*) golpeteo *m*
VT **1** (= *strike*) golpear • **to ~ a hole in sth** hacer *or* abrir un agujero en algo • **to ~ a nail into sth** clavar un clavo en algo • **to ~ sb on the head** golpear a algn en la cabeza • **to ~ one's head on/against sth** (*by accident*) dar con la cabeza contra algo; (*deliberately*) dar cabezazos contra algo • **I ~ed my elbow on** *or* **against the table** me di (un golpe) en el codo con la mesa • **to ~ sb to the ground** tirar *or* echar a algn al suelo • **to ~ sb unconscious** *or* **out** *or* **cold** dejar a algn sin sentido • **to ~ sth to the floor** dar con algo en el suelo • **he ~ed the knife out of her hand** le quitó el cuchillo de la mano de un golpe • **I ~ed the ball into the water** tiré la pelota al agua • **to ~ the bottom out of sth** [+ *box*] desfondar algo; (*fig*) [+ *argument*] dejar algo sin fundamentos • IDIOMS: • **to ~ sth on the head** (*Brit**) (= *put paid to*) [+ *idea*] echar algo por tierra • **to ~ some sense into sb*** hacer entrar en razón a algn • **to ~ sb sideways*** dejar de piedra *or* patidifuso a algn* • **to ~ spots off sb*** dar mil vueltas a algn*
2* (= *criticize*) criticar, hablar mal de
VI **1** (*strike*) golpear; (*at door*) llamar a la puerta • **"knock before entering"** "llamar a la puerta antes de entrar" • **he ~ed at the door/on the table** llamó a la puerta/dio un golpe en la mesa • **poverty was ~ing at his door** la pobreza llamaba a su puerta • **I can't give a job to everyone who comes ~ing on my door** no puedo dar trabajo a todos los que vienen pidiéndomelo *or* que llaman a mi puerta
2 (= *bump*) • **to ~ into sth/sb** chocar *or* tropezar con algo/algn • **to ~ against sth** chocar *or* dar con *or* contra algo
3 [*engine*] golpetear
▸ **knock about, knock around** VT + ADV
1 [+ *person*] pegar, maltratar; [+ *object*] golpear, maltratar • **the place was badly ~ed about** el lugar sufrió grandes estragos • **the car was rather ~ed about** el coche estaba en bastante mal estado
2 (= *discuss*) • **to ~ an idea around** dar vueltas a una idea
VI + ADV* • **he's ~ed about (the world) a bit** ha visto mucho mundo • **he's ~ing about somewhere** anda por algún lado • **she ~s around with a bad crowd** anda con malas compañías
▸ **knock back*** VT + ADV **1** [+ *drink*] beberse (de un trago) • **he can certainly ~ them back** sabe darle al trago*
2 (= *cost*) • **it ~ed me back £10** me costó 10 libras
3 (= *shock*) asombrar, pasmar* • **the smell ~s you back** el olor echa para atrás*
4* (= *reject*) [+ *offer*] rechazar; [+ *person*] rechazar, dar con la puerta en las narices a
▸ **knock down** VT + ADV **1** (= *pull, throw to the ground*) [+ *building*] derribar, demoler; [+ *person*] tirar al suelo; [+ *pedestrian*] atropellar; [+ *tree, door etc*] derribar, echar abajo; (*fig*) [+ *argument etc*] echar por tierra
2 (= *reduce*) [+ *price*] rebajar, reducir • **I ~ed him down to £20** conseguí que me rebajara el precio a 20 libras
3 (*at auction*) • **it was ~ed down to him for £200** se lo adjudicaron en 200 libras
▸ **knock in** VT + ADV clavar
▸ **knock off** VT + ADV **1** (= *make fall*) hacer caer; (*intentionally*) echar abajo
2 (= *deduct*) • **he ~ed £5 off** (*from price*) rebajó el precio en 5 libras, hizo un descuento de 5 libras • **to ~ three seconds off the record** mejorar el récord en tres segundos
3* (= *steal*) birlar*
4* (= *do quickly*) [+ *meal*] preparar enseguida; [+ *garment*] hacer enseguida; [+ *novel*] escribir rápidamente
5* (= *stop*) • **~ it off!** ¡déjalo ya!
6‡ (= *arrest*) detener, agarrar*; (= *kill*) cargarse*
7** [+ *woman*] tirarse a**
VI + ADV* • **he ~s off at five** sale del trabajo a las cinco • **I ~ off for lunch at one** dejo el trabajo a la una para (salir a) comer
▸ **knock on*** VI + ADV • **he's ~ing on a bit** es bastante viejo • **she's ~ing on for 60** va para los 60
▸ **knock out** VT + ADV **1** (= *stun*) dejar sin sentido, hacer perder el conocimiento; (*Boxing*) poner fuera de combate, dejar K.O.
2 (= *strike out*) [+ *nails*] extraer, sacar; (*in fight*) [+ *teeth*] romper
3 (*in competition*) eliminar
4* (= *make*) [+ *product*] producir, fabricar; [+ *garment*] hacer; [+ *novel*] escribir
5 (= *destroy*) [+ *enemy target*] destruir; (= *stop*) [+ *electricity supply, telephone lines*] cortar
6* (= *exhaust*) agotar, dejar para el arrastre*
7* (*shock*) dejar pasmado*
▸ **knock over** VT + ADV [+ *object*] tirar, voltear (*LAm*); [+ *pedestrian*] atropellar
▸ **knock together** VT + ADV **1** [+ *two objects*] golpear (uno contra otro) • **I ought to ~ your heads together!** ¡os debería dar una buena paliza!
2 = knock up
▸ **knock up** VT + ADV **1** (*Brit*) (= *waken*) despertar, llamar
2 (= *make hastily*) hacer; [+ *meal*] preparar
3 (*Brit**) (= *tire*) agotar; (= *make ill*) dejar enfermo • **he was ~ed up for a month** estuvo enfermo durante un mes
4‡ (= *make pregnant*) dejar embarazada
VI + ADV (*Tennis*) pelotear
knockabout [ˈnɒkəbaʊt] ADJ (*esp Brit*) bullicioso, tumultuoso • **~ comedy** farsa *f* bulliciosa
N (*Sport*) • **to have a ~** pelotear
knockback* [ˈnɒkbæk] N **1** (= *rejection*) rechazo *m*, feo* *m* • **to get the ~** sufrir un feo*
2 (= *setback*) revés *m*, duro golpe *m*
knockdown [ˈnɒkdaʊn] ADJ (= *reduced*) [*price*] de ganga, regalado
knocker [ˈnɒkəʳ] N **1** (*on door*) aldaba *f*
2* (= *critic*) detractor(a) *m/f*, crítico/a *m/f*
3 knockers‡ tetas* *fpl*
knocker-up [ˈnɒkəˈrʌp] N (*Brit*) despertador *m*
knock-for-knock [ˈnɒkfəˈnɒk] ADJ • **knock-for-knock agreement** acuerdo *m* de pago respectivo
knocking [ˈnɒkɪŋ] N (= *sound*) golpes *mpl*, golpeteo *m*; (*at door*) golpe *m*, llamada *f*; (*Aut*) golpeteo *m*
CPD ▸ **knocking copy** contrapublicidad *f*, *anuncio destinado a denigrar el producto de otro*
knocking-off time* [ˌnɒkɪŋˈɒfˌtaɪm] N hora *f* de salir del trabajo
knocking-shop* [ˈnɒkɪŋʃɒp] N casa *f* de putas
knock-kneed [ˈnɒkˈniːd] ADJ patizambo; (*fig*) débil, irresoluto
knock-on [ˈnɒkˈɒn] N (*Rugby*) autopase *m*
CPD ▸ **knock-on effect** (*Brit*) repercusiones *fpl* • **the rise in interest rates will have a knock-on effect on the housing market** la subida en los tipos de interés repercutirá en el mercado inmobiliario
knockout [ˈnɒkaʊt] N **1** (*Boxing*) knock-out *m*, K.O. *m*, nocaut *m*
2 (= *competition*) concurso *m* eliminatorio, eliminatoria *f*
3* (= *stunner*) maravilla *f* • **she's a ~** es una chica alucinante* • **he's a ~!** ¡está buenísimo!*
CPD ▸ **knockout agreement** acuerdo *m* secreto para no hacerse competencia
▸ **knockout blow** golpe *m* aplastante
▸ **knockout competition** concurso *m* eliminatorio, eliminatoria *f* ▸ **knockout drops*** somnífero *msing*, calmante *msing*
▸ **knockout punch** = knockout blow
knock-up [ˈnɒkʌp] N (*Tennis*) (= *practice*) peloteo *m* • **to have a knock-up** pelotear
knoll [nəʊl] N otero *m*, montículo *m*
knot [nɒt] N **1** (*gen*) nudo *m* • **to tie a ~** hacer un nudo • **her hair was all in ~s** tenía el pelo enredado • IDIOMS: • **to tie sb up in ~s** enredar a algn • **to get tied up** *or* **tie o.s. up in ~s** armarse un lío* • **to tie the ~** casarse
2 (*Naut*) (= *unit of speed*) nudo *m*; ▹ rate
3 (*in wood*) nudo *m*; (= *group*) [*of people*] grupo *m*, corrillo *m*
VT anudar, atar • **to ~ sth together** anudar algo, atar algo con un nudo • **get ~ted!*** ¡fastídiate!*
VI hacerse un nudo
knotgrass [ˈnɒtgrɑːs] N (*Bot*) centinodia *f*
knothole [ˈnɒthəʊl] N agujero *m* (que deja un nudo en la madera)
knotted [ˈnɒtɪd] ADJ [*rope*] anudado, con nudos; [*scarf, tie*] atado con un nudo
knotty [ˈnɒtɪ] ADJ (COMPAR: **knottier**, SUPERL: **knottiest**) [*wood*] nudoso; (*fig*) [*problem*] espinoso
knout [naʊt] N knut *m*

know [nəʊ]

TRANSITIVE VERB
INTRANSITIVE VERB
NOUN

(PT: **knew**, PP: **known**)

TRANSITIVE VERB

Look up set combinations such as **know the ropes, know one's stuff, know sth backward** *at the other word.*

1 (= *be aware of*) **a** [+ *facts, dates etc*] saber • **to ~ the difference between ...** saber la diferencia entre ... • **she ~s a lot about chemistry** sabe mucho de química • **I don't ~ much about history** no sé mucho de historia • **I don't ~ much about that** no sé mucho de eso • **I ~ nothing about it** • **I don't ~ anything about it** no sé nada de eso • **he ~s all the answers** lo sabe todo • **one minute you're leaving school, then before you ~ it, you've got a family to support** dejas el colegio y al minuto siguiente, antes de darte cuenta, tienes una familia que mantener
b (*with clause*) • **to ~ that** saber que • **to ~ why/when/where/if** saber por qué/cuándo/dónde/si • **to ~ how to do sth** saber hacer algo • **do you ~ how he did that?** ¿sabes cómo lo hizo? • **you ~ how it is** ya sabes cómo son las cosas • **you don't ~ how glad I am to see you** no sabes cuánto me alegro de verte • **I'll** *or* **I'd have you ~ that ...** que sepas que ..., para que te enteres, ... • **you haven't time, as well he knew** no tienes tiempo, como él bien sabía • **you ~ as well as I do that ...** sabes tan bien como yo que ... • **to ~ what** saber qué *or* lo que • **I ~ what I said** ya sé qué *or* lo que dije

• **he doesn't ~ what to do** no sabe qué hacer • **I don't ~ whether or not you've heard, but ...** no sé si has oído o no pero ... • IDIOM: • **to ~ what's what** saber cuántas son cinco
c (*in exclamations*) • **I knew it!** ¡lo sabía! • **that's all you ~!*** ¡y más que podría yo contarte! • **don't I ~ it!** ¡a mí me lo vas a contar! • **"she's furious" — "don't I ~ it?"** —está furiosa —¡a mí me lo vas a contar! • **how was I to ~ that ...?** ¿cómo iba yo a saber que ...? • **I should have ~n you'd mess things up!** debería haberme figurado *or* imaginado que ibas a estropear las cosas • **do you ~ what, I think she did it!** ¿sabes una cosa? creo que lo hizo ella • **I ~ what, let's drop in on Daphne!** ¡ya sé! ¡vamos a pasarnos por casa de Daphne! • **you ~ what you can do with it!*** ¡métel o por donde te quepa!‡ • **(well,) what do you ~!*** ¿qué te parece?, ¡fíjate!, ¡mira nomás! (*LAm*) • **what does he ~ about dictionaries!** ¡qué sabrá él de diccionarios! • **Peter, wouldn't you ~ it, can't come!** Peter, como era de esperar, no puede venir
d • **to ~ to do sth***: **does he ~ to feed the rabbits?** ¿sabe que tiene que dar de comer a los conejos?

2 (*= be acquainted with*) [*+ person, place*] conocer; [*+ subject*] saber • **do you ~ him?** ¿lo conoces? • **to ~ French** saber francés • **to ~ one's classics/linguistic theory** saberse los clásicos/la teoría lingüística • **most of us ~ him only as a comedian** la mayoría de nosotros lo conocemos solo como comediante • **civilization as we ~ it** la civilización tal y como la conocemos • **don't you ~ me better than that!** ¿o es que no me conoces?, ¡como si no me conocieras! • **to ~ sb by sight/name** conocer a algn de vista/de nombre • **to ~ sb by reputation** haber oído hablar de algn • **she knew him for a liar and a cheat** sabía que era un mentiroso y un tramposo • **they ~ each other from university** se conocen de la universidad • **if I ~ him, he'll say no** me apuesto a que dice que no • **she ~s her own mind** sabe lo que quiere • PROVERB: • **it's not what you ~, it's who you ~** lo importante no es lo que sabes sino a quién conoces

3 (*with infinitive*) • **I ~ him to be a liar** sé que es un mentiroso • **he is ~n to have been there** se sabe que ha estado allí • **I've never ~n him to smile** nunca lo he visto sonreír • **I've never ~n her to be wrong** que yo sepa nunca se ha equivocado • **it has never been ~n to happen** no se tienen noticias de que haya pasado nunca • **I don't ~ him to speak to** no lo conozco personalmente

4 (*= understand*) • **I don't ~ how you can say that** no sé *or* no entiendo cómo puedes decir eso • **you ~ what I mean** ya me entiendes, ya sabes lo que quiero decir • **I ~ the problem!** conozco el problema • **I ~ the problems that arise when ...** sé los problemas que surgen cuando ...

5 (*= recognize*) reconocer • **he knew me at once** me reconoció en seguida • **I'd have ~n you anywhere** te hubiese reconocido en cualquier parte • **I knew him by his voice** le reconocí por la voz • **to ~ right from wrong** saber distinguir el bien del mal • IDIOM: • **she ~s a good thing when she sees it*** sabe reconocer algo bueno cuando lo ve

6 (*= be certain*) • **I don't ~ if it has made things any easier** no sé si ha facilitado las cosas • **I don't ~ if *or* that it's a very good idea** no sé si es una buena idea, no estoy seguro de que sea una buena idea • **I don't ~ if I can do it** no sé si puedo hacerlo

7 (*sexually*††) • **to ~ sb** conocer a algn

8 (*in set expressions*) **to get to know sb** (llegar a) conocer a algn • **I'd like to get to ~ you better** me gustaría (llegar a) conocerte mejor • **we got to ~ each other during military service** llegamos a conocernos bien durante la mili
to get to know sth • **as you get to ~ the piece better ...** cuando conoces mejor la pieza ..., cuando estás más familiarizado con la pieza ... • **get to ~ the area before buying a house** estudia bien la zona antes de comprar una casa
to let sb know ... • **I'll let you ~ the price as soon as I can** en cuanto sepa el precio te lo digo • **let us ~ if you need help** avísanos si necesitas ayuda • **let me ~ if you can't come** avísame si no puedes venir • **let me ~ how you get on** ya me contarás cómo te fue

INTRANSITIVE VERB

1 (*gen*) saber • **I don't ~** no (lo) sé • **yes, I ~** sí, ya lo sé • **Mummy ~s best** mamá sabe lo que te conviene • **he doesn't ~ any better** no sabe lo que hace • **he thinks he's going to get the job, but I ~ better** cree que va a conseguir el trabajo, pero yo sé mejor lo que cabe esperar • **you ought to ~ better than to ...** ya deberías saber que no se puede ... • **Mary ~s better than to risk upsetting me** Mary sabe demasiado bien que no le conviene que me enfade • **how should I ~?** ¿cómo iba yo a saberlo? • **I ~, let's ...** ya sé, vamos a ... • **one never ~s** • **you never ~** nunca se sabe • **there's no (way of) ~ing** no hay manera de saberlo • **afterwards they just don't want to ~** (*in relationships*) después "si te he visto no me acuerdo"; (*in business*) después no quieren saber nada del asunto • **who ~s?** ¿quién sabe? • **"was she annoyed about it?" — "I wouldn't ~"** —¿se enfadó por eso? —¿y yo que sé? • **it's not easy, you ~** no es fácil, sabes • **you ~, I think I'm beginning to like Richard** ¿sabes? creo que me está empezando a gustar Richard; ▹ **all**

2 (*in set expressions*) **to know about** • **to ~ about sth/sb: did you ~ about Paul?** ¿te has enterado de *or* sabes lo de Paul? • **I didn't ~ about the accident** no me había enterado de lo del accidente, no sabía nada de lo del accidente • **I'd ~n about his illness for some time** sabía lo de su enfermedad hacía tiempo • **everything you always wanted to ~ about sex** todo lo que siempre ha querido saber sobre el sexo • **she ~s about cats** ella entiende de gatos • **"you must be delighted!" — "I don't ~ about that"** ¡debes estar encantado! —no sé qué decirte • **"you're a genius!" — "oh, I don't ~ about that"** —¡eres un genio! —hombre, no sé qué decirte • **"I'm taking tomorrow off" — "I don't ~ about that!"** —mañana me tomo el día libre —no sé, habrá que ver • **I don't ~ about you, but I think it's terrible** a ti no sé, pero a mí me parece terrible
to get to know about sth enterarse de algo
to know of (*= be acquainted with*) conocer • **I ~ of a nice little café** conozco un pequeño café muy agradable • **I don't ~ him but I ~ of him** no lo conozco pero he oído hablar de él; (*= be aware of*) • **I ~ of no reason why he should have committed suicide** que yo sepa no tenía razones para suicidarse • **the first I knew of it was when Pete told me** lo primero que oí *or* supe del asunto fue lo que me dijo Pete • **that was the first I knew of it** esa fue la primera noticia que tuve del asunto • **not that I ~ of** que yo sepa, no
to let sb know • **we'll let you ~** ya te diremos lo que sea, ya te avisaremos • **I'll let you ~ on Monday** te diré lo que sea el lunes • **why didn't you let me ~?** ¿por qué no me lo dijiste?

NOUN

• **to be in the know*** (*= well-informed*) estar enterado; (*= privy to sth*) estar al tanto *or* al corriente • **those not in the ~** los que no lo sabían

knowable [ˈnəʊəbl] ADJ conocible
know-all [ˈnəʊɔːl] N (*Brit*) (*pej*) sabelotodo *mf inv*, sabihondo/a *m/f*
know-how [ˈnəʊhaʊ] N (*= knowledge*) conocimientos *mpl*; (*= experience*) experiencia *f*; (*= expertise*) pericia *f* • **technical know-how** conocimientos *mpl* técnicos
knowing [ˈnəʊɪŋ] ADJ (*= sharp*) astuto, sagaz; [*look, smile*] de complicidad
N • **there's no ~** no hay modo de saberlo • **there's no ~ what he'll do** es imposible adivinar lo que hará
knowingly [ˈnəʊɪŋlɪ] ADV **1** (*= intentionally*) a sabiendas, adrede
2 (*= archly*) [*smile, look, nod*] con complicidad
know-it-all [ˈnəʊɪtɔːl] N (*US*) (*pej*) sabelotodo *mf inv*, sabihondo/a *m/f*
knowledge [ˈnɒlɪdʒ] N **1** (*= information, awareness, understanding*) conocimiento *m* • **to deny all ~ of sth** negar tener conocimiento de algo • **to bring sth to sb's ~** poner a algn al tanto de algo • **it has come to my ~ that ...** me he enterado de que ... • **it is common ~ that ...** todo el mundo sabe que ..., es del dominio público que ... • **to have no ~ of sth** no tener conocimiento de algo • **to (the best of) my ~** a mi entender, que yo sepa • **not to my ~** que yo sepa, no • **without my ~** sin saberlo yo
2 (*= person's range of information*) conocimientos *mpl* • **my ~ of Spanish** mis conocimientos del español • **he has some ~ of computers** sabe algo de informática • **to have a working ~ of** dominar los principios esenciales de • **I have a working ~ of Portuguese** me defiendo en portugués • **to have a thorough ~ of history** conocer a fondo la historia
3 (*= learning*) saber *m* • **the pursuit of ~** la búsqueda del saber • **the advance of ~** el progreso de la ciencia
knowledgeable [ˈnɒlɪdʒəbl] ADJ [*person*] (*gen*) informado; (*in specific subject*) entendido (**about** en); [*remark*] erudito • **she's very ~ about antiques** es muy entendida en antigüedades, sabe mucho de antigüedades
knowledgeably [ˈnɒlɪdʒəblɪ] ADV con conocimiento de causa, de manera erudita
knowledge-based [ˈnɒlɪdʒbeɪst] N
1 [*society, economy*] del conocimiento; [*product*] basado en el conocimiento • **the shift from an industrial to a knowledge-based economy** el cambio de la economía industrial a la basada en el conocimiento
2 [*system*] experto
known [nəʊn] PP *of* **know**
ADJ **1** [*+ person, fact*] conocido • **he is ~ as Hercules** es conocido por el nombre de Hércules • **she wishes to be ~ as Jane Beattie** quiere que se la conozca como Jane Beattie • **he is ~ as a man of great charm** tiene fama de tener mucho encanto • **it soon became ~ that ...** tardó poco en saberse que ... • **to be ~ for sth** ser conocido por algo • **he is best ~ for his fiction** se le conoce sobre todo por sus obras de ficción • **he let it be ~ that ...** dio a entender que ... • **to make o.s. ~ to sb** presentarse a algn • **they made it ~ that they did not intend to prosecute** dieron a saber que no tenían intención de interponer una acción judicial • **to make**

one's presence ~ to sb hacer saber a algn que se ha llegado • **to make one's wishes ~** hacer que se sepa lo que uno desea • **he is ~ to be unreliable** tiene fama de no ser una persona en la que se pueda confiar • **the most dangerous snake ~ to man** la serpiente más peligrosa de todas las conocidas por el hombre • **it's well ~ that ...** es bien sabido que ..., es de todos conocido que ...; ▹ **know**
2 (= *acknowledged*) reconocido • **a ~ expert** un experto reconocido como tal • **an internationally ~ expert** un experto conocido en todo el mundo
knuckle ['nʌkl] (N) (*Anat*) nudillo *m*; [*of meat*] jarrete *m* • **to rap sb's ~s** • **rap sb over the ~s** echar un rapapolvo a algn* • IDIOM: • **it was a bit near the ~** rayaba en la indecencia
▸ **knuckle down*** (VI + ADV) • **to ~ down (to work)** ponerse a trabajar en serio
▸ **knuckle under** (VI + ADV) someterse, bajar la cerviz
knucklebone ['nʌkl,bəʊn] (N) nudillo *m*
knuckleduster ['nʌkl,dʌstəʳ] (N) puño *m* de hierro
knucklehead* ['nʌkl,hed] (N) cabeza *mf* hueca
knurl [nɜːl] (N) nudo *m*, protuberancia *f*; [*of coin*] cordón *m*
(VT) [+ *coin*] acordonar
knurled [nɜːld] (ADJ) nudoso; [*coin*] acordonado
KO* (N ABBR) = **knockout** (PL: **KO's**) K.O. *m*, nocaut *m*
(VT) (VB: PT, PP: **KO'd**) (*gen*) (*Boxing*) dejar K.O., dejar fuera de combate

koala [kəʊ'ɑːlə] (N) (*also* **koala bear**) koala *m*
kohl ['kəʊl] (N) kohl *m*
kohlrabi [kəʊl'rɑːbɪ] (N) (PL: **kohlrabies**) colinabo *m*
Kolkata [kɒl'kɑːtə] (N) Kolkata *f*
kook* [kuːk] (N) (*US*) majareta *mf* (*Sp**), excéntrico/a *m/f*
kookaburra ['kʊkə,bʌrə] (N) kookaburra *m*
kookie*, kooky* ['kuːkɪ] (ADJ) (COMPAR: **kookier**, SUPERL: **kookiest**) (*US*) [*person*] chiflado*, majareta (*Sp**); [*idea*] descabellado, disparatado
kopeck ['kəʊpek] (N) cópec *m*
Koran [kɒ'rɑːn] (N) Corán *m*, Alcorán *m*
Koranic [kɒ'rænɪk] (ADJ) coránico, alcoránico
Korea [kə'rɪə] (N) Corea *f* • **North/South ~** Corea *f* del Norte/Sur
Korean [kə'rɪən] (ADJ) coreano
(N) coreano/a *m/f*
korma ['kɔːʳmə] (N) *plato indio con nata y coco*
kosher ['kəʊʃəʳ] (ADJ) **1** (*lit*) autorizado por la ley judía, kosher
2* (= *genuine*) legal*
Kosova, Kosovo ['kɒsəvəʊ] (N) Kosovo *m*
Kosovan ['kɒsəvən], **Kosovar** ['kɒsəvɑːʳ] (ADJ) kosovar • **~ Albanian** albanokosovar *mf*
kowtow ['kaʊ'taʊ] (VI) (= *bow*) saludar humildemente; (= *be subservient*) • **to ~ to sb** bajar la cabeza *or* doblegarse ante algn
KP (N ABBR) **1** (*US*) (*Mil*) = **kitchen police**
2 (*Med*) = **Kaposi's sarcoma**
kph (ABBR) (= **kilometres per hour**) km/h, kph
Kraut‡ [kraʊt] (*offensive*) (ADJ) alemán
(N) alemán/ana *m/f*
Kremlin ['kremlɪn] (N) • **the ~** el Kremlin

Kremlinologist [,kremlɪ'nɒlədʒɪst] (N) kremlinólogo/a *m/f*
Kremlinology [,kremlɪ'nɒlədʒɪ] (N) kremlinología *f*
krill [krɪl] (N) (PL: **krill**) camarón *m* antártico
krona ['krəʊnə] (N) (= *old currency*) corona *f*
krone ['krəʊnə] (N) (= *old currency*) corona *f*
krugerrand ['kruːgə,rænd] (N) krugerrand *m*
krumhorn, krummhorn ['krʌmhɔːn] (N) cuerno *m*
Kruschev [kruːs'tʃɒf] (N) Jruschov
krypton [krɪptɒn] (N) criptón *m*
KS (ABBR) (*US*) = **Kansas**
Kt (ABBR) (*Brit*) = **Knight**
Kuala Lumpur ['kwɑːlə'lʊmpʊəʳ] (N) Kuala Lumpur *m*
kudos ['kjuːdɒs] (N) prestigio *m*
Ku Klux Klan ['kuː'klʌks'klæn] (N) • **the ~** el Ku Klux Klan
kummel ['kʊməl] (N) cúmel *m*, kummel *m*
kumquat ['kʌmkwɒt] (N) naranja *f* china
kung fu ['kʌŋ'fuː] (N) kung fu *m*
Kurd [kɜːd] (N) kurdo/a *m/f*
Kurdish ['kɜːdɪʃ] (ADJ) kurdo
(N) (*Ling*) kurdo *m*
Kurdistan [,kɜːdɪ'stæn] (N) Kurdistán *m*
Kuwait [kʊ'weɪt] (N) Kuwait *m*
Kuwaiti [kʊ'weɪtɪ] (ADJ) kuwaití
(N) kuwaití *mf*
kV, kv (ABBR) (= **kilovolt(s)**) kv
kW, kw (ABBR) (= **kilowatt(s)**) kw
kWh, kW/h (ABBR) (= **kilowatt-hour(s)**) kw/h
KY (ABBR) (*US*) = **Kentucky**
Kyrgyzstan [,kɜːgɪs'tɑːn] (N) Kirguizistán *m*

k

Ll

L, l [el] (N) (= *letter*) L, l *f* • **L for Lucy** L de Lorenzo
(ABBR) **1** (*in maps etc*) = **lake**
2 (*Aut*) = **learner** • **L-plate** (*Brit*) placa *f* de la L (*de conductor en prácticas*); ▹ **DRIVING LICENCE/DRIVER'S LICENSE**
3 (= *garment size*) = **large**
4 (= **left**) izq., izq.º
5 (= **litre(s)**) l
6 (*Ling*) = **Latin**
LA (ABBR) (*US*) **1** = **Los Angeles**
2 = **Louisiana**
La. (ABBR) **1** (*US*) = **Louisiana**
2 = **Lane**
Lab (ADJ ABBR), (N ABBR) (*Brit*) (*Pol*) = **Labour**
(ABBR) (*Canada*) = **Labrador**
lab* [læb] (N ABBR) (= **laboratory**) laboratorio *m*
(CPD) ▸ **lab coat** bata *f* de laboratorio ▸ **lab technician** técnico/a *m/f* de laboratorio
label ['leɪbl] (N) **1** (*on merchandise, luggage, clothing*) etiqueta *f* • **sticky ~** etiqueta *f* adhesiva • **warning ~** etiqueta *f* de advertencia; ▹ **address, luggage**
2 (= *brand*) marca *f* • **these products are sold under our own ~** estos productos se venden como parte de nuestra propia marca; ▹ **designer, own-label**
3 (*also* **record label**) sello *m* discográfico • **the LP is on the A & M ~** el elepé es del sello discográfico A & M
4 (*fig*) (= *classification*) etiqueta *f* • **it was comforting to be able to put a ~ on my illness** era reconfortante el poder ponerle una etiqueta a mi enfermedad
(VT) **1** (*lit*) etiquetar, poner etiqueta a • **I've just spent a whole day ~ling boxes** me he pasado el día etiquetando cajas *or* poniendo etiquetas a cajas • **the jar was not ~led** el bote no llevaba etiqueta, el bote no estaba etiquetado • **the bottle was ~led "poison"** la botella llevaba una etiqueta que decía "veneno" • **every packet must be clearly ~led** cada paquete debe llevar una etiqueta que indique claramente su contenido
2 (*fig*) • **to ~ sb (as) sth** calificar a algn de algo, tachar a algn de algo (*pej*) • **he was ~led (as) a troublemaker** lo calificaron *or* lo tacharon de alborotador
labelling, labeling (*US*) ['leɪbəlɪŋ] (N) etiquetaje *m*
labia ['leɪbɪə] (NPL) *of* **labium**
labial ['leɪbɪəl] (ADJ) labial
(N) labial *f*
labiodental [,leɪbɪəʊ'dentəl] (ADJ) labiodental
(N) labiodental *f*
labiovelar [,leɪbɪəʊ'viːləʳ] (ADJ) labiovelar
(N) labiovelar *f*
labium ['leɪbɪəm] (N) (PL: **labia**) labio *m*
labor ['leɪbəʳ] (*US*) (N), (VT), (VI) = **labour**
(CPD) ▸ **Labor Day** Día *m* del Trabajo *or* de los Trabajadores ▸ **labor union** sindicato *m*

> **LABOR DAY**
> El **Labor Day** (Día del Trabajo *or* de los Trabajadores) es una festividad nacional en honor al trabajo, que se celebra en Estados Unidos y en Canadá el primer lunes de septiembre. Fue instaurada en 1894 por el Congreso de los Estados Unidos, después de que los trabajadores la solicitaran durante más de doce años. En la actualidad, ya sin las connotaciones políticas de sus orígenes y coincidiendo con el final del verano y con el principio del curso escolar, se celebran desfiles, mítines y comidas campestres.

laboratory [lə'bɒrətərɪ,], (*US*) ['læbrə,tɔːrɪ] (N) laboratorio *m*; ▹ **language**
(CPD) de laboratorio ▸ **laboratory animal** animal *m* de laboratorio ▸ **laboratory assistant** ayudante *mf* de laboratorio ▸ **laboratory coat** bata *f* de laboratorio ▸ **laboratory equipment** equipo *m* de laboratorio ▸ **laboratory experiment** experimento *m* de laboratorio ▸ **laboratory technician** técnico/a *m/f* de laboratorio ▸ **laboratory test** prueba *f* de laboratorio
laborer ['leɪbərəʳ] (N) (*US*) = **labourer**
laboring ['leɪbərɪŋ] (ADJ) (*US*) = **labouring**
labor-intensive ['leɪbərɪn'tensɪv] (ADJ) (*US*) = **labour-intensive**
laborious [lə'bɔːrɪəs] (ADJ) [*task, work, process*] laborioso; [*written style*] farragoso, poco claro
laboriously [lə'bɔːrɪəslɪ] (ADV) [*work*] laboriosamente; (*pej*) [*write*] farragosamente
laborite ['leɪbəraɪt] (N) (*US*) = **labourite**
labor-saving ['leɪbə,seɪvɪŋ] (ADJ) (*US*) = **labour-saving**
labour, labor (*US*) ['leɪbəʳ] (N) **1** (= *work, toil*) trabajo *m* • **the division of ~** la división del trabajo • **hard ~** (*Jur*) trabajos *mpl* forzados • **five years' hard ~** cinco años de trabajos forzados • **Ministry of Labour** Ministerio *m* de Trabajo • **to withdraw one's ~** ponerse en huelga; ▹ **manual**
2 (= *effort*) (*usu pl*) trabajo *m*, esfuerzo *m* • **he is starting to see the fruits of his ~s** está empezando a ver los frutos de su trabajo *or* sus esfuerzos
3 (= *task*) trabajo *m*, tarea *f* • **a ~ of love** un trabajo realizado con amor, una tarea realizada con amor • **the ~s of Hercules** los trabajos de Hércules
4 (*Ind*) (= *workers*) obreros *mpl*; (= *workforce*) mano *f* de obra • **capital and ~** la empresa y los obreros • **women were used as a source of cheap ~** se utilizaba a las mujeres como mano de obra barata; ▹ **child, skilled**
5 • **Labour** (*Brit*) (*Pol*) el Partido Laborista, los laboristas • **to vote Labour** votar a los laboristas
6 (= *birth*) parto *m* • **to be in ~** estar de parto • **to go into ~** ponerse de parto
(VT) [+ *point*] insistir en • **I think that's ~ing the point a bit** creo que eso es insistir demasiado en ese punto • **I won't ~ the point** no insistiré en ello
(VI) **1** (= *work*) trabajar • **to ~ at sth** trabajar en algo • **the ~ing classes** las clases trabajadoras • **a ~ing job** un trabajo de peón • **to ~ to do sth** esforzarse *or* afanarse por hacer algo
2 (= *struggle*) [*engine*] sonar forzado • **to ~ up a hill** [*person, vehicle*] subir una cuesta con esfuerzo *or* dificultad • **you seem to be ~ing under a misapprehension** me parece que te estás equivocando • **to ~ under the misapprehension** *or* **illusion that** engañarse pensando que, creerse que
(CPD) ▸ **labour camp** campamento *m* de trabajos forzados ▸ **labour charges** gastos *mpl* de mano de obra ▸ **labour costs** costo *msing* de la mano de obra ▸ **Labour Day** Día *m* del Trabajo, Día *m* de los Trabajadores ▸ **labour dispute** conflicto *m* laboral ▸ **Labour Exchange** (*Brit*) (*formerly*) Bolsa *f* de Trabajo ▸ **labour force** (= *numbers, people*) mano *f* de obra ▸ **labour law** (*as study*) derecho *m* laboral ▸ **labour market** mercado *m* laboral, mercado *m* del trabajo ▸ **labour movement** movimiento *m* obrero ▸ **labour pains** (= *birth*) dolores *mpl* de parto ▸ **Labour Party** Partido *m* Laborista ▸ **labour relations** relaciones *fpl* laborales ▸ **labour supply** oferta *f* de mano de obra ▸ **labour unrest** agitación *f* social ▸ **labour ward** sala *f* de partos
laboured, labored (*US*) ['leɪbəd] (ADJ) [*breathing*] pesado; [*style*] forzado; [*text*] farragoso, recargado
labourer, laborer (*US*) ['leɪbərəʳ] (N) (*on roads etc*) peón *m*, obrero/a *m/f*; (= *farm labourer*) trabajador(a) *m/f* del campo, peón *m*; (= *day labourer*) jornalero/a *m/f*; (*Agr*) bracero/a *m/f* • **bricklayer's ~** peón *m* de albañil
labouring, laboring (*US*) ['leɪbərɪŋ] (ADJ) ▹ **labour**
labour-intensive, labor-intensive (*US*) ['leɪbərɪn'tensɪv] (ADJ) que emplea mucha mano de obra • **labour-intensive industry** industria *f* que emplea mucha mano de obra
labourite, laborite (*US*) ['leɪbəraɪt] (N) (*pej*) laborista *mf*
labour-saving, labor-saving (*US*) ['leɪbə,seɪvɪŋ] (ADJ) que ahorra trabajo • **labour-saving device** aparato *m* que ahorra trabajo
labrador ['læbrədɔː] (N) labrador *m*
laburnum [lə'bɜːnəm] (N) lluvia *f* de oro, codeso *m*
labyrinth ['læbərɪnθ] (N) laberinto *m*
labyrinthine [,læbə'rɪnθaɪn] (ADJ) laberíntico
lac [læk] (N) laca *f*
lace [leɪs] (N) **1** (= *open fabric*) encaje *m*; (*as trimming*) puntilla *f*; [*of gold, silver*] galón *m*
2 [*of shoe, corset*] cordón *m*, agujeta *f* (*Mex*)
(VT) **1** (*also* **lace up**) [+ *shoes*] atar (los

cordones de)
2 (= *fortify with spirits*) [+ *drink*] echar licor a • **a drink ~d with brandy** una bebida con un chorrito de coñac • **a drink ~d with cyanide** una bebida envenenada con *or* con dosis de cianuro
3 (*fig*) • **the story is ~d with irony** la historia tiene una vena irónica, la historia está teñida de ironía
(CPD) de encaje
▸ **lace into**‡ (VI + PREP) • **to ~ into sb** dar una paliza a algn
lace-maker ['leɪs,meɪkəʳ] (N) encajero/a *m/f*
lacemaking ['leɪs,meɪkɪŋ] (N) labor *f* de encaje
lacerate ['læsəreɪt] (VT) (*Med*) lacerar; [+ *feelings*] herir
lacerated ['læsəreɪtɪd] (ADJ) [*skin, body, flesh*] lacerado
laceration [,læsə'reɪʃən] (N) laceración *f*
lace-up ['leɪsʌp] (ADJ) (*Brit*) [*shoes etc*] de cordones, con cordones
lace-ups ['leɪsʌps] (NPL) (*Brit*) (*also* **lace-up shoes**) zapatos *mpl* con cordones
lacework ['leɪswɜːk] (N) (= *fabric*) encaje *m*; [*of gold and silver*] galón *m*
lachrymal ['lækrɪməl] (ADJ) lagrimal
lachrymose ['lækrɪməʊs] (ADJ) lacrimoso, lloroso
lacing ['leɪsɪŋ] (N) [*of shoe*] cordón *m*, agujeta *f* (*Mex*); [*of corset*] cordones *mpl* • **uniforms with gold ~** uniformes con adornos dorados • **tea with a ~ of rum** té con un chorrito de ron
lack [læk] (N) falta *f*; (*frm*) carencia *f* • **~ of funds** falta *f* de fondos • **there was no ~ of applicants for the job** no faltaban candidatos al puesto • **there is no ~ of money** no falta dinero • **despite his ~ of experience, he got the job** a pesar de su falta de experiencia, consiguió el trabajo • **there was a complete ~ of interest in my proposals** hubo una absoluta falta de interés por mis propuestas • **for ~ of**: • **the charges were dropped for ~ of evidence** retiraron la acusación por falta de pruebas • **malevolence, for ~ of a better word** malevolencia, a falta de una palabra mejor • **if I didn't get them to agree it wasn't for ~ of trying** si no conseguí que accedieran no fue por falta de intentarlo
(VT) • **he ~s confidence** le falta confianza en sí mismo, carece de confianza en sí mismo (*frm*) • **they ~ the necessary skills** les faltan los requisitos necesarios, carecen de los requisitos necesarios (*frm*) • **what he ~s in ability he makes up for in enthusiasm** lo que le falta en habilidad, lo suple con entusiasmo • **he does not ~ talent** talento no le falta, no carece de talento (*frm*)
(VI) 1 (= *be missing, deficient*) • **to be ~ing** faltar • **even if evidence is ~ing** incluso si faltan las pruebas, incluso si se carece de pruebas (*frm*) • **this information was ~ing from the report** esta información no figuraba *or* no constaba en el informe • **to be ~ing in sth**: • **he is ~ing in confidence** le falta confianza en sí mismo, carece de confianza en sí mismo (*frm*) • **he is completely ~ing in imagination** no tiene nada de imaginación, carece completamente de imaginación (*frm*) • **I find her singularly ~ing in charm** la encuentro especialmente falta *or* (*frm*) carente de encanto • **it is a quality that we find ~ing in so many politicians today** es una cualidad de la que nos parece que carecen tantos políticos hoy en día • **innovation has been sadly** *or* **sorely ~ing** ha habido una falta absoluta de innovación • **her education is sadly ~ing** su educación es muy deficiente
2 (= *want*) • **they ~ for nothing** no les falta nada, no carecen de nada (*frm*)
lackadaisical [,lækə'deɪzɪkəl] (ADJ) (= *careless*) descuidado, informal; (= *lazy*) perezoso, flojo (*LAm*); (= *dreamy*) distraído
lackey ['lækɪ] (N) (*gen*) lacayo *m* (*also fig*)
lacklustre, **lackluster** (*US*) ['læk,lʌstəʳ] (ADJ) 1 (= *dull*) [*surface*] sin brillo, deslustrado; [*eyes*] apagado
2 (*fig*) [*performance, style*] mediocre, deslucido • **he fought a ~ election campaign** realizó una campaña electoral mediocre *or* deslucida
laconic [lə'kɒnɪk] (ADJ) lacónico
laconically [lə'kɒnɪkəlɪ] (ADV) lacónicamente
lacquer ['lækəʳ] (N) laca *f*; (*also* **hair lacquer**) laca *f* (para el pelo); (*for nails*) esmalte *m* (de uñas), laca *f* (de uñas)
(VT) [+ *wood*] lacar, barnizar con laca • **to ~ one's hair** ponerse *or* echarse laca en el pelo • **to ~ one's nails** darse esmalte en las uñas
lacquered ['lækəd] (ADJ) [*surface*] lacado, laqueado, barnizado con laca; [*hair*] con laca; [*nails*] con esmalte
lacrosse [lə'krɒs] (N) lacrosse *m*
lactate ['lækteɪt] (VI) lactar
lactation [læk'teɪʃən] (N) lactancia *f*
lacteal ['læktɪəl] (ADJ) lácteo
lactic ['læktɪk] (ADJ) láctico
(CPD) ▸ **lactic acid** ácido *m* láctico
lacto-ovo-vegetarian [,læktəʊ,əʊvəʊ-,vedʒɪ'tɛərɪən] (N) lacto-ovo-vegetariano/a *m/f*
lactose ['læktəʊs] (N) lactosa *f*
lacto-vegetarian [,læktəʊ,vedʒɪ'tɛərɪən] (N) lacto-vegetariano/a *m/f*
lacuna [lə'kjuːnə] (N) (PL: **lacunas** *or* **lacunae** [lə'kjuːniː]) laguna *f*
lacustrine [lə'kʌstraɪn] (ADJ) lacustre
lacy ['leɪsɪ] (ADJ) (COMPAR: **lacier**, SUPERL: **laciest**) (= *of lace*) de encaje; (= *like lace*) como de encaje • **a ~ dress** un vestido lleno de encajes
lad [læd] (N) (= *young man, boy*) muchacho *m*, chico *m*, chaval *m* (*Sp**), pibe *m* (*S. Cone**), cabro *m* (*Chile**), chavo *m* (*Mex**); (*in stable etc*) mozo *m* • **come on, lads!** ¡vamos, muchachos! • **when I was a lad** cuando yo era un muchacho, cuando yo era joven • **he's only a lad** no es más que un muchacho, es aún muy joven • **you need some exercise, my lad** tú, chico *or* muchacho, necesitas hacer algo de ejercicio • **he's gone for a drink with the lads** (*Brit**) ha salido a tomar algo con los muchachos *or* (*Sp*) con sus amiguetes • **he just wants to be one of the lads** lo que quiere es que su círculo de amigos lo acepte • **he's a bit of a lad** (*Brit*) (*fig*) es un gamberrete, está hecho una buena pieza*
(CPD) ▸ **lad mag*** revista *f* masculina
ladder ['lædəʳ] (N) 1 escalera *f* de mano; ▹ **extension, rope**
2 (*fig*) escala *f*, jerarquía *f* • **the social ~** la escala social • **it's a first step up the ~** es el primer peldaño • **it's a first step up the ~ of success** es el primer paso hacia el éxito • **to be at the top of the ~** estar en la cumbre de su profesión *etc*
3 (*Brit*) (*in stockings*) carrera *f*
(VT) (*Brit*) [+ *stocking, tights*] hacer una carrera en
(VI) (*Brit*) [*stocking*] hacerse una carrera
ladderproof ['lædəpruːf] (ADJ) (*Brit*) [*stocking, tights*] indesmallable
laddie* ['lædɪ] (N) (*esp Scot*) = **lad**
laddish* ['lædɪʃ] (ADJ) (*Brit*) macho (*adj inv*)
lade [leɪd] (PT: **laded**, PP: **laden**) (VT) cargar (**with** de)
(VI) tomar cargamento
laden ['leɪdn] (ADJ) • **~ with** cargado de • **trucks ~ with arms** camiones *mpl* cargados (hasta los topes) de armas • **plates ~ with food** platos *mpl* hasta arriba de *or* repletos de comida • **she was ~ with shopping** iba cargando con un montón de compra • **the branches were ~ with fruit** las ramas estaban llenas *or* repletas de frutos • **a report heavily ~ with scientific jargon** un informe con una enorme cantidad de jerga científica
-laden [-,leɪdən] (SUFFIX) • **salt-laden air** aire cargado de sal • **a fat-laden meal** una comida con mucha grasa; ▹ **debt-laden**
la-di-da* ['lɑːdɪ'dɑː] (*pej*) (ADJ) [*person, voice*] afectado, cursi*, repipi (*Sp**)
(ADV) [*talk etc*] de manera afectada, con afectación
lading ['leɪdɪŋ] (N) cargamento *m*, flete *m* • **bill of ~** conocimiento *m* de embarque
ladle ['leɪdl] (N) (*Culin*) cazo *m*, cucharón *m*
(VT) (*also* **ladle out**) servir con cucharón
▸ **ladle out** (VT + ADV) (*fig*) [+ *money, advice*] repartir generosamente
ladleful ['leɪdlfʊl] (N) • **one ~** un cucharón lleno • **each pan holds ten ~s** en cada cacerola caben diez cucharones llenos
lady ['leɪdɪ] (N) 1 (= *woman*) señora *f*, dama *f* (*frm*) • **ladies' clothing** ropa *f* de señora • **ladies' hairdresser** peluquero/a *m/f* de señoras • **ladies first** las damas *or* las señoras primero • **ladies and gentlemen!** ¡señoras y señores!, ¡damas y caballeros! • **"ladies only"** "solo para Señoras" • **cleaning ~** mujer *f or* señora *f* de la limpieza • **First Lady** Primera Dama *f* • **the ~ of the house** la señora de la casa • **leading ~** (*Theat*) primera actriz *f*; (*Cine*) protagonista *f* • **I'm not used to being a ~ of leisure** no estoy acostumbrada a la vida ociosa • **he's a ladies' man** es un donjuán • **an old ~** una señora mayor • **a little old ~** una viejecita • **this is the young ~ who served me** esta es la señorita *or* la joven que me sirvió • **now listen here, young ~!** ¡escúchame, jovencita!
2 (= *educated woman, noblewoman*) dama *f* • **she's no ~** no es lo que se dice una dama • **she's a real ~** es toda una dama • **society ~** dama *f* de la alta sociedad
3 (*in titles*) • **Lady Jane Grey** Lady Jane Grey • IDIOMS: • **she liked to play Lady Bountiful** le gustaba hacerse la rumbosa • **she thinks she's Lady Muck!*** ¡se cree toda una duquesa!
4 (*US**) (*as form of address*) señora *f* • **what seems to be the trouble, ~?** ¿qué ocurre, señora?
5† (= *wife*) señora *f*, esposa *f* • **your good ~** su esposa, su señora • **my ~ wife** mi señora esposa
6 (*Rel*) • **Our Lady** Nuestra Señora
7 • **the ladies** (= *lavatory*) el servicio (de señoras), el baño (de señoras) (*LAm*) • **"Ladies"** "Señoras", "Damas"
(CPD) ▸ **ladies' room** servicio *m* de señoras, baño *m* de señoras (*LAm*) ▸ **Lady Chapel** (*Rel*) capilla *f* de la Virgen ▸ **Lady Day** (*Brit*) día *m* de la Anunciación (*25 de marzo*) ▸ **lady doctor** doctora *f*, médico *f* ▸ **lady friend** amiga *f* ▸ **lady mayoress** alcaldesa *f* ▸ **lady's fingers** (*Bot*) (*with sing or pl vb*) quingombó *m* ▸ **lady's maid** doncella *f*
ladybird ['leɪdɪbɜːd], **ladybug** (*US*) ['leɪdɪbʌg] (N) (= *beetle*) mariquita *f*, vaca *f* de San Antón*
ladyboy* ['leɪdɪbɔɪ] (N) (= *transvestite*) travesti *m*; (= *transsexual*) transexual *m*
ladyfinger ['leɪdɪ,fɪŋgəʳ] (N) (*US*) bizcocho *m* de soletilla, plantilla *f* (*Arg, Ven*)

L

lady-in-waiting ['leɪdɪɪn'weɪtɪŋ] (N) (PL: **ladies-in-waiting**) dama *f* de honor
ladykiller ['leɪdɪ,kɪləʳ] (N) ladrón *m* de corazones, donjuán* *m*, tenorio* *m*
ladylike ['leɪdɪlaɪk] (ADJ) elegante, fino
lady-love ['leɪdɪlʌv] (N) (*liter or hum*) amada *f*
ladyship ['leɪdɪʃɪp] (N) • **Her Ladyship/Your Ladyship** su señoría *f*
LAFTA ['læftə] (N ABBR) (= **Latin-American Free Trade Association**) ALALC *f*
lag¹ [læg] (N) (*also* **time lag**) (= *delay*) retraso *m*; (= *interval*) lapso *m* de tiempo, intervalo *m*
(VI) (*also* **lag behind**) (= *not progress*) quedarse atrás; (*in pace*) rezagarse, quedarse atrás • **we lag behind in space exploration** nos hemos quedado atrás en la exploración del espacio • **English students are lagging behind their European counterparts** los alumnos ingleses se están quedando atrás con respecto a sus homólogos europeos, los alumnos ingleses van a la zaga de sus homólogos europeos
lag² [læg] (VT) [+ *boiler, pipes*] revestir (**with** de)
lag³ [læg] (N) (*esp Brit*) • **old lag** (= *old prisoner*) (preso/a *m/f*) veterano/a *m/f*; (= *ex-prisoner*) ex-presidiario/a *m/f*
lager ['lɑːgəʳ] (N) cerveza *f* rubia
(CPD) ▸ **lager lout** (*Brit**) gamberro *m* borracho, gamberro *m* de la litrona (*Sp*)
laggard ['lægəd] (N) (= *having fallen behind*) rezagado/a *m/f*; (= *idler*) holgazán/ana *m/f*
lagging ['lægɪŋ] (N) (*Tech*) revestimiento *m* calorífugo
lagoon [lə'guːn] (N) laguna *f*
Lagos ['leɪgɒs] (N) Lagos *m*
lah [lɑː] (N) (*Mus*) la *m*
lah-di-dah [,lɑːdɪ'dɑː] = **la-di-da**
laicize ['leɪɪsaɪz] (VT) laicizar
laid [leɪd] (PT), (PP) *of* **lay¹**
laid-back* [,leɪd'bæk] (ADJ) [*person, attitude*] (= *easy-going*) relajado; (= *casual*) despreocupado; [*party*] tranquilo
lain [leɪn] (PP) *of* **lie²**
lair [lɛəʳ] (N) guarida *f*, cubil *m*
laird [lɛəd] (N) (*Scot*) terrateniente *m*
laissez faire ['leɪseɪ'fɛəʳ] (N) laissez-faire *m*, liberalismo *m* económico
(ADJ) [*attitude, approach, policy*] liberal, liberalista
laity ['leɪɪtɪ] (N) • **the** ~ los seglares, los legos
lake¹ [leɪk] (N) lago *m* • **the Lakes** (*Brit*) el País de los Lagos (*región de lagos en el noroeste de Inglaterra*) • **Lake Michigan** el lago Michigan • **the Great Lakes** los Grandes Lagos • **wine** ~ excedentes *mpl* de vino • IDIOM: • **oh! go and jump in a ~!*** ¡que te zurzan!*, ¡vete a freír espárragos!*
(CPD) ▸ **the Lake District** el País de los Lagos (*región de lagos en el noroeste de Inglaterra*) ▸ **lake dweller** (*Hist*) *habitante de una población lacustre* ▸ **lake dwelling** vivienda *f* lacustre
lake² [leɪk] (N) (= *colour*) laca *f*
lakeside ['leɪksaɪd] (N) ribera *f* de(l) lago, orilla *f* de(l) lago
(CPD) [*restaurant, village, home*] a la orilla del lago, junto al lago
La La Land* ['lɑːlɑːlænd] (N) (= *cloud-cuckoo land*) • **to be in** ~ estar en las nubes
Lallans ['lælənz] (N) *dialecto y lengua literaria de las Tierras Bajas (Lowlands) de Escocia*
lam¹* [læm] (VT) pegar, dar una paliza a
(VI) • **to lam into sb** dar una paliza a algn
lam²* [læm] (N) • **to be on the lam** (*US*) ser fugitivo de la justicia
lama ['lɑːmə] (N) lama *m*
lamb [læm] (N) (= *animal*) cordero *m*; (*older*) borrego *m*; (= *meat*) (carne *f* de) cordero *m* • **the Lamb of God** el Cordero de Dios • **my poor ~!** ¡pobrecito! • **he surrendered like a** ~ no ofreció la menor resistencia • **he took it like a** ~ ni siquiera rechistó • IDIOM: • **to go like a ~ to the slaughter** ir como borrego al matadero
(VI) parir
(CPD) ▸ **lamb chop** chuleta *f* de cordero ▸ **lamb's lettuce** valeriana *f* ▸ **lamb's wool** = **lambswool**
lambada [,læm'bɑːdə] (N) lambada *f*
lambast, lambaste [læm'beɪst] (VT) fustigar, despellejar
lambing ['læmɪŋ] (N) parición *f* de las ovejas, época *f* del parto de las ovejas • ~ **time** • **the ~ season** la parición de las ovejas, la época del parto de las ovejas
lamb-like ['læmlaɪk] (ADJ) manso como un cordero
lambskin ['læmskɪn] (N) (piel *f* de) cordero *m*
lambswool ['læmzwʊl] (N) lambswool *m*, lana *f* de cordero
lame [leɪm] (ADJ) (COMPAR: **lamer**, SUPERL: **lamest**) **1** (*physically*) cojo • **to be** ~ (*permanently*) ser cojo, cojear; (*temporarily*) cojear, estar cojo • **to go** ~ [*animal*] (*permanently*) quedar cojo; (*temporarily*) empezar a cojear • **to be ~ in one foot** (*permanently*) ser cojo de un pie, cojear de un pie; (*temporarily*) estar cojo de un pie, cojear de un pie • **to be left** ~ quedarse cojo
2 (= *weak*) [*excuse*] débil, pobre; [*attempt*] patético; [*joke*] malo; [*argument, performance*] flojo, pobre
(N) • **the** ~ los lisiados
(VT) lisiar, dejar lisiado • **to be ~d** quedar lisiado
(CPD) ▸ **lame duck** (= *person*) caso *m* perdido • **the project was a ~ duck** el proyecto estaba condenado al fracaso
lamé ['lɑːmeɪ] (N) lamé *m* • **gold** ~ lamé *m* de oro, lamé *m* dorado
lamely ['leɪmlɪ] (ADV) [*say*] de forma poco convincente; [*try*] sin convicción
lameness ['leɪmnɪs] (N) **1** [*of person, horse, leg*] cojera *f*, renquera *f*
2 (*fig*) pobreza *f*
lament [lə'ment] (N) (= *poem*) elegía *f*, endecha *f* (**for** por); (= *song*) canción *f* elegíaca, endecha *f*; (= *grief*) lamento *m*
(VT) [+ *absence, lack, loss*] llorar, lamentar • **she was ~ing her misfortune** se lamentaba de su infortunio • **to ~ sb** llorar la muerte de algn, llorar a algn • **it is much to be ~ed that ...** es de lamentar que ... (+ *subjun*)
(VI) • **to ~ over sth** [+ *passing, loss*] llorar algo, lamentarse de algo • **to ~ for sb** llorar a algn
lamentable ['læməntəbl] (ADJ) lamentable
lamentably ['læməntəblɪ] (ADV) lamentablemente • **there is, ~, nothing we can do** lamentablemente, no podemos hacer nada • **to fail ~ to do sth** fracasar estrepitosamente *or* de manera lamentable en el intento de hacer algo • **there are still ~ few women surgeons** es de lamentar *or* es lamentable que todavía existan muy pocas cirujanas
lamentation [,læmən'teɪʃən] (N) lamentación *f*
laminate (VT) ['læmɪneɪt] laminar
(N) ['læmɪnɪt] laminado *m*
laminated ['læmɪneɪtɪd] (ADJ) [*metal*] laminado; [*glass*] inastillable; [*wood*] contrachapado; [*document*] plastificado
laminator ['læmɪneɪtəʳ] (N) laminador *m*
lamp [læmp] (N) (= *table lamp, floor lamp*) lámpara *f*; (*hand-held*) linterna *f*; (*in street*) farol *m*, farola *f*; (*Aut, Rail etc*) faro *m*; (= *bulb*) bombilla *f*, bombillo *m* (*LAm*), foco *m* (*LAm*)
(CPD) ▸ **lamp bracket** brazo *m* de lámpara ▸ **lamp chimney, lamp glass** tubo *m* de lámpara ▸ **lamp holder** portalámparas *m inv* ▸ **lamp standard** poste *m* de farola
lampblack ['læmpblæk] (N) negro *m* de humo
lamplight ['læmplaɪt] (N) luz *f* de (la) lámpara; [*of street lamp*] luz *f* de(l) farol • **by** ~ • **in the** ~ a la luz de la lámpara/del farol
lamplighter ['læmp,laɪtəʳ] (N) (*Hist*) farolero *m*
lampoon [læm'puːn] (N) sátira *f*
(VT) satirizar
lamppost ['læmppəʊst] (N) farol *m*, farola *f*
lamprey ['læmprɪ] (N) lamprea *f*
lampshade ['læmpʃeɪd] (N) pantalla *f* (de lámpara)
LAN [læn] (N ABBR) (*Comput*) (= **local area network**) RAL *f*
Lancastrian [læŋ'kæstrɪən] (ADJ) de Lancashire
(N) nativo/a *m/f* de Lancashire, habitante *mf* de Lancashire
lance [lɑːns] (N) (= *weapon*) lanza *f*; (*Med*) lanceta *f*
(VT) (*Med*) abrir con lanceta
(CPD) ▸ **lance corporal** (*Brit*) soldado *mf* de primera
Lancelot ['lɑːnslət] (N) Lanzarote
lancer ['lɑːnsəʳ] (N) lancero *m* • **~s** (= *dance*) lanceros *mpl*
lancet ['lɑːnsɪt] (N) lanceta *f*
(CPD) ▸ **lancet arch** ojiva *f* aguda ▸ **lancet window** ventana *f* ojival
Lancs. [læŋks] (ABBR) (*Brit*) = **Lancashire**
land [lænd] (N) **1** (= *not sea*) tierra *f* • **~ ho** • **~ ahoy!** ¡tierra a la vista! • **to go/travel by** ~ ir/viajar por tierra • **dry** ~ tierra *f* firme • **on dry** ~ en tierra firme • **to make** ~ (*Naut*) tomar tierra • **there was action at sea, on ~, and in the air** se combatió en mar, tierra y aire • **to sight** ~ divisar tierra
2 (*Agr, Constr*) (= *ground*) tierra *f*, tierras *fpl* • **160 acres of** ~ 160 acres de tierra • **agricultural** ~ tierra(s) *f(pl)* agrícola(s), terreno *m* agrícola • **grazing** ~ tierra(s) *f(pl)* de pastoreo, tierra(s) *f(pl)* para pastos • **the lay** *or* **lie of the** ~ (*lit*) la configuración del terreno • **a piece/plot of** ~ un terreno, una parcela • **the** ~ (*Agr*) la tierra • **to live off the** ~ vivir de la tierra • **to work on the** ~ trabajar *or* cultivar la tierra • **the drift from the** ~ el éxodo rural • IDIOMS: • **to see how the ~ lies** • **get the lie** *or* **lay of the** ~ tantear el terreno; ▹ **arable**
3 (= *property*) tierras *fpl* • **get off my ~!** ¡fuera de mis tierras! • **to own** ~ poseer tierras
4 (*Geog*) (= *region*) • **desert/equatorial/temperate ~s** tierras *fpl* desérticas/ecuatoriales/templadas
5 (= *nation, country*) país *m* • **a ~ of opportunity/contrasts** un país de oportunidades/contrastes • **throughout the** ~ en todo el país • IDIOMS: • **to be in the ~ of the living** (*hum*) estar en el mundo de los vivos, estar vivito y coleando (*hum*) • **the ~ of milk and honey** el paraíso terrenal • **to be in the Land of Nod** (*hum*) estar dormido, estar roque (*Sp**); ▹ **fantasy, native, promise**
(VI) **1** (*after flight*) [*plane*] aterrizar; (*on water*) amerizar, amarizar; (*on moon*) alunizar • **to ~ on sth** [*bird, insect*] posarse en algo • **the Americans were the first to ~ on the moon** los americanos fueron los primeros en llegar a la luna
2 (*from boat*) [*passenger*] desembarcar
3 (*after fall, jump, throw*) caer • **I ~ed awkwardly** caí en una mala postura • **the hat ~ed in my lap** el sombrero me cayó en el regazo • **to ~ on one's back** caer de espaldas • **to ~ on one's feet** (*lit*) caer de pie; (*fig*) salir adelante

4* (*also* **land up**) (*in prison, hospital*) ir a parar* (**in** a), acabar (**in** en) • **he ~ed in hospital** fue a parar al hospital*, acabó en el hospital
(VT) **1** (= *disembark, unload*) [+ *passengers*] desembarcar; [+ *cargo*] descargar • **vessels will have to ~ their catch at designated ports** los buques tendrán que descargar la pesca en los puertos designados
2 (= *bring down*) [+ *plane*] hacer aterrizar
3 (= *catch*) [+ *fish*] pescar, conseguir pescar; (*fig*) [+ *job, contract*] conseguir; [+ *prize*] obtener
4* a (= *put, dump*) • **to ~ a blow on sb's chin** • **~ sb a blow on the chin** asestar a algn un golpe en la barbilla • **they ~ed the children on me** me endilgaron *or* endosaron a los niños*
b • **to ~ sb in sth**: • **his comments ~ed him in court** sus comentarios hicieron que acabara en los tribunales, sus comentarios hicieron que fuera a parar a los tribunales* • **his extravagant lifestyle soon ~ed him in debt** su estilo de vida extravagante pronto hizo que endeudase • **to ~ sb in it*** fastidiar *or* jorobar a algn pero bien* • **it ~ed me in a mess** me metió en un lío* • **to ~ sb in trouble** causar problemas a algn • **to ~ o.s. in trouble** meterse en problemas
c (= *encumber*) • **to ~ sb with sth/sb** endilgar algo/a algn a algn*, endosar algo/a algn a algn* • **I got ~ed with the job** me endilgaron *or* endosaron el trabajo* • **I got ~ed with him for two hours** me lo endilgaron *or* endosaron dos horas* • **getting overdrawn could ~ you with big bank charges** girar al descubierto te puede ocasionar enormes intereses bancarios • **how did you ~ yourself with all these debts?** ¿cómo acabaste tan endeudado? • **I've ~ed myself with a bit of a problem** me he metido en un apuro
(CPD) ▸ **land agent** administrador(a) *m/f* de fincas ▸ **land defences** defensas *fpl* de tierra ▸ **land forces** fuerzas *fpl* de tierra ▸ **land management** administración *f* de fincas ▸ **land reclamation** reclamación *f* de tierras ▸ **land reform** reforma *f* agraria ▸ **land register, land registry** (*Brit*) catastro *m*, registro *m* catastral, registro *m* de la propiedad inmobiliaria ▸ **Land Rover®** (*Aut*) (vehículo *m*) todo terreno *m* ▸ **land tax** contribución *f* territorial ▸ **land use** uso *m* de la tierra

▸ **land up*** (VI + ADV) (= *end up*) ir a parar*, acabar • **he ~ed up in prison** fue a parar a la cárcel*, acabó en la cárcel • **so eventually we ~ed up in Madrid** así es que al final fuimos a parar a Madrid*, así es que al final acabamos en Madrid
(VT + ADV) • **this sort of behaviour could ~ you up in prison** este tipo de comportamiento puede llevarte a la cárcel

> **LAND OF HOPE AND GLORY**
> **Land of Hope and Glory** es el título de una canción patriótica británica. Para muchos ciudadanos, sobre todo en Inglaterra, es un símbolo más del país, casi como el himno o la bandera nacional. Se suele entonar al final del congreso anual del Partido Conservador y en la última noche de los **Proms**, junto con otras conocidas canciones patrióticas.
> ▹ **PROM**

landau [ˈlændɔː] (N) landó *m*
landed [ˈlændɪd] (ADJ) [*person*] hacendado, que posee tierras
(CPD) ▸ **landed property** bienes *mpl* raíces *or* inmuebles ▸ **the landed gentry** los terratenientes, la aristocracia rural
landfall [ˈlændfɔːl] (N) (*Naut*) recalada *f*, aterrada *f*
landfill [ˈlændfɪl] (N) entierro *m* de basuras
(CPD) ▸ **landfill site** vertedero *m* de basuras
landholder [ˈlændˌhəʊldəʳ] (N) terrateniente *mf*
landing [ˈlændɪŋ] (N) **1** (*Aer*) [*of aircraft, spacecraft*] (*on land*) aterrizaje *m*; (*on sea*) amerizaje *m*, amarizaje *m*; (*on moon*) alunizaje *m*; ▹ **crash, emergency, forced**
2 (*Mil*) [*of troops*] desembarco *m* • **the Normandy ~s** (*Hist*) los desembarcos de Normandía
3 (*Archit*) (*in house*) descansillo *m*, rellano *m*
(CPD) ▸ **landing card** tarjeta *f* de desembarque ▸ **landing craft** lancha *f* de desembarco ▸ **landing field** campo *m* de aterrizaje ▸ **landing gear** (*Aer*) tren *m* de aterrizaje ▸ **landing ground** campo *m* de aterrizaje ▸ **landing lights** luces *fpl* de aterrizaje ▸ **landing net** (*Fishing*) salabardo *m*, manga *f*, cuchara *f* ▸ **landing party** (*Naut*) destacamento *m* de desembarco ▸ **landing run** recorrido *m* de aterrizaje ▸ **landing stage** (*Naut*) desembarcadero *m* ▸ **landing strip** (*Aer*) pista *f* de aterrizaje ▸ **landing wheels** (*Aer*) ruedas *fpl* de aterrizaje
landlady [ˈlændˌleɪdɪ] (N) [*of flat*] casera *f*, dueña *f*; (*Brit*) [*of boarding house*] patrona *f*; (*Brit*) [*of pub*] (= *owner*) dueña *f*, patrona *f*; (= *manager*) encargada *f*, jefa *f*
landless [ˈlændlɪs] (ADJ) [*peasant*] sin tierras
(NPL) • **the ~** los campesinos sin tierra
landlessness [ˈlændlɪsnɪs] (N) situación *f* de los desposeídos (de tierra)
landline [ˈlændlaɪn] (N) teléfono *m* fijo • **can I call you on your ~?** ¿te puedo llamar al fijo?
landlocked [ˈlændlɒkt] (ADJ) sin acceso al mar
landlord [ˈlændlɔːd] (N) [*of property, land*] propietario *m*, dueño *m*; [*of flat*] casero *m*, dueño *m*; (*Brit*) [*of boarding house*] patrón *m*; [*of inn*] posadero *m*, mesonero *m*; (*Brit*) [*of pub*] (= *owner*) dueño *m*, patrón *m*; (= *manager*) encargado *m*, jefe *m*
landlubber [ˈlændˌlʌbəʳ] (N) marinero *m* de agua dulce
landmark [ˈlændmɑːk] (N) **1** (*Naut*) marca *f*, señal *f* fija; (= *boundary mark*) mojón *m*
2 (= *well-known thing*) punto *m* de referencia
3 (= *important event*) hito *m* • **to be a ~ in history** marcar un hito en la historia, ser un hito histórico • **it was a ~ case** (*Jur*) el caso sentó precedente
landmass [ˈlændˌmæs] (N) masa *f* continental
landmine [ˈlændmaɪn] (N) mina *f* terrestre
landowner [ˈlændˌəʊnəʳ] (N) terrateniente *mf*, hacendado/a *m/f*
landowning [ˈlændəʊnɪŋ] (ADJ) terrateniente
landscape [ˈlænskeɪp] (N) **1** (= *scenery*) paisaje *m*
2 (*Art*) paisaje *m*
3 (*fig*) panorama *m* • **the political ~** el panorama político • **the entire ~ of broadcasting has changed** en el mundo de la radio- y tele-difusión el panorama ha cambiado por completo
(VT) [+ *terrain, grounds*] ajardinar; [+ *park, garden*] diseñar
(CPD) ▸ **landscape architect** arquitecto/a *m/f* paisajista ▸ **landscape architecture** arquitectura *f* paisajista ▸ **landscape format** (*Typ, Comput, Phot*) formato *m* apaisado • **in ~ format** en formato apaisado ▸ **landscape gardener** jardinero/a *m/f* paisajista ▸ **landscape gardening** jardinería *f* paisajista ▸ **landscape mode** = **landscape format** ▸ **landscape painter** paisajista *mf* ▸ **landscape painting** (= *picture*) paisaje *m*
landscaped [ˈlænskeɪpt] (ADJ) [*grounds, park, area*] ajardinado
(CPD) ▸ **landscaped gardens** zona *fsing* ajardinada
landscaping [ˈlænskeɪpɪŋ] (N) (= *subject*) arquitectura *f* paisajista; (= *land area*) arquitectura *f* del paisaje
landslide [ˈlændslaɪd] (N) corrimiento *m or* desprendimiento *m* de tierras, deslave *m* (*LAm*); (*Pol*) victoria *f* arrolladora *or* aplastante
(CPD) ▸ **landslide majority** mayoría *f* abrumadora • **to win a ~ majority** ganar por mayoría abrumadora ▸ **landslide victory** victoria *f* arrolladora *or* aplastante
landslip [ˈlændslɪp] (*esp Brit*) ▹ **landslide**
landward [ˈlændwəd] (ADJ) de hacia tierra, de la parte de la tierra
(ADV) hacia tierra • **to ~(s)** en la dirección de la tierra
landwards [ˈlændwədz] (ADV) (*Brit*) = **landward**
lane [leɪn] (N) **1** (*in country*) camino *m* • **a quiet country ~** un tranquilo camino *or* sendero rural; ▹ **memory**
2 (*in town*) callejuela *f*, callejón *m*
3 (*Aut*) carril *m*, vía *f* (*LAm*) • **bus ~** carril de autobuses • **to change ~s** cambiar de carril • **cycle ~** carril *m* bici, carril *m* de bicicletas • **the fast ~** (*Brit*) el carril de la derecha; (*most countries*) el carril de la izquierda • **the frenzied pace of life in the fast ~** el ritmo de vida frenético de los que viven a tope • **"get in ~"** "incorpórese al carril" • **the inside ~** (*Brit*) el carril de la izquierda; (*most countries*) el carril de la derecha • **"keep in ~"** "manténgase en su carril" • **the outside ~** (*Brit*) el carril de la derecha; (*most countries*) el carril de la izquierda • **traffic was reduced to a single ~** se pasó a circular por un solo carril • **a three-lane motorway** una autopista de tres carriles • **I'm in the wrong ~** no estoy en el carril donde debería estar
4 (*Naut*) ruta *f* • **sea ~** ruta *f* marítima • **shipping ~** ruta *f* de navegación
5 (*Aer*) (*also* **air lane**) corredor *m* aéreo, ruta *f* aérea
6 (*Sport*) calle *f* • **inside/outside ~** calle *f* de dentro/de fuera
(CPD) ▸ **lane closure** corte *m* de carril • **there will be ~ closures on the M1** habrá carriles cortados en la M1 ▸ **lane markings** líneas *fpl* divisorias
langlauf [ˈlɑːŋˌlaʊf] (N) esquí *m* nórdico
language [ˈlæŋgwɪdʒ] (N) **1** (= *faculty, style of speech*) lenguaje *m* • **the tone of his ~ was diplomatic and polite** se expresó de forma diplomática y educada
2 (= *national tongue*) lengua *f*, idioma *m* • **the Spanish ~** la lengua española, el idioma español • **he studies ~s** estudia idiomas *or* lenguas • **she can speak six ~s** habla seis idiomas • **first ~** lengua *f* materna • **modern ~s** lenguas *fpl* modernas • IDIOM: • **we don't talk the same ~** no hablamos el mismo idioma
3 (= *means of expression*) lenguaje *m* • **in plain ~** en lenguaje sencillo • **legal/technical ~** lenguaje *m* jurídico/técnico • **the ~ of violence** el lenguaje de la violencia
4 (*Comput*) lenguaje *m* • **computer ~** lenguaje *m* de ordenador *or* (*LAm*) computador(a)
5 (= *swear words*) • **watch your ~** no digas palabrotas • **that's no ~ to use to your mother!** ¡así no se habla a tu madre! • **bad ~** palabrotas *fpl*, lenguaje *m* grosero; ▹ **strong**
(CPD) ▸ **language acquisition** adquisición *f* del lenguaje ▸ **language barrier** barrera *f* del

idioma ▸ **language degree** título *m* en idiomas ▸ **language development** desarrollo *m* lingüístico ▸ **language laboratory** laboratorio *m* de idiomas ▸ **language school** academia *f* de idiomas ▸ **language skills** *(with foreign languages)* facilidad *f* para los idiomas ▸ **language student** estudiante *mf* de idiomas ▸ **language studies** estudios *mpl* de idiomas ▸ **language teacher** profesor(a) *m/f* de idiomas

languid [ˈlæŋgwɪd] (ADJ) lánguido

languidly [ˈlæŋgwɪdlɪ] (ADV) lánguidamente

languidness [ˈlæŋgwɪdnɪs] (N) languidez *f*

languish [ˈlæŋgwɪʃ] (VI) **1** *(= pine)* languidecer, consumirse
2 *(in prison)* pudrirse • **the results of her research ~ed for years before action was taken** los resultados de su investigación cayeron en el olvido durante años antes de que se tomaran medidas • **they are ~ing at the bottom of the second division** están pasando sus horas más bajas en los últimos puestos de la segunda división

languishing [ˈlæŋgwɪʃɪŋ] (ADJ) lánguido; *[look]* amoroso, sentimental

languor [ˈlæŋgəʳ] (N) languidez *f*

languorous [ˈlæŋgərəs] (ADJ) lánguido

languorously [ˈlæŋgərəslɪ] (ADV) lánguidamente

lank [læŋk] (ADJ) *[hair]* lacio; *[grass]* largo

lanky [ˈlæŋkɪ] (ADJ) (COMPAR: **lankier**, SUPERL: **lankiest**) *[person]* larguirucho*

lanolin, lanoline [ˈlænəʊlɪn] (N) lanolina *f*

lantern [ˈlæntən] (N) farol *m*, linterna *f*; *(Archit)* linterna *f*; *(Naut)* faro *m*, farol *m*; *[of lighthouse]* fanal *m*
(CPD) ▸ **lantern lecture** conferencia *f* con diapositivas ▸ **lantern slide** diapositiva *f*

lantern-jawed [ˈlæntənˈdʒɔːd] (ADJ) chupado de cara

lanyard [ˈlænjəd] (N) acollador *m*

Laos [laʊs] (N) Laos *m*

Laotian [ˈlaʊʃɪən] (ADJ) laosiano
(N) laosiano/a *m/f*

lap¹ [læp] (N) regazo *m* • **to sit on sb's lap** sentarse en el regazo *or* las rodillas de algn • **with her hands in her lap** con las manos en el regazo • **he expects the money to fall into his lap** espera que el dinero le caiga como llovido del cielo • **they dump everything in my lap and expect me to deal with it** lo echan todo a mis espaldas y pretenden que me encargue de ello • IDIOMS: • **the outcome is in the lap of the gods now** del resultado Dios dirá, la suerte está echada y ya veremos qué pasa • **to live in the lap of luxury** vivir *or* nadar en la abundancia
(CPD) ▸ **lap dancer** *bailarina erótica que baila cerca del regazo de los clientes* ▸ **lap dancing** *baile erótico que se realiza cerca del regazo de los clientes*

lap² [læp] (N) **1** *(Sport)* vuelta *f* • **lap of honour** *(esp Brit)* vuelta *f* de honor • **a ten-lap race** una carrera de diez vueltas
2 *(= stage)* etapa *f*, fase *f* • **we're on the last lap now** *(fig)* ya estamos en la recta final
(VT) • **to lap sb** doblar a algn
(VI) completar *or* dar una vuelta • **to lap at 190k.p.h.** completar *or* dar una vuelta a 190km/h
(CPD) ▸ **lap record** récord *m* del circuito

lap³ [læp] (N) *(= lick)* lengüetada *f*, lametazo *m*; *[of waves]* chapaleteo *m*
(VT) **1** *(= drink)* *[+ water, milk etc]* beber a lengüetazos
2 *(= touch)* *[waves, water, tide]* *[+ shore, cliff]* lamer, besar
(VI) **1** *[waves, water]* chapalear • **to lap at** *or* **against sth** lamer *or* besar algo
2 *[animal]* • **to lap at sth** beber algo a lengüetazos
▸ **lap up** (VT + ADV) *(lit)* beber a lengüetazos; *(fig)* *[+ compliments, attention]* disfrutar con

laparoscopy [ˌlæpəˈrɒskəpɪ] (N) laparoscopia *f*

laparotomy [ˌlæpəˈrɒtəmɪ] (N) laparotomía *f*

La Paz [laeˈpæz] (N) La Paz

LAPD *(US)* (N ABBR) = **Los Angeles Police Department**

lapdog [ˈlæpdɒg] (N) perro *m* faldero

lapel [ləˈpel] (N) solapa *f*
(CPD) ▸ **lapel badge** pin *m* de solapa, insignia *f* de solapa ▸ **lapel pin** insignia *f* de solapa

lapidary [ˈlæpɪdərɪ] (ADJ) lapidario
(N) lapidario/a *m/f*

lapis lazuli [ˈlæpɪsˈlæzjʊlaɪ] (N) lapislázuli *m*

Lapland [ˈlæplænd] (N) Laponia *f*

Laplander [ˈlæplændəʳ] (N) lapón/ona *m/f*

Lapp [læp] (ADJ) lapón
(N) **1** lapón/ona *m/f*
2 *(Ling)* lapón *m*

lapping [ˈlæpɪŋ] (N) *[of waves, water]* chapaleteo *m*

Lappish [ˈlæpɪʃ] (N) *(Ling)* lapón *m*

lapse [læps] (N) **1** *(= error)* fallo *m*, lapsus *m inv*; *(= lack)* falta *f* • **she has the occasional ~ of memory** de vez en cuando tiene fallos *or* lapsus de memoria • **it was a ~ of judgement on his part** fue un error de cálculo por su parte • **the accident was caused by a momentary ~ of** *or* **in concentration** el accidente lo provocó un despiste momentáneo, el accidente lo provocó una falta momentánea de concentración
2 *[of time]* lapso *m*, intervalo *m*, período *m* • **after a ~ of four months** después de un lapso *or* intervalo *or* período de cuatro meses, al cabo de cuatro meses • **there was a momentary ~ in the conversation** hubo un breve silencio en medio de la conversación
(VI) **1** *(= slip)* • **to ~ into one's old ways** volver a las andadas • **he ~d into silence** se calló, se quedó callado • **he ~d into unconsciousness** perdió el conocimiento • **he ~d into the vernacular** recurrió a la lengua vernácula
2 *(= expire)* *[season ticket]* caducar, vencer
3 *(= cease to exist)* • **our friendship ~d when she moved to London** dejamos de vernos cuando ella se fue a Londres
4 *(= decline)* *[standards]* entrar en declive
5 *(= pass)* *[time]* pasar, transcurrir

lapsed [læpst] (ADJ) *(Rel)* que ya no practica

laptop [ˈlæptɒp] (N) *(also* **laptop computer***)* ordenador *m or (LAm)* computador(a) *m/f* portátil

lapwing [ˈlæpwɪŋ] (N) avefría *f*

larboard [ˈlɑːbəd] (ADJ) de babor
(N) babor *m*

larcenous [ˈlɑːsənəs] (ADJ) de robo • **~ activities** actividades de robo

larceny [ˈlɑːsənɪ] (N) *(Jur)* hurto *m*, robo *m* • **grand ~** *(US)* hurto *m* mayor • **petty ~** hurto *m* menor

larch [lɑːtʃ] (N) *(also* **larch tree***)* alerce *m*

lard [lɑːd] (N) manteca *f* de cerdo
(VT) lardear, mechar; *(fig)* • **to ~ sth with** salpicar algo de, adornar algo con

larder [ˈlɑːdəʳ] (N) despensa *f*

lardy [ˈlɑːdɪ] (ADJ) mantecoso

large [lɑːdʒ] (ADJ) (COMPAR: **larger**, SUPERL: **largest**) **1** *(in size)* *[house, object, organization]* grande; *[person]* corpulento; *[area]* grande, extenso • **a ~ room** una gran habitación, una habitación grande • **in ~ doses the toxin is fatal** en grandes dosis, la toxina es mortal • **he has very ~ feet** tiene unos pies muy grandes • **do you have (it in) a ~r size?** ¿lo tiene en una talla más grande? • **by and ~** en general • **to grow ~r** crecer • **as ~ as life** en carne y hueso, en persona • **he was a ~r-than-life character** era una persona que se salía de lo corriente • **the central character is a ~r-than-life, cantankerous Italian** el personaje principal es un italiano exuberante y cascarrabias • **to make ~r** hacer más grande; *[+ premises etc]* ampliar, ensanchar • **in ~ part** en gran parte; ▹ **extent, measure**
2 *(in number)* *[family, group, army]* numeroso, grande; *[sum, amount]* grande, importante • **a ~ group of people** un grupo numeroso *or* grande de personas • **a ~ crowd had gathered** se había formado un gran gentío • **a ~ number of them** un gran número de ellos • **~ numbers of people came** vinieron muchísimas personas, vinieron gran número de personas • **a ~ proportion of** una gran proporción de • **a ~ quantity of** una gran cantidad de
3 *(Comm)* de tamaño grande • **"large"** *(on clothing label)* "grande"; *(on food packet, washing powder etc)* "tamaño familiar" • **a dozen ~ envelopes** una docena de sobres de tamaño grande; ▹ GREAT, BIG, LARGE
(N) • **at ~ 1** *(= in general)* • **the country/society at ~** el país/la sociedad en general
2 *(= on the loose)* • **to be at ~** *[dangerous person, animal]* andar suelto
(ADV) ▹ **loom²**
(CPD) ▸ **the large intestine** *(Anat)* el intestino grueso ▸ **large print** • **in ~ print** en letra grande

largely [ˈlɑːdʒlɪ] (ADV) **1** *(= mainly)* en gran parte, en gran medida • **the rest of the world has ~ ignored China's environmental problems** el resto del mundo, en gran parte *or* en gran medida, ha hecho caso omiso de los problemas medioambientales de China • **it is a ~ working-class area** es en su mayor parte una zona de clase obrera • **he was elected ~ because ...** se le eligió en gran parte porque ... • **this is ~ due to ...** esto se debe en gran parte *or* medida a ... • **to be ~ reponsible for sth** ser en gran parte *or* medida responsable de algo • **~ speaking** hablando en líneas generales
2 *(= prominently)* • **to figure ~ in sth** *[person]* tener un papel destacado en algo; *[theme, subject]* ocupar un papel destacado en algo

largeness [ˈlɑːdʒnɪs] (N) *[of person, thing]* gran tamaño *m*; *[of group, family]* lo numeroso • **the ~ of the sum** lo cuantioso *or* grande de la suma

large-print [ˈlɑːdʒprɪnt] (ADJ) en letra grande

large-scale [ˈlɑːdʒˈskeɪl] (ADJ) a *or* en gran escala

large-size, large-sized [ˈlɑːdʒˈsaɪz(d)] (ADJ) de gran tamaño, de tamaño extra

largesse [lɑːˈʒes] (N) generosidad *f*, liberalidad *f*; *(= gift)* dádiva *f* espléndida

largish [ˈlɑːdʒɪʃ] (ADJ) bastante grande, más bien grande

largo [ˈlɑːgəʊ] (N) *(Mus)* largo *m*

lariat [ˈlærɪət] (N) lazo *m*

lark¹ [lɑːk] (N) *(= bird)* alondra *f* • **to get up** *or* **rise with the ~** levantarse con las gallinas, madrugar mucho; ▹ **happy**

lark² [lɑːk] *(esp Brit)* (N) **1** *(= joke)* broma *f* • **what a ~!** ¡qué risa!, ¡qué divertido! • **to do sth for a ~** hacer algo por diversión *or* para divertirse • **to have a ~ with sb** gastar una broma *or* tomar el pelo a algn • **sod this for a ~!**‡ ¡vaya lío!*
2 *(= business, affair)* • **that ice-cream ~** ese asunto de los helados, ese tinglado de los helados* • **this dinner-jacket ~** esto de

ponerse esmoquin
▸ **lark about***, **lark around*** VI + ADV (*esp Brit*) (= *act foolishly*) hacer el tonto, hacer tonterías • **stop ~ing about!** ¡basta de bromas! • **to ~ about with sth** divertirse con algo, jugar con algo
larkspur ['lɑːkspɜːʳ] N espuela *f* de caballero
larky* ['lɑːkɪ] ADJ guasón*, bromista
Larry ['lærɪ] N *familiar form of* **Laurence, Lawrence**
larva ['lɑːvə] N (PL: **larvae** ['lɑːviː]) larva *f*
larval ['lɑːvəl] ADJ larvario
laryngeal [ˌlærɪn'dʒiːəl] ADJ laríngeo • **~ reflex** reflejo laríngeo
laryngitis [ˌlærɪn'dʒaɪtɪs] N laringitis *f inv*
larynx ['lærɪŋks] N (PL: **larynxes** *or* **larynges** [lə'rɪndʒiːz]) laringe *f*
lasagna, **lasagne** [lə'zænjə] N lasaña *f*
lascivious [lə'sɪvɪəs] ADJ lascivo
lasciviously [lə'sɪvɪəslɪ] ADV lascivamente
lasciviousness [lə'sɪvɪəsnɪs] N lascivia *f*, lujuria *f*
laser ['leɪzəʳ] N láser *m*
CPD ▸ **laser beam** rayo *m* láser ▸ **laser disc, laser disk** (*US*) disco *m* láser ▸ **laser disc player, laser disk player** (*US*) reproductor *m* de discos láser ▸ **laser gun** pistola *f* de rayos láser ▸ **laser light** luz *f* láser ▸ **laser printer** impresora *f* láser ▸ **laser show** espectáculo *m* con láser ▸ **laser surgery** cirujía *f* con láser
lash [læʃ] N **1** (= *eyelash*) pestaña *f*
2 (= *thong*) tralla *f*; (= *whip*) látigo *m*; (= *stroke*) latigazo *m*, azote *m*; [*of tail*] coletazo *m*
VT **1** (= *beat*) azotar, dar latigazos a; [+ *animal*] fustigar; [*rain, waves*] (*also* **lash against**) azotar • **the wind ~ed the trees** el viento azotaba los árboles • **the wind ~ed the sea into a fury** el viento encrespó con fuerza el mar • **it ~ed its tail** dio coletazos
2 (= *tie*) atar; (*Naut*) trincar, amarrar (**to** a)
VI • **to ~ about** [*person*] agitarse violentamente, dar bandazos • **the rain ~ed against the windows** la lluvia azotaba las ventanas • **he ~ed at the donkey** fustigaba *or* azotaba al burro
▸ **lash down** VT + ADV sujetar con cuerdas
VI + ADV [*rain*] caer con fuerza
▸ **lash out** VI + ADV **1** • **to ~ out** (*with fists*) repartir golpes a diestro y siniestro; (*with feet*) soltar patadas, tirar coces • **to ~ out at** *or* **against sb** (*lit, fig*) arremeter contra algn
2* (= *spend*) • **now we can really ~ out** ahora podemos gastar todo lo que queramos • **he ~ed out and bought himself a Rolls** tiró la casa por la ventana y se compró un Rolls • **I decided to ~ out on a new sofa** decidí tirar la casa por la ventana con un sofá nuevo
VT + ADV* (= *spend*) • **he had to ~ out £50** tuvo que desembolsar 50 libras
lashing ['læʃɪŋ] N **1** (= *beating*) azotes *mpl* • **to give sb a ~** azotar a algn
2 (= *tying*) atadura *f*; (*Naut*) trinca *f*, amarradura *f*
3 • **~s of** (*esp Brit**) montones de*
lash-up* ['læʃʌp] N arreglo *m* provisional, improvisación *f*
lass [læs] N (*esp Scot*) muchacha *f*, chica *f*, chavala *f* (*Sp**), cabra *f* (*Chile**), piba *f* (*S. Cone**), chamaca *f* (*CAm, Mex**); (= *country lass*) moza *f*, zagala *f*
lassie* ['læsɪ] N (*esp Scot*) = **lass**
lassitude ['læsɪtjuːd] N lasitud *f*
lasso [læ'suː] N (PL: **lassos** *or* **lassoes**) lazo *m*
VT lazar, coger con el lazo
last[1] [lɑːst] ADJ **1** (= *most recent*) último • **I've seen her twice in the ~ week** la he visto dos veces en la última semana • **the ~ few weeks have been hectic** las últimas semanas han sido muy ajetreadas • **over the ~ few months** durante los últimos meses • **he hasn't been seen these ~ two years** no se lo ha visto en los últimos dos años
2 (= *previous*) (*referring to specific occasion*) [*Christmas, Easter*] pasado; [*time, meeting, birthday*] último • **~ Christmas we went to my mother's** las Navidades pasadas fuimos a casa de mi madre • **the ~ time we went, it rained** la última vez que fuimos, llovió • **on Monday ~** (*frm*) el pasado lunes • **~ Friday/month/year** el viernes/el mes/el año pasado • **this time ~ year** el año pasado por estas fechas • **~ week** la semana pasada • **this time ~ week** la semana pasada a estas horas; ▹ **night**
3 (= *final*) último • **the ~ Friday of the month** el último viernes del mes • **the ~ Sunday before Christmas** el último domingo antes de Navidad • **the ~ door on the right** la última puerta a la derecha • **the ~ three pages of the book** las tres últimas paginas del libro • **he spent the ~ few years of his life here** pasó los últimos años de su vida aquí • **~ but one** penúltimo • **down to the ~ detail** hasta el más mínimo detalle, hasta el último detalle • **the Last Judg(e)ment** el Juicio Final • **to fight to the ~ man** (*lit, fig*) luchar hasta el último aliento • **I was the ~ person to arrive/to see him alive** fui la última en llegar/la última persona que lo vió vivo • **I'm down to my ~ pound** solo me queda una libra • **the ~ rites** (*Rel*) la extremaunción • **second to ~** antepenúltimo • **~ thing at night** antes de acostarse • **I'll finish it if it's the ~ thing I do** ¡lo terminaré aunque sea la última cosa que haga en esta vida! • **that was the ~ time I saw him** esa fue la última vez que lo vi • **for the ~ time, shut up!** ¡cállate, y que sea la última vez que te lo digo! • IDIOM: • **to be on it's/one's ~ legs*** estar en las últimas; ▹ **every, gasp, laugh, post, supper, resort, straw, word**
4 (= *least likely*) • **you're the ~ person I'd trust with it** lo confiaría a cualquiera menos a ti, eres la última persona a la que se lo confiaría • **I would be the ~ person to stand in your way** yo soy la que menos me interpondría en tu camino, yo soy la última persona que se interpondría en tu camino • **that was the ~ thing I expected** eso era lo que menos me esperaba • **at 32, retirement is the ~ thing on his mind** con 32 años, jubilarse es lo último en que piensa
PRON **1** (*of series*) último • **he was the ~ of the Tudors** fue el último de los Tudores • **that was the ~ I saw of him** después de aquello no volví a verlo más • **the ~ we heard of him he was in Rio** según las últimas noticias estaba en Río • **if we don't go we shall never hear the ~ of it** si no vamos no dejarán de recordárnoslo • **you haven't heard the ~ of this!** ¡esto no se acaba aquí!, ¡esto no se va a quedar así! • **to be the ~ (one) to do sth** ser el último en hacer algo • **we're always the ~ to know** siempre somos los últimos en enterarnos • **the ~ but one** el/la penúltimo/a • **to leave sth till ~** dejar algo para lo último *or* el final • **to look one's ~ on sth** (*liter*) ver algo por última vez • **to the ~** hasta el final; ▹ **breathe**
2 (= *previous one*) • **each one is better than the ~** son cada vez mejores • **the night before ~** anteanoche • **the week before ~** la semana anterior a la pasada, la semana pasada no, la anterior • **the Saturday before ~** el sábado anterior al pasado, el sábado pasado no, el anterior • **it was the question before ~ that I found difficult** la pregunta que me resultó difícil fue la penúltima
3 (= *all that remains*) • **this is the ~ of the bread/wine** esto es lo que queda de pan/vino • **he was the ~ of his kind, a true professional** fue el último de los de su clase, un verdadero profesional
4 • **at ~** por fin • **at long ~ the search was over** por fin la búsqueda había concluido
ADV **1** (= *finally*) • **~ of all, take out the screws** por último, saca los tornillos • **~ but not least** por último, pero no por ello menos importante
2 (= *in last place, at the end*) • **he was** *or* **came ~ in the 100 metres** terminó en último lugar *or* en última posición en los 100 metros • **to arrive ~** llegar el *or* (*LAm*) al último • **~ in, first out** los últimos en llegar son a los que despiden los primeros
3 (= *most recently*) • **when I ~ saw them** la última vez que las vi • **he was ~ seen in Brighton** se lo vio por última vez en Brighton • **I ~ saw her in 1987** la vi por última vez en 1987
last[2] [lɑːst] VI **1** (= *continue*) durar • **it ~s (for) two hours** dura dos horas • **the trial is expected to ~ (for) three weeks** se espera que el juicio dure tres semanas • **the symptoms can ~ (for) up to a week** los síntomas pueden persistir hasta una semana • **nothing ~s forever** nada dura para siempre • **it's too good to ~** • **it can't ~** esto no puede durar
2 (= *survive*) durar • **the previous boss only ~ed a week** el jefe anterior solamente duró una semana • **he wouldn't have ~ed ten minutes in those conditions** no hubiera durado *or* aguantado ni diez minutos en esas condiciones • **he won't ~ the night (out)** no sobrevivirá hasta la mañana
3 (= *be enough*) durar • **how long will the gas ~?** ¿hasta cuándo durará *or* alcanzará el gas? • **the town has enough water to ~ a fortnight** la ciudad tiene agua suficiente para dos semanas • **"only available while stocks ~"** (*Comm*) "solo hasta que se agoten las existencias"
4 (= *remain usable*) durar • **this material will ~ (for) years** esta tela durará años • **more expensive batteries ~ longer** las pilas más caras duran más • **made to ~** hecho para que dure
VT durar • **this amount should ~ you (for) a week** esta cantidad debería durarte una semana • **it will ~ you a lifetime** te durará toda la vida • **I've had enough publicity to ~ me a lifetime!** ¡me han dado publicidad suficiente para toda una vida!
▸ **last out** VI + ADV **1** [*money, resources*] alcanzar • **my money doesn't ~ out the month** el dinero no me alcanza para todo el mes
2 [*person*] aguantar • **I can't ~ out without something to eat** ya no aguanto a no ser que coma algo • **he won't ~ out the winter** no sobrevivirá el invierno
last[3] [lɑːst] N (*in shoemaking*) horma *f* • IDIOM: • **(shoemaker) stick to your ~!** ¡zapatero a tus zapatos!
last-ditch ['lɑːst'dɪtʃ] ADJ [*defence, attempt*] último, desesperado
last-gasp ['lɑːst'gɑːsp] ADJ de última hora
lasting ['lɑːstɪŋ] ADJ duradero, perdurable; [*shame*] eterno; [*colour*] sólido
lastly ['lɑːstlɪ] ADV por último, finalmente
last-minute ['lɑːst'mɪnɪt] ADJ de última hora
lat. ABBR = **latitude**
latch [lætʃ] N (= *bar*) cerrojo *m*, pestillo *m*; (= *lock*) pestillo *m* • **to drop the ~** echar el

cerrojo *or* pestillo • **the door is on the ~** la puerta no tiene echado el pestillo
(VT) 1 [+ *door*] echar el pestillo a
2 (= *fix, fasten*) sujetar, asegurar
▸ **latch on*** (VI + ADV) (= *understand*) comprender, darse cuenta
▸ **latch onto** (VI + PREP) 1 (= *cling*) (*to person, group*) pegarse a • **she ~ed onto his arm** se enganchó a su brazo
2 [+ *idea*] agarrarse a • **the media were quick to ~ onto the story** la prensa no tardó en recoger la noticia

latchkey ['lætʃki:] (N) llave *f*
(CPD) ▸ **latchkey child** niño/a *m/f* cuya madre trabaja

late [leɪt] (COMPAR: **later**, SUPERL: **latest**)
(ADV) 1 (= *towards end of period, day, month etc*) • **he had arrived ~ the previous evening** había llegado tarde la noche anterior • **~ at night** muy de noche, ya entrada la noche • **~ in the morning** a última hora de la mañana • **~ in the afternoon** a media tarde • **~ in the year** a finales del año • **~ in 1992/May** a finales del año 1992/de mayo • **symptoms appear only ~ in the disease** los síntomas aparecen solo cuando la enfermedad ya está muy avanzada • **it wasn't until ~ in his career that he became famous** solo al final de su carrera se hizo famoso, solo en los últimos años de su carrera se hizo famoso • **they scored ~ in the second half** metieron un gol ya bien entrado el segundo tiempo • **~ into the night** hasta bien entrada la noche • **~ that night I got a phone call** ya entrada la noche recibí una llamada de teléfono • **too ~** demasiado tarde • IDIOM: • **~ in the day** (= *at the last moment*) a última hora; (= *too late*) • **it's a bit ~ in the day to be changing your mind** es un poco tarde para cambiar de opinión
2 (= *after the usual time*) [*get up, go to bed*] tarde • **the chemist is open ~ on Thursdays** la farmacia cierra tarde los jueves • **everything is flowering very ~ this year** todo está floreciendo tardísimo este año • **she came ~ to acting** empezó a actuar ya mayor • **Liz had started learning German quite ~ in life** Liz había empezado a aprender alemán ya mayor • **to sleep ~** levantarse tarde • **to stay up ~** irse a la cama tarde, trasnochar • **to work ~** trabajar hasta tarde
3 (= *after arranged/scheduled time*) [*arrive*] tarde, con retraso • **he arrived ten minutes ~** llegó con diez minutos de retraso, llegó diez minutos tarde • **they arrived ~ for dinner** llegaron tarde *or* con retraso a la cena • **we're running ~ this morning** llevamos retraso esta mañana • **we're running about 40 minutes ~** llevamos unos 40 minutos de retraso, llevamos un retraso de unos 40 minutos • PROVERB: • **better ~ than never** más vale tarde que nunca
4 (= *recently*) • **as ~ as** aún en • **as ~ as 1950** aún en 1950 • **of ~** (*frm*) últimamente, recientemente • **Jane Smith, ~ of Bristol** (*frm*) Jane Smith, domiciliada hasta hace poco en Bristol
(ADJ) 1 (= *towards end of period, day, month etc*) • **~ morning** última hora *f* de la mañana • **~ afternoon** media tarde *f* • **~ evening** última hora *f* de la tarde • **~ 1989** finales de 1989 • **it was very ~ and I was tired** era muy tarde y estaba cansado • **in ~ September/spring** a finales de septiembre/de la primavera • **in the ~ 1960s** a finales de los años sesenta • **in the ~ 18th century** a fines del siglo XVIII • **to be in one's ~ thirties/forties** rondar los cuarenta/cincuenta, tener cerca de cuarenta/cincuenta años • **it's getting ~** se está haciendo tarde • **~ goal** gol *m* de última hora • **I apologize for arriving at this ~ hour** siento llegar a estas horas • **even at this ~ stage** incluso a estas alturas
2 (= *after arranged or scheduled time*) • **I apologize for my ~ arrival** perdone/perdonen mi retraso • **we apologize for the ~ arrival/departure of this train** les rogamos disculpen el retraso en la llegada/salida de este tren • **it was postponed to allow for ~ arrivals** se aplazó por si alguien llegaba tarde *or* con retraso • **our train was ~ again** nuestro tren se retrasó otra vez, nuestro tren llegó con retraso otra vez • **as usual, Jim was ~** como siempre, Jim llegó tarde *or* con retraso, como siempre, Jim se retrasó • **sorry I'm ~!** ¡siento llegar tarde *or* con retraso! • **you're ~!** ¡llegas tarde! • **the train is 20 minutes ~** el tren llega con 20 minutos de retraso, el tren lleva un retraso de 20 minutos • **she's 20 minutes ~** lleva 20 minutos de retraso • **I was already ten minutes ~** ya llegaba diez minutos tarde, ya llevaba diez minutos de retraso • **both my babies were ~** mis dos hijos nacieron más tarde de la fecha prevista • **he was ~ (in) finishing his essay** terminó la redacción con retraso • **she was ~ (in) returning from work** regresó tarde del trabajo • **I was ~ (in) paying my phone bill** me retrasé en pagar la factura del teléfono • **I'm ~ for my train** voy a perder el tren • **I'm ~ for work** voy a llegar tarde al trabajo • **I was half an hour ~ for my appointment** llegué con media hora de retraso a la cita • **a fault on the plane made us two hours ~** una avería en el avión nos retrasó dos horas • **you're going to make me ~ for my appointment** vas a hacer que llegue tarde a la cita • **we got off to a ~ start** empezamos tarde *or* con retraso • **I was ~ with the payments** me había retrasado en los pagos
3 (= *after usual or normal time*) [*reservation, booking*] de última hora; [*crop, flowers*] tardío • **we had a ~ breakfast/lunch** desayunamos/comimos tarde • **Easter is ~ this year** la Semana Santa cae tarde este año • **"~ opening till ten pm on Fridays"** "los viernes cerramos a las diez" • **my period is ~** se me está retrasando la regla • **spring is ~ this year** la primavera llega tarde este año; ▹ **night**
4 • **too ~** demasiado tarde • **they tried to operate, but it was too ~** intentaron operar, pero era demasiado tarde • **it's too ~ to change your mind** es demasiado tarde para cambiar de opinión • **it's not too ~ (for you) to change your mind** aún estás a tiempo para cambiar de opinión • **it's never too ~ to …** nunca es demasiado tarde para …; ▹ **little**
5 (*Hist, Art*) • **~ Baroque** barroco *m* tardío • **the ~ Middle Ages** la baja edad media • **a ~ Georgian house** una casa de finales del periodo Georgiano • **Beethoven's ~ symphonies** las últimas sinfonías de Beethoven • **Rembrandt's ~ work** las últimas obras de Rembrandt
6 (= *dead*) difunto • **the ~ Harry Brown** el difunto Harry Brown
7 (*frm*) (= *former*) antiguo • **the ~ Prime Minister** el antiguo primer ministro
(CPD) ▸ **late edition** edición *f* de última hora; ▹ **developer** ▸ **late trading** (*St Ex*) operaciones *fpl* tras el cierre

latecomer ['leɪtkʌməʳ] (N) rezagado/a *m/f*, el/la que llega tarde • **~s will not be admitted** no se permitirá la entrada una vez comenzado el acto/espectáculo • **the firm is a ~ to the industry** la empresa es nueva en el sector, la empresa acaba de establecerse en el sector

lateen [lə'ti:n] (N) vela *f* latina

late-lamented ['leɪtlə'mentɪd] (ADJ) malogrado, fallecido

lately ['leɪtlɪ] (ADV) últimamente, recientemente • **have you heard from her ~?** ¿has sabido algo de ella últimamente? • **(up) until** *or* **till ~** hasta hace poco • **it's only ~ that …** hace poco que …

latency ['leɪtənsɪ] (N) estado *m* latente

lateness ['leɪtnɪs] (N) [*of person, vehicle*] retraso *m*, tardanza *f*, atraso *m* (*LAm*); [*of hour*] lo avanzado • **he was fined for persistent ~** le sancionaron por llegar constantemente tarde

late-night ['leɪt'naɪt] (ADJ) • **late-night film** (*Cine*) película *f* de sesión de noche; (*TV*) película *f* de medianoche • **late-night show** *or* **performance** sesión *f* de noche • **late-night opening** *or* **shopping is on Thursdays** se abre hasta tarde los jueves • **is there a late-night bus?** ¿hay autobús nocturno?

latent ['leɪtənt] (ADJ) [*heat*] latente; [*tendency*] implícito • **~ defect** defecto *m* latente

later ['leɪtəʳ] (ADV) 1 más tarde • **the gun was ~ found in his flat** más tarde se encontró la pistola en su piso • **two years/ten minutes ~** dos años/diez minutos después *or* más tarde • **I'll do it ~** lo haré luego *or* más tarde • **~, when all the guests had left** luego *or* más tarde, cuando todos los invitados se habían marchado • **~ I discovered that he had lied** más tarde descubrí que había mentido • **several whiskies ~, I was rather the worse for wear** después de varios whiskies, se me empezaban a notar los efectos • **~ than expected** más tarde de lo esperado • **all essays should be handed in no ~ than Monday** todos los trabajos deben entregarse el lunes a más tardar • **only ~** solo más tarde • **it was only ~ that I learned the truth** no descubrí la verdad hasta más tarde, solo más tarde descubrí la verdad • **~ that day** más tarde *or* posteriormente ese día • **~ that morning/night** más tarde *or* posteriormente esa mañana/esa noche • **the results will be available ~ today** los resultados se sabrán hoy mismo más tarde; ▹ **see¹**, **sooner**
2 • **~ on** más tarde, más adelante • **we'll be dealing with this in more detail ~ on** trataremos esto a fondo más tarde *or* más adelante • **~ on that day/night** aquel día/aquella noche más tarde • **~ on in the play/film** más adelante en la obra/película • **~ on in the morning/afternoon/evening** más entrada la mañana/tarde/noche • **~ on in life** más adelante
(ADJ) [*chapter, version, work*] posterior • **I took a ~ flight/train** tomé un avión/tren que salía más tarde • **we plan to meet at a ~ date** tenemos intención de reunirnos más adelante • **in ~ life** más adelante • **at a ~ stage** más adelante

lateral ['lætərəl] (ADJ) lateral
(CPD) ▸ **lateral thinking** pensamiento *m* lateral

laterally ['lætərəlɪ] (ADV) lateralmente

latest ['leɪtɪst] (SUPERL *of* **late**) (ADJ) 1 (= *last*) [*flight, train, bus*] último • **the ~ (possible) date** la fecha límite • **the ~ possible moment** el último momento • **the ~ (possible) time** lo más tarde
2 (= *most recent*) [*figures, boyfriend, book*] último, más reciente • **the ~ in a series of** el último *or* el más reciente en una serie de • **the ~ fashion** la última moda • **it's the ~ model** es el último modelo • **the ~ news** las últimas noticias
(N) • **the ~** 1 (= *news*) • **have you heard the ~?** ¿te has enterado de la última noticia? • **for the ~ on where to go and what to do …** para

la información más actualizada acerca de dónde ir y qué hacer ... • **have you heard his ~? he broke his leg jumping off a wall** ¿has oído la última que ha hecho? se rompió una pierna saltando de un muro
2 (= *most modern type*) • **it's the ~ in food processors** es lo último en robots de cocina
3 (= *last possible time*) lo más tarde • **the ~ he can see you is Thursday** lo más tarde que puede verte es el jueves • **at the (very) ~** como muy tarde • **it has to be here by Friday at the (very) ~** tiene que estar aquí el viernes como muy tarde
4* (= *boyfriend, girlfriend*) • **have you seen her ~?** ¿has visto a su último ligue?*
latex ['leɪteks] (N) (PL: **latexes** *or* **latices** ['lætɪsi:z]) látex *m*
(CPD) ▸ **latex rubber** látex *m*
lath [lɑ:θ] (N) (PL: **laths** [lɑ:ðz]) listón *m*
lathe [leɪð] (N) torno *m*
lather ['læðəʳ] (N) espuma *f*; [*of sweat*] sudor *m* • **the horse was in a ~** el caballo estaba empapado en sudor • IDIOM: • **to be in/get into a ~ (about sth)** estar/ponerse frenético (por algo)
(VT) [+ *one's face*] enjabonarse
(VI) hacer espuma
latifundia [,lætɪ'fʊndɪə] (NPL) latifundios *mpl*
Latin ['lætɪn] (ADJ) latino
(N) 1 (= *person*) latino/a *m/f* • **the ~s** los latinos
2 (*Ling*) latín *m*
(CPD) ▸ **Latin lover** galán *m* latino ▸ **Latin quarter** barrio *m* latino
Latin America ['lætɪnə'merɪkə] (N) América *f* Latina, Latinoamérica *f*, Hispanoamérica *f*
Latin American ['lætɪnə'merɪkən] (ADJ) latinoamericano
(N) latinoamericano/a *m/f*
latinism ['lætɪnɪzəm] (N) latinismo *m*
latinist ['lætɪnɪst] (N) latinista *mf*
latinity [lə'tɪnɪtɪ] (N) latinidad *f*
latinization [,lætɪnaɪ'zeɪʃən] (N) latinización *f*
latinize ['lætɪnaɪz] (VT) latinizar
(VI) latinizar
latish ['leɪtɪʃ] (ADV) algo tarde
(ADJ) algo tardío
latitude ['lætɪtju:d] (N) 1 (*Geog*) latitud *f*
2 (*fig*) (= *freedom*) libertad *f*
latitudinal [,lætɪ'tju:dɪnl] (ADJ) latitudinal
Latium ['leɪʃɪəm] (N) Lacio *m*
latrine [lə'tri:n] (N) letrina *f*
latte ['lɑ:teɪ] (N) (= *coffee*) café *m* con leche
latter ['lætəʳ] (ADJ) 1 (= *last*) último • **the ~ part of the story** la última parte del relato • **in the ~ part of the century** hacia fines *or* finales del siglo
2 (*of two*) segundo
(N) • **the ~** (*sing*) este/esta; (*pl*) estos/estas • **the former ... the ~ ...** aquel ... este ...

> *In the past the standard spelling for* ***este/esta*** *and* ***aquel/aquella*** *as pronouns was with an accent (****éste/ésta*** *and* ***aquél/aquélla****). Nowadays the* ***Real Academia Española*** *advises that the accented form is only required where there might otherwise be confusion with the adjectives (****este/esta*** *and* ***aquel/aquella****).*

latter-day ['lætə'deɪ] (ADJ) moderno, de nuestros días • **the Latter-day Saints** (= *people*) los Mormones • **the Church of (Jesus Christ of) the Latter-day Saints** la Iglesia de Jesucristo de los Santos de los Últimos Días
latterly ['lætəlɪ] (ADV) últimamente, recientemente
lattice ['lætɪs] (N) enrejado *m*; (*on window*) reja *f*, celosía *f*
(CPD) ▸ **lattice window** ventana *f* de celosía
latticed ['lætɪst] (ADJ) [*window*] con reja
latticework ['lætɪswɜ:k] (N) enrejado *m*; (*on window*) celosía *f*
Latvia ['lætvɪə] (N) Letonia *f*, Latvia *f*
Latvian ['lætvɪən] (ADJ) letón, latvio
(N) letón/ona *m/f*, latvio/a *m/f*
laud [lɔ:d] (VT) (*liter*) alabar, elogiar
laudable ['lɔ:dəbl] (ADJ) loable, laudable
laudably ['lɔ:dəblɪ] (ADV) de modo loable
laudanum ['lɔ:dnəm] (N) láudano *m*
laudatory ['lɔ:dətərɪ] (ADJ) laudatorio
laugh [lɑ:f] (N) 1 (*lit*) risa *f*; (*loud*) carcajada *f*, risotada *f* • **he has a very distinctive ~** tiene una risa muy suya • **if you want a ~, read on** si te quieres reír, sigue leyendo • **she gave a little ~** soltó una risita • **to get a ~** hacer reír (a la gente) • **to have a (good) ~ about** *or* **over** *or* **at sth** reírse (mucho) de algo • **that sounds like a ~ a minute** (*iro*) suena como para mondarse de risa* (*iro*) • **to raise a ~** hacer reír (a la gente) • **"I'm not jealous," he said with a ~** —no estoy celoso —dijo riéndose • IDIOM: • **to have the last ~** ser el que ríe el último
2* (= *fun*) • **to be a ~**: • **he's a ~** es un tío gracioso *or* divertido*, es muy cachondo (*Sp**) • **you should come — it'll be a ~** deberías venir — será divertido • **life isn't a bundle of ~s just now** mi vida ahora mismo no es precisamente muy divertida *or* muy alegre • **to do sth for a ~** hacer algo por divertirse • **he's always good for a ~** siempre te ríes *or* te diviertes con él
3 (= *joke*) • **the ~ is on you*** te salió el tiro por la culata* • **that's a ~!** • **what a ~!** (*iro*) ¡no me hagas reír!
(VI) reírse, reír • **I tried not to ~** intenté no reír(me) • **I didn't know whether to ~ or cry** no sabía si reír(me) o llorar • **you may ~, but ...** tú te ríes, pero ... • **once we get this contract signed we're ~ing*** (*fig*) una vez que nos firmen este contrato, lo demás es coser y cantar • **to ~ about sth** reírse de algo • **we're still ~ing about the time that ...** todavía nos reímos de cuando ... • **there's nothing to ~ about** no es cosa de risa *or* (*LAm*) reírse • **to ~ at sb/sth** reírse de algn/algo • **he never ~s at my jokes** nunca se ríe de mis chistes • **to burst out ~ing** echarse a reír • **I thought I'd die ~ing** creí que me moría de (la) risa • **to ~ in sb's face** reírse de algn en su cara • **to fall about ~ing** troncharse *or* desternillarse de risa • **you have (got) to ~** hay que reírse • **to ~ like a drain/hyena** reírse como una hiena • **to make sb ~** hacer reír a algn • **don't make me ~** (*iro*) no me hagas reír • **to ~ out loud** reírse a carcajadas • **I ~ed till I cried** *or* **till the tears ran down my cheeks** me reí a más no poder, me tronché de (la) risa • **I ~ed to myself** me reí para mis adentros • IDIOMS: • **they'll be ~ing all the way to the bank** estarán contentísimos contando el dinero • **he'll soon be ~ing on the other side of his face** pronto se le quitarán las ganas de reír • **to ~ up one's sleeve** reírse por detrás • PROVERBS: • **~ and the world ~s with you, cry and you cry alone** si ríes todo el mundo te acompaña, pero si lloras nadie quiere saber nada • **he who ~s last ~s longest** *or* **best** quien ríe el último ríe mejor
(VT) • **"don't be silly," he ~ed** —no seas bobo —dijo riéndose • **he ~ed a nervous laugh** se rió nervioso • **to ~ sb to scorn** mofarse de algn • **to ~ o.s. silly** reírse a más no poder • IDIOMS: • **to ~ sth out of court**: • **his idea was ~ed out of court** se rieron de su idea • **to ~ one's head off*** partirse *or* desternillarse *or* troncharse de risa
(CPD) ▸ **laugh lines** arrugas *fpl* producidas al reír
▸ **laugh down** (VT + ADV) ridiculizar
▸ **laugh off** (VT + ADV) [+ *pain, accusation, suggestion*] tomarse a risa • **he tried to ~ it off** intentó tomárselo a risa
laughable ['lɑ:fəbl] (ADJ) [*sum, amount*] irrisorio; [*suggestion*] ridículo • **it's really quite ~ that ...** es realmente un poco ridículo *or* irrisorio que ...
laughably ['lɑ:fəblɪ] (ADV) 1 (*with adjective*) • **such ideas now seem ~ dated** esas ideas están ahora tan pasadas de moda que resultan ridículas • **the portions were ~ small** las raciones eran de tamaño irrisorio • **it's a ~ small amount of money** es una cantidad irrisoria *or* de risa
2 (*with verb*) ridículamente • **what was ~ called a double room** lo que ridículamente denominaban una habitación doble
laughing ['lɑ:fɪŋ] (ADJ) risueño, alegre • **it's no ~ matter** no tiene ninguna gracia, no es cosa de risa
(CPD) ▸ **laughing gas** gas *m* hilarante
▸ **laughing stock** hazmerreír *m*
laughingly ['lɑ:fɪŋlɪ] (ADV) • **he said ~** dijo riendo *or* riéndose • **what is ~ called progress** lo que se llama irónicamente el progreso
laughter ['lɑ:ftəʳ] (N) (*gen*) risa *f*, risas *fpl*; (= *guffaws*) risotadas *fpl*, carcajadas *fpl* • **their ~ could be heard in the next room** se oían sus risas *or* se les oía reír desde la habitación de al lado • **there was loud ~ at this remark** el comentario provocó carcajadas *or* grandes risas • **she let out a shriek of ~** soltó una sonora carcajada *or* risotada • **to burst into ~** soltar la carcajada • PROVERB: • **~ is the best medicine** la risa es el mejor antídoto; ▷ **roar**
(CPD) ▸ **laughter lines** arrugas *fpl* producidas al reír
Launcelot ['lɑ:nslət] (N) Lanzarote
launch [lɔ:ntʃ] (N) 1 (= *boat*) lancha *f* • **motor ~** lancha *f* motora
2 (= *act*) **a** (*lit*) [*of ship*] botadura *f*; [*of lifeboat, rocket, satellite*] lanzamiento *m*
b (= *introduction*) [*of campaign, product, book*] lanzamiento *m*; [*of film, play*] estreno *m*; [*of company*] creación *f*, fundación *f*; [*of shares*] emisión *f*
(VT) 1 (= *lit*) [+ *ship*] botar; [+ *lifeboat*] echar al mar; [+ *rocket, missile, satellite*] lanzar
2 (= *introduce*) [+ *campaign, product, book, attack*] lanzar; [+ *film, play*] estrenar; [+ *company*] crear, fundar; [+ *shares*] emitir
3 (= *start*) • **it was this novel that really ~ed him as a writer** fue esta novela la que lo lanzó a la fama como escritor • **to ~ sb on his/her way** iniciar a algn en su carrera • **once he's ~ed on that subject we'll never stop him** en cuanto se ponga a hablar de ese tema no habrá forma de pararlo
4 (= *hurl*) • **to ~ o.s. at sth/sb** abalanzarse *or* arrojarse sobre algo/algn • **to ~ o.s. into sth** meterse de lleno en algo, entregarse a algo
(VI) • **to ~ into sth: she ~ed into a long speech about patriotism** se puso a soltar *or* empezó un largo discurso sobre el patriotismo • **he ~ed into an attack on the president** emprendió un ataque contra el presidente, se puso a despotricar contra el presidente • **then the chorus ~es into the national anthem** entonces el coro la emprende con el himno nacional
(CPD) ▸ **launch attempt** intento *m* de lanzamiento ▸ **launch date** fecha *f* prevista para el lanzamiento ▸ **launch pad** (*lit*) rampa *f* or plataforma *f* de lanzamiento; (*fig*)

l

rampa *f* or plataforma *f* de lanzamiento, trampolín *m* ▸ **launch party** (*Comm, Media*) fiesta *f* de lanzamiento ▸ **launch site** lugar *m* del lanzamiento ▸ **launch vehicle** lanzadera *f*
▸ **launch forth** (VI + ADV) = launch
▸ **launch out** (VI + ADV) **1** (= *set out*) lanzarse • **the company needs to ~ out into new markets** la compañía necesita lanzarse a nuevos mercados • **he had ~ed out on sth for which he was ill-prepared** se había lanzado a algo para lo que no estaba preparado
2 (= *be extravagant*) • **now we can afford to ~ out a bit** ahora nos podemos permitir algunos lujos

launcher [ˈlɔːntʃəʳ] (N) (*also* **rocket launcher**) lanzacohetes *m inv*; (*also* **missile launcher**) lanzamisiles *m inv*, lanzadera *f* de misiles

launching [ˈlɔːntʃɪŋ] (N) [*of missile, satellite, lifeboat, company, product*] lanzamiento *m*; [*of ship*] botadura *f*
(CPD) ▸ **launching ceremony** ceremonia *f* de botadura ▸ **launching pad** rampa *f* or plataforma *f* de lanzamiento ▸ **launching site** lugar *m* del lanzamiento

launder [ˈlɔːndəʳ] (VT) **1** (*lit*) lavar y planchar **2** (*fig*) [+ *money*] blanquear, lavar (*LAm*)
(VI) • **this fabric ~s beautifully** esta tela queda muy bien después de lavarla (y plancharla)

launderette [ˌlɔːndəˈret] (N) lavandería *f* automática

laundering [ˈlɔːndərɪŋ] (N) **1** (*lit*) colada *f* **2** (*fig*) [*of money*] blanqueo *m*, lavado *m* (*LAm*) • **money ~** blanqueo *m* de dinero, lavado *m* de dinero (*LAm*)

laundress [ˈlɔːndrɪs] (N) lavandera *f*

Laundromat® [ˈlɔːndrəmæt] (N) (*US*) lavandería *f* automática

laundry [ˈlɔːndrɪ] (N) **1** (= *clothes*) (= *dirty*) ropa *f* sucia, ropa *f* para lavar; (= *clean*) ropa *f* lavada, colada *f* • **to do the ~** hacer la colada, lavar la ropa
2 (= *establishment*) lavandería *f*; (*domestic*) lavadero *m*
(CPD) ▸ **laundry basket** cesto *m* de la ropa sucia ▸ **laundry detergent** (*US*) jabón *m* en polvo, detergente *m* ▸ **laundry list** lista *f* de ropa para lavar ▸ **laundry mark** marca *f* de lavandería

laureate [ˈlɔːrɪɪt] (N) laureado *m* • **the Poet Laureate** (*Brit*) el Poeta Laureado

laurel [ˈlɒrəl] (N) laurel *m* • IDIOMS: • **to look to one's ~s** no dormirse en los laureles • **to rest on one's ~s** dormirse en los laureles • **to win one's ~s** cargarse de laureles, laurearse
(CPD) ▸ **laurel wreath** corona *f* de laurel

Laurence [ˈlɒrəns] (N) Lorenzo

Lausanne [ləʊˈzæn] (N) Lausana *f*

lav* [læv] (N) = **lavatory**

lava [ˈlɑːvə] (N) lava *f*
(CPD) ▸ **lava flow** torrente *m* or río *m* de lava ▸ **lava lamp** lámpara *f* de lava

lavatorial [ˌlævəˈtɔːrɪəl] (ADJ) [*humour*] cloacal, escatológico

lavatory [ˈlævətrɪ] (N) (= *room*) (*in house*) wáter *m* (*Sp*), baño *m* (*LAm*); (*in public place*) aseos *mpl*, servicio(s) *m(pl)* (*Sp*), baño(s) *m(pl)* (*LAm*); (= *appliance*) inodoro *m*, wáter *m* (*Sp*), taza *f* (*LAm*)
(CPD) ▸ **lavatory bowl, lavatory pan** taza *f* de wáter ▸ **lavatory paper** papel *m* higiénico ▸ **lavatory seat** asiento *m* de retrete

lavender [ˈlævɪndəʳ] (N) espliego *m*, lavanda *f*
(CPD) ▸ **lavender blue** azul *m* lavanda ▸ **lavender water** lavanda *f*

lavish [ˈlævɪʃ] (ADJ) **1** (= *sumptuous*) [*apartment, meal, production, costume*] suntuoso; [*lifestyle*] suntuoso, lleno de lujo
2 (= *generous*) [*gift, hospitality*] espléndido, generoso; [*praise*] profuso, abundante; [*amount*] abundante, generoso • **to be ~ with one's gifts** hacer regalos espléndidos or generosos • **to be ~ with one's money** gastar pródigamente el dinero, derrochar el dinero (*pej*) • **to be ~ in** or **with one's praise** ser pródigo en elogios, no escatimar elogios
(VT) • **to ~ sth on** or **upon sb** colmar a algn de algo • **to ~ attention on sb** colmar a algn de atenciones • **to ~ praise on sb** ser pródigo en elogios hacia algn

lavishly [ˈlævɪʃlɪ] (ADV) **1** (= *sumptuously*) [*decorated, furnished*] suntuosamente, fastuosamente
2 (= *generously*) [*entertain, pay*] espléndidamente, generosamente; [*praise*] profusamente

lavishness [ˈlævɪʃnɪs] (N) **1** (= *sumptuousness*) suntuosidad *f*, fastuosidad *f*
2 (= *generosity*) [*of person*] prodigalidad *f* • **the ~ of his praise** la profusión de sus elogios

law [lɔː] (N) **1** (= *piece of legislation*) ley *f* • **there's no law against it** no hay ley que lo prohíba • IDIOM: • **to be a law unto o.s.** dictar sus propias leyes; ▹ **pass**
2 (= *system of laws*) • **the law** la ley • **it's the law** es la ley • **to be above the law** estar por encima de la ley • **according to** or **in accordance with the law** según la ley, de acuerdo con la ley • **the bill became law on 6 August** el proyecto de ley se hizo ley el 6 de agosto • **by law** por ley, de acuerdo con la ley • **to be required by law to do sth** estar obligado por (la) ley a hacer algo • **civil/criminal law** derecho *m* civil/penal • **in law** según la ley • **the law of the land** la ley vigente • **officer of the law** agente *mf* de la ley • **the law on abortion** la legislación sobre el aborto • **law and order** el orden público • **the forces of law and order** las fuerzas del orden • **he is outside the law** está fuera de la ley • **to have the law on one's side** tener la justicia de su lado • **to keep** or **remain within the law** obrar legalmente • **his word is law** su palabra es ley • IDIOMS: • **to lay down the law*** imponer su criterio, obrar autoritariamente • **to take the law into one's own hands** tomarse la justicia por su mano
3 (= *field of study*) derecho *m* • **to study law** estudiar derecho
4 (= *profession*) abogacía *f* • **she is considering a career in law** está pensando dedicarse a la abogacía • **to practise law** ejercer de abogado, ejercer la abogacía
5 (= *legal proceedings*) • **court of law** tribunal *m* de justicia • **to go to law** recurrir a la justicia or a los tribunales • **to take a case to law** llevar un caso ante los tribunales
6 (= *rule*) [*of organization, sport*] regla *f* • **the laws of the game** las reglas del juego • **God's law** la ley de Dios
7 (= *standard*) norma *f* • **there seemed to be one law for the rich and another for the poor** parecía haber unas normas para los ricos y otras para los pobres
8 (*Sci, Math*) ley *f* • **the laws of physics** las leyes de la física • **by the law of averages** por la estadística, estadísticamente • **the law of gravity** la ley de la gravedad • **the law of supply and demand** la ley de la oferta y la demanda; ▹ **nature**
9* (= *police*) • **the law** la policía • **to have the law on sb** denunciar a algn a la policía, llevar a algn a los tribunales
(CPD) ▸ **law court** tribunal *m* de justicia ▸ **law enforcement** aplicación *f* de la ley ▸ **law enforcement agency** *organismo encargado de velar por el cumplimiento de la ley* ▸ **law enforcement officer** (*esp US*) policía *mf* ▸ **Law Faculty** (*Univ*) facultad *f* de Derecho ▸ **law firm** gabinete *m* jurídico, bufete *m* de abogados ▸ **Law Lord** (*Brit*) (*Pol*) juez *mf* lor • **the Law Lords** *jueces que son miembros de la Cámara de los Lores y constituyen el Tribunal Supremo* ▸ **law reports** repertorio *m* de jurisprudencia ▸ **law school** (*US*) facultad *f* de derecho ▸ **law student** estudiante *mf* de derecho

law-abiding [ˈlɔːəˌbaɪdɪŋ] (ADJ) (*lit*) cumplidor de la ley; (*fig*) decente

lawbreaker [ˈlɔːˌbreɪkəʳ] (N) infractor(a) *m/f* or transgresor(a) *m/f* de la ley

law-breaking [ˈlɔːˌbreɪkɪŋ] (ADJ) infractor or transgresor de la ley
(N) infracción *f* or transgresión *f* de la ley

lawful [ˈlɔːfʊl] (ADJ) [*owner, government*] legítimo; [*action, behaviour*] legítimo, lícito; [*contract*] legal, válido • **~ wedded husband** legítimo esposo *m* • **~ wedded wife** legítima esposa *f*

lawfully [ˈlɔːfəlɪ] (ADV) legalmente • **the children were not ~ theirs** los hijos no eran legalmente suyos • **he was judged to have acted ~** consideraron que había actuado legítimamente

lawfulness [ˈlɔːfʊlnɪs] (N) (= *legality*) legalidad *f*

lawgiver [ˈlɔːˌgɪvəʳ] (N) (*Brit*) legislador(a) *m/f*

lawless [ˈlɔːlɪs] (ADJ) [*act*] ilegal; [*person*] rebelde, que rechaza la ley; [*country*] ingobernable, anárquico

lawlessness [ˈlɔːlɪsnɪs] (N) [*of place*] desgobierno *m*, anarquía *f*; [*of act*] ilegalidad *f*, criminalidad *f*

lawmaker [ˈlɔːˌmeɪkəʳ] (N) (*US*) legislador(a) *m/f*

lawman [ˈlɔːmæn] (N) (PL: **lawmen**) (*US*) representante *m* de la ley, agente *m* del orden

lawn¹ [lɔːn] (N) césped *m*, pasto *m* (*LAm*)
(CPD) ▸ **lawn bowling** (*US*) bochas *fpl* ▸ **lawn tennis** tenis *m* sobre hierba

lawn² [lɔːn] (N) (= *cloth*) linón *m*

lawnmower [ˈlɔːnˌməʊəʳ] (N) cortacésped *m* (*Sp*), segadora *f* (*LAm*)

Lawrence [ˈlɒrəns] (N) Lorenzo

lawrencium [lɒˈrensɪəm] (N) laurencio *m*

lawsuit [ˈlɔːsuːt] (N) pleito *m*, juicio *m* • **to bring a ~ against sb** entablar demanda judicial contra algn

lawyer [ˈlɔːjəʳ] (N) abogado/a *m/f* • **a divorce ~** un abogado matrimonialista

LAWYERS

En el Reino Unido existen dos tipos diferentes de abogados: **solicitors** y **barristers** (estos últimos reciben el nombre de **advocates** en Escocia). Los **solicitors** defienden a sus clientes ante tribunales de menor importancia y se encargan de asuntos civiles tales como la compra o venta de propiedades, testamentos, divorcios o el cobro de deudas, aunque pueden ser contratados directamente por el cliente para que los representen en casos tanto civiles como penales. Por su parte, los **barristers** o **advocates** no tratan directamente con sus clientes sino que, en los asuntos legales particulares, asesoran solamente en aquellos casos que les son remitidos por los **solicitors**, ya que su formación va más bien dirigida para actuar ante el Tribunal Supremo.
▹ ATTORNEY

lax [læks] (ADJ) (COMPAR: **laxer**, SUPERL: **laxest**) (*pej*) [*person, discipline*] poco estricto, poco riguroso; [*standards, morals*] laxo, relajado • **things are very lax at the school** en el colegio hay poca disciplina • **to be lax about** *or* **on punctuality** ser negligente en la puntualidad • **to be morally lax** tener una moral laxa *or* relajada

laxative ['læksətɪv] ADJ laxante
N laxante *m*

laxity ['læksɪtɪ], **laxness** ['læksnɪs] N (*pej*) [*of person, discipline*] falta *f* de rigor; [*of standards*] relajamiento *m*, relajación *f* • **moral ~** relajamiento *m or* relajación *f* de la moral

lay[1] [leɪ] VT (PT, PP: **laid**) **1** (= *place, put*) poner, colocar; [+ *carpet, lino*] poner, extender; [+ *bricks*] poner, colocar; [+ *pipes*] (*in building*) instalar; [+ *cable, mains, track, trap*] tender; [+ *foundations*] echar; [+ *foundation stone*] colocar; [+ *bomb, explosives*] colocar; [+ *mines*] sembrar • **I haven't laid eyes on him for years** hace años que no lo veo • **I didn't lay a finger on it!** ¡no lo toqué! • **to lay sth flat** extender algo (sobre la mesa *etc*) • **I don't know where to lay my hands on …** no sé dónde echar mano a *or* conseguir … • **to lay sth over** *or* **on sth** extender algo encima de algo
2 (= *prepare*) [+ *fire*] preparar; [+ *plans*] hacer • **to lay the table** (*Brit*) poner la mesa • PROVERB: • **the best laid plans (of mice and men) can go astray** el hombre propone y Dios dispone
3 (= *present*) [+ *plan, proposal*] presentar (**before** a); [+ *accusation, charge*] hacer; [+ *complaint*] formular, presentar • **to lay a claim before sb** presentar una reivindicación a algn • **to lay the facts before sb** presentar los hechos a algn; ▹ **charge, claim**
4 (= *attribute*) [+ *blame*] echar; [+ *responsibility*] atribuir (**on** a) • **to lay the blame (for sth) on sb** echar la culpa (de algo) a algn
5 (= *flatten, suppress*) [+ *corn*] abatir, encamar; [+ *dust*] matar; [+ *doubts, fears*] acallar; [+ *ghost*] conjurar
6 (= *cause to be*) • **to lay a town flat** arrasar *or* destruir una ciudad • **he has been laid low with flu** la gripe lo ha tenido en cama • **to lay o.s. open to attack/criticism** exponerse al ataque/a la crítica • **to be laid to rest** ser enterrado
7 [+ *bet*] hacer; [+ *money*] apostar (**on** a) • **I'll lay you a fiver on it!** ¡te apuesto cinco libras a que es así! • **to lay that …** apostar a que … • **they're laying bets on who is going to leave next** hacen apuestas sobre quién será el próximo en marcharse; ▹ **odds**
8 [+ *egg*] [*bird, reptile*] poner; [*fish, amphibian, insect*] depositar • **it lays its eggs on/in …** [*fish, amphibian, insect*] deposita los huevos *or* desova en …
9‡ (= *have sex with*) tirarse a**, follarse a (*Sp***)
VI [*hen*] poner (huevos)
N **1** [*of countryside, district etc*] disposición *f*, situación *f* • **the lay of the land** (*US*) la configuración del terreno; (*fig*) la situación, el estado de las cosas
2 • **hen in lay** gallina *f* ponedora • **to come into lay** empezar a poner huevos • **to go out of lay** dejar de poner huevos
3‡ • **she's an easy lay** es una tía fácil* • **she's a good lay** se lo hace muy bien‡
4** (= *act*) polvo** *m*
CPD ▸ **lay days** (*Comm*) días *mpl* de detención *or* inactividad
▸ **lay about** VI + PREP • **to lay about one** dar palos de ciego, repartir golpes a diestro y siniestro
▸ **lay aside** VT + ADV **1** (= *save*) [+ *food, provisions*] guardar; [+ *money*] ahorrar
2 (= *put away*) [+ *book, pen*] dejar, poner a un lado
3 (= *abandon*) [+ *prejudices, differences*] dejar de lado
▸ **lay away** VT + ADV (*US*) = **lay aside**
▸ **lay by** VT + ADV = **lay aside**
▸ **lay down** VT + ADV **1** (= *put down*) [+ *book, pen*] dejar, poner a un lado; [+ *luggage*] dejar; [+ *burden*] posar, depositar en tierra; [+ *cards*] extender sobre el tapete; (= *lay flat*) [+ *person, body*] acostar, tender • **to lay o.s. down** tumbarse, echarse
2 [+ *ship*] colocar la quilla de
3 [+ *wine*] poner en bodega, guardar en cava
4 (= *give up*) [+ *arms*] deponer, rendir • **to lay down one's life for sth/sb** dar su vida por algo/algn
5 (= *establish*) [+ *condition*] establecer; [+ *precedent*] sentar, establecer; [+ *principle*] establecer, formular; [+ *policy*] trazar, formular; [+ *ruling*] dictar • **to lay it down that …** asentar que …, dictaminar que …; ▹ **law**
6 (= *impose*) [+ *condition*] imponer
VI + ADV (*Cards*) poner sus cartas sobre el tapete; (*Bridge*) (*as dummy*) tumbarse
▸ **lay in** VT + ADV [+ *food, fuel, water*] proveerse de, abastecerse de; (= *amass*) acumular; (= *buy*) comprar • **to lay in supplies** aprovisionarse • **to lay in supplies of sth** proveerse *or* abastecerse de algo
▸ **lay into*** VI + PREP [+ *person*] (*lit, fig*) arremeter contra; [+ *food*] lanzarse sobre, asaltar
▸ **lay off** VT + ADV [+ *workers*] (= *sack*) despedir; (*temporarily*) despedir *or* suspender (temporalmente por falta de trabajo)
VI + ADV **1** (*Naut*) virar de bordo
2* • **lay off, will you?** ¡déjalo!, ¡por Dios!
VI + PREP* • **to lay off sb** dejar a algn en paz • **to lay off cigarettes** dejar de fumar (cigarrillos) • **lay off it!** ¡ya está bien!, ¡déjalo por Dios!
▸ **lay on** VT + ADV **1** (*Brit*) (= *install*) instalar, conectar • **a house with water laid on** una casa con agua corriente
2 (= *provide*) [+ *food, drink*] proporcionar • **you rent the hall and we'll lay on the refreshments** usted alquila la sala y nosotros nos hacemos cargo de *or* ponemos los refrigerios • **everything's laid on** todo está dispuesto • **they laid on a car for me** pusieron un coche a mi disposición
3 [+ *paint*] poner, aplicar • IDIOM: • **to lay it on thick** *or* **with a trowel*** (= *exaggerate*) recargar las tintas*
4 [+ *tax, duty*] imponer
5 • **to lay it on sb*** dar una paliza a algn
▸ **lay out** VT + ADV **1** (= *dispose*) [+ *cloth, rug*] tender, extender; [+ *objects*] disponer, arreglar; [+ *goods for sale*] exponer; [+ *garden, town*] trazar, hacer el trazado de; [+ *page, letter*] presentar, diseñar; [+ *clothes*] preparar; [+ *ideas*] exponer, explicar • **the house is well laid out** la casa está bien distribuida • **the town is well laid out** la ciudad tiene un trazado elegante
2 [+ *corpse*] amortajar
3 [+ *money*] (= *spend*) gastar; (= *invest*) invertir, emplear (**on** en)
4* (= *knock out*) derribar; (*Boxing*) dejar K.O.
5 (*reflexive*) • **to lay o.s. out for sb** hacer lo posible por ayudar/complacer a algn • **he laid himself out to please** se volcó por complacerla/los *etc*
▸ **lay over** VI + ADV (*US*) pasar la noche, descansar
▸ **lay up** VT + ADV **1** (= *store*) guardar, almacenar; (= *amass*) acumular • **he's laying up trouble for himself** se está creando *or* buscando problemas
2 (= *put out of service*) [+ *ship*] meter en el dique seco; [+ *boat*] amarrar; [+ *car*] encerrar (en el garaje)
3 (*Med*) • **to be laid up (with sth)** estar en cama (con algo) • **she was laid up for weeks** tuvo que guardar cama durante varias semanas

lay[2] [leɪ] PT *of* **lie[2]**

lay[3] [leɪ] ADJ (*Rel*) laico, lego, seglar; (= *non-specialist*) lego, profano, no experto
CPD ▸ **lay brother** (*Rel*) donado *m*, lego *m*, hermano *m* lego ▸ **lay person** (*Rel*) lego/a *m/f*; (= *non-specialist*) profano/a *m/f* ▸ **lay preacher** predicador(a) *m/f* laico/a ▸ **lay reader** (*Rel*) *persona laica encargada de conducir parte de un servicio religioso* ▸ **lay sister** (*Rel*) donada *f*, lega *f*

lay[4] [leɪ] N (*Mus, Literat*) trova *f*, canción *f*

layabout* ['leɪəbaʊt] N holgazán/ana *m/f*, vago/a *m/f*

layaway ['leɪəweɪ] N (*US*) (*Comm*) *sistema por el cual se aparta o reserva mercancía mediante el pago de un depósito* • **to put sth on ~** apartar *or* reservar algo dejando un depósito

lay-by ['leɪbaɪ] N (*Aut*) área *f* de descanso, área *f* de estacionamiento

layer ['leɪəʳ] N **1** (*gen*) capa *f*; (*Geol*) estrato *m*; (*Agr*) acodo *m*
2 (= *hen*) gallina *f* ponedora • **to be a good ~** ser buena ponedora • **the best ~** la más ponedora
VT **1** (*Culin*) [+ *vegetables, pasta, pancakes*] poner en capas
2 (*Agr*) acodar

layered ['leɪəd] ADJ • **a ~ dress** un vestido de volantes • **a ~ haircut** un corte (de pelo) a capas

layette [leɪ'et] N canastilla *f*, ajuar *m*

laying ['leɪɪŋ] N (= *placing*) colocación *f*; [*of cable, track etc*] tendido *m*; [*of eggs*] puesta *f*, postura *f* • **~ on of hands** imposición *f* de manos

layman ['leɪmən] N (PL: **laymen**) **1** (*Rel*) seglar *mf*, lego/a *m/f*
2 (*fig*) profano(a) *m/f*, lego(a) *m/f* • **in ~'s terms** para entendernos, para los profanos en la materia

lay-off ['leɪɒf] N (= *act*) despido *m*; (= *period*) paro *m* (involuntario), baja *f*

layout ['leɪaʊt] N [*of building*] plan *m*, distribución *f*; [*of town*] trazado *m*; (*Typ*) composición *f*

layover ['leɪəʊvəʳ] N (*US*) parada *f* intermedia; (*Aer*) escala *f*

Lazarus ['læzərəs] N Lázaro

laze [leɪz] VI (*also* **laze about, laze around**) no hacer nada, descansar; (*pej*) holgazanear, gandulear • **we ~d in the sun for a week** pasamos una semana tirados al sol

lazily ['leɪzɪlɪ] ADV **1** (= *without effort*) perezosamente
2 (*fig*) [*drift, float*] perezosamente (*liter*), lentamente

laziness ['leɪzɪnɪs] N pereza *f*, flojera *f* (*esp LAm**)

lazy ['leɪzɪ] (COMPAR: **lazier**, SUPERL: **laziest**)
ADJ **1** (= *idle*) perezoso, vago • **to feel ~** tener pereza, tener flojera (*esp LAm**) • **to have a ~ eye** (*Med*) tener un ojo vago
2 (*pej*) (= *unconsidered*) [*assumption*] poco meditado • **it's another example of ~ thinking** es otro ejemplo de pensar sin cuestionar las cosas
3 (= *relaxed*) [*smile, gesture*] perezoso; [*meal, day*] relajado; [*holiday*] descansado • **we spent a ~ Sunday on the river** pasamos un domingo de lo más relajado en el río
4 (*liter*) [*river*] lento

lazybones ['leɪzɪ,bəʊnz] NSING gandul(a)

m/f, vago/a m/f, flojo/a m/f (LAm)
lazy Susan [ˌleɪzɪˈsuːzn] (N) (= *dish*) *bandeja giratoria para servir la comida en la mesa*
LB (ABBR) (*Canada*) = **Labrador**
lb (ABBR) (= **pound**) libra *f*
LBO (N ABBR) (*Econ*) = **leveraged buyout**
lbw (ABBR) (*Cricket*) (= **leg before wicket**) *expulsión de un jugador cuya pierna ha sido golpeada por la pelota que de otra forma hubiese dado en los palos*
LC (N ABBR) (*US*) = **Library of Congress**
lc, l.c. (ABBR) (*Typ*) (= **lower case**) min
L/C (N ABBR) (*Comm*) (= **letter of credit**) cta. cto.
LCD (N ABBR) **1** (= **liquid crystal display**) LCD *m*
2 = **lowest common denominator**
L-Cpl (ABBR) *of* **lance corporal**
Ld (ABBR) *of* **Lord**
LDS (N ABBR) **1** (*Univ*) = **Licentiate in Dental Surgery**
2 (= **Latter-day Saints**) Iglesia *f* de Jesucristo de los Santos de los Últimos Días
LEA (N ABBR) (*Brit*) (*Educ*) = **Local Education Authority**
lea [liː] (N) (*poet*) prado *m*
leach [liːtʃ] (VT) lixiviar
(VI) lixiviarse
lead¹ [led] (N) (= *metal*) plomo *m*; (*in pencil*) mina *f*; (*Naut*) sonda *f*, escandallo *m* • **my limbs felt like ~** *or* **as heavy as ~** los brazos y las piernas me pesaban como plomo • **they filled him full of ~*** lo acribillaron a balazos
• IDIOM: • **to swing the ~*** fingirse enfermo, racanear*, hacer el rácano*
(CPD) de plomo ▸ **lead acetate** acetato *m* de plomo ▸ **lead crystal** cristal *m* (que contiene óxido de plomo) ▸ **lead oxide** óxido *m* de plomo ▸ **lead paint** pintura *f* a base de plomo ▸ **lead pencil** lápiz *m* ▸ **lead pipe** tubería *f* de plomo ▸ **lead poisoning** saturnismo *m*, plumbismo *m*, intoxicación *f* por el plomo ▸ **lead replacement petrol** (gasolina *f*) súper *f* aditiva, (gasolina *f*) súper *f* con aditivos ▸ **lead shot** perdigonada *f* ▸ **lead weight** peso *m* plomo
lead² [liːd] (VB: PT, PP: **led**) (N) **1** (= *leading position*) (*Sport*) delantera *f*, cabeza *f*; (= *distance, time, points ahead*) ventaja *f* • **to be in the ~** (*gen*) ir a la *or* en cabeza, ir primero; (*Sport*) llevar la delantera; (*in league*) ocupar el primer puesto • **to have two minutes' ~ over sb** llevar a algn una ventaja de dos minutos • **to have a ~ of half a length** tener medio cuerpo de ventaja • **to take the ~** (*Sport*) tomar la delantera; (= *take the initiative*) tomar la iniciativa
2 (= *example*) ejemplo *m* • **to follow sb's ~** seguir el ejemplo de algn • **to give sb a ~** guiar a algn, dar el ejemplo a algn, mostrar el camino a algn
3 (= *clue*) pista *f*, indicación *f* • **the police have a ~** la policía tiene una pista • **to follow up a ~** seguir *or* investigar una pista
4 (*Theat*) papel *m* principal; (*in opera*) voz *f* cantante; (= *person*) primer actor *m*, primera actriz *f* • **to play the ~** tener el papel principal • **to sing the ~** llevar la voz cantante • **with Greta Garbo in the ~** con Greta Garbo en el primer papel
5 (= *leash*) cuerda *f*, traílla *f*, correa *f* (*LAm*) • **dogs must be kept on a ~** los perros deben llevarse con traílla
6 (*Elec*) cable *m*
7 (*Cards*) • **whose ~ is it?** ¿quién sale?, ¿quién es mano? • **it's my ~** soy mano, salgo yo • **it's your ~** tú eres mano, sales tú • **if the ~ is in hearts** si la salida es a corazones
8 (*Press*) primer párrafo *m*, entrada *f*
(VT) **1** (= *conduct*) llevar, conducir • **to ~ sb to a table** conducir a algn a una mesa • **kindly ~ me to him** haga el favor de conducirme a su presencia *or* de llevarme donde está • **they led him into the king's presence** lo condujeron ante el rey • **what led you to Venice?** ¿qué te llevó a Venecia?, ¿con qué motivo fuiste a Venecia? • **this road ~s you back to Jaca** por este camino se vuelve a Jaca • **this ~s me to an important point** esto me lleva a un punto importante • **this discussion is ~ing us nowhere** esta discusión no nos lleva a ninguna parte • **to ~ the way** (*lit*) ir primero; (*fig*) mostrar el camino, dar el ejemplo
2 (= *be the leader of*) [+ *government*] dirigir, encabezar; [+ *party*] encabezar, ser jefe de; [+ *expedition, regiment*] mandar; [+ *discussion*] conducir; [+ *team*] capitanear; [+ *league*] ir a la *or* en cabeza de, encabezar, ocupar el primer puesto en; [+ *procession*] ir a la *or* en cabeza de, encabezar; [+ *orchestra*] (*Brit*) ser el primer violín en; (*US*) dirigir
3 (= *be first in*) • **to ~ the field** (*Sport*) ir a la cabeza, llevar la delantera • **they ~ the field in this area of research** son los líderes en este campo de la investigación • **Britain led the world in textiles** Inglaterra era el líder mundial en la industria textil
4 (= *be in front of*) [+ *opponent*] aventajar • **Roberts ~s Brown by four games to one** Roberts le aventaja a Brown por cuatro juegos a uno • **they led us by 30 seconds** nos llevaban una ventaja de 30 segundos
5 [+ *life, existence*] llevar • **to ~ a busy life** llevar una vida muy ajetreada • **to ~ a full life** llevar *or* tener una vida muy activa, llevar *or* tener una vida llena de actividades • **to ~ sb a miserable life** amargar la vida a algn; ▹ **dance, life**
6 (= *influence*) • **to ~ sb to do sth** llevar *or* inducir *or* mover a algn a hacer algo • **we were led to believe that …** nos hicieron creer que … • **what led you to this conclusion?** ¿qué te hizo llegar a esta conclusión? • **he is easily led** es muy sugestionable • **to ~ sb into error** inducir a algn a error
(VI) **1** (= *go in front*) ir primero
2 (*in match, race*) llevar la delantera • **he is ~ing by an hour/ten metres** lleva una hora/diez metros de ventaja
3 (*Cards*) ser mano, salir • **you ~** sales tú, tú eres mano • **she led with the three of clubs** salió con el tres de tréboles
4 (= *be in control*) estar al mando • **we need someone who knows how to ~** necesitamos una persona que sepa estar al mando *or* que tenga dotes de mando
5 • **to ~ to** [*street, corridor*] conducir a; [*door*] dar a • **this street ~s to the station** esta calle conduce a la estación, por esta calle se va a la estación • **this street ~s to the main square** esta calle sale a *or* desemboca en la plaza principal • **this road ~s back to Burgos** por este camino se vuelve a Burgos
6 (= *result in*) • **to ~ to** llevar a • **it led to his arrest** llevó a su detención • **all my enquiries led nowhere** mis indagaciones no llevaron a nada • **it led to war** condujo a la guerra • **it led to a change** produjo un cambio • **one thing led to another …** una cosa nos/los *etc* llevó a otra … • **it all ~s back to the butler** todo nos lleva de nuevo al mayordomo (como sospechoso)
(CPD) ▸ **lead singer** cantante *mf* ▸ **lead story** reportaje *m* principal ▸ **lead time** plazo *m* de entrega
▸ **lead along** (VT + ADV) llevar (por la mano)
▸ **lead away** (VT + ADV) (*gen*) llevar • **he was led away by the police** se lo llevó la policía • **we must not be led away from the main issue** no nos apartemos del asunto principal
▸ **lead in** (VT + ADV) hacer entrar a
(VI + ADV) • **this is a way of ~ing in** esta es una manera de introducir (el argumento *etc*) • **to ~ in with** empezar con
▸ **lead off** (VT + ADV) **1** (= *take away*) llevar
2 (*fig*) (= *begin*) empezar (**with** con)
(VI + PREP) [*street*] salir de; [*room*] comunicar con • **the streets that ~ off (from) the square** las calles que salen de la plaza • **a room ~ing off (from) another** una habitación que comunica con otra
▸ **lead on** (VT + ADV) **1** (= *tease*) engañar, engatusar; (*amorously*) ir dando esperanzas a
2 (= *incite*) • **to ~ sb on (to do sth)** incitar a algn (a hacer algo)
(VI + ADV) ir primero, ir a la cabeza • **you ~ on** tú primero • **~ on!** ¡vamos!, ¡adelante!
▸ **lead out** (VT + ADV) (*outside*) llevar *or* conducir fuera; (*onto stage, dance floor*) sacar
▸ **lead up to** (VI + ADV + PREP) llevar a, conducir a • **what's all this ~ing up to?** ¿a dónde lleva *or* a qué conduce todo esto?, ¿a qué vas con todo esto? • **the years that led up to the war** los años que precedieron a la guerra • **the events that led up to the war** los sucesos que condujeron a la guerra
leaded [ˈledɪd] (ADJ) [*window*] emplomado
(CPD) ▸ **leaded lights** cristales *mpl* emplomados ▸ **leaded petrol** gasolina *f* con plomo
leaden [ˈledn] (ADJ) (= *of lead*) de plomo, plúmbeo; (*in colour*) plomizo; (*fig*) [*heart*] triste
leaden-eyed [ˌlednˈaɪd] (ADJ) • **to be leaden-eyed** tener los párpados pesados
leader [ˈliːdə[r]] (N) **1** [*of group, party*] líder *m/f*, jefe/a *m/f*; (= *guide*) guía *mf*, conductor(a) *m/f*; [*of rebels*] cabecilla *mf*; (*Mus*) [*of orchestra*] (*Brit*) primer violín *m*; (*US*) director(a) *m/f* • **our political ~s** nuestros líderes políticos • **he's a born ~** ha nacido para mandar • **Leader of the House** (*of Commons*) (*Pol*) Presidente/a *m/f* de la Cámara de los Comunes; (*of Lords*) Presidente/a *m/f* de la Cámara de los Lores • **Leader of the Opposition** jefe/a *m/f* de la oposición
2 (*in race, field etc*) primero/a *m/f*; (*in league*) líder *m*; (= *horse*) caballo *m* que va primero; ▹ **market, world**
3 (*in newspaper*) editorial *m*
4 (*Comm*) (= *company, product*) líder *m*
(CPD) ▸ **leader writer** (*Brit*) editorialista *mf*

LEADER OF THE HOUSE

Leader of the House es el término que, en el Reino Unido, hace referencia tanto al presidente de la Cámara de los Comunes como al presidente de la Cámara de los Lores. Ambos pertenecen al gobierno británico y son los encargados de organizar y hacer público el horario semanal de debates y otros asuntos en sus respectivas cámaras, previa consulta con su homólogo de la oposición o **Shadow Leader of the House** y con los **Whips** de cada partido.
▹ **WHIP, SPEAKER**

leaderene [ˌliːdəˈriːn] (N) (*hum*) líder *f*
leaderless [ˈliːdəlɪs] (ADJ) [*organization*] sin jefe; [*party, union, country*] sin líder; [*rebels, mob*] sin cabecilla
leadership [ˈliːdəʃɪp] (N) **1** (= *position*) dirección *f*, liderazgo *m* • **under the ~ of …** bajo la dirección *or* liderazgo de …
• **~ qualities** dotes *fpl* de mando • **to take over the ~ (of sth)** asumir la dirección (de algo)
2 (= *leaders*) dirección *f*, jefatura *f*

lead-free [ˌledˈfriː] ADJ sin plomo

lead-in [ˈliːdˈɪn] N introducción *f* (**to** a)

leading [ˈliːdɪŋ] ADJ **1** (= *foremost*) [*expert, politician, writer*] principal, más destacado; (*Ind*) [*producer*] principal; [*company, product, brand*] líder; (*Theat, Cine*) [*part, role*] principal, de protagonista • **one of Britain's ~ writers** uno de los principales *or* más destacados escritores británicos • **to play the ~ role** *or* **part in** [+ *film, play*] interpretar el papel principal *or* de protagonista en
2 (= *prominent*) [*expert, politician, writer*] destacado • **~ scientists believe it will be possible** destacados científicos creen que será posible • **a ~ member of the Sikh community** un miembro destacado de la comunidad sij • **a ~ industrial nation** un país industrializado líder, uno de los principales países industrializados • **to play a ~ role** *or* **part in sth** (*fig*) jugar un papel importante *or* destacado en algo
3 (*in race*) [*athlete, horse, driver*] en cabeza, que va a la cabeza; (*in procession, convoy*) que va a la cabeza
CPD ▸ **leading article** (*Brit*) (*Press*) artículo *m* de fondo, editorial *m* ▸ **leading edge** (*Aer*) [*of wing*] borde *m* anterior; (= *forefront*) vanguardia *f* • **to be at** *or* **on the ~ edge of** estar a la vanguardia de; ▹ **leading-edge** ▸ **leading lady** (*Theat*) primera actriz *f*; (*Cine*) protagonista *f* ▸ **leading light** figura *f* principal ▸ **leading man** (*Theat*) primer actor *m*; (*Cine*) protagonista *m* ▸ **leading question** pregunta *f* capciosa

leading-edge [ˌliːdɪŋˈedʒ] ADJ • **leading-edge technology** tecnología *f* de vanguardia, tecnología *f* punta

lead-up [ˈliːdʌp] N período *m* previo (**to** a) • **during the lead-up to the election ...** durante la precampaña electoral ... • **the lead-up to the wedding** los meses antes de la boda

leaf [liːf] N (PL: **leaves**) **1** [*of plant*] hoja *f* • **to come into ~** echar hojas; ▹ **shake**
2 [*of book*] página *f* • IDIOMS: • **to turn over a new ~** pasar página, hacer borrón y cuenta nueva • **to take a ~ out of sb's book** seguir el ejemplo de algn
3 [*of table*] ala *f*, hoja *f* abatible
CPD ▸ **leaf bud** yema *f* ▸ **leaf mould, leaf mold** (*US*) mantillo *m* (de hojas), abono *m* verde ▸ **leaf spinach** hojas *fpl* de espinaca ▸ **leaf tobacco** tabaco *m* en rama
▸ **leaf through** VI + PREP [+ *book*] hojear

leafless [ˈliːflɪs] ADJ sin hojas, deshojado

leaflet [ˈliːflɪt] N (*containing several pages*) folleto *m*; (= *single piece of paper*) octavilla *f*
VI repartir folletos
VT [+ *area, street*] repartir folletos en

leafleting [ˈliːflətɪŋ] N reparto *m* de folletos, volanteo *m* (*LAm*)
CPD ▸ **leafleting campaign** campaña *f* de reparto de folletos, campaña *f* de volanteo (*LAm*)

leafy [ˈliːfɪ] ADJ (COMPAR: **leafier**, SUPERL: **leafiest**) frondoso, con muchas hojas • **the ~ suburbs of the city** los barrios residenciales de la ciudad

league¹ [liːg] N (= *measure*) legua *f*

league² [liːg] N liga *f* (*also Sport*), sociedad *f*, asociación *f*, comunidad *f* • **League of Nations** Sociedad *f* de las Naciones • **he's not in the same ~** (*fig*) no está al mismo nivel • **they're not in the same ~** (*fig*) no hay comparación • **to be in ~ with sb** estar de manga con algn, haberse confabulado con algn
CPD ▸ **league champion(s)** campeón *msing* de liga ▸ **league championship** (*Brit*) (*Ftbl*) campeonato *m* de liga ▸ **league leader** líder *m* de la liga ▸ **league match** (*Brit*) (*Ftbl*) partido *m* de liga ▸ **league table** clasificación *f*

leak [liːk] N **1** (= *hole*) (*in roof*) gotera *f*; (*in pipe, radiator, tank*) rotura *f*; (*in boat*) vía *f* de agua; ▹ **spring**
2 (= *escape*) [*of gas, water, chemical*] escape *m*, fuga *f*
3 (*fig*) [*of information, document*] filtración *f*; ▹ **security**
4 • IDIOM: • **to go for** *or* **have** *or* **take a ~‡** echar una meada‡, mear‡
VI **1** (= *be leaky*) [*roof*] tener goteras; [*pipe, radiator, tank*] gotear, tener una fuga; [*boat*] hacer agua; [*pen*] perder tinta • **her shoes ~ed** le entraba agua en *or* por los zapatos • **the window is ~ing a bit** entra un poco de agua por la ventana • **my pen has ~ed onto my shirt** me ha caído tinta del bolígrafo en la camisa
2 (= *escape*) • **radioactive gas was ~ing from a reactor** había un escape *or* fuga de gas radiactivo en un reactor • **water was ~ing through the roof** entraba agua por el tejado, goteaba agua del tejado
VT **1** [+ *liquid*] (= *discharge*) perder; (= *pour out*) derramar • **a tanker has ~ed oil into the Baltic Sea** un petrolero ha derramado petróleo al mar Báltico • **it is feared that these weapons could ~ plutonium** se teme que se produzca un escape de plutonio de estas armas
2 (*fig*) [+ *information, document*] filtrar (**to** a) • **his letter was ~ed to the press** su carta se filtró a la prensa
▸ **leak in** VI + ADV [*liquid*] entrar
▸ **leak out** VI + ADV **1** (*lit*) [*gas, liquid*] salirse
2 (*fig*) [*secret, news, information*] filtrarse

leakage [ˈliːkɪdʒ] N **1** (*lit*) [*of gas, liquid*] escape *m*, fuga *f*
2 (*fig*) filtración *f*

leakproof [ˈliːkpruːf] ADJ [*container*] hermético; [*nappy, pants*] impermeable

leaky [ˈliːkɪ] ADJ (COMPAR: **leakier**, SUPERL: **leakiest**) [*roof*] con goteras; [*pipe, container*] que gotea, con fugas; [*boat*] que hace agua; [*pen*] que pierde tinta

lean¹ [liːn] ADJ (COMPAR: **leaner**, SUPERL: **leanest**) **1** (= *slim*) [*person, body*] delgado, enjuto; [*animal*] flaco • **companies will need to be ~er in order to compete** las compañías tendrán que racionalizarse para ser más competitivas
2 (= *not prosperous*) [*times*] difícil; [*harvest*] pobre • **to have a ~ time of it** pasar por una mala racha • **~ years** años *mpl* de vacas flacas
3 (= *not fatty*) [*meat*] magro, sin grasa
4 (*Aut*) • **~ mixture** mezcla *f* pobre
N (*Culin*) magro *m*
CPD ▸ **lean manufacturing, lean production** producción *f* ajustada

lean² [liːn] (PT, PP: **leaned** *or* **leant**) VI
1 (= *slope*) inclinarse, ladearse • **to ~ to(wards) the left/right** (*lit*) estar inclinado hacia la izquierda/derecha; (*fig*) (*Pol*) inclinarse hacia la izquierda/la derecha • **to ~ towards sb's opinion** inclinarse por la opinión de algn
2 (*for support*) apoyarse • **to ~ on/against sth** apoyarse en/contra algo • **to ~ on sb** (*lit*) apoyarse en algn; (*fig*) (= *put pressure on*) presionar a algn • **to ~ on sb for support** (*fig*) contar con el apoyo de algn
VT • **to ~ a ladder/a bicycle against a wall** apoyar una escala/una bicicleta contra una pared • **to ~ one's head on sb's shoulder** apoyar la cabeza en el hombro de algn
▸ **lean across** VI + ADV [*person*] inclinarse hacia un lado • **she ~ed across and opened the passenger door** se inclinó hacia un lado y abrió la puerta del asiento del pasajero
▸ **lean back** VI + ADV reclinarse, recostarse
▸ **lean forward** VI + ADV inclinarse hacia delante
▸ **lean out** VI + ADV asomarse • **to ~ out of the window** asomarse a *or* por la ventana
▸ **lean over** VI + ADV inclinarse • **to ~ over backwards to help sb** volcarse *or* desvivirse por ayudar a algn • **we've ~ed over backwards to get agreement** hemos hecho todo lo posible *or* nos hemos volcado para llegar a un acuerdo
VI + PREP inclinarse sobre

Leander [liːˈændəʳ] N Leandro

leaning [ˈliːnɪŋ] N inclinación *f* (**to, towards** hacia), tendencia *f* (**to, towards** a) • **she has leftish ~s** tiene inclinaciones *or* tendencias izquierdistas • **he has artistic ~s** tiene inclinaciones artísticas
ADJ inclinado • **the Leaning Tower of Pisa** la Torre Inclinada de Pisa

leanness [ˈliːnnɪs] N **1** [*of person, body*] delgadez *f*; [*of animal*] flacura *f*, flaqueza *f*
2 [*of meat*] lo magro • **the meat is valued for its ~** la carne es muy apreciada por lo magra que es

leant [lent] PT, PP *of* **lean²**

lean-to [ˈliːntuː] N (PL: **lean-tos**) cobertizo *m*

leap [liːp] (VB: PP, PT: **leaped** *or* **leapt**) N
1 (= *jump*) **a** (*lit*) salto *m*; (*showing exuberance*) salto *m*, brinco *m*
b (*fig*) salto *m* • **by ~s and bounds** a pasos agigantados • **a ~ in the dark** un salto al vacío • **his heart gave a ~** le dio un vuelco el corazón • **it doesn't take a great ~ of the imagination to foresee what will happen** no se requiere un gran esfuerzo de imaginación para prever lo que va a pasar • **she successfully made the ~ into films** dio el salto con éxito al mundo del cine • **to make** *or* **take a huge ~ forward** dar un gran salto *or* paso hacia adelante • **to make** *or* **take a ~ of faith** hacer un gran esfuerzo de fe, hacer profesión de fe • **mental ~** salto *m* mental • **a ~ into the unknown** un salto a lo desconocido
2 (= *increase*) subida *f* • **a 6% ~ in profits** una subida de un 6% en las ganancias
VI **1** (= *jump*) **a** (*lit*) saltar; (*exuberantly*) brincar, saltar • **to ~ about** dar saltos, brincar • **to ~ about with excitement** dar saltos *or* brincar de emoción • **the dog ~ed at the man, snarling** el perro saltó *or* se arrojó sobre el hombre gruñiendo • **he ~t down from his horse** se bajó del caballo de un salto • **the car ~t forward** el coche dio una sacudida • **he ~t from a moving train** saltó de un tren en marcha • **he ~ed into the river** saltó *or* se tiró al río • **he ~t off/onto the bus** bajó del/subió al autobús de un salto • **he suddenly ~t on top of me** de repente me saltó *or* se me tiró encima • **to ~ out of a car** bajarse *or* saltar de un coche • **she ~t out of bed** se levantó de la cama de un salto, saltó de la cama • **to ~ over** [+ *obstacle*] saltar por encima de; [+ *stream*] cruzar de un salto • **to ~ to one's feet** levantarse de un salto
b (*fig*) • **my heart ~ed** me dio un vuelco el corazón • **she ~t at the chance to play the part** no dejó escapar la oportunidad de representar el papel • **to ~ at an offer** aceptar una oferta al vuelo • **he ~t on my mistake** se lanzó sobre mi error • **the tabloids are quick to ~ on such cases** la prensa amarilla está a la que salta con estos casos • **the headline ~t out at her** el titular le saltó a la vista • **he ~t to his brother's defence** enseguida saltó a defender a su hermano

l

2 (= *increase*) • **sales ~t by one third** las ventas se incrementaron repentinamente en un tercio
VT [+ *fence, ditch*] saltar por encima de; [+ *stream, river*] cruzar de un salto
CPD ▸ **leap year** año *m* bisiesto
▸ **leap up** VI + ADV **1** [*person*] levantarse de un salto; [*flame*] subir • **the dog ~t up at him** el perro le saltó *or* se le echó encima
2 (= *increase*) [*profits, sales, prices, unemployment*] subir de repente
leapfrog ['li:pfrɒg] N pídola *f* • **to play ~** jugar a la pídola
VI jugar a la pídola • **to ~ over sth/sb** saltar por encima de algo/algn
VT saltar por encima de
leapt [lept] PT, PP *of* **leap**
learn [lɜ:n] (PT, PP: **learned** *or* **learnt**) VT
1 (*by study, practice etc*) [+ *language, words, skill*] aprender; [+ *instrument*] aprender a tocar • **you can ~ a lot by listening and thinking** se puede aprender mucho escuchando y pensando • **I ~t a lot from her** aprendí mucho de ella • **you must ~ patience** tienes que aprender a tener paciencia • **to ~ (how) to do sth** aprender a hacer algo • **to ~ sth by heart** aprender(se) algo de memoria • IDIOM: • **to ~ one's lesson** aprender la lección, escarmentar; ▹ **line[1], rope**
2 (= *find out*) enterarse de • **to ~ that** enterarse de que
3‡ (= *show, teach*) (*incorrect usage*) enseñar • **that'll ~ you** para que escarmientes *or* aprendas, te está bien empleado • **I'll ~ you!** ¡yo te enseñaré!
VI **1** (*by study, practice etc*) aprender • **it's never too late to ~** nunca es tarde para aprender • **he'll ~!** ¡un día aprenderá!, ¡ya aprenderá! • **we are ~ing about the Romans** estamos estudiando los romanos • **to ~ from experience** aprender por experiencia • **to ~ from one's mistakes** aprender de los errores (cometidos)
2 (= *find out*) • **to ~ of** *or* **about sth** enterarse de algo
▸ **learn off** VT + ADV aprender de memoria
▸ **learn up** VT + ADV esforzarse por aprender, empollar
learned ['lɜ:nɪd] ADJ [*person*] docto, erudito; [*remark, speech, book*] erudito; [*profession*] liberal • **my ~ friend** (*frm*) mi distinguido colega
CPD ▸ **learned body** academia *f* ▸ **learned society** sociedad *f* científica
learnedly ['lɜ:nɪdlɪ] ADV eruditamente
learner ['lɜ:nə^r] N (= *novice*) principiante *mf*; (= *student*) estudiante *mf*; (*also* **learner driver**) (*Brit*) conductor(a) *m/f* en prácticas, aprendiz(a) *m/f* de conductor(a) • **to be a slow ~** tener dificultades de aprendizaje • **to be a fast ~** aprender con mucha rapidez
CPD ▸ **learner driver** (*Brit*) conductor(a) *m/f* en prácticas, aprendiz(a) *m/f* de conductor(a) ▸ **learner's permit** (*US, Australia*) (= *provisional driving licence*) permiso *m* de conducir provisional
learner-centred, learner-centered (*US*) ['lɜ:nə,sentəd] ADJ centrado en el alumno
learning ['lɜ:nɪŋ] N **1** (= *act*) aprendizaje *m*
2 (= *knowledge*) conocimientos *mpl*, saber *m*; (= *erudition*) saber *m*, erudición *f* • **man of ~** sabio *m*, erudito *m* • **seat of ~** centro *m* de estudios
CPD ▸ **learning curve** proceso *m* de aprendizaje • **it's a ~ curve** hay que ir aprendiendo poco a poco • **it's going to be a steep ~ curve** va a ser un proceso de aprendizaje rápido ▸ **learning difficulties** dificultades *fpl* de aprendizaje ▸ **learning disability** • **to have a ~ disability** tener dificultades de aprendizaje • **people with ~ disabilities** personas con dificultades de aprendizaje
learning-disabled [,lɜ:nɪŋdɪs'eɪbld] ADJ (*US*) con dificultades de aprendizaje • **to be learning-disabled** tener dificultades de aprendizaje
learnt [lɜ:nt] (*esp Brit*) PT, PP *of* **learn**
lease [li:s] N contrato *m* de arrendamiento • **to take a house on a 99-year ~** alquilar una casa con un contrato de arrendamiento de 99 años • **to let sth out on ~** arrendar algo, dar algo en arriendo • IDIOMS: • **to give sb a new ~ of life** hacer revivir a algn • **to take on a new ~ of life** [*person*] recobrar su vigor; [*thing*] renovarse
VT (= *take*) arrendar (**from** de), tomar en arriendo; (= *rent*) alquilar; (= *give*) (*also* **lease out**) arrendar, alquilar, dar en arriendo
▸ **lease back** VT + ADV subarrendar
leaseback ['li:sbæk] N rearrendamiento *m* al vendedor, subarriendo *m*
leasehold ['li:shəʊld] N (= *contract*) derechos *mpl* de arrendamiento; (= *property*) inmueble *m* arrendado
CPD [*property, house, flat*] arrendado, alquilado ▸ **leasehold reform** reforma *f* del sistema de arriendos
leaseholder ['li:shəʊldə^r] N arrendatario/a *m/f*
leash [li:ʃ] N correa *f*, traílla *f*; ▹ **strain[1]**
leasing ['li:sɪŋ] N (= *option to buy*) alquiler *m* con opción a compra, leasing *m*; (= *renting*) arrendamiento *m*, alquiler *m*; (*Econ*) arrendamiento *m* financiero
least [li:st] ADJ **1** (*superl of* **little[2]**) **a** (= *minimum, smallest amount of*) menor • **with the ~ possible delay** con el menor retraso posible, a la mayor brevedad posible (*frm*) • **choose yoghurts which contain the ~ fat** elija los yogures que contengan la menor cantidad de grasa • **he didn't have the ~ difficulty deciding** no le costó nada decidir
b (= *smallest, slightest*) [*idea, hint, complaint*] más mínimo • **she wasn't the ~ bit jealous** no estaba celosa en lo más mínimo • **we haven't the ~ idea where he is** no tenemos la más mínima *or* la menor idea de dónde está • **the ~ thing upsets her** se ofende a la mínima *or* por lo más mínimo; ▹ **last[1], line[1]**
2 (*in comparisons*) menos • **he has the ~ money** es el que menos dinero tiene
PRON **1** (*superl of* **little[2]**) **a** (= *the very minimum*) (*gen*) lo menos; (= *amount*) lo mínimo • **"thanks, anyway" — "it was the ~ I could do"** —gracias de todas formas —era lo menos que podía hacer • **what's the ~ you are willing to accept?** ¿qué es lo mínimo que estás dispuesto a aceptar? • **that's the ~ of it** eso es lo de menos • **the ~ said the better** cuanto menos se hable de eso mejor • **accommodation was basic to say the ~** el alojamiento era muy sencillo, por no decir otra cosa • PROVERB: • **~ said, soonest mended** cuanto menos se diga, antes se arregla
b (*in comparisons*) • **the country that spends the ~ on education** el país que menos (se) gasta en materia de enseñanza • **that's the ~ of my worries** eso es lo que menos me preocupa
2 • **in the ~**: • **I don't mind in the ~** no me importa lo más mínimo • **Pete wasn't in the ~ in love with me** Pete no estaba ni mucho menos enamorado de mí • **"don't you mind?" — "not in the ~"** —¿no te importa? —en absoluto *or* —para nada
3 • **at ~ a** (= *not less than*) por lo menos, como mínimo, al menos • **I must have slept for at ~ 12 hours** debo de haber dormido por lo menos *or* como mínimo *or* al menos 12 horas • **he earns at ~ as much as you do** gana por lo menos *or* al menos tanto como tú
b (= *if nothing more*) al menos, por lo menos • **we can at ~ try** al menos *or* por lo menos podemos intentarlo
c (= *for all that*) por lo menos, al menos • **it's rather laborious but at ~ it is not dangerous** requiere bastante trabajo pero por lo menos *or* al menos no es peligroso
d (= *anyway*) al menos, por lo menos • **Etta appeared to be asleep, at ~ her eyes were shut** Etta parecía estar dormida, al menos *or* por lo menos tenía los ojos cerrados
e • **at the (very) ~** como mínimo, como poco
ADV menos • **the ~ expensive car** el coche menos caro • **they're the ones who need it the ~** son los que menos lo necesitan • **when ~ expected** cuando menos se espera • **~ of all me** y yo menos, yo menos que nadie • **no one knew, ~ of all me** nadie lo sabía, y yo menos • **for a variety of reasons, not ~ because it is cheap** por toda una serie de razones, entre ellas que es barato
leastways* ['li:stweɪz] ADV de todos modos
leastwise ['li:stwaɪz] ADV por lo menos
least-worst ['li:stwɜ:st] ADJ menos malo • **the least-worst scenario** el panorama menos malo (de todos)
leather ['leðə^r] N **1** (= *hide*) cuero *m*, piel *f*
2 (= *washleather*) gamuza *f*
3 leathers (*for motorcyclist*) ropa *f* de cuero
VT (= *thrash*) zurrar*
CPD de cuero, de piel ▸ **leather goods** artículos *mpl* de cuero ▸ **leather jacket** cazadora *f* de cuero *or* de piel
leather-bound ['leðə,baʊnd] ADJ encuadernado en cuero
leatherette [,leðə'ret] N cuero *m* sintético, piel *f* sintética, polipiel *f*
leathering* ['leðərɪŋ] N • **to give sb a ~** dar una paliza a algn
leathern (*liter*) ['leðə(:)n] ADJ de cuero
leatherneck* ['leðənek] N (*US*) infante *m* de marina
leathery ['leðərɪ] ADJ [*meat*] correoso; [*skin*] curtido
leave [li:v] (VB: PT, PP: **left**) N **1** (*frm*) (= *permission*) permiso *m* • **to ask ~ to do sth** pedir permiso para hacer algo • **by your ~†** con permiso de usted • **without so much as a "by your ~"** sin pedir permiso a nadie • **I take ~ to doubt it** me permito dudarlo
2 (= *permission to be absent*) permiso *m*; (*Mil*) (*brief*) permiso *m*; (*lengthy, compassionate*) licencia *f* • **~ of absence** permiso *m* para ausentarse • **to be on ~** estar de permiso *or* (*S. Cone*) licenciado
3 (= *departure*) • **to take (one's) ~ (of sb)** despedirse (de algn) • **to take ~ of one's senses** perder el juicio • **have you taken ~ of your senses?** ¿te has vuelto loco?
VT **1** (= *go away from*) dejar, marcharse de; [+ *room*] salir de, abandonar; [+ *hospital*] salir de; [+ *person*] abandonar, dejar • **I'll ~ you at the station** te dejo en la estación • **I must ~ you** tengo que despedirme *or* marcharme • **you may ~ us** (*frm*) puede retirarse (*frm*) • **she ~s home at 8am** sale de casa a las ocho • **he left home when he was 18** se fue de casa a los 18 años • **to ~ one's post** (*improperly*) abandonar su puesto • **to ~ the rails** descarrilar, salirse de las vías • **the car left the road** el coche se salió de la carretera • **to ~ school** (= *finish studies*) terminar el colegio • **to ~ the table** levantarse de la mesa • **he has left his wife** ha dejado *or* abandonado a su mujer

2 (= *forget*) dejar, olvidar
3 (= *bequeath*) dejar, legar
4 (= *allow to remain*) dejar • **to ~ two pages blank** dejar dos páginas en blanco • **to ~ things lying about** dejar las cosas de cualquier modo • **it's best to ~ him alone** es mejor dejarlo solo • **to ~ sb alone** *or* **in peace** dejar a algn en paz • **let's ~ it at that** dejémoslo así, ¡ya está bien (así)! • **this left me free for the afternoon** eso me dejó la tarde libre • **to ~ one's greens** no comer las verduras • **to ~ a good impression on sb** producir a algn una buena impresión • **it ~s much to be desired** deja mucho que desear • **to ~ one's supper** dejar la cena sin comer • **take it or ~ it** lo tomas o lo dejas • **~ it to me!** ¡yo me encargo!, ¡tú, déjamelo a mí! • **I'll ~ it up to you** lo dejo a tu criterio • **I ~ it to you to judge** júzguelo usted • **he ~s a wife and a child** le sobreviven su viuda y un hijo, deja mujer y un hijo • **to ~ sth with sb** dejar algo en manos de algn, entregar algo a algn • **I left the children with my mother** dejé los niños con mi madre • **~ it with me** yo me encargaré del asunto
5 • **to be left** (= *remain*) quedar • **there's nothing left** no queda nada • **how many are (there) left?** ¿cuántos quedan? • **we were left with four** quedamos con cuatro, nos quedaron cuatro • **nothing was left for me but to sell it** no tuve más remedio que venderlo • **there are three left over** sobran tres • **all the money I have left** todo el dinero que me queda
6 (*Math*) • **three from ten ~s seven** diez menos tres son siete, de tres a diez van siete
VI (*go out*) salir; (*go away*) [*person*] irse, marcharse, partir; [*train, bus*] salir • **the train is leaving in ten minutes** el tren sale dentro de diez minutos

▸ **leave about, leave around** VT + ADV dejar tirado
▸ **leave aside** VT + ADV dejar de lado • **leaving that aside, let's consider ...** dejando eso de lado, consideremos ...
▸ **leave behind** VT + ADV **1** (= *not take*) [+ *person*] dejar, no llevar consigo • **we had to ~ the furniture behind** no pudimos llevarnos los muebles • **we have left all that behind us** (*fig*) todo eso ha quedado atrás *or* ya es historia
2 (= *forget*) olvidarse
3 (= *outdistance*) dejar atrás
▸ **leave in** VT + ADV [+ *passage, words*] dejar tal como está/estaba, conservar; [+ *plug*] dejar puesto
▸ **leave off** VT + ADV **1** omitir, no incluir
2 [+ *lid*] no poner, dejar sin poner; [+ *clothes*] no ponerse
3 [+ *gas*] no poner, no encender; [+ *light*] dejar apagado
4* (= *stop*) [+ *work*] terminar, suspender • **to ~ off smoking** dejar de fumar • **to ~ off working** dejar *or* terminar de trabajar • **when it ~s off raining** cuando deje de llover • **we'll carry on where we left off last time** continuaremos por donde quedamos la última vez
VI + ADV* (= *stop*) parar • **when the rain ~s off** cuando deje de llover • **~ off, will you!** ¡déjalo!
▸ **leave on** VT + ADV [+ *clothes*] dejar puesto, no quitarse; [+ *light, TV*] dejar encendido *or* (*LAm*) prendido • **to ~ one's hat on** seguir con el sombrero puesto, no quitarse el sombrero
▸ **leave out** VT + ADV **1** (= *omit*) [+ *word, passage*] (*on purpose*) omitir; (*accidentally*) omitir, saltarse; [+ *person*] dejar fuera, excluir • **nobody wanted to be left out** nadie quería quedar fuera • **he feels left out** se siente excluido • IDIOM: • **~ it out!** (*Brit*‡) ¡venga ya!*, ¡no me vengas con esas!*, ¡tírate de la moto! (*Sp*‡)
2 (= *not put back*) no devolver a su lugar, no guardar; (= *leave outside*) dejar fuera • **it got left out in the rain** quedó fuera bajo la lluvia • **the cat was left out all night** el gato pasó toda la noche fuera
3 (= *leave ready*) [+ *food, meal*] dejar preparado
▸ **leave over** VT + ADV **1** (*after use*) • **she saved whatever was left over of her wages** ahorraba lo que le sobraba del sueldo • **there is some wine left over from the party** queda un poco de vino de la fiesta • **these are hang-ups left over from his childhood** eso son traumas de su niñez; ▹ **leave**
2 (= *postpone*) dejar, aplazar

leaven ['levn] N levadura *f*; (*fig*) toque *m*
VT leudar; (*fig*) (= *enliven*) aligerar
leavening ['levnɪŋ] N levadura *f*; (*fig*) toque *m*
leaves [li:vz] NPL *of* **leaf**
leave-taking ['li:vˌteɪkɪŋ] N despedida *f*
leaving ['li:vɪŋ] N (= *departure*) salida *f*
CPD [*ceremony, present*] de despedida
leavings ['li:vɪŋz] NPL sobras *fpl*, restos *mpl*
Lebanese [ˌlebə'ni:z] ADJ libanés
N libanés/esa *m/f*
Lebanon ['lebənən] N • **the ~** el Líbano
lech* [letʃ] N libidinoso *m*
VI • **to ~ after sb: he's ~ing after his secretary** se le van los ojos detrás de su secretaria*, se le alegran las pajarillas cuando ve a su secretaria (*hum*)
lecher ['letʃəʳ] N libidinoso *m*
lecherous ['letʃərəs] ADJ lascivo, lujurioso
lecherously ['letʃərəslɪ] ADV lascivamente
lechery ['letʃərɪ] N lascivia *f*, lujuria *f*
lectern ['lektə(:)n] N atril *m*; (*Rel*) facistol *m*
lector ['lektɔ:ʳ] N (*Univ*) profesor(a) *m/f* de universidad
lecture ['lektʃəʳ] N **1** (*Univ*) clase *f*; (*by visitor*) conferencia *f*; (*less formal*) charla *f* • **to attend ~s on** dar *or* recibir clases de, seguir un curso sobre *or* de • **to give a ~** dar una conferencia; (*less formal*) dar una charla
2 (*fig*) sermón *m* • **I gave him a ~ on good manners** le eché un sermón sobre buenos modales
VI • **to ~ (in** *or* **on sth)** dar clases (de algo) • **she ~s in Law** da clases de derecho • **he ~s at Princeton** es profesor en Princeton
VT (= *scold*) sermonear
CPD ▸ **lecture hall** (*Univ*) aula *f*; (*gen*) sala *f* de conferencias ▸ **lecture notes** apuntes *mpl* de clase ▸ **lecture room, lecture theatre** = **lecture hall**
lecturer ['lektʃərəʳ] N (= *visitor*) conferenciante *mf*; (*Brit*) (*Univ*) profesor(a) *m/f*
lectureship ['lektʃəʃɪp] N cargo *m or* puesto *m* de profesor (adjunto)
LED N ABBR = **light-emitting diode**
led [led] PT, PP *of* **lead²**
-led [-ˌled] SUFFIX **1** (*controlled by a specific group*) • **student-led** dirigido por estudiantes • **German-led** bajo dirección alemana
2 (*influenced by a particular factor*) • **export-led growth** crecimiento debido a las exportaciones • **a market-led economy** una economía dominada por el mercado
ledge [ledʒ] N (*on wall, of window*) alféizar *m*; (= *shelf*) repisa *f*, anaquel *m*; (*on mountain*) saliente *m*, cornisa *f*
ledger ['ledʒəʳ] N libro *m* mayor
ledger line ['ledʒəˌlaɪn] N línea *f* suplementaria
lee [li:] N sotavento *m*; (= *shelter*) abrigo *m*, socaire *m* • **in the lee of** al socaire *or* abrigo de
ADJ de sotavento
leech [li:tʃ] N sanguijuela *f* (*also fig*) • IDIOM: • **to stick to sb like a ~** pegarse a algn como una lapa*
leek [li:k] N puerro *m*
leer [lɪəʳ] N mirada *f* lasciva • **he said with a ~** dijo con una sonrisa lasciva
VI mirar de manera lasciva • **to ~ at sb** lanzar una mirada lasciva a algn
leery ['lɪərɪ] ADJ (= *cautious*) cauteloso; (= *suspicious*) receloso • **to be ~ of sth/sb** recelar de algo/algn
lees [li:z] NPL heces *fpl*, poso *m*
leeward ['li:wəd] ADJ (*Naut*) de sotavento
ADV a sotavento
N (*Naut*) sotavento *m* • **to ~** a sotavento (**of** de)
Leeward Isles ['li:wədˌaɪlz] NPL islas *fpl* de Sotavento
leeway ['li:weɪ] N (*Naut*) deriva *f*; (*fig*) (= *scope*) libertad *f* de acción • **that doesn't give me much ~** (= *scope*) eso no me deja mucha libertad de acción; (= *time to spare*) eso no me deja mucho margen de tiempo
left¹ [left] PT, PP *of* **leave**
left² [left] ADJ **1** izquierdo • **~ shoe** zapato *m* (del pie) izquierdo • **take a ~ turn** gira a la izquierda • IDIOM: • **to have two ~ feet*** ser un patoso*
2 (*Pol*) de izquierda, de izquierdas (*Sp*)
ADV [*turn, look*] a la izquierda • IDIOMS: • **~, right and centre** • **~ and right** (*US*) a diestra y siniestra, a diestro y siniestro (*Sp*) • **they owe money ~, right and centre** deben dinero a todos, tienen deudas por doquier
N **1** (= *left side*) izquierda *f* • **turn it to the ~** [+ *key, knob*] gíralo a la izquierda • **pictured from ~ to right are ...** de izquierda a derecha vemos a ... • **the third from the ~** el tercero empezando por la izquierda • **on** *or* **to my, your** *etc* **~** a mi, tu *etc* izquierda • **on the ~** a la izquierda • **it's on the ~ as you go in** está a la izquierda según entras • **it's the first/second door on the ~** es la primera/segunda puerta a la izquierda • **to drive on the ~** conducir *or* (*LAm*) manejar por la izquierda • **"keep left"** "manténgase a la izquierda"
2 (= *left turning*) • **take the next ~** toma la próxima a la izquierda
3 (*Boxing*) (= *left hand*) izquierda *f*; (= *punch*) izquierdazo *m*, golpe *m* de izquierda *or* con la izquierda
4 • **the ~** (*Pol*) la izquierda • **the parties of the ~** los partidos de izquierda *or* (*Sp*) izquierdas
CPD ▸ **left back** (*Sport*) (= *player*) lateral *mf* izquierdo/a; (= *position*) lateral *m* izquierdo ▸ **left field** (*Baseball*) (= *area*) jardín *m* izquierdo; (= *position*) jardinero/a *m/f* izquierdo/a • **to come out of ~ field** (*esp US**) (*fig*) • **his question/decision came out of ~ field** su pregunta/decisión me/le *etc* pilló desprevenido ▸ **left half** (*Sport*) (= *player*) lateral *mf* izquierdo/a; (= *position*) lateral *m* izquierdo ▸ **left wing** (*Sport*) banda *f* izquierda; (*Pol*) ala *f* izquierda; ▹ **left-wing**
left-click ['leftklɪk] VI cliquear con la parte izquierda del ratón (**on** en)
VT • **to ~ an icon** cliquear en un icono con la parte izquierda del ratón
left-hand ['lefthænd] ADJ • **left-hand drive: a left-hand drive car** un coche con el volante a la izquierda • **is it a left-hand drive?** ¿tiene el volante a la izquierda? • **left-hand page** página *f* izquierda • **left-hand side** lado *m* izquierdo, izquierda *f* • **the house is on the left-hand side** la casa está a la izquierda *or* en el lado izquierdo • **on the left-hand side of the road** en el lado izquierdo de la carretera • **left-hand turn** vuelta *f* a la izquierda • **to make a left-hand turn** girar a

la izquierda
left-handed ['left'hændɪd] ADJ [*person*] zurdo; [*shot, stroke*] (realizado) con la (mano) izquierda; [*tool*] para zurdos; (*fig*) [*compliment*] con doble sentido, ambiguo
left-hander [,left'hændəʳ] N (= *person*) zurdo/a *m/f*; (= *blow*) izquierdazo *m*
leftie* ['leftɪ] N (*Brit*) izquierdista *mf*
leftish ['leftɪʃ] ADJ izquierdista • **his views are ~** es de ideas izquierdistas
leftism ['leftɪzəm] N izquierdismo *m*
leftist ['leftɪst] ADJ, N izquierdista *mf*
left-justify ['left,dʒʌstɪfaɪ] VT justificar a la izquierda
left-luggage ['left'lʌgɪdʒ] N (*also* **left-luggage office**) (*Brit*) consigna *f*
CPD ▸ **left-luggage locker** (*Brit*) consigna *f* automática ▸ **left-luggage office** consigna *f*
leftover ['leftəʊvəʳ] ADJ sobrante, restante • **we used up the ~ turkey** usamos el pavo que había sobrado
N **1** (= *relic*) • **a ~ from another age** una reliquia de otra edad
2 leftovers sobras *fpl*, restos *mpl*
leftward ['leftwəd] ADJ [*movement*] a *or* hacia la izquierda
ADV [*move*] a *or* hacia la izquierda
leftwards ['leftwədz] ADV (*esp Brit*) = **leftward**
left-wing ['left,wɪŋ] ADJ (*Pol*) de izquierda, izquierdista, de izquierdas (*Sp*)
left-winger ['left'wɪŋəʳ] N (*Pol*) izquierdista *mf*; (*Sport*) delantero/a *m/f* izquierdo/a
lefty* ['leftɪ] N (*Brit*) izquierdista *mf*, rojillo/a *m/f*
leg [leg] N **1** [*of person*] pierna *f*; [*of animal, bird, insect*] pata *f*; [*of furniture*] (= *one of set*) pata *f*; (= *central support*) pie *m*; [*of trousers*] pernera *f*; [*of stocking*] caña *f* • **artificial leg** pierna *f* ortopédica *or* artificial • **wooden leg** pierna *f* de madera, pata *f* de palo* • **he was the fastest thing on two legs** era rápido donde los haya • **to give sb a leg up** (*Brit**) (*lit*) aupar a algn; (*fig*) dar un empujoncito a algn*, echar un cable a algn* • IDIOMS: • **to get one's** *or* **a leg over**‡ (*hum*) (= *have sex*) darse un revolcón* • **to have legs*** (= *have potential*) tener potencial; (= *be promising*) prometer • **to be on its/one's last legs*** estar en las últimas • **the company is on its last legs** la compañía está en las últimas* • **the washing machine is on its last legs** la lavadora está en las últimas* • **to pull sb's leg** tomar el pelo a algn • **to shake a leg** (= *hurry*) espabilarse; (= *dance*) menear *or* mover el esqueleto* • **show a leg!*** ¡a levantarse! • **he hasn't got a leg to stand on** (*in case, argument*) no tiene donde agarrarse*
2 (*Culin*) [*of lamb, mutton, pork*] pierna *f*; [*of chicken, turkey*] muslo *m*, pata *f* • **frogs' legs** ancas *fpl* de rana
3 (= *stage*) [*of journey*] tramo *m*, etapa *f*; [*of race*] etapa *f*, manga *f*; [*of championship*] vuelta *f*
VT* • **to leg it** (= *go on foot*) ir a pata*; (= *run*) echarse una carrera*; (= *run away*) salir por piernas *or* patas*
CPD ▸ **leg bone** tibia *f* ▸ **leg iron** (*Med*) aparato *m* ortopédico ▸ **leg irons** (*for prisoner*) grilletes *mpl* ▸ **leg muscles** músculos *mpl* de las piernas ▸ **leg room** sitio *m* para las piernas
legacy ['legəsɪ] N legado *m*; (*fig*) legado *m*, herencia *f* • **this inflation is a ~ of the previous government** esta inflación es un legado del gobierno anterior
legal ['li:gəl] ADJ **1** (= *judicial*) [*error*] judicial; [*document*] legal; [*firm*] de abogados; [*question, matter*] legal, jurídico • **to take ~ action** poner una denuncia • **to take ~ action against sb** poner una denuncia a algn, presentar una demanda (judicial) contra algn • **to take ~ advice** consultar a un abogado • **~ adviser** asesor(a) *m/f* jurídico/a • **~ battle** contienda *f* judicial *or* legal, pleito *m* • **~ costs** *or* **fees** costas *fpl*, gastos *mpl* judiciales • **~ department** (*of bank, company*) departamento *m* jurídico • **to be above** *or* **over the ~ limit** estar por encima del límite permitido por ley • **to be below** *or* **under the ~ limit** estar por debajo del límite permitido por ley • **~ loophole** laguna *f* en la legislación, resquicio *m* legal • **~ proceedings** procedimiento *m* jurídico, pleito *m* • **to start** *or* **initiate ~ proceedings against sb** entablar un pleito contra algn • **the ~ process** el proceso judicial *or* jurídico • **the ~ profession** la abogacía • **to enter the ~ profession** hacerse abogado • **they were allowed no ~ representation** no les permitieron que un abogado les representara
2 (= *lawful*) [*activity, action*] legal, legítimo; [*owner*] legítimo; (= *under the law*) [*right, protection*] legal • **to be ~ to do sth** ser legal hacer algo • **to have the ~ authority to do sth** tener la autoridad *or* el poder legal para hacer algo • **to make sth ~** legalizar algo • **they decided to make it ~*** (= *get married*) decidieron formalizar *or* legalizar su relación
CPD ▸ **legal aid** asistencia *f* de un abogado de oficio ▸ **legal currency** = **legal tender** ▸ **legal high** droga *f* legal ▸ **legal holiday** (*US*) fiesta *f* oficial, día *m* festivo oficial, (día *m*) feriado *m* (*LAm*) ▸ **legal offence, legal offense** (*US*) delito *m* contra la ley ▸ **legal opinion** dictamen *m* jurídico ▸ **legal system** sistema *m* jurídico ▸ **legal tender** (*Econ*) moneda *f* de curso legal
legalese [,li:gə'li:z] N jerga *f* legal
legalistic [,li:gə'lɪstɪk] ADJ legalista
legality [lɪ'gælɪtɪ] N legalidad *f*
legalization [,li:gəlaɪ'zeɪʃən] N legalización *f*
legalize ['li:gəlaɪz] VT [+ *document, political party*] legalizar; [+ *drugs, euthanasia, abortion*] legalizar, despenalizar • **to ~ one's position** legalizar la situación
legally ['li:gəlɪ] ADV **1** (= *from a legal point of view*) [*obliged, required*] por ley; [*entitled*] legalmente, según la ley • **~, the whole issue is a nightmare** desde el punto de vista legal, toda esa cuestión es una pesadilla • **this contract is ~ binding** el contrato vincula jurídicamente, el contrato implica obligatoriedad jurídica • **to be ~ responsible for sth/sb** ser legalmente responsable *or* el/la responsable legal de algo/algn
2 (= *lawfully*) legalmente • **their wealth was ~ acquired** consiguieron su riqueza por medios legales *or* legalmente
legate ['legɪt] N legado *m*
legatee [,legə'ti:] N legatario/a *m/f*
legation [lɪ'geɪʃən] N legación *f*
legato [lɪ'gɑ:təʊ] (*Mus*) ADJ ligado
ADV ligado
N ligadura *f*
legend ['ledʒənd] N leyenda *f* • **she was a ~ in her own lifetime** fue una leyenda en su vida, fue un mito viviente
legendary ['ledʒəndərɪ] ADJ legendario
legerdemain ['ledʒədə'meɪn] N juego *m* de manos, prestidigitación *f*
-legged ['legɪd] ADJ (*ending in compounds*) [*person*] de piernas…; [*animal*] de patas…; [*stool*] de tres patas • **long-legged** de piernas largas, zancudo • **three-legged** de tres piernas
leggings ['legɪŋz] NPL mallas *fpl*, leotardos *mpl*; (*baby's*) pantalones *mpl* polainas
leggo‡ [le'gəʊ] EXCL = **let go** ▹ **go**
leggy ['legɪ] ADJ (COMPAR: **leggier**, SUPERL: **leggiest**) [*person*] de piernas largas, patilargo*; (= *attractive*) [*girl*] de piernas bonitas, de piernas atractivas
Leghorn ['leg'hɔ:n] N Livorno *m*; (*Hist*) Liorna *f*
legibility [,ledʒɪ'bɪlɪtɪ] N legibilidad *f*
legible ['ledʒəbl] ADJ legible
legibly ['ledʒəblɪ] ADV legiblemente
legion ['li:dʒən] N legión *f* (*also fig*) • **they are ~** son legión, son muchos

LEGION
La **American Legion** es una organización de veteranos de las Fuerzas Armadas estadounidenses. Se fundó después de la Primera Guerra Mundial y se encarga del cuidado y la reintegración de los veteranos de guerra y sus familias. También es un órgano de presión ante el Congreso en favor de los intereses de los veteranos y de un sólido sistema de defensa nacional. A otro nivel, la **American Legion** ha creado clubs sociales para sus miembros.
En el Reino Unido el equivalente de la **American Legion** es la **British Legion** que, todos los años en noviembre, recauda fondos mediante la venta de amapolas de papel.
▹ **POPPY DAY**

legionary ['li:dʒənərɪ] ADJ legionario
N legionario *m*
legionnaire [,li:dʒə'nɛəʳ] N legionario *m*
• **~'s disease** enfermedad *f* del legionario, legionella *f*
legislate ['ledʒɪsleɪt] VI legislar • **one cannot ~ for every case** es imposible legislarlo todo
VT • **to ~ sth out of existence** hacer que algo desaparezca a base de legislación
legislation [,ledʒɪs'leɪʃən] N (= *law*) ley *f*; (= *body of laws*) legislación *f*
legislative ['ledʒɪslətɪv] ADJ legislativo
CPD ▸ **legislative action** acción *f* legislativa ▸ **legislative body** cuerpo *m* legislativo
legislator ['ledʒɪsleɪtəʳ] N legislador(a) *m/f*
legislature ['ledʒɪslətʃəʳ] N asamblea *f* legislativa, legislatura *f* (*LAm*)
legist ['li:dʒɪst] N legista *mf*
legit* [lə'dʒɪt] ADJ • **I checked him out, he's ~** he hecho averiguaciones y es de fiar, he hecho averiguaciones y es un tipo legal (*Sp**) • **to go ~** legalizar la situación
legitimacy [lɪ'dʒɪtɪməsɪ] N **1** (= *lawfulness*) [*of government, action, birth*] legitimidad *f*
2 (= *justifiableness*) [*of concern*] justificación; [*of argument*] validez *f* • **there can be no doubt as to the ~ of such claims** no cabe duda de que estas reclamaciones están justificadas
legitimate [lɪ'dʒɪtɪmɪt] ADJ **1** (= *lawful*) [*government, right, power*] legítimo; [*business*] legal • **he has a ~ claim to the property** tiene el derecho legítimo de reivindicar la propiedad
2 (= *valid*) [*reason, argument, target*] válido; [*complaint, conclusion*] justificado; [*interest*] legítimo • **it is perfectly ~ to ask questions** preguntar está perfectamente justificado
3 (*Jur*) [*son, daughter*] legítimo
VT = **legitimize**
legitimately [lɪ'dʒɪtɪmɪtlɪ] ADV **1** (= *lawfully*) legítimamente
2 (= *justifiably*) [*expect*] justificadamente • **you could ~ argue that …** sería justo *or* estaría justificado argumentar que … • **he can ~ claim to speak for all South Africans** tiene sobradas razones para erigirse en portavoz

de todos los sudafricanos • **he has demanded, quite ~, that …** ha exigido, con toda la razón, que …

legitimation [lɪˌdʒɪtɪˈmeɪʃn] N legitimación *f*

legitimize [lɪˈdʒɪtɪmaɪz] VT legitimar; [*+ child, birth*] legalizar

legless [ˈleglɪs] ADJ **1** (= *without legs*) [*person*] sin piernas; [*animal*] sin patas
2 (*Brit**) (= *drunk*) como una cuba*

legman [ˈlegmæn] N (PL: **legmen**) reportero/a *m/f*

leg-pull* [ˈlegpʊl] N broma *f*, tomadura *f* de pelo*

leg-puller* [ˈlegpʊləʳ] N bromista *mf*

leg-pulling* [ˈlegˌpʊlɪŋ] N tomadura *f* de pelo*

legroom [ˈlegru:m] N sitio *m* para las piernas

legume [ˈlegju:m] N (= *species*) legumbre *f*; (= *pod*) vaina *f*

leguminous [leˈgju:mɪnəs] ADJ leguminoso

legwarmers [ˈlegˌwɔ:məz] NPL calentadores *mpl* (de piernas)

legwork [ˈlegwɜ:k] N trabajo *m* de campo, preparativos *mpl* • **to do the ~** hacer los preparativos

Leics. ABBR (*Brit*) = **Leicestershire**

leisure [ˈleʒəʳ], (*US*) [ˈli:ʒəʳ] N ocio *m* • **a life of ~** una vida de ocio, una vida ociosa • **do it at your ~** hazlo cuando tengas tiempo *or* te convenga • **to have the ~ to do sth** disponer de tiempo para hacer algo; ▹ **lady**
CPD ▸ **leisure activities** pasatiempos *mpl* ▸ **leisure centre** (*Brit*), **leisure complex** polideportivo *m* ▸ **leisure industry** sector *m* del ocio ▸ **leisure occupations, leisure pursuits** = leisure activities ▸ **leisure suit** chandal *m* ▸ **leisure time** tiempo *m* libre • **in one's ~ time** en sus ratos libres, en los momentos de ocio ▸ **leisure wear** ropa *f* de sport

leisured [ˈleʒəd] ADJ [*pace*] pausado; [*class*] acomodado

leisurely [ˈleʒəlɪ] ADJ [*stroll, swim, meal*] relajado, sin prisas • **at a ~ pace** sin prisas
ADV despacio, con calma

leitmotiv [ˈlaɪtməʊˌti:f] N leitmotiv *m*

lemma [ˈlemə] (PL: **lemmas** *or* **lemmata** [ˈlemətə]) N lema *m*

lemmatization [ˌlemətaɪˈzeɪʃən] N lematización *f*

lemmatize [ˈlemətaɪz] VT lematizar

lemmatizer [ˈlemətaɪzəʳ] N lematizador *m*

lemming [ˈlemɪŋ] N lem(m)ing *m* • **they were jumping over the side of the ship like ~s** se lanzaban por la borda uno tras otro

lemon [ˈlemən] N **1** (= *fruit*) limón *m*; (= *tree*) limonero *m*; (= *drink*) limonada *f*
2* bobo/a *m/f* • **I felt a bit of a ~** me sentí como un auténtico imbécil • **you ~!** ¡bobo!
ADJ [*colour*] amarillo limón (*inv*)
CPD ▸ **lemon cheese, lemon curd** crema *f* de limón ▸ **lemon grass** citronela *f*, hierba *f* (de) limón, caña *f* santa, caña *f* (de) limón, zacate *m* (de) limón (*Mex, CAm*) ▸ **lemon grove** limonar *m* ▸ **lemon juice** zumo *m or* (*LAm*) jugo *m* de limón ▸ **lemon squash** limonada *f* (*sin burbujas*) ▸ **lemon sole** (*Brit*) platija *f* ▸ **lemon squeezer** exprimelimones *m inv*, exprimidor *m* ▸ **lemon tea** té *m* con limón ▸ **lemon tree** limonero *m* ▸ **lemon yellow** amarillo limón *m inv*; ▹ **lemon-yellow**

lemonade [ˌleməˈneɪd] N limonada *f*, gaseosa *f* (*Sp*)

lemony [ˈlemənɪ] ADJ a limón • **the salad dressing was too ~** el aliño de la ensalada sabía demasiado a limón

lemon-yellow [ˌlemənˈjeləʊ] ADJ amarillo limón (*inv*) • **a lemon-yellow blouse** una blusa amarillo limón; ▹ **lemon yellow**

lemur [ˈli:məʳ] N lémur *m*

Len [len] N *familiar form of* **Leonard**

lend [lend] (PT, PP: **lent**) VT **1** (*as favour*) prestar, dejar • **to ~ sb sth** • **~ sth to sb** prestar algo a algn, dejar algo a algn
2 (*Econ*) [*bank, building society*] prestar
3 (= *give*) • **to ~ credibility to sth** conceder credibilidad a algo; ▹ **ear, hand, name, weight**
4 (*reflexive*) • **the system does not ~ itself to rapid reform** el sistema no se presta a una reforma rápida • **he refused to ~ himself to their scheming** se negó a colaborar en sus intrigas, no quiso prestarse a sus intrigas
VI (*Econ*) prestar dinero
▸ **lend out** VT + ADV prestar

lender [ˈlendəʳ] N **1** prestador(a) *m/f*; ▹ **borrower**
2 (*professional*) (= *person*) prestamista *mf*; (= *bank, building society*) entidad *f* crediticia *or* de crédito; ▹ **mortgage**

lending [ˈlendɪŋ] CPD ▸ **lending library** biblioteca *f* de préstamo ▸ **lending limit** límite *m* de crédito *or* de préstamos ▸ **lending policy** política *f* crediticia *or* de préstamos ▸ **lending rate** tipo *m* de interés sobre los préstamos

length [leŋ(k)θ] N **1** (= *size*) largo *m*, longitud *f* • **what is its ~?** • **what ~ is it?** ¿cuánto tiene *or* mide de largo? • **two pieces of cable of roughly equal** *or* **the same ~** dos trozos *mpl* de cable de aproximadamente el mismo largo *or* la misma longitud • **the tail was at least twice the ~ of the body** el rabo medía por lo menos el doble que el cuerpo • **his trousers were never the right ~ for him** los pantalones nunca le quedaban bien de largo • **it was two metres in ~** tenía *or* medía dos metros de largo • **they range in ~ from three to six metres** su longitud varía entre los tres y los seis metros • **they vary in ~** son de diferentes medidas; ▹ **measure**
2 (= *extent*) **a** [*of street, river, house*] • **the room runs the ~ of the house** la habitación tiene el largo de la casa • **he walked the ~ of the beach** recorrió toda la orilla de la playa • **I walked the entire ~ of the street** recorrí la calle de una punta a la otra • **I have travelled the ~ and breadth of the country** he viajado a lo largo y ancho del país, he viajado por todo el país; ▹ **arm¹**
b [*of book, letter, essay*] extensión *f* • **an essay 4,000 words in ~** un ensayo de 4.000 palabras (de extensión)
c • IDIOM: • **to go to great ~s to do sth** esforzarse mucho para hacer algo • **I'd go to any ~(s) to protect her** haría cualquier cosa por protegerla • **they went to extraordinary ~s to keep their relationship secret** llegaron a extremos insospechables para mantener su relación en secreto
3 (= *duration*) duración *f* • **a concert two hours in ~** un concierto de dos horas de duración • **~ of service** antigüedad *f*, años *mpl* de servicio • **we must reduce the ~ of time patients have to wait** tenemos que reducir el tiempo de espera de los pacientes • **you couldn't keep that effort up for any ~ of time** un esfuerzo así no se puede mantener (durante) mucho tiempo • **if you were outside for any ~ of time you'd freeze to death** si te quedases en la calle más de un cierto tiempo, morirías congelado
4 • **at ~** (= *finally*) finalmente, por fin; (= *in detail*) [*discuss*] detenidamente; [*explain*] con mucho detalle; [*write*] extensamente; (= *for a long time*) largo y tendido • **she spoke at (some) ~** habló largo y tendido • **he would quote Shakespeare at great ~** se recreaba dando interminables citas de Shakespeare
5 (= *piece*) [*of rope, wire, tubing*] trozo *m*, pedazo *m*; [*of cloth*] largo *m*, corte *m*; [*of track, road*] tramo *m* • **dress ~** largo *m* para vestido
6 [*of vowel, syllable*] duración *f*, cantidad *f* (*Tech*)
7 (*Sport*) (*in horse races*) cuerpo *m*; (*in rowing*) largo *m*; [*of pool*] largo *m* • **to win by half a ~/four ~s** ganar por medio cuerpo/cuatro cuerpos
CPD ▸ **length mark** (*Ling*) signo *m* de vocal larga

-length [leŋ(k)θ] ADJ (*ending in compounds*) • **ankle-length skirt** falda *f* por los tobillos • **elbow-length sleeves** medias mangas *fpl*; ▹ **feature-length, knee-length, shoulder-length**

lengthen [ˈleŋ(k)θən] VT [*+ dress, trousers*] alargar; [*+ term, period, life, jail sentence*] prolongar, alargar; (*Ling*) [*+ vowel*] alargar • **to ~ one's stride** alargar el paso
VI [*shadows, queue, skirts, days, nights*] alargarse; [*silence*] prolongarse • **the odds on us succeeding are ~ing** las probabilidades de que lo consigamos están disminuyendo

lengthily [ˈleŋ(k)θɪlɪ] ADV [*speak*] largo y tendido; [*write*] extensamente

lengthways [ˈleŋ(k)θˌweɪz], **lengthwise** [ˈleŋ(k)θˌwaɪz] ADV longitudinalmente, a lo largo • **to measure sth ~** medir el largo de algo
ADJ longitudinal, de largo

lengthy [ˈleŋ(k)θɪ] ADJ (COMPAR: **lengthier**, SUPERL: **lengthiest**) **1** (= *long-lasting*) [*war, illness, process*] largo, prolongado; [*investigation*] largo, extenso • **~ delays** retrasos *mpl* considerables • **he still has a ~ wait for his treatment** aún tiene que esperar mucho para su tratamiento
2 (= *extensive*) [*article, speech, interview*] largo, extenso
3 (= *long and boring*) interminable

lenience [ˈli:nɪəns], **leniency** [ˈli:nɪənsɪ] N indulgencia *f*, benevolencia *f* • **to show leniency to** *or* **towards sb** ser *or* mostrarse indulgente con *or* hacia algn

lenient [ˈli:nɪənt] ADJ [*sentence, treatment*] benévolo, poco severo; [*person, attitude*] indulgente, poco severo • **to be ~ with sb** ser indulgente *or* poco severo con algn

leniently [ˈli:nɪəntlɪ] ADV con indulgencia, con benevolencia

Leningrad [ˈlenɪngræd] N (*Hist*) Leningrado *m*

Leninism [ˈlenɪnɪzəm] N leninismo *m*

Leninist [ˈlenɪnɪst] ADJ leninista
N leninista *mf*

lenitive [ˈlenɪtɪv] ADJ lenitivo

lens [lenz] N [*of spectacles*] lente *m or f*; [*of camera*] objetivo *m*; (= *handlens*) (*for stamps etc*) lupa *f*; (*Anat*) cristalino *m* • **contact ~** lente *m or f* de contacto, lentilla *f*
CPD ▸ **lens cap** tapa *f* de objetivo ▸ **lens hood** parasol *m* de objetivo

Lent [lent] N Cuaresma *f*

lent [lent] PT, PP *of* **lend**

Lenten [ˈlentən] ADJ cuaresmal

lentil [ˈlentl] N lenteja *f*
CPD ▸ **lentil soup** sopa *f* de lentejas

Leo [ˈli:əʊ] N **1** (= *sign, constellation*) Leo *m*
2 (= *person*) leo *mf* • **she's (a) Leo** es leo

Leon [ˈli:ɒn] N León *m*

Leonese [li:əˈni:z] ADJ leonés
N **1** (= *person*) leonés/esa *m/f*
2 (*Ling*) leonés *m*

leonine [ˈli:ənaɪn] ADJ leonino

leopard [ˈlepəd] N leopardo *m* • PROVERB: • **the ~ cannot change its spots** genio y figura hasta la sepultura

l

leopardess [ˈlepədes] (N) leopardo *m* hembra
leopardskin [ˈlepədskɪn] (N) piel *f* de leopardo • **a ~ coat** un abrigo de piel de leopardo
leotard [ˈlɪətɑːd] (N) malla *f*
leper [ˈlepəʳ] (N) leproso/a *m/f* (*also fig*)
(CPD) ▸ **leper colony** leprosería *f*, colonia *f* de leprosos
lepidoptera [ˌlepɪˈdɒptərə] (NPL) lepidópteros *mpl*
lepidopterist [ˌlepɪˈdɒptərɪst] (N) lepidopterólogo/a *m/f*
leprechaun [ˈleprəkɔːn] (N) (*Irl*) duende *m*
leprosy [ˈleprəsɪ] (N) lepra *f*
leprous [ˈleprəs] (ADJ) leproso
lesbian [ˈlezbɪən] (ADJ) lesbiano, lésbico
(N) lesbiana *f*
lesbianism [ˈlezbɪənɪzəm] (N) lesbianismo *m*
lesbo‡ [ˈlezbəʊ] (N) (PL: **lesbos**) (*pej*) tortillera* *f*, arepera *f* (*Col, Ven**), volteada *f* (*Mex**)
lèse-majesté, lese-majesty [ˈleɪzˈmæʒəstɪ] (N) lesa majestad *f*
lesion [ˈliːʒən] (N) lesión *f*
Lesotho [lɪˈsuːtuː] (N) Lesoto *m*
less [les] (ADJ) (COMPAR *of* **little²**) menos • **now we eat ~ bread** ahora comemos menos pan • **she has ~ time to spare now** ahora tiene menos tiempo libre • **of ~ importance** de menos importancia • **St James the Less** Santiago el Menor • **no ~ a person than the bishop** no otro que el obispo, el mismísimo obispo • **that was told me by the minister no ~** eso me lo dijo el mismo ministro
(PRON) menos • **it's ~ than you think** es menos de lo que piensas • **can't you let me have it for ~?** ¿no me lo puedes dar en menos? • **~ than £1/a kilo/three metres** menos de una libra/un kilo/tres metros • **at a price of ~ than £1** a un precio inferior *or* menor a una libra • **~ than a week ago** hace menos de una semana • **a tip of £10, no ~!** ¡una propina de 10 libras, nada menos! • **nothing ~ than** nada menos que • **it's nothing ~ than a disaster** es un verdadero *or* auténtico desastre • **the ~ ... the ~ ...** cuanto menos ... menos ... • **the ~ he works the ~ he earns** cuanto menos trabaja menos gana • **the ~ said about it the better** cuanto menos se hable de eso mejor
(ADV) menos • **to go out ~ (often)** salir menos • **you work ~ than I do** trabajas menos que yo • **grief grows ~ with time** la pena disminuye a medida que pasa el tiempo • **in ~ than an hour** en menos de una hora • **it's ~ expensive than the other one** cuesta menos que el otro • **~ and ~** cada vez menos • **that doesn't make her any ~ guilty** no por eso es menos culpable • **even ~** • **still ~** todavía menos, menos aún • **the problem is ~ one of capital than of personnel** el problema más que de capitales es de personal
(PREP) menos • **the price ~ 10%** el precio menos 10 por ciento • **the price ~ VAT** el precio excluyendo el IVA • **a year ~ four days** un año menos cuatro días

> **LESS THAN, FEWER THAN**
>
> **"Menos ... que" or "menos ... de"?**
>
> ▹ *Use* **menos** *with* **que** *before nouns and pronouns (provided they are not followed by clauses) as well as before adverbs and prepositions:*
>
> **He has less money than his sister**
> Tiene menos dinero que su hermana
> **He sells less/fewer than I do** *or* **than me**
> Vende menos que yo
> **These days I'm much less shy than before**
> Hoy en día soy mucho menos tímido que antes
>
> ▹ *Use* **menos ... de lo que/del que/de la que/de los que/de las que** *with following clauses:*
>
> **He earns less than I thought**
> Gana menos de lo que yo creía
> **They have 16 seats — five fewer than they had before these elections**
> Tienen 16 escaños — cinco menos de los que tenían antes de estas elecciones
> **It provides the body with fewer calories than it needs**
> Proporciona al organismo menos calorías de las que necesita
>
> ▹ *Use* **menos** *with* **de** *before* **lo** + *adjective/past participle:*
>
> **The price of wheat went up less than expected**
> El precio del trigo subió menos de lo previsto
>
> ▹ *Use* **menos** *with* **de** *in comparisons involving numbers or quantity:*
>
> **... in less than eight seconds ...**
> ... en menos de ocho segundos ...
> **You won't get it for less than 4,000 euros**
> No lo conseguirás por menos de 4.000 euros
>
> *NOTE: But use* **que** *instead in emphatic expressions like* **nada menos que** *and* **ni más ni menos que** *even when followed by numbers:*
>
> **They offered him no less than 100,000 euros a year!**
> ¡Le ofrecieron nada menos que *or* ni más ni menos que 100.000 euros al año!
>
> **A lot less, far fewer**
>
> ▹ *When translating* **a lot less, far fewer** *etc remember to make the* **mucho** *in* **mucho menos** *agree with any noun it describes or refers to:*
>
> **These bulbs use a lot less electricity than conventional ones**
> Estas bombillas gastan mucha menos electricidad que las normales
> **They have had far fewer opportunities than wealthy people**
> Han gozado de muchas menos oportunidades que la gente rica
>
> *For further uses and examples, see* **fewer, less**

...less [lɪs] (SUFFIX) sin • **coatless** sin abrigo • **hatless** sin sombrero
lessee [leˈsiː] (N) [*of house*] inquilino/a *m/f*; [*of land*] arrendatario/a *m/f*
lessen [ˈlesn] (VT) [+ *risk, danger*] reducir; [+ *pain*] aliviar; [+ *cost, stature*] rebajar • **it will ~ your chances of getting the job** disminuirá las posibilidades que tienes de conseguir el puesto
(VI) [*noise, anger, love*] disminuir; [*pain*] aliviarse
lessening [ˈlesnɪŋ] (N) disminución *f*, reducción *f*
lesser [ˈlesəʳ] (ADJ) (COMPAR *of* **less**) menor • **to a ~ extent** *or* **degree** en menor grado • **he pleaded guilty to the ~ charge** se declaró culpable del cargo menor • **the ~ of two evils** el menor de dos males
lesser-known [ˌlesəˈnəʊn] (ADJ) menos conocido
lesson [ˈlesn] (N) **1** (= *class*) clase *f* • **a French/tennis ~** una clase de francés/tenis • **to give swimming/piano ~s** dar clases de natación/piano • **to give (sb) private ~s in maths** dar (a algn) clases particulares de matemáticas • **she's having driving ~s** le están dando clases de conducir
2 (*in textbook*) lección *f*
3 (*fig*) lección *f* • **if there is a single ~ to be drawn from this, it is that ...** si hay algo que podemos aprender de esto, es que ... • **there are ~s to be learnt from this terrible tragedy** esta terrible tragedia nos debe servir de lección • **let that be a ~ to you!** ¡que te sirva de lección!, ¡para que aprendas! • **to teach sb a ~** dar una lección a algn • **his courage is a ~ to us all** su valor debe servirnos a todos de lección; ▹ **learn**
4 (*Rel*) lectura *f*
(CPD) ▸ **lesson plan** plan *m* de estudio
lessor [leˈsɔːʳ] (N) arrendador(a) *m/f*
lest [lest] (CONJ) (*frm or liter*) **1** (= *in order to prevent*) para que no (+ *subjun*) • **~ we forget** para que no nos olvidemos, no sea que nos olvidemos • **~ he catch me unprepared** para que no me coja *or* (*LAm*) agarre desprevenido
2 (= *in case*) • **I feared ~ he should fall** temía que fuera a caerse • **I didn't do it ~ somebody should object** no lo hice por miedo a que alguien pusiera peros
let¹ [let] (VT) (PT, PP: **let**) **1** (= *allow to*) **a** (*gen*) dejar, permitir (*more frm*) • **to let sb do sth** dejar *or* (*more frm*) permitir que algn haga algo, dejar *or* (*more frm*) permitir a algn hacer algo • **my parents wouldn't let me go out with boys** mis padres no dejaban que saliera con chicos, mis padres no me dejaban salir con chicos • **let me help you** déjeme ayudarle *or* que le ayude • **let me take your coat** permítame que tome su abrigo • **let me think** déjame pensar, a ver que piense • **don't let me forget to post the letters** recuérdame que eche las cartas al correo • **she wanted to help but her mother wouldn't let her** quería ayudar, pero su madre no la dejaba • **pride wouldn't let him talk about the situation** su orgullo no le permitía hablar de la situación • **to let o.s. be persuaded** dejarse persuadir • **don't let me catch you cheating again!** ¡no quiero volver a pillarte haciendo trampa!, ¡que no vuelva a pillarte haciendo trampa! • **you must let me be the judge of that** eso tengo que juzgarlo yo • **don't let me keep you** no quiero entretenerle • **now let me see** ¿a ver?, déjame que vea • **it's hard work, let me tell you** es mucho trabajo, te lo aseguro; ▹ **alone, be, go, rip**
b (*in prayers, wishes*) • **please don't let it rain** por favor, que no llueva • **don't let him die, she prayed** no dejes que se muera, le pidió a Dios
2 (= *cause to*) • **when can you let me have it?** ¿cuándo me lo puedes dejar? • **I'll let you have it back tomorrow** te lo devuelvo mañana • **he really let her have it about being late*** le echó una buena bronca por llegar tarde* • **to let it be known that** hacer saber que; ▹ **slip**
3 (+ *prep, adv*) • **they won't let you into the country** no te dejarán entrar en el país • **he let himself into the flat** entró en el piso • **he wouldn't let me past** no me dejaba pasar • **the barrier rose to let the car through** la barrera subió para dejar pasar el coche • **they wouldn't let us through the gate** no nos dejaban pasar en la entrada; ▹ **let in, let out, secret**
4 (= *forming imperative*) **a** (1st *person plural*) • **her**

then boyfriend (let's call him Dave) ... el entonces novio suyo (llamémosle *or* vamos a llamarle Dave) ... • **let's get out here** bajémonos aquí • **let's go!** ¡vámonos! • **let's go for a walk** vamos a dar un paseo • **let's not** *or* **don't let's jump to conclusions** no nos precipitemos a sacar conclusiones • **let us pray** (*frm*) oremos • **if you weigh, let's say, 175 pounds ...** si pesas, digamos, 175 libras ... • **let's say I'm very pleased with the results** digamos que estoy muy satisfecha con los resultados • **let's see, what was I saying?** a ver *or* déjame ver, ¿qué decía yo? • **"shall we eat now?" — "yes, let's"** —¿comemos ahora? —sí, venga *or* —sí, vale • **"shall we go home now?" — "yes, let's"** —¿nos vamos a casa ahora? —¡sí, vamos! *or* —¡sí, vámonos!
b (*forming 3rd-person imperative*) • **let them wait** que esperen • **"people may complain" — "let them"** —puede que la gente se queje —pues que lo hagan • **let people say what they will, we know we are right** que la gente diga lo que quiera, nosotros sabemos que tenemos razón • **let that be a lesson to you!** ¡que eso te sirva de lección! • **let there be light** hágase la luz • **never let it be said that ...** que nunca se diga que ...
5 (*Math*) • **let X be 6** supongamos que X equivale a 6
6 (*esp Brit*) (= *rent out*) alquilar, arrendar (**to** a) • **"to let"** "se alquila"
7 (= *put*) • **a plaque let into a wall** una lápida empotrada en una pared
8 (*Med*) [+ *blood*] sacar
(N) • **we're converting the barn for holiday lets** estamos remodelando el granero para alquilarlo durante las vacaciones
• **long/short let** alquiler *m* a corto/largo plazo
▸ **let away** (VT + ADV) • **to let sb away with sth** dejar a algn salirse con la suya, dejar a algn que se salga con la suya
▸ **let by** (VT + ADV) dejar pasar
▸ **let down** (VT + ADV) **1** (= *lower*) [+ *window*] bajar; [+ *hair*] soltar, dejar suelto; (*on rope*) bajar • IDIOM: • **to let one's hair down** soltarse la melena*
2 (= *lengthen*) [+ *dress, hem*] alargar
3 (= *deflate*) [+ *tyre*] desinflar
4 (*fig*) **a** (= *disappoint*) defraudar; (= *fail*) fallar • **the weather let us down** el tiempo nos defraudó • **we all felt let down** todos nos sentimos defraudados • **I trusted you and you let me down** confié en ti y me fallaste • **I was badly let down** me llevé un gran chasco • **this car has never let me down yet** hasta ahora este coche nunca me ha fallado • **my backhand lets me down** el revés me falla • **to let o.s. down** quedar mal • IDIOM: • **to let the side down:** • **she would never let the side down** jamás nos haría quedar mal, jamás nos fallaría
b • **to let sb down gently** amortiguarle el golpe a algn
▸ **let in** (VT + ADV) **1** • **to let sb in** (= *allow to enter*) dejar entrar a algn; (= *usher in*) hacer pasar a algn; (= *open door to*) abrir la puerta a algn • **who let him in?** ¿quién le ha dejado entrar?, ¿quién le ha abierto la puerta? • **let him in!** ¡que pase! • **your mother let me in** tu madre me abrió la puerta
2 (= *allow to come through*) • **shoes which let the water in** zapatos que dejan calar el agua • **a glass roof to let in the light** un tejado de cristal para dejar entrar la luz

> **LET**
>
> **Meaning "allow"**
>
> ▹ *Translate using either* **dejar**, *especially in informal contexts, or* **permitir**, *especially in more formal contexts. Both verbs can be followed either by an infinitive or by* **que** + *subjunctive:*
>
> **Let me do it**
> Déjame hacerlo, Déjame que lo haga
> **Let her have a look**
> Deja que ella lo vea, Déjale verlo
> **We must not let the children see this**
> No debemos permitir que los niños vean esto *or* permitir a los niños ver esto
>
> **Imperative**
>
> ***First person plural***
>
> ▹ *Translate* **let's** *and* **let us** + *verb using either* **vamos a** + *infinitive or using the present subjunctive of the main verb. The second construction is used particularly in formal language and when translating* **let's not**:
>
> **Let's go for a walk!**
> Vamos a dar un paseo
> **Let's consider the implications of the Government's decision**
> Consideremos las implicaciones de la decisión del Gobierno
> **Let's not waste any more time**
> No perdamos ya más tiempo
>
> *To translate* **let's go**, *use* **vamos** *or* **vámonos** *on its own without a following infinitive:*
>
> **Let's go to the theatre**
> ¡Vamos al teatro!
>
> ▹ *When* **let's** *is used on its own to reply to a suggestion, translate using* **vamos** *or* **vámonos** *if the verb in the suggestion was* **ir**. *Use* **vale** *or* **venga** *if not:*
>
> **"Shall we go?" — "Yes, let's"**
> "¿Nos vamos?" — "¡Sí, vamos!" *or* "¡Sí, vámonos!"
> **"Shall we watch the match?" — "Yes, let's"**
> "¿Vemos el partido?" — "Sí, vale" *or* "Sí, venga"
>
> ***Third person***
>
> ▹ *When* **let** *introduces a command, suggestion or wish in the third person, translate using* **que** + *subjunctive:*
>
> **Let him come up!**
> ¡Que suba!
> **Let there be no misunderstanding about this**
> ¡Que no haya ningún malentendido sobre esto!
> **Let them do as they like**
> ¡Que hagan lo que quieran!
>
> ▹ *Be careful to distinguish between the "permission" sense of* **let sb do something** *and the "command" sense:*
>
> **Please let them stay here** (*i.e. Please allow them to stay*)
> Déjalos que se queden aquí *or* Déjalos quedarse aquí, por favor
> **Let them stay here!** (*i.e. expressing a decision or an order*)
> ¡Que se queden aquí!
>
> *When* **que** *is used in this sense, it never takes an accent.*
>
> *For further uses and examples, see main entry.*

3 • **to let sb in on sth: to let sb in on a secret** contar un secreto a algn • **to let sb in on a deal** dejar que algn participe en un negocio
4 • **to let o.s. in for sth: you don't know what you're letting yourself in for** no sabes bien a lo que te estás exponiendo, no sabes bien en lo que te estás metiendo • **you may find you've let yourself in for a lot of extra work** puede que encuentres que te has expuesto a un montón de trabajo extra
5 (*Aut*) [+ *clutch*] soltar
▸ **let off** (VT + ADV) **1** (= *cause to explode, fire*) [+ *bomb*] hacer explotar; [+ *firework*] tirar; [+ *firearm*] disparar
2 (= *release*) • **to let off steam** [*boiler, engine*] soltar vapor; [*person**] (*fig*) (= *release anger*) desahogarse; (= *unwind*) relajarse
3 (= *allow to leave*) dejar salir • **they let the children off early today** hoy han dejado salir a los niños antes de la hora
4 (= *exempt*) perdonar • **it's your turn to do the washing up but I'll let you off this time** te toca fregar a ti pero esta vez te perdono
5 (= *not punish*) perdonar • **to let sb off lightly** ser demasiado blando con algn • **the headmaster let him off with a warning** el director le dejó escapar con solo una advertencia
(VT + PREP) **1** (= *release from*) • **can I let the dog off the lead?** ¿puedo soltar al perro?; ▹ **hook**
2 (= *exempt*) perdonar • **I'll let you off the £5 you owe me** te perdono las 5 libras que me debes • **the authorities let him off National Service** las autoridades le permitieron librarse del servicio militar
▸ **let on*** (VI + ADV) (= *say*) • **he's not letting on** no dice nada • **don't let on!** ¡no digas nada!, ¡no te vayas de la lengua!* • **don't let on (to her) about what they did** no (le) digas lo que hicieron
(VT + ADV) **1** • **to let on that a** (= *reveal*) decir que • **she didn't let on that she'd seen me** no dijo que me había visto
b (= *pretend*) fingir que • **I let on that the tears in my eyes were because of the onions** fingí que las lágrimas que tenía en los ojos se debían a la cebolla
2 (= *allow on board*) dejar subir
▸ **let out** (VT + ADV) **1** (= *allow to leave*) [+ *visitor*] acompañar a la puerta; [+ *prisoner*] poner en libertad; [+ *penned animal*] dejar salir • **I'll let you out** te acompaño a la puerta • **the watchman let me out** el vigilante me abrió la puerta (para que pudiera salir) • **let me out!** ¡déjenme salir! • **he let himself out quietly** salió sin hacer ruido • **can you let yourself out?** ¿hace falta que te acompañe a la puerta? • **they are let out of school at four** salen de la escuela a las cuatro • **to let the air out of a tyre** desinflar *or* deshinchar un neumático • **to let the water out of the bath** dejar salir el agua de la bañera • IDIOM: • **to let the cat out of the bag** descubrir el pastel
2 (= *reveal*) [+ *secret, news*] contar, revelar • **don't let it out that ...** no digas que ..., no cuentes que ...
3 (= *release*) dispensar, eximir • **they won't let me out of the contract** no me van a dispensar *or* eximir de las obligaciones contractuales
4 (= *enlarge*) [+ *dress, skirt*] ensanchar • **to let out a seam** soltar una costura
5 (*esp Brit*) (= *rent out*) alquilar
6 (= *utter*) • **to let out a cry/sigh** dar un grito/un suspiro
7 (*Aut*) [+ *clutch*] soltar
▸ **let up** (VI + ADV) **1** (= *moderate*) [*bad weather*] mejorar; [*storm, wind*] amainar • **when the rain lets up** cuando deje de llover tanto
2 (= *do less*) • **in spite of his health, he did not**

let up a pesar de su salud, no aflojó el ritmo (*del trabajo, de las actividades etc*) • **she can't afford to let up on her studies** no puede permitirse aflojar en los estudios
3 (= *stop*) • **he never lets up** (*talking*) no deja de hablar, habla sin parar; (*working*) trabaja sin descanso
4 (= *show leniency*) • **to let up on sb: though she protested, her mother would not let up on her** aunque ella protestaba, su madre no cedía

let[2] [let] N **1** (*Tennis*) dejada *f*, let *m*
2 (*Jur*) • **without let or hindrance** sin estorbo ni obstáculo

letch* [letʃ] = **lech**

letdown ['letdaʊn] N decepción *f*, desilusión *f*

lethal ['li:θəl] ADJ **1** (= *deadly*) [*weapon*] mortífero, letal; [*blow*] mortal; [*dose, injection, effects*] mortal, letal; [*force*] letal • **it is ~ to rats** tiene un efecto mortal en las ratas
2 (*fig*) (= *very dangerous*) [*opponent*] muy peligroso; [*weather conditions*] nefasto • **the roads are ~ in these conditions** las carreteras son nefastas en estas condiciones • **this coffee is ~** (*hum*) este café es un veneno (*hum*) • **this schnapps is ~** (*hum*) este aguardiente es mortal (*hum*) • **his driving is ~** (*hum*) es un peligro público al volante (*hum*)
CPD ▸ **lethal injection** inyección *f* letal • **he was executed by ~ injection** lo ejecutaron mediante inyección letal

lethargic [lɪ'θɑ:dʒɪk] ADJ letárgico, aletargado; [*response*] apático • **to feel ~** [*person*] sentirse somnoliento *or* aletargado • **the market/trading was ~** (*St Ex*) el mercado/el volumen de contratación apenas se movió

lethargically [lɪ'θɑ:dʒɪkəlɪ] ADV (= *unenergetically*) de manera letárgica; (= *without interest*) apáticamente

lethargy ['leθədʒɪ] N letargo *m*

Lethe ['li:θi:] N Lete(o) *m*

let-out ['letaʊt] N (*Brit*) escapatoria *f*
CPD ▸ **let-out clause** cláusula *f* que incluye una escapatoria

let's [lets] ▹ **let**

Lett [let] = **Latvian**

letter ['letəʳ] N **1** [*of alphabet*] letra *f* • **the ~ G** la letra G • **small ~** (letra *f*) minúscula *f* • **capital ~** (letra *f*) mayúscula *f* • **the ~ of the law** la ley escrita • **to follow instructions to the ~** cumplir las instrucciones al pie de la letra
2 (= *missive*) carta *f* • **~s of Galdós** (*as published*) epistolario *m* de Galdós • **~ of acknowledgement** carta *f* de acuse de recibo • **~ of advice** carta *f* de aviso, notificación *f* • **~ of application** instancia *f*, carta *f* de solicitud • **~ of appointment** carta *f* de confirmación de un puesto de trabajo • **~ of attorney** *or* **proxy** (carta *f* de) poder *m* • **by ~** por carta, por escrito • **covering ~** carta *f* adjunta • **~s of credence** cartas *fpl* credenciales • **~ of credit** carta *f* de crédito • **documentary/irrevocable ~ of credit** carta *f* de crédito documentaria/irrevocable • **~ of intent** carta *f* de intenciones • **~ of introduction** carta *f* de presentación • **~ of lien** carta *f* de gravamen • **~s patent** título *m* de privilegio, patente *f* (de invención) • **~ of protest** carta *f or* escrito *m* de protesta • **~ of recommendation/reference** carta *f* de recomendación
3 letters (= *learning*) letras *fpl* • **man of ~s** hombre *m* de letras, literato *m*
VT estampar con letras • **~ed in gold** estampado con letras doradas • **a hand-lettered sign** un cartel escrito a mano • **the boxes were ~ed according to country** las cajas estaban ordenadas por letras según los países
CPD ▸ **letter bomb** carta *f* bomba ▸ **letter card** (*Brit*) carta-tarjeta *f* ▸ **letter carrier** (*US*) cartero/a *m/f* ▸ **letter opener** abrecartas *m inv* ▸ **letter quality** calidad *f* carta ▸ **letter quality printer** impresora *f* calidad carta ▸ **letter writer** corresponsal *mf* • **I'm not much of a ~ writer** apenas escribo cartas

letterbox ['letəbɒks] N (*esp Brit*) buzón *m*

lettered ['letəd] ADJ [*person*] culto

letterfile ['letəfaɪl] N carpeta *f*, guardacartas *m*

letterhead ['letəhed] N membrete *m*

lettering ['letərɪŋ] N letras *fpl*, inscripción *f*

letterpress ['letəpres] N (= *method, printed image*) impresión *f* tipográfica

letting ['letɪŋ] N arrendamiento *m*, alquiler *m*
CPD ▸ **letting agency** agencia *f* de alquiler

lettuce ['letɪs] N lechuga *f*

let-up* ['letʌp] N descanso *m*; (*fig*) tregua *f*; (= *reduction*) reducción *f*, disminución *f* (**in** de) • **we worked five hours without a let-up** trabajamos cinco horas sin descanso *or* sin interrupción • **if there is a let-up in the rain** si deja un momento de llover • **there has been no let-up in the fighting** se ha luchado sin descanso *or* sin tregua

leucocyte ['lu:kəˌsaɪt] N leucocito *m*

leukaemia, leukemia (*US*) [lu:'ki:mɪə] N leucemia *f*

Levant [lɪ'vænt] N Oriente *m* Medio

Levantine ['levəntaɪn] ADJ levantino
N levantino/a *m/f*

levee[1] ['leveɪ] N (*Hist*) (= *reception*) besamanos *m inv*, recepción *f*

levee[2] ['levɪ] N (= *bank*) ribero *m*, dique *m*

level ['levl] ADJ **1** (*lit*) (= *not sloping*) nivelado; (= *not uneven*) plano, llano • **place on a ~ surface** (= *not sloping*) colocar en una superficie nivelada; (= *not uneven*) colocar en una superficie plana *or* llana • **a ~ spoonful** (*Culin*) una cucharada rasa • IDIOMS: • **to compete on a ~ playing field** competir en igualdad de condiciones • **to do one's ~ best to do sth*** hacer todo lo posible para hacer algo
2 (= *at same height, position*) • **to be ~ (with sb)** (*in race*) estar *or* ir igualado (con algn); (*in league, competition*) estar *or* ir empatado (con algn) • **the teams were ~ at the end of extra time** los equipos estaban *or* iban empatados al terminar la prórroga • **to be ~ (with sth)** (= *at same height*) estar a la misma altura (que algo) • **to be ~ with the ground** estar a ras del suelo • **she knelt down so that their eyes were ~** se agachó para que sus ojos estuvieran a la misma altura • **to draw ~ with sth/sb** (*esp Brit*) (*gen, also in race*) alcanzar algo/a algn; (*in league, competition*) empatar con algo/algn
3 (= *steady*) [*voice, tone*] sereno; [*gaze*] penetrante • **she spoke in a ~ voice** habló con voz serena, habló sin alterar la voz • **to keep a ~ head** no perder la cabeza
N **1** (= *amount, degree*) nivel *m* • **we have the lowest ~ of inflation for some years** tenemos el nivel de inflación más bajo que hemos tenido en varios años • **the exercises are graded according to their ~ of difficulty** los ejercicios están ordenados por nivel *or* grado de dificultad • **bankruptcies have reached record ~s** el número de bancarrotas ha alcanzado cifras récord • **~ of unemployment** índice *m* de paro; ▹ **poverty**
2 (= *height*) nivel *m* • **the water reached a ~ of ten metres** el agua alcanzó un nivel de diez metros • **at eye ~** a la altura de los ojos • **to be on a ~ with sth** (*lit*) estar al nivel *or* a la altura de algo; ▹ **ground[1]**, **sea**
3 (= *floor*) [*of building*] piso *m*
4 (= *rank, grade*) nivel *m* • **talks at ministerial ~** conversaciones *fpl* a nivel ministerial • **at advanced/elementary ~** a nivel avanzado/elemental • **at local/national/international ~** a nivel local/nacional/internacional • **on one ~** (*fig*) por un lado, de cierta manera • **to be on a ~ with** (*fig*) estar a la altura de • **some people put him on a ~ with von Karajan** algunos lo equiparan con *or* a von Karajan • IDIOM: • **to come down to sb's ~** rebajarse al nivel de algn; ▹ **high-level, low-level, top-level**
5 (= *flat place*) llano *m* • **on the ~** en superficie plana *or* llana • **a car which can reach speeds of 300 miles per hour on the ~** un coche que puede alcanzar velocidades de unas 300 millas por hora en superficie plana *or* llana • IDIOM: • **to be on the ~*** [*person*] ser de fiar, ser un tipo cabal* • **it's on the ~** es un negocio serio *or* limpio
6 (*also* **spirit level**) nivel *m* de burbuja
VT **1** (= *make level*) [+ *ground, site*] nivelar, allanar • IDIOM: • **to ~ the playing-field** igualar las condiciones
2 (= *raze*) [+ *building, city*] arrasar
3 (*Sport*) (= *equalize*) [+ *match, game*] igualar • **to ~ the score(s)** igualar el marcador
4 (= *direct*) • **he has denied the charges ~led against him** ha negado las acusaciones que se han hecho en su contra • **he has not responded to the criticism ~led at him** no ha reaccionado ante las críticas que se le han dirigido • **to ~ a gun at sb** apuntar a *or* contra algn con una pistola
VI (*esp US**) • **I'll ~ with you** te voy a hablar con franqueza, te voy a ser franco • **you didn't ~ with me** no has sido franco conmigo
CPD ▸ **level crossing** (*Brit*) paso *m* a nivel
▸ **level down** VT + ADV nivelar (*al nivel más bajo*)
▸ **level off** VI + ADV [*ground, road*] nivelarse; [*prices, rate of growth*] estabilizarse; [*aircraft*] tomar una trayectoria horizontal, nivelarse
VT + ADV (= *make flat*) nivelar, allanar
▸ **level out** VI + ADV [*road, ground*] nivelarse; [*prices, rate of growth*] estabilizarse
VT + ADV (= *make flat*) nivelar, allanar

level-headed ['levl'hedɪd] ADJ sensato, equilibrado

leveller, leveler (*US*) ['levələʳ] N *persona en pro de la igualdad de derechos*

levelling, leveling (*US*) ['levlɪŋ] N nivelación *f*
CPD ▸ **levelling process** proceso *m* de nivelación

levelling-off [ˌlevəlɪŋ'ɒf] N nivelación *f*

levelly ['levəlɪ] ADV [*gaze etc*] con compostura, con ecuanimidad, sin emocionarse

level-peg [ˌlevl'peg] VI • **they were level-pegging** iban empatados

level-pegging [ˌlevl'pegɪŋ] N igualdad *f*, situación *f* de empate • **it's level-pegging** now van muy iguales, están empatados

lever ['li:vəʳ] N (*also fig*) palanca *f*
VT • **to ~ sth up/out/off** levantar/sacar/quitar algo con palanca

leverage ['li:vərɪdʒ] N apalancamiento *m*; (*fig*) influencia *f*, palanca *f*

leveraged buy-out [ˌli:vərɪdʒd'baɪaʊt] N *compra de todas las acciones de una compañía pagándolas con dinero prestado a cambio de asegurar que las acciones serán compradas*

leveret ['levərɪt] N lebrato *m*

leviathan [lɪ'vaɪəθən] N (*Bible*) leviatán *m*; (= *ship*) buque *m* enorme

Levi's® ['li:vaɪz] (NPL) vaqueros *mpl*, levis® *mpl*
levitate ['levɪteɪt] (VT) elevar por levitación (VI) levitar
levitation [ˌlevɪ'teɪʃən] (N) levitación *f*
Levite ['li:vaɪt] (N) levita *m*
Leviticus [lɪ'vɪtɪkəs] (N) Levítico *m*
levity ['levɪtɪ] (N) (*frm*) (= *frivolity*) ligereza *f*, frivolidad *f*
levy ['levɪ] (N) **1** (= *act*) exacción *f* (*de tributos*); (= *tax*) impuesto *m*
2 (*Mil*) leva *f*
(VT) **1** (= *impose*) [+ *tax, fine*] imponer (**on** a); (= *collect*) [+ *contribution*] recaudar
2 (*Mil*) reclutar
lewd [lu:d] (ADJ) (COMPAR: **lewder**, SUPERL: **lewdest**) [*person*] lascivo; [*song, story*] verde, colorado (*LAm*)
lewdly ['lu:dlɪ] (ADV) lascivamente
lewdness ['lu:dnɪs] (N) lascivia *f*; [*of song, story*] lo verde
lexeme ['leksi:m] (N) lexema *m*
lexical ['leksɪkəl] (ADJ) léxico
lexicalize ['leksɪkəlaɪz] (VT) lexicalizar
lexicographer [ˌleksɪ'kɒgrəfəʳ] (N) lexicógrafo/a *m/f*
lexicographical [ˌleksɪkəʊ'græfɪkəl] (ADJ) lexicográfico
lexicography [ˌleksɪ'kɒgrəfɪ] (N) lexicografía *f*
lexicologist [ˌleksɪ'kɒlədʒɪst] (N) lexicólogo/a *m/f*
lexicology [ˌleksɪ'kɒlədʒɪ] (N) lexicología *f*
lexicon ['leksɪkən] (N) léxico *m*
lexis ['leksɪs] (N) vocabulario *m*
Leyden ['laɪdn] (N) Leiden
(CPD) ▸ **Leyden jar** botella *f* de Leiden
LGBT (ADJ ABBR) (= *lesbian, gay, bisexual, and transgender*) LGBT
LGV (N ABBR) (= **Large Goods Vehicle**) *vehículo pesado*
l.h. (ABBR) (= **left hand**) izq
l.h.d. (ABBR) (= **left-hand drive**) ▹ **left-hand**
LI (ABBR) (*US*) = **Long Island**
liability [ˌlaɪə'bɪlɪtɪ] (N) **1** (= *responsibility*) responsabilidad *f* • **to admit/deny ~ (for sth)** admitir/negar ser responsable (de algo)
2 (= *obligation, debt*) • **tax ~** carga *f* fiscal • **current liabilities** pasivo *msing* circulante • **long-term liabilities** pasivo *msing* (exigible) a largo plazo • **they failed to meet their liabilities** no hicieron frente a sus obligaciones; ▹ **limited, unlimited**
3 (= *risk, burden*) • **I do not want to be a ~ to you** no quiero ser una carga *or* un estorbo para ti • **this car's a bit of a ~** este coche da muchos problemas
4 (= *propensity*) predisposición *f*, propensión *f* (**to** a) **to have an increased ~ to infection** tener una mayor predisposición *or* propensión a las infecciones
(CPD) ▸ **liability insurance** seguro *m* de daños a terceros, seguro *m* de responsabilidad civil (*Sp*)
liable ['laɪəbl] (ADJ) **1** (= *likely*) • **to be ~ to do sth: he's ~ to do something stupid** puede fácilmente hacer alguna tontería, es muy posible que haga una tontería • **he's ~ to have an accident** es probable que tenga un accidente • **it's ~ to rain at any moment** puede empezar a llover en cualquier momento
2 (= *prone*) • **we are all ~ to make mistakes** todos podemos cometer errores • **some people are more ~ to depression than others** algunas personas son más propensas a la depresión *or* tienen más tendencia a la depresión que otras
3 (= *responsible*) • **to be ~ for** [+ *debt, loan*] ser responsable de, deber responder de • **the company is ~ for damages** la compañía es responsable de los daños, la compañía debe pagar los daños • **to hold sb ~ for sth** considerar a algn responsable de algo
4 (= *subject*) • **to be ~ for/to sth: the programme is ~ to change without notice** el programa puede cambiar sin previo aviso • **to be ~ to duty** (*Comm*) [*goods*] estar sujeto a derechos de aduana, deber pagar impuestos de aduana • **to be ~ for military service** estar obligado a hacer el servicio militar • **to be ~ to prosecution** poder ser procesado • **to be ~ to** *or* **for tax** [*person*] deber pagar impuestos; [*thing*] estar sujeto a impuestos, ser gravable • **any savings you have are ~ for tax** todos sus ahorros están sujetos a impuestos *or* son gravables • **he is not ~ for tax** no tiene que pagar impuestos, está exento de pagar impuestos
liaise [lɪ'eɪz] (VI) • **to ~ with** (*Brit*) trabajar en colaboración con • **police ~d with the customs authorities to make the arrest** la policía trabajó en colaboración con las autoridades aduaneras para efectuar la detención • **the agency will ~ between youth groups and the government** la agencia servirá de puente *or* enlace entre los grupos juveniles y el gobierno
liaison [lɪ'eɪzɒn] (N) (= *coordination*) enlace *m*, coordinación *f*; (*fig*) (= *relationship*) relación *f*
(CPD) ▸ **liaison committee** comité *m* de enlace ▸ **liaison officer** oficial *mf* de enlace
liana [lɪ'ɑ:nə] (N) bejuco *m*, liana *f*
liar ['laɪəʳ] (N) mentiroso/a *m/f*, embustero/a *m/f* • **liar!** ¡mentira!
Lib. [lɪb] (N ABBR) (*Pol*) **1** = **Liberal**
2 = **Liberation** • **Women's ~** (= *Women's Liberation Movement*) Movimiento *m* de Liberación de la Mujer
libation [laɪ'beɪʃən] (N) libación *f*
libber* ['lɪbəʳ] (N) • **women's ~** feminista *mf* • **animal ~** defensor(a) *m/f* de los animales
Lib Dem [ˌlɪb'dem] (N) liberal demócrata *mf* • **the ~s** los liberales demócratas
libel ['laɪbəl] (N) (*Jur*) difamación *f*, calumnia *f* (**on** de); (*written*) escrito *m* difamatorio, libelo *m* • **it's a ~!** (*hum*) ¡es mentira!
(VT) difamar, calumniar
(CPD) ▸ **libel action** pleito *m* por difamación ▸ **libel laws** leyes *fpl* contra la difamación ▸ **libel suit** = **libel action**
libellous, libelous (*US*) ['laɪbələs] (ADJ) difamatorio, calumnioso
liberal ['lɪbərəl] (ADJ) **1** (= *tolerant*) [*person, view, education, regime*] liberal
2 (= *generous*) [*quantity, amount*] abundante, generoso; [*portion*] generoso • **to be ~ with sth** ser generoso con algo • **he is very ~ with his money** es muy generoso con el dinero • **she was rather ~ with the mayonnaise** puso mucha mayonesa • **he is not ~ with his praise** no es muy pródigo con los elogios
3 (*Brit*) (*Pol*) (= *of the Liberal Party*) • **Liberal** [*MP*] del partido liberal; [*government, policy*] liberal
4 (= *free*) [*interpretation, translation*] libre
(N) **1** (= *broad-minded person*) liberal *mf*
2 (*Brit*) (*Pol*) • **Liberal** liberal *mf*
(CPD) ▸ **the liberal arts** (*esp US*) (*Univ*) las humanidades, las artes liberales ▸ **Liberal Democrat** (*Brit*) (*Pol*) demócrata *mf* liberal ▸ **the Liberal Democratic Party** (*Brit*) el Partido Democrático Liberal ▸ **the Liberal Party** (*Brit*) el Partido Liberal ▸ **liberal studies** (*esp Brit*) *asignatura de letras complementaria para aquellos que estudian ciencias*
liberalism ['lɪbərəlɪzəm] (N) liberalismo *m*
liberality [ˌlɪbə'rælɪtɪ] (N) (= *generosity*) liberalidad *f*, generosidad *f*
liberalization [ˌlɪbərəlaɪ'zeɪʃən] (N) liberalización *f*
liberalize ['lɪbərəlaɪz] (VT) liberalizar
liberally ['lɪbərəlɪ] (ADV) **1** (= *generously*) [*give*] generosamente; [*apply, spread, sprinkle*] abundantemente, generosamente • **his language is ~ sprinkled with swear words** su lenguaje está salpicado de abundantes palabrotas
2 (= *tolerantly*) con tolerancia • **the political prisoners have generally been treated more ~** por lo general, los prisioneros políticos han sido tratados con más tolerancia • **they treated their children too ~** eran demasiado tolerantes con sus hijos
3 (= *freely*) [*interpret, translate*] libremente
liberal-minded ['lɪbərəl'maɪndɪd] (ADJ) tolerante, liberal
liberal-mindedness ['lɪbərəl'maɪndɪdnɪs] (N) tolerancia *f*, amplitud *f* de miras
liberate ['lɪbəreɪt] (VT) (= *free*) liberar, libertar (**from** de); [+ *prisoner, slave*] poner en libertad; [+ *gas etc*] dejar escapar
liberated ['lɪbəreɪtɪd] (ADJ) liberado • **a ~ woman** una mujer liberada
liberating ['lɪbəreɪtɪŋ] (ADJ) liberador • **a ~ experience** una experiencia liberadora
liberation [ˌlɪbə'reɪʃən] (N) liberación *f*
(CPD) ▸ **liberation theology** teología *f* de la liberación ▸ **Women's Liberation Movement** movimiento *m* de liberación de la mujer; ▹ **Lib**
liberator ['lɪbəreɪtəʳ] (N) libertador(a) *m/f*
Liberia [laɪ'bɪərɪə] (N) Liberia *f*
Liberian [laɪ'bɪərɪən] (ADJ) liberiano
(N) liberiano/a *m/f*
libertarian [ˌlɪbə'tɛərɪən] (ADJ) libertario
(N) libertario/a *m/f*
libertarianism [ˌlɪbə'tɛərɪənɪzəm] (N) (= *philosophy*) libertarismo *m*, doctrina *f* libertaria; (= *personal philosophy*) ideas *fpl* libertarias
libertinage ['lɪbətɪnɪdʒ] (N) libertinaje *m*
libertine ['lɪbəti:n] (N) libertino/a *m/f*
liberty ['lɪbətɪ] (N) **1** (= *freedom*) libertad *f* • **individual/personal ~** libertad *f* individual/personal • **to be at ~** (= *free*) estar en libertad • **to be at ~ to do sth** tener libertad para hacer algo, ser libre de hacer algo • **I'm not at ~ to say who it was** no puedo decir quién fue
2 (= *presumption, impertinence*) atrevimiento *m* • **that was rather a ~ on his part** eso fue un atrevimiento por su parte • **what a ~!*** ¡qué atrevimiento *or* descaro! • **to take liberties with sb** (= *be cheeky*) tomarse libertades *or* demasiadas confianzas con algn; (*sexually*) propasarse con algn • **to take the ~ of doing sth** tomarse la libertad de hacer algo
(CPD) ▸ **liberty bodice**† camiseta *f* interior
libidinous [lɪ'bɪdɪnəs] (ADJ) libidinoso
libido [lɪ'bi:dəʊ] (N) libido *f*
Libor ['li:bɔʳ] (N ABBR) = **London inter-bank offered rate**
Libra ['li:brə] (N) **1** (= *sign, constellation*) Libra *f*
2 (= *person*) libra *mf* • **he's (a) ~** es libra
Libran ['li:brən] (N) libra *mf*
librarian [laɪ'brɛərɪən] (N) bibliotecario/a *m/f*; (*professionally qualified*) bibliotecólogo/a *m/f*
librarianship [laɪ'brɛərɪənʃɪp] (N) (*esp Brit*)
1 (= *post*) puesto *m* de bibliotecario
2 (= *science*) bibliotecología *f*, biblioteconomía *f*
library ['laɪbrərɪ] (N) (*also Comput*) biblioteca *f* • **newspaper ~** hemeroteca *f* • **public ~** biblioteca *f* pública; ▹ **film, video**
(CPD) ▸ **library book** libro *m* de biblioteca ▸ **library card** = **library ticket** ▸ **library pictures** (*TV*) imágenes *fpl* de archivo ▸ **library science** = **librarianship** ▸ **library ticket** carnet *m* de biblioteca

l

LIBRARY OF CONGRESS
La Biblioteca del Congreso es la biblioteca nacional de EE.UU. y tiene su sede en Washington D.C. Se fundó en 1800 como fuente de referencia para los miembros del Congreso y actualmente registra también los derechos de autor de todos los libros publicados en Estados Unidos, por lo que recibe dos ejemplares de cada publicación. Posee un fondo inmenso de libros y manuscritos históricos, así como partituras, mapas, películas, grabaciones sonoras y microfilmes.

librettist [lɪˈbretɪst] N libretista *mf*

libretto [lɪˈbretəʊ] N (PL: **librettos** *or* **libretti** [lɪˈbreti:]) libreto *m*

Libya [ˈlɪbɪə] N Libia *f*

Libyan [ˈlɪbɪən] ADJ libio
N libio/a *m/f*

lice [laɪs] NPL *of* **louse**

licence, license[1] (US) [ˈlaɪsəns] N **1** (= *permit*) permiso *m*, licencia *f*; (*Aut*) permiso *m* de conducir, carnet *m* (de conducir) • **dog ~** licencia *f* para tener licencia • **export ~** permiso *m or* licencia *f* de exportación • **fishing ~** permiso *m or* licencia *f* de pesca • **full ~** (*Aut*) carnet *m or* permiso *m* de conducir (definitivo) • **import ~** licencia *f or* permiso *m* de importación • **he lost his ~** (*Aut*) le retiraron el carnet *or* permiso • **provisional ~** (*Aut*) *permiso o licencia de conducir que se obtiene antes de sacarse el carnet definitivo* • **they were married by special ~** se casaron con una licencia especial • **to manufacture sth under ~** fabricar algo bajo licencia; ▹ **driving, television**
2 (= *freedom*) **a** (*pej*) • **such a policy would give people a ~ to break the law** una política semejante serviría de excusa para que la gente violase la ley • IDIOMS: • **to give sb a ~ to kill** darle a algn licencia para matar • **it's a ~ to print money** es una mina de oro
b (*Art, Literat*) licencia *f* • **artistic/poetic ~** licencia artística/poética • **you can allow some ~ in translation** se pueden aceptar algunas libertades al traducir
3 (= *immorality*) libertinaje *m*
CPD ▸ **licence fee** (*Brit*) (*TV*) *cuota que debe pagarse para el uso de un televisor* ▸ **licence holder** (*Aut*) titular *mf* del carnet *or* permiso de conducir ▸ **licence number, licence plate** (*Aut*) matrícula *f*, placa *f*, patente *f* (*S. Cone*)

license[2] [ˈlaɪsəns] VT **1** (= *issue with license*) [+ *drug, medicine*] autorizar la comercialización de; [+ *vehicle*] conceder el permiso de circulación a; [+ *gun*] autorizar la licencia de; [+ *dog, company, operator*] registrar; [+ *surgeon, practitioner*] otorgarle la licencia de ejercer a • **to be ~d to do sth** tener licencia para hacer algo, estar autorizado para hacer algo • **we are not ~d to sell alcohol** no tenemos licencia para vender bebidas alcohólicas, no estamos autorizados para vender bebidas alcohólicas • **he is ~d to drive this vehicle** está autorizado para conducir este vehículo • **to be ~d to carry a gun** tener licencia para llevar un revólver
2 (= *authorize*) [+ *sale, use*] autorizar
N (US) = **licence**
CPD ▸ **license plate** (US) (*Aut*) matrícula *f*, placa *f*, patente *f* (*S. Cone*)

licensed [ˈlaɪsənst] ADJ [*dealer*] autorizado; [*restaurant, premises*] autorizado para la venta de bebidas alcohólicas
CPD ▸ **licensed trade** comercio *m* autorizado, negocio *m* autorizado ▸ **licensed victualler** vendedor(a) *m/f* de bebidas alcohólicas

licensee [ˌlaɪsənˈsi:] N concesionario/a *m/f*; (*Brit*) [*of bar*] patrón/ona *m/f*

licensing [ˈlaɪsənsɪŋ] N [*of drug*] permiso *m* de comercialización; (*Med*) [*of practitioner*] concesión *f* de licencia para el ejercicio; (*Aut*) matrícula *f*
CPD ▸ **licensing agreement** acuerdo *m* de licencia ▸ **licensing hours** horas *fpl* durante las cuales se permite la venta y consumo de alcohol (*en un bar etc*) ▸ **licensing laws** (*Brit*) leyes *fpl* reguladoras de la venta y consumo de alcohol

licentiate [laɪˈsenʃɪɪt] N (= *person*) licenciado/a *m/f*; (= *title*) licencia *f*, licenciatura *f*

licentious [laɪˈsenʃəs] ADJ licencioso

lichee [ˌlaɪˈtʃi:] = **lychee**

lichen [ˈlaɪkən] N liquen *m*

lich gate [ˈlɪtʃgeɪt] N entrada *f* de cementerio

licit [ˈlɪsɪt] ADJ lícito

lick [lɪk] VT **1** lamer • **flames were ~ing (at) the door** las llamas empezaron a lamer la puerta • **to ~ one's wounds** (*lit*) lamerse las heridas; (*fig*) curarse las heridas • IDIOMS: • **to ~ sb's boots*** hacer la pelota *or* dar coba a algn* • **to ~ sth into shape*** poner algo a punto
2* (= *defeat*) dar una paliza a*
N **1** (*with tongue*) lametazo *m*, lengüetada *f* • IDIOM: • **a ~ and a promise*** una lavada a la carrera *or* de cualquier manera
2 (*fig*) • **a ~ of paint** una mano de pintura • **a ~ of polish** un poquito de cera
3* (= *speed*) • **to go at a good** *or* **a fair old ~** ir a buen tren* • **at full ~** a todo gas*, a toda mecha*

▸ **lick off** VT + ADV quitar de un lametazo

▸ **lick up** VT + ADV beber a lengüetadas

licking [ˈlɪkɪŋ] N **1** lamedura *f*
2* paliza* *f* • **to give sb a ~** dar una paliza a algn*

lickspittle* [ˈlɪkspɪtl] N cobista* *mf*, pelotillero/a* *m/f*

licorice [ˈlɪkərɪs] N = **liquorice**

lid [lɪd] N **1** tapa *f*; (= *hat**) gorro *m* • IDIOMS: • **he's flipped his lid*** ha perdido la chaveta* • **that puts the lid on it!** ¡esto es el colmo *or* el acabóse! • **to take the lid off** [+ *scandal*] exponer a la luz pública
2 (= *eyelid*) párpado *m*

lidded [ˈlɪdɪd] ADJ **1** [*pot etc*] con tapa
2 • **heavily ~ eyes** ojos *mpl* con párpados gruesos

lidless [ˈlɪdləs] ADJ **1** [*jar*] sin tapa
2 [*eyes*] sin párpados

lido [ˈli:dəʊ] N (*swimming*) piscina *f* (al aire libre), alberca *f* pública (*Mex*), pileta *f* pública (*Arg*); (*boating*) centro *m* de balandrismo; (= *resort*) balneario *m*

lie[1] [laɪ] N mentira *f* • **it's a lie!** ¡(es) mentira! • **to tell lies** mentir • **white lie** mentira *f* piadosa • IDIOM: • **to give the lie to** [+ *report, theory*] desmentir; [+ *person*] dar el mentís a; ▹ **pack**
VI mentir
VT • **to lie one's way out of it** salir del apuro mintiendo
CPD ▸ **lie detector** detector *m* de mentiras ▸ **lie-detector test** prueba *f* con el detector de mentiras

lie[2] [laɪ] (PT: **lay**, PP: **lain**) VI **1** [*person, animal*] (= *act*) echarse, acostarse, tenderse, tumbarse; (= *state*) estar echado *or* acostado *or* tendido *or* tumbado; (*in grave*) yacer, estar enterrado, reposar (*liter*) • **don't lie on the grass** no te eches sobre el césped • **he lay where he had fallen** se quedó donde había caído • **to lie asleep/in bed** estar dormido/en la cama • **to lie dead** yacer muerto • **to lie helpless** estar tumbado sin poder ayudarse • **here lies ...** aquí yace ... • **to let things lie** dejar estar las cosas como están • **to lie resting** estar descansando • **to lie still** quedarse inmóvil • IDIOM: • **to lie low** mantenerse a escondidas
2 (= *be situated*) [*object*] estar; [*town, house*] estar situado, encontrarse, ubicarse (*LAm*); (= *remain*) quedarse; (= *stretch*) extenderse • **the book lay on the table** el libro estaba sobre la mesa • **our road lay along the river** nuestro camino seguía a lo largo del río • **the plain lay before us** la llanura se extendía delante de nosotros • **where does the difficulty lie?** ¿en qué consiste *or* radica la dificultad? • **the factory lay idle** la fábrica estaba parada • **the town lies in a valley** el pueblo está situado *or* ubicado en un valle • **England lies in third place** Inglaterra está en tercer lugar *or* ocupa la tercera posición • **the money is lying in the bank** el dinero sigue en el banco • **how does the land lie?** ¿cuál es el estado actual de las cosas? • **obstacles lie in the way** hay obstáculos por delante • **the problem lies in his refusal** el problema estriba en su negativa • **the snow lay half a metre deep** había medio metro de nieve • **the snow did not lie** la nieve se derritió • **the book lay unopened** el libro quedaba sin abrir • **the fault lies with you** la culpa es tuya, tú eres el culpable • **it lies with you to change things** te corresponde a ti cambiar las cosas
N [*of ball*] posición *f* • **the lie of the land** (*Geog*) la configuración del terreno; (*fig*) el estado de las cosas

▸ **lie about, lie around** VI + ADV [*objects*] estar por ahí tirado; [*person*] pasar el tiempo sin hacer nada • **we lay about on our beds** nos quedamos tumbados en las camas • **it must be lying about somewhere** estará por aquí, debe de andar por aquí

▸ **lie back** VI + ADV recostarse (**against, on** sobre) • **lie back and think of England!** ¡relájate y hazlo por la patria!

▸ **lie behind** VI + PREP (*fig*) • **what lies behind his attitude?** ¿cuál es la verdadera razón de su actitud? • **I wonder what lies behind all this** me pregunto qué hay detrás de todo esto

▸ **lie down** VI + ADV echarse, acostarse, tenderse, tumbarse • **lie down!** (*to dog*) ¡échate! • IDIOMS: • **to lie down on the job** gandulear • **to take sth lying down** aguantar *or* soportar algo sin rechistar • **he's not one to take things lying down** no es de los que se callan, no es de los que tragan con todo* • **we're not going to take this lying down** no nos vamos a callar con este tema, no vamos a permitir que esto se quede así

▸ **lie in** VI + ADV (= *stay in bed*) quedarse en la cama hasta tarde

▸ **lie over** VI + ADV quedar aplazado *or* en suspenso

▸ **lie to** VI + ADV (*Naut*) (= *act*) ponerse a la capa; (= *state*) estar a la capa

▸ **lie up** VI + ADV (= *hide*) esconderse; (= *rest*) descansar; (= *be out of use*) quedar fuera de uso; (*Naut*) estar amarrado

lie-abed [ˈlaɪəbed] N dormilón/ona *m/f*

Liechtenstein [ˈlɪktənstaɪn] N Liechtenstein *m*

lied [li:d] (PL: **lieder** [ˈli:dəʳ]) N lied *m*

lie-down [ˌlaɪˈdaʊn] N descanso *m* • **I must have a lie-down** necesito echarme un rato

lief†† [li:f] ADV • **I'd as ~ not go** igual me da no ir, de igual gana no voy

liege [li:dʒ] N (= *lord*) señor *m* feudal; (= *vassal*) vasallo *m* • **yes, my ~** sí, (mi) señor

CPD ▸ **liege lord** señor *m* feudal
Liège [lɪ'eɪʒ] N Lieja *f*
liegeman ['li:dʒmæn] N (PL: **liegemen**) vasallo *m*
lie-in [,laɪ'ɪn] N • **to have a lie-in** quedarse en la cama hasta tarde
lien [lɪən] N derecho *m* de retención (**on** de) • **banker's ~** gravamen *m* bancario • **general ~** embargo *m* preventivo, gravamen *m* general • **vendor's ~** gravamen *m* del vendedor
lieu [lu:] N • **in ~ of** en lugar de, en vez de
Lieut. ABBR (= **Lieutenant**) Tte
lieutenant [lef'tenənt], (US) [lu:'tenənt] N (*Mil*) teniente *mf*; (*Naut*) teniente *mf* de navío; (= *deputy*) lugarteniente *mf*
CPD ▸ **lieutenant colonel** teniente *mf* coronel ▸ **lieutenant commander** capitán/ana *m/f* de corbeta ▸ **lieutenant general** (*Mil*) teniente *mf* general
life [laɪf] N (PL: **lives**) **1** (= *animate state*) vida *f* • **~ on earth** la vida en la tierra • **bird ~** los pájaros • **there is not much insect ~ here** aquí hay pocos insectos • **plant ~** vida *f* vegetal, las plantas *fpl* • **to bring sb back to ~** resucitar *or* reanimar a algn • **a matter of ~ and death** cosa *f* de vida o muerte • **I don't believe in ~ after death** no creo en la vida después de la muerte • **to risk ~ and limb** jugarse la vida
2 (= *existence*) vida *f* • **the ~ of an ant** la vida de una hormiga • **how's ~?*** ¿cómo te va (la vida)?, ¿qué hubo? (*Mex, Chile*) • **I do have a ~ outside of work, you know** yo hago otras cosas en mi vida aparte de trabajar ¿sabes? • **to begin ~ as ...** empezar la vida como ... • **~ begins at 40** la vida comienza a los 40 • **to depart this ~** (*liter*) partir de esta vida • **in early/later ~** en los años juveniles/maduras • **I can't for the ~ of me remember*** por más que lo intento no puedo recordar • **I clung on for dear ~** me agarré como si me fuera la vida en ello • **she was fighting for her ~** se debatía entre la vida y la muerte • **run for your ~!** ¡sálvese quien pueda! • **to be on trial for one's ~** ser acusado de un crimen capital • **you gave me the fright of my ~!** ¡qué susto me diste! • **~ goes on** *or* **must go on** la vida sigue • **to lay down one's ~** dar su vida, entregar su vida • **to lose one's ~** perder la vida • **how many lives were lost?** ¿cuántas víctimas hubo? • **three lives were lost** murieron tres • **never in my ~** en mi vida • **in the next ~** en el más allá, en la otra vida • **to have a ~ of its own** [*object, machine*] tener vida propia • **in real ~** en la vida real • **to see ~** ver mundo • **to spend one's ~ doing sth** pasar la vida haciendo algo • **to take sb's ~** quitar la vida a algn • **to take one's own ~** quitarse la vida, suicidarse • **you'll be taking your ~ in your hands if you climb up there** subir allí es jugarse la vida • **at my time of ~** a mi edad, con los años que yo tengo • **his ~ won't be worth living** más le valdría morirse • **it's more than my ~'s worth** sería jugarme la vida; ▹ **bed, private, save'**
3 (= *way of living*) • **country/city ~** la vida de la ciudad/del campo • **the good ~** una vida agradable; (*Rel*) la vida santa • **it's a good ~** es una vida agradable • **I've had a good ~** la vida me ha tratado bien • **it's a hard ~** la vida es muy dura • **to make a new ~ for o.s.** • **to start a new ~** comenzar una vida nueva • **to live one's own ~** ser dueño de su propia vida • **to lead a quiet ~** llevar una vida tranquila; ▹ **Riley**
4 (*in exclamations*) • **get a ~!*** ¡espabílate y haz algo! • **(upon) my ~!**† ¡Dios mío! • **not on your ~!*** ¡ni hablar! • **such is ~!** • **that's ~!** ¡así es la vida! • **this is the ~!** ¡esto sí que es vida!, ¡esto es jauja! • **what a ~!** (= *bad*) ¡qué vida esta!; (= *good*) ¡vaya vida!, ¡eso sí que es vivir bien!
5 (= *liveliness*) vida *f* • **his acting brought the character to ~** su actuación dio vida al personaje • **she brought the party to ~** animó la fiesta • **to come to ~** animarse • **to put** *or* **breathe new ~ into sth/sb** infundir nueva vida a algo/algn • **you need to put a bit of ~ into it** tienes que ponerle un poco de garra • **the ~ and soul of the party** el alma de la fiesta
6 (= *lifespan*) [*of person*] vida *f*; [*of licence*] vigencia *f*, validez *f*; [*of battery*] vida *f*, duración *f* • **during the ~ of this government** durante el mandato de este gobierno • **friends for ~** amigos *mpl* para siempre • **scarred for ~** con una cicatriz de por vida • **a job for ~** un trabajo para toda la vida • **these birds mate for ~** estas aves tienen una sola pareja en su vida • **it was her ~'s work** fue el trabajo de toda su vida
7* (= *life imprisonment*) • **to do ~** cumplir una condena de cadena *or* reclusión perpetua • **to get ~** • **be sentenced to ~** ser condenado a cadena *or* reclusión perpetua
8 (*Art*) • **to paint from ~** pintar del natural • **true to ~** fiel a la realidad
9 (= *biography*) vida *f*
10 (*US‡*) [*of prostitute*] • **she's in the ~** hace la calle*, es una mujer de la vida
CPD ▸ **life and death struggle** lucha *f* a vida o muerte ▸ **life annuity** pensión *f or* anualidad *f* vitalicia ▸ **life assurance** seguro *m* de vida ▸ **life class** (*Art*) clase *f* de dibujo al natural ▸ **life coach** *profesional encargado de mejorar la situación laboral y personal de sus clientes* ▸ **life cycle** ciclo *m* vital ▸ **life drawing** dibujo *m* del natural ▸ **life expectancy** esperanza *f* de vida ▸ **life force** fuerza *f* vital ▸ **life form** forma *f* de vida ▸ **Life Guards** (*Brit*) (*Mil*) *regimiento de caballería* ▸ **life history** [*of person*] (historia *f* de la) vida *f*; (*hum, iro*) vida *f* y milagros* *mpl* • **the ~ history of the salmon** (la historia de) la vida del salmón ▸ **life imprisonment** cadena *f* perpetua ▸ **life insurance** = **life assurance** ▸ **life interest** usufructo *m* vitalicio ▸ **life jacket** chaleco *m* salvavidas ▸ **life member** miembro *m* vitalicio ▸ **life membership** • **to take out a ~ membership** inscribirse como miembro vitalicio *or* de por vida ▸ **life peer** (*Brit*) (*Parl*) *miembro de la Cámara de los Lores de carácter no hereditario* ▸ **life preserver** (*Brit*) cachiporra *f*; (*US*) chaleco *m* salvavidas ▸ **life president** presidente *mf* de por vida ▸ **life raft** balsa *f* salvavidas ▸ **life sciences** ciencias *fpl* de la vida ▸ **life sentence** condena *f* a perpetuidad ▸ **life span** [*of person*] vida *f*; [*of product*] vida *f* útil ▸ **life story** biografía *f* ▸ **life vest** (*US*) chaleco *m* salvavidas
life-affirming ['laɪfəfɜ:mɪŋ] ADJ [*film, book, comedy*] optimista
lifebelt ['laɪfbelt] N salvavidas *m inv*, flotador *m*
lifeblood ['laɪfblʌd] N sangre *f* vital; (*fig*) alma *f*, sustento *m*
lifeboat ['laɪfbəʊt] N (*from shore*) lancha *f* de socorro; (*from ship*) bote *m* salvavidas
CPD ▸ **lifeboat station** estación *f* de lanchas de socorro
lifeboatman ['laɪfbəʊtmən] N (PL: **lifeboatmen**) tripulante *mf* de una lancha de socorro
lifebuoy ['laɪfbɔɪ] N boya *f* salvavidas, guindola *f*
life-enhancing ['laɪfɪn'hɑ:nsɪŋ] ADJ [*experience*] edificante; [*drug*] que alarga la vida
life-giving ['laɪfgɪvɪŋ] ADJ que da vida, vivificante
lifeguard ['laɪfgɑ:d] N (*on beach*) salvavidas *mf inv*, socorrista *mf*
lifeless ['laɪflɪs] ADJ [*body*] sin vida, exánime; [*streets*] sin vida, desolado; [*face, voice, eyes*] apagado, sin vida; [*hair*] sin cuerpo, lacio
lifelessly ['laɪflɪslɪ] ADV • **she lay ~ on the floor** yacía inerte en el suelo
lifelessness ['laɪflɪsnɪs] N (*fig*) falta *f* de vida
lifelike ['laɪflaɪk] ADJ natural; (= *seemingly real*) que parece vivo • **her photo is so ~** la foto es el vivo retrato de ella
lifeline ['laɪflaɪn] N cuerda *f* de salvamento; (*fig*) cordón *m* umbilical, sustento *m*
lifelong ['laɪflɒŋ] ADJ de toda la vida
lifer* ['laɪfəʳ] N presidiario *m* de por vida, condenado/a *m/f* a cadena perpetua
life-saver ['laɪf,seɪvəʳ] N salvador(a) *m/f*; (= *lifeguard*) socorrista *mf*
life-saving ['laɪfseɪvɪŋ] N salvamento *m*; (= *training for life-saving*) socorrismo *m*
ADJ [*equipment*] de salvamento, salvavidas; (*Med*) [*operation*] a vida o muerte • **she was rushed to hospital for a life-saving operation** la ingresaron de urgencia en el hospital para operarla a vida o muerte
life-size ['laɪf'saɪz], **life-sized** ['laɪf'saɪzd] ADJ de tamaño natural
lifestyle ['laɪfstaɪl] N estilo *m* de vida
life-support ['laɪfsə,pɔ:t] ADJ • **life-support system** sistema *m* de respiración asistida (*pulmón artificial etc*)
CPD ▸ **life-support machine** (*Brit*) máquina *f* de respiración asistida • **to be on a life-support machine** estar conectado a una máquina de respiración asistida • **he's on a life-support machine** está conectado a una máquina de respiración asistida
life-threatening ['laɪfθretnɪŋ] ADJ [*disease, injury, emergency*] de vida o muerte • **a life-threatening heart condition** una grave afección cardíaca
lifetime ['laɪftaɪm] N **1** (= *lifespan*) vida *f* • **in my ~** durante mi vida, en el curso de mi vida • **in the ~ of this parliament** en el transcurso de esta legislatura • **within my ~** mientras viva • **the chance of a ~** una oportunidad única en la vida • **once in a ~** una vez en la vida • **the work of a ~** el trabajo de toda una vida
2 (*fig*) eternidad *f* • **it seemed a ~** pareció una eternidad
CPD ▸ **lifetime achievement** • **an award for ~ achievement** • **a ~ achievement award** un premio a toda una vida • **a prize for ~ achievement in the arts** un premio a toda una vida en el mundo de las artes
lifework ['laɪf'wɜ:k] N trabajo *m* de toda la vida
LIFO ['laɪfəʊ] ABBR (= **last in, first out**) UEPS
lift [lɪft] N **1** (*Brit*) (= *elevator*) ascensor *m*; (*for goods*) montacargas *m inv*
2 (*esp Brit*) (*in car*) • **never accept ~s from strangers** nunca te montes en un coche con extraños • **can I give you a ~?** ¿quiere que le lleve (en coche)?, ¿quiere que le dé aventón? (*Mex*), ¿quiere que le dé un aventón? (*Col*) • **she gave me a ~ home** me llevó a casa en coche, me acompañó con su coche a casa; ▹ **hitch**
3 (*fig*) (= *boost*) • **to give sb a ~** (*psychologically*) levantar el ánimo a algn; (*physically*) dar fuerzas a algn
4 (*Aer*) propulsión *f*
VT **1** (= *raise, pick up*) [+ *cover, box, head*]

levantar; [+ *phone, receiver*] descolgar, coger (*Sp*); [+ *child*] tomar en brazos, coger en brazos (*Sp*), alzar; [+ *invalid*] mover • **this suitcase is too heavy for me to ~** esta maleta pesa demasiado para que yo la levante • **he ~ed his eyes and looked out of the window** levantó *or* alzó la vista y miró por la ventana • **the wind ~ed the balloon into the air** el viento se llevó el globo por los aires • **he ~ed the lid off the pan** levantó la tapadera de la olla, destapó la olla • **he ~ed the child onto his knee** alzó *or* (*Sp*) cogió al niño y lo sentó en su rodilla • **to ~ sb's spirits** levantar el ánimo a algn • **she ~ed her glass to her lips** se llevó el vaso a los labios • **to ~ weights** (*Sport*) hacer *or* levantar pesas • IDIOMS: • **she never ~s a finger to help** no mueve un dedo para ayudar • **to ~ the lid on sth** destapar algo
2 (= *remove*) [+ *restrictions, sanctions*] levantar
3 (= *dig up*) [+ *potatoes, carrots*] recoger
4 (= *improve*) mejorar • **they need to ~ their game to win** tienen que mejorar su juego si quieren ganar
5* (= *steal*) [+ *goods, money*] mangar*, birlar*; [+ *idea, quotation*] copiar, plagiar • **the article was ~ed from a newspaper** el artículo fue copiado *or* plagiado de un periódico
(VI) **1** (= *rise*) levantarse, alzarse (*LAm*)
2 (= *raise*) • **a bra which ~s and separates** un sujetador que realza y separa el busto
3 (= *disappear*) [*mist, fog*] disiparse; [*depression*] desaparecer • **his mood seemed to have ~ed** parecía estar de mejor humor
4 (= *cheer up*) • **his spirits ~ed at the thought of seeing her** se le levantaron los ánimos al pensar que iba a verla
(CPD) ▸ **lift attendant** (*Brit*) ascensorista *mf* ▸ **lift cage** (*Brit*) caja *f* de ascensor ▸ **lift operator** (*Brit*) = **lift attendant** ▸ **lift shaft** (*Brit*) caja *f or* hueco *m* del ascensor
▸ **lift down** (VT + ADV) bajar • **to ~ sth down from a shelf** bajar algo de una estantería
▸ **lift off** (VT + ADV) [+ *lid, cover*] quitar, levantar
(VI + ADV) **1** (= *gen*) levantarse • **the top ~s off** la parte de arriba se levanta
2 [*spacecraft*] despegar
▸ **lift out** (VT + ADV) **1** (*gen*) sacar • **he ~ed the child out of his playpen** sacó al niño del parque
2 (*Mil*) [+ *troops*] evacuar
▸ **lift up** (VT + ADV) [+ *object, cover*] levantar; [+ *head, person*] levantar, alzar • **to ~ up one's eyes** levantar *or* alzar la vista
(VI + ADV) levantarse • **the seat ~s up to reveal storage space** el asiento se levanta dejando ver un espacio para guardar cosas

lift-off ['lɪftɒf] (N) despegue *m*

ligament ['lɪgəmənt] (N) ligamento *m*

ligature ['lɪgətʃəʳ] (N) (*Med, Mus*) ligadura *f*; (*Typ*) ligado *m*

light¹ [laɪt] (VB: PT, PP: **lit** *or* **lighted**) (N)
1 (= *not darkness*) luz *f* • **she was sitting with her back to the ~** *or* **with the ~ behind her** estaba sentada de espaldas a la luz • **the ~ was beginning to fade** estaba empezando a oscurecer • **her hair is almost black in certain ~s** según como le da la luz tiene el pelo casi negro • **against the ~** al trasluz • **to hold sth against the ~** acercar algo a la luz, mirar algo al trasluz • **by the ~ of the moon/a candle** a la luz de la luna/de una vela • **at first ~** al rayar el día • **you're (standing) in my ~** me quitas la luz, me haces sombra • • **~ and shade** luz y sombra; (*Art*) claroscuro *m* • **to hold sth up to the ~** acercar algo a la luz, mirar algo al trasluz • IDIOMS: • **to see (a) ~ at the end of the tunnel** ver la salida del túnel, ver una solución al problema • **to bring sth to ~** sacar algo a la luz • **to shed** *or* **throw** *or* **cast ~ on sth** arrojar luz sobre algo • **in the cold ~ of day** a la luz del día; (*fig*) pensándolo con calma • **to come to ~** salir a la luz (pública) • **new facts have come to ~** han salido a la luz nuevos datos • **(the) ~ dawned on him/her** se dio cuenta, comprendió • **to hide one's ~ (under a bushel)** quitarse importancia, ser modesto • **he was the ~ of her life** era la niña de sus ojos • **to see the ~** (*Rel*) ver la luz; (= *understand*) abrir los ojos, ver la luz (*hum*) • **to see the ~ (of day)** ver la luz (del día); ▹ **leading**
2 (= *lamp*) luz *f* • **in the distance I could see the ~s of a town** a lo lejos veía las luces de una ciudad • **to switch on** *or* **turn on the ~** encender la luz • **to switch off** *or* **turn off the ~** apagar la luz • IDIOM: • **to go out like a ~*** (= *fall asleep*) dormirse al instante; (= *lose consciousness*) caer (en) redondo*; ▹ **bright, runway**
3 (= *electricity*) luz *f* • **electric ~** luz *f* eléctrica
4 (*Aut*) (*on vehicle*) luz *f* • **rear** *or* **tail ~s** pilotos *mpl*, luces *fpl* traseras, calaveras *fpl* (*Mex*) • **reversing ~s** luces *fpl* de marcha atrás
5 (= *traffic signal*) semáforo *m* • **a red/green/amber ~** un semáforo en rojo/verde/ámbar • **to go through a red ~** saltarse un semáforo en rojo • **the ~s** el semáforo • **the ~s were at** *or* **on red** el semáforo estaba en rojo • **the ~s were against us all the way** nos tocaron todos los semáforos en rojo; ▹ **green**
6 (= *viewpoint*) • **according to** *or* **by sb's ~s** (*frm*) según el parecer de algn • **to see things/look at sth in a different** *or* **new ~** ver las cosas/mirar algo con una perspectiva distinta *or* desde otro punto de vista • **I began to see my friends in a new ~** empecé a ver a mis amigos con otros ojos • **to show** *or* **portray sth/sb in a good/bad ~** dar una buena/mala imagen de algo/algn • **this shows our country in a bad ~** esto da una mala imagen de nuestro país • **in the ~ of what you have said ...** en vista de *or* a la luz de lo que has dicho ...
7 (= *glint, twinkle*) brillo *m* • **there was a strange ~ in his eye** había un brillo extraño en su mirada
8 (= *flame*) • **have you got a ~?** (*for cigarette*) ¿tienes fuego? • **to set ~ to sth** (*Brit*) prender fuego a algo; ▹ **strike**
9 (*Archit*) cristal *m*, vidrio *m*
(ADJ) (COMPAR: **lighter**, SUPERL: **lightest**)
1 (= *bright*) [*room, hallway*] con bastante luz • **her house is ~ and airy** su casa tiene bastante luz y ventilación • • **~ summer evenings** las claras tardes de verano • **while it's still ~** mientras es de día *or* hay luz • **to get ~** hacerse de día
2 (= *pale*) [*colour*] claro; [*hair*] rubio, güero (*CAm, Mex*); [*skin*] blanco • • **~ blue/green** azul/verde claro • • **in colour** de color claro
(VT) **1** (= *illuminate*) iluminar • **she appeared at a ~ed window** se asomó a la ventana de una habitación iluminada • **to ~ the way for sb** alumbrar (el camino) a algn
2 (= *ignite*) [+ *match, candle, fire*] encender, prender; [+ *cigarette*] encender
(VI) (= *ignite*) encenderse, prender • **the fire wouldn't ~** el fuego no se encendía, el fuego no prendía
(CPD) ▸ **light bulb** bombilla *f*, foco *m* (*And*), bombillo *m* (*Col, Ven*) ▸ **light fitting** *instalación eléctrica donde se colocan bombillas, tubos fluorescentes etc* ▸ **light meter** (*Phot*) fotómetro *m* ▸ **light pen** lápiz *m* óptico ▸ **light show** espectáculo *m* de luces ▸ **lights out** hora *f* de apagar las luces • **what time is ~s out?** ¿a qué hora se apagan las luces? ▸ **light switch** interruptor *m* ▸ **light wave** onda *f* luminosa ▸ **light year** año *m* luz • **3000 ~ years away** a una distancia de 3000 años luz
▸ **light out**†* (VI + ADV) largarse* (**for** para)
▸ **light up** (VI + ADV) **1** (*gen*) iluminarse • **her face lit up** se le iluminó la cara
2* (= *light cigarette*) encender un cigarrillo
(VT + ADV) iluminar

light² [laɪt] (ADJ) (COMPAR: **lighter**, SUPERL: **lightest**) **1** (*in weight*) [*object, clothing, equipment*] ligero, liviano (*LAm*); [*step*] ligero • **I want to be ten pounds ~er** quiero adelgazar diez libras • **I'm ten pounds ~er than I was** peso diez libras menos que antes • **to be ~ on one's feet** ser ligero de pies • **with a ~ heart** (= *cheerfully*) con el corazón alegre; (= *without thinking*) a la ligera • **you need a ~ touch to make good pastry** necesitas manos de seda para conseguir una buena masa • IDIOM: • **as ~ as a feather** ligero como una pluma
2 (= *scanty, slight*) [*breeze*] leve, suave; [*shower*] ligero • **a ~ rain was falling** lloviznaba • **a ~ fall of snow** una ligera nevada • **trading was ~ on the Stock Exchange** hubo poca actividad en la Bolsa • **traffic was ~** había poco tráfico • **the speech was ~ on content** el discurso tenía poco contenido
3 (*Culin*) [*meal, food, cake*] ligero, liviano (*LAm*)
4 (= *low-alcohol*) de bajo contenido alcohólico, de bajo contenido en alcohol; (= *low-calorie*) light, bajo en calorías; (= *low-tar*) light, de bajo contenido en alquitrán
5 (= *soft*) [*sound*] leve; [*voice*] suave • **there was a ~ tapping on the door** se oyeron unos golpecitos a la puerta
6 (= *not demanding*) [*work, duties*] ligero • **she can only manage ~ work** solo puede realizar tareas ligeras • IDIOM: • **to make ~ work of sth** hacer algo con facilidad
7 (= *not serious*) [*novel, music*] ligero • **to make ~ of sth** quitar importancia a algo • **on a ~er note** hablando de cosas menos serias • **take along some ~ reading** llévate algo fácil de leer
8 (= *not harsh*) [*sentence*] leve
9 (= *shallow*) • **she had drifted into a ~ sleep** se había quedado medio dormida • **to be a ~ sleeper** tener el sueño ligero
10 (= *loose*) [*soil*] poco denso
(ADV) • **to travel ~** viajar con poco equipaje
(N) **1 lights** (*Culin*†) pulmones *mpl*
2 (= *cigarette*) cigarrillo *m* light, cigarrillo *m* de bajo contenido en alquitrán
(CPD) ▸ **light aircraft** avión *m* ligero ▸ **light ale, light beer** (*US*) cerveza *f* rubia, cerveza *f* clara ▸ **light cream** (*US*) (= *single cream*) nata *f* líquida ▸ **light entertainment** (*TV*) programas *mpl* de variedades • **a stand-up comedian provided ~ entertainment** un humorista amenizó la velada ▸ **light heavyweight** (= *cruiserweight*) peso *m* semipesado ▸ **light industry** industria *f* ligera ▸ **light infantry** infantería *f* ligera ▸ **light opera** (= *show*) opereta *f*; (= *genre*) género *m* lírico ▸ **light verse** poesías *fpl* festivas

light³ [laɪt] (PT, PP: **lit** *or* **lighted**) (VI) • **to ~ on sth** (*liter*) dar con algo, tropezar con algo, encontrar algo

light-coloured ['laɪt'kʌləd] (ADJ) claro, de color claro

light-emitting diode [,laɪtɪmɪtɪŋ'daɪəʊd] (N) diodo *m* luminoso

lighten¹ ['laɪtn] (VT) [+ *room*] iluminar más; [+ *sky*] iluminar; [+ *color*] hacer más claro
(VI) [*sky*] clarear; (*Met*) relampaguear

lighten² ['laɪtn] (VT) [+ *load*] aligerar, hacer menos pesado; (*fig*) (= *make cheerful*)

[+ *atmosphere*] relajar; [+ *heart*] alegrar; (= *reduce*) [+ *cares*] aliviar
(VI) [*load*] aligerarse, hacerse menos pesado; [*heart*] alegrarse

lighter[1] ['laɪtə^r] (N) (*also* **cigarette lighter**) encendedor *m*, mechero *m*
(CPD) ▸ **lighter flint** piedra *f* de mechero ▸ **lighter fuel** gas *m* de encendedor

lighter[2] ['laɪtə^r] (N) (*Naut*) gabarra *f*, barcaza *f*

lightfast ['laɪtfɑːst] (ADJ) que no se descolora con la luz

light-fingered ['laɪt'fɪŋgəd] (ADJ) con las manos muy largas • **to be light-fingered** tener las manos muy largas, ser muy amigo de lo ajeno

light-footed ['laɪt'fʊtɪd] (ADJ) ligero (de pies)

light-haired ['laɪt'hɛəd] (ADJ) rubio, güero (*CAm, Mex*)

light-headed ['laɪt'hedɪd] (ADJ) (*by temperament*) ligero de cascos*; (= *dizzy*) mareado; (*with fever*) delirante; (*with excitement*) exaltado • **wine makes me light-headed** el vino se me sube a la cabeza

light-hearted ['laɪt'hɑːtɪd] (ADJ) desenfadado, alegre; [*remark*] poco serio, dicho en tono festivo

light-heartedly ['laɪt'hɑːtɪdlɪ] (ADV) alegremente

lighthouse ['laɪthaʊs] (N) (PL: **lighthouses** ['laɪthaʊzɪz]) faro *m*
(CPD) ▸ **lighthouse keeper** farero/a *m/f*, torrero/a *m/f*

lighting ['laɪtɪŋ] (N) (= *act*) iluminación *f*; [*of fire*] encendimiento *m*; [*of cigarette*] encendido *m*; (= *system*) alumbrado *m*; (*at pop show*) equipo *m* de luces, iluminación *f*; (*Theat*) iluminación *f*
(CPD) ▸ **lighting effects** efectos *mpl* luminosos ▸ **lighting engineer** luminotécnico/a *m/f*

lighting-up time [,laɪtɪŋ'ʌptaɪm] (N) hora *f* de encender los faros

lightless ['laɪtlɪs] (ADJ) oscuro, sin luz

lightly ['laɪtlɪ] (ADV) **1** (= *gently, softly*) [*touch, knock*] suavemente; [*tread, walk*] con paso ligero • **she kissed him ~ on the forehead** le dio un beso con suavidad en la frente • **brush ~ with beaten egg** extienda una ligera capa de huevo batido
2 (= *slightly*) levemente, ligeramente • **~ clad** ligero de ropa, con muy poca ropa • **season ~ with salt and pepper** sazone con un poquito de sal y pimienta • **a ~ boiled egg** un huevo poco cocido, un huevo pasado por agua • **to touch ~ on a matter** mencionar un asunto de paso
3 (= *frivolously*) a la ligera • **this is not a charge to be made ~** este tipo de acusación no se hace a la ligera • **to get off ~** librarse de una buena • **to speak ~ of danger** despreciar el peligro

lightness[1] ['laɪtnɪs] (N) **1** (= *brightness*) [*of room*] luminosidad *f*
2 (= *paleness*) [*of colour*] claridad *f*

lightness[2] ['laɪtnɪs] (N) **1** (*in weight*) ligereza *f*, liviandad *f* (*LAm*); (*Culin*) [*of pastry, mixture*] ligereza *f*, suavidad *f* • **a feeling of ~ came over her** le invadió una sensación de ligereza • **her ~ of step** la ligereza *or* agilidad de sus pasos
2 (= *undemanding nature*) [*of duties*] ligereza *f*
3 [*of tone, voice*] suavidad *f*
4 [*of sentence*] levedad *f*

lightning ['laɪtnɪŋ] (N) (= *flash*) relámpago *m*; (= *stroke*) rayo *m* • **a flash of ~** un relámpago • **where the ~ struck** donde cayó el rayo • IDIOMS: • **as quick as ~** • **like (greased) ~*** como un rayo • PROVERB: • **~ never strikes twice in the same place** desgracias así no suelen repetirse
(CPD) ▸ **lightning attack** ataque *m* relámpago ▸ **lightning bug** (*US*) (= *firefly*) luciérnaga *f* ▸ **lightning conductor**, **lightning rod** (*US*) pararrayos *m inv* ▸ **lightning strike** huelga *f* relámpago ▸ **lightning visit** visita *f* relámpago

lightproof ['laɪtpruːf] (ADJ) a prueba de luz

lightship ['laɪtʃɪp] (N) buque-faro *m*

light-skinned [,laɪt'skɪnd] (ADJ) de piel blanca

lightweight ['laɪtweɪt] (ADJ) (*gen*) ligero, de poco peso, liviano (*esp LAm*); (*Boxing*) de peso ligero
(N) (*Boxing*) peso *m* ligero; (*fig*) (*pej*) persona *f* de poco peso *or* sin importancia

ligneous ['lɪgnɪəs] (ADJ) leñoso

lignite ['lɪgnaɪt] (N) lignito *m*

lignum vitae ['lɪgnəm'viːtaɪ] (N) palo *m* santo; (= *tree*) guayaco *m*

Ligures ['lɪgjʊəz] (NPL) ligures *mpl*

Ligurian [lɪ'gjʊərɪən] (ADJ) ligur
(N) ligur *mf*

likable ['laɪkəbl] = **likeable**

like[1] [laɪk] (ADJ) (*frm*) (= *similar*) parecido, semejante • **snakes, lizards and ~ creatures** serpientes *fpl*, lagartos *mpl* y criaturas *fpl* parecidas *or* semejantes • **to be of ~ mind** tener ideas afines • **she and a group of friends of ~ mind** ella y un grupo de amigos con ideas afines • **he was very intolerant towards people not of a ~ mind** era muy intransigente con las personas que no le daban la razón • IDIOM: • **they are as ~ as two peas (in a pod)** se parecen como dos gotas de agua
(PREP) **1** (= *similar to*) como • **what's he ~?** ¿cómo es (él)? • **you know what she's ~** ya la conoces, ya sabes cómo es • **what's Spain ~?** ¿cómo es España? • **what's the weather ~?** ¿qué tiempo hace? • **a house ~ mine** una casa como la mía, una casa parecida a la mía • **I found one ~ it** encontré uno parecido *or* igual • **she was ~ a sister to me** fue (como) una hermana para mí • **we heard a noise ~ someone sneezing** nos pareció oír a alguien estornudar, oímos como un estornudo • **I never saw anything ~ it** nunca he visto cosa igual *or* semejante • **what's he ~ as a teacher?** ¿qué tal es como profesor? • **to be ~ sth/sb** parecerse a algo/algn, ser parecido a algo/algn • **you're so ~ your father** (*in looks, character*) te pareces mucho a tu padre, eres muy parecido a tu padre • **this portrait is not ~ him** en este retrato no parece él • **it was more ~ a prison than a house** se parecía más a una cárcel que a una casa • **the figure is more ~ 300** la cifra se acerca más bien a 300 • **why can't you be more ~ your sister?** ¿por qué no aprendes de tu hermana? • **that's more ~ it!*** ¡así está mejor!, ¡así me gusta! • **there's nothing ~ real silk** no hay nada como la seda natural • **something ~ that** algo así, algo por el estilo • **I was thinking of giving her something ~ a doll** pensaba en regalarle algo así como una muñeca, pensaba en regalarle una muñeca o algo por el estilo • **they earn something ~ £50,000 a year** ganan alrededor de 50.000 libras al año • **people ~ that can't be trusted** esa clase *or* ese tipo de gente no es de fiar; ▹ **feel, look, smell, sound**[1], **taste**
2 (= *typical of*) • **it's not ~ him to do that** no es propio de él hacer eso • **isn't it just ~ him!** ¡no cambia!, ¡eso es típico de él! • **(it's) just ~ you to grab the last cake!** ¡qué típico que tomes *or* (*Sp*) cojas tú el último pastelito!
3 (= *similarly to*) como • **he thinks ~ us** piensa como nosotros • **~ me, he is fond of Brahms** igual que a mí, le gusta Brahms • **she behaved ~ an idiot** se comportó como una idiota • **just ~ anybody else** igual que cualquier otro • **~ this/that** así • **it wasn't ~ that** no fue así, no ocurrió así • **I'm sorry to intrude on you ~ this** siento importunarte de este modo • **stop pacing ~ that** deja de dar vueltas • **he got up and left, just ~ that** se levantó y se marchó, así, sin más • PROVERB: • **~ father ~ son** de tal palo tal astilla; ▹ **anything, crazy, hell, mad**
4 (= *such as*) como • **large cities ~ New York** las grandes urbes como Nueva York • **the basic necessities of life, ~ food and drink** las necesidades básicas de la vida, como la comida y la bebida
(ADV) **1** (= *comparable*) • **on company advice, well, orders, more ~** siguiendo los consejos de la empresa, bueno, más bien sus órdenes • **it's nothing ~ as hot as it was yesterday** no hace tanto calor como ayer, ni mucho menos • **£500 will be nothing ~ enough** 500 libras no serán suficientes, ni mucho menos
2 (= *likely*) • **(as) ~ as not**: • **they'll be down the pub (as) ~ as not** lo más probable es que estén en el bar
(CONJ)* **1** (= *as*) como • **~ we used to (do)** como solíamos (hacer) • **do it ~ I do** hazlo como yo • **it's just ~ I say** es como yo digo* • IDIOM: • **to tell it ~ it is** decir las cosas como son
2 (= *as if*) como si • **he behaved ~ he was afraid** se comportaba como si tuviera miedo • **you look ~ you've seen a ghost** parece que acabas de ver un fantasma
(N) • **we shall not see his ~ again** (*frm, liter*) no volveremos a ver otro igual • **the exchange was done on a ~-for-like basis** el intercambio se hizo basándose en dos cosas parecidas • **did you ever see the ~ (of it)?** ¿has visto cosa igual? • **I've no time for the ~s of him*** no soporto a la gente como él • **sparrows, starlings and the ~** *or* **and such ~** gorriones, estorninos y otras aves por el estilo • **to compare ~ with ~** comparar dos cosas semejantes • IDIOM: • **~ attracts ~** Dios los cría y ellos se juntan

like[2] [laɪk] (VT) **1** (= *find pleasant*) • **I ~ dancing/football** me gusta bailar/el fútbol • **I ~ bright colours** me gustan los colores vivos • **which do you ~ best?** ¿cuál es el que más te gusta? • **your father won't ~ it** esto no le va a gustar a tu padre • **I ~ oysters but they don't ~ me*** me gustan las ostras pero no me sientan muy bien • **we ~ it here** nos gusta este sitio • **I ~ him** me cae bien *or* simpático • **I don't ~ him at all** me resulta antipático, no me cae nada bien • **I've come to ~ him** le he llegado a tomar *or* (*Sp*) coger cariño • **don't you ~ me just a little bit?** ¿no me quieres un poquitín? • **you know he ~s you very much** sabes que te tiene mucho cariño *or* que te quiere mucho • **I don't think they ~ each other** creo que no se caen bien • **I don't ~ the look of him** no me gusta su aspecto, no me gusta la pinta que tiene* • **I ~ your nerve!*** ¡qué frescura!, ¡qué cara tienes! • **well, I ~ that!*** (*iro*) ¡será posible!, ¡habráse visto! • **she is well ~d here** aquí se la quiere mucho
2 (= *feel about*) • **how do you ~ Cadiz?** ¿qué te parece Cádiz? • **how do you ~ it here?** ¿qué te parece este sitio? • **how would you ~ to go to the cinema?** ¿te apetece *or* (*LAm*) se te antoja ir al cine? • **how would you ~ it if somebody did the same to you?** ¿cómo te sentirías si alguien te hiciera lo mismo? • **how do you ~ that! I've been here five years and he doesn't know my name** ¡qué te parece!, llevo

cinco años trabajando aquí y no sabe ni cómo me llamo

3 (= *have a preference for*) • **I ~ my whisky neat** me gusta el whisky solo • **this plant doesn't ~ sunlight** a esta planta no le gusta la luz • **I ~ to know the facts before I form opinions** me gusta conocer los hechos antes de formarme una opinión • **I ~ to be obeyed** me gusta que me obedezcan • **she ~s him to be home by ten** le gusta que esté en casa antes de las diez • **I ~ to think I'm not prejudiced** creo que no tengo prejuicios • **I ~ to think of myself as a humanitarian** me considero una persona humanitaria

4 (= *want*) • **I didn't ~ to say no** no quise decir que no; (*because embarrassed*) me dio vergüenza decir que no • **take as much as you ~** toma *or* coge todo lo que quieras • **he thinks he can do as he ~s** cree que puede hacer lo que quiera, cree que puede hacer lo que le de la gana* • **whether he ~s it or not** le guste o no (le guste), quiera o no (quiera) • **whenever you ~** cuando quieras

5 • **would/should ~ a** (*specific request, offer, desire*) • **would you ~ a drink?** ¿quieres tomar algo? • **I'd ~ you to do it** quiero que lo hagas • **would you ~ me to wait?** ¿quiere que espere? • **I'd** *or* **I would** *or* (*frm*) **I should ~ an explanation** quisiera una explicación, me gustaría que me dieran una explicación • **I'd ~ to think we're still friends** quisiera creer que todavía somos amigos • **I'd ~ to take this opportunity to thank you all** quisiera aprovechar esta oportunidad para darles las gracias a todos • **I'd ~ the roast chicken, please** (me trae) el pollo asado, por favor • **I'd ~ three pounds of tomatoes, please** (me da) tres libras de tomates, por favor

b (*wishes, preferences*) • **I'd ~ a bigger flat** me gustaría tener un piso más grande • **he'd ~ to have met her** le hubiera gustado conocerla • **I should ~ to have been there** • **I should have ~d to be there** (*frm*) me hubiera gustado estar allí

VI querer • **as you ~** como quieras • **"shall we go now?" — "if you ~"** —¿nos vamos ya? —si quieres

N **likes** gustos *mpl* • **~s and dis~s** aficiones *fpl* y fobias *or* manías, cosas *fpl* que gustan y cosas que no • **he has distinct ~s and dis~s where food is concerned** con respecto a la comida tiene claras preferencias *or* sabe muy bien lo que le gusta y lo que no (le gusta)

LIKE

Verb

"Gustar" better avoided

▷ *While* **gustar** *is one of the main ways of translating* **like**, *its use is not always appropriate. Used to refer to people, it may imply sexual attraction. Instead, use expressions like* **caer bien** *or* **parecer/resultar simpático/agradable**. *These expressions work like* **gustar** *and need an indirect object:*

I like Francis very much
Francis me cae muy bien *or* me parece muy simpático *or* agradable
She likes me, but that's all
(A ella) le caigo bien, pero nada más

Like + verb

▷ *Translate* **to like doing sth** *and* **to like to do sth** *using* **gustar** + *infinitive:*

Doctors don't like having to go out to visit patients at night
A los médicos no les gusta tener que salir a visitar pacientes por la noche
My brother likes to rest after lunch
A mi hermano le gusta descansar después de comer

▷ *Translate* **to like sb doing sth** *and* **to like sb to do sth** *using* **gustar** + **que** + *subjunctive:*

My wife likes me to do the shopping
A mi mujer le gusta que haga la compra
I don't like Irene living so far away
No me gusta que Irene viva tan lejos

"How do you like ...?"

▷ *Use* **qué** + **parecer** *to translate* **how do/did you like** *when asking someone's opinion:*

How do you like this coat?
¿Qué te parece este abrigo?
How did you like the concert?
¿Qué te ha parecido el concierto?

▷ *But use* **cómo** + **gustar** *when using* **how do you like** *more literally:*

How do you like your steak?
¿Cómo le gusta la carne?

Would like

▷ *When translating* **would like**, *use* **querer** *with requests and offers and* **gustar** *to talk about preferences and wishes:*

Would you like a glass of water?
¿Quiere un vaso de agua?
What would you like me to do about the tickets?
¿Qué quieres que haga respecto a los billetes?
I'd very much like to go to Spain this summer
Me gustaría mucho ir a España este verano

Literal translations of **I'd like** *are better avoided when making requests in shops and restaurants. Use expressions like the following:*

I'd like steak and chips
¿Me pone un filete con patatas fritas?, (Yo) quiero un filete con patatas fritas

For further uses and examples, see main entry.

...like, -like [laɪk] SUFFIX parecido a, como • **birdlike** como un pájaro • **with queenlike dignity** con dignidad de reina; ▷ **catlike** *etc*

likeable [ˈlaɪkəbl] ADJ simpático, agradable

likeableness [ˈlaɪkəblnɪs] N simpatía *f*

likelihood [ˈlaɪklɪhʊd] N probabilidad *f* • **what is the ~ of a successful outcome?** ¿qué probabilidad hay de que el resultado sea favorable? • **there is no ~ of infection** no hay probabilidad de infección • **there is little/every ~ that he'll come** es poco/muy probable que venga • **there is a strong ~ they'll be elected** es muy probable que salgan elegidos • **in all ~ the explosion was caused by a bomb** lo más probable es que una bomba causase la explosión

likely [ˈlaɪklɪ] ADJ (COMPAR: **likelier**, SUPERL: **likeliest**) **1** (= *probable*) [*outcome, consequences*] probable • **what kind of changes are ~?** ¿qué tipo de cambios son probables? • **snow is ~ on high ground** es probable que nieve en zonas altas • **it is ~ that** es probable que (+ *subjun*) • **it is ~ to rain later on** es probable que llueva más tarde • **they are not ~ to come** no es probable que vengan • **he's ~ to do anything** puede hacer cualquier cosa • **he's the man most ~ to win** es el que más probabilidades tiene de ganar • **a ~ story** *or* **tale!** (*iro*) ¡menudo cuento!, ¡y yo que me lo creo! (*iro*)

2 (= *suitable*) • **this seems a ~ spot for a picnic** este parece un buen sitio para hacer un picnic • **she's the most ~ candidate** es la candidata que parece más idónea • **here comes a ~-looking character** aquí viene un tipo que parece adecuado *or* que bien puede servir

ADV (= *probably*) • **she will very** *or* **most ~ arrive late** lo más probable es que llegue tarde • **some prisoners will ~ be released soon** (*US*) es probable que pronto se deje en libertad a algunos prisioneros • **(as) ~ as not he'll arrive early** lo más probable es que llegue pronto, seguramente llegará pronto • **this is more than ~ true** lo más probable *or* seguro es que sea cierto • **"I expect she'll be re-elected" — "yes, more than ~"** —me imagino que la volverán a elegir —sí, seguramente • **not ~!*** ¡ni hablar!*

like-minded [ˈlaɪkˈmaɪndɪd] ADJ con ideas afines, de igual parecer

liken [ˈlaɪkən] VT comparar (**to** con)

likeness [ˈlaɪknɪs] N **1** (= *resemblance*) semejanza *f*, parecido *m* • **family ~** aire *m* de familia

2 (= *appearance*) aspecto *m* • **in the ~ of ...** a imagen y semejanza de ... • **to assume the ~ of ...** tomar la forma de ..., adoptar la apariencia de ...

3 (= *portrait*) retrato *m* • **it's a good ~** se parece mucho

likewise [ˈlaɪkwaɪz] ADV (= *also*) asimismo, igualmente, también; (= *the same*) lo mismo, igualmente • **~ it is true that ...** asimismo es verdad que ... • **to do ~** hacer lo mismo

liking [ˈlaɪkɪŋ] N (*for thing*) gusto *m* (**for** por), afición *f* (**for** a); (*for person*) simpatía *f*, aprecio *m* (*LAm*) • **to have a ~ for sth** ser aficionado *or* tener afición a algo • **to have a ~ for sb** tener simpatía a algn • **to be to sb's ~** ser del gusto de algn • **to take a ~ to sth/to doing sth** tomar *or* coger gusto a algo/a hacer algo • **to take a ~ to sb** tomar *or* coger simpatía a algn • **it's too strong for my ~** para mí es demasiado fuerte, es demasiado fuerte para mi gusto

lilac [ˈlaɪlək] N (*Bot*) lila *f*; (= *colour*) lila *m*, color *m* lila
ADJ de color lila

Lille [liːl] N Lila *f*

Lilliputian [ˌlɪlɪˈpjuːʃɪən] ADJ liliputiense
N liliputiense *mf*

Lilo® [ˈlaɪləʊ] N colchoneta *f* inflable

lilt [lɪlt] N (*in voice*) tono *m* cantarín; (*in song*) ritmo *m* alegre • **a song with a ~ to it** una canción de ritmo alegre

lilting [ˈlɪltɪŋ] ADJ [*voice*] cantarín

lily [ˈlɪlɪ] N lirio *m*, azucena *f* • **~ of the valley** muguete *m*, lirio *m* de los valles
CPD ▸ **lily pad** hoja *f* de nenúfar

lily-livered [ˈlɪlɪˈlɪvəd] ADJ cobarde, pusilánime

lily-white [ˈlɪlɪwaɪt] ADJ blanco como la azucena

Lima [ˈliːmə] N Lima *f*

lima bean [ˈliːməˌbiːn] N (*US*) fríjol *m* de media luna, judía *f* de la peladilla

limb [lɪm] N (*Anat*) miembro *m*, extremidad *f*; [*of tree*] rama *f* • **to lose a ~** perder uno de los miembros *or* una de las extremidades • IDIOMS: • **to be/go out on a ~** (*in danger*) estar/quedar en peligro; (= *be isolated*) estar/quedarse aislado; (= *take risk*) correr el riesgo • **to tear sb ~ from ~** despedazar a algn; ▷ **life**

-limbed [lɪmd] ADJ (*ending in compounds*)

▹ **long-limbed**

limber¹ [ˈlɪmbəʳ] (ADJ) [*person*] ágil; [*material*] flexible

▸ **limber up** (VI + ADV) (*Sport*) entrar en calor, hacer ejercicios preparatorios; (*fig*) entrenarse, prepararse

limber² [ˈlɪmbəʳ] (N) (*Mil*) armón *m* (de artillería)

limbless [ˈlɪmlɪs] (ADJ) (que está) falto de un brazo *or* una pierna

limbo [ˈlɪmbəʊ] (N) (*Rel*) (*also* **Limbo**) limbo *m*; (= *dance*) limbo *m* • IDIOM: • **to be in ~** [*person*] quedarse nadando entre dos aguas

lime¹ [laɪm] (N) (*Geol*) cal *f*; (*birdlime*) liga *f* (VT) (*Agr*) abonar con cal

lime² [laɪm] (N) (*Bot*) (*also* **lime tree**) (= *linden*) tilo *m*

lime³ [laɪm] (N) (*Bot*) (= *citrus fruit*) lima *f*; (= *tree*) limero *m*; (= *colour*) verde *m* lima (CPD) ▸ **lime cordial** refresco *m* de lima ▸ **lime juice** zumo *m or* (*LAm*) jugo *m* de lima

lime-green [ˌlaɪmˈgriːn] (ADJ) verde lima (*inv*)

limekiln [ˈlaɪmkɪln] (N) horno *m* de cal

limelight [ˈlaɪmlaɪt] (N) luz *f* de calcio • IDIOMS: • **to be in the ~** ser el centro de atención, estar en el candelero • **to hog the ~** acaparar *or* llevarse todo el protagonismo • **he never sought the ~** no trató nunca de acaparar la atención

limerick [ˈlɪmərɪk] (N) *especie de quintilla jocosa*

LIMERICK

Un **limerick** es un poema burlón que consta de cinco versos con rima **aabba**. Las composiciones suelen ir dirigidas a una persona y el tono es normalmente bastante grosero o surrealista. A menudo comienzan con las palabras **there was a...** y contienen dos versos largos seguidos de otros dos cortos más un remate incisivo que puede llevar una rima torpe o inesperada a propósito. A continuación mostramos un ejemplo de **limerick**: **There once was a man from North Wales, Who bought a trombone in the sales; But he found, when he tried it, There was something inside it: Fifty pence and a packet of nails.**

limescale [ˈlaɪmskeɪl] (N) (= *deposit*) cal *f*

limestone [ˈlaɪmstəʊn] (N) (piedra *f*) caliza *f* (CPD) ▸ **limestone pavement** pavimento *m* de piedra caliza

limewash [ˈlaɪmwɒʃ] (VT) cubrir con lechada de cal (N) lechada *f* de cal

limey* [ˈlaɪmɪ] (N) (*US, Canada*) (*pej*) inglés/esa *m/f*

limit [ˈlɪmɪt] (N) **1** (= *cut-off point, furthest extent*) límite *m* • **there is a ~ to my patience** mi paciencia tiene un límite • **there's a ~ to what doctors can do in such cases** lo que pueden hacer los médicos en estos casos es limitado • **to be at the ~ of one's endurance** ya no poder más • **to be at the ~ of one's patience** haber agotado la paciencia • **behaviour beyond the ~s of acceptability** comportamiento *m* que va más allá de los límites de lo aceptable • **to know no ~s** no tener límite(s) • **these establishments are off ~s to ordinary citizens** los ciudadanos de a pie tienen prohibido el acceso a estos establecimientos • **that sort of question is off ~s** ese tipo de pregunta se sale de los límites • **that is outside the ~s of my experience** eso va más allá de los límites de mi experiencia • **it is important that parents set ~s for their children** es importante que los padres les pongan límites a sus hijos • **she tried my patience to the ~** puso mi paciencia a prueba • **it is true within ~s** es verdad dentro de ciertos límites; ▹ **city, sky, stretch**
2 (= *permitted maximum*) límite *m* • **there is no ~ on** *or* **to the amount you can import** no existe un límite con respecto a la cantidad que se puede importar • **one glass of wine's my ~** con un vaso de vino me basta y me sobra • **he was three times over the ~** (*Aut*) había ingerido tres veces más de la cantidad de alcohol permitida (para conducir); ▹ **age, credit, speed, spending, time, weight**
3 • **the ~: it's the ~!*** (= *too much*) ¡es el colmo!, ¡es demasiado! • **he's the ~!** ¡es el colmo!, ¡es el no va más!
4 (*Math*) límite *m*
(VT) [+ *numbers, power, freedom*] limitar; [+ *spending*] restringir • **try to ~ your fat intake** procura limitar el consumo de grasas • **are you ~ed as to time?** ¿tienes el tiempo limitado? • **he ~ed questions to 25 minutes** limitó las preguntas a 25 minutos • **to ~ o.s. to sth** limitarse a algo • **he ~ed himself to a few remarks** se limitó a hacer algunas observaciones • **I ~ myself to ten cigarettes a day** me permito solo diez cigarrillos al día

limitation [ˌlɪmɪˈteɪʃən] (N) limitación *f*, restricción *f*; (*Jur*) prescripción *f* • **he has his ~s** tiene sus limitaciones, tiene sus puntos flacos • **there is no ~ on exports** no hay restricción a las exportaciones

limited [ˈlɪmɪtɪd] (ADJ) **1** (= *small*) [*number, space*] limitado; [*resources*] limitado, escaso; [*range, scope*] limitado, reducido • **we only have a ~ amount of time** solo contamos con una cantidad de tiempo limitada • **to a ~ extent** hasta cierto punto • **"for a limited period only"** "solo por un periodo limitado"
2 (= *restricted*) limitado • **she feels very ~ in her job** se siente muy limitada en su trabajo • **he has ~ use of one arm** tiene algo de movilidad en un brazo • **the choice is ~** hay poca elección
3 (*esp Brit*) (*Jur, Comm*) (*in company names*) • **Hourmont Travel Limited** Hourmont Travel, Sociedad Anónima
(CPD) ▸ **limited company** (*esp Brit*) (*Comm, Jur*) sociedad *f* anónima, sociedad *f* limitada ▸ **limited edition** [*of book*] edición *f* limitada; [*of picture, record*] tirada *f* limitada; [*of car*] serie *f* limitada ▸ **limited liability** (*esp Brit*) (*Jur*) responsabilidad *f* limitada ▸ **limited partnership** (*Comm*) sociedad *f* limitada, sociedad *f* en comandita; ▹ **public**

limiter [ˈlɪmɪtəʳ] (N) **1** (= *limitation*) limitador *m*
2 (*Elec*) limitador *m* de amplitud

limiting [ˈlɪmɪtɪŋ] (ADJ) restrictivo

limitless [ˈlɪmɪtlɪs] (ADJ) ilimitado, sin límites

limo* [ˈlɪməʊ] (N) = **limousine**

limousine [ˈlɪməziːn] (N) limusina *f*

limp¹ [lɪmp] (N) cojera *f* • **to walk with a ~** cojear
(VI) cojear, renguear (*LAm*) • **he ~ed to the door** fue cojeando a la puerta • **the ship managed to ~ to port** el buque llegó con dificultad al puerto

limp² [lɪmp] (ADJ) (COMPAR: **limper**, SUPERL: **limpest**) **1** [*person, body*] sin fuerzas; [*penis*] flácido; [*hair*] lacio; [*handshake*] flojo • **a piece of ~ lettuce** un trozo de lechuga mustia • **she fell ~ at their feet** cayó sin fuerzas a sus pies • **his arms hung ~** los brazos le colgaban muertos *or* como si fueran de trapo • **his body went ~** se le fueron las fuerzas del cuerpo • **she went ~ in his arms** se dejó caer en sus brazos
2 (= *unconvincing*) [*excuse*] pobre, poco convincente
3 (= *soft*) [*book binding*] blando, flexible

limpet [ˈlɪmpɪt] (N) lapa *f* • **like a ~** como una lapa
(CPD) ▸ **limpet mine** mina *f* lapa

limpid [ˈlɪmpɪd] (ADJ) [*water*] límpido, cristalino; [*air*] diáfano, puro; [*eyes*] claro

limply [ˈlɪmplɪ] (ADV) **1** (= *without energy*) [*lie*] sin fuerzas • **his arms hung ~ at his sides** los brazos le colgaban muertos a los lados • **her hair hung ~ over her face** el pelo lacio le caía sin gracia sobre la cara
2 (*fig*) (= *unconvincingly*) [*say*] de manera poco convincente; [*applaud*] sin entusiasmo

limpness [ˈlɪmpnɪs] (N) [*of body, limb*] flojedad *f*; [*of excuse*] lo pobre, lo poco convincente

limp-wristed* [ˈlɪmpˈrɪstɪd] (ADJ) inútil; (*pej*) (= *gay*) de la acera de enfrente, sarasa‡

limy [ˈlaɪmɪ] (ADJ) calizo

linage [ˈlaɪnɪdʒ] (N) (*Press*) número *m* de líneas • **advertising ~** espacio *m* destinado a publicidad

linchpin [ˈlɪntʃpɪn] (N) (*lit*) pezonera *f*; (*fig*) eje *m*

Lincs [lɪŋks] (ABBR) (*Brit*) = **Lincolnshire**

linctus [ˈlɪŋktəs] (N) (PL: **linctuses**) jarabe *m* para la tos

linden [ˈlɪndən] (N) = **lime²**

line¹ [laɪn] (N) **1** (*gen*) línea *f*; (*drawn*) raya *f* • **to draw a ~** trazar una línea • **there's a fine** *or* **thin ~ between genius and madness** la línea que separa la genialidad de la locura es muy sutil • **~ of latitude/longitude** línea *f* de latitud/longitud • **to put a ~ through sth** tachar *or* (*LAm*) rayar algo • **the Line** (*Geog*) el ecuador • IDIOMS: • **to draw the ~ at sth** no tolerar *or* aceptar algo • **one must draw the ~ somewhere** hay que fijar ciertos límites • **to know where to draw the ~** saber dónde pararse • **to draw a ~ under** [+ *episode, event*] poner punto final a • **to be on the ~:** • **his job is on the ~** su puesto está en peligro, se expone a perder su puesto • **to lay it on the ~** decirlo claramente, hablar con franqueza • **to lay** *or* **put one's reputation on the ~** arriesgar su reputación • **to put one's neck on the ~*‡** • **to put one's ass on the ~** (*US‡*) jugársela*
2 (= *rope*) cuerda *f*; (= *fishing line*) sedal *m*; (= *clothes line, washing line*) cuerda *f* para tender la ropa • **they threw a ~ to the man in the sea** le lanzaron un cable *or* una cuerda al hombre que estaba en el agua
3 (= *wrinkle*) (*on face etc*) arruga *f*; (*in palmistry*) raya *f*, línea *f*
4 [*of print, verse*] renglón *m*, línea *f* • **"new ~"** (*in dictation*) "otra línea" • **drop me a ~*** (*fig*) escríbeme • **to learn one's ~s** (*Theat*) aprenderse el papel • IDIOM: • **to read between the ~s** leer entre líneas
5 (= *row*) hilera *f*, fila *f*, línea *f* • **~ of traffic** fila *f or* cola *f* de coches • **the traffic stretched for three miles in an unbroken ~** había una caravana *or* cola de coches de tres millas • **a ~ of winning numbers** (*in bingo, lottery etc*) una línea ganadora • **to be in ~ with** estar de acuerdo con, ser conforme a • **to be in ~ for promotion** estar bajo consideración para un ascenso • **public sector pay is in ~ to rise** está previsto que suban los salarios del sector público • **to keep the party in ~** mantener la disciplina del partido • **to keep people in ~** mantener a la gente a raya • **to bring sth into ~ with sth** poner algo de acuerdo con algo • **to fall** *or* **get into ~** (*abreast*) meterse en fila • **to fall into ~ with sb** estar de acuerdo con algn • **to fall into ~ with sth** ser conforme a algo • **to be out of ~ with** no ser

L

conforme con • he was completely out of ~ to suggest that ...* estaba totalmente fuera de lugar que propusiera que ... • IDIOMS: • all along the ~ desde principio a fin • somewhere along the ~ we went wrong en algún punto nos hemos equivocado • to reach *or* come to the end of the ~ llegar al final; ▹ step
6 (= *series*) serie *f* • the latest in a long ~ of tragedies la última de una larga serie *or* lista de tragedias
7 (= *lineage*) linaje *m* • ~ of descent linaje *m* • the title is inherited through the male/female ~ el título se hereda por línea paterna/materna • he comes from a long ~ of artists proviene de un extenso linaje de artistas • the royal ~ el linaje real
8 (= *hierarchy*) • ~ of command cadena *f* de mando
9 (*Mil*) línea *f* • ~ of battle línea de batalla • the (battle) ~s are drawn (*fig*) la guerra está declarada • the first ~ of defence (*lit*) la primera línea de retaguardia; (*fig*) el primer escudo protector • behind enemy ~s tras las líneas enemigas • ship of the ~ navío *m* de línea; ▹ front
10 (*esp US*) (= *queue*) cola *f* • to form a ~ hacer una cola • to get into ~ ponerse en la cola *or* a la cola • to stand in ~ hacer cola
11 (= *direction*) línea *f* • the main *or* broad ~s [*of story, plan*] las líneas maestras • along *or* on the ~s of algo por el estilo de • something along those *or* the same ~s algo por el estilo • along *or* on political/racial ~s según criterios políticos/raciales • on the right ~s por buen camino • ~ of argument argumento *m* • ~ of attack (*Mil*) modo *m* de ataque; (*fig*) planteamiento *m* • in the ~ of duty en cumplimiento de sus deberes • it's all in the ~ of duty es una parte normal del deber • in the ~ of fire (*Mil*) en la línea de fuego • ~ of flight [*of bird*] trayectoria *f* de vuelo; [*of object*] trayectoria *f* • ~ of inquiry línea *f* de investigación • ~ of sight *or* vision visual *f* • ~ of thought hilo *m* del pensamiento
12 (*Elec*) (= *wire*) cable *m* • to be/come on ~ (*Comput*) estar/entrar en (pleno) funcionamiento
13 (*Telec*) línea *f* • can you get me a ~ to Chicago? ¿me puede poner con Chicago? • it's a very bad ~ se oye muy mal • ~s of communication líneas *fpl* de comunicación • to keep the ~s of communication open with sb mantener todas las líneas de comunicación abiertas con algn • the ~'s gone dead se ha cortado la línea • the ~s are down no hay línea • the ~ is engaged *or* (*US*) busy está comunicando • hold the ~ please no cuelgue, por favor • Mr. Smith is on the ~ (for you) El Sr. Smith está al teléfono (y quiere hablar con usted) • the ~s are open from six o'clock onwards las líneas están abiertas de seis en adelante; ▹ hot
14 (= *pipe*) (*for oil, gas*) conducto *m*
15 (= *shape*) (*usu pl*) • the rounded ~s of this car la línea redondeada *or* el contorno redondeado de este coche
16 (= *field, area*) • what ~ (of business) are you in? ¿a qué se dedica? • we're in the same ~ (of business) nos dedicamos a lo mismo, trabajamos en el mismo campo • ~ of research campo *m* de investigación • it's not my ~ (= *speciality*) no es de mi especialidad • fishing's more (in) my ~ me interesa más la pesca, de pesca sí sé algo
17 (= *stance, attitude*) actitud *f* • to take a strong *or* firm ~ on sth adoptar una actitud firme sobre algo • to take the ~ that ... ser de la opinión que ... • what ~ is the government taking? ¿cuál es la actitud del gobierno? • to follow *or* take the ~ of least resistance conformarse con la ley del mínimo esfuerzo • this is the official ~ esta es la versión oficial • IDIOM: • to toe the ~ acatar las normas • to toe *or* follow the party ~ conformarse a *or* seguir la línea del partido; ▹ hard
18 (*Comm*) (= *product*) línea *f* • a new/popular ~ una línea nueva/popular • that ~ did not sell at all esa línea de productos se vendió muy mal • we have a nice ~ in spring hats tenemos un bonito surtido de sombreros para primavera • he's got a nice ~ in rude jokes lo suyo son los chistes verdes
19 (*Rail*) (= *route*) línea *f*; (= *track*) vía *f* • down ~ vía descendente • up ~ vía ascendente • the ~ to Palencia el ferrocarril de Palencia, la línea de Palencia • to cross the ~(s) cruzar la vía • to leave the ~(s) descarrilar
20 (*also* shipping line) (= *company*) naviera *f*; (= *route*) línea *f* marítima, ruta *f* marítima
21 (= *clue, lead*) pista *f* • to give sb a ~ on sth poner a algn sobre la pista de algo • the police have a ~ on the criminal la policía anda *or* está sobre la pista del delincuente
22 (= *spiel*) • IDIOM: • to feed sb a ~ (about sth)* soltar un rollo *or* contar un cuento chino a algn (sobre algo)*; ▹ shoot
23 (*Ind*) (= *assembly line*) línea *f*
24 [*of cocaine etc*] raya *f*
VT (= *cross with lines*) [+ *paper*] rayar; [+ *field*] surcar; [+ *face*] arrugar
CPD ▸ **line dancing** *danza folclórica en que los que bailan forman líneas y filas* ▸ **line drawing** dibujo *m* lineal ▸ **line editing** corrección *f* por líneas ▸ **line feed** avance *m* de línea ▸ **line fishing** pesca *f* con caña ▸ **line judge** (*Tennis*) juez *mf* de fondo ▸ **line manager** (*Brit*) (*Ind*) jefe/a *m/f* de línea ▸ **line printer** impresora *f* de línea
▸ **line up** VT + ADV **1** (= *stand in line*) poner en fila
2 (= *arrange*) • I wonder what he's got ~d up for us me pregunto qué nos tendrá preparado • have you got something ~d up for this evening? ¿tienes algún plan para esta noche? • I had a job and house all ~d up, all I needed was my plane ticket ya tenía un trabajo y una casa esperándome, solo me faltaba el billete de avión • have you got someone ~d up for the job? ¿tienes pensado *or* tienes en mente a alguien para el puesto?
VI + ADV (*in queue*) hacer cola; (*in row*) ponerse en fila; (*behind one another*) formar fila • they ~d up in opposition to *or* against the chairman hicieron frente común contra el presidente • they ~d up behind *or* with the head agruparon para apoyar al director

line² [laɪn] VT **1** (= *put lining in*) [+ *garment*] forrar (with de); (*Tech*) revestir (with de); [+ *brakes*] guarnecer; [*bird*] [+ *nest*] cubrir • eat something to ~ your stomach come algo para no tener el estómago vacío; ▹ pocket
2 (= *border*) • streets ~d with trees calles *fpl* bordeadas de árboles • to ~ the route alinearse a lo largo de la ruta • to ~ the streets ocupar las aceras • portraits ~d the walls las paredes estaban llenas de retratos

lineage [ˈlɪnɪɪdʒ] N **1** (= *line of descent*) linaje *m*
2 (*Press*) = linage

lineal [ˈlɪnɪəl] ADJ lineal, en línea recta; [*descent*] en línea directa

lineament [ˈlɪnɪəmənt] N lineamento *m*

linear [ˈlɪnɪəʳ] ADJ [*design*] lineal; [*measure*] de longitud

linebacker [ˈlaɪnbækəʳ] N (*US*) defensa *mf* (*en fútbol americano*)

lined¹ [laɪnd] ADJ [*paper*] de rayas, pautado; [*face*] arrugado • to become ~ arrugarse

lined² [laɪnd] ADJ [*garment*] forrado, con forro; (*Tech*) revestido

-lined [-ˌlaɪnd] SUFFIX • tree-lined bordeado de árboles

lineman [ˈlaɪnmən] N (PL: **linemen**) **1** (*US*) (*Rail*) guardavías *m*
2 (*Telec*) técnico *m* de mantenimiento de redes
3 (*American Ftbl*) defensa *m*

linen [ˈlɪnɪn] N **1** (= *cloth*) lino *m*
2 (= *household linen*) ropa *f* blanca; (= *bed linen*) ropa *f* de cama; (= *table linen*) mantelería *f* • clean ~ ropa *f* limpia • dirty ~ ropa *f* sucia *or* para lavar • IDIOM: • to wash one's dirty ~ in public (*Brit*) sacar a relucir los trapos sucios
CPD de lino ▸ **linen basket** canasta *f or* cesto *m* de la ropa ▸ **linen closet, linen cupboard** armario *m* para la ropa blanca

line-out [ˈlaɪnaʊt] N saque *m* de banda

liner¹ [ˈlaɪnəʳ] N (= *ship*) transatlántico *m*

liner² [ˈlaɪnəʳ] N (= *bin liner*) bolsa *f* (para basura); (= *eyeliner*) lápiz *m* de ojos; (*US*) (= *record sleeve*) portada *f*, funda *f*; ▹ nappy
CPD ▸ **liner note** (*US*) *comentario en la portada de un disco*

linesman [ˈlaɪnzmən] N (PL: **linesmen**)
1 (*Sport*) juez *m* de línea, linier *m*
2 (*Rail, Telec*) guardavía *mf*
3 (*Elec*) celador *m*, recorredor *m* de la línea

line-up [ˈlaɪnʌp] N (*Sport*) formación *f*, alineación *f*; (*Theat, Cine*) [*of actors*] reparto *m*, elenco *m*; (*Mus*) [*of band*] formación *f*, integrantes *mfpl*; (*US*) (= *suspects*) rueda *f* de reconocimiento; (= *queue*) cola *f*

ling¹ [lɪŋ] N (PL: **ling** *or* **lings**) (= *fish*) abadejo *m*

ling² [lɪŋ] N (*Bot*) brezo *m*

linger [ˈlɪŋgəʳ] VI **1** (= *be unwilling to go*) rezagarse, tardar en marcharse
2 (*also* **linger on**) (*in dying*) tardar en morirse; [*pain*] persistir, durar; [*doubts*] persistir, quedar; [*smell*] persistir, tardar en desaparecer; [*tradition*] sobrevivir; [*memory*] pervivir, seguir vivo
3 (= *take one's time*) • to ~ on a subject dilatarse con un tema • I let my eye ~ on the scene seguía sin apartar los ojos de la escena • to ~ over doing sth tardar *or* no darse prisa en hacer algo • to ~ over a meal comer despacio

lingerie [ˈlænʒəriː] N lencería *f*, ropa *f* interior femenina

lingering [ˈlɪŋgərɪŋ] ADJ [*smell*] persistente; [*doubt*] persistente, que no se desvanece; [*look*] fijo; [*death*] lento

lingo* [ˈlɪŋgəʊ] N (PL: **lingoes**) (= *language*) lengua *f*, idioma *m*; (= *specialist jargon*) jerga *f*

lingua franca [ˌlɪŋgwəˈfræŋkə] N (PL: **lingua francas** *or* **linguae francae** [ˌlɪŋgwiːˈfrænsiː]) lengua *f* franca

linguist [ˈlɪŋgwɪst] N **1** (= *speaker of languages*) • he's an accomplished ~ domina varios idiomas • I'm no ~ se me dan mal los idiomas, no puedo con los idiomas • the company needs more ~s la compañía necesita más gente que sepa idiomas
2 (= *specialist in linguistics*) lingüista *mf*; (*Univ*) estudiante *mf* de idiomas

linguistic [lɪŋˈgwɪstɪk] ADJ [*ability, skills*] lingüístico • a child with good ~ skills un niño con mucha aptitud lingüística • we need people with good ~ skills necesitamos gente que tenga facilidad para los idiomas

linguistically [lɪŋˈgwɪstɪkəlɪ] ADV [*able, skilled*] desde el punto de vista lingüístico • she's very gifted ~ tiene mucha facilidad para los idiomas • ~ speaking lingüísticamente hablando, hablando desde un punto de vista lingüístico

linguistician [ˌlɪŋgwɪsˈtɪʃən] N lingüista *mf*, especialista *mf* en lingüística

linguistics [lɪŋˈgwɪstɪks] NSING lingüística *f*

liniment [ˈlɪnɪmənt] N linimento *m*

lining [ˈlaɪnɪŋ] N [*of garment*] forro *m*; (*Tech*) revestimiento *m*; [*of brake*] guarnición *f*

link [lɪŋk] N **1** [*of chain*] eslabón *m* • **the last ~ in the chain** (*fig*) el último eslabón en la cadena • **the missing ~** (*fig*) el eslabón perdido • **weak ~** (*fig*) punto *m* débil
2 (= *connection*) relación *f*, conexión *f* • **the ~ between smoking and lung cancer** la relación *or* conexión entre el tabaco y el cáncer de pulmón
3 (= *tie, association*) vínculo *m*, lazo *m* • **cultural ~s** vínculos *mpl or* lazos *mpl* culturales • **to have ~s with sth/sb** tener vínculos *or* lazos con algo/algn • **we now have closer ~s with overseas universities** ahora tenemos vínculos *or* lazos más estrechos con universidades extranjeras • **the district has strong ~s with Charles Dickens** la región está muy vinculada a Charles Dickens • **trade ~s** vínculos *mpl or* lazos *mpl* comerciales
4 (*Travel*) enlace *m*, conexión *f* • **rail/air/road ~s** enlaces *mpl* ferroviarios/aéreos/por carretera, conexiones *fpl* ferroviarias/aéreas/por carretera
5 (*Telec, TV, Rad*) • **radio/telephone/satellite ~** conexión *f* radiofónica/telefónica/vía satélite
6 (*Internet*) enlace *m*; ▹ **links**
VT **1** (= *join, connect*) [+ *parts, units*] unir (**to** a), conectar (**to** con); [+ *computers*] conectar (**to** con); [+ *towns, buildings*] comunicar, conectar • **the Channel Tunnel ~s Britain and France** el túnel del Canal de la Mancha comunica *or* conecta Gran Bretaña con Francia, el túnel del Canal de la Mancha une a Gran Bretaña y Francia • **to ~ arms** tomarse del brazo, cogerse del brazo (*Sp*) • **to be ~ed into a system** (*Comput*) estar conectado a un sistema • **to ~ two machines together** conectar dos máquinas
2 (= *relate*) relacionar • **the evidence ~ing smoking with early death** las pruebas que relacionan *or* que establecen una relación entre el tabaco y las muertes prematuras • **there is evidence ~ing the group to a series of terrorist attacks** hay pruebas que implican al grupo en una serie de atentados terroristas
VI **1** • **to ~ together** [*parts, components*] encajar
2 • **to ~ into sth** (*Comput*) conectar con algo
▸ **link up** VI + ADV [*people*] unirse; [*companies*] unir fuerzas; [*spacecraft*] acoplarse; [*railway lines, roads*] empalmar • **this ~s up with another problem** esto tiene relación con otro problema • **to ~ up with sb** juntarse a algn • **we are ~ing up with another firm for this project** vamos a unir fuerzas con otra empresa para llevar a cabo este proyecto
VT + ADV conectar • **to ~ sth up to sth** conectar algo a algo

linkage [ˈlɪŋkɪdʒ] N **1** conexión *f*, enlace *m*
2 (*Tech*) articulación *f*, acoplamiento *m*; (*Comput*) enlace *m*

linked [lɪŋkt] ADJ [*problems, concepts*] relacionado, vinculado

linking verb [ˈlɪŋkɪŋˌvɜːb] N verbo *m* copulativo

linkman [ˈlɪŋkmæn] N (PL: **linkmen**) (*Rad, TV*) locutor *m* de continuidad

links [lɪŋks] NPL **1** (= *golf links*) campo *msing or* (*LAm*) cancha *fsing* de golf
2 (= *cuff links*) gemelos *mpl*, mancuernas *fpl* (*CAm, Mex*)

linkup [ˈlɪŋkʌp] N conexión *f*, vinculación *f*; (= *meeting*) encuentro *m*, reunión *f*; [*of roads*] empalme *m*; [*of spaceships*] acoplamiento *m*; (*Rad, TV*) conexión *f*, enlace *m*

linnet [ˈlɪnɪt] N pardillo *m* (común)

lino [ˈlaɪnəʊ], **linoleum** [lɪˈnəʊlɪəm] N (*Brit*) linóleo *m*

Linotype® [ˈlaɪnəʊtaɪp] N linotipia *f*

linseed [ˈlɪnsiːd] N linaza *f*
CPD ▸ **linseed oil** aceite *m* de linaza

lint [lɪnt] N hilas *fpl*

lintel [ˈlɪntl] N dintel *m*

lion [ˈlaɪən] N león *m*; (*fig*) celebridad *f*
• IDIOMS: • **the ~'s share** la parte del león, la mejor parte • **to beard the ~ in his den** entrar en el cubil de la fiera • **to put one's head in the ~'s mouth** meterse en la boca del lobo • **to throw sb to the ~s** abandonar a algn a su suerte
CPD ▸ **lion cub** cachorro *m* de león ▸ **lion tamer** domador(a) *m/f* de leones

lioness [ˈlaɪənɪs] N leona *f*

lion-hearted [ˌlaɪənˈhɑːtɪd] ADJ valiente

lionize [ˈlaɪənaɪz] VT • **to ~ sb** tratar a algn como una celebridad

lip [lɪp] N **1** (*Anat*) labio *m*; [*of cup, crater*] borde *m*; [*of jug etc*] pico *m* • **to bite one's lip** (*lit*) morderse el labio; (*fig*) morderse la lengua • **to lick** *or* **smack one's lips** relamerse • **to read sb's lips** leer en los labios de algn • **my lips are sealed** (= *I won't tell*) soy una tumba; (= *I can't tell*) no puedo contar nada • IDIOM: • **to pay lip service to an ideal** defender un ideal de boquilla • **he's just paying lip service** todo lo que dice es boquilla; ▹ **stiff**
2* (= *insolence*) impertinencia *f*, insolencia *f* • **none of your lip!** ¡cállate la boca!*
CPD ▸ **lip balm** = **lip salve** ▸ **lip gloss** brillo *m* de labios ▸ **lip salve** (*Brit*) vaselina *f*, cacao *m*, protector *m* labial

lipid [ˈlaɪpɪd] N lípido *m*

lipo* [ˈlɪpəʊ, ˈlaɪpəʊ] N liposucción *f*

liposuction [ˈlɪpəʊˌsʌkʃən, ˈlaɪpəʊˌsʌkʃən] N liposucción *f*

lippy* [ˈlɪpɪ] ADJ (*Brit*) contestón*, descarado

lip-read [ˈlɪpriːd] VT leer los labios a
VI leer los labios

lip-reading [ˈlɪpˌriːdɪŋ] N lectura *f* de labios

lipstick [ˈlɪpstɪk] N lápiz *m* de labios, barra *f* de labios • **to put (one's) ~ on** pintarse los labios

liquefaction [ˌlɪkwɪˈfækʃən] N licuefacción *f*

liquefy [ˈlɪkwɪfaɪ] VT licuar
VI licuarse

liqueur [lɪˈkjʊəʳ] N licor *m*
CPD ▸ **liqueur chocolate** bombón *m* de licor ▸ **liqueur glass** copa *f* de licor

liquid [ˈlɪkwɪd] ADJ **1** (*lit*) líquido; [*measure*] para líquidos • IDIOM: • **to have a ~ lunch** (*hum*) remojar el gaznate*
2 (*fig*) [*sound*] claro, puro; (*Phon*) líquido
N líquido *m*; (*Phon*) líquida *f*
CPD ▸ **liquid assets** (*Econ*) activo *msing* líquido ▸ **liquid crystal** cristal *m* líquido ▸ **liquid crystal display** LCD *m*, pantalla *f* de cristal líquido ▸ **liquid nitrogen** nitrógeno *m* líquido ▸ **Liquid Paper®** Tipp-Ex® *m* ▸ **liquid waste** vertidos *mpl* líquidos

liquidate [ˈlɪkwɪdeɪt] VT (*all senses*) liquidar

liquidation [ˌlɪkwɪˈdeɪʃən] N liquidación *f* • **to go into ~** entrar en liquidación

liquidator [ˈlɪkwɪdeɪtəʳ] N liquidador(a) *m/f*

liquidity [lɪˈkwɪdɪtɪ] N (*Econ*) liquidez *f*
CPD ▸ **liquidity ratio** tasa *f or* coeficiente *m* de liquidez

liquidize [ˈlɪkwɪdaɪz] VT licuar
VI licuarse

liquidizer [ˈlɪkwɪdaɪzəʳ] N (*Brit*) (*Culin*) licuadora *f*

liquor [ˈlɪkəʳ] N (*Brit*) (*frm*) licores *mpl*; (*US*) alcohol *m* • **hard ~** licores *mpl* espiritosos, bebidas *fpl* fuertes • **to be in ~** estar borracho • **to be the worse for ~** haber bebido más de la cuenta, estar algo borracho
CPD ▸ **liquor cabinet** (*US*) mueble *m* bar ▸ **liquor license** (*US*) licencia *f* (para la venta) de bebidas alcohólicas ▸ **liquor store** (*US*) bodega *f*, tienda *f* de bebidas alcohólicas, licorería *f* (*LAm*)

liquorice [ˈlɪkərɪs] N regaliz *m*, orozuz *m*
CPD ▸ **liquorice all-sorts** (*Brit*) gominolas *fpl* de regaliz

lira [ˈlɪərə] N (PL: **lire** [ˈlɪərɪ]) lira *f*

Lisbon [ˈlɪzbən] N Lisboa *f*

lisle [laɪl] N hilo *m* de Escocia

lisp [lɪsp] N ceceo *m* • **to speak with a ~** cecear
VI cecear
VT decir ceceando

lissom, lissome [ˈlɪsəm] ADJ ágil, flexible

list¹ [lɪst] N (*gen*) lista *f*; (= *catalogue*) catálogo *m* • **price ~** lista *f* de precios • **waiting ~** lista *f* de espera • **to be on the active ~** (*Mil*) estar en activo • **that job is at the top of my ~** para mí ese trabajo es lo primero *or* lo más importante
VT (= *include in list*) poner en una/la lista; (= *make a list of*) hacer una lista de; (*verbally*) enumerar; (*Econ*) cotizar (**at** a); (*Comput*) listar • **it is not ~ed** no aparece en la lista • **he began to ~ all he had been doing** empezó a enumerar todas las cosas que había hecho
CPD ▸ **list price** precio *m* de catálogo ▸ **list renting** alquiler *m* de listas de posibles clientes

list² [lɪst] N (*Naut*) escora *f* • **to have a ~ of 20°** escorar a un ángulo de 20°
VI (*Naut*) escorar (**to port** a babor) • **to ~ badly** escorar de modo peligroso

listed [ˈlɪstɪd] ADJ • **~ building** (*Brit*) edificio *m* protegido • **~ company** empresa *f* con cotización • **~ securities** valores *mpl* registrados en bolsa

listen [ˈlɪsn] VI **1** (= *try to hear*) escuchar • **~! can't you hear something?** ¡escucha! ¿no oyes algo? • **I ~ed outside the bedroom door** me quedé escuchando en la puerta del dormitorio • **we ~ed for footsteps approaching** estuvimos atentos por si oíamos venir a alguien
2 (= *pay attention*) escuchar • **he wouldn't ~** no quiso escuchar • **~, I finish at one, why don't we have lunch together?** mira, yo termino a la una, ¿por qué no almorzamos juntos? • **~ (here), young lady, I've had enough of your cheek!** ¡escúchame *or* mira jovencita, ya estoy harto de tu cara dura! • **~ carefully, and repeat after me** escuchen con atención y repitan • **to ~ to sth/sb** escuchar algo/a algn • **I like ~ing to music** me gusta escuchar música • **I love ~ing to the rain** me encanta oír el sonido de la lluvia • **the only person she will ~ to is her father** la única persona a la que escucha es a su padre • **now just you ~ to me!** ¡escúchame! • **I don't have to ~ to this!** ¡no tengo por qué escuchar esta bazofia! • **will you ~ to him! who does he think he is?** ¡fíjate cómo habla! ¡quién se habrá creído que es! • **you never ~ to a word I say!** ¡nunca escuchas nada de lo que te digo!, ¡nunca me haces caso! • **~ to yourself, you're getting paranoid!** ¡será posible lo que estás diciendo! ¡te estás volviendo

paranoico! • IDIOM: • **to ~ with both ears** aguzar el oído; ▹ **reason**

(N) • **to have a ~ (to sth)*** escuchar (algo)

▸ **listen in** (VI + ADV) **1** (*Rad*) • **to ~ in to sth** escuchar algo

2 (= *eavesdrop*) escuchar • **to ~ in on** *or* **to a conversation** escuchar una conversación a hurtadillas

3 (= *attend, observe*) • **I would like to ~ in on** *or* **to your discussion** me gustaría participar en tu discusión en calidad de oyente

▸ **listen out** (VI + ADV) • **to ~ out for sth/sb: can you ~ out for the postman?** ¿podrías estar atento por si viene el cartero?

listener [ˈlɪsnəʳ] (N) (*gen*) oyente *mf*; (*Rad*) radioyente *mf* • **to be a good ~** saber escuchar • **dear ~s!** (*Rad*) ¡queridos radioyentes *or* oyentes!

listening [ˈlɪsnɪŋ] (N) • **good ~!** ¡que disfruten de la emisión! • **we don't do much ~ now** ahora escuchamos muy poco la radio

(CPD) ▸ **listening comprehension test** ejercicio *m* de comprensión oral ▸ **listening device** aparato *m* auditivo ▸ **listening post** puesto *m* de escucha

listeria [lɪsˈtiːərɪə] (N) listeria *f*

listeriosis [lɪsˌtɪərɪˈəʊsɪs] (N) listeriosis *f*

listing [ˈlɪstɪŋ] (N) **1** (*gen*) (*Comput*) listado *m*

2 (*Comm*) • **they have a ~ on the Stock Exchange** cotizan en Bolsa

3 listings (= *publication*) cartelera *f*, guía *fsing* del ocio

listless [ˈlɪstlɪs] (ADJ) **1** (= *without energy*) lánguido

2 (= *without direction*) apático, indiferente

listlessly [ˈlɪstlɪslɪ] (ADV) **1** (= *without energy*) lánguidamente

2 (= *without direction*) con apatía, con desgana

listlessness [ˈlɪstlɪsnɪs] (N) **1** (= *lack of energy*) languidez *f*

2 (= *lack of direction*) apatía *f*, desgana *f*

lists [lɪsts] (NPL) (*Hist*) liza *f* • **to enter the ~ (against sth/sb)** (*fig*) salir *or* saltar a la palestra (contra algo/algn)

lit [lɪt] (PT) (PP *of* **light**[1]) • **to be lit up*** estar achispado*

Lit., **lit.**[1]* [lɪt] (N ABBR) = **literature**

lit.[2] (ABBR) = **literal(ly)**

litany [ˈlɪtənɪ] (N) letanía *f*

lite* [laɪt] (ADJ) **1** (*Culin*) (= *low-fat*) bajo en calorías, light (*inv*)

2 (*fig*) (= *mild*) descafeinado, light (*inv*)

liter [ˈliːtəʳ] (N) (*US*) = **litre**

literacy [ˈlɪtərəsɪ] (N) alfabetismo *m*, capacidad *f* de leer y escribir • **~ is low in Burkina Faso** el grado de alfabetización es bajo en Burkina Faso

(CPD) ▸ **literacy campaign** campaña *f* de alfabetización ▸ **literacy hour** (*Scol*) hora *f* de lectura y escritura ▸ **literacy project**, **literacy scheme** programa *m* de alfabetización ▸ **literacy test** prueba *f* básica de lectura y escritura

literal [ˈlɪtərəl] (ADJ) **1** [*sense, translation*] literal • **they follow a ~ interpretation of the Bible** siguen la Biblia al pie de la letra • **to be ~ about sth** tomar algo al pie de la letra • **he's a very ~ person** es una persona que todo se lo toma al pie de la letra; ▹ **literal-minded**

2 (*as intensifier*) • **a ~ fact** un hecho real • **the ~ truth** la pura verdad

(N) (*Typ*) errata *f*

literally [ˈlɪtərəlɪ] (ADV) **1** (= *actually*) literalmente • **I was quite ~ living on bread and water** estaba literalmente viviendo a base de pan y agua • **he's crazy, I mean ~** está loco, y lo digo en el verdadero sentido de la palabra • **they were quite ~ in fear of their lives** temían realmente por sus vidas • **to take sth ~** tomarse algo al pie de la letra • **she ~ flew out the door** (*as intensifier*) (= *almost*) salió casi volando por la puerta

2 (= *word for word*) [*translate, mean*] literalmente, palabra por palabra

literal-minded [ˈlɪtərəlˈmaɪndɪd] (ADJ) sin imaginación, poco imaginativo

literary [ˈlɪtərərɪ] (ADJ) [*prize, award*] de literatura, literario • **~ circles** círculos *mpl* literarios • **a ~ man** un hombre de letras • **it's a ~ masterpiece** es una obra maestra de la literatura • **the ~ scene** el ambiente literario, los círculos literarios • **a ~ work** una obra literaria *or* de literatura

(CPD) ▸ **literary agent** agente *mf* literario/a ▸ **literary critic** crítico/a *m/f* literario/a ▸ **literary criticism** crítica *f* literaria ▸ **literary history** historia *f* de la literatura ▸ **literary studies** estudios *mpl* de literatura, estudios *mpl* literarios ▸ **literary theory** teoría *f* de la literatura, teoría *f* literaria

literate [ˈlɪtərɪt] (ADJ) que sabe leer y escribir • **highly ~** culto • **not very ~** (*fig*) poco culto, que tiene poca cultura

literati [ˌlɪtəˈrɑːtiː] (NPL) literatos *mpl*

literature [ˈlɪtərɪtʃəʳ] (N) **1** (= *writings*) literatura *f*

2* (= *promotional material*) información *f*, publicidad *f*

3 (= *learned studies of subject*) estudios *mpl*, bibliografía *f*

lithe [laɪð] (ADJ) ágil

lithium [ˈlɪθɪəm] (N) litio *m*

litho* [ˈlaɪθəʊ] (N ABBR) = **lithograph**

lithograph [ˈlɪθəʊgrɑːf] (N) litografía *f*

(VT) litografiar

lithographer [lɪˈθɒgrəfəʳ] (N) litógrafo/a *m/f*

lithographic [lɪθəʊˈgræfɪk] (ADJ) litográfico

lithography [lɪˈθɒgrəfɪ] (N) litografía *f*

Lithuania [ˌlɪθjʊˈeɪnɪə] (N) Lituania *f*

Lithuanian [ˌlɪθjʊˈeɪnɪən] (ADJ) lituano

(N) **1** (= *person*) lituano/a *m/f*

2 (*Ling*) lituano *m*

litigant [ˈlɪtɪgənt] (N) litigante *mf*

litigate [ˈlɪtɪgeɪt] (VI) litigar, pleitear

litigation [ˌlɪtɪˈgeɪʃən] (N) litigio *m*, pleito *m*

litigator [ˈlɪtɪgeɪtəʳ] (N) (= *litigant*) litigante *mf*; (= *lawyer*) abogado/a *m/f* litigante

litigious [lɪˈtɪdʒəs] (ADJ) litigioso

litmus [ˈlɪtməs] (N) tornasol *m*

(CPD) ▸ **litmus paper** papel *m* de tornasol ▸ **litmus test** prueba *f* de tornasol; (*fig*) prueba *f* de fuego

litre, **liter** (*US*) [ˈliːtəʳ] (N) litro *m*

litter [ˈlɪtəʳ] (N) **1** (= *rubbish*) basura *f*; (= *papers*) papeles *mpl* (tirados); (= *wrappings*) envases *mpl* • **"no litter"** "prohibido arrojar basura"

2 (= *untidiness*) desorden *m* • **in a ~** en desorden • **a ~ of books** un montón desordenado de libros, un revoltijo de libros

3 (*Zool*) camada *f*

4 (= *vehicle*) litera *f*; (*Med*) camilla *f*

5 (= *bedding*) lecho *m*, cama *f* de paja

6 (*for animal*) lecho *m* de paja; ▹ **cat**

(VT) **1** (= *make untidy*) • **to ~ the streets** tirar basura por la calle • **to ~ papers about a room** • **~ a room with papers** esparcir papeles por un cuarto, dejar papeles esparcidos por un cuarto • **he ~ed the floor with all his football gear** dejó toda la ropa de fútbol tirada por el suelo • **the lorry ~ed the road with rubbish** el camión dejó basura esparcida por toda la carretera, el camión dejó la carretera sembrada de basura • **a pavement ~ed with papers** una acera sembrada de papeles • **a room ~ed with books** un cuarto con libros por todas partes • **a page ~ed with mistakes** una página plagada de errores

2 (= *provide with bedding*) [+ *animal*] dar cama de paja a

3 (= *give birth to*) [*animal*] parir

(VI) [*cat*] parir

(CPD) ▸ **litter basket**, **litter bin** (*Brit*) papelera *f* ▸ **litter box** (*US*) = **litter tray** ▸ **litter lout** *persona que tira papeles o basura a la vía pública* ▸ **litter tray** (*esp Brit*) *lecho de arena higiénica para animales domésticos*

litterbug [ˈlɪtəbʌg] (N) (*US*) = **litter lout**

little[1] [ˈlɪtl] (ADJ) **1** (= *small*) pequeño, chico (*LAm*) • **a ~ house** una casa pequeña *or* (*LAm*) chica • **a ~ book** un libro pequeño *or* (*LAm*) chico • **she had a ~ girl yesterday** ayer tuvo una niñita • **when I was ~** cuando era pequeña, de pequeña • **the ~ ones** (= *children*) los pequeños

2 (= *short*) corto • **a ~ walk** un paseo corto • **we went for a ~ holiday** nos fuimos para unas vacaciones cortitas

3 (= *diminutive*) (*in cpds*) -ito • **a ~ book/boat/piece** *etc* un librito/barquito/trocito *etc* • **a ~ house** una casita • **a ~ girl** una niñita, una chiquita • **a ~ fish** un pececillo, un pececito • **a ~ sip** un sorbito • **the ~ woman** (*hum*) (= *wife*) la costilla*, la parienta (*Sp**) • **it's the ~ man who suffers** (= *small trader*) el pequeño comerciante es el que sale perdiendo • **it's just a ~ something*** no es más que una cosita de poco valor

4 (= *younger*) • **her ~ brother** su hermano menor, su hermanito

(CPD) ▸ **little end** (*Brit*) (*Aut*) pie *m* de biela ▸ **Little Englander** (*Brit*) (*Hist*) *en el siglo XIX, persona con ideas opuestas a la ampliación del imperio británico*; (= *chauvinist*) patriotero/a *m/f*; (= *anti-European*) anti-europeoísta *mf* ▸ **little finger** dedo *m* meñique, meñique *m* ▸ **the little folk** (= *fairies*) los duendecillos ▸ **Little League** (*US*) *liga de béisbol aficionado para jóvenes de entre 6 y 18 años* ▸ **the little people** (= *fairies*) los duendecillos ▸ **little toe** dedo *m* pequeño del pie

little[2] [ˈlɪtl] (COMPAR: **less**, SUPERL: **least**)

(PRON) **1** (= *not much*) poco • **he knows ~** sabe poco • **to see/do ~** ver/hacer poco • **there was ~ we could do** apenas había nada que hacer • **he had ~ to say** poco fue lo que tenía que decir • **that has ~ to do with it!** ¡eso tiene poco que ver! • **as ~ as £5** 5 libras, nada más • **there's very ~ left** queda muy poco • **to make ~ of sth** (= *play down*) quitarle importancia a algo; (= *fail to exploit*) desaprovechar algo • **they made ~ of loading the huge boxes** (= *accomplish easily*) cargaron las enormes cajas como si nada • **~ of what he says is true** poco de lo que dice es verdad • **~ or nothing** poco o nada • **to spend ~ or nothing** gastar poco o nada • **he lost weight because he ate so ~** adelgazó porque comía muy poco • **I know too ~ about him to have an opinion** no lo conozco lo suficiente para poder opinar • **too ~ too late** muy poco y muy tarde

2 (= *some*) • **give me a ~** dame un poco • **I had a ~ of everything** comí un poco de todo • **~ by ~** poco a poco • **however ~ you give, we'll be grateful** agradeceremos su donativo, por pequeño que sea • **a ~ less/more milk** un poco menos/más de leche • **a ~ more slowly** un poco más despacio • **the ~ I have seen is excellent** lo poco que he visto me ha parecido excelente • **I did what ~ I could** hice lo poco que pude; ▹ **every**

3 (= *short time*) • **they'll have to wait a ~** tendrán que esperar un poco • **for a ~** un rato, durante un rato

(ADJ) **1** (= *not much*) poco • **there is ~ hope of finding them alive** hay pocas esperanzas de encontrarlos con vida • **with ~ difficulty** sin

problema *or* dificultad • **so much to do, so ~ time** tanto que hacer y en tan poco tiempo • **I have so ~ time for reading** tengo muy poco tiempo para leer • **he gave me too ~ money** me dio poquísimo dinero • **I have very ~ money** tengo muy poco dinero
2 (= *some*) • **a ~ wine** un poco de vino • **I speak a ~ Spanish** hablo un poco de español • **a ~ bit (of)** un poquito (de) • **with no ~ trouble** con bastante dificultad, con no poca dificultad
3 (= *short*) • **for a ~ time** *or* **while** un ratito
(ADV) **1** (= *not much*) poco • **he reads ~** lee poco • **they spoke very ~ on the way home** hablaron muy poco de camino para casa • **try to move as ~ as possible** intenta moverte lo menos posible • **(as) ~ as I like him, I must admit that …** aunque me gusta muy poco, debo admitir que … • **a ~ known fact** un hecho poco conocido • **~ more than** poco más que • **~ more than a month ago** hace poco más de un mes • **a ~ read book** un libro poco leído, un libro que se lee poco • **it's ~ short of a miracle** es casi un milagro
2 (= *somewhat*) algo • **we were a ~ surprised/happier** nos quedamos algo sorprendidos/más contentos • **a ~ better** un poco mejor, algo mejor • **a ~ less/more than …** un poco menos/más que … • **we were not a ~ worried** nos inquietamos bastante, quedamos muy inquietos
3 (= *not at all*) • **~ does he know that …** no tiene la menor idea de que …
4 (= *rarely*) poco • **I watch television very ~ nowadays** ahora veo la televisión muy poco • **it occurs very ~ in small companies** raramente ocurre *or* es raro que ocurra en empresas pequeñas

littleness [ˈlɪtlnɪs] (N) (*in size*) pequeñez *f*; (*fig*) mezquindad *f*
littoral [ˈlɪtərəl] (ADJ) litoral
(N) litoral *m*
liturgical [lɪˈtɜːdʒɪkəl] (ADJ) litúrgico
liturgy [ˈlɪtədʒɪ] (N) liturgia *f*
livable [ˈlɪvəbl] (ADJ) [*house*] habitable; [*life*] llevadero
livable-in [ˈlɪvəbl,ɪn] (ADJ) habitable
livable-with [ˈlɪvəbl,wɪð] (ADJ) [*person*] tratable
live[1] [lɪv] (VI) **1** (= *exist*) vivir • **the times we ~ in** los tiempos en que vivimos, los tiempos que corremos • **she has only six months to ~** solo le quedan seis meses de vida • **to ~ from day to day** vivir de día en día • **to ~ in fear** vivir atemorizado • **she ~s in fear of her life/that she may be found out** vive temiendo por su vida/que la descubran • **to ~ for sth**: • **I'm living for the day (when) I retire** vivo esperando a que llegue el día en que me jubile • **she ~d for her work** vivía por y para su trabajo • **to ~ for today** *or* **the moment** vivir al día • **I've got nothing left to ~ for** no tengo nada por lo que vivir • IDIOM: • **to ~ and let ~** vivir y dejar vivir • PROVERBS: • **we should eat to ~, not ~ to eat** deberíamos comer para vivir, y no vivir para comer • **you ~ and learn** nunca te acostarás sin saber una cosa más; ▷ **hand, happily, hope, long**[1]**, shadow, style**
2 (= *survive*) • **the doctor said she would ~** el médico dijo que sobreviviría • **you'll ~!** (*hum*) ¡de esta no te mueres! (*hum*) • **he ~d to a ripe old age/to be 103** llegó a viejo/a cumplir 103 años • **she'll never ~ to see it** no vivirá para verlo; ▷ **regret**
3 (= *conduct o.s.*) vivir • **she ~s by her own rules** vive según sus propias normas • **men who ~d by the gun** hombres cuya ley era la pistola • **to ~ modestly/well** vivir modestamente/bien • IDIOM: • **to ~ like a king** *or* **a lord** vivir a cuerpo de rey; ▷ **dangerously, sin**
4 (= *earn one's living*) vivir • **to ~ by hunting** vivir de la caza; ▷ **pen**[1]**, wit**[1]
5 (= *reside*) vivir • **where do you ~?** ¿dónde vives? • **to ~ in a flat/in London** vivir en un piso/en Londres • **she ~s in Station Road** vive en Station Road • **this is a nice place to ~** este es un buen sitio para vivir • **this house isn't fit to ~ in** esta casa está en pésimas condiciones
6 (*Brit**) (= *go, belong*) ir, guardarse • **where does the teapot ~?** ¿dónde va *or* se guarda la tetera?
7 (= *enjoy life*) • **let's ~ a little!*** ¡vivamos la vida un poquito!* • **she really knows how to ~** sabe disfrutar muy bien de la vida • **if you've never been to an opera, you haven't ~d*** si no has ido nunca a la ópera no sabes lo qué es vivir
(VT) **1** [+ *life*] (*gen*) vivir; (*in particular way*) llevar • **to ~ life to the full** vivir la vida al máximo • **to ~ a happy life** llevar una vida feliz • **to ~ a life of luxury/crime** llevar una vida de lujos/de delincuencia • **to ~ a life of hardship** vivir pasando penurias • **how you ~ your life is your business** tu vida es cosa tuya
2 (*Theat*) • **to ~ the part** vivir el personaje *or* el papel
▸ **live down** (VT + ADV) • **I thought I'd never ~ it down** pensé que no se iba a olvidar nunca • **he was unable to ~ down his reputation as a drunk** no consiguió librarse de su fama de borracho
▸ **live in** (VI + ADV) [*servant, nanny*] vivir en la casa
▸ **live off** (VI + PREP) **1** (= *depend financially on*) vivir a costa de; (= *support o.s. on*) vivir de • **he ~s off his uncle** vive a costa de su tío • **she ~s off the income from her investments** vive de las rentas de sus inversiones; ▷ **land**
2 (= *eat*) alimentarse de
▸ **live on** (VI + PREP) **1** (= *subsist on*) • **what does he ~ on?** ¿de qué vive? • **he ~s on £50 a week** vive con 50 libras por semana • **we have just enough to ~ on** tenemos lo justo para vivir • IDIOM: • **to ~ on borrowed time** tener los días contados
2 (= *feed on*) alimentarse de • **she ~s on cheese** vive solo a base de queso • **she absolutely ~s on chocolate** no come otra cosa más que chocolate
(VI + ADV) (= *go on living*) [*person, memory, tradition*] seguir vivo • **his memory ~s on within us** su recuerdo sigue vivo en nosotros • **Lenin ~s on in the minds and hearts of many people** Lenin sigue vivo en las mentes y corazones de muchas personas
▸ **live out** (VI + ADV) [*servant*] vivir fuera
(VT + ADV) **1** (= *live to the end of*) • **she won't ~ the year out** no vivirá hasta fin de año, no llegará a fin de año • **the house where he ~d out his last three years** la casa donde vivió sus últimos tres años • **he ~d out the war in the country** mientras duró la guerra vivió en el campo • **he wanted to ~ out his life in his own home** quería vivir *or* pasar el resto de sus días en su propia casa • **he ~d out his days in a mental asylum** acabó sus días en un psiquiátrico
2 (= *act out*) [+ *fantasy*] vivir
▸ **live through** (VI + PREP) **1** (= *experience*) vivir • **she has ~d through two world wars** ha vivido dos guerras mundiales
2 (= *survive*) sobrevivir • **he won't ~ through the winter** no sobrevivirá el invierno
▸ **live together** (VI + ADV) (*in amity*) convivir; (*as lovers*) vivir juntos
▸ **live up** (VT + ADV) • IDIOM: • **to ~ it up*** (= *have fun*) pasárselo en grande*; (= *live in luxury*) darse la gran vida*
▸ **live up to** (VI + PREP) **1** (= *be true to*) [+ *principles*] vivir de acuerdo con; [+ *promises*] cumplir
2 (= *be equal to*) [+ *reputation, expectations*] estar a la altura de • **marriage failed to ~ up to her expectations** el matrimonio no estuvo a la altura de *or* defraudó sus expectativas • **his brother's success will give him something to ~ up to** el éxito de su hermano le dará algo que igualar • **the new president has not ~d up to their hopes** el nuevo presidente ha defraudado sus esperanzas • **the product doesn't ~ up to its name** el producto no hace honor a su nombre
▸ **live with** (VI + PREP) **1** (= *coexist with*) [+ *person, memory*] vivir con • **he's not an easy person to ~ with** no es una persona con la que se pueda vivir fácilmente • **to ~ with the knowledge that …** vivir sabiendo que … • **I'd never be able to ~ with myself if I let that happen** jamás podría vivir tranquila *or* vivir con mi conciencia si dejara que pasara eso
2 (= *accept*) aceptar • **you'll have to learn to ~ with it** tendrás que aprender a aceptarlo
live[2] [laɪv] (ADJ) **1** (= *living*) [*animal, person*] vivo • **experiments on ~ animals** experimentos *mpl* con animales vivos • **a real ~ crocodile** un cocodrilo de verdad • **a real ~ duke** un duque de carne y hueso • **9.1 deaths per thousand ~ births** 9,1 muertes por cada mil bebés nacidos vivos
2 (= *topical*) [*issue*] de actualidad, candente
3 (*Rad, TV*) [*broadcast, coverage*] en vivo, en directo; [*performance, show, recording*] en vivo • **the bar has ~ entertainment at weekends** el bar tiene espectáculos en vivo los fines de semana • **performed before a ~ audience** interpretado delante del público
4 (= *not blank*) [*shell, ammunition*] cargado; [*bomb*] sin explotar
5 (= *still burning*) [*coal*] encendido, prendido (*LAm*)
6 (*Elec*) [*cable, wire, appliance*] conectado, con corriente • **is this cable ~?** ¿está conectado *or* tiene corriente este cable?
(ADV) **1** (*Rad, TV*) en vivo, en directo • **the match is brought to you ~ from Madrid** le ofrecemos el partido en vivo *or* en directo desde Madrid • **here, ~ from New York, is our reporter Malcolm McDonald** aquí tenemos a nuestro corresponsal Malcolm McDonald que nos habla en directo desde Nueva York • **we'll be going ~ to Montreal later on** conectaremos con Montreal en directo más adelante
2 • **to go ~** (= *come into operation*) entrar en funcionamiento • **the new computer system will go ~ next week** el nuevo ordenador entrará en funcionamiento la semana que viene
(CPD) ▸ **live bait** (*Fishing*) cebo *m* vivo ▸ **live coal** brasa *f*, ascua *f* ▸ **live export** [*of livestock*] exportación *f* en pie ▸ **live oak** roble *m* de Virginia ▸ **live rail** raíl *m* electrizado ▸ **live weight** [*of livestock*] peso *m* en pie ▸ **live wire** (*Elec*) alambre *m* conectado, alambre *m* con corriente; (*fig**) torbellino* *m* • **he's a real ~ wire!** ¡es un torbellino!*, ¡tiene mucha marcha!* ▸ **live yoghurt** yogur *m* con biocultivos
liveblog [ˈlaɪvblɒg] (N) blog *m* en directo
(VT), (VI) bloguear en directo
lived-in [ˈlɪvd,ɪn] (ADJ) • **the blinds and cushions give the room a lived-in look** las persianas y los cojines le dan un aspecto acogedor a la habitación
live-in [ˈlɪv,ɪn] (ADJ) • **live-in lover** compañero/a *m/f* • **live-in maid** criada *f* interna

livelihood [ˈlaɪvlɪhʊd] (N) sustento *m* • **rice is their ~** el arroz es su único sustento • **to earn a** *or* **one's ~** ganarse la vida *or* el sustento

liveliness [ˈlaɪvlɪnɪs] (N) [*of person, mind, imagination*] vivacidad *f*; [*of atmosphere, party, place*] animación *f*; [*of conversation, discussion*] lo animado; [*of description, account, style*] lo vívido

livelong [ˈlɪvlɒŋ] (ADJ) • **all the ~ day** todo el santo día

lively [ˈlaɪvlɪ] (ADJ) (COMPAR: **livelier**, SUPERL: **liveliest**) **1** (*gen*) [*person, personality*] vivaz, alegre; [*atmosphere, conversation, party, town*] animado; [*bar, street, market*] animado, bullicioso; [*dog*] juguetón; [*tune*] alegre; [*performance*] enérgico • **things are a little livelier in June** la cosa se anima más en junio
2 (= *heated*) [*debate, discussion*] animado • **the meeting promises to be a ~ affair** la reunión promete ser animada • **things were getting quite ~** el ambiente se estaba caldeando
3 (= *fast*) [*pace, speed*] rápido • **look ~!** ¡espabila!
4 (= *keen*) [*mind*] vivaz, inquieto; [*imagination*] vivo; [*sense of humour*] agudo • **she took a ~ interest in everything** ponía un gran interés en todo
5 (= *vivid*) [*description, account, style*] vivo, vívido

liven [ˈlaɪvn] (VT) • **to ~ up** animar
(VI) • **to ~ up** animarse

liver[1] [ˈlɪvəʳ] (N) (*Anat*) hígado *m*
(CPD) [*pâté, sausage*] de hígado; [*disease*] hepático, del hígado ▸ **liver complaint** mal *m* de hígado, afección *f* hepática ▸ **liver pâté** foie gras *m*, paté *m* de hígado ▸ **liver salts** sal *fsing* de fruta ▸ **liver sausage** salchicha *f* de hígado ▸ **liver spots** manchas *fpl* de la vejez

liver[2] [ˈlɪvəʳ] (N) • **fast ~** calavera* *m* • **good ~** (= *lover of good food*) gastrónomo/a *m/f*; (= *lover of the good life*) persona *f* que se da buena vida

liveried [ˈlɪvərɪd] (ADJ) en librea

liverish [ˈlɪvərɪʃ] (ADJ) • **to be** *or* **feel ~** sentirse mal del hígado

Liverpudlian [ˌlɪvəˈpʌdlɪən] (ADJ) de Liverpool
(N) nativo/a *m/f* de Liverpool, habitante *mf* de Liverpool

liverwort [ˈlɪvəˌwɜːt] (N) hepática *f*

liverwurst [ˈlɪvəwɜːst] (N) (*esp US*) embutido *m* de hígado

livery [ˈlɪvərɪ] (N) librea *f*; (*liter*) ropaje *m*
(CPD) ▸ **livery company** (*Brit*) gremio *m* (*antiguo de la Ciudad de Londres*) ▸ **livery stable** cuadra *f* de caballos de alquiler

lives [laɪvz] (NPL) *of* **life**

livestock [ˈlaɪvstɒk] (N) ganado *m*; (*also* **livestock farming**) ganadería *f*

livestream [ˈlaɪvstriːm] (N) transmisión *f* en directo
(VT) transmitir en directo

livid [ˈlɪvɪd] (ADJ) **1*** (= *furious*) furioso, furibundo* • **to be ~ about** *or* **at sth** estar furioso por algo, estar furibundo por algo*
2 (= *purple*) [*bruise, scar*] amoratado; [*colour, sky*] morado • **his face was ~** su rostro estaba lívido • **to be ~ with rage** estar lívido de rabia • **the sky was a ~ blue** el cielo era de un azul tirando a morado • **the scar was a ~ red** la cicatriz tenía un color rojo amoratado

living [ˈlɪvɪŋ] (ADJ) **1** (= *alive*) [*person, creature, plant*] vivo • **I have no ~ relatives** no tengo ningún pariente vivo • **Ireland's greatest ~ playwright** el mejor dramaturgo irlandés vivo *or* aún con vida • **a ~ death** (*liter*) un infierno • **~ faith** fe *f* viva • **he's the ~ image of his uncle** es el retrato vivo *or* la imagen viva de su tío • **~ language** lengua *f* viva • **the worst drought in** *or* **within ~ memory** la peor sequía que se recuerda • **the San Francisco earthquake is still within ~ memory** el terremoto de San Francisco tuvo lugar en nuestro tiempo • **~ proof** prueba *f* evidente *or* palpable • **I didn't see a ~ soul** no vi a un alma • **I promised I wouldn't tell a ~ soul** prometí que no se lo diría a nadie • **there wasn't a ~ thing to be seen** no se veía a ningún ser vivo; ▹ **daylight**
2 (= *for living in*) [*area*] destinado a la vivienda • **our ~ accommodation was pretty basic** el lugar donde vivíamos era bastante modesto
(N) **1** (= *livelihood*) • **to earn a ~** ganarse la vida • **what do you do for a ~?** ¿cómo te ganas la vida?, ¿en qué trabajas? • **now he has to work for a ~** ahora tiene que trabajar para ganarse la vida • **to make a ~** ganarse la vida • **he thinks the world owes him a ~** piensa que tiene derecho a que se lo den todo regalado
2 (= *way of life*) vida *f* • **the quality of urban ~** la calidad de la vida en la ciudad • **clean ~** vida *f* ordenada • **loose ~** vida *f* disipada, vida *f* disoluta; ▹ **cost, standard**
(NPL) • **the ~** los vivos
(CPD) ▸ **living area** zona *f* destinada a la vivienda ▸ **living conditions** condiciones *fpl* de vida ▸ **living expenses** gastos *mpl* de mantenimiento ▸ **living quarters** (*for students*) residencia *f*; (*for soldiers, servants, staff*) dependencias *fpl* ▸ **living room** sala *f* de estar, living *m* ▸ **living space** espacio *m* vital (*also fig*) ▸ **living standards** nivel *m* de vida • **a fall in ~ standards** un descenso del nivel de vida ▸ **living wage** *salario de subsistencia* • **£20 a week isn't a ~ wage** con 20 libras a la semana no se puede vivir ▸ **living will** declaración *f* de últimas voluntades (*por la que el declarante se niega a que su vida sea prolongada por medios artificiales en caso de encontrarse enfermo en fase terminal*)

Livy [ˈlɪvɪ] (N) Tito Livio

Liz [lɪz] (N) *familiar form of* **Elizabeth**

lizard [ˈlɪzəd] (N) (*large*) lagarto *m*; (*small*) lagartija *f*

ll. (ABBR) = **lines**

llama [ˈlɑːmə] (N) llama *f*

LLB (N ABBR) (*Univ*) (= **Legum Baccalaureus**) (= *Bachelor of Laws*) Ldo/a en Dcho

LLD (N ABBR) (*Univ*) (= **Legum Doctor**) (= *Doctor of Laws*) Dr. en Dcho, Dra. en Dcho

LM (N ABBR) = **lunar module**

LMS (N ABBR) = **local management of schools**

LMT (N ABBR) (*US*) = **Local Mean Time**

LNG (N ABBR) = **liquefied natural gas**

lo [ləʊ] (EXCL) • **lo and behold the result!** ¡he aquí el resultado! • **and lo and behold there it was** y mira por dónde ahí estaba

loach [ləʊtʃ] (N) locha *f*

load [ləʊd] (N) **1** (= *cargo*) carga *f*; (= *weight*) peso *m* • **the lorry had a full ~** el camión iba lleno • **I put another ~ in the washing machine** puse otra colada a lavar *or* en la lavadora • **I had three ~s of coal delivered** me repartieron tres cargas de carbón • **they were forced to carry heavy ~s** les obligaron a cargar con pesos pesados • **"maximum load: 17 tons"** "carga máxima: 17 toneladas"
2 (*fig*) (= *burden*) carga *f* • **he finds his new responsibilities a heavy ~** sus nuevas responsabilidades le resultan una gran carga • **she's taking some of the ~ off the secretaries** está aligerándoles la carga de trabajo a las secretarias • **that's (taken) a ~ off my mind!** ¡eso me quita un peso de encima!; ▹ **caseload, workload**
3 (*Elec, Tech*) (*also of firearm*) carga *f*
4 loads* cantidad* *f*, un montón* • **we've got ~s of time** tenemos cantidad *or* un montón de tiempo* • **I've got ~s (of them) at home** tengo cantidad *or* un montón en casa*
5 • **a ~ of***: **the book is a ~ of rubbish** el libro es una basura*, el libro no vale nada • **he talks a ~ of rubbish** no dice más que tonterías • **they're just a ~ of kids** no son más que un hatajo *or* una panda de críos* • **get a ~ of this!** (= *look*) ¡échale un vistazo a esto!*, ¡mírame esto!; (= *listen*) ¡escucha esto!
(VT) **1** [+ *lorry, washing machine, gun*] cargar • **the gun is not ~ed** la pistola no está cargada • **do you know how to ~ this program?** ¿sabes cómo cargar este programa?
2 (= *weigh down*) • **to be ~ed with sth**: • **we're ~ed with debts** estamos cargados *or* agobiados de deudas • **the branch was ~ed with fruit** la rama estaba cargada de fruta • **her words were ~ed with meaning** sus palabras estaban llenas *or* cargadas de significado • **the whole thing is ~ed with problems** el asunto está erizado de dificultades
3 (= *bias*) • **the dice were ~ed** los dados estaban cargados • **the dice are ~ed against him** (*fig*) todo está en su contra • **the situation is ~ed in our favour** la situación se inclina a nuestro favor
(VI) **1** [*lorry, ship*] cargar • **"loading and unloading"** "permitido carga y descarga"
2 [*gun, camera*] cargarse • **how does this gun/camera ~?** ¿cómo se carga esta pistola/cámara?
3 [*person*] cargar • **load!** ¡carguen armas!
(CPD) ▸ **load factor** (*Elec, Aer*) factor *m* de carga ▸ **load line** (*Naut*) línea *f* de carga
▸ **load down** (VT + ADV) • **to be ~ed down with sth: she was ~ed down with shopping** iba cargada de bolsas de la compra • **we're ~ed down with work** estamos hasta arriba de trabajo • **he was ~ed down with debt** estaba cargado *or* agobiado de deudas
▸ **load up** (VT + ADV) [+ *vehicle, animal, person*] cargar (**with** de)
(VI + ADV) [*vehicle*] cargarse; [*person*] cargar • **to ~ up on sth** cargarse de algo

load-bearing [ˈləʊdˌbɛərɪŋ] (ADJ) [*beam*] maestro • **a load-bearing wall** un muro de carga

loaded [ˈləʊdɪd] (ADJ) **1** [*gun, camera, vehicle*] cargado
2 [*remark, question*] lleno de implicaciones, cargado de implicaciones
3 (= *weighted*) [*dice*] cargado
4* (= *rich*) • **to be ~** estar forrado de dinero*, estar podrido de dinero*
5* (= *drunk*) • **to be ~** estar como una cuba*, estar tomado (*LAm**)
6 • IDIOM: • **to be ~ for bear** (*US*) estar preparado para el ataque

loader [ˈləʊdəʳ] (N) cargador(a) *m/f*

loading [ˈləʊdɪŋ] (N) (*Insurance*) sobreprima *f*
(CPD) ▸ **loading bay, loading dock** área *m* de carga y descarga ▸ **loading ramp** rampa *f* de carga

loadstar [ˈləʊdstɑːʳ] (N) = **lodestar**

loadstone [ˈləʊdstəʊn] (N) = **lodestone**

loaf[1] [ləʊf] (N) (PL: **loaves**) **1** [*of bread*] (*unsliced*) pan *m* de molde; (*sliced*) pan *m* de molde (en rebanadas); (= *French bread*) barra *f* • **use your ~!** (*Brit**) ¡espabílate! • PROVERB: • **half a ~ is better than no bread** menos da una piedra, peor es nada; ▹ RHYMING SLANG
2 [*of sugar*] pan *m*, pilón *m*
(CPD) ▸ **loaf sugar** pan *m* de azúcar ▸ **loaf tin** bandeja *f* de horno

loaf[2] [ləʊf] (VI) (*also* **loaf about, loaf around**) holgazanear, flojear (*LAm*)

loafer [ˈləʊfəʳ] (N) **1** (= *person*) gandul(a) *m/f*, vago/a *m/f*

2 (= *shoe*) mocasín *m*

loam [ləʊm] N marga *f*

loamy [ˈləʊmɪ] ADJ margoso

loan [ləʊn] N (= *thing lent between persons*) préstamo *m*; (*from bank*) crédito *m*, préstamo *m* • **it's on ~** está prestado • **I had it on ~ from the company** me lo prestó la empresa • **she is on ~ to another department** presta temporalmente sus servicios en otra sección • **to raise a ~** (= *money*) obtener *or* conseguir un préstamo • **to subscribe a ~** suscribir un préstamo • **I asked for the ~ of the book** le pedí prestado el libro
VT prestar
CPD ▸ **loan account** cuenta *f* de crédito ▸ **loan agreement** acuerdo *m* de crédito ▸ **loan capital** capital *m* en préstamo ▸ **loan fund** fondo *m* de crédito para empréstitos ▸ **loan guarantee** garantía *f* de préstamo ▸ **loan repayment** reembolso *m* del préstamo ▸ **loan shark** prestamista *mf* usurero/a, tiburón *m* ▸ **loan translation** calco *m* lingüístico ▸ **loan word** préstamo *m*

▸ **loan out** VT + ADV (*gen*) prestar; [+ *player*] ceder

loath [ləʊθ] ADJ • **to be ~ to do sth** estar poco dispuesto a hacer algo, ser reacio a hacer algo • **to be ~ for sb to do sth** no querer en absoluto que algn haga algo • **nothing ~** de buena gana

loathe [ləʊð] VT [+ *thing, person*] detestar, odiar • **I ~ doing it** detesto *or* odio hacerlo • **he ~s being corrected** detesta que se le corrija

loathing [ˈləʊðɪŋ] N odio *m* • **it fills me with ~** me repugna • **the ~ which I felt for him** el odio que sentía hacia *or* por él

loathsome [ˈləʊðsəm] ADJ [*thing, person*] detestable, odioso; [*smell, disease*] repugnante

loathsomeness [ˈləʊðsəmnɪs] N [*of person, thing*] lo detestable, lo odioso; [*of smell, disease*] lo repugnante

loaves [ləʊvz] NPL *of* **loaf**[1]

lob [lɒb] VT [+ *ball*] volear por alto • **to lob sth over to sb** tirar *or* echar algo a algn
N lob *m*, globo *m*
VI lanzar un globo

lobby [ˈlɒbɪ] N **1** (= *entrance hall*) vestíbulo *m*; (= *corridor*) pasillo *m*; (= *anteroom*) antecámara *f*; (= *waiting room*) sala *f* de espera
2 (*Pol*) (*for public*) vestíbulo *m* público, antecámara *f*; (= *division lobby*) (*for voting*) sala *f* de votantes
3 (= *pressure group*) grupo *m* de presión • **the environmental ~** el grupo de presión ecologista
VT • **to ~ one's member of parliament** ejercer presiones sobre su diputado
VI ejercer presiones, presionar • **to ~ for a reform** presionar para conseguir una reforma
CPD ▸ **lobby correspondent** (*Brit*) corresponsal *mf* parlamentario/a

lobbyer [ˈlɒbɪəʳ] N (*US*) = **lobbyist**

lobbying [ˈlɒbɪɪŋ] N cabildeo *m*

lobbyist [ˈlɒbɪɪst] N cabildero/a *m/f*

lobe [ləʊb] N lóbulo *m*

lobed [ləʊbd] ADJ lobulado

-lobed [-ˌləʊbd] SUFFIX • **three-lobed** trilobulado

lobelia [ləʊˈbiːlɪə] N lobelia *f*

lobotomy [ləʊˈbɒtəmɪ] N lobotomía *f*

lobster [ˈlɒbstəʳ] N (*also* **rock lobster, spiny lobster**) langosta *f*; (*with large pincers*) langosta *f*, bogavante *m* (*Sp*)
CPD ▸ **lobster pot** nasa *f*, langostera *f*

local [ˈləʊkəl] ADJ **1** (= *in or of the area*) [*custom, newspaper, radio*] local; [*school, shop, doctor*] del barrio; [*bus, train*] urbano; [*news, weather forecast*] regional • **the ~ community** el vecindario, el barrio; (*wider*) la zona, el área • **~ currency** moneda *f* local, moneda *f* del país • **to be of ~ interest** ser de interés local • **he's a ~ man** es de aquí • **~ residents have complained to the council** los residentes del barrio *or* de la zona se han quejado al ayuntamiento • **~ train services have been cut** han reducido los servicios locales de tren • **whatever you do, don't drink the ~ wine** hagas lo que hagas no bebas el vino del lugar
2 (= *municipal*) [*administration, taxes, elections*] municipal • **at (the) ~ level** a nivel municipal *or* local
3 (*Med*) [*pain*] localizado
N **1*** (= *local resident*) • **the ~s** los vecinos; (*wider*) la gente de la zona • **he's a ~** es de aquí
2 (*Brit**) (= *pub*) *bar de la zona donde alguien vive*
3 (*Med**) (= *local anaesthetic*) anestesia *f* local
4 (*US*) (*Rail*) *tren, autobús etc que hace parada en todas las estaciones*
CPD ▸ **local anaesthetic, local anesthetic** (*US*) anestesia *f* local • **under ~ anaesthetic** bajo anestesia local ▸ **local area network** red *f* de área local ▸ **local authority** (*Brit, New Zealand*) gobierno *m* local; [*of city, town*] ayuntamiento *m* ▸ **local call** (*Telec*) llamada *f* local ▸ **local colour, local color** (*US*) (*esp Literat, Cine*) ambiente *m* local, ambiente *m* del lugar ▸ **local council** ayuntamiento *m*, municipio *m* ▸ **local education authority** secretaría *f* municipal de educación ▸ **local government** (*Brit*) administración *f* municipal ▸ **local government elections** elecciones *fpl* municipales ▸ **local government expenditure** gastos *mpl* municipales ▸ **local politics** la vida política local ▸ **local time** hora *f* local

locale [ləʊˈkɑːl] N (= *place*) lugar *m*; (= *scene*) escenario *m*

localism [ˈləʊkəˌlɪzəm] N **1** (= *local preference*) provincianismo *m*
2 (*Pol*) descentralización *f*

locality [ləʊˈkælɪtɪ] N localidad *f*

localization [ˌləʊkəlaɪˈzeɪʃən] N (*also Comput*) localización *f*

localize [ˈləʊkəlaɪz] VT localizar

localized [ˈləʊkəlaɪzd] ADJ localizado, local

locally [ˈləʊkəlɪ] ADV **1** (= *in the area*) [*live, work*] en las cercanías; [*make, produce*] en la región (*or* la zona, la localidad *etc*); [*buy*] en las tiendas del barrio (*or* la zona, la localidad *etc*) • **to be known ~ as** conocerse localmente como • **she's very well known ~** es muy conocida en el barrio (*or* la zona, la localidad *etc*) • **I prefer to shop ~** prefiero comprar en las tiendas del barrio *or* del pueblo
2 (= *at local level*) [*decide, vote*] a nivel local • **both nationally and ~** tanto a nivel nacional como regional

locate [ləʊˈkeɪt] VT **1** (= *place*) situar, ubicar (*esp LAm*) • **to be ~d at** estar situado en, estar ubicado en (*esp LAm*)
2 (= *find*) localizar • **we ~d it eventually** por fin lo encontramos

location [ləʊˈkeɪʃən] N **1** (= *place*) lugar *m* • **the house is set in** *or* **has a beautiful ~** la casa está situada en un lugar precioso
2 (= *placing*) [*of building*] situación *f*, ubicación *f* • **"central ~ near the sea"** (*in brochure*) "situación *f or* ubicación *f* céntrica próxima al mar" • **this would be an ideal spot for the ~ of the hotel** este sería un lugar ideal para la ubicación del hotel
3 (= *exact position*) [*of missing person, suspect*] paradero *m*; [*of airplane, ship*] posición *f* • **what's your ~?** ¿cuál es tu posición?
4 (= *finding*) localización *f*
5 (*Cine*) • **to be on ~ in Mexico** estar rodando exteriores en México • **to film on ~** filmar en exteriores

locative [ˈlɒkətɪv] N locativo *m*

loch [lɒx] N (*Scot*) lago *m*; (= *sea loch*) ría *f*, brazo *m* de mar

loci [ˈləʊsaɪ] NPL *of* **locus**

lock[1] [lɒk] N [*of hair*] mecha *f*, mechón *m*; (= *ringlet*) bucle *m*; **locks** (*poet*) cabellos *mpl*

lock[2] [lɒk] N **1** (*on door, box, safe*) cerradura *f*, chapa *f* (*LAm*); (*Aut*) (*on steering wheel*) tope *m*, retén *m*; (= *bolt*) cerrojo *m*; (*also* **padlock**) candado *m*; [*of gun*] llave *f* • **under ~ and key** bajo siete llaves • **to put sth under ~ and key** guardar algo bajo llave • **~, stock, and barrel** (*fig*) con todo incluido
2 (*on canal*) esclusa *f*; (= *pressure chamber*) cámara *f* intermedia
3 (*Aut*) (= *steering lock*) ángulo *m* de giro
4 (*Wrestling*) llave *f*
VT **1** (*with key*) cerrar con llave; (*with bolt*) cerrar con cerrojo; (*with padlock*) cerrar con candado • **to ~ sth/sb in a place** encerrar algo/a algn en un lugar
2 (*Mech*) trabar; [+ *steering wheel*] (*to prevent theft*) bloquear, inmovilizar; (= *jam*) bloquear; (*Comput*) [+ *screen*] desactivar
3 (= *entwine*) (*usu pass*) • **they were ~ed in each other's arms** estaban unidos en un abrazo • **the armies were ~ed in combat** los ejércitos luchaban encarnizadamente • IDIOM: • **to ~ horns with sb** enzarzarse en una disputa *or* pelea con algn
VI **1** (*with key*) cerrarse con llave
2 (*Mech*) trabarse • **the front wheels of the car ~ed** las ruedas delanteras se trabaron
CPD ▸ **lock gate** puerta *f* de esclusa ▸ **lock keeper** esclusero/a *m/f* ▸ **lock picker** espadista *m*

▸ **lock away** VT + ADV (*gen*) guardar bajo llave; [+ *criminal, mental patient*] encerrar

▸ **lock in** VT + ADV dejar encerrado dentro

▸ **lock on to** VI + PREP (*Mech*) acoplarse a, unirse a

▸ **lock out** VT + ADV cerrar la puerta a, dejar fuera con la puerta cerrada • **to find o.s. ~ed out** estar fuera sin llave para abrir la puerta • **the workers were ~ed out** los obreros se quedaron sin trabajo por cierre patronal

▸ **lock up** VT + ADV [+ *object*] guardar bajo llave; [+ *house*] cerrar con llave; [+ *criminal*] encarcelar; [+ *funds*] inmovilizar • **you ought to be ~ed up!** ¡irás a parar a la cárcel!
VI + ADV echar la llave

lockable [ˈlɒkəbl] ADJ que se puede cerrar con llave

lockage [ˈlɒkɪdʒ] N **1** (= *canal lock*) esclusa *f*
2 (= *toll*) derechos *mpl* de esclusa
3 (= *passage of ship*) paso *m* por una esclusa

lockdown [ˈlɒkdaʊn] N cierre *m* de emergencia • **to be in** *or* **under ~** [*place*] estar cerrado (*por emergencia*) • **to be in** *or* **on ~** [*prisoner*] estar recluido *or* aislado

locked [lɒkt] ADJ [*door, suitcase, drawer*] cerrado con llave

locker [ˈlɒkəʳ] N cajón *m* con llave; (*for left luggage*) casillero *m* (de consigna), consigna *f* automática; (*US*) cámara *f* de frío; [*of gymnasium*] taquilla *f*
CPD ▸ **locker room** vestuario *m*

locket [ˈlɒkɪt] N relicario *m*, guardapelo *m*

locking [ˈlɒkɪŋ] ADJ [*door, container, cupboard*] que se cierra con llave • **~ petrol cap** (*Aut*) tapón *m* de gasolina con llave

lockjaw [ˈlɒkdʒɔː] N trismo *m*

locknut [ˈlɒknʌt] N contratuerca *f*

lockout [ˈlɒkaʊt] N cierre *m* patronal

locksmith [ˈlɒksmɪθ] N cerrajero/a *m/f*

lock-up [ˈlɒkʌp] N **1** (*US*) (= *prison*) cárcel *f*
2 (*Brit*) (*also* **lock-up garage**) garaje *m*, cochera *f* (*LAm*)
3 (*Brit*) (= *shop*) tienda *f* sin trastienda
CPD ▸ **lock-up stall** (*US*) garaje *m*, cochera *f* (*LAm*)

loco[1]* [ˈləʊkəʊ] N = **locomotive**

loco[2] [ˈləʊkəʊ] ADV • ~ **Southampton** *precio cotizado en Southampton, y la mercancía se halla en Southampton como lugar de origen*; (*Comm*)
CPD ▸ **loco price** *precio cotizado en un lugar (aceptando el comprador todos los costos y riesgos al trasladar la mercancía a otro lugar)*

locomotion [ˌləʊkəˈməʊʃən] N locomoción *f*

locomotive [ˌləʊkəˈməʊtɪv] ADJ locomotor
N (*Rail*) locomotora *f*, máquina *f*

locum [ˈləʊkəm] N (*also* **locum tenens**) (*Brit*) (*frm*) interino/a *m/f*

locus [ˈləʊkəs] N (PL: **loci**) punto *m*, sitio *m*; (*Math*) lugar *m* (geométrico)

locust [ˈləʊkəst] N **1** (*Zool*) langosta *f*
2 (*Bot*) algarroba *f*
CPD ▸ **locust tree** (= *false acacia*) acacia *f* falsa; (= *carob*) algarrobo *m*

locution [ləˈkjuːʃən] N locución *f*

locutory [ˈlɒkjʊtərɪ] N locutorio *m*

lode [ləʊd] N filón *m*, veta *f*

lodestar [ˈləʊdstɑːʳ] N estrella *f* polar; (*fig*) norte *m*

lodestone [ˈləʊdstəʊn] N piedra *f* imán

lodge [lɒdʒ] N (*at gate of park*) casa *f* del guarda; [*of porter*] portería *f*; (*Freemasonry*) logia *f*; (= *hunting lodge*) pabellón *m* de caza; (*Univ*) (*master's*) rectoría *f*
VT [+ *person*] alojar, hospedar; [+ *object*] colocar, meter; [+ *complaint*] presentar; [+ *statement*] prestar; (*Jur*) [+ *appeal*] interponer • **to ~ sth with sb** dejar algo en manos de algn, entregar algo a algn • **the bullet is ~d in the lung** la bala se ha alojado en el pulmón
VI (= *reside*) alojarse, hospedarse (**with** con, en casa de); [*object*] (= *get stuck*) alojarse, meterse • **where do you ~?** ¿dónde estás alojado? • **the bullet ~d in the lung** la bala se alojó en el pulmón • **a bomb ~d in the engine room** una bomba se penetró en la sala de máquinas

lodger [ˈlɒdʒəʳ] N inquilino/a *m/f* (*de habitación en una casa particular*), huésped(a) *m/f* • **I was a ~ there once** hace tiempo me hospedé allí • **she takes ~s** alquila habitaciones en su casa

lodging [ˈlɒdʒɪŋ] N alojamiento *m*, hospedaje *m* • **they gave me a night's ~** me dieron alojamiento; **lodgings** alojamiento *msing* • **to look for ~s** buscar alojamiento • **we took ~s with Mrs P** nos hospedamos en casa de la Sra. P • **are they good ~s?** ¿es buena la pensión?
CPD ▸ **lodging house** pensión *f*, casa *f* de huéspedes

loess [ˈləʊɪs] N loess *m*

loft [lɒft] N (= *attic*) desván *m*; (= *hay loft*) pajar *m*; (*in church*) galería *f*; (= *apartment*) loft *m*, *aprovechamiento doméstico de un espacio industrial*
VT [+ *ball*] lanzar por lo alto
CPD ▸ **loft conversion** (*Brit*) (= *accommodation*) apartamento *m* abuhardillado (*renovado*)

loftily [ˈlɒftɪlɪ] ADV [*say, look*] con altivez, con altanería • **"I know what I'm doing," she said ~** —sé lo que estoy haciendo —dijo muy altanera *or* con altivez

loftiness [ˈlɒftɪnɪs] N [*of ceiling, mountain, tower*] altura *f*; [*of aim, ideal*] nobleza *f*, lo elevado; [*of person, attitude*] altanería *f*, altivez *f*; [*of tone*] ampulosidad *f*, grandilocuencia *f*

lofty [ˈlɒftɪ] ADJ (COMPAR: **loftier**, SUPERL: **loftiest**) **1** (*liter*) (= *high*) [*ceiling, building, tower*] alto, elevado; [*mountain*] alto; [*room*] de techo alto • **he rose to a ~ position within the organization** ascendió a una posición elevada dentro de la organización
2 (= *noble*) [*aim, ideal*] elevado, noble
3 (= *haughty*) [*person, attitude*] altivo, altanero • ~ **air/manner** aire *m* de superioridad, altivez *f* • ~ **contempt/disdain** altivo desdén *m*
4 (= *grandiose*) [*rhetoric*] grandilocuente

log[1] [lɒg] N **1** [*of wood*] tronco *m*, leño *m*
2 = **logbook**
VT **1** (*Naut, Aer*) anotar, apuntar
2 (*Aut*) (*also* **log up**) [+ *distance*] recorrer • **we logged 50 kilometres that day** ese día recorrimos *or* cubrimos 50 kilómetros
VI cortar (y transportar) troncos
CPD ▸ **log cabin** cabaña *f* de troncos *or* de madera ▸ **log fire** fuego *m* de leña
▸ **log in** (*Comput*) VI + ADV acceder al sistema, entrar en el sistema
VT + ADV meter en el sistema
▸ **log off** VI + ADV, VT + ADV = **log out**
▸ **log on** VI + ADV, VT + ADV = **log in**
▸ **log out** (*Comput*) VI + ADV salir del sistema, terminar de operar
VT + ADV sacar del sistema
▸ **log up** VT + ADV (*Aut*) [+ *distance*] recorrer • **we logged up 50 kilometres that day** ese día recorrimos *or* cubrimos 50 kilómetros

log[2] [lɒg] N ABBR (*Math*) (= **logarithm**) logaritmo *m*
CPD ▸ **log tables** tablas *fpl* de logaritmos

loganberry [ˈləʊgənbərɪ] N (= *fruit*) frambuesa *f* norteamericana; (= *bush*) frambueso *m* norteamericano

logarithm [ˈlɒgərɪðəm] N logaritmo *m*

logarithmic [ˌlɒgəˈrɪðmɪk] ADJ logarítmico

logbook [ˈlɒgbʊk] N (*Naut*) cuaderno *m* de bitácora, diario *m* de navegación; (*Aer*) diario *m* de vuelo; (*Aut*) documentación *f*; (*Tech*) cuaderno *m* de trabajo

logger [ˈlɒgəʳ] N **1** (= *dealer*) maderero/a *m/f*, negociante *mf* en maderas
2 (*US*) (= *lumberjack*) leñador(a) *m/f*

loggerheads [ˈlɒgəhedz] NPL • **to be at ~ with sb** estar a matar con algn, estar picado con algn

loggia [ˈlɒdʒə] N (PL: **loggias** *or* **loggie** [ˈlɒdʒe]) logia *f*

logging [ˈlɒgɪŋ] N explotación *f* forestal
CPD ▸ **logging company** empresa *f* maderera

logic [ˈlɒdʒɪk] N lógica *f* • **I can't see the ~ of it** no le veo la lógica
CPD ▸ **logic circuit** (*Comput*) circuito *m* lógico

logical [ˈlɒdʒɪkəl] ADJ lógico • **she's the ~ choice for the job** es lógico que sea ella la elegida para el puesto • **to take sth to its ~ conclusion** llevar algo a su lógica conclusión • **she has a ~ mind** es una persona lógica • **it seemed a ~ step** parecía el paso lógico • **it is ~ that** es lógico que • **he is incapable of ~ thinking** es incapaz de razonar con lógica *or* de manera lógica
CPD ▸ **logical positivism** positivismo *m* lógico

logically [ˈlɒdʒɪkəlɪ] ADV **1** (= *by a logical process*) lógicamente
2 (= *rationally*) [*think, speak, act*] de manera lógica, de forma lógica; [*designed, laid out*] con lógica • **I'm not thinking ~** no estoy pensando de manera *or* forma lógica, no estoy pensando con lógica • ~ **(enough), the controls are on the right** como es lógico, los controles están a la derecha

logician [lɒˈdʒɪʃən] N lógico/a *m/f*

login [ˈlɒgɪn] N login *m*

logistic [lɒˈdʒɪstɪk] ADJ logístico

logistical [lɒˈdʒɪstɪkəl] ADJ = **logistic**

logistically [lɒˈdʒɪstɪkəlɪ] ADV logísticamente, desde el punto de vista logístico

logistics [lɒˈdʒɪstɪks] NSING logística *f*

logjam [ˈlɒgdʒæm] N (*fig*) atolladero *m* • **to clear the ~** desbloquear la situación, salir del atolladero

logo [ˈləʊgəʊ] N logo *m*, logotipo *m*

log-off [ˈlɒgˈɒf] N (*Comput*) salida *f* del sistema

log-on [ˈlɒgˈɒn] N (*Comput*) entrada *f* al sistema

logrolling [ˈlɒgˌrəʊlɪŋ] N (*US*) intercambio *m* de favores políticos, sistema *m* de concesiones mutuas

logy [ˈləʊgɪ] ADJ (COMPAR: **logier**, SUPERL: **logiest**) (*US*) torpe, lerdo

loin [lɔɪn] N **1** [*of meat*] lomo *m*
2 loins (*Anat*) (*liter*) lomos *mpl* • **to gird (up) one's ~s** (*fig*) aprestarse a luchar, apretarse los machos*
CPD ▸ **loin chop** (*Culin*) chuleta *f* de lomo

loincloth [ˈlɔɪnklɒθ] N taparrabo *m*, taparrabos *m inv*

Loire [lwɑːr] N Loira *m*

loiter [ˈlɔɪtəʳ] VI (= *idle*) perder el tiempo; (= *lag behind*) rezagarse; (= *dally*) entretenerse • **don't ~ on the way!** ¡no te entretengas! • **to ~ (with intent)** (*Jur*) merodear con fines sospechosos *or* delictivos
▸ **loiter about** VI + ADV merodear
▸ **loiter away** VT + ADV • **to ~ away the time** perder el tiempo

loiterer [ˈlɔɪtərəʳ] N (= *idler*) holgazán/ana *m/f*, ocioso/a *m/f*; (= *straggler*) rezagado/a *m/f*

LOL*, **lol***[lɒl] ABBR (= **laugh out loud, laughing out loud**) me parto

loll [lɒl] VI [*head*] colgar, caer • **to ~ against** recostarse en
▸ **loll about, loll around** VI + ADV repantigarse
▸ **loll back** VI + ADV • **to ~ back on** recostarse en
▸ **loll out** VI + ADV • **his tongue was ~ing out** le colgaba la lengua

lollipop [ˈlɒlɪpɒp] N pirulí *m*, piruleta *f* (*Sp*), chupaleta *f* (*Mex*), chupetín *m* (*Arg, Uru*); (*iced*) polo *m*, paleta *f* helada (*LAm*)
CPD ▸ **lollipop lady** (*Brit**) *mujer encargada de ayudar a los niños a cruzar la calle* ▸ **lollipop man** (*Brit**) *hombre encargado de ayudar a los niños a cruzar la calle*

LOLLIPOP LADY/MAN

Se llama **lollipop man** o **lollipop lady** a la persona encargada de parar el tráfico en las calles cercanas a los colegios en el Reino Unido, para que los niños las crucen sin peligro. Suelen ser personas ya jubiladas, que van vestidas con una gabardina fosforescente y que llevan una señal de stop en un poste portátil, lo que recuerda por su forma a una piruleta, y de ahí su nombre.

lollop [ˈlɒləp] VI moverse desgarbadamente • **to ~ along** moverse torpemente, arrastrar los pies

lolly [ˈlɒlɪ] N **1** = **lollipop**
2 (*Brit**) (= *money*) pasta* *f*, lana *f* (*LAm**)

Lombard [ˈlɒmbɑːd] ADJ lombardo
N lombardo/a *m/f*

Lombardy [ˈlɒmbədɪ] N Lombardía *f*
CPD ▸ **Lombardy poplar** chopo *m* lombardo

London [ˈlʌndən] N Londres *m*

CPD londinense ▸ **London pride** (*Bot*) corona *f* de rey

Londoner ['lʌndənəʳ] N londinense *mf*

lone [ləʊn] ADJ (= *solitary*) solitario • **to play a ~ hand** (*fig*) actuar solo; ▹ **lonely**
CPD ▸ **lone parent** = **single parent** ▸ **lone parent family** = **single-parent family** ▸ **lone ranger** llanero *m* solitario ▸ **lone wolf** (*fig*) lobo *m* solitario

loneliness ['ləʊnlɪnɪs] N soledad *f*

lonely ['ləʊnlɪ] ADJ **1** (COMPAR: **lonelier**, SUPERL: **loneliest**) (= *without company*) • **he was a sad and ~ man** era un hombre triste y solitario • **to feel ~** sentirse solo • **I was ~ and didn't know what to do** me sentía solo y no sabía qué hacer
2 (= *solitary*) [*life, place, period of time*] solitario • **the ~ hours of the night** las horas nocturnas de soledad, las solitarias horas de la noche • **it's ~ at the top** uno se siente muy solo en la cumbre
3 (= *remote*) [*village, house*] solitario, aislado; [*road*] solitario
4 (*liter*) (= *mournful*) [*sound*] lúgubre y solitario (*liter*)
NPL • **the ~** las personas que están solas
CPD ▸ **lonely hearts club** club *m* de corazones solitarios ▸ **lonely hearts (column)** sección *f* de corazones solitarios

lone-parent ['ləʊn,pɛərənt] CPD ▸ **lone-parent family** (*Brit*) familia *f* monoparental

loner ['ləʊnəʳ] N solitario/a *m/f*

lonesome ['ləʊnsəm] (*esp US*) ADJ [*person*] solo; [*place*] (= *isolated*) aislado, solitario • **to be/feel ~** sentirse solo

long[1] [lɒŋ] (COMPAR: **longer**, SUPERL: **longest**) ADJ **1** (*in size*) [*dress, hair, journey*] largo • **it's six metres ~** tiene seis metros de largo • **it's a very ~ book** es un libro muy largo • **he has ~ legs** tiene las piernas largas • **it's a ~ distance from the school** está (muy) lejos del colegio • **to make** *or* **pull a ~ face** poner cara larga • **to get ~er** [*queue*] hacerse más largo; [*hair*] crecer (más) • **how ~ is it?** (*table, hallway, piece of material, stick*) ¿cuánto mide de largo?; (*more precisely*) ¿qué longitud tiene?; (*river*) ¿qué longitud tiene? • **how ~ is her hair?** ¿cómo tiene el pelo de largo? • **to be ~ in the leg** [*trousers*] tener piernas largas • **the speech was ~ on rhetoric and short on details** el discurso tenía mucha retórica y pocos detalles • IDIOMS: • **the ~ arm of the law** el brazo de la ley, el alcance de la ley • **a list as ~ as your arm** una lista larguísima • **not by a ~ chalk** ni con mucho • **he's a bit ~ in the tooth*** es bastante viejo ya; ▹ **suit**
2 (*in distance*) • **it's a ~ way** está lejos • **it's a ~ way to the shops** las tiendas están lejos • **we walked a ~ way** caminamos mucho
3 (*in time*) [*film*] largo; [*visit*] prolongado; [*wait*] largo, prolongado • **two hours ~** de dos horas • **the course is six months ~** el curso es de seis meses, el curso dura seis meses • **a ~ walk** un paseo largo • **a ~ holiday** unas vacaciones largas • **it has been a ~ day** (*fig*) ha sido un día muy atareado • **there will be ~ delays** habrá grandes retrasos, habrá retrasos considerables • **he took a ~ drink of water** se bebió un vaso grande de agua • **the days are getting ~er** los días se están alargando • **how ~ is the film?** ¿cuánto (tiempo) dura la película? • **how ~ are the holidays?** ¿cuánto duran las vacaciones? • **to be ~ in doing sth** tardar en hacer algo • **the reply was not ~ in coming** la respuesta no tardó en llegar • **it will be a ~ job** será un trabajo que llevará mucho tiempo • **at ~ last** por fin • **to take a ~ look at sth** mirar algo detenidamente • **he has a ~ memory** (*fig*) es de los que no perdonan fácilmente • **in the ~ run** (*fig*) a la larga • **a ~ time ago** hace mucho tiempo • **it takes a ~ time** lleva mucho tiempo • **I've been waiting a ~ time** llevo esperando mucho tiempo • **~ time no see!*** ¡cuánto tiempo sin verte! • **it's a good place to go for a ~ weekend** es un buen sitio para ir durante un fin de semana largo • IDIOM: • **he's not ~ for this world*** no le queda mucho de vida; ▹ **term, long-term, view**
4 (*Ling*) [*vowel*] largo
ADV **1** (= *a long time*) • **don't be ~!** ¡vuelve pronto! • **I shan't be ~** (*in finishing*) termino pronto, no tardo; (*in returning*) vuelvo pronto, no tardo • **will you be ~?** ¿vas a tardar mucho? • **we didn't stay ~** nos quedamos poco tiempo • **he hasn't been gone ~** no hace mucho que se ha ido • **have you been waiting ~?** ¿hace mucho que espera? • **I have ~ believed that …** creo desde hace tiempo que …, hace tiempo que creo que … • **this method has ~ been used in industry** este método se viene usando desde hace mucho tiempo en la industria • **~ after he died** mucho tiempo después de morir • **he died ~ after his wife** murió mucho tiempo después que su mujer • **~ ago** hace mucho (tiempo) • **how ~ ago was it?** ¿cuánto tiempo hace de eso? • **as ~ ago as 1930** ya en 1930 • **not ~ ago** no hace mucho (tiempo) • **~ before** mucho antes • **not ~ before** poco antes • **~ before now** hace mucho tiempo • **~ before you came** mucho antes de que llegaras • **not ~ before the war** poco antes de la guerra • **not ~ before his wife died** poco antes de que muriera su mujer • **they left before ~** se marcharon muy pronto • **I only had ~ enough to buy a paper** solo tuve tiempo para comprar un periódico • **we won't stay for ~** nos quedamos un rato nada más • **are you going away for ~?** ¿te vas para mucho tiempo? • **he hesitated, but not for ~** dudó, pero solo por un instante • **"are you still in London?" — "yes, but not for much ~er"** —¿todavía estás en Londres? —sí, pero por poco tiempo ya • **how ~ will you be?** (*in finishing*) ¿cuánto (tiempo) tardarás?; (*in returning*) ¿cuánto tiempo te quedarás? • **how ~ have you been here?** ¿cuánto tiempo llevas aquí? • **how ~ will it take?** ¿cuánto tiempo llevará? • **how ~ did he stay?** ¿cuánto tiempo se quedó? • **how ~ have you been learning Spanish?** ¿desde cuándo llevas aprendiendo español? • **how ~ is it since you saw her?** ¿cuánto tiempo hace que no la ves? • **it didn't last ~** fue cosa de unos pocos minutos *or* días *etc* • **to live ~** tener una vida larga • **women live ~er than men** las mujeres son más longevas que los hombres • **he hasn't ~ to live** no le queda mucho de vida • **~ live the King!** ¡viva el rey! • **it's not ~ since he died** • **he died not ~ since** no hace mucho que murió, murió hace poco • **~ since dead** muerto hace mucho • **so ~!** (*esp US**) ¡hasta luego! • **it won't take ~** no tardará mucho • **it didn't take him ~ to realize that …** no tardó en darse cuenta de que … • **he talked ~ about politics** habló largamente de política
2 • **~er** más tiempo • **we stayed ~er than you** quedamos más tiempo que vosotros • **wait a little ~er** espera un poco más • **how much ~er can you stay?** ¿hasta cuándo podéis quedaros? • **how much ~er do we have to wait?** ¿hasta cuándo tenemos que esperar? • **two hours ~er** dos horas más • **I can't stay any ~er** no me puedo quedar por más tiempo • **I can't stand it any ~er** ya no lo aguanto más • **no ~er** ya no • **he no ~er comes** ya no viene
3 • **~est: six months at the ~est** seis meses, como máximo *or* como mucho
4 • **as ~ as** • **so ~ as** (= *while*) mientras • **as ~ as the war lasts** mientras dure la guerra • **as ~ as I live** mientras viva • **stay (for) as ~ as you like** quédate hasta cuando quieras • **as ~ as (is) necessary** el tiempo que haga falta, lo que haga falta
5 • **as ~ as** • **so ~ as** (= *provided that*) siempre que (+ *subjun*) • **you can borrow it as ~ as John doesn't mind** lo puedes tomar prestado siempre que a John no le importe *or* si a John no le importa
6 (= *through*) • **all day ~** todo el (santo) día • **all night ~** toda la noche • **all summer ~** todo el verano
N **1** • **the ~ and the short of it is that …** (*fig*) en resumidas cuentas, es que …, concretamente, es que …
2 longs (*Econ*) valores *mpl* a largo plazo
CPD ▸ **long division** (*Math*) división *f* larga ▸ **long drink** refresco *m*, bebida *f* no alcohólica ▸ **long johns** calzoncillos *mpl* largos ▸ **long jump** salto *m* de longitud ▸ **long jumper** saltador(a) *m/f* de longitud ▸ **long shot** (*Cine*) toma *f* a distancia; (*in race*) desconocido/a *m/f* • **it's a ~ shot*** dudo que resulte • IDIOM: • **not by a ~ shot** ni con mucho ▸ **long sight** presbicia *f*, hipermetropía *f* • **to have ~ sight** ser présbita ▸ **the long term** • **in** *or* **over the ~ term** a largo plazo ▸ **long trousers** (*as opposed to shorts*) pantalones *mpl* largos ▸ **the long vacation, the long vac*** (*Brit*) (*Univ*) las vacaciones de verano ▸ **long wave** (*Rad*) onda *f* larga; (*used as adj*) de onda larga

long[2] [lɒŋ] VI • **to ~ for sth** anhelar algo, desear algo • **to ~ for sb** suspirar por algn, añorar a algn • **to ~ to do sth** tener muchas ganas de hacer algo, estar deseando hacer algo • **to ~ for sb to do sth** desear que algn haga algo

-long [lɒŋ] ADJ (*ending in compounds*) • **month-long** de un mes de duración

long. ABBR = **longitude**

long-armed ['lɒŋ'ɑːmd] ADJ de brazos largos

long-awaited ['lɒŋə'weɪtɪd] ADJ largamente esperado

longboat ['lɒŋbəʊt] N lancha *f*

longbow ['lɒŋbəʊ] N arco *m*

long-dated ['lɒŋ'deɪtɪd] ADJ a largo plazo

long-distance ['lɒŋ'dɪstəns] ADJ [*flight*] largo, de larga distancia; [*race, runner*] de fondo; [*train*] de largo recorrido
ADV • **to call sb long-distance** poner una conferencia a algn
CPD ▸ **long-distance call** llamada *f* interurbana *or* de larga distancia, conferencia *f* ▸ **long-distance bus** autocar *m*, coche *m* de línea ▸ **long-distance runner** corredor(a) *m/f* de fondo, fondista *mf*

long-drawn-out ['lɒŋdrɔːn'aʊt] ADJ interminable

long-eared ['lɒŋ'ɪəd] ADJ orejudo, de orejas largas

longed-for ['lɒŋdfɔːʳ] ADJ ansiado

longevity [lɒn'dʒevɪtɪ] N longevidad *f*

long-forgotten ['lɒŋfə'gɒtn] ADJ olvidado hace mucho tiempo

long-grain ['lɒŋgreɪn] ADJ [*rice*] de grano largo

long-haired ['lɒŋ'hɛəd] ADJ de pelo largo

longhand ['lɒŋhænd] N • **in ~** escrito a mano
ADJ escrito a mano
ADV a mano

long-haul ['lɒŋ,hɔːl] ADJ [*flight*] de larga distancia

longhorn ['lɒŋhɔːn] N res *f* de cuernos largos

long-hours culture [ˌlɒŋ'aʊəz,kʌltʃəʳ] (N) (*Comm*) cultura *f* de trabajar muchas horas

longing ['lɒŋɪŋ] (N) (= *yearning*) (*for place*) nostalgia *f*, añoranza *f*; (*for past time*) añoranza *f*; (*for person, thing*) anhelo *m* • **she felt a ~ for her childhood days** añoraba los días de su infancia • **he felt a ~ for his homeland** sentía nostalgia por su país, añoraba su país • **people have a ~ for normality** la gente anhela la normalidad • **she gazed at him with ~** lo miró con anhelo (ADJ) [*look*] anhelante

longingly ['lɒŋɪŋlɪ] (ADV) [*look, gaze*] con anhelo, con ansia • **she thought ~ of those days in Madrid** pensó con nostalgia *or* añoranza en aquellos días en Madrid

longish ['lɒŋɪʃ] (ADJ) bastante largo

longitude ['lɒŋgɪtjuːd] (N) longitud *f*

longitudinal [ˌlɒŋgɪ'tjuːdɪnl] (ADJ) longitudinal

longitudinally [ˌlɒŋgɪ'tjuːdɪnəlɪ] (ADV) longitudinalmente

long-lasting ['lɒŋ'lɑːstɪŋ] (ADJ) [*material, memory, effect*] duradero

long-legged ['lɒŋ'legɪd] (ADJ) [*person*] de piernas largas; [*animal*] de patas largas; [*bird*] zancudo

long-life ['lɒŋ'laɪf] (ADJ) de larga duración

long-limbed [ˌlɒŋ'lɪmd] (ADJ) patilargo

long-list, longlist ['lɒŋlɪst] (N) [*of candidates*] (*for job, award*) preselección *f* (VT) [+ *candidates*] (*for job, award*) preseleccionar • **to be long-listed** estar en una lista de preselección • **she was long-listed for the senior team** estaba en la lista de preselección para el equipo senior

long-lived ['lɒŋ'lɪvd] (ADJ) [*person, species*] longevo, de larga vida; [*plant*] duradero; [*rumour*] duradero, persistente • **women are more long-lived than men** las mujeres son más longevas que los hombres

long-lost ['lɒŋ'lɒst] (ADJ) perdido hace mucho tiempo

long-playing ['lɒŋ'pleɪɪŋ] (ADJ) • **long-playing record** (*abbr LP*) disco *m* de larga duración, elepé *m*

long-range ['lɒŋ'reɪndʒ] (ADJ) [*gun, missile*] de largo alcance; [*aircraft*] para vuelos de larga distancia; [*weather forecast, plan*] a largo plazo

long-running ['lɒŋ'rʌnɪŋ] (ADJ) [*dispute*] largo; [*play*] taquillero, que se mantiene mucho tiempo en la cartelera; [*programme*] que lleva mucho tiempo en antena

longship ['lɒŋʃɪp] (N) (*Viking*) barco *m* vikingo

longshoreman ['lɒŋʃɔːmən] (N) (PL: **longshoremen**) (*esp US*) estibador *m*, obrero *m* portuario

long-sighted ['lɒŋ'saɪtɪd] (ADJ) (*Med*) hipermétrope, présbita; (*fig*) previsor

long-sightedness ['lɒŋ'saɪtɪdnɪs] (N) (*Med*) presbicia *f*, hipermetropía *f*; (*fig*) previsión *f*, clarividencia *f*

long-sleeved ['lɒŋsliːvd] (ADJ) de manga larga

long-standing ['lɒŋ'stændɪŋ] (ADJ) [*agreement, dispute, friendship*] antiguo

long-stay ['lɒŋsteɪ] (ADJ) [*hospital*] para enfermos de larga duración; [*patient*] de larga duración; [*car park*] para aparcamiento *or* (*LAm*) estacionamiento prolongado

long-suffering ['lɒŋ'sʌfərɪŋ] (ADJ) sufrido

long-term ['lɒŋ'tɜːm] (ADJ) [*effect, investment, care, solution*] a largo plazo • **joining the army is a long-term commitment** entrar en el ejército significa comprometerse a largo plazo • **the drug's long-term effects** los efectos del medicamento a largo plazo • **this will have a long-term effect on unemployment** esto tendrá un efecto a largo plazo sobre el desempleo • **they're in a long-term relationship** llevan tiempo juntos • **I've had several long-term relationships** he tenido varias relaciones sentimentales duraderas • **the long-term unemployed** *las personas que llevan mucho tiempo sin trabajo* • **long-term unemployment** el desempleo de larga duración
(CPD) ▸ **long-term car park** parking *m* para aparcamiento *or* (*LAm*) estacionamiento prolongado ▸ **long-term memory** memoria *f* a largo plazo

long-time ['lɒŋ'taɪm] (ADJ) [*friend*] viejo, de muchos años; [*partner*] de muchos años

longueur [lɒŋ'gɜːʳ] (N) (*in novel, play etc*) parte *f* larga y aburrida

longways ['lɒŋweɪz] (ADV) a lo largo, longitudinalmente

long-wearing [ˌlɒŋ'weərɪŋ] (ADJ) (*US*) resistente

long-winded ['lɒŋ'wɪndɪd] (ADJ) [*person*] prolijo; [*speech, explanation*] prolijo, interminable

long-windedly ['lɒŋ'wɪndɪdlɪ] (ADV) prolijamente

loo* [luː] (N) (= *toilet*) retrete *m*, wáter *m* (*Sp*), baño *m* (*LAm*)

loofah ['luːfəʳ] (N) esponja *f* de lufa

look [lʊk] (N) **1** (= *glance*) mirada *f*, vistazo *m* • **to have a ~ at sth** echar un vistazo a algo • **let me have a ~** déjame ver • **have a ~ at this!** ¡mira esto!, ¡échale un vistazo a esto! • **shall we have a ~ round the town?** ¿damos una vuelta por la ciudad? • **to have a ~ round a house** inspeccionar una casa • **to take a ~ at sth** echar un vistazo a algo • **take a ~ at this!** ¡míra esto!, ¡échale un vistazo a esto! • **to take a good ~ at sth** mirar algo detenidamente • **to take a long hard ~ at o.s.** (*fig*) examinarse a sí mismo detenidamente • **take a long hard ~ before deciding** antes de decidir conviene pensar muchísimo • **do you want a ~?** ¿quieres verlo?
2 (= *expression*) mirada *f* • **she gave me a dirty ~** me echó una mirada de odio • **he gave me a furious ~** me miró furioso, me lanzó una mirada furiosa • **a ~ of despair** una cara de desesperación • **we got some very odd ~s** la gente nos miró extrañada • **if ~s could kill*...** si las miradas mataran ...
3 (= *search*) • **to have a ~ for sth** buscar algo • **I've had a good ~ for it already** lo he buscado ya en todas partes • **have another ~!** ¡vuelve a buscar!
4 (= *air, appearance*) aire *m*, aspecto *m*, pinta* *f* • **there's a mischievous ~ about that child** ese niño tiene pinta de pillo* • **he had a sad ~** tenía un aspecto *or* aire triste • **he had the ~ of a sailor** tenía aire de marinero • **by the ~(s) of it** *or* **things** a juzgar por las apariencias • **by the ~(s) of him ...** viéndole, se diría que ... • **you can't go by ~s alone** es arriesgado juzgar por las apariencias nada más • **to like the ~ of sb/sth**: • **I don't like the ~ of him** me cae mal, no me fío de él • **I don't like the ~ of it** no me gusta nada
5 looks (= *attractiveness*) • **~s aren't everything** la belleza no lo es todo • **good ~s** belleza *fsing* • **she has kept her ~s** sigue tan guapa como siempre • **she's losing her ~s** no es tan guapa como antes
6 (= *fashion*) moda *f*, estilo *m* • **the 1999 ~** la moda de 1999 • **the new ~** la nueva moda • **I need a new ~** quiero cambiar de imagen
(VI) **1** (= *see, glance*) mirar • **look!** ¡mira! • **~ here!** ¡oye! • **just ~!** ¡mira!, ¡fíjate! • **I'll ~ and see** voy a ver • **~ how she does it** fíjate cómo lo hace • **~ who's here!** ¡mira quién está aquí! • **to ~ into sb's eyes** mirarle a los ojos a algn • **to ~ the other way** (*lit*) mirar para el otro lado; (*fig*) hacer como que no se da cuenta • **to be ~ing over sb's shoulder** (*fig*) estar siempre vigilando a algn • IDIOM: • **to ~ down one's nose at sth/sb** menospreciar algo/a algn • PROVERB: • **~ before you leap** mira bien lo que haces
2 (= *search*) • **~ again!** ¡vuelve a buscar! • **you can't have ~ed far** no has mirado mucho • **you should have ~ed more carefully** tendrías que haber mirado mejor
3 (= *seem, appear*) parecer, verse (*LAm*) • **he ~s about 60 (years old)** aparenta tener alrededor de los 60 años • **to ~ one's age** aparentar *or* representar su edad • **she doesn't ~ her age** no aparenta *or* representa la edad que tiene • **it ~s all right to me** me parece que está bien • **it will ~ bad** (*fig*) quedará mal • **he wanted to ~ his best for the interview** quería estar lo mejor (arreglado) posible para la entrevista • **I don't ~ my best first thing in the morning** cuando me levanto por la mañana no estoy muy guapa que digamos • **he just does it to ~ big*** lo hace solo para impresionar • **they made me ~ a fool** me hicieron quedar como un idiota • **they made me ~ foolish** me hicieron quedar en ridículo • **he ~s good in a uniform** está muy guapo en uniforme • **Manchester United are ~ing good for the championship** el Manchester United tiene muchas posibilidades de ganar el campeonato • **it ~s good on you** te sienta bien • **he ~s happy** parece contento • **she wasn't ~ing herself** parecía otra, no parecía la misma • **how does it ~ to you?** ¿qué te parece? • **how do I ~?** ¿cómo estoy? • **she's 70 but doesn't ~ it** tiene 70 años pero no los aparenta *or* representa • **~ lively!*** ¡muévete!* • **that cake ~s nice** ese pastel tiene buena pinta* • **that hairstyle makes her ~ old** ese peinado la hace parece mayor • **to ~ the part** (*fig*) parecerlo • **she ~ed prettier than ever** estaba más guapa que nunca • **how pretty you ~!** ¡qué guapa estás! • **it ~s promising** parece prometedor • **to make sb ~ small** (*fig*) rebajar a algn • **he ~ed surprised** hizo un gesto de extrañeza • **he ~s tired** parece cansado • **to ~ well** [*person*] tener buena cara • **it ~s well** parece muy bien, tiene buena apariencia
4 • **to ~ like a** (= *be in appearance*) • **what does she ~ like?** ¿cómo es físicamente?
b • **to ~ like sb** (= *resemble*) parecerse a algn • **he ~s like his brother** se parece a su hermano • **this photo doesn't ~ like him** la foto no se le parece, en esta foto no parece él
c (= *seem*) • **it ~s like cheese to me** a mí me parece (que es) queso • **the festival ~s like being lively** la fiesta se anuncia animada • **it ~s like rain** parece que va a llover • **it certainly ~s like it** parece que sí
5 • **to ~ as if** *or* **as though: it ~s as if** *or* **as though the train will be late** parece que el tren va a llegar tarde • **try to ~ as if** *or* **as though you're glad to see me** haz como que te alegras de verme • **it doesn't ~ as if** *or* **as though he's coming** parece que no va a venir
6 (= *face*) • **it ~s south** [*house*] mira hacia el sur, está orientada hacia el sur
7 (= *seek*) • **they are ~ing to make a profit** quieren sacar ganancias
(VT) **1** (= *look at*) mirar • **to ~ sb (straight) in the eye(s)** *or* **in the face** mirar directamente a los ojos de algn • **I would never be able to ~ her in the eye(s)** *or* **face again** no podría resistir su mirada, siempre me avergonzaría al verla • **to ~ sb up and down** mirar a algn de arriba abajo

2 (= *pay attention to*) • **~ what you've done now!** ¡mira lo que has hecho! • **~ where you're going!** ¡fíjate por donde vas!

▸ **look about** (VI + ADV), (VI + PREP) = **look around**

▸ **look after** (VI + PREP) **1** (= *take care of*) [+ *invalid, animal, plant*] cuidar, cuidar de; [+ *one's possessions*] velar por • **he can ~ after himself** sabe cuidar de *or* valerse por sí mismo • **she can't ~ after herself any more** ya no puede valerse por sí misma
2 (= *mind*) [+ *child*] vigilar, cuidar; [+ *shop, business*] encargarse de
3 • **to ~ after sth for sb** (= *watch over*) [+ *luggage, house*] vigilar algo a algn; (= *keep temporarily*) guardar algo a algn

▸ **look ahead** (VI + ADV) (*in front*) mirar hacia delante; (*to future*) hacer proyectos para el futuro

▸ **look around** (VI + ADV) echar una mirada alrededor • **to ~ around for sth** buscar algo • **we're ~ing around for a house** estamos buscando casa
(VI + PREP) • **to ~ around one** mirar a su alrededor

▸ **look at** (VI + PREP) **1** (= *observe*) mirar • **to ~ hard at** [+ *person*] observar detenidamente; [+ *idea*] estudiar cuidadosamente • **just ~ at this mess!** ¡mira qué desorden! • **to ~ at him you would never think that ...** por la apariencia nunca pensarías que ... • **it isn't much to ~ at** • **it's nothing to ~ at** no es muy bonito • **~ at how she does it** fíjate cómo lo hace
2 (= *consider*) [+ *alternatives*] considerar, examinar; [+ *problem*] estudiar • **it depends (on) how you ~ at it** depende de cómo se enfoca la cuestión, depende del punto de vista de uno • **whichever way you ~ at it** se mire por donde se mire
3 (= *check*) [+ *patient, wound, heart*] examinar; [+ *engine, spelling*] revisar • **will you ~ at the engine?** ¿podría revisar el motor? • **I'll ~ at it tomorrow** lo miraré mañana
4 (= *accept*) • **I wouldn't even ~ at the job** no aceptaría el puesto por nada del mundo • **the landlady won't ~ at students** la patrona no aguanta los estudiantes
5* (= *have in prospect*) • **you're ~ing at a minimum of £200** calcula 200 libras como mínimo

▸ **look away** (VI + ADV) apartar la mirada (from de)

▸ **look back** (VI + ADV) **1** (= *look behind*) mirar hacia atrás
2 (= *remember*) pensar en el pasado • **~ing back, I'm surprised I didn't suspect anything** pensándolo ahora, me sorprende que no hubiera sospechado nada • **to ~ back on** *or* **at** [+ *event, period*] recordar, rememorar • **after that he never ~ed back** (*fig*) desde entonces todo le ha ido sobre ruedas

▸ **look down** (VI + ADV) (= *lower eyes*) bajar la mirada; (= *look downward*) mirar hacia abajo • **to ~ down at sb/sth** mirar abajo hacia algn/algo

▸ **look down on** (VI + PREP) **1** (*fig*) (= *despise*) despreciar
2 (= *overlook*) • **the castle ~s down on the town** el castillo domina la ciudad

▸ **look for** (VI + PREP) **1** (= *seek*) buscar • **to be ~ing for trouble*** andar buscando camorra*
2 (= *expect*) [+ *praise, reward*] esperar

▸ **look forward** (VI + ADV) (= *plan for the future*) mirar hacia el futuro

▸ **look forward to** (VI + ADV + PREP) [+ *event*] esperar con ansia, esperar con impaciencia • **we're ~ing forward to the journey** el viaje nos hace mucha ilusión • **we had been ~ing forward to it for weeks** durante semanas enteras veníamos pensando en eso con mucha ilusión • **I'm really ~ing forward to the holidays** estoy deseando que lleguen las vacaciones • **I'm not ~ing forward to it at all** no me hace ninguna ilusión • **to ~ forward to doing sth** tener muchas ganas de *or* estar deseando hacer algo • **~ing forward to hearing from you ...** (*in letter*) a la espera de sus noticias ...

▸ **look in** (VI + ADV) **1** (= *see in*) mirar por dentro
2 (= *visit*) pasar por casa, caer por casa • **to ~ in on sb** pasar a ver a algn

▸ **look into** (VI + PREP) (= *examine*) [+ *matter, possibility*] estudiar, investigar

▸ **look on** (VI + ADV) mirar (como espectador)
(VI + PREP) (= *consider*) considerar • **I ~ on him as a friend** lo considero un amigo • **we do not ~ on it with favour** no nos merece una buena opinión • **to ~ kindly on sth/sb** mirar algo/a algn con buenos ojos • **to ~ on the bright side (of things)** mirar el lado bueno (de las cosas)

▸ **look onto** (VI + PREP) (= *face*) [*building, room*] dar a • **it ~s onto the garden** da al jardín

▸ **look out** (VI + ADV) **1** (= *look outside*) mirar fuera • **to ~ out of the window** mirar por la ventana • **it ~s out on to the garden** da al jardín
2 (= *take care*) tener cuidado • **~ out!** ¡cuidado!, ¡aguas! (*Mex*)
(VT + ADV) (*Brit*) (= *search for*) buscar; (= *find*) encontrar

▸ **look out for** (VI + PREP) **1** (= *watch for*) • **to ~ out for sth/sb** esperar algo/a algn, estar atento a algo/algn • **do ~ out for pickpockets** ten mucho ojo con los carteristas • **~ out for special deals** estáte al tanto de las gangas
2* (= *look after*) [+ *person*] cuidar • **to ~ out for o.s.** cuidar de sí mismo, cuidarse • **he's only ~ing out for himself** (*pej*) solo mira sus propios intereses • **we ~ out for each other** nos cuidamos el uno al otro, cuidamos el uno del otro
3 (= *seek*) buscar

▸ **look over** (VT + ADV) [+ *document, list*] echar un vistazo a; [+ *person, goods, produce*] echar un vistazo a; (*carefully*) examinar; [+ *town, building*] echar un vistazo a; (*carefully*) inspeccionar

▸ **look round** (VI + ADV) **1** (= *look about one*) mirar a su alrededor
2 (= *turn*) volver la cabeza, volverse • **I called him and he ~ed round** lo llamé y volvió la cabeza, lo llamé y se volvió
3 (*in shop*) mirar • **we're just ~ing round** estamos mirando solamente • **do you mind if we ~ round?** ¿le importa que echemos un vistazo?
4 (= *search*) • **to ~ round for** buscar
(VI + PREP) [+ *town, factory*] visitar, recorrer • **to ~ round an exhibition** visitar una exposición • **I like ~ing round the shops** me gusta ir a ver tiendas

▸ **look through** (VI + PREP) **1** [+ *window*] mirar por
2 (= *search*) registrar; (= *leaf through*) hojear; (= *examine closely*) examinar detenidamente; (= *re-read*) [+ *notes*] revisar
3 (*fig*) (= *ignore*) • **he ~ed right through me** me miró sin verme, me miró como si no existiera

▸ **look to** (VI + PREP) **1** (*fig*) (= *turn to*) contar con, recurrir a • **it's no good ~ing to me for help** es inútil recurrir a mí en busca de ayuda • **to ~ to sb to do sth** esperar que algn haga algo, contar con algn para hacer algo
2 (= *think of*) • **we must ~ to the future** tenemos que pensar en el futuro *or* mirar hacia delante
3 (= *attend to*) ocuparse de, mirar por

▸ **look up** (VI + ADV) **1** (= *glance*) levantar la vista, alzar la vista
2 (= *improve*) mejorar • **things are ~ing up** las cosas van mejor
(VT + ADV) **1** [+ *information*] buscar • **if you don't know a word, ~ it up in the dictionary** si no conoces una palabra, búscala en el diccionario
2 (= *visit*) [+ *person*] ir a visitar

▸ **look upon** (VI + PREP) = **look on**

▸ **look up to** (VI + PREP) • **to ~ up to sb** (*fig*) respetar a algn, admirar a algn

> **LOOK FOR**
>
> **Omission of article**
>
> ▷ *Don't translate the article "a" in sentences like* **I'm looking for a flat,** *when the number of such things is not significant since people normally only look for one at a time:*
> **I'm looking for a flat**
> Estoy buscando piso
> **He's looking for a secretary**
> Busca secretaria
>
> *The personal* **a** *is not used before people when the article is omitted as above.*
>
> ▷ *Do translate the article when the thing or person is qualified:*
> **He's looking for a little flat**
> Busca un piso pequeño
>
> *NOTE: When translating examples like* **I'm looking for someone to ...** *translate the English to-infinitive using* **que** + *subjunctive:*
> **I'm looking for someone to help with the children**
> Busco a alguien que me ayude con los niños
> **I'm looking for a mechanic to repair my car**
> Busco a un mecánico que me arregle el coche
>
> *For further uses and examples, see main entry.*

lookalike ['lʊkə,laɪk] (N) doble *mf*

looked-for ['lʊktfɔːʳ] (ADJ) esperado, deseado

looker* ['lʊkəʳ] (N) bombón* *f*

looker-on ['lʊkərˈɒn] (N) (PL: **lookers-on**) espectador(a) *m/f*

look-in* ['lʊkɪn] (N) • **to get a look-in** (*Brit*) tener una oportunidad, tener chance (*LAm*) • **we never got** *or* **had a look-in** no nos dejaron participar; [*losers*] nunca tuvimos posibilidades de ganar

-looking ['lʊkɪŋ] (ADJ) (*ending in compounds*) • **strange-looking** de aspecto raro • **mad-looking** con pinta de loco*

looking-glass† ['lʊkɪŋglɑːs] (N) (*frm*) espejo *m*

lookout ['lʊkaʊt] (N) **1** (= *act*) observación *f*, vigilancia *f* • **to keep a ~ for sth** • **be on the ~ for sth** estar atento a *or* al acecho de algo • **keep a ~ for the postman** estáte atento por si viene el cartero • **to keep a sharp ~** estar ojo avizor
2 (= *viewpoint*) mirador *m*; (= *person*) centinela *mf*; (= *place*) = **lookout post**
3 (= *prospect*) perspectiva *f* • **it's a grim** *or* **poor ~ for us/for education** la perspectiva es desalentadora para nosotros/para la educación • **that's his ~!** ¡eso es asunto suyo!, ¡allá él!
(CPD) ▸ **lookout post** atalaya *f*, puesto *m* de observación

L

look-see* ['lʊksiː] N vistazo *m* • **to have a look-see** echar un vistazo

look-up ['lʊkʌp] N consulta *f*
CPD ▸ **look-up table** tabla *f* de consulta

loom¹ [luːm] N (*for weaving*) telar *m*

loom² [luːm] VI **1** (*also* **loom up**) (= *appear*) surgir, aparecer • **the ship ~ed (up) out of the mist** el barco surgió de la neblina
2 (= *threaten*) amenazar • **dangers ~ ahead** se vislumbran los peligros que hay por delante • **to ~ large** cernerse, pender amenazadoramente

LOOM N ABBR (US) (= **Loyal Order of Moose**) *asociación benéfica*

looming ['luːmɪŋ] ADJ [*danger*] que amenaza, inminente

loon [luːn] N **1*** (= *fool*) bobo/a *m/f*
2 (= *bird*) somorjugo *m*

loony* ['luːnɪ] ADJ (COMPAR: **loonier**, SUPERL: **looniest**) loco, chiflado*
N loco/a *m/f*
CPD ▸ **loony bin** manicomio *m* ▸ **the loony left** (*Brit*) (*Pol*) (*pej*) la izquierda radical

loop [luːp] N **1** (*in string, ribbon*) lazo *m*, lazada *f*; (*Naut*) gaza *f*; (= *bend*) curva *f*, recodo *m* • **to knock sb for a ~** (*US**) dejar a algn pasmado
2 (*Comput*) bucle *m*
3 (*Elec*) circuito *m* cerrado
4 (= *informed group*) • **to be in the ~** estar en el grupo de gente informada • **to be out of the ~** estar fuera del grupo de gente informada
5 (*Sew*) presilla *f*
6 (*Aer*) rizo *m* • **to ~ the ~** hacer el rizo, rizar el rizo
VT • **to ~ round** dar vuelta a • **to ~ a rope round a post** pasar una cuerda alrededor de un poste
VI [*rope, ribbon, cable*] formar un lazo; [*line, road*] serpentear
CPD ▸ **loop line** (*Rail*) desviación *f*

loophole ['luːphəʊl] N **1** (*Mil*) aspillera *f*, tronera *f*
2 (*fig*) escapatoria *f*; (*in law*) laguna *f*, resquicio *m* legal • **every law has a ~** hecha la ley, hecha la trampa

loopy* ['luːpɪ] ADJ (COMPAR: **loopier**, SUPERL: **loopiest**) chiflado*

loose [luːs] ADJ (COMPAR: **looser**, SUPERL: **loosest**) **1** (= *not firmly attached*) [*thread, wire, screw, brick, page*] suelto; [*handle, knob*] desatornillado; [*tooth*] flojo, que se mueve • **this button is ~** este botón está a punto de caerse • **to come** *or* **get** *or* **work ~** [*thread, wire, brick*] soltarse; [*screw*] aflojarse; [*page*] desprenderse; [*knob, handle*] aflojarse, desatornillarse; ▹ **screw, connection**
2 (= *not tied back*) [*hair*] suelto • **to wear one's hair ~** llevar el pelo suelto
3 (= *not tight*) [*clothes*] holgado, amplio; [*bandage, tie*] flojo • **these trousers are too ~ round the waist** estos pantalones son muy anchos de cintura
4 (= *not taut*) [*skin*] flácido, colgón*
5 (= *not dense*) [*mixture, soil, powder*] suelto • **to be of a ~ consistency** tener poca consistencia
6 (= *not tied up*) [*animal*] suelto • **he was chased by a ~ dog** le persiguió un perro que andaba suelto • **to let** *or* **set sth/sb ~** soltar algo/a algn • **when the cub had recovered it was set ~ in the wild** cuando el cachorro se recuperó lo soltaron *or* lo dejaron en libertad • **the affair has let ~ dangerous political forces** el asunto ha desatado fuerzas políticas peligrosas • **inexperienced doctors were let ~ on seriously ill patients** se dejó que médicos sin experiencia trataran a pacientes gravemente enfermos; ▹ **break, cut, hell**
7 (= *flexible*) [*alliance, coalition, grouping*] libre; [*organization*] poco rígido; [*arrangement*] flexible • **a ~ confederation of sovereign republics** una confederación libre de repúblicas soberanas
8 (= *imprecise*) [*meaning, expression*] poco preciso, vago; [*style, interpretation*] libre; [*translation*] aproximado • **he despised ~ thinking** odiaba toda forma de pensar vaga • **in ~ terms, it could be called a religion** haciendo un uso un tanto libre del término, podría llamarse religión
9 (= *not packaged*) [*carrots, potatoes*] suelto, a granel; (*Comm*) • **to buy/sell sth ~** vender algo suelto *or* a granel
10† (*pej*) (= *immoral*) [*behaviour, attitudes*] disoluto; [*morals*] disoluto, libertino • **a ~ woman** una mujer de vida alegre (*pej*), una mujer fácil†; ▹ **living**
11 (*Med*) • **to have ~ bowels** tener el vientre suelto
12 (= *readily available*) [*funds*] disponible • **~ cash** dinero *m* en efectivo • **~ change** dinero *m* suelto
VT **1** (*liter*) (= *release*) [+ *animal*] soltar; [+ *prisoner*] poner en libertad, soltar • **they ~d the dogs on him** le soltaron los perros
2 (= *fire*) (*also* **loose off**) [+ *arrow, missile*] lanzar; [+ *gun, cannon*] disparar • **to ~ (off) a volley of abuse at sb** soltar una sarta de insultos a algn
3 (= *unfasten*) • **to ~ a boat from its moorings** soltar las amarras de un barco
N • **to be on the ~** [*person, gang*] andar suelto
ADV • **stay** *or* **hang ~!** (*US**) ¡tranqui!*, ¡relájate!; ▹ **play**
CPD ▸ **loose box** establo *m* móvil ▸ **loose cannon** (*fig*) bomba *f* de relojería ▸ **loose chippings** (*on roadway*) gravilla *fsing* suelta ▸ **loose connection** (*Elec*) mala conexión *f* ▸ **loose cover** (*Brit*) (*for furniture*) funda *f* lavable, funda *f* que se puede quitar ▸ **loose end** (*fig*) cabo *m* suelto • **to tie up ~ ends** atar los cabos sueltos • **to be at a ~ end*** (*fig*) no saber qué hacer ▸ **loose scrum** (*Rugby*) melé *f* abierta *or* espontánea ▸ **loose talk** palabrería *f* ▸ **loose tongue** • **to have a ~ tongue** tener la lengua suelta, ser ligero de lengua ▸ **loose weave** tejido *m* abierto

▸ **loose off** VT + ADV (*esp Brit*) [+ *ammunition, bullet*] disparar • **he ~d off two shots at the oncoming car** disparó dos tiros contra el coche que venía
VI + ADV • **to ~ off at sb/sth** disparar a *or* contra algn/algo

loose-fitting ['luːs'fɪtɪŋ] ADJ [*clothes*] holgado

loose-leaf ['luːs'liːf] ADJ [*book*] de hojas sueltas
CPD ▸ **loose-leaf binder** carpeta *f* de anillas ▸ **loose-leaf folder** = **loose-leaf binder**

loose-limbed ['luːs'lɪmd] ADJ ágil

loose-living ['luːs'lɪvɪŋ] ADJ de vida airada, de vida inmoral

loosely ['luːslɪ] ADV **1** (= *not tightly*) [*fasten, tie*] con un nudo flojo, ligeramente; [*hold*] sin apretar, ligeramente • **a ~ tied bandage** un vendaje poco apretado • **cover the dish ~ with foil** cubrir la fuente ligeramente con papel de plata • **to hang ~** [*arms*] colgar relajado; [*skin, flesh*] colgar fláccido • **his shirt hung ~ from his shoulders** la camisa le caía ancha de hombros
2 (= *not precisely*) [*translated*] libremente • **a novel ~ based on the life of Shakespeare** una novela basada, en términos generales, sobre la vida de Shakespeare • **it is ~ defined as …** en términos generales se define como …, sin ser muy precisos *or* rigurosos se define como … • **~ speaking** hablando en términos generales • **what is ~ termed socialist realism** lo que se denomina, de forma poco precisa, realismo socialista
3 (= *informally*) [*organized, structured*] sin mucha rigidez, con bastante flexibilidad • **groups ~ connected to the Hizbollah movement** grupos *mpl* que tienen cierta conexión con el movimiento Hezbolá

loosely-knit [ˌluːslɪ'nɪt] ADJ [*group, alliance*] flexible

loosen ['luːsn] VT **1** (= *slacken*) aflojar; (= *untie*) desatar • **to ~ one's grip on sth** dejar de apretar algo con tanta fuerza
2 [+ *restrictions*] aflojar, reducir
VI (= *come unfastened*) soltarse, desatarse; (= *get slack*) aflojarse

▸ **loosen up** VI + ADV (*gen*) desentumecerse; (*before game*) desentumecer los músculos, entrar en calor; (= *relax**) soltarse, relajarse • **to ~ up on sb** (*fig*) tratar a algn con menos severidad
VT + ADV [+ *muscles*] desentumecer

looseness ['luːsnɪs] N **1** (*gen*) [*of bandage, tie*] lo flojo; [*of clothes*] holgura *f*, amplitud *f*; [*of soil*] lo suelto • **~ of the bowels** (*Med*) diarrea *f*
2 (= *imprecision*) [*of meaning, expression*] imprecisión *f*; [*of translation*] lo aproximado
3 (= *immorality*) [*of behaviour, morals*] lo disoluto

loosening ['luːsnɪŋ] N [*of controls, regulations*] relajamiento *m*

loot [luːt] N botín *m*, presa *f*; (= *money**) pasta* *f*, plata *f* (*LAm**)
VT saquear
VI entregarse al saqueo

looter ['luːtəʳ] N saqueador(a) *m/f*

looting ['luːtɪŋ] N saqueo *m*

lop [lɒp] VT **1** [+ *tree*] mochar, desmochar
2 (*also* **lop away, lop off**) [+ *branches*] podar; (*fig*) cortar

lope [ləʊp] VI • **to ~ along** andar a grandes zancadas, correr dando grandes zancadas • **to ~ off** alejarse con paso largo

lop-eared ['lɒpˌɪəd] ADJ de orejas caídas

loping ['ləʊpɪŋ] ADJ [*step*] firme • **his long, ~ walk** su paso largo y firme

lopsided ['lɒp'saɪdɪd] ADJ (*gen*) torcido, ladeado, chueco (*LAm*); [*table*] cojo; (*fig*) [*view*] desequilibrado

loquacious [lə'kweɪʃəs] ADJ (*frm*) locuaz

loquacity [lə'kwæsɪtɪ] N (*frm*) locuacidad *f*

lord [lɔːd] N **1** (= *nobleman*) señor *m*; (= *British title*) lord *m* • **Lord (John) Smith** (*Brit*) Lord (John) Smith • **the (House of) Lords** (*Brit*) (*Pol*) la Cámara de los Lores • **my Lord** (*to bishop*) Ilustrísima; (*to noble*) señor; (*to judge*) señoría, señor juez • **my ~ bishop of Tooting** su Ilustrísima el obispo de Tooting • **~ of the manor** señor *m* feudal • **~ and master** dueño y señor
2 (*Rel*) • **the Lord** el Señor • **Our Lord** Nuestro Señor • **good Lord!** ¡Dios mío! • **the Lord's Prayer** el padrenuestro • **Lord knows where …!*** ¡Dios sabe dónde …!
VT • **to ~ it** mandar despóticamente • **to ~ it over sb*** ser muy mandón con algn
CPD ▸ **Lord Chancellor** *jefe de la administración de la justicia en Inglaterra y Gales, y presidente de la Cámara de los Lores* ▸ **Lord Lieutenant** *representante de la Corona en un condado* ▸ **Lord Mayor** (*Brit*) alcalde *m* ▸ **Lord Mayor's Show** (*Brit*) desfile *m* del alcalde de Londres (*el día de su inauguración*) ▸ **Lord Provost** (*Scot*) alcalde *m*

LORD
El título de **Lord** se les da a los miembros masculinos de la nobleza británica, especialmente a los marqueses, condes, vizcondes y barones, personas que ocupan un escaño en la Cámara de los Lores. El término forma parte también del nombre de algunos cargos oficiales: el **Lord Chancellor** es la máxima autoridad judicial en Inglaterra y Gales, el **Lord Chief Justice** es el cargo inmediatamente inferior, mientras que en Escocia el encargado del sistema judicial es el **Lord Advocate**. Por su parte, el **Lord Chamberlain** es el encargado del mantenimiento de las residencias oficiales de la realeza británica.

lordliness ['lɔ:dlɪnɪs] (N) lo señorial, carácter *m* señorial; (*pej*) altivez *f*, arrogancia *f*

lordly ['lɔ:dlɪ] (ADJ) (COMPAR: **lordlier**, SUPERL: **lordliest**) [*house, vehicle*] señorial, señoril; [*manner*] altivo, arrogante; [*command*] imperioso

lords-and-ladies ['lɔ:dzənd'leɪdɪz] (N) (*Bot*) aro *m*

lordship ['lɔ:dʃɪp] (N) señoría *f* • **your Lordship** Señoría

lore [lɔ:ʳ] (N) saber *m* popular • **in local ~** según la tradición local • **he knows a lot about plant ~** sabe mucho de plantas

lorgnette [lɔ:'njet] (N) impertinentes *mpl*

Lorraine [lɒ'reɪn] (N) Lorena *f*

lorry ['lɒrɪ] (*Brit*) (N) camión *m* • **it fell off the back of a ~*** (*euph*) es de trapicheo*
(CPD) ▸ **lorry driver** camionero/a *m/f* ▸ **lorry load** carga *f*

lose [lu:z] (PT, PP: **lost**) (VT) **1** (= *mislay, fail to find*) perder • **he's always losing things** siempre está perdiendo las cosas • **I've lost my pen** he perdido el bolígrafo • **I lost him in the crowd** lo perdí entre la muchedumbre
2 (= *be deprived of*) perder • **you've got nothing to ~** no tienes nada que perder • **you've nothing to ~ by helping him** no vas a perder nada ayudándole • **what have you got to ~?** ¿qué tienes tú que perder?, ¿qué vas a perder? • **he lost £1,000 on that deal** perdió 1.000 libras en ese trato • **I lost my father when I was ten** perdí a mi padre cuando tenía diez años • **I don't want to ~ you** no quiero perderte • **he's lost his licence** le han retirado el carnet • **to ~ one's life** perder la vida • **to ~ a patient** no lograr salvar a un paciente • **to ~ the use of an arm** perder el uso de un brazo; ▹ **breath, voice**
3 (= *fail to keep*) perder • **the poem lost a lot in the translation** el poema perdió mucho en la traducción • **she's lost her figure/her looks** ha perdido la línea/su belleza • IDIOM: • **to ~ it*** perder los papeles, perder el control; ▹ **interest, rag¹, sight, temper**
4 (= *fail to win*) [+ *game, war, election*] perder
5 (= *miss*) • **to ~ one's way** (*lit*) perderse; (*fig*) perder el rumbo
6 (= *waste*) perder • **there was not a moment to ~** no había ni un momento que perder • **I wouldn't ~ any sleep over it!** ¡no pierdas el sueño por ello!, ¡no te preocupes por ello! • **to ~ no time in doing sth**: • **she lost no time in making up her mind** se decidió enseguida, no le costó nada decidirse • **I lost no time in telling him exactly what I thought of him** no vacilé en decirle exactamente lo que pensaba de él
7* (= *get rid of*) [+ *unwanted companion*] deshacerse de; [+ *pursuers*] zafarse de • **to ~ weight** perder peso, adelgazar • **I lost two kilos** perdí *or* adelgacé dos kilos
8 (= *fall behind*) [*watch, clock*] atrasarse • **this watch ~s five minutes every day** este reloj se atrasa cinco minutos cada día
9 (= *cause loss of*) • **it lost him the job/the match** le costó el puesto/el partido, le hizo perder el puesto/el partido • **that deal lost me £5,000** ese negocio me costó *or* me hizo perder 5.000 libras
10* (= *confuse*) confundir • **you've lost me there** ahora sí que me has confundido, ahora sí que no te entiendo
11 • **to ~ o.s. in sth** (*a book, music, memories*) ensimismarse en algo
(VI) **1** [*player, team*] perder • **he's losing (by) two sets to one** va perdiendo (por) dos sets a uno • **they lost (by) three goals to two** perdieron (por) tres goles a dos • **to ~ to sb** perder contra algn • **you can't ~** no tienes pérdida, tienes que forzosamente salir ganando • **he lost on the deal** salió perdiendo en el negocio • **the story did not ~ in the telling** el cuento no perdió en la narración • **it ~s in translation** pierde en la traducción
2 [*watch, clock*] atrasarse
▸ **lose out** (VI + ADV) salir perdiendo • **you've never been in love? don't you think you've lost out on something?** ¿nunca has estado enamorada? ¿no piensas que te has perdido algo? • **in the long run CD-ROMs may ~ out to cable television** a largo plazo, es posible que los CD-ROMs vayan perdiendo mercado frente a la televisión por cable

loser ['lu:zəʳ] (N) (= *person*) perdedor(a) *m/f*; (= *card*) carta *f* perdedora • **he's a born ~** siempre sale perdiendo, es un perdedor nato • **to be a bad ~** no saber perder, tener mal perder • **to be a good ~** saber perder, tener buen perder • **to come off the ~** salir perdiendo

losing ['lu:zɪŋ] (ADJ) perdedor • **the ~ team** el equipo perdedor • **to fight a ~ battle** luchar por una causa perdida • **she was fighting a ~ battle against her depression** luchaba en vano *or* sin éxito contra su depresión • **to be on the ~ side** estar en el lado de los perdedores *or* vencidos • **to be on a ~ streak** estar pasando por una racha de mala suerte • **to be on a ~ wicket*** (*fig*) llevar las de perder
(N) **losings** (= *money*) pérdidas *fpl*

loss [lɒs] (N) **1** [*of possessions, blood, sight*] pérdida *f* • **the factory closed with the ~ of 300 jobs** la fábrica cerró, con la pérdida de 300 puestos de trabajo • **it's your ~** el que sales perdiendo eres tú • **~ of appetite** pérdida *f* del apetito • **his death was a great ~ to the company** su muerte fue una gran pérdida para la empresa • **he's no great ~** no vamos a perder nada con su marcha • **the army suffered heavy ~es** el ejército sufrió pérdidas cuantiosas • **we want to prevent further ~ of life** queremos evitar que se produzcan más muertes *or* que se pierdan más vidas • **~ of memory** amnesia *f*, pérdida *f* de la memoria • **to feel a sense of ~** sentir un vacío; ▹ **hair, heat, job, weight**
2 (*Econ, Comm*) pérdida *f* • **at a ~**: • **the factory was operating at a ~** la fábrica estaba funcionando con pérdida de capital • **to sell sth at a ~** vender algo con pérdida • **the company made a ~ in 1999** la empresa tuvo un balance adverso en 1999 • **the company made a ~ of £2 million** la empresa sufrió pérdidas de 2 millones de libras • IDIOM: • **to cut one's ~es** cortar por lo sano; ▹ **dead, profit**
3 (= *death*) pérdida *f*, muerte *f* • **our sadness at the ~ of a loved one** nuestra tristeza por la pérdida *or* muerte de un ser querido • **since the ~ of his wife** desde que perdió a su mujer, desde que falleció su mujer
4 • IDIOM: • **to be at a ~**: • **they are at a ~ to explain how such a mistake could have been made** no se explican cómo se pudo haber cometido semejante error • **to be at a ~ for words** no encontrar palabras con qué expresarse • **he's never at a ~ for words** tiene mucha facilidad de palabra • **I was at a ~ (as to) what to do next** no sabía qué hacer después
(CPD) ▸ **loss adjuster** (*Insurance*) ajustador(a) *m/f* de pérdidas, tasador(a) *m/f* de pérdidas ▸ **loss leader** (*Comm*) artículo *m* de lanzamiento

lossless ['lɒslɪs] (ADJ) sin pérdidas

lossmaker ['lɒs,meɪkəʳ] (N) (= *business*) negocio *m* nada rentable, negocio *m* deficitario; (= *product*) producto *m* nada rentable

lossmaking ['lɒs,meɪkɪŋ] (ADJ) [*enterprise*] deficitario

lost [lɒst] (PP), (PT) *of* **lose**
(ADJ) **1** (= *unable to find one's way*) perdido • **I'm ~** me he perdido, estoy perdido • **the ~ child was taken to the security desk** llevaron al niño perdido al mostrador de seguridad • **to get ~** [*person*] perderse; [*issue, fact*] olvidarse • **to tell sb to get ~*** mandar a algn al cuerno *or* a la porra‡ • **get ~!*** ¡vete al cuerno!‡, ¡vete a la porra!‡ • IDIOM: • **to be ~ for words** no tener palabras, no saber qué decir • **I had thought of so many things I wanted to say, but now I'm ~ for words** había tantas cosas que quería decir, pero ahora no tengo palabras • **I was ~ for words when I heard the news** me quedé mudo cuando me enteré de la noticia
2 (= *missing, mislaid*) [*thing, animal*] perdido, extraviado • **he was looking for a ~ contact lens** buscaba una lentilla que se le había perdido • **to get ~** perderse, extraviarse • **to give sb up for ~** dar a algn por desaparecido • **to give sth up for ~** dar algo por perdido • **thousands of credit cards are reported ~ each day** cada día se denuncia la pérdida de miles de tarjetas de crédito • **she is ~ to us forever** (*fig*) la hemos perdido para siempre
3 (= *bewildered*) perdido, desorientado • **I felt ~ and lonely in a strange town** me sentía perdido *or* desorientado y solo en una ciudad desconocida • **it's too difficult to understand, I'm ~** es demasiado difícil de entender, estoy perdido • **with a ~ expression/look** con la confusión pintada en el rostro
4 (= *completely absorbed*) • **to be ~ in sth** estar absorto en algo • **I was ~ in thought** estaba absorto en mis pensamientos • **she was ~ in the music** estaba absorta en la música • **to be ~ to the world** estar en otro mundo
5 (= *wasted*) [*opportunity, income, output*] perdido • **to catch up on** *or* **make up for ~ time** recuperar el tiempo perdido • **to be ~ on sb**: • **the message is often ~ on drug users** el mensaje a menudo no hace eco en los drogadictos • **the meaning of that was ~ on me** no entendí *or* no capté el significado de eso • **an irony/a fact which was not ~ on me** una ironía/un hecho que no se me escapaba
6 (= *former*) [*youth, job, homeland*] perdido • **he pined for his ~ youth** suspiraba por su juventud perdida
7 (= *vanished*) [*civilization*] desaparecido; [*skill, art*] desaparecido, perdido
8 (= *not won*) [*battle, campaign, struggle*] perdido • **all is not ~!** ¡no se ha perdido todo!
9 (= *dead*) • **she grieved for her ~ son** lloraba al hijo que había perdido • **we are all ~!** (*liter*) ¡estamos perdidos! • **to be ~ at sea** desaparecer en el mar

10† (*euph*) • **~ woman** mujer *f* perdida
CPD ▸ **lost and found** (*US*) = **lost property**
▸ **lost cause** causa *f* perdida ▸ **the lost generation** (*liter*) *generación de escritores a la que pertenecieron autores como Scott Fitzgerald y Hemingway y que produjeron sus obras después de la Primera Guerra Mundial* ▸ **lost property** (= *belongings*) objetos *mpl* perdidos; (= *office*) oficina *f* de objetos perdidos ▸ **lost property office** oficina *f* de objetos perdidos ▸ **lost sheep** (*fig*) oveja *f* perdida, oveja *f* descarriada ▸ **lost soul** alma *f* perdida

lost-and-found department ['lɒstən'faʊnd-dɪ,pɑ:tmənt] N (*US*) = **lost property office**

lot [lɒt] N **1** (= *large quantity*) • **a lot of money** mucho dinero • **a lot of people** mucha gente • **we have lots of flowers (that we don't want)** nos sobran flores, tenemos flores de sobra • **an awful lot of things to do** la mar de cosas que hacer • **I'd give a lot to know** me gustaría muchísimo saberlo • **quite/such a lot of books** bastantes/tantos libros • **quite/such a lot of noise** bastante/tanto ruido • **there wasn't a lot we could do** apenas había nada que pudiéramos hacer
2 • **a lot** (*as adv*) mucho • **I read a lot** leo mucho • **we don't go out a lot** no salimos mucho • **things have changed a lot** las cosas han cambiado mucho • **he drinks an awful lot** bebe una barbaridad • **not a lot**: • **"do you like football?" — "not a lot"** —¿te gusta el fútbol? —no mucho • **thanks a lot!** ¡muchísimas gracias!, ¡muy agradecido!
3 lots* • **lots of people** mucha gente, cantidad de gente* • **she has lots of friends** tiene muchos amigos, tiene un montón de *or* (*LAm*) hartos amigos* • **he feels lots better** se encuentra mucho mejor • **take as much as you want, I've got lots** llévate cuanto quieras, tengo un montón *or* (*LAm*) harto(s)*
4* (= *group*) • **a fine lot of students** un buen grupo de estudiantes • **Melissa's friends? I don't like that lot** ¿los amigos de Melissa? no me cae bien ese grupo
5 • **the lot*** (= *all, everything*) todo • **he took the lot** se lo llevó todo • **that's the lot** eso es todo • **the (whole) lot of them** todos • **big ones, little ones, the lot!** ¡los grandes, los pequeños, todos!
6 (= *destiny*) suerte *f*, destino *m* • **his lot was different** su suerte fue otra • **the common lot** la suerte común • **it fell to my lot (to do sth)** me cayó en suerte (hacer algo) • **it falls to my lot to do it** me corresponde a mí hacerlo • **to throw in one's lot with sb** unirse a la suerte de algn
7 (= *random selection*) • **to decide sth by lot** determinar algo por sorteo • **to draw lots (for sth)** echar suertes (para algo)
8 (*at auction*) lote *m* • IDIOM: • **he's a bad lot** es un mal sujeto • **I'll send it in three lots** (*Comm*) se lo mando en tres paquetes *or* tandas
9 (= *plot*) (*esp US*) terreno *m*, solar *m*; (*Cine*) solar *m*
10 (= *share*) porción *f*, parte *f*; ▹ **fat**

loth [ləʊθ] ADJ = **loath**

lotion ['ləʊʃən] N loción *f*

lottery ['lɒtərɪ] N lotería *f*

lotto ['lɒtəʊ] N (= *game*) lotería *f*

lotus ['ləʊtəs] N loto *m*
CPD ▸ **lotus position** postura *f* del loto

louche [lu:ʃ] ADJ [*person, place*] de mala fama

loud [laʊd] (COMPAR: **louder**, SUPERL: **loudest**) ADJ **1** (= *noisy*) [*music*] alto, fuerte; [*applause, noise, explosion, scream*] fuerte • **she has a ~ voice** tiene una voz muy fuerte • **in a ~ voice** en voz alta • **the music is too ~** la música está demasiado fuerte *or* alta • **he's a bit ~*** (*pej*) es un poco escandaloso • **to be ~ in one's support for sth** dar grandes muestras de apoyo a algo • **to be ~ in one's condemnation of sth** condenar algo enérgicamente
2 (*pej*) (= *garish*) [*colour*] chillón, llamativo; [*pattern, clothes*] llamativo • **a ~ check jacket** una llamativa chaqueta de cuadros
ADV [*speak*] alto; [*laugh, shout*] fuerte • **you'll have to speak ~er** tendrás que hablar más fuerte *or* alto • **she likes to listen to her music ~** le gusta escuchar la música muy fuerte *or* alta • **"Nevermind" is one of those records you play ~** "Nevermind" es uno de esos discos que tienes que poner a todo volumen • **~ and clear**: • **I am reading** *or* **receiving you ~ and clear** (*Telec*) te recibo perfectamente • **I hear you ~ and clear, but I don't agree** te entiendo perfectamente, pero no estoy de acuerdo • **out ~** [*think, wonder, read, laugh*] en voz alta; ▹ **cry out**

loudhailer ['laʊd'heɪləʳ] N megáfono *m*

loudly ['laʊdlɪ] ADV **1** (= *not quietly*) [*say*] en voz alta; [*talk, speak*] alto, en voz alta; [*sing, shout, scream*] fuerte; [*laugh, knock*] con fuerza; [*complain, proclaim*] enérgicamente • **don't speak so ~!** ¡no hables tan alto! • **he cleared his throat ~** se aclaró la garganta ruidosamente • **a band that plays very ~ and badly** un grupo que toca muy alto y muy mal • **the audience applauded ~** el público aplaudía con fuerza • **she has been ~ applauded for ...** (*fig*) ha recibido grandes muestras de aprobación por ...
2 (= *garishly*) [*dress*] llamativamente

loudmouth* ['laʊdmaʊθ] N bocazas* *mf inv*

loudmouthed ['laʊd'maʊðd] ADJ bocazas*

loudness ['laʊdnɪs] N **1** [*of bang, explosion*] estrépito *m* • **we couldn't hear because of the ~ of the music** la música estaba tan alta que no nos dejaba oír
2 [*of clothes, colour*] lo llamativo

loudspeaker ['laʊd'spi:kəʳ] N altavoz *m*, altoparlante *m* (*LAm*)

lough [lɒx] N (*Irl*) lago *m*; (= *sea lough*) ría *f*, brazo *m* de mar

Louis ['lu:ɪ] N Luis

Louisiana [lʊ,i:zɪ'ænə] N Luisiana *f*

lounge [laʊndʒ] N (*in house*) salón *m*, sala *f* de estar, living *m* (*LAm*); (*at airport*) sala *f*; (*on liner*) salón *m*
VI (= *be idle*) gandulear, pasar el rato sin hacer nada • **we spent a week lounging in Naples** pasamos una semana en Nápoles sin hacer nada • **to ~ against a wall** apoyarse distraídamente en una pared
CPD ▸ **lounge bar** salón-bar *m* ▸ **lounge lizard*** *persona a la que le gusta frecuentar lugares de postín* ▸ **lounge suit** traje *m* de calle, terno *m* de calle (*LAm*)

▸ **lounge about, lounge around** VI + ADV gandulear, holgazanear

▸ **lounge back** VI + ADV • **to ~ back in a chair** repanchigarse en un asiento

lounger ['laʊndʒəʳ] N gandul *m*, haragán/ana *m/f*

loupe [lu:p] N (*for jewellers and watchmakers*) lupa *f*

louse [laʊs] N (PL: **lice**) **1** (= *insect*) piojo *m*
2* (*pej*) (= *person*) canalla* *mf*, sinvergüenza *mf*

▸ **louse up*** VT + ADV fastidiar, echar a perder

lousy ['laʊzɪ] ADJ (COMPAR: **lousier**, SUPERL: **lousiest**) **1** (= *louse-ridden*) piojoso
2* (= *very bad*) [*climate, food*] asqueroso*; [*secretary, driver*] malísimo, pésimo • **it was a ~ meal** fue una comida asquerosa • **I'm a ~ player** juego fatal* • **all for a few ~ quid** todo por unas cochinas libras* • **we had a ~ time** lo pasamos fatal* • **what a ~ trick!** ¡qué cerdada!* • **I feel ~** me siento fatal*
3 • **to be ~ with money‡** (= *rich*) estar forrado*, estar podrido de dinero*

lout [laʊt] N gamberro *m*

loutish ['laʊtɪʃ] ADJ grosero, maleducado

Louvain ['lu:veɪn] N Lovaina

louvre, louver (*US*) ['lu:vəʳ] N (*Archit*) lumbrera *f*; (= *blind*) persiana *f*

louvred (*US*) ['lu:vəd], **louvered** ADJ [*shutters, windows*] de láminas, de listones

lovable ['lʌvəbl] ADJ adorable

lovage ['lʌvɪdʒ] N (*Bot*) perejil *m* silvestre

love [lʌv] N **1** (= *affection*) [*of person*] amor *m* • **I no longer feel any ~ for** *or* **towards him** ya no siento amor *or* cariño por él • **it was ~ at first sight** fue amor a primera vista, fue un flechazo • **her ~ for** *or* **of her children** su amor *m* por sus hijos • **her children's ~ for her** el amor de sus hijos por ella • **don't give me any money, I'm doing it for ~** no me des dinero, lo hago por amor al arte (*hum*) • **to marry for ~** casarse por amor • **for ~ of her son** • **out of ~ for her son** por amor a su hijo, por el amor que le tiene/tenía a su hijo • **for the ~ of God** *or* **Mike!** ¡por el amor de Dios! • **to be/fall in ~ (with sb)** estar enamorado/enamorarse (de algn) • **they are in ~ (with each other)** están enamorados (el uno del otro) • **to make ~ (with/to sb)** (*euph*) (= *have sex*) hacer el amor (con algn) • **to make ~ to sb**† (= *woo*) hacer la corte *or* el amor a algn • IDIOMS: • **there is no ~ lost between them** no se pueden ver • **I wouldn't do it for ~ nor money** no lo haría por nada del mundo • **it wasn't to be had for ~ nor money** era imposible conseguirlo
2 (= *liking*) [*of activity, food, place*] afición *f*, pasión *f* • **her ~ of colour comes out in her garden** su afición *f or* pasión *f* por el colorido se refleja en su jardín • **he studies history for the ~ of it** estudia historia por pura afición
3 (*in greetings, letters*) • **(with) ~ (from) Jim** con cariño (de) Jim, besos (de) Jim • **all my ~, Jim** con todo mi cariño, Jim • **give him my ~** dale *or* mándale recuerdos míos • **lots of ~, Jim** muchos besos, Jim • **he sends (you) his ~** te da *or* manda recuerdos
4 (= *person loved*) amor *m*; (= *thing loved*) pasión *f* • **she was my first ~** fue mi primer amor • **football was his first ~** el fútbol era su principal pasión • **the theatre was her great ~** el teatro era su gran pasión • **he was the ~ of her life** fue el amor de su vida
5 (*as term of address*) cariño *m* • **yes, ~** sí, cariño • **thanks, ~** (*to woman*) gracias, guapa *or* (*Sp*) maja; (*to man*) gracias, guapo *or* (*Sp*) majo; (*to child*) gracias, cielo *or* cariño • **my ~** amor mío, mi vida
6 (= *adorable person*) • **he's a little ~** es un cielo, es un encanto • **be a ~ and make us a cup of tea** venga, cielo *or* cariño, prepáranos una taza de té
7 (*Tennis*) • **~ all** cero cero • **15 ~** 15 a cero
VT **1** (= *feel affection for*) querer, amar (*frm*) • **you don't ~ me any more** ya no me quieres • **I ~d that boy as if he were my own son** quería a ese chico como si fuera mi hijo • **~ thy neighbour as thyself** ama al prójimo como a ti mismo (*frm*) • **she ~s her children/her cat/that car** quiere mucho a *or* siente mucho cariño por sus hijos/su gato/ese coche • **she ~d him dearly** lo quería muchísimo, lo amaba profundamente • **I must ~ you and leave you** (*hum*) me despido que me tengo que marchar • **~ me, ~ my dog** quien quiere a Beltrán quiere a su can • IDIOM: • **she ~s me, she ~s me not** me quiere, no me quiere
2 (= *like very much*) • **I ~ strawberries** me

encantan las fresas • **I ~ Madrid** me encanta Madrid, me gusta muchísimo Madrid • **"would you like a drink?" — "I'd ~ one"** —¿quieres tomar algo? —¡sí, por favor! • **I'd ~ a beer** daría cualquier cosa por una cerveza • **he ~s swimming** • **he ~s to swim** le encanta nadar, le gusta muchísimo nadar • **I'd ~ to come** me encantaría ir, me gustaría muchísimo ir • **I'd ~ to!** ¡con mucho gusto!, ¡yo, encantado!

(CPD) ▸ **love affair** aventura *f* (sentimental), amorío *m*; (*fig*) pasión *f* • **her ~ affair with France began in 1836** su pasión por Francia comenzó en 1836 • **she had a ~ affair with a younger man** tuvo una aventura (sentimental) *or* un amorío con un hombre más joven que ella ▸ **love child** hijo/a *m/f* natural ▸ **love game** (*Tennis*) juego *m* en blanco ▸ **love handles**‡ agarraderas‡ *fpl* ▸ **love letter** carta *f* de amor ▸ **love life** (*emotional*) vida *f* sentimental; (*sexual*) vida *f* sexual • **how's your ~ life these days?** ¿qué tal te va la vida últimamente en el campo sentimental *or* romántico? ▸ **love match** matrimonio *m* por amor ▸ **love nest** nido *m* de amor ▸ **love potion** filtro *m* (de amor), bebedizo *m* (de amor) ▸ **love scene** escena *f* de amor ▸ **love seat** confidente *m*, canapé *m* ▸ **love song** canción *f* de amor ▸ **love story** historia *f* de amor ▸ **love token** prenda *f* de amor, prueba *f* de amor ▸ **love triangle** triángulo *m* amoroso

LOVE

Love *can usually be translated by* **querer**.

▷ *With people, pets and native lands,* **querer** *is the most typical translation:*

I love you
Te quiero
Timmy loves his mother more than his father
Timmy quiere más a su madre que a su padre
When he lived abroad he realized how much he loved his country
Cuando vivió en el extranjero, se dio cuenta de lo mucho que quería a su país

▷ **Querer** *is commonly used with* **mucho** *in statements like the following:*

I love my parents
Quiero mucho a mis padres
He loved his cat and was very depressed when it died
Quería mucho a su gato y tuvo una gran depresión cuando murió

▷ *Use* **amar**, *especially in formal language, to talk about spiritual or elevated forms of love:*

To love God above everything else
Amar a Dios sobre todas las cosas
Their duty was to love and respect their parents
Su deber era amar y respetar a sus padres

▷ *Use the impersonal* **encantarle a uno** *to talk about things and people that you like very much:*

He loved playing tennis
Le encantaba jugar al tenis
I love children
(A mí) me encantan los niños

For further uses and examples, see main entry.

lovebird [ˈlʌvbɜːd] (N) periquito *m*; **lovebirds** (*fig*) (*hum*) palomitos *mpl*, tórtolos *mpl*
lovebite [ˈlʌvˌbaɪt] (N) mordisco *m* amoroso
-loved [lʌvd] (ADJ) (*ending in compounds*) • **much-loved** muy querido • **best-loved** más querido
loved ones [ˈlʌvdwʌnz] (NPL) seres *mpl* queridos
love-hate [ˈlʌvheɪt] (CPD) ▸ **love-hate relationship** relación *f* de amor-odio
loveless [ˈlʌvlɪs] (ADJ) sin amor
loveliness [ˈlʌvlɪnɪs] (N) [*of woman*] hermosura *f*, belleza *f*; [*of thing, place, landscape*] belleza *f* • **a vision of ~** (*liter*) la viva imagen de la belleza
lovelorn [ˈlʌvlɔːn] (ADJ) *perdidamente enamorado y sin ser correspondido* • **to be ~** sufrir de mal de amores
lovely [ˈlʌvlɪ] (ADJ) (COMPAR: **lovelier**, SUPERL: **loveliest**)
(ADJ) **1** (= *beautiful*) [*face, figure, thing*] precioso, muy bonito, lindo (*LAm*); [*woman*] hermoso, bello; [*day*] precioso, bueno; [*morning*] precioso, bonito; [*food, meal*] delicioso, riquísimo • **look at these ~ flowers!** ¡mira que flores más bonitas! • **the house was full of ~ things** la casa estaba llena de detalles preciosos, la casa estaba llena de detalles monísimos* • **she has two ~ sons** tiene dos hijos preciosos • **what ~ children/puppies!** ¡qué niños/cachorros tan preciosos!, ¡qué niños/cachorros más ricos *or* monos!* • **this is a ~ place for a holiday** este es un lugar precioso para venir de vacaciones • **it's a ~ day!** hace un día precioso *or* muy bueno • **it's a ~ day for a walk** hace un día precioso para dar un paseo • **it was a ~ sunny day** hacía un día de sol precioso • **we had a ~ day** pasamos un día muy agradable • **you look ~, Maria** estás preciosa, María • **it's ~ to see you again** que alegría volver a verte • **what a ~ surprise!** ¡qué sorpresa más agradable! • **what ~ weather!** ¡hace un tiempo estupendo *or* buenísimo!
2 (= *kind*) [*person, family, character*] encantador, amoroso (*LAm*) • **he's got a ~ face** tiene una cara muy dulce • **you do say some ~ things** dices unas cosas preciosas
3 (*as intensifier*) • **it's ~ and cool in here** hace un fresquito muy agradable aquí dentro • **it's ~ and hot/cold** [*drink, water*] está calentito/fresquito; [*air*] hace calorcito/fresquito
(N)* (*liter, hum*) belleza *f* • **swim-suited lovelies** bellezas *fpl* en bañador
lovemaking [ˈlʌvˌmeɪkɪŋ] (N) (= *courting*) galanteo *m*; (= *sexual intercourse*) relaciones *fpl* sexuales
lover [ˈlʌvəʳ] (N) **1** (*sexually*) amante *mf*; (*romantically*) enamorado/a *m/f* • **the ~s** los amantes • **we were ~s for two years** durante dos años fuimos amantes • **he became her ~** se hizo su amante • **so she took a ~** así que se echó un amante
2 (= *fan*) aficionado/a *m/f* • **music ~** • **~ of music** aficionado/a *m/f* a la música, amante *mf* de la música • **cinema ~s** los aficionados al cine, los amantes del cine • **he is a great ~ of the violin** es un gran aficionado al *or* amante del violín
(CPD) ▸ **lover boy** (*hum, iro*) macho *m*
lovesick [ˈlʌvsɪk] (ADJ) enfermo de amor
lovestruck [ˈlʌvstrʌk] (ADJ) perdidamente enamorado
lovey-dovey* [ˌlʌvɪˈdʌvɪ] (ADJ) tierno, sentimental
loving [ˈlʌvɪŋ] (ADJ) cariñoso, tierno • **with ~ care** con amoroso cuidado • **~ kindness** bondad *f* • **(from) your ~ wife, Elizabeth**† (*in letters*) (de) tu esposa que te quiere, Elizabeth
(CPD) ▸ **loving cup** copa *f* de la amistad (*que circula en una cena en que beben todos*)
-loving [ˈlʌvɪŋ] (ADJ) (*ending in compounds*) • **money-loving** amante del dinero, aficionado al dinero
lovingly [ˈlʌvɪŋlɪ] (ADV) **1** (= *affectionately*) [*look, speak*] cariñosamente, tiernamente; (*stronger*) amorosamente
2 (= *carefully*) [*cook, prepare, inscribe*] con cariño • **~ restored** cuidadosamente restaurado
low¹ [ləʊ] (ADJ) (COMPAR: **lower**, SUPERL: **lowest**) **1** (*in height*) [*wall, shelf, seat, level*] bajo; [*bow*] profundo; [*blow*] sucio • **on low ground** a nivel del mar, en tierras bajas • **a dress with a low neckline** un vestido escotado
2 (= *quiet*) [*voice, TV, radio*] bajo
3 (= *low-pitched*) [*voice, musical note*] grave, bajo
4 [*number*] bajo; [*price, income*] reducido, bajo; [*stock, supplies*] escaso • **five at the lowest** cinco como mínimo • **the battery is low** la batería se está acabando • **fuel is getting low** está empezando a escasear la gasolina • **stocks are running low** las existencias empiezan a escasear
5 (*in intensity*) [*light, rate, speed, temperature*] bajo • **the temperature is in the low 40s** la temperatura es de 40 grados y alguno más • **to cook on a low heat** cocer a fuego lento
6 (= *inferior*) [*standard, quality*] inferior
7 (= *humble*) [*rank*] humilde; [*card*] pequeño
8 (*Aut*) • **in low gear** en primera *or* segunda
9 [*health*] débil, malo; [*diet*] deficiente • **to feel low** • **be low in spirits** sentirse deprimido, estar bajo de moral
10 [*character, behaviour, opinion*] malo; [*comedian*] grosero; [*character*] vil; [*joke, song*] verde; [*trick*] sucio, malo; ▷ **tide**
(ADV) (COMPAR: **lower**, SUPERL: **lowest**)
1 [*aim, fly, sing*] bajo; [*swing*] bajo, cerca de la tierra • **to bow low** hacer una reverencia profunda • **a dress cut low in the back** un vestido muy escotado de espalda • **to fall low** (*fig*) caer bajo • **England never fell so low** Inglaterra nunca cayó tan bajo • **to be laid low with flu** ser postrado por la gripe • **to lay sb low** derribar a algn, poner a algn fuera de combate • **to lie low** (= *hide*) mantenerse escondido; (= *be silent*) mantenerse quieto • **to sink low** (*fig*) caer bajo
2 [*quietly*] [*say, sing*] bajo, en voz baja
3 • **to turn the lights/the volume down low** bajar las luces/el volumen
4 (*Cards*) • **to play low** poner pequeño
(N) **1** (*Met*) área *f* de baja presión
2 (*Aut*) primera *or* segunda (marcha) *f*
3 (*fig*) (= *low point*) punto *m* más bajo • **to reach a new *or* an all-time low** estar más bajo que nunca • **this represents a new low in deceit** esta es la peor forma de vileza; ▷ **all-time**
(CPD) ▸ **low beam headlights** (*US*) luces *fpl* de cruce ▸ **Low Church** *sector de la Iglesia Anglicana de tendencia más protestante* ▸ **low comedy** farsa *f* ▸ **the Low Countries** los Países Bajos ▸ **low heels** (= *shoes*) tacones *mpl* bajos ▸ **Low Latin** bajo latín *m* ▸ **low mass** misa *f* rezada ▸ **low point** punto *m* (más) bajo ▸ **low salt** sal *f* dietética ▸ **low season** (*esp Brit*) temporada *f* baja ▸ **Low Sunday** Domingo *m* de Cuasimodo ▸ **low tide** marea *f* baja ▸ **low vowel** vocal *f* grave ▸ **low water** bajamar *f* ▸ **low water mark** línea *f* de bajamar
low² [ləʊ] (VI) mugir
(N) mugido *m*
low-alcohol [ˈləʊˈælkəhɒl] (ADJ) con baja graduación
lowborn [ˈləʊˈbɔːn] (ADJ) de humilde cuna
lowbrow [ˈləʊbraʊ] (ADJ) poco culto
(N) persona *f* nada intelectual, persona *f* de poca cultura
low-budget [ˌləʊˈbʌdʒɪt] (ADJ) de bajo

presupuesto • **low-budget film** película *f* de presupuesto modesto

low-cal* [ˌləʊˈkæl] ADJ = **low-calorie**

low-calorie [ˌləʊˈkæləri] ADJ [*diet, menu, food*] bajo en calorías, con pocas calorías; [*beer, cola*] light (*inv*)

low-carb* [ˈləʊˌkɑːb] ADJ [*diet, meal*] bajo en carbohidratos

low-carbohydrate [ˌləʊkɑːbəʊˈhaɪdrət] ADJ [*diet, meal*] bajo en carbohidratos

low-class [ˈləʊˌklɑːs] ADJ de clase baja

low-cost [ˈləʊˈkɒst] ADJ económico

low-cut [ˈləʊˈkʌt] ADJ [*dress*] escotado

low-density [ˌləʊˈdensɪtɪ] ADJ de baja densidad

low-down [ˈləʊdaʊn] N* informes *mpl* confidenciales • **he gave me the low-down on it** me contó todo sobre el tema • **come on, give us the low-down** venga, cuéntanos todo lo que sabes
ADJ rastrero, bajo

lower[1] [ˈləʊəʳ] ADJ ▹ **low 1** (= *bottom*) [*part, section, floors, windows*] de abajo, inferior; [*slopes*] inferior, bajo • **the ~ of the two** el de más abajo de los dos • **the ~ bunk** la litera de abajo • **the ~ left corner** la esquina inferior izquierda • **the ~ half/part of** la mitad/parte inferior de, la mitad/parte de abajo de
2 (= *less important*) [*level, rank, caste*] inferior • **the ~ chamber** (*Parl*) la cámara baja • **the ~ court** (*Jur*) los tribunales inferiores • **the ~ middle class(es)** la clase media baja • **a ~ middle-class family** una familia de clase media baja • **soldiers in the ~ ranks** soldados *mpl* de menor rango *or* de rango inferior • **the ~ school** el segundo ciclo
3 (*Anat*) inferior • **the ~ abdomen/back** la parte inferior del abdomen/de la espalda • **she suffered severe cuts on her ~ leg** sufrió cortes de gravedad en la parte inferior de la pierna • **the ~ limbs** los miembros inferiores
4 (*Zool*) inferior
5 (*Geog*) (*in names*) • **Lower Egypt** el Bajo Egipto • **the Lower Rhine** el Bajo Rin • **~ Manhattan** el sur de Manhattan; ▹ **reach**
VT (*gen*) bajar; [+ *boat*] echar al agua; [+ *flag, sail*] arriar; (= *reduce*) [+ *price*] bajar, rebajar • **to ~ o.s.** (*fig*) rebajarse • **I wouldn't ~ myself to do such a thing** no me rebajaría a hacer algo así • **to ~ one's guard** bajar la guardia • **to ~ one's headlights** (*US*) poner las luces de cruce • **to ~ one's voice** bajar la voz
VI bajar
CPD ▸ **lower case** (*Typ*) minúsculas *fpl* • **in ~ case** en minúsculas; ▹ **lower-case** ▸ **lower class** • **the ~ class** *or* **classes** la clase baja; ▹ **lower-class** ▸ **lower deck** [*of bus*] piso *m* de abajo; (*Naut*) (= *part of ship*) cubierta *f* inferior • **the ~ deck*** (= *personnel*) los marineros ▸ **the Lower House** (*Parl*) la Cámara Baja ▸ **lower jaw** mandíbula *f* inferior ▸ **lower lip** labio *m* inferior ▸ **lower sixth** (*Brit*) ≈ 1º de Bachillerato *f* • **he's in the ~ sixth** está en 1º de Bachillerato ▸ **lower vertebrates** vertebrados *mpl* inferiores

lower[2] [ˈlaʊəʳ] VI [*person*] fruncir el entrecejo, fruncir el ceño; [*sky*] encapotarse

lower-case [ˈləʊəˌkeɪs] ADJ minúsculo • **lower-case letter** minúscula *f*; ▹ **lower**[1]

lower-class [ˈləʊəˌklɑːs] ADJ de (la) clase baja • **a lower-class family** una familia de clase baja

lower-income [ˌləʊərˈɪnkʌm] ADJ [*group, family*] de renta baja

lowering [ˈlaʊərɪŋ] ADJ [*expression, glance*] ceñudo; [*sky*] encapotado

lowest [ˈləʊɪst] ADJ SUPERL *of* **low**
N • **activity is at its ~** las actividades están en su punto más bajo
CPD ▸ **lowest common denominator** (*Math*) mínimo común denominador *m*; (*fig*) • **to appeal to the ~ common denominator** dirigirse al estrato social más bajo ▸ **lowest common multiple** mínimo común múltiplo *m*

low-fat [ˈləʊˈfæt] ADJ [*margarine, cheese*] bajo en grasas; [*milk, yoghurt*] desnatado
CPD ▸ **low-fat foods** alimentos *mpl* bajos en grasas

low-flying [ˈləʊˌflaɪɪŋ] ADJ que vuela bajo

low-grade [ˈləʊˌgreɪd] ADJ de baja calidad

low-heeled [ˈləʊˈhiːld] ADJ [*shoes*] bajos, de tacón bajo

lowing [ˈləʊɪŋ] N mugidos *mpl*

low-key* [ˌləʊˈkiː] ADJ discreto

lowland [ˈləʊlənd] N tierra *f* baja; **the Lowlands** las tierras bajas de Escocia
ADJ de tierra baja

lowlander [ˈləʊləndəʳ] N habitante *mf* de tierra baja

low-level [ˈləʊˈlevl] ADJ de bajo nivel
CPD ▸ **low-level language** (*Comput*) lenguaje *m* de bajo nivel

low-life [ˈləʊlaɪf] N bajos fondos *mpl*
ADJ de los bajos fondos

lowlights [ˈləʊlaɪts] NPL **1** (*Hairdressing*) reflejos *mpl* oscuros, mechas *fpl* oscuras
2 (*esp hum*) [*of TV programme, football match*] momentos *mpl* más aburridos

lowliness [ˈləʊlɪnɪs] N humildad *f*

low-loader [ˌləʊˈləʊdəʳ] N (*Aut*) camión *m* de plataforma de carga baja

lowly [ˈləʊlɪ] ADJ (COMPAR: **lowlier**, SUPERL: **lowliest**) humilde

low-lying [ˈləʊˌlaɪɪŋ] ADJ bajo

low-minded [ˈləʊˈmaɪndɪd] ADJ vil, mezquino

low-necked [ˈləʊˈnekt] ADJ escotado

lowness [ˈləʊnɪs] N [*of shelf, voice, number, temperature*] lo bajo; [*of note*] lo grave; [*of stocks, supplies*] escasez *f*; [*of rank*] lo bajo; [*of character*] vileza *f*, bajeza *f*; [*of joke, song*] lo verde • **~ of spirits** abatimiento *m*

low-paid [ˌləʊˈpeɪd] ADJ [*work*] mal pagado, de baja remuneración (*more frm*); [*worker*] mal pagado, mal remunerado (*more frm*)
NPL • **the low-paid** los mal pagados *or* (*more frm*) remunerados

low-pitched [ˈləʊpɪtʃt] ADJ [*note, voice*] bajo; [*campaign, speech*] en tono menor

low-powered [ˈləʊpaʊəd] ADJ de baja potencia

low-pressure [ˈləʊˈpreʃəʳ] ADJ de baja presión

low-priced [ˌləʊˈpraɪst] ADJ barato, económico

low-profile [ˈləʊˈprəʊfaɪl] ADJ [*activity*] discreto

low-ranking [ˌləʊˈræŋkɪŋ] ADJ (*Mil*) [*official*] de baja graduación

low-rent [ˈləʊrent] ADJ **1** (*lit*) [*housing, flat*] de renta baja, de alquiler bajo
2 (*fig**) de tres al cuarto*, de pacotilla*

low-rise [ˈləʊraɪz] ADJ de baja altura

low-risk [ˌləʊˈrɪsk] ADJ de bajo riesgo

low-slung [ˈləʊslʌŋ] ADJ [*chair*] con el asiento bajo; [*sports car*] con el suelo bajo

low-spirited [ˈləʊˈspɪrɪtɪd] ADJ desanimado

low-tar [ˈləʊˌtɑːʳ] ADJ [*cigarette*] bajo en alquitrán

low-tech [ˈləʊtek] ADJ de tecnología poco avanzada

low-tension [ˈləʊˈtenʃən] ADJ de baja tensión

lox [lɒks] N (*esp US*) salmón *m* ahumado

Loya Jirga [ˌlɔːjəˈdʒɜːgə] N (*in Afghanistan*) Loya Jirga *f*

loyal [ˈlɔɪəl] ADJ [*friend, subject, employee, wife, supporter*] leal, fiel; [*customer, reader*] fiel • **a ~ servant of the Party** un leal *or* fiel servidor del partido • **he has a ~ following** tiene seguidores leales *or* fieles • **to be/remain ~ to** [+ *leader, government*] ser/permanecer leal a; [+ *beliefs, principles*] ser/permanecer fiel a
CPD ▸ **the loyal toast** (*Brit*) *el brindis por el rey/la reina*

loyalist [ˈlɔɪəlɪst] N (*gen*) partidario/a *m/f* del régimen; (*in Spain 1936*) republicano/a *m/f*; (*in Northern Ireland*) (*Pol*) unionista *mf* • **~ paramilitaries** (*in Northern Ireland*) paramilitares *mpl* unionistas

loyally [ˈlɔɪəlɪ] ADV lealmente, fielmente • **she ~ continued to support her husband** continuó apoyando lealmente *or* fielmente a su marido

loyalty [ˈlɔɪəltɪ] N **1** (= *quality*) (*to leader, government*) lealtad *f* (**to** a); (*to beliefs, principles*) fidelidad *f* (**to** a)
2 (*often pl*) (= *feeling*) • **he has divided loyalties** tiene un conflicto de lealtades • **she is a woman of fierce loyalties** es una mujer muy leal
CPD ▸ **loyalty card** (*Brit*) (*Comm*) *tarjeta que reparten los hipermercados a sus clientes, mediante la que se acumulan puntos u otras ventajas*

lozenge [ˈlɒzɪndʒ] N **1** (*Med*) pastilla *f*
2 (*Math*) rombo *m*; (*Heraldry*) losange *m*

LP N (ABBR) (= **long-playing record**) elepé *m*

LPG N (= **liquefied petroleum gas**) GPL *m*

L-plate [ˈelpleɪt] N (placa *f* de) la L; ▹ DRIVING LICENCE/DRIVER'S LICENSE

LPN N ABBR (*US*) (*Med*) (= **Licensed Practical Nurse**) *enfermero/a practicante*

LPU N ABBR (= **least publishable unit**) cuanto *m* de publicación

LRAM N ABBR (*Brit*) = **Licentiate of the Royal Academy of Music**

LRCP N ABBR (*Brit*) = **Licentiate of the Royal College of Physicians**

LRCS N ABBR (*Brit*) = **Licentiate of the Royal College of Surgeons**

LRP N ABBR (= **lead replacement petrol**) LRP *f*

LSAT N ABBR (*US*) (*Univ*) = **Law School Admission Test**

LSD N ABBR **1** (*Drugs*) (= **lysergic acid diethylamide**) LSD *m*
2 (*Brit*) (*formerly*) (= **librae, solidi, denarii**) (= *pounds, shillings and pence*) *antigua moneda británica*

LSE N ABBR (*Brit*) = **London School of Economics**

L-shaped [ˈelʃeɪpt] ADJ [*room*] en L

LSI N ABBR = **large-scale integration**

LST N ABBR (*US*) = **Local Standard Time**

LT ABBR (*Elec*) = **low tension**

Lt ABBR (= **lieutenant**) Tte

LTA ABBR = **Lawn Tennis Association**

Lt.-Col. ABBR = **lieutenant-colonel**

Ltd ABBR (*Brit*) (*Comm etc*) (= **limited**) S.A.

Lt.-Gen. ABBR = **lieutenant-general**

lube* [luːb] (*US*) N lubricación *f*; (*Med*) lubricante *m*
VT lubricar

lubricant [ˈluːbrɪkənt] ADJ lubricante
N lubricante *m*

lubricate [ˈluːbrɪkeɪt] VT lubricar, engrasar

lubricating [ˈluːbrɪkeɪtɪŋ] ADJ lubricante
CPD ▸ **lubricating oil** aceite *m* lubricante

lubrication [ˌluːbrɪˈkeɪʃən] N (*Aut*) lubricación *f*, engrase *m*

lubricator [ˈluːbrɪkeɪtəʳ] N lubricador *m*

lubricious [luːˈbrɪʃəs] ADJ (*frm or liter*) (= *lewd*) lascivo

lubricity [luːˈbrɪsɪtɪ] N (*frm or liter*) (= *lewdness*) lascivia *f*

Lucan [ˈluːkən] N Lucano

lucerne [luːˈsɜːn] N (*esp Brit*) alfalfa *f*

lucid [ˈluːsɪd] ADJ lúcido • **~ interval** intervalo *m* de lucidez

lucidity [luːˈsɪdɪtɪ] N lucidez *f*

lucidly [ˈluːsɪdlɪ] ADV claramente, con claridad

Lucifer [ˈluːsɪfəʳ] N Lucifer

luck [lʌk] N suerte *f* • **some people have all the ~** los hay con suerte, algunos parece que nacen de pie* • **I couldn't believe my ~** no me podía creer la suerte que tenía • **good/bad ~** buena/mala suerte *f* • **good ~!** ¡(buena) suerte! • **bad** *or* **hard** *or* **tough ~!** ¡(qué) mala suerte!, ¡qué pena! • **to bring (sb) (good) ~/bad ~** traer buena/mala suerte (a algn) • **to have the (good) ~/bad ~ to do sth** tener la (buena) suerte/mala suerte de hacer algo • **it's good/bad ~ to see a black cat** cruzarse con un gato negro trae buena/mala suerte • **any ~?** ¿hubo suerte? • **beginner's ~** suerte *f* del principiante • **best of ~!** ¡muchísima suerte!, ¡que tengas suerte! • **and the best of ~!** (*iro*) ¡Dios te la depare buena! (*iro*) • **better ~ next time!** ¡a la tercera va la vencida! • **that was a bit of ~!** ¡eso fue un golpe de suerte! • **for ~: to keep sth for ~** guardar algo por si trae suerte • **once more for ~!** ¡una vez más por si trae suerte! • **I think this is going to be a great photo, I'll take one more for ~** creo que este va a ser una foto bonita, tomaré una más por si acaso • **as ~ would have it** ... quiso la suerte que ... • **his ~ held and no one detected him** siguió con su racha de buena suerte y nadie lo descubrió • **here's ~!** (*in toast*) ¡salud! • **to be in ~** estar de *or* con suerte • **it would be just my ~ to meet the boss** mira que toparme con el jefe ... ¡solo me pasan a mí estas cosas! • **knowing my ~** con la suerte que tengo • **no such ~!** ¡ojalá! • **if it's money you want you're out of ~** si lo que quieres es dinero, me temo que no estás de suerte • **to push one's ~** tentar a la suerte • **to have ~ on one's side** tener la suerte de su parte • **~ was on their side** la suerte estaba de su parte • **that was a stroke of ~!** ¡eso fue un golpe de suerte! • **to trust to ~** hacer las cosas a la buena de Dios • **wish me ~!** ¡deséame suerte! • **I wish them all the ~ in the world** les deseo toda la suerte del mundo • **with (any) ~** con (un poco de) suerte • **worse ~** desgraciadamente • IDIOMS: • **to have the ~ of the devil** • **have the devil's own ~** tener la suerte de los tontos • **it's the ~ of the draw** es cuestión de suerte • **to be down on one's ~** estar de mala racha; ▹ try

▸ **luck out*** VI + ADV (US) tener un golpe de suerte

luckily [ˈlʌkɪlɪ] ADV afortunadamente, por suerte • **~ for me, he believed my story** afortunadamente *or* por suerte para mí, creyó mi historia

luckless [ˈlʌklɪs] ADJ desdichado, desafortunado

lucky [ˈlʌkɪ] (COMPAR: **luckier**, SUPERL: **luckiest**) ADJ **1** (= *fortunate*) [*person*] afortunado, suertudo (*esp LAm**); [*coincidence, shot*] afortunado • **he's a ~ chap** es un tipo afortunado *or* con suerte • **it was just a ~ guess** acerté de casualidad • **to be ~** [*person*] tener suerte • **I'm ~ to have** *or* **in having an excellent teacher** tengo la suerte de tener un profesor excelente • **he is ~ to be alive** tiene suerte de seguir vivo • **he will be ~ to get £5 for it** con mucha suerte conseguirá 5 libras por ello • **he was ~ that I didn't kill him** tuvo suerte de que no lo matara • **it's ~ (that) it didn't rain** es una suerte *or* menos mal que no haya llovido • **it was ~ for them that** ... afortunadamente para ellos ... • **she's very ~ at cards** tiene mucha suerte jugando a las cartas • **to be born ~** nacer con suerte • **a ~ break** un golpe de suerte • **it's your ~ day** es tu día de suerte • **~ devil!*** ¡qué suertudo!* • **he was ~ enough to get a seat** tuvo la suerte de conseguir un sitio • **to have a ~ escape** salvarse de milagro • **to get ~*** tener suerte • **to be ~ in life** tener suerte en la vida, tener buena estrella* • **to be ~ in love** tener suerte *or* ser afortunado en el amor • **who's the ~ man/woman?*** ¿quién es el afortunado/la afortunada? • **you should be so ~!*** ¡ya quisieras!*, ¡ojalá!* • **~ winner** afortunado/a ganador(a) *m/f* • **~ (old) you!*** ¡qué suerte!, ¡vaya *or* menuda suerte la tuya!* • **you'll be ~!*** ¡sería un milagro!*; ▹ count, strike, third

2 (= *bringing luck*) [*number, shirt*] de la suerte • **seven is his ~ number** el siete es su número de la suerte • **a ~ rabbit's foot** un amuleto de pata de conejo • **~ charm** amuleto *m*; ▹ star

CPD ▸ **lucky dip** (*Brit*) (*at fair*) caja *f* de las sorpresas; (*fig*) • **taking in lodgers can be something of a ~ dip** tener inquilinos es un poco una lotería

lucrative [ˈluːkrətɪv] ADJ lucrativo

lucre [ˈluːkəʳ] N (= *profit*) lucro *m* • **filthy ~** (*hum*) el vil metal

Lucretia [luːˈkriːʃə] N Lucrecia

Lucretius [luːˈkriːʃəs] N Lucrecio

lucubration [ˌluːkjʊˈbreɪʃən] N lucubración *f*

Lucy [ˈluːsɪ] N Lucía

Luddite [ˈlʌdaɪt] ADJ ludita, ludista N ludita *mf*, ludista *mf*

ludic [ˈluːdɪk] ADJ lúdico

ludicrous [ˈluːdɪkrəs] ADJ ridículo, absurdo

ludicrously [ˈluːdɪkrəslɪ] ADV ridículamente, absurdamente

ludicrousness [ˈluːdɪkrəsnɪs] N ridiculez *f*, lo absurdo

ludo [ˈluːdəʊ] N (*Brit*) ludo *m*

luff [lʌf] N orza *f* VI orzar

luffa [ˈlʌfə] N (US) esponja *f* de lufa

lug* [lʌg] VT (= *drag*) arrastrar, jalar (*LAm*); (= *carry*) cargar (*con trabajo*) • **I've been lugging this camera around with me all day** llevo cargando con esta cámara todo el día • **they lugged him off to the theatre** lo llevaron a rastras al teatro • **he lugged the cases upstairs** llevó a rastras las maletas al piso de arriba N **1** (= *projecting part*) oreja *f*, agarradera *f*; (*Tech*) orejeta *f*

2* (= *ear*) oreja *f*

3 (= *loop*) (*on harness*) *lazada de cuero de los arreos*

4 = **lugsail**

luge [luːʒ] N luge *m*

luggage [ˈlʌgɪdʒ] N equipaje *m*

CPD ▸ **luggage boot** (*Brit*) (*Aut*) maletero *m*, portaequipajes *m inv* ▸ **luggage car** (US) = **luggage van** ▸ **luggage carrier** portaequipajes *m inv*, baca *f* ▸ **luggage checkroom** (US) consigna *f* ▸ **luggage grid** = **luggage carrier** ▸ **luggage handler** despachador(a) *m/f* de equipaje ▸ **luggage label** etiqueta *f* de equipaje ▸ **luggage locker** consigna *f* automática ▸ **luggage rack** (*on train etc*) rejilla *f*, redecilla *f*; (*Aut*) baca *f*, portaequipajes *m inv* ▸ **luggage van** (*Brit*) furgón *m* de equipajes

lugger [ˈlʌgəʳ] N lugre *m*

lughole* [ˈlʌghəʊl] N oreja *f*; (= *inner ear*) oído *m*

lugsail [ˈlʌgsl] N vela *f* al tercio

lugubrious [luːˈguːbrɪəs] ADJ lúgubre

lugubriously [luːˈguːbrɪəslɪ] ADV lúgubremente

lugworm [ˈlʌgˌwɜːm] N lombriz *f* de tierra

Luke [luːk] N Lucas

lukewarm [ˈluːkwɔːm] ADJ **1** (= *slightly warm*) [*water, food, coffee*] tibio

2 (*fig*) [*reception, applause, support*] tibio, poco entusiasta • **the report was given a ~ reception** el informe tuvo una tibia acogida *or* una acogida poco entusiasta • **he was ~ about the idea** no le entusiasmaba la idea

lull [lʌl] N (*in storm, wind*) pausa *f*, momento *m* de calma; (*in fighting, bombardment*) tregua *f*; (*in activity*) respiro *m*, pausa *f* • **during a ~ in the conversation** en una pausa de la conversación • IDIOM: • **this was just the ~ before the storm** esto era solo la calma que precede a la tempestad VT [+ *person*] calmar; [+ *fears*] calmar, sosegar • **to ~ sb to sleep** arrullar a algn, adormecer a algn • IDIOM: • **he was ~ed into a false sense of security** se le inspiró un falso sentimiento de seguridad

lullaby [ˈlʌləbaɪ] N canción *f* de cuna, nana *f*

lumbago [lʌmˈbeɪgəʊ] N lumbago *m*

lumbar [ˈlʌmbəʳ] ADJ lumbar

lumber¹ [ˈlʌmbəʳ] N **1** (= *wood*) (*esp US*) maderos *mpl*

2 (*esp Brit**) (= *junk*) trastos *mpl* viejos VT **1** (*Brit**) (= *encumber*) • **to ~ sb with sth** hacer que algn cargue con algo, endilgar algo a algn • **he got ~ed with the job** le endilgaron el trabajo • **I got ~ed with the girl for the afternoon** tuve que cargar toda la tarde con la chica, me endilgaron a la chica toda la tarde

2 (= *fill*) [+ *space, room*] • **to ~ sth with sth** atiborrar algo de algo VI cortar y aserrar árboles, explotar los bosques

CPD ▸ **lumber company** empresa *f* maderera ▸ **lumber jacket** chaqueta *f* de leñador ▸ **lumber mill** aserradero *m* ▸ **lumber room** trastero *m* ▸ **lumber yard** (US) almacén *m* de madera

lumber² [ˈlʌmbəʳ] VI (*also* **lumber about**) moverse pesadamente; (*also* **lumber along**) avanzar pesadamente

lumbering¹ [ˈlʌmbərɪŋ] N (US) explotación *f* forestal

lumbering² [ˈlʌmbərɪŋ] ADJ [*gait, run*] pesado, torpe

lumberjack [ˈlʌmbədʒæk] N leñador(a) *m/f*

CPD ▸ **lumberjack shirt** camisa *f* de leñador

lumberjacket [ˈlʌmbəˌdʒækɪt] N chaqueta *f* de leñador, cazadora *f* de leñador (*Sp*)

lumberman [ˈlʌmbəmən] N (PL: **lumbermen**) = **lumberjack**

luminary [ˈluːmɪnərɪ] N lumbrera *f*

luminescence [ˌluːmɪˈnesns] N luminiscencia *f*

luminescent [ˌluːmɪˈnesnt] ADJ luminescente

luminosity [ˌluːmɪˈnɒsɪtɪ] N luminosidad *f*

luminous [ˈluːmɪnəs] ADJ luminoso

lummet‡ [ˈlʌmɪ] EXCL (*Brit*) = **lummy**

lummox* [ˈlʌməks] N (US) bobo/a* *m/f*

lummy†‡ [ˈlʌmɪ] EXCL (*Brit*) ¡caray!*

lump [lʌmp] N [*of sugar*] terrón *m*; [*of cheese, earth, clay, ice*] trozo *m*, pedazo *m*; (= *swelling*) bulto *m*, hinchazón *f*; (*on surface*) bulto *m*, protuberancia *f*; (= *person**) (*pej*) zoquete* *mf* • **he had a nasty ~ on his head** tenía un buen chichón en la cabeza • **with a ~ in one's throat** con un nudo en la garganta • **I get a ~ in my throat** se me hace un nudo en la garganta VT* (= *endure*) aguantar • **if he doesn't like it he can ~ it** si no le gusta que se aguante

CPD ▸ **lump sugar** azúcar *m* en terrones ▸ **lump sum** cantidad *f* or suma *f* global

▸ **lump together** VT + ADV [+ *things*]

amontonar; [+ *persons*] agrupar • **these problems can't be ~ed together under any one heading** estos problemas no pueden agruparse *or* englobarse bajo el mismo encabezamiento • **excellent wine is ~ed together with plonk** un vino excelente aparece junto a un vino peleón

lumpen ['lʌmpən] (*esp Brit*) ADJ [*person*] necio

lumpish ['lʌmpɪʃ] ADJ torpe, pesado

lumpy ['lʌmpɪ] ADJ (COMPAR: **lumpier**, SUPERL: **lumpiest**) [*sauce*] grumoso, lleno de grumos; [*bed*] desigual; [*soil*] aterronado

lunacy ['lu:nəsɪ] N (*fig*) locura *f* • **it's sheer ~!** ¡es una locura!

lunar ['lu:nəʳ] ADJ lunar
CPD ▸ **lunar eclipse** eclipse *m* lunar ▸ **lunar landing** alunizaje *m*, aterrizaje *m* lunar ▸ **lunar module** módulo *m* lunar ▸ **lunar month** mes *m* lunar

lunatic ['lu:nətɪk] N loco/a *m/f*
ADJ [*person*] loco; [*plan, scheme*] descabellado; [*smile, grin*] de loco • **the ~ fringe** el sector más fanático *or* radical
CPD ▸ **lunatic asylum** manicomio *m*

lunch [lʌntʃ] N comida *f*, almuerzo *m*, lonche *m* (*Mex*) • **to have ~** comer, almorzar • IDIOM: • **to be out to ~** (*US**) (*hum*) estar como una regadera *or* cabra*
CPD ▸ **lunch break** = **lunch hour** ▸ **lunch counter** (*US*) (= *café*) *cafetería donde se sirven comidas*; (= *counter*) *mostrador o barra donde se come* ▸ **lunch hour** hora *f* de la comida *or* del almuerzo *or* (*Mex*) del lonche; ▷ **lunchroom**

lunchbox ['lʌntʃbɒks] N **1** fiambrera *f*, tartera *f*
2* (*hum*) paquete‡ *m*

luncheon ['lʌntʃən] N (*frm*) comida *f*, almuerzo *m*
CPD ▸ **luncheon meat** fiambre *m* en conserva ▸ **luncheon voucher** (*Brit*) vale *m or* (*LAm*) tíquet *m* de comida

luncheonette [,lʌntʃə'net] N bar *m* para almuerzos

lunchpail ['lʌntʃpeɪl] N (*US*) fiambrera *f*, tartera *f*

lunchroom, **lunch room** ['lʌntʃru:m] N (*US*) comedor *m*

lunchtime ['lʌntʃtaɪm] N hora *f* del almuerzo *or* (*Mex*) del lonche, hora *f* de comer *or* de la comida

lung [lʌŋ] N pulmón *m*
CPD ▸ **lung cancer** cáncer *m* de pulmón ▸ **lung disease** enfermedad *f* pulmonar

lunge [lʌndʒ] N arremetida *f*, embestida *f*; (*Fencing*) estocada *f*
VI (*also* **lunge forward**) arremeter, embestir; (*Fencing*) dar una estocada • **to ~ at sth/sb (with sth)** arremeter contra algo/algn (con algo), lanzarse *or* abalanzarse sobre algo/algn (con algo)

lupin ['lu:pɪn] N altramuz *m*, lupino *m*

lupus ['lu:pəs] N lupus *m inv*

lurch¹ [lɜ:tʃ] N sacudida *f*, tumbo *m*; (*Naut*) bandazo *m* • **to give a ~** dar una sacudida *or* un tumbo
VI [*person*] tambalearse; [*vehicle*] (*continually*) dar sacudidas, dar tumbos; (*once*) dar una sacudida, dar un tumbo; (*Naut*) dar un bandazo • **the bus ~ed forward** el autobús avanzó dando tumbos/dando un tumbo • **he ~ed in/out** entró/salió tambaleándose

lurch² [lɜ:tʃ] N • IDIOM: • **to leave sb in the ~** dejar a algn en la estacada

lure [ljʊəʳ] N (= *decoy*) señuelo *m*; (= *bait*) cebo *m*; (*fig*) atractivo *m*, aliciente *m*, encanto *m*
VT [+ *person*] atraer; [+ *animal*] atraer (con un señuelo) • **to ~ sb into a trap** hacer que algn caiga en una trampa • **they ~d him into the house** consiguieron con artimañas que entrara en la casa • **he was ~d away from the company by a more lucrative offer** dejó la empresa atraído por una oferta más lucrativa

lurex ['lʊəreks] N lúrex *m*

lurgy* ['lɜ:gɪ] N (*Brit*) (*hum*) • **I've got the dreaded ~ again** he pillado algo malo otra vez

lurid ['ljʊərɪd] ADJ **1** (= *sordid, prurient*) [*description, novel, photo, crime*] morboso, escabroso; [*imagination, headline*] morboso • **in ~ detail** sin omitir los detalles más escabrosos
2 (= *garish*) [*colour, tie, shirt*] chillón • **a ~ pink dress** un vestido (de color) rosa chillón
3 (= *unnaturally colourful*) [*sky, sunset, light*] refulgente

luridly ['ljʊərɪdlɪ] ADV **1** (= *pruriently*) con morbosidad, morbosamente
2 (= *garishly*) • **~ coloured** (de color) chillón

lurk [lɜ:k] VI [*person*] (= *lie in wait*) estar al acecho, merodear; (= *hide*) estar escondido • **I saw him ~ing around the building** lo vi merodeando *or* al acecho por el edificio • **a doubt ~s in my mind** una duda persiste en mi mente • **danger ~s round every corner** el peligro acecha en cada esquina

lurking ['lɜ:kɪŋ] ADJ [*fear, doubt*] vago, indefinible

luscious ['lʌʃəs] ADJ [*scent, breeze, wine*] delicioso; [*fruit*] suculento; [*girl*] deliciosa, atractiva

lusciously ['lʌʃəslɪ] ADV deliciosamente • **~ coated in thick cream** cubierto con una deliciosa crema espesa

lusciousness ['lʌʃəsnɪs] N exquisitez *f*; [*of fruit*] suculencia *f*

lush [lʌʃ] ADJ (COMPAR: **lusher**, SUPERL: **lushest**) **1** (= *luxuriant*) [*vegetation*] exuberante, lozano; [*pastures*] rico
2 (= *opulent*) opulento, lujoso
N* (= *alcoholic*) borracho/a *m/f*

lushness ['lʌʃnɪs] N **1** (= *luxuriance*) lozanía *f*, exuberancia *f*
2 (= *opulence*) opulencia *f*, lujo *m*

lust [lʌst] N (= *greed*) codicia *f*; (*sexual*) lujuria *f* • **~ for power/revenge** ansia *f or* sed *f* de poder/venganza • **~ for money** codicia *f*
▸ **lust after**, **lust for** VI + PREP • **to ~ after** *or* **for sth** codiciar algo • **to ~ after sb** desear a algn

luster ['lʌstəʳ] N (*US*) = **lustre**

lusterless ['lʌstəlɪs] ADJ (*US*) = **lustreless**

lustful ['lʌstfʊl] ADJ lujurioso, libidinoso; [*look*] lascivo, lleno de deseo

lustfully ['lʌstfəlɪ] ADV lujuriosamente, libidinosamente; [*look*] lascivamente

lustfulness ['lʌstfʊlnɪs] N lujuria *f*, lascivia *f*

lustily ['lʌstɪlɪ] ADV [*sing*] animadamente

lustre, **luster** (*US*) ['lʌstəʳ] N lustre *m*, brillo *m*

lustreless, **lusterless** (*US*) ['lʌstəlɪs] ADJ [*hair*] deslustrado; [*eyes*] apagado

lustrous ['lʌstrəs] ADJ [*hair*] brillante, lustroso; [*eyes*] brillante; [*gold*] reluciente

lusty ['lʌstɪ] ADJ (COMPAR: **lustier**, SUPERL: **lustiest**) [*person*] vigoroso, lozano; [*cry, cheer*] fuerte • **he has a ~ appetite** tiene buen apetito

lute [lu:t] N laúd *m*

lutetium [lʊ'ti:ʃɪəm] N lutecio *m*

Luther ['lu:θəʳ] N Lutero

Lutheran ['lu:θərən] ADJ luterano
N luterano/a *m/f*

Lutheranism ['lu:θərənɪzəm] N luteranismo *m*

luv* [lʌv] N (*Brit*) = **love** • **yes, luv** sí, cariño

luvvies* ['lʌvɪz] NPL (*Brit*) (*pej*) (= *actors*) gente *f* de la farándula

Luxembourg ['lʌksəmbɜ:g] N Luxemburgo *m*

Luxembourger ['lʌksəmbɜ:gəʳ] N luxemburgués/esa *m/f*

luxuriance [lʌg'zjʊərɪəns] N exuberancia *f*

luxuriant [lʌg'zjʊərɪənt] ADJ exuberante, lozano

luxuriantly [lʌg'zjʊərɪəntlɪ] ADV exuberantemente, de manera exuberante

luxuriate [lʌg'zjʊərɪeɪt] VI [*plant*] crecer con exuberancia; [*person*] disfrutar • **to ~ in** disfrutar (de), deleitarse con, entregarse al lujo de

luxurious [lʌg'zjʊərɪəs] ADJ [*house, apartment, hotel, furnishings*] lujoso, de lujo; [*life*] de lujo

luxuriously [lʌg'zjʊərɪəslɪ] ADV lujosamente

luxury ['lʌkʃərɪ] N (= *opulence*) lujo *m*; (= *extravagance, treat*) lujo *m*; (= *article*) artículo *m* de lujo • **to live in ~** vivir con mucho lujo • **a holiday is a ~ we can't afford** unas vacaciones son un lujo que no nos podemos permitir
CPD [*goods, apartment*] de lujo ▸ **luxury tax** impuesto *m* de lujo

LV N ABBR = **luncheon voucher**

LW N ABBR (*Rad*) (= **long wave**) OL *f*

lyceum [laɪ'si:əm] N liceo *m*

lychee [,laɪ'tʃi:] N lichi *m*

lych gate ['lɪtʃ geɪt] N *entrada techada a un cementerio*

Lycra® ['laɪkrə] N licra® *f*

lye [laɪ] N lejía *f*

lying ['laɪɪŋ] ADJ [*statement, story*] falso • **you ~ son-of-a-bitch!**** ¡mentiroso hijo de puta!**
N mentiras *fpl*

lying-in† ['laɪɪŋ'ɪn] (*Med*) N (PL: **lyings-in**) parto *m*
CPD ▸ **lying-in ward** sala *f* de maternidad

lymph [lɪmf] N linfa *f*
CPD ▸ **lymph gland** ganglio *m* linfático ▸ **lymph node** ganglio *m* linfático

lymphatic [lɪm'fætɪk] ADJ linfático
N vaso *m* linfático

lymphocyte ['lɪmfəʊ,saɪt] N linfocito *m*

lynch [lɪntʃ] VT linchar
CPD ▸ **lynch law** ley *f* del linchamiento ▸ **lynch mob** *muchedumbre dispuesta a linchar a alguien*

lynching ['lɪntʃɪŋ] N linchamiento *m*

lynchpin ['lɪntʃpɪn] = **linchpin**

lynx [lɪŋks] N (PL: **lynxes** *or* **lynx**) lince *m*

lynx-eyed ['lɪŋksaɪd] ADJ con ojos de lince

Lyons ['laɪənz] N Lyón *m*

lyre ['laɪəʳ] N lira *f*

lyrebird ['laɪəbɜ:d] N ave *f* lira

lyric ['lɪrɪk] ADJ lírico
N (= *poem*) poema *m* lírico; (= *genre*) lírica *f*; **lyrics** (= *words of song*) letra *fsing*

lyrical ['lɪrɪkəl] ADJ (*lit*) lírico; (*fig*) entusiasmado • **to wax** *or* **become ~ about** *or* **over sth** deshacerse en elogios a algo • **he was waxing ~ about my roast beef** se deshacía en elogios a mi rosbif, estaba entusiasmado con mi rosbif

lyrically ['lɪrɪkəlɪ] ADV (= *poetically*) [*speak, write, describe*] líricamente, con lirismo

lyricism ['lɪrɪsɪzəm] N lirismo *m*

lyricist ['lɪrɪsɪst] N letrista *mf*

lysergic acid [lɪ'sɜ:dʒɪk 'æsɪd] N ácido *m* lisérgico

Lysol® ['laɪsɒl] N lisol® *m*

Mm

M¹, m¹ [em] (N) (= *letter*) M, m *f* • **M for Mary** M de Madrid

M², m² (ABBR) **1** = **million(s)**
2 (= **medium**) (= *garment size*) M
3 (= **married**) se casó con
4 (= **metre(s)**) m
5 = **mile(s)**
6 (= **male**) m
7 (= **minute(s)**) m
8 (*Brit*) = **motorway** • **the M8** ≈ la A8

MA (N ABBR) (*Univ*) (= **Master of Arts**)
▷ DEGREE
(ABBR) **1** (*US*) = **Massachusetts**
2 (*US*) = **Military Academy**

ma* [mɑː] (N) mamá *f*

ma'am [mæm] (N) (*esp US*) = **madam**

Maastricht Treaty ['mɑːstrɪkt'triːtɪ] (N) • **the ~** el Tratado de Maastricht

mac* [mæk] (N) **1** (*Brit*) (= *mackintosh*) impermeable *m*; (= *cagoule*) chubasquero *m*
2 (*esp US*) • **this way, Mac!** ¡por aquí, amigo!

macabre [mə'kɑːbr] (ADJ) macabro

macadam [mə'kædəm] (N) macadán *m*

macadamize [mə'kædəmaɪz] (VT) macadamizar

macaque [mə'kɑːk] (N) (= *monkey*) macaco *m*

macaroni [,mækə'rəʊnɪ] (N) macarrones *mpl*
(CPD) ▸ **macaroni cheese** macarrones *mpl* gratinados (con queso)

macaronic [,mækə'rɒnɪk] (ADJ) macarrónico

macaroon [,mækə'ruːn] (N) macarrón *m*, mostachón *m*

macaw [mə'kɔː] (N) guacamayo *m*

mace¹ [meɪs] (N) (= *ceremonial staff*) maza *f*

mace² [meɪs] (N) (= *spice*) macis *f*

macebearer ['meɪs,beərəʳ] (N) macero *m*

Macedonia [,mæsɪ'dəʊnɪə] (N) Macedonia *f*

Macedonian [,mæsɪ'dəʊnɪən] (ADJ) macedonio/a *m/f*
(N) **1** (= *person*) macedonio/a *m/f*
2 (*Ling*) macedonio *m*

macerate ['mæsəreɪt] (VT) macerar
(VI) macerar(se)

Mach [mæk] (N) mach *m*

machete [mə'tʃeɪtɪ] (N) machete *m*

Machiavelli [,mækɪə'velɪ] (N) Maquiavelo

Machiavellian [,mækɪə'velɪən] (ADJ) maquiavélico

machinations [,mækɪ'neɪʃənz] (NPL) maquinaciones *fpl*, intrigas *fpl*, manipulaciones *fpl*

machine [mə'ʃiːn] (N) **1** (*gen*) máquina *f*, aparato *m*; (= *machinery*) maquinaria *f*
2 (*referring to particular appliance*) (= *car, motorbike*) máquina *f*; (= *aeroplane*) aparato *m*; (= *cycle*) bicicleta *f*; (= *washing machine*) lavadora *f*
3 (*Pol*) organización *f*, aparato *m*
(VT) (*Tech*) elaborar a máquina; (*Sew*) coser a máquina
(CPD) mecánico, (hecho) a máquina
▸ **machine age** era *f* de las máquinas ▸ **machine code** (*Comput*) lenguaje *m* (de) máquina ▸ **machine error** error *m* de la máquina ▸ **machine gun** ametralladora *f*; ▷ **machine-gun** ▸ **machine gunner** ametrallador *m* ▸ **machine intelligence** inteligencia *f* artificial ▸ **machine language** lenguaje *m* (de) máquina ▸ **machine operator** operario/a *m/f*, maquinista *mf* ▸ **machine pistol** metralleta *f* ▸ **machine shop** taller *m* de máquinas ▸ **machine time** tiempo *m* de máquina ▸ **machine tool** máquina *f* herramienta ▸ **machine translation** traducción *f* automática

machine-assisted translation [mə,ʃiːnə-,sɪstɪd,træns'leɪʃən] (N) traducción *f* asistida por ordenador

machine-gun [mə'ʃiːngʌn] (VT) ametrallar

machine-made [mə'ʃiːnmeɪd] (ADJ) hecho a máquina

machine-readable [mə'ʃiːn'riːdəbl] (ADJ) legible por máquina • **in machine-readable form** en forma legible por máquina • **machine-readable code** código *m* legible por máquina

machinery [mə'ʃiːnərɪ] (N) **1** (= *machines*) maquinaria *f*; (= *mechanism*) mecanismo *m*
2 (*fig*) maquinaria *f*, aparato *m*

machine-stitch [mə'ʃiːn,stɪtʃ] (VT) coser a máquina

machine-wash [mə'ʃiːnwɒʃ] (VT) lavar a máquina

machine-washable [mə'ʃiːn'wɒʃəbl] (ADJ) lavable en la lavadora

machinist [mə'ʃiːnɪst] (N) (*Tech*) operario/a *m/f*; (*Sew*) costurero/a *m/f* a máquina

machismo [mæ'tʃɪzməʊ] (N) machismo *m*

macho ['mætʃəʊ] (ADJ) muy de macho, muy masculino • **a ~ man** un tipo muy macho, un macho
(N) macho *m*

mackerel ['mækrəl] (N) (PL: **mackerel** *or* **mackerels**) caballa *f*
(CPD) ▸ **mackerel sky** cielo *m* aborregado

mackintosh ['mækɪntɒʃ] (N) impermeable *m*; (= *cagoule*) chubasquero *m*

macramé [mə'krɑːmɪ] (N) macramé *m*

macro ['mækrəʊ] (N ABBR) (*Comput*) (= **macro-instruction**) macro *m*

macro... ['mækrəʊ] (PREFIX) macro...

macrobiotic [,mækrəʊbaɪ'ɒtɪk] (ADJ) macrobiótico

macrobiotics [,mækrəʊbaɪ'ɒtɪks] (N) macrobiótica *f*

macrocosm ['mækrəʊkɒzəm] (N) macrocosmo *m*

macroeconomic [,mækrəʊ,iːkə'nɒmɪk] (ADJ) macroeconómico

macroeconomics [,mækrəʊ,iːkə'nɒmɪks] (NSING) macroeconomía *f*

macroeconomy [,mækrəʊɪ'kɒnəmɪ] (N) macroeconomía *f*

macroscopic [,mækrə'skɒpɪk] (ADJ) macroscópico

> **MACY'S THANKSGIVING PARADE**
> **Macy's Thanksgiving Parade** es una cabalgata anual que tiene lugar en Nueva York el Día de Acción de Gracias, el cuarto jueves de noviembre. Patrocinado por los grandes almacenes **Macy's**, este desfile de globos con personajes de dibujos animados, bandas de música y grupos de personas que vienen de todas las partes de EE.UU. recorre las calles de Broadway a la vez que se televisa a todo el país. En el desfile son típicas unas carrozas profusamente adornadas llamadas **floats**, en las que van montados cantantes famosos y estrellas de Broadway. A pesar de que se celebra el Día de Acción de Gracias, el tema del desfile es la Navidad y Santa Claus siempre va en la última carroza.
> ▷ THANKSGIVING

MAD (N ABBR) (*US*) (*Mil*) = **mutual(ly) assured destruction**

mad [mæd] (ADJ) (COMPAR: **madder**, SUPERL: **maddest**) **1** [*person*] **a** (= *mentally ill*) loco • **to drive sb mad** (= *make insane*) volver loco a algn • **captivity drives some animals mad** la cautividad vuelve locos a algunos animales • **to go mad** (= *become insane*) volverse loco; ▷ **raving, stark**
b* (= *crazy, foolish*) loco • **are you mad?** ¿estás loco? • **you must be mad!** ¡tú estás loco *or* mal de la cabeza! • **to drive sb mad** (= *irritate*) volver loco a algn • **she drove me mad with her constant questions** me volvió loco con sus constantes preguntas • **don't go mad! we've only got £100** ¡no te pases! solo tenemos 100 libras • **I worked/ran/pedalled like mad** trabajé/corrí/pedaleé como (un) loco • **they fancy her like mad** les gusta horrores *or* una barbaridad* • **to be mad with grief** estar loco de dolor
c* (= *angry*) furioso • **I was really mad when I found out** me puse furiosísimo *or* (*Sp*) me enfadé muchísimo *or* (*esp LAm*) me enojé muchísimo cuando me enteré • **to be mad at sb** estar furioso con algn, estar muy enfadado con algn (*Sp*), estar muy enojado con algn (*esp LAm*) • **to get** *or* **go mad** ponerse furioso • **he gets** *or* **goes mad when he loses** se pone furioso *or* hecho una fiera cuando pierde • **it makes her mad when you do that** cuando haces eso la sacas de quicio • **to be mad with sb** estar furioso con algn, estar muy enfadado con algn (*Sp*), estar muy enojado con algn (*esp LAm*) • **I was mad with him for breaking my window** estaba muy enfadado con él porque me había roto la ventana
d* (= *keen*) • **to be mad about sb** estar loco por algn • **to be mad about** *or* **on sth**: • **he's mad about** *or* **on football** el fútbol le vuelve loco, es un fanático del fútbol • **she's mad on Chinese food** le pirra *or* le chifla la comida china* • **I can't say I'm mad about** *or* **on the idea** no es precisamente que la idea me

vuelva loco • **to go mad**: • **he walked onstage and the audience went mad** salió al escenario y el público se puso como loco
e • IDIOMS: • **to be barking mad** estar loco de remate*, estar loco de atar • **to be (as) mad as a hatter** *or* **March hare** estar más loco que una cabra* • **to be mad as hell** (= *furious*) estar cabreadísimo‡; ▷ **hop¹**
2 [*thing*] **a** (= *silly, irresponsible*) [*plan, idea, scheme*] descabellado, de locos • **this is bureaucracy gone mad** esto es la burocracia llevada al extremo del ridículo
b (= *frantic, uncontrolled*) [*race*] desenfrenado • **the daily mad dash to work** la desenfrenada carrera diaria por llegar al trabajo • **there was a mad rush for the exit** todo el mundo corrió *or* se lanzó desenfrenado hacia la salida, todo el mundo corrió como loco hacia la salida • **after the news came through the phones went mad** tras saberse la noticia los teléfonos sonaban como locos
ADV (= *very*) • **she's mad keen to go** tiene unas ganas locas de ir • **I can't say I'm mad keen on the idea** no es precisamente que la idea me vuelva loco
CPD ▸ **mad cow disease*** enfermedad *f* de las vacas locas*, encefalopatía *f* espongiforme bovina ▸ **mad dog** (*with rabies*) perro *m* rabioso (*con la enfermedad de la rabia*)

-mad [mæd] ADJ (*ending in compounds*) • **he's football-mad** el fútbol le vuelve loco, es un fanático del fútbol • **football-mad boys** chicos *mpl* con la manía del fútbol • **pony-mad teenagers** quinceañeras *fpl* locas por los caballitos

Madagascar [ˌmædəˈɡæskəʳ] N Madagascar *m*

madam [ˈmædəm] N (PL: **madams** *or* **mesdames** [ˈmeɪdæm]) **1** señora *f* • **yes, ~** sí, señora; ▷ **dear**
2 (*Brit**) (= *girl*) niña *f* malcriada, niña *f* repipi
3 [*of brothel*] madama *f*, dueña *f*

madame [ˈmædəm] N (PL: **mesdames** [ˈmeɪdæm]) **1** madama *f*, señora *f* • **Madame Dupont** la señora de Dupont
2 [*of brothel*] madama *f*, dueña *f*

madcap [ˈmædkæp] ADJ alocado, disparatado
N locuelo/a *m/f*, tarambana *mf*

MADD ABBR = **mothers against drunk driving**

madden [ˈmædn] VT (= *infuriate*) enfurecer, sacar de quicio; (= *make demented*) enloquecer • **it ~s me** me pone furioso, me enfurece, me saca de quicio • **a ~ed bull** un toro enloquecido

maddening [ˈmædnɪŋ] ADJ [*delay, habit, trait*] exasperante • **she had a ~ smirk on her face** su rostro tenía una sonrisita exasperante • **it's (quite) ~!** ¡es desesperante!, ¡es como para desesperarse! • **he can be absolutely ~ at times** a veces puede sacarte de quicio

maddeningly [ˈmædnɪŋlɪ] ADV [*smile, grin*] de forma exasperante • **progress was ~ slow** se progresaba con una lentitud exasperante *or* desesperante • **he was always ~ punctual** siempre fue de una puntualidad exasperante *or* desesperante

made [meɪd] PT, PP *of* **make**

-made [-ˈmeɪd] SUFFIX • **British-made** fabricado en el Reino Unido • **specially-made** hecho a medida • **factory-made** manufacturado

made-for-mobile [ˌmeɪdfəˈməʊbaɪl] ADJ para móviles (*Sp*), para celulares (*LAm*)

Madeira [məˈdɪərə] N Madeira *f*; (= *wine*) (vino *m* de) madeira *m*

made-to-measure [ˌmeɪdtəˈmeʒəʳ] ADJ hecho a (la) medida

made-to-order [ˌmeɪdtəˈɔːdəʳ] ADJ (*Brit*) hecho de encargo; (*US*) hecho a (la) medida

made-up [ˈmeɪdˈʌp] ADJ **1** (= *wearing make-up*) [*face*] maquillado; [*eyes*] pintado, maquillado • **she was heavily made-up** llevaba mucho maquillaje, iba muy pintada
2 (= *invented*) [*story, character*] inventado, ficticio; [*word*] inventado
3 (= *ready-made*) [*mixture, solution*] preparado

Madge [mædʒ] N *familiar form of* **Margaret**

madhouse* [ˈmædhaʊs] N (PL: **madhouses** [ˈmædhaʊzɪz]) manicomio *m*, casa *f* de locos • **this is a ~!** ¡esto es una casa de locos!

madly [ˈmædlɪ] ADV **1** (= *crazily*) [*scream, laugh, wave, rush*] (*one person*) como (un) loco/(una) loca; (*more than one person*) como locos • **my heart was beating ~** mi corazón latía como loco
2 (= *very*) • **he was ~ jealous of his sister** estaba terriblemente celoso de su hermana • **they were ~ in love with each other** estaban locamente *or* perdidamente enamorados uno del otro • **she found her new life ~ exciting** su nueva vida le parecía terriblemente excitante • **life is not ~ exciting at the moment** en este momento mi vida no es muy emocionante

madman [ˈmædmən] N (PL: **madmen**) loco *m*

madness [ˈmædnɪs] N **1** (= *mental illness*) locura *f*, demencia *f*
2 (= *foolishness*) locura *f* • **it would be sheer ~ to continue** sería una auténtica locura seguir • **it's ~!** ¡es una locura!

Madonna [məˈdɒnə] N Virgen *f*

madrasah, madrassa [məˈdræsə] N madraza *f*

Madrid [məˈdrɪd] N Madrid *m*
ADJ madrileño

madrigal [ˈmædrɪɡəl] N madrigal *m*

madwoman [ˈmædwʊmən] N (PL: **madwomen**) loca *f*

maelstrom [ˈmeɪlstrəʊm] N torbellino *m*, remolino *m*

maestro [ˈmaɪstrəʊ] N (PL: **maestros** *or* **maestri** [ˈmaɪstrɪ]) maestro *m*

Mae West [ˈmeɪˈwest] N (*Aer*) (*hum*) chaleco *m* salvavidas

MAFF N ABBR (*Brit*) (= **Ministry of Agriculture, Fisheries and Food**) ≈ MAPA *m*

mafia [ˈmæfɪə] N mafia *f*

mafioso [ˌmæfɪˈəʊsəʊ] N (PL: **mafiosi** [ˌmæfɪˈəʊsɪ]) mafioso *m*

mag* [mæɡ] N ABBR (*Brit*) (= **magazine**) revista *f*

magazine [ˌmæɡəˈziːn] N **1** (= *journal*) revista *f*
2 (*TV, Rad*) (*also* **magazine programme**) magazine *m*, programa *m* magazine
3 (*in rifle*) recámara *f*; (*in slide projector*) (*round*) carrusel *m*; (*elongated*) carro *m*, bandeja *f*
4 (*Mil*) (= *store*) almacén *m*; (*for powder*) polvorín *m*; (*Naut*) santabárbara *f*
CPD ▸ **magazine rack** portarrevistas *m inv*

Magdalen [ˈmæɡdəlɪn] N Magdalena

Magellan [məˈɡelən] N Magallanes
CPD ▸ **Magellan Straits** estrecho *m* de Magallanes

magenta [məˈdʒentə] N magenta *m*
ADJ magenta (*inv*)

Maggie [ˈmæɡɪ] N *familiar form of* **Margaret**

maggot [ˈmæɡət] N cresa *f*, gusano *m*

maggoty [ˈmæɡətɪ] ADJ agusanado, lleno de gusanos

Maghrib [ˈmʌɡrəb] N Magreb *m*

Magi [ˈmeɪdʒaɪ] NPL • **the ~** los Reyes Magos

magic [ˈmædʒɪk] N (*lit, fig*) magia *f* • **as if by ~** como por arte de magia, como por encanto • **this bath oil works ~ for tired and aching limbs** este aceite de baño es mágico para brazos y piernas doloridos y cansados • **the ~ of Hollywood** la magia de Hollywood • **the old ~ was still there** (*in relationship*) todavía existía algo especial entre ellos/nosotros; ▷ **black, white**
ADJ **1** (*relating to spells, sorcery*) [*solution, word*] mágico • **you just have to say the ~ word and we'll forget all about it** basta con que digas la palabra mágica y olvidaremos todo el asunto • **there is no ~ formula for success** no existe una fórmula mágica para el éxito
2 (= *captivating*) [*moment*] especial • **he hasn't lost his ~ touch** no ha perdido ese toque especial suyo
3* (= *super*) fabuloso, estupendo • **"did you enjoy it?" — "it was ~"** —¿te gustó? —fue fabuloso *or* estupendo
CPD ▸ **magic bullet** (*Med*) (*also fig*) panacea *f* ▸ **magic carpet** alfombra *f* mágica ▸ **magic circle** círculo *m* mágico ▸ **magic lantern** linterna *f* mágica ▸ **magic mushrooms*** setas *fpl* alucinógenas, hongos *mpl* alucinógenos ▸ **magic realism** (*Literat*) realismo *m* mágico ▸ **magic spell** hechizo *m*, encanto *m* ▸ **magic square** (*Math*) cuadrado *m* mágico ▸ **magic trick** truco *m* de magia ▸ **magic wand** varita *f* mágica
▸ **magic away** VT + ADV hacer desaparecer como por arte de magia
▸ **magic up** VT + ADV hacer aparecer como por arte de magia

magical [ˈmædʒɪkəl] ADJ **1** (*lit*) [*powers, properties*] mágico
2 (*fig*) **a** (= *captivating*) [*experience, moment*] mágico
b (= *miraculous*) [*transformation*] milagroso • **she had undergone a ~ transformation** había sufrido una transformación milagrosa

magically [ˈmædʒɪkəlɪ] ADV como por arte de magia • **a bottle of champagne was ~ produced** apareció una botella de champán como por arte de magia

magician [məˈdʒɪʃən] N **1** (= *sorcerer*) mago/a *m/f*
2 (= *conjuror*) prestidigitador(a) *m/f*

magisterial [ˌmædʒɪsˈtɪərɪəl] ADJ magistral

magisterially [ˌmædʒɪsˈtɪərɪəlɪ] ADV autoritariamente • **he waves his hand ~** saluda con la mano autoritariamente

magistracy [ˈmædʒɪstrəsɪ] N magistratura *f*

magistrate [ˈmædʒɪstreɪt] N magistrado/a *m/f*, juez *mf*
CPD ▸ **magistrates' court** (*in England*) juzgado *m* de primera instancia

maglev [ˈmæɡlev] N (*Rail*) tren *m* de levitación magnética

magma [ˈmæɡmə] N (PL: **magmas** *or* **magmata** [ˈmæɡmətə]) magma *m*

Magna Carta, Magna Charta [ˈmæɡnəˈkɑːtə] N (*Brit*) Carta *f* Magna

magnanimity [ˌmæɡnəˈnɪmɪtɪ] N magnanimidad *f*

magnanimous [mæɡˈnænɪməs] ADJ magnánimo (*frm*), generoso • **to be ~ in victory** mostrarse magnánimo con los perdedores • **to be ~ to sb** mostrarse magnánimo con algn (*frm*), mostrarse generoso con algn

magnanimously [mæɡˈnænɪməslɪ] ADV (*gen*) magnánimamente; [*say*] con magnanimidad, magnánimamente

magnate [ˈmæɡneɪt] N magnate *mf*, potentado/a *m/f*

magnesia [mæɡˈniːʃə] N magnesia *f*

magnesium [mæɡˈniːzɪəm] N magnesio *m*

(CPD) ▸ **magnesium sulphate** sulfato *m* magnésico

magnet [ˈmæɡnɪt] (N) (*lit, fig*) imán *m*
(CPD) ▸ **magnet school** (*US*) *colegio público que ofrece cursos especializados*

magnetic [mæɡˈnetɪk] (ADJ) magnético; (*fig*) carismático
(CPD) ▸ **magnetic card reader** lector *m* de tarjeta magnética ▸ **magnetic disk** disco *m* magnético ▸ **magnetic field** campo *m* magnético ▸ **magnetic mine** mina *f* magnética ▸ **magnetic needle** aguja *f* magnética ▸ **magnetic north** norte *m* magnético ▸ **magnetic pole** polo *m* magnético ▸ **magnetic resonance imaging** resonancia *f* magnética, imagen *f* por resonancia magnética ▸ **magnetic resonance imaging scan** resonancia *f* magnética ▸ **magnetic resonance imaging system** sistema *m* de imágenes por resonancia magnética ▸ **magnetic resonance imaging technology** tecnología *f* de imágenes por resonancia magnética ▸ **magnetic storm** tormenta *f* magnética ▸ **magnetic strip, magnetic stripe** banda *f* magnética ▸ **magnetic tape** cinta *f* magnética

magnetically [mæɡˈnetɪkəlɪ] (ADV) magnéticamente

magnetism [ˈmæɡnɪtɪzəm] (N) magnetismo *m*; (*fig*) magnetismo *m*, atractivo *m*

magnetizable [ˌmæɡnɪˈtaɪzəbl] (ADJ) magnetizable

magnetize [ˈmæɡnɪtaɪz] (VT) **1** (*lit*) magnetizar, imantar
2 (*fig*) magnetizar

magneto [mæɡˈniːtəʊ] (N) magneto *f*

magnetometer [ˌmæɡnɪˈtɒmɪtəʳ] (N) magnetómetro *m*

magnetosphere [mæɡˈniːtəʊˌsfɪəʳ] (N) magnetosfera *f*

Magnificat [mæɡˈnɪfɪkæt] (N) Magníficat *m*

magnification [ˌmæɡnɪfɪˈkeɪʃən] (N) **1** (*Opt*) aumento *m*, ampliación *f* • **high ~** gran aumento *m* • **low ~** pequeño aumento *m*
2 (*fig*) exageración *f*

magnificence [mæɡˈnɪfɪsəns] (N) magnificencia *f*

magnificent [mæɡˈnɪfɪsənt] (ADJ) [*display, performance, achievement, animal, view*] magnífico, espléndido; [*building*] espléndido • **he has done a ~ job** ha hecho un trabajo magnífico *or* espléndido • **the princess looked ~** la princesa estaba esplendorosa

magnificently [mæɡˈnɪfɪsəntlɪ] (ADV) magníficamente • **they played/performed ~** tocaron/actuaron magníficamente (bien)

magnifier [ˈmæɡnɪfaɪəʳ] (N) **1** (= *magnifying glass*) lupa *f*
2 (*Elec*) amplificador *m*

magnify [ˈmæɡnɪfaɪ] (VT) **1** (*Opt*) aumentar, ampliar • **to ~ sth seven times** aumentar algo siete veces
2 (= *exaggerate*) exagerar
(CPD) ▸ **magnifying glass** lupa *f* ▸ **magnifying power** aumento *m*

magnitude [ˈmæɡnɪtjuːd] (N) **1** (*gen*) magnitud *f*; (= *importance*) magnitud *f*, envergadura *f* • **in operations of this ~** en operaciones de esta magnitud *or* envergadura
2 (*Astron*) magnitud *f* • **a star of the first ~** una estrella de primera magnitud

magnolia [mæɡˈnəʊlɪə] (N) magnolia *f*

magnox reactor [ˈmæɡnɒksriːˈæktəʳ] (N) reactor *m* magnox

magnum [ˈmæɡnəm] (N) (PL: **magnums**) (= *bottle*) botella *f* doble
(ADJ) • **~ opus** obra *f* maestra

magpie [ˈmæɡpaɪ] (N) urraca *f*, marica *f*

Magyar [ˈmæɡjɑːʳ] (ADJ) magiar
(N) magiar *mf*

maharajah [ˌmɑːhəˈrɑːdʒə] (N) maharajá *m*

maharani [ˌmɑːhəˈrɑːniː] (N) maharaní *f*

Mahdi [ˈmɑːdɪ] (N) mahdi *m*

mahjong, mahjongg [ˌmɑːˈdʒɒŋ] (N) dominó *m* chino

mahogany [məˈhɒɡənɪ] (N) caoba *f*
(ADJ) de caoba

Mahomet [məˈhɒmɪt] (N) Mahoma

Mahometan‡ [məˈhɒmɪtən] (ADJ) mahometano
(N) mahometano/a *m/f*

maid [meɪd] (N) **1** (= *servant*) criada *f*, muchacha *f* (*S. Cone*), mucama *f* (*S. Cone*), recamarera *f* (*Mex*); (*in hotel*) camarera *f* • **lady's ~** doncella *f*
2 (= *young girl††*) doncella *f*; ▹ **old**
(CPD) ▸ **maid of honor** (*US*) dama *f* de honor ▸ **maid service** (*in hotel, holiday accommodation*) servicio *m* de camarera

maiden [ˈmeɪdn] (N) (*liter*) doncella *f*
(ADJ) [*flight, speech*] inaugural, de inauguración
(CPD) ▸ **maiden aunt** tía *f* solterona ▸ **maiden lady†** soltera *f* ▸ **maiden name** apellido *m* de soltera ▸ **maiden over** (*Cricket*) *serie de seis lanzamientos en que no se anota ninguna carrera*

maidenhair [ˈmeɪdnheəʳ] (N) (*also* **maidenhair fern**) cabello *m* de Venus, culantrillo *m*

maidenhead [ˈmeɪdnhed] (N) virginidad *f*, himen *m*

maidenhood [ˈmeɪdnhʊd] (N) doncellez *f*

maidenly [ˈmeɪdnlɪ] (ADJ) (= *virginal*) virginal; (= *demure*) recatado, modesto

maid-of-all-work [ˌmeɪdəvˈɔːlˌwɜːk] (N) chica *f* para todo

maidservant [ˈmeɪdˌsɜːvənt] (N) criada *f*, sirvienta *f*

mail[1] [meɪl] (N) **1** (= *postal system*) correo *m* • **by** *or* **through the ~** por correo; ▹ **airmail**
2 (= *letters*) cartas *fpl*, correspondencia *f* • **is there any ~ for me?** ¿hay alguna carta para mí?
3 = **email**
(VT) **1** (*esp US*) (= *post*) echar al correo; (= *send by mail*) enviar por correo
2 = **email**
(CPD) ▸ **mail boat** vapor *m* correo ▸ **mail bomb** (*US*) (= *letter bomb*) carta *f* bomba; (= *parcel bomb*) paquete *m* bomba ▸ **mail car** (*US*) (*Rail*) furgón *m* postal, vagón *m* correo ▸ **mail carrier** (*US*) cartero/a *m/f* ▸ **mail coach** (*Hist*) diligencia *f*, coche *m* correo; (*Rail*) furgón *m* postal, vagón *m* correo ▸ **mail merge** combinación *f* de correspondencia ▸ **mail order** (= *system*) venta *f* por correo; (= *order*) pedido *m* por correo; ▹ **mail-order** ▸ **mail room** sala *f* de correo, departamento *m* de registro (de entradas y salidas) ▸ **mail server** (*Comput*) servidor *m* de correo ▸ **mail train** tren *m* correo ▸ **mail truck** (*US*) camioneta *f* de correos ▸ **mail van** (*Brit*) (*Aut*) camioneta *f* de correos; (*Rail*) furgón *m* postal, vagón *m* correo

mail[2] [meɪl] (N) (*Mil*) malla *f*, cota *f* de malla

mailbag [ˈmeɪlbæɡ] (N) saca *f* de correos

mailbox [ˈmeɪlbɒks] (N) (*US*) (*in street*) buzón *m*; (*in office etc*) casilla *f*; (*Comput*) buzón *m*

maildrop [ˈmeɪldrɒp] (N) (= *act*) entrega *f* de correo; (= *address*) dirección *f* para correo

mailed fist [ˌmeɪldˈfɪst] (N) • **the ~** la mano dura

mailing [ˈmeɪlɪŋ] (N) envío *m*
(CPD) ▸ **mailing address** (*US*) dirección *f* postal, dirección *f* de correo ▸ **mailing list** lista *f* de direcciones • **I'll put you on our ~ list** le incluiré en nuestra lista de direcciones para enviarle información

mailman [ˈmeɪlmæn] (N) (PL: **mailmen**) (*US*) cartero *m*

mail-order [ˈmeɪlˌɔːdəʳ] (CPD) ▸ **mail-order catalogue, mail-order catalog** (*US*) catálogo *m* de venta por correo ▸ **mail-order firm, mail-order house** empresa *f* de venta por correo; ▹ **mail**

mailshot [ˈmeɪlʃɒt] (N) (*Brit*) mailing *m*

mailwoman [ˈmeɪlˌwʊmən] (N) (PL: **mailwomen**) cartera *f*

maim [meɪm] (VT) mutilar, lisiar • **to be ~ed for life** quedar lisiado de por vida

main [meɪn] (ADJ) [*reason, problem, aim, concern*] principal, fundamental; [*gate, entrance*] principal • **that was my ~ reason for doing it** esa fue la razón principal *or* fundamental por (la) que lo hice • **the ~ thing is that no one was hurt** lo principal es que nadie resultó herido • **the ~ thing is not to panic** lo principal es no dejarse llevar por el pánico
(N) **1** (= *pipe*) cañería *f* principal, conducto *m* principal; (= *cable*) cable *m* principal • **gas/water ~** cañería *or* conducto principal del gas/agua • **the ~s** (*Elec*) la red, la red de suministro; (*for gas, water*) la red de suministro • **the water in this tap comes from the ~s** el agua de este grifo viene de la red de suministro • **to turn the gas/water off at the ~s** cerrar la llave principal del gas/agua • **to turn the electricity off at the ~s** apagar la electricidad • **this radio works on batteries or off the ~s** esta radio funciona con pilas o conectada a la red
2 (*liter*) • **the ~** (= *open sea*) la mar océana • **the Spanish Main** el mar Caribe
3 • **in the ~** (= *generally speaking*) por lo general, por regla general, en general; (= *in the majority*) por lo general, en su mayoría, en su mayor parte • **the people she met were, in the ~, wealthier than her** la gente que conoció era, por lo general *or* en su mayoría *or* en su mayor parte, más rica que ella
4 ▹ **might[2]**
(CPD) ▸ **main beam** (*Archit*) viga *f* maestra; (*Aut*) luces *fpl* largas, luz *f* larga ▸ **main clause** (*Gram*) oración *f* principal ▸ **main course** plato *m* principal ▸ **main deck** (*Naut*) cubierta *f* principal ▸ **the main drag*** (*US*) la calle principal ▸ **main line** (*Rail*) línea *f* principal; ▹ **mainline** ▸ **main man*** (*US*) (= *friend*) mejor colega* *m* ▸ **main memory** (*Comput*) memoria *f* central ▸ **main office** (= *headquarters of organization*) sede *f*, oficina *f* central ▸ **main road** carretera *f* principal ▸ **main sheet** (*Naut*) escota *f* mayor ▸ **main street** calle *f* mayor ▸ **the mains supply** el suministro de la red

mainbrace [ˈmeɪnbreɪs] (N) braza *f* de mayor

mainframe [ˈmeɪnfreɪm] (N) (*also* **mainframe computer**) ordenador *m* or computadora *f* central

mainland [ˈmeɪnlənd] (N) tierra *f* firme, continente *m* • **they want to move to the ~** [*islanders*] quieren trasladarse a Inglaterra/Francia *etc*
(CPD) ▸ **mainland Britain** (la isla *f* principal de) Gran Bretaña *f* • **the coast of ~ Britain** la costa de la isla principal de Gran Bretaña

mainline [ˈmeɪnlaɪn] (ADJ) **1** (*Rail*) [*service, station*] principal, interurbano
2 (= *mainstream*) tradicional, al uso
(VT) (*Drugs**) chutarse‡, picarse‡, inyectarse • **to ~ heroin** chutarse *or* picarse heroína‡, meterse un chute *or* pico de heroína‡

m

(VI) (*Drugs**) chutarse‡, inyectarse

mainly ['meɪnlɪ] (ADV) **1** (= *fundamentally*) principalmente, fundamentalmente; (= *for the greater part*) mayormente, principalmente • **they have stayed together ~ because of their children** han seguido juntos principalmente *or* fundamentalmente por sus hijos • **he lives ~ in Paris** vive mayormente *or* principalmente en París • **it was ~ his idea** fue mayormente *or* principalmente idea suya
2 (= *in the majority*) en su mayoría, en su mayor parte • **her customers are ~ women** sus clientes son en su mayoría *or* en su mayor parte mujeres

mainmast ['meɪnmɑːst] (N) palo *m* mayor

mainsail ['meɪnsl] (N) vela *f* mayor

mainspring ['meɪnsprɪŋ] (N) [*of watch*] muelle *m* real; (*fig*) motivo *m* principal, principal resorte *m*

mainstay ['meɪnsteɪ] (N) (*Naut*) estay *m* mayor; (*fig*) sostén *m* principal, pilar *m*

mainstream ['meɪnstriːm] (N) [*of ideology, philosophy, literature*] corriente *f* principal • **his work diverges sharply from the ~ of English fiction** su trabajo se aparta radicalmente de la corriente principal de la novela inglesa • **our policies aim to bring these young people into the ~ of American life** nuestra política tiene como objetivo hacer que estos jóvenes adopten la forma de vida del ciudadano medio americano • **they remain outside the political ~** permanecen fuera de la escena política mayoritaria
(ADJ) [*political party*] mayoritario; [*press, media, culture*] dominante; [*fashion*] de masas; [*education*] convencional • **they remain on the margins of ~ society** siguen estando marginados con respecto al ciudadano medio • **the rise of the right in ~ politics** el ascenso de la derecha dentro de la corriente política dominante • **the mindlessness of much ~ cinema** la estupidez de gran parte de la corriente dominante en el cine
(VT) (*US*) (*Scol*) integrar

maintain [meɪn'teɪn] (VT) **1** (= *keep up*) [+ *attitude, correspondence, order, speed, advantage*] mantener; [+ *silence*] guardar; [+ *war*] sostener, continuar • **the two countries ~ friendly relations** los dos países mantienen relaciones amistosas • **he ~ed his opposition to the plan** se mantuvo contrario al plan
2 (= *support*) [+ *family, dependents*] mantener; [+ *army*] mantener, costear
3 (= *keep in good condition*) [+ *road, building, car, machine*] mantener en buen estado • **the house costs a fortune to ~** el mantenimiento de la casa cuesta un dineral, cuesta un dineral mantener la casa en buen estado
4 (= *have, retain*) [+ *house, property*] poseer, tener • **as well as his house in London he ~s one in New York and one in France** además de su casa en Londres, posee *or* tiene una en Nueva York y otra en Francia
5 (= *claim*) [+ *one's innocence*] mantener, sostener • **he ~ed that the earth was round** mantenía *or* sostenía que la tierra era redonda

maintained school [meɪn'teɪnd,skuːl] (N) (*Brit*) colegio *m* estatal *or* público

maintenance ['meɪntɪnəns] (N) **1** (= *upkeep*) [*of machine, car*] mantenimiento *m*; [*of house, building*] manutención *f*, cuidado *m*
2 (= *money paid to ex-wife and family*) pensión *f* alimenticia
(CPD) ▸ **maintenance agreement** contrato *m* de mantenimiento ▸ **maintenance allowance** pensión *f* alimenticia ▸ **maintenance contract** = **maintenance agreement** ▸ **maintenance costs** gastos *mpl* de mantenimiento ▸ **maintenance crew** personal *m* de servicios ▸ **maintenance grant** (*Univ*) beca *f* ▸ **maintenance order** *orden judicial que obliga al pago de una pensión alimenticia* ▸ **maintenance payments** pago *msing* de la manutención ▸ **maintenance staff** personal *m* del servicio de mantenimiento

Mainz [maɪnts] (N) Maguncia *f*

maisonette [,meɪzə'net] (N) (*esp Brit*) dúplex *m inv*

maître d' [,metrə'diː] (PL: **maîtres d'**), **maître d'hôtel** [,metrədəʊ'tel] (N) (PL: **maîtres d'hôtel**) maître *mf*

maize [meɪz] (N) (*Brit*) maíz *m* • **ear of ~** mazorca *f*, elote *m* (*Mex*), choclo *m* (*And, S. Cone*)
(CPD) ▸ **maize field** maizal *m*

Maj. (ABBR) = **Major**

majestic [mə'dʒestɪk] (ADJ) majestuoso

majestically [mə'dʒestɪkəlɪ] (ADV) majestuosamente

majesty ['mædʒɪstɪ] (N) majestad *f* • **His/Her Majesty** Su Majestad • **Your Majesty** (Vuestra) Majestad

Maj.-Gen. (ABBR) = **Major-General**

major ['meɪdʒə^r] (ADJ) **1** (= *large, important*) [*city, company*] muy importante; [*change, role*] fundamental, muy importante; [*factor*] clave, muy importante, fundamental; [*problem*] serio, grave; [*worry*] enorme; [*breakthrough*] de enorme importancia • **the result was a ~ blow to the government** el resultado fue un duro golpe para el gobierno • **it is a ~ cause of death** causa un enorme número de muertes • **to be a ~ factor in sth** ser un factor clave *or* muy importante *or* fundamental en algo • **of ~ importance** de la mayor importancia • **three ~ issues remained unresolved** quedaron sin resolver tres temas fundamentales *or* tres temas de enorme importancia • **the ~ issues which affect our lives** las principales cuestiones que afectan nuestras vidas, las cuestiones de mayor importancia *or* más importantes que afectan nuestras vidas • **nothing ~ has happened** no ha pasado nada de importancia • **a hysterectomy is a ~ operation** la histerectomía es una operación seria *or* grave • **getting him off to school is a ~ operation** (*hum*) llevarlo al colegio es una operación a gran escala (*hum*) • **this represents a ~ step forward** esto representa un enorme paso hacia delante • **he is recovering after ~ surgery** se está recuperando de una operación seria *or* grave
2 (= *principal*) [*cities, political parties*] más importante • **Brazil's ~ cities** las ciudades más importantes de Brasil • **our ~ concern is the welfare of the hostages** nuestra principal preocupación es el bienestar de los rehenes
3 (*Mus*) [*chord, key*] mayor • **C ~** do mayor
4 (*Brit*) (*Scol*†) • **Jones Major** Jones el mayor
(N) **1** (*Mil*) comandante *m*, mayor *m* (*LAm*)
2 (*US*) (*Univ*) **a** (= *subject*) asignatura *f* principal
b (= *student*) • **he's a Spanish ~** estudia español como asignatura principal
3 (*US*) (*Baseball*) • **the ~s** las grandes ligas
(VI) • **to ~ in sth** (*US*) (*Univ*) especializarse en algo
(CPD) ▸ **major general** (*Mil*) general *m* de división ▸ **major league** (*US*) liga *f* principal; ▹ **major-league** ▸ **major suit** (*Bridge*) palo *m* mayor

Majorca [mə'jɔːkə] (N) Mallorca *f*

Majorcan [mə'jɔːkən] (ADJ) mallorquín
(N) **1** (= *person*) mallorquín/ina *m/f*
2 (*Ling*) mallorquín *m*

majordomo [,meɪdʒə'dəʊməʊ] (N) mayordomo *m*

majorette [,meɪdʒə'ret] (N) majorette *f*, batonista *f*

majority [mə'dʒɒrɪtɪ] (N) **1** mayoría *f* • **a two-thirds ~** una mayoría de las dos terceras partes • **they won by a ~** ganaron por mayoría • **in the ~ of cases** en la mayoría *or* la mayor parte de los casos • **such people are in a ~** la mayoría de la gente es así, predomina la gente así • **to be in a ~ of three** formar parte de una mayoría de tres • **the vast ~** la inmensa mayoría • **the great ~ of lecturers** la mayoría *or* la mayor parte de los conferenciantes
2 (*Jur*) • **to attain one's ~** llegar a la mayoría de edad
(CPD) ▸ **majority decision** • **by a ~ decision** por decisión mayoritaria *or* de la mayoría ▸ **majority interest** interés *m* mayoritario ▸ **majority opinion** (*US*) opinión *f* mayoritaria ▸ **majority rule** gobierno *m* mayoritario, gobierno *m* en mayoría ▸ **majority (share)holding** accionariado *m* mayoritario ▸ **majority verdict** • **by a ~ verdict** por fallo *or* veredicto mayoritario ▸ **majority vote** • **by a ~ vote** por la mayoría de los votos

> **MAJORITY, MOST**
>
> **Singular or plural verb?**
>
> *When* **mayoría** *is the subject of a verb, the verb can be in the singular or the plural, depending on the context.*
>
> ▹ *When translating* **majority** *rather than* **most**, *put the verb in the singular if* **majority** *is seen as a unit rather than a collection of individuals:*
>
> **The socialist majority voted against the four amendments**
> La mayoría socialista votó en contra de las cuatro enmiendas
>
> ▹ *If* **la mayoría** *is seen as a collection of individuals, particularly when it is followed by* **de** *+ plural noun, the plural form of the verb is more common than the singular, though both are possible:*
>
> **The majority still wear this uniform**
> La mayoría siguen vistiendo *or* sigue vistiendo este uniforme
> **Most scientists believe it is a mistake**
> La mayoría de los científicos creen *or* cree que se trata de un error
>
> ▹ *The plural form must be used when* **la mayoría** *or* **la mayoría de** *+ plural noun is followed by* **ser** *or* **estar** *+ plural complement:*
>
> **Most of them are men**
> La mayoría son hombres
> **Most of the dead were students**
> La mayoría de los muertos eran estudiantes
> **Most of the children were black**
> La mayoría de los niños eran negros
>
> *For further uses and examples, see* **majority, most**

major-league [,meɪdʒə'liːg] (CPD) (*US*) ▸ **major-league baseball** béisbol *m* de la liga principal

majorly ['meɪdʒəlɪ] (ADV) (= *extremely*) extremamente, sumamente

make [meɪk]

TRANSITIVE VERB
INTRANSITIVE VERB
NOUN
PHRASAL VERBS

(PT, PP: **made**)

When **make** *is part of a set combination, eg* **make an attempt, make a bow, make a case, make sure**, *look up the other word.*

TRANSITIVE VERB

1 (*= create, prepare*) [*+ fire, bed, tea, will, remark, plan, suggestion*] hacer; [*+ dress*] hacer, confeccionar; [*+ shelter*] construir; [*+ meal*] hacer, preparar; [*+ record*] grabar; [*+ film*] rodar; (*= manufacture*) [*+ tool, machine*] fabricar, hacer • **I'm going to ~ a cake** voy a hacer un pastel • **I ~ my bed every morning** me hago la cama cada mañana • **he made it himself** lo hizo él mismo • **God made man** Dios hizo al hombre • **don't ~ a noise** no hagas ruido • **"made in Spain"** [*+ tool, machine*] "fabricado en España"; [*+ dress*] "confeccionado en España"; [*+ nougat, chocolate*] "elaborado en España" • **he's as cunning as they make 'em*** es de lo más astuto que hay • **this car isn't made to carry eight people** este coche no está pensado para ocho personas • **they don't ~ songs like that any more** ya no componen canciones como las de antes • **they were made for each other** estaban hechos el uno para el otro • **her shoes weren't made for walking** llevaba unos zapatos poco adecuados para caminar • **we had the curtains made to measure** nos hicieron las cortinas a medida • **it's made of gold** es de oro, está hecho de oro; ▹ **show**

2 (*= carry out*) [*+ journey, effort*] hacer; [*+ speech*] pronunciar; [*+ payment*] efectuar; [*+ error*] cometer • **I'd like to ~ a phone call** quisiera hacer una llamada • **he made an agreement to pay off the arrears** se comprometió a pagar los atrasos

3 (*= earn*) ganar • **how much do you ~?** ¿cuánto ganas? • **he ~s £350 a week** gana 350 libras a la semana • **the deal made him £500** ganó 500 libras con el negocio, el negocio le reportó 500 libras • **the film made millions** la película recaudó millones

4 (*= reach, achieve*) [*+ place*] llegar a • **will we ~ Paris before lunch?** ¿llegaremos a París antes de la hora de comer? • **Lara made a hundred** (*Cricket*) Lara hizo *or* se anotó 100 carreras • **the novel made the bestseller list** la novela entró en las listas de libros más vendidos • **we made it just in time** llegamos justo a tiempo • **can you ~ it by 10?** ¿puedes llegar a las 10? • **sorry, I can't ~ it** lo siento, no puedo *or* no me va bien • **do you think he'll ~ (it to) university?** ¿crees que conseguirá ir a la universidad? • **he made (it into) the first team** consiguió entrar en el primer equipo • **you've got the talent to ~ it** con tu talento llegarás muy lejos • **to ~ it with sb*** (*sexually*) hacérselo con algn* • **to ~ land** (*Naut*) llegar a tierra • **to ~ port** (*Naut*) tomar puerto • IDIOM: • **he's got it made*** tiene el éxito asegurado

5 (*= say, agree*) • **let's ~ it 9 o'clock** pongamos las 9 • **another beer, please, no, ~ that two** otra cerveza por favor, no, que sean dos

6 (*= cause to succeed*) • **this film made her** esta película la consagró • **he was made for life** se aseguró un porvenir brillante • IDIOM: • **to ~ or break sth/sb**: • **this deal will ~ or break him** con este negocio o fracasa o se asegura el éxito • **sex can ~ or break a relationship** el sexo es determinante en una relación, el sexo puede afianzar una relación o hacer que fracase

7 (*= constitute*) • **this log ~s a good seat** este tronco va muy bien de asiento • **he'll ~ somebody a good husband** va a ser *or* hará un buen marido para algn • **it'll ~ a (nice) change not to have to cook every day** lo de no tener que cocinar cada día estará muy bien, ¡qué descanso, no tener que cocinar cada día! • **they ~ a lovely couple** hacen muy buena pareja • **he'll ~ a good footballer** será buen futbolista • **it ~s pleasant reading** es una lectura amena • **it still doesn't ~ a set** todavía no completa un juego entero • **it made a nice surprise** fue una sorpresa agradable

8 (*= equal*) • **two and two ~ four** dos y dos son cuatro • **this one ~s 20** con este son *or* hacen 20 • **how much does that ~ (altogether)?** ¿a cuánto sube (en total)? • **8 pints ~ a gallon** 8 pintas hacen *or* son un galón

9 (*= calculate*) calcular • **what do you ~ the total?** ¿cuánto calculas que es el total? • **how many do you ~ it?** ¿cuántos calculas que hay? • **I ~ the total 17** calculo que hay 17 en total • **what time do you ~ it** • **what do you ~ the time?** ¿qué hora tienes? • **I ~ it 6 o'clock** yo tengo las 6

10 (*Cards*) [*+ trick*] ganar, hacer; (*Bridge*) [*+ contract*] cumplir

11 (*in set structures*) **to make sb sth** (*= cause to be*) • **to ~ sb king** hacer rey a algn • **he made her his wife** la hizo su esposa • **they've made Owen secretary** han nombrado secretario a Owen • **he made her a star** hizo de ella una estrella

to make sb/sth (*+ adjective/past participle*) • **to ~ sb happy** hacer feliz a algn • **to ~ sb angry** poner furioso a algn • **to ~ o.s. heard** hacerse oír • **the noise made concentration difficult** *or* **made it difficult to concentrate** con ese ruido era difícil concentrarse • **why ~ things difficult for yourself?** ¿por qué te complicas la vida?; ▹ **ill, sick, unhappy**

to make sth/sb into sth convertir algo/a algn en algo • **we made the guest room into a study** convertimos la habitación de los invitados en estudio • **they have made him into a cult figure** lo han convertido en un ídolo • **the fibres are made into rope** con las fibras se hace cuerda

to make sb do sth (*= cause to do sth*) hacer a algn hacer algo; (*= force to do sth*) hacer a algn hacer algo, obligar a algn a hacer algo • **to ~ sb laugh/cry** hacer reír/llorar a algn • **now look what you've made me do!** ¡mira lo que me has hecho hacer! • **what made you say that?** ¿cómo se te ocurrió decir eso?, ¿por qué dijiste eso? • **what ~s you do it?** ¿qué es lo que te lleva a hacerlo? • **it ~s you think, doesn't it?** da que pensar ¿no? • **he made me apologize to the teacher** me hizo pedir perdón *or* me obligó a pedir perdón al profesor • **you can't ~ me (do it)** no puedes obligarme (a hacerlo) • **I was made to wait for an hour** me hicieron esperar una hora

to make o.s. do sth obligarse a hacer algo • **I have to ~ myself (do it)** tengo que obligarme (a hacerlo), tengo que hacer un esfuerzo (por hacerlo) • **she made herself look him in the eye** tuvo que obligarse a mirarle a los ojos

to make sth do, make do with sth arreglárselas *or* apañárselas con algo • **I'll ~ do with what I've got** me las arreglaré con lo que tengo

12 (*in set expressions*) **to make good** [*+ promise*] cumplir; [*+ accusation*] hacer bueno, probar; [*+ claim*] justificar; [*+ loss*] compensar; [*+ damage*] reparar; (*= pay*) pagar; ▹ **make**

to make sth of sth (*= understand*) • **I don't know what to ~ of it** no sé qué pensar • **what do you ~ of Anna?** ¿qué piensas de Anna?, ¿qué te parece Anna? • **what do you ~ of this?** ¿qué te parece esto? • **I can't ~ anything of this letter** no entiendo nada de lo que pone esta carta, no saco nada en claro de esta carta; (*= give importance to*) • **I think you're making rather too much of what I said** creo que le estás dando demasiada importancia a lo que dije; ▹ **issue**

INTRANSITIVE VERB

(*in set expressions*) • **to ~ after sb** perseguir a algn, correr tras algn • **he made as if to** (*+ infin*) hizo como si (*+ subjun*), hizo ademán de (*+ infin*) • **he made as if to strike me** hizo como si me fuera a pegar, hizo ademán de pegarme • **to ~ good** [*ex-criminal*] rehabilitar, reformar • **he was making like he didn't have any money** (*US**) hacía como si no tuviera dinero • IDIOM: • **it's ~ or break time for the England team** al equipo inglés le ha llegado la hora de la verdad

NOUN

(*= brand*) marca *f* • **what ~ of car was it?** ¿qué marca de coche era? • **they are our own ~** son de nuestra propia marca • **they have rifles of Belgian ~** tienen fusiles de fabricación belga • IDIOM: • **to be on the ~*** (*for money*) estar intentando sacar tajada*; (*for power*) ser muy ambicioso; (*for sex*) ir a la caza*, ir de ligoteo*

▸ **make away** (VI + ADV) = make off

▸ **make away with** (VI + PREP) (*= murder*) • **to ~ away with sb** eliminar a algn • **to ~ away with o.s.** (*euph†*) quitarse la vida, suicidarse

▸ **make for** (VI + PREP) **1** (*= go towards*) [*+ place*] dirigirse hacia *or* a • **he made for the door** se dirigió hacia la puerta • **police think he may be making for Sweden** la policía cree que puede estar de camino a Suecia
2 (*= attack*) • **to ~ for sb** atacar a algn, abalanzarse sobre algn
3 (*= contribute to*) contribuir a; (*= lead to*) conducir a • **it ~s for an easy life** contribuye a hacer la vida más fácil • **it doesn't ~ for good customer relations** no conduce a una buena relación con los clientes

▸ **make off** (VI + ADV) irse rápidamente, largarse* • **to ~ off with sth** llevarse algo, escaparse con algo, largarse con algo*

▸ **make out** (VT + ADV) **1** (*= write out*) [*+ cheque*] hacer, extender; [*+ receipt, list*] hacer; [*+ document*] redactar; (*= fill in*) [*+ form*] llenar • **to ~ a cheque out to somebody** hacer *or* extender un cheque a favor de algn • **the cheque should be made out to Pérez** el cheque debe extenderse a nombre de Pérez
2 (*= see, discern*) [*+ distant object*] distinguir, divisar
3 (*= decipher*) [*+ writing*] descifrar
4 (*= understand*) entender, comprender • **I can't ~ her out at all** no la entiendo *or* comprendo en absoluto • **can you ~ out what they're saying?** ¿entiendes lo que dicen? • **I can't ~ it out at all** no consigo entenderlo
5 (*= claim, imply*) • **you ~ him out to be better than he is** lo haces parecer mejor de lo que es en realidad • **he's not as rich as people ~ out** no es tan rico como dice la gente • **the situation is not so bad as you ~ it out to be** la situación no es tan grave como la pintas • **the play ~s him out to be a fool** en la obra aparece como una idiota • **to ~ out that** dar a entender que • **they're making out it was my fault** están dando a entender que fue

m

culpa mía • **all the time he made out he was working** estuvo todo el tiempo haciéndonos creer que estaba trabajando • **she made out it was a wrong number** hizo como que se había equivocado de número
(VI + ADV)* (= *get on*) (*with person*) llevarse • **how do you ~ out with your neighbours?** ¿cómo te llevas con tus vecinos? • **how did you ~ out at the audition?** ¿qué tal te fue en la audición? • **how are you making out on your pension?** ¿cómo te las arreglas con la pensión? • **to ~ out with sb** (*US**) (*sexually*) hacérselo con algn*

▸ **make over** (VT + ADV) **1** (= *assign*) ceder, traspasar (to a) • **he had made over the farm to his son** le había cedido *or* traspasado la granja a su hijo
2 (= *revamp*) [+ *organization*] modernizar, poner al día • **to ~ o.s. over** cambiar de imagen

▸ **make up** (VT + ADV) **1** (= *invent*) inventar(se) • **he made up the whole story** (se) inventó toda la historia • **you're making it up!** ¡te lo estás inventando!
2 (= *put together, prepare*) [+ *list*] hacer, preparar; [+ *parcel, bed*] hacer; [+ *medicine*] preparar; [+ *collection*] formar, reunir; [+ *sweater, dress*] montar y coser • **I'll ~ up a bed for him on the sofa** le haré una cama en el sofá • **the chemist's where I went to get the prescription made up** la farmacia a la que fui para que me preparasen la medicina • **I made the papers up into bundles** hice paquetes con los periódicos
3 (= *settle*) • **to ~ up one's differences (with sb)** resolver sus diferencias (con algn) • **to ~ it up with sb** hacer las paces con algn, reconciliarse con algn • **they'd made up their quarrel** se habían reconciliado
4 (= *complete*) completar • **I paid £200 and my parents made up the difference** pagué 200 libras y mis padres pusieron la diferencia • **we need someone to ~ up the numbers** necesitamos a alguien para completar el grupo
5 (= *decide*) • **to ~ up one's mind** decidirse
6 (= *compensate for, replace*) [+ *loss*] compensar; [+ *deficit*] cubrir • **if I take time off I have to ~ up the hours later** si me tomo tiempo libre después tengo que recuperar las horas • **I'd like to ~ it up to him for spoiling his birthday** me gustaría compensarle por haberle estropeado el cumpleaños • **he tried to ~ it up to her by buying her a bunch of flowers** intentó hacerse perdonar comprándole un ramo de flores • **to ~ up (lost) time** recuperar el tiempo perdido
7 (= *constitute*) componer • **women ~ up 13% of the police force** las mujeres componen el 13% del cuerpo de policía • **it is made up of 6 parts** lo componen 6 partes, está compuesto de 6 partes • **the group was made up of parents, teachers and doctors** el grupo lo componían *or* integraban padres, profesores y médicos • **the blood is made up of red and white cells** la sangre se compone de glóbulos rojos y glóbulos blancos
8 (*with cosmetics*) [+ *actor*] maquillar • **to ~ o.s. up** maquillarse, pintarse
9 [+ *fire*] (*with coal*) echar carbón a; (*with wood*) echar madera *or* leña a
(VI + ADV) **1** (*after quarrelling*) hacer las paces, reconciliarse
2 (= *apply cosmetics*) maquillarse, pintarse

▸ **make up for** (VI + PREP) (= *compensate for*) compensar • **her willingness to learn more than made up for her lack of experience** sus ganas de aprender compensaban con creces su falta de experiencia • **we hope this ~s up for the inconvenience caused** esperamos que esto compense los inconvenientes que podamos haberles causado • **to ~ up for lost time** recuperar el tiempo perdido

▸ **make up on** (VI + PREP) alcanzar, coger

▸ **make up to*** (VI + PREP) • **to ~ up to sb** (procurar) congraciarse con algn, (procurar) ganarse el favor de algn

make-believe [ˈmeɪkbɪˌliːv] (ADJ) fingido, simulado; [*world etc*] de ensueño, de fantasía • **make-believe play/games** juegos *mpl* de fantasía
(N) • **don't worry, it's just make-believe** no te preocupes, no es de verdad • **a land** *or* **world of make-believe** un mundo de ensueño *or* fantasía • **to play at make-believe** jugar a ser personajes imaginarios
(VI) fingir
(VT) • **to make-believe that …** fingir que …, hacer que …

makeover [ˈmeɪkəʊvəʳ] (N) **1** (*lit*) (*by beautician*) sesión *f* de maquillaje y peluquería
2 (*fig*) lavado *m* de cara

maker [ˈmeɪkəʳ] (N) **1** (= *craftsman*) creador(a) *m/f*, artífice *mf*
2 (= *manufacturer*) fabricante *mf*
3 (*Rel*) • **Maker** Creador *m*, Hacedor *m* • **she has gone to meet her Maker** ha pasado a mejor vida, Dios la ha llamado a su seno • **prepare to meet your Maker** prepárate a morir

makeshift [ˈmeɪkʃɪft] (ADJ) (= *improvised*) improvisado; (= *provisional*) provisional
(N) arreglo *m* provisional

make-up [ˈmeɪkʌp] (N) **1** (= *cosmetics*) maquillaje *m*, pintura *f* • **she touched up her make-up** se retocó el maquillaje • **she was wearing hardly any make-up** llevaba muy poco maquillaje, iba casi sin maquillar • **to put on one's make-up** maquillarse, pintarse
2 (= *composition*) composición *f*; (= *structure*) estructura *f*; (= *character*) carácter *m*, modo *m* de ser • **the racial make-up of a country** la composición racial de un país
3 [*of clothes*] confección *f*
4 (*Typ*) compaginación *f*, ajuste *m*
(CPD) ▸ **make-up artist** maquillador(a) *m/f* ▸ **make-up bag** neceser *m* del maquillaje ▸ **make-up girl** maquilladora *f* ▸ **make-up remover** desmaquillador *m*, desmaquillante *m*

makeweight [ˈmeɪkweɪt] (N) **1** (= *weight, object*) contrapeso *m*
2 (*fig*) (= *person*) suplente *mf*, sustituto/a *m/f*; (*pej*) parche *m*, elemento *m* de relleno

making [ˈmeɪkɪŋ] (N) **1** (= *production*) fabricación *f*; (= *preparation*) preparación *f*; (= *cutting and assembling*) [*of clothes*] confección *f* • **I wasn't involved in the ~ of the film** no colaboré en el rodaje de la película • **the building has been five years in the ~** llevan cinco años construyendo el edificio • **it's a disaster in the ~** es un desastre en potencia • **it's history in the ~** esto pasará a la historia • **the mistake was not of my ~** no soy yo el responsable del error • **she was caught in a trap of her own ~** había caído en su propia trampa • **it was the ~ of him** fue lo que lo consagró
2 makings elementos *mpl* (necesarios), ingredientes *mpl* • **a chain of events that had all the ~s of a Hollywood epic** una cadena de acontecimientos que tenía todos los elementos *or* ingredientes de una epopeya de Hollywood • **I have the ~s of a meal in the fridge** con lo que tengo en la nevera puedo hacer una comida • **he has the ~s of an actor** tiene madera de actor

Malachi [ˈmæləˌkaɪ] (N) Malaquías *m*
malachite [ˈmæləˌkaɪt] (N) malaquita *f*
maladjusted [ˈmæləˈdʒʌstɪd] (ADJ) (*Psych*) inadaptado
maladjustment [ˈmæləˈdʒʌstmənt] (N) (*Psych*) inadaptación *f*, desajuste *m*
maladministration [ˈmælədˌmɪnɪsˈtreɪʃən] (N) mala administración *f*
maladroit [ˈmæləˈdrɔɪt] (ADJ) torpe
maladroitly [ˈmæləˈdrɔɪtlɪ] (ADV) torpemente
maladroitness [ˈmæləˈdrɔɪtnɪs] (N) torpeza *f*
malady [ˈmælədɪ] (N) mal *m*, enfermedad *f*
Malagasy [ˈmæləgɑːzɪ] (ADJ) madagascarí
(N) madagascarí *mf*
malaise [mæˈleɪz] (N) malestar *m*
malapropism [ˈmæləprɒpɪzəm] (N) lapsus *m inv* linguae, equivocación *f* de palabras
malaria [məˈlɛərɪə] (N) malaria *f*, paludismo *m*
(CPD) ▸ **malaria control** lucha *f* contra la malaria
malarial [məˈlɛərɪəl] (ADJ) palúdico
malarkey* [məˈlɑːkɪ] (N) (= *messing about*) payasadas* *fpl*; (= *nonsense*) majaderías* *fpl*; (= *goings-on*) tejemanejes* *mpl*
Malawi [məˈlɑːwɪ] (N) Malawi *m*, Malaui *m*
Malawian [məˈlɑːwɪən] (ADJ) malawiano, malauiano
(N) malawiano/a *m/f*, malauiano/a *m/f*
Malay [məˈleɪ] (ADJ) malayo
(N) **1** (= *person*) malayo/a *m/f*
2 (*Ling*) malayo *m*
Malaya [məˈleɪə] (N) (*Hist*) Malaya *f*
Malayan [məˈleɪən] (ADJ) malayo
(N) malayo/a *m/f*
Malaysia [məˈleɪzɪə] (N) Malaisia *f*
Malaysian [məˈleɪzɪən] (ADJ) malaisio
(N) malaisio/a *m/f*
malcontent [ˈmælkənˈtent] (ADJ) malcontento, desafecto, revoltoso
(N) malcontento/a *m/f*, desafecto/a *m/f*, revoltoso/a *m/f*
Maldives [ˈmɔːldaɪvz], **Maldive Islands** [ˌmɔːldaɪvˈaɪləndz] (NPL) (islas *fpl*) Maldivas *fpl*
male [meɪl] (N) (= *animal, plant*) macho *m*; (= *person*) varón *m* • **white ~s aged 35 to 40** varones de raza blanca de edades comprendidas entre los 35 y 40 años • **I don't need a ~ to support me** no necesito un hombre para que me mantenga
(ADJ) **1** [*rat, spider, plant*] macho; [*baby, child*] varón; [*friend, worker, colleague*] del sexo masculino; [*population, hormone, sex, attitude, behaviour*] masculino; [*voice*] de hombre, masculino • **please indicate whether you are ~ or female** por favor indique si es hombre *or* mujer
2 (*Tech*) [*plug*] macho
(CPD) ▸ **male chauvinism** machismo *m* ▸ **male chauvinist** machista *m* ▸ **the male member** (*euph*) el miembro viril, el miembro masculino ▸ **male menopause** menopausia *f* masculina, andropausia *f* ▸ **male model** modelo *m* del sexo masculino ▸ **male nurse** enfermero *m* ▸ **male prostitute** prostituto *m* ▸ **male voice choir** coro *m* masculino *or* de hombres; ▹ **supremacist**
malediction [ˌmælɪˈdɪkʃən] (N) maldición *f*
male-dominated [ˈmeɪlˈdɒmɪneɪtɪd] (ADJ) dominado por los hombres
malefactor [ˈmælɪfæktəʳ] (N) (*frm*) malhechor(a) *m/f*
maleness [ˈmeɪlnɪs] (N) **1** (= *state of being male*) masculinidad *f*
2 (= *masculinity, virility*) masculinidad *f*, virilidad *f*

malevolence [mə'levələns] N malevolencia *f*

malevolent [mə'levələnt] ADJ malévolo

malevolently [mə'levələntlɪ] ADV con malevolencia

malfeasance [mæl'fi:zəns] N (*Jur*) infracción *f*

malformation ['mælfɔ:'meɪʃən] N malformación *f*, deformidad *f*

malformed [,mæl'fɔ:md] ADJ malformado, deforme

malfunction [mæl'fʌŋkʃən] N [*of machine*] fallo *m*, mal funcionamiento *m*
VI funcionar mal

malice ['mælɪs] N **1** (= *grudge*) rencor *m*; (= *badness*) malicia *f* • **to bear sb ~** guardar rencor a algn • **I bear him no ~** no le guardo rencor • **out of ~** por malicia • **with ~ toward none** sin mala intención hacia nadie
2 (*Jur*) intención *f* delictuosa, dolo *m*
• **~ aforethought** premeditación *f*

malicious [mə'lɪʃəs] ADJ [*person, remark*] malicioso
CPD ▸ **malicious damage** (*Jur*) daños *mpl* intencionados ▸ **malicious libel** difamación *f* intencionada, calumnia *f* intencionada

maliciously [mə'lɪʃəslɪ] ADV maliciosamente, con malicia

malign [mə'laɪn] ADJ maligno, malévolo
VT [+ *person, reputation*] calumniar, difamar • **you ~ me** eso no es justo

malignancy [mə'lɪgnənsɪ] N malignidad *f*

malignant [mə'lɪgnənt] ADJ (= *evil*) malvado; (*Med*) maligno

malignity [mə'lɪgnɪtɪ] N malignidad *f*

malinger [mə'lɪŋgə^r] VI fingirse enfermo, hacer la encorvada*

malingerer [mə'lɪŋgərə^r] N enfermo/a *m/f* fingido/a

mall [mɔ:l], (*US*) [mæl] N **1** (= *avenue*) alameda *f*, paseo *m*
2 (= *pedestrian street*) calle *f* peatonal
3 (*also* **shopping mall**) centro *m* comercial
CPD ▸ **mall rat*** (*US*) *joven que se pasa el día vagando por los centros comerciales*

mallard ['mæləd] N (PL: **mallard(s)**) ánade *m* real

malleability [,mælɪə'bɪlɪtɪ] N maleabilidad *f*

malleable ['mælɪəbl] ADJ maleable, dúctil

mallet ['mælɪt] N (*Carpentry, Sport*) mazo *m*

mallow ['mæləʊ] N malva *f*

malnourished [,mæl'nʌrɪʃt] ADJ desnutrido

malnutrition ['mælnjʊ'trɪʃən] N desnutrición *f*

malodorous [mæ'ləʊdərəs] ADJ maloliente, hediondo

malpractice ['mæl'præktɪs] N (= *negligence*) negligencia *f* profesional; (= *wrongdoing*) práctica *f* abusiva
CPD ▸ **malpractice suit** (*US*) (*Jur*) juicio *m* por negligencia profesional

malt [mɔ:lt] N malta *f*
VT [+ *barley*] maltear; [+ *drink etc*] preparar con malta
CPD ▸ **malt extract** extracto *m* de malta ▸ **malt liquor** (*US*) cerveza *f* ▸ **malt vinegar** vinagre *m* de malta ▸ **malt whisky** whisky *m* de malta

Malta ['mɔ:ltə] N Malta *f*

malted ['mɔ:ltɪd] ADJ malteado
CPD ▸ **malted barley** cebada *f* malteada, malta *f* de cebada ▸ **malted milk** leche *f* malteada

Maltese ['mɔ:l'ti:z] ADJ maltés
N (PL: **Maltese**) **1** (= *person*) maltés/esa *m/f*
2 (*Ling*) maltés *m*
CPD ▸ **Maltese Cross** cruz *f* de Malta

malthusianism [mæl'θju:zɪə,nɪzəm] N malt(h)usianismo *m*

malting barley [,mɔ:ltɪŋ'bɑ:lɪ] N cebada *f* para maltear

maltreat [mæl'tri:t] VT maltratar, tratar mal

maltreatment [mæl'tri:tmənt] N maltrato *m*, maltratamiento *m*, malos tratos *mpl*

Malvinas [mæl'vi:nəs] N • **the ~** las Malvinas

malware ['mælwεə^r] N (*Comput*) malware *m*, software *m* malicioso

mam* [mæm] N (*Brit*) (*dialect*) mamá *f*

mama†* [mə'mɑ:] N mamá *f*

mamba ['mæmbə] N (*Zool*) mamba *f*

mambo ['mæmbəʊ] N mambo *m*

mamma* ['mɑ:mə] N (*esp US*) mamá *f*

mammal ['mæməl] N mamífero *m*

mammalian [mæ'meɪlɪən] ADJ mamífero

mammaries ['mæmərɪz] NPL (*hum*) pechos *mpl*

mammary ['mæmərɪ] ADJ mamario
CPD ▸ **mammary gland** mama *f*, glándula *f* mamaria

mammogram ['mæməgræm] N mamografía *f*

mammography [mæ'mɒgrəfɪ] N mamografía *f*

Mammon ['mæmən] N Mammón

mammoplasty ['mæməʊ,plæstɪ] N mamoplastia *f*

mammoth ['mæməθ] N (*Zool*) mamut *m*
ADJ descomunal, gigante

mammy ['mæmɪ] N **1*** mami *f*, mamaíta *f*, mamacita *f* (*LAm*)
2 (*US*) (= *black nurse*) nodriza *f* negra

man [mæn] N (PL: **men**) **1** (= *not woman*) hombre *m*; (= *husband*) marido *m*; (= *boyfriend*) novio *m*; (= *servant*) criado *m*; (= *workman*) obrero *m*; (= *ordinary soldier*) soldado *m*; (= *ordinary sailor*) marinero *m* • **he's been a different man since he got married** es otro hombre desde que se casó • **the man who does the garden** el señor que hace el jardín • **when a man needs a wash** cuando uno necesita lavarse • **her man is in the army** (*husband*) su marido está en el ejército; (*boyfriend*) su novio está en el ejército • **officers and men** (= *soldiers*) oficiales y soldados; (= *sailors*) oficiales y marineros • **he's not the man to do it** él no es la persona adecuada para hacerlo • **I've lived here man and boy** vivo aquí desde pequeño • **he's not the man for the job** no es el más indicado para esa tarea • **man of God** religioso *m*, clérigo *m* • **good man!** ¡bravo!, ¡muy bien! • **my good man**† buen hombre, amigo mío • **all good men and true** (*liter*) todos los que merecen llamarse hombres • **man of letters** literato *m* • **it's got to be a local man** tiene que ser uno de aquí • **to make a man of sb** hacer un hombre de algn • **the army will make a man out of him** el ejército le hará un hombre • **man of means** hombre *m* acaudalado • **the man in the moon** el rostro de (mujer en) la luna • **to feel (like) a new man** sentirse como nuevo • **look here, old man**† mira, amigo • **my old man*** el viejo* • **the man on the Clapham omnibus** el hombre de la calle • **our man in Washington** (= *agent*) nuestro agente en Washington; (= *representative*) nuestro representante en Washington; (= *ambassador*) nuestro embajador en Washington • **man of parts** hombre *m* de talento • **man of property** hombre *m* acaudalado • **man of straw** (= *person of no substance*) monigote *m*, títere *m*; (*esp US*) (= *front man*) hombre *m* de paja, testaferro *m* • **the man in the street** el hombre de la calle • **the strong man of the government** el hombre fuerte del gobierno • **that man Jones** aquel Jones • **man to man** de hombre a hombre • **he's a man about town** es un gran vividor • **man and wife** marido y mujer • **to live as man and wife** vivir como casados *or* en matrimonio • **a man of the world** un hombre de mundo • **a young man** un joven • **her young man** su novio • IDIOMS: • **this will separate** *or* **sort the men from the boys** con esto se verá quiénes son hombres y quiénes no • **to be man enough to do sth** ser lo bastante hombre *or* tener valor suficiente como para hacer algo • **to reach man's estate** (*frm*) llegar a la edad viril; ▹ **best, cloth, grand**
2 (= *humanity in general*) (*also* **Man**) el hombre • PROVERB: • **man proposes, God disposes** el hombre propone y Dios dispone
3 (= *individual, person*) persona *f* • **what else could a man do?** ¿es que se podía hacer otra cosa? • **men say that ...** se dice que ... • **any man** cualquiera, cualquier hombre • **no man** ninguno, nadie • **as one man** como un solo hombre • **one man one vote** un voto para cada uno • **they agreed to a man** no hubo voz en contra • **they're communists to a man** todos sin excepción son comunistas • **then I'm your man** entonces soy la persona que estás buscando
4 (= *type*) • **he's a six pints a night man** es de los que se beben seis pintas en una noche • **he's a Celtic man** es del Celtic • **I'm not a drinking man** yo no bebo • **he's a family man** (= *with family*) es padre de familia; (= *home-loving*) es muy casero • **I'm not a football man** no soy aficionado al fútbol, no me gusta mucho el fútbol • **he's a man's man** es un hombre estimado entre otros hombres • **he's his own man** es un hombre muy fiel a sí mismo • **I'm a whisky man myself** yo prefiero el whisky
5 (*Chess*) pieza *f*; (*Draughts*) ficha *f*
6* (*excl*) • **hey man!** ¡oye, tronco!* • **you can't do that, man** hombre, no puedes hacer eso • **man, was I startled!** ¡vaya susto que me dio!, ¡qué susto me pegué!
VT [+ *ship*] tripular; [+ *fortress, watchtower*] guarnecer; [+ *guns*] servir; [+ *pumps*] acudir a, hacer funcionar • **the gun is manned by four soldiers** cuatro soldados manejan el cañón • **the telephone is manned all day** el teléfono está atendido todo el día; ▹ **manned**
CPD ▸ **man day** (*Comm, Ind*) día-hombre *m* ▸ **man flu*** (*pej*) resfriado *m* ▸ **man Friday** criado *m* fiel ▸ **men's doubles** (*Tennis*) dobles *mpl* masculinos ▸ **men's final** (*Sport*) final *f* masculina ▸ **men's room** (*esp US*) lavabo *m* de caballeros

-man [-'mæn] SUFFIX (= *-person*) • **a four-man crew** un equipo de cuatro personas • **a two-man tent** una tienda para dos personas

Man. ABBR (*in Canada*) = **Manitoba**

manacle ['mænəkl] N **1** manilla *f*
2 manacles esposas *fpl*, grillos *mpl*
VT esposar, poner esposas a • **they were ~d together** iban esposados (juntos) • **his hands were ~d** llevaba esposas en las muñecas

manage ['mænɪdʒ] VT **1** (= *direct*) [+ *firm, economy, shop*] dirigir, administrar; [+ *employees, team*] dirigir; [+ *time, property, money*] administrar; [+ *household*] llevar; (*Comput*) [+ *system, network*] gestionar • **he's been managing my affairs for years** lleva años encargándose de mis asuntos, hace años que lleva mis asuntos • **~d currency** moneda *f* controlada *or* dirigida • **~d**

m

economy economía *f* planificada *or* dirigida • **~d fund** fondo *m* controlado *or* dirigido
2 (= *cope with, control*) [+ *situation*] manejar; [+ *suitcases, packages*] poder con; [+ *animal*] dominar • **you ~d the situation very well** manejaste muy bien la situación • **can you ~ the cases?** ¿puedes con las maletas? • **he has no idea how to ~ children** no tiene ni idea de cómo manejar *or* controlar a los niños • **he's clever at managing people** se le da bien manejar a la gente
3 (= *achieve*) • **they've ~d only one win this season** solo han conseguido una victoria esta temporada • **can you ~ two more in the car?** ¿te caben dos más en el coche? • **can you ~ eight o'clock?** ¿puedes estar para las ocho? • **I can't ~ Friday** el viernes no puedo • **to ~ to do sth** lograr hacer algo, conseguir hacer algo • **how did you ~ not to spill it?** ¿cómo lograste *or* conseguiste no derramarlo? • **he ~d not to get his feet wet** logró *or* consiguió no mojarse los pies • **he ~d to annoy everybody** consiguió irritar a todo el mundo • **£20 is all I can ~** 20 libras es todo lo que puedo dar *or* pagar • **can you ~ another cup?** ¿quieres otra taza? • **I couldn't ~ another mouthful** no podría comer ni un bocado más • **£20 is the most I can ~** 20 libras es todo lo que puedo dar *or* pagar
4 (*pej*) (= *manipulate*) [+ *news, election*] manipular
VI **1** (= *cope*) (*with situation*) arreglárselas; (*financially*) arreglarse, arreglárselas • **can you ~?** (= *deal with situation*) ¿puedes arreglártelas?; (= *carry sth*) ¿puedes con eso? • **thanks, I can ~** gracias, yo puedo • **she ~s on her pension/on £60 a week** se (las) arregla con la pensión/con 60 libras a la semana • **to ~ without sth/sb**: • **"do you need the car?" — "I can ~ without it"** —¿necesitas el coche? —me (las) puedo arreglar *or* apañar sin él • **I don't know how we'd have ~d without her** no sé cómo nos (las) hubiéramos arreglado *or* apañado sin ella
2 (= *direct, administrate*) dirigir

manageable [ˈmænɪdʒəbl] ADJ
1 (= *controllable*) [*size, number, level, rate*] razonable; [*situation*] controlable; [*problem*] que se puede solucionar; [*vehicle*] manejable, fácil de maniobrar; [*hair*] dócil • **she reduces complex issues to ~ proportions** reduce cuestiones muy complejas a algo de proporciones manejables
2 (= *achievable*) [*task*] que se puede realizar • **this cycle ride is quite ~, even for children** este recorrido en bicicleta es fácil de realizar, incluso para los niños
3 (= *docile*) [*person, child, animal*] dócil

management [ˈmænɪdʒmənt] N
1 (= *process*) [*of firm*] dirección *f*, administración *f*, gestión *f*
2 (= *people*) directivos *mpl*; (= *managing body*) [*of firm*] dirección *f*, gerencia *f*; (*Theat*) empresa *f* • **"under new management"** "bajo nueva dirección" • **~ and workers** empresarios y trabajadores • **almost always ~ is at fault** casi siempre lo que falla es la gestión
3 (= *handling*) [*of situation*] manejo *m*
4 (*Univ*) (*also* **management studies**) administración *f* de empresas
CPD ▸ **management accounting** contabilidad *f* de gestión ▸ **management audit** evaluación *f* administrativa *or* de gestión ▸ **management buyout** adquisición *f* de una empresa por sus ejecutivos ▸ **management chart** organigrama *m* de gestión ▸ **management committee** comité *m* directivo ▸ **management company** sociedad *f* gestora ▸ **management consultancy** consultoría *f* de gestión ▸ **management consultant** consultor(a) *m/f* en gestión de empresas ▸ **management fee** honorarios *mpl* de dirección ▸ **management review** revisión *f* de gestión (de la gerencia) ▸ **management services** servicios *mpl* de administración ▸ **management skills** dotes *mpl* de gestión ▸ **management style** estilo *m* de gestión ▸ **management team** [*of company*] equipo *m* de dirección • **the firm's ~ team** la dirección de la empresa ▸ **management trainee** ejecutivo/a *m/f* en formación ▸ **management training** formación *f* de mandos

manager [ˈmænɪdʒəʳ] N [*of firm, bank, hotel*] director(a) *m/f*, gerente *mf*; [*of estate*] administrador(a) *m/f*; [*of football team*] director(a) *m/f* técnico/a; [*of restaurant, shop*] encargado/a *m/f*; [*of farm*] capataz(a) *m/f*, mayoral(a) *m/f*; [*of actor, singer*] representante *mf*, mánager *mf*; [*of boxer*] mánager *mf* • **she's a good ~** es buena administradora; ▹ **sale**

manageress [ˌmænɪdʒəˈres] N [*of restaurant, shop*] encargada *f*

managerial [ˌmænəˈdʒɪərɪəl] ADJ directivo, de gestión • **the ~ class** el empresariado, la patronal • **at ~ level** a nivel directivo • **~ responsibilities** obligaciones *fpl* directivas • **~ staff** personal *m* directivo *or* de gerencia • **~ structure** estructura *f* administrativa • **~ style** estilo *m* de gestión

managing [ˈmænɪdʒɪŋ] CPD ▸ **managing director** (*Brit*) director(a) *m/f* gerente ▸ **managing editor** director(a) *m/f* editorial ▸ **managing partner** socio *mf* gerente

man-at-arms [ˈmænətˈɑːmz] N (PL: **men-at-arms**) hombre *m* de armas

manatee [ˌmænəˈtiː] N manatí *m*

Manchuria [mænˈtʃʊərɪə] N Manchuria *f*

Manchurian [mænˈtʃʊərɪən] ADJ manchuriano
N manchuriano/a *m/f*

Mancunian [mænˈkjuːnɪən] ADJ de Manchester
N (= *native*) nativo/a *m/f* de Manchester; (= *inhabitant*) habitante *mf* de Manchester

mandarin [ˈmændərɪn] N **1** (= *person*) (*lit, fig*) mandarín *m*
2 (*also* **mandarin orange**) mandarina *f*
3 • **Mandarin** (*Ling*) mandarín *m*

mandate [ˈmændeɪt] N **1** (= *authority*) mandato *m* • **the UN troops have no ~ to intervene in the fighting** las tropas de la ONU no tienen mandato para intervenir en el conflicto • **he does not have a ~ to rule this country** carece de autoridad para gobernar este país
2 (= *country*) territorio *m* bajo mandato
VT **1** (= *authorize*) [+ *person*] encomendar, encargar; [+ *elections*] autorizar
2 [+ *country*] asignar bajo mandato (**to** a)
3 (*US*) (= *make mandatory*) exigir

mandated [ˈmændeɪtɪd] ADJ **1** [*territory*] bajo mandato
2 [*delegate*] encargado

mandatory [ˈmændətərɪ] ADJ
1 (= *compulsory*) obligatorio • **each article contained the ~ quota of rude jokes** (*iro*) cada artículo contenía la cuota obligatoria de chistes verdes • **it is ~ that you complete levels one and two** es obligatorio que usted realice los niveles uno y dos, tiene usted que realizar los niveles uno y dos obligatoriamente
2 (*Jur*) [*sentence, penalty, fine*] preceptivo, obligatorio

Mandelbrot set [ˈmændəlˌbrɒtˌset] N (*Math*) conjunto *m* de Mandelbrot

mandible [ˈmændɪbl] N mandíbula *f*

mandolin, mandoline [ˈmændəlɪn] N mandolina *f*, bandolina *f* (*LAm*)

mandrake [ˈmændreɪk] N mandrágora *f*

mandrill [ˈmændrɪl] N mandril *m*

mane [meɪn] N [*of lion, person*] melena *f*; [*of horse*] crin *f*, crines *fpl*

man-eater [ˈmænˌiːtəʳ] N **1** (= *animal*) fiera *f* devoradora de hombres
2* (= *woman*) devoradora *f* de hombres

man-eating [ˈmænˌiːtɪŋ] ADJ antropófago

maneuver *etc* [məˈnuːvəʳ] (*US*) = **manoeuvre** *etc*

manful [ˈmænfʊl] ADJ valiente, resuelto

manfully [ˈmænfəlɪ] ADV valientemente, resueltamente

manga [ˈmæŋgə] N manga *m*

manganese [ˌmæŋgəˈniːz] N (*Chem*) manganeso *m*
CPD ▸ **manganese oxide** óxido *m* de manganeso ▸ **manganese steel** acero *m* al manganeso

mange [meɪndʒ] N sarna *f*

mangel [ˈmæŋgl], **mangel-wurzel** [ˈmæŋglˈwɜːzl] N remolacha *f* forrajera

manger [ˈmeɪndʒəʳ] N pesebre *m*

mangetout [ˈmɒnʒˈtuː] N (*also* **mangetout pea**) tirabeque *m*, arveja *f* china

mangle[1] [ˈmæŋgl] N (= *device*) escurridor *m*
VT (= *wring*) pasar por el escurridor

mangle[2] [ˈmæŋgl] VT (= *crush*) aplastar; [+ *text etc*] mutilar, estropear

mangled [ˈmæŋgld] ADJ **1** [*body*] mutilado
2 • **the ~ wreckage** [*of car*] los restos destrozados (del coche)

mango [ˈmæŋgəʊ] N (PL: **mangoes**) (= *fruit, tree*) mango *m*

mangold [ˈmæŋgəld], **mangold-wurzel** [ˈmæŋgəldˈwɜːzl] N remolacha *f* forrajera

mangrove [ˈmæŋgrəʊv] N mangle *m*
CPD ▸ **mangrove swamp** manglar *m*

mangy [ˈmeɪndʒɪ] ADJ (COMPAR: **mangier**, SUPERL: **mangiest**) roñoso, sarnoso

manhandle [ˈmænˌhændl] VT **1** (*esp Brit*) (= *move by hand*) mover a base de brazos • **we ~d the dinghy out of the shed** sacamos la barca del cobertizo a base de brazos
2 (*fig*) maltratar • **the police admitted manhandling the prisoners** la policía admitió haber maltratado a los presos • **the men were ~d into the back of the van** metieron a los hombres de muy malos modos en la trasera de la furgoneta

manhole [ˈmænhəʊl] N boca *f* de alcantarilla, registro *m* de alcantarilla
CPD ▸ **manhole cover** tapa *f* de registro, tapa *f* de alcantarilla

manhood [ˈmænhʊd] N **1** (= *age of majority*) mayoría *f* de edad, madurez *f* • **to reach ~** alcanzar la mayoría de edad, llegar a la madurez
2 (= *manliness*) hombría *f*, virilidad *f*
3 (*frm*) (= *men*) hombres *mpl* • **English ~** • **England's ~** (*liter*) todos los ingleses, todos los hombres de Inglaterra
4 (*euph*) (= *penis*) miembro *m* viril

man-hour [ˈmænaʊəʳ] N hora *f* hombre • **1000 man-hours** 1000 horas hombre

manhunt [ˈmænhʌnt] N búsqueda *f* (*de delincuente, desaparecido*)

mania [ˈmeɪnɪə] N manía *f* • **to have a ~ for (doing) sth** tener la manía de hacer algo

maniac [ˈmeɪnɪæk] ADJ maníaco
N **1** maníaco/a *m/f* • **he drives like a ~** conduce como un loco
2 (*fig*) (= *enthusiast*) fanático/a *m/f*, maniático/a *m/f* • **these sports ~s** estos

fanáticos *or* maniáticos del deporte

maniacal [mə'naɪəkəl] ADJ maníaco

maniacally [mə'naɪəkəlɪ] ADV [*work, laugh*] (*one person*) como (un) loco/(una) loca; (*more than one person*) como locos

manic ['mænɪk] ADJ **1** (= *insane*) [*person, behaviour*] maníaco; [*smile, laughter, stare*] de maníaco
2 (= *frenetic*) [*activity, energy*] frenético
CPD ▸ **manic depression** maniacodepresión *f* • **she suffers from ~ depression** sufre maniacodepresión, es maniacodepresiva ▸ **manic depressive** maniacodepresivo/a *m/f*

manically ['mænɪklɪ] ADV [*work, laugh, search*] (*one person*) como (un) loco/(una) loca; (*more than one person*) como locos • **he was pacing ~ up and down** se paseaba arriba y abajo como si estuviera loco • **he is ~ tidy** es un maniático del orden

Manichaean, Manichean [,mænɪ'ki:ən] ADJ maniqueo
N maniqueo/a *m/f*

Manichaeism, Manicheism [,mænɪ'ki:ɪzəm] N maniqueísmo *m*

manicure ['mænɪkjʊəʳ] N manicura *f*
VT [+ *person*] hacer la manicura a; [+ *nails*] limpiar, arreglar
CPD ▸ **manicure case, manicure set** estuche *m* de manicura

manicured ['mænɪkjʊəd] ADJ **1** [*nails, hands*] muy cuidado
2 [*lawn, garden*] muy cuidado

manicurist ['mænɪkjʊərɪst] N manicuro/a *m/f*

manifest ['mænɪfest] ADJ manifiesto, patente • **to make sth ~** poner algo de manifiesto
VT manifestar • **to ~ itself** manifestarse
N (*Naut, Comm*) manifiesto *m*

manifestation [,mænɪfes'teɪʃən] N manifestación *f*

manifestly ['mænɪfestlɪ] ADV evidentemente

manifesto [,mænɪ'festəʊ] N (PL: **manifesto(e)s**) manifiesto *m*

manifold ['mænɪfəʊld] ADJ (= *numerous*) múltiple; (= *varied*) diverso
N (*Aut*) colector *m* de escape

manikin ['mænɪkɪn] N = **mannikin**

Manila [mə'nɪlə] N Manila *f*

manila, manilla [mə'nɪlə] ADJ [*envelope, paper*] manila

manioc ['mænɪɒk] N mandioca *f*, yuca *f*

manipulate [mə'nɪpjʊleɪt] VT **1** [+ *tool, machine, vehicle*] manipular, manejar
2 (*fig*) [+ *facts, figures*] manipular; [+ *public opinion, person*] manipular

manipulation [mə,nɪpjʊ'leɪʃən] N **1** [*of tool, machine, vehicle*] manipulación *f*, manejo *m*
2 (*fig*) [*of facts, figures, public opinion, person*] manipulación *f*

manipulative [mə'nɪpjʊlətɪv] ADJ (*fig*) [*person, behaviour*] manipulador

manipulator [mə'nɪpjʊleɪtəʳ] N manipulador(a) *m/f*

mankind [mæn'kaɪnd] N humanidad *f*, género *m* humano

manky* ['mæŋkɪ] ADJ (*Brit*) asqueroso

manlike ['mænlaɪk] ADJ **1** (= *manly*) varonil
2 (= *like man*) parecido al hombre

manliness ['mænlɪnɪs] N masculinidad *f*, hombría *f*, virilidad *f*

manly ['mænlɪ] (**manlier, manliest**) ADJ **1** (= *masculine*) [*person, physique*] varonil, viril; [*quality, pursuit*] masculino, varonil • **it wasn't ~ to talk about one's emotions** hablar de los propios sentimientos no era cosa de hombres
2 (= *courageous*) valiente

man-made ['mæn'meɪd] ADJ [*material*] sintético, artificial; [*lake, island, environment*] artificial; [*gas, chemical*] producido por el hombre • **man-made fibres** fibras *fpl* sintéticas • **man-made disasters such as Chernobyl** desastres provocados por el hombre como Chernobyl

manna ['mænə] N maná *m* • IDIOM: • **~ from heaven** maná *m* caído del cielo

manned [mænd] ADJ tripulado • **a fully ~ ship** un buque con toda su tripulación *or* dotación
CPD ▸ **manned space flight** vuelo *m* espacial tripulado

mannequin ['mænɪkɪn] N **1** (= *dressmaker's dummy*) maniquí *m*
2 (= *fashion model*) modelo *f*, maniquí *f*
CPD ▸ **mannequin parade** desfile *m* de modelos

manner ['mænəʳ] N **1** (= *mode, way*) manera *f*, modo *m* • **after** *or* **in this ~** de esta manera • **after** *or* **in the ~ of Van Gogh** a la manera *or* al estilo de Van Gogh • **a princess (as) to the ~ born** una princesa nata • **in like ~** de la misma manera • **~ of payment** modo *m* de pago, forma *f* de pago • **in a ~ of speaking** (= *so to speak*) por así decirlo, como si dijéramos; (= *up to a point*) hasta cierto punto, en cierto modo • **it's a ~ of speaking** es solo una manera *or* forma de hablar • **in such a ~ that …** de tal manera que …
2 (= *behaviour etc*) forma *f* de ser, comportamiento *m* • **I don't like his ~** no me gusta su forma de ser • **there's something odd about his ~** tiene un aire algo raro • **he had the ~ of an old man** tenía aire de viejo
3 (= *class, type*) clase *f* • **what ~ of man is he?** ¿qué clase *or* tipo de hombre es? • **all ~ of** toda clase *or* suerte de • **by no ~ of means** de ningún modo • **no ~ of doubt** sin ningún género de duda
4 manners: **a** [*of person*] modales *mpl*, educación *fsing* • **bad ~s** falta *f* de educación, malos modos *mpl* • **to have bad ~s** ser maleducado • **it's bad ~s to yawn** es de mala educación bostezar • **to forget one's ~s** perder la compostura • **aren't you forgetting your ~s?** (*to child*) no seas maleducado • **good ~s** educación *f*, buenos modales *mpl* • **good ~s demand that …** la educación exige que … • **it's good ~s to say "please"** se dice "por favor" • **he's got no ~s** es un maleducado • **road ~s** comportamiento *m* en la carretera • **to teach sb ~s** enseñar a algn a comportarse
b [*of society*] costumbres *fpl* • **a novel of ~s** una novela costumbrista *or* de costumbres • PROVERB: • **~s maketh (the) man** la conducta forma al hombre

mannered ['mænəd] ADJ **1** (= *affected*) [*style*] amanerado
2 (= *camp*) cursi

-mannered ['mænəd] ADJ (*ending in compounds*) de modales …; ▸ **bad-mannered** *etc*

mannerism ['mænərɪzəm] N **1** (= *gesture etc*) gesto *m*
2 (*Art, Literat*) (*also* **Mannerism**) manierismo *m*; (*pej*) amaneramiento *m*

mannerist ['mænərɪst] ADJ manierista
N manierista *mf*

mannerliness ['mænəlɪnɪs] N (buena) educación *f*, crianza *f*, cortesía *f*

mannerly ['mænəlɪ] ADJ educado, formal

mannikin ['mænɪkɪn] N **1** (= *dressmaker's dummy*) maniquí *m*
2 (= *fashion model*) modelo *f*, maniquí *f*
3 (*frm*) (= *dwarf*) enano *m*

manning levels ['mænɪŋlevlz] NPL niveles *mpl* de personal

mannish ['mænɪʃ] ADJ hombruno

manoeuvrability, maneuverability (*US*) [mə,nu:vrə'bɪlɪtɪ] N maniobrabilidad *f*

manoeuvrable, maneuverable (*US*) [mə'nu:vrəbl] ADJ manejable

manoeuvre, maneuver (*US*) [mə'nu:vəʳ] N **1** (*Mil*) maniobra *f* • **to be on ~s** estar de maniobras
2 (*fig*) (= *clever plan*) maniobra *f*, estratagema *f* • **this leaves us little room for ~** esto apenas nos deja margen de maniobra
VT (*gen*) maniobrar • **to ~ a gun into position** colocar un cañón en posición • **I was ~d into it** me embaucaron para que lo hiciera • **to ~ sb into doing sth** manipular a algn para que haga algo
VI maniobrar

manoeuvring, maneuvering (*US*) [mə'nu:vrɪŋ] N el maniobrar • **political ~s** maniobras *fpl* políticas

man-of-war ['mænəv'wɔ:ʳ] N (PL: **men-of-war**) buque *m* de guerra

manometer [mə'nɒmɪtəʳ] N manómetro *m*

manor ['mænəʳ] N **1** (*feudal*) señorío *m*; (*modern*) finca *f*
2 (*Brit*) (*Police**) distrito *m*, barrio *m*
CPD ▸ **manor house** casa *f* solariega, casa *f* señorial

manorial [mə'nɔ:rɪəl] ADJ señorial

manpower ['mænpaʊəʳ] N mano *f* de obra; (*Mil*) soldados *mpl*
CPD ▸ **manpower planning** planificación *f* de recursos humanos *or* mano de obra

manqué ['mɔ:ŋkeɪ] ADJ • **a novelist ~** un novelista frustrado

manse [mæns] N (*esp Brit*) casa *f* del pastor (protestante)

manservant ['mæn,sɜ:vənt] N (PL: **manservants** *or* **menservants** ['men,sɜ:vənts]) criado *m*

mansion ['mænʃən] N mansión *f*; [*of ancient family*] casa *f* solariega
CPD ▸ **Mansion House** (*Brit*) *residencia del alcalde de Londres*

man-sized ['mænsaɪzd] ADJ **1** (*lit*) de tamaño de hombre
2 (*fig*) bien grande, grandote

manslaughter ['mæn,slɔ:təʳ] N homicidio *m* involuntario

mantelpiece ['mæntlpi:s] N repisa *f* (de chimenea)

mantelshelf† ['mæntlʃelf] N (PL: **mantelshelves** ['mæntlʃelvz]) = **mantelpiece**

mantilla [mæn'tɪlə] N mantilla *f*, velo *m*

mantis ['mæntɪs] N (PL: **mantises** *or* **mantes** ['mænti:z]) • **praying ~** mantis *f inv* religiosa

mantle ['mæntl] N **1** (= *layer*) capa *f*; (= *blanket*) manto *m* • **a ~ of snow** una capa de nieve
2 (= *gas mantle*) manguito *m* incandescente, camisa *f* incandescente
3†† (= *cloak*) manto *m*
4 • **he accepted the ~ of leader** asumió el liderazgo, aceptó el cargo de líder • **the ~ of responsibility** la plena responsabilidad
VT (*liter*) cubrir (**in** de), envolver (**in** en)

mantlepiece ['mæntlpi:s] N = **mantelpiece**

mantleshelf† ['mæntlʃelf] N (PL: **mantleshelves** ['mæntlʃelvz]) = **mantelpiece**

man-to-man ['mæntə'mæn] ADJ de hombre a hombre
ADV de hombre a hombre

mantra ['mæntrə] N mantra *m*

mantrap ['mæntræp] N cepo *m*

manual ['mænjʊəl] ADJ manual • **~ labour** *or* (*US*) **labor** trabajo *m* manual • **~ training** enseñanza *f* de artes y oficios • **~ worker**

trabajador(a) *m/f* manual
N **1** (= *book*) manual *m*
2 (*Mus*) teclado *m*

manually [ˈmænjʊəlɪ] ADV manualmente, a mano

manufacture [ˌmænjʊˈfæktʃəʳ] N **1** (= *act*) fabricación *f*
2 (= *manufactured item*) producto *m* manufacturado
VT **1** (*Ind*) fabricar • **~d goods** productos *mpl* manufacturados
2 (*fig*) fabricar, inventar

manufacturer [ˌmænjʊˈfæktʃərəʳ] N fabricante *mf*

manufacturing [ˌmænjʊˈfæktʃərɪŋ] N fabricación *f*
CPD [*town, city, sector*] industrial, manufacturero/a ▸ **manufacturing base** base *f* industrial ▸ **manufacturing capacity** capacidad *f* de fabricación ▸ **manufacturing costs** costes *mpl* de fabricación ▸ **manufacturing industries** industrias *fpl* manufactureras ▸ **manufacturing plant** planta *f* de fabricación ▸ **manufacturing process** proceso *m* de fabricación

manure [məˈnjʊəʳ] N estiércol *m*, abono *m*
VT estercolar, abonar
CPD ▸ **manure heap** estercolero *m*

manuscript [ˈmænjʊskrɪpt] N manuscrito *m*; (= *original of book, article*) original *m*
ADJ manuscrito

Manx [mæŋks] ADJ de la isla de Man
N **1** (*Ling*) lengua *f* de la isla de Man
2 • **the ~** (= *people*) los nativos de la isla de Man
CPD ▸ **Manx cat** *gato rabón de pelo corto*

Manxman [ˈmæŋksmən] N (PL: **Manxmen**) nativo *m* de la isla de Man

Manxwoman [ˈmæŋkswʊmən] N (PL: **Manxwomen**) nativa *f* de la isla de Man

many [ˈmenɪ] ADJ muchos/as • **~ people** mucha gente, muchas personas • **in ~ cases** en muchos casos • **a good** *or* **a great ~ houses** muchas *or* (*LAm*) bastantes casas • **however ~ books you have** por muchos libros que tengas • **not ~ people** poca gente • **so ~** tantos/as • **so ~ flies** tantas moscas • **ever so ~ people** la mar de gente, tantísimas personas • **~ a time I've seen him act** • **~'s the time I've seen him act** muchas veces lo he visto actuar • **too ~** demasiados/as • **too ~ difficulties** demasiadas dificultades
PRON muchos/as • **~ of them came** muchos (de ellos) vinieron • **he has as ~ as I have** tiene tantos como yo • **he has three times as ~ as I have** tiene tres veces más que yo • **there were as ~ as 100 at the meeting** asistieron a la reunión hasta cien personas • **as ~ again** otros tantos • **and as ~ more** y otros tantos • **how ~ are there?** ¿cuántos hay? • **how ~ there are!** ¡cuántos hay! • **however ~ you have** por muchos que tengas • **not ~** pocos • **not ~ came** vinieron pocos
N • **the ~** la mayoría

many-coloured, many-colored (*US*) [ˈmenɪˈkʌləd] ADJ multicolor

many-sided [ˈmenɪˈsaɪdɪd] ADJ **1** [*figure*] multilátero
2 (*fig*) [*talent, personality*] multifacético, polifacético; [*problem*] complicado

Maoism [ˈmaʊɪzəm] N maoísmo *m*

Maoist [ˈmaʊɪst] ADJ maoísta
N maoísta *mf*

Maori [ˈmaʊrɪ] ADJ maorí
N **1** (= *person*) maorí *mf*
2 (*Ling*) maorí *m*

Mao Tse-tung [ˈmaʊtseɪˈtʊŋ], **Mao Zedong** [ˈmaʊtzeɪˈdʊŋ] N Mao Zedong

map [mæp] N [*of town*] plano *m*; [*of world, country*] mapa *m*; (= *chart*) carta *f* • IDIOMS: • **this will put us on the map** esto nos dará a conocer • **it's right off the map** está en el quinto infierno
VT • **to map an area** levantar un mapa de una zona
CPD ▸ **map reference** coordenadas *fpl*
▸ **map onto** VT + PREP • **to map sth onto sth** transferir algo a algo
▸ **map out** VT + ADV **1** (*lit*) indicar en un mapa
2 (= *organize*) [+ *strategy, future*] planificar, planear; [+ *schedule*] elaborar, confeccionar; [+ *plan*] trazar

maple [ˈmeɪpl] N (*also* **maple tree**) arce *m*
CPD ▸ **maple leaf** hoja *f* de arce ▸ **maple sugar** azúcar *m* de arce ▸ **maple syrup** jarabe *m* de arce

mapmaker [ˈmæpˌmeɪkəʳ] N cartógrafo/a *m/f*

mapmaking [ˈmæpˌmeɪkɪŋ], **mapping** [ˈmæpɪŋ] N cartografía *f*

mar [mɑːʳ] VT estropear, echar a perder • **to mar sb's enjoyment** aguar la fiesta a algn

Mar ABBR (= **March**) mar.

marabou [ˈmærəbuː] N marabú *m*

maracas [məˈrækəs] NPL maracas *fpl*

maraschino [ˌmærəsˈkiːnəʊ] N marrasquino *m*
CPD ▸ **maraschino cherries** guindas *fpl* en conserva de marrasquino

marathon [ˈmærəθən] N (*Sport*) maratón *m*
ADJ (*fig*) maratoniano
CPD ▸ **marathon runner** corredor(a) *m/f* de maratón

maraud [məˈrɔːd] VI merodear

marauder [məˈrɔːdəʳ] N merodeador(a) *m/f*, intruso/a *m/f*

marauding [məˈrɔːdɪŋ] ADJ merodeador, intruso
N merodeo *m*

marble [ˈmɑːbl] N **1** (= *material*) mármol *m*
2 (= *work in marble*) obra *f* en mármol
3 (= *glass ball*) canica *f*, bolita *f* (*And, S. Cone*), metra *f* (*Ven*) • **to play ~s** jugar a las canicas • IDIOM: • **to lose one's ~s*** perder la chaveta*
CPD marmóreo, de mármol ▸ **marble quarry** cantera *f* de mármol ▸ **marble staircase** escalera *f* de mármol

marbled [ˈmɑːbld] ADJ **1** (= *covered with marble*) [*floor, pillar, room*] revestido de mármol
2 (= *patterned, streaked*) [*paper, tabletop, work surface*] marmolado; [*meat*] con vetas de grasa; [*soap*] con vetas • **~ effect** efecto *m* marmolado

March [mɑːtʃ] N marzo *m*; ▸ **July**

march[1] [mɑːtʃ] N (*Mil, Mus*) marcha *f*; (*fig*) (= *long walk*) marcha *f*, caminata *f* • **forced ~** marcha *f* forzada • **an army on the ~** un ejército en marcha • **we were on the ~ to the capital** marchábamos hacia *or* sobre la capital • **it's a day's ~ from here** está a un día de marcha desde aquí; (*fig*) eso queda lejísimos; ▹ **quick, steal**
VT **1** [+ *soldiers*] hacer marchar, llevar • **I was ~ed into an office** me llevaron a un despacho, me hicieron entrar en un despacho
2 [+ *distance*] recorrer (marchando)
VI **1** (*Mil*) marchar • **forward ~!** de frente ¡ar! • **quick ~!** al trote ¡ar! • **to ~ past** desfilar • **to ~ past sb** desfilar ante algn
2 (= *demonstrate*) manifestarse, hacer una manifestación
3 (*fig*) • **to ~ into a room** entrar resueltamente en un cuarto • **to ~ up to sb** abordar a algn
CPD ▸ **march past** (*Mil*) desfile *m*
▸ **march in** VI + ADV entrar (resueltamente *etc*)
▸ **march off** VT + ADV • **to ~ sb off** llevarse a algn
VI + ADV irse (resueltamente *etc*)
▸ **march on** VI + PREP marchar sobre
VI + ADV seguir marchando
▸ **march out** VI + ADV salir (airado, resueltamente *etc*)

march[2] [mɑːtʃ] N (*Hist*) marca *f* • **the Spanish March** la Marca Hispánica • **the Welsh ~es** la marca galesa

marcher [ˈmɑːtʃəʳ] N (*on demonstration*) marchista *mf*, manifestante *mf*

marching [ˈmɑːtʃɪŋ] ADJ [*song*] de marcha
CPD ▸ **marching orders** (*Mil*) orden *fsing* de ponerse en marcha • IDIOMS: • **to get one's ~ orders*** ser despedido • **to give sb his ~ orders*** despedir a algn, poner a algn en la calle*

marchioness [ˈmɑːʃənɪs] N marquesa *f*

Mardi Gras [ˌmɑːdɪˈgrɑː] N martes *m* de Carnaval

mare [mɛəʳ] N yegua *f*
CPD ▸ **mare's nest** (*fig*) parto *m* de los montes

marg* [mɑːdʒ] N (*Brit*) = **margarine**

Margaret [ˈmɑːgərɪt] N Margarita

margarine [ˌmɑːdʒəˈriːn] N margarina *f*

margarita [ˌmɑːgəˈriːtə] N (= *drink*) margarita *f*

Marge [mɑːdʒ] N *familiar form of* **Margaret, Marjory**

marge* [mɑːdʒ] N (*Brit*) = **margarine**

margin [ˈmɑːdʒɪn] N **1** (*on page*) margen *m* • **to write sth in the ~** escribir algo al margen
2 (*fig*) margen *m* • **~ of error** margen *m* de error • **~ of safety** margen *m* de seguridad • **to win by a wide/narrow ~** vencer por un amplio/estrecho margen • **they live on the ~(s) of society** viven al margen *or* marginados de la sociedad
3 (*Comm*) (*also* **profit margin, margin of profit**) margen *m* de beneficios

marginal [ˈmɑːdʒɪnl] ADJ **1** (= *very small*) [*benefit, improvement, difference, increase*] mínimo, insignificante; [*role*] marginal, menor • **to be of ~ importance** *or* **significance** tener una importancia menor
2 (= *peripheral*) [*issue*] menor; [*character, public figure*] marginal, al margen • **these points are ~ to the issue of sovereignty** estos puntos son tangenciales respecto a la cuestión de la soberanía • **they are made to feel ~ to the rest of society** se les hace sentirse al margen de la sociedad
3 (*Brit*) (*Parl*) [*seat*] obtenido con escasa mayoría • **~ constituency** *distrito electoral en la que un determinado partido ha ganado con escasa mayoría*
4 (*Econ*) [*cost, utility, productivity*] marginal • **~ tax rate** tasa *f* impositiva marginal
5 (*Agr*) [*land*] poco rentable
N (*Brit*) (*Parl*) (*also* **marginal seat**) *escaño obtenido por escasa mayoría*; ▹ MARGINAL SEAT; (*also* **marginal constituency**) *distrito electoral en el que un determinado partido ha ganado con escasa mayoría*

marginalization [ˌmɑːdʒɪnəlaɪˈzeɪʃən] N marginalización *f*

marginalize [ˈmɑːdʒɪnəlaɪz] VT marginar

marginally [ˈmɑːdʒɪnəlɪ] ADV ligeramente • **sales were ~ better in November** las ventas fueron ligeramente mejores en noviembre • **wholemeal loaves are only ~ more expensive than white ones** las barras de pan integral son solo ligeramente más caras que las de pan blanco • **they were only ~ affected by the war** la guerra apenas los afectó

MARGINAL SEAT
En el Reino Unido se llama **marginal seat** o **marginal constituency** al escaño (y al distrito electoral correspondiente) que se gana por escaso margen, con lo cual en las siguientes elecciones hay muchas posibilidades de que pueda ganarlo a su vez la oposición. Debido a esto, si dicho escaño queda vacante por fallecimiento o dimisión de un parlamentario y se convocan elecciones parciales con carácter excepcional para cubrirlo (**by-election**), el resultado de las mismas será tomado por los medios de comunicación como un indicador de la popularidad del gobierno. Por el contrario, el escaño que un partido suele ganar por amplia mayoría, debido a la homogeneidad en la tendencia política de los electores, se conoce como **safe seat**.
▷ **BY-ELECTION**

marguerita [ˌmɑːgəˈriːtə] N = margarita
marguerite [ˌmɑːgəˈriːt] N (*Bot*) margarita *f*
Maria [məˈriːə] N María
Marian [ˈmɛərɪən] ADJ mariano
mariculture [ˈmærɪˌkʌltʃəʳ] N maricultura *f*
Marie Antoinette [məˈriːæntwɑːˈnet] N María Antonieta
marigold [ˈmærɪgəʊld] N (*Bot*) maravilla *f*
marijuana, marihuana [ˌmærɪˈhwɑːnə] N marihuana *f*, mariguana *f*
marimba [məˈrɪmbə] N marimba *f*
marina [məˈriːnə] N puerto *m* deportivo
marinade [ˌmærɪˈneɪd] N adobo *m*
VT adobar
VI estar en adobo
marinate [ˈmærɪneɪt] VT adobar
VI estar en adobo
marine [məˈriːn] N **1** (*Mil*) (= *person*) infante *m* de marina • **the Marines** (*Brit*) la infantería de marina; (*US*) los marines • IDIOM: • **tell that to the ~s!**†* ¡a otro perro con ese hueso!*
2 (= *fleet*) marina *f* • **the merchant** *or* **mercantile ~** la marina mercante
ADJ **1** (= *sea*) [*creature, plant, pollution*] marino
2 (= *maritime*) [*law, warfare*] marítimo
CPD ▸ **marine biologist** biólogo/a *m/f* marino/a ▸ **marine biology** biología *f* marina ▸ **Marine Corps** (*US*) Infantería *f* de Marina ▸ **marine engineer** ingeniero/a *m/f* naval ▸ **marine engineering** ingeniería *f* naval ▸ **marine insurance** seguro *m* marítimo ▸ **marine life** vida *f* marina, flora y fauna *f* marina ▸ **marine science** ciencia *f* marina ▸ **marine scientist** científico/a *m/f* marino/a
mariner [ˈmærɪnəʳ] N marinero *m*, marino *m*
Mariolatry [ˌmɛərɪˈɒlətrɪ] N mariolatría *f*
Mariology [ˌmɛərɪˈɒlədʒɪ] N mariología *f*
marionette [ˌmærɪəˈnet] N títere *m*, marioneta *f*
marital [ˈmærɪtl] ADJ [*home, bliss*] conyugal; [*problems*] matrimonial, conyugal • **the ~ bed** el lecho conyugal
CPD ▸ **marital counselling** orientación *f* sobre problemas matrimoniales ▸ **marital rape** violación *f* dentro del matrimonio ▸ **marital status** estado *m* civil
maritime [ˈmærɪtaɪm] ADJ marítimo
CPD ▸ **maritime law** derecho *m* marítimo
marjoram [ˈmɑːdʒərəm] N mejorana *f*, orégano *m*
Mark [mɑːk] N Marcos • **~ Antony** Marco Antonio
mark[1] [mɑːk] N (= *currency*) marco *m*
mark[2] [mɑːk] N **1** (= *stain, spot etc*) mancha *f* • **the ~s of violence** las señales de violencia • **he left the ring without a ~ on his body** salió del cuadrilátero sin llevar señal alguna en el cuerpo
2 (= *written symbol on paper etc*) señal *f*, marca *f*; (*instead of signature*) signo *m*, cruz *f*; (*fig*) (= *imprint, trace*) huella *f* • **to make one's ~** (*lit*) firmar con una cruz; (*fig*) dejar huella, distinguirse • IDIOM: • **to make/leave one's ~ on sth** dejar huella en algo • **he has certainly made his ~ on British politics** no cabe duda de que ha dejado huella en la política británica
3 (= *indication*) señal *f*; (= *proof*) prueba *f* • **as a ~ of my disapproval** en señal de mi desaprobación • **as a ~ of our gratitude** en señal de nuestro agradecimiento • **it's the ~ of a gentleman** es señal de un caballero • **it bears the ~ of genius** lleva la marca de un genio
4 (*in exam*) nota *f*, calificación *f* • **52 ~s** 52 puntos, 52 por cien • **to get high ~s in French** sacar buena nota en francés • **to get no ~s at all as a cook** (*fig*) ser un desastre como cocinero • **there are no ~s for guessing** (*fig*) las simples conjeturas no merecen punto alguno; ▷ **full, top[1]**
5 (= *target*) blanco *m* • **to hit the ~** (*lit*) alcanzar el objetivo, acertar; (*fig*) dar en el clavo • **to be wide of the ~** (*lit*) errar el tiro; (*fig*) estar lejos de la verdad • IDIOMS: • **he's way off the ~** no acierta ni con mucho • **he's on the ~** ha dado en el blanco, está en lo cierto
6 (*Sport*) (= *line*) raya *f* • **to be quick/slow off the ~** ser rápido/lente al salir; (*fig*) ser muy vivo/parado • **on your ~s, get set, go!** ¡preparados, listos, ya!
7 (= *level, standard*) • **to hit the £1000 ~** alcanzar el total de 1000 libras • **gas ~ 1** (*Culin*) número 1 del gas • IDIOMS: • **to be up to the ~** [*person*] estar a la altura de las circunstancias; [*work*] alcanzar el nivel necesario • **to come up to the ~** alcanzar el nivel que era de esperar; ▷ **overstep**
8 (= *model*) • **a Spitfire Mark 1** un Spitfire (de) primera serie
9 (*Comm*) (= *label*) marca *f*
10 (= *distinction*) • **of ~** de categoría, de cierta distinción
VT **1** (= *make a mark on*) marcar • **~ it with an asterisk** ponga un asterisco allí
2 (= *stain*) manchar • **he wasn't ~ed at all** no mostraba señal alguna de golpe
3 [+ *bird, animal*] • **a bird ~ed with red** un pájaro manchado de rojo, un pájaro con manchas rojas
4 (= *label*) rotular; (= *price*) indicar el precio de • **this exhibit is not ~ed** este objeto no lleva rótulo • **the chair is ~ed at £12** la silla tiene un precio de 12 libras
5 (= *indicate*) señalar, indicar; (= *characterize*) señalar, distinguir; [+ *anniversary etc*] señalar, celebrar; [+ *birthday*] festejar • **stones ~ the path** unas piedras señalan el camino • **this ~s the frontier** esto marca la frontera • **it ~s a change of policy** indica un cambio de política • **this ~s him as a future star** esto le señala como un as futuro • **it's not ~ed on the map** no está indicado en el mapa • **we must do something special to ~ the occasion** tenemos que hacer algo especial para celebrarlo
6 (= *note down*) apuntar; (= *notice*) advertir, observar; (= *heed*) prestar atención a • **did you ~ where it fell?** (*frm*) ¿has notado dónde cayó? • **~ what I say** escucha lo que te digo • **~ my words!** ¡fíjese *or* acuérdese bien de lo que le digo!, ¡te lo advierto! • **~ you** ahora (bien)
7 [+ *exam*] calificar; [+ *candidate*] dar nota a • **to ~ sth right** aprobar algo • **to ~ sth wrong** rechazar *or* (*LAm*) reprobar algo • **we ~ed him (as) first class** le dimos nota de sobresaliente
8 (*Ftbl*) marcar, doblar
9 (*Mus*) [+ *rhythm*] marcar • **to ~ time** (*Mil*) marcar el paso; (*fig*) estancarse
VI mancharse
CPD ▸ **mark reader, mark scanner** lector *m* de marcas ▸ **mark reading, mark scanning** lectura *f* de marcas
▸ **mark down** VT + ADV **1** (= *note down*) apuntar, anotar
2 (*Comm*) [+ *prices, goods*] rebajar
3 [+ *student*] bajar la nota a • **you'll be ~ed down for poor handwriting** te van a bajar la nota por mala caligrafía
4 (= *identify*) • **he was immediately ~ed down as a troublemaker** enseguida fue identificado como un alborotador • **I had him ~ed down as a friend of hers** pensé que era un amigo suyo, lo tomé por un amigo suyo
▸ **mark off** VT + ADV **1** (= *separate*) separar, dividir
2 (= *distinguish*) distinguir, diferenciar • **her clothes ~ed her off from the rest of the delegates** su atuendo la distinguía *or* diferenciaba del resto de los delegados
3 [+ *items on list etc*] (= *tick off*) marcar, poner una señal contra; (= *cross out*) tachar
▸ **mark out** VT + ADV **1** [+ *road etc*] marcar, jalonar • **the track is ~ed out by flags** el camino está marcado con *or* jalonado de banderas
2 (= *single out*) señalar; (= *distinguish*) distinguir, señalar • **he's ~ed out for promotion** se le ha señalado para un ascenso • **his red hair ~ed him out from the others** como era pelirrojo se le distinguía claramente de los demás
▸ **mark up** VT + ADV **1** (= *write up*) (*on board, paper etc*) apuntar
2 (*Comm*) [+ *price*] subir; [+ *goods*] subir el precio de
3 [+ *student*] subir la nota a
markdown [ˈmɑːkdaʊn] N (*Comm*) rebaja *f*, reducción *f*
marked [mɑːkt] ADJ **1** (= *noticeable*) [*improvement, increase, deterioration, reduction*] marcado, notable; [*difference, change*] acusado, marcado; [*contrast*] acusado, fuerte; [*accent*] marcado, fuerte; [*effect*] acusado, notable; [*reluctance*] notable, evidente • **the difference has become more ~** la diferencia se ha vuelto más acusada *or* marcada, la diferencia se acusa cada vez más • **he was a quiet boy, in ~ contrast to his raucous brothers** era un chico callado, muy diferente a sus escandalosos hermanos
2 (= *targeted*) • **to be a ~ man** ser un hombre marcado
markedly [ˈmɑːkɪdlɪ] ADV **1** (*with adj/adv*) [*different*] notablemente, marcadamente; [*better, worse*] visiblemente, notablemente • **their second album has been ~ more/less successful than their first** su segundo álbum ha tenido notablemente más/menos éxito que el primero
2 (*with verb*) [*increase, improve, decline*] notablemente, sensiblemente; [*differ, change, contrast*] notablemente
marker [ˈmɑːkəʳ] N **1** (= *indicator*) (*also Bio*) marcador *m*; (*in field*) jalón *m*; (= *signpost*)

m

poste *m* indicador • **to put down a ~** (*fig*) dejar una señal, marcar un lugar
2 (*also* **marker pen**) rotulador *m*
3 (= *bookmark*) marca *f*, señal *f*
4 (*Ftbl*) (= *person*) marcador(a) *m/f*, secante *mf*
5 (*Scol*) (= *person*) examinador(a) *m/f*
6 (*Billiards etc*) marcador *m*; (*in other games*) ficha *f*
7 (*Comput*) bandera *f*

market ['mɑːkɪt] (N) **1** (= *place*) mercado *m* • **to go to ~** ir al mercado
2 (= *trade*) mercado *m* • **overseas/domestic ~** mercado exterior/nacional • **to corner the ~ in maize** acaparar el mercado del maíz • **to flood the ~ with sth** inundar el mercado de algo • **strawberries are flooding the ~** las fresas inundan el mercado • **to be in the ~ for sth** estar dispuesto a comprar algo • **to be on the ~** estar en venta *or* a la venta • **it's the dearest shirt on the ~** es la camisa más cara del mercado • **to bring** *or* **put a product on(to) the ~** lanzar un producto al mercado • **to come on(to) the ~** salir a la venta *or* al mercado, ponerse en venta • **to rig the ~** manipular la lonja; ▹ **open**
3 (= *demand*) demanda *f* • **there is a ready ~ for video games** hay una gran demanda de videojuegos • **there's no ~ for pink socks** los calcetines de color rosa no encuentran salida • **to find a ready ~** venderse fácilmente, tener fácil salida
4 (= *stock market*) bolsa *f* (de valores) • **to play the ~** jugar a la bolsa
(VT) **1** (= *sell*) comercializar, poner en venta
2 (= *promote*) publicitar
(VI) (*esp US*) hacer la compra
(CPD) ▸ **market analysis** análisis *m inv* de mercado(s) ▸ **market day** día *m* de mercado ▸ **market demand** demanda *f* del mercado ▸ **market economy** economía *f* de mercado ▸ **market forces** fuerzas *fpl* del mercado, tendencias *fpl* del mercado ▸ **market garden** (*Brit*) (*small*) huerto *m*; (*large*) huerta *f* ▸ **market gardener** (*Brit*) hortelano/a *m/f* ▸ **market gardening** (*Brit*) horticultura *f* ▸ **market intelligence** información *f* del mercado ▸ **market leader** líder *m* del mercado ▸ **market opportunity** oportunidad *f* comercial ▸ **market penetration** penetración *f* del mercado ▸ **market place** plaza *f* (del mercado); (= *world of trade*) mercado *m* ▸ **market potential** potencial *m* comercial ▸ **market price** precio *m* de mercado ▸ **market rates** precios *mpl* del mercado; (*Econ*) cotizaciones *fpl* ▸ **market research** estudios *mpl* de mercados ▸ **market researcher** investigador(a) *m/f* de mercados ▸ **market share** cuota *f* de mercado ▸ **market study, market survey** estudio *m* de mercado ▸ **market town** mercado *m* ▸ **market trends** tendencias *fpl* de mercado ▸ **market value** valor *m* de mercado

marketability [ˌmɑːkɪtəˈbɪlɪtɪ] (N) comerciabilidad *f*, vendibilidad *f*

marketable ['mɑːkɪtəbl] (ADJ) **1** (= *saleable*) [*commodity, product*] vendible, comercializable • **of ~ quality** de valor comercial
2 (*fig*) [*skill*] con mucha salida • **the more specialized your skill, the more ~ you are** cuanto más especializado estés, mayores posibilidades tendrás en el mercado laboral • **he is one of our most ~ young actors** es uno de nuestros actores jóvenes con más posibilidades en el mercado cinematográfico

market-driven ['mɑːkɪtˌdrɪvən] (ADJ) determinado por el mercado

marketeer [ˌmɑːkɪ'tɪə^r] (N) (*Brit*) (*Pol*) (*also* **pro-Marketeer**) partidario/a *m/f* del Mercado Común; ▹ **black**

marketing ['mɑːkɪtɪŋ] (N) márketing *m*, mercadotecnia *f*
(CPD) ▸ **marketing agreement** acuerdo *m* de comercialización ▸ **marketing department** departamento *f* de márketing ▸ **marketing director** jefe/a *m/f* de márketing ▸ **marketing manager** director(a) *m/f* de márketing ▸ **marketing mix** marketing mix *m* ▸ **marketing plan** plan *m* de comercialización ▸ **marketing strategy** estrategia *f* de comercialización

marketize ['mɑːkɪtaɪz] (VT) mercantilizar

market-led ['mɑːkɪt'led] (ADJ) dominado por el mercado

marking ['mɑːkɪŋ] (N) **1** (= *mark*) señal *f*, marca *f*; (*on animal*) pinta *f*; (= *colouration*) coloración *f*
2 (*Brit*) (*Scol*) corrección *f* (*de exámenes, deberes*)
3 (*Ftbl*) marcaje *m*
(CPD) ▸ **marking ink** tinta *f* indeleble ▸ **marking pen** rotulador *m*

marksman ['mɑːksmən] (N) (PL: **marksmen**) tirador *m*

marksmanship ['mɑːksmənʃɪp] (N) puntería *f*

markswoman ['mɑːksˌwʊmən] (N) (PL: **markswomen**) tiradora *f*

mark-up ['mɑːkʌp] (N) (= *profit*) margen *m* (de beneficio); (= *price increase*) aumento *m* de precio

marl [mɑːl] (N) marga *f*

marlin ['mɑːlɪn] (N) (PL: **marlin** *or* **marlins**) (= *fish*) aguja *f*

marlin, marline ['mɑːlɪn] (N) (*Naut*) merlín *m*, empalmadura *f*, trincafía *f*
(CPD) ▸ **marlin(e) spike** pasador *m*

marly ['mɑːlɪ] (ADJ) margoso

marmalade ['mɑːməleɪd] (N) mermelada *f* (de naranja amarga *or* limón)
(CPD) ▸ **marmalade orange** naranja *f* amarga

marmoreal [mɑː'mɔːrɪəl] (ADJ) marmóreo

marmoset ['mɑːməzet] (N) tití *m*

marmot ['mɑːmət] (N) marmota *f*

maroon¹ [mə'ruːn] (ADJ) granate *inv*
(N) (= *colour*) granate *m*

maroon² [mə'ruːn] (VT) [+ *castaway*] abandonar (en una isla desierta); (*fig*) aislar, dejar aislado • **we were ~ed by floods** quedamos aislados debido a las inundaciones

maroon³ [mə'ruːn] (N) (= *distress signal*) petardo *m*

marque [mɑːk] (N) marca *f*

marquee [mɑː'kiː] (N) (*esp Brit*) (= *tent*) carpa *f*; (*open-sided*) entoldado *m*; (*US*) (*over doorway*) marquesina *f*

marquess ['mɑːkwɪs] (N) marqués *m*

marquetry ['mɑːkɪtrɪ] (N) marquetería *f*

marquis ['mɑːkwɪs] (N) = **marquess**

Marrakech, Marrakesh [ˌmærə'keʃ] (N) Marraquech *m*, Marraqués *m*, Marrakech *m*

marriage ['mærɪdʒ] (N) **1** (= *state of being married*) matrimonio *m* • **aunt by ~** tía *f* política • **to be related by ~** estar emparentados • **to become related by ~ to sb** emparentar con algn • **~ of convenience** matrimonio *m* de conveniencia • **to give sb in ~ to** casar a algn con, dar a algn en matrimonio a
2 (= *wedding*) boda *f*, casamiento *m*; (*fig*) unión *f*
(CPD) ▸ **marriage bed** lecho *m* nupcial, tálamo *m* (*frm*) ▸ **marriage bonds** lazos *mpl or* vínculos *mpl* matrimoniales ▸ **marriage broker** casamentero/a *m/f* ▸ **marriage bureau** agencia *f* matrimonial ▸ **marriage ceremony** ceremonia *f* nupcial, matrimonio *m* ▸ **marriage certificate** partida *f* matrimonial *or* de matrimonio ▸ **marriage counseling** (*US*) = **marriage guidance** ▸ **marriage counselor** (*US*) = **marriage guidance counsellor** ▸ **marriage guidance** orientación *f* matrimonial ▸ **marriage guidance counsellor** consejero/a *m/f* matrimonial ▸ **marriage licence, marriage license** (*US*) licencia *f* matrimonial ▸ **marriage lines** (*Brit*) partida *f* matrimonial *or* de matrimonio ▸ **marriage partner** cónyuge *mf*, consorte *mf* ▸ **marriage rate** (índice *m* de) nupcialidad *f* ▸ **marriage settlement** contrato *m* matrimonial; (*Jur*) capitulaciones *fpl* (matrimoniales) ▸ **marriage vows** votos *mpl* matrimoniales

marriageable ['mærɪdʒəbl] (ADJ) casadero • **of ~ age** en edad de casarse

married ['mærɪd] (ADJ) [*person*] casado; [*love*] conyugal • **~ man** (hombre *m*) casado *m* • **~ woman** (mujer *f*) casada *f* • **~ couple** matrimonio *m* • **~ life** vida *f* matrimonial • **the ~ state** el estado matrimonial • **twice-married** casado por segunda vez *or* en segundas nupcias • **"just married"** "recién casados"
(CPD) ▸ **married name** nombre *m* de casada ▸ **married quarters** (*Mil*) casa *fsing* cuartel, residencia *fsing* para matrimonios

marrow ['mærəʊ] (N) **1** (*Anat*) médula *f*, tuétano *m*; (*as food*) tuétano *m* de hueso • IDIOMS: • **a Spaniard to the ~** un español de pura cepa, un español hasta la médula • **to be frozen to the ~** estar helado hasta los huesos
2 (*Brit*) (*Bot*) (*also* **vegetable marrow**) calabacín *m* • **baby ~** calabacín *m*, calabacita *f*

marrowbone ['mærəʊbəʊn] (N) hueso *m* con tuétano

marrowfat ['mærəʊfæt] (N) (*also* **marrowfat pea**) *tipo de guisante*

marry ['mærɪ] (VT) **1** (= *take in marriage*) casarse con • **to be married to sb** estar casado con algn • **we have been married for 14 years** llevamos 14 años (de) casados • **to ~ money** casarse con alguien de dinero
2 (= *give or join in marriage*) casar • **they were married by the village priest** los casó el cura del pueblo • **he has three daughters to ~ (off)** tiene tres hijas por casar
3 (*fig*) conjugar, aunar • **a style which marries beauty and practicality** un estilo que conjuga *or* aúna belleza y pragmatismo • **he's married to his job** vive por y para el trabajo, vive para trabajar *or* para el trabajo
(VI) (*also* **get married**) casarse • **to ~ again** volver a casarse, casarse en segundas nupcias • **to ~ beneath one** casarse con alguien de rango inferior • **to ~ into a rich family** emparentar con una familia rica • **to ~ into the peerage** casarse con alguien de la nobleza
▸ **marry up** (VT + ADV) (*fig*) conjugar

Mars [mɑːz] (N) Marte *m* • **~ landing** • **landing on ~** amartizaje *m*

Marseillaise [ˌmɑːsə'leɪz] (N) • **the ~** la Marsellesa

Marseilles [mɑː'seɪ] (N) Marsella *f*

marsh [mɑːʃ] (N) pantano *m*, ciénaga *f*; (= *salt marsh*) marisma *f*
(CPD) ▸ **marsh fever** paludismo *m* ▸ **marsh gas** gas *m* de los pantanos, metano *m* ▸ **marsh marigold** botón *m* de oro ▸ **marsh warbler** papamoscas *m inv*

marshal ['mɑːʃəl] (N) **1** (*Mil*) mariscal *m*
2 (*at demonstration, meeting*) oficial *m*
3 (*US*) alguacil *m*, oficial *m* de justicia
(VT) **1** [+ *soldiers, procession*] formar
2 [+ *facts etc*] ordenar; [+ *evidence*] presentar

marshalling yard ['mɑːʃəlɪŋ,jɑːd] (N) (*Rail*) área *f* de clasificación
marshland ['mɑːʃlænd] (N) pantanal *m*
marshmallow ['mɑːʃmæləʊ] (N) (*Bot*) malvavisco *m*; (= *sweet*) esponja *f*, dulce *m* de merengue blando
marshy ['mɑːʃɪ] (ADJ) (COMPAR: **marshier**, SUPERL: **marshiest**) pantanoso
marsupial [mɑː'suːpɪəl] (ADJ) marsupial
(N) marsupial *m*
mart [mɑːt] (N) (*esp US*) (= *trade centre*) emporio *m*; (= *market*) mercado *m*; (= *auction room*) martillo *m*; (= *property mart*) (*in newspaper*) bolsa *f* de la propiedad
marten ['mɑːtɪn] (N) (PL: **martens** *or* **marten**) marta *f*
Martial ['mɑːʃəl] (N) Marcial
martial ['mɑːʃəl] (ADJ) marcial • **~ bearing** porte *m* militar, aire *m* marcial
(CPD) ▸ **martial arts** artes *fpl* marciales
▸ **martial law** ley *f* marcial
Martian ['mɑːʃɪən] (ADJ) marciano
(N) marciano/a *m/f*
Martin ['mɑːtɪn] (N) Martín
martin ['mɑːtɪn] (N) avión *m*, vencejo *m*
martinet [,mɑːtɪ'net] (N) ordenancista *mf*, rigorista *mf*
Martini® [mɑː'tiːnɪ] (N) **1** (= *vermouth*) vermú *m*
2 (= *cocktail*) martini *m* (*vermú seco con ginebra*)
Martinique [,mɑːtɪ'niːk] (N) Martinica *f*
Martinmas ['mɑːtɪnməs] (N) día *m* de San Martín (*11 noviembre*)
martyr ['mɑːtəʳ] (N) mártir *mf* • **to be a ~ to arthritis** ser víctima de la artritis
(VT) martirizar
martyrdom ['mɑːtədəm] (N) martirio *m*
martyrize ['mɑːtɪraɪz] (VT) martirizar
marvel ['mɑːvəl] (N) maravilla *f* • **you're a ~** eres una maravilla • **it's a ~ to me how she does it** no llego a entender cómo lo hace • **if he gets there it will be a ~** si llega será un milagro
(VI) maravillarse, asombrarse (**at** de)
marvellous, marvelous (*US*) ['mɑːvələs] (ADJ) maravilloso, estupendo • **marvellous!** ¡magnífico! • **isn't it ~?** (*also iro*) ¡qué bien!
marvellously, marvelously (*US*) ['mɑːvələslɪ] (ADV) maravillosamente, de maravilla
Marxism ['mɑːksɪzəm] (N) marxismo *m*
Marxist ['mɑːksɪst] (ADJ) marxista
(N) marxista *mf*
Mary ['mɛərɪ] (N) María *f* • **~ Magdalen** la Magdalena • **~ Queen of Scots** • **~ Stuart** María Estuardo
marzipan [,mɑːzɪ'pæn] (N) mazapán *m*
masc. (ABBR) (= **masculine**) m
mascara [mæs'kɑːrə] (N) rímel® *m*
mascaraed [mæs'kɑːrəd] (ADJ) pintado con rímel
mascot ['mæskət] (N) mascota *f*
masculine ['mæskjʊlɪn] (ADJ) **1** [*qualities, voice etc*] masculino
2 (*esp pej*) [*woman, image, appearance*] masculino, hombruno (*pej*)
3 (*Gram*) masculino
(N) (*Gram*) masculino *m*
masculinist ['mæskjʊlɪnɪst] (ADJ) masculino
masculinity [,mæskjʊ'lɪnɪtɪ] (N) masculinidad *f*
masculinization [,mæskjʊlɪnaɪ'zeɪʃən] (N) masculinización *f*
masculinize ['mæskjʊlɪnaɪz] (VT) (*frm*) masculinizar
MASH [mæʃ] (N ABBR) (*US*) (= **mobile army surgical unit**) *unidad quirúrgica móvil del ejército*
mash [mæʃ] (N) **1** (= *mixture*) mezcla *f*; (= *pulp*) pasta *f*, amasijo *m*
2 (*Brit**) (= *mashed potatoes*) puré *m* de patata(s) *or* (*LAm*) papas
3 (*in brewing*) malta *f* remojada
4 (*for animals*) afrecho *m*
(VT) **1** (= *crush*) triturar, machacar
2 (= *purée*) [+ *potatoes*] hacer puré de
mashed [mæʃt] (ADJ) • **~ potatoes** puré *m* de patatas, puré *m* de papas (*LAm*)
masher ['mæʃəʳ] (N) *utensilio para aplastar las patatas al hacer puré*
mashie ['mæʃɪ] (N) (*Golf*) hierro *m* número 5
mask [mɑːsk] (N) **1** (*as disguise*) (*also fig*) máscara *f*; (*just covering eyes and nose*) antifaz *m* • **the man in the ~ produced a gun** el hombre enmascarado *or* que llevaba la máscara sacó una pistola • **his talk is a ~ for his ignorance** habla para enmascarar su ignorancia
2 (*ornamental, ritual*) máscara *f*, careta *f*
3 (*also* **face mask**) (*protective, cosmetic*) mascarilla *f*; (*surgeon's*) mascarilla *f*, barbijo *m*; ▹ **death, face, gas, oxygen**
4 (*in baseball, fencing, ice-hockey*) careta *f*
(VT) **1** [+ *person, face*] enmascarar
2 [+ *object*] ocultar • **a thick grey cloud ~ed the sun** una nube espesa y gris ocultó el sol
3 (*fig*) [+ *taste, smell*] enmascarar; [+ *truth, feelings, motives*] ocultar, encubrir; [+ *effect of drug*] enmascarar
4 (*during painting, spraying*) cubrir
masked [mɑːskt] (ADJ) enmascarado; [*terrorist, attacker*] encapuchado
(CPD) ▸ **masked ball** baile *m* de máscaras
masking tape ['mɑːskɪŋ,teɪp] (N) cinta *f* adhesiva protectora (*del margen del área a pintar*)
masochism ['mæsəʊkɪzəm] (N) masoquismo *m*
masochist ['mæsəʊkɪst] (N) masoquista *mf*
masochistic [,mæsəʊ'kɪstɪk] (ADJ) masoquista
mason ['meɪsn] (N) **1** (= *builder*) albañil *mf*; (= *stonework specialist*) mampostero/a *m/f*
2 (= *monumental mason*) marmolista *mf* (de monumentos funerarios)
3 (*in quarry*) cantero/a *m/f*
4 (= *freemason*) masón *m*, francmasón *m*

MASON-DIXON LINE
La línea **Mason-Dixon** o **Mason and Dixon** es la que divide simbólicamente el norte y el sur de Estados Unidos y que, hasta el final de la Guerra Civil, marcaba la separación entre aquellos estados en donde existía la esclavitud y aquellos en los que no. Esta línea de demarcación, que se extiende a lo largo de 377 kilómetros, fue establecida por Charles Mason y Jeremiah Dixon en el siglo XVIII con el fin de solucionar un conflicto que ya duraba 80 años sobre la frontera entre Maryland y Pensilvania. En 1779 la línea se extendió para demarcar la frontera entre Pensilvania y Virginia (hoy Virginia del Oeste); en la actualidad aún sirve como referencia del sur en general y en las canciones de **country & western** los cantantes hablan con nostalgia de "cruzar la línea" para volver a sus tierras sureñas.

masonic [mə'sɒnɪk] (ADJ) (*also* **Masonic**) masónico
masonry ['meɪsnrɪ] (N) **1** (= *building trade*) albañilería *f*
2 (= *stonework*) mampostería *f*
3 (= *rubble*) escombros *mpl*
4 (= *freemasonry*) masonería *f*, francmasonería *f*
masque [mɑːsk] (N) mascarada *f*
masquerade [,mæskə'reɪd] (N) **1** (= *pretence*) farsa *f*, mascarada *f*
2 (= *fancy-dress ball*) baile *m* de máscaras, mascarada *f*
(VI) • **to ~ as** hacerse pasar por
mass¹ [mæs] (N) (*Rel*) misa *f* • **to go to ~** ir a misa, oír misa • **to hear ~** oír misa • **to say ~** decir misa
mass² [mæs] (N) **1** (= *concentration*) masa *f* • **the garden was a ~ of colour** el jardín era una masa de color • **she had a ~ of auburn hair** tenía una mata de pelo castaño rojizo • **he's a ~ of bruises** está cubierto de cardenales • **the (great) ~ of the population** la (gran) masa de la población • **in the ~** en conjunto; ▹ **air, critical**
2 masses* (= *great quantity*) montones* *mpl*, cantidad* *fsing* • **there's ~es of work for her to do** hay montones* *or* cantidad* de trabajo para ella • **~es of people crowded inside** una masa de gente entró en tropel
3 • **the ~es** (= *ordinary people*) las masas
4 (*Phys*) masa *f*
(VT) concentrar
(VI) [*people, crowds, troops*] concentrarse; [*clouds*] agruparse
(CPD) [*movement, action*] de masas; [*protest, unemployment, support*] masivo; [*suicide*] colectivo; [*tourism*] en masa ▸ **mass destruction** destrucción *f* masiva ▸ **mass exodus** éxodo *m* masivo *or* en masa ▸ **mass grave** fosa *f* común ▸ **mass hysteria** histeria *f* colectiva ▸ **mass killing** matanza *f*, masacre *f* ▸ **mass market** mercado *m* popular ▸ **mass marketing** comercialización *f* en masa ▸ **mass media** medios *mpl* de comunicación (de masas) ▸ **mass meeting** concentración *f* de masas ▸ **mass movement** movimiento *m* de masas ▸ **mass murder** matanza *f*, masacre *f* ▸ **mass murderer** autor(a) *m/f* de una matanza *or* masacre ▸ **mass noun** sustantivo *m or* nombre *m* no contable ▸ **mass number** número *m* de masa ▸ **mass production** fabricación *f* en serie ▸ **mass transit** (*US*) transporte *m* público
Mass. (ABBR) (*US*) = **Massachusetts**
massacre ['mæsəkəʳ] (N) **1** (= *killing*) masacre *f*, carnicería *f*
2* (= *defeat*) derrota *f* aplastante, paliza* *f*
(VT) **1** (= *kill*) masacrar, aniquilar
2* (= *defeat*) aplastar, dar una paliza a*
massage ['mæsɑːʒ] (N) (*lit*) masaje *m* • **"massage"** (*euph*) "Relax"
(VT) **1** (*lit*) dar un masaje a
2* [+ *figures*] maquillar*
(CPD) ▸ **massage parlour, massage parlor** (*US*) (*lit*) sala *f* de masaje; (*euph*) sala *f* de relax
massed [mæst] (ADJ) • **the ~ ranks of the enemy** las pobladas filas del enemigo • **~ ranks of reporters** una masa de periodistas • **~ choirs** grandes agrupaciones *fpl* corales
masseur [mæ'sɜːʳ] (N) masajista *mf*
masseuse [mæ'sɜːz] (N) masajista *f*
massif [mæ'siːf] (N) macizo *m*
massive ['mæsɪv] (ADJ) [*wall*] macizo, sólido; [*boulder, increase, dose, support*] enorme; [*person, head, body*] enorme, gigantesco*; [*explosion, effort*] enorme, grande; [*job losses*] cuantioso; [*intervention, influx*] masivo • **~ heart attack** infarto *m* masivo • **on a ~ scale** a gran escala
massively ['mæsɪvlɪ] (ADV) [*overweight*] tremendamente; [*popular*] tremendamente, enormemente; [*invest*] a gran escala; [*increase*] enormemente
massiveness ['mæsɪvnɪs] (N) [*of wall*] solidez *f*, lo macizo; [*of increase, dose, explosion, effort*] enormidad *f*; [*of person, head, body, boulder*] lo gigantesco
mass-produce ['mæsprə'djuːs] (VT)

fabricar en serie, producir en serie

mass-produced ['mæsprə,dju:st] (ADJ) fabricado en serie, producido en serie

mast[1] [mɑ:st] (N) **1** (*Naut*) mástil *m*, palo *m* • **ten years before the ~** (*liter*) diez años de servicio como marinero
2 (*Rad*) torre *f*

mast[2] [mɑ:st] (N) (*Bot*) [*of oak*] bellota *f*; [*of beech*] hayuco *m*

mastectomy [mæ'stektəmɪ] (N) (*Med*) mastectomía *f* • **she had to have a ~** tuvieron que hacerle una mastectomía

-masted ['mɑ:stɪd] (ADJ) (*ending in compounds*) de ... palos • **three-masted** de tres palos

master ['mɑ:stə[r]] (N) **1** [*of the house*] señor *m*, amo *m*; [*of dog, servant*] amo *m*; (*in address*) señor *m* • **the ~ is not at home** el señor no está • **the young ~** el señorito • **to be ~ in one's own house** mandar en su propia casa • **to be one's own ~** ser dueño de sí mismo • **I am (the) ~ now** ahora mando yo • **to be ~ of the situation** dominar la situación • **to be ~ of one's fate** decidir su propio destino • IDIOMS: • **to meet one's ~** ser derrotado por fin, tener que sucumbir por fin • **to serve two ~s** servir a Dios y al diablo
2 (*Naut*) [*of ship*] capitán *m*
3 (= *musician, painter etc*) maestro *m*; ▷ **old**
4 (= *expert*) experto/a *m/f* • **he is a ~ at (the art of) making money** es un experto en el arte de hacer dinero; ▷ **past**
5† (= *teacher*) (*primary*) maestro *m*; (*secondary*) profesor *m* • **the music ~** el profesor de música
6 (*Univ*) • **Master of Arts/Science** (= *qualification*) master *m* en letras/ciencias; (= *person*) *persona que posee un master en letras/ciencias* • **she's working for her Master's (degree)** está estudiando para sacarse el máster; ▷ DEGREE
(VT) [+ *subject, situation, technique*] dominar • **to ~ the violin** llegar a dominar el violín
(CPD) ▸ **master baker** maestro *m* panadero ▸ **master bedroom** dormitorio *m* principal ▸ **master builder** maestro *m* de obras ▸ **master card** carta *f* maestra ▸ **master class** clase *f* magistral ▸ **master copy** original *m* ▸ **master disk** disco *m* maestro ▸ **master file** fichero *m* maestro ▸ **master key** llave *f* maestra ▸ **master mariner** capitán *m* ▸ **master mason** albañil *mf* maestro/a ▸ **master of ceremonies** maestro *m* de ceremonias; [*of show*] presentador *m*, animador *m* ▸ **master of foxhounds** cazador *m* mayor ▸ **Master of the Rolls** (*Brit*) juez *mf* del tribunal de apelación ▸ **master plan** plan *m* maestro, plan *m* rector ▸ **master sergeant** (*US*) sargento *mf* mayor ▸ **master spy** jefe *mf* de espías, controlador(a) *m/f* de espías ▸ **master switch** interruptor *m* general ▸ **master tape** máster *m*, cinta *f* maestra

masterful ['mɑ:stəfʊl] (ADJ) **1** (= *skilful*) [*performance*] magistral; [*swordsman, horseman*] diestro; [*leadership*] capaz
2 (= *imperious*) imperioso, autoritario; [*personality*] dominante

masterfully ['mɑ:stəfəlɪ] (ADV) magistralmente

masterly ['mɑ:stəlɪ] (ADJ) magistral, genial • **she is ~ in describing life in Victorian London** describe de forma magistral la vida en el Londres de la época victoriana

mastermind ['mɑ:stəmaɪnd] (N) (= *genius*) genio *m*; (*in crime etc*) cerebro *m*
(VT) dirigir, planear

masterpiece ['mɑ:stəpi:s] (N) obra *f* maestra

Mastersingers ['mɑ:stə,sɪŋəz] (NPL) • **"the Mastersingers"** "los maestros cantores"

masterstroke ['mɑ:stə,strəʊk] (N) golpe *m* maestro

masterwork ['mɑ:stəwɜ:k] (N) obra *f* maestra

mastery ['mɑ:stərɪ] (N) **1** (= *understanding*) [*of subject, technique*] dominio *m*
2 (= *skill*) maestría *f* • **his ~ on the football field** su maestría en el terreno de juego
3 (= *control*) (*over competitors etc*) dominio *m*, superioridad *f* • **to gain the ~ of** (= *dominate*) llegar a dominar; (= *take over*) hacerse el señor de

masthead ['mɑ:sthed] (N) **1** (*Naut*) tope *m*
2 [*of newspaper*] mancheta *f*

mastic ['mæstɪk] (N) masilla *f*

masticate ['mæstɪkeɪt] (VT) masticar

mastiff ['mæstɪf] (N) mastín *m*, alano *m*

mastitis [mæs'taɪtɪs] (N) mastitis *f inv*

mastodon ['mæstədən] (N) mastodonte *m*

mastoid ['mæstɔɪd] (ADJ) mastoides (*inv*)
(N) mastoides *f inv*

masturbate ['mæstəbeɪt] (VI) masturbarse
(VT) masturbar

masturbation [,mæstə'beɪʃən] (N) masturbación *f*

masturbatory ['mæstə'beɪtərɪ] (ADJ) masturbatorio

mat[1] [mæt] (N) **1** (*on floor*) estera *f*, esterilla *f*; (*also* **doormat**) felpudo *m*
2 (*also* **tablemat**) (mantel *m*) individual *m*; (*in centre of table*) salvamanteles *m inv*
(VT) enmarañar
(VI) enmarañarse

mat[2] [mæt] (ADJ) = **matt**

MAT (N ABBR) (= **machine-assisted translation**) TAO *f*

matador ['mætədɔ:[r]] (N) matador *m*, diestro *m*

match[1] [mætʃ] (N) (*for lighting*) fósforo *m*, cerilla *f*, cerillo *m* (*Mex*) • **a box of ~es** una caja de fósforos *or* cerillas

match[2] [mætʃ] (N) **1** (*esp Brit*) (*Tennis, Cricket*) partido *m*; (*Ftbl*) partido *m*, encuentro *m*; (*Boxing*) combate *m*; (*Fencing*) asalto *m* • **boxing ~** combate *m* de boxeo; ▷ **shooting, shouting, test**
2 (= *complement*) • **the skirt is a good ~ for the jumper** la falda hace juego *or* queda bien con el jersey • **I'm looking for a ~ for these curtains** estoy buscando un color que haga juego con estas cortinas • **the two of them make** *or* **are a good ~** hacen una buena pareja
3 (= *equal*) • **to be a ~/no ~ for sb** estar/no estar a la altura de algn • **he was more than a ~ for Paul** venció fácilmente a Paul • **he's a ~ for anybody** puede competir con el más pintado, está a la altura del más pintado • **to meet one's ~ (in sb)** encontrar la horma de su zapato (en algn)
4 (= *marriage*) casamiento *m*, matrimonio *m*; (= *potential partner*) partido *m* • **he's a good ~** es un buen partido • **she made a good ~** se casó bien
(VT) **1** (= *pair off*) emparejar • **they're well ~ed** [*couple*] hacen buena pareja • **the teams were well ~ed** los equipos estaban muy igualados *or* (*esp LAm*) eran muy parejos • **they ~ your skills with employers' requirements** emparejan tus aptitudes con los requisitos de las empresas • **the children were asked to ~ the pictures with the words** se pidió a los niños que emparejaran las imágenes con las palabras • **they ~ed fibres to the suspect's clothes** encontraron fibras que se correspondían con la ropa del sospechoso; ▷ **evenly**
2 (= *equal*) igualar • **her performance would be hard to ~** su actuación sería difícil de igualar • **I can ~ any offer** puedo igualar cualquier oferta • **for sheer cheek there's no one to ~ him** en cuanto a cara dura no hay quien le iguale • **the results did not ~ our expectations** los resultados no estuvieron a la altura de nuestras expectativas
3 (= *correspond to*) ajustarse a, corresponder a • **a man ~ing the police description** un hombre que se ajustaba a *or* que correspondía a la descripción de la policía
4 (= *put in opposition to*) enfrentar • **to ~ sth/sb against sth/sb** enfrentar algo/a algn a *or* con algo/algn • **she ~ed her wits against his strength** enfrentó *or* midió su ingenio con la fuerza de él • **Scotland has been ~ed against France in the final** Escocia se enfrentará a *or* con Francia en la final
5 (= *tone with*) [+ *clothes, colours*] combinar con, hacer juego con
6 (*also* **match up**) (= *find sth similar to*) • **can you ~ (up) this material?** (*with sth exactly same*) ¿puedes encontrar algo que iguale este tejido?; (*with sth which goes well*) ¿puedes encontrar algo que vaya bien con este tejido?
(VI) **1** (= *go together*) [*colours*] combinar bien; [*clothes*] hacer juego • **I dyed the shoes to ~** teñí los zapatos para que hicieran juego • **with a skirt to ~** con una falda a tono *or* que hace juego • **he has a vicious tongue and a temper to ~** tiene una lengua viperina y un genio de mil demonios*
2 (= *be the same*) corresponderse, coincidir
(CPD) ▸ **match point** (*Tennis*) bola *f* de partido, match point *m* ▸ **match report** informe *m* sobre el partido

▸ **match up** (VT + ADV) (= *bring together*) [+ *two objects*] emparejar, aparear; [+ *two people*] emparejar; (= *group*) [+ *objects, people*] agrupar; [+ *pattern*] hacer coincidir • **to ~ sth up with sth** [+ *pairs*] emparejar *or* aparear algo con algo; [+ *colours*] (= *coordinate*) conjuntar algo con algo • **they ~ up your skills with employers' requirements** emparejan tus aptitudes con los requisitos de las empresas • **they ~ed up fibres to the suspect's clothes** encontraron fibras que se correspondían con la ropa del sospechoso; ▷ **match**
(VI + ADV) **1** (= *be the same, fit*) [*numbers, pattern*] coincidir • **check the numbers against your card to see if they ~ up** compruebe los números con los de su cartón para ver si coinciden • **his fingerprints don't ~ up exactly with the murderer's** sus huellas dactilares no coinciden exactamente con *or* no corresponden exactamente a las del asesino
2 (= *perform*) responder
3 (= *compare*) • **his record ~es up well against those of previous presidents** su historial se puede comparar al de presidentes anteriores

▸ **match up to** (VI + PREP) estar a la altura de

matchbook ['mætʃbʊk] (N) (*esp US*) librito *m* de cerillas

matchbox ['mætʃbɒks] (N) caja *f* de fósforos *or* cerillas

matching ['mætʃɪŋ] (ADJ) haciendo juego, a juego (*Sp*) • **a blue silk dress with ~ shoes** un vestido de seda azul con zapatos haciendo juego *or* (*Sp*) a juego
(CPD) ▸ **matching funds** (*US*) fondos *mpl* de contrapartida

matchless ['mætʃlɪs] (ADJ) sin par *or* igual, incomparable

matchmaker ['mætʃ,meɪkə[r]] (N) casamentero/a *m/f*, alcahuete/a *m/f*

matchmaking ['mætʃ,meɪkɪŋ] (N) actividades *fpl* de casamentero
(ADJ) casamentero

matchplay ['mætʃpleɪ] (N) partido *m* oficial
matchstick ['mætʃstɪk] (N) fósforo *m*
match-up, matchup ['mætʃʌp] (N) (= *head-to-head, competition*) duelo *m*
matchwood ['mætʃwʊd] (N) astillas *fpl* • **to smash sth to ~** hacer algo añicos • **to be smashed to ~** hacerse añicos
mate¹ [meɪt] (*Chess*) (N) mate *m*
(VT) dar jaque mate a, matar
(VI) dar jaque mate, matar • **white plays and ~s in two** blanco juega y mata en dos
mate² [meɪt] (N) **1** (*Zool*) (*male*) macho *m*; (*female*) hembra *f*
2* (*hum*) (= *husband, wife*) compañero/a *m/f*
3 (= *assistant*) ayudante *mf*, peón *m*; ▹ **plumber**
4 (*Brit*) (*Naut*) primer(a) oficial *mf*; (*US*) segundo/a *m/f* de a bordo
5 (*at work*) compañero/a *m/f*, colega *mf*
6 (*Brit**) (= *friend*) amigo/a *m/f*, compinche* *mf*, colega* *mf*, cuate/a *m/f* (*Mex*) • **John and his ~s*** John y sus amiguetes *or* colegas • **look here, ~*** mire, amigo
(VT) **1** (*Zool*) aparear
2 (*hum*) unir
(VI) (*Zool*) aparearse • PROVERB: • **age should not ~ with youth** no debe casarse el viejo con la joven
maté ['mɑːteɪ] (N) mate *m* (cocido), yerba *f* mate • **~ kettle** pava *f*
mater ['meɪtəʳ] (N) (*Brit*) (*frm*) madre *f*
material [mə'tɪərɪəl] (ADJ) **1** (= *physical*) [*goods, needs, comforts, benefits, damage*] material • **to do sth for ~ gain** hacer algo para obtener un beneficio material • **~ possessions** bienes *mpl* materiales • **the ~ world** el mundo físico
2 (= *important*) [*reason*] importante, de peso, fundamental
3 (*Jur*) (= *relevant*) [*fact*] pertinente; [*witness*] primordial, principal • **~ evidence** pruebas *fpl* sustanciales • **to be ~ to sth** ser pertinente a algo
(N) **1** (= *cloth*) tela *f*, tejido *m*
2 (= *substance*) materia *f*, material *m* • **natural ~s** materias *fpl* naturales, materiales *mpl* naturales • **raw ~s** materias *fpl* primas
3 materials (= *equipment, components*) material(es) *m(pl)* • **building ~s** material(es) *m(pl)* de construcción • **teaching ~s** material(es) *m(pl)* didácticos • **writing ~s** artículos *mpl* de escritorio
4 (= *information*) datos *mpl*, información *f* • **they researched a lot of background ~ for the book** recogieron muchos datos *or* mucha información antes de escribir el libro • **she was busy gathering ~ for her article** estaba ocupada recogiendo datos *or* información para su artículo
5 (= *potential*) • **he is university ~** tiene madera de universitario • **he is not management ~** no tiene madera de jefe
materialism [mə'tɪərɪəlɪzəm] (N) materialismo *m*
materialist [mə'tɪərɪəlɪst] (N) materialista *mf*
(ADJ) materialista
materialistic [mə'tɪərɪə'lɪstɪk] (ADJ) materialista
materialize [mə'tɪərɪəlaɪz] (VI) **1** (= *come into being*) [*idea, hope etc*] realizarse
2 (= *appear*) aparecer • **the funds haven't ~d so far** hasta ahora no han aparecido los fondos
3 [*spirit*] materializarse
(VT) materializar
materially [mə'tɪərɪəlɪ] (ADV) **1** (= *physically*) materialmente • **~ and emotionally** material y emocionalmente
2 (= *importantly*) sustancialmente, sensiblemente • **interest rates now are not ~ different from last year** los tipos de interés actuales no son sustancialmente *or* sensiblemente diferentes de los del año pasado • **they are not ~ different** no hay grandes diferencias entre ellos, no hay diferencias sustanciales *or* fundamentales entre ellos • **that does not ~ alter things** eso no afecta la situación de modo sustancial
materiel [mə,tɪərɪ'el] (N) (*US*) material *m* bélico
maternal [mə'tɜːnl] (ADJ) **1** (= *motherly*) [*woman, behaviour, instinct*] maternal; [*feelings, love*] maternal, de madre
2 (= *on the mother's side*) materno (*por parte de madre*) • **~ aunt** tía *f* materna (*por parte de madre*) • **~ grandfather** abuelo *m* materno (*por parte de madre*)
maternity [mə'tɜːnɪtɪ] (N) maternidad *f*
(CPD) ▸ **maternity allowance** subsidio *m* de maternidad ▸ **maternity benefit** (*Brit*) subsidio *m* de maternidad ▸ **maternity dress** vestido *m* premamá ▸ **maternity home, maternity hospital** maternidad *f* ▸ **maternity leave** baja *f* por maternidad ▸ **maternity pay** (*Brit*) *salario durante la baja por maternidad* ▸ **maternity ward** sala *f* de maternidad
mateship ['meɪtʃɪp] (N) (*esp Australia*) compañerismo *m*, compadreo *m* (*esp LAm*)
matey* ['meɪtɪ] (ADJ) (*Brit*) [*person*] afable, simpático; [*atmosphere*] acogedor; [*gathering*] informal, familiar • **she's quite ~ with my wife** es bastante amiga con mi mujer
(N) (*Brit*) (*in direct address*) chico, hijo
math* [mæθ] (N ABBR) (*US*) = **mathematics**; mates* *fpl*
mathematical [,mæθə'mætɪkəl] (ADJ) matemático • **I'm not very ~** no se me dan bien las matemáticas • **he's a ~ genius** es un genio para las matemáticas
(CPD) ▸ **mathematical error** error *m* matemático ▸ **mathematical model** modelo *m* matemático
mathematically [,mæθə'mætɪkəlɪ] (ADV) matemáticamente
mathematician [,mæθəmə'tɪʃən] (N) matemático/a *m/f*
mathematics [,mæθə'mætɪks] (NSING) matemáticas *fpl*
Mathilda [mə'tɪldə] (N) = **Matilda**
maths* [mæθs] (NSING ABBR) (*Brit*) = **mathematics**; mates* *fpl*
Matilda [mə'tɪldə] (N) Matilde
matinée ['mætɪneɪ] (N) función *f* de tarde, matiné(e) *f* (*S. Cone*)
(CPD) ▸ **matinée coat** (*Brit*) abriguito *m* de lana ▸ **matinée idol** ídolo *m* del público ▸ **matinée jacket** = **matinée coat**
matiness* ['meɪtɪnɪs] (N) [*of person*] afabilidad *f*, simpatía *f*; [*of gathering*] ambiente *m* informal, carácter *m* familiar
mating ['meɪtɪŋ] (N) **1** (*Zool*) apareamiento *m*
2 (*fig*) unión *f*
(CPD) ▸ **mating call** aullido *m*/rugido *m* de la época de celo ▸ **mating season** época *f* de celo
matins ['mætɪnz] (NSING OR NPL) maitines *mpl*
matriarch ['meɪtrɪɑːk] (N) matriarca *f*
matriarchal [,meɪtrɪ'ɑːkl] (ADJ) matriarcal
matriarchy ['meɪtrɪɑːkɪ] (N) matriarcado *m*
matric* [mə'trɪk] (N) (*Brit*) (*formerly*) = **matriculation**
matrices ['meɪtrɪsiːz] (NPL) *of* **matrix**
matricide ['meɪtrɪsaɪd] (N) **1** (= *act*) matricidio *m*
2 (= *person*) matricida *mf*
matriculate [mə'trɪkjʊleɪt] (VT) matricular
(VI) matricularse
matriculation [mə,trɪkjʊ'leɪʃən] (N)
1 matriculación *f*
2 (*Brit*) (*Univ*) (*formerly*) examen *m* de ingreso
matrimonial [,mætrɪ'məʊnɪəl] (ADJ) [*problems*] matrimonial; [*vow, bed*] de matrimonio; [*life*] conyugal • **the ~ home** el domicilio conyugal
matrimony ['mætrɪmənɪ] (N) matrimonio *m*
matrix ['meɪtrɪks] (N) (PL: **matrixes** *or* **matrices**) (*all senses*) matriz *f*
matron ['meɪtrən] (N) **1** (*in nursing home*) supervisora *f*
2† (*in hospital*) enfermera *f* jefe
3 (*in school*) enfermera *f*
4 (= *married woman*) matrona *f*
(CPD) ▸ **matron of honour** dama *f* de honor (*casada*)
matronly ['meɪtrənlɪ] (ADJ) matronal, de matrona; [*figure*] maduro y algo corpulento
matt [mæt] (ADJ) mate
(CPD) ▸ **matt emulsion** pintura *f* mate
matted ['mætɪd] (ADJ) enmarañado y apelmazado • **~ hair** greñas *fpl*, pelo *m* enmarañado y apelmazado • **~ with blood** enmarañado y apelmazado por la sangre
matter ['mætəʳ] (N) **1** (= *substance*) materia *f*, sustancia *f*
2 (*Typ, Publishing*) material *m* • **advertising ~** material *m* publicitario • **printed ~** impresos *mpl*
3 (*Med*) (= *pus*) pus *m*, materia *f*
4 (*Literat*) (= *content*) contenido *m* • **form and ~** la forma y el contenido
5 (= *question, affair*) asunto *m*, cuestión *f* • **in this ~** en este asunto • **that's quite another ~** • **that's another ~ altogether** esa es otra cuestión, eso es totalmente distinto • **business ~s** negocios *mpl* • **the ~ is closed** el asunto está concluido • **as a ~ of course** automáticamente • **it's a ~ of course with us** con nosotros es cosa de cajón • **that's a very different ~** esa es otra cuestión, eso es totalmente distinto • **it's an easy ~ to phone him** es cosa fácil llamarle • **it will be no easy ~** no será fácil • **as a ~ of fact ...**: • **as a ~ of fact I know her very well** de hecho *or* en realidad la conozco muy bien • **I don't like it, as a ~ of fact I'm totally against it** no me gusta, de hecho estoy totalmente en contra • **"don't tell me you like it?" — "as a ~ of fact I do"** —no me digas que te gusta —pues sí, la verdad es que sí • **as a ~ of fact we were just talking about you** precisamente estábamos hablando de ti • **for that ~** en realidad • **it's a ~ of form** es pura formalidad • **the ~ in hand** la cuestión del momento • **money ~s** asuntos *mpl* financieros • **it is no great ~** es poca cosa, no importa • **in the ~ of** en cuanto a, en lo que se refiere • **there's the ~ of my wages** queda el asunto de mi sueldo • **it will be a ~ of a few weeks** será cuestión de unas semanas • **a ~ of minutes** cosa de minutos • **it's a ~ of a couple of hours** es cosa de un par de horas • **in a ~ of ten minutes** en cosa de diez minutos • **it's a ~ of great concern to us** es motivo de gran preocupación para nosotros • **it's a ~ of taste** es cuestión de gusto • **it's a serious ~** es cosa seria; ▹ **laughing, mince**
6 (= *importance*) • **no ~!** • **it makes no ~** (*frm*) ¡no importa!, ¡no le hace! (*LAm*) • **no ~ how you do it** no importa cómo lo hagas • **no ~ how big it is** por grande que sea • **no ~ how hot it is** por mucho calor que haga • **get one, no ~ how** procura uno, del modo que sea • **no ~ what he says** diga lo que diga • **what ~?** (*frm*) ¿qué importa? • **no ~ when** no importa cuándo • **no ~ who goes** quienquiera que vaya

m

7 (= *difficulty, problem etc*) • **what's the ~?** ¿qué pasa?, ¿qué hay? • **what's the ~ with you?** ¿qué te pasa?, ¿qué tienes? • **what's the ~ with Tony?** ¿qué le pasa a Tony? • **something's the ~ with the lights** algo les pasa a las luces, algo pasa con las luces • **what's the ~ with my hat?** ¿qué pasa con mi sombrero? • **what's the ~ with singing?** ¿por qué no se puede cantar?, ¿es que está prohibido cantar? • **nothing's the ~** no pasa nada • **as if nothing were the ~** como si no hubiese pasado nada, como si tal cosa
8 matters (= *things*) situación *fsing* • **as ~s stand** tal como están las cosas • **to make ~s worse** para colmo de males
VI importar • **does it ~ to you if I go?** ¿te importa que yo vaya? • **why should it ~ to me?** ¿a mí qué me importa *or* qué más me da? • **it doesn't ~** (*unimportant*) no importa; (*no preference*) (me) da igual *or* lo mismo • **what does it ~?** ¿qué más da?, ¿y qué? • **some things ~ more than others** algunas cosas son más importantes que otras

matter-of-fact [ˈmætərəvˈfækt] ADJ [*style*] prosaico; [*person*] (*practical*) práctico
Matthew [ˈmæθjuː] N Mateo
matting [ˈmætɪŋ] N estera *f*
mattins [ˈmætɪnz] NSING OR NPL = **matins**
mattock [ˈmætək] N azadón *m*
mattress [ˈmætrɪs] N colchón *m*
maturation [ˌmætjʊˈreɪʃən] N (*frm*) maduración *f*
mature [məˈtjʊəʳ] ADJ (COMPAR: **maturer**, SUPERL: **maturest**) **1** (*emotionally*) maduro • **she's very ~ for her age** es muy madura para su edad
2 (*physically*) [*animal, plant*] adulto • **to be physically ~** estar desarrollado • **of ~ years** de edad madura
3 [*wine, whisky*] añejo; [*cheese*] curado
4 (*Econ*) [*insurance policy, investment*] vencido
VI **1** [*person*] (*emotionally*) madurar; [*child, young animal*] (*physically*) desarrollarse • **she had ~d into a self-possessed young woman** se había convertido en una joven dueña de sí misma • **her style had not yet ~d** su estilo aún no había madurado
2 [*wine, whisky*] añejarse; [*cheese*] curarse
3 (*Econ*) [*insurance policy, investment*] vencer
VT [+ *wine, whisky*] añejar; [+ *cheese*] curar
CPD ▸ **mature student** estudiante *mf* mayor
maturely [məˈtjʊəlɪ] ADV de manera juiciosa, con madurez
maturity [məˈtjʊərɪtɪ] N **1** (*emotional*) madurez *f*
2 (*physical*) [*of person, animal*] madurez *f*, pleno desarrollo *m*; [*of plant*] pleno desarrollo *m* • **to reach physical ~** alcanzar su pleno desarrollo
3 (*Econ*) [*of insurance policy, bond*] vencimiento *m*
matzo [ˈmætsəʊ] N matzá *m*
maudlin [ˈmɔːdlɪn] ADJ (= *weepy*) llorón; (= *sentimental*) sensiblero
maul [mɔːl] VT **1** (*lit*) [*tiger, bear*] atacar y malherir • **to ~ sb to death** atacar y matar a algn
2 (*fig*) [+ *writer, play*] vapulear; [+ *text*] destrozar, arruinar; [+ *team, competitor, candidate*] dar una paliza a • **he got badly ~ed in the press** la prensa lo vapuleó, la prensa lo puso como un trapo*
N (*Rugby*) melé *f* espontánea
mauling [ˈmɔːlɪŋ] N • **to get a ~** [*player, team*] recibir una paliza; [*author, book*] ser vapuleado
maunder [ˈmɔːndəʳ] VI divagar
Maundy [ˈmɔːndɪ] CPD ▸ **Maundy money** (*Brit*) *dinero que reparte el monarca a los pobres el Jueves Santo* ▸ **Maundy Thursday** Jueves *m* Santo
Maurice [ˈmɒrɪs] N Mauricio
Mauritania [ˌmɔːrɪˈteɪnɪə] N Mauritania *f*
Mauritanian [ˌmɔːrɪˈteɪnɪən] ADJ mauritano
N mauritano/a *m/f*
Mauritian [məˈrɪʃən] ADJ mauriciano
N mauriciano/a *m/f*
Mauritius [məˈrɪʃəs] N (isla *f*) Mauricio *m*
mausoleum [ˌmɔːsəˈliːəm] N (PL: **mausoleums** *or* **mausolea** [ˌmɔːsəˈliːə]) mausoleo *m*
mauve [məʊv] ADJ malva
N malva *m*
maverick [ˈmævərɪk] N **1** (*US*) (*Agr*) res *f* sin marcar
2 (= *nonconformist*) inconformista *mf*; (*Pol etc*) disidente *mf*
ADJ (= *nonconformist*) inconformista; (*Pol*) disidente
maw [mɔː] N **1** (*Anat*) estómago *m*; [*of cow etc*] cuajar *m*; [*of bird*] molleja *f*, buche *m*
2 (*fig*) fauces *fpl*
mawkish [ˈmɔːkɪʃ] ADJ empalagoso, sensiblero, insulso
mawkishness [ˈmɔːkɪʃnɪs] N sensiblería *f*, insulsez *f*
max [mæks] ABBR (= **maximum**) máx. • **a couple of weeks, max** dos semanas como máximo
N • **to do sth to the max*** hacer algo al máximo, hacer algo a tope*
maxi* [ˈmæksɪ] N (= *skirt*) maxifalda *f*, maxi* *f*
maxi... [ˈmæksɪ] PREFIX maxi...
maxilla [mækˈsɪlə] N (PL: **maxillae** [mækˈsɪliː]) maxilar *m* superior
maxillary [mækˈsɪlərɪ] ADJ (*Anat*) maxilar
maxim [ˈmæksɪm] N máxima *f*
maxima [ˈmæksɪmə] NPL *of* **maximum**
maximal [ˈmæksɪməl] ADJ máximo
maximization [ˌmæksɪmaɪˈzeɪʃən] N [*of profits, assets, potential*] maximización *f*
maximize [ˈmæksɪmaɪz] VT [+ *profits, assets, potential, opportunities*] maximizar
maximum [ˈmæksɪməm] ADJ [*amount, temperature, speed, load, efficiency*] máximo • **for ~ benefit, use once a week** para obtener un beneficio máximo úsese una vez a la semana • **for ~ effect** para conseguir el máximo efecto • **to use sth to ~ effect** usar algo de manera muy efectiva • **~ expenditure** gasto *m* máximo • **a ~ security prison/hospital** una prisión/un hospital de máxima seguridad • **~ sentence** condena *f* máxima
N (PL: **maximums** *or* **maxima**) máximo *m* • **20 kilos is the ~** el máximo son 20 kilos • **at the ~** como máximo, a lo sumo • **up to a ~ of £20** hasta 20 libras como máximo • **to the ~** al máximo
ADV como máximo • **you should drink two cups of coffee a day ~** deberías beber dos tazas de café al día como máximo, deberías beber un máximo de dos tazas de café al día
maxi-single [ˈmæksɪˈsɪŋgəl] N (*Mus*) maxisingle *m*
maxiskirt [ˈmæksɪˌskɜːt] N maxifalda *f*
May [meɪ] N mayo *m*; ▹ **July**
CPD ▸ **May Day** el primero de mayo ▸ **May Queen** reina *f* de mayo
may¹ [meɪ] (PT, COND: **might**) MODAL VB **1** (*of possibility*) • **it may rain** puede *or* es posible que llueva • **it may be that he has had to go out** puede (ser) que haya tenido que salir • **he may not be hungry** a lo mejor no tiene hambre • **they may well be related** puede que sean parientes • **that's as may be** eso puede ser • **be that as it may** sea como sea • **they may have gone out** puede que hayan salido, a lo mejor han salido • **he may not have spoken to her yet** a lo mejor no ha hablado con ella todavía, puede que no haya hablado con ella todavía • **I may have said so** es posible que lo haya dicho • **yes, I may** sí, es posible, sí, a lo mejor • **I might have said so** pudiera haberlo dicho • **as you might expect** como era de esperar, según cabía esperar • **who might you be?** ¿quién es usted? • **how old might you be?** ¿cuántos años tendrás? • **such a policy as might bring peace** una política que pudiera traernos la paz
2 (*of permission*) poder • **yes, you may** sí, puedes, ¡cómo no! • **if I may** si me lo permites • **may I?** ¿me permite?, con permiso • **may I go now?** ¿puedo irme ya? • **may I see it?** ¿se puede ver?, ¿puedo verlo? • **may I come in?** ¿se puede?, con permiso • **you may smoke** se permite fumar • **you may not smoke** se prohíbe fumar • **if I may advise you** si permites que te dé un consejo • **might I suggest that ...?** me permito sugerir que ...
3 (*in wishes*) • **may you have a happy life together** ¡que seáis felices! • **may God bless you** ¡Dios te bendiga! • **may you be forgiven!** ¡que Dios te perdone! • **long may he reign!** ¡que reine muchos años! • **or may I never eat prawns again** o que no vuelva nunca a comer gambas
4 (*frm or liter*) • **I hope he may succeed** espero que tenga éxito • **I hoped he might succeed this time** esperaba que lo lograra esta vez
5 • **might a** (*suggesting*) • **you might try Smith's** podrías probar en la tienda de Smith • **mightn't it be better to ...?** (+ *infin*) ¿no sería mejor ...? (+ *infin*)
b (*criticizing*) • **you might shut the door!** ¡podrías *or* podías cerrar la puerta! • **he might have offered to help** podría haberse prestado a ayudar • **you might have told me!** ¡habérmelo dicho!
6 (*in phrases*) • **we may** *or* **might as well go** vámonos ya *or* de una vez • **run as he might** por mucho que corriese
may² [meɪ] N (*Bot*) (= *blossom*) flor *f* del espino; (*Brit*) (= *tree*) espino *m*
Maya [ˈmaɪjə], **Mayan** [ˈmaɪjən] ADJ maya
N maya *mf*
maybe [ˈmeɪbiː] ADV a lo mejor, quizá(s), tal vez • **~ he'll come tomorrow** a lo mejor viene mañana, puede que *or* quizá(s) *or* tal vez venga mañana • **~ I should grow a moustache** a lo mejor debería dejarme bigote • **there were ~ ten people in the room** habría unas diez personas en la habitación • **maybe, maybe not** puede que sí, puede que no, a lo mejor sí, a lo mejor no
Mayday [ˈmeɪdeɪ] N (= *distress call*) socorro *m*, SOS *m*
mayfly [ˈmeɪflaɪ] N cachipolla *f*, efímera *f*
mayhem [ˈmeɪhem] N **1** alboroto *m*, caos *m*
2 (*US*) (*Jur*) mutilación *f* criminal
mayn't [meɪnt] = **may not**
mayo* [ˈmeɪəʊ] N (*US*) = **mayonnaise**
mayonnaise [meɪəˈneɪz] N mayonesa *f*; ▹ **garlic**
mayor [mɛəʳ] N alcalde *m*, alcaldesa *f*, intendente *mf* (*S. Cone, Mex*), regente *mf* (*Mex*) • **Mr Mayor** Señor Alcalde • **Madam Mayor** Señora Alcaldesa
mayoral [ˈmɛərəl] ADJ [*candidate, election*] para alcalde, para la alcaldía
mayoralty [ˈmɛərəltɪ] N alcaldía *f*
mayoress [ˈmɛəres] (*Brit*) N (= *lady mayor, wife of mayor*) alcaldesa *f*, intendente *f* (*S. Cone, Mex*), regente *f* (*Mex*)
maypole [ˈmeɪpəʊl] N mayo *m*

maze [meɪz] (N) laberinto *m*
MB (N ABBR) **1** (*Brit*) (*Univ*) = **Bachelor of Medicine**
2 (*Canada*)
(ABBR) = **Manitoba**
Mb (N ABBR) (*Comput*) (= **megabyte**) Mb
MBA (N ABBR) (*Univ*) (= **Master of Business Administration**) ▹ DEGREE
m-banking ['em,bæŋkɪŋ] (N) banca *f* móvil
MBBS, MBChB (N ABBR) (*Univ*) = **Bachelor of Medicine and Surgery**
MBE (N ABBR) (= **Member of the Order of the British Empire**) *título ceremonial británico*; ▹ HONOURS LIST
MBO (N ABBR) (*Econ*) = **management buyout**
m-book ['embʊk] (N) libro *m* para el móvil (*Sp*), libro *m* para el celular (*LAm*)
MC (N ABBR) **1** = **Master of Ceremonies**
2 (*US*) = **Member of Congress**
3 (*Brit*) (*Mil*) = **Military Cross**
MCA (ABBR) = **maximum credible accident**
MCAT (N ABBR) (*US*) (*Univ*) = **Medical College Admissions Test**
McCarthyism [mə'kɑːθɪɪzəm] (N) (*US*) (*Pol*) macartismo *m*
McCoy [mə'kɔɪ] (N) ▹ **real**
m-commerce ['em,kɒmɜːs] (N) comercio *m* móvil
MCP‡ (N ABBR) (= **male chauvinist pig**) ▹ **chauvinist**
m/cycle (ABBR) = **motorcycle**
MD (N ABBR) **1** = **Doctor of Medicine**
2 = **managing director**
3 (= **MiniDisc**®) minidisc *m*
(ABBR) **1** = **mentally deficient**
2 (*US*) = **Maryland**
(CPD) ▸ **MD player** minidisc *m*
MDF [,ɛmdiː'ɛf] (N ABBR) (= **medium-density fibreboard**) MDF *m*
MDMA (N ABBR) MDMA *m*
MDT (N ABBR) (*US*) = **Mountain Daylight Time**
ME (N ABBR) **1** = **myalgic encephalomyelitis**
2 (*US*) = **medical examiner**
(ABBR) (*US*) = **Maine**
me[1] [miː] (PRON) **1** (*direct/indirect object*) me; (*after prep*) mí • **he loves me** me quiere • **look at me!** ¡mírame! • **could you lend me your pen?** ¿me prestas tu bolígrafo? • **without me** sin mí • **come with me** ven conmigo • **like me** como yo • **dear me!** ¡vaya!
2 (*emphatic, in comparisons, after verb "to be"*) yo • **who, me?** ¿quién, yo? • **what, me?** ¿cómo, yo? • **he's taller than me** es más alto que yo • **it's me** soy yo • **it's me, Paul** (*identifying self*) soy Paul
me[2] [miː] (N) (*Mus*) mi *m*
Me. (ABBR) (*US*) = **Maine**
mead [miːd] (N) aguamiel *f*, hidromiel *m*
meadow ['medəʊ] (N) prado *m*, pradera *f*; (*esp water meadow*) vega *f*
meadowland ['medəʊlænd] (N) prados *mpl*
meadowlark ['medəʊlɑːk] (N) pradero *m*
meadowsweet ['medəʊswiːt] (N) reina *f* de los prados
meagre, meager (*US*) ['miːgə'] (ADJ) [*amount, salary, rations*] escaso, exiguo • **he eked out a ~ existence as a labourer** a duras penas se ganaba la vida trabajando de peón • **his salary is a ~ £350 a month** gana unas míseras 350 libras al mes
meagrely ['miːgəlɪ], **meagerly** (*US*) (ADV) escasamente, pobremente
meal[1] [miːl] (N) comida *f* • **to go for a ~** ir a comer fuera • **to have a (good) ~** comer (bien) • **I don't eat between ~s** no como entre horas • **~s on wheels** servicio *m* de comidas a domicilio (*para ancianos*) • IDIOM: • **to make a ~ of sth*** (= *dramatize*) exagerar algo; (= *make the most of*) sacar todo el jugo posible a algo; (= *take time over*) tardar lo suyo en hacer algo
(CPD) ▸ **meal ticket** (*lit*) vale *m* de comida; (*fig*) • **she's just looking for a ~ ticket** solo busca a alguien que la mantenga
meal[2] [miːl] (N) (= *flour*) harina *f*
mealie meal ['miːlɪmiːl] (N) harina *f* de maíz, maicena *f* (*Sp*), Maizena® *f* (*Sp*)
mealtime ['miːltaɪm] (N) hora *f* de comer
mealworm ['miːlwɜːm] (N) gusano *m* de la harina
mealy ['miːlɪ] (ADJ) harinoso
mealy-mouthed ['miːlɪ'maʊðd] (ADJ) modoso, evasivo • **let us not be mealy-mouthed about it** hablemos claro sobre esto
mean[1] [miːn] (ADJ) (COMPAR: **meaner**, SUPERL: **meanest**) **1** (= *stingy*) tacaño, agarrado*, amarrete (*And, S. Cone**) • **you ~ thing!** ¡qué tacaño eres!
2 (= *nasty*) malo • **don't be ~!** ¡no seas malo! • **you ~ thing!** ¡qué malo eres! • **a ~ trick** una jugarreta, una mala pasada • **that was pretty ~ of them** se han portado bastante mal • **you were ~ to me** te portaste fatal *or* muy mal conmigo
3 (= *vicious*) malo
4 (= *of poor quality*) inferior; (= *shabby*) humilde, vil; (= *humble*) [*birth*] humilde, pobre • **the ~est citizen** el ciudadano más humilde • **obvious to the ~est intelligence** obvio para cualquiera con un mínimo de sentido común • **she's no ~ cook** es una cocinera excelente
5 (*US*) formidable, de primera • **he plays a ~ game** juega estupendamente
mean[2] [miːn] (N) (= *middle term*) término *m* medio; (= *average*) promedio *m*; (*Math*) media *f* • **the golden** *or* **happy ~** el justo medio
(ADJ) medio • **~ life** (*Phys*) vida *f* media
mean[3] [miːn] (PT, PP: **meant**) (VT) **1** [*word, sign*] (= *signify*) significar, querer decir • **what does this word ~?** ¿qué significa *or* quiere decir esta palabra? • **"vest" ~s something different in America** en América "vest" tiene otro significado *or* significa otra cosa • **you know what it ~s to hit a policeman?** ¿usted sabe qué consecuencias trae el golpear a un policía? • **what do you ~ by that?** ¿qué quieres decir con eso? • **it ~s a lot to have you with us** significa mucho tenerte con nosotros • **your friendship ~s a lot to me** tu amistad es muy importante *or* significa mucho para mí • **a pound ~s a lot to her** para ella una libra es mucho dinero • **it ~s a lot of expense for us** supone un gasto muy fuerte para nosotros • **the name ~s nothing to me** el nombre no me suena • **the play didn't ~ a thing to me** no saqué nada en claro de la obra; ▹ **know**
2 [*person*] **a** (= *imply*) querer decir; (= *refer to*) referirse a • **what do you ~?** ¿qué quieres decir? • **18, I ~ 19** 18, digo 19 • **do you ~ me?** ¿te refieres a mí?
b (= *signify*) significar • **don't I ~ anything to you?** ¿no significo yo nada para ti?
c (= *be determined about*) • **I ~ what I say** lo digo en serio • **you can't ~ it!** ¡no lo dirás en serio! • **I ~ it** va en serio
d (= *intend*) • **to ~ to do sth** pensar hacer algo • **what do you ~ to do?** ¿qué piensas hacer? • **I ~t to help** pensaba ayudar, tenía la intención de ayudar • **I ~ to have it** pienso *or* me propongo obtenerlo • **he didn't ~ to do it** lo hizo sin querer • **I ~ to have you sacked** voy a encargarme de que te despidan • **sorry, I didn't ~ you to do it** lo siento, mi intención no era que lo hicieras tú • **I ~ to be obeyed** insisto en que se me obedezca • **if he ~s to be awkward** si quiere complicar las cosas • **I ~t it as a joke** lo dije en broma • **was the remark ~t for me?** ¿el comentario iba por mí? • **I ~t no harm by what I said** no lo dije con mala intención • **he ~t no offence** no tenía intención de ofender a nadie • **he ~s well** tiene buenas intenciones
3 (= *suppose*) suponer • **to be ~t to do sth**: • **it's ~t to be a good car** este coche se supone que es bueno • **parents are ~t to love their children** se supone que los padres quieren a sus hijos • **the teacher is ~t to do it** se supone que el profesor lo debe hacer • **we were ~t to arrive at eight** se suponía que llegaríamos a las ocho • **this picture is ~t to tell a story** este cuadro se propone contar una historia • **this portrait is ~t to be Anne** este retrato es de Anne, aunque no lo parezca • **perhaps you weren't ~t to be a vet** quizá lo tuyo no sea la veterinaria • **I wasn't ~t to work for my living!** ¡yo no estoy hecho para trabajar! • **you're not ~t to drink it!** ¡no es para beber!
meander [mɪ'ændə'] (VI) **1** [*river*] serpentear
2 [*person*] (= *roam*) deambular, vagar; (*in speech*) divagar
(N) meandro *m* • **~s** (*fig*) meandros *mpl*
meandering [mɪ'ændərɪŋ] (ADJ) **1** (*lit*) [*river*] con meandros; [*road*] serpenteante
2 (*fig*) [*account, speech etc*] lleno de digresiones
meanderings [mɪ'ændərɪŋz] (NPL) (*fig*) divagaciones *fpl*
meanie* ['miːnɪ] (N) • **he's an old ~** es un tío agarrado*
meaning ['miːnɪŋ] (N) **1** (= *sense*) [*of word*] significado *m*, acepción *f*; [*of phrase*] significado *m*; [*of life, work*] sentido *m* • **this word has lots of ~s** esta palabra tiene muchos significados *or* muchas acepciones • **life has no ~ for her now** ahora para ella la vida no tiene sentido • **double ~** doble sentido • **do you get my ~?** ¿me entiendes?, ¿me comprendes? • **he doesn't know the ~ of the word** (*fig*) ni sabe lo que eso significa • **what's the ~ of "hick"?** ¿qué significa "hick"?, ¿qué quiere decir "hick"? • **what's the ~ of this?** (*as reprimand*) ¿se puede saber qué significa esto?
2 (= *intention*) intención *f*, propósito *m* • **a look full of ~** una mirada llena de intención • **to mistake sb's ~** malinterpretar la intención de algn
(ADJ) [*look etc*] significativo, lleno de intención
meaningful ['miːnɪŋfʊl] (ADJ)
1 (= *worthwhile*) [*discussion, negotiations*] valioso, positivo; [*experience*] valioso, significativo; [*relationship*] serio, significativo; [*activity*] que merece la pena; [*question, explanation*] coherente, que tiene sentido; [*comment, analogy*] que tiene sentido • **to lead a ~ life** vivir una vida que tenga sentido • **nothing ~ is ever discussed at these meetings** en estas reuniones nunca se discute nada de trascendencia *or* nada que merezca la pena
2 (= *eloquent*) [*smile, look*] significativo, elocuente
meaningfully ['miːnɪŋfəlɪ] (ADV) **1** (= *in a worthwhile way*) • **to spend one's time ~** emplear el tiempo en algo que valga la pena
2 (= *eloquently*) [*smile, look, say*] de manera significativa
meaningless ['miːnɪŋlɪs] (ADJ) (*gen*) sin sentido • **in this situation it is ~** en esta situación no tiene sentido • **to write "xybj" is ~** escribir "xybj" carece de sentido
meanly ['miːnlɪ] (ADV) **1** (= *stingily*) mezquinamente
2 (= *nastily*) maliciosamente

m

meanness ['mi:nnɪs] (N) **1** (= *stinginess*) tacañería *f*, mezquindad *f*
2 (= *nastiness*) maldad *f*, vileza *f*
3 (= *humbleness*) humildad *f*

means [mi:nz] (N) **1** (*with sing vb*) (= *way*) manera *fsing*, modo *msing*; (= *method*) medio *msing* • **by any ~** de cualquier manera, del modo que sea • **not by any ~** de ninguna manera *or* ningún modo • **by any ~ possible** como sea/fuera posible, a como dé/diera lugar (*CAm, Mex*) • **there is no ~ of doing it** no hay manera *or* modo de hacerlo • **by some ~ or other** de alguna manera u otra, de algún modo u otro • **by this ~** de esta manera, de este modo • **a ~ to an end** un medio para conseguir algo *or* un fin • **by ~ of** por medio de • **it moves by ~ of a pulley system** se mueve por medio de poleas • **~ of transport** medio *m* de transporte; ▷ **fair¹**
2 (*in phrases*) • **by all ~!** ¡claro que sí!, ¡por supuesto! • **by all ~ take one** por favor toma uno • **"is she a friend of yours?" — "by no means"** —¿es amiga suya? —de ninguna manera *or* ningún modo • **they're by no ~ rich** no son ricos, ni mucho menos • **it is by no ~ difficult** no es nada difícil • **by no manner of ~** en absoluto
3 (*with pl vb*) (*Econ*) recursos *mpl*, medios *mpl* • **we haven't the ~ to do it** no contamos con los recursos *or* los medios para hacerlo • **to live beyond one's ~** vivir por encima de sus posibilidades, gastar más de lo que se gana • **a man of ~** un hombre acaudalado • **private ~** rentas *fpl* (particulares) • **to live within one's ~** vivir de acuerdo con sus posibilidades
(CPD) ▸ **means test** prueba *f* de haberes (*para determinar si una persona tiene derecho a determinada prestación*); ▷ **means-test**

mean-spirited [,mi:n'spɪrɪtɪd] (ADJ) malintencionado

means-test ['mi:nztest] (VT) • **this benefit is means-tested** este subsidio se otorga después de averiguar los recursos económicos del solicitante; ▷ **means**

meant [ment] (PT), (PP) *of* **mean³**

meantime ['mi:n'taɪm] (ADV) entretanto, mientras tanto
(N) • **for the ~** (*referring to now*) por ahora, de momento; (*referring to past*) entretanto • **in the ~** (*referring to now*) mientras tanto; (*referring to past*) en el ínterin • **in the ~ she had had two children** en el ínterin había tenido dos hijos

meanwhile ['mi:n'waɪl] (ADV) entretanto, mientras tanto
(N) • **in the ~** entretanto, mientras tanto

measles ['mi:zlz] (NSING) sarampión *m*

measly* ['mi:zlɪ] (ADJ) (COMPAR: **measlier**, SUPERL: **measliest**) miserable, mezquino

measurable ['meʒərəbl] (ADJ) **1** (*lit*) mensurable, que se puede medir
2 (= *perceptible*) apreciable, perceptible

measurably ['meʒərəblɪ] (ADV) sustancialmente; (= *perceptibly*) apreciablemente

measure ['meʒəʳ] (N) **1** (= *system*) medida *f* • **liquid/dry ~** medida para líquidos/áridos • **a suit made to ~** un traje hecho a (la) medida • IDIOMS: • **beyond ~**: • **our knowledge has increased beyond ~** nuestros conocimientos han aumentado enormemente *or* de manera inconmensurable • **he irritated her beyond ~** la irritaba hasta más no poder • **to have the ~ of sb** tener a algn calado* • **the government had failed to get the ~ of the crisis** el gobierno no había apreciado la magnitud de la crisis; ▷ **made-to-measure**
2 (= *measuring device*) (= *rule*) metro *m*; (= *glass*) probeta *f* graduada; ▷ **tape**
3 (= *indication*) indicativo *m* • **it is a ~ of how serious the situation is** es un indicativo de lo grave de la situación
4 (= *amount measured*) cantidad *f* • **I poured two equal ~s into the glasses** eché dos cantidades iguales en los vasos • **to give (sb) good** *or* **full ~** dar la medida exacta (a algn) • **to give (sb) short ~** dar una medida escasa (a algn) • IDIOM: • **for good ~**: • **he gave me a few extra for good ~** me dio unos pocos más por añadidura • **I repeated my question for good ~** repetí la pregunta por si acaso
5 (= *step*) medida *f* • **to take ~s against sb** tomar medidas contra algn • **to take ~s to do sth** tomar medidas para hacer algo • **they took no ~s to avoid the disaster** no tomaron ninguna medida para evitar el desastre
6 (= *extent*) • **we had some ~ of success** tuvimos cierto éxito • **it gives a ~ of protection** da cierta protección • **in large ~** en gran parte *or* medida • **this is due in no small ~ to the problems we have had** esto se debe en gran parte *or* medida a los problemas que hemos tenido • **in some ~** hasta cierto punto, en cierta medida
7 [*of spirits*] cantidad *f*; (*sold in pub*) medida *f*
8 (*Mus*) (= *beat*) ritmo *m*; (= *bar*) compás *m*
(VT) **1** [+ *object, speed, length, width, height*] medir; [+ *person*] (*for height*) medir; (*for clothes*) tomar las medidas a • **to ~ the height of sth** medir la altura de algo • **I have to be ~d for my costume** me tienen que tomar las medidas para el traje • **how can you ~ success?** ¿cómo puedes medir el éxito? • **to ~ one's length (on the floor/ground)** caerse todo lo largo que se es (al suelo); ▷ **word**
2 (= *compare*) • **to ~ sth/sb against sth/sb** comparar algo/a algn con algo/algn • **I don't like being ~d against other people** no me gusta que se me compare con otra gente • **the competition will be a chance for him to ~ himself against the best** la competición será una ocasión para medirse con los mejores
(VI) medir • **what does it ~?** ¿cuánto mide? • **the room ~s four metres across** la habitación mide cuatro metros de ancho

▸ **measure off** (VT + ADV) medir

▸ **measure out** (VT + ADV) **1** [+ *solid ingredients*] pesar; [+ *liquid, piece of ground, length*] medir
2 (= *give out*) repartir, distribuir

▸ **measure up** (VT + ADV) **1** [+ *wood, material*] medir
2 (= *evaluate*) [+ *sb's intentions*] averiguar; [+ *situation*] evaluar
(VI + ADV) **1** (= *take measurements*) tomar medidas • **she ~d up for the curtains** tomó medidas para las cortinas
2 (= *fulfil expectations*) dar la talla, estar a la altura • **to ~ up to sth** estar a la altura de algo

measured ['meʒəd] (ADJ) [*tread, pace*] acompasado; [*tone, way of talking, statement*] mesurado, comedido

measureless ['meʒəlɪs] (ADJ) inmensurable, inmenso

measurement ['meʒəmənt] (N) **1** (= *size*) medida *f* • **bust/hip ~** contorno *m* de pecho/de caderas • **inside leg ~** largo *m* de entrepierna • **waist ~** cintura *f*, talle *m* • **to take sb's ~s** tomar las medidas a algn
2 (= *act, system*) medición *f*

measuring ['meʒərɪŋ] (N) medición *f*
(CPD) ▸ **measuring chain** cadena *f* de agrimensor ▸ **measuring cup** taza *f* para medir ▸ **measuring jug** jarra *f* medidora *or* graduada ▸ **measuring rod** vara *f* de medir ▸ **measuring spoon** cuchara *f* medidora ▸ **measuring tape** cinta *f* métrica, metro *m*

meat [mi:t] (N) **1** (*gen*) carne *f*; (= *cold meat*) fiambre *m* • IDIOM: • **it's ~ and drink to me** no puedo vivir sin ello • PROVERB: • **one man's ~ is another man's poison** lo que a uno cura a otro mata
2 (*fig*) enjundia *f*, sustancia *f* • **a book with some ~ in it** un libro con enjundia *or* sustancia
(CPD) ▸ **meat eater** (= *person*) persona *f* que come carne; (*Zool*) carnívoro/a *m/f* • **we're not ~ eaters** no comemos carne ▸ **meat extract** extracto *m* de carne ▸ **meat grinder** (*US*) máquina *f* de picar carne ▸ **meat hook** gancho *m* carnicero ▸ **meat industry** industria *f* cárnica ▸ **meat loaf** *rollo de carne picada sazonado, cocido y servido como fiambre* ▸ **meat pie** pastel *m* de carne; (*individual*) empanada *f* ▸ **meat products** productos *mpl* cárnicos ▸ **meat safe** (*Brit*) fresquera *f*

meatball ['mi:t'bɔ:l] (N) albóndiga *f*

meat-eating ['mi:t,i:tɪŋ] (ADJ) carnívoro

meatfly ['mi:tflaɪ] (N) mosca *f* de la carne

meathead‡ ['mi:thed] (N) (*US*) idiota *mf*, gilipollas** *mf*

meatless ['mi:tlɪs] (ADJ) [*diet*] sin carne • **~ day** día *m* de vigilia

meatpacking ['mi:tpækɪŋ] (N) (*US*) (*Comm*) procesado *m* de la carne; (= *industry*) industria *f* cárnica
(CPD) ▸ **meatpacking industry** industria *f* cárnica

meaty ['mi:tɪ] (ADJ) (COMPAR: **meatier**, SUPERL: **meatiest**) **1** [*soup, filling*] con carne; [*flavour*] a carne
2 (*fig*) **a** (= *substantial*) [*argument, book*] sustancioso, enjundioso; [*part, role*] importante, de peso
b (= *fleshy*) [*arm, hand*] rollizo

Mecca ['mekə] (N) La Meca; (*fig*) • **a ~ for tourists** una de las mecas del turismo

Meccano® [mɪ'kɑ:nəʊ] (N) (*Brit*) mecano® *m*

mechanic [mɪ'kænɪk] (N) mecánico/a *m/f*

mechanical [mɪ'kænɪkəl] (ADJ) **1** [*toy, problem, failure, device*] mecánico
2 (*fig*) (= *unthinking*) [*behaviour, reply*] mecánico, maquinal
(CPD) ▸ **mechanical drawing** diseño *m* mecánico ▸ **mechanical engineer** ingeniero/a *m/f* mecánico/a ▸ **mechanical engineering** ingeniería *f* mecánica

mechanically [mɪ'kænɪkəlɪ] (ADV) **1** [*operated, driven*] mecánicamente • **I'm not ~ minded** no se me da muy bien la mecánica, no tengo cabeza para las cosas mecánicas
2 (*fig*) (= *unthinkingly*) [*behave, reply*] mecánicamente, maquinalmente

mechanics [mɪ'kænɪks] (NSING) (*Tech, Phys*) mecánica *f*
(NPL) (= *machinery*) mecanismo *msing*; (*fig*) mecánica *f*

mechanism ['mekənɪzəm] (N) **1** (*gen*) mecanismo *m*
2 (*Philos*) mecanicismo *m*

mechanistic [,mekə'nɪstɪk] (ADJ) **1** (*gen*) mecánico, maquinal
2 (*Philos*) mecanístico

mechanization [,mekənaɪ'zeɪʃən] (N) mecanización *f*

mechanize ['mekənaɪz] (VT) [+ *process, task*] mecanizar; [+ *factory*] automatizar

mechanized ['mekənaɪzd] (ADJ) [*process*] mecanizado; [*troops, unit*] motorizado

MEd [em'ed] (N ABBR) (*Univ*) = **Master of Education**

Med* [med] (N) • **the Med** el Mediterráneo

med., med (ABBR) = **medium**

medal ['medl] (N) medalla *f* • **he deserves a ~ for it** merece que le den una medalla por ello

medallion [mɪˈdælɪən] (N) medallón *m*
medallist, medalist (US) [ˈmedəlɪst] (N) medallista *mf* • **Olympic ~** medallista *mf* olímpico/a • **bronze/silver/gold ~** medalla *mf* de bronce/plata/oro
medal-winner [ˈmedəlwɪnəʳ] (N) medallista *mf*
meddle [ˈmedl] (VI) **1** (= *interfere*) (entro)meterse (**in en**) • **who asked you to ~?** ¿quién te manda a ti meterte en esto? • **he's always meddling** es un entrometido **2** • **to ~ with sth** (= *touch*) toquetear algo, manosear algo; (*causing damage*) estropear algo
meddler [ˈmedləʳ] (N) entrometido/a *m/f*
meddlesome [ˈmedlsəm] (ADJ) entrometido
meddlesomeness [ˈmedlsəmnɪs] (N) entrometimiento *m*
meddling [ˈmedlɪŋ] (N) intromisión *f* (ADJ) = **meddlesome**
Mede [mi:d] (N) medo *m* • **the ~s and the Persians** los medos y los persas
media [ˈmi:dɪə] (N) (*pl of* **medium**) • **the ~** los medios de comunicación (de masas) (CPD) ▸ **media analysis** análisis *m inv* de los medios ▸ **media circus*** circo *m* mediático ▸ **media coverage** cobertura *f* informativa ▸ **media event** acontecimiento *m* periodístico ▸ **media group** grupo *m* de medios de comunicación ▸ **media hype** • **the ~ hype surrounding the royals** el bombo que los medios de comunicación le dan a la familia real ▸ **media man** (= *journalist*) periodista *m*; (*in advertising*) agente *m* de publicidad ▸ **media person** (= *journalist*) periodista *mf*; (*in advertising*) agente *mf* de publicidad; (= *personality*) personaje *mf* de los medios de comunicación ▸ **media research** investigación *f* de los medios de comunicación ▸ **media studies** (*Univ*) ciencias *fpl* de la información (*frm*), periodismo* *msing*
mediaeval [ˌmedɪˈi:vəl] (ADJ) = **medieval**
medial [ˈmi:dɪəl] (ADJ) medial
median [ˈmi:dɪən] (ADJ) mediano (N) **1** (US) (*also* **median strip**) mediana *f*, franja *f* central **2** (*Math*) (*gen*) mediana *f*; (= *number*) número *m* medio; (= *point*) punto *m* medio
mediate [ˈmi:dɪeɪt] (VI) mediar (**between** entre, **in** en) (VT) [+ *talks*] mediar en, actuar de mediador en; [+ *dispute*] mediar en, arbitrar; [+ *agreement*] conseguir mediante mediación
mediating [ˈmi:dɪeɪtɪŋ] (ADJ) [*role, efforts*] mediador • **to play a ~ role** actuar como mediador, tener un papel de mediador
mediation [ˌmi:dɪˈeɪʃən] (N) mediación *f*
mediator [ˈmi:dɪeɪtəʳ] (N) mediador(a) *m/f*
mediatory [ˈmi:dɪətərɪ] (ADJ) mediador • **in a ~ capacity** en calidad de mediador
medic* [ˈmedɪk] (N) **1** (= *doctor*) médico/a *m/f* **2** (= *student*) estudiante *mf* de medicina
Medicaid [ˈmedɪˌkeɪd] (N) (US) *seguro médico estatal para personas de bajos ingresos*
medical [ˈmedɪkəl] (ADJ) [*care, facilities, staff, treatment*] médico; [*records*] médico, clínico; [*student*] de medicina; [*problems*] de salud • **to seek ~ advice** consultar a un médico • **he is in urgent need of ~ attention** necesita atención médica urgente • **she suffered from a rare ~ condition** sufría una enfermedad rara *or* poco frecuente • **on ~ grounds** por razones de salud • **the ~ history of a patient** el historial médico *or* clínico de un paciente, la historia clínica de un paciente • **it made ~ history** pasó a la historia de la medicina • **~ opinion is divided on the subject** la opinión médica está dividida con respecto a este tema • **the ~ profession** la profesión médica (N) reconocimiento *m* médico, revisión *f* médica, examen *m* médico • **to have a ~** someterse a un reconocimiento médico *or* a un examen médico *or* a una revisión médica (CPD) ▸ **medical board** (*Mil*) consejo *m* de médicos ▸ **medical certificate** certificado *m* médico ▸ **medical ethics** ética *f* médica ▸ **medical examination** reconocimiento *m* médico, revisión *f* médica, examen *m* médico ▸ **medical examiner** (US) médico/a *m/f* forense ▸ **medical insurance** seguro *m* médico ▸ **medical officer** médico/a *m/f*; (*Mil*) oficial *mf* médico/a; [*of town*] jefe *mf* de sanidad municipal ▸ **medical practice** (= *practice of medicine*) práctica *f* de la medicina; (= *place*) consultorio *m* médico ▸ **medical practitioner** (*frm*) médico/a *m/f* ▸ **medical records** historial *msing* médico ▸ **Medical Research Council** (*Brit*) • **the Medical Research Council** *organismo británico dedicado a la investigación médica* ▸ **medical school** facultad *f* de medicina ▸ **medical science** medicina *f*, ciencia *f* médica
medicalization [ˌmedɪkəlaɪˈzeɪʃən] (N) medicalización *f*
medicalize [ˈmedɪkəlaɪz] (VT) medicalizar
medically [ˈmedɪkəlɪ] (ADV) [*prove, explain, treat*] médicamente • **he was ~ examined** se le hizo un reconocimiento médico *or* un exámen médico *or* una revisión médica • **it is recognized ~ as being a good diet** se considera una buena dieta desde el punto de vista médico • **he was pronounced ~ fit** dictaminaron que estaba sano *or* que su salud era buena; (*for army*) los médicos lo declararon apto • **~ qualified** titulado en medicina • **~ speaking** desde el punto de vista médico
medicament [meˈdɪkəmənt] (N) medicamento *m*
Medicare [ˈmedɪkeəʳ] (N) (US) *seguro médico estatal para ancianos y minusválidos*
medicate [ˈmedɪkeɪt] (VT) [+ *patient*] medicar; [+ *wound*] curar; [+ *dressing, bandage*] impregnar (**with de**)
medicated [ˈmedɪkeɪtɪd] (ADJ) medicinal (CPD) ▸ **medicated soap** jabón *m* medicinal ▸ **medicated shampoo** champú *m* medicinal ▸ **medicated cough sweets** caramelos *mpl* para la tos
medication [ˌmedɪˈkeɪʃən] (N) (= *drugs*) medicación *f*
medicinal [meˈdɪsɪnl] (ADJ) medicinal
medicinally [meˈdɪsɪnəlɪ] (ADV) [*use*] con fines médicos
medicine [ˈmedsɪn, ˈmedɪsɪn] (N) **1** (= *drug*) medicina *f*, medicamento *m* • IDIOMS: • **to give sb a dose** *or* **taste of his own ~** pagar a algn con la misma moneda • **to take one's ~** cargar con *or* arrostrar las consecuencias **2** (= *science*) medicina *f* (CPD) ▸ **medicine ball** (*Sport*) balón *m* medicinal ▸ **medicine box, medicine cabinet, medicine chest** botiquín *m* ▸ **medicine man** hechicero *m*
medico* [ˈmedɪkəʊ] (N) médico/a *m/f*
medieval [ˌmedɪˈi:vəl] (ADJ) medieval
medievalism [ˌmedɪˈi:vəlɪzəm] (N) medievalismo *m*
medievalist [ˌmedɪˈi:vəlɪst] (N) medievalista *mf*
mediocre [ˌmi:dɪˈəʊkəʳ] (ADJ) mediocre
mediocrity [ˌmi:dɪˈɒkrɪtɪ] (N) **1** (= *quality*) mediocridad *f* **2** (= *person*) mediocre *mf*
meditate [ˈmedɪteɪt] (VI) (= *think*) reflexionar, meditar (**on sobre**); (*spiritually*) meditar (VT) meditar
meditation [ˌmedɪˈteɪʃən] (N) (= *thought*) meditación *f*, reflexión *f*; (*spiritual*) meditación
meditative [ˈmedɪtətɪv] (ADJ) meditativo
meditatively [ˈmedɪtətɪvlɪ] (ADV) meditativamente, pensativamente
Mediterranean [ˌmedɪtəˈreɪnɪən] (ADJ) mediterráneo • **the ~ Sea** el mar Mediterráneo (N) • **the ~** (= *region, sea*) el Mediterráneo
medium [ˈmi:dɪəm] (ADJ) **1** (= *not small or large*) [*object*] mediano; [*length, size*] mediano, medio • **available in small, ~ and large** disponible en talla pequeña, mediana y grande • **of ~ build** de constitución mediana *or* media • **cook over a ~ heat** cocinar a fuego medio • **of ~ height** de estatura regular **2** (*Culin*) • **a ~ steak** un filete no muy hecho (N) **1** (PL: **media, mediums**) **a** (= *means of communication*) medio *m* • **the advertising media** los medios publicitarios *or* de publicidad • **through the ~ of television/the press** por medio de la televisión/la prensa, a través de la televisión/la prensa **b** (= *intervening substance*) medio *m*; (= *environment*) medio ambiente *m* • **air is a ~ for sound** el aire es un medio de transmisión del sonido **c** (*for growing culture*) caldo *m* de cultivo; (*for preserving specimens*) *sustancia usada para conservar muestras de laboratorio* **d** (= *solvent*) diluyente *m* **e** (*Art*) (= *technique, materials used*) medio *m* **f** (= *midpoint*) • **happy ~** término *m* medio **2** (PL: **mediums**) (= *spiritualist*) médium *mf* (CPD) ▸ **medium wave** (*Rad*) onda *f* media
medium-dry [ˌmi:dɪəmˈdraɪ] (ADJ) [*wine*] semi seco
medium-fine [ˌmi:dɪəmˈfaɪn] (ADJ) entrefino
medium-priced [ˌmi:dɪəmˈpraɪst] (ADJ) de precio medio
medium-range [ˌmi:dɪəmˈreɪndʒ] (ADJ) [*missile*] de alcance medio; [*weather forecast*] a medio plazo
medium-rare [ˌmi:dɪəmˈrɛəʳ] (ADV) [*steak*] en su punto, no muy hecho (*Sp*), más bien jugoso (*Arg, Uru*)
medium-size [ˌmi:dɪəmˈsaɪz], **medium-sized** [ˌmi:dɪəmˈsaɪzd] (ADJ) de tamaño mediano *or* medio • **medium-sized business** empresa *f* mediana
medium-sweet [ˌmi:dɪəmˈswi:t] (ADJ) [*wine*] semidulce
medium-term [ˈmi:dɪəmtɜ:m] (ADJ) a medio plazo
medlar [ˈmedləʳ] (N) (= *fruit, tree*) níspero *m* • **oriental** *or* **Japanese ~** níspero *m* del Japón
medley [ˈmedlɪ] (N) (= *mixture*) mezcla *f*; (= *miscellany*) miscelánea *f*; (*Mus*) popurrí *m*
medulla [meˈdʌlə] (N) (PL: **medullas** *or* **medullae** [meˈdʌli:]) medula *f*
meek [mi:k] (ADJ) (COMPAR: **meeker**, SUPERL: **meekest**) (= *submissive*) [*person*] sumiso, dócil, manso (*liter*); [*voice, acceptance*] sumiso • IDIOMS: • **~ and mild** como una malva • **as ~ as a lamb** más manso que un cordero (NPL) • **the ~** (*Rel*) los mansos • **blessed are the ~** bienaventurados los mansos
meekly [ˈmi:klɪ] (ADV) [*say, accept, follow*] sumisamente, dócilmente, mansamente (*liter*)
meekness [ˈmi:knɪs] (N) docilidad *f*, mansedumbre *f* (*liter*)
meerschaum [ˈmɪəʃəm] (N) **1** (= *material*) espuma *f* de mar **2** (*also* **meerschaum pipe**) pipa *f* de espuma de mar

m

meet[1] [mi:t] (PT, PP: **met**) VT **1** (*by arrangement*) quedar con, verse con; (*by chance*) encontrarse con, tropezarse con • **I'm ~ing them for lunch tomorrow** he quedado para almorzar con ellos mañana • **I had arranged to ~ her in town** había quedado con ella en el centro, había acordado en verla en el centro • **I'll ~ you outside the cinema** te veré en la entrada del cine • **you'll never guess who I met on the bus today!** ¿a que no sabes con quién me encontré *or* me tropecé hoy en el autobús? • **we will be ~ing the ambassador tomorrow to discuss the situation** mañana tendremos un encuentro *or* una reunión con el embajador para discutir la situación, mañana nos entrevistaremos *or* nos reuniremos con el embajador para discutir la situación
2 (= *go/come to get*) ir/venir a buscar; (= *welcome*) recibir • **we met her at the station** la fuimos a buscar a la estación • **I'm being met at the airport** me vendrán a buscar al aeropuerto • **she ran out to ~ us** salió corriendo a recibirnos • **to ~ sb off the train** ir a esperar a algn a la estación • **don't bother to ~ me** no os molestéis en venir a esperarme • **the bus for Aix ~s the ten o'clock train** el autobús que va a Aix conecta con el tren de las diez; ▹ **halfway**
3 (= *get to know, be introduced to*) conocer • **I never met him** no lo llegué a conocer • **I met my wife in 1988** conocí a mi mujer en 1988 • **~ my brother** quiero presentarte a mi hermano • **he's the kindest person I've ever met** es la persona más amable que he conocido jamás • **nice to have met you!** ¡encantado de conocerlo! • **pleased to ~ you!** ¡mucho gusto!, ¡encantado de conocerlo!
4 (= *come together with*) • **where the sea ~s the horizon** donde el mar se junta con el horizonte • **the box met the ground with an almighty thud** la caja se estrelló ruidsosamente contra el suelo • **the sound which met his ears** el sonido que llegó a sus oídos • **I could not ~ his eye** no podía mirarle a los ojos • **her eyes met her sister's across the table** tropezó con la mirada de su hermana al otro lado de la mesa • **what a scene met my eyes!** ¡el escenario que se presentó ante mis ojos!; ▹ **eye**
5 (= *come across*) [+ *problem*] encontrarse con • **almost all retired people ~ this problem** casi todos los jubilados se encuentran con este problema
6 (= *confront*) [+ *opponent*] enfrentarse con; (*in duel*) batirse con; [+ *problem*] hacer frente a • **he met his death** *or* **his end in 1800** halló *or* encontró la muerte en 1800 • **to ~ death calmly** enfrentarse con la muerte con tranquilidad • **to ~ sth head-on** enfrentarse de lleno con algo, hacer frente *or* plantar cara directamente a algo • **this suggestion was met with angry protests** la gente reaccionó con protestas de indignación ante la sugerencia; ▹ **match**[2]
7 (= *satisfy*) [+ *need*] satisfacer, cubrir; [+ *demand*] atender a, satisfacer; [+ *wish*] satisfacer; [+ *requirement*] cumplir con; [+ *debt*] pagar; [+ *expense, cost*] correr con, hacer frente a; [+ *obligation*] atender a, cumplir con; [+ *target, goal*] alcanzar; [+ *challenge*] hacer frente a; [+ *expectations*] estar a la altura de • **he offered to ~ the full cost of the repairs** se ofreció a correr con *or* hacer frente a todos los gastos de la reparación • **it did not ~ our expectations** no estuvo a la altura de nuestras expectativas
VI **1** (= *encounter each other*) (*by arrangement*) quedar, verse; (*by chance*) encontrarse; (= *hold meeting*) reunirse; [*ambassador, politician*] (*with interested parties*) entrevistarse, reunirse • **we could ~ for a drink after work** podríamos vernos *or* quedar para tomar una copa después del trabajo • **what time shall we ~?** ¿a qué hora quieres que quedemos *or* nos veamos? • **let's ~ at eight** quedemos para las ocho • **they arranged to ~ at ten** quedaron en verse a las diez • **the two ministers met to discuss the treaty** los dos ministros se entrevistaron *or* se reunieron para discutir el tratado • **to ~ again** volver a verse • **until we ~ again!** ¡hasta la vista!, ¡hasta pronto!
2 (= *convene*) [*Parliament, club, committee*] reunirse • **the society ~s at eight** la sociedad se reúne a las ocho
3 (= *get to know one another, be introduced*) conocerse • **we met in Seville** nos conocimos en Sevilla • **we have met before** nos conocemos ya • **have we met?** ¿nos conocemos de antes?
4 (= *come together, join*) [*two ends*] unirse; [*rivers*] confluir; [*roads*] empalmar • **our eyes met** cruzamos una mirada • **their lips met** sus labios se encontraron; ▹ **end, twain**
5 (= *confront each other*) [*teams, armies*] enfrentarse • **Bilbao and Valencia will ~ in the final** el Bilbao se enfrentará con el Valencia en la final, Bilbao y Valencia se disputarán la final • **to ~ (sb) in battle** librar batalla (con algn)
N (*Hunting*) cacería *f*; (*esp US*) (*Sport*) encuentro *m*
▸ **meet up** VI + ADV **1** • **to ~ up (with sb)** (*by arrangement*) quedar (con algn), verse (con algn); (*by chance*) encontrarse (con algn), tropezarse (con algn) • **they promised to ~ up again in a year's time** prometieron volver a verse *or* quedar un año después • **we ~ up for lunch occasionally** de vez en cuando quedamos para almorzar juntos • **where did you two ~ up?** (*for 1st time*) ¿dónde os conocisteis?
2 (= *join*) empalmar • **this road ~s up with the motorway** esta carretera empalma con la autopista
▸ **meet with** VI + PREP **1** (= *experience*) [+ *hostility*] experimentar; [+ *difficulties*] encontrarse con, tropezar con; [+ *kindness*] encontrarse con; [+ *accident*] tener, sufrir; [+ *success*] tener • **we hope the idea ~s with your approval** esperamos que la idea reciba su aprobación • **the idea met with a cool response** la idea fue acogida *or* recibida con frialdad • **efforts to contact her met with no response** los esfuerzos para ponerse en contacto con ella fracasaron • **attempts to find them have met with failure** los intentos de encontrarlos han fracasado
2 (*esp US*) [+ *person*] (*by arrangement*) quedarse con, verse con; (*by chance*) encontrarse con, tropezarse con; (*formally*) reunirse con; [+ *politician, ambassador*] entrevistarse con, reunirse con

meet[2] [mi:t] ADJ [*liter*] conveniente, apropiado • **it is ~ that ...** conviene que ... (+ *subjun*) • **to be ~ for** ser apto para

meeting ['mi:tɪŋ] N **1** (= *assembly, business meeting*) reunión *f*; [*of legislative body*] sesión *f*; (= *popular gathering*) mitin *m*, mitín *m* • **to address a ~** tomar la palabra en una reunión • **to call a ~** convocar una reunión • **I have a ~ at ten** tengo una reunión a las diez • **the Council had a ~ on Thursday** el Consejo se reunió el jueves • **to hold a ~** celebrar una reunión • **I'm afraid Jeremy's in a ~** ahora mismo Jeremy está reunido *or* está en una reunión • **to open a ~** abrir una sesión
2 (*between 2 people*) (*arranged*) cita *f*, compromiso *m*; (*accidental*) encuentro *m*; (*with politician, person in authority*) entrevista *f*, encuentro *m* • **I liked him from our first ~** me gustó desde el día que le conocí *or* desde nuestro primer encuentro • **to have a ~**: • **the minister had a ~ with the ambassador** el ministro se entrevistó con el embajador • **I had a ~ with the headmistress today** hoy he tenido una entrevista *or* reunión con la directora • **a ~ of minds** un encuentro de inteligencias
3 (*Athletics*) competición *f*; (*Horse racing*) jornada *f*; (*between two teams*) encuentro *m*
4 [*of rivers*] confluencia *f*
CPD ▸ **meeting house** (*gen*) centro *m* *or* sala *f* de reuniones; (*Rel*) templo *m* (de los cuáqueros) ▸ **meeting place** [*of 2 people*] lugar *m* de cita; [*of many*] lugar *m* de reunión *or* encuentro • **this bar was their usual ~ place** solían citarse en este bar, acostumbraban reunirse en este bar ▸ **meeting point** (*lit*) punto *m* de reunión, punto *m* de encuentro; (*fig*) punto *m* de convergencia • **the ~ point between East and West** el punto de convergencia entre Oriente y Occidente

Meg [meg] N *familiar form of* **Margaret**
meg* [meg] N (*Comput*) mega* *m*
mega* ['megə] ADJ súper*
mega... ['megə] PREFIX mega...
megabit ['megəbɪt] N megabit *m*
megabucks* ['megə͵bʌks] N (*esp US*) • **now he's making ~** ahora está ganando un dineral*, ahora se está forrando* • **we're talking ~** hablamos de un montón *or* porrón de dinero*
megabyte ['megə͵baɪt] N megabyte *m*, mega *m*
megacycle ['megə͵saɪkl] N megaciclo *m*
megadeath ['megə͵deθ] N muerte *f* de un millón de personas
megahertz ['megə͵hɜ:ts] N (PL: **megahertz**) megahercio *m*
megalith ['megəlɪθ] N megalito *m*
megalithic [͵megə'lɪθɪk] ADJ megalítico
megalomania ['megələʊ'meɪnɪə] N megalomanía *f*
megalomaniac ['megələʊ'meɪnɪæk] N megalómano/a *m/f*
megalopolis [͵megə'lɒpəlɪs] N megalópolis *f inv*
megaphone ['megəfəʊn] N megáfono *m*
megapixel ['megəpɪksəl] N megapíxel *m*
megastar ['megə͵stɑ:ʳ] N superestrella *f*
megastore ['megəstɔ:ʳ] N macrotienda *f*
megaton ['megətʌn] N megatón *m*
megavolt ['megəvəʊlt] N megavoltio *m*
megawatt ['megəwɒt] N megavatio *m*
meh [me] EXCL bah
meiosis [maɪ'əʊsɪs] N (PL: **meioses** [maɪ'əʊsi:z]) **1** (*Bio*) meiosis *f*
2 (= *litotes*) lítote *f*
melamine ['meləmi:n] N melamina *f*
melancholia [͵melən'kəʊlɪə] N melancolía *f*
melancholic [͵melən'kɒlɪk] ADJ melancólico
melancholically [͵melən'kɒlɪklɪ] ADV melancólicamente
melancholy ['melənkəlɪ] ADJ [*person, mood*] melancólico; [*duty, sight*] triste
N melancolía *f*
melange, mélange [me'lɑ:nʒ] N mezcla *f*
melanin ['melənɪn] N melanina *f*
melanism ['melənɪzəm] N melanismo *m*
melanoma [͵melə'nəʊmə] N (PL: **melanomas** *or* **melanomata** [͵melə'nəʊmətə]) melanoma *m*
Melba toast ['melbə'təʊst] N tostada *f* delgada
meld [meld] VT fusionar • **to ~ sth into sth** fusionar algo con algo

VI fusionarse
N fusión *f*
Meldrew ['meldru:] N (*Brit*) *persona frustrada y desilusionada con la sociedad actual (apellido de un protagonista de telecomedia)*
melée ['meleɪ] N **1** (= *confusion*) tumulto *m* • **it got lost in the ~** se perdió en el tumulto • **there was such a ~ at the booking office** la gente se apiñaba delante de la taquilla
2 (= *fight*) pelea *f* confusa, refriega *f*
mellifluous [me'lɪfluəs] ADJ melifluo
Mellotron® ['melətrɒn] N Mellotron® *m*
mellow ['meləʊ] ADJ (COMPAR: **mellower**, SUPERL: **mellowest**) **1** (= *pleasant, smooth*) [*wine, whisky*] suave, añejo; [*fruit*] maduro, dulce; [*colour, light*] suave y dorado, tenue y dorado; [*instrument*] melodioso; [*voice, tone, sound*] dulce, meloso
2 [*person*] **a** (= *calm*) apacible, sosegado • **he has grown more ~ over the years** los años le han suavizado el carácter, se ha vuelto más afable con los años
b (= *relaxed*) • **to be ~** (*after eating, drinking*) estar relajado • **to get ~*** (= *tipsy*) achisparse* • **to be in a ~ mood** sentirse relajado
VI **1** (= *soften*) • **he has ~ed with age** los años le han suavizado el carácter, con los años se ha vuelto más afable
2 (= *relax*) relajarse
3 [*wine, whisky*] añejarse; [*fruit*] madurar; [*colour, light, voice, character*] suavizarse; [*views*] moderarse • **to ~ with age** [*wine, whisky*] mejorar con los años
VT **1** (= *soften*) • **old age has ~ed him** la vejez le ha suavizado el carácter *or* lo ha hecho más afable
2 (= *relax*) relajar
3 [+ *wine*] añejar
mellowing ['meləʊɪŋ] N [*of fruit*] maduración *f*; [*of wine*] añejamiento *m*
mellowness ['meləʊnɪs] N (= *smoothness*) [*of wine, brandy*] suavidad *f*, añejez *f*; [*of fruit*] dulzura *f*; [*of colour, light*] suavidad *f*; [*of instrument*] lo melodioso
melodic [mɪ'lɒdɪk] ADJ melódico
melodious [mɪ'ləʊdiəs] ADJ melodioso
melodiously [mɪ'ləʊdɪəslɪ] ADV melodiosamente
melodrama ['meləʊ,drɑːmə] N melodrama *m*
melodramatic [,meləʊdrə'mætɪk] ADJ melodramático
melodramatically [,meləʊdrə'mætɪklɪ] ADV melodramáticamente
melody ['melədɪ] N melodía *f*
melon ['melən] N melón *m*
melt [melt] VT **1** (*lit*) [+ *snow, chocolate, butter*] derretir, fundir; [+ *metal*] fundir; [+ *chemical*] disolver
2 (*fig*) (= *soften*) ablandar
VI **1** (*lit*) [*snow, chocolate, butter*] derretirse, fundirse; [*metal*] fundirse; [*chemical*] disolverse • **it ~s in the mouth** se deshace en la boca; ▹ **butter**
2 (*fig*) **a** [*person*] (= *soften*) ablandarse • **to ~ into tears** deshacerse en lágrimas • IDIOM: • **her heart ~ed with pity** se le ablandó el corazón de lástima
b (= *disappear*) • **the gunman ~ed into the crowd** el pistolero desapareció entre la multitud • **night ~ed into day** la noche dio paso al día
▸ **melt away** VI + ADV **1** (*lit*) derretirse
2 (*fig*) [*confidence*] desvanecerse; [*money*] evaporarse; [*crowd*] dispersarse; [*person*] esfumarse, escabullirse
▸ **melt down** VT + ADV fundir
meltdown ['meltdaʊn] N **1** (*lit*) fusión *f* de un reactor, fundido *m*
2 (*fig*) cataclismo *m*, debacle *f*
melting ['meltɪŋ] ADJ [*look*] tierno, dulce
CPD ▸ **melting point** punto *m* de fusión ▸ **melting pot** (*lit, fig*) crisol *m* • IDIOM: • **to be in the ~ pot** (*Brit*) estar sobre el tapete
meltwater ['meltwɔːtəʳ] N agua *f* de fusión de la nieve
member ['membəʳ] N **1** [*of organization, committee*] miembro *mf*; [*of society, club*] miembro *mf*, socio/a *m/f*; [*of political party, trade union*] miembro *mf*, afiliado/a *m/f* • **"members only"** "solo para socios", "reservado para los socios" • **the ~ for Woodford** el diputado por Woodford • **if any ~ of the audience ...** si cualquiera de los espectadores ..., si cualquier miembro del público ... • **she's a ~ of our church** es una feligresa *or* es miembro de nuestra iglesia • **~ of Congress** (*US*) miembro *mf* del Congreso • **~ of the crew** • **crew ~** tripulante *mf* • **a ~ of the family** • **a family ~** un miembro de la familia • **full ~** miembro *mf* de pleno derecho • **Member of Parliament** (*Brit*) diputado/a *m/f*, parlamentario/a *m/f* • **Member of the European Parliament** diputado/a *m/f* del Parlamento Europeo, eurodiputado/a *m/f* • **a ~ of the public** un ciudadano/una ciudadana • **the library is open to ~s of the public** la biblioteca está abierta al público • **~ of staff** empleado/a *m/f*; (*Univ, Scol*) miembro *mf* del profesorado
2 (*Anat, Bot, Math*) miembro *m*; ▹ **male**
CPD ▸ **member country** país *m* miembro ▸ **member state** estado *m* miembro
membership ['membəʃɪp] N **1** (= *members*) [*of club, society*] socios *mpl*, miembros *mpl*; [*of political party*] miembros *mpl*, militancia *f*, afiliados *mpl*; [*of trade union*] afiliados *mpl*, miembros *mpl*
2 (= *position*) • **~ carries certain rights** el ser socio *or* miembro conlleva ciertos derechos • **~ of the union is compulsory** es obligatorio afiliarse a *or* hacerse miembro del sindicato • **I've paid for a year's ~** he pagado la cuota anual de socio *or* miembro • **to apply for ~** solicitar el ingreso como socio *or* miembro • **Spain's ~ of** *or* (*US*) **in the Common Market** (= *state*) la pertenencia de España al Mercado Común; (= *act*) el ingreso de España en el Mercado Común
3 (= *numbers*) número *m* de miembros *or* socios *etc*, membresía *f* (*Mex*) • **a ~ of more than 800** más de 800 socios *or* miembros • **trade union ~ has declined** el número de afiliados a los sindicatos ha disminuido
CPD ▸ **membership card** [*of club, society*] tarjeta *f or* carné *m* de socio; [*of political party, trade union*] tarjeta *f or* carné *m* de afiliación ▸ **membership fee** cuota *f* de socio ▸ **membership list** relación *f* de socios
membrane ['membreɪn] N membrana *f*
membranous [mem'breɪnəs] ADJ membranoso
meme [miːm] N (*Internet, Sociol*) meme *m*
memento [mɪ'mentəʊ] N (PL: **mementos** *or* **mementoes**) recuerdo *m*
memo* ['meməʊ] N ABBR (= **memorandum**) memo *m*
CPD ▸ **memo pad** bloc *m* de notas
memoir ['memwɑːʳ] N **1 memoirs** (= *autobiography*) memorias *fpl*, autobiografía *fsing*
2 (= *biographical note*) nota *f* biográfica
3 (= *essay*) memoria *f*
memorabilia [,memərə'bɪlɪə] N (= *objects*) recuerdos *mpl*
memorable ['memərəbl] ADJ memorable
memorably ['memərəblɪ] ADV memorablemente
memorandum [,memə'rændəm] N (PL: **memorandums** *or* **memoranda** [,memə'rændə]) memorándum *m*; (= *personal reminder*) apunte *m*, nota *f*
memorial [mɪ'mɔːrɪəl] ADJ conmemorativo
N **1** (= *monument*) monumento *m* conmemorativo
2 (= *document*) memorial *m*
CPD ▸ **Memorial Day** (*US*) día *m* de los caídos en la guerra (*último lunes de mayo*) ▸ **memorial park** (*US*) cementerio *m* ▸ **memorial service** ≈ misa *f* de difuntos
memorialize [mɪ'mɔːrɪəlaɪz] VT conmemorar
memorize ['meməraɪz] VT memorizar, aprender de memoria
memory ['memərɪ] N **1** (= *faculty*) memoria *f* • **to commit sth to ~** aprender algo de memoria • **to lose one's ~** perder la memoria • **I have a bad ~ for faces** se me olvida la cara de la gente • **he recited the poem from ~** recitó el poema de memoria • **if my ~ serves me** si mi memoria no me falla, si mal no recuerdo • **to the best of my ~** que yo recuerde • IDIOM: • **to have a ~ like a sieve** tener malísima memoria
2 (= *recollection*) recuerdo *m* • **of blessed ~** de feliz recuerdo, de grata memoria • **"Memories of a country childhood"** "Recuerdos de una infancia campestre" • **to have happy memories of sth** tener *or* guardar buenos recuerdos de algo • **to keep sb's ~ alive** guardar el recuerdo de algn, mantener vivo el recuerdo de algn
3 (= *remembrance*) • **in ~ of** • **to the ~ of** en memoria de
4 (*Comput*) memoria *f*
CPD ▸ **memory bank** banco *m* de memoria ▸ **memory capacity** capacidad *f* de memoria ▸ **memory card** tarjeta *f* de memoria ▸ **memory chip** chip *m* de memoria ▸ **memory lane** mundo *m* de los recuerdos (sentimentales) • IDIOM: • **to take a trip down ~ lane** adentrarse en el mundo de los recuerdos ▸ **memory loss** pérdida *f* de memoria ▸ **memory management** gestión *f* de la memoria ▸ **memory stick** (*for camera*) memory stick *m*; (= *USB flash drive*) llave *f* de memoria, memoria *f* USB
memsahib ['mem,sɑːhɪb] N (*India*) mujer *f* casada
men [men] NPL *of* **man**
menace ['menɪs] N **1** (*no pl*) (= *intimidation*) • **a voice full of ~** una voz amenazadora
2 (= *danger*) peligro *m*, amenaza *f*
3 (= *threat*) amenaza *f*
4* (= *person*) • **he's a ~** (*child*) es un diablillo*; (*adult*) es un peligro público
VT amenazar
menacing ['menɪsɪŋ] ADJ amenazador
menacingly ['menɪsɪŋlɪ] ADV de modo amenazador
ménage [me'nɑːʒ] N hogar *m* • **~ à trois** trío *m* amoroso, ménage à trois *m*
menagerie [mɪ'nædʒərɪ] N casa *f or* colección *f* de fieras
mend [mend] N (= *patch*) remiendo *m*; (= *darn*) zurcido *m* • IDIOM: • **to be on the ~** ir mejorando
VT **1** (= *repair*) [+ *watch, toy, wall*] arreglar, reparar; [+ *shoes*] arreglar; (= *darn*) remendar, zurcir
2 (= *improve*) • **to ~ matters** mejorar las cosas • IDIOM: • **to ~ one's ways** enmendarse
VI (= *improve*) mejorar
mendacious [men'deɪʃəs] ADJ (*frm*) mendaz
mendacity [men'dæsɪtɪ] N (*frm*) mendacidad *f*
mendelevium [,mendɪ'liːvɪəm] N mendelevio *m*

m

Mendelian [men'di:lɪən] (ADJ) mendeliano
Mendelianism [men'di:lɪənɪzəm] (N), **Mendelism** ['mendəlɪzəm] (N) mendelismo *m*
mendicancy ['mendɪkənsɪ] (N) mendicidad *f*
mendicant ['mendɪkənt] (*frm*) (ADJ) mendicante
(N) mendicante *mf*
mendicity [men'dɪsɪtɪ] (N) (*frm*) mendicidad *f*
mending ['mendɪŋ] (N) **1** (= *act*) reparación *f*, arreglo *m*; [*of clothes*] zurcido *m* • **invisible ~** zurcido *m* invisible
2 (= *clothes to be mended*) ropa *f* para remendar
Menelaus [,menɪ'leɪəs] (N) Menelao
menfolk ['menfəʊk] (NPL) hombres *mpl*
menhir ['menhɪəʳ] (N) menhir *m*
menial ['mi:nɪəl] (ADJ) (= *lowly*) servil; (= *domestic*) doméstico, de la casa • **~ work** trabajo *m* de baja categoría
(N) (= *servant*) sirviente/a *m/f*
meningitis [,menɪn'dʒaɪtɪs] (N) meningitis *f inv*
meniscus [mə'nɪskəs] (N) (PL: **meniscuses** *or* **menisci** [mɪ'nɪsaɪ]) menisco *m*
menopausal [,menəʊ'pɔ:zəl] (ADJ) menopáusico
menopause ['menəʊpɔ:z] (N) menopausia *f*
menorrhagia [,menɔ:'reɪdʒɪə] (N) menorragia *f*
menservants ['men,sɜ:vənts] (NPL) *of* **manservant**
menses ['mensi:z] (NPL) menstruo *msing*
menstrual ['menstrʊəl] (ADJ) menstrual
(CPD) ▸ **menstrual cycle** ciclo *m* menstrual
menstruate ['menstrʊeɪt] (VI) menstruar, tener la menstruación
menstruation [,menstrʊ'eɪʃən] (N) menstruación *f*
mensuration [,mensjʊə'reɪʃən] (N) medición *f*, medida *f*, mensuración *f*
menswear ['menzwɛəʳ] (N) ropa *f* de caballero
mental ['mentl] (ADJ) **1** (= *not physical*) [*development, health, effort*] mental • **the stigma attached to ~ illness** el estigma vinculado con las enfermedades mentales • **I formed a ~ picture of what he looked like** me formé una imagen mental de cómo era • **to make a ~ note of sth** tomar nota mentalmente de algo
2 (*Brit**) (= *crazy*) chiflado* • **he must be ~** debe estar chiflado*
(CPD) ▸ **mental age** edad *f* mental ▸ **mental arithmetic** cálculos *mpl* mentales ▸ **mental block** bloqueo *m* mental ▸ **mental cruelty** crueldad *f* mental ▸ **mental handicap** retraso *m* mental ▸ **mental healing** (*US*) cura *f* mental ▸ **mental home, mental hospital** hospital *m* psiquiátrico, manicomio *m* ▸ **mental institution** institución *f* para enfermos mentales ▸ **mental patient** paciente *mf* psiquiátrico/a ▸ **mental powers** poderes *mpl* mentales
mentality [men'tælɪtɪ] (N) mentalidad *f*
mentally ['mentəlɪ] (ADV) **1** (= *not physically*) mentalmente • **to be ~ disturbed** estar trastornado • **to be ~ handicapped** ser un disminuido psíquico • **to be ~ ill** tener una enfermedad mental, ser un enfermo mental
2 (= *in the mind*) [*calculate, formulate*] mentalmente • **~, I tried to picture what the house must have looked like** intenté formarme una imagen mental de cómo debía haber sido la casa
menthol ['menθɒl] (N) mentol *m*
(CPD) [*cigarette, sweet*] mentolado
mentholated ['menθəleɪtɪd] (ADJ) mentolado
mention ['menʃən] (N) **1** mención *f* • **the mere ~ of his name exasperates me** la sola mención de su nombre me saca de quicio • **at the ~ of food, she looked up** al oír que se mencionaba comida, levantó la vista • **it got a ~ in the news** lo mencionaron en las noticias • **to make ~ of sth/sb** mencionar algo/a algn, hacer mención de algo/algn • **there was no ~ of any surcharge** no se mencionó ningún recargo adicional, no se hizo mención de ningún recargo adicional; ▹ **honourable**
2 (*Mil*) citación *f*
(VT) mencionar • **I will ~ it to him** se lo mencionaré, se lo diré • **he ~ed to me that you were coming** me mencionó *or* comentó que venías • **I've never heard him ~ his father** nunca le he oído mencionar *or* mentar a su padre • **too numerous to ~** demasiado numerosos para mencionar • **he has been ~ed as a potential candidate** se ha hecho alusión a él *or* se le ha aludido como posible candidato • **don't ~ it to anyone** no se lo digas a nadie • **don't ~ it!** (*in reply to thanks*) ¡de nada!, ¡no hay de qué! • **I need hardly ~ that …** ni que decir tiene que …, no es necesario decir que … • **just ~ my name** basta con decir mi nombre • **he didn't ~ any names** no dijo *or* dio los nombres • **they make so much mess, not to ~ the noise** lo dejan todo patas arriba, y no digamos ya el ruido que arman • **to ~ sb in one's will** dejar algo a algn en el testamento, legar algo a algn • **it's worth ~ing that …** merece la pena mencionar que …; ▹ **dispatch**
mentor ['mentɔ:ʳ] (N) mentor *m*
menu ['menju:] (N) **1** (= *list*) carta *f*; (= *set meal*) menú *m*
2 (*Comput*) menú *m*
menu-driven ['menju:,drɪvn] (ADJ) (*Comput*) guiado por menú
meow [mɪ'aʊ] (N) maullido *m*, miau *m*
(VI) maullar
MEP (N ABBR) (*Brit*) (= **Member of the European Parliament**) eurodiputado/a *m/f*
Mephistopheles [,mefɪs'tɒfɪli:z] (N) Mefistófeles
Mephistophelian [,mefɪstə'fi:lɪən] (ADJ) mefistofélico
mercantile ['mɜ:kəntaɪl] (ADJ) mercantil
mercantilism ['mɜ:kəntɪlɪzəm] (N) mercantilismo *m*
mercenary ['mɜ:sɪnərɪ] (ADJ) mercenario
(N) mercenario/a *m/f*
merchandise ['mɜ:tʃəndaɪz] (N) mercancías *fpl*
(VT) comercilizar
merchandiser, merchandizer (*US*) ['mɜ:tʃəndaɪzəʳ] (N) minorista *mf*, detallista *mf*
merchandising, merchandizing ['mɜ:tʃəndaɪzɪŋ] (N) **1** (= *objects*) merchandising *m*
2 (= *activity*) comercialización *f*
merchandize ['mɜ:tʃəndaɪz] (VT) = **merchandise**
merchant ['mɜ:tʃənt] (N) **1** (= *trader, dealer*) comerciante *mf*; (= *retailer*) minorista *mf*, detallista *mf* • **a diamond ~** un comerciante de diamantes • **a wine ~** un vinatero • **"The Merchant of Venice"** "El Mercader de Venecia"
2* tío* *m*, sujeto *m*
(CPD) ▸ **merchant bank** banco *m* mercantil *or* comercial ▸ **merchant banker** (*Brit*) ejecutivo/a *m/f* de un banco mercantil *or* comercial ▸ **merchant fleet** flota *f* mercante ▸ **merchant marine** (*US*), **merchant navy** marina *f* mercante ▸ **merchant seaman** marino *m* mercante ▸ **merchant ship** buque *m* mercante ▸ **merchant shipping** marina *f* mercante; (= *ships*) buques *mpl* mercantes
merchantable ['mɜ:tʃəntəbl] (ADJ) comercializable • **of ~ quality** de calidad comerciable
merchantman ['mɜ:tʃəntmən] (N) (PL: **merchantmen**) buque *m* mercante
merciful ['mɜ:sɪfʊl] (ADJ) **1** (= *compassionate*) [*god*] misericordioso, clemente, compasivo; [*person*] clemente, compasivo • **to be ~ to** *or* **towards sb** ser clemente con algn, mostrarse compasivo con algn
2 (= *blessed*) • **death came as a ~ release** la muerte fue como una bendición
mercifully ['mɜ:sɪfəlɪ] (ADV) **1** (= *kindly*) con clemencia, con compasión
2 (= *fortunately*) afortunadamente, gracias a Dios
merciless ['mɜ:sɪlɪs] (ADJ) [*person, attack*] despiadado, cruel; [*killing, beating*] cruel; [*sun, heat*] implacable • **he's famous for his ~ treatment of hecklers** tiene fama de tratar despiadadamente a los que interrumpen con preguntas o comentarios molestos
mercilessly ['mɜ:sɪlɪslɪ] (ADV) [*beat, punish, treat*] despiadadamente, sin piedad • **Joe teased his sister ~** Joe se burló de su hermana despiadadamente *or* sin piedad
mercurial [mɜ:'kjʊərɪəl] (ADJ) **1** (*Chem*) mercúrico, mercurial
2 (= *lively*) vivo; (= *changeable*) veleidoso, voluble
Mercury ['mɜ:kjʊrɪ] (N) (*Astron, Myth*) Mercurio *m*
mercury ['mɜ:kjʊrɪ] (N) mercurio *m*, azogue *m*
mercy ['mɜ:sɪ] (N) **1** (= *compassion*) misericordia *f*; (= *clemency*) clemencia *f*, piedad *f* • **to beg for ~** pedir clemencia • **to have ~ on sb** tener misericordia *or* piedad de algn, tener clemencia para con algn • **have ~!** ¡por piedad! • **God in His ~** el Señor en su infinita bondad • **to show sb no ~** no mostrarse misericordioso *or* clemente con algn • **no ~ was shown to the rioters** no hubo clemencia para los revoltosos
2 (= *discretion*) • **to be at the ~ of sth/sb** estar a merced de algo/algn • **to be left to the tender mercies of sb** (*esp hum*) quedar a merced de algn • IDIOM: • **to throw o.s. on sb's ~** ponerse en (las) manos de algn
3 (= *blessing*) • **his death was a ~** su muerte fue una bendición • **it's a ~ that no-one was hurt*** es un milagro que nadie resultara herido, menos mal que nadie resultó herido • **we should be grateful for small mercies** y demos gracias, porque podría haber sido peor; ▹ **thankful**
(CPD) ▸ **mercy flight** vuelo *m* de ayuda (*para ayudar a alguien necesitado en una guerra etc*) ▸ **mercy killing** eutanasia *f*
mere¹ [mɪəʳ] (N) lago *m*
mere² [mɪəʳ] (ADJ) (SUPERL: **merest**) mero, simple • **the ~ fact that …** el mero *or* simple hecho de que … • **the merest jolt can upset the balance of the wheels** la más mínima sacudida puede desequilibrar las ruedas • **it was sold for a ~ £45** lo vendieron por apenas 45 libras • **a ~ child could do it** incluso un niño podría hacerlo • **I was a ~ child when I married him** no era más que una niña cuando me casé con él, era solamente una niña cuando me casé con él • **a ~ formality** una mera *or* pura *or* simple formalidad • **the merest hint of a smile** apenas un atisbo de sonrisa • **a ~ man** un hombre nada más *or* (*LAm*) nomás • **it's way beyond the abilities of ~ mortals like us** está más allá de la

capacidad del común de los mortales como nosotros • **a ~ nothing** casi nada • **the ~ sight of blood is enough to make her faint** solo con ver la sangre *or* con solo ver la sangre se desmaya • **the merest suggestion of sth** la mera sugerencia de algo; ▹ **mention**

merely [ˈmɪəlɪ] (ADV) simplemente, solamente • **she's ~ a secretary** es simplemente *or* solamente una secretaria, no es más que una secretaria • **I was ~ suggesting that ...** estaba simplemente *or* solamente sugiriendo que ... • **this ~ aggravates the problem** esto lo único que hace es agravar el problema • **I ~ said that ...** solo dije que ..., lo único que dije era que ... • **she ~ shrugged** ella se limitó a encogerse de hombros • **she ~ smiled** sonrió nada más, se limitó a sonreír

meretricious [ˌmerɪˈtrɪʃəs] (ADJ) [*charm, attraction*] superficial, aparente; [*style, writing*] rimbombante

merge [mɜːdʒ] (VT) **1** (*Comm*) fusionar, unir
2 (*Comput*) [+ *text, files*] fusionar
(VI) **1** [*colours, sounds, shapes*] fundirse; [*roads*] empalmar • **to ~ into the background** confundirse con el fondo • **the bird ~d into its background of leaves** el pájaro se confundía *or* mimetizaba con el fondo de hojas • **this question ~s into a bigger one** esta cuestión queda englobada en otra mayor
2 [*companies, organizations, parties*] fusionarse • **to ~ with another company** fusionarse con otra empresa
(N) (*Comput*) fusión *f*

merger [ˈmɜːdʒəʳ] (N) (*Comm*) fusión *f*

meridian [məˈrɪdɪən] (N) **1** (*Astron, Geog*) meridiano *m*
2 (*fig*) cenit *m*, auge *m*

meridional [məˈrɪdɪənl] (ADJ) meridional

meringue [məˈræŋ] (N) merengue *m*

merino [məˈriːnəʊ] (ADJ) merino
(N) (= *sheep, wool*) merino *m*

merit [ˈmerɪt] (N) mérito *m* • **it has the ~ of being clear** tiene el mérito de ser claro • **to treat a case on its ~s** juzgar un caso según sus propios méritos • **to look** *or* **inquire into the ~s of sth** estudiar los aspectos positivos de algo • **a work of great ~** un trabajo de mucho mérito, un trabajo muy meritorio
(VT) merecer • **this ~s further discussion** esto (se) merece mayor discusión
(CPD) ▸ **merit increase** aumento *m* por méritos ▸ **merit pay** (*US*) plus *m* por méritos ▸ **merit system** (*US*) (*in the workplace*) *sistema de ascensos y contrataciones por méritos*

meritocracy [ˌmerɪˈtɒkrəsɪ] (N) meritocracia *f*

meritocrat [ˈmerɪtəʊkræt] (N) meritócrata *mf*

meritocratic [ˌmerɪtəˈkrætɪk] (ADJ) meritocrático

meritorious [ˌmerɪˈtɔːrɪəs] (ADJ) meritorio

meritoriously [ˌmerɪˈtɔːrɪəslɪ] (ADV) merecidamente

merlin [ˈmɜːlɪn] (N) esmerejón *m*

mermaid [ˈmɜːmeɪd] (N) sirena *f*
(CPD) ▸ **mermaid tears** (= *plastic waste*) residuos *mpl* plásticos en el mar

merman [ˈmɜːmæn] (N) (PL: **mermen**) tritón *m*

Merovingian [ˌmerəʊˈvɪndʒɪən] (ADJ) merovingio
(N) merovingio/a *m/f*

merrily [ˈmerɪlɪ] (ADV) **1** (= *cheerfully*) [*laugh, say, dance*] alegremente
2 (= *blithely*) • **she quite ~ wrote out a cheque for £3,000** extendió tranquilamente *or* tan tranquila un cheque por 3.000 libras

merriment [ˈmerɪmənt] (N) alegría *f*, regocijo *m*; (= *laughter*) risas *fpl* • **at this there was much ~** esto provocó muchas risas

merry [ˈmerɪ] (ADJ) (COMPAR: **merrier**, SUPERL: **merriest**) **1** (= *cheerful*) [*laughter, face, tune*] alegre • **they were in a very ~ mood** estaban de muy buen humor • **Robin Hood and his ~ men** Robin Hood y sus valientes compañeros • **Merry Christmas!** ¡Feliz Navidad! • **to make ~** (*liter*) divertirse
• IDIOMS: • **to go one's (own) ~ way**: • **whatever advice you give her she just goes her own ~ way** (*iro*) le des el consejo que le des, ella sigue haciendo su santa voluntad* • **to lead sb a ~ dance** (*Brit*) (*iro*) enredar a algn; ▹ **hell, more**
2 (*Brit**) (= *tipsy*) achispado, alegre • **to get ~** achisparse, ponerse alegre

merry-go-round [ˈmerɪgəʊˌraʊnd] (N) tiovivo *m*, caballitos *mpl*, calesita(s) *f(pl)* (*And, S. Cone*)

merrymaker [ˈmerɪˌmeɪkəʳ] (N) juerguista *mf*, parrandero/a *m/f*

merrymaking [ˈmerɪˌmeɪkɪŋ] (N) (= *party*) fiesta *f*; (= *enjoyment*) diversión *f*; (= *happiness*) alegría *f*, regocijo *m*

mesa [ˈmeɪsə] (N) (*US*) colina *f*, baja duna *f*

mescal [ˈmeskæl] (N) mezcal *m*

mescaline [ˈmeskəlɪn] (N) mescalina *f*

mesentery [ˈmeːzəntrɪ] (N) mesenterio *m*

meseta [məˈseɪtə] (N) meseta *f*

mesh [meʃ] (N) **1** (= *spacing*) malla *f*
2 (= *netting*) • **wire ~** tela *f* metálica, malla *f* metálica
3 (= *network, net, also fig*) red *f*
4 (= *gears etc*) • **in ~** engranado
(VT) • **to get ~ed** enredarse (**in** en)
(VI) (*Tech*) engranar (**with** con)

mesmeric [mezˈmerɪk] (ADJ) mesmeriano

mesmerism [ˈmezmərɪzəm] (N) mesmerismo *m*

mesmerize [ˈmezməraɪz] (VT) hipnotizar; (*fig*) fascinar

mesmerizing [ˈmezməraɪzɪŋ] (ADJ) fascinante, hipnotizante • **she has a ~ smile** tiene una sonrisa fascinante *or* hipnotizante

mesolith [ˈmesəʊlɪθ] (N) mesolito *m*

mesolithic [ˌmesəʊˈlɪθɪk] (ADJ) mesolítico
(N) • **the Mesolithic** el Mesolítico

mesomorph [ˈmesəʊˌmɔːf] (N) mesomorfo *m*

meson [ˈmiːzɒn] (N) mesón *m*

Mesopotamia [ˌmesəpəˈteɪmɪə] (N) Mesopotamia *f*

mesotherapy [ˌmesəʊˈθerəpɪ] (N) mesoterapia *f*

Mesozoic [ˌmesəʊˈzəʊɪk] (ADJ) mesozoico
(N) • **the ~** el Mesozoico

mess [mes] (N) **1** (*untidy*) desorden *m*; (*dirty*) porquería *f*; (= *shambles*) desastre *m*, desbarajuste *m*; (= *predicament*) lío* *m*, follón* *m*; (= *bad job*) chapuza* *f*, desastre *m* • **excuse the ~** perdone el desorden • **to be a ~**: • **this place is a ~** esta casa es un desastre • **her hair is a ~** tiene el pelo hecho un desastre • **this page is a ~, rewrite it** esta página es una chapuza* *or* un desastre, vuélvela a escribir • **the economy is a ~** la economía es un desastre • **her life is a ~** su vida es un desastre *or* un desbarajuste • **you can clean that ~ up** ya puedes ir limpiando esta pena • **to be in a ~**: • **the house was in a ~** la casa estaba hecha un desastre • **the toys were in a ~** había un desorden de juguetes • **to leave things in a ~** dejarlo todo desordenado *or* hecho un desastre • **the economy is in a ~** la economía es un desastre • **her life is in a ~** su vida es un desastre *or* un desbarajuste • **his face was in a bit of a ~** (*after fight, accident*) tenía la cara que daba pena • **we're in a ~** estamos metidos en un lío *or* un follón* • **to get (o.s.) into a ~** (*fig*) meterse en un lío *or* un follón* • **a fine** *or* **nice ~ you got us into!** ¡en menudo lío *or* follón nos has metido!* • **you look (such) a ~** vas hecho un desastre • **look at the ~ you've made of this room** mira cómo has dejado esta habitación de desordenada • **to make a ~**: • **look what a ~ you've made!** ¡mira cómo lo has puesto todo! • **he made a ~ of his audition** la audición le fue fatal* • **I've made such a ~ of my life** he arruinado *or* echado a perder mi vida • **you've made a real ~ of things, haven't you?** has liado bien las cosas ¿no crees?*
2 (*euph*) (= *excrement*) caca *f* • **dog ~** caca *f* de perro • **the cat's made a ~ in the kitchen** el gato ha hecho caca en la cocina
3 (*Mil*) comedor *m* • **officers' ~** comedor *m* de oficiales
(VI) **1** (*Mil*) (= *eat*) hacer rancho, comer (juntos)
2* • **no ~ing!** ¡sin bromas!, ¡nada de tonterías! • **no ~ing?** ¿en serio?
3 (= *soil o.s.*) hacerse caca encima*
(VT) • **to ~ one's pants/trousers** hacerse caca encima*
(CPD) ▸ **mess deck** sollado *m* ▸ **mess hall** comedor *m* ▸ **a mess of pottage** (*Bible*) un plato de lentejas ▸ **mess tin** plato *m* de campaña

▸ **mess about, mess around*** (VT + ADV) (*Brit*) • **all they do is ~ me about, they won't give me a straight answer** no hacen más que jugar conmigo, no me dan una respuesta concreta • **they were ~ing me about so much over the dates that I told them to forget it** me querían cambiar las fechas tantas veces que les dije que se olvidaran del asunto
(VI + ADV) (= *play the fool*) hacer tonterías; (= *do nothing in particular*) pasar el rato, gandulear; (= *waste time*) perder el tiempo • **"what are you doing?" — "just ~ing about"** —¿qué haces? —nada, pasando el rato • **we ~ed about in Paris for two days** pasamos dos días en París haciendo esto y lo otro • **he enjoys ~ing about in boats** le gusta entretenerse con las barcas • **she's not one to ~ about, she gets on with the job** no es de las que pierde el tiempo, saca el trabajo adelante • **I don't want him ~ing about here** no le quiero fisgoneando por aquí • **stop ~ing about!** ¡déjate de tonterías! • **to ~ about with sb**: • **he isn't the kind of guy you ~ about with** no es de los que se deja enredar *or* tomar el pelo • **he ~ed about with some lads from college for a while** salió con unos tíos de la universidad durante un tiempo • **she'd been ~ing about with other men** había estado liada con otros hombres* • **to ~ about with sth**: • **he was ~ing about with his watchstrap** estaba jugueteando con la correa del reloj • **who's been ~ing about with the video?** ¿quién ha estado manoseando *or* toqueteando el vídeo?

▸ **mess up** (VT + ADV) **1** (= *disarrange*) [+ *books, papers*] descolocar; [+ *hair*] desarreglar; [+ *room, house*] desordenar, desarreglar
2 (= *dirty*) ensuciar
3 (= *ruin*) [+ *plans, arrangements*] estropear, echar por tierra; [+ *piece of work*] estropear
4 (*US*) (= *beat up*) zurrar*, dar una paliza a*
(VI + ADV)* meter la pata*

▸ **mess with*** (VI + PREP) **1** (= *challenge, confront*) meterse con* • **if he ever ~es with me again I'll kill him** si vuelve a meterse conmigo lo mato*
2 (= *interfere with*) interferir con • **the system works well so don't ~ with it** el sistema

m

funciona bien así que no interfieras con él
3 (= *get involved with*) • **I used to ~ with drugs** estaba metido en drogas*

message ['mesɪdʒ] (N) recado *m*; (*frm*) (*fig*) (*Comput*) mensaje *m* • **to leave a ~** dejar un recado • **would you like to leave him a ~?** ¿quiere dejarle algún recado? • **a secret ~** un mensaje secreto • **the ~ of the film** el mensaje de la película • IDIOM: • **to get the ~***: • **do you think he got the ~?*** ¿crees que lo comprendió *or* entendió?
(CPD) ▸ **message board** (*Internet*) tablero *m* de mensajes ▸ **message switching** (*Comput*) conmutación *f* de mensajes

messaging ['mesɪdʒɪŋ] (N) mensajería *f*

messenger ['mesɪndʒəʳ] (N) mensajero/a *m/f*
(CPD) ▸ **messenger boy** recadero *m*

Messiah [mɪ'saɪə] (N) Mesías *m*

messianic [,mesɪ'ænɪk] (ADJ) mesiánico

Messieurs ['mesəz] (NPL) señores *mpl*

messily ['mesɪlɪ] (ADV) **1** (= *creating mess*) • **babies eat ~** los bebés lo dejan todo perdido *or* lo ensucian todo cuando comen • **try not to write so ~** intenta que lo que escribes te salga más limpio
2 (= *awkwardly*) • **the divorce ended ~** el divorcio terminó de mala manera

messmate ['mesmeɪt] (N) **1** (*in army etc*) compañero *m* de rancho, comensal *m*
2 (= *friend*) amigo *m*

Messrs ['mesəz] (NPL ABBR) (*Brit*) (= **Messieurs**) Srs., Sres.

mess-up* ['mesʌp] (N) (*Brit*) follón* *m*, lío* *m* • **we had a mess-up with the trains** nos hicimos un lío con los trenes*

messy ['mesɪ] (ADJ) (COMPAR: **messier**, SUPERL: **messiest**) **1** (= *creating mess*) [*person*] desordenado; [*animal, activity, job*] sucio • **he's such a ~ eater** lo deja todo perdido *or* lo ensucia todo cuando come
2 (= *dirty, untidy*) [*place, room*] desordenado; [*clothes*] desarreglado, desordenado; [*hair*] despeinado • **"this is a ~ piece of work," said the teacher** —la presentación de este trabajo es un desastre —dijo el profesor • **she was penalized for ~ work** la castigaron por presentar un trabajo sucio y descuidado
3 (= *confused and awkward*) [*situation, divorce, relationship*] turbio, turbulento; [*process, dispute*] enrevesado, complicado • **she is locked in a ~ legal battle with her landlord** está metida en un pleito muy enrevesado con su casero

mestizo [mɪs'ti:zəʊ] (N) (PL: **mestizos** *or* **mestizoes**) (*US*) mestizo/a *m/f*

Met [met] (ADJ ABBR) (*Brit*) = **meteorological** • **the Met Office** el instituto meteorológico británico
(N ABBR) **1** (*Brit*) (= **Metropolitan Police**) *la policía de Londres*
2 (*US*) = **Metropolitan Opera**

met [met] (PT), (PP) *of* **meet**

meta... ['metə] (PREFIX) meta...

metabolic [,metə'bɒlɪk] (ADJ) metabólico • **~ rate** ciclo *m* metabólico

metabolism [me'tæbəlɪzəm] (N) metabolismo *m*

metabolize [me'tæbəlaɪz] (VT) metabolizar

metacarpal [,metə'kɑ:pl] (N) metacarpiano *m*

metacarpus [,metə'kɑ:pəs] (N) (PL: **metacarpi** [,metə'kɑ:paɪ]) metacarpo *m*

metal ['metl] (N) **1** (*Chem, Phys*) metal *m*
2 (*Brit*) (*on road*) grava *f*
3 (*Brit*) (*Rail*) **metals** rieles *mpl*
4 (*fig*) = **mettle**
(ADJ) metálico, de metal
(VT) (*Brit*) [+ *road*] engravar
(CPD) ▸ **metal detector** detector *m* de metales ▸ **metal fatigue** fatiga *f* del metal ▸ **metal polish** abrillantador *m* de metales

metalanguage ['metə,læŋgwɪdʒ] (N) metalenguaje *m*

metalinguistic [,metəlɪŋ'gwɪstɪk] (ADJ) metalingüístico

metalinguistics [,metəlɪŋ'gwɪstɪks] (NSING) metalingüística *f*

metalled ['metəld] (ADJ) (*esp Brit*) [*road, path*] de grava

metallic [mɪ'tælɪk] (ADJ) metálico

metallurgic [,metə'lɜ:dʒɪk] (ADJ) = **metallurgical**

metallurgical [,metə'lɜ:dʒɪkəl] (ADJ) metalúrgico

metallurgist [me'tælədʒɪst] (N) metalúrgico/a *m/f*

metallurgy [me'tælədʒɪ] (N) metalurgia *f*

metalwork ['metlwɜ:k] (N) (= *craft*) metalistería *f*

metalworker ['metlwɜ:kəʳ] (N) trabajador(a) *m/f* del metal, metalúrgico/a *m/f*

metalworking ['metlwɜ:kɪŋ] (N) metalurgia *f*

metamorphic [,metə'mɔ:fɪk] (ADJ) metamórfico

metamorphose [,metə'mɔ:fəʊz] (VT) metamorfosear (**into** en)
(VI) metamorfosearse (**into** en)

metamorphosis [,metə'mɔ:fəsɪs] (N) (PL: **metamorphoses** [,metə'mɔ:fəsi:z]) metamorfosis *f inv*

metaphor ['metəfɔ:ʳ] (N) metáfora *f*; ▹ **mixed**

metaphoric [,metə'fɒrɪk] (ADJ) = **metaphorical**

metaphorical [,metə'fɒrɪkəl] (ADJ) metafórico

metaphorically [,metə'fɒrɪkəlɪ] (ADV) metafóricamente

metaphysical [,metə'fɪzɪkəl] (ADJ) metafísico

metaphysics [,metə'fɪzɪks] (NSING) metafísica *f*

metastasis [mɪ'tæstəsɪs] (N) (PL: **metastases** [mɪ'tæstəsi:z]) metástasis *f inv*

metatarsal [,metə'tɑ:sl] (N) metatarsiano *m*

metatarsus [,metə'tɑ:səs] (N) (PL: **metatarsi** [,metə'tɑ:saɪ]) metatarso *m*

metathesis [me'tæθəsɪs] (N) (PL: **metatheses** [me'tæθəsi:z]) metátesis *f inv*

mete [mi:t] (VT) • **to ~ out** [+ *punishment, justice*] imponer; [+ *challenge*] asignar

metempsychosis [,metəmsaɪ'kəʊsɪs] (N) metempsicosis *f inv*

meteor ['mi:tɪəʳ] (N) meteoro *m*
(CPD) ▸ **meteor shower** lluvia *f* de meteoritos

meteoric [,mi:tɪ'ɒrɪk] (ADJ) **1** (*lit*) meteórico
2 (*fig*) rápido, meteórico

meteorite ['mi:tɪəraɪt] (N) meteorito *m*

meteoroid ['mi:tɪərɔɪd] (N) meteoroide *m*

meteorological [,mi:tɪərə'lɒdʒɪkəl] (ADJ) meteorológico
(CPD) ▸ **the Meteorological Office** (*Brit*) *el instituto meteorológico británico*

meteorologically [,mi:tɪərə'lɒdʒɪklɪ] (ADV) meteorológicamente, en lo que se refiere a la meteorología

meteorologist [,mi:tɪə'rɒlədʒɪst] (N) meteorólogo/a *m/f*

meteorology [,mi:tɪə'rɒlədʒɪ] (N) meteorología *f*

meter¹ ['mi:təʳ] (N) contador *m*, medidor *m* (*LAm*); (*in taxi*) taxímetro *m* • **gas/electricity ~** contador de gas/de electricidad • **parking ~** parquímetro *m*
(CPD) ▸ **meter reader** lector(a) *m/f* de contadores

meter² ['mi:təʳ] (N) (*US*) = **metre**

meterage ['mi:tərɪdʒ] (N) metraje *m*

metermaid ['mi:tə,meɪd] (N) (*US*) controladora *f* de estacionamiento

methadone ['meθə,dəʊn] (N) metadona *f*

methamphetamine [,meθæm'fetəmi:n] (N) metanfetamina *f*

methane ['mi:θeɪn] (N) metano *m*

methanol ['meθənɒl] (N) metanol *m*

methinks [mɪ'θɪnks] (ADV) †† a mi parecer, a mi entender

method ['meθəd] (N) **1** (= *manner, way*) método *m*; (= *procedure*) procedimiento *m* • **~ of payment** forma *f* de pago • IDIOM: • **there's ~ in his madness** no está tan loco como parece
2 (= *technique*) técnica *f*
(CPD) ▸ **method acting** método *m* Stanislavski ▸ **method actor** actor *m* adepto del método Stanislavski ▸ **method actress** actriz *f* adepta del método Stanislavski

methodical [mɪ'θɒdɪkəl] (ADJ) metódico

methodically [mɪ'θɒdɪkəlɪ] (ADV) metódicamente

Methodism ['meθədɪzəm] (N) metodismo *m*

Methodist ['meθədɪst] (ADJ), (N) metodista *mf*

methodological [,meθədə'lɒdʒɪkəl] (ADJ) metodológico

methodologically [,meθədə'lɒdʒɪkəlɪ] (ADV) metodológicamente, desde el punto de vista metodológico

methodology [,meθə'dɒlədʒɪ] (N) metodología *f*

meths* [meθs] (*Brit*) (N ABBR) = **methylated spirit(s)**
(CPD) ▸ **meths drinker** bebedor(a) *m/f* de alcohol metilado

Methuselah [mɪ'θju:zələ] (N) Matusalén

methylamphetamine [,meθɪlæm'fetəmi:n] (N) metanfetamina *f*

methylated spirit ['meθɪleɪtɪd'spɪrɪt], **methylated spirits** (N) (*Brit*) alcohol *msing* desnaturalizado

meticulous [mɪ'tɪkjʊləs] (ADJ) meticuloso

meticulously [mɪ'tɪkjʊləslɪ] (ADV) meticulosamente

meticulousness [mɪ'tɪkjʊləsnɪs] (N) meticulosidad *f*

métier ['meɪtɪeɪ] (N) (= *trade*) oficio *m*; (= *strong point*) fuerte *m*; (= *speciality*) especialidad *f*

Met-man* ['metmæn] (N) (PL: **Met-men**) meteorólogo *m*

metre, meter (*US*) ['mi:təʳ] (N) metro *m*

metric ['metrɪk] (ADJ) métrico • **to go ~** pasar al sistema métrico
(CPD) ▸ **metric system** sistema *m* métrico ▸ **metric ton** tonelada *f* métrica (= 1.000kg)

metrical ['metrɪkəl] (ADJ) (*Poetry*) métrico

metrication [,metrɪ'keɪʃən] (N) conversión *f* al sistema métrico

metrics ['metrɪks] (N) métrica *f*

metro ['metrəʊ] (N) metro *m*

metrological [,metrə'lɒdʒɪkəl] (ADJ) metrológico

metronome ['metrənəʊm] (N) metrónomo *m*

metronomic [,metrə'nɒmɪk] (ADJ) metronómico

metropolis [mɪ'trɒpəlɪs] (N) metrópoli *f*

metropolitan [,metrə'pɒlɪtən] (ADJ) metropolitano
(CPD) ▸ **the Metropolitan Police** *la policía de Londres*

metrosexual [metrə'seksjʊəl] (ADJ) metrosexual
(N) metrosexual *m*

mettle ['metl] (N) ánimo *m*, valor *m* • **to be on one's ~** estar dispuesto a demostrar su

valía • **to put sb on his ~** picar a algn en el amor propio *or* en el orgullo • **to show one's ~** mostrar lo que uno vale
mettlesome ['metlsəm] (ADJ) animoso, brioso
Meuse [mɜːz] (N) Mosa *m*
mew [mjuː] (N) maullido *m*
(VI) maullar, hacer miau
mewl [mjuːl] (VI) [*cat*] maullar, hacer miau; [*baby*] lloriquear
mews [mjuːz] (*Brit*) (NSING) callejuela *f*
(CPD) ▸ **mews cottage** *casa acondicionada en antiguos establos o cocheras*
Mexican ['meksɪkən] (ADJ), (N) mexicano/a *m/f*
(CPD) ▸ **Mexican wave** (*Brit*) ola *f* (mexicana)
Mexico ['meksɪkəʊ] (N) México *m*
(CPD) ▸ **Mexico City** (Ciudad *f* de) México *m*
mezzanine ['mezəniːn] (N) entresuelo *m*
mezzo-soprano ['metsəʊsə'prɑːnəʊ] (N) (= *singer*) mezzosoprano *f*; (= *voice*) mezzosoprano *m*
mezzotint ['metsəʊtɪnt] (N) grabado *m* mezzotinto
MF (N ABBR) = **medium frequency**
MFA (N ABBR) (*US*) (*Univ*) = **Master of Fine Arts**
MFH (N ABBR) (*Brit*) = **Master of Foxhounds**
MFN (N ABBR) (*US*) (= **most favored nation**) nación *f* más favorecida • **MFN treatment** trato *m* de nación más favorecida
mfr, mfrs (ABBR) (= **manufacturer(s)**) fab
MG (ABBR) (= **machine gun**) ametralladora *f*
mg (ABBR) (= **milligram(s)**) mg.
Mgr (ABBR) (*Rel*) (= **Monseigneur** *or* **Monsignor**) Mons.
mgr (ABBR) = **manager**
MHR (N ABBR) (*US*) = **Member of the House of Representatives**
MHz (ABBR) (*Rad*) (= **megahertz**) MHz
MI (N ABBR) = **machine intelligence**
(ABBR) (*US*) = **Michigan**
mi [miː] (N) (*Mus*) mi *m*
mi. (ABBR) = **mile(s)**
MI5 [,emaɪ'faɪv] (N ABBR) (*Brit*) (= **Military Intelligence 5**) *servicio de inteligencia contraespionaje*
MI6 [,emaɪ'sɪks] (N ABBR) (*Brit*) (= **Military Intelligence 6**) *servicio de inteligencia*
MIA (ADJ ABBR) (*Mil*) = **missing in action**
miaow [miː'aʊ] (N) maullido *m*
(VI) maullar, hacer miau
miasma [mɪ'æzmə] (N) (PL: **miasmas** *or* **miasmata** [mɪ'æzmətə]) miasma *m*
miasmic [mɪ'æzmɪk] (ADJ) miasmático
mica ['maɪkə] (N) mica *f*
mice [maɪs] (NPL) *of* **mouse**
Mich. (ABBR) (*US*) = **Michigan**
Michael ['maɪkl] (N) Miguel
Michaelmas ['mɪklməs] (N) fiesta *f* de San Miguel (*29 setiembre*)
(CPD) ▸ **Michaelmas daisy** margarita *f* de otoño ▸ **Michaelmas term** (*Brit*) (*Jur, Univ*) trimestre *m* de otoño, primer trimestre *m*
Michelangelo [,maɪkəl'ændʒɪləʊ] (N) Miguel Ángel
Mick [mɪk] (N) *familiar form of* **Michael**
Mickey ['mɪkɪ] (CPD) ▸ **Mickey Finn** bebida *f* drogada ▸ **Mickey Mouse** el ratón Mickey • **it's a ~ Mouse set-up** es una empresa poco seria
mickey* ['mɪkɪ] (N) • **to take the ~ (out of sb)** tomar el pelo (a algn)
micra ['maɪkrə] (NPL) *of* **micron**
micro ['maɪkrəʊ] (N) **1** (*Comput*) microcomputadora *f*, microordenador *m* (*Sp*)
2* (= *microwave*) microondas *m*
micro... ['maɪkrəʊ] (PREFIX) micro...
microbe ['maɪkrəʊb] (N) microbio *m*
microbial [maɪ'krəʊbɪəl] (ADJ) microbiano
microbiological [,maɪkrəʊbaɪə'lɒdʒɪkəl] (ADJ) microbiológico
microbiologist [,maɪkrəʊbaɪ'ɒlədʒɪst] (N) microbiólogo/a *m/f*
microbiology [,maɪkrəʊbaɪ'ɒlədʒɪ] (N) microbiología *f*
microblog ['maɪkrəʊ,blɒg] (N) microblog *m*
(CPD) ▸ **microblog post** entrada *f* de un microblog
microblogger ['maɪkrəʊ,blɒgəʳ] (N) microbloguero/a *m/f*
microbrewery ['maɪkrəʊ,bruːərɪ] (N) pequeña fábrica *f* de cerveza
microbus ['maɪkrəʊ,bʌs] (N) (*Aut*) microbús *m*
microcar ['maɪkrəʊ,kɑːʳ] (N) microcoche *m* (*Sp*), microcarro *m* (*LAm*)
microchip ['maɪkrəʊ,tʃɪp] (N) microchip *m*
microcircuit ['maɪkrəʊ,sɜːkɪt] (N) microcircuito *m*
microcircuitry ['maɪkrəʊ'sɜːkɪtrɪ] (N) microcircuitería *f*
microclimate ['maɪkrəʊ,klaɪmɪt] (N) microclima *m*
microcomputer [,maɪkrəʊkəm'pjuːtəʳ] (N) microcomputador *m*, microcomputadora *f*, microordenador *m* (*Sp*)
microcomputing ['maɪkrəʊkəm'pjuːtɪŋ] (N) microcomputación *f*
microcosm ['maɪkrəʊkɒzəm] (N) microcosmo *m*
microcredit ['maɪkrəʊ,kredɪt] (N) microcrédito *m*
microdot ['maɪkrəʊ,dɒt] (N) micropunto *m*
microeconomic [,maɪkrəʊ,iːkə'nɒmɪk] (ADJ) microeconómico
microeconomics ['maɪkrəʊ,iːkə'nɒmɪks] (NSING) microeconomía *f*
microelectronic ['maɪkrəʊ,ɪlek'trɒnɪk] (ADJ) microelectrónico
microelectronics ['maɪkrəʊ,ɪlek'trɒnɪks] (NSING) microelectrónica *fsing*
microfibre, microfiber (*US*) ['maɪkrəʊ,faɪbəʳ] (N) microfibra *f*
microfiche ['maɪkrəʊ,fiːʃ] (N) microficha *f*
(CPD) ▸ **microfiche reader** lector *m* de microfichas
microfilm ['maɪkrəʊfɪlm] (N) microfilm *m*
(VT) microfilmar
(CPD) ▸ **microfilm reader** lector *m* de microfilms
microform ['maɪkrəʊ,fɔːm] (N) microforma *f*
microgravity [,maɪkrəʊ'grævɪtɪ] (N) microgravedad *f*
microgroove ['maɪkrəʊgruːv] (N) microsurco *m*
microlight, microlite ['maɪkrəʊ,laɪt] (N) (*also* **microlight aircraft**) avión *m* ultraligero, ultraligero *m*
micromesh ['maɪkrəʊmeʃ] (ADJ) [*stockings*] de malla fina
micrometer [maɪ'krɒmɪtəʳ] (N) micrómetro *m*
micron ['maɪkrɒn] (N) (PL: **microns** *or* **micra** ['maɪkrə]) micrón *m*
microorganism ['maɪkrəʊ'ɔːgənɪzəm] (N) microorganismo *m*
microphone ['maɪkrəfəʊn] (N) micrófono *m*
microprocessor [,maɪkrəʊ'prəʊsesəʳ] (N) microprocesador *m*
microprogramming, microprograming (*US*) [,maɪkrəʊ'prəʊgræmɪŋ] (N) microprogramación *f*
micro-scooter ['maɪkrəʊ,skuːtəʳ] (N) patinete *m*
microscope ['maɪkrəskəʊp] (N) microscopio *m*
microscopic [,maɪkrə'skɒpɪk], **microscopical** [,maɪkrə'skɒpɪkəl] (ADJ) microscópico
microscopically [,maɪkrəʊ'skɒpɪklɪ] (ADV) microscópicamente • **~ small** microscópico • **to examine sth ~** (*with microscope*) examinar algo al microscopio
microscopy [maɪ'krɒskəpɪ] (N) microscopía *f*
microsecond ['maɪkrəʊ,sekənd] (N) microsegundo *m*
microspacing [,maɪkrəʊ'speɪsɪŋ] (N) microespaciado *m*
microstructural [,maɪkrəʊ'strʌktʃərəl] (ADJ) microestructural
microstructure ['maɪkrəʊ,strʌktʃəʳ] (N) microestructura *f*
microsurgery [,maɪkrəʊ'sɜːdʒərɪ] (N) microcirugía *f*
microsurgical [,maɪkrəʊ'sɜːdʒɪkəl] (ADJ) microquirúrgico
microtechnology [,maɪkrəʊtek'nɒlədʒɪ] (N) microtecnología *f*
microtransmitter [,maɪkrəʊtrænz'mɪtəʳ] (N) microtransmisor *m*
microwavable, microwaveable ['maɪkrəʊ,weɪvəbl] (ADJ) apto para microondas
microwave ['maɪkrəʊ,weɪv] (N) **1** (*Phys*) microonda *f*
2 (*also* **microwave oven**) (horno *m*) microondas *m inv*
(VT) (= *cook*) cocinar con microondas; (= *heat*) calentar en el microondas
microwaveable ['maɪkrəʊ,weɪvəbl] (ADJ) = **microwavable**
micturate ['mɪktjʊəreɪt] (VI) (*frm*) orinar
micturition [,mɪktjʊ'rɪʃən] (N) (*frm*) micción *f*
mid [mɪd] (ADJ) • **in mid June** a mediados de junio • **he's in his mid twenties** tiene unos veinticinco años, tiene veinte y tantos años • **in mid afternoon** a media tarde • **in mid channel** en medio del canal • **in mid course** (*during academic year*) a mitad de curso; (*of degree course*) a mitad de carrera • **in mid journey** a medio camino • **in mid morning** a media mañana • **in mid ocean** en alta mar, en mitad del océano
(PREP) (*liter, poet*) = **amid**
mid-air ['mɪdeəʳ] (N) • **to catch sth in mid-air** agarrar *or* atrapar algo al vuelo • **to refuel in mid-air** repostar combustible en pleno vuelo • IDIOM: • **to leave sth in mid-air** dejar algo a medio hacer
(ADJ) • **mid-air collision** colisión *f* en el aire
Midas ['maɪdəs] (N) Midas • IDIOM: • **he has the ~ touch** todo lo que toca se convierte en dinero
mid-Atlantic [mɪdət'læntɪk] (ADJ) [*accent*] de mitad del Atlántico
midbrain ['mɪdbreɪn] (N) mesencéfalo *m*, cerebro *m* medio
midday ['mɪd'deɪ] (N) mediodía *m* • **at ~** a(l) mediodía
(CPD) ▸ **the midday sun** el sol de(l) mediodía
midden ['mɪdn] (N) muladar *m*
middle ['mɪdl] (N) **1** [*of object, area*] centro *m*, medio *m* • **in the ~ of the table/the room** en medio *or* en el centro de la mesa/la habitación • **he was in the ~ of the road** estaba en medio *or* en (la) mitad de la carretera • **the potatoes were raw in the ~** las patatas estaban crudas por el centro • **to cut sth down the ~** cortar algo por el medio *or* por la mitad • **we agreed to split the bill down the ~** acordamos dividir la cuenta por la mitad • **the party is split down the ~ on this issue** el partido está dividido en dos facciones con respecto a este tema • **in the ~**

m

of nowhere quién sabe dónde, en el quinto pino (*Sp**) • **right in the ~** • **in the very ~** (*physically*) en el mismo centro
2 [*of period*] • **in the ~ of the night** en mitad de la noche • **in the ~ of summer** en pleno verano • **in** *or* **about** *or* **towards the ~ of May** a mediados de mayo • **in the ~ of the morning** a media mañana • **the heat in the ~ of the day was intense** el calor del mediodía era intenso • **he was in his ~ thirties** tenía unos treinta y cinco años, tenía treinta y tantos años
3 [*of activity*] • **to be in the ~ of sth** estar en mitad de algo • **we were in the ~ of dinner** estábamos en mitad de la cena • **I'm in the ~ of a conversation** estoy en mitad de una conversación • **to be in the ~ of doing sth: I'm in the ~ of reading it** lo estoy leyendo • **I'm right in the ~ of getting lunch** justo ahora estoy preparando la comida; ▹ **week**
4* (= *waist*) cintura *f* • **she wore it round her ~** lo llevaba alrededor de la cintura • **he was in the water up to his ~** el agua le llegaba por la cintura
(ADJ) **1** (= *central*) • **the ~ shelf of the oven** la bandeja del medio del horno • **my ~ daughter** mi segunda hija, mi hija de en medio • **~ ground** terreno *m* neutral • **in the ~ years of the nineteenth century** a mediados del siglo diecinueve • **women in their ~ years** mujeres de mediana edad • IDIOM: • **to steer** *or* **take a ~ course** tomar por la calle de en medio
2 (= *average*) mediano • **a man of ~ size** un hombre de mediana estatura
(CPD) ▸ **middle age** madurez *f* ▸ **the Middle Ages** la Edad Media ▸ **Middle America** (= *Central America*) Mesoamérica *f*, Centroamérica *f*; (*US*) (*Geog*) el centro de los Estados Unidos; (*fig*) (*US*) (= *middle class*) la clase media norteamericana ▸ **middle C** (*Mus*) do *m* (*en medio del piano*) ▸ **the middle class(es)** la clase media • **the ~ classes** la clase media • **the upper/lower ~ class(es)** la clase media alta/baja; ▹ **middle-class** ▸ **middle distance** • **in the ~ distance** (*gen*) a una distancia intermedia; (*Art*) en segundo plano; ▹ **middle-distance** ▸ **middle ear** oído *m* medio ▸ **the Middle East** el Oriente Medio ▸ **Middle English** *la lengua inglesa de la edad media* ▸ **middle finger** dedo *m* corazón ▸ **middle management** mandos *mpl* medios ▸ **middle manager** mando *mf* medio ▸ **middle name** segundo nombre *m* de pila • IDIOM: • **"discretion" is my ~ name** soy la discreción en persona ▸ **middle school** (*Brit*) *colegio para niños de ocho o nueve a doce o trece años*; (*US*) *colegio para niños de doce a catorce años* ▸ **the Middle West** (*US*) *la región central de los Estados Unidos*

middle-aged ['mɪdl'eɪdʒd] (ADJ) de mediana edad

middlebrow ['mɪdlbraʊ] (ADJ) de *or* para gusto medianamente culto, de gusto entre intelectual y plebeyo
(N) persona *f* de gusto medianamente culto, persona *f* de cultura mediana

middle-class ['mɪdl'klɑ:s] (ADJ) de (la) clase media; (= *bourgeois*) burgués; ▹ **middle**

middle-distance [ˌmɪdl'dɪstəns] (CPD) ▸ **middle-distance race** carrera *f* de medio fondo ▸ **middle-distance runner** mediofondista *mf*

Middle-Eastern [ˌmɪdl'i:stən] (ADJ) de Oriente Medio

middle-grade manager ['mɪdlgreɪdˌmænɪdʒəʳ] (N) (*US*) mando *m* intermedio

middle-income [ˌmɪdl'ɪnkʌm] (ADJ) [*family*] de ingresos medios

middleman ['mɪdlmæn] (N) (PL: **middlemen**) (*Comm*) intermediario/a *m/f*

middle-of-the-road ['mɪdləvðə'rəʊd] (ADJ) moderado; (*pej*) mediocre

middle-ranking ['mɪdl'ræŋkɪŋ] (ADJ) [*official*] medio

middle-sized ['mɪdlˌsaɪzd] (ADJ) mediano

middleware ['mɪdlwɛəʳ] (N) middleware *m*

middleweight ['mɪdlweɪt] (N) peso *m* medio • **light ~** peso *m* medio ligero
(CPD) ▸ **middleweight champion** campeón/ona *m/f* de peso medio, campeón/ona *m/f* de los pesos medios

middling ['mɪdlɪŋ] (ADJ) mediano; (*pej*) regular • **"how are you?" — "middling"** —¿qué tal estás? —regular; ▹ **fair**[1]
(ADV)* • **~ good** medianamente bueno, regular

Middx (ABBR) (*Brit*) = **Middlesex**

middy* ['mɪdɪ] (N) = **midshipman**

Mideast [mɪd'i:st] (*US*) (N) • **the ~** el Oriente Medio
(ADJ) del Oriente Medio • **a ~ peace conference** una conferencia de paz del Oriente Medio

midfield ['mɪdfi:ld] (N) centro *m* del campo
(CPD) ▸ **midfield player** centrocampista *mf*

midfielder [mɪd'fi:ldəʳ] (N) (*Ftbl*) centrocampista *mf*

midge [mɪdʒ] (N) mosquito *m* pequeño

midget ['mɪdʒɪt] (N) ‡ enano/a *m/f*
(ADJ) en miniatura, en pequeña escala; [*submarine*] de bolsillo

MIDI ['mɪdɪ] (= **musical instrument digital interface**) (N ABBR) MIDI *m*
(ADJ ABBR) MIDI

midi ['mɪdɪ] (ADJ) • **~ hi-fi** • **~ system** minicadena *f*
(N) = **midiskirt**

midiskirt ['mɪdɪskɜ:t] (N) midi *m*, midifalda *f*

midland ['mɪdlənd] (ADJ) del interior, del centro

Midlander ['mɪdləndəʳ] (N) *nativo or habitante de la región central de Inglaterra*

Midlands ['mɪdləndz] (NPL) • **the ~** *la región central de Inglaterra*

midlife ['mɪdˌlaɪf] (CPD) ▸ **midlife crisis** crisis *f inv* de los cuarenta

mid-morning ['mɪd'mɔ:nɪŋ] (ADJ) de media mañana • **mid-morning coffee** café *m* de media mañana, café *m* de las once

midmost ['mɪdməʊst] (ADJ) (*liter*) el/la más cercano/a al centro

midnight ['mɪdnaɪt] (N) medianoche *f* • **at ~** a medianoche • IDIOM: • **to burn the ~ oil** quemarse las pestañas
(CPD) ▸ **midnight blue** negro *m* azulado ▸ **midnight feast** banquete *m* a medianoche ▸ **midnight mass** misa *f* del gallo ▸ **the midnight sun** el sol de medianoche

midpoint ['mɪdˌpɔɪnt] (N) punto *m* medio

mid-range ['mɪdreɪndʒ] (ADJ) [*service*] de categoría media; [*product*] de gama media • **comfortable mid-range accommodation** un alojamiento cómodo de categoría media • **a mid-range family car** un coche familiar de gama media

midriff ['mɪdrɪf] (N) estómago *m*; (*Med*) diafragma *m*

midsection ['mɪdsekʃən] (N) sección *f* de en medio

midshipman ['mɪdʃɪpmən] (N) (PL: **midshipmen**) guardia *mf* marina, alférez *mf* de fragata

midships ['mɪdʃɪps] (ADV) en medio del navío

midsized ['mɪdsaɪzd], **midsize** ['mɪdsaɪz] (ADJ) mediano

midst [mɪdst] (N) • **in the ~ of** (*place*) en medio de, a mitad de (*LAm*) • **in the ~ of the battle** (*fig*) en plena batalla • **in our ~** entre nosotros
(PREP) (*liter*) = **amidst**

midstream ['mɪd'stri:m] (N) (*lit*) centro *m* de la corriente/del río • **in ~** (*lit*) en el medio de la corriente/del río; (*fig*) antes de terminar, a mitad de camino • **he stopped talking in ~** dejó de hablar a mitad de la frase
(ADV) en medio de la corriente/del río

midsummer ['mɪd'sʌməʳ] (N) pleno verano *m* • **in ~** en pleno verano • **"A Midsummer Night's Dream"** "El sueño de una noche de verano"
(CPD) ▸ **Midsummer('s) Day** Día *m* de San Juan (*24 junio*) ▸ **midsummer madness** locura *f* pasajera

midterm ['mɪd'tɜ:m] (ADJ) • **~ exam** examen *m* de mitad del trimestre • **~ elections** (*US*) elecciones *fpl* a mitad del mandato (presidencial)

midtown ['mɪdˌtaʊn] (N) centro *m* de la ciudad
(CPD) ▸ **midtown shops** tiendas *fpl* del centro de la ciudad

mid-Victorian ['mɪdvɪk'tɔ:rɪən] (ADJ) (*Brit*) de mitades de la época victoriana

midway ['mɪd'weɪ] (ADV) a mitad de camino, a medio camino • **~ between Edinburgh and Glasgow** a mitad de camino *or* a medio camino entre Edimburgo y Glasgow • **we are now ~** ahora estamos a mitad de camino *or* a medio camino • **~ through the interview, Taggart got up** Taggart se levantó a mitad de la entrevista
(ADJ) • **the ~ point between X and Y** el punto medio entre X y Y
(N) (*US*) avenida *f* central, paseo *m* central

midweek ['mɪd'wi:k] (ADV) entre semana
(ADJ) de entre semana

Midwest [mɪd'west] (N) (*US*) mediooeste *m* (*llanura central de EEUU*)

Midwestern ['mɪdˌwestən] (ADJ) (*US*) del mediooeste (*de EEUU*)

Midwesterner [mɪd'westənəʳ] (N) (*US*) *nativo/habitante del Midwest*

midwife ['mɪdwaɪf] (N) (PL: **midwives**) comadrona *f*, partera *f*

midwifery ['mɪdˌwɪfərɪ] (N) partería *f*

midwinter ['mɪd'wɪntəʳ] (N) pleno invierno *m* • **in ~** en pleno invierno
(CPD) de pleno invierno

midwives ['mɪdwaɪvz] (NPL) *of* **midwife**

mien [mi:n] (N) (*liter*) aire *m*, porte *m*, semblante *m*

miff* [mɪf] (N) disgusto *m*
(VT) disgustar, ofender • **he was pretty ~ed about it** se ofendió bastante por eso

might[1] [maɪt] (PT), (COND) *of* **may**

might[2] [maɪt] (N) poder *m*, fuerza *f* • **with all one's ~** con todas sus fuerzas • **with ~ and main** a más no poder, esforzándose muchísimo

might-have-been ['maɪtəvˌbi:n] (N) esperanza *f* no cumplida

mightily ['maɪtɪlɪ] (ADV) **1**† (= *greatly*) [*rejoice*] tremendamente, enormemente; [*impressive*] sumamente • **to be ~ impressed/relieved** estar tremendamente *or* sumamente impresionado/aliviado • **I was ~ surprised** me sorprendí enormemente
2 (*liter*) (= *powerfully*) [*strike, hit*] con fuerza • **they heaved ~** tiraron con todas sus fuerzas

mightiness ['maɪtɪnɪs] (N) (= *strength*) fuerza *f*; (= *power*) poder *m*, poderío *m*

mightn't ['maɪtnt] = **might not**

mighty ['maɪtɪ] (ADJ) (COMPAR: **mightier**, SUPERL: **mightiest**) (*liter*) **1** (= *powerful*) [*blow*] tremendo*; [*effort*] grandísimo; [*nation*]

poderoso • **he shook his ~ fist** agitó su poderoso puño • **God's ~ power** la omnipotencia de Dios; ▷ **high**
2 (= *loud*) [*bang, roar*] enorme
3 (= *large*) [*river, fortress, wall*] enorme, inmenso
ADV (*US**) (= *very*) • **I'm ~ glad to hear it** me alegro muchísimo de saberlo • **she's a ~ fine-looking woman** es una mujer muy guapa • **we were ~ worried** estábamos la mar de preocupados* • **it's a ~ long way to Southfork** Southfork está tremendamente lejos *or* está lejísimos
NPL • **the ~** los poderosos • IDIOM: • **how the ~ have fallen!** ¡cómo han caído los poderosos!
mignonette [ˌmɪnjəˈnet] N reseda *f*
migraine [ˈmi:greɪn] N jaqueca *f*, migraña *f* • **I've got a ~** tengo jaqueca *or* migraña
CPD ▸ **migraine attack** ataque *m* de jaqueca *or* migraña ▸ **migraine sufferer** • **this will benefit ~ sufferers** esto beneficiará a los que padecen de jaqueca *or* migraña
migrant [ˈmaɪgrənt] ADJ migratorio
N emigrante *mf*; (= *bird*) ave *f* migratoria *or* de paso • **economic ~** emigrante *mf* económico/a, emigrante *mf* por razones económicas
CPD ▸ **migrant worker** trabajador(a) *m/f* emigrado/a
migrate [maɪˈgreɪt] VI [*animals, people*] emigrar
migration [maɪˈgreɪʃən] N migración *f*
migratory [maɪˈgreɪtərɪ] ADJ migratorio
Mike [maɪk] N (*familiar form of* **Michael**) • **for the love of ~!*** ¡por Dios!
mike* [maɪk] N ABBR (= **microphone**) micro *m*
mil* [mɪl] N ABBR (= *million*) millón *m*
milady [mɪˈleɪdɪ] N miladi *f*
Milan [mɪˈlæn] N Milán *m*
milch cow [ˈmɪltʃkaʊ] N vaca *f* lechera
mild [maɪld] ADJ (COMPAR: **milder**, SUPERL: **mildest**) **1** (= *not severe*) [*winter*] moderado, poco frío; [*weather, climate, evening*] templado • **it's very ~ for the time of year** no hace mucho frío para esta época del año
2 (= *not strong*) [*cheese, cigar, detergent, shampoo, sedative*] suave; [*curry*] suave, no muy picante; [*protest*] moderado; [*criticism*] suave, moderado • **he issued a ~ rebuke to his Republican opponents** reprendió a sus oponentes republicanos con cierta suavidad
3 (= *not serious*) [*fever*] ligero; [*infection*] pequeño; [*symptoms*] leve • **he had a ~ stroke last year** tuvo un derrame cerebral de poca seriedad el año pasado • **I had a ~ case of food poisoning** tuve una ligera intoxicación
4 (= *slight*) [*pain*] leve, ligero • **they listened with ~ interest** escuchaban con cierto interés • **he turned to Mona with a look of ~ confusion/surprise** se volvió hacia Mona y la miró ligeramente confundido/sorprendido
5 (= *pleasant*) [*person, voice*] afable, dulce; [*words*] dulce; [*disposition*] tranquilo, apacible; [*manner*] afable
N (*Brit*) (= *beer*) *cerveza suave y de color oscuro*
CPD ▸ **mild steel** *acero con bajo contenido carbónico*
mildew [ˈmɪldju:] N (*on plants*) añublo *m*; (*on food, leather etc*) moho *m*
mildewed [ˈmɪldju:d] ADJ mohoso
mildly [ˈmaɪldlɪ] ADV **1** (= *gently*) [*say, reply*] suavemente, con suavidad
2 (= *slightly*) [*amusing, surprised, interested, irritated*] ligeramente
3 (= *weakly*) [*protest*] débilmente; [*rebuke*] con suavidad, suavemente • **he was only ~ criticized for his actions** solo recibió críticas moderadas por sus acciones
4 • **to put it ~**: **to put it ~, I was cross** decir que estaba enfadado es quedarse corto • **he's a low-down thief, and that's putting it ~** es un cochino ladrón por no decir algo peor
mild-mannered [ˈmaɪldˈmænəd] ADJ apacible
mildness [ˈmaɪldnɪs] N **1** (*Met*) [*of weather, climate*] lo templado
2 (= *weakness*) [*of cigar, detergent, shampoo, rebuke, criticism*] suavidad *f*; [*of symptoms*] levedad *f*
3 (= *pleasantness*) [*of person, disposition*] afabilidad *f*, placidez *f*; [*of words*] dulzura *f*; [*of manner*] gentileza *f*, afabilidad *f*
mile [maɪl] N **1** milla *f* (= *1609,33m*) • **30 ~s a** *or* **to the gallon** 30 millas por galón • **50 ~s per** *or* **an hour** 50 millas por hora • **we walked ~s!*** ¡anduvimos millas y millas! • **people came from ~s around** la gente vino de millas a la redonda • **they live ~s away** viven lejísimos de aquí • **you could see for ~s** se veía hasta lejísimos • IDIOMS: • **to be ~s away**: • **sorry, I was ~s away** lo siento, estaba pensando en otra cosa • **by a ~** • **by ~s**: • **the shot missed by a ~** *or* **by ~s** el disparo falló por mucho • **the best hotel by a ~** *or* **by ~s is the Inglaterra** el mejor hotel con mucho es el Inglaterra • **to go the extra ~** dar el paso siguiente* • **not a million ~s from here** (*hum*) no muy lejos de aquí • **a ~ off**: • **you can smell/see it a ~ off** eso se huele/se ve a la legua • **to run a ~**: • **as soon as he sees me coming, he runs a ~** en cuanto me ve venir sale pitando* • **it stands** *or* **sticks out a ~** salta a la vista, se ve a la legua; ▷ **inch**, **miss**[1], IMPERIAL SYSTEM
2* **miles** (= *very much*) • **she's ~s better than I am at maths** las matemáticas se le dan cien mil veces mejor que a mí • **the sleeves are ~s too long** las mangas no me van largas, me van larguísimas
CPD ▸ **Mile High City** Denver; ▷ CITY NICKNAMES
-mile [maɪl] ADJ (*ending in compounds*) • **a 50-mile bike ride** un paseo en bici de 50 millas
mileage [ˈmaɪlɪdʒ] N **1** distancia *f* en millas; (*on mileometer*) ≈ kilometraje *m* • **what ~ does your car do?** ≈ ¿cuántos kilómetros hace tu coche por galón de gasolina?, ¿cuántas millas hace tu coche por galón de gasolina? • **what ~ has this car done?** ≈ ¿qué kilómetraje tiene este coche?, ¿cuántas millas/cuántos kilómetros tiene este coche?
2 (*fig*) • **there's no ~ in this story** esta historia solo tiene un interés pasajero • **he got a lot of ~ out of it** le sacó mucho partido
CPD ▸ **mileage allowance** dietas *fpl* por desplazamiento en vehículo propio, ≈ dietas *f* por kilometraje ▸ **mileage indicator** ≈ cuentakilómetros *m inv* ▸ **mileage rate** tarifa *f* por distancia
mileometer [maɪˈlɒmɪtəʳ] N (*Brit*) (*Aut*) ≈ cuentakilómetros *m inv*
milepost [ˈmaɪlpəʊst] N (*Hist*) poste *m* miliar, mojón *m*
miler [ˈmaɪləʳ] N corredor(a) *m/f* (*etc que se especializa en las pruebas de una milla*)
milestone [ˈmaɪlstəʊn] N **1** (*on road*) mojón *m*
2 (*fig*) hito *m* • **these events are ~s in our history** estos acontecimientos marcan un hito en *or* de nuestra historia
milieu [ˈmi:ljɜ:] (PL: **milieus** *or* **milieux** [ˈmi:ljɜ:]) N medio *m*, entorno *m*
militancy [ˈmɪlɪtənsɪ] N [*of group, trade union*] militancia *f*, combatividad *m*; [*of person, attitude*] combatividad *m*
militant [ˈmɪlɪtənt] ADJ [*group, trade union*] militante, combativo; [*person, attitude*] combativo • **to be in (a) ~ mood** estar combativo
N militante *mf* • **to be a party ~** militar en un partido
militantly [ˈmɪlɪtəntlɪ] ADV [*react, behave*] de forma agresiva *or* combativa; [*nationalist*] radicalmente • **to be ~ opposed to sth** oponerse radicalmente a algo
militarily [ˈmɪlɪtərɪlɪ] ADV [*intervene, respond*] militarmente; [*significant, useful, effective*] desde un punto de vista militar
militarism [ˈmɪlɪtərɪzəm] N militarismo *m*
militarist [ˈmɪlɪtərɪst] ADJ militarista
N militarista *mf*
militaristic [ˌmɪlɪtəˈrɪstɪk] ADJ militarista
militarize [ˈmɪlɪtəraɪz] VT militarizar
military [ˈmɪlɪtərɪ] ADJ [*intervention, government, history, bearing*] militar • **he retired with full ~ honours** se retiró con todos los honores militares • **to do sth with ~ precision** hacer algo con una precisión militar
NPL • **the ~** los militares
CPD ▸ **military academy** academia *f* militar ▸ **military base** base *f* militar ▸ **military police** policía *f* militar ▸ **military policeman** policía *m* militar ▸ **military service** servicio *m* militar • **to do (one's) ~ service** hacer *or* prestar el servicio militar, hacer la mili*
militate [ˈmɪlɪteɪt] VI • **to ~ against** militar en contra de
militia [mɪˈlɪʃə] N milicia(s) *f(pl)*
CPD ▸ **the militia reserves** (*US*) las reservas (territoriales)
militiaman [mɪˈlɪʃəmən] (PL: **militiamen**) N miliciano *m*
milk [mɪlk] N leche *f* • **skim(med) ~** leche *f* desnatada • **powdered ~** leche *f* en polvo • **~ of magnesia** (*Med*) leche de magnesia • **the ~ of human kindness** la compasión personificada • PROVERB: • **it's no good crying over spilt ~** a lo hecho pecho
VT **1** [+ *cow*] ordeñar
2 (*fig*) exprimir; [+ *applause*] arrancar del público, sacar todo el partido a • **they're ~ing the company for all they can get** chupan todo lo que pueden de la compañía
VI dar leche
CPD ▸ **milk bar** cafetería *f* ▸ **milk chocolate** chocolate *m* con leche ▸ **milk churn** lechera *f* ▸ **milk cow** vaca *f* lechera ▸ **milk diet** dieta *f* láctea ▸ **milk duct** (*Anat*) conducto *m* galactóforo ▸ **milk float** carro *m* de la leche ▸ **milk jug** jarrita *f* para la leche ▸ **milk pan** cazo *m* *or* cacerola *f* para la leche ▸ **milk products** productos *mpl* lácteos ▸ **milk pudding** arroz *m* con leche ▸ **milk round** (*lit*) recorrido *m* del lechero; (*Brit*) (*Univ*) *recorrido anual de las principales empresas por las universidades para entrevistar a estudiantes del último curso con vistas a una posible contratación* ▸ **milk run** (*Aer*) vuelo *m* rutinario ▸ **milk saucepan** cazo *m* *or* cacerola *f* para la leche ▸ **milk shake** batido *m*, malteada *f* (*LAm*) ▸ **milk tooth** diente *m* de leche ▸ **milk truck** (*US*) = **milk float**
milk-and-water [ˈmɪlkənˈwɔ:təʳ] ADJ (*fig*) débil, flojo
milkiness [ˈmɪlkɪnɪs] N lechosidad *f*
milking [ˈmɪlkɪŋ] ADJ lechero, de ordeño
N ordeño *m*
CPD ▸ **milking machine** ordeñadora *f* mecánica
milkmaid [ˈmɪlkmeɪd] N lechera *f*
milkman [ˈmɪlkmən] N (PL: **milkmen**) lechero *m*, repartidor *m* de leche
milksop [ˈmɪlksɒp] N marica *m*
milkweed [ˈmɪlkwi:d] N algodoncillo *m*

milk-white ['mɪlk'waɪt] ADJ blanco como la leche

milky ['mɪlkɪ] (COMPAR: **milkier**, SUPERL: **milkiest**) ADJ **1** (= *pale white*) [*lotion, liquid, eyes, skin*] lechoso; [*green, blue*] blanquecino • **the leaves yield a ~ juice if broken** si se parten las hojas sueltan un jugo lechoso
2 (*containing a lot of milk*) [*tea, coffee*] con mucha leche • **I like my coffee nice and ~** me gusta el café con mucha leche • **this tea is too ~ for my liking** este té tiene mucha leche para mi gusto • **it tastes ~** sabe mucho a leche • **a ~ drink helps you sleep at night** una bebida hecha con leche te ayuda a dormir por la noche
CPD ▸ **the Milky Way** (*Astron*) la Vía Láctea

mill [mɪl] N **1** (= *textile factory*) fábrica *f* (de tejidos); (= *sugar mill*) ingenio *m* de azúcar; (= *spinning mill*) hilandería *f*; (= *steel mill*) acería *f*
2 (= *machine*) molino *m*; (*for coffee, pepper*) molinillo *m*; (*Tech*) fresadora *f* • IDIOM: • **to put sb through the ~**: • **they put me through the ~** me las hicieron pasar canutas *or* moradas
VT moler; [+ *metal*] pulir; (*coin*) acordonar
CPD ▸ **mill worker** (*in textile mill*) obrero/a *m/f* de fábrica de tejidos • **she was a ~ worker** era obrera de una fábrica de tejidos • **a ~ workers' union** un sindicato de obreros de fábricas de tejidos
▸ **mill about, mill around** VI + ADV arremolinarse
VI + PREP • **people were ~ing about the booking office** la gente se apiñaba delante de la taquilla

milled [mɪld] ADJ [*grain*] molido; [*coin, edge*] acordonado

millenarian [ˌmɪlə'nɛərɪən] ADJ milenario

millenarianism [ˌmɪlə'nɛərɪənɪzəm] N milenarismo *m*

millenary [mɪ'lenərɪ] ADJ milenario
N milenario *m*

millennial [mɪ'lenɪəl] ADJ milenario

millennium [mɪ'lenɪəm] N (PL: **millenniums** *or* **millennia** [mɪ'lenɪə]) milenio *m* • **the ~** el milenio
CPD ▸ **the millennium bug** (*Comput*) el (problema del) efecto 2000 ▸ **millennium fund** (*Brit*) *fondo de financiación y desarrollo para el nuevo milenio*

millepede ['mɪlɪˌpiːd] N = **millipede**

miller ['mɪləʳ] N molinero/a *m/f*

millet ['mɪlɪt] N mijo *m*

millhand ['mɪlhænd] N obrero/a *m/f*, operario/a *m/f*

milli... ['mɪlɪ] PREFIX mili...

milliamp ['mɪlɪæmp] N miliamperio *m*

milliard ['mɪlɪɑːd] N (*Brit*) mil millones *mpl*

millibar ['mɪlɪbɑːʳ] N milibar *m*

milligram, milligramme ['mɪlɪgræm] N miligramo *m*

millilitre, milliliter (*US*) ['mɪlɪˌliːtəʳ] N mililitro *m*

millimetre, millimeter (*US*) ['mɪlɪˌmiːtəʳ] N milímetro *m*

millimole ['mɪlɪməʊl] N milimol *m*

milliner ['mɪlɪnəʳ] N sombrerero/a *m/f* • **~'s (shop)** sombrerería *f*

millinery ['mɪlɪnərɪ] N sombrerería *f*, sombreros *mpl* de señora

milling ['mɪlɪŋ] N **1** (= *grinding*) molienda *f*
2 (*on coin*) cordoncillo *m*
CPD ▸ **milling machine** fresadora *f*

million ['mɪljən] N millón *m* • **four ~ dogs** cuatro millones de perros • **I've got ~s of letters to write*** tengo miles de cartas que escribir • **I've told you ~s of times*** te lo he dicho infinidad de veces • IDIOMS: • **to feel like a ~ dollars** *or* (*US*) **bucks*** sentirse a las mil maravillas • **she's one in a ~*** es única, es fuera de lo común

millionaire [ˌmɪljə'nɛəʳ] N millonario/a *m/f*

millionairess [mɪljə'nɛəres] N millonaria *f*

millionth ['mɪljənθ] ADJ millonésimo
N millonésimo *m*

millipede ['mɪlɪpiːd] N milpiés *m inv*

millisecond ['mɪlɪˌsekənd] N milésima *f* de segundo, milisegundo *m*

millpond ['mɪlpɒnd] N represa *f* de molino

millrace ['mɪlreɪs] N caz *m*

millstone ['mɪlstəʊn] N piedra *f* de molino, muela *f* • **it's a ~ round his neck** es una cruz que lleva a cuestas

millstream ['mɪlstriːm] N corriente *f* del caz

millwheel ['mɪlwiːl] N rueda *f* de molino

milometer [maɪ'lɒmɪtəʳ] N = **mileometer**

milord [mɪ'lɔːd] N milord *m*

milt [mɪlt] N lecha *f*

mime [maɪm] N (= *acting*) mimo *m*, mímica *f*; (= *play*) teatro *m* de mimo; (= *actor*) mimo *mf*
VT imitar, remedar
VI (= *act*) hacer mímica • **to ~ to a song** cantar una canción haciendo playback
CPD ▸ **mime artist** mimo *mf*

Mimeograph® ['mɪmɪəgrɑːf] N mimeógrafo® *m*
VT mimeografiar

mimetic [mɪ'metɪk] ADJ (*frm*) [*dance*] mimético; [*theatre*] de mimo; [*re-enactment*] mímico

mimic ['mɪmɪk] N mímico/a *m/f*
VT imitar, remedar

mimicry ['mɪmɪkrɪ] N mímica *f*; (*Bio*) mimetismo *m*

mimosa [mɪ'məʊzə] N mimosa *f*

Min. ABBR (*Brit*) (= **Ministry**) Min

min. ABBR **1** (= **minute(s)**) m
2 (= **minimum**) mín

minaret [mɪnə'ret] N alminar *m*, minarete *m*

minatory ['mɪnətərɪ] ADJ (*liter*) amenazador

mince [mɪns] N (*Brit*) (*Culin*) (*also* **minced meat**) carne *f* picada
VT **1** [+ *meat*] picar
2 (*fig*) • **well, not to ~ matters** bueno, para decirlo francamente • IDIOM: • **not to ~ one's words** no tener pelos en la lengua
VI (*in walking*) andar con pasos medidos; (*in talking*) hablar remilgadamente
CPD ▸ **mince pie** pastel *m* de picadillo de fruta

minced [mɪnsd] ADJ **1** [*meat, onion*] picado
2 (*Brit**) (= *drunk*) mamado*

mincemeat ['mɪnsmiːt] N (= *dried fruit*) conserva *f* de picadillo de fruta; (*Brit*) (= *minced meat*) carne *f* picada • IDIOM: • **to make ~ of sb*** hacer picadillo *or* pedazos a algn

mincer ['mɪnsəʳ] N (= *machine*) máquina *f* de picar carne

mincing ['mɪnsɪŋ] ADJ remilgado, afectado; [*step*] menudito
CPD ▸ **mincing machine** máquina *f* de picar carne

mind [maɪnd]

NOUN
TRANSITIVE VERB
INTRANSITIVE VERB
COMPOUNDS
PHRASAL VERB

NOUN

1 (= *brain, head*) mente *f* • **a logical/creative ~** una mente racional/creativa • **he has the ~ of a five-year-old** tiene la edad mental de un niño de cinco años • **it's all in the ~** es pura sugestión • **at the back of my ~ I had the feeling that ...** tenía la remota sensación de que ... • **to bring one's ~ to bear on sth** concentrarse en algo • **it came to my ~ that ...** se me ocurrió que ... • **I'm not clear in my ~ about it** todavía no lo tengo claro *or* no lo llego a entender • **it crossed my ~ (that)** se me ocurrió (que) • **yes, it had crossed my ~** sí, eso se me había ocurrido • **does it ever cross your ~ that ...?** ¿piensas alguna vez que ...? • **my ~ was elsewhere** tenía la cabeza en otro sitio • **it never entered my ~** jamás se me pasó por la cabeza • **I can't get it out of my ~** no me lo puedo quitar de la cabeza • **to go over sth in one's ~** repasar algo mentalmente • **a triumph of ~ over matter** un triunfo del espíritu sobre la materia • **it's a question of ~ over matter** es cuestión de voluntad • **to have one's ~ on sth** estar pensando en algo • **I had my ~ on something else** estaba pensando en otra cosa • **to have sth on one's ~** estar preocupado por algo • **what's on your ~?** ¿qué es lo que te preocupa? • **you can put that right out of your ~** conviene no pensar más en eso • **if you put your ~ to it** si te concentras en ello • **knowing that he had arrived safely set my ~ at ease** *or* **rest** el saber que había llegado sano y salvo me tranquilizó • **if you set your ~ to it** si te concentras en ello • **the thought that springs to ~ is ...** lo que primero se le ocurre a uno es ... • **state of ~** estado *m* de ánimo • **that will take your ~ off it** eso te distraerá • **to be uneasy in one's ~** quedarse con dudas • **he let his ~ wander** dejó que los pensamientos se le fueran a otras cosas • IDIOM: • **~'s eye** imaginación *f* • **in my ~'s eye I could still see her sitting there** mentalmente todavía la veía allí sentada • **that's a load** *or* **weight off my ~!** ¡eso me quita un peso de encima!; ▹ **blank, read, presence**

2 (= *memory*) • **to bear sth/sb in ~** tener en cuenta algo/a algn • **we must bear (it) in ~ that ...** debemos tener en cuenta que ..., tenemos que recordar que ... • **I'll bear you in ~** te tendré en cuenta • **to keep sth/sb in ~** tener presente *or* en cuenta algo/a algn • **he puts me in ~ of his father** me recuerda a su padre • **to pass out of ~** caer en el olvido • **time out of ~** tiempo *m* inmemorial • **it went right** *or* **clean out of my ~** se me fue por completo de la cabeza • **to bring** *or* **call sth to ~** recordar algo, traer algo a la memoria • **that calls something else to ~** eso me trae otra cosa a la memoria; ▹ **slip, stick**

3 (= *intention*) • **you can do it if you have a ~ to** puedes lograrlo si de verdad estás empeñado en ello • **I have a good ~ to do it** ganas de hacerlo no me faltan • **I have half a ~ to do it** estoy tentado *or* me dan ganas de hacerlo • **nothing was further from my ~** nada más lejos de mi intención • **to have sth in ~** tener pensado algo • **she wrote it with publication in ~** lo escribió con la intención de publicarlo • **to have sb in ~** tener a algn en mente • **who do you have in ~ for the job?** ¿a quién piensas darle el puesto *or* tienes en mente para el puesto? • **to have in ~ to do sth** tener intención de hacer algo

4 (= *opinion*) opinión *f*, parecer *m* • **to change one's ~** cambiar de opinión *or* idea *or* parecer • **to change sb's ~** hacer que algn cambie de opinión • **to have a closed ~** tener una mente cerrada • **to know one's own ~** saber lo que uno quiere • **to make up one's ~** decidirse • **we can't make up our ~s about selling the house** no nos decidimos a vender la casa • **I can't make up my ~ about him** todavía tengo ciertas dudas con respecto a él • **he has made up his ~ to leave home** ha decidido irse de casa, está decidido a irse de casa • **to my ~** a mi juicio • **to be of one ~** estar de acuerdo • **with one ~** unánimemente • **with an open ~** con espíritu abierto *or* mentalidad abierta • **to keep an open ~ on a subject** mantener una mentalidad abierta con relación a un tema • **to have a ~ of one's own** [*person*] (= *think for o.s.*) pensar por sí mismo; (*hum*) [*machine etc*] tener voluntad propia, hacer lo que quiere • **to be of the same ~** ser de la misma opinión, estar de acuerdo • **I was of the same ~ as my brother** yo estaba de acuerdo con mi hermano, yo era de la misma opinión que mi hermano • IDIOM: • **to be in** *or* (*US*) **of two ~s** dudar, estar indeciso; ▹ **piece, speak**

5 (= *mental balance*) juicio *m* • **his ~ is going** está perdiendo facultades mentales • **to lose one's ~** perder el juicio • **nobody in his right ~ would do it** nadie que esté en su sano juicio lo haría • **of sound ~** en pleno uso de sus facultades mentales • **of unsound ~** mentalmente incapacitado • IDIOM: • **to be out of one's ~** estar loco, haber perdido el juicio • **you must be out of your ~!** ¡tú debes estar loco! • **we were bored out of our ~s** estábamos muertos de aburrimiento • **to go out of one's ~** perder el juicio, volverse loco • **to go out of one's ~ with worry/jealousy** volverse loco de preocupación/celos

6 (= *person*) mente *f*, cerebro *m* • **one of the finest ~s of the period** uno de los cerebros privilegiados de la época • PROVERB: • **great ~s think alike** (*hum*) los sabios siempre pensamos igual

TRANSITIVE VERB

1 (= *be careful of*) tener cuidado con • **~ you don't fall** ten cuidado, no te vayas a caer • **~ you don't get wet!** ten cuidado, no te vayas a mojar • **~ your head!** ¡cuidado con la cabeza! • **~ how you go!*** (*as farewell*) ¡cuídate! • **~ your language!** ¡qué manera de hablar es esa! • **~ your manners!** ¡qué modales son esos! • **~ the step!** ¡cuidado con el escalón! • **~ what you're doing!** ¡cuidado con lo que haces! • **~ where you're going!** ¡mira por dónde vas! • **~ yourself!** ¡cuidado, no te vayas a hacer daño!

2 (= *make sure*) • **~ you get there first** procura llegar primero • **~ you do it!** ¡hazlo sin falta!, ¡no dejes de hacerlo!

3 (= *pay attention to*) hacer caso de • **~ what I say!** ¡hazme caso!, ¡escucha lo que te digo! • **~ your own business!** ¡no te metas donde no te llaman! • **don't ~ me** por mí no se preocupe • **don't ~ me!** (*iro*) ¡y a mí que me parta un rayo!* • **never ~ that now** olvídate de eso ahora • **never ~ him** no le hagas caso • **~ you, it was raining at the time** claro que *or* te advierto que en ese momento llovía • **it was a big one, ~ you** era grande, eso sí

4 (= *look after*) cuidar • **could you ~ the baby this afternoon?** ¿podrías cuidar al niño esta tarde? • **could you ~ my bags for a few minutes?** ¿me cuidas *or* guardas las bolsas un momento?

5 (= *dislike, object to*) • **I don't ~ the cold** a mí no me molesta el frío • **I don't ~ four, but six is too many** cuatro no me importa, pero seis son muchos • **I don't ~ waiting** no me importa esperar • **if you don't ~ my** *or* **me saying so, I think you're wrong** perdona que te diga pero estás equivocado, permíteme que te diga que te equivocas • **I don't ~ telling you, I was shocked** estaba horrorizado, lo confieso • **I wouldn't ~ a cup of tea** no me vendría mal un té

6 (*in requests*) • **do you ~ telling me where you've been?** ¿te importa decirme dónde has estado? • **would you ~ opening the door?** ¿me hace el favor de abrir la puerta?, ¿le importa(ría) abrir la puerta?

7 (*dialect*) (= *remember*) acordarse de, recordar • **I ~ the time when ...** me acuerdo de cuando ...

INTRANSITIVE VERB

1 (= *be careful*) tener cuidado • **~!** ¡cuidado!, ¡ojo!, ¡abusado! (*Mex*)

2 (= *object*) • **do you ~?** ¿te importa? • **do you ~!** (*iro*) ¡por favor! • **do you ~ if I open the window?** ¿te molesta que abra *or* si abro la ventana? • **do you ~ if I come?** ¿te importa que yo venga? • **I don't ~** me es igual • **"do you ~ if I take this book?" — "I don't ~ at all"** —¿te importa si me llevo *or* que me lleve este libro? —en absoluto • **if you don't ~, I won't come** si no te importa, yo no iré • **please, if you don't ~** si no le importa, si es tan amable • **close the door, if you don't ~** hazme el favor de cerrar la puerta • **"cigarette?" — "I don't ~ if I do"** —¿un cigarrillo? —pues muchas gracias *or* bueno *or* no digo que no • **never ~** (= *don't worry*) no te preocupes; (= *it makes no odds*) es igual, da lo mismo; (= *it's not important*) no importa • **I can't walk, never ~ run** no puedo andar, ni mucho menos correr

3 (*qualifying comment*) • **he didn't do it, ~** pero en realidad no lo hizo, la verdad es que no lo hizo

COMPOUNDS

▸ **mind game** juego *m* psicológico ▸ **mind map** mapa *m* mental

▸ **mind out** (VI + ADV) tener cuidado • **~ out!** ¡cuidado!, ¡ojo!, ¡abusado! (*Mex*)

---

mind-altering [ˈmaɪnd,ɔːltərɪŋ] (ADJ) [*drug, substance, effect*] psicotrópico

mind-bender* [ˈmaɪnd,bendəʳ] (N) (*US*) 1 (= *drug*) alucinogénico *m*, droga *f* alucinogénica 2 (= *revelation*) noticia *f* or escena *f etc* alucinante*

mind-bending* [ˈmaɪnd,bendɪŋ], **mind-blowing*** [ˈmaɪnd,bləʊɪŋ], **mind-boggling*** [ˈmaɪnd,bɒglɪŋ] (ADJ) increíble, alucinante*

mind-bogglingly [ˈmaɪnd,bɒglɪŋlɪ] (ADV) increíblemente, alucinantemente

minded [ˈmaɪndɪd] (ADJ) • **if you are so ~** si estás dispuesto a hacerlo, si quieres hacerlo

-minded [ˈmaɪndɪd] (ADJ) (*ending in compounds*) • **fair-minded** imparcial • **an industrially-minded nation** una nación de mentalidad industrial • **scientifically-minded** con aptitudes científicas • **a romantically-minded girl** una joven con una vena romántica *or* con ideas románticas

minder* [ˈmaɪndəʳ] (N) 1 guardaespaldas *mf inv*, acompañante *mf*, escolta *mf* 2 (*esp Brit*) = **childminder**

mind-expanding [ˈmaɪndɪks,pændɪŋ] (ADJ) [*drug*] visionario

mindful [ˈmaɪndfʊl] (ADJ) • **to be ~ of** tener presente *or* en cuenta • **we must be ~ of the risks** hay que tener presentes *or* en cuenta los riesgos

mindfulness [ˈmaɪndfʊlnɪs] (N) atención *f* or conciencia *f* plena

mindless [ˈmaɪndlɪs] (ADJ) 1 (*Brit*) (= *senseless*) [*violence, vandalism, killing*] sin sentido 2 (= *unchallenging*) [*work, routine*] mecánico; [*entertainment*] sin sentido, absurdo 3 (= *unintelligent*) [*person*] tonto • **they're a bunch of ~ hooligans** son un atajo de gamberros salvajes 4 (= *heedless*) • **~ of sth** (*frm*) haciendo caso omiso de algo

mindlessly [ˈmaɪndlɪslɪ] (ADV) (= *unchallengingly*) [*entertaining*] tontamente; (= *without thinking*) sin pensar; (= *stupidly*) estúpidamente

mind-numbing [ˈmaɪnd,nʌmɪŋ] (ADJ) soporífero

mind-reader [ˈmaɪnd,riːdəʳ] (N) adivinador(a) *m/f* de pensamientos • **I'm not a mind-reader, you know!*** ¿tú te crees que yo soy adivino?*

mind-reading [ˈmaɪnd,riːdɪŋ] (N) adivinación *f* de pensamientos

mind-set [ˈmaɪndset] (N) actitud *f*, disposición *f*

mine[1] [maɪn] (POSS PRON) (*referring to singular possession*) (el/la) mío/a; (*referring to plural possession*) (los/las) míos/as • **that car is ~** ese coche es mío • **is this glass ~?** ¿es mío este vaso?, ¿este vaso es mío? • **a friend of ~** un amigo mío • **"is this your coat?" — "no, ~ is black"** —¿es este tu abrigo? —no, el mío es negro • **which is ~?** ¿cuál es el mío? • **your parents and ~** tus padres y los míos • **I think that brother of ~ is responsible*** creo que mi hermano es el que tiene la culpa, creo que el responsable es mi hermano • **be ~!†** (*also hum*) ¡cásate conmigo! • **the house became ~** la casa pasó a ser mía *or* de mi propiedad • **it's no business of ~** no es asunto mío, no tiene que ver conmigo • **I want to make her ~** quiero que sea mi mujer • **~ and thine** lo mío y lo tuyo • **what's ~ is yours** todo lo mío es tuyo (también)

mine[2] [maɪn] (N) 1 mina *f* • **a coal ~** una mina de carbón • **to work down the ~s** trabajar en la mina; ▹ **diamond, gold, salt** 2 (*Mil, Naut etc*) mina *f* • **to lay ~s** poner minas • **to sweep ~s** dragar *or* barrer minas 3 (*fig*) • **the book is a ~ of information** este libro es una mina de información; ▹ **useless**
(VT) 1 [+ *minerals*] extraer; [+ *area*] explotar 2 (*Mil, Naut*) minar, poner minas en
(VI) extraer mineral • **to ~ for sth** abrir una mina para extraer algo
(CPD) ▸ **mine detector** detector *m* de minas

minefield [ˈmaɪnfiːld] (N) 1 (*lit*) campo *m* de minas 2 (*fig*) avispero *m*, campo *m* minado

minehunter [ˈmaɪn,hʌntəʳ] (N) cazaminas *m*

minelayer [ˈmaɪn,leɪəʳ] (N) minador *m*

miner [ˈmaɪnəʳ] (N) minero/a *m/f*

mineral [ˈmɪnərəl] (N) mineral *m*
(CPD) ▸ **mineral deposit** yacimiento *m* minero ▸ **mineral oil** aceite *m* mineral ▸ **mineral rights** derechos *mpl* al subsuelo ▸ **mineral supplement** complemento *m* mineral ▸ **mineral water** agua *f* mineral

mineralogist [,mɪnəˈrælədʒɪst] (N) mineralogista *mf*

mineralogy [,mɪnəˈrælədʒɪ] (N) mineralogía *f*

Minerva [mɪˈnɜːvə] (N) Minerva

mineshaft [ˈmaɪnʃɑːft] (N) pozo *m* de mina

minestrone [,mɪnɪˈstrəʊnɪ] (N) minestrone *f* • **~ soup** sopa *f* minestrone

minesweeper [ˈmaɪnswiːpəʳ] (N) dragaminas *m inv*

Ming [mɪŋ] (ADJ) Ming • **the ~ Dynasty** la dinastía Ming • **a ~ vase** un jarrón Ming

minger‡ [ˈmɪŋəʳ] (N) (*Brit*) (*ugly and*

unattractive) aborto‡ m; (dirty) cerdo‡ m
minging‡ ['mɪŋɪŋ] ADJ (= ugly and unpleasant) cerdo‡; (= bad) [decision, game etc] lamentable; (= smelly) apestoso
mingle ['mɪŋgl] VT mezclar
VI 1 (= mix) mezclarse
2 (= become indistinguishable) [sounds] confundirse (**in, with** con) • **to ~ with the crowd** perderse entre la multitud
3 (socially) • **she ~d for a while and then sat down with her husband** alternó con los invitados durante un rato y luego se sentó junto a su marido • **he ~d with people of all classes** se asociaba con personas de todas las clases
mingy* ['mɪndʒɪ] ADJ (COMPAR: **mingier**, SUPERL: **mingiest**) [person] tacaño; [amount, portion] mísero, miserable
Mini ['mɪnɪ] N (Aut) Mini m
mini ['mɪnɪ] N (= miniskirt) minifalda f
mini... ['mɪnɪ] PREFIX mini..., micro...
miniature ['mɪnɪtʃəʳ] N miniatura f • **in ~** en miniatura
ADJ (= not full-sized) (en) miniatura; (= tiny) diminuto • **~ clocks** relojes en miniatura • **a ~ bottle of whisky** una botellita de whisky
CPD ▸ **miniature golf** minigolf m ▸ **miniature poodle** caniche mf enano/a ▸ **miniature railway** ferrocarril m en miniatura ▸ **miniature submarine** submarino m de bolsillo
miniaturist ['mɪnɪtʃərɪst] N miniaturista mf
miniaturization [ˌmɪnɪtʃəraɪ'zeɪʃən] N miniaturización f
miniaturize ['mɪnɪtʃəraɪz] VT miniaturizar
minibar ['mɪnɪbɑːʳ] N minibar m
minibreak ['mɪnɪˌbreɪk] N minivacaciones fpl
minibudget ['mɪnɪˌbʌdʒɪt] N presupuesto m interino
minibus ['mɪnɪbʌs] N microbús m, micro m
minicab ['mɪnɪkæb] N radiotaxi m
minicam ['mɪnɪkæm] N minicámara f
minicomputer [ˌmɪnɪkəm'pjuːtəʳ] N minicomputadora f, miniordenador m (Sp)
minicourse ['mɪnɪˌkɔːs] N (US) cursillo m
MiniDisc®, minidisc ['mɪnɪdɪsk] N (= system, disc) MiniDisc® m, minidisc m
CPD ▸ **MiniDisc® player, minidisc player** (reproductor m) MiniDisc® m or minidisc m
minidress ['mɪnɪdres] N minivestido m
minim ['mɪnɪm] N blanca f
CPD ▸ **minim rest** (Mus) silencio m de blanca
minima ['mɪnɪmə] NPL of **minimum**
minimal ['mɪnɪml] ADJ mínimo
minimalism ['mɪnɪməlɪzəm] N minimalismo m
minimalist ['mɪnɪməlɪst] ADJ, N minimalista mf
minimally ['mɪnɪməlɪ] ADV • **he was paid, but only ~** le pagaron, pero solo lo mínimo • **I was ~ successful** tuve un éxito mínimo, apenas tuve éxito
minimarket ['mɪnɪˌmɑːkɪt], **minimart** ['mɪnɪˌmɑːt] N autoservicio m
minimize ['mɪnɪmaɪz] VT 1 (= reduce) reducir al mínimo, minimizar
2 (= belittle) menospreciar
minimum ['mɪnɪməm] ADJ [amount, charge, age, temperature] mínimo
N (PL: **minimums** or **minima**) mínimo m • **to reduce sth to a ~** reducir algo al mínimo • **to keep costs down to a** or **the ~** mantener los costos al mínimo • **he's someone who always does the bare ~** es una persona que siempre sigue la ley del mínimo esfuerzo • **with a ~ of effort** con un mínimo de esfuerzo • **with the ~ of clothing** sin apenas ropa
CPD ▸ **minimum lending rate** tipo m de interés mínimo ▸ **minimum wage** salario m mínimo ▸ **minimum security prison** cárcel f abierta
mining ['maɪnɪŋ] N 1 minería f, explotación f de minas
2 (Mil, Naut) minado m
CPD ▸ **mining engineer** ingeniero/a m/f de minas ▸ **mining industry** industria f minera ▸ **mining town** población f minera
minion ['mɪnjən] N (= follower) secuaz mf; (= servant) paniaguado m
minipill ['mɪnɪˌpɪl] N minipíldora f
miniscule ['mɪnɪsˌkjuːl] = **minuscule**
miniseries ['mɪnɪˌsɪərɪz] N (PL: **miniseries**) (TV) miniserie f
miniskirt ['mɪnɪskɜːt] N minifalda f
minister ['mɪnɪstəʳ] N 1 (Pol) ministro/a m/f, secretario/a m/f (Mex) • **Prime Minister** primer(a) ministro/a m/f • **the Minister for Education** el/la Ministro/a de Educación
2 (Rel) pastor(a) m/f, clérigo/a m/f;
▹ CHURCHES OF ENGLAND/SCOTLAND
VI • **to ~ to sb** atender a algn • **to ~ to sb's needs** atender or satisfacer las necesidades de algn
CPD ▸ **Minister of Health** ministro/a m/f de Sanidad ▸ **Minister of State** (Brit) ≈ Secretario/a m/f de Estado
ministerial [ˌmɪnɪs'tɪərɪəl] ADJ 1 (Pol) [meeting] del gabinete; [post, career, duties] ministerial; [changes] en el gabinete • **at ~ level** a nivel ministerial
2 (Rel) [duties, meeting] pastoral
ministration [ˌmɪnɪs'treɪʃən] N (frm) ayuda f, agencia f, servicio m; (Rel) ministerio m
ministry ['mɪnɪstrɪ] N 1 (Pol) ministerio m, secretaría f (Mex)
2 (Rel) sacerdocio m • **to enter the ~** hacerse sacerdote; (Protestant) hacerse pastor
CPD ▸ **Ministry of Defence** (Brit) ministerio m de Defensa ▸ **Ministry of the Interior** ministerio m del Interior ▸ **Ministry of Transport** ministerio m de Transporte
minium ['mɪnɪəm] N minio m
minivan ['mɪnɪˌvæn] N (US) (= people carrier) monovolumen m
mink [mɪŋk] N (PL: **mink** or **minks**) 1 (Zool) visón m
2 (= fur) piel f de visón
3 (= coat) abrigo m de visón
CPD ▸ **mink coat** abrigo m de visón ▸ **mink farm** criadero m de visones
Minn. ABBR (US) = **Minnesota**
minnow ['mɪnəʊ] N (PL: **minnow** or **minnows**) pececillo m (de agua dulce)
minor ['maɪnəʳ] ADJ 1 (= small, unimportant) [problem] de poca importancia; [adjustment, detail] menor, de poca importancia; [change, damage, poet, work] menor; [role] (in film, play) secundario; (in negotiations) de poca importancia; [road] secundario • **of ~ importance** de poca importancia
2 (= not serious) [injury] leve; [illness] poco grave; [surgery, operation] de poca importancia
3 (Mus) [chord] menor • **in F ~** en fa menor • **in a ~ key** en clave menor
4 (Brit) (Scol†) • **Smith ~** Smith el pequeño, Smith el menor
N 1 (Jur) menor mf (de edad)
2 (US) (Univ) asignatura f secundaria
VI (US) (Univ) • **to ~ in sth** estudiar algo como asignatura secundaria
CPD ▸ **minor league** (Baseball) liga f menor; ▹ **minor-league** ▸ **minor offence** (Brit), **minor offense** (US) delito m de menor cuantía
Minorca [mɪ'nɔːkə] N Menorca f
Minorcan [mɪ'nɔːkən] ADJ menorquín
N menorquín/ina m/f
minority [maɪ'nɒrɪtɪ] N 1 (= small number) minoría f • **only a small ~ of children contract the disease** solo una pequeña minoría de niños contraen la enfermedad • **to be in a** or **the ~** ser minoría, estar en minoría • **you're in a ~ of one, there!** (hum) ¡te has quedado más solo que la una!
2 (= community) minoría f • **ethnic ~** minoría f étnica
3 (Jur) (= age) minoría f de edad
ADJ 1 [group, interest, view, government] minoritario • **~ language** lengua f minoritaria • **~ rights** (Pol) derechos mpl de las minorías
2 (Econ) • **~ interest** • **~ stake** participación f minoritaria • **~ shareholder** accionista mf minoritario • **~ shareholding** accionado m minoritario
3 (US) (Pol) • **Minority Leader** líder mf de la oposición • **House Minority Leader** líder mf de la oposición del Congreso • **Senate Minority Leader** líder mf de la oposición del Senado

MINORITY

Singular or plural verb?

*When **minoría** is the subject of a verb, the verb can be in the singular or the plural, depending on the context:*

▹ *Put the verb in the singular if **minority** is seen as a unit rather than a collection of individuals:*
A minority should always be respected, however small it may be
Una minoría, aunque sea pequeña, debe ser respetada siempre

▹ *If **la minoría** is seen as a collection of individuals, particularly when it is followed by **de** + plural noun, the plural form of the verb is more common than the singular, though both are possible:*
A minority of agitators want to introduce anarchy
Una minoría de agitadores quieren or quiere traer la anarquía

▹ *The plural form must be used when **la minoría** or **la minoría de** + plural noun is followed by **ser** or **estar** + plural complement:*
Only a minority of the demonstrators were students
Solo una minoría de los manifestantes eran estudiantes

For further uses and examples, see main entry.

minor-league [maɪnəʳliːg] CPD ▸ **minor-league baseball** (US) béisbol m de liga menor ▸ **minor-league criminals** criminales mpl de segundo orden, criminales mpl de segunda
Minotaur ['maɪnətɔːʳ] N Minotauro m
minster ['mɪnstəʳ] N (= cathedral) catedral f; (= church) iglesia f de un monasterio
minstrel ['mɪnstrəl] N juglar m
minstrelsy ['mɪnstrəlsɪ] N (= music) música f; (= song) canto m; (= art of epic minstrel) juglaría f; (= art of lyric minstrel) gaya ciencia f
mint[1] [mɪnt] N casa f de la moneda • **Royal Mint** (Brit) Real Casa f de la Moneda • IDIOM: • **to be worth a ~ (of money)** valer un dineral
ADJ • **in ~ condition** como nuevo, en perfecto estado

(VT) acuñar • **newly ~ed** [*coin*] recién acuñado; (*fig*) [*graduate*] recién salido de la universidad

mint[2] [mɪnt] (N) **1** (*Bot*) hierbabuena *f*, menta *f*
2 (= *sweet*) pastilla *f* de menta
(CPD) ▸ **mint julep** (*US*) julepe *m* de menta, (bebida *f* de) whisky *m* con menta ▸ **mint sauce** salsa *f* de menta ▸ **mint tea** té *m* de menta

minuet [ˌmɪnjʊˈet] (N) minué *m*

minus [ˈmaɪnəs] (PREP) **1** menos • **nine ~ six** nueve menos seis
2 (= *without, deprived of*) sin • **he appeared ~ his trousers** apareció sin pantalón
(ADJ) [*number*] negativo • **it's ~ 20 outside** fuera hace una temperatura de 20 bajo cero • **I got a B ~ for my French** me pusieron un notable bajo en francés
(N) (= *sign*) signo *m* menos; (= *amount*) cantidad *f* negativa
(CPD) ▸ **minus sign** signo *m* menos

minuscule [ˈmɪnəskjuːl] (ADJ) minúsculo

minute[1] [ˈmɪnɪt] (N) **1** (= *60 secs*) minuto *m* • **it is twenty ~s past two** son las dos y veinte (minutos) • **a 10-minute break** un descanso de 10 minutos • **every ~ counts** no hay tiempo que perder • **it won't take five ~s** es cosa de pocos minutos • **it's a few ~s walk from the station** está a unos minutos de la estación andando • **they were getting closer by the ~** se nos estaban acercando por minutos • **at six o'clock to the ~** a las seis en punto • **her schedule was planned to the ~** su horario estaba planeado hasta el último minuto • **they were on the scene within ~s** llegaron al lugar de los hechos a los pocos minutos • PROVERB: • **there's one born every ~!*** ¡hay cada tonto por ahí suelto!*
2 (= *short time*) momento *m* • **I shan't be a ~** (*on going out*) vuelvo enseguida; (*when busy*) termino enseguida • **will you shut up for a ~!** ¿te callas un momento? • **have you got a ~?** ¿tienes un momento? • **I'll come in a ~** ahora voy, vengo dentro de un momento • **just a ~!** • **wait a ~!** ¡espera un momento!, ¡un momento!, ¡momentito! (*LAm*)
3 (= *instant*) instante *m* • **it was all over in a ~** todo esto ocurrió en un instante • **I haven't had a ~ to myself all day** no he tenido ni un instante *or* momento para mí en todo el día • **we expect him (at) any ~** le esperamos de un momento a otro • **any ~ now he's going to fall off there** se va caer en cualquier momento • **at that ~ the phone rang** en ese momento sonó el teléfono • **I bet you loved every ~ of it!** ¡seguro que te lo pasaste en grande! • **at the last ~** a última hora, en el último momento • **to leave things until the last ~** dejar las cosas hasta última hora *or* hasta el último momento • **one ~ she was there, the next she was gone** estaba allí, y al momento se había ido • **we caught the train without a ~ to spare** cogimos el tren justo a tiempo • **at that ~ my father came in** en ese momento entró mi padre • **tell me the ~ he arrives** avísame en cuanto llegue • **sit down this ~!** ¡siéntate ya! • **I've just this ~ heard** me acabo de enterar • **(at) this very ~** ahora mismo • IDIOM: • **I don't believe him for a** *or* **one ~** no le creo para nada *or* en absoluto; ▹ **soon**
4 (= *official note*) nota *f*, minuta *f*
5 minutes [*of meeting*] acta *f* • **to take the ~s (of a meeting)** levantar (el) acta (de una reunión)
(VT) [+ *meeting*] levantar (el) acta de; [+ *remark, fact*] registrar • **I want that ~d** quiero que eso conste en acta • **you don't need to ~ that** no hace falta que registres *or* anotes eso
(CPD) ▸ **minute book** libro *m* de actas ▸ **minute hand** minutero *m* ▸ **minute steak** biftec *m* pequeño (que se hace rápidamente)

minute[2] [maɪˈnjuːt] (ADJ) **1** (= *very small*) [*amount, change*] mínimo; [*particles*] diminuto
2 (= *rigorous*) [*examination, scrutiny*] minucioso • **in ~ detail** hasta el mínimo detalle

minutely [maɪˈnjuːtlɪ] (ADV) **1** (= *in detail*) [*describe*] detalladamente, minuciosamente; [*examine*] minuciosamente • **a ~ detailed account** un relato extremadamente detallado *or* completo hasta en los más pequeños detalles
2 (= *by a small amount*) [*move, change, differ*] mínimamente • **anything ~ resembling a fish** cualquier cosa mínimamente parecida a un pez

minutiae [mɪˈnjuːʃiː] (NPL) detalles *mpl* minuciosos

minx [mɪŋks] (N) picaruela *f*, mujer *f* descarada • **you ~!** ¡lagarta!

Miocene [ˈmaɪəsiːn] (ADJ) mioceno
(N) mioceno *m*

MIPS [mɪps] (NPL ABBR) (= **millions of instructions per second**) MIPS *mpl*

miracle [ˈmɪrəkl] (N) (*Rel*) (*also fig*) milagro *m* • **it's a ~ that you weren't hurt!** ¡fue un milagro que salieras ileso! • **by some ~ he passed his exam** milagrosamente aprobó el examen
(CPD) ▸ **miracle cure** remedio *m* milagroso ▸ **miracle drug** medicamento *m* milagro ▸ **miracle play** auto *m* sacramental ▸ **miracle worker** • **I'm not a ~ worker, you know*** yo no puedo hacer milagros

miraculous [mɪˈrækjʊləs] (ADJ) **1** (*Rel*) [*powers, healing*] milagroso
2 (= *extraordinary*) [*escape, recovery*] milagroso; [*change, result*] extraordinario • **he made a ~ recovery** tuvo una recuperación milagrosa, se recuperó de forma milagrosa • **his escape was nothing short of ~** la forma en que logró escaparse fue un verdadero *or* auténtico milagro

miraculously [mɪˈrækjʊləslɪ] (ADV) [*survive, escape, transform*] milagrosamente • **casualties were ~ light** las bajas resultaron ser milagrosamente escasas • **~, he escaped unhurt** milagrosamente, salió ileso

mirage [ˈmɪrɑːʒ] (N) espejismo *m*

MIRAS [ˈmaɪræs] (N ABBR) (*Brit*) = **mortgage interest relief at source**

mire [maɪə^{r}] (N) fango *m*, lodo *m*
(VT) (*US*) • **to get ~d in** quedar atascado *or* preso en

mirror [ˈmɪrə^{r}] (N) espejo *m* • **driving ~** retrovisor *m*, espejo *m* retrovisor • **to look at o.s. in the ~** mirarse en el *or* al espejo • **she got in the car and adjusted the ~** entró en el coche y ajustó el retrovisor
(VT) reflejar
(CPD) ▸ **mirror image** reflejo *m* exacto ▸ **mirror site** (*on the internet*) sitio *m* espejo

mirth [mɜːθ] (N) (= *good humour*) alegría *f*, júbilo *m*; (= *laughter*) risas *fpl*

mirthful [ˈmɜːθfʊl] (ADJ) alegre

mirthless [ˈmɜːθlɪs] (ADJ) triste, sin alegría

mirthlessly [ˈmɜːθlɪslɪ] (ADV) tristemente

miry [ˈmaɪrɪ] (ADJ) fangoso, lodoso • **~ place** lodazal *m*

MIS (N ABBR) = **management information system**

misadventure [ˌmɪsədˈventʃə^{r}] (N) desgracia *f*, contratiempo *m* • **death by ~** (*Jur*) muerte *f* accidental

misalliance [ˌmɪsəˈlaɪəns] (N) casamiento *m* inconveniente

misanthrope [ˈmɪzənθrəʊp] (N) misántropo *m*

misanthropic [ˌmɪzənˈθrɒpɪk] (ADJ) misantrópico

misanthropist [mɪˈzænθrəpɪst] (N) misántropo/a *m/f*

misanthropy [mɪˈzænθrəpɪ] (N) misantropía *f*

misapplication [ˌmɪsæplɪˈkeɪʃən] (N) mala aplicación *f*, uso *m* indebido

misapply [ˌmɪsəˈplaɪ] (VT) (*gen*) usar indebidamente; [+ *funds*] malversar; [+ *efforts, talents*] malgastar

misapprehend [ˌmɪsæprɪˈhend] (VT) entender mal, comprender mal

misapprehension [ˌmɪsæprɪˈhenʃən] (N) malentendido *m* • **there seems to be some ~** parece haber algún malentendido • **to be under a ~** estar equivocado

misappropriate [ˌmɪsəˈprəʊprɪeɪt] (VT) malversar, desfalcar

misappropriation [ˌmɪsəprəʊprɪˈeɪʃən] (N) malversación *f*, desfalco *m*

misbegotten [ˌmɪsbɪˈgɒtn] (ADJ) bastardo, ilegítimo; [*plan etc*] descabellado, llamado a fracasar

misbehave [ˌmɪsbɪˈheɪv] (VI) portarse mal, comportarse mal

misbehaviour, misbehavior (*US*) [ˌmɪsbɪˈheɪvjə^{r}] (N) mala conducta *f*, mal comportamiento *m*

misc. (ABBR) = **miscellaneous**

miscalculate [ˌmɪsˈkælkjʊleɪt] (VT) calcular mal
(VI) calcular mal

miscalculation [ˌmɪskælkjʊˈleɪʃən] (N) error *m* de cálculo

miscall [ˌmɪsˈkɔːl] (VT) llamar equivocadamente

miscarriage [ˈmɪsˌkærɪdʒ] (N) **1** (*Med*) aborto *m* (natural)
2 • **~ of justice** error *m* judicial

miscarry [mɪsˈkærɪ] (VI) **1** (*Med*) abortar
2 (= *fail*) [*plans*] fracasar, malograrse (*Peru*)

miscast [ˌmɪsˈkɑːst] (PT, PP: **miscast**) (VT) • **to ~ sb** (*Theat*) dar a algn un papel que no le va • **he was ~ as Othello** no fue muy acertado darle el papel de Otelo

miscegenation [ˌmɪsɪdʒɪˈneɪʃən] (N) (*frm*) mestizaje *m*, cruce *m* de razas

miscellaneous [ˌmɪsɪˈleɪnɪəs] (ADJ) [*objects*] variado, de todo tipo; [*writings, collection*] variado • **a ~ collection of objects** una variada colección de objetos • **categorized** *or* **classified as ~** catalogado *or* clasificado en concepto de "varios" • **~ expenses** gastos *mpl* diversos

miscellany [mɪˈselənɪ] (N) [*of objects*] miscelánea *f*; [*of writings*] antología *f*

mischance [mɪsˈtʃɑːns] (N) desgracia *f*, mala suerte *f* • **by some ~** por desgracia

mischief [ˈmɪstʃɪf] (N) **1** (= *naughtiness*) travesura *f*, diablura *f* • **he's up to some ~** está haciendo alguna travesura • **he's always getting into ~** siempre anda haciendo travesuras • **keep out of ~!** (*to child*) ¡no hagas travesuras!; (*to adult*) (*hum*) ¡pórtate bien! • **to keep sb out of ~** evitar que algn haga travesuras
2 (= *harm*) daño *m* • **to do o.s. a ~*** hacerse daño
3 (= *malicious behaviour*) • **to make ~** causar daño

mischief-maker [ˈmɪstʃɪfˌmeɪkə^{r}] (N) (= *trouble-maker*) revoltoso/a *m/f*; (= *gossip*) chismoso/a *m/f*

mischievous [ˈmɪstʃɪvəs] (ADJ) **1** (= *impish*) [*person, smile*] pícaro; (= *naughty*) [*child, kitten*] travieso • **the ~ tricks the children used to get up to** las travesuras que los niños solían hacer

2 (= *malicious*) [*person, glance, rumour*] malicioso

mischievously ['mɪstʃɪvəslɪ] ADV
1 (= *impishly*) [*say, smile*] con picardía, pícaramente; [*tease*] juguetonamente, pícaramente
2 (= *maliciously*) [*say, smile*] maliciosamente; [*tease*] con malicia

mischievousness ['mɪstʃɪvəsnɪs] N travesuras *fpl*

misconceive [,mɪskən'si:v] VT entender mal, comprender mal

misconceived [,mɪskən'si:vd] ADJ • **a ~ plan** un proyecto descabellado

misconception [,mɪskən'sepʃən] N malentendido *m*, concepto *m* erróneo • **but this is a ~** pero esta idea es errónea

misconduct N [mɪs'kɒndʌkt] mala conducta *f*; (*professional*) falta *f* de ética profesional, mala conducta *f* profesional
VT [,mɪskən'dʌkt] manejar mal, dirigir mal • **to ~ o.s.** portarse *or* conducirse mal

misconstruction ['mɪskəns'trʌkʃən] N (= *misinterpretation*) mala interpretación *f*; (*deliberate*) tergiversación *f* • **words open to ~** palabras *fpl* que se prestan a ser malinterpretadas

misconstrue [,mɪskən'stru:] VT interpretar mal, malinterpretar

miscount VT [,mɪs'kaʊnt] contar mal, equivocarse en la cuenta de
VI [,mɪs'kaʊnt] contar mal
N ['mɪskaʊnt] • **there was a ~** hubo un error en el recuento

miscreant ['mɪskrɪənt] N sinvergüenza *mf*, bellaco/a *m/f*

misdate [,mɪs'deɪt] VT [+ *letter*] poner la fecha equivocada a

misdeal [,mɪs'di:l] N reparto *m* erróneo
VT [+ *cards*] dar mal, repartir mal

misdeed [,mɪs'di:d] N fechoría *f*

misdemeanour, misdemeanor (US) [,mɪsdɪ'mi:nəʳ] N fechoría *f*; (*Jur*) delito *m* menor, falta *f*

misdiagnose [,mɪs'daɪəg,nəʊz] VT [+ *illness, patient, problem, situation*] diagnosticar erróneamente

misdiagnosis [,mɪsdaɪəg'nəʊsɪs] N (PL: **misdiagnoses**) [*of illness, problem*] diagnóstico *m* erróneo

misdial ['mɪs'daɪəl] VT, VI (*Telec*) • **to ~ (the number)** equivocarse al marcar (el número)

misdirect [,mɪsdɪ'rekt] VT [+ *operation*] manejar mal; [+ *letter*] poner las señas mal en; [+ *person*] informar mal

misdirected [,mɪsdɪ'rektɪd] ADJ
1 (= *misguided*) desacertado, equivocado
2 [*mail*] con la dirección equivocada

misdirection [,mɪsdɪ'rekʃən] N [*of operation, scheme*] mala dirección *f*; [*of resources*] mala administración *f*, mal manejo *m*

miser ['maɪzəʳ] N avaro/a *m/f*

miserable ['mɪzərəbl] ADJ 1 (= *unhappy*) [*person*] abatido, con el ánimo por los suelos; [*face*] triste • **to feel ~** tener el ánimo por los suelos, sentirse abatido *or* deprimido • **Sheila was looking ~** a Sheila se la veía abatida • **don't look so ~!** ¡alegra esa cara! • **to make sb ~** hacer a algn sentirse deprimido • **my job was making me really ~** mi trabajo me estaba deprimiendo
2 (= *depressing*) [*place, life, weather*] deprimente; [*childhood*] desdichado, infeliz • **it was wet and ~ outside** fuera hacía un tiempo lluvioso y deprimente • **it was a ~ business** era un asunto deprimente *or* lamentable • **to make sb's life ~** • **make life ~ for sb** amargar la vida a algn • **to have a ~ time** pasarlo mal, pasarlo fatal*
3 (= *wretched*) [*hovel, shantytown, beggar*] mísero • **the ~ conditions they were living in** la miseria en la que vivían
4 (= *contemptible, mean*) • **you ~ (old) thing!** ¡viejo ruin!
5 (= *paltry*) [*offer*] mísero, mezquino; [*pay*] miserable; [*meal*] triste, mísero • **a ~ two pounds** dos miserables libras • **they gave me a ~ piece of bread for lunch** me dieron un triste trozo de pan para comer
6 (= *complete*) • **to be a ~ failure** [*attempt, play*] ser un fracaso espantoso *or* rotundo, ser un triste fracaso; [*person*] ser un fracaso total

miserably ['mɪzərəblɪ] ADV 1 (= *unhappily*) [*say, think, nod*] tristemente, con desconsuelo
2 (= *depressingly*) [*furnished, decorated*] miserablemente, míseramente • **the supplies were ~ inadequate** los suministros eran miserablemente escasos • **it was ~ cold** hacía un frío deprimente • **our wages are ~ low** nos pagan una miseria
3 (= *completely*) • **to fail ~** fracasar rotundamente

misère [mɪ'zɛəʳ] N (*Cards*) nulos *mpl* • **to go ~** jugar a nulos

miserliness ['maɪzəlɪnɪs] N tacañería *f*

miserly ['maɪzəlɪ] ADJ 1 (= *mean*) [*person*] mezquino, ruin, tacaño
2 (= *paltry*) [*sum*] mísero

misery ['mɪzərɪ] N 1 (= *sadness*) tristeza *f*, pena *f*
2 (= *poverty*) miseria *f*, pobreza *f* • **to live in ~** vivir en la miseria
3 (= *misfortune*) desgracia *f* • **a life of ~** una vida desgraciada
4 (= *suffering*) sufrimiento *m*, dolor *m* • **to put an animal out of its ~** rematar a un animal (para que no sufra) • **to put sb out of his/her ~** (*fig*) sacar a algn de la incertidumbre • **to make sb's life a ~** amargar la vida a algn
5 (*Brit**) (= *person*) aguafiestas *mf inv*
CPD ▸ **misery guts*** aguafiestas *mf inv*, amargado/a *m/f*

misfile [,mɪs'faɪl] VT [+ *papers*] archivar incorrectamente

misfire [,mɪs'faɪəʳ] VI [*plan, engine*] fallar; [*gun*] encasquillarse

misfit ['mɪsfɪt] N (= *person*) inadaptado/a *m/f* • **he's always been a ~ here** no se ha adaptado nunca a las condiciones de aquí, en ningún momento ha estado realmente contento aquí

misfortune [mɪs'fɔ:tʃən] N desgracia *f* • **companion in ~** compañero/a *m/f* en la desgracia • **I had the ~ to meet him** tuve la desgracia de conocerlo • **it is his ~ that he is lame** tiene la mala suerte de ser cojo • **that's your ~!** ¡mala suerte!

misgiving [mɪs'gɪvɪŋ] N recelo *m*, duda *f* • **not without some ~** no sin cierto recelo • **I had ~s about the scheme** tuve mis dudas sobre el proyecto

misgovern [,mɪs'gʌvən] VT, VI gobernar mal

misgovernment [,mɪs'gʌvənmənt] N desgobierno *m*, mal gobierno *m*

misguided [,mɪs'gaɪdɪd] ADJ [*attempt*] torpe; [*belief, view*] equivocado; [*person*] descaminado, desacertado; [*actions*] desacertado, equivocado • **a ~ sense of loyalty** un sentido desacertado *or* equivocado de la lealtad • **in the ~ belief that ...** creyendo, equivocadamente *or* erróneamente, que ... • **he was ~ enough to believe he could get away with it** era tan insensato como para creer que podría salirse con la suya • **poor ~ fool!** ¡pobre infeliz!

misguidedly [,mɪs'gaɪdɪdlɪ] ADV [*believe*] equivocadamente, erróneamente; [*tell*] erróneamente

mishandle [,mɪs'hændl] VT 1 (= *treat roughly*) [+ *object, goods*] maltratar
2 (= *mismanage*) [+ *situation*] llevar mal, manejar mal; [+ *problem*] no saber tratar

mishandling [,mɪs'hændlɪŋ] N 1 [*of object, goods*] mal trato *m*
2 [*of situation, problem*] mal manejo *m*

mishap ['mɪshæp] N contratiempo *m* • **without ~** sin contratiempos • **to have a ~** tener un accidente • **we had a slight ~** tuvimos un pequeño contratiempo

mishear [,mɪs'hɪəʳ] (PT, PP: **misheard** [,mɪs'hɜ:d]) VT oír mal
VI oír mal

mishit N ['mɪshɪt] golpe *m* defectuoso
VT [,mɪs'hɪt] golpear mal

mishmash ['mɪʃmæʃ] N revoltijo *m*, batiburrillo* *m*

misinform [,mɪsɪn'fɔ:m] VT informar mal

misinformation [,mɪsɪnfə'meɪʃən] N (= *wrong information*) mala información *f*, información *f* errónea; (= *deliberate act*) desinformación *f*

misinterpret [,mɪsɪn'tɜ:prɪt] VT interpretar mal, malinterpretar; (*deliberately*) tergiversar

misinterpretation [,mɪsɪntɜ:prɪ'teɪʃən] N mala interpretación *f*; (*deliberate*) tergiversación *f*

misjudge [,mɪs'dʒʌdʒ] VT 1 (= *miscalculate*) calcular mal • **the driver ~d the bend** el conductor no calculó bien la curva • **she ~d the distance** calculó mal la distancia
2 (= *judge wrongly*) [+ *person*] juzgar mal • **I may have ~d him** a lo mejor lo juzgué mal

misjudgement [,mɪs'dʒʌdʒmənt] N 1 [*of distance etc*] mal cálculo *m*
2 [*of person*] juicio *m* erróneo

mislay [mɪs'leɪ] (PT, PP: **mislaid** [mɪs'leɪd]) VT extraviar, perder • **I've mislaid my glasses** no sé dónde he puesto las gafas

mislead [mɪs'li:d] (PT, PP: **misled**) VT
1 (= *give wrong idea*) engañar • **I wouldn't like to ~ you** no quisiera inducirle a error, no me gustaría que se hiciera una idea equivocada • **I'm afraid you have been misled** me temo que le han dado una idea equivocada
2 (= *misdirect*) despistar
3 (= *lead into bad ways*) corromper

misleading [mɪs'li:dɪŋ] ADJ engañoso

misleadingly [mɪs'li:dɪŋlɪ] ADV engañosamente

misled [mɪs'led] PT, PP *of* **mislead**

mismanage [,mɪs'mænɪdʒ] VT [+ *business, estate, shop*] administrar mal; [+ *situation*] llevar mal, manejar mal

mismanagement [,mɪs'mænɪdʒmənt] N [*of business*] mala administración *f*; [*of situation*] manejo *m* inadecuado

mismatch [,mɪs'mætʃ] VT emparejar mal
N • **there is a ~ between the skills offered by people and the skills needed by industry** la preparación ofrecida por la gente no coincide con lo que la industria precisa • **a ~ of styles/colours** una falta de armonía en los estilos/colores

misname [,mɪs'neɪm] VT llamar equivocadamente • **this grotesquely ~d society** esta sociedad con su nombre grotescamente inapropiado

misnomer [,mɪs'nəʊməʳ] N nombre *m* equivocado *or* inapropiado • **that is a ~** ese nombre es impropio

misogamist [mɪ'sɒgəmɪst] N misógamo/a *m/f*

misogamy [mɪ'sɒgəmɪ] N misogamia *f*

misogynist [mɪ'sɒdʒɪnɪst] ADJ misógino
N misógino/a *m/f*

misogynistic [mɪ,sɒdʒɪ'nɪstɪk] ADJ misógino

misogyny [mɪ'sɒdʒɪnɪ] (N) misoginia *f*
misplace [,mɪs'pleɪs] (VT) perder • **he frequently ~s important documents** con frecuencia traspapela *or* pierde documentos importantes • **I'm sorry, I seem to have ~d the address** perdona, no sé dónde he puesto las señas
misplaced [,mɪs'pleɪst] (ADJ)
1 (= *inappropriate*) [*confidence, trust*] inmerecido; [*enthusiasm*] que no viene a cuento; [*good humour*] fuera de lugar, inoportuno • **I realize now that my confidence/trust in you was ~** ahora me doy cuenta de que me equivoqué al confiar en ti • **a ~ sense of duty/loyalty** un sentido desacertado *or* equivocado del deber/de la lealtad
2 (= *wrongly positioned*) [*accent, comma*] mal colocado, puesto en el lugar equivocado
misprint (N) ['mɪsprɪnt] error *m* de imprenta, errata *f*
(VT) [mɪs'prɪnt] imprimir mal
mispronounce [,mɪsprə'naʊns] (VT) pronunciar mal
mispronunciation [,mɪsprənʌnsɪ'eɪʃən] (N) mala pronunciación *f*
misquotation [,mɪskwəʊ'teɪʃən] (N) cita *f* equivocada
misquote [,mɪs'kwəʊt] (VT) citar incorrectamente • **he was ~d in the press** la prensa no reprodujo con exactitud sus palabras
misread [,mɪs'ri:d] (PT, PP: **misread** [,mɪs'red]) (VT) (= *read wrongly*) leer mal; (= *misinterpret*) interpretar mal, malinterpretar
misreading [,mɪs'ri:dɪŋ] (N) [*of situation, opinion*] mala interpretación *f*
misrepresent [,mɪsreprɪ'zent] (VT) [+ *person*] dar una imagen falsa de; [+ *views, situation*] tergiversar • **he was ~ed in the papers** los periódicos tergiversaron sus palabras
misrepresentation [,mɪsreprɪzen'teɪʃən] (N) [*of facts*] tergiversación *f*, desfiguración *f*; (*Jur*) declaración *f* falsa • **this report is a ~ of what I said** este informe tergiversa mis palabras
misrule [,mɪs'ru:l] (N) desgobierno *m*, mal gobierno *m*
(VT) desgobernar, gobernar mal
miss¹ [mɪs] (N) **1** [*of shot*] fallo *m* • **he scored three hits and two ~es** tuvo tres lanzamientos acertados y dos fallos, acertó tres tiros y falló dos • **he had two bad ~es in the first half** falló dos tiros fáciles en el primer tiempo • PROVERB: • **a ~ is as good as a mile** lo mismo da librarse por poco que por mucho; ▹ **near**
2 • IDIOM: • **to give sth a ~**: • **you could give rehearsals a ~ for once** por una vez podrías faltar a los ensayos • **I'll give the wine a ~ this evening** esta noche no tomaré vino
(VT) **1** (= *fail to hit*) [+ *target*] no dar en • **the arrow ~ed the target** la flecha no dio en el blanco • **the shot just ~ed me** la bala me pasó rozando • **the plane just ~ed the tower** faltó poco para que el avión chocara con la torre
2 (= *escape, avoid*) evitar • **if we go that way we can ~ Burgos** si tomamos esa ruta podemos evitarnos pasar por Burgos • **it seems we ~ed the bad weather** parece que nos hemos escapado del mal tiempo • **he narrowly ~ed being run over** por poco lo atropellan, faltó poco para que lo atropellaran
3 (= *fail to find, take, use etc*) [+ *aim, shot*] fallar; [+ *bus, train, plane, flight*] perder; [+ *opportunity, chance*] dejar pasar, perder; [+ *meeting, class, appointment*] faltar a, no asistir a; [+ *film, match*] perderse • **I ~ed the meeting last week** falté a *or* no asistí a la reunión la semana pasada • **I haven't ~ed a rehearsal in five years** no he faltado a un ensayo en cinco años, no me he perdido un solo ensayo en cinco años • **don't ~ this film** no te pierdas *or* no dejes de ver esta película • **we ~ed our lunch because we were late** nos quedamos sin comer porque llegamos tarde • **she ~ed her holiday last year** el año pasado no pudo tomarse las vacaciones • **you haven't ~ed much!** ¡no te has perdido mucho! • **I ~ed you at the station** no te vi en la estación • **I ~ed you by five minutes** si hubiera llegado cinco minutos antes te hubiera visto, si hubiera llegado cinco minutos antes te hubiera cogido (*Sp**) • **they ~ed each other in the crowd** no lograron encontrarse entre tanta gente • **to ~ one's cue** (*Theat*) entrar a destiempo • **we ~ed the tide** nos perdimos la pleamar • **to ~ one's vocation** equivocarse de vocación • **to ~ one's way** equivocarse de camino • IDIOM: • **to ~ the boat** *or* **bus*** perder el tren (*fig*)
4 (= *skip*) [+ *meal*] saltarse • **I think you've ~ed a page** creo que te has saltado una página • **my heart ~ed a beat** me dio un vuelco el corazón
5 (= *overlook*) • **you've ~ed that bit in the corner** se te ha pasado por alto ese trozo en la esquina • **you ~ed our anniversary again** se te volvió a olvidar *or* pasar nuestro aniversario
6 (= *fail to understand*) no entender, no coger (*Sp*) • **she seems to have ~ed the joke** parece que no ha entendido *or* cogido el chiste • **you're ~ing the point** no lo entiendes
7 (= *fail to hear, see*) • **I ~ed what you said** no he oído lo que has dicho • **you don't ~ much, do you?** no se te escapa nada ¿verdad? • **you can't ~ the house** la casa no tiene pérdida • **I ~ed the step and fell flat on my face** no vi el escalón y me caí de bruces • **he ~ed the turning** se pasó de cruce; ▹ **trick**
8 (= *long for*) echar de menos, extrañar (*esp LAm*) • **I ~ you so (much)** te echo tanto de menos, te extraño tanto • **they're ~ing one another** se echan de menos *or* se extrañan • **he won't be (much) ~ed** no se le echará de menos *or* no se le echará en falta que digamos • **I ~ having a garden** echo de menos tener un jardín
9 (= *notice absence of*) echar en falta • **then I ~ed my wallet** entonces eché en falta la cartera • **we're ~ing eight dollars** nos faltan ocho dólares
(VI) **1** (= *not hit*) [*shot*] errar el blanco; [*person*] fallar, errar el tiro • **you can't ~!** ¡es imposible fallar!, ¡es imposible errar el tiro!
2 (= *not function properly*) [*motor*] fallar
3 (= *not attend*) faltar • **I've not ~ed once in ten years** en diez años no he faltado ni una sola vez
▸ **miss out** (VT + ADV) (*esp Brit*) [+ *word, line, page*] saltarse • **tell me if I ~ anybody out** decidme si me salto a algn • **he was ~ed out in the promotions** en los ascensos le pasaron por encima
(VI + ADV) • **I'm glad you can come, I wouldn't want you to ~ out** me alegro de que puedas venir, no quisiera que te lo perdieras • **don't ~ out, order your copy today** no se lo pierda, pida su ejemplar hoy
▸ **miss out on** (VI + PREP) [+ *opportunity*] dejar pasar, perder • **he ~ed out on several good deals** dejó pasar varias ocasiones buenas • **did you think you were ~ing out on something?** ¿creías que te estabas perdiendo algo?
miss² [mɪs] (N) señorita *f*; (*in address*) Srta. • **Miss Peters wants to see you** la señorita Peters quiere verte • **the Misses Smith**† las señoritas Smith • **Miss Spain** Miss España • **a modern ~** una señorita moderna • **she's a cheeky little ~!** ¡es una niña muy creidita!; ▹ **MR, MRS, MISS**
(CPD) ▸ **Miss World** Miss Mundo *f* • **the Miss World contest** el concurso de Miss Mundo
Miss. (ABBR) (*US*) = **Mississippi**
missal ['mɪsəl] (N) misal *m*
mis-sell [,mɪs'sel] (VT) [+ *pension, insurance*] vender de forma abusiva
mis-selling [,mɪs'selɪŋ] (N) [*of pension, insurance*] venta *f* abusiva
misshapen [,mɪs'ʃeɪpən] (ADJ) deforme
missile ['mɪsaɪl] (N) **1** (*Mil*) misil *m* • **guided ~** misil teledirigido
2 (= *object thrown*) proyectil *m*
(CPD) ▸ **missile base** base *f* de misiles ▸ **missile launcher** lanzamisiles *m inv*
missing ['mɪsɪŋ] (ADJ) **1** (= *lost*) [*object*] perdido; [*child, cat*] desaparecido, extraviado; [*fisherman, explorer*] desaparecido • **some companies help with ~ luggage** algunas compañías te ayudan cuando se te pierde *or* extravía equipaje • **an important document was found to be ~** se descubrió que faltaba un importante documento • **to go ~** desaparecer
2 (*Mil*) [*soldier, plane*] desaparecido • **~ (and) presumed dead** desaparecido y dado por muerto • **~ in action** desaparecido en combate • **reported ~** declarado como desaparecido
3 (= *lacking*) [*piece, button, tooth*] que falta • **fill in the ~ words** complete las palabras que faltan • **to be ~** faltar • **two pieces are ~** faltan dos piezas • **your shirt has a button ~** te falta un botón en la camisa
(CPD) ▸ **the missing link** (*Anthropology, Zool*) el eslabón perdido; (= *detail*) la pieza que faltaba ▸ **missing person** desaparecido/a *m/f* • **I want to report a ~ person** quiero denunciar una desaparición ▸ **Missing Persons Bureau** *oficina que se encarga de coordinar las investigaciones sobre personas desaparecidas*
mission ['mɪʃən] (N) **1** (= *duty, purpose etc*) misión *f* • **it's her ~ in life** es su misión en la vida • **to send sb on a secret ~** enviar a algn en misión secreta
2 (= *people on mission*) misión *f*
3 (*Rel*) (= *building*) misión *f*
(CPD) ▸ **mission control** centro *m* de control ▸ **mission controller** controlador(a) *m/f* de (la) misión ▸ **mission statement** (*Comm, Ind*) (*of a business*) declaración *f* de objetivos; (*of an organization*) declaración *f* de intenciones
missionary ['mɪʃənrɪ] (N) (*Rel*) misionero/a *m/f*
(CPD) ▸ **missionary position** (*hum*) postura *f* del misionero ▸ **missionary society** sociedad *f* misionera ▸ **missionary zeal** fervor *m* apostólico
missis* ['mɪsɪz] (N) • **my ~** • **the ~** mi mujer, la parienta (*Sp**), la patrona (*S. Cone**) • **John and his ~** John y su mujer • **is the ~ in?** ¿está la señora?
Mississippi [,mɪsɪ'sɪpɪ] (N) Misisipí *m*
missive ['mɪsɪv] (N) misiva *f*
Missouri [mɪ'zʊərɪ] (N) Misuri *m*
misspell [,mɪs'spel] (PT, PP: **misspelled, misspelt**) (VT) escribir mal
misspelling [,mɪs'spelɪŋ] (N) error *m* de ortografía
misspend [,mɪs'spend] (PT, PP: **misspent**) (VT) malgastar, desperdiciar
misspent [,mɪs'spent] (ADJ) • **a ~ youth** una juventud malgastada *or* desperdiciada

misstate [ˌmɪsˈsteɪt] VT declarar erróneamente; (*deliberately*) declarar falsamente
misstatement [ˌmɪsˈsteɪtmənt] N declaración *f* errónea; (*deliberate*) declaración *f* falsa
missus* [ˈmɪsɪz] N = **missis**
missy* [ˈmɪsɪ] N (*hum or pej*) = **miss²**
mist [mɪst] N neblina *f*; (= *rain*) llovizna *f*, garúa *f* (*LAm*); (*at sea*) bruma *f*; (*in liquid*) nube *f*; (*on glass etc*) vaho *m* • **through a ~ of tears** (*fig*) a través de un velo de lágrimas • **lost in the ~s of time** (*liter*) perdido en la noche de los tiempos
VI (*also* **mist over, mist up**) [*scene, landscape*] nublarse; [*mirror, window*] empañarse; [*eyes*] llenarse de lágrimas
mistakable [mɪsˈteɪkəbl] ADJ confundible
mistake [mɪsˈteɪk] (VB: PT: **mistook**, PP: **mistaken**) N **1** error *m* • **there must be some ~** debe de haber algún error • **by ~**: • **he has been arrested by ~** lo detuvieron por error *or* equivocación • **he fired the gun by ~** disparó la pistola sin querer • **he took my hat in ~ for his** confundió mi sombrero con el suyo • **to make a ~** (*gen*) cometer un error; (= *be mistaken*) equivocarse • **they made the ~ of asking too much** cometieron el error de pedir demasiado • **the doctor must have made a ~** el médico debe de haberse equivocado • **make no ~ about it** • **let there be no ~ about it** y que no quepa la menor duda • **my ~!** ¡la culpa es mía!, es culpa mía • **she's pretty and no ~*** es guapa de verdad *or* con ganas*
2 (*in piece of work*) error *m*, fallo *m* • **his essay was full of ~s** su trabajo estaba lleno de errores *or* fallos • **if you make a ~, start again** si te equivocas, vuelve a empezar • **spelling ~** falta *f* de ortografía
VT **1** (= *misunderstand*) [+ *meaning, remark*] malinterpretar • **I'm sorry, I mistook your meaning** perdón, te malinterpreté *or* no te entendí bien • **there was no mistaking his intention** su intención estaba clarísima
2 (= *mix up, confuse*) [+ *time, road*] equivocarse de • **I mistook the turning to your house** me equivoqué al torcer para ir a tu casa • **to ~ sth/sb for sth/sb** confundir algo/a algn con algo/algn • **he is often ~n for Peter** se le confunde muchas veces con Peter • **she mistook his attention for interest** erróneamente, interpretó su atención como interés • **she could easily be ~n for a boy** se la podría confundir fácilmente con un chico • **there's no mistaking her voice** su voz es inconfundible
mistaken [mɪsˈteɪkən] PP *of* **mistake**
ADJ [*belief, idea*] equivocado, falso • **in the ~ belief that ...** creyendo, equivocadamente *or* erróneamente, que ... • **to be ~** equivocarse, estar equivocado • **you must be ~** debes de estar equivocado • **if I'm not ~** si no me equivoco, a no ser que me equivoque • **unless I'm very much ~** si no me equivoco, o mucho me equivoco o ... • **unless I'm very much ~, that's him** si no me equivoco, ese es él, o mucho me equivoco o es él • **I see I was ~ about you** veo que me equivoqué contigo • **he was ~ in his belief that he was irreplaceable** se equivocaba *or* estaba equivocado al creer que era irreemplazable • **~ identity** identificación *f* errónea
mistakenly [mɪsˈteɪkənlɪ] ADV **1** (= *wrongly*) [*believe, assume*] equivocadamente, erróneamente
2 (= *accidentally*) por equivocación, por error
mister [ˈmɪstəʳ] N **1** (*gen abbr Mr*) señor *m* (*gen abbr Sr.*)
2 (*in direct address*) • **hey, ~!** ¡oiga, usted!
mistime [ˈmɪsˈtaɪm] VT • **to ~ sth** hacer algo a destiempo
mistiming [ˌmɪsˈtaɪmɪŋ] N • **the ~ of his statement was spectacular** la inoportunidad de su declaración fue monumental • **the ~ of the attack** la inoportunidad del momento del ataque
mistle thrush [ˈmɪslˌθrʌʃ] N zorzal *m* charlo, tordo *m* mayor
mistletoe [ˈmɪsltəʊ] N muérdago *m*
mistook [mɪsˈtʊk] PT *of* **mistake**
mistral [mɪˈstrɑːl] N mistral *m*
mistranslate [ˌmɪstrænsˈleɪt] VT traducir mal
mistranslation [ˌmɪstrænsˈleɪʃən] N mala traducción *f*
mistreat [mɪsˈtriːt] VT maltratar
mistreatment [mɪsˈtriːtmənt] N maltrato *m*, malos tratos *mpl*
mistress [ˈmɪstrɪs] N **1** [*of household, servant*] señora *f*, ama *f* • **to be one's own ~** ser independiente • **to be ~ of the situation** ser dueña de la situación
2 (= *lover*) amante *f*, querida *f*, amasia *f* (*Mex*)
3 (*Brit†*) (= *teacher*) (*in primary school*) maestra *f*; (*in secondary school*) profesora *f* • **our English ~** nuestra profesora de inglés
4†† (= *Mrs*) señora *f* de ...
mistrial [ˌmɪsˈtraɪəl] N (*US, Brit*) (*invalidated*) juicio *m* viciado de nulidad; (*US*) (*inconclusive*) juicio *m* nulo por desacuerdo del jurado
mistrust [ˌmɪsˈtrʌst] N desconfianza *f*
VT desconfiar de
mistrustful [ˌmɪsˈtrʌstfʊl] ADJ desconfiado, receloso • **to be ~ of sth/sb** desconfiar de algo/algn
misty [ˈmɪstɪ] ADJ (COMPAR: **mistier**, SUPERL: **mistiest**) [*day, morning*] neblinoso; [*valley, shore*] cubierto de neblina; [*mirror, window*] empañado; [*memories*] vago; [*outline*] borroso, difuso; [*eyes*] empañado, lloroso • **it is ~** (*Met*) hay neblina; (*US*) está lloviznando
misty-eyed [ˈmɪstɪˌaɪd] ADJ sentimental
misunderstand [ˌmɪsʌndəˈstænd] (PT, PP: **misunderstood**) VT entender mal • **sorry, I misunderstood you** lo siento, te entendí mal, lo siento, malinterpreté tus palabras • **don't ~ me** entiéndeme, no me entiendas mal
misunderstanding [ˌmɪsʌndəˈstændɪŋ] N (= *confusion*) malentendido *m*; (= *mistake*) equivocación *f*; (= *disagreement*) desacuerdo *m* • **there must be some ~** (= *confusion*) debe de haber algún malentendido; (= *mistake*) debe de haber alguna equivocación
misunderstood [ˌmɪsʌndəˈstʊd] PT, PP *of* **misunderstand**
ADJ incomprendido
misuse N [ˌmɪsˈjuːs] [*of power, drug*] abuso *m*; [*of machine*] mal uso *m or* manejo *m*; [*of word, language*] uso *m* incorrecto; [*of funds*] malversación *f*
VT [ˌmɪsˈjuːz] [+ *power, drug*] abusar de; [+ *machine*] usar *or* manejar mal; [+ *word, language*] utilizar *or* emplear mal; [+ *funds*] malversar
MIT N ABBR (*US*) = **Massachusetts Institute of Technology**
mite¹ [maɪt] N (= *insect*) ácaro *m*, acárido *m*
mite² [maɪt] N **1** (= *small quantity*) pizca *f* • **a ~ of consolation** una pizca de consuelo • **there's not a ~ left** (*scrap*) no queda ni pizca; (*drop*) no queda ni una sola gota • **well, just a ~ then** bueno, un poquitín • **we were a ~ surprised** nos quedamos un tanto sorprendidos
2 (= *child*) chiquillo/a *m/f*, criatura *f* • **poor little ~!** ¡pobrecito!
3 (= *coin*) ardite *m*; (*as contribution*) óbolo *m*
miter [ˈmaɪtəʳ] N (*US*) = **mitre**
Mithraic [mɪθˈreɪɪk] ADJ mitraico
Mithraism [ˈmɪθreɪɪzəm] N mitraísmo *m*
Mithras [ˈmɪθræs] N Mitra
mitigate [ˈmɪtɪgeɪt] VT aliviar, mitigar • **mitigating circumstances** circunstancias *fpl* atenuantes
mitigation [ˌmɪtɪˈgeɪʃən] N mitigación *f*, alivio *m* • **to say a word in ~** decir algo en descargo
mitochondrial [ˌmaɪtəʊˈkɒndrɪəl] ADJ mitocondrial
mitre, miter (*US*) [ˈmaɪtəʳ] N **1** (*Rel*) mitra *f*
2 (*Tech*) (*also* **mitre joint**) inglete *m*, ensambladura *f* de inglete
VT (*Tech*) ingletear
CPD ▸ **mitre box** caja *f* de ingletes ▸ **mitre joint** inglete *m*, ensambladura *f* de inglete
mitt [mɪt] N **1** (*glove*) mitón *m*
2 (= *baseball glove*) guante *m* de béisbol
3* (= *hand*) zarpa* *f* • **get your ~s off my dictionary!** ¡quita tus zarpas de mi diccionario!* • **keep your ~s off my sweets!** ¡no se te ocurra poner tus zarpas en mis caramelos!*
mitten [ˈmɪtn] N **1** (= *glove*) mitón *m*, manopla *f*
2 (*Boxing*) guante *mpl* de boxeo
mix [mɪks] VT **1** [+ *ingredients, colours, liquids*] mezclar; [+ *concrete, plaster, cocktail*] preparar; [+ *salad*] remover • **mix all the ingredients together** mezcle todos los ingredientes • **never mix your drinks!** ¡no mezcle nunca bebidas! • **mix the eggs into the sugar** añada los huevos al azúcar y mézclelos • **to mix and match sth** combinar algo • **mix to a smooth paste** mezcle hasta que se forme una pasta sin grumos • **to mix sth with** *or* **and sth** mezclar algo con algo • **mix the cinnamon with the sugar** mezcle la canela con el azúcar • **to mix business and** *or* **with pleasure** mezclar los negocios con el placer
• IDIOM: • **to mix it (with sb)** (*Brit**) buscar camorra (con algn)*
2 [+ *recording, sound*] mezclar
VI **1** [*things*] **a** (= *combine*) mezclarse • **oil and water don't mix** el aceite y el agua no se mezclan • **politics and sport don't mix** la política y el deporte no hacen buena combinación
b (= *go together well*) [*colours*] combinar (bien), pegar
2 [*people*] (= *socialize*) alternar • **to mix in high society** alternar con la alta sociedad • **she mixes with all kinds of people** se mezcla con toda clase de gente
N **1** (= *combination*) mezcla *f* • **there was a good mix of people at the party** había una mezcla variada *or* una buena variedad de gente en la fiesta
2 (= *ingredients*) mezcla *f*; (*commercially prepared*) preparado *m* • **a cake mix** un preparado para pasteles
3 [*of recording, sound*] mezcla *f*
▸ **mix in** VT + ADV (= *add*) [+ *ingredients*] añadir; (= *intersperse*) mezclar • **pieces of grit mixed in with the rice** piedrecitas mezcladas con el arroz
▸ **mix up** VT + ADV **1** (= *prepare*) [+ *paint, paste*] preparar
2 (= *combine*) [+ *ingredients*] mezclar
3 (= *jumble up*) mezclar • **don't mix up your clothes with mine** no mezcles tu ropa con la mía • **the letter got mixed up with my things** la carta se mezcló con mis cosas
4 (= *confuse*) [+ *person*] confundir • **you've got me all mixed up** me has confundido, me has hecho un lío*
5 (= *mistake*) [+ *names, dates, person*] confundir • **she tends to mix up her words** tiende a

m

equivocar las palabras al hablar • **we got the dates mixed up** confundimos las fechas • **I'm mixing you up with somebody else** te estoy confundiendo con otra persona
6 (= *involve*) • **to be/get mixed up in sth** estar metido/meterse en algo • **are you mixed up in this?** ¿tú andas metido en esto?, ¿tú tienes que ver con esto? • **how could David be mixed up in a murder?** ¿cómo puede David estar involucrado en un asesinato? • **he's got mixed up with a bad crowd** se ha mezclado con mala gente, anda con malas compañías • **why did I ever get mixed up with you?** ¿cómo acabé relacionándome contigo?, ¿cómo acabé liada contigo?* • **to mix sb up in sth** meter *or* mezclar a algn en algo
7 • IDIOM: • **to mix it up (with sb)** (*US**) (= *cause trouble*) buscar camorra (con algn)*

mixed [mɪkst] (ADJ) **1** (= *varied*) [*selection*] variado; (= *assorted*) [*biscuits, sweets, vegetables*] surtido, variado • **a ~ crowd turned up** apareció un grupo muy variopinto, apareció un grupo con gente de todo tipo • IDIOMS: • **a ~ bag*** (= *some good, some bad*) un poco de todo, una mezcla de todo; (= *with good variety*) una gran variedad • **a ~ bunch*** un grupo variopinto, un batiburrillo de gente • **my class were a ~ bunch** mi clase era un grupo variopinto
2 (= *both good and bad*) [*reviews, reactions*] diverso • **to be a ~ blessing** tener su lado bueno y su lado malo • **~ feelings** sentimientos *mpl* encontrados • **to have ~ feelings about sth** no tener muy claro algo, tener sus dudas acerca de algo • **the government's proposals have had a ~ reception** las propuestas del gobierno han sido recibidas con reservas *or* han tenido una acogida desigual • **with ~ results** con resultados desiguales *or* diversos • **we had ~ weather** el tiempo fue variable
3 (= *of different races*) [*parentage, marriage*] mixto • **of ~ race** mestizo
4 (= *for both sexes*) [*school, education, bathing*] mixto • **in ~ company** con personas de ambos sexos • **I wouldn't say it in ~ company** no lo diría delante de personas del otro sexo
(CPD) ▸ **mixed ability class** clase *f* con niveles de aptitud distintos ▸ **mixed doubles** (*Sport*) (dobles *mpl*) mixtos *mpl* ▸ **mixed economy** economía *f* mixta ▸ **mixed farming** agricultura *f* mixta ▸ **mixed forest** bosque *m* mixto ▸ **mixed fruit** frutas *fpl* surtidas ▸ **mixed grill** (*Brit*) parrillada *f* mixta ▸ **mixed herbs** surtido *m* de hierbas ▸ **mixed marriage** matrimonio *m* mixto (*de esposos de religión o raza distintas*) ▸ **mixed martial arts** artes *fpl* marciales mixtas ▸ **mixed metaphor** metáfora *f* disparada ▸ **mixed salad** ensalada *f* mixta ▸ **mixed spice** mezcla *f* de especias

mixed-media [ˌmɪkst'mi:dɪə] (ADJ) multimedia (*inv*)

mixed-up ['mɪkst'ʌp] (ADJ) [*person, idea*] confuso; [*things*] revuelto • **he's very mixed-up** (= *disturbed*) es una persona con problemas (psicológicos); (= *confused*) está muy confuso; ▹ **mix up**

mixer ['mɪksəʳ] (N) **1** (*Culin*) batidora *f*
2 (= *cement mixer*) hormigonera *f*
3 (*Rad*) mezclador(a) *m/f*
4 (= *sociable person*) • **he's a good ~** tiene don de gentes • **he's not much of a ~** no le gusta alternar, no tiene don de gentes
5 (= *drink*) refresco *m* (*para mezclar con licores*)
6 (*US*) (*Univ*) fiesta *f* de bienvenida para nuevos estudiantes
(CPD) ▸ **mixer tap** (*Brit*) (grifo *m*) monobloque *m*

mixing bowl ['mɪksɪŋbəʊl] (N) cuenco *m* grande

mixture ['mɪkstʃəʳ] (N) (*also Culin*) mezcla *f*; (*Med*) preparado *m*, compuesto *m* • **the ~ as before** la misma receta que antes; (*fig*) lo de siempre; ▹ **cough**

mix-up ['mɪks'ʌp] (N) lío *m*, confusión *f* • **there was a mix-up over the tickets** hubo un lío *or* una confusión con las entradas • **we got in a mix-up with the trains** nos hicimos un lío con los trenes

mizzen ['mɪzn] (N) mesana *f*

mizzenmast ['mɪznmɑ:st] (N) palo *m* de mesana

mizzle* ['mɪzl] (*dialect*) (VI) lloviznar

Mk, mk (ABBR) (= **mark**) Mk

mkt (ABBR) = **market**

ml (ABBR) (= **millilitre(s)**) ml

MLA (N ABBR) (*Brit*) (*Pol*) (= **Member of the Legislative Assembly**) *miembro de la asamblea legislativa*

m-learning ['em,lɜ:nɪŋ] (N) aprendizaje *m* electrónico móvil

MLitt [em'lɪt] (N ABBR) (*Univ*) **1** = **Master of Literature**
2 = **Master of Letters**

MLR (N ABBR) = **minimum lending rate**

MLS (N ABBR) **1** (*St Ex*) = **multiple listing system**
2 (*US*) (*Univ*) (= **Master of Library Science**) *título de bibliotecario*

M'lud [mə'lʌd] (N ABBR) (*Brit*) (*Jur*) = **My Lord**

MM (ABBR) (= **Messieurs**) Srs., Sres.

mm¹ (ABBR) (= **millimetre(s)**) mm

mm² [mm] (EXCL) esto, pues, vamos a ver

MMC (N ABBR) (*Brit*) = **Monopolies and Mergers Commission**

MME (N ABBR) (*US*) (*Univ*) **1** = **Master of Mechanical Engineering**
2 = **Master of Mining Engineering**

MMR vaccine [ˌemem'ɑ:ˌvæksi:n] (N) (*against measles, mumps, rubella*) vacuna *f* triple vírica

MMS (N) (= **multimedia messaging service**) *MMS m*

MN (N ABBR) (*Brit*) = **Merchant Navy**
(ABBR) (*US*) = **Minnesota**

mnemonic [nɪ'mɒnɪk] (ADJ) mnemotécnico, nemotécnico
(N) *figura o frase etc mnemotécnica*

mnemonics [nɪ'mɒnɪks] (NSING) mnemotécnica *f*, nemotécnica *f*

MO (N ABBR) = **medical officer**
(ABBR) **1** (*US*) = **Missouri**
2 (*esp US**) (= **modus operandi**) *manera de actuar*

mo (ABBR) (= **month**) m.

mo'* [məʊ] (N ABBR) = **moment**

Mo. (ABBR) = **Missouri**

m.o. (ABBR) (= **money order**) g.p., g/

moan [məʊn] (N) **1** (= *groan*) [*of person, wind, trees*] gemido *m*
2 (= *complaint*) queja *f*
(VI) **1** (= *groan*) gemir
2 (= *complain*) quejarse • **they're ~ing about the food again** han vuelto a quejarse de la comida • **she's always ~ing about something** siempre se está quejando de algo
(VT) **1** (= *groan*) decir gimiendo, decir con un gemido
2 (= *complain*) • **"why does it always have to be me?" he ~ed** —¿por qué siempre me toca a mí? —se quejó

moaner* ['məʊnəʳ] (N) protestón/ona* *m/f*

moaning ['məʊnɪŋ] (N) **1** (= *groans*) gemidos *mpl*
2 (= *complaints*) quejas *fpl*, protestas *fpl*

moat [məʊt] (N) foso *m*

moated ['məʊtɪd] (ADJ) con foso, rodeado de un foso

mob [mɒb] (N) **1** (= *crowd*) multitud *f*, muchedumbre *f*, bola *f* (*Mex*); (= *rabble*) populacho *m*, turba *f* (*esp LAm*) • **some houses were burnt by the mobs** unas casas fueron incendiadas por el populacho • **the army has become a mob** el ejército se ha transformado en una turba incontrolada • **they went in a mob to the town hall** fueron en tropel al ayuntamiento • **to join the mob** echarse a las calles • **they're a hard-drinking mob** son una pandilla de borrachos
2 • **the mob** (*pej*) (= *the masses*) el populacho
3* (= *criminal gang*) pandilla *f* • **Joe and his mob** Joe y su pandilla • **the Mob** (*US*) la Mafia
4 (*Mil*) • **which mob were you in?** ¿en qué regimiento estuviste?
(VT) **1** (= *attack*) asaltar
2 (= *surround*) • **he was mobbed whenever he went out** al salir siempre se veía acosado por la gente • **the minister was mobbed by journalists** los periodistas se apiñaban en torno al ministro
(CPD) ▸ **mob boss** capo *m* de la mafia ▸ **mob oratory** demagogia *f* populachera ▸ **mob rule** ley *f* de la calle ▸ **mob violence** violencia *f* colectiva

mobcap ['mɒbkæp] (N) cofia *f*

mob-handed* [ˌmɒb'hændɪd] (ADV) en masa, en tropel, con mogollón de gente (*Sp**)

mobile ['məʊbaɪl] (ADJ) (= *movable*) [*theatre, shop*] ambulante; [*missile launcher*] portátil, transportable; [*workforce*] que tiene movilidad; [*society*] con movilidad; (= *expressive*) [*face, features*] expresivo • **I'm still very ~** todavía me muevo bastante • **now that we're ~*** ahora que tenemos coche, ahora que estamos motorizados*; ▹ **upwardly**
(N) **1** (*Art*) móvil *m*
2* (= *mobile phone*) móvil *m* (*Sp**), (teléfono *m*) celular *m* (*LAm*)
(CPD) ▸ **mobile commerce** comercio *m* móvil ▸ **mobile home** caravana *f*, casa *f* rodante (*S. Cone, Ven*) ▸ **mobile library** biblioteca *f* ambulante, bibliobús *m* ▸ **mobile number** número *m* del móvil (*Sp*), número *m* del celular (*LAm*) ▸ **mobile phone** teléfono *m* móvil (*Sp*), teléfono *m* celular (*LAm*) ▸ **mobile phone mast** antena *f* de telefonía móvil, antena *f* de telefonía celular (*LAm*) ▸ **mobile TV** televisión *f* móvil ▸ **mobile unit** unidad *f* móvil

mobility [məʊ'bɪlɪtɪ] (N) [*of person, joint, society*] movilidad *f*; [*of face, features*] expresividad *f* • **~ of labour** movilidad *f* de la mano de obra • **social ~** movilidad *f* social
(CPD) ▸ **mobility allowance** (*Brit*) *subsidio que reciben ciertos minusválidos para cubrir sus gastos de desplazamiento*; ▹ **upward**

mobilization [ˌməʊbɪlaɪ'zeɪʃən] (N) movilización *f*

mobilize ['məʊbɪlaɪz] (VT) movilizar
(VI) movilizarse

mobster* ['mɒbstəʳ] (N) (*US*) gángster *m*, pandillero *m*

moccasin ['mɒkəsɪn] (N) mocasín *m*

mocha ['mɒkə] (N) moca *m*

mock [mɒk] (VT) (= *ridicule*) mofarse de, burlarse de; (= *mimic*) imitar, remedar • **you shouldn't ~ other people's beliefs** no hay que mofarse *or* burlarse de las creencias de la gente
(VI) mofarse, burlarse • **to ~ at sth/sb** mofarse de algo/algn, burlarse de algo/algn
(ADJ) (= *feigned*) [*solemnity, terror*] fingido, simulado; (= *imitation*) [*leather, fur*] de imitación • **in ~ despair** fingiendo

desesperación • **in ~ horror** fingiendo estar horrorizado
(N) **1** • **to make a ~ of sth** poner algo en ridículo
2 mocks (*Brit*) (*Scol**) exámenes *mpl* de prueba
(CPD) ▸ **mock battle** simulacro *m* (de batalla) ▸ **mock exam** examen *m* de prueba ▸ **mock orange** (*Bot*) jeringuilla *f*, celinda *f* ▸ **mock trial** juicio *m* de prueba
mocker ['mɒkəʳ] (N) **1** (= *scoffer*) mofador(a) *m/f*
2 • IDIOM: • **to put the ~s on sth** dar al traste con algo • **to put the ~s on sb‡** hacer que algn fracase
mockery ['mɒkərɪ] (N) **1** (= *derision*) burla *f*, mofa *f*
2 (= *farce*) • **this is a ~ of justice** esto es una negación de la justicia • **it was a ~ of a trial** fue un simulacro de juicio • **to make a ~ of sth** poner algo en ridículo
mock-heroic ['mɒkhɪ'rəʊɪk] (ADJ) heroicoburlesco
mocking ['mɒkɪŋ] (ADJ) burlón, socarrón
(N) burlas *fpl*
mockingbird ['mɒkɪŋbɜːd] (N) sinsonte *m*, zenzontle *m* (*LAm*)
mockingly ['mɒkɪŋlɪ] (ADV) [*say*] en tono burlón, con sorna; [*smile, look*] burlonamente, con sorna
mock-Tudor [ˌmɒk'tjuːdəʳ] (ADJ) [*house, mansion*] de estilo Tudor • **a mock-Tudor mansion** una mansión de estilo Tudor
mock-up ['mɒkʌp] (N) maqueta *f*, modelo *m* a escala
MOD (N ABBR) (*Brit*) (= **Ministry of Defence**) ≈ Min. de D.
modal ['məʊdl] (ADJ) modal
modality [məʊ'dælɪtɪ] (N) modalidad *f*
mod cons* [ˌmɒd'kɒnz] (NPL) = **modern conveniences** ▹ **modern**
modding‡ ['mɒdɪŋ] (N) [*of cars*] modding‡ *m*
mode [məʊd] (N) **1** (= *way, manner*) manera *f*, modo *m*
2 (= *fashion*) moda *f*
3 (*Comput*) función *f*, modalidad *f*
(CPD) ▸ **mode of transport** medio *m* de transporte
model ['mɒdl] (N) **1** (= *small-scale representation*) modelo *m* a escala, maqueta *f*
2 (= *example*) modelo *m* • **to hold sth/sb up as a ~** presentar algo/a algn como modelo (a seguir) • **a tribunal is to be set up on the ~ of Nuremberg** se constituirá un tribunal según el modelo de *or* a la manera del de Nuremberg
3 (= *paragon*) modelo *m* • **he is a ~ of good behaviour/patience** es un modelo de buen comportamiento/paciencia
4 (= *person*) (*Art*) modelo *mf*; (*Fashion*) modelo *mf*, maniquí *mf*
5 (*Comm*) (= *design*) modelo *m*
(ADJ) **1** (= *miniature*) [*railway, village*] en miniatura, a escala • **~ aeroplane** aeromodelo *m*
2 (= *prototype*) [*home*] piloto
3 (= *perfect*) modelo (*inv*) • **a ~ husband/wife** un marido/una esposa modelo
(VT) **1** • **to ~ sth on sth: their new socialist state is ~led on that of China** su nuevo estado socialista toma como modelo el de China • **the gardens are ~led on those at Versailles** los jardines están inspirados en los de Versalles • **to ~ o.s. on sb** tomar a algn como modelo • **children usually ~ themselves on their parents** los niños normalmente toman como modelo a sus padres • **he ~s himself on James Dean** imita a James Dean, su modelo a imitar es James Dean
2 (*Art*) modelar
3 (*Fashion*) • **Jane is ~ling a design by Valentino** Jane luce un modelo de Valentino • **her daughter ~s children's clothes** su hija es modelo de ropa de niños
(VI) **1** (*Art*) (= *make models*) modelar
2 (*Phot, Art*) posar; (*Fashion*) ser modelo, trabajar de modelo
modeller, modeler (*US*) ['mɒdləʳ] (N) modelador(a) *m/f*
modelling, modeling (*US*) ['mɒdlɪŋ] (N)
1 (= *making models*) (*by shaping*) modelado *m*; (*by building*) modelismo *m*, construcción *f* de maquetas
2 (= *modelling clothes*) profesión *f* de modelo • **my daughter does ~** mi hija es modelo
(CPD) ▸ **modelling clay** plastilina® *f*
modem ['məʊdem] (N) módem *m*
moderate (ADJ) ['mɒdərɪt] **1** (= *not excessive*) [*amount, speed, wind, heat, success*] moderado; [*price*] módico; [*ability*] regular, mediano; [*improvement, achievement*] regular • **bake the fish in a ~ oven** hacer el pescado al horno a una temperatura moderada • **she is a ~ drinker** bebe con moderación
2 (*Pol*) (= *not extreme*) [*leader, views, policies*] moderado
(N) ['mɒdərɪt] (*Pol*) moderado/a *m/f*
(VT) ['mɒdəreɪt] **1** (= *adjust*) [+ *speed, behaviour, language, temperature*] moderar; [+ *anger*] aplacar
2 (= *reduce*) [+ *one's demands*] moderar
3 (= *act as moderator for*) [+ *discussion, debate*] moderar
(VI) ['mɒdəreɪt] **1** [*weather*] moderarse; [*anger*] aplacarse; [*wind, storm*] amainar, calmarse
2 (= *arbitrate*) moderar, hacer de moderador
moderately ['mɒdərɪtlɪ] (ADV) [*good, wealthy*] medianamente; [*drink, eat*] con moderación • **he was a ~ successful actor** fue un actor de cierto *or* relativo éxito • **she did ~ well in her exams** los exámenes le salieron medianamente bien • **~ priced** de precio módico
moderation [ˌmɒdə'reɪʃən] (N) moderación *f* • **in ~** con moderación
moderator ['mɒdəreɪtəʳ] (N) **1** (*Brit*) (*Univ*) árbitro *mf*, asesor(a) *m/f*
2 • **Moderator** (*Rel*) *presidente de la asamblea de la Iglesia Presbiteriana Escocesa y de otras iglesias protestantes*; ▹ CHURCHES OF ENGLAND/SCOTLAND
modern ['mɒdən] (ADJ) moderno • **"all modern conveniences"** "todo confort"
(CPD) ▸ **modern art** arte *m* moderno ▸ **modern history** historia *f* contemporánea ▸ **modern languages** (*esp Brit*) lenguas *fpl* modernas ▸ **modern literature** literatura *f* contemporánea
modernism ['mɒdənɪzəm] (N) modernismo *m*
modernist ['mɒdənɪst] (ADJ) modernista
(N) modernista *mf*
modernistic [ˌmɒdə'nɪstɪk] (ADJ) modernista
modernity [mɒ'dɜːnɪtɪ] (N) modernidad *f*
modernization [ˌmɒdənaɪ'zeɪʃən] (N) modernización *f*
modernize ['mɒdənaɪz] (VT) [+ *methods, system*] modernizar, actualizar; [+ *building*] modernizar
(VI) modernizarse, actualizarse
modest ['mɒdɪst] (ADJ) **1** (= *humble*) modesto • **don't be so ~!** ¡no seas tan modesto! • **he's just being ~** está siendo modesto • **to be ~ about sth** ser modesto con algo
2 (= *small*) [*garden, income*] modesto, pequeño; [*amount, sum*] módico, modesto; [*increase, improvement, reform*] moderado • **on a ~ scale** a escala moderada
3 (= *chaste, proper*) [*person, clothes*] púdico, recatado
modestly ['mɒdɪstlɪ] (ADV) **1** (= *humbly*) modestamente
2 (= *moderately*) con moderación • **~ priced** de precio módico • **~ sized** de tamaño medio
3 (= *chastely*) pudorosamente, con pudor
modesty ['mɒdɪstɪ] (N) **1** (= *humbleness*) modestia *f* • **in all ~, I think I could do the job better** modestamente *or* con toda modestia, creo yo que podría hacer mejor el trabajo • **I can't tell you, ~ forbids** no puedo decírtelo, pecaría de poco modesto; ▹ **false**
2 (= *propriety*) pudor *m*, recato *m*
modicum ['mɒdɪkəm] (N) • **a ~ of** un mínimo de
modifiable ['mɒdɪfaɪəbl] (ADJ) modificable
modification [ˌmɒdɪfɪ'keɪʃən] (N) modificación *f* (**to** de)
modifier ['mɒdɪfaɪəʳ] (N) modificante *m*
modify ['mɒdɪfaɪ] (VT) **1** (= *change*) modificar
2 (= *moderate*) moderar
3 (*Ling*) modificar
modifying ['mɒdɪfaɪɪŋ] (ADJ) [*note, term, factor*] modificador, modificante
(N) modificación *f*
modish ['məʊdɪʃ] (ADJ) muy de moda, sumamente elegante
modishly ['məʊdɪʃlɪ] (ADV) elegantemente • **to be ~ dressed** ir vestido con suma elegancia
modiste [məʊ'diːst] (N) modista *f*
Mods* [mɒdz] (N ABBR) (*at Oxford university*) (= **(Honour) Moderations**) *examen de la licenciatura de la universidad de Oxford*
modular ['mɒdjʊləʳ] (ADJ) modular
(CPD) ▸ **modular program(m)ing** programación *f* modular
modularity [ˌmɒdjʊ'lærɪtɪ] (N) modularidad *f*
modularization [ˌmɒdjʊləraɪ'zeɪʃən] (N) modularización *f*
modularize ['mɒdjʊləraɪz] (VT) modularizar
modularized ['mɒdjʊləraɪzd] (ADJ) modularizado
modulate ['mɒdjʊleɪt] (VT) (*Mus, Phys*) modular
modulated ['mɒdjʊleɪtɪd] (ADJ) modulado
modulation [ˌmɒdjʊ'leɪʃən] (N) (*Mus, Phys*) modulación *f*
module ['mɒdjuːl] (N) **1** (*Space*) módulo *m*
2 (*Brit*) (*Univ*) módulo *m*
3 (*Constr*) módulo *m*
4 (*Comput*) módulo *m*
modus operandi ['məʊdəsˌɒpə'rændiː] (N) modo *m* de proceder, modus operandi *m inv*
modus vivendi ['məʊdəsvɪ'vendiː] (N) modus *m* vivendi
Mogadishu [ˌmɒgə'dɪʃuː] (N) Mogadiscio *m*
moggy* ['mɒgɪ] (N) (*Brit*) gatito/a *m/f*, michino/a* *m/f*
mogul ['məʊgəl] (N) **1** (*Hist*) mo(n)gol(a) *m/f* • **the Great Mogul** el Gran Mogol
2 (*fig*) magnate *m* • **film ~** magnate *m* de la cinematografía
MOH (N ABBR) (*Brit*) = **Medical Officer of Health**
mohair ['məʊhɛəʳ] (N) mohair *m*
Mohammed [məʊ'hæmed] (N) Mahoma *m*
Mohammedan [məʊ'hæmɪdən] (ADJ) mahometano
(N) mahometano/a *m/f*
Mohammedanism [məʊ'hæmɪdənɪzəm] (N) mahometanismo *m*
Mohican [məʊ'hiːkən] (N) (PL: **Mohicans** *or* **Mohican**) **1** (= *Native American*) mohicano/a *m/f*
2 (= *hairstyle*) cresta *f* mohicana

m

moiré ['mwɑːreɪ] N muaré *m*
moist [mɔɪst] ADJ (COMPAR: **moister**, SUPERL: **moistest**) [*atmosphere, soil, cloth*] húmedo; [*cake*] esponjoso • **his hands were ~ with perspiration** tenía las manos húmedas del sudor • **her eyes were ~ with tears** tenía los ojos llorosos
moisten ['mɔɪsn] VT (= *wet*) humedecer, mojar • **to ~ one's lips** humedecerse los labios • **~ with olive oil** imprégnese de aceite de oliva
VI humedecerse, mojarse
moistness ['mɔɪstnɪs] N = **moisture**
moisture ['mɔɪstʃəʳ] N (= *dampness*) humedad *f*; (*on glass, mirror*) vaho *m*
moisturize ['mɔɪstʃəraɪz] VT hidratar
moisturizer ['mɔɪstʃəraɪzəʳ] N crema *f* hidratante
moisturizing cream ['mɔɪstʃəraɪzɪŋ,kriːm] N crema *f* hidratante
mojo* ['məʊdʒəʊ] N magnetismo *m* personal
molar ['məʊləʳ] N muela *f*
molasses [mə'læsɪz] NSING melaza *f*
mold *etc* [məʊld] (US) N = **mould** *etc*
Moldavia [mɒl'deɪvɪə] N (*formerly*) Moldavia *f*
Moldavian [mɒl'deɪvɪən] (*formerly*) ADJ moldavo
N moldavo/a *m/f*
Moldova [mɒl'dəʊvə] N Moldova *f*
Moldovan [mɒl'dəʊvən] ADJ moldavo
N moldavo/a *m/f*
mole¹ [məʊl] N (*Anat*) lunar *m*
mole² [məʊl] N **1** (*Zool*) topo *m*
2 (*fig*) (= *spy*) topo *m*, espía *mf*
mole³ [məʊl] N (*Naut*) espigón *m*, rompeolas *m inv*
molecular [mə'lekjʊləʳ] ADJ molecular
CPD ▸ **molecular biologist** biólogo/a *m/f* molecular ▸ **molecular biology** biología *f* molecular
molecule ['mɒlɪkjuːl] N (*Chem*) molécula *f*
molehill ['məʊlhɪl] N topera *f*; ▹ **mountain**
moleskin ['məʊlskɪn] N piel *f* de topo
molest [məʊ'lest] VT **1** (*sexually*) (= *attack*) agredir sexualmente; (= *abuse*) abusar de
2 (= *bother*) importunar, molestar
molestation [,məʊles'teɪʃən] N **1** (= *sexual abuse*) abusos *mpl* sexuales, abusos *mpl* deshonestos
2 (= *trouble*) importunidad *f*
molester [mə'lestəʳ] N (*also* **child molester**) *persona que abusa sexualmente de niños*
moll* [mɒl] N • **gangster's ~** compañera *f* de gángster
mollify ['mɒlɪfaɪ] VT aplacar, apaciguar • **he was somewhat mollified by this** esto lo aplacó *or* apaciguó un poco, con esto se calmó un poco
mollusc, mollusk (US) ['mɒləsk] N molusco *m*
mollycoddle ['mɒlɪkɒdl] VT mimar, sobreproteger
mollycoddling ['mɒlɪ,kɒdlɪŋ] N mimo *m*
Molotov cocktail [,mɒlətɒf'kɒkteɪl] N cóctel *m* Molotov
molt [məʊlt] VI, VT, N (US) = **moult**
molten ['məʊltən] ADJ fundido, derretido; [*lava*] líquido
molybdenum [mɒ'lɪbdɪnəm] N molibdeno *m*
mom* [mɒm] (US) N mamá* *f*
CPD ▸ **mom and pop store** tienda *f* de la esquina, pequeño negocio *m*
moment ['məʊmənt] N **1** (*in time*) momento *m*, al rato • **a ~ ago** hace un momento • **they should be arriving any ~ (now)** deberían llegar ahorita (*LAm*) *or* de un momento a otro • **at the ~** en este momento • **I could lose my job at any ~** podría perder mi trabajo en cualquier momento • **at this/that ~** en este/ese momento, en este/ese instante • **at this ~ in time** en este mismo momento • **I shan't be a ~** (*on going out*) vuelvo en seguida, ahorita vuelvo (*LAm*); (*when busy*) termino en un momento, ahorita acabo (*LAm*) • **for the ~** por el momento, por lo pronto • **he didn't hesitate for a ~** no vaciló ni un momento *or* instante • **not for a** *or* **one ~ did I believe it** no me lo creí ni por un momento • **I'm not saying for a ~ you're wrong** no digo que no tengas razón ni mucho menos • **not for a ~ did I think that ...** en ningún momento pensaba que ... • **from the ~ I saw him** desde el momento en que lo vi • **from ~ to ~** al momento • **from that ~ on** desde entonces, desde ese *or* aquel momento • **the play has its ~s** la obra tiene sus momentos • **yes, in a ~!** ¡sí en seguida! • **I'll come in a ~** vengo en seguida, vengo dentro de un momento • **it was all over in a ~** todo ocurrió en un instante • **in ~s, I was asleep** en seguida me quedé dormido • **just a ~!** ¡un momento! • **I've just this ~ heard** acabo de enterarme • **at the last ~** a última hora, en el último momento • **to leave things until the last ~** dejar las cosas hasta última hora, dejarlo todo para lo último • **a ~ later** un momento después • **the next ~ he collapsed** al instante se desplomó • **he was weeping one ~, laughing the next** tan pronto lloraba como se reía • **the man of the ~** el hombre del momento • **one ~!** ¡un momento! • **I was waiting for the right ~ to tell him** estaba esperando el momento adecuado *or* oportuno para decírselo • **it won't take a ~** no tardará ni un momento, es cosa de un momento • **tell me the ~ he arrives** avísame en cuanto llegue • **the ~ of truth** la hora de la verdad • **I did it in a ~ of weakness** lo hice en un momento de debilidad
2 (*Phys*) momento *m*
3 (*frm*) (= *importance*) importancia *f* • **of great/little ~** de gran/poca importancia
momenta [məʊ'mentə] NPL *of* **momentum**
momentarily ['məʊməntərɪlɪ] ADV **1** (= *for a moment*) por un momento, momentáneamente • **he paused ~ to ...** paró un momento para ...
2 (US) (= *at any moment*) de un momento a otro, en seguida, ahorita (*LAm*)
momentary ['məʊməntərɪ] ADJ [*hesitation, silence, weakness*] momentáneo; [*feeling*] pasajero • **there was a ~ calm** hubo un momento de calma
momentous [məʊ'mentəs] ADJ trascendental, de gran trascendencia
momentousness [məʊ'mentəsnɪs] N trascendencia *f*, suma importancia *f*
momentum [məʊ'mentəm] N (PL: **momentums** *or* **momenta** [məʊ'mentə]) (*Phys*) momento *m*; (*fig*) ímpetu *m*, impulso *m* • **to gather** *or* **gain ~** (*lit*) cobrar velocidad; (*fig*) ganar fuerza
momma* ['mɒmə] N (US), **mommy*** ['mɒmɪ] N (US) mamá* *f*
Mon. ABBR (= **Monday**) lun.
Monaco ['mɒnəkəʊ] N Mónaco *m*
monad ['mɒnæd] N mónada *f*
Mona Lisa ['məʊnə'liːzə] N • **the ~** la Gioconda, la Mona Lisa
monarch ['mɒnək] N monarca *mf*
monarchic [mɒ'nɑːkɪk] ADJ = **monarchical**
monarchical [mɒ'nɑːkɪkəl] ADJ monárquico
monarchism ['mɒnəkɪzəm] N (= *system*) monarquía *f*; (= *advocacy of monarchy*) monarquismo *m*
monarchist ['mɒnəkɪst] ADJ monárquico
N monárquico/a *m/f*
monarchy ['mɒnəkɪ] N monarquía *f*
monastery ['mɒnəstrɪ] N monasterio *m*
monastic [mə'næstɪk] ADJ monástico
CPD ▸ **monastic order** orden *f* monástica ▸ **monastic vows** votos *mpl* monásticos
monasticism [mə'næstɪsɪzəm] N monacato *m*, vida *f* monástica
Monday ['mʌndɪ] N lunes *m inv*; ▹ **Tuesday**
Monegasque [mɒnə'gæsk] ADJ monegasco
N monegasco/a *m/f*
monetarism ['mʌnɪtərɪzəm] N monetarismo *m*
monetarist ['mʌnɪtərɪst] ADJ monetarista
N monetarista *mf*
monetary ['mʌnɪtərɪ] ADJ monetario
CPD ▸ **monetary policy** política *f* monetaria ▸ **monetary reserves** reservas *fpl* monetarias ▸ **monetary system** sistema *m* monetario ▸ **monetary unit** unidad *f* monetaria
monetization [,mʌnɪtaɪ'zeɪʃən] N monetización *f*
monetize ['mʌnɪtaɪz] VT monetizar
money ['mʌnɪ] N **1** (*gen*) dinero *m* • **Spanish ~** dinero español • **there's ~ in second-hand cars** los coches de segunda mano son (un) buen negocio • **"~ back if not satisfied"** "si no queda satisfecho le devolvemos su dinero" • **to bring in ~** aportar dinero • **to come into ~** heredar dinero • **when do I get my ~?** ¿cuándo me vas a pagar? • **to earn good ~** ganar un buen sueldo, ganar su buen dinero *or* dinerito*, ganar sus buenos dineros *or* dineritos* • **I paid** *or* **gave good ~ for it** pagué un buen dinero por ello • **I'd rather be paid in ~** prefiero que me paguen en dinero • **your ~ or your life!** ¡la bolsa o la vida! • **to make ~** [*person*] ganar dinero; [*business*] rendir, dar dinero • **he made his ~ by dealing in cotton** ganó el dinero que tiene comerciando con algodón • **to put ~ into sth** invertir dinero en algo • **it was ~ well spent** fue dinero bien empleado
• IDIOMS: • **bad ~ drives out good** el dinero malo echa fuera al bueno • **~ doesn't grow on trees** el dinero no cae del cielo *or* de los árboles • **to have ~ to burn** estar cargado *or* podrido de dinero* • **~ isn't everything** el dinero no lo es todo • **it's ~ for jam** *or* **~ for old rope** (*Brit**) es dinero regalado* • **to throw good ~ after bad** echar la soga tras el caldero • **to be in the ~** estar bien de dinero • **to be made of ~** ser millonario, tener un banco • **for my ~:** • **that's the one for my ~!** ¡yo apostaría por ese! • **I'd put ~ on it:** • **he'll be back, I'd put ~ on it** apuesto (lo que sea) a que volverá • **my ~ is on Fred** yo apuesto por Fred • **to put one's ~ where one's mouth is** predicar con el ejemplo • **to spend ~ like water** tener un agujero en el bolsillo, ser un/una manirroto/a • **to throw one's ~ about** *or* **around** tirar *or* derrochar el dinero • **to throw ~ at a problem** intentar solucionar un problema a base de dinero • **to get one's ~'s worth** sacar partido a su dinero • **he certainly gives the audience its ~'s worth** la verdad es que con él el público sale contento • PROVERBS: • **~ can't buy happiness** el dinero no da *or* trae la felicidad • **~ makes ~** dinero llama dinero • **~ makes the world go round** el dinero mueve montañas • **(the love of) ~ is the root of all evil** el dinero es la raíz de todos los males • **~ talks** poderoso caballero es don Dinero; ▹ **burn¹, coin, colour, even, hand, licence, marry, ready**
2 (*Jur*) **monies** *or* **moneys** (*pl*) sumas *fpl* de

dinero • **public monies** dinero *m* público
CPD [*worries, problems*] de dinero, económico ▸ **money back guarantee** garantía *f* de devolución (del dinero) ▸ **money belt** riñonera *f* ▸ **money economy** economía *f* monetaria ▸ **money laundering** blanqueo *m* de dinero ▸ **money laundering operation** operación *f* de blanqueo de dinero ▸ **money laundering scandal** escándalo *m* de blanqueo de dinero ▸ **money laundering scheme** sistema *m* de blanqueo de dinero ▸ **money market** bolsa *f or* mercado *m* de valores, mercado *m* monetario ▸ **money matters** asuntos *mpl* financieros ▸ **money order** (*US*) giro *m* postal ▸ **money prize** premio *m* en metálico ▸ **money spider** araña *f* de la suerte ▸ **the money supply** la oferta *or* masa monetaria, el volumen de moneda

moneybags* ['mʌnɪbægz] N • **he's a ~** está forrado*

moneybox ['mʌnɪbɒks] N hucha *f*

moneychanger ['mʌnɪˌtʃeɪndʒəʳ] N cambista *mf*

moneyed ['mʌnɪd] ADJ adinerado

moneygrubber ['mʌnɪˌgrʌbəʳ] N avaro/a *m/f*

money-grubbing ['mʌnɪˌgrʌbɪŋ] ADJ avaro

moneylender ['mʌnɪˌlendəʳ] N prestamista *mf*

moneylending ['mʌnɪˌlendɪŋ] N préstamo *m*

moneymaker ['mʌnɪˌmeɪkəʳ] N fuente *f* de ganancias

money-making ['mʌnɪˌmeɪkɪŋ] ADJ [*business etc*] rentable
N ganancia *f*, lucro *m*

money-purchase [ˌmʌnɪ'pɜːtʃɪs] ADJ [*pension, plan*] con cotizaciones definidas • **money-purchase scheme** pensión con cotizaciones definidas

money-spinner ['mʌnɪˌspɪnəʳ] N (*Brit*) = **moneymaker**

-monger ['mʌŋgəʳ] N (*ending in compounds*) • **rumour-monger** *persona que se dedica a difundir rumores*; ▹ **fishmonger, warmonger**

Mongol ['mɒŋgəl] N **1** (= *person*) mongol(a) *m/f*
2 (*Ling*) mongol *m*

mongol‡* ['mɒŋgəl] (*offensive*) N mongólico/a *m/f*
ADJ mongólico

Mongolia [mɒŋ'gəʊlɪə] N Mongolia *f*

Mongolian [mɒŋ'gəʊlɪən] ADJ mongol
N **1** (= *person*) mongol(a) *m/f*
2 (*Ling*) mongol *m*

mongolism‡* ['mɒŋgəlɪzəm] N mongolismo *m*

Mongoloid ['mɒŋgəlɔɪd] ADJ (*Anthropology*) mongólico

mongoloid‡* ['mɒŋgəlɔɪd] ADJ mongoloide, mongólico

mongoose ['mɒŋguːs] N (PL: **mongooses**) mangosta *f*

mongrel ['mʌŋgrəl] N (*also* **mongrel dog**) perro *m* mestizo, perro *m* cruzado
ADJ [*dog*] mestizo, cruzado

monicker‡ ['mɒnɪkəʳ] N (= *name*) nombre *m*; (= *nickname*) apodo *m*; (= *signature*) firma *f*; (= *initials*) iniciales *fpl*

monied ['mʌnɪd] ADJ = **moneyed**

monitor ['mɒnɪtəʳ] N **1** (*TV, Comput, Med*) monitor *m*
2 (= *person*) supervisor(a) *m/f*; (*Rad*) radioescucha *mf*; (*Scol*) encargado/a *m/f* (*de la disciplina*) • **human rights ~s** supervisores de los derechos humanos
VT **1** (= *control, check*) [+ *progress, process*] seguir (la marcha de), controlar; [+ *elections*] observar; (*with machine*) monitorizar, monitorear • **we are ~ing the situation closely** estamos observando *or* controlando la situación de cerca
2 (*Rad*) [+ *foreign broadcasts, station*] escuchar

monitoring ['mɒnɪtərɪŋ] N **1** [*of process, situation*] supervisión *f*, control *m*; [*of patient, elections*] observación *f*; [*of agreement, law*] supervisión *f*
2 (*Electronics*) monitorización *f*
3 (*Rad*) [*of broadcasts, station*] escucha *f*
CPD [*body, responsibility*] de observación, de verificación

monk [mʌŋk] N monje *m*

monkey ['mʌŋkɪ] N (*Zool*) mono *m*; (*fig*) (= *child*) diablillo *m* • IDIOMS: • **I don't give a ~'s**‡ me importa un rábano* • **to make a ~ out of sb** poner a algn en ridículo
CPD ▸ **monkey bars** *estructura en la cual los niños juegan trepando* ▸ **monkey business*** (*dishonest*) trapisondas *fpl*, tejemanejes *mpl*; (*mischievous*) travesuras *fpl*, diabluras *fpl* ▸ **monkey nut** (*Brit*) cacahuete *m*, maní *m* (*LAm*), cacahuate *m* (*Mex*) ▸ **monkey puzzle** (*Bot*) araucaria *f* ▸ **monkey shines** (*US*) = **monkey tricks** ▸ **monkey suit*** traje *m* de etiqueta, esmoquin *m* ▸ **monkey tricks** travesuras *fpl* ▸ **monkey wrench** llave *f* inglesa

▸ **monkey about, monkey around** VI + ADV hacer tonterías • **to ~ about** *or* **around with sth** juguetear con algo

monkfish ['mʌŋkfɪʃ] (PL: **monkfish** *or* **monkfishes**) N rape *m*, pejesapo *m*

monkish ['mʌŋkɪʃ] ADJ monacal, monástico; (*pej*) frailuno

monkshood ['mʌŋkshʊd] N acónito *m*

mono ['mɒnəʊ] ADJ ABBR (= **monophonic**) mono (*inv*), monoaural, monofónico • **~ system** sistema *m* monoaural
N • **in ~** en mono

mono... ['mɒnəʊ] PREFIX mono...

monochrome ['mɒnəkrəʊm] ADJ monocromo
N monocromo *m*

monocle ['mɒnəkl] N monóculo *m*

monoculture ['mɒnəʊˌkʌltʃəʳ] N monocultivo *m*

monogamist [mɒ'nɒgəmɪst] N monógamo/a *m/f*

monogamous [mɒ'nɒgəməs] ADJ monógamo

monogamy [mɒ'nɒgəmɪ] N monogamia *f*

monogenetic [mɒnəʊdʒɪ'netɪk] ADJ monogenético

monoglot ['mɒnəʊglɒt] ADJ monolingüe
N monolingüe *mf*

monogram ['mɒnəgræm] N monograma *m*, iniciales *fpl*

monogrammed ['mɒnəgræmd] ADJ con monograma

monograph ['mɒnəgræf] N monografía *f*

monohull ['mɒnəʊˌhʌl] N monocasco *m*

monokini [ˌmɒnəʊ'kiːniː] N monokini *m*

monolingual [ˌmɒnəʊ'lɪŋgwəl] ADJ monolingüe

monolingualism [ˌmɒnəʊ'lɪŋgwəlɪzəm] N monolingüismo *m*

monolith ['mɒnəʊlɪθ] N monolito *m*

monolithic [ˌmɒnəʊ'lɪθɪk] ADJ monolítico

monologue, monolog (*US*) ['mɒnəlɒg] N monólogo *m*

monomania [ˌmɒnəʊ'meɪnɪə] N monomanía *f*

monomaniac [ˌmɒnəʊ'meɪnɪæk] ADJ monomaníaco
N monomaníaco/a *m/f*

mononucleosis [ˌmɒnəʊˌnjuːklɪ'əʊsɪs] N (*US*) (*also* **infectious mononucleosis**) mononucleosis *f* infecciosa

monophonic [ˌmɒnəʊ'fɒnɪk] ADJ monoaural, monofónico

monoplane ['mɒnəpleɪn] N monoplano *m*

monopolist [mə'nɒpəlɪst] N monopolista *mf*

monopolistic [məˌnɒpə'lɪstɪk] ADJ monopolístico

monopolization [məˌnɒpəlaɪ'zeɪʃən] N monopolización *f*

monopolize [mə'nɒpəlaɪz] VT (*lit, fig*) monopolizar

monopoly [mə'nɒpəlɪ] N (*lit, fig*) monopolio *m*
CPD ▸ **Monopolies and Mergers Commission** (*Brit*) *organismo regulador de monopolios y fusiones encargado de velar por la libre competencia*

monopsony [mə'nɒpsənɪ] N monopsonio *m*

monorail ['mɒnəʊreɪl] N monocarril *m*, monorraíl *m*

monoski ['mɒnəʊˌskiː] N monoesquí *m*

monoskier ['mɒnəʊˌskiːəʳ] N monoesquiador(a) *m/f*

monoskiing ['mɒnəʊˌskiːɪŋ] N monoesquí *m*

monosodium glutamate [ˈmɒnəʊˌsəʊdɪəm-ˈgluːtəmeɪt] N glutamato *m* monosódico

monosyllabic ['mɒnəʊsɪ'læbɪk] ADJ **1** (*lit*) [*word*] monosílabo
2 (*fig*) (= *reticent*) lacónico

monosyllable ['mɒnəˌsɪləbl] N monosílabo *m*

monotheism ['mɒnəʊˌθiːɪzəm] N monoteísmo *m*

monotheist ['mɒnəʊˌθiːɪst] N monoteísta *mf*

monotheistic [ˌmɒnəʊθiː'ɪstɪk] ADJ monoteísta

monotherapy ['mɒnəʊˌθerəpɪ] N monoterapia *f*

monotone ['mɒnətəʊn] N monotonía *f* • **to speak in a ~** hablar en un solo tono

monotonous [mə'nɒtənəs] ADJ monótono • **he gets drunk with ~ regularity** se emborracha con indefectible regularidad

monotonously [mə'nɒtənəslɪ] ADV de forma monótona, monótonamente • **~ reliable** tediosamente fiable • **~ punctual** de una puntualidad religiosa

monotony [mə'nɒtənɪ] N monotonía *f* • **she decided to go away for the weekend, just to break the ~** decidió irse el fin de semana, solo para romper la monotonía *or* salir de la rutina

Monotype® ['mɒnəʊtaɪp] N monotipia® *f*
CPD ▸ **Monotype machine** (máquina *f*) monotipo® *m*

monoxide [mɒ'nɒksaɪd] N (*Chem*) monóxido *m*

Mons ABBR (*Rel*) (= **Monseigneur** *or* **Monsignor**) Mons.

monseigneur [ˌmɒnsen'jɜːʳ] N monseñor *m*

monsignor [mɒn'siːnjəʳ] N (PL: **monsignors** *or* **monsignori**) monseñor *m*

monsoon [mɒn'suːn] N monzón *m*
CPD ▸ **the monsoon rains** las lluvias monzónicas ▸ **monsoon season** época *f* monzónica, estación *f* de los monzones

monster ['mɒnstəʳ] ADJ* (= *enormous*) enorme, gigantesco
N monstruo *m*; (= *big animal, plant, thing**) monstruo *m*, gigante *m* • **a real ~ of a fish** un pez verdaderamente enorme

monstrance ['mɒnstrəns] N custodia *f*

monstrosity [mɒns'trɒsɪtɪ] N monstruosidad *f*

monstrous ['mɒnstrəs] ADJ **1** (= *huge*) enorme, gigantesco
2 (= *dreadful*) monstruoso • **it is ~ that ...** es

una verdadera vergüenza *or* un auténtico escándalo que (+ *subjun*)

monstrously ['mɒnstrəslɪ] ADV enormemente • **~ unfair** terriblemente injusto

Mont. ABBR (*US*) = **Montana**

montage [mɒn'tɑːʒ] N montaje *m*

Mont Blanc [ˌmɔ̃'blɑ̃] N el Mont Blanc

Montenegrin [mɒntɪ'niːgrən] ADJ montenegrino
N montenegrino/a *m/f*

Montenegro [mɒntə'niːgrəʊ] N Montenegro *m*

month [mʌnθ] N mes *m* • **in the ~ of May** en el mes de mayo • **a deposit of two ~s' rent** un depósito equivalente a dos meses de alquiler • **a ~'s unlimited rail travel** uso ilimitado del tren por el periodo de un mes • **an eight-month-old baby** un bebé de ocho meses • **three times a ~** tres veces al mes • **30 dollars a ~** 30 dólares al mes, 30 dólares mensuales • **at the beginning of the ~** a principios de mes • **I get paid by the ~** me pagan mensualmente • **what** *or* **which day of the ~ is it?** ¿a cuántos estamos? • **at the end of the ~** a fin *or* finales de mes • **every ~** todos los meses • **she was here for a ~** estuvo aquí un mes • **it went on for ~s** duró meses y meses • **I was able to walk for the first time in ~s** por primera vez después de meses pude andar • **I'm off to Mexico in a ~'s time** *or* **in a ~** me voy a México dentro de un mes • **last ~** el mes pasado • **a ~ later** al mes, un mes más tarde • **next ~** el mes que viene • **six ~s pregnant** embarazada de seis meses • **in recent ~s** en los últimos meses • **this ~** este mes • **it's that time of the ~*** tiene/tengo la regla • IDIOM: • **not** *or* **never in a ~ of Sundays** ni de casualidad; ▸ **calendar, lunar**

monthly ['mʌnθlɪ] ADJ [*publication, salary, rainfall*] mensual • **on a ~ basis** mensualmente, todos los meses • **~ instalment** *or* **payment** mensualidad *f*, cuota *f* mensual
ADV [*publish*] mensualmente, todos los meses; [*pay*] mensualmente, por meses • **they meet ~** se reúnen todos los meses *or* cada mes • **twice ~** dos veces al mes
N (= *journal*) publicación *f* mensual
CPD ▸ **monthly cycle** (*menstrual*) ciclo *m* menstrual ▸ **monthly period** (*menstrual*) periodo *m* (menstrual)

Montreal [ˌmɒntrɪ'ɔːl] N Montreal *f*

monty* ['mɒntɪ] N • **the full ~** todo completo, el paquete *or* lote completo*

monument ['mɒnjʊmənt] N monumento *m* (**to** a)

monumental [ˌmɒnjʊ'mentl] ADJ
1 (= *grand*) [*building, sculpture, arch*] monumental
2 (= *huge*) [*task, success, effort*] monumental, colosal; [*blunder, error*] garrafal • **of ~ proportions** de proporciones monumentales • **on a ~ scale** a una escala gigantesca
CPD ▸ **monumental mason** marmolista *mf* (funerario/a)

monumentally [ˌmɒnjʊ'mentəlɪ] ADV [*dull, popular*] enormemente, tremendamente • **~ important** enormemente importante, de tremenda importancia

moo [muː] N mugido *m*
VI mugir
EXCL ¡mu!

MOOC [muːk] N (= **massive open online course**) curso *m* en línea masivo y abierto

mooch* [muːtʃ] VI • **to ~ about** *or* **around the shops** pasear por las tiendas • **to ~ about** *or* **around the house** dar vueltas por la casa • **to ~ along** andar arrastrando los pies

moo-cow* ['muːkaʊ] N (*baby talk*) vaca *f*

mood¹ [muːd] N (*Ling*) modo *m*

mood² [muːd] N humor *m* • **that depends on his ~** eso es según el *or* depende del humor que tenga • **to be in the ~ for sth/to do sth** tener ganas de algo/de hacer algo, estar de humor para algo/para hacer algo • **he plays well when he's in the ~** toca bien cuando está en vena *or* por la labor • **are you in a ~ for chess?** ¿te apetece una partida de ajedrez?, ¿quieres jugar al ajedrez? • **I'm not in the ~** no tengo ganas, no me apetece • **I'm not in the ~ for games** no estoy (de humor) para juegos • **he's in a bit of a ~** está de mal humor • **to be in a bad ~** estar de mal humor • **to be in a forgiving ~** estar dispuesto a perdonar • **to be in a generous ~** sentirse generoso • **to be in a good ~** estar de buen humor • **he has ~s** (*angry*) tiene arranques de cólera; (*gloomy*) tiene sus rachas de melancolía • **I'm in no ~ to argue** no tengo ganas de discutir, no estoy (de humor) para discutir • **to be in no laughing ~** *or* **in no ~ for laughing** no tener ganas de reír • **she's in one of her ~s** está de malas, está con un humor de perros • **to be in an ugly ~** [*person*] estar de muy mal humor; [*crowd*] tener los ánimos muy exaltados *or* encendidos
CPD ▸ **mood disorder** trastorno *m* del humor ▸ **mood enhancer** antidepresivo *m* ▸ **mood music** música *f* de fondo *or* de ambiente ▸ **mood swing** cambio *m* de humor

mood-altering ['muːdˌɒltərɪŋ] ADJ [*drug, substance, effect, experience*] que cambia el humor

moodily ['muːdɪlɪ] ADV malhumoradamente

moodiness ['muːdɪnɪs] N (= *variability*) humor *m* variable; (= *bad mood*) mal humor *m*

moody ['muːdɪ] ADJ (COMPAR: **moodier**, SUPERL: **moodiest**) (= *variable*) (de carácter) variable, temperamental; (= *bad-tempered*) malhumorado • **he's very ~** es muy temperamental, es de humor muy variable

moola‡, moolah‡ ['muːlɑː] N (*US*) pasta* *f*, parné‡ *m*

moon [muːn] N luna *f* • **full ~** luna *f* llena • **there's a full ~ tonight** esta noche hay luna llena • **new ~** luna *f* nueva • **there was no ~** no había luna • **by the light of the ~** a la luz de la luna • **many ~s ago** (*liter or hum*) hace mucho tiempo • IDIOMS: • **to ask for the ~** pedir la luna • **once in a blue ~** de Pascuas a Ramos • **to be over the ~*** estar loco de contento, estar en el séptimo cielo • **to promise the ~** prometer la luna *or* el oro y el moro; ▸ **phase**
VI* enseñar el culo*
CPD ▸ **moon buggy** vehículo *m* lunar ▸ **moon landing** alunizaje *m*

▸ **moon about, moon around** VI + ADV mirar a las musarañas

▸ **moon over** VI + PREP • **she was ~ing over the photo** miraba amorosamente la foto, contemplaba extasiada la foto

moonbeam ['muːnbiːm] N rayo *m* de luna

moonboots ['muːnbuːts] NPL botas *fpl* altas acolchadas

moon-faced ['muːnfeɪst] ADJ con la cara redonda

Moonie ['muːnɪ] N miembro *mf* de la Iglesia de la Unificación

moonless ['muːnlɪs] ADJ sin luna

moonlight ['muːnlaɪt] N luz *f* de la luna • **by ~** • **in the ~** a la luz de la luna
VI* practicar el pluriempleo • **he ~s as a taxi driver** en sus ratos libres trabaja de taxista
CPD ▸ **moonlight flit** (*Brit*) mudanza *f* a la chita callando • **to do a ~ flit** largarse a la chita callando*

moonlighter* ['muːnlaɪtəʳ] N pluriempleado/a *m/f*

moonlighting* ['muːnlaɪtɪŋ] N pluriempleo *m*

moonlit ['muːnlɪt] ADJ [*object*] iluminado por la luna; [*night*] de luna

moonrise ['muːnraɪz] N salida *f* de la luna

moonscape ['muːnskeɪp] N paisaje *m* lunar

moonshine ['muːnʃaɪn] N **1** (= *moonlight*) luz *f* de la luna
2* (= *nonsense*) pamplinas *fpl*
3 (*US*) (= *illegal spirits*) licor *m* destilado ilegalmente

moonshiner* ['muːnʃaɪnəʳ] N (*US*)
1 (= *distiller*) fabricante *mf* de licor ilegal
2 (= *smuggler*) contrabandista *mf*

moonshot ['muːnʃɒt] N **1** (= *vessel*) nave *f* espacial con destino a la luna
2 (= *launch*) lanzamiento *m* de una nave espacial con destino a la luna

moonstone ['muːnstəʊn] N feldespato *m*, labradorita *f*

moonstruck ['muːnstrʌk] ADJ chiflado

moony* ['muːnɪ] ADJ • **to be ~** estar distraído, estar soñando despierto

Moor [mʊəʳ] N moro/a *m/f*

moor¹ [mʊəʳ] N (*esp Brit*) páramo *m*, brezal *m*

moor² [mʊəʳ] VT amarrar
VI echar las amarras

moorhen ['mʊəhen] N polla *f* de agua

mooring ['mʊərɪŋ] N **1** (= *place*) amarradero *m*
2 moorings (= *ropes, fixtures*) amarras *fpl*

Moorish ['mʊərɪʃ] ADJ [*person*] moro; [*culture, influence, invasion*] árabe; [*architecture*] morisco

moorland ['mʊələnd] N páramo *m*, brezal *m*

moose [muːs] N (PL: **moose**) alce *m*

moot [muːt] ADJ • **it's a ~ point** *or* **question** es un punto discutible
VT • **it has been ~ed that ...** se ha sugerido que ... • **when the question was first ~ed** cuando se discutió la cuestión por primera vez
N (*Hist*) junta *f*, asamblea *f*

mop [mɒp] N **1** (*for floor*) fregona *f*, trapeador *m* (*LAm*); (*for dishes*) estropajo *m*
2* • **mop of hair** pelambrera *f*, melena *f*
VT [+ *floor*] fregar, trapear (*LAm*); [+ *brow*] enjugar • **to mop one's face** enjugarse la cara

▸ **mop up** VT + ADV **1** [+ *spilt water*] secar; [+ *floor, surface*] limpiar • **you can always mop up the sauce with your bread** siempre puedes rebañar *or* mojar la salsa con el pan
2 (*Mil*) acabar con
VI + ADV (= *clean*) limpiar; (*with mop*) pasar la fregona

mope [məʊp] VI quedar abatido • **to ~ for sb** estar triste por la pérdida de algn

▸ **mope about, mope around** VI + ADV andar con cara mustia

moped ['məʊped] N (*esp Brit*) ciclomotor *m*

mopping-up ['mɒpɪŋ'ʌp] N limpieza *f*
CPD ▸ **mopping-up operation** (*Mil*) operación *f* de limpieza, barrida *f*; (*after flood, storm*) operaciones *fpl* de limpieza y reconstrucción

mopy* ['məʊpɪ] ADJ depre* • **I'm feeling a bit ~ today** hoy me siento un poco depre*

moquette [mə'ket] N moqueta *f*

MOR ADJ ABBR (*Mus*) (= **middle-of-the-road**) para el gran público

moraine [mɒ'reɪn] (N) morena *f*

moral ['mɒrəl] (ADJ) [*values, principles, issue, dilemma*] moral • **I have a ~ responsibility for what happened** me siento moralmente responsable de lo que ocurrió • **a fall in ~ standards** una decadencia moral • **~ fibre** fibra *f* moral • **on ~ grounds** por razones morales • **the ~ majority** la mayoría moral
(N) **1** (= *lesson*) moraleja *f*
2 morals moralidad *f* • **he has no ~s** no tiene moralidad
(CPD) ▸ **moral support** apoyo *m* moral • **I went along with her for ~ support** fui con ella para darle apoyo moral ▸ **moral victory** victoria *f* moral

morale [mɒ'rɑːl] (N) moral *f* • **~ was at an all-time low** la moral estaba más baja que nunca • **to raise/lower sb's ~** levantar/bajar la moral a algn, animar/desanimar a algn

morale-booster [mɒ'rɑːl,buːstəʳ] (N) inyección *f* de moral • **his recent win was a great morale-booster** su reciente victoria le levantó mucho la moral

morale-boosting [mə'rɑːl,buːstɪŋ] (ADJ) [*win, victory*] que supone una inyección de moral

moralist ['mɒrəlɪst] (N) moralizador(a) *m/f*; (= *philosopher, teacher*) moralista *mf*

moralistic [,mɒrə'lɪstɪk] (ADJ) moralizador

morality [mə'rælɪtɪ] (N) moralidad *f*, moral *f*
(CPD) ▸ **morality play** moralidad *f*

moralize ['mɒrəlaɪz] (VI) moralizar

moralizer ['mɒrəlaɪzəʳ] (N) moralizador(a) *m/f*

moralizing ['mɒrəlaɪzɪŋ] (ADJ) moralizador
(N) instrucción *f* moral, predicación *f* sobre la moralidad

morally ['mɒrəlɪ] (ADV) [*superior, responsible*] moralmente; [*right, wrong*] desde el punto de vista moral; [*act, behave*] moralmente, éticamente • **a ~ bankrupt society** una sociedad en bancarrota moral

morass [mə'ræs] (N) cenagal *m*, pantano *m* • **a ~ of problems** un laberinto de problemas • **a ~ of figures** un mar de cifras

moratorium [,mɒrə'tɔːrɪəm] (N) (PL: **moratoriums** *or* **moratoria** [,mɒrə'tɔːrɪə]) moratoria *f*

Moravia [mə'reɪvɪə] (N) Moravia *f*

moray ['mɒreɪ] (N) (= *fish*) morena *f*

morbid ['mɔːbɪd] (ADJ) **1** (= *perverse*) morboso, malsano • **don't be so ~!** ¡no seas morboso! • **~ curiosity** curiosidad *f* malsana
2 (*Med*) mórbido
(CPD) ▸ **morbid obesity** obesidad *f* mórbida

morbidity [mɔː'bɪdɪtɪ] (N) **1** (= *perverseness*) morbosidad *f*, lo malsano
2 (*Med*) morbosidad *f*

morbidly ['mɔːbɪdlɪ] (ADV) [*talk*] morbosamente, con morbo; [*think*] morbosamente

morbidness ['mɔːbɪdnɪs] (N) = **morbidity**

mordacity [mɔːdæsɪtɪ] (N) mordacidad *f*

mordant ['mɔːdənt] (ADJ) mordaz

mordent ['mɔːdənt] (N) mordente *m*

more [mɔːʳ] (ADJ) más • **there's ~ tea in the cupboard** hay más té en el aparador • **is there any ~ wine in the bottle?** ¿queda vino en la botella? • **a few ~ weeks** unas semanas más • **it'll take a few ~ days** llevará unos cuantos días más • **many ~ people** muchas más personas • **much ~ butter** mucha más mantequilla • **I have no ~ money** no me queda más dinero • **no ~ singing, I can't bear it!** ¡que no se cante más, no lo aguanto! • **do you want some ~ tea?** ¿quieres más té? • **you have ~ money than I** tienes más dinero que yo • **it's two ~ miles to the house** faltan dos millas para llegar a la casa
(N), (PRON) **1** más • **four ~** cuatro más • **we can't afford ~** no podemos pagar más • **is there any ~?** ¿hay más? • **there isn't any ~** ya no hay más • **a bit ~?** ¿un poco más? • **a few ~** algunos más • **a little ~** un poco más • **many ~** muchos más • **much ~** mucho más • **there isn't much ~ to do** no hay *or* queda mucho más que hacer • **there's no ~ left** no queda (nada) • **let's say no ~ about it!** ¡no se hable más del asunto! • **she's no ~ a duchess than I am** tan duquesa es como mi padre • **he no ~ thought of paying me than of flying to the moon** antes iría volando a la luna que pensar pagarme a mí • **I shall have ~ to say about this** volveré a hablar de esto • **some ~** más • **he's got ~ than me!** ¡él tiene más que yo! • **it's ~ than a job** es (algo) más que un trabajo • **~ than ever** más que nunca • **~ than half** más de la mitad • **~ than one/ten** más de uno/diez • **not ~ than 15** no más de quince • **not much ~ than £20** poco más de 20 libras • **it cost ~ than we had expected** costó más de lo que esperábamos • **and what's ~ ...** y además ... • **there's ~ where that came from!** ¡esto no es más que el principio!
2 • **(all) the ~** tanto más • **it makes me (all) the ~ ashamed** tanto más vergüenza me da • **all the ~ so because** *or* **as** *or* **since ...** tanto más cuanto que ... • **the ~ you give him the ~ he wants** cuanto más se le da, (tanto) más quiere • **the ~ he drank the thirstier he got** cuanto más bebía más sed tenía • **the ~ the better** • **the ~ the merrier** cuantos más mejor
(ADV) **1** más • **~ difficult** más difícil • **~ easily** con mayor facilidad • **more and more** cada vez más • **if he says that any ~** si vuelve a decir eso, si dice eso otra vez • **if he comes here any ~** si vuelve por aquí • **~ or less** más o menos • **neither ~ nor less** ni más ni menos • **"I don't understand it" — "no ~ do I"** —no lo comprendo —ni yo tampoco • **he's ~ intelligent than me** es más inteligente que yo • **the house is ~ than half built** la casa está más que medio construida • **I had ~ than carried out my obligation** había cumplido con creces mi obligación • **it will ~ than meet the demand** satisfará ampliamente la demanda • **he was ~ surprised than angry** más que enfadarse se sorprendió • **it's ~ a short story than a novel** más que novela es un cuento
2 (= *again*) • **once ~** otra vez, una vez más
3 (= *longer*) • **he doesn't live here any ~** ya no vive aquí • **Queen Anne is no ~** la reina Ana ya no existe • **we shall see her no ~** no la volveremos a ver

> **MORE THAN**
>
> **"Más ... que" or "más ... de"?**
>
> ▸ *Use* **más** *with* **que** *before nouns and personal pronouns (provided they are not followed by clauses) as well as before adverbs and prepositions:*
>
> **It was much more than a book**
> Era mucho más que un libro
> **She knows more than I do about such things**
> Ella sabe más que yo de esas cosas
> **Spain won more medals than ever before**
> España logró más medallas que nunca
>
> ▸ *Use* **más ... de lo que/del que/de la que/de los que/de las que** *with following clauses:*
>
> **It's much more complicated than you think**
> Es mucho más complicado de lo que te imaginas
> **There's much more violence now than there was in the seventies**
> Hay mucha más violencia ahora de la que había en los setenta
>
> ▸ *Use* **más** *with* **de** *before* **lo** *+ adjective/past participle:*
>
> **You'll have to work more quickly than usual**
> Tendrás que trabajar más rápido de lo normal
> **It was more difficult than expected**
> Fue más difícil de lo previsto
>
> ▸ *Use* **más** *with* **de** *in comparisons involving numbers or quantity:*
>
> **There were more than twenty people there**
> Había más de veinte personas allí
> **More than half are women**
> Más de la mitad son mujeres
> **They hadn't seen each other for more than a year**
> No se veían desde hacía más de un año
>
> ▸ *But* **más ... que** *can be used with numbers in more figurative comparisons:*
>
> **A picture is worth more than a thousand words**
> Una imagen vale más que mil palabras
>
> **Más ... que** *can be used before numbers in the construction* **no ... más que**, *meaning "only". Compare the following:*
>
> No gana más que 1000 euros al mes
> **He only earns 1000 euros a month**
> No gana más de 1000 euros al mes
> **He earns no more than 1000 euros a month**
>
> **A lot more**
>
> ▸ *When translating* **a lot more, far more** *etc remember to make the* **mucho** *in* **mucho más** *agree with any noun it describes or refers to:*
>
> **We eat much more junk food than we used to**
> Tomamos mucha más comida basura que antes
> **It's only one sign. There are a lot** *or* **many more**
> Solo es una señal. Hay muchas más
> **A lot more research will be needed**
> Harán falta muchos más estudios
>
> *For further uses and examples, see* **more**

moreish* ['mɔːrɪʃ] (ADJ) apetitoso

morello [mə'reləʊ] (N) (*also* **morello cherry**) guinda *f*

moreover [mɔː'rəʊvəʳ] (ADV) además, es más • **he discovered, moreover, that this was not the first time** descubrió, además, que esta no era la primera vez, es más, descubrió que esta no era la primera vez • **moreover, there were the children to consider** por otra parte *or* además, había que tener en cuenta a los niños

mores ['mɔːreɪz] (NPL) costumbres *fpl*

morganatic [,mɔːgə'nætɪk] (ADJ) morganático

morganatically [,mɔːgə'nætɪkəlɪ] (ADV) • **he married her ~** se casó con ella en casamiento morganático

morgue [mɔːg] (N) depósito *m* de cadáveres, morgue *f* (*esp LAm*)

MORI ['mɔːrɪ] (N ABBR) (= **Market & Opinion Research Institute**) *empresa británica que realiza sondeos de opinión y estudios de mercado*

moribund ['mɒrɪbʌnd] ADJ moribundo

Mormon ['mɔːmən] ADJ mormón
N mormón/ona *m/f*

Mormonism ['mɔːmənɪzəm] N mormonismo *m*

morn [mɔːn] N (*poet*) (= *morning*) mañana *f*; (= *dawn*) alborada *f*

morning ['mɔːnɪŋ] N mañana *f*; (*before dawn*) madrugada *f* • **he's generally out ~s*** por las mañanas no suele estar • **the ~ after** (*hum*) la mañana después de la juerga • **good ~!** ¡buenos días! • **in the ~** (= *during the morning*) por la mañana, en la mañana (*LAm*); (*tomorrow*) mañana por la mañana • **early in the ~** a primera hora de la mañana, muy de mañana • **at seven o'clock in the ~** a las siete de la mañana • **at three in the ~** a las tres de la madrugada • **the next ~** la mañana siguiente • **on Saturday ~** el sábado por la mañana • **tomorrow ~** mañana por la mañana • **yesterday ~** ayer por la mañana
CPD ▸ **morning coat** chaqué *m* ▸ **morning dress** chaqué *m*, traje *m* de etiqueta ▸ **morning glory** dondiego *m* de día, ipomea *f* ▸ **morning mist** bruma *f* del alba ▸ **morning paper** diario *m or* periódico *m* de la mañana ▸ **morning prayers** oficio *m* matinal ▸ **morning sickness** (*Med*) náuseas *fpl* del embarazo ▸ **morning star** lucero *m* del alba ▸ **morning tea** té *m* mañanero

morning-after ['mɔːnɪŋ'ɑːftəʳ] CPD ▸ **the morning-after pill** la píldora (anticonceptiva) del día después

Moroccan [mə'rɒkən] ADJ marroquí
N marroquí *mf*

Morocco [mə'rɒkəʊ] N Marruecos *m*

morocco [mə'rɒkəʊ] N (*also* **morocco leather**) marroquí *m*, tafilete *m*

moron ['mɔːrɒn] N **1*** (= *idiot*) imbécil *mf*
2 (*Med, Psych*†) retrasado/a *m/f* mental

moronic [mə'rɒnɪk] ADJ imbécil

morose [mə'rəʊs] ADJ malhumorado

morosely [mə'rəʊslɪ] ADV malhumoradamente, morbosamente

morph [mɔːf] N morfo *m*

morpheme ['mɔːfiːm] N morfema *m*

morphemic [mɔː'fiːmɪk] ADJ morfímico

morphia ['mɔːfɪə], **morphine** ['mɔːfiːn] N morfina *f*

morphing ['mɔːfɪŋ] N (*Cine*) morphing *m*, mutación *f* con efectos especiales

morphological [,mɔːfə'lɒdʒɪkəl] ADJ morfológico

morphologically [,mɔːfə'lɒdʒɪkəlɪ] ADV morfológicamente

morphologist [mɔː'fɒlədʒɪst] N morfólogo/a *m/f*

morphology [mɔː'fɒlədʒɪ] N morfología *f*

morphosyntax [,mɔːfəʊ'sɪntæks] N morfosintaxis *f inv*

morris dance ['mɒrɪs,dɑːns] N *baile tradicional inglés de hombres en el que estos llevan cascabeles en la ropa*

morris dancer ['mɒrɪs,dɑːnsəʳ] N *bailarín de un baile tradicional inglés de hombres en el que estos llevan cascabeles en la ropa*

morris dancing ['mɒrɪs,dɑːnsɪŋ] N (*Brit*) *baile tradicional inglés de hombres en el que estos llevan cascabeles en la ropa*

morrow ['mɒrəʊ] N • **on the ~** (*liter*) al día siguiente

Morse [mɔːs] N morse *m*
CPD ▸ **Morse code** alfabeto *m* Morse

morsel ['mɔːsl] N [*of food*] bocado *m*; (*fig*) pedazo *m*

mort. ABBR = **mortgage**

mortadella [,mɔːtə'delə] N mortadela *f*

mortal ['mɔːtl] ADJ **1** (= *destined to die*) mortal
2 (*liter*) (= *fatal*) [*wound, blow*] mortal
3 (= *deadly*) [*enemy*] mortal
4 (= *extreme*) [*terror*] espantoso • **she screamed in ~ terror** gritó aterrorizada • **to be in ~ danger** estar en peligro de muerte • **to live in ~ fear that ...** vivir aterrorizado de que ...
N mortal *mf* • **they are now reduced to the status of ordinary ~s** quedan ahora reducidos al estatus de simples mortales; ▹ **mere[2]**
CPD ▸ **mortal combat** combate *m* a muerte ▸ **mortal remains** restos *mpl* mortales ▸ **mortal sin** pecado *m* mortal

mortality [mɔː'tælɪtɪ] N **1** (= *condition*) mortalidad *f*
2 (= *fatalities*) mortandad *f*, número *m* de víctimas
CPD ▸ **mortality rate** tasa *f* de mortalidad ▸ **mortality table** tabla *f* de mortalidad

mortally ['mɔːtəlɪ] ADV **1** (= *fatally*) • **to be ~ wounded** estar herido de muerte, estar mortalmente herido
2 (= *extremely*) • **~ afraid** muerto de miedo • **he was ~ embarrassed** estaba terriblemente avergonzado, estaba cortadísimo* • **~ offended** profundamente ofendido

mortar ['mɔːtəʳ] N **1** (= *cannon*) mortero *m*
2 (= *cement*) argamasa *f*, mortero *m*; ▹ **brick**
3 (= *bowl*) mortero *m*
VT (*Mil*) bombardear con morteros

mortarboard ['mɔːtəbɔːd] N (*Univ*) birrete *m* cuadrado

mortgage ['mɔːgɪdʒ] N hipoteca *f* • **to pay off a ~** amortizar *or* liquidar *or* redimir una hipoteca • **to raise a ~** • **take out a ~** obtener una hipoteca (**on** sobre)
VT hipotecar
CPD ▸ **mortgage bank** banco *m* hipotecario, sociedad *f* de crédito hipotecario ▸ **mortgage broker** especialista *mf* en hipotecas ▸ **mortgage company** (*US*) = **mortgage bank** ▸ **mortgage lender** sociedad *f* hipotecaria ▸ **mortgage loan** préstamo *m* hipotecario ▸ **mortgage payment** pago *m* de la hipoteca, plazo *m* de la hipoteca ▸ **mortgage rate** tipo *m* de interés hipotecario

mortgageable ['mɔːgədʒəbl] ADJ hipotecable

mortgagee [,mɔːgə'dʒiː] N acreedor(a) *m/f* hipotecario/a

mortgager, mortgagor ['mɔːgədʒəʳ] N deudor(a) *m/f* hipotecario/a

mortice ['mɔːtɪs] N = **mortise**

mortician [mɔː'tɪʃən] N (*US*) director(a) *m/f* de pompas fúnebres

mortification [,mɔːtɪfɪ'keɪʃən] N mortificación *f*, humillación *f*, vergüenza *f*

mortify ['mɔːtɪfaɪ] VT avergonzar • **I was mortified (to find that ...)** me moría de vergüenza (al descubrir que ...)
VI (*Med*) gangrenarse

mortifying ['mɔːtɪfaɪɪŋ] ADJ humillante

mortise ['mɔːtɪs] N mortaja *f*
CPD ▸ **mortise lock** cerradura *f* de muesca

mortuary ['mɔːtjʊərɪ] N depósito *m* de cadáveres
ADJ mortuorio

Mosaic [məʊ'zeɪɪk] ADJ mosaico

mosaic [məʊ'zeɪɪk] N mosaico *m*

Moscow ['mɒskəʊ] N Moscú *m*

Moselle [məʊ'zel] N Mosela *m*

Moses ['məʊzɪs] N Moisés
CPD ▸ **Moses basket** moisés *m*

mosey ['məʊzɪ] VI • **to ~ along*** pasearse • **to ~ down to the shops** ir dando un paseo a las tiendas

Moslem ['mɒzlem] ADJ musulmán
N musulmán/ana *m/f*

mosque [mɒsk] N mezquita *f*

mosquito [mɒs'kiːtəʊ] N (PL: **mosquitoes**) mosquito *m*, zancudo *m* (*LAm*)
CPD ▸ **mosquito bite** picadura *f* de mosquito ▸ **mosquito coil** espiral *f* repelente ▸ **mosquito net** mosquitero *m*, mosquitera *f* ▸ **mosquito netting** mosquitero *m*, mosquitera *f* • **the ~ netting over the windows** el mosquitero en las ventanas ▸ **mosquito repellent** repelente *m* antimosquitos

moss [mɒs] N (*Bot*) musgo *m*; ▹ **rolling**
CPD ▸ **moss stitch** punto *m* de musgo

Mossad ['mɒsæd] N Mossad *m*

mossy ['mɒsɪ] ADJ musgoso, cubierto de musgo

most [məʊst] ADJ SUPERL **1** (*making comparisons*) más • **who has (the) ~ money?** ¿quién tiene más dinero? • **for the ~ part** por lo general
2 (= *the majority of*) la mayoría de, la mayor parte de • **~ men** la mayoría de *or* la mayor parte de los hombres • **~ people go out on Friday nights** la mayoría de *or* la mayor parte de la gente sale los viernes por la noche
N, PRON • **~ of it** la mayor parte • **~ of them** la mayoría de ellos, la mayor parte de ellos • **~ of the money** la mayor parte del dinero • **~ of the time** la mayor parte del tiempo, gran parte del tiempo • **~ of those present** la mayoría de *or* la mayor parte de los asistentes • **~ of her friends** la mayoría de *or* la mayor parte de sus amigos • **do the ~ you can** haz lo que puedas • **at (the) ~** • **at the very ~** como máximo, a lo sumo • **20 minutes at the ~** 20 minutos como máximo *or* a lo sumo • **to get the ~ out of a situation** sacar el máximo partido a una situación • **to make the ~ of sth** (= *make good use of*) aprovechar algo al máximo, sacar el máximo partido a algo; (= *enjoy*) disfrutar algo al máximo • **to make the ~ of one's advantages** aprovechar al máximo las propias ventajas • **he made the ~ of the story** explotó todas las posibilidades del cuento
ADV **1** (*superl*) más • **he spent ~** él gastó más • **the ~ difficult question** la pregunta más difícil • **which one did it ~ easily?** ¿quién lo hizo con mayor facilidad?
2 (= *extremely*) sumamente, muy • **~ holy** santísimo • **a ~ interesting book** un libro interesantísimo *or* sumamente interesante • **you have been ~ kind** ha sido usted muy amable • **~ likely** lo más probable;
▹ MAJORITY, MOST

...most [məʊst] SUFFIX más • **centremost** más central • **furthermost** más lejano

mostly ['məʊstlɪ] ADV (= *mainly*) en su mayoría, en su mayor parte • **they are ~ women** en su mayoría *or* en su mayor parte son mujeres, la mayoría *or* casi todas son mujeres • **this part of the country is ~ unspoiled** esta zona del país conserva, en su mayor parte, su belleza natural • **owls hunt ~ at night** el búho caza principalmente *or* sobre todo de noche • **~ because ...** principalmente porque ..., sobre todo porque ... • **it's ~ finished** está casi terminado

MOT (*Brit*) N ABBR **1** (= **Ministry of Transport**) ≈ Ministerio *m* de Transportes
2 (*Aut*) (*also* **MOT test**) (= **Ministry of Transport test**) *examen anual de coches obligatorio*, ≈ Inspección *f* Técnica de Vehículos (*Sp*), ≈ ITV *f* (*Sp*) • **to pass the MOT** (*Aut*) ≈ pasar la ITV (*Sp*) • **MOT certificate** ≈ certificado *m* de la ITV (*Sp*)
VT • **I got my car MOT'd last month** ≈ el coche pasó la ITV el mes pasado • **car for**

sale, MOT'd till June ≈ se vende coche, ITV válida hasta junio

mote [məʊt] N átomo *m*, mota *f* • **to see the ~ in our neighbour's eye and not the beam in our own** ver la paja en el ojo ajeno y no la viga en el propio

motel [məʊ'tel] N motel *m*

motet [məʊ'tet] N motete *m*

moth [mɒθ] N mariposa *f* nocturna; (= *clothes moth*) polilla *f*
CPD ▸ **moth repellent** antipolilla *m*

mothball ['mɒθbɔːl] N bola *f* de naftalina • **in ~s** (*Naut*) en la reserva • **to put sth in ~s** [+ *project*] aparcar algo, dejar algo aparcado
VT [+ *ship*] poner en la reserva; [+ *project*] aparcar, dejar aparcado

moth-eaten ['mɒθ,iːtn] ADJ apolillado

mother ['mʌðəʳ] N madre *f* • **to be like a ~ to sb** ser como una madre para algn
VT (= *care for*) cuidar como una madre; (= *spoil*) mimar, consentir; (= *give birth to*) parir, dar a luz
CPD ▸ **mother country** patria *f*; (*more sentimentally*) madre patria *f* ▸ **Mother Earth** la madre tierra ▸ **mother figure** figura *f* materna, figura *f* de la madre ▸ **Mother Goose** la Oca ▸ **mother hen** gallina *f* madre ▸ **mother love** amor *m* maternal ▸ **Mother Nature** la madre Naturaleza ▸ **Mother's Day** Día *m* de la Madre ▸ **mother's help** niñera *f* ▸ **Mother of God** madre *f* de Dios ▸ **mother ship** buque *m* nodriza ▸ **Mother Superior** madre *f* superiora ▸ **mother tongue** lengua *f* materna

motherboard ['mʌðə,bɔːd] N (*Comput*) placa *f* base

mothercraft ['mʌðəkrɑːft] N arte *m* de cuidar a los niños pequeños, arte *m* de ser madre

motherfucker** ['mʌðə,fʌkəʳ] N (*US*) hijoputa** *m*, hijaputa** *f*

motherfucking** ['mʌðə,fʌkɪŋ] ADJ (*US*) pijotero‡, condenado*

motherhood ['mʌðəhʊd] N maternidad *f* • **to prepare for ~** prepararse para ser madre

mothering ['mʌðərɪŋ] N cuidados *mpl* maternales
CPD ▸ **Mothering Sunday** (*Brit*) fiesta *f* de la Madre

mother-in-law ['mʌðərɪnlɔː] N (PL: **mothers-in-law**) suegra *f*

motherland ['mʌðəlænd] N patria *f*; (*more sentimentally*) madre patria *f*

motherless ['mʌðəlɪs] ADJ huérfano de madre, sin madre

motherly ['mʌðəlɪ] ADJ maternal

mother-of-pearl ['mʌðərəv'pɜːl] N madreperla *f*, nácar *m*
ADJ nacarado

mother-to-be ['mʌðətə'biː] N (PL: **mothers-to-be**) futura madre *f*

moth-hole ['mɒθhəʊl] N apolilladura *f*

mothproof ['mɒθpruːf] ADJ a prueba de polillas

motif [məʊ'tiːf] N (*Art, Mus*) motivo *m*; [*of speech etc*] tema *m*; (*Sew*) adorno *m*

motion ['məʊʃən] N **1** (= *movement*) movimiento *m* • **to be in ~** (*lit*) estar en movimiento • **plans are already in ~ for a new opera house** ya hay planes en marcha para la construcción de un nuevo teatro de la ópera • **to set in ~** [+ *mechanism*] poner en marcha • **the strike set in ~ a chain of events which led to his overthrow** la huelga desencadenó una serie de acontecimientos que condujeron a su derrocamiento
• IDIOMS: • **to go through the ~s (of doing sth)**: • **he was just going through the ~s of living** estaba viviendo maquinalmente, vivía por inercia • **they went through the ~s of consulting members** siguieron la formalidad de consultar a los miembros • **to set the wheels in ~ (to do sth)** poner las cosas en marcha (para hacer algo);
▹ **perpetual, slow, time**
2 (= *gesture*) gesto *m*, ademán *m* • **he made a chopping ~ with his hand** hizo un gesto como si fuera a cortar algo con la mano, hizo un ademán de cortar algo con la mano
3 (= *proposal*) moción *f* • **the ~ was carried/defeated** la moción fue aprobada/rechazada • **to propose** *or* (*US*) **make a ~ (that ...)** presentar una moción (para que (+ *subjun*) • **to propose** *or* (*US*) **make a ~ (to do sth)** presentar una moción (para hacer algo) • **to vote on a ~** votar una moción
4 (*US*) (*Jur*) petición *f* • **to file a ~ (for sth/to do sth)** presentar una petición (para algo/para hacer algo)
5 (*Brit*) (*frm*) (*also* **bowel motion**) (= *action*) evacuación *f*; (= *stool*) deposición *f* • **to have** *or* **pass a ~** evacuar el vientre
6 [*of watch, clock*] mecanismo *m*
VT • **he ~ed me to a chair/to sit down** con un gesto indicó que me sentara, hizo señas para que me sentara • **to ~ sb in(side)/out(side)** señalar *or* indicar a algn con un gesto que entre/salga
VI • **he ~ed for the doors to be opened** hizo un gesto *or* hizo señas para que se abrieran las puertas • **to ~ to sb to do sth** indicar a algn con un gesto que haga algo, hacer señas a algn para que haga algo
CPD ▸ **motion of censure** (*Parl*) moción *f* de censura ▸ **motion picture** (*esp US*) película *f* ▸ **motion picture camera** (*esp US*) cámara *f* cinematográfica, cámara *f* de cine ▸ **the motion picture industry** la industria cinematográfica ▸ **motion picture theater** (*US*) cine *m* ▸ **motion sickness** mareo *m*

motionless ['məʊʃənlɪs] ADJ inmóvil • **to remain ~** permanecer inmóvil, permanecer sin moverse

motivate ['məʊtɪveɪt] VT motivar • **to be ~d to do sth** tener motivación *or* estar motivado para hacer algo • **he is highly ~d** tiene una fuerte motivación, está muy motivado • **the campaign is politically ~d** la campaña tiene una motivación política

motivation [,məʊtɪ'veɪʃən] N motivación *f*

motivational [,məʊtɪ'veɪʃənl] ADJ [*problem, factor*] de motivación
CPD ▸ **motivational research** estudios *mpl* motivacionales

motive ['məʊtɪv] N motivo *m*; (*for crime*) móvil *m* • **what can his ~ have been?** ¿qué motivos habrá tenido? • **my ~s were of the purest** lo hice con la mejor intención
ADJ motor (*fem: motora/motriz*)
CPD ▸ **motive power** fuerza *f* motriz

motiveless ['məʊtɪvlɪs] ADV sin motivo, inmotivado

motley ['mɒtlɪ] ADJ (= *many-coloured*) multicolor, abigarrado; (= *ill-assorted*) [*collection, bunch*] variopinto • **they were a ~ crew** era una pandilla de lo más variopinto
N botarga *f*, traje *m* de colores

motocross ['məʊtəkrɒs] N motocross *m*

motor ['məʊtəʳ] N **1** (= *engine*) motor *m*
2* (= *car*) coche *m*, automóvil *m*, carro *m* (*LAm*), auto *m* (*esp LAm*)
VI † ir en coche *etc* • **we ~ed down to Ascot** fuimos en coche a Ascot • **we ~ed over to see them** fuimos a visitarlos (en coche)
ADJ (= *giving motion*) [*nerve, muscle*] motor (*fem: motora/motriz*); (= *motorized*) automóvil
CPD ▸ **motor accident** accidente *m* de circulación ▸ **motor home** autocaravana *f* ▸ **motor industry** industria *f* automovilística ▸ **motor insurance** seguro *m* de automóvil ▸ **motor launch** lancha *f* motora ▸ **motor mechanic** mecánico/a *m/f* de automóviles ▸ **motor neurone disease, motor neuron disease** esclerosis *f* lateral amiotrófica ▸ **motor oil** aceite *m* para motores ▸ **motor racing** (*Sport*) carreras *fpl* de coches, automovilismo *m* ▸ **motor racing track** pista *f* de automovilismo, circuito *m* de automovilismo ▸ **motor scooter** Vespa® *f*, escúter *m*, motoneta *f* (*LAm*) ▸ **motor show** feria *f* de automóviles • **the Paris ~ show** el salón del automóvil de París ▸ **motor trade** • **the ~ trade** el sector automovilístico ▸ **motor transport** transporte *m* rodado, transporte *m* motorizado ▸ **motor vehicle** automóvil *m* ▸ **motor vessel** motonave *f*

motorail ['məʊtəreɪl] N motorraíl *m*

motorbike ['məʊtəbaɪk] N motocicleta *f*, moto *f*

motorboat ['məʊtəbəʊt] N lancha *f* motora, motora *f*

motorcade ['məʊtəkeɪd] N desfile *m* de automóviles

motorcar ['məʊtəkɑːʳ] N (*frm*) coche *m*, automóvil *m*

motorcoach ['məʊtəkəʊtʃ] N autocar *m*, autobús *m*, camión *m* (*Mex*), micro *m* (*Arg*)

motorcycle ['məʊtə,saɪkl] N motocicleta *f*, moto *f*
CPD ▸ **motorcycle combination** motocicleta *f* con sidecar ▸ **motorcycle racing** carreras *fpl* de motos

motorcycling ['məʊtə,saɪklɪŋ] N motociclismo *m*, motorismo *m*

motorcyclist ['məʊtə,saɪklɪst] N motociclista *mf*, motorista *mf*

motor-driven ['məʊtə'drɪvn] ADJ automóvil, propulsado por motor

-motored ['məʊtəd] ADJ (*ending in compounds*) • **four-motored** cuatrimotor • **petrol-motored** de gasolina

motoring ['məʊtərɪŋ] ADJ [*accident*] de tráfico, de circulación • **~ holiday** vacaciones *fpl* en coche • **the ~ public** los automovilistas
N automovilismo *m* • **school of ~** autoescuela *f*, escuela *f* de manejo (*LAm*)
CPD ▸ **motoring offence** infracción *f* de tráfico ▸ **motoring organization** asociación *f* de automovilistas

motorist ['məʊtərɪst] N conductor(a) *m/f*, automovilista *mf*

motorization [,məʊtəraɪ'zeɪʃən] N motorización *f*

motorize ['məʊtəraɪz] VT motorizar

motorized ['məʊtəraɪzd] ADJ motorizado • **to be ~** tener coche, estar motorizado* • **now that we're ~*** ahora que tenemos coche, ahora que estamos motorizados* • **to get ~** comprarse un coche, motorizarse*

motorman ['məʊtəmən] N (PL: **motormen**) (*US*) conductor *m* de locomotora eléctrica *etc*, maquinista *m*

motormouth‡ ['məʊtəmaʊθ] N cotorra* *f*

motor-mower ['məʊtə,məʊəʳ] N cortacésped *m* a motor

motorway ['məʊtəweɪ] N (*Brit*) autopista *f*
CPD ▸ **motorway madness** locura *f* en la autopista ▸ **motorway service area** área *f* de servicios de autopista ▸ **motorway services** servicios *mpl* en autopista

mottled ['mɒtld] ADJ [*egg*] moteado; [*leaf, colour*] jaspeado; [*marble*] jaspeado, veteado; [*complexion, skin*] con manchas • **~ blue and white** moteado/jaspeado de azul y blanco • **~ with brown** con manchas marrones

motto ['mɒtəʊ] N (PL: **mottoes** *or* **mottos**) **1** [*of family, person*] lema *m*
2 (*Heraldry*) divisa *f*

3 (= *watchword*) consigna *f*
4 (*in cracker*) (= *joke*) chiste *m*
mould¹, **mold** (*US*) [məʊld] N (= *fungus*) moho *m*; (= *iron mould*) orín *m*
mould², **mold** (*US*) [məʊld] N (*Art, Culin, Tech etc*) molde *m* • **cast in a heroic ~** de carácter heroico • IDIOM: • **to break the ~**: • **they broke the ~ when they made him** rompieron el molde después de hacerlo a él
VT 1 (= *fashion*) moldear; (= *cast*) vaciar • **~ed plastics** plásticos *mpl* moldeados
2 (*fig*) formar • **it is ~ed on ...** está hecho según ... • **to ~ o.s. on sb** tomar a algn como ejemplo
mould³, **mold** (*US*) [məʊld] N (= *soil*) mantillo *m*
moulder, **molder** (*US*) ['məʊldəʳ] VI (*also* **moulder away**) desmoronarse; (*fig*) desmoronarse, decaer
mouldering, **moldering** (*US*) ['məʊldərɪŋ] ADJ [*house*] que se está desmoronando; [*leaves*] podrido
mouldiness, **moldiness** (*US*) ['məʊldɪnɪs] N moho *m*, lo mohoso
moulding, **molding** (*US*) ['məʊldɪŋ] N
1 (*Archit*) moldura *f*
2 (= *process*) moldeado *m*
3 (= *cast*) vaciado *m*
4 (*fig*) amoldamiento *m*, formación *f*
mouldy, **moldy** (*US*) ['məʊldɪ] ADJ (COMPAR: **mouldier**, SUPERL: **mouldiest**)
1 (= *covered with mould*) [*cheese, bread*] mohoso, enmohecido; [*mattress, clothing*] enmohecido, lleno de moho • **to go ~** enmohecerse, criar moho • **to smell ~** oler a moho *or* a humedad
2 (*Brit†**) (= *lousy*) cochino*
moult, **molt** (*US*) [məʊlt] VI [*bird*] mudar las plumas; [*mammal*] mudar el pelo; [*snake*] mudar la piel
VT [+ *feathers, hair*] mudar
N muda *f*
mound [maʊnd] N 1 (= *pile*) montón *m*
2 (= *hillock*) montículo *m*; (= *burial mound*) túmulo *m*; (= *earthwork*) terraplén *m*
mount¹ [maʊnt] N 1 (*liter*) monte *m* • **the Sermon on the Mount** el Sermón de la Montaña
2 (*in names*) monte *m* • **the Mount of Olives** el monte de los Olivos • **Mount Sinai** el monte Sinaí • **Mount Everest** el Everest
mount² [maʊnt] N 1 (= *horse*) montura *f*, caballería *f* (*frm*)
2 (= *support, base*) [*of machine*] soporte *m*, base *f*; [*of jewel*] engaste *m*, montura *f*; (*for stamps*) fijasellos *m inv*; (*for photograph in album*) fijafotografías *m inv* adhesivo; (*for transparency*) marco *m*; [*of specimen, exhibit*] soporte *m*; (= *microscope slide*) portaobjetos *m inv*; (= *backing for picture*) fondo *m*
VT 1 [+ *horse*] montar; [+ *bicycle*] montar en; [+ *platform, stage, podium, throne*] subir a; [+ *stairs, hill*] subir • **the vehicle ~ed the pavement** el vehículo se subió a la acera
2 [+ *jewel*] engastar; [+ *stamp, exhibit, specimen, TV, speakers*] fijar; [+ *picture*] poner un fondo a; [+ *gun, engine*] montar
3 [+ *exhibition, campaign, event*] montar, organizar; [+ *play*] montar, poner en escena; [+ *attack, offensive, defence*] preparar
4 • **to ~ guard (on** *or* **over sth/sb)** montar (la) guardia (para vigilar algo/a algn)
5 (*in mating*) cubrir, montar
6 (= *provide with horse*) proveer de caballo
VI 1 (= *climb*) subir • **the blood ~ed to his cheeks** la sangre (se) le subió a los carrillos
2 (*also* **mount up**) (= *get on horse*) montar
3 (= *increase*) [*prices, temperature*] subir, aumentar; [*excitement, tension*] crecer, aumentar
4 (*also* **mount up**) (= *accumulate*) [*bills, debts, problems*] amontonarse
mountain ['maʊntɪn] N (*lit*) montaña *f*; (*fig*) [*of work etc*] montón *m* • **in the ~s** en la montaña • IDIOM: • **to make a ~ out of a molehill** hacer una montaña de un grano de arena
CPD ▸ **mountain ash** serbal *m* ▸ **mountain bike** bicicleta *f* de montaña ▸ **mountain chain** (*large*) cordillera *f*, cadena *f* montañosa; (*smaller*) sierra *f* ▸ **mountain climber** alpinista *mf*, montañero/a *m/f* ▸ **mountain dew*** *whisky destilado clandestinamente* ▸ **mountain goat** cabra *f* montés ▸ **mountain hut** albergue *m* de montaña ▸ **mountain lion** puma *m* ▸ **mountain pass** puerto *m* *or* paso *m* de montaña ▸ **mountain range** (*large*) cordillera *f*; (*smaller*) sierra *f* ▸ **mountain refuge** albergue *m* de montaña ▸ **mountain rescue** servicio *m* de rescate de montaña ▸ **mountain rescue team** equipo *m* de rescate de montaña ▸ **mountain sickness** mal *m* de montaña, puna *f* (*LAm*), soroche *m* (*LAm*)
mountainboarding ['maʊntɪn,bɔːdɪŋ] N mountainboarding *m*
mountaineer [,maʊntɪ'nɪəʳ] N alpinista *mf*, andinista *mf* (*LAm*)
VI dedicarse al montañismo, hacer alpinismo
mountaineering [,maʊntɪ'nɪərɪŋ] N alpinismo *m*, andinismo *m* (*LAm*)
CPD montañero, alpinista
mountainous ['maʊntɪnəs] ADJ 1 (*lit*) montañoso
2 (*fig*) gigantesco
mountainside ['maʊntɪnsaɪd] N ladera *f* de montaña, falda *f* de montaña
mountaintop ['maʊntɪntɒp] N cima *f* de la montaña, cumbre *f* de la montaña
mountebank ['maʊntɪbæŋk] N saltabanco *m*, saltimbanqui *m*
mounted ['maʊntɪd] ADJ 1 (*on horseback*) montado • **the ~ police** la policía montada
2 [*photograph*] montado
Mountie* ['maʊntɪ] N (*Canada*) miembro *m* de la policía montada canadiense • **the ~s** la policía montada canadiense
mounting ['maʊntɪŋ] N 1 (= *act*) [*of machine*] montaje *m*
2 (= *support, base*) = **mount²**
ADJ [*concern, tension, excitement, opposition, unemployment*] creciente; [*debts*] cada vez mayor • **we watched with ~ horror as ...** observábamos cada vez más aterrorizados como ... • **to be under ~ pressure to do sth** encontrarse cada vez más presionado para hacer algo • **there is ~ evidence that ...** hay pruebas, cada vez más concluyentes, de que ...
mourn [mɔːn] VT [+ *person*] (= *grieve for*) llorar (la muerte de); (= *be in mourning for*) estar de luto *or* duelo por; [+ *death, loss*] lamentar, sentir • **Conservatives ~ the passing of family values** los conservadores se lamentan de la desaparición de los valores familiares
VI (= *be in mourning*) estar de luto *or* duelo • **when a relative dies one needs time to ~** (= *grieve*) cuando un pariente muere se necesita tiempo para llorarlo *or* llorar su muerte • **to ~ for sb** llorar a algn, llorar la muerte de algn • **it is no use ~ing for what might have been** no sirve de nada lamentarse por lo que podría haber sido • **he was ~ing over his lost love** lloraba por su amor perdido
mourner ['mɔːnəʳ] N doliente *mf*; (*hired*) plañidero/a *m/f*
mournful ['mɔːnfʊl] ADJ [*person*] afligido; [*tone, sound*] triste, lúgubre; [*occasion*] triste, luctuoso
mournfully ['mɔːnfəlɪ] ADV tristemente
mournfulness ['mɔːnfʊlnɪs] N [*of expression, sigh*] tristeza *f*; [*of person*] aflicción *f*
mourning ['mɔːnɪŋ] N luto *m*, duelo *m*; (= *dress*) luto *m* • **to be in ~ (for sb)** estar de luto *or* duelo (por algn) • **to wear ~** llevar luto • **to come out of ~** dejar el luto • **to plunge a town into ~** poner de luto a una ciudad
CPD ▸ **mourning clothes** luto *m*
mouse [maʊs] N (PL: **mice**) 1 (*Zool*) ratón *m*
2 (*Comput*) ratón *m*
VI cazar ratones
CPD ▸ **mouse mat**, **mouse pad** (*Comput*) alfombrilla *f*, almohadilla *f*
mousehole ['maʊshəʊl] N ratonera *f*
mouser ['maʊsəʳ] N cazador *m* de ratones
mousetrap ['maʊstræp] N ratonera *f*
CPD ▸ **mousetrap cheese*** queso *m* corriente
mousey ['maʊsɪ] ADJ = mousy
moussaka [mʊ'sɑːkə] N musaca *f*
mousse [muːs] N 1 (*Culin*) mousse *m* *or* *f* • **chocolate ~** mousse *m* *or* *f* de chocolate
2 (*for hair*) espuma *f*
moustache, **mustache** (*US*) [mə'stɑːʃ] N bigote *m* • **to wear a ~** tener bigote • **he's got a ~** tiene bigote • **a tall man with a ~** un hombre alto con bigote
moustachioed, **mustachioed** (*US*) [mə'stɑːʃɪəʊd] ADJ bigotudo
mousy ['maʊsɪ] ADJ (COMPAR: **mousier**, SUPERL: **mousiest**) [*person*] tímido; [*colour, hair*] pardusco
mouth [maʊθ] N (PL: **mouths** [maʊðz]) (*Anat*) boca *f*; [*of bottle*] boca *f*, abertura *f*; [*of cave*] entrada *f*; [*of river*] desembocadura *f*; [*of channel*] embocadero *m*; [*of wind instrument*] boquilla *f* • **to foam** *or* **froth at the ~** espumajear • **to open one's ~** (*lit, fig*) abrir la boca • **he never opened his ~ at the meeting** en la reunión no abrió la boca • **she didn't dare to open her ~** no se atrevió a decir ni pío • IDIOMS: • **he's all ~ and (no) trousers** (*Brit**) se le va (toda) la fuerza por la boca*, es un fanfarrón *or* un fantasma* • **to be down in the ~** estar deprimido • **to shoot one's ~ off*** hablar más de la cuenta • **to keep one's ~ shut*** callarse, no decir ni esta boca es mía • **shut your ~!‡** ¡cállate ya! • **to stop sb's ~‡** hacer callar a algn • **watch your ~!‡** ¡cuidadito con lo que dices! • **to put words into sb's ~** poner palabras en boca de algn; ▹ **big**
VT [maʊð] (*insincerely*) soltar; (*affectedly*) pronunciar con afectación, articular con rimbombancia • **"go away!" she ~ed** —¡vete de aquí! —dijo moviendo mudamente los labios
CPD [maʊθ] ▸ **mouth organ** (*esp Brit*) armónica *f*
-mouthed [maʊðd] ADJ (*ending in compounds*) de boca ..., que tiene la boca ... • **big-mouthed** de boca grande
mouthful ['maʊθfʊl] N [*of food*] bocado *m*; [*of drink*] trago *m*; [*of smoke, air*] bocanada *f* • **the name is a bit of a ~** es un nombre kilométrico • **you said a ~** (*US**) ¡y que lo digas!, ¡tú lo has dicho!
mouthpiece ['maʊθpiːs] N 1 (*Mus*) boquilla *f*
2 [*of telephone*] micrófono *m*
3 (= *person, publication*) portavoz *mf*
mouth-to-mouth ['maʊθtə'maʊθ] CPD ▸ **mouth-to-mouth resuscitation** (respiración *f*) boca a boca *m*
mouthwash ['maʊθwɒʃ] N elixir *m* bucal

m

mouthwatering ['maʊθ'wɔːtərɪŋ] ADJ muy apetitoso, que hace la boca agua

mouthy* ['maʊðɪ] ADJ • **to be ~** ser charlatán

movable ['muːvəbl] ADJ movible, móvil • **~ feast** fiesta *f* movible • **not easily ~** nada fácil de mover
NPL • **~s** muebles *mpl*, mobiliario *msing*; (*Jur*) bienes *mpl* muebles

move [muːv] N **1** (= *movement*) movimiento *m* • **to watch sb's every ~** observar a algn sin perder detalle, acechar a algn cada movimiento • **to get a ~ on (with sth)*** (= *hurry up*) darse prisa *or* (*LAm*) apurarse (con algo) • **get a ~ on!*** ¡date prisa!, ¡apúrate! (*LAm*) • **to make a ~** (= *start to leave, go*) ponerse en marcha • **it was midnight and no-one had made a ~** era medianoche pero nadie daba señales de irse • **it's time we made a ~** es hora de irnos • **to be on the ~** (= *travelling*) estar de viaje; [*troops, army*] estar avanzando • **to be always on the ~** [*nomads, circus*] andar siempre de aquí para allá; [*animal, child*] no saber estar quieto • **Spain is a country on the ~** España es país en marcha
2 (*in game*) (= *turn*) jugada *f* • **whose ~ is it?** ¿a quién le toca jugar? • **it's my ~** es mi turno, me toca a mí • **to have the first ~** salir
3 (*fig*) (= *step, action*) • **the government's first ~** la primera gestión del gobierno • **what's the next ~?** ¿qué hacemos ahora?, y ahora ¿qué? • **that was a bad ~** fue una mala decisión • **there was a ~ to defeat the proposal** se tomaron medidas para rechazar la propuesta • **to make a ~/the first ~** dar un/el primer paso • **it's up to him to make the first ~** le toca a él dar el primer paso • **without making the least ~ to** (+ *infin*) sin hacer la menor intención de (+ *infin*)
4 (= *house removal*) mudanza *f*; (*to different job*) traslado *m* • **it's our third ~ in two years** esta es la tercera vez en dos años que nos mudamos
VT **1** (= *change place of*) cambiar de lugar, cambiar de sitio; [+ *part of body*] mover; [+ *chess piece etc*] jugar, mover; (= *transport*) transportar, trasladar • **you've ~d all my things!** ¡has cambiado de sitio todas mis cosas! • **if we can ~ the table a few inches** si podemos mover la mesa unos centímetros • **can you ~ your fingers?** ¿puedes mover los dedos? • **to ~ house** mudarse • **~ your chair nearer the fire** acerca *or* arrima la silla al fuego • **~ the cupboard out of the corner** saca el armario del rincón • **he ~d his family out of the war zone** trasladó a su familia fuera de la zona de guerra • **he asked to be ~d to London/to a new department** pidió el traslado a Londres/a otro departamento
2 (= *cause sth to move*) mover • **the breeze ~d the leaves gently** la brisa movía *or* agitaba dulcemente las hojas • **to ~ one's bowels** hacer de vientre, evacuar • **~ those children off the grass!** ¡quite esos niños del césped!; ▷ **heaven**
3 (= *change timing of*) • **to ~ sth forward/back** [+ *event, date*] adelantar/aplazar algo • **we'll have to ~ the meeting to later in the week** tendremos que aplazar la reunión para otro día de la semana
4 (*fig*) (= *sway*) • **he will not be easily ~d** no se dejará convencer • **"we shall not be ~d"** "no nos moverán"
5 (= *motivate*) • **to ~ sb to do sth** mover *or* inducir a algn a hacer algo • **I'll do it when the spirit ~s me** (*hum*) lo haré cuando sienta la revelación divina (*hum*)
6 (*emotionally*) conmover, emocionar • **to be ~d** estar conmovido • **to be easily ~d** ser impresionable, ser sensible • **to ~ sb to tears/anger** hacer llorar/enfadar a algn • **to ~ sb to pity** provocar la compasión de algn
7 (*frm*) (= *propose*) • **to ~ a resolution** proponer una resolución • **to ~ that ...** proponer que ...
8 (*Comm*) [+ *merchandise*] colocar, vender
VI **1** (*gen*) moverse • **she ~s beautifully** se mueve con elegancia • **move!** ¡muévete!, ¡menéate! • **don't ~!** ¡no te muevas! • **I saw something moving in the bushes** vi moverse algo entre los arbustos • **you can't ~ for books in that room*** hay tantos libros en esa habitación que es casi imposible moverse • **to ~ freely** [*piece of machinery*] tener juego; [*person, traffic*] circular libremente • **I won't ~ from here** no me muevo de aquí • **to ~ in high society** frecuentar la buena sociedad • **let's ~ into the garden** vamos al jardín • **he has ~d into another class** se ha cambiado de clase • **they hope to ~ into the British market** quieren introducirse en *or* penetrar el mercado británico • **keep moving!** ¡no te pares!; (*order from traffic policeman*) ¡circulen! • **the policeman kept the traffic moving** el policía mantuvo la circulación fluida • **the procession ~d slowly out of sight** la procesión avanzaba lentamente hasta que desapareció en la distancia • **it's time we were moving** es hora de irnos • **she ~d to the next room** pasó a la habitación de al lado • **he ~d slowly towards the door** avanzó *or* se acercó lentamente hacia la puerta • **to ~ to** *or* **towards independence** avanzar *or* encaminarse hacia la independencia
2 (= *move house*) mudarse, trasladarse • **the family ~d to a new house** la familia se mudó *or* se trasladó a una casa nueva • **to ~ to the country** mudarse *or* trasladarse al campo • **the company has ~d to larger offices** la empresa se ha trasladado *or* mudado a oficinas mayores
3 (= *travel*) ir; (= *be in motion*) estar en movimiento • **the bus was moving at 50kph** el autobús iba a 50kph • **the car was not moving** el coche no estaba en movimiento • **do not get out while the bus is moving** no se baje mientras el autobús esté en marcha • **he was certainly moving!*** ¡iba como el demonio!
4 (*Comm*) [*goods*] venderse
5 (= *progress*) • **things are moving at last** por fin se empiezan a mover las cosas • **he certainly knows how to get things moving** ese sí que sabe poner las cosas en marcha
6 (*in games*) jugar, hacer una jugada • **who ~s next?** ¿a quién le toca jugar? • **it's you to ~** te toca a ti jugar • **white ~s** (*Chess*) blanco juega • **the knight ~s like this** el caballo se mueve así
7 (= *take steps*) dar un paso, tomar medidas • **the government must ~ first** el gobierno ha de dar el primer paso • **the council ~d to stop the abuse** el consejo tomó medidas para corregir el abuso • **we'll have to ~ quickly if we want to get that contract** tendremos que actuar inmediatamente si queremos hacernos con ese contrato

▸ **move about, move around** VT + ADV **1** (= *place in different position*) cambiar de sitio
2 (= *employee*) trasladar de un sitio a otro
VI + ADV **1** (= *fidget*) moverse
2 (= *walk about*) andar
3 (= *travel*) viajar de un sitio a otro • **to ~ about freely** circular libremente

▸ **move along** VT + ADV [+ *crowd*] hacer circular
VI + ADV **1** [*crowd*] circular • **~ along there!** ¡circulen!
2 (= *move forward*) avanzar, adelantarse
3 (*on bench etc*) correrse, hacerse a un lado

▸ **move aside** VT + ADV apartar
VI + ADV apartarse, ponerse a un lado, quitarse de en medio

▸ **move away** VT + ADV **1** (*gen*) apartar, alejar
2 (= *move to another place*) mover
VI + ADV **1** (= *move aside*) apartarse
2 (= *leave*) irse, marcharse • **to ~ away (from)** marcharse (de)
3 (= *move house*) mudarse

▸ **move back** VT + ADV **1** [+ *crowd*] hacer retroceder
2 (*to former place*) volver, regresar
3 [+ *employee*] volver a trasladar
4 (= *postpone*) aplazar, posponer • **let's ~ the meeting back to Friday** vamos a aplazar *or* posponer la reunión hasta el viernes
VI + ADV **1** (= *withdraw*) retroceder, retirarse
2 (*to former place*) volver, regresar
3 (= *move house*) • **they ~d back to Burgos again** volvieron a mudarse a Burgos

▸ **move down** VT + ADV **1** [+ *person, object*] bajar
2 (*on bench etc*) hacer correrse
3 (*Scol*) [+ *pupil*] • **I may have to ~ you down (a group)** puede que tenga que ponerte en un nivel más bajo
VI + ADV **1** [*person, object*] bajar
2 (*on bench etc*) correrse
3 (*Scol*) [*pupil*] • **he has had to ~ down one class** ha tenido que cambiarse al curso inmediatamente inferior
4 (*Sport*) (*in league*) descender (a la división inferior *etc*)

▸ **move forward** VT + ADV **1** avanzar
2 (= *bring forward*) [+ *date, meeting*] adelantar • **to ~ the clocks forward** adelantar los relojes
VI + ADV adelantarse

▸ **move in** VT + ADV (= *take inside*) meter, llevar hacia dentro
VI + ADV **1** (*into accommodation*) instalarse • **to ~ in with sb** irse a vivir con algn
2 (= *start operations*) ponerse manos a la obra, intervenir; (*Comm*) (*to new market*) introducirse • **drug dealers soon ~d in** los traficantes de drogas se pusieron rápidamente manos a la obra
3 (= *come closer*) acercarse (**on** a); [*army*] avanzar (**on** sobre)

▸ **move off** VT + ADV sacar
VI + ADV **1** (= *go away*) irse, marcharse
2 (= *start moving*) ponerse en marcha

▸ **move on** VT + ADV **1** [+ *crowd etc*] hacer circular
2 [+ *hands of clock*] adelantar
VI + ADV **1** [*person, vehicle*] circular
2 (*fig*) **a** [*time*] pasar
b (*to new job*) • **this training will prove useful when you want to ~ on** esta formación te resultará útil cuando quieras cambiar de trabajo • **she wanted to ~ on to a bigger company** quería irse a trabajar a una empresa mayor
c (*in discussion*) pasar (**to** a) • **let's leave it there and ~ on (to the next point)** dejémoslo aquí y pasemos al punto siguiente
d (= *change*) cambiar • **things have ~d on since your visit** las cosas han cambiado desde tu visita

▸ **move out** VT + ADV **1** [+ *person, object*] sacar
2 [+ *troops*] retirar
VI + ADV **1** (= *leave accommodation*) mudarse • **to ~ out of an area** marcharse de un barrio • **to ~ out of a flat** mudarse de un piso *or* (*LAm*) departamento
2 (= *withdraw*) [*troops*] retirarse

▸ **move over** VT + ADV hacer a un lado, correr
VI + ADV **1** (*on bench, seat*) correrse, hacerse a

un lado • ~ over! ¡córrete!
2 (*fig*) • **if he can't do the job, he should ~ over to let someone else have a chance** si no sabe hacerlo, debería dejarlo para que otro lo intente • **we should ~ over to a different system** nos convendría cambiar de sistema
▸ **move up** (VT + ADV) **1** [+ *object, person*] subir
2 [+ *troops*] trasladar al frente
3 (= *promote*) ascender
(VI + ADV) **1** (= *make room*) correrse
2 (= *increase*) [*shares, rates etc*] subir
3 (= *be promoted*) ascender, ser ascendido • **to ~ up a class** [*pupil*] pasar de curso, pasar al curso inmediatamente superior

moveable ['mu:vəbl] = **movable**

movement ['mu:vmənt] (N) **1** (= *motion*) movimiento *m*; [*of part*] juego *m*, movimiento *m*; [*of traffic*] circulación *f*; (*on stock exchange*) actividad *f* • **upward/downward ~** movimiento ascendente/descendente • **to be in ~** estar en movimiento • **there was a ~ towards the door** algunos se dirigieron hacia la puerta • **the police questioned him about his ~s** la policía le pidió informes sobre sus actividades • **~ of capital** movimiento de capitales
2 (= *gesture*) gesto *m*, ademán *m*
3 (*political, artistic etc*) movimiento *m*
4 (*Mech*) mecanismo *m*
5 (*Mus*) tiempo *m*, movimiento *m*
6 (*Med*) (*also* **bowel movement**) evacuación *f*

mover ['mu:vəʳ] (N) **1** [*of motion*] promotor(a) *m/f*
2 (*US*) agente *m* de mudanzas
3* • **he's a lovely ~** se mueve con mucho garbo, baila/anda con mucha elegancia

movie ['mu:vɪ] (*esp US*) (N) película *f*, film(e) *m* • **the ~s** el cine • **to go to the ~s** ir al cine
(CPD) ▸ **movie camera** cámara *f* cinematográfica ▸ **movie house** = **movie theatre** ▸ **the movie industry** la industria cinematográfica ▸ **movie star** estrella *f* de cine ▸ **movie theatre** cine *m*

moviegoer ['mu:vɪgəʊəʳ] (N) (*US*) aficionado/a *m/f* al cine

movieland ['mu:vɪlænd] (N) (*US*) (= *dreamworld*) mundo *m* de ensueño creado por el cine; (*eg Hollywood*) centro *m* de la industria cinematográfica

moving ['mu:vɪŋ] (ADJ) **1** (= *not fixed*) móvil • **~ part** pieza *f* móvil
2 (= *not stationary*) [*vehicle*] en marcha, en movimiento; [*target*] móvil, en movimiento
3 (= *touching*) [*book, story, film, sight, event*] conmovedor, emotivo
4 (*fig*) (= *instigating*) motor (*fem: motora/motriz*), impulsor • **the ~ force behind sth** la fuerza motora *or* motriz *or* impulsora de algo • **the ~ spirit behind sth** el espíritu impulsor de algo
(N) (= *relocation*) • **~ is a very stressful experience** mudarse *or* una mudanza de casa es una experiencia muy estresante
(CPD) ▸ **moving company** (*US*) empresa *f* de mudanzas ▸ **moving pavement, moving sidewalk** (*US*) cinta *f* móvil ▸ **moving picture**† película *f* ▸ **moving staircase** escalera *f* mecánica ▸ **moving van** (*US*) camión *m* de mudanzas ▸ **moving walkway** cinta *f* móvil

movingly ['mu:vɪŋlɪ] (ADV) [*speak, write*] emotivamente, de manera conmovedora

mow [məʊ] (PT: **mowed**, PP: **mown, mowed**) (VT) **1** • **to mow the lawn** cortar el césped
2 (*Agr*) segar, cortar • **to mow sb down** (*fig*) acabar con algn, segar la vida de algn

mower ['məʊəʳ] (N) **1** (*also* **lawn mower**) cortacésped *m*
2 (*Agr*) (= *machine*) segadora *f*; (= *person*) segador(a) *m/f*

mowing ['məʊɪŋ] (N) siega *f*
(CPD) ▸ **mowing machine** segadora *f* (mecánica)

mown [məʊn] (PP) *of* **mow**

moxie‡, moxy‡ ['mɒksɪ] (N) (*US*) (= *courage*) valor *m*; (= *nerve*) sangre fría *f*; (= *vigour*) vigor *m*, dinamismo *m*

Mozambican [,məʊzəm'bi:kən] (ADJ), (N) mozambiqueño/a *m/f*

Mozambique [,məʊzəm'bi:k] (N) Mozambique *m*

Mozarab [mɒz'ærəb] (N) mozárabe *mf*

Mozarabic [mɒz'ærəbɪk] (ADJ) mozárabe
(N) mozárabe *m*

mozzarella [,mɒtsə'relə] (N) mozzarella *f*

MP (N ABBR) **1** (*Brit*) (= **member of parliament**) Dip., diputado/a *m/f*, parlamentario/a *m/f*
2 (*Mil*) (= **military police**) PM *f*
3 (*Canada*) = **mounted police**

MP3 [,empi:'θri:] (N) MP3 *m*
(CPD) ▸ **MP3 player** reproductor *m* (de) MP3, lector *m* (de) MP3

MP4 [,empi:'fɔ:] (N) MP4 *m*
(CPD) ▸ **MP4 player** reproductor *m* (de) MP4, lector *m* (de) MP4

m-payment ['em,peɪmənt] (N) pago *m* a través del móvil (*Sp*), pago *m* a través del celular (*LAm*)

MPEG ['empeg] (N) MPEG *m*

mpg (N ABBR) (*Aut*) (= **miles per gallon**) ≈ k.p.l.

mph (N ABBR) (= **miles per hour**) ≈ km/h, ≈ k.p.h.

MPhil [em'fɪl] (N ABBR) (*Univ*) = **Master of Philosophy**

MPS (N ABBR) (*Brit*) = **Member of the Pharmaceutical Society**

MPV (N ABBR) = **multipurpose vehicle**

Mr ['mɪstəʳ] (N ABBR) (PL: **Messrs**) (= **Mister**) Sr., señor • **Mr Jones wants to see you** el señor Jones quiere verte • **yes, Mr Brown** sí, señor Brown; ▸ **big, right**

MR, MRS, MISS

Use of article

▹ *Use the article with* **Sr./señor, Sra./señora, Srta./señorita** *when you are talking about someone rather than to them:*
Mr Smith is not at home
El Sr. Smith no está en casa
Mr and Mrs Crespo are on holiday
Los Sres. (de) Crespo están de vacaciones
Have you seen Miss Barrios this morning?
¿Ha visto a la Srta. Barrios esta mañana?

The abbreviated form is more common than the full form in writing.

▹ *Don't use the article before* **Sr./señor, Sra./señora, Srta./señorita** *when addressing someone directly:*
Good morning, Mrs Ramírez
Buenos días, Sra. Ramírez
Mr López, there's a telephone call for you
Sr. López, le llaman por teléfono

Capitalization

▹ *Write the full forms* **señor, señora** *and* **señorita** *with a small "s", even when using them as titles:*
El señor Smith no está en casa
Estaba hablando con la señora (de) Williams

Addressing correspondence

▹ *Use* **Sr. Don/Sra. Doña (Sr. D./Sra. Dña.)** *rather than* **Sr./Sra.** *when giving both forename and surname. Don't use the article:*
Mr Bernardo García
Sr. Don *or* Sr. D. Bernardo García
Mrs Teresa Álvarez Serrano
Sra. Doña *or* Sra. Dña. Teresa Álvarez Serrano

For further uses and examples, see **miss², mister, Mrs**

MRC (N ABBR) (*Brit*) (= **Medical Research Council**) *depto. estatal que controla la investigación médica*

MRCP (N ABBR) (*Brit*) = **Member of the Royal College of Physicians**

MRCS (N ABBR) (*Brit*) = **Member of the Royal College of Surgeons**

MRCVS (N ABBR) (*Brit*) = **Member of the Royal College of Veterinary Surgeons**

MRD (N ABBR) = **machine-readable dictionary**

MRI (N) (= **magnetic resonance imaging**) RM *f*
(CPD) ▸ **MRI scan** resonancia *f* magnética

MRP (N ABBR) = **manufacturer's recommended price**

Mrs ['mɪsɪz] (N ABBR) (*pl inv*) (= **Mistress**) Sra., señora • **Mrs Pitt wants to see you** la señora (de) Pitt quiere verte • **yes, Mrs Brown** sí, señora Brown; ▹ MR, MRS, MISS
(CPD) ▸ **Mrs Mop*** (*Brit*) (*hum*) la maruja*

MRSA (N ABBR) (= **methicillin-resistant Staphylococcus aureus**) *virus asesino sin tratamiento conocido*

MS (N ABBR) **1** = **multiple sclerosis**
2 (*US*) = **Master of Science**
(ABBR) **1** (*US*) = **Mississippi**
2 (*also* **ms**) = **manuscript**

Ms [mɪz, məz] (N ABBR) (= **Miss** *or* **Mrs**) *prefijo de nombre de mujer que evita expresar su estado civil* • **Ms Sinclair is not at home** la señora Sinclair no está en casa

MS

La fórmula de tratamiento **Ms** es el equivalente femenino de **Mr** y se utiliza frecuentemente en la actualidad para evitar la distinción que los términos tradicionales establecían entre mujer casada (**Mrs**) y soltera (**Miss**). Las formas **Ms** y **Miss** nunca llevan punto, pero **Mr** y **Mrs** a veces sí.

MSA (N ABBR) (*US*) (*Univ*) = **Master of Science in Agriculture**

MSC (N ABBR) (*Brit*) (*formerly*) = **Manpower Services Commission**

MSc (N ABBR) (*Brit*) (*Univ*) (= **Master of Science**) ▹ DEGREE

MS-DOS [,emes'dɒs] (N ABBR) = **Microsoft Disk Operating System**

MSF (N ABBR) (*Brit*) = **Manufacturing, Science, Finance**

MSG (N ABBR) = **monosodium glutamate**

Msgr (ABBR) (= **Monsignor**) Mons.

m-shopping ['em,ʃɒpɪŋ] (N) compras *fpl* a través de dispositivos móviles

MSI (N ABBR) = **medium-scale integration**

MSP (N ABBR) (*Brit*) = **Member of the Scottish Parliament**

MSS (ABBR) = **manuscripts**

MST (N ABBR) (*US*) = **Mountain Standard Time**

MSW (N ABBR) (*US*) (*Univ*) = **Master of Social Work**

MT (N ABBR) = **machine translation**

m

(ABBR) (*US*) = **Montana**

Mt (ABBR) (*Geog*) (= **Mount, Mountain**) m.

MTB (N ABBR) = **motor torpedo boat**

mth (ABBR) (= **month**) m.

MTV (N ABBR) = **music television**

much [mʌtʃ] (ADJ) mucho • **there isn't ~ time** no tenemos mucho tiempo, tenemos poco tiempo • **~ crime goes unreported** hay muchos crímenes que no se denuncian • **I haven't got as ~ energy as you** no tengo tanta energía como tú • **how ~ sugar do you want?** ¿cuánto azúcar quieres? • **so ~ tea** tanto té • **she's got so ~ energy** tiene tanta energía • **too ~ jam** demasiada mermelada *f* • **we haven't got too ~ time** no tenemos demasiado tiempo • **very ~** mucho • **we haven't very ~ time** no tenemos mucho tiempo, tenemos poco tiempo • **without ~ money** sin mucho dinero
(ADV) **1** (= *a lot*) mucho; (*before pp*) muy • **she doesn't go out ~** no sale mucho • **it doesn't ~ matter** • **it doesn't matter ~** no importa mucho • **I ~ regret that ...** siento mucho que ... • **it won't finish ~ before midnight** no terminará mucho antes de la media noche • **~ better** mucho mejor • **he's ~ richer than I am** *or* **than me** es mucho más rico que yo • **~ pleased** muy satisfecho • **~ as I would like to go** a pesar de que me gustaría mucho ir, aunque me gustaría mucho ir • **~ as I should like to** por mucho que quisiera • **~ as I like him** aunque *or* a pesar de que me gusta mucho • **~ as he hated the idea ...** a pesar de lo que odiaba la idea ... • **~ as I respect her ideas, I still think she's wrong** a pesar de que respeto mucho sus ideas *or* aunque respeto mucho sus ideas, creo que está equivocada • **however ~ he tries** por mucho que se esfuerce • **I hardly know her, ~ less her mother** apenas la conozco, y mucho menos a su madre • **not ~** no mucho • **thank you (ever) so ~** muchísimas gracias, muy agradecido • **I feel ever so ~ better** me siento muchísimo mejor • **~ though I like him** por mucho que él me guste • **~ though he hated the idea, he knew that ...** a pesar de lo que odiaba la idea, sabía que ... • **he had reservations about the scheme, ~ though he valued Alison's opinions** tenía sus dudas respecto al plan, a pesar de que valoraba mucho las opiniones de Alison • **~ to my astonishment** para gran sorpresa mía • **he talks too ~** habla demasiado • **very ~** mucho • **I enjoyed myself very ~** me divertí mucho
2 (= *by far*) con mucho • **~ the biggest** con mucho el más grande • **I would ~ rather stay** prefiero mucho más quedarme
3 (= *more or less*) más o menos, casi • **they're ~ the same size** tienen más o menos el mismo tamaño • **they are ~ of an age** tienen casi la misma edad
(PRON) mucho • **there isn't ~ to do** no hay mucho que hacer • **but ~ remains to be done** pero queda mucho que *or* por hacer • **you've got as ~ as she has** tienes tanto como ella • **it didn't cost as ~ as I had expected** no costó tanto como yo me esperaba • **it can cost as ~ as $2,000** puede llegar a costar 2.000 dólares • **that's a bit ~!*** ¡eso es demasiado! • **there isn't ~ in it** (*between alternatives*) no hay mucha diferencia, no va mucho de uno a otro • **how ~ is it a kilo?** ¿cuánto vale el kilo? • **how ~ does it cost?** ¿cuánto cuesta? • **she won but there wasn't ~ in it** ganó, pero no por mucho • **she's not ~ to look at** físicamente no vale mucho • **to make ~ of sth** dar mucha importancia a algo • **~ of this is true** gran parte de esto es verdad • **we don't see ~ of each other** no nos vemos mucho • **we haven't heard ~ of him lately** últimamente apenas sabemos nada de él • **I'm not ~ of a musician** sé muy poco de música, entiendo poco de música • **I'm not ~ of a cook** no cocino muy bien • **he's not ~ of a player** como jugador no vale mucho • **that wasn't ~ of a dinner** eso apenas se podía llamar cena • **we spent so ~** gastamos tanto • **I've got so ~ to do** tengo tantísimo que hacer • **that's too ~** eso es demasiado • **it's not up to ~*** no vale gran cosa

muchness ['mʌtʃnɪs] (N) • **they're much of a ~** son poco más o menos lo mismo

mucilage ['mju:sɪlɪdʒ] (N) mucílago *m*

mucilaginous [,mju:sɪ'lædʒɪnəs] (ADJ) mucilaginoso

muck [mʌk] (N) **1** (= *dirt*) suciedad *f*, mugre *f*; (= *manure*) estiércol *m*; ▹ **lady**
2 (*fig*) porquería *f*

▸ **muck about***, **muck around*** (VT + ADV) • **to ~ sb about** *or* **around** fastidiar *or* (*LAm**) fregar a algn
(VI + ADV) **1** (= *lark about*) hacer tonterías; (= *do nothing in particular*) gandulear • **he enjoys ~ing about in boats** le gusta hacer el gandul navegando • **stop ~ing about!** ¡déjate de tonterías!
2 (= *tinker*) manosear

▸ **muck in*** (VI + ADV) compartir el trabajo, arrimar el hombro

▸ **muck out** (VT + ADV) (*Brit*) limpiar • **to ~ out a stable** limpiar una cuadra

▸ **muck up*** (VT + ADV) **1** (= *dirty*) ensuciar
2 (= *spoil*) echar a perder, fastidiar

mucker‡ ['mʌkəʳ] (N) compinche *m*

muckheap ['mʌk,hi:p] (N) estercolero *m*

muckiness ['mʌkɪnɪs] (N) suciedad *f*

muckrake* ['mʌkreɪk] (VI) (*pej*) (= *dig up past*) revelar los trapos sucios; (= *pry*) buscar y revelar cosas vergonzosas en la vida de otros, escarbar vidas ajenas

muckraker* ['mʌk,reɪkəʳ] (N) (*pej*) escarbador(a) *m/f* de vidas ajenas

muckraking* ['mʌk,reɪkɪŋ] (N) (*pej*) (= *digging up the past*) revelación *f* de trapos sucios; (*in journalism*) amarillismo *m*, sensacionalismo *m*

muck-up* ['mʌkʌp] (N) lío *m* grande • **that muck-up with the timetable** ese lío que nos armamos con el horario • **what a muck-up!** ¡qué faena!*

mucky ['mʌkɪ] (ADJ) (COMPAR: **muckier**, SUPERL: **muckiest**) (= *muddy*) lleno de barro, embarrado; (= *filthy*) sucio, asqueroso, mugroso (*LAm*) • **keep your ~ paws off!*** (*hum*) ¡no toques con esas manazas tan sucias!* • **to get ~** (= *muddy*) llenarse de barro, embarrarse; (= *filthy*) ponerse hecho un asco*, ensuciarse • **to get sth ~** (= *muddy*) llenar algo de barro, embarrar algo; (= *filthy*) dejar algo hecho un asco*, ensuciar algo • IDIOM: • **you're a ~ pup!*** (*hum*) ¡qué cochinote eres!*

mucous ['mju:kəs] (ADJ) mucoso
(CPD) ▸ **mucous membrane** mucosa *f*

mucus ['mju:kəs] (N) moco *m*

mud [mʌd] (N) barro *m*, lodo *m* • **to stick in the mud** [*cart*] quedarse atascado en el barro; [*ship*] embarrancar • IDIOMS: • **(here's) mud in your eye!*** (*toast*) ¡salud y pesetas! • **to drag sb's name through the mud** ensuciar el nombre de algn • **his name is mud** tiene muy mala fama • **to sling** *or* **throw mud at sb** vilipendiar *or* insultar a algn, poner a algn como un trapo *or* por los suelos
(CPD) ▸ **mud bank** banco *m* de lodo ▸ **mud bath** baño *m* de lodo ▸ **mud flap** cortina *f* ▸ **mud hut** choza *f* de barro ▸ **mud pack** mascarilla *f* de barro ▸ **mud pie** bola *f* de barro ▸ **mud wall** tapia *f* ▸ **mud wrestling** *espectáculo de lucha sobre un cuadrilátero de barro*

muddle ['mʌdl] (N) (*untidy*) desorden *m*, lío* *m*; (= *tricky situation*) lío* *m*, follón *m* (*Sp**); (= *mix-up*) confusión *f* • **what a ~!** (*looking at mess*) ¡qué desorden!, ¡qué lío!; (*situation*) ¡qué lío!*, ¡qué follón! (*Sp**) • **there's been a ~ over the seats** ha habido una confusión con las localidades • **to be in a ~** [*room, books*] estar en desorden, estar revuelto, estar hecho un desbarajuste*; [*person*] estar confuso, estar hecho un lío* • **the arrangements are all in a ~** hay un verdadero lío con los preparativos* • **to get into a ~** [*things*] desordenarse, revolverse; [*person*] hacerse un lío* • **to get sth into a ~** desordenar algo, revolver algo
(VT) (*also* **muddle up**) **1** (= *jumble*) [+ *photos, papers*] revolver, desordenar • **you've ~d (up) all my papers!** ¡has revuelto *or* desordenado todos mis papeles! • **she'd got all the papers ~d (up)** había revuelto todos los papeles • **to get ~d (up)** [*things*] desordenarse, revolverse
2 (= *confuse*) [+ *person, details*] confundir • **to get ~d (up)** [*person*] confundirse, hacerse un lío*, liarse*; ▹ **muddle up**

▸ **muddle along** (VI + ADV) arreglárselas de alguna manera, ir tirando*

▸ **muddle on** (VI) hacer las cosas al tuntún

▸ **muddle through** (VI + ADV) arreglárselas de alguna manera, ir tirando* • **I expect we shall ~ through** espero que lo logremos de algún modo u otro

▸ **muddle up** (VT + ADV) **1** (= *jumble*) ▹ **muddle**
2 (= *confuse*) • **I kept getting my words ~d up** no hacía más que confundirme al hablar • **the copies had got ~d up with the original documents** las copias se habían mezclado *or* confundido con los documentos originales • **you're getting me ~d up with the other Julie** me estás confundiendo con la otra Julie; ▹ **muddle**

muddled ['mʌdld] (ADJ) [*account, explanation*] confuso, lioso*; [*ideas, article, thinking*] confuso, poco claro; [*person*] confundido, liado* • **I'm afraid I'm a little ~** me temo que estoy un poco confundido, me temo que estoy un poco liado*

muddleheaded ['mʌdl,hedɪd] (ADJ) [*person*] despistado, atolondrado; [*ideas*] confuso

muddler ['mʌdləʳ] (N) atolondrado/a *m/f*

muddy ['mʌdɪ] (ADJ) (COMPAR: **muddier**, SUPERL: **muddiest**) **1** (= *covered in mud*) [*clothes, hands, floor, carpet, track, field*] lleno de barro, embarrado; [*water, stream*] turbio
2 (= *dull*) [*brown, green*] sucio; [*skin, complexion*] terroso
3 (= *confused*) [*ideas, thinking*] confuso, poco claro
(VT) **1** (= *make dirty*) [+ *floor, carpet*] llenar de barro; [+ *hands, dress*] manchar de barro; [+ *water, stream*] enturbiar
2 (= *make confused*) • **to ~ the issue** confundir el tema *or* la cuestión, enredar las cosas • IDIOM: • **to ~ the waters** confundir el tema *or* la cuestión, enredar las cosas

mudflats ['mʌdflæts] (NPL) marisma *f*

mudguard ['mʌdgɑ:d] (N) guardabarros *m inv*

mudlark ['mʌdlɑ:k] (N) galopín *m*

mudslide ['mʌdslaɪd] (N) alud *m* de lodo

mudslinging ['mʌd,slɪŋɪŋ] (N) injurias *fpl* • **there won't be any ~ in this campaign** no habrá ataques personales en esta campaña

muesli ['mju:zlɪ] (N) muesli *m*

muezzin [mu:'ezɪn] (N) almuecín *m*, almuédano *m*

muff[1] [mʌf] (N) (*for hands*) manguito *m*

muff[2] [mʌf] (VT) [+ *shot, catch etc*] fallar; (*Theat*) [+ *entrance, lines*] estropear • **to ~ a**

chance desperdiciar una oportunidad, echar a perder una oportunidad • **to ~ it** fastidiarla, hacerlo fatal

muffin [ˈmʌfɪn] (N) **1** (= *cake*) magdalena *f* *(generalmente con sabor a chocolate o con trocitos de fruta)*
2 (*eaten with butter*) (*Brit*) ≈ mollete *m*; (*US*) *especie de pan dulce*, ≈ bollo *m*

muffle [ˈmʌfl] (VT) **1** (= *deaden*) [+ *sound*] amortiguar
2 (= *wrap warmly*) (*also* **muffle up**) abrigar • **to ~ o.s. (up)** abrigarse
3 (= *cover*) [+ *oars, drum, hooves*] enfundar *(para amortiguar el ruido)* • **he ~d the receiver** (*Telec*) tapó el auricular con la mano

muffled [ˈmʌfld] (ADJ) **1** (= *deadened*) [*sound, shot, cry, sob*] sordo, apagado; [*voice*] apagado
2 (= *warmly wrapped*) envuelto, abrigado • **children ~ up in scarves and woolly hats** niños envueltos *or* abrigados con bufandas y gorros de lana
3 (= *covered*) [*oars, drum, hooves*] enfundado *(para amortiguar el ruido)*

muffler [ˈmʌfləʳ] (N) **1** (= *scarf*) bufanda *f*
2 (*Mus*) sordina *f*
3 (*US*) (*Aut*) silenciador *m*, mofle *m* (*LAm*)

mufti [ˈmʌftɪ] (N) • **in ~** (vestido) de paisano

mug [mʌg] (N) **1** (= *cup*) tazón *m* (*más alto que ancho*) • **do you want a cup or a mug?** ¿quieres una taza normal o una taza grande?
2 (= *glass*) jarra *f* • **a beer mug** una jarra de *or* para cerveza
3‡ (= *dupe*) bobo/a *m/f*, primo/a *m/f* • **what a mug I've been!** ¡mira que he sido bobo! • **smoking is a mug's game** fumar es cosa de bobos
4‡ (= *face*) jeta* *f*, careto *m* (*Sp*‡) • **what a mug she's got!** ¡qué jeta tiene!*
(VT) (= *attack and rob*) atracar, asaltar • **he was mugged in the city centre** lo atracaron en el centro de la ciudad
(CPD) ▸ **mug shot*** fotografía *f* para las fichas

▸ **mug up*** (VT + ADV) **1** (*Brit*) (*also* **mug up on**) empollar
2 • **to mug it up** (*US*) (= *grimace*) gesticular, hacer muecas; (*Theat*) actuar exagerando

mugger [ˈmʌgəʳ] (N) atracador(a) *m/f*, asaltante *mf*

mugging [ˈmʌgɪŋ] (N) atraco *m* (callejero)

muggins* [ˈmʌgɪnz] (N) (*Brit*) • **~ will do it** lo haré yo, como un tonto

muggy [ˈmʌgɪ] (ADJ) (COMPAR: **muggier**, SUPERL: **muggiest**) [*weather*] bochornoso • **it's ~ today** hoy hace bochorno

mugwump [ˈmʌgwʌmp] (N) (*US*) votante *mf* independiente

Muhammad [mʊˈhæməd] (N) = Mohammed

mujaheddin [ˈmu:dʒəhəˈdi:n] (NPL) mujaidines *mpl*

mulatto*‡ [mju:ˈlætəʊ] (ADJ) mulato
(N) (PL: **mulattos** *or* **mulattoes**) mulato/a *m/f*

mulberry [ˈmʌlbərɪ] (N) (= *fruit*) mora *f*; (= *tree*) morera *f*, moral *m*

mulch [mʌltʃ] (N) capote *m*, mantillo *m*
(VT) cubrir con capote, cubrir con mantillo

mulct [mʌlkt] (VT) **1** (= *fine*) multar
2 (= *cheat*) • **to ~ sb of sth** quitar algo a algn, privar a algn de algo

mule¹ [mju:l] (N) (= *animal*) mulo/a *m/f*; (*fig*) (= *person*) testarudo/a *m/f* • IDIOM: • **(as) stubborn as a ~** terco como una mula
(CPD) ▸ **mule track** camino *m* de herradura

mule² [mju:l] (N) (= *slipper*) babucha *f*

muleteer [ˌmju:lɪˈtɪəʳ] (N) arriero *m*

mulish [ˈmju:lɪʃ] (ADJ) terco, testarudo

mulishness [ˈmju:lɪʃnɪs] (N) terquedad *f*, testarudez *f*

mull [mʌl] (VT) calentar con especias • **~ed wine** ponche *m*

▸ **mull over** (VT + ADV) reflexionar sobre, meditar

mullah [ˈmʌlə] (N) mullah *m*

mullet [ˈmʌlɪt] (N) • **grey ~** mújol *m* • **red ~** salmonete *m*

mulligatawny [ˌmʌlɪgəˈtɔ:nɪ] (N) *especie de caldo de pollo o carne al curry*

mullion [ˈmʌlɪən] (N) parteluz *m*

mullioned [ˈmʌlɪənd] (ADJ) [*window*] dividido con parteluz

multi... [ˈmʌltɪ] (PREFIX) multi...

multi-access [ˌmʌltɪˈækses] (ADJ) (*Comput*) multiacceso (*inv*), de acceso múltiple
(N) acceso *m* múltiple

multicellular [ˌmʌltɪˈseljʊləʳ] (ADJ) multicelular

multichannel [ˈmʌltɪˈtʃænl] (ADJ) (*TV*) multicanal

multicoloured, multicolored (*US*) [ˈmʌltɪˈkʌləd] (ADJ) multicolor

multicultural [ˌmʌltɪˈkʌltʃərəl] (ADJ) multicultural

multiculturalism [ˌmʌltɪˈkʌltʃərəlɪzəm] (N) multiculturalismo *m*

multidimensional [ˌmʌltɪdɪˈmenʃənl] (ADJ) multidimensional

multidirectional [ˌmʌltɪdɪˈrekʃənl] (ADJ) multidireccional

multidisciplinary [ˌmʌltɪˈdɪsɪplɪnərɪ] (ADJ) multidisciplinario

multifaceted [ˌmʌltɪˈfæsɪtɪd] (ADJ) [*person*] multifacético; [*job*] con múltiples aspectos

multifarious [ˌmʌltɪˈfeərɪəs] (ADJ) múltiple, vario

multifocals [ˈmʌltɪˌfəʊkəlz] (NPL) multifocales *fpl*

multiform [ˈmʌltɪfɔ:m] (ADJ) multiforme

multifunctional [ˈmʌltɪˈfʌŋkʃnəl] (ADJ) multifuncional

multifunctionality [ˌmʌltɪˌfʌŋkʃˈnælɪtɪ] (N) multifuncionalidad *f*

multigrain [ˈmʌltɪgreɪn] (ADJ) multigrano

multigym [ˈmʌltɪdʒɪm] (N) estación *f* de musculación

multihull [ˈmʌltɪhʌl] (N) multicasco *m*

multilateral [ˈmʌltɪˈlætərəl] (ADJ) (*Pol*) multilateral

multilayer [ˌmʌltɪˈleɪəʳ], **multilayered** [ˌmʌltɪˈleɪəd] (ADJ) multicapa

multilevel [ˌmʌltɪˈlevl] (ADJ) (*US*) de muchos pisos

multilingual [ˌmʌltɪˈlɪŋgwəl] (ADJ) plurilingüe

multilingualism [ˌmʌltɪˈlɪŋgwəlɪzəm] (N) plurilingüismo *m*, multilingüismo *m*

multimedia [ˈmʌltɪˈmi:dɪə] (ADJ) [*aids, presentation*] (*also Comput*) multimedia (*inv*)
(CPD) ▸ **multimedia machine** ordenador *m* multimedia

multimillion [ˈmʌltɪˈmɪljən] (ADJ) multimillonario

multimillionaire [ˈmʌltɪmɪljəˈnɛəʳ] (N) multimillonario/a *m/f*

multi-million-pound [ˌmʌltɪˈmɪljənˌpaʊnd] (ADJ) [*deal, fraud etc*] de (varios) millones de libras, multimillonario

multi-nation [ˈmʌltɪˈneɪʃən] (ADJ) [*treaty, agreement*] multinacional

multinational [ˌmʌltɪˈnæʃənl] (N) compañía *f* multinacional, multinacional *f*
(ADJ) multinacional

multi-pack [ˈmʌltɪpæk] (N) multipack *m*

multi-party [ˌmʌltɪˈpɑ:tɪ] (ADJ) (*Pol*) [*system, democracy*] multipartidista, multipartidario • **multi-party talks** conversaciones *fpl* entre partidos

multiple [ˈmʌltɪpl] (ADJ) múltiple • **he died of ~ injuries** murió tras sufrir heridas múltiples • **~ accident** (*Aut*) colisión *f* múltiple *or* en cadena • **~ birth** parto *m* múltiple
(N) **1** (*Math*) múltiplo *m* • **lowest common ~** mínimo común múltiplo *m*
2 (= *shop*) (*also* **multiple store**) (sucursal *f* de una cadena de) grandes almacenes *mpl*
(CPD) ▸ **multiple choice question** pregunta *f* de elección múltiple, pregunta *f* tipo test ▸ **multiple choice test** examen *m* de elección múltiple, examen *m* tipo test ▸ **multiple ownership** multipropiedad *f* ▸ **multiple personality (disorder)** (*Psych*) personalidad *f* múltiple ▸ **multiple sclerosis** esclerosis *f* múltiple ▸ **multiple store** (sucursal *f* de una cadena de) grandes almacenes *mpl*

multiple-entry visa [ˌmʌltɪplˌentrɪˈvi:zə] (N) visado *m* para múltiples entradas

multiplex [ˈmʌltɪˌpleks] (N) (*also* **multiplex cinema**) multicines *mpl*

multiplexor [ˈmʌltɪˌpleksəʳ] (N) multiplexor *m*

multiplicand [ˌmʌltɪplɪˈkænd] (N) multiplicando *m*

multiplication [ˌmʌltɪplɪˈkeɪʃən] (N) multiplicación *f*
(CPD) ▸ **multiplication sign** signo *m* de multiplicar ▸ **multiplication table** tabla *f* de multiplicar

multiplicity [ˌmʌltɪˈplɪsɪtɪ] (N) multiplicidad *f* • **for a ~ of reasons** por múltiples razones • **a ~ of solutions** una gran diversidad *or* variedad de soluciones

multiplier [ˈmʌltɪˌplaɪəʳ] (N) (*Math*) multiplicador *m*

multiply [ˈmʌltɪplaɪ] (VT) (*Math*) multiplicar • **to ~ eight by seven** multiplicar ocho por siete
(VI) **1** (*Math*) multiplicar
2 (= *reproduce o.s.*) multiplicarse

multiprocessing [ˌmʌltɪˈprəʊsesɪŋ] (N) multiprocesamiento *m*

multiprocessor [ˌmʌltɪˈprəʊsesəʳ] (N) multiprocesador *m*

multiprogramming, multiprograming (*US*) [ˌmʌltɪˈprəʊgræmɪŋ] (N) multiprogramación *f*

multipurpose [ˌmʌltɪˈpɜ:pəs] (ADJ) multiuso

multiracial [ˈmʌltɪˈreɪʃəl] (ADJ) multirracial

multirisk [ˈmʌltɪrɪsk] (CPD) ▸ **multirisk insurance** seguro *m* multirriesgo, seguro *m* a todo riesgo

multistorey [ˌmʌltɪˈstɔ:rɪ], **multistoreyed, multistoried** (*US*) [ˌmʌltɪˈstɔ:rɪd] (ADJ) de varias plantas, de varios pisos
(CPD) ▸ **multistorey car park** aparcamiento *m* de varias plantas

multistrike [ˈmʌltɪˌstraɪk] (CPD) ▸ **multistrike ribbon** cinta *f* de múltiples impactos

multisystem [ˈmʌltɪˌsɪstəm] (ADJ) [*TV*] multisistema (*inv*)

multitask [ˈmʌltɪˌtɑ:sk] (VI) **1** [*person*] realizar simultáneamente diferentes tareas
2 (*Comput*) trabajar en multitarea

multitasker [ˌmʌltɪˈtɑ:skəʳ] (N) experto/a *m/f* en realizar simultáneamente diferentes tareas

multitasking [ˈmʌltɪˈtɑ:skɪŋ] (N) **1** (*by person*) *realización simultánea de diferentes tareas*
2 (*Comput*) multitarea *f*

multitrack [ˈmʌltɪˌtræk] (ADJ) • **~ recording** grabación *f* en bandas múltiples

multitude [ˈmʌltɪtju:d] (N) **1** (= *crowd*) multitud *f*, muchedumbre *f* • **they came in ~s** acudieron en tropel • **the ~** (*pej*) las masas, la plebe
2 (*fig*) • **a ~ of problems** una infinidad de

m

problemas, multitud de problemas • **there are a ~ of reasons why we shouldn't do it** hay multitud de razones por las que no deberíamos hacerlo • **for a ~ of reasons** por múltiples razones

multitudinous [ˌmʌltɪˈtjuːdɪnəs] ADJ muy numeroso, numerosísimo

multiuser [ˌmʌltɪˈjuːzəʳ] ADJ multiusuario • **~ system** sistema *m* multiusuario

mum¹* [mʌm] N (*Brit*) (= *mother*) mamá* *f*, mamaíta* *f*, mamacita* *f* (*LAm*) • **I'll ask Mum** le preguntaré a mamá • **my mum** mi mamá

mum²* [mʌm] ADJ • **to keep mum (about sth)** guardar silencio (sobre algo) • **everybody is keeping mum about it** nadie suelta prenda sobre el asunto • **mum's the word!** ¡punto en boca!, ¡ni una palabra a nadie!

Mumbai [mʊmˈbaɪ] N Bombay *f*, Mumbai *f*

mumble [ˈmʌmbl] VI mascullar
VT mascullar
N • **he said in a ~** masculló, dijo entre dientes

mumbo jumbo [ˈmʌmbəʊˈdʒʌmbəʊ] N (= *nonsense*) galimatías *m inv*

mummer [ˈmʌməʳ] N *actor o actriz enmascarado en una representación teatral tradicional, por lo general mímica*

mummery [ˈmʌmərɪ] N *representación teatral tradicional, por lo general mímica, en que se usan máscaras*

mummification [ˌmʌmɪfɪˈkeɪʃən] N momificación *f*

mummify [ˈmʌmɪfaɪ] VT momificar
VI momificarse

mummy¹ [ˈmʌmɪ] N (= *preserved corpse*) momia *f*

mummy²* [ˈmʌmɪ] N (*Brit*) = **mum¹**

mumps [mʌmps] NSING paperas *fpl* • **my brother's got ~** mi hermano tiene paperas

mumsy* [ˈmʌmzɪ] ADJ [*appearance, hair*] de señora • **she's much more ~ now** se la ve más maternal ahora

munch [mʌntʃ] VT mascar, masticar
VI mascar, masticar

Münchhausen's Syndrome [ˈmʌntʃaʊzənzˈsɪndrəʊm] N síndrome *m* de Munchhausen

munchies* [ˈmʌntʃɪz] NPL (*US*) **1** (= *snacks*) algo para picar
2 • **to have the ~** tener hambre

mundane [ˌmʌnˈdeɪn] ADJ (= *humdrum*) [*task*] rutinario; [*matter, problem*] trivial; [*existence*] prosaico • **on a more ~ level** a modo de trivialidad

municipal [mjuːˈnɪsɪpəl] ADJ municipal
CPD ▸ **municipal court** (*US*) juzgado *m* municipal

municipality [mjuːˌnɪsɪˈpælɪtɪ] N (= *place*) municipio *m*

municipally [mjuːˈnɪsɪpəlɪ] ADV • **~ owned** de propiedad municipal

munificence [mjuːˈnɪfɪsns] N munificencia *f*

munificent [mjuːˈnɪfɪsnt] ADJ munífico, munificente

muniments [ˈmjuːnɪmənts] NPL documentos *mpl* (probatorios)
CPD ▸ **muniments room** archivos *mpl*

munitions [mjuːˈnɪʃənz] NPL municiones *fpl*
CPD ▸ **munitions dump** polvorín *m*, depósito *m* de municiones ▸ **munitions factory** fábrica *f* de municiones

muppet* [ˈmʌpɪt] N (*Brit*) (= *idiot*) berzotas* *mf inv*

mural [ˈmjʊərəl] ADJ mural
N mural *m*, pintura *f* mural

murder [ˈmɜːdəʳ] N **1** asesinato *m*; (*Jur*) homicidio *m* • **accused of ~** acusado de homicidio • **to commit ~** cometer un asesinato *or* un crimen • **first-degree ~** • **~ in the first degree** homicidio *m* premeditado, homicidio *m* en primer grado • **second-degree ~** • **~ in the second degree** homicidio *m* en segundo grado • **the ~ weapon** el arma homicida • PROVERB: • **~ will out** todo termina por saberse; ▹ **attempted, mass²**
2* • **"did you have a good holiday?" — "no, it was ~!"** —¿pasaste unas buenas vacaciones? —¡no, lo pasé fatal* *or* fueron horribles! • **the noise/heat in here is ~** el ruido que hay aquí/el calor que hace aquí es insoportable • **the roads were ~** las carreteras estaban hasta los topes* • IDIOMS: • **to scream** *or* **shout blue** *or* **bloody ~** poner el grito en el cielo • **to get away with ~**: • **she lets the children get away with ~** a los niños les consiente todo, a los niños les deja hacer lo que les da la gana*
VT **1** [+ *person*] asesinar, matar, ultimar (*LAm*) • **the ~ed man** el hombre asesinado
2 (*fig**) [+ *song, music, play, language*] destrozar, cargarse*; [+ *opponent*] aniquilar*
3* (= *really enjoy*) • **I could ~ a beer/a cup of tea** daría cualquier cosa por una cerveza/una taza de té
VI cometer asesinatos, matar
CPD ▸ **murder case** caso *m* de asesinato *or* homicidio ▸ **murder charge** acusación *f* por asesinato *or* homicidio • **he is wanted on ~ charges** lo buscan por asesinato ▸ **murder hunt** caza *f* al asesino ▸ **murder mystery** historia *f* policial ▸ **Murder Squad** brigada *f* de homicidios ▸ **murder trial** juicio *m* por asesinato ▸ **murder victim** víctima *f* de un asesinato *or* homicidio

murderer [ˈmɜːdərəʳ] N asesino/a *m/f*; (*as Jur term*) homicida *mf*

murderess [ˈmɜːdərɪs] N asesina *f*; (*as Jur term*) homicida *f*

murderous [ˈmɜːdərəs] ADJ **1** (= *homicidal*) homicida; (*fig*) cruel, feroz, sanguinario; [*look*] asesino, homicida • **I felt ~** (*lit, fig*) me vinieron pensamientos homicidas
2* (= *terrible*) • **this heat is ~** este calor es cruel

murderously [ˈmɜːdərəslɪ] ADV **1** [*glare*] de manera asesina
2* (= *terribly*) terriblemente • **the bags were ~ heavy** las bolsas pesaban terriblemente *or* de forma matadora

murk [mɜːk] N oscuridad *f*, tinieblas *fpl*

murkiness [ˈmɜːkɪnɪs] [ˈmɜːkɪ] N (= *darkness*) oscuridad *f*; (*fig*) lo turbio, tenebrosidad *f*; [*of water, river*] lo turbio

murky [ˈmɜːkɪ] ADJ (COMPAR: **murkier**, SUPERL: **murkiest**) **1** (= *dark and cloudy*) [*night, evening*] tenebroso, oscuro; [*water*] turbio; [*fog*] espeso; [*brown, green*] sucio
2 (*fig*) [*past*] turbio • **the ~ depths of Soviet politics** los turbios entresijos de la política soviética

murmur [ˈmɜːməʳ] N (= *soft speech*) murmullo *m*; [*of water, leaves*] murmullo *m*, susurro *m*; [*of distant traffic*] rumor *m* • **there were ~s of disagreement** hubo un murmullo de desaprobación • **without a ~** sin una queja; ▹ **heart**
VI [*person*] murmurar; [*water*] murmurar, susurrar • **to ~ about sth** (= *complain*) quejarse de algo, murmurar de algo
VT murmurar, decir en voz baja

Murphy [ˈmɜːfɪ] N • **~'s law** ley *f* de la indefectible mala voluntad de los objetos inanimados

MusB, MusBac N ABBR (*Univ*) = **Bachelor of Music**

muscat [ˈmʌskæt] N (*also* **muscat grape**) uva *f* de moscatel

muscatel [ˌmʌskəˈtel] ADJ moscatel
N moscatel *m*

muscle [ˈmʌsl] N **1** (*Anat*) músculo *m* • **to flex one's ~s** tensar los músculos • **he never moved a ~** ni se inmutó
2 (*fig*) fuerza *f* • **political ~** poder *m* político
CPD ▸ **muscle tissue** tejido *m* muscular
▸ **muscle in*** VI + ADV • **to ~ in (on sth)** meterse por la fuerza (en algo)

musclebound [ˈmʌslbaʊnd] ADJ exageradamente musculoso

muscleman* [ˈmʌslmæn] N (PL: **musclemen**) forzudo *m*

muscle-wasting [ˈmʌslˌweɪstɪŋ] ADJ • **muscle-wasting disease** enfermedad *f* de desgaste muscular

muscly* [ˈmʌslɪ] ADJ musculoso

Muscovite [ˈmʌskəvaɪt] N moscovita *mf*
ADJ moscovita

muscular [ˈmʌskjʊləʳ] ADJ **1** (*Med, Physiol*) [*tissue, pain, control*] muscular
2 (= *brawny*) [*person, body*] musculoso
CPD ▸ **muscular dystrophy** distrofia *f* muscular

musculature [ˈmʌskjʊlətjʊəʳ] N musculatura *f*

MusD, MusDoc N ABBR (*Univ*) = **Doctor of Music**

Muse [mjuːz] N musa *f* • **the ~s** las Musas

muse [mjuːz] VI • **to ~ on** *or* **about sth** reflexionar sobre algo, meditar algo
VT • **"should we?" he ~d** —¿debemos hacerlo? —dijo pensativo

museum [mjuːˈzɪəm] N museo *m*
CPD ▸ **museum piece** (*lit*) pieza *f* de museo; (*fig*) antigualla *f*, pieza *f* de museo

mush¹ [mʌʃ] N **1** (*Culin*) gachas *fpl*
2 (*fig*) sensiblería *f*, sentimentalismo *m*

mush²‡ [mʊʃ] N **1** (= *face*) jeta* *f*, careto *m* (*Sp‡*)
2 (*in direct address*) • **hey, ~!** ¡hola, tronco!*

mushroom [ˈmʌʃrʊm] N (*Culin*) (*round-topped*) champiñón *m*; (*flat-topped*) seta *f*; (*Bot*) seta *f*, hongo *m*, callampa *f* (*Chile*) • **a great ~ of smoke** un enorme hongo de humo • **to grow like ~s** crecer como hongos • **to spring up like ~s** (*fig*) surgir como hongos
VI [*town etc*] crecer vertiginosamente • **the cloud of smoke went ~ing up** una nube de humo ascendió en forma de hongo
CPD [*salad, omelette etc*] de champiñones ▸ **mushroom cloud** hongo *m* nuclear ▸ **mushroom growth** crecimiento *m* vertiginoso ▸ **mushroom town** ciudad *f* que crece vertiginosamente

mushrooming [ˈmʌʃruːmɪŋ] N crecimiento *m* vertiginoso

mushy [ˈmʌʃɪ] ADJ (COMPAR: **mushier**, SUPERL: **mushiest**) **1** (*lit*) pulposo, mollar • **~ peas** (*Brit*) puré *m* de guisantes *or* (*LAm*) arvejas, chícharos *mpl* aguados (*Mex*)
2 (*fig*) sensiblero, sentimentaloide

music [ˈmjuːzɪk] N música *f* • **to set a work to ~** poner música a una obra • IDIOMS: • **it was ~ to my ears** daba gusto escucharlo, me sonaba a música celestial • **to face the ~** afrontar las consecuencias
CPD ▸ **music box** (*esp US*) caja *f* de música ▸ **music centre** equipo *m* estereofónico ▸ **music critic** crítico/a *m/f* musical ▸ **music director** director(a) *m/f* musical ▸ **music festival** festival *m* de música ▸ **music hall** teatro *m* de variedades ▸ **music lesson** (*instrumental*) clase *f* de música; (*vocal*) clase *f* de solfeo ▸ **music lover** aficionado/a *m/f* a la música, amante *mf* de la música ▸ **music paper** papel *m* de música, papel *m* pautado ▸ **music stand** atril *m* ▸ **music video**

videoclip *m*
musical ['mju:zɪkəl] ADJ **1** (= *relating to music*) [*career, taste, style, accompaniment, composition*] musical; [*talent, ability*] musical, para la música
2 (= *musically talented*) [*person, child*] dotado para la música, con aptitudes musicales • **he came from a ~ family** venía de una familia de músicos *or* dotada para la música
3 (= *melodious*) [*laugh, voice*] musical
N (*Cine, Theat*) musical *m*
CPD ▸ **musical box** caja *f* de música ▸ **musical chairs** juego *msing* de las sillas, juego *msing* del stop • **to play ~ chairs** jugar a las sillas, jugar al stop ▸ **musical comedy** (*esp US*) comedia *f* musical ▸ **musical director** = music director ▸ **musical instrument** instrumento *m* musical ▸ **musical interlude** interludio *m* (musical) ▸ **musical score** (= *written music*) partitura *f*; (= *soundtrack*) banda *f* sonora
musicale [,mju:zɪ'kɑ:l] N velada *f* musical
musicality [,mju:zɪ'kælɪtɪ] N musicalidad *f*
musically ['mju:zɪkəlɪ] ADV **1** (= *from a musical point of view*) • **I'm ~ trained** tengo formación musical • **she was incredibly gifted ~** tenía un talento increíble para la música, tenía un talento musical increíble • **~, the piece cannot be faulted** desde el punto de vista musical, no se le pueden sacar defectos a la pieza
2 (= *melodiously*) [*say*] con un tono musical, melodiosamente
musician [mju:'zɪʃən] N músico/a *m/f* • **he's a ~** es músico
musicianship [mju:'zɪʃənʃɪp] N maestría *f* musical
musicologist [,mju:zɪ'kɒlədʒɪst] N musicólogo/a *m/f*
musicology [,mju:zɪ'kɒlədʒɪ] N musicología *f*
musingly ['mju:zɪŋlɪ] ADV [*say etc*] con aire distraído, pensativamente
musings ['mju:zɪŋz] NPL meditaciones *fpl*
musk [mʌsk] N (= *substance*) almizcle *m*; (= *scent*) perfume *m* de almizcle; (*Bot*) almizcleña *f*
CPD ▸ **musk ox** buey *m* almizclado ▸ **musk rose** (*Bot*) rosa *f* almizcleña
musket ['mʌskɪt] N mosquete *m*
musketeer [,mʌskɪ'tɪəʳ] N mosquetero *m*
musketry ['mʌskɪtrɪ] N (= *muskets*) mosquetes *mpl*; (= *firing*) fuego *m* de mosquetes, tiros *mpl*
muskrat ['mʌskræt] N ratón *m* almizclero
musky ['mʌskɪ] ADJ almizcleño, almizclado; [*smell*] a almizcle
Muslim N ['mʊslɪm] (PL: **Muslims** *or* **Muslim**) = Moslem
muslin ['mʌzlɪn] N muselina *f*
ADJ de muselina
musquash ['mʌskwɒʃ] N **1** (= *animal*) = muskrat
2 (= *fur*) piel *f* de ratón almizclero
muss* [mʌs] VT (*also* **muss up**) [+ *hair*] despeinar; [+ *dress*] arrugar
mussel ['mʌsl] N mejillón *m*
CPD ▸ **mussel bed** criadero *m* de mejillones
must¹ [mʌst] N = mustiness
must² [mʌst] MODAL VB **1** (*obligation*) deber, tener que • **I ~ do it** debo hacerlo, tengo que hacerlo • **the patient ~ have complete quiet** el enfermo debe tener *or* tiene que tener *or* requiere silencio absoluto • **I ~ buy some presents** tengo que comprar unos regalos • **you ~ come again next year** tienes que volver el año que viene • **you ~n't forget to send her a card** no te vayas a olvidar de mandarle una tarjeta • **you ~n't touch it** no debes tocarlo • **"must not be switched off"** "no debe apagarse" • **I'll do it if I ~** si me obligan, lo haré, lo haré si es necesario • **do it if you ~** hazlo si es necesario • **if you ~ know, I'm Portuguese** para que lo sepa, soy portugués • **one ~ not be too hopeful** no hay que ser demasiado optimista • **I really ~ go now** de verdad que me tengo que ir ya • **I ~ say, he's very irritating** tengo que decir que es muy irritante • **why ~ you always be so rude?** ¿por qué tienes que ser siempre tan maleducado?
2 (*probability*) deber de • **you ~ be tired** debes de estar cansado • **it ~ be cold up there** debe de hacer frío allí arriba • **he ~ be there by now** ya debe de estar allí • **it ~ be eight o'clock by now** ya deben de ser las ocho • **but you ~ have seen her!** ¡pero debes de haberla visto! • **there ~ be a reason** debe de haber *or* tiene que haber una razón
N* • **this programme is a ~** no hay que perderse este programa, este programa hay que verlo
must-* [mʌst-] PREFIX • **a must-see movie** una película que hay que ver, una película que no puede perderse • **leather jeans are the must-have fashion item of the season** los vaqueros de cuero son la prenda de moda imprescindible de la temporada • **a must-read** un libro obligado • **it's a must-visit** es una visita obligada
mustache ['mʌstæʃ] N (*US*) = **moustache**
mustachioed [mʌ'stæʃɪəʊd] ADJ (*US*) = **moustachioed**
mustang ['mʌstæŋ] N potro *m*, mesteño mustang(o) *m*
mustard ['mʌstəd] N (*Bot, Culin*) mostaza *f* • IDIOM: • **he doesn't cut the ~*** no da la talla
ADJ • **a ~ (yellow) dress** un vestido color mostaza
CPD ▸ **mustard gas** (*Chem, Mil*) gas *m* mostaza ▸ **mustard plaster** sinapismo *m*, cataplasma *f* de mostaza ▸ **mustard pot** mostacera *f* ▸ **mustard powder** harina *f* de mostaza ▸ **mustard seed** semilla *f* de mostaza
muster ['mʌstəʳ] N (*esp Mil*) revista *f* • IDIOM: • **to pass ~** ser aceptable
VT (= *call together, collect*) reunir; (*also* **muster up**) [+ *courage*] armarse de; [+ *strength*] cobrar • **the club can ~ 20 members** el club cuenta con 20 miembros, el club consta de 20 miembros
VI juntarse, reunirse
mustiness ['mʌstɪnɪs] N [*of room*] olor *m* a cerrado, olor *m* a humedad
mustn't ['mʌsnt] = **must not** ▹ **must²**
musty ['mʌstɪ] ADJ (COMPAR: **mustier**, SUPERL: **mustiest**) [*room etc*] que huele a humedad, que huele a cerrado; (*fig*) anticuado
mutability [,mju:tə'bɪlɪtɪ] N mutabilidad *f*
mutable ['mju:təbl] ADJ mudable
mutagen ['mju:tədʒən] N mutagene *m*
mutant ['mju:tənt] ADJ mutante
N mutante *mf*
mutate [mju:'teɪt] VT (*Bio*) mutar; (= *change*) transformar
VI (*Bio*) mutarse, sufrir mutación; (= *change*) transformarse
mutation [mju:'teɪʃən] N mutación *f*
mute [mju:t] ADJ mudo • **to become ~** enmudecer • **with H ~** con hache muda
N **1** (= *person*) mudo/a *m/f*
2 (*Mus*) sordina *f*
3 (*Ling*) letra *f* muda
VT (*Mus*) poner sordina a; [+ *noise*] amortiguar; [+ *feelings etc*] acallar
muted ['mju:tɪd] ADJ [*noise*] sordo; [*criticism*] callado, silencioso
mutilate ['mju:tɪleɪt] VT mutilar
mutilation [,mju:tɪ'leɪʃən] N mutilación *f*
mutineer [,mju:tɪ'nɪəʳ] N amotinado *m*, amotinador *m*
mutinous ['mju:tɪnəs] ADJ (*lit*) amotinado; (*fig*) rebelde • **we were feeling pretty ~** estábamos hartos ya, estábamos dispuestos a rebelarnos
mutiny ['mju:tɪnɪ] N motín *m*
VI amotinarse
mutt* [mʌt] N **1** (= *fool*) bobo *m*
2 (= *dog*) chucho *m*
mutter ['mʌtəʳ] N murmullo *m* • **a ~ of voices** un murmullo de voces
VT murmurar, decir entre dientes • **"yes," he ~ed** —sí —dijo entre dientes
VI (*gen*) murmurar; [*guns, thunder*] retumbar a lo lejos; (= *complain*) quejarse
mutton ['mʌtn] N cordero *m* • **a leg of ~** una pierna de cordero • IDIOM: • **~ dressed as lamb** vejestorio *m* emperifollado
CPD ▸ **mutton chop** chuleta *f* de cordero
muttonhead‡ ['mʌtn,hed] N cabeza *mf* de chorlito*
mutual ['mju:tjʊəl] ADJ **1** (= *reciprocal*) [*affection, help*] mutuo • **the feeling is ~** el sentimiento es mutuo • **they had a ~ understanding not to bring up the subject** tenían el mutuo acuerdo de no sacar el tema
2 (= *common*) [*friend, cousin*] común • **they had a ~ interest in rugby** tenían un interés común *or* compartían su interés por el rugby • **it is to our ~ benefit** *or* **advantage** es beneficioso para ambos • **by ~ consent** de mutuo *or* común acuerdo
CPD ▸ **mutual benefit society** mutualidad *f*, mutua *f*, mutual *f* (*Chile, Peru, Bol*) ▸ **mutual fund** (*US*) fondo *m* de inversión mobiliaria ▸ **mutual insurance** seguro *m* mutuo ▸ **mutual savings bank** caja *f* mutua de ahorros
mutuality [,mju:tjʊ'ælɪtɪ] N mutualidad *f*
mutually ['mju:tjʊəlɪ] ADV **1** (= *reciprocally*) mutuamente • **these views are ~ exclusive** estas opiniones se excluyen mutuamente
2 (= *for/by both parties involved*) • **we arranged to meet at a ~ convenient time** acordamos vernos a una hora que nos viniera bien a los dos • **such a move would be ~ beneficial to the two companies** esta medida resultaría beneficiosa para ambas empresas • **we ~ agreed that …** decidimos de mutuo *or* común acuerdo que …
Muzak® ['mju:zæk] N hilo *m* musical
muzzle ['mʌzl] N **1** (= *snout*) hocico *m*
2 [*of gun*] boca *f*
3 (= *restraint for dog*) bozal *m*
VT **1** [+ *dog*] poner bozal a
2 (*fig*) [+ *person*] amordazar
CPD ▸ **muzzle loader** arma *f* que se carga por la boca ▸ **muzzle velocity** velocidad *f* inicial
muzzy ['mʌzɪ] ADJ (COMPAR: **muzzier**, SUPERL: **muzziest**) [*outline, ideas*] borroso; [*person*] atontado, confuso
MVP N ABBR (*US*) = **most valuable player**
MW N ABBR **1** (*Rad*) (= **medium wave**) OM *f*
2 (*Elec*) = **megawatt(s)**
my [maɪ] POSS ADJ (*with singular noun*) mi; (*with plural noun*) mis • **my friend** mi amigo • **my books** mis libros • **my two best friends** mis dos mejores amigos • **my own car** mi propio coche • **they stole my car** me robaron el coche • **I'm washing my hair** me estoy lavando la cabeza • **I took off my coat** me quité el abrigo
EXCL ¡caramba!
myalgia [maɪ'ældʒɪə] N mialgia *f*
myalgic encephalomyelitis [maɪ'ældʒɪk-en,sefələʊmaɪə'laɪtɪs] N encefalomielitis *f*

m

inv miálgica
Myanmar ['maɪænma:ʳ] (N) Myanmar *f*
mycology [maɪ'kɒlədʒɪ] (N) micología *f*
myopia [maɪ'əʊpɪə] (N) (*frm*) miopía *f*
myopic [maɪ'ɒpɪk] (ADJ) (*frm*) miope
myriad ['mɪrɪəd] (*frm*) (ADJ) • **a ~ flies** un sinnúmero *or* una miríada de moscas
(N) miríada *f* • **the ~ of problems we face** la miríada de problemas a la que nos enfrentamos
myrmidon ['mɜ:mɪdən] (N) (*pej, hum*) secuaz *m* fiel, satélite *m*, esbirro *m*
myrrh [mɜ:ʳ] (N) mirra *f*
myrtle ['mɜ:tl] (N) arrayán *m*, mirto *m*
myself [maɪ'self] (PRON) **1** (*reflexive*) me • **I've hurt ~** me he hecho daño • **I couldn't see ~ in the mirror** no pude verme en el espejo
2 (*emphatic*) yo mismo/a; (*after prep*) mí, mí mismo/a • **I made it ~** lo hice yo mismo • **I went ~** fui en persona • **I talked mainly about ~** hablé principalmente de mí (mismo)
3 (*phrases*) • **by ~** solo/a • **I did it all by ~** lo hice yo solo • **I don't like travelling by ~** no me gusta viajar solo • **don't leave me all by ~!** ¡no me dejes aquí solo! • **a beginner like ~** un principiante como yo • **I'm not ~** no me encuentro nada bien • **I was talking to ~** hablaba solo
mysterious [mɪs'tɪərɪəs] (ADJ) **1** (= *puzzling*) [*disappearance, illness, circumstances*] misterioso • **there is nothing ~ about it** no tiene nada de misterioso, no tiene ningún misterio • PROVERB: • **the Lord moves in ~ ways** los designios del Señor son inescrutables
2 (= *enigmatic*) [*person, object*] misterioso; [*smile*] misterioso, lleno de misterio • **why are you being so ~?** ¿por qué andas con tanto misterio?, ¿a qué viene tanto misterio?
mysteriously [mɪs'tɪərɪəslɪ] (ADV) [*say, smile, behave*] misteriosamente, de forma misteriosa; [*disappear, appear, arrive*] misteriosamente
mystery ['mɪstərɪ] (N) **1** (*also Rel*) misterio *m* • **there's no ~ about it** no tiene ningún misterio • **to make a great ~ out of a matter** rodear un asunto con un halo de misterio • **it's a ~ to me where it can have gone** no entiendo dónde puede haberse metido • **it's a ~ how I lost it** no entiendo cómo lo pude perder
2 (*Literat*) (*also* **mystery story**) novela *f* de misterio
3 (*Rel, Theat*) (*also* **mystery play**) auto *m* sacramental, misterio *m*
(CPD) ▸ **mystery man** hombre *m* misterioso ▸ **mystery play** auto *m* sacramental, misterio *m* ▸ **mystery ship** buque *m* misterioso ▸ **mystery story** novela *f* de misterio ▸ **mystery tour, mystery trip** viaje *m* sorpresa
mystic ['mɪstɪk] (ADJ) místico
(N) místico/a *m/f*
mystical ['mɪstɪkəl] (ADJ) místico
mysticism ['mɪstɪsɪzəm] (N) misticismo *m*; (= *doctrine, literary genre*) mística *f*
mystification [,mɪstɪfɪ'keɪʃən] (N)
1 (= *mystery*) misterio *m* • **why all the ~?** ¿por qué tanto misterio?
2 (= *confusion*) perplejidad *f* • **my ~ increased** creció mi perplejidad
mystified ['mɪstɪfaɪd] (ADJ) perplejo, desconcertado • **I was ~** me quedé perplejo *or* desconcertado • **he had a ~ look on his face** se le notaba en la cara que estaba perplejo *or* desconcertado, tenía cara de perplejidad *or* desconcierto
mystify ['mɪstɪfaɪ] (VT) dejar perplejo, desconcertar
mystifying ['mɪstɪfaɪɪŋ] (ADJ) desconcertante
mystique [mɪs'ti:k] (N) mística *f*
myth [mɪθ] (N) (= *story*) mito *m*; (= *imaginary person, thing*) mito *m*, ilusión *f* • **a Greek ~** un mito griego • **that's a ~** eso es un mito • **it's a ~ that boiling water freezes faster than cold water** es un mito que el agua hirviendo se congela más rápidamente que el agua fría; ▹ **urban**
mythic ['mɪθɪk] (ADJ) = **mythical**
mythical ['mɪθɪkəl] (ADJ) (*Myth*) [*beast, creature*] mítico; (= *imaginary*) imaginario
mythological [,mɪθə'lɒdʒɪkəl] (ADJ) mitológico
mythology [mɪ'θɒlədʒɪ] (N) mitología *f*
myxomatosis [,mɪksəʊmə'təʊsɪs] (N) mixomatosis *f inv*

m

Nn

N[1], n [en] N (= *letter*) N *f*, n *f* • **N for Nellie** N de Navarra • **there are n ways of doing it** hay X maneras de hacerlo; ▹ **nth**

N[2] ABBR (= **north**) N

'n'‡ [ən] CONJ = **and**

NA N ABBR (*US*) **1** = **Narcotics Anonymous** **2** = **National Academy**

n/a ABBR **1** (= **not applicable**) no interesa **2** (*Banking*) = **no account** **3** (*Comm*) = **not available**

NAACP N ABBR (*US*) = **National Association for the Advancement of Colored People**

> **NAACP**
> La **NAACP**, siglas que corresponden a **National Association for the Advancement of Colored People** (Asociación Nacional para el Progreso de la Gente de Color), es una organización voluntaria estadounidense fundada en 1910 que se opone a la discriminación racial y que lucha por conseguir leyes que protejan los derechos de los ciudadanos de color. En 1953, la **NAACP** anunció que la integración en las escuelas era su objetivo prioritario, y este se vio cumplido cuando al año siguiente el Tribunal Supremo de los Estados Unidos prohibió las escuelas segregadas conocidas como **separate but equal**. Esta asociación siempre ha propugnado la no violencia y rechazó el **black power movement** de los años sesenta. El movimiento cuenta con el apoyo de cientos de miles de estadounidenses, muchos de ellos de raza blanca.

NAAFI [ˈnæfɪ] N ABBR (*Brit*) (*Mil*) (= **Navy, Army and Air Force Institute**) (*servicio de*) *cantinas, economatos etc para las fuerzas armadas*

naan [ˈnɑːn] N = **nan bread**

nab* [næb] VT (= *grab*) [+ *thing*] agarrar; [+ *person*] pillar*; (= *arrest*) pescar*, coger, agarrar (*LAm*); (= *steal*) robar, mangar (*Sp**)

nabob [ˈneɪbɒb] N nabab *m*

nacelle [næˈsel] N barquilla *f*, góndola *f*

nacho [ˈnɑːtʃəʊ] N (PL: **nachos**) nacho *m*

nacre [ˈneɪkəʳ] N nácar *m*

nacreous [ˈneɪkrɪəs] ADJ nacarino, nacarado, de nácar

NACU N ABBR (*US*) = **National Association of Colleges and Universities**

nada* [ˈnɑːdə] PRON (= *nothing*) na*

nadir [ˈneɪdɪəʳ] N (*Astron*) nadir *m*; (*fig*) punto *m* más bajo, nadir *m*

naevus, nevus (*US*) [ˈniːvəs] N (PL: **naevi,** (*US*) **nevi** [ˈniːvaɪ]) nevo *m*

naff* [næf] ADJ (COMPAR: **naffer**, SUPERL: **naffest**) (= *in poor taste*) de mal gusto, hortera (*Sp**); (= *inferior*) ordinario, inferior

▸ **naff off*** VI + ADV • **~ off** vete a paseo*, vete al cuerno*

NAFTA [ˈnæftə] N ABBR (= **North American Free Trade Agreement**) TLC *m*

nag[1] [næɡ] N (= *horse*) rocín *m*, jaco *m*

nag[2] [næɡ] VT **1** (= *annoy*) fastidiar, dar la lata* • **stop nagging me!** ¡deja ya de fastidiarme!, ¡deja ya de darme la lata!* • **she nags me all day long** se pasa el día fastidiándome, se pasa el día dándome la lata* • **to nag sb to do sth • nag sb into doing sth** dar la lata a algn para que haga algo*, fastidiar a algn para que haga algo* **2** (= *scold*) regañar • **to nag sb for doing sth** regañar a algn por hacer algo **3** (= *torment*) • **his conscience was nagging him** le remordía la conciencia • **he was nagged by doubts** lo acosaban las dudas

VI **1** (= *annoy*) fastidiar, dar la lata* **2** (= *scold*) regañar

N gruñón/ona *m/f*

▸ **nag at** VI + PREP **1** [*feeling*] angustiar; [*doubt*] inquietar • **a thought nagged at him** le angustiaba un pensamiento • **a feeling of doubt had been nagging at him ever since** desde entonces, le inquietaba una duda • **the worries that nag at every pregnant woman** las preocupaciones que inquietan a todas las embarazadas **2** • **to nag at sb to do sth** [*person*] dar la lata a algn para que haga algo* • **my girlfriend has been nagging at me to cut my hair** mi novia me ha estado dando la lata para que me corte el pelo*

nagger [ˈnæɡəʳ] N gruñón/ona *m/f*

nagging [ˈnæɡɪŋ] ADJ [*person*] gruñón; [*pain, doubt, fear*] persistente; [*conscience*] intranquilo

N quejas *fpl*, críticas *fpl*

nah [næ*] EXCL (*Brit*) ¡no!

NAHT N ABBR (*Brit*) (= **National Association of Head Teachers**) *sindicato de profesores*

naiad [ˈnaɪæd] N (PL: **naiads** *or* **naiades** [ˈnaɪədiːz]) náyade *f*

nail [neɪl] N **1** (*Anat*) uña *f* • **to bite one's ~s** morderse las uñas **2** (*metal*) clavo *m* • IDIOMS: • **a ~ in sb's coffin**: • **this is another ~ in his coffin** este es otro paso hacia su destrucción • **to hit the ~ on the head** dar en el clavo • **to pay (cash) on the ~** pagar en el acto, pagar a tocateja (*Sp**); ▹ **hard**

VT **1** (= *fix with nails*) clavar, sujetar con clavos • **to ~ two things together** fijar *or* unir dos cosas con clavos **2*** (= *catch, get hold of*) agarrar, pillar* **3** (= *expose*) [+ *lie*] poner al descubierto; [+ *rumour*] demostrar la falsedad de **4** (= *define*) definir, precisar

CPD ▸ **nail bomb** bomba *f* de metralla ▸ **nail clippers** cortauñas *m inv* ▸ **nail enamel** (*US*) esmalte *m* de uñas ▸ **nail extension** prótesis *f* de uña ▸ **nail file** lima *f* (para las uñas) ▸ **nail polish** esmalte *m* de uñas ▸ **nail polish remover** quitaesmalte *m* ▸ **nail scissors** tijeras *fpl* para las uñas ▸ **nail varnish** esmalte *m* de uñas ▸ **nail varnish remover** quitaesmalte *m*

▸ **nail down** VT + ADV **1** (= *secure with nails*) clavar, sujetar con clavos **2** (*fig*) [+ *person*] obligar a concretar • **you can't ~ him down** es imposible hacerle concretar • **we ~ed him down to a date** le forzamos a fijar una fecha

▸ **nail up** VT + ADV (= *fix*) (*on wall*) clavar; (= *close*) [+ *window*] condenar (*claveteándole tablas*)

nail-biting [ˈneɪlˌbaɪtɪŋ] ADJ [*tension*] angustioso; [*contest, finish*] emocionantísimo

N *mala costumbre de morderse las uñas*

nailbrush [ˈneɪlbrʌʃ] N cepillo *m* de uñas

nailgun [ˈneɪlɡʌn] N pistola *f* de clavos

Nairobi [naɪˈrəʊbɪ] N Nairobi *m*

naïve, naive [naɪˈiːv] ADJ **1** [*person*] ingenuo; [*argument*] simplista; [*attitude, views*] ingenuo, cándido **2** (*Art*) naïf

naïvely, naively [naɪˈiːvlɪ] ADV ingenuamente

naïveté, naivety [naɪˈiːvtɪ] N ingenuidad *f*, candor *m*

naked [ˈneɪkɪd] ADJ **1** (= *unclothed*) [*person, body, flesh*] desnudo; [*breasts*] desnudo, al descubierto • **visible/invisible to the ~ eye** visible/invisible a simple vista; ▹ **stark, strip** **2** (*fig*) (= *defenceless*) • **to go ~ into battle** entrar en combate a cuerpo descubierto **3** (= *without grass, plants etc*) [*earth*] pelado, yermo (*liter*); [*tree, branches*] pelado, desnudo (*liter*) **4** (= *exposed*) [*light bulb*] sin pantalla; [*wire*] pelado; [*sword*] desenvainado • **~ flame** llama *f* **5** (= *undisguised*) [*hatred, misery*] manifiesto, visible; [*ambition*] patente, ostensible • **the ~ pursuit of power** la carrera manifiesta por el poder • **the ~ truth** la verdad al desnudo, la pura verdad

nakedly [ˈneɪkɪdlɪ] ADV (= *unashamedly*) (*with adj*) manifiestamente, ostensiblemente; (*with verb*) de manera ostensible

nakedness [ˈneɪkɪdnɪs] N (*lit*) desnudez *f*; [*of aggression, ambition*] lo patente

NALGO [ˈnælɡəʊ] N ABBR (*Brit*) (*formerly*) (= **National and Local Government Officers' Association**) *sindicato de funcionarios*

NAM N ABBR (*US*) = **National Association of Manufacturers**

Nam*, 'Nam* [næm] N (*US*) (= *Vietnam*) Vietnam

namby-pamby [ˈnæmbɪˈpæmbɪ] ADJ soso, ñoño*

N persona *f* sosa, ñoño/a* *m/f*

name [neɪm] N **1** [*of person, firm*] nombre *m*; (= *surname*) apellido *m*; [*of book, film*] título *m* • **what's your ~?** ¿cómo te llamas? • **my ~ is Peter** me llamo Peter • **what ~ shall I say?** (*Telec*) ¿de parte de quién?; (*announcing arrival*) ¿a quién debo anunciar? • **what ~ are they giving the child?** ¿qué nombre le van a poner al niño? • **they married to give the child a ~** se casaron para darle nombre *or* legitimar al

niño • **to take sb's ~ and address** apuntar el nombre y las señas de algn • **by ~** de nombre • **I know him by ~ only** lo conozco solamente de nombre • **Pérez by ~** de apellido Pérez, apellidado Pérez • **a lady by the ~ of Dulcinea** una dama llamada Dulcinea • **we know it by another ~** lo conocemos por otro nombre • **to go by the ~ of** ser conocido por el nombre de • **in ~**: • **he was king in ~ only** era rey tan solo de nombre • **it exists in ~ only** no existe más que de nombre • **at least in ~** al menos nominalmente • **she's the boss in all but ~** para jefa solo le falta el nombre • **in the ~ of peace** en nombre de la paz • **I thank you in the ~ of all those present** le doy las gracias en nombre de todos los presentes • **he signed on in the ~ of Smith** se inscribió en el paro *or* desempleo con el apellido Smith • **open up, in the ~ of the law!** ¡abran en nombre de la ley! • **what's in a ~?** ¿qué importa un nombre? • **to lend one's ~ to** prestar su nombre a • **I'll do it, or my ~'s not Bloggs!** ¡como que me llamo Bloggs que lo haré! • **to put one's ~ down for** [+ *new car etc*] apuntarse para; [+ *school, course*] inscribirse en • **he had his ~ taken** (*Sport*) el árbitro apuntó su nombre • **we know it under another ~** lo conocemos por otro nombre • **to go under the ~ of** ser conocido por el nombre de • IDIOMS: • **that's the ~ of the game*** (= *the norm*) así son las cosas; (= *what's important*) eso es lo importante • **he hasn't a penny to his ~** no tiene donde caerse muerto; ▹ **Christian, first, maiden, middle, pet**
2 names (= *insults*) • **to call sb ~s** insultar a algn
3 (= *reputation*) reputación *f*, fama *f* • **to get (o.s.) a bad ~** crearse mala reputación *or* fama • **he's giving the place a bad ~** le está dando mala fama al lugar • **he has a ~ for carelessness** tiene fama de descuidado • **the firm has a good ~** la casa tiene buena reputación • **to make a ~ for o.s.** hacerse famoso • **to make one's ~** llegar a ser famoso
4 (= *person*) • **big ~*** (gran) figura *f*, personaje *m* importante • **he's one of the big ~s in the business** es uno de los grandes en este negocio • **this show has no big ~s** este show no tiene figuras famosas
(VT) **1** (= *call*) llamar; [+ *person*] (*at birth*) poner • **a man ~d Jack** un hombre llamado Jack • **they ~d the child Mary** a la niña le pusieron María • **to ~ sth/sb after** *or* (*US*) **for sth/sb: they ~d him Winston after Churchill** le pusieron Winston por Churchill • **she was ~d after her grandmother** la llamaron como a su abuela, le pusieron el nombre de su abuela • **they ~d the street after Nelson Mandela** a la calle le pusieron el nombre de Nelson Mandela
2 (= *mention*) • **you were not ~d in the speech** no se te nombró *or* mencionó en el discurso • **he is not ~d in this list** no figura en esta lista • **~ the third president of the USA** diga el nombre del tercer presidente de EE.UU. • **~ 20 British birds** nómbrame 20 pájaros británicos • **first-named** primero • **last-named** último • **you ~ it, we've got it** cualquier cosa que pidas, la tenemos • **to name names** dar *or* mencionar nombres
3 (= *fix*) [+ *date, price*] fijar • **have you ~d the day yet?** ¿han fijado ya la fecha de la boda? • **they're so keen to buy it you can ~ your price** tienen tanto afán por comprarlo que puedes pedirles lo que quieras *or* decir el precio que quieras
4 (= *nominate*) nombrar • **he was ~d ambassador to Warsaw** lo nombraron embajador en Varsovia
(CPD) ▸ **name day** (*Rel*) día *m* del santo, fiesta *f* onomástica; (*Econ*) día *m* de ajuste de cuentas ▸ **name tape** etiqueta *f* con el nombre

name-calling [ˈneɪmkɔːlɪŋ] (N) insultos *mpl*, ofensas *fpl*

namecheck [ˈneɪmtʃek] (N) alusión *f* directa, referencia *f* directa (*en una canción, película etc*) • **he gets a ~ in the first song** hay una referencia directa a él en la primera canción
(VT) aludir directamente a, mencionar

name-drop [ˈneɪmdrɒp] (VI) dárselas de conocer gente importante • **I don't want to name-drop, but I did get to meet Madonna** no quiero dármelas de que conozco a gente importante, pero llegué a conocer a Madonna

name-dropper [ˈneɪmˌdrɒpəʳ] (N) • **he's a name-dropper** siempre está mencionando a la gente importante que conoce

name-dropping [ˈneɪmˈdrɒpɪŋ] (N) • **there was a good deal of name-dropping** todo el mundo se las daba de conocer a gente importante

nameless [ˈneɪmlɪs] (ADJ) **1** (= *anonymous*) anónimo, sin nombre • **someone, who shall be ~ …** cierta persona, cuyo nombre me callo …
2 (= *indefinable*) [*dread, grief*] indescriptible; [*crime*] horrendo, indescriptible

namely [ˈneɪmlɪ] (ADV) a saber, concretamente • **another possibility, ~ that it was not working** otra posibilidad, a saber, que no funcionaba

nameplate [ˈneɪmpleɪt] (N) (*on door*) placa *f* (del nombre); (*on goods*) placa *f* del fabricante

namesake [ˈneɪmseɪk] (N) tocayo/a *m/f*, homónimo/a *m/f*

name-tag [ˈneɪmtæg] (N) placa *f* de identificación

Namibia [nɑːˈmɪbɪə] (N) Namibia *f*

Namibian [nɑːˈmɪbɪən] (ADJ) namibio
(N) namibio/a *m/f*

naming [ˈneɪmɪŋ] (N) nombramiento *m*

nan* [næn], **nana*** [ˈnænə] (N) (*Brit*) (= *grandmother*) abuelita* *f*, yaya* *f*

nan bread [ˈnɑːnbred] (N) *pan indio sin apenas levadura*

nance‡ [næns], **nancy**‡ [ˈnænsɪ], **nancy-boy**‡ [ˈnænsɪbɔɪ] (N) (*Brit*) (*pej*) maricón‡ *m*

nandrolone [ˈnændrələʊn] (N) nandrolona *f* • **to test positive for ~** dar positivo de nandrolona

nanny [ˈnænɪ] (N) **1** (= *childminder*) niñera *f*
2* (= *grandmother*) abuelita* *f*, yaya* *f*
(CPD) ▸ **nanny goat** cabra *f* ▸ **nanny state** (*esp Brit*) papá-estado *m*

nannying [ˈnænɪɪŋ] (N) **1** (= *job*) profesión *f* de niñera
2 (*pej*) (= *mollycoddling*) protección *f* excesiva

nano- [ˈnænəʊ] (PREFIX) nano-

nanobacteria [ˈnænəʊbækˌtɪərɪə] (NPL) nanobacterias *fpl*

nanobacterium [ˈnænəʊbækˌtɪərɪəm] (N) (PL: **nanobacteria**) nanobacteria *f*

nanobot [ˈnænəʊˌbɒt] (N) nanorobot *m*

nanometre [ˈnænəʊˌmiːtəʳ] (N) nanómetro *m*

nanoscale [ˈnænəʊˌskeɪl] (N) nanoescala *f*

nanoscience [ˈnænəʊˌsaɪəns] (N) nanociencia *f*

nanosecond [ˈnænəʊˌsekənd] (N) nanosegundo *m*

nanotechnology [ˌnænəʊtekˈnɒlədʒɪ] (N) nanotecnología *f*

nanotube [ˈnænəʊˌtjuːb] (N) nanotubo *m*

Naomi [ˈneɪəmɪ] (N) Naomi

nap¹ [næp] (N) sueñecito *m*; (*in afternoon*) siesta *f* • **to have** *or* **take a nap** echar un sueñecito/una siesta
(VI) dormitar • IDIOMS: • **to catch sb napping** pillar a algn desprevenido • **to be caught napping** estar desprevenido

nap² [næp] (N) (*on cloth*) lanilla *f*, pelusa *f*

nap³ [næp] (N) (*Cards*) (= *game*) napolitana *f* • **to go nap** jugarse el todo (**on** a)

NAPA (N ABBR) (*US*) (= **National Association of Performing Artists**) *sindicato de trabajadores del espectáculo*

napalm [ˈneɪpɑːm] (N) napalm *m*

nape [neɪp] (N) (*also* **nape of the neck**) nuca *f*, cogote *m*

naphtha [ˈnæfθə] (N) nafta *f*

naphthalene [ˈnæfθəliːn] (N) naftalina *f*

napkin [ˈnæpkɪn] (N) (= *table napkin*) servilleta *f*; (*Brit*) (*baby's*) pañal *m*; (*US*) (= *sanitary towel*) compresa *f* higiénica, paño *m* higiénico
(CPD) ▸ **napkin ring** servilletero *m*

Naples [ˈneɪplz] (N) Nápoles *m*

Napoleon [nəˈpəʊlɪən] (N) Napoleón

Napoleonic [nəˌpəʊlɪˈɒnɪk] (ADJ) napoleónico

nappa [ˈnæpə] (N) napa *f*

napper* [ˈnæpəʳ] (N) (= *head*) coca* *f*

nappy [ˈnæpɪ] (N) (*Brit*) pañal *m* • **the baby's got a dirty ~** el niño tiene caca • **leave the dirty nappies to soak** pon los pañales sucios a remojo
(CPD) ▸ **nappy liner** gasa *f* ▸ **nappy rash** irritación *f* • **to have ~ rash** estar escaldado

Narbonne [nɑːˈbɒn] (N) Narbona *f*

narc* [nɑːk] (N) (*US*) agente* *mf* de la brigada de los narcóticos

narcissi [nɑːˈsɪsaɪ] (NPL) *of* **narcissus**

narcissism [nɑːˈsɪsɪzəm] (N) narcisismo *m*

narcissist [ˈnɑːsɪˌsɪst] (N) narcisista *mf*

narcissistic [ˌnɑːsɪˈsɪstɪk] (ADJ) narcisista

Narcissus [nɑːˈsɪsəs] (N) Narciso

narcissus [nɑːˈsɪsəs] (N) (PL: **narcissi** *or* **narcissuses** [nɑːˈsɪsaɪ]) (*Bot*) narciso *m*

narcolepsy [ˈnɑːkəʊlepsɪ] (N) narcolepsia *f*

narcoleptic [ˌnɑːkəʊˈleptɪk] (ADJ) narcoléptico
(N) narcoléptico/a *m/f*

narcosis [nɑːˈkəʊsɪs] (N) narcosis *f*, narcotismo *m*

narco-terrorism [ˌnɑːkəʊˈterərɪzəm] (N) narcoterrorismo *m*

narcotic [nɑːˈkɒtɪk] (N) **1** (*Med*) narcótico *m*
2 (*esp US*) (= *illegal drug*) **narcotics** estupefacientes *mpl*, narcóticos *mpl*
(ADJ) narcótico • **~ drug** narcótico *m*
(CPD) ▸ **narcotics agent** agente *mf* de narcóticos ▸ **Narcotics Anonymous** Narcóticos *mpl* Anónimos ▸ **narcotics charge** • **to be on a ~s charge** estar acusado de traficar con drogas ▸ **narcotics trafficker** narcotraficante *mf*, traficante *mf* de drogas ▸ **narcotics trafficking** narcotráfico *m*, tráfico *m* de estupefacientes *or* drogas

narcotism [ˈnɑːkəˌtɪzəm] (N) narcotismo *m*

narcotize [ˈnɑːkətaɪz] (VT) narcotizar

narco-trafficker [ˌnɑːkəʊˈtræfɪkəʳ] (N) narcotraficante *mf*

narco-trafficking [ˌnɑːkəʊˈtræfɪkɪŋ] (N) narcotráfico *m*

nard [nɑːd] (N) nardo *m*

nark* [nɑːk] (N) soplón/ona* *m/f*
(VT) (*Brit*) • **~ it!** (= *stop it*) ¡déjalo!; (= *go away*) ¡lárgate!*

narked* [nɑːkt] (ADJ) (*Brit*) (= *annoyed*) cabreado* • **to be ~** estar cabreado* (**at sth** por algo) • **to get ~** cabrearse* • **he got really ~** se cabreó de lo lindo*

narky* [ˈnɑːkɪ] (ADJ) • **to get ~** (*Brit*) cabrearse*

narrate [nəˈreɪt] (VT) [+ *documentary*] narrar, hacer los comentarios de; [+ *story*] narrar, relatar

narration [nəˈreɪʃən] (N) [*of documentary*] narración *f*, comentarios *mpl*; [*of story*] narración *f*, relato *m*
narrative [ˈnærətɪv] (ADJ) narrativo
(N) (= *act*) narración *f*; (= *story*) narración *f*, relato *m*
narrator [nəˈreɪtəʳ] (N) [*of story*] narrador(a) *m/f*; [*of documentary*] narrador(a) *m/f*, comentarista *mf*
narrow [ˈnærəʊ] (ADJ) (COMPAR: **narrower**, SUPERL: **narrowest**) **1** (*in width*) [*street, passage, room, stairs*] estrecho, angosto; [*bed, channel, face*] estrecho, angosto (*LAm*) • **to become** *or* **get ~(er)** estrecharse, angostarse (*LAm*)
2 (= *limited*) [*range*] reducido, limitado; [*definition*] restringido • **prices rose and fell within a ~ band** los precios subieron y bajaron dentro de una estrecha banda • **in a ~ sense** en sentido estricto
3 (= *small, slight*) [*margin, majority*] escaso; [*victory, defeat*] por un escaso margen • **to have a ~ escape** salvarse de milagro, salvarse por los pelos* • **to have a ~ lead (over sb)** llevar una pequeña ventaja (a algn)
4 (*pej*) (= *restricted*) [*person*] de miras estrechas, intolerante; [*mind*] estrecho de miras; [*view, idea*] cerrado
(VI) **1** (= *become less wide*) [*road, path, river*] estrecharse, angostarse (*LAm*)
2 (= *almost close*) [*eyes*] entrecerrarse
3 (= *diminish*) [*gap, majority*] reducirse
(VT) **1** (= *reduce*) [+ *gap*] reducir; [+ *differences*] solventar en cierta medida
2 (= *almost close*) • **to ~ one's eyes** entrecerrar los ojos
(N) **1** ▹ **straight**
2 narrows estrecho *msing*
(CPD) ▸ **narrow boat** (*Brit*) barcaza *f* ▸ **narrow gauge** (*Rail*) vía *f* estrecha; (*before noun*) de vía estrecha
▸ **narrow down** (VT + ADV) [+ *search, investigation, possibilities*] restringir, limitar • **I've ~ed the guest list down to 30** he reducido la lista de invitados a 30
(VI + ADV) [*road, path, valley*] estrecharse, angostarse (*LAm*); [*search, investigation*] restringirse • **the list of candidates has ~ed down to four** la lista de candidatos se ha reducido a cuatro
narrow-gauge [ˌnærəʊˈgeɪdʒ] (ADJ) (*Rail*) [*train, railway*] de vía estrecha
• **narrow-gauge line** línea *f* de vía estrecha
narrowing [ˈnærəʊɪŋ] (N) [*of road, path, channel*] estrechamiento *m* • **the ~ of the gap between rich and poor** el acortamiento de la distancia que separa a ricos y pobres
narrowly [ˈnærəʊlɪ] (ADV) **1** (= *just*) [*escape, avoid, miss, fail*] por poco; [*defeat*] por un escaso margen • **to be ~ defeated** (*in election*) ser derrotado por un escaso margen; (*Sport*) perder por poco
2 (= *restrictively*) [*define*] de forma restringida • **to be ~ based** [*organization*] tener una base limitada • **these exams are too ~ vocational** estos exámenes tienen un enfoque demasiado vocacional
3 (= *closely*) [*watch*] de cerca; [*observe*] atentamente
narrow-minded [ˈnærəʊˈmaɪndɪd] (*pej*) (ADJ) [*person*] estrecho de miras, de mentalidad cerrada; [*views*] intolerante, cerrado; [*ideas, outlook*] cerrado
narrow-mindedness [ˈnærəʊˈmaɪndɪdnɪs] (N) estrechez *f* de miras, intolerancia *f*
narrowness [ˈnærəʊnɪs] (N) **1** [*of road, path, channel*] estrechez *f*
2 [*of victory, defeat*] escaso margen *m*
3 [*of attitude*] lo cerrado • **~ of mind** estrechez *f* de miras
narwhal [ˈnɑːwəl] (N) narval *m*

NAS (N ABBR) (*US*) = **National Academy of Sciences**
NASA [ˈnæsə] (N ABBR) (*US*) (= **National Aeronautics and Space Administration**) NASA *f*
nasal [ˈneɪzəl] (ADJ) **1** (*Anat*) nasal
2 (= *twanging*) gangoso
(N) nasal *f*
nasality [neɪˈzælɪtɪ] (N) nasalidad *f*
nasalization [ˌneɪzəlaɪˈzeɪʃən] (N) nasalización *f*
nasalize [ˈneɪzəlaɪz] (VT) nasalizar; (*twangingly*) pronunciar con timbre gangoso
nasally [ˈneɪzəlɪ] (ADV) nasalmente, por la nariz • **to speak ~** hablar por la nariz
nascent [ˈnæsnt] (ADJ) [*industry, democracy*] naciente
Nassau [ˈnæsɔː] (N) Nassau *m*
nastily [ˈnɑːstɪlɪ] (ADV) [*speak, behave*] con maldad
nastiness [ˈnɑːstɪnɪs] (N) **1** (= *unpleasantness*) [*of weather, situation*] lo desagradable; [*of taste, smell*] lo desagradable, lo repugnante
2 (= *spitefulness*) maldad *f*
nasturtium [nəsˈtɜːʃəm] (N) (*Bot*) capuchina *f*
nasty [ˈnɑːstɪ] (ADJ) (COMPAR: **nastier**, SUPERL: **nastiest**) **1** (= *unpleasant*) [*situation, experience, surprise*] desagradable; [*taste, smell*] desagradable, repugnante; [*habit, weather*] desagradable, feo, malo • **it was a ~ business** fue un asunto desagradable • **I've got a ~ feeling that ...** tengo la horrible sensación de que ... • **history has a ~ habit of repeating itself** la historia tiene la mala costumbre de repetirse • **he had a ~ shock** se llevó un susto terrible • **the situation turned ~** la situación se puso fea; ▹ **taste**
2 (= *serious*) [*accident*] serio, grave; [*cut, wound*] feo; [*infection*] fuerte; [*disease*] peligroso • **a ~ case of** un caso grave de • **she had a ~ fall** tuvo una mala caída
3 (= *difficult*) [*question*] difícil; [*bend, junction*] peligroso; [*problem*] complicado • **there was one ~ moment when ...** se produjo un momento de tensión cuando ...
4 (= *spiteful*) [*person, remark*] cruel, desagradable; [*joke*] de mal gusto, grosero • **a nasty-looking individual** un individuo mal encarado • **he's a ~ piece of work** es un canalla* • **to be ~ to sb** ser cruel con algn • **don't be ~ to your little brother** no seas malo con tu hermanito • **a ~ trick** una mala jugada • **he turned ~ and started to shout** se puso agresivo y empezó a gritar
(N)* • **there were a few hidden nasties in my bill** había unas cuantas sorpresas desagradables en mi cuenta; ▹ **video**
NAS/UWT (N ABBR) (*Brit*) (= **National Association of Schoolmasters/Union of Women Teachers**) *sindicato de profesores*
nat (ABBR) (= **national**) nal.
Natal [nəˈtæl] (N) Natal *m*
natal [ˈneɪtl] (ADJ) natal
natality [nəˈtælɪtɪ] (N) natalidad *f*
natatorium [ˌneɪtəˈtɔːrɪəm] (N) (PL: **natatoria** [ˌneɪtəˈtɔːrɪə]) (*US*) piscina *f*
natch‡ [nætʃ] (EXCL) naturalmente, naturaca‡
NATFHE (N ABBR) (*Brit*) (= **National Association of Teachers in Further and Higher Education**) *sindicato de la enseñanza superior*
nation [ˈneɪʃən] (N) (*Pol*) nación *f*; (= *people*) pueblo *m*, nación *f*
(CPD) ▸ **Nation of Islam** (*US*) Nación *f* del Islam
national [ˈnæʃənl] (ADJ) **1** (= *of one nation*) nacional
2 (= *nationwide*) [*newspaper, economy*] nacional; [*election, campaign*] a nivel nacional • **the ~ average** la media nacional
(N) **1** (= *person*) ciudadano/a *m/f*
2 (= *newspaper*) periódico *m* nacional
(CPD) ▸ **National Aeronautics and Space Administration** (*US*) NASA *f* ▸ **national anthem** himno *m* nacional ▸ **National Assistance** (*Brit*) (*formerly*) *subsidio (al necesitado)* ▸ **national bank** (*state-owned*) banco *m* nacional, banco *m* estatal; (*US*) (*commercial*) *banco que forma parte del Sistema de Reservas Federal* ▸ **national costume** traje *m* típico nacional ▸ **National Curriculum** (*Brit*) *plan de estudios oficial que se sigue en las escuelas de enseñanza pública de Inglaterra y País de Gales* ▸ **national debt** deuda *f* pública ▸ **national dress** = **national costume** ▸ **the National Front** (*Brit*) el Frente Nacional (británico) (*partido político de extrema derecha e ideología racista*) ▸ **national government** gobierno *m* nacional ▸ **national grid** red *f* eléctrica nacional ▸ **the National Guard** (*US*) la Guardia Nacional ▸ **the National Health (Service)** (*Brit*) *servicio de asistencia pública sanitaria* • **to have an operation done on the National Health (Service)** ≈ operarse por la Seguridad Social *or* el Seguro ▸ **national heritage** patrimonio *m* nacional ▸ **national holiday** (*esp US*) fiesta *f*, día *m* festivo, (día *m*) feriado *m* (*LAm*) ▸ **National Insurance** (*Brit*) ≈ Seguridad *f* Social ▸ **National Insurance contributions** cotizaciones *fpl* a la Seguridad Social, aportes *mpl* a la Seguridad Social (*S. Cone*) ▸ **National Insurance number** número *m* de la Seguridad Social ▸ **the National Lottery** (*Brit*) ≈ la lotería primitiva ▸ **national monument** monumento *m* nacional ▸ **national park** parque *m* nacional ▸ **national press** prensa *f* nacional ▸ **National Savings (Bank)** (*Brit*) ≈ caja *f* postal de ahorros ▸ **National Savings Certificate** (*Brit*) ≈ bono *m* del Estado ▸ **national security** seguridad *f* nacional ▸ **the National Security Council** (*US*) el Consejo para la Seguridad Nacional ▸ **national service** (*Mil*) servicio *m* militar • **to do (one's) ~ service** hacer el servicio militar, hacer la mili* ▸ **National Socialism** nacionalsocialismo *m* ▸ **the National Trust** (*Brit*) ≈ la Dirección General del Patrimonio Nacional

NATIONAL GUARD
La **National Guard** (Guardia Nacional) es una organización estadounidense que recluta voluntarios no profesionales a los que se prepara para colaborar con el ejército profesional y las fuerzas aéreas en tiempos de crisis. Los requisitos para alistarse son los mismos que para el ejército normal y, aunque su preparación la dirige el gobierno federal, sus miembros pueden ser movilizados para ayudar en situaciones de emergencia, catástrofes naturales y el control de situaciones excepcionales de violencia civil. Los miembros de la **National Guard** tienen que prestar juramento de fidelidad a los EE. UU. y al estado al que pertenecen.

NATIONAL TRUST
El **National Trust** es una organización benéfica británica que se dedica a la conservación de lugares del patrimonio histórico-artístico o de parajes naturales. Se financia a través de donaciones, aportaciones de los socios, y dinero procedente de la venta de entradas, souvenirs y de las cafeterías o restaurantes que suele haber en muchos de estos lugares.

n

nationalism ['næʃnəlɪzəm] N nacionalismo *m*
nationalist ['næʃnəlɪst] ADJ nacionalista
N nacionalista *mf*
nationalistic [,næʃnə'lɪstɪk] ADJ nacionalista
nationality [,næʃə'nælɪtɪ] N **1** (= *citizenship*) nacionalidad *f*, ciudadanía *f* • **she took/adopted French ~** adquirió/adoptó la nacionalidad *or* ciudadanía francesa
2 (= *national group*) nacionalidad *f* • **the city is home to 20 different nationalities** la ciudad alberga hasta 20 nacionalidades distintas
nationalization [,næʃnəlaɪ'zeɪʃən] N nacionalización *f*
nationalize ['næʃnəlaɪz] VT nacionalizar • **~d industry** industria *f* nacionalizada
nationally ['næʃnəlɪ] ADV [*distributed*] por todo el país, a escala nacional; [*available*] en todo el país • **this is the case locally, but not ~** eso es cierto a nivel local, pero no a nivel nacional • **a ~ recognized qualification** una titulación reconocida a nivel nacional *or* en todo el país
nationhood ['neɪʃənhʊd] N carácter *m* de nación • **they have a strong sense of ~** poseen un acusado sentimiento nacionalista • **to achieve ~** llegar a constituir una nación, llegar a tener categoría de nación
nation-state ['neɪʃən'steɪt] N estado-nación *m*
nationwide ['neɪʃənwaɪd] ADJ [*survey, poll*] a nivel nacional; [*campaign, strike, debate*] a escala nacional; [*interest, support*] en todo el país; [*network, referendum*] nacional; [*tour*] por todo el país • **police have initiated a ~ hunt for the killer** la policía ha comenzado una búsqueda del asesino por todo el país
ADV [*deliver*] en todo el territorio nacional, por todo el país • **we now have over 300 branches ~** ya tenemos más de 300 sucursales por todo el país • **the film will be released ~ on 28th** la película se estrena en todo el país el día 28
native ['neɪtɪv] ADJ **1** (= *of one's birth*) [*town, country, soil*] natal • **~ Britons** los nacidos en Gran Bretaña
2 (= *indigenous*) **a** [*inhabitant, culture, population*] indígena • **the ~ peoples of the Amazon** los pueblos indígenas del Amazonas • **to go ~** adoptar las costumbres del lugar
b [*plant, animal, species*] autóctono, originario del lugar • **to be ~ to** ser originario de
3 (= *innate*) [*ability, talent*] natural, innato • **~ wit** ingenio *m*
N **1** (*referring to birth or nationality*) nativo/a *m/f* • **he speaks German like a ~** habla alemán como un nativo • **he was a ~ of Seville** nació en Sevilla
2† (*freq pej*) (= *member of indigenous people*) indígena *mf*
3 (= *plant, animal*) • **to be a ~ of** ser originario de
CPD ▸ **native country, native land** patria *f* ▸ **native language** lengua *f* materna ▸ **native son** (*liter*) hijo *m* predilecto ▸ **native speaker** hablante *mf* nativo/a • **a Spanish ~ speaker** • **a ~ speaker of Spanish** un hablante nativo de español ▸ **native tongue** = **native language**
Native American [,neɪtɪvə'merɪkən] ADJ americano nativo
N americano/a *m/f* nativo/a
nativity [nə'tɪvɪtɪ] N **1** (*gen*) natividad *f*
2 (*Rel*) • **the Nativity** la Natividad
3 (*Art*) • **Nativity** nacimiento *m*
CPD ▸ **Nativity play** auto *m* de Navidad ▸ **Nativity scene** belén *m*, nacimiento *m*

NATO ['neɪtəʊ] N ABBR (= **North Atlantic Treaty Organization**) OTAN *f*
NATSOPA [,næt'səʊpə] N ABBR (*Brit*) (= **National Society of Operative Printers, Graphical and Media Personnel**) *sindicato de tipógrafos*
natter* ['nætəʳ] (*Brit*) N charla *f*, plática *f* (*Mex*) • **to have a ~** charlar, estar de palique (*Sp**), platicar (*Mex*) (**with** con) • **we had a good old ~** estuvimos charlando un buen rato
VI (= *chat*) charlar, platicar (*Mex*); (= *chatter*) parlotear, hablar mucho
natterer* ['nætərəʳ] N charlatán/ana *m/f*, cotorra* *mf*
NATTKE N ABBR (*Brit*) (= **National Association of Television, Theatrical and Kinematographic Employees**) *sindicato de empleados de televisión, teatro y cine*
natty* ['nætɪ] ADJ (COMPAR: **nattier**, SUPERL: **nattiest**) **1** (= *smart*) [*suit, tie*] elegante, elegantoso (*esp LAm**) • **he looked ~ in his white uniform** iba de lo más elegantoso *or* elegantón con su uniforme blanco* • **to be a ~ dresser** ir siempre muy elegantoso *or* elegantón*
2 (= *handy*) [*gadget*] ingenioso
natural ['nætʃrəl] ADJ **1** (= *occurring naturally*) [*environment, substance, disaster, remedy*] natural • **she isn't a ~ blonde** no es rubia natural • **he died of ~ causes** murió de muerte natural • **the rest of his ~ life** el resto de sus días; ▹ **die¹**
2 (= *understandable*) [*reaction, behaviour, feeling*] natural, normal; [*mistake*] comprensible; [*explanation*] lógico y natural • **it's a perfectly ~ mistake to make** es un error totalmente comprensible • **there is a perfectly ~ explanation** hay una explicación perfectamente lógica y natural • **it's only ~** es normal *or* natural • **it's only ~ that she should be upset** es normal *or* natural que esté disgustada
3 (= *inborn*) [*ability, talent*] innato; [*reaction, fear*] instintivo • **he had a ~ flair for business** tenía un don innato para los negocios • **she is a ~ leader/athlete** es una líder/atleta innata • **~ instinct** instinto *m* natural
4 (= *relaxed, unforced*) [*person, manner, charm*] natural • **I was able to be very ~ with him** con él pude ser yo mismo
5 (= *biological*) [*father, mother, child*] biológico
6 (*Mus*) natural
N **1** (= *person*) • **she's a ~ with computers** tiene un don innato para los ordenadores
2 (*Mus*) (= *note*) nota *f* natural; (= *sign*) becuadro *m*
CPD ▸ **natural causes** • **to die of ~ causes** morir de muerte natural ▸ **natural childbirth** parto *m* natural ▸ **natural disaster** desastre *m* natural ▸ **natural gas** gas *m* natural ▸ **natural history** historia *f* natural ▸ **natural law** ley *f* natural ▸ **natural number** (*Math*) número *m* natural ▸ **natural philosophy** filosofía *f* natural ▸ **natural resources** recursos *mpl* naturales ▸ **natural science** (*uncount*) ciencias *fpl* naturales; (*count*) ciencia *f* de la naturaleza ▸ **natural selection** selección *f* natural • **by ~ selection** por selección natural ▸ **natural wastage** (*Brit*) (*Ind*) *bajas voluntarias de los empleados de una empresa, y cuyos puestos quedan sin cubrir* • **the jobs will be lost through ~ wastage** los puestos irán despareciendo a medida que se produzcan bajas voluntarias
naturalism ['nætʃrəlɪzəm] N naturalismo *m*
naturalist ['nætʃrəlɪst] N naturalista *mf*
naturalistic [,nætʃrə'lɪstɪk] ADJ naturalista

naturalization [,nætʃrəlaɪ'zeɪʃən] N naturalización *f*
CPD ▸ **naturalization papers** carta *fsing* de ciudadanía
naturalize ['nætʃrəlaɪz] VT [+ *person*] naturalizar; [+ *plant, animal*] aclimatar, establecer
VI [*person*] naturalizarse; [*plant etc*] aclimatarse, establecerse
naturalized ['nætʃrəlaɪzd] ADJ (*Brit*) [*citizen*] naturalizado • **to become ~** [*person*] naturalizarse; [*plant, animal*] aclimatarse, establecerse
naturally ['nætʃrəlɪ] ADV **1** (= *by a natural process*) [*happen, develop*] de forma natural • **beans are ~ high in minerals** las alubias tienen de por sí un alto contenido de minerales • **to die ~** morir de muerte natural • **to give birth ~** tener un parto natural
2 (= *by nature*) [*cheerful, cautious*] por naturaleza • **her hair is ~ curly** tiene el pelo rizado natural • **he is a ~ gifted singer** es un cantante con un talento innato • **playing the violin seems to come ~ to her** parece que hubiera nacido sabiendo tocar el violín • **I just do what comes ~** simplemente hago lo que me sale • **winning seems to come ~ to him** se diría que ganar no le supone ningún esfuerzo
3 (= *unaffectedly*) [*behave, speak*] con naturalidad, con espontaneidad
4 (= *as a consequence*) [*follow, lead*] como consecuencia natural
5 (= *obviously*) naturalmente, por supuesto • **~, I understand your feelings** naturalmente *or* por supuesto, sé cómo te sientes • **"did you tell him?" — "naturally"** —¿se lo dijiste? —por supuesto • **~ enough** como es natural, lógicamente
naturalness ['nætʃrəlnɪs] N naturalidad *f*
nature ['neɪtʃəʳ] N **1** (= *essential quality*) [*of things*] naturaleza *f* • **the ~ and extent of the damage is still not known** aún se desconoce la naturaleza y el alcance de los daños • **the project is experimental in ~** el proyecto es de carácter experimental • **his comment was in the ~ of a compliment** su comentario fue algo así como un cumplido • **in the ~ of things it's impossible** desde el punto de vista lógico es imposible • **we were unaware of the serious ~ of his illness** ignorábamos que su enfermedad fuera tan grave • **the true ~ of his intentions** sus verdaderas intenciones • **by its very ~** por su propia naturaleza; ▹ **human**
2 (= *character*) [*of person*] carácter *m* • **she trusted people, that was her ~** se fiaba de la gente, era así por naturaleza • **to appeal to sb's better ~** apelar al buen corazón de algn • **to be cautious by ~** ser cauteloso por naturaleza • **she took all their teasing with good ~** aceptó todas sus burlas de buen grado • **to take advantage of sb's good ~** abusar de la amabilidad de algn • **it is not in his ~ to lie** mentir no es propio de él; ▹ **second¹**
3 (= *kind, type*) • **something of that ~** algo por el estilo • **documents of a technical ~** documentos *mpl* de carácter técnico • **"nature of contents"** (*Comm*) "descripción *f* del contenido"
4 (= *natural life, environment*) naturaleza *f* • **it's against ~** es antinatural, es contrario a la naturaleza • **the beauties of ~** las maravillas de la naturaleza • **to draw/paint from ~** dibujar/pintar del natural • **to get back to ~** [*person*] volver a la naturaleza • **the laws of ~** las leyes de la naturaleza • **to return to ~** [*area*] volver a su estado natural • **fever is ~'s**

way of fighting infection la fiebre es el mecanismo natural para combatir la infección; ▸ call, freak, mother
CPD ▸ nature conservation protección f de la naturaleza ▸ nature cure curación f natural ▸ nature lover amante mf de la naturaleza ▸ nature reserve reserva f natural ▸ nature study estudio m de la historia natural, historia f natural ▸ nature trail ruta f para el estudio de la naturaleza
-natured ['neɪtʃəd] ADJ (*ending in compounds*) de carácter ... • good-natured de carácter bondadoso • ill-natured de mal carácter
naturism ['neɪtʃərɪzəm] N (*esp Brit*) naturismo *m*
naturist ['neɪtʃərɪst] N (*esp Brit*) naturista *mf*
naturopath ['neɪtʃərə,pæθ] N naturópata *mf*
naturopathy [,neɪtʃə'rɒpəθɪ] N naturopatía *f*
naught [nɔ:t] N 1 (*Math*) = nought
2 (*liter*) (= *nothing*) nada *f* • all for ~ todo en balde • to come to ~ [*hopes*] frustrarse; [*project*] malograrse • to set at ~ no hacer caso de, despreciar; ▹ nought
naughtily ['nɔ:tɪlɪ] ADV 1 (*of child*) traviesamente; [*behave*] mal
2 (*of adult*) [*say*] con picardía
naughtiness ['nɔ:tɪnɪs] N 1 (= *mischief*) travesuras *fpl*; (= *bad behaviour*) mala conducta *f*
2 (= *risqué character*) atrevimiento *m*; [*of joke, song etc*] lo verde
naughty ['nɔ:tɪ] ADJ (COMPAR: naughtier, SUPERL: naughtiest) 1 [*child*] travieso, malo • you've been very ~ has sido muy malo • that was very ~ of you • that was a ~ thing to do eso ha estado muy feo • you ~ boy! (*angrily*) ¡mira que eres malo *or* travieso!; (*indulgently*) ¡anda, pillín *or* picaruelo!*
2 (*of adult*) • I'm going to be very ~ and have two cakes voy a portarme mal y comerme dos pasteles • it was a bit ~ of you to leave without telling anyone no estuvo nada bien que te marcharas sin decir nada
3 (= *risqué*) [*joke, song*] verde, colorado (*LAm*) • she gave me a ~ look me miró con picardía • ~ bits* (*hum*) (= *male genitals*) paquete‡ *m* • the ~ bits* (*in film etc*) las escenas picantes • the Naughty Nineties la Bella Época
nausea ['nɔ:sɪə] N (*Med*) náusea *f* • his remarks filled me with ~ (*fig*) sus comentarios me dieron náuseas *or* asco
nauseam ['nɔ:sɪæm] ▹ ad nauseam
nauseate ['nɔ:sɪeɪt] VT (*lit*) dar náuseas a; (*fig*) repugnar, asquear, dar asco a • I was ~d by her attitude su actitud me repugnó *or* asqueó
nauseating ['nɔ:sɪeɪtɪŋ] ADJ [*smell*] nauseabundo; [*crime, violence, hypocrisy*] repugnante, asqueroso • it was ~ to see it era repugnante *or* asqueroso verlo
nauseatingly ['nɔ:sɪeɪtɪŋlɪ] ADV • the film is ~ violent la película es de una violencia repugnante • he is ~ virtuous es tan perfecto que da asco
nauseous ['nɔ:sɪəs] ADJ 1 (*lit*) • to feel ~ sentir náuseas • the sight of food made me (feel) ~ solo de ver la comida me daban náuseas
2 [*colour, smell*] nauseabundo
nautical ['nɔ:tɪkəl] ADJ [*terms, matters, charts*] náutico, marítimo
CPD ▸ nautical almanac almanaque *m* náutico ▸ nautical mile milla *f* marina
nautically ['nɔ:tɪkəlɪ] ADV [*superior*] náuticamente
nautilus ['nɔ:tɪləs] N (PL: nautiluses *or* nautili ['nɔ:tɪ,laɪ]) nautilo *m*
Navaho ['nævəhəʊ] ADJ navajo
N 1 (*also* Navaho Indian) Navajo *mf*
2 (*Ling*) Navajo *m*
naval ['neɪvəl] ADJ [*warfare, strength, base*] naval; [*affairs, forces*] de la marina; [*officer*] de marina; [*power*] marítimo • Britain's ~ tradition la tradición naval británica
CPD ▸ naval academy escuela *f* naval ▸ naval architect ingeniero/a *m/f* naval ▸ naval attaché agregado *m* naval ▸ naval base base *f* naval ▸ naval college escuela *f* naval ▸ naval officer oficial *mf* de marina
Navarre [nə'vɑ:ʳ] N Navarra *f*
Navarrese [,nævə'ri:z] ADJ navarro
N 1 navarro/a *m/f*
2 (*Ling*) navarro *m*
nave¹ [neɪv] N (*Archit*) nave *f*
nave² [neɪv] N (= *wheel*) cubo *m* • ~ plate (*Aut*) tapacubos *m inv*
navel ['neɪvəl] N ombligo *m*
CPD ▸ navel orange naranja *f* navel
navel-gazing ['neɪvəlgeɪzɪŋ] N (*pej*) ombliguismo *m*, autocontemplación *f*
navigable ['nævɪgəbl] ADJ 1 [*river*] navegable
2 [*ship, balloon*] gobernable, dirigible
navigate ['nævɪgeɪt] VT 1 [+ *ship, plane*] conducir; (*fig*) conducir, guiar • to ~ a bill through parliament lograr que un proyecto de ley se tramite en el parlamento
2 [+ *sea, river*] navegar por
VI 1 (*at sea*) navegar • navigating officer oficial *mf* de derrota *or* navegación
2 (*in car*) hacer de copiloto
navigation [,nævɪ'geɪʃən] N 1 (= *act*) [*of ship, plane*] navegación *f* • to do the ~ (*Aut*) hacer de copiloto
2 (= *science*) náutica *f*, navegación *f*
CPD ▸ navigation lights (*on ship*) luces *fpl* de navegación; (*in harbour*) baliza *f*
navigational [,nævɪ'geɪʃənl] ADJ [*instruments, system*] de navegación • ~ aids ayudas *fpl* a la navegación
navigator ['nævɪgeɪtəʳ] N 1 (*Naut*) (= *officer on ship*) oficial *mf* de derrota, oficial *mf* de navegación; (*Aer*) navegante *mf*; (*Aut*) copiloto *mf*
2 (*Hist*) (= *seafarer*) navegador *m*, navegante *m*
navvy ['nævɪ] N (*Brit*) peón *m* caminero
navy ['neɪvɪ] N 1 (= *ships*) armada *f*, flota *f*
2 (= *organization*) marina *f* de guerra
3 (= *colour*) (*also* navy blue) azul *m* marino
ADJ (= *dark blue*) azul marino
CPD ▸ navy blue azul *m* marino; ▹ navy-blue ▸ Navy Department (*US*) Ministerio *m* de Marina ▸ navy yard (*US*) astillero *m* naval
navy-blue ['neɪvɪ'blu:] ADJ azul marino
nay [neɪ] ADV 1†† (= *no*) no
2 (*liter*) (= *or rather*) más aún, mejor dicho • bad, nay terrible malo, mejor dicho horrible • dozens, nay hundreds docenas, más aún centenares
N (= *refusal*) negativa *f*; (*in voting*) voto *m* negativo, voto *m* en contra • to say sb nay indicar lo contrario a algn; ▹ yea
Nazarene [,næzə'ri:n] ADJ nazareno
N nazareno/a *m/f*
Nazareth ['næzərəθ] N Nazaret *m*
Nazi ['nɑ:tsɪ] ADJ nazi, nazista
N nazi *mf*
Nazism ['nɑ:tsɪzəm] N nazismo *m*
NB ABBR 1 (= nota bene) (= *note well*) N.B.
2 (*Canada*) = New Brunswick
NBA N ABBR 1 (*US*) = National Basketball Association
2 (*US*) = National Boxing Association
3 (*Brit*) (*formerly*) = Net Book Agreement
NBC N ABBR (*US*) = National Broadcasting Company
NBS N ABBR (*US*) = National Bureau of Standards
NC ABBR 1 (*US*) = North Carolina
2 (*Comm etc*) = no charge
NCB N ABBR (*Brit*) (*formerly*) = National Coal Board
NCC N ABBR 1 (*Brit*) (= Nature Conservancy Council) ≈ ICONA *m*, ≈ Icona *m*
2 (*US*) = National Council of Churches
NCCL N ABBR (*Brit*) = National Council for Civil Liberties
NCIS N ABBR (*Brit*) (= National Criminal Intelligence Service) *servicio nacional de inteligencia criminal del Reino Unido*
NCO N ABBR (*Mil*) (= non-commissioned officer) suboficial *m*
NCV ABBR = no commercial value
ND ABBR (*US*) = North Dakota
n.d. ABBR (= no date) s.f.
N.Dak. ABBR (*US*) = North Dakota
NDP N ABBR (= Net Domestic Product) PIN *m*
NE ABBR 1 (*Geog*) (= north east) NE
2 (*US*) = Nebraska
3 (*US*) = New England
NEA N ABBR (*US*) = National Educational Association
Neanderthal [nɪ'ændətɑ:l] N (*Geog*) Neanderthal *m*
ADJ Neanderthal, de Neanderthal • ~ man hombre *m* de Neanderthal
neap [ni:p] N (*also* neap tide) marea *f* muerta
Neapolitan [nɪə'pɒlɪtən] ADJ napolitano • ~ ice-cream helado *m* napolitano
N napolitano/a *m/f*
near [nɪəʳ] ADV 1 (*in place*) cerca • he lives quite ~ vive bastante cerca • don't come any ~er! ¡no te acerques más! • so ~ and yet so far: • the shore was so ~ and yet so far la orilla estaba al alcance de la mano pero llegar a ella era imposible • victory was so ~ and yet so far la victoria parecía estar asegurada pero ese último esfuerzo para obtenerla les resultó imposible
2 (*in time*) • the agreement brings peace a little ~er este acuerdo nos acerca un poco más a la paz • winter is drawing ~ el invierno se acerca • the ~er it gets to the election the more they look like losing a medida que se acercan las elecciones mayor parece la posibilidad de que pierdan • to be ~ at hand [*object*] estar al alcance de la mano; [*event, season*] estar a la vuelta de la esquina
3 (*in level, degree*) • the ~est I ever came to feeling that was when ... la única vez que llegué a sentir algo parecido fue cuando ... • you as ~ as dammit killed me* no me mataste, pero por un pelo* • that's ~ enough (*numbers*) no merece la pena precisar más; (*amount*) con eso vale • you won't get any ~er than that to what you want no vas a encontrar otra cosa que se aproxime más a lo que buscas • the ~est I ever got to winning lo más cerca que estuve de ganar • it's nowhere ~ enough* con eso no basta ni mucho menos • "have you finished it yet?" — "nowhere ~" —¿has terminado ya? —qué va, me falta muchísimo • as ~ as I can recall que yo recuerde
4 (= *almost*) casi • I came ~ to telling her everything llegué casi a decírselo todo • ~ on 3,000 people casi 3.000 personas • it's in ~ perfect condition está casi en perfectas condiciones • I could hardly see it in the ~ total darkness apenas lo veía en la oscuridad que era casi total
PREP (*also* near to) 1 (*of place*) cerca de • I live ~ Liverpool vivo cerca de Liverpool • is there a bank ~ here? ¿hay algún banco por aquí cerca? • I sat ~ the fire me senté cerca

de la chimenea • **the schools ~ where I live** los colegios de mi barrio • **the person ~est the door** la persona que está más cerca de la puerta • **he won't let anyone ~ his toys** no deja que nadie se acerque a sus juguetes • **we don't live anywhere ~ Lincoln** vivimos bastante *or* muy lejos de Lincoln • **if you come ~ me I'll kill you** como te me acerques, te mato • **nobody comes anywhere ~ him at swimming** en natación nadie le llega ni a la suela del zapato • **the passage is ~ the end of the book** el trozo viene hacia el final del libro • **don't go ~ the edge** no te acerques al borde • **we were nowhere ~ the station** estábamos bastante *or* muy lejos de la estación
2 (*in time*) • **her birthday is ~ mine** su cumpleaños cae cerca del mío • **~ the end of the century** hacia fines del siglo
3 (= *almost*) • **the sun was ~ to setting** el sol estaba a punto de ponerse • **we were ~ to being drowned** por poco nos morimos ahogados • **she was ~ death** estaba al borde de la muerte, tocaba a su fin (*liter*) • **~ to tears** a punto de llorar
(ADJ) 1 (*in place*) cercano • **my house is ~ enough to walk** mi casa está muy cerca, se puede ir andando • **where's the ~est service station?** ¿dónde está la gasolinera más cercana? • **these glasses make things look ~er** con estas gafas todo parece estar más cerca • **£250 or ~est offer** 250 libras o precio a discutir • **calculate to the ~est decimal place** para el cálculo solo utilicen el primer decimal • **he calculated the price to the ~est pound** redondeó el precio a la libra entera
2 (*in time*) próximo • **in the ~ future** en un futuro cercano • **the time is ~ when …** falta poco cuando …
3 (*in level, degree*) • **it's the ~est thing to heaven I can think of** para mí esto es como estar en el séptimo cielo • **that's the ~est thing to a compliment you'll get from him** (*iro*) eso es lo más parecido a un elogio que vas a conseguir de él • IDIOM: • **a ~ thing**: • **she won, but it was a ~ thing** ganó, pero por los pelos
4 [*relative*] cercano • **your ~est and dearest** tus seres más allegados y queridos
(VT) 1 (*in space*) acercarse a
2 (*in time*) • **it was ~ing lunchtime** faltaba poco para la hora de comer • **I'm ~ing the end of my contract** falta poco para que venza mi contrato • **he is ~ing 50** frisa en los 50, tiene casi 50 años
3 (*in level, degree*) • **the building is ~ing completion** el edificio está casi terminado • **the country is ~ing total anarchy** el país está al borde de la anarquía total
(VI) acercarse
(CPD) ▸ **the Near East** el Cercano Oriente ▸ **near miss** [*of planes*] casi colisión *f*; (*when aiming*) casi acierto *m*; (*in competition*) (= *near-victory*) casi victoria *f* • **he had a ~ miss** (*Aer*) no se estrelló por poco; (*Aut*) no se chocó por poco • **it was a ~ miss** (*target*) no dio en el blanco por poco ▸ **near money** (*Comm*) activos *mpl* realizables

nearby [ˈnɪəˈbaɪ] (ADV) cerca • **there's a church ~** hay una iglesia cerca
(ADJ) cercano • **we had a drink in a ~ pub** tomamos una copa en un bar cercano *or* que había cerca

near-death experience [ˌnɪədeθɪkˈspɪərɪəns] (N) *experiencia extracorpórea sufrida por una persona que ha estado clínicamente muerta*

near-Earth object [ˌnɪərɜːθˈɒbdʒɪkt] (N) objeto *m* próximo a la Tierra

nearly [ˈnɪəlɪ] (ADV) 1 (= *almost*) casi • **it's ~ three o'clock** son casi las tres • **she's ~ 40** tiene casi 40 años • **it was ~ dark** era casi de noche • **I've ~ finished** casi he terminado • **I ~ fell over** casi me caigo • **she was ~ as tall as he was** era casi tan alta como él • **we are ~ there** casi hemos llegado • **I ~ lost it** casi lo pierdo, por poco lo pierdo • **very ~** casi • **he (very) ~ succeeded** estuvo a punto de conseguirlo
2 (*with negative*) • **not ~** ni con mucho, ni mucho menos • **these drugs are not ~ as effective as the others** estos medicamentos no son ni con mucho *or* ni mucho menos tan eficaces como los otros • **that's not ~ enough** eso no es ni mucho menos suficiente • **your work isn't ~ good enough** tu trabajo no es ni con mucho satisfactorio • **it's not ~ ready** falta mucho para que esté listo

nearness [ˈnɪənɪs] (N) (*in place*) proximidad *f*, cercanía *f*; (*in time*) proximidad *f*, inminencia *f* • **because of its ~ to the station** por estar tan cerca de la estación, por su cercanía a la estación

near real-time [nɪəˈrɪəltaɪm] (ADJ) casi en tiempo real

nearside [ˈnɪəsaɪd] (*Aut*) (N) (*Brit*) lado *m* izquierdo; (*most other countries*) lado *m* derecho
(ADJ) [*door, verge, lane*] (*Brit*) de la izquierda; (*most other countries*) de la derecha

near-sighted [ˈnɪəˈsaɪtɪd] (ADJ) miope, corto de vista

near-sightedness [ˈnɪəˈsaɪtɪdnɪs] (N) miopía *f*

neat [niːt] (ADJ) (COMPAR: **neater**, SUPERL: **neatest**) 1 (= *tidy in appearance*) [*room, desk, row, pile*] ordenado; [*garden*] bien cuidado; [*appearance*] cuidado, pulcro, prolijo (*S. Cone*); [*clothes*] muy cuidado; [*work*] bien presentado • **everything looks ~ and tidy** todo parece muy ordenado • **she always looks very ~** siempre va muy arreglada • **her hair is always very ~** siempre va muy bien peinada • **he has very ~ handwriting** tiene muy buena letra
2 (= *tidy by nature*) [*person*] ordenado, pulcro, prolijo (*S. Cone*)
3 (= *compact*) [*figure*] bien proporcionado; [*waist, waistline*] delgado • **a ~ little car** un coche pequeño y de línea sencilla
4 (= *clever*) [*solution*] ingenioso, bueno; [*plan*] ingenioso; [*division, category, explanation*] claro
5 (*US**) (= *wonderful*) genial* • **that's a ~ idea** esa es una idea genial • **those new apartments are really ~** esos nuevos apartamentos son muy chulos*
6 (*Brit*) (= *undiluted*) [*whisky, brandy etc*] solo • **I take it ~** lo tomo solo • **half a litre of ~ whisky** medio litro de whisky puro

neaten [ˈniːtn] (VT) [+ *desk*] arreglar, ordenar; [+ *handwriting*] esmerarse con • **she ~ed her skirt** se alisó la falda • **to ~ one's hair** arreglarse el pelo, retocarse el peinado

'neath [niːθ] (PREP) (*liter*) = **beneath**

neatly [ˈniːtlɪ] (ADV) 1 (= *carefully, tidily*) [*arrange, put, fold*] con cuidado, cuidadosamente, con esmero; [*write, type*] claramente • **she is always very ~ dressed** siempre va muy arreglada • **a ~ kept garden** un jardín bien cuidado
2 (= *cleverly*) [*summarize, explain*] con claridad, bien; [*avoid*] ingeniosamente, con habilidad • **as you so ~ put it** como tú muy bien dijiste • **it was very ~ put** estaba muy bien expresado
3 (= *conveniently*) [*fit*] perfectamente; [*divide*] claramente, fácilmente • **they do not fit ~ into categories** no se los puede encasillar tan fácilmente • **everything worked out very ~** todo se resolvió muy bien

neatness [ˈniːtnɪs] (N) 1 (= *tidiness*) [*of room, garden, things*] orden *m*; [*of handwriting, typing*] claridad *f*; [*of person's appearance*] pulcritud *f*, prolijidad *f* (*S. Cone*)
2 (= *cleverness*) habilidad *f*, destreza *f*
3 (= *clarity*) [*of division*] claridad *f*

NEB (N ABBR) 1 (*Brit*) = **National Enterprise Board**
2 = **New English Bible**

Nebr. (ABBR) (*US*) = **Nebraska**

Nebuchadnezzar [ˌnebjʊkədˈnezəʳ] (N) Nabucodonosor

nebula [ˈnebjʊlə] (N) (PL: **nebulas** *or* **nebulae** [ˈnebjʊliː]) nebulosa *f*

nebulizer [ˈnebjʊˌlaɪzəʳ] (N) nebulizador *m*

nebulous [ˈnebjʊləs] (ADJ) (*fig*) vago, nebuloso

NEC (N ABBR) = **National Executive Committee**

necessarily [ˈnesɪsərɪlɪ] (ADV) necesariamente, forzosamente • **"you will have to resign" — "not ~"** —tendrás que dimitir —no necesariamente • **it doesn't ~ follow that …** no implica necesariamente *or* por fuerza que … • **this is not ~ the case** esto no tiene por qué ser así

necessary [ˈnesɪsərɪ] (ADJ) 1 (= *required*) necesario • **is that really ~?** ¿es eso realmente *or* verdaderamente necesario? • **to be ~ to do sth** ser necesario *or* preciso hacer algo • **is it ~ for us to go?** ¿es necesario *or* preciso que vayamos? • **if ~** si es necesario *or* preciso • **don't do more than is ~** no hagas más de lo necesario • **do whatever (is) ~ to find him** haz todo lo posible para encontrarlo • **when/where ~** cuando/donde sea necesario *or* preciso
2 (= *inevitable*) [*consequence, conclusion*] inevitable • **a ~ evil** un mal necesario
(N) 1 (= *what is required*) • **the ~** lo necesario • **I'll do the ~** haré lo que haga falta, haré lo que sea necesario
2* (= *money*) • **have you got the ~?** ¿tienes la pasta?*
3 **necessaries** (= *essentials*) • **the necessaries of life** las necesidades básicas (de la vida) • **there are shops nearby for all the necessaries** hay tiendas cerca para todo lo necesario

necessitate [nɪˈsesɪteɪt] (VT) requerir, exigir

necessitous [nɪˈsesɪtəs] (ADJ) (*frm*) necesitado, indigente

necessity [nɪˈsesɪtɪ] (N) 1 (= *need*) necesidad *f* • **I don't see the ~ of it** no veo la necesidad de eso • **there is no ~ for you to do it** no es necesario que lo hagas • **she works from economic ~** trabaja por necesidad • **of ~** necesariamente, forzosamente, por fuerza • **out of sheer ~** por pura necesidad • PROVERB: • **~ is the mother of invention** la necesidad agudiza el ingenio
2 (= *necessary thing*) necesidad *f* • **necessities such as food and clothing were in short supply** escaseaban artículos de primera necesidad tales como la comida y la ropa • **the basic necessities of life** las necesidades básicas (de la vida); ▹ **bare**
3 (= *unavoidable thing*) • **the curfew was seen as a regrettable ~** el toque de queda era visto como un mal necesario

neck [nek] (N) 1 [*of person*] cuello *m*; [*of animal*] pescuezo *m*, cuello *m* • **the rain ran down my ~** la lluvia me corría por el cuello • **~ and ~** a la par, parejos • **to be ~ and ~** [*horses, runners, competitors*] ir a la par, ir parejos • **the back of the ~** la nuca • **to break one's ~** (*lit*) desnucarse • **to break sb's ~** (*fig*) romper *or* partir el cuello a algn • **to win by a ~** ganar por una cabeza • **they threw him out ~ and crop** le pusieron de patitas en la calle* • **she fell on his ~** se le colgó del cuello • **to risk one's ~** jugarse el pellejo *or* el tipo* • **to save one's ~** salvar el pellejo *or* el tipo* • **to be in sth up to one's ~*** (*trouble, plot etc*) estar metido hasta el cuello en algo* • **to be up to one's ~ (in work)*** estar hasta arriba de trabajo* • **to wring sb's ~*** (*fig*) retorcer el pescuezo a algn* • **I'll wring your ~!*** ¡te voy a retorcer el pescuezo!* • **to wring a chicken's ~** retorcer el pescuezo a un pollo • IDIOMS: • **to breathe down sb's ~*** no dejar a algn ni a sol ni a sombra* • **to have sb breathing down one's ~** tener a algn encima • **to get it in the ~*** (= *be punished*) cargársela*; (= *be told off*) llevarse una buena bronca *or* un buen rapapolvo* • **to stick one's ~ out** arriesgarse; ▹ **stiff**

2 [*of dress, T-shirt etc*] cuello *m*, escote *m*

3 [*of bottle*] cuello *m*, gollete *m*

4 (*Geog*) [*of land*] istmo *m* • **in your ~ of the woods*** por tu zona • **in this ~ of the woods*** por estos pagos*

5 (*Mus*) [*of guitar*] cuello *m*; [*of violin*] mástil *m*

6 (*Anat*) [*of uterus, bladder*] cuello *m*

7 (*Brit**) = **nerve**

VI * [*couple*] besuquearse*

neckband [ˈnekbænd] N tirilla *f*

neckcloth†† [ˈneklɒθ] N fular *m*

neckerchief [ˈnekətʃiːf] N pañuelo *m*

necking* [ˈnekɪŋ] N besuqueo* *m*

necklace [ˈneklɪs] N collar *m*

necklet [ˈneklɪt] N collar *m*

neckline [ˈneklaɪn] N escote *m* • **with a low ~** escotado

necktie [ˈnektaɪ] N corbata *f*

necrological [ˌnekrəʊˈlɒdʒɪkəl] ADJ necrológico

necrology [neˈkrɒlədʒɪ] N necrología *f*

necromancer [ˈnekrəʊmænsəʳ] N nigromante *m*

necromancy [ˈnekrəʊmænsɪ] N nigromancia *f*, nigromancía *f*

necrophile [ˈnekrəʊˌfaɪl] N necrófilo/a *m/f*

necrophilia [ˌnekrəʊˈfɪlɪə] N necrofilia *f*

necrophiliac [ˌnekrəʊˈfɪlɪæk] ADJ necrófilo N necrófilo/a *m/f*

necropolis [neˈkrɒpəlɪs] N (PL: **necropolises** *or* **necropoleis** [neˈkrɒpəˌleɪs]) necrópolis *f inv*

necrosis [neˈkrəʊsɪs] N necrosis *f inv*

necrotising fasciitis [ˈnekrəʊtaɪzɪŋfæʃɪˈaɪtɪs] N (*Med*) fascitis *f* necrotizante

nectar [ˈnektəʳ] N néctar *m*

nectarine [ˈnektəriːn] N nectarina *f*

ned‡ [ned] N (*esp Scot*) chorizo/a‡ *m/f*, gamberro/a *m/f*

NEDC N ABBR (*Brit*) (*formerly*) = **National Economic Development Council**

Neddy* [ˈnedɪ] N ABBR (*Brit*) (*formerly*) = **National Economic Development Council**

née [neɪ] ADJ • **Mary Green, née Smith** Mary Green, de soltera Smith

need [niːd] N **1** (= *necessity*) necesidad *f* (**for, of de**) • **I see no ~** no veo la necesidad • **without the ~ to pay so much** sin necesidad de pagar tanto • **staff are always available, in case of ~** siempre hay personal disponible en caso de necesidad • **there is a ~ for qualified staff** hay demanda de personal cualificado • **there is every ~ for discretion in this matter** es muy necesario mantener discreción en este asunto • **a house in ~ of painting** una casa que hace falta pintar • **to be in ~ of • have ~ of • stand in ~ of** necesitar • **when I'm in ~ of a drink** cuando necesito un trago, cuando me hace falta tomar algo • **there's no ~ to worry** no hay por qué preocuparse • **there's no ~ for you to go** no hace falta *or* no es preciso que vayas • **there's no ~ for that sort of language!** ¡no hay ninguna necesidad de usar ese vocabulario!, ¡no hace falta usar ese vocabulario! • **I have no ~ of advice** no me hacen falta consejos, no necesito consejos • **in times of ~** en momentos de apuro *or* necesidad; ▹ **needs**

2 (= *poverty*) necesidad *f*, indigencia *f* • **to be in ~** estar necesitado

3 (= *thing needed*) necesidad *f* • **the ~s of industry** las necesidades de la industria • **my ~s are few** es poco lo que necesito • **bodily ~s** necesidades *fpl* corporales • **a holiday that caters for every ~** unas vacaciones que satisfacen todas las necesidades • **they tended to my every ~** procuraban que no me faltase de nada • **to supply sb's ~s** proveer lo que necesita algn

VT **1** [*person*] necesitar • **I ~ a bigger car** necesito *or* me hace falta un coche más grande • **I ~ two more to make up the series** me faltan dos para completar la serie • **I ~ to get some petrol** tengo que echar gasolina • **she ~s to go to the toilet** tiene que ir al servicio *or* (*LAm*) al baño • **he ~s to be told everything twice** hay que decírselo todo dos veces • **they don't ~ to be told all the details** no es preciso *or* no hace falta contarles todos los detalles • **you only ~ed to ask** tenía más que pedírmelo • **he ~s watching** hay que vigilarlo • **that's all I ~! • that's just what I ~!** (*iro*) ¡solo me faltaba eso! (*iro*), ¡lo que me faltaba! (*iro*) • **it's just what I ~ed** es precisamente lo que necesitaba • **I ~ this like I ~ a hole in the head** esto es lo último que necesitaba • **a much ~ed holiday** unas vacaciones muy necesarias • **he ~ed no asking** no se hizo de rogar • **who ~s more motorways?** ¿para qué queremos más autopistas?

2 (= *require*) [+ *concentration, effort, skill*] requerir • **it ~s care** requiere cuidado • **a visa is ~ed** se requiere un visado • **this room ~s painting** este cuarto hay que *or* hace falta pintarlo • **I gave it a much ~ed wash** le di un buen lavado, que era lo que necesitaba • **the report ~s no comment** el informe no deja lugar a comentarios • **this will ~ some explaining** no va a ser fácil explicar esto

3 (*impersonal*) • **it doesn't ~ to be done now** no hace falta hacerlo ahora • **it doesn't ~ me to tell him** no hace falta que yo se lo diga • **it ~ed a war to alter that** fue necesaria una guerra para cambiar eso

MODAL VB • **~ I go?** ¿es necesario que vaya?, ¿tengo que ir? • **I ~ hardly remind you that …** no hace falta que les recuerde que … • **~ I say that this is untrue?** ni que decir tiene que esto no es cierto • **it ~ not follow that …** lo que no significa necesariamente que … • **I ~n't have bothered** fue trabajo perdido

needful [ˈniːdfʊl] ADJ necesario N • **the ~*** el cumquibus*

neediness [ˈniːdɪnɪs] N necesidad *f*, pobreza *f*

needle [ˈniːdl] N **1** (*for sewing*) aguja *f* • IDIOMS: • **to get the ~*** ponerse negro* • **to give sb the ~*** pinchar a algn, meterse con algn • **it's like looking for a ~ in a haystack** es como buscar una aguja en un pajar; ▹ **knitting, pin**

2 (*Bot*) aguja *f*, acícula *f* • **pine ~** aguja *f* de pino

3* rivalidad *f*, pique *m*

4‡ (= *drugs*) droga *f*

VT **1*** pinchar*, fastidiar

2 (*US*‡) [+ *drink*] añadir alcohol a

CPD ▸ **needle case** alfiletero *m* ▸ **needle exchange** (centro *m*) de intercambio *m* de jeringuillas ▸ **needle match** partido *m* de máxima rivalidad

needlecord [ˈniːdlkɔːd] N (*Brit*) pana *f* fina

needlecraft [ˈniːdlkrɑːft] N arte *m* de la costura

needlepoint [ˈniːdlpɔɪnt] N bordado *m* sobre cañamazo, cañamazo *m*

needle-sharp [ˈniːdlˈʃɑːp] ADJ afiladísimo; (*fig*) agudísimo, muy penetrante

needless [ˈniːdlɪs] ADJ innecesario, superfluo • **~ to say …** huelga decir que …, ni qué decir tiene que … • **he was, ~ to say, drunk** ni qué decir tiene que estaba borracho

needlessly [ˈniːdlɪslɪ] ADV innecesariamente • **you worry quite ~** te inquietas sin motivo alguno

needlessness [ˈniːdlɪsnɪs] N [*of action*] carácter *m* innecesario, innecesariedad *f*; [*of remark*] inoportunidad *f*

needlewoman [ˈniːdlˌwʊmən] N (PL: **needlewomen**) costurera *f* • **to be a good ~** coser bien

needlework [ˈniːdlwɜːk] N (= *sewing*) labor *f* de aguja; (= *embroidery*) bordado *m* • **to do ~** hacer costura

needn't [niːdnt] = **need not**

needs [niːdz] ADV • **if ~ be I'll go on my own** si es necesario *or* si hace falta iré solo • **if ~ must** si hace falta • **oh well, ~ must!** ¡qué le vamos a hacer!, ¡qué se le va a hacer! • **one or the other must ~ prevail** uno de los dos habrá de ganar • **we must ~ walk** no tenemos más remedio que ir andando

need-to-know [ˌniːdtəˈnəʊ] ADJ • **on a need-to-know basis:** • **we operate on a need-to-know basis** solo informamos de lo estrictamente necesario

needy [ˈniːdɪ] ADJ (COMPAR: **needier**, SUPERL: **neediest**) necesitado NPL • **the ~** los necesitados

ne'er [nɛəʳ] ADV (*poet*) nunca

ne'er-do-well [ˈnɛəduˌwel] ADJ inútil N inútil *mf*

nefarious [nɪˈfɛərɪəs] ADJ nefario, vil, inicuo

nefariousness [nɪˈfɛərɪəsnɪs] N vileza *f*

neg. ABBR = **negative**

negate [nɪˈgeɪt] VT anular, invalidar

negation [nɪˈgeɪʃən] N **1** (*gen*) (*Ling*) negación *f*

2 (= *denial, refusal*) negativa *f*

negative [ˈnegətɪv] ADJ (*all senses*) negativo • **a ~ answer** *or* **reply** *or* **response** una negativa, una respuesta negativa • **the test proved ~** el análisis dio negativo • **~ cash flow** liquidez *f* negativa • **~ feedback** reacción *f* desfavorable

N **1** (= *negative reply*) negativa *f* • **he answered in the ~** contestó negativamente, contestó que no

2 (*Ling*) negación *f* • **in the ~** en negativo

3 (*Phot*) negativo *m*

4 (*Elec*) polo *m* negativo

VT (= *veto*) poner veto a; (= *vote down*) rechazar, desaprobar; [+ *statement*] negar, desmentir; [+ *effect*] anular

CPD ▸ **negative equity** valor *m* líquido negativo

negatively [ˈnegətɪvlɪ] ADV **1** [*reply, think, affect*] negativamente • **to answer ~** contestar negativamente, contestar que no

2 (*Phys*) • **~ charged** con carga negativa

negativity [ˌnegəˈtɪvɪtɪ] N (*Psych*) negatividad *f*

neglect [nɪˈglekt] N (= *carelessness*) descuido *m*; (= *negligence*) negligencia *f*; (*in appearance*) dejadez *f*; [*of rules, duty*] incumplimiento *m*; (= *neglected state*) abandono *m*; (*towards others*) desatención *f*

• **the garden was in a state of ~** el jardín estaba muy descuidado *or* abandonado • **the plants had died of ~** las plantas se habían muerto de no cuidarlas
VT **1** [+ *obligations*] descuidar, desatender; [+ *duty*] no cumplir con, faltar a; [+ *friends, family*] desatender; [+ *opportunity*] desperdiciar, desaprovechar; [+ *work, garden*] descuidar
2 (= *omit*) • **to ~ to do sth** omitir hacer algo • **they ~ed to mention this fact** omitieron mencionar este hecho, no mencionaron este hecho

neglected [nɪˈglektɪd] ADJ [*child*] desatendido; [*house, garden*] descuidado, abandonado; [*appearance*] (*of person*) descuidado, desaliñado; [*promise*] incumplido • **he is a much ~ composer** es un compositor insuficientemente *or* poco reconocido

neglectful [nɪˈglektfʊl] ADJ negligente • **to be ~ of** [+ *family, children*] desatender a; [+ *work*] descuidar; [+ *duty*] no cumplir con • **they were ~ of the needs of the community** desatendían las necesidades de la comunidad

neglectfully [nɪˈglektfəlɪ] ADV negligentemente

negligee [ˈneglɪʒeɪ] N **1** (= *nightdress etc*) salto *m* de cama, negligé *m*
2 (= *housecoat*) bata *f*, negligé *m*

negligence [ˈneglɪdʒəns] N **1** (= *carelessness*) negligencia *f* • **through ~** por negligencia
2 (*Jur*) negligencia *f*

negligent [ˈneglɪdʒənt] ADJ **1** (= *careless*) negligente • **to be ~ in doing sth** pecar de negligencia al hacer algo • **she had been ~ of her duties** había faltado a sus deberes
2 (*liter*) [*gesture*] despreocupado

negligently [ˈneglɪdʒəntlɪ] ADV
1 (= *carelessly*) con negligencia
2 (= *casually*) despreocupadamente

negligible [ˈneglɪdʒəbl] ADJ [*amount*] insignificante; [*damage, difference*] insignificante, sin importancia • **a by no means ~ opponent** un adversario nada despreciable

negotiable [nɪˈgəʊʃɪəbl] ADJ **1** (*Comm*) negociable • **this is our position and it is not ~** esta es nuestra postura y no es negociable
2 [*road etc*] transitable; [*river*] salvable
CPD ▸ **negotiable instrument** instrumento *m* negociable

negotiate [nɪˈgəʊʃɪeɪt] VT **1** (= *arrange*) [+ *treaty*] negociar; [+ *loan, deal*] negociar, gestionar
2 (= *get round, over*) [+ *bend*] tomar; [+ *hill*] subir; [+ *obstacle*] salvar, franquear; [+ *river, stream*] pasar, cruzar
VI negociar • **to ~ for** negociar para obtener • **to ~ for peace** negociar para obtener la paz, entablar negociaciones de paz • **to ~ with sb** negociar con algn

negotiating [nɪˈgəʊʃɪeɪtɪŋ] N negociación *f*
CPD [*strategy*] negociador; [*skills*] de negociación ▸ **negotiating table** mesa *f* de negociaciones • **to sit (down) at the ~ table** sentarse a la mesa de negociaciones

negotiation [nɪˌgəʊʃɪˈeɪʃən] N **1** (= *act of negotiating*) negociación *f*; [*of loan, deal*] negociación *f*, gestión *f* • **to be in ~(s) with sb** estar en negociaciones con algn • **the treaty is under ~** el tratado está siendo negociado • **that will be a matter for ~** eso tendrá que ser negociado, eso tendrá que someterse a negociación
2 negotiations (= *talks*) negociaciones *fpl*, tratativas *fpl* (*S. Cone*) • **to break off ~s** romper las negociaciones • **to enter into ~s with sb** entrar en negociaciones con algn

negotiator [nɪˈgəʊʃɪeɪtəʳ] N negociador(a) *m/f*

Negress‡ [ˈniːgres] N (*pej in US*) negra *f*

Negro‡ [ˈniːgrəʊ] (*pej in US*) ADJ negro
N (PL: **Negroes**) negro *m*
CPD ▸ **Negro spiritual** espiritual *m*

negroid‡ [ˈniːgrɔɪd] ADJ negroide

neigh [neɪ] N relincho *m*
VI relinchar

neighbour, **neighbor** (*US*) [ˈneɪbəʳ] N vecino/a *m/f*; (= *fellow being*) prójimo/a *m/f*, semejante *m* • **Israel and its Arab ~s** Israel y sus vecinos árabes; ▸ **next-door**
VI • **to ~ (up)on** (= *adjoin*) colindar con, estar contiguo a; (= *be almost*) rayar en • **to ~ with sb** (*US*) comportarse como buen vecino de algn
CPD ▸ **Good Neighbour Policy** (*US*) Política *f* del Buen Vecino ▸ **neighbor states** (*US*) estados *mpl* vecinos

neighbourhood, **neighborhood** (*US*) [ˈneɪbəhʊd] N **1** (= *area*) barrio *m*, vecindario *m* • **not a very nice ~** un barrio poco atractivo • **somewhere in the ~** por allí
2 (= *surrounding area*) alrededores *mpl*, cercanías *fpl* • **anyone in the ~ of the crime** cualquier persona que estuviera en las cercanías del lugar del crimen • **in the ~ of £80** alrededor de (las) 80 libras
3 (= *people*) vecindario *m*, vecinos *mpl*
CPD [*supermarket, chemist*] de(l) barrio; [*policeman*] de barrio ▸ **neighbourhood watch** (*Brit*), **neighborhood watch** (*US*) *vigilancia de barrio llevada a cabo por los propios vecinos* ▸ **neighbourhood watch scheme** grupo *m* de vigilancia de los (propios) vecinos

neighbouring, **neighboring** (*US*) [ˈneɪbərɪŋ] ADJ [*town, villages*] cercano, vecino; [*houses, streets, fields*] cercano, de las proximidades; [*state, country*] vecino • **the people at the ~ table** la gente de la mesa de al lado • **in ~ Latvia** en el país vecino de Letonia

neighbourliness, **neighborliness** (*US*) [ˈneɪbəlɪnɪs] N • **good ~** buena vecindad *f*

neighbourly, **neighborly** (*US*) [ˈneɪbəlɪ] ADJ [*person*] amable; [*attitude*] de buen vecino, amable • **she was full of ~ concern** era de lo más atenta

neighing [ˈneɪɪŋ] N relinchos *mpl*

neither [ˈnaɪðəʳ] ADV • **~ … nor** ni … ni • **~ he nor I can go** ni él ni yo podemos ir • **he ~ smokes nor drinks** ni fuma ni bebe • **that's ~ here nor there** (*fig*) eso no viene al caso
CONJ tampoco • **if you aren't going, ~ am I** si tú no vas, yo tampoco • **"I don't like it" — "~ do I"** —a mí no me gusta —a mí tampoco • **~ will he agree to sell it** ni consiente en venderlo tampoco
PRON • **~ of them has any money** ninguno de los dos tiene dinero, ni el uno ni el otro tiene dinero • **~ of them saw it** ni el uno ni el otro lo vio
ADJ ninguno de los/las dos • **~ car is for sale** ninguno de los dos coches está a la venta

nelly* [ˈnelɪ] N • **not on your ~!*** ¡ni hablar!*

nelson [ˈnelsən] N (*Wrestling*) • **full ~** llave *f* • **half ~** media llave *f* • **to put a half ~ on sb** (*fig*) ponerle trabas a algn

nem. con. ABBR (= **nemine contradicente**) (= *no one contradicting*) nemine discrepante

nemesis [ˈnemɪsɪs] N (PL: **nemeses**) (justo) castigo *m* • **AIDS is our collective ~** SIDA representa nuestro castigo colectivo

neo… [ˈniːəʊ] PREFIX neo…

neoclassical [ˈniːəʊˈklæsɪkəl] ADJ neoclásico

neoclassicism [ˈniːəʊˈklæsɪsɪzəm] N neoclasicismo *m*

neocolonialism [ˌniːəʊkəˈləʊnɪəˌlɪzəm] N neocolonialismo *m*

neocon* [ˈniːəʊkɒn] (*US*) N neocon *mf inv*, neoconservador(a) *m/f*
ADJ neocon (*inv*), neoconservador

neo-conservatism [ˌniːəʊkənˈsɜːvətɪzəm] N neoconservadurismo *m*

neo-conservative [ˌniːəʊkənˈsɜːvətɪv] N neoconservador(a) *m/f*
ADJ neoconservador

neodymium [ˌniːəʊˈdɪmɪəm] N neodimio *m*

neofascism [ˈniːəʊˈfæʃɪzəm] N neofascismo *m*

neofascist [ˈniːəʊˈfæʃɪst] ADJ neofascista
N neofascista *mf*

neo-Gothic [ˌniːəʊˈgɒθɪk] ADJ neogótico

neo-liberal [ˌniːəʊˈlɪbərəl] N neoliberal *mf*
ADJ neoliberal

neo-liberalism [ˌniːəʊˈlɪbərəlɪzəm] N neoliberalismo *m*

neolithic [ˌniːəʊˈlɪθɪk] ADJ neolítico
CPD ▸ **Neolithic Age** • **the Neolithic Age** el Neolítico

neological [ˌnɪəˈlɒdʒɪkəl] ADJ neológico

neologism [nɪˈɒlədʒɪzəm] N neologismo *m*

neomycin [ˌniːəʊˈmaɪsɪn] N neomicina *f*

neon [ˈniːɒn] N neón *m*
CPD ▸ **neon light** luz *f* de neón ▸ **neon sign** anuncio *m* de neón

neonatal [ˈniːəʊˌneɪtl] ADJ neonatal

neonazi [ˈniːəʊˈnɑːtsɪ] ADJ neonazi, neonazista
N neonazi *mf*

neophyte [ˈniːəʊfaɪt] N neófito/a *m/f*

neoplatonic [ˈniːəʊpləˈtɒnɪk] ADJ neoplatónico

neoplatonism [ˈniːəʊˈpleɪtənɪzəm] N neoplatonismo *m*

neoplatonist [ˈniːəʊˈpleɪtənɪst] N neoplatonista *mf*

Neozoic [ˌniːəʊˈzəʊɪk] ADJ neozoico

Nepal [nɪˈpɔːl] N Nepal *m*

Nepalese [ˌnepɔːˈliːz] ADJ nepalés
N nepalés/esa *m/f*

nephew [ˈnevjuː] N sobrino *m*

nephrectomy [nɪˈfrektəmɪ] N nefrectomía *f*

nephritic [neˈfrɪtɪk] ADJ nefrítico

nephritis [neˈfraɪtɪs] N nefritis *f*

nephrology [nɪˈfrɒlədʒɪ] N nefrología *f*

nephrosis [nɪˈfrəʊsɪs] N nefrosis *f*

nepotism [ˈnepətɪzəm] N nepotismo *m*

Neptune [ˈneptjuːn] N Neptuno *m*

neptunium [nepˈtjuːnɪəm] N neptunio *m*

nerd‡ [nɜːd] N pazguato/a *m/f*

nerdy‡ [ˈnɜːdɪ] ADJ (COMPAR: **nerdier**, SUPERL: **nerdiest**) pazguato, timorato

nereid [ˈnɪərɪɪd] N nereida *f*

Nero [ˈnɪərəʊ] N Nerón

nerve [nɜːv] N **1** (*Anat, Bot*) nervio *m* • **my ~s are on edge** tengo los nervios de punta • **it/he gets on my ~s** me pone los nervios de punta *or* me saca de quicio • **to be living on one's ~s** vivir en estado de tensión constante • **to have ~s of steel** tener nervios de acero • **to strain every ~ to do sth** hacer un esfuerzo supremo por hacer algo
2 nerves (= *tension*) nerviosismo *m*, nervios *mpl*, excitabilidad *f* nerviosa • **she suffers from ~s** padece de los nervios, sufre trastornos nerviosos • **a fit of ~s** un ataque de nervios • **to be in a state of ~s** estar muy nervioso, estar hipertenso
3 (= *courage*) valor *m* • **he didn't have the ~ to do it** no tuvo el valor de hacerlo • **I wouldn't have the ~ to do that!** ¡yo no me atrevería a hacer eso! • **to hold** *or* **keep one's ~**

mantenerse firme, no amilanarse • **to lose one's ~** perder el valor, rajarse* • **it takes some ~ to do that** hace falta mucho valor *or* mucha sangre fría para hacer eso
4 (= *cheek*) caradura* *f*, cara* *f* • **of all the ~!** • **the ~ of it!** • **what a ~!** ¡qué caradura!*, ¡qué frescura!* • **you've got a ~!** ¡qué cara tienes!*, ¡eres un caradura!* • **he had the ~ to ask for money** tuvo la cara de pedir dinero*
VT • **to ~ o.s. to do sth** armarse de valor para hacer algo
CPD ▸ **nerve agent** agente *m* neurotóxico ▸ **nerve cell** neurona *f*, célula *f* nerviosa ▸ **nerve centre, nerve center** (US) centro *m* nervioso; (*fig*) punto *m* neurálgico ▸ **nerve ending** terminación *f* nerviosa ▸ **nerve gas** gas *m* nervioso ▸ **nerve specialist** neurólogo/a *m/f*

nerveless ['nɜːvlɪs] ADJ (*fig*) [*grasp*] flojo; [*person*] enervado, débil, soso

nerve-racking ['nɜːvˌrækɪŋ] ADJ [*wait, experience*] angustioso; [*drive, journey, interview*] estresante

nerviness ['nɜːvɪnɪs] N nerviosidad *f*, nerviosismo *m*

nervosa [nɜː'vəʊsə] ▸ **anorexia**

nervous ['nɜːvəs] ADJ **1** (= *tense*) nervioso • **to be/feel ~** estar nervioso; (= *frightened*) tener miedo • **I was ~ about the meeting** estaba nervioso pensando en la reunión, la reunión me tenía nervioso • **I was ~ about speaking in public** me asustaba hablar en público • **to be of a ~ disposition** ser nervioso • **to get ~** ponerse nervioso • **to make sb ~** poner nervioso a algn; (= *frighten*) dar miedo a algn • **to be ~ of sth/sb** tener miedo a algo/algn • **he was in a highly ~ state** estaba muy nervioso, tenía los nervios a flor de piel • **to be a ~ wreck*** (*temporarily*) ser un manojo de nervios; (*more permanently*) estar hecho polvo de los nervios*
2 (*Med*) nervioso
CPD ▸ **nervous breakdown** crisis *f inv* nerviosa ▸ **nervous collapse** colapso *m* nervioso ▸ **nervous exhaustion** agotamiento *m* nervioso ▸ **nervous system** sistema *m* nervioso

nervously ['nɜːvəslɪ] ADV nerviosamente • **he laughed ~** soltó una risa nerviosa, rió nerviosamente • **I waited ~ in the hall** esperé nervioso en el hall

nervousness ['nɜːvəsnɪs] N (= *apprehension, timidity*) nerviosismo *m*; (= *fear*) miedo *m* • **his ~ of flying** su miedo a volar

nervy ['nɜːvɪ] ADJ (COMPAR: **nervier**, SUPERL: **nerviest**) **1** (*Brit*) (= *tense*) nervioso
2 (US) (= *cheeky*) descarado, caradura*

nest [nest] N **1** [*of bird*] nido *m*; [*of hen*] nidal *m*; [*of rat, fox*] madriguera *f*; [*of mouse*] ratonera *f*; [*of wasps, hornets*] avispero *m*; [*of ants*] hormiguero *m* • IDIOMS: • **to fly the ~**: • **when the children have flown the ~** cuando los hijos dejen el nido • **to feather one's ~** barrer hacia adentro, arrojar piedras al tejado propio • **to foul one's own ~** manchar el propio nido
2 (*fig*) [*of thieves, spies*] guarida *f*
3 (= *set*) [*of boxes, tables*] juego *m*
4 (= *gun emplacement*) • **a machine-gun ~** un nido de ametralladoras
VI **1** [*bird*] anidar, hacer su nido
2 [*collector*] buscar nidos
CPD ▸ **nest egg** (*fig*) ahorros *mpl*

nesting ['nestɪŋ] N (*Orn*) nidificación *f*, anidación *f*
CPD ▸ **nesting box** (*for hen*) nidal *m*, ponedero *m*; (*for wild bird*) caja *f* anidadera ▸ **nesting season** época *f* de puesta, época *f* de nidificación, época *f* de anidación ▸ **nesting site** zona *f* de nidificación, zona *f* de anidación

nestle ['nesl] VI • **to ~ against** *or* **up to sb** arrimarse *or* acurrucarse junto a algn • **to ~ down in bed** acurrucarse en la cama • **to ~ down among the blankets** hacerse un ovillo entre las mantas • **to ~ among leaves** hacerse un nido entre las hojas • **a village nestling among hills** un pueblo abrigado por las colinas
VT • **she ~d the kitten on her lap** le hizo un hueco al gato en su regazo

nestling ['neslɪŋ] N polluelo *m*

NET N ABBR (US) = **National Educational Television**

net¹ [net] N **1** (*for catching fish, butterflies*) red *f*; (*for hair*) redecilla *f*; (= *fabric*) tul *m* • IDIOMS: • **to cast one's net wider** ampliar el campo de acción • **to fall into the net** caer en la trampa • **to slip through the net** escapar de la red
2 (*Tennis, Ftbl*) red *f*
3 (= *network*) red *f* • **the net** (= *internet*) (el *or* la) Internet • **to surf the net** navegar por Internet
VT [+ *fish*] pescar (con red); [+ *criminal*] atrapar
VI (*Sport*) (= *score goal*) marcar
CPD ▸ **net curtain** visillo *m* ▸ **net phone** teléfono *m* por Internet ▸ **net phone call** llamada *f* telefónica por Internet ▸ **net surfer** internauta *mf* ▸ **net surfing** navegación *f* por Internet

net² [net] ADJ **1** (*Comm*) [*price, interest, salary*] neto • **net of tax** deducidos los impuestos • **at a net profit of 5%** con un beneficio neto del 5% • **net weight** peso *m* neto
2 [*result, effect*] final, global
VT (*Comm*) (= *earn*) ganar en limpio; (= *produce*) producir en limpio • **the new tax will net the government £50m** el nuevo impuesto le supondrá al gobierno unos ingresos netos de 50 millones de libras • **the deal netted him £50,000** se embolsó 50.000 libras en el negocio
CPD ▸ **net assets** activo *msing* neto ▸ **net income** renta *f* neta ▸ **net loss** pérdida *f* neta ▸ **net payment** importe *m* neto

netball ['netbɔːl] N *especie de baloncesto jugado especialmente por mujeres*

nether ['neðəʳ] ADJ inferior, más bajo • **~ lip** labio *m* inferior • **~ regions** (= *hell*) infierno *m*; (*hum*) (= *buttocks*) trasero *m*, regiones *fpl* donde la espalda pierde su casto nombre (*hum*)

Netherlander ['neðəˌlændəʳ] N holandés/esa *m/f*, neerlandés/esa *m/f*

Netherlands ['neðələndz] NPL • **the ~** los Países Bajos

nethermost† ['neðəməʊst] ADJ SUPERL el más bajo/la más baja

netherworld ['neðəwɜːld] N (*liter*) infiernos *mpl*

netiquette ['netɪket] N (*Internet*) netiqueta *f*, *normas de conducta oficiosas para navegar por Internet*

netizen ['netɪzən] N (*Comput*) ciudadano/a *m/f* de la red

netspeak*, net-speak* ['netspiːk] N (= *internet jargon*) jerga *f* de Internet

net-surfer, netsurfer ['netsɜːfəʳ] N internauta *mf*

net-surfing, netsurfing [netsɜːfɪŋ] N navegación *f* por Internet

nett [net] = **net²**

netting ['netɪŋ] N (= *wire*) malla *f*; (= *nets*) redes *fpl*; (*Sew*) malla *f*; ▸ **wire**

nettle ['netl] N (*Bot*) ortiga *f* • IDIOM: • **to grasp the ~** (*Brit*) agarrar el toro por los cuernos
VT* picar*, molestar • **somewhat ~d by this** algo molesto por esto
CPD ▸ **nettle rash** urticaria *f* ▸ **nettle sting** picadura *f* de ortiga

network ['netwɜːk] N (*also Comput*) red *f*; (*Rad, TV*) red *f*, cadena *f* • **the national railway ~** la red nacional de ferrocarriles • **a ~ of spies** una red de espías
VT (*Rad, TV*) difundir por la red de emisoras, emitir en cadena; (*Comput*) conectar a la red
VI hacer contactos (*en el mundo de los negocios*)
CPD ▸ **network card, network interface card** (*Comput*) tarjeta *f* de red ▸ **network provider** (*for mobile phones*) proveedor *m* de red ▸ **Network Standard** (US) estándar *m* de red

networking ['netwɜːkɪŋ] N (*Comput*) conexión *f* de redes; (= *making contacts*) establecimiento *m* de contactos
CPD ▸ **networking site** sitio *m* de redes sociales

neural ['njʊərəl] ADJ neural • **~ network** (*Comput*) red *f* neural

neuralgia [njʊə'rældʒə] N neuralgia *f*

neuralgic [njʊ'rældʒɪk] ADJ neurálgico

neurasthenia [ˌnjʊərəs'θiːnɪə] N neurastenia *f*

neurasthenic [ˌnjʊərəs'θenɪk] ADJ neurasténico

neuritis [njʊə'raɪtɪs] N neuritis *f*

neuro... ['njʊərəʊ] PREFIX neuro...

neurobiology [ˌnjʊərəʊbaɪ'ɒlədʒɪ] N neurobiología *f*

neurochemistry [ˌnjʊərəʊ'kemɪstrɪ] N neuroquímica *f*

neurolinguistic programming ['njʊərəʊlɪŋ'gwɪstɪk'prəʊgræmɪŋ] N programación *f* neurolingüística

neurological [ˌnjʊərə'lɒdʒɪkəl] ADJ neurológico

neurologist [njʊə'rɒlədʒɪst] N neurólogo/a *m/f*

neurology [njʊə'rɒlədʒɪ] N neurología *f*

neuron ['njʊərɒn] N neurona *f*

neuropath ['njʊərəpæθ] N neurópata *mf*

neuropathic [njʊərə'pæθɪk] ADJ neuropático

neuropathology ['njʊərəʊpə'θɒlədʒɪ] N neuropatología *f*

neuropathy [njʊ'rɒpəθɪ] N neuropatía *f*

neurophysiological [ˌnjʊərəʊˌfɪzɪə'lɒʒɪkəl] ADJ neurofisiológico

neurophysiologist [ˌnjʊərəʊˌfɪzɪ'ɒlədʒɪst] N neurofisiólogo/a *m/f*

neurophysiology [ˌnjʊərəʊˌfɪzɪ'ɒlədʒɪ] N neurofisiología *f*

neuropsychiatric [ˌnjʊərəʊˌsaɪkɪ'ætrɪk] ADJ neuropsiquiátrico

neuropsychiatrist [ˌnjʊərəʊsaɪ'kaɪətrɪst] N neuropsiquiatra *mf*

neuropsychiatry [ˌnjʊərəʊsaɪ'kaɪətrɪ] N neuropsiquiatría *f*

neuropsychology ['njʊərəʊsaɪ'kɒlədʒɪ] N neuropsicología *f*

neurosis [njʊə'rəʊsɪs] N (PL: **neuroses** [njʊə'rəʊsiːz]) neurosis *f inv* • **he's got so many neuroses and hang-ups** es un neurótico lleno de complejos

neurosurgeon [ˌnjʊərəʊ'sɜːdʒən] N neurocirujano/a *m/f*

neurosurgery [ˌnjʊərəʊ'sɜːdʒərɪ] N neurocirugía *f*

neurosurgical [ˌnjʊərəʊ'sɜːdʒɪkəl] ADJ neuroquirúrgico

neurotic [njʊ'rɒtɪk] ADJ neurótico
N neurótico/a *m/f*

neurotically [njʊ'rɒtɪkəlɪ] ADV neuróticamente

neuroticism [njʊ'rɒtɪsɪzəm] N neuroticismo *m*

neurotoxin [ˌnjʊərəʊ'tɒksɪn] N (*Pharm*) neurotoxina *f*

neurotransmitter [ˌnjʊərəʊtrænz'mɪtəʳ] N neurotransmisor *m*

neurovascular [ˌnjʊərəʊ'væskjʊləʳ] ADJ neurovascular

neuter ['nju:təʳ] ADJ **1** (*Ling*) neutro
2 [*cat*] castrado
3 (*Bot*) [*plant*] asexuado
N **1** (*Ling*) neutro *m* • **in the ~** en género neutro
2 (= *cat*) macho *m* castrado
3 (= *insect*) insecto *m* asexuado
VT [+ *cat*] castrar, capar

neutral ['nju:trəl] ADJ **1** (= *impartial*) [*person, country, opinion*] neutral • **to remain ~** permanecer neutral
2 (= *not controversial*) [*language, term*] neutro • **I kept my questions ~** el tono de mis preguntas era neutro
3 (= *unemotional*) [*manner, expression, voice*] neutro
4 (= *indistinct*) [*shade, colour, accent*] neutro • **~ shoe cream** betún *m* incoloro
5 (*Elec, Chem etc*) neutro
N **1** (*Pol*) (= *person*) persona *f* neutral; (= *country*) país *m* neutral
2 (*Aut*) • **in ~** en punto muerto

neutralism ['nju:trəlɪzəm] N neutralismo *m*

neutralist ['nju:trəlɪst] ADJ neutralista
N neutralista *mf*

neutrality [nju:'trælɪtɪ] N neutralidad *f*

neutralization [ˌnju:trəlaɪ'zeɪʃən] N neutralización *f*

neutralize ['nju:trəlaɪz] VT neutralizar

neutron ['nju:trɒn] N neutrón *m*
CPD ▸ **neutron bomb** bomba *f* de neutrones ▸ **neutron star** estrella *f* de neutrones

Nev. ABBR (*US*) = **Nevada**

never ['nevəʳ] ADV **1** (= *not ever*) nunca • **"have you ever been to Argentina?" "no, ~"** —¿has estado alguna vez en Argentina? —no, nunca • **~ leave valuables in your car** no dejen nunca objetos de valor en el coche • **you ~ saw anything like it** nunca se ha visto nada parecido • **I ~ believed him** nunca le creí • **never!** ¡jamás! • **~ in all my life have I been so embarrassed** en mi vida *or* jamás en la vida he pasado tanta vergüenza • **~ again!** ¡nunca más! • **scenes ~ before shown on TV** imágenes *fpl* nunca vistas con anterioridad en televisión • **it had ~ been tried before** no se había intentado antes • **~, ever do that again!** ¡no vuelvas a hacer eso nunca jamás! • **it's a lesson he'll ~, ever forget** es una lección que nunca jamás olvidará • **I've ~ yet known him to fail** no lo he visto nunca fracasar
2 (*emphatic negative*) • **never!*** ¿en serio?, ¡no puede ser! • **I had a free ticket but I ~ went** tenía una entrada gratis pero no llegué a ir • **I ~ expected to see him again** no contaba con volverlo a ver • **surely you ~ bought it?** ¿pero lo has comprado de verdad? • **you ~ did!*** ¿en serio?, ¡no puede ser! • **~ mind** no importa, no te preocupes • **~ a one** ni uno siquiera • **well I ~!*** ¡no me digas!, ¡no me lo puedo creer! • **~ a word did he say** no dijo ni una sola palabra

never-ending ['nevər'endɪŋ] ADJ [*search, struggle, procession*] interminable, inacabable

never-failing ['nevə'feɪlɪŋ] ADJ [*method*] infalible; [*supply, source*] inagotable

nevermore ['nevə'mɔ:ʳ] ADV nunca más

never-never ['nevə'nevəʳ] N • **to buy sth on the never-never** (*Brit**) comprar algo a plazos
CPD ▸ **never-never land** país *m* del ensueño

nevertheless [ˌnevəðə'les] ADV sin embargo, no obstante • **~, it is true that …** • **it is ~ true that …** sin embargo *or* no obstante es verdad que … • **he is ~ my brother** sin embargo, es mi hermano • **I don't like him but I appreciate his qualities ~** no me cae bien, pero a pesar de todo sé apreciar

never-to-be-forgotten ['nevətəbi:ˌfə'gɒtn] ADJ inolvidable

nevus ['ni:vəs] N (PL: **nevi** ['ni:vaɪ]) (*US*) = **naevus**

new [nju:] ADJ (COMPAR: **newer**, SUPERL: **newest**) **1** (= *unused*) [*purchase, acquisition*] nuevo • **I've bought a new house/coat** me he comprado una casa nueva/un abrigo nuevo • **I've put in new batteries** he puesto pilas nuevas • **I'll open a new packet of biscuits** abriré otro paquete de galletas • **she sold it as new** lo vendió que parecía nuevo • **new for old insurance** seguro *m* de valor de nuevo • **it's as good as new** está como nuevo • **it looks like new** parece nuevo
2 (= *novel, different*) [*idea, theory, boyfriend*] nuevo • **it's a new way of thinking** es una nueva forma de pensar • **I feel like a new man** me siento como nuevo • **she's been a new woman since she got divorced** desde que se ha divorciado parece otra • **new face** (= *person*) cara *f* nueva; (= *image*) • **the new face of** la nueva imagen de • **that's nothing new** eso no es ninguna novedad • **there's nothing new under the sun** no hay nada nuevo bajo el sol • **that's a new one on me!** ¡la primera vez que lo oigo! • **that's something new!** (*iro*) ¡qué *or* vaya novedad! • **hi, what's new?*** hola, ¿que hay de nuevo? • **so what's new?*** (*iro*) ¡qué *or* vaya novedad!
3 (= *recently arrived*) [*recruit, student, worker*] nuevo • **the new people at number five** los nuevos vecinos del número cinco • **new boy** (*Scol*) alumno *m* nuevo • **new girl** (*Scol*) alumna *f* nueva • **are you new here?** ¿eres nuevo aquí? • **the new rich** los nuevos ricos • **I'm new to the area** hace poco que vivo aquí • **he's new to the office/job** es nuevo en la oficina/el trabajo
4 (= *freshly produced*) [*bread*] recién hecho; [*wine*] joven; [*crop*] nuevo • **new potatoes** patatas *f* nuevas • **have you read her new book?** ¿has leído el libro que acaba de publicar?
5 (= *young*) [*shoot, bud*] nuevo
CPD ▸ **new age** new age *f*; (*before noun*) [*music, philosophy*] new age (*adj inv*) ▸ **new blood** (*in team, organization*) savia *f* nueva ▸ **New Brunswick** Nuevo Brunswick *m* ▸ **new build** nueva construcción *f* ▸ **New Caledonia** Nueva Caledonia *f* ▸ **New Delhi** Nueva Delhi *f* ▸ **New England** Nueva Inglaterra *f* ▸ **New Englander** *habitante o nativo de Nueva Inglaterra* ▸ **New Guinea** Nueva Guinea *f* ▸ **New Hampshire** Nuevo Hampshire *m*, Nueva Hampshire *f* ▸ **the New Hebrides** las Nuevas Hébridas ▸ **New Jersey** Nueva Jersey *f* ▸ **New Labour** (*Brit*) (= *ideology*) Nuevo Laborismo *m*; (= *party*) Nuevo Partido *m* Laborista ▸ **new man** *hombre de ideas modernas que se ocupa de tareas tradicionalmente femeninas como el cuidado de la casa y de los niños* ▸ **New Mexico** Nuevo México *m* ▸ **new moon** luna *f* nueva ▸ **New Orleans** Nueva Orleáns *f* ▸ **new rave** new rave *f* ▸ **New Scotland Yard** Nuevo Scotland Yard *m* ▸ **New South Wales** Nueva Gales *f* del Sur ▸ **the New Testament** el Nuevo Testamento ▸ **new town** (*Brit*) *ciudad recién creada de la nada* ▸ **new wave** nueva ola *f*; (*before noun*) [*music, film*] de la nueva ola ▸ **the New World** el Nuevo Mundo ▸ **New Year** año *m* nuevo • **to bring** *or* **see in the New Year** celebrar el año nuevo • **happy New Year!** ¡feliz año nuevo! ▸ **New Year resolutions** buenos propósitos *mpl* del año nuevo ▸ **New Year's** (*US**) (= *New Year's Eve*) Nochevieja *f*; (= *New Year's Day*) el día de año nuevo ▸ **New Year's Day** el día de año nuevo ▸ **New Year's Eve** Nochevieja *f* ▸ **New Year's Eve party** fiesta *f* de fin de año ▸ **New Year's resolutions** buenos propósitos *mpl* del año nuevo ▸ **New York** Nueva York *f*; (*before noun*) neoyorquino ▸ **New Yorker** neoyorquino/a *m/f* ▸ **New Zealand** Nueva Zelanda *f*, Nueva Zelandia *f* (*LAm*); (*before noun*) neocelandés, neozelandés ▸ **New Zealander** neocelandés/esa *m/f*, neozelandés/esa *m/f*

> **NEW**
>
> **Position of "nuevo"**
>
> **Nuevo** *tends to follow the noun when it means* **new** *in the sense of "brand-new" and to precede the noun when it means* **new** *in the sense of "another", "replacement" or "latest":*
>
> **... the sales of new cars ...**
> ... las ventas de automóviles nuevos ...
> **... the new prime minister ...**
> ... el nuevo primer ministro ...
> **... the new model ...**
> ... el nuevo modelo ...
>
> *For further uses and examples, see main entry.*

new... [nju:] PREFIX recién

newbie* ['nju:bɪ] N novato/a *m/f*, principiante *mf*

newborn ['nju:bɔ:n] ADJ [*baby*] recién nacido

new-build ['njubɪld] ADJ [*property, apartment, house*] de nueva construcción
N nueva construcción *f*

newcomer ['nju:ˌkʌməʳ] N recién llegado/a *m/f* • **they were ~s to the area** eran nuevos en la zona, en la zona eran unos recién llegados

newel ['nju:əl], **newel post** [ˌnju:əl'pəʊst] N poste *m* (*de una escalera*)

new-fangled ['nju:ˌfæŋgld] ADJ (*pej*) [*idea, theory, gadget*] moderno, tan de moda

new-found ['nju:ˌfaʊnd] ADJ [*talent*] recién descubierto; [*wealth, freedom*] recién adquirido; [*friend*] nuevo • **his new-found zeal** su recién estrenado entusiasmo

Newfoundland ['nju:fəndlənd] N **1** (*Geog*) Terranova *f*
2 (*also* **Newfoundland dog**) perro *m* de Terranova

Newfoundlander ['nju:fəndləndəʳ] N habitante *mf* de Terranova

newish ['nju:ɪʃ] ADJ bastante nuevo

new-laid ['nju:'leɪd] ADJ [*egg*] fresco, recién puesto
CPD ▸ **new-laid egg** huevo *m* fresco, huevo *m* recién puesto

new-look [ˌnju:'lʊk] ADJ nuevo, renovado • **the new-look Labour Party** el nuevo *or* renovado Partido Laborista

newly ['nju:lɪ] ADV (= *recently*) recién • **~ made/arrived/elected** recién hecho/llegado/elegido • **the ~ independent countries of Africa** los países de África que acababan de conseguir la independencia

newly-minted [ˌnju:li'mɪntɪd] ADJ [*coin, term*] recién acuñado; [*champion, minister etc*] nuevo

newlyweds ['nju:lɪwedz] NPL recién

casados *mpl*

new-mown ['nju:'məʊn] ADJ recién segado, recién cortado

newness ['nju:nɪs] N **1** [*of car, clothes etc*] lo nuevo
2 [*of idea, fashion*] novedad *f*
3 [*of bread*] lo fresco; [*of wine*] lo joven

news [nju:z] NSING **1** • **that's wonderful ~!** ¡qué buena noticia! • **some sad ~** • **a sad piece of ~** una triste noticia • **what ~?** • **what's the ~?** ¿qué hay de nuevo? • **a 700th anniversary is ~** un 700 aniversario es noticia • **so you think you're going out tonight? well, I've got ~ for you!** (*iro*) si crees que vas a salir esta noche, te vas a llevar una sorpresa • **to be bad ~*** [*person*] ser un ave de mal agüero; [*thing*] ser mal asunto* • **to break the ~ to sb** dar la noticia a algn • **when the ~ broke** al saberse la noticia • **that's good ~** es una buena noticia • **they're in the ~** son de actualidad • **a piece of ~** una noticia • **it was ~ to me** me pilló de nuevas* • PROVERBS: • **bad ~ travels fast** las malas noticias llegan muy rápido • **no ~ is good ~** la falta de noticias es una buena señal
2 (*Press, Rad, TV*) noticias *fpl* • **the ~** (*Rad*) las noticias, el noticiario; (*TV*) las noticias, el telediario (*Sp*), el noticiero (*LAm*), el noticioso (*And*) • **the foreign ~ pages** la sección *or* las páginas de noticias internacionales • **News in Brief** (= *section in newspaper*) Noticias *fpl* Breves, Breves *fpl*
CPD ▸ **news agency** agencia *f* de noticias ▸ **news blackout** apagón *m* informativo ▸ **news broadcast** noticias *fpl* ▸ **news bulletin** boletín *m* informativo ▸ **news conference** rueda *f* de prensa ▸ **news dealer** (*US*) vendedor(a) *m/f* de periódicos ▸ **news desk** redacción *f* ▸ **news editor** jefe *mf* de redacción ▸ **the news headlines** (*TV, Rad*) el resumen de las noticias ▸ **news item** noticia *f* ▸ **news magazine** revista *f* de actualidad ▸ **news media** medios *mpl* de comunicación ▸ **news programme, news program** (*US*) programa *m* de actualidad ▸ **news release** (*esp US*) = **press release** ▸ **news sheet** hoja *f* informativa ▸ **news vendor** vendedor(a) *m/f* de periódicos

newsagent ['nju:z,eɪdʒənt] N (*Brit*) vendedor(a) *m/f* de periódicos • **~'s** tienda *f or* quiosco *m* de periódicos

newsboy ['nju:zbɔɪ] N (= *deliverer*) chico *m* que reparte periódicos; (= *seller*) chico *m* que vende periódicos, voceador *m* (*Mex*)

newscast ['nju:zkɑ:st] N noticiario *m*, noticiero *m* (*LAm*), noticioso *m* (*And*)

newscaster ['nju:z'kɑ:stəʳ] N locutor(a) *m/f*

newscopy ['nju:zkɒpɪ] N (*Press*) texto *m* de la noticia; (*TV, Rad*) resumen *m* de la noticia

newsdealer ['nju:z'di:ləʳ] N (*US*) vendedor(a) *m/f* de periódicos

newsflash ['nju:zflæʃ] N flash *m*, noticia *f* de última hora

news-gathering ['njʊ:zgæðərɪŋ] N recopilación *f* de noticias, recolección *f* de información

newsgirl ['nju:zgɜ:l] N (*US*) (= *deliverer*) chica *f* que reparte periódicos; (= *seller*) chica *f* que vende periódicos, voceadora *f* (*Mex*)

newsgroup ['nju:zgru:p] N (*on internet*) grupo *m* de discusión, grupo *m* de noticias

newshound* ['nju:zhaʊnd] N reportero/a *m/f*

newsletter ['nju:z,letəʳ] N boletín *m* informativo

newsman ['nju:zmæn] N (PL: **newsmen**) (*esp US*) (= *journalist*) periodista *m*, reportero *m*; (= *newsreader*) locutor *m*; (= *anchor*) presentador *m* de informativos

newspaper ['nju:s,peɪpəʳ] N (*gen*) periódico *m*; (= *daily*) diario *m*; (= *material*) papel *m* de periódico
CPD ▸ **newspaper clipping, newspaper cutting** recorte *m* de periódico ▸ **newspaper office** redacción *f* (de periódico) ▸ **newspaper report** reportaje *m*

newspaperman ['nju:z,peɪpəmæn] N (PL: **newspapermen**) periodista *m*, reportero *m*

newspaperwoman ['nju:z,peɪpəwʊmən] N (PL: **newspaperwomen**) periodista *f*, reportera *f*

newspeak ['nju:spi:k] N neolengua *f*

newsprint ['nju:zprɪnt] N papel *m* prensa, papel *m* continuo • **acres of ~ have been devoted to the subject** han corrido ríos de tinta sobre el asunto

newsreader ['nju:z,ri:dəʳ] N (*Brit*) (*TV*) locutor(a) *m/f*

newsreel ['nju:zri:l] N noticiario *m*, documental *m* de actualidades, ≈ Nodo *m* (*Sp*)

newsroom ['nju:zrʊm] N sala *f* de redacción

newsstand ['nju:zstænd] N (*US*) quiosco *m* de periódicos y revistas

newswoman ['nju:z,wʊmən] N (PL: **newswomen**) (*esp US*) (= *journalist*) periodista *f*, reportera *f*; (= *newsreader*) locutora *f*; (= *anchor*) presentadora *f* de informativos

newsworthiness ['nju:z,wɜ:ðɪnɪs] N interés *m* periodístico

newsworthy ['nju:z,wɜ:ðɪ] ADJ de interés periodístico • **it's not ~** no es noticia, no tiene interés periodístico

newsy* ['nju:zɪ] ADJ lleno de noticias

newt [nju:t] N tritón *m*; ▷ **pissed**

newton ['nju:tn] N newton *m*, neutonio *m*

Newtonian [nju:'təʊnɪən] ADJ newtoniano

next [nekst] ADJ **1** (*of time*) (*in future*) próximo; (*in past*) siguiente • **he retires ~ January** se jubila el enero próximo • **the ~ five days will be crucial** los próximos cinco días serán decisivos • **the ~ five days were very busy** los cinco días siguientes fueron muy ajetreados • **~ month/year** (*in future*) el mes/año que viene, el mes/año próximo, el mes/año entrante (*esp LAm*) • **the ~ month/year** (*in past*) el mes/año siguiente • **(the) ~ day/morning** al día/a la mañana siguiente • **unemployment is predicted to fall both this year and ~** se prevé que el desempleo disminuirá este año y el próximo *or* el siguiente • **she'll have been gone six months ~ Friday** el viernes que viene *or* el viernes próximo hará seis meses que se marchó • **on 4 May ~** (*frm*) el 4 de mayo próximo • **the week after ~** la semana que viene no *or* la semana próxima no, la siguiente • **he died ten years ago ~ week** la semana que viene *or* la semana próxima hará diez años que murió *or* se cumplen diez años de su muerte • **the ~ thing I knew he was gone** cuando me quise dar cuenta se había ido • **this time ~ week** la semana que viene a estas horas • **this time ~ year** el año que viene por estas fechas • **~ time** la próxima vez • **(the) ~ time you see him** la próxima vez que lo veas • **from one moment/day to the ~** de un momento/día para otro; ▷ **moment**
2 (*of order*) próximo, siguiente • **I get out at the ~ stop** me bajo en la próxima *or* siguiente parada • **who's ~?** ¿a quién le toca ahora?, ¿quién sigue? • **I'm/you're ~** me/te toca (a mí/ti) • **~ please!** ¡el siguiente por favor! • **she was ~** *or* **the ~ person to arrive** ella fue la próxima *or* siguiente en llegar • **I'm as much against violence as the ~ person, but ...** estoy tan en contra de la violencia como cualquiera, pero ... • **he's ~ after me** es el primero después de mí • **it's the ~ road but one** es la segunda calle después de esta • **the ~ life** la otra vida • **on the ~ page** en la siguiente página • **the ~ size up/down** (*in clothes*) una talla más grande/más pequeña; (*in shoes*) un número más grande/más pequeño
3 (= *adjacent*) • **~ door** (en la casa de) al lado • **~ door's dog** el perro de (los vecinos de) al lado • **I went ~ door to the bathroom** fui al baño que estaba (en el cuarto de) al lado • **(the) ~ door but one** no la puerta de al lado, sino la siguiente • **~ door to** al lado de • **we live ~ door to each other** vivimos uno al lado del otro • **I live ~ door to her** vivo en la casa de al lado de la suya *or* contigua a la suya • **the ~ house** la casa de al lado • **I could hear them talking in the ~ room** les oía hablar en el cuarto de al lado • **she lives in the ~ street to me** vive en la calle contigua a la mía • IDIOM: • **the girl/boy ~ door** la hija/el hijo del vecino
ADV **1** (*in past*) después, luego • **what did he do ~?** ¿qué hizo después *or* luego? • **when I ~ saw him** cuando lo volví a ver • **I ~ saw him in Rome** la siguiente vez que lo vi fue en Roma
2 (*in future*) • **what do we do ~?** ¿y ahora qué hacemos? • **~ we put the salt in** a continuación *or* ahora añadimos la sal • **when you ~ see him** • **when ~ you see him** cuando lo vuelvas a ver, la próxima vez que lo veas • **whatever ~!** ¡lo que faltaba!
3 (*of place, order*) • **who's the ~ tallest boy?** ¿quién le sigue en altura? • **the ~ smaller size** la talla más pequeña a continuación de esta • **it's the ~ best thing to having your own swimming pool** si no puedes tener tu propia piscina, esto es lo mejor • **what comes ~?** ¿qué viene ahora?, ¿qué sigue?
4 • **~ to a** (= *beside*) al lado de • **his room is ~ to mine** su habitación está al lado de la mía • **I was sitting ~ to her** estaba sentada a su lado • **to wear silk ~ to one's skin** llevar seda en contacto directo con la piel
b (= *after*) después de • **~ to Spain, what country do you like best?** ¿después de España, cuál es tu país preferido?
c (= *compared to*) al lado de • **~ to her I felt totally inept** al lado de ella, me sentía totalmente inútil
d (= *second*) • **he finished the race ~ to last** terminó la carrera en el penúltimo lugar • **the ~ to last row** la penúltima fila
e (= *almost*) casi • **it's ~ to impossible** es casi imposible • **I know ~ to nothing about computers** no sé casi nada de ordenadores, sé poquísimo de ordenadores • **we got it for ~ to nothing** lo conseguimos por poquísimo dinero
CPD ▸ **next of kin** familiar(es) *m(pl)* más cercano(s), pariente(s) *m(pl)* más cercano(s)

next-door ['neks'dɔ:ʳ] ADJ • **next-door flat** piso *m* de al lado • **next-door neighbour** vecino/a *m/f* de al lado

nexus ['neksəs] N nexo *m*

NF N ABBR (*Brit*) (*Pol*) = **National Front**
ABBR (*Canada*) = **Newfoundland**

n/f ABBR (*Banking*) = **no funds**

NFL N ABBR (*US*) = **National Football League**

Nfld. ABBR (*Canada*) = **Newfoundland**

NFS N ABBR (*Brit*) = **National Fire Service**

NFT N ABBR (*Brit*) = **National Film Theatre**

NFU N ABBR (*Brit*) = **National Farmers' Union**

NG ABBR (US) = **National Guard**

NGA N ABBR (Brit) (= **National Graphical Association**) *sindicato de tipógrafos*

NGO N ABBR (= **non-governmental organization**) ONG *f*

NH ABBR **1** (US) = **New Hampshire**
2 = **National Health**

NHI ABBR = **National Health Insurance**

NHL N ABBR (US) = **National Hockey League**

NHS N ABBR (Brit) (= **National Health Service**) Sistema *m* Nacional de Salud

NI ABBR **1** = **Northern Ireland**
2 = **National Insurance**

niacin ['naɪəsɪn] N ácido *m* nicotínico

Niagara [naɪ'ægrə] N Niágara *m*
CPD ▸ **Niagara Falls** Cataratas *fpl* del Niágara

nib [nɪb] N punta *f*; [*of fountain pen*] plumilla *f*, plumín *m*

nibble ['nɪbl] N **1** (= *little bite*) mordisquito *m* • **I never had a ~ all day** (*Fishing*) el corcho no se movió en todo el día
2 (= *food*) bocado *m* • **I feel like a ~** me apetece comer algo, no me vendría mal un bocado
3 nibbles (*at party etc*) comida *fsing* para picar
VT [*person*] mordisquear, mordiscar; [*fish*] picar; [*rat, mouse*] roer; [*horse*] rozar
VI • **to ~ (at)** [+ *food*] picar • **to ~ at an offer** mostrar cierto interés por una oferta

nibs [nɪbz] N • **his ~*** (*hum*) su señoría

NIC N ABBR **1** (Brit) (= **National Insurance Contribution**) *contribuciones a la Seguridad Social*
2 = **newly industrialized** *or* **industrializing country**

NICAM ['naɪkæm] N ABBR = **near-instantaneous companding audio multiplex**

Nicaragua [,nɪkə'rægjʊə] N Nicaragua *f*

Nicaraguan [,nɪkə'rægjʊən] ADJ nicaragüense
N nicaragüense *mf*

Nice [ni:s] N Niza *f*

nice [naɪs] ADJ (COMPAR: **nicer**, SUPERL: **nicest**) **1** (= *pleasant*) [*book, holiday, evening*] bueno, agradable, lindo (*LAm*); [*weather*] bueno; [*food, aroma*] rico • **it's very ~ here** se está muy bien aquí • **it would be ~ to speak a foreign language** estaría bien poder hablar otro idioma • **it was ~ to see you** me ha alegrado mucho verte, fue un placer verte (*frm*) • **it's not a very ~ day, is it?** (*weather-wise*) no hace un día muy bueno, ¿verdad? • **did you have a ~ day?** (*at work*) ¿qué tal te fue el día?; (*on trip*) ¿lo pasaste bien? • **it's a ~ idea, but ...** es buena idea, pero ... • **it would be ~ if you came too** me gustaría que tú también vinieses • **~ one!*** (*also iro*) ¡estupendo!, ¡genial!* • **it smells ~** huele bien • **it doesn't taste at all ~** no sabe nada bien • **did you have a ~ time at the party?** ¿te lo pasaste bien en la fiesta?
2 (= *likeable*) simpático, majo*, buena gente* • **he's a really ~ guy** es muy simpático, es muy majo (*Sp**), es muy buena gente (*LAm**)
3 (= *kind*) amable • **he was very ~ about it** se mostró *or* (*LAm*) se portó muy amable al respecto • **it was ~ of you to help us** fuiste muy amable ayudándonos • **to say ~ things about sb** hablar bien de algn • **to be ~ to sb** ser amable con algn, tratar bien a algn
4 (= *attractive*) [*person*] guapo, lindo (*LAm*); [*thing, place, house*] bonito, lindo (*LAm*) • **~ car!** ¡vaya coche!, ¡qué auto más lindo! (*LAm*) • **you look ~!** ¡qué guapa estás!, ¡qué bien te ves! (*LAm*) • **she has a ~ smile** tiene una sonrisa muy bonita
5 (= *polite*) fino, educado • **that's not ~** eso no está bien, eso no se hace • **~ girls don't smoke** las chicas finas *or* bien educadas no fuman • **he has ~ manners** es muy educado • **what a ~ young man** que joven más agradable y educado
6 (*emphatic*) bien • **a ~ cold drink** una bebida bien fría • **a ~ little house** una casita muy mona* • **it's ~ and convenient** resulta muy conveniente • **~ and early** bien temprano • **just take it ~ and easy** tú tómatelo con calma • **it's ~ and warm here** aquí hace un calorcito muy agradable
7 (*iro*) (= *not nice*) • **that's a ~ thing to say!** ¡hombre, muy amable! • **~ friends you've got, they've just walked off with my radio** vaya amigos que tienes *or* menudos amigos tienes, acaban de llevarse mi radio • **here's a ~ state of affairs!** ¡dónde hemos ido a parar!
8 (= *subtle*) [*distinction, point*] sutil; [*judgment*] acertado
9 (*frm*) (= *fastidious*) remilgado

nice-looking ['naɪs'lʊkɪŋ] ADJ atractivo, lindo (*LAm*); [*person*] bien parecido, guapo

nicely ['naɪslɪ] ADV **1** (= *well*) bien • **~ browned** bien dorado • **she is coming along ~ at school** en el colegio le va bien • **that will do ~** así está perfecto *or* bien • **your driver's licence will do ~** su carnet de conducir sirve *or* vale • **he's doing very ~ (for himself)** le van muy bien las cosas • **to be ~ placed (to do sth)** estar en buena posición (para hacer algo)
2 (= *attractively*) [*arranged, decorated, furnished*] bien, con gusto • **she dresses ~** viste con muy buen gusto
3 (= *politely*) [*ask, say*] bien, con educación

niceness ['naɪsnɪs] N **1** (= *pleasantness*) [*of place, thing*] lo agradable
2 (= *likeableness*) [*of person*] simpatía *f*
3 (= *kindness*) amabilidad *f*
4 (= *politeness*) finura *f*
5 (= *subtlety*) sutileza *f*

nicety ['naɪsɪtɪ] N sutileza *f* • **niceties** detalles *mpl*, sutilezas *fpl* • **legal niceties** pormenores *mpl* legales • **she went through the social niceties** realizó las formalidades *or* los cumplidos de rigor • **to judge sth to a ~** juzgar algo con precisión *or* al detalle

niche [ni:ʃ] N (*Archit*) nicho *m*, hornacina *f*; (*fig*) hueco *m* • **to find a ~ for o.s.** hacerse con una buena posición *or* un huequito*
CPD ▸ **niche market** mercado *m* de nicho • **a profitable ~ market** un mercado de nicho rentable

Nicholas ['nɪkələs] N Nicolás

Nick [nɪk] N (*familiar form of* **Nicholas**) • **Old ~** (*hum*) Pedro Botero* (*hum*)

nick [nɪk] N **1** (= *cut*) muesca *f*, mella *f*; (= *crack*) hendedura *f*
2 (*Brit**) (= *prison*) chirona* *f*, trullo *m* (*Sp‡*); (= *police station*) comisaría *f*
3 • IDIOM: • **in the ~ of time** justo a tiempo
4* (= *condition*) • **in good ~** en buen estado
VT **1** (= *cut*) hacer una muesca en, mellar • **he ~ed his chin shaving** se hizo un corte en la barbilla afeitándose • **the bullet had ~ed the bone** la bala le había hendido el hueso • **the film does no more than ~ the surface of this thorny issue** la película no hace más que tocar muy de refilón este espinoso asunto • **to ~ o.s.** cortarse
2* (= *steal*) robar, afanar*; (= *arrest*) agarrar*, trincar (*Sp**), apañar (*Mex**) • **you're ~ed!** ¡estás detenido!

nickel ['nɪkl] N **1** (= *metal*) níquel *m*
2 (*US*) (= *coin*) moneda *f* de cinco centavos
CPD ▸ **nickel silver** plata *f* alemana

nickel-plated ['nɪkl'pleɪtɪd] ADJ niquelado

nicker‡ ['nɪkəʳ] N (*Brit*) libra *f* esterlina

nickname ['nɪkneɪm] N apodo *m*, mote *m*
VT apodar, dar el apodo de • **they ~d him Nobby** le dieron el apodo de Nobby

Nicosia [,nɪkəʊ'si:ə] N Nicosia *f*

nicotine ['nɪkəti:n] N nicotina *f*
CPD ▸ **nicotine patch** parche *m* de nicotina
▸ **nicotine poisoning** nicotinismo *m*
▸ **nicotine replacement therapy** terapia *f* de sustitución de la nicotina

nicotinic [,nɪkə'tɪnɪk] ADJ • **~ acid** ácido *m* nicotínico

niece [ni:s] N sobrina *f*

niff‡ [nɪf] N (*Brit*) olorcito *m* (**of** a); (*unpleasant*) tufillo *m*

niffy‡ ['nɪfɪ] ADJ (*Brit*) maloliente, apestoso

nifty* ['nɪftɪ] ADJ (COMPAR: **niftier**, SUPERL: **niftiest**) **1** (= *excellent*) [*person*] sensacional*, chachi (*Sp**); [*place, car*] chulo*; [*gadget, idea*] ingenioso, chulo*
2 (= *skilful*) diestro, hábil
3 (= *quick*) • **you'd better be ~ about it!** ¡ya puedes ir ligerito!, ¡más vale que te des prisa!
4 (= *elegant*) (= *stylish*) [*outfit*] elegante, chulo*

Niger ['naɪdʒəʳ] N (= *country, river*) Níger *m*

Nigeria [naɪ'dʒɪərɪə] N Nigeria *f*

Nigerian [naɪ'dʒɪərɪən] ADJ nigeriano
N nigeriano/a *m/f*

niggardliness ['nɪgədlɪnɪs] N tacañería *f*

niggardly ['nɪgədlɪ] ADJ [*person*] tacaño; [*allowance*] miserable

nigger‡* ['nɪgəʳ] N (*offensive*) negro/a *m/f* • IDIOM: • **to be the ~ in the woodpile†** ser lo que lo estropea todo

niggle ['nɪgl] VI (= *complain*) quejarse
VT **1** (= *worry*) preocupar • **it's something that has always ~d me** es algo que siempre me ha tenido inquieto
2 (= *find fault with*) criticar continuamente
N (= *complaint*) queja *f*; (= *worry*) preocupación *f*
▸ **niggle at** VI + PREP **1** (= *worry*) preocupar
2 (= *find fault with*) criticar continuamente

niggling ['nɪglɪŋ] ADJ [*detail*] engorroso; [*doubt, suspicion*] persistente, constante; [*injury*] molesto, molestoso (*LAm*); [*person*] quisquilloso
N (= *complaints*) quejas *fpl*

nigh† [naɪ] (*liter*) ADJ (= *imminent*) próximo, cercano • **the end is ~** el final se avecina *or* está muy próximo
ADV **1** (= *near*) cerca • **when winter draws ~** cuando se acerca el invierno
2 • **~ on** (= *nearly*) casi • **it's ~ on finished** está casi terminado

night [naɪt] N **1** (= *time of day*) noche *f* • **it is ~** (*liter*) es de noche • **Monday ~** el lunes por la noche • **a Beethoven ~** un concierto dedicado a Beethoven • **all ~ (long)** toda la noche • **at ~** por la noche, de noche • **11 o'clock at ~** las 11 de la noche • **last thing at ~** lo último antes de acostarse • **to stay up late at ~** trasnochar • **to have a bad ~** dormir mal, pasar una mala noche • **the ~ before the ceremony** la víspera de la ceremonia • **by ~** de noche, por la noche • **~ and day** noche y día • **to have an early ~** acostarse temprano • **good ~!** ¡buenas noches! • **in the ~** durante la noche • **last ~** (= *late*) anoche; (= *in the evening*) ayer por la tarde • **the ~ before last** anteanoche • **to have a late ~** acostarse muy tarde • **you've had too many late ~s** llevas muchos días acostándote muy tarde • **we decided to make a ~ of it and go to a club afterwards** decidimos prolongar la velada e irnos a una discoteca después • **to have a ~ out** salir por la noche • **I can't sleep ~s** (*US*) no puedo dormir la noche • **to spend the ~** pasar la noche • **to spend the ~ together** (*euph*) (= *to have sex*) pasar la noche juntos • **tomorrow ~** mañana por la noche • **to work ~s** trabajar de noche
2 (*Theat*) • **first ~** estreno *m* • **last ~** última

representación *f*
(CPD) ▸ **night bird** ave *f* nocturna ▸ **night blindness** ceguera *f* nocturna ▸ **night bus** autobús *m* nocturno ▸ **night fighter** caza *m* nocturno, cazabombardero *m* nocturno ▸ **night nurse** enfermera *f* de noche ▸ **night out** • **girls' ~ out** salida *f* de chicas • **boys' ~ out** salida *f* de chicos • **he was returning home after a ~ out with friends when ...** volvía a casa después de haber salido con los amigos cuando ... ▸ **night owl*** (*fig*) ave *f* nocturna ▸ **night porter** guarda *m* nocturno ▸ **night safe** caja *f* de seguridad nocturna ▸ **night school** escuela *f* nocturna ▸ **night shelter** albergue *m* ▸ **night shift** turno *m* nocturno, turno *m* de noche ▸ **night stand** (*US*) = **night table** ▸ **night storage heater** acumulador *m* eléctrico nocturno ▸ **night table** mesita *f* de noche ▸ **night vision** visión *f* nocturna; ▹ **night-vision** ▸ **night watch** (= *shift*) turno *m* de noche; (*Hist*) ronda *f* nocturna; (= *individual*) = **night watchman** ▸ **night watchman** (*in factory*) vigilante *m* nocturno; (*in street*) sereno *m* ▸ **night work** trabajo *m* nocturno

nightcap ['naɪtkæp] (N) **1** (= *hat*) gorro *m* de dormir
2 (= *drink*) *bebida que se toma antes de acostarse*

nightclothes ['naɪtˌkləʊðz] (N) ropa *fsing* de dormir

nightclub ['naɪtklʌb] (N) club *m* nocturno, discoteca *f*

nightclubber ['naɪtklʌbəʳ] (N) discotequero/a *m/f*

nightclubbing ['naɪtklʌbɪŋ] (N) salidas *fpl* (nocturnas) a discotecas • **to go ~** ir de discotecas

nightdress ['naɪtdres] (N) (*esp Brit*) camisón *m* de noche

nightfall ['naɪtfɔːl] (N) anochecer *m* • **at ~** al anochecer • **by ~** antes del anochecer

nightgown ['naɪtgaʊn] (N) (*esp US*) camisón *m* de noche

nighthawk ['naɪthɔːk] (N) chotacabras *m inv*

nightie* ['naɪtɪ] (N) = **nightdress**

nightingale ['naɪtɪŋgeɪl] (N) ruiseñor *m*

nightjar ['naɪtdʒɑːʳ] (N) chotacabras *m inv*

nightlife ['naɪtlaɪf] (N) vida *f* nocturna

night-light ['naɪtlaɪt] (N) lamparilla *f*, mariposa *f*

nightlong ['naɪtlɒŋ] (ADJ) de toda la noche, que dura toda la noche

nightly ['naɪtlɪ] (ADV) todas las noches
(ADJ) de noche, nocturno; (*regular*) de todas las noches

nightmare ['naɪtmɛəʳ] (N) (*also fig*) pesadilla *f* • IDIOM: • **to be sb's worst ~** ser la peor pesadilla de algn
(CPD) ▸ **nightmare scenario** • **a hung parliament would be the ~ scenario for the market** el peor panorama para el mercado sería un parlamento en el cual ningún partido tiene la mayoría absoluta

nightmarish ['naɪtmɛərɪʃ] (ADJ) de pesadilla, espeluznante

night-night* ['naɪtˌnaɪt] (EXCL) (= *goodnight*) buenas noches

nightshade ['naɪtʃeɪd] (N) dulcamara *f*, hierba *f* mora • **deadly ~** belladona *f*

nightshirt ['naɪtʃɜːt] (N) camisa *f* de dormir

night-sight ['naɪtsaɪt] (N) visor *m* nocturno

nightspot ['naɪtˌspɒt] (N) local *m* nocturno

nightstick ['naɪtstɪk] (N) (*US*) porra *f* (de policía)

night-time ['naɪttaɪm] (N) noche *f* • **at night-time** por la noche, de noche • **in the night-time** durante la noche, por la noche
(CPD) [*visit, call*] nocturno

night-vision ['naɪtvɪʒən] (ADJ) [*goggles, binoculars, equipment*] de vigilancia nocturna

nightwear ['naɪtwɛəʳ] (N) ropa *f* de dormir

nig-nog‡* ['nɪgnɒg] (N) (*offensive*) negro/a *m/f*

NIH (N ABBR) (*US*) = **National Institutes of Health**

nihilism ['naɪɪlɪzəm] (N) nihilismo *m*

nihilist ['naɪɪlɪst] (N) nihilista *mf*

nihilistic [ˌnaɪɪ'lɪstɪk] (ADJ) nihilista

Nikkei average [nɪˌkeɪ'ævərɪdʒ], **Nikkei index** [nɪˌkeɪ'ɪndeks] (N) índice *m* Nikkei

nil [nɪl] (N) (= *nothing*) nada *f*; (*Sport*) cero *m* • **Granada beat Murcia two-nil** el Granada venció al Murcia dos-cero *or* por dos a cero • **they drew nil-nil** empataron a cero; ▹ ZERO
(ADJ) nulo • **its merits are nil** sus méritos son nulos, no tiene mérito alguno
(CPD) ▸ **nil balance** (*Econ*) balance *m* nulo

Nile [naɪl] (N) Nilo *m*

nimble ['nɪmbl] (ADJ) (COMPAR: **nimbler**, SUPERL: **nimblest**) [*person, mind*] ágil; [*feet*] ligero; [*fingers*] hábil, diestro • **~-fingered** de dedos hábiles • **~-footed** de pies ligeros

nimbleness ['nɪmblnɪs] (N) [*of person*] agilidad *f*; [*of feet*] ligereza *f*; [*of fingers*] destreza *f*

nimbly ['nɪmblɪ] (ADV) **1** [*jump, skip*] ágilmente; [*dance*] con ligereza
2 [*stitch, fasten*] con destreza

nimbostratus [ˌnɪmbəʊ'streɪtəs] (N) (PL: **nimbostrati** [ˌnɪmbəʊstreɪtaɪ]) nimbostrato *m*

nimbus ['nɪmbəs] (N) (PL: **nimbi** *or* **nimbuses**) nimbo *m*

NIMBY ['nɪmbɪ] (= **not in my backyard**) (N ABBR) *persona que se opone a la ubicación de cualquier tipo de construcción o proyecto problemático en su vecindario*
(ADJ) *de oposición a la ubicación de cualquier tipo de construcción o proyecto problemático en un vecindario concreto*

nimbyism, NIMBYism ['nɪmbɪzəm] (N) *oposición a la ubicación de cualquier tipo de construcción o proyecto problemático en un vecindario concreto*

nincompoop†* ['nɪŋkəmpuːp] (N) bobo/a *m/f*

nine [naɪn] (ADJ), (PRON) nueve • **~-to-five job** trabajo *m* de nueve a cinco • **~ times out of ten** casi siempre, en el noventa por ciento de los casos • IDIOM: • **a ~ days' wonder** una maravilla de un día
(N) (= *numeral*) nueve *m* • **to work ~ to five** trabajar (la) jornada completa • IDIOMS: • **to be dressed up to the ~s** (*Brit**) ir de punta en blanco • **to get dressed up to the ~s** ponerse de punta en blanco; ▹ **five**

9-11, Nine-Eleven [ˌnaɪnɪ'levn] (N) 11-S *m*

999, nine nine nine [ˌnaɪnnaɪn'naɪn] (N) (*Brit*) *número de urgencias y emergencias* • **to dial 999** • **call 999** *llamar al número de urgencias y emergencias*

911, nine one one [ˌnaɪnwʌn'wʌn] (N) (*US*) *número de urgencias y emergencias* • **to call 911** • **dial 911** *llamar al número de urgencias y emergencias*

ninepins ['naɪnpɪnz] (NPL) (= *game*) juego *m* de bolos; (= *objects*) bolos *mpl* • IDIOM: • **to go down like ~** caer como bolos en bolera

nineteen ['naɪn'tiːn] (ADJ), (PRON) diecinueve
(N) (= *numeral*) diecinueve *m* • IDIOM: • **to talk ~ to the dozen*** hablar por los codos*; ▹ **five**

nineteenth ['naɪn'tiːnθ] (ADJ) decimonoveno, decimonono • **the ~ century** el siglo diecinueve • IDIOM: • **the ~ (hole)** (*hum*) el bar; ▹ **fifth**

ninetieth ['naɪntɪɪθ] (ADJ) nonagésimo • **the ~ anniversary** el noventa aniversario; ▹ **fifth**

ninety ['naɪntɪ] (ADJ), (PRON) noventa
(N) (= *numeral*) noventa *m* • **the nineties** los años noventa • **to be in one's nineties** tener más de noventa años, ser un noventón/una noventona • **temperatures were in the nineties** ≈ las temperaturas superaban los treinta grados centígrados; ▹ **five**

ninny* ['nɪnɪ] (N) bobo/a *m/f*

ninth [naɪnθ] (ADJ) noveno, nono • **Pius IX** Pío Nono; ▹ **fifth**
(N) noveno *m*
(ADV) en novena posición • **to come in ~** llegar el noveno *or* en novena posición

ninth-grader [ˌnaɪnθ'greɪdəʳ] (N) (*US*) alumno/a *m/f* de noveno curso (*de entre 14 y 15 años*)

niobium [naɪ'əʊbɪəm] (N) niobio *m*

Nip‡ [nɪp] (N) (*pej*) japonés/esa *m/f*

nip¹ [nɪp] (N) (= *pinch*) pellizco *m*; (= *bite*) mordisco *m* • **there's a nip in the air** hace bastante frío • **it was nip and tuck throughout the match** (= *neck and neck*) el encuentro estuvo muy reñido *or* igualado
(VT) (= *pinch*) pellizcar, pinchar; (= *bite*) mordiscar, mordisquear; [*frost*] [+ *plant*] quemar; [*wind*] [+ *one's face*] cortar; (*also* **nip off**) [+ *flowers, buds*] cortar • **to nip one's fingers in a door** pillarse los dedos en una puerta • IDIOM: • **to nip sth in the bud** cortar algo de raíz
(VI) (*Brit**) • **to nip inside** entrar un momento • **to nip in and out of the traffic** colarse por entre el tráfico • **to nip off/out/down** irse/salir/bajar un momento • **I nipped round to the shop** hice una escapadita a la tienda • **we were nipping along at 100kph** íbamos a 100kph

▸ **nip at** (VI + PREP) (= *bite*) mordisquear • **the dog nipped at his heels** el perro le mordisqueó los talones

▸ **nip down** (VI + ADV) (*Brit**) bajar un momento • **I'll just nip down and post these letters** bajaré un momento a echar estas cartas

▸ **nip into** (VI + PREP) (*Brit**) acercarse a • **to nip into a shop** acercarse a una tienda

▸ **nip out** (VI + ADV) (*Brit**) salir • **shall I nip out and get some groceries?** ¿quieres que salga a comprar algo de comer?

▸ **nip to** (VI + PREP) (*Brit**) acercarse un momento a • **I'm just nipping to the shop** me voy a acercar un momento a la tienda

▸ **nip up** (VI + ADV) (*Brit**) subir un momento • **I'll just nip up to the loo** subo un momento al baño

nip² [nɪp] (N) [*of drink*] trago *m*, traguito* *m*

nipper* ['nɪpəʳ] (N) (*Brit*) chiquillo/a *m/f*

nipple ['nɪpl] (N) **1** (*Anat*) [*of female*] pezón *m*; [*of male*] tetilla *f*; (*on baby's bottle*) tetina *f*
2 (*Mech*) boquilla *f* roscada, manguito *m* de unión; (*for greasing*) engrasador *m*, pezón *m* de engrase

nippy* ['nɪpɪ] (ADJ) (COMPAR: **nippier**, SUPERL: **nippiest**) **1** (= *quick*) [*person*] ágil, rápido; [*car*] rápido • **be ~ about it!** ¡date prisa! • **we shall have to be ~** tendremos que darnos prisa, tendremos que apurarnos *or* movernos (*LAm*)
2 (= *cold*) [*weather*] fresquito

niqab [nɪ'kaːb] (N) nicab *m*

NIREX ['naɪreks] (N ABBR) (*Brit*) = **Nuclear Industry Radioactive Waste Executive**

nirvana [nɪə'vaːnə] (N) nirvana *m*

nisi ['naɪsaɪ] (CONJ) ▹ **decree**

nit [nɪt] (N) **1** (*Zool*) liendre *f*
2 (*Brit**) (= *idiot*) imbécil *mf*, bobo/a *m/f*, zonzo/a *m/f* (*LAm*) • **you nit!** ¡imbécil!

nite* ['naɪt] (N) (= *night*) noche *f*

niter ['naɪtəʳ] (N) (*US*) = **nitre**

nitpick* ['nɪtˌpɪk] (VI) (*pej*) sacarle faltas a todo, buscarle tres pies al gato*

nit-picker* ['nɪtˌpɪkəʳ] N criticón/ona *m/f*, quisquilloso/a *m/f*
nit-picking* ['nɪtˌpɪkɪŋ] ADJ [*question, criticism*] quisquilloso; [*objection*] puntilloso
N quisquillosidad *f*
nitrate ['naɪtreɪt] N nitrato *m*
nitration [naɪ'treɪʃən] N nitratación *f*, nitración *f*
nitre, niter (*US*) ['naɪtəʳ] N nitro *m*
nitric ['naɪtrɪk] ADJ • **~ acid** ácido *m* nítrico • **~ oxide** óxido *m* nítrico
nitrite ['naɪtraɪt] N nitrito *m*
nitro- ['naɪtrəʊ-] PREFIX nitro-
nitrobenzene [ˌnaɪtrəʊben'ziːn] N nitrobenceno *m*
nitrogen ['naɪtrədʒən] N nitrógeno *m*
CPD ▸ **nitrogen cycle** ciclo *m* del nitrógeno ▸ **nitrogen dioxide** dióxido *m* de nitrógeno ▸ **nitrogen oxide** óxido *m* de nitrógeno
nitrogenous [naɪ'trɒdʒɪnəs] ADJ nitrogenado
nitroglycerin, nitroglycerine ['naɪtrəʊ'glɪsəriːn] N nitroglicerina *f*
nitrous ['naɪtrəs] ADJ nitroso • **~ acid** ácido *m* nitroso • **~ oxide** óxido *m* nitroso
nitty-gritty* [ˌnɪtɪgrɪtɪ] N • **the nitty-gritty** lo esencial, el meollo • IDIOM: • **to get down to the nitty-gritty** ir al grano
nitwit* ['nɪtwɪt] N imbécil *mf*, bobo/a *mf*, zonzo/a *m/f* (*LAm*)
nix‡ [nɪks] N nada
EXCL ¡ni hablar!
NJ ABBR (*US*) = **New Jersey**
NLF N ABBR = **National Liberation Front**
NLP N ABBR = **neurolinguistic programming**
NLQ N ABBR (*Comput*) (= **near letter quality**) calidad *f* casi de correspondencia
NLRB N ABBR (*US*) = **National Labor Relations Board**
NM ABBR (*US*) = **New Mexico**
N. Mex. ABBR (*US*) = **New Mexico**
NMR N ABBR = **nuclear magnetic resonance**
NNE ABBR (= **north-northeast**) NNE
NNP N ABBR (= **net national product**) PNN *m*
NNR N ABBR (*Brit*) = **National Nature Reserve**
NNW ABBR (= **north-northwest**) NNO
no [nəʊ] ADV **1** (*answer*) no
2 (*emphatic*) no
3 (*in comparisons*) • **I am no taller than you** yo no soy más alto que tú
ADJ **1** (= *not any*) ningún • **they've got no friends in London** no tienen ningún conocido en Londres • **there are no trains after midnight** no hay trenes después de medianoche • **I have no money/furniture** *etc* no tengo dinero/muebles *etc* • **"no admittance"** • **"no entry"** "se prohíbe la entrada" • **"no parking"** "no aparcar", "no estacionarse" (*esp LAm*) • **"no smoking"** "prohibido fumar" • **it's no good** es inútil • **details of little or no interest** detalles *mpl* sin interés • **there is no coffee left** no queda café • **we'll be there in no time** llegamos en un dos por tres, no tardamos nada • **it's no trouble** no es molestia • **no two of them are alike** no hay dos iguales • **it's no use** es inútil
2 (= *quite other than*) • **he's no film star! that's the man who lives at number 54** ¡ese no es una *or* no es ninguna estrella de cine! es el señor que vive en el número 54 • **he's no fool** no es tonto, ni mucho menos, no es ningún tonto • **he's no friend of mine** no es precisamente amigo mío
3 (= *no way of*) • **there's no denying it** es imposible negarlo • **there's no getting out of it** no hay posibilidad de evitarlo • **there's no pleasing him** es imposible contentarle; ▹ doubt, end, joke
4 • **no place*** (*adv*) = **nowhere**
N (PL: **noes**) **1** (= *refusal*) no *m* • **I won't take no for an answer** no acepto un no por respuesta
2 (*Pol*) voto *m* en contra • **the noes have it** se ha rechazado la moción
CPD ▸ **no entry sign** (= *traffic sign*) señal *f* de prohibido el paso; (*on gate, door*) cartel *m* de "prohibido el paso" ▸ **no throw** (*Sport*) lanzamiento *m* nulo
No., no. ABBR (= **number**) núm, N.º, n.º • **we live at No. 23** vivimos en el (número) 23
no-account* ['nəʊə'kaʊnt] (*US*) ADJ insignificante, inútil
N cero *m* a la izquierda
Noah ['nəʊə] N Noé • **~'s ark** arca *f* de Noé
nob1‡ [nɒb] N (*Anat*) mollera* *f*, coco* *m*, cholla *f* (*Mex‡*)
nob2‡ [nɒb] N (*Brit*) (= *toff, person of importance*) potentado/a *m/f*
nobble* ['nɒbl] (*Brit*) VT **1** [+ *person*] (= *waylay*) pescar*; (= *bribe*) sobornar, comprar
2 (= *drug*) [+ *horse*] drogar
3 (= *arrest*) agarrar, pescar*
4 (= *steal*) birlar*, afanar*
Nobel [nəʊ'bel] CPD ▸ **Nobel prize** premio *m* Nobel ▸ **Nobel prizewinner** ganador(a) *m/f* del premio Nobel
nobelium [nəʊ'biːlɪəm] N nobelio *m*
nobility [nəʊ'bɪlɪtɪ] N (*all senses*) nobleza *f*
noble ['nəʊbl] ADJ (COMPAR: **nobler**, SUPERL: **noblest**) **1** (*by birth*) noble; [*title*] de nobleza
2 (= *generous, praiseworthy*) magnánimo, generoso
N noble *mf*, aristócrata *mf*; (*Spanish Hist*) hidalgo *m*
CPD ▸ **the noble art** el boxeo ▸ **noble rot** [*of wine*] podredumbre *f* noble ▸ **noble savage** buen salvaje *m*
nobleman ['nəʊblmən] N (PL: **noblemen**) noble *m*, aristócrata *m*; (*Spanish Hist*) hidalgo *m*
noble-minded [ˌnəʊbl'maɪndɪd] ADJ generoso, magnánimo
nobleness ['nəʊblnɪs] N nobleza *f*
noblewoman ['nəʊblwʊmən] N (PL: **noblewomen**) noble *f*, aristócrata *f*
nobly ['nəʊblɪ] ADV noblemente, con nobleza; (*fig*) generosamente, con generosidad
nobody ['nəʊbədɪ] PRON nadie • **~ spoke** nadie habló, no habló nadie • **~ has more right to it than she has** nadie tiene más derecho a ello que ella
N • **a mere ~** un don nadie • **I knew him when he was ~** lo conocí cuando no era nadie
no-brainer‡ [ˌnəʊ'breɪnəʳ] N • **it's a no-brainer** no tiene ningún misterio
no-claim bonus [ˌnəʊ'kleɪmˌbəʊnəs], **no-claims bonus** [ˌnəʊ'kleɪmzˌbəʊnəs] N prima *f* de no reclamación
no-claim discount [ˌnəʊ'kleɪmˌdɪskaʊnt], **no-claims discount** [ˌnəʊ'kleɪmzˌdɪskaʊnt] N (*US*) = **no-claim bonus**
nocturnal [nɒk'tɜːnl] ADJ nocturno
nocturne ['nɒktɜːn] N (*Mus*) nocturno *m*
nod [nɒd] N inclinación *f* de la cabeza • **give me a nod when you want me to start** hazme una señal con la cabeza cuando quieras que empiece • **he gave a nod** (*answering yes*) asintió con la cabeza • **with a nod (of the head)**: • **he answered with a nod** contestó con una inclinación de la cabeza • **he agreed with a nod** asintió con la cabeza • **she greeted me with a nod** me saludó con la cabeza • IDIOMS: • **to give sth/sb the nod** dar luz verde a algo/algn • **to go through** *or* **be accepted on the nod** ser aprobado sin discusión • **a nod is as good as a wink (to a blind horse)** a buen entendedor (pocas palabras bastan) • **the Land of Nod** el país de los sueños
VT **1** • **to nod (one's) agreement** asentir con la cabeza • **to nod (one's) approval** hacer un gesto *or* una señal de aprobación con la cabeza • **he nodded a greeting** nos saludó con la cabeza • **she nodded her head** inclinó la cabeza; (*saying yes*) asintió con la cabeza • **he was nodding his head in time to the music** movía la cabeza al son de la música • **the porter nodded us through** el conserje nos hizo una señal con la cabeza para que pasáramos
2 (*Sport*) [+ *ball*] cabecear
VI **1** (= *move one's head*) inclinar la cabeza; (*in agreement*) asentir con la cabeza • **she said nothing but simply nodded** no dijo nada, se limitó a hacer una inclinación de cabeza • **he nodded in the direction of the house** señaló la casa con la cabeza • **she nodded to me to come forward** me indicó con la cabeza que me adelantara • **to nod in agreement** asentir con la cabeza • **to nod in approval** hacer un gesto *or* una señal de aprobación con la cabeza • **she nodded to him in greeting** lo saludó con la cabeza
2 (= *sway*) [*flowers, plumes*] mecerse
3 (= *doze*) dar cabezadas, cabecear
4 (*as adj*) • **he has a nodding acquaintance with German** habla un poco de alemán • **he has a nodding acquaintance with this author** conoce superficialmente las obras de este autor • **we're on nodding terms** nos conocemos de vista
▸ **nod at** VI + PREP **1** (= *greet*) saludar con la cabeza
2 (= *indicate*) señalar con la cabeza a • **does it work? he asked, nodding at the piano** ¿funciona?, preguntó señalando con la cabeza al piano
▸ **nod off** VI + ADV dormirse, quedarse dormido • **I must have nodded off for a moment** me he debido dormir *or* quedar dormido un momento • **he was nodding off (to sleep) in an armchair** estaba dando cabezadas en un sillón
▸ **nod through** VT + ADV (*Pol*) • **the delegates were nodded through** los delegados fueron aprobados sin votación
▸ **nod to** VI + PREP **1** (= *greet*) saludar con la cabeza • **I nodded to the ladies and sat down** saludé con la cabeza a las señoras y me senté
2 (= *give a signal*) • **to nod to sb to do sth** hacer una señal con la cabeza a algn para que haga algo • **he lifted the end of the canoe, nodding to me to take up mine** levantó el extremo de la canoa y me hizo una señal con la cabeza para que levantase el otro
▸ **nod towards** VI + PREP (*indicating*) señalar con la cabeza • **"ask him," said Rob, nodding towards Stevens** "pregúntale a él" dijo Rob, señalando con la cabeza a Stevens
nodal ['nəʊdəl] ADJ nodal • **~ point** (*fig*) punto *m* nodal
noddle* ['nɒdl] N mollera* *f*, coco* *m*
node [nəʊd] N (*Anat, Astron, Phys*) nodo *m*; (*Bot*) nudo *m*
nodular ['nɒdjʊləʳ] ADJ nodular
nodule ['nɒdjuːl] N nódulo *m*
Noel [nəʊ'el] N Navidad *f*
no-fault ['nəʊ'fɔːlt] ADJ • **no-fault agreement** acuerdo *m* de pago respectivo • **no-fault divorce** divorcio *m* en el que no se culpa a ninguno de los esposos • **no-fault insurance** seguro *m* en el que no entra el

factor de culpabilidad

no-fly zone [ˌnəʊˈflaɪˌzəʊn] N zona *f* de exclusión aérea

no-frills [ˈnəʊˌfrɪlz] ADJ [*house*] sin adornos, sin lujo; [*wedding*] sencillo

noggin [ˈnɒgɪn] N **1** (= *glass*) vaso *m* pequeño; (*loosely*) vaso *m*, caña *f* (de cerveza) • **let's have a ~** (*Brit*) tomemos algo
2 (= *measure*) *medida de licor (= 1,42 decilitros)*
3 (*US**) (= *head*) coco* *m*, calabaza‡ *f*

no-go [ˌnəʊˈgəʊ] ADJ • **no-go area** (*Brit*) zona *f* prohibida

no-good* [ˈnəʊgʊd] ADJ (*US*) inútil

no-growth [ˈnəʊˈgrəʊθ] ADJ • **no-growth economy** economía *f* sin crecimiento *or* de crecimiento cero

no-holds-barred [ˌnəʊhəʊldzˈbɑːd] ADJ [*book, interview, performance*] sin tapujos • **she wrote a no-holds-barred account of her 11-year relationship** relató sin tapujos sus 11 años de relación

no-hoper* [ˈnəʊˌhəʊpəʳ] N nulidad *f*

nohow* [ˈnəʊhaʊ] ADV de ninguna manera

noise [nɔɪz] N **1** (= *sound*) ruido *m* • **she jumps at the slightest ~** el menor ruido la hace sobresaltarse • **I heard a scuffling ~** oí el ruido de algo que correteaba • **I heard a creaking ~** oí un ruido chirriante • **he was making choking ~s in his throat** hacía ruidos con la garganta como si se estuviera ahogando; ▸ **background**
2 (= *loud sound*) ruido *m* • **he hates ~** odia el ruido • **stop that ~!** ¡deja de hacer ese ruido! • **to make a ~** hacer ruido • **tell them not to make any ~** diles que no hagan ruido
3* (*fig*) • **to make a ~ about sth** protestar por algo • **they made a lot of ~ about it** protestaron mucho por ello • **she made ~s about wanting to go home early** quería irse pronto a casa y estuvo soltando indirectas • **she showed polite interest and made all the right ~s** se mostró interesada y cortés y dijo todo lo correcto • **I just made sympathetic ~s and said what a shame it was** me limité a mostrarme comprensiva y dije que era una lástima
4* (= *person*) • **a big ~** un pez gordo*
5 (*Rad, TV, Telec, Comput*) interferencia *f*
VT • **to ~ sth about** *or* **abroad** divulgar algo, correr la voz de algo • **we don't want it ~d abroad** no queremos que se corra la voz
CPD ▸ **noise abatement** reducción *f* del ruido ▸ **noise level** nivel *m* del ruido ▸ **noise pollution** contaminación *f* acústica

noiseless [ˈnɔɪzlɪs] ADJ silencioso

noiselessly [ˈnɔɪzlɪslɪ] ADV silenciosamente, en silencio, sin (hacer) ruido

noisemaker [ˈnɔɪzˌmeɪkəʳ] N (*US*) matraca *f*

noisily [ˈnɔɪzɪlɪ] ADV ruidosamente

noisiness [ˈnɔɪzɪnɪs] N ruido *m*, lo ruidoso

noisome [ˈnɔɪsəm] ADJ (= *disgusting*) asqueroso; (= *smelly*) fétido, maloliente; (= *harmful*) nocivo

noisy [ˈnɔɪzɪ] ADJ (COMPAR: **noisier**, SUPERL: **noisiest**) [*neighbours, children, crowd*] ruidoso, escandaloso; [*music*] ruidoso, estridente • **it's very ~ here** hay mucho ruido aquí • **don't be too ~** no hagáis mucho ruido

no-jump [ˈnəʊˌdʒʌmp] N salto *m* nulo

nomad [ˈnəʊmæd] N nómada *mf*

nomadic [nəʊˈmædɪk] ADJ nómada

nomadism [ˈnəʊmædɪzəm] N nomadismo *m*

no-man's land [ˈnəʊmænzlænd] N tierra *f* de nadie

nom de plume [ˈnɒmdəˈpluːm] N (PL: **noms de plume**) seudónimo *m*, nombre *m* artístico

nomenclature [nəʊˈmenklətʃəʳ] N nomenclatura *f*

nomenklatura [ˌnəʊmenkləˈtʊərə] N • **the ~** la nomenklatura

nominal [ˈnɒmɪnl] ADJ (= *in name*) [*Christian, Catholic*] solamente de nombre, nominal; (= *token*) [*sum, charge*] simbólico
CPD ▸ **nominal partner** socio/a *m/f* nominal ▸ **nominal value** valor *m* nominal ▸ **nominal wage** salario *m* nominal

nominalism [ˈnɒmɪnəlɪzəm] N nominalismo *m*

nominalist [ˈnɒmɪnəlɪst] ADJ nominalista
N nominalista *mf*

nominalization [ˌnɒmɪnəlaɪˈzeɪʃən] N nominalización *f*

nominalize [ˈnɒmɪnəlaɪz] VT nominalizar

nominally [ˈnɒmɪnəlɪ] ADV nominalmente, solo de nombre

> *In the past the standard spelling for solo as an adverb was with an accent (**sólo**). Nowadays the **Real Academia Española** advises that the accented form is only required where there might otherwise be confusion with the adjective **solo**.*

nominate [ˈnɒmɪneɪt] VT (= *propose*) proponer; (= *appoint*) nombrar • **to ~ sb as** *or* **for chairman** proponer a algn como candidato a la presidencia • **to ~ sb for a job** nombrar a algn para un cargo • **she was ~d for an Oscar** la nominaron para un Oscar

nomination [ˌnɒmɪˈneɪʃən] N (= *proposal*) propuesta *f*; (= *appointment*) nombramiento *m* • **the race for the presidential ~** (*US*) la carrera por la candidatura a la presidencia

nominative [ˈnɒmɪnətɪv] ADJ (*Ling*) nominativo • **~ case** nominativo *m*
N nominativo *m*

nominator [ˈnɒmɪneɪtəʳ] N *persona que propone o nombra a un candidato*

nominee [ˌnɒmɪˈniː] N (= *person proposed*) candidato/a *m/f*; (= *person appointed*) persona *f* nombrada • **the Democratic ~** el candidato propuesto por los demócratas

non- [nɒn] PREFIX no..., des..., in...

non-academic [ˈnɒnˌækəˈdemɪk] ADJ [*staff*] no docente

non-acceptance [ˈnɒnəkˈseptəns] N rechazo *m*, no aceptación *f*

non-achiever [ˈnɒnəˈtʃiːvəʳ] N *persona que no alcanza lo que se espera de ella*

non-addictive [ˈnɒnəˈdɪktɪv] ADJ que no crea dependencia

nonagenarian [ˌnɒnədʒɪˈneərɪən] ADJ nonagenario
N nonagenario/a *m/f*

non-aggression [ˈnɒnəˈgreʃən] N no agresión *f*
CPD ▸ **non-aggression pact** pacto *m* de no agresión

non-alcoholic [ˈnɒnælkəˈhɒlɪk] ADJ no alcohólico
CPD ▸ **non-alcoholic drink** bebida *f* no alcohólica

non-aligned [ˈnɒnəˈlaɪnd] ADJ [*country*] no alineado

non-alignment [ˈnɒnəˈlaɪnmənt] N no alineamiento *m*

non-allergenic [ˌnɒnæləˈdʒenɪk] ADJ no alergénico

non-appearance [ˈnɒnəˈpɪərəns] N ausencia *f*; (*Jur*) no comparecencia *f*

non-arrival [ˈnɒnəˈraɪvəl] N ausencia *f* • **the non-arrival of the mail** el hecho de no haber llegado el correo

non-attendance [ˈnɒnəˈtendəns] N ausencia *f*, no asistencia *f*

non-availability [ˈnɒnəˌveɪləˈbɪlɪtɪ] N no disponibilidad *f*

non-believer [ˈnɒnbɪˈliːvəʳ] N no creyente *mf*

non-belligerent [ˈnɒnbɪˈlɪdʒərənt] ADJ no beligerante
N no beligerante *mf*

non-biological [ˈnɒnbaɪəʊˈlɒdʒɪkl] ADJ no biológico

non-breakable [ˈnɒnˈbreɪkəbl] ADJ irrompible

non-cash [ˈnɒnˈkæʃ] ADJ • **non-cash assets** activo *m* no líquido • **non-cash payment** pago *m* no dinerario

non-Catholic [ˈnɒnˈkæθəlɪk] ADJ no católico, acatólico
N no católico/a *m/f*

nonce [nɒns] ADV • **for the ~** por el momento
N‡ (= *sexual offender*) delincuente *mf* sexual

nonce-word [ˈnɒnswɜːd] N hápax *m inv* (*palabra efímera creada para un caso especial*)

nonchalance [ˈnɒnʃələns] N **1** (= *casualness*) despreocupación *f* • **with affected ~** con un descuido afectado
2 (= *indifference*) falta *f* de interés

nonchalant [ˈnɒnʃələnt] ADJ **1** (= *casual*) [*person, attitude, manner*] despreocupado • **I tried to look ~** intenté adoptar un aire despreocupado • **she gave a ~ wave of her hand** agitó la mano con desenfado
2 (= *indifferent*) indiferente • **she was very ~ about it** actuó como si no tuviera ninguna importancia para ella

nonchalantly [ˈnɒnʃələntlɪ] ADV (= *casually*) con aire despreocupado; (= *with indifference*) con indiferencia

non-Christian [ˌnɒnˈkrɪstɪən] ADJ, N no cristiano/a *m/f*

non-combatant [ˈnɒnˈkɒmbətənt] ADJ, N no combatiente *mf*

non-combustible [ˈnɒnkəmˈbʌstɪbl] ADJ incombustible

non-commercial [ˈnɒnkəˈmɜːʃl] ADJ no comercial, no lucrativo

non-commissioned [ˈnɒnkəˈmɪʃənd] ADJ • **non-commissioned officer** suboficial *mf*

non-committal [ˈnɒnkəˈmɪtl] ADJ [*person*] que no se compromete; [*answer*] evasivo • **he was rather noncommittal** no dijo ni que sí ni que no, no se comprometió a nada • **to be non-committal about sth** no definirse con respecto a algo

non-committally [ˌnɒnkəˈmɪtlɪ] ADV sin comprometerse

non-completion [ˈnɒnkəmˈpliːʃən] N incumplimiento *m*

non-compliance [ˈnɒnkəmˈplaɪəns] N incumplimiento *m* (**with** de)

non compos mentis [ˈnɒnˈkɒmpəsˈmentɪs] ADJ (*Jur*) (*also hum*) desposeído de sus facultades mentales

non-conductor [ˈnɒnkənˈdʌktəʳ] N (*Elec*) aislante *m*, no conductor *m*, mal conductor *m*

nonconformism [ˈnɒnkənˈfɔːmɪzəm] N inconformismo *m*

nonconformist [ˈnɒnkənˈfɔːmɪst] ADJ inconformista
N inconformista *mf* • **Nonconformist** (*Brit*) (*Rel*) no conformista *mf*

nonconformity [ˈnɒnkənˈfɔːmɪtɪ] N inconformismo *m*

non-consensual [ˌnɒnkənˈsenʃuəl] ADJ sin consentimiento • **non-consensual sex** relaciones sexuales no consentidas

non-contagious [ˈnɒnkənˈteɪdʒəs] ADJ no contagioso

non-contributory [ˌnɒnkənˈtrɪbjʊtərɪ] ADJ • **non-contributory pension scheme** plan *m* de jubilación no contributivo

(costeado por la empresa)

non-controversial ['nɒnkɒntrə'vɜːʃl] ADJ no conflictivo, no polémico

non-conventional ['nɒnkən'venʃənəl] ADJ no convencional

non-convertible ['nɒnkən'vɜːtɪbl] ADJ *[currency]* no convertible

non-cooperation ['nɒnkəʊ,ɒpə'reɪʃən] N *(Pol)* no cooperación *f*

non-cooperative [,nɒnkəʊ'ɒpərətɪv] ADJ no cooperativo

non-cumulative ['nɒn'kjuːmjʊlətɪv] ADJ no cumulativo

non-custodial sentence ['nɒnkʌs'təʊdɪəl 'sentəns] N *sentencia que no implica privación de libertad*

non-delivery [,nɒndɪ'lɪvərɪ] N no entrega *f*

non-denominational ['nɒndɪnɒmɪ'neɪʃənl] ADJ aconfesional

nondescript ['nɒndɪskrɪpt] ADJ *[person, clothes, face]* (= *unremarkable*) anodino; (= *uninteresting*) insulso, soso*; *[building, furniture]* corriente; *[colour]* indefinido

nondiscrimination [,nɒndɪskrɪmɪ'neɪʃən] N no discriminación *f* • **~ principle** principio de la no discriminación

nondiscriminatory [,nɒndɪs'krɪmɪnətərɪ] ADJ no discriminatorio

non-distinctive [,nɒndɪs'tɪŋktɪv] ADJ *(Ling)* no distintivo

non-dom* ['nɒn'dɒm] *(Brit)* N no domiciliado/a *m/f*

CPD ▸ **non-dom status** estatus *m* de no domiciliado

non-domiciled [,nɒn'dɒmɪ,saɪld] ADJ no domiciliado

non-drinker ['nɒn'drɪŋkəʳ] N no bebedor(a) *m/f* • **she is a non-drinker** no bebe

non-drip ['nɒn'drɪp] ADJ que no gotea

non-durable ['nɒn'djʊərəbl] ADJ perecedero

non-dutiable ['nɒn'djuːtɪəbl] ADJ libre de aranceles, no sujeto a derechos de aduana

none [nʌn] PRON **1** (= *person*) nadie, ninguno; (= *thing*) nada, ninguno • **~ of them** ninguno de ellos • **~ of you can tell me** ninguno de vosotros sabe decirme • **we have ~ of your books** no tenemos ninguno de tus libros *or* ningún libro tuyo • **~ of this is true** nada de esto es verdad • **"any news?" — "none!"** —¿alguna noticia? —¡nada! *or* ¡ninguna!, —¿se sabe algo? —¡nada! • **there are ~ left** no queda ninguno • **I want ~ of your lectures!** ¡no quiero que me sermonees! • **we'll have ~ of that!** ¡vale ya! • **he would have ~ of it, he insisted on paying** no hubo forma de convencerlo, insistió en pagar • **everyone wanted her to win, ~ more so than I** todos querían que ganara, y yo más que nadie • **it was ~ other than the bishop** fue el obispo mismo

2 *(liter)* • **~ can tell** nadie lo sabe • **~ but he knows of this** solo lo sabe él • **reply came there ~** no hubo respuesta

ADV • **I was ~ too comfortable** no me sentía nada cómodo • **he did ~ too well in his exams** los exámenes no le fueron nada bien • **it was ~ too soon** ya era hora • **it's ~ the worse for that** no es peor por eso

nonentity [nɒ'nentɪtɪ] N (= *person*) nulidad *f*, cero *m* a la izquierda

non-essential ['nɒnɪ'senʃəl] ADJ no esencial

N cosa *f* secundaria

nonetheless [,nʌnðə'les] ADV sin embargo, aún así

non-EU [,nɒniː'juː] ADJ *[citizen, passport]* no comunitario; *[imports]* de fuera de la Unión Europea

non-event [,nɒnɪ'vent] N fracaso *m*, fiasco *m* • **it was a non-event** fue un fiasco

non-executive [,nɒnɪg'zekjʊtɪv] ADJ • **non-executive director** vocal *mf*, consejero/a *m/f (no ejecutivo)*

non-existence ['nɒnɪg'zɪstəns] N inexistencia *f*, no existencia *f*

non-existent ['nɒnɪg'zɪstənt] ADJ inexistente

non-fattening [,nɒn'fætnɪŋ] ADJ que no engorda

non-ferrous ['nɒn'ferəs] ADJ no ferroso, no férreo

non-fiction ['nɒn'fɪkʃən] N literatura *f* no novelesca

non-finite [,nɒn'faɪnaɪt] ADJ • **non-finite verb** verbo *m* no conjugado

non-flammable ['nɒn'flæməbl] ADJ ininflamable

non-fulfilment ['nɒnfʊl'fɪlmənt] N incumplimiento *m*

non-governmental ['nɒn,gʌvn'mentl] ADJ no gubernamental

CPD ▸ **non-governmental organization** organización *f* no gubernamental

nonhereditary ['nɒnhɪ,redɪtərɪ] ADJ no hereditario

non-infectious ['nɒn,ɪn'fekʃəs] ADJ no infeccioso

non-inflammable ['nɒnɪn'flæməbl] ADJ ininflamable

non-interference [,nɒnɪntə'fɪərəns] N no intervención *f*

non-intervention ['nɒn,ɪntə'venʃən] N no intervención *f*

non-iron ['nɒn'aɪən] ADJ que no necesita plancha

non-laddering ['nɒn'lædərɪŋ] ADJ *[stocking]* indesmallable

non-lethal ['nɒn'liːθl] ADJ *[weapon]* no mortífero; *[wound]* no mortal

non-malignant ['nɒnmə'lɪgnənt] ADJ no maligno

non-member ['nɒn,membəʳ] N no miembro *mf*

non-metal [,nɒn'metl] ADJ no metálico

non-negotiable [,nɒnnɪ'gəʊʃɪəbl] ADJ *[demand]* innegociable

non-nuclear ['nɒn'njuːklɪəʳ] ADJ *[defence, policy]* no nuclear; *[area]* desnuclearizado

no-no* ['nəʊnəʊ] N • **that's a no-no** (= *undesirable*) eso no se hace; (= *not an option*) no existe tal posibilidad

non-observance ['nɒnəb'zɜːvns] N no observancia *f*, incumplimiento *m*

non obst. ABBR (= **non obstante**) (= *notwithstanding*) no obstante

no-nonsense [,nəʊ'nɒnsəns] ADJ sensato

non-operational ['nɒn,ɒpə'reɪʃənl] ADJ (= *not working*) que no funciona; *(Mil)* no operacional

nonpareil ['nɒnpərəl] ADJ sin par

N (= *person*) persona *f* sin par; (= *thing*) cosa *f* sin par; *(Typ)* nomparell *m*

non-participating ['nɒnpɑː'tɪsɪpeɪtɪŋ] ADJ no participante

nonpartisan ['nɒn,pɑːtɪ'zæn] ADJ imparcial

non-party ['nɒn'pɑːtɪ] ADJ *(Pol)* independiente

non-paying ['nɒn'peɪɪŋ] ADJ que no paga

non-payment ['nɒn'peɪmənt] N falta *f* de pago, impago *m* • **sued for non-payment of debts** demandado por no pagar sus deudas

non-perishable [,nɒn'perɪʃəbl] ADJ no perecedero

non-person ['nɒn'pɜːsn] N persona *f* que no existe, ser *m* inexistente

non-playing [,nɒn'pleɪɪŋ] ADJ *[captain]* no jugador

nonplus ['nɒn'plʌs] (PT, PP: **nonplussed**) VT dejar perplejo, desconcertar • **he was completely ~sed** estaba totalmente perplejo *or* desconcertado

non-poisonous [,nɒn'pɔɪznəs] ADJ *[substance]* no tóxico, atóxico; *[snake]* no venenoso

non-political [,nɒnpə'lɪtɪkəl] ADJ apolítico

non-polluting ['nɒnpə'luːtɪŋ] ADJ no contaminante

non-practising ['nɒn'præktɪsɪŋ] ADJ no practicante

non-printing ['nɒn,prɪntɪŋ] ADJ que no se imprime • **non-printing character** carácter que no se imprime

non-productive [,nɒnprə'dʌktɪv] ADJ improductivo

non-professional ['nɒnprə'feʃnəl] ADJ no profesional, aficionado

non-profit [,nɒn'prɒfɪt] *(US)* ADJ = **non-profit-making**

non-profit-making ['nɒn'prɒfɪtmeɪkɪŋ] ADJ no lucrativo

non-proliferation [,nɒnprəlɪfə'reɪʃən] N *[of nuclear weapons]* no proliferación *f*

CPD ▸ **non-proliferation treaty** tratado *m* de no proliferación

non-radioactive [,nɒnreɪdɪəʊ'æktɪv] ADJ *[substance]* no radioactivo

non-recurring ['nɒnrɪ'kɜːrɪŋ] ADJ que no se repite, único

CPD ▸ **non-recurring expenditure** gasto *m* ocasional

non-resident ['nɒn'rezɪdənt] ADJ *[citizen, population]* no residente, transeúnte; *[status]* de no residente; *[staff, workers]* no fijo

N *[of hotel etc]* no residente *mf*; *[of country]* no residente *mf*, transeúnte *mf*

non-residential ['nɒn,rezɪ'denʃl] ADJ no residencial

non-returnable [,nɒnrɪ'tɜːnəbl] ADJ *[deposit]* no reembolsable • **non-returnable bottle** envase *m* no retornable

non-scheduled ['nɒn'ʃedjuːld] ADJ *[flight, plane]* no regular

non-sectarian ['nɒnsek'teərɪən] ADJ no sectario

nonsense ['nɒnsəns] N tonterías *fpl* • **(what) ~!** ¡tonterías!, ¡qué tontería! • **but that's ~!** ¡eso es absurdo!, ¡eso es ridículo! • **it is ~ to say that ...** es absurdo *or* ridículo decir que ... • **I've never heard such ~!** ¡vaya (una) tontería!, ¡jamás oí (una) tontería igual! • **to make (a) ~ of** *[+ claim, system, law]* quitar sentido a; *[+ pledge]* convertir en papel mojado • **a piece of ~** una tontería • **I'll stand no ~ from you!** • **I won't take any ~ from you!** ¡no voy a tolerar tus tonterías! • **to talk ~** decir tonterías *or* disparates • **stop this ~!** ¡ya vale de tonterías!

CPD ▸ **nonsense verse** disparates *mpl* (en verso), versos *mpl* disparatados

nonsensical [nɒn'sensɪkəl] ADJ absurdo

nonsensically [nɒn'sensɪkəlɪ] ADV absurdamente

non seq. ABBR = **non sequitur**

non sequitur [,nɒn'sekwɪtəʳ] N incongruencia *f*, falta *f* de lógica

non-sexist ['nɒn'seksɪst] ADJ no sexista

non-shrink ['nɒn'ʃrɪŋk] ADJ que no encoge

non-skid ['nɒn'skɪd] ADJ *[surface]* antideslizante, antirresbaladizo

non-skilled ['nɒn'skɪld] ADJ *[worker]* no cualificado; *[work]* no especializado

non-slip ['nɒn'slɪp] ADJ = **non-skid**

non-smoker ['nɒn'sməʊkəʳ] N (= *person*) no fumador(a) *m/f* • **I've always been a non-smoker** no he fumado nunca

non-smoking ['nɒn'sməʊkɪŋ] ADJ *[person]* no fumador; *[compartment, area]* de no fumadores; *[flight]* para no fumadores

non-specialist ['nɒn'speʃəlɪst] N no

especialista *mf*

non-specific [ˌnɒnspəˈsɪfɪk] ADJ **1** (*Med*) no específico, sin causa *or* sintomatolgía específica
2 (= *imprecise*) indeterminado, vago

non-standard [ˌnɒnˈstændəd] ADJ (*Ling*) no estándar

non-starter [ˌnɒnˈstɑːtəʳ] N • **that idea is a non-starter** esa idea es imposible

non-stick [ˌnɒnˈstɪk] ADJ [*pan*] antiadherente, que no se pega; [*coating*] antiadherente

non-stop [ˈnɒnˈstɒp] ADV (= *without a pause*) sin cesar, sin parar; (*Rail*) sin hacer paradas; (*Aer*) sin hacer escalas • **he talks non-stop** no para de hablar
ADJ (= *without a pause*) continuo; [*flight*] directo • **80 minutes of non-stop music** 80 minutos de música ininterrumpida

non-taxable [ˈnɒnˈtæksəbl] ADJ no sujeto a impuestos, exento de impuestos • **non-taxable income** ingresos *mpl* exentos de impuestos

non-teaching [ˈnɒnˈtiːtʃɪŋ] ADJ [*staff*] no docente

non-technical [ˈnɒnˈteknɪkl] ADJ no técnico

non-toxic [ˈnɒnˈtɒksɪk] ADJ no tóxico

non-trading [ˈnɒnˈtreɪdɪŋ] ADJ • **non-trading partnership** sociedad *f* no mercantil

non-transferable [ˈnɒntrænsˈfɜːrəbl] ADJ intransferible

non-U* [ˌnɒnˈjuː] ADJ (*Brit*) (= **non-upper class**) *que no pertenece a la clase alta*

non-union [ˈnɒnˈjuːnjən], **non-unionized** [ˈnɒnˈjuːnjənaɪzd] ADJ no sindicado

non-verbal [ˈnɒnˈvɜːbl] ADJ sin palabras

non-viable [ˈnɒnˈvaɪəbl] ADJ inviable

non-violence [ˈnɒnˈvaɪələns] N no violencia *f*

non-violent [ˈnɒnˈvaɪələnt] ADJ no violento, pacífico

non-volatile memory [ˈnɒnˌvɒlətaɪlˈmemərɪ] N (*Comput*) memoria *f* permanente

non-voting [ˌnɒnˈvəʊtɪŋ] ADJ [*delegate*] sin derecho a voto • **non-voting shares** (*Comm*) acciones *fpl* sin derecho a voto

non-white [ˌnɒnˈwaɪt] ADJ de color
N persona *f* de color

non-yielding [ˈnɒnˈjiːldɪŋ] ADJ improductivo

noodle[1]* [ˈnuːdl] N **1** (= *head*) cabeza *f*
2 (= *fool*) bobo/a *m/f*

noodle[2] [ˈnuːdl] NPL **noodles** fideos *mpl*, tallarines *mpl*
CPD ▸ **noodle soup** sopa *f* de fideos

nook [nʊk] N rincón *m* • **we looked in every ~ and cranny** buscamos hasta el último rincón

nookie [ˈnʊkɪ] N • **to have a bit of ~**‡ echarse un polvo‡

noon [nuːn] N mediodía *m* • **at ~** a mediodía • **high ~** (= *midday*) mediodía *m*; (*fig*) (= *peak*) apogeo *m*, punto *m* culminante; (= *critical point*) momento *m* crucial
CPD de mediodía

noonday [ˈnuːndeɪ] ADJ (= *midday*) [*sun*, *heat*] de mediodía

no-one, no one [ˈnəʊwʌn] PRON = **nobody**

noontime [ˈnuːntaɪm] (*esp US*) N mediodía *m* • **at ~** al mediodía
ADJ [*meal*, *sun*, *class*] del mediodía

noose [nuːs] N (= *loop*) nudo *m* corredizo; (*for animal*, *as trap*) lazo *m*; [*of hangman*] soga *f*
• IDIOM: • **to put one's head in the ~** ponerse la soga al cuello
VT coger con lazo

no-par securities [ˌnəʊpɑːsɪˈkjʊərɪtɪz] NPL títulos *mpl* sin valor nominal

nope* [nəʊp] EXCL no

nor [nɔːʳ] CONJ **1** (*following "neither"*) ni • **neither Sarah nor Tamsin is coming to the party** no vienen ni Sarah ni Tamsin a la fiesta, ni Sarah ni Tamsin vienen a la fiesta • **she neither eats nor drinks** ni come ni bebe • **he was neither fat nor thin** no estaba ni gordo ni delgado
2 (*as complement to neg statement*) • **"I don't work here" — "nor do I"** —yo no trabajo aquí —ni yo (tampoco) *or* —yo tampoco • **"I didn't like the film" — "nor did I"** —no me gustó la película —a mí tampoco *or* —ni a mí • **"we haven't seen him" — "nor have we"** —no lo hemos visto —nosotros tampoco *or* —ni nosotros • **I don't know, nor can I guess** ni lo sé, ni (tampoco) lo puedo adivinar, no lo sé y tampoco lo puedo adivinar • **nor does it seem likely** ni tampoco parece probable • **nor was this all** y esto no fue todo

Nordic [ˈnɔːdɪk] ADJ nórdico
CPD ▸ **Nordic walking** caminata *f* nórdica

Norf ABBR (*Brit*) = **Norfolk**

norm [nɔːm] N **1** (= *pattern of behaviour*, *official standard*) norma *f* • **in the West monogamy is the ~** la monogamia es la norma en Occidente • **small families have become the ~** las familias pequeñas han pasado a ser lo normal
2 (= *average*) • **the ~** lo normal • **larger than the ~** más grande de lo normal; (*Bio*) más grande que el tipo

normal [ˈnɔːməl] ADJ **1** (= *usual*) normal • **it's perfectly ~ to feel that way** es muy normal sentirse así, no hay nada raro en sentirse así • **above/below ~** por encima/debajo de lo normal • **to carry on as ~** seguir haciendo todo como de costumbre • **to get back** *or* **return to ~** [*situation*] normalizarse, volver a la normalidad • **"normal service will be resumed as soon as possible"** "se reanudará la emisión lo antes posible" • **I woke at the ~ time** me desperté a la hora de siempre • **he bought a return ticket instead of the ~ single** compró un billete de ida y vuelta en vez del de solo ida que solía comprar
2 (= *well-adjusted*) [*person*] normal
3 (= *healthy*) [*baby*] normal; [*pregnancy*] sin complicaciones
4 (*Math*, *Chem*) normal
CPD ▸ **normal school** (*US*†) escuela *f* normal ▸ **normal time** (*Sport*) (= *regulation time*) tiempo *m* reglamentario • **at the end of ~ time** al final del tiempo reglamentario

normalcy [ˈnɔːməlsɪ] N (*esp US*) normalidad *f*

normality [nɔːˈmælɪtɪ] N normalidad *f*

normalization [ˌnɔːməlaɪˈzeɪʃən] N normalización *f*

normalize [ˈnɔːməlaɪz] VT normalizar

normally [ˈnɔːməlɪ] ADV normalmente • **he ~ arrives at seven o'clock** normalmente llega a las siete, suele llegar a las siete • **the trains are running ~** los trenes están funcionando con normalidad

Norman [ˈnɔːmən] ADJ normando • **the ~ Conquest** la conquista de los normandos • **~ architecture** arquitectura *f* románica
N normando/a *m/f*

Normandy [ˈnɔːməndɪ] N Normandía *f*

normative [ˈnɔːmətɪv] ADJ normativo

norovirus [ˈnɔːrəʊvaɪrəs] N norovirus *m*

Norse [nɔːs] ADJ nórdico, escandinavo • **~ mythology** mitología *f* nórdica
N (*Ling*) nórdico *m*

Norseman [ˈnɔːsmən] N (PL: **Norsemen**) escandinavo *m*

north [nɔːθ] N norte *m* • **in the ~ of the country** al norte *or* en el norte del país • **to live in the ~** vivir en el norte • **the wind is from the** *or* **in the ~** el viento sopla *or* viene del norte • **North and South** (*Pol*) el Norte y el Sur
ADJ del norte, norteño, septentrional
ADV (= *northward*) hacia el norte; (= *in the north*) al norte, en el norte • **we were travelling ~** viajábamos hacia el norte • **this house faces ~** esta casa mira al norte *or* tiene vista hacia el norte • **my window faces ~** mi ventana da al norte • **~ of the border** al norte de la frontera • **it's ~ of London** está al norte de Londres
CPD ▸ **North Africa** África *f* del Norte; ▹ **North African** ▸ **North America** Norteamérica *f*, América *f* del Norte; ▹ **North American** ▸ **North Atlantic** • **the North Atlantic** el Atlántico Norte ▸ **North Atlantic Drift** Corriente *f* del Golfo ▸ **North Atlantic route** ruta *f* del Atlántico Norte ▸ **the North Atlantic Treaty Organization** la Organización del Tratado del Atlántico Norte ▸ **North Carolina** Carolina *f* del Norte ▸ **North Korea** Corea *f* del Norte; ▹ **North Korean** ▸ **the North Pole** el Polo Norte ▸ **the North Sea** el mar del Norte ▸ **North Sea gas** gas *m* del mar del Norte ▸ **North Sea oil** petróleo *m* del mar del Norte ▸ **north star** estrella *f* polar, estrella *f* del norte ▸ **North Vietnam** Vietnam *m* del Norte; ▹ **North Vietnamese**

North African [ˈnɔːθˈæfrɪkən] ADJ norteafricano
N norteafricano/a *m/f*

North American [ˈnɔːθəˈmerɪkən] ADJ norteamericano
N norteamericano/a *m/f*

Northants [nɔːˈθænts] ABBR (*Brit*) = **Northamptonshire**

northbound [ˈnɔːθbaʊnd] ADJ [*traffic*] en dirección norte; [*carriageway*] de dirección norte, en dirección norte

north-country [ˈnɔːθˌkʌntrɪ] ADJ del norte de Inglaterra

Northd ABBR (*Brit*) = **Northumberland**

northeast [ˈnɔːθˈiːst] N nor(d)este *m*
ADJ [*point*, *direction*] nor(d)este; [*wind*] del nor(d)este
ADV (= *northeastward*) hacia el nor(d)este; [*situated*] al nor(d)este, en el nor(d)este

northeasterly [ˈnɔːθˈiːstəlɪ] ADJ [*wind*] del nor(d)este • **we were headed in a ~ direction** íbamos rumbo al nor(d)este *or* en dirección nor(d)este
N viento *m* del nor(d)este

northeastern [ˈnɔːθˈiːstən] ADJ nor(d)este, del nor(d)este • **in ~ Spain** al nor(d)este *or* en el nor(d)este de España • **the ~ coast** la costa nororiental *or* nor(d)este

northeastward [ˈnɔːθˈiːstwəd] ADV
ADJ [*movement*, *migration*] hacia el nor(d)este, en dirección nor(d)este (*also* **northeastwards**) hacia el nor(d)este

northeastwards [ˈnɔːθˈiːstwədz] ADV (*esp Brit*) = **northeastward**

northerly [ˈnɔːðəlɪ] ADJ [*wind*] del norte • **the most ~ point in Europe** el punto más al norte *or* más septentrional de Europa • **we were headed in a ~ direction** íbamos hacia el norte *or* rumbo al norte *or* en dirección norte
N viento *m* del norte

northern [ˈnɔːðən] ADJ del norte, norteño, septentrional • **the ~ part of the island** la parte norte *or* septentrional de la isla • **the ~ coast** la costa septentrional *or* (del) norte • **in ~ Spain** al norte *or* en el norte de España, en la España septentrional
CPD ▸ **the northern hemisphere** el hemisferio norte, el hemisferio boreal ▸ **Northern Ireland** Irlanda *f* del Norte ▸ **the**

northern lights la aurora boreal

northerner ['nɔːðənə^r] N norteño/a *m/f*; (*US*) (*Hist*) nordista *mf* • **he's a ~** es del norte • **~s like this sort of thing** a la gente del norte le gusta este tipo de cosas

Northern Irish [ˌnɔːðən'aɪərɪʃ] ADJ norirlandés
NPL • **the ~** los norirlandeses

northernmost ['nɔːðənməʊst] ADJ más septentrional, más al norte • **the ~ town in Europe** la ciudad más al norte *or* más septentrional de Europa

north-facing ['nɔːθ,feɪsɪŋ] ADJ orientado hacia el norte • **north-facing slope** vertiente *f* norte

North Korean ['nɔːθkə'rɪən] ADJ norcoreano
N norcoreano/a *m/f*

northland ['nɔːθlənd] N (*US*) región *f* septentrional

Northman ['nɔːθmən] N (PL: **Northmen**) vikingo *m*, escandinavo *m*

north-northeast [ˌnɔːθ,nɔːθ'iːst] N nornor(d)este *m*
ADJ nornor(d)este
ADV (= *toward north-northeast*) hacia el nornor(d)este; [*situated*] al nornor(d)este, en el nornor(d)este

north-northwest [ˌnɔːθ,nɔːθ'west] N nornoroeste *m*
ADJ nornoroeste
ADV (= *toward north-northwest*) hacia el nornoroeste; [*situated*] al nornoroeste, en el nornoroeste

Northumb ABBR (*Brit*) = **Northumberland**

Northumbria [nɔː'θʌmbrɪə] N *región del nordeste de Inglaterra*

Northumbrian [nɔː'θʌmbrɪən] ADJ de Northumbria
N habitante *mf* de Northumbria, nativo/a *m/f* de Northumbria

North Vietnamese ['nɔːθvɪetnə'miːz] ADJ norvietnamita
N norvietnamita *mf*

northward ['nɔːθwəd] ADJ [*movement, migration*] hacia el norte, en dirección norte
ADV (*also* **northwards**) hacia el norte, en dirección norte

northwards ['nɔːθwədz] ADV (*esp Brit*) = **northward**

northwest ['nɔːθ'west] N noroeste *m*
ADJ [*point, direction*] noroeste; [*wind*] del noroeste
ADV (= *northwestward*) hacia el noroeste; [*situated*] al noroeste, en el noroeste

northwesterly ['nɔːθ'westəlɪ] ADJ [*wind*] del noroeste • **we were headed in a ~ direction** íbamos hacia el noroeste *or* rumbo al noroeste *or* en dirección noroeste
N viento *m* del noroeste

northwestern ['nɔːθ'westən] ADJ noroeste, del noroeste • **the ~ part of the island** la parte noroeste *or* noroccidental de la isla • **the ~ coast** la costa noroeste *or* noroccidental • **in ~ Spain** en el noroeste *or* al noroeste de España, en la España noroccidental

northwestward ['nɔːθ'westwəd] ADJ [*movement, migration*] hacia el noroeste, en dirección noroeste
ADV (*also* **northwestwards**) hacia el noroeste, en dirección noroeste

northwestwards ['nɔːθ'westwədz] ADV (*esp Brit*) = **northwestward**

Norway ['nɔːweɪ] N Noruega *f*
CPD ▸ **Norway lobster** cigala *f*

Norwegian [nɔː'wiːdʒən] ADJ noruego
N **1** (= *person*) noruego/a *m/f*
2 (*Ling*) noruego *m*

Nos., nos. ABBR (= **numbers**) núms

no-score draw [ˌnəʊskɔː'drɔː] N empate *m* a cero

nose [nəʊz] N **1** (*Anat*) [*of person*] nariz *f*; [*of animal*] hocico *m* • **his ~ was bleeding** le sangraba la nariz, le salía sangre de la nariz • **to have one's ~ in a book** estar enfrascado en un libro • **get your ~ out of that book and come and help me** deja el libro un momento y ven a ayudarme • **to hold one's ~** (*lit*) taparse la nariz • **to talk** *or* **speak through one's ~** ganguear, hablar con voz gangosa • IDIOMS: • **you wouldn't recognize an opportunity if it bit you on the ~** no reconocerías una buena oportunidad ni aunque te topases con ella de frente • **to keep one's ~ clean*** no meterse en problemas *or* líos* • **to cut off one's ~ to spite one's face** tirar piedras a su tejado • **to get/have one's ~ in front** coger/tener la delantera • **he gets up my ~*** me revienta* • **to keep one's ~ out (of sth)** no entrometerse (en algo) • **to lead sb by the ~** tener a algn agarrado por las narices • **you shouldn't let them lead you by the ~** no deberías permitirles que te manejen a su antojo • **to look down one's ~ at sth/sb*** despreciar algo/a algn, mirar a algn por encima del hombro • **(right) on the ~** en el clavo • **that's it! you've hit it on the ~!** ¡eso es! ¡has dado en el clavo! • **to pay through the ~ (for sth)*** pagar un ojo de la cara (por algo)*, pagar un dineral (por algo) • **she paid through the ~ (for it)** le costó un ojo de la cara*, pagó un dineral (por ello)* • **to make sb pay through the ~** hacer pagar a algn un dineral* • **to poke** *or* **stick one's ~ into sth*** meter las narices en algo*, meterse en algo • **who asked you to poke your ~ in?** ¿quién te manda meter las narices* *or* meterte en esto? • **he's always poking his ~ (in) where it's not wanted** siempre está metiendo las narices *or* metiéndose en lo que no le incumbe* • **to put sb's ~ out of joint** molestar a algn • **to see no further than the end of one's ~** no ver más allá de sus narices • **to turn up one's ~ at sth** hacerle ascos a algo • **under sb's ~: it's right under your ~** lo tienes delante de las narices* • **she did it under his very ~** *or* **right under his ~** lo hizo delante de sus narices; ▹ **bloody, blow², follow, grindstone, joint, pick, plain, thumb**
2 (= *distance*) • **to win by a ~** [*horse*] ganar por una nariz; (*fig*) ganar por los pelos
3 (= *front part*) [*of aeroplane, car*] morro *m*, parte *f* delantera; [*of boat*] proa *f* • **the traffic was ~ to tail** los coches iban pegados unos a otros
4 (= *sense of smell*) olfato *m* • **I have a sensitive ~** tengo un olfato muy fino
5 (= *instinct*) • **to have a (good) ~ for** tener (buen) olfato para • **she has a keen ~ for facts** tiene buena intuición para saber lo que ha ocurrido realmente • **she's got a (good) ~ for a story** tiene (buen) olfato para lo que es noticia
6 [*of wine*] aroma *m*, buqué *m*
VI • **the car ~d forward** el coche se abrió paso lentamente • **the coach ~d out into the traffic** el autocar se incorporó lentamente al tráfico
VT **1** (= *move*) • **he ~d his car into the garage** metió el coche en el garaje maniobrando con cuidado • **a van ~d its way past** una furgoneta pasó despacio
2 (= *nuzzle, nudge*) • **the horse ~d my palm** el caballo me olfateó la palma de la mano • **the dog managed to ~ the door open** el perro consiguió abrir la puerta con el hocico • **they just ~d us into second place** por muy poco nos dejaron en segundo lugar
CPD ▸ **nose cone** [*of missile*] ojiva *f*; [*of racing car*] cabeza *f* separable ▸ **nose drops** gotas *fpl* para la nariz ▸ **nose job*** • **to have a ~ job** operarse la nariz ▸ **nose ring** [*of animal*] argolla *f* (en el hocico); [*of person*] pendiente *m* en la nariz ▸ **nose stud** piercing *m* de *or* en la nariz • **to have a ~ stud** tener un piercing en la nariz

▸ **nose about, nose around** VI + ADV curiosear, fisgonear
VI + PREP curiosear por, fisgonear por • **the police came nosing about your house last night** anoche la policía estuvo curioseando *or* fisgoneando por tu casa

▸ **nose out** VT + ADV **1** (= *smell*) [*dog, fox*] olfatear
2 (= *discover*) [+ *secret, truth*] averiguar, lograr descubrir; [+ *fugitive*] encontrar

nosebag ['nəʊzbæg] N morral *m*

noseband ['nəʊzbænd] N muserola *f*

nosebleed ['nəʊzbliːd] N hemorragia *f* nasal (*Med*) • **to have a ~** sangrar *or* echar sangre por la nariz, tener una hemorragia nasal (*Med*) • **you have a ~** estás sangrando *or* echando sangre por la nariz, te está sangrando la nariz

-nosed [nəʊzd] ADJ (*ending in compounds*) de nariz ... • **Roman/snub-nosed** de nariz aguileña/chata • **red-nosed** de nariz coloradota*; ▹ **hard-nosed, toffee-nosed**

nose-dive ['nəʊzdaɪv] N **1** (*Aer*) picado *m* vertical
2 (*fig*) caída *f* súbita • **to take a nose-dive** [*profits, shares, sales, reputation*] caer en picado
VI **1** (*Aer*) descender en picado
2 (*fig*) [*profits, shares, sales, reputation*] caer en picado • **the shares nose-dived 11p to 511p** las acciones cayeron 11 peniques de golpe y pasaron a cotizar 511 peniques

nosegay ['nəʊzgeɪ] N ramillete *m*

nosewheel ['nəʊzwiːl] N (*Aer*) rueda *f* delantera de aterrizaje

nosey* ['nəʊzɪ] ADJ (COMPAR: **nosier**, SUPERL: **nosiest**) entrometido • **don't be so ~!** ¡no seas tan entrometido!

nosey-parker* ['nəʊzɪ'pɑːkə^r] N metomentodo/a* *m/f*

nosh* [nɒʃ] N (*Brit*) comida *f*, papeo‡ *m*, manduca *f* (*Sp**) • **~ up!** ¡a comer!
VI comer, papear‡

no-show ['nəʊ'ʃəʊ] N ausente *mf* (*persona que no ocupa una plaza reservada previamente*)

nosh-up‡ ['nɒʃʌp] N (*Brit*) comilona* *f*, tragadera *f* (*LAm**)

nosily ['nəʊzɪlɪ] ADV entrometidamente

nosiness ['nəʊzɪnɪs] N entrometimiento *m*

no-smoking ['nəʊ,sməʊkɪŋ] ADJ [*area, carriage*] de no fumadores; [*policy*] de prohibición del tabaco

nostalgia [nɒ'stældʒɪə] N nostalgia *f*, añoranza *f*

nostalgic [nɒ'stældʒɪk] ADJ nostálgico

nostalgically [nɒ'stældʒɪkəlɪ] ADV [*look back*] con nostalgia

nostril ['nɒstrɪl] N (*Anat*) [*of person, dog, lion*] ventana *f* de la nariz, orificio *m* nasal (*frm*); [*of horse*] ollar *m* • **~s** narices *fpl*

nostrum ['nɒstrəm] N (= *remedy*) remedio *m* secreto, panacea *f*; (*fig*) panacea *f*

nosy* ['nəʊzɪ] = **nosey**

nosy-parker* ['nəʊzɪ'pɑːkə^r] N = **nosey-parker**

not [nɒt] ADV **1** (*with vb*)

The word **not** *is often contracted to* **n't** *on the end of modals, auxiliaries and parts of the verb* **to be** *in everyday language.*

no • **I'm not sure** no estoy seguro • **he's not here** • **he isn't here** no está aquí • **it wasn't**

me yo no fui • **it's too late, isn't it?** es demasiado tarde, ¿no? • **you owe me money, don't you?** me debes dinero, ¿verdad? *or* (*esp LAm*) ¿no es cierto? • **she won't go** • **she will not go** no irá • **I don't think she'll come now** ya no creo que venga • **he asked me not to do it** me pidió que no lo hiciera • **fear not!** ¡no temas! • **I hope not** espero que no • **I suppose not** supongo que no • **to tell sb not to do sth** decir a algn que no haga algo • **I think not** creo que no • **not thinking that ...** sin pensar que ...
2 (*with pronoun etc*) • **not one** ni uno • **not me/you** *etc* yo/tú *etc* no • **not I!** ¡yo no! • **not everybody can do it** no lo puede hacer cualquiera, no todos pueden hacerlo • **not any more** ya no; ▹ **even**
3 (*in expressions*) • **absolutely not!** ¡en absoluto! • **not at all** (*after verb*) no ... en absoluto; (*responding to thanks*) ¡de nada!, ¡no hay de qué! • **I don't mind at all** no me importa en absoluto • **it doesn't hurt at all** no duele nada de nada, no duele para nada • **"are you cold?" — "not at all!"** —¿tienes frío? —¡en absoluto! *or* —¡qué va! • **"you don't mind?" — "not at all!"** —¿no te importa? —¡en absoluto! • **he's not at all selfish** no es nada egoísta • **certainly not!** ¡en absoluto! • **of course not!** ¡claro que no! • **not a few ...** no pocos ... • **not for anything (in the world)** por nada (del mundo) • **not guilty** no culpable • **the not inconsiderable sum of £30,000** la nada despreciable suma de 30.000 libras • **not likely!** ¡ni hablar! • **with not a little surprise** con no poca sorpresa • **are you coming or not?** ¿vienes o no? • **whether you go or not** tanto si vas como si no • **"did you like it?" — "not really"** —¿te gustó? —no mucho • **big, not to say enormous** grande, por no decir enorme • **the young and the not so young** los jóvenes y los no tan jóvenes • **I shan't be sorry to see the last of him** no voy a sentirlo cuando lo pierda de vista • **not that I don't like him** no es que no me guste • **not that I know of** no que yo sepa • **why not?** ¿por qué no? • **not without some regrets** no sin cierto pesar • **not yet** todavía no • **they haven't arrived yet** todavía no han llegado; ▹ **likely, mention, much, only**

notability [ˌnəʊtəˈbɪlɪtɪ] (N) **1** [*of person*] notabilidad *f*
2 (= *person*) notabilidad *f*, personaje *m*

notable [ˈnəʊtəbl] (ADJ) [*person*] destacado • **to be ~ for** distinguirse por • **it is ~ that ...** es de notar que ...
(N) persona *f* importante, personaje *m* • **~s** personas *fpl* importantes, notables *mpl*

notably [ˈnəʊtəblɪ] (ADV) **1** (= *in particular*) particularmente, en particular • **several countries, ~ France and Spain** varios países, particularmente *or* en particular Francia y España • **later religions, most ~ Christianity ...** posteriores religiones, muy en particular *or* sobre todo el cristianismo ...
2 (= *noticeably*) notablemente

notarial [nəʊˈtɛərɪəl] (ADJ) notarial

notarize [ˈnəʊtəraiz] (VT) (*US*) dar fe pública de, autenticar mediante acta notarial

notary [ˈnəʊtərɪ] (N) (*also* **notary public**) notario/a *m/f*

notate [nəʊˈteɪt] (VT) (*Mus*) notar

notation [nəʊˈteɪʃən] (N) (*Math, Mus*) notación *f*

notch [nɒtʃ] (N) **1** (= *cut*) corte *m*, muesca *f*
2 (*US*) (= *mountain pass*) desfiladero *m*
(VT) hacer una muesca en, hacer un corte en

▸ **notch up** (VT + ADV) apuntarse

note [nəʊt] (N) **1** (= *written reminder, record*) **a** (*short*) nota *f* • **keep a ~ of all your expenses** detalla *or* anota todos tus gastos • **to make** *or* **take a ~ of sth** apuntar *or* anotar algo • **I must make a ~ to buy some more** tengo que hacer una nota para que no se me olvide comprar más; ▹ **mental**
b notes apuntes *mpl*, notas *fpl* • **to speak from ~s** hablar con la ayuda de apuntes *or* notas • **to make ~s** hacer anotaciones • **to take ~s** tomar apuntes • **to speak without ~s** hablar sin la ayuda de apuntes *or* notas • IDIOM: • **to compare ~s (about sth)** intercambiar impresiones (acerca de algo); ▹ **lecture**
2 (*on text*) anotación *f*, nota *f*; (*more detailed*) comentario *m* • **see ~ 16 on page 223** véase nota número 16 en la página 223 • **with an introduction and ~s by ...** con introducción y comentarios de ... • **author's ~** nota del autor; ▹ **programme, sleeve**
3 (= *letter, message*) nota *f* • **I left him a ~ saying where I was** le dejé una nota diciéndole dónde estaba • **just a quick ~ to tell you ...** solo una nota para decirte que ...; ▹ **delivery, sick, suicide**
4 (*official, diplomatic*) nota *f*
5 (= *tone*) (*gen*) nota *f*; (*in voice*) dejo *m*, deje *m* • **the only discordant ~ was the bad feeling between his two brothers** la única nota discordante fue la animosidad entre sus dos hermanos • **there was a ~ of nostalgia in her voice** había un dejo *or* deje de nostalgia en su voz • **there was a ~ of bitterness in her voice** había cierto resentimiento en su voz • **the talks ended on a ~ of optimism** las negociaciones se cerraron con una nota de optimismo • **the 1980s/evening ended on a high ~** la década de los ochenta/la velada se cerró con un broche de oro • **on a more positive ~ ...** mirando el lado positivo ... • **to sound a ~ of caution** llamar a la prudencia • **he tried to strike a ~ of optimism in his speech** intentó que su discurso sonara optimista • **his speech struck the right/wrong ~** su discurso fue/no fue acertado
6 (*Mus*) (= *sound*) nota *f*; (= *key*) tecla *f*
7 (= *bank note*) billete *m* • **a five-pound ~** un billete de cinco libras
8 (= *importance*) • **a writer/an artist of ~** un escritor/un artista destacado *or* de renombre • **nothing of ~** nada digno de mención • **this is a first novel of some ~** esta es una primera novela que merece atención
9 (= *notice*) • **to take ~ (of sth/sb)**: • **the government should take ~ of this survey** el gobierno debería tomar nota del resultado de esta encuesta • **they will take ~ of what you say** tendrán en cuenta lo que digas • **people began to take ~ of him** la gente empezó a tenerlo en cuenta *or* prestarle atención • **worthy of ~** digno de mención
(VT) **1** (= *observe*) • **~ the statue by Rodin in the entrance hall** tomen nota de *or* fíjense en la estatua de Rodin en el vestíbulo • **to ~ that** notar que • **she ~d that his hands were dirty** notó que tenía las manos sucias, se dio cuenta de que tenía las manos sucias • **please ~ that there are a limited number of tickets** les informamos que el número de entradas es limitado
2 (= *point out*) • **the report ~s that this trend is on the increase** el informe señala *or* indica que esta tendencia se está extendiendo
3 (= *record officially*) tomar nota de • **your remarks have been ~d** hemos tomado nota de sus observaciones
4 (= *write down*) anotar, apuntar
(CPD) ▸ **note issue** emisión *f* fiduciaria

▸ **note down** (VT + ADV) anotar, apuntar

notebook [ˈnəʊtbʊk] (N) **1** (= *notepad, jotter*) libreta *f*, bloc *m*; (= *exercise book*) cuaderno *m*
2 (*also* **notebook computer**) ordenador *m* portátil, computador *m* portátil (*LAm*)

note-case [ˈnəʊtkeɪs] (N) (*Brit*) cartera *f*, billetero *m*

noted [ˈnəʊtɪd] (ADJ) [*historian, writer*] destacado, renombrado • **to be ~ for sth** ser conocido *or* famoso por algo • **a man not ~ for his generosity** un hombre que no es precisamente conocido *or* famoso por su generosidad

notelet [ˈnəʊtlɪt] (N) tarjeta *f* en díptico (*de felicitación, agradecimiento*)

notepad [ˈnəʊtpæd] (N) bloc *m*, libreta *f* para notas

notepaper [ˈnəʊtˌpeɪpəʳ] (N) papel *m* de carta

note-perfect [ˌnəʊtˈpɜːfɪkt] (ADJ) [*performance*] sublime

noteworthiness [ˈnəʊtˌwɜːðɪnɪs] (N) notabilidad *f*

noteworthy [ˈnəʊtˌwɜːðɪ] (ADJ) notable, digno de atención • **it is ~ that ...** es notable que ..., es de notar que ...

nothing [ˈnʌθɪŋ] (PRON) nada *f*; (= *nought*) cero *m* • **I have ~ to give you** no tengo nada que darte • **to have ~ to do with** no tener nada que ver con • **there's ~ mean about him** no tiene nada de tacaño • **~ but** solamente • **to come to ~** parar en nada, quedarse en aguas de borraja • **~ doing!** ¡de ninguna manera!, ¡ni hablar! • **~ else** nada más • **there's ~ to fear** no hay de qué tener miedo • **for ~** (= *free*) gratis; (= *unpaid*) sin sueldo; (= *in vain*) en vano, en balde • **it is not for ~ that ...** no es sin motivo que ..., por algo será que ... • **there was ~ for it but to pay** no había más remedio *or* (*LAm*) no nos quedaba otra que pagar • **to build up a business from ~** crear un negocio de la nada • **he is ~ if not careful** es de lo más cauteloso • **there is ~ in the rumours** los rumores no tienen nada de verdad • **there's ~ in it for us** de esto no vamos a sacar ningún provecho • **there's ~ in it** (*in race*) van muy iguales • **I could make ~ of what he said** no entendí nada *or* no pude sacar nada en claro de lo que dijo • **a mere ~** una nimiedad • **it's ~ more than a rumour** es simplemente un rumor • **~ much** poco, no mucho • **there's ~ much to be said** poco hay que decir • **next to ~** casi nada • **I'm ~ of a swimmer** yo nado bastante mal • **to have ~ on** (= *naked*) estar desnudo; (= *not busy*) estar libre • **it's ~ to be proud of** no es motivo para enorgullecerse • **to say ~ of ...** sin mencionar ..., amén de ... • **to get something for ~** obtener algo gratis • **there's ~ special about it** no tiene nada de particular • **to stop at ~** no pararse en barras • **to stop at ~ to do sth** emplear sin escrúpulo todos los medios para hacer algo • **to think ~ of** tener en poco • **he thinks ~ of walking 30km** para él no tiene importancia *or* no es nada recorrer 30km a pie • **think ~ of it!** ¡no hay de qué!, ¡no tiene cuidado! (*LAm*) • **there's ~ to it!** ¡es facilísimo! • **she is ~ to him** ella le es indiferente • **it's ~ to me whether he comes or not** no me importa que venga o no • IDIOM: • **he has ~ on her** (*comparison*) no le llega ni a la suela del zapato*; ▹ **all, do with, kind, like, next, short, sort, ZERO**
(ADV) • **~ daunted** sin inmutarse • **it's ~ like him** el retrato no se le parece en nada • **it was ~ like as expensive as we thought** era mucho menos caro de lo que nos imaginábamos; ▹ **less**
(N) • **a mere ~** una friolera, una bagatela • **to her he was a ~** para ella él no tenía ningún valor • IDIOM: • **to whisper sweet ~s to sb**

decir ternezas a los oídos de algn

nothingness ['nʌθɪŋnɪs] (N) (= *non-existence*) nada *f*; (= *emptiness*) vacío *m*

notice ['nəʊtɪs] (N) **1** (= *intimation, warning*) aviso *m* • **~ to appear** (*Jur*) citación *f* judicial, orden *f* de comparecencia • **we require 28 days' ~ for delivery** se requieren 28 días para la entrega • **until further ~** hasta nuevo aviso • **to give sb ~ to do sth** avisar a algn que haga algo • **~ is hereby given that ...** se pone en conocimiento del público que ... • **at a moment's ~** en seguida, inmediatamente, luego (*Mex*), al tiro (*Chile*) • **important decisions often have to be taken at a moment's ~** a menudo las decisiones importantes se han de tomar en seguida *or* inmediatamente • **you must be ready to leave at a moment's ~** tienes que estar listo para salir en cuanto te avisen • **we had no ~ of it** no nos habían avisado • **~ to quit** aviso *or* notificación de desalojo • **at short ~** con poca antelación • **sorry, I know it's short ~, but ...** lo siento, sé que es avisar con poca antelación, pero ... • **to give sb at least a week's ~** avisar a algn por lo menos con una semana de antelación • **I must have at least a week's ~ if you want to ...** me tienes que avisar con una semana de antelación si quieres ... • **without previous ~** sin previo aviso
2 (= *order to leave job etc*) (*by employer*) despido *m*; (*by employee*) dimisión *f*, renuncia *f*; (= *period*) preaviso *m* • **to get one's ~** ser despedido • **to give sb ~** despedir a algn • **to give sb a week's ~** despedir a algn con una semana de preaviso *or* plazo • **to hand in one's ~** dimitir, renunciar • **a week's wages in lieu of ~** el salario de una semana en lugar del plazo *or* de preaviso • **to be under ~** estar despedido • **to dismiss sb without ~** despedir a algn sin preaviso
3 (= *announcement*) (*in press*) anuncio *m*, nota *f*; [*of meeting*] convocatoria *f*, llamada *f*; (= *sign*) letrero *m*; (= *poster*) cartel *m* • **birth/marriage ~** anuncio *m* de nacimiento/matrimonio • **death ~** nota *f* necrológica, esquela *f* • **to give out a ~** anunciar algo, comunicar algo • **the ~ says "keep out"** el letrero dice "prohibida la entrada"
4 (= *review*) [*of play, opera etc*] reseña *f*, crítica *f*
5 (= *attention*) atención *f* • **to attract sb's ~** atraer *or* llamar la atención de algn • **to bring a matter to sb's ~** llamar la atención de algn sobre un asunto • **it has come to my ~ that ...** ha llegado a mi conocimiento que ... • **to escape ~** pasar inadvertido • **to take ~ of sb** hacer caso a algn • **to take no ~ of sth/sb** no hacer caso de algo/a algn, ignorar algo/a algn (*esp LAm*) • **to take ~ of sth** hacer caso de algo • **take no ~!** ¡no hagas caso! • **I was not taking much ~ at the time** en ese momento no estaba prestando mucha atención • **a fat lot of ~ he takes of me!*** ¡maldito el caso que me hace!* • **to sit up and take ~** (*fig*) aguzar el oído
6 (= *interest*) interés *m* • **it has attracted a lot of ~** ha suscitado gran interés
(VT) (= *perceive*) fijarse en, notar; (= *realize*) darse cuenta de; (= *recognize*) reconocer • **did you ~ the bloodstain on the wall?** ¿te fijaste en *or* te diste cuenta de *or* notaste la mancha de sangre que había en la pared? • **I don't ~ such things** no me fijo en tales cosas • **eventually he deigned to ~ me** por fin se dignó a reconocerme • **have you ever ~d how slowly time passes when you're flying?** ¿te has fijado en *or* te has dado cuenta de lo lento que pasa el tiempo cuando vas en avión? • **I ~ you've removed the bookcase** veo que has quitado la estantería
(VI) fijarse, darse cuenta • **I never ~d** no me había fijado • **don't worry about the mark, he won't ~** no te preocupes por la mancha, no se fijará *or* no se dará cuenta • **yes, so I've ~d!** (*iro*) ¡sí, ya me he dado cuenta *or* ya lo he notado!
(CPD) ▸ **notice board** (*esp Brit*) tablón *m* de anuncios

noticeable ['nəʊtɪsəbl] (ADJ) [*difference, change, effect, increase*] sensible, perceptible • **it is ~ that** se nota que, es evidente que, está claro que • **it isn't ~** [*mark, stain*] no se nota • **a ~ smell of burning** un fuerte olor a quemado • **a ~ lack of enthusiasm** una evidente falta de entusiasmo

noticeably ['nəʊtɪsəblɪ] (ADV) [*different, changed, improved*] sensiblemente, perceptiblemente • **the next day it was ~ warmer** al día siguiente se notaba que hacía más calor • **they are ~ less well-off than before** se nota que tienen menos dinero que antes • **she looks ~ worse than when I last saw her** está sensiblemente peor que la última vez que la vi, se la nota peor que la última vez que la vi

notifiable ['nəʊtɪfaɪəbl] (ADJ) de declaración obligatoria

notification [ˌnəʊtɪfɪ'keɪʃən] (N) (= *warning, prior notice*) notificación *f*, aviso *m*; (= *announcement*) anuncio *m*

notify ['nəʊtɪfaɪ] (VT) avisar • **you must ~ the police** debes avisar a la policía, debes notificarlo a la policía • **to ~ sb of sth** comunicar *or* notificar algo a algn

notion ['nəʊʃən] (N) **1** (= *idea*) idea *f*; (= *view*) opinión *f*, noción *f*; (= *whim*) capricho *m* • **I have a ~ that ...** tengo la idea de que ... • **I had no ~ that he was planning to leave** no tenía ni idea de que tuviera pensado marcharse • **to have no ~ of** no tener ni idea de • **I haven't the slightest ~** no tengo ni idea • **to have a ~ to do sth** estar inclinado a hacer algo
2 notions (*Sew*) artículos *mpl* de mercería, mercería *f*

notional ['nəʊʃənl] (ADJ) **1** (*Econ*) [*value, profit, amount, capital, income*] hipotético, teórico
2 (= *hypothetical*) • **it is purely ~** es pura hipótesis *or* teoría *or* especulación
3 (*Ling*) [*word*] nocional

notionally ['nəʊʃənəlɪ] (ADV) teóricamente, en teoría, hipotéticamente

notoriety [ˌnəʊtə'raɪətɪ] (N) mala fama *f*, mala reputación *f* • **to achieve** *or* **gain ~** adquirir mala fama *or* reputación

notorious [nəʊ'tɔːrɪəs] (ADJ) [*criminal*] muy conocido, celebérrimo; [*area, town, prison*] de mala fama, de mala reputación; [*comment, speech*] desgraciadamente famoso; [*case, crime*] muy sonado • **a ~ womanizer** un hombre con fama de donjuán • **she's a ~ flirt** tiene fama de que le gusta flirtear • **Prussia was ~ in this respect** Prusia tenía mala fama en este sentido • **to be ~ as sth** tener fama de ser algo • **to be ~ for sth** ser conocido por algo, tener fama de algo • **he's ~ for cheating at cards** tiene fama de hacer trampas jugando a las cartas

notoriously [nəʊ'tɔːrɪəslɪ] (ADJ) • **anorexia nervosa is ~ difficult to treat** tratar la anorexia nerviosa es de notoria dificultad, es bien sabido que tratar la anorexia nerviosa entraña gran dificultad • **she is ~ difficult to work with** tiene fama de ser una persona con la que resulta difícil trabajar • **he is ~ unreliable** tiene fama de informal

no-trumps ['nəʊ'trʌmps] (N) • **to bid four no-trumps** marcar cuatro sin triunfos

Notts [nɒts] (N ABBR) (*Brit*) = **Nottinghamshire**

notwithstanding [ˈnɒtwɪðˈstændɪŋ] (PREP) a pesar de, no obstante • **the weather ~** a pesar del tiempo
(ADV) sin embargo, no obstante
(CONJ) (*also* **notwithstanding that**) a pesar de que, por más que (+ *subjun*)

nougat ['nuːgɑː] (N) turrón *m*

nought [nɔːt] (N) **1** (*esp Brit*) (*Math*) cero *m* • **~s and crosses** (*Brit*) tres *m* en raya; ▷ ZERO
2† (*liter*) (= *nothing*) nada *f*

noun [naʊn] (N) (*Ling*) nombre *m*, sustantivo *m*
(CPD) ▸ **noun clause** oración *f* sustantiva, cláusula *f* nominal ▸ **noun phrase** frase *f* nominal

nourish ['nʌrɪʃ] (VT) **1** (*lit*) alimentar, nutrir • **to ~ sb on sth** alimentar a algn con algo
2 (*fig*) fomentar, nutrir

nourishing ['nʌrɪʃɪŋ] (ADJ) nutritivo, alimenticio

nourishment ['nʌrɪʃmənt] (N) **1** (= *food*) alimento *m* • **to derive ~ from** sustentarse de
2 (= *nutrition*) nutrición *f*

nous* [naʊs] (N) (*Brit*) cacumen* *m*, chirumen* *m*

nouveau riche [ˌnuːvəʊ'riːʃ] (N) (PL: **nouveaux riches**) nuevo/a rico/a *m/f*

nouvelle cuisine ['nuːvelkwiː'ziːn] (N) nueva cocina *f*, nouvelle cuisine *f*

Nov (ABBR) (= **November**) nov., N.

nova ['nəʊvə] (N) (PL: **novas** *or* **novae**) nova *f*

Nova Scotia ['nəʊvə'skəʊʃə] (N) Nueva Escocia *f*

Nova Scotian ['nəʊvə'skəʊʃən] (ADJ) de Nueva Escocia
(N) habitante *mf* de Nueva Escocia

novel ['nɒvəl] (ADJ) [*idea, suggestion, method*] original, novedoso • **it was a ~ experience for him** era una experiencia nueva para él
(N) novela *f*

novelette [ˌnɒvə'let] (N) novela *f* corta; (*pej*) novela *f* sentimental, novela *f* sin valor

novelettish [ˌnɒvə'letɪʃ] (ADJ) sentimental, romántico

novelist ['nɒvəlɪst] (N) novelista *mf*

novella [nəʊ'velə] (N) (PL: **novellas** *or* **novelle** [nəʊ'veleɪ]) novela *f* corta

novelty ['nɒvəltɪ] (N) (= *quality, thing*) novedad *f* • **once the ~ has worn off** cuando pase la novedad
(CPD) ▸ **novelty value** novedad *f*

November [nəʊ'vembəʳ] (N) noviembre *m*; ▷ July

novena [nəʊ'viːnə] (N) (PL: **novenae** [nəʊ'viːniː]) novena *f*

novice ['nɒvɪs] (N) principiante *mf*, novato/a *m/f*; (*Rel*) novicio/a *m/f*; (*Sport*) principiante *mf*, novato/a *m/f* • **he's no ~** no es ningún principiante • **to be a ~ at a job** ser nuevo en un oficio
(ADJ) • **a ~ painter** un pintor principiante, un aspirante a pintor

noviciate, novitiate [nəʊ'vɪʃɪɪt] (N) **1** (*Rel*) (= *period, place*) noviciado *m*
2 (*fig*) período *m* de aprendizaje

novocaine ['nəʊvəʊkeɪn] (N) novocaína *f*

NOW [naʊ] (N ABBR) (*US*) = **National Organization for Women**

now [naʊ] (ADV) **1** (*of present, immediate future*)
a (= *at this time*) ahora • **what shall we do now?** ¿qué hacemos ahora? • **now for something completely different** y ahora algo totalmente distinto • **not now, dear** ahora no, querido • **right now all I want to do is ...** en este momento *or* ahora mismo, lo único que me apetece es ... • **the time is now eight o'clock** son las ocho
b (= *these days*) hoy en día, ahora • **nobody would think of doing that now** hoy en día *or* ahora a nadie se le ocurriría hacer eso

c (= *at last, already*) ya • **the fire is now under control** el incendio ya está controlado • **can I go now?** ¿ya me puedo ir? • **I must be off now** ya me tengo que marchar
d (= *immediately*) ahora; (*more emphatic*) ya • **if we leave now, we'll be there by six** si salimos ahora *or* ya, estaremos allí para las seis • **it's now or never** es ahora o nunca • **I'll do it right now** lo haré ahora mismo
2 (*of duration up to present*) • **they've been married now for 30 years** ya llevan 30 años casados, hace 30 años que se casaron • **it's some days now since I heard anything** hace varios días que no sé nada
3 (*in accounts of past events*) ahora • **it had once been the pantry but was now his office** tiempo atrás había sido la despensa, pero ahora era su estudio
4 (*after prep*) • **as of now** a partir de ahora • **before now** (= *already*) ya, antes; (= *in the past*) antes de ahora; (= *till this moment*) hasta ahora, antes • **you should have done that before now** ya tendrías que haber hecho eso, tendrías que haber hecho eso antes • **I've gone hungry before now to feed my children** ya he pasado hambre antes de ahora para poder alimentar a mis hijos • **she should have arrived long before now** hace tiempo que tenía que haber llegado • **between now and next Tuesday** entre hoy y el martes que viene • **by now**: • **they must be there by now** ya deben haber llegado • **by now it was clear that ...** en ese momento ya estaba claro que ... • **by now everybody was tired** para entonces ya estaban todos cansados • **that will be all for now** • **that will do for now** por ahora *or* por el momento basta con eso • **(in) three weeks/100 years from now** dentro de tres semanas/100 años • **from now on** (*with present, future tense*) a partir de ahora, de ahora en adelante; (*with past tense*) a partir de entonces • **till now** • **until now** • **up to now** (= *till this moment*) hasta ahora; (= *till that moment*) hasta entonces • **I've always done it this way up to now** hasta ahora siempre lo había hecho así
5 (= *in these circumstances*) **a** (*gen*) ya • **it's raining, now we won't be able to go** está lloviendo, ya no podemos ir • **it's too late now** ya es demasiado tarde • **how can I believe you now?** ¿cómo puedo seguir confiando en ti? • **now what (do we do)?** ¿y ahora, qué (hacemos)? • **they won't be long now** no tardarán en venir, al rato vienen (*Mex*)
b (*emphatic*) • **now you've gone and done it!*** ¡ahora sí que la has hecho buena!* • **now look what you've done!** ¡mira lo que has hecho!
6 (*in phrases relating to time*) • **(every) now and again** de vez en cuando • **any minute** *or* **moment now** de un momento a otro • **any day now** cualquier día de estos • **just now** (= *at this moment*) ahora mismo, en este momento; (= *a moment ago*) hace un momento • **I'm busy just now** ahora mismo *or* en este momento estoy ocupado • **plums are in season just now** es temporada de ciruelas • **I saw him come in just now** lo he visto entrar hace un momento, acabo de verlo entrar • **(every) now and then** de vez en cuando; ▹ **here**
7 (*without temporal force*) **a** (*introducing new topic*) bien, bueno • **now, as you all know ...** bien *or* bueno, como todos sabéis ... • **now, some people may disagree but ...** bien *or* bueno, puede que algunos no estén de acuerdo pero ...
b (*commenting on previous statement*) • **now there's a coincidence!** ¡eso sí que es una coincidencia! • **now there's a thought** pues no es mala idea
c (*asking question*) • **now, what's everyone drinking?** a ver, ¿qué queréis tomar?
d (*remonstrating, pacifying*) • **now Fred, you don't really mean that** vamos Fred, no lo dices en serio • **now, now, don't get so upset!** ¡venga, no te pongas así! • **now, now, we'll have none of that!** ¡vale ya, nada de tonterías! • **come now, you must be hungry** venga ya, no me digas que no tienes hambre • **hush now, don't cry** shh, no llores • **now then, what's the trouble?** ¡entonces a ver! ¿cuál es el problema? • **now then, don't tease!** ¡ya está bien, deja de burlarte! • **well now, what have we here!** ¡vamos a ver! ¿qué tenemos aquí?
8 • **now ..., now ...: now she dances, now she sings** (*liter*) tan pronto está bailando como cantando
(PRON) • **now is the best time to go to Scotland** esta es la mejor época para ir a Escocia • **now is your chance to talk to him** está es tu oportunidad de hablar con él; ▹ **here**
(CONJ) • **now (that)** ahora que • **now that she was retired she had more time** ahora que estaba jubilada disponía de más tiempo • **now you (come to) mention it** ahora que lo dices
(ADJ) actual • **the now president** el presidente actual

nowadays ['naʊədeɪz] (ADV) hoy (en) día, en la actualidad
noways* ['nəʊweɪz] (ADV) (*US*) de ninguna manera
nowhere ['nəʊwɛəʳ] (ADV) **1** (*lit*) [*be*] en ninguna parte; [*go*] a ninguna parte • **you're going ~** no vas a ninguna parte • **they have ~ to go** no tienen dónde ir • **there was ~ to hide** no había dónde esconderse • **there is ~ more romantic than Paris** no hay lugar más romántico que París • **it's ~ you know** no es ningún sitio que conoces • **it's ~ you'll ever find it** está en un sitio donde no lo encontrarás nunca • • **~ else** en/a ninguna otra parte • **she had ~ else to go** no tenía otro lugar a donde ir • **from ~** de la nada • • **~ in Europe** en ninguna parte de Europa • **he was ~ to be seen** • **he was ~ in sight** no se le veía por ninguna parte
2 (*fig*) • **without me he would be ~** sin mí no habría llegado a ninguna parte • **he came from ~ to take the lead in the race** pasó de ir muy a la zaga a tomar la delantera en la carrera • **the party came from ~ to win the election** el partido surgió de la nada y ganó las elecciones • **we're getting ~** no estamos consiguiendo nada • **I'm getting ~ with this analysis** no estoy logrando nada con este análisis • **he got ~ with her** no consiguió nada con ella • **this is getting us ~** esto no nos lleva • **flattery will get you ~** con halagos no vas a conseguir nada • **a fiver goes ~ these days** cinco libras no se hace nada hoy en día • **it's ~ near as big** no es tan grande ni con mucho • **it's ~ near as good** no es tan bueno ni con mucho, dista mucho de ser tan bueno • **£10 is ~ near enough** 10 libras no bastan, ni mucho menos
no-win ['nəʊ'wɪn] (ADJ) • **a no-win situation** una situación imposible *or* sin salida
no-win, no-fee [nəʊ'wɪnnəʊ,fiː] (ADJ) [*basis, arrangement, scheme*] *basado en el principio de "si no se gana no se cobra" mediante el cual un abogado no cobra sus honorarios si su cliente no gana el caso*
nowise ['nəʊwaɪz] (ADV) (*US*) de ninguna manera
nowt [naʊt] (N) (*Brit*) (*dialect*) = **nothing**
noxious ['nɒkʃəs] (ADJ) nocivo
nozzle ['nɒzl] (N) [*of hose, vacuum cleaner etc*] boquilla *f*; [*of spray*] pulverizador *m*; (*Mech*) tobera *f*, inyector *m*
NP (N ABBR) = **notary public**
n.p. (ABBR) (= **new paragraph**) punto *m* y aparte
NPD (N ABBR) (*Comm*) = **new product development**
n.p. or d. (ABBR) (= **no place or date**) s.l. ni f.
NPV (N ABBR) (*Econ*) = **net present value**
nr (ABBR) = **near**
NRA (N ABBR) **1** (*Brit*) = **National Rivers Authority**
2 (*US*) = **National Rifle Association of America**

NRA
La **National Rifle Association of America** o **NRA** (Asociación Nacional del Rifle) es uno de los grupos de presión más controvertidos y poderosos frente al Congreso de Estados Unidos. Cuenta con varios millones de socios, propietarios de armas de fuego para la caza o el tiro deportivo. La **NRA** promueve estos deportes al mismo tiempo que la conservación de la fauna, y organiza competiciones de tiro a nivel nacional. También se encarga de dar clases de seguridad para el uso de armas y apoya el derecho de todo estadounidense a tener armas de fuego para su propia defensa. La **NRA** ha recibido bastantes críticas por su oposición a las leyes de control de armas de fuego.

NRT (N ABBR) (= **nicotine replacement therapy**) terapia *f* de sustitución de la nicotina
NRV (N ABBR) (*Econ*) = **net realizable value**
NS (ABBR) (*Canada*) = **Nova Scotia**
n/s (N ABBR) = **nonsmoker**
(ADJ ABBR) = **nonsmoking**
NSB (N ABBR) (*Brit*) = **National Savings Bank**
NSC (N ABBR) **1** (*US*) (*Pol*) = **National Security Council**
2 (*Brit*) = **National Safety Council**
NSF (N ABBR) (*US*) = **National Science Foundation**
NSPCA (N ABBR) (*Brit*) = **National Society for the Prevention of Cruelty to Animals**
NSPCC (N ABBR) (*Brit*) = **National Society for the Prevention of Cruelty to Children**
NSU (N ABBR) (*Med*) = **nonspecific urethritis**
NSW (ABBR) = **New South Wales**
NT (N ABBR) **1** (= **New Testament**) N.T.
2 (*Brit*) = **National Trust**
nth [enθ] (ADJ) enésimo • **to the nth power** *or* **degree** a la enésima potencia • **for the nth time*** por enésima vez
NUAAW (N ABBR) (*Brit*) = **National Union of Agricultural and Allied Workers**
nuance ['njuːɑ̃ːns] (N) matiz *m*
nub [nʌb] (N) (= *piece*) pedazo *m*, trozo *m*; (= *protuberance*) protuberancia *f*; (*fig*) lo esencial, parte *f* esencial • **that's the nub of the question** ahí está el quid del asunto
NUBE (N ABBR) (*Brit*) = **National Union of Bank Employees**
nubile ['njuːbaɪl] (ADJ) [*girl, woman*] núbil; (*hum*) joven y guapa
nubuck ['njuːbʌk] (N) nobuk *m*
(CPD) [*boots, jacket etc*] de nobuk ▸ **nubuck leather** nobuk *m*
nuclear ['njuːklɪəʳ] (ADJ) (*Phys, Mil*) nuclear
(CPD) ▸ **nuclear age** era *f* nuclear ▸ **nuclear bomb** bomba *f* nuclear ▸ **nuclear capability** capacidad *f* nuclear ▸ **nuclear deterrent** fuerza *f* disuasiva nuclear ▸ **nuclear**

disarmament desarme *m* nuclear ▸ **nuclear energy** energía *f* nuclear ▸ **nuclear family** familia *f* nuclear ▸ **nuclear fission** fisión *f* nuclear ▸ **nuclear fuel** combustible *m* nuclear ▸ **nuclear fusion** fusión *f* nuclear ▸ **the nuclear industry** la industria nuclear ▸ **Nuclear Non-Proliferation Treaty** Tratado *m* de No Proliferación Nuclear ▸ **nuclear physicist** físico/a *m/f* nuclear ▸ **nuclear physics** física *f* nuclear ▸ **nuclear power** energía *f* nuclear ▸ **nuclear power station, nuclear (power) plant** central *f* nuclear ▸ **nuclear reaction** reacción *f* nuclear ▸ **nuclear reactor** reactor *m* nuclear ▸ **nuclear scientist** científico/a *m/f* nuclear ▸ **nuclear shelter** refugio *m* antinuclear ▸ **nuclear submarine** submarino *m* nuclear ▸ **nuclear test** prueba *f* nuclear ▸ **nuclear testing** pruebas *fpl* nucleares ▸ **nuclear war** guerra *f* nuclear ▸ **nuclear waste** desechos *mpl* nucleares ▸ **nuclear weapon** arma *f* nuclear ▸ **nuclear winter** invierno *m* nuclear

nuclear-free ['nju:klɪə,fri:] ADJ desnuclearizado, no nuclear
CPD ▸ **nuclear-free zone** zona *f* desnuclearizada

nuclear-powered [,nju:klɪə'paʊəd] ADJ nuclear

nuclei ['nju:klɪaɪ] NPL *of* **nucleus**

nucleic acid [nju:,kli:ɪk'æsɪd] N ácido *m* nucleico

nucleo... ['nju:klɪəʊ] PREFIX nucleo...

nucleus ['nju:klɪəs] N (PL: **nuclei** *or* **nucleuses** ['nju:klɪaɪ]) núcleo *m* • **the ~ of a library** el núcleo de una biblioteca • **we have the ~ of a crew** tenemos los elementos indispensables para formar una tripulación

NUCPS N ABBR (*Brit*) = **National Union of Civil and Public Servants**

nude [nju:d] ADJ desnudo • **to sunbathe ~** tomar el sol desnudo
N **1** (*Art*) desnudo *m* • **a ~ by Goya** un desnudo de Goya
2 (= *person*) hombre *m* desnudo, mujer *f* desnuda
3 (= *state*) • **in the ~** desnudo/a
CPD ▸ **nude scene** (*Cine*) desnudo *m*, escena *f* de desnudo ▸ **nude study** desnudo *m*

nudge [nʌdʒ] N codazo *m* • **to give sb a ~** dar un codazo a algn • **he said she's his secretary, ~ ~** dijo que era su secretaria, tú ya me entiendes
VT dar un codazo a • **to ~ sb's memory** refrescar la memoria a algn

nudie‡ ['nju:dɪ] N (*also* **nudie magazine**) revista *f* porno*

nudism ['nju:dɪzəm] N nudismo *m*

nudist ['nju:dɪst] N (des)nudista *mf*
CPD ▸ **nudist camp, nudist colony** colonia *f* nudista

nudity ['nju:dɪtɪ] N desnudez *f*

nugatory ['nju:gətərɪ] ADJ (*frm*) (= *trivial*) insignificante; (= *useless*) ineficaz, fútil, baladí

nugget ['nʌgɪt] N (*Min*) pepita *f* • **gold ~** pepita de oro

NUGMW N ABBR (*Brit*) = **National Union of General and Municipal Workers**

nuisance ['nju:sns] N **1** (= *state of affairs, thing*) fastidio *m*, lata* *f* • **what a ~!** ¡qué lata!* • **it's a ~ having to shave!** ¡qué lata tener que afeitarse!* • **the ~ of having to shave** el fastidio de tener que afeitarse
2 (= *person*) pesado/a *m/f*, latoso/a* *m/f* • **what a ~ you are!** ¡eres un pesado!, ¡eres un latoso!* • **you're being a ~** me estás dando la lata* • **to make a ~ of o.s.** dar la lata*, ponerse pesado
3 (*Jur*) perjuicio *m*; ▹ **public**
CPD ▸ **nuisance call** llamada *f* molesta ▸ **nuisance caller** acosador(a) *m/f* telefónico/a ▸ **nuisance value** • **he's only of ~ value** no hace más que fastidiar *or* incordiar, solo vale para crear problemas

NUJ N ABBR (*Brit*) = **National Union of Journalists**

nuke* [nju:k] (*esp US*) VT atacar con arma nuclear
N bomba *f* atómica

null [nʌl] ADJ nulo, inválido • **to render sb's efforts ~** invalidar los esfuerzos de algn • **~ and void** (*Jur*) nulo

nullification [,nʌlɪfɪ'keɪʃən] N anulación *f*, invalidación *f*

nullify ['nʌlɪfaɪ] VT anular, invalidar

nullity ['nʌlɪtɪ] N nulidad *f*

NUM N ABBR (*Brit*) = **National Union of Mineworkers**

numb [nʌm] ADJ **1** (*with cold*) entumecido • **my legs feel ~** (*from bad circulation etc*) se me han dormido las piernas • **my fingers have gone ~** (*gen*) se me han dormido los dedos; (*with cold*) se me han entumecido los dedos • **my feet were ~ with cold** tenía los pies entumecidos de frío
2 (*fig*) (*with fear, shock*) paralizado • **to be ~ with fright** estar paralizado de miedo • **when I heard about the accident I just felt ~** cuando me enteré del accidente me quedé atontado *or* sin poder reaccionar
VT **1** (= *deaden*) (*with injection*) adormecer • **the cold wind ~ed my face** el viento frío me dejó la cara entumecida • **alcohol was the only thing that ~ed the pain** (*fig*) el alcohol era la única cosa que aplacaba el dolor • **repeated images of violence have ~ed people to the reality of war** la continua exposición a escenas violentas ha insensibilizado a la gente frente a la realidad de la guerra
2 (= *stun*) atontar • **I was ~ed by the news of his death** la noticia de su muerte me dejó atontado *or* sin poder reaccionar

numbed [nʌmd] ADJ **1** (*with cold*) entumecido
2 (*fig*) (*with fear, shock*) paralizado • **after the accident I felt ~** tras el accidente me sentía incapaz de reaccionar

number ['nʌmbəʳ] N **1** (*Math*) número *m* • **think of a ~, any ~** piensa un número, uno cualquiera • **an even/odd ~** un número par/impar • **to do sth by ~s** *or* (*US*) **by the ~s** (*fig*) hacer algo como es debido • **painting by ~s** pintar siguiendo los números • **to play the ~s** (*US**) jugar a la lotería; ▹ **lucky, prime, round**
2 (= *identification number*) [*of house, room, page*] (*also Telec*) número *m*; [*of car*] (*also* **registration number**) matrícula *f* • **we live at ~ 15** vivimos en el número 15 • **my ~ is 414 3925** mi (número de) teléfono es el 414 3925 • **the ~ 49 bus** el autobús número 49 • **I don't know her room ~** no sé su número de habitación • **did you get his ~?** ¿has apuntado la matrícula? • **his ~ came up** (*in lottery, raffle*) su número salió premiado • **reference ~** número de referencia • **Number Ten** (*Brit*) (*Pol*) *la casa del Primer Ministro británico* • **you've got the wrong ~** (*Telec*) se ha equivocado de número • IDIOMS: • **to have sb's ~*:** • **I've got his ~ now*** ya lo tengo calado* • **his ~ is up*** le ha llegado la hora; ▹ **registration, serial, telephone**
3 (*in hierarchy*) • **it's (at) ~ three in the charts** está tercero *or* es el número tres en la lista de éxitos • **~ one:** • **she's the world ~ one** es la campeona mundial • **the ~ one Spanish player** el mejor jugador español, el número uno de los jugadores españoles • **I'm your ~ one fan** soy su más rendido admirador • **it's my ~ one priority** es lo más importante para mí • **he's my ~ two** es mi inferior inmediato • IDIOM: • **to look after** *or* **look out for ~ one** anteponer el propio interés • **he only thinks of ~ one** solo piensa en sí mismo; ▹ **opposite, public**
4 (= *quantity, amount*) número *m* • **equal ~s of women and men** el mismo número de mujeres y hombres • **the slump in student ~s** la caída en picado del número de estudiantes • **a ~ of** (= *several*) varios • **on a ~ of occasions** en varias ocasiones • **a ~ of people have mentioned it** varias personas lo han mencionado • **in a large ~ of cases** en muchos casos, en un gran número de casos • **in a small ~ of cases** en contados *or* unos pocos casos • **I've had a fair/an enormous ~ of letters** he recibido bastantes/muchísimas cartas • **there must be any ~ of people in my position** debe haber gran cantidad de personas en mi situación • **any ~ can play** puede jugar cualquier número de personas • **they were eight/few in ~** eran ocho/pocos • **to make up the ~s** hacer bulto • **times without ~** (*liter*) un sinfín de veces; ▹ **force, safety**
5 (= *group*) • **one of their ~** uno de ellos • **I include myself in their ~** me considero uno de ellos
6 (= *edition*) número *m* • **the January ~** el número de enero; ▹ **back**
7 (= *song, act*) número *m* • **and for my next ~ I shall sing ...** ahora voy a cantar ... • IDIOM: • **to do a ~ on sb** (*US**) hacer una jugada a algn*
8* (= *item of clothing*) modelo *m* • **that little ~ is by Dior** ese modelito es de Dior
9* (= *person*) • **she's a nice little ~** está como un tren*, está más buena que el pan*
10* (= *product*) • **this wine is a nice little ~** este vino no está nada mal
11* (= *job, situation*) • **a cushy ~** un buen chollo (*Sp**)
12 (*Gram*) número *m*
13 Numbers (*in Bible*) • **(the Book of) Numbers** (el libro de) Números
VT **1** (= *assign number to*) numerar • **they are ~ed from one to ten** están numerados del uno al diez • **~ed (bank) account** cuenta *f* (bancaria) numerada
2 (= *amount to*) • **they ~ 700** son 700, hay 700 • **the dead ~ed several hundred** el número de muertos ascendía a varios centenares • **the library ~s 30,000 books** la biblioteca cuenta con 30.000 libros
3 (= *include*) contar • **to ~ sb among one's friends** contar a algn entre sus amigos • **he ~ed Beethoven among his pupils** Beethoven era uno de sus discípulos • **to be ~ed among** figurar entre
4 (= *count in numbers*) contar • IDIOM: • **his days are ~ed** tiene los días contados
VI • **to ~ among** figurar entre
CPD ▸ **number cruncher*** (= *machine*) procesador *m* de números; (= *person*) encargado/a *m/f* de hacer los números* ▸ **number crunching** cálculo *m* numérico ▸ **number plate** (*Brit*) (*Aut*) matrícula *f*, placa *f* (*esp LAm*), chapa *f* (de matrícula) (*S. Cone*) ▸ **numbers game, numbers racket** (*US*) (= *lottery*) lotería *f*; (*illegal*) *lotería clandestina* • **to play the ~s game** jugar a la lotería; (*fig*) (*pej*) dar cifras ▸ **number theory** teoría *f* numérica

numbering ['nʌmbərɪŋ] N numeración *f*
CPD ▸ **numbering machine** numerador *m*

numberless ['nʌmbəlɪs] ADJ innumerable, sin número • **~ friends** un sinfín de amigos

numbhead* ['nʌmhed] N (US) tonto/a *m/f*, bobo/a *m/f*

numbly ['nʌmlɪ] ADV [*watch, gaze, say*] aturdido

numbness ['nʌmnɪs] N **1** (*lit*) • **I had a feeling of ~ in my legs** se me habían dormido las piernas; (*from cold*) tenía las piernas entumecidas
2 (*fig*) (*from grief, fear, shock*) atontamiento *m* • **a feeling of ~ overcame me** me quedé atontado

numbskull, numskull ['nʌmskʌl] N zoquete* *m*, majadero* *m* • **you ~!** ¡majadero!

numeracy ['nju:mərəsɪ] N conocimientos *mpl* básicos de aritmética

numeral ['nju:mərəl] N número *m*
ADJ numeral

numerate ['nju:mərɪt] ADJ con conocimientos básicos de aritmética • **to be ~** tener conocimientos básicos de aritmética

numeration [,nju:mə'reɪʃən] N numeración *f*

numerator ['nju:məreɪtəʳ] N numerador *m*

numeric [nju'merɪk] ADJ numérico
CPD ▸ **numeric field** campo *m* numérico ▸ **numeric keypad** teclado *m* numérico

numerical [nju:'merɪkəl] ADJ numérico • **in ~ order** por orden numérico

numerically [nju:'merɪkəlɪ] ADV numéricamente • **~ superior to** con superioridad numérica a, superiores en cuanto a su número a

numerological [,nju:mərə'lɒdʒɪkəl] ADJ numerológico

numerology [,nju:mə'rɒlədʒɪ] N numerología *f*

numerous ['nju:mərəs] ADJ numeroso • **in ~ cases** en numerosos casos • **~ people believe that ...** mucha gente cree que ...

numismatic [,nju:mɪz'mætɪk] ADJ numismático

numismatics [,nju:mɪz'mætɪks] N numismática *f*

numismatist [nju:'mɪzmətɪst] N numismático/a *m/f*, numísmata *mf*

numskull ['nʌmskʌl] N = **numbskull**

nun [nʌn] N monja *f*, religiosa *f* • **to become a nun** hacerse monja, meterse (a) monja*

nunciature ['nʌnʃɪətjʊəʳ] N nunciatura *f*

nuncio ['nʌnʃɪəʊ] N (*also* **papal nuncio**) nuncio *m* apostólico

nunnery ['nʌnərɪ] N convento *m* de monjas

NUPE ['nju:pɪ] N ABBR (*Brit*) (*formerly*) = **National Union of Public Employees**

nuptial ['nʌpʃəl] ADJ nupcial

nuptials ['nʌpʃəlz] NPL (*hum*) nupcias *fpl*

NUR N ABBR (*Brit*) (*formerly*) = **National Union of Railwaymen**

nurd* [nɜ:d] N = **nerd**

nurse [nɜ:s] N **1** (*in hospital, clinic*) enfermero/a *m/f* • **male ~** enfermero *m* • **student ~** estudiante *mf* de enfermería • **veterinary ~** auxiliar *mf* de veterinaria; ▹ **staff**
2 (*children's*) niñera *f*; ▹ **wet**
VT **1** [+ *patient*] cuidar, atender • **she ~d him back to health** lo cuidó hasta que se repuso • **to ~ a cold** curarse de un resfriado
2 [+ *baby*] (= *suckle*) amamantar; (= *cradle*) mecer
3 (*fig*) [+ *anger, grudge*] alimentar; [+ *hope*] abrigar • **to ~ one's constituency** (*Brit*) (*Parl*) cuidar de los intereses de los electores de su circunscripción electoral • **to ~ a business along** fomentar un negocio

nursemaid† ['nɜ:smeɪd] N niñera *f*, aya *f* • **to play ~ to sb** hacer de niñera de algn

nursery ['nɜ:srɪ] N **1** (*where small children are looked after*) guardería *f*, jardín *m* de infancia; (= *school*) parvulario *m*, escuela *f* de párvulos, escuela *f* infantil (*Sp*), kínder *m* (*LAm*); (= *room at home*) cuarto *m* del bebé, habitación *f* del bebé
2 (*Agr, Hort*) vivero *m*
3 (*Zool*) criadero *m*
CPD ▸ **nursery education** educación *f* preescolar ▸ **nursery nurse** puericultor(a) *m/f* ▸ **nursery rhyme** canción *f* infantil ▸ **nursery school** parvulario *m*, escuela *f* de párvulos, escuela *f* infantil (*Sp*), kínder *m* (*LAm*) ▸ **nursery schooling** = **nursery education** ▸ **nursery school teacher** = **nursery teacher** ▸ **nursery slopes** (*Brit*) (*Ski*) pistas *fpl* para principiantes ▸ **nursery teacher** maestro/a *m/f* de parvulario, maestro/a *m/f* de preescolar

nurseryman ['nɜ:srɪmən] N (PL: **nurserymen**) horticultor *m*

nursing ['nɜ:sɪŋ] N **1** (= *career, course, profession*) enfermería *f* • **to go in for ~** hacerse enfermero/a, dedicarse a la enfermería
2 (= *care*) [*of patient*] asistencia *f*, cuidado *m*
3 (= *suckling*) lactancia *f*
CPD ▸ **nursing auxiliary** (*Brit*) auxiliar *mf* de enfermería ▸ **nursing bottle** (*US*) biberón *m* ▸ **nursing college** escuela *f* de enfermería ▸ **nursing home** (*for elderly*) hogar *m* de ancianos; (*for convalescents*) clínica *f* (particular) ▸ **nursing mother** madre *f* que amamanta ▸ **nursing officer** enfermero/a *m/f* ▸ **nursing staff** personal *m* de enfermería

nursling ['nɜ:slɪŋ] N lactante *mf*, niño/a *m/f* de pecho

nurture ['nɜ:tʃəʳ] VT **1** (= *bring up*) criar, educar
2 (= *nourish*) nutrir, alimentar
N **1** (= *bringing-up*) educación *f*, crianza *f* • **nature or ~** naturaleza o educación
2 (= *nourishment*) nutrición *f*

NUS N ABBR (*Brit*) **1** = **National Union of Students**
2 (*formerly*) = **National Union of Seamen**

NUT N ABBR (*Brit*) = **National Union of Teachers**

nut [nʌt] N **1** (*Tech*) tuerca *f* • IDIOM: • **the nuts and bolts of a scheme** los aspectos prácticos de un proyecto
2 (*Bot*) nuez *f* • IDIOM: • **to be a hard** *or* **tough nut:** • **it's a hard** *or* **tough nut to crack** es un hueso duro de roer • **he's a tough nut** es un tipo duro
3* (= *head*) coco* *m* • IDIOMS: • **to do one's nut** (*Brit*) salirse de sus casillas* • **to be off one's nut** estar chiflado *or* chalado* • **you must be off your nut!** ¿tú estás chalado o qué?*
4* (= *crazy person*) chiflado/a* *m/f*, chalado/a* *m/f*
5 nuts** (= *testicles*) cojones** *mpl*, huevos** *mpl*
6 nuts!* ¡narices!*
CPD ▸ **nut allergy** alergia *f* a los frutos secos ▸ **nut chocolate** chocolate *m* de nueces ▸ **nut tree** (= *hazel*) avellano *m*; (= *walnut*) nogal *m*

nut-brown ['nʌt'braʊn] ADJ café avellana (*adj inv*); [*hair*] castaño claro

nutcase* ['nʌtkeɪs] N chiflado/a* *m/f*, chalado/a* *m/f*

nutcracker ['nʌtkrækəʳ] N cascanueces *m inv* • **The Nutcracker** (*Mus*) El Cascanueces

nutcrackers ['nʌt,krækəz] NPL cascanueces *m inv* • **a pair of ~** un cascanueces

nuthatch ['nʌthætʃ] N trepador *m*, trepatroncos *m*

nuthouse‡ ['nʌthaʊs] N (PL: **nuthouses** ['nʌthaʊzɪz]) manicomio *m*

nutmeg ['nʌtmeg] N nuez *f* moscada
CPD ▸ **nutmeg grater** rallador *m* de nuez moscada

nutrasweet® ['nju:trəswi:t] N edulcorante *m*, sacarina *f*

nutrient ['nju:trɪənt] N nutriente *m*
ADJ nutritivo

nutriment ['nju:trɪmənt] N nutrimento *m*, alimento *m*

nutrition [nju:'trɪʃən] N nutrición *f*, alimentación *f*

nutritional [nju:'trɪʃənl] ADJ [*value*] nutritivo, nutricional

nutritionist [nju:'trɪʃənɪst] N nutricionista *mf*

nutritious [nju:'trɪʃəs], **nutritive** ['nju:trətɪv] ADJ nutritivo, alimenticio

nuts* [nʌts] ADJ chiflado*, chalado* • **to be ~ about sth/sb** estar chiflado por algo/algn* • **to drive sb ~** volver loco a algn • **to go ~** volverse loco

nutshell ['nʌtʃel] N cáscara *f* de nuez • IDIOM: • **in a ~** en pocas palabras • **to put it in a ~** para decirlo en pocas palabras

nutter‡ ['nʌtəʳ] N (*Brit*) chiflado/a* *m/f*, chalado/a* *m/f*

nutty ['nʌtɪ] ADJ (COMPAR: **nuttier**, SUPERL: **nuttiest**) **1** [*cake*] con nueces; [*taste*] a nuez; [*sherry*] almendrado, avellanado; [*colour*] de nuez
2* (= *crazy*) chiflado* • **to be ~ about sth** estar loco por algo*

nuzzle ['nʌzl] VT acariciar con el hocico
VI arrimarse
▸ **nuzzle up against** VI + PREP **1** (= *cuddle up to*) acurrucarse contra
2 (*with snout*) acariciar con el hocico

NV ABBR (*US*) = **Nevada**

NVQ N ABBR (*Brit*) = **National Vocational Qualification**

> **NVQ**
> La **National Vocational Qualification** o **NVQ** es una titulación profesional dirigida sobre todo a personas que ya han entrado en el mundo laboral, aunque en algunos casos puede cursarse también durante el período escolar, a la vez que o en vez de algún otro título académico como los **GCSEs** o los **A-levels**. La evaluación se hace a través del trabajo práctico realizado durante el curso y a través de exámenes orales y escritos. Este sistema funciona en Inglaterra, Gales e Irlanda del Norte, mientras que en Escocia funciona un sistema similar, el llamado **Scottish Vocational Qualification** o **SVQ**.
> ▹ **GCSE, SVQ**

NW ABBR (= **north-west**) NO

NWT ABBR (*Canada*) = **Northwest Territories**

NY ABBR (*US*) = **New York**

NYC ABBR (*US*) = **New York City**

nylon ['naɪlɒn] N **1** (= *fabric*) nilón *m*, nailon *m*
2 nylons medias *fpl* de nilón *or* nailon
ADJ de nilón, de nailon

nymph [nɪmf] N ninfa *f*

nymphet, nymphette [nɪm'fet] N nínfula *f*

nympho* ['nɪmfəʊ] ADJ ninfómano
N ninfómana *f*

nymphomania [,nɪmfəʊ'meɪnɪə] N ninfomanía *f*

nymphomaniac [,nɪmfəʊ'meɪnɪæk] N ninfómana *f*
ADJ ninfómano

NYPD N ABBR (*US*) = **New York Police Department**

NYSE N ABBR (*US*) = **New York Stock Exchange**

NZ, N. Zeal ABBR = **New Zealand**

Oo

O, o [əʊ] N **1** (= *letter*) O, o *f* • **O for Oliver** O de Oviedo
2 (= *number*) (*Telec etc*) cero *m*
EXCL (*poet*) ¡oh!
CPD ▸ **O Grade** (*Scot*) (*Scol*) (*formerly*) ≈ bachillerato *m* elemental (*examen oficial que se solía realizar en el cuarto curso de secundaria*) ▸ **O level** (*Brit*) (*Scol*) (*formerly*) ≈ bachillerato *m* elemental (*examen oficial que se solía realizar en el cuarto curso de secundaria*)
o' [əʊ] PREP (= **of**) de; ▹ **o'clock**
o/a ABBR = **on account**
oaf [əʊf] N zoquete* *mf*
oafish ['əʊfɪʃ] ADJ zafio
oak [əʊk] N roble *m*; (= *evergreen*) encina *f*
• PROVERB: • **great oaks from little acorns grow** *las grandes cosas siempre suelen comenzar de forma modesta*
CPD [*table, furniture*] de roble ▸ **oak apple** agalla *f* (de roble)
oaked ['əʊkt] ADJ [*wine*] con sabor a roble
oaken ['əʊkən] ADJ (*liter*) de roble
oakum ['əʊkəm] N estopa *f* (de calafatear)
oakwood ['əʊkwʊd] N robledo *m*
O & M N ABBR = **Organization and Methods**
OAP N ABBR **1** = **old age pension**
2 = **old age pensioner**
OAPEC [əʊ'eɪpek] N ABBR (= **Organization of Arab Petroleum-Exporting Countries**) OPAEP *f*
oar [ɔːʳ] N **1** (= *paddle*) remo *m* • **to ship the oars** desarmar los remos • **to lie** *or* **rest on one's oars** dejar de remar; (*fig*) descansar, dormir sobre sus laureles • IDIOM: • **to put** *or* **shove one's oar in*** entrometerse, meter las narices*
2 (= *person*) remero/a *m/f* • **to be a good oar** ser buen remero, remar bien
oared [ɔːd] ADJ (= *having oars*) provisto de remos
-oared [ɔːd] ADJ (*ending in compounds*) de ... remos • **eight-oared** de ocho remos
oarlock ['ɔːlɒk] N (*US*) tolete *m*, escálamo *m*, chumacera *f*
oarsman ['ɔːzmən] N (PL: **oarsmen**) remero *m*
oarsmanship ['ɔːzmənʃɪp] N arte *m* de remar
oarswoman ['ɔːz,wʊmən] N (PL: **oarswomen**) remera *f*
OAS N ABBR (= **Organization of American States**) OEA *f*
oasis [əʊ'eɪsɪs] N (PL: **oases** [əʊ'eɪsiːz]) (*lit, fig*) oasis *m inv*
oast house ['əʊsthaʊs] N (PL: **oast houses** ['əʊsthaʊzɪz])
N secadero *m* para lúpulo
oat bran ['əʊt'bræn] N (*US*) salvado *m* de avena
oatcake ['əʊtkeɪk] N torta *f* de avena
oaten ['əʊtn] ADJ de avena
oatfield ['əʊtfiːld] N avenal *m*
oath [əʊθ] N (PL: **oaths** [əʊðz]) **1** (= *solemn promise etc*) juramento *m* • **under ~** • **on ~** bajo juramento • **to administer an ~ to sb** tomar juramento a algn • **to break one's ~** romper su juramento • **to put sb on ~** hacer prestar juramento a algn • **to swear on (one's) ~** jurar • **to take the ~** prestar juramento • **to take an ~ that ...** jurar que ... • **to take an ~ of allegiance** (*Mil*) jurar la bandera
2 (= *swear word*) palabrota *f*, grosería *f* (*esp LAm*), lisura *f* (*And, S. Cone*); (= *curse*) blasfemia *f*, maldición *f*
oatmeal ['əʊtmiːl] N harina *f* de avena
ADJ [*colour*] (color) avena (*adj inv*)
oats [əʊts] NPL avena *fsing* • IDIOMS: • **to be off one's ~** estar desganado, haber perdido el apetito • **to get one's ~** (*Brit‡*) echarse polvos (con regularidad)**‡; ▹ **wild**
OAU N ABBR (= **Organization of African Unity**) OUA *f*
OB N ABBR (*TV*) = **outside broadcast**
ob. ABBR (= **obit**) (= *died*) m.
Obadiah [,əʊbə'daɪə] N Abdías
obbligato [,ɒblɪ'gɑːtəʊ] (*Mus*) ADJ obligado
N (PL: **obbligatos** *or* **obbligati**) obligado *m*
obduracy ['ɒbdjʊrəsɪ] N (= *stubbornness*) obstinación *f*, terquedad *f*; (= *inflexibility*) inflexibilidad *f*
obdurate ['ɒbdjʊrɪt] ADJ (= *stubborn*) obstinado, terco; (= *unyielding*) inflexible, firme
obdurately ['ɒbdjʊrɪtlɪ] ADV (= *stubbornly*) obstinadamente; (= *unyieldingly*) inflexiblemente • **she remained ~ silent** se quedó obstinadamente callada
OBE N ABBR (*Brit*) (= **Officer of the Order of the British Empire**) *título ceremonial*; ▹ HONOURS LIST
obedience [ə'biːdɪəns] N obediencia *f* • **to command ~** inspirar obediencia • **to owe ~ to sb** (*frm*) deber obediencia a algn • **to show ~ to sb/sth** obedecer a algn/algo • **in ~ to your orders** (*frm*) conforme a *or* en cumplimiento de sus órdenes • **in ~ to your wishes** (*frm*) obedeciendo a sus deseos
CPD ▸ **obedience training** adiestramiento *m*
obedient [ə'biːdɪənt] ADJ obediente • **he was a very ~ child** era un niño muy obediente • **to be ~ to sth/sb** obedecer a algo/algn • **to be ~ to sb's wishes** obedecer los deseos de algn • **your ~ servant**† (*frm*) (*in letters*) su humilde servidor (*frm*)
obediently [ə'biːdɪəntlɪ] ADV obedientemente
obeisance [əʊ'beɪsəns] N (*frm*) **1** (= *homage*) homenaje *m* • **to do** *or* **make** *or* **pay ~ to** tributar homenaje a
2 (= *bow etc*) reverencia *f*; (= *salutation*) saludo *m*
obelisk ['ɒbɪlɪsk] N obelisco *m*
obese [əʊ'biːs] ADJ obeso
obeseness [əʊ'biːsnɪs] N = **obesity**
obesity [əʊ'biːsɪtɪ] N obesidad *f*
obesogenic [əʊ'biːsə,dʒenɪk] ADJ obesogénico
obey [ə'beɪ] VT [+ *person*] obedecer; [+ *law*] observar, acatar; [+ *order*] cumplir; [+ *instruction*] seguir; [+ *summons*] acudir a; [+ *need, controls*] responder a • **I like to be ~ed** exijo obediencia
VI obedecer
obfuscate ['ɒbfəskeɪt] VT (*frm*) ofuscar
obit* ['ɒbɪt] N = **obituary**
obituarist [ə'bɪtjʊərɪst] N escritor(a) *m/f* de necrologías
obituary [ə'bɪtjʊərɪ] N necrología *f*, obituario *m*
CPD ▸ **obituary column** sección *f* necrológica ▸ **obituary notice** necrología *f*, esquela *f* de defunción
object¹ ['ɒbdʒɪkt] N **1** (= *item*) objeto *m* • **I was forbidden to lift heavy ~s** tenía prohibido levantar objetos pesados; ▹ **sex**
2 (= *focus*) objeto *m* • **the economy was the ~ of heated discussion** la economía fue el objeto de una acalorada discusión • **the ~ of her hatred/love** el objeto de su odio/su amor • **she was an ~ of pity to all** era objeto de conmiseración para todos • **he became an ~ of ridicule** quedó en ridículo
3 (= *aim*) objetivo *m* • **their main ~ was to make money** su principal objetivo era hacer dinero • **what's the ~ of doing that?** • **what ~ is there in doing that?** ¿de qué sirve hacer eso? • **the ~ of the exercise is to raise money for charity** lo que se persigue con esto es recaudar dinero con fines benéficos • **that's the whole ~ of the exercise** de eso precisamente se trata • **with this ~ in mind** *or* **in view** con este objetivo *or* propósito en mente
4 (= *obstacle*) • **I want the best, money is no ~** quiero lo mejor, no importa cuánto cueste • **I want to have a great holiday, money is no ~** quiero tirarme unas vacaciones estupendas, el dinero no es problema • **money is no ~ to him** el dinero no es problema *or* obstáculo para él
5 (*Gram*) complemento *m* • **direct/indirect ~** complemento *m* directo/indirecto
CPD ▸ **object clause** (*Gram*) proposición *f* en función de complemento ▸ **object language** (*Comput*) lengua *f* objeto ▸ **object lesson** (*fig*) • **it was an ~ lesson in how not to drive a car** fue un perfecto ejemplo de cómo no conducir un coche ▸ **object pronoun** (*Gram*) pronombre *m* que funciona como objeto • **direct/indirect ~ pronoun** pronombre *m* que funciona como objeto directo/indirecto
object² [əb'dʒekt] VT objetar • **"you can't do that," he ~ed** —no puedes hacer eso —objetó • **he ~ed that there wasn't enough time** puso la objección de que *or* objetó que no tenían suficiente tiempo
VI **1** (= *disapprove*) oponerse • **I won't go if you ~** no iré si te opones • **if you don't ~** si no tiene inconveniente • **to ~ to sth: a lot of people will ~ to the book** mucha gente se

o

opondrá al libro • **I wouldn't ~ to a bite to eat** no diría que no a algo que comer • **to ~ to sb: she ~s to my friends** no le gustan mis amigos • **I would ~ to Paul but not to Robert as chairman** me opondría a que Paul fuera presidente, pero no a que lo fuera Robert • **to ~ to sb doing sth: he ~s to her drinking** no le gusta que beba • **do you ~ to my smoking?** ¿le molesta que fume? • **do you ~ to my going?** ¿te importa que vaya?
2 (= *protest*) oponerse, poner objeciones • **he didn't ~ when …** no su opuso *or* no puso objeciones cuando … • **he ~ed in the strongest possible terms** se opuso de la manera más enérgica • **I ~!** (*frm*) ¡protesto! • **we ~ed strongly but were outvoted** nos opusimos enérgicamente pero perdimos la votación • **I ~ to that remark!** ¡ese comentario no lo tolero!
3 (*Jur*) • **the prosecution ~s to splitting the cases** la acusación se opone a dividir los casos • **the defence can ~ to three jurors** la defensa puede objetar a tres miembros del jurado

objection [əb'dʒekʃən] N 1 (= *aversion*) • **do you have any ~ to my smoking?** ¿le molesta que fume? • **I have no ~ to people having a celebration, but …** no tengo nada en contra de que la gente celebre cosas, pero …
2 (= *opposing view*) objeción *f*; (= *problem*) inconveniente *m* • **are there any ~s?** ¿alguna objeción?, ¿alguien en contra? • **what is your ~?** ¿qué objeción tienes? • **we have no ~ to the plan** no tenemos ninguna objeción al plan • **I have no ~** no tengo inconveniente • **do you have any ~ to my going?** ¿tienes algún inconveniente en que vaya (yo)? • **they had no ~ to our being present** no tuvieron ningún inconveniente en que *or* no pusieron ninguna objeción a que estuviéramos presentes • **she made no ~** no puso ninguna objeción • **it met with no ~** nadie se opuso • **to raise ~s (to sth)** poner objeciones (a algo) • **I see no ~** no veo inconveniente
3 (*Jur*) • **objection!** ¡protesto! • **~ overruled!** no ha lugar a la protesta • **~ sustained!** ha lugar a la protesta

objectionable [əb'dʒekʃnəbl] ADJ [*person*] grosero, desagradable; [*behaviour, attitude, remark*] inaceptable; [*language*] (= *indecent*) grosero, soez; (= *offensive*) ofensivo; [*smell*] desagradable, molesto • **the language used in the programme was ~ to many viewers** el lenguaje que se usa en el programa les resultó ofensivo a muchos telespectadores • **I find your tone highly ~** su tono me resulta totalmente inaceptable *or* muy ofensivo

objective [əb'dʒektɪv] ADJ 1 (= *impartial*) [*person, view, assessment, opinion*] objetivo • **friends may not be able to be ~** puede que los amigos no sean capaces de ser objetivos • **to take an ~ look at sth** mirar algo desde un punto de vista objetivo
2 (= *real*) [*evidence, facts*] objetivo
3 (*Gram*) [*pronoun, genitive*] de complemento directo • **~ case** acusativo *m*
N 1 (= *aim*) objetivo *m*, propósito *m* • **if we achieve our ~** si alcanzamos nuestro objetivo, si conseguimos nuestro propósito • **military ~** objetivo *m* militar
2 (*Phot*) objetivo *m*
3 (*Gram*) acusativo *m*

objectively [əb'dʒektɪvlɪ] ADV
1 (= *impartially*) objetivamente, de manera objetiva • **stand back and look ~ at the problem** distánciate y estudia el problema objetivamente *or* de manera objetiva • **~, such criticism is hardly fair** objetivamente *or* desde un punto de vista objetivo, críticas semejantes no son lo que se dice justas
2 (= *actually*) realmente • **whether this was ~ true or not, I felt it was** tanto si esto era realmente verdad como si no, yo creí que lo era

objectivism [əb'dʒektɪvɪzəm] N objetivismo *m*

objectivity [ˌɒbdʒɪk'tɪvɪtɪ] N objetividad *f*

objector [əb'dʒektəʳ] N opositor(a) *m/f*; ▹ **conscientious**

object-oriented ['ɒbdʒɪktˌɔːrɪentɪd], **object-orientated** ['ɒbdʒɪktˌɔːrɪənteɪtɪd] ADJ (*Comput*) orientado a objeto

objet d'art [ˌɒbʒeɪ'dɑːʳ] N objeto *m* de arte

objurgate ['ɒbdʒɜːgeɪt] VT (*frm*) increpar, reprender

objurgation [ˌɒbdʒɜː'geɪʃən] N (*frm*) increpación *f*, reprensión *f*

oblation [əʊ'bleɪʃən] N (*Rel*) oblación *f*; (= *offering*) oblata *f*, ofrenda *f*

obligate ['ɒblɪgeɪt] VT (*frm*) • **to ~ sb to do sth** obligar a algn a hacer algo • **to be ~d to do sth** estar obligado a hacer algo

obligation [ˌɒblɪ'geɪʃən] N obligación *f* • **without ~** (*in advert*) sin compromiso • **"no obligation to buy"** "sin compromiso a comprar" • **it is your ~ to see that …** le cumple a usted comprobar que (+ *subjun*) • **to be under an ~ to sb/to do sth** estar comprometido con algn/a hacer algo • **to lay *or* put sb under an ~** poner a algn bajo una obligación • **to meet/fail to meet one's ~s** hacer frente a/faltar a sus compromisos • **of ~** (*Rel*) de precepto

obligatory [ɒ'blɪgətərɪ] ADJ obligatorio • **to make it ~ for sb to do sth** hacer obligatorio que algn haga algo

oblige [ə'blaɪdʒ] VT 1 (= *compel*) obligar, forzar • **to ~ sb to do sth** obligar a algn a hacer algo • **to be ~d to do sth** estar *or* verse obligado a hacer algo • **you are not ~d to do it** no estás obligado a hacerlo
2 (= *gratify*) complacer, hacer un favor a • **he did it to ~ us** lo hizo como favor *or* para complacernos • **to ~ sb with a match** hacer a algn el favor de ofrecerle una cerilla • **anything to ~!*** ¡cualquier cosa!, ¡con mucho gusto! • **to be ~d to sb for sth** (= *grateful*) estarle agradecido a algn por algo; (= *under obligation*) deber un favor a algn por algo • **much ~d!** ¡muchísimas gracias!, ¡muy agradecido! • **I should be much ~d if …** agradecería que (+ *subjun*) • **I am ~d to you for your help** le agradezco mucho su ayuda

obligee [ˌɒblɪ'dʒiː] N (*Jur*) tenedor(a) *m/f* de una obligación

obliging [ə'blaɪdʒɪŋ] ADJ amable, atento • **she's a very ~ person** es una persona muy amable *or* muy atenta *or* muy solícita • **it was very ~ of them** fue muy amable de su parte

obligingly [ə'blaɪdʒɪŋlɪ] ADV amablemente, atentamente • **he very ~ helped us** nos ayudó muy amablemente *or* atentamente • **he ~ held the door open** sostuvo la puerta con mucha amabilidad • **the baby had been asleep, but he ~ opened his eyes now** el bebé había estado durmiendo, pero ahora amablemente abría los ojos

oblique [ə'bliːk] ADJ 1 [*angle etc*] oblicuo
2 (*fig*) [*reference*] indirecto, tangencial; [*reply*] evasivo
N (*Typ*) oblicua *f*

obliquely [ə'bliːklɪ] ADV (*lit*) oblicuamente; (*fig*) indirectamente

obliqueness [ə'bliːknɪs] N [*of angle*] oblicuidad *f*; (*fig*) [*of reference*] lo indirecto, lo tangencial; [*of reply*] evasividad *f*

obliquity [ə'blɪkwɪtɪ] N = **obliqueness**

obliterate [ə'blɪtəreɪt] VT 1 (= *destroy*) arrasar con, destruir
2 (= *blot out*) borrar; (= *hide*) ocultar

obliteration [əˌblɪtə'reɪʃən] N
1 (= *destruction*) arrasamiento *m*, destrucción *f*
2 (= *occlusion*) eliminación *f*

oblivion [ə'blɪvɪən] N olvido *m* • **to cast into ~** echar al olvido • **to fall *or* sink into ~** caer en el olvido

oblivious [ə'blɪvɪəs] ADJ • **~ of *or* to** inconsciente de • **he was ~ to the pain he caused** no se daba cuenta *or* era inconsciente del dolor que causaba

obliviously [ə'blɪvɪəslɪ] ADV • **to carry on ~** continuar inconscientemente

obliviousness [ə'blɪvɪəsnɪs] N • **his ~ to the danger he was in** su falta de consciencia del peligro que estaba corriendo

oblong ['ɒblɒŋ] ADJ rectangular, oblongo
N rectángulo *m*

obloquy ['ɒbləkwɪ] N (*frm*) (= *abuse*) injurias *fpl*, calumnia *f*; (= *shame*) deshonra *f* • **to cover sb with ~** llenar a algn de injurias

obnoxious [əb'nɒkʃəs] ADJ [*person, behaviour, smell*] repugnante, asqueroso • **it is ~ to me to** (+ *infin*) me repugna (+ *infin*), me es odioso (+ *infin*)

obnoxiously [ɒb'nɒkʃəslɪ] ADV repugnantemente, asquerosamente

o.b.o. ABBR (*US*) (= **or best offer**) abierto ofertas

oboe ['əʊbəʊ] N oboe *m*

oboist ['əʊbəʊɪst] N oboe *mf*

obscene [əb'siːn] ADJ 1 (= *indecent*) [*gesture, language, remark*] obsceno, soez; [*phone call, act*] obsceno, indecente
2 (= *shocking*) [*profit, salary*] escandaloso
CPD ▸ **obscene publication** (*Jur*) publicación *f* pornográfica ▸ **Obscene Publications Act** (*Brit*) (*Jur*) ley *f* de las publicaciones pornográficas ▸ **Obscene Publications Squad** (*Brit*) brigada *f* en contra de las publicaciones pornográficas

obscenely [əb'siːnlɪ] ADV 1 (= *indecently*) [*gesture, remark*] obscenamente • **to talk/write ~** decir/escribir obscenidades • **he was swearing ~** estaba soltando tacos y obscenidades
2 (= *shockingly*) [*fat*] repugnantemente; [*rich, expensive*] escandalosamente • **she earns ~ large amounts of money** gana unas cantidades de dinero escandalosas

obscenity [əb'senɪtɪ] N 1 (= *indecency*) obscenidad *f*, indecencia *f*
2 (= *word*) palabrota *f*, grosería *f* (*esp LAm*), lisura *f* (*And, S. Cone*) • **to utter obscenities** proferir obscenidades
3 (*fig*) • **that thing is an ~** esa cosa es una aberración
CPD ▸ **the obscenity laws** las leyes de obscenidad

obscurantism [ˌɒbskjʊə'ræntɪzəm] N oscurantismo *m*

obscurantist [ˌɒbskjʊə'ræntɪst] ADJ oscurantista
N oscurantista *mf*

obscure [əb'skjʊəʳ] ADJ 1 (= *not well-known*) [*book, artist, poet*] poco conocido, oscuro; [*village*] recóndito, perdido • **some ~ disease we had never heard of before** una enfermedad poco conocida de la que nunca habíamos oído hablar antes • **Norris himself has remained relatively ~** el mismo Norris sigue siendo hasta cierto punto un desconocido
2 (= *not obvious*) [*word, jargon, terminology*] de difícil comprensión; [*origins*] oscuro, poco claro • **the meaning is ~** el significado es

oscuro *or* poco claro • **for some ~ reason** por alguna extraña razón • **to make ~ references to sth** referirse de forma críptica a algo
3 (= *indistinct*) [*shape, figure*] borroso
VT **1** (= *hide*) [+ *object, face, truth*] ocultar • **some clouds ~d the sun** algunas nubes ocultaron el sol • **the house is ~d by trees** la casa está escondida detrás de unos árboles • **my view was ~d by a lady in a large hat** una señora con un sombrero enorme no me dejaba ver • **his article ~s the facts** su artículo oscurece los hechos • **this news should not be allowed to ~ the fact that ...** no se debería permitir que esta noticia impida ver claramente que ..., no se debería permitir que esta noticia vele el hecho de que ...
2 (= *complicate*) complicar • **it served only to ~ the matter further** sirvió para complicar aun más el asunto

obscurely [əbˈskjʊəlɪ] ADV **1** (= *out of the public eye*) [*live, die*] en la oscuridad
2 (= *cryptically*) [*describe*] de forma poco clara; [*argue, write*] de manera que confunde; [*refer, say*] de forma críptica

obscurity [əbˈskjʊərɪtɪ] N **1** (= *the unknown*) oscuridad *f* • **to live in ~** vivir en la oscuridad • **she rose from ~ to be a leading name in fashion** salió de la nada para llegar a ser un nombre destacado del mundo de la moda • **the band faded into ~** el grupo cayó en el olvido
2 (= *complexity*) [*of language, idea*] oscuridad *f* • **obscurities** (*in a book*) puntos *mpl* oscuros
3 (*liter*) (= *darkness*) oscuridad *f*

obsequies [ˈɒbsɪkwɪz] NPL (*frm*) exequias *fpl*

obsequious [əbˈsiːkwɪəs] ADJ servil, sumiso

obsequiously [əbˈsiːkwɪəslɪ] ADV servilmente, de forma sumisa

obsequiousness [əbˈsiːkwɪəsnɪs] N servilismo *m*, sumisión *f*

observable [əbˈzɜːvəbl] ADJ [*benefit, consequence, effect*] visible; [*phenomenon*] observable, perceptible; [*rise, fall, improvement, increase*] apreciable, perceptible • **these are ~ facts** estos son hechos visibles • **the ~ universe** el universo visible • **there is no ~ difference** no hay ninguna diferencia apreciable *or* perceptible • **the same pattern is ~ in Georgia** la misma pauta puede apreciarse en Georgia

observably [əbˈzɜːvəblɪ] ADV visiblemente

observance [əbˈzɜːvəns] N **1** [*of rule etc*] observancia *f* (**of** de), cumplimiento *m* (**of** de); [*of customs, rites etc*] práctica *f*
2 (= *rite etc*) práctica *f*; (= *custom*) costumbre *f* • **religious ~s** prácticas *fpl* religiosas

observant [əbˈzɜːvənt] ADJ **1** (= *watchful*) observador; (= *attentive*) atento • **the child is very ~** el niño es muy observador
2 (= *strict in obeying rules*) observante, cumplidor

observation [ˌɒbzəˈveɪʃən] N **1** (= *perception*) observación *f* • **he is under ~ in hospital** lo tienen en observación en el hospital • **the police are keeping him under ~** la policía lo tiene vigilado • **we can keep the valley under ~ from here** desde aquí dominamos el valle • **powers of ~** capacidad *fsing* de observación • **to escape ~** pasar inadvertido
2 (= *remark*) observación *f*, comentario *m* • **"Observations on Sterne"** "Apuntes *mpl* sobre Sterne"
3 [*of rule etc*] observancia *f*, cumplimiento *m*
CPD ▸ **observation car** (*Rail*) vagón-mirador *m*, coche *m* panorámico ▸ **observation deck** terraza *f* panorámica ▸ **observation post** (*Mil*) puesto *m* de observación ▸ **observation tower** torre *f* de vigilancia ▸ **observation ward** sala *f* de observación

observatory [əbˈzɜːvətrɪ] N observatorio *m*

observe [əbˈzɜːv] VT **1** (= *see, notice*) observar, ver • **I ~d him steal the duck** vi cómo robaba el pato
2 (= *watch carefully, study*) observar, mirar; [+ *suspect*] vigilar • **now ~ this closely** ahora fijaos bien en esto
3 (= *remark*) observar, comentar • **"it looks like rain," he ~d** —parece que va a llover —observó *or* comentó él • **I ~d to him that ...** le hice observar que ... • **as Jeeves ~d** como observó Jeeves
4 (= *obey*) [+ *rule, custom*] observar; [+ *Sabbath, silence*] guardar • **failure to ~ the law** incumplimiento *m* de la ley
5 [+ *anniversary*] celebrar

observer [əbˈzɜːvəʳ] N observador(a) *m/f*

obsess [əbˈses] VT obsesionar
VI obsesionarse (**about, over** con, por) • **to ~ about sth** estar obsesionado con algo

obsessed [əbˈsest] ADJ obsesionado • **you're ~!** ¡estás obsesionado! • **to be ~ with sb/sth** estar obsesionado con algn/algo • **he's ~ with the idea** está obsesionado con la idea, le obsesiona la idea • **he's ~ with cleanliness** está obsesionado con la limpieza, tiene obsesión *or* manía con la limpieza • **she's ~ with becoming rich** está obsesionada con (la idea de) hacerse rica

obsession [əbˈseʃən] N obsesión *f* • **to become an ~** convertirse en una obsesión • **to have an ~ about sth** estar obsesionado con algo • **his ~ with her** su obsesión con ella • **his ~ with punctuality** su obsesión *or* manía con la puntualidad • **football is an ~ with him** está obsesionado con el fútbol, el fútbol es una obsesión para él

obsessional [əbˈseʃənəl] ADJ [*behaviour, love, hatred, thought*] obsesivo • **to be ~ about sth** estar obsesionado con algo

obsessive [əbˈsesɪv] ADJ [*behaviour, jealousy, interest, need*] obsesivo; [*love, gambler*] obsesivo, enfermizo; [*fear*] enfermizo • **his ~ tidiness was driving her crazy** su obsesión *or* manía con *or* por la limpieza la estaba sacando de quicio • **he was an ~ reader** la lectura era una obsesión para él • **to be ~ about sth** estar obsesionado con algo • **to become ~** [*person*] obsesionarse; [*thing*] volverse una obsesión • **to become ~ about sth** obsesionarse con algo • **dieting can become ~** hacer dieta puede volverse una obsesión
N (*Psych*) obsesivo/a *m/f*
CPD ▸ **obsessive compulsive disorder** (*Psych*) trastorno *m* obsesivo-compulsivo ▸ **obsessive neurosis** (*Psych*) neurosis *f inv* obsesiva

obsessively [əbˈsesɪvlɪ] ADV [*work*] de (una) forma obsesiva; [*love, hate*] de (una) forma obsesiva, de (una) forma enfermiza • **to be ~ concerned about sth** estar preocupado de (una) forma obsesiva por algo • **she is ~ tidy** tiene obsesión *or* manía con *or* por la limpieza • **she was ~ devoted to her mother** tenía una devoción obsesiva por su madre

obsidian [ɒbˈsɪdɪən] N obsidiana *f*

obsolescence [ˌɒbsəˈlesns] N caída *f* en desuso, obsolescencia *f* • **planned ~** obsolescencia *f* planificada

obsolescent [ˌɒbsəˈlesnt] ADJ que está cayendo en desuso • **to be ~** estar cayendo en desuso

obsolete [ˈɒbsəliːt] ADJ [*weapon, equipment, machine*] obsoleto; [*attitude, idea, system*] obsoleto, anticuado; [*process, practice, word, law*] obsoleto, en desuso; [*ticket*] caduco • **to become ~** (*gen*) quedarse obsoleto, caer en desuso; [*ticket*] caducar

obstacle [ˈɒbstəkl] N obstáculo *m*; (= *hindrance*) estorbo *m*, impedimento *m* • **one of the ~s is money** uno de los obstáculos *or* impedimentos es el dinero • **to be an ~ to sth/sb** ser un obstáculo para algo/algn • **to put an ~ in the way of sth/sb** crear dificultades *or* poner obstáculos a algo/algn • **that is no ~ to our doing it** eso no impide que lo hagamos • **~s to independence** los factores que dificultan la independencia
CPD ▸ **obstacle course** pista *f* de obstáculos ▸ **obstacle race** (*Sport*) carrera *f* de obstáculos

obstetric [ɒbˈstetrɪk] ADJ obstétrico

obstetrical [ɒbˈstetrɪkəl] ADJ = **obstetric**

obstetrician [ˌɒbstəˈtrɪʃən] N tocólogo/a *m/f*, obstetra *mf*

obstetrics [ɒbˈstetrɪks] NSING obstetricia *f*, tocología *f*

obstinacy [ˈɒbstɪnəsɪ] N [*of person*] obstinación *f*, terquedad *f*; [*of resistance*] tenacidad *f*; [*of illness*] persistencia *f*

obstinate [ˈɒbstɪnɪt] ADJ **1** (= *stubborn*) [*person*] obstinado, terco • **to be ~ about sth** obstinarse en algo, ser obstinado con algo
2 (= *tenacious*) [*resistance*] tenaz; [*illness*] persistente

obstinately [ˈɒbstɪnɪtlɪ] ADV obstinadamente, tercamente

obstreperous [əbˈstrepərəs] ADJ [*person, behaviour*] escandaloso • **he became ~** empezó a desmandarse

obstreperously [əbˈstrepərəslɪ] ADV escandalosamente

obstruct [əbˈstrʌkt] VT **1** (= *block*) obstruir; [+ *pipe*] atascar; [+ *road*] cerrar, bloquear; [+ *view*] tapar
2 (= *hinder*) [+ *person*] estorbar, impedir; [+ *plan, progress etc*] dificultar, obstaculizar; (*Parl, Sport*) obstruir, bloquear
VI estorbar

obstruction [əbˈstrʌkʃən] N **1** (= *blockage*) obstrucción *f*; (*in pipe, road*) atasco *m*; (*Med*) oclusión *f* • **to cause an ~** estorbar; (*Aut*) obstruir el tráfico
2 (= *obstacle*) (*to progress*) dificultad *f*, obstáculo *m*
3 (*Ftbl*) obstrucción *f*, bloqueo *m*
CPD ▸ **obstruction of justice** obstrucción *f* a la justicia

obstructionism [əbˈstrʌkʃənɪzəm] N obstruccionismo *m*

obstructionist [əbˈstrʌkʃənɪst] ADJ obstruccionista
N obstruccionista *mf*

obstructive [əbˈstrʌktɪv] ADJ obstruccionista • **he's just being ~** está poniendo dificultades nada más

obstructiveness [əbˈstrʌktɪvnɪs] N obstruccionismo *m*

obtain [əbˈteɪn] VT obtener, conseguir; (= *acquire*) adquirir • **his uncle ~ed the job for him** su tío le consiguió el puesto • **oil can be ~ed from coal** se puede extraer aceite del carbón
VI (*frm*) [*price, law*] regir; [*theory*] prevalecer, predominar • **the price which ~s now** el precio que rige ahora • **in the conditions then ~ing** en las condiciones que imperaban entonces • **that did not ~ in my day** en mis tiempos eso no era así

obtainable [əbˈteɪnəbl] ADJ (= *on sale*) a la venta; (= *accessible*) asequible • **"obtainable at all chemists"** "de venta en todas las farmacias" • **it is no longer ~** ya no se puede conseguir

obtrude [əbˈtruːd] (*frm*) VT [+ *tongue etc*] sacar • **to ~ sth on sb** imponer algo a algn

O

VI [*person*] entrometerse • **he does not let his opinions ~** no hace gala de sus opiniones, no impone sus opiniones a los demás

obtrusion [əb'tru:ʒən] N (= *imposition*) [*of opinions*] imposición *f*; (= *interference, intrusion*) entrometimiento *m*, importunidad *f*

obtrusive [əb'tru:sɪv] ADJ [*presence, person*] molesto; [*smell*] penetrante; [*colours*] llamativo; [*building*] demasiado prominente • **the background music was very ~** la música de fondo resultaba muy molesta • **that lamp/painting is too ~** esa lámpara/ese cuadro es demasiado prominente

obtrusively [əb'tru:sɪvlɪ] ADV [*do sth*] de (una) forma que resulta molesta

obtuse [əb'tju:s] ADJ **1** (*Math*) obtuso **2** (= *stupid, insensitive*) [*person*] obtuso, torpe; [*remark*] desacertado, poco inteligente • **he can be very ~ at times** a veces puede ser muy obtuso • **now you're just being ~** te empeñas en no comprender

obtuseness [əb'tju:snɪs] N (*fig*) torpeza *f*, obtusidad *f*

obverse ['ɒbvɜ:s] ADJ del anverso N anverso *m*; (*fig*) complemento *m*

obviate ['ɒbvɪeɪt] VT obviar, evitar • **to ~ the need for sth** evitar *or* ahorrar la necesidad de algo

obvious ['ɒbvɪəs] ADJ **1** (= *clear, perceptible*) [*disadvantage, solution*] obvio, claro; [*danger*] evidente; [*question*] obvio • **to be ~ that** estar claro que, ser obvio *or* evidente que • **it's ~ that he's unhappy/we can't win** está claro *or* es evidente que es infeliz/no podemos ganar • **he isn't going to resign, that much is ~** no va a dimitir, eso está claro *or* es evidente • **it's ~, isn't it?** es obvio, ¿no? • **it was by no means ~ who would win** no estaba claro en absoluto quién iba a ganar • **her confusion was ~** era evidente que estaba confusa • **she made it very ~ that she didn't like him** dejó muy claro que no le gustaba, hizo patente que no le gustaba • **he's the ~ man for the job** es la persona obvia para el puesto • **it was painfully ~ that she hadn't studied for the exam** estaba clarísimo que no había estudiado para el examen • **it's perfectly ~ that he has no intention of coming** está perfectamente claro *or* es más que evidente que no tiene intención de venir • **for ~ reasons** por razones obvias *or* evidentes • **it's the ~ thing to do** está claro que es eso lo que hay que hacer • **it was ~ to everyone that it had been a mistake** todo el mundo se daba cuenta de que había sido un error • **it's not that ~ to me** para mí no está tan claro **2** (= *unsubtle*) [*ploy*] evidente, obvio; [*lie*] descarado; [*symbolism*] poco sutil • **we mustn't be too ~ about it** no conviene que se nos note demasiado • **her rather ~ charms** sus encantos poco sutiles N • **to state the ~** afirmar lo obvio

obviously ['ɒbvɪəslɪ] ADV **1** (= *clearly*) obviamente • **it's ~ the best** obviamente es el mejor, es evidente que es el mejor • **he was ~ very angry/tired** se notaba que estaba muy enfadado/cansado, estaba claro *or* era evidente *or* era obvio que estaba muy enfadado/cansado • **he was ~ not drunk** estaba claro *or* era evidente *or* era obvio que no estaba borracho • **he was not ~ drunk** no se le notaba que estaba borracho • **~, I am delighted** lógicamente *or* por supuesto, estoy encantado • **obviously!** ¡por supuesto!, ¡lógico!, ¡obvio! • **"aren't they coming?" — "~ not!"** —¿no vienen? —¡evidentemente no *or* obviamente no! • **it's ~ true** está claro que es verdad **2** (= *unsubtly*) burdamente • **she asked him rather too ~ where he had been** le preguntó sin mucha delicadeza (que) dónde había estado

obviousness ['ɒbvɪəsnɪs] N [*of answer, solution, idea*] obviedad *f*

OC N ABBR (= **Officer Commanding**) jefe *m*

o/c ABBR = **overcharge**

ocarina [,ɒkə'ri:nə] N ocarina *f*

OCAS N ABBR (= **Organization of Central American States**) ODECA *f*

occasion [ə'keɪʒən] N **1** (= *particular time*) ocasión *f* • **(on) the first ~ that it happened** la primera vez que ocurrió • **that was the first ~ that we had met** esa fue la ocasión en que nos conocimos • **this would be a good ~ to try it out** esta sería una buena oportunidad *or* ocasión para probarlo • **on ~** de vez en cuando • **on one ~** una vez • **on other ~s** otras veces • **on previous ~s** en ocasiones previas • **on rare ~s** rara vez • **he went back on three separate ~s** volvió en tres ocasiones • **on that ~** esa vez, en aquella ocasión • **on the ~ of his retirement** con motivo de su jubilación • **as (the) ~ requires** si la ocasión lo requiere • **he was waiting for a suitable ~ to apologize** esperaba el momento adecuado para disculparse, esperaba una oportunidad *or* ocasión para disculparse • **to take (the) ~ to do sth** aprovechar la oportunidad para hacer algo **2** (= *event*) acontecimiento *m* • **it was quite an ~** fue todo un acontecimiento • **what's the ~?** ¿qué se celebra? • **I wasn't dressed for the ~** no estaba vestida de forma adecuada para la ocasión • **to rise** *or* **be equal to the ~** ponerse a la altura de las circunstancias • **I keep it for special ~s** lo guardo para las grandes ocasiones; ▹ **sense** **3** (= *reason*) razón *f*, motivo *m* • **there is no ~ for alarm** • **there is no ~ to be alarmed** no hay razón *or* motivo para alarmarse • **should the ~ arise** • **if the ~ arises** si se da el caso • **to give (sb) ~ to do sth** (= *opportunity*) dar ocasión a algn de hacer algo; (= *reason*) dar motivo a algn para hacer algo • **to give (sb) ~ for sth** (= *opportunity*) dar ocasión a algn para algo; (= *reason*) dar motivo a algn para algo • **to have ~ to do sth** (= *opportunity*) tener ocasión de hacer algo; (= *reason*) tener motivo para hacer algo • **you had no ~ to say that** no había necesidad de que dijeras eso, no había motivo para decir eso VT (*frm*) ocasionar (*frm*), causar • **losses ~ed by bad weather** pérdidas ocasionadas por el mal tiempo (*frm*), pérdidas causadas por el mal tiempo

occasional [ə'keɪʒənl] ADJ **1** (= *infrequent*) [*lapse, meeting*] esporádico; [*rain, showers*] ocasional, aislado • **she made ~ visits to England** hacía alguna que otra visita a Inglaterra, hacía visitas esporádicas a Inglaterra • **I like the** *or* **an ~ cigarette** me gusta fumar un cigarrillo de vez en cuando • **I have the** *or* **an ~ drink** tomo una copa de vez en cuando • **they had passed the ~ car on the road** de vez en cuando pasaban algún coche en la carretera • **he smokes only the** *or* **a very ~ cigar** solo muy de vez en cuando *or* muy de tarde en tarde se fuma un puro **2** (*frm*) (= *created for special event*) [*poem, music*] compuesto especialmente para la ocasión • **it was written as an ~ piece for the Coronation** se escribió la pieza especialmente con ocasión de la coronación CPD ▸ **occasional table** mesa *f* auxiliar ▸ **occasional worker** (*US*) jornalero/a *m/f*, temporero/a *m/f*

occasionally [ə'keɪʒnəlɪ] ADV de vez en cuando, a veces, ocasionalmente (*frm*), cada cuando (*LAm*) • **he ~ drinks wine but never beer** de vez en cuando *or* a veces bebe vino pero nunca cerveza • **very ~** muy de vez en cuando, muy de tarde en tarde • **we see each other (only) very ~** nos vemos (solo) muy de vez en cuando *or* muy de tarde en tarde

occident ['ɒksɪdənt] N occidente *m*

occidental [,ɒksɪ'dentl] ADJ occidental

occipital [ɒk'sɪpɪtəl] ADJ occipital

occiput ['ɒksɪpʌt] N (PL: **occiputs** *or* **occipita**) occipucio *m*

occlude [ɒ'klu:d] VT ocluir

occluded front [ɒ,klu:dɪd'frʌnt] N (*Met*) oclusión *f*, frente *m* ocluido

occlusion [ɒ'klu:ʒən] N oclusión *f*

occlusive [ɒ'klu:sɪv] ADJ oclusivo N oclusiva *f*

occult [ɒ'kʌlt] ADJ (= *mystic*) oculto; [*reason etc*] oculto, misterioso N • **the ~** lo oculto • **to study the ~** dedicarse al ocultismo, estudiar las ciencias ocultas

occultism ['ɒkəltɪzəm] N ocultismo *m*

occultist ['ɒkəltɪst] N ocultista *mf*

occupancy ['ɒkjʊpənsɪ] N ocupación *f*; (= *tenancy*) inquilinato *m*; [*of post*] tenencia *f*

occupant ['ɒkjʊpənt] N **1** (= *tenant*) inquilino/a *m/f* **2** [*of boat, car etc*] ocupante *mf* • **all the ~s were killed** perecieron todos los ocupantes *or* pasajeros **3** [*of job, post*] titular *mf*

occupation [,ɒkjʊ'peɪʃən] N **1** (= *employment*) empleo *m*, profesión *f* • **what is his ~?** ¿cuál es su profesión? • **he's a joiner by ~** es carpintero de profesión • **it gives ~ to 50 men** emplea a 50 hombres, proporciona empleo a 50 hombres **2** (= *pastime*) pasatiempo *m* • **a harmless enough ~** un pasatiempo inocente • **this will give some ~ to your mind** esto te mantendrá la mente ocupada **3** (*Mil etc*) ocupación *f* • **army of ~** ejército *m* de ocupación • **the ~ of Paris** la ocupación de París • **under (military) ~** ocupado por el ejército **4** [*of house etc*] tenencia *f* • **to be in ~** ocupar • **we found them already in ~** vimos que ya se habían instalado allí • **the house is ready for ~** la casa está lista para habitar • **a house unfit for ~** una casa inhabitable, una casa carente de las condiciones mínimas de habitabilidad **5** [*of post, office*] tenencia *f*

occupational [,ɒkjʊ'peɪʃənl] ADJ (*gen*) profesional CPD ▸ **occupational accident** accidente *m* laboral ▸ **occupational disease** enfermedad *f* profesional ▸ **occupational guidance** orientación *f* profesional ▸ **occupational hazard** [*of job*] riesgo *m* laboral; (*hum*) gaje *m* del oficio ▸ **occupational health** salud *f* laboral ▸ **occupational pension scheme** plan *m* de jubilación ▸ **occupational risk** = **occupational hazard** ▸ **occupational therapist** terapeuta *mf* ocupacional ▸ **occupational therapy** terapia *f* ocupacional ▸ **occupational training** formación *f* profesional, formación *f* ocupacional

occupationally [,ɒkjʊ'peɪʃənəlɪ] ADV profesionalmente • **equality for women politically and ~** igualdad para las mujeres política y profesionalmente

occupier ['ɒkjʊpaɪə[r]] N [*of house, land*] inquilino/a *m/f*; [*of post*] titular *mf*

occupy ['ɒkjʊpaɪ] VT **1** [+ *house*] habitar, vivir en; [+ *office, seat*] ocupar • **is this seat occupied?** ¿está ocupado este asiento?

O

2 (*Mil etc*) ocupar • **in occupied France** en la Francia ocupada (por los alemanes)
3 [+ *post, position*] ocupar
4 (= *take up, fill*) [+ *space, time*] ocupar • **this job occupies all my time** este trabajo me ocupa *or* absorbe todo el tiempo • **he is occupied in research** se dedica a la investigación
5 (= *keep busy*) ocupar • **to be occupied with sth/in doing sth** estar ocupado con algo/haciendo algo • **he is very occupied at the moment** está muy ocupado en este momento • **she occupies herself by knitting** se entretiene haciendo punto
6 (*US*) (*Telec*) • **to be occupied** estar comunicando

occur [əˈkɜːʳ] VI 1 (= *happen*) ocurrir, suceder • **to ~ again** volver a suceder, repetirse • **don't let it (ever) ~ again** que no se vuelva a repetir (nunca) • **if a vacancy ~s** si se produce una vacante • **if the opportunity ~s** si se presenta la oportunidad
2 (= *be found*) darse, encontrarse • **the plant ~s all over Spain** la planta se da en todas partes en España
3 (= *come to mind*) • **to ~ to sb** ocurrírsele a algn • **it ~s to me that ...** se me ocurre que ... • **it ~red to me to ask him** se me ocurrió preguntárselo • **such an idea would never have ~red to her** semejante idea jamás se le hubiera ocurrido *or* pasado por la mente

occurrence [əˈkʌrəns] N 1 (= *happening*) suceso *m*, hecho *m* • **it's an everyday ~** es cosa de todos los días, es un hecho cotidiano • **a common ~** un hecho frecuente • **that is a common ~** eso sucede a menudo
2 (= *existence*) existencia *f* • **its ~ in the south is well known** se sabe que existe en el sur

OCD N ABBR (= *obsessive compulsive disorder*) TOC *m*

ocean [ˈəʊʃən] N océano *m* • **~s of*** (*fig*) la mar de*
CPD [*climate, region*] oceánico ▸ **ocean bed** fondo *m* del océano ▸ **ocean cruise** crucero *m* ▸ **ocean liner** transatlántico *m*

oceanarium [ˌəʊʃəˈnɛərɪəm] N (PL: **oceanariums** *or* **oceanaria** [ˌəʊʃəˈnɛərɪə]) oceanario *m*

ocean-going [ˈəʊʃən,gəʊɪŋ] ADJ [*ship*] transatlántico

Oceania [ˌəʊʃɪˈeɪnɪə] N Oceanía *f*

oceanic [ˌəʊʃɪˈænɪk] ADJ oceánico

oceanographer [ˌəʊʃəˈnɒgrəfəʳ] N oceanógrafo/a *m/f*

oceanographic [ˌəʊʃənəˈgræfɪk] ADJ oceanográfico

oceanography [ˌəʊʃəˈnɒgrəfɪ] N oceanografía *f*

ocelot [ˈəʊsɪlɒt] N ocelote *m*

och [ɒx] EXCL (*Scot*) ¡oh!

ochre, ocher (*US*) [ˈəʊkəʳ] N ocre *m* • **red ~** ocre *m* rojo, almagre *m* • **yellow ~** ocre *m* amarillo

ochreous [ˈəʊkrɪəs] ADJ de color ocre

o'clock [əˈklɒk] ADV 1 (*time*) • **it is seven ~** son las siete • **it is one ~** es la una • **at nine ~ (exactly)** a las nueve (en punto) • **it is just after two ~** son las dos pasadas, son un poco más de las dos • **it is nearly eight ~** son casi las ocho • **the six ~ (train/bus)** el (tren/autobús) de las seis • **the nine ~ news** las noticias de las nueve
2 (*Aer, Mil*) (*direction*) • **aircraft approaching at five ~** se aproxima un aparato a las cinco

OCR N ABBR (*Comput*) 1 (= **optical character reader**) LOC *m*
2 (= **optical character recognition**) ROC *m*

Oct. ABBR (= **October**) oct.

octagon [ˈɒktəgən] N octágono *m*

octagonal [ɒkˈtægənl] ADJ octagonal

octahedron [ˈɒktəˈhiːdrən] N (PL: **octahedrons** *or* **octahedra** [ˈɒktəˈhiːdrə]) octaedro *m*

octal [ˈɒktəl] ADJ octal
N octal *m*

octane [ˈɒkteɪn] N octano *m*
CPD ▸ **octane number, octane rating** grado *m* octánico

octave [ˈɒktɪv] N (*Mus, Poetry*) octava *f*

Octavian [ɒkˈteɪvɪən] N Octavio

octavo [ɒkˈteɪvəʊ] ADJ en octavo
N (PL: **octavos**) libro *m* en octavo

octet, octette [ɒkˈtet] N octeto *m*

October [ɒkˈtəʊbəʳ] N octubre *m*; ▹ **July**

octogenarian [ˌɒktəʊdʒɪˈnɛərɪən] ADJ octagenario
N octagenario/a *m/f*

octopus [ˈɒktəpəs] N (PL: **octopuses**) pulpo *m*

octosyllabic [ˈɒktəʊsɪˈlæbɪk] ADJ octosílabo

octosyllable [ˈɒktəʊˈsɪləbl] N octosílabo *m*

ocular [ˈɒkjʊləʳ] ADJ ocular

oculist [ˈɒkjʊlɪst] N oculista *mf*

OD¹, O/D ABBR 1 = **on demand**
2 = **overdraft**
3 = **overdrawn**

OD²‡ [əʊˈdiː] (= **overdose**) N sobredosis *f*
VI 1 (*lit*) tomar una sobredosis
2 (*fig*) (*hum*) • **to OD on TV** ver demasiada tele

odalisk, odalisque [ˈəʊdəlɪsk] N odalisca *f*

odd [ɒd] ADJ (COMPAR: **odder**, SUPERL: **oddest**) 1 (= *strange*) raro, extraño • **he's got rather odd lately** recientemente se ha vuelto algo raro • **that's very odd, I could have sworn I'd left my keys here** qué raro *or* qué cosa más rara, juraría que había dejado aquí mis llaves • **how odd!** ¡qué raro!, ¡qué curioso!, ¡qué extraño! • **how odd that we should meet here** qué raro *or* qué extraño que nos hayamos encontrado aquí • **it was odd of him to leave suddenly like that** fue raro que se fuese así, tan de repente • **the odd thing about it is ...** lo raro *or* lo extraño que tiene es que ... • **he says some odd things** dice cosas muy raras *or* extrañas; ▹ STRANGE, RARE
2 (= *occasional*) algún que otro • **he has written the odd article** ha escrito algún que otro artículo • **there will be the odd shower later** caerá algún que otro chaparrón más tarde • **he enjoys the odd glass of champagne** le gusta tomar una copa de champán de vez en cuando, le gusta tomar alguna que otra copa de champán • **at odd moments** en los ratos *or* momentos libres
3 (*Math*) [*number*] impar • **odd or even** par o impar
4 (= *unpaired*) [*shoe, sock*] desparejado, sin pareja • **you're wearing odd socks** llevas los calcetines desparejados, llevas dos calcetines distintos
5 (= *extra, left over*) • **to be the odd one out** (= *be over*) ser el que sobra, estar de más; (= *be different*) ser distinto • **these clowns are all identical except one — which is the odd one out?** estos payasos son todos iguales excepto uno, ¿cuál es distinto? • **but everybody will be wearing a tie, I don't want to be the odd one** *or* **man out** pero todo el mundo va a llevar corbata, yo no quiero ser la excepción • **would you like the odd penny?** ¿quiere el penique? • **£5 and some odd pennies** cinco libras y algunos peniques • **any odd piece of wood** cualquier trozo de madera • **an odd piece of material** un retal • **an odd scrap of paper** un trozo de papel
6* (*with approximate numbers*) • **30 odd** treinta y pico, treinta y tantos • **she must be 40 odd** debe tener cuarenta y tantos *or* y pico años • **£20 odd** unas 20 libras • **I haven't seen him for forty odd years** llevo cuarenta y tantos *or* cuarenta y pico años sin verlo
ADV • **he acted a bit odd when I told him** reaccionó de forma rara cuando se lo dije
CPD ▸ **odd jobs** trabajillos *mpl* • **he did some odd jobs around the house for us** nos hizo algunos trabajillos *or* pequeños arreglos en la casa ▸ **odd lot** (*St Ex*) cantidad *f* irregular (y normalmente pequeña) de acciones *or* valores

oddball* [ˈɒdbɔːl] N bicho *m* raro*, excéntrico/a *m/f*
ADJ raro, excéntrico

oddbod* [ˈɒd,bɒd] N = **oddball**

oddity [ˈɒdɪtɪ] N 1 (= *odd thing*) cosa *f* rara; (= *odd trait*) manía *f* • **he has his oddities** tiene sus manías • **he's a real ~** es un tipo realmente raro • **one of the oddities of the situation** uno de los aspectos raros de la situación
2 (= *strangeness*) rareza *f*

odd-job man [ɒdˈdʒɒb,mæn] N (PL: **odd-job men**) *hombre que se dedica a hacer pequeños trabajos u arreglos*, manitas *m inv* (*Sp, Mex**)

odd-looking [ˈɒd,lʊkɪŋ] ADJ de aspecto singular

oddly [ˈɒdlɪ] ADV [*behave, act*] de (una) manera rara, de (una) manera extraña, en forma extraña (*LAm*) • **he's behaving very ~** se está comportando de (una) manera muy rara *or* extraña • **~ attractive/calm** extrañamente atractivo/tranquilo • **an ~ shaped room** una habitación con una forma rara *or* extraña • **they are ~ similar** tienen un extraño parecido • **~ enough, you're right** por extraño que parezca, tienes razón

oddment [ˈɒdmənt] N artículo *m* suelto; (*Brit*) (*Comm*) resto *m*; **oddments** [*of fabric*] retazos *mpl*, retales *mpl*

oddness [ˈɒdnɪs] N rareza *f*

odds [ɒdz] NPL 1 (*in betting*) puntos *mpl* de ventaja • **to give ~ of 3 to 1** ofrecer 3 puntos de ventaja a 1 • **what ~ will you give me?** ¿cuánta ventaja me da? • **the ~ on the horse are 5 to 1** las apuestas al caballo están a 5 contra 1 • **short/long ~** pocas/muchas probabilidades • **to lay ~ on sth** (*fig*) hacer apuestas sobre algo • IDIOM: • **to pay over the ~** (*Brit*) pagar en demasía
2 (= *chances for or against*) probabilidades *fpl* • **the ~ are in his favour** lo tiene todo a su favor • **to fight against overwhelming ~** luchar con todo en contra • **to succeed against all the ~** tener éxito en contra de todas las predicciones • **the ~ are that ...** lo más probable es que ... • **the ~ are too great** llevamos mucha desventaja es • **the ~ are against it** es poco probable
3* (= *difference*) • **what's the ~?** ¿qué importa?, ¿qué más da? • **it makes no ~** da lo mismo, da igual • **it makes no ~ to me** me da igual
4 (= *variance, strife*) • **to be at ~ with sb over sth** estar reñido *or* en desacuerdo con algn por algo • **to set two people at ~** enemistar a dos personas
5 • **~ and ends** (= *bits and pieces*) trozos *mpl*, pedacitos *mpl*, corotos *mpl* (*Col, Ven*); [*of cloth etc*] retazos *mpl*, retales *mpl*; [*of food*] restos *mpl*, sobras *fpl* • **there were ~ and ends of machinery** había piezas sueltas de máquinas
6 • **all the ~ and sods‡** todo quisque*, todo hijo de vecina*

odds-on [ˈɒdzˈɒn] ADJ • **it's odds-on he won't come** lo más probable es que no venga
CPD ▸ **odds-on favourite** caballo *m* favorito, caballo *m* con puntos de ventaja • **he's odds-on favourite for the job** él tiene

las mejores posibilidades de ganar el puesto
odd-sounding ['ɒd,saʊndɪŋ] (ADJ) [*name*] raro • **odd-sounding words** palabras que suenan raras
ode [əʊd] (N) oda *f*
odious ['əʊdɪəs] (ADJ) [*person, task*] odioso, detestable; [*behaviour, crime*] detestable; [*comparison*] odioso
odiously ['əʊdɪəslɪ] (ADV) odiosamente, de forma detestable
odium ['əʊdɪəm] (N) (*frm*) odio *m* • **to bring ~ on sb** hacer que algn sea odiado • **to incur the ~ of having done sth** suscitar el odio de la gente por haber hecho algo
odometer [ɒ'dɒmɪtəʳ] (N) (*US*) cuentakilómetros *m inv*
odontologist [,ɒdɒn'tɒlədʒɪst] (N) odontólogo/a *m/f*
odontology [,ɒdɒn'tɒlədʒɪ] (N) odontología *f*
odor ['əʊdəʳ] (N) (*US*) = **odour**
odoriferous [,əʊdə'rɪfərəs] (ADJ) odorífero
odorless ['əʊdəlɪs] (ADJ) (*US*) = **odourless**
odorous ['əʊdərəs] (ADJ) oloroso
odour, **odor** (*US*) ['əʊdəʳ] (N) olor *m* (**of** a); (*fig*) sospecha *f* • **bad ~** mal olor • **~ of sanctity** olor de santidad • IDIOMS: • **to be in bad ~** (= *bad repute*) tener mala fama • **to be in bad ~ with sb** estar mal con algn
odourless, **odorless** (*US*) ['əʊdəlɪs] (ADJ) inodoro
Odysseus [ə'dɪsjuːs] (N) Odiseo
Odyssey ['ɒdɪsɪ] (N) (*Myth*) Odisea *f* • **odyssey** (*fig*) odisea *f*
OE (N ABBR) (*Ling*) = **Old English**
OECD (N ABBR) (= **Organization for Economic Cooperation and Development**) OCDE *f*
oecumenical [,iːkjuː'menɪkəl] (ADJ) ecuménico
oedema [ɪ'diːmə] (N) (PL: **oedemata** [ɪ'diːmətə]) edema *m*
oedipal ['iːdɪpl] (ADJ) [*conflict, situation*] edípico
Oedipus ['iːdɪpəs] (N) Edipo
(CPD) ▸ **Oedipus complex** (*Psych*) complejo *m* de Edipo
OEEC (N ABBR) (= **Organization for European Economic Cooperation**) OECE *f*
oenologist, **enologist** (*US*) [iː'nɒlədʒɪst] (N) enólogo/a *m/f*
oenology, **enology** (*US*) [iː'nɒlədʒɪ] (N) enología *f*
oenophile, **enophile** (*US*) ['iːnəʊfaɪl] (N) enófilo/a *m/f*
o'er ['əʊəʳ] (*poet*) = **over**
oesophagus, **esophagus** (*US*) [iː'sɒfəgəs] (N) esófago *m*
oestrogen, **estrogen** (*US*) ['iːstrəʊdʒən] (N) estrógeno *m*
oestrous, **estrous** (*US*) ['iːstrəs] (ADJ) en celo
(CPD) ▸ **oestrous cycle** ciclo *m* de celo
oestrus, **estrus** (*US*) ['iːstrəs] (N) estro *m*
oeuvre ['ɜːvrə] (N) obra *f*
of [ɒv, əv] (PREP) **1** (*indicating possession*) de • **the house of my uncle** la casa de mi tío • **the love of God** el amor de Dios • **a friend of mine** un amigo mío • **it's no business of yours** aquí no te metas, no tienes que ver con esto
2 (*objective genitive*) a, hacia • **hatred of injustice** odio a la injusticia • **love of country** el amor a la patria
3 (*partitive etc*) de • **a pound of flour** una libra de harina • **how much of this do you need?** ¿cuánto necesitas de eso? • **there were four of them** eran cuatro • **all of them** todos ellos • **of the 12, two were bad** de los 12, dos estaban pasados • **you of all people ought to know** debieras saberlo más que nadie • **most of all** sobre todo, más que nada • **we're the best of friends** somos muy (buenos) amigos • **the book of books** el libro de los libros • **king of kings** rey de reyes
4 (*indicating cause*) por, de • **out of fear** por temor • **out of anger** de rabia • **of itself** de por sí • **of necessity** por necesidad • **to die of pneumonia** morir de pulmonía
5 (*agent*) • **beloved of all** querido de todos • **it was rude of him to say that** fue de mala educación que dijese eso • **it was nice of him to offer** fue muy amable ofreciéndose • **that was very kind of you** fue muy amable de su parte
6 (*indicating material*) de • **made of steel/paper** hecho de acero/papel
7 (*descriptive*) de • **the City of New York** la ciudad de Nueva York • **a boy of eight** un niño de ocho años • **a man of great ability** un hombre de gran talento • **that idiot of a minister** ese idiota de ministro • **by the name of Green** llamado Green • **a real palace of a house** una casa que es un verdadero palacio • **a tragedy of her own making** una tragedia que ella misma había labrado, una tragedia de su propia cosecha • **bright of eye** de ojos claros • **hard of heart** duro de corazón
8 (= *concerning*) de • **what do you think of him?** ¿qué piensas de él? • **what of it?** ¿y a ti qué (te) importa?, ¿y qué?
9 (*indicating deprivation, riddance*) • **loss of faith** pérdida de fe • **lack of water** falta de agua
10 (*indicating separation in space or time*) de • **south of Glasgow** al sur de Glasgow • **it's a quarter of six** (*US*) son las seis menos cuarto, falta un cuarto para las seis (*LAm*)
11 (*in time phrases*) • **I go to the pub of an evening*** al pub suelo ir por las noches • **he died of a Friday** (*frm*) murió un viernes • **it was fine of a morning*** por la mañana hacía buen tiempo
12 (*with certain verbs*) • **to dream of sth** soñar con algo • **to judge of sth** juzgar algo, opinar sobre algo • **he was robbed of his watch** le robaron el reloj, se le robó el reloj • **to smell of sth** oler a algo

off [ɒf]

ADVERB
ADJECTIVE
PREPOSITION
NOUN
INTRANSITIVE VERB
TRANSITIVE VERB
COMPOUNDS

*When **off** is the second element in a phrasal verb, eg **get off**, **keep off**, **take off**, look up the verb. When it is part of a set combination, eg **off duty/work**, **far off**, look up the other word.*

ADVERB
1 (= *distant*) • **a place two miles off** un lugar a dos millas (de distancia) • **it landed not 50 metres off** cayó a menos de 50 metros • **it's some way off** está algo lejos • **noises off** (*gen*) ruidos *mpl* de fondo; (*Theat*) efectos *mpl* sonoros • **a voice off** una voz de fondo; (*Cine*) una voz en off
2 (*in time*) • **the game is 3 days off** faltan 3 días para el partido
3 (= *removed*) • **the lid is off** la tapa está quitada • **there are two buttons off** faltan dos botones • **he had his coat off** no llevaba el abrigo puesto • **with his shoes off** descalzo, sin zapatos • **with his hat off** con el sombrero quitado • **hats off!** ¡descúbranse! • **hands off!** ¡fuera las manos!, ¡sin tocar! • **off with those wet socks!** ¡quítate esos calcetines mojados! • **off with his head!** ¡que le corten la cabeza!
4 (= *departing*) • **to be off** irse, marcharse • **it's time I was off** es hora de irme, es hora de marcharme • **I must be off** tengo que irme, tengo que marcharme • **I'm off** me voy, me marcho • **I'm off to Paris** me voy a París, me marcho a París, salgo para París • **where are you off to?** ¿a dónde te vas? • **she's off at 4** sale del trabajo a las 4 • **be off!** ¡fuera de aquí!, ¡lárgate! • **they're off!** (*race*) ¡ya salen! • **he's off fishing** ha ido a pescar • **off with you!** (= *go away*) ¡fuera de aquí!, ¡lárgate!; (*affectionately*) ¡vete ya! • **off we go!** ¡vamos! • **he's off on his favourite subject again** está otra vez dale que dale con su tema favorito*
5 (= *not at work*) • **to be off** (= *away*) estar fuera, no estar • **Ana is off sick today** (= *indisposed*) Ana no ha venido a trabajar hoy porque está enferma; (= *with doctor's note*) Ana está de baja hoy • **she's off on Tuesdays** los martes no viene (a trabajar) • **are you off this weekend?** ¿vas a estar fuera este fin de semana? • **to have** *or* **take a day off** tomarse un día de descanso • **I've got this afternoon off** tengo esta tarde libre • **he gets two days off each week** tiene dos días libres a la semana
6 (*Elec, Mech etc*) • **to be off** [*apparatus, radio, TV, light*] estar apagado; [*tap*] estar cerrado; [*water etc*] estar cortado; [*brake*] no estar puesto, estar quitado; [*machinery*] estar parado
7 (*Comm*) • **"10% off"** "descuento del 10 por ciento" • **I'll give you 5% off** te hago el 5 por ciento de descuento, te hago un descuento del 5 por ciento
8 (*in phrases*) • **off and on** de vez en cuando, a ratos • **right off** • **straight off** inmediatamente, enseguida • **3 days straight off** 3 días seguidos

ADJECTIVE
1 (*Brit*) (= *bad*) • **to be off** [*fish, yoghurt, meat*] estar malo *or* pasado; [*milk*] estar cortado
2 (= *cancelled*) • **the game is off** se ha cancelado el partido • **the talks are off** se han cancelado las conversaciones • **sorry, but the party's off** lo siento, pero no hay fiesta • **their engagement is off** han roto el noviazgo • **salmon is off** (*on menu*) ya no hay salmón, se acabó el salmón
3* (= *not right*) • **the timing is a bit off** resulta un poco inoportuno • **it's a bit off, isn't it?** (*fig*) eso no está muy bien ¿no? • **it was a bit off, him leaving like that** no estuvo muy bien de su parte marcharse así • **I thought his behaviour was rather off** me pareció que su forma de comportarse fue una salida de tono *or* estuvo fuera de lugar • **she's feeling rather off** se siente bastante mal
4 (*for money, supplies, time*) • **how are you off for money?** ¿qué tal andas de dinero? • **how are you off for bread?** ¿qué tal andas de pan? • **how are we off for time?** ¿qué tal vamos de tiempo?; ▹ **badly, better, well-off**
5 (*Sport*) = **offside**
6 (*Elec, Mech etc*) • **in the off position** en posición de apagado

PREPOSITION
1 (= *from*) de • **to fall off a table** caer de una mesa • **to fall off a cliff** caer por un precipicio • **to eat off a dish** comer en un plato • **to dine off fish** cenar pescado
2 (= *near*) • **a street off the square** una calle que sale de la plaza • **a flat just off the high street** un piso junto a la calle mayor

3 (= away from) • **a house off the main road** una casa algo apartada de la carretera • **height off the ground** altura del suelo, altura sobre el suelo • **he ran towards the car and was 5 yards off it when ...** corrió hacia el coche y estaba a cinco metros de él cuando ... • **to be off air** (*Rad, TV*) no estar en el aire • **to go off air** (= *finish for day*) cerrar la emisión; (= *cease being broadcast*) dejar de emitirse • **our programme was taken off air ten days ago** nuestro programa dejó de emitirse hace diez días

4 (Naut) • **off Portland Bill** a la altura de Portland Bill, frente a Portland Bill

5 (= missing from) • **there are two buttons off my coat** a mi chaqueta le faltan dos botones • **the lid was off the tin** la lata tenía la tapa quitada

6 (= absent from) • **he was off work for 3 weeks** estuvo sin poder ir a trabajar 3 semanas • **to take 3 days off work** tomarse 3 días libres

7 (Comm) • **to take 5% off the price** rebajar el precio en un 5 por ciento

8 (= not taking) • **he's been off drugs for a year** hace un año que no prueba las drogas, dejó las drogas hace un año • **I'm off coffee** (= *not taking*) he dejado de tomar café; (= *disliking*) tengo aborrecido el café, no puedo ver el café • **to be off one's food** no tener apetito

NOUN

* (= *start*) comienzo *m*; (*Sport*) salida *f* • **at the off** en la salida • **ready for the off** listos para comenzar; (*Sport*) listos para salir

INTRANSITIVE VERB

(*esp US*‡) (= *leave*) largarse*

TRANSITIVE VERB

(*US*‡) (= *kill*) cargarse‡, ventilarse‡

COMPOUNDS

▸ **off day** • **to have an off day** tener un día malo ▸ **off season** temporada *f* baja • **in the off season** fuera de temporada

offal [ˈɒfəl] (N) asaduras *fpl*, menudillos *mpl*

off-beam* [ˌɒfˈbiːm] (ADJ) [*statement, person*] desacertado

offbeat [ˈɒfˌbiːt] (ADJ) excéntrico, original

Off-Broadway [ˌɒfˈbrɔːdweɪ] (ADJ) *que no pertenece a las superproducciones de Broadway*

OFF-BROADWAY

Off-Broadway es el término que se utiliza en la jerga del teatro para referirse a las producciones teatrales de Nueva York que no se representan en los famosos escenarios de Broadway. La primera vez que se utilizó esta expresión fue en los años cincuenta, al hablar de obras de bajo presupuesto pero con gran originalidad de dramaturgos como Tennessee Williams o Edward Albee. Estas producciones - tanto las amateur como las más profesionales - suelen representarse en teatros con poco aforo y las entradas suelen ser bastante asequibles. También existe el término **off-off Broadway**, para referirse a los teatros que presentan obras aún más vanguardistas.

off-campus [ˌɒfˈkæmpəs] (*Univ*) (ADJ), (ADV) fuera del campus

off-centre, off-center (US) [ˌɒfˈsentəʳ] (ADJ) descentrado

off-chance [ˈɒftʃɑːns] (N) • **(let's go) on the off-chance** (vamos) por si acaso • **he bought it on the off-chance that it would come in useful** lo compró pensando que tal vez resultaría útil

off-colour, off-color (US) [ˌɒfˈkʌləʳ] (ADJ) 1 (*Brit*) (= *ill*) indispuesto, pachucho (*Sp**) • **to feel/be off-colour** sentirse/estar indispuesto

2 [*joke, remark*] subido de tono

offcut [ˈɒfkʌt] (N) 1 trozo *m*

2 **offcuts** restos *mpl*, sobras *fpl*

offence, offense (US) [əˈfens] (N) 1 (= *crime*) delito *m*; (*moral*) pecado *m*, falta *f*; (*Sport*) falta *f* • **first ~** primer delito • **second ~** reincidencia *f* • **to commit an ~** cometer un delito • **it is an ~ to ...** está prohibido ..., se prohíbe ...

2 (= *insult*) ofensa *f*, agravio *m* • **no ~! • no ~ meant** sin ánimo de ofender • **no ~ was intended • he intended no ~** no tenía intención de ofender a nadie • **it is an ~ to the eye** hace daño a la vista • **to give** *or* **cause ~ (to sb)** ofender (a algn) • **to take ~ (at sth)** ofenderse *or* sentirse ofendido (por algo)

offend [əˈfend] (VT) ofender • **to be ~ed** ofenderse • **he is easily ~ed** se ofende fácilmente • **don't be ~ed** no te vayas a ofender • **to be ~ed at or by sth** ofenderse por algo • **to become ~ed** ofenderse • **it ~s my ears/eyes** me hace daño al oído/a la vista • **to feel ~ed** sentirse ofendido • **to look ~ed** poner cara de ofendido • **to ~ reason** ir en contra de la razón • **it ~s my sense of justice** atenta contra mi sentido de la justicia

(VI) 1 (= *cause offence*) ofender • **scenes that may ~** escenas que pueden ofender • **to ~ against** [+ *good taste*] atentar contra; [+ *law*] infringir • **to ~ against God** pecar contra Dios

2 (*criminally*) (= *commit an offence*) cometer una infracción; (= *commit offences*) cometer infracciones • **girls are less likely to ~ than boys** las chicas son menos propensas a cometer infracciones que los chicos • **to ~ again** reincidir

offender [əˈfendəʳ] (N) 1 (= *lawbreaker*) delincuente *mf*; (*against traffic regulations etc*) infractor(a) *m/f* • **first ~** delincuente *mf* sin antecedentes penales

2 (*moral*) transgresor(a) *m/f*, pecador(a) *m/f* • **regarding air pollution, industry is the worst ~** en lo que se refiere a la contaminación atmosférica, la industria es la mayor culpable

3 (= *insulter*) ofensor(a) *m/f*

offending [əˈfendɪŋ] (ADJ) (*esp hum*) • **the dentist proceeded to fill the ~ tooth** el dentista procedió a empastar el diente culpable • **the book was withdrawn for the ~ passages to be deleted** el libro fue retirado para eliminar los pasajes responsables de la controversia • **he put the ~ object out of sight** guardó el objeto causante del conflicto • **he put the ~ jacket back in the wardrobe** puso de nuevo en el armario la chaqueta que según parecía era un atentado contra el buen gusto

(CPD) ▸ **offending behaviour** [*of criminal, delinquent*] conducta *f* delictiva

offense [əˈfens] (N) (US) = **offence**

offensive [əˈfensɪv] (ADJ) 1 (= *causing offence, unpleasant*) [*behaviour, book, joke*] ofensivo; [*remark, language*] ofensivo, insultante; [*smell*] muy desagradable • **to find sth/sb ~** encontrar algo/a algn ofensivo • **he doesn't mean to be ~** no pretende ofender • **to be ~ to sb** ofender a algn

2 (*Mil*) [*operation, action, capability*] ofensivo

3 (*Sport*) [*player, play*] de ataque

(N) (*Comm, Mil, Sport*) ofensiva *f* • **an advertising ~** una ofensiva publicitaria • **to be on the ~** estar a la ofensiva • **to go on the ~** pasar a la ofensiva, pasar al ataque • **to launch an ~** lanzar una ofensiva • **a sales ~** una ofensiva de ventas • **to take the ~** tomar la ofensiva

(CPD) ▸ **offensive material** (*on internet etc*) contenido *m* inapropiado ▸ **offensive weapon** (*Jur*) arma *f* ofensiva; (*Mil*) arma *f* de ataque

offensively [əˈfensɪvlɪ] (ADV) 1 (= *abusively*) [*behave, shout*] de manera ofensiva, de modo ofensivo • **~ rude/sexist** de un grosero/sexista que ofende

2 (= *unpleasantly*) • **to smell ~** tener un olor muy desagradable • **the music had become ~ loud** la música estaba ya tan alta que molestaba

3 (*Mil*) • **to use/deploy sth ~** usar/hacer uso de algo para atacar • **~, they are superior to us** desde el punto de vista ofensivo, son superiores a nosotros

4 (*Sport*) • **they played ~ in the first half** en la primera mitad realizaron un juego de ataque • **to be good/poor ~** ser bueno/malo en el ataque

offer [ˈɒfəʳ] (N) (*also Comm*) oferta *f* • **"offers over £25"** "ofertas a partir de 25 libras" • **"£50 or nearest offer"** "50 libras, negociable" • **he has had a good ~ for the house** le han hecho una buena oferta por la casa • **introductory ~** oferta *f* de lanzamiento • **to make (sb) an ~ (for sth)** hacer una oferta (a algn) (por algo) • **they made me an ~ I couldn't refuse** me hicieron una oferta que no pude rechazar • **~s of help are flooding in** están lloviendo las ofertas de ayuda • **I accepted his ~ of a lift** acepté cuando se ofreció a llevarme en coche • **~ of marriage** propuesta *f* de matrimonio • **to be on ~** (*Comm*) estar de oferta • **"on offer this week"** "de oferta esta semana" • **it's the only entertainment on ~ in this town** es la única atracción en esta ciudad • **there are so many courses on ~** existe tal oferta de cursillos • **~ of peace • peace ~** ofrecimiento *m* de paz • **I might take you up on that ~** puede que acepte tu oferta • **the house is under ~** tenemos una oferta para la casa pendiente de formalizar el contrato; ▸ **job, open, share, special**

(VT) 1 (= *invite to*) • **can I ~ you sth to drink?** ¿quieres tomar algo? • **"can I get you a drink?" she ~ed** —¿te sirvo algo? —preguntó ofreciéndose

2 (= *make available*) [+ *help, services, money*] ofrecer; [+ *information, advice*] dar, ofrecer • **to have a lot to ~** tener mucho que ofrecer • **to ~ sb sth • ~ sth to sb** ofrecer algo a algn • **the island has little to ~ the tourist** la isla no tiene mucho que ofrecer al turista • **I ~ed her a fair price for the land** le ofrecí un buen precio por el terreno • **to ~ to do sth** ofrecerse a hacer algo • **I ~ed to pay for her** me ofrecí a pagar lo suyo • **one of the group ~ed himself as spokesman** uno del grupo se prestó *or* se ofreció a ser el portavoz • **to ~ one's hand** (*to shake*) tender la mano

3 (= *express, make*) [+ *opinion*] expresar; [+ *comment, remark, suggestion*] hacer • **if I may ~ a suggestion ...** si me permite hacer una sugerencia ... • **to ~ an apology** ofrecer disculpas, disculparse • **he ~ed no explanation** no dio ninguna explicación • **the President has ~ed his sympathy to relatives** el presidente ha expresado sus condolencias a los familiares

4 (= *afford*) [+ *opportunity, prospect, solution*] ofrecer • **the country ~s a wealth of opportunities for investment** el país ofrece *or* brinda muchas oportunidades de inversión • **the hotel ~s magnificent views over the lake** el hotel tiene unas magníficas vistas al lago • **it seemed to ~ a solution to**

our problem parecía ofrecer *or* brindar una solución a nuestro problema
5 (= *show*) • **he ~ed no resistance** no opuso resistencia
6 (*Rel*) (*also* **offer up**) [+ *sacrifice*] ofrecer • **to ~ (up) a prayer for sb** rezar una oración por algn • **to ~ (up) a prayer to Saint Anthony** ofrecer *or* rezar una oración a San Antonio • **she ~ed (up) a silent prayer of thanks** rezó en silencio dando gracias
VI 1 (= *volunteer*) ofrecerse • **I could have done with some help but no one ~ed** me hubiera venido bien algo de ayuda pero nadie se ofreció
2 (= *become available*) presentarse • **she promised to do it when opportunity ~ed** prometió hacerlo cuando se presentara la oportunidad
CPD ▸ **offer price** (*St Ex*) precio *m* de oferta
offering [ˈɒfərɪŋ] N 1 (*gen*) ofrenda *f*; (= *gift*) regalo *m*
2 (*Rel*) exvoto *m*; (= *sacrifice*) sacrificio *m*
offertory [ˈɒfətərɪ] N (*Rel*) (= *part of service*) ofertorio *m*; (= *collection*) colecta *f*
CPD ▸ **offertory box** cepillo *m*
offhand [ɒfˈhænd] ADJ 1 (= *casual*) • **he was very ~ about his achievements** no daba importancia a sus logros • **"it was nothing," he said in an ~ manner** —no fue nada —dijo como quitándole importancia • **"it could have been worse," said Hamish, in an ~ tone** —podría haber sido peor —dijo Hamish en tono despreocupado • **his attitude to work/punctuality is very ~** se toma el trabajo/la puntualidad muy a la ligera
2 (= *cavalier*) displicente • **the next day he was very ~ with her** al día siguiente estuvo muy displicente con ella • **to treat sb in an ~ manner** tratar a algn con displicencia
ADV (= *without some thought*) sin pensarlo • **I can't tell you ~** no te lo puedo decir así de pronto *or* sin pensarlo un poco *or* (*LAm*) así nomás • **~, I'd say that there were around 40** así, a ojo, diría que eran unos cuarenta • **do you know ~ where the copies are kept?** ¿sabes por casualidad dónde se guardan las copias? • **do you know her phone number ~?** ¿te sabes de memoria su número de teléfono?
offhanded [ɒfˈhændɪd] ADJ = **offhand**
offhandedly [ɒfˈhændɪdlɪ] ADV
1 (= *casually*) a la ligera • **he dealt with the whole matter very ~** trató todo el asunto muy a la ligera • **"we were just playing," I said as ~ as I could** —solo estábamos jugando —dije en el tono más despreocupado que pude
2 (= *cavalierly*) [*reply, behave*] displicentemente • **to treat sb ~** tratar a algn con displicencia
offhandedness [ɒfˈhændɪdnɪs] N
1 (= *casualness*) • **the ~ with which he handled the matter** la forma tan a la ligera en la que trató el asunto
2 (= *cavalier manner*) displicencia *f*
office [ˈɒfɪs] N 1 (= *place*) oficina *f*; (= *room*) despacho *m*; [*of lawyer*] bufete *m*; (*US*) [*of doctor*] consultorio *m*
2 (= *part of organization*) sección *f*, departamento *m*; (= *ministry*) ministerio *m*; (= *branch*) sucursal *f*; ▹ **foreign, head**
3 (= *public position*) cargo *m*; (= *duty, function*) función *f* • **it is my ~ to** (+ *infin*) tengo el deber de (+ *infin*), me incumbe (+ *infin*) • **to perform the ~ of sb** hacer las veces de algn • **to be in/hold ~** [*person*] desempeñar *or* ocupar un cargo; [*political party*] ocupar el poder • **to be out of ~** no estar en el poder • **to come into** *or* **take ~** [*person*] tomar posesión del cargo (**as** de); [*political party*] acceder al poder • **to leave ~** [*person*] dejar el cargo; [*government*] salir del poder; ▹ **remove**
4 **offices** (*frm*) • **through his good ~s** mediante sus buenos oficios • **through the ~s of** por mediación *or* medio de
5 (*Rel*) oficio *m* • **Office for the Dead** oficio de difuntos
CPD de oficina ▸ **office automation** ofimática *f*, buromática *f* ▸ **office bearer** titular *mf* (de una cartera) ▸ **office block** (*Brit*) bloque *m* de oficinas ▸ **office boy** recadero *m*, mandadero *m* (*LAm*) ▸ **office building** = **office block** ▸ **office equipment** mobiliario *m* de oficina ▸ **office furniture** mobiliario *m* de oficina ▸ **office holder** funcionario/a *m/f* ▸ **office hours** (*Brit*) horas *fpl* de oficina; (*US*) horas *fpl* de consulta ▸ **office job** trabajo *m* de oficina ▸ **office junior** auxiliar *m/f* de oficina ▸ **office manager** gerente *mf* ▸ **Office of Fair Trading** (*Brit*) *departamento encargado de mantener las normas comerciales establecidas* ▸ **Office of Management and Budget** (*US*) *organismo encargado de elaborar el presupuesto del Estado* ▸ **office party** fiesta *f* de la oficina ▸ **office politics** intrigas *fpl* de oficina ▸ **office staff** personal *m* de oficina ▸ **office supplies** material *m* de oficina ▸ **office work** trabajo *m* de oficina ▸ **office worker** (*gen*) oficinista *mf*; (= *civil servant etc*) funcionario/a *m/f*
officer [ˈɒfɪsəʳ] N 1 (*Mil, Naut, Aer*) oficial *mf* • **an ~ and a gentleman** un oficial y un caballero
2 (= *official*) funcionario/a *m/f*; [*of company*] directivo(a) *m/f* • **the ~s of a company** los directivos *or* la junta directiva de una empresa
3 (= *police officer*) policía *mf*, agente *mf* de policía • **excuse me, ~** perdone agente
VT (= *command*) mandar; [+ *staff*] proveer de oficiales • **to be well ~ed** tener buena oficialidad
CPD ▸ **officer of the day** (*Mil*) oficial *mf* del día ▸ **officer of the watch** (*Naut*) oficial *mf* de guardia ▸ **officers' mess** comedor *m* de oficiales ▸ **Officer Training Corps** (*Brit*) *cuerpo del ejército británico que proporciona adiestramiento militar a estudiantes universitarios*
official [əˈfɪʃəl] ADJ oficial • **is that ~?** ¿es oficial?, ¿se ha confirmado eso oficialmente? • **it's ~: working mothers are stressed** está confirmado: las madres que trabajan están estresadas • **the phone was answered by an ~ sounding voice** una voz con un tono oficioso contestó el teléfono • **~ channels** conductos *mpl* *or* vías *fpl* oficiales • **to do sth through (the) ~ channels** hacer algo por los conductos *or* vías oficiales • **"for official use only"** "solo para uso oficial"
N (*in civil service*) funcionario/a *m/f*; (*elsewhere*) oficial *mf* • **government ~** funcionario/a *m/f* del estado • **trade union ~** representante *mf* sindical
CPD ▸ **official receiver** síndico *m* ▸ **Official Secrets Act** (*Brit*) *ley relativa a los secretos de Estado* ▸ **official strike** huelga *f* oficial
officialdom [əˈfɪʃəldəm] N (*pej*) burocracia *f*
officialese [əˌfɪʃəˈliːz] N (*pej*) jerga *f* burocrática
officially [əˈfɪʃəlɪ] ADV oficialmente
officiate [əˈfɪʃɪeɪt] VI oficiar • **to ~ as Mayor** ejercer las funciones de alcalde • **to ~ at a marriage** oficiar un enlace *or* una boda
officious [əˈfɪʃəs] ADJ oficioso
officiously [əˈfɪʃəslɪ] ADV oficiosamente
officiousness [əˈfɪʃəsnɪs] N oficiosidad *f*
offing [ˈɒfɪŋ] N • **to be in the ~** (*Naut*) haber a la vista; (*fig*) haber en perspectiva
offish* [ˈɒfɪʃ] ADJ distante
off-key [ɒfˈkiː] ADJ desafinado
ADV desentonadamente, fuera de tono
off-licence [ˈɒfˌlaɪsəns] N (*Brit*) (= *shop*) bodega *f*, tienda *f* de licores (*LAm*)
off-limits [ɒfˈlɪmɪts] ADJ 1 (*US*) (*Mil*) prohibido, de acceso prohibido
2 (*fig*) [*activity, substance*] prohibido
offline [ɒfˈlaɪn] ADJ (*Comput*) off-line, fuera de línea; (= *switched off*) desconectado
ADV fuera de línea, off-line
offload [ˈɒfləʊd] VT 1 [+ *goods*] descargar; [+ *passengers*] desembarcar, hacer bajar
2 (= *get rid of*) librarse de
off-message [ˈɒfˌmesɪdʒ] ADJ descentrado en cuanto al mensaje • **to be off-message** no centrarse en el mensaje adecuado, transmitir el mensaje erróneo
off-peak [ɒfˈpiːk] ADJ (*gen*) fuera de las horas punta (*Sp*), fuera de las horas pico (*LAm*); [*tickets*] de menor demanda; [*holiday*] de temporada baja; [*times*] de tarifa reducida, valle (*inv*); [*rate*] reducido, valle (*inv*)
ADV (*gen*) fuera de las horas punta, en horario de tarifa reducida; [*travel, have holiday*] en temporada baja; [*telephone, consume electricity*] en horas de menor consumo, en horario de tarifa reducida
off-piste [ɒfˈpiːst] ADJ, ADV fuera de pista
offprint [ˈɒfprɪnt] N separata *f*, tirada *f* aparte
off-putting [ˈɒfˌpʊtɪŋ] ADJ (= *dispiriting*) desalentador; (= *unpleasant*) [*taste, smell etc*] desagradable; [*behaviour*] desagradable, chocante; (= *unfriendly*) [*person*] difícil, poco amable; [*reception*] nada amistoso • **it's very off-putting to see him do that** es muy desagradable verlo hacer eso
off-ramp [ˈɒfræmp] N (*US*) (= *on freeway*) carril *m* de salida
off-road [ˈɒfrəʊd] ADJ [*driving, racing*] todoterreno
CPD ▸ **off-road vehicle** vehículo *m* todoterreno
off-roader* [ˈɒfrəʊdəʳ] N todoterreno *m*
off-roading [ˌɒfˈrəʊdɪŋ] N offroad *m*
off-sales [ˈɒfseɪlz] (*Brit*) N (= *shop*) tienda *f* de bebidas alcohólicas
NPL (= *sales of alcohol*) venta *f* de bebidas alcohólicas para llevar
off-screen [ˈɒfskriːn] (*Cine, TV*) ADJ real, en la vida privada
ADV fuera de la pantalla, en la vida privada
off-season [ˈɒfˌsiːzn] N temporada *f* baja • **I take my holidays (in the) off-season** me voy de vacaciones en temporada baja
ADJ [*rates, prices*] de temporada baja
ADV [*travel, have holiday*] en temporada baja
offset [ˈɒfset] (VB: PT, PP: **offset**) N
1 (= *counterbalancing factor*) compensación *f*
2 (*Typ*) offset *m*
3 (*Hort*) (= *layer*) acodo *m*; (= *bulb*) bulbo *m* reproductor
4 (*Archit*) retallo *m*
VT 1 (= *compensate for*) compensar • **higher prices will be ~ by wage increases** los aumentos de precios serán compensados por incrementos salariales
2 (= *counteract*) contrarrestar, contrapesar • **to ~ A against B** contrapesar A y B
CPD ▸ **offset lithography** = **offset printing** ▸ **offset press** prensa *f* offset ▸ **offset printing** impresión *f* con offset
offshoot [ˈɒfʃuːt] N (*Bot*) vástago *m*; (*Comm*) rama *f*; (*fig*) ramificación *f*
offshore [ˌɒfˈʃɔːʳ] ADJ 1 (= *near the shore*) [*island*] cercano a la costa, del litoral; [*waters*] de la costa, del litoral • **~ fishing** pesca *f* de bajura
2 (= *out at sea*) [*rig, platform, drilling*] off-shore

(adj inv), costa afuera; *[well]* submarino • **~ oil** petróleo *m* de costa afuera • **~ oilfield** campo *m* petrolífero submarino
3 (= *from land*) *[breeze]* que sopla de la tierra, terral
4 (*Econ*) *[account, fund]* en un paraíso fiscal/en paraísos fiscales, offshore *(inv)* (*Tech*) • **he has an ~ account** tiene una cuenta en un paraíso fiscal, tiene una cuenta offshore (*Tech*) • **people with ~ accounts** la gente con cuentas en paraísos fiscales, la gente con cuentas offshore (*Tech*) • **~ banking** operaciones *fpl* bancarias en paraísos fiscales • **~ investments** inversiones *fpl* en paraísos fiscales
(ADV) **1** (= *near the coast*) *[lie, anchor, fish]* cerca de la costa • **they were just ~** estaban en las inmediaciones de la costa
2 (= *out at sea*) *[drill]* off-shore, costa afuera
3 (= *away from the shore*) • **the current carried him ~** la corriente lo alejaba de la costa *or* hacia el interior del mar • **they were rescued 20 miles ~** los rescataron a 20 millas de la costa
4 (*Econ*) *[invest]* en un paraíso fiscal/en paraísos fiscales • **people who invest ~** la gente que invierte en paraísos fiscales

offside [ˌɒfˈsaɪd] (ADJ) **1** (*Sport*) *[player, goal]* en fuera de juego • **to be ~** estar fuera de juego, estar orsay *or* offside • **in an ~ position** fuera de juego • **the ~ rule** la regla de fuera de juego • **the ~ trap** la trampa de fuera de juego
2 (*Aut*) *[door, verge, lane]* (= *left-hand*) del lado izquierdo, del lado del conductor; (*Brit*) (= *right-hand*) del lado derecho, del lado del conductor
(ADV) (*Sport*) en fuera de juego • **Wallace was caught ~** cogieron a Wallace en fuera de juego
(N) **1** (*Ftbl*) fuera de juego *m*, orsay *m*, offside *m*
2 (*Aut*) (= *left-hand*) lado *m* izquierdo, lado del conductor; (*Brit*) (= *right-hand*) lado *m* derecho, lado *m* del conductor
(EXCL) ¡fuera de juego!, ¡orsay!, ¡offside!

offspring [ˈɒfsprɪŋ] (N) *(pl inv)* descendencia *f*, prole* *f* • **to die without ~** morir sin dejar descendencia

offstage [ˌɒfˈsteɪdʒ] (ADJ) de entre bastidores
(ADV) entre bastidores, fuera del escenario

off-street parking [ˌɒfstriːtˈpɑːkɪŋ] (N) aparcamiento *m or* estacionamiento *m* fuera de la vía pública

off-the-cuff [ˌɒfðəˈkʌf] (ADJ) *[remark]* espontáneo, dicho sin pensar; *[speech]* improvisado
(ADV) de improviso

off-the-job training [ˌɒfðədʒɒbˈtreɪnɪŋ] (N) formación *f* fuera del trabajo

off-the-peg [ˌɒfðəˈpeg], **off-the-rack** (*US*) [ˈɒfðəˈræk] (ADJ) confeccionado, de percha

off-the-record [ˌɒfðəˈrekɔd] (ADJ) no oficial, extraoficial

off-the-wall* [ˌɒfðəˈwɔːl] (ADJ) *[idea etc]* disparatado

off-white [ˌɒfˈwaɪt] (ADJ) de color hueso *(adj inv)*, blanquecino

Ofgas [ˈɒfgæs] (N ABBR) (*Brit*) (= **Office of Gas Supply**) *organismo que controla a las empresas del gas en Gran Bretaña*

Oflot [ˈɒflɒt] (N ABBR) (*Brit*) (= **Office of the National Lottery**) *organismo regulador de la lotería nacional en Gran Bretaña*, ≈ Organismo Nacional de Loterías y Apuestas del Estado, ≈ ONLAE *m* (*Sp*)

Ofsted [ˈɒfsted] (N ABBR) (= **Office for Standards in Education**) (*Brit*) *organismo regulador de los centros escolares*

OFT (N ABBR) (*Brit*) = **Office of Fair Trading**

oft [ɒft] (ADV) (*poet*) = **often** • **many a time and oft** repetidas veces

Oftel [ˈɒftel] (N ABBR) (*Brit*) (= **Office of Telecommunications**) *organismo que controla a las telecomunicaciones británicas*

often [ˈɒfən] (ADV) a menudo, con frecuencia, seguido (*LAm*) • **I've ~ wondered why you turned the job down** me he preguntado muchas veces *or* a menudo *or* con frecuencia por qué no aceptaste el trabajo • **it's not ~ that I ask you to help me** no es frecuente que te pida ayuda • **we ~ meet here** solemos reunirnos aquí • **do you ~ argue?** ¿discutís mucho?, ¿discutís muy a menudo? • **we visit her as ~ as possible** la visitamos tanto como nos es posible • **twice as ~ as** dos veces más que • **women consult doctors twice as ~ as men** las mujeres consultan a un médico dos veces más que los hombres • **as ~ as not** la mitad de las veces • **every so ~** (*of time*) de vez en cuando; (*of distance, spacing*) de trecho en trecho, cada cierta distancia • **we see each other every so ~** nos vemos de vez en cuando, nos vemos alguna que otra vez • **how ~?** (= *how many times*) ¿con qué frecuencia?; (= *at what intervals*) ¿cada cuánto? • **how ~ do you see him?** ¿cada cuánto lo ves?, ¿con qué *or* cuánta frecuencia lo ves? • **how ~ have I warned you that this would happen?** ¿cuántas veces te he advertido de que iba a pasar esto? • **how ~ she had asked herself that very question!** ¡cuántas veces se había hecho esa misma pregunta! • **he saw her less ~ now that she had a job** la veía con menos frecuencia ahora que tenía un trabajo • **more ~ than not** la mayoría de las veces, las más de las veces • **he's read it so ~ he knows it off by heart** lo ha leído tantas veces que se lo sabe de memoria • **(all) too ~** con demasiada frecuencia, demasiado a menudo, demasiadas veces • **you've been drunk on duty once too ~** ha estado borracho una y otra vez estando de servicio • **very ~** muchísimas veces, muy a menudo

OFTEN

In statements

▷ *When* **often** *means "on many occasions", you can usually translate it using* **con frecuencia** *or* **a menudo**:
He often came to my house
Venía con frecuencia *or* a menudo a mi casa
She doesn't often get angry
No se enfada con frecuencia *or* a menudo
You are late too often
Llegas tarde con demasiada frecuencia *or* demasiado a menudo

▷ *In informal contexts, particularly when* **often** *can be substituted by* **a lot** *or* **much** *with no change of meaning,* **mucho** *is an alternative translation:*
He doesn't often come to see me
No viene mucho a verme
He often hangs out in this bar
Para mucho en este bar

▷ **Muchas veces** *is another possible translation, but it should be used with the present only if the time, place or activity is restricted in some way:*
I've often heard him talk about the need for this law
Le he oído muchas veces hablar de la necesidad de esta ley
It can often be difficult to discuss this subject with one's partner
Muchas veces es difícil hablar con la pareja sobre este tema

▷ *When* **often** *describes a predictable, habitual or regular action, you can often translate it using the present or imperfect of* **soler** *as applicable:*
In England it is often cold in winter
En Inglaterra suele hacer frío en invierno
I often have a glass of sherry before dinner
Suelo tomar un jerez antes de cenar
We often went out for a walk in the evening
Solíamos salir por la tarde a dar un paseo

▷ *Use* **soler** *also when* **often** *means "in many cases":*
This heart condition is often very serious
Esta enfermedad cardíaca suele ser muy grave

In questions

▷ *You can usually use* **con frecuencia** *in questions, though there are other possibilities:*
How often do you go to Madrid?
¿Con qué frecuencia vas a Madrid?
Do you often go to Spain?
¿Vas a España con frecuencia?, ¿Vas a menudo *or* mucho a España?

For further uses and examples, see main entry.

oftentimes [ˈɒfəntaɪmz] (ADV) (*US*) (= *often*) a menudo, con frecuencia

oft-times [ˈɒftaɪmz] (ADV) (*liter*) a menudo

Ofwat [ˈɒfwɒt] (*Brit*) (N ABBR) (= **Office of Water Services**) *organismo que controla a las empresas suministradores de agua en Inglaterra y Gales*

ogival [əʊˈdʒaɪvəl] (ADJ) ojival

ogive [ˈəʊdʒaɪv] (N) ojiva *f*

ogle [ˈəʊgl] (VT) comerse con los ojos
▸ **ogle at** (VI + PREP) • **to ~ at sb** comerse a algn con los ojos

O-grade [ˈəʊgreɪd] (N ABBR) (*Scot*) (*Scol*) (= **Ordinary grade**) ≈ BUP *m*

ogre [ˈəʊgəʳ] (N) ogro *m*

OH (ABBR) (*US*) = **Ohio**

oh [əʊ] (EXCL) **1** (*gen*) ¡ah! • **oh is he?** ¿en serio? • **oh dear, I've spilt the milk!** ¡ay, se me ha caído la leche! • **oh for a horse!** ¡quién tuviera un caballo! • **oh good!** ¡qué bien! • **oh no you don't!** ¡eso sí que no!, ¡de eso nada! • **oh really?** ¿no me digas?, ¿de veras? • **oh really!** ¡no puede ser! • **oh to be in Paris!** ¡ojalá estuviera en París! • **oh what a surprise!** ¡qué sorpresa! • **oh yes?** ¿ah sí?
2 (= *cry of pain*) ¡ay!
3 (*vocative*) • **oh king!** ¡oh rey!

ohm [əʊm] (N) ohmio *m*, ohm *m*

OHMS (ABBR) (*Brit*) = **On Her** *or* **His Majesty's Service**

OHP (N ABBR) (= **overhead projector**) retroproyector *m*

oi* [ˈɔɪ] (EXCL) (*Brit*) ¡eh!

oik* [ɔɪk] (N) (*Brit*) palurdo *m*, patán *m*

oil [ɔɪl] (N) **1** (*also Aut*) aceite *m*; (= *holy oil*) crisma *f*, santo óleo *m* • **to check the oil** (*Aut etc*) revisar el nivel del aceite • IDIOMS: • **to pour oil on troubled waters** calmar los ánimos • **to pour oil on the flames** echar más leña al fuego; ▹ **midnight**
2 (*Geol*) (*as mineral*) petróleo *m* • **to strike oil** encontrar petróleo; (*fig*) encontrar un filón
3 (*Art*) óleo *m* • **an oil by Rembrandt** un óleo de Rembrandt • **to paint in oils** pintar al óleo

(VT) lubricar, engrasar • IDIOMS: • **to oil the wheels** allanar el terreno • **to be well oiled*** ir a la vela*
(CPD) ▸ **oil change** (*Aut*) cambio *m* de aceite ▸ **oil colours** (*Art*) óleos *mpl* ▸ **oil deposits** (*Geol*) yacimientos *mpl* de petróleo ▸ **oil embargo** embargo *m* petrolífero ▸ **oil filter** (*Aut*) filtro *m* de aceite ▸ **oil gauge** (*Aut*) indicador *m* de(l) aceite ▸ **oil industry** industria *f* del petróleo ▸ **oil lamp** lámpara *f* de aceite, quinqué *m* ▸ **oil level** nivel *m* del aceite ▸ **oil paint** (*Art*) óleo *m*, pintura *f* al óleo ▸ **oil painting** (*Art*) pintura *f* al óleo • **she's no oil painting*** no es ninguna belleza ▸ **oil pipeline** oleoducto *m* ▸ **oil platform** plataforma *f* petrolífera ▸ **oil pollution** contaminación *f* petrolífera ▸ **oil pressure** (*Aut*) presión *f* del aceite ▸ **oil refinery** refinería *f* de petróleo ▸ **oil rig** torre *f* de perforación; (*Naut*) plataforma *f* de perforación submarina ▸ **oil slick** (*large*) marea *f* negra; (*small*) mancha *f* de petróleo, capa *f* de petróleo (en el agua) ▸ **oil spill** (= *act*) fuga *f* de petróleo; (= *substance*) = **oil slick** ▸ **oil stove** (*for cooking*) cocina *f* de petróleo; (*for heating*) estufa *f* de petróleo ▸ **oil tanker** petrolero *m* ▸ **oil terminal** terminal *f* petrolífera ▸ **oil well** pozo *m* de petróleo

oil-based ['ɔɪlbeɪst] (ADJ) [*product*] derivado del petróleo

oil-burning ['ɔɪl,bɜːnɪŋ] (ADJ) (alimentado) al petróleo, de petróleo

oilcake ['ɔɪlkeɪk] (N) torta *f* de borujo, torta *f* de linaza

oilcan ['ɔɪlkæn] (N) aceitera *f*

oilcloth ['ɔɪlklɒθ] (N) hule *m*, encerado *m*

oildrum ['ɔɪldrʌm] (N) bidón *m* de aceite

oiler ['ɔɪləʳ] (N) **1** (= *ship*) petrolero *m*; (= *can*) lata *f* de aceite, lata *f* de lubricante; (= *person*) engrasador(a) *m/f*
2 oilers (*US*) (= *clothes*) hule *m*

oilfield ['ɔɪlfiːld] (N) yacimiento *m* petrolífero

oil-fired ['ɔɪlfaɪəd] (ADJ) de fuel-oil
(CPD) ▸ **oil-fired central heating** calefacción *f* central al petróleo ▸ **oil-fired power-station** central *f* térmica de fuel

oiliness ['ɔɪlɪnɪs] (N) **1** (= *greasiness*) [*of food*] lo aceitoso, lo grasiento; [*of skin, hair*] lo grasiento, lo graso; [*of substance*] oleaginosidad *f*
2 (*pej*) [*of manners, tone*] zalamería *f*, lo empalagoso

oilman ['ɔɪlmæn] (N) (PL: **oilmen**) (= *worker*) petrolero *m*; (= *magnate*) magnate *m* del petróleo

oilpan ['ɔɪlpæn] (N) (*US*) (*Aut*) cárter *m*

oilseed rape [,ɔɪlsiːd'reɪp] (N) (*Brit*) colza *f*

oilskin ['ɔɪlskɪn] (N) **1** (= *oilcloth*) hule *m*, encerado *m*
2 oilskins (*Brit*) (= *clothes*) chubasquero *m*, impermeable *m*

oily ['ɔɪlɪ] (ADJ) (COMPAR: **oilier**, SUPERL: **oiliest**) **1** (= *greasy*) [*food*] aceitoso, grasiento, grasoso (*LAm*); [*hands, rag*] grasiento, lleno de aceite; [*skin, hair*] graso, grasoso (*LAm*); [*road, beach*] lleno de aceite; [*substance, liquid*] oleaginoso
2 (= *smarmy*) [*person, voice*] zalamero, empalagoso
(CPD) ▸ **oily fish** (*Culin*) pescado *m* azul

oink [ɔɪŋk] (VI) gruñir
(EXCL) ¡oink!

ointment ['ɔɪntmənt] (N) ungüento *m*, pomada *f*

o.j. (N ABBR) (*esp US*) (= **orange juice**) zumo *m* de naranja (*Sp*), jugo *m* de naranja (*LAm*)

OJT (N ABBR) (*US*) (= **on-the-job training**) aprendizaje *m* en el trabajo

OK¹* ['əʊ'keɪ] (EXCL) (= *all right*) ¡está bien!, ¡okey! (*LAm*); (= *yes*) ¡sí!; (= *understood*) ¡comprendo!; (= *I agree*) ¡vale!; (= *enough*) ¡basta ya!, ¡ya estuvo bueno! (*LAm*) • **OK, OK!** ¡vale, vale!, ¡ya, ya! • **OK, the next item on the agenda is ...** bueno, el siguiente punto en el orden del día es ...
(ADJ) **1** (= *undamaged, in good health*) bien • **is the car OK?** ¿anda bien el coche?
2 (= *agreed*) • **it's OK with** *or* **by me** yo estoy de acuerdo, por mí vale • **is it OK with you if ...?** ¿te importa si ...?, ¿te molesta que ...? • **OK it's difficult, but ...** estoy de acuerdo que es difícil pero ... • **I'm coming too, OK?** vengo yo también, ¿vale *or* (*LAm*) okey?
3 (= *acceptable*) • **that may have been OK last year** eso puede haber estado bien el año pasado
4 (= *well provided for*) • **are you OK for money/time?** ¿andas *or* (*esp LAm*) vas bien de dinero/tiempo? • **"do you want another drink?" — "I'm OK, thanks"** —¿te apetece otro trago? —no quiero más, gracias
5 (= *likeable*) • **he's OK** • **he's an OK guy** es un buen tipo*, es un tío majo (*Sp**)
(ADV) • **he's doing OK** las cosas le van bien
(N) visto *m* bueno • **to give sth the OK** dar el visto bueno a algo, aprobar algo
(VT) dar el visto bueno a, aprobar

OK² (ABBR) (*US*) = **Oklahoma**

okapi [əʊ'kɑːpɪ] (N) (PL: **okapis** *or* **okapi**) okapi *m*

okay* [əʊ'keɪ] = **OK**¹

okey-doke‡ [,əʊkɪ'dəʊk], **okey-dokey‡** [,əʊkɪ'dəʊkɪ] (EXCL) bueno, vale*

Okla (ABBR) (*US*) = **Oklahoma**

okra ['əʊkrə] (N) kimbombó *m*

ol'* [əʊl] (ADJ) (*esp US*) = **old**

old [əʊld] (ADJ) (COMPAR: **older**, SUPERL: **oldest**) **1** (= *not young*) [*person*] viejo; (*more respectful*) mayor, anciano; [*animal*] viejo; [*civilization*] antiguo • **an old man** un viejo, un anciano • **an old woman** una vieja, una anciana • **he's a bit of an old woman** es un poco Doña Remilgos • **an old lady** una señora mayor *or* anciana • **a little old lady** una viejecita, una ancianita • **old people** • **old folks*** los viejos; (*more respectful*) los ancianos, las personas mayores • **to live to be old** llegar a una edad avanzada • **if I live to be that old** si llego a esa edad • **to be old before one's time** hacerse mayor antes de tiempo • **to be old beyond one's years** ser maduro para la edad que se tiene • **he's old for his age** *or* **for his years** [*child*] es muy maduro para su edad • **that dress is too old for you** ese vestido es para alguien mayor que tú, ese vestido no es apropiado para tu edad • **to get** *or* **grow old** envejecer • **he's afraid of getting** *or* **growing old** tiene miedo a envejecer • **he's getting old** se está haciendo viejo • **to get older** envejecer • **as we get older ...** según envejecemos ... • **to look old** parecer viejo, estar avejentado • **she's not as old as she looks** no es tan vieja como parece • IDIOMS: • **as old as Methuselah** más viejo que Matusalén • **he/she has an old head on young shoulders** es maduro/a para su edad; ▹ **dirty, fogey, fool, teach**
2 (*relating to ages*) • **how old are you?** ¿cuántos años tienes?, ¿qué edad tienes? • **Laura is six weeks/months/years old** Laura tiene seis semanas/meses/años • **she's three years old today** hoy cumple tres años • **he'll be six weeks old tomorrow** cumplirá seis semanas mañana • **a six-week-old baby** un niño de seis semanas • **a five-year-old (child)** un niño de cinco años • **the building is 300 years old** el edificio tiene 300 años • **the company is a century old** la compañía existe desde hace un siglo • **at ten months old she was already walking** cuando tenía diez meses ya andaba • **she is two years older than you** tiene dos años más que tú • **you'll understand when you are older** cuando seas mayor lo entenderás • **when you are older it's harder to change jobs** cuando eres mayor es más difícil cambiar de trabajo • **their oldest child** su hijo mayor • **she is the oldest** es la mayor • **she is the oldest teacher in the school** es la profesora de más edad del colegio • **to be old enough for sth/to do sth** tener edad para algo/para hacer algo • **she's old enough to go alone** ya tiene edad para ir sola • **he's old enough to know better** (*to have more sense*) a su edad debería tener más sentido común, ya es mayorcito para saber lo que está bien y lo que está mal; (*to behave better*) a su edad debería portarse mejor • **she's old enough to be your mother** con la edad que tiene, podría ser tu madre • **you're as old as you feel** eres tan viejo como te sientes; ▹ **generation**
3 (= *not new*) **a** (= *antique*) [*painting, book, building*] antiguo; [*wine*] añejo • **the old part of Glasgow** la parte vieja *or* antigua de Glasgow • IDIOMS: • **to be as old as the hills** • **be as old as Adam** ser de tiempos de Maricastaña, ser más viejo que el mundo; ▹ **chip**
b [*clothes, furniture*] (= *tatty*) viejo; (= *worn*) usado, gastado • **it's too old to be any use** es demasiado viejo para servir de algo
4 (= *long-standing*) viejo • **he's an old friend of mine** es un viejo amigo mío • **that's an old problem** eso no es nada nuevo, eso ya viene de atrás • **it's a very old tradition/custom** es una vieja tradición/costumbre, es una tradición/costumbre antigua • **the old ways survived in some country areas** las viejas costumbres perduraron en algunas partes del campo • **an old family** una familia de abolengo; ▹ **score**
5 (= *former*) antiguo • **my old flat was very small** mi antiguo piso era muy pequeño • **the old country** la madre patria, la patria • **in the old days** antaño, en los viejos tiempos • **the good old days** los viejos tiempos • **it's not as good as our old one** no es tan bueno como el anterior • **my old school** mi antiguo *or* viejo colegio • **of the old school** (*fig*) de la vieja escuela • **for old times' sake** por los viejos tiempos
6* (*expressing affection*) • **here's old Peter coming** ahí viene el bueno de Peter • **good old Mike!** ¡este Mike! • **come on, old man!**† ¡venga hombre! • **she's a funny old thing** es rarita • **my** *or* **the old lady** *or* **woman** (= *mother*) mi *or* la vieja‡; (= *wife*) la parienta* • **my** *or* **the old man** (= *father*) mi *or* el viejo‡; (= *husband*) mi marido
7* (*as intensifier*) • **what a load of old rubbish!** ¡qué cantidad de chorradas!* • **any old**: • **any old thing will do** cualquier cosa sirve • **it's not just any old painting, it's a Rembrandt** no es un cuadro cualquiera, es un Rembrandt • **just put it any old where** ponlo en cualquier parte • **he leaves his things any old how** deja sus cosas de cualquier manera • **I parked the car any old how** aparqué el coche de cualquier manera • **we had a high old time** hacía tiempo que no nos divertíamos tanto • **it's the same old story** es la misma historia de siempre
(N) **1** • **the old** los viejos *mpl*, los ancianos *mpl* • **their music appeals to old and young alike** su música gusta tanto a jóvenes como a viejos • **the circus appeals to old and young**

alike el circo gusta igualmente a grandes y pequeños

2 (*liter*) • **of old: to know sb of old** conocer a algn desde hace tiempo • **knights/legends of old** los caballeros/las leyendas de antaño (*liter*) • **in days of old** antaño (*liter*), en los tiempos antiguos

(CPD) ▸ **old age** vejez *f* • **in one's old age** en la vejez • **perhaps I'm going soft in my old age** quizá me estoy ablandando al hacerme viejo *or* en la vejez • **he is unable to travel much because of old age** no puede viajar mucho debido a su edad; ▹ **ripe** ▸ **old age pension** subsidio *m* de la tercera edad, pensión *f* ▸ **old age pensioner** pensionista *mf*, jubilado/a *m/f* ▸ **the Old Bailey** (*Brit*) *el tribunal de lo penal de más alto rango de Inglaterra* ▸ **the Old Bill‡** (*Brit*) la poli*, la pasma (*Sp‡*) ▸ **old boy** (= *former pupil*) ex-alumno *m*, antiguo alumno *m*†;* (= *old chap*) amigo *m* mío • **the old-boy network** (*esp pej*) el amiguismo ▸ **the old brigade** los veteranos ▸ **old campaigner** veterano *m* ▸ **old chestnut*** (= *joke*) broma *f* muy pasada; (= *story*) historia *f* muy pasada ▸ **Old Dominion** (*US*) *el estado de Virginia* ▸ **Old English** inglés *m* antiguo; ▹ **ANGLO-SAXON** ▸ **Old English sheepdog** perro *m* pastor ovejero inglés ▸ **old flame** antiguo amor *m* ▸ **old folks' home** residencia *f* de ancianos ▸ **old girl** (= *former pupil*) ex-alumna *f*, antigua alumna *f*; (= *elderly woman*) (*†) señora *f*, abuelita* *f* ▸ **Old Glory** (*US*) *bandera de los Estados Unidos* ▸ **old gold** oro *m* viejo ▸ **the old guard** la vieja guardia ▸ **old hand** veterano/a *m/f* • **he's an old hand at photography** es un veterano de la fotografía ▸ **old lag*** (= *old prisoner*) (preso/a *m/f*) veterano/a *m/f*; (= *ex-prisoner*) ex-presidiario/a *m/f* ▸ **old maid** (*pej*) solterona *f* • **she'll end up an old maid** se quedará para vestir santos ▸ **Old Man River** (*US*) *el río Mississippi* ▸ **old master** (= *work*) obra *f* maestra de la pintura clásica; (= *painter*) gran maestro *m* de la pintura clásica ▸ **old money** dinero *m* de familia ▸ **Old Nick*** (*hum*) Pedro Botero* (*hum*) ▸ **old people's home** residencia *f* de ancianos ▸ **old salt** (*Naut*) viejo lobo *m* de mar ▸ **old school tie** (*Brit*) (*lit*) *corbata con los colores representativos de la escuela a la que alguien ha asistido* • **the old school tie** (*fig*) el amiguismo ▸ **old soldier** veterano *m*, excombatiente *m* ▸ **the Old South** (*US*) el viejo sur ▸ **old stager** veterano/a *m/f* ▸ **Old Testament** Antiguo Testamento *m* ▸ **old wives' tale** cuento *m* de viejas, patraña *f* ▸ **the Old World** el Viejo Mundo, el Viejo Continente; ▹ **old-world**

> **OLD**
>
> **Position of "viejo" and "antiguo"**
>
> **Viejo** *and* **antiguo** *can go either before or after the noun, depending on their meaning.*
>
> **Viejo**
>
> ▹ *Put* **viejo** *after the noun when you are referring to age:*
>
> **... boxes full of old clothes ...**
> ... cajas llenas de ropa vieja ...
> **Old cars are the ones that pollute the environment most**
> Son los coches viejos los que más contaminan el medio ambiente
>
> ▹ *Put* **viejo** *before the noun when you mean* **old** *in the sense of "long-standing" or "well-established":*
>
> **They got in touch with an old friend**
> Se pusieron en contacto con un viejo amigo
> **Many of the old customs have changed with the passing of time**
> Muchas de las viejas costumbres han cambiado con el paso del tiempo
>
> **Antiguo**
>
> ▹ *Generally put* **antiguo** *after the noun to translate* **ancient** *or* **old** *in the sense of "ancient":*
>
> **... one of Canada's most beautiful old houses ...**
> ... una de las más bellas casas antiguas de Canadá ...
> **... the old part of the town ...**
> ... el barrio antiguo de la ciudad ...
>
> ▹ *Put* **antiguo** *before the noun to translate* **former** *or* **old** *in the sense of "former":*
>
> **My old colleagues are no longer my friends**
> Mis antiguos compañeros ya no son mis amigos
> **... the former British colonies ...**
> ... las antiguas colonias británicas ...
>
> *For further uses and examples, see main entry.*

olden [ˈəʊldən] (ADJ) (*liter*) antiguo • **in ~ times** *or* **days** antaño (*liter*), antiguamente

old-established [ˈəʊldɪˈstæblɪʃt] (ADJ) antiguo

olde-worlde [ˈəʊldɪˈwɜːldɪ] (ADJ) (*hum*) viejísimo, antiquísimo • **with olde-worlde lettering** con letras al estilo antiguo • **a very olde-worlde interior** un interior pintoresco de antaño • **Stratford is terribly olde-worlde** Stratford tiene sabor arcaico en exceso

old-fashioned [ˈəʊldˈfæʃnd] (ADJ)
1 (= *outmoded*) [*thing*] anticuado, pasado de moda; [*person, attitude*] anticuado, chapado a la antigua • **good old-fashioned honesty** la honestidad de toda la vida
2 (*Brit*†) (= *disapproving*) • **to give sb an old-fashioned look** mirar a algn con extrañeza

oldie* [ˈəʊldɪ] (N) **1** (= *song*) melodía *f* del ayer; (= *joke*) chiste *m* anticuado
2 (*Brit*) (= *old person*) vejete/a *m/f*

oldish [ˈəʊldɪʃ] (ADJ) algo viejo, más bien viejo, que va para viejo

old-looking [ˈəʊld,lʊkɪŋ] (ADJ) de aspecto viejo

old-maidish [ˈəʊldˈmeɪdɪʃ] (ADJ) (= *spinsterish*) de solterona; (= *fussy*) remilgado

oldster [ˈəʊldstəʳ] (N) (*US*) viejo/a *m/f*, anciano/a *m/f*

old-style [ˈəʊldˈstaɪl] (ADJ) antiguo, al estilo antiguo, a la antigua • **old-style calendar** calendario *m* juliano

old-time [ˈəʊldtaɪm] (ADJ) de antaño
(CPD) ▸ **old-time dancing** baile *m* antiguo, baile *m* de antaño

old-timer [,əʊldˈtaɪməʳ] (N) veterano/a *m/f*; (*US**) (= *old person*) viejo/a *m/f*, anciano/a *m/f*

old-world [ˈəʊldˈwɜːld] (ADJ) **1** (= *traditional*) antiguo; [*style*] clásico; [*manners*] anticuado • **the old-world charm of Toledo** el sabor antiguo *or* arcaico de Toledo
2 (*Geog*) del Viejo Mundo; ▹ **old**

OLE (N ABBR) (*Comput*) = **object linking and embedding**

oleaginous [əʊlɪˈædʒɪnəs] (ADJ) oleaginoso

oleander [,əʊlɪˈændəʳ] (N) adelfa *f*

oleo... [ˈəʊlɪəʊ] (PREFIX) oleo...

O-level [ˈəʊ,levl] (N) (*Brit*) (*Scol*) (*formerly*) (= **Ordinary level**) ≈ BUP *m*

olfactory [ɒlˈfæktərɪ] (ADJ) olfativo, olfatorio

oligarchic [,ɒlɪˈɡɑːkɪk] (ADJ) oligárquico

oligarchical [,ɒlɪˈɡɑːkɪkəl] (ADJ) = **oligarchic**

oligarchy [ˈɒlɪɡɑːkɪ] (N) oligarquía *f*

oligo... [ˈɒlɪɡəʊ] (PREFIX) oligo...

Oligocene [ˈɒlɪɡəʊsiːn] (ADJ) oligocénico
(N) • **the ~** el Oligoceno

oligopoly [,ɒlɪˈɡɒpəlɪ] (N) oligopolio *m*

oligopsony [,ɒlɪˈɡɒpsənɪ] (N) oligopsonio *m*

olive [ˈɒlɪv] (N) (= *fruit*) aceituna *f*, oliva *f*; (*also* **olive tree**) olivo *m* • **eating ~** aceituna *f* de mesa
(ADJ) (*also* **olive-green**) [*complexion, skin*] [*shirt, paint*] verde oliva (*inv*)
(CPD) ▸ **olive branch** rama *f* de olivo • **IDIOM**: • **to hold out an ~ branch** hacer un gesto de paz ▸ **olive green** verde *m* oliva ▸ **olive grove** olivar *m* ▸ **olive grower** oleicultor(a) *m/f* ▸ **olive growing** oleicultura *f*; ▹ **olive-growing** ▸ **olive oil** aceite *m* de oliva ▸ **olive tree** olivo *m*

olive-green [ˈɒlɪvˈɡriːn] (ADJ) verde oliva • **olive-green uniforms** uniformes *mpl* verde oliva

olive-growing [ˈɒlɪv,ɡrəʊɪŋ] (ADJ) • **olive-growing region** región *f* olivera; ▹ **olive**

Oliver [ˈɒlɪvəʳ] (N) Oliverio

Olympia [əˈlɪmpɪə] (N) Olimpia *f*

Olympiad [əʊˈlɪmpɪæd] (N) olimpíada *f*

Olympian [əʊˈlɪmpɪən] (ADJ) olímpico
(N) (*Sport*) olímpico/a *m/f*

Olympic [əʊˈlɪmpɪk] (ADJ) olímpico
(N) • **the ~s** las Olimpiadas
(CPD) ▸ **the Olympic Games** las Olimpiadas ▸ **Olympic medallist** medallero/a *m/f* olímpico/a ▸ **Olympic torch** antorcha *f* olímpica

Olympus [əʊˈlɪmpəs] (N) Olimpo *m*

OM (N ABBR) (*Brit*) (= **Order of Merit**) *título ceremonial*

Oman [əʊˈmɑːn] (N) Omán *m*

Omani [əʊˈmɑːnɪ] (ADJ) omaní
(N) omaní *mf*

OMB (N ABBR) (*US*) (= **Office of Management and Budget**) *servicio que asesora al presidente en materia presupuestaria*

ombudsman [ˈɒmbʊdzmən] (N) (PL: **ombudsmen**) ≈ defensor *m* del pueblo

> **OMBUDSMAN**
>
> Se conoce con el nombre de **ombudsman** al funcionario encargado de investigar las quejas de los ciudadanos contra una institución determinada. En el Reino Unido, el **ombudsman** que se ocupa de los casos de administración fraudulenta en los ministerios del gobierno, el **NHS** y otros organismos institucionales es el **Parliamentary Commissioner for Administration**. Su jurisdicción se limita al área administrativa del gobierno, pero no afecta a su política o legislación. Otros **ombudsmen** se nombran para estudiar las quejas que provienen de los clientes de instituciones financieras, como por ejemplo el **Financial Ombudsman**, el **Building Societies Ombudsman** o el **Insurance Ombudsman**. En Estados Unidos, los **ombudsmen** llevan a cabo labores similares de investigación de instituciones, tanto en el sector público como en el privado.

omega [ˈəʊmɪɡə] (N) omega *f*

omelette, omelet (*esp US*) [ˈɒmlɪt] (N) tortilla *f* francesa, torta *f* de huevos (*Mex*) • **PROVERB**: • **you can't make an ~ without breaking eggs** no se puede hacer tortillas sin romper huevos

CPD ▸ **omelette pan, omelet pan** (*esp US*) sartén *f* para tortillas

omen [ˈəʊmen] N augurio *m*, presagio *m* • **it is a good ~ that ...** es un buen presagio que ... • **bird of ill ~** ave *f* de mal agüero

OMG* [ˌəʊemˈdʒiː] EXCL (= *oh my God!*) ¡Dios mío!

ominous [ˈɒmɪnəs] ADJ [*development, event*] de mal agüero; [*silence*] que no augura nada bueno, que no presagia nada bueno; [*sound*] siniestro; [*cloud*] amenazador; [*tone*] (= *sinister*) amenazador; (= *worrying*) inquietante • **that's ~** eso es una mala señal • **it was an ~ sign** era una señal de mal agüero • **to look/sound ~** no augurar *or* presagiar nada bueno

ominously [ˈɒmɪnəslɪ] ADV • **"we have a problem," she said ~** —tenemos un problema —dijo en un tono que resultaba inquietante • **"I would not do that if I were you," he said ~** —yo que tú no haría eso —dijo con un tono inquietante *or* en tono amenazador • **the men marched ~ up the street** los hombres marchaban calle arriba de una forma que no presagiaba *or* auguraba nada bueno • **the thunder rumbled ~** los truenos retumbaban amenazadores • **Steve was ~ quiet** era inquietante lo tranquilo que estaba Steve • **the deadline was drawing ~ close** la fecha límite se acercaba amenazadora • **this sounded ~ like a declaration of war** esto guardaba un siniestro parecido con una declaración de guerra

omission [əʊˈmɪʃən] N (= *act of omitting*) omisión *f*; (= *mistake*) descuido *m* • **it was an ~ on my part** fue un descuido mío

omit [əʊˈmɪt] VT (*on purpose*) suprimir; (*by accident*) olvidarse de; [+ *person, person's name*] pasar por alto • **to ~ to do sth** (*on purpose*) omitir hacer algo, decidir no hacer algo; (*by accident*) olvidarse de hacer algo

omni... [ˈɒmnɪ] PREFIX omni...

omnibus [ˈɒmnɪbəs] N **1**† (= *bus*) ómnibus *m*, autobús *m*, camión *m* (*Mex*) **2** (= *book*) antología *f*, tomo *m* de obras escogidas

ADJ general, para todo

CPD ▸ **omnibus edition** (*Literat*) edición *f* antológica, edición *f* de obras escogidas; (*Brit*) (*TV, Rad*) programa *m* especial (*que incluye varios episodios*)

omnidirectional [ˌɒmnɪdɪˈrekʃənl] ADJ omnidireccional

omnipotence [ɒmˈnɪpətəns] N omnipotencia *f*

omnipotent [ɒmˈnɪpətənt] ADJ omnipotente

omnipresence [ˈɒmnɪˈprezəns] N omnipresencia *f*

omnipresent [ˈɒmnɪˈprezənt] ADJ omnipresente

omniscience [ɒmˈnɪsɪəns] N omnisciencia *f*

omniscient [ɒmˈnɪsɪənt] ADJ omnisciente

omnivore [ˈɒmnɪvɔːʳ] N omnívoro/a *m/f*

omnivorous [ɒmˈnɪvərəs] ADJ omnívoro • **she is an ~ reader** es una lectora insaciable

ON ABBR (*Canada*) = **Ontario**

on [ɒn]

> *When* **on** *is the second element in a phrasal verb, eg* **have on, get on, go on**, *look up the verb. When it is part of a set combination, such as* **broadside on, further on**, *look up the other word.*

PREP **1** (*indicating place, position*) en, sobre • **on the ceiling** sobre el techo • **on the Continent** en Europa • **with her hat on her head** con el sombrero puesto • **on page two** en la página dos • **on the right** a la derecha • **on the high seas** en alta mar • **on all sides** por todas partes, por todos lados • **a house on the square** una casa en la plaza • **on the table** en *or* sobre la mesa • **a meal on the train** una comida en el tren • **hanging on the wall** colgado en la pared

2 (*indicating time*) • **on Friday** el viernes • **on Fridays** los viernes • **on May 14th** el catorce de mayo • **on or about the 8th** el día 8 o por ahí • **on and after the 15th** el día 15 y a partir de la misma fecha • **on a day like this** (en) un día como este • **on the next day** al día siguiente • **on some days it is** hay días cuando lo es • **on the evening of July 2nd** el 2 de julio por la tarde

3 (= *at the time of*) • **on seeing him** al verlo • **on my arrival** al llegar, a mi llegada • **on my calling to him** al llamarle yo

4 (= *about, concerning*) sobre, acerca de • **a book on physics** un libro de *or* sobre física • **he lectured on Keats** dio una conferencia sobre Keats • **Eden on the events of 1956** lo que dice Eden acerca de los acontecimientos de 1956 • **have you read Purnell on Churchill?** ¿has leído los comentarios de Purnell sobre Churchill? • **have you heard the boss on the new tax?** ¿has oído lo que dice el jefe acerca de la nueva contribución? • **while we're on the subject** como hablamos de esto

5 (= *towards, against*) • **the march on Rome** la marcha sobre Roma • **an attack on the government** un ataque contra el gobierno

6 (= *earning, receiving*) • **he's on £6,000 a year** gana seis mil libras al año • **a student on a grant** un estudiante con beca • **many live on less than that** muchos viven con menos

7 (= *taking, consuming*) • **I'm on a milk diet** sigo un régimen lácteo • **he's back on drugs** ha vuelto a drogarse • **he's on heroin** está enganchado a la heroína • **I'm on three pills a day** tomo tres píldoras al día; ▹ **live on**

8 (= *engaged in*) • **I'm on a new project** trabajo sobre un nuevo proyecto • **we're on irregular verbs** estamos con los verbos irregulares • **he's away on business** está en viaje de negocios • **to be on holiday** estar de vacaciones • **the company is on tour** la compañía está en gira

9 (*indicating membership*) • **he's on the committee** es miembro del comité • **he's on the permanent staff** es de plantilla

10 (= *playing*) • **with Louis Armstrong on trumpet** con Louis Armstrong a la trompeta • **all the children play on the piano** todos los chicos saben tocar el piano • **he played it on the violin** lo tocó al violín

11 (*TV, Rad*) • **on the radio** en *or* por la radio • **on television** en *or* por (la) televisión • **there's a good film on TV tonight** esta noche dan una buena película en la tele • **on video** en vídeo

12 (= *about one's person*) • **I haven't any money on me** no llevo dinero encima

13 (= *after, according to*) • **on this model** según este modelo

14 (= *compared to*) • **prices are up on last year('s)** los precios han subido frente a los del año pasado

15 (= *at the expense of*) • **this round's on me** esta ronda la pago yo, invito yo • **the tour was on the Council** la gira la pagó el Consejo, corrió el Consejo con los gastos de la gira • IDIOM: • **it's on the house** la casa invita

16 (*liter*) • **woe on woe** dolor sobre dolor • **snow on snow** nieve y más nieve

17 (*phrases*) • **on account of** a causa de • **on good authority** de buena tinta • **on his authority** con su autorización • **on average** por término medio • **to swear on the Bible** prestar juramento sobre la Biblia • **on a charge of murder** acusado de homicidio • **on foot** a pie • **on horseback** a caballo • **on pain of** so pena de • **on sale** de venta • **on the telephone** por teléfono • **on time** a la hora, a tiempo; ▹ **base**

ADV **1** (= *in place*) [*lid etc*] puesto • **the lid is on** la tapa está puesta • **it's not on properly** no está bien puesto; ▹ **screw on**

2 (*with clothes*) • **to have one's boots on** llevar las botas puestas • **to have one's coat on** tener el abrigo puesto • **what's she got on?** ¿qué lleva puesto?, ¿cómo va vestida? • **she had not got much on** iba muy ligera de ropa

3 (*indicating time*) • **from that day on** a partir de aquel día, de aquel día en adelante • **on and off** de vez en cuando, a intervalos • **it was well on in the evening** estaba ya muy entrada la tarde • **well on in June** bien entrado junio • **they talked well on into the night** hablaron hasta bien entrada la noche • **well on in years** entrado en años, que va para viejo; ▹ **further, later**

4 (*indicating continuation*) • **to go/walk on** seguir adelante • **to read on** seguir leyendo • **he rambled on and on** estuvo dale que dale*, estuvo dale y dale (*esp LAm*) • **and so on** (= *and the rest*) y demás; (= *etc*) etcétera • **on with the show!** ¡que empiece *or* continúe el espectáculo! • **on with the dancing girls!** ¡que salgan las bailarinas!

5 (*in phrases*) • **what are you on about?*** ¿de qué (me) hablas? • **he's always on at me about it*** me está majando continuamente con eso*; ▹ **go on**

ADJ **1** (= *functioning, in operation*) • **to be on** [*engine*] estar encendido, estar en marcha; [*switch*] estar encendido *or* conectado; [*machine*] estar encendido *or* funcionando; [*light*] estar encendido, estar prendido (*LAm*); [*TV set etc*] estar encendido, estar puesto, estar prendido (*LAm*); [*tap*] estar abierto; [*brake etc*] estar puesto, estar echado • **in the on position** [*tap*] abierto, en posición de abierto; (*Elec*) encendido, puesto, prendido (*LAm*)

2 (= *being performed, shown*) • **the show is now on** ha comenzado el espectáculo • **the show is on in London** se ha estrenado el espectáculo en Londres • **the show was on for only two weeks** el show estuvo solamente 15 días en cartelera • **what's on at the cinema?** ¿qué ponen en el cine? • **what's on at the theatre?** ¿qué dan en el teatro? • **"what's on in London"** "cartelera de los espectáculos londinenses" • **the programme is on in a minute** el programa empieza dentro de un minuto • **there's a good film on tonight** hay una película buena esta noche

3 (= *taking place*) • **is the meeting still on tonight?** ¿sigue en pie la reunión de esta noche?, ¿se lleva a cabo siempre la reunión de esta noche? (*LAm*) • **the deal is on** se ha cerrado el trato

4 (= *arranged*) • **have you got anything on this evening?** ¿tienes compromiso para esta noche? • **sorry, I've got something on tonight** lo siento, esta noche tengo un compromiso

5 (= *performing, working*) • **to be on** [*actor*] estar en escena • **you're on in five minutes** sales en cinco minutos • **are you on next?** ¿te toca a ti la próxima vez? • **are you on tomorrow?** (= *on duty*) ¿trabajas mañana?, ¿estás de turno mañana? • **to have one day on and the next off** trabajar un día y el otro no

6* (*indicating agreement, acceptance*) • **you're**

O

on! ¡te tomo la palabra! • **are you still on for dinner tomorrow night?** ¿sigo contando contigo para cenar mañana? • **that's not on** *(Brit)* eso no se hace, no hay derecho

EXCL ¡adelante!

onanism [ˈəʊnənɪzəm] N onanismo *m*

on-board [ˌɒnˈbɔːd] ADJ *[computer, entertainment]* de a bordo

ONC N ABBR *(Brit) (Scol)* (= **Ordinary National Certificate**) *título escolar*

on-campus [ˌɒnˈkæmpəs] *(Univ)* ADJ, ADV en el campus

once [wʌns] ADV **1** (= *on one occasion*) una vez • **you ~ said you'd never do that** una vez dijiste que nunca harías eso • **he walked away without looking back ~** se alejó caminando sin mirar atrás ni una sola vez • **~ a thief, always a thief** quien roba una vez roba veinte • **~ a smoker, always a smoker** el que es fumador no lo deja de ser nunca • **~ a week** una vez a la *or* por semana • **~ again** otra vez, una vez más • **~ and for all** de una vez (por todas) • **we were here ~ before** ya estuvimos aquí una vez antes • **~ every two days** una vez cada dos días • **for ~** por una vez • **~ more** otra vez, una vez más • **more than ~** más de una vez • **it never ~ occurred to me** ni se me occurrió • **~ only** solo una vez, una sola vez • **~ or twice** un par de veces, una o dos veces • **(every) ~ in a while** de vez en cuando, de cuando en cuando, cada cuando *(LAm)*; ▹ **blue**

2 (= *formerly*) antes • **it had ~ been white** antes había sido blanco • **a ~ powerful nation** un país que antes *or* en su día había sido poderoso • **the ~ opulent city** la que en su día fuera una opulenta ciudad, la otrora opulenta ciudad *(frm)* • **the ring ~ belonged to my father** el anillo había pertenecido en tiempos a mi padre • **~ when we were young** hace tiempo cuando éramos jóvenes • **Texas was ~ ruled by Mexico** Tejas estuvo en su tiempo gobernada por México • **I knew him ~** le conocí hace tiempo • **~ upon a time there was** *(as start of story)* érase una vez ..., había una vez ... • **~ upon a time they used to hang people for stealing sheep** (= *in the old days*) hubo un tiempo en que solían ahorcar a la gente que robaba ovejas

3 • **at ~ a** (= *immediately*) inmediatamente; (= *now*) ahora mismo • **remove from the heat and serve at ~** retirar del fuego y servir inmediatamente • **he read the letter at ~** leyó la carta inmediatamente *or* en seguida • **we'd better leave at ~** mejor que nos vayamos ahora mismo • **stop it at ~!** ¡deja de hacer eso ahora mismo *or* inmediatamente!

b (= *simultaneously*) a la vez, al mismo tiempo • **everybody was talking at ~** todo el mundo hablaba a la vez *or* al mismo tiempo • **his style is at ~ original and stimulating** su estilo es al mismo tiempo original y estimulante • **all at ~** (= *suddenly*) de repente, de pronto; (= *simultaneously*) a la vez, al mismo tiempo • **all at ~ she felt afraid** de repente *or* de pronto le entró miedo • **a number of things then happened all at ~** una serie de cosas sucedieron a la vez *or* al mismo tiempo • **don't eat it all at ~** no te lo comas todo de un golpe • **you don't have to pay it all at ~** no tienes que pagar todo de un golpe

CONJ una vez que • **~ you give him the chance** una vez que le des la oportunidad, si le das la oportunidad • **~ they finish, we can start** una vez que *or* en cuanto ellos terminen podemos empezar nosotros • **~ the sun had set, the air turned cold** en cuanto se ocultó el sol, el aire se volvió frío • **~ inside her flat, she opened the letter** una vez dentro del piso, abrió la carta

N • **I met her just the ~** solo la he visto una vez • **just this ~** esta vez solo, esta vez nada más

once-only [ˈwʌnsˌəʊnlɪ] ADJ • **a once-only offer** una oferta irrepetible

once-over* [ˈwʌnsˌəʊvəʳ] N (= *search etc*) • **to give sth/sb the once-over** echar un vistazo a algo/algn • **they gave the house the once-over** registraron superficialmente la casa

oncologist [ɒŋˈkɒlədʒɪst] N oncólogo/a *m/f*

oncology [ɒŋˈkɒlədʒɪ] N oncología *f*

oncoming [ˈɒnˌkʌmɪŋ] ADJ **1** *[car, traffic]* que viene en el sentido opuesto

2 *[event]* que se aproxima, venidero

on-costs [ˈɒnkɒsts] NPL *(Brit) (Comm)* gastos *mpl* generales

OND N ABBR *(Brit) (Scol)* (= **Ordinary National Diploma**) *título escolar*

one [wʌn] ADJ **1** (= *number*) un/una; *(before sing noun)* un • **one man** un hombre • **one man out of two** uno de cada dos hombres • **the baby is one (year old)** el bebé tiene un año • **it's one (o'clock)** es la una • **for one reason or another** por diferentes razones • **the last but one** el penúltimo/la penúltima • **one or two people** algunas personas • **that's one way of doing it** esa es una forma *or* una de las maneras de hacerlo

2 *(indefinite)* un/una, cierto • **one day** un día, cierto día • **one cold winter's day** un día frío de invierno • **one hot July evening** una tarde de julio de mucho calor • **one Pérez** un tal Pérez

3 (= *sole*) único • **his one worry** su única preocupación • **the one way to do it** la única forma de hacerlo • **no one man could do it** ningún hombre podría hacerlo por sí solo • **the one and only difficulty** la única dificultad • **the one and only Charlie Chaplin** el único e incomparable Charlot

4 (= *same*) mismo • **all in one direction** todos en la misma dirección • **it's all one** es lo mismo • **it's all one to me** me da igual, me da lo mismo • **they are one and the same** son el mismo • **they are one and the same person** son la misma persona • **it is one and the same thing** es la misma cosa

5 (= *united*) • **God is one** Dios es uno • **they all shouted as one** todos gritaron a una • **to become one** casarse • **to be one with sth** formar un conjunto con algo

N (= *figure*) uno *m* • **I belted him one*** le di un guantazo • **one and six(pence)** *(Brit†)* un chelín y seis peniques • **to be at one (with sb)** estar completamente de acuerdo (con algn) • **to be at one with o.s.** estar en paz consigo mismo • **to go one better than sb** tomar la ventaja *or* la delantera a algn • **but John went one better** pero Juan lo hizo mejor • **she's cook and housekeeper in one** es a la vez cocinera y ama de llaves • **it's made all in one** está hecho en una sola pieza • **you've got it in one!*** ¡y que lo digas!* • **in ones and twos** en pequeños grupos • **they came in ones and twos** vinieron uno a uno y en parejas • **to be one up** *(Sport etc)* llevar un punto/gol *etc* de ventaja • **that puts us one up** *(Sport etc)* eso nos da un punto/gol *etc* de ventaja • **to be one up on sb** llevar ventaja a algn; ▹ **fast, quick, road**

PRON **1** *(indefinite)* uno/una • **have you got one?** ¿tienes uno? • **there is only one left** queda uno solamente • **his message is one of pessimism** su mensaje es pesimista, el suyo es un mensaje pesimista • **one after the other** uno tras otro • **one and all** todos sin excepción, todo el mundo • **one by one** uno tras otro, uno a uno • **I for one am not going** yo, por mi parte, no voy • **not one** ni uno • **one of them** uno de ellos • **any one of us** cualquiera de nosotros • **he's one of the group** es del grupo, forma parte del grupo • **he's one of the family now** ya es de la familia • **the one ..., the other ...** uno ..., el otro ... • **you can't buy one without the other** no se puede comprar el uno sin el otro • **price of one** precio *m* de la unidad • **two for the price of one** dos por el precio de uno • **one or two** unos pocos

2 *(specific)* • **this one** este/esta • **that one** ese/esa, aquel/aquella • **this one is better than that one** este es mejor que ese • **which one do you want?** ¿cuál quieres? • **the white dress and the grey one** el vestido blanco y el gris • **who wants these red ones?** ¿quién quiere estos colorados? • **what about this little one?** ¿y este pequeñito *or* (*esp LAm*) chiquito? • **that's a difficult one** esa sí que es difícil

> *In the past the standard spelling for **este/esta, ese/esa** and **aquel/aquella** as pronouns was with an accent (**éste/ésta, ése/ésa** and **aquél/aquélla**). Nowadays the **Real Academia Española** advises that the accented forms are only required where there might otherwise be confusion with the adjectives (**este/esta, ese/esa** and **aquel/aquella**).*

3 *(relative)* • **the one who** • **the one that** el/la que • **the ones who** • **the ones that** los/las que • **they were the ones who told us** ellos fueron quienes nos lo dijeron • **he looked like one who had seen a ghost** tenía el aspecto del que acababa de ver un fantasma • **to one who can read between the lines** para el que sabe leer entre líneas • **the one on the floor** el que está en el suelo • **one more sensitive would have fainted** una persona de mayor sensibilidad se hubiera desmayado

4 (= *person*) • **he's a clever one** es un taimado • **he's the troublesome one** él es el revoltoso • **you are a one!** ¡qué cosas dices/haces! • **our dear ones** nuestros seres queridos • **the Evil One** el demonio • **you're a fine one!*** ¡menuda pieza estás tú hecho!* • **he's one for the ladies** tiene éxito con las mujeres • **he's a great one for chess** es muy bueno al ajedrez • **he's a great one for arguing** es de los que les encanta discutir • **the little ones** los pequeños, los chiquillos • **never a one** ni uno siquiera • **he is not one to protest** no es de los que protestan • **he's not much of a one for sweets** no le gustan mucho los dulces

5 • **one another**: • **they kissed one another** se besaron (el uno al otro) • **they all kissed one another** se besaron (unos a otros) • **do you see one another much?** ¿se ven mucho? • **it's a year since we saw one another** hace un año que no nos vemos

6 *(impers)* uno/una • **one never knows** nunca se sabe • **one must eat** hay que comer • **one has one's pride** uno tiene cierto amor propio • **one's life is not really safe** la vida de uno no tiene seguridad • **one's opinion does not count** la opinión de uno no cuenta • **to cut one's finger** cortarse el dedo

one- [wʌn] PREFIX de un ..., de un solo ..., uni-, un- • **a one-line message** un mensaje de una sola línea • **a one-celled animal** un animal unicelular • **a one-day excursion** *(US)* un billete de ida y vuelta en un día

one-act [ˈwʌnˈækt] ADJ de un solo acto

one-armed [ˈwʌnˈɑːmd] ADJ manco

CPD ▸ **one-armed bandit*** máquina *f* tragamonedas, máquina *f* tragaperras *(Sp)*

one-day [ˈwʌnˌdeɪ] ADJ *[seminar, course]* de un día

one-dimensional [ˌwʌndaɪˈmenʃənl] ADJ
1 (*Math*) unidimensional
2 [*character*] simplista
one-eyed [ˈwʌnˌaɪd] ADJ tuerto
one-handed [ˈwʌnˈhændɪd] ADV • **to catch the ball one-handed** recoger la pelota con una sola mano
ADJ manco
one-hit wonder [ˌwʌnhɪtˈwʌndəʳ] N (= *artist*) artista *mf* de un día; (= *song*) éxito *m* único
one-horse [ˈwʌnˈhɔːs] ADJ 1 [*carriage*] de un solo caballo
2* insignificante, de poca monta • **one-horse town** pueblucho* *m*
3 • **a one-horse race** (*fig*) una contienda en la que no hay color, un paseo triunfal
one-hundred share index [wʌnˌhʌndrəd-ˈʃeərɪˌndeks] N índice *m* Footsie-100
one-legged [ˈwʌnˈlegɪd] ADJ con una sola pierna
one-liner [ˌwʌnˈlaɪnəʳ] N chiste *m* breve
one-man [ˈwʌnˈmæn] ADJ 1 (= *solo*) individual; [*job*] para una sola persona; [*business*] llevado por una sola persona
2 (= *monogamous*) • **she's a one-man woman** es (una) mujer de un solo hombre
CPD ▸ **one-man band** (*Mus*) hombre *m* orquesta • **it's a one-man band*** (*fig*) lo hace todo uno solo ▸ **one-man exhibition, one-man show** exposición *f* individual
oneness [ˈwʌnnɪs] N (= *unity*) unidad *f*; (= *identity*) identidad *f*
one-night stand [ˌwʌnnaɪtˈstænd] N
1 (*Theat*) función *f* de una sola noche, representación *f* única
2 (*fig*) ligue *m* de una noche
one-of-a-kind [ˌwʌnəvəˈkaɪnd] ADJ (*esp US*) (= *unique*) único en su género
one-off* [ˈwʌnɒf] (*Brit*) N intento *m* único • **it's a one-off** es un caso único
ADJ [*appearance, exhibition, show*] aislado; [*payment*] único • **it was just a one-off job, I don't think there will be any more** fue un trabajo aislado, no creo que haya más de ese tipo
one-on-one [wʌnɒnˈwʌn] ADJ, ADV (*US*) = **one-to-one**
one-parent family [ˌwʌnpeərəntˈfæmɪlɪ] N familia *f* monoparental
one-party [ˌwʌnˈpɑːtɪ] ADJ [*state etc*] de partido único
CPD ▸ **one-party system** sistema *m* unipartidista
one-piece [ˌwʌnˈpiːs] ADJ de una pieza
N (= *swimsuit*) bañador *m* de una pieza
onerous [ˈɒnərəs] ADJ [*debt*] oneroso; [*task, duty*] pesado
oneself [wʌnˈself] PRON 1 (*reflexive*) se • **to wash ~** lavarse
2 (*for emphasis*) uno/a mismo/a; (*after prep*) sí mismo/a • **it's quicker to do it ~** es más rápido si lo hace uno mismo
3 (*phrases*) • **to be ~** (= *behave naturally*) conducirse con naturalidad • **to be by ~** estar solo *or* a solas • **to do sth by ~** hacer algo solo *or* por sí solo • **it's nice to have the museum to ~** es agradable tener el museo para uno mismo • **to look out for ~** mirar por sí • **to say to ~** decir para sí, decirse a uno mismo • **to see for ~** ver por sí mismo • **to talk to ~** hablar solo • IDIOM: • **to come to ~** volver en sí
one-shot* [ˌwʌnʃɒt] (*US*) N, ADJ = **one-off**
one-sided [ˌwʌnˈsaɪdɪd] ADJ [*view etc*] parcial; [*decision*] unilateral; [*contest*] desigual
one-sidedness [ˌwʌnˈsaɪdɪdnɪs] N [*of view etc*] parcialidad *f*; [*of decision*] carácter *m* unilateral; [*of contest*] desigualdad *f*

onesie [ˈwʌnzɪ] N pelele *m*
one-size [ˈwʌnsaɪz] ADJ [*garment*] de talla única
one-size-fits-all [ˌwʌnsaɪzfɪtsˈɔːl] ADJ [*policy, approach*] que no tiene en cuenta las diferencias individuales • **a one-size-fits-all approach** un enfoque que no tiene en cuenta las diferencias individuales
one-stop shop [ˌwʌnstɒpˈʃɒp] N *empresa que ofrece múltiples servicios o productos en un mismo lugar*
one-stop shopping [ˌwʌnstɒpˈʃɒpɪŋ] N tiendas *fpl* y servicios *mpl* bajo el mismo techo
one-time [ˈwʌntaɪm] ADJ antiguo, ex • **one-time prime minister** ex primer ministro/a *m/f* • **one-time butler to Lord Yaxley** antiguo mayordomo *m* de Lord Yaxley • **the one-time revolutionary** el otrora revolucionario
one-to-one [ˈwʌntəˈwʌn], **one-on-one** (*US*) [wʌnɒnˈwʌn] ADJ [*equivalence, correspondence*] exacto; [*relationship, conversation*] de uno a uno; [*meeting*] entre dos; [*teaching*] individual, individualizado • **on a one-to-one basis** [*teach*] individualmente; [*talk*] de uno a uno
ADV [*discuss, talk*] de uno a uno
one-track [ˈwʌntræk] ADJ (*Rail*) de vía única • **to have a one-track mind** no tener más que una idea en la cabeza
one-two [ˈwʌnˈtuː] N 1 (*Brit*) (*Ftbl*) pared *f* • **to play a one-two with sb** hacer la pared con algn
2 (*Boxing*) un-dos *m*
one-upmanship [wʌnˈʌpmənʃɪp] N arte *m* de aventajar a los demás, arte *m* de llevar siempre la delantera
one-way [ˈwʌnweɪ] ADJ 1 [*street*] de dirección única, de sentido único (*esp LAm*); [*ticket*] de ida, sencillo (*Mex*) • **one-way journey** viaje *m* sin retorno • **"one-way traffic"** "dirección única", "dirección obligatoria"
2 (*fig*) [*admiration etc*] no correspondido
one-woman [ˌwʌnˈwʊmən] ADJ 1 (= *solo*) individual • **one-woman business** empresa *f* dirigida por una sola mujer
2 (= *monogamous*) • **he's a one-woman man** es (un) hombre de una sola mujer
CPD ▸ **one-woman exhibition, one-woman show** exposición *f* individual
one-year [ˈwʌnjɪəʳ] ADJ de *or* para un año • **one-year unconditional warranty** garantía *f* incondicional de un año
ongoing [ˈɒnˌgəʊɪŋ] ADJ (= *in progress*) en curso; (= *continuing*) en desarrollo; (= *current*) corriente
onion [ˈʌnjən] N cebolla *f* • IDIOM: • **to know one's ~s** (*Brit**) conocer a fondo su oficio, conocer el paño*
CPD de cebolla ▸ **onion dome** (*Archit*) cúpula *f* bulbosa ▸ **onion gravy** salsa *f* de cebollas ▸ **onion rings** aros *mpl* de cebolla rebozados ▸ **onion skin** (= *paper*) papel *m* de cebolla ▸ **onion soup** sopa *f* de cebolla
onion-shaped [ˈʌnjənʃeɪpd] ADJ acebollado, con forma de cebolla
online [ˈɒnlaɪn] ADJ (*Comput*) on-line, en línea; (= *switched on*) conectado
ADV on-line, en línea • **to go ~** conectarse • **to shop ~** comprar on-line *or* en línea • **it's available ~** está disponible on-line *or* en línea
CPD ▸ **online banking** banca *f* on-line *or* en línea ▸ **online gaming** juegos *mpl* on-line *or* en línea ▸ **online retailer** tienda *f* on-line *or* en línea ▸ **online shopping** compras *fpl* on-line *or* en línea ▸ **online store** tienda *f* on-line *or* en línea

onlooker [ˈɒnˌlʊkəʳ] N espectador(a) *m/f*; (*esp pej*) mirón/ona *m/f* • **I was a mere ~** yo era un simple espectador
only [ˈəʊnlɪ] ADJ único • **your ~ hope is to hide** la única posibilidad que te queda es esconderte • **it's the ~ one left** es el único que queda • **"I'm tired" — "you're not the ~ one!"** —estoy cansado —¡no eres el único! • **the ~ thing I don't like about it is ...** lo único que no me gusta de esto es ...
ADV

> *The adverb **only** commonly translates as **solo**. In the past, when this was used as an adverb, it was usually written with an accent (**sólo**). Nowadays the **Real Academia Española** advises that the accented form is only required where there might otherwise be confusion with the adjective **solo**.*

1 (= *no more than*) solo, sólo, solamente • **he's ~ ten** solo *or* solamente tiene diez años • **we ~ have five** solo *or* solamente tenemos cinco • **what, ~ five?** ¿cómo, cinco nada más?, ¿cómo, solo *or* solamente cinco?
2 (= *merely*) • **I'm ~ the porter** no soy más que el portero • **I'm ~ a porter** soy un simple portero • **I ~ touched it** no hice más que tocarlo • **it's ~ to be expected** cabe de esperar • **he raced onto the platform ~ to find the train pulling out** llegó corriendo al andén para encontrarse con que el tren estaba saliendo • **you ~ have to ask** • **you have ~ to ask** no tienes más que pedirlo, solo tienes que pedirlo • **it's ~ fair to tell him** lo mínimo que puedes hacer es decírselo • **I was ~ joking** lo he dicho en broma • **that ~ makes matters worse** eso solo empeora las cosas • **I will ~ say that ...** diré solamente que ..., solo diré que ... • **I ~ wish he were here now** ojalá estuviese ahora aquí
3 (= *exclusively*) solo • **a ticket for one person ~** un billete para una persona solo • **"members only"** "solo socios" • **God ~ knows!‡** ¡Dios sabe! • **~ time will tell** solo el tiempo puede decirlo • **a women-only therapy group** un grupo de terapia solo para mujeres
4 (= *not until*) • **I've ~ recently met him** hace poco que lo conocí
5 (= *no longer ago than*) • **I saw her ~ yesterday** ayer mismo la vi, la vi ayer nomás (*LAm*), recién ayer la vi (*LAm*) • **it seems like ~ yesterday that ...** parece que fue ayer cuando ...
6 (*in phrases*) • **~ just:** • **the hole was ~ just big enough** el agujero era lo justo • **I've ~ just arrived** acabo de llegar ahora mismo, no he hecho más que llegar • **it fits him, but ~ just** le cabe pero le queda muy justo • **not ~ ... but also:** • **not ~ was he late but he also forgot the tickets** no solo llegó tarde sino que además olvidó las entradas • **a machine that is not ~ efficient but looks good as well** una máquina que no solo es eficaz sino también atractiva • **~ too:** • **I'd be ~ too pleased to help** estaría encantado de *or* me encantaría poder ayudar(les) • **it is ~ too true** por desgracia es verdad *or* cierto • **I knew ~ too well what would happen** sabía demasiado bien lo que iba a pasar; ▹ **if**
CONJ solo que, pero • **it's a bit like my house, ~ nicer** es un poco como mi casa, solo que *or* pero más bonita • **I would gladly do it, ~ I shall be away** lo haría de buena gana, solo que *or* pero voy a estar fuera
CPD ▸ **only child** hijo/a *m/f* único/a; ▹ **one**
on-message [ˈɒnˌmesɪdʒ] ADJ centrado en el mensaje adecuado • **to be on-message** centrarse en el mensaje adecuado,

O

transmitir el mensaje adecuado
o.n.o. ABBR (= **or near(est) offer**) abierto ofertas
on-off switch [ˌɒnɒfˈswɪtʃ] N botón *m* de conexión
onomastic [ˌɒnəʊˈmæstɪk] ADJ onomástico
onomastics [ˌɒnəʊˈmæstɪks] NSING onomástica *f*
onomatopoeia [ˌɒnəʊmætəʊˈpiːə] N onomatopeya *f*
onomatopoeic [ˌɒnəʊmætəʊˈpiːɪk] ADJ, **onomatopoetic** [ˌɒnəʊmætəʊpəʊˈetɪk] ADJ onomatopéyico
on-ramp [ˈɒnræmp] N (*US*) (= *on freeway*) carril *m* de incorporación
onrush [ˈɒnrʌʃ] N [*of water*] oleada *f*; (*fig*) oleada *f*, avalancha *f*
onrushing [ˈɒnˌrʌʃɪŋ] ADJ [*vehicle*] embalado, sin freno; [*water*] creciente • **the ~ tide of immigrants** la creciente oleada de inmigrantes
on-screen [ˌɒnˈskriːn] ADJ **1** (*Comput etc*) en pantalla
2 (*Cine, TV*) [*romance, kiss*] cinematográfico
ADV (*Cine, TV*) en la pantalla
onset [ˈɒnset] N (= *beginning*) principio *m*, comienzo *m*; [*of disease*] aparición *f* • **the ~ of winter** el comienzo del invierno
onshore [ˈɒnʃɔːˈ] ADV tierra adentro
ADJ [*breeze*] que sopla del mar hacia la tierra
onside [ˈɒnsaɪd] ADJ **1** (*Aut*) (*in Britain*) izquierdo; (*in most other countries*) derecho
2 (*Ftbl etc*) • **to be ~** estar en posición correcta
N (*Aut*) (*in Britain*) lado *m* izquierdo; (*in most other countries*) lado *m* derecho
on-site [ˈɒnˌsaɪt] ADJ in situ
onslaught [ˈɒnslɔːt] N (*gen*) ataque *m*, arremetida *f* • **to make a furious ~ on a critic** atacar violentamente a un crítico
on-street parking [ˌɒnstriːtˈpɑːkɪŋ] N aparcamiento *m* en la vía pública
Ont. ABBR (*Canada*) = **Ontario**
on-the-job training [ˌɒnðədʒɒbˈtreɪnɪŋ] N formación *f* en el trabajo, formación *f* sobre la práctica
on-the-spot [ˈɒnðəˈspɒt] ADJ [*decision*] instantáneo; [*investigation*] sobre el terreno; [*report*] inmediato; [*fine*] en el acto • **our on-the-spot reporter** nuestro reportero en el lugar de los hechos
onto [ˈɒntʊ] PREP **1** (= *on top of*) a, sobre, en, arriba de (*LAm*) • **he got ~ the table** se subió a la mesa
2 (= *on track of*) • **to be ~ sth** haber encontrado algo, seguir una pista interesante • **he knows he's ~ a good thing** sabe que ha encontrado algo que vale la pena • **the police are ~ the villain** la policía tiene una pista que le conducirá al criminal • **we're ~ them** les conocemos el juego • **they were ~ him at once** le calaron en seguida, le identificaron en el acto
3 (= *in touch with*) • **I'll get ~ him about it** insistiré con él, se lo recordaré
ontological [ˌɒntəˈlɒdʒɪkəl] ADJ ontológico
ontology [ɒnˈtɒlədʒɪ] N ontología *f*
onus [ˈəʊnəs] N (PL: **onuses**) responsabilidad *f* • **the ~ is upon the makers** la responsabilidad es de los fabricantes • **the ~ is upon him to prove it** es suya la responsabilidad de demostrarlo, le incumbe a él demostrarlo • **the ~ of proof is on the prosecution** le incumbe al fiscal probar la acusación
onward [ˈɒnwəd] ADJ [*march etc*] progresivo, hacia adelante; [*flight, journey*] de conexión; [*connection*] posterior
ADV (*also* **onwards**) adelante, hacia adelante • **from that time ~** desde entonces • **from the 12th century ~** desde el siglo doce en adelante, a partir del siglo doce • **~!** ¡adelante!
CPD ▸ **onward progress** avance *m*
onwards [ˈɒnwədz] ADV (*esp Brit*) = **onward**
▷ ADV
onyx [ˈɒnɪks] N ónice *m*, ónix *m*
oodles* [ˈuːdlz] NPL • **we have ~ (of)** tenemos cantidad *or* montones (de)*
ooh [uː] EXCL ¡oh!
VI exclamar con placer
oolite [ˈəʊəlaɪt] N oolito *m*
oolitic [ˌəʊəˈlɪtɪk] ADJ oolítico
oompah* [ˈuːmpɑː] N chumpa *f*
oomph‡ [ʊmf] N brío *m*, marcha* *f* • **it will put the ~ back into your sex life** dará nuevos bríos a su vida sexual
oophorectomy [ˌəʊəfəˈrektəmɪ] N ooforectomía *f*, ovariotomía *f*
oops* [ʊps] EXCL ¡ay!
ooze [uːz] N cieno *m*, limo *m*; [*of blood*] pérdida *f*, salida *f*
VI [*liquid*] rezumar(se); [*blood*] salir; (= *leak*) gotear
VT rezumar; (*fig*) rebosar • **the wound was oozing blood** la herida sangraba lentamente • **he simply ~s confidence** rebosa confianza
▸ **ooze away** VI + ADV rezumarse
▸ **ooze out** VI + ADV rezumarse
op¹* [ɒp] N ABBR **1** (*Med, Mil*) = **operation**
2 = **opportunity**
CPD ▸ **op shop** (*Australia*) *tienda de artículos de segunda mano que destina parte de su recaudación a causas benéficas*
op² ABBR (*Mus*) = **opus**
opacity [əʊˈpæsɪtɪ] N [*of lens, substance*] opacidad *f*; [*of statement etc*] hermetismo *m*, ininteligibilidad *f*
opal [ˈəʊpəl] N ópalo *m*
opalescence [ˌəʊpəˈlesns] N opalescencia *f*
opalescent [ˌəʊpəˈlesnt] ADJ opalescente
opaque [əʊˈpeɪk] ADJ [*glass, lens, substance*] opaco; [*statement etc*] poco claro, ininteligible
op art [ˈɒpɑːt] N op-art *m*
op.cit. [ˈɒpˈsɪt] ABBR (= **opere citato**) (= *in the work cited*) ob. cit.
OPEC [ˈəʊpek] N ABBR (= **Organization of Petroleum-Exporting Countries**) OPEP *f*
Op-Ed [ˈɒpˈed] (*esp US*) ADJ ABBR, N ABBR (*Press*) = **opposite editorial** • **Op-Ed (page)** página *f* de tribuna
open [ˈəʊpən] ADJ **1** (*gen*) [*book, grave, pores, wound etc*] abierto; [*bottle, tin etc*] destapado • **the book was ~ at page seven** el libro estaba abierto por la página siete • **the door is ~** la puerta está abierta • **to break a safe ~** forzar una caja fuerte • **to cut a bag ~** abrir una bolsa rajándola • **to fling** *or* **throw a door ~** abrir una puerta de golpe *or* de par en par • **wide ~** (*door etc*) abierto de par en par • IDIOM: • **to welcome sb with ~ arms** dar la bienvenida *or* recibir a algn con los brazos abiertos; ▷ **book, arm**
2 [*shop, bank etc*] abierto (al público) • **the shop is still not ~** la tienda sigue cerrada
3 (= *unfolded*) desplegado; (= *unfastened*) desabrochado • **the map was ~ on the table** el mapa estaba desplegado sobre la mesa • **with his shirt ~** (= *unbuttoned*) con la camisa desabotonada • **a shirt ~ at the neck** una camisa con el cuello desabrochado
4 (= *not enclosed*) descubierto, abierto; [*car*] descapotable • **in the ~ air** al aire libre • **~ country** campo *m* raso • **on ~ ground** en un claro; (= *waste ground*) en un descampado • **~ sea** mar *m* abierto • **with ~ views** con amplias *or* extensas vistas
5 (= *not blocked*) abierto, sin obstáculos • **the way to Paris lay ~** el camino de París quedaba abierto • **the speed permitted on the ~ road** la velocidad permitida circulando en carretera • **road ~ to traffic** carretera abierta al tráfico, vía libre
6 (= *public, unrestricted*) [*championship, race, scholarship, ticket*] abierto; [*trial*] público • **books on ~ access** libros *mpl* en libre acceso • **in ~ court** en juicio público • **to keep ~ house** tener mesa franca *or* casa abierta • **we had an ~ invitation to visit them** nos habían invitado a visitarles cuando quisiéramos • **~ to the public on Mondays** abierto al público los lunes • **the competition is ~ to all** todos pueden participar en el certamen, el certamen se abre a todos • **membership is not ~ to women** la sociedad no admite a las mujeres
7 (= *available, permissible*) • **what choices are ~ to me?** ¿qué posibilidades *or* opciones me quedan? • **it is ~ to you to** (+ *infin*) puedes perfectamente (+ *infin*), tienes derecho a (+ *infin*)
8 (= *not biased or prejudiced*) abierto • **to be ~ to sth: I am ~ to advice** escucho de buena gana los consejos • **I am ~ to offers** estoy dispuesto a recibir ofertas • **I am ~ to persuasion** se me puede convencer
9 (= *declared, frank*) abierto; [*person, admiration*] franco; [*hatred*] declarado • **an ~ enemy of the Church** un enemigo declarado de la Iglesia • **to be in ~ revolt** estar en abierta rebeldía • **it's an ~ secret that ...** es un secreto a voces que ... • **to be ~ with sb** ser franco con algn
10 (= *undecided*) por resolver, por decidir; [*race, contest*] muy abierto, muy igualado • **to leave the matter ~** dejar el asunto pendiente • **~ question** cuestión *f* pendiente *or* sin resolver • **it's an ~ question whether ...** está por ver si ...; ▷ **mind**
11 (= *exposed, not protected*) abierto, descubierto; [*town*] abierto; (*Mil*) expuesto, vulnerable • **to be ~ to sth: it is ~ to criticism on several counts** se le puede criticar por diversas razones, es criticable desde diversos puntos de vista • **to lay o.s. ~ to criticism/attack** exponerse a ser criticado/atacado • **it is ~ to doubt whether ...** queda la duda sobre si ... • **~ to the elements** desprotegido, desabrigado • **~ to influence from advertisers** accesible a la influencia de los anunciantes • **it is ~ to question whether ...** es cuestionable que ... • **~ to every wind** expuesto a todos los vientos
N **1** • **(out) in the ~** (= *out of doors*) al aire libre; (= *in the country*) en campo *m* raso *or* abierto • **to sleep (out) in the ~** dormir al raso, dormir a cielo abierto • **to bring a dispute (out) into the ~** hacer que una disputa llegue a ser del dominio público • **their true feelings came (out) into the ~** sus verdaderos sentimientos se dejaron adivinar • **why don't you come (out) into the ~ about it?** ¿por qué no lo declara abiertamente?
2 (*Golf, Tennis*) • **the Open** el (Torneo) Abierto, el Open
VT **1** (*gen*) [+ *eyes, case, letter etc*] abrir; [+ *parcel*] abrir, desenvolver; [+ *bottle etc*] destapar; [+ *legs*] abrir, separar; [+ *abscess*] cortar; [+ *pores*] dilatar • **I didn't ~ my mouth** ni abrí la boca, no dije ni pío
2 [+ *shop*] (*for daily business*) abrir; (= *set up*) abrir, poner
3 (= *unfold*) [+ *map*] desplegar, extender; [+ *newspaper*] desplegar
4 (= *unblock*) • **to ~ a road to traffic** abrir una carretera al público

5 (= *begin*) [+ *conversation, debate, negotiations*] entablar, iniciar • **to ~ three hearts** (*Bridge*) abrir de tres corazones • **to ~ a bank account** abrir una cuenta en el banco • **to ~ the case** (*Jur*) exponer los detalles de la acusación • **to ~ fire** (*Mil*) romper *or* abrir el fuego
6 (= *declare open, inaugurate*) inaugurar • **the exhibition was ~ed by the Queen** la exposición fue inaugurada por la Reina • **to ~ Parliament** abrir la sesión parlamentaria
7 (= *reveal, disclose*) [+ *mind, heart*] abrir; [+ *feelings, intentions*] revelar; ▹ **mind**
8 (= *make*) • **to ~ a road through a forest** abrir una carretera a través de un bosque • **to ~ a hole in a wall** hacer un agujero en una pared
VI **1** [*door, flower*] abrirse; [*pores*] dilatarse • **the door ~ed** se abrió la puerta • **this room ~s into a larger one** este cuarto se comunica con *or* se junta con otro más grande • **a door that ~s onto the garden** una puerta que da al jardín • IDIOM: • **the heavens ~ed** se abrieron los cielos
2 (*for business*) [*shop, bank*] abrir • **the shops ~ at nine** las tiendas abren a las nueve
3 (= *begin*) dar comienzo, iniciarse; [*speaker*] comenzar; (*Theat*) [*play*] estrenarse; (*Cards, Chess*) abrir • **the season ~s in June** la temporada comienza en junio • **when we ~ed in Bradford** (*Theat*) cuando dimos la primera representación en Bradford • **to ~ for the Crown** (*Jur*) exponer los detalles de la acusación, presentar los hechos en que se basa la acusación • **the play ~ed to great applause** el estreno de la obra fue muy aplaudido • **the book ~s with a long description** el libro empieza con una larga descripción • **to ~ with two hearts** (*Bridge*) abrir de dos corazones
CPD ▸ **open cheque** (*Brit*) cheque *m* sin cruzar ▸ **open day** día *m* abierto a todos ▸ **open fire** chimenea *f*, hogar *m* ▸ **open government** política *f* de transparencia gubernamental ▸ **open learning** aprendizaje *m* abierto ▸ **open learning centre** centro *m* de aprendizaje abierto ▸ **open letter** carta *f* abierta ▸ **open market** (*in town*) mercado *m* al aire libre; (*Econ*) mercado *m* libre, mercado *m* abierto • **he bought it on the ~ market** lo compró en el mercado público ▸ **open pit** (*US*) mina *f* a cielo abierto ▸ **open policy** (*Insurance*) póliza *f* abierta ▸ **open primary** (*US*) *elección primaria abierta a aquellos que no son miembros de un partido* ▸ **open prison** cárcel *f* abierta ▸ **open sandwich** sandwich *m* sin tapa, sandwich *m* abierto (*esp LAm*) ▸ **open shop** (*Ind*) empresa *f* con personal agremiado y no agremiado ▸ **open source** código *m* abierto ▸ **open source software** software *m* de código abierto ▸ **Open University** (*Brit*) ≈ Universidad *f* Nacional de Enseñanza a Distancia ▸ **open verdict** (*Jur*) juicio *m* en el que se determina el crimen sin designar el culpable
▸ **open out** VT + ADV abrir; (= *unfold*) [+ *map*] desplegar, extender
VI + ADV **1** [*flower*] abrirse
2 [*passage, tunnel, street*] ensancharse; [*view, panorama*] extenderse
3 (*fig*) (= *develop, unfold*) desarrollarse; [*new horizons*] abrirse
4 (*Brit*) (*emotionally*) abrirse
▸ **open up** VT + ADV **1** [+ *box, jacket*] abrir; [+ *map*] extender, desplegar
2 [+ *house, shop*] abrir
3 [+ *new business*] abrir, poner
4 [+ *route*] abrir; [+ *blocked road*] franquear, despejar; [+ *country*] explorar; [+ *secret, new vista*] revelar; [+ *new possibility*] crear • **to ~ up a market** abrirse un mercado, conquistar un mercado • **to ~ up a country for trade** incorporar un país al comercio • **when the oilfield was ~ed up** cuando se empezó a explotar el campo petrolífero
VI + ADV **1** [*flower*] abrirse; [*new shop, business*] abrir, inaugurarse • **~ up!** ¡abran!; (*police order*) ¡abran a la autoridad!
2 (*fig*) [*prospects etc*] abrirse, desplegarse
3 (*emotionally*) abrirse, confiarse
4 (*Mil*) (= *start shooting*) romper el fuego
5* (= *accelerate*) [*car*] acelerar (a fondo)

OPEN UNIVERSITY
La **Open University** o **OU** es el nombre que recibe en el Reino Unido la universidad a distancia para adultos, fundada en 1969. No se exigen requisitos formales de acceso para los primeros cursos y los alumnos estudian desde casa, con el apoyo de algunos programas de radio y televisión emitidos por la **BBC**, cursos por correspondencia y tutores en su localidad. Además, sobre todo en verano, se organizan algunos cursos a los que los alumnos tienen que asistir en persona.

open-air [ˌəʊpnˈɛəʳ] ADJ al aire libre
open-and-shut case [ˌəʊpənənʃʌtˈkeɪs] N caso *m* claro, caso *m* evidente
open-cast [ˈəʊpənˌɑːst] ADJ • **open-cast mining** minería *f* a cielo abierto
open-door [ˌəʊpənˈdɔːʳ] ADJ • **open-door policy** política *f* de puerta abierta
open-ended [ˌəʊpənˈendɪd] ADJ (*fig*) [*contract, offer etc*] indefinido, sin plazo definido; [*discussion*] sin desarrollo preestablecido
open-end trust [ˌəʊpənendˈtrʌst] N (*US*) sociedad *f* inversionista
opener [ˈəʊpnəʳ] N **1** abridor *m*; (= *bottle opener*) sacacorchos *m inv*; (= *can opener*) abrelatas *m inv*
2 (*Theat etc*) primer número *m*
3 • **for ~s** (*US**) de entrada
open-eyed [ˌəʊpnˈaɪd] ADJ con los ojos abiertos; (= *amazed*) con ojos desorbitados
open-handed [ˌəʊpənˈhændɪd] ADJ
1 (= *liberal*) liberal
2 (= *generous*) generoso
open-handedness [ˌəʊpənˈhændɪdnɪs] N (= *liberal attitude*) liberalidad *f*; (= *generosity*) generosidad *f*
open-hearted [ˌəʊpənˈhɑːtɪd] ADJ franco, generoso
open-heart surgery [ˌ] N cirugía *f* a corazón abierto
opening [ˈəʊpnɪŋ] ADJ [*remark*] primer(o); [*ceremony, speech*] de apertura, inaugural; [*price*] inicial
N **1** (= *gap*) abertura *f*; (*in wall*) brecha *f*, agujero *m*; (*in clouds, trees*) claro *m*
2 (= *beginning*) comienzo *m*, principio *m*; (*Cards, Chess*) apertura *f*; (= *first showing*) (*Theat*) estreno *m*; [*of exhibition*] inauguración *f*; [*of parliament*] apertura *f*
3 (= *chance*) oportunidad *f*; (= *post*) puesto *m* vacante, vacante *f* • **to give one's opponent an ~** dar una oportunidad *or* (*LAm*) darle chance al adversario • **to give sb an ~ for sth** dar a algn la oportunidad de hacer algo
CPD ▸ **opening act** (*at concert, event*) telonero/a *m/f* ▸ **opening arguments** (*US*) alegaciones *fpl* iniciales ▸ **opening balance** saldo *m* inicial, saldo *m* de apertura ▸ **opening batsman** (*Cricket*) primer bateador *m* ▸ **opening batswoman** (*Cricket*) primera bateadora *f* ▸ **opening bowler** (*Cricket*) primer(a) lanzador(a) *m/f* ▸ **opening gambit** (= *opening tactic*) táctica *f* inicial; (= *conversational opener*) táctica *f* para entablar conversación ▸ **opening hours** horas *fpl* de abrir ▸ **opening night** (*Theat*) noche *f* de estreno; [*of club etc*] inauguración *f* ▸ **opening price** cotización *f* de apertura ▸ **opening stock** existencias *fpl* iniciales ▸ **opening time** hora *f* de apertura
open-jaw [ˌəʊpənˈdʒɔː] ADJ [*ticket*] de circuito abierto (*que permite viajar hasta una ciudad y regresar desde otra*)
openly [ˈəʊpənlɪ] ADV (= *frankly*) abiertamente, francamente; (= *publicly*) públicamente
open-minded [ˈəʊpnˈmaɪndɪd] ADJ libre de prejuicios, de miras amplias • **I'm still open-minded about it** no me he decidido todavía
open-mindedness [ˈəʊpnˈmaɪndɪdnɪs] N ausencia *f* de prejuicios, imparcialidad *f*
open-mouthed [ˈəʊpnˈmaʊðd] ADJ boquiabierto
open-necked [ˈəʊpnˈnekt] ADJ sin corbata
openness [ˈəʊpnnɪs] N (= *frankness*) franqueza *f*
open-plan [ˈəʊpnˌplæn] ADJ [*house, office etc*] sin tabiques, de planta abierta
open-top [ˈəʊpənˌtɒp] ADJ [*car, bus*] descubierto
openwork [ˈəʊpnwɜːk] N (*Sew*) calado *m*, enrejado *m*
opera¹ [ˈɒpərə] N ópera *f*
CPD ▸ **opera company** compañía *f* de ópera ▸ **opera glasses** gemelos *mpl* de teatro ▸ **opera hat** clac *m* ▸ **opera house** teatro *m* de la ópera ▸ **opera singer** cantante *mf* de ópera
opera² [ˈɒpərə] NPL *of* **opus**
operable [ˈɒpərəbl] ADJ (*Med*) operable
opera-goer [ˈɒpərəˌgəʊəʳ] N aficionado/a *m/f* a la ópera
operand [ˈɒpərænd] N operando *m*
operate [ˈɒpəreɪt] VT **1** (= *work*) [+ *machine, vehicle, switchboard*] manejar; [+ *switch, lever*] accionar • **can you ~ this machine?** ¿sabes manejar esta máquina? • **this switch ~s a fan** este interruptor activa un ventilador
2 (= *run, manage*) [+ *company*] dirigir; [+ *service*] ofrecer; [+ *system*] aplicar; [+ *mine, oil well, quarry*] explotar • **they ~ a system of flexible working hours** aplican un horario flexible de trabajo
VI **1** (= *function*) [*machine, system, principle, mind*] funcionar; [*person*] actuar, obrar; [*law*] regir • **she knows how to ~ in a crisis** sabe cómo actuar *or* obrar en los momentos difíciles • **we ~ on the principle that …** partimos del principio de que … • **special laws ~ in Northern Ireland** en Irlanda del Norte rigen leyes especiales
2 (= *act, influence*) [*drug, propaganda*] actuar (**on** sobre); [*factors*] intervenir • **advertising ~s on the subconscious** la publicidad actúa sobre el subconsciente
3 (= *carry on one's business*) [*person*] trabajar; [*company, factory, criminal, service*] operar; [*airport*] funcionar • **we shall be operating under difficult conditions** trabajaremos en unas condiciones difíciles • **we were operating at a loss** estábamos operando con déficit • **an airline operating out of Heathrow** una compañía aérea con base en Heathrow *or* que opera desde Heathrow • **a drug ring operating in New York** una red de narcotráfico que opera en Nueva York • **this service does not ~ on Sundays** este servicio no opera *or* no funciona los domingos • **all flights are operating normally** todos los vuelos están operando con normalidad
4 (*Med*) operar • **to ~ on sb (for sth)** operar a algn (de algo) • **she was ~d on for appendicitis** la operaron de apendicitis • **to ~ on sb's back/eyes** operar a algn de la

espalda/de la vista

operatic [ˌɒpəˈrætɪk] (ADJ) operístico

operating [ˈɒpəreɪtɪŋ] (ADJ) **1** (*Comm*) [*budget, assets*] de explotación • **~ costs** *or* **expenses** gastos *mpl* de explotación • **~ loss** pérdida *f* de explotación • **~ profit** beneficio *m* de explotación
2 (*Comput*) • **~ system** sistema *m* operativo
3 (*Tech*) • **~ conditions** condiciones *fpl* de funcionamiento
(CPD) ▸ **operating instructions** modo *msing* de empleo ▸ **operating manual** manual *m* de empleo ▸ **operating room** (*US*) (*Med*) quirófano *m*, sala *f* de operaciones ▸ **operating software** software *m* operativo ▸ **operating table** (*Med*) mesa *f* de operaciones ▸ **operating theatre** (*Med*) quirófano *m*, sala *f* de operaciones

operation [ˌɒpəˈreɪʃən] (N) **1** (= *functioning*) funcionamiento *m* • **to be in ~** [*machine, system, business*] estar en funcionamiento *or* en marcha, estar funcionando; [*law*] ser vigente, estar en vigor • **to come into ~** [*machine, system*] entrar en funcionamiento; [*law*] entrar en vigor • **the system is designed to come into ~ in 2003** está previsto que el sistema entre en funcionamiento en 2003 • **to put sth into ~** [+ *plan, factory*] poner algo en funcionamiento *or* en marcha
2 (= *use*) [*of controls, machine*] manejo *m*; [*of system*] uso *m*
3 (= *activity*) operación *f* • **United Nations peacekeeping ~s** las operaciones de paz de las Naciones Unidas • **our ~s in Egypt** [*of company*] nuestras operaciones en Egipto; [*of mine, oil well*] nuestras operaciones *or* explotaciones en Egipto • **moving house is an expensive ~** mudarse de casa resulta caro; ▹ **rescue**
4 (*Med*) operación *f*, intervención *f* quirúrgica (*frm*) • **a liver ~** una operación de hígado • **will I need an ~?** ¿hará falta que me operen? • **to have** *or* (*frm*) **undergo an ~ for appendicitis** operarse de apendicitis • **to have** *or* (*frm*) **undergo an ~ to remove a tumour** someterse a una operación *or* una intervención quirúrgica para extirpar un tumor (*frm*) • **to perform an ~ on sb** operar a algn
5 (*Comm*) (= *business*) operación *f*
6 (*Mil*) operación *f* • **Operation Torch** Operación Antorcha
7 (*Econ, St Ex*) (= *transaction*) operación *f* • **~s on the Stock Exchange** las operaciones bursátiles, la actividad bursátil
8 (*Math, Comput*) operación *f*
(CPD) ▸ **operation code** código *m* de operación ▸ **operations centre, operations center** (*US*) (*Police*) centro *m* de coordinación; (*Mil*) centro *m* de operaciones ▸ **operations director** director(a) *m/f* de operaciones ▸ **operations manager** director(a) *m/f* de operaciones ▸ **operations research** investigaciones *fpl* operativas *or* operacionales ▸ **operations room** (*Police*) centro *m* de coordinación; (*Mil*) centro *m* de operaciones

operational [ˌɒpəˈreɪʃənl] (ADJ) **1** (= *relating to operations*) [*control, plan*] operativo, de operaciones; [*problems, cost, expenses*] de funcionamiento; [*staff*] de servicio • **~ research** investigaciones *fpl* operacionales • **for ~ reasons** por necesidades operativas
2 (= *ready for use or action*) [*aircraft, service, airport*] en funcionamiento; [*bus, train*] en servicio; [*troops*] operacional • **the bridge could be ~ in three years' time** el puente podría entrar en funcionamiento dentro de tres años • **to be fully ~** estar en pleno funcionamiento

operationally [ˌɒpəˈreɪʃənəlɪ] (ADV) [*use*] de forma operativa • **the device had been used ~ some months previously** habían usado el dispositivo de forma operativa hacía algunos meses

operative [ˈɒpərətɪv] (ADJ) **1** (*gen*) operativo • **the ~ word** la palabra clave
2 (*Jur*) • **to be ~** estar en vigor • **to become ~ from the 9th** entrar en vigor a partir del 9
3 (*Med*) operatorio
(N) (= *worker*) obrero/a *m/f*; (*with a special skill*) operario/a *m/f*, obrero/a *m/f* especializado/a

operator [ˈɒpəreɪtəʳ] (N) **1** [*of machine etc*] operario/a *m/f*; (= *machinist*) maquinista *mf*; (*Cine*) operador(a) *m/f*; (*Telec*) telefonista *mf*
2* (*fig*) • **a smooth ~** (*in business*) un tipo hábil; (*in love*) un engatusador • **he's a very clever ~** es un tipo muy vivo*

operetta [ˌɒpəˈretə] (N) zarzuela *f*, opereta *f*

Ophelia [ɒˈfiːlɪə] (N) Ofelia

ophthalmia [ɒfˈθælmɪə] (N) oftalmía *f*

ophthalmic [ɒfˈθælmɪk] (ADJ) oftálmico

ophthalmologist [ˌɒfθælˈmɒlədʒɪst] (N) oftalmólogo/a *m/f*

ophthalmology [ˌɒfθælˈmɒlədʒɪ] (N) oftalmología *f*

ophthalmoscope [ɒfˈθælməskəʊp] (N) oftalmoscopio *m*

opiate [ˈəʊpɪɪt] (N) opiata *f*

opine [əʊˈpaɪn] (VI) opinar

opinion [əˈpɪnjən] (N) **1** (= *belief, view*) opinión *f* • **what's your ~ of him?** ¿qué opinas de él?, ¿qué opinión te merece? • **what's your ~ of this book?** ¿qué opinas de este libro?, ¿qué opinión te merece este libro? • **well, that's my ~** por lo menos eso pienso yo • **to ask sb's ~ (on** *or* **about sth)** pedir a algn su opinión *or* parecer (sobre *or* acerca de algo) • **when I want your ~ I'll ask for it!** ¡cuando quiera saber tu opinión, te la pediré! • **if you ask my ~, he's hiding something** mi opinión es que está ocultando algo • **there are differences of ~ as to what happened** hay discordancia *or* discrepancia de opiniones respecto a lo que pasó • **to form an ~ of sth/sb** formarse una opinión sobre algo/algn • **to have** *or* **hold an ~ on** *or* **about sth** tener una opinión sobre *or* acerca de algo • **many people have very strong ~s about this** mucha gente tiene opiniones muy definidas sobre *or* acerca de esto • **she held the ~ that ...** opinaba que ... • **to have a high** *or* **good ~ of sth/sb** tener un alto concepto de algo/algn, tener muy buena opinión de algo/algn • **to have a poor** *or* **low ~ of sth/sb** tener un bajo concepto de algo/algn, tener muy mala opinión de algo/algn • **she has a very low ~ of herself** tiene un concepto muy bajo de sí misma • **I haven't much of an ~ of him** no tengo un alto concepto de él, no tengo muy buena opinión de él • **in my ~** en mi opinión, a mi juicio • **it's a matter of ~** es cuestión de opiniones • **to be of the ~ that ...** opinar que ...
2 (= *judgment*) opinión *f* • **we need an expert ~** necesitamos la opinión de un experto • **could you give us your professional ~?** ¿nos puede dar su opinión (como) profesional? • **to seek a second ~** pedir una segunda opinión
3 (= *the prevailing view*) opinión *f* • **he is in a position to influence ~** está en una posición en la que puede ejercer influencia sobre las opiniones • **medical ~ was divided over the case** la opinión médica estaba dividida con respecto al caso • **they are trying to turn world ~ against the United States** están intentando poner al mundo entero en contra de Estados Unidos; ▹ **consensus, public**
(CPD) ▸ **opinion former, opinion maker** formador(a) *m/f* de opinión ▸ **opinion poll** sondeo *m* (de opinión) ▸ **opinion survey** encuesta *f* de opinión

opinionated [əˈpɪnjəneɪtɪd] (ADJ) testarudo

opium [ˈəʊpɪəm] (N) opio *m*
(CPD) ▸ **opium addict** opiómano/a *m/f* ▸ **opium addiction** opiomanía *f* ▸ **opium den** fumadero *m* de opio ▸ **opium poppy** adormidera *f* ▸ **opium war** guerra *f* del opio

opossum [əˈpɒsəm] (N) (PL: **opossums** *or* **opossum**) zarigüeya *f*

opp. (ABBR) = **opposite**

opponent [əˈpəʊnənt] (N) adversario/a *m/f*, contrincante *mf*; (*in debate, discussion*) oponente *mf*, adversario/a *m/f*

opportune [ˈɒpətjuːn] (ADJ) [*arrival, event, remark*] oportuno • **at an ~ moment** *or* **time** en un momento oportuno

opportunely [ˈɒpətjuːnlɪ] (ADV) [*remark, intervene*] oportunamente; [*arrive, call*] en un momento oportuno

opportunism [ˌɒpəˈtjuːnɪzəm] (N) oportunismo *m*

opportunist [ˌɒpəˈtjuːnɪst] (ADJ) oportunista
(N) oportunista *mf*

opportunistic [ˌɒpətjʊˈnɪstɪk] (ADJ) oportunista

opportunistically [ˌɒpətjuːˈnɪstɪkəlɪ] (ADV) [*act, exploit*] de forma oportunista

opportunity [ˌɒpəˈtjuːnɪtɪ] (N) oportunidad *f*, ocasión *f* • **at the earliest ~** en la primera oportunidad, cuanto antes • **equality of ~** igualdad *f* de oportunidades • **he criticized her at every ~** la criticaba siempre que se le presentaba la ocasión *or* en cuanto podía • **at the first ~** en la primera oportunidad, cuanto antes • **opportunities for promotion** oportunidades de promoción • **when I get the ~** cuando se me presente la oportunidad *or* la ocasión, cuando tenga ocasión • **we were given no ~ to prepare ourselves** no se nos ofreció la oportunidad *or* la ocasión de prepararnos • **given the ~, he'll watch TV all day** si le dejases, se pasaría el día entero viendo la tele • **to have the/an ~ to do sth • have the/an ~ of doing sth** tener la oportunidad de hacer algo • **I haven't had an ~ of talking to him** no he tenido la oportunidad de hablar con él • **to miss one's ~** perder la oportunidad • **he never missed an ~ to criticize her** nunca dejaba pasar la oportunidad de criticarla • **to seize the/one's ~** aprovechar la oportunidad *or* ocasión • **to take the ~ to do sth • take the ~ of doing sth** aprovechar la oportunidad *or* la ocasión para hacer algo; ▹ **equal, job, photo**
(CPD) ▸ **opportunity shop** (*Australia*) *tienda de artículos de segunda mano que destina parte de su recaudación a causas benéficas*

oppose [əˈpəʊz] (VT) **1** (= *disagree with*) oponerse a, estar en contra de • **67% are in favour of the measure and 33% ~ it** el 67% está a favor de la medida y el 33% restante se opone *or* está en contra • **they ~d the motion** se opusieron a la moción
2 (= *combat*) luchar contra, combatir • **I have no wish to ~ progress** no deseo luchar contra *or* combatir el progreso • **he may decide to ~ him at the next election** puede que decida enfrentarse a él en las próximas elecciones

opposed [əˈpəʊzd] (ADJ) **1** (= *in disagreement*) • **to be ~ to sth** oponerse a algo, estar en contra de algo • **he is strongly ~ to the use of force** se opone enérgicamente al uso de la

fuerza, está totalmente en contra del uso de la fuerza • **they have diametrically ~ views on abortion** tienen opiniones diametralmente opuestas sobre el aborto
2 • **as ~ to** (= *rather than*) en vez de; (= *compared to*) a diferencia de • **why did you become a Republican, as ~ to a Democrat?** ¿por qué te hiciste republicano, en vez de demócrata? • **savings as ~ to investments** los ahorros a diferencia de las inversiones

opposing [əˈpəʊzɪŋ] ADJ [*views, ideas*] opuesto, contrario; [*team*] contrario; [*army*] enemigo • **we've always had ~ views on politics** nuestras ideas políticas siempre han sido opuestas *or* contrarias • **they found themselves on ~ sides in the war** en la guerra se encontraron luchando en bandos contrarios

opposite [ˈɒpəzɪt] ADV enfrente • **I looked at the director, sitting ~** miré al director que estaba sentado enfrente (de mí) • **please fill in the box ~** por favor, rellene la casilla de al lado • **they live directly** *or* **immediately ~** viven justo enfrente
PREP (*also* **opposite to**) **1** (= *across from*) frente a, enfrente de • **~ the library** frente a *or* enfrente de la biblioteca • **Lynn was sitting ~ him** Lynn estaba sentada frente a él *or* enfrente de él • **they sat ~ one another** se sentaron uno frente a(l) otro, se sentaron frente a frente
2 (= *next to*) junto a, al lado de • **~ his name was a question mark** junto a *or* al lado de su nombre había una interrogación • **to play ~ sb** (*Theat*) aparecer junto a algn
ADJ **1** (*in position*) de enfrente • **the house ~** la casa de enfrente • **on the ~ bank** en la ribera opuesta • **on the ~ page** en la página opuesta *or* de al lado • **to be facing the ~ way** estar mirando al otro lado, estar de cara al otro lado
2 (= *far*) [*end, corner*] opuesto • **we sat at ~ ends of the sofa** nos sentamos cada uno a un extremo del sofá, nos sentamos en extremos opuestos del sofá
3 (= *contrary*) contrario, opuesto • **in the ~ direction** en dirección contraria *or* opuesta, en sentido contrario *or* opuesto • **it had the ~ effect** produjo el efecto contrario *or* opuesto • **~ number** homólogo/a *m/f* • **the ~ sex** el otro sexo, el sexo opuesto • **they were on ~ sides in the war** lucharon en bandos contrarios *or* opuestos en la guerra • **she presented the ~ view** presentó el punto de vista contrario *or* opuesto • **we take the ~ view** nosotros pensamos lo contrario
N • **the ~** lo contrario • **she said the exact ~** • **she said just the ~** dijo exactamente lo contrario • **my brother is just the ~** mi hermano es justo lo contrario • **it's the ~ of what we wanted** es lo contrario de lo que queríamos • **he says the ~ of everything I say** me lleva la contraria en todo • **quite the ~!** ¡todo lo contrario! • **the ~ is true** la verdad es todo lo contrario

opposition [ˌɒpəˈzɪʃən] N **1** (= *resistance*) resistencia *f*, oposición *f*; (= *people opposing*) oposición *f*; (*Sport*) (= *team*) equipo *m* contrario • **to advance a kilometre without ~** avanzar un kilómetro sin encontrar resistencia • **there is a lot of ~ to the new law** hay mucha oposición a la nueva ley • **he made his ~ known** indicó su disconformidad • **to be in ~** estar en la oposición • **in ~ to** (= *against*) en contra de; (= *unlike*) a diferencia de • **to start up a business in ~ to another** montar un negocio en competencia con otro • **to act in ~ to the chairman** obrar en oposición al presidente
2 (*Brit*) (*Pol*) • **the Opposition** los partidos de la oposición, la oposición • **leader of the Opposition** líder *mf* de la oposición • **the party in ~** el partido de la oposición
CPD [*member, party*] de la oposición ▸ **the Opposition benches** los escaños de la Oposición, la Oposición

oppositionist [ˌɒpəˈzɪʃənɪst] N (*Pol*) militante *mf* de la oposición clandestina

oppress [əˈpres] VT **1** (*Mil, Pol etc*) oprimir • **the ~ed** los oprimidos
2 [*heat, anxiety etc*] agobiar • **~ed with worry** angustiado/a

oppression [əˈpreʃən] N opresión *f*

oppressive [əˈpresɪv] ADJ **1** (= *unjust*) [*regime, law, system*] opresivo; [*tax*] gravoso
2 (= *stifling*) [*heat, air, atmosphere*] sofocante, agobiante; [*mood, feeling, silence*] opresivo, agobiante • **the little room was ~** la pequeña habitación resultaba opresiva *or* agobiante

oppressively [əˈpresɪvlɪ] ADV **1** (= *unjustly*) [*rule, govern*] de manera opresiva, de modo opresivo
2 (= *stiflingly*) • **the room was ~ hot** en la habitación hacía un calor sofocante *or* agobiante • **it was ~ humid** hacía una humedad agobiante • **the city is ~ drab and grey** la ciudad es tan monótona y gris que resulta opresiva *or* agobiante

oppressiveness [əˈpresɪvnɪs] N **1** [*of regime, system*] opresión *f*
2 [*of heat, climate, taxes*] lo agobiante

oppressor [əˈpresəʳ] N opresor(a) *m/f*

opprobrious [əˈprəʊbrɪəs] ADJ (*frm*) oprobioso

opprobrium [əˈprəʊbrɪəm] N (*frm*) oprobio *m*

opt [ɒpt] VI • **to opt for sth** optar por algo • **to opt to do sth** optar por hacer algo
▸ **opt in** VI + ADV (= *join*) optar por participar • **they can't opt out, because they never opted in** no pueden retirarse porque nunca han optado por participar • **at present individuals must opt in by putting their names on the register** en estos momentos las personas deben solicitar ser incluidos escribiendo sus nombres en la lista
▸ **opt into** VI + PREP (= *join*) optar por participar en
▸ **opt out** VI + ADV **1** (= *decide against*) • **to opt out of doing sth** optar por no hacer algo • **I think I'll opt out of going** creo que optaré por no ir
2 (= *withdraw*) retractarse

optative [ˈɒptətɪv] ADJ optativo
N optativo *m*

optic [ˈɒptɪk] ADJ óptico • **~ nerve** nervio *m* óptico

optical [ˈɒptɪkəl] ADJ óptico • **~ disk** disco *m* óptico • **~ fibre** fibra *f* óptica • **~ illusion** ilusión *f* óptica • **~ (character) reader** lector *m* óptico (de caracteres) • **~ character recognition** reconocimiento *m* óptico de caracteres

optician [ɒpˈtɪʃən] N óptico/a *m/f* • **~'s** óptica *f*

optics [ˈɒptɪks] NSING óptica *f*

optimal [ˈɒptɪml] ADJ óptimo

optimally [ˈɒptɪməlɪ] ADV de manera óptima, óptimamente

optimism [ˈɒptɪmɪzəm] N optimismo *m* • **the Prime Minister has expressed ~ about the outcome of the talks** el primer ministro ha expresado su optimismo acerca del resultado de las negociaciones • **there is some cause for ~** hay algunas razones para ser optimistas

optimist [ˈɒptɪmɪst] N optimista *mf* • **he's the eternal ~** es el eterno optimista

optimistic [ˌɒptɪˈmɪstɪk] ADJ optimista • **to be ~ that** ser optimista respecto a que • **to be ~ about sth** ser optimista acerca de *or* con respecto a algo • **to keep** *or* **remain ~** mantener el optimismo • **to be in an ~ mood** sentirse optimista • **to end on an ~ note** terminar con una nota de optimismo; ▹ **cautiously**

optimistically [ˌɒptɪˈmɪstɪklɪ] ADV con optimismo

optimization [ˌɒptɪmaɪˈzeɪʃən] N optimización *f*

optimize [ˈɒptɪmaɪz] VT optimizar

optimum [ˈɒptɪməm] ADJ [*level, number*] óptimo • **in ~ conditions** en las condiciones óptimas *or* más favorables • **within the ~ time** dentro del tiempo ideal • **for ~ health** para gozar de buena salud
N (PL: **optimums** *or* **optima** [ˈɒptɪmə]) • **the ~** lo óptimo, lo mejor • **they are not functioning at their ~** no están funcionando lo mejor que pueden, no están funcionando al nivel óptimo

option [ˈɒpʃən] N **1** (= *choice*) opción *f* • **what are my ~s?** ¿qué opciones tengo? • **you have a number of ~s** tienes varias opciones • **I have no ~** no tengo más *or* otro remedio, no tengo otra opción • **she had no ~ but to leave** no tuvo más remedio que irse • **to have the ~ of doing sth** tener la posibilidad de hacer algo • **imprisonment without the ~ of bail** (*Jur*) prisión *f* preventiva • **to keep one's ~s open** no descartar ninguna posibilidad
2 (*Comm*) opción *f* • **at the ~ of the purchaser** a opción del comprador • **stock ~** (*Econ*) compra *f* opcional de acciones • **to take out an ~ on another 100** suscribir una opción para la compra de otros 100 • **with the ~ to buy** con opción de compra • **with an ~ on ten more aircraft** con opción para la compra de otros diez aviones
3 (*Scol, Univ*) asignatura *f* optativa • **I'm doing geology as my ~** tengo geología como asignatura optativa
CPD ▸ **options market** mercado *m* de opciones

optional [ˈɒpʃənl] ADJ [*course, subject*] optativo, facultativo; [*part, accessory*] opcional • **that is completely ~** eso es completamente opcional • **~ extra** (*Aut*) accesorio *m* opcional, extra *m* • **"dress optional"** "no se requiere (ir de) etiqueta"

optionally [ˈɒpʃənlɪ] ADV opcionalmente

optometrist [ɒpˈtɒmətrɪst] N optometrista *mf*

optometry [ɒpˈtɒmətrɪ] N optometría *f*

opt-out [ˈɒptaʊt] ADJ **1** (*Brit*) [*school, hospital*] autónomo (*transferido de la administración local al gobierno central*)
2 (*esp Brit*) • **opt-out clause** cláusula *f* de exclusión voluntaria, cláusula *f* de no participación
N (*from agreement, treaty*) opción *f* de exclusión voluntaria, opción *f* de no participación

opulence [ˈɒpjʊləns] N opulencia *f*

opulent [ˈɒpjʊlənt] ADJ opulento

opus [ˈəʊpəs] N (PL: **opuses** *or* **opera**) (*Mus*) opus *m*

OR ABBR **1** = **operations** *or* **operational research**
2 (*US*) = **Oregon**
3 (*Sport*) = **Olympic record**

or [ɔːʳ] CONJ **1** (*giving alternative*) o; (*before o-, ho-*) u; (*between numerals*) ó • **would you like tea or coffee?** ¿quieres té o café? • **seven or eight** siete u ocho • **men or women** mujeres u hombres • **15 or 16** 15 ó 16 • **let me go or I'll scream!** ¡suélteme, o me pongo a gritar! • **hurry up or you'll miss the bus** date prisa, que vas a perder el autobús • **rain or no rain, you've got to go** con lluvia o sin lluvia,

O

tienes que ir • **not ... or ...** no ... ni ... • **he didn't write or telephone** no escribió ni telefoneó • **I don't eat meat or fish** no como carne ni pescado • **she can't dance or sing** no sabe bailar ni cantar • **20 or so** unos veinte, veinte más o menos • **an hour or so** una hora más o menos • **without relatives or friends** sin parientes ni amigos; ▸ **either, else**
2 (= *that is*) es decir • **botany, or the science of plants** botánica, es decir la ciencia que estudia las plantas • **or rather ...** o mejor dicho ..., o más bien ...

> **OR**
>
> **"U" and "ó" instead of "o"**
>
> ▸ *While* **or** *is usually translated by* **o**, *use* **u** *instead before words beginning with* **o** *and* **ho**:
>
> **... two or three photos ...**
> ... dos o tres fotos ...
> **... for one reason or another ...**
> ... por un motivo u otro ...
> **She was accused of parricide or homicide**
> Se le acusó de parricidio u homicidio
>
> ▸ *Write* **ó** *instead of* **o** *between numerals to prevent confusion with zero:*
>
> **... 5 or 6 ...**
> ... 5 ó 6 ...
>
> NOTE: *Remember to use* **ni** *with negatives.*
>
> *For further uses and examples, see main entry.*

o.r. (ABBR) = **at owner's risk**
oracle ['ɒrəkl] (N) oráculo *m*
oracular [ɒ'rækjʊlə^r] (ADJ) profético, fatídico
oral ['ɔːrəl] (ADJ) **1** (= *spoken*) [*history, tradition, exam*] oral; (*Jur*) [*agreement, evidence*] verbal
2 (*Med, Anat*) [*contraceptive, vaccine, sex*] oral; [*hygiene*] bucal
(N) (*also* **oral exam, oral examination**) examen *m* oral
(CPD) ▸ **oral examiner** examinador(a) *m/f* en la prueba oral
orally ['ɔːrəlɪ] (ADV) **1** (= *verbally*) verbalmente, oralmente
2 (*Med*) por vía oral
orange ['ɒrɪndʒ] (N) (= *fruit*) naranja *f*; (*also* **orange tree**) naranjo *m*; (= *colour*) naranja *m*; (= *orangeade*) naranjada *f* (*con burbujas*); (= *orange squash*) naranjada *f* (*sin burbujas*)
(ADJ) **1** (*in colour*) naranja (*inv*), (de) color naranja (*inv*) • **bright ~** naranja fuerte *or* chillón, (de) color naranja fuerte *or* chillón
2 (*in taste*) [*flavour*] a naranja
(CPD) ▸ **orange blossom** azahar *m*, flor *f* de naranjo ▸ **orange box, orange crate** (*US*) caja *f* de fruta ▸ **orange drink** refresco *m* de naranja ▸ **orange flower water** agua *f* de azahar ▸ **orange grove** naranjal *m* ▸ **orange juice** zumo *m* de naranja (*Sp*), jugo *m* de naranja (*LAm*) ▸ **orange marmalade** mermelada *f* de naranja ▸ **orange peel** *or* **rind** cáscara *f* de naranja ▸ **orange sauce** salsa *f* de naranja ▸ **orange squash** naranjada *f* (*sin burbujas*) ▸ **orange stick** palito *m* de naranjo ▸ **orange tree** naranjo *m*
orangeade ['ɒrɪndʒ'eɪd] (N) (*natural*) naranjada *f*; (*fizzy*) refresco *m* de naranja
orange-coloured, orange-colored (*US*) ['ɒrɪndʒ,kʌləd] (ADJ) naranja (*inv*), (de) color naranja (*inv*)
Orangeman ['ɒrɪndʒmən] (N) (PL: **Orangemen**) *miembro de las logias protestantes de la Orden de Orange*
orangery ['ɒrɪndʒərɪ] (N) invernadero *m* de naranjos
orangey ['ɒrɪndʒɪ] (ADJ) naranjilla, anaranjado
orang-outang [ɔː,ræŋuː'tæŋ], **orang-utan** [ɔː,ræŋuː'tæn] (N) orangután *m*
orate [ɔː'reɪt] (VI) (*hum*) perorar
oration [ɔː'reɪʃən] (N) (= *speech*) discurso *m*; (= *peroration*) arenga *f* • **funeral ~** oración *f* fúnebre
orator ['ɒrətə^r] (N) orador(a) *m/f*
oratorical [,ɒrə'tɒrɪkəl] (ADJ) oratorio, retórico
oratorio [,ɒrə'tɔːrɪəʊ] (N) (PL: **oratorios**) (*Mus*) oratorio *m*
oratory[1] ['ɒrətərɪ] (N) (= *art of speaking*) oratoria *f*
oratory[2] ['ɒrətərɪ] (N) (*Rel*) oratorio *m*
orb [ɔːb] (N) (= *sphere*) esfera *f*, globo *m*; (*in regalia*) orbe *m*
orbit ['ɔːbɪt] (N) órbita *f* • **to be in/go into ~ (round the earth/moon)** estar en/entrar en órbita (alrededor de la tierra/luna) • **it's outside my ~** (*fig*) está fuera de mi competencia, que da fuera de mi ámbito
(VI) [*satellite*] orbitar, girar; [*astronaut*] estar en órbita
(VT) [+ *earth, moon*] girar alrededor de
orbital ['ɔːbɪtl] (ADJ) **1** (*Space*) orbital • **~ space station** estación *f* orbital
2 (*Brit*) (*Aut*) • **~ motorway/road** autopista *f*/ carrera *f* de circunvalación
orbiter ['ɔːbɪtə^r] (N) (*Space*) orbitador *m*
orchard ['ɔːtʃəd] (N) huerto *m* • **apple ~** manzanar *m*, manzanal *m*
orchestra ['ɔːkɪstrə] (N) orquesta *f* • **symphony ~** orquesta *f* sinfónica • **string ~** orquesta *f* de cuerdas • **chamber ~** orquesta *f* de cámara
(CPD) ▸ **orchestra pit** foso *m* de orquesta ▸ **orchestra stalls** (*Theat*) luneta *fsing*, platea *fsing*
orchestral [ɔː'kestrəl] (ADJ) orquestal
orchestrate ['ɔːkɪstreɪt] (VT) **1** (*Mus*) orquestar
2 (*fig*) [+ *rebellion*] tramar; [+ *campaign*] organizar
orchestration [,ɔːkɪs'treɪʃən] (N) (*lit, fig*) orquestación *f*
orchid ['ɔːkɪd] (N) orquídea *f*
orchis ['ɔːkɪs] (N) orquídea *f*
ordain [ɔː'deɪn] (VT) **1** (= *order*) ordenar, decretar; [*God*] mandar, disponer • **it was ~ed that ...** se dispuso que ...
2 (*Rel*) ordenar • **to ~ sb priest** ordenar a algn sacerdote • **to be ~ed** ordenarse
(VI) mandar, disponer • **as God ~s** según manda Dios, como Dios manda
ordeal [ɔː'diːl] (N) **1** (= *bad experience*) terrible experiencia *f* • **it was a terrible ~** fue una experiencia terrible • **after such an ~** después de tan terrible experiencia • **exams are an ~ for me** para mí los exámenes son un suplicio
2 (*Hist*) ordalías *fpl* • **~ by fire** ordalías *fpl* del fuego
order ['ɔːdə^r] (N) **1** (= *sequence*) orden *m* • **in ~** en orden, por orden • **what ~ should these documents be in?** ¿en qué orden deben estar estos documentos? • **in alphabetical ~** por *or* en orden alfabético • **"cast in order of appearance"** (*Theat, Cine*) "por orden de aparición" • **in chronological ~** por orden cronológico • **in ~ of merit** ordenado según el mérito • **they are out of ~** están mal ordenados • **to get out of ~** desarreglarse • **put these in the right ~** ponga estos por orden • **in ~ of seniority** por orden de antigüedad • **word ~** orden *m* de las palabras • **they are in the wrong ~** están mal ordenados
2 (= *system*) orden *m* • **a new political/social ~** un nuevo orden político/social • **she has no ~ in her life** lleva un régimen de vida muy desorganizado • **the old ~ is changing** el viejo orden está cambiando • **it is in the ~ of things** es ley de vida • **a new world ~** un nuevo orden mundial
3 (= *good order*) buen estado *m*, orden *m* • **in ~** (*legally*) en regla; [*room*] en orden, ordenado • **his papers are in ~** tiene los papeles en regla • **everything is in ~** todo está en regla • **is this passport in ~?** ¿este pasaporte está en regla? • **to put a matter in ~** arreglar un asunto • **to put one's affairs in ~** poner sus asuntos en orden • **in good ~** en buen estado, en buenas condiciones • **a machine in working** *or* **running ~** una máquina en buen estado • **to be out of ~** [*machine*] estar estropeado *or* (*LAm*) descompuesto • **the line is out of ~** (*Telec*) no hay línea, la línea no funciona • **"out of order"** "no funciona"
4 (= *peace, control*) orden *m* • **the forces of ~** las fuerzas del orden • **to keep ~** mantener el orden • **she can't keep ~** es incapaz de imponer la disciplina, no puede hacerse obedecer • **to keep children in ~** mantener a los niños en orden
5 (= *command*) orden *f*; [*of court etc*] sentencia *f*, fallo *m* • **~s are ~s** las órdenes no se discuten • **bankruptcy ~** orden *f* de quiebra • **by ~ of** por orden de • **Order in Council** (*Brit*) (*Parl*) Orden *f* Real • **~ of the court** sentencia *f* del tribunal • **deportation ~** orden *f* de deportación • **till further ~s** hasta nueva orden • **to give ~s** dar órdenes • **to give sb ~s to do sth** ordenar *or* mandar a algn hacer algo • **he gave the ~ for it to be done** ordenó que se hiciera • **to obey ~s** cumplir órdenes • **on the ~s of** a las órdenes de • **to take ~s from sb** recibir órdenes de algn • **I don't take ~s from anyone** a mí no me da órdenes nadie • **that's an ~!** ¡es una orden! • **under ~s** bajo órdenes • **we are under ~s not to allow it** tenemos orden de no permitirlo • **to be under the ~s of** estar bajo el mando de • IDIOM: • **to get one's marching ~s*** ser despedido; ▸ **starter**
6 (= *correct procedure*) (*at meeting, Parliament etc*) orden *m* • **order (, order)!** ¡orden! • **to call sb to ~** llamar a algn al orden • **to call the meeting to ~** abrir la sesión • **~ of the day** (*Mil*) orden del día; (*fig*) moda *f*, estilo *m* del momento • **strikes are the ~ of the day** las huelgas están a la orden del día • **to be in ~** [*action, request*] ser procedente • **a beer would be in ~** sería indicado tomarse una cerveza • **it seems congratulations are in ~!** ¡enhorabuena! • **is it in ~ for me to go to Rome?** ¿(le) es inconveniente si voy a Roma? • **it is not in ~ to discuss Ruritania** Ruritania está fuera de la cuestión • **to be out of ~*** (= *unacceptable*) [*remark*] estar fuera de lugar; [*person*] comportarse mal • **to rule a matter out of ~** decidir que un asunto no se puede discutir • **a point of ~** una cuestión de procedimiento
7 (*Comm*) pedido *m*, encargo *m* • **we have it on ~ for you** está pedido para usted • **we will put it on ~ for you** se lo pediremos para usted al fabricante • **to place an ~ for sth with sb** encargar *or* hacer un pedido de algo a algn • **repeat ~** pedido *m* de repetición • **rush ~** pedido *m* urgente • **made to ~** hecho a medida • **we can't do things to ~** no podemos proveer en seguida todo cuanto se nos pide • IDIOM: • **that's rather a tall ~** eso es mucho pedir
8 (*in restaurant*) • **the waiter took our ~** el camarero tomó nota de lo que íbamos a comer • **an ~ of French fries** una ración de patatas fritas

9 • **in ~ to do sth** para *or* a fin de hacer algo • **in ~ that he may stay** para que pueda quedarse
10 [*of society etc*] clase *f*, categoría *f*; (*Bio*) orden *m* • **Benedictine Order** Orden *f* de San Benito • **the present crisis is of a different ~** la crisis actual es de un orden distinto • **talents of the first ~** talentos *mpl* de primer orden • **holy ~s** órdenes *fpl* sagradas • **to be in/take (holy) ~s** ser/ordenarse sacerdote • **the lower ~s** las clases bajas *or* (*LAm*) populares • **of the ~ of 500** del orden de los quinientos • **something in** *or* **of** *or* (*US*) **on the ~ of £3,000** unos 3.000, alrededor de 3.000 • **~ of magnitude** magnitud *f*
11 (*Econ*) libranza *f*; (*postal*) giro *m* • **pay to the ~ of** páguese a la orden de
12 (*Archit*) orden *m* • **Doric ~** orden *m* dórico
13 • **in short ~** (*US*) rápidamente
14 (*Mil*) • **in battle ~** en orden de batalla • **in close ~** en filas apretadas • **in marching ~** en orden de marchar
(VT) **1** (= *command*) mandar, ordenar • **to ~ sb to do sth** mandar *or* ordenar a algn hacer algo • **to be ~ed to pay costs** ser condenado en costas • **he was ~ed to be quiet** le ordenaron que se callara • **he ~ed that the army should advance** ordenó que el ejército avanzara, dio órdenes de que el ejército avanzara • **the referee ~ed the player off the field** el árbitro expulsó al jugador del campo • **to ~ sb in/up** *etc* mandar entrar/subir *etc* a algn, hacer entrar/subir *etc* a algn • **are you ~ing me out of my own house?** ¿me estás echando de mi propia casa?
2 (= *put in order*) ordenar, poner en orden • **they are ~ed by date/size** están ordenados por fecha/tamaño
3 (= *organize*) organizar, arreglar • **to ~ one's life properly** organizar bien su vida, vivir de acuerdo a cierto método
4 [+ *goods, meal, taxi*] pedir, encargar • **to ~ a suit** mandar hacer un traje • **we ~ed steak and chips** pedimos un filete con patatas fritas
(VI) (*in restaurant*) pedir • **are you ready to ~?** ¿han decidido qué van a pedir?
(CPD) ▸ **order book** (*Comm*) libro *m* de pedidos, cartera *f* de pedidos ▸ **order department** (*Comm*) sección *f* de pedidos ▸ **order form** (*Comm*) hoja *f* de pedido ▸ **order number** (*Comm*) número *m* de pedido ▸ **Order of Merit** (*Brit*) • **the Order of Merit** la Orden del Mérito ▸ **order paper** (*Brit*) (*Parl etc*) orden *m* del día; ▹ **garter**
▸ **order about, order around** (VT + ADV) dar órdenes a, mandonear* • **she was fed up with being ~ed about** estaba harta de que le dieran órdenes
▸ **order back** (VT + ADV) mandar volver
ordered [ˈɔːdəd] (ADJ) ordenado, metódico, disciplinado
ordering [ˈɔːdərɪŋ] (N) (*Comm*) pedido *m*
orderliness [ˈɔːdəlɪnɪs] (N) orden *m*, método *m*, disciplina *f*
orderly [ˈɔːdəlɪ] (ADJ) [*queue, row, room*] ordenado; [*person, mind*] ordenado, metódico; [*crowd*] pacífico; [*class*] obediente, disciplinado • **in an ~ fashion** *or* **way** *or* **manner** de forma *or* manera ordenada
(N) (*Mil*) ordenanza *mf*; (*Med*) celador(a) *m/f*
(CPD) ▸ **orderly room** (*Mil*) oficina *f*
ordinal [ˈɔːdɪnl] (ADJ) ordinal • **~ number** número *m* ordinal
(N) ordinal *m*
ordinance [ˈɔːdɪnəns] (N) decreto-ley *m*, reglamento *m*
ordinand [ˈɔːdɪnænd] (N) ordenando *m*
ordinarily [ɔːdɪˈnɛərɪlɪ] (ADV) por lo común, generalmente
ordinary [ˈɔːdnrɪ] (ADJ) **1** (= *usual, normal*) [*milk, coffee*] normal, corriente • **it has 25 calories less than ~ ice cream** tiene 25 calorías menos que el helado normal *or* corriente • **my ~ doctor** el médico al que voy normalmente • **I'd rather wear my ~ clothes** prefiero usar mi ropa normal • **the heat made ~ life almost impossible** el calor hacía la vida normal casi imposible • **in ~ use** usado normalmente • **in the ~ way** normalmente
2 (= *unremarkable, average*) normal y corriente • **it was just an ~ weekend for us** para nosotros no era más que un fin de semana cualquiera *or* un fin de semana normal y corriente • **he's a normal, ~ guy** es un tipo normal y corriente • **it's not what you'd call an ~ present** no es lo que se dice un regalo de todos los días • **an ~ citizen** un simple ciudadano, un ciudadano de a pie • **it was no ~ bar** no era un bar corriente • **your life since then must have seemed very ~** tu vida desde entonces debe de haberte parecido demasiado normal • **the meal was very ~** (*pej*) la comida fue bastante mediocre, la comida no fue nada del otro mundo *or* del otro jueves
(N) • **a man above the ~** un hombre fuera de serie, un hombre excepcional • **a cut above the ~** fuera de serie • **out of the ~** fuera de lo común, extraordinario
(CPD) ▸ **ordinary degree** (*Brit*) (*Univ*) diploma *m*, *título universitario de categoría inferior al Honours degree*; ▹ DEGREE ▸ **Ordinary Grade** (*Scot*) (*formerly*) *nivel medio de la enseñanza secundaria*, ≈ Bachillerato *m* Unificado y Polivalente (*Sp*) ▸ **Ordinary Level** (*Brit*) (*formerly*) *nivel medio de la enseñanza secundaria*, ≈ Bachillerato *m* Unificado y Polivalente (*Sp*) ▸ **Ordinary National Certificate** (*Brit*) ≈ diploma *m* de técnico especialista ▸ **Ordinary National Diploma** (*Brit*) *diploma profesional*, ≈ diploma *m* de técnico especialista ▸ **ordinary seaman** (*Brit*) (*Navy*) marinero *m* ▸ **ordinary shares** acciones *fpl* ordinarias
ordination [ˌɔːdɪˈneɪʃən] (N) (*Rel*) ordenación *f*
ordnance [ˈɔːdnəns] (*Mil*) (N) (= *guns*) artillería *f*; (= *supplies*) pertrechos *mpl* de guerra, material *m* de guerra
(CPD) ▸ **Ordnance Corps** Cuerpo *m* de Armamento y Material ▸ **ordnance factory** fábrica *f* de artillería ▸ **Ordnance Survey** (*Brit*) *servicio estatal de cartografía* ▸ **Ordnance Survey map** (*Brit*) mapa *m* del servicio estatal de cartografía
Ordovician [ˌɔːdəʊˈvɪʃən] (ADJ) ordoviciense
ordure [ˈɔːdjʊəʳ] (N) (*lit, fig*) inmundicia *f*
ore [ɔːʳ] (N) mineral *m*, mena *f* • **copper ore** mineral *m* de cobre
Ore. (ABBR) (*US*) = **Oregon**
ore-carrier [ˈɔːkærɪəʳ] (N) mineralero *m*
Oreg. (ABBR) (*US*) = **Oregon**
oregano [ˌɒrɪˈɡɑːnəʊ], (*US*) [əˈreɡənəʊ] (N) orégano *m*
organ [ˈɔːɡən] (N) **1** (*Mus*) órgano *m*; (= *barrel organ*) organillo *m*
2 (*Anat*) órgano *m*
3 (= *mouthpiece*) [*of opinion*] órgano *m*, portavoz *mf*
(CPD) ▸ **organ donor** donante *m/f* de órganos ▸ **organ loft** tribuna *f* del órgano, galería *f* del órgano ▸ **organ pipe** cañón *m* de órgano ▸ **organ stop** registro *m* de órgano ▸ **organ transplant** transplante *m* de órganos
organdie, organdy (*US*) [ˈɔːɡəndɪ] (N) organdí *m*
organ-grinder [ˈɔːɡənˌɡraɪndəʳ] (N) organillero/a *m/f*
organic [ɔːˈɡænɪk] (ADJ) **1** (= *living*) [*matter, waste*] orgánico; [*fertiliser*] orgánico, natural
2 (= *not chemical*) [*farmer, farm, methods*] ecológico; [*vegetables, produce*] de cultivo biológico, biológico; [*meat*] ecológico; [*flour*] integral; [*wine, beer*] sin sustancias artificiales • **~ food** alimentos *mpl* biológicos, alimentos *mpl* de cultivo biológico • **~ farming** agricultura *f* ecológica *or* biológica • **~ restaurant** restaurante *m* de cocina natural
3 (*Chem*) orgánico • **~ chemistry** química *f* orgánica
4 (*frm*) (= *natural*) [*growth, development, change*] natural; (= *united*) [*society, state, community*] orgánico
organically [ɔːˈɡænɪkəlɪ] (ADV) **1** (*Agr*) [*grow, produce, farm*] biológicamente, sin utilizar pesticidas ni fertilizantes artificiales • **~ grown foods** alimentos *mpl* biológicos, alimentos *mpl* de cultivo biológico • **an ~ rich soil** un suelo orgánicamente rico
2 (*Med*) • **the surgeons could find nothing ~ wrong** los cirujanos no encontraban nada que estuviera mal desde el punto de vista físico
3 (*fig*) [*grow, develop, integrate*] de forma natural
organism [ˈɔːɡənɪzəm] (N) (*Bio*) organismo *m*
organist [ˈɔːɡənɪst] (N) organista *mf*
organization [ˌɔːɡənaɪˈzeɪʃən] (N) **1** (= *act*) organización *f*
2 (= *body*) organización *f*, organismo *m*
(CPD) ▸ **organization chart** organigrama *m*
organizational [ˌɔːɡənaɪˈzeɪʃənl] (ADJ) organizativo
organize [ˈɔːɡənaɪz] (VT) **1** (= *arrange*) [+ *event, activity*] organizar • **they ~d demonstrations against the closures** organizaron manifestaciones en contra de los cierres • **can you ~ some food for us?** ¿puedes encargarte de nuestra comida? • **I will ~ transport** yo me encargaré del transporte
2 (= *put in order*) • **she tried to ~ her thoughts** intentó ordenar *or* poner en orden sus pensamientos • **she ~s her time very well** administra muy bien su tiempo, se organiza muy bien (el tiempo) • **she's always organizing people** siempre le está diciendo a la gente qué hacer • **stop trying to ~ my life** deja de intentar organizar mi vida • **to get (o.s.) ~d** • **~ o.s.** organizarse
3 (*Ind*) sindicar, organizar en sindicatos
(VI) **1** (= *make arrangements*) organizar • **we have ~d for every eventuality** lo hemos organizado todo para cualquier eventualidad • **he's ~d for us to meet the director** lo ha organizado para que nos reunamos con el director
2 (*Ind*) sindicarse
organized [ˈɔːɡənaɪzd] (ADJ) **1** (= *methodical*) [*person*] organizado • **it was ~ chaos** era un caos organizado *or* ordenado
2 (= *planned*) [*crime, event, tour*] organizado
3 (*Ind*) • **~ labour** trabajadores *mpl or* obreros *mpl* sindicados
(CPD) ▸ **organized religion** religión *f* organizada
organizer [ˈɔːɡənaɪzəʳ] (N) organizador(a) *m/f*
organizing [ˈɔːɡənaɪzɪŋ] (ADJ) • **she has excellent ~ ability** tiene una aptitud excelente para organizar • **the ~ principle** el principio organizador
(CPD) ▸ **organizing committee** comité *m* organizador, comisión *f* organizadora
organophosphate [ɔːˌɡænəʊˈfɒsfeɪt] (N) organofosfato *m*

organza [ɔːˈgænzə] N organza *f*, organdí *m* de seda

orgasm [ˈɔːgæzəm] N orgasmo *m* • **to bring sb to ~** hacer llegar al orgasmo a algn
VI tener un orgasmo, llegar al orgasmo

orgasmic [ɔːˈgæzmɪk] ADJ orgásmico

orgiastic [ˌɔːdʒɪˈæstɪk] ADJ orgiástico

orgy [ˈɔːdʒɪ] N (*lit, fig*) orgía *f* • **an ~ of destruction** una orgía de destrucción

oriel [ˈɔːrɪəl] N mirador *m*

Orient [ˈɔːrɪənt] N Oriente *m*

orient [ˈɔːrɪənt] VT = **orientate**

oriental [ˌɔːrɪˈentəl] ADJ oriental, de Oriente
N • **Oriental**† oriental *mf*

orientalism [ˌɔːrɪˈentəlɪzəm] N orientalismo *m*

orientalist [ˌɔːrɪˈentəlɪst] ADJ orientalista
N orientalista *mf*

orientate [ˈɔːrɪenteɪt] VT orientar; (*fig*) encaminar • **to ~ o.s.** orientarse

orientated [ˈɔːrɪənteɪtɪd], **oriented** [ˈɔːrɪentɪd] ADJ • **to be ~ to sth** [*person*] inclinarse por algo • **to be ~ towards sth** [*thing*] estar orientado hacia algo

-orientated [ˈɔːrɪenteɪtɪd], **-oriented** [ˈɔːrɪentɪd] ADJ (*ending in compounds*) • **career-orientated** orientado hacia una carrera • **commercially-orientated** orientado hacia el comercio

orientation [ˌɔːrɪenˈteɪʃən] N orientación *f*
CPD ▸ **orientation course** curso *m* de orientación

oriented [ˈɔːrɪentɪd] ▹ **orientated**

-oriented [ˈɔːrɪentɪd] ADJ (*ending in compounds*) ▹ **-orientated**

orienteering [ˌɔːrɪənˈtɪərɪŋ] N (= *sport*) carrera *f* con mapa y brújula

orifice [ˈɒrɪfɪs] N orificio *m*

origami [ˌɒrɪˈgɑːmɪ] N papiroflexia *f*

origin [ˈɒrɪdʒɪn] N [*of belief, rumour, language, person*] origen *m*; [*of river*] nacimiento *m* • **country of ~** país *m* de origen *or* de procedencia • **to be of humble ~** • **have humble ~s** ser de origen humilde

original [əˈrɪdʒɪnl] ADJ **1** (= *first, earliest*) [*version, size, colour, owner, intention, idea*] original; [*inhabitants*] primero, primitivo • **of the ~ twenty, only twelve remained** de los veinte iniciales, solo quedaban doce • **one of the ~ members** uno de los primeros miembros
2 (= *not copied*) [*document, painting*] original • **an ~ Picasso** un Picasso original
3 (= *unusual, creative*) [*person, idea*] original • **he's an ~ thinker** es un pensador original • **he has an ~ mind** tiene una mente original
N **1** (= *manuscript, painting, document*) original *m* • **he reads Homer in the ~** lee a Homero en versión original • **in the ~ French** en la versión original francesa
2 (= *person*) • **he was something of an ~** era un tanto original
CPD ▸ **original sin** pecado *m* original

originality [əˌrɪdʒɪˈnælɪtɪ] N originalidad *f*

originally [əˈrɪdʒənəlɪ] ADV **1** (= *at first*) originariamente, en un principio • **they were in Athens originariamente** *or* **en un principio estuvieron en Atenas** • **Lucy had ~ intended to be a doctor** Lucy tenía inicialmente la intención de ser médico, Lucy en un principio tenía la intención de ser médico • **he's ~ from Armenia** es originario de Armenia
2 (= *in an original way*) con originalidad, de manera original • **she dresses very ~** es muy original vistiendo, viste con mucha originalidad *or* de manera muy original • **it is quite ~ written** está escrito con bastante originalidad

originate [əˈrɪdʒɪneɪt] VT producir, originar; [*person*] idear, crear
VI • **to ~ (from** *or* **in)** originarse (en), tener su origen (en); (= *begin*) empezar (en *or* con) • **where did the fire ~?** ¿dónde se originó el incendio? • **these oranges ~ from Israel** estas naranjas son de Israel • **where do you ~ from?** ¿de dónde eres? • **with whom did the idea ~?** ¿quién tuvo la idea primero?

originator [əˈrɪdʒɪneɪtəʳ] N inventor(a) *m/f*, creador(a) *m/f*

oriole [ˈɔːrɪəʊl] N • **golden ~** oropéndola *f*

Orkney [ˈɔːknɪ] N (*also* **the Orkney Islands**) las (Islas) Órcadas

Orlon® [ˈɔːlɒn] N orlón® *m*

ormolu [ˈɔːməʊluː] N similor *m*, bronce *m* dorado

ornament N [ˈɔːnəmənt] (*gen*) adorno *m*, ornamento *m*; (= *vase etc*) objeto *m* de adorno, adorno *m*
VT [ˈɔːnəment] adornar

ornamental [ˌɔːnəˈmentl] ADJ decorativo, de adorno; (*Bot*) ornamental

ornamentation [ˌɔːnəmenˈteɪʃən] N (= *act*) ornamentación *f*, decoración *f*; (= *ornaments*) adornos *mpl*

ornate [ɔːˈneɪt] ADJ [*decor*] ornamentado; [*building, ceiling, vase, architectural style*] ornamentado, ricamente decorado; [*written style, language*] florido, recargado (*pej*) • **the room is too ~ for my taste** la habitación está demasiado recargada para mi gusto

ornately [ɔːˈneɪtlɪ] ADV [*carved, painted, designed*] con muchos adornos, de manera elaborada; [*written*] en un estilo florido *or* (*pej*) recargado

ornateness [ɔːˈneɪtnɪs] N [*of decor, ceiling, building, vase*] lo ornamentado; [*of language*] lo florido, estilo *m* florido, recargamiento *m* (*pej*)

ornithological [ˌɔːnɪθəˈlɒdʒɪkəl] ADJ ornitológico

ornithologist [ˌɔːnɪˈθɒlədʒɪst] N ornitólogo/a *m/f*

ornithology [ˌɔːnɪˈθɒlədʒɪ] N ornitología *f*

orphan [ˈɔːfən] N huérfano/a *m/f*
ADJ huérfano
VT • **to be ~ed** quedarse huérfano • **she was ~ed at the age of nine** quedó huérfana a los nueve años • **the children were ~ed by the accident** el accidente dejó huérfanos a los niños

orphanage [ˈɔːfənɪdʒ] N **1** (= *institution*) orfanato *m*, orfanatorio *m* (*Mex*)
2 (= *state*) orfandad *f*

Orpheus [ˈɔːfjuːs] N Orfeo

ortho... [ˈɔːθəʊ] PREFIX orto...

orthodontic [ɔːθəʊˈdɒntɪk] ADJ de ortodoncia, ortodoncista

orthodontics [ˌɔːθəʊˈdɒntɪks] NSING ortodoncia *f*

orthodontist [ˌɔːθəʊˈdɒntɪst] N ortodoncista *mf*

orthodox [ˈɔːθədɒks] ADJ ortodoxo
CPD ▸ **Orthodox Church** • **the Orthodox Church** la Iglesia Ortodoxa ▸ **orthodox Jew** judío/a *m/f* ortodoxo/a

orthodoxy [ˈɔːθədɒksɪ] N ortodoxia *f*

orthographic [ˌɔːθəˈgræfɪk] ADJ ortográfico

orthographical [ˌɔːθəˈgræfɪkəl] ADJ = **orthographic**

orthography [ɔːˈθɒgrəfɪ] N ortografía *f*

orthopaedic, orthopedic (*US*) [ˌɔːθəʊˈpiːdɪk] ADJ ortopédico • **~ surgeon** ortopedista *mf*, traumatólogo/a *m/f* • **~ surgery** cirujía *f* ortopédica

orthopaedics, orthopedics (*US*) [ˌɔːθəʊˈpiːdɪks] NSING ortopedia *f*

orthopaedist, orthopedist (*US*) [ˌɔːθəʊˈpiːdɪst] N ortopedista *mf*, traumatólogo/a *m/f*

orthoptic [ɔːˈθɒptɪk] ADJ (*Med*) ortóptico • **~ exercises** ejercicios ortópticos

oryx [ˈɒrɪks] N (PL: **oryxes** *or* **oryx**) orix *m*, órix *m*

OS ABBR **1** (*Brit*) (*Geog*) (= **Ordnance Survey**) *servicio oficial de topografía*
2 (*Brit*) (*Navy*) = **Ordinary Seaman**
3 (*Hist*) (= **old style**) según el calendario juliano

O/S ABBR = **out of stock**

o/s ABBR (*Comm*) (= **outsize**) de tamaño extraordinario

Oscar [ˈɒskəʳ] N (*Cine*) Oscar *m*
CPD ▸ **Oscar ceremony, Oscars ceremony** ceremonia *f* de los Oscar(s)

oscillate [ˈɒsɪleɪt] VI **1** (*Phys*) oscilar; [*compass, needle etc*] oscilar, fluctuar
2 (*fig*) oscilar • **he ~s between boredom and keenness** pasa del aburrimiento al entusiasmo, oscila entre el aburrimiento y el entusiasmo
VT hacer oscilar

oscillating [ˈɒsɪleɪtɪŋ] ADJ oscilante

oscillation [ˌɒsɪˈleɪʃən] N **1** (*Phys*) oscilación *f*; [*of prices*] fluctuación *f*
2 (*fig*) oscilación *f*

oscillator [ˈɒsɪleɪtəʳ] N oscilador *m*

oscillatory [ˌɒsɪˈleɪtərɪ] ADJ oscilatorio

oscilloscope [ɒˈsɪləˌskəʊp] N osciloscopio *m*

osculate [ˈɒskjʊleɪt] (*hum*) VT besar
VI besar, besarse

osculation [ˌɒskjʊˈleɪʃən] N (*hum*) ósculo *m*

OSD ABBR (*Rel*) (= **Order of Saint Dominic**) O.P.

OSHA N ABBR (*US*) = **Occupational Safety and Health Administration**

osier [ˈəʊʒəʳ] N mimbre *m or f*
CPD ▸ **osier bed** mimbrera *f*

Oslo [ˈɒzləʊ] N Oslo *m*

osmium [ˈɒzmɪəm] N osmio *m*

osmosis [ɒzˈməʊsɪs] N ósmosis *f inv*, osmosis *f inv*

osmotic [ɒzˈmɒtɪk] ADJ osmótico

osprey [ˈɒspreɪ] N águila *f* pescadora

osseous [ˈɒsɪəs] ADJ óseo

ossification [ˌɒsɪfɪˈkeɪʃən] N osificación *f*

ossify [ˈɒsɪfaɪ] VI (*lit*) osificarse; (*fig*) anquilosarse
VT osificar

ossuary [ˈɒsjʊərɪ] N osario *m*

OST N ABBR (*US*) = **Office of Science and Technology**

Ostend [ɒsˈtend] N Ostende *m*

ostensible [ɒsˈtensəbl] ADJ aparente

ostensibly [ɒsˈtensəblɪ] ADV aparentemente, en apariencia

ostensive [ɒˈstensɪv] ADJ ostensivo

ostentation [ˌɒstenˈteɪʃən] N ostentación *f*, boato *m*

ostentatious [ˌɒstenˈteɪʃəs] ADJ [*behaviour, car, clothes*] ostentoso; [*surroundings, style of living*] suntuoso, fastuoso

ostentatiously [ˌɒstenˈteɪʃəslɪ] ADV ostentosamente, con ostentación

osteo... [ˈɒstɪəʊ] PREFIX osteo...

osteoarthritis [ˈɒstɪəʊɑːˈθraɪtɪs] N osteoartritis *f*

osteomalacia [ˌɒstɪəʊməˈleɪʃɪə] N osteomalacia *f*

osteomyelitis [ˌɒstɪəʊmaɪˈlaɪtɪs] N osteomielitis *f*

osteopath [ˈɒstɪəpæθ] N osteópata *mf*

osteopathy [ˌɒstɪˈɒpəθɪ] N osteopatía *f*

osteoporosis [ˌɒstɪəʊpɔːˈrəʊsɪs] N osteoporosis *f inv*

ostler†† [ˈɒsləʳ] N (*esp Brit*) mozo *m* de cuadra

ostmark ['ɒstːmaːk] (N) marco *m* de la antigua RDA
ostracism ['ɒstrəsɪzəm] (N) ostracismo *m*
ostracize ['ɒstrəsaɪz] (VT) condenar al ostracismo
ostrich ['ɒstrɪtʃ] (N) (PL: **ostriches** *or* **ostrich**) avestruz *m*
(CPD) ▸ **ostrich egg** huevo *m* de avestruz
OT (N ABBR) **1** (= **Old Testament**) A.T.
2 (*Med*) = **occupational therapy**
OTB (N ABBR) (*US*) (= **off-track betting**) *apuestas ilegales hechas fuera del hipódromo*
OTC (ADV ABBR) (*Comm*) = **over the counter**
(N ABBR) (*Brit*) = **Officer Training Corps**
OTE (NPL ABBR) (*Brit*) (= **on-target earnings**) beneficios *mpl* según los objetivos
Othello [ə'θeləʊ] (N) Otelo
other ['ʌðəʳ] (ADJ) otro • **all the ~ books have been sold** todos los otros *or* los demás libros se han vendido • **the ~ five** los otros cinco • **the ~ day** el otro día • **every ~ day** cada dos días • **together with every ~ woman** así como todas las mujeres • **if there are no ~ questions ...** si no hay más preguntas ... • **the ~ one** el otro/la otra • **some actor or ~** un actor cualquiera • **~ people** los otros, los demás • **~ people have done it** otros lo han hecho • **some ~ people have still to arrive** todavía no han llegado todos, aún tienen que llegar algunos más • **~ people's property** la propiedad ajena • **~ people's ideas** las ideas ajenas • **on the ~ side of the street** al otro lado de la calle • **among ~ things she is a writer** entre otras cosas es escritora • **some ~ time** en otro momento, en otra ocasión • **there must be some ~ way of doing it** debe haber alguna otra forma de hacerlo
(PRON) • **the ~** el otro/la otra • **the ~s** los otros/las otras, los/las demás • **the ~s are going but I'm not** los demás van, pero yo no • **some do, ~s don't** algunos sí, otros no • **and these five ~s** y estos otros cinco • **we must respect ~s' rights** hay que respetar los derechos ajenos • **one after the ~** uno tras otro • **among ~s** entre otros • **are there any ~s?** (*gen*) ¿hay algún otro?; (= *any unaccounted for*) ¿falta alguno?; (= *anybody unaccounted for*) ¿falta alguien? • **you and no ~** solamente tú • **no book ~ than this** ningún libro que no sea este • **he had no clothes ~ than those he stood up in** no tenía más ropa que la que llevaba puesta • **it was no ~ than the bishop** fue el obispo en persona • **none ~ than** el mismísimo/la mismísima • **one or ~ of them will come** uno de ellos vendrá • **somebody or ~** alguien, alguno • **some fool or ~** algún tonto; ▹ **every**
(ADV) • **somewhere or ~** en alguna parte, en algún lado • **~ than him** aparte de él • **he could not have acted ~ than he did** no le quedaba otro recurso que hacer lo que hizo • **I wouldn't wish him ~ than he is** no quisiera que fuera distinto de como es
otherness ['ʌðənɪs] (N) alteridad *f*
otherwise ['ʌðəwaɪz] (CONJ) (= *if not*) si no, de lo contrario • **let's go with them, ~ we shall have to walk** vámonos con ellos, si no *or* de lo contrario tendremos que ir a pie • **of course I'm interested, I wouldn't be here ~** claro que me interesa, si no *or* de lo contrario no estaría aquí
(ADV) **1** (= *another way, differently*) de otra manera • **it cannot be ~** (*frm*) no puede ser de otra manera • **they may be arrested or ~ persecuted** puede que los detengan o que los persigan de otra manera • **unless your doctor advises ~** a menos que el médico le recomiende otra cosa • **it's true, and nothing you can say will convince me ~** es verdad, y nada que puedas decir me convencerá de lo contrario • **she was ~ engaged** (*frm or hum*) tenía otro compromiso • **Miller, ~ known as Dusty** Miller, también conocido como Dusty • **until proven** *or* **proved ~** hasta que se demuestre lo contrario • **except where** *or* **unless ~ stated** (*frm*) salvo indicación de lo contrario (*frm*), a no ser que se indique lo contrario • **we had no reason to think ~** no teníamos motivo para creer otra cosa
2 (= *in other respects*) aparte de esto, por lo demás • **it's an ~ excellent piece of work** aparte de esto *or* por lo demás es un trabajo excelente • **she was a little thinner, but ~ unchanged** estaba un poco más delgada, pero aparte de eso *or* por lo demás seguía igual
3 (= *in other circumstances*) en otras circunstancias • **people who might ~ have died will live** gente que en otras circunstancias hubiera muerto, vivirá • **it's more expensive than I would ~ have bought** es más caro de lo que hubiera gastado normalmente
4 (= *of another sort*) • **he would do it by any means, legal or ~** lo haría por todos los medios, legales o no • **it may not be transmitted by any means, electronic or ~** está prohibida su transmisión por cualquier medio, ya sea electrónico o de otra clase
otherworldliness [,ʌðə'wɜːldlɪnɪs] (N) [*of person, attitude*] espiritualidad *f*
other-worldly ['ʌðə'wɜːldlɪ] (ADJ) **1** [*person*] muy espiritual
2 [*experience*] (como) de otro mundo; [*being*] extraterrestre
otiose ['əʊtɪəʊs] (ADJ) ocioso, inútil
otitis [əʊ'taɪtɪs] (N) otitis *f*
OTT* (ADJ ABBR) = **over the top**
Ottawa ['ɒtəwə] (N) Ottawa *f*
otter ['ɒtəʳ] (N) (PL: **otters** *or* **otter**) nutria *f*
Otto ['ɒtəʊ] (N) Otón
Ottoman ['ɒtəmən] (ADJ) otomano
(N) otomano/a *m/f*
ottoman ['ɒtəmən] (N) (PL: **ottomans**) otomana *f*
OU (N ABBR) (*Brit*) (= **Open University**) ≈ UNED *f*; ▹ **OPEN UNIVERSITY**
ouch [aʊtʃ] (EXCL) ¡ay!
ought¹ [ɔːt] (MODAL VB) **1** (*moral obligation*) deber • **I ~ to do it** debería hacerlo, debiera hacerlo • **one ~ not to do it** no se debiera hacer • **I ~ to have done it** debiera haberlo hecho • **you ~ to have warned me** me deberías haber avisado • **he ~ to have known** debía saberlo • **I th~ I ~ to tell you** me creí en el deber de decírselo • **to behave as one ~** comportarse como se debe
2 (*vague desirability*) • **you ~ to go and see it** vale la pena ir a verlo • **you ~ to have seen him!** ¡tenías que haberle visto!
3 (*probability*) deber • **he ~ to win** debería ganar • **that ~ to be enough** con eso debería ser suficiente • **he ~ to have arrived by now** debería de haber llegado ya
ought² [ɔːt] (N) = **aught**
Ouija® ['wiːdʒə] (N) (*also* **Ouija board**) tabla *f* de espiritismo
ounce [aʊns] (N) **1** (= *measure*) onza *f*; ▹ **IMPERIAL SYSTEM**
2 (*fig*) pizca *f* • **there's not an ~ of truth in it** en eso no hay ni una pizca de verdad • **if you had an ~ of common sense** si tuvieras una gota de sentido común
our [aʊəʳ] (POSS ADJ) (*with singular noun*) nuestro/a; (*with plural noun*) nuestros/as • **our house** nuestra casa • **our neighbours are very nice** nuestros vecinos son muy simpáticos • **we took off our coats** nos quitamos los abrigos • **they stole our car** nos robaron el coche
ours [aʊəz] (POSS PRON) (*referring to singular possession*) (el/la) nuestro/a; (*referring to plural possession*) (los/las) nuestros/as • **this house is ~** esta casa es nuestra • **a friend of ~** un amigo nuestro • **your car is much bigger than ~** vuestro coche es mucho más grande que el nuestro • **"our teachers are strict" — "~ are too"** —nuestros profesores son estrictos —los nuestros también
ourself [aʊə'self] (PERS PRON) (*frm*) (*singular use relating esp to royal or editorial 'we'*) nosotros
ourselves [,aʊə'selvz] (PERS PRON) **1** (*reflexive*) nos • **we couldn't see ~ in the photo** no podíamos vernos en la foto • **we really enjoyed ~** nos divertimos mucho
2 (*emphatic*) nosotros/as (mismos/as); (*after prep*) nosotros/as (mismos/as) • **we built our garage ~** nos construimos el garaje nosotros mismos • **we went ~** fuimos en persona • **let's not talk about ~ any more** no hablemos más de nosotros (mismos) • **we said to ~** nos dijimos
3 (*phrases*) • **we were talking among ~** hablábamos entre nosotros • **by ~** solos/as • **we prefer to be by ~** preferimos estar solos • **we did it (all) by ~** lo hicimos nosotros mismos
oust [aʊst] (VT) (*gen*) expulsar, echar; (*from house*) desahuciar, desalojar • **we ~ed them from the position** les hicimos abandonar su posición • **to ~ sb from a post** hacer que algn renuncie a un puesto
out [aʊt] (ADV)

*When **out** is the second element in a phrasal verb, eg **go out**, **put out**, **walk out**, look up the verb.*

1 (= *not in*) fuera, afuera • **it's cold out** fuera *or* afuera hace frío • **they're out in the garden** están fuera *or* afuera en el jardín • **to be out** (= *not at home*) no estar (en casa) • **Mr Green is out** el señor Green no está *or* (*LAm*) no se encuentra • **he's out for the afternoon** no estará en toda la tarde • **he's out a good deal** pasa bastante tiempo fuera • **"way out"** "salida" • **to be out and about again** estar bien otra vez (*después de una enfermedad*) • **to have a day out** pasar un día fuera de casa • **out you go!** ¡fuera! • **it's cold out here** hace frío aquí fuera • **the journey out** el viaje de ida • **to have a night out** salir por la noche (a divertirse); (*drinking*) salir de juerga *or* (*LAm*) de parranda • **to run out** salir corriendo • **it's dark out there** está oscuro ahí fuera • **the tide is out** la marea está baja • **out with him!** ¡fuera con él!, ¡que le echen fuera!; ▹ **second**¹
2 (= *on strike*) • **the railwaymen are out** los ferroviarios están en huelga
3 (*indicating distance*) • **she's out in Kuwait** se fue a Kuwait, está en Kuwait • **the boat was ten km out** el barco estaba a diez kilómetros de la costa • **three days out from Plymouth** (*Naut*) a tres días de Plymouth • **it carried us out to sea** nos llevó mar adentro
4 • **to be out**: • **when the sun is out** cuando brilla el sol • **the dahlias are out** las dalias están en flor • **to come out**: • **when the sun comes out** cuando sale el sol • **the roses are coming out** los rosales están floreciendo
5 (= *in existence*) que hay, que ha habido • **it's the biggest swindle out*** es la mayor estafa que se ha conocido jamás • **when will the magazine be out?** ¿cuándo sale la revista? • **the book is out** se ha publicado el libro, ha salido el libro • **the film is now out on video** la película ya ha salido en vídeo
6 (= *in the open*) conocido/a, fuera • **your secret's out** tu secreto se ha descubierto *or* ha salido a la luz • **out with it!**

¡desembucha!, ¡suéltalo ya!, ¡suelta la lengua! (*LAm*)
7 (= *to or at an end*) terminado/a • **before the week was out** antes de que terminara la semana
8 [*lamp, fire, gas*] apagado/a • **all the lights are out** todas las luces están apagadas • **"lights out at ten pm"** "se apagan las luces a las diez" • **my pipe is out** se me ha apagado la pipa
9 (= *not in fashion*) pasado/a de moda • **long dresses are out** ya no se llevan los vestidos largos, los vestidos largos están pasados de moda
10 (= *not in power*) • **now that the Liberals are out** ahora que los liberales están fuera del poder
11 (*Sport*) [*player*] fuera de juego; [*boxer*] fuera de combate; [*loser*] eliminado/a • **that's it, Liverpool are out** ya está, Liverpool queda eliminado • **you're out** (*in games*) quedas eliminado • **the ball is out** el balón está fuera del terreno • **out!** ¡fuera!
12 (*indicating error*) equivocado/a • **he was out in his reckoning** calculó mal • **I was not far out** por poco acierto • **your watch is five minutes out** su reloj lleva cinco minutos de atraso/de adelanto • **I'm two dollars out** he perdido dos dólares en el cálculo
13 (*indicating loudness, clearness*) en voz alta, en alto • **speak out (loud)!** ¡habla en voz alta *or* fuerte!; ▹ **right, straight**
14 (*indicating purpose*) • **he's out to make money** lo que busca es hacerse rico • **out for** en busca de • **to be out for sth** buscar algo • **he's out for all he can get** busca sus propios fines, anda detrás de lo suyo • **they're out for trouble** quieren armar un escándalo
15 • **to be out** (= *unconscious*) estar inconsciente; (= *drunk*) estar completamente borracho; (= *asleep*) estar durmiendo como un tronco • **he was out cold** estuvo completamente sin conocimiento • **I was out for some minutes** estuve inconsciente durante varios minutos, estuve varios minutos sin conocimiento
16 • **out and away** con mucho
17 (= *worn through*) • **the coat is out at the elbows** la chaqueta está rota por los codos
18 • **out of**

> *When **out of** is part of a set combination, eg **out of danger, out of proportion, out of sight**, look up the other word.*

a (= *outside, beyond*) fuera de • **out of town** fuera de la ciudad • **he lives out of town** vive fuera de la ciudad • **three kilometres out of town** a tres kilómetros de la ciudad • **to go out of the house** salir de la casa • **to look out of the window** mirar por la ventana • **to throw sth out of a window** tirar algo por una ventana • **to turn sb out of the house** echar a algn de la casa • **we're well out of it*** de buena nos hemos librado • IDIOM: • **to feel out of it*** sentirse aislado *or* fuera de contacto; ▹ **danger, proportion, range, season, sight**
b (*cause, motive*) por • **out of curiosity** por curiosidad • **out of respect for you** por el respeto que te tengo • **to do sth out of sympathy** hacer algo por compasión; ▹ **necessity, spite**
c (*origin*) de • **to copy sth out of a book** copiar algo de un libro • **to drink sth out of a cup** beber algo de una taza • **to take sth out of a drawer** sacar algo de un cajón • **a box made out of wood** una caja (hecha) de madera • **it was like something out of a nightmare** era como de una pesadilla • **a chapter out of a novel** un capítulo de una novela • **to read out of a novel** leer en una novela
d (= *from among*) de cada • **one out of every three smokers** uno de cada tres fumadores • **in nine cases out of ten** en nueve de cada diez casos
e (= *without*) sin • **we're out of petrol** nos hemos quedado sin gasolina • **we're out of milk** se nos ha acabado la leche • **it's out of stock** (*Comm*) está agotado • **to be out of hearts** (*Cards*) tener fallo a corazones; ▹ **breath**
f (*Vet*) • **Blue Ribbon, by Black Rum out of Grenada** el caballo Blue Ribbon, hijo de Black Rum y de la yegua Grenada
(N) ▹ **in**
(VT) (= *expose as homosexual*) revelar la homosexualidad de
(VI) • **the truth will out** se descubrirá la verdad • **murder will out** el asesinato se descubrirá

outa‡ ['aʊtə] (ABBR) (*esp US*) = **out of**
outage ['aʊtɪdʒ] (N) (*esp US*) (*Elec*) apagón *m*, corte *m*
out-and-out ['aʊtən'aʊt] (ADJ) **1** (= *absolute*) [*liar, villain*] redomado, empedernido; [*defeat, lie*] absoluto
2 (= *dedicated*) acérrimo
outback ['aʊtbæk] (N) (*in Australia*) despoblado *m*, campo *m*
outbid [aʊt'bɪd] (PT, PP: **outbid**) (VT) pujar más alto que
outboard ['aʊtbɔːd] (ADJ) fuera borda
(N) • **~ (motor)** motor *m* fuera borda *or* bordo
outbound ['aʊt,baʊnd] (US) (ADV) hacia fuera, hacia el exterior
(ADJ) que va hacia fuera, que va hacia el exterior; [*flight*] de ida
outbox [aʊt'bɒks] (VT) boxear mejor que
outbreak ['aʊtbreɪk] (N) [*of war*] declaración *f*; [*of hostilities*] comienzo *m*; [*of disease*] brote *m*; [*of crimes*] ola *f*; [*of violence*] arranque *m*; [*of spots*] erupción *f*
• **a salmonella ~** un brote de salmonelosis
• **at the ~ of war** al estallar la guerra
outbuilding ['aʊt,bɪldɪŋ] (N) (= *outhouse*) dependencia *f*; (= *shed*) cobertizo *m*, galpón *m* (*S. Cone*)
outburst ['aʊtbɜːst] (N) (*gen*) estallido *m*, explosión *f*; [*of anger*] arrebato *m*, arranque *m*; [*of applause*] salva *f* • **forgive my ~ last week** perdona que perdiera los estribos la semana pasada
outcast ['aʊtkɑːst] (N) (= *rejected person*) paria *mf*; (*in exile*) desterrado/a *m/f* • **he's a social ~** vive marginado por la sociedad
outclass [aʊt'klɑːs] (VT) aventajar a, superar
outcome ['aʊtkʌm] (N) (= *result*) resultado *m*; (= *consequences*) consecuencias *fpl*
outcrop ['aʊtkrɒp] (N) afloramiento *m*
(VI) aflorar
outcry ['aʊtkraɪ] (N) (= *protest*) protesta *f*, clamor *m*; (= *noise*) alboroto *m* • **to raise an ~ about sth** levantar fuertes protestas por algo • **there was a great ~** hubo fuertes protestas
outdated [aʊt'deɪtɪd] (ADJ) anticuado, pasado de moda
outdid [,aʊt'dɪd] (PT) *of* **outdo**
outdistance [aʊt'dɪstəns] (VT) dejar atrás
outdo [aʊt'duː] (PT: **outdid** [aʊt'dɪd]) (PP: **outdone** [aʊt'dʌn]) (VT) • **to ~ sb (in sth)** superar a algn (en algo) • **he was not to be outdone** no quiso quedarse atrás • **not to be outdone, he added ...** ni corto ni perezoso, añadió que ...
outdoor ['aʊtdɔːʳ] (ADJ) [*sports, work, market*] al aire libre; [*swimming pool, tennis court*] descubierto, al aire libre; [*clothes, shoes*] de calle; [*plant*] de exterior • **the ~ life** la vida al aire libre • **for ~ use** para uso al aire libre • **she's definitely the ~ type** es definitivamente una persona a la que le gusta estar al aire libre *or* a la que le gustan las actividades al aire libre
outdoors ['aʊt'dɔːz] (ADV) **1** (= *outside*) fuera • **go and play ~** id a jugar fuera • **to go ~** salir fuera • **~, there are three heated swimming pools** afuera, hay tres piscinas climatizadas
2 (= *in the open air*) [*exercise, bathe*] al aire libre; [*sleep*] al raso
(N) campo *m* abierto • **the great ~** (*hum*) la naturaleza
outer ['aʊtəʳ] (ADJ) **1** (= *exterior*) [*layer, surface*] exterior; [*skin, shell*] de fuera; [*wall, door*] exterior, de fuera; [*garment*] externo
• **remove the ~ leaves from the cabbage** quite las hojas de la parte de fuera de la col
• **the ~ world** el mundo exterior
2 (= *peripheral*) [*edge, limit*] exterior; [*suburbs*] periférico, del extrarradio • **the ~ reaches of the solar system** los extremos del sistema solar
(CPD) ▸ **Outer Hebrides** Hébridas *fpl* Exteriores ▸ **Outer London** *área administrativa que comprende los barrios situados fuera del centro de Londres* ▸ **Outer Mongolia** Mongolia *f* Exterior ▸ **outer space** espacio *m* exterior, espacio *m* sideral
outermost ['aʊtəməʊst] (ADJ) [*place*] más extremo, más remoto; [*cover, layer*] más externo, más exterior
outface [aʊt'feɪs] (VT) desafiar
outfall ['aʊtfɔːl] (N) [*of drain*] desagüe *m*, desaguadero *m*; [*of river*] desembocadura *f*
outfield ['aʊtfiːld] (N) (*Sport*) parte *f* más lejana del campo; (*Baseball*) jardín *m*
outfielder ['aʊtfiːldəʳ] (N) (*Baseball, Cricket*) *jugador en el extremo del campo*
outfight [,aʊt'faɪt] (VT) (PT, PP: **outfought**) vencer
outfit ['aʊtfɪt] (N) **1** (= *clothes*) traje *m*; (= *uniform*) uniforme *m*; (= *costume*) conjunto *m* • **a cowboy ~** un traje de vaquero • **why are you wearing that ~?** ¿por qué te has trajeado así?
2 (= *equipment*) equipo *m*; (= *tools*) juego *m* de herramientas • **a complete camper's ~** un equipo completo de campista
3* (= *organization*) grupo *m*, organización *f*; (*Mil*) unidad *f*, cuerpo *m* • **when I joined this ~** cuando vine a formar parte de esta unidad
outfitter ['aʊtfɪtəʳ] (N) camisero *m*
• **gentlemen's ~'s** (= *shop*) tienda *f* de ropa para caballero • **sports ~'s** (= *shop*) tienda *f* de artículos deportivos
outflank [aʊt'flæŋk] (VT) (*Mil*) flanquear, rebasar; (*fig*) superar en táctica, burlar
outflow ['aʊtfləʊ] (N) efusión *f*; [*of capital etc*] fuga *f*, salida *f*; (*Mech*) tubo *m* de salida
outfox [aʊt'fɒks] (VT) ser más listo que
outgeneral [aʊt'dʒenərəl] (VT) superar en estrategia, superar en táctica
outgo ['aʊtgəʊ] (N) (*US*) gastos *mpl*
outgoing ['aʊt,gəʊɪŋ] (ADJ) **1** [*president*] saliente; [*government*] cesante; [*boat, train, mail*] de salida; [*flight*] de ida; [*tide*] que baja
2 [*character*] extrovertido, sociable
outgoings ['aʊt,gəʊɪŋz] (NPL) gastos *mpl*
outgrow [aʊt'grəʊ] (PT: **outgrew** [aʊt'gruː]) (PP: **outgrown** [aʊt'grəʊn]) (VT) (*lit*) crecer más que; [+ *habit etc*] perder con la edad; [+ *defect, illness*] curarse de ... con la edad • **to ~ one's clothes** quedarle pequeña la ropa a algn • **she has ~n her gloves** se le han quedado pequeños los guantes • **we've ~n all that** todo eso ha quedado ya atrás
outgrowth ['aʊt,grəʊθ] (N) excrecencia *f*; (*fig*) extensión *f*
outguess [aʊt'ges] (VT) adelantarse a,

demostrar ser más rápido que
outgun [ˌaʊtˈɡʌn] VT (*Mil*) sobrepasar en potencia de fuego a; (*fig*) vencer
outhouse [ˈaʊthaʊs] N (PL: **outhouses** [ˈaʊthaʊzɪz]) **1** (*Brit*) = **outbuilding**
2 (*US*) (= *toilet*) retrete *m* fuera de la casa
outing [ˈaʊtɪŋ] N **1** (= *trip*) excursión *f*, paseo *m* (*LAm*) • **everyone went on an ~ to Toledo** todos fueron de excursión a Toledo
2 (= *walk*) paseo *m* • **I took a little ~** di un pequeño paseo, di una vuelta
outlandish [aʊtˈlændɪʃ] ADJ [*appearance, clothes*] estrafalario, extravagante; [*behaviour, ideas*] extraño, disparatado; [*prices*] estrafalario
outlandishly [ˌaʊtˈlændɪʃlɪ] ADV [*decorated, portrayed, dressed*] estrafalariamente, extravagantemente; [*expensive*] ridículamente; [*behave*] estrafalariamente
outlast [aʊtˈlɑːst] VT durar más tiempo que; [+ *person*] sobrevivir a
outlaw [ˈaʊtlɔː] N (= *fugitive*) prófugo/a *m/f*, fugitivo/a *m/f*; (= *bandit*) bandido/a *m/f*, matrero/a *m/f* (*And, S. Cone*); (*in Westerns*) forajido/a *m/f*
VT proscribir; [+ *drug etc*] ilegalizar; [+ *practice etc*] declarar ilegal
CPD ▸ **outlaw regime** régimen *m* fuera de la ley ▸ **outlaw state** estado *m* fuera de la ley
outlawry [ˈaʊtlɔːrɪ] N bandolerismo *m*
outlay [ˈaʊtleɪ] N desembolso *m*, gastos *mpl*
outlet [ˈaʊtlet] N **1** (*for water etc*) salida *f*; (= *drain*) desagüe *m*, distribuidora *f*; [*of river*] desembocadura *f*
2 (*Comm*) (= *shop*) tienda *f*; (= *agency*) sucursal *f*; (= *market*) mercado *m*, salida *f* • **to find an ~ for a product** encontrar una salida *or* un mercado para un producto
3 (*US*) (*Elec*) toma *f*
4 (*fig*) (*for emotion, talents etc*) desahogo *m* • **it provides an ~ for his energies** ofrece una válvula de escape para su energía
CPD (*Tech*) de salida; [*drain*] de desagüe; [*valve*] de escape ▸ **outlet mall** (*esp US*) centro *m* comercial de outlets ▸ **outlet pipe** conducto *m* de desagüe ▸ **outlet store** outlet *m* ▸ **outlet village** (*esp Brit*) centro *m* comercial de outlets
outline [ˈaʊtlaɪn] N **1** (= *shape*) contorno *m*, perfil *m*
2 (= *draft*) [*of book, film, plan, theory*] esbozo *m*, boceto *m*; (= *summary*) [*of events, facts*] resumen *m* • **parliament gave ~ approval to the new law** el parlamento aprobó en principio el nuevo proyecto de ley • **I'll give you the broad** *or* **general ~ of what we mean to do** te voy a explicar a grandes rasgos lo que pensamos hacer, te voy a resumir lo que pensamos hacer • **in ~, the story goes like this** en resumen, la historia es así
VT **1** (= *sketch*) esbozar, bosquejar; (= *silhouette*) perfilar • **the mountain was ~d against the sky** la montaña se perfilaba *or* recortaba contra el cielo • **she ~s her eyes with a dark pencil** se perfila los ojos con un lápiz de ojos oscuro
2 (= *summarize*) [+ *policy, situation, plan*] resumir, explicar a grandes rasgos
CPD ▸ **outline drawing** esbozo *m*, bosquejo *m* ▸ **outline planning permission** (*Brit*) (*for building*) permiso *m* provisional de obras ▸ **outline sketch** = **outline drawing**
outlive [aʊtˈlɪv] VT sobrevivir a • **the agreement has ~d its original purpose** el acuerdo ha durado más tiempo de lo que se había planeado • **she dropped men as soon as they ~d their usefulness** abandonaba a los hombres tan pronto como dejaban de resultarle útiles
outlook [ˈaʊtlʊk] N **1** (= *view*) vista *f*, perspectiva *f*
2 (= *prospects*) perspectivas *fpl*, panorama *m* • **the ~ for the economy/the wheat crop is good** las perspectivas económicas/de la cosecha de trigo son favorables • **it's a grim ~** las perspectivas no son nada halagüeña
3 (= *opinion*) punto *m* de vista; (*on life*) actitud *f* • **she has a very positive ~ on life** tiene una actitud muy positiva ante la vida • **his ~ is always pessimistic** su actitud siempre es pesimista • **a person with a broad ~** una persona de amplias miras
4 (*Met*) • **the ~ for next Saturday is sunny** la previsión para el próximo sábado es que hará sol
outlying [ˈaʊtˌlaɪɪŋ] ADJ (= *distant*) [*towns, villages*] remoto, lejano; (= *surrounding*) [*areas*] periférico; [*suburb*] periférico, circundante
outmanoeuvre, outmaneuver (*US*) [ˌaʊtməˈnuːvəʳ] VT (*Mil*) [+ *enemy*] superar tácticamente; (*fig*) [+ *opposition, competition*] superar a
outmatch [aʊtˈmætʃ] VT superar, aventajar
outmoded [aʊtˈməʊdɪd] ADJ = **outdated**
outnumber [aʊtˈnʌmbəʳ] VT exceder en número, ser más numeroso que • **the actors ~ed the audience** había más actores que público • **we were ~ed ten to one** ellos eran diez veces más que nosotros
out-of-body experience [ˌaʊtəvˌbɒdɪɪkˈspɪərɪəns] N experiencia *f* extracorporal
out-of-bounds [ˌaʊtəvˈbaʊndz] ADJ ▸ **bound¹**
out-of-court [aʊtəvˈkɔːt] ADJ • **an out-of-court settlement** un arreglo sin acudir a los tribunales
out-of-date [ˈaʊtəvˈdeɪt] ADJ [*ideas*] anticuado; [*clothes*] pasado de moda; [*passport, ticket*] caducado, vencido
out-of-doors [ˈaʊtəvˈdɔːz] ADV = **outdoors**
out-of-pocket [ˈaʊtəvˈpɒkɪt] ADJ • **out-of-pocket expenses** gastos *mpl* varios
out-of-school [ˌaʊtəvˈskuːl] ADJ • **out-of-school activities** actividades *fpl* extraescolares
out-of-the-way [ˈaʊtəvðəˈweɪ] ADJ **1** (= *remote*) remoto, apartado; (= *inaccessible*) inaccesible
2 (= *unusual*) poco conocido, poco común, poco corriente
out-of-towner [ˌaʊtəvˈtaʊnəʳ] N (*US*) forastero/a *m/f*
outpace [aʊtˈpeɪs] VT dejar atrás
outpatient [ˈaʊtˌpeɪʃənt] N paciente *mf* externo/a • **~s' department** sección *f* de pacientes externos *or* no hospitalizados
outperform [ˈaʊtpəˈfɔːm] VT hacer mejor que, superar a; [*shares, investment fund*] dar mayores beneficios que
outplacement [ˈaʊtpleɪsmənt] N recolocación *f*
CPD ▸ **outplacement agency** agencia *f* de recolocación
outplay [aʊtˈpleɪ] VT jugar mejor que • **we were ~ed in every department** ellos resultaron ser mejores que nosotros en todos los aspectos del juego, nos dominaron por completo
outpoint [ˌaʊtˈpɔɪnt] VT (*Boxing*) ganar por puntos a
outpost [ˈaʊtpəʊst] N **1** (*Mil*) avanzada *f*, puesto *m* avanzado
2 (*fig*) avanzada *f*
outpouring [ˈaʊtˌpɔːrɪŋ] N efusión *f* • **an ~ of emotion** una efusión de emoción • **the ~s of a sick mind** los desahogos de una mente enferma
output [ˈaʊtpʊt] N [*of factory*] producción *f*; [*of person, machine*] rendimiento *m*; (*Comput*) salida *f*; (*Elec*) potencia *f* de salida • **to raise ~** aumentar la producción
VT (*Comput*) imprimir
CPD ▸ **output bonus** prima *f* por rendimiento ▸ **output device** dispositivo *m* de salida
outrage [aʊtˈreɪdʒ] N **1** (= *wicked, violent act*) atrocidad *f* • **bomb ~** atentado *m* (con bomba)
2 (= *indecency*) ultraje *m*, escándalo *m*; (= *injustice*) atropello *m*, agravio *m* • **a public ~** un escándalo público • **an ~ against good taste** un atentado al buen gusto • **it's an ~!** ¡es un escándalo!, ¡qué barbaridad! • **to commit an ~ against** *or* **on sb** [*terrorists*] cometer un atentado contra algn
VT [+ *person*] ultrajar; [+ *standards, decency*] atentar contra • **it ~s justice** es un atentado a la justicia • **to be ~d by sth** indignarse ante algo
outrageous [aʊtˈreɪdʒəs] ADJ **1** (= *shocking, intolerable*) [*conduct, decision, accusation*] escandaloso; [*price, demands*] exorbitante, escandaloso; [*act, crime*] atroz, monstruoso • **it's ~! I won't stand for it** ¡qué barbaridad! *or* ¡es escandaloso! no lo pienso consentir • **it is ~ that taxpayers will have to foot the bill** es escandaloso que sean los contribuyentes los que tengan que pagar
2 (= *extravagant*) [*clothes, fashion*] extravagante, estrafalario; [*idea, story*] estrambótico • **she has an ~ sense of humour** su sentido del humor es de escándalo • **he's ~!** ¡es increíble *or* imposible!
outrageously [aʊtˈreɪdʒəslɪ] ADV **1** (= *shockingly, intolerably*) [*behave*] de manera escandalosa • **she flirted with him ~** era escandaloso cómo flirteaba con él, flirteaba de manera escandalosa con él
2 (= *extravagantly*) [*dress*] de forma extravagante, de forma estrafalaria
3 (= *extremely*) [*unfair, racist*] terriblemente; [*expensive*] escandalosamente • **his latest comedy is ~ funny** su última comedia es para desternillarse
outran [ˌaʊtˈræn] PT *of* outrun
outrank [aʊtˈræŋk] VT ser de rango superior a
outré [ˈuːtreɪ] ADJ extravagante, estrafalarío
outreach [ˈaʊtriːtʃ] CPD ▸ **outreach programme, outreach program** (*US*) *programa de acercamiento destinado a usuarios potenciales de determinados servicios sociales* ▸ **outreach work** trabajo *m* de acercamiento (*destinado a usuarios potenciales de determinados servicios sociales*) ▸ **outreach worker** *trabajador social que realiza un trabajo de acercamiento destinado a usuarios potenciales de determinados servicios sociales*
outrider [ˈaʊtˌraɪdəʳ] N motociclista *mf* de escolta
outrigger [ˈaʊtˌrɪɡəʳ] N (= *beam, spar*) batanga *f*, balancín *m*; (= *rowlock*) portarremos *m* exterior; (= *boat*) bote *m* con batanga, bote *m* con portarremos exterior
outright [aʊtˈraɪt] ADJ **1** (= *complete*) [*failure*] completo, total; [*winner, victory*] absoluto; [*lie*] descarado; [*owner*] absoluto (*sin hipotecas*); [*refusal, rejection*] rotundo, absoluto
2 (= *open, forthright*) franco; [*rudeness, hostility*] abierto, franco; [*contempt, scorn*] declarado; [*compliment*] sin ambages
ADV **1** (= *completely*) [*own*] en su totalidad; [*win*] de manera absoluta; [*refuse, reject*] rotundamente, de pleno • **to buy sth ~** comprar algo en su totalidad • **to reject an offer ~** rechazar una oferta de pleno • **they won the cup ~** ganaron la copa indiscutiblemente • **he was killed ~** murió

en el acto
2 (*= openly, forthrightly*) abiertamente, francamente • **why don't you tell her ~?** ¿por qué no se lo dices abiertamente *or* francamente? • **to laugh ~ at sth** reírse abiertamente de algo
outrun [aʊt'rʌn] (PT: **outran**, PP: **outrun**) VT dejar atrás; (*fig*) exceder, sobrepasar
outsell [ˌaʊtsel] (PT, PP: **outsold**) VT venderse más que • **this product ~s all the competition** este producto se vende más que todos los competidores
outset ['aʊtset] N principio *m*, comienzo *m* • **at the ~** al principio *or* comienzo • **from the ~** desde el principio *or* comienzo
outshine [aʊt'ʃaɪn] (PT, PP: **outshone** [aʊt'ʃɒn]) VT (*fig*) eclipsar
outside ['aʊt'saɪd] ADV fuera, afuera (*esp LAm*) • **to be/go ~** estar/salir fuera • **seen from ~** visto desde fuera
PREP (*also* **outside of**) 1 (*= not inside*) fuera de, afuera de (*LAm*); (*= beyond*) más allá de • **~ the city** fuera de la ciudad, en las afueras de la ciudad • **it's ~ the normal range** cae fuera del alcance normal • **the car ~ the house** el coche que está frente a la casa • **he waited ~ the door** esperó en la puerta
2 (*= not within*) fuera de • **this matter is ~ their jurisdiction** este asunto queda fuera de su competencia • **that's ~ our terms of reference** eso no entra dentro de nuestro cometido • **it's ~ my experience** no tengo experiencia en eso
ADJ 1 (*= exterior*) [*wall*] exterior; [*door*] que da a la calle; (*= outdoors*) [*patio, swimming pool*] descubierto, al aire libre; (*= alien*) [*influence*] externo • **~ broadcast** (*Rad, TV*) retransmisión *f* desde exteriores • **~ call** llamada *f* de fuera • **the ~ lane** (*Brit*) (*Aut*) el carril de la derecha; (*most other countries*) el carril de la izquierda • **~ line** (*Telec*) línea *f* exterior • **an ~ seat** un asiento al lado del pasillo • **his parents shielded him from the ~ world** sus padres le protegieron del mundo exterior
2 (*= unlikely*) • **an ~ chance** una posibilidad remota
3 (*= of another organization, person*) • **~ contractor** contratista *mf* independiente • **to get an ~ opinion** pedir una opinión independiente
N 1 (*= outer part*) exterior *m*, parte *f* exterior • **judging from the ~** a juzgar por las apariencias • **to open a window from the ~** abrir una ventana desde fuera • **on the ~** por fuera • **to overtake on the ~** (*Brit*) (*Aut*) adelantar *or* (*Mex*) rebasar por la derecha; (*most other countries*) adelantar *or* (*Mex*) rebasar por la izquierda
2 (*= maximum*) • **at the (very) ~** a lo sumo, como máximo
CPD ▸ **outside toilet** retrete *m* exterior
outside-forward ['aʊtsaɪd'fɔːwəd] N delantero/a *m/f* extremo/a
outside-left ['aʊtsaɪd'left] N extremo/a *m/f* izquierdo/a
outsider ['aʊt'saɪdəʳ] N 1 (*= stranger*) forastero/a *m/f*, desconocido/a *m/f*; (*pej*) intruso/a *m/f*
2 (*= independent*) persona *f* independiente, persona *f* ajena al asunto • **I'm an ~ in these matters** soy un profano en estos asuntos
3 (*in horse race*) caballo *m* que no figura entre los favoritos; (*in election*) candidato *m* poco conocido; (*pej*) segundón *m*
outside-right ['aʊtsaɪd'raɪt] N extremo/a *m/f* derecho/a
outsize ['aʊtsaɪz] ADJ [*clothes*] de talla muy grande; (*= huge*) enorme
outskirts ['aʊtskɜːts] NPL [*of town*] afueras *fpl*, alrededores *mpl*; [*of wood*] cercanías *fpl*
outsmart [aʊt'smɑːt] VT • **to ~ sb** ser más listo que algn; (*= deceive*) engañar a algn
outsold [ˌaʊt'səʊld] PT, PP ▸ **outsell**
outsource [ˌaʊt'sɔːs] VT [*+ work*] externalizar
outsourcing ['aʊtsɔːsɪŋ] N (*Comm*) [*of labour*] contratación *f* externa • **the ~ of components** la adquisición de componentes de fuentes externas
outspend [aʊt'spend] (PT, PP: **outspent**) VT • **to ~ sb** gastar más que algn
outspoken [aʊt'spəʊkən] ADJ [*criticism*] franco, abierto; [*opponent, critic*] declarado • **to be ~** ser muy franco, no tener pelos en la lengua*
outspokenly [aʊt'spəʊkənlɪ] ADV francamente, abiertamente
outspokenness [aʊt'spəʊkənnɪs] N franqueza *f*
outspread ['aʊt'spred] ADJ [*wings*] extendido, desplegado; [*legs, feet*] extendido • **with ~ arms** con los brazos abiertos
outstanding [aʊt'stændɪŋ] ADJ
1 (*= exceptional*) [*person, achievement, contribution, feature*] destacado; [*beauty, performance, service*] excepcional, extraordinario; [*example*] sobresaliente • **he was the most ~ scientist of his generation** fue el científico más destacado de su generación • **an area of ~ natural beauty** una zona de excepcional belleza natural
2 (*= not settled*) [*issue, problem*] pendiente, por resolver; [*bill*] por cobrar; [*debt, balance, account*] pendiente; [*shares*] en circulación, en manos del público • **a lot of work is still ~** aún queda mucho trabajo pendiente *or* por hacer • **amount ~** saldo *m* pendiente
outstandingly [aʊt'stændɪŋlɪ] ADV [*beautiful, effective, well-written*] excepcionalmente, extraordinariamente • **an ~ gifted musician** un músico de excepcional *or* extraordinario talento • **she performed ~ well in the exam** hizo el examen extraordinariamente bien
outstare [ˌaʊt'stɛəʳ] VT • **I ~d him** lo miré tan fijamente que tuvo que bajar *or* apartar la vista
outstation ['aʊtˌsteɪʃən] N dependencia *f*
outstay [aʊt'steɪ] VT quedarse más tiempo que • **to ~ one's welcome** quedarse más de lo debido • **I don't want to ~ my welcome** no quiero quedarme más de lo debido, no quiero abusar de su hospitalidad
outstretched ['aʊtstretʃt] ADJ [*arms, legs, hands, wings*] extendido
outstrip [aʊt'strɪp] VT dejar atrás, aventajar; (*fig*) aventajar, adelantarse a
out-take ['aʊtˌteɪk] N trozo *m* de película desechado
out-tray ['aʊtˌtreɪ] N bandeja *f* de salida
outturn ['aʊttɜːn] N (*US*) rendimiento *m*, producción *f*
outvote [aʊt'vəʊt] VT [*+ proposal*] rechazar (por mayoría de votos); [*+ party, person*] vencer (en la votación) • **but I was ~d** pero en la votación perdí
outward ['aʊtwəd] ADJ 1 (*= going out*) [*flight, ship, freight*] de salida, de ida; [*movement*] hacia fuera • **on the ~ journey** en el viaje de ida
2 (*= exterior*) [*appearance etc*] exterior, externo • **with an ~ show of concern** haciendo gala de *or* (*LAm*) luciendo preocupación
ADV hacia fuera • **~ bound (from/for)** saliendo (de/con rumbo a) • **the ship was ~ bound from/for Vigo** el barco salía de/iba con rumbo a Vigo
outward-looking ['aʊtwədˌlʊkɪŋ] ADJ [*person, organization, country*] abierto al exterior; [*policy, attitude*] abierto, expansivo
outwardly ['aʊtwədlɪ] ADV por fuera, aparentemente
outwards ['aʊtwədz] ADV (*esp Brit*) = **outward**
outwear [aʊt'wɛəʳ] (PT: **outwore**, PP: **outworn**) VT 1 (*= last longer than*) durar más tiempo que
2 (*= wear out*) gastar
outweigh [aʊt'weɪ] VT pesar más que, tener mayor peso que; (*fig*) pesar más que • **the advantages ~ the disadvantages** las ventajas pesan más que *or* superan a las desventajas • **this ~s all other considerations** esto pesa más *or* tiene mayor peso que todos los demás factores
outwit [aʊt'wɪt] VT ser más listo que
outwith [ˌaʊt'wɪθ] PREP (*Scot*) ▸ **outside**
outworker ['aʊtwɜːkəʳ] N *persona que trabaja en su propio domicilio*
outworn [aʊt'wɔːn] PP *of* **outwear**
ADJ [*expression*] trillado, manido; [*idea, custom*] anticuado, caduco; [*joke, slogan*] muy viejo, muy visto; [*superstition*] viejo, antiguo
ouzo ['uːzəʊ] N ouzo *m*
ova ['əʊvə] NPL *of* **ovum**
oval ['əʊvəl] ADJ oval, ovalado • **the Oval Office** (*US*) el Despacho Oval
N óvalo *m*
ovarian [əʊ'vɛərɪən] ADJ ovárico
CPD ▸ **ovarian cancer** cáncer *m* de ovario, cáncer *m* ovárico
ovary ['əʊvərɪ] N ovario *m*
ovate ['əʊveɪt] ADJ aovado
ovation [əʊ'veɪʃən] N ovación *f* • **to give sb an ~** ovacionar a algn • **to receive an ~** ser ovacionado • **to give sb a standing ~** ponerse en pie *or* levantarse para ovacionar a algn • **she got a standing ~ from the audience** el público se puso en pie *or* se levantó para ovacionarla, el público puesto en pie la ovacionó
oven ['ʌvn] N horno *m* • **it's like an ~ in there** aquello es un horno
CPD ▸ **oven glove** guante *m* para el horno, manopla *f* para el horno ▸ **oven tray** bandeja *f* para horno
ovenproof ['ʌvnpruːf] ADJ [*dish*] refractario, (a prueba) de horno
oven-ready [ˌʌvn'redɪ] ADJ listo para el horno
ovenware ['ʌvnwɛəʳ] N vajilla *f* refractaria

over ['əʊvəʳ]

ADVERB
PREPOSITION
ADJECTIVE
NOUN

*When **over** is the second element in a phrasal verb, eg **come over**, **go over**, **start over**, **turn over**, look up the verb.*

ADVERB
1 (*= across*) por encima, por arriba (*LAm*) • **this one goes under and that one goes ~** este pasa por debajo y ese por encima
2 (*= here, there*) • **I'll be ~ at 7 o'clock** estaré ahí a las 7 • **they're ~ for the day** han venido a pasar el día • **when you're next ~ this way** la próxima vez que pases por aquí

*With prepositions and adverbs **over** is usually not translated*

• **they're ~ from Canada for the summer** han venido desde Canadá a pasar el verano

• ~ **here** aquí • **how long have you lived ~ here?** ¿cuánto tiempo llevas viviendo aquí? • **when you're next ~ here** la próxima vez que vengas • **he's ~ in the States at the moment** en este momento está en Estados Unidos • ~ **in the States, people reacted differently** (allí) en Estados Unidos la gente reaccionó de otra manera • **it's ~ on the other side of town** está al otro lado de la ciudad • ~ **there** allí • **how long were you ~ there?** ¿cuánto tiempo estuviste allí? • **the next time you're ~ there** la próxima vez que vayas (allí) • **the baby crawled ~ to its mother** el bebé gateó hacia su madre • **to drive ~ to the other side of town** ir en coche al otro lado de la ciudad • ~ **to you!** (*to speak*) ¡te paso la palabra! • **so now it's ~ to you** (*to decide*) así que ahora te toca a ti decidir • **now ~ to our Paris correspondent** ahora damos paso a nuestro corresponsal en París

3 (*indicating repetition*) • **it happened all ~ again** volvió a ocurrir, ocurrió otra vez • **to start (all) ~ again** volver a empezar • ~ **and ~ (again)** repetidas veces, una y otra vez • **several times ~** varias veces seguidas • **we did it two or three times ~** lo volvimos a hacer dos o tres veces

4 (US) (= *again*) otra vez • **to do sth ~** volver a hacer algo, hacer algo otra vez

5 (= *remaining*) • **there are three (left) ~** sobran *or* quedan tres • **there were two slices each and one (left) ~** había dos rebanadas para cada uno y sobraba una • **is there any cake left ~?** ¿queda *or* sobra (algo de) pastel? • **when they've paid the bills there's nothing (left) ~ for luxuries** después de pagar las facturas no les sobra *or* queda nada para caprichos • **4 into 29 goes 7 and 1 ~** 29 dividido entre 4 son 7 y me llevo 1

6 (= *more*) • **sums of £50,000 and ~** cantidades iguales *or* superiores a 50.000 libras • **persons of 21 and ~** las personas de veintiún años para arriba

7 (*Telec*) • **over!** ¡cambio! • ~ **and out!** ¡cambio y corto!

8 (*in set expressions*) • ~ **against** (*lit*) contra; (*fig*) frente a • ~ **against the wall** contra la pared • **the importance of faith ~ against good works** la importancia de la fe frente a las buenas obras • **the (whole) world ~** en *or* por todo el mundo, en el mundo entero

PREPOSITION

1 (*indicating position*) (= *situated above*) encima de, arriba de (*LAm*); (= *across*) por encima de, por arriba de (*LAm*) • **there's a mirror ~ the washbasin** encima del lavabo hay un espejo • **a washbasin with a mirror ~ it** un lavabo con un espejo encima • **the water came ~ his knees** el agua le llegaba por encima de las rodillas • **the ball went ~ the wall** la pelota pasó por encima del muro • **to jump ~ sth** saltar por encima de algo • **the bridge ~ the river** el puente sobre el río • **pour some sauce ~ it** échale un poco de salsa por encima • **I put a blanket ~ her** le eché una manta por encima • **she put an apron on ~ her dress** se puso un delantal encima del vestido • **to spread a sheet ~ sth** extender una sábana sobre *or* por encima de algo; ▹ **all, head, hill**

2 (= *superior to*) • **he's ~ me (in the company)** está por encima mío (en la empresa)

3 (= *on the other side of*) • **the bar ~ the road** el bar de enfrente • **it's ~ the river** está en la otra orilla del río • **the noise came from ~ the wall** el ruido venía del otro lado de la pared • ~ **the page** en la página siguiente

4 (= *more than*) más de • ~ **two hundred** más de doscientos • **well ~ 200 people** bastante más de 200 personas • **he must be ~ 60** debe de tener más de 60 años • **(the) ~-18s** los mayores de 18 años • **an increase of 5% ~ last year** un aumento del 5 por ciento respecto al año pasado • **spending has gone up by 7% ~ and above inflation** el gasto ha aumentado un 7% por encima de la inflación • **this was ~ and above his normal duties** eso iba más allá de sus deberes habituales • ~ **and above normal requirements** además de los requisitos normales • **yes, but ~ and above that, we must ...** sí, pero además de eso, debemos ... • ~ **and above the fact that ...** además de que ...; ▹ **well**

5 (= *during*) durante • ~ **the last few years** durante los últimos años • **payments spread ~ some years** pagos espaciados durante varios años • ~ **Christmas** durante las Navidades • ~ **the winter** durante *or* en el invierno • **why don't we discuss it ~ dinner?** ¿por qué no vamos a cenar y lo hablamos? • **they talked ~ a cup of coffee** hablaron mientras se tomaban un café • **how long will you be ~ it?** ¿cuánto tiempo te va a llevar? • **he took** *or* **spent hours ~ the preparations** dedicó muchas horas a los preparativos; ▹ **linger**

6 (= *because of*) por • **to cry ~ sth** llorar por algo • **they fell out ~ money** se pelearon por una cuestión de dinero

7 (= *about*) sobre • **the two sides disagreed ~ how much should be spent** ambas partes discrepaban sobre cuánto debería gastarse

8 (= *recovered from*) • **he's not ~ that yet** (*illness*) todavía no se ha repuesto de aquello; (*shock*) todavía no se ha repuesto de *or* sobrepuesto a aquello • **she's ~ it now** (*illness*) se ha repuesto de eso ya • **it'll take her years to get ~ it** (*shock*) tardará años en sobreponerse • **I hope you'll soon be ~ your cold** espero que se te pase pronto el resfriado, espero que te repongas pronto del resfriado • **she's still not ~ her last boyfriend** aún no ha olvidado a su último novio • **we're ~ the worst now** ya pasó lo peor

9 (*indicating means of communication*) por • ~ **the telephone** por teléfono • ~ **the loudspeaker** por los altavoces • **I heard it ~ the radio** lo escuché *or* oí por la radio

10 (= *contrasted with*) • **the issue of quality ~ economy** la cuestión de la calidad en contraposición a la rentabilidad

ADJECTIVE

(= *finished*) • **when** *or* **after the war is ~, we'll go ...** cuando (se) acabe la guerra, nos iremos ... • **I'll be happy when the exams are ~** seré feliz cuando (se) hayan acabado *or* terminado los exámenes • **our troubles are ~** (se) han acabado nuestros problemas • **the danger was soon ~** el peligro pasó pronto • **it's all ~** se acabó • **it's all ~ between us** lo nuestro se acabó • **I'll be glad when it's all ~ and done with** estaré contento cuando todo (se) haya acabado *or* terminado • **for us the incident was ~ and done with** nosotros dábamos el incidente por zanjado • **to get sth ~ and done with: if we've got to tell her, best get it ~ and done with** si tenemos que decírselo, cuanto antes (lo hagamos) mejor

NOUN

(*Cricket*) serie *f* de seis lanzamientos

---

over... ['əʊvəʳ] PREFIX **1** sobre..., super...; (= *too much*) demasiado • **overabundant** sobreabundante, superabundante • **overambitious** demasiado ambicioso **2** (*with neg*) • **I'm not overkeen on Szymanowski's music** no me entusiasma demasiado la música de Szymanowski

overabundance [,əʊvərə'bʌndəns] N sobreabundancia *f*, superabundancia *f*

overabundant [,əʊvərə'bʌndənt] ADJ sobreabundante, superabundante

overachieve [,əʊvərə'tʃiːv] VI rendir más allá de lo normal • **a society which encourages people to ~** una sociedad que alienta a las personas a que rindan más allá de lo normal

overachiever [,əʊvərə'tʃiːvəʳ] N *persona que obtiene resultados más allá de lo normal*

overact [,əʊvər'ækt] VI sobreactuar, exagerar (el papel)

overacting [,əʊvər'æktɪŋ] N sobreactuación *f*, exageración *f* (del papel)

overactive [,əʊvər'æktɪv] ADJ calenturienta; [*thyroid*] hiperactivo

overage ['əʊvərɪdʒ] N (US) (*Comm*) excedente *m* de mercancías

over-age [,əʊvər'eɪdʒ] ADJ demasiado mayor, mayor de la edad permitida

overall¹ ADJ ['əʊvərɔːl] [*study, view*] de conjunto, global; [*width, length, cost*] total • ~ **dimensions** (*Aut*) dimensiones *fpl* exteriores • **what was your ~ impression?** ¿cuál fue tu impresión general?
ADV [,əʊvər'ɔːl] en conjunto, en su totalidad • **~, we are well pleased** en términos generales estamos muy contentos
CPD ['əʊvərɔːl] ▸ **overall majority** mayoría *f* absoluta

overall² ['əʊvərɔːl] N **1** (*esp Brit*) (= *protective overcoat*) guardapolvo *m*, bata *f*
2 overalls (*Brit*) (= *boiler suit*) mono *msing* (*Sp*), overol *msing* (*LAm*); (*US*) (= *dungarees*) peto *msing* (*Sp*), overol *msing* (*LAm*), mameluco *m* (*S. Cone*)

overambitious [,əʊvəræm'bɪʃəs] ADJ demasiado ambicioso

overanxious [,əʊvər'æŋkʃəs] ADJ
1 (= *worried*) demasiado preocupado
2 (= *eager*) • **he was ~ to give a good impression** estaba demasiado preocupado por causar buena impresión • **I'm not ~ to go** tengo pocas ganas de ir

overarching [,əʊvər'ɑːtʃɪŋ] ADJ [*question*] global; [*desire*] general

overarm ['əʊvərɑːm] ADV [*throw, bowl*] por encima de la cabeza

overate [,əʊvə'reɪt] PT *of* **overeat**

overawe [,əʊvər'ɔː] VT intimidar • **I was ~d by his presence** me sentía intimidado en su presencia • **I was ~d by the occasion** me sentía sobrecogido por la ocasión

overbalance [,əʊvə'bæləns] VI [*person*] perder el equilibrio; [*boat, car*] volcar
VT [+ *person*] hacer perder el equilibrio; [+ *thing*] hacer volcar

overbearing [,əʊvə'bɛərɪŋ] ADJ (= *imperious*) imperioso, autoritario; (= *despotic*) despótico

overbid (VB: PT, PP: **overbid**) N ['əʊvəbɪd] (*at auction*) mejor oferta *f*, mejor postura *f*; (*Bridge*) sobremarca *f*
VT [,əʊvə'bɪd] (*at auction*) hacer mejor oferta que, pujar más que; (*Bridge*) marcar más que
VI [,əʊvə'bɪd] (*Bridge*) hacer una sobremarca; (*foolishly*) declarar demasiado

overbill [,əʊvə'bɪl] VT (US) = **overcharge**

overblown [,əʊvə'bləʊn] ADJ **1** [*flower*] marchito, pasado
2 [*style*] pomposo, pretencioso

overboard ['əʊvəbɔːd] ADV (*Naut*) por la borda • **to fall ~** caer al agua *or* por la borda • **man ~!** ¡hombre al agua! • IDIOM: • **to go ~**: • **let's not go ~** no hay que exagerar, no nos pasemos* • **she went ~ with the lace and sequins** se pasó con los encajes y las lentejuelas* • **to go ~ for sb** volverse loco por algn

overbold [ˌəʊvəˈbəʊld] ADJ demasiado atrevido

overbook [ˌəʊvəˈbʊk] VT hacer overbooking en

overbooked [ˌəʊvəˈbʊkt] ADJ con overbooking, con sobreventa de plazas • **the plane is ~** el avión tiene overbooking

overbooking [ˌəʊvəˈbʊkɪŋ] N overbooking *m (reserva de habitaciones en un hotel, plazas en un vuelo etc, que sobrepasa al número real de las mismas)*

overburden [ˌəʊvəˈbɜːdn] VT sobrecargar; (*fig*) agobiar, abrumar • **~ed with worries** abrumado *or* agobiado por las preocupaciones

overbuy [ˌəʊvəˈbaɪ] (PT, PP: **overbought**) VT, VI sobrecomprar

overcall [ˌəʊvəˈkɔːl] VT, VI = **overbid**

overcame [ˌəʊvəˈkeɪm] PT *of* **overcome**

over-capacity [ˌəʊvəkəˈpæsɪtɪ] N sobrecapacidad *f*

overcapitalization [ˌəʊvəkæpɪtəlaɪˈzeɪʃən] N sobrecapitalización *f*, capitalización *f* inflada

overcapitalize [ˌəʊvəˈkæpɪtəlaɪz] VI sobrecapitalizar

overcast [ˈəʊvəkɑːst] ADJ [*sky*] encapotado, cubierto; [*day*] nublado • **to grow ~** nublarse

overcautious [ˌəʊvəˈkɔːʃəs] ADJ demasiado cauteloso

overcautiousness [ˌəʊvəˈkɔːʃəsnɪs] N excesiva cautela *f*

overcharge [ˌəʊvəˈtʃɑːdʒ] VT **1** • **to ~ sb for sth** cobrar a algn de más por algo
2 (*Elec*) sobrecargar, poner una carga excesiva a
VI cobrar de más

overcharging [ˌəʊvəˈtʃɑːdʒɪŋ] N • **the firm has been accused of ~** la empresa ha sido acusada de cobrar de más

overcoat [ˈəʊvəkəʊt] N abrigo *m*, sobretodo *m*

overcome [ˌəʊvəˈkʌm] (PT: **overcame**, PP: **overcome**) VT **1** (= *conquer*) [+ *enemy, opposition*] vencer; [+ *problem, temptation, inhibitions*] superar, vencer; [+ *rage, fear, disgust*] superar, dominar • **the book is an account of how she overcame cancer** el libro describe cómo superó *or* venció el cáncer • **her curiosity finally overcame her shyness** finalmente, su curiosidad superó *or* venció su timidez
2 (= *overwhelm*) [*feeling*] adueñarse de; [*sleep, fatigue*] vencer • **a sense of total inadequacy overcame him** una sensación de ineptitud total se adueñó de él • **sleep overcame him** lo venció el sueño • **to be ~ by sth**: • **I was ~ by the heat** el calor me agobió, me sentí agobiado por el calor • **he was ~ by the smoke** el humo le impidió respirar • **she was quite ~ by the occasion** la ocasión la conmovió mucho • **~ by curiosity, he reached out to touch it** vencido *or* dominado por la curiosidad, extendió la mano para tocarlo • **to be ~ with sth**: • **she was ~ with remorse** le abrumaba el remordimiento • **he was ~ with grief** estaba abrumado *or* postrado de dolor • **she was so ~ with emotion she couldn't answer** estaba tan conmovida que no podía responder • **you don't seem exactly ~ with joy** no parece que estés rebosante de alegría
VI vencer, triunfar • **we shall ~!** ¡venceremos!

overcommit [ˌəʊvəkəˈmɪt] VT • **to ~ o.s.** (*financially*) contraer cargas financieras en exceso; (*at work*) comprometerse a trabajar más de lo que se puede

WE SHALL OVERCOME

We Shall Overcome (Venceremos) es el título de una canción cantada por los miembros del llamado **US Civil Rights Movement** (movimiento por los derechos civiles en Estados Unidos). Se cantaba sobre todo en los años 50 y 60 durante las protestas contra la discriminación racial y aún hoy la usan quienes protestan en contra de la injusticia.

overcompensate [ˌəʊvəˈkɒmpenˌseɪt] VI • **to ~ for sth** compensar algo en exceso

overcompensation [ˌəʊvəkɒmpenˈseɪʃən] N compensación *f* excesiva

overconfidence [ˌəʊvəˈkɒnfɪdəns] N confianza *f* excesiva, exceso *m* de confianza

overconfident [ˌəʊvəˈkɒnfɪdənt] ADJ demasiado confiado (**of** en); (= *conceited*) presumido

overconsumption [ˌəʊvəkənˈsʌmpʃən] N superconsumo *m*, exceso *m* de consumo

overcook [ˌəʊvəˈkʊk] VT cocer demasiado, recocer

overcritical [ˌəʊvəˈkrɪtɪkəl] ADJ hipercrítico • **let's not be ~** seamos justos en nuestra crítica

overcrowded [ˌəʊvəˈkraʊdɪd] ADJ [*room, bus, train*] atestado de gente; [*road, suburb*] congestionado; [*city, country*] superpoblado • **they live in ~ conditions** viven hacinados

overcrowding [ˌəʊvəˈkraʊdɪŋ] N [*of housing, prison*] hacinamiento *m*; [*of bus, train*] abarrotamiento *m*; [*of town*] superpoblación *f*

overdependence [ˌəʊvədɪˈpendəns] N dependencia *f* excesiva

overdependent [ˌəʊvədɪˈpendənt] ADJ excesivamente dependiente (**on** de)

overdeveloped [ˌəʊvədɪˈveləpt] ADJ (*gen*) excesivamente desarrollado; (*Phot*) sobreprocesado, sobrerrevelado

overdevelopment [ˌəʊvədɪˈveləpmənt] N superdesarrollo *m*

overdo [ˌəʊvəˈduː] (PT: **overdid** [ˌəʊvəˈdɪd]) (PP: **overdone**) VT **1** (= *exaggerate*) exagerar; (= *use to excess*) pasarse con* • **I overdid the garlic** me he pasado con el ajo*, se me ha ido la mano con el ajo* • **don't ~ the smoking** no fumes demasiado • **she rather ~es the scent** tiende a ponerse demasiado perfume • **to ~ it** *or* **things** (= *work too hard*) trabajar demasiado; (= *exaggerate*) exagerar; (*in description, sentiment etc*) cargar las tintas
2 (= *cook too long*) cocer demasiado, recocer

overdone [ˌəʊvəˈdʌn] PP *of* **overdo**
ADJ (= *exaggerated*) exagerado; (= *overcooked*) recocido, muy hecho

overdose [ˈəʊvədəʊs] N
N sobredosis *f inv*
VI tomar una sobredosis (**on** de) • **she ~d on the chocolate** comió demasiado chocolate

overdraft [ˈəʊvədrɑːft] N (*Econ*) sobregiro *m*, giro *m* en descubierto; (*on account*) saldo *m* deudor • **to have an ~** tener la cuenta en descubierto
CPD ▸ **overdraft charges** cargos *mpl* por descubierto ▸ **overdraft facility** crédito *m* al descubierto ▸ **overdraft limit** límite *m* del descubierto

overdraw [ˌəʊvəˈdrɔː] (PT: **overdrew** [ˌəʊvəˈdruː]) (PP: **overdrawn** [ˌəʊvəˈdrɔːn])
VT girar en descubierto • **your account is ~n (by £50)** su cuenta tiene un saldo deudor (de 50 libras) • **I'm ~n** tengo un descubierto

overdress [ˌəʊvəˈdres] VI vestirse con demasiada elegancia

overdressed [ˌəʊvəˈdrest] ADJ • **to be ~** ir demasiado arreglado • **he makes me feel ~** me hace sentir como si fuera demasiado arreglado

overdrive [ˈəʊvədraɪv] N (*Aut*) superdirecta *f* • **to go into ~** (*fig*) ponerse *or* empezar a funcionar a toda marcha • **phones and fax machines went into ~ when the crisis struck** los faxes y teléfonos empezaron a funcionar a toda marcha *or* se dispararon cuando se produjo la crisis

overdue [ˌəʊvəˈdjuː] ADJ [*salary, wages*] atrasado; [*bill*] vencido y no pagado; [*train, plane*] retrasado, con retraso • **the plane was already ~** el avión ya iba retrasado *or* con retraso • **the train is 30 minutes ~** el tren tiene *or* lleva 30 minutos de retraso • **the baby is two weeks ~** el niño tenía que haber nacido hace quince días • **her period was ~** se le había atrasado la regla • **this book is five days ~** el plazo de préstamo de este libro venció hace cinco días • **that change was long ~** ese cambio tenía que haberse hecho hace tiempo • **that coat is long ~ for replacement** hace tiempo que tenía que haber reemplazado ese abrigo por uno nuevo

over-eager [ˌəʊvərˈiːgəʳ] ADJ [*person*] demasiado preocupado; [*efforts*] demasiado entusiasta • **to be over-eager (to do sth)** estar demasiado preocupado (por hacer algo) • **she was not over-eager to help** tenía pocas ganas de ayudar

overeat [ˌəʊvərˈiːt] (PT: **overate**, PP: **overeaten** [ˈəʊvərˈiːtn]) VI comer en exceso

overeating [ˌəʊvərˈiːtɪŋ] N comida *f* excesiva

over-egg [ˌəʊvərˈeg] VT (= *exaggerate*) exagerar • IDIOM: • **to over-egg the pudding** exagerar

overelaborate [ˌəʊvərɪˈlæbərɪt] ADJ [*instructions, mechanism*] demasiado complicado; [*attempts*] demasiado esforzado; [*analysis*] rebuscado; [*courtesy*] estudiado

overemphasis [ˌəʊvərˈemfəsɪs] N énfasis *m* excesivo

overemphasize [ˌəʊvərˈemfəsaɪz] VT poner demasiado énfasis en

overemphatic [ˌəʊvərɪmˈfætɪk] ADJ demasiado enfático

overemployment [ˌəʊvərɪmˈplɔɪmənt] N superempleo *m*

overenthusiastic [ˌəʊvərɪnθjuːzɪˈæstɪk] ADJ demasiado entusiasta

overenthusiastically [ˌəʊvərɪnθuːzɪˈæstɪkəlɪ] ADV con demasiado entusiasmo

overestimate N [ˌəʊvərˈestɪmɪt] sobreestimación *f*, estimación *f* excesiva; (*Econ*) presupuesto *m* excesivo
VT [ˌəʊvərˈestɪmeɪt] [+ *importance, value, cost, person*] sobreestimar • **to ~ one's strength/ability** creerse uno más fuerte/capaz de lo que es

overestimation [ˌəʊvərestɪˈmeɪʃən] N [*of power, importance*] sobreestimación *f*

overexcite [ˌəʊvərɪkˈsaɪt] VT sobreexcitar

overexcited [ˌəʊvərɪkˈsaɪtɪd] ADJ sobreexcitado; (= *nervous*) muy nervioso

overexcitement [ˌəʊvərɪkˈsaɪtmənt] N sobreexcitación *f*

overexercise [ˌəʊvərˈeksəsaɪz] VT ejercitar en exceso
VI hacer ejercicio en exceso • **the dangers of overexercising** los peligros de hacer ejercicio en exceso

overexert [ˌəʊvərɪgˈzɜːt] VT • **to ~ o.s.** hacer un esfuerzo excesivo

overexertion [ˌəʊvərɪgˈzɜːʃən] N (= *effort*) esfuerzo *m* excesivo; (= *weariness*) fatiga *f*,

agotamiento *m*
overexpenditure [ˌəʊvəɪksˈpendɪtʃəʳ] (N) gasto *m* excesivo
overexploit [ˌəʊvərɪksˈplɔɪt] (VT) sobreexplotar
overexpose [ˌəʊvərɪksˈpəʊz] (VT) [+ *photo*] sobreexponer
overexposed [ˌəʊvərɪksˈpəʊzd] (ADJ) [*photo*] sobreexpuesto
overexposure [ˌəʊvərɪksˈpəʊʒəʳ] (N) sobreexposición *f* • **~ to the sun** exposición *f* excesiva al sol • **their cause is suffering from ~ in the media** su caso está siendo afectado negativamente por aparecer demasiado en los medios de comunicación
overextended [ˌəʊvərɪkˈstendɪd] (ADJ) [*person, organization*] desbordado (por las obligaciones)
overfamiliar [ˌəʊvəfəˈmɪlɪəʳ] (ADJ) (= *too well-known*) demasiado conocido • **to get ~ with sb** tomarse demasiadas libertades *or* confianzas con algn
overfeed [ˌəʊvəˈfiːd] (PT, PP: **overfed** [ˌəʊvəˈfed]) (VT) sobrealimentar, dar demasiado de comer a
overfeeding [ˌəʊvəˈfiːdɪŋ] (N) sobrealimentación *f*
overfill [ˌəʊvəˈfɪl] (VT) llenar en exceso
overfish [ˌəʊvəˈfɪʃ] (VT) [+ *the sea etc*] sobreexplotar los recursos pesqueros de
overfishing [ˌəʊvəˈfɪʃɪŋ] (N) sobrepesca *f*, captura *f* abusiva (*de pescado*)
overflight [ˈəʊvəflaɪt] (N) sobrevuelo *m*
overflow (N) [ˈəʊvəfləʊ] (= *pipe*) desagüe *m*, tubo *m* de desagüe; (= *outlet, hole*) rebosadero *m*; (= *liquid*) exceso *m* de líquido, líquido *m* derramado; [*of people*] exceso *m* • **they made an extra room available for the ~ from the meeting** acomodaron otra sala para dar cabida al exceso de asistentes a la reunión
(VI) [ˌəʊvəˈfləʊ] [*liquid*] rebosar, derramarse; [*container, room, hall*] rebosar; [*river*] desbordarse • **people ~ed from the hall into the streets outside** la gente desbordó la sala, inundando las calles del alrededor • **to fill a cup to ~ing** llenar una taza hasta rebosar • **the crowd filled the stadium to ~ing** el estadio estaba a rebosar de público • **she was ~ing with joy** estaba rebosante de alegría
(VT) [ˌəʊvəˈfləʊ] [+ *banks*] desbordarse de, salir de; [+ *fields, surrounding area*] inundar
(CPD) ▸ **overflow meeting** reunión *f* para el exceso de público ▸ **overflow pipe** desagüe *m*, tubo *m* de desagüe
overfly [ˌəʊvəˈflaɪ] (PT: **overflew** [ˌəʊvəˈfluː]) (PP: **overflown** [ˌəʊvəˈfləʊn]) (VT) sobrevolar
overfond [ˌəʊvəˈfɒnd] (ADJ) • **he's rather ~ of criticizing people** le gusta demasiado criticar a la gente • **she is not ~ of dogs** no le dislocan los perros, no se vuelve loca por los perros
overfull [ˌəʊvəˈfʊl] (ADJ) demasiado lleno, rebosante (**of** de)
overgenerous [ˌəʊvəˈdʒenərəs] (ADJ) [*person*] demasiado generoso; [*helping, portion*] excesivamente grande • **they were ~ in their praise of him** lo elogiaron con exceso
overground [ˈəʊvəgraʊnd] (ADJ) de superficie
(ADV) por la superficie, a cielo abierto
overgrown [ˌəʊvəˈgrəʊn] (ADJ) **1** [*garden*] descuidado, cubierto de malas hierbas • **~ with** cubierto *or* revestido de • **the path is quite ~ now** la senda está ya casi cubierta de vegetación
2 [*child, adolescent*] demasiado grande para su edad • **he's just an ~ schoolboy** es como un niño grande
overhand [ˈəʊvəhænd] (US) (ADJ) [*stroke*] dado por encima de la cabeza
(ADV) por encima de la cabeza
overhang (VB: PT, PP: **overhung**) (N) [ˈəʊvəhæŋ] proyección *f*; [*of roof*] alero *m*; (*in rock climbing*) saliente *m*, extraplomo *m*
(VT) [ˌəʊvəˈhæŋ] sobresalir por encima de • **a beach overhung with palm trees** una playa sobre la que se inclinan las palmeras • **the mists that overhung the valley** la neblina que flotaba sobre el valle
(VI) [ˌəʊvəˈhæŋ] sobresalir
overhanging [ˌəʊvəˈhæŋɪŋ] (ADJ) [*cliff, rock*] saliente; [*branches, trees, balcony*] que sobresale
overhastily [ˌəʊvəˈheɪstɪlɪ] (ADV) apresuradamente, precipitadamente
overhasty [ˌəʊvəˈheɪstɪ] (ADJ) apresurado, precipitado
overhaul (N) [ˈəʊvəhɔːl] repaso *m* general, revisión *f*
(VT) [ˌəʊvəˈhɔːl] **1** (= *check*) [+ *machine*] revisar, repasar, dar un repaso general a; [+ *plans etc*] volver a pensar, rehacer, replantear
2 (= *overtake*) alcanzar, adelantarse a
overhead (ADV) [ˌəʊvəˈhed] por lo alto, en alto, por encima de la cabeza • **a bird flew ~** pasó un pájaro
(ADJ) [ˈəʊvəhed] de arriba, encima de la cabeza; [*crane*] de techo; [*railway*] elevado, suspendido; [*camshaft*] en cabeza
(N) [ˈəʊvəhed] • **~** (US) • **~s** (Brit) gastos *mpl* generales
(CPD) [ˈəʊvəhed] ▸ **overhead cable** línea *f* eléctrica aérea ▸ **overhead costs, overhead expenses** gastos *mpl* generales ▸ **overhead kick** chilena *f*, tijereta *f* ▸ **overhead light** luz *f* de techo ▸ **overhead locker** (*on plane, train*) compartimento *m* superior (*para el equipaje de mano*) ▸ **overhead projector** retroproyector *m*
overhear [ˌəʊvəˈhɪəʳ] (PT, PP: **overheard** [ˌəʊvəˈhɜːd]) (VT) oír (por casualidad) • **I couldn't help ~ing their conversation** no pude evitar oír su conversación • **she was ~d complaining** se la oyó quejarse
(VI) • **be careful, someone might ~** ten cuidado, alguien podría oírnos
overheat [ˌəʊvəˈhiːt] (VT) **1** (*lit*) recalentar, sobrecalentar • **to get ~ed** recalentarse
2 (*Econ*) (*also fig*) sobrecalentar
(VI) recalentarse
overheating [ˌəʊvəˈhiːtɪŋ] (N) recalentamiento *m* (*also fig*) (*also Econ*)
overhung [ˌəʊvəˈhʌŋ] (PT), (PP) *of* **overhang**
overindulge [ˌəʊvərɪnˈdʌldʒ] (VT) [+ *child*] mimar, consentir; [+ *passion*] dar rienda suelta a, dejarse llevar por
(VI) excederse • **everyone ~s at Christmas** todo el mundo se excede en Navidades • **to ~ in alcohol** abusar del alcohol
overindulgence [ˌəʊvərɪnˈdʌldʒəns] (N) **1** (= *excess*) abuso *m* (**in** de)
2 (*with children*) exceso *m* de tolerancia (**towards** con)
overindulgent [ˌəʊvərɪnˈdʌldʒənt] (ADJ) demasiado indulgente, demasiado blando (**toward, with** con)
overinvestment [ˌəʊvərɪnˈvestmənt] (N) sobreinversión *f*
overissue [ˈəʊvərɪʃuː] (*St Ex*) (N) emisión *f* excesiva
(VT) emitir con exceso
overjoyed [ˌəʊvəˈdʒɔɪd] (ADJ) lleno de alegría (**at** por), contentísimo (**at** de) • **he was ~ at the news** no cabía en sí de contento con la noticia • **she will be ~ to see you** estará encantada de verte
overkill [ˈəʊvəkɪl] (N) **1** (*Mil*) capacidad *f* excesiva de destrucción
2 (*fig*) • **there is a danger of ~ here** corremos peligro de excedernos
overladen [ˌəʊvəˈleɪdn] (ADJ) sobrecargado (**with** de)
overland (ADV) [ˌəʊvəˈlænd] por tierra, por vía terrestre
(ADJ) [ˈəʊvəlænd] terrestre
overlap (N) [ˈəʊvəlæp] **1** (*lit*) superposición *f* (parcial)
2 (*fig*) coincidencia *f* (parcial) • **there is some ~ between the two categories** las dos categorías coinciden en parte
(VI) [ˌəʊvəˈlæp] **1** (*lit*) superponerse (parcialmente) • **it is made of ~ping strips of bark** está hecho de tiras de corteza parcialmente superpuestas
2 (*fig*) coincidir (en parte) • **our jobs ~ in some areas** nuestros trabajos coinciden en parte
(VT) [ˌəʊvəˈlæp] colocar parcialmente unos sobre otros • **~ the tomato slices as you place them on the plate** coloque las rodajas de tomate en la fuente de manera que queden parcialmente cubiertas unas por otras
overlay (PT, PP: **overlaid** [ˌəʊvəˈleɪd]) (VT) [ˌəʊvəˈleɪ] cubrir (**with** con), revestir (**with** de) • **to get overlaid with** formarse una capa de, cubrirse con
(N) [ˈəʊvəleɪ] capa *f* sobrepuesta, revestimiento *m*; (= *applied decoration*) incrustación *f*; (*on map etc*) transparencia *f* superpuesta
overleaf [ˌəʊvəˈliːf] (ADV) al dorso • **"see overleaf"** "véase al dorso"
overlie [ˌəʊvəˈlaɪ] (VT) recubrir
overload (N) [ˈəʊvələʊd] sobrecarga *f*
(VT) [ˌəʊvəˈləʊd] sobrecargar (**with** de) • **to be ~ed with** estar sobrecargado de; (*with work*) estar agobiado de
overlong [ˌəʊvəˈlɒŋ] (ADJ) demasiado largo
overlook [ˌəʊvəˈlʊk] (VT) **1** [*building*] tener vista a, dar a • **the house ~s the park** la casa tiene vistas al parque • **the garden is not ~ed** el jardín no tiene ningún edificio al lado que lo domine
2 (= *leave out*) pasar por alto; (= *not notice*) pasar por alto, no darse cuenta de; (= *tolerate*) pasar por alto, dejar pasar; (= *turn a blind eye to*) hacer la vista gorda a • **we'll ~ it this time** por esta vez lo pasaremos por alto *or* lo dejaremos pasar • **the plant is easily ~ed** es fácil pasar por alto *or* no ver la planta
3 (= *watch over*) vigilar; (= *inspect*) inspeccionar, examinar
overlord [ˈəʊvəlɔːd] (N) (*feudal*) señor *m*; (= *leader*) jefe *m* supremo
overlordship [ˈəʊvəlɔːdʃɪp] (N) (*feudal*) señoría *f*; (= *leadership*) jefatura *f* suprema
overly [ˈəʊvəlɪ] (ADV) (*esp US*) demasiado • **he's not ~ fond of cucumber** no le gusta demasiado el pepino, no le vuelve loco el pepino
overman [ˌəʊvəˈmæn] (VT) proveer exceso de mano de obra a • **an ~ned industry** una industria con exceso de mano de obra
overmanning [ˌəʊvəˈmænɪŋ] (N) exceso *m* de mano de obra
overmuch [ˌəʊvəˈmʌtʃ] (ADV) demasiado, en demasía
(ADJ) demasiado
overnice [ˌəʊvəˈnaɪs] (ADJ) melindroso, remilgado
overnight [ˌəʊvəˈnaɪt] (ADV) **1** (= *through the night*) • **we drove ~** condujimos durante la noche • **we'd like to keep him in ~ for observation** nos gustaría que se quedase la noche en observación • **soak the beans ~** deje las judías a remojo toda la noche • **we stayed ~ in Pisa/at John's place** pasamos la

noche en Pisa/en casa de John, hicimos noche en Pisa/en casa de John
2 (= quickly) [disappear, spring up] de la noche a la mañana • **the plants came up almost ~** las plantas salieron prácticamente de la noche a la mañana
ADJ 1 (= night-time) • **~ accommodation is included** el precio de la estancia por la noche está incluido • **it involved a lot of ~ driving** supuso conducir muchas horas durante la noche • **an ~ journey** un viaje de noche • **to make an ~ journey** viajar de noche • **the operation requires an ~ stay in hospital** esta operación requiere que se quede una noche *or* que haga noche en el hospital • **we arrived in Rio after an ~ stop in Madrid** llegamos a Río tras hacer noche en Madrid
2 (= quick) [change, transformation] repentino • **the film that turned her into an ~ sensation** la película que la convirtió en una sensación de la noche a la mañana • **he became an ~ success in America** de la noche a la mañana, se convirtió en una estrella en América
CPD ▸ **overnight bag** bolso *m* de viaje

overoptimistic [ˌəʊvərɒptɪˈmɪstɪk] ADJ demasiado optimista

overpaid [ˌəʊvəˈpeɪd] ADJ con un sueldo excesivo, que cobra demasiado • **grossly ~** con un sueldo escandaloso

overparticular [ˌəʊvəpəˈtɪkjʊləʳ] ADJ melindroso, escrupuloso en exceso • **he's not ~ about money** le importa poco el dinero; (*pej*) es poco escrupuloso en asuntos de dinero • **he's not ~ about hygiene** no es muy escrupuloso en cuestiones de higiene

overpass [ˈəʊvəpɑːs] N (US) paso *m* elevado *or* (LAm) a desnivel

overpay [ˌəʊvəˈpeɪ] (PT, PP: **overpaid** [ˌəʊvəˈpeɪd]) VT [+ person] pagar demasiado a

overpayment [ˌəʊvəˈpeɪmənt] N pago *m* excesivo

overplay [ˌəʊvəˈpleɪ] VT [+ issue, problem] exagerar • **to ~ (one's hand)** pasarse, ir demasiado lejos

overpopulated [ˌəʊvəˈpɒpjʊleɪtɪd] ADJ superpoblado

overpopulation [ˌəʊvəpɒpjʊˈleɪʃən] N superpoblación *f*

overpower [ˌəʊvəˈpaʊəʳ] VT 1 (= subdue physically) dominar; (= defeat) [+ enemy, opponent] derrotar, vencer • **it took ten guards to ~ him** se necesitaron diez guardas para dominarlo *or* para poder con él
2 (*fig*) [heat] agobiar, sofocar; [sound] aturdir; [emotion] embargar; [guilt, shame] abrumar; [sleep, tiredness] vencer; [flavour] dominar • **a sudden dizziness ~ed him** un mareo repentino se apoderó de él • **that piece of furniture ~s the room** ese mueble domina la habitación • **I was ~ed by feelings of guilt** me sentía abrumado por un sentimiento de culpabilidad

overpowering [ˌəʊvəˈpaʊərɪŋ] ADJ 1 (= very strong, intense) [smell] penetrante, intensísimo; [perfume] embriagado; [heat] asfixiante, sofocante; [sound] ensordecedor; [force] arrollador; [flavour] fortísimo; [desire] irresistible; [need] acuciante • **the noise was ~** el ruido era ensordecedor
2 (= intimidating) [person, manner] apabullante, abrumador

overpraise [ˌəʊvəˈpreɪz] VT elogiar demasiado

overprescribe [əʊvəprɪsˈkraɪb] (Pharm, Med) VI recetar demasiados medicamentos VT recetar sin control

overprice [ˌəʊvəˈpraɪs] VT cargar demasiado sobre el precio de • **these goods are ~d** el precio de estas mercancías es excesivo, estas mercancías son demasiado caras para lo que son

overprint [ˌəʊvəˈprɪnt] N sobrecarga *f* VT sobrecargar (**with de**)

overproduce [ˌəʊvəprəˈdjuːs] VT, VI producir demasiado

overproduction [ˌəʊvəprəˈdʌkʃən] N superproducción *f*, exceso *m* de producción

overprotect [ˌəʊvəprəˈtekt] VT proteger demasiado

overprotection [ˌəʊvəprəˈtekʃən] N exceso *m* de protección, sobreprotección *f*

overprotective [ˌəʊvəprəˈtektɪv] ADJ excesivamente protector

overqualified [ˌəʊvəˈkwɒlɪfaɪd] ADJ con titulación que excede la exigida

overran [ˌəʊvəˈræn] PT of **overrun**

overrate [ˌəʊvəˈreɪt] VT sobrevalorar, sobre(e)stimar • **I think his success has been ~d** creo que sus logros se han sobrevalorado *or* sobre(e)stimado

overrated [ˌəʊvəˈreɪtɪd] ADJ sobre(e)stimado, sobrevalorado

overreach [ˌəʊvəˈriːtʃ] VT • **to ~ o.s.** ir más allá de las propias posibilidades • **the company has ~ed itself and made unwise investments** la compañía ha ido más allá de sus propias posibilidades y ha hecho inversiones poco sensatas

overreact [ˌəʊvərɪˈækt] VI reaccionar de manera exagerada

overreaction [ˌəʊvərɪˈækʃən] N reacción *f* exagerada

overreliance [ˌəʊvərɪˈlaɪəns] N dependencia *f* excesiva (**on de**)

overreliant [ˌəʊvərɪˈlaɪənt] ADJ • **to be ~ on sth/sb** depender demasiado de algo/algn

over-represented [ˌəʊvəreprɪˈzentɪd] ADJ • **to be over-represented** estar sobrerrepresentado

override [ˌəʊvəˈraɪd] (PT: **overrode**, PP: **overridden** [ˌəʊvəˈrɪdn]) VT 1 (= ignore) hacer caso omiso de, ignorar; (= cancel) anular, invalidar • **the court can ~ all earlier decisions** el tribunal puede anular *or* invalidar cualquier toda decisión anterior • **this fact ~s all others** este hecho invalida todos los demás • **our protests were overridden** hicieron caso omiso de nuestras protestas, ignoraron nuestras protestas
2 (Tech) anular, invalidar

overriding [ˌəʊvəˈraɪdɪŋ] ADJ (gen) [need, importance, reason] primordial; [principle] fundamental

overripe [ˌəʊvəˈraɪp] ADJ demasiado maduro, pasado

overrode [ˌəʊvəˈrəʊd] PT of **override**

overrule [ˌəʊvəˈruːl] VT [+ judgment, decision] anular, invalidar; [+ request] denegar, rechazar; [+ objection] ignorar • **his suggestion was ~d** denegaron *or* rechazaron su propuesta • **but we were ~d** pero rechazaron nuestra propuesta • **"objection ~d"** (Jur) "objeción desestimada"

overrun [ˌəʊvəˈrʌn] (PT: **overran**, PP: **overrun**) VT 1 (Mil) [+ country] invadir • **the field is ~ with weeds** las malas hierbas han invadido el campo, el campo está cubierto de maleza • **the town is ~ with tourists** el pueblo está inundado de turistas
2 (= exceed) [+ time limit] rebasar, exceder
VI [ˌəʊvəˈrʌn] [meeting, speech, TV programme] exceder el tiempo previsto • **his speech overran by 15 minutes** su discurso se excedió al tiempo previsto en 15 minutos
N [ˈəʊvərʌn] (on costs) exceso *m* (en relación a lo previsto) • **the project has suffered huge cost ~s** el proyecto ha excedido en mucho los costes previstos

overscrupulous [ˌəʊvəˈskruːpjʊləs] ADJ = **overparticular**

overseas [ˌəʊvəˈsiːz] ADV [be, live] en el extranjero, allende el mar (*liter*) • **to go ~** ir al extranjero • **to travel ~** viajar por el extranjero • **visitors from ~** visitas *fpl* del extranjero • **to be posted ~** ser destinado al extranjero
ADJ [student] extranjero; [duty, trade] exterior; (Mil) [service] en el extranjero, en ultramar • **~ market** mercado *m* exterior • **a company with ~ interests** una empresa con intereses en el extranjero • **she was given an ~ posting/assignment** la destinaron al extranjero

oversee [ˌəʊvəˈsiː] (PT: **oversaw** [ˌəʊvəˈsɔː]) (PP: **overseen** [ˌəʊvəˈsiːn]) VT supervisar

overseer [ˌəʊvəsɪəʳ] N (= foreman) capataz *mf*; (= supervisor) supervisor(a) *m/f*

oversell [ˌəʊvəˈsel] (PT, PP: **oversold**) VT [+ product] hacer una propaganda excesiva a favor de; (*fig*) alabar en exceso

oversensitive [ˌəʊvəˈsensɪtɪv] ADJ hipersensible, demasiado susceptible

oversexed [ˌəʊvəˈsekst] ADJ de deseo sexual excesivo; (*hum*) sexualmente obsesionado

overshadow [ˌəʊvəˈʃædəʊ] VT 1 (*lit*) hacer sombra a
2 (*fig*) eclipsar • **it was ~ed by greater events** fue eclipsado por sucesos de mayor trascendencia • **the event was ~ed by his death** su muerte ensombreció el acontecimiento

overshoe [ˈəʊvəʃuː] N chanclo *m*

overshoot [ˌəʊvəˈʃuːt] (PT, PP: **overshot** [ˌəʊvəˈʃɒt]) VT [+ destination] ir más allá de; [+ turning] pasarse de • **to ~ the runway** salirse de la pista de aterrizaje • **we overshot (the target) by 40 tons** producimos 40 toneladas más de lo previsto • IDIOM: • **to ~ (the mark)** pasarse de la raya, excederse

oversight [ˈəʊvəsaɪt] N 1 (= omission) descuido *m* • **it was an ~** fue un descuido • **by an ~** por descuido
2 (= supervision) supervisión *f*

oversimplification [ˌəʊvəsɪmplɪfɪˈkeɪʃən] N simplificación *f* excesiva

oversimplified [ˌəʊvəˈsɪmplɪfaɪd] ADJ demasiado simplificado

oversimplify [ˌəʊvəˈsɪmplɪfaɪ] VT simplificar demasiado

oversize [ˌəʊvəˈsaɪz], **oversized** [ˌəʊvəˈsaɪzd] ADJ demasiado grande, descomunal; (US) [clothes] de talla muy grande

oversleep [ˌəʊvəˈsliːp] (PT, PP: **overslept** [ˌəʊvəˈslept]) VI quedarse dormido, no despertar(se) a tiempo • **I overslept** me quedé dormido, no (me) desperté a tiempo

overspecialization [əʊvəspeʃəlaɪˈzeɪʃən] N especialización *f* excesiva

overspend [ˌəʊvəˈspend] (PT, PP: **overspent** [ˌəʊvəˈspent]) VT • **to ~ one's allowance** gastar más de lo que permite su asignación
VI gastar demasiado *or* más de la cuenta • **we have overspent by 50 dollars** hemos gastado 50 dólares de más *or* más de lo que debíamos

overspending [ˌəʊvəˈspendɪŋ] N gasto *m* excesivo

overspill [ˈəʊvəspɪl] N (= population) exceso *m* de población • **an ~ town** una ciudad satélite

overstaffed [ˌəʊvəˈstɑːft] ADJ con exceso de personal, con exceso de plantilla

overstaffing [ˌəʊvəˈstɑːfɪŋ] N exceso *m* de personal, exceso *m* de plantilla

overstate [ˌəʊvəˈsteɪt] VT exagerar • **to ~ one's case** exagerar sus argumentos

overstatement [ˌəʊvəˈsteɪtmənt] N exageración *f*

overstay [ˌəʊvəˈsteɪ] VT • **to ~ one's leave**

quedarse más tiempo de lo que la licencia permite • **to ~ one's welcome** quedarse más tiempo de lo debido • **I don't want to ~ my welcome** no quiero ser un pesado, no quiero abusar de su hospitalidad

oversteer [ˌəʊvəˈstɪəʳ] VI [*driver*] girar demasiado el volante

overstep [ˌəʊvəˈstep] VT (*fig*) [*+ boundary*] traspasar; [*+ authority*] excederse en el ejercicio de • IDIOM: • **to ~ the mark** pasarse de la raya, excederse

overstock [ˌəʊvəˈstɒk] VT abarrotar • **to be ~ed with** tener existencias excesivas de

overstrain [ˌəʊvəˈstreɪn] N fatiga *f* excesiva; (*nervous*) hipertensión *f*
VT [*+ person*] (= *tire*) fatigar excesivamente; (= *overstress*) provocar una hipertensión en; [*+ metal*] deformar, torcer; [*+ resources*] estirar • **to ~ o.s.** fatigarse excesivamente

overstretch [ˌəʊvəˈstretʃ] VT **1** (*lit*) [*+ muscles, legs*] forzar demasiado
2 (*fig*) [*+ resources, budget, finances*] estirar; [*+ abilities*] forzar demasiado • **to ~ o.s.** exigirse demasiado; (*financially*) ponerse en una situación (económica) comprometida

overstretched [ˌəʊvəˈstretʃt] ADJ [*system, service, hospital*] desbordado, que funciona al límite de su capacidad • **the ~ air traffic control system could reach breaking point** el sistema de control del tráfico aéreo está desbordado *or* funciona al límite de su capacidad y podría llegar a una situación límite • **to be ~** [*system, service, hospital*] estar desbordado, funcionar al límite de su capacidad • **the crime rate is rising rapidly at present and the police force is ~** actualmente, el índice de criminalidad aumenta rápidamente y la policía está desbordada • **my budget is ~** he estirado al máximo mi presupuesto

overstrict [ˌəʊvəˈstrɪkt] ADJ [*person*] demasiado estricto; [*regime, schedule*] excesivamente riguroso

overstrike [ˌəʊvəˈstraɪk] N (*on printer*) superposición *f*
VT superponer

overstrung [ˌəʊvəˈstrʌŋ] ADJ [*person*] sobre(e)xcitado, hipertenso; [*piano*] *con dos grupos de cuerdas que se cruzan formando un ángulo oblicuo*

oversubscribed [ˌəʊvəsəbˈskraɪbd] ADJ • **the course is heavily ~** existe un exceso enorme de solicitudes para el curso • **the issue was ~** se pidieron más acciones de las que había • **the issue was ~ four times** la solicitud de acciones rebasó cuatro veces la cantidad de títulos ofrecidos

oversupply [ˌəʊvəsəˈplaɪ] VT proveer en exceso (**with** de) • **we are oversupplied with cars** tenemos exceso de coches

overt [əʊˈvɜːt] ADJ [*racism, discrimination, hostility*] manifiesto, patente; [*criticism*] abierto, manifiesto • **there were no ~ signs of ...** no había signos manifiestos *or* patentes de ...

overtake [ˌəʊvəˈteɪk] (PT: **overtook** [ˌəʊvəˈtʊk]) (PP: **overtaken** [ˌəʊvəˈteɪkən])
VT **1** (= *pass*) [*+ car*] adelantar, rebasar (*Mex*); [*+ runner*] adelantar, dejar atrás; [*+ competition, rival*] tomar la delantera a • **he doesn't want to be ~n** no quiere dejarse adelantar • **you can't ~ that car on the bend** no puedes adelantar ese coche en la curva • **we overtook a lorry near Burgos** cerca de Burgos adelantamos un camión • **Swift has ~n Metmark in steel production** Swift le ha tomado la delantera a Metmark en la producción de acero
2 (*fig*) pillar desprevenido • **we have been ~n by events** los sucesos nos pillaron desprevenidos *or* de sorpresa
VI (*Aut*) adelantar, rebasar (*Mex*) • **"no overtaking"** "prohibido adelantar", "prohibido rebasar" (*Mex*)

overtaking [ˌəʊvəˈteɪkɪŋ] N (*Aut*) adelantamiento *m*, rebase *m* (*Mex*)

overtax [ˌəʊvəˈtæks] VT **1** (*Econ*) gravar en exceso
2 (*fig*) [*+ strength, patience*] agotar, abusar de • **to ~ o.s.** exigirse demasiado a sí mismo

overtaxed [ˌəʊvəˈtækst] ADJ (= *paying too much tax*) [*people, country*] que paga demasiados impuestos

over-the-counter [ˈəʊvəðəˈkaʊntəʳ] ADJ [*method*] limpio, honrado • **over-the-counter drugs** medicamentos *mpl* sin receta • **over-the-counter market** (*St Ex*) mercado *m* de acciones no cotizadas en la bolsa

overthrow [ˌəʊvəˈθrəʊ] (VB: PT: **overthrew** [ˌəʊvəˈθruː]) (PP: **overthrown** [ˌəʊvəˈθrəʊn])
N [*of president, dictator, government*] derrocamiento *m*
VT [*+ system*] echar abajo, derribar; [*+ president, dictator, government*] derrocar

overtime [ˈəʊvətaɪm] N **1** (*Ind*) horas *fpl* extra(s) • **to do/work ~** hacer/trabajar horas extra(s) • **we shall have to work ~ to catch up** (*fig*) tendremos que esforzarnos al máximo para recuperar lo que hemos perdido • **your imagination has been working ~!** ¡tienes una imaginación demasiado activa!
2 (*US*) (*Sport*) prórroga *f*, tiempo *m* suplementario
CPD ▸ **overtime ban** prohibición *f* de horas extra(s) ▸ **overtime pay** pago *m* de horas extra(s)

overtired [ˌəʊvəˈtaɪəd] ADJ agotado

overtly [əʊˈvɜːtlɪ] ADV abiertamente

overtone [ˈəʊvətəʊn] N **1** (= *hint, element*) • **a speech with a hostile ~** un discurso con cierto tono hostil • **the strike has political ~s** la huelga tiene un trasfondo político • **a play with religious ~s** una obra con connotaciones religiosas • **a wine with citrus ~s** un vino con un cierto sabor cítrico
2 (= *connotation*) [*of word, phrase*] connotación *f*
3 (= *insinuation*) insinuación *f* • **his behaviour was full of sexual ~s** no paraba de insinuarse
4 (*Mus*) armónico *m*

overtook [ˌəʊvəˈtʊk] PT *of* **overtake**

overtop [ˌəʊvəˈtɒp] VT descollar sobre

overtrain [ˌəʊvəˈtreɪn] VT, VI entrenar en exceso • **~ed** que ha entrenado en exceso

overtrick [ˈəʊvətrɪk] N baza *f* de más

overtrump [ˌəʊvəˈtrʌmp] VT contrafallar

overture [ˈəʊvətjʊəʳ] N **1** (*Mus*) obertura *f*
2 (*fig*) • **to make ~s to sb** (*Pol, Comm*) hacer una propuesta a algn; (*sexual*) hacer insinuaciones a algn • **they had made ~s to Fox, but without success** le hicieron una propuesta a Fox, pero no se llegó a nada • **the government made peace ~s to the rebels** el gobierno les hizo una propuesta de paz a los rebeldes

overturn [ˌəʊvəˈtɜːn] VT [*+ car, boat, saucepan*] volcar; [*+ government*] derrocar, derribar; [*+ decision, ruling*] anular • **they managed to have the ruling ~ed** lograron hacer anular la decisión
VI [*car*] volcar, dar una vuelta de campana; [*boat*] zozobrar

overuse [ˌəʊvəˈjuːz] VT usar demasiado

overused [ˌəʊvəˈjuːzd] ADJ (= *overworked*) [*word*] manido, trillado

overvalue [ˌəʊvəˈvæljuː] VT sobrevalorar

overview [ˈəʊvəvjuː] N visión *f* de conjunto

overweening [ˌəʊvəˈwiːnɪŋ] ADJ arrogante, presuntuoso, altivo • **~ pride** desmesurado orgullo *m*

overweight [ˌəʊvəˈweɪt] ADJ [*person*] gordo • **to be ~** [*parcel, luggage*] pesar demasiado, tener exceso de peso; [*person*] estar demasiado gordo • **he is 8 kilos ~** pesa 8 kilos de más • **the suitcase is a kilo ~** la maleta tiene un exceso de peso de un kilo
N exceso *m* de peso, sobrepeso *m*

overwhelm [ˌəʊvəˈwelm] VT **1** (= *defeat*) [*+ opponent, team*] arrollar, aplastar
2 (= *overcome*) [*difficulties, fear, loneliness*] abrumar • **sorrow ~ed him** estaba abrumado por el dolor • **try not to let panic ~ you** intenta que el pánico no se apodere de ti • **I felt ~ed by events/her** me sentía abrumado por los acontecimientos/por ella • **he was ~ed by their kindness** su amabilidad le dejó abrumado *or* le conmovió profundamente • **she was ~ed with grief** estaba sumida en la tristeza • **she was ~ed with joy** rebosaba de alegría
3 (= *inundate, overload*) (*with work*) abrumar, agobiar; (*with questions, requests, information*) atosigar • **you shouldn't ~ the customer with too much information** no deberías atosigar al cliente con demasiada información • **we have been ~ed with offers of help** nos han inundado las ofertas de ayuda

overwhelming [ˌəʊvəˈwelmɪŋ] ADJ [*defeat, victory*] arrollador, aplastante; [*success*] arrollador; [*majority*] abrumador, aplastante; [*heat*] agobiante; [*pressure, urge*] irresistible; [*desire*] irresistible, imperioso; [*emotion*] incontenible • **one's ~ impression is of heat** lo que más impresiona es el calor

overwhelmingly [ˌəʊvəˈwelmɪŋlɪ] ADV • **they voted ~ for Blake** una mayoría aplastante *or* arrolladora votó por Blake, la inmensa mayoría votó por Blake • **the proposal was ~ defeated** la propuesta fue rechazada por una mayoría abrumadora *or* aplastante • **the legal profession is ~ male** en la abogacía la inmensa mayoría son hombres

overwind [ˌəʊvəˈwaɪnd] (PT, PP: **overwound**) VT [*+ watch*] dar demasiada cuerda a

overwork [ˌəʊvəˈwɜːk] N agotamiento *m* por trabajo excesivo
VT [*+ person*] hacer trabajar demasiado; [*+ eye, part of body*] exigir un esfuerzo excesivo a; [*+ word, concept*] desgastar (*a base de utilizarlo en exceso*) • **"ecological" has become the most ~ed adjective there is** "ecológico" se ha convertido en el adjetivo más desgastado *or* manido que hay
VI trabajar demasiado

overworked [ˌəʊvəˈwɜːkt] ADJ • **we're ~** tenemos demasiado trabajo, nos hacen trabajar demasiado

overwrite [ˌəʊvəˈraɪt] (PT: **overwrote** [ˌəʊvəˈrəʊt]) (PP: **overwritten** [ˌəʊvəˈrɪtn])
VT **1** exagerar • **this passage is overwritten** este pasaje tiene un estilo recargado
2 (*Comput*) sobreescribir
VI exagerar

overwrought [ˌəʊvəˈrɔːt] ADJ • **to be ~** estar crispado

overzealous [ˌəʊvəˈzeləs] ADJ demasiado entusiasta

Ovid [ˈɒvɪd] N Ovidio

oviduct [ˈəʊvɪdʌkt] N oviducto *m*

oviform [ˈəʊvɪfɔːm] ADJ oviforme

ovine [ˈəʊvaɪn] ADJ ovino

oviparous [əʊˈvɪpərəs] ADJ ovíparo

ovoid [ˈəʊvɔɪd] ADJ ovoide
N ovoide *m*

ovulate [ˈɒvjʊleɪt] VI ovular

ovulation [ˌɒvjʊˈleɪʃən] N ovulación *f*

ovule ['əʊvju:l] N óvulo *m*
ovum ['əʊvəm] N (PL: **ova** ['əʊvə]) óvulo *m*
ow [aʊ] EXCL ¡ay!
owe [əʊ] VT (*gen*) deber • **to owe sb £2** deber dos libras a algn • **I'll owe it to you** te lo quedo a deber • **to owe sb for a meal** deber a algn una comida • **he claims he is still owed for the work** asegura que todavía se le debe dinero por el trabajo • **he owes his life to a lucky chance** debe su vida a una casualidad • **he owes his talent to his mother** le debe su talento a su madre • **to what do I owe the honour of your visit?** ¿a qué debo el honor de su visita? • **you owe it to yourself to come** venir es un deber que tienes contigo mismo • **I owe it to her to confess** mi deber con ella me obliga a confesarlo • **I think I owe you an explanation** creo que es necesaria una explicación; ▸ **allegiance**
VI tener deudas • **he owed for three coffees** debía tres cafés
owing ['əʊɪŋ] ADJ • **how much is ~ to you now?** ¿cuánto se le debe ahora? • **I think an explanation is ~** creo que se debe dar una explicación
PREP • **~ to** (= *due to*) debido a, a causa de • **~ to the bad weather** debido al mal tiempo • **it is ~ to lack of time** se debe a la falta de tiempo
owl [aʊl] N (= *barn owl*) lechuza *f*; (= *little owl*) mochuelo *m*; (= *long-eared owl*) búho *m*; (= *tawny owl*) cárabo *m*
owlet ['aʊlɪt] N mochuelo *m*
owlish ['aʊlɪʃ] ADJ [*look, eyes*] de búho; [*face*] solemne
own¹ [əʊn] VT **1** (= *possess*) [+ *object, goods*] tener, poseer; [+ *land, house, company*] ser dueño de, poseer • **he owns two tractors** tiene *or* posee dos tractores • **he owns three newspapers** es dueño de tres periódicos • **do you own your own house?** ¿tienes casa propia?, ¿tienes una casa de tu propiedad? • **who owns the newspaper?** ¿quién es el propietario *or* dueño del periódico? • **who owns this pen?** ¿de quién es esta pluma? • **a cat nobody wants to own** un gato que nadie quiere reclamar • **as if he owned the place** como si dueño del lugar • **you don't own me!** ¡no te pertenezco!
2 (= *admit*) reconocer, admitir • **I own I was wrong** reconozco *or* admito que me equivoqué • **he owned the child as his** reconoció al niño como suyo
VI • **to own to sth** confesar *or* reconocer algo
▸ **own up** VI + ADV confesar (**to sth** algo) • **own up!** ¡confiésalo! • **they owned up to having stolen the apples** confesaron haber robado las manzanas
own² [əʊn] ADJ propio • **the house has its own garage** la casa tiene garaje propio • **in her own house** en su propia casa • **it's all my own money** todo el dinero es mío
PRON • **my/his/her** *etc* **own: the house is her own** la casa es de su propiedad *or* le pertenece • **my time is my own** dispongo de mi tiempo como quiero • **we all look after our own** todos cuidamos lo nuestro • **he has a style all his own** tiene un estilo muy suyo *or* propio • **I'm so busy I can scarcely call my time my own** estoy tan ocupado que apenas dispongo de mi tiempo • **without a chair to call my own** sin una silla que pueda decir que es mía • **can I have it for my own?** ¿puedo quedarme con él? • **he made the theory his own** hizo suya la teoría, adoptó la teoría • **she has money of her own** tiene su propio dinero • **a place of one's own** (una) casa propia • **I'll give you a copy of your own** te daré una copia para ti • **for reasons of his own** él sabrá por qué • **to be on one's own** estar solo • **now we're on our own** ya estamos solos *or* a solas • **if I can get him on his own** si puedo hablar con él a solas • **to do sth on one's own** (= *unaccompanied*) hacer algo por su cuenta; (= *unaided*) hacer algo solo *or* sin ayuda (de nadie) • **you'll have a room of your very own** tendrás una habitación para ti solo • IDIOMS: • **to get one's own back (on sb)** vengarse (de algn) • **to come into one's own**: • **women came into their own during the Second World War** las mujeres no se hicieron valer hasta la Segunda Guerra Mundial • **his ideas really came into their own in the sixties** hasta los años sesenta no se valoraron de verdad sus ideas • **to hold one's own** defenderse; (= *not give in*) no cejar, mantenerse firme • **he can hold his own with the best of them** no le va a la zaga ni al mejor de ellos • **I can hold my own in German** me defiendo en alemán • PROVERB: • **each to his own** cada uno a lo suyo, cada cual a lo suyo
CPD ▸ **own brand** (*Comm*) marca *f* propia (*de un supermercado etc*); ▸ **own-brand** ▸ **own goal** (*Brit*) (*Sport*) autogol *m*; (*fig*) • **the campaign was considered a public relations own goal for the government** la campaña se consideró un perjuicio que el gobierno se ha hecho a sí mismo *or* un gol que el gobierno se ha marcado a sí mismo en el ámbito de las relaciones públicas ▸ **own label** = own brand
own-brand ['əʊn,brænd] ADJ • **own-brand products** productos *mpl* de marca propia (*de un supermercado etc*)
owner ['əʊnəʳ] N [*of goods*] dueño/a *m/f*; [*of land, property, company*] dueño/a *m/f*, propietario/a *m/f*; ▸ **home**
CPD ▸ **owner driver** conductor(a) *m/f* propietario/a ▸ **owner occupancy** • **there's a growing level of ~ occupancy** hay cada vez más propietarios de la vivienda ▸ **owner occupier** ocupante *mf* propietario/a
ownerless ['əʊnəlɪs] ADJ sin dueño
owner-occupied [,əʊnə'ɒkjʊpaɪd] ADJ (*Brit*) [*property, house*] ocupado por el dueño, ocupado por el propietario
ownership ['əʊnəʃɪp] N propiedad *f* • **they abolished private ~ of the means of production** abolieron la propiedad privada de los medios de producción • **the ~ of the land is in dispute** está en disputa la propiedad de la tierra • **"under new ownership"** "nuevo propietario", "nuevo dueño" • **under his ~ the business flourished** el negocio prosperó mientras fue de su propiedad
own-label [,əʊn'leɪbl] ADJ = **own-brand**
ownsome* ['əʊnsəm] N • **on one's ~** a solas, solito*
owt [aʊt] N (*Brit*) (*dialect*) algo, alguna cosa
ox [ɒks] N (PL: **oxen**) buey *m*
oxalic [ɒk'sælɪk] ADJ • **~ acid** ácido *m* oxálico
oxblood ['ɒksblʌd] ADJ de color rojo oscuro
oxbow ['ɒks,bəʊ], **oxbow lake** N lago *m* en forma de herradura
Oxbridge ['ɒksbrɪdʒ] N (*Brit*) *Universidades de Oxford y Cambridge*

OXBRIDGE

Oxbridge se usa para hacer referencia a las universidades de **Oxford** y **Cambridge**, sobre todo cuando se quiere destacar el ambiente de privilegio al que se las asocia, originado por su posición como las dos universidades más antiguas y prestigiosas del Reino Unido y por el hecho de que muchos licenciados de **Oxbridge** suelen acabar en puestos muy influyentes del ámbito empresarial, político o diplomático. Muchos estudiantes de estas universidades todavía provienen de institutos privados, aunque ambas instituciones tratan de aumentar el número de alumnos de centros estatales.

oxcart ['ɒkskɑ:t] N carro *m* de bueyes
oxen ['ɒksən] NPL *of* **ox**
ox-eye daisy [,ɒksaɪ'deɪzɪ] N margarita *f*
Oxfam ['ɒksfæm] N ABBR = **Oxford Committee for Famine Relief**

OXFAM

Oxfam es una organización benéfica cuyas siglas significan en inglés **Oxford Committee for Famine Relief**, muy conocida por sus campañas para recaudar fondos, su trabajo de ayuda al Tercer Mundo y su intento de promocionar el uso de tecnología básica y de los recursos locales renovables. Además, el nombre **Oxfam** se asocia también a una cadena de tiendas gestionadas por esta organización, en las que se puede adquirir ropa y otros artículos de segunda mano, así como objetos hechos en talleres y cooperativas del Tercer Mundo.

oxford ['ɒksfəd] N (*US*) zapato *m* (de tacón bajo)
oxhide ['ɒkshaɪd] N cuero *m* de buey
oxidation [,ɒksɪ'deɪʃən] N oxidación *f*
oxide ['ɒksaɪd] N óxido *m*
oxidize ['ɒksɪdaɪz] VT oxidar
VI oxidarse
oxlip ['ɒkslɪp] N prímula *f*
Oxon ABBR = **Oxfordshire**
Oxon. ['ɒksən] ADJ ABBR (*Brit*) (= **Oxoniensis**) (= *of Oxford*) de Oxford
Oxonian [ɒk'səʊnɪən] ADJ oxoniense
N oxoniense *mf*
oxtail ['ɒksteɪl] N • **~ soup** sopa *f* de rabo de buey
oxter ['ɒkstəʳ] N (*Scot*) axila *f*
oxyacetylene ['ɒksɪə'setɪli:n] ADJ oxiacetilénico • **~ burner** *or* **lamp** *or* **torch** soplete *m* oxiacetilénico • **~ welding** soldadura *f* oxiacetilénica
oxygen ['ɒksɪdʒən] N oxígeno *m* • IDIOM: • **to give sb the ~ of publicity** hacer propaganda gratuita a algn
CPD ▸ **oxygen cylinder** botella *f* de oxígeno, bombona *f* de oxígeno ▸ **oxygen mask** máscara *f* de oxígeno, mascarilla *f* de oxígeno ▸ **oxygen tank** tanque *m* de oxígeno ▸ **oxygen tent** cámara *f* de oxígeno
oxygenate [ɒk'sɪdʒəneɪt] VT oxigenar
oxygenation [,ɒksɪdʒə'neɪʃən] N oxigenación *f*
oxymoron [,ɒksɪ'mɔ:rɒn] N (PL: **oxymora** [,ɒksɪ'mɔ:rə]) oxímoron *m*
oyez [əʊ'jez] EXCL ¡oíd!
oyster ['ɔɪstəʳ] N ostra *f*; ▸ **world**
CPD ▸ **oyster cracker** (*US*) galletita *f* salada ▸ **oyster farm** criadero *m* de ostras ▸ **oyster farming** ostricultura *f*, cría *f* de ostras ▸ **oyster shell** concha *f* de ostra
oysterbed ['ɔɪstəbed] N criadero *m* de ostras, vivero *m* de ostras
oystercatcher ['ɔɪstə,kætʃəʳ] N ostrero *m*
Oz‡ [ɒz] N ABBR = **Australia**
oz ABBR = **ounce(s)**
ozone ['əʊzəʊn] N ozono *m*
CPD ▸ **ozone hole** agujero *m* de ozono ▸ **ozone layer** capa *f* de ozono
ozone-friendly ['əʊzəʊn,frendlɪ], **ozone-safe** ['əʊzəʊn,seɪf] ADJ que no daña la capa de ozono
ozonosphere [əʊ'zəʊnə,sfɪəʳ] N ozonosfera *f*

Pp

P¹, p¹ [piː] N (*= letter*) P, p *f* • **P for Peter** P de Pedro • IDIOM: • **to mind** *or* **watch one's Ps and Qs*** cuidarse *or* tener mucho cuidado de no meter la pata*
P² ABBR = **parking**
p² ABBR **1** = **penny, pence**
2 (= **page**) p., pág.
P. ABBR **1** (= **president**) P.
2 (= **prince**) P.
P45 [piːfɔːtɪ'faɪv] N (*Brit*) *formulario que se entrega al trabajador a la finalización de una relación laboral*
PA N ABBR **1** = **personal assistant**
2 = **public address system**
3 = **Press Association**
ABBR **1** (*US*) = **Pennsylvania**
2 (*Theat etc*) = **personal appearance**
Pa. ABBR (*US*) = **Pennsylvania**
pa* [pɑː] N papá* *m*
p.a. ABBR (= **per annum**) (= *yearly*) por año, al año
PAC N ABBR (*US*) = **political action committee**
pace¹ ['peɪs] N **1** (= *step*) paso *m* • **I took a couple of ~s forward/back** di un par de pasos hacia delante/atrás • **the tiger was only a few ~s away** el tigre estaba a solo unos pasos • **to go through one's ~s** [*performer*] demostrar de lo que se es capaz • **to put sb through his/her ~s** poner a algn a prueba • **to put a horse through its ~s** ejercitar un caballo
2 (= *speed*) **a** (*when walking, running*) paso *m*, ritmo *m* • **I could hardly keep ~ (with him)** apenas podía seguirle el ritmo *or* el paso • **to set the ~** (*Sport*) marcar el paso *or* el ritmo • **they walked at a steady ~ • their ~ was steady** marchaban a un paso *or* ritmo constante; ▷ **quicken, slacken, snail, walking**
b (*fig*) ritmo *m* • **to do sth at one's own ~** hacer algo a su (propio) ritmo • **the economy is growing at a brisk ~** la economía está creciendo a un ritmo rápido • **the ~ of change/life** el ritmo de cambio/vida • **I can't keep ~ with events** no puedo seguir el ritmo de los acontecimientos • **salaries are not keeping ~ with inflation** los sueldos no avanzan al mismo ritmo *or* paso que la inflación, los sueldos no siguen el ritmo de la inflación • **her novels lack ~** el ritmo de sus novelas es demasiado lento • **this company is setting the ~ in new technology** esta empresa está marcando la pauta en nueva tecnología • **he can't stand** *or* **stay the ~** las cosas se desarrollan demasiado rápidamente para él; ▷ **force**
VT **1** (*anxiously*) • **to ~ the floor** ir *or* andar de un lado para otro • **Harry was pacing the room** Harry iba *or* andaba de un lado para otro de la habitación
2 (= *set pace of*) • **to ~ sb** (*Sport*) marcar el ritmo a algn • **to ~ o.s.: it was a tough race and I had to ~ myself** era una carrera difícil y tuve que tener cuidado de no gastar toda mi energía al principio • **you should ~ yourself and not attempt too much at once** tienes que tomártelo poco a poco y no intentar hacer demasiado de una vez • **he knows how to ~ the action** (*Cine, Theat*) sabe cómo marcar el ritmo de la acción
• **a fast-paced world/life** un mundo/una vida de ritmo trepidante • **a well-paced drama** un drama con el ritmo de la acción bien marcado
VI • **Alan was pacing nervously** Alan se paseaba nervioso (de un lado para otro), Alan iba *or* andaba de un lado para otro nervioso • **to ~ back and forth • ~ up and down** ir *or* pasearse de un lado para otro
CPD ▸ **pace bowler** (*Cricket*) *jugador de críquet que normalmente lanza la bola rápido* ▸ **pace bowling** (*Cricket*) *lanzamiento rápido de la bola*
▸ **pace around** VI + ADV dar vueltas
VI + PREP [+ *room*] dar vueltas por • **Roger ~d around his office until they arrived** Roger daba vueltas por su oficina hasta que llegaron
▸ **pace out, pace off** VT + ADV [+ *distance*] medir en *or* con pasos • **to ~ out ten metres** medir diez metros en *or* con pasos • **he ~d out the length of the field** midió la longitud del campo en *or* con pasos
pace² ['peɪsɪ] PREP (*frm*) según, de acuerdo con
pacemaker ['peɪsˌmeɪkəʳ] N **1** (*Med*) marcapasos *m inv*
2 (*Sport*) liebre *f*
3 (*in market, business*) = **pacesetter**
pacer ['peɪsəʳ] N (*US*) (*Sport*) liebre *f*
pacesetter ['peɪsˌsetəʳ] N **1** (*Sport*) liebre *f*
2 (*in market, business*) persona *f* que marca la pauta
pacey, pacy ['peɪsɪ] ADJ (COMPAR: **pacier**, SUPERL: **paciest**) **1** [*production, thriller*] rápido, con buen ritmo
2 (*Sport*) [*player*] rápido, con buen ritmo
pachyderm ['pækɪdɜːm] N paquidermo *m*
Pacific [pə'sɪfɪk] ADJ pacífico • **the ~ region** la región del Pacífico
N • **the ~ (Ocean)** el (Océano) Pacífico
CPD ▸ **the Pacific Rim** los países de la Costa del Pacífico ▸ **Pacific Standard Time** (*US*) hora *f* oficial de la región del Pacífico
pacific [pə'sɪfɪk] ADJ pacífico
pacifically [pə'sɪfɪkəlɪ] ADV pacíficamente
pacification [ˌpæsɪfɪ'keɪʃən] N pacificación *f*
pacifier ['pæsɪfaɪəʳ] N (*US*) (= *dummy*) chupete *m*
pacifism ['pæsɪfɪzəm] N pacifismo *m*
pacifist ['pæsɪfɪst] ADJ pacifista
N pacifista *mf*
pacifistic ['pæsɪ'fɪstɪk] ADJ pacifista
pacify ['pæsɪfaɪ] VT (= *calm*) [+ *person*] apaciguar, calmar; [+ *country*] pacificar • **we managed to ~ him eventually** por fin logramos apaciguarlo *or* calmarlo
pack [pæk] N **1** (= *packet*) (*gen*) paquete *m*; (*esp US*) [*of cigarettes*] paquete *m*, cajetilla *f*; (= *wrapping*) envase *m* • **a six-pack of beer** un paquete de seis cervezas • **she smokes a ~ and a half a day** fuma un paquete y medio *or* una cajetilla y media de tabaco al día • **for sell-by date see back of ~** para la fecha de caducidad ver el reverso del envase; ▷ **economy, information**
2 (*traveller's*) (*also* **backpack**) mochila *f*; (*on animal*) fardo *m*
3 [*of cards*] baraja *f* • **a ~ of cards** una baraja de cartas • **the roof collapsed like a ~ of cards** el tejado se derrumbó como una baraja de cartas • **he told me a ~ of lies** me contó una sarta *or* (*LAm*) bola de mentiras • **it's a ~ of lies!** ¡es una sarta *or* (*LAm*) bola de mentiras!, ¡son todo mentiras!
4 (= *dressing*) (*Med*) compresa *f* • **cold ~** compresa *f* fría; ▷ **face, ice, mud**
5 [*of hounds, dogs*] jauría *f*; [*of wolves*] manada *f* • **a ~ of hounds** una jauría (de perros) • **a ~ of wolves** una manada de lobos
6 [*of people*] **a** (= *bunch*) [*of tourists, reporters*] manada *f*; [*of idiots, fools*] hatajo *m* • **with a ~ of cameramen in hot pursuit** con una manada de cámaras pisándoles los talones • **they're like a ~ of kids** son como un hatajo de críos*; ▷ **rat**
b [*of brownies, cubs*] patrulla *f*
c [*of runners, cyclists*] pelotón *m*; (*fig*) • **they are way ahead of the ~ in electronic gadgetry** están muy a la cabeza del pelotón en materia de aparatos electrónicos
7 (*Rugby*) • **the ~** (= *forwards*) los delanteros; (= *scrum*) el pack
VT **1** (= *put in container*) **a** [+ *possessions*] (*in case, bag etc*) • **I decided to ~ a few things** decidí meter algunas cosas en la maleta • **have you ~ed the salt and pepper for the picnic?** ¿has metido *or* puesto la sal y la pimienta para el picnic? • **~ your things and get out!** ¡coge tus cosas *or* haz la maleta (con tus cosas) y lárgate de aquí!*
b [+ *goods, products for transport*] (*in package*) empaquetar; (*in crate, container*) embalar, empacar (*esp LAm*) • **he was ~ing plates and wine glasses into** *or* **in boxes** estaba metiendo *or* empaquetando platos y copas en cajas
c (*Comm*) (*in individual packaging*) envasar • **she spent the summer ~ing apricots** se pasó el verano envasando albaricoques • **they come ~ed in dozens** vienen en cajas de una docena
2 (= *fill*) [+ *box, crate*] llenar • **he has a job ~ing boxes in a warehouse** trabaja en un almacén llenando cajas • **to ~ one's bags** (*lit*) hacer las maletas • **to ~ one's bags (and go** *or* **leave)** (*fig*) coger sus cosas e irse, coger sus cosas y largarse* • **to ~ one's/a (suit)case** hacer la maleta • **Eleanor was ~ing her trunk** Eleanor estaba metiendo sus cosas en el baúl • **a crate ~ed with books** una caja llena de libros • **~ your shoes with paper so they**

P

don't lose their shape** mete papel en los zapatos para que no pierdan la forma
3 (*= fill tightly*) [*+ hall, stadium*] llenar a rebosar • **they ~ed the hall to see him** llenaron la sala a rebosar para verlo • **a fun-packed holiday** unas vacaciones llenas *or* repletas de diversión • **to ~ a jury** *formar un jurado con personas que simpatizan con el interesado* • **a thrill-packed evening** una tarde muy emocionante; ▹ **action-packed**
4 (*= press tightly*) • **to ~ sth/sb into sth**: • **we ~ed the children into the car** apretujamos a los niños en el coche • **they've ~ed enough information into this guide to satisfy every need** han incluído suficiente información en esta guía como para satisfacer las necesidades de todo el mundo • **to ~ sth round sth** encajar algo alrededor de algo • **to ~ earth round a plant** acollar una planta; ▹ **packed**
5* (*= carry*) • **he ~s a gun** lleva un revólver • **he ~s a powerful punch** (*lit*) pega duro • **this play ~s a powerful punch** esta es una obra con mucho impacto emocional • **drinks that ~ quite a punch** bebidas *fpl* que pegan fuerte
(VI) **1** (*lit*) **a** (*= do one's packing*) hacer la(s) maleta(s) • IDIOM: • **to send sb ~ing*** [*+ visitor, caller*] echar a algn con cajas destempladas; (*from job*) despedir a algn sin contemplaciones
b (*= fit*) caber • **these books will ~ easily into that box** estos libros cabrán bien en esa caja • **do you think all this will ~ into one suitcase?** ¿crees que todo esto cabrá *or* se podrá meter en una maleta?
2 (*= cram*) [*people*] • **to ~ into a room/theatre** apiñarse *or* apretujarse en una habitación/un teatro • **the five of us ~ed into her Mini** los cinco nos apiñamos *or* apretujamos en su Mini, los cinco nos metimos apretujados en su Mini • **they ~ed round the speaker** se apiñaron *or* se apretujaron en torno al orador
3 (*= compact*) [*snow*] hacerse una masa compacta
(CPD) ▸ **pack animal** bestia *f or* animal *m* de carga ▸ **pack ice** banco *m* de hielo, masa *f* flotante de hielo ▸ **pack leader** (*Rugby*) delantero/a *m/f* principal; (*fig*) líder *mf* de la panda *or* del grupo
▸ **pack away** (VT + ADV) (*lit*) guardar • **I ~ed the tools away** guardé las herramientas • **he can certainly ~ away food, can't he?*** da buena cuenta de la comida ¿verdad?*
(VI + ADV) dejarse guardar • **his umbrella wouldn't ~ away correctly** su paraguas no se dejaba guardar bien
▸ **pack down** (VT + ADV) (*gen*) apretar, comprimir; (*with feet*) apisonar
(VI + ADV) (*Rugby*) formar la melé *or* el scrum
▸ **pack in*** (VT + ADV) **1** (*= cram*) [*+ people*] • **airlines make money by ~ing people in** las compañías aéreas hacen dinero metiendo a un montón de gente en los aviones • **they were ~ed in like sardines** estaban como sardinas en lata • **the show's ~ing them in** el espectáculo llena la sala al completo *or* a rebosar • **we ~ed a lot of sightseeing into those two days** metimos un montón de visitas turísticas en esos dos días
2 (*= stop doing*) [*+ job, activity*] dejar • **it's time we ~ed it in** ya es hora de dejarlo • **let's ~ it in for the day** dejémoslo por hoy • **~ it in!** ¡déjalo ya!
▸ **pack off** (VT + ADV) (*= send away*) largar* • **I ~ed him off in a taxi** lo despaché en un taxi, lo largué en un taxi* • **they ~ed him off to London** lo enviaron sin más a Londres • **to ~ a child off to bed/school** mandar a un niño a la cama/al colegio

▸ **pack out** (VT + ADV) [*+ stadium, hall*] llenar a rebosar, llenar hasta los topes*
▸ **pack up** (VI + ADV) **1*** (*= cease to function*) [*washing-machine, car*] estropearse, descomponerse (*esp Mex*); [*battery*] agotarse; [*engine*] averiarse, estropearse
2* [*person*] **a** (*= stop activity*) • **let's ~ up now** vamos a dejarlo *or* terminar ya
b (*= collect things together*) recoger (mis, tus, sus *etc* cosas) • **they just ~ed up and left** recogieron (sus cosas) y se marcharon
(VT + ADV) **1** (*= put away*) [*+ belongings*] recoger
2* (*= give up*) dejar
package ['pækɪdʒ] (N) **1** (*= parcel, container*) paquete *m*
2 (*US*) (*= packet*) paquete *m* • **the ingredients were clearly listed on the ~** los ingredientes estaban enumerados claramente en el paquete
3 (*fig*) **a** (*= deal*) oferta *f* • **a generous remuneration ~** una generosa oferta de remuneración • **the ~ includes two nights in a hotel** la oferta incluye dos noches en un hotel
b [*of measures, aid*] paquete *m* • **an economic aid ~** un paquete de ayuda económica; ▹ **rescue**
c (*= holiday*) viaje *m* organizado, vacaciones *fpl* organizadas • **the price of a ~ has gone up by 8% since last year** el precio de un viaje organizado *or* de las vacaciones organizadas ha subido un 8% desde el año pasado
4 (*Comput*) paquete *m*; ▹ **software**
(VT) **1** (*US*) (*Comm*) (*also* **package up**) (*in paper, packet*) empaquetar, embalar, empacar (*LAm*); (*in bottle, jar*) envasar • **~d foods** alimentos *mpl* envasados
2 (*fig*) presentar • **it depends how you ~ the proposal** depende de la forma en que presentes la propuesta
(CPD) ▸ **package deal** (*= holiday*) viaje *m* organizado, vacaciones *fpl* organizadas; (*= deal*) oferta *f*; (*= agreement*) acuerdo *m* global ▸ **package holiday** (*Brit*), **package vacation** (*US*) viaje *m* organizado, vacaciones *fpl* organizadas • **to go on** *or* **take a ~ holiday** hacer un viaje organizado ▸ **package store** (*US*) *tienda con licencia para vender bebidas alcohólicas* ▸ **package tour** viaje *m* organizado
packager ['pækɪdʒəʳ] (N) (*Publishing, TV*) productora *f*
packaging ['pækɪdʒɪŋ] (N) **1** (*= packet, box etc*) embalaje *m*; (*= wrapping*) envoltorio *m*
2 (*Comm*) (*= presentation*) presentación *f* • **if the image and the ~ are right, consumers will buy anything** si la imagen y la presentación son las adecuadas, los clientes comprarán cualquier cosa
(CPD) ▸ **packaging company, packaging plant** envasadora *f* ▸ **packaging industry** industria *f* del empaquetado *or* del envase ▸ **packaging machine** máquina *f* empaquetadora *or* envasadora ▸ **packaging material** material *m* de envasado *or* de empaquetado
packed [pækt] (ADJ) **1** (*= crowded*) (*with people, vehicles*) lleno, repleto, a rebosar; (*more emph*) atestado • **the bus was ~ (with people)** el autobús estaba lleno *or* repleto *or* a rebosar *or* atestado (de gente) • **the lecture was ~** la conferencia llenó la sala a rebosar • **the show played to ~ houses for 12 weeks** el espectáculo tuvo lleno completo durante 12 semanas • **the place was ~ (out)** el local estaba repleto *or* a tope* *or* hasta arriba*; ▹ **jam-packed**
2 (*= filled*) lleno, repleto • **crates ~ with books** cajones *mpl* de embalaje llenos *or* repletos de libros • **the book is ~ with interesting facts** el libro está lleno de datos interesantes • **~ full of sth** repleto de algo, completamente lleno de algo
3 (*= with luggage ready*) • **she was ~ and ready to leave** ya había hecho la(s) maleta(s) y estaba lista para irse
4 (*= compressed*) [*snow*] • **the snow was ~ hard** la nieve se había convertido en una masa compacta
(CPD) ▸ **packed lunch** bolsa *f* de bocadillos • **I usually take a ~ lunch to work** me suelo preparar algo de comida y llevarla al trabajo, me suelo preparar unos bocadillos y llevarlos al trabajo
packer ['pækəʳ] (N) empacador(a) *m/f*
packet ['pækɪt] (N) **1** (*= carton*) cajita *f*; [*of cigarettes*] cajetilla *f*; [*of seeds, needles*] sobre *m*; [*of crisps etc*] bolsa *f*; (*= small parcel*) paquete *m*
2 (*fig*) • **a new ~ of proposals** un paquete de nuevas propuestas • **a whole ~ of trouble** la mar de disgustos*
3 (*Brit**) (*= large sum*) dineral *m* • **to make a ~** ganar un dineral *or* una fortuna • **that must have cost a ~** eso habrá costado un dineral
4 (*Naut*) (*also* **packet boat**) paquebote *m*
(CPD) ▸ **packet switching** (*Comput*) conmutación *f* de paquetes
packhorse ['pækhɔːs] (N) caballo *m* de carga
packing ['pækɪŋ] (N) **1** (*Comm*) (*= product wrapping, act of packing*) embalaje *m*; ▹ **postage**
2 [*of suitcase*] • **to do one's ~** hacer la(s) maleta(s)
(CPD) ▸ **packing box** (*esp US*) caja *f* de embalaje ▸ **packing case** caja *f* de embalaje ▸ **packing density** (*Comput*) densidad *f* de compacidad ▸ **packing department** (*for mail, transport*) departamento *m* de embalaje ▸ **packing house** envasadora *f* ▸ **packing list** *lista de lo que se va a meter o ya se ha metido en la maleta* ▸ **packing plant** envasadora *f* ▸ **packing slip** hoja *f* de embalaje
packsack ['pæksæk] (N) (*US*) mochila *f*
packsaddle ['pækˌsædl] (N) albarda *f*
pact [pækt] (N) **1** (*between two people*) pacto *m* • **to make a ~ (with sb)** hacer un pacto (con algn) • **to make a ~ with the Devil** hacer un pacto con el diablo • **to make a ~ (not) to do sth** acordar (no) hacer algo, pactar (no) hacer algo; ▹ **suicide**
2 (*Pol, Comm*) pacto *m*; (*esp Econ, Ind*) convenio *m* • **electoral ~** pacto *m* electoral • **non-aggression ~** pacto *m* de no agresión
pacy ['peɪsɪ] (ADJ) = **pacey**
pad¹ [pæd] (N) **1** (*to prevent friction etc*) almohadilla *f*, cojinete *m*; (*for ink*) tampón *m*; (*= brake pad*) zapata *f*
2 (*= shoulder pad*) hombrera *f*; (*= knee pad*) rodillera *f*; (*= elbow pad*) codera *f*; (*= shin pad*) espinillera *f*
3 (*= note pad, writing pad*) bloc(k) *m*, cuaderno *m*; (*= blotting pad*) secafirmas *m*
4 (*for helicopter*) plataforma *f*; (*= launch pad*) plataforma *f* de lanzamiento
5 [*of animal's foot*] almohadilla *f*
(VT) **1** [*+ shoulders etc*] acolchonar, poner hombreras a; [*+ armour*] enguatar
2 (*= stuff*) rellenar; (*fig*) [*+ book, speech etc*] meter paja en
(VI) • **to pad about** andar *or* (*esp LAm*) caminar sin hacer ruido • **to pad in** entrar sin hacer ruido
▸ **pad out** (VT + ADV) [*+ speech, essay*] meter paja en • **the essay was padded out with references to ...** el trabajo estaba inflado de referencias a ...
pad²* [pæd] (N) (*= home*) casa *f*; (*= flat*) piso *m*, departamento *m* (*LAm*); (*= room*) agujero‡ *m*, habitación *f*
padded ['pædɪd] (ADJ) [*bra*] reforzado; [*cell*]

P

acolchonado; [*dashboard etc*] almohadillado; [*armour*] enguatado; [*envelope*] acolchado
CPD ▸ **padded shoulders** hombreras *fpl*
padding ['pædɪŋ] N **1** (= *material*) relleno *m*, almohadilla *f*
2 (*fig*) (*in speech etc*) paja *f*, borra *f*
paddle ['pædl] N **1** (= *oar*) zagual *m*, pala *f*, remo *m* (*LAm*); (= *blade of wheel*) paleta *f*; (= *wheel*) rueda *f* de paletas
2 (*US*) (= *bat*) raqueta *f*
3 • **to go for** *or* **have a ~** ir a chapotear, ir a mojarse los pies
VT **1** [+ *boat*] remar con pala
2 (*US**) (= *spank*) azotar, zurrar*
3 • **to ~ one's feet in the sea** mojarse los pies en el mar
VI **1** (*in boat*) remar con pala • **they ~d to the bank** dirigieron el bote a la orilla
2 (= *walk in water*) mojarse los pies
CPD ▸ **paddle boat, paddle steamer** vapor *m* de ruedas *or* paletas ▸ **paddle wheel** rueda *f* de paletas
paddling pool ['pædlɪŋpu:l] N (*Brit*) piscina *f* para niños
paddock ['pædək] N (= *field*) potrero *m*; [*of racecourse*] paddock *m*; (*Motor racing*) parque *m*
Paddy ['pædɪ] N **1** *familiar form of* **Patrick**
2 (*pej‡*) irlandés *m*
paddy¹ ['pædɪ] N (= *rice*) arroz *m*; (= *field*) arrozal *m*
CPD ▸ **paddy field** arrozal *m*
paddy²* ['pædɪ] N (= *anger*) rabieta* *f* • **to get into a ~** coger una rabieta
paddy waggon* ['pædɪ,wægən] N (*US*) coche *m* celular
paddywhack* ['pædɪwæk] N rabieta* *f*
padlock ['pædlɒk] N candado *m*
VT cerrar con candado
padre ['pɑ:drɪ] N (*Mil*) capellán *m* militar; (*Univ*) capellán *m* de colegio; (*in direct address*) padre
paean ['pi:ən] N himno *m* de alegría • **~s of praise** alabanzas *fpl*
paederast ['pedəræst] N = **pederast**
paediatric, pediatric (*US*) [,pi:dɪ'ætrɪk] ADJ de pediatría, pediátrico
CPD ▸ **paediatric ward** sala *f* de pediatría
paediatrician, pediatrician (*US*) [,pi:dɪə'trɪʃən] N pediatra *mf*
paediatrics, pediatrics (*US*) [,pi:dɪ'ætrɪks] NSING pediatría *f*
paedological, pedological (*US*) [,pi:də'lɒdʒɪkl] ADJ pedológico
paedology, pedology (*US*) [pɪ'dɒlədʒɪ] N pedología *f*
paedophile, pedophile (*US*) ['pi:dəʊfaɪl] N pedófilo/a *m/f*, pederasta *mf*
CPD ▸ **paedophile ring, pedophile ring** (*US*) red *f* de pedófilos
paedophilia, pedophilia (*US*) [,pi:dəʊ'fɪlɪə] N pedofilia *f*, pederastia *f*
paella [paɪ'elə] N paella *f*
pagan ['peɪgən] ADJ pagano
N pagano/a *m/f*
paganism ['peɪgənɪzəm] N paganismo *m*
page¹ [peɪdʒ] N [*of book, newspaper etc*] página *f* • **see ~ 20** véase en la página 20 • **a glorious ~ in our history** una página gloriosa de nuestra historia • **back ~** contraportada *f* • **the picture on the facing ~ shows …** el dibujo de la página de en frente muestra … • **financial ~** página *f* de economía *or* de negocios • **front ~** primera plana *f*, primera página *f* • **it made front ~ news** salió en primera plana *or* página • **on ~ 14** en la página 14 • **over the ~** en la página siguiente • **a ~ three girl** (*Brit**) *una chica de las que aparecen en la página tres de los periódicos de prensa amarilla británicos*; ▹ **inside, title, yellow**
CPD ▸ **page break** salto *m* de página ▸ **page design** diseño *m* de página ▸ **page proofs** (*Typ*) pruebas *fpl* de página

PAGE THREE
Durante años, en la página tres del periódico **The Sun**, el diario sensacionalista de más venta en el Reino Unido, aparecía una foto a toda página de una chica en topless, conocida como la **page three girl**. De ahí que el término haya pasado a usarse también, en sentido extenso, para referirse a las modelos que posan semidesnudas en otros periódicos sensacionalistas.

page² [peɪdʒ] N **1** (*also* **pageboy**) (*in hotel*) botones *m inv*
2 (*US*) (*at wedding*) paje *m*
3 (*US*) (*in Congress*) mensajero *m*
4 (*Hist*) escudero *m*
VT • **to ~ sb** (*over public address*) llamar a algn por megafonía; (*with pager*) llamar a algn por el busca (*Sp*) *or* por el localizador
-page [peɪdʒ] ADJ (*ending in compounds*) • **a 4-page pamphlet** un folleto de 4 páginas
pageant ['pædʒənt] N (= *show*) espectáculo *m*; (= *procession*) desfile *m* • **a ~ of Elizabethan times** una representación de la época isabelina en una serie de cuadros • **the town held a ~ to mark the anniversary** la ciudad organizó una serie de fiestas públicas para celebrar el aniversario
pageantry ['pædʒəntrɪ] N pompa *f*, boato *m* • **it was celebrated with much ~** se celebró con gran boato • **the ~ of the occasion** lo espectacular *or* vistoso del acontecimiento • **all the ~ of history** todo el esplendor de la historia
pageboy ['peɪdʒbɔɪ] N **1** (*in hotel*) botones *m inv*; (*Brit*) (*at wedding*) paje *m*
2 (*also* **pageboy hairstyle**) estilo *m* paje
pager ['peɪdʒə^r] N localizador *m*, busca *m* (*Sp*)
CPD ▸ **pager message** mensaje *m* del localizador *or* (*Sp*) del busca
page-turner ['peɪdʒtɜ:nə^r] N libro *m* que engancha
pageview ['peɪdʒvju:] N página *f* vista • **the site now receives about 80 million ~s a month** el sitio recibe ahora unas 80 millones de páginas vistas al mes
paginate ['pædʒɪneɪt] VT paginar
pagination [,pædʒɪ'neɪʃən] N paginación *f* • **without ~** sin paginar
paging ['peɪdʒɪŋ] N (*Comput*) paginación *f*
CPD ▸ **paging device** localizador *m*, busca* *m*
pagoda [pə'gəʊdə] N pagoda *f*
pah† [pæ] EXCL ¡bah!
paid [peɪd] PT, PP *of* **pay**
ADJ **1** [*official*] asalariado, que recibe un sueldo; [*work*] remunerado, rentado (*S. Cone*); [*bill, holiday etc*] pagado • **a ~ hack** un escritorzuelo a sueldo*
2 • **to put ~ to sth** (*Brit*) acabar con *or* poner fin a algo
paid-up ['peɪd'ʌp] ADJ **1** [*member*] con sus cuotas pagadas *or* al día
2 (*Econ*) [*share*] liberado • **fully paid-up share** acción *f* totalmente liberada
CPD ▸ **paid-up capital** capital *m* pagado
pail [peɪl] N balde *m*, cubo *m*; (*child's*) cubito *m*
pailful ['peɪlfʊl] N cubo *m*, contenido *m* de un cubo
paillasse ['pælɪæs] N jergón *m*
pain [peɪn] N **1** (*physical*) dolor *m* • **she winced with ~** hizo una mueca de dolor • **where is the ~?** ¿dónde le duele? • **in order to ease the ~** para aliviar el dolor • **back/chest/muscle ~** dolor *m* de espalda/pecho/músculos • **I have a ~ in my leg** me duele la pierna • **to be in ~** sufrir dolor(es), tener dolor(es) • **I was in excruciating ~** sufría *or* tenía unos dolores horribles • PROVERB: • **no ~, no gain** el que algo quiere, algo le cuesta; ▹ **growing, labour, period**
2 (*mental*) dolor *m* • **his harsh words caused her much ~** sus duras palabras le causaron mucho dolor *or* la hicieron sufrir mucho
3* (= *nuisance*) • **to be a ~** [*person*] ser un pesado*; [*situation*] ser una lata*, ser un rollo* • **he's a real ~** es un verdadero pesado* • **don't be such a ~!** ¡no fastidies!*, ¡no seas tan pesada!* • **what a ~!** ¡qué lata!*, ¡qué rollo!* • **he's a ~ in the arse** *or* (*US*) **ass‡** es un coñazo‡ • **he's a ~ in the neck*** es insoportable
4 pains (= *efforts*) • **to be at ~s to do sth** esforzarse al máximo por hacer algo, intentar por todos los medios hacer algo • **for my ~s** después de todos mis esfuerzos • **to take ~s to do sth** poner especial cuidado en hacer algo • **he took infinite ~s with his job** se esmeraba *or* se esforzaba muchísimo en su trabajo • **I had taken great ~s with my appearance** me había esmerado *or* esforzado mucho con mi apariencia
5 (= *penalty*) • **on** *or* **under ~ of sth** bajo pena de algo, so pena de algo
VT (*mentally*) doler, hacer sufrir • **it ~s me to think of you struggling all alone** me duele pensar que estás luchando sola, pensar que estás luchando sola me hace sufrir • **it ~s me to tell you** me duele decírtelo • **it ~ed him that his father talked like that** le dolía que su padre hablara así
CPD ▸ **pain barrier** • IDIOM: • **to go through the ~ barrier** (*Brit*) [*player*] sobreponerse al dolor • **England's World Cup hero is determined to play through the ~ barrier** el héroe del Mundial de Inglaterra está decidido a jugar sobreponiéndose al dolor ▸ **pain clinic** unidad *f* del dolor ▸ **pain relief** alivio *m* contra el dolor ▸ **pain threshold** resistencia *f* al dolor
pained [peɪnd] ADJ [*expression*] dolorido, de dolor; [*voice*] afligido • **Frank gave him a ~ look** Frank le dirigió una mirada dolorida *or* de dolor
painful ['peɪnfʊl] ADJ **1** (*physically*) [*injury, swelling*] doloroso • **a slow and ~ death** una muerte lenta y dolorosa • **my ankle is still ~** todavía me duele el tobillo • **her wrist was ~ to the touch** la muñeca le dolía al tocarla • **was it very ~?** ¿te dolió mucho? • **he received a ~ blow on the back** recibió un golpe en la espalda que le causó un intenso dolor
2 (*mentally*) [*memory, reminder, experience*] doloroso; [*task, decision*] penoso • **it will be a long and ~ process** será un proceso largo y doloroso *or* penoso • **his embarrassment was ~ to witness** daba pena ver lo abochornado que estaba • **it is my ~ duty to tell you that …** es mi penoso deber comunicarle que …, tengo el desagradable deber de comunicarle que …
3* (= *embarrassingly bad*) fatal*, de pena* • **her acting was so bad it was ~ to watch** su actuación era tan mala que daba vergüenza ajena presenciarla, su actuación era de pena*
painfully ['peɪnfəlɪ] ADV **1** (*lit*) • **his tooth throbbed ~** la muela le producía un dolor punzante • **he felt the muzzle of the revolver dig ~ into his side** sintió el dolor que le causaba el revólver clavándose en el costado • **I hope he dies slowly and ~** espero que tenga una muerte lenta y dolorosa
2 (*emphatic*) (= *extremely*) • **to be ~ aware of**

P

sth/that ... ser plenamente consciente de algo/de que ... • **it was ~ clear that ...** estaba penosamente claro que ... • **she was ~ shy/thin** era tan tímida/delgada que daba pena • **our economic recovery will be ~ slow** nuestra recuperación económica va a ser un proceso lento y penoso *or* doloroso
3 (= *laboriously*) con mucho trabajo *or* esfuerzo

painkiller [ˈpeɪnkɪləʳ] (N) analgésico *m*

painkilling [ˈpeɪn,kɪlɪŋ] (ADJ) [*drug*] analgésico

painless [ˈpeɪnlɪs] (ADJ) **1** (= *without pain*) indoloro, sin dolor • **~ childbirth** parto *m* sin dolor
2 (*fig*) (= *easy*) sin mayores dificultades

painlessly [ˈpeɪnlɪslɪ] (ADV) (= *without pain*) sin causar dolor; (*fig*) (= *easily*) fácilmente

painstaking [ˈpeɪnz,teɪkɪŋ] (ADJ) [*task, research etc*] esmerado, concienzudo; [*person*] meticuloso, esmerado

painstakingly [ˈpeɪnz,teɪkɪŋlɪ] (ADV) laboriosamente, concienzudamente, esmeradamente

paint [peɪnt] (N) **1** (= *substance*) pintura *f* • **a coat of ~** una mano de pintura • **the ~ was flaking off the walls** la pintura de las paredes se estaba descascarillando • **"wet paint"** "(ojo,) recién pintado"; ▹ **face, finger, gloss[2], oil, poster, spray**
2 paints pinturas *fpl* • **a box of ~s** una caja de pinturas
(VT) **1** (*Art*) [+ *picture, subject*] pintar; [+ *slogan, message*] escribir con pintura
2 (= *apply paint to*) [+ *wall, fence etc*] pintar • **to ~ sth blue** pintar algo de azul • IDIOM: • **to ~ the town red** irse de juerga *or* parranda*
3 (= *make up*) [+ *nails, lips*] pintarse • **she ~ed her fingernails red** se pintó las uñas rojas *or* de rojo • **to ~ one's face** pintarse, maquillarse
4 (*fig*) (= *portray*) describir, pintar • **to ~ a grim/gloomy/bleak picture of sth** describir algo en términos sombríos/deprimentes/desalentadores, pintar algo muy negro • **pro-democracy activists ~ quite a different picture of the situation** los activistas en pro de la democracia describen la situación en términos muy diferentes • **to ~ a rosy picture of sth** pintar algo de color de rosa • **to ~ a vivid picture of sth** describir algo gráficamente
5 • **to ~ sth on** [+ *varnish, dye*] aplicar algo • **~ the solution on with a clean brush** aplicar la solución con un pincel limpio
6 (*Med*) • **treatment involves ~ing the sores with iodine solution** el tratamiento requiere aplicar una solución de yodo en las heridas
(VI) pintar • **to ~ in oils** pintar al óleo • **to ~ in watercolours** pintar con acuarelas
(CPD) ▸ **paint bomb** bomba *f* de pintura • **~ bombs were thrown** arrojaron bombas de pintura ▸ **paint remover** quitapintura *f* ▸ **paint roller** rodillo *m* (pintor) ▸ **paint scraper** raspador *m* de paredes ▸ **paint spray** pistola *f* (rociadora) de pintura ▸ **paint stripper** (= *substance*) quitapintura *f*; (= *tool*) raspador *m* de paredes ▸ **paint thinner** disolvente *m*
▸ **paint in** (VT + ADV) (= *add*) pintar
▸ **paint out** (VT + ADV) tapar con pintura
▸ **paint over** (VT + ADV) **1** = **paint out**
2 (= *repaint*) pintar otra vez encima, volver a pintar

paintball [ˈpeɪntbɔː] (N) bola *f* de pintura, paintball *m*

paintbox [ˈpeɪntbɒks] (N) caja *f* de pinturas

paintbrush [ˈpeɪntbrʌʃ] (N) (*Art*) pincel *m*; (*for decorating*) brocha *f*

painter[1] [ˈpeɪntəʳ] (N) (*Art*) pintor(a) *m/f*; (= *decorator*) pintor(a) *m/f* de brocha gorda
(CPD) ▸ **painter and decorator** pintor(a) *m/f* y decorador(a) *m/f* (de interiores)

painter[2] [ˈpeɪntəʳ] (N) (*Naut*) amarra *f* • **to cut the ~** (*lit*) cortar las amarras; (*fig*) independizarse

painterly [ˈpeɪntəlɪ] (ADJ) [*style, talents*] pictoricista

painting [ˈpeɪntɪŋ] (N) **1** (*Art*) (= *picture*) cuadro *m*, pintura *f*; (= *activity, genre*) pintura *f* • **to study ~** estudiar pintura • **French Impressionist ~** la pintura impresionista francesa; ▹ **oil**
2 (= *decorating*) pintura *f* • **~ and decorating** pintura *f* y decoración

paintpot [ˈpeɪntpɒt] (N) bote *m* de pintura

paintwork [ˈpeɪntwɜːk] (N) pintura *f*

pair [pɛəʳ] (N) **1** (= *set*) [*of gloves, shoes, socks etc*] par *m* • **these socks are not a ~** estos calcetines no son del mismo par • **a ~ of binoculars** unos prismáticos • **a ~ of glasses** *or* **spectacles** unas gafas, unos anteojos • **we need another ~ of hands** necesitamos otro par de manos • **I've only got one ~ of hands** solo tengo dos manos • **a ~ of pyjamas** un pijama • **a ~ of scissors** unas tijeras, un par de tijeras • **six ~s of scissors** seis tijeras • **a ~ of trousers** un pantalón, unos pantalones, un par de pantalones
2 (= *group of 2 things*) pareja *f* • **a ~ of aces** una pareja de ases • **to arrange in ~s** [+ *glasses, chairs*] colocar de dos en dos; [+ *related words, pictures*] colocar en parejas; ▹ **heel[1]**
3 [*of people*] (= *group of 2*) par *m*; (= *couple*) pareja *f* • **a ~ of teenage boys were smoking** un par de quinceañeros estaban fumando • **a ~ of identical twins** una pareja de gemelos • **get out of my sight, the ~ of you!** ¡fuera de mi vista, los dos! • **the happy ~** la feliz pareja, los novios • **to do sth in ~s** hacer algo en parejas *or* de dos en dos • **those two make a right ~!** ¡vaya par!, ¡vaya pareja! • **they make an unlikely ~** forman una insólita pareja, hacen *or* forman una extraña pareja
4 [*of animals, birds*] pareja *f* • **a carriage and ~** un carruaje con dos caballos, un landó con dos caballos
5 (= *counterpart*) **a** (*gen*) pareja *f* • **can I try on the ~ to this please?** ¿puedo probarme la pareja, por favor?
b (*Brit*) (*Parl*) *uno de los dos miembros de partidos opuestos que se ponen de acuerdo para ausentarse de una votación y, de esa forma, anularse mutuamente*
6 (*Sport*) **pairs** dobles *mpl* • **~s skating** patinaje *m* en parejas
(VT) **1** (*Zool*) aparear
2 (= *put together*) [+ *socks, gloves*] emparejar • **long skirts ~ed with knitted jackets** faldas *fpl* largas a juego *or* haciendo juego con rebecas de punto • **ginger biscuits are delicious ~ed with glasses of lemonade** las galletas de jengibre están buenísimas acompañadas de vasos de limonada • **to ~ sb with sb: trainees will be ~ed with experienced managers** a los aprendices se les pondrá formando pareja con gerentes con experiencia • **I was ~ed with Henry in the general knowledge competition** me pusieron formando pareja con *or* de compañero de Henry en el concurso de cultura general
(VI) **1** (*gen*) formar pareja(s) (**with** con) • **when a Y chromosome ~s with an X chromosome** cuando el cromosoma Y forma pareja con el cromosoma X • **beer ~s well with many New Zealand dishes** la cerveza acompaña bien a muchos platos de Nueva Zelanda
2 (*Zool*) aparearse (**with** con), formar pareja(s) (**with** con)
(CPD) ▸ **pair bonding** unión *f* de pareja, emparejamiento *m*
▸ **pair off** (VT + ADV) **1** (*as couple*) emparejar • **everyone was ~ed off** todo el mundo estaba emparejado *or* tenía pareja • **they are always trying to ~ her off** siempre están intentando buscarle pareja
2 (= *group in twos*) agrupar por parejas • **people are ~ed off according to their level of competence** se agrupa a las personas por parejas de acuerdo con su nivel de aptitud
(VI + ADV) **1** (*as a couple, team*) formar pareja(s)
2 (*Zool*) aparearse, formar pareja
▸ **pair up** (VI + ADV) formar pareja(s) • **~ up with the person next to you** forme pareja con la persona de al lado
(VT + ADV) [+ *socks, shoes, gloves*] emparejar; [+ *people*] poner formando pareja • **in the final I was ~ed up with a French teacher** me pusieron formando pareja con un profesor de francés para la final

pairing [ˈpɛərɪŋ] (N) **1** (= *team*) pareja *f*, dúo *m*
2 (*Zool*) apareamiento *m*

paisley [ˈpeɪzlɪ] (N) (= *fabric, design*) cachemira *f*
(CPD) ▸ **paisley shawl** chal *m* de cachemira

pajama [pəˈdʒɑːmə] (N) (*US*) = **pyjama**

pajamas [pəˈdʒɑːməz] (NPL) (*US*) = **pyjamas**

Paki** [ˈpækɪ] (N ABBR) (*Brit*) (*offensive*) = **Pakistani**

Pakistan [,pɑːkɪsˈtɑːn] (N) Pakistán *m*, Paquistán *m*

Pakistani [,pɑːkɪsˈtɑːnɪ] (ADJ) pakistaní, paquistaní
(N) pakistaní *mf*, paquistaní *mf*

pakora [pəˈkɔːrə] (N) (PL: **pakora** *or* **pakoras**) *plato indio consistente en bolas de cebolla fritas en pasta de harina de garbanzos*

PAL [pæl] (N ABBR) (*TV*) = **phase alternation line**

pal* [pæl] (N) amigo/a *m/f*, compinche* *mf*, cuate/a *m/f* (*Mex**), pata *mf* (*Peru**) • **be a pal!** ¡venga, pórtate como un amigo! • **they're great pals** son muy amigos • **old pals' act** acto *m* de amiguismo*
▸ **pal up*** (VI + ADV) hacerse amigos • **to pal up with sb** hacerse amigo de algn

palace [ˈpælɪs] (N) (*lit*) palacio *m*; (*fig*) (= *grand house etc*) palacio *m* • **the Palace has refused to comment** (*Brit*) la Casa Real se ha negado a hacer comentarios
(CPD) ▸ **palace revolution** (*fig*) revolución *f* de palacio ▸ **palace spokesman** portavoz *mf* de la Casa Real

palaeographer [,pælɪˈɒgrəfəʳ] (N) paleógrafo/a *m/f*

palaeography [,pælɪˈɒgrəfɪ] (N) paleografía *f*

palaeolithic [,pælɪəʊˈlɪθɪk] (ADJ) paleolítico
(N) • **the Paleolithic** el Paleolítico

palaeontologist [ˈpælɪɒnˈtɒlədʒɪst] (N) paleontólogo/a *m/f*

palaeontology [,pælɪɒnˈtɒlədʒɪ] (N) paleontología *f*

Palaeozoic [,pælɪəʊˈzəʊɪk] (*Geol*) (ADJ) paleozoico
(N) • **the ~** el Paleozoico

palatability [,pælətəˈbɪlɪtɪ] (N) **1** [*of food*] carácter *m* sabroso
2 (*fig*) aceptabilidad *f*

palatable [ˈpælətəbl] (ADJ) **1** (= *tasty*) sabroso, apetitoso; (= *just passable*) comible
2 (*fig*) aceptable (**to a**) • **it may not be ~ to the government** puede no ser del gusto *or* agrado del gobierno

palatal [ˈpælətl] (ADJ) palatal
(N) palatal *f*

palatalize [ˈpælətəlaɪz] (VT) palatalizar
(VI) palatalizarse

palate [ˈpælɪt] (N) (*Anat*) paladar *m* • **to have**

a delicate ~ tener un paladar delicado • **to have no ~ for wine** no tener paladar para el vino • **I have no ~ for that kind of activity** no aguanto *or* no puedo tragar ese tipo de actividad • **hard ~** paladar *m* • **soft ~** velo *m* del paladar

palatial [pəˈleɪʃəl] ADJ suntuoso, espléndido

palatinate [pəˈlætɪnɪt] N palatinado *m*

palaver* [pəˈlɑːvəʳ] N **1** (= *fuss*) jaleo *m*, desmadre* *m*; (= *trouble*) molestias *fpl*, trámites *mpl* engorrosos; (*US*) (= *chatter*) palabrería *f* • **what a ~!** ¡qué jaleo! • **why all the ~!** ¡no es para tanto! • **that ~ about the car** aquel jaleo que se armó con el coche • **can't we do it without a lot of ~?** ¿no podemos hacerlo sin meternos en tantos líos?*
2 (= *conference*) conferencia *f*, parlamento *m*
VI parlamentar

pale¹ [peɪl] ADJ (COMPAR: **paler**, SUPERL: **palest**) **1** [*person, face*] (*naturally*) blanco; (*from illness, shock*) pálido • **she had ~ skin** tenía la piel muy blanca • **she looked ~** se la veía pálida • **you look very ~** estás muy pálido • **she was deathly ~** estaba pálida como la muerte • **to go** *or* **grow** *or* **turn ~** [*person*] palidecer, ponerse pálido • **her face went ~ with shock** paledeció *or* se puso pálida del susto
2 (= *not bright*) [*light, daylight*] tenue, pálido; [*moon*] pálido • **the ~ light of dawn** la tenue *or* pálida luz del alba • **a ~ imitation** una burda imitación
3 (= *not dark*) [*colour*] claro • **a ~ blue dress** un vestido azul claro
VI **1** [*person*] palidecer, ponerse pálido • **his face ~d with fear** palideció *or* se puso pálido de miedo
2 (*fig*) (= *seem insignificant*) • **it ~s into insignificance beside …** se vuelve insignificante en comparación con *or* al compararse con … • **her beauty ~d beside her mother's** su belleza perdía esplendor al lado de la de su madre
CPD ▸ **pale ale** (*Brit*) cerveza *f* rubia suave

pale² [peɪl] N (= *stake*) estaca *f* • IDIOM: • **to be beyond the ~** ser inaceptable

paleface** [ˈpeɪlfeɪs] N rostropálido/a *m/f*; (*US*) blanco/a *m/f*

pale-faced [ˌpeɪlˈfeɪst] ADJ pálido

palely [ˈpeɪllɪ] ADV [*shine, lit*] pálidamente

paleness [ˈpeɪlnɪs] N palidez *f*; [*of skin*] blancura *f*

paleo- *etc* [ˈpælɪəʊ] PREFIX = **palaeo-** *etc*

pale-skinned [ˌpeɪlˈskɪnd] ADJ de piel pálida

Palestine [ˈpælɪstaɪn] N Palestina *f*

Palestinian [ˌpæləsˈtɪnɪən] ADJ palestino
N palestino/a *m/f*

palette [ˈpælɪt] N paleta *f*
CPD ▸ **palette knife** espátula *f*

palfrey [ˈpɔːlfrɪ] N palafrén *m*

palimony* [ˈpælɪmənɪ] N alimentos *mpl* pagados a una ex compañera

palimpsest [ˈpælɪmpsest] N palimpsesto *m*

palindrome [ˈpælɪndrəʊm] N palíndromo *m*

paling [ˈpeɪlɪŋ] N (= *stake*) estaca *f*; (= *fence*) estacada *f*, (em)palizada *f*

palisade [ˌpælɪˈseɪd] N **1** palizada *f*, estacada *f*
2 palisades (*US*) (= *cliffs*) acantilado *msing*

pall¹ [pɔːl] N **1** (*on coffin*) paño *m* mortuorio; (*Rel*) (= *robe*) palio *m*
2 (*fig*) manto *m*, capa *f* • **a ~ of smoke** una cortina de humo • **to cast a ~ over sth** empañar algo

pall² [pɔːl] VI perder el interés (**on** para), dejar de gustar (**on a**) • **it ~s after a time** después de cierto tiempo deja de gustar • **it never ~s** nunca pierde su interés • **I found the book ~ed** encontré que el libro empezaba a aburrirme

palladium [pəˈleɪdɪəm] N paladio *m*

pallbearer [ˈpɔːlˌbɛərəʳ] N portador(a) *m/f* del féretro

pallet [ˈpælɪt] N **1** (*for goods*) paleta *f*
2 (= *bed*) jergón *m*, catre *m*
CPD ▸ **pallet truck** carretilla *f* elevadora de paletas

palletization [pælɪtaɪˈzeɪʃən] N paletización *f*

palliasse [ˈpælɪæs] N = **paillasse**

palliate [ˈpælɪeɪt] VT (*frm*) paliar, mitigar

palliative [ˈpælɪətɪv] ADJ paliativo
N paliativo *m*, lenitivo *m*
CPD ▸ **palliative care** cuidado *m* paliativo

pallid [ˈpælɪd] ADJ pálido

pallidness [ˈpælɪdnɪs] N = **pallor**

pallor [ˈpæləʳ] N palidez *f*

pally* [ˈpælɪ] ADJ (COMPAR: **pallier**, SUPERL: **palliest**) • **to be ~ with sb** ser muy amigo de algn • **they're very ~** son muy amigos

palm¹ [pɑːm] N (*Bot*) (*also* **palm tree**) palma *f*, palmera *f*; (= *English sallow*) sauce *m*; (*as carried at Easter*) ramo *m* • **coconut ~** cocotero *m*
CPD ▸ **palm grove** palmar *m*, palmeral *m* ▸ **palm oil** aceite *m* de palma ▸ **Palm Sunday** Domingo *m* de Ramos ▸ **palm tree** palma *f*, palmera *f*

palm² [pɑːm] N (*Anat*) palma *f* • **to read sb's ~** leer la mano a algn • **you must cross the gipsy's ~ with silver** hay que pagar a la gitana con una moneda de plata • IDIOMS: • **to grease sb's ~** untar la mano a algn • **to have sb in the ~ of one's hand** tener a algn en la palma de la mano • **to have an itching** *or* **itchy ~** ser muy codicioso; (= *be bribable*) estar dispuesto a dejarse sobornar
VT [+ *card*] escamotear
CPD ▸ **palm reader** quiromántico/a *m/f*
▸ **palm off*** VT + ADV • **to ~ sth off on sb** encajar algo a algn* • **I managed to ~ the visitor off on John** le encajé la visita a Juan* • **I ~ed him off with the excuse that …** me lo saqué de encima con la excusa de que …

palmcorder [ˈpɑːmkɔːdəʳ] N videocámara *f* portátil, minicámara *f* de vídeo

palmetto [pælˈmetəʊ] N palmito *m*

palmist [ˈpɑːmɪst] N quiromántico/a *m/f*, palmista *mf*

palmistry [ˈpɑːmɪstrɪ] N quiromancia *f*

palmtop [ˈpɑːmtɒp] N (*also* **palmtop computer**) ordenador *m* de bolsillo, computador *m or* computadora *f* de bolsillo (*LAm*), palmtop *m*

palmy [ˈpɑːmɪ] ADJ próspero, feliz • **those ~ days** aquellos días tan prósperos

palomino [pæləˈmiːnəʊ] N (PL: **palominos**) *caballo de color tostado con crin y cola blancas*

palpable [ˈpælpəbl] ADJ **1** (= *tangible*) palpable
2 (*fig*) [*lie, mistake*] obvio, patente

palpably [ˈpælpəblɪ] ADV **1** (*lit*) palpablemente
2 (*fig*) (= *manifestly*) • **a ~ unjust sentence** una condena manifiestamente injusta • **that is ~ untrue** eso es a todas luces falso

palpate [ˈpælpeɪt] VT (*Med*) palpar

palpitate [ˈpælpɪteɪt] VI [*heart*] palpitar

palpitating [ˈpælpɪteɪtɪŋ] ADJ palpitante

palpitation [ˌpælpɪˈteɪʃən] N palpitación *f* • **to have ~s** tener palpitaciones

palsied [ˈpɔːlzɪd] ADJ paralítico

palsy [ˈpɔːlzɪ] N perlesía *f*, parálisis *f inv*

paltry [ˈpɔːltrɪ] (COMPAR: **paltrier**, SUPERL: **paltriest**) ADJ ínfimo, miserable • **for a few ~ pennies** por unos miserables peniques • **for some ~ reason** por alguna nimiedad

pampas [ˈpæmpəs] NPL pampa *fsing* • **the Pampas** la Pampa
CPD ▸ **pampas grass** hierba *f* de la Pampa

pamper [ˈpæmpəʳ] VT mimar, consentir

pampered [ˈpæmpəd] ADJ [*child etc*] mimado, consentido; [*life*] regalado • **he had a ~ childhood** se crió entre algodones

pamphlet [ˈpæmflɪt] N (*informative, brochure*) folleto *m*; (*political, handed out in street*) volante *m*, panfleto *m*; (*Literat*) panfleto *m*

pamphleteer [ˌpæmflɪˈtɪəʳ] N folletista *mf*, panfletista *mf*

pan¹ [pæn] N **1** (*for cooking*) cacerola *f*; (= *large pot*) olla *f*; (= *frying pan*) sartén *f* (*m in LAm*)
2 [*of scales*] platillo *m*; [*of lavatory*] taza *f*; [*of firearm*] cazoleta *f* • IDIOM: • **to go down the pan‡** irse al traste*
VT **1** [+ *gold*] lavar con batea
2* (= *criticize*) [+ *play etc*] dejar por los suelos*
VI • **to pan for gold** cribar oro
CPD ▸ **pan lid** tapa *f* de (la) cacerola ▸ **pan scrub, pan scrubber** estropajo *m* (*para sartenes*)
▸ **pan out** VI + ADV resultar, salir (bien *etc*) • **if it pans out as we hope** si sale como nosotros lo esperamos • **it didn't pan out at all well** no dio ningún resultado satisfactorio • **we must wait and see how it pans out** tenemos que esperar hasta ver cómo sale esto

pan² [pæn] (*Cine*) VI tomar panorámicas *or* vistas pan
VT • **a television camera panned the stadium** una cámara de televisión recorrió el estadio

pan- [pæn] PREFIX pan- • **pan-Arabic** panárabe

panacea [ˌpænəˈsɪə] N panacea *f*

panache [pəˈnæʃ] N garbo *m*, gracia *f* • **to do sth with ~** hacer algo con garbo

Pan-African [ˈpænˈæfrɪkən] ADJ panafricano

Pan-Africanism [ˈpænˈæfrɪkənɪzəm] N panafricanismo *m*

Panama [ˈpænəmɑː] N Panamá *m*
CPD ▸ **Panama Canal** Canal *m* de Panamá ▸ **Panama hat** (sombrero *m* de) jipijapa *f*, panamá *m*

Panamanian [ˌpænəˈmeɪnɪən] ADJ panameño
N panameño/a *m/f*

Pan-American [ˈpænəˈmerɪkən] ADJ panamericano
CPD ▸ **Pan-American Union** Unión *f* Panamericana

Pan-Americanism [ˈpænəˈmerɪkənɪzəm] N panamericanismo *m*

Pan-Asian [ˈpænˈeɪʃn] ADJ panasiático

panatella [ˌpænəˈtelə] N cigarro *m* largo

pancake [ˈpænkeɪk] N tortita *f*, panqueque *m* (*LAm*); ▷ **flat¹**
CPD ▸ **Pancake Day** (*Brit*) martes *m inv* de carnaval ▸ **pancake landing** (*Aer*) aterrizaje *m* de panza ▸ **pancake roll** (*Brit*) rollito *m* de primavera

panchromatic [ˈpænkrəʊˈmætɪk] ADJ pancromático

pancreas [ˈpæŋkrɪəs] N páncreas *m*

pancreatic [ˌpæŋkrɪˈætɪk] ADJ pancreático

panda [ˈpændə] N panda *m*
CPD ▸ **panda car** (*Brit*) coche *m* patrulla

pandemic [pænˈdemɪk] ADJ pandémico
N pandemia *f*

pandemonium [ˌpændɪˈməʊnɪəm] N (= *chaos*) jaleo *m*, desmadre* *m* • **at this there was ~** en esto se armó un tremendo jaleo, en esto se armó las de Caín • **it's sheer ~!** ¡es

P

un desmadre!*

pander ['pændəʳ] VI • **to ~ to sb** consentir a algn • **to ~ to sb's desire for sth** complacer el deseo de algn por algo • **this is ~ing to the public's worst tastes** esto es condescender con los peores gustos del público

p & h ABBR (US) (= **postage and handling**) gastos *mpl* de envío

P & L N ABBR (= **profit and loss**) Pérd. y Gan.

Pandora [pæn'dɔːrə] N • **~'s box** caja *f* de Pandora

p & p N ABBR (= **postage and packing**) gastos *mpl* de envío

pandrop ['pændrɒp] N (*Scot*) pastilla *f* de menta

pane [peɪn] N cristal *m*, vidrio *m*

panegyric [,pænɪ'dʒɪrɪk] N panegírico *m*

panel ['pænl] N **1** [*of wall*] panel *m*; [*of door*] entrepaño *m*; [*of ceiling*] artesón *m*
2 [*of instruments, switches*] tablero *m*
3 (*Sew*) paño *m*; (*Art*) tabla *f*
4 [*of judges, in a competition*] jurado *m*; (*TV, Rad*) panel *m*
5 (*Brit*) (*Med*) (*formerly*) lista *f* de pacientes
VT [+ *wall, door*] revestir con entrepaños de madera
CPD ▸ **panel beater** carrocero/a *m/f* ▸ **panel beating** chapistería *f* ▸ **panel discussion** mesa *f* redonda ▸ **panel game** programa *m* concurso para equipos ▸ **panel pin** clavo *m* de espiga ▸ **panel truck, panel van** (*US*) furgoneta *f*

panelled, **paneled** (*US*) ['pænld] ADJ con paneles

panelling, **paneling** (*US*) ['pænəlɪŋ] N paneles *mpl*

panellist, **panelist** (*US*) ['pænəlɪst] N miembro *mf* del jurado/de la mesa redonda

Pan-European ['pæn,jʊərə'piːən] ADJ paneuropeo

pan-fried [,pæn'fraɪd] ADJ pochado

pan-fry [,pæn'fraɪ] VT pochar

pang [pæŋ] N **1** (= *pain*) punzada *f* • **~s of childbirth** dolores *mpl* de parto • **~s of hunger** • **hunger ~s** dolores *mpl* de hambre
2 (*fig*) • **I felt a ~ of conscience** me remordió la conciencia • **to feel a ~ of remorse** sentir remordimiento

panhandle ['pænhændl] (*US*) N (*Geog*) *faja angosta de territorio de un estado que entra en el de otro*
VI* (= *beg*) mendigar, pedir limosna

panhandler* ['pænhændləʳ] N (*US*) (= *beggar*) pordiosero/a *m/f*

panic ['pænɪk] (VB: PT, PP: **panicked**) N
1 (= *fear*) pánico *m* • **an earthquake hit the capital, spreading ~ among the population** un terremoto azotó la capital, sembrando el pánico entre la población • **to be in a (state of) ~** ser presa del pánico • **I phoned my mum in a ~** llamé a mi madre muerto de miedo*, llamé a mi madre presa del pánico • **a patient rang me in a state of ~ because her baby had swallowed a key** me llamó una paciente muy asustada porque su hijo se había tragado una llave • **I was in a blind ~** estaba ofuscado por el pánico • **to flee in ~** huir aterrado, huir presa del pánico • **if I asked the simplest question, she would go into** *or* **get into a ~** si le hacía la pregunta más simple le entraba el pánico • **to send** *or* **throw sb into a ~**: • **her sudden arrival threw him into a ~** su inesperada llegado hizo que le entrase el pánico • **the country was thrown into a ~** cundió el pánico en el país • **the explosion threw the crowd into a ~** la explosión provocó el pánico entre la multitud • IDIOM: • **it was ~ stations*** reinaba el pánico
2* (= *rush*) • **there's no ~, tomorrow will do no** es que haya prisa, mañana vale • **we've had a bit of a ~ on here and it slipped my mind till now** hemos ido un poco de cabeza por aquí y se me ha olvidado hasta ahora
VI dejarse llevar por el pánico • **I refused to ~** me negué a dejarme llevar por el pánico • **industry is ~king about the recession** la recesión tiene a la industria presa del pánico • **don't ~!** ¡calma!, ¡cálmate! • **don't ~, sit still and keep calm** no te dejes llevar por el pánico, quédate sentado y mantén la calma
VT [+ *crowd, population*] provocar el pánico entre; [+ *person*] provocar *or* infundir el pánico en, llenar de pánico a • **the sound of the gun ~ked the elephants** el sonido del rifle provocó el pánico en *or* entre los elefantes • **he had been ~ked into the decision** había tomado la decisión impulsado por el pánico
CPD ▸ **panic alarm** alarma *f* antipánico ▸ **panic attack** ataque *m* de pánico • **to have a ~ attack** tener *or* sufrir un ataque de pánico ▸ **panic button** (*lit*) botón *m* de alarma • **to press** *or* **hit** *or* **push the ~ button** (*fig*) perder el control *or* la calma ▸ **panic buying** • **~ buying has caused shortages of some foodstuffs** las compras provocadas por el pánico han provocado escasez de algunos alimentos ▸ **panic measures** medidas *fpl* inducidas por el pánico ▸ **panic reaction** reacción *f* motivada por el pánico ▸ **panic stations*** • IDIOM: • **it was ~ stations** reinaba el pánico

panicky ['pænɪkɪ] ADJ [*person, behaviour*] nervioso; [*decision, action*] motivado por el pánico *or* el nerviosismo; [*reaction*] nervioso, motivado por el pánico *or* el nerviosismo • **to get ~** dejarse llevar por el pánico

panic-stricken ['pænɪk,strɪkən] ADJ [*person*] presa del pánico, aterrorizado; [*behaviour*] causado *or* motivado por el pánico • **to be panic-stricken** ser presa del pánico, estar aterrorizado

panini [pæ'niːniː] N (PL: **panini** *or* **paninis**) panini *m*

panjandrum [pæn'dʒændrəm] N jefazo *m*, mandamás *m inv* • **he's the great ~** es el archipámpano

pannier ['pænɪəʳ] N (*for horse etc*) cuévano *m*; (*for cycle etc*) (*also* **pannier bag**) cartera *f*, bolsa *f*

panoply ['pænəplɪ] N (= *armour*) panoplia *f*; (*fig*) (= *array*) despliegue *m*

panorama [,pænə'rɑːmə] N panorama *m*

panoramic [,pænə'ræmɪk] ADJ panorámico
CPD ▸ **panoramic screen** pantalla *f* panorámica ▸ **panoramic view** visión *f* panorámica

panpipes ['pænpaɪps] NPL zampoña *f*

pansy ['pænzɪ] N **1** (*Bot*) pensamiento *m*
2‡ (*pej*) (= *homosexual man*) marica* *m* (*pej*)

pant¹ [pænt] N (= *gasp*) jadeo *m*, resuello *m*
VI jadear, resollar • **to ~ for breath** jadear
VT (*also* **pant out**) decir jadeando, decir de manera entrecortada
▸ **pant for** VI + PREP (*fig*) suspirar por, anhelar • **he was ~ing for a drink** jadeaba de sed • **to ~ with desire for sth** desear algo ardientemente

pant² [pænt] CPD ▸ **pant leg** (*US*) pierna *f* del pantalón, pernera *f* • **the children were tugging at his ~ leg** los niños le tiraban del pantalón

pantaloons ['pæntəluːns] NPL (pantalones *mpl*) bombachos *mpl*

pantechnicon [pæn'teknɪkən] N (*Brit*) camión *m* de mudanzas

pantheism ['pænθiːɪzəm] N panteísmo *m*

pantheist ['pænθiːɪst] N panteísta *mf*

pantheistic [,pænθiː'ɪstɪk] ADJ panteísta

pantheon ['pænθɪən] N panteón *m*

panther ['pænθəʳ] N (PL: **panthers** *or* **panther**) pantera *f*, jaguar *m* (*LAm*)

panties ['pæntɪz] NPL bragas *fpl* (*Sp*), calzones *mpl* (*LAm*) • **a pair of ~** unas bragas, unos calzones (*LAm*)

pantihose ['pæntɪhəʊz] NPL = **pantyhose**

pantile ['pæntaɪl] N (= *tile*) teja *f* mixta

panting ['pæntɪŋ] N jadeo *m*

panto* ['pæntəʊ] N ABBR (*Brit*) (*Theat*) = **pantomime**

pantomime ['pæntəmaɪm] N **1** (*Theat*) (= *mime*) pantomima *f* • **to explain sth in ~** explicar algo por gestos
2 (*Brit*) (*at Christmas*) revista *f* musical navideña
3 (*Brit*) (*fig*) (= *farce*) • **what a ~!** ¡qué farsa! • **it was a real ~** fue una verdadera comedia
CPD ▸ **pantomime dame** (*Brit*) *papel femenino en comedia musical navideña, tradicionalmente interpretado por un hombre*

PANTOMIME

Una **pantomime**, abreviada en inglés como **panto**, es una obra teatral que se representa normalmente en Navidades ante un público familiar. Suele estar basada en un cuento de hadas u otra historia conocida y en ella nunca faltan personajes como la dama (**dame**), papel que siempre interpreta un actor, el protagonista joven (**principal boy**), normalmente interpretado por una actriz, y el malvado (**villain**). Aunque es un espectáculo familiar dirigido fundamentalmente a los niños, en él se alienta la participación de todo el público y posee una gran dosis de humor para adultos.

pantry ['pæntrɪ] N despensa *f*

pants [pænts] NPL (*Brit*) (*man's*) calzoncillos *mpl*; (*woman's*) bragas *fpl* (*Sp*), calzones *mpl* (*LAm*); (*US*) pantalones *mpl* • **a pair of ~** (*Brit*) (*man's*) unos calzoncillos; (*woman's*) unas bragas, unos calzones (*LAm*); (*US*) un pantalón, unos pantalones • IDIOMS: • **to bore the ~ off sb*** aburrir terriblemente a algn • **to catch sb with his ~ down*** pillar a algn desprevenido • **she wears the ~*** ella es la que manda
ADJ (*Brit‡*) (= *bad*) • **to be ~** ser una porquería • **I thought his performance was ~** me pareció que su actuación fue una porquería
CPD ▸ **pants press** (*US*) prensa *f* para pantalones ▸ **pants suit** (*US*) = **pantsuit**

pantsuit ['pæntsuːt] N (*US*) traje *m* de chaqueta y pantalón

panty girdle ['pæntɪ,gɜːdl] N faja *f* pantalón

pantyhose ['pæntɪhəʊz] NPL (*esp US*) pantys *mpl*, pantimedias *fpl*

panty liner ['pæntɪ,laɪnəʳ] N protege-slip *m*, salva-slip *m*

Panzer ['pæntsəʳ] N • **the ~s** las tropas motorizadas
CPD motorizado ▸ **Panzer division** división *f* motorizada

pap [pæp] N (*Culin*) papilla *f*, gachas *fpl*; (*fig*) (*pej*) bazofia* *f*

papa [pə'pɑː] N papá *m*

papacy ['peɪpəsɪ] N papado *m*, pontificado *m*

papadum ['pæpədəm] N torta *f* india

papal ['peɪpəl] ADJ papal, pontificio
CPD ▸ **papal nuncio** nuncio *m* apostólico

paparazzi [,pæpə'rætsiː] N (PL: **paparazzi**) paparazzi *mpl*

papaya [pə'paɪə] N (= *fruit*) papaya *f*; (= *tree*)

árbol *m* de papaya
paper ['peɪpəʳ] N **1** (= *material*) papel *m*; (= *wallpaper*) papel *m* pintado • **a piece of ~** un papel, una hoja (de papel) • **to put sth down on ~** • **commit sth to ~** poner algo por escrito • **on ~** (*fig*) en teoría, sobre el papel • **it's not worth the ~ it's written on** no vale para nada
2 (= *newspaper*) periódico *m*, diario *m* • **to write to the ~ about sth** escribir una carta al director de un periódico sobre algo • **the ~s** los periódicos, la prensa • **to write for the ~s** colaborar en los periódicos, escribir artículos para los periódicos • **it came out in the ~s** salió en los periódicos
3 papers (= *writings, documents*) papeles *mpl*; (= *identity papers*) documentación *f*, papeles *mpl* • **your ~s, please** la documentación, por favor • **Churchill's private ~s** los papeles personales de Churchill • **his divorce ~s have just come through** han llegado los papeles de su divorcio • **ship's ~s** documentación *f* del barco
4 (*Univ etc*) (= *essay*) ejercicio *m*, ensayo *m*; (= *exam*) examen *m* • **to do a good ~ in maths** hacer un buen examen de matemáticas • **to set a ~ in physics** poner un examen de física
5 (*scholarly*) (*written*) artículo *m*; (*read aloud*) ponencia *f*, comunicación *f* • **we heard a good ~ on place names** escuchamos una buena ponencia sobre toponimia
6 (*Parl*) documento *m* base • **a government ~ on European policy** un documento base gubernamental sobre política europea
VT [+ *wall, room*] empapelar, tapizar (*Mex*)
CPD de papel ▸ **paper advance** (*on printer*) avance *m* de papel ▸ **paper bag** bolsa *f* de papel • IDIOM: • **he couldn't fight his way out of a ~ bag*** (*hum*) es un gallina* ▸ **paper chain** cadeneta *f* de papel ▸ **paper chase** rallye-paper *m* ▸ **paper clip** clip *m*, sujetapapeles *m inv* ▸ **paper credit** (*Econ*) papel *m* crédito ▸ **paper cup** vaso *m* de cartón ▸ **paper currency** papel *m* moneda ▸ **paper fastener** grapa *f* ▸ **paper feed(er)** alimentador *m* de papel ▸ **paper handkerchief, paper hankie** pañuelo *m* de papel ▸ **paper industry** industria *f* papelera ▸ **paper knife** abrecartas *m inv* ▸ **paper lantern** farolillo *m* de papel ▸ **paper loss** (*Econ*) *pérdida que tiene lugar cuando baja el valor de una acción etc sin venderse esta* ▸ **paper mill** fábrica *f* de papel, papelera *f* ▸ **paper money** (*gen*) papel *m* moneda; (= *banknotes*) billetes *mpl* de banco ▸ **paper napkin** servilleta *f* de papel ▸ **paper profit** (*Econ*) beneficio *m* no realizado ▸ **paper qualifications** títulos *mpl* ▸ **paper round** reparto *m* de periódicos • **to do a ~ round** repartir periódicos ▸ **paper shop** (*Brit*) tienda *f* de periódicos, quiosco *m* ▸ **paper tape** cinta *f* de papel ▸ **paper tiger** (*fig*) tigre *m* de papel ▸ **paper tissue** pañuelo *m* de papel, tisú *m* ▸ **paper towel** toallita *f* de papel ▸ **paper trail** (*esp US*) pruebas *fpl* documentales
▸ **paper over** VI + PREP **1** (*lit*) empapelar
2 (*fig*) disimular • IDIOM: • **to ~ over the cracks** (*Brit*) guardar las apariencias; ▹ **crack**
paperback ['peɪpəbæk] N (*gen*) libro *m* en rústica; (*small*) libro *m* de bolsillo • **in ~** en rústica
CPD ▸ **paperback book** (*gen*) libro *m* en rústica; (*small*) libro *m* de bolsillo ▸ **paperback edition** edición *f* rústica
paperbacked ['peɪpəbækt] ADJ en rústica
paperbound ['peɪpəbaʊnd] ADJ = **paperbacked**
paperboy ['peɪpəbɔɪ] N repartidor *m* de periódicos
papergirl ['peɪpəgɜ:l] N repartidora *f* de periódicos
paperhanger ['peɪpəˌhæŋəʳ] N (*Brit*) empapelador(a) *m/f*
paperless ['peɪpəlɪs] ADJ sin papel • **the ~ society** la sociedad sin papel
paper-thin ['peɪpəˌθɪn] ADJ [*slice*] muy fino; (*iro*) casi transparente; [*wall*] de papel; (*fig*) [*majority, lead*] estrecho
paperweight ['peɪpəweɪt] N pisapapeles *m inv*
paperwork ['peɪpəwɜ:k] N trabajo *m* administrativo; (*pej*) (= *bureaucracy*) papeleo* *m*
papery ['peɪpərɪ] ADJ parecido al papel
papier-mâché ['pæpɪeɪ'mæʃeɪ] N cartón *m* piedra
CPD de cartón piedra
papism ['peɪpɪzəm] N (*pej*) papismo *m*
papist ['peɪpɪst] (*pej*) ADJ papista
N papista *mf*
papistry ['peɪpɪstrɪ] N (*pej*) papismo *m*
papoose [pə'pu:s] N **1** (= *baby*) niño/a *m/f* indio/a norteamericano/a
2 (= *baby sling*) mochila *f* portabebés
pappy* ['pæpɪ] N (*US*) papi* *m*
paprika ['pæprɪkə] N pimentón *m*, paprika *f*
Pap smear ['pæpˌsmɪəʳ], **Pap test** ['pæpˌtest] N frotis *m* (cervical)
Papua New Guinea ['pæpjʊənju:'gɪnɪ] N Papúa *f* Nueva Guinea, Nueva Guinea *f* Papúa
Papua New Guinean ['pæpjʊənju:'gɪnɪən] ADJ de Papúa Nueva Guinea, papú
N papú *mf*
papyrus [pə'paɪərəs] N (PL: **papyruses** *or* **papyri** [pə'paɪəraɪ]) papiro *m*
par[1] [pɑ:ʳ] N **1** (*Econ*) par *f* • **to be above/below par** estar sobre/bajo la par • **to be at par** estar a la par
2 (*Golf*) par *m* • **two over par** dos sobre par • **five under par** cinco bajo par
3 (*fig*) • **to be on a par with sth/sb** estar en pie de igualdad con algo/algn • **to place sth on a par with** parangonar *or* equiparar algo con • **to be under** *or* **below par** (= *ill*) sentirse mal, estar indispuesto • **to not be up to par** ser inferior a la calidad normal • IDIOM: • **that's par for the course** eso es lo más normal
CPD ▸ **par value** (*Econ*) valor *m* a la par
par[2]* ABBR (*Press*) (= **paragraph**) párr.
para ABBR (= **paragraph**) párr.
paraben ['pærəˌben] N parabeno *m*
parable ['pærəbl] N parábola *f*
parabola [pə'ræbələ] N parábola *f*
parabolic [ˌpærə'bɒlɪk] ADJ parabólico
CPD ▸ **parabolic aerial** antena *f* parabólica
paracetamol [pærə'si:təmɒl] N paracetamol *m*
parachute ['pærəʃu:t] N paracaídas *m inv*
VT lanzar en paracaídas • **to ~ food to sb** suministrar víveres a algn en paracaídas
VI (*also* **parachute down**) lanzarse *or* saltar en paracaídas • **to ~ to safety** salvarse utilizando el paracaídas
CPD ▸ **parachute drop** lanzamiento *m* en paracaídas ▸ **parachute jump** salto *m* en paracaídas ▸ **parachute regiment** regimiento *m* de paracaidistas
parachuting ['pærəʃu:tɪŋ] N paracaidismo *m*; ▹ **freefall parachuting**
parachutist ['pærəʃu:tɪst] N paracaidista *mf*
Paraclete ['pærəkli:t] N • **the ~** el Paráclito
parade [pə'reɪd] N **1** (= *procession*) desfile *m*; (*Mil*) desfile *m*, parada *f*; [*of models*] desfile *m*, pase *m* • **to be on ~** (*Mil*) estar en formación; (*fig*) estar a la vista de todos; ▹ **fashion**
2 (*fig*) • **a ~ of** (= *exhibition*) una exhibición de; (= *series*) una serie de • **to make a ~ of** (= *show off*) hacer alarde de
3 (*esp Brit*) (= *road*) paseo *m* • **a ~ of shops** una calle de tiendas
VT **1** [+ *troops*] hacer desfilar; [+ *streets*] recorrer, desfilar por; [+ *placard etc*] pasear (**through the streets** por las calles)
2 (= *show off*) [+ *learning, wealth, new clothes*] hacer alarde de, lucir
VI **1** (*Mil etc*) desfilar • **the strikers ~d through the town** los huelguistas desfilaron por la ciudad
2* pasearse • **she ~d up and down with the hat on** se paseaba de un lado a otro con el sombrero puesto, andaba de acá para allá luciendo el sombrero
CPD ▸ **parade ground** (*Mil*) plaza *f* de armas
▸ **parade about***, **parade around*** VI + ADV pavonearse
paradigm ['pærədaɪm] N paradigma *m*
CPD ▸ **paradigm shift** cambio *m* de paradigma
paradigmatic [ˌpærədɪg'mætɪk] ADJ paradigmático
paradisaic [ˌpærədɪ'seɪɪk] ADJ = **paradisiacal**
paradise ['pærədaɪs] N paraíso *m* • **this is ~!** ¡esto es el paraíso!; ▹ **fool**[1], **earthly**
paradisiacal [ˌpærədɪ'saɪəkəl] ADJ paradisíaco
paradox ['pærədɒks] N paradoja *f*
paradoxical ['pærə'dɒksɪkəl] ADJ paradójico
paradoxically [ˌpærə'dɒksɪkəlɪ] ADV paradójicamente
paraffin ['pærəfɪn] N (*Brit*) (*also* **paraffin oil**) petróleo *m* (de alumbrado), queroseno *m*; (= *wax*) parafina *f*
CPD ▸ **paraffin heater** estufa *f* de parafina ▸ **paraffin lamp** quinqué *m* ▸ **paraffin wax** parafina *f*
paraglide ['pærəglaɪd] VI hacer parapente
paraglider ['pærəˌglaɪdəʳ] N **1** (= *person*) parapentista *mf*
2 (= *object*) parapente *m*
paragliding ['pærəˌglaɪdɪŋ] N parapente *m*
paragon ['pærəgən] N modelo *m*, dechado *m* • **a ~ of virtue** un dechado de virtudes
paragraph ['pærəgrɑ:f] N párrafo *m*, (punto) acápite *m* (*LAm*); (*in law etc*) aparte *m*; (= *short article in newspaper*) suelto *m* • **"new ~"** "(punto y) aparte"
VT dividir en párrafos
Paraguay ['pærəgwaɪ] N Paraguay *m*
Paraguayan [ˌpærə'gwaɪən] ADJ paraguayo
N paraguayo/a *m/f*
parakeet ['pærəki:t] N perico *m*, periquito *m*
paralanguage ['pærəˌlæŋgwɪdʒ] N paralenguaje *m*
paralegal [ˌpærə'li:gəl] N ayudante *mf* de abogado
ADJ que trabaja como ayudante de abogado
paralinguistic [ˌpærəlɪŋ'gwɪstɪk] ADJ paralingüístico
parallax ['pærəlæks] N paralaje *m*
parallel ['pærəlel] ADJ **1** (*Geom*) paralelo (**to a**); (*Comput, Elec*) en paralelo • **in a ~ direction to** en dirección paralela a • **to run ~ to** ir en línea paralela a, correr paralelo con
2 (*fig*) análogo (**to a**) • **this is a ~ case to the last one** este caso es análogo al anterior
N **1** (*Geom*) paralela *f* • **in ~** (*Elec*) en paralelo
2 (*Geog*) paralelo *m* • **the 49th ~** el paralelo 49
3 (*fig*) • **a case without ~** un caso inaudito *or* único • **it has no ~ as far as I know** que yo

P

sepa no tiene paralelo *or* no hay nada parecido • **to draw a ~ between X and Y** establecer un paralelo entre X y Y • **these things occur in ~** estas cosas corren parejas (**with** con), estas cosas ocurren paralelamente
VT (*fig*) (= *compare*) comparar (**with** con); (= *equal*) igualar (**with** a) • **it is ~ed by ...** es parejo a ..., tiene su paralelo en ... • **his talent ~s his brother's** su talento es comparable *or* parejo al de su hermano
CPD ▸ **parallel bars** (*Sport*) paralelas *fpl* ▸ **parallel printer** impresora *f* en paralelo ▸ **parallel processing** (*Comput*) procesamiento *m* en paralelo

parallelepiped [ˌpærəˌlelə'paɪped] N paralelepípedo *m*

parallelism ['pærəlelɪzəm] N paralelismo *m*

parallelogram [ˌpærə'leləʊgræm] N paralelogramo *m*

Paralympic [pærə'lɪmpɪk] ADJ paralímpico
NPL **the Paralympics** los juegos paralímpicos
CPD ▸ **the Paralympic Games** los juegos paralímpicos

paralysation, paralyzation (*US*) [pærəlaɪ'zeɪʃən] N paralización *f*

paralyse, paralyze (*US*) ['pærəlaɪz] VT (*lit, fig*) paralizar • **to be ~d in both legs** estar paralizado de las dos piernas • **to be ~d with fright** estar paralizado de miedo • **the factory was ~d by the strike** la fábrica quedó paralizada por la huelga

paralysing ['pærəlaɪzɪŋ], **paralyzing** (*US*) ADJ (*lit, fig*) paralizador, paralizante

paralysis [pə'ræləsɪs] N (PL: **paralyses** [pə'ræləsi:z]) (*Med*) parálisis *f inv*; (*fig*) paralización *f*, parálisis *f inv*

paralytic [ˌpærə'lɪtɪk] ADJ **1** (*Med*) paralítico
2 (*Brit‡*) (= *drunk*) como una cuba*
N paralítico/a *m/f*

paralyzation [ˌpærəlaɪ'zeɪʃən] N (*US*) = **paralysation**

paralyze ['pærəlaɪz] VT (*US*) = **paralyse**

paralyzing ['pærəlaɪzɪŋ] ADJ (*US*) = **paralysing**

paramedic [ˌpærə'medɪk] N paramédico/a *m/f*

paramedical [ˌpærə'medɪkəl] ADJ paramédico

parameter [pə'ræmɪtəʳ] N parámetro *m*

paramilitary [ˌpærə'mɪlɪtərɪ] ADJ paramilitar
N paramilitar *mf*

paramount ['pærəmaʊnt] ADJ **1** (= *utmost*) sumo • **of ~ importance** de suma importancia
2 (= *of prime importance*) primordial • **solvency must be ~** la solvencia es primordial *or* lo más importante

paramountcy ['pærəmaʊntsɪ] N carácter *m* primordial

paramour ['pærəmʊəʳ] N (*liter*) amante *mf*, querido/a *m/f*

paranoia [ˌpærə'nɔɪə] N paranoia *f*

paranoiac [ˌpærə'nɔɪɪk] ADJ paranoico
N paranoico/a *m/f*

paranoid ['pærənɔɪd] ADJ paranoide
N paranoico/a *m/f*

paranormal [ˌpærə'nɔ:məl] ADJ paranormal
N • **the ~** lo paranormal

parapet ['pærəpɪt] N [*of balcony, roof*] pretil *m*, antepecho *m*; [*of fortification*] parapeto *m* • IDIOMS: • **to put one's head above the ~** (*Brit*) arriesgar el cuello • **to keep one's head below the ~** (*Brit*) mantenerse al margen

paraphernalia [ˌpærəfə'neɪlɪə] N parafernalia *f*

paraphrase ['pærəfreɪz] N paráfrasis *f inv*
VT parafrasear

paraplegia [ˌpærə'pli:dʒə] N paraplejía *f*

paraplegic [ˌpærə'pli:dʒɪk] ADJ parapléjico
N parapléjico/a *m/f*

parapsychological [ˌpærəsaɪkə'lɒdʒɪkəl] ADJ parapsicológico

parapsychologist [ˌpærəsaɪ'kɒlədʒɪst] N parapsicólogo/a *m/f*

parapsychology [ˌpærəsaɪ'kɒlədʒɪ] N parapsicología *f*

Paraquat® ['pærəkwɒt] N herbicida *m*

Paras* ['pærəz] NPL ABBR (= **Parachute Regiment**) paras* *mpl*, paracas* *mpl*

parasailing ['pærəˌseɪlɪŋ] N parasail *m*, paravela *f*

parascending ['pærəsendɪŋ] N *esquí acuático con paracaídas* • **to go ~** *hacer esquí acuático con paracaídas*

parasite ['pærəsaɪt] N (*lit, fig*) parásito/a *m/f* (**on** de)

parasitic [ˌpærə'sɪtɪk] ADJ parásito, parasitario • **to be ~ on** ser parásito de

parasitical [ˌpærə'sɪtɪkəl] ADJ = **parasitic**

parasitism ['pærəsɪtɪzəm] N parasitismo *m*

parasitize ['pærəsɪˌtaɪz] VT parasitar (en)

parasitologist [ˌpærəsaɪ'tɒlədʒɪst] N parasitólogo/a *m/f*

parasitology [ˌpærəsɪ'tɒlədʒɪ] N parasitología *f*

parasol ['pærəsɒl] N sombrilla *f*, parasol *m*

parasuicide [ˌpærə'sʊɪsaɪd] N parasuicidio *m*

parataxis [ˌpærə'tæksɪs] N parataxis *f*

paratroop ['pærətru:p] ADJ [*regiment, unit, officer*] de paracaidistas

paratrooper ['pærətru:pəʳ] N paracaidista *mf*

paratroops ['pærətru:ps] NPL paracaidistas *mpl*

paratyphoid ['pærə'taɪfɔɪd] N paratifoidea *f*

parboil ['pɑ:bɔɪl] VT sancochar, cocer a medias

Parcae ['pɑ:ki:] NPL • **the ~** las Parcas

parcel ['pɑ:sl] N **1** (= *package*) paquete *m* • **pass the ~** (*Brit*) *juego infantil en que los niños van desenvolviendo un paquete haciéndolo pasar de mano en mano*; ▹ **part**
2 [*of land*] parcela *f*, lote *m*
3 (*Brit**) (= *quantity*) • **a ~ of nonsense** una sarta de disparates • **a ~ of idiots** una panda de idiotas*
CPD ▸ **parcel bomb** paquete-bomba *m* ▸ **parcel office** departamento *m* de paquetes ▸ **parcel post** servicio *m* de paquetes postales ▸ **parcel shelf** (*in car*) bandeja *f* cubremaletero
▸ **parcel out** VT + ADV repartir; [+ *land*] parcelar
▸ **parcel up** VT + ADV empaquetar; (*large size*) embalar

parch [pɑ:tʃ] VT secar, resecar, agostar
VI secarse

parched [pɑ:tʃt] ADJ [*land etc*] abrasado, reseco; (= *thirsty**) reseco, muerto de sed • **I'm ~** me muero de sed

parchment ['pɑ:tʃmənt] N pergamino *m*

parchment-like ['pɑ:tʃməntˌlaɪk] ADJ apergaminado

pardner* ['pɑ:dnəʳ] N (*US*) (*hum*) compadre* *m*, comadre* *f*, cuate *mf* (*CAm, Mex**)

pardon ['pɑ:dn] N **1** perdón *m* • **to beg sb's ~** pedir perdón a algn • **I do beg your ~!** ¡perdone usted!, ¡disculpe! (*esp LAm*) • **I beg your ~, but could you ...?** perdone *or* (*esp LAm*) disculpe la molestia, pero ¿podría usted ...? • **(I beg your) ~?** (= *what?*) ¿perdón?, ¿cómo?, ¿mande? (*Mex*)
2 (*Jur*) indulto *m* • **free ~** indulto *m* absoluto • **general ~** amnistía *f*
VT **1** (= *forgive*) perdonar, disculpar (*esp LAm*) • **to ~ sb sth** perdonar algo a algn • **~ me, but could you ...?** perdone *or* (*esp LAm*) disculpe la molestia, pero ¿podría usted ...? • **~ me!** ¡perdone!, ¡ay, perdone! • **~ me?** (*US*) ¿perdón?, ¿cómo?, ¿mande? (*Mex*) • **~ my mentioning it** siento tener que decirlo, perdone que se lo diga
2 (*Jur*) indultar

pardonable ['pɑ:dnəbl] ADJ perdonable, disculpable

pardonably ['pɑ:dnəblɪ] ADV • **he was ~ angry** era fácil disculpar su enojo, se comprende fácilmente que se encolerizara

pare [pɛəʳ] VT [+ *nails*] cortar; [+ *fruit etc*] pelar
▸ **pare down** VT + ADV reducir • **to ~ sth down to the minimum** reducir algo al mínimo
▸ **pare off** VT + ADV [+ *slice*] cortar; [+ *rind, skin*] pelar • **he took out a slab of cheese and ~d off a slice** sacó un trozo de queso y cortó una loncha • **he gently ~d off the rind and took a bite** peló la cáscara con cuidado y le dio un bocado

pared-down [ˌpɛəd'daʊn] ADJ **1** (= *not elaborate*) [*style*] minimalista • **her style is pared-down and simple** su estilo es sencillo y minimalista
2 [*organization*] restringido

parent ['pɛərənt] N padre *m*/madre *f*; **parents** padres *mpl*
ADJ • **the ~ plant** la planta madre
CPD ▸ **parent body** [*of organization*] organización *f* matriz ▸ **parent company** casa *f* matriz ▸ **parent group** [*of company*] empresa *f* matriz ▸ **parents' evening** reunión *f* de padres ▸ **parent teacher association** asociación *f* de padres de familia y profesores

parentage ['pɛərəntɪdʒ] N familia *f* • **of humble ~** de nacimiento humilde • **of unknown ~** de padres desconocidos

parental [pə'rentl] ADJ [*care etc*] de los padres
CPD ▸ **parental authority** patria potestad *f* ▸ **parental guidance** los consejos de los padres ▸ **parental leave** permiso *m* parental

parenteral [pæ'rentərəl] ADJ parenteral

parenthesis [pə'renθɪsɪs] N (PL: **parentheses** [pə'renθɪsi:z]) paréntesis *m inv* • **in ~** entre paréntesis

parenthetic [ˌpærən'θetɪk] ADJ = **parenthetical**

parenthetical [ˌpærən'θetɪkəl] ADJ entre paréntesis

parenthetically [ˌpærən'θetɪkəlɪ] ADV entre paréntesis

parenthood ['pɛərənthʊd] N paternidad *f* • **planned ~** planificación *f* familiar, paternidad *f* responsable

parenting ['pɛərəntɪŋ] N el ser padres • **shared ~** participación *f* conjunta en la vida familiar • **~ is a full-time occupation** el cuidar de los hijos es una labor de plena dedicación

parent-teacher meeting [ˌpɛərənt'ti:tʃəˌmi:tɪŋ] N reunión *f* de padres y profesores

parer ['pɛərəʳ] N pelalegumbres *m inv*

par excellence [ˌpɑ:r'eksəlɑ̃:ns] ADV por excelencia

pariah ['pærɪə] N paria *mf*

parietal [pə'raɪɪtl] ADJ parietal

paring knife ['pɛərɪŋˌnaɪf] N cuchillo *m* de mondar

parings ['pɛərɪŋz] (NPL) [*of fruit, vegetables*] peladuras *fpl*; [*of nails*] trozos *mpl*

pari passu ['pærɪ'pæsu:] (ADV) a ritmo parecido, al igual • **~ with** a ritmo parecido al de, al igual que

Paris ['pærɪs] (N) París *m*
(ADJ) parisiense, parisino

parish ['pærɪʃ] (N) parroquia *f*
(CPD) parroquial, de la parroquia ▸ **parish church** iglesia *f* parroquial ▸ **parish council** concejo *m* parroquial ▸ **parish hall** salón *m* parroquial ▸ **parish magazine** revista *f* parroquial ▸ **parish priest** párroco *m* ▸ **parish records** registros *mpl* parroquiales ▸ **parish register** libro *m* parroquial

parishioner [pə'rɪʃənəʳ] (N) feligrés/esa *m/f*

parish-pump ['pærɪʃ'pʌmp] (ADJ) (*Brit*) (*pej*) pueblerino, de campanario, de aldea • **parish-pump attitude** mentalidad *f* pueblerina, espíritu *m* de campanario • **parish-pump politics** política *f* pueblerina

Parisian [pə'rɪzɪən] (ADJ) parisiense, parisino
(N) parisiense *mf*

parity ['pærɪtɪ] (N) (*Econ etc*) paridad *f*; [*of wages, conditions*] igualdad *f* • **exchange at ~** cambio *m* a la par

park [pɑ:k] (N) **1** (= *public gardens*) parque *m*;
▹ **business, science**
2 (*Brit*) (*Sport**) (= *field*) campo *m*
(VT) **1** (*Aut*) aparcar (*Sp*), estacionar (*esp LAm*) • **can I ~ my car here?** ¿puedo aparcar mi coche aquí?
2* (= *put*) poner, dejar • **she ~ed herself on the sofa** se colocó en el sofá
(VI) (*Aut*) aparcar (*Sp*), estacionarse (*esp LAm*)
(CPD) ▸ **park bench** banco *m* de parque ▸ **park keeper** guardián/ana *m/f* (de parque), guardabosque *mf* ▸ **park ranger** guarda *mf* forestal
▸ **park up** (VI + ADV) aparcar (*Sp*), estacionar (*esp LAm*)
(VT + ADV) aparcar (*Sp*), estacionar (*esp LAm*) • **he ~ed up his Range-Rover** aparcó (*Sp*) or estacionó (*esp LAm*) su Range-Rover

parka ['pɑ:kə] (N) chaquetón *m* acolchado con capucha, anorak *m*

park-and-ride [,pɑ:kənd'raɪd] (N) *aparcamiento en estaciones periféricas conectadas con el transporte urbano colectivo*

parked ['pɑ:kt] (ADJ) aparcado (*Sp*), estacionado (*esp LAm*) • **my sister was ~ near the cinema** mi hermana estaba aparcada (*Sp*) or estacionada (*esp LAm*) cerca del cine

parking ['pɑ:kɪŋ] (N) aparcamiento *m* (*Sp*), parking *m*, estacionamiento *m* (*esp LAm*) • **"parking for 50 cars"** "parking para 50 coches" • **"no parking"** "prohibido aparcar", "prohibido estacionarse" (*esp LAm*) • **"ample parking available"** "amplio aparcamiento or (*LAm*) estacionamiento para coches"
(CPD) ▸ **parking attendant** guardacoches *mf inv* ▸ **parking bay** área *f* de aparcamiento or (*esp LAm*) estacionamiento de coches ▸ **parking brake** (*US*) freno *m* de mano ▸ **parking fine** multa *f* de aparcamiento (*Sp*), multa *f* por estacionamiento indebido (*esp LAm*) ▸ **parking garage** (*US*) parking *m* ▸ **parking lights** luces *fpl* de estacionamiento ▸ **parking lot** (*US*) aparcamiento *m* (*Sp*), (playa *f* de) estacionamiento *m* (*esp LAm*) ▸ **parking meter** parquímetro *m* ▸ **parking offence** infracción *f* por aparcamiento or (*esp LAm*) estacionamiento indebido ▸ **parking permit** permiso *m* de aparcamiento or (*esp LAm*) estacionamiento ▸ **parking place, parking space** aparcamiento *m* (*Sp*), parking *m*, estacionamiento *m* (*esp LAm*) ▸ **parking ticket** multa *f* de aparcamiento (*Sp*), multa *f* por estacionamiento indebido (*esp LAm*) ▸ **parking violation** (*US*) = **parking offence**

Parkinson's disease ['pɑ:kɪnsənzdɪ,zi:z] (N) enfermedad *f* de Parkinson

Parkinson's law ['pɑ:kɪnsənz,lɔ:] (N) ley *f* de Parkinson

parkland ['pɑ:klænd] (N) parques *mpl*

parkour ['pɑ:kɔ:ʳ] (N) parkour *m*

park-ride [,pɑ:k'raɪd] (N) = **park-and-ride**

parkway ['pɑ:kweɪ] (N) (*US*) alameda *f*

parky‡ ['pɑ:kɪ] (ADJ) (*Brit*) • **it's a bit ~** está haciendo fresco

parlance ['pɑ:ləns] (N) lenguaje *m* • **in common ~** en lenguaje corriente • **in technical ~** en lenguaje técnico

parley ['pɑ:lɪ] (N) parlamento *m*
(VI) parlamentar (**with** con)

parliament ['pɑ:ləmənt] (N) parlamento *m*, ≈ Cortes *fpl* (*Sp*), ≈ Congreso *m* (*LAm*); (= *period between elections*) legislatura *f* • **to go into** or **enter ~** ser elegido diputado or senador
(CPD) ▸ **parliament building** parlamento *m* ▸ **parliament house** parlamento *m*

parliamentarian [,pɑ:ləmen'tɛərɪən] (ADJ) parlamentario
(N) parlamentario/a *m/f*

parliamentary [,pɑ:lə'mentərɪ] (ADJ) parlamentario
(CPD) ▸ **parliamentary agent** agente *mf* parlamentario/a ▸ **parliamentary candidate** candidato/a *m/f* parlamentario/a • **the ~ candidate for Blackburn** el candidato parlamentario por Blackburn ▸ **parliamentary democracy** democracia *f* parlamentaria ▸ **parliamentary election** elecciones *fpl* parlamentarias ▸ **parliamentary government** gobierno *m* parlamentario ▸ **parliamentary immunity** inmunidad *f* parlamentaria ▸ **parliamentary inquiry** investigación *f* parlamentaria ▸ **parliamentary privilege** privilegio *m* parlamentario

parlour, **parlor** (*US*) ['pɑ:ləʳ] (N) (*in house*) sala *f*, salón *m* • **beauty ~** salón *m* de belleza • **ice-cream ~** heladería *f*
(CPD) ▸ **parlor car** (*US*) coche-salón *m* ▸ **parlour game, parlor game** (*US*) juego *m* de salón

parlourmaid, **parlormaid** (*US*) ['pɑ:ləmeɪd] (N) camarera *f*

parlous ['pɑ:ləs] (ADJ) [*state*] lamentable, crítico, pésimo

Parma ham [,pɑ:mə'hæm] (N) jamón *m* de Parma

Parma violet [,pɑ:mə'vaɪəlɪt] (N) violeta *f* de Parma

Parmesan [,pɑ:mɪ'zæn] (N) parmesano *m*
(CPD) ▸ **Parmesan cheese** queso *m* parmesano

Parnassus [pɑ:'næsəs] (N) Parnaso *m*

parochial [pə'rəʊkɪəl] (ADJ) (*Rel*) parroquial; (*pej*) (= *provincial*) provinciano; (= *narrow-minded*) de miras estrechas
(CPD) ▸ **parochial school** (*US*) escuela *f* parroquial

parochialism [pə'rəʊkɪəlɪzəm] (N) (*pej*) mentalidad *f* provinciana or pueblerina

parodic [pə'rɒdɪk] (ADJ) paródico

parodist ['pærədɪst] (N) parodista *mf*

parody ['pærədɪ] (N) parodia *f*
(VT) parodiar

parole [pə'rəʊl] (N) (= *word*) palabra *f* (de honor); (*Jur*) libertad *f* condicional • **to be on ~** estar en libertad condicional • **to break one's ~** quebrantar las condiciones impuestas por la libertad condicional • **to put sb on ~** poner a algn en libertad condicional
(VT) dejar en libertad condicional
(CPD) ▸ **parole board** ≈ comisión *f* de libertad condicional ▸ **parole hearing** audiencia *f* de libertad condicional ▸ **parole officer** ≈ agente *mf* de la condicional ▸ **parole violation** violación *f* de la libertad condicional

paroxysm ['pærəksɪzəm] (N) paroxismo *m* • **she broke into a ~ of coughing** le dio un ataque muy fuerte de tos • **it sent him into ~s of mirth/rage** le hizo troncharse de risa/le produjo un ataque de ira

parquet ['pɑ:keɪ] (N) parquet *m*, parqué *m*
(CPD) ▸ **parquet floor** suelo *m* de parquet, suelo *m* de parqué ▸ **parquet flooring** suelo *m* de parquet, suelo *m* de parqué

parquetry ['pɑ:kɪtrɪ] (N) (= *floor*) entarimado *m*; (= *activity*) obra *f* de entarimado

parrakeet ['pærəki:t] = **parakeet**

parricide ['pærɪsaɪd] (N) **1** (= *act*) parricidio *m*
2 (= *person*) parricida *mf*

parrot ['pærət] (N) loro *m*, papagayo *m* • **they repeated it like ~s** lo repitieron como loros;
▹ **sick**
(VT) [+ *words*] repetir como un loro

parrot-cry ['pærətkraɪ] (N) cantinela *f*, eslogan *m* (*que se repite mecánicamente*)

parrot-fashion ['pærət,fæʃən] (ADV) [*learn*] como un loro

parrotfish ['pærət,fɪʃ] (N) pez *m* loro • **two ~** dos peces loro

parry ['pærɪ] (VT) (*Fencing*) parar; [+ *blow*] parar, desviar; [+ *attack*] rechazar, defenderse de; (*fig*) esquivar, eludir

parse [pɑ:z] (VT) analizar (sintácticamente)

parsec ['pɑ:sek] (N) parsec *m*

Parsee [pɑ:'si:] (N) parsi *mf*

parser ['pɑ:zəʳ] (N) analizador *m* sintáctico

parsimonious [,pɑ:sɪ'məʊnɪəs] (ADJ) parco, excesivamente frugal

parsimoniously [,pɑ:sɪ'məʊnɪəslɪ] (ADV) parcamente

parsimony ['pɑ:sɪmənɪ] (N) parquedad *f*, excesiva frugalidad *f*

parsing ['pɑ:zɪŋ] (N) análisis *m inv* sintáctico or gramatical

parsley ['pɑ:slɪ] (N) perejil *m*
(CPD) ▸ **parsley sauce** salsa *f* de perejil

parsnip ['pɑ:snɪp] (N) chirivía *f*, pastinaca *f*

parson ['pɑ:sn] (N) clérigo *m*, cura *m*; (*Protestant*) pastor *m*
(CPD) ▸ **parson's nose** [*of chicken*] rabadilla *f*

parsonage ['pɑ:snɪdʒ] (N) casa *f* del párroco, parroquia *f*

parsonical [pɑ:'sɒnɪkəl] (ADJ) (*hum*) frailuno

part [pɑ:t] (N) **1** (= *portion, proportion*) parte *f* • **the ~s of the body** las partes del cuerpo • **it was all ~ of the job** todo formaba parte del trabajo • **this was only ~ of the story** esta no era la historia completa, esto solo era parte de la historia • **~ of me wanted to apologize** por un lado quería pedir perdón, una parte de mí quería pedir perdón • **it went on for the best ~ of an hour** continuó durante casi una hora • **you haven't heard the best ~ yet** todavía no has oído lo mejor • **in the early ~ of this century** a principios de este siglo • **the funny ~ of it is that nobody seemed to notice** lo gracioso es que nadie pareció darse cuenta • **a good ~ of sth** gran parte de algo • **in great ~** en gran parte • **in ~** en parte • **the book is good in ~s** hay partes del libro que son buenas, el libro es bueno en partes • **a large ~ of sth** gran parte de algo • **in large ~** en gran parte • **for the most ~** (*proportion*) en su mayor parte; (*number*) en su mayoría; (= *usually*) por lo general • **for the most ~, this is still unexplored terrain** en su mayor parte, este es un territorio aún no explorado • **the locals are, for the most ~, very friendly** los habitantes son, en su mayoría, muy

simpáticos • **the work is, for the most ~, quite well paid** el trabajo está, por lo general, bastante bien pagado • IDIOMS: • **a man of (many) ~s** un hombre de muchas facetas • **to be ~ and parcel of sth** ser parte integrante de algo • **suffering and death are ~ and parcel of life** el sufrimiento y la muerte son parte integrante de la vida; ▹ **furniture, private, sum**
2 (= *measure*) parte *f* • **one ~ alcohol to two ~s water** una parte de alcohol por cada dos partes de agua • **mix together equal ~s of salt and flour** mezcle partes iguales de sal y harina
3 (= *share, role*) • **to do one's ~** poner de su parte • **he had no ~ in stealing it** no intervino *or* no participó en el robo • **work plays an important ~ in her life** el trabajo juega un papel importante en su vida • **to take ~ (in sth)** tomar parte (en algo), participar (en algo) • **I want no ~ of this** no quiero tener nada que ver con esto
4 (*Theat, Cine*) papel *m* • **to look the ~** vestir el cargo • **to play the ~ of Hamlet** hacer el papel de Hamlet • **he's just playing a ~** está fingiendo; ▹ **bit**
5 (= *region*) [*of city*] parte *f*, zona *f*; [*of country, world*] región *f* • **I don't know this ~ of London very well** no conozco esta parte *or* esta zona de Londres muy bien • **a lovely ~ of the country** una región hermosa del país • **what ~ of Spain are you from?** ¿de qué parte de España eres? • **delegates from all ~s of the country** delegados de todos los rincones del país • **in some ~s of the world** en algunas regiones del mundo • **in this/that ~ of the world** en esta/esa región • **in foreign ~s** en el extranjero • **in** *or* **round these ~s** por aquí, por estos pagos* • **he's not from these ~s** no es de por aquí
6 (= *side*) • **for my ~, I do not agree** en lo que a mí se refiere *or* por mi parte, no estoy de acuerdo • **to take sth in good ~** tomarse algo bien • **it was bad organization on their ~** fue mala organización por su parte • **to take sb's ~** ponerse de parte de algn, tomar partido por algn
7 (*Mech*) pieza *f*
8 (*Gram*) parte *f* • **~ of speech** parte *f* de la oración, categoría *f* gramatical • **what ~ of speech is "of"?** ¿qué parte de la oración es "de"?, ¿a qué categoría gramatical pertenece "de"?
9 (*Mus*) parte *f* • **the soprano ~** la parte de soprano • **a song in four ~s** • **a four-part song** una canción a cuatro voces
10 (= *instalment*) [*of journal*] número *m*; [*of serialized publication*] fascículo *m*; (*TV, Rad*) (= *episode*) parte *f*
11 (*US*) (*in hair*) raya *f* • **side/center ~** raya *f* al lado/al medio
ADV (= *partly*) en parte • **it is ~ fiction and ~ fact** es en parte ficción y en parte realidad, contiene partes ficticias y partes reales • **the cake was ~ eaten** el pastel estaba empezado *or* medio comido • **she is ~ French** tiene algo de sangre francesa
VT **1** (= *separate*) separar • **it would kill her to be ~ed from him** le mataría estar separada de él • **market traders try to ~ the tourists from their money** los dueños de los puestos en los mercados intentan sacar dinero de los turistas
2 (= *open*) [+ *curtains*] abrir, correr; [+ *legs, lips*] abrir
3 (= *divide*) • **to ~ one's hair on the left/right** peinarse con raya a la izquierda/derecha • **his hair was ~ed at the side/in the middle** tenía raya al lado/al medio
VI **1** (= *separate*) [*people*] separarse • **they couldn't bear to ~** no soportaban la idea de separarse • **we ~ed on good terms** lo dejamos como amigos • **to ~ from sb** separarse de algn
2 (= *move to one side*) [*crowd, clouds*] apartarse
3 (= *open*) [*lips, curtains*] abrirse
4 (= *break*) [*rope*] romperse, partirse
CPD ▸ **part exchange** • **they take your old car in ~ exchange** aceptan tu coche viejo como parte del pago • **they offer ~ exchange on older vehicles** aceptan vehículos más antiguos como parte del pago de uno nuevo ▸ **part owner** copropietario/a *m/f* ▸ **part payment** pago *m* parcial • **to accept sth as ~ payment for sth** aceptar algo como parte del pago *or* como pago parcial de algo ▸ **part song** canción *f* a varias voces
▸ **part with** VI + PREP [+ *possession*] desprenderse de, deshacerse de; [+ *person*] separarse de; [+ *money*] gastar, soltar* • **I hate ~ing with it** me duele tener que desprenderme *or* deshacerme de él • **she couldn't bear to ~ with the baby** fue incapaz de separarse del bebé

part- [ˈpɑːt-] PREFIX (*Brit*) • **part-Irish, part-Australian** medio irlandés, medio australiano • **part-baked** precocido

partake [pɑːˈteɪk] (PT: **partook**, PP: **partaken**) VI (*frm*) **1** (= *consume*) • **to ~ of** [+ *food*] comer; [+ *drink*] beber
2 (= *participate*) • **to ~ in an activity** tomar parte *or* participar en una actividad • **are you partaking?** ¿va a tomar parte?

parterre [pɑːˈteə] N (= *garden*) parterre *m*

parthenogenesis [ˈpɑːθɪnəʊˈdʒenɪsɪs] N partenogénesis *f inv*

Parthenon [ˈpɑːθənɒn] N Partenón *m*

partial [ˈpɑːʃəl] ADJ **1** (= *not complete*) parcial
2 (= *biased*) parcial (**towards** hacia)
3 • **to be ~ to sth** (= *like*) tener debilidad por algo • **he's ~ to a cigar after dinner** le gusta fumarse un puro después de cenar

partiality [ˌpɑːʃɪˈælɪtɪ] N **1** (= *bias*) parcialidad *f* (**towards** hacia)
2 (= *liking*) debilidad *f* (**for, to** por), gusto *m* (**for, to** por)

partially [ˈpɑːʃəlɪ] ADV **1** (= *partly*) parcialmente, en parte • **~ deaf** con deficiencia auditiva • **the accident had left him ~ deaf** el accidente lo dejó parcialmente sordo • **~ sighted** con deficiencia visual • **~ sighted students** alumnos con deficiencia visual • **to be ~ sighted** tener deficiencia visual
2 (= *with bias*) con parcialidad

participant [pɑːˈtɪsɪpənt] N (*in debate, fight, argument*) participante *mf*; (*in competition*) concursante *mf*

participate [pɑːˈtɪsɪpeɪt] VI participar, tomar parte (**in** en) • **participating countries** países *mpl* participantes • **to ~ in a sport** practicar un deporte

participation [pɑːˌtɪsɪˈpeɪʃən] N participación *f* (**in** en); ▹ **audience**

participative [pɑːˈtɪsɪpətɪv] ADJ [*management, democracy*] participativo

participator [pɑːˈtɪsɪpeɪtəʳ] N participante *mf*

participatory [pɑːtɪsɪˈpeɪtərɪ] ADJ [*democracy, sport*] participativo

participial [ˌpɑːtɪˈsɪpɪəl] ADJ participial

participle [ˈpɑːtɪsɪpl] N participio *m* • **past ~** participio *m* pasado *or* pasivo • **present ~** participio *m* activo *or* (de) presente

particle [ˈpɑːtɪkl] N **1** (*gen*) partícula *f*; [*of dust*] partícula *f*, grano *m*; (*fig*) pizca *f* • **there's not a ~ of truth in it** eso no tiene ni pizca de verdad
2 (*Phys, Gram*) partícula *f*
CPD ▸ **particle accelerator** acelerador *m* de partículas ▸ **particle board** (*US*) madera *f* aglomerada ▸ **particle physics** física *f* de partículas

parti-coloured, parti-colored (*US*) [ˈpɑːtɪˌkʌləd] ADJ de diversos colores, multicolor, abigarrado

particular [pəˈtɪkjʊləʳ] ADJ **1** (= *special*) especial • **the flowers had been chosen with ~ care** se habían escogido las flores con especial cuidado • **she's a ~ friend of mine** es muy amiga mía • **is there anything ~ you want?** ¿quieres algo en particular *or* en concreto? • **to pay ~ attention to sth** prestar especial atención a algo • **nothing ~ happened** no pasó nada en especial
2 (= *specific*) • **in this ~ case** en este caso concreto • **at this ~ point in time** en este preciso momento • **is there any ~ food you don't like?** ¿hay algún alimento en particular *or* en especial *or* en concreto que no te guste? • **the people living in a ~ area** la gente que vive en una zona determinada • **for no ~ reason** por ninguna razón especial *or* en particular *or* en concreto
3 (= *fussy*) • **to be ~ about sth**: • **he's very ~ about his food** es muy exigente con *or* especial para la comida • **I'm rather ~ about my friends** escojo mis amigos con cierto cuidado • **she's not very ~ about her appearance** no se preocupa mucho por su aspecto • **they weren't too ~ about where the money came from** no les importaba *or* preocupaba mucho de dónde viniera el dinero
4 (= *insistent*) • **he was most ~ that I shouldn't go to any trouble** insistió mucho en que no me tomara ninguna molestia
N **1** (*frm*) (*usu pl*) (= *detail*) detalle *m* • **her account was accurate in every ~** su versión fue exacta en todos los detalles • **please give full ~s** se ruega hacer constar todos los detalles • **for further ~s apply to ...** para más información escriba a ... • **the nurse took her ~s** la enfermera le tomó sus datos personales
2 • **in ~**: **I remember one incident in ~** recuerdo un incidente en particular *or* en concreto • **are you looking for anything in ~?** ¿busca usted algo en particular *or* en concreto? • **"are you doing anything tonight?" — "nothing in ~"** —¿vas a hacer algo esta noche? —nada en particular *or* en especial
3 • **the ~** lo particular; ▹ **general**

particularity [pəˌtɪkjʊˈlærɪtɪ] N particularidad *f*

particularize [pəˈtɪkjʊləraɪz] VT pormenorizar, especificar
VI entrar en detalles

particularly [pəˈtɪkjʊləlɪ] ADV **1** (= *especially*) especialmente • **in many countries, ~ France** en muchos países, especialmente *or* particularmente en Francia • **he ~ dislikes quiz shows** siente especial aversión por los concursos televisivos • **he was not ~ pleased** no se puso loco de contento que digamos • **"do you want to see it?" — "not ~"** —¿quieres verlo? —no especialmente
2 (= *specifically*) • **do you want it ~ for tomorrow?** ¿lo necesitas expresamente *or* precisamente para mañana?

particulate [pɑːˈtɪkjʊlət] ADJ [*emissions, filter*] de partículas
NPL **particulates** partículas *fpl*

parting [ˈpɑːtɪŋ] ADJ de despedida • **his ~ words** sus palabras de despedida • **~ shot** (*fig*) golpe *m* de gracia
N **1** (= *separation*) separación *f*, despedida *f* • **the ~ of the ways** (*fig*) la encrucijada, el momento de la separación
2 (*in hair*) raya *f* • **side/centre ~** raya *f* al

lado/al medio
partisan [ˌpɑːtɪˈzæn] (ADJ) (= *one-sided*) parcial; (= *of party*) partidista; (*Mil*) guerrillero
(N) partidario/a *m/f* (**of** de); (*Mil*) partisano/a *m/f*, guerrillero/a *m/f*
(CPD) ▸ **partisan warfare** guerra *f* partisana
partisanship [ˌpɑːtɪˈzænʃɪp] (N) partidismo *m*
partition [pɑːˈtɪʃən] (N) **1** (= *wall*) tabique *m*
2 (*Pol*) partición *f*, división *f*
(VT) **1** (= *divide*) [+ *country*] partir, dividir; (= *share*) repartir (**among** entre)
2 [+ *room, area*] tabicar, dividir con tabiques
▸ **partition off** (VT + ADV) separar con tabiques
partitive [ˈpɑːtɪtɪv] (ADJ) partitivo
partly [ˈpɑːtlɪ] (ADV) en parte • **that is only ~ true** eso es verdad solo en parte • **I am ~ to blame** en parte es culpa mía • **he is ~ responsible for this** en parte él es responsable de esto • **it was ~ destroyed** quedó parcialmente destruido • **the film is ~ a romance, ~ a comedy** la película es en parte romántica y en parte cómica, la película tiene partes románticas y partes cómicas
partner [ˈpɑːtnəʳ] (N) **1** (*in activity*) compañero/a *m/f* • **work with a ~ for this exercise** realizar este ejercicio con un compañero *or* en pareja • **~(s) in crime** (*lit*) (*hum*) cómplice(s) *m(pl)*
2 (*in dance, tennis, golf, cards*) pareja *f*; (= *co-driver*) copiloto *mf*
3 (*Comm, Pol*) socio/a *m/f* • **junior ~** socio/a *m/f* menor • **senior ~** socio/a *m/f* principal, socio/a *m/f* mayoritario/a (*Sp*); ▹ **sleeping, trading**
4 (*in relationship*) pareja *f*, compañero/a *m/f*; (*in sex*) pareja *f* • **marriage ~** cónyuge *mf* (*frm*); ▹ **sexual**
(VT) **1** (= *be partner of*) • **to ~ sb in a waltz** bailar un vals con algn • **he ~ed her at bridge** jugó al bridge en pareja con ella, fue su pareja al bridge
2 (= *pair*) • **to ~ sb with sb** juntar a algn con algn (como pareja)
partnership [ˈpɑːtnəʃɪp] (N) **1** (= *relationship*) asociación *f*; (= *couple*) relación *f* de pareja • **a stable, loving ~** una relación de pareja estable y llena de cariño • **our relationship wasn't just a marriage, it was a ~** nuestra relación no era solo un matrimonio sino una asociación • **their ~ was based on mutual respect** su relación se basaba en el respeto mutuo • **the ~ between government and industry** la alianza entre el gobierno y la industria
2 (*Comm*) (= *company*) sociedad *f* colectiva • **to be in ~ with sb** estar asociado con algn • **to go** *or* **enter into ~ (with sb)** asociarse (con algn) • **we work in ~ with our clients** trabajamos conjuntamente con nuestros clientes; ▹ **limited**
3 (= *position as partner*) • **they've offered me a ~** me han ofrecido hacerme socio
(CPD) ▸ **partnership agreement** contrato *m* de sociedad
partook [pɑːˈtʊk] (PT) *of* **partake**
partridge [ˈpɑːtrɪdʒ] (N) (PL: **partridges** *or* **partridge**) perdiz *f*
part-time [ˈpɑːtˈtaɪm] (ADV) a tiempo parcial (*Sp*), medio tiempo (*LAm*) • **to work part-time** trabajar a tiempo parcial *or* (*LAm*) medio tiempo
(ADJ) [*worker, job*] de media jornada, a tiempo parcial (*Sp*), de medio tiempo (*LAm*)
(N) (*Ind*) jornada *f* reducida • **to be on part-time** trabajar en horario de jornada reducida
part-timer [ˌpɑːtˈtaɪməʳ] (N) trabajador(a) *m/f* a tiempo parcial (*Sp*), trabajador(a) *m/f* a medio tiempo (*LAm*)
parturition [ˌpɑːtjʊəˈrɪʃən] (N) (*frm*) parturición *f*, parto *m*
partway [ˈpɑːtˌweɪ] (ADV) • **~ through the week** a mitad de la semana • **the wood had been sawn ~ through** la madera había sido serrada parcialmente • **I'll walk ~ with you** caminaré un trozo contigo • **it goes ~ toward explaining his strange behaviour** explica en parte su extraño comportamiento • **we're only ~ into** *or* **through the work** hemos hecho solo una parte del trabajo
party [ˈpɑːtɪ] (N) **1** (= *celebration*) fiesta *f* • **to give** *or* **have** *or* **throw a ~** dar *or* (*frm*) ofrecer una fiesta • IDIOM: • **the ~'s over** se acabó la fiesta; ▹ **house**
2 (*Pol*) partido *m* • **to join a ~** afiliarse a un partido, hacerse miembro de un partido
3 (= *group*) grupo *m* • **a ~ of tourists** un grupo de turistas • **we were only a small ~** éramos pocos, éramos un grupo pequeño
4 (*in dispute, contract*) parte *f* • **the parties concerned** los interesados, las partes interesadas • **the guilty/injured/innocent ~** la parte culpable/perjudicada/inocente • **to be (a) ~ to sth**: • **I will not be a ~ to any violence** no me voy a prestar a la violencia • **to be (a) ~ to an agreement** ser parte en un acuerdo • **to be (a) ~ to a crime** ser cómplice en un delito • **the parties to a dispute** las partes involucradas en una querella; ▹ **third, warring**
(VI)* (= *go to parties*) ir a fiestas; (= *have a good time*) irse de juerga*, irse de marcha (*Sp**) • **let's ~!** ¡vámonos de juerga!*, ¡vámonos de marcha! (*Sp**) • **where shall we ~ tonight?** ¿a qué fiesta vamos esta noche?
(CPD) ▸ **party animal** fiestero/a *m/f*, juerguista *mf* ▸ **party dress** vestido *m* de fiesta ▸ **party food** (= *nibbles*) canapés *mpl* ▸ **party game** (*for children*) juego *m* de fiestas; (*for adults*) juego *m* de sociedad ▸ **party hat** sombrero *m* de fiesta, gorro *m* de fiesta ▸ **party line** (*Telec*) línea *f* compartida • **the ~ line** (*Pol*) la línea del partido ▸ **party member** miembro *m* del partido ▸ **party mood** (= *mood for enjoying o.s.*) ganas *fpl* de fiesta • **to be in the ~ mood** tener ganas de fiesta ▸ **party music** música *f* de fiesta ▸ **party official** (*Pol*) funcionario/a *m/f* de partido ▸ **party piece** numerito *m* (de fiesta)* • **to do one's ~ piece** hacer su numerito* ▸ **party politics** (*gen*) política *fsing* de partido; (*pej*) partidismo *msing* (*pej*), politiqueo *msing* (*pej*) ▸ **party pooper*** aguafiestas *mf inv* ▸ **party spirit** espíritu *m* festivo • **we entered into the ~ spirit** nos empezó a entrar el espíritu festivo ▸ **party time** • **it's ~ time!** ¡es hora de fiesta! ▸ **party trick** truco *m* ▸ **party wall** pared *f* medianera
party-giver [ˈpɑːtɪgɪvəʳ] (N) • **they are great party-givers** organizan muchas fiestas
party-goer [ˈpɑːtɪˌgəʊəʳ] (N) (*gen*) asiduo/a *m/f* a fiestas; (*on specific occasion*) invitado/a *m/f* • **I'm not much of a party-goer** yo voy poco a las fiestas
party-going [ˈpɑːtiˌgəʊɪŋ] (N) • **he spends his time party-going instead of working** se pasa el tiempo yendo a fiestas en lugar de trabajar
partying* [ˈpɑːtɪɪŋ] (N) • **I'm not a great one for ~** no me gustan mucho las fiestas
party political [ˌpɑːtɪpəˈlɪtɪkəl] (ADJ) [*advantage, issue*] de(l) partido • **~ broadcast** emisión *f* de propaganda política, ≈ espacio *m* electoral
parvenu [ˈpɑːvənjuː] (N) advenedizo/a *m/f*
paschal [ˈpɑːskəl] (ADJ) pascual • **the Paschal Lamb** el cordero pascual
pas de deux [ˈpɑːdəˈdɜː] (N) paso *m* a dos
pasha [ˈpæʃə] (N) bajá *m*, pachá *m*
pashmina [pæʃˈmiːnə] (N) **1** (= *wool*) pashmina *f*
2 (= *shawl*) chal *m* de pashmina
(ADJ) [*scarf, shawl*] de pashmina
Pashtun [pʌʃˈtʊn] (ADJ) pashtún (*inv*)
(N) pashtún *mf inv*
pass [pɑːs] (N) **1** (= *permit*) (*gen*) pase *m*; (*Mil*) permiso *m*, pase *m* • **bus ~** abono *m or* pase *m* de autobús • **overnight ~** permiso *m or* pase *m* de pernocta • **press ~** pase *m* de prensa • **rail ~** abono *m or* pase *m* de ferrocarril • **security ~** pase *m* de seguridad • **visitor's ~** pase *m* de visitas • **weekend ~** permiso *m or* pase *m* de fin de semana; ▹ **boarding**
2 (*Sport*) pase *m* • **back ~** pase *m* hacia atrás • **forward ~** pase *m* adelantado
3 (*in exam*) aprobado *m* • **a ~ in biology** un aprobado en biología • **to get a ~ (in sth)** aprobar (algo) • **she got seven ~es** aprobó siete asignaturas
4 (*by conjuror*) pase *m*; (*by aircraft*) pasada *f*
5 (= *situation*) • **things have come to a pretty ~** ¡hasta dónde hemos llegado! • **things had reached such a ~ that …** las cosas habían llegado a tal extremo que …
6 (= *sexual approach*) • **to make a ~ at sb*** tirarle a algn los tejos*, intentar ligar con algn*
7 (*Geog*) puerto *m*, paso *m*; (*small*) desfiladero *m* • **mountain ~** puerto *m or* paso *m* de montaña
(VT) **1** (= *go past*) pasar; (= *go in front of*) pasar por delante de; (= *cross paths with*) cruzarse con; (*Aut*) (= *overtake*) adelantar, pasar, rebasar (*Mex*) • **the road ~es a farmyard** la carretera pasa por un corral • **the procession ~ed the royal stand** el desfile pasó por delante de la tribuna de Sus Majestades • **I ~ed them on the stairs** me crucé con ellos en las escaleras • **they ~ed each other on the way** se cruzaron en el camino • **he looked the other way as he ~ed me** miró al otro lado cuando nos cruzamos • **he tried to ~ me on the inside** (*Aut*) intentó adelantarme *or* pasarme por la derecha; (*in UK*) intentó adelantarme *or* pasarme por la izquierda
2 (= *surpass*) superar • **total membership has ~ed the six million mark** el número total de miembros supera los seis millones
3 (= *cross*) [+ *barrier, frontier, customs*] cruzar • **not a word has ~ed my lips** de mí no ha salido una palabra, no he dicho ni una palabra
4 (= *convey, transfer*) (*gen*) pasar; (*Sport*) [+ *ball*] pasar • **the gas is then ~ed along a pipe** el gas luego se pasa por una tubería • **to ~ sth down the line** pasar algo de mano en mano • **to ~ a dish round the table** pasar un plato entre todos los que están a la mesa • **to ~ sb sth** • **~ sth to sb** pasar algo a algn • **~ me the salt, please** ¿me pasas *or* alcanzas la sal, por favor? • **my application was ~ed to another department** pasaron mi solicitud a otro departamento; ▹ **buck, parcel, word**
5 (= *move in given direction*) pasar • **he ~ed his handkerchief over his face** se pasó el pañuelo por la cara • **to ~ a cloth over sth** limpiar algo con un paño • **he ~ed the rope round the axle/through the ring** pasó la cuerda por el eje/por el aro
6 (= *spend*) [+ *time*] pasar • **it ~es the time** ayuda a pasar el rato • IDIOM: • **to ~ the time of day with sb** charlar un rato con algn
7 (= *not fail*) [+ *exam, essay, candidate*] aprobar; [+ *inspection*] pasar • **he has just ~ed his driving test** acaba de aprobar el examen de

P

conducir; ▸ fit¹, muster
8 (Cine) [+ film] [censor] aprobar • the censors felt they could not ~ the film los censores sintieron que no podían aprobar la película • the film failed to ~ the censors la película no consiguió pasar la censura
9 (= approve) [+ law, bill motion] aprobar
10 (= express) [+ remark, comment] hacer • it would be unfair to ~ comment on his private life no sería justo hacer comentarios sobre su vida privada • to ~ (an) opinion on sth expresar una opinión acerca de algo • to ~ sentence (Jur) fallar, dictar sentencia • to ~ sentence on sb sentenciar or condenar a algn; ▸ judgment
11 (Med) [+ blood] echar • to ~ a stone expulsar un cálculo • to ~ a stool realizar una deposición, defecar • to ~ urine orinar • to ~ wind expulsar ventosidades or una ventosidad (frm); ▸ water
12 (criminally) [+ counterfeit money, stolen goods] pasar
VI 1 (= go past) pasar; (Aut) (= overtake) pasar, adelantar, rebasar (Mex) • I stood aside to let her ~ me puse a un lado para dejarle pasar • we ~ed in the corridor nos cruzamos en el pasillo • the procession was still ~ing an hour later seguían desfilando una hora más tarde; ▸ ship
2 (= move, go) pasar • to ~ behind/in front of sth/sb pasar por detrás/por delante de algo/algn • she ~ed right in front of me pasó justo por delante mío or de mí • messages ~ed back and forth between them se intercambiaban mensajes entre sí, se mandaban mensajes el uno al otro • ~ down the bus please! ¡vayan hacia el fondo del autobús, por favor! • to ~ into oblivion pasar al olvido • control of the business ~ed out of my hands la dirección de la empresa pasó a otras manos • to ~ out of sight perderse de vista • the bullet ~ed through her shoulder la bala le atravesó el hombro • ~ through the gate and turn left cruce la verja y gire a la izquierda • she knew what was ~ing through his mind sabía lo que se le estaba pasando por la cabeza • words ~ed between them intercambiaron algunas palabras (fuertes)
3 (= be transferred) pasar • the estate ~ed to my brother la herencia pasó a mi hermano
4 (Sport) hacer un pase
5 (= happen) • all that ~ed between them todo lo que hubo entre ellos • it came to ~ that ... (liter) aconteció que ... (liter)
6 (= go by) [time, deadline] pasar • as the years ~ed a medida que pasaban los años, con el paso de los años • how time ~es! ¡como pasa el tiempo! • the months ~ed into years los meses se convirtieron en años
7 (= disappear) [storm, pain, danger] pasar • it'll ~ eso pasará, eso se olvidará • once the danger had ~ed una vez pasado el peligro • the old order is ~ing el antiguo orden está desapareciendo • the rain had ~ed había dejado de llover
8 (in exam) aprobar
9 (= be approved) [bill, amendment] ser aprobado
10 (= be accepted) pasar • "will this do?" — "oh, it'll ~" —¿esto servirá? —bueno, pasará • what ~es in New York may not be good enough here lo que es aceptable en Nueva York puede no serlo aquí • to ~ for sth pasar por algo • she could easily ~ for 20 podría pasar fácilmente por una chica de 20 años • or what ~es nowadays for a hat o lo que pasa por or se llama sombrero hoy día • let it ~ no hagas caso, pásalo por alto • we can't let that ~! ¡eso no lo podemos consentir or pasar por alto!; ▸ unnoticed
11 (at cards, in quiz) • (I) ~! ¡paso! • I'm afraid I don't know, I'll have to ~ on that one me temo que no lo sé, no puedo contestar esa pregunta • I think I'll ~ on the hiking next time* creo que la próxima vez voy a pasar de la excursión*
CPD ▸ **pass degree** (Brit) título universitario inferior al "honours degree" (licenciatura) ▸ **pass key** llave f maestra ▸ **pass mark** aprobado m, nota f de aprobado ▸ **pass rate** índice m de aprobados

▸ **pass around, pass round** VT + ADV • a bottle of whisky was ~ed around se pasaron una botella de whisky de mano en mano or de uno a otro • you ~ round the biscuits pasa las galletas entre todos • to ~ round the hat pasar la gorra

▸ **pass away** VI + ADV 1 (euph) (= die) fallecer
2 (= disappear) desaparecer

▸ **pass back** VT + ADV 1 (= return) devolver • glass can be collected and ~ed back to glass manufacturers for recycling se puede recoger y devolver el vidrio al fabricante para su reciclaje • the benefits must be ~ed back to the consumer los beneficios deben repercutir en el consumidor
2 [+ message] transmitir
3 [+ ball] volver a pasar

▸ **pass by** VI + ADV 1 (= go past) pasar • I was just ~ing by and I saw your car estaba pasando por aquí y he visto tu coche • she would beg from the people ~ing by pedía limosna a la gente que pasaba
2 [time, occasion] pasar • as the hours ~ed by a medida que pasaban las horas
VT + ADV • life has ~ed her by la vida se le ha pasado sin enterarse, no ha disfrutado de la vida • fortune seemed to have ~ed him by la fortuna parecía haberle dejado de lado • don't let this opportunity ~ you by no dejes pasar (por alto) esta oportunidad
VI + PREP pasar por • I'll ~ by your place to pick you up pasaré por tu casa para recogerte

▸ **pass down** VT + ADV 1 (= transfer) [+ custom, disease, trait] pasar, transmitir; [+ inheritance] pasar • these beliefs were ~ed down from generation to generation estas creencias se fueron pasando or transmitiendo de generación en generación • it's been ~ed down through the family se ha ido heredando en la familia • the painting was ~ed down to my father and he ~ed it down to me el cuadro lo heredó mi padre y luego me lo pasó a mí • my clothes were always ~ed down from my elder sister yo siempre heredaba la ropa de mi hermana mayor • when you grow out of this coat you can ~ it down to your brother cuando este abrigo te quede pequeño se lo puedes pasar or dar a tu hermano
2 (= convey downwards) pasar • he ~ed the bags down to me me pasó las bolsas
VI + ADV 1 (= be transferred) [custom] pasar, transmitirse
2 (= be inherited) • the farm ~ed down to me yo heredé la granja

▸ **pass off** VI + ADV 1 (= happen) transcurrir • it all ~ed off without incident todo transcurrió sin percances
2 (= wear off) [headache, bad mood] pasarse • her headache ~ed off after an hour el dolor de cabeza se le pasó una hora después
VT + ADV 1 (= present as genuine) • to ~ sth/sb off as sth hacer pasar algo/a algn por algo • he ~ed the girl off as his sister hizo pasar a la chica por su hermana • to ~ o.s. off as sth hacerse pasar por algo • she tried to ~ herself off as an 18-year-old intentó hacerse pasar por una chica de 18 años
2 (= dismiss) • he tried to ~ it off as a joke intentó quitarle importancia haciendo ver que lo había dicho en broma

▸ **pass on** VT + ADV 1 (= transfer) [+ information] pasar, comunicar, dar; [+ message] (written) dar, pasar; (spoken) dar, comunicar; [+ object] pasar; [+ disease] [person] contagiar; [animal] transmitir • I didn't want her to ~ her cold on to me no quería que me contagiara el constipado • they ~ the increase on to the consumer hacen que el consumidor cargue con el incremento • we ~ our savings on to the customer los ahorros redundan en favor de nuestros clientes • Sheila's having a party, ~ it on!* Sheila va a dar una fiesta, ¡corre la voz!
2 (= put in contact) [+ person] • to ~ sb on to sb poner a algn en contacto con algn; (on telephone) poner a algn con algn • I was ~ed on to another doctor me mandaron a otro médico, me pusieron en contacto con otro médico • I'll ~ you on to my supervisor le pongo a mi supervisor
VI + ADV 1 (= proceed) pasar (to a) • they ~ed on to other matters pasaron a discutir otros asuntos • the man lowered his eyes and ~ed on el hombre bajó la vista y pasó de largo
2 (euph) (= die) fallecer

▸ **pass out** VI + ADV 1 (= faint) perder el conocimiento, desmayarse
2 (Mil) graduarse
VT + ADV (= distribute) repartir

▸ **pass over** VI + ADV 1 (= move overhead) • a flock of geese ~ed over una bandada de gansos voló por encima nuestro
2 (= cross over) • we ~ed over into France under cover of night cruzamos a Francia al amparo de la noche
3 (euph) (= die) fallecer
VT + ADV 1 (= omit) pasar por alto, omitir • he had ~ed over an important point había pasado por alto or omitido un punto muy importante • he was ~ed over for promotion a la hora de los ascensos lo dejaron de lado
2 (= hand over) dar, pasar • ~ over that butter, will you? ¿me das or pasas la mantequilla?

▸ **pass round** VT + ADV = pass around

▸ **pass through** VI + ADV 1 (= not stay) estar de paso • I'm just ~ing through estoy de paso nada más
2 (= go through) pasar • he wouldn't let me ~ through without identification no me dejaba pasar sin documentación
VI + PREP [+ town, country, gap] pasar por; [+ phase, crisis] pasar por, atravesar; [+ barrier] pasar

▸ **pass up** VT + ADV 1 (= forgo) echar a perder, desperdiciar • an opportunity like this was too good to ~ up una oportunidad así era demasiado buena para echarla a perder or desperdiciarla
2 (lit) [+ object] pasar

passable ['pɑːsəbl] ADJ 1 (= tolerable) pasable
2 [road] transitable

passably ['pɑːsəblɪ] ADV pasablemente • he spoke ~ good French hablaba francés bastante bien • she's doing ~ well at school los estudios le van bastante bien

passage ['pæsɪdʒ] N 1 (= corridor) pasillo m; (between buildings, underground) pasaje m; (= alley) callejón m • a house full of secret ~s una casa llena de pasadizos secretos
2 (Anat) conducto m • nasal ~s conductos nasales; ▸ back
3 (= voyage) travesía f, viaje m; (= fare) pasaje m • to work one's ~ trabajar a bordo a cambio del pasaje
4 (= access, way through) paso m • his

bodyguards forced a ~ through the crowds sus guardaespaldas se abrieron camino *or* paso entre la muchedumbre • **their win has given them an easy ~ to the final** han llegado fácilmente a la final tras esta victoria • **free ~** paso *m* libre • **right of ~** derecho *m* de paso • **safe ~** salvoconducto *m*
5 (= *progress*) paso *m* • **his ~ through life had not been easy** su paso por la vida no había sido fácil • **the opposition was giving the bill a rough ~ through Parliament** la oposición estaba obstruyendo la aprobación del proyecto de ley en el Parlamento • **the ~ of time** el paso del tiempo • **with the ~ of time** con el (paso del) tiempo; ▹ **bird**
6 (= *transition*) paso *m* • **one's ~ into womanhood/manhood** el paso de uno a la edad adulta • **the ~ of summer into autumn** el paso del verano al otoño • **the book charts her ~ into madness** el libro recoge su descenso a la locura • **to ease their ~ from a socialist to a market economy** para facilitar la transición *or* el paso de una economía socialista a una de mercado; ▹ **rite**
7 (= *section*) [*of book, music*] pasaje *m*
(CPD) ▸ **passage money**† pasaje *m*

passageway ['pæsɪdʒweɪ] (N) (*in house*) pasillo *m*, corredor *m*; (*between buildings etc*) pasaje *m*

passbook ['pɑːsbʊk] (N) libreta *f* de ahorros

passcard ['pɑːskɑːd] (N) (*also Internet*) tarjeta *f* de acceso

passé ['pæseɪ] (ADJ) pasado de moda

passel ['pæsəl] (N) (*US*) muchedumbre *f*

passenger ['pæsndʒə^{r}] (N) **1** pasajero/a *m/f*; ▹ **fellow, foot**
2 (*pej*) parásito *m* • **I felt like a ~** me sentía como un parásito • **there's no room for ~s in this company** en esta empresa no hay lugar para los gandules
(CPD) [*jet, ship, train*] de pasajeros ▸ **passenger door** (*Aut*) puerta *f* del pasajero ▸ **passenger enquiries** información *fsing* (para pasajeros) ▸ **passenger ferry** ferry *m* (de pasajeros) ▸ **passenger list** lista *f* de pasajeros ▸ **passenger miles** millas-pasajero *fpl* ▸ **passenger seat** (*Aut*) asiento *m* del pasajero ▸ **passenger ship** barco *m* de pasajeros ▸ **passenger side** [*of car*] lado *m* del pasajero • **he smashed into the ~ side of the car** chocó contra el lado del pasajero • **on the ~ side** en el lado del pasajero ▸ **passenger traffic** tráfico *m* de pasajeros

passe-partout ['pæspɑːtuː] (N) paspartú *m*, passe partout *m*

passer-by [ˈpɑːsəˈbaɪ] (N) (PL: **passers-by**) transeúnte *mf*

passim ['pæsɪm] (ADV) passim

passing ['pɑːsɪŋ] (ADJ) [*fad*] pasajero; [*glance*] rápido, superficial; [*remark*] hecho de paso • **a ~ car** un coche que pasaba • **with each ~ day it gets more difficult** cada día se hace más difícil • **~ fancy** capricho *m* • **the story aroused no more than ~ interest** la noticia no despertó más que un interés pasajero • **the speech made only a ~ reference to the Middle East** el discurso hizo solo una breve alusión a Oriente Medio • **he bears more than a ~ resemblance to Rock Hudson** su parecido con Rock Hudson es notable
(N) **1** (= *disappearance*) [*of custom, tradition*] desaparición *f*; (*euph*) (= *death*) fallecimiento *m* • **with the ~ of the years** con el paso de los años, conforme van pasando los años • **to mention sth in ~** mencionar algo de paso *or* pasada
2 (*US*) (*Aut*) adelantamiento *m*
3 (*Parl*) aprobación *f*
(CPD) ▸ **passing bell** toque *m* de difuntos ▸ **passing lane** (*US*) (*Aut*) carril *m* de adelantamiento ▸ **passing place** (*Brit*) (*Aut*) apartadero *m* ▸ **passing shot** (*Tennis*) tiro *m* pasado

passing-out [ˌpɑːsɪŋˈaʊt] (N) graduación *f*
(CPD) ▸ **passing-out parade** desfile *m* de promoción

passion ['pæʃən] (N) **1** (= *love*) (*sexual, fig*) pasión *f* • **his ~ for accuracy** su pasión por la exactitud • **I have a ~ for shellfish** el marisco me apasiona; ▹ **crime**
2 (= *fervour, emotion*) pasión *f* • **he spoke with great ~** habló con gran pasión • **political ~s are running high** las pasiones políticas están caldeadas • **she has taken to golf with a ~** ha empezado a jugar al golf y le apasiona
3 (= *anger*) cólera *f*, pasión *f* • **to be in a ~** estar encolerizado • **to do sth in a fit of ~** hacer algo en un arrebato *or* un arranque de cólera *or* pasión • **to fly into a ~** montar en cólera, encolerizarse
4 (*Rel*) • **the Passion** la Pasión • **the St John/St Matthew Passion** la Pasión según San Juan/San Mateo
(CPD) ▸ **passion fruit** granadilla *f* ▸ **passion killer** • **there's no greater ~ killer than predictability** nada acaba con la pasión más rápidamente que la previsibilidad ▸ **Passion play** misterio *m* ▸ **Passion Sunday** Domingo *m* de Pasión

passionate ['pæʃənɪt] (ADJ) [*affair, love, kiss*] apasionado; [*believer, supporter*] ardiente, ferviente; [*desire*] ardiente, vehemente; [*speech*] apasionado, vehemente; [*belief*] inquebrantable; [*interest*] enorme • **he is ~ in his desire to achieve this** tiene un deseo ardiente *or* vehemente de conseguir esto • **to be ~ about sth** ser un apasionado de algo • **we're both ~ gardeners** a los dos nos apasiona *or* entusiasma la jardinería • **she has a ~ hatred of conservatism** odia a muerte el conservadurismo

passionately ['pæʃənɪtlɪ] (ADV) [*love, embrace, kiss*] apasionadamente, con pasión; [*believe, desire*] ardientemente, fervientemente • **she argued ~ in his defence** abogó con vehemencia en su favor, lo defendió con vehemencia • **he was ~ devoted to his sister** sentía una devoción ciega por su hermana • **I was ~ in love with him** estaba locamente enamorada de él, lo amaba apasionadamente *or* con pasión

passionflower ['pæʃən,flaʊə^{r}] (N) pasionaria *f*

passionless ['pæʃənlɪs] (ADJ) [*relationship*] sin pasión, frío

passive ['pæsɪv] (ADJ) (*gen*) pasivo; (= *inactive*) inactivo
(N) (*Ling*) voz *f* pasiva
(CPD) ▸ **passive resistance** resistencia *f* pasiva ▸ **passive smoking** fumar *m* pasivo

passively ['pæsɪvlɪ] (ADV) pasivamente

passiveness ['pæsɪvnɪs] (N), **passivity** [pæ'sɪvɪtɪ] (N) pasividad *f*

Passover ['pɑːsəʊvə^{r}] (N) Pascua *f* (judía)

passphrase ['pɑːsfreɪz] (N) contraseña *f* (*en forma de frase*)

passport ['pɑːspɔːt] (N) pasaporte *m* • **the ~ to fame** el pasaporte a la fama • **the money was his ~ to a new life** el dinero le abrió las puertas a una nueva vida
(CPD) ▸ **passport control** control *m* de pasaportes ▸ **passport holder** • **British ~ holder** titular *mf* de pasaporte británico ▸ **passport office** oficina *f* de pasaportes ▸ **passport photo(graph)** foto *f* de pasaporte

password ['pɑːswɜːd] (N) (*gen*) contraseña *f*, santo *m* y seña; (*Comput*) contraseña *f* de acceso

past [pɑːst] (ADV) **1** (*in place*) • **she walked ~ slowly** pasó despacio • **the days flew ~** los días pasaron volando • **to march ~** desfilar • **to run/rush ~** pasar corriendo/precipitadamente
2 (*in time*) • **it's ten ~** son y diez • **I've been waiting since half ~** llevo esperando desde y media
(PREP) **1** (*in place*) **a** (= *passing by*) por delante de • **we went ~ your house** pasamos por delante de tu casa • **we drove ~ a flock of sheep** pasamos al lado de un rebaño de ovejas con el coche
b (= *beyond*) más allá de • **just ~ the town hall** un poco más allá del Ayuntamiento • **it's the first house ~ the park** es la primera casa después del parque • **first you have to get ~ a fierce dog** antes de entrar vas a tener que vértelas con un perro fiero • **we couldn't get ~ the crowds of people** no pudimos abrirnos paso entre la muchedumbre • **she just pushed ~ me** pasó pegándome un empujón • **to run ~ sb** pasar a algn corriendo
2 (*in time*) • **quarter/half ~ four** las cuatro y cuarto/media • **at twenty ~ four** a las cuatro y veinte • **it's ~ twelve** son las doce pasadas • **it's long ~ the time he normally gets back** él normalmente hubiese llegado hace tiempo • **it's ~ your bedtime** ya tenías que estar durmiendo
3 (= *beyond the limits of*) • **he's ~ 40** tiene más de 40 años • **it's ~ mending** ya no tiene remedio • **it's ~ belief** es increíble • **I'm ~ caring** ya me trae sin cuidado • **it's ~ endurance** es intolerable • IDIOMS: • **to be ~ it*** [*person*] estar para el arrastre* • **those jeans are a bit ~ it** esos vaqueros ya están como para jubilarlos* • **I wouldn't put it ~ him*** no me extrañaría en él, lo creo capaz hasta de eso
(ADJ) **1** (= *previous*) [*occasion*] anterior • **~ experience tells me not to trust him** sé por experiencia que no debo fiarme de él • **I'm not interested in his ~ life** no me interesa su pasado • **we must have met in a ~ life** seguro que nos hemos conocido en una vida anterior • **in ~ years** en años anteriores
2 (= *former*) antiguo • **~ president of ...** antiguo presidente de ..., ex presidente de ... • **her ~ and present pupils** sus alumnos de ayer y de hoy
3 (= *most recent, last*) último • **the ~ few weeks have been hell** las últimas semanas han sido un verdadero infierno • **she has got worse in the ~ few days** su condición ha empeorado en los últimos días • **what has happened over the ~ week/year?** ¿qué ha pasado en la última semana/el último año?
4 (= *over*) • **all that is ~ now** todo eso ya ha pasado, todo eso ya ha quedado atrás • **what's ~ is ~** lo pasado, pasado (está) • **those days are ~ now** aquellos tiempos pasaron ya • **for some time ~** de un tiempo a esta parte • **in times ~** antiguamente, antaño (*liter*)
(N) **1** (= *past times*) • **the ~** el pasado • **you mustn't dwell on the ~** no debes pensar demasiado en el pasado • **you can't change the ~** no puedes cambiar el pasado • **in the ~ it was considered bad manners to ...** antes *or* antiguamente se consideraba de mala educación hacer ... • **I've always done it like this in the ~** yo siempre lo he hecho así • **you're living in the ~** estás viviendo en el pasado • **it's a thing of the ~** pertenece a la historia
2 [*of person*] pasado *m*; [*of place*] historia *f* • **a woman with a ~** una mujer con pasado • **a town with a ~** una ciudad con historia
3 (*Ling*) pasado *m*, pretérito *m*
(CPD) ▸ **past master** (*Brit*) • IDIOM: • **to be a ~**

master at (doing) sth ser un(a) maestro/a consumado/a en (el arte de hacer) algo ▸ **past participle** (*Ling*) participio *m* pasado *or* pasivo ▸ **past perfect** (*Ling*) pluscuamperfecto *m* ▸ **past tense** (*Ling*) (tiempo *m*) pasado *m*

pasta [ˈpæstə] (N) pasta(s) *f(pl)*

paste [peɪst] (N) **1** (= *substance, consistency*) pasta *f*; (*Culin*) pasta *f*; (= *glue*) engrudo *m*, cola *f* • **anchovy ~** pasta *f* de anchoas • **fish ~** paté *m* de pescado • **tomato ~** concentrado *m* de tomate
2 (= *diamond-like material*) estrás *m*; (= *costume jewellery*) bisutería *f*, joyas *fpl* de imitación *or* de fantasía • **it's only ~** es bisutería
(VT) **1** (= *put paste on*) engomar, encolar; (= *stick with paste*) pegar • **to ~ sth into/onto sth** pegar algo a algo • **to ~ sth to a wall** pegar algo a una pared
2* (= *beat*) pegar; (*Sport*) cascar*, dar una paliza a*
(CPD) [*jewellery*] (*lit*) de estrás; (*costume*) de fantasía
▸ **paste up** (VT + ADV) [+ *notice*] pegar; (*Typ*) armar

pasteboard [ˈpeɪstbɔːd] (N) cartón *m*
(CPD) de cartón

pastel [ˈpæstəl] (N) **1** (= *crayon, colour*) pastel *m*; (= *drawing*) pintura *f* al pastel
2 pastels (= *crayons*) pasteles *mpl*; (= *colours*) colores *mpl* pastel
(ADJ) [*colour, shade, blue*] pastel; [*drawing*] al pastel

pastern [ˈpæstɜːn] (N) cuartilla *f* (del caballo)

pasteurization [ˌpæstəraɪˈzeɪʃən] (N) paste(u)rización *f*

pasteurize [ˈpæstəraɪz] (VT) paste(u)rizar

pasteurized [ˈpæstəraɪzd] (ADJ) paste(u)rizado

pastiche [pæsˈtiːʃ] (N) pastiche *m*, imitación *f*

pastille [ˈpæstɪl] (N) pastilla *f*

pastime [ˈpɑːstaɪm] (N) pasatiempo *m*

pasting* [ˈpeɪstɪŋ] (N) paliza *f* • **to give sb a ~** dar una paliza a algn • **the city took a ~ during the war** la ciudad fue muy castigada durante la guerra • **he got a ~ from the critics** los críticos fueron muy duros con él

pastor [ˈpɑːstəʳ] (N) pastor(a) *m/f*

pastoral [ˈpɑːstərəl] (ADJ) [*care, economy*] pastoral; (*Rel*) pastoral; (*Literat*) pastoril • **~ letter** (*Rel*) pastoral *f*
(N) (*Rel*) pastoral *f*

pastrami [pəˈstrɑːmɪ] (N) *especie de embutido ahumado a base de carne de vaca con especias*

pastry [ˈpeɪstrɪ] (N) (= *dough*) masa *f*; (= *cake*) pastel *m*
(CPD) ▸ **pastry board** tabla *f* de amasar ▸ **pastry brush** cepillo *m* de repostería ▸ **pastry case** cobertura *f* de pasta ▸ **pastry chef, pastry cook** repostero/a *m/f*, pastelero/a *m/f* ▸ **pastry cutter** cortador *m* de masa ▸ **pastry shop** pastelería *f*, repostería *f*

pasturage [ˈpɑːstjʊrɪdʒ] (N) = **pastureland**

pasture [ˈpɑːstʃəʳ] (N) (= *field*) pasto *m*, prado *m*; (= *pastureland*) tierra(s) *f(pl)* de pastoreo • **to put animals out to ~** apacentar *or* pastorear el ganado • **they're putting me out to ~** (*fig*) (*hum*) me echan al pasto (como a caballo viejo) • IDIOM: • **to seek ~s new** buscar nuevos horizontes
(VT) [+ *animals*] apacentar, pastorear; [+ *grass*] comer, pacer
(VI) pastar, pacer

pastureland [ˈpɑːstʃəlænd] (N) pradera *f*, tierra(s) *f(pl)* de pastoreo

pasty¹ [ˈpæstɪ] (N) (*Brit*) (= *pie*) pastel *m* (de carne), empanada *f*

pasty² [ˈpeɪstɪ] (ADJ) (COMPAR: **pastier**, SUPERL: **pastiest**) [*substance*] pastoso; [*complexion*] pálido • **to look ~** estar pálido

pasty-faced [ˈpeɪstɪˌfeɪst] (ADJ) pálido, de cara pálida

pat¹ [pæt] (N) **1** (= *light blow*) palmadita *f*, golpecito *m*; (= *caress*) caricia *f* • **to give sb a pat on the back** (*lit*) dar a algn una palmada en la espalda; (*fig*) felicitar a algn • **to give o.s. a pat on the back** (*fig*) felicitarse a sí mismo
2 [*of butter*] porción *f*
(VT) (= *touch*) [+ *hair, face etc*] tocar, pasar la mano por; (= *tap*) dar una palmadita en; [+ *child's head, dog*] acariciar

pat² [pæt] (ADV) • **he knows it (off) pat** lo sabe al dedillo *or* de memoria • **he always has an excuse just pat** siempre tiene su excusa lista • **the answer came too pat** dio su respuesta con demasiada prontitud • IDIOM: • **to stand pat** (*US*) mantenerse firme *or* en sus trece
(ADJ) [*answer*] fácil

Pat [pæt] (N) *familiar form of* **Patrick, Patricia**

pat. (ABBR) (= **patent(ed)**) pat.

Patagonia [ˌpætəˈgəʊnɪə] (N) Patagonia *f*

Patagonian [ˌpætəˈgəʊnɪən] (ADJ) patagón, patagónico
(N) patagón/ona *m/f*

patch [pætʃ] (N) **1** (= *mend*) (*on clothing*) remiendo *m*, parche *m*; (*on tyre, wound*) parche *m* • IDIOM: • **this book's not a ~ on the other one*** este libro no tiene ni punto de comparación con el otro
2 (= *stain*) mancha *f*; (= *small area*) pedazo *m* • **a ~ of oil** una mancha de aceite • **a ~ of blue sky** un pedazo de cielo azul, un claro • **a ~ of blue flowers** un área de flores azules • **the team is going through a bad ~** el equipo está pasando por una mala racha • **then we hit a bad ~ of road** dimos luego con un tramo de carretera bastante malo
3 (= *piece of land*) parcela *f*, terreno *m*; ▹ **vegetable**
4* (= *territory*) territorio *m* • **but this is their ~** pero este es territorio de ellos • **they must get off our ~** tienen que largarse de nuestro territorio*
5 (*Comput*) ajuste *m*
(VT) [+ *garment, hole*] remendar, poner remiendos a • **a pair of ~ed jeans** unos vaqueros con remiendos
▸ **patch together** (VT + ADV) [+ *solution, agreement, coalition, government*] improvisar
▸ **patch up** (VT + ADV) [+ *clothes*] remendar provisionalmente; [+ *car, machine*] arreglar provisionalmente; [+ *cut, wound*] vendar; [+ *marriage, relationship*] salvar • **the doctor soon ~ed him up** el doctor enseguida le curó las heridas • **to ~ things up (with sb)** hacer las paces (con algn) • **they ~ed up their differences** resolvieron sus diferencias

patchwork [ˈpætʃwɜːk] (N) **1** labor *f* de retazos, arpillería *f* (*LAm*)
2 (*fig*) • **a ~ of fields** un mosaico de campos • **their policy is a ~ of half-measures** su política es un conjunto fragmentario de medias tintas
(CPD) ▸ **patchwork quilt** edredón *m* de retazos multicolores

patchy [ˈpætʃɪ] (ADJ) (COMPAR: **patchier**, SUPERL: **patchiest**) [*performance*] desigual, poco uniforme; [*knowledge*] incompleto; [*clouds*] disperso; [*fog*] discontinuo

pate† [peɪt] (N) mollera *f*, testa *f* • **bald ~** calva *f*

pâté [ˈpæteɪ] (N) paté *m*

patella [pəˈtelə] (N) (PL: **patellae** [pəˈteliː]) rótula *f*

paten [ˈpætən] (N) patena *f*

patent [ˈpeɪtənt] (ADJ) **1** (*frm*) (= *obvious*) patente, evidente
2 (= *patented*) [*invention*] patentado
(N) patente *f* • **~ applied for** • **~ pending** patente en trámite • **to take out a ~** obtener una patente
(VT) patentar
(CPD) ▸ **patent agent** agente *mf* de patentes ▸ **Patent and Trademark Office** (*US*) = **Patent Office** ▸ **patent infringement** violación *f* de patentes ▸ **patent law** derecho *m* de patentes ▸ **patent leather** charol *m* ▸ **patent medicine** específico *m* ▸ **patent office** oficina *f* de patentes ▸ **Patent Office** (*Brit*) *registro de la propiedad industrial* ▸ **patent rights** derechos *mpl* de patente

patentable [ˈpeɪtəntəbl] (ADJ) patentable

patentee [ˌpeɪtənˈtiː] (N) poseedor(a) *m/f* de patente

patently [ˈpeɪtəntlɪ] (ADV) evidentemente • **to be ~ obvious** saltar a la vista, ser evidente • **a ~ untrue statement** una declaración de evidente falsedad

patentor [ˈpeɪtəntəʳ] (N) *individuo u organismo que otorga una patente*

pater†* [ˈpeɪtəʳ] (N) (*esp Brit*) • **the ~** el viejo*

paterfamilias [ˈpeɪtəfəˈmɪlɪæs] (N) (PL: **patresfamilias** [ˌpɑːtreɪzfəˈmɪlɪæs]) padre *m* de familia

paternal [pəˈtɜːnl] (ADJ) **1** (= *fatherly*) [*love, feelings*] paterno, paternal; [*authority*] paterno; [*pride*] de padre
2 (= *on the father's side*) [*grandparent*] paterno, por parte de padre
(CPD) ▸ **paternal grandfather** abuelo *m* paterno, abuelo *m* por parte del padre ▸ **paternal grandmother** abuela *f* paterna, abuela *f* por parte del padre

paternalism [pəˈtɜːnəlɪzəm] (N) paternalismo *m*

paternalist [pəˈtɜːnəlɪst] (ADJ) paternalista

paternalistic [pəˌtɜːnəˈlɪstɪk] (ADJ) paternalista

paternally [pəˈtɜːnəlɪ] (ADV) paternalmente • **he said ~** dijo paternal

paternity [pəˈtɜːnɪtɪ] (N) paternidad *f*
(CPD) ▸ **paternity leave** permiso *m* por paternidad, licencia *f* de paternidad ▸ **paternity suit** (*Jur*) litigio *m* de paternidad ▸ **paternity test** prueba *f* de la paternidad

paternoster [ˈpætəˈnɒstəʳ] (N) padrenuestro *m*

path [pɑːθ] (N) (PL: **paths** [pɑːðz]) **1** (*also* **pathway, footpath**) (= *track*) (*surfaced*) camino *m*; (*unsurfaced*) camino *m*, sendero *m* • **feet had worn a ~ in the rock** las pisadas habían formado un camino *or* un sendero sobre la piedra • **they hacked a ~ through the jungle** se abrieron camino a machetazos a través de la jungla; ▹ **cycle, garden**
2 (= *course*) [*of person, vehicle*] camino *m*; [*of missile, sun, storm*] trayectoria *f* • **the earth's ~ round the sun** la trayectoria de la tierra alrededor del sol • **the hurricane destroyed everything in its ~** el huracán destruyó todo a su paso • **he stepped into the ~ of an oncoming car** se cruzó en el camino de un coche que se acercaba; ▹ **flight**
3 (= *way forward*) paso *m* • **a group of reporters blocked his ~** un grupo de periodistas le cerraba el paso
4 (*fig*) **a** (= *route*) camino *m* • **I hope never to cross ~s with him again** espero no volvérmelo a encontrar nunca, espero no volver a toparme con él nunca • **our ~s first crossed in Milan** nuestros caminos se cruzaron por primera vez en Milán, la primera vez que coincidimos fue en Milán • **these measures helped smooth the ~ to**

independence estas medidas ayudaron a allanar *or* facilitar el camino hacia la independencia • IDIOM: • **to beat a ~ to sb's door** asediar a algn; ▹ **garden, primrose**
b (= *course of action*) • **I wouldn't go down that ~ if I were you** yo en tu lugar no haría eso

path-breaking ['pɑːθbreɪkɪŋ] (ADJ) (*esp US*) revolucionario

pathetic [pə'θetɪk] (ADJ) **1** (= *piteous*) [*sight*] patético, lastimoso; [*smile*] conmovedor • **it was ~ to see him like that** daba verdadera lástima *or* pena verlo así • **a ~ creature** un pobre infeliz
2* (= *useless*) [*excuse, attempt*] pobre • **it was a ~ performance** fue una actuación penosa *or* que daba pena • **~, isn't it?** da pena ¿no?
(CPD) ▸ **pathetic fallacy** (*Literat*) engaño *m* sentimental, falacia *f* patética

pathetically [pə'θetɪklɪ] (ADV) **1** (= *piteously*) [*whimper, moan*] lastimeramente; [*say*] con voz lastimera • **~ thin/weak** tan delgado/débil que da/daba pena • **she was ~ grateful** su gratitud resultaba penosa
2 (= *uselessly*) [*play, perform*] que da/daba pena • **a ~ inadequate answer** una respuesta patética

pathfinder ['pɑːθ,faɪndəʳ] (N) explorador(a) *m/f*; (*Mil*) *avión o paracaidista que indica un objetivo militar dejando caer bengalas*

path lab ['pæθlæb] (N) (= **pathology laboratory**) laboratorio *m* de patología

pathogen ['pæθədʒen] (N) patógeno *m*

pathogenic [pæθə'dʒenɪk] (ADJ) patógeno

pathological [,pæθə'lɒdʒɪkəl] (ADJ) (*lit, fig*) patológico

pathologically [,pæθə'lɒdʒɪkəlɪ] (ADV) patológicamente • **to be ~ jealous** tener celos patológicos

pathologist [pə'θɒlədʒɪst] (N) patólogo/a *m/f*

pathology [pə'θɒlədʒɪ] (N) patología *f*

pathos ['peɪθɒs] (N) patetismo *m*

pathway ['pɑːθweɪ] (N) camino *m*, sendero *m*; = **path**

patience ['peɪʃəns] (N) **1** paciencia *f* • **my ~ is exhausted** se me ha acabado *or* agotado la paciencia • **you must have ~** hay que tener paciencia • **I have no ~ with you** ya no te aguanto más • **he has no ~ with fools** no soporta a los tontos • **to lose one's ~ (with sth/sb)** perder la paciencia (con algo/algn) • **to try sb's ~** poner a prueba la paciencia de algn • IDIOMS: • **to have the ~ of a saint** tener más paciencia que un santo • **to possess one's soul in ~** armarse de paciencia
2 (*Brit*) (*Cards*) solitario *m* • **to play ~** hacer un solitario

patient¹ ['peɪʃənt] (ADJ) [*person*] paciente; [*explanation*] detallado • **to be ~** tener paciencia • **you must be ~** hay que tener paciencia • **we have been ~ long enough!** ¡se nos está acabando *or* agotando la paciencia! • **to be ~ with sb** tener paciencia con algn

patient² ['peɪʃənt] (N) (*on doctor's list*) paciente *mf*; (*having medical treatment*) enfermo/a *m/f*; ▹ **cancer, mental**
(CPD) ▸ **patient care** cuidado *m* de los enfermos ▸ **patient confidentiality** confidencialidad *f* del paciente

patiently ['peɪʃəntlɪ] (ADV) con paciencia, pacientemente

patina ['pætɪnə] (N) pátina *f*

patio ['pætɪəʊ] (N) patio *m*
(CPD) ▸ **patio doors** puertas *fpl* que dan al patio ▸ **patio furniture** muebles *mpl* de jardín ▸ **patio heater** estufa *f* de terraza

patisserie [pə'tiːsərɪ] (N) **1** (= *shop*) pastelería *f*
2 (= *cakes and pastries*) pasteles *mpl*

patois ['pætwɑː] (N) (PL: **patois**) dialecto *m*, jerga *f*

pat. pend. (ABBR) = **patent pending**

patriarch ['peɪtrɪɑːk] (N) (*Rel*) patriarca *m*

patriarchal [,peɪtrɪ'ɑːkəl] (ADJ) patriarcal

patriarchy ['peɪtrɪ,ɑːkɪ] (N) patriarcado *m*

Patricia [pə'trɪʃə] (N) Patricia

patrician [pə'trɪʃən] (ADJ) patricio
(N) patricio/a *m/f*

patricide ['pætrɪsaɪd] (N) (= *crime*) patricidio *m*; (= *person*) patricida *mf*

Patrick ['pætrɪk] (N) Patricio

patrimony ['pætrɪmənɪ] (N) patrimonio *m*

patriot ['peɪtrɪət] (N) patriota *mf*

patriotic [,pætrɪ'ɒtɪk] (ADJ) patriótico

patriotically [pætrɪ'ɒtɪkəlɪ] (ADV) patrióticamente

patriotism ['pætrɪətɪzəm] (N) patriotismo *m*

patrol [pə'trəʊl] (N) (*gen*) patrulla *f*; (= *night patrol*) ronda *f*; (*in Scouts*) patrulla *f* • **to be on ~** estar de patrulla
(VT) [+ *streets*] patrullar por; [+ *frontier*] patrullar • **the frontier is not ~led** la frontera no tiene patrullas
(VI) patrullar • **he ~s up and down** se pasea de un lado a otro
(CPD) ▸ **patrol boat** patrullero *m*, (lancha *f*) patrullera *f* ▸ **patrol car** (*Brit*) coche *m* patrulla ▸ **patrol leader** jefe *m* de patrulla ▸ **patrol wagon** (*US*) coche *m* celular

patrolman [pə'trəʊlmən] (N) (PL: **patrolmen**) **1** (*US*) guardia *m*, policía *m*
2 (*Aut*) *mecánico del servicio de ayuda en carretera*

patrolwoman [pə'trəʊl,wʊmən] (N) (PL: **patrolwomen**) **1** (*US*) mujer *f* policía
2 (*Brit*) (*Aut*) *mecánica del servicio de ayuda en carretera*

patron ['peɪtrən] (N) [*of charity, society*] patrocinador(a) *m/f*; (*Comm*) [*of shop, hotel*] cliente/a *m/f* • **a ~ of the arts** un mecenas
(CPD) ▸ **patron saint** patrono/a *m/f*

patronage ['pætrənɪdʒ] (N) (= *support*) patrocinio *m*; (= *clients*) clientela *f*; [*of the arts*] mecenazgo *m*; (*political*) apoyo *m*; (*Rel*) patronato *m* • **under the ~ of** patrocinado por, bajo los auspicios de

patroness ['peɪtrənes] (N) [*of enterprise*] patrocinadora *f*; [*of the arts*] mecenas *f*

patronize ['pætrənaɪz] (VT) **1** (= *treat condescendingly*) tratar con condescendencia
2 (= *be customer of*) [+ *shop*] ser cliente de, comprar en; [+ *hotel, cinema*] frecuentar; [+ *services*] usar, utilizar • **the shop is well ~d** la tienda tiene mucha clientela, la tienda está muy acreditada
3 (= *support*) [+ *enterprise*] patrocinar, apoyar

patronizing ['pætrənaɪzɪŋ] (ADJ) [*person, attitude*] condescendiente • **a few ~ remarks** unas cuantas observaciones dichas en tono condescendiente

patronizingly ['pætrənaɪzɪŋlɪ] (ADV) con condescendencia

patronymic [,pætrə'nɪmɪk] (ADJ) patronímico
(N) patronímico *m*

patsy* ['pætsɪ] (N) (*US*) bobo/a *m/f*, primo* *m*

patten ['pætn] (N) zueco *m*, chanclo *m*

patter¹* ['pætəʳ] (N) (= *talk*) labia *f*; [*of salesman*] rollo* *m*, discursito* *m* • **the guy has some very clever ~** el tipo *or* (*Sp*) el tío tiene unos argumentos muy hábiles
(VI) (*also* **patter on**) charlar, parlotear (**about de**)

patter² ['pætəʳ] (N) [*of feet*] golpeteo *m*; [*of rain*] tamborileo *m* • **we shall soon hear the ~ of tiny feet** (*hum*) pronto habrá un niño en la casa
(VI) [*feet*] golpetear; (*rain*) golpetear, tamborilear; (*also* **patter about**) [*person, small animal*] corretear • **he ~ed over to the door** fue con pasos ligeros a la puerta

pattern ['pætən] (N) **1** (= *design*) dibujo *m* • **a fabric in** *or* **with a floral ~** una tela con un dibujo *or* diseño floral • **to draw a ~** hacer un dibujo
2 (*Sew, Knitting*) patrón *m*, molde *m* (*S. Cone*)
3 (*fig*) (= *system, order*) • **a clear ~ began to emerge** empezaron a surgir unas pautas definidas • **behaviour ~** modelo *m* de comportamiento • **a healthy eating ~** unos hábitos alimenticios sanos • **the ~ of events** el curso de los hechos • **to follow a ~** seguir unas pautas • **my daily routine doesn't follow any set ~** mi rutina diaria no sigue unas pautas definidas • **it is following the usual ~** se está desarrollando como siempre *or* según las pautas • **a system of government on the British ~** un sistema de gobierno basado en el modelo británico • **it set a ~ for other conferences** marcó las pautas para otros congresos, creó el modelo para otros congresos • **sleep ~(s)** hábitos *mpl* de dormir • **weather ~(s)** condiciones *fpl* meteorológicas • **work ~(s)** costumbres *fpl* de trabajo
(VT) **1** (= *model*) • **to ~ sth after** *or* **on sth**: • **a building ~ed after a 14th century chapel** un edificio modelado sobre una capilla del siglo XIV • **action movies ~ed on Rambo** películas *fpl* de acción que siguen el modelo de Rambo
2 (= *mark*) estampar
(CPD) ▸ **pattern book** [*of wallpaper, fabrics*] muestrario *m*; (*Sew, Knitting*) libro *m* de patrones ▸ **pattern recognition** reconocimiento *m* de formas

patterned ['pætənd] (ADJ) estampado

patterning ['pætənɪŋ] (N) diseño *m*, dibujo *m*

pattern-maker ['pætən'meɪkəʳ] (N) carpintero/a *m/f* modelista

patty ['pætɪ] (N) empanada *f*
(CPD) ▸ **patty pan** molde *m* para empanadas

paucity ['pɔːsɪtɪ] (N) escasez *f*, insuficiencia *f*

Paul [pɔːl] (N) Pablo; (= *Saint*) Pablo; (= *Pope*) Paulo; ▹ **John**

Pauline¹ ['pɔːlaɪn] (ADJ) • **the ~ Epistles** las Epístolas de San Pablo

Pauline² ['pɔːliːn] (N) Paulina

paunch [pɔːntʃ] (N) panza* *f*, barriga* *f* • **to have a ~** tener panza*, ser barrigón*

paunchy ['pɔːntʃɪ] (ADJ) (COMPAR: **paunchier**, SUPERL: **paunchiest**) panzudo*, barrigudo*

pauper ['pɔːpəʳ] (N) pobre *mf*, indigente *mf* • **~'s grave** fosa *f* común

pauperism ['pɔːpərɪzəm] (N) pauperismo *m*

pauperization [,pɔːpəraɪ'zeɪʃən] (N) pauperización *f*, empobrecimiento *m*

pauperize ['pɔːpəraɪz] (VT) pauperizar, empobrecer

pause [pɔːz] (N) **1** (= *interruption*) pausa *f* (*also Mus*); (= *silence*) silencio *m*; (= *rest*) descanso *m* • **after a moment's ~ he went on speaking** tras una breve pausa continuó hablando • **there was a ~ while the rest came in** se hizo una pausa mientras entraban los demás • **there was a ~ for refreshments** hubo un descanso para tomar refrigerios • **there was an awkward ~ in the conversation** se produjo un silencio incómodo en medio de la conversación • **to give sb ~** • **give ~ to sb** hacer vacilar a algn • **to give sb ~ for thought** dar que pensar a algn • **without (a) ~** sin interrupción
2 (*on cassette-player*) botón *m* de pausa
(VI) (*in activity*) hacer un descanso; (*when speaking*) callarse (momentáneamente), detenerse; (*when moving*) detenerse • **we ~d for a break half-way through the afternoon** paramos a descansar a media tarde • **let's ~ here** hagamos un descanso aquí • **it made**

P

him ~ le hizo vacilar • **to ~ for breath** detenerse para tomar aliento
CPD ▸ **pause button** botón *m* de pausa
pave [peɪv] VT (*gen*) pavimentar; (*with flagstones*) enlosar; (*with stones*) adoquinar, empedrar; (*with bricks*) enladrillar • **the streets are ~d with gold** se atan los perros con longaniza • IDIOM: • **to ~ the way for sth/sb** preparar el terreno para algo/algn
paved [peɪvd] ADJ [*road*] asfaltado, pavimentado; (*with flagstones, tiles*) [*garden, courtyard, path*] enlosado
pavement ['peɪvmənt] N (*Brit*) acera *f*, vereda *f* (*LAm*), andén *m* (*CAm, Col*), banqueta *f* (*Mex*); (*US*) calzada *f*, pavimento *m* • **brick ~** enladrillado *m* • **stone ~** empedrado *m*, adoquinado *m* • **to leave the ~** (*US*) (*Aut*) salir de la calzada
CPD ▸ **pavement artist** pintor(a) *m/f* callejero/a ▸ **pavement café** café *m* con terraza, café *m* al aire libre
pavilion [pə'vɪlɪən] N (*for band*) quiosco *m*; (*Sport*) caseta *f*, vestuario *m*; (*at trade fair*) pabellón *m*
paving ['peɪvɪŋ] N [*of concrete*] pavimento *m*; [*of flagstones*] enlosado *m*; [*of stones*] adoquinado *m*, empedrado *m*; [*of brick*] enladrillado *m*
CPD ▸ **paving slab** losa *f* ▸ **paving stone** adoquín *m*, baldosa *f* (*LAm*); (= *flagstone*) losa *f*
pavlova [pæv'ləʊvə] N pavlova *f*
Pavlovian [pæv'ləʊvɪən] ADJ pavloviano
paw [pɔː] N **1** [*of animal*] pata *f*; [*of cat*] garra *f*; [*of lion*] zarpa *f*, garra *f*
2* (= *hand*) manaza* *f*
VT **1** [*animal*] tocar con la pata; [*lion*] dar zarpazos a • **to paw the ground** [*horse*] piafar
2 (*pej*) (= *touch*) [+ *person*] manosear, tocar; (*amorously*) sobar • **stop pawing me!** ¡fuera las manos!
VI • **to paw at sth** [*animal*] tocar algo con la pata; (*to wound*) dar zarpazos a algo
pawl [pɔːl] N trinquete *m*
pawn¹ [pɔːn] N (*Chess*) peón *m*; (*fig*) instrumento *m* • **they simply used me as a ~** se aprovecharon de mí como mero instrumento • **he was just a ~ in their game** era solo un títere en sus manos
pawn² [pɔːn] N • **to be in ~** estar en prenda, estar empeñado • **the country is in ~ to foreigners** el país está empeñado a extranjeros • **to leave** *or* **put sth in ~** dejar algo en prenda, empeñar algo
VT empeñar
CPD ▸ **pawn ticket** papeleta *f* de empeño
pawnbroker ['pɔːn,brəʊkə^r] N prestamista *mf* • **~'s** = **pawnshop**
pawnshop ['pɔːnʃɒp] N monte *m* de piedad, casa *f* de empeños
pawpaw ['pɔːpɔː] N **1** (*Brit*) = **papaya**
2 (*US*) asimina *f*, chirimoya *f*
pay [peɪ] (VB: PT, PP: **paid**) N (= *wages*) [*of professional person*] sueldo *m*; [*of worker*] salario *m*, sueldo *m*; [*of day labourer*] jornal *m*; (= *payment*) paga *f* • **the pay's not very good** no pagan muy bien • **to draw** *or* **get one's pay** cobrar • **to be in sb's pay** estar al servicio de algn • **agents in the enemy's pay** agentes *mpl* al servicio del enemigo
VT **1** [+ *bill, duty, fee*] pagar; [+ *account*] liquidar; [+ *debt*] saldar, liquidar; [+ *employee, worker*] pagar a • **to pay sb £10** pagar 10 libras a algn • **how much is there to pay?** ¿cuánto hay que pagar? • **to pay sb to do a job** pagar a algn para que haga un trabajo • **"paid"** (*on receipted bill*) "pagado" • **to pay sth on account** pagar algo a cuenta • **a badly paid worker** un obrero mal pagado • **to pay cash (down)** pagar al contado • **I paid £5 for that record** pagué 5 libras por ese disco • **how much did you pay for it?** ¿cuánto pagaste por él?, ¿cuánto te costó? • **that's what you're paid for** para eso te pagan • **it's a service that has to be paid for** es un servicio que hay que pagar • **to be** *or* **get paid on Fridays** cobrar los viernes • **when do you get paid?** ¿cuándo cobras? • **does your current account pay interest?** ¿le rinde intereses su cuenta corriente? • **to pay money into an account** ingresar dinero en una cuenta • **to pay one's way** pagarse los gastos; ▹ **paid**
2 (= *be profitable to*) • **it wouldn't pay him to do it** (*lit*) no le compensaría hacerlo; (*fig*) no le valdría la pena hacerlo • **but it paid him in the long run** pero a la larga le fue provechoso
3 [+ *attention*] prestar (**to** a); [+ *homage*] rendir (**to** a); [+ *respects*] ofrecer, presentar • **to pay sb a visit** *or* **call** • **to pay a visit to** *or* **a call on sb** ir a ver a algn; ▹ **heed, penalty, respect**
VI **1** pagar • **don't worry, I'll pay** no te preocupes, lo pago yo • **to pay in advance** pagar por adelantado • **can I pay by cheque?** ¿puedo pagar con cheque? • **to pay for sth** pagar algo • **they paid for her to go** pagaron para que fuera • **to pay in full** pagarlo todo, pagar la cantidad íntegra • **to pay in instalments** pagar a plazos
2 [*job*] • **his job pays well** tiene un buen sueldo, el trabajo le paga bien
3 (= *be profitable*) [*business*] rendir, ser rentable • **the business doesn't pay** el negocio no es rentable • **it pays to advertise** compensa hacer publicidad • **it pays to be courteous/tell the truth** vale la pena ser cortés/decir la verdad; ▹ **crime**
4 (*fig*) (= *suffer*) pagar • **she paid for it with her life** le costó la vida • **they made him pay dearly for it** le hicieron pagarlo muy caro • **you'll pay for this!** ¡me las pagarás!
CPD ▸ **pay as you earn** (*Brit*) retención *f* fiscal (hecha por la empresa) ▸ **pay award** adjudicación *f* de aumento de salarios ▸ **pay bargaining** negociación *f* salarial ▸ **pay bed** cama *f* de pago ▸ **pay cheque** cheque *m* de la paga; (= *salary*) sueldo *m* ▸ **pay claim** reivindicación *f* salarial ▸ **pay cut** reducción *f* salarial ▸ **pay deal** acuerdo *m* salarial • **the union wants a better pay deal** el sindicato pide un mejor acuerdo salarial ▸ **pay desk** caja *f* ▸ **pay dirt** (*US*) grava *f* provechosa • IDIOM: • **to hit** *or* **strike pay dirt** dar con un filón de oro ▸ **pay dispute** conflicto *m* salarial ▸ **pay envelope** (*US*) sobre *m* de la paga ▸ **pay increase** incremento *m* salarial ▸ **pay negotiations** negociaciones *fpl* salariales ▸ **pay offer** propuesta *f* de aumento (de sueldo) ▸ **pay office** caja *f*, pagaduría *f* ▸ **pay packet** (*Brit*) sobre *m* de la paga ▸ **pay pause†** congelación *f* de sueldos y salarios ▸ **pay phone** (*Brit*) teléfono *m* público ▸ **pay policy** política *f* salarial ▸ **pay raise** (*US*), **pay rise** incremento *m* salarial ▸ **pay round** serie *f* de negociaciones salariales ▸ **pay scale** escala *f* salarial ▸ **pay slip** nómina *f*, hoja *f* salarial *or* de sueldo ▸ **pay station** (*US*) teléfono *m* público; (*for parking*) parquímetro *m* ▸ **pay structure** estructura *f* salarial ▸ **pay talks** = **pay negotiations** ▸ **pay television** televisión *f* de pago
▸ **pay back** VT + ADV **1** [+ *money*] devolver; (*frm*) restituir, reintegrar; [+ *loan*] pagar
2 [+ *person*] • **to pay sb back for sth/doing sth: I'll pay you back for the meal tomorrow** te devuelvo el dinero de la comida mañana • **I'll never be able to pay you back for all you've done** nunca podré corresponderte por todo lo que has hecho • **I'll pay you back for betraying me!** te voy a hacer pagar caro tu traición • **I'll pay you back for this!** ¡me las vas a pagar! • IDIOM: • **to pay sb back in his own coin** pagar a algn con la misma moneda
▸ **pay down** VT + ADV [+ *cash*] pagar al contado; [+ *deposit*] pagar como desembolso inicial
▸ **pay in** VT + ADV [+ *money*] ingresar, depositar; [+ *cheque*] ingresar, abonar
VI + ADV (*at bank*) ingresar dinero
▸ **pay off** VT + ADV **1** [+ *debt*] liquidar, saldar; [+ *mortgage*] amortizar • **to pay sth off in instalments** pagar algo a plazos • **to pay off old scores** ajustar cuentas
2 [+ *workers, crew*] pagar y despedir
VI + ADV merecer *or* valer la pena • **the gamble paid off** mereció *or* valió la pena arriesgarse • **his efforts paid off** sus esfuerzos merecieron *or* valieron la pena • **the investment paid off handsomely** la inversión bien mereció la pena *or* dio muy buenos frutos • **when do you think it will begin to pay off?** ¿cuándo piensas que empezará a dar resultado?
▸ **pay out** VT + ADV **1** [+ *money*] (*for purchase*) gastar, desembolsar; (*to shareholder, prizewinner*) pagar
2 [+ *rope*] ir soltando
3† (*fig*) desquitarse con • **I'll pay you out for this!** ¡me las pagarás!
VI + ADV • **to pay out on a policy** pagar una póliza
▸ **pay up** VT + ADV [+ *insurance premiums, subscription*] abonar • **first you must pay up what you owe** primero debe abonar la deuda • **I was not worried because I knew my insurance policy was paid up** no estaba preocupada porque sabía que los pagos de mi póliza de seguros estaban al día
VI + ADV pagar (lo que se debe) • **pay up!** ¡a pagar!
payable ['peɪəbl] ADJ pagadero • **~ to bearer** pagadero al portador • **~ on demand** pagadero a presentación *or* a vista • **to make a cheque ~ to sb** extender un cheque a favor de algn
pay-and-display [,peɪəndɪs'pleɪ] ADJ (*Brit*) [*car park*] *de pago colocando el ticket en el interior del parabrisas*
pay-as-you-go [,peɪəzjʊ'gəʊ] N (*US*) (*Tax*) retención *f* fiscal (hecha por la empresa)
ADJ [*mobile phone*] de tarjeta prepago
payback ['peɪbæk] N restitución *f*
CPD ▸ **payback period** período *m* de restitución ▸ **payback time** (= *time to face the consequences*) • **they did wrong and this summer will be ~ time** hicieron mal y este verano pagarán las consecuencias; (= *time for reward*) • **this will repay his faith in us. It's ~ time** esto le devolverá la fe en nosotros. Es hora de recompensarle
paycheck ['peɪtʃek] N (*US*) cheque *m* de la paga; (= *salary*) sueldo *m*
payday ['peɪdeɪ] N día *m* de paga
CPD ▸ **payday lender** empresa *f* de préstamos del día de pago, empresa *f* de préstamos de corto plazo ▸ **payday lending** préstamos *mpl* del día de pago, préstamos *mpl* de corto plazo ▸ **payday loan** préstamo *m* del día de pago, préstamo *m* a corto plazo
PAYE N ABBR (*Brit*) (= **pay as you earn**) ▹ **pay**
payee [peɪ'iː] N portador(a) *m/f*, tenedor(a) *m/f*; (*on cheque*) beneficiario/a *m/f* • **"account payee only"** (*on cheque*) "cuenta nominal"
payer ['peɪə^r] N pagador(a) *m/f* • **slow ~** • **bad ~** moroso/a *m/f*
paying ['peɪɪŋ] ADJ provechoso, rentable • **it's a ~ proposition** es un negocio provechoso
CPD ▸ **paying bank** banco *m* pagador ▸ **paying guest** huésped(a) *m/f* (de pago),

pensionista *mf*
paying-in slip [ˌpeɪɪŋˈɪnˌslɪp], **pay-in slip** [ˌpeɪˈɪnˌslɪp] N hoja *f* de ingreso
payload [ˈpeɪləʊd] N carga *f* útil
paymaster [ˈpeɪmɑːstəʳ] N **1** (oficial *m*) pagador *m*
2 (*pej*) • **the ~s of terrorism** los mecenas del terrorismo
CPD ▸ **Paymaster General** (*Brit*) *encargado del departamento del ministerio de Hacienda a través del que se paga a los funcionarios públicos*
payment [ˈpeɪmənt] N **1** [*of salary, debt, invoice*] pago *m*; (*for services*) remuneración *f* • **~ of this invoice is now due** ya hay que hacer efectivo el pago de esta factura • **I don't expect ~ for my help** no espero que me paguen por mi ayuda, no espero remuneración por mi ayuda • **as ~ for your help** como pago por tu ayuda • **in ~ for/of** en pago por/de • **to make a ~** efectuar un pago • **to make a ~ into one's account** hacer un depósito *or* (*Sp*) un ingreso en cuenta • **on ~ of £5** mediante pago de cinco libras, pagando cinco libras • **to present sth for ~** presentar algo para el cobro; ▹ **advance, kind, maintenance**
2 (= *instalment*) plazo *m* • **ten monthly ~s of £50** diez plazos mensuales *or* diez mensualidades de 50 libras • **to fall behind with one's/the ~s** atrasarse en los pagos • **to keep up one's/the ~s** mantenerse al día con los pagos
3 (*fig*) (= *reward*) recompensa *f*, retribución *f* • **a stream of abuse was the only ~ he received** la única recompensa *or* retribución que recibió fue una sarta de insultos
CPD ▸ **payment card** tarjeta *f* de pago ▸ **payment holiday** período *m* de carencia • **you can also underpay or take ~ holidays if you choose** también puede optar por pagar menos o acogerse a períodos de carencia
payoff* [ˈpeɪɒf] N **1** (= *payment*) pago *m*; [*of debt*] liquidación *f* (total)
2 (= *reward*) recompensa *f*, beneficios *mpl*
3 (= *vengeance*) ajuste *m* de cuentas, castigo *m*
4 (= *bribe*) soborno *m*, coima *f* (*And, S. Cone*), mordida *f* (*CAm, Mex*)
5 (= *final outcome, climax*) momento *m* decisivo, desenlace *m*
payola* [peɪˈəʊlə] N (*US*) soborno *m*, coima *f* (*And, S. Cone*), mordida *f* (*CAm, Mex*)
payout [ˈpeɪaʊt] N pago *m*; (= *share-out*) reparto *m*; (*in competition*) premio *m* en metálico; (*from insurance*) indemnización *f*
pay-per-click [peɪpəˈklɪk] N pago *m* por click
ADJ de pago por click
pay-per-view [ˌpeɪpəˈvjuː] ADJ de pago
payphone [ˈpeɪfəʊn] N teléfono *m* público
payroll [ˈpeɪrəʊl] N nómina *f* (de sueldos) • **to be on a firm's ~** estar en la nómina de una empresa • **he has 1000 people on his ~** tiene una nómina de 1000 empleados
CPD ▸ **payroll tax** impuesto *m* sobre la nómina
pay-TV [ˈpeɪtiːˌviː] N televisión *f* de pago
paywall [ˈpeɪwɔːl] N (*Internet*) muro *m* de pago, sistema *m* de pago por contenidos • **behind a ~** tras un muro de pago
PB ABBR (*Sport*) (= **personal best**) marca *f* personal
PBAB ABBR = **please bring a bottle**
PBS N ABBR (*US*) = **Public Broadcasting Service**
PBX N ABBR (*Telec*) (= **private branch exchange**) *centralita para extensiones*
PC N ABBR **1** (= **personal computer**) PC *m*, OP *m*
2 (*Brit*) (= **police constable**) policía *mf*
3 (*Brit*) = **Privy Councillor**
ADJ ABBR* = **politically correct**
pc N ABBR = **postcard**
p.c. ABBR (= **per cent**) p.c.
P/C, p/c ABBR **1** (*St Ex*) (= **prices current**) cotizaciones *fpl*
2 (*Comm*) = **petty cash**
PCA N ABBR **1** (*Brit*) = **Police Complaints Authority**
2 = **Professional Chess Association**
PCB N ABBR **1** (= **printed circuit board**) TCI *f*
2 (= **polychlorinated biphenyl**) PCB *m*
PCC N ABBR (*Brit*) = **Press Complaints Commission**
PCFC N ABBR = **Polytechnics and Colleges Funding Council**
PCI N ABBR (= **Peripheral Component Interconnect**) PCI *m*
pcm ADV ABBR (= **per calendar month**) p/mes
PCP N ABBR **1** (*Drugs*)® (= **phencyclidine**) fenciclidina *f*
2 (*Med*) = **pneumocystis carinii pneumonia**
PD N ABBR (*US*) = **police department**
pd ABBR (= **paid**) pgdo.
PDA N ABBR (= **personal digital assistant**) agenda *f* electrónica, PDA *m*
PDF N ABBR (= **Portable Document Format**) PDF *m*
PDO ABBR (= **Protected Designation of Origin**) D.O.P. *f*
pdq* ADV ABBR (= **pretty damn(ed) quick**) en un santiamén*
PDSA N ABBR (*Brit*) = **People's Dispensary for Sick Animals**
PDT N ABBR (*US*) = **Pacific Daylight Time**
PE N ABBR (= **physical education**) ed. física
ABBR (*Canada*) = **Prince Edward Island**
CPD ▸ **PE teacher** profesor(a) *m/f* de E.F.
pea [piː] N guisante *m* (*Sp*), chícharo *m* (*CAm*), arveja *f* (*LAm*), alverja *f* (*LAm*) • **sweet pea** guisante *m* de olor (*Sp*), clarín *m* (*Chile*); ▹ **like¹**
CPD ▸ **pea jacket** chaquetón *m* ▸ **pea soup** sopa *f* de guisantes *etc*
peace [piːs] N **1** paz *f*
2 • **to be at ~** (*euph*) (= *dead*) descansar en paz • **Egypt is at ~ with Israel** Egipto está en paz con Israel • **a world at ~** un mundo donde reine la paz *or* donde haya paz • **I am at ~ with my conscience** estoy en paz con mi conciencia • **to be at ~ with o.s.** estar en paz consigo mismo • **we come in ~†** (*also hum*) venimos en son de paz • **to disturb the ~** perturbar la paz; (*Jur*) alterar el orden público • **he gave her no ~ until she agreed** no la dejó tranquila *or* en paz hasta que accedió • **to hold** *or* **keep one's ~** guardar silencio • **speak now or forever hold your ~** hable ahora o calle para siempre • **to keep the ~** (*gen*) mantener la paz *or* el orden; (*Jur*) [*citizen*] respetar el orden público; [*police*] mantener el orden público • **to leave sb in ~** dejar a algn tranquilo *or* en paz • **to live in ~ (with sb)** vivir en paz (con algn) • **to make ~ (with sb)** hacer las paces (con algn) • **~ of mind** tranquilidad *f* (de espíritu) • **anything for the sake of ~ and quiet** lo que sea por un poco de tranquilidad • **the ~ and quiet of the woods** la tranquilidad del bosque • **in times of ~** en tiempos de paz; ▹ **breach, rest¹**
CPD [*agreement, plan, settlement*] de paz; [*campaign, conference*] por la paz ▸ **peace accord** acuerdo *m* de paz ▸ **peace activist** activista *mf* por la paz ▸ **peace camp** campamento *m* por la paz ▸ **peace campaigner** *persona que participa en una campaña por la paz* ▸ **peace conference** conferencia *f* de paz ▸ **Peace Corps** (*US*) Cuerpo *m* de Paz ▸ **peace dividend** beneficios *mpl* reportados por la paz ▸ **peace envoy** enviado/a *m/f* de paz ▸ **peace initiative** iniciativa *f* de paz ▸ **peace movement** movimiento *m* pacifista ▸ **peace offering** (*fig*) prenda *f* de paz ▸ **peace pipe** pipa *f* de la paz ▸ **the peace process** el proceso de paz ▸ **peace settlement** acuerdo *m* de paz ▸ **peace sign** señal *f* de paz ▸ **peace studies** (*Univ*) estudios *mpl* de la paz ▸ **peace talks** negociaciones *fpl* por la paz ▸ **peace treaty** tratado *m* de paz
peaceable [ˈpiːsəbl] ADJ pacífico
peaceably [ˈpiːsəblɪ] ADV [*live, settle*] pacíficamente
peaceful [ˈpiːsfʊl] ADJ **1** (= *non-violent*) [*person, tribe, nation*] pacífico; [*demonstration, protest*] pacífico, no violento • **to live in ~ coexistence (with sb)** convivir pacíficamente (con algn) • **to change society by** *or* **through ~ means** cambiar la sociedad por medios pacíficos • **to seek a ~ solution to a conflict** buscar una solución pacífica a un conflicto • **the ~ uses of atomic energy** los usos de la energía atómica para fines pacíficos
2 (= *calm, untroubled*) [*place, life*] tranquilo • **on a ~ June evening** una tranquila tarde de junio • **it's very ~ here** este es un lugar muy tranquilo • **the streets are ~ after yesterday's fighting** las calles están tranquilas después de las confrontaciones de ayer • **they say it's a ~ way to go** dicen que es una forma de morir sin nada de sufrimiento *or* sin sufrir dolores • **she's had a ~ night** ha pasado buena noche
peacefully [ˈpiːsfəlɪ] ADV **1** (= *non-violently*) [*demonstrate, live, co-exist*] pacíficamente
2 (= *calmly*) tranquilamente • **he was sleeping ~** dormía tranquilamente • **to die ~** morir sin sufrir
peacefulness [ˈpiːsfʊlnɪs] N (= *calmness*) tranquilidad *f*, paz *f*; (= *non-violent nature*) carácter *m* pacífico
peacekeeper [ˈpiːsˌkiːpəʳ] N (*Mil*) tropas *fpl* encargadas de mantener la paz • **UN ~s** tropas *fpl* de las Naciones Unidas encargadas de mantener la paz
peace-keeping [ˈpiːsˌkiːpɪŋ] N mantenimiento *m* de la paz
CPD ▸ **peace-keeping force(s)** fuerzas *fpl* encargadas de mantener la paz ▸ **peace-keeping operation** operación *f* para mantener la paz
peace-loving [ˈpiːsˌlʌvɪŋ] ADJ amante de la paz
peacemaker [ˈpiːsˌmeɪkəʳ] N (= *pacifier*) pacificador(a) *m/f*; (= *conciliator*) conciliador(a) *m/f*
peacemaking [ˈpiːsmeɪkɪŋ] N pacificación *f*, negociaciones *mpl* por la paz
ADJ [*efforts, process, role*] pacificador, de conciliación
peacenik* [ˈpiːsnɪk] N pacifista *mf*, milikaka *mf* (*Sp**)
peacetime [ˈpiːstaɪm] N tiempos *mpl* de paz
peach [piːtʃ] N **1** (= *fruit*) melocotón *m* (*Sp*), durazno *m* (*LAm*); (= *tree*) melocotonero *m* (*Sp*), duraznero *m* (*LAm*)
2* • **she's a ~** es un bombón *or* una monada*, es una belleza (*LAm*) • **it's a ~ of a job** es un trabajo muy cómodo, es un chollo (*Sp**)
3 (= *colour*) color *m* (de) melocotón *or* (*LAm*) durazno
ADJ de color melocotón *or* (*LAm*) durazno
CPD ▸ **peach tree** melocotonero *m* (*Sp*), duraznero *m* (*LAm*)
peachy* [ˈpiːtʃɪ] ADJ (*esp US*) (= *nice*) genial • **everything in her life is just ~** todo en su vida es simplemente genial
peacock [ˈpiːkɒk] N (PL: **peacocks** *or* **peacock**) pavo *m* real

CPD ▸ **peacock blue** azul *m* (de) pavo real ▸ **peacock feather** pluma *f* de pavo real

peacock-blue [,pi:kɒk'blu:] ADJ azul (*inv*) (de) pavo real

pea-green ['pi:'gri:n] ADJ verde claro

peahen ['pi:hen] N pava *f* real

peak [pi:k] N **1** [*of mountain*] cumbre *f*, cima *f*; (= *mountain itself*) pico *m*; (= *point*) (*also of roof*) punta *f*; (*on graph*) pico *m* • **beat the egg whites until stiff ~s form** bata las claras de huevo a punto de nieve
2 [*of cap*] visera *f*
3 (= *high point*) [*of career, fame, popularity*] cumbre *f*, cúspide *f* • **during the ~ of the war in Nicaragua** cuando la guerra en Nicaragua era más intensa • **she died at the ~ of her career** murió cuando estaba en la cumbre *or* la cúspide de su carrera • **to be at the ~ of fitness** estar en condiciones óptimas, estar en plena forma • **coffee is at its ~ just after grinding** cuando mejor está el café es recién molido • **at the ~ of the morning rush hour** en el momento de mayor intensidad de la hora punta matinal • **the heyday of drugs has passed its ~** ya ha pasado la época de máximo apogeo de las drogas • **house prices reached a ~ in 1988** el precio de las viviendas alcanzó su nivel máximo en 1988 • **computer technology has not yet reached its ~** la tecnología informática aún no ha alcanzado su cumbre *or* cúspide • **discontent had reached its ~** el descontento había alcanzado su momento crítico • **~s and troughs** auges *mpl* y depresiones *fpl*; ▹ **widow**
VI [*temperatures*] alcanzar su punto más alto; [*inflation, sales*] alcanzar su nivel máximo; [*crisis*] alcanzar su momento crítico; [*career*] alcanzar su cumbre *or* su cúspide; [*sportsperson*] alcanzar su mejor momento
ADJ (*before noun*) **1** (= *top*) • **in ~ condition** (*athlete*) en óptimas condiciones, en plena forma; (*animal*) en óptimas condiciones
2 (= *busiest*) • **~ hours** (*of traffic*) horas *fpl* punta; (*Elec*) horas *fpl* de mayor consumo • **~ period** (*Telec, Internet, Elec*) período *m* de mayor demanda; (*for holidays*) temporada *f* alta • **~ time** (*TV*) horas *fpl* de máxima audiencia; (*Telec, Elec*) horas *fpl* de máxima demanda; (= *rush hour*) horas *fpl* punta • **it is more expensive to call at ~ times** resulta más caro llamar durante las horas de máxima demanda • **~ viewing time** horas *fpl* de máxima audiencia
CPD ▸ **peak rate** (*Telec*) tarifa *f* alta ▸ **peak season** temporada *f* alta

peaked¹ [pi:kt] ADJ • **~ cap** gorra *f* de visera

peaked² [pi:kt] ADJ = **peaky**

peak-hour ['pi:k'aʊər] ADJ en hora punta • **they took a detour to avoid peak-hour traffic** dieron un rodeo para evitar el tráfico en hora punta • **we need to improve peak-hour train services** es necesario mejorar el servicio de trenes en hora punta

peak-time ['pi:ktaɪm] ADJ (*Brit*) (*TV*) • **a peak-time television film** una película que se emite durante las horas de máxima audiencia; (*Telec*) • **peak-time calls** llamadas *fpl* telefónicas durante las horas de máxima demanda

peaky* ['pi:kɪ] ADJ (COMPAR: **peakier**, SUPERL: **peakiest**) paliducho* • **to look ~** estar paliducho*

peal [pi:l] N (= *sound of bells*) repique *m* • **a ~ of bells** (= *set*) un carillón • **a ~ of thunder** un trueno • **the ~ of the organ** el sonido del órgano • **~s of laughter** carcajadas *fpl*
VT (*also* **peal out**) repicar, tocar a vuelo
VI [*church bell*] repicar, tocar a vuelo; [*doorbell, organ*] sonar

peanut ['pi:nʌt] N **1** cacahuete *m* (*Sp*), maní *m* (*LAm*), cacahuate *m* (*Mex*)
2 peanuts* (= *very small amount*) una miseria* • **he gets paid ~s** le pagan una miseria
CPD ▸ **peanut allergy** alergia *f* a los cacahuetes (*Sp*), alergia *f* a los maníes (*LAm*), alergia *f* a los cacahuates (*Mex*) ▸ **peanut butter** mantequilla *f or* crema *f* de cacahuete (*Sp*), mantequilla *f* de maní (*LAm*), manteca *f* de maní (*Arg, Uru*), mantequilla *f* de cacahuate (*Mex*) ▸ **peanut oil** aceite *m* de cacahuete (*Sp*), aceite *m* de maní (*LAm*), aceite *m* de cacahuate (*Mex*)

peanut-butter sandwich [,pi:nʌtbʌtər'sænwɪdʒ] N sándwich *m* de mantequilla de cacahuete (*Sp*), sándwich *m* de mantequilla de maní (*LAm*), sándwich *m* de manteca de maní (*Arg, Uru*), sándwich *m* de mantequilla de cacahuate (*Mex*)

peapod ['pi:pɒd] N vaina *f* de guisante (*Sp*), vaina *f* de arveja (*LAm*), vaina *f* de chícharo (*CAm*)

pear [pɛər] N (= *fruit*) pera *f*; (*also* **pear tree**) peral *m*

pearl [pɜ:l] N perla *f*; (= *mother-of-pearl*) nácar *m*, madreperla *f* • **~ of wisdom** (*fig*) joya *f* de sabiduría • IDIOM: • **to cast ~s before swine** echar margaritas a los cerdos
CPD [*earring, button*] de perla(s); (*in colour*) color de perla ▸ **pearl barley** cebada *f* perlada ▸ **pearl button** botón *m* de nácar ▸ **pearl diver** pescador(a) *m/f* de perlas ▸ **pearl necklace** collar *m* de perlas ▸ **pearl oyster** ostra *f* perlífera

pearl-grey ['pɜ:l'greɪ] ADJ gris perla

pearly ['pɜ:lɪ] ADJ (COMPAR: **pearlier**, SUPERL: **pearliest**) [*teeth*] de perla; [*colour*] color de perla • **~ white/pink** blanco/rosa perla • **the Pearly Gates** (*hum*) las puertas del cielo

pear-shaped ['pɛəʃeɪpt] ADJ (*lit*) en forma de pera • IDIOM: • **to go pear-shaped** (*Brit**) irse a la porra*, fastidiarse* • **things started to go pear-shaped** las cosas empezaron a ir mal

peasant ['pezənt] N campesino/a *m/f*; (*pej*) palurdo/a *m/f* • **a ~ revolt** un levantamiento campesino *or* del campesinado
CPD ▸ **peasant farmer** campesino *m* ▸ **peasant woman** campesina *f*

peasantry ['pezəntrɪ] N campesinado *m*, campesinos *mpl*

peashooter ['pi:ʃu:tər] N cerbatana *f*

pea-souper* ['pi:'su:pər] N niebla *f* muy densa

peat [pi:t] N turba *f*
CPD ▸ **peat bog** turbera *f*, turbal *m*

peaty ['pi:tɪ] ADJ (COMPAR: **peatier**, SUPERL: **peatiest**) turboso

pebble ['pebl] N guijarro *m* • IDIOM: • **you're not the only ~ on the beach*** no eres el único
CPD ▸ **pebble beach** playa *f* de guijarros

pebbledash [,pebl'dæʃ] N enguijarrado *m*
VT enguijarrar

pebbly ['peblɪ] ADJ guijarroso

pecan ['pi:kæn] N pacana *f*
CPD ▸ **pecan pie** tarta *f* de pacanas

peccadillo [,pekə'dɪləʊ] N (PL: **peccadillos** *or* **peccadilloes**) pecadillo *m*, falta *f* leve

peccary ['pekərɪ] N (PL: **peccary** *or* **peccaries**) (*Zool*) saíno *m*, pecarí *m* (*LAm*), pécari *m* (*LAm*)

peck¹ [pek] N picotazo *m*; (= *kiss*) besito *m*, beso *m* rápido
VT picotear; (= *kiss*) dar un besito a, dar un beso rápido a
VI picotear • **to ~ at** [*bird*] picar • **he ~ed at his food** picaba la comida (con desgana)

peck² [pek] N *medida de áridos (= 9,087 litros)*; (*fig*) montón *m* • **he got himself in a ~ of trouble** se metió en un buen lío*

pecker ['pekər] N **1** (*Brit**) • IDIOM: • **to keep one's ~ up** no dejarse desanimar • **keep your ~ up!** ¡ánimo!
2 (*US***) polla *f* (*Sp***)

pecking order ['pekɪŋ'ɔ:dər] N (*fig*) jerarquía *f*

peckish* ['pekɪʃ] ADJ con ganas de comer algo • **I'm** *or* **I feel a bit ~** tengo ganas de comer algo

pecs* [peks] NPL ABBR (= **pectorals**) pectorales *mpl*

pectin ['pektɪn] N pectina *f*

pectoral ['pektərəl] ADJ pectoral
NPL **pectorals** (músculos *mpl*) pectorales *mpl*

peculate ['pekjʊleɪt] VI desfalcar

peculation [,pekjʊ'leɪʃən] N desfalco *m*, peculado *m*

peculiar [pɪ'kju:lɪər] ADJ **1** (= *strange*) extraño, raro • **it's really most ~** es realmente extraño • **how very ~!** ¡qué extraño!, ¡qué raro! • **I'm feeling a bit ~** me siento algo raro, no me siento del todo bien; ▹ **funny**
2 (= *exclusive, special*) peculiar • **everyone has their own ~ likes and dislikes** cada uno tiene sus gustos y manías peculiares *or* particulares • **a species ~ to Africa** una especie que existe únicamente en África • **the style of dress ~ to that period in history** la forma de vestir peculiar *or* característica *or* propia de esa época de la historia • **this is not a problem ~ to Britain** este no es un problema exclusivamente británico • **in his/her own ~ way** a su modo • **in her own ~ way she was very fond of him** a su modo le tenía mucho cariño

peculiarity [pɪ,kjʊlɪ'ærɪtɪ] N
1 (= *strangeness*) rareza *f*
2 (= *specific quality*) peculiaridad *f* • **it's a ~ of hers that she always wears black** ir vestida siempre de negro es una peculiaridad suya • **he has his peculiarities** tiene sus rarezas *or* manías
3 (= *unusual thing*) rasgo *m* singular • **his only ~ is a missing arm** su único rasgo singular es que le falta un brazo

peculiarly [pɪ'kju:lɪəlɪ] ADV **1** (= *strangely*) de forma rara • **he's been acting very ~** se ha estado comportando de una forma rarísima
2 (= *specifically*) típicamente, peculiarmente • **it's a ~ French trait** es un rasgo típicamente *or* peculiarmente francés
3 (= *unusually, exceptionally*) particularmente, especialmente • **he was ~ quiet that day** ese día estuvo particularmente *or* especialmente callado

pecuniary [pɪ'kju:nɪərɪ] ADJ (*frm*) [*advantage, benefit*] pecuniario

pedagogic [,pedə'gɒdʒɪk] ADJ = **pedagogical**

pedagogical [,pedə'gɒdʒɪkəl] ADJ pedagógico

pedagogically [,pedə'gɒdʒɪkəlɪ] ADV pedagógicamente

pedagogue, pedagog (US) ['pedəgɒg] N pedagogo/a *m/f*

pedagogy ['pedəgɒgɪ] N pedagogía *f*

pedal ['pedl] N pedal *m* • **loud ~** (*Mus*) pedal *m* fuerte • **soft ~** (*Mus*) sordina *f*
VI pedalear • **he was ~ling furiously** estaba dándole duro a los pedales
VT [+ *bicycle*] darle a los pedales de
CPD ▸ **pedal (bi)cycle** bicicleta *f* a pedales ▸ **pedal bin** cubo *m* de la basura con pedal ▸ **pedal boat** = **pedalo** ▸ **pedal car** cochecito *m* con pedales

pedalo ['pedələʊ] N (PL: **pedalos** *or*

pedaloes) patín *m* a pedal
pedant [ˈpedənt] (N) pedante *mf*
pedantic [pɪˈdæntɪk] (ADJ) pedante
pedantically [pɪˈdæntɪkəlɪ] (ADV) con pedantería
pedantry [ˈpedəntrɪ] (N) pedantería *f*
peddle [ˈpedl] (VT) (= *sell*) ir vendiendo (de puerta en puerta); [+ *drugs*] pasar*; (*fig*) [+ *ideas*] difundir
peddler [ˈpedləʳ] (N) (*US*) = **pedlar** ▹ **drug**
pederast [ˈpedəræst] (N) pederasta *mf*
pederasty [ˈpedəræstɪ] (N) pederastia *f*
pedestal [ˈpedɪstl] (N) pedestal *m*, basa *f* • IDIOMS: • **to put sb on a ~** poner a algn sobre un pedestal • **to knock sb off his ~** bajar los humos *or* el copete a algn*
(CPD) ▸ **pedestal basin** lavabo *m or* lavamanos *m inv* con pie central ▸ **pedestal desk** escritorio *m* con cajones a ambos lados ▸ **pedestal lamp** lámpara *f* de pie
pedestrian [pɪˈdestrɪən] (N) peatón/ona *m/f*
(ADJ) (= *dull, commonplace*) [*style, speech*] prosaico, pedestre
(CPD) ▸ **pedestrian area** = **pedestrian precinct** ▸ **pedestrian crossing** (*Brit*) paso *m* de peatones ▸ **pedestrian mall** (*US*), **pedestrian precinct** (*Brit*) zona *f* peatonal ▸ **pedestrian traffic** circulación *f* de peatones ▸ **pedestrian zone** (*US*) zona *f* peatonal
pedestrianize [pɪˈdestrɪənaɪz] (VT) peatonizar • **~d street** calle *f* peatonal
pedi* [ˈpedɪ] (N) = **pedicure**
pediatric *etc* [ˌpi:dɪˈætrɪk] (*US*) = **paediatric** *etc*
pedicab [ˈpedɪˌkæb] (N) bicitaxi *m*
pedicure [ˈpedɪkjʊəʳ] (N) pedicura *f*
pedigree [ˈpedɪgri:] (N) (= *lineage*) linaje *m*, genealogía *f*; [*of animal*] pedigrí *m*; (= *family tree*) árbol *m* genealógico; (= *document*) certificado *m* de genealogía; (*fig*) (= *record*) historial *m*
(CPD) (*lit*) de raza, de casta; (*fig*) certificado, garantizado
pediment [ˈpedɪmənt] (N) frontón *m*
pedlar [ˈpedləʳ] (N) vendedor(a) *m/f* ambulante, buhonero† *m*
pedological *etc* [ˌpi:dəˈlɒdʒɪkl] (ADJ) (*US*) = **paedological** *etc*
pedometer [prˈdɒmɪtəʳ] (N) podómetro *m*
pedophile [ˈpi:dəʊfaɪl] (N) (*US*) = **paedophile**
pedophilia [ˈpi:dəʊˈfɪlɪə] (N) (*US*) = **paedophilia**
pee* [pi:] (N) pipí* *m* • **to go for a pee** ir a hacer pipí* • **to have a pee** hacer pipí*
(VI) hacer pipí* • **the dog peed on my shoe** el perro se me meó en el zapato*
(VT) • **to pee one's pants** hacerse pipí encima
peek [pi:k] (N) ojeada *f*, miradita *f*, mirada *f* furtiva • **to take** *or* **have a ~ at** echar una ojeada *or* miradita a; (*furtively*) echar una mirada furtiva a, mirar a hurtadillas
(VI) (= *glance*) echar una ojeada *or* miradita; (*furtively*) mirar (a hurtadillas) • **no ~ing!** ¡sin mirar! • **I opened the door a crack and ~ed in/out** abrí la puerta un poquito y miré (a hurtadillas)
▸ **peek over** (VI + PREP) [+ *fence, wall*] echar un vistazo por encima de • • **~ over the fence to see what your neighbour is doing** echa un vistazo por encima de la valla para ver que está haciendo tu vecino
peekaboo [ˌpi:kəˈbu:] (N) *juego para hacer reír a un niño que consiste en esconderse y reaparecer repentinamente diciendo "peekaboo"*
(EXCL) ¡bu!
peel [pi:l] (N) (= *skin*) piel *f*; [*of citrus fruit*] cáscara *f*; [*of apple, potato*] piel *f*; (*removed*) [*of citrus fruit*] cáscaras *fpl*; [*of apple, potato*] peladuras *fpl*, mondas *fpl*
(VT) [+ *fruit, vegetable*] pelar; [+ *layer of paper*] quitar • **to ~ the bark from a tree** descortezar un árbol, quitar la corteza de un árbol
(VI) [*wallpaper*] despegarse, desprenderse; [*paint*] desconcharse; [*skin, person*] pelarse • **I'm ~ing** me estoy pelando
▸ **peel away** (VI + ADV) [*paint*] desconcharse; [*wallpaper*] despegarse, desprenderse; [*skin*] pelarse
(VT + ADV) quitar, despegar
▸ **peel back** (VT + ADV) quitar, despegar
▸ **peel off** (VT + ADV) [+ *layer, paper*] quitar, despegar; [+ *clothes*] quitarse rápidamente *or* lisamente
(VI + ADV) **1** (= *separate*) separarse (**from** de); (= *leave formation*) [*vehicle, plane*] despegarse • **he ~ed off to the east** se desvió hacia el este
2* desnudarse rápidamente
peeler [ˈpi:ləʳ] (N) **1** (*also* **potato peeler**) pelapatatas *m inv*
2 (*Brit*††*) (= *policeman*) polizonte* *m*
peelie-wally‡ [ˈpi:lɪˈwælɪ] (ADJ) • **to be peelie-wally** (*Scot*) tener mala cara
peeling [ˈpi:lɪŋ] (N) (*Med*) [*of face etc*] descamación *f*; (*cosmetic trade*) peeling *m*; **peelings** [*of apple, potato*] peladuras *fpl*, mondas *fpl*; [*of citrus fruit*] cáscaras *fpl*
peep¹ [pi:p] (N) ojeada *f*, miradita *f* • **to get a ~ at sth** lograr ver algo brevemente • **to take** *or* **have a ~ (at sth)** echar una ojeada *or* miradita (a algo)
(VI) **1** (= *look*) mirar rápidamente; (*furtively*) mirar furtivamente *or* a hurtadillas • **to ~ at** echar una ojeada *or* miradita a • **I lifted the lid and ~ed inside** levanté la tapa y eché una miradita • **he ~ed through the curtains** se asomó a ver por detrás de las cortinas • **to ~ through the window** asomarse a la ventana para mirar
2 (= *stick out*) asomar(se) • **a head ~ed out** se asomó una cabeza • **the sun ~ed out from behind the clouds** el sol se asomó tras las nubes • **her shoes ~ed from beneath her skirt** los zapatos se le asomaban por debajo de la falda
peep² [pi:p] (N) **1** [*of bird*] pío *m*; [*of whistle*] silbido *m*
2* • **there hasn't been a ~ out of them** no han dicho ni pío* • **we can't get a ~ out of them** no les podemos sacar nada • **I don't want to hear ~ out of you!** ¡tú ni chistar!, ¡tú ni pío!*
(VI) piar
peep-bo* [ˌpi:pˈbəʊ] (EXCL) ¡cucú!
peepers* [ˈpi:pəz] (NPL) ojos *mpl*
peephole [ˈpi:phəʊl] (N) mirilla *f*, atisbadero *m*
Peeping Tom [ˌpi:pɪŋˈtɒm] (N) mirón *m*
peeps‡ [pi:ps] (NPL) (= *people*) gente *fsing*
peepshow [ˈpi:pʃəʊ] (N) (= *device*) mundonuevo *m*; (= *show*) vistas *fpl* sicalípticas, espectáculo *m* deshonesto
peeptoe [ˈpi:ptəʊ] (ADJ) [*sandal, shoe*] abierto
peer¹ [pɪəʳ] (N) **1** (= *noble*) par *m*, lord *m* • **he was made a life ~** le concedieron un título vitalicio
2 (= *equal*) (*in status*) par *mf*, igual *mf*; (*in age*) coetáneo/a *m/f* • **as a musician he has no ~** como músico no tiene par *or* igual • **children like to feel accepted by their ~s** a los niños les gusta sentirse aceptados por sus coetáneos
(CPD) ▸ **peer evaluation** = **peer review** ▸ **peer group** grupo *m* paritario ▸ **peer pressure, peer-group pressure** presión *f* ejercida por los iguales *or* (*frm*) por el grupo paritario ▸ **peer review** evaluación *f* por los iguales
peer² [pɪəʳ] (VI) • **to ~ at sth/sb** (*short-sightedly*) mirar algo/a algn con ojos de miope; (*closely*) escudriñar algo/a algn • **the old man ~ed at the book** el anciano miraba el libro con ojos de miope • **he ~ed at his reflection in the water** escudriñaba su reflejo en el agua • **we went up to the window and ~ed in** fuimos hasta la ventana y nos asomamos para ver lo que pasaba dentro • **to ~ into sb's face** escudriñar la cara a algn • **I ~ed over her shoulder** miré por encima de su hombro • **we ~ed over the wall** nos asomamos para mirar por encima de la pared
peerage [ˈpɪərɪdʒ] (N) nobleza *f* • **he was given a ~** le otorgaron un título de nobleza • **to marry into the ~** casarse con un título • **to be raised to the ~** obtener un título de nobleza
peeress [ˈpɪərɪs] (N) paresa *f*
peerless [ˈpɪəlɪs] (ADJ) sin par, incomparable
peeve* [pi:v] (VT) molestar, irritar
peeved* [pi:vd] (ADJ) picado*, molesto
peevish [ˈpi:vɪʃ] (ADJ) [*look, glance*] malhumorado; [*tone*] de irritación • **he gave her a ~ look** la miró malhumorado
peevishly [ˈpi:vɪʃlɪ] (ADV) malhumoradamente, con mal humor • **he said ~** dijo malhumorado
peevishness [ˈpi:vɪʃnɪs] (N) mal humor *m*
peewee* [ˈpi:wi:] (ADJ) (*US*) diminuto, pequeñito
peewit [ˈpi:wɪt] (N) avefría *f*
peg [peg] (N) **1** (*in ground, tent peg*) estaca *f*; (= *clothes peg*) pinza *f*, broche *m* (*LAm*); (*Mus*) (= *tuning peg*) clavija *f*; (*in board game*) ficha *f*; (*in barrel*) estaquilla *f*; (*Croquet*) piquete *m*; (*Climbing*) clavija *f* • IDIOM: • **to take** *or* **bring sb down a peg (or two)*** bajar los humos *or* el copete a algn*; ▹ **square**
2 (*for coat, hat*) gancho *m*, colgador *m* • **off the peg** (*Brit*) confeccionado, de confección • **an off-the-peg suit** un traje confeccionado *or* de confección • **he always buys clothes off the peg** siempre compra ropa confeccionada *or* de confección
3 (= *pretext*) pretexto *m* • **use the new law as a peg for the question** utiliza la nueva ley como pretexto para hacer la pregunta • **a peg on which to hang a theory** un punto de apoyo para justificar una teoría
(VT) **1** (= *secure*) (*gen*) fijar; [+ *clothes*] (*on line*) tender; [+ *tent*] fijar con estacas, sujetar con estacas; ▹ **peg out**
2 (*fig*) **a** (= *fix*) [+ *prices, wages*] fijar, estabilizar (**at, to** en) • **the Bank wants to peg rates at 9%** el banco quiere fijar *or* estabilizar las tasas en el 9%
b (= *link*) vincular (**to a**) • **they continue to peg their currencies to the dollar** siguen vinculando su moneda al dólar
c* (= *categorize*) [+ *person*] encasillar • **here you're pegged by what you wear** aquí te encasillan por la ropa que llevas • **his accent pegged him as an Englishman** su acento lo delataba como inglés
d • **to peg one's hopes on sth** depositar *or* cifrar sus esperanzas en algo
(CPD) ▸ **peg leg** pata *f* de palo
▸ **peg away*** (VI + ADV) machacar* • **just keep pegging away until you feel more confident** sigue machacando hasta que te sientas más seguro* • **to peg away at sth** machacar algo*, darle duro a algo*
▸ **peg back** (VT + ADV) • **Villa were pegged back to a 1-1 draw** Villa perdió su ventaja y terminó empatado a uno
▸ **peg down** (VT + ADV) **1** (= *fasten down*) [+ *tent*] fijar con estacas, sujetar con estacas
2 (= *force to agree*) • **I pegged him down to**

P

saying how much he wanted for it conseguí que me dijera exactamente por cuánto lo quería vender • **I pegged him down to £10 an hour** conseguí que aceptara 10 libras por hora

▸ **peg out*** VI + ADV (*= die*) estirar la pata*; (*= collapse*) caerse redondo*
VT + ADV (*= mark out*) [*+ area*] marcar con piquetes; (*= secure*) sujetar *or* fijar con estacas; (*= hang out*) [*+ clothes*] tender (con pinzas)

Pegasus ['pegəsəs] N Pegaso *m*

pegboard ['pegbɔːd] N tablero *m* de clavijas

PEI ABBR (*Canada*) = **Prince Edward Island**

peignoir ['peɪnwɑːʳ] N bata *f* (de señora), peinador *m*

pejorative [pɪ'dʒɒrətɪv] ADJ peyorativo, despectivo

pejoratively [pɪ'dʒɒrətɪvlɪ] ADV peyorativamente, de manera peyorativa, despectivamente

peke* [piːk] N pequinés/esa *m/f*

Pekin [piː'kɪn], **Peking** [piː'kɪŋ] N Pekín *m*

pekinese [ˌpiːkɪ'niːz], **pekingese** N pequinés/esa *m/f*

pelagic [pɪ'lædʒɪk] ADJ pelágico

pelican ['pelɪkən] N pelícano *m*
CPD ▸ **pelican crossing** semáforo *m* sonoro

pellagra [pə'lægrə] N pelagra *f*

pellet ['pelɪt] N (*= little ball*) bolita *f*; (*for gun*) perdigón *m*; [*of fertilizer*] gránulo *m*; (*Med*) píldora *f*
CPD ▸ **pellet gun** pistola *f* de perdigones

pell-mell ['pel'mel] ADV [*rush*] en tropel, atropelladamente • **their belongings were piled pell-mell into the trucks** metieron de cualquier manera sus pertenencias en los camiones

pellucid [pe'luːsɪd] ADJ diáfano, cristalino

pelmet ['pelmɪt] N (*Brit*) galería *f* (para cubrir la barra de las cortinas)

Peloponnese [ˌpeləpə'niːs] N • **the ~** el Peloponeso

Peloponnesian [ˌpeləpə'niːʃən] ADJ peloponense

pelota [pɪ'ləʊtə] N pelota *f* (vasca)
CPD ▸ **pelota player** pelotari *mf*

pelt¹ [pelt] VT • **to ~ sb with eggs** arrojar *or* tirar huevos a algn • **to ~ sb with stones** apedrear a algn • **they ~ed him with questions** lo acribillaron a preguntas
VI* **1** (*= fall fast*) • **it's ~ing with rain** está lloviendo a cántaros, está diluviando
2 (*= go fast*) • **to go ~ing off** salir como un rayo
N • **to go full ~** ir a todo correr, ir a toda pastilla*

▸ **pelt down*** VI + ADV (*= rain*) llover a cántaros • **it's ~ing down** está lloviendo a cántaros, está diluviando • **the rain was ~ing down outside** estaba diluviando fuera
VI + PREP [*person*] • **to ~ down the stairs** salir disparado *or* pitando escaleras abajo • **to ~ down the street** bajar la calle a toda prisa *or* pitando

pelt² [pelt] N (*= fur*) piel *f*; (*= skin*) pellejo *m*

pelvic ['pelvɪk] ADJ pélvico
CPD ▸ **pelvic floor** suelo *m* pélvico ▸ **pelvic floor exercise** ejercicio *m* para fortalecer el suelo pélvico ▸ **pelvic floor muscles** músculos *mpl* del suelo pélvico

pelvis ['pelvɪs] N (PL: **pelvises** *or* **pelves**) pelvis *f*

pen¹ [pen] N (*= fountain pen*) (pluma *f*) estilográfica *f*, pluma *f*, pluma *f* fuente (*LAm*); (*= ballpoint*) bolígrafo *m*; (*= felt tip*) rotulador *m* • **to live by the** *or* **one's pen** ganarse la vida escribiendo • **to put pen to paper** ponerse a escribir • **to wield a pen** (*liter*) menear cálamo; ▹ **marker, slip**
VT [*+ letter, article, book*] escribir; [*+ poem, song*] componer
CPD ▸ **pen-and-ink drawing** dibujo *m* a pluma ▸ **pen drive** (*Comput*) llave *f* de memoria *or* de datos ▸ **pen friend** amigo/a *m/f* por correspondencia ▸ **pen name** seudónimo *m*, nombre *m* de guerra ▸ **pen nib** punta *f* (de pluma) ▸ **pen pal*** = **pen friend** ▸ **pen wiper** limpiaplumas *m inv*

pen² [pen] N **1** (*= enclosure*) (*for cattle*) corral *m*; (*for sheep*) redil *m*, aprisco *m*; (*for bulls*) toril *m*; (*= playpen*) parque *m* (de niño), corral *m*
2 (*US**) (*= prison*) (*also* **penitentiary**) cárcel *f*, chirona *f* (*Sp**)
VT [*+ animal*] encerrar, acorralar; [*+ person*] • **I've been penned in the kitchen all day** he estado metida en la cocina todo el día

▸ **pen in** VT + ADV [*+ animal*] encerrar, acorralar • **she was penned in by the crowd** se encontraba acorralada por la muchedumbre • **the French had the enemy penned in** los franceses tenían al enemigo cercado

▸ **pen up** VT + ADV [*+ animal*] = **pen in**

pen³ [pen] N (*Orn*) cisne *m* hembra

penal ['piːnl] ADJ **1** [*reform, policy, system*] penal
2 (*= harsh*) [*rate, charges*] muy gravoso, perjudicial
CPD ▸ **penal code** código *m* penal ▸ **penal colony** colonia *f* penal ▸ **penal servitude** trabajos *mpl* forzados

penalization [ˌpiːnəlaɪ'zeɪʃən] N castigo *m*

penalize ['piːnəlaɪz] VT (*= punish*) castigar; (*by law*) penar; (*accidentally, unfairly*) perjudicar; (*Sport*) sancionar, penalizar • **to be ~d for a foul** ser penalizado por una falta • **we are ~d by not having a car** somos perjudicados por no tener coche • **the decision ~s those who …** la decisión perjudica a quienes …

penalty ['penəltɪ] N **1** (*Jur*) (*= punishment*) pena *f*, castigo *m*; (*= fine*) multa *f*; (*Comm*) recargo *m*; (*fig*) (*= disadvantage*) desventaja *f* • **there is a ~ for paying the loan off early** se cobra un recargo si se paga el préstamo antes de que venza • **"penalty £50"** "multa de 50 libras" • **telling the truth can have its penalties** decir la verdad puede tener sus desventajas • **the ~ for this is death** esto se castiga con la muerte • **on** *or* **under ~ of dismissal** so *or* bajo pena de ser despedido • **to pay the ~ (for** *or* **of sth/for doing sth)** pagar las consecuencias (de algo/de haber hecho algo) • **we were paying the ~ of success** estábamos pagando las consecuencias del éxito; ▹ **death**
2 (*Ftbl*) penalti *m*, penalty *m*; (*Golf*) penalización *f*; (*Bridge*) multa *f*, castigo *m* • **there is a 7-second ~ for each error** se quitan 7 segundos por cada error • **the final was decided on penalties** la final se decidió con penaltis • **to take a ~** lanzar penalti *or* penalty
CPD ▸ **penalty area, penalty box** (*Ftbl*) área *f* de castigo *or* de penalti *or* de penalty; (*Ice hockey*) banquillo *m* ▸ **penalty clause** cláusula *f* penal ▸ **penalty corner** (*Hockey*) córner *m* de penalti *or* penalty ▸ **penalty goal** gol *m* de penalti *or* penalty ▸ **penalty kick** penalti *m*, penalty *m* ▸ **penalty point** (*on driving licence, in showjumping*) punto *m* de castigo ▸ **penalty shoot-out** desempate *m* a penaltis ▸ **penalty shot** penalti *m*, penalty *m* ▸ **penalty spot** punto *m* de penalti *or* penalty

penance ['penəns] N **1** (*= atonement*) penitencia *f* • **to do ~ for** hacer penitencia por
2 (*= punishment*) castigo *m*

pence [pens] NPL *of* **penny**

penchant [ˌpɑ̃ːŋʃɑ̃ːŋ] N predilección *f* (por), inclinación *f* (**for** hacia, por) • **to have a ~ for** tener predilección por

pencil ['pensl] N lápiz *m*, lapicero *m*; (*= propelling pencil*) lapicero *m* • **to draw in ~** dibujar con lápiz • **to write in ~** escribir a lápiz; ▸ **eyebrow**
VT (*also* **pencil in**) escribir a lápiz • **a ~led note** una nota escrita a lápiz
CPD ▸ **pencil box** cajita *f* para lápices ▸ **pencil case** estuche *m* (para lápices), plumero *m*, plumier *m* (*Sp*) ▸ **pencil drawing** dibujo *m* a lápiz ▸ **pencil pusher*** (*US*) chupatintas* *mf inv* ▸ **pencil sharpener** sacapuntas *m inv* ▸ **pencil skirt** falda *f* tubo ▸ **pencil torch** linterna *f* muy fina

▸ **pencil in** VT + ADV apuntar (con lápiz); (*fig*) [*+ appointment*] apuntar con carácter provisional • **I'll ~ you in for Thursday** de momento te apunto para el jueves

pendant ['pendənt] N colgante *m*

pendent ['pendənt] ADJ colgante • **~ lamp** lámpara colgante

pending ['pendɪŋ] ADJ pendiente • **to be ~** estar pendiente *or* en trámite • **and other matters ~** y otros asuntos todavía por resolver
PREP • **~ the arrival of …** hasta que llegue … • **~ your decision** mientras se decida usted • **he has been suspended ~ further investigation** ha sido suspendido en espera de que continúe la investigación
CPD ▸ **pending tray** cajón *m* de asuntos pendientes

pendulous ['pendjʊləs] ADJ colgante

pendulum ['pendjʊləm] N péndulo *m*

Penelope [pə'neləpɪ] N Penélope

penes ['piːniːz] NPL *of* **penis**

penetrable ['penɪtrəbl] ADJ penetrable

penetrate ['penɪtreɪt] VT **1** (*= go right through*) [*+ skin, armour*] penetrar (por), traspasar
2 (*Mil*) [*+ defences*] infiltrar, penetrar; [*+ territory*] penetrar en
3 (*= enter, infiltrate*) [*+ organization*] infiltrarse en; (*Comm*) [*+ market*] introducirse en, entrar en
4 (*= understand*) [*+ mystery*] penetrar; [*+ sb's mind, thoughts*] penetrar en
5 (*during sex*) penetrar
VI (*= go right through*) atravesar; (*= spread, permeate*) [*idea, ideology*] trascender, infiltrarse; (*= get inside*) penetrar; (*= be understood*) entrar, penetrar • **to ~ into** [*+ territory*] penetrar en • **these ideas have ~d into our everyday life** estas ideas han trascendido a *or* se han infiltrado en nuestra vida cotidiana

penetrating ['penɪtreɪtɪŋ] ADJ [*eyes, sound*] penetrante; [*mind*] perspicaz

penetratingly ['penɪtreɪtɪŋlɪ] ADV de manera penetrante, con penetración

penetration [ˌpenɪˌtreɪʃən] N (*gen*) penetración *f*; [*of analysis, observation*] agudeza *f*

penetrative ['penɪtrətɪv] ADJ penetrante
CPD ▸ **penetrative sex** relaciones *fpl* sexuales con penetración

penguin ['peŋgwɪn] N pingüino *m*

penholder ['penˌhəʊldəʳ] N portaplumas *m inv*

penicillin [ˌpenɪ'sɪlɪn] N penicilina *f*
CPD ▸ **penicillin tablet** comprimido *m* de penicilina

penile ['piːnaɪl] ADJ del pene

peninsula [pɪ'nɪnsjʊlə] N península *f*

peninsular [pɪ'nɪnsjʊləʳ] ADJ peninsular • **the Peninsular War** la Guerra de Independencia

penis ['piːnɪs] (N) (PL: **penises** *or* **penes**) pene *m*
penitence ['penɪtəns] (N) penitencia *f*
penitent ['penɪtənt] (ADJ) arrepentido; (*Rel*) penitente
(N) penitente *mf*
penitential [ˌpenɪ'tenʃəl] (ADJ) penitencial
penitentiary [ˌpenɪ'tenʃərɪ] (N) (*esp US*) (= *prison*) penitenciaría *f*
penitently ['penɪtəntlɪ] (ADV) arrepentidamente, compungidamente; (*Rel*) penitentemente
penknife ['pennaɪf] (N) (PL: **penknives**) navaja *f*, cortaplumas *m inv*
penman ['penmən] (N) (PL: **penmen**) calígrafo *m*, pendolista *m*
penmanship ['penmənʃɪp] (N) caligrafía *f*
Penn, Penna (ABBR) (US) = **Pennsylvania**
pennant ['penənt] (N) banderín *m*; (*Naut*) gallardete *m*
pennies ['penɪz] (NPL) *of* **penny**
penniless ['penɪlɪs] (ADJ) [*aristocrat, immigrant*] sin dinero • **to be ~** no tener un céntimo *or* un centavo • **to be left ~** quedarse sin un céntimo *or* un centavo
Pennine ['penaɪn] (N) • **the ~s** los (Montes) Peninos
pennon ['penən] (N) pendón *m*
Pennsylvania [ˌpensɪl'veɪnɪə] (N) Pensilvania *f*
Penny ['penɪ] (N) *familiar form of* **Penelope**
penny ['penɪ] (N) (= *value*) (PL: **pence**), (= *coins*) (PL: **pennies**) (*Brit*) penique *m*; (*US*) (= *cent*) centavo *m*; (*Spanish equivalent*) perra *f* gorda • **it costs five pence** cuesta cinco peniques • **I have five pennies** tengo cinco peniques • **I don't owe you a ~** no te debo nada • **it cost £500 but it was worth every ~** costó 500 libras, pero mereció la pena pagarlas • **£20, not a ~ more, not a ~ less** 20 libras, ni un penique más ni menos • **new ~** *penique del sistema monetario británico actual que es la centésima parte de una libra* • **old ~** *penique del sistema monetario británico antiguo equivalente a 0,4 peniques actuales* • **a ten-pence piece** *or* **coin** una moneda de diez peniques • IDIOMS: • **he turns up like a bad ~** está hasta en la sopa • **to count the pennies** mirar el dinero • **then the ~ dropped** por fin cayó en la cuenta • **he hasn't a ~ to his name** • **he hasn't two pennies to rub together** no tiene dónde caerse muerto • **(a) ~ for your thoughts** • **a ~ for them*** ¿en qué estás pensando? • **for two pence I'd tell her what I think of her** por menos de nada le digo lo que pienso de ella • **to be two** *or* **ten a ~** haberlo a montones • **he thinks jobs are two a ~** cree que hay trabajos a montones • **to watch the pennies** mirar el dinero • PROVERBS: • **in for a ~, in for a pound** de perdidos, al río • **take care of the pennies and the pounds will take care of themselves** muchos pocos hacen un montón • **a ~ saved is a ~ gained** si pagas aunque sea solo un céntimo *or* un poco menos, eso que te ahorras; ▷ **honest, pretty, spend**
(CPD) ▸ **penny arcade** (*US*) galería *f* de máquinas tragaperras ▸ **penny black** *primer sello de correos británico, que data del 1830* ▸ **penny dreadful** *libro o revista escabroso o sensacionalista* ▸ **penny farthing** velocípedo *m* ▸ **penny loafer** (*US*) mocasín *m* ▸ **penny whistle** flauta *f* metálica
penny-a-liner ['penɪə'laɪnəʳ] (N) escritorzuelo/a* *m/f* (*pej*), gacetillero/a *m/f* (*pej*)
penny-in-the-slot machine [ˌpenɪɪnðə'slɒtməʃiːn] (N) (máquina *f*) tragaperras *f inv*
penny-pinching ['penɪˌpɪntʃɪŋ] (N) tacañería *f*
(ADJ) [*person*] tacaño, avaro
pennyweight ['penɪweɪt] (N) *peso de 24 granos (= 1,555 gramos)*
penny-wise [ˌpenɪ'waɪz] (ADJ) • **to be penny-wise** mirar el dinero • IDIOM: • **to be penny-wise and pound-foolish** mirar tanto el dinero que se acaba gastando un dineral
pennyworth ['penəθ] (N) (*Hist*) • **a ~ of sweets** un penique de caramelos • IDIOM: • **to put in one's two ~** meter baza* • **you've had your two ~** tú metiste baza*
penologist [piː'nɒlədʒɪst] (N) penalista *mf*, criminólogo/a *m/f*
penology [piː'nɒlədʒɪ] (N) ciencia *f* penal, criminología *f*
penpusher ['penˌpʊʃəʳ] (N) (*Brit*) (*pej*) chupatintas* *m inv*
pension¹ ['penʃən] (N) pensión *f* • **to claim/draw one's** *or* **a ~** solicitar/estar cobrando una pensión • **to retire on a ~** jubilarse • **to retire on full ~** retirarse con toda la jubilación • **company ~** plan *m* de pensiones de la empresa • **disability/ invalidity ~** pensión *f* de invalidez • **old age ~** (pensión *f* de) jubilación *f*, retiro *m* • **personal** *or* **private ~** plan *m* de pensiones personal • **retirement ~** retiro *m*, (pensión *f* de) jubilación *f* • **state ~** pensión *f* estatal • **war ~** pensión *f* de guerra • **widow's ~** pensión *f* de viudedad
(VT) (= *allow to retire*) jubilar; (= *give pension*) pagar una pensión a
(CPD) ▸ **pension benefits** pensión *f*, *dinero que se cobra de la misma* ▸ **pension book** libreta *f* de pensión ▸ **pension contributions** aportaciones *mpl* a la pensión ▸ **pension fund** fondo *m* de pensiones ▸ **pension plan** plan *m* de pensiones ▸ **pension provider** (= *company*) proveedor *m* de pensiones ▸ **pension provision** (*by state, employers*) cobertura *f* de pensiones ▸ **pension rights** derechos *mpl* de pensión ▸ **pension scheme** plan *m* de pensiones
▸ **pension off** (VT + ADV) (*lit*) jubilar • **isn't it time you ~ed off that car of yours?*** ¿no va siendo hora de que jubiles ese coche?*
pension² ['pɒ̃sjɔ̃] (N) (= *hotel*) pensión *f*
pensionable ['penʃənəbl] (ADJ) [*age*] de jubilación; [*post*] con derecho a pensión
pensioner ['penʃənəʳ] (N) pensionado/a *m/f*, pensionista *mf*; (= *old age pensioner*) jubilado/a *m/f*
pensive ['pensɪv] (ADJ) (*gen*) pensativo, meditabundo
pensively ['pensɪvlɪ] (ADV) pensativamente
pent [pent] (ADJ) ▷ **pent-up**
pentagon ['pentəgən] (N) pentágono *m* • **the Pentagon** (*Washington*) el Pentágono
pentagonal [pen'tægənl] (ADJ) pentagonal
pentagram ['pentəgræm] (N) estrella *f* de cinco puntas
pentameter [pen'tæmɪtəʳ] (N) pentámetro *m*
Pentateuch ['pentətjuːk] (N) Pentateuco *m*
pentathlete [pen'tæθliːt] (N) pentatleta *mf*
pentathlon [pen'tæθlən] (N) pentatlón *m*
pentatonic [ˌpentə'tɒnɪk] (ADJ) pentatónico
(CPD) ▸ **pentatonic scale** escala *f* pentatónica
Pentecost ['pentɪkɒst] (N) (*Rel*) Pentecostés *m*
Pentecostal [ˌpentɪ'kɒstl] (ADJ) de Pentecostés
Pentecostalism [ˌpentɪ'kɒstlɪzəm] (N) pentecostalismo *m*
penthouse ['penthaʊs] (N) (PL: **penthouses** ['penthaʊzɪz]) ático *m*
Pentium processor® [ˌpentɪəm'prəʊsesəʳ] (N) procesador *m* Pentium
pent-up ['pentʌp] (ADJ) [*rage*] contenido, reprimido; [*emotion, frustration, energy*] contenido • **pent-up demand** demanda *f* reprimida
penult [pɪ'nʌlt] (N) penúltima *f*
penultimate [pɪ'nʌltɪmɪt] (ADJ) penúltimo
penumbra [pɪ'nʌmbrə] (N) (PL: **penumbras** *or* **penumbrae** [pɪ'nʌmbriː]) penumbra *f*
penurious [pɪ'njʊərɪəs] (ADJ) miserable, pobrísimo
penury ['penjʊrɪ] (N) miseria *f*, penuria *f* • **to live in ~** vivir en la penuria *or* miseria • **to be reduced to ~** quedarse en la miseria
peon ['piːən] (N) peón *m*
peonage ['piːənɪdʒ] (N) condición *f* de peón; (*fig*) servidumbre *f*, esclavitud *f*
peony ['pɪənɪ] (N) peonía *f*
people ['piːpl] (N) **1** (*with pl vb*) **a** (*seen as a mass*) gente *f* • **what will ~ think?** ¿qué va a pensar la gente? • **they stole from ~'s houses** robaban las casas de la gente • **the place was full of ~** el local estaba lleno de gente • **country ~** la gente del campo • **I like the ~ here** la gente de aquí me cae bien • **here ~ quarrel a lot** aquí se riñe mucho • **they don't mix much with the local ~** no se tratan mucho con la gente del lugar • **what a lot of ~!** ¡cuánta gente! • **old ~** los ancianos, la gente mayor • **~ say that …** dicen que …, la gente dice que … • **young ~** los jóvenes, la gente joven
b (= *persons, individuals*) personas *fpl* • **20 ~** 20 personas • **millions of ~** millones *mpl* de personas • **~ are more important than animals** las personas son más importantes que los animales • **how many ~ are there in your family?** ¿cuántos sois en tu familia? • **he got a knighthood, him of all ~!** le han nombrado sir, ¡precisamente a él! • **you of all ~ should understand** tú deberías entenderlo mejor que nadie • **the ~ concerned** la gente *or* las personas en cuestión • **English ~** los ingleses • **two English ~** dos ingleses • **the gas ~ are coming tomorrow** los del gas vienen mañana • **~ like you are not welcome** no queremos gente como tú • **many ~ think that …** mucha gente cree que …, muchos creen que … • **most ~ like it** a la mayoría de la gente le gusta • **several ~ have told me** me lo han dicho varias personas • **some ~ are born lucky** hay gente que nace de pie, hay gente con suerte • **they're strange ~** son gente rara • **what do you ~ think?** y ustedes ¿qué opinan?; ▷ **little¹**
c (= *inhabitants*) habitantes *mpl* • **Madrid has over four million ~** Madrid tiene más de cuatro millones de habitantes • **the ~ of London** los habitantes de Londres, los londinenses • **the ~ of Angola** los habitantes *or* la gente de Angola • **the ~ of this country are fed up** la gente de este país está harta • **a leader who will serve the country and its ~** un líder al servicio del país y de su gente
d (= *citizens, public*) pueblo *m* • **the ~** el pueblo • **the will of the ~** la voluntad popular *or* del pueblo • **the British ~** el pueblo británico • **the king and his ~** el rey y su pueblo *or* sus súbditos • **a ~'s army/democracy/republic** un ejército/una democracia/una república popular • **government by the ~** el gobierno del pueblo • **the ~ at large** el pueblo en general • **a man of the ~** un hombre del pueblo • **power to the ~** poder *m* para el pueblo • **a ~'s tribunal** un tribunal popular • IDIOM: • **to go to the ~** consultar la opinión popular; ▷ **common**
e (= *family*) gente *f*, familia *f* • **my ~ come from the north** mi familia *or* mi gente es del

norte • **have you met his ~?** ¿conoces a su familia?
f (= *colleagues*) • **I asked one of our ~ in Boston to handle it** pedí a uno de los nuestros en Boston que se encargara de ello
2 (*with sing vb*) (= *ethnic group*) pueblo *m* • **an oppressed ~** un pueblo oprimido • **the ~s of the former Soviet Union** los pueblos de la antigua Unión Soviética • **Spanish-speaking ~s** los pueblos *or* las gentes de habla hispana
VT poblar • **the country is ~d by nomads** el país está poblado *or* habitado por nómadas • **his novels are ~d with outlandish characters** sus novelas están pobladas de personajes extravagantes
CPD ▸ **people carrier** monovolumen *m* ▸ **people mover** (*US*) cinta *f* transbordadora, pasillo *m* móvil ▸ **people skills** • **to have good ~ skills** tener habilidades sociales • **"good people skills are essential"** "fundamental tener facilidad para relacionarse", "fundamental tener habilidades sociales" ▸ **people trafficking** tráfico *m* de personas

PEP [pep] N ABBR (*Brit*) (*Econ*) = **personal equity plan**

pep* [pep] N energía *f*, dinamismo *m*
CPD ▸ **pep pill** estimulante *m* ▸ **pep rally** (*US*) *encuentro de motivación* ▸ **pep talk** palabras *fpl* que motivan, palabras *fpl* para levantar la moral • **to give sb a pep talk** hablar a algn para motivarle *or* levantarle la moral
▸ **pep up** VT + ADV [+ *person*] (= *encourage*) animar, estimular; (= *revive*) dar un nuevo impulso a; [+ *drink*] hacer más fuerte • **how to pep up your love life** cómo dar un nuevo impulso a su vida amorosa

PEP RALLY
Pep rally es un término usado en Estados Unidos para referirse a las concentraciones que se realizan antes de la celebración de un partido de fútbol americano o baloncesto en los institutos de enseñanza secundaria o en la universidad. En estas celebraciones, que tienen lugar uno o varios días antes del partido, participan animadores de grupo, una banda de música y tanto los jugadores como los entrenadores tienen que pronunciar unas palabras ante los demás. También se emplea a veces el término **pep rally** con referencia a los mítines políticos o a encuentros entre los miembros de una empresa para alentar la motivación entre sus afiliados o empleados por medio de la adulación pública o el anuncio de nuevos proyectos o de éxitos futuros.

pepper ['pepəʳ] N **1** (= *spice*) pimienta *f* • **black/white ~** pimienta *f* negra/blanca; ▹ **cayenne**
2 (= *vegetable*) pimiento *m*, pimentón *m* (*S. Cone*) • **green ~** pimiento *m* verde, pimentón *m* verde (*LAm*) • **red ~** (= *capsicum*) pimiento *m* rojo, pimiento *m* morrón, pimentón *m* rojo (*LAm*); ▹ **chili**
VT **1** (*lit*) echar *or* poner pimienta a, sazonar con pimienta
2 (*fig*) **a** (= *bombard*) acribillar • **the walls were ~ed with bullet holes** las paredes habían sido acribilladas a balazos • **to ~ sth/sb with bullets** acribillar algo/a algn a balazos • **to ~ sb with questions** acribillar a algn a preguntas
b (= *sprinkle*) salpicar • **his English is heavily ~ed with Americanisms** su inglés está salpicado de americanismos • **to ~ a work with quotations** salpicar una obra de citas • **his hair is ~ed with grey** tiene el pelo salpicado de canas
CPD ▸ **pepper mill** molinillo *m* de pimienta ▸ **pepper plant** pimentero *m* ▸ **pepper pot, pepper shaker** (*US*) pimentero *m* ▸ **pepper spray** aerosol *m* de pimienta ▸ **pepper steak** filete *m* a la pimienta

peppercorn ['pepəkɔːn] N grano *m* de pimienta
CPD ▸ **peppercorn rent** alquiler *m* nominal

peppermint ['pepəmɪnt] N (*Bot*) menta *f*; (= *sweet*) caramelo *m* de menta; (= *lozenge*) pastilla *f* de menta • **~ flavour ice cream** helado *m* con sabor a menta

pepperoni [pepə'rəʊnɪ] N salchichón *m* a la pimienta, pepperoni *m*

peppery ['pepərɪ] ADJ (= *hot, sharp*) picante; (= *tasting of pepper*) con sabor a pimienta; (*fig*) (= *short-tempered*) enojadizo • **~ taste** sabor *m* a pimienta; (*hot, sharp*) sabor *m* picante

peppy* ['pepɪ] ADJ lleno de vida

pepsin ['pepsɪn] N pepsina *f*

peptic ['peptɪk] ADJ péptico
CPD ▸ **peptic ulcer** úlcera *f* péptica

peptide ['peptaɪd] N péptido *m*
CPD ▸ **peptide bond** enlace *m* peptídico ▸ **peptide chain** cadena *f* peptídica

peptone ['peptəʊn] N peptona *f*

per [pɜːʳ] PREP por • **per annum** al año • **we shall proceed as per instructions** procederemos de acuerdo con las instrucciones • **as per invoice** de acuerdo con *or* según la factura • **£10 per dozen** 10 libras la docena • **30 miles per gallon** 30 millas por cada galón • **per head** por cabeza • **per head of population** por habitante • **60 miles per hour** 60 millas por hora • **per person** por persona • **£15 per person per night** 15 libras por persona y por noche • **per se** de por sí • **£7 per week** 7 libras a la semana; ▹ **per cent, usual**

perambulate [pə'ræmbjʊleɪt] VT recorrer
VI pasearse, deambular

perambulation [pə,ræmbjʊ'leɪʃən] N (*frm, hum*) (= *stroll*) paseo *m*; (= *journey*) viaje *m*; (= *visit*) visita *f* de inspección

perambulator† ['præmbjʊleɪtəʳ] N (*Brit*) (*frm*) cochecito *m* de niño

perborate [pə'bɔːreɪt] N perborato *m*

per capita [pə'kæpɪtə] ADV per cápita
CPD ▸ **per capita consumption** consumo *m* per cápita • **the ~ consumption of alcohol** el consumo de alcohol per cápita ▸ **per capita income** ingresos *mpl* per cápita

perceivable [pə'siːvəbl] ADJ perceptible • **barely ~** apenas perceptible

perceive [pə'siːv] VT **1** (= *see, hear*) percibir; (= *realize*) darse cuenta de, notar • **now I ~ that ...** ahora veo que ... • **do you ~ anything strange?** ¿notas algo raro? • **~d need/interest** necesidad *f*/interés *m* que se ha detectado
2 (= *understand*) comprender • **I do not ~ how it can be done** no comprendo cómo se puede hacer
3 (= *consider*) considerar • **their action may be ~d as a threat** su actuación puede considerarse *or* puede verse como una amenaza • **the things children ~ as being important** las cosas que los niños consideran importantes • **they ~ themselves as rebels** se ven a sí mismos como rebeldes, se consideran a sí mismos rebeldes

per cent [pə'sent] N por ciento • **20 ~** el 20 por ciento • **it has increased by eight ~** ha aumentado (en) un ocho por ciento • **there's a ten ~ discount** hay un descuento del diez por cien(to), hay un diez por ciento de descuento • **the population is 90 ~ Roman Catholic** el 90 por ciento de la población es católica • **a half (a) ~ cut in interest rates** un recorte de un cero coma cinco por ciento en los tipos de interés • **100 ~** cien por cien • **he's not feeling a hundred ~ today** hoy no se encuentra al cien por cien

percentage [pə'sentɪdʒ] N **1** (= *proportion*) porcentaje *m* • **what is the ~ of nitrogen in air?** ¿cuál es el porcentaje de nitrógeno en el aire? • **a large ~ of people are immune** un gran porcentaje de la gente es inmune • **the figure is expressed as a ~** la cifra está expresada en tantos por ciento • **on a ~ basis California lost more jobs than any other state** según los porcentajes California perdió más puestos de trabajo que ningún otro estado • **a high ~ are girls** un alto *or* elevado porcentaje son chicas • **in ~ terms** proporcionalmente
2 (= *commission*) porcentaje *m* • **my ~ is deducted beforehand** mi porcentaje se deduce antes • **to get a ~ on all sales** recibir un tanto por ciento sobre todas las ventas • **on a ~ basis** a porcentaje
3* (= *rake-off*) tajada* *f* • **all they're after is their ~** lo único que buscan es llevarse una tajada*
4 (= *advantage, benefit*) • **there's no ~ in doing that** haciendo eso no se saca nada • **what ~ is there in it for me?** ¿y yo qué saco?
CPD ▸ **percentage increase** aumento *m* porcentual ▸ **percentage point** punto *m* porcentual ▸ **percentage sign** signo *m* del tanto por ciento

percentile [pə'sentaɪl] N percentil *m*

perceptible [pə'septəbl] ADJ (= *appreciable*) sensible; (= *discernible*) perceptible

perceptibly [pə'septəblɪ] ADV (= *appreciably*) sensiblemente; (= *discernibly*) perceptiblemente • **it has improved ~** ha mejorado sensiblemente

perception [pə'sepʃən] N **1** (= *act*) percepción *f* • **it changes one's ~ of time** cambia la percepción que uno tiene del tiempo • **sense ~** percepción *f* sensorial
2 (= *impression*) impresión *f* • **what is your ~ of the situation?** ¿qué impresión tienes de la situación? • **her ~ was that she had done sth wrong** tenía la impresión de haberse equivocado en algo • **the public ~ is that ...** la gente tiene la impresión de que ...
3 (= *insight*) perspicacia *f*, agudeza *f*

perceptive [pə'septɪv] ADJ [*person*] perspicaz; [*remark*] perspicaz, agudo; [*function*] perceptivo

perceptively [pə'septɪvlɪ] ADV [*say, write*] con perspicacia

perceptiveness [pə'septɪvnɪs] N (= *insight*) perspicacia *f*, agudeza *f*; (= *ability to perceive*) facultad *f* perceptiva

perceptual [pə'septjʊəl] ADJ [*skills, problems*] de percepción, perceptual

perch¹ [pɜːtʃ] N [*of bird*] percha *f*; (*fig*) [*of person*] posición *f* elevada • IDIOM: • **to knock sb off his ~** bajar los humos *or* el copete a algn*
VT encaramar • **we ~ed the child on the wall** encaramamos al niño en la tapia • **the village is ~ed on a hilltop** el pueblo está encaramado en lo alto de una colina • **he ~ed his hat on his head** se colocó el sombrero en la cabeza
VI [*bird*] posarse (**on** en); [*person*] (= *sit*) sentarse (**on** en); (*high up*) encaramarse (**on** en) • **she ~ed on the arm of my chair** se sentó en el brazo de mi sillón • **we ~ed in a tree to see the procession** nos encaramamos *or* subimos a un árbol para ver el desfile

perch² [pɜːtʃ] N (PL: **perch, perches**) (= *fish*) perca *f*

perch³ [pɜːtʃ] N *medida de longitud, = 5,029m*

perchance [pəˈtʃɑːns] ADV (*liter*) (= *by chance*) por ventura, acaso; (= *perhaps*) acaso, tal vez • **to sleep, ~ to dream** dormir, acaso or tal vez soñar • **are they ~ afraid of me?** ¿acaso les doy miedo?

percipient [pəˈsɪpɪənt] ADJ = **perceptive**

percolate [ˈpɜːkəleɪt] VT filtrar; [+ *coffee*] hacer (*en una cafetera de filtro*) • **~d coffee** café *m* (de) filtro
VI **1** (*lit, fig*) filtrarse • **to ~ down to** filtrarse hasta • **to ~ through (sth)** [*water*] filtrarse (por algo); [*ideas*] propagarse (por algo) • **these ideas may eventually ~ through to the top of the organization** puede que al final estas ideas se propaguen por la cúpula de la organización
2 [*coffee*] hacerse (*en una cafetera de filtro*)

percolator [ˈpɜːkəleɪtəʳ] N cafetera *f* de filtro

percuss [pəˈkʌs] VT (*Med*) percutir

percussion [pəˈkʌʃən] N **1** (= *impact, noise*) percusión *f*
2 (*Mus*) percusión *f* • **to play ~** ser percusionista
CPD ▸ **percussion cap** cápsula *f* fulminante ▸ **percussion instrument** instrumento *m* de percusión ▸ **percussion section** percusión *f*, sección *f* de percusión

percussionist [pəˈkʌʃənɪst] N percusionista *mf*

percussive [pəˈkʌsɪv] ADJ de percusión

per diem [ˈpɜːˈdiːem] ADV por día
N (= *allowance*) complemento *m* para gastos diarios

perdition [pɜːˈdɪʃən] N (*liter*) perdición *f*

peregrination [ˌperɪgrɪˈneɪʃən] N peregrinación *f*; **peregrinations** (*hum*) periplo *m*, peregrinaje *m*

peregrine [ˈperɪgrɪn] N halcón *m* común, neblí *m*
CPD ▸ **peregrine falcon** halcón *m* peregrino

peremptorily [pəˈremptərɪlɪ] ADV [*say, refuse*] en tono perentorio, en tono imperioso • **they were ~ sacked** los despidieron sin más

peremptory [pəˈremptərɪ] ADJ [*tone*] perentorio, imperioso; [*person*] imperioso, autoritario

perennial [pəˈrenɪəl] ADJ (*Bot*) perenne; [*problem*] perenne, eterno • **~ youth** la juventud eterna • **it's a ~ complaint** es una queja constante
N (*Bot*) planta *f* perenne, planta *f* vivaz

perennially [pəˈrenɪəlɪ] ADV perennemente, constantemente • **they are ~ short of staff** les falta personal constantemente

perestroika [perəˈstrɔɪkə] N perestroika *f*

perfect [ˈpɜːfɪkt] ADJ **1** (= *faultless*) perfecto • **nobody is ~** nadie es perfecto • **everything was ~ on the day** ese día todo salió perfecto • **in ~ condition** en perfectas condiciones • **he spoke ~ English** • **his English was ~** hablaba un inglés perfecto • **his Spanish is far from ~** su español dista mucho de ser perfecto • **you're in ~ health** se encuentra perfectamente de salud; ▹ **practice, word-perfect**
2 (= *ideal*) [*moment, solution, place*] ideal, perfecto • **a job like that would be ~ for you** un trabajo como ese sería ideal or perfecto para ti • **Saturday morning would be ~** el sábado por la mañana sería ideal or perfecto • **he's the ~ man for the job** es el hombre idóneo or ideal or perfecto para el cargo • **his expertise made him the ~ choice** su experiencia hacía de él la persona idónea or ideal or perfecta • **in a ~ world** en un mundo ideal
3 (= *exact*) perfecto • **a ~ circle** un círculo perfecto • **a ~ copy** una copia perfecta • **the jacket was a ~ fit** la chaqueta me estaba perfecta or me quedaba perfectamente • **my watch keeps ~ time** mi reloj siempre marca la hora exacta
4 (= *absolute, utter*) • **a ~ fool/stranger** un perfecto idiota/desconocido • **I have a ~ right to be here** estoy en el perfecto derecho de estar aquí • **she's a ~ pest** es una verdadera pesada* • **it makes ~ sense to me** me parece completamente or totalmente lógico
5 (*Gram*) perfecto; ▹ **future, present, past**
6 (*Mus*) [*fourth, fifth, octave*] perfecto • **a ~ fifth** una quinta perfecta
N [ˈpɜːfɪkt] (*Gram*) • **the ~** el tiempo perfecto; ▹ **future, present, past**
VT [pəˈfekt] perfeccionar • **she wanted to ~ her English** quería perfeccionar su inglés • **to ~ the art of doing sth** perfeccionar el arte de hacer algo
CPD [ˈpɜːfɪkt] ▸ **perfect number** (*Math*) número *m* perfecto ▸ **perfect pitch** (*Mus*) oído *m* perfecto • **to have ~ pitch** tener el oído perfecto ▸ **perfect tense** (*also* **present perfect tense**) • **the ~ tense** el tiempo perfecto

perfectibility [pəˌfektɪˈbɪlɪtɪ] N perfectibilidad *f*

perfectible [pəˈfektəbl] ADJ perfectible

perfection [pəˈfekʃən] N perfección *f* • **the peak of ~** el súmmum de la perfección • **cooked to ~** cocinado a la perfección

perfectionism [pəˈfekʃənɪzm] N perfeccionismo *m*

perfectionist [pəˈfekʃənɪst] N perfeccionista *mf*

perfective [pəˈfektɪv] ADJ [*aspect, verb*] perfectivo
N perfectivo *m*

perfectly [ˈpɜːfɪktlɪ] ADV **1** (= *very well*) perfectamente • **the plan worked ~** el plan salió perfectamente or a la perfección • **he is ~ placed to understand the situation** está en la posición perfecta para comprender la situación • **you timed your arrival ~** has llegado en el momento preciso • **one of the most ~ preserved medieval towns in the world** uno de los pueblos medievales mejor conservados del mundo
2 (= *absolutely, entirely*) [*honest, frank, normal*] totalmente • **to be ~ honest, I hate classical music** si te soy totalmente sincero, odio la música clásica • **I'll be ~ frank with you** te voy a ser totalmente franco • **it's ~ disgusting!** ¡es verdaderamente asqueroso! • **I'm ~ all right** estoy perfectamente • **well, actually, we're ~ happy about it** pues, la verdad, no nos importa en absoluto • **there may be some ~ innocent explanation** puede que esto tenga una explicación totalmente inocente • **it is ~ possible to eat well on a diet** es muy posible alimentarse bien aunque se esté a régimen • **you'll be ~ safe here** aquí no correrás ni el más mínimo peligro • **we're ~ satisfied with this** estamos plenamente satisfechos con esto • **look, it's ~ simple** mira, es de lo más sencillo • **you know ~ well what my answer will be** bien sabes or sabes muy bien qué respuesta te voy a dar

perfidious [pɜːˈfɪdɪəs] ADJ (*liter*) pérfido

perfidiously [pɜːˈfɪdɪəslɪ] ADV (*liter*) pérfidamente

perfidy [ˈpɜːfɪdɪ] N (*liter*) perfidia *f*

perforate [ˈpɜːfəreɪt] VT perforar • **to ~ holes in sth** practicar agujeros en algo

perforated [ˈpɜːfəreɪtɪd] ADJ [*stamp*] dentado
CPD ▸ **perforated line** línea *f* perforada ▸ **perforated ulcer** (*Med*) úlcera *f* perforada

perforation [ˌpɜːfəˈreɪʃən] N (*gen*) perforación *f*; [*of stamp*] perforado *m*

perforce [pəˈfɔːs] ADV (*liter*) forzosamente

perform [pəˈfɔːm] VT **1** (*Theat, Mus*) [+ *play*] representar; [+ *part, piece, song, dance*] interpretar • **it meant a lot to her to have her music ~ed here** significó mucho para ella el que interpretaran su música aquí • **she will ~ a series of sonatas by Mozart** interpretará or ejecutará varias sonatas de Mozart
2 (= *carry out*) [+ *task, experiment, feat*] realizar, llevar a cabo; [+ *operation, autopsy*] practicar, realizar, llevar a cabo; [+ *duty*] cumplir con; [+ *function, role*] desempeñar, cumplir; [+ *rite, ritual, ceremony*] celebrar; [+ *miracle*] realizar, hacer • **they ~ed a great service to their country** prestaron un gran servicio a su país • **to ~ surgery** or **an operation on sb** operar a algn, practicar una operación quirúrgica a algn (*frm*)
VI **1** (*Theat, Mus*) [*entertainer, actor*] actuar; [*musician*] tocar; [*orchestra, pop group*] actuar, tocar; [*singer*] cantar; [*dancer*] bailar; [*trained animal*] hacer trucos, realizar trucos • **he ~ed brilliantly as Hamlet** interpretó brillantemente el papel de Hamlet, se lució en el papel de Hamlet • **the band will be ~ing live** el grupo actuará or tocará en concierto • **and ~ing for us tonight on the violin is Rebecca Hunt** y esta noche Rebecca Hunt nos tocará el violín
2 (= *respond, behave*) [*vehicle, machine*] responder, funcionar; [*team, athlete, horse*] responder; [*investment, shares*] rendir; [*metal, material*] comportarse; [*worker*] (= *be productive*) rendir; (= *react*) responder • **how did the company ~ last year?** ¿qué resultados dio la empresa el año pasado? • **the party ~ed abysmally at the last election** el partido obtuvo unos resultados pésimos en las últimas elecciones • **he ~ed well at school** rendía en los estudios • **he did not ~ very well in his exams** no obtuvo muy buenos resultados en los exámenes, los exámenes no le salieron muy bien • **our economy has been ~ing well recently** últimamente, nuestra economía ha estado produciendo buenos resultados
3* (*esp hum*) (= *go to toilet*) [*child, dog*] hacer sus menesteres
4* (*sexually*) cumplir*

performance [pəˈfɔːməns] N **1** (*Theat, Mus etc*) **a** (= *session*) (*Theat*) función *f*; (*Cine*) sesión *f* • **tonight's ~ will end at 9.45 pm** (*Theat*) la función de esta noche terminará a las 21.45 • **the late ~** (*Theat*) la función de noche; (*Cine*) la sesión de noche • **two ~s nightly** (*Theat*) dos funciones or representaciones por noche; (*Cine*) dos sesiones por noche • **no ~ tonight** esta noche no hay función, no hay representación esta noche
b (= *presentation*) [*of play, opera, ballet*] representación *f*; [*of piece of music*] interpretación *f* • **it has not had a ~ since 1950** (*Theat*) no se ha representado desde 1950; (*Mus*) no se ha interpretado desde 1950 • **the play ran for over 300 ~s** la obra tuvo más de 300 representaciones • **first ~** estreno *m* • **video footage of the band in ~** unas secuencias en vídeo del grupo en concierto
c (*by actor, singer*) actuación *f*, interpretación *f*; (*by pianist, orchestra*) interpretación *f*; (*by comedian*) actuación *f* • **his ~ as Don Juan was excellent** su actuación en el papel or su interpretación

del papel de Don Juan fue excelente • **this will be her first ~ at Covent Garden** esta será su primera actuación en Covent Garden; ▹ **gala, virtuoso**
2 (= *effectiveness*) [*of investment, worker*] rendimiento *m*; [*of currency*] comportamiento *m*; [*of team, athlete, racehorse*] actuación *f*; [*of company*] resultados *mpl*; [*of vehicle*] rendimiento *m*, performance *f* (*LAm*); [*of machine*] (= *productivity*) rendimiento *m*; (= *working*) funcionamiento *m* • **the ~ of the pound against the mark** el comportamiento de la libra con respecto al marco • **we judge people on ~ rather than age** juzgamos a las personas por su rendimiento y no por su edad • **the party's disastrous ~ in the elections** los pésimos resultados del partido en las elecciones • **Britain's poor economic ~ in the 1970s** el poco rendimiento de la economía británica en los setenta • **on past ~, an England victory seems unlikely** si nos basamos en las actuaciones anteriores, parece poco probable que Inglaterra vaya a ganar • **her poor ~ in French** su poco rendimiento en francés, sus malos resultados en francés • **he didn't put up a very good ~ in the exams** no obtuvo muy buenos resultados en los exámenes, los exámenes no le salieron muy bien • **the team gave** *or* **put up a poor ~** el equipo tuvo una actuación pobre; ▹ **high-performance, performance-related**
3 (= *execution*) [*of task*] realización *f*, ejecución *f*; [*of duty*] cumplimiento *m*; [*of function*] ejercicio *m*; [*of rite, ritual*] práctica *f*, celebración *f* • **she has to rely on others for the ~ of the simplest tasks** tiene que depender de otros para realizar *or* ejecutar las tareas más sencillas • **in the ~ of his duties** en el ejercicio de su cargo
4* (= *bother, rigmarole*) follón* *m*, jaleo* *m* • **it's such a ~ getting here** llegar aquí supone tal follón *or* jaleo* • **what a ~ it is to get a visa!** ¡conseguir un visado es un verdadero follón *or* jaleo!*
5* (= *fuss about nothing*) numero* *m* • **what a ~ she made of making the tea** vaya numero que montó para hacer el té*
6 (*Ling*) actuación *f*
CPD ▸ **performance art** performance art *m* ▸ **performance bonus** prima *f* de productividad ▸ **performance car** coche *m* de alto rendimiento ▸ **performance figures** cifras *fpl* de productividad ▸ **performance indicator** (*Comm, Econ*) indicador *m* del rendimiento ▸ **performance target** objetivo *m* de rendimiento

performance-enhancing [pəˈfɔːmənsɪn,hɑːnsɪŋ] ADJ • **performance-enhancing drug** sustancia *f* que potencia el rendimiento

performance-related [pəˈfɔːmənsrɪˈleɪtɪd] ADJ [*bonus, scheme*] en relación con los resultados • **performance-related pay** remuneración *f* con arreglo al rendimiento

performative [pəˈfɔːmətɪv] N • **~ (verb)** (verbo *m*) performativo *m*

performer [pəˈfɔːməʳ] N (*Theat*) actor/actriz *m/f*, artista *mf*; (*Mus*) intérprete *mf* • **a skilled ~ on the piano** un pianista experto • **this fund has been one of the best ~s in recent years** este fondo de inversiones ha sido de los que han dado mejores resultados en los últimos años • **he was a poor ~ at school** no le iba muy bien en el colegio

performing [pəˈfɔːmɪŋ] ADJ [*animal*] amaestrado
CPD ▸ **performing arts** artes *fpl* de la interpretación

perfume [ˈpɜːfjuːm] N perfume *m*
VT [pəˈfjuːm] perfumar

perfumed [ˈpɜːfjuːmd] [pəˈfjuːmd] ADJ perfumado

perfumer [pəˈfjuːməʳ] N (= *maker*) perfumista *mf*; (= *seller*) vendedor(a) *m/f* de perfumes; (= *device*) perfumero *m*

perfumery [pəˈfjuːmərɪ] N perfumería *f*; (= *perfumes*) perfumes *mpl*

perfunctorily [pəˈfʌŋktərɪlɪ] ADV [*inspect*] superficialmente, someramente; [*reply*] a la ligera; [*kiss*] con indiferencia, mecánicamente

perfunctory [pəˈfʌŋktərɪ] ADJ [*inspection, glance*] superficial, somero; [*reply*] dado a la ligera; [*kiss*] indiferente, mecánico • **he gave a ~ performance** tocó *etc* por cumplir

pergola [ˈpɜːgələ] N pérgola *f*

perhaps [pəˈhæps] ADV quizá(s), tal vez • **~ he'll come** quizá *or* tal vez venga, a lo mejor viene • **"will you be seeing her later?" — "perhaps"** —¿la vas a ver después? —a lo mejor *or* —tal vez *or* —puede que sí • **~ not** puede que no • **~ so** puede que sí, puede que así sea, quizá sea así • **there were ~ 50 people there** habría quizás unas 50 personas allí, puede que hubiese unas 50 personas allí

peri... [ˈperɪ] PREFIX peri...

pericardium [,perɪˈkɑːdɪəm] N (PL: **pericardia** [,perɪˈkɑːdɪə]) pericardio *m*

peridot [ˈperɪdɒt] N peridotita *f*

perigee [ˈperɪdʒiː] N perigeo *m*

peril [ˈperɪl] N riesgo *m*, peligro *m* • **to be in ~** estar en *or* correr peligro • **she was in ~ of her life** su vida estaba en peligro, corría el riesgo *or* peligro de perder la vida • **do it at your ~** hágalo por su cuenta y riesgo

perilous [ˈperɪləs] ADJ peligroso, arriesgado • **it would be ~ to attempt it** sería peligroso *or* arriesgado intentarlo

perilously [ˈperɪləslɪ] ADV peligrosamente • **the film comes ~ close to kitsch** la película roza peligrosamente lo cursi • **he came ~ close to being caught** por poco lo agarran

perimeter [pəˈrɪmɪtəʳ] N perímetro *m*
CPD ▸ **perimeter fence** valla *f* que rodea el recinto ▸ **perimeter wall** muro *m* que rodea el recinto

perinatal [,perɪˈneɪtl] ADJ perinatal

perineum [,perɪˈniːəm] N (PL: **perinea**) perineo *m*

period [ˈpɪərɪəd] N **1** (= *length of time*) período *m*; (= *time limit*) plazo *m*; (= *era*) época *f*; (= *stage*) (*in career, development etc*) etapa *f*; (*Sport*) tiempo *m* • **for a ~ of three weeks** durante (un período de) tres semanas • **within a three month ~** en tres meses, dentro de un plazo de tres meses • **for a limited ~** por un periodo limitado • **at that ~ (of my life)** en aquella época (de mi vida) • **the holiday ~** el período de vacaciones • **the postwar ~** la posguerra • **the Victorian ~** la época victoriana • **a painting from his early ~** un cuadro de su primera época
2 (*Scol*) clase *f*, hora *f* • **we have two French ~s** tenemos dos clases *or* horas de francés
3 (*Gram*) período *m*; (= *full stop*) (*esp US*) punto *m* • **I said no, ~** he dicho que no, y punto
4 (= *menstruation*) período *m*, regla *f* • **I've got my ~** estoy con la regla
CPD ▸ **period cost** costo *m* fijo ▸ **period costume** traje *m* de época ▸ **period drama** (= *play*) drama *m* histórico ▸ **period dress** traje(s) *mpl* de época ▸ **period furniture** muebles *mpl* de época ▸ **period instrument** instrumento *m* de época ▸ **period pain** dolores *fpl* menstruales ▸ **period piece** (= *film*) película *f* de época; (= *novel*) novela *f* de época

periodic [,pɪərɪˈɒdɪk] ADJ periódico
CPD ▸ **periodic table** tabla *f* periódica

periodical [,pɪərɪˈɒdɪkəl] ADJ periódico
N revista *f*, publicación *f* periódica
CPD ▸ **periodicals library** hemeroteca *f*

periodically [,pɪerɪˈɒdɪkəlɪ] ADV (= *at regular intervals*) periódicamente; (= *from time to time*) cada cierto tiempo, de vez en cuando

periodicity [,pɪərɪəˈdɪsɪtɪ] N periodicidad *f*

periodontal [perɪˈdɒntl] ADJ periodontal

peripatetic [,perɪpəˈtetɪk] ADJ [*salesman*] ambulante; [*teacher*] con trabajo en varios colegios; (*Philos*) peripatético • **to lead a ~ existence** cambiar mucho de domicilio, no tener residencia fija

peripheral [pəˈrɪfərəl] ADJ **1** (*Med*) [*vision*] periférico
2 (= *outer, surrounding*) [*area*] periférico, de la periferia
3 (= *minor*) [*role, concern*] secundario
N (*Comput*) periférico *m*, unidad *f* periférica
CPD ▸ **peripheral device** dispositivo *m* periférico

peripheralize [pəˈrɪfərəlaɪz] VT marginar

periphery [pəˈrɪfərɪ] N periferia *f*

periphrasis [pəˈrɪfrəsɪs] N (PL: **periphrases** [pəˈrɪfrəsiːz]) perífrasis *f inv*

periphrastic [,perɪˈfræstɪk] ADJ perifrástico

periscope [ˈperɪskəʊp] N periscopio *m*

perish [ˈperɪʃ] VI **1** [*person*] perecer, fallecer • **we shall do it or ~ in the attempt** lo conseguiremos o moriremos intentándolo • **he ~ed at sea** murió en el mar • **~ the thought!** ¡Dios me libre!
2 [*food, material*] deteriorarse, estropearse
VT deteriorar, estropear • **to be ~ed (with cold)*** estar helado*

perishable [ˈperɪʃəbl] ADJ perecedero
N **perishables** productos *mpl* perecederos

perisher†‡ [ˈperɪʃəʳ] N (*Brit*) tío* *m* • **you little ~!** ¡ay, tunante!*

perishing [ˈperɪʃɪŋ] ADJ **1*** (= *freezing*) • **it's ~ (cold)** hace un frío de muerte*, hace un frío que pela* • **I'm ~** estoy helado*
2 (*Brit*‡) condenado*

peristalsis [,perɪˈstælsɪs] N (PL: **peristalses** [,perɪˈstælsiːz]) peristalsis *f*

peristyle [ˈperɪstaɪl] N peristilo *m*

peritoneum [,perɪtəˈniːəm] N (PL: **peritoneums** *or* **peritonea** [,perɪtəˈniːə]) peritoneo *m*

peritonitis [,perɪtəˈnaɪtɪs] N peritonitis *f*

periwig [ˈperɪwɪg] N peluca *f*

periwinkle [ˈperɪ,wɪŋkl] N (*Bot*) vincapervinca *f*; (*Zool*) caracol *m* de mar, bígaro *m*

perjure [ˈpɜːdʒəʳ] VT • **to ~ o.s.** jurar en falso, perjurar

perjured [ˈpɜːdʒəd] ADJ [*evidence*] falso

perjurer [ˈpɜːdʒərəʳ] N perjuro/a *m/f*

perjury [ˈpɜːdʒərɪ] N perjurio *m* • **to commit ~** cometer perjurio

perk[1]* [pɜːk] N (= *money*) beneficio *m* adicional • **it's one of the ~s of the job** es uno de los incentivos *or* las ventajas del puesto • **there are no ~s in this job** en este puesto no hay nada aparte del sueldo • **company ~s** beneficios *mpl* corporativos

perk[2]* [pɜːk] VI (= **percolate**) [*coffee*] filtrarse

▸ **perk up** VT + ADV [+ *person*] animar • **this will ~ you up!** ¡esto te animará! • **it ~s up the flavour of frozen vegetables** da vida a *or* anima las verduras congeladas
VI + ADV [*person*] reanimarse; (*in health*) sentirse mejor • **business is ~ing up** el

negocio va mejorando • **ears ~ed up when his name was mentioned** todo el mundo aguzó el oído cuando se mencionó su nombre • **share prices ~ed up as a result of the deal** la cotización de las acciones aumentó como resultado del trato

perkily ['pɜːkɪlɪ] ADV (= *cheerfully*) alegremente; (= *cheekily*) con descaro *or* frescura

perkiness ['pɜːkɪnɪs] N alegría *f*, vida *f*; (= *cheekiness*) frescura *f*

perky ['pɜːkɪ] ADJ (COMPAR: **perkier**, SUPERL: **perkiest**) (= *cheerful, bright*) alegre, animado; (= *cheeky*) fresco

perm¹* [pɜːm] N (*Brit*) permanente *f* • **she's got a ~** lleva permanente • **to have a ~** hacerse una permanente
VT • **to ~ sb's hair** hacer una permanente a algn • **to have one's hair ~ed** hacerse una permanente

perm² [pɜːm] N ABBR = **permutation**
VT ABBR = **permute**

perma- ['pɜːmə-] PREFIX • **perma-tanned** de bronceado permanente • **perma-grin** sonrisa *f* permanente

permafrost ['pɜːməfrɒst] N permagel *m*

permalink ['pɜːməlɪŋk] N permalink *m*, enlace *m* permanente

permanence ['pɜːmənəns] N permanencia *f*

permanency ['pɜːmənənsɪ] N permanencia *f*; (= *permanent arrangement*) arreglo *m* permanente

permanent ['pɜːmənənt] ADJ **1** (= *fixed, unchangeable*) [*limp*] permanente; [*damage*] irreparable; [*finish on steel*] inalterable • **we cannot make any ~ arrangements** no podemos arreglar las cosas de modo definitivo • **on a ~ basis** de forma permanente • **he has become a ~ fixture in her life** se ha convertido en una figura permanente en su vida
2 (= *stable, lasting*) [*job*] estable, fijo; [*relationship*] estable • **they have made their ~ home in Paris** se han establecido de forma permanente en París • **I'm not ~ here** (*in job*) no estoy fijo aquí
3 (= *constant*) continuo, permanente • **I lived in a ~ state of fear** vivía en un estado de miedo continuo *or* permanente
N (*US*) = **perm¹**
CPD ▸ **permanent address** domicilio *m* permanente ▸ **permanent magnet** imán *m* permanente ▸ **Permanent Secretary** (*Brit*) (*Admin*) Secretario/a *m/f* Permanente (*alto cargo de la Administración en Gran Bretaña*) ▸ **permanent staff** personal *m* de plantilla ▸ **Permanent Under-secretary** (*Brit*) (*Admin*) Subsecretario/a *m/f* Permanente (*alto cargo de la Administración en Gran Bretaña*) ▸ **permanent wave** permanente *f*

permanently ['pɜːmənəntlɪ] ADV [*live, go away, come back*] permanentemente; [*damage*] irreparablemente, de forma permanente; [*stain, disqualify, ban*] para siempre • **the accident left him ~ brain-damaged** el accidente le produjo un daño cerebral irreparable, el accidente le dejó dañado el cerebro para siempre • **his face seemed to be ~ fixed in a scowl** parecía tener siempre el ceño fruncido • **he is ~ drunk** está siempre *or* permanentemente borracho

permanent-press [,pɜːmənənt'pres] ADJ [*trousers*] de raya permanente; [*skirt*] inarrugable

permanganate [pɜː'mæŋgənɪt] N permanganato *m* • **~ of potash** permanganato *m* de potasio

permeability [,pɜːmɪə'bɪlɪtɪ] N permeabilidad *f*

permeable ['pɜːmɪəbl] ADJ permeable

permeate ['pɜːmɪeɪt] VT **1** [*liquid*] penetrar, impregnar; [*smell*] impregnar; [*substance, chemical*] penetrar • **to be ~d with** estar impregnado de
2 (*fig*) [*ideology, corruption*] estar presente en • **this way of thinking ~s all areas of society** esta forma de pensar está presente en *or* impregna todos los niveles sociales
VI **1** • **to ~ through sth** [*liquid*] penetrar a través de algo, impregnar algo; [*smell*] impregnar algo; [*substance, chemical*] penetrar a través de algo
2 (*fig*) [*ideology, corruption*] extenderse, propagarse (**through** por)

permed [pɜːmd] ADJ [*hair*] permanentado

permissible [pə'mɪsəbl] ADJ lícito • **it is not ~ to do that** no se permite hacer eso • **would it be ~ to say that ...?** ¿podríamos decir que ...?

permission [pə'mɪʃən] N permiso *m* • **no ~ is needed** no hay que pedir permiso • **I'd like your ~ to go ahead with the deal** me gustaría que me diera permiso *or* su autorización para seguir adelante con el trato • **to ask (sb's) ~ to do sth** pedir permiso (a algn) para hacer algo • **by kind ~ of Pérez Ltd** con el permiso amablemente concedido por Pérez, S. A. • **"reprinted by permission of the publisher"** reimprimido con permiso *or* autorización de la editorial • **to get ~ from sb (to do sth)** obtener permiso de algn (para hacer algo) • **to give** *or* **grant ~ (for sth)** dar *or* conceder permiso (para algo) • **to give** *or* **grant sb ~ (to do sth)** dar permiso a algn (para hacer algo) • **you have my ~ to use the car** tienes mi permiso para utilizar el coche • **could I have ~ to leave early?** ¿podría salir antes? • **his widow was refused ~ to live in Britain** a su viuda se le negó el permiso de residencia en Gran Bretaña • **to seek ~ (from sb) to do sth** pedir permiso (a algn) para hacer algo • **with your ~** con su permiso • **he borrowed my car/left the country without ~** se llevó mi coche/se marchó del país sin permiso; ▹ **planning**

permissive [pə'mɪsɪv] ADJ (= *tolerant*) [*attitude, law*] permisivo • **the ~ society** la sociedad permisiva

permissively [pə'mɪsɪvlɪ] ADV permisivamente

permissiveness [pə'mɪsɪvnɪs] N permisividad *f*

permit N ['pɜːmɪt] (= *licence*) permiso *m*, licencia *f*; (= *pass*) pase *m*; (= *permission*) permiso *m* • **do you have a ~ to carry that gun?** ¿tienes permiso *or* licencia para llevar esa pistola? • **building ~** permiso *m* de de obras; ▹ **parking, residence**
VT [pə'mɪt] permitir • **I won't ~ it** no lo permitiré • **is smoking ~ted?** ¿se permite *or* está permitido fumar?, ¿se puede fumar? • **"smoking is not permitted on the car deck"** "está prohibido fumar *or* no se permite fumar en la cubierta de automóviles" • **the law ~s the sale of this substance** la ley autoriza *or* permite la venta de esta sustancia • **he ~ted himself one cigar a day** se permitía (fumar) un cigarro al día • **to ~ sb to do sth** permitir a algn hacer algo, permitir que algn haga algo • **~ me to give you some advice** (*frm*) permítame aconsejarle *or* que le aconseje • **if I may be ~ted to make a suggestion** (*frm*) si se me permite hacer una sugerencia, si me permite que haga una sugerencia
VI [pə'mɪt] • **if time ~s** si hay tiempo (suficiente) • **weather ~ting** si el tiempo lo permite • **to ~ of sth** (*frm*) admitir algo, dar posibilidad a algo • **the crime ~s of no defence** el crimen no admite defensa alguna, el crimen no da posibilidad a defensa alguna
CPD ['pɜːmɪt] ▸ **permit holder** titular *mf* de un permiso

permutation [,pɜːmjʊ'teɪʃən] N **1** (*Math*) [*of number*] permutación *f*
2 (= *variety, combination*) combinación *f*

permute [pə'mjuːt] VT permutar

pernicious [pɜː'nɪʃəs] ADJ **1** [*idea, influence*] pernicioso • **the ~ custom of ...** la perniciosa *or* funesta costumbre de ...
2 (*Med*) pernicioso
CPD ▸ **pernicious anaemia** anemia *f* perniciosa

perniciously [pɜː'nɪʃəslɪ] ADV perniciosamente

pernickety* [pə'nɪkɪtɪ] ADJ [*person*] quisquilloso, remilgado; [*task*] delicado • **she's ~ about food** es exigente para la comida • **he's terribly ~ about punctuality** tiene la manía de la puntualidad

perorate ['perə,reɪt] VI (*liter*) (= *speak at length*) perorar; (= *conclude a speech*) hacer una peroración

peroration [,perə'reɪʃən] N (*frm, iro*) perorata *f*

peroxide [pə'rɒksaɪd] N peróxido *m*
CPD ▸ **peroxide blonde** rubia *f* de bote, rubia *f* oxigenada

perp* [pɜːp] N = **perpetrator**

perpendicular [,pɜːpən'dɪkjʊlə^r] ADJ **1** (*Math*) perpendicular
2 (*Archit*) *perteneciente al estilo gótico de los siglos XIV y XV en Gran Bretaña*
N perpendicular *f* • **to be out of (the) ~** salir de la perpendicular, no estar a plomo

perpendicularly [,pɜːpən'dɪkjʊləlɪ] ADV perpendicularmente, de manera perpendicular

perpetrate ['pɜːpɪtreɪt] VT cometer; (*Jur*) perpetrar

perpetration [,pɜːpɪ'treɪʃən] N comisión *f*; (*Jur*) perpetración *f*

perpetrator ['pɜːpɪtreɪtə^r] N autor(a) *m/f*, responsable *mf*

perpetual [pə'petjʊəl] ADJ (= *eternal*) [*youth*] eterno; [*smile, snow*] perpetuo; (= *continuous*) [*complaints*] continuo, constante • **he has a ~ grin on his face** tiene una sonrisa perpetua *or* permanente *or* (*hum*) perenne en la cara • **she is in a state of ~ anxiety** está en un perpetuo estado de preocupación • **it was a ~ reminder of her dependency on him** era un constante recordatorio de su dependencia de él • **his ~ nagging gets on my nerves** sus quejas constantes *or* continuas me ponen de los nervios
CPD ▸ **perpetual calendar** calendario *m* perpetuo ▸ **perpetual motion** movimiento *m* continuo

perpetually [pə'petjʊəlɪ] ADV (= *eternally*) permanentemente; (= *continually*) constantemente, continuamente • **we were ~ hungry** teníamos siempre hambre

perpetuate [pə'petjʊeɪt] VT perpetuar

perpetuation [pə,petjʊ'eɪʃən] N perpetuación *f*

perpetuity [,pɜːpɪ'tjuːɪtɪ] N perpetuidad *f* • **in ~** a perpetuidad

Perpignan ['pɜːpiːnjɒn] N Perpiñán *m*

perplex [pə'pleks] VT (= *puzzle*) dejar perplejo; (= *confuse*) desconcertar, confundir; [+ *situation, issue*] complicar

perplexed [pə'plekst] ADJ perplejo, confuso • **we were ~** nos quedamos perplejos, estábamos confusos • **to look ~** parecer confuso

perplexedly [pə'pleksɪdlɪ] ADV perplejamente

P

perplexing [pəˈpleksɪŋ] ADJ [*person*] desconcertante; [*issue, question, problem*] complicado • **it's all very ~** es todo muy complicado

perplexingly [pəˈpleksɪŋlɪ] ADV • **a ~ difficult problem** un problema de una dificultad desconcertante

perplexity [pəˈpleksɪtɪ] N perplejidad *f*, confusión *f*

per pro. ABBR (= **per procurationem**) (= *by proxy*) p.p.

perquisite [ˈpɜːkwɪzɪt] N beneficio *m* adicional, gaje *m*; **perquisites** gajes *mpl* y emolumentos *mpl*

perry [ˈperɪ] N sidra *f* de peras

persecute [ˈpɜːsɪkjuːt] VT perseguir; (= *harass*) acosar • **they were ~d under the Nazis** sufrieron persecución bajo los nazis • **to ~ sb with questions** acosar a algn con preguntas

persecution [ˌpɜːsɪˈkjuːʃən] N persecución *f*
CPD ▸ **persecution complex** (*Psych*) complejo *m* persecutorio ▸ **persecution mania** (*Psych*) manía *f* persecutoria

persecutor [ˈpɜːsɪkjuːtəʳ] N perseguidor(a) *m/f*

Persephone [pəˈsefənɪ] N Perséfone *f*

Perseus [ˈpɜːsjuːs] N Perseo *m*

perseverance [ˌpɜːsɪˈvɪərəns] N perseverancia *f*

persevere [ˌpɜːsɪˈvɪəʳ] VI perseverar, persistir (**in** en) • **to ~ with** perseverar con, continuar con

persevering [ˌpɜːsɪˈvɪərɪŋ] ADJ perseverante, tenaz

perseveringly [ˌpɜːsɪˈvɪərɪŋlɪ] ADV con perseverancia, perseverantemente

Persia [ˈpɜːʃə] N (*Hist*) Persia *f*

Persian [ˈpɜːʃən] ADJ persa
N **1** (= *person*) persa *mf*
2 (*Ling*) persa *m*
CPD ▸ **Persian carpet** alfombra *f* persa ▸ **Persian cat** gato *m* persa ▸ **Persian Gulf** golfo *m* Pérsico ▸ **Persian lamb** (= *animal*) oveja *f* caracul; (= *skin*) caracul *m*

persiflage [ˌpɜːsɪˈflɑːʒ] N burlas *fpl*, guasa* *f*

persimmon [pɜːˈsɪmən] N placaminero *m*, caqui *m*

persist [pəˈsɪst] VI **1** (= *continue to exist*) [*belief, rumour, symptoms*] persistir • **this sort of attitude ~s even today** este tipo de actitud persiste incluso hoy en día
2 (= *insist*) • **we shall ~ in our efforts to do it** seguiremos esforzándonos por hacerlo • **he ~s in calling me at all hours of the day** se empeña *or* insiste en llamarme a todas horas del día

persistence [pəˈsɪstəns], **persistency** [pəˈsɪstənsɪ] N **1** (= *tenacity*) perseverancia *f* • **as a reward for her ~** como premio a su perseverancia
2 (= *continuing to exist*) [*of symptoms, disease*] persistencia *f*

persistent [pəˈsɪstənt] ADJ **1** (= *tenacious*) [*person*] insistente • **he is most ~** es muy insistente
2 (= *continuing*) [*rumours, rain, headache*] persistente; [*problem*] continuo, que persiste
3 (= *repeated, constant*) [*questions, refusal, denial*] continuo, constante • **despite our ~ warnings** a pesar de nuestras continuas advertencias
CPD ▸ **persistent offender** multirreincidente *mf*, delincuente *mf* habitual ▸ **persistent vegetative state** estado *m* vegetativo persistente

persistently [pəˈsɪstəntlɪ] ADV **1** (= *tenaciously*) persistentemente, con persistencia
2 (= *continually*) constantemente • **he ~ refuses to help** se niega constantemente a prestar su ayuda • **the main problem is ~ high inflation** el principal problema es un nivel de inflación constantemente elevado

persnickety* [pəˈsnɪkɪtɪ] ADJ (*US*) = **pernickety**

person [ˈpɜːsn] N **1** (PL: **people** *or* (*frm*) **persons**) (= *individual*) persona *f* • **who would be the best ~ to ask?** ¿quién es la persona más indicada para preguntarle? • **she is a very caring ~** es (una persona) muy comprensiva • **Jane was the last ~ to see him** Jane fue la última (persona) que lo vio • **I don't know of any such ~** no conozco a tal persona • **there is no such ~ as Father Christmas** no hay tal Papá Noel • **who is this Ford ~ she keeps talking about?** ¿quién es este tal Ford del que habla constantemente? • **the right of accused ~s to remain silent** (*frm*) el derecho de los acusados a no declarar • **two-person households** viviendas *fpl* de dos personas • **I like him as a ~, but not as a politician** me gusta como persona, pero no como político • **a certain ~, who shall be nameless ...** (*hum*) cierta persona, a quien no voy a nombrar ... (*hum*) • **to call sb ~ to ~** (*Telec*) llamar a algn de persona a persona • **murder by ~ or ~s unknown** (*Jur*) homicidio *m* a manos de persona *or* personas sin identificar; ▹ **people, per, single, third, young, person-to-person**
2 (PL: **persons**) (= *body, physical presence*) persona *f* • **crimes** *or* **offences against the ~** (*Jur*) crímenes *mpl or* ofensas *fpl* contra la persona • **to have a weapon concealed on** *or* **about one's ~** (*frm*) llevar encima una arma oculta • **in ~** en persona • **give it to him in ~** dáselo a él en persona • **he found one new problem in the ~ of Max Steel** encontró un nuevo problema en la persona de Max Steel
3 (PL: **people***) (= *type*) • **I'm not much of a city ~ myself** no soy de los que les gusta la ciudad* • **Steve is a cat ~** Steve es un amante de los gatos
4 (PL: **persons**) (*Gram*) persona *f* • **the first ~ singular** la primera persona del singular • **in the first/third ~** en primera/tercera persona

persona [pɜːˈsəʊnə] N (PL: **personae** [pɜːˈsəʊnaɪ]) **1** (= *character*) personaje *m*
2 (= *image*) imagen *f*
3 • **~ grata** persona *f* grata • **~ non grata** persona *f* no grata

personable [ˈpɜːsnəbl] ADJ bien parecido

personage [ˈpɜːsnɪdʒ] N personaje *m*

personal [ˈpɜːsnl] ADJ **1** (= *individual*) personal • **I will give it my ~ attention** me encargaré personalmente • **I know from ~ experience that it's not easy** sé por experiencia personal que no es fácil • **it's an attack on their ~ freedom** es un ataque contra su libertad personal • **he was a ~ friend** era un amigo íntimo *or* personal • **to have/take a ~ interest in sth** tener un interés personal en *or* por algo, interesarse personalmente en *or* por algo • **my ~ opinion is that ...** en mi opinión personal ... • **it is a matter of ~ preference** es una cuestión de preferencia personal • **are you willing to take ~ responsibility for her?** ¿estás dispuesto a responsabilizarte personalmente de ella? • **if you continue with this investigation you do so at great ~ risk** si continúa con esta investigación correrá usted un gran riesgo contra su persona • **to give sth the ~ touch** dar a algo el toque personal
2 (= *private*) personal • **"personal"** (*on letter*) "confidencial" • **~ belongings** efectos *mpl or* cosas *fpl* personales • **they don't allow ~ calls on the office phone** no permiten que se hagan llamadas particulares en el teléfono de la oficina • **she refused to discuss her ~ life** se negó a discutir su vida personal *or* privada • **this was a ~ matter, something between us two** este era un asunto personal, algo entre nosotros dos • **for ~ reasons** por razones personales • **~ space** espacio *m* vital • **to invade sb's ~ space** acercarse demasiado a algn • **two telephones, one for ~ use and the other for business** dos teléfonos, uno para uso personal y el otro para los negocios
3 (= *in person*) [*visit, interview*] en persona • **to make a ~ appearance** hacer acto de presencia
4 (= *against the person*) [*abuse, insult*] de carácter personal • **there's no need to get ~** no hace falta llevar las cosas al terreno personal • **they are suing for ~ injury** van a denunciar por daños contra la persona • **I have nothing ~ against him** no tengo nada personal en contra suya • **to ask ~ questions** hacer preguntas personales *or* de carácter personal • **to make ~ remarks (about sb)** hacer comentarios de carácter personal acerca de *or* sobre algn
5 (= *physical*) personal • **~ appearance** aspecto *m* (físico) • **~ cleanliness** aseo *m* personal • **~ hygiene** higiene *f* personal
N (*US*) (*Journalism*) (= *advert*) anuncio *m* personal, aviso *m* personal (*LAm*)
CPD ▸ **personal account** (*Econ*) cuenta *f* personal ▸ **personal ad*** anuncio *m* personal, aviso *m* personal (*LAm*) ▸ **personal allowance** (*for tax*) desgravación *f* personal ▸ **personal assets** bienes *mpl* muebles ▸ **personal assistant** ayudante *mf* personal (**to** de) ▸ **personal best** (*Sport*) marca *f* personal ▸ **personal bodyguard** guardaespaldas *mf inv* personal • **one of her ~ bodyguards** uno de sus guardaespaldas personales ▸ **personal care** (*for the elderly or infirm*) asistencia *f* personal ▸ **personal chair** (*Brit*) • **to have a ~ chair** ser titular de una cátedra ▸ **personal cleanliness** higiene *f* personal, aseo *m* personal ▸ **personal column** (*Brit*) (*for births, deaths and marriages*) (páginas *fpl*) sociales *fpl* (y necrológicas); (*for lonely hearts*) (sección *f* de) anuncios *mpl* personales ▸ **personal computer** ordenador *m or* (*LAm*) computadora *f* personal ▸ **personal details** (= *name, address*) datos *mpl* personales • **please fill in your ~ details on the attached form** por favor, rellene el formulario adjunto con sus datos personales ▸ **personal digital assistant** agenda *f* electrónica, PDA *m* ▸ **personal effects** efectos *mpl* personales ▸ **personal finance** finanzas *fpl* personales ▸ **personal foul** falta *f* personal ▸ **personal growth** crecimiento *m* personal ▸ **personal identification number** número *m* de identificación personal ▸ **personal income** ingresos *mpl* personales ▸ **personal income tax** impuesto *m* sobre la renta de las personas físicas ▸ **personal injury** daños *mpl* y perjuicios ▸ **personal insurance** seguro *m* personal ▸ **personal loan** préstamo *m* personal ▸ **personal organizer** (*paper*) agenda *f* personal; (*electronic*) agenda *f* personal electrónica ▸ **personal pronoun** pronombre *m* personal ▸ **personal property** (*Jur*) bienes *mpl* (muebles); (*private*) cosas *fpl* personales ▸ **personal relationships** relaciones *fpl* personales ▸ **personal secretary** secretario/a *m/f* personal ▸ **personal security** (= *safety*) seguridad *f* personal; (*on loan*) garantía *f* personal

▸ **personal shopper** asistente *mf* personal de compras ▸ **personal stereo** Walkman® *m*, equipo *m* de música personal ▸ **personal trainer** preparador(a) *m/f* ▸ **personal tuition** clases *fpl* particulares

personality [ˌpɜːsəˈnælɪtɪ] (N) **1** (= *nature*) personalidad *f* • **she reached the top through sheer force of ~** alcanzó la cima simplemente gracias a su fuerte personalidad; ▹ **dual, multiple, split**
2 (= *charisma*) personalidad *f* • **a woman of great ~** una mujer de gran personalidad • **some people find him lacking in ~** algunos encuentran que le falta personalidad
3 (= *celebrity*) figura *f*, personalidad *f* • **politicians and other prominent personalities** políticos *mpl* y otras prominentes figuras *or* personalidades • **a well-known TV ~** una conocida figura de la TV • **a sports** *or* **sporting ~** una figura de los deportes
4 (= *remarkable person*) personaje *m* • **the old fellow is a real ~** el viejo es todo un personaje
5 personalities (= *personal remarks*) personalismos *mpl* • **the debate degenerated into personalities** el debate degeneró y se entró en personalismos
(CPD) ▸ **personality clash** incompatibilidad *f* de caracteres ▸ **personality cult** culto *m* a la personalidad ▸ **personality disorder** trastornos *mpl* mentales ▸ **personality test** test *m* psicotécnico ▸ **personality trait** rasgo *m* de personalidad

personalize [ˈpɜːsənəlaɪz] (VT) **1** [+ *garment, accessory*] marcar con iniciales
2 [+ *argument, issue*] llevar al terreno de lo personal

personalized [ˈpɜːsənəlaɪzd] (ADJ) [*garment, accessory*] con las iniciales; [*stationery*] con membrete; [*service*] personalizado, individualizado • **a ~ exercise programme** un programa de ejercicios personalizado • **~ number plate** *matrícula personalizada, que contiene, por ejemplo, las iniciales del propietario*

personally [ˈpɜːsnəlɪ] (ADV) **1** (= *individually*) personalmente • **~ I think that ...** personalmente creo que ... • **I wasn't referring to you ~** no me estaba refiriendo a ti personalmente • **I know her ~** la conozco personalmente • **I hold you ~ responsible for what has happened/for her safety** lo declaro responsable personalmente de lo que ha ocurrido/de su seguridad
2 (= *in person*) en persona, personalmente • **the manager saw me ~** el gerente habló conmigo en persona *or* personalmente
3 (= *unkindly*) • **I didn't mean it ~** no pretendía ofenderte • **don't take it too ~** no te lo tomes a mal

personalty [ˈpɜːsnltɪ] (N) bienes *mpl* muebles

personate [ˈpɜːsəneɪt] (VT) (= *impersonate*) hacerse pasar por; (*Theat*) hacer el papel de

personification [pɜːˌsɒnɪfɪˈkeɪʃən] (N) personificación *f* • **he is the ~ of evil/kindness** es el mal personificado/la amabilidad personificada, es la personificación del mal/de la amabilidad

personify [pɜːˈsɒnɪfaɪ] (VT) (= *epitomize*) personificar; (= *represent as person*) personificar • **he is greed personified** es la codicia personificada *or* en persona, es la personificación de la codicia • **he personified the spirit of resistance** encarnó el espíritu de la resistencia

personnel [ˌpɜːsəˈnel] (N) **1** (= *staff*) personal *m*
2 (= *department*) departamento *m* de personal, sección *f* de personal • **head of ~** jefe/a *m/f* de personal
3 (*Mil*) personal *m* • **military ~** personal *m* militar; ▹ **antipersonnel**
(CPD) ▸ **personnel agency** agencia *f* de personal ▸ **personnel carrier** vehículo *m* militar para transporte de tropas • **armoured** *or* (*US*) **armored ~ carrier** camión *m* blindado ▸ **personnel department** departamento *m* de personal, sección *f* de personal ▸ **personnel director** director(a) *m/f* de personal ▸ **personnel file** historial *m* personal ▸ **personnel management** administración *f* de personal, gestión *f* de personal ▸ **personnel manager** jefe/a *m/f* de personal ▸ **personnel officer** jefe/a *m/f* de personal (*subordinado al "personnel manager" si lo hay*) ▸ **personnel policy** política *f* en materia de personal ▸ **personnel record** historial *m* personal

person-to-person [ˌpɜːsntəˈpɜːsn] (ADJ) • **person-to-person call** (*Telec*) llamada *f* (de) persona a persona

perspective [pəˈspektɪv] (N) **1** (*lit*) **a** (*Art*) perspectiva *f* • **to be in/out of ~** estar/no estar en perspectiva
b (= *view*) vista *f*
2 (*fig*) perspectiva *f* • **it has given him a new ~ on life** le ha dado una nueva perspectiva *or* visión de la vida • **I would like to offer a historical ~** me gustaría ofrecer una perspectiva histórica • **from our ~** desde nuestro punto de vista • **let's get things in ~** pongamos las cosas en su sitio • **he gets things out of ~** ve las cosas distorsionadas • **to keep sth in ~** guardar algo en su justa medida • **to look at** *or* **see sth in ~** mirar *or* ver algo en su justa medida • **it helped me put things into ~** me ayudó a ver las cosas con cierta perspectiva *or* en su justa medida • **that puts things in a different ~** eso le da otro cariz a las cosas • **try to keep a sense of ~** trata de ser objetivo

Perspex® [ˈpɜːspeks] (N) (*esp Brit*) plexiglás® *m*

perspicacious [ˌpɜːspɪˈkeɪʃəs] (ADJ) (*frm*) perspicaz

perspicacity [ˌpɜːspɪˈkæsɪtɪ] (N) (*frm*) perspicacia *f*

perspicuity [ˌpɜːspɪˈkjʊːɪtɪ] (N) (*frm*) perspicuidad *f*

perspicuous [ˌpəˈspɪkjʊəs] (ADJ) (*frm*) perspicuo

perspiration [ˌpɜːspəˈreɪʃən] (N) transpiración *f* (*frm*), sudor *m* • **beads of ~** gotas *fpl* de sudor • **to be bathed in ~** estar bañado en sudor, estar todo sudoroso

perspire [pəsˈpaɪəʳ] (VI) transpirar (*frm*), sudar • **to ~ freely** transpirar *or* sudar mucho

perspiring [pəsˈpaɪərɪŋ] (ADJ) sudoroso

persuadable [pəˈsweɪdəbl] (ADJ) influenciable, persuasible • **he may be ~** quizá lo podamos persuadir

persuade [pəˈsweɪd] (VT) convencer, persuadir (*frm*) • **they would not be ~d** no había quien los convenciera *or* persuadiera • **she is easily ~d** se deja convencer *or* persuadir fácilmente • **she didn't need any persuading** no hizo falta insistirle, no hizo falta que la persuadieran *or* convencieran • **he is not ~d of the need for electoral reform** la necesidad de una reforma electoral no lo convence • **to ~ sb that** convencer a algn de que • **I am ~d that ...** estoy convencido de que ... • **he tried to ~ himself that it did not matter** intentó convencerse de que no tenía importancia • **to ~ sb to do sth** convencer a algn de que *or* para que haga algo, persuadir a algn para que haga algo • **I wanted to help but they ~d me not to** quise ayudar pero me convencieron de que *or* para que no lo hiciera, quise ayudar pero me persuadieron para que no lo hiciera

persuasion [pəˈsweɪʒən] (N) **1** (= *act*) persuasión *f* • **his powers of ~ were formidable** sus dotes de persuasión *or* convicción eran extraordinarios • **all he needs is a little gentle** *or* **friendly ~** (*lit, fig*) solo hace falta aplicarle unas suaves técnicas de persuasión • **I wouldn't need much ~ to stop working nights** costaría poco convencerme de *or* para que dejara de trabajar por la noche
2 (= *belief*) (*Rel*) creencia *f*; (*Pol*) ideología *f* • **sport brings people of all races and ~s together** el deporte une a la gente de todas las razas y creencias • **politicians of every ~** políticos *mpl* de todas las ideologías • **I'm not of that ~** no soy de esa opinión, no es esa mi opinión

persuasive [pəˈsweɪsɪv] (ADJ) [*person, voice, tone*] persuasivo; [*argument, evidence*] convincente

persuasively [pəˈsweɪsɪvlɪ] (ADV) de modo persuasivo

persuasiveness [pəˈsweɪsɪvnɪs] (N) persuasiva *f*

PERT [pɜːt] (N ABBR) = **programme evaluation and review technique**

pert [pɜːt] (ADJ) **1** (= *coquettish*) [*young woman, hat*] coqueto
2 (= *neat, firm*) [*nose*] respingón; [*breasts*] levantado
3 (= *rude*) [*reply*] un tanto descarado

pertain [pɜːˈteɪn] (VI) (*frm*) • **to ~ to** (= *concern*) concernir a, estar relacionado con; (= *belong to*) pertenecer a; (= *be the province of*) incumbir a • **and other matters ~ing to it** y otros asuntos relacionados

pertinacious [ˌpɜːtɪˈneɪʃəs] (ADJ) pertinaz

pertinaciously [ˌpɜːtɪˈneɪʃəslɪ] (ADV) con pertinacia

pertinacity [ˌpɜːtɪˈnæsɪtɪ] (N) pertinacia *f*

pertinence [ˈpɜːtɪnəns] (N) pertinencia *f*

pertinent [ˈpɜːtɪnənt] (ADJ) [*information, facts*] pertinente • **evidence ~ to the case** pruebas *f* pertinentes al *or* que guardan relación con el caso • **that is not ~ to the discussion** eso no es pertinente a *or* no está relacionado con la discusión • **he asked some very ~ questions** hizo unas preguntas muy pertinentes

pertinently [ˈpɜːtɪnəntlɪ] (ADV) [*say, reply*] oportunamente, con tino • **where had he learned all this, or, more ~, why had he remembered it?** ¿dónde había aprendido todo esto, o, lo que es más importante, por qué lo recordó?

pertly [ˈpɜːtlɪ] (ADV) [*reply*] descaradamente; [*sit, pose*] con coquetería

pertness [ˈpɜːtnɪs] (N) **1** [*of sb's figure*] elegancia *f*
2 [*of reply*] descaro *m*

perturb [pəˈtɜːb] (VT) **1** (= *distress*) inquietar, preocupar • **we are all very ~ed** estamos todos muy inquietos *or* preocupados • **he didn't seem in the least ~ed** no parecía estar inquieto *or* preocupado en lo más mínimo
2 (= *disturb*) [+ *calm, harmony*] perturbar

perturbation [ˌpɜːtɜːˈbeɪʃən] (N) **1** (= *distress*) inquietud *f*, preocupación *f*
2 (= *disturbance*) (*esp Phys, Astron*) perturbación *f*

perturbing [pəˈtɜːbɪŋ] (ADJ) inquietante, preocupante

Peru [pəˈruː] (N) Perú *m*

perusal [pəˈruːzəl] (N) examen *m* • **after a brief/careful ~ of the document** tras un somero/detenido examen del documento, tras una somera/detenida lectura del

P

documento • **a copy is enclosed for your ~** adjunta se ha enviado una copia para que la examine

peruse [pəˈru:z] VT [+ *book, menu*] leer detenidamente, examinar con detenimiento; [+ *crowd*] examinar con detenimiento; [+ *exhibition*] ver con detenimiento

Peruvian [pəˈru:vɪən] ADJ peruano
N peruano/a *m/f*
CPD ▸ **Peruvian bark** quina *f*

perv‡ [pɜ:v] N pervertido/a *m/f*

pervade [pɜ:ˈveɪd] VT [*smell*] extenderse por; [*light*] difundirse por; [*feeling, atmosphere*] impregnar; [*influence, ideas*] extenderse por • **the smell of burnt food ~d the whole house** el olor a comida quemada se extendió por toda la casa • **this prejudice ~s our society** este prejuicio está extendido en nuestra sociedad; ▷ **all-pervading**

pervasive [pɜ:ˈveɪsɪv] ADJ [*smell*] penetrante; [*feeling, influence*] dominante; [*superstition, belief, presence*] generalizado

pervasively [pɜ:ˈveɪsɪvlɪ] ADV • **to spread ~** [*smell etc*] esparcirse de manera penetrante; [*ideas, mood etc*] extenderse de manera dominante

perverse [pəˈvɜ:s] ADJ (= *contrary*) retorcido; (= *obstinate*) terco, contumaz; (= *wicked*) perverso • **human nature is ~** el hombre es perverso por naturaleza • **I took a ~ pleasure in his predicament** verlo en un aprieto me producía un placer perverso

perversely [pəˈvɜ:slɪ] ADV (= *irrationally*) sin ninguna lógica; (= *obstinately*) tercamente; (= *wickedly*) con perversidad

perverseness [pəˈvɜ:snɪs] N = **perversity**

perversion [pəˈvɜ:ʃən] N (*Med, Psych*) perversión *f*; [*of justice*] deformación *f*; [*of truth, facts*] tergiversación *f*

perversity [pəˈvɜ:sɪtɪ] N (= *contrariness*) contrariedad *f*; (= *obstinacy*) terquedad *f*, contumacia *f*

pervert VT [pəˈvɜ:t] **1** (= *corrupt*) pervertir
2 (= *twist*) [+ *words*] torcer, desvirtuar; [+ *facts, truth*] distorsionar, tergiversar • **to ~ the course of justice** (*Jur*) torcer el curso de la justicia
N [ˈpɜ:vɜ:t] pervertido/a *m/f*

perverted [pəˈvɜ:tɪd] ADJ (*all senses*) pervertido

pervious [ˈpɜ:vɪəs] ADJ permeable (**to** a)

pervy* [ˈpɜ:vɪ] ADJ (*Brit*) pervertido

peseta [pəˈsetə] N peseta *f*

pesky* [ˈpeskɪ] ADJ (COMPAR: **peskier**, SUPERL: **peskiest**) (*US*) molesto

peso [ˈpeɪsəʊ] N peso *m*

pessary [ˈpesərɪ] N pesario *m*

pessimism [ˈpesɪmɪzəm] N pesimismo *m*

pessimist [ˈpesɪmɪst] N pesimista *mf*

pessimistic [ˌpesɪˈmɪstɪk] ADJ pesimista • **he is ~ about the future** es pesimista en lo que al futuro se refiere

pessimistically [ˌpesɪˈmɪstɪkəlɪ] ADV con pesimismo

pest [pest] N **1** (*Zool*) plaga *f*; (= *insect*) insecto *m* nocivo; (= *animal*) animal *m* dañino, animal *m* nocivo
2 (*fig*) (= *person*) pelma *mf* (*Sp**), pelmazo/a *m/f* (*Sp**), fregón/ona *m/f* (*LAm**); (= *thing*) lata* *f*, fastidio *m* • **what a ~ that child is!** ¡cómo me fastidia ese niño! • **it's a ~ having to go** es una lata tener que ir*
CPD ▸ **pest control** lucha *f* contra las plagas de insectos y ratas ▸ **pest control department** servicio *m* de control de plagas (de insectos y ratas) ▸ **pest control officer** funcionario/a *m/f* del departamento de lucha contra plagas de insectos y ratas

pester [ˈpestəʳ] VT molestar, fregar (*LAm*) • **is this man ~ing you?** ¿la está molestando este hombre? • **he's always ~ing me** siempre me está dando la lata* • **she ~ed me for the book** estuvo dando la lata para que le prestara el libro* • **he ~s me with his questions** me fastidia con sus preguntas • **to ~ sb to do sth** dar la lata a algn para que haga algo*

pesticide [ˈpestɪsaɪd] N pesticida *m*

pestilence [ˈpestɪləns] N pestilencia *f*, peste *f*

pestilent [ˈpestɪlənt] ADJ **1** (= *infected, diseased*) apestado
2* (= *annoying*) latoso*

pestilential [ˌpestɪˈlenʃəl] ADJ **1** [*disease*] mortal; [*smell*] pestilente
2* (= *annoying*) latoso*

pestle [ˈpesl] N mano *f* (de mortero)

pesto [ˈpestəʊ] N pesto *m*

PET [pet] (*Med*) N ABBR (= **positron emission tomography**) tomografía *f* por emisión de positrones
CPD ▸ **PET scan** PET *f*, TEP *f*

pet[1] [pet] N **1** (= *animal*) animal *m* doméstico, mascota *f* • **have you got a pet?** ¿tenéis algún animal en casa?, ¿tenéis mascota? • **family/household pet** animal *m* doméstico • **to keep sth as a pet** tener algo como animal doméstico *or* mascota • **"no pets allowed"** "no se admiten animales"
2 (= *favourite*) preferido/a *m/f* • **she's teacher's pet** es la preferida de la profesora, es la enchufada de la profesora*
3* (*as term of address*) cielo *m*, amor *m* • **come here, (my) pet** ven aquí mi cielo *or* amor
4* (= *lovable person*) cielo *m* • **be a pet and fetch me my glasses** sé un cielo y alcánzame las gafas • **he's rather a pet** es un cielo
ADJ **1** [*animal*] • **she keeps two pet snakes** tiene dos serpientes en casa • **he had a pet monkey which had been trained to do tricks** tenía un mono domesticado al que habían enseñado a hacer gracias • **he lives alone with his pet dog** vive solo con su perro • **he was always hanging around her like a pet dog** iba siempre con ella como un perro mascota
2 (= *favourite*) [*theory, project*] preferido, favorito • **once she gets onto her pet subject there's no stopping her** una vez empieza con su tema preferido *or* predilecto no hay quien la pare • **pet hate** • **pet aversion** pesadilla *f* • **my pet hate is smoking** lo que más detesto es el tabaco, el tabaco es mi pesadilla • **pet name** nombre *m* cariñoso; (= *short form*) diminutivo *m* cariñoso
VT **1** (= *indulge*) mimar, consentir
2 (= *fondle*) acariciar
VI (*sexually*) sobarse, acariciarse
CPD ▸ **pet door** (*US*) gatera *f* ▸ **pet food** comida *f* para animales ▸ **pet insurance** seguro *m* para mascotas ▸ **pet owner** dueño/a *m/f* de animal ▸ **pet passport** pasaporte *m* para animales de compañía ▸ **pet shop, pet store** (*US*) pajarería *f*

pet[2] [pet] N • **to be in a pet** estar enfurruñado • **to get into a pet** enfurruñarse

petal [ˈpetl] N pétalo *m*

petard [peˈtɑ:d] N petardo *m* • IDIOM: • **he was hoist with his own ~** le salió el tiro por la culata*

Pete [pi:t] N (*familiar form of* **Peter**) Perico • **for ~'s sake!*** ¡por (el amor de) Dios!

peter[1] [ˈpi:təʳ] VI • **to ~ out** [*supply*] irse agotando; [*conversation*] irse acabando; [*road, stream*] perderse, desaparecer; [*interest, excitement*] desvanecerse, decaer; [*plan*] quedar en nada; [*song, noise, voice*] apagarse • **the road ~ed out into a track** la carretera dio paso a un camino, la carretera se transformó en camino

peter[2]** [ˈpi:təʳ] N (*US*) verga** *f*, picha** *f*

peter[3]‡ [ˈpi:təʳ] N (= *safe*) caja *f* de caudales; (= *cell*) celda *f*

Peter [ˈpi:təʳ] N Pedro • **~ the Great** Pedro el Grande • **~ Rabbit** el Conejo Peter • IDIOM: • **to rob ~ to pay Paul** desnudar a un santo para vestir a otro

Peter Pan [ˌpi:təˈpæn] N Peter Pan *m*, niño *m* eterno

pethidine [ˈpeθɪdi:n] N petidina *f*

petit bourgeois [ˌpetɪˈbʊəʒwɑ:] ADJ pequeñoburgués
N pequeñoburgués/esa *m/f*

petite [pəˈti:t] ADJ chiquita

petite bourgeoisie [pəˌti:tˌbʊəʒwɑ:ˈzi:] N pequeña burguesía *f*

petit four [ˌpetɪˈfɔ:] N pastelito *m* de mazapán

petition [pəˈtɪʃən] N **1** (= *list of names*) petición *f* • **to sign a ~** firmar una petición
2 (*frm*) (= *request*) solicitud *f*; (*Jur*) demanda *f*; (= *entreaty*) súplica *f* • **~ for divorce** demanda *f* de divorcio • **to file a ~** presentar una demanda
VT [+ *authorities*] solicitar a; (*Jur*) [+ *court*] elevar una petición a • **to ~ sb to do sth** (*Jur*) elevar una petición a algn para que haga algo
VI • **to ~ for sth** (*gen*) solicitar algo; (*Jur*) elevar una petición pidiendo algo • **to ~ for divorce** presentar una demanda de divorcio

petitioner [pəˈtɪʃnəʳ] N (*gen*) peticionario/a *m/f*; (*Jur*) demandante *mf*

petits pois [ˈpeti:ˈpwɑ] NPL petits pois *mpl*, *guisantes pequeños y dulces*

Petrarch [ˈpetrɑ:k] N Petrarca

Petrarchan [peˈtrɑ:kən] ADJ petrarquista

Petrarchism [ˈpetrɑ:kɪzəm] N petrarquismo *m*

petrel [ˈpetrəl] N petrel *m*, paíño *m*

petrifaction [ˌpetrɪˈfækʃən], **petrification** [ˌpetrɪfɪˈkeɪʃən] N petrificación *f*

petrified [ˈpetrɪfaɪd] ADJ petrificado

petrify [ˈpetrɪfaɪ] VT **1** (*lit*) petrificar • **to become petrified** petrificarse
2 (*fig*) aterrorizar, horrorizar • **we were petrified** nos quedamos aterrorizados *or* horrorizados • **to be petrified with fear** estar muerto de miedo • **she's petrified of losing** le aterroriza *or* horroriza perder
VI petrificarse

petrifying [ˈpetrɪfaɪɪŋ] ADJ (= *terrifying*) aterrador

petro... [ˈpetrəʊ] PREFIX petro...

petrochemical [ˌpetrəʊˈkemɪkəl] ADJ petroquímico
N **petrochemicals** productos *mpl* petroquímicos

petrochemistry [ˌpetrəʊˈkemɪstrɪ] N petroquímica *f*

petrodollar [ˈpetrəʊˌdɒləʳ] N petrodólar *m*

petrol [ˈpetrəl] (*Brit*) N gasolina *f*, nafta *f* (*Arg*), bencina *f* (*Chile*); (*for lighter*) bencina *f* • **4-star ~** gasolina *f* súper • **to run out of ~** quedarse sin gasolina
CPD ▸ **petrol bomb** bomba *f* de gasolina ▸ **petrol can** bidón *m* de gasolina ▸ **petrol cap** tapón *m* del depósito ▸ **petrol engine** motor *m* de gasolina ▸ **petrol filler cap** tapón *m* del depósito ▸ **petrol gauge** indicador *m* de nivel de gasolina ▸ **petrol pump** (*at garage*) surtidor *m* de gasolina; (*in engine*) bomba *f* de gasolina ▸ **petrol station** gasolinera *f*, estación *f* de servicio, bencinera *f* (*Chile*), surtidor *m* (*Bol*), grifo *m* (*Peru*) ▸ **petrol tank** depósito *m* de gasolina ▸ **petrol tanker** camión *m* cisterna

petroleum [pɪˈtrəʊlɪəm] N petróleo *m*

P

(CPD) ▸ **petroleum jelly** vaselina *f* ▸ **petroleum products** derivados *mpl* del petróleo

petrolhead* [ˈpetrəlhed] (N) fanático/a *m/f* del automovilismo

petrology [peˈtrɒlədʒɪ] (N) petrología *f*

petticoat [ˈpetɪkəʊt] (N) enagua(s) *f(pl)*; (= *slip*) combinación *f*

pettifogging [ˈpetɪfɒgɪŋ] (ADJ) [*detail*] insignificante, nimio; [*lawyer*] pedante; [*suggestion*] hecho para entenebrecer el asunto

pettily [ˈpetɪlɪ] (ADV) mezquinamente

pettiness [ˈpetɪnɪs] (N) (= *small-mindedness*) mezquindad *f*, estrechez *f* de miras; (= *triviality*) insignificancia *f*, nimiedad *f*

petting* [ˈpetɪŋ] (N) caricias *fpl*, manoseo *m* (*pej*), magreo *m* (*Sp*‡) (*pej*)

pettish [ˈpetɪʃ] (ADJ) malhumorado

petty [ˈpetɪ] (ADJ) (COMPAR: **pettier**, SUPERL: **pettiest**) **1** (= *trivial*) [*detail*] insignificante, nimio; [*squabble, rivalry, concerns*] pequeño, trivial
2 (= *minor*) [*offence*] menor
3 (= *small-minded, spiteful*) mezquino • **you're being very ~ about it** te estás portando de manera muy mezquina
(CPD) ▸ **petty cash** dinero *m* para gastos menores, caja *f* chica* ▸ **petty cash book** libro *m* de caja auxiliar ▸ **petty crime** delito *m* menor ▸ **petty criminal** delincuente *mf* de poca monta ▸ **petty larceny** robo *m* de menor cuantía ▸ **petty officer** suboficial *mf* de marina ▸ **petty sessions** tribunal *msing* de primera instancia ▸ **petty theft** robo *m* de poca monta ▸ **petty thief** ladrón/ona *m/f* de poca monta

petulance [ˈpetjʊləns] (N) mal humor *m*, irritabilidad *f*

petulant [ˈpetjʊlənt] (ADJ) [*person, voice, tone*] malhumorado, irritable; [*gesture*] malhumorado, de irritación

petulantly [ˈpetjʊləntlɪ] (ADV) de mal humor, con irritación • **"I'm too busy!" she said ~** —¡estoy demasiado ocupada! —dijo malhumorada *or* irritada

petunia [prˈtjuːnɪə] (N) petunia *f*

pew [pjuː] (N) (*in church*) banco *m* (de iglesia) • **take a pew!*** (*hum*) ¡siéntate!

pewter [ˈpjuːtəʳ] (N) peltre *m*
(CPD) de peltre

peyote [peɪˈəʊtɪ] (N) peyote *m*

PFC (ABBR) (*US*) (*Mil*) = **private first class**

PFI (N ABBR) (*Brit*) (= **private finance initiative**) *plan de incentivos y potenciación de la iniciativa privada en el sector público*

PFLP (N ABBR) (= **Popular Front for the Liberation of Palestine**) FPLP *m*

PG (ABBR) **1** (*Cine*) (*film censor's rating*) (= **Parental Guidance**) ≈ menores acompañados
2 = **paying guest**

PG13 [ˌpiːdʒiːθɜːˈtiːn] (ABBR) (*US*) (= **Parental Guidance 13**) no apto para menores de 13 años

PGA (N ABBR) = **Professional Golfers' Association**

PGCE (N ABBR) (*Brit*) (= **Postgraduate Certificate in Education**) ≈ C.A.P. *m*

PH (ABBR) (*US*) (*Mil*) (= **Purple Heart**) *decoración otorgada a los heridos de guerra*

pH (ABBR) (= **potential of hydrogen**) pH *m*
(CPD) ▸ **pH balance** equilibrio *m* del pH

PHA (N ABBR) (*US*) = **Public Housing Administration**

phablet [ˈfæblɪt] (N) tabléfono *m*

phage [ˈfeɪdʒ] (N) (= **bacteriophage**) fago *m*

phagocyte [ˈfægəʊsaɪt] (N) fagocito *m*

phalange [ˈfælændʒ] (N) falange *f* • **the Phalange** (*in Spain*) la Falange

phalangist [fæˈlændʒɪst] (ADJ), (N) falangista *mf*

phalanx [ˈfælæŋks] (N) (PL: **phalanges** [fæˈlændʒiːz]) falange *f*

phalarope [ˈfælərəʊp] (N) falaropo *m*

phallic [ˈfælɪk] (ADJ) fálico
(CPD) ▸ **phallic symbol** símbolo *m* fálico

phallocentric [ˌfæləʊˈsentrɪk] (ADJ) falocéntrico

phallus [ˈfæləs] (N) (PL: **phalluses** *or* **phalli** [ˈfælaɪ]) falo *m*

phantasm [ˈfæntæzəm] (N) fantasma *m*

phantasmagoria [ˌfæntæzməˈgɔːrɪə] (N) fantasmagoría *f*

phantasmagoric [ˌfæntæzməˈgɒrɪk] (ADJ) fantasmagórico

phantasmal [fænˈtæzməl] (ADJ) fantasmal

phantasy [ˈfæntəzɪ] (N) fantasía *f*

phantom [ˈfæntəm] (N) fantasma *m*
(CPD) [*form, shape*] fantasmal; [*bank account*] fantasma ▸ **phantom limb** extremidad *f* imaginaria ▸ **phantom pregnancy** embarazo *m* psicológico ▸ **phantom ship** buque *m* fantasma

Pharaoh [ˈfɛərəʊ] (N) Faraón *m*

Pharisaic [ˌfærɪˈseɪɪk], **Pharisaical** [ˌfærɪˈseɪɪkəl] (ADJ) farisaico

Pharisee [ˈfærɪsiː] (N) fariseo *m*

pharmaceutical [ˌfɑːməˈsjuːtɪkəl] (ADJ) farmacéutico
(N) producto *m* farmacéutico
(CPD) ▸ **pharmaceuticals company** empresa *f* farmacéutica

pharmaceutics [ˌfɑːməˈsjuːtɪks] (NSING) (= *dispensing drugs*) farmacia *f*
(NPL) (= *pharmaceutical remedies*) productos *mpl* farmacéuticos

pharmacist [ˈfɑːməsɪst] (N) farmacéutico/a *m/f* • **to go to the ~'s** ir a la farmacia

pharmacological [ˌfɑːməkəˈlɒdʒɪkəl] (ADJ) farmacológico

pharmacologist [ˌfɑːməˈkɒlədʒɪst] (N) farmacólogo/a *m/f*

pharmacology [ˌfɑːməˈkɒlədʒɪ] (N) farmacología *f*

pharmacopoeia, pharmacopeia (*US*) [ˌfɑːməkəˈpiːə] (N) farmacopea *f*

pharmacy [ˈfɑːməsɪ] (N) farmacia *f*

pharming [ˈfɑːmɪŋ] (N) pharming *m*, *redirección fraudulenta a otro dominio*

pharyngeal [ˌfærɪnˈdʒiːəl], **pharyngal** [ˌfærɪŋgəl] (ADJ) faríngeo

pharyngitis [ˌfærɪnˈdʒaɪtɪs] (N) faringitis *f*

pharynx [ˈfærɪŋks] (N) (PL: **pharynxes** *or* **pharynges** [fæˈrɪndʒiːz]) faringe *f*

phase [feɪz] (N) **1** etapa *f*, fase *f* • **she'll get over it, it's just a ~ (she's going through)** se le pasará, es algo pasajero • **a passing ~** una etapa pasajera • **to be in ~** (*Tech, Elec*) estar en fase • **to be out of ~** (*Tech, Elec*) estar fuera de fase *or* desfasado; (*fig*) estar desfasado • **their policies were increasingly out of ~ with a rapidly changing society** su política estaba cada vez más desfasada en una sociedad que cambiaba con rapidez
2 (*Astron*) fase *f* • **the ~s of the moon** las fases de la luna
(VT) **1** (= *introduce gradually*) escalonar, llevar a cabo de forma escalonada • **the redundancies will be ~d over two years** los despidos se llevarán a cabo de forma escalonada durante dos años
2 (= *coordinate*) organizar • **~d development** desarrollo *m* por etapas • **~d withdrawal** retirada *f* progresiva
▸ **phase in** (VT + ADV) [+ *change, increase*] introducir progresivamente
▸ **phase out** (VT + ADV) [+ *machinery, product*] retirar progresivamente; [+ *job*] eliminar por etapas; [+ *subsidy*] eliminar progresivamente; [+ *production*] parar progresivamente; [+ *factory, plant*] cerrar progresivamente

phase-in [ˈfeɪzɪn] (N) introducción *f* progresiva • **phase-in period** periodo *m* de introducción progresiva

phase-out [ˈfeɪzaʊt] (N) retirada *f* progresiva

phat‡ [fæt] (ADJ) fenomenal*, super*

phatic [ˈfætɪk] (ADJ) fático

PhD (N ABBR) (= **Doctor of Philosophy**) (= *qualification*) doctorado *m*; (= *person*) doctor(a) *m/f* en filosofía • **to have a PhD in ...** tener un doctorado en ...; ▸ **DEGREE**
(CPD) ▸ **PhD student** estudiante *mf* de doctorado ▸ **PhD thesis** tesis *f inv* doctoral

pheasant [ˈfeznt] (N) faisán *m*

phenobarbitone [ˈfiːnəʊˈbɑːbɪtəʊn] (N) fenobarbitona *f*

phenol [ˈfiːnɒl] (N) fenol *m*

phenomena [fɪˈnɒmɪnə] (NPL) *of* **phenomenon**

phenomenal [fɪˈnɒmɪnl] (ADJ) [*memory, success, strength*] extraordinario; [*speed*] espectacular

phenomenally [fɪˈnɒmɪnəlɪ] (ADV) extraordinariamente • **to be ~ successful** tener un éxito extraordinario

phenomenological [fəˌnɒmənəˈlɒdʒɪkəl] (ADJ) fenomenológico

phenomenologist [fəˌnɒməˈnɒlədʒɪst] (N) fenomenólogo/a *m/f*

phenomenology [fɪˈnɒmɪˈnɒlədʒɪ] (N) fenomenología *f*

phenomenon [fɪˈnɒmɪnən] (N) (PL: **phenomenons** *or* **phenomena**) fenómeno *m*

phenotype [ˈfiːnəʊˌtaɪp] (N) fenotipo *m*

pheromone [ˈferəməʊn] (N) feromona *f*

phew [fjuː] (EXCL) ¡uf!, ¡puf!

phial [ˈfaɪəl] (N) ampolla *f*, redoma *f*

Phi Beta Kappa [ˌfaɪbeɪtəˈkæpə] (N) (*US*) (*Univ*) *asociación de antiguos alumnos sobresalientes*

PHI BETA KAPPA

La sociedad honorífica **Phi Beta Kappa** fue fundada en Estados Unidos en 1776 para estudiantes universitarios con aptitudes académicas sobresalientes. Los miembros se eligen durante el tercer o cuarto año de sus estudios y el nombre proviene de las iniciales griegas que forman el lema de la asociación: **philosophia biou kubernetes (la filosofía como motor de vida)**. A cada miembro se lo conoce como un **Phi Beta Kappa** o un **Phi Beta Kappa student**.

Phil [fɪl] (N) *familiar form of* **Philip**

Phil. [fɪl] (ABBR) = **Philadelphia**

Philadelphia [ˌfɪləˈdelfɪə] (N) Filadelfia *f*

philander [fɪˈlændəʳ] (VI) flirtear, ejercer de Don Juan (**with** con)

philanderer [fɪˈlændərəʳ] (N) Don Juan *m*, tenorio *m*

philandering [fɪˈlændərɪŋ] (ADJ) que le gusta flirtear, que le gusta ejercer de Don Juan
(N) flirteo *m*

philanthropic [ˌfɪlənˈθrɒpɪk] (ADJ) filantrópico

philanthropically [ˌfɪlənˈθrɒpɪkəlɪ] (ADV) de manera filantrópica

philanthropist [fɪˈlænθrəpɪst] (N) filántropo/a *m/f*

philanthropy [fɪˈlænθrəpɪ] (N) filantropía *f*

philatelic [ˌfɪləˈtelɪk] (ADJ) filatélico

philatelist [fɪˈlætəlɪst] (N) filatelista *mf*

philately [fɪˈlætəlɪ] (N) filatelia *f*

...phile [faɪl] (SUFFIX) ...filo • **francophile**

francófilo/a *m/f*
philharmonic [fɪlɑːˈmɒnɪk] ADJ filarmónico • **the Berlin Philharmonic (Orchestra)** la (Orquesta) Filarmónica de Berlín
...philia [ˈfɪlɪə] SUFFIX ...filia • **francophilia** francofilia *f*
Philip [ˈfɪlɪp] N Felipe
philippic [fɪˈlɪpɪk] N filípica *f*
Philippine [ˈfɪlɪpiːn] ADJ filipino
N filipino/a *m/f*
Philippines [ˈfɪlɪpiːnz] NPL • **the ~** (las) Filipinas *fpl* • **the Philippine Islands** las islas Filipinas
Philistine [ˈfɪlɪstaɪn] ADJ **1** (*lit*) filisteo
2 (*fig*) inculto
N **1** (*lit*) filisteo/a *m/f*
2 (*fig*) inculto/a *m/f*
philistinism [ˈfɪlɪstɪnɪzəm] N filisteísmo *m*
Phillips screw® [ˌfɪlɪpsˈskruː] N tornillo *m* de cabeza cruciforme
Phillips screwdriver® [ˌfɪlɪpsˈskruːdraɪvəʳ] N destornillador *m* cruciforme
philological [ˌfɪləˈlɒdʒɪkəl] ADJ filológico
philologist [fɪˈlɒlədʒɪst] N filólogo/a *m/f*
philology [fɪˈlɒlədʒɪ] N filología *f*
philosopher [fɪˈlɒsəfəʳ] N filósofo/a *m/f* • **~'s stone** piedra *f* filosofal
philosophic [ˌfɪləˈsɒfɪk] ADJ = **philosophical**
philosophical [ˌfɪləˈsɒfɪkəl] ADJ filosófico • **she was ~ about the delay** se tomó el retraso con filosofía
philosophically [ˌfɪləˈsɒfɪkəlɪ] ADV [*important, disputable*] filosóficamente; (= *from a philosophical point of view*) desde el punto de vista filosófico; (= *with resignation*) [*accept*] con filosofía • **to be ~ inclined** *or* **minded** tener inclinaciones filosóficas
philosophize [fɪˈlɒsəfaɪz] VI filosofar
philosophizing [fɪˈlɒsəfaɪzɪŋ] N • **he was anxious to cut short the ~ and get down to more urgent problems** estaba deseando terminar con tanto filosofar y ponerse a tratar problemas de mayor urgencia
philosophy [fɪˈlɒsəfɪ] N filosofía *f* • **her ~ of life** su filosofía de la vida
philtre, philter (US) [ˈfɪltəʳ] N filtro *m*
phishing [ˈfɪʃɪŋ] (*Internet*) N phishing *m*
CPD ▸ **phishing attack** ataque *m* (de) phishing
phiz* [fɪz] N jeta* *f*
phlebitis [flɪˈbaɪtɪs] N flebitis *f*
phlebotomy [flɪˈbɒtəmɪ] N flebotomía *f*
phlegm [flem] N **1** (*Med*) (= *mucus*) flema *f*
2 (= *equanimity*) flema *f*
phlegmatic [flegˈmætɪk] ADJ flemático
phlegmatically [flegˈmætɪkəlɪ] ADV con flema • **he said ~** dijo flemático
phlox [flɒks] N (PL: **phlox** *or* **phloxes**) flox *m*
Phnom Penh, Pnom Penh [ˈnɒmˈpen] N Phnom Penh *m*
...phobe [fəʊb] SUFFIX ...fobo • **francophobe** francófobo/a *m/f*
phobia [ˈfəʊbɪə] N fobia *f*
...phobia [ˈfəʊbɪə] SUFFIX ...fobia • **anglophobia** anglofobia *f*
phobic [ˈfəʊbɪk] ADJ fóbico
Phoebus [ˈfiːbəs] N Febo
Phoenicia [fɪˈnɪʃɪə] N Fenicia *f*
Phoenician [fɪˈnɪʃɪən] ADJ fenicio
N fenicio/a *m/f*
phoenix [ˈfiːnɪks] N fénix *m*
phone [fəʊn] N teléfono *m* • **the ~ hasn't stopped ringing all afternoon** el teléfono no ha dejado de sonar toda la tarde • **he can't come to the ~ just now** ahora no puede ponerse *or* venir al teléfono • **by ~** por teléfono • **to get off the ~** colgar (el teléfono) • **to be on the ~** (*Brit*) (= *have a telephone*) tener teléfono; (= *be in conversation*) estar hablando por teléfono • **who was that on the ~?** ¿con quién estabas hablando por teléfono? • **there's someone on the ~ for you** te llama alguien por teléfono, hay alguien al teléfono que quiere hablar contigo • **I spent an hour on the ~ trying to sort things out** me pasé una hora al teléfono intentando resolver las cosas • **Dennis sounded very excited on the ~** Dennis parecía muy entusiasmado por teléfono • **he immediately got on the ~ to his solicitor** llamó por teléfono a su abogado inmediatamente • **I can't talk about it over the ~** no puedo hablar de ello por teléfono • **public ~** teléfono *m* público • **to put down the ~** colgar el teléfono; ▹ **car, mobile, pay**
VT [+ *person*] llamar (por teléfono); [+ *number*] llamar a • **to ~ the hospital/office** llamar al hospital/a la oficina • **I have to ~ Helsinki again** tengo que hablar con Helsinki otra vez • **I tried phoning the emergency number** intenté llamar al número de emergencia • **write to us or ~ 0171 586 4034** escríbanos o llámenos al 0171 586 4034
VI llamar (*por teléfono*) • **she ~d to say she would be late** llamó para decir que llegaría tarde • **shall I ~ for a taxi?** ¿llamo a un taxi?, ¿quieres que llame a *or* pida un taxi?
CPD ▸ **phone bill** cuenta *f* del teléfono, factura *f* del teléfono • **he ran up a £240 ~ bill** gastó 240 libras de teléfono ▸ **phone book** guía *f* (telefónica) • **she's not in the ~ book** su número no viene en la guía ▸ **phone booth** cabina *f* (telefónica) ▸ **phone box** (*Brit*) cabina *f* (telefónica) ▸ **phone call** llamada *f* (telefónica) • **there's a ~ call for you** tienes una llamada (telefónica) • **to make a ~ call** hacer una llamada (telefónica) ▸ **phone company** compañía *f* telefónica ▸ **phone line** línea *f* de teléfono • **the ~ lines are busy** las líneas de teléfono están ocupadas ▸ **phone number** número *m* de teléfono • **we need your daytime ~ number** nos hace falta un número de teléfono en el que se lo pueda contactar durante el día ▸ **phone tap** escucha *f* telefónica • **he assured them that ministers were not subjected to ~ taps** les aseguró que los ministros no estaban siendo sometidos a escuchas telefónicas ▸ **phone tapping** intervención *f* telefónica, pinchazo *m* de teléfono*
▸ **phone back** VT + ADV (= *return call*) llamar; (= *call again*) volver a llamar
VI + ADV (*return call*) llamar; (= *call again*) volver a llamar • **they asked you to ~ back – urgently** te pidieron que llamaras – urgentemente • **he's not here, could you ~ back tomorrow?** no está aquí, ¿podría volver a llamar mañana?
▸ **phone down** VI + ADV • **just wait while I ~ down to reception** espere un momento mientras llamo (abajo) a la recepción
▸ **phone in** VI + ADV llamar • **listeners can ~ in with their views** los oyentes pueden llamar para expresar sus puntos de vista • **~ in to base if you change your plans** si cambia de planes, llame por teléfono para comunicárselo a la base • **you could always ~ in sick** siempre podrías llamar diciendo que estás enfermo
VT + ADV • **she had ~d in a message for Wade to call her** había llamado dejando un mensaje para Wade de que la llamara • **our reporter ~d in this account of what had happened** nuestro reportero nos mandó por teléfono esta versión de lo ocurrido • **you can ~ in your order on 0898 060606** puede hacer su pedido llamando al 0898 060606
▸ **phone out** VI + ADV llamar al exterior
▸ **phone round** VI + ADV llamar a varios sitios
VI + PREP • **he ~d round all his friends** llamó a todos sus amigos
▸ **phone through** VT + ADV • **~ through your order on our special credit card line** haga su pedido por teléfono a través de nuestra línea especial para tarjetas de crédito
VI + ADV llamar • **I still haven't managed to ~ through to my wife** aún no he conseguido llamar a mi esposa
▸ **phone up** VT + ADV llamar • **I must ~ her up tonight** debo llamarla esta noche
VI + ADV llamar
phonecam [ˈfəʊnkæm] N móvil *m* con cámara (*Sp*), celular *m* con cámara (*LAm*)
phonecard [ˈfəʊnkɑːd] N tarjeta *f* telefónica
phone-in [ˈfəʊnɪn] N (*also* **phone-in programme**) (*Brit*) *programa de radio or televisión con participación telefónica del público*
phoneme [ˈfəʊniːm] N fonema *m*
phonemic [fəʊˈniːmɪk] ADJ fonémico
phonetap evidence [ˈfəʊntæpˌevɪdəns] N pruebas *fpl* a partir de escuchas telefónicas
phonetic [fəʊˈnetɪk] ADJ fonético
phonetically [fəʊˈnetɪkəlɪ] ADV fonéticamente
phonetician [ˌfəʊnɪˈtɪʃən] N fonetista *mf*
phonetics [fəʊˈnetɪks] N fonética *f*
phoney*, phony* (US) [ˈfəʊnɪ] ADJ [*moustache*] falso, postizo; [*name, document, smile*] falso; [*accent*] fingido • **there's sth ~ about it** esto huele a camelo* • **the ~ war** (1939) la guerra ilusoria
N (PL: **phoneys**) (= *person*) farsante* *mf*; (= *thing*) falsificación *f*
phonic [ˈfɒnɪk] ADJ fónico
phonics [ˈfɒnɪks] N (*used in the teaching of reading*) ≈ fonología *f* • **they are taught to read using ~** les están enseñando a leer utilizando la fonología
phono... [ˈfəʊnəʊ] PREFIX fono...
phonograph [ˈfəʊnəgrɑːf] N (US) fonógrafo *m*, tocadiscos *m inv*
phonological [ˌfəʊnəˈlɒdʒɪkəl] ADJ fonológico
phonologically [ˌfəʊnəˈlɒdʒɪklɪ] ADV fonológicamente
phonologist [fəˈnɒlədʒɪst] N fonólogo/a *m/f*
phonology [fəʊˈnɒlədʒɪ] N fonología *f*
phony [ˈfəʊnɪ] (US) = **phoney**
phooey* [ˈfuːɪ] EXCL (= *rubbish*) ¡bobadas!; (*annoyance*) ¡qué tonto soy!; (*disappointment*) ¡ay!
phosgene [ˈfɒzdʒiːn] N fosgeno *m*
phosphate [ˈfɒsfeɪt] N fosfato *m*
phosphene [ˈfɒsfiːn] N fosfeno *m*
phosphide [ˈfɒsfaɪd] N fosfito *m*
phosphine [ˈfɒsfiːn] N fosfino *m*
phosphoresce [ˌfɒsfəˈres] VI fosforecer
phosphorescence [ˌfɒsfəˈresns] N fosforescencia *f*
phosphorescent [ˌfɒsfəˈresnt] ADJ fosforescente
phosphoric [fɒsˈfɒrɪk] ADJ fosfórico
CPD ▸ **phosphoric acid** ácido *m* fosfórico
phosphorous [ˈfɒsfərəs] ADJ fosforoso
phosphorus [ˈfɒsfərəs] N fósforo *m*
photo [ˈfəʊtəʊ] N (PL: **photos**) foto *f* • **to take a ~** hacer *or* (*esp LAm*) sacar una foto • **I took a ~ of the bride and groom** les hice una foto a los novios
CPD ▸ **photo album** álbum *m* de fotos ▸ **photo booth** cabina *f* de fotos, fotomatón *m* (*Sp*) ▸ **photo gallery** galería *f* de fotos ▸ **photo ID** identificación *f* fotográfica ▸ **photo opportunity** sesión *f* de fotos

P

▸ **photo session** sesión *f* de fotos ▸ **photo shoot** sesión *f* de fotos
photo... ['fəʊtəʊ] PREFIX **1** (= *relating to photography*) foto... • **photo-montage** fotomontaje *m*
2 (= *relating to light*) foto... • **photosynthesis** fotosíntesis *f*
photobomb* ['fəʊtəʊbɒm] VT colarse en la foto de
N foto *f* estropeada por entrometidos
photocall ['fəʊtəʊkɔːl] N sesión *f* de fotos
photocard ['fəʊtəʊkɑːd] N documento *m* de identidad (*con foto*)
photocell ['fəʊtəʊˌsel] N célula *f* fotoeléctrica
photochemical [ˌfəʊtəʊ'kemɪkəl] ADJ fotoquímico
photocompose [ˌfəʊtəʊkəm'pəʊz] VT fotocomponer
photocomposer [ˌfəʊtəʊkəm'pəʊzəʳ] N fotocomponedora *f*
photocomposition [ˌfəʊtəʊkɒmpə'zɪʃən] N fotocomposición *f*
photocopier ['fəʊtəʊ'kɒpɪəʳ] N fotocopiadora *f*
photocopy ['fəʊtəʊˌkɒpɪ] N fotocopia *f*
VT fotocopiar
photocopying ['fəʊtəʊˌkɒpɪɪŋ] N • **to do some ~** hacer algunas fotocopias • **the ~ of this publication is forbidden without prior permission** se prohíbe fotocopiar esta publicación sin permiso previo
photocoverage ['fəʊtəʊˌkʌvərɪdʒ] N reportaje *m* gráfico
photodegradable [ˌfəʊtəʊdɪ'greɪdəbl] ADJ fotodegradable
photodisk ['fəʊtəʊˌdɪsk] N fotodisco *m*
photoelectric ['fəʊtəʊɪ'lektrɪk] ADJ fotoeléctrico
CPD ▸ **photoelectric cell** célula *f* fotoeléctrica
photoelectron [ˌfəʊtəʊɪ'lektrɒn] N fotoelectrón *m*
photoengrave [ˌfəʊtəʊɪn'greɪv] VT fotograbar
photoengraving ['fəʊtəʊen'greɪvɪŋ] N fotograbado *m*
photo-finish ['fəʊtəʊ'fɪnɪʃ] N resultado *m* comprobado por fotocontrol; (*fig*) final *m* muy reñido
Photofit® ['fəʊtəʊfɪt] N (*Brit*) (*also* **Photofit picture**) retrato *m* robot
photogenic [ˌfəʊtəʊ'dʒenɪk] ADJ fotogénico
photograph ['fəʊtəgræf] N fotografía *f*, foto *f* • **it's a very good ~ of her** es una fotografía muy buena de ella • **to take a ~ (of sth/sb)** hacer *or* (*esp LAm*) sacar una foto (a algo/algn)
VT fotografiar, hacer *or* (*esp LAm*) sacar una foto(grafía) a • **I hate being ~ed** odio que me hagan fotos • **"~ed by Paul Smith"** "fotografía de Paul Smith"
VI • **to ~ well** ser fotogénico
CPD ▸ **photograph album** álbum *m* de fotos
photographer [fə'tɒgrəfəʳ] N fotógrafo/a *m/f* • **an amateur ~** un fotógrafo amateur • **he's a keen ~** es muy aficionado a la fotografía • **a ~'s** (= *shop*) una tienda de fotografía; ▹ press
photographic [ˌfəʊtə'græfɪk] ADJ fotográfico • **to have a ~ memory** tener una memoria fotográfica
photographically [ˌfəʊtə'græfɪkəlɪ] ADV fotográficamente
photography [fə'tɒgrəfɪ] N fotografía *f*
photogravure [ˌfəʊtəgrə'vjʊəʳ] N fotograbado *m*
photojournalism [ˌfəʊtəʊ'dʒɜːnəlɪzəm] N fotoperiodismo *m*
photojournalist [ˌfəʊtəʊ'dʒɜːnəlɪst] N fotoperiodista *mf*
photokit ['fəʊtəʊkɪt] N retrato *m* robot
photolitho [ˌfəʊtəʊ'laɪθəʊ] N fotolito *m*
photolithograph [ˌfəʊtəʊ'lɪθəˌgrɑːf] N grabado *m* fotolitográfico
photolithography [ˌfəʊtəʊlɪ'θɒgrəfɪ] N fotolitografía *f*
photometer [fə'tɒmɪtəʳ] N fotómetro *m*
photometric [ˌfəʊtə'metrɪk] ADJ fotométrico
photometry [fəʊ'tɒmɪtrɪ] N fotometría *f*
photomontage [ˌfəʊtəʊmɒn'tɑːʒ] N fotomontaje *m*
photon ['fəʊtɒn] N fotón *m*
photorealism [ˌfəʊtəʊ'rɪəlɪzəm] N (*Art, Comput*) fotorrealismo *m*
photorealistic [ˌfəʊtəʊrɪə'lɪstɪk] ADJ (*Art, Comput*) fotorrealista
photosensitive [ˌfəʊtəʊ'sensɪtɪv] ADJ fotosensible
photosensitivity [ˌfəʊtəʊsensɪ'tɪvɪtɪ] N fotosensibilidad *f*
photosensitize [ˌfəʊtəʊ'sensɪˌtaɪz] VT fotosensibilizar
Photoshop® ['fəʊtəʊʃɒp] N Photoshop® *m*
VT editar con Photoshop®
photostat† ['fəʊtəʊstæt] N (= *machine*) fotocopiadora *f*; (= *photocopy*) fotocopia *f*
VT fotocopiar
photosynthesis [ˌfəʊtəʊ'sɪnθəsɪs] N fotosíntesis *f*
phototropism ['fəʊtəʊ'trəʊpɪzəm] N fototropismo *m*
phototype ['fəʊtəʊˌtaɪp] N fototipo *m*
phototypesetting [ˌfəʊtəʊ'taɪpˌsetɪŋ] N (*US*) (*Typ*) fotocomposición *f*
phototypography [ˌfəʊtəʊtaɪ'pɒgrəfɪ] N fototipografía *f*
photovoltaic [ˌfəʊtəʊvɒl'teɪɪk] ADJ fotovoltaico
CPD ▸ **photovoltaic cell** célula *f* fotovoltaica
phrasal ['freɪzəl] ADJ frasal
CPD ▸ **phrasal verb** verbo *m* con preposición *or* adverbio
phrase [freɪz] N **1** (*Gram, Mus*) frase *f* • **noun/verb ~** frase *f* nominal/verbal
2 (= *expression*) frase *f* • **she had picked up some useful ~s** había aprendido algunas frases útiles • **I think, to use** *or* **to borrow your ~, that ...** creo que, usando tus propias palabras, ...
3 (= *idiom*) locución *f*, giro *m*; ▹ **catch, coin, set, stock, turn**
VT **1** (*orally*) expresar, formular • **I should have ~d that better** debería haberlo expresado *or* formulado mejor
2 (*in writing*) redactar, expresar • **can we ~ that differently?** ¿podemos redactar *or* expresar eso de otro modo? • **a carefully ~d letter** una carta redactada con cuidado
3 (*Mus*) frasear
CPD ▸ **phrase book** libro *m* de frases ▸ **phrase marker** (*Ling*) marcador *m* de frase ▸ **phrase structure** (*Ling*) estructura *f* de frase
phrasemonger ['freɪzmʌŋgəʳ] N (*pej*) creador(a) *m/f* de frases grandilocuentes
phraseology [ˌfreɪzɪ'ɒlədʒɪ] N fraseología *f*
phrasing ['freɪzɪŋ] N (= *act*) redacción *f*; [*of question*] formulación *f*; (= *style*) estilo *m*, términos *mpl*; (*Mus*) fraseo *m* • **the ~ is rather unfortunate** la forma en que está expresado es bastante desafortunada
phrenetic [frɪ'netɪk] ADJ frenético
phrenic ['frenɪk] ADJ (*Anat*) diafragmático
phrenologist [frɪ'nɒlədʒɪst] N frenólogo/a *m/f*
phrenology [frɪ'nɒlədʒɪ] N frenología *f*
phthisis ['θaɪsɪs] N tisis *f*
phut* [fʌt] ADJ • **to go ~** estropearse, hacer kaput*; (*fig*) fracasar
phyla ['faɪlə] NPL *of* **phylum**
phylactery [fɪ'læktərɪ] N filacteria *f*
phylloxera [ˌfɪlɒk'sɪərə] N filoxera *f*
phylum ['faɪləm] N (PL: **phyla**) (*Bio*) filo *m*, phylum *m*
physalis [faɪ'seɪlɪs] N (*Bot*) uchuva *f*, aguaymanto *m* (*Peru*)
physic†† ['fɪzɪk] N medicina *f*
physical ['fɪzɪkəl] ADJ **1** (= *of the body*) [*condition, disability, contact, violence*] físico; [*punishment*] corporal
2 (= *material*) [*properties, characteristics*] físico; [*world*] material • **~ environment** entorno *m* físico • **~ evidence** pruebas *fpl* materiales • **it's a ~ impossibility** es materialmente imposible • **his ~ presence repelled her** su mera presencia le repugnaba
3 (= *involving physical contact, effort*) físico • **he's a very ~ man** es un hombre que recurre mucho al contacto físico • **rugby is a very ~ sport** el rugby es un deporte muy físico *or* con mucho contacto físico • **there was some very ~ play from both teams** hubo mucho juego duro por parte de los dos equipos • **he has been ordered not to do any ~ work** le han dicho que no haga ninguna clase de trabajo que requiera esfuerzo físico • **to get ~** (*sexually*) pasar al plano físico; (= *be rough*) emplear la fuerza física, llegar a las manos*
4 (= *of physics*) físico • **the ~ sciences** las ciencias físicas
N (*also* **physical examination**) reconocimiento *m* físico
CPD ▸ **physical chemistry** fisicoquímica *f* ▸ **physical education** educación *f* física ▸ **physical examination** reconocimiento *m* físico ▸ **physical exercise** ejercicio *m* (físico) ▸ **physical fitness** (buena) forma *f* física • **a ~ fitness programme** un programa de ejercicios físicos ▸ **physical geography** geografía *f* física ▸ **physical handicap** impedimento *m* físico ▸ **physical jerks*** (*Brit*) gimnasia *fsing*, ejercicios *mpl* (físicos) ▸ **physical science** ciencia *f* física ▸ **physical therapist** (*US*) fisioterapeuta *mf* ▸ **physical therapy** (*US*) fisioterapia *f* ▸ **physical training** entrenamiento *m*, ejercicio *m* (físico)
physicality [ˌfɪzɪ'kælɪtɪ] N fisicalidad *f*
physically ['fɪzɪkəlɪ] ADV físicamente • **I don't find him ~ attractive** no me parece físicamente atractivo • **it's very ~ demanding work** es un trabajo que requiere mucho esfuerzo físico • **you need to be ~ fit to attempt this climb** tienes que estar en buena forma (física) para intentar esta escalada • **it's ~ impossible** es materialmente imposible • **he had to be ~ removed from the premises** lo tuvieron que sacar del local por la fuerza • **the thought of food made me ~ sick** solo pensar en comer me daba náuseas
physician [fɪ'zɪʃən] N médico/a *m/f*
physician-assisted suicide [fɪˌzɪʃənəˌsɪstɪd 'suːɪsaɪd] N eutanasia *f* asistida
physicist ['fɪzɪsɪst] N físico/a *m/f*
physics ['fɪzɪks] NSING física *f*
physio* ['fɪzɪəʊ] N (*Sport*) = **physiotherapist** (*Brit*) = **physiotherapy**
physio... ['fɪzɪəʊ] PREFIX fisio...
physiognomy [ˌfɪzɪ'ɒnəmɪ] N fisonomía *f*
physiological ['fɪzɪə'lɒdʒɪkəl] ADJ fisiológico
physiologically ['fɪzɪə'lɒdʒɪkəlɪ] ADV fisiológicamente

physiologist [ˌfɪzɪˈɒlədʒɪst] (N) fisiólogo/a *m/f*
physiology [ˌfɪzɪˈɒlədʒɪ] (N) fisiología *f*
physiotherapeutic [ˈfɪzɪəˌθerəˈpjuːtɪk] (ADJ) fisioterapéutico
physiotherapist [ˌfɪzɪəˈθerəpɪst] (N) fisioterapeuta *mf*
physiotherapy [ˌfɪzɪəˈθerəpɪ] (N) fisioterapia *f*
physique [fɪˈziːk] (N) físico *m*
phytobiology [ˌfaɪtəʊbaɪˈɒlədʒɪ] (N) fitobiología *f*
phytofagous [faɪˈtɒfəgəs] (ADJ) fitófago
phytopathology [ˌfaɪtəʊpəˈθɒlədʒɪ] (N) fitopatología *f*
phytosterol [ˌfaɪtəʊˈsterɒl] (N) fitoesterol *m*
PI (N ABBR) (= **private investigator**) investigador(a) *m/f* privado/a
pi [paɪ] (N) (PL: **pis**) (*Math*) pi *f*
pianist [ˈpɪənɪst] (N) pianista *mf*
piano [ˈpjɑːnəʊ] (N) (PL: **pianos**) piano *m*
(CPD) ▸ **piano accordion** acordeón-piano *m* ▸ **piano concerto** concierto *m* para piano ▸ **piano duet** pieza *f* para piano a cuatro manos ▸ **piano lesson** lección *f* de piano ▸ **piano piece** pieza *f* para piano ▸ **piano player** pianista *mf* ▸ **piano stool** taburete *m* de piano ▸ **piano teacher** profesor(a) *m/f* de piano ▸ **piano tuner** afinador(a) *m/f* de pianos
pianoforte [ˌpjɑːnəʊˈfɔːtɪ] (N) = **piano**
pianola® [pɪəˈnəʊlə] (N) pianola *f*
piastre, piaster (US) [pɪˈæstəʳ] (N) piastra *f*
piazza [pɪˈætsə] (N) (US) pórtico *m*, galería *f*; (= *square*) plaza *f*
pic* [pɪk] (PL: **pics, pix**) (N ABBR) **1** (= **picture**) (= *photo*) foto *f*
2 (= *movie*) película *f*
3 pics (= *cinema*) cine *m* • **to go to the pics** ir al cine
pica [ˈpaɪkə] (N) (*Med, Vet*) pica *f*; (*Typ*) cícero *m*
picador [ˈpɪkədɔː] (N) picador *m*
Picardy [ˈpɪkədɪ] (N) Picardía *f*
picaresque [ˌpɪkəˈresk] (ADJ) picaresco
picayune* [ˌpɪkəˈjuːn] (US) (ADJ) insignificante, de poca monta
piccalilli [ˈpɪkəˌlɪlɪ] (N) legumbres *fpl* en escabeche, encurtidos *mpl* picantes
piccaninny†✿ [ˈpɪkəˌnɪnɪ] (N) negrito/a *m/f*
piccolo [ˈpɪkələʊ] (N) (PL: **piccolos**) flautín *m*, píccolo *m*
pick [pɪk] (N) **1** (= *choice*) • **to have one's ~ of sth** escoger *or* elegir lo que uno quiere de algo • **take your ~!** ¡escoja *or* elija lo que quiera! • **take your ~ of** *or* **from ten luxury hotels** escoja *or* elija el que quiera de entre diez hoteles de lujo
2 (= *best*) • **the ~ of sth** lo mejor de algo, la flor y nata de algo • **the ~ of the bunch** *or* **the crop** (*fig*) lo mejor de grupo
3 (*also* **pickaxe**) (= *tool*) pico *m*, piqueta *f*
4 (*US*) (= *plectrum*) púa *f*; ▸ **toothpick**
(VT) **1** (= *choose*) (*gen*) escoger, elegir; [+ *team, candidate*] seleccionar • **~ a card, any card** escoge *or* elige una carta, cualquiera • **to ~ a fight (with sb)** (*lit*) buscar pelea *or* pleito (con algn); (*fig*) (= *argue*) discutir (con algn) • **to ~ one's way through/across sth** abrirse camino cuidadosamente a través de algo • **to ~ a winner** (*lit*) escoger *or* elegir un ganador; (*fig*) escoger bien • **I think she ~ed a winner with her new boyfriend** creo que con su nuevo novio escogió bien; ▸ **quarrel**
2 (= *gather*) [+ *flowers, fruit, tea, cotton*] coger, recoger (*LAm*) • **to go strawberry ~ing** ir a coger fresas
3 (= *lift, remove*) • **to ~ sth off the ground** recoger algo del suelo • **let me ~ that bit of fluff off your collar** deja que te quite esa pelusa del cuello • **to ~ o.s. off the floor** *or* **ground** levantarse del suelo • **to ~ names out of a hat** sacar nombres de un sombrero
4 (= *make*) [+ *hole*] hacer; ▸ **hole**
5 [+ *scab, spot*] toquetear; [+ *lock*] forzar *or* abrir con ganzúa; [+ *guitar, banjo*] puntear • **to ~ sb's brains** exprimir el coco a algn* • **their bones had been ~ed clean by the birds** los pájaros habían dejado limpios los huesos • **to ~ one's nose** hurgarse la nariz • **to ~ sb's pocket** robar algo a algn del bolsillo • **to ~ one's teeth** mondarse *or* escarbarse los dientes; ▸ **bone, piece**
(VI) **1** (= *choose*) escoger, elegir • **to ~ and choose** ponerse a escoger *or* elegir, ser muy exigente • **you can't ~ and choose** no puedes ponerte a escoger *or* elegir, no puedes ser muy exigente
2 (= *examine*) • **dogs ~ through the garbage on the streets** los perros hurgan en *or* por la basura de las calles; ▸ **pick over**
▸ **pick at** (VI + PREP) **1** (= *toy with*) • **try not to ~ at your spots** intenta no toquetearte las espinillas • **to ~ at one's food** comer con poca gana, picar la comida
2 (= *criticize*) • **she used to ~ at everything** solía meterse con todo *or* ponerle faltas a todo
3 (*US**) = **pick on**
▸ **pick off** (VT + ADV) **1** (= *remove*) [+ *leaves, fluff, paint*] quitar; [+ *scab*] arrancar
2 (= *shoot*) cargarse*, liquidar*; (= *eliminate*) [+ *opponents*] acabar uno a uno con
▸ **pick on** (VI + PREP) **1** (= *choose, single out*) escoger, elegir • **I can't think why he ~ed on that wallpaper** no logro entender por qué escogió *or* eligió ese papel para la pared • **they ~ed on me to go and tell him** me escogieron *or* eligieron a mí para que se lo dijera • **why ~ on me?** ¿por qué yo (y no otro)?
2* (= *harass*) meterse con* • **stop ~ing on me** deja de meterte conmigo* • **~ on someone your own size!** ¡métete con alguien de tu tamaño!*
▸ **pick out** (VT + ADV) **1** (= *choose*) elegir, escoger • **~ out two or three you would like to keep** elige *or* escoge dos o tres con los que te gustaría quedarte
2 (= *single out*) escoger • **there are so many great pianists it's difficult to ~ one out** hay tantos grandes pianistas que es difícil escoger a uno
3 (= *draw out*) sacar • **I took the hat and ~ed out a raffle ticket** cogí el sombrero y saqué uno de los boletos de la rifa
4 (= *discern*) distinguir • **I could just ~ out the letters ALG** solo podía distinguir y con dificultad, las letras ALG
5 (= *identify*) reconocer • **can you ~ me out in this photo?** ¿eres capaz de reconocerme en esta foto?
6 (= *highlight*) resaltar • **the name is ~ed out in gold letters** el nombre está resaltado en letras doradas • **his headlights ~ed out the cyclist in front** los faros de su coche iluminaron al ciclista que tenía delante
7 (= *play*) [+ *tune*] tocar de oído
▸ **pick over** (VT + ADV) • **~ over the raspberries** escoge las frambuesas que estén mejor • **she was ~ing over the shirts in the sale** estaba seleccionando las camisas en las rebajas • **it's no good ~ing over the past** de nada sirve remover el pasado
▸ **pick up** (VT + ADV) **1** (= *lift*) [+ *box, suitcase, cat*] levantar; [+ *dropped object*] recoger, coger; (= *take hold of*) tomar, coger, agarrar (*LAm*) • **I saw her fall and ran to ~ her up** la vi caerse y corrí a levantarla • **that child is always wanting to be ~ed up** ese niño siempre quiere que lo cojan *or* (*LAm*) levanten • **she bent to ~ up her glove** se agachó para recoger *or* coger su guante • **she ~ed up a pencil and fiddled with it** tomó *or* cogió *or* (*LAm*) agarró un lápiz y se puso a enredar con él • **you can't ~ up a newspaper these days without reading about her** últimamente no puedes coger *or* (*LAm*) agarrar un periódico que no hable de ella • **to ~ up the bill** *or* **tab (for sth)*** pagar la cuenta (de algo) • **to ~ o.s. up** (*lit*) levantarse, ponerse de pie; (*fig*) recuperarse, reponerse; ▸ **piece**
2 (= *collect*) [+ *person*] recoger, ir a buscar (*esp LAm*); (= *give lift to*) [+ *hitch-hiker, passenger*] recoger, coger • **did you ~ up my laundry?** ¿recogiste mi colada?
3 (= *learn*) [+ *language, skill*] aprender; [+ *accent, habit*] coger, agarrar (*LAm*), adquirir (*frm*) • **you'll soon ~ it up again** pronto lo volverás a aprender • **I ~ed up a bit of news about him today** hoy me enteré de algunas cosas sobre él
4 (= *buy*) comprar; (= *find*) [+ *bargain*] encontrar; (= *catch*) [+ *disease*] coger, agarrar (*LAm*), pillar* • **an old car he ~ed up for £250** un coche viejo que compró por 250 libras • **I'll ~ up some beer on the way back** compraré unas cervezas a la vuelta • **I may ~ up some useful ideas for my book** puede que encuentre algunas ideas útiles para mi libro
5* (= *earn, gain*) ganar, sacarse • **she ~s up £400 a week** gana *or* se saca 400 libras a la semana • **it ~ed up the best musical award** ganó *or* se llevó el premio al mejor musical • **to ~ up speed** acelerar, coger velocidad, tomar velocidad (*LAm*)
6* (*sexually*) ligarse a* • **are you trying to ~ me up?** ¿estás intentando ligar conmigo?
7 (*Rad, TV*) [+ *station, channel*] captar, coger; (*Tech*) [+ *signal*] captar, registrar • **we can ~ up Italian television** podemos captar *or* coger la televisión italiana
8 (= *notice, detect*) • **he ~ed up ten misprints** encontró diez erratas • **she ~ed up every mistake** no se le escapó ni un error • **I had no difficulty ~ing up the signals he was sending me** (*fig*) no tuve problemas para captar las indirectas que me estaba mandando; ▸ **scent**
9 (= *resume*) [+ *conversation, narrative*] continuar; [+ *relationship*] reanudar; ▸ **thread**
10 (= *focus on*) • **I'd like to ~ up the point David made** quisiera volver al punto que planteó David • **the papers ~ed up the story** los periódicos publicaron la historia
11 (= *reprimand*) reñir, reprender • **she ~ed him up for using bad language** le riñó *or* le reprendió por decir palabrotas
12 (= *correct*) • **he ~ed me up on my grammar** me señaló diversas faltas de gramática • **if I may ~ you up on that point** si me permites corregirte en ese punto
13 (= *rescue*) recoger, rescatar
14 (= *arrest*) detener
15 (= *revive*) [+ *person*] reanimar • **this tonic will soon ~ you up** este tónico te reanimará pronto
16 (*US**) (= *tidy*) [+ *room, house*] recoger
(VI + ADV) **1** (= *improve*) [*conditions, weather, sales*] mejorar; [*market, economy*] reponerse; [*business, trade*] ir mejor; [*prices*] volver a subir • **the game ~ed up in the second half** el partido mejoró en el segundo tiempo
2 (= *increase*) [*wind*] levantarse
3 (= *continue*) • **to ~ up where one left off** [+ *activity, conversation, relationship*] continuar donde se había dejado
4 (= *notice, react to*) • **I was getting nervous**

and he ~ed up on that me estaba poniendo nervioso y él lo captó *or* se dio cuenta • the press did not ~ up on it la prensa no reaccionó ante la noticia
5* (= *become involved with*) • to ~ up with sb juntarse con algn • she's ~ed up with a bad crowd se ha juntado con una gente no muy recomendable
6 (= *tidy up*) • to ~ up after sb ir recogiendo detrás de algn • he expects me to ~ up after him espera que vaya recogiendo detrás suyo
pickaback ['pɪkəbæk] N, ADV = **piggyback**
pick-and-mix [,pɪkn'mɪks] ADJ = **pick 'n' mix**
pickaxe, pickax (US) ['pɪkæks] N pico *m*, piqueta *f*
picked [pɪkt] ADJ escogido, selecto
picker ['pɪkəʳ] N [*of fruit, tea*] recolector(a) *m/f*
picket ['pɪkɪt] N 1 (= *stake*) estaca *f*
2 (= *strikers*) piquete *m*; (*Mil*) (= *sentry*) piquete *m*; (= *group*) pelotón *m*
VT [+ *factory*] poner piquetes a la puerta de, piquetear (*LAm*)
VI formar piquetes, piquetear (*LAm*)
CPD ▸ **picket duty** • to be on ~ duty estar de guardia ▸ **picket fence** estacada *f*, cerca *f* ▸ **picket line** piquete *m* • to cross a ~ line no hacer caso de un piquete
picketer ['pɪkɪtəʳ] N miembro *mf* de un piquete
picketing ['pɪkɪtɪŋ] N formación *f* de piquetes
picking ['pɪkɪŋ] N 1 [*of fruit etc*] recolección *f*, cosecha *f*; (= *act of choosing*) elección *f*, selección *f*
2 **pickings** (= *leftovers*) restos *mpl*, sobras *fpl*; (= *profits*) ganancias *fpl* • there are rich ~s for bargain hunters at these sales en esta liquidación hay pingües beneficios para los que van a la caza de gangas
pickle ['pɪkl] N 1 (= *condiment*) (*also* **pickles**) encurtidos *mpl*; (= *liquid*) escabeche *m*
2* (= *plight*) lío* *m*, apuro *m*, aprieto *m* • to be in a ~ estar en un apuro *or* aprieto • to get into a ~ meterse en un lío*
VT encurtir, escabechar
pickled ['pɪkld] ADJ 1 [*food*] escabechado, encurtido, en conserva
2 • to be ~* (= *drunk*) estar jumado*
CPD ▸ **pickled onions** cebollas *fpl* en vinagre ▸ **pickled herrings** arenques *mpl* en escabeche ▸ **pickled walnuts** nueces *fpl* adobadas
pickling onions ['pɪklɪŋ,ʌnjənz] NPL cebollitas *fpl*
picklock ['pɪklɒk] N ganzúa *f*
pick-me-up ['pɪkmiːʌp] N estimulante *m*; (= *drink*) bebida *f* tonificante; (*Med*) tónico *m*, reconstituyente *m* • he tends to pop into the pub on the way home for a pick-me-up suele pasarse por el pub de camino a casa para ponerse a tono • this bath oil is the ideal pick-me-up after a hard day at work esta esencia de baño te deja como nuevo después de un día duro de trabajo
pick 'n' mix [,pɪkn'mɪks] ADJ [*selection*] misceláneo; (*also* **pick 'n' mix counter**) *mostrador de caramelos variados*
pickpocket ['pɪk,pɒkɪt] N carterista *mf*, bolsista *mf* (*Mex*)
pick-up ['pɪkʌp] N 1 (*Mus*) **a** (*on instrument*) pastilla *f*; (*on microphone*) toma *f* de sonidos **b** (*also* **pick-up arm**) brazo *m* (del tocadiscos)
2 (*also* **pick-up truck**) furgoneta *f*, camioneta *f*
3 (= *collection*) • to make a pick-up [*truck driver, drug runner*] recoger algo • the bus made three pick-ups el autobús hizo tres paradas para recoger a gente
4 (= *recovery*) (*in economy, trade, sales*) mejora *f*; (*in prices*) subida *f*
5* (= *pick-me-up*) estimulante *m*
6* (*sexual*) • to him it was just a pick-up él no quería más que ligar con ella* • a pick-up joint un garito de ligue*
7 (*Aut*) (= *acceleration*) facilidad *f* de aceleración
CPD ▸ **pick-up joint*** bar *m* de ligoteo* ▸ **pick-up point** (*for people*) parada *f*; (*for goods*) punto *m* de recogida
picky* ['pɪkɪ] ADJ (US) (COMPAR: **pickier**, SUPERL: **pickiest**) 1 (= *critical*) criticón
2 (= *choosy*) melindroso, quisquilloso
picnic ['pɪknɪk] (VB: PT, PP: **picnicked**) N comida *f* en el campo, picnic *m* (*esp LAm*) • to go on a ~ ir de picnic, ir a comer al campo • we found a nice place for a ~ encontramos un buen sitio para comer al aire libre • it was no ~* (= *unpleasant*) fue muy desagradable; (= *difficult*) no fue nada fácil
VI comer en el campo • we ~ked by the river merendamos junto al río
CPD ▸ **picnic basket** cesta *f or* (*LAm*) canasta *f* de la merienda *or* comida *etc* ▸ **picnic lunch** (= *outdoor meal*) picnic *m*; (*provided by hotel*) comida *f* picnic ▸ **picnic site** lugar *m* destinado para picnics ▸ **picnic table** mesa *f* de picnic
picnicker ['pɪknɪkəʳ] N excursionista *mf*
pics* [pɪks] NPL ABBR (*Brit*) = **pictures**
Pict [pɪkt] N picto/a *m/f*
Pictish ['pɪktɪʃ] ADJ picto
N picto *m*
pictogram ['pɪktəʊgræm] N pictograma *m*
pictograph ['pɪktəgrɑːf] N 1 (= *record, chart*) pictografía *f*
2 (*Ling*) (= *symbol*) pictograma *m*; (= *writing*) pictografía *f*
pictorial [pɪk'tɔːrɪəl] ADJ (*Art*) pictórico; [*record, history*] gráfico; [*magazine*] ilustrado
N revista *f* ilustrada
pictorially [pɪk'tɔːrɪəlɪ] ADV (= *from a pictorial point of view*) pictóricamente; [*represent*] gráficamente, por imágenes
picture ['pɪktʃəʳ] N 1 (*Art*) (= *print, engraving*) cuadro *m*; (= *drawing*) dibujo *m*; (= *painting*) cuadro *m*, pintura *f*; (= *portrait*) retrato *m* • to draw a ~ (of sth/sb) hacer un dibujo (de algo/algn) • to paint a ~ (of sth/sb) pintar un cuadro (de algo/algn) • he painted a black ~ of the future nos pintó un cuadro muy negro del porvenir • to paint sb's ~ pintar un retrato de algn, pintar a algn • PROVERBS: • every ~ tells a story detrás de cada imagen hay una historia • a ~ is worth a thousand words una imagen vale más que mil palabras; ▹ **pretty**
2 (= *photo*) foto *f*, fotografía *f* • to take a ~ of sth/sb hacer *or* (*esp LAm*) sacar una foto a algo/algn • we all had our ~s taken todos nos hicimos *or* (*esp LAm*) sacamos fotos
3 (= *illustration*) (*in book*) ilustración *f*; (*in magazine*) ilustración *f*, foto *f*
4 (= *personification*) • he looked the ~ of health era la salud personificada
5 (= *wonderful sight*) • the garden is a ~ in June el jardín es una preciosidad en junio • his face was a ~ ¡vaya cara que puso!, ¡vieras *or* hubieras visto su cara! (*LAm*)
6 (= *situation*) panorama *m* • the overall ~ is encouraging el panorama general es alentador • you have to look at the whole ~ tienes que considerar la situación *or* el panorama en conjunto • where do I come *or* fit into the ~?* ¿qué pinto yo *or* dónde encajo yo en todo esto?*, ¿cuál es mi papel en todo esto? • to get the ~* comprender • I get the ~ ya comprendo • do you get the ~? ¿te enteras?*, ¿lo captas?* • he was a bit unsure in the job at first but he soon got the ~ al principio no se sentía muy seguro de cómo hacer su trabajo pero pronto le cogió el truco* • to put sb in the ~ (about sth) poner a algn al corriente *or* al tanto (de algo)
7 (= *idea*) • these figures give the general ~ estas cifras ofrecen una idea general *or* una visión de conjunto • I have a ~ in my mind of how I want it to look tengo una imagen mental del aspecto que quiero que tenga
8 (*TV*) imagen *f*
9 (*esp US*) (*Cine*) película *f*; (*Brit*†) • the ~s el cine • to go to the ~s ir al cine; ▹ **motion**
VT 1 (= *imagine*) imaginarse • I never ~d you as a family man nunca te imaginé *or* te vi como hombre de familia • ~ the scene figuraos la escena • ~ yourself lying on the beach imagínate que estás tumbado en la playa
2 (= *portray*) (*in painting, film, novel*) representar; (*in photograph*) • his wife, ~d with him above su mujer, que figura con él en la foto de arriba • the documentary ~d the police as good-natured fools el documental pintaba a la policía como si fueran un hatajo de tontos con buen corazón, el documental representaba a la policía como un hatajo de tontos con buen corazón
CPD ▸ **picture book** libro *m* ilustrado ▸ **picture frame** marco *m* ▸ **picture gallery** (= *shop*) galería *f* de arte; (= *museum*) museo *m* de pintura, pinacoteca *f*; (*in stately home*) galería *f* de cuadros ▸ **picture hat** pamela *f* ▸ **picture house**† cine *m* ▸ **picture library** biblioteca *f* fotográfica ▸ **picture message** mensaje *m* con foto ▸ **picture messaging** (envío *m* de) mensajes *mpl* con foto ▸ **picture palace**† cine *m* ▸ **picture phone** teléfono *m* con cámara ▸ **picture postcard** (tarjeta *f*) postal *f* ▸ **picture rail** *moldura para colgar cuadros* ▸ **picture tube** (*TV*) tubo *m* de imagen ▸ **picture window** ventanal *m*
picturegoer ['pɪktʃə,gəʊəʳ] N aficionado/a *m/f* al cine
picture-in-picture [,pɪktʃərɪn'pɪktʃəʳ] N (*TV, Comput*) imagen *f* dentro de la imagen
picture-postcard [,pɪktʃə'pəʊstkɑːd] ADJ [*village*] de postal
picturesque [,pɪktʃə'resk] ADJ (= *quaint*) [*village*] pintoresco; [*name, title*] pintoresco, peculiar; (= *vivid*) [*language*] expresivo, vívido
picturesquely [,pɪktʃə'resklɪ] ADV de modo pintoresco
picturesqueness [,pɪktʃə'resknɪs] N [*of village*] lo pintoresco, pintoresquismo *m*; [*of language, description*] expresividad *f*
piddle* ['pɪdl] N • to have a ~ hacer pipí *or* pis*
VI hacer pipí*, hacer pis*
piddling* ['pɪdlɪŋ] ADJ ridículo, irrisorio
pidgin ['pɪdʒɪn] N (*also* **pidgin English**) (*formerly*) *lengua franca (inglés-chino) comercial del Lejano Oriente* • he used his ~ French to chat up the girls recurrió a su francés macarrónico para ligar con las chicas*
pie [paɪ] N [*of fruit*] tarta *f*, pay *m* (*LAm*); [*of meat, fish etc*] (= *large*) pastel *m*; (= *small*) empanada *f* • IDIOMS: • it's as easy as pie* es pan comido* • it's all pie in the sky son castillos en el aire, es pura ilusión • to eat humble pie tragarse el orgullo y pedir perdón, morder el polvo; ▹ **finger**
CPD ▸ **pie chart** (*Math, Comput*) gráfico *m* de sectores, gráfico *m* circular ▸ **pie dish** molde *m* para pasteles
piebald ['paɪbɔːld] ADJ pío, picazo
N caballo *m* pío, picazo *m*
piece [piːs] N 1 (= *fragment*) trozo *m*, pedazo *m* • to come to ~s hacerse pedazos,

P

romperse • **to fall to ~s** caerse a pedazos, romperse • **my watch lay in ~s on the pavement** mi reloj quedó destrozado en la acera, mi reloj quedó en la acera hecho pedazos • **his life lay in ~s** su vida estaba destrozada • **a ~ of sth**: • **a ~ of bread** un trozo *or* un pedazo de pan • **a ~ of cake** una porción *or* un trozo de tarta • **another ~ of cake?** ¿quieres más tarta? • **a ~ of cheese/glass** un trozo de queso/cristal • **a ~ of paper** un trozo *or* una hoja de papel, un papel • **a ~ of string** un trozo de cuerda, un cabo • **a ~ of toast** una tostada • **I've got a ~ of grit in my eye** tengo una mota en el ojo • **(all) in one ~**: • **the vase is still in one ~** el jarrón sigue intacto • **we got back all in one ~** llegamos sanos y salvos • **he had a nasty fall but he's still in one ~** sufrió una mala caída pero no le pasó nada • **it is made (all) in one ~** está hecho de una sola pieza • **to pick** *or* **pull sth to ~s** [*+ argument, theory*] echar por tierra algo • **to smash (sth) to ~s**: • **the glass fell off the table and smashed to ~s** el vaso se cayó de la mesa y se hizo añicos • **I smashed the vase to ~s** rompí el jarrón en mil pedazos, hice el jarrón añicos • **the boat was smashed to ~s on the rocks** el barco se estrelló contra las rocas y se hizo añicos • IDIOMS: • **to go to ~s** [*person*] (*= break down*) quedar deshecho, quedar hecho pedazos; (*= lose one's grip*) desquiciarse • **she went to ~s when Arnie died** quedó deshecha *or* hecha pedazos cuando Arnie murió • **every time he's faced with a problem he goes to ~s** cada vez que se ve ante un problema se desquicia *or* el pánico se apodera de él • **it's a ~ of cake*** es pan comido* • **to give sb a ~ of one's mind** decir cuatro verdades a algn, cantar las cuarenta a algn* • **he got a ~ of my mind** le dije cuatro verdades, le canté las cuarenta* • **to pick up the ~s**: • **they always leave me to pick up the ~s** siempre me toca sacarles las castañas del fuego, siempre dejan que sea yo el que pague los platos rotos • **she never picked up the ~s after her fiancé died** nunca logró superar la muerte de su prometido, nunca rehizo realmente su vida después de la muerte de su prometido; ▸ **action, nasty, thrill**

2 (*= part, member of a set*) pieza *f* • **~ by ~** pieza por *or* a pieza • **it comes to ~s** se desmonta, es desmontable • **(all) of a ~**: • **Dostoyevsky's life and work are of a ~** la vida y las obras de Dostoyevsky son uno y lo mismo • **Amy was putting the ~s together now** ahora Amy estaba juntando *or* atando los cabos • **to take sth to ~s** desmontar *or* desarmar algo

3 (*as suffix*) • **a four-piece band** un grupo de cuatro músicos • **a three-piece suit** un traje con chaleco • **a three-piece suite** un juego de sofá y dos butacas, un tresillo (*Sp*) • **a fifteen-piece tea set** un juego de té de quince piezas

4 (*= item*) • **a ~ of advice** un consejo • **to sell sth by the ~** vender algo suelto • **a ~ of clothing** una prenda (de vestir) • **a ~ of equipment** un aparato • **a ~ of evidence** una prueba • **a ~ of furniture** un mueble • **a ~ of information** un dato • **a ~ of legislation** una ley • **you are allowed two ~s of luggage** se le permite llevar dos bultos • **a ~ of news** una noticia • **your essay was a sloppy ~ of work** tu redacción deja mucho que desear; ▸ **history, land**

5 (*= instance*) • **it was a ~ of luck** fue una suerte • **what a ~ of luck you called round** qué suerte que te hayas pasado por aquí

6 (*= composition*) (*Press*) artículo *m*; (*Mus, Art, Theat*) pieza *f* • **a piano ~** una pieza para piano • IDIOM: • **to say one's ~** decir uno lo que tiene que decir; ▸ **museum, party, period**

7 (*Mil*) • **artillery ~s** • **~s of artillery** piezas *fpl* de artillería

8 (*in chess*) pieza *f*; (*in draughts, backgammon*) ficha *f*

9 (*= coin*) moneda *f* • **a 10 pence ~** una moneda de 10 peniques • **a ~ of eight** un real de a ocho

10 (*US**) (*= distance*) • **his place is down the road a ~** su casa está un poco más allá bajando la calle

11†* (*offensive*) (*= woman*) tipa* *f*, tía *f* (*Sp**) • **a nice little ~** una tía buena (*Sp**), una tipaza*

CPD ▸ **piece of research** trabajo *m* de investigación • **a ~ of research on the effects of the drug** un trabajo de investigación sobre los efectos del fármaco ▸ **piece rate** (*Comm*) tarifa *f* por pieza • **they are on ~ rates** les pagan por pieza *or* a destajo

▸ **piece together** VT + ADV [*+ jigsaw puzzle, events*] reconstruir; [*+ plan, strategy*] concebir • **she ~d together the torn-up letter** reconstruyó la carta que estaba hecha pedazos • **we eventually ~d together what had happened** por fin logramos atar todos los cabos de lo que había pasado

pièce de résistance [ˌpjesdərezɪsˈtɑ̃:s] N [*of programme, exhibition*] atracción *f* principal; (*on menu*) plato *m* principal; [*of author, director*] (*= novel, film*) obra *f* maestra • **his ~ was a goal in the 89th minute** dio la campanada con un gol en el minuto 89

piecemeal [ˈpi:smi:l] ADV (*= gradually*) poco a poco, por partes; (*= unsystematically*) de manera poco sistemática
ADJ [*approach, reform*] poco sistemático • **a ~ solution** una solución de compromiso

piecework [ˈpi:swɜ:k] N trabajo *m* a destajo • **to be on/do ~** trabajar a destajo

pieceworker [ˈpi:swɜ:kəʳ] N destajista *mf*

piecrust [ˈpaɪkrʌst] N (*= base*) fondo *m* de masa; (*= top*) tapa *f* de masa
CPD ▸ **piecrust pastry** (*US*) pasta *f* quebradiza

pied [paɪd] ADJ [*horse*] pío, picazo; [*bird*] pinto • **the Pied Piper of Hamelin** el flautista de Hamelin

pied-à-terre [ˌpeɪdɑ:ˈtɛəʳ] N (PL: **pieds-à-terre** [ˌpeɪdɑ:ˈtɛəʳ]) segunda vivienda *f* (*en una ciudad*)

Piedmont [ˈpi:dmɒnt] N Piamonte *m*

Piedmontese [ˌpi:dmɒnˈti:z] ADJ piamontés
N piamontés/esa *m/f*

pie-eyed* [ˈpaɪˈaɪd] ADJ como una cuba*, jumado*

pier [pɪəʳ] N **1** (*= amusement centre*) *paseo marítimo situado como zona de ocio sobre un muelle o malecón*; (*= landing-stage*) embarcadero *m*, muelle *m*

2 (*Archit*) pilar *m*, columna *f*; [*of bridge*] estribo *m*, pila *f*

pierce [pɪəs] VT (*= puncture*) perforar; (*= go right through*) atravesar, traspasar; (*= make hole in*) agujerear; (*fig*) [*sound*] desgarrar, penetrar • **the broken rib ~d his lung** la costilla rota le perforó el pulmón • **the thorn ~d his heel** la espina se le clavó en el talón • **the dagger ~d her heart/the armour** el puñal le atravesó el corazón/atravesó la armadura • **to ~ a hole in sth** hacer un agujero en algo • **to have one's ears ~d** hacerse los agujeros de las orejas • **a nail ~d the tyre** un clavo pinchó el neumático • **a cry ~d the silence** un grito desgarró *or* penetró el silencio • **a light ~d the darkness** una luz hendió la oscuridad • **the cold ~d their bones** el frío les penetraba hasta los huesos • **the news ~d him to the heart** la noticia le hirió en el alma

piercer [ˈpɪəsəʳ] N (*= body piercer*) perforador(a) *m/f* corporal

piercing [ˈpɪəsɪŋ] ADJ penetrante, agudo; [*eyes, gaze*] penetrante; [*cry*] desgarrador; [*wind*] cortante; [*cold*] penetrante; [*pain*] punzante
N (*in body art*) piercing *m*

piercingly [ˈpɪəsɪŋlɪ] ADV [*stare*] de modo penetrante; [*blow*] de modo cortante • **it was ~ cold** el frío se te metía hasta los huesos

pierhead [ˈpɪəhed] N punta *f* del muelle

pierrot [ˈpɪərəʊ] N pierrot *m*

pietism [ˈpaɪətɪzəm] N piedad *f*, devoción *f*; (*pej*) beatería *f*, mojigatería *f*

pietistic [paɪəˈtɪstɪk] ADJ (*pej*) pietista, beato, mojigato

piety [ˈpaɪətɪ] N piedad *f*, devoción *f*; (*= affected piety*) beatería *f*

piffle* [ˈpɪfl] N tonterías *fpl*, paparruchas* *fpl* • **piffle!** ¡tonterías!, ¡bobadas!

piffling* [ˈpɪflɪŋ] ADJ [*dispute, task*] de poca monta, insignificante; [*excuse*] absurdo, ridículo; [*sum, amount*] ridículo, irrisorio

pig [pɪg] N **1** cerdo *m*, chancho *m* (*LAm*) • **roast pig** lechón *m* asado *or* al horno • **wild pig** cerdo *m* de monte • IDIOMS: • **he made a right pig's ear of it*** le salió muy mal, le salió un verdadero churro (*Sp**), le salió una auténtica cagada‡ • **in a pig's eye!** (*US**) ¡ni hablar! • **yes, and pigs might fly!** cuando las ranas críen pelo • **to buy a pig in a poke** comprar algo a ciegas • **to sell sb a pig in a poke** dar gato por liebre a algn

2* (*= person*) (*dirty, nasty*) cerdo/a* *m/f*, puerco/a* *m/f*, chancho/a* *m/f* (*LAm*); (*greedy*) comilón/ona* *m/f*, tragón/ona* *m/f* • **you pig!** (*hum*) ¡bandido! • IDIOM: • **to make a pig of o.s.** darse un atracón*, ponerse las botas*

3‡ (*= policeman*) poli* *m* • **the pigs** la poli*, la pasma (*Sp*‡), la cana (*S. Cone*‡)

4* (*= sth difficult or unpleasant*) • **it was a pig of a job** fue un trabajo de lo más puñetero* • **this car's a pig to start** a este puñetero coche le cuesta lo suyo arrancar*

5 (*Metal*) lingote *m*

VT • **to pig it** vivir como cerdos

CPD ▸ **pig farm** granja *f* porcina ▸ **pig farmer** criador(a) *m/f* de cerdos ▸ **pig iron** hierro *m* en lingotes

▸ **pig out*** VI + ADV • **to pig out (on sth)** darse un atracón *or* ponerse las botas (de algo)*

pig-breeding [ˈpɪgˌbri:dɪŋ] N cría *f* de cerdos

pigeon [ˈpɪdʒən] N **1** (*gen*) paloma *f*; (*as food*) pichón *m*; ▸ **clay**

2* • **that's his ~** allá él • **it's not my ~** eso no tiene que ver conmigo

CPD ▸ **pigeon fancier** colombófilo/a *m/f* ▸ **pigeon fancying** colombofilia *f* ▸ **pigeon house, pigeon loft** palomar *m* ▸ **pigeon post** correo *m* de palomas • **by ~ post** por paloma mensajera ▸ **pigeon shooting** tiro *m* de pichón

pigeonhole [ˈpɪdʒənhəʊl] N casilla *f*; (*= set of pigeonholes*) casillero *m*, casillas *fpl*
VT (*= classify*) encasillar, clasificar; (*= store away*) archivar; (*= shelve*) dar carpetazo a

pigeon-toed [ˈpɪdʒənˈtəʊd] ADJ • **to be pigeon-toed** tener los pies torcidos hacia dentro

piggery [ˈpɪgərɪ] N **1** (*= pig farm*) granja *f* porcina

2 (*= pigsty*) pocilga *f*, porqueriza *f*

3 (*= greediness*) glotonería *f*

piggish [ˈpɪgɪʃ] ADJ (*in manners*) cochino, puerco; (*= greedy*) glotón; (*= stubborn*) tozudo, testarudo

piggy [ˈpɪgɪ] N cerdito *m*, chanchito *m* (*LAm*) • **to play ~ in the middle** jugar al balón

prisionero • IDIOM: • **to be ~ in the middle** (= *powerless to act, influence*) estar entre dos fuegos
(ADJ) • **with little ~ eyes** con ojos pequeños como de cerdo
(CPD) ▸ **piggy bank** hucha *f* (*Sp*) (en forma de cerdito), alcancía *f* (*LAm*)

piggyback [ˈpɪgɪbæk] (N) • **to give sb a ~** llevar a algn a cuestas
(ADV) • **to carry sb ~** llevar a algn a cuestas
▸ **piggyback on** (VI + PREP) aprovecharse de • **I was just ~ing on Wilson's idea** simplemente me estaba aprovechando de la idea de Wilson

pigheaded [ˈpɪgˈhedɪd] (ADJ) [*person*] terco, testarudo; [*attitude*] obstinado

pigheadedly [ˈpɪgˈhedɪdlɪ] (ADV) tercamente

pigheadedness [ˈpɪgˈhedɪdnɪs] (N) terquedad *f*, testarudez *f*

pig-ignorant* [ˌpɪgˈɪgnərənt] (ADJ) bruto

piglet [ˈpɪglɪt] (N) cerdito *m*, lechón *m*, chanchito *m* (*LAm*)

pigman [ˈpɪgmæn] (N) (PL: **pigmen**) porquerizo *m*, porquero *m*

pigmeat [ˈpɪgmiːt] (N) carne *f* de cerdo

pigment [ˈpɪgmənt] (N) pigmento *m*

pigmentation [ˌpɪgmənˈteɪʃən] (N) pigmentación *f*

pigmented [pɪgˈmentɪd] (ADJ) pigmentado

pigmy [ˈpɪgmɪ] (ADJ), (N) = **pygmy**

pigpen [ˈpɪgpen] (N) (*US*) = **pigsty**

pigskin [ˈpɪgskɪn] (N) piel *f* de cerdo, cuero *m* de chancho (*LAm*)

pigsty [ˈpɪgstaɪ] (N) pocilga *f*, porqueriza *f*

pigswill [ˈpɪgswɪl] (N) bazofia *f* (*also fig*)

pigtail [ˈpɪgteɪl] (N) (= *plait*) trenza *f*; (*of Chinese, bullfighter etc*) coleta *f*

pike¹ [paɪk] (N) (*Mil*) pica *f*

pike² [paɪk] (N) (PL: **pike** *or* **pikes**) (= *fish*) lucio *m*

pikeman [ˈpaɪkmən] (N) (PL: **pikemen**) (*Hist*) piquero *m*

pikeperch [ˈpaɪkpɜːtʃ] (N) (*Zool*) lucioperca *f*

piker‡ [ˈpaɪkəʳ] (N) (*US*) (= *stingy person*) agarrado/a* *m/f*, roñoso/a* *m/f*; (= *unimportant person*) pelagatos* *mf inv*; (= *coward*) gallina* *mf*

pikestaff [ˈpaɪkstɑːf] (N) ▹ **plain**

pilaf, **pilaff** [ˈpɪlæf] (N) *plato oriental a base de arroz*

pilaster [pɪˈlæstəʳ] (N) pilastra *f*

Pilate [ˈpaɪlət] (N) Pilatos

Pilates [pɪˈlɑːtiːz] (N) Pilates *m*

pilau [pɪˈlaʊ] (N) = **pilaf**

pilchard [ˈpɪltʃəd] (N) sardina *f*

pile¹ [paɪl] (N) **1** (= *heap*) [*of books, clothes*] montón *m* • **to put things in a ~** amontonar cosas, juntar cosas en un montón • **the building was reduced to a ~ of rubble** el edificio quedó reducido a un montón *or* una pila de escombros
2* (= *large amount*) montón* *m* • **I've got ~s of work to do** tengo un montón *or* tengo montones de trabajo que hacer*
3* (= *fortune*) dineral* *m*, fortuna *f* • **he made a ~ on this deal** ganó un dineral *or* una fortuna con el trato, se hizo de oro con el trato • **he made his ~ in oil** hizo su fortuna con el petróleo
4* (*hum*) (= *building*) mole *f* (*hum*) • **some stately ~ in the country** una mole de casa *or* un caserón en el campo
5 (*Phys*) pila *f*; ▹ **atomic**
(VT) amontonar, apilar • **he ~d the plates onto the tray** amontonó *or* apiló los platos en la bandeja • **we ~d more coal on the fire** echamos más carbón al fuego • **the tables were ~d high with food** en las mesas había montones *or* montañas de comida • **her hair was ~d high on her head** llevaba el pelo recogido con un tocado alto • **I ~d the children into the car*** metí a los niños apretujados en el coche
(VI)* **1** (= *squeeze*) • **we all ~d into the car** nos metimos todos apretujados en el coche • **we ~d off the bus** salimos en avalancha *or* en tropel del autobús • **they ~d onto the bus** se metieron apretujados en el autobús
2 (= *attack*) • **they ~d into him** se abalanzaron sobre él
3 (= *crash*) • **his car ~d into the tree** su coche se estrelló contra el árbol • **12 cars had ~d into each other** 12 coches se habían estrellado en cadena
▸ **pile in*** (VI + ADV) **1** (= *get in*) • **~ in!** ¡súbanse como puedan!
2 (= *intervene*) lanzarse al ataque
▸ **pile off*** (VI + ADV) [*people*] salir en avalancha *or* en tropel
▸ **pile on*** (VI + ADV) (= *crowd on*) meterse a empujones, meterse apretujados
(VT + ADV) • **he ~d on more branches** echó más ramas • **they really ~ the work on, don't they?** te dan muchísimo trabajo, ¿verdad? • **to ~ on the agony** multiplicar el martirio* • **he does rather ~ it on*** es un exagerado • **they were piling it on** estaban exagerando; ▹ **pressure**
▸ **pile out*** (VI + ADV) [*people*] salir en avalancha *or* en tropel
▸ **pile up** (VI + ADV) **1** (= *accumulate*) [*work*] amontonarse, acumularse • **black clouds were piling up on the horizon** el horizonte se estaba cargando *or* se llenaba de nubes negras
2 (= *crash*) [*vehicle*] estrellarse, chocar; [*vehicles*] estrellarse en cadena, chocar en cadena
(VT + ADV) **1** (= *put in heap*) [+ *books, clothes*] apilar, amontonar
2 (= *accumulate*) [+ *possessions*] acumular; [+ *debts*] acumular, llenarse de

pile² [paɪl] (N) (*Constr*) pilote *m*, pilar *m*
(CPD) ▸ **pile driver** martinete *m* ▸ **pile dwelling** (*Hist*) vivienda *f* construida sobre pilotes

pile³ [paɪl] (N) [*of carpet, cloth*] pelo *m*; ▹ **shag⁴**

piles [paɪlz] (NPL) (*Med*) almorranas *fpl*, hemorroides *fpl*

pile-up* [ˈpaɪlʌp] (N) (*Aut*) accidente *m* múltiple, choque *m* en cadena • **there was a pile-up on the motorway** chocaron varios coches en cadena en la autopista, hubo un accidente múltiple en la autopista

pilfer [ˈpɪlfəʳ] (VT) ratear*, hurtar, robar; (*esp by servant*) robar, sisar (*Sp**)
(VI) ratear*, robar cosas

pilferage [ˈpɪlfərɪdʒ] (N) ratería* *f*, hurto *m*, robo *m*

pilferer [ˈpɪlfərəʳ] (N) ratero/a* *m/f*, ladronzuelo/a* *m/f*

pilfering [ˈpɪlfərɪŋ] (N) ratería* *f*, hurto *m*, robo *m*

pilgrim [ˈpɪlgrɪm] (N) peregrino/a *m/f*, romero/a *m/f*
(CPD) ▸ **the Pilgrim Fathers** los primeros colonos de Nueva Inglaterra

> **PILGRIM FATHERS**
> Los **Pilgrim Fathers** fueron un grupo de puritanos que abandonaron Inglaterra en 1620 huyendo de las persecuciones religiosas y que, después de cruzar el Atlántico en el **Mayflower**, fundaron una colonia en Nueva Inglaterra (New Plymouth, Massachusetts), dando así comienzo a la colonización británica en Norteamérica. Se los considera como los fundadores de Estados Unidos y el éxito de su primera cosecha se conmemora cada año en el Día de Acción de Gracias (**Thanksgiving Day**).
> ▹ **THANKSGIVING**

pilgrimage [ˈpɪlgrɪmɪdʒ] (N) peregrinación *f* • **to go on a ~** • **make a ~ (to)** ir de peregrinación (a)
(CPD) ▸ **pilgrimage site** lugar *m* de peregrinación

piling [ˈpaɪlɪŋ] (N) (= *post*) pilote *m*

pill [pɪl] (N) **1** (*Med*) (*also fig*) píldora *f*, pastilla *f* • **to take a ~** tomar una píldora • IDIOM: • **to sugar** *or* **sweeten the ~** dorar la píldora; ▹ **bitter**, **pop**
2 (= *contraceptive*) • **the ~** la píldora (anticonceptiva) • **to be on/take the ~** tomar la píldora (anticonceptiva) • **to go on/come off the ~** empezar a/dejar de tomar la píldora • **birth control** *or* **contraceptive ~** píldora *f* anticonceptiva
(CPD) ▸ **pill bottle** frasco *m* de pastillas

pillage [ˈpɪlɪdʒ] (N) pillaje *m*, saqueo *m*
(VT), (VI) saquear

pillaging [ˈpɪlɪdʒɪŋ] (N) pillaje *m*

pillar [ˈpɪləʳ] (N) pilar *m*, columna *f* • **a ~ of smoke** una columna de humo • **the Pillars of Hercules** las Columnas de Hércules • **~ of salt** (*Bible*) estatua *f* de sal • **a ~ of the church** (*fig*) un pilar de la iglesia • IDIOMS: • **to be a ~ of strength** ser firme como una roca • **to go from ~ to post** ir de la Ceca a la Meca
(CPD) ▸ **pillar box** (*Brit*) buzón *m*

pillar-box red [ˌpɪləbɒksˈred] (ADJ) carmesí (*inv*)
(N) carmesí *m*

pillared [ˈpɪləd] (ADJ) [*building*] con pilares

pillbox [ˈpɪlbɒks] (N) (*Med*) pastillero *m*; (*Mil*) fortín *m*; (*also* **pillbox hat**) casquete *m* (*gorro*)

pillion [ˈpɪljən] (N) (*also* **pillion seat**) asiento *m* trasero
(ADV) • **to ride ~** ir en el asiento trasero
(CPD) ▸ **pillion passenger** pasajero/a *m/f* de atrás

pillock‡ [ˈpɪlək] (N) (*Brit*) imbécil *mf*, gili *mf* (*Sp**)

pillory [ˈpɪlərɪ] (N) picota *f*
(VT) poner en ridículo

pillow [ˈpɪləʊ] (N) almohada *f*
(VT) apoyar • **she ~ed her head on my shoulder** apoyó la cabeza en mi hombro
(CPD) ▸ **pillow fight** lucha *f* de almohadas ▸ **pillow talk** conversaciones *fpl* de alcoba

pillowcase [ˈpɪləʊkeɪs], **pillowslip** [ˈpɪləʊslɪp] (N) funda *f* de almohada

pilot [ˈpaɪlət] (N) **1** (*Aer*) piloto *mf*; ▹ **airline**, **automatic**, **fighter**, **test**
2 (*Naut*) práctico *mf*, piloto *mf*
3 = **pilot light**
4 = **pilot programme**
(VT) **1** (*Aer*, *Naut*) pilotar, pilotear (*esp LAm*)
2 (*fig*) (= *guide*) conducir; (= *test*) [+ *scheme*] poner a prueba • **he ~ed the negotiations through** condujo las negociaciones a buen fin • **to ~ a bill through the House** asegurar la aprobación de un proyecto de ley
(CPD) [*project*, *scheme*] piloto (*inv*), experimental ▸ **pilot boat** barco *m* del práctico ▸ **pilot episode** (*TV*) episodio *m* piloto ▸ **pilot error** • **the airline blamed ~ error for the crash** la compañía achacó el accidente a un error del piloto ▸ **pilot fish** pez *m* piloto ▸ **pilot house** (*Naut*) timonera *f* ▸ **pilot's licence** licencia *f* de piloto ▸ **pilot light** piloto *m* ▸ **pilot officer** oficial *m* piloto ▸ **pilot plant** (*Ind*) planta *f* de prueba, planta *f* piloto ▸ **pilot programme** (*TV*) programa *m* piloto ▸ **pilot scheme**

proyecto *m* piloto ▸ **pilot study** estudio *m* piloto ▸ **pilot whale** calderón *m* negro

pilotless [ˈpaɪlətlɪs] (ADJ) sin piloto

pimento [pɪˈmentəʊ] (N) (PL: **pimentos**) pimiento *m*, pimentón *m* morrón (*S. Cone*)

pimiento [pɪˈmjentəʊ] (N) pimiento *m* morrón, ají *m* morrón (*S. Cone*)

pimp [pɪmp] (N) proxeneta *m* (*frm*), chulo *m* (de putas) (*Sp**), cafiche *m* (*S. Cone**)
(VI) • **to ~ for sb** ejercer de proxeneta de algn

pimpernel [ˈpɪmpənel] (N) murajes *mpl*, pimpinela *f*

pimping [ˈpɪmpɪŋ] (N) proxenetismo *m*

pimple [ˈpɪmpl] (N) (*gen*) grano *m*; (*on face*) espinilla *f* • **she came out in ~s** le salieron granos

pimply [ˈpɪmplɪ] (ADJ) (COMPAR: **pimplier**, SUPERL: **pimpliest**) lleno de granos, cubierto de granos • **a ~ youth** (*fig*) un mozalbete, un mocoso (*pej*)

PIMS (N ABBR) = **personal information management system**

PIN [pɪn] (N ABBR) = **personal identification number** • **PIN number** NPI *m*

pin [pɪn] (N) **1** (*Sew*) alfiler *m*; (*also* **safety pin**) imperdible *m*, seguro *m* (*CAm, Mex*); (*also* **hairpin**) horquilla *f*; (*also* **hatpin**) alfiler *m* (de sombrero); (= *brooch*) alfiler *m*; (*also* **drawing pin**) chincheta *f*, chinche *m* or *f* (*LAm*); (*also* **clothes pin**) (*US*) pinza *f* (de la ropa) • **pins and needles** hormigueo *msing* • IDIOMS: • **to be on pins and needles** (*US*) estar hecho un manojo de nervios, estar en *or* sobre ascuas • **you could have heard a pin drop** se oía el vuelo de una mosca • **like a new pin** • **as neat as a (new) pin** (= *clean*) como una patena, limpio como un espejo; (= *tidy*) pulcro y muy ordenado • **for two pins I'd knock his head off*** por menos de nada le rompería la crisma • **it doesn't matter two pins to me** • **I don't care two pins** me importa un rábano *or* comino*; ▷ **bobby pin**, **lapel**, **panel**
2 (*Tech*) [*of metal*] clavija *f*; [*of wood*] espiga *f*, clavija *f*; (= *bolt*) perno *m*; (= *cotter*) chaveta *f*
3 (*Elec*) [*of plug*] polo *m* • **three-pin plug** clavija *f* de tres polos, clavija *f* tripolar
4 (*Med*) (*in limb*) clavo *m*
5 (*on grenade*) anilla *f*
6 (*Bowls*) bolo *m*; (*Golf*) banderín *m*
7 pins (*hum**) (= *legs*) patas* *fpl*, bielas‡ *fpl*
(VT) **1** [+ *fabric, seam, hem*] prender *or* sujetar con alfileres • **there was a note pinned on** *or* **to the door** había una nota clavada en la puerta • **to pin a medal to sb's uniform** prender una medalla al uniforme de algn • **she had pinned her hair into a bun** se había hecho un moño con horquillas
2 (*Tech*) (*with bolt*) sujetar (con perno)
3 (*fig*) • **to pin one's hopes on sth/sb** cifrar *or* depositar sus esperanzas en algo/algn • **the Democrats are pinning their hopes on the next election** los demócratas tienen cifradas sus esperanzas en las próximas elecciones • **you can't pin the blame on me** no podéis cargarme con la culpa • **they're trying to pin the murder on us** tratan de culparnos del asesinato • **there was nothing they could pin on him** no podían acusarlo *or* culparlo de nada
4 (= *immobilize*) • **two men pinned him to the floor** dos hombres lo sujetaron en el suelo • **his arms were pinned to his sides** llevaba los brazos sujetos a los costados • **they pinned me against the wall** me sujetaron contra la pared
(CPD) ▸ **pin money** dinero *m* para gastos menores ▸ **pin table** millón *m*, flíper *m*

▸ **pin back** (VT + ADV) [+ *fabric*] doblar hacia atrás y sujetar con alfileres; [+ *hair*] recogerse; [+ *window, door*] sujetar; (*Med*) [+ *ears, skin*] operarse de • IDIOM: • **to pin one's ears back*** escuchar muy atento

▸ **pin down** (VT + ADV) **1** (= *fasten or hold down*) sujetar • **he pinned me down by my wrists** me sujetó por las muñecas • **I was pinned down by a fallen tree** quedé atrapado bajo un árbol caído
2 (*fig*) **a** (= *oblige to be specific*) • **to pin sb down** hacer que algn concrete • **she is really hard to pin down** es difícil hacerla concretar • **the minister refused to be pinned down on the timing of the reforms** el ministro no quiso comprometerse a dar fechas específicas para las reformas • **you can't pin him down to a date** es imposible lograr que nos dé una fecha concreta
b (= *identify*) [+ *problem*] identificar; [+ *concept*] precisar, definir; [+ *reason*] dar con; [+ *date*] precisar • **the idea is rather hard to pin down** es un concepto difícil de precisar *or* definir • **there's something wrong but I can't pin it down** algo va mal pero no sé exactamente qué
3 (*Mil*) [+ *troops*] atrapar • **our men were pinned down by artillery fire** nuestros hombres se vieron atrapados por fuego de artillería

▸ **pin on** (VT + ADV) prender, poner

▸ **pin together** (VT + ADV) [+ *fabric pieces, papers*] sujetar, prender

▸ **pin up** (VT + ADV) [+ *notice*] poner, pegar; [+ *clothing*] recoger con alfileres; (*with safety pin*) recoger con imperdible; [+ *hem*] sujetar con alfileres; [+ *hair*] recoger (con horquilla)

pina colada [ˈpiːnəkəˈlɑːdə] (N) piña *f* colada

pinafore [ˈpɪnəfɔːʳ] (N) (= *overall, apron*) delantal *m*, mandil *m*
(CPD) ▸ **pinafore dress** jumper *m*, pichi *m* (*Sp*)

pinball [ˈpɪnbɔːl] (N) (*also* **pinball machine**) millón *m*, flíper *m* • **to play ~** jugar al millón *or* al flíper

pinboard [ˈpɪnbɔːd] (N) tablón *m* de anuncios

pince-nez [ˈpeːnsneɪ] (NPL) quevedos *mpl*

pincer [ˈpɪnsəʳ] (N) **1** (*Zool*) pinza *f*
2 (*Tech*) **pincers** tenazas *fpl*, pinzas *fpl* • **a pair of ~s** unas tenazas
(CPD) ▸ **pincer movement** (*Mil*) movimiento *m* de pinza *or* tenaza

pinch [pɪntʃ] (N) **1** (*with fingers*) pellizco *m* • **to give sb a ~ on the arm** dar a algn un pellizco en el brazo, pellizcar el brazo a algn
2 (= *small quantity*) pizca *f* • **a ~ of salt** una pizca de sal • **a ~ of snuff** un polvo de rapé • IDIOM: • **to take sth with a ~ of salt** tomarse algo con reservas, no creerse algo a pies juntillas
3 (*fig*) apuro *m* • **at a ~** en caso de apuro *or* necesidad • **if it comes to the ~** en un caso extremo • IDIOM: • **to feel the ~** (empezar a) pasar apuros *or* estrecheces • **to feel the ~ of poverty** saber lo que significa ser pobre
(VT) **1** (*with fingers*) pellizcar; [*shoe*] apretar • **to ~ one's finger in the door** pillarse el dedo en la puerta • **to ~ off** *or* **out** *or* **back a bud** arrancar un brote con los dedos
2* (= *steal*) robar, birlar*, guindar (*Sp**) • **I had my pen ~ed** me robaron la pluma, me birlaron la pluma* • **he ~ed that idea from Shaw** esa idea la robó de Shaw • **he ~ed Mike's girl** le pisó *or* levantó la novia a Mike*
3* (= *arrest*) pescar*, coger, agarrar (*LAm*) • **he got ~ed for a parking offence** lo pescaron en una infracción de aparcamiento*, le metieron un paquete por aparcamiento indebido*
(VI) [*shoe*] apretar • **to ~ and scrape** privarse de lo necesario • **they ~ed and scraped to send her to college** se privaron de muchas cosas para poder enviarla a la universidad

pinchbeck [ˈpɪntʃbek] (N) similor *m*
(CPD) de similor; (*fig*) falso

pinched [ˈpɪntʃt] (ADJ) **1** (= *drawn*) • **to look ~** tener un aspecto demacrado • **to be ~ with cold** estar aterido de frío
2 (= *short*) • **to be ~ for money** andar escaso de dinero • **we're very ~ for space** tenemos muy poco espacio

pinch-hit [ˈpɪntʃhɪt] (VI) (*US*) batear de suplente; (*fig*) • **to pinch-hit for sb** sustituir a algn en un apuro

pinchpenny† [ˈpɪntʃpenɪ] (ADJ) tacaño

pincushion [ˈpɪn,kʊʃən] (N) acerico *m*, almohadilla *f*

Pindar [ˈpɪndəʳ] (N) Píndaro

Pindaric [pɪnˈdærɪk] (ADJ) pindárico

pine¹ [paɪn] (N) pino *m*
(CPD) ▸ **pine cone** piña *f* ▸ **pine grove** pinar *m* ▸ **pine kernel** piñón *m* ▸ **pine marten** marta *f* ▸ **pine needle** aguja *f* de pino ▸ **pine nut** piñón *m* ▸ **pine tree** pino *m*

pine² [paɪn] (VI) (*also* **pine away**) consumirse, languidecer • **to ~ for sth/sb** suspirar por algo/algn

pineal body [ˈpɪnɪəl,bɒdɪ], **pineal gland** [ˈpɪnɪəl,glænd] (N) glándula *f* pineal

pineapple [ˈpaɪn,æpl] (N) piña *f*, ananá *m* (*esp Arg, Uru*)
(CPD) ▸ **pineapple juice** zumo *m* de piña (*Sp*), jugo *m* de piña (*LAm*), jugo *m* de ananá (*esp Arg, Uru*)

pinewood [ˈpaɪnwʊd] (N) pinar *m*

ping [pɪŋ] (N) (*on striking*) sonido *m* metálico; [*of bullet*] silbido *m*; [*of bell*] tintín *m*
(VI) (*on striking*) producir un sonido metálico; [*bullet*] silbar; [*bell*] tintinear, hacer tintín

ping-pong® [ˈpɪŋpɒŋ] (N) ping-pong® *m*, tenis *m* de mesa
(CPD) ▸ **ping-pong ball** pelota *f* de ping-pong

pinhead [ˈpɪnhed] (N) **1** (*lit*) cabeza *f* de alfiler
2* (*pej*) (= *idiot*) mentecato *m*, cabeza *f* de chorlito*

pinheaded* [ˈpɪn,hedɪd] (ADJ) tonto*, sin seso*

pinhole [ˈpɪnhəʊl] (N) agujero *m* de alfiler
(CPD) ▸ **pinhole camera** cámara *f* de agujero de alfiler

pinion¹ [ˈpɪnjən] (N) (*poet*) ala *f*
(VT) [+ *bird*] cortar las alas a; [+ *person*] atar los brazos a • **he was ~ed against the wall** lo tenían inmovilizado contra la pared

pinion² [ˈpɪnjən] (N) (*Mech*) piñón *m*

pink¹ [pɪŋk] (N) **1** (= *colour*) rosa *m*, rosado *m* (*LAm*) • **~ doesn't suit her** el rosa no le sienta bien • IDIOMS: • **to be in the ~** (= *healthy*) rebosar salud; (= *happy*) estar feliz y contento • **to be in the ~ of condition** estar en perfecto estado; ▷ **dusty**, **rose**, **salmon**, **shocking**
2 (*Bot*) clavel *m*, clavelina *f*
3 (*Snooker*) bola *f* rosa
(ADJ) (COMPAR: **pinker**, SUPERL: **pinkest**)
1 (= *colour*) (*gen*) (color de) rosa, rosado (*LAm*); [*cheeks, face*] sonrosado • **we painted the nursery ~** pintamos el cuarto de los niños de rosa • **their little faces were ~ with excitement** tenían las caritas encendidas de entusiasmo • **his face was ~ with rage** estaba rojo de furia • **his cheeks were flushed ~ from the wine** el vino le había sonrosado las mejillas • **to turn** *or* **go ~** [*person*] (*with embarrassment*) ponerse colorado, sonrojarse; [*sky, liquid*] ponerse rosa • **she turned ~ with pleasure** se sonrojó

de placer; ▹ tickle
2 (*Pol**) rojillo*
3* (= *gay*) [*pound, vote*] homosexual, gay (*inv*)
CPD ▸ **pink gin** ginebra *f* con angostura ▸ **pink grapefruit** *variedad de pomelo de pulpa rojiza* ▸ **pink lady** pink lady *m* ▸ **pink salmon** salmón *m* del Pacífico ▸ **pink slip** (*US*) notificación *f* de despido ▸ **pink champagne** champán *m* rosado

pink[2] [pɪŋk] VT (*Sew*) rematar con tijeras dentadas; (= *make holes in*) [+ *fabric*] calar; (*Fencing*) herir levemente
VI (*Brit*) (*Aut*) [*engine*] picar

pinkeye ['pɪŋkaɪ] N (*Med*) conjuntivitis *f* aguda

pinkie* ['pɪŋkɪ] N (*Scot, US*) (dedo *m*) meñique *m*

pinking ['pɪŋkɪŋ] N (*Brit*) (*Aut*) piqueteo *m*

pinking shears ['pɪŋkɪŋ,ʃiːəz] NPL tijeras *fpl* dentadas

pinkish ['pɪŋkɪʃ] ADJ rosáceo; (*Pol*) rojillo*

pinkness ['pɪŋknɪs] N rojez *f* • **meat which has been cooked thoroughly shows no traces of ~** un carne bien cocinada no queda roja por dentro

pinko* ['pɪŋkəʊ] (*Pol*) (*pej*) ADJ rojillo*
N (PL: **pinkos** *or* **pinkoes**) rojillo/a* *m/f*

pinnace ['pɪnɪs] N pinaza *f*

pinnacle ['pɪnəkl] N (*Archit*) pináculo *m*; (= *peak*) [*of rock*] punta *f*; [*of mountain*] cumbre *f*, cima *f*; (*fig*) cumbre *f*, cúspide *f* • **the ~ of fame/success** la cumbre *or* la cúspide de la fama/del éxito

pinny* ['pɪnɪ] N = **pinafore**

Pinocchio [pɪ'nɒkɪəʊ] N Pinocho

pinpoint ['pɪnpɔɪnt] N [*of light*] puntito *m*
VT (= *identify*) [+ *location, source, problem*] identificar, determinar; [+ *cause*] precisar, señalar con precisión • **it's difficult to ~ when it first started happening** resulta difícil precisar cuándo empezó a ocurrir por primera vez • **we ~ed the issues that need priority attention** determinamos qué cuestiones necesitan atención prioritaria
CPD ▸ **pinpoint accuracy** (= *extreme accuracy*) precisión *f* milimétrica • **the ~ accuracy of the bombing campaign** la precisión milimétrica de la campaña de atentados

pinprick ['pɪnprɪk] N (*lit*) pinchazo *m*; (*fig*) pequeña molestia *f*

pinstripe ['pɪnstraɪp] ADJ de raya diplomática
N (= *suit*) traje *m* de raya diplomática; (= *fabric*) tela *f* de raya diplomática; (= *stripe*) raya *f* diplomática
CPD ▸ **pinstripe suit** traje *m* de raya diplomática

pinstriped ['pɪnstraɪpt] ADJ de raya diplomática

pint [paɪnt] N **1** (= *measure*) pinta *f* ((*Brit*) = *0,57 litros*; (*US*) = *0,47 litros*); ▹ IMPERIAL SYSTEM
2 (*Brit**) [*of beer*] • **a ~** una cerveza • **to go for a ~** salir a tomar una cerveza • **we had a few ~s** bebimos *or* (*LAm*) tomamos unas cervezas, bebimos unas cañas (*Sp*), bebimos *or* (*LAm*) tomamos unas cuantas*

pinta* ['paɪntə] N pinta *f* de leche

pintail ['pɪnteɪl] N ánade *m* rabudo

pinto bean ['pɪntəʊbiːn] N judía *f or* alubia *f* pinta

pint-size* ['paɪntsaɪz], **pint-sized*** ['paɪntsaɪzd] ADJ diminuto, pequeñito*

pin-up ['pɪnʌp] N *foto o póster de un famoso, de una chica atractiva etc.*
CPD ▸ **pin-up girl** chica *f* de revista (*modelo*)

pinwheel ['pɪn,wiːl] N (*esp US*) rueda *f* catalina

Pinyin [,pɪn'jɪn] N pinyin *m*

pioneer [,paɪə'nɪəʳ] N (= *explorer*) explorador(a) *m/f*, pionero/a *m/f*; (= *early settler*) colonizador(a) *m/f*, pionero/a *m/f*; (= *initiator*) pionero/a *m/f*, precursor(a) *m/f*; (*Mil*) zapador(a) *m/f* • **he was a ~ in the study of bats** fue uno de los primeros en estudiar los murciélagos
VT [+ *technique*] ser el/la primero/a en utilizar • **he ~ed the use of vitamin B in the treatment of mental illness** fue el primero en utilizar la vitamina B para el tratamiento de enfermedades mentales
VI explorar, abrir nuevos caminos
CPD ▸ **pioneer corps** cuerpo *m* de zapadores ▸ **pioneer spirit** espíritu *m* pionero ▸ **pioneer work** trabajo *m* pionero

pioneering [,paɪə'nɪərɪŋ] ADJ [*work, research, study, surgeon*] pionero, innovador

pious ['paɪəs] ADJ piadoso, pío; (*pej*) santurrón, beato
CPD ▸ **pious hope** esperanza *f* infundada

piously ['paɪəslɪ] ADV piadosamente, devotamente; (*pej*) vanamente

piousness ['paɪəsnɪs] N piedad *f*; (*pej*) santurronería *f*, beatería *f*

pip[1] [pɪp] N **1** (*Bot*) pepita *f*, pepa *f* (*esp LAm*); (*on card, dice*) punto *m*; (*Brit*) (*Mil**) (*on uniform*) estrella *f*; (*on radar screen*) señal *f*
2 (= *sound*) bip *m*, pitido *m* • **the pips** (*Telec*) la señal • **wait till you hear the pips** espere a que oiga la señal

pip[2]†* [pɪp] (*Brit*) N • IDIOM: • **to give sb the pip** sacar de quicio a algn • **it's enough to give you the pip** es para volverse loco • **he's got the pip** está de muy mal humor

pip[3] [pɪp] VT • IDIOM: • **to be pipped at** *or* **to the post** (*Brit**) perder por un pelo* • **Baby Boy pipped Omar at** *or* **to the post** Baby Boy le ganó a Omar por un pelo*

pipe [paɪp] N **1** (= *tube*) tubo *m*, caño *m*; (*larger, system of pipes*) tubería *f*, cañería *f* • **a length of copper ~** una tubería de cobre; ▹ overflow, waste
2 (*Mus*) [*of organ*] cañón *m*, tubo *m*; (= *wind instrument*) flauta *f*, caramillo *m*; **pipes** (*also* **bagpipes**) gaita *f*; (*boatswain's*) silbato *m* • **the ~s of Pan** la flauta de Pan • **to play the ~s** tocar la gaita
3 (*smoker's*) pipa *f*, cachimba *f* (*esp LAm*) • IDIOM: • **put that in your ~ and smoke it!*** ¡chúpate esa!*; ▹ peace
VT **1** (= *convey*) [+ *water*] canalizar por tuberías; [+ *gas*] llevar por gasoducto; [+ *oil*] llevar por oleoducto • **sewage from the villages is ~d into the river** las aguas residuales de los pueblos son canalizadas y vertidas al río • **most of the houses here don't have ~d water** la mayoría de las casas aquí no tienen agua corriente • **the oil is ~d across the desert** el petróleo es conducido a través del desierto por un oleoducto
2 (= *broadcast*) [+ *music*] emitir • **~d music** música *f* ambiental, hilo *m* musical (*Sp*)
3 (= *play*) [+ *tune*] tocar (en flauta *or* gaita) • **they ~d the admiral aboard** con el silbato avisaron al almirante de que subiera a bordo
4 (*Culin*) [+ *cake*] adornar con manga; [+ *icing, cream*] poner con manga • **to ~ cream on a cake** adornar una tarta con nata *or* (*LAm*) crema usando la manga
5 (*Sew*) ribetear con cordoncillo • **a jacket ~d with blue at the seams** una chaqueta con cordoncillo azul en las costuras
6 (= *say*) decir con voz de pito; (= *sing*) cantar con tono agudo • **"but I want to help," she ~d** —pero es que yo quiero ayudar —dijo ella con voz de pito
VI (*Mus*) tocar el caramillo/la flauta/la gaita; (*Naut*) tocar el silbato; [*bird*] trinar
CPD ▸ **pipe band** banda *f* de gaiteros ▸ **pipe bomb** *bomba de mano casera en forma de tubo* ▸ **pipe cleaner** (escobilla *f*) limpiapipas *m inv* ▸ **pipe dream** sueño *m* imposible ▸ **pipe organ** órgano *m* de tubos ▸ **pipe rack** soporte *m* para pipas ▸ **pipe smoker** fumador(a) *m/f* de pipa ▸ **pipe stem** cañón *m* de la pipa ▸ **pipe tobacco** tabaco *m* de pipa
▸ **pipe down*** VI + ADV callarse, cerrar el pico* • **~ down, will you!** ¡cerrad ya el pico!*
▸ **pipe up*** VI + ADV meter baza*, saltar • **then somebody ~d up with another question** y entonces alguien metió baza con otra pregunta*
VT + ADV soltar de sopetón* • **"can I come too?" ~d up a little voice** —¿puedo ir yo también? —soltó de sopetón una vocecilla

pipeclay ['paɪpkleɪ] N albero *m*
VT blanquear con albero

pipefitter ['paɪp,fɪtəʳ] N fontanero/a *m/f*

pipeful ['paɪpfʊl] N pipa *f* • **a ~ of tobacco** una pipa de tabaco

pipeline ['paɪplaɪn] N (*for water*) tubería *f*, cañería *f*; (*for oil*) oleoducto *m*; (*for gas*) gasoducto *m* • IDIOM: • **it's in the ~** está en proyecto, se está tramitando • **a sequel to the series is in the ~** ya hay planes para una segunda parte de la serie

piper ['paɪpəʳ] N (*on bagpipes*) gaitero/a *m/f* • PROVERB: • **he who pays the ~ calls the tune** quien paga, manda

pipette [pɪ'pet] N pipeta *f*

pipework ['paɪpwɜːk] N tuberías *fpl*, cañerías *fpl*

piping ['paɪpɪŋ] N **1** (*in house, building*) tubería *f*, cañería *f* • **two metres of copper ~** dos metros de tubería de cobre
2 (*Mus*) música *f* de gaita/de flauta, sonido *m* del caramillo; [*of bird*] trinar *m*, trinos *mpl*
3 (*Sew*) ribete *m*, cordoncillo *m*
ADJ [*voice*] agudo
ADV • **~ hot** bien caliente
CPD ▸ **piping bag** (*for icing, cream, mashed potato*) manga *f* pastelera

pipistrelle [,pɪpɪ'strel] N pipistrelo *m*

pipit ['pɪpɪt] N bisbita *f*, pitpit *m*

pipkin ['pɪpkɪn] N ollita *f* de barro

pippin ['pɪpɪn] N camuesa *f*, manzana *f* reineta

pipsqueak ['pɪpskwiːk] N fantoche *m*, pintamonas* *mf inv*

piquancy ['piːkənsɪ] N lo fuerte, gusto *m* fuerte; [*of situation*] chispa *f*, gracia *f*

piquant ['piːkənt] ADJ [*taste*] fuerte; [*humour*] corrosivo, ácido; [*situation*] con chispa, con gracia

piquantly ['piːkəntlɪ] ADV (*of taste*) con fuerza; (= *interestingly, provocatively*) con chispa

pique [piːk] N resentimiento *m* • **to be in a ~** estar resentido • **to do sth in a fit of ~** hacer algo por resentimiento *or* por despecho
VT **1** (= *offend*) • **I was ~d at his refusal to acknowledge me** me ofendió que se negara a saludarme
2 (= *arouse*) [+ *interest, appetite*] despertar; [+ *curiosity*] picar

piquet [pɪ'ket] N piquet *m*

piracy ['paɪərəsɪ] N (*lit*) piratería *f*; [*of book*] publicación *f* pirata; [*of tape, video, software*] reproducción *f* pirata

piranha [pɪ'rɑːnə] N piraña *f*

pirate ['paɪərɪt] N pirata *mf* (*also in publishing*)
VT [+ *book, tape, video, software*] piratear
CPD pirata (*inv*) ▸ **pirate broadcasting** emisión *f* pirata ▸ **pirate copy** copia *f* pirata ▸ **pirate radio** emisión pirata ▸ **pirate radio station** emisora *f* pirata ▸ **pirate ship** barco *m* pirata

pirated ['paɪərɪtɪd] ADJ [*book, tape, video,*

software] pirata (inv), pirateado

piratical [paɪ'rætɪkəl] ADJ pirático

pirogue [pɪ'rəʊg] N (= dug-out canoe) piragua f

pirouette [,pɪrʊ'et] N pirueta f
VI piruetear

Piscean ['paɪsɪən] N piscis mf • to be a ~ ser piscis

Pisces ['paɪsi:z] N 1 (= sign, constellation) Piscis m
2 (= person) piscis mf • he's (a) ~ es piscis

pisciculture ['pɪsɪ,kʌltʃəʳ] N (frm) piscicultura f

piss** [pɪs] N (= urine) meados** mpl; (= act) meada** f • to have or take a ~ mear**, echar una meada** • to take the ~ out of sb (Brit) tomar el pelo a algn, cachondearse de algn (Sp*) • it's ~ easy or a piece of ~ (Brit) está tirado*, está chupado (Sp*)
VI mear** • it's ~ing with rain or ~ing down (Brit) están cayendo chuzos de punta*
VT • to ~ o.s. mearse (encima)** • to ~ o.s. (laughing or with laughter) (Brit) mearse de (la) risa**
CPD ▸ piss artist** (Brit) borracho/a m/f, curda‡ mf

▸ piss about**, piss around** VI + ADV
1 (Brit) (= play the fool) hacer el tonto, hacer el indio (Sp*)
2 (= waste time) perder el tiempo
VT + ADV [+ treat flippantly] jugar con • all they do is ~ me about, I want the truth no hacen más que jugar conmigo, quiero que me digan la verdad

▸ piss off** VT + ADV reventar*, cabrear‡, joder** • it really ~es me off when he does that me revienta cuando hace eso*, me cabrea cuando hace eso‡, me jode cuando hace eso** • he's feeling ~ed off (= depressed) está fastidiado*, está jodido**; (= fed up) está hasta las narices*, está hasta los cojones** • to be ~ed off (with sth/sb) estar hasta las narices (de algo/algn)*, estar hasta los cojones (de algo/algn)**, estar cabreado (por algo/con algn)‡
VI + ADV (= go away) largarse* • ~ off! ¡vete a la mierda!**, ¡vete al cuerno!*

pissed‡ [pɪst] ADJ 1 • to be ~ (Brit) (= drunk) estar mamado‡ • to be as ~ as a newt or a fart • be ~ out of one's mind tener un buen pedo‡, estar (borracho) como una cuba*
2 (US) • to be ~ (at sth/sb) (= angry) estar cabreado (por algo/con algn)‡, estar de mala leche (por algo/con algn)**

pisshead‡ ['pɪshed] N (Brit) borrachín/ina* m/f

piss-poor‡ [,pɪs'pʊəʳ] ADJ (Brit) nefasto

piss-take‡ ['pɪsteɪk] N broma f, tomadura f de pelo*

piss-up** ['pɪsʌp] N (Brit) juerga f de borrachera • IDIOM: • he couldn't organize a piss-up in a brewery no tiene ni pajolera idea de cómo organizar algo*

pistachio [pɪs'tɑ:ʃɪəʊ] N (PL: pistachios) pistacho m; (= tree) pistachero m; (= colour) color m de pistacho

piste [pi:st] N (Ski) pista f

pistil ['pɪstɪl] N pistilo m

pistol ['pɪstl] N pistola f, revólver m • at ~ point a punta de pistola
CPD ▸ pistol shot pistoletazo m • to be within ~ shot estar a tiro de pistola

pistol-whip ['pɪstlwɪp] VT golpear con una pistola

piston ['pɪstən] N pistón m, émbolo m; (Mus) pistón m, llave f
CPD ▸ piston engine motor m a pistón ▸ piston ring aro m or segmento m de pistón ▸ piston rod biela f ▸ piston stroke carrera f del émbolo

piston-engined ['pɪstən,endʒɪnd] ADJ con motor de pistón

pit[1] [pɪt] N 1 (= hole in ground) hoyo m, foso m; (as grave) fosa f; (as trap) trampa f; (fig) abismo m • he felt himself in a pit of despair se hallaba sumido en un abismo de desesperación • the pit (= hell) el infierno • the pit of hell lo más profundo del infierno • the pit of one's stomach la boca del estómago; ▹ bear[1], clay, gravel, snake
2 (Min) mina f (de carbón); (= quarry) cantera f • to go down the pit(s) (lit) bajar a la mina; (= start work there) ir a trabajar a la mina
3 (Aut) (also inspection pit) foso m de reparación
4 • the pits a (Motor racing) los boxes
b (US*) • to be in the pits [person, economy] estar por los suelos*
c (Brit) (= awful) • this town really is the pits este pueblo es para echarse a llorar • he's the pits es insoportable
5 (Brit) (Theat) • the pit el patio de butacas, la platea; ▹ orchestra
6 (for cockfighting) cancha f, reñidero m
7 (US) (St Ex) parquet m de la Bolsa • the cotton pit la bolsa del algodón
8 (= small depression) (in metal, glass) muesca f, marca f; (on face) marca f, picadura f
9 (Brit*) (= bed) catre* m, piltra f (Sp*)
VT 1 (= mark) [+ surface] picar, marcar • a car pitted with rust un coche con marcas de óxido • his face was pitted with pockmarks tenía la cara picada de viruelas • the tarmac was pitted with craters la calzada estaba llena de hoyos
2 (fig) • her argument is pitted with flaws su argumento está plagado de defectos
CPD ▸ pit bull (terrier) pit bull terrier m, bull terrier m de pelea ▸ pit closure cierre m de pozos (mineros) ▸ pit lane (Motor racing) recta f de boxes ▸ pit pony poney usado antiguamente en las minas ▸ pit stop (Motor racing) entrada f* en boxes; (on journey) parada f en ruta • to make a pit stop (Motor racing) entrar en boxes;* (on journey) hacer una parada ▸ pit worker minero/a m/f

▸ pit against VT + PREP enfrentar con • the war pitted American against American la guerra enfrentó a americanos con americanos • salesmen are pitted against each other a los vendedores se los enfrenta • he was pitting himself against the authorities se estaba enfrentando a las autoridades • to pit one's strength against sb medir sus fuerzas con algn • to pit one's wits against sb poner a prueba su inteligencia frente a algn • here is your chance to pit your wits against the experts es tu oportunidad de poner a prueba tu inteligencia frente a los expertos

pit[2] [pɪt] (US) N (in fruit) pepita f, hueso m, pepa f (esp LAm)
VT deshuesar, quitar el hueso a

pita ['pɪtə] N (also pita bread) = pitta

pitapat ['pɪtə'pæt] ADV • to go ~ [feet, rain] golpetear • my heart went ~ el corazón me latía con fuerza

pitch[1] [pɪtʃ] N 1 (esp Brit) (Ftbl, Cricket, Hockey) (= area of play) campo m, cancha f (LAm)
2 (Baseball) (= throw) lanzamiento m, tiro m
3 [of note, voice, instrument] tono m; ▹ concert, perfect, queer
4 (esp Brit) [of market trader] puesto m; [of homeless person] sitio m
5 (= height, degree) extremo m, punto m • matters reached such a ~ that ... las cosas llegaron a tal extremo or a tal punto que ... • excitement is at a high ~ la emoción está al rojo vivo; ▹ fever
6* (= sales talk) rollo* m • she stood up and made her ~ se levantó y soltó su rollo • he made a ~ for the women's vote procuró hacerse con or acaparar los votos de las mujeres; ▹ sale
7 (= slope) (gen) grado m de inclinación; [of roof] pendiente f
8 (Naut) cabezada f
VT 1 (= throw) [+ ball] lanzar; [+ person] arrojar • he was ~ed off his horse salió disparado del caballo • the impact ~ed her over the handlebars el impacto la arrojó por encima del manillar
2 (Mus) [+ note] dar; [+ instrument] graduar el tono de
3 (= present) • it must be ~ed at the right level for the audience el tono ha de ajustarse al público • today he ~ed the plan to business leaders hoy presentó el plan ante los dirigentes de negocios • to ~ one's aspirations too high picar demasiado or muy alto • you're ~ing it a bit high! or strong! ¡estás recargando las tintas!
4 (= set up) [+ tent] armar, montar • to ~ camp acampar, montar el campamento
VI 1 (= fall) [person] caer, caerse • he ~ed head-first over the wall se cayó or cayó de cabeza por el muro • the ball ~ed in front of him la pelota cayó delante de él or vino a parar a sus pies • the aircraft ~ed into the sea el avión se precipitó en el mar • to ~ forward: • the passengers ~ed forward as the coach stopped los pasajeros salieron despedidos hacia adelante cuando se paró el autocar • he went down on his knees, then ~ed forward se cayó or cayó de rodillas y luego de bruces
2 (Naut, Aer) cabecear • the ship was ~ing and rolling or tossing el barco cabeceaba de un lado para otro
3 (Baseball) lanzar • IDIOM: • to be in there ~ing (esp US*) seguir en la brecha*, seguir al pie del cañón*
CPD ▸ pitch inspection (Brit) (Sport) inspección f del terreno de juego • we have arranged a ~ inspection by a referee for 9am on Wednesday morning hemos dispuesto que un árbitro inspeccione el terreno de juego el miércoles a las nueve de la mañana ▸ pitch invasion (Brit) invasión f de campo • there was a peaceful ~ invasion after Juventus's eighth goal después del octavo gol de la Juventus hubo una pacífica invasión de campo ▸ pitch pipe (Mus) diapasón m ▸ pitch shot (Golf) pitch m

▸ pitch in* VI + ADV 1 (= start to eat) empezar a comer • ~ in! ¡venga, a comer!
2 (= start work) • we all ~ed in together todos nos pusimos manos a la obra, todos nos pusimos a trabajar juntos
3 (= cooperate) echar una mano, arrimar el hombro • we all ~ed in to help todos echamos una mano, todos arrimamos el hombro • the company has ~ed in with a pledge of £50,000 la compañía ha contribuido con un donativo de 50,000 libras

▸ pitch into VI + PREP 1 (= start) [+ food] atacar • they ~ed into the work with enthusiasm se pusieron a trabajar con entusiasmo
2 (= attack) (physically) atacar, arremeter contra; (verbally) criticar, arremeter contra
VT + PREP • to ~ sb into sth lanzar a algn a algo • this ~ed him into the political arena esto lo lanzó al mundillo de la política

▸ pitch up VI + ADV aparecer

pitch[2] [pɪtʃ] N (= tar) brea f, pez f • it was ~ black outside afuera estaba oscuro como boca de lobo • his face was ~ black with coal dust tenía la cara toda tiznada de polvo de carbón

CPD ▸ **pitch blackness** oscuridad *f* total ▸ **pitch pine** (= *wood*) pino *m* de tea

pitch-and-putt [ˌpɪtʃən'pʌt] N minigolf *m*

pitch-and-toss [ˌpɪtʃən'tɒs] N (juego *m* de) cara *f* o cruz, chapas *fpl*

pitch-black ['pɪtʃ'blæk] ADJ [*night*] oscuro como boca de lobo; [*water, sea*] muy oscuro

pitchblende ['pɪtʃblend] N pec(h)blenda *f*

pitch-dark ['pɪtʃ'dɑːk] ADJ oscuro como boca de lobo

pitched [pɪtʃt] ADJ • **~ battle** (*Mil*) (*also fig*) batalla *f* campal • **a ~ roof** un tejado a dos aguas

pitcher¹ ['pɪtʃəʳ] N (*esp US*) (= *jar*) cántaro *m*, jarro *m*

pitcher² ['pɪtʃəʳ] N (*Baseball*) pítcher *mf*, lanzador(a) *m/f*; ▸ BASEBALL

pitchfork ['pɪtʃfɔːk] N horca *f*
VT (*fig*) (= *thrust unwillingly or unexpectedly*) • **he was ~ed into the job** le encasquetaron el trabajo, lo metieron en el trabajo a la fuerza • **she was ~ed onto the front pages from total obscurity** saltó del más absoluto anonimato a las primeras planas de los periódicos

piteous ['pɪtɪəs] ADJ [*cry*] lastimero; [*expression, story*] lastimoso • **it was a ~ sight** daba lástima verlo

piteously ['pɪtɪəslɪ] ADV lastimeramente

pitfall ['pɪtfɔːl] N (*fig*) (= *danger*) peligro *m*; (= *problem*) dificultad *f*, escollo *m* • **there are many ~s ahead** hay muchos peligros por delante • **it's a ~ for the unwary** es una trampa para los imprudentes • **how to avoid the ~s involved in buying a house** cómo evitar las dificultades *or* los escollos que conlleva la compra de una casa • **"Pitfalls of English"** "Escollos *mpl* del Inglés"

pith [pɪθ] N (*Bot*) *parte interna blanquecina (endocarpo) de la cáscara de los cítricos*, blanco *m* de la cáscara; (*fig*) (= *core*) meollo *m*
CPD ▸ **pith helmet** salacot *m*

pithead ['pɪthed] N bocamina *f*

pithily ['pɪθɪlɪ] ADV de manera concisa, sucintamente

pithiness ['pɪθɪnɪs] N (= *terseness*) lo sucinto, concisión *f*

pithy ['pɪθɪ] ADJ (COMPAR: **pithier**, SUPERL: **pithiest**) (*Bot*) con mucho blanco en la cáscara; (*fig*) (= *terse*) [*statement, comment, style*] sucinto, conciso

pitiable ['pɪtɪəbl] ADJ [*condition*] lastimoso; [*attempt*] penoso • **age had reduced him to a ~ figure** la edad lo había reducido a una figura digna de compasión

pitiably ['pɪtɪəblɪ] ADV [*low, small, weak*] lamentablemente

pitiful ['pɪtɪfʊl] ADJ **1** (= *moving to pity*) [*sight*] lastimoso, penoso; [*cry*] lastimero
2 (= *contemptible*) [*efforts*] lamentable; [*sum, amount*] irrisorio
3 (= *dreadful*) pésimo, lamentable • **it was a ~ performance** fue una actuación pésima *or* lamentable

pitifully ['pɪtɪfəlɪ] ADV **1** (= *pathetically*) lastimosamente • **she was ~ thin** estaba tan delgada que daba lástima • **she was crying most ~** lloraba que daba lástima
2 (= *contemptibly*) lamentablemente • **~ inadequate supplies** equipamiento *m* de una pobreza lamentable

pitiless ['pɪtɪlɪs] ADJ [*enemy*] despiadado; [*sun, storm*] implacable

pitilessly ['pɪtɪlɪslɪ] ADV despiadadamente; [*shine*] [*sun, light*] implacablemente

pitman ['pɪtmən] N (PL: **pitmen**) (*Brit*) minero *m*

piton ['piːtɒn] N pitón *m*, clavija *f* de escala

pit-prop ['pɪtprɒp] N puntal *m*, peón *m*

pitta ['pɪtə] N (*also* **pitta bread**) pan *m* árabe

pittance ['pɪtəns] N miseria *f* • **she gets paid a ~** le pagan una miseria

pitted ['pɪtɪd] ADJ **1** [*skin*] picado (de viruelas); [*surface*] picado
2 (*US*) [*fruit*] deshuesado, sin hueso

pitter-patter ['pɪtə'pætəʳ] N = **patter²**

pituitary [pɪ'tjuːɪtərɪ] ADJ pituitario
N glándula *f* pituitaria
CPD ▸ **pituitary gland** glándula *f* pituitaria

pity ['pɪtɪ] N **1** piedad *f*, compasión *f* • **to feel (no) ~ for sb** (no) sentir compasión por algn • **have ~ on us** ten piedad de nosotros • **to move sb to ~** mover a algn a compasión, dar lástima a algn • **I did it out of ~ for him** se lo hice por compasión • **for ~'s sake!** ¡por piedad!; (*less seriously*) ¡por el amor de Dios! • **to take ~ on sb** compadecerse *or* apiadarse de algn
2 (= *cause of regret*) lástima *f*, pena *f* • **what a ~!** ¡qué lástima!, ¡qué pena! • **what a ~ he didn't see it** ¡qué pena que no lo viera! • **more's the ~** desgraciadamente, pero ¿qué le vamos a hacer? • **it is a ~ that ...** es una lástima que (+ *subjun*), es una pena que (+ *subjun*) • **it is a ~ that you can't come** es una lástima *or* una pena que no puedas venir • **the ~ of it was that ...** lo lamentable fue que ..., lo peor del caso fue que ... • **it is a thousand pities that ...** es muy de lamentar que (+ *subjun*)
VT compadecer(se de), tener lástima a • **I think he is more to be pitied than feared** yo creo que da más lástima que miedo • **I don't want you to ~ me** no quiero que me tengas lástima • **I ~ you when she finds out!** ¡pobre de ti cuando se entere!

pitying ['pɪtɪɪŋ] ADJ (= *compassionate*) [*look, smile*] lleno de compasión, compasivo; (= *contemptuous*) [*look, smile*] de desprecio

pityingly ['pɪtɪɪŋlɪ] ADV (= *compassionately*) compasivamente, con lástima; (= *contemptuously*) con desprecio

Pius ['paɪəs] N Pío

pivot ['pɪvət] N (*Mil, Tech*) pivote *m*; (*fig*) eje *m* (central) • **she is the ~ around which the community revolves** ella es el eje sobre el que gira toda la comunidad
VT (= *mount on pivot*) montar sobre un pivote; (= *cause to turn*) hacer girar • **he ~ed it on his hand** lo hizo girar sobre la mano
VI girar (**on** sobre) • **she ~ed in front of the mirror** se dio una vuelta frente al espejo • **to ~ on sth** (*fig*) girar alrededor de algo, depender de algo

pivotal ['pɪvətl] ADJ (*fig*) central, fundamental

pix* [pɪks] = **pics**

pixel ['pɪksel] N (*Comput*) pixel *m*, punto *m*

pixelate ['pɪksɪleɪt] VT pixelar

pixelation [ˌpɪksɪ'leɪʃən] N pixelación *f*

pixie ['pɪksɪ] N duendecillo *m*
CPD ▸ **pixie hat, pixie hood** caperucita *f*

pizazz, pizzazz* [pə'zæz] N energía *f*, dinamismo *m*

pizza ['piːtsə] N pizza *f*
CPD ▸ **pizza delivery** reparto *m* de pizzas ▸ **pizza delivery service** servicio *m* de reparto de pizzas ▸ **pizza delivery shop** pizzería *f* de entrega a domicilio ▸ **pizza parlour, pizza parlor** (*US*) pizzería *f* ▸ **pizza restaurant** (restaurante *m*) pizzería *f*

pizzeria [ˌpiːtsə'rɪə] N pizzería *f*

pizzicato [ˌpɪtsɪ'kɑːtəʊ] ADJ, ADV pizzicato

pjs*, pj's* ['piːdʒeɪz] NPL (= **pyjamas**) pijama *msing*

pkt ABBR (= **packet**) paquete *m*

Pl. ABBR (= **Place**) Plaza *f*

PL a/c ABBR = **profit and loss account**

placard ['plækɑːd] N (*on wall*) cartel *m*; (= *sign, announcement*) letrero *m*; (*carried in demonstration*) pancarta *f*
VT • **the wall is ~ed all over** la pared está llena de carteles • **the flats are ~ed as luxury residences** los pisos *or* (*LAm*) los departamentos aparecen anunciados como viviendas de lujo

placate [plə'keɪt] VT aplacar, apaciguar

placatory [plə'keɪtərɪ] ADJ [*act, gesture, smile*] apaciguador

place [pleɪs] N **1** (*gen*) lugar *m*, sitio *m* • **this is the ~** este es el lugar, aquí es • **we came to a ~ where ...** llegamos a un lugar donde ... • **the furniture was all over the ~** los muebles estaban todos manga por hombro • **we're all over the ~** tenemos un lío que no nos aclaramos • **in another** *or* **some other ~** en otra parte • **any ~ will do** cualquier lugar vale *or* sirve • **it all began to fall into ~** todo empezó a tener sentido • **when the new law/system is in ~** cuando la nueva ley/el nuevo sistema entre en vigor • **a blue suit, worn in ~s** un traje azul, raído a retazos • **the snow was a metre deep in ~s** había tramos *or* trozos en que la nieve cubría un metro • **this is no ~ for you** este no es sitio para ti • **there was no ~ to hide** no había donde esconderse • **to run in ~** (*US*) correr en parada • **it must be some ~ else** (*US*) estará en otra parte • **a ~ in the sun** (*fig*) una posición envidiable
2 (*specific*) lugar *m* • **~ of amusement** lugar *m* de diversión • **~ of birth** lugar *m* de nacimiento • **~ of business** [*of employment*] lugar *m* de trabajo; (= *office*) oficina *f*, despacho *m*; (= *shop*) comercio *m* • **~ of refuge** refugio *m*, asilo *m* • **~ of residence** domicilio *m*, residencia *f* • **~ of worship** templo *m*, lugar *m* de culto
3 (= *town, area*) lugar *m*, sitio *m* • **it's a small ~** es un pueblo pequeño • **to go ~s** (*US*) (= *travel*) viajar, conocer mundo • **he's going ~s*** (*fig*) llegará lejos • **we like to go ~s at weekends** durante los fines de semana nos gusta salir de excursión • **from ~ to ~** de un sitio a otro • **he drifted from ~ to ~, from job to job** iba de un sitio a otro, de trabajo en trabajo
4 (= *house*) casa *f*; (= *building*) sitio *m* • **his ~ in the country** su casa de campo • **they have a new ~ now** tienen una nueva casa ya • **we were at Peter's ~** estuvimos en casa de Pedro, estuvimos donde Pedro* • **come to our ~** ven (a visitarnos) a casa • **my ~ or yours?** ¿en mi casa o en la tuya? • **I helped him out when he had no ~ to go** yo le eché una mano cuando no tenía donde ir • **there's a new pizza ~ in town** han abierto un sitio de pizzas en el centro • **I must be mad, working in this ~** debo de estar loca para trabajar en este sitio *or* lugar
5 (*in street names*) plaza *f*
6 (= *proper or natural place*) sitio *m*, lugar *m* • **does this have a ~?** ¿tiene esto un sitio determinado? • **this isn't the ~ to discuss politics** no es el lugar más indicado para hablar de política • **his troops were in ~** sus tropas estaban en su sitio • **he checked that his tie was in ~** comprobó que llevaba bien puesta *or* colocada la corbata • **the final arrangements are now in ~** ya se han ultimado los preparativos que faltaban • **everything in its ~** cada cosa en su lugar • **to hold sth in ~** sujetar algo en su lugar • **to put sth back in its ~** devolver algo a su sitio • **to be out of ~** estar fuera de lugar • **it looks out of ~ here** aquí parece que está fuera de

(su) lugar • **that remark was quite out of ~** aquella observación estaba fuera de lugar • **I feel rather out of ~ here** me siento como que estoy de más aquí, aquí me siento un poco fuera de lugar • **to laugh in** *or* **at the right ~** reírse en el momento oportuno
7 (*in book*) página *f* • **to find/lose one's ~** encontrar/perder la página • **to mark one's ~** poner una marca (de por dónde se va) en un libro
8 (= *seat*) asiento *m*; (*in cinema, theatre*) localidad *f*; (*at table*) cubierto *m*; (*in queue*) turno *m*; (*in school, university, on trip*) plaza *f*; (*in team*) puesto *m* • **are there any ~s left?** ¿quedan plazas? • **is this ~ taken?** ¿está ocupado este asiento? • **he managed to keep his ~ in the team** logró conservar su puesto en el equipo • **a university ~** una plaza en la universidad • **to change ~s with sb** cambiar de sitio con algn • **to give ~ to** dar paso a • **to lay an extra ~ for sb** poner otro cubierto para algn • **to lose one's ~** (*in queue*) perder su turno
9 (= *job, vacancy*) puesto *m* • **his uncle found him a ~ in the firm** su tío le buscó un puesto en la compañía • **~s for 500 workers** 500 puestos de trabajo • **to seek a ~ in publishing** buscarse una colocación *or* un puesto en una casa editorial
10 (= *position*) lugar *m* • **it is not my ~ to do it** no me toca a mí hacerlo • **put yourself in my ~** ponte en mi lugar • **if I were in your ~** yo en tu lugar, yo que tú • **your ~ is to obey orders** lo tuyo es obedecer órdenes • **I wouldn't mind changing ~s with her!** ¡no me importaría estar en su lugar! • **friends in high ~s** amigos *mpl* bien situados • **to know one's ~** saber cuál es su lugar • **racism has no ~ here** aquí no hay sitio para el racismo • **she occupies a special ~ in the heart of the British people** ocupa un rincón especial en el corazón del pueblo británico • **to take the ~ of sth/sb** sustituir *or* suplir algo/a algn • **nobody could ever take his ~** nadie sería capaz de sustituirlo • **I was unable to go so Sheila took my ~** yo no pude ir, así que Sheila lo hizo por mí
11 (*in series, rank*) posición *f*, lugar *m* • **to work sth out to three ~s of decimals** calcular algo hasta las milésimas *or* hasta con tres decimales • **Madrid won, with Bilbao in second ~** ganó Madrid, con Bilbao en segunda posición *or* segundo lugar • **she took second ~ in the race/Latin exam** quedó la segunda en la carrera/el examen de Latín • **he didn't like having to take second ~ to his wife in public** delante de la gente no le gustaba quedar en un segundo plano detrás de su mujer • **for her, money takes second ~ to job satisfaction** para ella un trabajo gratificante va antes que el dinero • IDIOM: • **to put sb in his ~** poner a algn en su lugar, bajar los humos a algn*
12 (*other phrases*) • **in the first/second ~** en primer/segundo lugar • **in ~ of** en lugar de, en vez de • **to take ~** tener lugar • **the marriage will not now take ~** ahora la boda no se celebrará, ahora no habrá boda • **there are great changes taking ~** están ocurriendo *or* se están produciendo grandes cambios
VT **1** (= *put*) (*gen*) poner; (*more precisely*) colocar • **she ~d the dish on the table** puso el plato en la mesa • **~ the mask over your nose and mouth** colóquese la mascarilla sobre la nariz y la boca • **to ~ a matter in sb's hands** dejar un asunto en manos de algn • **the drought is placing heavy demands on the water supply** la sequía está poniendo en serios apuros al suministro de agua • **his job ~s heavy demands on him** su trabajo le exige mucho • **unemployment ~s a great strain on families** el desempleo somete a las familias a una fuerte presión
2 (= *give, attribute*) [+ *blame*] echar (**on** a); [+ *responsibility*] achacar (**on** a); [+ *importance*] dar, otorgar (*more frm*) (**on a**) • **I had no qualms about placing my confidence in him** no tenía ningún reparo en depositar mi confianza en él • **they ~ too much emphasis on paper qualifications** le dan demasiada importancia a los títulos • **we should ~ no trust in that** no hay que fiarse de eso
3 (= *situate*) situar, ubicar • **the house is well ~d** la casa está bien situada • **we are better ~d than a month ago** estamos en mejor situación que hace un mes • **he is well ~d to see it all** está en una buena posición para observarlo todo • **we are well ~d to attack** estamos en una buena posición para atacar • **how are you ~d for money?** ¿qué tal andas de dinero?
4 (*Comm*) [+ *order*] hacer; [+ *goods*] colocar; (*Econ*) [+ *money, funds*] colocar, invertir • **goods that are difficult to ~** mercancías *fpl* que no encuentran salida • **to ~ an advert in a paper** poner un anuncio en un periódico • **to ~ a contract for machinery with a French firm** firmar un contrato con una compañía francesa para adquirir unas máquinas • **to ~ an order (for sth) (with sb)** hacer un pedido (de algo) (a algn); ▹ **bet**
5 (= *find employment for*) [*agency*] encontrar un puesto a, colocar; [*employer*] ofrecer empleo a, colocar; (= *find home for*) colocar • **the child was ~d with a loving family** el niño fue (enviado) a vivir con una familia muy cariñosa
6 (*of series, rank*) colocar, clasificar • **to be ~d** (*in horse race*) llegar colocado • **they are currently ~d second in the league** actualmente ocupan el segundo lugar de la clasificación • **Vigo is well ~d in the League** Vigo tiene un buen puesto en la Liga • **she was ~d in the top group for maths** en matemáticas la colocaron en el grupo de los mejores
7 (= *recall, identify*) recordar; (= *recognize*) reconocer; (= *identify*) identificar, ubicar (*LAm*) • **I can't ~ her** no recuerdo de dónde la conozco, no la ubico (*LAm*)
VI (*US*) (*in race, competition*) • **to ~ second** quedar segundo, quedar en segundo lugar
CPD ▸ **place card** *tarjeta que indica el lugar de alguien en la mesa* ▸ **place kick** (*Rugby*) puntapié *m* colocado; (*Ftbl*) tiro *m* libre ▸ **place mat** bajoplato *m*, salvamanteles *m inv* individual ▸ **place name** topónimo *m*; **place names** (*as study, in general*) toponimia *f* • **the ~ names of Aragon** la toponimia aragonesa ▸ **place setting** cubierto *m*

placebo [plə'si:bəʊ] N (PL: **placebos** *or* **placeboes**) placebo *m*
CPD ▸ **placebo effect** efecto *m* placebo

placeholder ['pleɪs,həʊldə[r]] N (*Comput, Math*) marcador *m* de posición

placeman ['pleɪsmæn] N (PL: **placemen**) (*Brit*) (*pej*) adlátere *mf*, hombre *m* de confianza

placement ['pleɪsmənt] N (= *positioning*) colocación *f* (*Comm*), emplazamiento *m* • **students come to our company on work ~s** en la empresa tenemos estudiantes en prácticas
CPD ▸ **placement office** (*US*) oficina *m* de empleo ▸ **placement test** (*US*) test *m* de nivel

placenta [plə'sentə] N (PL: **placentas** *or* **placentae** [plə'senti:]) placenta *f*

placid ['plæsɪd] ADJ [*person*] apacible, plácido; [*face*] tranquilo, sosegado; [*water*] apacible, tranquilo

placidity [plə'sɪdɪtɪ] N placidez *f*, apacibilidad *f*, tranquilidad *f*

placidly ['plæsɪdlɪ] ADV [*sit*] plácidamente, apaciblemente; [*say, reply*] tranquilamente, sosegadamente

placing ['pleɪsɪŋ] N (= *act*) colocación *f*; (= *placing in league, rank*) puesto *m*, clasificación *f*

placket ['plækɪt] N jareta *f*

plagal ['pleɪgəl] ADJ plagal

plagiarism ['pleɪdʒɪərɪzəm] N plagio *m*

plagiarist ['pleɪdʒɪərɪst] N plagiario/a *m/f*

plagiarize ['pleɪdʒɪəraɪz] VT plagiar

plague [pleɪg] N (= *disease*) peste *f*; (*fig*) plaga *f*, fastidio *m* • **a ~ of rats** una plaga de ratas • **the ~** la peste • **to avoid sth/sb like the ~** huir de algo/algn como de la peste, evitar algo a toda costa
VT (*lit*) infestar; (*fig*) plagar; [+ *person*] atormentar • **the area is ~d with malaria** la zona está infestada de malaria • **the thought has been plaguing me** la idea me viene atormentando • **the project has been ~d with problems from the beginning** el proyecto se ha visto plagado de problemas desde el comienzo • **a country ~d by recession** un país asolado por la recesión • **to ~ sb with questions** acosar a algn con preguntas

plague-ridden ['pleɪg,rɪdn], **plague-stricken** ['pleɪg,strɪkən] ADJ apestado

plaguey* ['pleɪgɪ] ADJ latoso*, engorroso

plaice [pleɪs] N (PL: **plaice** *or* **plaices**) platija *f*

plaid [plæd] N (= *cloth*) tela *f* escocesa *or* a cuadros; (= *cloak*) manta *f* escocesa, plaid *m*
CPD [*skirt, trousers, shirt*] escocés

plain [pleɪn] ADJ (COMPAR: **plainer**, SUPERL: **plainest**) **1** (= *clear, obvious*) claro, evidente • **it is ~ that** es evidente *or* obvio que, está claro que • **to make sth ~ (to sb)** poner algo de manifiesto (a algn), dejar algo claro • **you have made your feelings ~** has puesto tus sentimientos de manifiesto, has dejado claros tus sentimientos • **her guilt was ~ to see** saltaba a la vista que era culpable • IDIOM: • **it's as ~ as a pikestaff** *or* **as the nose on your face** *or* **as day*** está más claro que el agua
2 (= *outspoken, honest*) franco • **I shall be ~ with you** le hablaré con toda franqueza, seré franco con usted • **let me be ~ with you** déjeme que le hable claramente *or* sin rodeos, permítame que le hable con franqueza (*frm*) • **~ dealing** negocios *mpl* limpios
3 (= *unadorned*) [*answer*] franco; [*living*] sencillo, sin lujo; [*food, cooking*] sencillo, corriente; [*language, style*] sencillo, llano; [*envelope*] en blanco; [*paper*] liso; [*fabric*] de un solo color, liso • **he drank ~ water** bebió agua nada más • **they're very ~ people** es gente muy sencilla *or* llana • **she used to be ~ Miss Jones** antes se llamaba la Srta. Jones sin más • **it's just ~ common sense** es de sentido común • **in ~ clothes** [*policeman*] (vestido) de civil *or* paisano • **in ~ English** *or* **language** (= *understandably*) en lenguaje claro *or* sencillo; (= *frankly*) (hablando) sin rodeos • **the ~ truth** la verdad lisa y llana • IDIOM: • **it's ~ sailing from now on*** a partir de ahora es pan comido*
4 (= *not pretty*) poco atractivo • **she's terribly ~** no es nada atractiva • IDIOM: • **to be a ~ Jane** ser una chica poco atractiva, ser más bien fea
ADV **1*** (= *completely*) • **he's ~ wrong** no tiene razón, y punto • **it's just ~ stupid** es una ridiculez absoluta *or* total

2 (= *simply*) claramente, con toda claridad • **I can't put it ~er than that** más claramente no lo puedo decir, no lo puedo decir con más claridad • **he told me quite ~ that ...** me dijo claramente *or* con toda claridad que ...
N 1 (*Geog*) llanura *f*, llano *m* • **the Great Plains** (*US*) las Grandes Llanuras
2 (*Knitting*) punto *m* sencillo
CPD ▸ **plain chocolate** chocolate *m* amargo *or* sin leche ▸ **plain flour** harina *f* sin levadura ▸ **plain speaking** franqueza *f* • **she has a reputation for ~ speaking** tiene fama de ser franca ▸ **plain yogurt** yogur *m* natural
plainchant ['pleɪntʃɑːnt] N = plainsong
plain-clothes ['pleɪn'kləʊðz] ADJ • **plain-clothes policeman** policía *mf* de civil *or* de paisano
plainly ['pleɪnlɪ] ADV 1 (= *clearly*) • **~ I was not welcome** estaba claro *or* era evidente *or* era obvio que no era bienvenido • **I can remember it all quite ~** lo recuerdo con todo detalle *or* perfectamente
2 (= *frankly*) • **to put it ~, he's not wanted** hablando claro *or* sin rodeos, él sobra • **to speak ~ to sb** hablar claro a algn, hablar a algn sin rodeos
3 (= *simply*) con sencillez, sencillamente • **she dresses ~** viste con sencillez *or* sencillamente
plainness ['pleɪnnɪs] N 1 (= *clarity*) claridad *f*; (= *frankness*) franqueza *f*; (= *simplicity*) sencillez *f*
2 (= *unattractiveness*) falta *f* de atractivo
plainsman ['pleɪnzmən] N (PL: **plainsmen**) llanero *m*, hombre *m* de la llanura
plainsong ['pleɪnsɒŋ] N canto *m* llano
plain-spoken ['pleɪn'spəʊkən] ADJ franco, llano
plaint [pleɪnt] N (*liter*) 1 (= *complaint*) queja *f*
2 (= *cry*) lamento *m* • **the moans and ~s of their children** los gemidos y lamentos de sus hijos
plaintiff ['pleɪntɪf] N demandante *mf*, querellante *mf*
plaintive ['pleɪntɪv] ADJ lastimero, quejumbroso
plaintively ['pleɪntɪvlɪ] ADV lastimeramente, con dolor
plait [plæt] (*esp Brit*) N trenza *f* • **in ~s** trenzado, en trenzas • **she wears her hair in ~s** lleva trenzas
VT trenzar
plan [plæn] N 1 (= *scheme*) proyecto *m*, plan *m* • **~ of action • action ~** plan *m* de acción • **~ of attack/campaign** (*Mil*) (*also fig*) plan *m* de ataque/de campaña • **to draw up a ~** elaborar un proyecto, hacer *or* redactar un plan • **an exercise ~** una tabla *or* un programa de ejercicios • **a five-year ~** un plan quinquenal • **to make ~s for the future** hacer planes *or* planear para el futuro • **a peace ~** un proyecto *or* un plan de paz; ▹ **business, instalment, master, pension**
2 (= *idea, intention*) plan *m* • **do you have any ~s for the weekend?** ¿tienes planes para el fin de semana? • **the ~ is to come back later** pensamos volver más tarde • **there are ~s to modernize the building** tienen planeado modernizar el edificio • **if everything goes according to ~** si todo sale como está previsto *or* planeado • **the best ~ is to call first** lo mejor es llamar primero • **a change of ~** un cambio de planes • **to change one's ~s** cambiar de planes
3 (= *diagram, map*) plano *m*; ▹ **seating**
4 (= *outline*) [*of story, essay*] esquema *m*
5 (*Archit, Tech*) (*often pl*) plano *m*
VT 1 (= *organize*) [+ *schedule, event, crime*] planear; [+ *party, surprise*] preparar; [+ *route*] planificar, planear; [+ *essay*] hacer un esquema de, planear; [+ *family*] planificar • **as ~ned** según lo previsto, como estaba planeado • **things didn't work out as ~ned** las cosas no salieron según lo previsto *or* como estaban planeadas
2 (= *intend*) • **I had been ~ning a trip to New York** había estado pensando en *or* planeando un viaje a Nueva York • **how long do you ~ to stay?** ¿cuánto tiempo piensas quedarte? • **what do you ~ to do after college?** ¿qué tienes pensado hacer después de la universidad?, ¿qué te has propuesto hacer después de la universidad?
3 (= *design*) diseñar • **the art of ~ning a garden** el arte de diseñar un jardín
VI hacer planes • **to ~ ahead** planear con antelación • **to ~ for sth:** • **it is advisable to ~ for retirement** es aconsejable que se hagan planes para la jubilación • **to ~ for the future** hacer planes *or* planear para el futuro • **I hadn't ~ned for so many people** no había contado con que viniese tanta gente
▸ **plan on** VI + PREP 1 (= *intend*) • **to ~ on doing sth** tener pensado hacer algo • **I don't ~ on dying just yet** (*iro*) todavía no tengo pensado morirme • **we're ~ning on getting married in July** tenemos pensado casarnos en julio
2 (= *expect*) contar con • **I hadn't ~ned on the bad weather** no había contado con el mal tiempo
▸ **plan out** VT + ADV planear detalladamente • **I haven't even ~ned out the route yet** todavía no he planeado la ruta detalladamente • **he's got it all ~ned out** lo tiene todo planeado *or* planificado
planchette [plɑːn'ʃet] N tabla *f* de escritura espiritista
plane [pleɪn] N 1 (= *aeroplane, airplane*) avión *m* • **to go by ~** ir en avión • **to send goods by ~** enviar mercancías por avión
2 (*Art, Math, Constr*) plano *m* • **vertical/horizontal ~** plano *m* vertical/horizontal
3 (*fig*) nivel *m* • **he seems to exist on another ~** parece vivir en otro nivel *or* en una esfera distinta • **on the ideological ~** en el plano ideológico • **she tried to lift the conversation onto a higher ~** trató de llevar la conversación a un nivel más elevado
4 (= *tool*) (= *small*) cepillo *m* (de carpintero); (= *large*) garlopa *f*
5 (*Bot*) (*also* **plane tree**) plátano *m*
ADJ (*Geom*) plano • **a ~ surface** una superficie plana
VT cepillar • **to ~ sth down** cepillar *or* desbastar algo
VI [*bird, glider*] planear; [*boat, car*] deslizarse
CPD ▸ **plane crash** accidente *m* de avión ▸ **plane geometry** geometría *f* plana ▸ **plane journey** viaje *m* en avión ▸ **plane ticket** billete *m* *or* pasaje *m* de avión
planeload ['pleɪnləʊd] N cargamento *f* aéreo • **they've sent four ~s of relief supplies to the affected areas** han enviado cuatro cargamentos aéreos de ayuda a las zonas afectadas
planet ['plænɪt] N planeta *m* • **the ~ Earth** el planeta Tierra
planetarium [ˌplænɪ'tɛərɪəm] N (PL: **planetariums** *or* **planetaria** [ˌplænɪ'tɛərɪə]) planetario *m*
planetary ['plænɪtərɪ] ADJ planetario
planetoid ['plænɪtɔɪd] N (*Astron*) asteroide *m*
plangent ['plændʒənt] ADJ plañidero
plank [plæŋk] N 1 [*of wood*] tabla *f*, tablón *m* • **deck ~s** tablazón *fsing* de la cubierta • **to walk the ~** pasear por la tabla (sobre los tiburones) • IDIOM: • **to be as thick as two short ~s*** ser más bruto que un arado*
2 (*fig*) [*of policy*] punto *m*
VT 1 • **to ~ sth down** tirar algo violentamente, arrojar algo violentamente • **to ~ o.s. down** sentarse *etc* de modo agresivo
2 (*Naut*) [+ *hull, deck*] entablar, entarimar
planking ['plæŋkɪŋ] N tablas *fpl*, tablaje *m*; (*Naut*) tablazón *f* de la cubierta
plankton ['plæŋktən] N plankton *m*
planned [plænd] ADJ [*economy*] dirigido; [*development, redundancy*] programado; [*crime, murder*] premeditado; [*pregnancy*] deseado
planner ['plænəʳ] N planificador(a) *m/f*; ▹ **town**
planning ['plænɪŋ] N planificación *f* • **the trip needs careful ~** hay que planear bien el viaje • **we're still in the ~ stage(s)** *or* **at the ~ stage** estamos todavía en la etapa de la planificación; ▹ **family, town**
CPD [*committee, department, process*] de planificación ▸ **planning application** (*Brit*) solicitud *f* de permiso de obras ▸ **planning board** (*US*) comisión *f* planificadora ▸ **planning department** área *f* de urbanismo ▸ **planning officer** funcionario/a *m/f* de urbanismo ▸ **planning permission** permiso *m* de obra ▸ **planning regulations** normas *fpl* urbanísticas
plant [plɑːnt] N 1 (*Bot*) planta *f*
2 (*no pl*) (= *machinery*) maquinaria *f*; (*fixed*) instalaciones *fpl* • **heavy ~** maquinaria *f* pesada
3 (= *factory*) fábrica *f*, planta *f*; (= *power station*) planta *f*, central *f*
4* (= *misleading evidence*) • **it's a ~** esto es una trampa para incriminarnos
5* (= *infiltrator*) infiltrado/a *m/f*, espía *mf*
VT 1 (*Bot*) [+ *tree, flower, crop*] plantar; [+ *seed, garden, field*] sembrar • **to ~ sth with sth** sembrar algo de algo • **the field is ~ed with wheat** el campo está sembrado de trigo • **they plan to ~ the area with grass and trees** tienen pensado plantar la zona de árboles y poner césped
2 (= *put*) • **he stood with his feet ~ed apart** se quedó de pie con los pies separados • **he ~ed himself right in her path** se le plantó en el camino*, se plantó en mitad de su camino* • **to ~ an idea in sb's mind** meter a algn una idea en la cabeza • **to ~ a kiss on sb's cheek** plantar un beso en la mejilla a algn* • **she ~ed a punch right on his nose** le plantó un puñetazo en la nariz*
3 (*furtively*) [+ *bomb, evidence*] colocar, poner; [+ *informer, spy*] poner, infiltrar • **to ~ sth on sb** colocar algo a algn para incriminarle
VI plantar
CPD ▸ **plant food** fertilizante *m* (para plantas) ▸ **plant life** vida *f* vegetal, las plantas ▸ **plant pot** maceta *f*, tiesto *m*
▸ **plant out** VT + ADV [+ *seedlings*] trasplantar
plantain ['plæntɪn] N llantén *m*, plátano *m* (*LAm*)
plantation [plæn'teɪʃən] N [*of tea, sugar etc*] plantación *f*; (= *large estate*) hacienda *f*; [*of trees*] arboleda *f*; [*of young trees*] plantel *m*; (*Hist*) colonia *f*
planter ['plɑːntəʳ] N (= *person*) plantador(a) *m/f*; (= *plantation owner*) hacendado/a *m/f* (*esp LAm*); (*Hist*) (= *settler*) colono/a *m/f*; (= *machine*) plantadora *f*; (= *pot*) tiesto *m*, maceta *f*
planting ['plɑːntɪŋ] N • **flooding has delayed ~** las inundaciones han retrasado la plantación
CPD ▸ **planting season** estación *f* de plantar
plaque [plæk] N (= *plate*) placa *f*; (*on teeth*) sarro *m*, placa *f* (dental)
plash [plæʃ] (*liter*) = splash
plasm ['plæzəm] N = plasma

P

plasma ['plæzmə] (N) plasma *m*
(ADJ) [*screen, monitor, television*] de plasma
(CPD) ▸ **plasma screen** pantalla *f* de plasma
▸ **plasma TV** televisor *m* de plasma

plaster ['plɑːstəʳ] (N) **1** (*Constr*) yeso *m*; (= *layer on wall*) enlucido *m*
2 (*Med*) (*for broken limb*) escayola *f*, yeso *m* (*LAm*) • **with his leg in ~** con la pierna escayolada *or* (*LAm*) enyesada
3 (*Brit*) (= *sticking plaster*) esparadrapo *m*, tirita *f*, curita *f* (*LAm*)
4 • **~ of Paris** yeso *m* mate
(VT) **1** (*Constr*) enyesar; [+ *wall*] enyesar, enlucir • **to ~ over a hole** llenar *or* tapar un hoyo con yeso
2 (= *cover*) cubrir, llenar • **to ~ a wall with posters** cubrir *or* llenar una pared de carteles • **the children came back ~ed with mud** los niños volvieron cubiertos de lodo
3 (= *stick*) pegar • **to ~ posters on a wall** pegar carteles en una pared • **the story was ~ed all over the front page** el reportaje llenaba toda la primera plana
4* dar una paliza a*
(CPD) [*model, statue*] de yeso ▸ **plaster cast** (*Med*) escayola *f*, enyesado *m* (*LAm*); (= *model, statue*) vaciado *m* de yeso
▸ **plaster down** (VT + ADV) [*hair*] aplastar • **his hair was ~ed down to his scalp by the rain** se le aplastó el pelo con la lluvia

plasterboard ['plɑːstəbɔːd] (N) cartón *m* de yeso, pladur® *m* (*Sp*)

plastered* ['plɑːstəd] (ADJ) (= *drunk*) • **to be ~** estar como una cuba*, estar tomado (*LAm**) • **to get ~** ponerse como una cuba*

plasterer ['plɑːstərəʳ] (N) yesero/a *m/f*, enlucidor(a) *m/f*

plastering ['plɑːstərɪŋ] (N) enlucido *m*

plastic ['plæstɪk] (N) **1** plástico *m* • **to be made of ~** ser de plástico
2 plastics (materiales *mpl*) plásticos *mpl*
3 (= *credit cards*) plástico *m*
(ADJ) **1** (= *made of plastic*) [*container etc*] de plástico
2 (= *flexible*) plástico
3 (*pej**) (= *artificial*) [*smile*] falso, de plástico; [*person*] de plástico, superficial
(CPD) ▸ **the plastic arts** las artes plásticas ▸ **plastic bag** bolsa *f* de plástico ▸ **plastic bullet** bala *f* de goma ▸ **plastic explosive** goma *f* dos ▸ **plastic mac** (*Brit*) impermeable *m* ▸ **plastic money** dinero *m* de plástico ▸ **plastic sheeting** plástico *m* en planchas ▸ **plastics industry** industria *f* del plástico ▸ **plastic surgeon** cirujano/a *m/f* plástico/a ▸ **plastic surgery** cirugía *f* plástica *or* estética • **to have ~ surgery** hacerse la cirugía plástica *or* estética ▸ **plastic wrap** (*US*) film *m* adherente (*para envolver alimentos*)

Plasticine® ['plæstɪsiːn] (N) plastelina® *f*, plastilina® *f*, arcilla *f* de modelar

plasticity [plæs'tɪsɪtɪ] (N) plasticidad *f*

plastinate ['plæstɪneɪt] (VT) plastinar

Plate [pleɪt] (N) • **the River ~** el Río de la Plata

plate [pleɪt] (N) **1** (= *flat dish*) plato *m*; [*of metal etc*] lámina *f*, plancha *f*; (*for church collection*) platillo *m*; (= *plateful*) plato *m* • IDIOMS: • **to hand sth to sb on a ~*** ofrecer algo a algn en bandeja (de plata) • **to have a lot on one's ~*** estar muy atareado
2 (*on cooker*) quemador *m*, fuego *m*; (= *warming plate*) plancha *f* (eléctrica)
3 (= *silverware etc*) vajilla *f* • **gold/silver ~** vajilla *f* de oro/plata
4 (= *plaque*) (*on wall, door*) placa *f*
5 [*of microscope*] placa *f*
6 (*Aut*) (= *number plate*) matrícula *f*, placa *f*
7 (= *dental plate*) dentadura *f* (postiza)
8 (= *book illustration*) lámina *f*, grabado *m*
9 (*Geol*) placa *f*
10 (*Horse racing*) (= *prize*) premio *m*
11 (*US*) (*Baseball*) plato *m* • **to go to the ~** entrar a batear
12 plates (*Brit‡*) (= *feet*) tachines‡ *mpl*
(VT) **1** (*with gold*) dorar; (*with silver*) platear; (*with nickel*) niquelar; ▹ **chromium-plated**
2 (*with armour*) blindar
(CPD) ▸ **plate armour, plate armor** (*US*) blindaje *m* ▸ **plate glass** vidrio *m* cilindrado, cristal *m* cilindrado (*Sp*), luna *f* ▸ **plate rack** escurreplatos *m inv* ▸ **plate tectonics** (*Geol*) tectónica *f* de placas ▸ **plate warmer** calentador *m* de platos

plateau ['plætəʊ] (N) (PL: **plateaus** *or* **plateaux** ['plætəʊz]) **1** (*Geog*) meseta *f* • **high ~** (*in LAm*) altiplano *m*
2 (*fig*) estancamiento *m*, punto *m* muerto

plated ['pleɪtɪd] (ADJ) **1** [*metal, jewellery*] chapado (**with** en); (*with nickel*) niquelado
2 (= *armoured*) blindado

plateful ['pleɪtfʊl] (N) plato *m*

plate-glass window [ˌpleɪtglɑːs'wɪndəʊ] (N) ventana *f* de vidrio

plateholder ['pleɪtˌhəʊldəʳ] (N) (*Phot*) portaplacas *m inv*

platelayer ['pleɪtˌleɪəʳ] (N) obrero *m* (de ferrocarriles)

platelet ['pleɪtlɪt] (N) plaqueta *f*

platen ['plætən] (N) rodillo *m*

platform ['plætfɔːm] (N) **1** (*gen*) (= *structure*) plataforma *f*; (*roughly-built*) tarima *f*, tablado *m*; [*of oil rig*] plataforma *f* base; [*of bus*] plataforma *f*; (*for band etc*) estrado *m*; (*at meeting*) plataforma *f*, tribuna *f* • **last year they shared a ~** el año pasado ocuparon la misma tribuna
2 (*Rail*) andén *m*, vía *f* • **the 5.15 is at** *or* **on ~ eight** el tren de las 5.15 está en la vía número ocho
3 (*fig*) (*to express one's views*) plataforma *f*
4 (*Pol*) programa *m*
5 platforms* = **platform shoes**
(CPD) ▸ **platform shoes** zapatos *mpl* de plataforma ▸ **platform soles** suelas *fpl* de plataforma ▸ **the platform speakers** los oradores de la tribuna ▸ **platform ticket** (*Brit*) (*Rail*) billete *m* *or* (*LAm*) boleto *m* de andén

plating ['pleɪtɪŋ] (N) (= *layer of metal*) capa *f* metálica • **silver ~** plateado *m* • **gold ~** dorado *m* • **nickel ~** niquelado *m*; ▹ **armour**

platinum ['plætɪnəm] (N) platino *m*
(CPD) ▸ **platinum blonde** (= *colour*) rubio *m* platino; (= *woman*) rubia *f* platino • **~ blond(e) hair** pelo *m* rubio platino ▸ **platinum disc** (= *award*) disco *m* de platino

platitude ['plætɪtjuːd] (N) tópico *m*, lugar *m* común • **it is a ~ to say that ...** es un tópico decir que ...

platitudinize [ˌplætɪ'tjuːdɪnaɪz] (VI) decir tópicos

platitudinous [ˌplætɪ'tjuːdɪnəs] (ADJ) [*speech*] lleno de lugares comunes; [*speaker*] aficionado a los lugares comunes, que peca por exceso de tópicos

Plato ['pleɪtəʊ] (N) Platón

platonic [plə'tɒnɪk] (ADJ) platónico
(CPD) ▸ **platonic love** amor *m* platónico

Platonism ['pleɪtənɪzəm] (N) platonismo *m*

Platonist ['pleɪtənɪst] (N) platonista *mf*

platoon [plə'tuːn] (N) (*Mil*) pelotón *m*, sección *f*

platter ['plætəʳ] (N) **1** (*esp US*) (= *dish*) fuente *f*
2 (= *meal, course*) plato *m* • **a cheese ~** una tabla de quesos
3 (*US**) (= *record*) disco *m*

platypus ['plætɪpəs] (N) ornitorrinco *m*

plaudits ['plɔːdɪts] (NPL) aplausos *mpl*

plausibility [ˌplɔːzə'bɪlɪtɪ] (N) [*of argument*] verosimilitud *f*; [*of person*] credibilidad *f* • **his ~ is such that ...** habla tan bien que ...

plausible ['plɔːzəbl] (ADJ) [*argument etc*] verosímil, plausible; [*person*] convincente

plausibly ['plɔːzəblɪ] (ADV) de modo verosímil, de forma plausible • **he tells it most ~** lo cuenta de la manera más verosímil

play [pleɪ] (N) **1** (= *recreation*) juego *m* • **to be at ~** estar jugando • **to do/say sth in ~** hacer/decir algo en broma
2 (*Sport*) juego *m*; (= *move, manoeuvre*) jugada *f*, movida *f* • **neat ~** una bonita jugada • **a clever piece of ~** una hábil jugada • **~ began at three o'clock** el partido empezó a las tres • **to be in ~** [*ball*] estar en juego • **to be out of ~** [*ball*] estar fuera de juego; ▹ **fair¹**, **foul**
3 (*Theat*) obra *f* (de teatro), pieza *f*; **plays** teatro *msing* • **the ~s of Lope** las obras dramáticas de Lope, el teatro de Lope • **radio/television ~** obra *f* para radio/televisión • **to be in a ~** [*actor*] actuar en una obra; ▹ **radio**
4 (*Tech etc*) juego *m* • **there's not enough ~ in the rope** la cuerda no da lo suficiente • **there's too much ~ in the clutch** el embrague tiene demasiada holgura *or* va demasiado suelto
5 (*fig*) (= *interaction*) • **the ~ of light on the water** el rielar de la luz sobre el agua • **the ~ of light and dark in this picture** el efecto de luz y sombra en este cuadro • **the free ~ of market forces** la libre interacción de los mercados • **the ~ of ideas in the film is fascinating** el abanico de ideas en la película es fascinante
6 (*figurative phrases*) • **to bring** *or* **call into ~** poner en juego • **to come into ~** entrar en juego • **to make a ~ for sth/sb** intentar conseguir algo/conquistar a algn • **to make (a) great ~ of sth** insistir en algo, hacer hincapié en algo • **a ~ on words** un juego de palabras
(VT) **1** [+ *football, tennis, chess, bridge, cards, board game etc*] jugar a; [+ *game, match*] jugar, disputar • **do you ~ football?** ¿juegas al fútbol? • **what position does he ~?** ¿de qué juega? • **to ~ centre-forward/centre-half** *etc* jugar de delantero centro/medio centro *etc* • **they ~ed him in goal** lo pusieron en la portería • **to ~ a game of tennis** jugar un partido de tenis • **to ~ a game of cards (with sb)** echar una partida de cartas (con algn) • **the children were ~ing a game in the garden** los niños estaban jugando (a un juego) en el jardín • **don't ~ games with me!** (*fig*) ¡no me vengas con jueguecitos!, ¡no trates de engañarme! • IDIOMS: • **to ~ the field*** (= *have many girlfriends, boyfriends*) darse al ligue* • **to ~ the game** (= *get involved*) tomar parte, mojarse*; (= *play fair*) acatar las normas
2 [+ *team, opponent*] jugar contra • **I ~ed him twice** jugué contra él dos veces • **last time we ~ed Sunderland ...** la última vez que jugamos contra Sunderland ... • **to ~ sb at chess** jugar contra algn al ajedrez • **I'll ~ you for the drinks** quien pierde paga
3 [+ *card*] jugar; [+ *ball*] golpear; [+ *chess piece etc*] mover; [+ *fish*] dejar que se canse, agotar • **he ~ed the ball into the net** (*Tennis*) estrelló *or* golpeó la pelota contra la red • **to ~ the market** (*St Ex*) jugar a la bolsa • IDIOMS: • **to ~ one's cards right** *or* **well** jugar bien sus cartas • **he ~ed his ace** sacó el as que llevaba escondido en la manga • **to ~ ball (with sb)** (= *cooperate*) colaborar (con algn)
4 (= *perform*) [+ *role, part*] hacer, interpretar; [+ *work*] representar; (= *perform in*) [+ *town*]

actuar en • **what part did you ~?** ¿qué papel tuviste? • **when we ~ed "Hamlet"** cuando representamos "Hamlet" • **when I ~ed Hamlet** cuando hice el papel de Hamlet • **we shall be ~ing the West End** pondremos la obra en el West End • **when we last ~ed Blackpool** cuando actuamos la última vez en Blackpool • **let's ~ it for laughs** hagámoslo de manera burlesca • **to ~ the peacemaker/the devoted husband** (*fig*) hacer el papel de pacificador/de marido amantísimo • **we could have ~ed it differently** (*fig*) podríamos haber actuado de otra forma • IDIOMS: • **to ~ it cool*** mantener el tipo, actuar como si nada • **to ~ (it) safe** obrar con cautela, ser prudente; ▹ **book, fool, trick**

5 (*Mus etc*) [+ *instrument, note*] tocar; [+ *tune, concerto*] tocar, interpretar (*more frm*); [+ *tape, CD*] poner, tocar • **to ~ the piano/violin** tocar el piano/el violín • **they ~ed the 5th Symphony** tocaron *or* (*more frm*) interpretaron la Quinta Sinfonía • **they were ~ing Beethoven** tocaban *or* (*more frm*) interpretaban algo de Beethoven • **I can't ~ a note** no tengo ni idea de música

6 (= *direct*) [+ *light, hose*] dirigir • **to ~ hoses on a fire** dirigir mangueras sobre un incendio • **to ~ a searchlight on an aircraft** dirigir un reflector hacia un avión, hacer de un avión el blanco de un reflector

VI **1** (= *amuse o.s.*) [*child*] jugar; [*puppy, kitten etc*] jugar, juguetear • **to go out to ~** salir a jugar • **to ~ with a stick** juguetear con un palo • **to ~ with an idea** dar vueltas a una idea, barajar una idea • **to ~ with one's food** comiscar • **to ~ with fire** (*fig*) jugar con fuego • **he's got money to ~ with** tiene dinero de sobra • **how much time/money do we have to ~ with?** ¿con cuánto tiempo/dinero contamos?, ¿de cuánto tiempo/dinero disponemos? • **he's just ~ing with you** se está burlando de ti • **to ~ with o.s.*** (*euph*) tocarse, masturbarse

2 (*Sport*) (*at game, gamble*) jugar • **play!** ¡listo! • **who ~s first?** ¿quién juega primero? • **are you ~ing today?** ¿tu juegas hoy? • **I've not ~ed for a long time** hace mucho tiempo que no juego • **England are ~ing against Scotland in the final** Inglaterra jugará contra *or* se enfrentará a Escocia en la final • **to ~ at chess** jugar al ajedrez • **they're ~ing at soldiers** están jugando a (los) soldados • **he's just ~ing at it** lo hace para pasar el tiempo nada más • **the little girl ~s at being a woman** la niña juega a ser mujer • **what are you ~ing at?*** pero ¿qué haces?, ¿qué te pasa? • **to ~ by the rules** (*fig*) acatar las normas • **to ~ fair** jugar limpio • **he ~s for Liverpool** juega en el Liverpool • **to ~ for money** jugar por dinero • **to ~ for high stakes** (*lit*) apostar muy alto; (*fig*) poner mucho en juego • **to ~ in defence/goal** (*Sport*) jugar de defensa/de portero • **he ~ed into the trees** (*Golf*) mandó la bola a la zona de árboles • IDIOMS: • **to ~ for time** tratar de ganar tiempo • **to ~ into sb's hands** hacer el juego a algn • **to ~ to one's strengths** sacar partido a sus cualidades

3 (*Mus*) [*person*] tocar; [*instrument, record etc*] sonar • **do you ~?** ¿sabes tocar? • **a record was ~ing in the background** de fondo sonaba un disco • **when the organ ~s** cuando suena el órgano • **will you ~ for us?** ¿nos tocas algo? • **to ~ on the piano** tocar el piano • **to ~ to sb** tocar para algn

4 (*Theat, Cine*) (= *act*) actuar • **to ~ in a film** trabajar en una película • **we have ~ed all over the South** hemos representado en todas partes del Sur • **the film now ~ing at the Odeon** la película que se exhibe *or* proyecta en el Odeon • IDIOMS: • **to ~ hard to get** hacerse de rogar; [*woman*] hacerse la difícil • **to ~ dead** hacerse el muerto; ▹ **gallery**

5 (= *move about, form patterns*) correr • **the sun was ~ing on the water** rielaba el sol sobre el agua • **a smile ~ed on his lips** una sonrisa le bailaba en los labios

6 [*fountain*] correr, funcionar

CPD ▸ **play clothes** ropa *f* para jugar ▸ **play reading** lectura *f* (de una obra dramática)

▸ **play about** VI + ADV = **play around**

▸ **play along** VI + ADV • **to ~ along (with sb)** (*fig*) seguir el juego (a algn)

VT + ADV • **to ~ sb along** (*fig*) dar largas a algn*

▸ **play around** VI + ADV **1** (*also* **play about**) [*children*] jugar, divertirse

2* (= *sleep around*) dormir con cualquiera

3 • **to ~ around** *or* **about with sth** (= *fiddle with*) juguetear con algo; (= *tamper with*) toquetear algo • **I ~ed around with the programme till it worked** ensayé el programa de varias maneras hasta hacerlo funcionar bien • **to ~ around with an idea** dar vueltas a una idea, barajar una idea

▸ **play back** VT + ADV [+ *tape*] poner

▸ **play down** VT + ADV (= *downplay*) minimizar, quitar importancia a

▸ **play in** VT + ADV **1** • **the band ~ed the procession in** tocaba la orquesta mientras entraba el desfile

2 (*Sport etc*) • **to ~ o.s. in** acostumbrarse a las condiciones de juego

▸ **play off** VT + ADV • **to ~ one person off against another** enfrentar a una persona con otra

VI + ADV (*Sport*) jugar un partido de desempate

▸ **play on** VI + PREP (= *take advantage of*) aprovecharse de, explotar • **to ~ on sb's emotions** jugar con las emociones de algn • **to ~ on sb's credulity** explotar la credulidad de algn • **to ~ on words** jugar con las palabras • **to ~ on sb's nerves** (= *be irritating*) afectar los nervios a algn

VI + ADV (*Mus*) seguir tocando; (*Sport*) seguir jugando • **~ on!** ¡adelante!

▸ **play out** VT + ADV **1** (= *enact*) llevar a cabo; [+ *fantasy etc*] realizar • **they are ~ing out a drama of revenge** están representando un drama de venganza

2 • **to be ~ed out** [*person, argument*] estar agotado

3 • **the organ ~ed the congregation out** el órgano iba tocando mientras salían los fieles

▸ **play over, play through** VT + ADV • **to ~ a piece of music over** *or* **through** tocar una pieza entera

▸ **play up** VI + ADV **1** (*Brit**) (= *cause trouble*) [*children*] dar guerra* • **the car is ~ing up** el coche no anda bien • **my stomach is ~ing up again** el estómago me está dando problemas otra vez, mi estómago vuelve a darme problemas

2* (= *flatter*) • **to ~ up to sb** halagar a algn, dar coba a algn (*Sp**)

3 (*Sport*†) jugar mejor, jugar con más ánimo • **~ up!** ¡ánimo!, ¡aúpa!

VT + ADV **1** (*Brit**) (= *cause trouble to*) • **to ~ sb up** dar la lata a algn (*Sp**), fregar a algn (*LAm**) • **the kids ~ her up dreadfully** los chavales *or* (*LAm*) los chicos le dan guerra de mala manera* • **his rheumatism is ~ing him up** el reúma le está fastidiando

2 (= *exaggerate*) exagerar, encarecer

▸ **play upon** VI + PREP = **play on**

playability [ˌpleɪəˈbɪlɪtɪ] N [*of pitch, surface*] practicabilidad *f*; [*of game*] jugabilidad *f*

playable [ˈpleɪəbəl] ADJ [*pitch, surface*] practicable; [*game*] jugable

play-act [ˈpleɪækt] VI (*lit*) hacer teatro, actuar; (*fig*) (= *pretend*) hacer teatro

play-acting [ˈpleɪˌæktɪŋ] N (*lit*) actuación *f* teatral; (*fig*) teatro *m*, comedia *f* • **this is mere play-acting** (*fig*) esto es puro teatro, esto no es más que una comedia

play-actor [ˈpleɪˌæktəʳ] N (*lit, fig*) actor *m*, actriz *f*

playback [ˈpleɪbæk] N repetición *f*, reproducción *f*; (*TV etc*) playback *m*, previo *m*

playbill [ˈpleɪbɪl] N cartel *m*

playboy [ˈpleɪbɔɪ] N playboy *m*

Play-Doh® [ˈpleɪdəʊ] N ≈ plastilina® *f*

player [ˈpleɪəʳ] N **1** (*Sport*) jugador(a) *m/f* • **football ~** jugador(a) *m/f* de fútbol, futbolista *mf*

2 (*Theat*) actor *m*, actriz *f*

3 (*Mus*) músico/a *m/f* • **violin/piano ~** violinista *mf*/pianista *mf*

player-manager [ˈpleɪəˈmænɪdʒəʳ] N jugador(a) -entrenador(a) *m/f*

playfellow [ˈpleɪˌfeləʊ] N compañero/a *m/f* de juego

playful [ˈpleɪfʊl] ADJ [*person*] juguetón; [*mood*] alegre; [*remark*] dicho en broma, festivo

playfully [ˈpleɪfəlɪ] ADV (= *full of fun*) alegremente; (= *in jest*) en broma; (*as part of game*) jugando, en juego • **he said ~** dijo guasón

playfulness [ˈpleɪfʊlnɪs] N [*of person*] carácter *m* juguetón; [*of mood*] alegría *f*; [*of remark*] guasa *f*, tono *m* guasón

playgoer [ˈpleɪˌgəʊəʳ] N aficionado/a *m/f* al teatro • **we are regular ~s** vamos con regularidad al teatro

playground [ˈpleɪgraʊnd] N (*in school*) patio *m* de recreo; (*fig*) [*of millionaires*] paraíso *m*, lugar *m* favorito

playgroup [ˈpleɪˌgruːp] N jardín *m* de infancia, guardería *f*, kinder *m* (*LAm*)

playhouse [ˈpleɪhaʊs] N (PL: **playhouses** [ˈplaɪhaʊzɪz]) **1** (= *theatre*) teatro *m*

2 (*for children*) casa *f* de muñecas

playing [ˈpleɪɪŋ] N **1** (*Sport*) juego *m* • **~ in the wet is tricky** es difícil jugar cuando llueve

2 (*Mus*) • **the orchestra's ~ of the symphony was uninspired** la interpretación que hizo la orquesta de la sinfonía fue poco inspirada • **there was some fine ~ in the violin concerto** el concierto de violín estuvo muy bien interpretado

CPD ▸ **playing card** naipe *m* ▸ **playing field** campo *m* or (*LAm*) cancha *f* de deportes

playlet [ˈpleɪlɪt] N obra *f* corta de teatro

playlist [ˈpleɪlɪst] N (*Rad*) lista *f* discográfica

playmaker [ˈpleɪmeɪkəʳ] N (*Sport*) *jugador encargado de facilitar buenas jugadas a sus compañeros*

playmate [ˈpleɪmeɪt] N compañero/a *m/f* de juego

play-off [ˈpleɪɒf] N (*Sport*) (partido *m* de) desempate *m*; [*of top teams in league*] liguilla *f*

playpen [ˈpleɪpen] N parque *m*, corral *m*

playroom [ˈpleɪrʊm] N cuarto *m* de juego

playschool [ˈpleɪˌskuːl] N = **playgroup**

playsuit [ˈpleɪsuːt] N (*for baby*) pelele *m* (*Sp*), mameluco *m* (*LAm*)

plaything [ˈpleɪθɪŋ] N (*lit, fig*) juguete *m*

playtime [ˈpleɪtaɪm] N (*Scol*) (hora *f* de) recreo *m*

playwear [ˈpleɪwɛəʳ] N (*US*) (= *leisure wear*) ropa *f* de sport

playwright [ˈpleɪraɪt] N dramaturgo/a *m/f*

plaza [ˈplɑːzə] N **1** (= *public square*) plaza *f*

P

2 (*US*) (= *motorway services*) zona *f* de servicios; (= *toll*) peaje *m*

PLC, plc (N ABBR) (*Brit*) (= **public limited company**) S.A.

plea [pliː] (N) **1** (= *entreaty*) súplica *f*, petición *f* • **he made a ~ for mercy** pidió clemencia
2 (= *excuse*) pretexto *m*, disculpa *f*
3 (*Jur*) alegato *m*, defensa *f* • **a ~ of insanity** un alegato de desequilibrio mental • **a ~ of guilty/not guilty** una declaración de culpabilidad/inocencia • **to enter a ~ of innocent** declararse inocente
(CPD) ▸ **plea bargaining** (*Jur*) *acuerdo táctico entre fiscal y defensor para agilizar los trámites judiciales*

pleach [pliːtʃ] (VT) [+ *branches*] entretejer; [+ *hedge*] entrelazar

plead [pliːd] (PT, PP: (*esp US*) **pleaded, pled**)
(VT) **1** (= *argue*) • **to ~ sb's cause** hablar por algn, interceder por algn • **to ~ sb's case** (*Jur*) defender a algn en juicio
2 (*as excuse*) aducir, pretextar • **to ~ that** aducir *or* pretextar que • **to ~ ignorance** aducir *or* pretextar desconocimiento • **to ~ poverty** aducir *or* pretextar falta de medios económicos • **he ~ed certain difficulties** adujo *or* pretextó la existencia de ciertas dificultades
(VI) **1** (= *beg*) suplicar, rogar • **I ~ed and ~ed but it was no use** le supliqué mil veces pero de nada sirvió • **to ~ with sb (to do sth)** suplicar a algn (que haga algo) • **to ~ with sb for sth** rogar a algn que conceda algo • **the village has ~ed for a new bridge for ten years** hace diez años que el pueblo viene reclamando un nuevo puente
2 (*Jur*) (*as defendant*) presentar declaración; (*as barrister*) abogar • **how do you ~?** ¿cómo se declara el acusado? • **to ~ guilty/not guilty** declararse culpable/inocente

pleading [ˈpliːdɪŋ] (N) (= *entreaties*) súplicas *fpl*; (*Jur*) alegatos *mpl* • **special ~** argumentos *mpl* especiosos
(ADJ) [*tone etc*] suplicante, de súplica

pleadingly [ˈpliːdɪŋlɪ] (ADV) de manera suplicante

pleasant [ˈpleznt] (ADJ) **1** (= *agreeable*) [*place, experience, smell, taste, voice*] agradable; [*surprise*] grato, agradable; [*face*] agradable, simpático • **it's very ~ here** aquí se está muy bien • **it made a ~ change from our usual holiday** supuso un agradable cambio respecto a nuestras vacaciones habituales • **~ dreams!** ¡que sueñes con los angelitos! • **~-looking** de aspecto agradable
2 (= *friendly*) [*person*] agradable, simpático; [*style*] agradable • **he has a ~ manner** es agradable *or* simpático *or* amable • **try and be a bit more ~ to your sister** procura ser un poco más agradable con tu hermana

pleasantly [ˈplezntlɪ] (ADV) [*say*] amablemente, en tono agradable • **the evening passed ~ enough** la velada fue bastante agradable • **the room was ~ furnished** la habitación estaba amueblada con gusto • **it was ~ warm** hacía un calor agradable • **we were ~ surprised** fue una grata *or* agradable sorpresa para nosotros • **I was feeling ~ drowsy** tenía una agradable *or* placentera sensación de somnolencia

pleasantness [ˈplezntnɪs] (N) (= *agreeableness*) amenidad *f*, lo agradable; (= *friendliness*) simpatía *f*, amabilidad *f*

pleasantry [ˈplezntrɪ] (N) **1** (= *joke*) chiste *m*, broma *f*
2 (= *polite remark*) cumplido *m* • **to exchange pleasantries** intercambiar los cumplidos de rigor

please [pliːz] (EXCL) • **please!** ¡por favor!; (*as protest*) ¡por Dios! • **(yes,) ~** sí, gracias • **can you pass the salt, ~** me pasas la sal, por favor • **~ don't cry!** ¡no llores, (te lo pido) por favor! • **~ don't interfere, Boris** haz el favor de no meterte, Boris, no te metas, Boris, por favor • **~ be seated** (*said by interviewer, doctor etc*) siéntese; (*said over intercom, in plane, theatre etc*) les rogamos tomen asiento • **~ accept this book** le ruego acepte este libro • **oh, ~! not that song again!** ¡oh no! ¡esa canción otra vez no por favor! • **"may I?" — "~ do"** —¿puedo? —¡por supuesto! *or* —¡cómo no! • **"please do not smoke"** "se ruega no fumar"
(VI) **1** (= *like, prefer*) querer • **he does whatever he ~s** hace lo que quiere *or* lo que le place • **she can live where she ~s** puede vivir donde quiera *or* donde le plazca • **as you ~** como quieras • **do as you ~** haz lo que quieras, haz lo que te dé la gana* • **she came over casually as you ~ and picked up my diary*** se acercó con toda la tranquilidad del mundo y cogió mi agenda • **gentlemen, if you ~!** (*frm*) señores, por favor, señores, si son tan amables • **he wanted ten, if you ~!** quería llevarse diez, ¡a quién se le ocurre!, quería llevarse diez, ¡qué cara!* • **we'll have none of that language if you ~!** ¡mucho cuidadito con usar ese lenguaje!
2 (= *cause satisfaction*) • **we aim to ~** nuestro objetivo es complacer • **to be anxious** *or* **eager to ~** tener muchas ansias de quedar bien • **a gift that is sure to ~** un regalo que siempre gusta, un regalo que de seguro gustará
(VT) **1** (= *give pleasure to*) agradar, complacer; (= *satisfy*) complacer • **I did it just to ~ you** lo hice únicamente para agradarte *or* complacerte • **you can't ~ all of the people all of the time** no se puede complacer a todo el mundo todo el tiempo • **music that ~s the ear** una música grata al oído • **she is easily ~d** se contenta con cualquier cosa • **he is hard to ~** es difícil de contentar *or* complacer • **there's no pleasing him** no hay manera de contentarlo • **~ yourself!** ¡haz lo que quieras!, ¡haz lo que te dé la gana!*
2 (*frm*) (= *be the will of*) • **may it ~ Your Majesty** sea esta la voluntad de su Majestad
(N) • **she just took it without so much as a ~ or a thank you** lo cogió sin ni siquiera dignarse a pedirlo por favor ni a dar las gracias

pleased [pliːzd] (ADJ) **1** • **to be ~** (= *happy*) estar contento; (= *satisfied*) estar satisfecho • **we will be ~ to answer any questions** contestaremos, encantados *or* con mucho gusto, todas sus preguntas • **I am ~ to hear it** me alegra saberlo • **~ to meet you!** mucho gusto (en conocerlo), encantado (de conocerlo) • **we are ~ to inform you that ...** nos complace *or* nos es grato comunicarle que ... • **I'm so ~ you could make it** cómo me alegro de que hayas podido venir • **he wasn't too ~ that I had sold it** no le hizo mucha gracia que lo hubiese vendido • **to be ~ about/at sth:** • **I am ~ at the decision** me alegro de la decisión • **we were ~ at the news** la noticia nos alegró • **I'm not very ~ about it** no me hace mucha gracia • **I'm really ~ for you** me alegro mucho por ti • **what are you looking so ~ about?** ¿a qué se debe esa cara de alegría? • **to be ~ with sb/sth** estar contento con algn/algo • **he was ~ with my progress** estaba contento con *or* satisfecho de mis progresos • **he is/looks very ~ with himself** está/parece estar muy satisfecho de sí mismo *or* consigo mismo • **you needn't look so ~ with yourself** esa cara de satisfacción que tienes sobra; ▹ **Punch**
2 (*with noun*) • **he glanced at her with a ~ smile** la miró, sonriendo satisfecho • **there was a look of ~ surprise on her face** se le veía en la cara que se había llevado una grata *or* agradable sorpresa

pleasing [ˈpliːzɪŋ] (ADJ) [*manner*] agradable; [*news*] grato; [*result*] satisfactorio • **aesthetically ~** agradable desde el punto de vista estético • **~ to the ear/eye** grato *or* agradable al oído/a la vista

pleasingly [ˈpliːzɪŋlɪ] (ADV) • **the surface was ~ smooth to the touch** la superficie era lisa y agradable *or* grata al tacto

pleasurable [ˈpleʒərəbl] (ADJ) agradable, grato

pleasurably [ˈpleʒərəblɪ] (ADV) agradablemente, deleitosamente • **we were ~ surprised** para nosotros fue una grata sorpresa

pleasure [ˈpleʒəʳ] (N) **1** (= *satisfaction*) placer *m*, gusto *m*; (= *happiness*) alegría *f* • **to be fond of ~** ser amante de los placeres • **sexual ~** placer *m* sexual • **my ~!** • **the ~ is mine!** (*frm*) (*returning thanks*) ¡de nada!, ¡no hay de qué! (*esp LAm*) • **what ~ can you find in shooting partridges?** ¿qué placer encuentras en matar perdices? • **to do sth for ~** hacer algo por gusto *or* placer • **is this trip for business or ~?** ¿este viaje es de negocios o de placer? • **to get ~ from sth** disfrutar con algo • **to give sb ~** dar gusto a algn • **if it gives you any ~** si te gusta • **I have much ~ in informing you that ...** tengo el gran placer de comunicarles que ... • **may I have the ~?** (*frm*) (*at dance*) ¿quiere usted bailar? • **Mr and Mrs Brown request the ~ of your company** (*frm*) (*on invitation*) los Sres. Brown tienen el placer de solicitar su asistencia • **to take ~ in books** disfrutar leyendo • **I take great ~ in watching them grow** disfruto muchísimo viéndolos crecer • **to take ~ in teasing sb** disfrutar tomando el pelo a algn • **with ~** con mucho gusto
2 (= *source of pleasure*) placer *m*, gusto *m* • **it's a real ~** es un verdadero placer • **all the ~s of London** todos los placeres de Londres • **it's a ~ to see her** da gusto verla • **it's a ~ to know that ...** es un motivo de satisfacción saber que ...
3 (*frm*) (= *will*) voluntad *f* • **what is your ~, sir?** ¿en qué puedo servirle, señor?, ¿qué manda el señor? • **at sb's ~** según la voluntad de algn • **to be detained during her Majesty's ~** (*Jur*) quedar encarcelado a disposición del Estado
(VT) (*sexually*) dar placer a • **to ~ o.s.** (*euph*) (= *masturbate*) masturbarse
(CPD) ▸ **pleasure boat, pleasure craft** barco *m* de recreo ▸ **pleasure cruise** crucero *m* de recreo ▸ **pleasure ground** parque *m* de atracciones ▸ **pleasure seeker** hedonista *mf* ▸ **pleasure steamer** vapor *m* de recreo ▸ **pleasure trip** viaje *m* de placer

pleasure-loving [ˈpleʒəˌlʌvɪŋ],
pleasure-seeking [ˈpleʒəˌsiːkɪŋ] (ADJ) hedonista

pleat [pliːt] (N) pliegue *m*, doblez *m*; [*of skirt*] tabla *f*
(VT) plisar, plegar

pleated [ˈpliːtɪd] (ADJ) [*skirt*] plisado

pleather [ˈpleðəʳ] (*US*) (N) cuero *m* sintético, piel *f* sintética (*Mex, Sp*)
(ADJ) de cuero sintético, de piel sintética (*Mex, Sp*)

pleb* [pleb] (*Brit*) (N) plebeyo/a *m/f* • **the ~s** la plebe
(ADJ) plebeyo, aplebeyado

plebby* [ˈplebɪ] (ADJ) (*pej*) ordinario, naco (*Mex**)

plebeian [plɪˈbiːən] (ADJ) plebeyo; (*pej*) ordinario

P

N plebeyo/a *m/f*

plebiscite ['plebɪsɪt] N plebiscito *m*

plectrum ['plektrəm] N (PL: **plectrums** *or* **plectra** ['plektrə]) púa *f*, plectro *m*

pled [pled] (*US*) PT, PP *of* **plead**

pledge [pledʒ] N **1** (= *promise, assurance*) (*gen*) compromiso *m*, promesa *f*; [*of money*] promesa *f* de donación • **a company's ~ of satisfaction to its customers** el compromiso *or* la promesa por parte de una empresa de satisfacer a sus clientes • **he received ~s of support from more than 100 MPs** más de 100 parlamentarios se comprometieron a *or* prometieron apoyarlo • **the Pledge of Allegiance** (*US*) ≈ la jura de la bandera • **to break a ~** romper una promesa • **to give (sb) a ~ to do sth** prometer (a algn) hacer algo • **to honour** *or* **keep a ~** cumplir una promesa • **the government will honour its ~s** el gobierno cumplirá sus promesas, el gobierno hará honor a sus compromisos • **to make (sb) a ~ to do sth** prometer (a algn) hacer algo • **he made a ~ not to raise taxes** prometió no subir los impuestos • IDIOM: • **to sign** *or* **take the ~**†* (*hum*) jurar renunciar al alcohol

2 (= *token*) • **he sent his brother as a ~ of his sincerity** envió a su hermano en señal *or* como muestra de su sinceridad

3 (= *surety*) prenda *f*, garantía *f*; (*left in pawn*) prenda *f*

4 (= *toast*) brindis *m inv*

5 (*US*) (*Univ*) *promesa que hace un estudiante universitario en los Estados Unidos para convertirse en miembro de una hermandad*

VT **1** (= *promise*) [+ *money, donation*] prometer • **the government has ~d that it will not increase taxes** el gobierno ha prometido no subir los impuestos • **to ~ to do sth** prometer hacer algo • **to ~ o.s. to do sth** comprometerse a hacer algo • **to ~ (one's) support (for sth/sb)** comprometerse a prestar apoyo (a algo/algn) • **I am ~d to secrecy** he jurado *or* prometido guardar (el) secreto; ▸ **allegiance**

2 (= *give as security*) [+ *property*] entregar como garantía; [+ *one's word*] dar

3 (= *pawn*) empeñar, dejar en prenda

4 (*US*) (*Univ*) [+ *fraternity*] hacerse miembro de

PLEDGE OF ALLEGIANCE

El **Pledge of Allegiance** es un juramento de lealtad a la nación, considerado como un elemento de gran importancia en la educación norteamericana. Fue escrito en 1892 y desde entonces lo recitan diariamente los alumnos estadounidenses (especialmente en los centros de educación primaria) mirando a la bandera y con la mano en el corazón.

Pleiades ['plaɪədi:z] NPL Pléyades *fpl*

plenary ['pli:nərɪ] ADJ plenario • **in ~ session** en sesión plenaria

N (*also* **plenary paper**) ponencia *f* en sesión plenaria, ponencia *f* general

plenipotentiary [ˌplenɪpə'tenʃərɪ] ADJ plenipotenciario

N plenipotenciario/a *m/f*

plenitude ['plenɪtju:d] N plenitud *f*

plenteous ['plentɪəs] ADJ (*frm*) = **plentiful**

plentiful ['plentɪfʊl] ADJ [*wildlife, game, hair*] abundante • **a ~ supply of ...** un suministro abundante de ... • **eggs are now ~** *or* **in ~ supply** ahora hay abundancia de huevos, ahora abundan los huevos

plentifully ['plentɪfəlɪ] ADV en abundancia, abundantemente

plenty ['plentɪ] N abundancia *f* • **in ~** en abundancia • **the land of ~** la tierra de la abundancia

PRON **1** (= *lots*) • **that's ~, thanks** ¡así basta, gracias! • **she's got ~ to do** tiene muchas cosas que hacer, tiene un montón que hacer* • **there are ~ like me** hay mucha gente *or* hay muchos como yo • **there's ~ more where that came from** aún queda más de esto

2 • **~ of** (= *much, a good deal of*) mucho/a; (= *many*) muchos/as • **it takes ~ of courage** requiere mucho valor • **they have ~ of money** tienen mucho dinero • **we've got ~ of time to get there** tenemos tiempo de sobra para llegar • **I've got ~ of work to be getting on with** tengo trabajo más que suficiente para empezar • **drink ~ of fluids** beba muchos líquidos • **there are ~ of them** los hay en cantidad • **~ of people are self-employed nowadays** hoy en día hay mucha gente que trabaja de autónomo • **we see ~ of Mum and Dad** vemos a mis padres con frecuencia, vemos mucho a mis padres

ADV (*esp US**) • **it's ~ big enough** es bastante grande • **we like it ~** nos gusta mucho

plenum ['pli:nəm] N (PL: **plenums** *or* **plena**) pleno *m*

pleonasm ['pli:ənæzəm] N pleonasmo *m*

pleonastic [plɪə'næstɪk] ADJ pleonástico

plethora ['pleθərə] N plétora *f*

plethoric [ple'θɒrɪk] ADJ pletórico

pleurisy ['plʊərɪsɪ] N pleuresía *f*, pleuritis *f*

Plexiglas® ['pleksɪglɑ:s] N plexiglás® *m*

pliability [ˌplaɪə'bɪlɪtɪ] N (*also fig*) flexibilidad *f*

pliable ['plaɪəbl] ADJ (*also fig*) flexible

pliant ['plaɪənt] ADJ (*fig*) dócil, flexible

pliers ['plaɪəz] NPL alicates *mpl* • **a pair of ~** unos alicates

plight¹ [plaɪt] N situación *f* grave • **the country's economic ~** la grave situación económica del país • **the ~ of the shellfish industry** la crisis de la industria marisquera • **to be in a sad** *or* **sorry ~** estar en un estado lamentable

plight²† [plaɪt] VT [+ *word*] dar, empeñar • **to ~ one's troth** prometerse, dar su palabra de casamiento (**to** a)

plimsoll ['plɪmsəl] N (*Brit*) zapatilla *f* de tenis, playera *f*

CPD ▸ **Plimsoll line, Plimsoll mark** (*Naut*) línea *f* de máxima carga

plinth [plɪnθ] N plinto *m*

Pliny ['plɪnɪ] N Plinio • **~ the Elder** Plinio el Viejo • **~ the Younger** Plinio el Joven

PLO N ABBR (= **Palestine Liberation Organization**) OLP *f*

plod [plɒd] N **1** • **to go at a steady ~** caminar a un ritmo lento pero constante

2 • **it's a long ~ to the village** hay mucho camino hasta llegar al pueblo

VT • **we ~ded our way homeward** volvimos penosamente hacia casa

VI **1** (*lit*) andar con paso pesado • **to ~ along** *or* **on** ir andando con paso lento • **keep ~ding!** ¡ánimo!, ¡no os dejéis desanimar!

2 (*fig*) (*at work etc*) • **to ~ away at a task** seguir dándole a un trabajo • **we must ~ on** tenemos que seguir trabajando

plodder* ['plɒdəʳ] N *trabajador diligente pero lento*

plodding ['plɒdɪŋ] ADJ [*pace*] lento y pesado; [*student, worker*] más aplicado que brillante

plonk¹ [plɒŋk] (*esp Brit*) N (= *sound*) golpe *m* seco, ruido *m* seco • **it fell with a ~ to the floor** cayó al suelo con un ruido seco

ADV* • **he went ~ into the stream** cayó ¡zas! en el arroyo • **it landed ~ on his cheek** le dio de lleno en la mejilla • **~ in the middle** justo en el medio

VT* **1** (*Mus*) puntear

2 (*also* **plonk down**) dejar caer • **to ~ o.s. down** dejarse caer

EXCL* plaf

plonk²* [plɒŋk] N (*Brit*) (= *wine*) vino *m* peleón*

plonker‡ ['plɒŋkəʳ] N (*Brit*) imbécil *mf*, gilipollas *mf inv* (*Sp‡*)

plop [plɒp] N plaf *m*

VI hacer plaf

VT (*also* **plop down**) arrojar dejando oír un plaf

EXCL plaf

plosive ['pləʊsɪv] ADJ explosivo

N explosiva *f*

plot¹ [plɒt] N (*Agr*) parcela *f*, terreno *m*; [*of vegetables, flowers etc*] cuadro *m* • **a ~ of grass** un cuadro de césped • **a ~ of land** (*gen*) un terreno; (*for building*) un solar, un lote (*esp LAm*) • **a vegetable ~** un cuadro de hortalizas

plot² [plɒt] N **1** (= *conspiracy*) complot *m*, conjura *f*

2 (*Literat, Theat*) trama *f*, argumento *m* • IDIOMS: • **to lose the ~*** perderse, perder el hilo • **the ~ thickens** la cosa se complica

VT **1** (*on graph etc*) [+ *progress, course, position*] trazar • **to ~ A against Z** trazar A como función de Z

2 [+ *downfall, ruin etc*] urdir, fraguar

VI maquinar, conspirar • **to ~ to do sth** conspirar para hacer algo

▸ **plot out** VT + ADV [+ *course, route*] trazar; [+ *strategy, plan*] marcar, trazar

plotless ['plɒtlɪs] ADJ [*film, play, novel*] sin argumento, carente de argumento

plotline ['plɒtlaɪn] N trama *f*

plotter¹ ['plɒtəʳ] N (= *conspirator*) conspirador(a) *m/f*

plotter² ['plɒtəʳ] N (*Comput*) trazador *m* (de gráficos)

plotting ['plɒtɪŋ] N intrigas *fpl*, maquinaciones *fpl*

CPD ▸ **plotting board** tablero *m* trazador ▸ **plotting paper** (*US*) papel *m* cuadriculado ▸ **plotting table** mesa *f* trazadora

plough, plow (*US*) [plaʊ] N (*Agr*) arado *m* • **the Plough** (*Astron*) el Carro, la Osa Mayor

VT **1** (*Agr*) arar

2 (*fig*) • **to ~ money into a project** invertir (grandes cantidades de) dinero en un proyecto • **to ~ one's way through the snow** abrirse paso con dificultad por la nieve • **to ~ one's way through a book** leer un libro con dificultad • **I ~ed my way through it eventually** por fin acabé de leerlo pero resultó pesadísimo

3 (*Brit*) (*Univ*†*) dar calabazas a*, cargar (*Sp**) • **I was ~ed in German** • **they ~ed me in German** me dieron calabazas en alemán*

VI **1** (*Agr*) arar

2 (*fig*) • **the car ~ed into the wall** el coche dio fuerte(mente) contra la pared • **the lorry ~ed into the crowd** el camión se metió en la multitud • **to ~ through the mud** abrirse camino con dificultad a través del lodo

3 (*Brit*) (*Univ*†*) • **I ~ed again** volvieron a suspenderme *or* (*LAm*) reprobarme, volvieron a cargarme (*Sp**)

CPD ▸ **plough horse** caballo *m* de labranza

▸ **plough back** VT + ADV [+ *profits*] reinvertir

▸ **plough in, plough under** VT + ADV cubrir arando, enterrar arando

▸ **plough up** VT + ADV [+ *field*] arar, roturar; [+ *bushes etc*] arrancar con el arado; [+ *pathway*] hacer desaparecer arando • **the train ~ed up the track for 100 metres** el tren destrozó unos 100 metros de vía

ploughing, plowing (*US*) ['plaʊɪŋ] N arada *f* • **~ back of profits** reinversión *f* de ganancias

ploughland, **plowland** (*US*) ['plaʊlænd] N tierra *f* de labrantío, tierra *f* labrantía

ploughman, **plowman** (*US*) ['plaʊmən] N (PL: **ploughmen**) arador *m*, labrador *m*
CPD ▸ **ploughman's lunch** (*Brit*) pan *m* con queso y cebolla

ploughshare, **plowshare** (*US*) ['plaʊʃɛəʳ] N reja *f* del arado

plover ['plʌvəʳ] N chorlito *m*

plow *etc* [plaʊ] (*US*) = **plough** *etc*

ploy [plɔɪ] N truco *m*, estratagema *f*

PLP N ABBR (*Brit*) = **Parliamentary Labour Party**

PLR N ABBR (*Brit*) (*Admin*) = **Public Lending Right**

pls ABBR (= **please**) (*gen*) porfa (*por favor*); (*in texting*) xfa (*por favor*)

pluck [plʌk] N **1** (= *tug*) tirón *m*
2 (= *courage*) valor *m*, ánimo *m*; (= *guts*) agallas *fpl* • **it takes ~ to do that** hace falta mucho valor para hacer eso • **he's got plenty of ~** tiene muchas agallas • **I didn't have the ~ to own up** no tuve el valor para confesar
VT [+ *fruit, flower*] (*liter*) arrancar; [+ *bird*] desplumar; [+ *guitar*] pulsar, puntear • **to ~ one's eyebrows** depilarse las cejas • **the helicopter ~ed him from the sea** el helicóptero lo recogió del mar • **it's an idea I've just ~ed out of the air** es una idea que he tenido al vuelo • **he was ~ed from obscurity to star in the show** fue rescatado del anonimato para protagonizar el espectáculo
VI • **to ~ at** tirar de, dar un tirón a • **to ~ at sb's sleeve** tirar a algn de la manga
▸ **pluck off**, **pluck out** VT + ADV arrancar con los dedos, arrancar de un tirón
▸ **pluck up** VT + ADV (= *summon up*) • **to ~ up (one's) courage** armarse de valor • **to ~ up the courage to do sth** armarse de valor para hacer algo

pluckily ['plʌkɪlɪ] ADV valientemente

pluckiness ['plʌkɪnɪs] N (= *courage*) valor *m*, ánimo *m*; (= *guts*) agallas *fpl*

plucky ['plʌkɪ] ADJ (COMPAR: **pluckier**, SUPERL: **pluckiest**) valiente, valeroso

plug [plʌg] N **1** (*in bath, basin, barrel, for leak*) tapón *m* • **a ~ of cotton wool** un tampón (de algodón) • IDIOM: • **to pull the ~ on sth***: • **the bank pulled the ~ on my overdraft** el banco me cerró el grifo del descubierto
2 (*Elec*) (*on flex, apparatus*) enchufe *m*, clavija *f*; (= *socket*) toma *f* de corriente; (*Telec*) clavija *f*; (*Aut*) (= *spark plug*) bujía *f* • **2-/3-pin ~** clavija *f* bipolar/tripolar, clavija *f* de dos/tres polos
3 [*of tobacco*] rollo *m*, tableta *f* (de tabaco de mascar)
4* (= *piece of publicity*) publicidad *f* • **to give sth/sb a ~** dar publicidad a algo/algn • **to get/put in a ~ for a product** lograr anunciar un producto (de modo solapado)
VT **1** (*also* **plug up**) [+ *hole*] llenar, tapar; [+ *leak*] cubrir; (*Archit*) rellenar • **~ this cloth into the hole** tapa el agujero con este trapo • **to ~ a tooth** empastar una muela • **to ~ a loophole** (*fig*) cerrar una escapatoria • **to ~ the drain on the reserves** (*fig*) acabar con la pérdida de reservas
2 (= *insert*) introducir • **to ~ a lead into a socket** enchufar un hilo en una toma
3* (= *publicize*) dar publicidad a
4* (= *advocate, put forward*) insistir *or* hacer hincapié en • **he's been ~ging that line for years** hace años que viene diciendo lo mismo
5‡ (= *hit*) pegar; (= *shoot*) pegar un tiro a
▸ **plug away*** VI + ADV • **to ~ away (at sth)** perseverar (en algo), darle (a algo)*
▸ **plug in** VT + ADV (*Elec*) enchufar, conectar • **to ~ in a radio** conectar una radio
VI + ADV **1** (*Elec*) enchufar
2* (*fig*) ponerse en la onda* • **to ~ in to** ponerse en la onda de*, sintonizar con
▸ **plug up** VT + ADV (= *fill*) tapar, taponar

plug-and-play [ˌplʌgən'pleɪ] ADJ (*Comput*) fácil de conectar

plughole ['plʌghəʊl] N desagüe *m*, desaguadero *m* • IDIOM: • **to go down the ~*** irse al traste • **all that work has gone down the ~** todo ese trabajo se ha ido al traste

plug-in ['plʌg'ɪn] ADJ (*Elec*) enchufable, con enchufe

plug-ugly* [ˌplʌg'ʌglɪ] ADJ feísimo, horrendo

plum [plʌm] N **1** (= *fruit*) ciruela *f*; (*also* **plum tree**) ciruelo *m* • IDIOM: • **to speak with** *or* **have a ~ in one's mouth** (*Brit**) (*hum*) hablar muy engoladamente
2 (= *colour*) color *m* ciruela *or* (*LAm*) guinda
3 (*fig**) • **it's a real ~ (of a) job** es un trabajo fantástico, es un chollo (*Sp**)
CPD ▸ **plum pudding** pudín *m* or budín *m* de pasas ▸ **plum tomato** tomate *m* pera ▸ **plum tree** ciruelo *m*

plumage ['plu:mɪdʒ] N plumaje *m*

plumb [plʌm] N plomo *m*
ADJ vertical, a plomo
ADV **1** (= *vertically*) verticalmente, a plomo
2 (*US**) (= *wholly*) totalmente, completamente • **~ crazy** completamente loco • **he's ~ stupid** es un tonto perdido
3 • **~ in the middle** en el mismo *or* (*Mex*) mero centro • **it hit him ~ on the nose** le dio de lleno en las narices
VT **1** (= *descend to*) sondar
2 (*fig*) sondear • **to ~ the depths of the human mind** penetrar en las profundidades de la mente humana • **to ~ the depths of despair** conocer la mayor desesperación
3 (= *connect plumbing in*) [+ *building*] instalar la fontanería de, instalar las tuberías de
CPD ▸ **plumb bob** plomo *m* ▸ **plumb line** plomada *f*
▸ **plumb in** VT + ADV conectar (con el suministro de agua)

plumbago [plʌm'beɪgəʊ] N (PL: **plumbagos**) plombagina *f*

plumber ['plʌməʳ] N fontanero/a *m/f*, plomero/a *m/f* (*LAm*), gasfitero/a *m/f* (*Chile*)
CPD ▸ **plumber's helper** (*US*), **plumber's mate** (*Brit*) (= *tool*) desatascador *m* de fregaderos; (= *assistant*) ayudante *mf* or aprendiz *mf* de fontanero

plumbic ['plʌmbɪk] ADJ plúmbico, plúmbeo

plumbing ['plʌmɪŋ] N **1** (= *craft*) fontanería *f*, plomería *f* (*LAm*), gasfitería *f* (*Chile*)
2 (= *piping*) tuberías *fpl*, cañerías *fpl*; (= *bathroom fittings*) aparatos *mpl* sanitarios
CPD ▸ **plumbing fixtures** grifería *f*

plumbline ['plʌmlaɪn] N plomada *f*

plume [plu:m] N (= *feather*) pluma *f*; (*on helmet*) penacho *m*; (*fig*) [*of smoke etc*] columna *f*, hilo *m*
VT • **the bird ~s itself** el ave se limpia *or* se arregla las plumas

plumed [plu:md] ADJ [*hat*] con plumas; [*helmet*] empenachado

plummet ['plʌmɪt] N plomada *f*
VI [*bird, plane etc*] caer en picado *or* (*LAm*) en picada; [*temperature, price, sales*] bajar de golpe; [*spirits, morale*] caer a plomo

plummeting ['plʌmɪtɪŋ] ADJ [*prices, profits, sales*] que cae(n) en picado *or* (*LAm*) en picada; [*popularity*] que se va a pique; [*temperatures*] que baja(n) drásticamente

plummy* ['plʌmɪ] ADJ (COMPAR: **plummier**, SUPERL: **plummiest**) (*Brit*) [*voice*] engolado

plump¹ [plʌmp] ADJ (COMPAR: **plumper**, SUPERL: **plumpest**) [*person*] relleno, rollizo; [*face*] llenito, rollizo; [*baby*] rechoncho; [*animal*] gordo; [*fruit, vegetable*] gordo, orondo
VT (= *fatten*) engordar; (= *swell*) hinchar
▸ **plump up** VT + ADV (= *cause to swell*) hinchar; [+ *pillow*] mullir

plump² [plʌmp] ADV de lleno • **it fell ~ on the roof** cayó de lleno en el techo • **to run ~ into sb** dar de cara con algn
VI (= *fall*) caer pesadamente, dejarse caer pesadamente
▸ **plump down** VT + ADV dejar caer • **to ~ o.s. down** desplomarse, dejarse caer pesadamente
VI + ADV • **to ~ down on to a chair** desplomarse en un sillón, dejarse caer pesadamente en un sillón
▸ **plump for*** VI + PREP (= *choose*) decidirse por, optar por; (= *vote for*) votar por

plumpness ['plʌmpnɪs] N [*of person*] lo rollizo, gordura *f*; [*of face*] lo regordete, lo rollizo; [*of fruit, vegetable*] gordura *f*, lo orondo

plunder ['plʌndəʳ] N (= *act*) pillaje *m*, saqueo *m*; (= *loot*) botín *m*
VT pillar, saquear; [+ *tomb*] robar; [+ *safe*] robar (el contenido de) • **they ~ed my cellar** me saquearon la bodega

plunderer ['plʌndərəʳ] N saqueador(a) *m/f*

plundering ['plʌndərɪŋ] N saqueo *m*

plunge [plʌndʒ] N **1** (= *dive*) (*from bank etc*) salto *m*; (*under water*) zambullida *f*; (*by professional diver*) inmersión *f*; (= *bathe*) baño *m* • **the diver rested after each ~** el buzo descansaba después de cada inmersión • **he had a ~ before breakfast** se fue a bañar antes de desayunar
2 (*fig*) [*of currency etc*] caída *f* repentina, desplome *m* • IDIOM: • **to take the ~** aventurarse, dar el paso decisivo; (*hum*) (= *get married*) decidir casarse • **I took the ~ and bought it** me armé de valor y lo compré
3* (= *rash investment*) inversión *f* arriesgada
VT **1** (= *immerse*) sumergir, hundir (**into** en) • **he ~d his hands into the water** hundió las manos en el agua
2 (= *thrust*) arrojar • **he ~d his hand into his pocket** metió la mano bien dentro del bolsillo • **to ~ a dagger into sb's chest** clavar un puñal en el pecho de algn
3 (*fig*) • **to ~ a room into darkness** sumir un cuarto en la oscuridad • **New York was suddenly ~d into darkness** Nueva York se encontró de repente sumida en la oscuridad • **we were ~d into gloom by the news** la noticia nos hundió en la tristeza • **to ~ sb into debt** arruinar a algn
VI **1** (= *dive*) arrojarse, tirarse; (*into water*) lanzarse, zambullirse • **then the submarine ~d** luego el submarino se sumergió • **she ~d into ten metres of water** se zambulló en diez metros de agua
2 (= *fall*) caer, hundirse; [*road, cliff*] precipitarse • **he ~d to his death** tuvo una caída mortal • **he ~d from a fifth storey window** (= *threw himself*) se arrojó desde una ventana del quinto piso; (= *fell*) cayó desde una ventana del quinto piso • **the aircraft ~d into the sea off Dover** el avión cayó al *or* se precipitó en el mar a la altura de Dover
3 [*ship*] cabecear; [*horse*] corcovear
4 [*share prices, currency etc*] desplomarse • **to ~ into debt** sumirse en un mar de deudas
5 (*fig*) (= *rush*) lanzarse, precipitarse • **to ~ forward** precipitarse hacia adelante • **to ~ into one's work** sumirse en el trabajo • **to ~ heedlessly into danger** meterse alegremente en un peligro • **he ~d into a monologue on Plato** se puso a soltar *or* emprendió un monólogo sobre Platón
CPD ▸ **plunge pool** (*in sauna*) piscina *f* de contraste

▸ **plunge down** (VI + PREP) [+ *slope, embankment, ravine*] precipitarse por • **he ~d down a ravine and was trapped** se precipitó por un barranco y quedó atrapado
▸ **plunge in** (VT + ADV) [+ *head, hands*] (= *immerse*) sumergir, hundir; (= *thrust*) hundir
(VI + ADV) **1** (*into water*) zambullirse
2 (*fig*) (= *rush*) lanzarse
plunger ['plʌndʒəʳ] (N) (*Tech*) émbolo *m*; (*for clearing drain*) desatascador *m*
plunging ['plʌndʒɪŋ] (ADJ) • **~ neckline** escote *m* muy bajo
plunk [plʌŋk] (N) (*US*) = **plonk¹**
pluperfect ['plu:'pɜ:fɪkt] (N) (*Ling*) pluscuamperfecto *m*
plural ['plʊərəl] (ADJ) plural • **the ~ form of the noun** la forma del sustantivo en plural
(N) plural *m* • **in the ~** en (el) plural
pluralism ['plʊərəlɪzəm] (N) pluralismo *m*
pluralist ['plʊərəlɪst] (ADJ) pluralista
(N) pluralista *mf*
pluralistic [,plʊərə'lɪstɪk] (ADJ) pluralista
plurality [,plʊə'rælɪtɪ] (N) pluralidad *f* • **by a ~ of votes** por mayoría (simple) de votos
plus [plʌs] (PREP) **1** (*Math*) más, y • **3 ~ 4** 3 más 4 • **we're ~ 500** (*Bridge*) tenemos una ventaja de 500 puntos
2 (= *on top of*) • **~ what I have to do already** además de lo que ya tengo que hacer
(ADJ) **1** (*Math, Elec*) positivo • **a ~ factor** (*fig*) un factor a favor
2 • **twenty ~** veinte y pico, veintitantos • **two pounds ~** dos libras y algo más, más de dos libras • **on earnings of £40,000 ~** de un sueldo de 40.000 libras en adelante
(N) **1** (*Math*) (= *plus sign*) signo *m* (de) más, signo *m* de sumar
2 (*fig*) (= *advantage*) punto *m* a favor • **that is a ~ for him** es un punto a su favor
(CONJ) (= *moreover*) además • **~ we haven't got the money** además, no tenemos el dinero
(CPD) ▸ **plus fours** pantalones *mpl* de golf, pantalones *mpl* holgados de media pierna ▸ **plus one*** acompañante *mf* ▸ **plus point** ventaja *f* • **a ~ point for families is the nearby retail park** una ventaja para las familias es la proximidad de un parque comercial ▸ **plus sign** signo *m* (de) más, signo *m* de sumar
plush [plʌʃ] (N) (= *fabric*) felpa *f*
(ADJ) afelpado; (*fig*) de mucho lujo
plushly ['plʌʃlɪ] (ADV) lujosamente • **a ~ appointed room in an exclusive club** una habitación en un club exclusivo lujosamente terminada *or* con lujoso terminado
plushy* ['plʌʃɪ] (ADJ) de mucho lujo
Plutarch ['plu:tɑ:k] (N) Plutarco
Pluto ['plu:təʊ] (N) (*Astron, Myth*) Plutón *m*
plutocracy [,plu:'tɒkrəsɪ] (N) plutocracia *f*
plutocrat ['plu:təʊkræt] (N) plutócrata *mf*
plutocratic [,plu:təʊ'krætɪk] (ADJ) plutocrático
plutonium [plu:'təʊnɪəm] (N) plutonio *m*
pluviometer [,plu:vɪ'ɒmɪtəʳ] (N) pluviómetro *m*
ply [plaɪ] (VT) **1** [+ *needle, tool*] manejar, emplear; [+ *oars*] emplear; [+ *river, route*] navegar por; (*liter*) [+ *sea*] navegar por, surcar (*liter*) • **to ply one's trade** ejercer su profesión
2 • **to ply sb for information** importunar a algn pidiéndole información • **to ply sb with questions** acosar a algn con preguntas • **to ply sb with drink** no parar de ofrecer de beber a algn
(VI) • **to ply between** ir y venir de • **to ply for hire** ir en busca de clientes
-ply [plaɪ] (ADJ) (*ending in compounds*) • **three-ply wood** madera *f* de tres capas • **three-ply wool** lana *f* de tres cabos
plywood ['plaɪwʊd] (N) madera *f* contrachapada
PM (N ABBR) **1** (*Brit*) = **Prime Minister**
2 (*Jur, Med*) = **post mortem**
3 (= *private message*) MP *m*, privado *m*
(VT ABBR) (= *private message*) mandar un PM *or* un privado a
pm (ADV ABBR) (= **post meridiem**) p.m., de la tarde
PMG (N ABBR) **1** (*Brit*) = **Paymaster General**
2 = **Postmaster General**
PMQs [pi:em'kju:z] (NPL ABBR) (*Brit*) (= **Prime Minister's Questions**) preguntas *fpl* al Primer Ministro
PMS (N ABBR) (= **premenstrual syndrome**) SPM *m*
PMT (N ABBR) (= **premenstrual tension**) SPM *m*
PN, P/N (N ABBR) (= **promissory note**) pagaré *m*
PND (N ABBR) = **postnatal depression**
pneumatic [nju:'mætɪk] (ADJ) neumático
(CPD) ▸ **pneumatic drill** taladradora *f* neumática
pneumatically [nju:'mætɪkəlɪ] (ADV) neumáticamente • **a ~ operated drill** un taladro neumático
pneumococcal vaccine [,nju:məʊkɒkəl'væksi:n] (N) vacuna *f* contra el neumococo
pneumoconiosis [,nju:məʊ,kəʊnɪ'əʊsɪs] (N) neumoconiosis *f*
pneumonia [nju:'məʊnɪə] (N) pulmonía *f*, neumonía *f*
Pnom Penh ['nɒm'pen] (N) = **Phnom Penh**
PO (N ABBR) **1** (= **Post Office**) oficina *f* de correos • **PO Box** apdo., aptdo., CP (*LAm*)
2 (*Aer*) (= **Pilot Officer**) oficial *m* piloto
3 (*Naut*) (= **Petty Officer**) suboficial *m* de marina
po‡ [pəʊ] (N) (*Brit*) orinal *m*
p.o. (N ABBR) (*Brit*) (= **postal order**) g.p., g/p
POA (N ABBR) (*Brit*) (= **Prison Officers' Association**) *sindicato de empleados de cárcel*
(ABBR) (*Comm*) (= **price on application**) el precio a solicitud
poach¹ [pəʊtʃ] (VT) (*Culin*) [+ *egg*] escalfar; [+ *fish etc*] hervir
poach² [pəʊtʃ] (VT) **1** (= *hunt*) cazar en vedado; (= *fish*) pescar en vedado
2 (*fig**) (= *steal*) birlar*, quitar
(VI) (= *hunt*) cazar furtivamente; (= *fish*) pescar furtivamente • **IDIOM:** • **to ~ on sb's preserves** *or* **territory** invadir *or* pisar el terreno a algn
poached [pəʊtʃt] (ADJ) [*egg*] escalfado; [*fish etc*] hervido
poacher¹ ['pəʊtʃəʳ] (N) (= *person*) cazador(a) *m/f* furtivo/a • **~ turned gamekeeper** (*Brit*) (*fig*) *persona que abandona una actividad para hacer todo lo contrario*
poacher² ['pəʊtʃəʳ] (N) (*for eggs*) escalfador *m*
poaching ['pəʊtʃɪŋ] (N) caza *f*/pesca *f* furtiva
POB (ABBR) (= **post office box**) apdo
pochard ['pəʊtʃəd] (N) porrón *m* común
pock [pɒk] (N) (= *pustule*) pústula *f*; (*also* **pockmark**) (= *scar*) picadura *f*, hoyuelo *m*
pocked [pɒkt] (ADJ) = **pockmarked**
pocket ['pɒkɪt] (N) **1** (*in trousers etc*) bolsillo *m*, bolsa *f* (*Mex*) • **with his hands in his ~s** con las manos (metidas) en los bolsillos • **IDIOMS:** • **to have sth/sb in one's ~** tener algo/a algn en el bolsillo • **to line one's ~s** forrarse • **to live in each other's** *or* **one another's ~s** (*Brit*) vivir el uno para el otro, no dejarse ni a sol ni a sombra • **to put one's hand in one's ~** echar mano al bolsillo; ▹ **pick**
2 (*fig*) (= *finances, budget*) • **to have deep ~s** tener muchos posibles, tener las espaldas bien cubiertas • **that hurts his ~** eso le duele en el bolsillo • **to be in ~** salir ganando • **to be £5 in ~** haber ganado 5 libras • **to be out of ~** salir perdiendo • **to be £5 out of ~** haber perdido 5 libras
3 (*Billiards*) tronera *f*
4 (*fig*) • **~ of resistance** foco *m* de resistencia • **~ of warm air** bolsa *f* de aire caliente
(VT) **1** (*lit*) meter *or* guardar en el bolsillo • **IDIOM:** • **to ~ one's pride** aguantarse, tragarse el orgullo
2 (*Billiards*) entronerar
3 (*fig*) embolsar • **he ~ed half the takings** se embolsó la mitad de la recaudación
(CPD) de bolsillo ▸ **pocket battleship** acorazado *m* de bolsillo ▸ **pocket billiards** (*US*) billar *m* americano ▸ **pocket calculator** calculadora *f* de bolsillo ▸ **pocket diary** agenda *f* de bolsillo ▸ **pocket dictionary** diccionario *m* de bolsillo ▸ **pocket edition** edición *f* de bolsillo ▸ **pocket handkerchief** pañuelo *m* (de bolsillo) ▸ **pocket money** dinero *m* para gastos (personales); (*children's*) dinero *m* de bolsillo
pocketbook ['pɒkɪtbʊk] (N) **1** (= *notebook*) cuaderno *m*
2 (*US*) (= *handbag*) bolso *m*, cartera *f* (*LAm*); (= *wallet*) cartera *f*, billetero *m*; (= *purse*) monedero *m*
pocketful ['pɒkɪtfʊl] (N) (PL: **pocketfuls**) • **a ~ of nuts** un bolsillo (lleno) de nueces
pocketknife ['pɒkɪtnaɪf] (N) (PL: **pocketknives**) navaja *f*
pocket-size ['pɒkɪtsaɪz], **pocket-sized** ['pɒkɪtsaɪzd] (ADJ) de bolsillo
pockmark ['pɒkmɑ:k] (N) picadura *f*, hoyuelo *m*
pockmarked ['pɒkmɑ:kt] (ADJ) [*face*] picado de viruelas; [*surface*] marcado de hoyos • **to be ~ with** estar marcado *or* acribillado de
POD (ABBR) = **payment on delivery**
pod [pɒd] (N) vaina *f*
podcast ['pɒdkɑ:st] (PT, PP: **podcast**) (N) podcast *m*
(VI) hacer podcasts *or* un podcast
(VT) • **the show was ~ yesterday** el podcast del programa fue emitido ayer
podcasting ['pɒdkɑ:stɪŋ] (N) podcasting *m*
podgy* ['pɒdʒɪ] (ADJ) (COMPAR: **podgier**, SUPERL: **podgiest**) (*esp Brit*) gordinflón*; [*face*] mofletudo*
podiatrist [pɒ'di:ətrɪst] (N) (*US*) pedicuro/a *m/f*
podiatry [pɒ'di:ətrɪ] (N) (*US*) pedicura *f*
podium ['pəʊdɪəm] (N) (PL: **podiums, podia** ['pəʊdɪə]) podio *m*
podunk ['pəʊdʌŋk] (N) (*US*) (*pej*) (= *backwater, boring provincial town*) pueblucho *m*, pueblo *m* de mala muerte
POE (ABBR) **1** = **port of embarkation**
2 = **port of entry**
poem ['pəʊɪm] (N) (*short*) poesía *f*; (*long, narrative*) poema *m* • **Lorca's ~s** las poesías de Lorca, la obra poética de Lorca
poet ['pəʊɪt] (N) poeta *mf*
(CPD) ▸ **poet laureate** (PL: **poets laureate**) poeta *mf* laureado/a

> **POET LAUREATE**
> El poeta de la Corte, denominado **Poet Laureate**, ocupa un puesto vitalicio al servicio de la Casa Real británica. Era tradición que escribiera poemas conmemorativos para ocasiones oficiales, aunque hoy día esto es poco frecuente. El primer poeta así distinguido fue Ben Jonson, en 1616.

poetaster [,pəʊɪ'tæstəʳ] (N) poetastro *m*
poetess† ['pəʊɪtes] (N) poetisa *f*

P

poetic [pəʊ'etɪk] (ADJ) poético
(CPD) ▸ **poetic justice** justicia *f* divina
▸ **poetic licence, poetic license** (US) licencia *f* poética
poetical [pəʊ'etɪkəl] (ADJ) poético
poetically [pəʊ'etɪkəlɪ] (ADV) poéticamente
poeticize [pəʊ'etɪsaɪz] (VT) (= *enhance*) poetizar, adornar con detalles poéticos; (= *translate into verse*) hacer un poema *or* una versión poética de
poetics [pəʊ'etɪks] (NSING) poética *f*
poetry ['pəʊɪtrɪ] (N) poesía *f* • IDIOM: • ~ **in motion** poesía *f* en movimiento
(CPD) ▸ **poetry magazine** revista *f* de poesía
▸ **poetry reading** recital *m or* lectura *f* de poesías
po-faced* [,pəʊ'feɪst] (ADJ) que mira con desaprobación, severo
pogo ['pəʊgəʊ] (N) (*Mus*) pogo *m*
(VI) (= *dance*) bailar pogo
pogrom ['pɒgrəm] (N) pogrom *m*
poignancy ['pɔɪnjənsɪ] (N) patetismo *m*
poignant ['pɔɪnjənt] (ADJ) conmovedor, patético
poignantly ['pɔɪnjəntlɪ] (ADV) [*describe, write, speak*] de modo conmovedor
poinsettia [pɔɪn'setɪə] (N) flor *f* de pascua
point [pɔɪnt] (N) **1** (*Geom*) (= *dot*) punto *m*; (= *decimal point*) punto *m* decimal, coma *f* • **two ~ six (2.6)** dos coma seis (2,6)
2 (*on scale, thermometer*) punto *m* • **boiling/ freezing ~** punto de ebullición/congelación • **the thermometer went up three ~s** el termómetro subió tres grados • **the index is down three ~s** el índice bajó tres enteros • **the shares went down two ~s** las acciones bajaron dos enteros
3 (*on compass*) cuarta *f*, grado *m* • **from all ~s of the compass** desde los cuatro rincones del mundo
4 [*of needle, pencil, knife etc*] punta *f*; [*of pen*] puntilla *f* • **to put a ~ on a pencil** sacar punta a un lápiz • **a star with five ~s** una estrella de cinco puntas • **at the ~ of a sword** a punta de espada • **with a sharp ~** puntiagudo • IDIOM: • **not to put too fine a ~ on it** (= *frankly*) hablando sin rodeos
5 (= *place*) punto *m*, lugar *m* • **he had reached the ~ of resigning** había llegado al punto de la dimisión • **this was the low/high ~ of his career** este fue el momento más bajo/el momento cumbre de su carrera • **at all ~s** por todas partes, en todos los sitios • **delivered free to all ~s in Spain** entrega gratuita en cualquier punto de España • **the train stops at Carlisle and all ~s south** el tren para en Carlisle y todas las estaciones al sur • **at this ~** (*in space*) aquí, allí; (*in time*) en este *or* aquel momento • **when it comes to the ~** en el momento de la verdad • **when it came to the ~ of paying ...** cuando llegó la hora de pagar ..., a la hora de pagar ... • **there was no ~ of contact between them** no existía ningún nexo de unión entre ellos • **to be on** *or* **at the ~ of death** estar a punto de morir • **~ of departure** (*lit, fig*) punto *m* de partida • **~ of entry** (*into a country*) punto *m* de entrada, paso *m* fronterizo • **from that ~ on ...** de allí en adelante ... • **to reach the ~ of no return** (*lit, fig*) llegar al punto sin retorno • **to be on the ~ of doing sth** estar a punto de hacer algo • **abrupt to the ~ of rudeness** tan brusco que resulta grosero • **up to a ~** (= *in part*) hasta cierto punto, en cierta medida • **at the ~ where the road forks** donde se bifurca el camino
6 (= *counting unit*) (*in Sport, test*) punto *m* • **~s against** puntos *mpl* en contra • **~s for** puntos *mpl* a favor • **to win on ~s** ganar por puntos • **to give sth/sb ~s out of ten** dar a algo/algn un número de puntos sobre diez • **to score ten ~s** marcar diez puntos
7 (= *most important thing*) • **the ~ is that ...** el caso es que ... • **that's the whole ~** • **that's just the ~!** ¡eso es!, ¡ahí está! • **the ~ of the joke/story** la gracia del chiste/cuento • **to be beside the ~** no venir al caso • **it is beside the ~ that ...** no importa que (+ *subjun*) • **do you get the ~?** ¿entiendes por dónde voy *or* lo que quiero decir? • **to miss the ~** no comprender • **that's not the ~** esto no viene al caso, no es eso • **to get off the ~** salirse del tema • **his remarks were to the ~** sus observaciones venían al caso • **an argument very much to the ~** un argumento muy a propósito • **that is hardly to the ~** eso apenas hace al caso • **to come** *or* **get to the ~** ir al grano • **to get back to the ~** volver al tema • **to keep** *or* **stick to the ~** no salirse del tema • **to speak to the ~** (= *relevantly*) hablar acertadamente, hablar con tino
8 (= *purpose, use*) [*of action, visit*] finalidad *f*, propósito *m* • **it gave ~ to the argument** hizo ver la importancia del argumento • **there's little ~ in telling him** no merece la pena *or* no tiene mucho sentido decírselo • **there's no ~ in staying** no tiene sentido quedarse • **a long story that seemed to have no ~ at all** una larga historia que no parecía venir al caso en absoluto • **to see the ~ of sth** encontrar *or* ver sentido a algo, entender el porqué de algo • **I don't see the ~ of** *or* **in doing that** no veo qué sentido tiene hacer eso • **what's the ~?** ¿para qué?, ¿a cuento de qué? • **what's the ~ of** *or* **in trying?** ¿de qué sirve intentar?
9 (= *detail, argument*) punto *m* • **the ~s to remember are ...** los puntos a retener son los siguientes ... • **to carry** *or* **gain** *or* **win one's ~** salirse con la suya • **five-point plan** proyecto *m* de cinco puntos • **to argue ~ by ~** razonar punto por punto • **in ~ of fact** en realidad, el caso es que • **I think she has a ~** creo que tiene un poco de razón • **you've got** *or* **you have a ~ there!** ¡tienes razón!, ¡es cierto! (*LAm*) • **the ~ at issue** el asunto, el tema en cuestión • **to make one's ~** convencer • **you've made your ~** nos *etc* has convencido • **he made the following ~s** dijo lo siguiente • **to make the ~ that ...** hacer ver *or* comprender que ... • **to make a ~ of doing sth** • **make it a ~ to do sth** poner empeño en hacer algo • **on this ~** sobre este punto • **on that ~** en cuanto a eso • **on that ~ we agree** sobre eso estamos de acuerdo • **to differ on a ~** no estar de acuerdo en un particular • **to press the ~** insistir (**that** en que) • **to stretch a ~** hacer una excepción • **I take your ~** acepto lo que dices • **~ taken!** ¡de acuerdo!
10 • **~ of view** punto *m* de vista • **from the ~ of view of** desde el punto de vista de • **to see** *or* **understand sb's ~ of view** comprender el punto de vista de algn • **to look at a matter from all ~s of view** considerar una cuestión bajo todos sus aspectos • **to come round to sb's ~ of view** adoptar el criterio de algn
11 (= *matter*) cuestión *f* • **~ of detail** detalle *m* • **~ of honour** cuestión *f or* punto *m* de honor • **~ of interest** punto *m* interesante • **~ of law** cuestión *f* de derecho • **~ of order** cuestión *f* de procedimiento • **a ~ of principle** una cuestión de principios
12 (= *characteristic*) cualidad *f* • **what ~s should I look for?** ¿qué puntos debo buscar? • **bad ~s** cualidades *fpl* malas • **good ~s** cualidades *fpl* buenas • **he has his ~s** tiene algunas cualidades buenas • **tact isn't one of his strong ~s** la discreción no es uno de sus (puntos) fuertes • **it was always his strong ~** siempre ha sido su punto fuerte • **weak ~** flaco *m*, punto *m* flaco, punto *m* débil
13 points (*Brit*) (*Rail*) agujas *fpl*; (*Aut*) platinos *mpl*
14 (*Brit*) (*Elec*) (*also* **power point**) toma *f* de corriente, tomacorriente *m* (*S. Cone*)
15 (*Geog*) punta *f*, promontorio *m*, cabo *m*
16 (*Typ*) (= *punctuation mark*) punto *m* • **9 ~ black** (*Typ*) negritas *fpl* del cuerpo 9
17 (*Ballet*) (*usu pl*) punta *f* • **to dance on ~s** bailar sobre las puntas
(VT) **1** (= *aim, direct*) apuntar (**at** a) • **to ~ a gun at sb** apuntar a algn con un fusil • **to ~ one's finger at sth/sb** señalar con el dedo algo/a algn • **to ~ one's toes** hacer puntas • **he ~ed the car towards London** puso el coche rumbo a Londres • IDIOM: • **to ~ the finger at sb** señalar con el dedo a algn
2 (= *indicate, show*) señalar, indicar • **would you ~ me in the direction of the town hall?** ¿me quiere decir dónde está el ayuntamiento? • **we ~ed him in the right direction** le indicamos el camino • **to ~ the moral that ...** subrayar la moraleja de que ... • **to ~ the way** (*lit, fig*) señalar el camino
3 (*Constr*) [+ *wall*] rejuntar
4 [+ *text*] puntuar; [+ *Hebrew etc*] puntar
(VI) **1** (*lit*) señalar • **to ~ at** *or* **towards sth/sb** (*with finger*) señalar algo/a algn con el dedo • **the car isn't ~ing in the right direction** el coche no va en la dirección correcta • **it ~s (to the) north** apunta hacia el norte • **the hands ~ed to midnight** las agujas marcaban las 12 de la noche
2 (*fig*) (= *indicate*) indicar • **everything ~s that way** todo parece indicarlo • **this ~s to the fact that ...** esto indica que ... • **the evidence ~s to her** las pruebas indican que ella es la culpable • **everything ~s to his success** todo anuncia su éxito • **everything ~s to the festival being a lively one** el festival se anuncia animado
3 • **to ~ to sth** (= *call attention to*) señalar algo
4 [*dog*] mostrar la caza, parar
(CPD) ▸ **point duty** (*Brit*) (*Police*) control *m* de la circulación • **to be on ~ duty** dirigir la circulación *or* el tráfico ▸ **point man** (= *spokesman*) portavoz *m* ▸ **point of reference** punto *m* de referencia ▸ **point of sale** punto *m* de venta ▸ **points decision** (*Boxing*) decisión *f* a los puntos ▸ **points failure** (*Brit*) (*Rail*) fallo *m* en el sistema de agujas ▸ **points system** (*gen*) sistema *m* de puntos; (*Aut*) *sistema de penalización por las infracciones cometidas por un conductor que puede llevar a determinadas sanciones (p. ej. la retirada del permiso de conducir)* ▸ **points victory, points win** victoria *f* a los puntos; ▹ **point-of-sale**
▸ **point out** (VT + ADV) **1** (= *show*) señalar • **to ~ out sth to sb** señalar algo a algn
2 (= *explain*) señalar • **to ~ out sb's mistakes** señalar los errores de algn • **to ~ out that** señalar que • **to ~ out to sb the advantages of a car** señalar *or* hacer notar a algn las ventajas de tener coche • **may I ~ out that ...** permítaseme observar que ...
▸ **point up** (VT + ADV) subrayar, destacar
point-and-click [,pɔɪntənd'klɪk] (ADJ) de señalar y hacer clic • **the familiar point-and-click interface** la interfaz familiar del tipo señalar y hacer clic
point-and-shoot camera [,pɔɪntənd'ʃu:t,kæmərə] (N) cámara *f* de apuntar y disparar
point-blank ['pɔɪnt'blæŋk] (ADJ) **1** [*shot*] (hecho) a quemarropa • **at point-blank range** a bocajarro, a quemarropa
2 [*question*] directo; [*refusal*] rotundo, categórico
(ADV) [*shoot*] a bocajarro, a quemarropa;

[demand] tajantemente, categóricamente; *[refuse]* rotundamente, categóricamente • **to ask sb sth point-blank** preguntar algo a algn a quemarropa

point-by-point ['pɔɪntbaɪ'pɔɪnt] ADJ punto por punto

pointed ['pɔɪntɪd] ADJ **1** *(lit) [chin, nose, shoes]* puntiagudo; *[stick]* de punta afilada; *[hat]* de pico; *(Archit) [arch, window, roof]* apuntado, ojival
2 *(fig) [remark]* mal intencionado; *[criticism]* mordaz; *[question]* directo; *[look]* penetrante • **the book makes ~ reference to his numerous affairs** el libro hace alusiones directas a sus numerosas aventuras amorosas

pointedly ['pɔɪntɪdlɪ] ADV *[say]* intencionadamente; *[ask]* sin rodeos, directamente • **he was staring ~ at the clock** miraba fijamente al reloj sin ocultar su prisa *(or* aburrimiento *etc)* • **she ~ ignored him** lo ignoró intencionadamente *or* aposta • **he was ~ left off the guest list** se lo excluyó de la lista de invitados intencionadamente

pointer ['pɔɪntəʳ] N **1** *(= indicator)* indicador *m*, aguja *f*; *[of balance]* fiel *m*
2 *(= stick)* puntero *m*
3 *(= dog)* perro *m* de muestra
4 *(= clue, indication)* indicación *f*, pista *f* • **it is a ~ to a possible solution** es una indicación *or* pista para una posible solución • **there is at present no ~ to the outcome** por ahora nada indica qué resultado tendrá • **this is a ~ to the guilty man** es una pista que conducirá al criminal
5 *(= advice)* consejo *m*

pointillism ['pwæntɪlɪzəm] N puntillismo *m*

pointing ['pɔɪntɪŋ] N *(Constr) (= action)* rejuntado *m*; *(= mortar)* juntas *fpl*

pointless ['pɔɪntlɪs] ADJ **1** *(= useless)* inútil • **it is ~ to complain** es inútil quejarse, de nada sirve quejarse
2 *(= motiveless)* sin motivo, inmotivado • **an apparently ~ crime** en apariencia, un crimen inmotivado
3 *(= meaningless)* sin sentido • **a ~ existence** una vida sin sentido, una vida que carece de propósito

pointlessly ['pɔɪntlɪslɪ] ADV *(= vainly)* inútilmente; *(= without motive)* sin motivo

pointlessness ['pɔɪntlɪsnɪs] N falta *f* de sentido, inutilidad *f* • **the ~ of war** la insensatez de la guerra

point-of-sale [,pɔɪntəv'seɪl] ADJ *[advertising etc]* en el punto de venta

pointsman ['pɔɪntsmən] N (PL: **pointsmen**) *(Rail)* encargado *m* del cambio de agujas

point-to-point ['pɔɪnttə'pɔɪnt] N *(also* **point-to-point race**) *carrera de caballos a campo traviesa*

pointy* ['pɔɪntɪ] ADJ *[hat, ears, shoes]* picudo, puntiagudo

pointy-headed‡ [,pɔɪntɪ'hedɪd] ADJ *(pej)* intelectual

poise [pɔɪz] N **1** *(= balance)* equilibrio *m*
2 *(= carriage of head, body)* porte *m* • **she dances with such ~** baila con tal elegancia *or* tal garbo
3 *(= composure or dignity of manner)* elegancia *f*, aplomo *m* • **she does it with great ~** lo hace con el mayor aplomo • **he lacks ~** le falta confianza en sí mismo *or* aplomo
VT **1** *(= hold ready or balanced)* equilibrar, balancear • **the rock was ~d on the edge of the cliff** la roca se balanceaba al borde del precipicio • **the hawk was ~d in the air, about to swoop on its prey** el águila se cernía inmóvil en el aire, a punto de caer sobre su presa • **a waitress approached, pencil ~d** se acercó una camarera, lápicero en ristre • **he remained ~d between life and death** permanecía debatiéndose entre la vida y la muerte
2 • **to be ~d** *(fig) (= ready, all set)* estar listo • **they are ~d to attack** *or* **for the attack** están listos para atacar

poised [pɔɪzd] ADJ *(= self-possessed)* sereno, ecuánime

poison ['pɔɪzn] N *(lit, fig)* veneno *m* • **to die of ~** morir envenenado • **to take ~** envenenarse • **they hate each other like ~** se odian a muerte • IDIOM: • **what's your ~?*** *(hum)* ¿qué toma?
VT **1** envenenar; *(chemically)* intoxicar • **the wells were ~ed** habían echado sustancias tóxicas a los pozos
2 *(fig)* envenenar, emponzoñar • **to ~ sb's mind (against sth/sb)** envenenar la mente de algn (contra algo/algn) • **a ~ed chalice** *(esp Brit)* un arma de doble filo
CPD ▸ **poison gas** gas *m* tóxico ▸ **poison ivy** *(= plant)* hiedra *f* venenosa; *(= rash)* urticaria *f* ▸ **poison oak** *(= plant)* zumaque *m* venenoso; *(loosely)* = **poison ivy** ▸ **poison pen letter** anónimo *m* ofensivo

poisoner ['pɔɪznəʳ] N envenenador(a) *m/f*

poisoning ['pɔɪznɪŋ] N *(lit, fig)* envenenamiento *m*, intoxicación *f* • **to die of ~** morir envenenado *or* intoxicado

poisonous ['pɔɪznəs] ADJ **1** *[snake etc]* venenoso; *[substance, plant, fumes etc]* tóxico
2 *(fig) (= damaging)* pernicioso; *(= very bad)* horrible, malísimo • **this ~ propaganda** esta propaganda perniciosa • **the play was ~** la obra fue horrible • **he's a ~ individual** es una persona odiosa

poke¹ [pəʊk] N **1** *(= jab)* empujón *m*, empellón *m*; *(with elbow)* codazo *m*; *(with poker)* hurgonada *f*, hurgonazo *m* • **he gave me a ~ in the ribs** *(with finger)* me hincó el dedo en las costillas; *(with elbow)* me dio un codazo en las costillas • **to give the fire a ~** atizar la lumbre, remover la lumbre
2 • **to have a ~** *(Brit**)* *(= have sex)* echar(se) un polvo**
VT **1** *(= jab with stick, finger etc)* pinchar, clavar; *[+ fire]* hurgar, atizar, remover • **to ~ sb in the ribs** hincar el dedo a algn en las costillas • **to ~ sb with a stick** dar a algn un empujón con un palo • **you nearly ~d me in the eye with that!** ¡casi me saltas un ojo con eso!
2 *(= thrust)* introducir • **to ~ a rag into a tube** meter un trapo en un tubo • **to ~ a stick into a crack** meter un palo en una grieta • **to ~ a stick into the ground** clavar un palo en el suelo • **to ~ one's head out (of a window)** sacar *or* asomar la cabeza (por una ventana); ▹ **nose**
3 *[+ hole]* hacer • **to ~ a hole in a picture** hacer un agujero en un cuadro
4 • **to ~ fun at sb** reírse de algn
5 *(US*) (= punch)* pegar un puñetazo a
VI • **to ~ at sth with a stick** hurgar algo con un bastón

▸ **poke about*, poke around*** VI + ADV *(in drawers, attic etc)* fisgonear, hurgar; *(round shops)* curiosear; *(pej)* fisgar, hacer indagaciones a hurtadillas • **we spent a day poking about in the shops** pasamos un día curioseando en las tiendas • **and now you come poking about!** ¡y ahora te metes a husmear!*

▸ **poke out** VI + ADV *(= stick out)* salir
VT + ADV • **you almost ~d my eye out** casi me saltas el ojo

poke² [pəʊk] N *(esp Scot) (= bag)* saco *m*, bolsa *f*; ▹ **pig**

poker¹ ['pəʊkəʳ] N *(for fire)* atizador *m*, hurgón *m*

poker² ['pəʊkəʳ] N *(Cards)* póker *m*, póquer *m* • IDIOM: • **to have a ~ face** tener una cara impasible, tener una cara de póker; ▹ **stiff**

poker-faced ['pəʊkə'feɪst] ADJ de cara impasible, con cara de póquer • **they looked on poker-faced** miraron impasibles *or* sin expresión

pokerwork ['pəʊkəwɜːk] N *(Brit)* pirograbado *m*

pokeweed ['pəʊkwiːd] N *(US)* hierba *f* carmín

poky ['pəʊkɪ] ADJ (COMPAR: **pokier**, SUPERL: **pokiest**) *(pej)* • **a ~ room** un cuartucho* • **a ~ town** un pueblucho*

pol* [pɒl] N *(US) (= politician)* político/a *m/f*

Polack‡ ['pəʊlæk] N *(pej)* polaco/a *m/f*

Poland ['pəʊlənd] N Polonia *f*

polar ['pəʊləʳ] ADJ *(Elec, Geog)* polar
CPD ▸ **polar bear** oso *m* polar ▸ **polar (ice) cap** casquete *m* polar ▸ **Polar Circle** Círculo *m* Polar

polarity [pəʊ'lærɪtɪ] N **1** *(Elec, Phys)* polaridad *f*
2 *(frm) (fig) (between tendencies, opinions, people)* polaridad *f*

polarization [,pəʊləraɪ'zeɪʃən] N **1** *(Elec, Phys)* polarización *f*
2 *(frm) (fig) [of tendencies, opinions, people]* polarización *f*

polarize ['pəʊləraɪz] VT polarizar
VI polarizarse

Polaroid® ['pəʊlərɔɪd] ADJ Polaroid®
N **1** *(also* **Polaroid camera**) Polaroid® *f*; *(= photograph)* foto *f* de Polaroid®
2 Polaroids *(also* **Polaroid sunglasses**) gafas *fpl* de sol antirreflectantes

polder ['pəʊldəʳ] N pólder *m*

pole¹ [pəʊl] N **1** *(= rod)* palo *m*; *(= flag pole)* asta *f*; *(= telegraph pole)* poste *m*; *(= tentpole)* mástil *m*; *(= curtain pole)* barra *f*; *(for gymnastics)* percha *f*; *(for vaulting, punting)* pértiga *f*, garrocha *f (LAm)*; *(for fencing)* estaca *f*; *[of cart]* vara *f*, lanza *f* • IDIOM: • **to be up the ~†*** estar chiflado*
2 *(= archaic measure) medida de longitud, equivalente a 5,029 m*
VT *[+ punt etc]* impeler con pértiga
CPD ▸ **pole bean** *(US)* judía *f* trepadora ▸ **pole dancer** bailarina *f* de barra (americana) ▸ **pole dancing** baile *m* en barra (americana) ▸ **pole jump** salto *m* de pértiga ▸ **pole position** *(Motor racing)* posición *f* de cabeza en la parrilla de salida, pole *f*; *(fig)* posición *f* de ventaja ▸ **pole vault** salto *m* de pértiga ▸ **pole vaulter** saltador(a) *m/f* de pértiga, pertiguista *mf* ▸ **pole vaulting** salto *m* de pértiga; ▹ **pole-vault**

pole² [pəʊl] N *(Elec, Geog, Astron)* polo *m* • **North/South Pole** Polo *m* Norte/Sur • **from ~ to ~** de polo a polo • IDIOM: • **to be ~s apart** ser polos opuestos
CPD ▸ **Pole Star** Estrella *f* Polar

Pole [pəʊl] N polaco/a *m/f*

poleaxe, poleax *(US)* ['pəʊlæks] VT desnucar; *(fig*)* pasmar, aturdir

poleaxed* ['pəʊlækst] ADJ • IDIOM: • **to be pole-axed** *(esp Brit)* quedarse pasmado

polecat ['pəʊlkæt] N (PL: **polecats** *or* **polecat**) *(Brit)* turón *m*; *(US)* mofeta *f*

Pol. Econ., pol. econ. N ABBR = **political economy**

polemic [pɒ'lemɪk] ADJ polémico
N polémica *f*

polemical [pɒ'lemɪkəl] ADJ polémico

polemicist [pɒ'lemɪsɪst] N polemista *mf*

polemics [pɒ'lemɪks] NSING polémica *f*

pole-vault ['pəʊlvɔːlt] VI saltar con pértiga

P

police [pəˈliːs] NPL policía *fsing* • **to join the ~** hacerse policía • **more than a hundred ~ were called in** más de cien policías hicieron acto de presencia
VT [+ *frontier*] vigilar, patrullar por; [+ *area*] mantener el orden público en; [+ *process*] vigilar, controlar • **the frontier is ~d by UN patrols** la frontera la vigilan las patrullas de la ONU • **the area used to be ~d by Britain** la zona estaba antes bajo control de Gran Bretaña
CPD de policía ▸ **police brutality** violencia *f* policial ▸ **police captain** (*US*) subjefe *mf* ▸ **police car** coche *m* de policía ▸ **police cell** celda *f* (*de una comisaría*) ▸ **police chief** (*Brit*) ≈ jefe/a *m/f* de policía; (*US*) ≈ comisario/a *m/f* ▸ **police constable** (*Brit*) guardia *mf*, policía *mf* ▸ **police court** tribunal *m* de policía, tribunal *m* correccional ▸ **police custody** • **in ~ custody** bajo custodia policial ▸ **police department** (*US*) policía *f* ▸ **police dog** perro *m* policía ▸ **police escort** escolta *f* policial ▸ **police force** cuerpo *m* de policía ▸ **police headquarters** cuartel *m* general de la policía ▸ **police helicopter** helicóptero *m* de la policía ▸ **police inspector** inspector(a) *m/f* de policía ▸ **police officer** policía *mf* ▸ **police presence** presencia *f* policial • **a greater ~ presence is needed to combat street crime** para combatir la delincuencia callejera es necesaria una mayor presencia policial ▸ **police protection** protección *f* policial ▸ **police record** antecedentes *mpl* penales ▸ **police state** estado *m* policía ▸ **police station** comisaría *f* ▸ **police work** trabajo *m* policial *or* de la policía

policeman [pəˈliːsmən] N (PL: **policemen**) policía *m*

policewoman [pəˈliːsˌwʊmən] N (PL: **policewomen**) policía *f*, mujer *f* policía

policing [pəˈliːsɪŋ] N [*of area*] mantenimiento *m* del orden público *or* del servicio de policía; [*of process*] vigilación *f*, control *m*

policy[1] [ˈpɒlɪsɪ] N **1** (*gen, principles*) política *f*; [*of party, at election*] programa *m*; [*of newspaper*] normas *fpl* de conducta • **it's a matter of ~** es cuestión de política • **that's not my ~** ese no es mi sistema • **to change one's ~** cambiar de táctica • **it is a good/bad ~** es buena/mala táctica • **it would be contrary to public ~ to do this** iría en contra del interés nacional hacer esto
2† (= *prudence, prudent procedure*) discreción *f* • **it is ~ to wait a few days** es prudente esperar unos días
CPD ▸ **policy adviser, policy advisor** (*to organization, prime minister*) consejero/a *m/f* político/a ▸ **policy decision** decisión *f* de principio ▸ **policy priority** prioridad *f* política ▸ **policy statement** declaración *f* de política

policy[2] [ˈpɒlɪsɪ] N (*also* **insurance policy**) póliza *f* • **to take out a ~** sacar una póliza, hacerse un seguro

policy-holder [ˈpɒlɪsɪˌhəʊldəʳ] N (*Insurance*) asegurado/a *m/f*

policy-maker [ˈpɒlɪsɪˌmeɪkəʳ] N diseñador(a) *m/f* de políticas

policy-making [ˈpɒlɪsɪˌmeɪkɪŋ] N elaboración *f* de la política a seguir
ADJ [*body, process*] que organiza la política a seguir; [*role*] en la organización de la política a seguir

polio [ˈpəʊlɪəʊ] N poliomielitis *f*, polio *f*
CPD ▸ **polio vaccine** vacuna *f* contra la polio ▸ **polio virus** virus *m inv* de la polio

poliomyelitis [ˈpəʊlɪəʊmaɪəˈlaɪtɪs] N poliomielitis *f*

Polish [ˈpəʊlɪʃ] ADJ polaco
N **1** (*Ling*) polaco *m*
2 • **the ~** (= *people*) los polacos

polish [ˈpɒlɪʃ] N **1** (= *shoe polish*) betún *m*, bola *f* (*Mex*); (= *furniture polish, floor polish*) cera *f*; (= *metal polish*) líquido *m* para limpiar metales; (= *nail polish*) esmalte *m or* laca *f* (para las uñas)
2 (= *act*) • **my shoes need a ~** mis zapatos necesitan una limpieza • **to give sth a ~** dar brillo a algo
3 (= *shine*) lustre *m*, brillo *m* • **high ~** lustre *m* brillante • **the buttons have lost their ~** los botones han perdido su brillo *or* se han deslustrado • **to put a ~ on sth** sacar brillo a algo • **the water takes the ~ off** el agua quita el brillo
4 (*fig*) (= *refinement*) refinamiento *m*; [*of artistry etc*] elegancia *f* • **he lacks ~** le falta refinamiento
VT **1** (*gen*) pulir; [+ *shoes*] limpiar, lustrar (*esp LAm*), bolear (*Mex*), embolar (*Chile*); [+ *floor, furniture*] encerar; [+ *pans, metal, silver*] pulir; (*mechanically, industrially*) pulimentar
2 (*fig*) (*also* **polish up**) (= *improve*) perfeccionar; [+ *manners*] refinar; [+ *style etc*] pulir, limar; [+ *one's Spanish etc*] pulir, perfeccionar
▸ **polish off*** VT + ADV [+ *work, food, drink*] despacharse; [+ *person etc*] liquidar*
▸ **polish up** VT + ADV = polish

polished [ˈpɒlɪʃt] ADJ **1** (*lit*) [*metal, wood*] pulido
2 (*fig*) [*style etc*] pulido, elegante; [*person*] culto, refinado; [*manners*] refinado

polisher [ˈpɒlɪʃəʳ] N (= *person*) pulidor(a) *m/f*; (= *machine*) enceradora *f*

polishing machine [ˈpɒlɪʃɪŋməˌʃiːn] N pulidor *m*; (*for floors*) enceradora *f*

Politburo [ˈpɒlɪtbjʊərəʊ] N Politburó *m*

polite [pəˈlaɪt] ADJ [*person*] cortés, educado; [*smile*] cortés, amable; [*request*] cortés • **he was very ~ to me** fue muy cortés *or* educado conmigo • **I was too ~ to ask** no pregunté por educación *or* cortesía • **he said he liked it but I think he was just being ~** dijo que le gustaba pero creo que lo hizo solo por cumplir • **it's ~ to ask permission** es de buena educación pedir permiso • **it's not ~ to stare** es una falta de educación *or* es de mala educación quedarse mirando a la gente • **his speech received ~ applause** su discurso recibió el aplauso de rigor *or* cortesía • **that's not the sort of thing you do in ~ company** ese no es el tipo de cosa que harías entre gente educada *or* fina • **they sat there making ~ conversation** estaban ahí sentados, dando conversación para quedar bien • **he showed a ~ interest in my work** mostró interés en mi trabajo solo por cumplir • **in ~ society** en la buena sociedad • **that's not a very ~ thing to say** esas cosas no se dicen • **I was trying to think of a ~ way to say no** buscaba una forma de decir "no" sin ofender • **"cosy" is the ~ word for the flat's dimensions** (*iro*) siendo generoso, podría decirse que las dimensiones del piso lo hacen acogedor

politely [pəˈlaɪtlɪ] ADV **1** (= *courteously*) [*ask, listen, refuse*] cortésmente; [*smile*] cortésmente, amablemente • **I sent them a ~ worded letter** les mandé una carta muy correcta
2 (= *out of politeness*) por cortesía • **I ~ overlooked his bad manners** por cortesía, pasé por alto su falta de educación

politeness [pəˈlaɪtnɪs] N cortesía *f*, educación *f* • **to do sth out of ~** hacer algo por cortesía

politic [ˈpɒlɪtɪk] ADJ prudente

political [pəˈlɪtɪkəl] ADJ **1** (*gen*) político
2 (= *politically aware*) • **she was always very ~** siempre tuvo mucha conciencia política • **I'm not ~** no me interesa mucho la política • **the play is very ~** esta obra tiene mucho contenido político
3 (= *expedient, tactical*) estratégico
CPD ▸ **political asylum** asilo *m* político ▸ **political correctness** progresismo *m* ideológico ▸ **political correspondent** corresponsal *mf* político/a ▸ **political economy** economía *f* política ▸ **political editor** editor(a) *m/f* político/a ▸ **political levy** impuesto *m* político ▸ **political party** partido *m* político ▸ **political prisoner** preso/a *m/f* político/a ▸ **political process** proceso *m* político ▸ **political science** ciencias *fpl* políticas ▸ **political scientist** experto/a *m/f* en ciencias políticas

politically [pəˈlɪtɪkəlɪ] ADV políticamente • **~ correct** [*person, attitude, terminology*] políticamente correcto • **~ incorrect** políticamente incorrecto • **~ motivated** [*violence, killing, attack, prosecution*] de carácter político • **to be ~ motivated** [*killing, attack*] tener un carácter político

POLITICALLY CORRECT
Se dice que una persona o su comportamiento es **politically correct** o **PC** cuando sus actitudes o palabras no reflejan ningún desprecio o insulto hacia grupos minoritarios o con algún tipo de desventaja física o social, tales como disminuidos físicos o psíquicos, minorías étnicas, homosexuales, mujeres etc. Los que propugnan el uso de este tipo de lenguaje y actitud políticamente correctos creen que con ello desafían los valores que la sociedad occidental ha tratado de imponer sobre el resto del mundo a lo largo de la historia. Sin embargo, el término **politically correct** se emplea también de forma irónica por las personas que se burlan de este tipo de lenguaje y actitudes por considerarlas excesivas. Entre las expresiones políticamente correctas, algunas de las más conocidas son: **Native American** en vez de **Red Indian** (indio americano), **visually impaired** en vez de **blind** (ciego) y **vertically challenged** en vez de **short** (bajo).

politician [ˌpɒlɪˈtɪʃən] N político/a *m/f*

politicization [pəˌlɪtɪsaɪˈzeɪʃən] N politización *f*

politicize [pəˈlɪtɪsaɪz] VT politizar

politicized [pəˈlɪtɪsaɪzd] ADJ politizado

politicking [ˈpɒlɪtɪkɪŋ] N (*pej*) politiqueo *m*

politico* [pəˈlɪtɪkəʊ] N (PL: **politicos**) político *mf*

politics [ˈpɒlɪtɪks] NSING (= *subject, career*) política *f* • **to go into ~** dedicarse a la política, meterse en política* • **to talk ~** hablar de política
NPL **1** (= *views*) postura *fsing* política • **office ~** relaciones *fpl* de poder en la oficina; ▹ **sexual**
2 (= *political aspects*) • **the ~ of health care** la política *or* los aspectos políticos de la asistencia médica

polity [ˈpɒlɪtɪ] N (= *form of government*) gobierno *m*, forma *f* de gobierno; (= *politically organized state*) estado *m*

polka [ˈpɒlkə] N (PL: **polkas**) (= *dance*) polca *f*
CPD ▸ **polka dot** dibujo *m* de puntos

poll [pəʊl] N **1** (= *voting*) votación *f*; (= *election*) elecciones *fpl* • **in the ~ of 1945** en las elecciones de 1945 • **a ~ was demanded** exigieron una votación, insistieron en que se llevara a cabo una votación • **to head the**

~ obtener la mayoría de los votos • **to take a ~ on sth** someter algo a votación • **a ~ was taken among those present** se llevó a cabo una votación entre los asistentes
2 (= *total votes*) votos *mpl*, votación *f* • **there was a ~ of 84%** el 84% del electorado acudió a las urnas • **the candidate achieved a ~ of 5000 votes** el candidato obtuvo 5000 votos • **the ~ has been a heavy one** ha votado un elevado porcentaje del electorado
3 polls (= *voting place*) urnas *fpl* • **to go to the ~s** acudir a las urnas
4 (= *opinion poll*) encuesta *f*, sondeo *m*; (*Telec*) interrogación *f* • **to take a ~** hacer una encuesta; ▸ **Gallup poll**
(VT) **1** [+ *votes*] obtener • **he ~ed only 50 votes** obtuvo solamente 50 votos
2 (*in opinion poll*) encuestar • **1068 people were ~ed** encuestaron a 1068 personas
3 (= *remove horns from*) [+ *cattle*] descornar
(VI) • **he ~ed badly** obtuvo pocos votos, tuvo escaso apoyo • **we expect to ~ well** esperamos obtener muchos votos
(CPD) ▸ **poll rating** resultado *m* obtenido en las encuestas ▸ **poll taker** (*US*) encuestador(a) *m/f* ▸ **poll tax** (contribución *f* de) capitación *f*; (*Brit*) (*formerly*) impuesto *m* municipal por cabeza

pollack [ˈpɒlək] (N) (PL: **pollacks** *or* **pollack**) abadejo *m*

pollard [ˈpɒləd] (N) árbol *m* desmochado
(VT) desmochar

pollen [ˈpɒlən] (N) polen *m*
(CPD) ▸ **pollen allergy** alergia *f* polínica ▸ **pollen count** recuento *m* polínico ▸ **pollen grain** grano *m* de polen

pollinate [ˈpɒlɪneɪt] (VT) polinizar

pollination [ˌpɒlɪˈneɪʃən] (N) polinización *f*

pollinator [ˈpɒlɪneɪtəʳ] (N) (*Zool*) polinizador(a) *m/f*

polling [ˈpəʊlɪŋ] (N) votación *f* • **~ will be on Thursday** las elecciones se celebrarán el jueves, se votará el jueves • **~ has been heavy** ha votado un elevado porcentaje de los electores
(CPD) ▸ **polling booth** cabina *f* electoral ▸ **polling day** día *m* de las elecciones ▸ **polling place** (*US*) = **polling station** ▸ **polling station** centro *m* electoral

polliwog [ˈpɒlɪwɒg] (N) (*US*) (*Zool*) renacuajo *m*

pollster [ˈpəʊlstəʳ] (N) encuestador(a) *m/f*

pollutant [pəˈluːtənt] (N) contaminante *m*, agente *m* contaminador

pollute [pəˈluːt] (VT) **1** contaminar • **to become ~d** contaminarse (**with** de)
2 (*fig*) corromper

polluted [pəˈluːtɪd] (ADJ) [*water, air, land*] contaminado • **to be ~ with sth** estar contaminado con algo

polluter [pəˈluːtəʳ] (N) contaminador(a) *m/f*

pollution [pəˈluːʃən] (N) **1** contaminación *f*, polución *f*
2 (*fig*) corrupción *f*
(CPD) ▸ **pollution control** control *m* de la contaminación ▸ **pollution levels** niveles *mpl* de contaminación

polly* [ˈpɒlɪ] (N) (*Australia*) (= *politician*) político/a *m/f*

Pollyanna [pɒlɪˈænə] (N) optimista *mf* redomado/a

pollywog [ˈpɒlɪwɒg] (N) = **polliwog**

polo [ˈpəʊləʊ] (N) (*Sport*) polo *m*
(CPD) ▸ **polo neck (sweater)** (jersey *m* de) cuello *m* vuelto *or* cisne ▸ **polo player** jugador(a) *m/f* de polo ▸ **polo pony** poney *m* de polo ▸ **polo shirt** polo *m*

polonaise [ˌpɒləˈneɪz] (N) polonesa *f*

polo-necked [ˈpəʊləʊnekt] (ADJ) con cuello cisne *or* vuelto

polonium [pəˈləʊnɪəm] (N) polonio *m*

poltergeist [ˈpɔːltəgaɪst] (N) duende *m*

poltroon†† [pɒlˈtruːn] (N) cobarde *mf*

poly* [ˈpɒlɪ] (N) (*Brit*) = **polytechnic**

poly... [pɒlɪ] (PREFIX) poli..., multi...

polyamorous [ˌpɒlɪˈæmərəs] (ADJ) [*relationship, lifestyle, person*] poliamor (*inv*)

polyamory [ˌpɒlɪˈæmərɪ] (N) poliamor *m*

polyandrous [ˌpɒlɪˈændrəs] (ADJ) poliándrico

polyandry [ˈpɒlɪændrɪ] (N) poliandria *f*

polyanthus [ˌpɒlɪˈænθəs] (N) prímula *f*, primavera *f*, hierba *f* de San Pablo mayor

poly bag* [ˈpɒlɪbæg] (N) bolsa *f* de plástico *or* polietileno

polychromatic [ˌpɒlɪkrəʊˈmætɪk] (ADJ) policromo

polyclinic [ˌpɒlɪˈklɪnɪk] (N) policlínico *m*

polycotton [ˈpɒlɪˌkɒtən] (N) polycotton *m*, *mezcla de algodón y poliester*

polyester [ˌpɒlɪˈestəʳ] (N) poliéster *m*
(ADJ) de poliéster

polyethylene [ˌpɒlɪˈeθəliːn] (N) polietileno *m*

polygamist [pɒˈlɪgəmɪst] (N) polígamo *m*

polygamous [pɒˈlɪgəməs] (ADJ) polígamo

polygamy [pɒˈlɪgəmɪ] (N) poligamia *f*

polygenesis [ˌpɒlɪˈdʒenɪsɪs] (N) poligénesis *f*

polyglot [ˈpɒlɪglɒt] (ADJ) polígloto
(N) políglota/a *m/f*

polygon [ˈpɒlɪgən] (N) polígono *m*

polygonal [pɒˈlɪgənl] (ADJ) poligonal

polygraph [ˈpɒlɪgrɑːf] (N) polígrafo *m*, detector *m* de mentiras
(CPD) ▸ **polygraph test** prueba *f* del polígrafo

polyhedron [ˌpɒlɪˈhiːdrən] (N) (PL: **polyhedrons** *or* **polyhedra** [ˌpɒlɪˈhiːdrə]) poliedro *m*

polymath [ˈpɒlɪmæθ] (N) polímata *mf*, erudito/a *m/f*

polymer [ˈpɒlɪməʳ] (N) polímero *m*

polymeric [ˌpɒlɪˈmerɪk] (ADJ) polimérico

polymerization [ˈpɒlɪməraɪˈzeɪʃən] (N) polimerización *f*

polymorphic [ˌpɒlɪˈmɔːfɪk] (ADJ) polimorfo

polymorphism [ˌpɒlɪˈmɔːfɪzəm] (N) polimorfismo *m*

Polynesia [ˌpɒlɪˈniːzɪə] (N) Polinesia *f*

Polynesian [ˌpɒlɪˈniːzɪən] (ADJ) polinesio
(N) polinesio/a *m/f*

polynomial [ˌpɒlɪˈnəʊmɪəl] (ADJ) polinomio
(N) polinomio *m*

polyp [ˈpɒlɪp] (N) (*Med*) pólipo *m*

Polyphemus [ˌpɒlɪˈfiːməs] (N) Polifemo

polyphonic [ˌpɒlɪˈfɒnɪk] (ADJ) (*Mus*) polifónico

polyphonist [pəˈlɪfənɪst] (N) (*Mus*) polifonista *mf*

polyphony [pəˈlɪfənɪ] (N) polifonía *f*

polypropylene [ˌpɒlɪˈprɒpɪliːn] (N) polipropileno *m*

polypus [ˈpɒlɪpəs] (N) (PL: **polypi** [ˈpɒlɪpaɪ]) (*Zool*) pólipo *m*

polysemic [ˌpɒlɪˈsiːmɪk], **polysemous** [pəˈlɪsəməs] (ADJ) polisémico

polysemy [pəˈlɪsəmɪ] (N) polisemia *f*

polystyrene [ˌpɒlɪˈstaɪriːn] (N) (*esp Brit*) poliestireno *m*
(ADJ) de poliestireno

polysyllabic [ˈpɒlɪsɪˈlæbɪk] (ADJ) polisílabo

polysyllable [ˈpɒlɪˌsɪləbl] (N) polisílabo *m*

polytechnic [ˌpɒlɪˈteknɪk] (N) (*Brit*) (*formerly*) escuela *f* politécnica, politécnico *m*

polytheism [ˈpɒlɪθiːɪzəm] (N) politeísmo *m*

polytheistic [ˌpɒlɪθiːˈɪstɪk] (ADJ) politeísta

polythene [ˈpɒlɪθiːn] (*Brit*) (N) polietileno *m*
(CPD) ▸ **polythene bag** bolsa *f* de plástico *or* polietileno

polyunsaturate [ˌpɒlɪʌnˈsætʃərɪt] (N) poliinsaturado *m*

polyunsaturated [ˌpɒlɪʌnˈsætʃəreɪtɪd] (ADJ) poliinsaturado

polyurethane [ˌpɒlɪˈjʊərɪθeɪn] (N) poliuretano *m*

polyvalent [pəˈlɪvələnt] (ADJ) polivalente

polyvinyl [ˈpɒlɪvaɪnl] (N) polivinilo *m*

pom[1]* [pɒm] (N) = **pommy**

pom[2]* [pɒm] (N) (= *dog*) perro *m* de Pomerania, lulú *mf* (de Pomerania)

pomade [pəˈmɑːd] (N) pomada *f*

pomander [pəʊˈmændəʳ] (N) *recipiente de porcelana que contiene hierbas aromáticas*

pomegranate [ˈpɒməgrænɪt] (N) (= *fruit*) granada *f*; (= *tree*) granado *m*

pomelo [ˈpɒmɪˌləʊ] (N) (PL: **pomelos**) pomelo *m*

Pomeranian [ˌpɒməˈreɪnɪən] (N) (= *dog*) pomerano *m*

pommel [ˈpʌml] (N) pomo *m*
(VT) = **pummel**

pommy‡ [ˈpɒmɪ] (*Australia*) (*pej*) (ADJ) inglés
(N) inglés/esa *m/f*

pomp [pɒmp] (N) pompa *f* • **~ and circumstance** pompa *f* y solemnidad

pompadour [ˈpɒmpədʊəʳ] (N) (*Hist*) (= *hairstyle*) peinado *m* pompadour

Pompeii [pɒmˈpeɪɪ] (N) Pompeya *f*

Pompey [ˈpɒmpɪ] (N) Pompeyo

pom-pom [ˈpɒmpɒm], **pom-pon** [ˈpɒmpɒn] (N) (*on hat etc*) borla *f*, pompón *m*

pomposity [pɒmˈpɒsɪtɪ] (N) pomposidad *f*

pompous [ˈpɒmpəs] (ADJ) [*person*] pretencioso; [*occasion*] ostentoso; [*language*] ampuloso, inflado

pompously [ˈpɒmpəslɪ] (ADV) [*strut, stride*] pomposamente; [*reply, speak*] pomposamente, ampulosamente

ponce‡ [pɒns] (*Brit*) (N) **1** (= *pimp*) proxeneta *m*, chulo *m* (*Sp**)
2 (*pej*) (= *homosexual*) marica* *m*
▸ **ponce about‡**, **ponce around‡** (VI + ADV) (*Brit*) chulear*

poncho [ˈpɒntʃəʊ] (N) (PL: **ponchos**) poncho *m*, manta *f*, ruana *f* (*Col, Ven*), sarape *m* (*Mex*), jorongo *m* (*Mex*)

poncy‡ [ˈpɒnsɪ] (ADJ) (*Brit*) cursi*

pond [pɒnd] (N) (= *natural*) charca *f*; (*artificial*) estanque *m* • IDIOM: • **he's a big fish** *or* (*US*) **big frog in a small ~** es el tuerto en el país de los ciegos, es un reyezuelo (*en algún lugar o en algo poco importante*)
(CPD) ▸ **pond life** fauna *f* de las charcas/estanques ▸ **pond weed** planta *f* acuática

ponder [ˈpɒndəʳ] (VT) considerar, sopesar
(VI) reflexionar *or* meditar (**on, over** sobre)

ponderable [ˈpɒndərəbl] (ADJ) ponderable

ponderous [ˈpɒndərəs] (ADJ) pesado

ponderously [ˈpɒndərəslɪ] (ADV) pesadamente; [*say etc*] en tono pesado, lentamente y con énfasis

ponderousness [ˈpɒndərəsnəs] (N) (= *slow laboriousness*) lentitud *f* y torpeza; (= *heaviness*) pesadez *f*

pone [pəʊn] (N) (*US*) pan *m* de maíz

pong* [pɒŋ] (*Brit*) (N) peste *f*
(VI) apestar

pongy* [ˈpɒŋɪ] (ADJ) (*Brit*) foche*, maloliente

poniard [ˈpɒnjəd] (N) (= *liter*) puñal *m*

pontiff [ˈpɒntɪf] (N) pontífice *m*

pontifical [pɒnˈtɪfɪkəl] (ADJ) pontificio, pontifical; (*fig*) dogmático, autoritario

pontificate (N) [pɒnˈtɪfɪkɪt] (*Rel*) pontificado *m*
(VI) [pɒnˈtɪfɪkeɪt] pontificar

Pontius Pilate [ˈpɒnʃəsˈpaɪlət] (N) Poncio Pilato

pontoon[1] [pɒnˈtuːn] (N) pontón *m*
(CPD) ▸ **pontoon bridge** puente *m* de

P

pontones
pontoon[2] ['pɒn'tu:n] N (*Brit*) (*Cards*) veintiuna *f*
pony ['pəʊnɪ] N **1** poney *m*, potro *m*
2 (*Brit‡*) ≈ 25 libras
3 (*US**) (*Scol*) chuleta* *f*
CPD ▸ **pony club** *club ecuestre donde se monta en poni* ▸ **pony trekking** excursión *f* en poney
ponytail ['pəʊnɪteɪl] N cola *f* de caballo, coleta *f*
poo‡ [pu:] (*Brit*) (*baby talk*) N caca‡ *f* • **to do a poo** hacer caca‡
VT • **to poo one's pants** hacerse caca encima*
VI hacer caca*
pooch* [pu:tʃ] N perro *m*
poodle ['pu:dl] N caniche *mf*
poof‡ [pʊf] N (*Brit*) (*pej*) maricón*‡ *m*
poofter‡ ['pʊftəʳ] N (*Brit*) (*pej*) = **poof**
poofy‡ ['pʊfɪ] ADJ (*Brit*) (*pej*) de maricón*‡
pooh [pu:] EXCL ¡bah!
N, VT, VI = **poo**
pooh-pooh [pu:'pu:] VT despreciar; [+ *proposal etc*] rechazar con desdén; [+ *danger etc*] menospreciar, negar la importancia de
pool[1] [pu:l] N **1** (*natural*) charca *f*; (*artificial*) estanque *m*; (= *swimming pool*) piscina *f*, alberca *f* (*Mex*), pileta *f* (de natación) (*S. Cone*); (*in river*) pozo *m*
2 [*of spilt liquid*] charco *m*; (*fig*) [*of light*] foco *m*
CPD ▸ **pool attendant** encargado/a *m/f* de la piscina
pool[2] [pu:l] N **1** (= *common fund*) fondo *m* (común); (*Cards*) polla *f*
2 (= *supply, source*) reserva *f*; [*of genes etc*] fondo *m*, reserva *f* • **an untapped ~ of ability** una reserva de inteligencia no utilizada; ▹ **car, typing**
3 • **the ~s** (*Brit*) (= *football pools*) las quinielas (*Sp*) • **to do the (football) ~s** hacer las quinielas
4 (= *form of snooker*) billar *m* americano • **to shoot ~** (*US*) jugar al billar americano • IDIOM: • **that's dirty ~** (*US**) eso no es jugar limpio
5 (*Comm*) fondos *mpl* comunes; (*US*) (= *monopoly, trust*) consorcio *m* • **coal and steel ~** comunidad *f* de carbón y acero
VT juntar, poner en común
CPD ▸ **pool hall, pool room** sala *f* de billar ▸ **pool player** jugador(a) *m/f* de billar americano ▸ **pool table** mesa *f* de billar
poop[1] [pu:p] (*Naut*) N popa *f*
CPD ▸ **poop deck** toldilla *f*, castillo *m* de popa
poop[2]**‡** [pu:p] N (= *excrement*) caca‡ *f*
poop[3]***** [pu:p] N (*US*) (= *information*) onda* *f*, información *f*
pooped‡ [pu:pt] ADJ • **to be ~** (*esp US*) (= *tired*) estar hecho polvo*; (= *drunk*) estar ajumado*
pooper-scooper* ['pu:pə,sku:pəʳ], **poop-scoop*** ['pu:psku:p] N caca-can* *m*
poo-poo‡ ['pu:'pu:] N caca‡ *f*
poor [pʊəʳ] ADJ (COMPAR: **poorer**, SUPERL: **poorest**) **1** (= *not rich*) [*person, family, country*] pobre • **a ~ woman** una mujer pobre • **a ~ man** un pobre • **~ people** gente *f* pobre, personas *fpl* pobres • **pewter was the ~ man's silver** el peltre era la plata de los pobres • **they thought that cinema was a** *or* **the ~ relation of theatre** pensaban que el cine era el pariente pobre del teatro • **to be the ~er (for sth)**: • **the nation is the ~er for her death** la nación ha sufrido una gran pérdida con su muerte • **it left me £5 the ~er** me dejó con 5 libras de menos • IDIOM: • **to be as ~ as a church mouse** ser más pobre que las ratas
2 (= *inferior, bad*) [*goods, service*] malo, de mala calidad • **the wine was ~** el vino era malo *or* de mala calidad • **Britain's ~ economic performance** el bajo rendimiento económico obtenido por Gran Bretaña • **she has a very ~ attendance record** su expediente es muy malo en lo que a asistencia se refiere • **they had made a ~ job of it** habían hecho una chapuza* • **to be a ~ imitation of sth** ser una burda *or* pobre imitación de algo • **his decision shows ~ judgment** su decisión denota poco juicio • **to have a ~ opinion of sb** tener un concepto poco favorable de algn • **to come a ~ second (to sth/sb)**: • **he came a ~ second in the final race** quedó el segundo en la carrera final, a bastante distancia del primero • **his family comes a ~ second to his career** su familia queda relegada a segundo lugar tras su carrera
3 (= *deficient*) [*memory*] malo; [*soil*] pobre, estéril; [*harvest*] pobre, escaso • **I had a ~ education** la educación que recibí no fue muy buena • **many people eat a ~ diet** mucha gente tiene una dieta pobre • **"poor"** (*Scol*) (*as mark*) "deficiente" • **soils that are ~ in zinc** suelos que son pobres en zinc *or* que tienen bajo contenido en zinc
4 (= *untalented*) • **he was a ~ actor** era un actor flojo • **I'm a ~ traveller** lo de viajar no lo llevo muy bien • **she was a very ~ swimmer** no era buena nadadora • **to be ~ at maths** no ser muy bueno en matemáticas • **we are ~ at marketing ourselves** no somos muy buenos a la hora de darnos publicidad
5 (= *unfortunate*) pobre • **the ~ child was hungry** el pobre niño tenía hambre • **~ little thing!** ¡pobrecito!, ¡pobre criaturita! • **~ (old) you!** • **you ~ (old) thing!** ¡pobrecito! • **~ Mary's lost all her money** la pobre María ha perdido todo su dinero • **he's very ill, ~ chap** está grave el pobre • **a ~ little rich girl** una pobre niña rica; ▹ **devil**
NPL • **the ~** los pobres • **the rural/urban ~** los pobres de las zonas rurales/urbanas
CPD ▸ **poor box** cepillo *m* de las limosnas ▸ **poor law** (*Hist*) ley *f* de asistencia pública ▸ **poor white** (*US*) *persona pobre de raza blanca*; ▹ **relief**

> **POOR**
>
> **Position of "pobre"**
>
> *You should generally put* **pobre** *after the noun when you mean* **poor** *in the sense of "not rich" and before the noun in the sense of "unfortunate":*
>
> **It's a poor area**
> Es una región pobre
> **The poor boy was trembling**
> El pobre chico estaba temblando
>
> *For further uses and examples, see main entry.*

poorhouse ['pʊəhaʊs] N (PL: **poorhouses** ['pʊəhaʊzɪz]) asilo *m* de los pobres
poorly ['pʊəlɪ] ADV **1** (= *badly*) [*designed, equipped*] mal • **the shares have performed ~** el rendimiento de las acciones ha sido bajo • **to do ~**: • **she did ~ in history** sacó mala nota en historia • **she did ~ at school** sacaba malas notas en el colegio • **the room/road was ~ lit** la habitación/la carretera estaba mal iluminada • **the job was ~ paid** el trabajo estaba mal pagado • **he was ~ paid** le pagaban poco • **his army was ~ trained** su ejército estaba poco capacitado
2 (= *meagrely, shabbily*) pobremente • **to be ~ dressed** ir pobremente vestido
ADJ (*esp Brit*) (= *ill*) enfermo • **to be/feel ~** estar/encontrarse mal, estar/encontrarse pachucho *or* malucho* • **to look ~** tener mal aspecto
poorness ['pʊənɪs] N **1** (= *poverty*) pobreza *f*
2 (= *poor quality*) mala calidad *f* • **~ of spirit** apocamiento *m*, mezquindad *f*
poor-spirited ['pʊə'spɪrɪtɪd] ADJ apocado, mezquino
poove‡ [pu:v] N (*Brit*) = **poof**
pop[1] [pɒp] N **1** (= *sound*) pequeño estallido *m*; [*of cork*] taponazo *m*; [*of fastener etc*] ruido *m* seco; (= *imitative sound*) ¡pum!
2* (= *drink*) refresco *m*, gaseosa *f* (*Sp*)
3 (= *try*) • **to have** *or* **take a pop at (doing) sth*** probar (a hacer) algo
4 • **to have** *or* **take a pop at sth/sb*** (= *criticize*) criticar algo/a algn
5 • **the drinks go for $3.50 a pop** (*esp US**) las bebidas se venden a 3.50 dólares cada una
ADV • **to go pop** [*balloon*] reventar, hacer ¡pum!; [*cork*] salir disparado, hacer ¡pum!
VT **1** [+ *balloon*] hacer reventar; [+ *cork*] hacer saltar • IDIOM: • **to pop one's clogs** (*Brit**) (*hum*) estirar la pata*
2* (= *put*) poner (rápidamente) • **to pop sth into a drawer** meter algo (rápidamente) en un cajón • **to pop pills** drogarse (con pastillas) • IDIOM: • **to pop the question** declararse
3‡ (= *pawn*) empeñar
VI **1** [*balloon*] reventar; [*cork*] saltar, salir disparado • **there were corks popping all over** los tapones saltaban por todas partes • **to make sb's eyes pop** (*fig*) dejar a algn con los ojos fuera de órbita • **his eyes nearly popped out of his head** (*in amazement*) se le saltaban los ojos • **my ears popped on landing** al aterrizar se me taponaron los oídos
2* (= *go quickly or suddenly*) • **we popped over to see them** fuimos a hacerles una breve visita • **let's pop round to Joe's** vamos un momento a casa de Joe
▸ **pop back*** VT + ADV [+ *lid etc*] poner de nuevo, volver a poner
VI + ADV volver un momento
▸ **pop in*** VI + ADV entrar un momento • **to pop in to see sb** pasar por casa de algn • **I just popped in** no tuve la intención de quedarme • **I just popped in to say hello** solo vine a saludarte
▸ **pop off*** VI + ADV **1** (= *die*) estirar la pata*
2 (= *leave*) irse, marcharse
▸ **pop on*** VT + ADV [+ *light, oven*] poner, encender; [+ *kettle*] poner (a calentar); [+ *clothing*] ponerse (de prisa) • **I'll just pop my hat on** voy a ponerme el sombrero
▸ **pop out*** VT + ADV • **she popped her head out** asomó de repente la cabeza
VI + ADV salir un momento • **he popped out for some cigarettes** salió un momento a comprar cigarrillos • **he popped out from his hiding place** salió de repente de su escondite
▸ **pop up*** VI + ADV aparecer inesperadamente
pop[2]***** [pɒp] (= **popular**) N (música *f*) pop *m* • **to be top of the pops** ser el número uno en la lista de éxitos
CPD ▸ **pop art** pop-art *m*, arte *f* pop ▸ **pop band** grupo *m* (de) pop ▸ **pop concert** concierto *m* de pop ▸ **pop group** grupo *m* (de) pop ▸ **pop music** música *f* pop ▸ **pop quiz** (*US*) (= *surprise test*) examen *m* sorpresa ▸ **pop singer** cantante *mf* de pop ▸ **pop socks** (*Brit*) calcetas *fpl* ▸ **pop song** canción *f* pop ▸ **pop star** estrella *f* de la música pop
pop[3]***** [pɒp] N (*esp US*) (= *dad*) papá* *m*
pop. ABBR (= **population**) h.
popcorn ['pɒpkɔ:n] N palomitas *fpl* de maíz, alborotos *mpl* (*S. Cone, Peru*), cabritas *fpl*

P

(*S. Cone, Peru*)

pope [pəʊp] N papa *m* • **Pope John XXIII** el Papa Juan XXIII

popemobile* ['pəʊpməʊ,bi:l] N papamóvil *m*

popery ['pəʊpərɪ] N (*pej*) papismo *m* • **no ~!** ¡abajo el papa!, ¡papa no!

pop-eyed ['pɒp'aɪd] ADJ (*permanently*) de ojos saltones *or* desorbitados • **they were pop-eyed with amazement** se les desorbitaron los ojos con el asombro • **they looked at me pop-eyed** me miraron con los ojos desorbitados

popgun ['pɒpgʌn] N pistola *f* de juguete (de aire comprimido)

popinjay† ['pɒpɪndʒeɪ] N pisaverde *mf*

popish ['pəʊpɪʃ] ADJ (*pej*) papista

poplar ['pɒplə^r] N (*black*) chopo *m*, álamo *m*; (*white*) álamo *m* blanco

poplin ['pɒplɪn] N popelina *f*

popmobility [,pɒpməʊ'bɪlɪtɪ] N gym-jazz *m*

popover ['pɒp,əʊvə^r] N (*US*) *especie de panecillo hecho con harina y huevo*

poppa* ['pɒpə] N (*US*) papá* *m*

poppadum ['pɒpədəm] N = **papadum**

popper ['pɒpə^r] N **1** (*Brit**) (= *press-stud*) corchete *m*
2 (*Drugs*‡) *cápsula de nitrito amílico*

poppet* ['pɒpɪt] N (*Brit*) encanto *m*, cielo *m* • **yes, my ~** sí, hija, sí, querida • **she is a ~** es un cielo • **the boss is a ~** el jefe es un encanto

poppy ['pɒpɪ] N amapola *f*
CPD ▸ **Poppy Day** (*Brit*) *día en el que se recuerda a las caídos en las dos guerras mundiales* ▸ **poppy seed** semilla *f* de amapola

> **POPPY DAY**
> **Poppy Day** es la expresión coloquial para referirse al **Remembrance Day** o **Remembrance Sunday**, día en que se recuerdan los caídos en las dos grandes guerras mundiales del siglo XX. La celebración se hace el segundo domingo de noviembre y en los días que preceden a este día se venden amapolas de papel con el fin de recaudar fondos destinados a las instituciones de caridad que prestan ayuda a los veteranos de guerra y a sus familias. Las amapolas representan las que florecieron en los campos franceses, donde tantos soldados perecieron durante la Primera Guerra Mundial.
> ▹ **LEGION**

poppycock* ['pɒpɪkɒk] N paparruchas* *fpl*, tonterías *fpl* • **poppycock!** ¡paparruchas!*

pops* ['pɒps] N (*esp US*) (= *daddy*) papi* *m*

Popsicle® ['pɒpsɪkl] N (*US*) polo *m* (*Sp*), paleta *f* (helada) (*LAm*)

popsy‡ ['pɒpsɪ] N chica *f*

populace ['pɒpjʊlɪs] N (*gen*) pueblo *m*; (= *mob*) populacho *m*, turba *f*

popular ['pɒpjʊlə^r] ADJ **1** (= *well-liked*) • **the show is proving very ~** el espectáculo está gozando de mucho éxito *or* goza de mucha popularidad • **I'm not very ~ in the office just now** en este momento no gozo de mucha simpatía en la oficina • **this is one of our most ~ lines** (*Comm*) esta es una de nuestras líneas más vendidas • **to be ~ with sb**: • **he's ~ with the girls** tiene éxito con las chicas • **I'm not very ~ with her at the moment** en este momento no soy santo de su devoción • **she's very ~ with her colleagues** goza de mucha simpatía entre sus colegas • **the area is ~ with holidaymakers** es una zona muy frecuentada por los turistas
2 (= *fashionable*) de moda • **long skirts are ~** las faldas largas están de moda
3 (= *widespread*) [*image, belief*] generalizado • **contrary to ~ belief** *or* **opinion** en contra de *or* contrario a lo que comúnmente se cree • **by ~ demand** *or* **request** a petición del público, respondiendo a la demanda general • **it's a ~ misconception that ...** mucha gente piensa equivocadamente que ...
4 (= *of the people*) [*unrest, support*] popular; [*uprising*] popular, del pueblo • **he has great ~ appeal** goza del favor del público • **~ feeling is against him** el sentir popular *or* del pueblo está en su contra • **~ opinion** la opinión general
5 (= *appealing to the layman*) [*culture, music, art, version*] popular
CPD ▸ **popular culture** cultura *f* popular ▸ **popular front** frente *m* popular ▸ **popular music** música *f* pop ▸ **the popular press** la prensa popular ▸ **the popular vote** el voto popular

popularist ['pɒpjʊlərɪst] ADJ popularista

popularity [,pɒpjʊ'lærɪtɪ] N popularidad *f* • **to gain** *or* **grow in ~** gozar de una popularidad cada vez mayor

popularization [,pɒpjʊləraɪ'zeɪʃən] N (= *making well-liked, acceptable*) popularización *f*; (= *making available*) vulgarización *f*

popularize ['pɒpjʊləraɪz] VT **1** (= *make well-liked, acceptable*) popularizar
2 (= *make available to the people*) divulgar

popularizer ['pɒpjʊləraɪzə^r] N • **he is a great ~ of political/scientific ideas** es un gran divulgador de ideas políticas/científicas

popularly ['pɒpjʊləlɪ] ADV **1** (= *generally*) • **it is ~ thought that ...** comúnmente se cree que ... • **Albert, ~ known as Bertie** Albert, corrientemente conocido como Bertie
2 (= *by the people*) • **the country's first ~ elected president** el primer presidente del país que ha sido elegido por el pueblo

populate ['pɒpjʊleɪt] VT poblar

populated ['pɒpjʊleɪtɪd] ADJ [*area*] poblado • **a heavily ~ area** una zona muy poblada • **rural areas are sparsely ~** las zonas rurales están muy poco pobladas

population [,pɒpjʊ'leɪʃən] N
1 (= *inhabitants*) población *f* • **what is the ~ of Mexico?** ¿qué población tiene México?, ¿cuántos habitantes hay en México? • **they go to the cinema more often than the general ~** van al cine con más frecuencia que la población en general • **75% of the male ~** el 75% de la población masculina • **the student ~** la población estudiantil; ▹ **prison**
2 (= *settling*) población *f*
CPD ▸ **population centre** núcleo *m or* centro *m* de población ▸ **population control** control *m* demográfico ▸ **population density** densidad *f* de población ▸ **population explosion** explosión *f* demográfica ▸ **population growth** crecimiento *m* demográfico

populism ['pɒpjʊlɪzəm] N populismo *m*

populist ['pɒpjʊlɪst] ADJ populista
N populista *mf*

populous ['pɒpjʊləs] ADJ populoso • **the most ~ city in the world** la ciudad más populosa del mundo

pop-up ['pɒpʌp] ADJ (*Comput*) [*window, menu, advertisement*] emergente
N (*Comput*) ventana *f* emergente, (ventana *f*) pop-up *m*
CPD ▸ **pop-up book** libro *m* desplegable ▸ **pop-up menu** menú *m* emergente ▸ **pop-up toaster** tostador *m* automático

porage ['pɒrɪdʒ] N = **porridge**

porcelain ['pɔ:slɪn] N porcelana *f*
CPD de porcelana

porch [pɔ:tʃ] N [*of church*] pórtico *m*; [*of house*] porche *m*, portal *m*; (*US*) (= *veranda*) porche *m*, terraza *f*

porcine ['pɔ:saɪn] ADJ porcino, porcuno

porcupine ['pɔ:kjʊpaɪn] N puerco *m* espín
CPD ▸ **porcupine fish** pez *m* globo

pore¹ [pɔ:^r] N (*Anat, Zool*) poro *m*

pore² [pɔ:^r] VI • **to ~ over sth** escudriñar algo • **we ~d over it for hours** lo estudiamos durante horas y horas

pork [pɔ:k] N carne *f* de cerdo *or* puerco *or* (*LAm*) chancho
CPD ▸ **pork barrel*** (*US*) • IDIOM: • **the ~ barrel** el electoralismo • **principles go out of the window and the ~ barrel comes in** desaparecen los principios y entra en juego el electoralismo ▸ **pork barrel politician** (*US*) político/a *m/f* electoralista ▸ **pork barrel politics** (*US*) política *f* electoralista ▸ **pork barrel project** (*US*) proyecto *m* electoralista ▸ **pork butcher** charcutero/a *m/f*, chanchero/a *m/f* (*LAm*) ▸ **pork chop** chuleta *f* de cerdo *or* puerco ▸ **pork pie** (*Culin*) empanada *f* de carne de cerdo; (*Brit*‡) = **porky** ▸ **pork sausage** salchicha *f* de cerdo *or* puerco ▸ **pork scratchings** chicharrones *mpl*

porker ['pɔ:kə^r] N cerdo *m*, cochino *m*

porky ['pɔ:kɪ] ADJ* gordo, gordinflón*
N (*Brit*‡) (= *lie*) bola* *f*, mentira *f*

porn* [pɔ:n] N pornografía *f*, porno* *m* • **hard/soft ~** pornografía *f* dura/blanda
CPD [*magazine, video, actor*] porno* (*inv*) ▸ **porn merchant** traficante *mf* en pornografía ▸ **porn shop** tienda *f* de pornografía

porno* ['pɔ:nəʊ] ADJ = **porn**

pornographer [pɔ:'nɒgrəfə^r] N pornografista *mf*

pornographic [,pɔ:nə'græfɪk] ADJ pornográfico

pornography [pɔ:'nɒgrəfɪ] N pornografía *f*

porosity [pɔ:'rɒsɪtɪ] N porosidad *f*

porous ['pɔ:rəs] ADJ poroso

porousness ['pɔ:rəsnɪs] N porosidad *f*

porphyria [pɔ:'fɪrɪə] N porfirismo *m*

porphyry ['pɔ:fɪrɪ] N pórfido *m*

porpoise ['pɔ:pəs] N (PL: **porpoise** *or* **porpoises**) marsopa *f*, puerco *m* de mar

porridge ['pɒrɪdʒ] N **1** (*Culin*) avena *f* (cocida), ≈ atole *m* (*Mex*); (*baby's*) papilla *f*
2 • **to do two years' ~** (*Brit**) pasar dos años a la sombra*
CPD ▸ **porridge oats** copos *mpl* de avena

port¹ [pɔ:t] N **1** (= *harbour*) puerto *m* • **to come** *or* **put into ~** tomar puerto • **to leave ~** hacerse a la mar, zarpar • **~ of call** puerto *m* de escala • **his next ~ of call was the chemist's** (*fig*) luego fue a la farmacia • **where is your next ~ of call?** (*fig*) ¿adónde va ahora? • **~ of entry** puerto *m* de entrada • IDIOM: • **any ~ in a storm** la necesidad carece de ley
2 (= *city or town with a port*) puerto *m*
CPD portuario ▸ **port authority** autoridad *f* portuaria ▸ **port dues** derechos *mpl* de puerto ▸ **port facilities** facilidades *fpl* portuarias

port² [pɔ:t] (*Naut, Aer*) N (*also* **port side**) babor *m* • **the sea to ~** la mar a babor • **land to ~!** ¡tierra a babor!
ADJ de babor • **on the ~ side** a babor
VT • **to ~ the helm** poner el timón a babor, virar a babor

port³ [pɔ:t] N **1** (*Naut*) (= *porthole*) portilla *f*
2 (*Comput*) puerta *f*, puerto *m*, port *m*
3 (*Mech*) lumbrera *f*
4 (*Mil*††) tronera *f*

port⁴ [pɔːt] N (= *wine*) oporto *m*
portability [ˌpɔːtəˈbɪlɪtɪ] N (*esp Comput*) portabilidad *f*; [*of software*] transferibilidad *f*
portable [ˈpɔːtəbl] ADJ portátil
N máquina *f*/televisor *m etc* portátil
portage [ˈpɔːtɪdʒ] N porteo *m*
Portakabin® [ˈpɔːtəˌkæbɪn] N (*gen*) caseta *f* prefabricada; (= *extension to office etc*) anexo *m* prefabricado; (= *works office etc*) barracón *m* de obras
portal [ˈpɔːtl] N portal *m*
portcullis [pɔːtˈkʌlɪs] N rastrillo *m*
portend [pɔːˈtend] VT (*liter*) augurar, presagiar • **what does this ~?** ¿qué significa esto?
portent [ˈpɔːtent] N **1** (= *omen*) augurio *m*, presagio *m* • **a ~ of doom** un presagio de la catástrofe
2 (= *prodigy*) portento *m*
portentous [pɔːˈtentəs] ADJ **1** (= *ominous, prodigious*) portentoso
2 (= *pompous*) pomposo
portentously [pɔːˈtentəslɪ] ADV
1 (= *ominously*) portentosamente
2 (= *pompously*) pomposamente
porter [ˈpɔːtəʳ] N **1** (*Rail, Aer*) maletero *m*, mozo *m* de cuerda *or* de estación, changador *m* (*S. Cone*); (*US*) (*Rail*) mozo *m* de los coches-cama, camarero *m* (*LAm*); (*touting for custom*) mozo *m* de cuerda
2 (*Brit*) [*of hotel, office etc*] portero/a *m/f*
3 (= *Sherpa*) porteador *m*
4 (*in hospital*) camillero/a *m/f*
5† (= *beer*) cerveza *f* negra
CPD ▸ **porter's lodge** portería *f*, conserjería *f*
porterage [ˈpɔːtərɪdʒ] N porte *m*
porterhouse [ˈpɔːtəhaʊs] N (PL: **porterhouses** [ˈpɔːtəhaʊzɪz]) **1** (*Brit*) (*also* **porterhouse steak**) biftec *m* de filete
2†† mesón *m*
portfolio [pɔːtˈfəʊlɪəʊ] N (PL: **portfolios**) (= *file*) carpeta *f*; [*of artist, designer*] carpeta *f*, portafolio *m*; [*of business, politician*] cartera *f* • **~ of shares** cartera *f* de acciones • **minister without ~** ministro/a *m/f* sin cartera
CPD ▸ **portfolio management** gestión *f* de carteras ▸ **portfolio manager** gestor(a) *m/f* de carteras
porthole [ˈpɔːthəʊl] N portilla *f*
Portia [ˈpɔːʃə] N Porcia
portico [ˈpɔːtɪkəʊ] N (PL: **porticoes** *or* **porticos**) pórtico *m*
portion [ˈpɔːʃən] N **1** (= *part, piece*) porción *f*, parte *f*; [*of food*] ración *f*; [*of cake*] porción *f*, trozo *m*
2 (= *quantity, in relation to a whole*) porción *f*, porcentaje *m*
3 (*also* **marriage portion**) dote *f*
VT (*also* **portion out**) repartir, dividir
portliness [ˈpɔːtlɪnɪs] N gordura *f*, corpulencia *f*
portly [ˈpɔːtlɪ] ADJ grueso, corpulento
portmanteau [pɔːtˈmæntəʊ] N (PL: **portmanteaus, portmanteaux** [pɔːtˈmæntəʊz]) baúl *m* de viaje
CPD ▸ **portmanteau word** palabra *f* combinada
Porto Rico [ˌpɔːtəʊˈriːkəʊ] = **Puerto Rico** *etc*
portrait [ˈpɔːtrɪt] N retrato *m* • **to have one's ~ painted** • **sit for one's ~** hacerse un retrato
CPD ▸ **portrait format** (*Comput, Publishing*) formato *m* vertical ▸ **portrait gallery** museo *m* de retratos, galería *f* iconográfica ▸ **portrait mode** • **to print** *or* **output sth in ~ mode** imprimir algo en vertical ▸ **portrait painter** retratista *mf*
portraitist [ˈpɔːtrɪtɪst] N retratista *mf*
portraiture [ˈpɔːtrɪtʃəʳ] N (= *portrait*) retrato *m*; (= *portraits collectively*) retratos *mpl*; (= *art of portraiture*) arte *m* de retratar • **Spanish ~ in the 16th century** retratos *mpl* españoles del siglo XVI
portray [pɔːˈtreɪ] VT **1** (= *paint etc portrait of*) retratar
2 (= *describe, paint etc*) representar, pintar
portrayal [pɔːˈtreɪəl] N **1** (*Art*) retrato *m*
2 (= *description*) descripción *f*, representación *f* • **a most unflattering ~** una representación nada halagadora *or* favorecedora
portress [ˈpɔːtrɪs] N portera *f*
Portugal [ˈpɔːtjʊgəl] N Portugal *m*
Portuguese [ˌpɔːtjʊˈgiːz] ADJ portugués
N (PL: **Portuguese**) **1** (= *person*) portugués/esa *m/f*
2 (*Ling*) portugués *m*
CPD ▸ **Portuguese man-of-war** (*Zool*) *especie de medusa*
POS N ABBR (= **point of sale**) punto *m* de venta
pos. ABBR = **positive**
pose [pəʊz] N **1** [*of body*] postura *f*, actitud *f*
2 (*fig*) afectación *f*, pose *f* • **it's only a ~** es pura pose
VT **1** (= *position*) hacer posar • **he ~d the model in the position he wanted** hizo que la modelo posara como él quería
2 [+ *problem, question, difficulty*] plantear; [+ *threat*] representar, encerrar
VI **1** (= *place o.s.*) colocarse; (*for artist etc*) posar • **she once ~d for Picasso** una vez posó para Picasso
2 (*affectedly*) presumir, hacer pose
3 • **to ~ as** (= *pretend to be*) hacerse pasar por; (= *disguise o.s. as*) disfrazarse de
Poseidon [pəˈsaɪdən] N Poseidón
poser* [ˈpəʊzəʳ] N **1** (= *problem*) problema *m* *or* pregunta *f* difícil
2 (= *person*) = **poseur**
poseur [pəʊˈzɜːʳ] N persona *f* afectada
posh* [pɒʃ] ADJ (COMPAR: **posher**, SUPERL: **poshest**) (= *high-class*) elegante, pijo (*Sp**); (= *affected*) [*accent etc*] afectado; [*wedding etc*] de mucho rumbo; [*school*] de buen tono • **a ~ car/hotel** un coche/un hotel de lujo • **~ people** gente *f* bien • **it's a very ~ neighbourhood** es un barrio de lo más elegante
ADV • **to talk ~** hablar con acento afectado
▸ **posh up*** VT + ADV • **to ~ a place up** procurar que un local parezca más elegante, renovar la pintura *etc* de un local • **it's all ~ed up** está totalmente renovado, se ha reformado por completo • **to ~ o.s. up** arreglarse, ataviarse, emperejilarse
poshness* [ˈpɒʃnɪs] N elegancia *f*, pijería *f* (*Sp**); [*of accent*] afectación *f*
posing pouch [ˈpəʊzɪŋˌpaʊtʃ] N tanga *m*, marcapaquete* *m*
posit [ˈpɒzɪt] VT proponer como principio (**that** que), postular
position [pəˈzɪʃən] N **1** (= *location*) [*of object, person*] posición *f*; [*of house, town*] situación *f*, ubicación *f* (*LAm*) • **the ship radioed its ~** el barco transmitió su posición por radio • **the house is in a very exposed ~** la casa está situada *or* (*LAm*) ubicada en un lugar muy expuesto • **to be in ~** estar en su sitio • **to get into ~** ponerse en posición • **the troops are moving into ~** las tropas están ocupando posiciones • **to be out of ~** [*object*] estar desplazado *or* desencajado; (*Sport*) [*player*] estar fuera de sitio • **to take up ~(s)**: • **troops have taken up ~s near the border** las tropas se han apostado cerca de la frontera • **he took up his usual ~ in front of the fire** ocupó su sitio *or* lugar habitual frente a la chimenea • **I took up my lookout ~ on the bow** ocupé mi puesto *or* posición de vigilancia en la proa
2 (= *posture*) (*gen*) posición *f*, postura *f*; (*sexual*) postura *f* • **to change (one's) ~** cambiar de posición *or* postura • **he had raised himself to a sitting ~** se había incorporado
3 (*Sport*) • **what ~ do you play (in)?** ¿de qué juegas?
4 (*Mil*) [*of troops*] posición *f*; (*for gun*) emplazamiento *m* • **the enemy ~s** las posiciones enemigas *or* del enemigo
5 (*in race, competition*) puesto *m*, posición *f*, lugar *m*; (*in class, league*) puesto *m* • **he finished in third ~** terminó en tercer puesto *or* lugar, terminó en tercera posición; ▸ **pole**
6 (*in society*) posición *f* • **she gave up career, social ~, everything** renunció a su profesión, a su posición social, a todo
7 (= *post*) (*gen*) puesto *m*; (*high-ranking*) cargo *m* • **a high ~ in government** un alto cargo en el gobierno • **to take up a ~** aceptar un puesto • **a ~ of trust** un puesto de confianza
8 (= *situation, circumstance*) situación *f* • **this is the ~** la situación es esta • **it puts me in a rather difficult ~** me pone en una situación bastante delicada • **the country's economic ~** la situación económica del país • **put yourself in my ~** ponte en mi lugar • **(if I were) in his ~, I'd say nothing** yo que él *or* yo en su lugar no diría nada • **what is my legal ~?** desde el punto de vista legal, ¿cuál es mi situación? • **we are in a strong negotiating ~** estamos en una buena posición para negociar • **what's the ~ on deliveries/sales?** ¿cuál es la situación respecto a las entregas/ventas? • **they were in a ~ to help** su situación les permitía ayudar • **he's in no ~ to criticize** no es quién para criticar, él no está en condiciones de criticar; ▸ **consider, jockey**
9 (= *opinion*) postura *f* (**on** con respecto a) • **you must make your ~ clear** tienes que dejar clara tu postura • **what is our ~ on Greece?** ¿cuál es nuestra política *or* postura con respecto a Grecia?
10 (= *window*) (*in bank, post office*) ventanilla *f* • **"position closed"** "ventanilla cerrada"
VT **1** (= *place in position*) [+ *furniture, object*] colocar; [+ *police, troops*] apostar • **soldiers have been ~ed around the building** se han apostado soldados rodeando el edificio • **to ~ o.s.** (*lit*) colocarse, situarse; (*fig*) (= *take a stance*) adoptar una postura • **France is ~ing itself for offensive action** Francia está adoptando una postura de ataque
2 (*Sport*) [+ *ball, shuttlecock*] colocar
3 • **to be ~ed** (= *located*) **a** (*lit*) • **the house was strategically ~ed** la casa estaba situada *or* ubicada de forma estratégica • **it was a difficult shot from where she was ~ed** era un tiro difícil desde donde estaba situada *or* colocada
b (*fig*) • **he is well ~ed to act as intermediary** está en una buena posición para hacer de intermediario
CPD ▸ **position paper** informe *m* sintetizado • **the ministers will be examining a ~ paper outlining options** los ministros estudiarán un informe sintetizado que resuma las opciones
positional [pəˈzɪʃənəl] ADJ posicional • **his tactical and ~ play need improving** necesita mejorar su juego táctico y posicional
positive [ˈpɒzɪtɪv] ADJ **1** (= *sure, certain*) seguro • **you don't sound very ~** no pareces estar muy seguro • **"are you sure?" — "yes, ~"** —¿estás seguro? —segurísimo *or* —no me cabe la menor duda • **he's ~ about it** está seguro de ello • **we have ~ proof that ...**

tenemos pruebas concluyentes de que ...; ▹ **proof**
2 (= *affirmative, constructive*) [*attitude, view, influence*] positivo; [*criticism*] constructivo; [*person*] que tiene una actitud positiva • **she's a ~ sort of person** es una persona que tiene una actitud positiva • **I think this news is a ~ sign** creo que esta noticia es prometedora • **she made a very ~ impression with us** nos causó muy buena impresión • **to take ~ action** tomar medidas firmes • **~ discrimination** discriminación *f* positiva • **on the ~ side** en el lado positivo • **~ vetting** investigación *f* de antecedentes
3 (= *real*) [*disgrace, disadvantage*] verdadero, auténtico • **he's a ~ nuisance** es un verdadero *or* auténtico pelmazo*
4 (*Elec, Phot, Ling*) positivo; (*Med*) [*result*] positivo; (*Math*) [*number*] positivo • **~ cash flow** flujo *m* positivo de caja
(N) (= *plus point*) aspecto *m* positivo; (*Phot*) positivo *m*; (*Math*) número *m* positivo, valor *m* positivo • **the ~s outweigh the negatives** los aspectos positivos tienen más peso que *or* superan a los negativos • **to give a false ~** (*Med*) dar un resultado positivo falso
(ADV) • **to test ~** dar positivo • **you have to think ~** hay que ser positivo
(CPD) ▸ **positive thinking** pensamiento *m* positivo • **the benefits of ~ thinking** los beneficios del pensamiento positivo • **these people believe ~ thinking can cure diseases** estas personas creen que pensar positivamente puede curar las enfermedades

positively [ˈpɒzɪtɪvlɪ] (ADV) **1** (= *with certainty*) [*guarantee*] con seguridad; (= *categorically*) [*refuse*] tajantemente • **the body has been ~ identified** se ha hecho una identificación definitiva del cadáver
2 (= *affirmatively*) [*respond, act*] de manera positiva • **most employees view the new system ~** la mayoría de los empleados ha reaccionado favorablemente al nuevo sistema, la mayoría de los empleados ve el nuevo sistema con buenos ojos • **you must think and act ~** debes tener una actitud positiva • **they are contributing ~ to the development of their community** están participando activamente en el desarrollo de su comunidad
3* (= *really, absolutely*) [*amazed, delighted*] realmente, verdaderamente • **the food was ~ disgusting!** ¡la comida daba auténtico *or* verdadero asco!, ¡la comida era realmente *or* verdaderamente asquerosa! • **this is ~ the last time I'm going to tell you** está sí que es la última vez que te lo digo • **Miguel knows ~ nothing about business** Miguel no sabe absolutamente nada de negocios
4 (*Elec*) • **a ~ charged ion** un ión con carga positiva

positiveness [ˈpɒzɪtɪvnɪs] (N) **1** (= *certainty*) certeza *f*, certidumbre *f*; [*of voice*] seguridad *f*; [*of evidence*] certeza *f* • **her ~ that he was innocent** su certeza de que era inocente
2 (= *constructiveness*) positividad *f*, constructividad *f* • **I was reassured by the ~ of his attitude** me tranquilicé por lo positivo de su actitud

positivism [ˈpɒzɪtɪvɪzəm] (N) positivismo *m*

positivist [ˈpɒzɪtɪvɪst] (ADJ) positivista
(N) positivista *mf*

positivistic [pɒzɪtɪˈvɪstɪk] (ADJ) positivista

positron [ˈpɒzɪˌtrɒn] (N) positrón *m*

poss* [pɒs] (ADJ ABBR) = **possible** • **as soon as ~** cuanto antes, lo más pronto posible
(ADV ABBR) = **possibly**

posse [ˈpɒsɪ] (N) (*esp US*) pelotón *m*

possess [pəˈzes] (VT) **1** (= *have*) tener, poseer; (= *own*) [+ *property*] poseer, ser dueño de • **it ~es many advantages** tiene *or* posee muchas ventajas • **to ~ a large collection** poseer una gran colección • **to ~ o.s. of** (*frm*) tomar posesión de; (*violently*) apoderarse de • IDIOM: • **to ~ o.s.** *or* **one's soul in patience** (*liter or hum*) armarse de paciencia
2 (= *control, take over*) • **to be ~ed by an idea** estar poseído por una idea • **whatever can have ~ed you?** ¿cómo se te ocurrió? • **what can have ~ed you to think like that?** ¿cómo has podido pensar así?

possessed [pəˈzest] (ADJ) poseso, poseído • **to be ~ by demons** estar poseso *or* poseído por los demonios • **like one ~** como un poseído

possession [pəˈzeʃən] (N) **1** (= *act, state*) posesión *f* • **to come into ~ of** adquirir • **to come** *or* **pass into the ~ of** pasar a manos de • **to get ~ of** [+ *building, property*] ganar derecho de entrada a • **to get/have ~ of the ball** (*Sport*) hacerse con/tener el balón • **to have sth in one's ~** tener algo (en su posesión *or* sus manos) • **to be in ~ of sth** estar en posesión de algo • **to be in full ~ of one's faculties** estar en pleno uso de sus facultades mentales • **to be in the ~ of** estar en posesión *or* manos de • **to take ~ of sth** (*Jur*) tomar posesión de algo; (*by force*) apoderarse de algo • **a house with vacant ~** una casa (que se vende) desocupada • **"with vacant possession"** "llave en mano" • PROVERB: • **~ is nine points** *or* **tenths of the law** la posesión es lo que cuenta
2 (= *thing possessed*) posesión *f*; **possessions** posesiones *fpl*, bienes *mpl* • **Spain's overseas ~s** las posesiones de España en ultramar
3 (*illegal*) [*of drugs*] posesión *f* • **~ of arms** tenencia *f* de armas
4 (*by devil*) posesión *f*
(CPD) ▸ **possession order** (*Brit*) (*Jur*) orden *f* de posesión

possessive [pəˈzesɪv] (ADJ) **1** [*person*] posesivo; [*love etc*] dominante, tiránico • **to be ~ about sth/towards sb** ser posesivo con algo/algn
2 (*Ling*) posesivo
(N) (*Ling*) posesivo *m*
(CPD) ▸ **possessive adjective** adjetivo *m* posesivo ▸ **possessive pronoun** pronombre *m* posesivo

possessively [pəˈzesɪvlɪ] (ADV) • **she slipped her arm into his ~** le tomó del brazo de manera posesiva

possessiveness [pəˈzesɪvnɪs] (N) posesividad *f*

possessor [pəˈzesəʳ] (N) poseedor(a) *m/f*, dueño/a *m/f* • **to be the proud ~ of sth** ser el orgulloso dueño *or* poseedor de algo

posset [ˈpɒsɪt] (N) (= *drink*) *bebida de leche caliente cortada con vino o cerveza más algunas especias*

possibility [ˌpɒsəˈbɪlɪtɪ] (N) **1** (= *chance, likelihood*) posibilidad *f* • **is there any ~ (that) they could help?** ¿hay alguna posibilidad de que nos ayuden? • **there is a strong ~ I'll be late** es muy posible que me retrase, hay muchas posibilidades de que me retrase • **beyond/within the bounds of ~**: • **it is within the bounds of ~** está dentro de lo posible • **it is not beyond the bounds of ~ that he'll succeed** cabe dentro de lo posible *or* no es imposible que lo consiga • **there is no ~ of his agreeing to it** no existe ninguna posibilidad de que lo consienta; ▹ **distinct**
2 (= *option*) posibilidad *f* • **the possibilities are endless** hay infinidad de posibilidades • **she's a strong ~ for the nomination** tiene muchas posibilidades de ser nominada
3 (*usu pl*) (= *potential*) • **the scheme has real possibilities** es un plan que promete, es un plan de gran potencial • **it's a job with great possibilities** es un trabajo con mucho futuro *or* porvenir

possible [ˈpɒsəbl] (ADJ) **1** (= *feasible*) posible • **she scored seven points out of a ~ nine** obtuvo siete puntos de los nueve posibles • **will it be ~ for me to leave early?** ¿hay algún inconveniente en que me vaya antes de la hora? • **as ... as ~**: • **try to make the lesson as interesting as ~** trata de que la lección sea lo más interesante posible • **you must practise as much as ~** debes practicar todo lo que puedas *or* todo lo posible • **as soon as ~** cuanto antes, lo antes posible • **we provide the best ~ accommodation for our students** nuestros estudiantes disponen del mejor de los alojamientos • **if (at all) ~** si es posible, a ser posible • **to make sth ~**: • **improvements made ~ by new technology** mejoras *fpl* que la nueva tecnología ha hecho posible • **he made it ~ for me to go to Spain** gracias a él pude ir a España • **the new legislation would make it ~ for alcohol to be sold on Sundays** la nueva legislación posibilitaría la venta de alcohol los domingos • **I meant it in the nicest ~ way** lo dije con la mejor de las intenciones • **we will help whenever ~** ayudaremos siempre y cuando sea posible, ayudaremos siempre que podamos • **where ~** • **wherever ~** donde sea posible • **they have joined the job market at the worst ~ time** se han incorporado al mercado de trabajo en el peor momento posible *or* en el peor de los momentos; ▹ **world, as, far**
2 (= *likely*) posible • **a ~ candidate** un posible candidato
3 (= *conceivable*) posible • **what ~ motive could she have?** ¿qué motivo puede tener? • **there is no ~ excuse for his behaviour** su comportamiento no tiene excusa que valga • **it is ~ that he'll come** es posible que venga, puede (ser) que venga • **it's just ~ he may still be there** existe una pequeña posibilidad de que siga allí
(N) **1*** (= *suitable person*) (*for job*) candidato/a *m/f* • **he's a ~ for Saturday's match** es posible que juegue en el partido del sábado
2 • **the ~** lo posible

possibly [ˈpɒsəblɪ] (ADV) **1** (= *feasibly, conceivably*) • **if I ~ can** si me es posible, si puedo • **I go as often as I ~ can** voy siempre que puedo, voy lo más a menudo posible • **how can I ~ come tomorrow?** ¿cómo voy a poder venir mañana? • **could you ~ come another day?** ¿le sería posible venir otro día?, ¿podría venir otro día? • **I can't ~ eat all this** me es totalmente imposible comer todo esto • **I couldn't ~ allow it** de ninguna manera lo voy a permitir • **it can't ~ be true!** ¡no puede ser verdad! • **she will do everything she ~ can to help you** hará todo lo que esté en su mano *or* todo lo que pueda para ayudarte • **he never does it if he can ~ help it** siempre que puede evitarlo lo evita
2 (= *perhaps*) • **"will you be able to come?" — "possibly"** —¿podrás venir? —es posible *or* —puede que sí • **~ not** puede que no • **of the 200 who apply, ~ five may be accepted** de los 200 solicitantes, tal vez se elija a cinco

possum [ˈpɒsəm] (N) (*US*) zarigüeya *f* • IDIOM: • **to play ~** (= *sleeping*) fingir estar dormido; (= *dead*) hacerse el muerto

post¹ [pəʊst] (N) **1** [*of wood, metal*] poste *m*; (*also* **goalpost**) poste *m* (de la portería); (*for fencing, marking*) estaca *f*; ▹ **bedpost, deaf, doorpost, pillar**
2 (*Sport*) • **the starting/finishing ~** el poste de

P

salida/llegada • **the winning ~** la meta • IDIOM: • **to be left at the ~** quedar muy en desventaja; ▹ **first, pip³**
3 (*on Internet*) mensaje *m*
VT 1 (= *put up*) [+ *bill, notice*] (*also* **post up**) poner • **"post no bills"** "prohibido fijar carteles"
2 (= *announce*) [+ *exam results*] hacer público, sacar • **to ~ sth/sb (as) missing** dar algo/a algn por desaparecido
3 (*Comm*) (*also* **post up**) [+ *transaction*] anotar, registrar; (*US*) (*St Ex*) [+ *profit, loss*] registrar
4 (= *inform*) • **to keep sb ~ed (on** *or* **about sth)** tener *or* mantener a algn al corriente *or* al tanto *or* informado (de algo)
5 (*US*) (*Sport*) [+ *time, score*] registrar, obtener
6 (*Internet*) colgar, publicar
CPD ▸ **post hole** agujero *m* de poste

post² [pəʊst] N 1 (*Brit*) (= *mail service*) correo *m* • **by ~** *or* **through the ~** por correo • **first-class ~** correo *m* preferente • **your cheque is in the ~** su cheque está en el correo • **second-class ~** correo *m* normal; ▹ **first-class, registered, return**
2 (= *letters*) correo *m* • **is there any ~ for me?** ¿hay correo para mí?
3 (= *office*) correos *m*; (= *mailbox*) buzón *m* • **to drop** *or* **put sth in the ~** echar algo al correo *or* al buzón • **to drop or put sth in the ~ to sb** enviar *or* mandar algo a algn
4 (= *collection*) recogida *f*; (= *delivery*) entrega *f* • **the ~ goes at 8.30** la recogida del correo es a las 8.30, recogen el correo a las 8.30 • **the ~ is late** el correo se ha retrasado • **to catch the ~** echar el correo antes de la recogida • **first ~** (= *collection*) primera recogida *f*; (= *delivery*) primer reparto *m*, primera entrega *f* • **last ~** (= *collection*) última recogida • **to miss the ~** no llegar a tiempo para la recogida del correo • **it will arrive in the second ~** llegue en el segundo reparto
5 (= *cost*) gastos *mpl* de envío • **~ and packing** gastos *mpl* de envío
6 (*Hist*) (= *rider*) correo *m*; (= *coach*) posta *f*
VT (= *send by post*) (*also* **post off**) mandar *or* enviar por correo; (*Brit*) (= *put in mailbox*) echar al correo *or* al buzón • **this was ~ed on Monday** esto se echó al correo *or* al buzón el lunes • **to ~ sth to sb** mandar *or* enviar algo a algn por correo • **he ~ed a message to a newsgroup** (*Internet*) dejó un mensaje en un grupo de discusión
CPD ▸ **post horn** corneta *f* del correo ▸ **post office** oficina *f* de correos, correos *m*, correo *m* (*LAm*) • **I'm going to the ~ office** voy a correos, voy al correo (*LAm*) ▸ **the Post Office** ≈ la Dirección General de Correos ▸ **post office box** apartado *m* de correos, casilla *f* (postal *or* de correo(s) (*LAm*) ▸ **Post Office Savings Bank** ≈ Caja *f* Postal de Ahorros ▸ **post office worker** empleado/a *m/f* de correos

post³ [pəʊst] N 1 (= *job*) (*gen*) puesto *m*; (*high-ranking*) cargo *m* • **she's been offered a research ~** le han ofrecido un puesto *or* un trabajo de investigadora • **to hold a ~** (*gen*) ocupar un puesto; (*high-ranking*) ocupar un cargo • **to take up one's ~** (*gen*) ocupar el puesto; (*high-ranking*) entrar en funciones, ocupar el cargo • **she resigned to take up a ~ at the university** dimitió porque consiguió un puesto en la universidad
2 (*Mil*) (= *place of duty, stronghold*) puesto *m*; (*for gun*) emplazamiento *m* • **at one's ~** en su puesto • **border** *or* **frontier ~** puesto *m* fronterizo • **first ~** (toque *m* de) diana *f* • **last ~** (toque *m* de) retreta *f*; ▹ **command, customs, observation**
VT 1 (*Mil*) [+ *sentry, guard*] apostar
2 (*Brit*) (= *send*) [+ *diplomat, soldier*] destinar • **to ~ sb abroad** destinar a algn al extranjero
3 (*US*) (*Jur*) [+ *collateral*] pagar • **to ~ bail** pagar la fianza
CPD ▸ **post exchange** (*US*) (*Mil*) economato *m* militar, cooperativa *f* militar

POST N ABBR = **point-of-sale terminal**

post... [pəʊst] PREFIX post..., pos...

postage [ˈpəʊstɪdʒ] N franqueo *m*, porte *m* • **~ due** a pagar • **~ paid** porte *m* pagado
CPD ▸ **postage and packing** (*Brit*), **postage and handling** (*US*) gastos *mpl* de envío ▸ **postage costs** franqueo *msing*, gastos *mpl* de envío • **email really saves on ~ costs** el correo electrónico constituye un gran ahorro en franqueo ▸ **postage meter** (*US*) franqueadora *f* ▸ **postage rates** tarifa *fsing* de correo ▸ **postage stamp** sello *m* (de correos), estampilla *f* (*LAm*), timbre *m* (*Mex*)

postal [ˈpəʊstəl] ADJ postal
CPD ▸ **postal area, postal district** distrito *m* postal ▸ **postal charges** = **postal rates** ▸ **postal code** (*Brit*) código *m* postal ▸ **postal order** (*Brit*) giro *m* postal ▸ **postal rates** tarifa *fsing* de correo ▸ **postal service** servicio *m* postal ▸ **postal survey** encuesta *f* por correo ▸ **postal system** sistema *m* postal, correo *m* ▸ **postal vote** voto *m* postal ▸ **postal worker** empleado/a *m/f* de correos

postbag [ˈpəʊstbæg] N (*Brit*) (= *sack*) saco *m* postal; (= *letters*) correspondencia *f*, cartas *fpl* • **it arrived in my ~** llegó en mi correo • **he received a heavy ~** recibió muchas cartas

postbox [ˈpəʊstbɒks] N (*Brit*) buzón *m*

postcard [ˈpəʊstkɑːd] N (tarjeta *f*) postal *f*

postclassical [pəʊstˈklæsɪkəl] ADJ posclásico

postcode [ˈpəʊstkəʊd] N (*Brit*) código *m* postal
CPD ▸ **postcode prescribing** *situación arbitraria en la que algunas medicinas se recetan o no por la seguridad social según la zona donde se vive*

post-coital [pəʊstˈkəʊɪtəl] ADJ de después del coito

postdate [ˈpəʊstˈdeɪt] VT poner una fecha posterior a

postdated [ˈpəʊstˈdeɪtɪd] ADJ [*cheque*] con fecha posterior

post-doctoral [ˈpəʊstˈdɒktərəl] ADJ posdoctoral
CPD ▸ **post-doctoral fellow** becario/a *m/f* posdoctoral ▸ **post-doctoral fellowship** beca *f* posdoctoral

poster [ˈpəʊstəʳ] N cartel *m*, póster *m*, afiche *m* (*LAm*)
CPD ▸ **poster artist, poster designer** cartelista *mf* ▸ **poster child, poster boy/girl** (*esp US*) (*for cause, activity*) icono *m*; (*who appear on posters*) *persona imagen de una firma que aparece en los carteles publicitarios de la misma* • **she has become the ~ child for a whole generation of youths** se ha convertido en el icono de toda una generación de jóvenes • **she went out with a Calvin Klein ~ boy** salió con un modelo que es imagen de Calvin Klein ▸ **poster paint** pintura *f* al agua

poste restante [ˈpəʊstˈrestɑːnt] N (*esp Brit*) lista *f* de correos, poste *f* restante (*LAm*)

posterior [pɒsˈtɪərɪəʳ] ADJ (*frm*) posterior
N* (*hum*) trasero* *m*

posterity [pɒsˈterɪtɪ] N posteridad *f*

postern [ˈpəʊstɜːn] N postigo *m*

post-feminism [ˌpəʊstˈfemɪnɪzəm] N posfeminismo *m*

post-feminist [ˌpəʊstˈfemɪnɪst] ADJ [*people, attitudes*] posfeminista
N (= *person*) posfeminista *mf*

post-free [ˈpəʊstˈfriː] ADJ, ADV (con) porte pagado, libre de franqueo

postglacial [ˈpəʊstˈgleɪsɪəl] ADJ posglacial

postgrad* [ˈpəʊstˈgræd] = **postgraduate**

postgraduate [ˈpəʊstˈgrædjʊɪt] (*Brit*) N posgraduado/a *m/f*
CPD ▸ **postgraduate course** curso *m* para (pos)graduados ▸ **postgraduate student** ≈ estudiante *mf* de posgrado ▸ **postgraduate study, postgraduate studies** estudios *mpl* de posgrado

post-haste† [ˈpəʊstˈheɪst] ADV a toda prisa, con toda urgencia

post-holder [ˈpəʊsthəʊldəʳ] N titular *mf* de un puesto

posthumous [ˈpɒstjʊməs] ADJ póstumo

posthumously [ˈpɒstjʊməslɪ] ADV póstumamente, con carácter póstumo

postie* [ˈpəʊstɪ] N (*Brit*) cartero/a *m/f*

postilion [pəsˈtɪlɪən] N postillón *m*

post-imperial [ˈpəʊstɪmˈpɪərɪəl] ADJ posimperial

post-impressionism [ˈpəʊstɪmˈpreʃənɪzəm] N posimpresionismo *m*

post-impressionist [ˈpəʊstɪmˈpreʃənɪst] ADJ, N posimpresionista *mf*

post-industrial [ˌpəʊstɪnˈdʌstrɪəl] ADJ posindustrial

posting [ˈpəʊstɪŋ] N 1 (*Brit*) (*Mil etc*) destino *m*
2 (*Econ*) asiento *m*, traspaso *m* al libro mayor
3 (*on Internet*) mensaje *m*

postman [ˈpəʊstmən] N (PL: **postmen**) (*Brit*) cartero *m*
CPD ▸ **postman's knock** (= *game*) *juego de niños en que el que se intercambia un beso por una carta imaginaria*

postmark [ˈpəʊstmɑːk] N matasellos *m inv* • **date as ~** según fecha del matasellos
VT matasellar

postmarked [ˈpəʊstmɑːkt] ADJ • **the envelope was ~ Helsinki** el sobre tenía matasellos de Helsinki

postmaster [ˈpəʊstˌmɑːstəʳ] N administrador *m* de correos
CPD ▸ **postmaster general** (*Brit*) director *m* general de correos

postmistress [ˈpəʊstˌmɪstrɪs] N administradora *f* de correos

postmodern [ˈpəʊstˈmɒdən] ADJ posmoderno

postmodernism [ˈpəʊstˈmɒdənɪzəm] N posmodernismo *m*

postmodernist [ˈpəʊstˈmɒdənɪst] ADJ, N posmodernista *mf*

post-mortem [ˈpəʊstˈmɔːtəm] N (*gen*) autopsia *f* • **to carry out a post-mortem** practicar una autopsia • **to hold a post-mortem on sth** (*fig*) analizar los resultados de algo, hacer el balance de algo

post-natal [ˈpəʊstˈneɪtl] ADJ postnatal, pos(t)parto
CPD ▸ **post-natal depression** depresión *f* pos(t)parto

post-op* [ˈpəʊstˌɒp] ADJ (= *post-operative*) posoperatorio

postoperative [ˌpəʊstˈɒpərətɪv] ADJ posoperatorio

post-paid [ˈpəʊstˈpeɪd] ADV porte pagado, franco de porte

postpartum [pəʊstˈpɑːtəm] N postparto, posparto
CPD ▸ **postpartum depression** depresión *f* pos(t)parto

postpone [pəʊstˈpəʊn] VT aplazar, postergar (*LAm*) • **mightn't it be better to ~ it?** ¿no sería mejor aplazarlo? • **to ~ sth for a month** aplazar algo por un mes • **it has been ~d till Tuesday** ha sido aplazado hasta el martes

postponement [pəʊstˈpəʊnmənt] N aplazamiento *m*

postpositive [pəʊstˈpɒzɪtɪv] ADJ pospositivo

postprandial [ˈpəʊstˈprændɪəl] ADJ *[speech, talk etc]* de sobremesa; *[walk etc]* que se da después de comer

postproduction [ˌpəʊstprəˈdʌkʃən] N actividad *f* posterior a la producción CPD *[costs etc]* que sigue a la producción

postscript [ˈpəʊsskrɪpt] N *(to letter)* posdata *f*; *(fig)* epílogo *m* • **there is a ~ to this story** esta historia tiene epílogo

poststructuralism [ˈpəʊstˈstrʌktʃərəlɪzəm] N postestructuralismo *m*

poststructuralist [ˌpəʊstˈstrʌktʃərəlɪst] ADJ postestructuralista *(inv)* N postestructuralista *mf*

post-traumatic [ˌpəʊstrɔːˈmætɪk] ADJ postraumático CPD ▸ **post-traumatic stress** estrés *m* postraumático ▸ **post-traumatic stress disorder** síndrome *m* de estrés postraumático

postulant [ˈpɒstjʊlənt] N postulante/a *m/f*

postulate N [ˈpɒstjʊlɪt] postulado *m* VT [ˈpɒstjʊleɪt] postular

postulation [ˌpɒstjʊˈleɪʃən] N postulación *f*

postural [ˈpɒstʃərəl] ADJ *[habits, exercises]* postural

posture [ˈpɒstʃə(r)] N postura *f*, actitud *f* VI *(pej)* adoptar una postura afectada

posturing [ˈpɒstʃəˈrɪŋ] N pose *f* • **the threat to dispatch troops is mere ~** la amenaza de enviar tropas no es mas que una pose de cara al exterior • **there was a lot of political ~ going on** había mucho de fingimiento en las declaraciones políticas

post-viral fatigue syndrome [pəʊstˌvaɪərəlfəˈtiːgˌsɪndrəʊm], **post-viral syndrome** [pəʊstˈvaɪərəlˈsɪndrəʊm] N (= *ME*) síndrome *m* de fatiga crónica

postvocalic [ˌpəʊstvəʊˈkælɪk] ADJ posvocálico

post-war [ˈpəʊstˈwɔː(r)] ADJ de la posguerra • **the post-war period** la pos(t)guerra

postwoman [ˈpəʊstˌwʊmən] N (PL: **postwomen**) *(Brit)* cartera *f*

posy [ˈpəʊzɪ] N ramillete *m*

pot[1] [pɒt] N **1** *(for cooking)* cazuela *f*, olla *f* *(LAm)*; *(for jam)* tarro *m*, pote *m* *(S. Cone)*; *(for flowers)* tiesto *m*, maceta *f*; (= *teapot*) tetera *f*; (= *coffee pot*) cafetera *f*; (= *chamber pot*) orinal *m*; (= *piece of pottery*) cacharro *m* • **pots and pans** batería *fsing* de cocina, cacharros *mpl* • IDIOMS: • **to keep the pot boiling** (= *earn living*) ganarse la vida; (= *make things progress*) mantener las cosas en marcha • **to go to pot*** irse al traste* • **that's the pot calling the kettle black** el puchero le dijo a la sartén —apártate que me tiznas

2 (= *potful*) cazuela *f* • **a pot of coffee for two** café *m* para dos • **to make a pot of tea** hacer el té

3 *(Cards)* pozo *m*; *(esp US)* (= *kitty*) bote *m*

4 pots* (= *lots*) • **we have pots of it** tenemos montones* • **to have pots of money** estar forrado de dinero*

5 *(Sport*)* (= *prize*) copa *f*

6 *(Snooker, Billiards)* billa *f*

7* (= *shot*) • **he took a pot at the wolf** disparó contra el lobo

8* (= *stomach*) panza* *f*, barriga *f*

VT **1** *[+ jam, meat etc]* conservar en tarros

2 *[+ plant]* poner en tiesto *or* maceta; *(also* **pot up***)* *[+ seedling]* enmacetar

3 *(Snooker, Billiards)* meter en la tronera

4* (= *shoot*) *[+ duck, pheasant]* matar

VI (= *shoot*) • **to pot at sb** disparar sobre algn

CPD ▸ **pot belly** *(from overeating)* panza* *f*; *(from malnutrition)* barriga *f* hinchada ▸ **pot cheese** *(US)* ≈ requesón *m* ▸ **pot herb** hierba *f* aromática ▸ **pot luck** • **to take pot luck** conformarse con lo que haya ▸ **pot plant** planta *f* de interior ▸ **pot roast** carne *f* asada a la cazuela ▸ **pot scourer** *(metal)* estropajo *m* metálico, esponja *f* metálica ▸ **pot shot*** tiro *m* al azar • **to take a pot shot at sth** disparar contra algo al azar; ▹ **pot-bellied, pot-roast**

pot[2]‡ [pɒt] N (= *marijuana*) maría* *f*, chocolate* *m*, mota *f* *(LAm*)*

potable [ˈpəʊtəbl] ADJ potable

potage [ˈpɒtɑːʒ] N *(Culin)* potaje *m*

potash [ˈpɒtæʃ] N potasa *f*

potassium [pəˈtæsɪəm] N potasio *m* CPD ▸ **potassium cyanide** cianuro *m* de potasio ▸ **potassium nitrate** nitrato *m* de potasio ▸ **potassium sulphate** sulfato *m* potásico

potations [pəʊˈteɪʃənz] NPL *(frm)* libaciones *fpl*

potato [pəˈteɪtəʊ] N (PL: **potatoes**) patata *f*, papa *f* *(LAm)* • **baked ~** patata *f* al horno • **~es in their jackets** patatas *fpl* con su piel; ▹ **hot, small, sweet**

CPD ▸ **potato beetle** dorífora *f*, escarabajo *m* de la patata *or (LAm)* papa ▸ **potato blight** roña *f* de la patata *or (LAm)* papa ▸ **potato cake** croqueta *f* de patata *or (LAm)* papa ▸ **potato chip** *(US)* = **potato crisp** ▸ **potato crisp** patata *f* frita, papa *f* frita *(LAm)* ▸ **potato famine** hambruna *f* de la patata ▸ **potato field** patatal *m* ▸ **potato flour** fécula *f* de patata ▸ **potato masher** *utensilio para aplastar las patatas al hacer puré* ▸ **potato peeler** pelapatatas *m inv*, pelapapas *m inv (LAm)* ▸ **potato salad** ensalada *f* de patatas *or (LAm)* papas

pot-bellied [ˈpɒtˌbelɪd] ADJ *(from overeating)* barrigón*; *(from malnutrition)* de vientre hinchado

potboiler [ˈpɒtˌbɔɪlə(r)] N obra *f* (mediocre) *(escrita para ganar dinero)*

pot-bound [ˈpɒtbaʊnd] ADJ • **this plant is pot-bound** esta planta ya no cabe en la maceta, esta planta ha crecido demasiado para esta maceta

poteen [pɒˈtiːn, pɒˈtʃiːn] N aguardiente *m*, whiskey *m (irlandés, destilado ilegalmente)*

potency [ˈpəʊtənsɪ] N potencia *f*; *[of drink]* fuerza *f*; *[of remedy]* eficacia *f*; *(Physiol)* potencia *f*

potent [ˈpəʊtənt] ADJ potente, poderoso; *[drink]* fuerte; *[remedy]* eficaz

potentate [ˈpəʊtənteɪt] N potentado *m*

potential [pəˈtenʃəl] ADJ en potencia • **~ earnings** ganancias *fpl* potenciales • **a ~ prime minister** un primer ministro en ciernes • **a ~ threat** una posible amenaza

N **1** (= *possibilities*) potencial *m*; (= *ability*) capacidad *f* • **to have ~** mostrar gran potencial • **the war ~ of this country** el potencial bélico de este país • **our ~ for increasing production** nuestras posibilidades de incrementar la producción • **he hasn't yet realized his full ~** todavía no ha desarrollado plenamente su potencial • **to have the ~ to do sth** *[person]* tener aptitudes *or* capacidad para hacer algo • **the meeting has the ~ to be a watershed** la reunión puede llegar a ser un acontecimiento decisivo

2 *(Elec, Math, Phys)* potencial *m*

potentiality [pəˌtenʃɪˈælɪtɪ] N potencialidad *f*

potentially [pəˈtenʃəlɪ] ADV en potencia, potencialmente

potentiate [pəˈtenʃɪˌeɪt] VT *(frm)* potenciar

potful [ˈpɒtfʊl] N *[of tea]* tetera *f* llena; *[of coffee]* cafetera *f* llena

pothead‡ [ˈpɒthed] N fumador(a) *m/f* de marihuana, fumata *mf* *(Sp*)*, pichicatero/a *m/f* *(S. Cone*)*

pother [ˈpɒðə(r)] N lío *m* • **all this ~!** ¡qué lío! • **to make a ~ about sth** armar un lío a causa de algo

potholder [ˈpɒthəʊldə(r)] N *(US)* agarrador *m*, agarradera *f* *(LAm)*

pothole [ˈpɒthəʊl] N **1** *(in road)* bache *m* **2** *(Geol)* marmita *f* de gigante, gruta *f*; *(loosely)* cueva *f*, caverna *f*, profunda gruta *f*

pot-holed [ˈpɒtˌhəʊld] ADJ *[road]* lleno de baches

potholer [ˈpɒthəʊlə(r)] N *(Brit)* espeleólogo/a *m/f*

potholing [ˈpɒthəʊlɪŋ] N *(Brit)* espeleología *f* • **to go ~** hacer espeleología; *(on specific occasion)* ir de espeleología

pothook [ˈpɒthʊk] N **1** *(for pot)* gancho *m* **2** *(in writing)* garabato *m*

pothunter* [ˈpɒthʌntə(r)] N cazador(a) *m/f* de premios

potion [ˈpəʊʃən] N poción *f*, pócima *f*

potluck dinner [ˌpɒtlʌkˈdɪnə(r)] N *comida o cena en la que cada invitado aporta un plato de comida y la bebida*

potpie [ˈpɒtpaɪ] N *(US) guiso de carne y verduras cubierto de masa hojaldrada*

potpourri [pəʊˈpʊərɪ] N (PL: **potpourris**) **1** (= *flowers*) flores *fpl* secas aromáticas, popurrí *m* **2** *[of music, writing]* popurrí *m*

pot-roast [ˈpɒtrəʊst] VT asar

potsherd [ˈpɒtˌʃɜːd] N tiesto *m*, casco *m*

potted [ˈpɒtɪd] ADJ **1** *[food]* conservado en tarros; *[plant]* en tiesto, en maceta **2** (= *shortened*) *[history, version]* resumido

potter[1] [ˈpɒtə(r)] N alfarero/a *m/f*; *(artistic)* ceramista *mf* CPD ▸ **potter's clay** arcilla *f* de alfarería ▸ **potter's field** *(US)* cementerio *m* de pobres ▸ **potter's wheel** torno *m* de alfarero

potter[2] [ˈpɒtə(r)] VI *(Brit)* entretenerse haciendo un poco de todo • **I ~ed round the house all day** estuve todo el día en casa haciendo un poco de todo • **we ~ed round the shops** nos paseamos por las tiendas

▸ **potter about, potter around** VI + ADV *(Brit)* • **he likes ~ing about in the garden** le gusta entretenerse haciendo pequeños trabajos en el jardín

▸ **potter along** VI + ADV *(Brit)* hacerse el remolón* • **we ~ along** vamos tirando*

pottery [ˈpɒtərɪ] N **1** (= *craft*) alfarería *f*; (= *art*) cerámica *f* **2** (= *pots*) cerámica *f*; *[of fine quality]* loza *f* • **a piece of ~** una cerámica **3** (= *workshop*) alfar *m*, alfarería *f*

potting compost [ˈpɒtɪŋˌkɒmpɒst] N compost *m* para macetas

potting shed [ˈpɒtɪŋʃed] N cobertizo *m* de enmacetar

potty[1]* [ˈpɒtɪ] N orinal *m* de niño, bacinica *f* *(LAm)*

potty[2]* [ˈpɒtɪ] ADJ (COMPAR: **pottier**, SUPERL: **pottiest**) *(Brit)* **1** (= *mad*) chiflado* • **she's ~ about him** anda loca por él*, se chifla por él* • **you must be ~!** ¡tú estás loco! • **to drive sb ~** volver loco a algn • **it's enough to drive you ~** es para volverse loco **2** (= *small*) insignificante, miserable

potty-train [ˈpɒtɪtreɪn] *(Brit)* VT • **to potty-train sb** enseñar a algn a usar el orinal

potty-trained [ˈpɒtɪˌtreɪnd] ADJ *(Brit)* que ya no necesita pañales

potty-training [ˈpɒtɪtreɪnɪŋ] N *(Brit) adiestramiento de los niños pequeños en el uso del orinal para hacer sus necesidades*

pouch [paʊtʃ] N *(for tobacco)* petaca *f*; *(for ammunition)* cartuchera *f*; *(hunter's)* morral *m*;

(*Zool, Anat*) bolsa *f*

pouf, pouffe [pu:f] (N) **1** (= *seat*) puf(f) *m*
2 (*Brit*‡) = **poof**

poult [pəʊlt] (N) (*Agr*) **1** (= *chicken*) pollo *m* joven
2 (= *turkey*) pavo *m* joven
3 (= *pheasant*) faisán *m* joven

poulterer ['pəʊltərəʳ] (N) (*Brit*) pollero/a *m/f* • **~'s (shop)** pollería *f*

poultice ['pəʊltɪs] (N) cataplasma *f*, emplasto *m*
(VT) poner una cataplasma a, emplastar (**with** con)

poultry ['pəʊltrɪ] (N) (*alive*) aves *fpl* de corral; (*as food*) aves *fpl*
(CPD) ▸ **poultry breeding** avicultura *f* ▸ **poultry dealer** recovero/a *m/f*, pollero/a *m/f* ▸ **poultry farm** granja *f* avícola ▸ **poultry farmer** avicultor(a) *m/f* ▸ **poultry farming** avicultura *f* ▸ **poultry house** gallinero *m* ▸ **poultry keeper** = **poultry farmer** ▸ **poultry keeping** = **poultry farming** ▸ **poultry shop** (*US*) pollería *f*

pounce [paʊns] (N) salto *m*, ataque *m*; (*by bird*) calada *f*
(VI) abalanzarse (**on** sobre); [*bird*] calarse • **to ~ on sth/sb** (*lit*) abalanzarse sobre algo/algn, echarse encima de algo/algn • **to ~ on sb's mistake** saltar sobre el error de algn

pound¹ [paʊnd] (N) **1** (= *weight*) libra *f* (= *453,6gr*) • **half a ~** media libra • **two dollars a ~** dos dólares la libra • **they sell it by the ~** lo venden por libras • IDIOM: • **to demand one's ~ of flesh** exigir todo lo que le corresponde a uno; ▹ IMPERIAL SYSTEM
2 (= *money*) libra *f* • **one ~ sterling** una libra esterlina • **the ~** (*Econ*) la libra esterlina
(CPD) ▸ **pound coin** moneda *f* de una libra ▸ **pound cost averaging** costo *m* promedio en libras ▸ **pound note** billete *m* de una libra ▸ **pound shop** (*Brit*) ≈ tienda *f* de todo a un euro ▸ **pound sign** símbolo *m* de la libra esterlina • **all he can see is ~ signs** solo ve dinero

pound² [paʊnd] (VT) **1** (*strike*) **a** (*with fists*) [+ *door, table*] aporrear, golpear • **he ~ed the table with his fist** aporreó *or* golpeó la mesa con el puño • **to ~ one's fists against sth** golpear algo con los puños • **to ~ sth to pieces (with one's fists)** destrozar algo (a puñetazos *or* con los puños)
b (*with hammer*) martillear; (*with other instrument*) golpear • **he ~ed the stake into the ground with a rock** clavó la estaca en la tierra golpeándola con una piedra • **to ~ sth to pieces (with a hammer)** destrozar algo (a martillazos) • **they ~ed him into a pulp with their sticks** lo molieron a palos
c [*sea, waves*] azotar, batir contra • **the waves ~ed the boat to pieces** las olas batieron contra el bote hasta destrozarlo
d (*Mil*) • **day after day long-range artillery ~ed the city** día tras día fuego de artillería de largo alcance cayó sobre la ciudad causando estragos • **the bombs ~ed the city to rubble** las bombas redujeron la ciudad a escombros
2 (*Culin*) [+ *herbs, spices*] machacar; [+ *garlic, mixture*] machacar, majar; [+ *meat*] golpear; [+ *dough*] trabajar
3 (= *thump*) [+ *piano, typewriter*] aporrear
• IDIOMS: • **to ~ the beat*** rondar las calles (como policía) • **to ~ the pavement(s)** (*US**) patear las calles*
(VI) **1** (= *throb, pulsate*) [*head*] estar a punto de estallar; [*heart*] palpitar; [*music*] retumbar • **the blood ~ed in his ears** podía oír el pulso de la sangre en los oídos • **his heart ~ed with fear/joy/excitement** el corazón le palpitaba de miedo/de alegría/de emoción
2 (= *strike*) • **the sea ~ed against** *or* **on the rocks** el mar azotaba las rocas *or* batía contra las rocas • **somebody began ~ing at** *or* **on the door** alguien empezó a aporrear la puerta • **we listened to the rain ~ing on the roof** oíamos la lluvia cayendo con fuerza sobre el tejado
3 (= *move heavily*) • **he was ~ing along the road** corría con paso pesado *or* pesadamente por la carretera • **to ~ up/down the stairs** subir/bajar las escaleras con paso pesado *or* pesadamente • **the train ~ed past** el tren pasó retumbando
▸ **pound out** (VT + ADV) • **he was ~ing out a tune on the piano** aporreaba una canción en el piano • **the drums ~ed out the good news** los redobles de los tambores lanzaron a los cuatro vientos la buena noticia

pound³ [paʊnd] (N) (= *enclosure*) (*for dogs*) perrera *f*; (*for cars*) depósito *m* de coches

poundage ['paʊndɪdʒ] (N) *impuesto or comisión que se exige por cada libra esterlina or de peso*

-pounder ['paʊndəʳ] (N) (*ending in compounds*) • **four-pounder** (= *fish*) pez *m* de cuatro libras • **twenty-five-pounder** (*Mil*) cañón *m* de veinticinco

pounding ['paʊndɪŋ] (N) **1** (= *noise*) [*of feet, hooves*] pisadas *fpl*; [*of guns*] martilleo *m*; [*of sea, waves*] embate *m*; [*of heart*] palpitaciones *fpl*, latidos *mpl* violentos • **suddenly there was a furious ~ on the door** de repente empezaron a aporrear furiosamente la puerta
2 (= *pummelling*) (*from shells, bombs*) bombardeo *m* • **the city took a ~ last night** la ciudad fue muy castigada en el bombardeo de anoche
3* (*fig*) (= *thrashing*) • **Barcelona gave us a real ~** el Barcelona nos dio una paliza de las buenas* • **to take a ~** sufrir una (dura) derrota

pour [pɔ:ʳ] (VT) **1** (= *serve*) servir • **shall I ~ the tea?** ¿sirvo el té? • **to ~ sb a drink** • **~ a drink for sb** servir una copa a algn • **he ~ed himself some coffee** se sirvió café
2 (= *tip*) [+ *liquid*] verter, echar; [+ *salt, powder*] echar • **I ~ed the milk down the sink** vertí *or* eché la leche por el fregadero • **he ~ed some wine into a glass** vertió *or* echó un poco de vino en un vaso • **~ the sauce over the meat** vierta *or* eche la salsa sobre la carne; ▹ **cold, oil, scorn**
3 (= *invest*) • **they are ~ing millions into the Olympics** están invirtiendo millones en las Olimpiadas • **to ~ money into a project** invertir grandes cantidades de dinero en un proyecto • **we can't go on ~ing money into this project** no podemos seguir invirtiendo ese caudal en este proyecto
(VI) **1** (= *serve*) servir • **shall I ~?** ¿sirvo?
2 (= *tip*) • **this teapot doesn't ~ very well** es difícil servir con esta tetera
3 (= *flow*) • **water was ~ing down the walls** el agua caía a raudales por las paredes • **tears ~ed down his face** las lágrimas le resbalaban por la cara • **water ~ed from the broken pipe** el agua salía a raudales de la tubería rota • **blood ~ed from the wound** la sangre salía a borbotones de la herida • **water came ~ing into the room** el agua entraba a raudales en el cuarto • **the sweat was ~ing off him** sudaba a chorros
4 (*Met*) • **it's ~ing (with rain)** está lloviendo a cántaros, está diluviando; ▹ **pour down, rain**
5 (*fig*) • **smoke was ~ing from the window** grandes bocanadas de humo salían de la ventana • **passionate German prose ~ed from her lips** apasionadas palabras de prosa alemana le brotaban de los labios • **refugees ~ed into the country** entraban grandes cantidades de refugiados en el país • **sunshine ~ed into the room** el sol entraba a raudales en la habitación • **cars ~ed off the ferry** muchísimos coches salían del transbordador • **cars are ~ing off the assembly lines** grandes cantidades de coches están saliendo de las cadenas de montaje; ▹ **pour out**
▸ **pour away** (VT + ADV) tirar • **he had to ~ the wine away** tuvo que tirar el vino
▸ **pour down** (VI + ADV) • **it/the rain was ~ing down** llovía a cántaros • **the sun ~ed down on them** el sol les daba de lleno; ▹ **pour**
(VT + PREP) = **pour**
▸ **pour forth** (*liter*) (VT + ADV) (*lit*) [+ *smoke*] echar; (*fig*) [+ *words, abuse*] soltar • **the washing machine was ~ing forth water at an alarming rate** el agua se salía de la lavadora a una velocidad alarmante
(VI + ADV) (*lit*) [*smoke, gas*] salir en grandes cantidades; [*water, liquid*] salir a raudales; [*blood*] salir a borbotones; (*fig*) [*words, criticisms*] manar
▸ **pour in** (VI + ADV) **1** (*lit*) • **water was ~ing in** estaba entrando agua a raudales • **sunshine ~ed in from the courtyard** desde el patio el sol entraba a raudales en la habitación
2 (*fig*) [*people*] (*to country, area*) llegar a raudales; (*to shop, office*) entrar a raudales • **letters ~ed in from their fans** les llovían cartas de sus admiradores, llegaban avalanchas de cartas de sus admiradores • **as the results ~ed in ...** a medida que llegaba la avalancha de resultados ...
(VT + ADV) **1** (*lit*) [+ *liquid*] (*into mixture*) añadir; (*into container*) echar • **next, ~ in the milk** luego, añada la leche
2 (*fig*) • **we can't keep ~ing in capital** no podemos seguir invirtiendo tanto capital *or* ese caudal
▸ **pour off** (VT + ADV) (= *throw away*) tirar; (= *put aside*) apartar • **~ off the excess fat** tire el exceso de grasa • **~ off half the quantity** aparte la mitad
(VI + PREP) = **pour**
▸ **pour out** (VT + ADV) **1** (= *serve*) [+ *tea, milk, cornflakes*] servir • **shall I ~ you out some tea?** • **shall I ~ out some tea for you?** ¿te sirvo té?
2 (= *emit*) [+ *smoke, fumes*] arrojar
3 (= *produce*) • **the factory ~s out hundreds of cars a day** la fábrica produce cientos de coches al día
4 (*fig*) [+ *anger, emotion*] desahogar; [+ *words, abuse*] soltar • **he ~ed out a torrent of abuse (against them)** (les) soltó un torrente de insultos • **to ~ out one's feelings (to sb)** desahogarse (con algn) • **to ~ out one's heart to sb** desahogarse con algn, abrir su corazón a algn • **to ~ it all out** contarlo todo • **to ~ it all out to sb** contárselo todo a algn
(VI + ADV) **1** (*lit*) [*water, liquid*] salir a raudales; [*blood*] salir a borbotones • **he smashed the window and smoke ~ed out** rompió la ventana y salieron grandes bocanadas de humo
2 (= *come out in large numbers*) [*people, crowds*] salir en tropel • **the doors opened and thousands of fans ~ed out** las puertas se abrieron y miles de seguidores salieron en tropel • **they ~ed out into the streets** invadieron las calles
3 (= *gush out*) [*words*] brotar de la boca, manar de la boca • **once she started speaking, the ideas came ~ing out** una vez empezó a hablar, le fluyeron las ideas • **the words came ~ing out** las palabras brotaban *or* manaban de su boca • **once he started to talk it all came ~ing out** una vez empezó a

P

hablar, ya se desahogó del todo

pouring ['pɔːrɪŋ] (ADJ) **1** *[custard, cream etc]* líquido
2 *[rain]* torrencial • **we queued in the ~ rain for hours** hicimos cola durante horas bajo la lluvia torrencial

pout [paʊt] (N) puchero *m*, mohín *m*
(VI) hacer pucheros, hacer un mohín
(VT) • **"never!" she ~ed** —¡nunca! —dijo con gesto mohíno • **to ~ one's lips** hacer pucheros, hacer un mohín

poverty ['pɒvətɪ] (N) **1** (= *state of being poor*) pobreza *f* • **absolute/extreme/relative ~** pobreza *f* absoluta/extrema/relativa • **to live/die in ~** vivir/morir en la pobreza; ▹ **abject, grinding, plead, vow**
2 (= *lack*) pobreza *f*, escasez *f* • **~ of resources** pobreza *f or* escasez *f* de recursos • **~ of ideas** pobreza *f* de ideas • **~ of imagination** pobreza *f or* falta *f* de imaginación
3 (= *poor quality*) *[of soil]* pobreza *f*
(CPD) ▸ **poverty line, poverty level** *(US)* umbral *m* de pobreza • **to be** *or* **live above/below the ~ line** *or* **level** vivir por encima/por debajo del umbral de pobreza • **to be** *or* **live on the ~ line** vivir en el umbral de pobreza, vivir al borde de la pobreza ▸ **poverty trap** *(Brit)* trampa *f* de la pobreza

poverty-stricken ['pɒvətɪ,strɪkn] (ADJ) *[person]* muy pobre, indigente; *[area]* muy pobre • **to be poverty-stricken** estar en la miseria

POW (N ABBR) (= **prisoner of war**) prisionero/a *m/f* de guerra
(CPD) ▸ **POW camp** campo *m* de prisioneros de guerra

powder ['paʊdəʳ] (N) polvo *m*; (= *face powder, talcum powder*) polvos *mpl*; (= *gun powder*) pólvora *f* • **a fine white ~** un polvillo blanco • **to grind sth to (a) ~** reducir algo a polvo • IDIOM: • **to keep one's ~ dry** no gastar la pólvora en salvas, reservarse para mejor ocasión
(VT) **1** (= *reduce to powder*) pulverizar, reducir a polvo
2 (= *dust*) *(with face powder, talcum powder)* empolvar; *(Culin) (with flour, icing sugar)* espolvorear **(with de)** • **to ~ one's nose** *(lit)* empolvarse la nariz; *(euph)* ir al baño • **the ground was ~ed with snow** el terreno estaba salpicado de nieve
(VI) pulverizarse, hacerse polvo
(CPD) ▸ **powder blue** azul *m* pálido ▸ **powder blush, powder blusher** colorete *m* en polvo ▸ **powder compact** polvera *f* ▸ **powder horn** chifle *m*, cuerno *m* de pólvora ▸ **powder keg** barril *m* de pólvora • **the country is a ~ keg** el país es un polvorín ▸ **powder magazine** santabárbara *f* ▸ **powder puff** borla *f* ▸ **powder room** tocador *m*, aseos *mpl* (de señora) • **"powder room"** "señoras"

powder-blue ['paʊdə'bluː] (ADJ) azul pálido

powdered ['paʊdəd] (ADJ) en polvo
(CPD) ▸ **powdered milk** leche *f* en polvo ▸ **powdered sugar** *(US)* azúcar *m* glasé, azúcar *m* en polvo, azúcar *m* flor *(S. Cone)*

powdering ['paʊdərɪŋ] (N) *[of dust, sawdust]* fina capa *f*; *[of snow]* leve capa *f*

powdery ['paʊdərɪ] (ADJ) *[substance]* pulverulento; *[snow]* en polvo; *[surface]* polvoriento

power [paʊəʳ] (N) **1** (= *control*) poder *m*; *(physical strength)* fuerza *f* • **to have ~ over sb** tener poder sobre algn • **to have sb in one's ~** tener a algn en su poder • **to be in sb's ~** estar en poder de algn • **to have the ~ of life and death over sb** tener poder para decidir sobre la vida de algn • IDIOM: • **more ~ to your elbow!*** ¡qué tengas éxito!
2 *(Pol)* poder *m*, poderío *m* • **to be in ~** estar en el poder • **to come to ~** subir al poder • **to fall from ~** perder el poder • **~ to the people!** ¡el pueblo al poder!
3 *(Mil)* (= *capability*) potencia *f*, poderío *m* • **a nation's air/sea ~** la potencia aérea/naval de un país, el poderío aéreo/naval de un país
4 (= *authority*) poder *m*, autoridad *f* • **she has the ~ to act** tiene poder *or* autoridad para actuar • **they have no ~ in economic matters** carecen de autoridad en asuntos económicos • **it was seen as an abuse of his ~** se percibió como un abuso de poder por su parte • **~ of attorney** *(Jur)* poder *m*, procuración *f* • **that is beyond** *or* **outside my ~(s)** eso no es de mi competencia • **to exceed one's ~s** excederse en el ejercicio de sus atribuciones *or* facultades • **he has full ~s to negotiate a solution** goza de plenos poderes para negociar una solución • **~ of veto** derecho *m* de veto • **that does not fall within my ~(s)** eso no es de mi competencia
5 (= *ability, capacity*) • **it is beyond his ~ to save her** no está dentro de sus posibilidades salvarla, no puede hacer nada para salvarla • **~s of concentration** capacidad *f* de concentración • **to be at the height of one's ~s** estar en plenitud de facultades • **~s of imagination** capacidad *f* imaginativa • **to do all** *or* **everything in one's ~ to help sb** hacer todo lo posible por ayudar a algn • **~s of persuasion** poder *m* de persuasión *or* convicción; ▹ **purchasing**
6 (= *mental faculty*) facultad *f* • **his ~s are failing** decaen sus facultades • **mental ~s** facultades *fpl* mentales • **the ~ of speech** la facultad del habla
7 (= *nation*) potencia *f* • **the Great Powers** las grandes potencias • **one of the great naval ~s** una de las grandes potencias navales • **the leaders of the major world ~s** los líderes de las principales potencias mundiales
8 (= *person in authority*) • **he's a ~ in the land** es de los que mandan en el país • **they are the real ~ in the government** son los que ostentan el auténtico poder en el gobierno • **the Church is no longer the ~ it was** la Iglesia ha dejado de tener el poder que tenía • **the ~s that be** las autoridades, los que mandan • **the ~s of darkness** *or* **evil** las fuerzas del mal • IDIOM: • **the ~ behind the throne** la eminencia gris
9 (= *forcefulness*) *[of argument]* fuerza *f* • **the ~ of love/thought** el poder del amor/del intelecto • **a painting of great ~** un cuadro de gran impacto, un cuadro que causa honda impresión
10 *[of engine, machine]* potencia *f*, fuerza *f*; *[of telescope]* aumento *m*; (= *output*) rendimiento *m* • **microwave on full ~ for one minute** póngalo con el microondas a plena potencia durante un minuto • **engines at half ~** motores *mpl* a medio gas *or* a media potencia • **magnifying ~** capacidad *f* de aumento, número *m* de aumentos • **the ship returned to port under her own ~** el buque volvió al puerto impulsado por sus propios motores
11 (= *source of energy*) energía *f*; (= *electric power*) electricidad *f* • **they cut off the ~** cortaron la corriente • **nuclear ~** energía *f* nuclear
12 *(Math)* potencia *f* • **7 to the ~ (of) 3** 7 elevado a la 3ª potencia, 7 elevado al cubo • **to the nth ~** a la enésima potencia
13* (= *a lot of*) • **that holiday did me a ~ of good** esas vacaciones me hicieron mucho bien • **her words did their morale a ~ of good** sus palabras les levantaron un montón la moral • **the new training methods have done their game a ~ of good** el nuevo método de entrenamiento ha supuesto una notable mejoría en su juego
(VT) • **a plane ~ed by four jets** un avión propulsado por cuatro motores a reacción • **a racing car ~ed by a 4.2 litre engine** un coche de carreras impulsado por un motor de 4,2 litros • **a car ~ed by electricity** un coche eléctrico • **the electric lighting is ~ed by a generator** un generador se encarga de alimentar el alumbrado eléctrico; ▹ **-powered**
(CPD) ▸ **power base** base *f* de poder ▸ **power breakfast** desayuno *m* de negocios ▸ **power broker** *(Pol)* poder *m* en la sombra ▸ **power cable** cable *m* de energía eléctrica ▸ **power cut** *(Brit)* corte *m* de luz *or* de corriente, apagón *m* ▸ **power dressing** moda *f* de ejecutivo ▸ **power drill** taladro *m* eléctrico, taladradora *f* eléctrica ▸ **power failure** fallo *m* del suministro eléctrico ▸ **power game** *(esp Pol)* juego *m* del poder ▸ **power line** línea *f* de conducción eléctrica, cable *m* de alta tensión ▸ **power list** lista *f* de las personas más influyentes ▸ **power lunch** comida *f* de negocios ▸ **power outage** *(US)* = **power cut** ▸ **power pack** transformador *m* ▸ **power plant** (= *generator*) grupo *m* electrógeno; *(US)* = **power station** ▸ **power play** *(Sport)* demostración *f* de fuerza (en el juego ofensivo); *(from temporary suspension)* superioridad *f* (en el ataque); *(fig)* (= *use of power*) maniobra *f* de poder, demostración *f* de fuerza; (= *power struggle*) lucha *f* por el poder ▸ **power point** *(Brit) (Elec)* enchufe *m*, toma *f* de corriente ▸ **power politics** política *fsing* de fuerza ▸ **power saw** motosierra *f*, sierra *f* mecánica ▸ **power shovel** excavadora *f* ▸ **power shower** ducha *f* de hidromasaje ▸ **power station** central *f* eléctrica, usina *f* eléctrica *(S. Cone)* ▸ **power steering** *(Aut)* dirección *f* asistida ▸ **power structure** estructura *f* del poder ▸ **power struggle** lucha *f* por el poder ▸ **power supply** suministro *m* eléctrico ▸ **power surge** *(Elec)* subida *f* de tensión ▸ **power tool** herramienta *f* eléctrica ▸ **power trio** *(Mus)* trío *m* eléctrico ▸ **power unit** grupo *m* electrógeno ▸ **power vacuum** vacío *m* de poder ▸ **power walking** marcha *f* ▸ **power workers** trabajadores *mpl* del sector energético
▸ **power up** (VT + ADV) *[+ computer etc]* encender, conectar

power-assisted ['paʊərə,sɪstɪd] (ADJ) • **power-assisted brakes** servofrenos *mpl* • **power-assisted steering** dirección *f* asistida

powerboat ['paʊə,bəʊt] (N) lancha *f* a motor, motora *f*

powerboating ['paʊə,bəʊtɪŋ] (N) motonáutica *f*

power-driven ['paʊədrɪvn] (ADJ) *[machinery]* a motor; *[tool]* eléctrico

powered ['paʊəd] (ADJ) con motor • **the invention of ~ flight** la invención del vuelo a *or* con motor

-powered ['paʊəd] (ADJ) *(ending in compounds)* • **battery-powered** a pilas • **wind-powered** impulsado por el viento, que funciona con energía eólica

powerful ['paʊəfʊl] (ADJ) **1** (= *influential, controlling*) *[person, government, force, influence]* poderoso; ▹ **all-powerful**
2 (= *physically strong*) *[person]* fuerte, fornido; *[animal, physique, arms, muscles]* fuerte
3 (= *having great force or power*) *[engine, magnet, computer, explosive]* potente; *[kick, explosion, smell]* fuerte; *[voice]* potente, fuerte; *[swimmer]* resistente
4 (= *having a strong effect*) *[drug]* potente;

[emotion] intenso, profundo; *[argument]* poderoso, convincente; *[performance, film, novel]* impactante, que deja huella; *[speech]* conmovedor • **he gave a ~ performance** su actuación fue impactante *or* de las que deja huella • **we have ~ evidence for this** tenemos pruebas contundentes de esto • **this information is a ~ weapon against the government** esta información es un arma potente contra el gobierno

powerfully ['paʊəfəlɪ] ADV *[affect]* profundamente; *[speak, argue, express]* de forma convincente; *[hit, strike]* con fuerza • **it smelled ~ of sage** tenía un fuerte olor a salvia • **to be ~ built** ser de complexión fuerte

powerhouse ['paʊəhaʊs] N (PL: **powerhouses** ['paʊəhaʊzɪz]) **1** (*lit*) central *f* eléctrica
2 (*fig*) • **the town is the industrial ~ of Germany** el pueblo es el centro neurálgico de la industria alemana • **he's a ~ of ideas** es una fuente inagotable de ideas • **a hulking great ~ of a man** una auténtica mole de hombre*

powerless ['paʊəlɪs] ADJ impotente • **I felt ~ to resist** no tuve fuerzas para resistir, no pude resistir • **we are ~ to help you** no podemos hacer nada para ayudarle • **they are ~ in the matter** no tienen autoridad para intervenir en el asunto

powerlessness ['paʊəlɪsnɪs] N impotencia *f*

power-sharing ['paʊəʃeərɪŋ] N reparto *m* del poder
CPD *[arrangement, agreement]* de reparto del poder • **a power-sharing government** un gobierno de poder compartido

powwow ['paʊwaʊ] N *[of North American Indians] asamblea de indígenas norteamericanos*; (*fig**) asamblea *f*, reunión *f* • **we had a family ~ about it** hubo una asamblea *or* reunión familiar para discutirlo
VI *[North American Indians]* (*also fig*) reunirse en asamblea

pox* [pɒks] N • **the pox** (= *VD*) (la) sífilis; (= *smallpox*) (la) viruela • **a pox on them!**†† ¡malditos sean!

poxy‡ ['pɒksɪ] ADJ (*Brit*) puñetero‡

pp ABBR **1** (= **per procurationem**) (= *by proxy*) p.p.
2 = **parcel post**
3 = **post paid**
4 = **prepaid**

pp. ABBR (= **pages**) págs.

PPE ABBR (= **philosophy, politics, economics**) *grupo de asignaturas de la Universidad de Oxford*

ppm ABBR (= **parts per million**) ppm

PPP N ABBR = **personal pension plan**

pppn ABBR (= **per person per night**) p.p.p.n.

PPS N ABBR **1** (*Brit*) = **Parliamentary Private Secretary**
2 (= **post postscriptum**) posdata *f* adicional

PPV ABBR (= **pay-per-view**) de pago

PQ ABBR (*Canada*) = **Province of Quebec**

PR N ABBR **1** (*Pol*) = **proportional representation**
2 (*Comm*) (= **public relations**) R.P., RRPP *fpl*
ABBR (*US*) = **Puerto Rico**

Pr. ABBR (= **prince**) P.

practicability [,præktɪkə'bɪlɪtɪ] N viabilidad *f*, factibilidad *f*

practicable ['præktɪkəbl] ADJ practicable, viable, factible

practicably ['præktɪkəblɪ] ADV • **if it can ~ be done** si es factible hacerlo

practical ['præktɪkəl] ADJ **1** (= *not theoretical*) práctico • **the ~ applications of this research** las aplicaciones prácticas de estas investigaciones • **I did better in the written exam than in the ~ test** la prueba escrita me salió mejor que la práctica • **for all ~ purposes** a efectos prácticos • **in ~ terms** en términos prácticos • **to put one's knowledge to ~ use** hacer uso de *or* poner en práctica sus conocimientos • **the information was of no ~ use** la información no tenía ninguna utilidad práctica
2 (= *sensible*) *[person]* práctico • **let's be ~ (about this)** seamos prácticos (con respecto a esto)
3 (= *feasible*) factible • **what's the most ~ way of doing this?** ¿cuál es la forma más factible de hacer esto?
4 (= *useful, functional*) *[clothing, suggestion, guide]* práctico • **shoes which are both ~ and stylish** zapatos *mpl* que son prácticos y a la vez tienen estilo • **his clothes weren't very ~ for wet weather** su ropa no era muy práctica *or* apropiada *or* adecuada para la lluvia
5 (= *virtual*) • **it's a ~ certainty** es casi seguro
N (*Scol, Univ*) (= *exam*) examen *m* práctico; (= *lesson*) práctica *f*
CPD ▸ **practical joke** broma *f* • **to play a ~ joke on sb** gastar una broma a algn ▸ **practical joker** bromista *mf* ▸ **practical nurse** (*US*) enfermero/a *m/f* práctica *or* sin título

practicality [,præktɪ'kælɪtɪ] N *[of design, model]* utilidad *f*; *[of scheme, project]* lo factible; *[of person]* sentido *m* práctico • **practicalities** detalles *mpl* prácticos

practically ['præktɪklɪ] ADV **1** (= *almost*) casi, prácticamente • **~ everybody** casi todos, prácticamente todos • **the town was ~ deserted** el pueblo estaba casi *or* prácticamente desierto • **there has been ~ no rain** apenas ha llovido, casi no ha llovido • **you've eaten ~ nothing** apenas has comido, casi no has comido • **it ~ killed me** por poco me mata, casi me mata • **this disease has been ~ eliminated** esta enfermedad ha sido erradicada casi completamente
2 (= *sensibly*) con sentido práctico • **"how can we pay for it?" Bertha asked ~** —¿cómo vamos a pagarlo? —preguntó Bertha con sentido práctico
3 (= *in practical terms*) • **we are interested in how this might be used ~** nos interesa saber cómo se podría usar en la práctica, estamos interesados en las aplicaciones prácticas de esto • **what this means ~ is unclear** se desconocen las ramificaciones prácticas de esto, se desconoce lo que esto supondría en la práctica • **the work this term is more ~ based** el trabajo de este trimestre es más práctico • **~ speaking** en la práctica

practice ['præktɪs] N **1** (= *custom, tradition*) costumbre *f*, práctica *f*; (= *procedure*) práctica *f* • **ancient pagan ~s** las antiguas costumbres *or* prácticas paganas • **the ~ of sending young offenders to prison** la práctica de enviar a prisión a los menores que han cometido un delito • **it is not our ~ to do that** no tenemos por norma hacer eso • **unfair trade ~s** prácticas *fpl* de comercio desleales • **it is bad ~** no es una práctica recomendable • **these mistakes do not point to bad ~ in general** estos errores no apuntan a deficiencias en los métodos que se practican • **it is common ~ among modern companies to hire all their office equipment** entre las empresas modernas es una práctica muy extendida alquilar todo su material y mobiliario de oficina • **it is good ~ to interview several candidates before choosing one** es una práctica recomendable entrevistar a varios aspirantes antes de decidirse por uno • **to make a ~ of doing sth** acostumbrar a hacer algo • **it is normal** *or* **standard ~ for newspapers not to disclose such details** los periódicos tienen por norma no revelar ese tipo de detalles • **this procedure has become standard ~ in most hospitals** en la mayoría de los hospitales este procedimiento se ha convertido en norma; ▹ **business, restrictive, sharp**
2 (= *experience, drilling*) práctica *f* • **I need more ~** (= *practical experience*) necesito más práctica; (= *to practise more*) necesito practicar más • **it takes years of ~** requiere años de práctica • **he does six hours' piano ~ a day** practica el piano seis horas al día • **I haven't got a job yet but the interviews are good ~** aún no tengo trabajo pero las entrevistas me sirven de práctica • **skating's just a matter of ~** aprender a patinar es solo cuestión de práctica • **to be out of ~** (*at sport*) no estar en forma • **it gets easier with ~** resulta más fácil con la práctica • **PROVERB:** • **~ makes perfect** la práctica hace al maestro; ▹ **target, teaching**
3 (*Sport*) (= *training session*) sesión *f* de entrenamiento, entrenamiento *m*
4 (= *rehearsal*) ensayo *m* • **choir ~** ensayo *m* de coro
5 (= *reality*) práctica *f* • **we must combine theory with ~** tenemos que combinar la teoría con la práctica • **in ~** en la práctica • **to put sth into ~** poner algo en práctica
6 (= *exercise*) **a** *[of profession]* ejercicio *m* • **the ~ of medicine** el ejercicio de la medicina • **to be in ~ (as a doctor/lawyer)** ejercer (de médico/abogado) • **he is no longer in ~** ya no ejerce • **to go into ~** (*Med*) empezar a ejercer de médico • **to set up in ~** (*Med*) poner consulta; (*Jur*) poner bufete • **to set up in ~ as a doctor/solicitor** establecerse de *or* como médico/abogado
b *[of religion]* práctica *f*
7 (= *premises, firm*) (*Jur*) bufete *m*; (*Med*) consultorio *m*, consulta *f*; (*veterinary, dental*) clínica *f* • **a new doctor has just joined the ~** acaba de llegar un médico nuevo al consultorio; ▹ **family, general, group, private**
VT, VI (*US*) = **practise**
CPD ▸ **practice flight** vuelo *m* de entrenamiento ▸ **practice game** juego *m* de entrenamiento ▸ **practice manager** *[of medical practice]* director(a) *m/f* de clínica (médica) ▸ **practice match** partido *m* de entrenamiento ▸ **practice nurse** enfermero/a *m/f* del consultorio ▸ **practice run** (*Sport*) carrera *f* de entrenamiento ▸ **practice session** (*Sport*) sesión *f* de entrenamiento; (*Scol, Mus*) ensayo *m*

practiced ['præktɪst] ADJ (*US*) = **practised**

practicing ['præktɪsɪŋ] ADJ (*US*) = **practising**

practise, **practice** (*US*) ['præktɪs] VI **1** (*to improve skill*) (*Sport*) entrenar; (*Theat*) ensayar; (*Mus*) practicar • **he ~s for two hours every evening** entrena/ensaya/practica durante dos horas todas las tardes • **I've been practising with a ball on my own** he estado entrenando por mi cuenta con un balón • **I need someone to ~ on** necesito practicar con algn
2 (= *work professionally*) *[lawyer, doctor]* ejercer • **to ~ as a doctor/lawyer** ejercer de *or* como médico/abogado
VT **1** (= *put into practice*) *[+ medicine]* practicar; *[+ law]* ejercer; *[+ self-denial, one's religion, method]* practicar • **IDIOM:** • **to ~ what one preaches** predicar con el ejemplo

P

2 (= *work on*) (*Sport*) practicar; [+ *piano, language, technique*] practicar; [+ *song, speech*] ensayar • **I need to ~ my backhand** necesito practicar el revés • **~ giving your speech in front of a mirror** ensaye su discurso delante de un espejo • **I ~d my Spanish on her** practiqué el español con ella
practised, practiced (*US*) ['præktɪst] (ADJ) [*politician, surgeon, climber*] experto • **to be ~ in the art of (doing) sth** ser un experto en el arte de (hacer) algo • **with a ~ eye** con ojo experto
practising, practicing (*US*) ['præktɪsɪŋ] (ADJ) practicante • **he's a ~ homosexual** mantiene relaciones homosexuales
(CPD) ▸ **practising dentist** (*Brit*), **practicing dentist** (*US*) dentista *mf* practicante
▸ **practising doctor** (*Brit*), **practicing doctor** (*US*) médico/a *m/f* practicante
practitioner [præk'tɪʃənəʳ] (N) 1 [*of an art, a science*] practicante *mf*
2 (*Med*) médico/a *m/f*; ▹ **general**
praesidium [prɪ'sɪdɪəm] (N) (*Pol*) presidio *m*
praetorian [prɪ'tɔ:rɪən] (ADJ) pretoriano
(CPD) ▸ **praetorian guard** guardia *f* pretoriana
pragmatic [præg'mætɪk] (ADJ) pragmático
pragmatically [præg'mætɪklɪ] (ADV) pragmáticamente
pragmatics [præg'mætɪks] (NSING) pragmática *f* • **the ~ of the job in hand** las tareas prácticas del trabajo a realizar
pragmatism ['prægmətɪzəm] (N) pragmatismo *m*
pragmatist ['prægmətɪst] (N) pragmatista *mf*
Prague [prɑ:g] (N) Praga *f*
prairie ['prɛərɪ] (N) pradera *f*, llanura *f*, pampa *f* (*LAm*) • **the Prairies** (*US*) las Grandes Llanuras
(CPD) ▸ **prairie dog** perro *m* de las praderas
▸ **prairie oyster** (*US*) *huevo crudo y sazonado que se toma en una bebida alcohólica* ▸ **prairie wolf** coyote *m*
praise [preɪz] (N) 1 (= *approval, acclaim*) elogios *mpl*, alabanzas *fpl* • **I have nothing but ~ for her** merece todos mis elogios *or* alabanzas • **it's beyond ~** está por encima de todo elogio • **he is full of ~ for the medical staff** se deshace en elogios para con el personal médico • **let's give ~ where ~ is due** elogiemos a quienes se lo merecen • **to heap ~ on sb** colmar a algn de alabanzas • **that is high ~ indeed** eso sí que es un elogio de verdad • **he spoke in ~ of their achievements** elogió sus logros • **to be loud in ~ of** *or* **in one's ~s of sth** deshacerse en elogios para con algo; ▹ **damn, lavish, sing**
2 (*Rel*) alabanza *f* • **a hymn of ~** un himno de alabanza • **~ be to God!** ¡alabado sea Dios! • **let us give ~ (un)to the Lord** alabemos al Señor
(VT) 1 (= *applaud*) alabar, elogiar • **to ~ the virtues of sth** alabar *or* elogiar las virtudes de algo • IDIOM: • **to ~ sb to the skies** poner a algn por las nubes *or* los cielos; ▹ **sky**
2 (*Rel*) alabar • **to ~ God** *or* **the Lord** alabar a Dios *or* al Señor
praiseworthily ['preɪz,wɜ:ðɪlɪ] (ADV) loablemente, de modo digno de elogio
praiseworthiness ['preɪz,wɜ:ðɪnɪs] (N) lo loable, mérito *m*
praiseworthy ['preɪz,wɜ:ðɪ] (ADJ) [*conduct, effort, attempt*] loable, digno de elogio
praline ['prɑ:li:n] (N) praliné *m*
pram [præm] (N) (*Brit*) cochecito *m* (*de niño*)
prance [prɑ:ns] (VI) [*horse*] hacer cabriolas; [*person*] (*proudly*) pavonearse; (*gaily*) brincar, saltar • **he came prancing into the room** entró pavoneándose en la habitación
▸ **prance about, prance around** (VI + ADV) andar pavoneándose • **she was prancing around with nothing on** iba pavoneándose sin nada encima
prang†* [præŋ] (VT) (*Brit*) (= *crash*) [+ *car*] tener un accidente con; [+ *plane*] estrellar
prank [præŋk] (N) broma *f* • **a student ~** una broma estudiantil • **a childish ~** una travesura, una diablura • **to play a ~ on sb** gastar una broma a algn
prankish ['præŋkɪʃ] (ADJ) travieso, pícaro
prankster ['præŋkstəʳ] (N) bromista *mf*
praseodymium [,preɪzɪəʊ'dɪmɪəm] (N) praseodimio *m*
prat‡ [præt] (*Brit*) (N) (= *ineffectual person*) inútil* *mf*; (= *fool*) imbécil *mf* • **you ~!** ¡imbécil!
prate† [preɪt] (VI) parlotear, charlar • **to ~ about** hablar sin tasa de
pratfall‡ ['prætfɔ:l] (N) (*esp US*) culada‡ *f*, caída *f* de culo‡; (*fig*) (= *blunder*) metedura *f* de pata*
prating† ['preɪtɪŋ] (ADJ) parlanchín
prattle ['prætl] (N) parloteo *m*, cotorreo *m*; (*child's*) balbuceo *m*
(VI) parlotear, cotorrear; [*child*] balbucear
▸ **prattle on** (VI + ADV) parlotear
▸ **prattle on about** (VI + PREP) parlotear sobre
prattler ['prætləʳ] (N) (*pej*) (= *chatterbox*) parlanchín/ina *m/f*, cotorra* *f*
prawn [prɔ:n] (N) (*esp Brit*) (*medium*) gamba *f*, camarón *m* (*esp LAm*); (*small*) camarón *m*, quisquilla *f* (*Sp*); (= *Dublin Bay prawn, large prawn*) langostino *m*
(CPD) ▸ **prawn cocktail** cóctel *m* de gambas
▸ **prawn crackers** pan *msing* de gambas
pray [preɪ] (VI) (= *say prayers*) rezar, orar • **let us ~** oremos • **to ~ to God** rogar a Dios • **to ~ for sth/sb** rezar *or* rogar por algo/algn • **to ~ for sb's soul** rezar por el alma de algn • **we ~ed for rain** rezamos para que lloviera • **she's past ~ing for!*** ¡con ella ya no hay nada que hacer!, ¡no tiene salvación!
(VT) rogar, suplicar • **let me go, I ~ you!** (*liter*) ¡suélteme, se lo suplico! • **to ~ sb to do sth** rogar a algn que haga algo • **we ~ that it won't happen** rezamos para que no ocurra • **I was ~ing that he wouldn't notice** le pedía a Dios que no lo notara
(EXCL) • **~ be seated** (*frm*) siéntense, por favor • **~ tell me ...** (*frm*) le ruego decirme ... • **and what, ~, were you doing last night?** (*hum*) ¿y qué estabas tú haciendo anoche, si puede saberse?
prayer [prɛəʳ] (N) 1 (*Rel*) oración *f*, rezo *m*; (= *entreaty*) oración *f*, plegaria *f* • **a ~ for peace** una oración por la paz • **Lord, hear our ~** Señor, escucha nuestras plegarias *or* súplicas • **the Book of Common Prayer** la liturgia de la Iglesia Anglicana • **to be at one's ~s** estar rezando • **they offered (up) ~s of thanks** ofrecían rezos en acción de gracias • **to say one's ~s** orar, rezar • **say a ~ for me** reza por mí • **he didn't have a ~*** no tenía ni la menor posibilidad
2 (*as service*) oficio *m* • **morning/evening ~(s)** oficio *m* de maitines/vísperas
(CPD) ▸ **prayer beads** rosario *m* ▸ **prayer book** devocionario *m*, misal *m* ▸ **prayer mat** alfombra *f* de rezo ▸ **prayer meeting** reunión *f* de oraciones
praying mantis [,preɪɪŋ'mæntɪs] (N) mantis *f inv* religiosa
pre... [pri:] (PREFIX) 1 (= *before*) • **pre-Columbian** precolombino • **I had a pre-breakfast swim** me di un baño antes del desayuno
2 (= *beforehand*) • **a pre-recorded interview** una entrevista pregrabada
preach [pri:tʃ] (VT) 1 (*Rel*) predicar • **to ~ a sermon** dar un sermón • **to ~ the gospel** predicar el Evangelio
2 [+ *virtues*] predicar; [+ *patience*] aconsejar; ▹ **practise**
(VI) predicar • **to ~ at sb** sermonear a algn, dar un sermón a algn • IDIOM: • **to ~ to the converted** querer convertir a los que ya lo están
preacher ['pri:tʃəʳ] (N) [*of sermon*] predicador(a) *m/f*; (*US*) (= *minister*) pastor(a) *m/f*
preachify* ['pri:tʃɪfaɪ] (VI) sermonear largamente
preaching ['pri:tʃɪŋ] (N) predicación *f*; (*pej*) sermoneo *m*
preachy* ['pri:tʃɪ] (ADJ) [*person*] dado a sermonear; [*style, speech*] de predicador
preadolescent [,pri:ædə'lesənt] (ADJ) preadolescente
preamble [pri:'æmbl] (N) preámbulo *m*
preamplifier [,pri:'æmplɪfaɪəʳ] (N) preamplificador *m*
prearrange [,pri:ə'reɪndʒ] (VT) arreglar de antemano
prearranged [,pri:ə'reɪndʒd] (ADJ) [*time, location, signal*] convenido; [*meeting*] fijado
prearrangement [,pri:ə'reɪndʒmənt] (N) • **by ~** por previo acuerdo
prebend ['prebənd] (N) (= *stipend*) prebenda *f*; (= *person*) prebendado *m*
prebendary ['prebəndərɪ] (N) prebendado *m*
precarious [prɪ'kɛərɪəs] (ADJ) [*health, position*] precario • **they are in a ~ financial situation** se hallan en una situación económica precaria • **it could upset the ~ balance of the peace negotiations** podría alterar el precario equilibrio de las negociaciones de paz
precariously [prɪ'kɛərɪəslɪ] (ADV) precariamente
precariousness [prɪ'kɛərɪəsnɪs] (N) precariedad *f*
precast concrete [,pri:kɑ:st'kɒnkri:t] (N) hormigón *m* precolado
precaution [prɪ'kɔ:ʃən] (N) precaución *f* • **as a ~** como precaución, para mayor seguridad • **to take ~s** (*gen*) tomar precauciones; (= *use contraceptive*) usar anticonceptivos, tomar precauciones • **to take the ~ of doing sth** tomar la precaución de hacer algo • **he took the ~ of hiding the letter** tomó la precaución de esconder la carta
precautionary [prɪ'kɔ:ʃənərɪ] (ADJ) preventivo, de precaución • **as a ~ measure** como medida preventiva *or* de precaución
precede [prɪ'si:d] (VT) (*in space, time, rank*) preceder, anteceder • **he let me ~ him through the door** me dejó pasar por la puerta a mí primero • **the concert was ~d by a talk** el concierto vino precedido de una charla • **his reputation had ~d him** su reputación jugaba en contra de él • **for a month preceding this** durante un mes anterior a esto
precedence ['presɪdəns] (N) (*in rank*) precedencia *f*; (*in importance*) prioridad *f* • **in order of ~** (= *rank*) por orden de precedencia; (= *importance*) por orden de prioridad • **to take ~ over sth/sb** tener prioridad/precedencia sobre algo/algn • **this question must take ~ over all others** este asunto tiene prioridad con respecto a todos los demás • **they give ~ to people with language skills** le dan prioridad a la gente con idiomas
precedent ['presɪdənt] (N) precedente *m* (*also Jur*) • **according to ~** de acuerdo con los precedentes • **against all ~** contra todos los precedentes • **without ~** sin precedentes • **to**

P

break with ~ romper con todo precedente • **to establish** *or* **set a ~ (for sth)** sentar un precedente (para algo)

preceding [prɪ'siːdɪŋ] ADJ [*day, week, month, year*] anterior; [*chapter, paragraph, sentence*] precedente, anterior

precentor [prɪ'sentəʳ] N chantre *m*

precept ['priːsept] N precepto *m*

preceptor [prɪ'septəʳ] N preceptor *m*

pre-Christian [priː'krɪstʃən] ADJ precristiano

precinct ['priːsɪŋkt] N **1** (= *area*) recinto *m*; (*US*) (*Pol*) distrito *m* electoral, circunscripción *f*; (*US*) [*of police*] distrito *m* policial • **shopping ~** centro *m* comercial • **pedestrian ~** zona *f* peatonal
2 precincts (= *grounds, premises*) límites *mpl*; (= *environs*) alrededores *mpl*; [*of cathedral etc*] recinto *msing* • **within the ~s of** dentro de los límites de

preciosity [ˌpresɪ'ɒsɪtɪ] N (*frm*) preciosidad *f*

precious ['preʃəs] ADJ **1** (= *costly*) [*jewel, stone*] precioso; [*commodity, resource*] preciado; [*possession*] muy valioso • **we're wasting ~ time** estamos desperdiciando un tiempo precioso
2 (= *treasured*) preciado • **she savoured the ~ moments they spent together** saboreó esos momentos preciados que pasaron juntos • **her friendship is very ~ to me** aprecio *or* valoro mucho su amistad • **the book is very ~ to me** para mí el libro tiene gran valor
3 (= *artificial, affected*) [*person*] preciosista, afectado; [*style*] rebuscado
4 (*iro*) • **I couldn't care less about your ~ golf clubs** me traen sin cuidado tus queridos palos de golf (*iro*)
ADV* • **~ little/few** bien poco/pocos • **~ little has been gained** se ha logrado muy poco
N • **(my) ~!†** ¡querida!
CPD ▸ **precious metal** metal *m* precioso ▸ **precious stone** piedra *f* preciosa

precipice ['presɪpɪs] N precipicio *m*, despeñadero *m*

precipitance [prɪ'sɪpɪtəns] N (*frm*) = **precipitancy**

precipitancy [prɪ'sɪpɪtənsɪ] N (*frm*) precipitación *f*

precipitant [prɪ'sɪpɪtənt] N precipitante *m*
ADJ precipitado, apresurado

precipitate ADJ [prɪ'sɪpɪtɪt] precipitado, apresurado
VT [prɪ'sɪpɪteɪt] **1** (= *bring on*) precipitar, provocar • **an illness ~d by stress** una enfermedad provocada por el estrés • **the decision ~d her resignation** la decisión precipitó su dimisión
2 (= *hurl*) lanzar • **the civil war ~d the country into chaos** la guerra civil sumió al país en el caos
3 (*Chem*) precipitar; (*Met*) condensar
VI [prɪ'sɪpɪteɪt] (*Chem*) precipitarse; (*Met*) condensarse
N [prɪ'sɪpɪtɪt] (*Chem*) precipitado *m*

precipitately [prɪ'sɪpɪtɪtlɪ] ADV precipitadamente

precipitation [prɪˌsɪpɪ'teɪʃən] N (*all senses*) precipitación *f* • **the average annual ~** (*Met*) la media anual de precipitaciones

precipitous [prɪ'sɪpɪtəs] ADJ **1** (= *steep*) escarpado, cortado a pico
2 (= *hasty*) precipitado, apresurado

precipitously [prɪ'sɪpɪtəslɪ] ADV **1** (= *steeply*) • **the road fell away ~** la carretera descendía vertiginosamente • **prices have dropped ~** los precios han caído vertiginosamente
2 (= *hastily*) precipitadamente, apresuradamente

précis ['preɪsiː] N (PL: **précis**) resumen *m*
VT hacer un resumen de, resumir

precise [prɪ'saɪs] ADJ **1** (= *exact*) [*description, figure, measurements*] exacto; [*instructions*] preciso; [*details, information*] concreto • **he didn't give a ~ date** no precisó la fecha • **the timing had to be very ~** había que calcular el tiempo con mucha precisión • **there were five, to be ~** para ser exacto *or* preciso, fueron cinco • **can you be more ~?** ¿puedes ser más concreto? • **at that ~ moment** en ese preciso instante • **it achieved the ~ opposite of what we intended** con ello se consiguió exactamente *or* justamente lo contrario de lo que queríamos
2 (= *meticulous*) meticuloso

precisely [prɪ'saɪslɪ] ADV **1** (= *exactly*) exactamente • **we have ~ 17 minutes before the train leaves** tenemos exactamente 17 minutos antes de que salga el tren • **at four o'clock ~** • **at ~ four o'clock** a las cuatro en punto • **precisely!** ¡exactamente!, ¡efectivamente! • **~ what was it that you wanted?** ¿qué era lo que quería usted exactamente?
2 (= *expressly*) precisamente • **he liked her ~ because of her forthrightness** le caía bien precisamente por lo franca que era
3 (= *with precision*) [*calculate, measure*] con precisión
4 (= *meticulously*) meticulosamente

preciseness [prɪ'saɪsnɪs] N **1** (= *exactness*) precisión *f*, exactitud *f*
2 (= *meticulousness*) meticulosidad *f*, puntualidad *f*

precision [prɪ'sɪʒən] N (*gen*) precisión *f*; [*of calculations*] exactitud *f* • **~-made** [*product, instrument*] hecho con precisión
CPD ▸ **precision bombing** bombardeo *m* de precisión ▸ **precision engineering** ingeniería *f* de precisión ▸ **precision instrument** instrumento *m* de precisión

preclassical [priː'klæsɪkəl] ADJ preclásico

preclinical [ˌpriː'klɪnɪkəl] ADJ (*Med*) preclínico

preclude [prɪ'kluːd] VT (= *prevent*) impedir; [+ *possibility*] excluir • **this does not ~ the possibility of ...** esto no excluye *or* quita la posibilidad de ... • **so as to ~ all doubt** para disipar cualquier duda • **we are ~d from doing that** nos vemos imposibilitados para hacer eso

preclusion [prɪ'kluːʒən] N **1** [*of possibility*] exclusión *f*
2 (= *prevention*) prevención *f*

precocious [prɪ'kəʊʃəs] ADJ precoz

precociously [prɪ'kəʊʃəslɪ] ADV de modo precoz, con precocidad

precociousness [prɪ'kəʊʃəsnɪs], **precocity** [prɪ'kɒsɪtɪ] N precocidad *f*

precognition [ˌpriːkɒg'nɪʃən] N precognición *f*

pre-Columbian ['priːkə'lʌmbɪən] ADJ precolombino

preconceived ['priːkən'siːvd] ADJ preconcebido

preconception ['priːkən'sepʃən] N (= *idea*) preconcepción *f*, idea *f* preconcebida

preconcerted ['priːkən'sɜːtɪd] ADJ preconcertado

precondition ['priːkən'dɪʃən] N condición *f* previa

precook [ˌpriː'kʊk] VT precocinar

precooked [ˌpriː'kʊkt] ADJ precocinado

precool ['priː'kuːl] VT preenfriar

precursor [priː'kɜːsəʳ] N precursor(a) *m/f*

precursory [prɪ'kɜːsərɪ] ADJ preliminar

predate ['priː'deɪt] VT (= *put earlier date on*) poner fecha anterior a, antedatar; (= *precede*) preceder, ser anterior a

predator ['predətəʳ] N (= *animal*) depredador *m*; (= *bird*) ave *f* de presa, ave *f* rapaz

predatory ['predətərɪ] ADJ [*animal*] depredador; [*bird*] de presa, rapaz; [*person*] rapaz; [*look*] devorador

predecease ['priːdɪ'siːs] VT (*frm*) morir antes que

predecessor ['priːdɪsesəʳ] N predecesor(a) *m/f*, antecesor(a) *m/f*

predestination [priːˌdestɪ'neɪʃən] N predestinación *f*

predestine [priː'destɪn] VT predestinar • **to be ~d to do sth** estar predestinado a hacer algo

predetermination ['priːdɪˌtɜːmɪ'neɪʃən] N predeterminación *f*

predetermine ['priːdɪ'tɜːmɪn] VT (*Philos, Rel*) predeterminar; (= *arrange beforehand*) determinar de antemano

predetermined [ˌpriːdɪ'tɜːmɪnd] ADJ predeterminado

predeterminer [ˌpriːdɪ'tɜːmɪnəʳ] N predeterminante *m*

predicament [prɪ'dɪkəmənt] N apuro *m*, aprieto *m* • **to be in a ~** (= *in a fix*) estar en un apuro *or* un aprieto; (= *puzzled*) hallarse en un dilema • **what a ~ to be in!** ¡qué lío!

predicate N ['predɪkɪt] (*Ling*) predicado *m*
VT ['predɪkeɪt] **1** • **to be ~d (up)on** estar basado en, partir de
2 (= *imply*) implicar

predicative [prɪ'dɪkətɪv] ADJ predicativo

predicatively [prɪ'dɪkətɪvlɪ] ADV predicativamente

predict [prɪ'dɪkt] VT predecir, pronosticar, prever • **"it'll end in disaster," he ~ed** —será un desastre, —predijo *or* —pronosticó • **the ~ed fall in interest rates has not materialized** la bajada de los tipos de interés que estaba prevista aún no se ha materializado • **the motion was passed, as ~ed** la moción se aprobó como se había previsto *or* pronosticado • **I can't ~ the future** no puedo predecir *or* prever el futuro • **he ~ed a brilliant future for the child** le predijo un futuro brillante al niño • **to ~ that** predecir que, pronosticar que • **nobody can ~ what will happen** nadie puede predecir lo que va a pasar

predictability [prɪdɪktə'bɪlɪtɪ] N previsibilidad *f*

predictable [prɪ'dɪktəbl] ADJ [*result, outcome*] previsible • **his reaction was ~** su reacción era de esperar • **the contents of the report were entirely ~** el contenido del informe era totalmente previsible • **people were so ~** era tan fácil prever las reacciones de la gente • **you're so ~!** (= *always saying the same*) ¡siempre sales con las mismas!*; (= *always behaving the same*) ¡siempre estás igual! • **you men are so ~** siempre se sabe lo que los hombres vais a hacer/decir *etc*

predictably [prɪ'dɪktəblɪ] ADV [*behave, say, react*] como era de esperar • **his father was ~ furious** • **~, his father was furious** como era de esperar, su padre estaba furioso • **~ enough, share prices fell** de manera previsible *or* como era de esperar, el precio de las acciones bajó

prediction [prɪ'dɪkʃən] N **1** (= *forecast*) (*by expert, layman*) predicción *f*; (*by clairvoyant, oracle*) vaticinio *m*, profecía *f* • **their ~ that house prices would fall** su predicción de que el precio de la vivienda iba a bajar • **there were dire ~s that thousands would die of malnutrition** hubo predicciones alarmantes de que miles de personas morirían por desnutrición • **to make a ~ about sth** pronosticar *or* predecir algo
2 (= *act*) • **weather ~ has never been a perfect**

science pronosticar el tiempo nunca ha sido una ciencia exacta

predictive [prɪˈdɪktɪv] ADJ [*powers, ability*] de predicción
CPD ▸ **predictive text** texto *m* predictivo

predictor [prɪˈdɪktəʳ] N indicador *m*

predigested [ˌpriːdaɪˈdʒestɪd] ADJ predigerido

predilection [ˌpriːdɪˈlekʃən] N predilección *f* • **to have a ~ for** tener predilección por

predispose [ˈpriːdɪsˈpəʊz] VT predisponer • **some people are ~d to diabetes** hay gente propensa *or* predispuesta a la diabetes • **I was ~d to believe him** tenía predisposición a creerle

predisposition [ˈpriːˌdɪspəˈzɪʃən] N predisposición *f*

predominance [prɪˈdɒmɪnəns] N
1 (= *dominance*) primacía *f*; [*of flavour*] predominio *m*
2 (= *greater number*) predominio *m* • **the ~ of women in the labour force** el predominio de mujeres entre los trabajadores

predominant [prɪˈdɒmɪnənt] ADJ [*role, opinion, image*] predominante, preponderante; [*flavour, colour*] predominante • **the disease is much more ~ in women** la enfermedad es mucho más predominante en las mujeres

predominantly [prɪˈdɒmɪnəntlɪ] ADV (= *mainly*) predominantemente; (= *in the majority*) en su mayoría • **the emphasis is ~ on languages** se hace hincapié predominantemente en los idiomas • **a population of ~ Italian residents** una población en su mayoría de residentes italianos

predominate [prɪˈdɒmɪneɪt] VI predominar (**over** sobre)

predominately [prɪˈdɒmɪnətlɪ] = **predominantly**

pre-eclampsia [ˌpriːɪˈklæmpsɪə] N pre-eclampsia *f*

preemie* [ˈpriːmɪ] N (*US*) bebé *m* prematuro

pre-eminence [priːˈemɪnəns] N preeminencia *f*

pre-eminent [priːˈemɪnənt] ADJ preeminente

pre-eminently [priːˈemɪnəntlɪ] ADV • **his family were pre-eminently farmers** su familia era fundamentalmente campesina • **home ownership is a pre-eminently middle-class concern** la adquisición de la vivienda es una inquietud muy propia de la clase media • **it is also, and perhaps pre-eminently, a place of recreation** es además, y tal vez principalmente, un lugar de esparcimiento

pre-empt [priːˈempt] VT **1** [+ *person, attack, opposition*] adelantarse a, anticiparse a • **we found they had pre-empted us in buying it** encontramos que se nos habían adelantado a comprarlo • **I did it to pre-empt any family arguments** lo hice para evitar discusiones familiares
2 (*esp US*) [+ *public land*] *ocupar para ejercer la opción de compra prioritaria*

pre-emption [priːˈempʃən] N **1** (*Mil*) prevención *f*, anticipación *f*
2 (*Jur*) derecho *m* preferencial (de compra)

pre-emptive [priːˈemptɪv] ADJ [*measure*] preventivo; [*claim*] por derecho de prioridad, preferente
CPD ▸ **pre-emptive bid** oferta *f* hecha con intención de excluir cualquier otra ▸ **pre-emptive right** derecho *m* preferencial ▸ **pre-emptive strike** ataque *m* preventivo

preen [priːn] VT [+ *feathers*] arreglarse con el pico • **to ~ its feathers** *or* **itself** [*bird*] arreglarse las plumas con el pico • **to ~ o.s.** [*person*] pavonearse, atildarse • **to ~ o.s. on** enorgullecerse de, jactarse de

pre-establish [ˈpriːɪsˈtæblɪʃ] VT establecer de antemano

pre-established [ˈpriːɪsˈtæblɪʃt] ADJ establecido de antemano

pre-exist [ˈpriːɪgˈzɪst] VI preexistir

pre-existence [ˈpriːɪgˈzɪstəns] N preexistencia *f*

pre-existent [ˈpriːɪgˈzɪstənt] ADJ preexistente

prefab* [ˈpriːfæb] N casa *f* prefabricada

prefabricate [ˈpriːˈfæbrɪkeɪt] VT prefabricar

prefabricated [ˈpriːˈfæbrɪkeɪtɪd] ADJ prefabricado

prefabrication [priːˌfæbrɪˈkeɪʃən] N prefabricación *f*

preface [ˈprefɪs] N prólogo *m*, prefacio *m*
VT [+ *book*] prologar • **he ~d this by saying that …** a modo de prólogo a esto dijo que …, introdujo este tema diciendo que … • **the book is ~d by an essay** el libro tiene un ensayo a modo de prólogo • **he has the irritating habit of prefacing his sentences with …** tiene la molesta costumbre de comenzar las frases con …

prefaded [ˌpriːˈfeɪdɪd] ADJ [*jeans*] desteñido de origen

prefatory [ˈprefətərɪ] ADJ (*frm*) [*remarks, article, note*] preliminar, introductorio

prefect [ˈpriːfekt] N **1** (*Brit*) (*Scol*) monitor(a) *m/f*
2 (*Admin*) (*esp in France*) prefecto *m*

prefecture [ˈpriːfektjʊəʳ] N prefectura *f*

prefer [prɪˈfɜːʳ] VT **1** (= *like better*) preferir (**to** a) • **she ~s coffee to tea** prefiere el café al té • **which do you ~?** ¿cuál prefieres?, ¿cuál te gusta más? • **I ~red it the way it was** lo prefería tal como estaba • **"qualifications preferred but not essential"** "ser titulado es una ventaja pero no un requisito" • **to ~ doing sth** preferir hacer algo • **I ~ walking to going by car** prefiero ir andando *or* (*LAm*) caminando a ir en coche • **I'd ~ it if you didn't come with me** preferiría que no vinieras conmigo • **I much ~ Scotland** Escocia me gusta mucho más • **to ~ that** preferir que (+ *subjun*) • **we'd ~ that this visit be kept confidential** preferimos que esta visita se mantenga en secreto • **to ~ to do sth** preferir hacer algo • **"will you do it?" — "I'd ~ not to"** —¿lo harás? —preferiría no hacerlo • **he may ~ to discuss it with friends rather than with his family** puede que prefiera hablarlo con amigos a hacerlo con su familia • **to ~ sb to do sth** preferir que algn haga algo • **would you ~ me to drive?** ¿preferirías que condujera yo?
2 (*Jur*) • **to ~ charges (against sb)** presentar cargos (contra algn) • **our client may decide to ~ charges of assault** puede que nuestro cliente decida presentar cargos por agresión
3 (*esp Rel*) (= *promote*) ascender; (= *appoint*) nombrar • **he was ~red to the see of Toledo** lo nombraron arzobispo de Toledo
VI preferir • **as you ~** como usted quiera, como usted prefiera • **if you ~, we could leave it till tomorrow** si usted quiere *or* lo prefiere, lo podemos dejar para mañana

preferable [ˈprefərəbl] ADJ preferible (**to** a)

preferably [ˈprefərəblɪ] ADV de preferencia, preferentemente • **a large, ~ non-stick, frying pan** una sartén grande, preferentemente *or* a ser posible antiadherente

preference [ˈprefərəns] N **1** (= *greater liking or favour*) preferencia *f* • **he expressed a ~ for red wine** mostró su preferencia por el vino tinto • **she has a ~ for older men** prefiere a *or* tiene preferencia por los hombres maduros • **for ~** de preferencia • **in ~ to sth** antes que algo, más que algo
2 (= *thing preferred*) • **what is your ~?** ¿qué prefieres? • **I have no ~** no tengo preferencia
3 (= *priority*) • **to give ~ to sth/sb** dar prioridad a algo/algn • **to give sth ~ over sth else** anteponer algo a otra cosa
CPD ▸ **preference share** (*Econ*) acción *f* preferente, acción *f* privilegiada

preferential [ˌprefəˈrenʃəl] ADJ preferente, preferencial • **on ~ terms** con condiciones preferenciales • **to give a country ~ trade status** dar a un país un estatus comercial preferente

preferentially [ˌprefəˈrenʃəlɪ] ADV de manera preferente, de manera preferencial

preferment [prɪˈfɜːmənt] N (*esp Rel*) (= *promotion*) ascenso *m*, promoción *f*; (= *nomination*) nombramiento *m* (**to** a) • **to get ~** ser ascendido

preferred [prɪˈfɜːd] ADJ **1** (*gen*) preferido • **his ~ method of travel** su medio de transporte preferido • **our ~ method of payment is cash** preferimos pagar en efectivo
2 (*Econ*) [*creditor*] privilegiado
CPD ▸ **preferred stock** (*US*) (*Econ*) acciones *fpl* preferentes *or* privilegiadas

prefiguration [ˌpriːfɪgəˈreɪʃən] N prefiguración *f*

prefigure [priːˈfɪgəʳ] VT prefigurar

prefix [ˈpriːfɪks] N [*of word*] prefijo *m*; [*of phone number*] prefijo *m*
VT [priːˈfɪks] **1** (= *introduce*) introducir • **to ~ a statement with …** encabezar una declaración con …
2 (*Ling*) adjuntar un prefijo a

prefixed [ˈpriːfɪkst] ADJ • **to be ~ with sth** [+ *numbers, letters*] estar precedido de algo • **calls to Dublin should now be ~ with 003531** las llamadas a Dublín deberían ir ahora precedidas por los números 003531

preflight [ˈpriːˈflaɪt] ADJ anterior al despegue

prefrontal [priːˈfrʌntəl] ADJ prefrontal

preggers* [ˈpregəz] ADJ • **to be ~** estar con bombo*

pregnancy [ˈpregnənsɪ] N [*of woman*] embarazo *m*; [*of animal*] preñez *f*; ▹ **phantom**
CPD ▸ **pregnancy test** prueba *f* del embarazo

pregnant [ˈpregnənt] ADJ **1** (*lit*) **a** [*woman*] embarazada • **to be ~** estar embarazada • **to be six months ~** estar embarazada de seis meses • **to become** *or* **get ~ (by sb)** quedarse embarazada (de algn) • **Tina was ~ with their first son** Tina estaba embarazada de su primer hijo; ▹ **heavily**
b [*animal*] preñado
2 (*fig*) elocuente, significativo • **a ~ pause** una pausa elocuente *or* significativa • **~ with sth** cargado *or* preñado de algo

preheat [ˈpriːˈhiːt] VT precalentar

prehensile [prɪˈhensaɪl] ADJ prensil

prehistoric [ˈpriːhɪsˈtɒrɪk] ADJ prehistórico

prehistory [ˈpriːˈhɪstərɪ] N prehistoria *f*

preignition [ˌpriːɪgˈnɪʃən] N preignición *f*

prejudge [ˈpriːˈdʒʌdʒ] VT prejuzgar

prejudice [ˈpredʒʊdɪs] N **1** (= *biased opinion*) prejuicio *m* • **there's a lot of racial ~** hay muchos prejuicios raciales • **~ against women is widespread** los prejuicios machistas son moneda corriente • **to have a ~ against/in favour of sth/sb** estar predispuesto en contra de/a favor de algo/algn • **we all have our ~s** todos tenemos nuestros prejuicios • **he is quite without ~ in**

this matter sobre esto no tiene ningún prejuicio
2 (*Jur*) (= *injury, detriment*) perjuicio *m* • **to the ~ of** con perjuicio de, con menoscabo de • **without ~** (*Jur*) sin detrimento de sus propios derechos • **without ~ to** sin perjuicio de
VT 1 (= *bias*) predisponer, prevenir (**against** contra)
2 (= *damage*) perjudicar • **to ~ one's chances** perjudicar sus posibilidades

prejudiced ['predʒʊdɪst] ADJ [*view*] parcial, interesado • **he's very ~** tiene muchos prejuicios • **to be ~ against sth/sb** estar predispuesto en contra de algo/algn • **to be ~ in favour of sth/sb** estar predispuesto a favor de algo/algn

prejudicial [ˌpredʒʊ'dɪʃəl] ADJ perjudicial (**to** para) • **it would be ~ to her career** sería perjudicial para *or* perjudicaría a su carrera

prelate ['prelɪt] N prelado *m*

prelim ['pri:lɪm] N ABBR = **preliminary**

preliminary [prɪ'lɪmɪnərɪ] ADJ preliminar
N 1 prolegómeno *m* • **a background check is normally a ~ to a presidential appointment** la comprobación del historial personal es normalmente un prolegómeno al nombramiento de presidente • **let's dispense with the preliminaries and get down to business** dejémonos de prolegómenos *or* preámbulos y vayamos al grano
2 (*Sport*) fase *f* previa
CPD ▸ **preliminary hearing** audiencia *f* preliminar ▸ **Preliminary Scholastic Aptitude Test** (*US*) *test que determina la aptitud de un candidato para presentarse al examen de acceso a la universidad*

preloaded ['pri:ləʊdɪd] ADJ (*Comput*) [*program etc*] precargado

pre-loved [pri:'lʌvd] ADJ (*euph*) usado

prelude ['prelju:d] N preludio *m* (*also Mus*) (**to de**)
VT preludiar

prem* [prem] N (= *premature baby*) prematuro/a *m/f*

premarital ['pri:'mærɪtl] ADJ prematrimonial
CPD ▸ **premarital sex** relaciones *fpl* prematrimoniales

premature ['premətʃʊəʳ] ADJ [*baby, ageing, baldness*] prematuro; [*ejaculation*] precoz • **it would be ~ to conclude that ...** sería prematuro deducir que ... • **he was (born) five weeks ~** nació con cinco semanas de antelación • **I think you're being a little ~** creo que te estás adelantando a los acontecimientos

prematurely ['premətʃʊəlɪ] ADV prematuramente, antes de tiempo • **to be born ~** nacer prematuramente

pre-med ['pri:med] N (*Brit*) = **premedication**
ADJ (*US*) = **premedical** • **pre-med course** curso *m* preparatorio para ingresar en la Facultad de Medicina

premedication [ˌpri:medɪ'keɪʃən] N premedicación *f*, medicación *f* previa

premeditate [pri:'medɪteɪt] VT premeditar

premeditated [pri:'medɪteɪtɪd] ADJ premeditado

premeditation [pri:ˌmedɪ'teɪʃən] N premeditación *f*

premenstrual [ˌpri:'menstrʊəl] ADJ premenstrual
CPD ▸ **premenstrual syndrome** síndrome *m* premenstrual ▸ **premenstrual tension** tensión *f* premenstrual

premier ['premɪəʳ] ADJ primero, principal
N (= *prime minister*) primer(a) ministro/a *m/f*; (= *president*) presidente/a *m/f*
CPD ▸ **Premier Division** (*in Scotland*) primera división *f* ▸ **Premier League** (*Brit*) (*Ftbl*) primera división *f*

première [ˌpremɪ'ɛəʳ] N estreno *m* • **world ~** estreno *m* mundial • **the film had its ~** se estrenó la película
VT estrenar
CPD ▸ **première screening** premiere *f*

Premiership ['premɪəʃɪp] N (*Ftbl*) Primera División *f*

premiership ['premɪəʃɪp] N (*Pol*) cargo *m* del primer ministro, puesto *m* de primer ministro; (= *period in office*) mandato *m*

premise ['premɪs] N 1 (= *hypothesis*) premisa *f*
2 **premises** (*gen*) local *msing*; (= *shop, restaurant, hotel*) establecimiento *m*; (= *building*) edificio *m* • **they're moving to new ~s** se trasladan de local • **there is a doctor on the ~s at all times** hay un médico a todas horas en el edificio • **for consumption on the ~s** para consumirse en el local • **licensed ~s** local *msing* autorizado para la venta de bebidas alcohólicas • **to see sb off the ~s** echar a algn del local *or* establecimiento
VT (*frm*) • **to be ~d on** estar basado en, tener como premisa

premiss ['premɪs] N (= *hypothesis*) premisa *f*
VT (*frm*) • **to be ~ed on** estar basado en, tener como premisa

premium ['pri:mɪəm] N 1 (*Insurance*) prima *f*
2 (= *surcharge*) recargo *m* • **people will pay a ~ for quality** (*fig*) la gente está dispuesta a pagar más para adquirir calidad
3 (= *bonus*) prima *f*
4 (*US*) (= *gasoline*) súper *f*
5 (*in phrases*) • **to be at a ~** (*Comm*) estar por encima de la par; (= *be scarce*) estar muy solicitado • **space is at a ~ in our house** en casa no nos sobra espacio • **to sell sth at a ~** vender algo con prima • **to put** *or* **place a ~ on sth** (= *value*) valorar mucho algo; (= *make valuable*) hacer que suba el valor de algo; (= *make important*) hacer que se dé más importancia a algo • **I put a high ~ on privacy** valoro mucho la intimidad • **population pressure put land at a ~** la presión demográfica hizo que subiera el valor de la tierra • **the risk of disease puts a ~ on hygiene** el riesgo de enfermedad hace que se dé más importancia a la higiene
ADJ 1 (= *top quality*) [*brand, product*] de calidad superior, de primera calidad • **~ gasoline** (*US*) (gasolina *f*) súper *f*
2 (= *higher than normal*) • **~ price** precio *m* con prima, precio *m* más elevado • **~ rate** tarifa *f* de primas
CPD ▸ **premium bond** (*Brit*) *bono del estado que permite participar en una lotería nacional* ▸ **premium deal** oferta *f* especial ▸ **premium fuel** (*Brit*), **premium gasoline** (*US*) (gasolina *f*) súper *f*

premium-rate ['pri:mɪəmˌreɪt] ADJ (*Telec*) con aplicación de la máxima tarifa

premolar [pri:'məʊləʳ] N premolar *m*

premonition [ˌpremə'nɪʃən] N presentimiento *m*, premonición *f* • **to have a ~ that ...** presentir que ...

premonitory [prɪ'mɒnɪtərɪ] ADJ (*frm*) premonitorio

prenatal ['pri:'neɪtl] ADJ prenatal

prenuptial [ˌpri:'nʌpʃəl] ADJ prematrimonial, prenupcial
CPD ▸ **prenuptial agreement** contrato *m* matrimonial

preoccupation [pri:ˌɒkjʊ'peɪʃən] N preocupación *f* • **keeping warm was his main ~** su principal preocupación *or* lo que más le preocupaba era no pasar frío • **she was too busy with her own ~s to notice** estaba demasiado ensimismada en sus cosas para darse cuenta • **his incessant ~ with his appearance** su constante obsesión *or* preocupación por el aspecto

preoccupied [pri:'ɒkjʊpaɪd] ADJ (= *worried*) preocupado; (= *absorbed, distracted*) ensimismado, absorto • **he was too ~ to notice** estaba demasiado ensimismado *or* absorto para darse cuenta • **to be ~ about sth** estar preocupado por algo • **to be ~ with sth: Britain was ~ with the war in France** a Gran Bretaña le preocupaba la guerra en Francia • **you're too ~ with winning** estás demasiado obsesionado por ganar

preoccupy [pri:'ɒkjʊpaɪ] VT preocupar

pre-op* ['pri:'ɒp] ADJ preoperatorio • **pre-op medication** medicación *f* preoperatoria

preordain ['pri:ɔ:'deɪn] VT predestinar

preordained ['pri:ɔ:'deɪnd] ADJ predestinado

pre-owned ['pri:'əʊnd] ADJ seminuevo

prep [prep] ABBR (*Brit*) (*Scol*) (= **preparation**) (= *work*) tareas *fpl*, deberes *mpl*; (= *period*) tiempo *m* de estudio, hora *f* de los deberes
VI (*US**) • **to ~ for** prepararse para; (*Scol*) hacer el curso de preparación para (*los estudios universitarios*)
VT (*US**) preparar • **to ~ o.s.** prepararse
CPD ▸ **prep school** (*Brit*) ▹ **preparatory**

prepack [ˌpri:'pæk], **prepackage** [ˌpri:'pækɪdʒ] VT preempaquetar

prepacked [ˌpri:'pækt], **prepackaged** [ˌpri:'pækɪdʒd] ADJ (pre)empaquetado

prepaid [ˌpri:'peɪd] ADJ pagado con antelación; (*Comm*) [*order*] abonado por adelantado, pagado por adelantado; (*Econ*) [*interest*] cobrado por adelantado; [*envelope*] con franqueo pagado • **carriage ~** porte *m* pagado, franco de porte

preparation [ˌprepə'reɪʃən] N 1 (= *prior activity, development*) preparación *f* • **few things distracted him from the ~ of his lectures** pocas cosas le distraían de la preparación de sus clases • **the person responsible for food ~** la persona encargada de preparar la comida • **education should be a ~ for life** la educación debería servir de preparación para la vida • **her latest novel has been four years in ~** lleva cuatro años preparando su última novela • **he is learning French in ~ for his new job** está aprendiendo francés para prepararse para su nuevo trabajo
2 **preparations** preparativos *mpl* (**for** para), (de) • **I helped with the ~s for the party** ayudé con los preparativos para *or* de la fiesta • **to make ~s (for sth/to do sth)** hacer preparativos (para algo/para hacer algo) • **he'll have to make ~s for the funeral** tendrá que hacer los preparativos del *or* para el funeral
3 (*Culin, Pharm*) (= *substance*) preparado *m*
4 (*Brit*) (= *homework*) deberes *mpl*

preparatory [prɪ'pærətərɪ] ADJ preparatorio, preliminar • **~ to** como preparación para, antes de
CPD ▸ **preparatory school** (*Brit*) *escuela privada para niños de 6 a 13 años*; (*US*) colegio *m* privado; ▹ PREPARATORY SCHOOL

prepare [prɪ'pɛəʳ] VT [+ *meal, lesson, defence*] preparar; [+ *report*] redactar, preparar; [+ *plan, strategy*] idear, preparar • **to ~ sb for sth** preparar a algn para algo • **he had a tutor to ~ him for the exam** tenía un profesor particular para que lo preparara

para el examen • **nothing could have ~d me for this** nada hubiera podido ponerme en guardia contra esto • **she tried to ~ her children for her death** intentó preparar a sus hijos para su muerte *or* para que aceptaran su muerte • **to ~ o.s. for sth** prepararse para algo • **~ yourself for a shock** (*good*) prepárate para una sorpresa; (*bad*) prepárate para lo peor • **to ~ sth for sb** preparar algo a algn • **they had ~d a room for him** le habían preparado una habitación • IDIOM: • **to ~ the ground** *or* **way (for sth/sb)** preparar el terreno (para algo/algn)
(VI) prepararse • **to ~ for sth** prepararse para algo • **to ~ for an examination** prepararse para un examen • **we must ~ for war** tenemos que prepararnos para la guerra • **I think you'd better ~ for the worst** creo que deberías prepararte para lo peor • **to ~ to do sth** prepararse para hacer algo

PREPARATORY SCHOOL
En el Reino Unido una **preparatory school** o **prep school** es una escuela privada de educación primaria, normalmente no mixta, para alumnos de edades comprendidas entre los 6 y los 13 años. Estos centros exigen uniforme y su objetivo es preparar a los alumnos para que prosigan su formación en centros privados.
En Estados Unidos una **preparatory** o **prep school** es un centro privado de enseñanza secundaria que prepara a sus alumnos para su ingreso en la universidad. Tanto en el Reino Unido como en Estados Unidos las **preparatory schools** se asocian con las clases sociales más pudientes y privilegiadas. La palabra **preppy**, usada como sustantivo o adjetivo, designa a los alumnos de las **prep schools** estadounidenses o la forma de vestir y apariencia pulcra, discreta y conservadora que normalmente se les atribuye.

prepared [prɪˈpɛəd] (ADJ) **1** (= *ready*) preparado • **I am ~ for anything** estoy preparado para cualquier eventualidad • **we were ~ for it** íbamos preparados • **we were not ~ for this** esto no lo esperábamos, no contábamos con esto • **"be ~"** (*motto*) ¡siempre listos! • **to be ~ for the worst** estar preparado para lo peor
2 (= *made earlier*) **a** [*statement, answer*] preparado
b (*Culin*) • **supermarkets now stock ~ salads** ahora los supermercados venden ensaladas listas para comer *or* ensaladas preparadas • **~ foods** platos *m* precocinados, productos *mpl* previamente elaborados
3 (= *willing*) • **to be ~ to do sth** estar dispuesto a hacer algo • **he was ~ to be broadminded** estaba dispuesto a ser tolerante
preparedness [prɪˈpɛərɪdnɪs] (N) preparación *f*, estado *m* de preparación • **military ~** preparación *f* militar
prepay [ˈpriːˈpeɪ] (PT, PP: **prepaid**) (VT) (*Comm*) [+ *order*] abonar por adelantado, pagar por adelantado; (*Econ*) [+ *interest*] cobrar por adelantado; [+ *envelope*] emitir con franqueo pagado
prepayment [ˈpriːˈpeɪmənt] (N) pago *m* por adelantado, pago *m* anticipado
preponderance [prɪˈpɒndərəns] (N) preponderancia *f*, predominio *m*
preponderant [prɪˈpɒndərənt] (ADJ) preponderante, predominante
preponderantly [prɪˈpɒndərəntlɪ] (ADV) preponderantemente, predominantemente, de modo predominante
preponderate [prɪˈpɒndəreɪt] (VI) (*frm*) preponderar, predominar
preposition [ˌprepəˈzɪʃən] (N) (*Ling*) preposición *f*
prepositional [ˌprepəˈzɪʃənl] (ADJ) preposicional
(CPD) ▸ **prepositional phrase** locución *f* preposicional
prepositionally [ˌprepəˈzɪʃənəlɪ] (ADV) como preposición
prepossess [ˌpriːpəˈzes] (VT) (= *preoccupy*) preocupar; (= *bias, impress favourably*) predisponer
prepossessing [ˌpriːpəˈzesɪŋ] (ADJ) agradable, atractivo • **not very ~** no muy atractivo
preposterous [prɪˈpɒstərəs] (ADJ) absurdo, ridículo
preposterously [prɪˈpɒstərəslɪ] (ADV) absurdamente
preposterousness [prɪˈpɒstərəsnɪs] (N) lo absurdo
preppie*, **preppy*** [ˈprepɪ] (*US*) (ADJ) de muy buen tono
(N) **1** (= *prep school student*) *alumno de colegio secundario privado*
2 (= *rich kid*) niño/a *m/f* bien, niño/a *m/f* pera*, pijo/a* *m/f*
pre-prandial [ˌpriːˈprændɪəl] (ADJ) (*frm, hum*) • **a pre-prandial drink** un aperitivo
preprepared [ˌpriːprɪˈpɛəd] (ADJ) preprepareado
preprinted [ˈpriːˌprɪntɪd] (ADJ) preimpreso
preproduction [ˌpriːprəˈdʌkʃən] (N) preproducción *f*
(CPD) ▸ **preproduction model** prototipo *m* ▸ **preproduction trial** ensayo *m* con prototipo
preprogramme, **preprogram** (*esp US*) [ˌpriːˈprəʊgræm] (VT) preprogramar
preprogrammed, **preprogramed** (*US*) [ˌpriːˈprəʊgræmd] (ADJ) preprogramado
prepubescent [ˌpriːpjuːˈbesənt] (ADJ) prepúber
prepublication [ˌpriːpʌblɪˈkeɪʃən] (ADJ) de prepublicación
prepuce [ˈpriːpjuːs] (N) prepucio *m*
prequel [ˈpriːkwəl] (N) *película hecha para ser la primera parte de otra aparecida antes*
pre-Raphaelite [ˈpriːˈræfəlaɪt] (ADJ) prerrafaelista
(N) prerrafaelista *mf*
prerecord [ˈpriːrɪˈkɔːd] (VT) grabar de antemano, pregrabar
prerecorded [ˌpriːrɪˈkɔːdɪd] (ADJ) pregrabado, grabado de antemano
pre-release [ˈpriːrɪˈliːs] (ADJ) (*Cine*) [*copy*] promocional; [*publicity*] previo al estreno, promocional
(CPD) ▸ **pre-release showing** preestreno *m*
prerequisite [ˈpriːˈrekwɪzɪt] (N) requisito *m* indispensable, condición *f* previa • **a maths degree is a ~ for the job** la titulación en matemáticas es requisito indispensable para el puesto • **it's an essential ~ to success as an actor** es una condición *or* requisito indispensable para triunfar como actor
(ADJ) previamente necesario
prerogative [prɪˈrɒgətɪv] (N) prerrogativa *f* • **he can refuse if he wants to, that's his ~** puede negarse si quiere, está en su derecho
Pres (ABBR) (= **President**) Presidente/a *m/f*
presage [ˈpresɪdʒ] (*liter*) (N) presagio *m*
(VT) presagiar
Presbyterian [ˌprezbɪˈtɪərɪən] (ADJ) presbiteriano
(N) presbiteriano/a *m/f*
Presbyterianism [ˌprezbɪˈtɪərɪənɪzəm] (N) presbiterianismo *m*
presbytery [ˈprezbɪtərɪ] (N) casa *f* parroquial; (*Archit*) presbiterio *m*
preschool [ˈpriːˈskuːl] (ADJ) preescolar
(CPD) ▸ **preschool education** educación *f* preescolar
preschooler, pre-schooler [ˈpriːskuːləʳ] (N) preescolar *mf*
prescience [ˈpresɪəns] (N) clarividencia *f*
prescient [ˈpresɪənt] (ADJ) [*person, remark*] clarividente; [*dream*] profético
prescribable [prɪˈskraɪbəbl] (ADJ) [*medicine*] que se puede recetar
prescribe [prɪˈskraɪb] (VT) **1** (= *lay down, order*) prescribir, ordenar • **in the ~d way** en conformidad con lo prescrito • **~d books** lecturas *fpl* obligatorias • **the ~d punishment** la pena establecida *or* prescrita
2 [+ *medicine*] recetar • **to ~ sth for sb** • **~ sb sth** [+ *medicine*] recetar algo a algn • **the doctor ~d a course of antibiotics for me** el médico me recetó antibióticos • **he ~d complete rest** recomendó reposo absoluto • **the ~d dose** la dosis prescrita • **what do you ~?** ¿qué me recomienda?
(VI) (*Med*) recetar
prescription [prɪˈskrɪpʃən] (N) **1** (*Med*) receta *f* • **to make up** *or* (*US*) **fill a ~** preparar una receta • **"only available on prescription"** "de venta únicamente bajo receta"; ▹ **write**
2 (*Jur*) prescripción *f*
(CPD) ▸ **prescription charges** (*Brit*) precio *msing* de las recetas ▸ **prescription lenses** (*US*) lentillas *fpl* graduadas ▸ **prescription pad** talón *m* de recetas médicas
prescriptive [prɪˈskrɪptɪv] (ADJ) (*Jur*) [*title*] legal; (= *sanctioned by custom*) sancionado por la costumbre; (*Gram*) normativo
prescriptivism [prɪˈskrɪptɪˌvɪzəm] (N) prescriptivismo *m*
presealed [ˈpriːˈsiːld] (ADJ) precintado
pre-select [priːsɪˈlekt] (VT) preseleccionar
presence [ˈprezns] (N) **1** [*of person*] (*in place*) presencia *f*; (*at function*) asistencia *f* (**at** a) • **he was aware of her ~** era consciente de su presencia • **your ~ is requested** se ruega su asistencia • **to grace** *or* **honour sb with one's ~** (*also iro*) honrar a algn con su presencia • **in sb's ~** en presencia de algn, delante de algn • **he said it in the ~ of witnesses** lo dijo en presencia de *or* delante de testigos • **I felt comfortable in her ~** me sentía cómodo en su presencia *or* con ella • **to make one's ~ felt** hacerse notar *or* sentir
2 (*Mil, Police*) presencia *f* • **military ~** presencia *f* militar • **there was a massive police ~ at the match** hubo una importante presencia policial en el partido
3 (= *bearing, personality*) presencia *f* • **he had tremendous physical ~** tenía mucha presencia; ▹ **stage**
4 [*of thing, substance*] presencia *f* • **the ~ of a carcinogen in the water** la presencia de un carcinógeno en el agua • **metal rusts in the ~ of oxygen** el metal se oxida en presencia de oxígeno
5 • **~ of mind** presencia *f* de ánimo • **to have the ~ of mind to do sth** tener la suficiente presencia de ánimo como para hacer algo, tener la presencia de ánimo de hacer algo
6 (*ghostly*) presencia *f*
present[1] [ˈpreznt] (ADJ) **1** [*person*] • **to be ~** (*in place*) estar presente; (*at function*) asistir, estar presente • **he insisted on being ~** se empeñó en estar presente *or* en asistir • **the whole family was ~** estaba toda la familia presente • **how many others were ~?** ¿cuántos más había?, ¿cuántos más

estuvieron presentes? • **nobody else was ~** no había nadie más, nadie más estuvo presente • **is there a doctor ~?** ¿hay un médico (presente)? • **present!** ¡presente! • **ssh! there are ladies ~** ¡sss! hay señoras delante • **to be ~ at** [+ *function*] asistir a, estar presente en; [+ *scene, accident*] presenciar • **~ company excepted** exceptuando a los presentes • **all ~ and correct** (*Mil*) todos presentes; (*hum*) somos todos los que estamos y estamos todos los que somos • **those ~** los presentes
2 • **to be ~** [*thing, substance*] encontrarse • **in some areas, fluoride is naturally ~ in the water supply** en algunas zonas, el flúor se encuentra de forma natural en el agua • **to be ever ~** estar siempre presente
3 (= *current*) actual • **how long have you been in your ~ job?** ¿cuánto tiempo llevas en tu puesto actual? • **in its ~ form** en su forma actual • **the ~ government** el actual gobierno • **from Roman times to the ~ day** desde los tiempos romanos hasta nuestros días • **this tradition has continued to the ~ day** esta tradición sigue vigente • **a solution to the problems of the ~ day** una solución a los problemas actuales *or* de nuestros días • **at the ~ time** (= *at this instant*) en este momento; (= *currently*) actualmente, hoy día • **(up) to the ~ time** hasta nuestros días, hasta los tiempos actuales; ▹ **present-day**
4 (*Gram*) presente
N **1** (= *present time*) • **the ~** el presente • **for the ~** de momento, por lo pronto • **that will be all for the ~** de momento *or* por lo pronto esto es todo • **I'll say goodbye for the ~** me despido hasta la próxima • **up to the ~** hasta ahora • IDIOM: • **to live for the ~** vivir el momento • PROVERB: • **(there's) no time like the ~** no dejes para mañana lo que puedas hacer hoy
2 • **at ~** (= *at this instant*) en este momento; (= *currently*) ahora, actualmente • **Mr Young isn't here at ~** el Sr. Young no está aquí en este momento • **I don't want to get married at ~** de momento no me quiero casar • **as things are at ~** como están las cosas ahora, como están las cosas actualmente
3 (*Gram*) (tiempo *m*) presente *m*
4 (*Jur*) • **by these ~s** por los aquí presentes
CPD ▸ **the present continuous** el presente continuo ▸ **the present indicative** el presente de indicativo ▸ **present participle** participio *m* activo, participio *m* (de) presente ▸ **the present perfect** el pretérito perfecto ▸ **the present simple** el presente simple ▸ **the present subjunctive** el presente de subjuntivo ▸ **the present tense** el (tiempo) presente

present² ['preznt] N (= *gift*) regalo *m*, obsequio *m* (*frm*), presente *m* (*frm, liter*) • **it's for a ~** es para (un) regalo • **she gave me the book as a ~** me regaló el libro • **it was a ~ from Dad** era un regalo de papá • **to give sb a ~** hacer un regalo a algn • **to make sb a ~ of sth** regalar algo a algn; (*fig*) dar algo a algn medio regalado, servir algo a algn en bandeja; ▹ **birthday, Christmas, wedding**

present³ [prɪ'zent] VT **1** (= *give*) **a** [+ *prize, award*] entregar, hacer entrega de • **to ~ sth to sb** entregar algo a algn, hacer entrega de algo a algn • **they have ~ed a petition to Parliament** han hecho entrega de *or* han presentado una petición al parlamento
b [+ *gift*] • **to ~ sb with sth** • **~ sth to sb** regalar algo a algn, obsequiar a algn con algo (*more frm*), obsequiar algo a algn (*LAm*)
2 (= *introduce*) presentar • **may I ~ Miss Clark?** • **allow me to ~ Miss Clark** (*frm*) permítame presentarle a *or* le presento a la Srta. Clark • **it gives me great pleasure to ~ ...** es para mí un honor *or* placer presentarles a ... • **he ~ed Jane to his mother** presentó a Jane a su madre • **to be ~ed at court** (*Brit*) ser presentada en la corte
3 (= *offer formally*) • **to ~ one's apologies (to sb)** presentar sus excusas (ante algn) • **to ~ one's compliments (to sb)** presentar *or* ofrecer sus saludos (a algn) • **to ~ one's credentials (to sb)** [*diplomat*] presentar sus credenciales (ante algn)
4 (= *show*) [+ *documents, tickets*] presentar, mostrar
5 (= *put forward, communicate*) [+ *report, proposal, evidence*] presentar; [+ *case, argument*] exponer; (*Parl*) [+ *bill*] presentar • **figures can be ~ed in many ways** hay muchas maneras de presentar las cifras • **the party has to ~ a more professional image** el partido debe presentar *or* proyectar una imagen más profesional • **she ~ed her plan to the meeting** expuso su proyecto a la reunión
6 (= *pose*) [+ *challenge*] representar; [+ *opportunity*] presentar, ofrecer; [+ *sight*] ofrecer • **if you are old, getting fit can ~ a challenge** si es usted mayor, ponerse en forma puede representar un reto • **the bay ~s a magnificent sight** la bahía ofrece una vista maravillosa • **the boy ~s a problem** el chico nos plantea un problema • **the patrol ~ed an easy target** la patrulla era un blanco fácil
7 (= *provide, confront*) • **to ~ sb with sth: the author ~s us with a vivid chronicle of contemporary America** el autor nos brinda *or* ofrece una vívida crónica de la América contemporánea • **she bought a new car and ~ed me with the bill** se compró un coche nuevo y me pasó la factura • **to ~ sb with a daughter/son** (*frm, hum*) ofrecer a algn una hija/un hijo
8 (= *represent, portray*) presentar • **the report ~s her in a favourable light** el informe presenta una imagen favorable de ella
9 (*Comm*) (= *tender, submit*) [+ *bill*] presentar, pasar; [+ *cheque*] presentar • **the cheque was ~ed for payment on 24th** el cheque se presentó para el cobro el día 24
10 (*Rad, TV*) [+ *programme*] presentar; (*Theat*) [+ *play*] presentar, ofrecer el montaje de; (*Art*) [+ *exhibition*] exponer, presentar • **~ing Garbo as Mimi** con Garbo en el papel de Mimi
11 (*Mil*) • **to ~ arms** presentar las armas • **~ arms!** ¡presenten armas!
12 • **to ~ o.s.** [*person*] presentarse • **how you ~ yourself is extremely important** la manera de presentarse es muy importante • **to ~ o.s. as sth:** • **he ~s himself as a moderate, but he's not** se define a sí mismo como un moderado, pero no lo es • **she's thinking of ~ing herself as a candidate** está pensando en presentarse como candidata • **to ~ o.s. for examination** presentarse a (un) examen • **to ~ o.s. for (an) interview** presentarse a una entrevista
13 • **to ~ itself** [*opportunity, problem*] surgir, presentarse • **a problem has ~ed itself** ha surgido *or* se ha presentado un problema
VI (*Med*) • **to ~ with sth** [*patient*] presentarse con algo • **to ~ with** *or* **as sth** [*condition*] presentarse en forma de algo

presentable [prɪ'zentəbl] ADJ presentable • **are you ~?** (= *dressed*) ¿estás visible? • **to make sth ~** arreglar algo • **I must go and make myself ~** voy a arreglarme un poco

presentably [prɪ'zentəblɪ] ADV • **~ dressed** vestido de manera presentable

presentation [ˌprezən'teɪʃən] N **1** (= *act of presenting*) presentación *f*; (*Jur*) [*of case*] exposición *f* • **on ~ of the voucher** al presentar el vale
2 (*TV, Rad*) producción *f*; (*Theat*) representación *f*
3 (= *ceremony*) ceremonia *f* de entrega; (= *gift*) obsequio *m* • **to make the ~** hacer la presentación • **to make sb a ~ on his retirement** hacer un obsequio a algn con ocasión de su jubilación
CPD ▸ **presentation case** estuche *m* de regalo ▸ **presentation copy** ejemplar *m* con dedicatoria del autor ▸ **presentation skills** técnicas *fpl* de presentación

presentational [ˌprezən'teɪʃənəl] ADJ relativo a la presentación • **from a ~ point of view** desde el punto de vista de la presentación

present-day ['preznt'deɪ] ADJ actual, de hoy (en día) • **present-day Spain** la España actual *or* de hoy (en día)

presenter [prɪ'zentəʳ] N (*Rad*) locutor(a) *m/f*; (*TV*) presentador(a) *m/f*

presentiment [prɪ'zentɪmənt] N presentimiento *m* • **to have a ~ about sth** tener un presentimiento acerca de algo • **to have a ~ that ...** tener el presentimiento de que ..., presentir que ...

presently ['prezntlɪ] ADV **1** (= *shortly*) dentro de poco, al rato • **you'll feel better ~** enseguida te sentirás mejor • **~, he woke up** poco después se despertó
2 (*US*) (= *now*) en este momento, actualmente • **they're ~ on tour** actualmente están de gira

preservation [ˌprezə'veɪʃən] N [*of antiquities, food*] conservación *f*; [*of wildlife, land, buildings*] conservación *f*, preservación *f*; [*of order, democracy*] mantenimiento *m* • **in a good state of ~** en buen estado, bien conservado
CPD ▸ **preservation order** orden *f* de preservación ▸ **preservation society** (*Brit*) sociedad *f* para la preservación

preservationist [ˌprezə'veɪʃənɪst] N defensor(a) *m/f* del patrimonio

preservative [prɪ'zɜːvətɪv] N (*Culin*) conservante *m*
CPD [*function, substance*] conservante

preserve [prɪ'zɜːv] VT **1** (= *keep in existence*) [+ *endangered species, jobs, language*] proteger, preservar; [+ *customs, silence, reputation*] conservar, mantener; [+ *sense of humour, memory*] conservar • **we will do everything to ~ (the) peace** haremos todo lo posible por mantener la paz • **as a doctor, it was my duty to ~ life** como médico, era mi deber salvar vidas • **to ~ sb's anonymity** mantener a algn en el anonimato
2 (= *keep from decay*) [+ *object, environment, meat*] conservar • **perfectly ~d medieval houses** casas *fpl* medievales en perfecto estado • **to ~ one's looks** conservar el atractivo • **to ~ the status quo** mantener el statu quo • **the body was ~d in ice** el cuerpo se conservaba en hielo; ▹ **aspic, well-preserved**
3 (*esp Brit*) (*Culin*) (= *bottle, pickle etc*) [+ *fruit*] hacer conservas de; [+ *meat, fish*] conservar • **peppers and chillies may be ~d in oil** los pimientos y los chiles se pueden conservar en aceite • **to ~ sth in salt** conservar algo en sal
4 (= *protect*) **a** (*gen*) proteger • **to ~ sth from/against sth** proteger algo de algo • **paint the metal to ~ it from corrosion** pinte el metal para protegerlo de la corrosión
b (*in prayers, wishes*) • **may God ~ you** que Dios os ampare • **God** *or* **Heaven** *or* **saints ~ us!** ¡que Dios nos ampare! • **heaven ~ us from little boys** (*hum*) que Dios nos proteja de los niños

P

5 (*for private hunting, fishing*) [+ *game*] proteger
N 1 (Culin) (*singular*) (= *jam*) mermelada *f*, confitura *f*; (= *bottled fruit, chutney*) conserva *f* • **damson ~** mermelada *f* or confitura *f* de ciruela damascena
2 (Culin) **preserves** conservas *fpl*
3 (= *restricted area*) **a** (Hunting) coto *m*, vedado *m*; (*for wildlife*) reserva *f*; ▹ **game, wildlife**
b (*fig*) dominio *m* • **banking has remained almost exclusively a male ~** la banca sigue siendo casi exclusivamente del dominio masculino • **they are poaching on my ~** están invadiendo mi terreno

preserved [prɪˈzɜːvd] ADJ [*fruit, ginger*] en conserva • **you can use either fresh or ~ fruit** puede usar fruta fresca o en conserva or de lata • **~ foods** (*in bottles*) comida *f* en conserva; (*in cans*) comida *f* en conserva, comida *f* de lata

preset [ˈpriːˈset] (PT, PP: **preset**) VT programar

preshrunk [ˈpriːˈʃrʌŋk] ADJ ya lavado

preside [prɪˈzaɪd] VI presidir • **to ~ at** or **over a meeting/ceremony** presidir una reunión/ceremonia • **he ~d over the reunification of Germany** condujo la reunificación alemana • **a statue of him ~s over the main square of the town** una estatua suya preside la plaza mayor de la ciudad • **the presiding judge** el juez/la jueza presidente de sala

presidency [ˈprezɪdənsɪ] N 1 (= *office*) [*of country, organization, company*] presidencia *f* • **he is to be nominated for the ~** lo van a nombrar candidato a la presidencia
2 (= *period of office*) [*of country*] mandato *m* presidencial, presidencia *f*; [*of organization, company*] presidencia *f*, periodo *m* de gestión en la presidencia

president [ˈprezɪdənt] N [*of country, company, organization*] presidente/a *m/f*; (US) (Univ) rector(a) *m/f* • **~-elect** presidente/a *m/f* electo/a
CPD ▸ **Presidents' Day** (US) *día festivo en Estados Unidos (el tercer lunes de febrero) cuando se celebran los cumpleaños de los presidentes George Washington y Abraham Lincoln* ▸ **President's list** (US) (Univ) lista *f* de honor académica; ▹ **DEAN'S LIST**

presidential [ˌprezɪˈdenʃəl] ADJ [*palace, adviser, candidate*] presidencial • **~ election(s)** elecciones *fpl* presidenciales • **he will make his first ~ decision today** hoy tomará su primera decisión como presidente • **his ~ hopes** sus esperanzas de convertirse en presidente
CPD ▸ **presidential guard** guardia *f* presidencial

presiding officer [prɪˌzaɪdɪŋˈɒfɪsəʳ] N presidente/a *m/f*

presidium [prɪˈsɪdɪəm] N (Pol) presidio *m*

press [pres]

NOUN
TRANSITIVE VERB
INTRANSITIVE VERB
COMPOUNDS
PHRASAL VERBS

NOUN
1 Publishing **a** (= *newspapers collectively*) prensa *f* • **to get** or **have a good/bad ~** (*lit, fig*) tener buena/mala prensa • **the ~** (= *newspapers, journalists*) la prensa • **I saw it in the ~** lo vi en la prensa • **the ~ reported that ...** la prensa informó que ... • **member of the ~** periodista *mf*, miembro *mf* de la prensa • **the national/local ~** la prensa nacional/regional; ▹ **free, gutter**
b (= *printing press*) imprenta *f* • **to go to ~** entrar en prensa • **correct at the time of going to ~** correcto en el momento de impresión • **hot off the ~(es)** recién salido de la imprenta • **to be in ~** estar en prensa • **to pass sth for ~** aprobar algo para la prensa • **to set the ~es rolling** poner las prensas en marcha
c (= *publishing firm*) editorial *f*
2 = touch (*with hand*) apretón *m* • **at the ~ of a button** con solo apretar un botón
3 with iron • **to give sth a ~** planchar algo • **this skirt needs a ~** esta falda necesita un planchado
4 = apparatus, machine (*for wine, olives, cheese, moulding*) prensa *f*; (*also* **trouser press**) prensa *f* para planchar pantalones; (*for racket*) tensor *m* • **hydraulic ~** prensa *f* hidráulica; ▹ **cider, printing**
5 = crush apiñamiento *m*, agolpamiento *m* • **he lost his hat in the ~ to get out** perdió el sombrero en el apiñamiento *or* agolpamiento que se produjo a la salida
6 Weightlifting presa *f*
7 = cupboard armario *m*

TRANSITIVE VERB
1 = push, squeeze **a** [+ *button, switch, doorbell*] pulsar, apretar; [+ *hand, trigger*] apretar; [+ *accelerator*] pisar • **select the option required, then ~ "enter"** escoja la opción que desee, y luego pulse *or* apriete "intro" • **he ~ed his face against the window** apretó la cara contra el cristal • **she ~ed herself against me/the wall** se apretó contra mí/contra la pared • **she ~ed a note into his hand** le metió un billete en la mano • **she ~ed the lid on (to) the box** cerró la caja apretando la tapa • **he ~ed her to him** la atrajo hacia sí • **Dobbs ~ed his hand to his heart** Dobbs se llevó la mano al corazón • **he ~ed the revolver to Sally's head** le puso a Sally el revólver en la cabeza • **he ~ed his fingertips together** juntó las yemas de los dedos • IDIOM: • **to ~ the flesh** (US*) ir estrechando manos a diestro y siniestro
b (*painfully*) apretujar • **as the crowd moved back he found himself ~ed up against a wall** a medida que la multitud retrocedía, se vio apretujado contra una pared
2 using press [+ *grapes, olives, flowers*] prensar
3 = iron [+ *clothes*] planchar
4 Tech (= *make*) [+ *machine part*] prensar; [+ *record, disk*] imprimir
5 = pressurize presionar • **he didn't need much ~ing** no hubo que presionarle mucho • **when ~ed, she conceded the point** cuando la presionaron, les dio la razón • **to ~ sb for sth** exigir algo de algn • **to ~ sb for an answer** exigir una respuesta de algn • **he did not ~ her for further details** no le exigió más detalles • **to ~ sb for payment** insistir en que algn pague, exigir a algn el pago de lo que se debe • **to ~ sb into doing sth** obligar a algn a hacer algo • **I found myself ~ed into playing football with the children** me vi obligado a jugar al fútbol con los niños • **to ~ sb to do sth** (= *urge*) insistir en que algn haga algo; (= *pressurize*) presionar a algn para que haga algo • **he ~ed me to have a drink with him** insistió en que tomase una copa con él • **he didn't ~ her to go back to work** no la presionó para que volviera a trabajar • **the trade unions are ~ing him to stand firm** los sindicatos le están presionando para que se mantenga firme; ▹ **pressed**
6 = insist • **don't ~ me on this point** no me insistas sobre este punto • **she smiles coyly when ~ed about her private life** cuando insisten en querer saber sobre su vida privada, sonríe con coquetería • **he was being ~ed by creditors** le acosaban los acreedores
7 = force • **to ~ sth on sb** insistir en que algn acepte algo • **food and cigarettes were ~ed on him** le estuvieron ofreciendo insistentemente comida y cigarros
8 • **to be ~ed into service**: • **we were all ~ed into service** todos tuvimos que ponernos a trabajar • **the town hall has been ~ed into service as a school** se han visto obligados a usar el ayuntamiento como escuela • **Kenny had been ~ed into service to guard the door** habían convencido a Kenny para que vigilara la puerta
9 = pursue [+ *claim*] insistir en; [+ *demand*] exigir • **his officials have visited Washington to ~ their case for economic aid** sus representantes han ido a Washington para hacer presión a favor de la ayuda económica • **to ~ charges (against sb)** presentar cargos (contra algn) • **the champion failed to ~ home his advantage** el campeón no supo aprovechar su ventaja • **to ~ home an attack** sacar el máximo partido de un ataque • **I shan't ~ the point** no insistiré más sobre eso; ▹ **suit**

INTRANSITIVE VERB
1 = exert pressure apretar • **does it hurt when I ~ here?** ¿le duele cuando le aprieto aquí? • **I felt something hard ~ into my back** noté la presión de algo duro que se apretaba contra mi espalda • **the bone was ~ing on a nerve** el hueso estaba pinzando un nervio
2 = move, push • **he ~ed against her** se apretó contra ella • **his leg ~ed against her thigh** su pierna se apretaba contra su muslo • **the crowd ~ed round him** la muchedumbre se apiñó en torno a él • **he ~ed through the crowd** se abrió paso entre la muchedumbre • **the audience ~ed towards the exit** el público se apresuró hacia la salida
3 = urge, agitate • **to ~ for sth** exigir algo, insistir en algo • **he will ~ for the death penalty in this case** en este caso va a insistir en *or* exigir la pena de muerte • **a protest march in the capital to ~ for new elections** una marcha de protesta en la capital para exigir otras elecciones • **police may now ~ for changes in the law** puede que ahora la policía presione para que cambien las leyes • **to ~ for sb to resign** exigir la dimisión de algn, insistir en que algn dimita • **time is ~ing** el tiempo apremia
4 = weigh heavily • **to ~ on sb** pesar sobre algn • **the weight of guilt ~ed on her** el sentimiento de culpabilidad pesaba sobre ella

COMPOUNDS
▸ **press agency** agencia *f* de prensa ▸ **press agent** encargado/a *m/f* de prensa ▸ **press attaché** agregado/a *m/f* de prensa ▸ **press baron** magnate *m* de la prensa ▸ **press box** tribuna *f* de prensa ▸ **press briefing** rueda *f* de prensa, conferencia *f* de prensa ▸ **press card** pase *m* de periodista, carnet *m* de prensa ▸ **press clipping** = **press cutting** ▸ **press conference** rueda *f* de prensa, conferencia *f* de prensa • **to call a ~ conference** convocar una rueda *or* una conferencia de prensa • **to hold a ~ conference** celebrar una rueda *or* una conferencia de prensa ▸ **press corps** prensa *f* acreditada ▸ **press coverage** cobertura *f* periodística • **it's had a lot of ~ coverage** ha tenido mucha cobertura periodística ▸ **press cutting** recorte *m* (de periódico)

▸ **press gallery** tribuna *f* de prensa ▸ **press gang** (*Hist*) leva *f* ▸ **press kit** kit *m* de prensa ▸ **press launch** lanzamiento *m* de prensa ▸ **press office** oficina *f* de prensa ▸ **press officer** agente *mf* de prensa ▸ **press pack** (= *information pack*) dosier *m* de prensa; (*pej*) (= *group of reporters*) grupo *m* de reporteros; (= *sensationalist press*) prensa *f* amarilla ▸ **press pass** pase *m* de prensa ▸ **press photographer** fotógrafo/a *m/f* de prensa ▸ **press release** comunicado *m* de prensa • **to issue** *or* **put out a ~ release** publicar un comunicado de prensa ▸ **press report** nota *f* de prensa, reportaje *m* de prensa ▸ **press room** sala *f* de prensa ▸ **press run** (*US*) tirada *f* ▸ **press secretary** secretario/a *m/f* de prensa ▸ **press stud** (*Brit*) automático *m*, broche *m* de presión ▸ **press view** preestreno *m* (para prensa)

▸ **press ahead** (VI + ADV) seguir adelante (**with** con)

▸ **press back** (VT + ADV) [+ *crowd, enemy*] obligar a retroceder • **he ~ed himself back against the wall** se apretó contra la pared

▸ **press down** (VT + ADV) (= *depress*) [+ *button, knob, switch*] apretar, presionar; (= *flatten*) presionar hacia abajo • **seal the edges by ~ing them down** cierre los lados presionándolos hacia abajo, cierre los lados apretándolos • **he ~ed the lid down tight** apretó la tapa con fuerza
(VI + ADV) • **to ~ down on sth** (*gen*) presionar algo, hacer presión sobre algo; (*on pedal, accelerator*) pisar algo

▸ **press forward** (VI + ADV) **1** (= *push forward*) [*crowd*] avanzar en masa; [*individual*] abrirse camino (a base de empujones); [*troops*] avanzar
2 (= *advance*) seguir adelante (**with** con) • **they have decided to ~ forward with their economic reforms** han decidido seguir adelante con las reformas económicas

▸ **press on** (VI + ADV) (*with work, journey*) seguir adelante (**with** con), continuar (**with** con)

press-button ['pres,bʌtn] (N), (ADJ) = **push-button**

pressed [prest] (ADJ) • **to be ~ for money/time** andar muy escaso de dinero/tiempo; ▹ **hard-pressed**

press-gang ['presgæn] (VT) • **to press-gang sb into doing sth** forzar a algn a hacer algo

pressing ['presɪŋ] (ADJ) [*matter, problem*] urgente; [*request, invitation*] insistente

pressman ['presmæn] (N) (PL: **pressmen**)
1 (*Brit*) periodista *m*
2 (*US*) tipógrafo *m*

pressmark ['presmɑːk] (N) (*Brit*) signatura *f*

press-up ['presʌp] (N) (*Brit*) flexión *f*

pressure ['preʃəʳ] (N) **1** (*lit*) **a** (*Phys, Tech, Met*) presión *f* • **a ~ of 200kg to the square metre** una presión de 200kg por metro cuadrado • **oil/water ~** presión *f* del aceite/del agua • **at full ~** (*Tech*) a toda presión • **high/low ~** alta/baja presión *f* • **could you check the tyre ~?** ¿me puede mirar la presión de los neumáticos? • **under ~** a presión; ▹ **atmospheric, blood, diastolic, high-pressure, systolic**
b (*from hand, foot etc*) presión *f* • **he felt the ~ of her hand on his shoulder** notó la presión de su mano en el hombro • **it took a bit of ~ to make the lid close** se tuvo que hacer un poco de fuerza para cerrar la tapa • **to apply** *or* **put ~ (up)on sth** hacer *or* ejercer presión sobre algo
2 (*fig*) presión *f* • **because of parental ~** debido a la presión de los padres • **I left the job because I couldn't stand the ~** dejé el trabajo porque no aguantaba la presión • **the ~s of modern life** las presiones de la vida moderna • **to bring ~ to bear on sb (to do sth)** (*frm*) ejercer presión sobre algn (para que haga algo) • **to put ~ on sb (to do sth)** presionar a algn (para que haga algo) • **it will put intense ~ on our already overstretched resources** supondrá una gran carga sobre nuestros recursos, ya apurados al máximo • **to put the ~ on** • **pile on the ~*** apretar los tornillos* • **it will take some of the ~ off me** me aliviará un poco la carga • **the cut in interest rates will take the ~ off sterling** la reducción de los tipos de interés eliminará la presión existente sobre la libra esterlina • **~ of time prevented her from dealing with all the problems** el apremio del tiempo no le permitió tratar todos los problemas • **they were aware of the ~ of time** eran conscientes de que el tiempo se les echaba encima • **under ~:** • **to act/work under ~** obrar/trabajar bajo presión • **he is under ~ to sign the agreement** le están presionando para que firme el acuerdo • **the head resigned under ~ from parents** el director dimitió presionado por los padres • **he's under a lot of ~** está bajo mucha presión, está sometido a mucha presión • **I was unable to go due to ~ of work** no pude ir por razones de trabajo; ▹ **peer**
(VT) (= *pressurize*) presionar • **to ~ sb to do sth** presionar a algn para que haga algo • **to ~ sb into doing sth** obligar a algn a hacer algo
(CPD) ▸ **pressure cabin** (*Aer, Space*) cabina *f* presurizada ▸ **pressure cooker** (*lit*) olla *f* a presión, olla *f* exprés; (*fig*) polvorín *m* • **the country is a political ~ cooker** el país es un polvorín político ▸ **pressure feed** tubo *m* de alimentación a presión ▸ **pressure gauge** manómetro *m* ▸ **pressure group** grupo *m* de presión ▸ **pressure pan** (*US*) = **pressure cooker** ▸ **pressure point** (*Anat*) punto *m* de presión ▸ **pressure sore** úlcera *f* por presión ▸ **pressure suit** traje *m* de presión compensada

pressure-cook ['preʃə,kʊk] (VT) cocinar en olla a presión, cocinar en olla exprés

pressured ['preʃəd] (ADJ) [*life, environment*] lleno de presiones • **to feel ~** sentirse presionado

pressurization [,preʃəraɪ'zeɪʃən] (N) presurización *f*

pressurize ['preʃəraɪz] (VT) **1** (*Phys, Tech*) presurizar
2 (*fig*) presionar • **to ~ sb to do sth** presionar a algn para que haga algo • **to ~ sb into doing sth** obligar a algn a hacer algo

pressurized ['preʃəraɪzd] (ADJ) **1** (*lit*) [*cabin, aircraft*] presurizado; [*chamber, container*] cerrado a presión • **~ water reactor** reactor *m* de agua a presión
2 (*fig*) • **the island provides an escape from today's ~ world** la isla permite escapar del cúmulo de tensiones que es el mundo actual • **to feel ~** sentirse presionado

pressy*, **pressie*** ['prezɪ] (N) (*Brit*) (= *present*) regalito *m* • **Christmas pressies** regalitos *or* regalos de Navidad

Prestel® ['prestel] (N) videotex *m*

prestidigitation ['prestɪ,dɪdʒɪ'teɪʃən] (N) prestidigitación *f*

prestidigitator [,prestɪ'dɪdʒɪteɪtəʳ] (N) (*frm*) prestidigitador(a) *m/f*

prestige [pres'tiːʒ] (N) prestigio *m*

prestigious [pres'tɪdʒəs] (ADJ) prestigioso

presto ['prestəʊ] (ADV) • **hey ~!** ¡abracadabra!

prestressed ['priː'strest] (ADJ) • **~ concrete** hormigón *m* pretensado

presumable [prɪ'zjuːməbəl] (ADJ) presumible

presumably [prɪ'zjuːməblɪ] (ADV) • **~ he'll let us know** supongo *or* me imagino que nos avisará • **"will they be coming later?" — "presumably"** —¿vendrán más tarde? —es de suponer

presume [prɪ'zjuːm] (VT) **1** (= *suppose*) suponer, presumir • **his death must be ~d** es de suponer que ha muerto, hay que presumir que ha muerto • **to ~ that ...** suponer que ... • **it may be ~d that ...** es de suponer que ... • **to ~ sb to be innocent** suponer que algn es inocente • **Dr Livingstone, I ~** Dr Livingstone según creo
2 (= *venture*) • **to ~ to do sth** atreverse a hacer algo • **I wouldn't ~ to question your judgement** no me atrevería a poner en duda su buen criterio • **if I may ~ to advise you** si me permite ofrecerle un consejo
(VI) **1** (= *suppose*) suponer
2 (= *take liberties*) • **to ~ on sb's friendship** abusar de la amistad de algn • **you ~ too much** no sabes lo que pides, pides demasiado

presumption [prɪ'zʌmpʃən] (N)
1 (= *arrogance*) presunción *f*; (= *liberty-taking*) atrevimiento *m* • **pardon my ~** le ruego perdone mi atrevimiento
2 (= *thing presumed*) suposición *f*, presunción *f* • **the ~ is that ...** se supone que ..., es de suponer que ...

presumptive [prɪ'zʌmptɪv] (ADJ) [*heir*] presunto
(CPD) ▸ **presumptive evidence** pruebas *fpl* presuntivas

presumptuous [prɪ'zʌmptjʊəs] (ADJ) atrevido • **in that I was rather ~** en eso fui algo atrevido • **it would be ~ of me to express an opinion** sería osado por mi parte expresar una opinión

presumptuously [prɪ'zʌmptjʊəslɪ] (ADV) con atrevimiento, con osadía

presumptuousness [prɪ'zʌmptjʊəsnɪs] (N) (= *arrogance*) presunción *f*; (= *liberty-taking*) atrevimiento *m*

presuppose [,priːsə'pəʊz] (VT) presuponer

presupposition [,priːsʌpə'zɪʃən] (N) presuposición *f*

pre-tax [,priː'tæks] (ADJ) bruto • **pre-tax profits** beneficios *mpl* brutos *or* preimpositivos

pre-teen [,priː'tiːn] (*US*) (ADJ) preadolescente (NPL) • **the pre-teens** los preadolescentes

pretence, **pretense** (*US*) [prɪ'tens] (N)
1 (= *make-believe*) fingimiento *m*, simulación *f* • **to make a ~ of doing sth** fingir hacer algo • **it's all a ~*** todo es fingido
2 (= *claim*) pretensión *f* • **to make no ~ to learning** no pretender ser erudito
3 (= *pretext*) pretexto *m* • **on** *or* **under the ~ of doing sth** so pretexto de hacer algo; ▹ **false**
4 (= *display*) ostentación *f* • **without ~** • **devoid of all ~** sin ostentación

pretend [prɪ'tend] (VT) **1** (= *feign*) fingir, simular • **to ~ that ...** (querer) hacer creer que ... • **he's ~ing that he can't hear** finge no oír • **let's ~ that I'm the doctor and you're the nurse** (*child language*) yo era el médico y tú eras la enfermera • **to ~ to do sth** fingir hacer algo • **to ~ to be asleep** hacerse el dormido, fingir estar dormido • **to ~ to be mad** fingirse loco • **he ~s to be a poet** se las da de poeta, se dice poeta • **to ~ to go away** fingir marcharse • **to ~ not to be listening** hacerse el distraído • **to ~ not to understand** hacerse el desentendido
2 (= *claim*) pretender • **I don't ~ to know the answer** no pretendo saber la respuesta • **I don't ~ to understand art** no pretendo

entender de arte
VI 1 (= *feign*) fingir • **she is only ~ing** es de mentira • **we're only ~ing** (*to child*) es de mentirijillas* • **let's ~** imaginémoslo • **let's not ~ to each other** no nos engañemos uno a otro
2 (= *claim*) • **to ~ to the throne** pretender el trono • **to ~ to intelligence** afirmar tener inteligencia, pretender ser inteligente
ADJ* de mentira, fingido • **~ money*** dinero *m* de juego

pretended [prɪˈtendɪd] ADJ pretendido

pretender [prɪˈtendəʳ] N pretendiente *mf* • **~ to the throne** pretendiente *mf* al trono • **the Young Pretender** el joven Pretendiente

pretense [prɪˈtens] N (*US*) = **pretence**

pretension [prɪˈtenʃən] N 1 (= *claim*) pretensión *f* • **to have ~s to culture** tener pretensiones de cultura, pretender ser culto
2 (= *pretentiousness*) presunción *f*, pretenciosidad *f*

pretentious [prɪˈtenʃəs] ADJ (= *affected*) pretencioso; (= *ostentatious and vulgar*) cursi

pretentiously [prɪˈtenʃəslɪ] ADV con pretenciosidad

pretentiousness [prɪˈtenʃəsnɪs] N (= *affectedness*) pretenciosidad *f*; (= *vulgar ostentation*) cursilería *f*

preterite [ˈpretərɪt] N (*Ling*) pretérito *m*

preterm [ˌpriːˈtɜːm] ADJ prematuro
ADV prematuramente

preternatural [ˌpriːtəˈnætʃrəl] ADJ preternatural

preternaturally [ˌpriːtəˈnætʃrəlɪ] ADV (*frm*) preternaturalmente

pretext [ˈpriːtekst] N pretexto *m*, excusa *f* • **it's just a ~** no es más que un pretexto *or* una excusa • **on** *or* **under the ~ of doing sth** so pretexto *or* con la excusa de hacer algo

pretorian [prɪˈtɔːrɪən] ADJ = **praetorian**

pretrial [ˌpriːˈtraɪəl] ADJ (*Jur*) prejuicio *m*

prettify [ˈprɪtɪfaɪ] VT (*pej*) [+ *person*] emperifollar; [+ *object, place*] engalanar, adornar con mucho boato; [+ *facts, situation*] dulcificar

prettily [ˈprɪtɪlɪ] ADV [*smile, blush*] de forma encantadora; [*sit*] con gracia; [*arrange, lay out*] con elegancia • **~ patterned** con un diseño elegante *or* bonito • **her daughters were always ~ dressed** sus hijas siempre iban muy guapas *or* preciosas

prettiness [ˈprɪtɪnɪs] N [*of baby, woman, place, object*] belleza *f*

pretty [ˈprɪtɪ] ADJ (COMPAR: **prettier**, SUPERL: **prettiest**) 1 (= *attractive*) [*dress, object, baby*] bonito, mono*, lindo (*LAm*); [*girl*] bonito, guapo, lindo (*LAm*); [*name, smile*] bonito, lindo (*LAm*) • **what a ~ hat!** ¡qué sombrero más bonito!, ¡qué sombrero más mono!*, ¡qué monada de sombrero!* • **I'm not just a ~ face you know** para que te enteres, no soy tonta • **it'll cost you a ~ penny*** te va a costar un ojo de la cara *or* un dineral • **it was not a ~ sight** no era nada agradable de ver • IDIOM: • **she was as ~ as a picture** era preciosa • **the garden was as ~ as a picture** el jardín era de foto; ▷ **pass**
2* (= *large*) [*sum*] bonito*, importante
3 (*iro*) bueno • **a ~ mess you've got us into!** ¡en vaya *or* menudo *or* buen lío nos has metido!*
ADV bastante • **he got ~ cross** se enfadó bastante • **I have a ~ fair** *or* **good idea who did it** estoy casi seguro de quién lo hizo • **it sounds ~ far-fetched to me** me parece bastante inverosímil • **she got ~ good marks** sacó unas notas bastante buenas • **~ damn** *or* **damned quick*** bien pronto • **he's ~ damn stupid*** es bien estúpido • **it's ~ much the same** es mas o menos igual, es prácticamente lo mismo • **he goes there ~ nearly every day** va allí casi *or* prácticamente todos los días • **~ well:** • **I'm ~ well finished** ya casi he terminado • **that's ~ well everything** eso es todo más o menos; ▷ **sit**
N (*as excl*) • **gee up, my ~!** (*to horse*) ¡arre, caballito! • **I'll get you, my ~!** (*threatening*) ¡de mí no te escapas, preciosa *or* bonita!
▸ **pretty up** VT + ADV = **prettify**

pretty-pretty* [ˌprɪtɪˈprɪtɪ] ADJ (*pej*) • **he's very pretty-pretty** es un guapito de cara* • **she's very pretty-pretty** es una niña mona*

pretzel [ˈpretsl] N galleta *f* salada

prevail [prɪˈveɪl] VI 1 (= *gain mastery*) prevalecer • **finally good sense ~ed** por fin se impuso el buen sentido • **eventually peace ~ed** al final se restableció la paz • **to ~ against** *or* **over one's enemies** triunfar sobre los enemigos
2 (= *be current*) [*views, opinions*] predominar; (= *be in fashion*) estar de moda, estar en boga • **the conditions that now ~** las condiciones que ahora imperan
3 (= *persuade*) • **to ~ (up)on sb to do sth** convencer a algn para que haga algo • **he was eventually ~ed upon to do it** por fin lograron convencerlo de que lo hiciera • **she could not be ~ed upon** fue imposible persuadirla, no se convenció

prevailing [prɪˈveɪlɪŋ] ADJ [*opinion, wind*] predominante; [*price*] imperante • **the ~ fashion** la moda actual, la moda reinante • **under ~ conditions** bajo las condiciones actuales

prevalence [ˈprevələns] N 1 (= *dominance*) predominio *m*
2 (= *frequency*) frecuencia *f*

prevalent [ˈprevələnt] ADJ 1 (= *dominant*) dominante
2 (= *widespread*) extendido
3 (= *fashionable*) de moda; (= *present-day*) actual

prevaricate [prɪˈværɪkeɪt] VI responder con evasivas

prevarication [prɪˌværɪˈkeɪʃən] N evasivas *fpl*

prevaricator [prɪˈværɪkeɪtəʳ] N 1 (= *evasive person*) *persona que contesta con evasivas*
2 (= *liar*) mentiroso/a *m/f*
3 (*Jur*) prevaricador(a) *m/f*

prevent [prɪˈvent] VT 1 (= *avert*) (*by taking precautions*) [+ *accident, disaster, death, war, pregnancy*] prevenir, evitar; [+ *illness*] prevenir • **we want to ~ a recurrence of yesterday's violence** queremos evitar que la violencia desplegada ayer se repita, queremos prevenir *or* evitar una repetición de la violencia desplegada ayer
2 (= *impede, put a stop to*) [+ *crime, corruption*] impedir; [+ *attempt*] prevenir, impedir • **installations to ~ any attempt to escape** instalaciones *fpl* para prevenir *or* impedir cualquier intento de huida • **bodyguards ~ed his attempt to shoot the president** unos guardaespaldas hicieron fracasar su intento de disparar al presidente • **to ~ the spread of AIDS/nuclear weapons** impedir la propagación del SIDA/la proliferación de las armas nucleares • **to ~ sb (from) doing sth** • **~ sb's doing sth** impedir que algn haga algo • **I can't ~ him (from) leaving the country** • **I can't ~ his leaving the country** no puedo impedir que se vaya del país • **don't let this ~ you from going** no dejes que esto te impida ir • **she bit her lip to ~ herself from crying out** se mordió el labio para no gritar

preventable [prɪˈventəbl] ADJ evitable

preventative [prɪˈventətɪv] = **preventive**

prevention [prɪˈvenʃən] N prevención *f* • **the role of diet in cancer ~** el papel que desempeña la dieta en la prevención del cáncer • **the Government's commitment to crime ~** la dedicación del gobierno a la prevención de la delincuencia • **Society for the Prevention of Cruelty to Children/Animals** Sociedad *f* Protectora de Niños/Animales • PROVERB: • **~ is better than cure** más vale prevenir que curar

preventive [prɪˈventɪv] ADJ preventivo
N 1 (*Med*) (= *drug*) *medicamento que previene una enfermedad*
2 (= *measure*) • **fasting is sometimes recommended as a ~ against cancer** a veces se recomienda el ayuno como medida preventiva contra el cáncer
CPD ▸ **preventive dentistry** odontología *f* preventiva ▸ **preventive detention** arresto *m* preventivo ▸ **preventive measure** medida *f* preventiva ▸ **preventive medicine** medicina *f* preventiva

preview [ˈpriːvjuː] N [*of film*] preestreno *m* • **to give sb a ~ of sth** (*fig*) permitir a algn ver algo de antemano • **to have a ~ of sth** (*fig*) ver algo con anticipación, lograr ver algo antes que otros
VT preestrenar

previous [ˈpriːvɪəs] ADJ 1 (= *former, earlier*) [*night, day, year, page*] anterior; [*experience*] previo • **we met by ~ arrangement** nos reunimos acordando una cita previa *or* mediante cita previa • **I have a ~ engagement** tengo un compromiso previo • **in a ~ incarnation** *or* **life** en una vida anterior • **on ~ occasions** en ocasiones anteriores • **the car has had two ~ owners** el coche ha pasado por dos manos • **in ~ years** los años anteriores; ▷ **conviction**
2* (*hum*) (= *hasty*) prematuro • **this seems somewhat ~** esto parece algo prematuro • **you were a bit ~ in inviting him** te has precipitado un poco invitándole
PREP • **~ to: in the five years ~ to 1992** durante los cinco años anteriores a 1992 • **~ to that she had worked in London** antes de eso había trabajado en Londres

previously [ˈpriːvɪəslɪ] ADV (= *earlier, formerly*) antes, anteriormente; (= *in advance*) con antelación, previamente • **as ~ mentioned** como se ha mencionado antes *or* anteriormente • **~, the country had been divided in two** antes *or* anteriormente, el país había estado dividido en dos partes • **she read out a ~ prepared speech** leyó un discurso que había preparado con antelación *or* previamente

prewar [ˈpriːˈwɔːʳ] ADJ de antes de la guerra • **the ~ period** la preguerra

prewash [ˈpriːwɒʃ] N prelavado *m*

prey [preɪ] N (*lit, fig*) presa *f*, víctima *f* • **beast of ~** animal *m* de rapiña • **bird of ~** ave *f* de rapiña • **to be (a) ~ to** ser víctima de • **she is ~ to irrational fears** (*fig*) es presa de temores irracionales • **he fell (a) ~ to the disease** fue víctima de la enfermedad
VI • **to ~ on** [+ *animals*] (= *attack*) cazar; (= *feed on*) alimentarse de; [+ *person*] vivir a costa de • **rabbits are ~ed on by foxes** los conejos son presa de los zorros • **to ~ on sb's mind** traer preocupado *or* obsesionar a algn • **doubts ~ed on him** le obsesionaban las dudas • **the tragedy so ~ed on his mind that ...** la tragedia le obsesionó de tal modo que ...

prezzie*, **prezzy*** [ˈprezɪ] N (= **present**) regalo *m*

price [praɪs] N 1 (*Comm*) precio *m* • **an increase in the ~ of petrol** un aumento en el precio de la gasolina • **we pay top ~s for gold**

and silver pagamos los mejores precios por el oro y la plata • **who knows what the ~ will be in six months** quién sabe qué precio tendrá dentro de seis meses • **that's my ~, take it or leave it** eso es lo que pido, o lo tomas o lo dejas • **you can get it at a ~** se puede conseguir, pero pagando • **it's not for sale at any ~** no está a la venta a ningún precio • **their loyalty cannot be bought at any ~** su lealtad no tiene precio • **at a reduced ~** a (un) precio reducido, con rebaja • **at today's ~s** a los precios actuales • **it is beyond ~** no tiene precio • **for a ~**: • **he'll do it for a ~** él lo hará, pero será caro, lo hará si le pagan • **you can get anything you want for a ~** puedes conseguir todo lo que quieras pagando • **he would kill a man for the ~ of a packet of cigarettes** mataría a un hombre por el precio de una cajetilla de tabaco • **two for the ~ of one** (*lit, fig*) dos al *or* por el precio de uno • **can you give me a ~ for putting in a new window?** ¿cuánto me cobraría usted por colocar una ventana nueva? • **to go down** *or* **come down** *or* **fall in ~** bajar de precio • **to go up** *or* **rise in ~** subir de precio • **he got a good ~ for it** sacó una buena suma por ello • **everyone has their ~** todos tenemos un precio • **he's got** *or* **there's a ~ on his head** se ha puesto precio a su cabeza • **to name one's ~** fijar el precio, decir cuánto se quiere • **to put a ~ on sth** poner precio a algo • **you can't put a ~ on friendship** la amistad no tiene precio • **if the ~ is right**: • **he is prepared to make a comeback if the ~ is right** está dispuesto a volver si se le paga bien • **as long as the ~ is right, property will sell** si está a un buen precio, la propiedad se vende • **what ~ all his promises now?** (*iro*) ¿de qué sirven todas sus promesas ahora?; ▹ **closing, cut-price, fixed, half-price, retail**
2 (*Econ, St Ex*) (= *quotation*) cotización *f* • **stock ~s fell again on Wall Street** las cotizaciones en bolsa bajaron de nuevo en Wall Street
3 (*Betting*) (= *odds*) puntos *mpl* de ventaja • IDIOM: • **what ~ …?*** (= *what's the betting*) ¿qué apuestas …? • **what ~ she'll change her mind?** ¿qué apuestas a que cambia de opinión? • **what ~ war?** ¿qué apuestas a que estallará la guerra?
4 (= *sacrifice*) precio *m* • **that's the ~ we have to pay for progress** • **that's the ~ of progress** es el precio que tenemos que pagar por el progreso • **to pay the ~ (for sth)** cargar con *or* pagar las consecuencias (de algo) • **fame comes at a ~** la fama se paga cara • **he's famous now, but at what a ~!** ahora es famoso, ¡pero a qué precio! *or* ¡pero lo ha pagado caro! • **at any ~** (*with affirmative*) a toda costa • **they want peace at any ~** quieren la paz a toda costa; (*with negative*) • **a concert I wasn't going to miss at any ~** un concierto que no me iba a perder por nada del mundo • **to pay a high** *or* **heavy ~ for sth** pagar algo muy caro • **that's a small ~ to pay for independence/for keeping him happy** eso es poco sacrificio a cambio de la independencia/de tenerlo contento
(VT) 1 (= *fix price of*) • **retailers usually ~ goods by adding 100% to the wholesale ~** los minoristas normalmente ponen precio a sus productos añadiendo un cien por cien al precio de coste, los minoristas normalmente cargan un cien por cien al precio de coste de sus productos • **tickets, ~d £20, are now available** las entradas ya están a la venta a un precio de 20 libras • **it was ~d too high/low** su precio era demasiado alto/bajo • **this stylish fryer, competitively ~d at £29.99, can help you create new dishes** por solo £29.99, esta elegante freidora puede ayudarle a crear nuevos platos • **there is a very reasonably ~d menu** hay un menú a un precio muy razonable • IDIOM: • **to ~ sb out of the market** hacer que algn pierda competitividad (*rebajando uno sus precios artificialmente*) • **the restaurant has ~d itself out of the market** el restaurante ha subido demasiado los precios y ha perdido su competitividad en el mercado • **you'll ~ yourself out of a job if you go on demanding so much money** como sigas exigiendo tanto dinero, pondrás en peligro tu trabajo
2 (= *label with price*) • **the tins of salmon weren't clearly ~d** el precio de la latas de salmón no estaba claro *or* claramente indicado • **it was ~d at £15** estaba marcado a un precio de 15 libras
3 (= *estimate value of*) calcular el valor de • **it was ~d at £1,000** estaba valorado en mil libras
4 (= *find out price of*) comprobar el precio de
(CPD) ▸ **price bracket** • **he's looking for a property in the £70,000 ~ bracket** está buscando una vivienda que cueste alrededor de las setenta mil libras • **that is the normal ~ bracket for one of his creations** ese es el precio normal de *or* eso es lo que se paga normalmente por una de sus creaciones • **a traditional restaurant in the middle ~ bracket** un restaurante tradicional con precios de un nivel medio (dentro de la escala) ▸ **price control** control *m* de precios • **to impose ~ controls** aplicar control de precios ▸ **price cut** rebaja *f* ▸ **price cutting** reducción *f* de precios ▸ **price-earnings ratio** (*Econ*) relación *f* precio ganancias ▸ **price fixing** fijación *f* de precios ▸ **price freeze** congelación *f* de precios ▸ **price increase** subida *f* de precio ▸ **price index** (*Brit*) índice *m* de precios; ▹ **consumer** ▸ **price inflation** inflación *f* de los precios ▸ **price level** nivel *m* de precios ▸ **price limit** tope *m*, precio *m* tope ▸ **price list** lista *f* de precios ▸ **price point** rango *m* de precios • **no ~ point exists for the machine yet** todavía no se ha establecido ningún rango de precios para la máquina ▸ **price range** • **there are lots of good products in all ~ ranges** hay gran cantidad de productos de buena calidad en una amplia gama de precios • **in the medium** *or* **middle ~ range** dentro de un nivel medio de la escala de precios • **the upper/lower end of the ~ range** el nivel más alto/bajo en la escala de precios • **(with) in/out of one's ~ range** dentro de/fuera de las posibilidades de uno • **the hotel was somewhat out of my ~ range** el hotel estaba un tanto fuera de mis posibilidades ▸ **price rigging** fijación *f* fraudulenta de precios • **they were accused of ~ rigging** se les acusó de amañar los precios ▸ **price ring** cártel *m* (para la fijación de precios) ▸ **price rise** = **price increase** ▸ **prices and incomes policy** política *f* de precios y salarios, política *f* de precios y rentas ▸ **price support** subsidio *m* de precios ▸ **price tag** (*lit*) etiqueta *f* (del precio); (*fig*) precio *m* • **it doesn't justify the ~ tag of £17.5 million** no justifica un precio de 17,5 millones de libras ▸ **price war** guerra *f* de precios
▸ **price down** (VT + ADV) rebajar
▸ **price up** (VT + ADV) aumentar el precio de

-priced [praɪst] (ADJ) (*ending in compounds*) • **high-priced** muy caro; ▹ **low-priced**

priceless ['praɪslɪs] (ADJ) 1 [*picture, jewel*] inestimable
2* (= *amusing*) divertidísimo • **it was ~!** ¡fue para morirse de risa!*

pricey*, **pricy** ['praɪsɪ] (ADJ) (COMPAR: **pricier**, SUPERL: **priciest**) (*Brit*) carito*, caro

pricing ['praɪsɪŋ] (N) fijación *f* de precios
(CPD) ▸ **pricing policy** política *f* tarifaria

prick [prɪk] (N) 1 (= *act, sensation*) (*with pin, needle*) pinchazo *m*; [*of insect*] picadura *f*; [*of spur*] espolada *f*; (*with goad*) aguijonazo *m* • **~s of conscience** remordimientos *mpl* • IDIOM: • **to kick against the ~s** dar coces contra el aguijón
2** (= *penis*) polla *f* (*Sp***), picha *f* (*Sp***), pija *f* (*esp LAm***), pinga *f* (*esp LAm***)
3** (= *person*) gilipollas *mf inv* (*Sp*‡), cojudo/a *m/f* (*Bol, Peru*), boludo/a *m/f* (*Arg, Bol*)
(VT) 1 (= *puncture*) [*person, needle*] pinchar; [*insect*] picar; (*with spur*) dar con las espuelas a • **to ~ one's finger (with** *or* **on sth)** pincharse el dedo (con algo)
2 (= *goad*) aguijar
3 (= *make hole in*) agujerear; (= *mark with holes*) marcar con agujerillos
4 • **it ~ed his conscience** le remordía la conciencia
(VI) = **prickle**
▸ **prick out** (VT + ADV) (*Hort*) plantar
▸ **prick up** (VT + ADV) • **to ~ up one's ears** (*lit, fig*) aguzar el oído, parar la oreja (*LAm*)
(VI + ADV) • **the dog's ears ~ed up** al perro se le levantaron *or* aguzaron las orejas • **his ears ~ed up** (*fig*) aguzó el oído, pegó la oreja*

pricked [prɪkt] (ADJ) [*wine*] picado

prickings ['prɪkɪŋz] (NPL) • **~ of conscience** remordimientos *mpl*

prickle ['prɪkl] (N) 1 (*on plant, animal*) espina *f*
2 (= *sensation*) picor *m*, comezón *f*
(VT) picar
(VI) picar, hormiguear • **my eyes are prickling** me pican los ojos • **I could feel my skin prickling** me escocía la piel

prickly ['prɪklɪ] (ADJ) (COMPAR: **pricklier**, SUPERL: **prickliest**) 1 (= *spiky*) espinoso
2 (*fig*) [*person*] enojadizo • **he's rather ~ about that** sobre ese tema es algo quisquilloso
(CPD) ▸ **prickly heat** (*Med*) sarpullido *m* (causado por exceso de calor) ▸ **prickly pear** (= *plant*) chumbera *f*, nopal *m* (*LAm*); (= *fruit*) higo *m* chumbo, tuna *f* (*LAm*)

pricy ['praɪsɪ] (ADJ) ▹ **pricey**

pride [praɪd] (N) 1 (= *pleasure, satisfaction*) orgullo *m* • **civic/national ~** orgullo *m* cívico/nacional • **it is a source of ~ to us that …** es para nosotros un motivo de orgullo el que … • **to take (a) ~ in sth/in doing sth**: • **he takes a ~ in his appearance** se preocupa mucho por su aspecto • **she could take no ~ in what she had done** no podía enorgullecerse *or* estar orgullosa de lo que había hecho • **we take ~ in offering you the highest standards** nos enorgullecemos *or* estamos orgullosos de ofrecerle la mejor calidad • IDIOM: • **to have** *or* **take ~ of place** (*lit, fig*) ocupar el lugar de honor • **the photo takes ~ of place on the mantlepiece** la foto ocupa el lugar de honor en la repisa de la chimenea
2 (= *conceit*) orgullo *m*, soberbia *f*, arrogancia *f* • PROVERB: • **~ comes** *or* **goes before a fall** más dura será la caída
3 (= *self-respect*) orgullo *m*, amor *m* propio • **false ~** presuntuosidad *f* • **I wouldn't ask him any favours, I have my ~** no le pediría ningún favor, tengo mi orgullo *or* amor propio • **to hurt** *or* **wound sb's ~** herir a algn en su amor propio; ▹ **swallow**
4 (= *source of pride*) orgullo *m* • **he's the ~ of the family** es el orgullo de la familia • **his roses are his ~ and joy** sus rosas son su orgullo
5 [*of lions*] manada *f*
(VT) • **to ~ o.s. on sth: he ~s himself on his punctuality** se precia de ser puntual • **she ~s**

herself on not owning a TV está orgullosa de no tener televisor
priest [pri:st] (N) (*gen, pagan*) sacerdote *m*; (*Christian*) sacerdote *m*, cura *m* • **woman ~** diaconisa *f*; ▹ **high, ordain, parish**
priestess ['pri:stɪs] (N) sacerdotisa *f*; ▹ **high**
priesthood ['pri:sthʊd] (N) (= *function*) sacerdocio *m*; (= *priests collectively*) clero *m* • **to enter the ~** ordenarse sacerdote
priestly ['pri:stlɪ] (ADJ) sacerdotal
prig [prɪg] (N) gazmoño/a *m/f*, mojigato/a *m/f*
priggish ['prɪgɪʃ] (ADJ) gazmoño, mojigato
priggishness ['prɪgɪʃnɪs] (N) gazmoñería *f*, mojigatería *f*
prim [prɪm] (ADJ) (COMPAR: **primmer**, SUPERL: **primmest**) (*also* **prim and proper**) (= *formal*) formal, estirado; (= *demure*) remilgado, cursi; (= *prudish*) mojigato, gazmoño
primacy ['praɪməsɪ] (N) primacía *f*
prima donna [pri:mə'dɒnə] (N) (PL: **prima donna** *or* **prima donnas**) primadonna *f*, diva *f*; (*fig*) persona *f* difícil, persona *f* de reacciones imprevisibles
primaeval [praɪ'mi:vl] (ADJ) (*Brit*) = **primeval**
prima facie ['praɪmə'feɪʃɪ] (ADV) a primera vista
(ADJ) suficiente a primera vista • **~ evidence** prueba *f* semiplena • **to have a ~ case** (*Jur*) tener razón a primera vista • **he has a ~ case** (*fig*) a primera vista parece que tiene razón • **there are ~ reasons why ...** hay suficientes razones que justifican el que (+ *subjun*)
primal ['praɪməl] (ADJ) (= *first in time*) original; (= *first in importance*) principal • **~ scream** grito *m* primal
primarily ['praɪmərɪlɪ] (ADV) (= *chiefly*) ante todo, principalmente
primary ['praɪmərɪ] (ADJ) **1** (= *chief, main*) [*reason, purpose, source*] principal • **our ~ concern is the well-being of our children** nuestra mayor *or* principal preocupación es el bienestar de nuestros hijos • **that is not the ~ reason** esa no es la razón principal
2 (= *fundamental*) primordial • **to be of ~ importance** ser de primordial importancia
3 (= *first*) primario
4 (*esp Brit*) (*Scol*) (= *elementary*) primario
(N) **1** (*US*) (*also* **primary election**) elección *f* primaria, primaria *f*
2 (= *colour*) color *m* primario
3 = **primary school**
(CPD) ▸ **primary care, primary health care** atención *f* sanitaria primaria ▸ **primary colour** color *m* primario ▸ **primary education** (*esp Brit*) enseñanza *f* primaria, educación *f* primaria ▸ **primary election** (*US*) elección *f* primaria, primaria *f* ▸ **primary products** productos *mpl* primarios ▸ **primary school** (*Brit*) escuela *f* primaria; (*US*) escuela *f* primaria (de primer ciclo) (*6-9 años*) ▸ **primary school teacher** (*Brit*) profesor(a) *m/f* de enseñanza primaria, maestro/a *m/f* ▸ **primary storage** almacenamiento *m* primario ▸ **primary teacher** (*Brit*) profesor(a) *m/f* de enseñanza primaria, maestro/a *m/f*

PRIMARIES
Las elecciones primarias (**primaries**) sirven para preseleccionar a los candidatos de los partidos demócrata (**Democratic**) y republicano (**Republican**) durante la campaña que precede a las elecciones a la presidencia de Estados Unidos. Se inician en New Hampshire y tienen lugar en 35 estados entre los meses de febrero y junio. El número de votos obtenidos por cada candidato determina el número de delegados que votarán en el congreso general (**National Convention**) de julio y agosto, en el que se decide el candidato definitivo de cada partido.

primate ['praɪmeɪt] (N) **1** (*Zool*) primate *m*
2 (*Rel*) primado *m*
prime [praɪm] (ADJ) **1** (= *major, main*) [*cause, objective, target*] principal • **the/a ~ cause of stress in the workplace** la principal causa/una de las principales causas de estrés en el trabajo • **the ~ candidate to take over his job is May Reid** May Reid es la candidata con más posibilidades de sustituirle en el puesto • **our ~ concern is public safety** nuestra mayor *or* principal preocupación es la seguridad ciudadana • **to be of ~ importance** ser de primordial importancia, ser de fundamental importancia • **he's the ~ suspect** es el principal sospechoso
2 (= *top-quality, excellent*) [*real estate, property*] de primera; [*ingredient, cut*] de primera (calidad) • **to be in ~ condition** [*cattle, fruit, car*] estar en perfecto estado; [*athlete*] estar en plena forma • **~ quality beef** carne *f* de vaca de primera (calidad) • **~ rib(s)** costillas *fpl* de primera (calidad) • **a ~ site** un lugar privilegiado
3 (= *classic*) perfecto • **a ~ example of what to avoid** un perfecto ejemplo de lo que se debe evitar
4 (*Math*) [*number*] primo
(N) **1** (= *best years*) • **when trade unionism was in its ~** cuando el sindicalismo estaba en su apogeo • **to be in the ~** *or* **in the ~ of life** [*person*] estar en la flor de la vida • **to be cut off** *or* **cut down in one's ~** morir en la flor de la vida • **he's past his ~** ya ha dejado atrás los mejores años de su vida • **the hotel was past its ~** (*hum*) el hotel ya había dejado atrás sus días de gloria
2 (*Rel*) prima *f*
(VT) **1** (*prior to painting*) imprimar, preparar; (*with primer*) aplicar una capa de imprimación a; (*with undercoat*) aplicar una capa de (pintura) base a; (*with anticorrosive*) aplicar una capa de pintura anticorrosiva a
2 (*prior to use*) [+ *gun, pump*] cebar • **he ~d the bomb to go off at ten** cebó la bomba para que explotara a las diez • IDIOM: • **to ~ the pump** sacar las cosas adelante • **he was willing to ~ the pump by offering finance** estaba dispuesto a ofrecerse a financiarlo para que saliera adelante • **public investment is the best way of priming the pump of economic activity** la inversión pública es la mejor forma de promover la actividad económica
3 (= *prepare*) [+ *student, politician, soldier*] preparar • **she came well ~d for the interview** vino a la entrevista bien preparada • **they had been ~d to expect the worst** se les había preparado para lo peor • **to keep troops ~d for combat** tener a las tropas listas para el combate • **he had been ~d to say that** le habían dado instrucciones para que dijera eso
4 (*with drink*) • **he arrived well ~d** llegó ya bien bebido • **he ~d himself for the interview with a stiff whisky** se tomó un whisky fuerte como preparación para la entrevista
(CPD) ▸ **prime cost** coste *m* neto, coste *m* de producción ▸ **prime factor** factor *m* primordial, factor *m* principal ▸ **the prime meridian** (*Geog*) el meridiano de Greenwich ▸ **prime minister** primer(a) ministro/a *m/f* ▸ **prime ministership** (= *period of office*) mandato *m* como primer ministro; (= *office*) cargo *m* de(l) primer ministro ▸ **prime mover** (= *person*) promotor(a) *m/f*; (*Philos*) primer motor *m* • **a ~ mover in Middle East events** una de las promotoras de los acontecimientos en el Oriente Medio ▸ **prime number** (*Math*) número *m* primo ▸ **prime rate** tipo *m* de interés preferencial • **~ lending rate** tipo *m* de interés preferencial sobre los préstamos ▸ **prime time** (*TV*) horas *fpl* de máxima *or* mayor audiencia • **the programme was repeated in ~ time** el programa se repitió a una de las horas de máxima *or* mayor audiencia; ▹ **prime-time**
prime ministerial [ˌpraɪmɪnɪs'tɪərɪəl] (ADJ) [*decision, appointment*] del primer ministro; [*talks*] entre los primeros ministros
primer ['praɪmə^r] (N) **1** (= *textbook*) manual *m* básico • **a French ~** un manual básico de francés, un manual de francés elemental
2 (= *basic reader*) abecedario *m*
3 (= *paint*) pintura *f* base, imprimación *f*
4 [*of bomb*] iniciador *m*
prime-time ['praɪmtaɪm] (ADJ) de máxima audiencia, de mayor audiencia • **the documentary will be broadcast on prime-time television** el documental se emitirá por televisión durante las horas de máxima *or* mayor audiencia
primeval [praɪ'mi:vəl] (ADJ) primitivo
priming ['praɪmɪŋ] (N) preparación *f*; [*of pump*] cebo *m*; (*Art*) primera capa *f*
(CPD) ▸ **priming device** iniciador *m*
primitive ['prɪmɪtɪv] (ADJ) (*gen*) primitivo; (= *old-fashioned*) anticuado; (= *basic*) rudimentario, básico; (= *uncivilized*) inculto; (= *sordid*) miserable; (*Art*) primitivo
(N) (*Art*) (= *artist*) primitivista *mf*; (= *work*) obra *f* primitivista
primitivism ['prɪmɪtɪˌvɪzəm] (N) (*Art*) primitivismo *m*
primly ['prɪmlɪ] (ADV) (= *demurely*) remilgadamente, con remilgo; (= *prudishly*) con gazmoñería
primness ['prɪmnɪs] (N) (= *formality*) formalidad *f*, lo estirado; (= *demureness*) remilgo *m*, cursilería *f*; (= *prudishness*) mojigatería *f*, gazmoñería *f*
primogeniture [ˌpraɪməʊ'dʒenɪtʃə^r] (N) (*frm*) primogenitura *f*
primordial [praɪ'mɔ:dɪəl] (ADJ) primordial
primp [prɪmp] = **prink**
primrose ['prɪmrəʊz] (N) **1** (*Bot*) primavera *f*
2 (= *colour*) color *m* amarillo pálido
(ADJ) (*also* **primrose yellow**) amarillo pálido
(CPD) ▸ **primrose path** caminito *m* de rosas
primula ['prɪmjʊlə] (N) (*Bot*) prímula *f*
Primus® ['praɪməs], **Primus stove** (N) (*esp Brit*) cocina *f* de camping, camping-gas® *m*
prince [prɪns] (N) príncipe *m* • **Prince Charles** el príncipe Carlos • **Prince Charming** el Príncipe Azul, el Príncipe Encantador • **the Prince of Darkness** el príncipe de las tinieblas • **the Prince of Wales** el Príncipe de Gales (*heredero del trono del Reino Unido, equivalente al Príncipe de Asturias en España*); ▹ **crown**
(CPD) ▸ **Prince Consort** príncipe *m* consorte ▸ **Prince Regent** príncipe *m* regente
princely ['prɪnslɪ] (ADJ) (*lit*) principesco; (*fig*) magnífico, espléndido • **a ~ gesture** un gesto magnífico, un gesto digno de un príncipe • **the ~ sum of five dollars** (*iro*) la bonita suma de cinco dólares
princess [prɪn'ses] (N) (= *royal*) princesa *f* • **Princess Victoria** la Princesa Victoria • **the Princess Royal** la princesa real • **the Princess of Wales** la Princesa de Gales; ▹ **crown**
principal ['prɪnsɪpəl] (ADJ) **1** [*reason, cause, source*] principal • **our ~ concern is the**

P

well-being of our children nuestra mayor *or* principal preocupación es el bienestar de nuestros hijos
2 (*Mus*) primero
3 (*Econ*) • **~ amount** capital *m* principal, principal *m*
(N) **1** [*of school, college*] director(a) *m/f*; (*Univ*) rector(a) *m/f*
2 (*Theat*) protagonista *mf* principal
3 (*Mus*) primer(a) instrumentista *mf*
4 (*Econ*) capital *m*, principal *m* • **~ and interest** el principal y los intereses
(CPD) ▸ **principal boy** (*Brit*) (*Theat*) joven héroe *m* (*papel de actriz en la "pantomime" navideña*); ▹ PANTOMIME

principality ['prɪnsɪ'pælɪtɪ] (N) principado *m*

principally ['prɪnsɪpəlɪ] (ADV) principalmente

principle ['prɪnsəpl] (N) (*also Sci*) principio *m* • **the basic ~s of physics** los principios básicos de física • **the ~ that ...** el principio según el cual ... • **to lay it down as a ~ that ...** sentar el principio de que ... • **it is** *or* **it goes against my ~s** va (en) contra (de) mis principios • **to go back to first ~s** volver a los principios (fundamentales) • **to argue from first ~s** construir un argumento sobre los principios (fundamentales) • **to have high ~s** tener principios nobles • **in ~** en principio • **to reach an agreement in ~** llegar a un acuerdo de principio *or* en principio • **I make it a ~ never to lend money** tengo por norma no prestar nunca dinero, yo, por principio, nunca presto dinero • **as a matter of ~** por principio • **it's a matter of ~** es cuestión de principios • **a man/woman of (high) ~s** un hombre/una mujer de principios (nobles) • **on ~** por principio, por una cuestión de principios • **it's the ~ of the thing** es cuestión de principios; ▹ guiding

principled ['prɪnsɪpld] (ADJ) [*person*] de fuertes principios; [*behaviour, stand*] basado en fuertes principios

prink [prɪŋk] (VT) acicalar
(VI) acicalarse

print [prɪnt] (N) **1** (*Typ*) (= *letters*) letra *f*; (= *printed matter*) texto *m* impreso • **I can't read this ~, it's too small** no puedo leer esta letra, es demasiado pequeña • **columns of tiny ~** columnas *fpl* de letra pequeña *or* menuda • **it presents the reader with solid masses of ~** enfrenta al lector con largos párrafos de texto (impreso) ininterrumpido • **in bold ~** en negrita • **the fine ~** la letra pequeña *or* menuda • **to be in ~** (= *be published*) estar publicado; (= *be available*) estar a la venta • **to appear in ~** [*work*] publicarse • **the first time the term appeared in ~ was in 1530** la primera vez que apareció el término en una publicación fue en 1530 • **to get into ~** publicarse • **in large ~** con letra grande • **to be out of ~** estar agotado • **to go out of ~** agotarse • **to rush into ~** lanzarse a publicar • **in small ~** con letra pequeña *or* menuda • **read the small ~ before you sign** lea la letra pequeña *or* menuda antes de firmar
2 (= *mark, imprint*) [*of foot, finger, tyre*] huella *f*, marca *f*; (= *fingerprint*) huella *f* digital, huella *f* dactilar • **to take sb's ~s** tomar las huellas digitales *or* dactilares a algn
3 (= *fabric*) estampado *m* • **a cotton ~** un estampado de algodón; ▹ floral
4 (*Art*) (= *etching, woodcut, lithograph*) grabado *m*; (= *reproduction*) reproducción *f*
5 (*Phot, Cine*) copia *f*; ▹ contact
(VT) **1** (= *set in print*) [+ *letters, text*] imprimir; [+ *money*] emitir • **they ~ed 300 copies** hicieron una tirada de 300 ejemplares • **~ed in England** impreso en Inglaterra • **~ed by** impreso por • **to ~ sth on** *or* **onto sth** estampar algo en algo
2 (= *write in block letters*) escribir con *or* en letra de imprenta, escribir con *or* en letra de molde • **~ it in block capitals** escríbalo con *or* en mayúsculas
3 (*Phot*) [+ *negative*] imprimir; [+ *photo*] sacar una copia de; [+ *copy*] sacar
4 (*fig*) grabar • **her face was ~ed in my mind** su cara se me había quedado grabada en la mente
(VI) [*person*] escribir con *or* en letra de imprenta, escribir con *or* en letra de molde; [*machine*] imprimir; [*negative*] salir • **the book is ~ing now** el libro está en la imprenta en este momento
(CPD) ▸ **print dress** vestido *m* estampado ▸ **print journalist** periodista *mf* de prensa escrita ▸ **print media** medios *mpl* de comunicación impresos ▸ **print reporter** (*US*) = **print journalist** ▸ **print run** tirada *f* ▸ **print shop** (*Typ*) imprenta *f*; (= *art shop*) tienda *f* de grabados ▸ **print union** sindicato *m* de tipógrafos ▸ **print wheel** rueda *f* de tipos ▸ **print worker** tipógrafo/a *m/f*
▸ **print off** (VT + ADV) imprimir
▸ **print out** (VT + ADV) (*Comput*) imprimir

printable ['prɪntəbl] (ADJ) imprimible

printed ['prɪntɪd] (ADJ) **1** (*Publishing*) impreso • **the ~ book** el libro impreso • **~ matter** impresos *mpl* • **the ~ page** el impreso • **~ papers** impresos *mpl* • **~ paper rate** (*Brit*) tarifa *f* de impreso • **the ~ word** la palabra impresa
2 (*Textiles*) estampado • **a ~ cotton fabric** una tela de algodón estampada
3 (*Electronics*) • **~ circuit** circuito *m* impreso • **~ circuit board** placa *f* de circuito impreso

printer ['prɪntəʳ] (N) **1** (= *person*) impresor(a) *m/f* • **~'s ink** tinta *f* de imprenta • **~'s mark** pie *m* de imprenta
2 (*Comput*) (= *machine*) impresora *f*

printery ['prɪntərɪ] (N) imprenta *f*

printhead ['prɪnthed] (N) cabeza *f* impresora

printing ['prɪntɪŋ] (N) **1** (= *process*) impresión *f* • **fourth ~** cuarta impresión *f*
2 (= *craft, industry*) imprenta *f* • **"16th century ~ in Toledo"** "La imprenta en Toledo en el siglo XVI"
3 (= *block writing*) letras *fpl* de molde; (= *characters, print*) letra *f*
4 (= *quantity printed*) tirada *f* • **a ~ of 500 copies** una tirada de 500 ejemplares
(CPD) ▸ **printing error** error *m* de imprenta, errata *f* ▸ **printing frame** prensa *f* de copiar ▸ **printing ink** tinta *f* de imprenta ▸ **printing office** imprenta *f* ▸ **printing press** prensa *f* ▸ **printing queue** cola *f* de impresión ▸ **printing works** imprenta *f*

printmaker ['prɪnt,meɪkəʳ] (N) (= *artist*) grabador(a) *m/f*; (= *manufacturer*) fabricante *mf* de grabados

printmaking ['prɪntmeɪkɪŋ] (N) grabado *m*

printout ['prɪntaʊt] (N) (*Comput*) copia *f* impresa, listado *m*

prion ['praɪən] (N) prión *m*
(CPD) ▸ **prion protein** proteína *f* priónica

prior[1] ['praɪəʳ] (ADJ) **1** (= *previous*) previo • **I have a ~ engagement** tengo un compromiso previo • **to have a ~ claim to** *or* **on sth/sb**: • **there are others who have a ~ claim on my time** hay otros a los que tengo que dedicar mi tiempo que tienen prioridad *or* están antes • **she felt that her past connection with him gave her a ~ claim to him** le parecía que su pasada relación le daba ciertos derechos sobre él • **without ~ notice/warning** sin previo aviso
2 (= *earlier*) [*week, month, year*] anterior • **in ~ years** en años anteriores
(ADV) (*frm*) • **~ to sth** anterior *or* previo a algo • **~ to doing sth** antes de hacer algo • **~ to (his) leaving he hid the money** antes de marchar, escondió el dinero • **in the years ~ to his death** en los años anteriores *or* previos a su muerte • **~ to that day we had not met** antes de ese día no nos conocíamos, hasta ese día no nos conocimos • **~ to this/that** antes de esto/eso
(ADV) (*US*) antes • **it happened two days ~** ocurrió dos días antes

prior[2] ['praɪəʳ] (N) (*Rel*) prior *m*

prioress ['praɪərɪs] (N) priora *f*

prioritization [praɪ,ɒrɪtaɪ'zeɪʃən] (N) priorización *f* • **~ of these issues was a mistake** haberles dado prioridad a estos temas fue un error

prioritize [praɪ'ɒrɪtaɪz] (VT) (*esp US*) priorizar

priority [praɪ'ɒrɪtɪ] (N) **1** (= *precedence*) prioridad *f* • **to give sth/sb ~** • **give ~ to sth/sb** dar prioridad a algo/algn • **to give sth (a) high/low ~** dar mucha/poca importancia a algo • **to give sth top ~** dar máxima prioridad a algo • **housing must be given top ~** el problema de la vivienda debe tener máxima prioridad • **to have** *or* **take ~ (over sth/sb)** tener prioridad (sobre algo/algn) • **in (strict) order of ~** por (estricto) orden de prioridad
2 (= *concern, aim*) prioridad *f* • **try to decide what your priorities are** intenta establecer tu orden de prioridades • **it should be a ~ for all of us** tiene que ser prioridad de todos nosotros, debería ser lo más importante *or* lo principal para todos nosotros • **to set spending priorities** repartir los gastos por orden de prioridad • **our first ~ is to cut costs** nuestra máxima prioridad es reducir los gastos • **she made it clear where her priorities lay** dejó bien claro cuáles eran sus prioridades • **to be high/low on sb's list of priorities** ocupar un lugar alto/bajo en el orden de prioridades de algn • **my number one** *or* **top ~** lo más importante para mí • **we must get our priorities right** tenemos que tener claro cuáles son nuestras prioridades, tenemos que tener claro qué es lo más importante *or* lo principal para nosotros
3 (*on highway*) preferencia *f* de paso • **drivers on the right have ~** los conductores de la derecha tienen preferencia de paso
(CPD) ▸ **priority case** caso *m* prioritario ▸ **priority share** acción *f* prioritaria ▸ **priority treatment** trato *m* preferente

priory ['praɪərɪ] (N) priorato *m*

prise [praɪz] (VT) • **to ~ sth off** levantar algo haciendo palanca • **to ~ sth open** abrir algo haciendo palanca • **we had to ~ the secret out of him** tuvimos que sacarle el secreto a la fuerza • **to ~ sb out of his post** lograr que algn renuncie a su puesto, desahuciar a algn • **to ~ a lid up** levantar una tapa haciendo palanca

prism ['prɪzəm] (N) (*Geom, Tech*) prisma *m*

prismatic [prɪz'mætɪk] (ADJ) prismático

prison ['prɪzn] (N) **1** (= *place*) cárcel *f*, prisión *f* • **to be in ~** estar en la cárcel, estar en prisión • **to go to ~ for five years** (= *be sentenced*) ser condenado a cinco años de cárcel *or* prisión; (= *be imprisoned*) pasar cinco años en la cárcel *or* en prisión • **to put sb in ~** encarcelar a algn • **to release sb from ~** poner a algn en libertad, excarcelar a algn (*frm*) • **to send sb to ~** (= *imprison*) encarcelar a algn • **to send sb to ~ for two years** (= *sentence*) condenar a algn a dos años de

prisión; ▹ **maximum, open**
2 (= *imprisonment*) prisión *f*, cárcel *f* • **are there alternatives to ~?** ¿existen alternativas a la prisión *or* cárcel?
(CPD) ▸ **prison break** fuga *f* (de la cárcel) ▸ **prison camp** campamento *m* para prisioneros ▸ **prison cell** celda *f* de la cárcel *or* prisión ▸ **prison governor** director(a) *m/f* de (la) prisión ▸ **prison guard** (*US*) guardia *mf* de prisión ▸ **prison inmate** preso/a *m/f* ▸ **prison life** vida *f* en la cárcel ▸ **prison officer** carcelero/a *m/f* ▸ **prison population** número *m* de reclusos ▸ **prison riot** motín *m* carcelario ▸ **prison sentence** (*Brit*) condena *f*; ▹ **serve** ▸ **the prison service** los servicios penitenciarios ▸ **prison system** sistema *m* penitenciario ▸ **prison term** (*US*) = **prison sentence** ▸ **prison van** coche *m* celular ▸ **prison visitor** visitante *mf* de la prisión ▸ **prison warden** (*US*) = **prison governor** ▸ **prison warder** guardia *mf* de prisión ▸ **prison yard** patio *m* de (la) cárcel

prisoner [ˈprɪznəʳ] (N) **1** (*under arrest*) detenido/a *m/f*; (*in court*) acusado/a *m/f*; (*convicted*) preso/a *m/f*, reo/a *m/f*; (*Mil*) prisionero/a *m/f* • **~ of conscience** preso/a *m/f* de conciencia • **to hold sb ~** detener a algn • **to keep sb (a) ~** tener retenido a algn, tener prisionero a algn • **to take sb ~** tomar preso a algn, hacer prisionero a algn • **~ of war** prisionero/a *m/f* de guerra, preso/a *m/f* de guerra • IDIOM: • **to take no ~s** no andarse con miramientos, ir a por todas; ▹ **bar, political**
2 (*fig*) preso/a *m/f*, prisionero/a *m/f*

prisoner-of-war camp [ˌprɪznərəvwɔːˈkæmp] (N) campamento *m* para prisioneros de guerra

prissy* [ˈprɪsɪ] (ADJ) (COMPAR: **prissier**, SUPERL: **prissiest**) remilgado

pristine [ˈprɪstaɪn] (ADJ) prístino

prithee†† [ˈprɪðiː] (EXCL) le ruego

privacy [ˈprɪvəsɪ] (N) intimidad *f* • **they respected each other's ~** cada uno respetaba la intimidad del otro • **there is no ~** no se tiene intimidad • **in ~** en la intimidad • **in the ~ of one's own home** en la intimidad del hogar • **to invade sb's ~** invadir la intimidad *or* privacidad de algn • **lack of ~** falta *f* de intimidad
(CPD) ▸ **Privacy Act** ≈ Ley *f* del Derecho a la Intimidad ▸ **privacy law** ley *f* del derecho a la intimidad

private [ˈpraɪvɪt] (ADJ) **1** (= *not public*) [*conversation, visit, land, matter*] privado; [*letter, reason, opinion*] personal; [*language*] secreto; [*thoughts, grief, fantasy*] íntimo • **it was a ~ wedding** • **the wedding was ~** la boda se celebró en la intimidad • **"private"** (*on door*) "privado"; (*on envelope*) "confidencial" • **"private and confidential"** "confidencial" • **"private fishing"** "coto *m* de pesca" • **"private parking"** "aparcamiento *m* or (*LAm*) estacionamiento *m* privado" • **it's a silly ~ joke of ours** es un chiste tonto que solo nosotras entendemos • **to keep sth ~** [+ *beliefs*] no hablar de algo; [+ *opinions, views, doubts*] guardarse algo, reservarse algo • **I have always kept my political beliefs ~** nunca he hablado de mis ideas políticas • **he was diagnosed with AIDS in 1994 but kept it ~** en 1994 le diagnosticaron SIDA pero lo mantuvo en secreto • **I want to keep this ~** quiero que esto quede entre nosotros • **I've always tried to keep my ~ life ~** [*famous person*] siempre he intentado mantener mi vida privada alejada de la mirada del público; [*ordinary person*] siempre he intentado mantener mi vida privada fuera del alcance de los demás • **to be in ~ ownership** ser propiedad privada • **he's a very ~ person** es una persona muy reservada; ▹ **strictly**
2 (= *own, individual*) [*car, house, lesson, room*] particular; [*bank account*] personal • **76 bedrooms, all with ~ bathrooms** 76 habitaciones, cada una con su baño particular • **in a** *or* **one's ~ capacity** a título personal • **for your ~ information** únicamente para su información • **for ~ use** para el uso personal
3 (= *independent*) [*medicine, education, finance*] privado; [*school*] privado, particular; [*patient, tutor, teacher*] particular • **a ~ hospital** una clínica (privada), un hospital privado *or* particular • **he decided to take on ~ pupils** decidió dar clases particulares • **to go ~** [*patient*] ir por lo privado; [*dentist, doctor*] establecerse de forma privada; [*company*] dejar de cotizar en bolsa
4 (= *secluded*) [*place*] retirado • **is there somewhere we can be ~?** ¿hay algún sitio donde podamos hablar en privado?
(N) **1** (*Mil*) soldado *mf* raso • **Private Jones** el soldado Jones • **Private Jones!** ¡Jones!
2 • **in ~: could I talk to you in ~?** ¿te puedo hablar en privado? • **I have been told in ~ that ...** me han dicho confidencialmente *or* en confianza que ... • **the committee sat in ~** la comisión se reunió a puerta(s) cerrada(s) *or* en privado • **the wedding was held in ~** la boda se celebró en la intimidad • **what people do in ~ is up to them** lo que cada uno haga en su vida privada es asunto suyo
3 privates* (*euph, hum*) partes *fpl* pudendas
(CPD) ▸ **private citizen** (*Jur*) particular *mf* ▸ **private company** empresa *f* privada, compañía *f* privada ▸ **private detective** detective *mf* privado/a ▸ **private enterprise** (= *industry*) el sector privado; (= *initiative*) la iniciativa privada • **new employment laws which will hamper ~ enterprise** nuevas leyes *fpl* laborales que van a dificultar el crecimiento del sector privado ▸ **private enterprise economy** economía *f* capitalista, economía *f* de mercado ▸ **private equity fund** *fondo que invierte en compañías privadas que no cotizan en bolsa* ▸ **private eye** (*US**) detective *mf* privado/a ▸ **private finance initiative** (*Brit*) *plan de incentivos y potenciación de la iniciativa privada en el sector público* ▸ **private health care** servicio *m* médico privado ▸ **private health insurance** seguro *m* médico privado ▸ **private hearing** (*Jur*) vista *f* a puertas cerradas ▸ **private hotel** hotel *m* privado ▸ **private income** rentas *fpl* ▸ **private individual** (*Jur*) particular *mf* ▸ **private investigator** investigador(a) *m/f* privado/a ▸ **private law** derecho *m* privado ▸ **private life** vida *f* privada • **in ~ life** en su vida privada ▸ **private limited company** sociedad *f* limitada ▸ **private line** (*Telec*) línea *f* particular ▸ **private means** rentas *fpl* • **a man of ~ means** un hombre que vive de sus rentas ▸ **private member, Private Member** (*Brit*) (*Parl*) diputado/a *m/f* sin responsabilidades de gobierno ▸ **Private Member's Bill** *proyecto de ley presentado por un diputado a título personal* • **to introduce a Private Member's Bill** presentar un proyecto de ley a título personal ▸ **private parts** (*euph, hum*) partes *fpl* pudendas ▸ **private patient** paciente *mf* privado/a ▸ **private pension** pensión *f* personal ▸ **private pension plan** plan *m* de pensiones personal ▸ **private pension scheme** = **private pension plan** ▸ **private practice** (*Med*) consulta *f* privada • **to be in ~ practice** (*Med*) ejercer la medicina de forma privada • **he decided to set up in ~ practice** decidió establecerse como médico privado ▸ **private property** propiedad *f* privada ▸ **private property rights** derechos *mpl* de propiedad ▸ **private prosecution** (*Jur*) demanda *f* civil • **to bring a ~ prosecution against sb** presentar una demanda civil contra algn ▸ **private school** escuela *f* privada, escuela *f* particular ▸ **private secretary** secretario/a *m/f* particular ▸ **the private sector** el sector privado ▸ **private soldier** soldado *mf* raso ▸ **private study** (*Brit*) estudio *m* personal ▸ **private tuition** clases *fpl* particulares ▸ **private view, private viewing** visita *f* privada (a una exposición)

privateer [ˌpraɪvəˈtɪəʳ] (N) corsario *m*

privately [ˈpraɪvɪtlɪ] (ADV) **1** (= *not publicly*) en privado • **many politicians ~ admit that ...** en privado, muchos políticos admiten que ... • **the country may be publicly supporting sanctions while ~ violating them** puede que oficialmente el país esté apoyando las sanciones mientras que extraoficialmente las esté infringiendo • **is there anywhere where we can talk ~?** ¿hay algún sitio donde podamos hablar en privado? • **senior officials from the two sides met ~** altos funcionarios de ambas partes se reunieron en privado *or* a puerta(s) cerrada(s) • **~ he was furious at the prime minister's decision** aunque no lo demostró, estaba furioso con la decisión del primer ministro • **I tried to be understanding but ~ I was very angry with her** intenté ser comprensiva pero por dentro estaba muy enfadada con ella • **the Foreign Office was ~ appalled** extraoficialmente, el Ministerio de Exterior estaba horrorizado
2 (= *independently*) • **one in every four of these operations is now done ~** ahora una de cada cuatro operaciones de este tipo se hace en clínicas privadas • **he is being ~ educated** va a un colegio privado *or* particular • **~ financed projects** proyectos *mpl* de financiación privada • **~ funded organizations** organizaciones *fpl* fundadas por particulares • **~ owned land** tierras *fpl* que son propiedad privada

privation [praɪˈveɪʃən] (N) **1** (= *poverty*) miseria *f*, estrechez *f* • **to live in ~** vivir en la miseria
2 (= *hardship, deprivation*) privación *f* • **to suffer many ~s** pasar muchos apuros

privative [ˈprɪvətɪv] (ADJ), (N) privativo *m*

privatization [ˌpraɪvətaɪˈzeɪʃən] (N) privatización *f*

privatize [ˈpraɪvətaɪz] (VT) privatizar

privatized [ˈpraɪvətaɪzd] (ADJ) privatizado

privatizing [ˈpraɪvətaɪzɪŋ] (N) privatización *f*

privet [ˈprɪvɪt] (N) alheña *f*
(CPD) ▸ **privet hedge** seto *m* vivo

privilege [ˈprɪvɪlɪdʒ] (N) **1** (= *prerogative*) privilegio *m*; (*Jur, Parl*) inmunidad *f* • **members enjoy special ~s** los miembros gozan de privilegios especiales • **as the oldest son, he has certain ~s** como hijo mayor tiene ciertos privilegios • **that's your ~** estás en tu derecho • **to have parliamentary ~** gozar de inmunidad parlamentaria
2 (= *honour*) privilegio *m*, honor *m* • **I had the ~ of meeting her** tuve el privilegio *or* el honor de conocerla
(VT) **1** (= *favour*) privilegiar
2 • **to be ~d to do sth** tener el privilegio *or* el honor de hacer algo • **I am ~d to call him a friend** tengo el privilegio *or* el honor de poder decir que es amigo mío

privileged [ˈprɪvɪlɪdʒd] (ADJ) **1** (= *advantaged*)

P

[*position, life*] privilegiado • **for a ~ few** para unos pocos privilegiados *or* afortunados
2 (= *secret*) [*information*] confidencial
3 (*Jur*) [*communication*] privilegiado; [*document*] confidencial
N • **the ~** los privilegiados

privily ['prɪvɪlɪ] ADV [*speak*] privadamente, en privado; [*tell*] confidencialmente

privy ['prɪvɪ] ADJ • **to be ~ to sth** estar al tanto *or* enterado de algo
N retrete *m*, baño *m* (*LAm*)
CPD ▸ **Privy Council** (*Brit*) consejo *m* privado (del monarca), ≈ Consejo *m* de Estado ▸ **Privy Councillor** (*Brit*) consejero/a *m/f* privado/a (del monarca), ≈ consejero/a *m/f* de Estado ▸ **Privy Purse** (*Brit*) gastos *mpl* personales del monarca

PRIVY COUNCIL
El consejo de asesores de la Corona, conocido como **Privy Council**, tuvo su origen en la época de los normandos, y fue adquiriendo mayor importancia hasta ser substituido en 1688 por el actual Consejo de Ministros **Cabinet**. Hoy día sigue existiendo con un carácter fundamentalmente honorífico que se concede de forma automática a los ministros del gobierno, así como a otras personalidades políticas, eclesiásticas y jurídicas.

prize[1] [praɪz] N 1 (*in competition, lottery*) premio *m* • **to win a ~** (*in competition*) ganar un premio • **she won a ~ in the lottery** le tocó la lotería • **he won first ~** (*in race, competition*) se llevó el primer premio; (*in lottery*) le tocó el gordo • **to carry off the ~** • **win the ~** ganar el premio; ▸ **booby, cash, consolation, Nobel, star**
2 (*Sport*) (= *trophy*) trofeo *m*; (= *money*) premio *m*
3 (*fig*) premio *m*, galardón *m* (*frm*)
4 (*Naut*) presa *f*
ADJ 1 (= *outstanding*) de primera, de primera clase • **a ~ idiot*** un tonto de remate*
2 (= *prizewinning*) [*entry, rose*] galardonado, premiado; (*fig*) digno de premio
VT apreciar mucho, estimar mucho • **to ~ sth highly** estimar algo en mucho • **a ~d possession** un bien preciado
CPD ▸ **prize court** (*Naut*) tribunal *m* de presas marítimas ▸ **prize day** (*Scol*) día *m* de reparto de premios ▸ **prize draw** sorteo *m* con premio, tómbola *f* ▸ **prize fight** (*Boxing*) partido *m* (de boxeo) profesional ▸ **prize fighter** boxeador *m* profesional ▸ **prize fighting** boxeo *m* profesional ▸ **prize money** (= *cash*) premio *m* en metálico; (*Boxing*) bolsa *f*; (*Naut*) parte *f* de presa ▸ **prize ring** (*Boxing*) ring *m*

prize[2] [praɪz] VT (*US*) = **prise**

prize-giving ['praɪz,gɪvɪŋ] N reparto *m* de premios

prizewinner ['praɪz,wɪnəʳ] N premiado/a *m/f*

prizewinning ['praɪz,wɪnɪŋ] ADJ premiado

PRO N ABBR 1 (= **Public Record Office**) Archivo *m* Nacional
2 = **public relations officer**

pro[1] [prəʊ] PREFIX 1 (= *in favour of*) pro, en pro de • **pro-Soviet** pro-soviético • **pro-Spanish** hispanófilo • **pro-European** europeísta • **they were terribly pro-Franco** eran unos franquistas furibundos, eran partidarios acérrimos de Franco
2 • **pro rata** ▸ **pro rata**
3 • **pro tem** • **pro tempore** ▸ **pro tem**
N • **the pros and cons** los pros y los contras • **we are weighing up the pros and the cons** estamos estudiando los pros y los contras

pro[2]* [prəʊ] N (= *professional*) profesional *mf*

pro[3]* [prəʊ] N (= *prostitute*) puta *f*

pro-abortion [,prəʊə'bɔːʃən] ADJ pro-aborto, proabortista

pro-abortionist [,prəʊə'bɔːʃənɪst] N proabortista *mf*

proactive [prəʊ'æktɪv] ADJ proactivo

prob* [prɒb] N problema *m* • **no ~s** (= *of course*) claro; (= *it doesn't matter*) no hay problema, no importa

probabilistic [,prɒbəbə'lɪstɪk] ADJ probabilístico

probability [,prɒbə'bɪlɪtɪ] N (*also Math*) probabilidad *f* • **the ~ is that ...** es probable que ... (+ *subjun*) • **we calculated the probabilities of it happening** calculamos la probabilidad *or* las probabilidades de que ocurriera • **in all ~ he won't turn up** lo más probable es que no aparezca • **there is little ~ of anyone finding out** es muy poco probable que alguien se entere
CPD ▸ **probability theory** teoría *f* de la probabilidad

probable [əbl] ADJ 1 (= *likely*) probable • **wet roads were a ~ cause of the accident** una causa probable del accidente eran las carreteras mojadas • **it is ~ that ...** es probable que ... (+ *subjun*)
2 (= *credible*) verosímil • **her story didn't sound very ~ to me** su historia no me pareció muy verosímil

probably ['prɒbəblɪ] ADV probablemente • **she ~ forgot** se habrá olvidado, seguramente se ha olvidado, probablemente se haya olvidado • **he will ~ come** es probable que venga • **~ not** puede que no, quizá no • **very ~, but ...** es muy posible *or* bien puede ser, pero ...

probate ['prəʊbɪt] N (*Jur*) validación *f* de un testamento, validación *f* testamentaria • **to value sth for ~** evaluar algo para la validación testamentaria
CPD ▸ **probate court** tribunal *m* de testamentarías

probation [prə'beɪʃən] N (*Jur*) libertad *f* condicional • **to be on ~** estar en libertad condicional; (*in employment*) estar a prueba • **to put sb on ~** poner a algn en libertad provisional; (*fig*) asignar a algn un período a prueba • **to take sth on ~** (= *as a trial*) tomar algo a prueba • **release on ~** libertad *f* a prueba
CPD ▸ **probation officer** *funcionario que vigila a las personas que están en libertad condicional* ▸ **probation order** orden *f* de libertad condicional • **his jail sentence was reduced on appeal to a ~ order** le redujeron la condena en apelación a una orden de libertad condicional ▸ **probation service** • **the ~ service** el servicio de libertad condicional

probational [prə'beɪʃənl] ADJ probatorio • **~ period** período de prueba

probationary [prə'beɪʃnərɪ] ADJ de prueba
CPD ▸ **probationary period** (*Jur*) período *m* de libertad condicional; (*fig*) período *m* de prueba

probationer [prə'beɪʃnəʳ] N (*Jur*) persona *f* en libertad condicional; (*Med*) aprendiz *mf* de ATS (*Sp*), aprendiz *mf* de enfermero/a; (*Rel*) novicio/a *m/f*

probe [prəʊb] N 1 (*Med*) sonda *f*
2 (= *rocket*) cohete *m*, proyectil *m*; (*also* **space probe**) sonda *f* espacial
3 (= *inquiry*) investigación *f* • **a ~ into drug trafficking** una investigación del tráfico de drogas
VT 1 [+ *hole, crack*] (*with instrument, probe*) sondear; (*with hands*) palpar, tantear
2 (*Med*) sondar
3 (= *explore*) explorar
4 (= *investigate*) investigar • **the policeman kept probing me** el policía siguió sondeándome • **to ~ a mystery** investigar un misterio
VI investigar • **to ~ into sb's past** investigar el pasado de algn • **you should have ~d more deeply** deberías haber llevado a cabo una investigación más a fondo

probing ['prəʊbɪŋ] ADJ [*question*] agudo, penetrante
N 1 (*with probe, instrument*) sondeo *m*; (*with hands*) palpación *f*, tanteo *m*
2 (= *investigation*) investigación *f*
3 (= *exploration*) exploración *f*

probiotic [,prəʊbaɪ'ɒtɪk] N probiótico *m*
ADJ probiótico

probity ['prəʊbɪtɪ] N probidad *f*

problem ['prɒbləm] N (*gen*) (*also Math*) problema *m* • **what's the ~?** ¿cuál es el problema? • **that's your ~** eso es problema tuyo • **it's not my ~** no es problema mío • **loneliness isn't the ~** el problema no está en *or* no es la soledad • **the ~ is that she can't cook** el problema es que no sabe cocinar • **his ~ is that he's never satisfied** su problema es que nunca está satisfecho • **he has a drink ~** tiene problemas con la bebida, bebe demasiado • **she has a serious drug ~** tiene graves problemas con las drogas • **this will not solve America's drug ~** esto no solucionará el problema de las drogas en América • **the real ~ for the police is the lack of funding** el verdadero problema de la policía es la escasez de fondos • **that presents a big ~ for schools** eso supone un gran problema para las escuelas • **he shouldn't have a** *or* **any ~ finding a job** no le será difícil encontrar trabajo • **phone me if you have any ~s** llámame si tienes cualquier problema • **I had no ~ getting a mortgage** no tuve problemas para conseguir una hipoteca • **he's having ~s deciding what subjects to study** le está costando decidir qué asignaturas estudiar • **do you have a ~ with that?*** ¿te molesta? • **I have no ~ with the ordination of women** no tengo nada en contra de la ordenación de las mujeres • **health ~s** problemas *mpl* de salud • **to have a heart ~** tener problemas de corazón • **the housing ~** el problema de la vivienda • **no ~!*** (= *of course*) ¡claro!, ¡cómo no!; (= *it doesn't matter*) ¡no importa!, ¡no hay problema! • **the ~ of how to fund education** el problema de cómo financiar la enseñanza • **we've still got the ~ of what to give them for lunch** aún nos queda por solucionar el problema de qué darles para comer • **to have a weight ~** tener problemas de peso • **the ~ with men is that ...** lo malo de los hombres es que ...
CPD ▸ **problem area** (= *place*) zona *f* problemática; (*fig*) área *m* problemática • **travel insurance is another potential ~ area** el seguro de viaje es otra área problemática, el seguro de viaje es otro posible problema ▸ **problem case** (*Med, Sociol*) caso *m* difícil ▸ **problem child** niño/a *m/f* problemático/a ▸ **problem drinker** • **he's a ~ drinker** tiene problemas con la bebida ▸ **problem drinking** • **his ~ drinking is wrecking his marriage** sus problemas con la bebida están destrozando su matrimonio ▸ **problem family** familia *f* con problemas ▸ **problem page** consultorio *m* sentimental ▸ **problem play** drama *m* de tesis ▸ **problem solving** resolución *f* de problemas

problematic [,prɒblɪ'mætɪk] ADJ problemático • **it is ~ whether ...** es dudoso si ...

problematical [,prɒblɪ'mætɪkəl] ADJ

P

= problematic

problem-free ['prɒbləm,fri:] ADJ sin problemas

proboscis [prəʊ'bɒsɪs] N (PL: **proboscises** *or* **probocides** [prəʊ'bɒsɪdi:z]) probóscide *f*, trompa *f*; (*hum*) trompa* *f*

procedural [prə'si:djʊrəl] ADJ relativo al procedimiento; (*Jur*) procesal • **a ~ question** una cuestión de procedimiento

N (*also* **police procedural**) (= *novel*) novela *f* policíaca; (= *film*) película *f* policíaca

procedure [prə'si:dʒəʳ] N **1** (*gen*) procedimiento *m* • **what is the ~ for emergencies?** ¿cuál es el procedimiento a seguir *or* cómo se procede en caso de emergencia? • **the usual ~ is to write a letter** lo que se hace por lo general es escribir una carta • **the correct ~ would be to ...** lo correcto sería ... (+ *infin*); ▷ **complain, disciplinary, selection**

2 (*Admin*) trámites *mpl* • **what's the ~ for obtaining a visa?** ¿qué trámites *or* gestiones hay que hacer para conseguir un visado?

proceed [prə'si:d] VI **1** (*frm*) (= *go*) [*person, vehicle*] avanzar; [*plan, project*] desarrollarse; [*events*] transcurrir • **he was ~ing along the road** avanzaba por la calle • **things are ~ing according to plan** las cosas se están desarrollando conforme estaban previstas • **the march ~ed without incident** la marcha transcurrió sin incidentes

2 (= *go on, continue*) seguir, continuar • **proceed!** ¡siga!, ¡continúe!, ¡proceda! (*frm*) • **to ~ on one's way** seguir *or* continuar su camino • **before we ~ any further** antes de seguir adelante • **to ~ to sth: let us ~ to the next item** pasemos al siguiente punto • **to ~ to blows** llegar a las manos; (*to place*) • **we ~ed to London** proseguimos viaje a Londres • **we ~ed to the bar** nos dirigimos al bar • **to ~ to do sth** pasar a hacer algo • **she ~ed to outline my duties** pasó a hacerme un esquema de mis obligaciones • **he ~ed to drink the lot** acto seguido comenzó a bebérselo todo • **to ~ with sth** seguir adelante con algo • **they did not ~ with the charges against him** no siguieron adelante con los cargos contra él • **~ with your work** sigan con su trabajo

3 (= *act*) proceder, obrar • **we should ~ with caution** debemos proceder *or* obrar con precaución

4 (*frm*) (= *arise*) • **to ~ from sth:** • **sounds ~ed from the box** unos ruidos procedían *or* provenían *or* venían de la caja • **this ~s from ignorance** esto proviene de la ignorancia

5 (*Jur*) • **to ~ against sb** demandar a algn

VT (= *say*) proseguir • **"well," she ~ed** —bueno —prosiguió

proceeding [prə'si:dɪŋ] N **1** (= *action, course of action*) proceder *m* • **a somewhat dubious ~** un proceder sospechoso

2 (*Jur*) proceso *m* • **a criminal ~** un proceso criminal

3 proceedings (= *event*) acto *msing*; (= *record*) [*of learned society*] actas *fpl* • **the ~s began at seven o'clock** el acto comenzó a las siete • **hecklers attempted to disrupt the ~s** hubo gente que intentó perturbar el desarrollo del acto *or* de la reunión • **Proceedings of the Royal Society** Actas *fpl* de la Real Sociedad

4 proceedings (*esp Jur*) (= *measures*) medidas *fpl* • **legal ~s** proceso *msing* • **to take ~s (to do sth)** (*Jur*) abrir un proceso (para hacer algo) • **to start (legal) ~s (against sb)** (*Jur*) entablar pleito *or* una demanda (contra algn); ▷ **divorce, institute**

proceeds ['prəʊsi:dz] NPL [*of sale, transaction*] ganancias *fpl*; [*of insurance policy*] dinero *m* de una póliza • **all ~ will go to charity** toda la recaudación se destinará a obras benéficas • **he stole a wallet and got drunk on the ~** robó una cartera y se emborrachó con lo que sacó

process¹ ['prəʊses] N **1** (= *series of developments*) proceso *m* • **the production ~** el proceso de producción • **the ~es of government** los trámites gubernamentales • **the ageing ~** el envejecimiento • **I got what I wanted but made a lot of enemies in the ~** conseguí lo que quería pero a costa de crearme muchos enemigos • **in the ~ of:** • **it is in (the) ~ of construction** está en (vías de) construcción • **we are in the ~ of moving house** estamos en medio de una mudanza; ▷ **due, elimination**

2 (= *specific method*) proceso *m*, procedimiento *m* • **the Bessemer ~** el proceso de Bessemer

3 (*Jur*) (= *action*) proceso *m*; (= *summons*) citación *f* • **to bring a ~ against sb** demandar a algn • **to serve a ~ on sb** notificar una citación a algn

4 (*Anat, Bot, Zool*) protuberancia *f*

VT **1** (= *treat*) [+ *raw materials*] procesar; [+ *food*] (*industrially*) procesar, tratar; (*with food processor*) pasar por el robot de cocina • **to ~ sth into sth** procesar algo para convertirlo en algo

2 (= *deal with*) [+ *application, claim, order*] tramitar; [+ *applicants*] atender

3 (*Comput*) procesar

4 (*Phot*) revelar

CPD ▸ **process cheese** (*US*) queso *m* fundido ▸ **process server** agente *mf* judicial

process² [prə'ses] VI (*Brit*) (*frm*) (= *go in procession*) desfilar; (*Rel*) ir en procesión

processed ['prəʊsest], **process** (*US*) ['prəʊses] ADJ [*food*] procesado

CPD ▸ **processed cheese** queso *m* fundido ▸ **processed peas** guisantes *mpl* en conserva

processing ['prəʊsesɪŋ] N [*of raw materials*] procesamiento *m*, tratamiento *m*; [*of food*] procesamiento *m*; [*of application, claim, order*] tramitación *f*; (*Comput*) procesamiento *m*; (*Phot*) revelado *m*

CPD ▸ **processing plant** planta *f* de procesamiento ▸ **processing unit** unidad *f* de proceso

procession [prə'seʃən] N [*of people, cars etc*] desfile *m*; (= *ceremonial, funeral*) cortejo *m*; (*Rel*) procesión *f* • **to go** *or* **walk in ~** desfilar; (*Rel*) ir en procesión

processional [prə'seʃənl] ADJ procesional

processor ['prəʊsesəʳ] N (*Comput*) procesador *m*, unidad *f* de proceso; (*also* **food processor**) robot *m* de cocina

pro-choice [,prəʊ'tʃɔɪs] ADJ en favor de la libertad de elección

proclaim [prə'kleɪm] VT **1** (= *announce*) [+ *independence*] proclamar, declarar • **to ~ sb king** proclamar a algn rey • **to ~ one's innocence** declararse inocente • **to ~ one's loyalty to sb** declararse leal a algn • **to ~ one's support for sb** declarar que se apoya a algn

2 (= *reveal*) revelar, anunciar • **their faces ~ed their guilt** su culpabilidad se revelaba en las caras

proclamation [,prɒklə'meɪʃən] N (= *act*) proclamación *f*; (= *document*) proclama *f*

proclivity [prə'klɪvɪtɪ] N propensión *f*, proclividad *f* (**for, towards** a) • **sexual proclivities** tendencias *fpl* sexuales

proconsul [,prəʊ'kɒnsəl] N procónsul *m*

procrastinate [prəʊ'kræstɪneɪt] VI dejar las cosas para más tarde, aplazar las cosas • **to ~ over a decision** aplazar una decisión, buscar pretextos para no tomar una decisión • **stop procrastinating!** ¡hazlo ya!, ¡deja de buscar pretextos para no hacerlo!

procrastination [prəʊ,kræstɪ'neɪʃən] N indecisión *f*, falta *f* de resolución • **after months of ~** tras meses de indecisión

procrastinator [prəʊ,kræstɪ'neɪtəʳ] N • **he's too much of a ~** tiene una tendencia exagerada a dejar las cosas para más tarde

procreate ['prəʊkrɪeɪt] VT, VI procrear

procreation [,prəʊkrɪ'eɪʃən] N procreación *f*

Procrustean [prəʊ'krʌstɪən] ADJ de Procusto

Procrustes [prəʊ'krʌsti:z] N Procusto

proctor ['prɒktəʳ] N (*Jur*) procurador(a) *m/f*; (*Brit*) (*Univ*) censor(a) *m/f* (*oficial que cuida de la disciplina*); (*US*) (*Univ*) (= *invigilator*) celador(a) *m/f*

VT, VI (*US*) (= *invigilate*) vigilar

procurable [prə'kjʊərəbl] ADJ (*frm*) asequible • **easily ~** muy asequible

procurator ['prɒkjʊreɪtəʳ] N procurador(a) *m/f*

CPD ▸ **Procurator Fiscal** (*Scot*) fiscal *mf*

procure [prə'kjʊəʳ] VT **1** (*frm*) (= *obtain*) obtener, conseguir • **to ~ sb sth** • **~ sth for sb** conseguir *or* procurar algo para algn • **to ~ some relief** conseguir cierto alivio

2 (*frm*) (= *achieve*) [+ *freedom*] lograr, gestionar • **to ~ sb's release** lograr *or* gestionar la liberación de algn

3 (*for prostitution*) procurar

VI dedicarse al proxenetismo

procurement [prə'kjʊəmənt] N obtención *f*

CPD ▸ **procurement agency** agencia *f* de aprovisionamiento ▸ **procurement price** precio *m* al productor

procurer [prə'kjʊərəʳ] N proxeneta *m*, alcahuete *m*

procuress [prə'kjʊərɪs] N alcahueta *f*, proxeneta *f*

procuring [prə'kjʊərɪŋ] N proxenetismo *m*

Prod‡ [prɒd] N (*Irl, Scot*) (*pej*) protestante *mf*

prod [prɒd] N **1** (= *push*) empujón *m*; (*with elbow*) codazo *m*; (= *jab*) pinchazo *m* • **to give sb a ~** dar un pinchazo a algn • **he needs an occasional ~** (*fig*) hay que darle un empujón de vez en cuando

2 (*also* **cattle prod**) aguijada *f*, picana *f* (*LAm*)

VT (= *push*) empujar; (*with elbow*) codear, dar un codazo a; (= *jab*) pinchar, punzar; (*with goad*) agujar • **he needs to be ~ded all the time** (*fig*) hay que pincharlo *or* empujarlo constantemente • **to ~ sb into doing sth** instar a algn a hacer algo

VI • **he ~ded at the fire with a stick** atizó el fuego con un palo • **she ~ded gingerly at the sleeping dog** sacudió levemente y con cautela al perro que dormía

prodding ['prɒdɪŋ] N (= *prompting*) ánimo *m* • **without ~** por motu propio • **she did her chores without ~** hizo sus tareas sin necesidad de insistirle

prodigal ['prɒdɪgəl] ADJ pródigo • **~ of** (*frm*) pródigo con • **the ~ son** el hijo pródigo

N despilfarrador(a) *m/f*

prodigality [,prɒdɪ'gælɪtɪ] N prodigalidad *f*

prodigious [prə'dɪdʒəs] ADJ [*amount, quantity*] enorme, ingente; [*appetite*] enorme; [*memory, energy*] prodigioso • **she is a ~ reader** lee una barbaridad*

prodigiously [prə'dɪdʒəslɪ] ADV [*grow, read, eat*] una barbaridad* • **to be ~ talented** tener un talento prodigioso

prodigy ['prɒdɪdʒɪ] N prodigio *m* • **child ~** • **infant ~** niño/a *m/f* prodigio

produce VT [prə'dju:s] **1** (= *yield*) [+ *coal, crop, electricity, sound*] producir; [+ *milk*] [*farm*] producir; [*cow*] dar; [+ *interest*] rendir, producir; [+ *profit, benefits*] producir, reportar

P

• **the plant ~s three harvests a year** la planta da tres cosechas al año • **friction ~s heat** la fricción produce calor • **oil-producing countries** países *mpl* productores de petróleo
2 (*= manufacture*) [*+ cars, weapons, drugs*] fabricar, producir
3 (*= create*) [*+ novel*] escribir; [*+ magazine*] publicar; [*+ musical work*] componer • **she has ~d consistently good work at school** su trabajo escolar siempre ha sido bueno • **he is the most creative novelist this century has ~d** es el novelista más creativo que nos ha dado este siglo • **with this symphony he has ~d a masterpiece** ha compuesto una obra maestra con esta sinfonía
4 (*= give birth to*) [*+ offspring*] [*animal*] parir; [*woman*] tener, dar a luz a; [*parents*] tener
5 (*= bring out, supply*) [*+ gift, handkerchief, gun*] sacar; [*+ ticket, documents, evidence, proof*] presentar; [*+ argument*] dar, presentar; [*+ witness*] nombrar; [*+ meal*] preparar • **when challenged he ~d a knife** cuando se le paró sacó una navaja
6 (*Cine, Theat*) [*+ film, play, show*] producir; (*TV, Rad*) realizar; (*Publishing*) [*+ magazine*] publicar; (*Mus*) [*+ record*] producir
7 (*= cause*) [*+ symptoms*] producir, causar; [*+ response*] provocar, producir • **it ~d a sensation of drowsiness** producía *or* causaba una sensación de somnolencia • **the photographer used a special lens to ~ that effect** el fotógrafo usó una lente especial para producir ese efecto • **by combining the two kinds of paint you can ~ some interesting effects** combinando las dos clases de pintura puedes conseguir efectos interesantes • **you may find that just threatening this course of action will ~ the desired effect** puedes encontrarte con que amenazar este procedimiento producirá el efecto deseado • **she is optimistic that his visit could ~ results** piensa que su visita podría surtir efecto
8 (*Geom*) [*+ line, plane*] prolongar
VI [prəˈdjuːs] **1** [*mine, oil well, factory*] producir; [*land, tree*] dar fruto(s); [*cow*] dar leche; [*person*] rendir
2 (*Theat, Cine*) producir; (*TV, Rad*) realizar
N [ˈprɒdjuːs] (*Agr*) productos *mpl* agrícolas, productos *mpl* del campo • **"produce of Turkey"** "producto *m* de Turquía" • **"produce of more than one country"** "producto *m* elaborado en varios países"; ▹ **dairy, farm**
CPD [ˈprɒdjuːs] ▸ **produce counter** (*US*) mostrador *m* de verdura ▸ **produce store** (*US*) verdulería *f*

producer [prəˈdjuːsəʳ] N **1** [*of oil, coal, ore, crop*] productor(a) *m/f*; [*of product*] fabricante *mf*
2 (*Theat*) director(a) *m/f* de escena; (*Cine*) productor(a) *m/f*; (*TV*) realizador(a) *m/f*, productor(a) *m/f*

-producing [prəˈdjuːsɪŋ] ADJ (*ending in compounds*) productor de ... • **oil-producing** productor de petróleo

product [ˈprɒdʌkt] N **1** (*Comm, Ind*) producto *m* • **consumer ~s** productos *mpl* de consumo • **food ~s** productos *mpl* alimenticios; ▹ **end, finished, gross, waste**
2 (*fig*) producto *m*, fruto *m* • **it is the ~ of his imagination** es producto de su imaginación • **she is the ~ of a broken home** es el clásico producto de un hogar deshecho
3 (*Math, Chem*) producto *m*
CPD ▸ **product development** creación *f* de nuevos productos ▸ **product liability** responsabilidad *f* del fabricante ▸ **product line** línea *f* de productos ▸ **product manager** product manager *mf* ▸ **product placement** emplazamiento *m* ▸ **product range** gama *f* de productos ▸ **product research** investigación *f* del producto ▸ **product specification** descripción *f* del producto

production [prəˈdʌkʃən] N **1** (*= making*) producción *f*; (*= manufacture*) producción *f*, fabricación *f* • **the factory is in full ~** la fábrica trabaja a plena capacidad • **the car is due to go into ~ later this year** está previsto que el coche empiece a fabricarse este año • **this model went out of ~ in 1974** este modelo dejó de fabricarse en 1974 • **to put sth into ~** lanzar algo a la producción • **to take sth out of ~** [*+ product*] dejar de fabricar algo; [*+ land*] dejar de cultivar algo; ▹ **mass²**
2 (*= output*) (*Ind, Agr*) producción *f*; (*Art, Literat*) obra *f* • **the firm exports 90% of its ~** la empresa exporta el 90% de lo que produce *or* de su producción • **industrial/oil ~** producción *f* industrial/de aceite
3 (*= act of showing*) presentación *f* • **on ~ of this card** al presentar esta tarjeta
4 (*Media*) **a** (*= act of producing*) (*Theat*) producción *f*, puesta *f* en escena; (*Cine, TV, Rad*) realización *f* • **the series goes into ~ in March** la serie empezará a realizarse en marzo
b (*= play, film, programme*) (*Theat*) representación *f*, montaje *m*; (*Cine, TV*) producción *f* • **the opera has yet to receive its first ~** no se ha hecho nunca una representación *or* montaje de la ópera, la ópera nunca se ha representado • IDIOM: • **to make a ~ out of sth*** montar un show por algo* • **he made a real ~ out of it!** ¡montó un verdadero show!*
CPD [*process, department, costs, quota*] de producción ▸ **production agreement** (*US*) acuerdo *m* de productividad ▸ **production assistant** (*Cine, TV*) ayudante *mf* de realización ▸ **production company** (*TV*) (compañía *f*) productora *f* ▸ **production costs** costes *mpl* de producción ▸ **production line** cadena *f* de fabricación *or* montaje ▸ **production manager** (*Ind*) jefe/a *m/f* de producción; (*Cine, TV*) jefe/a *m/f* de realización ▸ **production run** serie *f* de producción

productive [prəˈdʌktɪv] ADJ **1** (*= efficient*) [*worker, land, industry*] productivo • **the factory is not yet fully ~** la fábrica todavía no trabaja a plena capacidad • **to be ~ of sth** (*frm*) producir algo, generar algo
2 (*= fruitful*) [*meeting, discussion*] fructífero • **I spent a ~ morning in the library** he tenido una mañana muy fructífera *or* provechosa en la biblioteca

productively [prəˈdʌktɪvlɪ] ADV [*use resources*] de manera productiva; [*spend time*] provechosamente

productivity [ˌprɒdʌkˈtɪvɪtɪ] N productividad *f*
CPD ▸ **productivity agreement, productivity deal** (*Brit*) acuerdo *m* sobre productividad ▸ **productivity bonus** prima *f* de productividad *or* rendimiento

proem [ˈprəʊem] N [*of book*] prefacio *m* m; [*of speech*] preámbulo *m*

Prof., prof.¹ [prɒf] N ABBR (= **professor**) Prof.

prof.² ADJ ABBR = **professional**

prof* [prɒf] N profe* *mf*

profanation [ˌprɒfəˈneɪʃən] N profanación *f*

profane [prəˈfeɪn] ADJ **1** (*= secular*) profano
2 (*= irreverent*) [*person, language*] blasfemo
VT profanar

profanity [prəˈfænɪtɪ] N (*= blasphemy*) blasfemia *f*; (*= oath*) blasfemia *f* • **to utter a string of profanities** soltar una sarta de blasfemias

profess [prəˈfes] VT **1** (*Rel*) [*+ faith, religion*] profesar
2 (*= state*) [*+ innocence*] declarar; [*+ regret, surprise*] manifestar; [*+ ignorance*] confesar • **he ~es a belief in the equality of women** se precia *or* presume de creer en la igualdad de las mujeres
3 (*= claim*) pretender • **I do not ~ to be an expert** no pretendo ser experto • **he ~es to be 25** dice *or* afirma tener 25 años • **he ~es to know all about it** afirma estar enterado de ello • **to ~ o.s. satisfied** declararse satisfecho • **to ~ o.s. unable to do sth** declararse incapaz de hacer algo

professed [prəˈfest] ADJ (*Rel*) profeso; (*= self-declared*) declarado; (*pej*) (*= supposed*) supuesto, ostensible

professedly [prəˈfesɪdlɪ] ADV (*= openly*) declaradamente; (*pej*) (*= supposedly*) supuestamente

profession [prəˈfeʃən] N **1** (*= calling*) profesión *f*, oficio *m* • **by ~** de profesión • **he is an engineer by ~** es ingeniero de profesión • **the oldest ~** (*euph*) el oficio más viejo
2 (*= body of people*) profesión *f*, cuerpo *m* profesional • **the ~s** las profesiones, los cuerpos profesionales • **to enter** *or* **join a ~** entrar a formar parte de una profesión *or* un cuerpo profesional • **the legal ~** el cuerpo de abogados • **the liberal ~s** las profesiones liberales • **the medical ~** la profesión médica, el cuerpo médico • **the teaching ~** el cuerpo docente • **a member of the teaching ~** un miembro del cuerpo docente • **to enter the teaching ~** entrar en la docencia *or* la enseñanza; ▹ **caring**
3 (*= declaration*) declaración *f*, manifestación *f* • **~ of faith** profesión *f* de fe

professional [prəˈfeʃənl] ADJ
1 (*= non-amateur*) [*sport, sportsperson, musician*] profesional; [*soldier*] de carrera • **she's a ~ singer** es cantante profesional • **he plays ~ football** se dedica al fútbol profesional • **that boy's a ~ trouble-maker*** (*iro, hum*) ese niño es un alborotador profesional • **to seek** *or* **take ~ advice** consultar a un profesional • **before spending any money you ought to seek ~ advice** deberías consultar a un profesional antes de gastar nada de dinero • **I have sought ~ advice and have been advised to go ahead with the case** he consultado a un abogado y me ha aconsejado seguir adelante con el caso • **she needs ~ help for her depression** necesita ayuda de un profesional para superar su depresión • **to turn** *or* **go ~** hacerse profesional, profesionalizarse
2 (*= employed in a profession*) • **the flat is ideal for the ~ single person** el piso es idóneo para el profesional soltero
3 (*= relating to a profession*) profesional • **he began his ~ life as an accountant** se inició en su vida profesional como contable • **his ~ conduct has come under scrutiny** se está investigando su conducta profesional
4 (*= appropriate to a professional*) • **I was impressed by his ~ approach** su profesionalidad me causó muy buena impresión • **that wasn't a very ~ thing to do** eso no fue propio de un profesional, eso fue una falta de profesionalidad
5 (*= competent, skilled*) • **it was a very ~ performance** fue una representación hecha con mucha profesionalidad • **a ~ job** obra *f* de un profesional *or* experto • **you could tell the burglary was a ~ job** se veía que el robo fue obra de un profesional *or* de un experto • **you've done a really ~ job of the decorating** has pintado la casa como un verdadero profesional *or* experto

(N) **1** (= *non-amateur*) profesional *mf*
2 (= *person employed in a profession*) profesional *mf* • **health ~** profesional *mf* de la medicina
3 (= *expert*) profesional *mf*, experto/a *m/f* • **the killing was the work of a ~** el asesinato fue obra de un profesional *or* de un experto • **Brenner was no ordinary thief, but a true ~** Brenner no era un ladrón cualquiera, sino un verdadero profesional *or* experto • **golf ~** golfista *mf* profesional
(CPD) ▸ **professional charges** honorarios *mpl* profesionales ▸ **the professional classes** la gente de carrera ▸ **professional fees** honorarios *mpl* profesionales ▸ **professional foul** falta *f* profesional ▸ **professional liability** responsabilidad *f* profesional ▸ **professional misconduct** falta *f* de ética profesional • **he was found guilty of ~ misconduct** se le declaró culpable de falta de ética profesional ▸ **professional practice** (= *method*) práctica *f* profesional; (= *career*) vida *f* profesional • **the ~ practice of homoeopathy** la práctica profesional de la homeopatía • **in his ~ practice he had come across many patients with similar symptoms** en su vida profesional había atendido a muchos pacientes con síntomas parecidos • **it is not good ~ practice** no es apropiado en el ejercicio de la profesión ▸ **professional qualification** título *m* profesional ▸ **professional school** (US) escuela *f* profesional superior ▸ **professional services** servicios *mpl* prestados por profesionales ▸ **professional skills** técnicas *fpl* de la profesión ▸ **professional standing** reputación *f* profesional ▸ **professional training** formación *f* profesional

professionalism [prəˈfeʃnəlɪzəm] (N) profesionalismo *m*

professionalization [prəˌfeʃənəlaɪˈzeɪʃən] (N) profesionalización *f*

professionalize [prəˈfeʃənəlaɪz] (VT) profesionalizar

professionally [prəˈfeʃnəlɪ] (ADV) **1** (*Sport, Mus*) [*play, sing*] profesionalmente • **he is known ~ as X** se le conoce profesionalmente como X
2 (= *in a professional capacity*) profesionalmente • **I only knew her ~** solo la traté profesionalmente • **to be ~ qualified** tener el título profesional
3 (= *expertly*) con profesionalidad, profesionalmente
4 (= *by an expert*) [*made, built*] por un profesional *or* un experto • **I advise you to have it done ~** te aconsejo que lo dejes en manos de un profesional *or* experto
5 (= *as befits a professional*) con profesionalidad • **she conducts her business very ~** lleva sus negocios con mucha profesionalidad

professor [prəˈfesəʳ] (N) **1** (*Brit, US*) (*Univ*) catedrático/a *m/f* (*de universidad*) • **Professor Cameron** el catedrático Cameron • **he is a ~ of economics** es catedrático de economía • **full ~** catedrático/a *m/f* (*de universidad*); ▹ **assistant, associate**
2 (US) (= *teacher*) profesor(a) *m/f* (universitario/a) • **a science ~** un profesor de ciencias

professorial [ˌprɒfəˈsɔːrɪəl] (ADJ) [*post, career*] de catedrático; [*tone, manner*] magistral

professorship [prəˈfesəʃɪp] (N) cátedra *f* • **to be appointed to a ~** ser nombrado a *or* obtener una cátedra

proffer [ˈprɒfəʳ] (VT) [+ *gift*] ofrecer; [+ *advice, help*] brindar, ofrecer; [+ *congratulations*] dar • **he ~ed his hand** me/le alargó la mano

proficiency [prəˈfɪʃənsɪ] (N) habilidad *f*, competencia *f* • **reading ~** habilidad *f* or competencia *f* como lector • **language ~** dominio *m* del idioma • **Cambridge Certificate of Proficiency** *diploma de inglés como lengua extranjera*
(CPD) ▸ **proficiency test** prueba *f* de aptitud

proficient [prəˈfɪʃənt] (ADJ) competente (**at, in** en) • **as you become more ~** según te vas haciendo más competente • **she was already ~ in German** tenía ya un gran dominio del alemán, dominaba ya el alemán

profile [ˈprəʊfaɪl] (N) **1** (= *side view, outline*) perfil *m* • **in ~** de perfil
2 (= *description, portrait*) reseña *f*, perfil *m*; (*TV programme*) perfil *m*; ▹ **customer**
3 (= *public image*) • **her work with the Fund has given her a very high ~** la labor que ha realizado para el Fondo ha dado gran relieve a su figura *or* la ha lanzado a un primer plano • **military men continued to have a high ~ in the administration** los militares seguían ocupando una posición destacada en la administración • **to keep** *or* **maintain a low ~** tratar de pasar desapercibido • **to raise the ~ of sth/sb** realzar la imagen de algo/algn; ▹ **high-profile**
(VT) **1** (= *show in profile*) perfilar
2 (= *describe*) [+ *situation, candidate*] describir; [+ *person's life*] hacer un perfil de

profiler [ˈprəʊfaɪləʳ] (N) **1** (*Police, Psych*) perfilador(a) *m/f*
2 (*Tech*) (= *profiling machine*) perfiladora *f*

profiling [ˈprəʊfaɪlɪŋ] (N) perfiles *mpl* • **psychological ~** perfiles psicológicos • **~ techniques** técnicas de elaboración de perfiles

profit [ˈprɒfɪt] (N) **1** (*Comm*) ganancias *fpl*, beneficios *mpl*, utilidades *fpl* (*LAm*) • **a 32% rise in ~s** un aumento del 32% en las ganancias *or* los beneficios • **at a ~**: • **to operate at a ~** ser rentable • **to sell (sth) at a ~** vender (algo) obteniendo una ganancia • **to make a ~** obtener ganancias *or* beneficios • **they made a ~ of two million** obtuvieron unas ganancias *or* unos beneficios de dos millones • **to make a ~ on** *or* **out of sth** obtener beneficios de algo • **to show a ~** registrar beneficios *or* ganancias • **to turn a ~** obtener ganancias *or* beneficios • **with ~s policy** (*Insurance*) póliza *f* con beneficios; ▹ **interim, trading**
2 (*fig*) utilidad *f*, beneficio *m* • **I could see no ~ in antagonizing them** no veía qué utilidad *or* beneficio tenía el enfadarles • **to turn sth to (one's) ~** sacar provecho *or* beneficio de algo
(VI) **1** (*financially*) obtener ganancia, obtener beneficio
2 (*fig*) • **to ~ by** *or* **from sth** aprovecharse de algo • **we do not want to ~ from someone else's misfortunes** no queremos aprovecharnos de las desgracias de otros • **I can't see how he hopes to ~ (by it)** no veo qué espera sacar (de ello)
(VT) † • **it will ~ him nothing** no le servirá de nada
(CPD) ▸ **profit and loss account** cuenta *f* de pérdidas y ganancias ▸ **profit centre, profit center** (US) centro *m* de beneficios ▸ **profit margin** margen *m* de beneficios ▸ **profit motive** afán *m* de lucro ▸ **profits tax** (*Brit*) impuesto *m* de beneficios ▸ **profit warning** advertencia *f* de beneficios

profitability [ˌprɒfɪtəˈbɪlɪtɪ] (N) rentabilidad *f*

profitable [ˈprɒfɪtəbl] (ADJ) (*Comm*) lucrativo; (= *economic to run*) rentable; (*fig*) (= *beneficial*) provechoso • **a ~ investment** una inversión lucrativa • **the line is no longer ~** la línea ya no es rentable • **a most ~ trip** un viaje sumamente provechoso • **you would find it ~ to read this** te beneficiarías de leer esto, te sería útil leer esto

profitably [ˈprɒfɪtəblɪ] (ADV) (*Comm*) [*run*] de forma rentable, obteniendo beneficios; [*sell*] con ganancia; (*fig*) (= *beneficially*) provechosamente

profiteer [ˌprɒfɪˈtɪəʳ] (N) especulador(a) *m/f* • **war ~** *persona que especula en tiempo de guerra*
(VI) especular, obtener ganancias excesivas

profiteering [ˌprɒfɪˈtɪərɪŋ] (N) especulación *f*

profiterole [prəˈfɪtərəʊl] (N) profiterol *m*

profitless [ˈprɒfɪtlɪs] (ADJ) inútil

profitlessly [ˈprɒfɪtlɪslɪ] (ADV) inútilmente

profit-making [ˈprɒfɪtˌmeɪkɪŋ] (ADJ) (= *profitable*) rentable; (= *aiming to make profit*) [*organization*] con fines lucrativos; ▹ **non-profit-making**

profit-related [ˈprɒfɪtrəˈleɪtɪd] (ADJ) [*pay, bonus*] proporcional a los beneficios

profit-seeking [ˈprɒfɪtˌsiːkɪŋ] (ADJ) [*activity*] con fines lucrativos

profit-sharing [ˈprɒfɪtˌʃɛərɪŋ] (N) reparto *m* de los beneficios

profit-taking [ˈprɒfɪtˌteɪkɪŋ] (N) (*St Ex*) venta *f* con beneficios, *venta de acciones tras una subida de precios en el mercado o antes de que se produzca una bajada de los mismos*

profligacy [ˈprɒflɪgəsɪ] (N) (= *dissoluteness*) libertinaje *m*; (= *extravagance*) prodigalidad *f*, despilfarro *m*

profligate [ˈprɒflɪgɪt] (ADJ) (= *dissolute*) libertino, disoluto; (= *extravagant*) despilfarrador, derrochador
(N) (= *degenerate*) libertino/a *m/f*; (= *spendthrift*) despilfarrador(a) *m/f*

pro-form [ˈprəʊˌfɔːm] (N) (*Ling*) pro forma *f*

pro forma [ˌprəʊˈfɔːmə] (ADJ) [*compliance, implementation*] puramente formal
(CPD) ▸ **pro forma invoice** factura *f* detallada que precede a la entrega ▸ **pro forma letter** carta *f* estándar

profound [prəˈfaʊnd] (ADJ) **1** (= *deep, intense*) [*emotion, silence*] profundo; [*effect, influence, changes*] profundo, grande
2 (= *meaningful*) [*ideas, thoughts*] profundo; [*person*] de ideas profundas; [*book, writing*] profundo • **her first novel is very ~** su primera novela es muy profunda

profoundly [prəˈfaʊndlɪ] (ADV) profundamente • **I was ~ affected by her ideas/her death** sus ideas me afectaron/su muerte me afectó profundamente • **he apologized ~ when he discovered his mistake** se deshizo en disculpas cuando se dio cuenta de su error • **to be ~ deaf** ser totalmente sordo • **I am ~ grateful to all the people who helped us** les estoy profundamente agradecido a todos los que nos ayudaron • **people are ~ ignorant about the law** la gente no sabe absolutamente nada acerca de la legislación

profundity [prəˈfʌndɪtɪ] (N) (*frm*) profundidad *f*

profuse [prəˈfjuːs] (ADJ) [*vegetation*] profuso, abundante; [*sweating*] copioso; [*bleeding*] intenso • **to be ~ in one's apologies** deshacerse en disculpas

profusely [prəˈfjuːslɪ] (ADV) [*grow*] con profusión, en abundancia • **he apologized ~** se deshizo en disculpas • **she thanked me ~** me dio las gracias efusivamente • **to sweat/bleed ~** sudar/sangrar profusamente *or* copiosamente

profusion [prəˈfjuːʒən] (N) profusión *f*, abundancia *f* • **there was a ~ of wines to choose from** había una gran profusión *or*

P

abundancia de vinos de entre los que elegir • **orchids bloomed in ~** las orquídeas florecieron profusamente *or* en abundancia • **a ~ of colour** un derroche de color, una gran profusión de color

prog.* [prɒg] (*Brit*) (*TV etc*) (N ABBR) (= **programme**) programa *m*

progenitor [prəʊ'dʒenɪtəʳ] (N) progenitor *m*

progeny ['prɒdʒɪnɪ] (N) progenie *f*

progesterone [prəʊ'dʒestərəʊn] (N) progesterona *f*

prognosis [prɒg'nəʊsɪs] (N) (PL: **prognoses** [prɒg'nəʊsi:z]) (*Med*) pronóstico *m*

prognostic [prɒg'nɒstɪk] (N) pronóstico *m*

prognosticate [prɒg'nɒstɪkeɪt] (VT) pronosticar

prognostication [prɒg,nɒstɪ'keɪʃən] (N) (= *act, art*) pronosticación *f*; (= *forecast*) pronóstico *m*

program, programme ['prəʊgræm] (*Comput*) (N) programa *m*
(VT) programar • **to ~ sth to do sth** programar algo para que haga algo
(VI) programar

programmable [prəʊ'græməbl] (ADJ) programable

programme, program (*esp US*) ['prəʊgræm] (N) **1** (= *plan, schedule*) programa *m* • **Iraq's nuclear weapons ~** el programa iraquí de armamento nuclear • **a training ~ for the unemployed** un programa de formación para los parados • **a ~ of meetings, talks and exhibitions** un programa de reuniones, discursos y exposiciones • **what's (on) the ~ for today?** ¿qué planes *or* programa tenemos para hoy?; ▸ **detoxification, space**
2 (*US*) (*Univ*) (= *syllabus*) plan *m* de estudios, programa *m*; (= *course*) curso *m*
3 (*TV, Rad*) programa *m* • **television ~** programa *m* de televisión; ▸ **magazine**
4 (= *performance details*) programa *m* • **they've put together an interesting ~ for tonight's concert** han conseguido reunir los elementos necesarios para un interesante programa de concierto esta noche • **can I have a look at the ~?** ¿puedo echarle un vistazo al programa?
5 (*Comput*) = **program**
6 (*on washing machine*) programa *m*
(VT) **1** (= *arrange*) programar, planear • **the broadcast was ~d for Sunday** la emisión estaba programada para el domingo
2 (*Comput*) = **program**
3 (*Elec*) (*also fig*) programar • **to ~ sth to do sth** programar algo para que haga algo • **to be ~d (to do sth)** [*machine, person*] estar programado (para hacer algo)
(VI) (*Comput*) = **program**
(CPD) ▸ **programme maker** (*TV*) realizador(a) *m/f* de televisión ▸ **programme music** música *f* de programa ▸ **programme notes** descripción *f* del programa (*en un concierto*)

programmed, programed (*US*) ['prəʊgræmd] (ADJ) programado
(CPD) ▸ **programmed learning, programmed teaching** enseñanza *f* programada

programmer, programer (*US*) ['prəʊgræməʳ] (N) programador(a) *m/f*

programming, programing (*US*) ['prəʊgræmɪŋ] (N) programación *f*
(CPD) ▸ **programming environment** entorno *m* de programación ▸ **programming language** lenguaje *m* de programación ▸ **programming skills** técnicas *fpl* de programación

progress (N) ['prəʊgres] **1** (= *forward movement*) avance *m* • **heavy snow slowed our ~** la espesa capa de nieve dificultó nuestro avance *or* nos retrasó • **we are making good ~** estamos avanzando rápidamente
2 (= *development*) [*of activity, student*] progresos *mpl*; [*of events*] marcha *f*, desarrollo *m*; [*of patient*] evolución *f*; [*of disease*] curso *m*, evolución *f* • **he briefed us on the ~ of the talks** nos informó sobre la marcha *or* el desarrollo de las negociaciones • **keep me informed on the patient's ~** manténganme informado de la evolución del paciente • **he came in to check on my ~** vino para ver cómo iba progresando • **to make ~** (*gen*) hacer progresos, progresar; [*patient*] mejorar • **China has made significant ~ in human rights** China ha hecho muchos progresos en lo que respecta a derechos humanos • **the two sides have made little ~ towards agreement** las dos partes apenas han avanzado hacia un acuerdo • **to make good/slow ~** avanzar rápidamente/lentamente; ▸ **chart**
3 (= *innovation*) progreso *m* • **it was all done in the name of ~** todo se hizo con la excusa del progreso
4 (= *course*) • **in ~**: • **the game was already in ~** había comenzado ya el partido • **negotiations are still in ~** aún se están manteniendo las negociaciones • **I went to see the work in ~** fui a ver cómo marchaba el trabajo • **"silence: exam in progress"** "silencio: examen"
(VI) [prə'gres] **1** (= *go forward*) [*work*] avanzar; [*events*] desarrollarse; [*disease*] evolucionar • **things are ~ing slowly** las cosas avanzan lentamente • **as the game ~ed** a medida que avanzaba *or* iba desarrollándose el partido • **as the evening ~ed** a medida que avanzaba la noche • **to ~ to sth**: • **he started sketching, then ~ed to painting** empezó haciendo bosquejos para luego pasar a pintar • **she has ~ed to a senior nursing position** ha ascendido a enfermera de rango superior
2 (= *improve*) [*student*] hacer progresos; [*patient*] mejorar • **her French is ~ing in leaps and bounds** avanza a pasos agigantados en francés
(VT) [prə'gres] (= *advance*) seguir adelante con
(CPD) ['prəʊgres] ▸ **progress report** (*Admin*) informe *m* sobre la marcha del trabajo; (*Med*) informe *m* médico; (*Scol*) informe *m* sobre el progreso del alumno

progression [prə'greʃən] (N) **1** [*of disease, career*] evolución *f*; [*of events*] desarrollo *m* • **arithmetical/geometric ~** progresión *f* aritmética/geométrica • **her ~ from awkward teenager to superstar** su evolución *or* paso de adolescente difícil a superestrella • **it's a natural ~** es lógico
2 (*Mus*) progresión *f* • **chord ~** progresión *f* de acordes

progressive [prə'gresɪv] (ADJ) **1** (= *increasing*) progresivo
2 (*Pol*) progresista
(N) (= *person*) progresista *mf*

progressively [prə'gresɪvlɪ] (ADV) progresivamente, poco a poco • **it diminishes ~** disminuye progresivamente *or* poco a poco • **it's getting ~ better** va mejorando poco a poco

progressiveness [prə'gresɪvnɪs] (N) carácter *m* progresista

prohibit [prə'hɪbɪt] (VT) **1** (= *forbid*) prohibir • **to ~ sb from doing sth** prohibir a algn hacer algo • **"it is prohibited to feed the animals"** "se prohíbe dar de comer a los animales" • **"smoking prohibited"** "se prohíbe *or* está prohibido fumar" • **~ed area** zona *f* prohibida
2 (= *prevent*) • **to ~ sb from doing sth** impedir a algn hacer algo • **his health ~s him from swimming** su salud le impide nadar

prohibition [,prəʊɪ'bɪʃən] (N) prohibición *f* • **Prohibition** (*US*) la ley seca, la Prohibición

prohibitionism [,prəʊɪ'bɪʃənɪzəm] (N) prohibicionismo *m*

prohibitionist [,prəʊɪ'bɪʃənɪst] (ADJ) prohibicionista
(N) prohibicionista *mf*

prohibitive [prə'hɪbɪtɪv] (ADJ) prohibitivo

prohibitively [prə'hɪbɪtɪvlɪ] (ADV) • **the car is ~ expensive** el precio del coche es prohibitivo, el coche es imposiblemente caro

prohibitory [prə'hɪbɪtərɪ] (ADJ) prohibitorio

project (N) ['prɒdʒekt] **1** (= *scheme, plan*) proyecto *m*
2 (*Scol, Univ*) trabajo *m*
3 (*also* **housing project**) (*US*) urbanización *f* *or* barrio *m* de viviendas protegidas; ▸ **housing**
(VT) [prə'dʒekt] **1** (= *estimate*) [+ *costs, expenditure*] hacer una proyección de
2 (= *forecast*) prever • **the population of Britain is ~ed to rise slowly over the next ten years** se prevé que la población de Gran Bretaña aumentará lentamente durante los próximos diez años • **a ~ed deficit of 2 million dollars** un déficit previsto de 2 millones de dólares
3 (= *plan*) (*usu passive*) • **there were demonstrations against his ~ed visit** hubo manifestaciones en contra de su programada *or* prevista visita • **it stood in the path of a ~ed motorway** estaba situado en un lugar por donde estaba previsto que pasara una autopista
4 (= *throw, send forward*) [+ *object*] (*frm*) lanzar; [+ *light*] proyectar • **the impact ~ed him forward onto the windscreen** con el impacto salió despedido contra el parabrisas • **to ~ one's voice** [*singer, actor*] proyectar la voz
5 (= *show*) [+ *slide, image*] proyectar
6 (= *communicate, represent*) [+ *image, personality*] proyectar • **he ~ed himself as the ideal family man** daba la imagen del hombre de familia ideal
7 (*Psych*) • **I ~ my own rage/fear onto the children** proyecto mi propia cólera/mi propio miedo en los niños
8 (*Math*) proyectar
(VI) [prə'dʒekt] **1** (= *jut out*) sobresalir • **a spit of land ~ed out from the shore** una lengua de tierra sobresalía de la orilla
2 (= *communicate, enunciate*) proyectarse • **his voice ~s very well** su voz se proyecta muy bien
(CPD) ['prɒdʒekt] ▸ **project leader** jefe/a *m/f* de proyecto ▸ **project management** administración *f* de proyectos ▸ **project manager** director(a) *m/f* de proyecto(s)

projectile [prə'dʒektaɪl] (N) proyectil *m*

projecting [prə'dʒektɪŋ] (ADJ) [*nail, branch*] saliente; [*cheekbones*] marcado, prominente; [*teeth*] salido, hacia fuera

projection [prə'dʒekʃən] (N) **1** [*of image, voice*] proyección *f*; ▸ **astral**
2 (= *overhang*) saliente *m*, resalto *m*; (= *knob*) protuberancia *f*
3 (= *forecast*) (*Econ*) pronóstico *m*
4 (*in cartography*) proyección *f*
5 (*Psych*) proyección *f*
(CPD) ▸ **projection booth** cabina *f* de proyección ▸ **projection room** (*Cine*) cabina *f* de proyección

projectionist [prə'dʒekʃnɪst] (N) (*Cine*) operador(a) *m/f* (de proyector), proyeccionista *mf*

projective [prəˈdʒektɪv] (ADJ) proyectivo • **~ geometry** geometría proyectiva
projector [prəˈdʒektəʳ] (N) (*Cine*) proyector *m*
prolapse [ˈprəʊlæps] (N) (*Med*) prolapso *m*
prole* [prəʊl] (N) (*Brit*) proletario/a *m/f* • **the ~s** los proletarios
proletarian [ˌprəʊləˈtɛərɪən] (ADJ) proletario (N) proletario/a *m/f*
proletarianize [ˌprəʊləˈtɛərɪənaɪz] (VT) proletarizar
proletariat [ˌprəʊləˈtɛərɪət] (N) proletariado *m*
pro-life [ˌprəʊˈlaɪf] (ADJ) pro-vida
proliferate [prəˈlɪfəreɪt] (VI) proliferar
proliferation [prəˌlɪfəˈreɪʃən] (N) proliferación *f* • **nuclear ~** proliferación *f* de armas nucleares
prolific [prəˈlɪfɪk] (ADJ) prolífico
prolix [ˈprəʊlɪks] (ADJ) prolijo
prolixity [prəʊˈlɪksɪtɪ] (N) prolijidad *f*
prologue, prolog (*US*) [ˈprəʊlɒg] (N) (*lit, fig*) prólogo *m* (**to** de)
prolong [prəˈlɒŋ] (VT) [*+ visit, life, war, recession*] prolongar, alargar • IDIOM: • **to ~ the agony**: • **this is just ~ing the agony** esto es solo prolongar la agonía
prolongation [ˌprəʊlɒŋˈgeɪʃən] (N) prolongación *f*
prolonged [prəˈlɒŋd] (ADJ) [*absence, silence, period, struggle, exposure*] prolongado • **~ use of the drug may lead to liver damage** un prolongado uso del medicamento puede ocasionar una lesión hepática • **there was ~ applause** el público aplaudió durante varios minutos
PROM (N ABBR) (*Comput*) = **Programmable Read Only Memory**
prom [prɒm] (N) **1** (*Brit**) (= *promenade*) paseo *m* marítimo
2 (*Brit**) = **promenade concert**
3 (*US*) *baile de gala bajo los auspicios de los alumnos de un colegio*

> **PROM**
> En Gran Bretaña el término **prom** es la forma abreviada de **promenade concert**, y hace referencia a un concierto de música clásica en el que una parte del público permanece de pie en una zona del auditorio reservada al efecto. La serie de conciertos de este tipo más conocida es la que se celebra cada verano en el **Royal Albert Hall** de Londres, y que tuvo su origen en 1895 a partir de una idea del director de orquesta Henry Wood. Actualmente convertidos en una institución nacional, destaca entre todas las actuaciones la llamada **Last Night of the Proms** en la que se interpretan piezas de carácter patriótico, entre otras de repertorio.
> En Estados Unidos un **prom** es un baile de gala que se celebra para los alumnos de un centro de educación secundaria o universitaria. De todos estos bailes el más famoso es el **senior prom**, al que asisten los alumnos del último año de una **high school** y que se considera un acontecimiento de gran importancia para los adolescentes estadounidenses. Los alumnos acuden normalmente con su pareja y visten de etiqueta: esmoquin los chicos y traje de noche las chicas.

promenade [ˌprɒmɪˈnɑːd] (N) **1** (= *act*) paseo *m*
2 (= *avenue*) paseo *m*, avenida *f*
3 (*at seaside*) paseo *m* marítimo
(VI) pasearse
(VT) pasear
(CPD) ▸ **promenade concert** *concierto en el que una parte del público permanece de pie*
▸ **promenade deck** cubierta *f* de paseo
promenader [ˌprɒmɪˈnɑːdəʳ] (N) **1** (= *walker*) paseante *mf*
2 (*Brit*) (*at concert*) *asistente a una "Prom" que permanece de pie*
Prometheus [prəˈmiːθjuːs] (N) Prometeo
prominence [ˈprɒmɪnəns] (N)
1 (= *importance*) importancia *f* • **to bring sth/sb to ~** hacer que algo/algn destaque *or* resalte • **to come (in)to** *or* **rise to ~** [*idea, subject*] adquirir importancia; [*person*] empezar a ser conocido • **he came to ~ in the Cuba affair** se le empezó a conocer cuando lo de Cuba • **to give ~ to sth** hacer que algo destaque *or* resalte
2 (= *conspicuousness*) prominencia *f* • **it was set in bold type to give it ~** para que destacara, aparecía en negrita
3 (= *hill*) prominencia *f*
prominent [ˈprɒmɪnənt] (ADJ) **1** (= *projecting*) [*nose*] prominente; [*cheekbones*] marcado, prominente; [*teeth*] salido, hacia fuera; [*eyes*] saltón
2 (= *conspicuous*) destacado, prominente • **put it in a ~ place** ponlo en un lugar destacado *or* prominente, ponlo donde salte a la vista • **the question of Bosnia was very ~ in their minds** la cuestión de Bosnia estaba muy presente en sus mentes
3 (= *important*) [*person*] destacado, prominente; [*position, role*] prominente, importante, destacado • **she is ~ in London society** es una figura destacada *or* prominente en la buena sociedad londinense • **to play a ~ part** *or* **role in sth** jugar un papel prominente *or* importante *or* destacado en algo
prominently [ˈprɒmɪnəntlɪ] (ADV)
1 (= *conspicuously*) • **to display sth ~** exponer algo muy a la vista • **the newspapers had carried the story ~** los periódicos habían publicado la historia en grandes titulares
2 (= *outstandingly*) • **he figured ~ in the case** desempeñó un papel prominente *or* importante *or* destacado en el juicio
promiscuity [ˌprɒmɪsˈkjuːɪtɪ] (N) promiscuidad *f*
promiscuous [prəˈmɪskjʊəs] (ADJ) promiscuo
promiscuously [prəˈmɪskjʊəslɪ] (ADV) promiscuamente
promise [ˈprɒmɪs] (N) **1** (= *pledge*) promesa *f* • **a ~ is a ~** lo prometido es deuda • **~s, ~s!** (*iro*) ¡mucho prometer y poco hacer! • **is that a ~?** ¿me lo prometes? • **to break one's ~** no cumplir su promesa, faltar a su promesa • **to hold** *or* **keep sb to his ~** obligar a algn a cumplir su promesa, hacer que algn cumpla su promesa • **to keep a/one's ~** cumplir una/su promesa • **to make (sb) a ~** hacer una promesa (a algn) • **I made him a ~ that I'd come and visit him** le hice la promesa de que *or* le prometí que vendría a visitarlo • **I might do it but I'm not making any ~s** puede que lo haga, pero no prometo nada • **~ of marriage** palabra *f* de matrimonio • **to release sb from his ~** absolver a algn de su promesa • **the party has received many ~s of support** al partido se le ha prometido mucho apoyo; ▸ **lick**
2 (= *hope, prospect*) • **full of ~** muy prometedor • **she fulfilled** *or* **lived up to the ~ she'd shown in the '84 Olympics** demostró estar a la altura de lo que prometía en las Olimpiadas del 84 • **America held (out) the ~ of a new life** América representaba la promesa de una nueva vida, América daba esperanzas de una nueva vida • **a young man of ~** un joven que promete • **she showed considerable ~ as a pianist** prometía mucho como pianista
(VT) **1** (= *pledge*) prometer • **the ~d aid had not been sent** no se había enviado la ayuda prometida • **to ~ (sb) that** prometer (a algn) que • **I ~d that I'd go** prometí que iría • **~ me you won't tell her** prométeme que no se lo dirás • **to ~ (sb) to do sth** prometer (a algn) hacer algo • **you must ~ me to do as I say** tienes que prometerme que harás lo que yo te diga • **he ~d faithfully to return it** dio su palabra de que lo devolvería • **I ~d myself I would go and visit her** me prometí que iría a visitarla • **buy that new dress you've been promising yourself** cómprate ese nuevo vestido que te habías hecho el propósito de comprarte • **she telephoned, as ~d** llamó, tal y como había prometido • **to ~ sb sth** • **~ sth to sb** prometer dar algo a algn • IDIOMS: • **to ~ sb the earth** *or* **the moon** prometer el oro y el moro a algn • **the Promised Land** la Tierra Prometida
2 (= *forecast, augur*) augurar • **their policies ~ little for the future** su política no augura un futuro muy prometedor • **those clouds ~ rain** esas nubes amenazan lluvia • **it ~s to be hot today** el día se presenta caluroso • **the debate ~s to be lively** el debate se presenta animado
3 (= *assure*) prometer, jurar • **there's no-one here, I ~ you** no hay nadie aquí, te lo prometo *or* juro
(VI) **1** (= *pledge*) prometer • **"(do you) ~?" — "all right, I ~"** —¿lo prometes? —bueno, lo prometo • **I can't ~ but I'll try** no te prometo nada, pero haré lo que pueda • **"I can't make it" "but you ~d!"** —no puedo —¡pero lo habías prometido!
2 (= *augur*) • **to ~ well**: • **such a good beginning ~s well for the future** un principio tan bueno resulta muy prometedor *or* augura un buen futuro
promising [ˈprɒmɪsɪŋ] (ADJ) [*student*] prometedor; [*future, prospect*] esperanzador, halagüeño • **a ~ young man** un joven que promete • **two ~ candidates** dos candidatos buenos • **it doesn't look very ~** no promete mucho, no parece muy prometedor
promisingly [ˈprɒmɪsɪŋlɪ] (ADV) de manera prometedora • **United began ~, with a goal in the second minute** el United tuvo un principio prometedor, con un gol en el segundo minuto
promissory note [ˈprɒmɪsərɪˌnəʊt] (N) (*esp US*) pagaré *m*
prommer*, Prommer* [ˈprɒməʳ] (N) *asistente a una "Prom" que permanece de pie*
promo* [ˈprəʊməʊ] (N) promo* *f*
(ADJ) [*material, work, tour*] promocional
(CPD) ▸ **promo video** vídeo *m or* (*LAm*) video *m* promocional
promontory [ˈprɒməntrɪ] (N) promontorio *m*
promote [prəˈməʊt] (VT) **1** (*in rank*) **a** [*+ employee*] ascender • **to be ~d** ser ascendido • **I got ~d from editor to editorial director** me ascendieron de redactor a jefe de redacción
b (*Mil*) ascender • **he was ~d (to) colonel** *or* **to the rank of colonel** lo ascendieron a coronel
c (*Sport*) [*+ team*] ascender • **Tarifa was ~d to the first division** el Tarifa subió *or* ascendió a primera división
d (*US*) (*Scol*) [*+ pupil*] • **I failed to get ~d and had to redo my year** no conseguí aprobar y tuve que repetir el curso
2 (= *encourage*) [*+ trade, cooperation, peace*] promover, fomentar; [*+ growth*] estimular; [*+ sales, campaign, project, cause*] promover; (*Parl*) [*+ bill*] presentar • **he has spent much of his fortune promoting the arts** ha gastado gran parte de su fortuna

promoviendo las artes • he was accused of promoting his own interests se le acusó de promover sus propios intereses
3 (= *advertise*) [+ *product*] promocionar, dar publicidad a • they will do a British tour to ~ their second album harán una gira por Gran Bretaña para promocionar su segundo álbum • the island is being ~d as a tourist destination se está dando publicidad a la isla como centro de interés turístico
4 (= *organize, put on*) [+ *concert, event*] organizar
5 (*Chem*) [+ *reaction*] provocar

promoter [prəˈməʊtəʳ] N (*gen*) promotor(a) *m/f*; (= *backer*) patrocinador(a) *m/f*; (*Boxing*) empresario/a *m/f*

promotion [prəˈməʊʃən] N 1 (*in rank*) a [*of employee*] ascenso *m*, promoción *f* • to get ~ ser ascendido (to a) • if I get ~, I have to move offices si me ascienden, tengo que trasladarme de oficina • to move up the ~ ladder subir en el escalafón
b (*Sport*) ascenso *m* • they narrowly missed ~ por muy poco no han ascendido a otra división • to win ~ ser promovido, ascender
c (*US*) (*Scol*) ascenso *m*
2 (= *encouragement*) [*of trade, peace*] fomento *m*, promoción *f*; [*of campaign, project*] apoyo *m*
3 (= *organization*) [*of concert, event*] organización *f*
4 (= *publicity, advertising*) promoción *f*; (= *advertising campaign*) campaña *f* (de promoción) • special ~ oferta *f* de promoción; ▹ sales
CPD ▸ promotion prospects perspectivas *fpl* de ascenso ▸ promotions manager *or* director director(a) *m/f* encargado/a de promoción

promotional [prəˈməʊʃənl] ADJ promocional, de promoción

prompt [prɒmpt] ADJ 1 (= *speedy*) [*delivery, reply, service*] rápido • it is not too late, but ~ action is needed no es demasiado tarde pero hay que actuar inmediatamente *or* es necesario tomar medidas inmediatas • if it hadn't been for her ~ action, we would all have drowned si no hubiera sido porque reaccionó con mucha rapidez, nos hubiéramos ahogado todos • they were ~ to offer their services ofrecieron sus servicios inmediatamente *or* rápidamente • the company was ~ in its response to these accusations la empresa reaccionó inmediatamente ante estas acusaciones, la empresa reaccionó con prontitud a estas acusaciones
2 (= *punctual*) puntual • she is always ~ and efficient siempre es puntual y eficiente • please be ~ se ruega puntualidad • there is a discount for ~ payment se hace un descuento por prontitud en el pago
ADV [*start, arrive*] puntualmente • at two o'clock ~ a las dos en punto
VT 1 (= *motivate*) empujar • I was ~ed by a desire to see justice done me movía el deseo de ver que se hiciera justicia • to ~ sb to do sth mover *or* incitar a algn a hacer algo • what ~ed you to do it? ¿qué te movió *or* incitó a hacerlo? • I felt ~ed to protest me vi forzado *or* empujado a protestar
2 (= *give rise to*) [+ *thought, question*] dar lugar a; [+ *reply, reaction, speculation*] provocar, dar lugar a • it has ~ed questions about his suitability ha dado lugar a que se cuestione su idoneidad • what ~ed that question? ¿cuál fue el motivo de esa pregunta? • my choice was ~ed by a number of considerations hay varias consideraciones que han influido en mi elección
3 (= *help with speech*) apuntar • don't ~ her! ¡no le apuntes!, ¡no le soples cosas al oído!*
4 (*Theat*) apuntar • she had to be ~ed three times tuvieron que apuntarle tres veces
VI (*Theat*) apuntar
N 1 (= *suggestion, reminder*) apunte *m*, palabra *f* clave (*que ayuda a recordar*)
2 (*Theat*) (= *person*) apuntador(a) *m/f* • to give sb a ~ apuntar a algn • I had to be given a ~ me tuvieron que apuntar
3 (*Comput*) aviso *m*
CPD ▸ prompt box (*Theat*) concha *f* (del apuntador) ▸ prompt side (*Theat*) lado *m* izquierdo (del actor)

prompter [ˈprɒmptəʳ] N (*Theat*) apuntador(a) *m/f*

prompting [ˈprɒmptɪŋ] N • without ~ (*lit*) sin tener que consultar el texto; (= *on one's own initiative*) por iniciativa propia, motu propio • the ~s of conscience los escrúpulos de la conciencia

promptitude [ˈprɒmptɪtjuːd] N = promptness

promptly [ˈprɒmptlɪ] ADV (= *immediately*) inmediatamente; (= *fast*) [*pay, deliver, reply*] rápidamente, con prontitud; (= *punctually*) [*start, arrive*] en punto, puntualmente • they left ~ at six partieron a las seis en punto • he flopped onto the sofa and ~ fell asleep se dejó caer en el sofá y se durmió inmediatamente

promptness [ˈprɒmptnɪs] N (= *punctuality*) puntualidad *f*; (= *speed*) rapidez *f*, prontitud *f*

promulgate [ˈprɒməlgeɪt] VT [+ *law, decree, constitution*] promulgar; [+ *idea, doctrine*] promulgar

promulgation [ˌprɒməlˈgeɪʃən] N [*of law, decree, constitution*] promulgación *f*; [*of idea, doctrine*] promulgación *f*

prone [prəʊn] ADJ 1 (= *face down*) • to be ~ estar postrado (boca abajo)
2 (= *liable*) • to be ~ to do sth ser propenso *or* tener tendencia a hacer algo • to be ~ to sth ser propenso a algo

proneness [ˈprəʊnnɪs] N propensión *f*, predisposición *f* (to a)

prong [prɒŋ] N [*of fork*] punta *f*, diente *m*

-pronged [prɒŋd] ADJ (*ending in compounds*) • three-pronged [*fork*] de tres puntas *or* dientes; [*attack*] por tres flancos

pronominal [prəʊˈnɒmɪnl] ADJ pronominal

pronoun [ˈprəʊnaʊn] N (*Ling*) pronombre *m*

pronounce [prəˈnaʊns] VT 1 [+ *letter, word*] pronunciar • how do you ~ it? ¿cómo se pronuncia? • the "k" in "knee" is not ~d la "k" de "knee" no se pronuncia
2 (= *declare*) declarar • they ~d him unfit to plead lo declararon incapaz de defenderse • he was ~d dead se dictaminó que estaba muerto • "I now ~ you man and wife" —y ahora os declaro marido y mujer • to ~ o.s. for/against sth declararse a favor de/en contra de algo • to ~ sentence (*Jur*) pronunciar *or* dictar sentencia
VI • to ~ in favour of/against sth pronunciarse a favor de/en contra de algo • to ~ on sth pronunciarse sobre algo

pronounceable [prəˈnaʊnsəbl] ADJ pronunciable

pronounced [prəˈnaʊnst] ADJ (= *marked*) [*tendency, influence*] marcado; [*limp*] fuerte, pronunciado; [*accent*] fuerte

pronouncement [prəˈnaʊnsmənt] N declaración *f*

pronto* [ˈprɒntəʊ] ADV en seguida

pronunciation [prəˌnʌnsɪˈeɪʃən] N pronunciación *f*

proof [pruːf] N 1 (= *evidence*) prueba(s) *f(pl)* • do you have any ~ of this? ¿tienes pruebas de esto? • it is ~ that he is innocent eso prueba su inocencia • as (a) *or* in ~ of como *or* en prueba de • the burden of ~ is *or* falls on him sobre él recae la tarea de demostrar su inocencia • by way of ~ a modo de prueba • to give *or* show ~ of sth/that … demostrar algo/que … • you will need ~ of identity necesitará algo que acredite su identidad • to be living ~ of sth ser prueba viviente de algo • ~ positive prueba *f* concluyente • to obtain a refund you must produce ~ of purchase para cualquier devolución necesitará el comprobante de compra
2 (= *test, trial*) prueba *f* • to put sth to the ~ poner algo a prueba • PROVERB: • the ~ of the pudding (is in the eating) para saber si algo es bueno hay que probarlo
3 (*Typ, Phot*) prueba *f* • to correct *or* read the ~s corregir las pruebas; ▹ galley, page¹
4 [*of alcohol*] graduación *f* (alcohólica) • it is 70 degrees ~ tiene una graduación del 40%; (*US*) tiene una graduación del 35% • over ~ con una graduación alcohólica superior al 57,1% • under *or* below ~ con una graduación alcohólica inferior al 57,1%
5 (= *security, safeguard*) protección *f* (against contra) • knowledge is no ~ against certain kinds of disaster el saber no es protección contra ciertas clases de desastre
6 (*Math, Geom*) prueba *f*
ADJ 1 [*alcohol*] de graduación normal
2 (= *secure*) • to be ~ against sth estar a prueba de algo • it is ~ against moisture está a prueba de la humedad • I'm not ~ against temptation no soy insensible a la tentación
VT 1 [+ *fabric, tent*] impermeabilizar
2 (= *proofread*) corregir las pruebas de
CPD ▸ proof copy copia *f* para la lectura de pruebas ▸ proof of postage resguardo *m* de envío ▸ proof sheet (*Typ, Phot*) prueba *f* ▸ proof spirit (*Brit, Canada*) licor *m* de graduación normal ▸ proof stage fase *f* de lectura de pruebas • to be at ~ stage estar en la fase de lectura de pruebas

-proof [pruːf] ADJ (*ending in compounds*) • bomb-proof a prueba de bombas • bullet-proof a prueba de balas • inflation-proof pension pensión *f* que no se ve afectada por la inflación; ▹ childproof, fireproof, foolproof *etc*

proofread [ˈpruːfriːd] (PT, PP: **proofread** [ˈpruːfred]) VT corregir las pruebas de

proofreader [ˈpruːfˌriːdəʳ] N corrector(a) *m/f* de pruebas

proofreading [ˈpruːfˌriːdɪŋ] N corrección *f* de pruebas

prop¹ [prɒp] N 1 (*lit*) (*Archit, Min*) puntal *m*; (*for clothesline*) palo *m*; (*Naut*) escora *f*; (*Aer**) (*also* propeller) hélice *f*; (*Rugby*) (*also* prop forward) pilier *m*; (*Theat*) (*also* property) accesorio *m*; props accesorios *mpl*, at(t)rezzo *msing*
2 (*fig*) sostén *m*, apoyo *m*
VT (= *support*) apuntalar; (= *rest, lean*) apoyar; (*fig*) sostener, apoyar • to ~ a ladder against a wall apoyar una escalera contra una pared • the door was ~ped open with a bucket habían puesto un cubo para que no se cerrara la puerta
CPD ▸ prop shaft* (*Aer*) (*also* propeller shaft) árbol *m* de la hélice
▸ **prop up** VT + ADV 1 (*lit*) [+ *roof, structure*] apuntalar • I ~ped him up with pillows le puse almohadas para que se recostara • she ~ped herself up on one elbow se enderezó apoyándose en el codo • he can usually be found ~ping up the bar (*hum*) te lo encuentras siempre en el bar empinando el codo*
2 (*fig*) [+ *economy, currency, regime*] respaldar • the company was ~ped up by a big loan la

compañía recibió el apoyo *or* el respaldo de un préstamo cuantioso, se respaldó a la compañía con un préstamo cuantioso

prop² (ABBR) (*Comm*) = **proprietor**

propaganda [ˌprɒpəˈgændə] (N) propaganda *f*
(CPD) [*leaflet, campaign*] de propaganda
▸ **propaganda machine** aparato *m* propagandístico

propagandist [ˌprɒpəˈgændɪst] (N) propagandista *mf*

propagandize [prɒpəˈgændaɪz] (VT) [+ *doctrine*] propagar; [+ *person*] hacer propaganda a
(VI) hacer propaganda

propagate [ˈprɒpəgeɪt] (VT) propagar
(VI) propagarse

propagation [ˌprɒpəˈgeɪʃən] (N) propagación *f*

propane [ˈprəʊpeɪn] (N) propano *m*
(CPD) ▸ **propane gas** gas *m* propano

propel [prəˈpel] (VT) [+ *vehicle, rocket*] impulsar, propulsar • **to ~ sth/sb along** impulsar algo/a algn • **they ~led him into the room** lo llevaron dentro de la habitación; (*more violently*) lo metieron en la habitación de un empujón

propellant, propellent [prəˈpelənt] (N) propulsor *m*; (= *aerosol etc*) propelente *m*

propeller [prəˈpeləʳ] (N) hélice *f*
(CPD) ▸ **propeller shaft** (*Aer*) árbol *m* de la hélice; (*Aut*) árbol *m or* eje *m* de transmisión; (*Naut*) eje *m* portahélice

propelling pencil [prəˈpelɪŋˈpensl] (N) lapicero *m*, portaminas *m inv*

propensity [prəˈpensɪtɪ] (N) propensión *f* (**to a**)

proper [ˈprɒpəʳ] (ADJ) **1** (= *right, suitable*) [*equipment, tools*] apropiado, adecuado • **that's not really the ~ tool for the job** esa no es la herramienta apropiada *or* adecuada para el trabajo • **at the ~ time** en el momento oportuno • **that's not the ~ way to do it** así no se hace • **you'll have to apply for a permit in the ~ way** tendrás que solicitar el permiso por las vías establecidas
2 (= *correct*) • **it was the ~ thing to say** fue lo que había que decir • **do as you think ~** haz lo que te parezca bien • **I thought it ~ to inform you** pensé que debía informarte; ▹ **right**
3 (= *actual, real*) propiamente dicho • **in the city ~** en la ciudad propiamente dicha, en la ciudad en sí • **he's never had a ~ job** nunca ha tenido un trabajo serio • **forget nouvelle cuisine, give me ~ food, any day** olvida la nueva cocina, dame todos los días comida como Dios manda • **in the ~ sense of the word** en el sentido estricto de la palabra
4* (= *complete, downright*) verdadero • **I felt a ~ idiot** me sentí como un perfecto *or* verdadero idiota • **we got a ~ beating** nos dieron una paliza de las buenas
5 (= *seemly*) [*person, behaviour*] correcto • **it wasn't considered ~ for a man to show his emotions** no se consideraba correcto *or* no estaba bien visto que un hombre mostrase sus emociones
6 (= *prim and proper*) correcto y formal
7 (= *peculiar, characteristic*) propio (**to de**)
(ADV) (*Brit**) • **he was ~ upset about it** estaba verdaderamente *or* realmente disgustado por ello • **she's a ~ stuck-up young lady** es una joven bien creída; ▹ **good**
(CPD) ▸ **proper fraction** (*Math*) fracción *f* propia ▸ **proper name, proper noun** nombre *m* propio

properly [ˈprɒpəlɪ] (ADV) **1** (= *suitably, adequately*) adecuadamente, apropiadamente • **the staff are not ~ trained** el personal no está adecuadamente *or* apropiadamente capacitado • **not ~ dressed** (*for occasion*) no vestido de la manera adecuada; (*for activity*) no vestido de la manera apropiada • **I had not eaten ~ for the past few days** hacía unos días que no comía como es debido
2 (= *correctly*) [*function, work*] bien • **sit up ~!** (*to child*) ¡siéntate como es debido! • **if you don't sit up ~ you can damage your back** si no te sientas correctamente, puedes fastidiarte la espalda • **if you can't behave ~ I'll have to take you home** si no te portas bien, tendremos que irnos a casa • **to do sth ~** hacer algo bien *or* como es debido • **we haven't got the money to do the job ~** no tenemos dinero para hacer bien el trabajo *or* para hacer el trabajo como es debido
• **~ speaking** hablando con propiedad, propiamente dicho • **the process is not ~ understood** no se sabe exactamente en qué consiste el proceso
3 (= *in seemly fashion*) correctamente • **to behave ~** portarse correctamente • **she very ~ refused** se negó a ello e hizo bien
4* (= *really, thoroughly*) verdaderamente • **we were ~ ashamed/puzzled** estábamos verdaderamente avergonzados/ confundidos

propertied [ˈprɒpətɪd] (ADJ) adinerado, acaudalado • **the ~ classes** la clase acaudalada

property [ˈprɒpətɪ] (N) **1** (= *possession*) propiedad *f* • **whose ~ is this?** ¿de quién es esto?, ¿a quién pertenece esto? • **it doesn't seem to be anyone's ~** no parece que tenga dueño • **she left her ~ to her daughter** dejó sus bienes a su hija • **common ~** propiedad *f* de todos • **government ~** propiedad *f* del gobierno • **personal ~** efectos *mpl or* objetos *mpl* personales • **you treat me as your personal ~** me tratas como si fuera de tu propiedad • **public ~** (= *land*) bien *m* público • **her success made her public ~ overnight** su éxito la convirtió en un personaje público de la noche a la mañana • **that news is public ~** eso lo saben todos ya, esa noticia es ya del dominio público • **he was charged with receiving stolen ~** se le acusó de comerciar con objetos robados; ▹ **intellectual, lost**
2 (= *land*) **a** (= *piece of land*) propiedad *f*, terreno *m* • **get off my ~** salga de mi propiedad • **"private property"** "propiedad *f* privada"
b (= *real estate*) propiedades *fpl* • **he owns ~ in Ireland** tiene propiedades en Irlanda • **a man/woman of ~** un hombre/una mujer acomodado/a; ▹ **real**
3 (= *building*) propiedad *f*, inmueble *m*
4 (= *ownership*) propiedad *f*
5 (= *phenomenon*) fenómeno *m*, estrella *f* • **he has become the hottest ~ in football** se ha convertido en el fenómemo futbolístico más importante
6 (*Theat*) accesorio *m*; **properties** accesorios *mpl*, at(t)rezzo *msing*
7 (= *quality*) (*gen pl*) propiedad *f* • **this plant has healing properties** esta planta tiene propiedades curativas
(CPD) ▸ **property company** compañía *f* inmobiliaria ▸ **property developer** promotor(a) *m/f* inmobiliario/a ▸ **property development** (= *activity*) promoción *f* inmobiliaria; (= *area*) lanzamiento *m* inmobiliario • **their father made a fortune out of ~ development** su padre ganó una fortuna con las promociones inmobiliarias ▸ **property insurance** seguro *m* inmobiliario ▸ **property ladder** • IDIOMS: • **to get on the ~ ladder** • **to get a foot on the ~ ladder** adquirir una propiedad ▸ **property law** ley *f* de la propiedad inmobiliaria ▸ **property manager** (*Theat*) accesorista *mf*, at(t)rezzista *mf* ▸ **property market, property mart** mercado *m* inmobiliario ▸ **property mistress** (*Theat*) accesorista *f*, at(t)rezzista *f* ▸ **property owner** (*rural*) terrateniente *mf*; (*urban*) dueño/a *m/f* de propiedades ▸ **property page(s)** sección *f* de ventas de inmuebles y viviendas (*de un periódico*) ▸ **property rights** derechos *mpl* sobre la propiedad ▸ **property speculation** especulación *f* inmobiliaria ▸ **property speculator** especulador(a) *m/f* inmobiliario/a ▸ **property tax** impuesto *m* sobre la propriedad

prophecy [ˈprɒfɪsɪ] (N) profecía *f*

prophesy [ˈprɒfɪsaɪ] (VT) (= *foretell*) profetizar; (= *predict*) predecir, vaticinar

prophet [ˈprɒfɪt] (N) profeta *m* • **a ~ of doom** (*fig*) un(a) catastrofista, un(a) agorero/a*

prophetess [ˈprɒfɪtɪs] (N) profetisa *f*

prophetic [prəˈfetɪk] (ADJ) profético

prophetically [prəˈfetɪkəlɪ] (ADV) proféticamente

prophylactic [ˌprɒfɪˈlæktɪk] (ADJ) profiláctico
(N) (= *contraceptive*) profiláctico *m*

prophylaxis [ˌprɒfɪˈlæksɪs] (N) profilaxis *f*

propinquity [prəˈpɪŋkwɪtɪ] (N) (*frm*) (= *nearness*) propincuidad *f*; (= *kinship*) consanguinidad *f*, parentesco *m*

propitiate [prəˈpɪʃɪeɪt] (VT) propiciar

propitiation [prəˌpɪʃɪˈeɪʃən] (N) propiciación *f*

propitiatory [prəˈpɪʃɪətərɪ] (ADJ) propiciatorio, conciliatorio

propitious [prəˈpɪʃəs] (ADJ) propicio, favorable

propitiously [prəˈpɪʃəslɪ] (ADV) de modo propicio, bajo signo propicio, favorablemente

propjet [ˈprɒpdʒet] (N) = **turboprop**

propman [ˈprɒpmæn] (N) (PL: **propmen**) (*Theat*) atrezista *m* (*Sp, Mex*), utilero *m* (*LAm*)

proponent [prəˈpəʊnənt] (N) defensor(a) *m/f*

proportion [prəˈpɔːʃən] (N) **1** (= *ratio*) proporción *f* • **the ~ of blacks to whites** la proporción entre negros y blancos • **in/out of ~** proporcionado/desproporcionado • **to be in/out of ~ (to one another)** estar en/no guardar proporción (el uno con el otro) • **to be in/out of ~ to** *or* **with sth** estar en/no guardar proporción con algo • **and the rest in ~** y lo demás en proporción; (*Comm*) y lo demás a prorrata • **in due ~** en su justa medida • **in ~ as** a medida que • **to see sth in ~** (*fig*) ver algo en su justa medida • **it has been magnified out of all ~** (*fig*) se ha exagerado mucho • **sense of ~** (*fig*) sentido *m* de la medida
2 (= *part, amount*) parte *f* • **in equal ~s** por partes iguales • **what ~ is in private hands?** ¿qué porción queda en manos de particulares?
3 proportions (= *size*) dimensiones *fpl*
(VT) • **to ~ sth to sth** [+ *charge, cost*] adecuar algo a algo • **well-proportioned** [*room*] de buenas proporciones; [*woman's figure*] bien proporcionado; [*man's figure*] bien armado

proportional [prəˈpɔːʃənl] (ADJ) proporcional (**to a**), en proporción (**to con**) • **X is not ~ to Y** X no guarda proporción con Y
(CPD) ▸ **proportional representation** (*Pol*) representación *f* proporcional ▸ **proportional spacing** (*on printer*) espaciado *m* proporcional

P

proportionality [ˌprəpɔːʃəˈnælɪtɪ] (N) proporcionalidad *f*

proportionally [prəˈpɔːʃnəlɪ] (ADV) proporcionalmente

proportionate [prəˈpɔːʃnɪt] (ADJ) proporcionado (**to** a)

proportionately [prəˈpɔːʃnɪtlɪ] (ADV) proporcionadamente, en proporción

proposal [prəˈpəʊzl] (N) **1** (= *offer, suggestion*) (*gen*) propuesta *f*, proposición *f*; (= *written submission*) propuesta *f* • **they have rejected the latest peace ~** han rechazado la última propuesta de paz • **to make sb an indecent ~** hacer una proposición deshonesta a algn • **let me make a ~** permítame hacer una propuesta *or* proposición • **I made the ~ that we should adjourn the meeting** propuse que levantásemos la sesión • **to put forward a ~** presentar una propuesta • **an advert asking for writers to submit ~s for a new TV series** un anuncio pidiendo a los escritores que mandaran propuestas para una nueva serie televisiva
2 (*also* **proposal of marriage**) proposición *f* de matrimonio, propuesta *f* de matrimonio

propose [prəˈpəʊz] (VT) **1** (= *suggest*) **a** (*gen*) proponer • **the idea was first ~d in 1789** la idea se propuso por primera vez en 1789 • **what do you ~?** ¿qué propones? • **to ~ sth to sb** proponer algo a algn • **to ~ doing sth**: • **I ~ writing her a letter** (= *I suggest I write*) me propongo escribirle una carta; (= *I suggest that someone writes*) yo propongo que se le escriba una carta • **to ~ that** proponer que (+ *subjun*) • **I ~ that we go and see her** propongo que vayamos a verla
b (*in meeting, parliament*) [+ *amendment*] proponer; [+ *motion*] presentar
c • **to ~ marriage to sb** proponer a algn en matrimonio, hacer una proposición *or* propuesta de matrimonio a algn
d • **to ~ sb's health** beber a la salud de algn, brindar por algn • **to ~ a toast (to sb)** proponer un brindis (por algn)
2 (= *nominate*) • **he ~d Smith as** *or* **for chairman** propuso a Smith como presidente • **to ~ sb for membership of a club** proponer a algn como socio de un club
3 (= *intend*) • **to ~ to do sth** • **~ doing sth** pensar hacer algo • **I do not ~ to discuss this matter any further** no pienso hablar más de este asunto • **what do you ~ doing?** ¿qué piensas hacer?
(VI) **1** (= *offer marriage*) • **to ~ to sb** proponer a algn en matrimonio, hacer una proposición de matrimonio a algn • **have you ~d yet?** ¿le has propuesto en matrimonio ya?, ¿le has hecho una proposición de matrimonio ya?
2 • PROVERB: • **man ~s, God disposes** el hombre propone y Dios dispone

proposed [prəˈpəʊzd] (ADJ) • **the ~ motorway** la autopista que se propone, la autopista propuesta • **your ~ solution** la solución que propusiste

proposer [prəˈpəʊzəʳ] (N) [*of motion*] proponente *mf*

proposition [ˌprɒpəˈzɪʃən] (N) **1** (= *proposal*) proposición *f*, propuesta *f* • **to make sb a ~** proponer algo a algn
2 (= *enterprise*) proposición *f* • **working as a freelance can be an attractive ~** trabajar por cuenta propia puede ser una proposición atractiva • **economically, it is not a viable ~** desde el punto de vista económico, no es una proposición viable
3 (= *opponent*) adversario/a *m/f*, contrincante *mf* • **he's a tough ~** es un adversario *or* contrincante fuerte
4 (*sexual*) • **she had received a number of unwanted sexual ~s** había sido objeto de varias proposiciones sexuales no deseadas
5 (*Math, Logic*) proposición *f*
(VT) hacer proposiciones deshonestas a

propound [prəˈpaʊnd] (VT) (*frm*) [+ *ideas etc*] exponer, plantear

proprietary [prəˈpraɪətərɪ] (ADJ) propietario; (*Comm*) patentado
(CPD) ▸ **proprietary brand** marca *f* comercial ▸ **proprietary goods** artículos *mpl* de marca ▸ **proprietary interest** interés *m* patrimonial ▸ **proprietary name** nombre *m* propietario

proprietor [prəˈpraɪətəʳ] (N) [*of shop, hotel etc*] dueño/a *m/f*; [*of land*] propietario/a *m/f*

proprietorial [prəˌpraɪəˈtɔːrɪəl] (ADJ) [*attitude etc*] protector

proprietorship [prəˈpraɪətəʃɪp] (N) propiedad *f*, posesión *f*

proprietress [prəˈpraɪətrɪs] (N) [*of shop, hotel etc*] dueña *f*

propriety [prəˈpraɪətɪ] (N) **1** (= *decency*) decoro *m*, decencia *f* • **breach of ~** ofensa *f* contra el decoro, incorrección *f* • **the proprieties** los cánones sociales • **to observe the proprieties** atenerse a los cánones sociales
2 (= *appropriateness*) conveniencia *f*

propulsion [prəˈpʌlʃən] (N) propulsión *f*; ▹ **jet**

pro rata [ˌprəʊˈrɑːtə] (ADV) a prorrateo • **the money will be shared out ~** el dinero será repartido a prorrateo, se prorrateará el dinero
(ADJ) a prorrateo • **a ~ agreement** (*US*) un acuerdo a prorrateo

prorate [ˈprəʊreɪt] (*US*) (N) prorrata *f*
(VT) prorratear

prorogation [ˌprəʊrəˈgeɪʃən] (N) prorrogación *f*

prorogue [prəˈrəʊg] (VT) prorrogar

prosaic [prəʊˈzeɪɪk] (ADJ) (= *dull*) prosaico

prosaically [prəʊˈzeɪɪkəlɪ] (ADV) prosaicamente

Pros. Atty. (ABBR) (*US*) = **prosecuting attorney**

proscenium [prəʊˈsiːnɪəm] (N) (PL: **prosceniums** *or* **proscenia** [prəʊˈsiːnɪə]) proscenio *m*
(CPD) ▸ **proscenium arch** embocadura *f* ▸ **proscenium box** palco *m* de proscenio

proscribe [prəʊsˈkraɪb] (VT) proscribir

proscription [prəʊsˈkrɪpʃən] (N) proscripción *f*

prose [prəʊz] (N) **1** (*Literat*) prosa *f*
2 (*Scol*) (*also* **prose translation**) texto *m* para traducir; (*also* **prose composition**) traducción *f* inversa
(CPD) ▸ **prose poem** poema *m* en prosa ▸ **prose writer** prosista *mf*

prosecute [ˈprɒsɪkjuːt] (VT) **1** (*Jur*) (= *try*) procesar, enjuiciar; (= *punish*) sancionar; [+ *claim*] demandar en juicio; [+ *case*] llevar a los tribunales • **to ~ sb for theft** procesar a algn por robo • **to be ~d for a traffic offence** ser procesado por una infracción de tráfico • **"trespassers will be prosecuted"** "se procederá contra los intrusos" • **the lawyer who will ~ the case** el/la fiscal
2 (*frm*) (= *carry on*) proseguir, llevar adelante
(VI) (*Jur*) interponer una acción judicial
• **prosecuting attorney** (*US*) fiscal *mf*
• **prosecuting counsel** (*Brit*) fiscal *mf*

prosecution [ˌprɒsɪˈkjuːʃən] (N) **1** (*Jur*) (= *act, proceedings*) proceso *m*, juicio *m*; (*in court*) (= *case, side*) acusación *f* • **counsel for the ~** fiscal *mf* • **to bring** *or* **start a ~ against sb** entablar juicio *or* una acción judicial contra algn
2 (*frm*) (= *furtherance*) prosecución *f* • **in the ~ of his duty** en el cumplimiento de su deber
(CPD) ▸ **prosecution case** acusación *f* ▸ **prosecution witness** testigo *mf* de cargo

prosecutor [ˈprɒsɪkjuːtəʳ] (N) (*Jur*) abogado/a *m/f* de la acusación; (*also* **public prosecutor**) fiscal *mf*

proselyte [ˈprɒsɪlaɪt] (N) prosélito/a *m/f*
(VT), (VI) (*US*) = **proselytize**

proselytism [ˈprɒsɪlɪtɪzəm] (N) proselitismo *m*

proselytize [ˈprɒsɪlɪtaɪz] (VI) ganar prosélitos
(VT) [+ *person*] convertir

prosody [ˈprɒsədɪ] (N) prosodia *f*

prospect (N) [ˈprɒspekt] **1** (= *outlook*) perspectiva *f* • **it was a daunting/pleasant ~** era una perspectiva desalentadora/agradable • **the ~s look grim** las perspectivas son desalentadoras • **~s for the harvest are poor** el panorama se anuncia más bien negro para la cosecha • **she was excited at the ~ of the China trip** estaba entusiasmada con la perspectiva de irse a China • **he was terrified at the ~** la perspectiva le aterraba • **to face the ~ of sth** • **be faced with the ~ of sth** verse ante la perspectiva de algo • **faced with the ~ of bankruptcy he committed suicide** ante la perspectiva de la ruina, se suicidó • **in ~** en perspectiva • **to have sth in ~** tener algo en perspectiva
2 (= *possibility*) posibilidad *f* • **the job held out the ~ of rapid promotion** el trabajo ofrecía la posibilidad de ascender con rapidez • **there is little ~ of his coming** hay pocas posibilidades de que venga • **he has little ~ of success/of succeeding** tiene pocas posibilidades de tener éxito • **I see no ~ of that (happening)** eso no lo creo probable • **he didn't relish the ~ of having to look for another job** no le entusiasmaba la posibilidad de tener que buscar otro trabajo
3 prospects (= *future possibilities*) porvenir *m*, futuro *m* • **a job with no ~s** un trabajo sin porvenir, un trabajo sin (perspectivas de) futuro • **what are his ~s?** ¿qué perspectivas de futuro tiene? • **job/promotion ~s** perspectivas *fpl* de trabajo/ascenso • **future ~s** perspectivas *fpl* de futuro • **she has good ~s** tiene buen porvenir *or* un buen futuro
4† (= *view*) panorama *m*, vista *f* • **a ~ of Toledo** un panorama de Toledo, una vista de Toledo
5 (= *prospective candidate, champion etc*) • **the company is not an attractive ~ for shareholders** la empresa no representa una opción *or* posibilidad atractiva para los accionistas • **the man who is Britain's best ~ for a gold medal in the Olympics** el hombre que tiene mayores posibilidades de conseguir una medalla de oro para Gran Bretaña en las Olimpiadas • **Steve is a great ~ for the future of British chess** Steve promete muchísimo para el futuro del ajedrez británico • **a salesman who considers everybody a ~** un vendedor que considera a todo el mundo como un potencial comprador
6 (= *marriage partner*) partido *m* • **he's/she's not much of a ~ for her/him** no es muy buen partido para ella/él
7 (*Min*) *zona donde es probable que haya yacimientos de minerales*
(VT) [prəsˈpekt] [+ *area, land*] hacer prospecciones en, prospectar
(VI) [prəsˈpekt] hacer prospecciones, prospectar • **oil companies are ~ing near here** las compañías petrolíferas están haciendo prospecciones *or* prospectando cerca de aquí • **to ~ for gold** buscar oro

prospecting [prəsˈpektɪŋ] (N) (*Min*) prospección *f*

prospective [prəsˈpektɪv] (ADJ) **1** (= *likely,*

P

possible) [*customer, candidate*] posible
2 (= *future*) [*son-in-law, home, legislation*] futuro; [*heir*] presunto
prospector [prəs'pektəʳ] (N) buscador(a) *m/f*, cateador(a) *m/f* (*LAm*) • **gold ~** buscador(a) *m/f* de oro • **oil ~s** prospectores *mpl* petroleros
prospectus [prəs'pektəs] (N) prospecto *m*
prosper ['prɒspəʳ] (VI) prosperar, medrar
(VT) (*frm*) favorecer, fomentar
prosperity [prɒs'perɪtɪ] (N) prosperidad *f*
prosperous ['prɒspərəs] (ADJ) próspero
prosperously ['prɒspərəslɪ] (ADV) prósperamente
prostaglandin [,prɒstə'glændɪn] (N) prostaglandina *f*
prostate ['prɒsteɪt] (N) (*also* **prostate gland**) próstata *f*
(CPD) ▸ **prostate cancer** cáncer *m* de próstata
prosthesis [prɒs'θi:sɪs] (N) (PL: **prostheses** [prɒs'θi:si:z]) prótesis *f*
prosthetic [prɒs'θetɪk] (ADJ) prostético
prostitute ['prɒstɪtju:t] (N) prostituto/a *m/f* • **to become a ~** prostituirse
(VT) (*fig*) prostituir • **to ~ o.s.** prostituirse
prostitution [,prɒstɪ'tju:ʃən] (N) (*lit, fig*) prostitución *f*
prostrate (ADJ) ['prɒstreɪt] **1** (*lit*) boca abajo, postrado; (*Bot*) procumbente
2 (*fig*) [*nation, country etc*] abatido; (= *exhausted*) postrado, abatido (**with** por)
(VT) [prɒs'treɪt] (*lit*) postrar; (*fig*) postrar, abatir • **to be ~d by grief** estar postrado por el dolor • **to ~ o.s.** (*lit, fig*) postrarse
prostration [prɒs'treɪʃən] (N) postración *f*; (*fig*) postración *f*, abatimiento *m*
prosy ['prəʊzɪ] (ADJ) (COMPAR: **prosier**, SUPERL: **prosiest**) prosaico, aburrido, monótono
Prot*, **prot*** [prɒt] (N ABBR) (*pej*) = **Protestant**
protagonist [prəʊ'tægənɪst] (N) protagonista *mf*
protean ['prəʊtɪən] (ADJ) proteico
protect [prə'tekt] (VT) proteger (**against** contra, **from** de) • **~ed species** especie *f* protegida
protection [prə'tekʃən] (N) **1** (*gen*) protección *f*, amparo *m* • **to be under sb's ~** estar bajo la protección de algn, estar amparado por algn
2 (*Insurance, Ind, Jur*) protección *f* • **the policy offers ~ against ...** la póliza protege contra ...
3 (= *contraception*) anticonceptivo *m* • **they didn't use any ~** no usaron ningún anticonceptivo, no se han cuidado
(CPD) ▸ **protection factor** [*of sun cream*] factor *m* de protección ▸ **protection money** • **he pays 200 dollars a week ~ money** paga 200 dólares de protección a la semana ▸ **protection order** ≈ orden *f* de alejamiento • **the hospital obtained an emergency ~ order to stop the parents removing their child from the hospital** el hospital ha conseguido una orden de alejamiento para evitar que los padres se llevasen al niño del hospital ▸ **protection racket** chantaje *m*
protectionism [prə'tekʃənɪzəm] (N) proteccionismo *m*
protectionist [prə'tekʃənɪst] (ADJ) proteccionista
(N) proteccionista *mf*
protective [prə'tektɪv] (ADJ) **1** (*physically*) [*layer, covering*] protector; [*clothing*] de protección
2 (*emotionally*) [*attitude, gesture*] protector • **Becky's fiercely ~ father, John** John, el padre de Becky, que tiene/tenía una actitud terriblemente protectora hacia ella • **to be ~ of sth** proteger algo • **to be/feel ~ towards** *or* **of sb** tener una actitud protectora hacia algn • **he's very ~ towards his little sister** tiene una actitud muy protectora hacia su hermanita, protege mucho a su hermanita
3 (*Econ*) [*tariffs*] proteccionista
(CPD) ▸ **protective cream** crema *f* protectora ▸ **protective custody** detención *f* preventiva
protectively [prə'tektɪvlɪ] (ADV) en actitud protectora, en actitud de protección
protectiveness [prə'tektɪvnɪs] (N) actitud *f* protectora
protector [prə'tektəʳ] (N) **1** (= *defender*) protector(a) *m/f*
2 (= *protective wear*) protector *m*
protectorate [prə'tektərɪt] (N) protectorado *m*
protectress [prə'tektrɪs] (N) protectora *f*
protégé ['prɒteʒeɪ] (N) protegido *m*, ahijado *m*
protégée ['prɒteʒeɪ] (N) protegida *f*, ahijada *f*
protein ['prəʊti:n] (N) proteína *f*
(CPD) ▸ **protein content** contenido *m* proteínico ▸ **protein deficiency** deficiencia *f* de proteínas
protein-rich ['prəʊti:nrɪtʃ] (ADJ) rico en contenido proteínico
pro tem ['prəʊ'tem], **pro tempore**† ['prəʊ'tempərɪ] (ADV) provisionalmente • **he's replacing the chairman ~** sustituye provisionalmente al presidente
(ADJ) interino • **the ~ chairman** el presidente interino • **on a ~ basis** de manera provisional
protest (N) ['prəʊtest] (*gen*) protesta *f*; (= *complaint*) queja *f* • **under ~** bajo protesta • **I'll do it but under ~** lo haré pero que conste mi protesta • **to make a ~** hacer una protesta
(VT) [prə'test] **1** (= *complain*) protestar • **to ~ that** protestar diciendo que
2 (*US*) (= *complain about*) protestar de
3 (= *dispute*) poner reparos a
4 (= *affirm*) [+ *one's love*] declarar, afirmar • **he ~ed his innocence** declaró enérgicamente su inocencia
(VI) [prə'test] protestar • **to ~ at** *or* **against** protestar de
(CPD) ['prəʊtest] ▸ **protest demonstration, protest march** manifestación *f or* marcha *f* (de protesta) ▸ **protest movement** movimiento *m* de protesta, movimiento *m* contestatario ▸ **protest song** canción *f* (de) protesta ▸ **protest vote** voto *m* de protesta
Protestant ['prɒtɪstənt] (ADJ) protestante
(N) protestante *mf*
Protestantism ['prɒtɪstəntɪzəm] (N) protestantismo *m*
protestation [,prɒtes'teɪʃən] (N)
1 (= *affirmation*) [*of love, loyalty etc*] afirmación *f*, declaración *f*
2 (= *protest*) protesta *f*
protester, protestor [prə'testəʳ] (N) protestador(a) *m/f*; (*on march, in demonstration etc*) manifestante *mf*
proto... ['prəʊtəʊ] (PREFIX) proto...
protocol ['prəʊtəkɒl] (N) protocolo *m*
proton ['prəʊtɒn] (N) protón *m*
protoplasm ['prəʊtəʊplæzəm] (N) protoplasma *m*
prototype ['prəʊtəʊtaɪp] (N) prototipo *m*
prototypical [,prəʊtə'tɪpɪkəl] (ADJ) prototípico
protozoan [,prəʊtə'zəʊən] (N) (PL: **protozoa** [,prəʊtə'zəʊə]) (*Bio*) protozoo *m*
(ADJ) protozoico
protozoon [,prəʊtə'zəʊən] (N) = **protozoan**
protract [prə'trækt] (VT) prolongar
protracted [prə'træktɪd] (ADJ) prolongado, (excesivamente) largo
protraction [prə'trækʃən] (N) prolongación *f*
protractor [prə'træktəʳ] (N) transportador *m*
protrude [prə'tru:d] (VI) salir, sobresalir
(VT) sacar fuera
protruding [prə'tru:dɪŋ] (ADJ) saliente, sobresaliente; [*eye, tooth*] saltón
protrusion [prə'tru:ʒən] (N) saliente *m*, protuberancia *f*
protrusive [prə'tru:sɪv] (ADJ) = **protruding**
protuberance [prə'tju:bərəns] (N) protuberancia *f*, saliente *m*
protuberant [prə'tju:bərənt] (ADJ) protuberante, saliente; [*eye, tooth*] saltón
proud [praʊd] (ADJ) (COMPAR: **prouder**, SUPERL: **proudest**) **1** (= *satisfied*) [*person*] orgulloso; [*expression, smile*] de orgullo • **he is the ~ father of a baby girl** es el orgulloso padre de una nena • **to be ~ that** estar *or* sentirse orgulloso de (que) • **I'm ~ that I did it on my own** estoy *or* me siento orgulloso de haberlo hecho solo • **to be ~ to do sth: I'm ~ to call her my friend** me enorgullece que sea mi amiga • **we are ~ to present ...** tenemos el honor de presentarles ... • **it was his ~ boast that he had never had a proper job** era un motivo de muchísimo orgullo para él el no haber tenido nunca un trabajo serio, presumía orgulloso de no haber tenido nunca un trabajo serio • **it makes you ~ to be a parent, doesn't it?** te hace sentirte orgulloso de ser padre, ¿verdad? • **to be ~ of sth/sb** estar orgulloso de algo/algn • **I'm working-class and ~ of it** soy de clase obrera y estoy orgulloso de ello • **that's nothing to be ~ of!** ¡esto no es motivo de orgullo! • **I'm not very ~ of myself** no estoy muy orgulloso *or* satisfecho de mí mismo • **I hope you're ~ of yourself!** (*iro*) ¡estarás orgulloso! • IDIOM: • **to do sb/o.s. ~***: • **the team have done their country ~** el equipo ha sido motivo de orgullo para su país • **his honesty did him ~** su honradez decía mucho en su favor • **the hotel did them ~** el hotel los trató a cuerpo de rey • **she did herself ~ in the piano competition** se lució en el concurso de piano
2 (= *self-respecting*) [*people, nation*] digno
3 (*pej*) (= *arrogant*) orgulloso, soberbio • **she's ~ and stubborn** es orgullosa *or* soberbia y terca • **he was flustered, but too ~ to show it** estaba nervioso pero era demasiado orgulloso para demostrarlo • **don't be too ~ to ask for help** no dejes que el orgullo te impida pedir ayuda • **I don't mind sitting on the floor, I'm not ~** no me importa sentarme en el suelo, no soy orgulloso, no me importa sentarme en el suelo, no se me caen los anillos*
4 (= *causing pride*) [*day, moment*] glorioso, de orgullo; [*history, reputation*] glorioso; [*possession, tradition*] preciado • **the locket was my ~est possession** el guardapelo era mi bien más preciado *or* mi mayor tesoro
5 (= *splendid, imposing*) espléndido, imponente
6 (*Brit*) (= *protruding*) • **to be/stand ~ (of sth)** sobresalir (de algo) • **that screw's still a bit ~ of the surface** ese tornillo aún sobresale un poco de la superficie
proudly ['praʊdlɪ] (ADV) (= *with satisfaction*) con orgullo; (= *arrogantly*) arrogantemente, con arrogancia; (= *splendidly, impressively*) de forma imponente • **he ~ showed me his drawing** orgulloso, me enseñó su dibujo, me enseñó con orgullo su dibujo
provable ['pru:vəbl] (ADJ) [*hypothesis, story,*

P

law] probable, demostrable; [*guilt, innocence*] probable, que se puede probar

prove [pru:v] (PT: **proved**, PP: **proved** *or* **proven**) VT **1** (= *give proof of*) [+ *theory, statement*] demostrar, probar; (*one's love, loyalty, strength*) demostrar • **my son was murdered, and I'm going to ~ it** a mi hijo lo asesinaron, y voy a demostrarlo *or* probarlo • **can you ~ it?** ¿lo puede demostrar *or* probar? • **statistics never ~ anything** las estadísticas nunca prueban *or* demuestran nada • **you say you love me, so ~ it** dices que me quieres, pues demuéstralo *or* pruébalo • **he wanted to ~ his love for her** quería demostrar su amor por ella • **you can't ~ anything against me** usted no tiene ninguna prueba en mi contra, usted no puede demostrar *or* probar nada en mi contra • **it just ~s how stupid he is** simplemente demuestra *or* prueba lo tonto que es • **to ~ sb's innocence** • **~ sb innocent** demostrar *or* probar la inocencia de algn • **to ~ one's point** demostrar que uno está en lo cierto *or* tiene razón • **she took him to court just to ~ a point** lo llevó a los tribunales simplemente para demostrar *or* probar que estaba en lo cierto *or* que ella tenía razón • **to ~ sb right** demostrar que algn tiene razón • **he was ~d right in the end** al fin se demostró que tenía razón • **it's been scientifically ~n** *or* **~d** se ha probado *or* demostrado científicamente, ha sido probado *or* demostrado científicamente • **to ~ that** demostrar que, probar que • **that ~s that she did it** eso demuestra *or* prueba que ella lo hizo • **she wants to ~ to herself that she can still hold down a job** quiere demostrarse a sí misma que todavía puede mantener un trabajo • **what are you trying to ~?** ¿qué intentas demostrar *or* probar? • **it's difficult to ~ what's going on** es difícil demostrar *or* probar lo que está pasando • **whether he was right remains to be ~d** aún falta por demostrar *or* probar si tenía razón • **to ~ sb wrong** demostrar que algn está equivocado • **everyone said that we would fail but we ~d them wrong** todo el mundo decía que fracasaríamos, pero demostramos que estaban equivocados • **she attempted to ~ their theory wrong** intentó encontrar pruebas que demostraran que su teoría estaba equivocada • IDIOM: • **the exception ~s the rule** la excepción confirma la regla

2 (= *verify*) comprobar • **you can ~ how effective this method is by trying it out yourself** puede comprobar la eficacia de este método probándolo usted mismo

3 • **to ~ o.s.** demostrar lo que uno vale • **you don't need to ~ yourself** no tienes que demostrar lo que vales • **he has ~d himself worthy of our trust** ha demostrado ser digno de nuestra confianza • **he has ~d himself to be a successful manager** ha demostrado ser un gerente eficaz

4 (= *test out*) poner a prueba, someter a prueba

5 (*Jur*) • **to ~ a will** homologar un testamento

VI **1** (= *turn out*) resultar • **it ~d (to be) useful** resultó (ser) útil • **if it ~s (to be) otherwise** si resulta (ser) lo contrario • **it may ~ difficult to secure funding** puede que resulte difícil conseguir fondos • **the news ~d false** resultó que la noticia era falsa • **the temptation ~d too much for her** la tentación resultó demasiado grande para ella, no pudo resistir la tentación

2 (*Culin*) [*dough*] leudarse

proven ['pru:vən] PP *of* **prove**

ADJ **1** (*gen*) [*formula, method*] de eficacia probada; [*abilities*] probado • **it's a ~ fact that ...** está probado *or* demostrado que ...; es un hecho comprobado que ...

2 ['prəʊvən] (*Scot*) (*Jur*) • **the case was found not ~** el acusado fue absuelto por falta de pruebas

provenance ['prɒvɪnəns] N procedencia *f*

Provençal [ˌprɒvɑ:n'sɑ:l] ADJ provenzal

N **1** (= *person*) provenzal *mf*

2 (*Ling*) provenzal *m*

Provence [prɒ'vɑ:ns] N Provenza *f*

provender ['prɒvɪndəʳ] N (*frm*) forraje *m*; (*hum*) provisiones *fpl*, comida *f*

proverb ['prɒvɜ:b] N refrán *m*, proverbio *m*

proverbial [prə'vɜ:bɪəl] ADJ proverbial

proverbially [prə'vɜ:bɪəlɪ] ADV proverbialmente

provide [prə'vaɪd] VT **1** (= *supply*) **a** [+ *materials, food*] proporcionar, suministrar; [+ *money, information, evidence*] proporcionar, facilitar; [+ *service*] prestar • **please place your litter in the receptacle ~d** por favor hagan uso de los recipientes que les hemos proporcionado *or* suministrado para depositar la basura • **the meeting ~d an opportunity to talk** la reunión les brindó *or* ofreció la oportunidad de hablar • **candidates must ~ their own pencils** los candidatos deben traer sus propios lápices • **to ~ sth for sb/sth**: • **I will ~ food for everyone** proveeré a todo el mundo de comida, proporcionaré *or* daré comida a todo el mundo • **it ~s accommodation for five families** provee a cinco familias de alojamiento, da *or* proporciona alojamiento a cinco familias • **the company ~s free health care for its employees** la empresa presta asistencia médica gratis a sus empleados • **it ~s shade for the cows** les da sombra a las vacas • **they've asked the United Nations to ~ protection for civilians** han pedido a las Naciones Unidas que faciliten protección a la población civil • **to ~ funding/money for sth** proporcionar *or* facilitar fondos/dinero para algo • **to ~ a solution (to sth)** ofrecer una solución (a algo)

b • **to ~ sb with sth** [+ *materials, food*] proveer a algn de algo, suministrar algo a algn; [+ *money, information, details*] proporcionar *or* facilitar algo a algn; [+ *service*] proporcionar algo a algn; [+ *means*] facilitar algo a algn; [+ *opportunity*] brindar algo a algn • **it ~s the plant with a continuous flow of nutrients** provee a la planta de *or* suministra a la planta un flujo continuo de nutrientes • **it ~d her with the opportunity she needed** le brindó la oportunidad que necesitaba

c • **to ~ o.s. with sth** proveerse de algo • **plants produce sugars and starch to ~ themselves with energy** las plantas producen azúcares y almidón para proveerse de energía • **he had forgotten to ~ himself with an alibi** se le había olvidado buscarse una coartada

2 (= *have available*) estar provisto de • **the field ~s plenty of space for a car park** el campo está provisto de muchísimo espacio para un aparcamiento de coches • **the car is ~d with a heater** el coche está provisto de un calentador

3 (= *stipulate*) • **the law ~s that ...** la ley estipula *or* dispone que ...

VI • IDIOM: • **the Lord will ~** Dios proveerá; ▹ **provide for**

▸ **provide against** VI + PREP (*frm*) [*person*] tomar precauciones contra, precaverse de; [*policy, insurance*] proporcionar protección contra, proporcionar cobertura contra

▸ **provide for** VI + PREP **1** (*financially*) **a** (= *support*) [+ *person, family*] mantener • **parents are expected to ~ for their children** se espera que los padres mantengan a sus hijos

b (= *make provision for*) • **he wanted to see that the children were well ~d for** quería asegurarse de que las necesidades de los niños estaban bien cubiertas • **his wife was left well ~d for in his will** en el testamento dejó a su mujer bien asegurado • **they are well ~d for** tienen medios de sobra • **individuals are encouraged to ~ for themselves by buying private insurance** se anima a las personas a que se aseguren el futuro *or* que hagan previsiones para el futuro comprando un seguro privado

2 (= *take care of*) prever • **the 50 employers which best ~ for the needs of women** los 50 empresarios que mejor prevén las necesidades de las mujeres • **we have ~d for that** eso lo hemos previsto • **it's impossible to ~ for all eventualities** es imposible prever todas las eventualidades *or* tomar precauciones contra toda eventualidad

3 (*Jur*) (= *make possible*) • **the accord ~s for greater police co-operation** en el acuerdo se prevé una mayor colaboración por parte de la policía • **the Act ~s for financial penalties to be imposed on all offenders** la ley estipula que se impongan multas a todos los transgresores • **as ~d for in the 1990 contract** de acuerdo con lo estipulado en el contrato de 1990

provided [prə'vaɪdɪd] CONJ • **~ (that)** con tal (de) que, a condición de que

providence ['prɒvɪdəns] N providencia *f* • Providence Divina Providencia *f*

provident ['prɒvɪdənt] ADJ providente, previsor, próvido

CPD ▸ **provident fund** fondo *m* de previsión ▸ **provident society** (*Brit*) sociedad *f* de socorro mutuo, mutualidad *f*

providential [ˌprɒvɪ'denʃəl] ADJ providencial; (= *fortunate*) afortunado, milagroso

providentially [ˌprɒvɪ'denʃəlɪ] ADV providencialmente; (= *fortunately*) afortunadamente, milagrosamente

providently ['prɒvɪdəntlɪ] ADV próvidamente

provider [prə'vaɪdəʳ] N proveedor(a) *m/f*

providing [prə'vaɪdɪŋ] CONJ = **provided**

province ['prɒvɪns] N **1** (*Geog*) provincia *f* • **they live in the ~s** viven en provincias

2 (*fig*) (= *area of knowledge, activity etc*) esfera *f*, campo *m*; (= *jurisdiction etc*) competencia *f* • **it's not within my ~** no es de mi competencia

3 (*Rel*) arzobispado *m*

provincial [prə'vɪnʃəl] ADJ provincial, de provincia; (*pej*) pueblerino, provinciano

N (*esp pej*) provinciano/a *m/f*

provincialism [prə'vɪnʃəlɪzəm] N provincialismo *m*

proving ground ['pru:vɪŋˌgraʊnd] N terreno *m* de prueba

provision [prə'vɪʒən] N **1** (= *act of providing*) [*of funds, accommodation, jobs*] provisión *f*; [*of food, water*] suministro *m*, abastecimiento *m*; [*of service, care*] prestación *f* • **~ of adequate toilet facilities on the site is essential** es esencial que la obra esté provista de aseos adecuados • **the ~ of care for the elderly** la prestación de asistencia social a los ancianos • **to get in** *or* **lay in a ~ of coal** abastecerse de carbón

2 (= *amount, number provided*) • **nursery ~ is usually poor in country areas** la provisión de guarderías es generalmente escasa en las zonas rurales, suele haber pocas

guarderías en las zonas rurales • **there is inadequate housing ~ for the poor** la provisión de viviendas para los pobres es insuficiente • **they have cut their ~ of grants to research students** han reducido la cantidad de ayudas destinadas a la investigación • **recent government policies have squeezed welfare ~** las recientes medidas gubernamentales han reducido las prestaciones en materia de bienestar social
3 (= *arrangements*) **a** (*gen*) previsiones *fpl* • **to make ~ for sth/sb** hacer previsiones para algo/algn • **the government had made no ~ for the refugees** el gobierno no había hecho previsiones para los refugiados
b (= *financial arrangements*) provisiones *fpl* • **to make ~ for sth/sb:** • **you must make ~ for your old age** debes hacer provisiones para la vejez • **to make ~ for one's family** asegurar el porvenir de su familia • **she would find some way of making proper ~ for her baby** ya encontraría alguna manera de proveer para su bebé • **he has made financial ~ for his son's education** ha hecho provisiones económicas para la educación de su hijo • **the state makes ~ for people without alternative resources** el estado hace provisiones para la gente que no tiene otras fuentes de ingreso • **he made no ~ in his will for his only child Violet** no incluyó a su única hija, Violet, en el testamento
4 provisions (= *food*) provisiones *fpl*, víveres *mpl*
5 (= *stipulation*) estipulación *f*, disposición *f* • **under** *or* **according to the ~s of the treaty** en virtud de las estipulaciones *or* disposiciones del tratado • **there is no ~ for this in the rules** • **the rules make no ~ for this** las reglas no disponen en previsión de esto • **it comes within the ~s of this law** está comprendido dentro de lo estipulado por esta ley, está comprendido dentro de las estipulaciones *or* disposiciones de esta ley
6 (= *condition, proviso*) condición *f* • **with the ~ that** con la condición de que • **she approved, with one ~: that ...** dio su aprobación con una condición: que ...
(VT) aprovisionar, abastecer • **to be ~ed with sth** (*frm*) estar provisto de algo

provisional [prəˈvɪʒənl] (ADJ) provisional, provisorio (*LAm*)
(N) • **Provisional** (*Pol*) (*in Ireland*) Provisional *mf* (*miembro de la tendencia activista del IRA*) • **the Provisionals** el IRA provisional
(CPD) ▸ **provisional driving licence** (*Brit*) permiso *m* de conducción provisional (*Sp*), licencia *f* provisional (*esp LAm*); ▷ DRIVING LICENCE/DRIVER'S LICENSE ▸ **the Provisional IRA** el IRA provisional

provisionally [prəˈvɪʒnəlɪ] (ADV) provisionalmente

proviso [prəˈvaɪzəʊ] (N) (PL: **provisos** *or* **provisoes**) (*gen*) salvedad *f* • **with the ~ that ...** a condición de que ...

provisory [prəˈvaɪzərɪ] (ADJ) **1** (= *with a proviso*) condicional • **a ~ clause** una cláusula condicional
2 (= *provisional*) provisional, provisorio (*LAm*)

Provo* [ˈprəʊvəʊ] (N) = **provisional**

provocateur [prəˌvɒkəˈtɜːʳ] (N) provocador(a) *m/f*

provocation [ˌprɒvəˈkeɪʃən] (N) provocación *f* • **she acted under ~** reaccionó a una provocación • **to suffer great ~** sufrir una gran provocación

provocative [prəˈvɒkətɪv] (ADJ)
1 (= *inflammatory*) [*remark, behaviour*] provocador; [*act*] de provocación, provocador
2 (= *thought-provoking*) [*book, film*] sugestivo, que hace reflexionar; [*title*] sugestivo
3 (= *seductive*) [*person*] seductor; [*clothing, look, smile*] provocativo

provocatively [prəˈvɒkətɪvlɪ] (ADV)
1 (= *aggressively*) [*act, behave*] de modo provocador; [*say*] provocadoramente
2 (= *seductively*) [*dress, smile*] de forma provocativa

provoke [prəˈvəʊk] (VT) **1** (= *cause*) [+ *reaction, response*] provocar; [+ *violence*] provocar, causar; [+ *crisis*] causar
2 (= *rouse, move*) incitar, mover (**to a**) • **it ~d us to action** nos incitó a obrar • **it ~d the town to revolt** incitó la ciudad a sublevarse • **to ~ sb into doing sth** incitar a algn a hacer algo
3 (= *anger*) provocar, irritar • **he is easily ~d** se irrita por cualquier cosa, se le provoca fácilmente

provoking [prəˈvəʊkɪŋ] (ADJ) irritante • **how very ~!** ¡qué fastidio!

provokingly [prəˈvəʊkɪŋlɪ] (ADV) (= *provocatively*) de manera provocadora

provost [ˈprɒvəst] (N) (*Univ*) rector(a) *m/f*; (*Scot*) alcalde/esa *m/f*
(CPD) ▸ **provost marshal** capitán *m* preboste

prow [praʊ] (N) (*Naut*) proa *f*

prowess [ˈpraʊɪs] (N) **1** (= *skill*) habilidad *f*, capacidad *f*
2 (= *courage*) valor *m*

prowl [praʊl] (N) ronda *f* (en busca de presa, botín *etc*) • **to be on the ~** merodear, rondar
(VI) (*also* **prowl about** *or* **around**) rondar, merodear • **he ~s round the house at night** (*outside*) ronda la casa de noche; (*inside*) se pasea por la casa de noche
(VT) • **to ~ the streets** rondar las calles
(CPD) ▸ **prowl car** (*US*) (*Police*) coche-patrulla *m*

prowler [ˈpraʊləʳ] (N) merodeador(a) *m/f*

prox. (ABBR) (= **proximo**) pr.fr.

proximate [ˈprɒksɪmət] (ADJ) **1** (= *next*) inmediato • **~ cause** causa inmediata
2 (= *close, very near*) contiguo
3 (= *forthcoming, imminent*) inminente
4 (= *approximate*) aproximado • **~ estimate** cálculo aproximado • **~ analysis** (*Chem*) análisis aproximado

proximity [prɒkˈsɪmɪtɪ] (N) proximidad *f* • **in ~ to** cerca *or* en las cercanías de

proximo [ˈprɒksɪməʊ] (ADV) (*Comm*) del mes próximo • **before the 7th ~** antes del 7 del mes que viene

proxy [ˈprɒksɪ] (N) (= *power*) poder *m*; (= *person*) apoderado/a *m/f* • **by ~** por poderes • **to be married by ~** casarse por poderes
(CPD) ▸ **proxy vote** voto *m* por poderes

Prozac® [ˈprəʊzæk] (N) Prozac® *m*

PRP (N ABBR) (*Brit*) **1** (= **performance-related pay**) *sistema salarial que incluye un plus de productividad*
2 (= **profit-related pay**) *sistema salarial en el que los empleados reciben un porcentaje de los beneficios de la empresa*

PRS (N ABBR) (= **Performing Rights Society**) *sociedad de derechos de autor*, ≈ SGAE *f*

prude [pruːd] (N) gazmoño/a *m/f*, mojigato/a *m/f*

prudence [ˈpruːdəns] (N) prudencia *f*

prudent [ˈpruːdənt] (ADJ) cauteloso, prudente

prudential [prʊˈdenʃəl] (ADJ) prudencial

prudently [ˈpruːdəntlɪ] (ADV) prudentemente, con prudencia

prudery [ˈpruːdərɪ] (N) mojigatería *f*, remilgo *m*

prudish [ˈpruːdɪʃ] (ADJ) mojigato, remilgado

prudishly [ˈpruːdɪʃlɪ] (ADV) [*say, behave*] de manera mojigata; [*dress*] pudorosamente

prudishness [ˈpruːdɪʃnɪs] (N) = **prudery**

prune¹ [pruːn] (N) **1** (= *fruit*) ciruela *f* pasa
2* (= *person*) bobo/a *m/f*, majadero/a* *m/f*

prune² [pruːn] (VT) [+ *tree, branches*] podar; (*fig*) reducir, recortar
▸ **prune away** (VT + ADV) [+ *branches*] podar; (*fig*) [+ *words*] cortar
▸ **prune back** (VT + ADV) [+ *plant*] podar

pruners [ˈpruːnəz] (NPL) podadera *fsing*, tijeras *fpl* de podar

pruning [ˈpruːnɪŋ] (N) [*of tree, branches*] poda *f*
(CPD) ▸ **pruning hook, pruning knife, pruning shears** podadera *f*

prurience [ˈprʊərɪəns] (N) salacidad *f*, lascivia *f*

prurient [ˈprʊərɪənt] (ADJ) salaz, lascivo

Prussia [ˈprʌʃə] (N) Prusia *f*

Prussian [ˈprʌʃən] (ADJ) prusiano
(N) prusiano/a *m/f*
(CPD) ▸ **Prussian blue** azul *m* de Prusia

prussic acid [ˌprʌsɪkˈæsɪd] (N) ácido *m* prúsico

pry¹ [praɪ] (VI) (= *snoop*) fisgonear, curiosear; (= *spy*) atisbar • **to pry into sb's affairs** (entro)meterse en los asuntos de algn • **to pry into sb's secrets** curiosear en los secretos de algn

pry² [praɪ] (VT) (*US*) = **prise**

prying [ˈpraɪɪŋ] (ADJ) (= *nosy*) fisgón; (= *meddling*) entrometido

PS (N ABBR) **1** (= **postscript**) P.D.
2 = **private secretary**

psalm [sɑːm] (N) salmo *m*

psalmist [ˈsɑːmɪst] (N) salmista *m*

psalmody [ˈsælmədɪ] (N) salmodia *f*

psalter [ˈsɔːltəʳ] (N) salterio *m*

PSAT (N ABBR) (*US*) = **Preliminary Scholastic Aptitude Test**

PSBR (N ABBR) (*Econ*) (= **public sector borrowing requirement**) *necesidades de endeudamiento del sector público*

psephologist [seˈfɒlədʒɪst] (N) psefólogo/a *m/f*

psephology [seˈfɒlədʒɪ] (N) psefología *f*

pseud* [sjuːd] (N) (*Brit*) farsante *mf*

pseudo* [ˈsjuːdəʊ] (ADJ) farsante, fraudulento; [*person*] fingido; (*person's character*) artificial, afectado

pseudo... [ˈsjuːdəʊ] (PREFIX) seudo... • **a pseudo-artist** un seudo artista

pseudonym [ˈsjuːdənɪm] (N) seudónimo *m*

pseudonymous [sjuːˈdɒnɪməs] (ADJ) seudónimo

pshaw† [pʃɔː] (EXCL) ¡bah!

PSHE (N ABBR) (*Brit*) (*Scol*) (= **personal, social and health education**) *formación social y sanitaria*

psi¹ (ABBR) (= **pounds per square inch**) ≈ kg/cm²

psi² [saɪ] (NPL) (= *psychic phenomena*) fenómenos *mpl* paranormales

psittacosis [ˌsɪtəˈkəʊsɪs] (N) psitacosis *f*

PSNI (N ABBR) (= **Police Service of Northern Ireland**) *servicio de policía de Irlanda del Norte*

psoriasis [səˈraɪəsɪs] (N) soriasis *f*

psst [pst] (EXCL) ¡oye!, ¡eh!

PST (N ABBR) (*US*) = **Pacific Standard Time**

PSV (N ABBR) (= **public service vehicle**) vehículo *m* de servicio público

psych* [saɪk] (VT) **1** (= *make uneasy*) (*also* **psych out**) poner nervioso • **that doesn't ~ me** no me da ni frío ni calor, me tiene sin cuidado
2 (= *prepare psychologically*) (*also* **psych up**) mentalizar
3 (= *guess, anticipate*) [+ *reactions etc*] adivinar, anticipar
▸ **psych out*** (VT + ADV) **1** (= *make uneasy*) poner nervioso
2 (*US*) (= *analyse, work out*) [+ *person*] calar* • **I ~ed it all out for myself** me di cuenta de

P

por dónde iban los tiros*
▸ **psych up*** (VT + ADV) • **to get o.s. ~ed up for sth** mentalizarse para algo • **he was all ~ed up to start, when ...** ya estaba mentalizado para empezar, cuando ...
psych... [saɪk] (PREFIX) psic..., psiqu..., sic..., siqu...
Psyche ['saɪkɪ] (N) Psique *f*
psyche ['saɪkɪ] (N) (*Psych*) psique *f*, psiquis *f*
psychedelic [,saɪkə'delɪk] (ADJ) psicodélico
psychiatric [,saɪkɪ'ætrɪk] (ADJ) psiquiátrico
psychiatrist [saɪ'kaɪətrɪst] (N) psiquiatra *mf*
psychiatry [saɪ'kaɪətrɪ] (N) psiquiatría *f*
psychic ['saɪkɪk] (ADJ) (*also* **psychical**)
1 (= *supernatural*) psíquico
2 (= *telepathic*) telepático • **you must be ~!*** ¿cómo lo adivinaste? • **I'm not ~!*** ¡no soy adivino!*
3 (*Psych*) psíquico
(N) (= *person*) vidente *mf*
psychical ['saɪkɪkəl] (ADJ) = **psychic**
psycho* ['saɪkəʊ] (N) psicópata *mf*
psycho... ['saɪkəʊ] (PREFIX) psico...
psychoactive [,saɪkəʊ'æktɪv] (ADJ) • **~ drug** droga *f* psicoactiva
psychoanalyse, psychoanalyze (*US*) [,saɪkəʊ'ænəlaɪz] (VT) psicoanalizar
psychoanalysis [,saɪkəʊə'nælɪsɪs] (N) psicoanálisis *m*
psychoanalyst [,saɪkəʊ'ænəlɪst] (N) psicoanalista *mf*
psychoanalytic [,saɪkəʊænə'lɪtɪk] (ADJ) psicoanalítico
psychoanalytical [,saɪkəʊænə'lɪtɪkəl] (ADJ) = **psychoanalytic**
psychoanalyze [,saɪkəʊ'ænəlaɪz] (VT) (*US*) = **psychoanalyse**
psychobabble* ['saɪkəʊ,bæbl] (N) verborrea *f*, jerga *f* de psicólogos
psychodrama ['saɪkəʊ,drɑːmə] (N) psicodrama *m*
psychodynamic [,saɪkəʊdaɪ'næmɪk] (ADJ) psicodinámico
psychodynamics [,saikəʊdaɪ'næmiks] (NSING) psicodinámica *f*
psychogenic [,saɪkəʊ'dʒenɪk] (ADJ) [*disease, complaint*] psicogénico
psychokinesis [,saɪkəʊkɪ'niːsɪs] (N) psicoquinesis *f*
psychokinetic [,saɪkəʊkɪ'netɪk] (ADJ) psicoquinético
psycholinguistic [,saɪkəʊlɪŋ'gwɪstɪk] (ADJ) psicolingüístico
psycholinguistics [,saɪkəʊlɪŋ'gwɪstɪks] (NSING) psicolingüística *f*
psychological [,saɪkə'lɒdʒɪkəl] (ADJ) psicológico • **it's only ~*** son cosas de la imaginación*
(CPD) ▸ **psychological block** bloqueo *m* psicológico ▸ **psychological make-up** perfil *m* psicológico ▸ **psychological moment** momento *m* psicológico ▸ **psychological profile** perfil *m* psicológico ▸ **psychological profiling** trazado *m* del perfil psicológico ▸ **psychological warfare** guerra *f* psicológica
psychologically [,saɪkə'lɒdʒɪkəlɪ] (ADV) psicológicamente
psychologist [saɪ'kɒlədʒɪst] (N) psicólogo/a *m/f*
psychology [saɪ'kɒlədʒɪ] (N) psicología *f*
psychometric ['saɪkəʊ'metrɪk] (ADJ) psicométrico
(CPD) ▸ **psychometric test** test *m* psicométrico ▸ **psychometric testing** tests *mpl* psicométricos
psychometrics ['saɪkəʊ'metrɪks] (NSING) psicometría *f*
psychometry [saɪ'kɒmɪtrɪ] (N) psicometría *f*
psychomotor ['saɪkəʊ'məʊtəʳ] (ADJ) psicomotor
psychoneurosis ['saɪkəʊnjʊə'rəʊsɪs] (N) (PL: **psychoneuroses** ['saɪkəʊnjʊə'rəʊsiːz]) psiconeurosis *f inv*
psychopath ['saɪkəʊpæθ] (N) psicópata *mf*
psychopathic [,saɪkəʊ'pæθɪk] (ADJ) psicopático
psychopathology ['saɪkəʊpə'θɒlədʒɪ] (N) psicopatología *f*
psychopathy [saɪ'kɒpəθɪ] (N) (= *Med*) psicopatía *f*
psychosexual [,saɪkəʊ'seksjʊəl] (ADJ) psicosexual
psychosis [saɪ'kəʊsɪs] (N) (PL: **psychoses** [saɪ'kəʊsiːz]) psicosis *f inv*
psychosocial ['saɪkəʊ'səʊʃəl] (ADJ) psicosocial
psychosociological ['saɪkəʊ,səʊsɪə'lɒdʒɪkəl] (ADJ) psicosociológico
psychosomatic ['saɪkəʊsəʊ'mætɪk] (ADJ) psicosomático
psychosurgery [,saɪkəʊ'sɜːdʒərɪ] (N) psicocirugía *f*
psychotherapeutic [,saɪkəʊ,θerə'pjuːtɪk] (ADJ) psicoterapéutico
psychotherapist [,saɪkəʊ'θerəpɪst] (N) psicoterapeuta *mf*
psychotherapy [,saɪkəʊ'θerəpɪ] (N) psicoterapia *f*
psychotic [saɪ'kɒtɪk] (ADJ) psicótico
(N) psicótico/a *m/f*
psychotropic [,saɪkəʊ'trɒpɪk] (ADJ) psicotrópico
PT† (N ABBR) (= **physical training**) gimnasia *f*, cultura *f* física
Pt (ABBR) (*Geog*) (= **Point**) Pta.
pt (ABBR) 1 = **part**
2 = **pint(s)**
3 = **point**
4 (*Comm*) = **payment**
P/T (ABBR) = **part-time**
PTA (N ABBR) 1 (= **Parent-Teacher Association**) ≈ APA *f*
2 (*Brit*) (= **Prevention of Terrorism Act**) *ley antiterrorista*
ptarmigan ['tɑːmɪgən] (N) (PL: **ptarmigans** *or* **ptarmigan**) perdiz *f* blanca
Pte (ABBR) (*Mil*) = **Private**
pterodactyl [,terəʊ'dæktɪl] (N) pterodáctilo *m*
PTO (ABBR) (= **please turn over**) sigue
Ptolemaic [,tɒlə'meɪɪk] (ADJ) • **~ system** sistema *m* de Tolomeo, sistema *m* tolemaico
Ptolemy ['tɒləmɪ] (N) Tolomeo
ptomaine ['təʊmeɪn] (N) (p)tomaína *f*
(CPD) ▸ **ptomaine poisoning** envenenamiento *m* (p)tomaínico
PTSD (N ABBR) = **post-traumatic stress disorder**
PTV (N ABBR) (*US*) 1 = **pay television**
2 = **public television**
pub [pʌb] (*Brit*) (N) pub *m*, bar *m*
(CPD) ▸ **pub crawl** • **to go on a pub crawl*** ir de chateo *or* de parranda (de bar en bar)*
▸ **pub lunch** comida *m* en un bar • **to go for a pub lunch** ir a comer a un bar ▸ **pub quiz** *concurso de preguntas y respuestas que se juega en un pub*
pub. (ABBR) = **published**
pube* [pjuːb] (N) (= *pubic hair*) pendejo* *m*
puberty ['pjuːbətɪ] (N) pubertad *f*
pubes‡ ['pjuːbiːz] (NPL) vello *m* púbico
pubescence [pjuː'besns] (N) pubescencia *f*
pubescent [pjuː'besnt] (ADJ) pubescente
(N) pubescente *mf*
pubic ['pjuːbɪk] (ADJ) púbico
(CPD) ▸ **pubic hair** vello *m* púbico
pubis ['pjuːbɪs] (N) (PL: **pubes**) pubis *m inv*
public ['pʌblɪk] (ADJ) 1 (= *of the State*) público • **they can hire expensive lawyers at ~ expense** pueden contratar abogados caros a costa de los contribuyentes • **to run for/hold ~ office** presentarse como candidato a/ostentar un cargo público • **the ~ purse** el erario público
2 (= *of, for, by everyone*) público • **they want to deflect ~ attention from the real issues** quieren desviar la opinión pública de los verdaderos problemas • **to be in the ~ eye** ser objeto del interés público • **he has kept his family out of the ~ eye** ha mantenido a su familia alejada de la atención pública • **I have decided to resign in the ~ interest** en el interés de los ciudadanos, he decidido dimitir • **in a bid to gain ~ support** en un intento de hacerse con el apoyo de la gente • IDIOM: • **~ enemy number one** enemigo *m* público número uno
3 (= *open, not private*) [*statement, meeting*] público; [*appearance*] en público • **it's too ~ here** aquí estamos demasiado expuestos al público, aquí no tenemos intimidad • **can we talk somewhere less ~?** ¿podemos hablar en algún sitio más privado *or* menos expuesto al público? • **to become ~** [*news, fact*] hacerse público • **to be in the ~ domain** (= *not secret*) ser de dominio público • **to go ~** (*Comm*) empezar a cotizar en bolsa • **they decided to go ~ about their relationship*** decidieron revelar su relación a la prensa *or* al público • **it is ~ knowledge** ya es de dominio público • **to retire from ~ life** retirarse de la vida pública • **to lead an active ~ life** llevar una vida pública activa • **to make sth ~** hacer público algo, publicar algo
4 (= *well-known*) • **a ~ figure** un personaje público
(N) 1 (= *people*) • **the ~** el público • **the house is open to the ~** la casa está abierta al público • **the general ~** el gran público • **a member of the ~** un ciudadano
2 (= *open place*) • **in ~** en público
3 (= *devotees*) público *m* • **she couldn't disappoint her ~** no podía decepcionar a su público • **the reading/sporting ~** los aficionados a la lectura/al deporte • **the viewing ~** los telespectadores
(CPD) ▸ **public access television** (*US*) *televisión abierta al público* ▸ **public address system** (sistema *m* de) megafonía *f*, altavoces *mpl*, altoparlantes *mpl* (*LAm*) ▸ **public affairs** actividades *fpl* públicas ▸ **public assistance** (*US*) asistencia *f* pública • **to be on ~ assistance** recibir asistencia pública ▸ **public bar** bar *m* ▸ **public body** organismo *m* público ▸ **public company** empresa *f* pública ▸ **public convenience** (*Brit*) (*frm*) servicios *mpl*, aseos *mpl* públicos ▸ **public debt** deuda *f* pública, deuda *f* del Estado ▸ **public defender** (*US*) defensor(a) *m/f* de oficio ▸ **public enemy** enemigo *m* público • IDIOM: • **to be Public Enemy No 1** *or* **number one** ser el enemigo público número uno ▸ **public enquiry** (*Brit*) = **public inquiry** ▸ **public expenditure** gasto *m* (del sector) público ▸ **public gallery** (*in parliament, courtroom*) tribuna *f* reservada al público ▸ **public health** salud *f* pública, sanidad *f* pública ▸ **public health inspector** inspector(a) *m/f* de salud *or* sanidad pública ▸ **Public Health Service** (*US*) ≈ Seguridad *f* Social, *servicio público de asistencia sanitaria* ▸ **public holiday** fiesta *f* nacional, fiesta *f* oficial, (día *m*) feriado *m* (*LAm*) ▸ **public house** (*Brit*) (*frm*) bar *m* ▸ **public housing** (*US*) viviendas *mpl* de protección oficial ▸ **public housing project** (*US*) proyecto *f* de viviendas de protección oficial ▸ **public**

inquiry investigación *f* oficial ▸ **public lavatory** aseos *mpl* públicos ▸ **public law** (= *discipline, body of legislation*) derecho *m* público; (*US*) (= *piece of legislation*) ley *f* pública ▸ **public library** biblioteca *f* pública ▸ **public limited company** sociedad *f* anónima ▸ **public money** fondos *mpl* públicos ▸ **public nuisance** (*Jur*) molestia *f* pública • **he's a ~ nuisance** siempre está causando problemas *or* molestias • **to cause a ~ nuisance** alterar el orden público ▸ **public opinion** opinión *f* pública ▸ **public opinion poll** sondeo *m* (de la opinión pública) ▸ **public ownership** • **to be taken into ~ ownership** pasar a ser propiedad del estado ▸ **public property** (= *land, buildings*) dominio *m* público; (*fig*) • **he couldn't handle being ~ property** no podía soportar ser un personaje público • **his private life is ~ property** su vida privada es de dominio público ▸ **public prosecutor** fiscal *mf* • **the Public Prosecutor's Office** la fiscalía; ▹ ATTORNEY ▸ **Public Record Office** (*Brit*) archivo *m* nacional ▸ **public relations** relaciones *fpl* públicas • **the police action was a ~ relations disaster** la actuación de la policía fue desastrosa para su imagen • **it's just a ~ relations exercise** es solo una operación publicitaria *or* de relaciones públicas ▸ **public relations officer** encargado/a *m/f* de relaciones públicas ▸ **public school** (*Brit*) colegio *m* privado; (= *boarding school*) internado *m* privado; (*US*) escuela *f* pública ▸ **the public sector** el sector público • **60,000 ~-sector jobs must be cut** se deben eliminar 60.000 puestos de funcionario, se deben eliminar 60.000 puestos en el sector público ▸ **public sector borrowing requirement** necesidades *fpl* de endeudamiento del sector público ▸ **public servant** funcionario/a *m/f* ▸ **public service** (= *Civil Service*) administración *f* pública; (*usu pl*) (= *community facility*) servicio *m* público • **she will be remembered for a lifetime of ~ service** se la recordará por cómo entregó su vida al servicio de la comunidad • **in doing this they were performing a ~ service** con esto estaban haciendo un servicio a la comunidad • **~ service announcement** comunicado *m* de interés público • **~ service jobs** puestos *mpl* de funcionario *or* en el sector público • **~ service vehicle** vehículo *m* de servicio público • **~ service worker** funcionario/a *m/f* ▸ **public service broadcasting** servicio *m* público de radio y televisión ▸ **public speaker** orador(a) *m/f* • **she is a good ~ speaker** habla muy bien en público, es una buena oradora ▸ **public speaking** oratoria *f* ▸ **public spending** gasto *m* (del sector) público ▸ **public television** (*US*) cadenas *fpl* públicas (de televisión) ▸ **public transport, public transportation** (*US*) transporte(s) *m(pl)* público(s) • **to ban smoking on ~ transport** prohibir fumar en los medios de transporte público ▸ **public utility** empresa *f* del servicio público ▸ **public works** obras *fpl* públicas

PUBLIC ACCESS TELEVISION

En Estados Unidos, el término **Public Access Television** hace referencia a una serie de cadenas no comerciales de televisión por cable que emiten programas de ámbito local o programas dedicados a organizaciones humanitarias sin ánimo de lucro. Entre sus emisiones se incluyen charlas sobre actividades escolares, programas sobre aficiones diversas e incluso discursos de organizaciones racistas. Estas emisiones de acceso público se crearon para dar cabida a temas de interés local e impedir que los canales por cable estuvieran dominados por unos cuantos privilegiados. En virtud de la Ley de Emisiones por Cable, el **Cable Act** de 1984, cualquier población en que haya algún canal por cable puede obligar a los propietarios de dicho canal a que instalen una cadena adicional de acceso público y provean el equipo, el estudio, los medios técnicos y el personal necesarios para la emisión.

publican [ˈpʌblɪkən] (N) **1** (*Brit*) dueño/a *m/f* *or* encargado/a *m/f* de un pub *or* bar
2 (*Bible*) publicano *m*

publication [ˌpʌblɪˈkeɪʃən] (N) (= *act*) publicación *f*, edición *f*; (= *published work*) publicación *f* • **this is not for ~** esto no está destinado a la publicación
(CPD) ▸ **publication date** fecha *f* de publicación ▸ **publication details** detalles *mpl* de publicación

publicist [ˈpʌblɪsɪst] (N) publicista *mf*

publicity [pʌbˈlɪsɪtɪ] (N) **1** publicidad *f*
2 (*Comm*) (= *advertising, advertisements*) publicidad *f*, propaganda *f*
(CPD) ▸ **publicity agent** agente *mf* de publicidad ▸ **publicity campaign** campaña *f* publicitaria ▸ **publicity manager** director(a) *m/f* de publicidad ▸ **publicity officer** directivo/a *m/f* de publicidad ▸ **publicity stunt** truco *m* publicitario

publicity-seeking [pʌbˈlɪsɪtɪˌsiːkɪŋ] (ADJ) [*stunt, ruse*] publicitario; [*person*] con motivos publicitarios
(N) • **she accused the lawyers of publicity-seeking** acusó a los abogados de albergar motivos publicitarios

publicity-shy [pʌbˈlɪsɪtɪʃaɪ] (ADJ) reacio a la publicidad

publicize [ˈpʌblɪsaɪz] (VT) **1** (= *make public*) publicar, divulgar
2 (= *advertise*) anunciar, hacer propaganda de

publicly [ˈpʌblɪklɪ] (ADV) [*acknowledge, criticize, accuse*] públicamente, en público; [*announce, state, humiliate*] públicamente; [*funded*] con fondos públicos • **land and buildings that are ~ owned** tierras *fpl* y edificios *mpl* que son propiedad pública *or* del Estado • **this information should be made ~ available** esta información se debería hacer pública

public-spirited [ˈpʌblɪkˈspɪrɪtɪd] (ADJ) [*act*] de espíritu cívico, solidario; [*person*] lleno de civismo, consciente del bien público

publish [ˈpʌblɪʃ] (VT) **1** [*newspaper*] [+ *article, photograph*] publicar; [*publisher*] [+ *book*] publicar, editar; [*publisher*] [+ *author*] publicar las obras de; [*author*] [+ *book*] publicar • **"published weekly"** "semanario"
2 (= *make public*) [+ *list, information*] divulgar, hacer público

publisher [ˈpʌblɪʃəʳ] (N) (= *person*) editor(a) *m/f*; (= *firm*) editorial *f*

publishing [ˈpʌblɪʃɪŋ] (N) (= *trade*) industria *f* editorial • **he's in ~** publica libros, está con una casa editorial
(CPD) ▸ **publishing company, publishing house** (casa *f*) editorial *f*

puce [pjuːs] (N) color *m* castaño rojizo
(ADJ) de color castaño rojizo; (*with shame etc*) colorado

puck¹ [pʌk] (N) (= *imp*) duende *m* (malicioso)

puck² [pʌk] (N) (*Sport*) puck *m*, disco *m*

pucker [ˈpʌkəʳ] (N) arruga *f*; (*Sew*) frunce *m*, fruncido *m*; (*accidentally formed*) buche *m*
(VT) (*also* **pucker up**) arrugar; [+ *brow, material*] fruncir
(VI) (*also* **pucker up**) arrugarse, formar buches

puckered [ˈpʌkəd] (ADJ) [*lips, brow, seam*] fruncido; [*skin*] arrugado

puckish [ˈpʌkɪʃ] (ADJ) malicioso, juguetón

pud* [pʊd] (N) (*Brit*) = **pudding**

pudding [ˈpʊdɪŋ] (N) (= *steamed pudding*) pudín *m*, budín *m*; (*Brit*) (= *dessert*) postre *m*; ▹ **black**
(CPD) ▸ **pudding basin** (*Brit*) cuenco *m* ▸ **pudding rice** arroz *m* redondo

puddingstone [ˈpʊdɪŋstəʊn] (N) (*Geol*) pudinga *f*

puddle [ˈpʌdl] (N) charco *m*
(VT) (*Tech*) pudelar

pudenda [pjuːˈdendə] (NPL) (*frm*) partes *fpl* pudendas

pudgy [ˈpʌdʒɪ] (ADJ) (COMPAR: **pudgier**, SUPERL: **pudgiest**) = **podgy**

pueblo [ˈpwebləʊ] (N) **1** (= *American Indian settlement*) poblado *m*
2 (= *town in Spanish-speaking America*) pueblo *m*

puerile [ˈpjʊəraɪl] (ADJ) pueril

puerility [pjʊəˈrɪlɪtɪ] (N) puerilidad *f*

puerperal [pjʊ(ː)ˈɜːpərəl] (ADJ) puerperal
(CPD) ▸ **puerperal fever** fiebre *f* puerperal ▸ **puerperal psychosis** psicosis *f inv* puerperal

Puerto Rican [ˈpwɜːtəʊˈriːkən] (ADJ) puertorriqueño
(N) puertorriqueño/a *m/f*

Puerto Rico [ˈpwɜːtəʊˈriːkəʊ] (N) Puerto Rico *m*

puff [pʌf] (N) **1** [*of breathing, engine*] resoplido *m*; [*of air*] soplo *m*; [*of wind*] racha *f*, ráfaga *f*; [*of smoke*] bocanada *f*; (*on cigarette, pipe*) chupada *f* • **I'm out of ~*** estoy sin aliento
2 (= *powder puff*) borla *f*
3 (*Culin*) • **cream ~** petisú *m*, pastel *m* de crema
4* (= *advert*) bombo* *m*
5 (*Drugs‡*) canabis *m*
(VT) **1** (= *blow*) soplar; [+ *pipe etc*] chupar • **to ~ smoke** echar bocanadas de humo • **to ~ smoke in sb's face** echar humo a la cara de algn
2 (*also* **puff up**) (= *inflate*) hinchar, inflar (*LAm*)
(VI) **1** (= *breathe heavily*) jadear, resoplar • **to ~ (away) at** *or* **on one's pipe** chupar la pipa
2 • **the train ~ed into/out of the station** el tren entró en/salió de la estación echando humo
(CPD) ▸ **puff adder** víbora *f* puff ▸ **puff paste** (*US*) = **puff pastry** ▸ **puff pastry** hojaldre *m* ▸ **puff sleeves** mangas *fpl* filipinas

▸ **puff along** (VI + ADV) [*train*] avanzar bufando; [*person*] correr jadeando

▸ **puff away** (VI + ADV) ▹ **puff**

▸ **puff out** (VT + ADV) **1** [+ *smoke etc*] echar, arrojar, despedir
2 [+ *cheeks, chest, sails*] hinchar, inflar (*LAm*); [+ *feathers*] erizar

▸ **puff up** (VT + ADV) **1** (= *inflate*) [+ *tyre etc*] hinchar, inflar (*LAm*)
2 = **puff out**
3* (*fig*) dar bombo a • **to ~ o.s. up** darse bombo, engreírse
(VI + ADV) hincharse

puffa jacket [ˈpʌfəˌdʒækɪt] (N) plumón *m*

puffball [ˈpʌfbɔːl] (N) bejín *m*, pedo *m* de lobo

puffed [pʌft] (ADJ) **1** (*also* **puffed up**) [*eye*] hinchado • **his face was all ~ (up)** tenía la cara hinchada • **to be ~ up with pride** (*fig*) hincharse de orgullo
2 • **I'm ~ (out)*** (= *out of breath*) me quedé sin aliento

P

puffer* [ˈpʌfəʳ] (N) locomotora *f*
puffin [ˈpʌfɪn] (N) frailecillo *m*
puffiness [ˈpʌfɪnɪs] (N) hinchazón *f*
puffy [ˈpʌfɪ] (ADJ) (COMPAR: **puffier**, SUPERL: **puffiest**) *[eye etc]* hinchado
pug [pʌg] (N) *(also* **pug dog**) doguillo *m*
(CPD) ▸ **pug nose** nariz *f* chata; ▹ **pug-nosed**
pugilism [ˈpjuːdʒɪlɪzəm] (N) pugilato *m*, pugilismo *m*
pugilist [ˈpjuːdʒɪlɪst] (N) púgil *m*, pugilista *m*
pugnacious [pʌgˈneɪʃəs] (ADJ) pugnaz, agresivo
pugnaciously [pʌgˈneɪʃəslɪ] (ADV) con pugnacidad, agresivamente
pugnacity [pʌgˈnæsɪtɪ] (N) pugnacidad *f*, agresividad *f*
pug-nosed [ˈpʌgˈnəʊzd] (ADJ) de nariz chata
puke‡ [pjuːk] (N) **1** (= *vomited matter*) vómito *m*
2 • **to have a ~** ▹ VI
(VI) *(also* **puke up**) devolver • **it makes me (want to) ~** *(fig)* me da asco
(VT) *(also* **puke up**) devolver*, vomitar
pukey‡ [ˈpjuːkɪ] (ADJ) *[colour]* de vómito
pukka* [ˈpʌkə] (ADJ) *(Brit)* (= *real*) auténtico, genuino; (= *posh*) esnob, elegante, lujoso
pulchritude [ˈpʌlkrɪtjuːd] (N) *(frm, liter)* belleza *f*
pulchritudinous [ˌpʌlkrɪˈtjuːdɪnəs] (ADJ) *(frm or liter)* bello

PULITZER
Los premios **Pulitzer** se conceden anualmente en Estados Unidos a trabajos periodísticos, literarios y musicales excepcionales, y gozan de un enorme prestigio. En periodismo se conceden trece premios, entre ellos los destinados al periodismo de investigación y crítica. En literatura existen seis categorías, entre las que destacan las de novela, poesía y teatro. Los premios llevan el nombre del editor periodístico norteamericano **Joseph Pulitzer** (1847-1911), quien inicialmente aportó el dinero de los premios.

pull [pʊl] (N) **1** (= *tug*) tirón *m*, jalón *m* *(LAm)*; *(with oar etc)* golpe *m* • **give the rope a ~** tira de la cuerda • **suddenly it gave a ~** de repente dio un tirón
2 *[of moon, magnet, sea etc]* (fuerza *f* de) atracción *f*; *[of current]* fuerza *f*, ímpetu *m*; *(fig)* (= *attraction*) atracción *f* • **the ~ of the south** la atracción del Sur, lo atractivo del Sur
3* (= *influence*) enchufe* *m*, palanca *f* *(LAm*)*; (= *advantage*) ventaja *f* • **he has ~ in the right places** tiene influencia donde hace falta • **they have a ~ over us now** ahora nos llevan ventaja • **he has a slight ~** tiene una pequeña ventaja
4 *(at pipe, cigarette)* chupada *f*; *(at drink)* trago *m* • **he took a ~ at his pipe** le dio una chupada a la pipa • **he took a ~ from the bottle** tomó un trago de la botella, dio un tiento a la botella *(Sp)*
5 (= *journey, drive etc*) • **it was a long ~** fue mucho camino *or* trecho • **we had a long ~ up the hill** nos costó mucho trabajo subir la cuesta
6 (= *handle of drawer etc*) tirador *m*; *[of bell]* cuerda *f*
7 *(Typ)* primeras pruebas *fpl*
8 *(Brit*)* • **to be on the ~** estar de ligue *(Sp*)*, estar chequeando *(LAm*)*
(VT) **1** (= *draw, drag*) tirar de, jalar *(LAm)* • **to ~ a door shut/open** cerrar/abrir una puerta de un tirón *or* *(LAm)* jalón • **the engine ~s six coaches** la locomotora arrastra seis vagones • **~ your chair over** acerca la silla • **his ideas ~ed me the same way** sus ideas me llevaron por el mismo camino; ▹ **punch, weight**
2 (= *tug*) tirar de, jalar *(LAm)*; *[+ trigger]* apretar; *[+ oar]* tirar de; *[+ boat]* remar; *(Naut)* *[+ rope]* halar, jalar; *[+ tooth]* sacar; *[+ weeds]* arrancar • **to ~ sb's hair** tirar *or* *(LAm)* jalar de los pelos a algn • IDIOM: • **~ the other one (it's got bells on)!**‡ ¡cuéntaselo a tu abuela!*; ▹ **leg**
3 (= *extract, draw out*) sacar, arrancar; *[+ beer]* servir • **to ~ a gun on sb** amenazar a algn con una pistola; ▹ **rank**
4 (= *injure*) • **to ~ a muscle** sufrir un tirón en un músculo
5 *[+ ball]* *(at golf etc)* golpear oblicuamente (a la izquierda)
6 *(Typ)* imprimir
7* (= *cancel*) *[+ TV programme]* suspender
8* (= *carry out, do*) • **what are you trying to ~?** ¿qué quieres conseguir?, ¿qué es lo que pretendes con esto? • **to ~ a fast one** *or* **a trick on sb** jugar una mala pasada a algn
9* (= *attract*) • **this will really ~ the punters** esto seguramente atraerá clientela • **he knows how to ~ the birds** *(Brit)* sabe ligar con las chicas*
(VI) **1** tirar, jalar *(LAm)* • **to ~ at** *or* **on a rope** tirar de una cuerda • **the car is ~ing to the right** el coche tira hacia la derecha • **the car isn't ~ing very well** el coche no tira
2 • **to ~ at** *or* **on one's pipe** dar chupadas a la pipa • **to ~ at a bottle** tomar un trago *or* *(Sp)* dar un tiento a una botella
3 (= *move*) *[vehicle]* ir; *[oarsmen etc]* remar • **he ~ed sharply to one side to avoid the lorry** torció bruscamente a un lado para no chocar con el camión • **the car ~ed slowly up the hill** el coche subía despacio la cuesta • **the train ~ed into the station** el tren entró en la estación • **he ~ed alongside the kerb** se acercó al bordillo • **it ~ed to a stop** se paró • **we ~ed for the shore** remamos hacia la orilla
4 *(Brit*)* ligar*, pillar (cacho) *(Sp‡)*
(CPD) ▸ **pull ring, pull tab** anilla *f*
▸ **pull about** (VT + ADV) (= *handle roughly*) maltratar, manosear
▸ **pull ahead** (VI + ADV) *(in race etc)* tomar la delantera; *(in poll, contest)* ponerse por delante • **to ~ ahead of sth/sb** *(in race etc)* tomar la delantera a algo/algn, dejar atrás algo/a algn; *(in poll, contest)* ponerse por delante de algo/algn
▸ **pull along** (VT + ADV) arrastrar • **to ~ o.s. along** arrastrarse
▸ **pull apart** (VT + ADV) **1** (= *separate*) separar; (= *take apart*) desmontar
2 *(fig*)* (= *search thoroughly*) registrar de arriba abajo, revolver
3 *(fig*)* (= *criticize*) deshacer, hacer pedazos
(VI + ADV) • **they ~ apart easily** se separan fácilmente
▸ **pull away** (VT + ADV) arrancar, quitar
(VI + ADV) **1** *[vehicle]* (= *move off*) salir, arrancar • **he soon ~ed away from the others** *(in race)* pronto dejó atrás a los demás
2 (= *draw back*) • **to ~ away from sb** apartarse bruscamente de algn
3 • **to ~ away at the oars** tirar (enérgicamente) de los remos
▸ **pull back** (VT + ADV) **1** *[+ lever etc]* tirar hacia sí; *[+ curtains]* descorrer
2 *(Sport*)* • **to ~ one back** remontar un gol
(VI + ADV) **1** (= *refrain*) contenerse
2 *(Mil)* (= *withdraw*) retirarse
▸ **pull down** (VT + ADV) **1** (= *lower*) *[+ blinds etc]* bajar • **he ~ed his hat down** se caló el sombrero, se encasquetó el sombrero*
2 (= *cause to fall*) *[+ person]* hacer caer, tumbar
3 (= *demolish*) derribar, demoler; *(fig)* *[+ government]* derribar
4 (= *weaken*) debilitar • **the mark in chemistry ~s her down** la nota de química es la que la perjudica *or* la que le baja la media
5 *(US*)* (= *earn*) ganar
▸ **pull in** (VT + ADV) **1** *[+ claws]* retraer; *[+ net]* recoger; *[+ rope]* cobrar
2 (= *rein in*) *[+ horse]* sujetar
3* (= *attract*) *[+ crowds]* atraer • **the film is ~ing them in** la película atrae un público numeroso, la película es muy popular • **this will ~ them in** esto les hará venir en masa
4* (= *take into custody*) detener
5* (= *earn*) ganar
(VI + ADV) (= *enter*) *(into station, harbour)* llegar; *(into driveway)* entrar; (= *stop, park*) parar
▸ **pull off** (VT + ADV) **1** (= *remove*) quitar, arrancar; *[+ clothes]* quitarse (de prisa)
2* (= *cause to succeed*) *[+ plan etc]* llevar a cabo, conseguir; *[+ deal]* cerrar, concluir con éxito • **to ~ it off** lograrlo
(VI + ADV) • **we ~ed off into a lay-by** *(Aut)* salimos de la carretera y paramos en un apartadero
(VT + PREP) • **the buses were ~ed off the road at once** en seguida los autobuses dejaron de circular
(VI + PREP) • **we ~ed off the road into a lay-by** salimos de la carretera y paramos en un apartadero
▸ **pull on** (VT + ADV) *[+ gloves etc]* ponerse (de prisa)
▸ **pull out** (VT + ADV) **1** (= *take out*) *(from pocket, drawer)* sacar; *(from ground)* arrancar; *[+ tooth]* sacar, extraer; (= *pull outwards*) *[+ lever etc]* tirar hacia fuera • **to ~ sb out of a river** sacar a algn de un río • **to ~ sb out of a hole** sacar a algn de un hoyo (a estirones)
2 (= *withdraw*) retirar • **everybody was ~ed out on strike** todos fueron llamados a la huelga
(VI + ADV) **1** *(Aut, Rail)* (= *come out*) salir • **the red car ~ed out from behind that black one** el coche rojo salió de detrás de aquel negro • **he ~ed out and disappeared into the traffic** arrancó y se perdió en el tráfico
2 *(Mil)* (= *withdraw*) retirarse (**from** de)
3 (= *leave*) salir, partir • **we're ~ing out** nos marchamos ya
4 • **it ~s out easily** *[drawer etc]* sale fácilmente
▸ **pull over** (VT + ADV) **1** (= *bring closer*) *[+ chair]* acercar
2 (= *topple*) volcar
3 *(Police)* *[+ car, driver]* parar
(VI + ADV) *(Aut)* hacerse a un lado
▸ **pull round** (VT + ADV) • **to ~ sb round** *[+ unconscious person]* reanimar a algn
(VI + ADV) *[unconscious person]* reanimarse, volver en sí
▸ **pull through** (VI + ADV) *(from illness)* reponerse, recobrar la salud; *(from difficulties etc)* reponerse
(VT + ADV) • **to ~ sb through** *[+ crisis]* sacar a algn del apuro; *[+ illness]* ayudar a algn a reponerse
▸ **pull together** (VT + ADV) **1** • **let me ~ together the threads of my argument** permítanme atar los cabos de mi razonamiento • **he has ~ed the team together** gracias a él los jugadores han recuperado su espíritu de equipo
2 • **to ~ o.s. together** calmarse, tranquilizarse • **~ yourself together!** ¡cálmate!
(VI + ADV) *(fig)* (= *cooperate*) ir todos a una
▸ **pull up** (VT + ADV) **1** (= *raise by pulling*) levantar, subir; *[+ socks etc]* subir
2 (= *bring closer*) *[+ chair]* acercar
3 (= *uproot*) sacar, arrancar • IDIOM: • **to ~ up one's roots** desarraigarse
4 (= *stop*) parar; *[+ horse]* refrenar • **the police**

~ed him up for speeding la policía lo paró por sobrepasar el límite de velocidad
5 (= *scold*) regañar
6 (= *strengthen*) fortalecer • **it has ~ed the pound up** ha fortalecido la libra • **his mark in French has ~ed him up** la nota de francés le ha subido la media
(VI + ADV) **1** (= *stop*) detenerse, parar; (*Aut*) parar(se)
2 (= *restrain o.s.*) contenerse
pull-back ['pʊlbæk] (N) (*Mil*) retirada *f*
pull-down ['pʊl,daʊn] (ADJ) • **pull-down menu** menú *m* desplegable
pullet ['pʊlɪt] (N) polla *f*, pollita *f*
pulley ['pʊlɪ] (N) polea *f*
pull-in ['pʊl,ɪn] (N) (*Brit*) (*Aut*) (= *lay-by*) apartadero *m*; (*for food*) café *m* de carretera, restaurante *m* de carretera
Pullman® ['pʊlmən] (N) (PL: **Pullmans**)
1 (*Brit*) (*also* **Pullman carriage**) vagón *m* de primera clase
2 (*US*) (*also* **Pullman car**) coche *m* cama
pull-off ['pʊlɒf] (N) (*US*) (*Aut*) apartadero *m*
pull-out ['pʊlaʊt] (N) **1** (*in magazine*) suplemento *m* separable
2 (*Mil etc*) retirada *f*
(CPD) [*magazine section*] separable; [*table leaf etc*] extensible
pullover ['pʊləʊvəʳ] (N) (*esp Brit*) jersey *m*, suéter *m*, chompa *f* (*Peru, Bol*)
pullulate ['pʌljʊleɪt] (VI) pulular
pull-up ['pʊlʌp] (N) **1** (*Brit*) = **pull-in**
2 (*US*) = **press-up**
pulmonary ['pʌlmənərɪ] (ADJ) pulmonar
(CPD) ▸ **pulmonary embolism** embolia *f* pulmonar
pulp [pʌlp] (N) **1** (= *paper pulp, wood pulp*) pasta *f*, pulpa *f*; (*for paper*) pulpa *f* de madera • **to reduce sth to ~** hacer algo papilla • **a leg crushed to ~** (*fig*) una pierna hecha trizas • **to beat sb to a ~*** (*fig*) dar a algn una tremenda paliza, hacer a algn papilla*
2 [*of fruit, vegetable*] pulpa *f*
(VT) reducir a pulpa
(CPD) ▸ **pulp literature** literatura *f* barata ▸ **pulp magazine** revista *f* amarilla
pulping ['pʌlpɪŋ] (N) reducción *f* a pulpa
pulpit ['pʊlpɪt] (N) púlpito *m*
pulpy ['pʌlpɪ] (ADJ) **1** pulposo
2* [*literature*] para tirar, de bajísima calidad
pulsar ['pʌlsɑːʳ] (N) pulsar *m*
pulsate [pʌl'seɪt] (VI) vibrar, palpitar
pulsating [pʌl'seɪtɪŋ] (ADJ) **1** [*heart*] palpitante; [*music*] vibrante
2 (*fig*) (= *exciting*) palpitante, excitante
pulsation [pʌl'seɪʃən] (N) pulsación *f*, latido *m*
pulse¹ [pʌls] (N) (*Anat*) pulso *m*; (*Phys*) pulsación *f*; (*fig*) [*of drums, music*] ritmo *m*, compás *m* • **to take sb's ~** tomar el pulso a algn • IDIOM: • **he keeps his finger on the company's ~** está tomando constantemente el pulso a la compañía, se mantiene al tanto de lo que pasa en la compañía
(VI) pulsar, latir
(CPD) ▸ **pulse beat** latido *m* del pulso ▸ **pulse rate** frecuencia *f* del pulso
pulse² [pʌls] (N) (*Bot, Culin*) legumbre *f*
pulverization [,pʌlvəraɪ'zeɪʃən] (N) pulverización *f*
pulverize ['pʌlvəraɪz] (VT) pulverizar; (*fig*) hacer polvo; (= *thrash**) hacer polvo a*
puma ['pjuːmə] (N) puma *m*
pumice ['pʌmɪs], **pumice stone** ['pʌmɪsstəʊn] (N) piedra *f* pómez
pummel ['pʌml] (VT) aporrear, apalear
(CPD) ▸ **pummel horse, pommel horse** potro *m*
pummelling, pummeling (*US*) ['pʌməlɪŋ] (N) • **to take a ~** (*lit*) recibir una paliza, llevarse una paliza; (*fig*) (*in debate etc*) recibir un vapuleo; (*in match etc*) recibir una paliza*
pump¹ [pʌmp] (N) **1** (*for liquid, gas, air*) bomba *f* • **foot/hand ~** bomba *f* de pie/de mano; ▹ **bicycle, bilge, petrol, suction**
2 (*also* **petrol pump**) surtidor *m* de gasolina
3 (= *act of pumping*) • **I gave the tyre a quick ~** le metí un poco de aire al neumático, inflé un poco el neumático • **after a few ~s water came gushing forth** después de darle a la bomba un par de veces, empezó a salir agua a borbotones
(VT) **1** (*lit*) **a** (*with a pump*) bombear • **gas is ~ed from under the sea bed** el gas se bombea desde el fondo del mar • **to ~ sth dry** [+ *well, river, lake*] secar algo, dejar algo seco • **the tank was ~ed full of water each day** el tanque se llenaba de agua todos los días • **to ~ gas** (*US*) echar *or* meter gasolina • **oil is ~ed into the house from a tank outside** el combustible se bombea a la casa desde un depósito que hay fuera • **a respirator ~ed oxygen into her lungs** un respirador le bombeaba oxígeno a los pulmones • **to ~ air into a tyre** inflar un neumático • **the factory just ~s its waste into the river** la fábrica simplemente vierte sus residuos al río • **they are ~ing oil out of the wrecked tanker** están bombeando el petróleo del buque cisterna siniestrado • **the heart ~s blood round the body** el corazón hace circular la sangre por el cuerpo • **to ~ sb's stomach** hacer un lavado de estómago a algn • IDIOM: • **to ~ sb dry** dejar a algn seco
b (*Naut*) • **to ~ (out) the bilges** achicar la sentina
2 (*fig*) • **we can't go on ~ing money into this project** no podemos seguir metiendo tanto dinero en *or* inyectándole tanto dinero a este proyecto • **he ~ed five bullets into her head** le metió cinco balas en la cabeza • **to ~ sb full of drugs** atiborrar a algn de drogas • **to ~ sb full of lead‡** acribillar *or* coser a algn a balazos*; ▹ **prime**
3 (= *move up and down*) [+ *pedal*] pisar repetidamente; [+ *handle*] darle repetidamente a • **he ~ed the accelerator** pisó repetidamente el pedal del acelerador, se puso a darle al pedal del acelerador • **to ~ sb's hand/arm** dar un fuerte apretón de manos a algn • IDIOM: • **to ~ iron*** hacer pesas
4* (= *question*) • **I ~ed him discreetly about his past** le sonsaqué discretamente todo lo que pude acerca de su pasado, le tiré de la lengua discretamente acerca de su pasado* • **to ~ sb for information** sonsacar información a algn
(VI) **1** [*person*] **a** (*at pump*) • **here's a bucket, get ~ing!** aquí tienes un balde, ¡a trabajar la bomba!
b (*on lever*) • **he was ~ing away on the lever** estaba moviendo la palanca de arriba abajo sin parar
c (*on pedal*) • **he was ~ing away, trying to get the car to start** pisaba repetidamente el pedal, intentando arrancar el coche
2 [*pump, machine*] • **the machine is ~ing (away) all the time** la máquina de bombeo está en funcionamiento constantemente • **the piston was ~ing up and down** el émbolo subía y bajaba
3 [*heart*] (= *circulate blood*) bombear la sangre; (= *beat*) latir; [*blood, adrenaline*] correr por las venas
4 [*liquid*] • **the oil was ~ing along the pipeline** el petróleo corría por el tubo • **blood ~ed from the severed artery** la sangre salía a borbotones de la arteria cortada
(CPD) ▸ **pump attendant** encargado/a *m/f* de la gasolinera ▸ **pump house** sala *f* de bombas ▸ **pump price** [*of petrol*] precio *m* de la gasolina • **a rise in ~ prices** una subida en los precios de la gasolina ▸ **pump room** sala *f* de bombas
▸ **pump in** (VT + ADV) **1** (*lit*) (*with pump*) bombear, meter *or* introducir con una bomba; (*with other device*) bombear • **~ some more air in** bombea más aire, introduce *or* mete más aire (con la bomba) • **they are having water ~ed in from surrounding areas** se les está bombeando agua de las zonas colindantes
2 (*fig*) [+ *money*] inyectar
▸ **pump out** (VT + ADV) **1** (= *extract, remove*) [+ *oil, water*] bombear, extraer *or* sacar con una bomba
2 (= *empty*) [+ *boat*] achicar el agua de; [+ *flooded cellar, building*] sacar el agua de • **it's no fun having your stomach ~ed out** un lavado de estómago no es nada divertido
3 (= *produce, emit*) **a** (*lit*) despedir • **the pipe was ~ing out raw sewage** el tubo estaba despidiendo aguas residuales sin tratar • **cars which ~ out deadly exhaust fumes** los coches que despiden gases letales
b (*fig**) • **the country is investing a lot of money into ~ing out more oil** el país está invirtiendo mucho dinero para producir más petróleo • **this station ~s out music 24 hours a day** esta cadena emite música las veinticuatro horas del día • **he ~s out articles each week** cada semana saca un artículo detrás de otro como si nada
(VI + ADV) manar • **oil was ~ing out from the ruptured tanks** el petróleo manaba de las cisternas rotas
▸ **pump up** (VT + ADV) **1** (= *inflate*) [+ *tyre*] hinchar, inflar (*LAm*)
2 (= *carry up*) [+ *water, oil*] bombear • **water is ~ed up from springs** se bombea el agua de los manantiales
3* (= *increase*) [+ *prices, profits*] inflar • **to ~ up the economy** reactivar la economía
4 (= *enhance*) mejorar • **we need to ~ up his image** tenemos que mejorar su imagen
5 (= *inspire*) [+ *person*] animar; [+ *morale*] subir, levantar
pump² [pʌmp] (N) (*esp Brit*) (= *sports shoe*) zapatilla *f*; (*esp US*) (= *dancing shoe*) bailarina *f*; (= *slip-on shoe*) zapato *m* de salón
pump-action shotgun [,pʌmpækʃən'ʃɒtgʌn] (N) escopeta *f* de pistón
pumper ['pʌmpəʳ] (N) (*US*) coche *m* bomba
pumpernickel ['pʌmpənɪkl] (N) pan *m* de centeno entero
pumping station ['pʌmpɪŋ,steɪʃən] (N) (*for water*) estación *f* de bombeo; (*for oil*) estación *f* de bombeo de crudo
pumpkin ['pʌmpkɪn] (N) (= *vegetable*) calabaza *f*, zapallo *m* (*And, S. Cone*); (= *plant*) calabacera *f*
(CPD) ▸ **pumpkin seed** semilla *f* de calabaza, semilla de zapallo (*And, S. Cone*)
pump-priming ['pʌmp'praɪmɪŋ] (N) (*fig*) inversión *f* inicial con carácter de estímulo; (*US*) *inversión estatal en nuevos proyectos que se espera beneficien la economía*
pun [pʌn] (N) juego *m* de palabras (**on** sobre), retruécano *m*, albur *m* (*Mex*)
(VI) hacer un juego de palabras (**on** sobre), alburear (*Mex*)
Punch [pʌntʃ] (N) (*Theat*) Polichinela *m* • IDIOM: • **to be as pleased as ~** estar como unas pascuas
(CPD) ▸ **Punch and Judy show** teatro *m* de títeres
punch¹ [pʌntʃ] (N) **1** (= *tool*) **a** (*for making holes*) (*in leather etc*) punzón *m*; (*in paper*)

P

perforadora *f*; (*in ticket*) máquina *f* de picar
b (*for stamping design*) troquel *m*, cuño *m*
c (*for driving in nails*) clavadora *f*
2 (= *blow*) puñetazo *m* • **he floored him with one ~** lo derribó de un solo puñetazo • **body ~** (*Boxing*) puñetazo *m* en el cuerpo • **a ~ in the face** un puñetazo en la cara • **to land a ~** asestar un puñetazo • **a ~ on** *or* **in the nose** un puñetazo en la nariz • **he packs a ~*** pega duro* • **to swing** *or* **throw a ~** soltar un puñetazo • **to take a ~** recibir un puñetazo • IDIOM: • **to pull one's ~es** andarse con miramientos • **he didn't pull any ~es** no se mordió la lengua; ▸ **knockout**
3 (*fig*) (= *vigour*) empuje *m*, garra *f* • **he has ~** tiene empuje *or* garra • **think of a phrase that's got some ~ to it** piensa una frase que tenga garra
VT **1** (= *perforate*) (*with tool*) [+ *paper, card, metal*] perforar; [+ *leather*] punzar; [+ *ticket*] picar; (*also* **punch out**) (*with die*) troquelar; (= *stamp*) [+ *design*] estampar • **~ed card** tarjeta *f* perforada • **to ~ the clock** fichar • **to ~ a hole in sth** (*in leather, paper, metal*) hacer un agujero a algo • **they ~ed holes in Arsenal's defence** encontraron huecos en la defensa del Arsenal • **~ed tape** cinta *f* perforada
2 (= *hit*) (*with fist*) dar un puñetazo a • **to ~ sb in the stomach/on the nose** dar un puñetazo a algn en el estómago/la nariz • **to ~ sb in the face** • **~ sb's face** dar un puñetazo a algn en la cara • **she ~ed the air in triumph** agitaba los brazos, triunfante • **I ~ed the ball into the net** metí el balón en la red de un manotazo • **he ~ed his fist through the glass** atravesó el cristal de un puñetazo • **he ~ed the wall angrily** golpeó la pared furioso
3 (= *press*) [+ *button, key*] presionar
4 (*US*) • **to ~ cattle** aguijonear al ganado
VI pegar (puñetazos) • **come on, you can ~ harder than that!** ¡venga, que puedes pegar con más fuerza! • **to ~ at sb** dar *or* pegar un puñetazo a algn
CPD ▸ **punch bag** (*Brit*) saco *m* de arena ▸ **punch card** tarjeta *f* perforada ▸ **punch line** remate *m* ▸ **punch operator** operador(a) *m/f* de máquina perforadora
▸ **punch in** VT + ADV **1** (= *beat up*) • **to ~ sb's face/head in*** romper la cara/la crisma a algn*
2 (= *key in*) [+ *code, number*] teclear • **you have to ~ the code in first** primero hay que teclear *or* introducir el código
VI + ADV (*on time clock*) fichar
▸ **punch out** VT + ADV **1** (*with tool*) [+ *hole*] perforar; (*with die*) [+ *machine parts*] troquelar
2 [+ *number, code*] teclear • **I picked up the phone and ~ed out a number** descolgué el teléfono y tecleé un número
3* (*with fist*) [+ *person*] pegar
VI + ADV (*on time clock*) fichar al salir
punch² [pʌntʃ] N (= *drink*) ponche *m*
punchball ['pʌntʃbɔːl] N **1** (*Brit*) pera *f*, punching-ball *m*
2 (*US*) (= *game*) *tipo de béisbol que se juega sin bate*
punchbowl ['pʌntʃbəʊl] N ponchera *f*
punch-drunk ['pʌntʃdrʌŋk] ADJ (*fig*) aturdido • **to be punch-drunk** estar grogui*
puncher ['pʌntʃəʳ] N **1** (= *tool*) perforadora *f*; (*for leather*) punzón *m*
2 (= *boxer etc*) • **he's a hard ~** pega fuerte
punching bag ['pʌntʃɪŋbæg] N (*US*) = **punch bag**
punch-up* ['pʌntʃʌp] N (*Brit*) pelea *f*, refriega *f*
punchy* ['pʌntʃɪ] ADJ (COMPAR: **punchier**, SUPERL: **punchiest**) [*person etc*] de empuje, con garra; [*phrase*] con garra; [*remark*] incisivo, contundente; [*style*] vigoroso

punctilio [pʌŋk'tɪlɪəʊ] N (PL: **punctilios**) (*frm*) puntillo *m*, etiqueta *f*
punctilious [pʌŋk'tɪlɪəs] ADJ puntilloso, quisquilloso
punctiliously [pʌŋk'tɪlɪəslɪ] ADV de modo puntilloso
punctual ['pʌŋktjʊəl] ADJ puntual • **you're very ~** (*now*) llegaste en punto; (*usually*) siempre llegas puntual • **"please be ~"** "se ruega la mayor puntualidad"
punctuality [ˌpʌŋktjʊ'ælɪtɪ] N puntualidad *f*
punctually ['pʌŋktjʊəlɪ] ADV puntualmente, en punto • **the bus arrived ~** el autobús llegó puntualmente *or* a la hora • **~ at six o'clock** a las seis en punto
punctuate ['pʌŋktjʊeɪt] VT (*Ling*) puntuar • **his speech was ~d by applause** los aplausos interrumpieron repetidamente su discurso
punctuation [ˌpʌŋktjʊ'eɪʃən] N (*Ling*) puntuación *f*
CPD ▸ **punctuation mark** signo *m* de puntuación
puncture ['pʌŋktʃəʳ] N (*in tyre, balloon*) pinchazo *m*, ponchadura *f* (*Mex*); (*in skin*) perforación *f*; (*Aut*) pinchazo *m*, ponchadura *f* (*Mex*) • **I have a ~** se me ha pinchado *or* (*Mex*) ponchado un neumático *or* (*esp LAm*) una llanta • **I had a ~ on the motorway** tuve un pinchazo en la autopista
VT [+ *tyre*] pinchar, ponchar (*Mex*); [+ *skin*] perforar • **this ~d his confidence** esto destruyó su confianza • **we'll see if it ~s his pride** veremos si esto le baja los humos
VI pincharse, poncharse (*Mex*)
CPD ▸ **puncture repair kit** kit *m* de reparación de pinchazos ▸ **puncture wound** herida *f* punzante
pundit ['pʌndɪt] N experto/a *m/f*
pungency ['pʌndʒənsɪ] N [*of smell, flavour*] acritud *f*; [*of remark*] mordacidad *f*
pungent ['pʌndʒənt] ADJ [*smell, flavour*] acre; [*remark, style*] mordaz
pungently ['pʌndʒəntlɪ] ADV [*smell*] acremente; [*remark, write*] mordazmente
Punic ['pjuːnɪk] ADJ púnico
N púnico *m*
punish ['pʌnɪʃ] VT **1** castigar • **to ~ sb for sth/for doing sth** castigar a algn por algo/por hacer algo • **they were severely ~ed for their disobedience** los castigaron severamente por su desobediencia
2 (*fig**) maltratar
punishable ['pʌnɪʃəbl] ADJ (*gen*) punible; (*Jur*) punible, sancionable • **a ~ offence** una infracción penada *or* sancionada por la ley • **a crime ~ by death** un delito castigado con la pena de muerte
punishing ['pʌnɪʃɪŋ] ADJ [*race, schedule*] duro, agotador
N castigo *m*; (*fig*) castigo *m*, malos tratos *mpl* • **to take a ~** recibir una paliza*; [*car, furniture etc*] recibir muchos golpes
punishment ['pʌnɪʃmənt] N **1** (= *punishing, penalty*) castigo *m* • **to make the ~ fit the crime** determinar un castigo acorde con la gravedad del crimen • **to take one's ~** aceptar el castigo
2 (*fig**) malos tratos *mpl* • **to take a lot of ~** (*Sport*) recibir una paliza*; [*car, furniture etc*] recibir muchos golpes
punitive ['pjuːnɪtɪv] ADJ punitivo; (*Jur*) [*damages*] punitorio
Punjab ['pʌndʒɑːb] N (*also* **the Punjab**) el Punjab
Punjabi [pʌn'dʒɑːbɪ] ADJ punjabí
N **1** (*Ling*) punjabí *m*
2 (= *person*) punjabí *mf*
punk [pʌŋk] N **1** (= *person*) (*also* **punk rocker**) punki *mf*, punk *mf*; (= *music*) (*also* **punk rock**) música *f* punk, punk *m*
2 (*US**) (= *hoodlum*) rufián *m*, matón *m* (*LAm*)
CPD ▸ **punk rock** música *f* punk, punk *m* • **a ~ rock band** un grupo punk
punnet ['pʌnɪt] N (*Brit*) canastilla *f*
punster ['pʌnstəʳ] N persona *f* aficionada a los juegos de palabras, equivoquista *mf*
punt¹ [pʌnt] N (= *boat*) batea *f*
VT [+ *boat*] impulsar (con percha); [+ *ball*] dar un puntapié a
VI • **to go ~ing** ir a pasear en batea
punt² [pʌnt] VI (= *bet*) apostar
punt³ [pʌnt] N puntapié *m* de volea
VT dar un puntapié de volea a
punt⁴ [pʊnt] N (= *currency*) libra *f* (irlandesa)
punter ['pʌntəʳ] (*esp Brit*) N **1** (*Brit*) (*Racing*) (= *gambler*) jugador(a) *m/f*, apostador(a) *m/f*
2* (= *customer*) cliente *mf*; [*of prostitute*] cliente *mf* • **the ~(s)** (*Brit*) (= *customer, member of public*) el público
puntpole ['pʌntpəʊl] N percha *f*, pértiga *f* (de batea)
puny ['pjuːnɪ] ADJ (COMPAR: **punier**, SUPERL: **puniest**) enclenque, endeble
PUP N ABBR (*Brit*) = **Progressive Unionist Party**
pup [pʌp] N (= *young*) [*of dog*] cachorro/a *m/f*; [*of other animal*] cría *f* • **seal pup** cría *f* de foca • IDIOM: • **to sell sb a pup** dar a algn gato por liebre
VI [*bitch*] parir
pupa ['pjuːpə] N (PL: **pupae** ['pjuːpiː]) crisálida *f*
pupate ['pjuːpeɪt] VI crisalidar
pupil¹ ['pjuːpl] N **1** (*in school*) alumno/a *m/f*, educando/a *m/f* (*frm*) • **last year ~ numbers increased by 46,100** el año pasado hubo un aumento de 46.100 en el número total de alumnos • **~-teacher ratio** proporción *f* de alumnos por maestro; ▸ **teacher-pupil ratio**
2 [*of musician, artist etc*] alumno/a *m/f*, discípulo/a *m/f*
CPD ▸ **pupil power** poder *m* de los alumnos
pupil² ['pjuːpl] N (*Anat*) pupila *f*
puppet ['pʌpɪt] N (*lit*) títere *m*, marioneta *f*; (*fig*) títere *m*
CPD ▸ **puppet government, puppet régime** gobierno *m* títere ▸ **puppet show** teatro *m* de títeres *or* marionetas ▸ **puppet theatre, puppet theater** (*US*) = **puppet show**
puppeteer [ˌpʌpɪ'tɪəʳ] N titiritero/a *m/f*
puppetry ['pʌpɪtrɪ] N títeres *mpl*, arte *m* del titiritero
puppy ['pʌpɪ] N cachorro/a *m/f*, perrito/a *m/f*
CPD ▸ **puppy fat** gordura *f* infantil ▸ **puppy love** amor *m* juvenil
purblind ['pɜːblaɪnd] ADJ cegato; (*fig*) ciego, falto de comprensión
purchasable ['pɜːtʃɪsəbl] ADJ comprable
purchase ['pɜːtʃɪs] N **1** (= *act, object*) compra *f*, adquisición *f* • **to make a ~** hacer una compra, efectuar una adquisición (*frm*)
2 (= *grip*) agarre *m*, asidero *m*; (= *leverage*) palanca *f* • **I got a ~ on the rope and pulled** me agarré de la cuerda y tiré • **I was trying to get a ~ on the cliff face** estaba intentando agarrarme a la pared del acantilado • **the wheels can't get a ~ on this surface** los neumáticos no se adhieren bien a esta superficie
VT (*frm*) comprar, adquirir • **to ~ sth from sb** comprar algo a algn • **he ~d his freedom at a great price** pagó muy cara su libertad
CPD ▸ **purchase order** orden *f* de compra ▸ **purchase price** precio *m* de compra ▸ **purchase tax** (*Brit*) (*formerly*) impuesto *m* sobre la venta
purchaser ['pɜːtʃɪsəʳ] N comprador(a) *m/f*

purchasing ['pɜːtʃɪsɪŋ] (N) compra *f*
(CPD) ▸ **purchasing department** departamento *m* de compras ▸ **purchasing officer** agente *mf* de compra ▸ **purchasing power** [*of person, currency*] poder *m* adquisitivo
purdah ['pɜːdə] (N) (*in India etc*) reclusión *f* femenina • **to be in ~** (*fig*) estar en cuarentena
pure [pjʊəʳ] (ADJ) (COMPAR: **purer**, SUPERL: **purest**) **1** (= *unadulterated*) [*wool, alcohol, substance*] puro; [*silk*] natural • **a ~ wool jumper** un jersey de lana pura • **it's blackmail, ~ and simple** esto es chantaje, lisa y llanamente
2 (= *clean, clear*) [*air, water, sound, light*] puro
3 (= *sheer*) [*pleasure, luck, coincidence, speculation*] puro • **the whole story was ~ invention** todo fue puro cuento • **by ~ chance** por pura casualidad
4 (= *theoretical*) puro • **~ mathematics/ science** matemáticas *fpl*/ciencias *fpl* puras
5 (= *virgin, blameless*) puro • **~ in** *or* **of heart** (*liter*) limpio de corazón • **~ in mind and body** de mente y cuerpo puros • IDIOM: • **as ~ as the driven snow** puro como la nieve
(CPD) ▸ **pure vowel** vocal *f* simple

> **PURE**
>
> **Position of "puro"**
>
> *You should generally put* **puro** *after the noun when you mean* **pure** *in the sense of "uncontaminated" or "unadulterated" and before the noun in the sense of "sheer" or "plain":*
>
> **... pure olive oil ...**
> ... aceite puro de oliva ...
> **It's pure coincidence**
> Es pura coincidencia
>
> *For further uses and examples, see main entry.*

purebred ['pjʊə'bred] (ADJ) [*horse*] de pura sangre; [*dog*] de raza
(N) animal *m* de raza; (= *horse*) pura sangre *mf*, purasangre *mf*
purée ['pjʊəreɪ] (N) (*Culin*) puré *m* • **apple ~** puré *m* de manzana • **tomato ~** puré *m* de tomate, concentrado *m* de tomate
purely ['pjʊəlɪ] (ADV) (= *wholly*) puramente • **their relationship was ~ physical** su relación era puramente física • **it is not a ~ physical illness** no es simplemente una enfermedad orgánica • **we met ~ by accident** nos conocimos por pura casualidad • **~ and simply** lisa y llanamente
pure-minded ['pjʊə'maɪndɪd] (ADJ) de mente pura
pureness ['pjʊənɪs] (N) pureza *f*
purgation [pɜː'geɪʃən] (N) purgación *f*
purgative ['pɜːgətɪv] (ADJ) (*Med*) purgante, purgativo
(N) (*Med*) purgante *m*
purgatorial [,pɜːgə'tɔːrɪəl] (ADJ) (*Rel*) [*concept*] del purgatorio; [*time, fire*] purgatorio, purgativo
purgatory ['pɜːgətərɪ] (N) (*Rel*) (*also fig*) purgatorio *m* • **it was ~!** ¡fue un purgatorio!
purge [pɜːdʒ] (N) (*all senses*) purga *f*, depuración *f*
(VT) (*all senses*) purgar, depurar
purification [,pjʊərɪfɪ'keɪʃən] (N) [*of air*] purificación *f*; [*of water*] depuración *f*
purifier ['pjʊərɪfaɪəʳ] (N) [*of air*] purificador *m*; [*of water*] depurador *m*
purify ['pjʊərɪfaɪ] (VT) [+ *air*] purificar; [+ *water*] depurar; [+ *metal*] acrisolar, refinar
Purim ['pʊərɪm] (N) Purim *m*
purism ['pjʊərɪzəm] (N) purismo *m*
purist ['pjʊərɪst] (N) purista *mf*
puritan ['pjʊərɪtən] (ADJ) puritano
(N) puritano/a *m/f*
puritanical [,pjʊərɪ'tænɪkəl] (ADJ) puritano
puritanism ['pjʊərɪtənɪzəm] (N) puritanismo *m*
purity ['pjʊərɪtɪ] (N) pureza *f*
purl [pɜːl] (N) punto *m* del revés
(VT) hacer punto del revés • **"~ two"** "dos del revés"
purler* ['pɜːləʳ] (N) • **to come a ~** caer pesadamente, caer aparatosamente; (*fig*) fracasar estrepitosamente, darse un batacazo*
purlieus ['pɜːljuːz] (NPL) (*frm, hum*) alrededores *mpl*, inmediaciones *fpl*
purloin [pɜː'lɔɪn] (VT) (*frm or hum*) robar
purple ['pɜːpl] (ADJ) morado • **to go ~ (in the face)** enrojecer • **Purple Heart** (*US*) (*Mil*) *decoración otorgada a los heridos de guerra* • **~ heart** (píldora *f* de) anfetamina *f* • **~ prose** prosa *f* de estilo inflado
(N) (= *colour*) púrpura *f*, morado *m*
(VT) purpurar
(CPD) ▸ **purple patch** estado *m* de gracia • **she's enjoying a ~ patch at the moment** en este momento está en estado de gracia
purplish ['pɜːplɪʃ] (ADJ) purpurino, algo purpúreo
purport (*frm*) (N) ['pɜːpət] **1** (= *meaning*) significado *m*, sentido *m*
2 (= *purpose*) intención *f*
(VT) [pɜː'pɔːt] • **to ~ to be** pretender ser
purported [pɜː'pɔːtɪd] (ADJ) [*benefit, reason*] supuesto • **many of the ~ benefits of legalized gambling are illusory** muchos de los supuestos beneficios del juego legalizado son ficticios
purportedly [pɜː'pɔːtɪdlɪ] (ADV) supuestamente
purpose ['pɜːpəs] (N) **1** (= *intention*) propósito *m*, objetivo *m* • **we all shared a common ~** todos teníamos el mismo propósito *or* objetivo • **she has a ~ in life** tiene un objetivo *or* una meta *or* un norte en la vida • **what was your ~ in going?** ¿con qué intención fuiste? • **"purpose of visit"** (*on official form*) "motivo del viaje" • **I put that there for a ~** he puesto eso ahí a propósito *or* por una razón • **this is good enough for our ~s** esto sirve para nuestros fines • **he exploited her talent for his own ~s** explotó su talento en beneficio propio • **for all practical ~s** en la práctica • **for the ~s of this meeting** para los fines de esta reunión • **for the ~ of doing sth** con el fin de hacer algo • **on ~** a propósito, adrede • **with the ~ of** con el fin de; ▹ **intent**
2 (= *use*) uso *m*, utilidad *f* • **what is the ~ of this tool?** ¿qué uso *or* utilidad tiene esta herramienta? • **it wasn't designed for this ~** no se diseñó para este fin *or* uso • **to good ~** provechosamente • **it was all to no ~** todo fue inútil *or* en vano • **you can adapt it to your own ~s** lo puede adaptar a sus necesidades • **it serves no useful ~** no tiene uso práctico, no tiene utilidad práctica; ▹ **serve**
3 (= *determination*) resolución *f*, determinación *f* • **to have a sense of ~** tener un rumbo en la vida • **he has no sense of ~** no tiene rumbo en la vida • **she has great strength of ~** tiene muchísima resolución *or* determinación, es muy resuelta; ▹ **infirm**
(VT) † • **to ~ doing sth/to do sth** proponerse *or* planear hacer algo
purpose-built [,pɜːpəs'bɪlt] (ADJ) construido especialmente
purposeful ['pɜːpəsfʊl] (ADJ) [*look, expression*] de determinación; [*manner, walk*] resuelto, decidido; [*work, activity*] con sentido
purposefully ['pɜːpəsfəlɪ] (ADV) resueltamente
purposefulness ['pɜːpəsfʊlnɪs] (N) resolución *f*
purposeless ['pɜːpəslɪs] (ADJ) [*person's character*] irresoluto; [*person's state*] indeciso; [*act*] sin propósito, sin objeto, sin finalidad
purposely ['pɜːpəslɪ] (ADV) a propósito, adrede, expresamente • **a ~ vague statement** una declaración realizada en términos vagos a propósito *or* adrede *or* expresamente
purposive ['pɜːpəsɪv] (ADJ) = **purposeful**
purr [pɜːʳ] (N) ronroneo *m*
(VI) [*cat, engine*] ronronear
(VT) (= *say*) susurrar, decir suavemente
purse [pɜːs] (N) **1** (*Brit*) (*for money*) monedero *m* • **a well-lined ~** una bolsa llena • **it is beyond my ~** mis recursos no llegan a tanto, está fuera de mi alcance • IDIOM: • **to hold the ~ strings** administrar el dinero; ▹ **public, silk**
2 (*US*) (= *handbag*) bolso *m*, cartera *f* (*LAm*)
3 (= *sum of money as prize*) premio *m* en metálico
(VT) • **to ~ one's lips** fruncir los labios
(CPD) ▸ **purse snatcher** (*US*) carterista *mf*
purser ['pɜːsəʳ] (N) (*Naut*) comisario/a *m/f*
pursuance [pə'sjuːəns] (N) (*frm*) • **in ~ of** [+ *plan, goal*] para la consecución de; [+ *duty*] en cumplimiento de
pursuant [pə'sjuːənt] (ADV) (*frm*) • **~ to** de acuerdo con, conforme a
pursue [pə'sjuː] (VT) **1** (= *chase*) perseguir, seguir • **they were being ~d by enemy planes** los aviones enemigos los perseguían *or* los seguían • **she was often ~d by fans** a menudo la perseguían *or* la acosaban sus admiradores • **he has been ~d by bad luck all his life** se ha visto perseguido por la mala suerte toda su vida
2 (= *engage in*) [+ *interests, career*] dedicarse a; [+ *studies, war, talks*] proseguir; [+ *profession*] ejercer, dedicarse a
3 (= *continue with*) [+ *course of action*] seguir; [+ *policy, reform*] aplicar • **he had been pursuing his own inquiries** había estado haciendo sus propias averiguaciones • **we have decided not to ~ the matter further** hemos decidido no seguir adelante con el asunto
4 (= *strive for*) [+ *aim, objective, peace*] luchar por; [+ *happiness, pleasure*] buscar; [+ *success, fame*] perseguir, buscar; [+ *rights*] reivindicar
pursuer [pə'sjuːəʳ] (N) perseguidor(a) *m/f*
pursuit [pə'sjuːt] (N) **1** (= *chase*) caza *f*, persecución *f*; (*fig*) [*of pleasure, happiness, knowledge*] busca *f*, búsqueda *f* • **the ~ of wealth** el afán de riqueza • **in (the) ~ of sth/sb** en busca de algo/algn • **to set out in ~ of sb** salir en busca de algn • **with two policemen in hot ~** con dos policías pisándole los talones
2 (= *occupation*) • **outdoor ~s** actividades *fpl* al aire libre • **literary ~s** intereses *mpl* literarios, actividades *fpl* literarias • **leisure ~s** pasatiempos *mpl*
(CPD) ▸ **pursuit plane** avión *m* de caza
purulence ['pjʊərʊləns] (N) purulencia *f*
purulent ['pjʊərʊlənt] (ADJ) purulento
purvey [pɜː'veɪ] (VT) (*frm*) proveer, suministrar, abastecer
purveyance [pɜː'veɪəns] (N) (*frm*) provisión *f*, suministro *m*, abastecimiento *m*
purveyor [pɜː'veɪəʳ] (N) (*frm*) proveedor(a) *m/f*, abastecedor(a) *m/f*
purview ['pɜːvjuː] (N) (*frm*) ámbito *m*, esfera *f* • **it comes within the ~ of the law** esta dentro del ámbito *or* la esfera de la ley

pus [pʌs] (N) pus *m*

push [pʊʃ] (N) **1** (= *shove*) empujón *m* • **with one ~** de un empujón • **the car needs a ~** hay que empujar el coche • **at the ~ of a button** con solo apretar *or* pulsar un botón • **to give sth/sb a ~** dar a algo/algn un empujón
2 (*Brit**) • **to get the ~**: • **he got the ~** [*worker*] lo pusieron de patitas en la calle*, lo echaron; [*lover*] ella lo plantó*, ella lo dejó • **to give sb the ~** [+ *worker*] poner a algn de patitas en la calle*, echar a algn; [+ *lover*] plantar a algn*, dejar a algn
3 (= *effort*) esfuerzo *m* • **in its ~ for economic growth ...** en su esfuerzo por desarrollar la economía ...
4 (= *encouragement*) empujoncito* *m* • **we need a ~ to take the first step** necesitamos un empujoncito para dar el primer paso*
5 (*Mil*) (= *offensive*) ofensiva *f* • **the allied ~ into occupied Kuwait** la ofensiva de los aliados en la zona ocupada de Kuwait
6* • **at a ~** a duras penas • **if** *or* **when it comes to the ~** en último caso, en el peor de los casos • IDIOM: • **when ~ comes to shove** a la hora de la verdad
7 (= *dynamism*) dinamismo *m*, empuje *m*, energía *f* • **he's got no ~** no tiene empuje, le falta energía • **he's a man with plenty of ~** es hombre de empuje
(VT) **1** (= *shove, move by pushing*) empujar • **don't ~ me!** ¡no me empujes! • **to ~ sb against a wall** empujar a algn contra una pared • **she ~ed him down the stairs** lo empujó escaleras abajo • **to ~ sb into a room** hacer entrar a algn en una habitación de un empujón • **to ~ a car into the garage** empujar un coche dentro del garaje • **to ~ one's finger into a hole** introducir el dedo en un agujero • **he ~ed the book into my hand** me metió el libro en la mano • **to ~ sb off the pavement** echar a algn de la acera a empujones • **he ~ed the books off the table** tiró los libros de la mesa de un empujón • **they ~ed the car off the cliff** empujaron el coche por el acantilado • **to ~ a door open/shut** abrir/cerrar una puerta empujándola *or* de un empujón • **he ~ed the thought to the back of his mind** intentó quitárselo de la cabeza • **to ~ one's way through the crowd** abrirse paso a empujones por la multitud • **he ~ed his head in through the window** metió la cabeza por la ventana • **he ~ed the box under the table** empujó *or* metió la caja debajo de la mesa
2 (= *press*) [+ *button etc*] apretar, pulsar
3 (*fig*) **a** (= *press, advance*) [+ *trade*] fomentar; [+ *product*] promover • **to ~ home one's advantage** aprovechar la ventaja • **don't ~ your luck!*** ¡no te pases!*, ¡no desafíes a la suerte!
b (= *put pressure on*) • **when we ~ed her, she explained it all** cuando la presionamos, nos lo explicó todo • **don't ~ her too far** no te pases con ella* • **to ~ sb for payment** ejercer presión sobre algn para que pague • **to ~ sb into doing sth** obligar a algn a hacer algo • **I was ~ed into it** me obligaron a ello • **that's ~ing it a bit*** eso es pasarse un poco*, eso es demasiado • **to ~ o.s.** (*in exercise, work etc*) esforzarse • **to be ~ed for time/money** andar justo de tiempo/escaso de dinero • **to ~ sb to do sth** presionar a algn para que haga algo • **we'll be (hard) ~ed to finish it** tendremos grandes dificultades para terminarlo
4* [+ *drugs*] pasar*
5* • **he's ~ing 50** raya en los 50
(VI) **1** (= *press*) empujar • **don't ~!** ¡no empujes! • **"push"** (*on door*) "empujar"; (*on bell*) "pulsar" • **he ~ed past me** pasó por mi lado dándome un empujón • **she ~ed through the crowd** se abrió paso entre la multitud a empujones
2 (*fig*) (= *make demands*) • **he ~es too much** insiste demasiado • **they're ~ing for better conditions** hacen campaña para mejorar sus condiciones (de trabajo)
3 (*Mil*) avanzar • **to ~ into enemy territory** avanzar en territorio enemigo

▸ **push about**, **push around*** (VT + ADV) (*fig*) (= *bully*) intimidar • **he's not one to be ~ed around** no se deja intimidar, no se deja mandonear* • **he likes ~ing people around** le gusta mandonear*, le gusta dar órdenes a la gente

▸ **push ahead** (VI + ADV) (= *make progress*) seguir adelante • **to ~ ahead with a plan** seguir adelante con un proyecto

▸ **push along** (VT + ADV) **1** [+ *object*] empujar
2 [+ *work*] acelerar, agilizar
(VI + ADV)* (= *leave*) marcharse

▸ **push aside** (VT + ADV) [+ *person, chair*] apartar, hacer a un lado; (*fig*) [+ *objection, suggestion*] hacer caso omiso de

▸ **push at** (VI + PREP) [+ *door etc*] empujar

▸ **push away** (VT + ADV) [+ *plate*] apartar; [+ *person*] apartar a un lado; (*more violently*) apartar de un empujón

▸ **push back** (VT + ADV) [+ *hair etc*] echar hacia atrás; [+ *enemy, crowd*] hacer retroceder • **he's ~ing back the frontiers of knowledge** está ampliando las fronteras del saber

▸ **push down** (VI + ADV) (= *press down*) apretar
(VT + ADV) **1** (= *press down*) apretar
2 (= *knock over*) derribar
3 (*fig*) [+ *prices, value*] hacer bajar

▸ **push forward** (VI + ADV) **1** (*Mil*) avanzar
2 • **to ~ forward with a plan** seguir adelante con un proyecto
(VT + ADV) [+ *person, object*] empujar hacia adelante; [+ *plan, work*] llevar adelante • **he tends to ~ himself forward** (*fig*) suele hacerse notar

▸ **push in** (VT + ADV) **1** [+ *screw etc*] introducir (a la fuerza)
2 (= *break*) [+ *window, door*] romper
3 [+ *person*] (*in lake etc*) empujar al agua
(VI + ADV) **1** (*in queue*) colarse
2 (*fig*) (= *interfere*) entrometerse

▸ **push off** (VT + ADV) **1** [+ *top etc*] quitar a la fuerza; [+ *person*] (*off wall etc*) hacer caer; [+ *object*] (*involuntarily*) tirar; (*intentionally*) hacer caer
2 (*Naut*) desatracar
(VI + ADV) **1** (*Naut*) desatracarse
2* (= *leave*) marcharse • **~ off!** ¡lárgate!*
3 • **the top ~es off** la tapa se quita empujando

▸ **push on** (VI + ADV) (= *carry on*) continuar; (*on journey*) seguir adelante • **to ~ on with sth** continuar con algo • **we ~ed on to the camp** seguimos hasta el campamento • **they ~ed on another five km** avanzaron cinco km más • **it's time we were ~ing on** es hora de ponernos en camino
(VT + ADV) **1** [+ *lid etc*] poner a la fuerza
2 (*fig*) (= *incite, urge on*) animar, alentar

▸ **push out** (VT + ADV) **1** (*of room, house*) echar a empujones; (*of car*) sacar a empujones
2 (*fig*) [+ *employee, member*] echar, expulsar
3 [+ *tentacle etc*] sacar, extender
4* (= *produce*) [+ *information, products*] producir
5 (*Naut*) [+ *boat*] desatracar
(VI + ADV) [*root etc*] extenderse

▸ **push over** (VT + ADV) **1** (= *cause to fall*) hacer caer, derribar
2 (= *knock over*) [+ *chair, table*] volcar

▸ **push through** (VT + ADV) **1** (*through door, hole*) introducir, meter • **I ~ed my way through** me abrí paso a empujones
2 (= *get done quickly*) [+ *deal*] expeditar, apresurar; (*Parl*) [+ *bill*] hacer aprobar
(VT + PREP) **1** (*lit*) • **he ~ed me through the door** me hizo entrar/salir (por la puerta) de un empujón • **he ~ed his hand through the bars** sacó la mano por entre los barrotes • **to ~ one's way through the crowd** abrirse paso a empujones entre la multitud
2 (*Parl*) • **the government ~ed the bill through Parliament** el gobierno hizo que el parlamento aprobara el proyecto de ley
(VI + ADV) [*plant*] abrirse paso
(VI + PREP) (*through crowd*) abrirse paso por

▸ **push to** (VT + ADV) [+ *door*] cerrar

▸ **push up** (VT + ADV) **1** [+ *lever, window*] levantar, subir; ▹ **daisy**
2 (*fig*) (= *raise, increase*) [+ *price, value*] hacer subir

push-bike [ˈpʊʃbaɪk] (N) (*Brit*) bicicleta *f*, bici* *f*

push-button [ˈpʊʃˌbʌtn] (N) pulsador *m*, botón *m* (de control *etc*)
(CPD) de mando de botón • **with push-button control** con mando de botón
▸ **push-button warfare** guerra *f* a control remoto

pushcart [ˈpʊʃkɑːt] (N) carretilla *f* de mano

pushchair [ˈpʊʃtʃɛəʳ] (N) (*Brit*) sillita *f* de paseo

pusher* [ˈpʊʃəʳ] (N) **1** [*of drugs*] camello* *mf*, traficante *mf*
2 (= *ambitious person*) ambicioso/a *m/f*

pushful [ˈpʊʃfʊl] (ADJ) (= *dynamic*) emprendedor, dinámico, enérgico; (= *ambitious*) ambicioso; (*pej*) agresivo

pushfulness [ˈpʊʃfʊlnɪs] (N) (= *dynamism*) empuje *m*, dinamismo *m*, espíritu *m* emprendedor; (= *ambition*) ambición *f*; (*pej*) agresividad *f*

pushiness* [ˈpʊʃɪnɪs] (N) prepotencia *f*

pushing [ˈpʊʃɪŋ] (ADJ) = **pushful**

pushover* [ˈpʊʃˌəʊvəʳ] (N) • **it's a ~** está tirado* • **he was a ~** era fácil convencerlo *or* sonsacarlo *etc* • **I'm a ~ when a woman asks me** no resisto cuando me lo pide una mujer

pushpin [ˈpʊʃpɪn] (N) (*esp US*) chincheta *f* (con cabeza de color) (*Sp*), chinche *m or f* (con cabeza de color) (*LAm*)

push-pull circuit [ˌpʊʃpʊlˈsɜːkɪt] (N) circuito *m* de contrafase, circuito *m* equilibrado

push-rod [ˈpʊʃrɒd] (N) (*Aut*) barra *f* de presión

push-up [ˈpʊʃʌp] (N) (*US*) = **press-up**

pushy* [ˈpʊʃɪ] (ADJ) (COMPAR: **pushier**, SUPERL: **pushiest**) (*pej*) agresivo, avasallador, prepotente (*esp LAm*)

pusillanimity [ˌpjuːsɪləˈnɪmɪtɪ] (N) pusilanimidad *f*

pusillanimous [ˌpjuːsɪˈlænɪməs] (ADJ) pusilánime

puss* [pʊs] (N) (= *cat*) minino* *m*, gatito *m* • **Puss in Boots** El Gato con Botas

pussy [ˈpʊsɪ] (N) **1** (*also* **pussycat***) (*child language*) minino* *m*, gatito *m*
2** (= *female genitals*) coño** *m*
(CPD) ▸ **pussy willow** sauce *m*

pussycat [ˈpʊsɪkæt] (N) (*child language*) minino* *m*, gatito *m*

pussyfoot* [ˈpʊsɪfʊt] (VI) (*esp US*) (*also* **pussyfoot around**) andar sigilosamente; (*fig*) no decidirse

pustule [ˈpʌstjuːl] (N) pústula *f*

put [pʊt]

TRANSITIVE VERB
INTRANSITIVE VERB
COMPOUND
PHRASAL VERBS

(PT, PP: **put**)

TRANSITIVE VERB

For set combinations consisting of **put** *+ noun, eg* ***put a price on, put a strain on, put an end to, put at risk, put out of business, put in touch with*** *look up the noun. For* **put** *+ adverb/preposition combinations, see also phrasal verbs.*

1 (= *place, thrust*) **a** (*physically*) poner; (*with precision*) colocar; (= *insert*) meter, introducir (*more frm*); (= *leave*) dejar • **I put a serviette by each plate** puse *or* coloqué una servilleta junto a cada plato • **put it in the drawer** ponlo en el cajón • **she put the chairs in a circle** puso *or* colocó las sillas en círculo • **shall I put milk in your coffee?** ¿te pongo leche en el café? • **you haven't put any salt in it** no le has puesto nada de sal • **to put an advertisement in the paper** poner un anuncio en el periódico • **he put a coin in the slot** puso *or* metió *or* (*more frm*) introdujo una moneda en la ranura • **he put the letter in his pocket** se metió la carta en el bolsillo • **he put the ball in the net** metió el balón en la red • **to put sb in a home** ingresar a algn en una residencia • **you should put your money in a bank** deberías poner *or* (*more frm*) depositar el dinero en un banco • **I put a sheet of paper into the typewriter** puse *or* coloqué una hoja de papel en la máquina de escribir • **I put my hand into the sack** metí la mano en el saco • **he put his keys on the table** puso *or* dejó las llaves en la mesa • **I put some more coal on the fire** puse *or* eché más carbón en el fuego • **she put her head on my shoulder** apoyó *or* recostó la cabeza en mi hombro • **my brother put me on the train** mi hermano me dejó en el tren • **to put a button on a shirt** coser un botón en una camisa • **she put her head out of the window** asomó la cabeza por la ventana • **he put his hand over his mouth** se tapó la boca con la mano, se puso la mano en la boca • **he put his head round the door** asomó la cabeza por la puerta • **put it there!*** (*handshake*) ¡chócala!* • **I put my fist through the window** rompí la ventana con el puño • **she put a bullet through his head** le metió una bala por la cabeza • **he put the shell to his ear** se puso *or* se acercó la concha al oído • IDIOMS: • **put yourself in my place** ponte en mi lugar • **I didn't know where to put myself*** creí que me moría de vergüenza, no sabía dónde meterme; ▹ **bed, flight², stay**

b (*with abstract nouns*)

Some **put** *+ noun combinations require a more specific Spanish verb. For very set combinations look up the noun.*

• **the syllabus puts a lot of emphasis on languages** el programa (de estudios) hace *or* pone mucho énfasis en los idiomas • **I wouldn't put any faith in what he says** yo no creería lo que dice, yo no tendría ninguna confianza en lo que dice • **you can put that idea out of your head** ya te puedes quitar esa idea de la cabeza • **this puts the responsibility on drivers to be aware of the law** esto responsabiliza a los conductores de estar enterados de la ley; ▹ **blame, figure, trust, tax**

2 (= *cause to be*) poner • **to put sb in a good/bad mood** poner a algn de buen/mal humor • **this puts me in a very awkward position** esto me pone *or* deja en una situación muy difícil • **his win today puts him in second place overall** la victoria de hoy le pone *or* coloca en segunda posición en la clasificación general • **to put sb in charge of sth** poner a algn a cargo de algo • **to put sb on a diet** poner a algn a dieta *or* a régimen • **the doctor has put me on antibiotics** el doctor me ha recetado antibióticos

3 (= *cause to undertake*) • **to put sb to sth: it put us to a lot of extra expense** nos supuso muchos gastos adicionales • **I don't want to put you to any trouble** no quiero causarte ninguna molestia • **she put him to work immediately** lo puso a trabajar en seguida

4 (= *express*) decir • **I don't quite know how to put this** la verdad, no sé cómo decir esto • **you can put all that in two words** todo eso se puede decir en dos palabras • **as Shakespeare puts it** como dice Shakespeare • **to put it bluntly** para decirlo claramente, hablando en plata* • **I find it hard to put into words** me resulta difícil expresarlo con palabras • **to put sth into French** traducir algo al francés • **how shall I put it?** ¿cómo lo diría? • **let me put it this way ...** digámoslo de esta manera ..., por decirlo de alguna manera ... • **to put it another way, it'll save you three hours** por decirlo de otra manera, te ahorrará tres horas • **try putting it another way** trata de decirlo de otra manera • **to put it simply** para decirlo sencillamente

5 (= *write*) poner, escribir • **what do you want me to put?** ¿qué quieres que ponga *or* escriba? • **put your name at the top of the paper** ponga *or* escriba su nombre en la parte superior del papel • **put the title in capital letters** pon *or* escribe el título en letras mayúsculas • **to put sth in writing** poner algo por escrito • **I've put you on the waiting list** le he puesto en la lista de espera • **put it on my account** (*Comm*) cárguelo a mi cuenta • **he put a line through the offending paragraph** tachó el párrafo controvertido • **to put one's signature to sth** firmar algo

6 (= *invest*) invertir • **to put money into a company** invertir dinero en una compañía • **he put all his savings into the project** invirtió todos sus ahorros en el proyecto • **I put most of the money into shares** invertí la mayor parte del dinero en acciones • **I've put a lot of time and effort into this** he invertido un montón de tiempo y esfuerzo en esto, le he dedicado a esto mucho tiempo y esfuerzo • **she has put a lot into the relationship** se ha esforzado mucho en su relación • **"I'm not getting much out of this course" — "well, you're not putting much into it, are you?"** —no estoy sacando mucho de este curso —tampoco es que te estés esforzando mucho, ¿no?

7 (= *contribute*) • **to put sth towards sth** contribuir (con) algo hacia algo • **I'll pay for the bike but you'll have to put something towards it** yo pagaré la bici pero tú tienes que contribuir con algo • **I'm going to put the money towards a holiday** voy a poner *or* guardar el dinero para unas vacaciones

8 (= *expound, submit*) [+ *views*] expresar, exponer • **this will give people an opportunity to put their views** esto dará a la gente la oportunidad de expresar *or* exponer sus puntos de vista • **he puts the case for a change in the law** plantea *or* expone argumentos a favor de un cambio en la ley • **she puts a convincing case** presenta *or* da argumentos convincentes • **the proposal was put before Parliament** la propuesta se presentó ante el parlamento • **to put sth to sb:** • **how will you put it to him?** ¿cómo se lo vas a decir *or* comunicar? • **put it to him gently** díselo suavemente • **I put it to you that ...** les sugiero que ... • **to put a question to sb** hacer una pregunta a algn • **the chairman put the proposal to the committee** el presidente sometió la propuesta a votación en el comité • **we shall have to put it to our members** tendremos que someterlo a la votación de nuestros miembros

9 (= *estimate*) • **they put the loss at around £50,000** calcularon *or* valoraron las pérdidas en unas 50.000 libras • **his fortune is put at 3 billion** se calcula *or* valora su fortuna en 3 billones • **the number of dead was put at 6,000** se calculó *or* estimó el número de muertos en 6.000 • **I would put him at 40** diría que tiene unos 40 años • **some put the figure as high as 20,000** algunos estiman que la cifra llega hasta 20.000

10 (= *rank*) • **he put himself above the law** creía estar por encima de la ley • **I wouldn't put him among the greatest poets** yo no le pondría entre los más grandes poetas • **we should never put money before happiness** no deberíamos nunca anteponer el dinero a la felicidad • **I put the needs of my children before anything else** para mí las necesidades de mis hijos van por delante de todo lo demás *or* son más importantes que todo lo demás • **she has always put her career first** para ella su carrera siempre ha sido lo primero

11 (= *set*) • **she put my brother against me** puso a mi hermano en contra mía • **to put a watch to the right time** poner un reloj en hora • **to put the words to music** poner música a la letra

12 (= *throw*) • **to put the shot** (*Sport*) lanzar el peso

13 (*St Ex*) (= *offer to sell*) [+ *stock, security*] declararse vendedor de

14 (= *bet*) ▹ **put on**

INTRANSITIVE VERB

(*Naut*) • **to put into port** entrar a puerto • **the ship put into Southampton** el barco entró a *or* en Southampton • **to put to sea** hacerse a la mar

COMPOUND

▸ **put option** (*St Ex*) opción *f* de venta a precio fijado

▸ **put about** (VT + ADV) **1** (*esp Brit*) [+ *rumour*] hacer correr • **to put it about that ...** hacer correr el rumor de que ...
2 (*Naut*) [+ *ship*] hacer virar
3* • **he's putting it about a bit** (*sexually*) se está ofreciendo a todo quisque* • **to put o.s. about** (= *make o.s. noticed*) hacerse notar
(VI + ADV) (*Naut*) cambiar de rumbo, virar

▸ **put across** (VT + ADV) **1** (= *communicate*) [+ *idea*] comunicar; [+ *meaning*] hacer entender • **he finds it hard to put his ideas across** le cuesta comunicar sus ideas • **the play puts the message across very well** la obra transmite el mensaje muy bien • **to put o.s. across** (= *present o.s.*) presentarse • **it all depends on how you put yourself across** todo depende de cómo te presentes a ti mismo • **to put o.s. across well** saber presentarse bien • **he puts himself across as a sympathetic, caring person** da la impresión de ser una persona comprensiva, compasiva • **to put sth across to sb** (= *explain*) explicar algo a algn; (= *convey*) hacer entender algo a algn
2 • **to put one across on sb*** engañar a algn

▸ **put aside** (VT + ADV) **1** (= *lay down*) dejar a un lado, poner a un lado • **he put the letter aside to read later** dejó *or* puso a un lado la carta para leerla más tarde
2 (= *save*) [+ *money*] ahorrar, guardar; [+ *time*] reservar; [+ *food*] apartar • **to have money**

put aside tener ahorros
3 (*in shop*) [+ *goods*] guardar, reservar, apartar • **could you put one aside for me?** ¿me podría guardar *or* reservar *or* apartar uno?
4 (= *ignore*) [+ *differences, feelings*] dejar de lado; [+ *fears*] apartar, desechar
5 (= *sacrifice*) [+ *career, personal interest*] sacrificar

▸ **put away** (VT + ADV) **1** (*in proper place*) [+ *clothes, toys, books*] guardar, poner en su sitio; [+ *shopping*] guardar, colocar; [+ *car*] poner en el garaje • **put that knife away!** ¡pon ese cuchillo en su sitio!
2* (= *confine*) (*in prison*) meter en la cárcel, encerrar; (*in asylum*) encerrar en un manicomio
3 (= *save*) [+ *money*] ahorrar, guardar
4* (= *consume*) [+ *food, drink*] tragarse*, zamparse* • **he can certainly put it away** ese sí sabe comer
5 (= *reject*) [+ *thought*] desechar, descartar; [+ *wife*] repudiar
6 (*Sport*) (= *score with*) [+ *ball*] meter, marcar; (*US*) (= *beat*) ganar a
7 = **put down**

▸ **put back** (VT + ADV) **1** (= *replace*) poner otra vez en su sitio; (*in pocket, drawer etc*) volver a guardar • **put it back when you've finished** ponlo otra vez en su sitio cuando hayas terminado • **put that back!** ¡deja eso en su sitio *or* donde estaba! • **the fresh air will put the colour back in your cheeks** el aire fresco te devolverá el color a las mejillas
2 (= *postpone*) aplazar, posponer • **the meeting has been put back till 2 o'clock** la reunión ha sido aplazada hasta las 2
3 (= *delay*) [+ *development, progress*] retrasar, atrasar • **this will put us back 10 years** esto nos retrasará 10 años • **he has been put back a class** *or* **year** (*Scol*) tiene que repetir el curso
4 (= *change*) [+ *clock*] • **to put a clock back one hour** atrasar *or* retrasar un reloj una hora • **don't forget to put your clocks back on Saturday** el sábado no olviden atrasar *or* retrasar los relojes • IDIOM: • **you can't put the clock back** no se puede volver al pasado
5 (= *move back*) • **he put his head back and roared with laughter** echó hacia atrás la cabeza y se puso a reír a carcajadas
6 (= *reinvest*) [+ *money, profits*] reinvertir (**into** en) • **the government didn't put enough money back into the economy** el gobierno no reinvirtió suficiente dinero en la economía
7* (= *drink*) beber, beberse • **he's already put back seven gins** se ha bebido ya siete copitas de ginebra
(VI + ADV) (*Naut*) volver, regresar • **to put back to port** volver *or* regresar a puerto

▸ **put back on** (VT + ADV) [+ *clothes, glasses*] volver a ponerse • **he put his trousers back on** volvió a ponerse los pantalones

▸ **put behind** (VT + PREP) **1** (*and forget*) • **you must put all that behind you now** ahora debes olvidar todo eso
2 (*providing support*) • **they're putting their money and expertise behind the scheme** están apoyando el plan con dinero y experiencia

▸ **put by** (VT + ADV) **1** (= *save*) ahorrar • **to have money put by** tener ahorros
2 (*in shop*) guardar, reservar, apartar • **I had it put by for you** se lo tenía guardado *or* reservado *or* apartado

▸ **put down** (VT + ADV) **1** [+ *object*] (= *leave*) dejar; (= *let go of*) soltar; [+ *telephone*] colgar; [+ *passenger*] dejar (bajar), dejar (apearse) • **she put her glass down and stood up** dejó el vaso y se levantó • **I'll put these bags down for a minute** voy a dejar estas bolsas en el suelo un momento • **put it down!** ¡déjalo!, ¡suéltalo! • **once I started the book I couldn't put it down** una vez que empecé el libro no podía dejarlo *or* dejar de leerlo • **put me down!** ¡bájame! • **the pilot wanted to put the plane down in Boston** el piloto quería aterrizar en Boston; ▸ **foot, root**
2 (= *lay*) [+ *carpets, poison, trap*] poner, colocar
3 (= *lower*) [+ *blinds, hand*] bajar
4 (= *close*) [+ *umbrella, parasol*] cerrar
5 (= *write down*) [+ *ideas*] anotar, apuntar; [+ *name on list*] poner, inscribir • **I've put down a few ideas** he anotado *or* apuntado algunas ideas • **I've put you down as unemployed** lo he inscrito *or* apuntado como desempleado • **put me down for £15** apúntame 15 libras • **put me down for two, please** por favor, apúntame dos • **he's put his son down for Eton** ha inscrito a su hijo en Eton (*internado privado*) • **I'll put you down for the interview on Radio 4, ok?** te apunto para la entrevista en Radio 4, ¿vale? • **I've put myself down for the computer course** me he inscrito para el curso de informática • **to put sth down in writing** *or* **on paper** poner algo por escrito • **put it down on my account** (*Comm*) cárguelo a mi cuenta
6 (= *suppress*) [+ *revolt*] reprimir, sofocar
7 (= *reduce in rank*) degradar; (*Sport etc*) pasar a una división inferior
8* (= *criticize, snub*) hacer de menos, rebajar • **he's always putting me down in front of my friends** siempre me está haciendo de menos *or* rebajando delante de mis amigos • **to put o.s. down** hacerse de menos, rebajarse • **you must stop putting yourself down** debes dejar de hacerte de menos *or* rebajarte
9 (= *pay*) • **to put down a deposit** dejar un depósito • **she put down £500 on the car** dejó una señal *or* un anticipo de 500 libras para el coche
10 (*Brit*) (*euph*) • **to have an animal put down** sacrificar a un animal
11 (= *put to bed*) [+ *baby*] acostar, poner a dormir
12 (= *table*) [+ *motion, amendment*] presentar
13 (= *store in cellar*) [+ *wine*] poner en cava
(VI + ADV) (*Aer*) aterrizar

▸ **put down as** (VT + PREP) • **to put sb down as sth** catalogar a algn como algo • **I had put him down as a complete fool** lo tenía catalogado como un tonto perdido • **I would put her down as about 30** le daría unos 30 años, debe tener unos 30 años

▸ **put down to** (VT + PREP) • **to put sth down to sth** atribuir algo a algo • **I put it down to his inexperience** lo atribuí a su inexperiencia

▸ **put forth** (VT + ADV) **1** (*liter*) [+ *leaves, roots, buds*] echar; [+ *hand*] tender, extender
2 (*frm*) = **put forward**

▸ **put forward** (VT + ADV) **1** (= *propose*) [+ *theory, idea*] presentar; [+ *plan, proposal*] presentar, proponer; [+ *suggestion*] hacer; [+ *argument*] presentar; [+ *opinion*] dar; [+ *name, candidate*] proponer • **to put o.s. forward for a job** presentarse como candidato para un puesto
2 (= *make earlier*) [+ *clock, meeting, starting time*] adelantar • **to put a clock forward one hour** adelantar un reloj una hora • **don't forget to put your clocks forward tonight** esta noche no olviden adelantar sus relojes • **the meeting was put forward (by half an hour) to 2 pm** la reunión se adelantó (media hora) a las 2 de la tarde

▸ **put in** (VT + ADV) **1** (*inside box, drawer, room*) meter • **she packed the camera but forgot to put the film in** cogió la cámara pero se le olvidó (meter) la película • **he put his head in at the window** metió la cabeza por la ventana • **I'll put some more sugar in** voy a poner más azúcar
2 (= *plant*) [+ *plants*] plantar; [+ *seeds*] sembrar
3 (*to garage, repair shop*) [+ *car*] • **I've put the car in for repairs** he llevado el coche a que lo reparen
4 (= *install*) [+ *central heating, double glazing*] instalar, poner
5 (= *include*) (*in book, speech*) incluir; (= *add*) agregar • **why don't you put a few jokes in?** ¿por qué no incluyes algunos chistes? • **did you put in your reasons for wanting to go?** ¿pusiste *or* incluiste las razones por las que quieres irte?
6 (= *interject*) interponer • **"I can't go either," put in James** —yo tampoco puedo ir —interpuso James
7 (= *submit*) [+ *request*] presentar • **to put in a claim for damages/expenses** presentar una demanda por daños/gastos • **to put sb in for an award** proponer a algn para un premio • **to put one's name in for sth** inscribirse para algo • **to put in a plea of not guilty** declararse inocente; ▸ **appearance**
8 (*Pol*) [+ *party, government, candidate*] elegir, votar a
9 (= *devote, expend*) [+ *time*] dedicar • **she puts in an hour a day at the piano** le dedica al piano una hora al día • **I've put in a lot of time on it** le he dedicado mucho tiempo a esto, he empleado mucho tiempo en esto • **I put in a couple of hours gardening** dediqué un par de horas a trabajar en el jardín, me pasé un par de horas trabajando en el jardín
10 (= *work*) trabajar • **can you put in a few hours at the weekend?** ¿puede trabajar unas horas el fin de semana? • **he puts in at least 40 hours a week** trabaja por lo menos 40 horas a la semana • **you've put in a good day's work** has trabajado bien hoy
(VI + ADV) (*Naut*) hacer escala (**at** en)
(VT + PREP) ▸ **put**

▸ **put in for** (VI + PREP) [+ *promotion, transfer, pay rise, divorce*] solicitar • **I've put in for a new job** he solicitado otro empleo

▸ **put off** (VT + ADV) **1** (= *postpone, delay*) [+ *departure, appointment, meeting, decision*] aplazar, posponer • **he put off writing the letter** pospuso *or* aplazó el escribir la carta • **I keep putting it off** no hago más que aplazarlo • **we shall have to put the guests off** tendremos que decir a los invitados que no vengan • **it's no good putting it off** (*sth unwelcome*) no tiene sentido eludirlo más • PROVERB: • **don't put off until tomorrow what you can do today** no dejes para mañana lo que puedes hacer hoy
2 (= *discourage*) • **her brusque manner puts some people off** desanima a la gente con sus maneras tan bruscas • **he's not easily put off** no es fácil apartarlo de su propósito, no es de los que se desaniman fácilmente
3 (= *distract*) distraer • **stop putting me off!** ¡deja ya de distraerme!
4 (= *dissuade*) disuadir
5 (= *fob off*) dar largas a • **to put sb off with an excuse** dar largas a algn con excusas • **she put him off with vague promises** le dio largas con vagas promesas
6 (= *switch off*) apagar
7 (= *set down*) [+ *passenger*] dejar; (*forcibly*) hacer bajar
8 (*esp liter*) (= *cast off*) • **once you put off that uniform you'll need a job** en cuanto dejes ese uniforme necesitarás un trabajo
(VT + PREP) **1** (= *cause not to like, want*) • **it almost put me off opera for good** casi mató

mi gusto por la ópera para siempre • **you quite put me off my meal** me has quitado el apetito • **it put me off going to Greece** me quitó las ganas de ir a Grecia
2 (*= dissuade from*) • **we tried to put him off the idea** intentamos quitarle la idea de la cabeza, intentamos disuadirlo • **I tried to put her off going by herself** intenté convencerla de que no fuera sola
3 (*Brit*) (*= distract from*) ▹ **stroke, scent**
VI + ADV (*Naut*) hacerse a la mar, salir (**from** de)
▸ **put on** VT + ADV **1** [*+ one's coat, socks, hat*] ponerse; [*+ ointment, cream*] ponerse, aplicarse (*more frm*) • **to put on one's make-up** ponerse maquillaje, maquillarse
2 (*= add, increase*) • **he's put on 3 kilos** ha engordado 3 kilos • **to put on speed** acelerar, cobrar velocidad • **to put on weight** engordar • **he has put on a lot of weight** ha engordado mucho
3 (*= organize*) [*+ concert*] presentar; [*+ exhibition*] montar; [*+ play*] representar, poner en escena; [*+ extra bus, train*] poner • **we're putting on "Bugsy Malone"** vamos a representar "Bugsy Malone"
4 (*= assume*) [*+ expression, air*] adoptar • **to put on a French accent** fingir (tener) un acento francés • **there's no need to put on an act, just be yourself** no tienes por qué fingir, sé tú mismo • **to put on an innocent expression** poner cara de inocente • **she's not ill, she's just putting it on** no está enferma, es puro teatro *or* está fingiendo • **she put on a show of enthusiasm** fingió entusiasmo • **the party put on a show of unity** el partido presentó una fachada de unidad; ▹ **air**
5 (*Telec*) • **"is John there, please?" — "I'll put him on"** —¿por favor, está John? —le pongo • **can you put me on to Mr Smith please** póngame con *or* (*esp LAm*) me comunica con el Sr. Smith, por favor
6 (*= switch on, start*) [*+ light, radio*] encender, prender (*LAm*); [*+ CD, tape, music*] poner; [*+ vegetables*] (*= begin to cook*) poner (a cocer); (*= begin to heat*) poner (a calentar) • **shall I put the heating on?** ¿enciendo la calefacción? • **to put the brakes on** frenar • **to put the kettle on** poner agua a hervir
7 [*+ clock*] adelantar • **to put a clock on one hour** adelantar un reloj una hora • **don't forget to put the clocks on tonight** esta noche no olviden adelantar los relojes
8 (*esp US**) (*= deceive*) engañar • **you're putting me on, aren't you?** me estás tomando el pelo, ¿verdad?
VT + PREP **1** (*= add to*) • **the proposal would put 5p on (to) a litre of petrol** la propuesta aumentaría en 5 peniques el litro de gasolina • **they put £2 on (to) the price** añadieron 2 libras al precio
2 (*= bet on*) • **to put money on a horse** apostar dinero a un caballo, jugarse dinero en un caballo • **he put £20 on Black Beauty to win** apostó *or* se jugó 20 libras a que Black Beauty ganaba • IDIOMS: • **I wouldn't put money on it!** yo no apostaría dinero • **he'll be back, I'd put money on it** volverá, me apuesto lo que quieras
▸ **put onto, put on to** VT + PREP • **to put sb onto sth/sb 1** (*= inform about*) • **who put the police onto him?** ¿quién lo denunció a la policía? • **somebody put the Inland Revenue onto his tax evasion** alguien informó a Hacienda de su evasión de impuestos
2 (*= put in touch with*) • **can you put me onto a good dentist?** ¿me puede recomendar un buen dentista? • **Sue put us onto you** Sue nos dio su nombre • **a fellow journalist put me onto the story** un compañero periodista me informó *or* me dio la pista de la historia; ▹ **put on**
▸ **put out** VT + ADV **1** (*= place outside*) [*+ rubbish*] sacar; [*+ cat*] sacar fuera, dejar afuera • **he put the cat out for the night** sacó al gato a que pasara la noche fuera, dejó al gato fuera para que pasara la noche • **to put the clothes out to dry** sacar la ropa a secar; ▹ **pasture**
2 (*= eject*) [*+ squatter, tenant, troublemaker*] echar, expulsar
3 (*= stretch out, push out*) [*+ hand*] alargar, tender; [*+ arm*] alargar, extender; [*+ tongue, claws, horns*] sacar; [*+ leaves, shoots*] echar • **he put out his arm to protect himself** se protegió con el brazo, puso el brazo para protegerse • **to put one's head out of a window** asomar la cabeza por una ventana; ▹ **feeler**
4 (*= lay out in order*) [*+ cards, chessmen, chairs*] disponer, colocar; [*+ clothes, best china*] sacar, poner
5 (*= publish*) [*+ book*] publicar, sacar; [*+ record*] sacar; [*+ appeal, statement, propaganda*] hacer; [*+ warning*] dar; (*= broadcast*) [*+ programme*] transmitir; (*= circulate*) [*+ rumour*] hacer circular, hacer correr • **they have put out a press release denying the allegations** han desmentido las alegaciones en un comunicado de prensa, han emitido un comunicado de prensa negando las alegaciones
6 (*= extinguish*) [*+ light, cigarette, fire*] apagar • **it took them five hours to put out the fire** tardaron cinco horas en apagar el incendio
7 (*= annoy, upset*) enfadar, enojar (*LAm*) • **he was very put out at finding her there** se enfadó mucho al encontrarla allí • **she looked very put out** parecía muy enfadada • **he's a bit put out that nobody came** le sentó mal que no viniera nadie
8 (*= disconcert*) desconcertar • **he didn't seem at all put out by the news** no parecía estar en absoluto desconcertado por las noticias
9 (*= inconvenience*) molestar • **to put o.s. out**: • **she really put herself out for us** se tomó muchas molestias por nosotros • **don't put yourself out, will you!** (*iro*) ¡tú, sobre todo, no hagas nada! • **I don't want to put you out** no quiero molestarle • **you mustn't put yourself out** no debes molestarte • **are you sure I'm not putting you out?** ¿está seguro de que no le causo ningún inconveniente?
10 (*= render incorrect*) [*+ calculations*] desbaratar, echar por tierra
11 (*Sport*) (*= eliminate*) [*+ team, contestant*] eliminar (**of** de) • **a knee injury put him out of the first two games** una lesión de rodilla lo eliminó de los primeros dos partidos
12 (*= dislocate*) [*+ shoulder, knee*] dislocar • **I put my back out lifting that box** me he hecho polvo la espalda levantando esa caja
13 (*= give anaesthetic to*) anestesiar, dormir
14 (*= lend*) [*+ money*] prestar • **to put money out at interest** prestar dinero con intereses
15 (*= subcontract*) • **to put sth out to tender** sacar algo a concurso *or* a licitación • **to put work out to contract** sacar una obra a contrata
16 (*Naut*) [*+ boat*] echar al mar
VI + ADV **1** (*Naut*) salir, zarpar (**from** de) • **to put out to sea** hacerse a la mar
2 (*US**) (*= agree to sex*) acceder, consentir
▸ **put over** VT + ADV **1** = **put across**
2 • **to put one over on sb*** (*= deceive*) engañar a algn, dar a algn gato por liebre*
▸ **put through** VT + ADV **1** (*= make, complete*) [*+ plan, reform, change*] llevar a cabo; [*+ deal*] cerrar; [*+ proposal*] hacer aceptar • **we put through 2,000 orders a week** despachamos 2.000 pedidos a la semana
2 (*Telec*) (*= connect*) [*+ call, caller*] pasar • **don't put any calls through for the next hour** no pases ninguna llamada en la próxima hora • **I'm putting you through now** ahora le paso *or* pongo • **who? Martha? all right, put her through** ¿quién? ¿Marta? bueno, ponme con ella • **can you put me through to Miss Blair, please** por favor, póngame *or* (*esp LAm*) me comunica con la Srta. Blair
VT + PREP **1** (*by providing finance*) • **she put two sons through university** mandó a dos hijos a la universidad
2 (*= make suffer*) • **she didn't want to put him through another ordeal like that** no quiso hacerle pasar por otra prueba tan dura como esa • **they really put him through it at the interview** se las hicieron pasar mal en la entrevista, se las hicieron pasar canutas en la entrevista* • IDIOM: • **to put sb through hell*** hacérselas pasar canutas a algn*; ▹ **pace**
▸ **put together** VT + ADV **1** (*= place together*) poner juntos, juntar • **put your feet together** pon los pies juntos, junta los pies • **don't put those two together, they fight** no pongas a esos dos juntos que se pelean • **if all the cigars in the world were put together end to end** si se unieran uno tras otro todos los puros del mundo • **put your hands together now for ...** démosle una calurosa bienvenida a ... • IDIOM: • **she's worth more than all the others put together** vale más que todos los demás juntos; ▹ **head, two**
2 (*= assemble*) [*+ model kit, piece of furniture*] armar, montar; [*+ meal*] preparar; [*+ collection*] juntar, reunir; [*+ team*] reunir, formar • **he took it apart piece by piece and put it back together again** lo desmontó pieza a pieza y lo volvió a montar otra vez • **the furniture had been put together out of old crates** habían hecho los muebles con viejos cajones de embalaje
3 (*= formulate*) [*+ plan, scheme*] formular, preparar; [*+ publication*] preparar • **she put together a convincing defence of her client** preparó una defensa de su cliente muy convincente • **he can't even put two sentences together** no sabe ni siquiera enhilar dos frases seguidas • **I need a few minutes to put my thoughts together** necesito unos minutos para pensarme las cosas un poco
▸ **put up** VT + ADV **1** (*= raise, lift up*) [*+ window, blinds*] subir; [*+ hand*] levantar; [*+ flag, sail*] izar; [*+ collar*] subirse • **if you have any questions, put your hand up** quien tenga alguna pregunta que levante la mano • **put 'em up!*** [*+ hands*] (*in surrender*) ¡manos arriba!; [*+ fists*] ¡pelea!; ▹ **back, foot**
2 (*= hang up*) [*+ picture, decorations*] colgar; [*+ notice, sign*] poner
3 (*= erect*) [*+ building, wall*] construir, levantar; [*+ statue, monument*] erigir, levantar; [*+ fence, barrier*] poner; [*+ tent*] montar; [*+ umbrella*] abrir; [*+ ladder*] montar, poner • **to put one's hair up** recogerse el pelo; (*stylishly*) hacerse un peinado alto
4 (*= send up*) [*+ satellite*] lanzar, mandar
5 (*= increase*) [*+ price, tax, sb's temperature, blood pressure*] aumentar, subir • **that puts the total up to over 1,000** con eso el total asciende a más de 1.000
6 (*= offer*) [*+ reward, prize, prayer*] ofrecer; [*+ resistance*] oponer • **the horse put up an excellent performance in today's race** el caballo hizo un papel excelente en la carrera de hoy • **he didn't put up much of a**

P

fight *or* **struggle** no se resistió mucho, no opuso mucha resistencia • **to put sth up for sale/auction** poner algo a la venta/a subasta, vender/subastar algo • **to put a child up for adoption** ofrecer un niño en adopción
7 (= *provide*) [+ *money*] poner, dar • **to put up the money for sth** poner *or* dar el dinero para algo
8 (= *give accommodation to*) alojar, hospedar • **we need volunteers to put up the visitors** se necesitan voluntarios para alojar *or* hospedar a los visitantes • **can you put me up for the night?** ¿me puedo quedar (en tu casa) esta noche?
9 (= *present, put forward*) [+ *plan, petition*] presentar; [+ *proposal, suggestion*] hacer; [+ *argument, case, defence*] presentar; [+ *candidate*] proponer (**for** para) • **he put up a spirited defence of the bill in Parliament** hizo una vehemente defensa del proyecto de ley en el parlamento • **we put him up for chairman** lo propusimos para presidente
10 (= *preserve*) [+ *fruit*] conservar
(VI + ADV) **1** (= *stay*) hospedarse, alojarse • **we put up for the night at a hotel** esa noche nos alojamos *or* hospedamos en un hotel
2 (*Pol*) (= *offer o.s.*) • **to put up for president** presentarse a presidente • **to put up for the Greens** presentarse como candidato de los Verdes
▸ **put upon** (VI + PREP) • **to put upon sb** (= *inconvenience*) molestar a algn, incomodar a algn; (= *impose on*) abusar de la amabilidad de algn
▸ **put up to** (VT + PREP) (= *incite*) • **to put sb up to sth: they said that she had put him up to the murder** dijeron que ella le había incitado *or* instigado al asesinato • **somebody must have put him up to it** alguien ha debido sugerírselo • **who put you up to this?** ¿quién te ha hecho hacer esto?
▸ **put up with** (VI + PREP) aguantar • **I can't put up with it any longer** ya no (lo) aguanto más • **you'll just have to put up with it** tendrás que aguantarte • **he has a lot to put up with** tiene que aguantar un montón • **she puts up with a lot** es muy tolerante, tiene mucho aguante

---

putative ['pju:tətɪv] (ADJ) supuesto; [*relation*] putativo
put-down* ['pʊt,daʊn] (N) (= *act*) humillación *f*; (= *words*) frase *f* despectiva
put-in ['pʊt,ɪn] (N) (*Rugby*) introducción *f*
put-on* ['pʊt,ɒn] (ADJ) (= *feigned*) fingido
(N) (= *pretence*) teatro* *m*; (= *hoax*) broma *f* (de mal gusto)
putrefaction [,pju:trɪ'fækʃən] (N) putrefacción *f*
putrefy ['pju:trɪfaɪ] (VI) pudrirse
(VT) pudrir
putrescence [pju:'tresns] (N) pudrición *f*
putrescent [pju:'tresnt] (ADJ) putrefacto
putrid ['pju:trɪd] (ADJ) **1** (= *rotten*) putrefacto, podrido
2 [*stench*] hediondo, pestilente
putsch [pʊtʃ] (N) golpe *m* de estado
putt [pʌt] (N) putt *m*
(VT) golpear
(VI) golpear la bola
putter¹ ['pʌtəʳ] (N) putter *m*
putter² ['pʌtəʳ] (VI) (*US*) = **potter²**
putting ['pʌtɪŋ] (N) minigolf *m*
(CPD) ▸ **putting green** (= *miniature golf*) campo *m* de minigolf; (*on golf course*) green *m*
putty ['pʌtɪ] (N) masilla *f* • IDIOM: • **to be ~ in sb's hands** ser el muñeco de algn
(CPD) ▸ **putty knife** espátula *f* para masilla
put-up ['pʊtʌp] (ADJ) • **put-up job*** chanchullo* *m* • **it was a put-up job to give him the post** fue un chanchullo para darle el puesto*
put-upon ['pʊtə,pɒn] (ADJ) • **she's feeling very put-upon** cree que los demás la están explotando
put-you-up ['pʊtjʊ,ʌp] (N) (*Brit*) cama *f* plegable, sofá-cama *m*
putz (N) (*US*) **1*** (= *person*) memo/a *m/f* (*Sp**), pendejo/a *m/f* (*LAm**)
2** (= *penis*) verga** *f*, polla *f* (*Sp***)
puzzle ['pʌzl] (N) **1** (= *game, jigsaw*) rompecabezas *m inv*; (= *crossword*) crucigrama *m*
2 (= *mystery*) misterio *m*, enigma *m*; (= *riddle*) acertijo *m*, adivinanza *f* • **it's a real ~** es un verdadero misterio *or* enigma
(VT) dejar perplejo, desconcertar • **that properly ~d him** eso lo dejó totalmente perplejo
(VI) • **to ~ about** *or* **over** dar vueltas (en la cabeza) a
(CPD) ▸ **puzzle book** libro *m* de puzzles
▸ **puzzle out** (VT + ADV) • **to ~ sth out** descifrar algo • **we're still trying to ~ out why he did it** seguimos tratando de comprender por qué lo hizo
puzzled ['pʌzld] (ADJ) perplejo • **you look ~!** ¡te has quedado perplejo! • **he gave her a ~ look** la miró perplejo • **to be ~ about sth** no entender algo • **I am ~ to know why** no llego a comprender por qué, no acabo de entender por qué
puzzlement ['pʌzlmənt] (N) perplejidad *f*
puzzler ['pʌzləʳ] (N) misterio *m*, enigma *m*
puzzling ['pʌzlɪŋ] (ADJ) desconcertante • **it is ~ that ...** es raro *or* curioso que ...
PVC (N ABBR) (= **polyvinyl chloride**) PVC *m*
PVR (ABBR) = **personal video recorder**
PVS (N ABBR) **1** = **postviral syndrome**
2 (= **persistent vegetative state**) estado *m* vegetativo persistente
Pvt. (ABBR) (*US*) (*Mil*) = **Private**
PW (N ABBR) **1** (*US*) (*Mil*) = **prisoner of war**
2 (*Brit*) = **policewoman**
pw (ABBR) (= **per week**) por semana, a la semana
PWR (N ABBR) = **pressurized water reactor**
PX (N ABBR) (*US*) (*Mil*) (= **Post Exchange**) *economato militar*
pygmy ['pɪgmɪ] (N) pigmeo/a *m/f*; (*fig*) enano/a *m/f*
(CPD) pigmeo; (*fig*) miniatura, minúsculo
pyjama [pɪ'dʒɑ:mə] (CPD) ▸ **pyjama bottoms** pantalón *msing* de pijama ▸ **pyjama top** parte *f* de arriba del pijama
pyjamas [pɪ'dʒɑ:məz] (NPL) pijama *msing*, piyama *msing* (*LAm*) • **a pair of ~** un pijama
pylon ['paɪlən] (N) (*Elec*) torre *f* de conducción eléctrica
pyorrhoea, pyorrhea (*US*) [,paɪə'rɪə] (N) piorrea *f*
pyramid ['pɪrəmɪd] (N) pirámide *f*
(CPD) ▸ **pyramid selling** venta *f* piramidal
pyramidal [pɪ'ræmɪdl] (ADJ) piramidal
pyre ['paɪəʳ] (N) pira *f*; (*fig*) hoguera *f*
Pyrenean [,pɪrə'ni:ən] (ADJ) pirenaico, pirineo
Pyrenees [,pɪrə'ni:z] (NPL) • **the ~** el Pirineo, los Pirineos
pyrethrum [paɪ'ri:θrəm] (N) piretro *m*
pyretic [paɪ'retɪk] (ADJ) pirético
Pyrex® ['paɪreks] (N) pyrex® *m*, pirex® *m*
(CPD) [*bowl, dish*] de pyrex® *or* pirex®
pyrites [paɪ'raɪti:z] (N) (PL: **pyrites**) pirita *f*
pyro... ['paɪərəʊ] (PREFIX) piro...
pyromania [,paɪrəʊ'meɪnɪə] (N) piromanía *f*
pyromaniac [,paɪərəʊ'meɪnɪæk] (N) pirómano/a *m/f*
pyrotechnic [,paɪərəʊ'teknɪk] (ADJ) pirotécnico
pyrotechnics [,paɪərəʊ'teknɪks] (NSING) pirotecnia *f*
Pyrrhic ['pɪrɪk] (ADJ) • **~ victory** victoria *f* pírrica
Pyrrhus ['pɪrəs] (N) Pirro
Pythagoras [paɪ'θægərəs] (N) Pitágoras
Pythagorean [paɪ,θægə'riən] (ADJ) pitagóreo
python ['paɪθən] (N) pitón *f*
Pythonesque [,paɪθə'nesk] (ADJ) pitonesco, del estilo de Monty Python
pyx [pɪks] (N) píxide *f*
pzazz* [pə'zæz] (N) = **pizazz**

Qq

Q¹, q [kjuː] (N) (= *letter*) Q, q *f* • **Q for Queen** Q de Quebec
Q² (ABBR) **1** = **Queen**
2 (= **question**) P
Q & A, Q and A [ˌkjuːən'eɪ] (N) preguntas y respuestas *fpl*
(ADJ) • **a ~ session** una sesión de preguntas y respuestas
Qatar [kæ'tɑːʳ] (N) Qatar *m*, Katar *m*
QC (N ABBR) (*Brit*) = **Queen's Counsel**

QC/KC
QC o **KC**, abreviaturas de **Queen's** o **King's Counsel**, es el título que se les da a los abogados de más alto rango en el Reino Unido. Los letrados denominados **barristers** (o **advocates** en Escocia) que hayan practicado la abogacía durante al menos diez años pueden solicitar este título al **Lord Chancellor**, quien a su vez los recomienda a la Corona para su designación. Pasar a ser un **QC** o **KC** se conoce como **taking silk** (recibir la seda), haciendo referencia al material de la túnica que llevan estos letrados.
▷ **LAWYERS**

QE2 [ˌkjuːiː'tuː] (N ABBR) (*Brit*) (*Naut*) = **Queen Elizabeth II**
QED (ABBR) (*Math*) (= **quod erat demonstrandum**) QED
QM (ABBR) = **Quartermaster**
qr (ABBR) = **quarter(s)**
QR code® [kjuː'ɑːkəʊd] (N) (= *Quick Response code*) código *m* QR
qt (ABBR) = **quart(s)**
q.t.* [kjuː'tiː] (ABBR) = **quiet** • **on the ~** a hurtadillas
qtr (ABBR) = **quarter**
qty (ABBR) (= **quantity**) ctdad
Qu. (ABBR) = **Queen**
qua [kweɪ] (PREP) (*frm*) en cuanto, como
quack¹ [kwæk] (N) [*of duck*] graznido *m*
(VI) [*duck*] graznar
quack²* [kwæk] (N) charlatán/ana *m/f*; (= *doctor*) curandero/a *m/f*; (*pej*) matasanos* *mf inv*
(CPD) [*remedy*] de curandero ▸ **quack doctor** medicucho/a* *m/f*, curandero/a *m/f*
quackery ['kwækərɪ] (N) charlatanismo *m*; (*Med*) curanderismo *m*
quack-quack ['kwæk'kwæk] (N) cuac cuac *m*
quad [kwɒd] (ABBR) **1** (*Archit**) ▹ **quadrangle**
2* = **quadruplet**
3 = **quadruple**
4 (*Typ*) cuadratín *m*
(CPD) ▸ **quad bike** quad *m*
Quadragesima [ˌkwɒdrə'dʒesɪmə] (N) Cuadragésima *f*
quadrangle ['kwɒdræŋgl] (N) **1** (*Geom*) (*with 4 angles*) cuadrilátero *m*, cuadrángulo *m*
2 (= *courtyard*) patio *m*
quadrangular [kwɒ'dræŋgjʊləʳ] (ADJ) cuadrangular

quadrant ['kwɒdrənt] (N) cuadrante *m*
quadraphonic [ˌkwɒdrə'fɒnɪk] (ADJ) cuatrifónico
quadratic [kwɒ'drætɪk] (ADJ) [*equation*] cuadrático, de segundo grado
quadrature ['kwɒdrətʃəʳ] (N) cuadratura *f*
quadrennial [kwɒ'drenɪəl] (ADJ) cuatrienal
quadriceps ['kwɒdrɪˌseps] (N) (PL: **quadriceps**) cuádriceps *m inv*
quadrilateral [ˌkwɒdrɪ'lætərəl] (ADJ) cuadrilátero
(N) cuadrilátero *m*
quadrille [kwə'drɪl] (N) cuadrilla *f*
quadrillion [kwɒ'drɪliən] (N) (*Brit*) cuatrillón *m*; (*US*) mil billones *mpl*
quadripartite ['kwɒdrɪ'pɑːtaɪt] (ADJ) cuadripartido
quadriplegia [ˌkwɒdrɪ'pliːdʒə] (N) cuadriplegia *f*, tetraplegia *f*
quadriplegic [ˌkwɒdrɪ'pliːdʒɪk] (ADJ) cuadripléjico, tetrapléjico
(N) cuadripléjico/a *m/f*, tetrapléjico/a *m/f*
quadrivium [kwɒ'drɪvɪəm] (N) cuadrivio *m*
quadroon** [kwɒ'druːn] (N) cuarterón *m*
quadrophonic [ˌkwɒdrə'fɒnɪk] (ADJ) = **quadraphonic**
quadruped ['kwɒdrʊped] (N) cuadrúpedo *m*
quadruple (ADJ) ['kwɒdrʊpl] cuádruple, cuádruplo • **in ~ time** (*Mus*) en compás de cuatro por cuatro
(N) ['kwɒdrʊpl] cuádruple *m*, cuádruplo *m*
(VT) [kwɒ'druːpl] cuadruplicar
(VI) [kwɒ'druːpl] cuadruplicarse
quadruplet [kwɒ'druːplɪt] (N) cuatrillizo/a *m/f*
quadruplicate (ADJ) [kwɒ'druːplɪkɪt] cuadruplicado
(N) [kwɒ'druːplɪkɪt] • **in ~** por cuadruplicado
(VT) [kwɒ'druːplɪkeɪt] cuadruplicar
quads* ['kwɒdz] (NPL) (= *quadriceps*) cuádriceps *mpl*
quaestor, questor (*US*) ['kwiːstəʳ] (N) cuestor *m*
quaff [kwɒf] (VT) † (*also hum*) beber(se), zamparse*
quagmire ['kwægmaɪəʳ] (N) cenagal *m*, lodazal *m*; (*fig*) atolladero *m*, cenagal *m*
quail¹ [kweɪl] (N) (PL: **quail** *or* **quails**) (= *bird*) codorniz *f*
quail² [kweɪl] (VI) (= *cower*) temblar (**at** ante) • **her heart ~ed** se le encogió el corazón
quaint [kweɪnt] (ADJ) (COMPAR: **quainter**, SUPERL: **quaintest**) **1** (= *picturesque*) [*building, street, village*] pintoresco
2 (= *odd*) [*custom, notion*] curioso; [*person*] peculiar, poco corriente • **how ~!** ¡qué curioso!
quaintly ['kweɪntlɪ] (ADV) **1** (= *charmingly*) [*decorated*] pintorescamente • **the building was ~ old-fashioned** el edificio parecía anticuado y pintoresco
2 (= *oddly*) • **the ~ named town of Normal** el pueblo denominado con el curioso nombre de Normal • **this may seem a ~ old-fashioned idea** puede que esta idea parezca extraña y anticuada • **he described it ~ as …** le dio la curiosa calificación de …
quaintness ['kweɪntnɪs] (N)
1 (= *picturesqueness*) [*of place, object*] lo pintoresco
2 (= *oddness*) [*of custom, word, idea, question*] lo curioso
quake [kweɪk] (VI) [*person*] (= *shake*) temblar; (*inwardly*) estremecerse • **to ~ with fright** temblar de miedo • **he was quaking at the knees** le temblaban las piernas • **I ~d at the prospect** esa posibilidad me hizo estremecer
(N)* (= *earthquake*) terremoto *m*, temblor *m*
quakeproof* ['kweɪkpruːf] (ADJ) [+ *building etc*] a prueba de terremotos, antisísmico
(VT) construir a prueba de terremotos
Quaker ['kweɪkəʳ] (ADJ) cuáquero
(N) cuáquero/a *m/f*
Quakerism ['kweɪkərɪzəm] (N) cuaquerismo *m*
qualification [ˌkwɒlɪfɪ'keɪʃən] (N)
1 (= *diploma*) título *m* • **he left school without any ~s** dejó la escuela sin sacarse ningún título • **what are his ~s?** ¿qué títulos tiene? • **a teaching ~** un título de profesor • **vocational ~s** títulos *mpl* de formación profesional
2 (*for a post*) requisito *m* • **she doesn't have the ~s for the post** no reúne los requisitos para el puesto • **the ~s for membership** lo que se requiere para ser socio
3 (= *description*) calificación *f*
4 (*Sport*) clasificación *f* • **they missed ~ for the finals** no consiguieron clasificarse para la final
5 (= *reservation*) reserva *f*; (= *modification*) salvedad *f* • **without ~** sin reserva • **this is true, with the ~ that …** esto es verdad, con la salvedad de que … • **by way of ~, I should point out that …** quisiera hacer la salvedad de que …
qualified ['kwɒlɪfaɪd] (ADJ) **1** (*in subject*) (*having exam passes, certificates*) titulado • **a ~ engineer** un ingeniero titulado • **~ ski instructors** instructores *mpl* de esquí titulados • **to be ~ to do sth** (*having passed exams*) estar titulado para hacer algo; (*having right expertise*) estar cualificado para hacer algo • **he was by far the best ~ for the task** era con mucho el mejor cualificado para la tarea • **a group of highly ~ young people** un grupo de jóvenes altamente cualificados • **a newly ~ accountant** un contable recién licenciado • **newly ~ drivers** conductores *mpl* que acaban de sacarse el carné • **to be properly ~** tener los títulos necesarios • **it can be difficult to find suitably ~ staff** a veces es difícil encontrar personal adecuadamente cualificado
2 (= *equipped, capable*) • **to be ~ to do sth** estar capacitado para hacer algo • **I don't feel ~ to judge that** no me siento capacitado para

juzgar eso • **no one is better ~ than Maria to do this** nadie está mejor capacitada que María para hacer esto
3 (= *eligible*) • **to be ~ to vote** reunir los requisitos necesarios para votar • **you are not ~ to receive benefit** usted no reúne los requisitos necesarios para recibir ayuda del estado
4 (= *limited*) • **he gave it his ~ approval** lo aprobó con reservas • **the committee gave a ~ endorsement to the plan** el comité aprobó el plan bajo ciertas condiciones • **it was a ~ success** fue un éxito relativo • **to give ~ support to sth** apoyar algo con reservas
CPD ▸ **qualified majority voting** votación *f* de mayoría mínima ▸ **qualified voter** elector(a) *m/f* habilitado/a

qualifier ['kwɒlɪfaɪəʳ] N **1** (*Sport*) (= *person*) clasificado/a *m/f*; (= *match, heat, round*) eliminatoria *f*
2 (*Gram*) calificador *m*

qualify ['kwɒlɪfaɪ] VI **1** (= *gain qualification*) (*degree*) terminar la carrera, sacar el título, recibirse (*LAm*); (*professional exams*) obtener la licencia para ejercer (como profesional) • **to ~ as an engineer** sacar el título de ingeniero
2 (= *meet criteria*) **a** • **to ~ as sth**: • **it may ~ as a medical expense** puede que cuente como gastos médicos • **to ~ as disabled, he must …** para ser declarado minusválido, tiene que … • **he hardly qualifies as a poet** apenas se le puede calificar de poeta
b • **to ~ for sth** (= *be eligible*) tener derecho a (recibir) algo • **she doesn't ~ for a grant** no tiene derecho a una beca, no puede optar a una beca
3 (*Sport*) clasificarse (**for** para) • **she qualified third** se clasificó en tercer lugar • **the winner qualifies for the second round** el ganador se clasifica para la segunda vuelta
VT **1** (= *give qualifications, knowledge to*) • **to ~ sb to do sth** capacitar a algn para hacer algo • **the basic course does not ~ you to practise as a therapist** el curso básico no le capacita para ejercer de terapeuta • **to ~ sb for sth** capacitar a algn para algo
2 (= *make eligible*) • **your age may ~ you for a special discount** puede que tu edad te dé derecho a un descuento especial • **that doesn't ~ him to speak on this** eso no le da derecho a hablar sobre esto
3 (= *modify*) [+ *statement*] matizar; (= *limit*) [+ *support, conclusion*] condicionar • **I think you should ~ that remark** creo que deberías matizar ese comentario
4 (= *describe*) **a** (*gen*) calificar (**as** de) • **some of her statements could be qualified as racist** algunos de sus comentarios se podrían calificar de racistas
b (*Gram*) calificar a • **the adjective qualifies the noun** el adjetivo califica al sustantivo

qualifying ['kwɒlɪfaɪɪŋ] ADJ **1** (*Univ, Sport*) [*exam, round, game*] eliminatorio; [*team, contestant*] clasificado • **~ heat** prueba *f* clasificatoria • **he failed to achieve the ~ time** (*Sport*) no consiguió el tiempo mínimo requerido para la clasificación • **after a four-month ~ period he will be able to play in the team** después del periodo de cuatro meses estipulado como requisito, podrá formar parte del equipo
2 (*Gram*) calificativo

qualitative ['kwɒlɪtətɪv] ADJ cualitativo

qualitatively ['kwɒlɪtətɪvlɪ] ADV [*different, new*] cualitativamente, desde un punto de vista cualitativo

quality ['kwɒlɪtɪ] N **1** (= *standard, high standard*) calidad *f* • **of good/high ~** de buena/alta calidad • **of poor/low ~** de mala/baja calidad • **a top-quality hotel** un hotel de primera calidad • **the ~ of life** la calidad de vida • **he has real ~** tiene verdadera calidad • **a product of ~** un producto de calidad • PROVERB: • **~ is more important than quantity** la calidad es más importante que la cantidad, lo que importa es la calidad, no la cantidad
2 (= *personal attribute*) cualidad *f* • **one of his good qualities** una de sus buenas cualidades • **one of his bad qualities** uno de sus defectos • **leadership qualities** cualidades *fpl* de líder
3 (= *physical property*) propiedad *f* • **the nutritional qualities of fruit** las propiedades nutritivas de la fruta
4 (= *nature, character*) cualidad *f* • **a childlike ~** una cualidad infantil
5 (= *tone*) [*of sound, voice*] timbre *m*, tono *m*
6 • **the qualities** (*Brit*) (*Press**) la prensa seria, los periódicos serios
CPD [*product, work*] de calidad; [*newspaper*] serio • **a ~ carpet** una alfombra de calidad ▸ **quality control** control *m* de calidad ▸ **quality controller** controlador(a) *m/f* de calidad ▸ **quality newspaper** periódico *m* serio ▸ **the quality papers** los periódicos serios ▸ **the quality press** la prensa seria; ▷ BROADSHEETS AND TABLOIDS ▸ **quality time** *tiempo dedicado a la familia y a los amigos* • **I need to spend some ~ time with my children** necesito pasar tiempo disfrutando con mis hijos • **if you don't spend ~ time studying you won't learn very much** si no dedicas tiempo en serio a estudiar no aprenderás mucho

qualm [kwɑːm] N **1** (= *scruple*) escrúpulo *m* • **he had no ~s about throwing them out on the street** no tuvo ningún escrúpulo para echarlos a la calle
2 (= *misgiving*) duda *f* • **she signed it without a ~** no tuvo ninguna duda al firmarlo • **he had ~s about their trustworthiness** tenía dudas acerca de su honradez • **I would have no ~s about doing the same again** no dudaría en hacer lo mismo otra vez
3 (*Med*) náusea *f*, mareo *m*

quandary ['kwɒndərɪ] N (= *dilemma*) dilema *m*; (= *difficult situation*) apuro *m* • **to be in a ~** estar en un dilema • **he was in a ~ about whether to accept** estaba en un dilema sobre si aceptar o no • **this put him in a ~** esto lo puso en un dilema • **to get sb out of a ~** sacar a algn de un apuro

quango ['kwæŋgəʊ] N (*Brit*) (= **quasi-autonomous non-governmental organization**) ONG *f*, *organización no gubernamental cuasi autónoma*

> **QUANGO**
> El término **quango**, que corresponde a las siglas de **quasi-autonomous non-governmental organization**, se empezó a usar en el Reino Unido para referirse a organizaciones tales como la **Equal Opportunities Commission** o la **Race Relations Board**, que fueron establecidas por el gobierno pero que no dependían de ningún ministerio. Algunos **quangos** poseen funciones ejecutivas, mientras que otros son meramente consultivos. La práctica de poner demasiadas responsabilidades en manos de **quangos** ha sido criticada debido al hecho de que sus miembros son a menudo nombrados a dedo por el gobierno y no tienen la obligación de responder de sus actividades ante el electorado.

quanta ['kwɒntə] NPL *of* **quantum**

quantifiable ['kwɒntɪfaɪəbl] ADJ cuantificable

quantification [ˌkwɒntɪfɪ'keɪʃən] N cuantificación *f*

quantifier ['kwɒntɪfaɪəʳ] N cuantificador *m*

quantify ['kwɒntɪfaɪ] VT cuantificar

quantitative ['kwɒntɪtətɪv] ADJ cuantitativo
CPD ▸ **quantitative easing** (*Econ*) expansión *f* cuantitativa

quantitatively ['kwɒntɪtətɪvlɪ] ADV cuantitativamente

quantity ['kwɒntɪtɪ] N cantidad *f* • **in large quantities** • **in ~** en grandes cantidades • **unknown ~** incógnita *f*
CPD ▸ **quantity discount** descuento *m* por cantidad ▸ **quantity mark** signo *m* prosódico ▸ **quantity surveyor** aparejador(a) *m/f*

quantum ['kwɒntəm] N (PL: **quanta**) cuanto *m*, quantum *m*
CPD ▸ **quantum leap** salto *m* espectacular ▸ **quantum mechanics** mecánica *f* cuántica ▸ **quantum number** número *m* cuántico ▸ **quantum physics** física *f* cuántica ▸ **quantum theory** teoría *f* cuántica

quarantine ['kwɒrəntiːn] N cuarentena *f* • **to be in ~** estar en cuarentena
VT poner en cuarentena

quark [kwɑːk] N (*Phys*) quark *m*

quarrel ['kwɒrəl] N (= *argument*) riña *f*, pelea *f* • **to have a ~ with sb** reñir *or* pelearse con algn • **I have no ~ with you** no tengo nada en contra de usted, no tengo queja de usted • **to pick a ~** buscar pelea *or* pleito • **to pick a ~ with sb** meterse con algn, buscar pelea *or* pleito con algn • **to take up sb's ~** ponerse de la parte de algn
VI reñir, pelearse • **we ~led and I never saw him again** reñimos y no volví a verlo • **they ~led about** *or* **over money** riñeron por cuestión de dinero • **to ~ with sb** reñir con algn • **I can't ~ with that** eso no lo discuto • **what we ~ with is …** en lo que discrepamos *or* no estamos de acuerdo es …

quarrelling, quarreling (*US*) ['kwɒrəlɪŋ] N riñas *fpl*, disputas *fpl*, peleas *fpl* • **there was constant ~** había riñas *or* disputas *or* peleas continuas

quarrelsome ['kwɒrəlsəm] ADJ pendenciero, peleón*

quarrelsomeness ['kwɒrəlsəmnɪs] N espíritu *m* pendenciero

quarrier ['kwɒrɪəʳ] N cantero *m*

quarry¹ ['kwɒrɪ] N (*Hunting*) presa *f*; (*fig*) presa *f*, víctima *f*

quarry² ['kwɒrɪ] N (= *mine*) cantera *f*
VT sacar, extraer
VI explotar una cantera, extraer piedra de una cantera • **to ~ for marble** abrir una cantera en busca de mármol
CPD ▸ **quarry tile** baldosa *f* (no vidriada)
▸ **quarry out** VT + ADV sacar, extraer

quarryman ['kwɒrɪmən] N (PL: **quarrymen**) cantero *m*, picapedrero *m*

quart [kwɔːt] N (*gen*) cuarto *m* de galón (*Brit* = *1,136 litros; US* = *0,946 litros*) • IDIOM: • **you're trying to get a ~ into a pint pot** está claro que no cabe

quarter ['kwɔːtəʳ] N **1** (= *fourth part*) [*of kilo, kilometre, second*] cuarto *m*; [*of price, population*] cuarta parte *f* • **a ~ of a mile** un cuarto de milla • **a ~ (of a pound) of tea** un cuarto de libra de té • **for a ~ of the price** por la cuarta parte del precio • **to divide sth into ~s** dividir algo en cuartos *or* en cuatro • **the tank was only a ~ full** el depósito solo estaba a un cuarto de su capacidad • **it's a ~ gone already** ya se ha gastado la cuarta parte • **I'm a ~ Spanish** tengo una cuarta parte de sangre española
2 (*in time*) cuarto *m* • **a ~ of an hour/century**

un cuarto de hora/siglo • **an hour and a ~** una hora y cuarto • **three ~s of an hour** tres cuartos de hora • **it's a ~ past** *or* (US) **after seven** son las siete y cuarto • **it's a ~ to** *or* (US) **of seven** son las siete menos cuarto, es un cuarto para las siete (*LAm*)
3 (*specific fourth parts*) **a** (*US, Canada*) (= *25 cents*) (moneda *f* de) cuarto *m* de dólar
b [*of year*] trimestre *m* • **to pay by the ~** pagar trimestralmente *or* al trimestre *or* cada tres meses
c [*of moon*] cuarto *m* • **when the moon is in its first/last ~** cuando la luna está en cuarto creciente/menguante
4 (= *part of town*) barrio *m* • **the business ~** el barrio comercial • **the old ~** el casco viejo *or* antiguo
5 (= *direction, area*) • **protest is growing in some ~s** las protestas aumentan en algunos círculos • **from all ~s** de todas partes • **at close ~s** de cerca • **he fired two shots at close ~s** disparó dos tiros a quemarropa • **they are spread over the four ~s of the globe** se extienden por todos los rincones *or* por todas partes del mundo • **help came from an unexpected ~** la ayuda nos llegó de un lugar inesperado
6 (*Naut, Geog*) [*of compass*] cuarta *f* • **the port/starboard ~** [*of ship*] la aleta de babor/estribor • **the wind was from the port ~** el viento soplaba de babor • **the wind is in the right ~** el viento sopla en dirección favorable
7 (*Heraldry*) cuartel *m*
8 (*frm*) (= *mercy*) clemencia *f* • **they knew they could expect no ~** sabían que no podían esperar clemencia • **to give (sb) no ~** no dar cuartel (a algn)
9 quarters (= *accommodation*) **a** (*for staff*) (= *building, section*) dependencias *fpl*; (= *rooms*) cuartos *mpl*, habitaciones *fpl* • **the servants' ~s** las dependencias del servicio • **they're living in very cramped ~s** viven hacinados • **the cramped ~s of the space capsule** el reducido espacio de la cápsula espacial; ▹ **living**
b (*Mil*) (= *barracks*) cuartel *msing*; (*also* **sleeping quarters**) barracones *mpl* • **the crew's/officers' ~s** (*on ship*) las dependencias de la tripulación/de los oficiales; ▹ **married**
(ADJ) cuarto • **he has a ~ share** tiene una cuarta parte • **a ~ pound/century** un cuarto de libra/siglo
(VT) **1** (= *divide into four*) [+ *apple, potato*] cortar en cuatro (trozos); [+ *carcass, body*] descuartizar; ▹ **hang**
2 (*Mil*) acuartelar, alojar • **our soldiers are ~ed in Ramsey** nuestros soldados están acuartelados en Ramsey
3 (= *range over*) [*person*] recorrer • **to ~ the ground** [*dog*] buscar olfateando; [*bird*] escudriñar el terreno
(CPD) ▸ **quarter day** (*gen*) *primer día del trimestre*; (*Econ*) *el día del vencimiento de un pago trimestral* ▸ **quarter light** (*Brit*) (*Aut*) ventanilla *f* direccional ▸ **quarter note** (*US*) (*Mus*) negra *f* ▸ **quarter pound** cuarto *m* de libra ▸ **quarter tone** cuarto *m* de tono ▸ **quarter turn** cuarto *m* de vuelta

quarterback ['kwɔːtəbæk] (N) (*US*) (*Ftbl*) mariscal *mf* de campo
quarterdeck ['kwɔːtədek] (N) alcázar *m*
quarter-final ['kwɔːtə,faɪnl] (N) cuarto *m* de final
quarter-finalist ['kwɔːtə'faɪnəlɪst] (N) cuartofinalista *mf*
quarter-hour ['kwɔːtə'aʊəʳ] (N) cuarto *m* de hora
quarter-hourly ['kwɔːtə'aʊəlɪ] (ADV) cada cuarto de hora
(ADJ) • **at quarter-hourly intervals** cada cuarto de hora
quartering ['kwɔːtərɪŋ] (N) (*Heraldry*) cuartel *m*
quarterlight ['kwɔːtəlaɪt] (N) (*Brit*) (*in vehicle*) ventanilla *f* triangular, ventanilla *f* giratoria
quarterly ['kwɔːtəlɪ] (ADV) trimestralmente, cada tres meses
(ADJ) trimestral
(N) publicación *f* trimestral
quartermaster ['kwɔːtə,mɑːstəʳ] (N) intendente *m*
(CPD) ▸ **quartermaster general** intendente *m* general ▸ **quartermaster sergeant** ≈ brigada *m*
quartern ['kwɔːtən] (N) cuarta *f*
(CPD) ▸ **quartern loaf** pan *m* de cuatro libras
quarter-pound [,kwɔːtə'paʊnd] (ADJ) de un cuarto de libra
quarter-pounder [,kwɔːtə'paʊndəʳ] (N) *hamburguesa que pesa un cuarto de libra*
quarterstaff ['kwɔːtəstɑːf] (N) (*Hist*) barra *f*
quartet, quartette [kwɔː'tet] (N) (*gen*) (*Mus*) cuarteto *m*
quartile ['kwɔːtaɪl] (N) cuartil *m*
quarto ['kwɔːtəʊ] (ADJ) [*volume*] en cuarto; [*paper*] tamaño *m* holandesa
(N) libro *m* en cuarto
quartz ['kwɔːts] (N) cuarzo *m*
(CPD) ▸ **quartz clock** reloj *m* de cuarzo ▸ **quartz crystal** cristal *m* de cuarzo ▸ **quartz lamp** lámpara *f* de cuarzo ▸ **quartz watch** reloj *m* de cuarzo
quartzite ['kwɔːtsaɪt] (N) cuarcita *f*
quasar ['kweɪzɑːʳ] (N) cuasar *m*, quásar *m*
quash [kwɒʃ] (VT) **1** [+ *rebellion*] sofocar
2 [+ *proposal*] rechazar; [+ *verdict*] anular, invalidar
quasi- ['kweɪzaɪ, 'kwɑːzɪ] (PREFIX) cuasi- • **quasi-religious** cuasi-religioso • **quasi-revolutionary** cuasi-revolucionario
quatercentenary [,kwɒtəsen'tiːnərɪ] (N) cuarto centenario *m*
quaternary [kwə'tɜːnərɪ] (ADJ) cuaternario
(N) cuaternario *m*
quatrain ['kwɒtreɪn] (N) cuarteto *m*, estrofa *f* de cuatro versos
quaver ['kweɪvəʳ] (N) (*when speaking*) temblor *m*; (*Mus*) (= *trill*) trémolo *m*; (*Brit*) (= *note*) corchea *f* • **with a ~ in her voice** con voz trémula
(VI) [*voice*] temblar
(VT) • **"yes," she ~ed** —sí —dijo con voz trémula *or* temblorosa
(CPD) ▸ **quaver rest** (*Brit*) pausa *f* de corchea
quavering ['kweɪvərɪŋ] (ADJ) trémulo, tembloroso
quavery ['kweɪvərɪ] (ADJ) = **quavering**
quay [kiː] (N) muelle *m* • **on the ~** en el muelle
quayside ['kiːsaɪd] (N) muelle *m*
Que. (ABBR) (*Canada*) = **Quebec**
queasiness ['kwiːzɪnɪs] (N) **1** (= *nausea*) náuseas *fpl*, sensación *f* de mareo • **the anaesthetic may cause a little ~** la anestesia puede producirle ligeras náuseas *or* una ligera sensación de mareo • **a feeling of ~** una sensación de mareo
2 (= *unease*) intranquilidad *f*
queasy ['kwiːzɪ] (ADJ) (COMPAR: **queasier**, SUPERL: **queasiest**) **1** (= *nauseous*) [*stomach*] revuelto • **his stomach was ~** tenía el estómago revuelto • **to be** *or* **feel ~** tener náuseas • **the food made her (feel) ~** la comida le revolvió el estómago • **the slight rocking made her feel ~** el ligero balanceo la mareó • **it made him (feel) ~ to watch it** se mareó al verlo, verlo le revolvió el estómago
2 (= *uneasy*) intranquilo • **I had a ~ feeling about the whole thing** todo este asunto me inquietaba *or* me hacía sentirme intranquilo
Quebec [kwɪ'bek] (N) Quebec *m*
queen [kwiːn] (N) **1** (= *monarch*) reina *f*; (*Chess*) reina *f*; (*Cards*) dama *f*; (*in Spanish pack*) caballo *m* • **she was ~ to Charles II** era la reina de Carlos II
2 (*Zool*) (*also* **queen bee**) abeja *f* reina; (= *ant*) hormiga *f* reina
3‡ marica‡ *m* (*pej*)
(VT) (*Chess*) [+ *pawn*] coronar • IDIOM: • **to ~ it** conducirse como una reina; (*fig*) pavonearse
(VI) (*Chess*) ser coronado
(CPD) ▸ **Queen's Bench** (*Brit*) *departamento del Tribunal Supremo de Justicia* ▸ **Queen's speech** (*Brit*) discurso *m* de la reina ▸ **queen mother** reina *f* madre ▸ **Queen's Counsel** (*Brit*) abogado *mf* (*de categoría superior*); ▹ **QC/KC**

QUEEN'S/KING'S SPEECH
En el Reino Unido, el **Queen's** o **King's speech** es el discurso que el monarca dirige cada año a las dos cámaras del Parlamento en la apertura del nuevo curso parlamentario. El discurso se retransmite por radio y televisión y es preparado por el gobierno, ya que en él se indican las directrices del programa de gobierno para el curso que comienza, así como la nueva legislación que se introducirá ese año. Para seguir con la tradición, en este discurso el monarca sigue refiriéndose al gobierno como **my government**.

queenly ['kwiːnlɪ] (ADJ) [*manner, bearing*] regio; [*responsibilities*] de reina
queen-size bed ['kwiːnsaɪz'bed], **queen-sized bed** ['kwiːnsaɪzd'bed] (N) cama *f* queen size
queer [kwɪəʳ] (ADJ) (COMPAR: **queerer**, SUPERL: **queerest**) **1** (= *odd*) raro, extraño • **there's something ~ going on** pasa algo raro *or* extraño • **there was a ~ noise coming from the kitchen** había un ruido raro en la cocina • **to be ~ in the head*** andar mal de la cabeza* • IDIOM: • **to be in Queer Street** (*Brit**) estar en apuros
2 (*Brit*†) (= *ill*) • **to feel ~** no sentirse bien, encontrarse mal • **to come over ~** ponerse malo
3†‡ (*pej*) (= *homosexual*) maricón‡, marica‡
(N)‡ (*pej*) (= *homosexual*) maricón‡ *m*, marica‡ *m*
(VT) • IDIOM: • **to ~ sb's pitch** fastidiar a algn
queer-bashing‡ ['kwɪə,bæʃɪŋ] (N) • **to go in for queer-bashing** atacar a homosexuales
queer-looking ['kwɪə,lʊkɪŋ] (ADJ) [*animal, plant, insect*] de aspecto extraño
queerly ['kwɪəlɪ] (ADV) [*behave, laugh, dress*] de modo raro *or* extraño, de forma rara *or* extraña
queerness ['kwɪənɪs] (N) (= *oddness*) lo raro, lo extraño
queer-sounding ['kwɪə,saʊndɪŋ] (ADJ) [*name*] raro
quell [kwel] (VT) [+ *uprising*] sofocar; [+ *opposition*] sobreponerse a, dominar; [+ *fears*] desechar
quench [kwentʃ] (VT) [+ *flames, thirst*] apagar; [+ *hope*] matar, sofocar; [+ *desire*] satisfacer; [+ *enthusiasm, passion*] enfriar
quenchless ['kwentʃlɪs] (ADJ) inapagable
quenelle [kə'nel] (N) (*Culin*) quenelle *f*
quern [kwɜːn] (N) molinillo *m* de mano
querulous ['kwerʊləs] (ADJ) quejumbroso
querulously ['kwerʊləslɪ] (ADV) quejumbrosamente; [*say*] en tono quejumbroso
query ['kwɪərɪ] (N) **1** (= *question*) pregunta *f*; (*fig*) (= *doubt*) duda *f*, interrogante *m or f* • **if**

you have any queries, please do not hesitate to call si tiene alguna pregunta, no dude en llamar • **there are many queries about his suitability for the job** hay muchos interrogantes acerca de su idoneidad para el puesto
2 (*Gram*) (= *question mark*) signo *m* de interrogación
VT (= *ask*) preguntar; (= *doubt*) dudar de, expresar dudas acerca de; (= *disagree with, dispute*) cuestionar, poner en duda; (*Comput*) interrogar • **to ~ sb about sth** preguntar a algn sobre algo • **to ~ whether ...** dudar si ... • **I would ~ that** dudo si eso es cierto, tengo mis dudas acerca de eso • **no one queried my decision** nadie cuestionó *or* puso en duda mi decisión • **they queried the bill** pidieron explicaciones sobre la factura • **do you ~ the evidence?** ¿tiene dudas acerca del testimonio?
CPD ▸ **query language** lenguaje *m* de interrogación

quest [kwest] N (*lit, fig*) búsqueda *f* (**for** de) • **to go in ~ of** ir en busca de
VI • **to ~ for sth** buscar algo

questing ['kwestɪŋ] ADJ [*mind*] inquisitivo

question ['kwestʃən] N **1** (= *query*) (*also in exam*) pregunta *f* • **(are there) any ~s?** ¿(hay) alguna pregunta? • **to ask (sb) a ~** hacer una pregunta (a algn) • **ask yourself this ~** hágase esta pregunta • **what a ~ to ask!** ¡vaya preguntita! • **there's a reward for the painting's return, no ~s asked** se ofrece una recompensa sin preguntas por la devolución del cuadro • **ask me no ~s and I'll tell you no lies** más vale que no me preguntes • **"why didn't you appoint him a year ago?" — "good ~"** —¿por qué no lo nombraste hace un año? —buena pregunta *or* —eso me pregunto yo • **he posed three ~s** hizo *or* planteó tres preguntas • **to put a ~ to sb** (*frm*) hacer una pregunta a algn • **to put down a ~ to** *or* **for sb** (*Parl*) formular una pregunta a algn • **to obey orders without ~** obedecer órdenes sin rechistar • IDIOM: • **the 64,000 dollar ~** la pregunta del millón; ▹ **leading, open, personal, pop, trick**
2 (= *matter, issue*) cuestión *f* • **the Palestinian ~** la cuestión palestina • **that is the ~** de eso se trata, esa es la cuestión • **that is not the ~** no se trata de eso, no es cuestión de eso • **at the time in ~** a la hora en cuestión • **it is not simply a ~ of money** no se trata simplemente de dinero, no es una simple cuestión de dinero • **this raises the ~ of her suitability** esto plantea la cuestión de si es la persona adecuada • **it's only a ~ of time before he finds out** solo es cuestión de tiempo que se entere; ▹ **beg**
3 (= *possibility*) posibilidad *f* • **there is no ~ of outside help** no hay posibilidad de ayuda externa • **there can be no ~ of your resigning** su dimisión no se puede admitir • **it's out of the ~!** ¡imposible!, ¡ni hablar! • **an interest rate cut is out of the ~** un recorte de los tipos de interés es imposible
4 (= *doubt*) duda *f* • **there is no ~ about it** no cabe la menor duda de esto • **as a manager, her ability is beyond ~** como directora, su capacidad está fuera de toda duda • **to bring** *or* **call sth into ~** poner algo en duda • **my integrity has been brought** *or* **called into ~** mi integridad se ha puesto en duda • **to be in ~** estar en duda • **your professional ability is not in ~** no es tu capacidad como profesional lo que se pone en duda • **his findings pose ~s about the future of these drugs** sus descubrimientos hacen que se planteen preguntas sobre el futuro de estas drogas • **this disaster raises ~s about air safety in the region** con el desastre se ha puesto en duda la seguridad aérea en la zona • **the ~ remains (as to) whether he can be trusted** la duda *or* la cuestión sigue siendo si se puede confiar en él • **the ~ remains: how did she escape?** la pregunta sigue ahí: ¿cómo escapó? • **there is some ~ as to whether he will sign** hay *or* existen ciertas dudas sobre si firmará • **without ~** sin duda, indudablemente
5 (*at meeting*) cuestión *f*, asunto *m* • **to move the previous ~** plantear la cuestión previa • **to put the ~ (to a vote)** someter la moción a votación
VT **1** (= *interrogate*) [+ *exam candidate, interviewee*] hacer preguntas a; [+ *suspect*] interrogar; (*Parl*) [+ *minister, secretary*] interpelar • **you will be ~ed on one of three topics** se te harán preguntas sobre uno de tres temas • **a suspect is being ~ed by police** la policía está interrogando a un sospechoso • **they ~ed him about his past** le hicieron preguntas *or* le preguntaron acerca de su pasado • **the minister was ~ed about his statement to Parliament** se interpeló al ministro sobre su declaración ante el Parlamento
2 (= *doubt*) [+ *honesty, loyalty, motives*] dudar de, poner en duda; [+ *decision, beliefs*] poner en duda, cuestionar
CPD ▸ **question mark** (*lit*) signo *m* de interrogación; (*fig*) interrogante *m or f* • **a big ~ mark hangs over his future** se plantea un enorme interrogante sobre su futuro
▸ **question master** interrogador *m*
▸ **question tag** coletilla *f* interrogativa
▸ **question time** (*Brit*) (*Parl*) sesión *f* de interpelaciones a los ministros

questionable ['kwestʃənəbl] ADJ
1 (= *uncertain, debatable*) [*assumption, significance, value*] discutible, cuestionable • **it is ~ whether ...** es discutible si ...
2 (= *morally dubious*) [*behaviour, method, practice*] cuestionable • **in ~ taste** de dudoso gusto

questionary ['kwestʃənərɪ] N cuestionario *m*, encuesta *f*

questioner ['kwestʃənə^r^] N interrogador(a) *m/f*; (*at meeting*) interpelante *mf*

questioning ['kwestʃənɪŋ] ADJ [*tone, mind*] inquisitivo, inquisidor • **she gave him a ~ look** le lanzó una mirada inquisitiva *or* inquisidora
N **1** (= *interrogation*) interrogatorio *m* • **he is wanted for ~ by police** la policía requiere su presencia para someterlo a un interrogatorio
2 (= *doubting*) cuestionamiento *m*, puesta *f* en duda

questioningly ['kwestʃənɪŋlɪ] ADV de manera inquisitiva *or* inquisidora

questionnaire [ˌkwestʃə'nɛə^r^] N cuestionario *m*

questor ['kwi:stə^r^] N (*US*) = **quaestor**

queue [kju:] (*esp Brit*) N cola *f* • **to form a ~** • **stand in a ~** hacer cola • **to jump the ~** colarse*, saltarse la cola
VI (*also* **queue up**) hacer cola • **to ~ for three hours** pasar tres horas haciendo cola • **we ~d for tickets** hicimos cola para comprar entradas

queue-jump ['kju:ˌdʒʌmp] VI (*Brit*) colarse*

queue-jumper ['kju:ˌdʒʌmpə^r^] N (*Brit*) colón/ona* *m/f*

queue-jumping ['kju:ˌdʒʌmpɪŋ] N (*Brit*) colarse *m* • **queue-jumping will not be tolerated** no se permitirá que nadie se cuele

quibble ['kwɪbl] N (= *trivial objection*) objeción *f* de poca monta • **he dismissed their objections as mere ~s** desestimó sus objeciones como si se trataran de simples nimiedades • **the deal was held up by some legal ~** se retrasó el acuerdo a causa de una pequeña objeción de carácter legal
VI hacer objeciones de poca monta • **he always ~s** es un quisquilloso • **to ~ over** *or* **about sth** discutir por algo sin importancia • **I'm not going to ~ over 20 pence** no voy a discutir por 20 peniques • **there's no point in quibbling about who's right and who's wrong** no sirve de nada discutir por quién tiene razón y quién no

quibbler ['kwɪblə^r^] N quisquilloso/a *m/f*

quibbling ['kwɪblɪŋ] ADJ quisquilloso
N objeciones *fpl* de poca monta

quiche [ki:ʃ] N quiche *m*

quick [kwɪk] ADJ (COMPAR: **quicker**, SUPERL: **quickest**) **1** (= *fast*) [*method, movement*] rápido • **this is the ~est way to do it** esta es la forma más rápida de hacerlo • **it's ~er by train** es más rápido ir en tren • **be ~!** ¡rápido!, ¡date prisa!, ¡apúrate! (*LAm*) • **to be ~ to do sth** hacer algo rápidamente • **he was ~ to see the possibilities** vio rápidamente las posibilidades • **his opponents were ~ to point out that ...** sus adversarios señalaron rápidamente que ... • **to be ~ to act** obrar con prontitud • **to be ~ to anger** enfadarse con facilidad • **to be ~ to take offence** ofenderse por nada • **and be ~ about it!** ¡y date prisa!, ¡y apúrate! (*LAm*) • **~ march!** (*Mil*) ¡marchando, ar! • **at a ~ pace** a un paso rápido • **he made a ~ recovery** se recuperó rápidamente • **in ~ succession** en rápida sucesión • **to have a ~ temper** tener un genio vivo • **he's a ~ worker** trabaja rápido, es un trabajador rápido; ▹ **draw, mark², uptake**
2 (= *with minimal delay*) [*answer, decision*] rápido • **we must have a ~ answer** necesitamos una respuesta rápida • **we are hoping for a ~ end to the bloodshed** esperamos que el derramamiento de sangre acabe pronto • **a ~ fix** una solución fácil • **the price has been reduced for a ~ sale** han reducido el precio para venderlo pronto
3 (= *not lengthy*) [*meal*] rápido • **he gave me a ~ kiss on the cheek** me dio un besito en la mejilla • **let's have a ~ look at that*** déjame echarle un vistazo rápido a eso • **to have a ~ one*** (= *drink*) tomarse un trago • **can I have a ~ word (with you)?** ¿puedo hablar un segundo contigo?, ¿podemos hablar un segundo?
4 (= *sharp*) [*person*] listo; [*wit*] agudo; [*mind, reflexes*] ágil, rápido • **he is very ~ at maths** es muy rápido para las matemáticas • **to have a ~ eye for sth** captar *or* coger algo al vuelo
N **1** (*Anat*) • **the ~**: • **her nails were bitten down to the ~** se había mordido las uñas hasta dejárselas como muñones • IDIOM: • **to cut sb to the ~** herir a algn en lo vivo
2†† (*liter*) • **the ~ and the dead** los vivos y los muertos
ADV deprisa, rápido • **~!** ¡deprisa!, ¡rápido! • **I left as ~ as I could** me fui lo más rápido *or* deprisa que pude • **come as ~ as you can** ven cuanto antes • IDIOM: • **as ~ as a flash** como un rayo *or* relámpago
CPD ▸ **quick thinking** reacción *f* rápida; ▹ **quick-thinking**

quick-acting ['kwɪk'æktɪŋ] ADJ de acción rápida

quick-change ['kwɪk'tʃeɪndʒ] ADJ (*Theat*) • **quick-change artist** transformista *mf*

quick-drying ['kwɪk'draɪɪŋ] ADJ [*paint, varnish*] de secado rápido

quick-eared ['kwɪk'ɪəd] ADJ de oído fino

quicken ['kwɪkən] VT (= *speed up*) acelerar, apresurar • **to ~ one's pace** apretar *or* acelerar el paso

VI [*breathing, pulse*] acelerarse; [*interest*] acrecentarse, avivarse; [*embryo*] empezar a moverse • **the pace ~ed** se aceleró el paso • **men's hearts ~ed whenever she appeared** cuando aparecía ella se les aceleraba el pulso a los hombres

quick-eyed ['kwɪk'aɪd] ADJ de vista aguda

quick-fire ['kwɪkfaɪəʳ] ADJ [*gun*] de tiro rápido; [*question*] rápido, hecho a quemarropa

quick-firing ['kwɪk,faɪərɪŋ] ADJ de tiro rápido

quick-freeze ['kwɪk'fri:z] VT congelar rápidamente

quickie* ['kwɪkɪ] N (= *question*) pregunta *f* cortita*; (= *drink*) copita* *f*; (= *sex*) polvito* *m* • **to have a ~** (= *drink*) tomarse una copita*; (= *sex*) echarse un polvito*
CPD ▸ **quickie divorce*** divorcio *m* exprés

quicklime ['kwɪklaɪm] N cal *f* viva

quickly ['kwɪklɪ] ADV **1** (= *fast*) [*move, work*] deprisa, rápidamente • **I'm working as ~ as I can** estoy trabajando lo más rápido *or* lo mas rápidamente que puedo, no puedo trabajar más deprisa • **he talks too ~ for me to understand** habla demasiado deprisa y no le entiendo
2 (= *with minimal delay*) [*arrive, answer, react*] en seguida, con prontitud (*more frm*) • **the police were ~ on the scene** la policía llegó en seguida • **they answered ~** contestaron pronto • **success ~ followed** el éxito llegó en seguida *or* muy poco después • **come as ~ as you can** ven cuanto antes
3 (= *not lengthily*) [*embrace, smile*] rápidamente • **he glanced ~ at the note** echó un vistazo rápido a la nota

quickness ['kwɪknɪs] N **1** (= *speed*) rapidez *f*, velocidad *f* • **his ~ on his feet** su velocidad
2 (= *lack of delay*) prontitud *f*
3 (= *sharpness*) agudeza *f* • **~ of mind** rapidez *f*, agilidad *f* mental

quick-release [,kwɪkrɪ'li:s] ADJ [*wheel, buckle, strap*] abrefácil (*inv*)

quicksand ['kwɪksænd] N arenas *fpl* movedizas

quickset ['kwɪkset] ADJ compuesto de plantas vivas (*esp de espinos*)
N (= *slip*) plantón *m*; (= *hawthorn*) espino *m*; (= *hedge*) seto *m* vivo (*esp de espinos*)

quick-setting ['kwɪk,setɪŋ] ADJ • **quick-setting glue** pegamento *m* rápido

quick-sighted ['kwɪk'saɪtɪd] ADJ de vista aguda; (*fig*) perspicaz

quicksilver ['kwɪk,sɪlvəʳ] N azogue *m*, mercurio *m*
ADJ (*fig*) [*moods, temperament*] inconstante, caprichoso
VT azogar

quickstep ['kwɪkstep] N (= *dance*) baile *formal a ritmo rápido*

quick-tempered ['kwɪk'tempəd] ADJ de genio vivo, irascible

quick-thinking [,kwɪk'θɪŋkɪŋ] ADJ [*person*] que reacciona rápidamente • **to be quick-thinking** reaccionar rápidamente; ▸ **quick thinking**

quickthorn ['kwɪkθɔ:n] N espino *m* albar

quick-witted ['kwɪk'wɪtɪd] ADJ agudo, perspicaz • **that was very quick-witted of you** en eso fuiste muy agudo

quid¹* [kwɪd] N (*Brit*) libra *f* (esterlina) • **three ~** tres libras • IDIOM: • **to be ~s in** haber ganado bastante

quid² [kwɪd] N [*of tobacco*] mascada *f* (de tabaco)

quiddity ['kwɪdɪtɪ] N (*Philos*) esencia *f*; (= *quibble*) sutileza *f*, sofistería *f*

quid pro quo ['kwɪdprəʊ'kwəʊ] N (PL: **quid pro quos**) compensación *f* (**for** por)

quiescence [kwaɪ'esns] N (*frm*) inactividad *f*, quietud *f*

quiescent [kwaɪ'esnt] ADJ (*frm*) inactivo, quieto

quiet ['kwaɪət] ADJ (COMPAR: **quieter**, SUPERL: **quietest**) **1** (= *not loud*) [*engine*] silencioso; [*music*] tranquilo, suave; [*tone*] bajo, quedo (*liter*); [*laughter*] suave • **he said in a ~ voice** dijo en(un) tono bajo
2 (= *silent*) **a** [*person*] callado • **to be ~** estar callado • **you're very ~ today** hoy estás muy callado • **be ~!** ¡cállate!, ¡silencio! • **to go ~** quedarse callado • **to keep** *or* **stay ~** (= *say nothing*) quedarse callado; (= *not make a noise*) no hacer ruido • **to keep ~ about sth** no decir nada acerca de algo • **to keep sb ~: they paid him £1,000 to keep him ~** le pagaron 1000 libras para que se callara • **that book should keep him ~ for a while** ese libro le tendrá entretenido durante un rato • **I gave him a biscuit to keep him ~** le di una galleta para que estuviese entretenido
b • **to keep sth ~: keep it ~** no se lo digas a nadie • **he managed to keep the whole thing ~** consiguió que nadie se enterara del asunto • **the government has tried to keep the matter ~** el gobierno ha intentado mantener el asunto en secreto
c [*place*] silencioso • **it was dark and the streets were ~** era de noche y las calles estaban silenciosas • **isn't it ~!** ¡qué silencio! • IDIOM: • **it was ~ as the grave** había un silencio sepulcral
3 (= *peaceful, not busy*) [*life, night, village, area*] tranquilo • **they lead a ~ life** llevan una vida tranquila • **he'll do anything for a ~ life** hará lo que sea para que lo dejen en paz • **the patient has had a ~ night** el paciente ha pasado una noche tranquila • **this town is too ~ for me** esta ciudad es demasiado tranquila para mí • **the shops will be ~er today** las tiendas estarán más tranquilas hoy, hoy habrá menos jaleo en las tiendas • **business is ~ at this time of year** hay poco movimiento en esta época • **everybody needs a ~ time** todo el mundo necesita un rato de tranquilidad • **those were ~ times** aquel fue un tiempo de tranquilidad • IDIOM: • **all ~ on the Western front** no hay moros en la costa
4 (= *calm, placid*) [*person*] callado; [*temperament*] tranquilo, sosegado; [*dog, horse*] manso • **my daughter is a very ~ girl** mi hija es una chica muy callada • **we have very ~ neighbours** tenemos unos vecinos muy tranquilos
5 (= *discreet*) [*manner, decor, style*] discreto; [*clothes, dress*] discreto, no llamativo; [*colour*] suave, apagado; [*despair*] callado; [*optimism*] comedido; [*ceremony*] íntimo • **the decoration was in ~ good taste** la decoración era de un gusto discreto • **with ~ humour he said ...** con un humor discreto dijo ... • **we had a ~ lunch/supper** comimos/cenamos en la intimidad • **it was a ~ funeral/wedding** el funeral/la boda se celebró en la intimidad • **to have a ~ dig at sb** burlarse discretamente de algn • **we had a ~ laugh over it** nos reímos en privado • **I'll have a ~ word with him** hablaré discretamente con él
N **1** (= *silence*) silencio *m* • **let's have complete ~ for a few minutes** vamos a tener unos minutos de completo silencio • **in the ~ of the night** en el silencio de la noche • **on the ~** a escondidas
2 (= *peacefulness*) tranquilidad *f* • **there was a period of ~ after the fighting** hubo un periodo de tranquilidad tras los enfrentamientos; ▸ **peace**
VT (*US*) = **quieten**
VI (*US*) = **quieten**

quieten ['kwaɪətn] VT (*also* **quieten down**) (= *calm*) calmar, tranquilizar; (*fig*) (= *silence*) [+ *fears*] acallar • **he managed to ~ the crowd** logró calmar a la multitud
VI (*also* **quieten down**) (= *calm down*) calmarse, tranquilizarse; (= *fall silent*) callarse; (*fig*) (*after unruly youth etc*) calmarse, sentar cabeza; (*after rage*) tranquilizarse

quietism ['kwaɪɪtɪzəm] N quietismo *m*

quietist ['kwaɪɪtɪst] N quietista *mf*

quietly ['kwaɪətlɪ] ADV **1** (= *not loudly*) [*say, whisper*] en voz baja; [*sing*] en voz baja, suavemente; [*drink, leave, walk, come in*] silenciosamente, sin hacer ruido • **this part should be played ~** (*Mus*) esta parte hay que tocarla bajo
2 (= *silently*) en silencio • **she said nothing, but listened ~** no dijo nada, sino que escuchó en silencio
3 (= *peacefully, calmly*) [*play, read*] tranquilamente • **I was ~ drinking a cup of coffee** estaba tomando café tranquilamente • **he refused to go ~** se negó a irse pacíficamente • **are you coming ~ or are you going to make trouble?** ¿nos acompaña usted pacíficamente o va a causar problemas? • **the house is ~ situated in attractive parkland** la casa está situada en una tranquila zona con jardines • **I'm ~ confident about the future** aunque no lo exteriorice, soy optimista respecto al futuro • **he was ~ content** estaba contento y tranquilo
4 (= *discreetly*) discretamente • **the president's plan had been ~ shelved** habían dejado de lado discretamente el plan del presidente • **she lives ~ in Suffolk** vive discretamente en Suffolk • **to be ~ dressed** vestirse con discreción • **he slipped off ~** se marchó sin que nadie lo notara • **let's get married ~** casémonos en la intimidad • **we dined ~ at home** cenamos en la intimidad del hogar

quietness ['kwaɪətnɪs] N **1** (= *softness*) [*of voice, music*] suavidad *f*
2 (= *silence*) silencio *m*
3 (= *calm*) tranquilidad *f*

quietude ['kwaɪətju:d] N quietud *f*

quietus [kwaɪ'i:təs] N (PL: **quietuses**) (*liter*) golpe *m* de gracia; (= *death*) muerte *f*; (*Comm*) quitanza *f*, finiquito *m*

quiff [kwɪf] N copete *m*

quill [kwɪl] N (= *feather*) pluma *f* de ave; (= *part of feather*) cañón *m* de pluma; [*of porcupine, hedgehog*] púa *f*; (= *pen*) pluma *f* (de ganso); (= *bobbin*) canilla *f*
CPD ▸ **quill pen** pluma *f* (de ganso)

quilt [kwɪlt] N edredón *m*; (*Brit*) (*also* **continental quilt**) edredón *m* (nórdico)
VT acolchar

quilted ['kwɪltɪd] ADJ acolchado

quilting ['kwɪltɪŋ] N (= *material*) tela *f* acolchada; (= *act, quilted work*) acolchado *m*

quim** [kwɪm] N coño** *m*

quin* [kwɪn] N (*Brit*) = **quintuplet**

quince [kwɪns] N membrillo *m*
CPD ▸ **quince cheese, quince jelly** (dulce *m* de) membrillo *m*

quincentenary [,kwɪnsen'ti:nərɪ] N quinto centenario *m*

quinine [kwɪ'ni:n] N quinina *f*

Quinquagesima [,kwɪŋkwə'dʒesɪmə] N Quincuagésima *f*

quinquennial [kwɪŋ'kwenɪəl] ADJ quinquenal

quinquennium [kwɪŋ'kwenɪəm] N (PL: **quinquennia** [kwɪŋ'kwenɪə]) quinquenio *m*

quinsy ['kwɪnzɪ] N angina *f*

p

quint* [kwɪnt] N (US) quintillizo/a *m/f*

quintessence [kwɪn'tesns] N quintaesencia *f*

quintessential [ˌkwɪntɪ'senʃəl] ADJ quintaesencial

quintessentially [ˌkwɪntɪ'senʃəlɪ] ADV típicamente

quintet, quintette [kwɪn'tet] N (*gen*) quinteto *m*

quintuple ADJ ['kwɪntjʊpl] quíntuplo
N ['kwɪntjʊpl] quíntuplo *m*
VT [kwɪn'tju:pl] quintuplicar
VI [kwɪn'tju:pl] quintuplicarse

quintuplet [kwɪn'tju:plɪt] N quintillizo/a *m/f*

quip [kwɪp] N ocurrencia *f*, salida *f*
VT • **"you'll have to go on a diet!" he ~ped** —¡tendrás que ponerte a dieta! —dijo bromeando
VI bromear

quipster ['kwɪpstəʳ] N bromista *mf*

quire ['kwaɪəʳ] N mano *f* (de papel)

quirk [kwɜ:k] N **1** (= *oddity*) rareza *f* • **it's just one of his little ~s** es una de sus rarezas • **by some ~ of fate/nature** por algún capricho del destino/de la naturaleza • **a statistical ~** una anomalía estadística
2 (*Art, Mus*) (= *flourish*) floritura *f*

quirkiness ['kwɜ:kɪnɪs] N rareza *f*

quirky ['kwɜ:kɪ] ADJ (COMPAR: **quirkier**, SUPERL: **quirkiest**) [*humour, behaviour, style*] raro, peculiar; [*person*] raro, estrafalario

quisling ['kwɪzlɪŋ] N colaboracionista *mf*

quit [kwɪt] (PT, PP: **quit, quitted**) VT
1 (= *cease*) • **to ~ doing sth** (*esp US*) dejar de hacer algo • **to ~ work** (*during job*) suspender el trabajo, dejar de trabajar; (*at end of day*) salir del trabajo • **~ stalling!** (*esp US**) ¡déjate de evasivas! • **~ fooling!** ¡déjate de tonterías!
2 (= *leave*) [+ *place*] abandonar, salir de; [+ *premises*] desocupar; (*Comput*) [+ *application*] abandonar • **to ~ one's job** dejar el trabajo, renunciar a su puesto
VI (*esp US*) (= *go away*) irse, marcharse; (= *resign*) dimitir, renunciar; (= *stop work*) suspender el trabajo, dejar de trabajar; (= *give up*) (*in game, task*) abandonar; (*Comput*) terminar, abandonar • **I ~!** ¡lo dejo!; (*from job*) ¡renuncio! • **I've been given notice to ~** he recibido una notificación de desahucio
ADJ • **to be ~ of sth/sb** haberse librado de algo/algn

quite [kwaɪt] ADV **1** (= *completely*) totalmente, completamente • **~ new** completamente nuevo • **I'm not ~ sure** no estoy del todo seguro • **I ~ agree with you** estoy totalmente de acuerdo contigo • **it's ~ clear that this plan won't work** está clarísimo que este plan no va a funcionar • **that's ~ enough for me** eso me basta a mí • **that'll be ~ enough of that!** ¡ya está bien! • **I can ~ believe that ...** no me cuesta creer que ... • **I ~ understand** comprendo perfectamente • **I don't ~ understand it** no acabo de entenderlo • **they are ~ simply the best** son simple y llanamente los mejores • **~ frankly, I can't stand him** para ser totalmente sincero, no lo aguanto • **you could ~ easily have killed yourself** podrías haberte matado con toda facilidad • **that's not ~ right** eso no es totalmente cierto • **he has not ~ recovered yet** no se ha repuesto todavía del todo • **it was ~ three months since she had called**† habían pasado por lo menos tres meses desde que llamó • **he's ~ grown up now** ahora está hecho todo un hombre
2 (= *exactly*) exactamente • **it's not ~ what we wanted** no es exactamente lo que queríamos • **we don't ~ know** no sabemos exactamente • **it's not ~ the same** no es exactamente lo mismo • **~ (so)!** ¡así es!, ¡exacto! • **not ~ as many as last time** no tantos como la última vez
3 (= *rather*) bastante • **it's ~ good/important** es bastante bueno/importante • **"how was the film?" — "~ good"** —¿qué tal la película? —bastante bien • **it was ~ a surprise** me sorprendió bastante • **it was ~ a shock** fue bastante chocante • **~ a lot** bastante • **I've been there ~ a lot** he ido allí bastante • **~ a lot of money** bastante dinero • **it costs ~ a lot to go abroad** es bastante caro salir al extranjero
4 (*emphatic use*) • **that's ~ a car!** ¡vaya coche! • **~ a hero** todo un héroe (*also iro*) • **there were ~ a few people there** había bastante gente allí • **~ suddenly, everything went black** de golpe, todo se volvió oscuro

Quito ['ki:təʊ] N Quito *m*

quits [kwɪts] ADJ • **to be ~ with sb** estar en paz con algn • **now we're ~!** ¡ahora estamos en paz! • **to call it ~** (= *give up*) rendirse • **let's call it ~** (*in argument*) hagamos las paces; (*when settling bill*) digamos que quedamos en paz

quitter* ['kwɪtəʳ] N (*pej*) rajado/a* *m/f* • **he's no ~** no es un rajado*

quiver¹ ['kwɪvəʳ] N [*of arrows*] carcaj *m*, aljaba *f*

quiver² ['kwɪvəʳ] N (= *trembling*) estremecimiento *m*
VI [*person,*] temblar, estremecerse (**with** de); [*voice, eyelids*] temblar

qui vive [ki:'vi:v] N • IDIOM: • **to be on the ~** estar alerta

Quixote ['kwɪksət] N Quijote • **Don ~** don Quijote

quixotic [kwɪk'sɒtɪk] ADJ quijotesco

quixotically [kwɪk'sɒtɪkəlɪ] ADV de manera quijotesca; [*behave*] como un quijote

quixotism ['kwɪksətɪzəm] N quijotismo *m*

quiz [kwɪz] N (PL: **quizzes**) (*TV, Rad*) concurso *m*; (*in magazine*) encuesta *f*; (*US*) test *m*, prueba *f*
VT (= *interrogate*) interrogar (**about** sobre)
CPD ▸ **quiz master** moderador *m* ▸ **quiz night** (*in pub*) *noche en la que se disputa un concurso de preguntas y respuestas* ▸ **quiz programme, quiz show** programa *m* concurso

quizzical ['kwɪzɪkəl] ADJ [*glance*] burlón, socarrón

quizzically ['kwɪzɪkəlɪ] ADV • **he looked at me ~** me miró de manera burlona, me miró socarronamente

quod‡ [kwɒd] N (*Brit*) chirona‡ *f*, cárcel *f*

quoin [kɔɪn] N (= *angle*) esquina *f*, ángulo *m*; (= *stone*) piedra *f* angular; (*Typ*) cuña *f*

quoit [kwɔɪt] N aro *m*, tejo *m*; **quoits** juego *msing* de los aros • **to play ~s** jugar a los aros

quondam†† ['kwɒndæm] ADJ antiguo

quorate ['kwɔ:reɪt] ADJ (*esp Brit*) • **the meeting was not ~** no había quórum en la reunión

Quorn® [kwɔ:n] N *alimento a base de proteínas vegetales*

quorum ['kwɔ:rəm] N quórum *m* • **what number constitutes a ~?** ¿cuántos constituyen quórum?

quot. ABBR = **quotation**

quota ['kwəʊtə] N (*gen*) cuota *f*; (*Comm etc*) cupo *m*, contingente *m*; [*of production*] cuota *f*, cupo *m* • **a fixed ~** un cupo fijo • **import ~** cupo *m* de importación • **I've done my ~ of chores** he hecho mi parte de las tareas • **I didn't get my full ~ of sleep last night** anoche no dormí las horas que necesito
CPD ▸ **quota system** sistema *m* de cuotas

quotability [ˌkwəʊtə'bɪlɪtɪ] N capacidad *f* de ser citado • **she has become renowned for her ~** ha pasado a ser conocida por sus citas

quotable ['kwəʊtəbl] ADJ citable, digno de citarse; (*Econ*) cotizable

quotation [kwəʊ'teɪʃən] N **1** (= *words, line*) cita *f* • **dictionary of ~s** diccionario *m* de citas famosas
2 (= *act of quoting*) • **he has a fondness for ~** le encanta citar
3 (*Comm*) (= *estimate*) presupuesto *m* • **shop around for the best insurance ~** pregunte en varias agencias hasta que encuentre la póliza más barata
4 (*St Ex*) cotización *f*
CPD ▸ **quotation marks** comillas *fpl* • **in ~ marks** (*lit, fig*) entre comillas • **I use the term "good" in ~ marks** utilizo el término "bueno" entre comillas • **single/double ~ marks** comillas *fpl* simples/dobles

quote [kwəʊt] VT **1** (= *cite*) [+ *writer, line, passage, source*] citar • **to ~ my aunt ...** para citar a mi tía ..., como decía mi tía ... • **you can ~ me** puedes decir que te lo he dicho yo • **don't ~ me on that** no te lo puedo decir a ciencia cierta • **he is ~d as saying that ...** se le atribuye haber dicho que ...
2 (= *mention*) [+ *example*] dar, citar; [+ *reference number*] indicar • **to ~ sth/sb as an example (of sth)** poner algo/a algn como ejemplo (de algo)
3 (*Comm*) (= *estimate*) • **he ~d/I was ~d a good price** me dio un presupuesto *or* precio muy razonable
4 (*Econ*) [+ *shares, company, currency*] cotizar (**at** a) • **last night, Hunt shares were ~d at 346 pence** anoche las acciones Hunt cotizaron a 346 peniques • **it is not ~d on the Stock Exchange** no se cotiza en la Bolsa • **~d company** empresa *f* que cotiza en Bolsa
VI **1** (= *recite, repeat*) citar • **to ~ from the Bible** citar de la Biblia • **he said, and I ~, ...** dijo, y cito sus propias palabras, ...
2 (*Comm*) • **to ~ for sth** hacer un presupuesto de algo, presupuestar algo • **I got several firms to ~ for the building work** pedí a varias empresas que me hicieran un presupuesto de *or* me presupuestaran la obra
N* **1** (= *line, passage*) cita *f*
2 (*Comm*) (= *estimate*) presupuesto *m*
3 (*St Ex*) cotización *f*
4 quotes (= *inverted commas*) comillas *fpl* • **in ~s** entre comillas
EXCL • **she said, ~, "he was as drunk as a lord", un~** sus palabras textuales fueron: —estaba como una cuba • **she died in a, ~, "accident", un~** murió en un accidente, entre comillas *or* por así decirlo • **"quote"** (*in dictation*) "comienza la cita"

quoth†† [kwəʊθ] VI • **~ I** dije yo • **~ he** dijo él

quotidian [kwəʊ'tɪdɪən] ADJ (*liter*) cotidiano

quotient ['kwəʊʃənt] N cociente *m*

Quran, Qur'an [kɔ:'rɑ:n] [kɔ:'ræn] N • **the ~** el Corán

Quranic, Qur'anic [kɔ:'rænɪk] ADJ coránico

q.v. ABBR (= **quod vide, which see**) véase, q.v.

qwerty keyboard [ˌkwɜ:tɪ'ki:bɔ:d] N teclado *m* QWERTY

Rr

R[1], r[1] [ɑː] (N) (= *letter*) R, r *f* • **R for Robert** R de Ramón • **the three Rs** (= *reading, writing and arithmetic*) *lectura, escritura y aritmética*; ▷ THREE RS

R[2], r[2] (ABBR) **1** (*Brit*) (= **Rex**) R
2 (*Brit*) (= **Regina**) R
3 (*Geog*) (= **river**) R
4 (= **right**) dcha, der, derº
5 = **Réaumur (scale)**
6 (*US*) (*Pol*) = **Republican**
(ADJ ABBR) (*US*) (*Cine*) (= **restricted**) ≈ solo mayores

® (N ABBR) (= **registered trade mark**) ®

RA (N ABBR) **1** (*Brit*) (= **Royal Academy of Arts**) ≈ Real Academia *f* de Bellas Artes
2 (*Brit*) (= **Royal Academician**) ≈ miembro *mf* de la Real Academia de Bellas Artes
3 (*Mil*) = **Royal Artillery**
4 = **Rear Admiral**

> **RA - ROYAL ACADEMY OF ARTS**
> La **Royal Academy of Arts** o **RA** es la más famosa de las fundaciones de arte británicas. Con sede en Londres, la **Royal Academy** presenta exposiciones de artistas modernos y de todas las épocas, y también imparte algunas clases a futuros artistas. Cada verano tiene lugar la **Summer Exhibition**, que es la mayor exposición abierta de arte contemporáneo en el mundo. Cualquier artista puede enviar su trabajo y la selección final de obras concentra una amplia gama de estilos, tanto de artistas consolidados como de principiantes. Los artistas miembros de la **Royal Academy of Arts** pueden escribir las iniciales **RA** después de sus nombres, como si de un título académico se tratase.

RAAF (N ABBR) = **Royal Australian Air Force**

Rabat [rəˈbɑːt] (N) Rabat *m*

rabbi [ˈræbaɪ] (N) rabino/a *m/f*; (*before name*) rabí *m* • **chief ~** gran rabino

Rabbinic [rəˈbɪnɪk] (N) (*Ling*) hebreo *m* rabínico

rabbinical [rəˈbɪnɪkəl] (ADJ) rabínico

rabbit [ˈræbɪt] (N) (PL: **rabbit** *or* **rabbits**) conejo *m*; ▷ **Welsh**
(VI) • **to go ~ing** ir a cazar conejos
(CPD) ▸ **rabbit burrow** madriguera *f* ▸ **rabbit ears*** (*US*) (*TV*) antena *f* de cuernos ▸ **rabbit food** (*lit, fig*) comida *f* para conejos ▸ **rabbit hole** madriguera *f* ▸ **rabbit hutch** conejera *f* ▸ **rabbit punch** golpe *m* de nuca ▸ **rabbit warren** conejera *f*, madriguera *f*
▸ **rabbit away*** (VI + ADV) (*Brit*) enrollarse
▸ **rabbit on*** (VI + ADV) enrollarse*

rabble [ˈræbl] (N) (= *disorderly crowd*) gentío *m*, muchedumbre *f*, mogollón *m* (*Sp**) • **the ~** (= *uncultured people*) la chusma • **a ~ of** una multitud turbulenta de

rabble-rouser [ˈræbl,raʊzəʳ] (N) demagogo/a *m/f*, agitador(a) *m/f*

rabble-rousing [ˈræblˈraʊzɪŋ] (N) demagogia *f*, agitación *f*
(ADJ) demagógico

Rabelaisian [,ræbəˈleɪzɪən] (ADJ) rabelasiano

rabid [ˈræbɪd] (ADJ) [*dog*] rabioso; (*fig*) [*person*] fanático

rabies [ˈreɪbiːz] (NSING) rabia *f* • **a dog with ~** un perro rabioso

RAC (N ABBR) (*Brit*) **1** (*Aut*) (= **Royal Automobile Club**) ≈ RACE *m* (*Sp*)
2 (*Mil*) = **Royal Armoured Corps**

raccoon [rəˈkuːn] (N) (PL: **raccoon** *or* **raccoons**) mapache *m*

race[1] [reɪs] (N) **1** (= *contest*) (*lit, fig*) carrera *f* • **it was a ~ to finish it in time** lo hicimos a la carrera para terminarlo a tiempo • **the ~ for the White House** la carrera hacia la Casa Blanca • **the election will be a very close ~** las elecciones van a estar muy reñidas • **a ~ against time/the clock** (*fig*) una carrera contra el tiempo/contra reloj • **the arms ~** la carrera armamentista • **boat ~** regata *f* • **cycle ~** carrera *f* ciclista • **horse ~** carrera *f* de caballos • **the ~ is on to find a donor** ha comenzado la carrera en busca de un donante • **to run (in) a ~** tomar parte en una carrera, participar en una carrera • **you ran a good ~** corriste muy bien • **the ~s** (= *horse races*) las carreras (de caballos) • **to go to the ~s** ir a las carreras
2 (= *swift current*) corriente *f* fuerte
(VT) **1** (= *enter in race*) [+ *horse*] presentar; [+ *car*] correr con • **they ~ vintage cars** hacen carreras de coches antiguos
2 (= *run against*) echarle una carrera a • **(I'll) ~ you home!** ¡te echo una carrera hasta casa!
3 • **to ~ an engine** acelerar un motor al máximo
(VI) **1** (= *compete*) [*driver, athlete, horse*] correr, competir • **to ~ against sb** competir con algn (en una carrera)
2 (= *go fast*) correr, ir a toda velocidad • **we ~d to get back home for eight o'clock** nos dimos prisa para estar en casa para las ocho • **to ~ against time/the clock (to do sth)** (*fig*) trabajar contra reloj (para hacer algo) • **to ~ ahead** ponerse a la cabeza • **he ~d down the street** bajó la calle corriendo *or* a toda velocidad • **we ~d for a taxi** corrimos a coger un taxi • **he ~d past us** nos pasó a toda velocidad *or* a toda carrera • **he ~d through the paperwork as quickly as he could** hizo el papeleo todo lo rápido que pudo
3 [*pulse, heart*] acelerarse; [*engine*] embalarse • **her heart ~d uncontrollably** el corazón se le aceleró descontrolado, el corazón le latía a un ritmo descontrolado • **my mind was racing** los pensamientos me invadían la mente
(CPD) ▸ **race car** (*US*) coche *m* de carreras ▸ **race (car) driver** (*US*) piloto *mf* de carreras, corredor(a) *m/f* de coches ▸ **race meeting** (*Brit*) carreras *fpl* (de caballos)
▸ **race back** (VI + ADV) (= *return quickly*) volver a toda prisa
▸ **race in** (VI + ADV) **1** (= *come in*) entrar corriendo
2 (= *run fast*) lanzarse a toda velocidad
▸ **race off** (VI + ADV) salir a toda velocidad
▸ **race out** (VI + ADV) (= *rush out*) [*person*] salir fuera rápidamente • **to ~ out of sth** [+ *house, school*] salir a toda prisa de algo
▸ **race towards** (VI + PREP) (= *head towards*) ir corriendo hacia

race[2] [reɪs] (N) (= *racial origin*) raza *f* • **discrimination on the grounds of ~** discriminación *f* por la raza *or* por motivos raciales • **people of mixed ~** (*esp of Indian and white descent*) gente *f* mestiza; (*of black and white descent*) gente *f* mulata • **the human ~** la raza humana, el género humano • **they looked on us as a ~ apart** nos consideraban otra casta
(CPD) ▸ **race card** baza *f* racial • **to play the ~ card** jugar la baza racial ▸ **race hatred, race hate** odio *m* racial, racismo *m* ▸ **race issue** asunto *m* racial • **a committee was set up to tackle ~ issues** se formó un comité para hacer frente a los asuntos *or* los problemas raciales ▸ **race relations** relaciones *fpl* interraciales ▸ **race riot** disturbio *m* racial

raceboat [ˈreɪsbəʊt] (N) (*Sport*) bote *m* de carreras

racecard [ˈreɪskɑːd] (N) programa *m* de carreras

racecourse [ˈreɪskɔːs] (N) hipódromo *m*

racegoer [ˈreɪsgəʊəʳ] (N) (*Brit*) aficionado/a *m/f* a las carreras

racehorse [ˈreɪshɔːs] (N) caballo *m* de carreras

raceme [ˈræsiːm] (N) racimo *m*

racer [ˈreɪsəʳ] (N) (= *runner*) corredor(a) *m/f*; (= *horse*) caballo *m* de carreras; (= *car*) coche *m* de carreras; (= *bike*) bicicleta *f* de carreras

racetrack [ˈreɪstræk] (N) (*for runners*) pista *f*; (*for horses*) hipódromo *m*; (*for cars*) circuito *m* de carreras; (*for cycles*) velódromo *m*

Rachel [ˈreɪtʃəl] (N) Raquel

rachitic [ræˈkɪtɪk] (ADJ) raquítico

racial [ˈreɪʃəl] (ADJ) racial
(CPD) ▸ **racial discrimination** discriminación *f* racial ▸ **racial harassment** acoso *m* racial ▸ **racial integration** integración *f* racial ▸ **racial profiling** *introducción de criterios raciales a la hora de investigar crímenes*

racialism [ˈreɪʃəlɪzəm] (N) (*esp Brit*) racismo *m*

racialist [ˈreɪʃəlɪst] (*esp Brit*) (ADJ) racista
(N) racista *mf*

racially [ˈreɪʃəlɪ] (ADV) racialmente • **children of ~ mixed parents** hijos *mpl* de padres de distintas razas • **~ motivated** [*attack, crime, incident*] por motivos racistas • **to be ~ motivated** [*attack, crime*] tener un origen racista

raciness [ˈreɪsɪnɪs] (N) lo picante

racing [ˈreɪsɪŋ] (N) carreras *fpl* • **greyhound/horse ~** carreras *fpl* de galgos/caballos

• **motor ~** carreras *fpl* automovilísticas *or* de coches • **the ~ world** el mundo de las carreras (de caballos); ▹ **flat**

CPD ▸ **racing bicycle**, **racing bike** bicicleta *f* de carreras ▸ **racing calendar** calendario *m* de carreras (de caballos) ▸ **racing car** coche *m* de carreras ▸ **racing circuit** autódromo *m*, pista *f* de carreras ▸ **racing commentator** comentarista *mf* hípico/a ▸ **racing correspondent** corresponsal *mf* hípico/a ▸ **racing cyclist** corredor(a) *m/f* ciclista ▸ **racing driver** piloto *mf* de carreras, corredor(a) *m/f* de carreras de coches ▸ **racing man** (*horse racing*) aficionado *m* a las carreras (de caballos) ▸ **racing pigeon** paloma *f* de carreras ▸ **racing yacht** yate *m* de regatas

racism ['reɪsɪzəm] N racismo *m*

racist ['reɪsɪst] ADJ racista
N racista *mf*

rack[1] [ræk] N **1** (= *dish rack*) escurridor *m*, escurreplatos *m inv*; (= *clothes rack*) perchero *m*, percha *f*; (= *luggage rack*) (*Rail*) portaequipajes *m inv*, rejilla *f*; (= *roof rack*) baca *f*, portaequipajes *m inv*, parrilla *f* (*And*); (= *mechanical rack*) cremallera *f* • **to buy clothes off the ~** (*US*) comprar ropa de percha
2 (*for torture*) potro *m* • **to be on the ~** (*fig*) estar en ascuas
3 (*Snooker, Pool*) triángulo *m*
VT **1** [*pain*] atormentar; [*cough*] sacudir • **to be ~ed by remorse** estar atormentado por el remordimiento • **to be ~ed by pains** estar atormentado por el dolor • IDIOM: • **to ~ one's brains** devanarse los sesos
2 [+ *wine*] (*also* **rack off**) trasegar
CPD ▸ **rack railway** ferrocarril *m* de cremallera ▸ **rack rent** alquiler *m* exorbitante
▸ **rack up** VT + ADV (= *accumulate*) acumular

rack[2] [ræk] N • **to go to ~ and ruin** [*building*] echarse a perder, venirse abajo; [*business*] arruinarse, tronar (*LAm*); [*country*] arruinarse; [*person*] dejarse ir

rack-and-pinion [,rækənd'pɪnjən] N (*Tech*) cremallera *f* y piñón
CPD ▸ **rack-and-pinion steering** cremallera *f*, piñón *m*

racket[1] ['rækɪt] N (*Sport*) raqueta *f*
CPD ▸ **racket sports** deportes *mpl* de raqueta

racket[2] ['rækɪt] N **1** (= *din*) [*of machine, engine*] estruendo *m*; (= *loud voices*) follón *m*, bulla *f* • **to kick up** *or* **make a ~** armar follón *or* bulla • **you never heard such a ~!** ¡menudo follón había!, ¡menuda bulla había!
2 (= *organized fraud*) estafa *f* • **the drug ~** el tráfico de drogas • **he was in on the ~** era de los que organizaron la estafa
VI (*make noise*) (*also* **racket about**) hacer ruido, armar un jaleo

racketeer [,rækɪ'tɪəʳ] N (*esp US*) estafador(a) *m/f*

racketeering [,rækɪ'tɪərɪŋ] N chantaje *m* sistematizado, crimen *m* organizado

racking ['rækɪŋ] ADJ [*pain*] atroz

raconteur [,rækɒn'tɜːʳ] N anecdotista *mf*

racoon [rə'kuːn] N = **raccoon**

racquet ['rækɪt] N = **racket**[1]

racquetball ['rækɪt,bɔːl] N ráquetbol *m*

racy ['reɪsɪ] ADJ (COMPAR: **racier**, SUPERL: **raciest**) [*style, speech, humour*] picante

rad‡ [ræd] ADJ (*esp US*) = **radical**

RADA ['rɑːdə] N ABBR (*Brit*) (= **Royal Academy of Dramatic Art**) ≈ C.D.N. *m*

radar ['reɪdɑːʳ] N radar *m*
CPD ▸ **radar scanner** antena *f* giratoria de radar ▸ **radar screen** pantalla *f* de radar ▸ **radar station** estación *f* de radar ▸ **radar trap** trampa *f* de radar

raddled ['rædld] ADJ depravado, decaído

radial ['reɪdɪəl] ADJ **1** [*engine, tyre*] radial
2 (*Med*) radial, del radio
N (*also* **radial tyre**) neumático *m* radial

radiance ['reɪdɪəns] N **1** (= *glow*) [*of face, personality, beauty*] lo radiante
2 (*liter*) (= *brightness*) [*of sun, colour, light*] resplandor *m*
3 (*Phys*) radiancia *m*

radiant ['reɪdɪənt] ADJ **1** (= *glowing*) [*smile, person, complexion*] radiante • **to look ~** estar radiante • **~ with joy** radiante *or* rebosante de alegría • **~ with health** rebosante de salud
2 (*liter*) (= *bright*) [*sunshine*] resplandeciente; [*colour*] radiante • **bathed in ~ sunshine** bañado en un sol radiante • **~ white robes** batas de un blanco radiante
3 (*Phys*) [*heat, light, energy*] radiante
N (*Astron, Math, Phys*) radiante *m*

radiantly ['reɪdɪəntlɪ] ADV **1** (= *glowingly*) • **to smile ~ at sb** dirigir una sonrisa radiante a algn • **he smiled ~** sonrió radiante • **she was ~ beautiful** era de una belleza deslumbrante • **she was/looked ~ happy** estaba radiante *or* rebosante de felicidad
2 (*liter*) (= *brightly*) • **to shine ~** resplandecer

radiate ['reɪdɪeɪt] VT (*lit, fig*) radiar, irradiar
VI • **to ~ from** [*lines, streets*] partir de • **light ~d from an opening in the tunnel roof** la luz se difundía por una abertura en el techo del túnel • **lines that ~ from the centre** líneas que parten del centro • **hostility ~d from him** irradiaba hostilidad

radiation [,reɪdɪ'eɪʃən] N radiación *f*
CPD ▸ **radiation sickness** enfermedad *f* por radiación ▸ **radiation therapy** radioterapia *f*, terapia *f* por radiaciones ▸ **radiation treatment** tratamiento *m* por radiaciones

radiator ['reɪdɪeɪtəʳ] N (*all senses*) radiador *m*
CPD ▸ **radiator cap** tapa *f* de radiador ▸ **radiator grille**, **radiator grill** rejilla *f* de radiador

radical ['rædɪkəl] ADJ **1** (*Pol*) [*idea, organization*] radical; [*person*] radical, de ideas radicales • **she's very ~** es muy radical, es de *or* tiene ideas muy radicales • **a ~ feminist** una feminista radical
2 (= *extreme, major*) [*change, measures, surgery, reduction*] radical; [*advance*] innovador
N (*Pol*) radical *mf*; (*Bot, Chem, Ling, Math*) radical *m*

radicalism ['rædɪkəlɪzəm] N (*Pol*) radicalismo *m*

radicalization [,rædɪkəlaɪ'zeɪʃən] N radicalización *f*

radicalize ['rædɪkə,laɪz] VT radicalizar

radically ['rædɪkəlɪ] ADV [*differ, change, improve, reduce, affect*] radicalmente, de forma radical; [*different, changed, new*] radicalmente • **to disagree with sb ~** estar en total desacuerdo con algn • **there's something ~ wrong with his knee** hay algo en su rodilla que no marcha bien en absoluto • **his assessment of the situation had been ~ wrong** su valoración de la situación había sido totalmente equivocada

radicchio [ræ'diːkɪəʊ] N achicoria *f* roja

radicle ['rædɪkl] N (*Bot*) radícula *f*; (*Chem*) radical *m*

radii ['reɪdɪaɪ] NPL *of* **radius**

radio ['reɪdɪəʊ] N **1** (= *set*) radio *f* • **over the ~** por radio • **on the ~** en *or* por la radio • **to talk on the ~** hablar por la radio
2 (*Telec*) radio *f*, radiofonía *f* • **by ~** por radio
VI • **to ~ to sb** enviar un mensaje a algn por radio • **to ~ for help** pedir socorro por radio
VT [+ *information, news*] radiar, transmitir por radio
CPD ▸ **radio alarm**, **radio alarm clock** radio-reloj *m* despertador ▸ **radio announcer** locutor(a) *m/f* de radio ▸ **radio astronomy** radioastronomía *f* ▸ **radio beacon** radiofaro *m* ▸ **radio beam** radiofaro *m* ▸ **radio broadcast** emisión *f* de radio ▸ **radio cab** = radio taxi ▸ **radio car** estudio *m* móvil de radio ▸ **radio cassette (player)** (*esp Brit*), **radio cassette recorder** (*Brit*) radiocasete *m* ▸ **radio communication**, **radio contact** comunicación *f* por radio ▸ **radio engineer** radiotécnico *mf* ▸ **radio engineering** radiotécnica *f* ▸ **radio frequency** frecuencia *f* de radio ▸ **radio ham** radioaficionado/a *m/f* ▸ **radio link** enlace *m* radiofónico ▸ **radio mast** torre *f* de radio ▸ **radio network** cadena *f or* red *f* de emisoras ▸ **radio operator** radiotelegrafista *mf* ▸ **radio play** obra *f* de teatro para la radio ▸ **radio programme**, **radio program** (*US*) programa *m* de radio ▸ **radio set** radio *f* ▸ **radio silence** silencio *m* radiofónico ▸ **radio station** emisora *f* (de radio) ▸ **radio taxi** radiotaxi *m* ▸ **radio telephone** radioteléfono *m* ▸ **radio telescope** radiotelescopio *m* ▸ **radio tower** = **radio mast** ▸ **radio transmitter** radiotransmisor *m* ▸ **radio wave** onda *f* de radio

radio... ['reɪdɪəʊ] PREFIX radio...

radioactive [,reɪdɪəʊ'æktɪv] ADJ radiactivo, radioactivo
CPD ▸ **radioactive waste** residuos *mpl* radiactivos

radioactively [,reɪdɪəʊ'æktɪvlɪ] ADV de manera radioactiva, radioactivamente • **~ contaminated** contaminado de manera radioactiva, contaminado radioactivamente

radioactivity [,reɪdɪəʊæk'tɪvɪtɪ] N radiactividad *f*, radioactividad *f*

radiobiology [,reɪdɪəʊbaɪ'ɒlədʒɪ] N radiobiología *f*

radiocarbon [,reɪdɪəʊ'kɑːbən] N radiocarbono *m*
CPD ▸ **radiocarbon analysis** análisis *m inv* por radiocarbono ▸ **radiocarbon dating** datación *f* por radiocarbono ▸ **radiocarbon test** test *m* por radiocarbono

radio-controlled ['reɪdɪəʊkən,trəʊld] ADJ [*car*] teledirigido

radiogram ['reɪdɪəʊgræm] N **1** (*Brit*) (= *combined radio and gramophone*) radiogramola *f*
2† (= *message*) radiograma *m*, radiotelegrama *m*
3 (= *X-ray picture*) radiografía *f*

radiograph ['reɪdɪəʊgrɑːf] N radiografía *f*
VT radiografiar

radiographer [,reɪdɪ'ɒgrəfəʳ] N radiógrafo/a *m/f*

radiography [,reɪdɪ'ɒgrəfɪ] N radiografía *f*

radioisotope ['reɪdɪəʊ'aɪsətəʊp] N radioisótopo *m*

radiolocation [,reɪdɪəʊlə'keɪʃən] N radiolocalización *f*

radiological [,reɪdɪə'lɒdʒɪkəl] ADJ radiológico

radiologist [,reɪdɪ'ɒlədʒɪst] N radiólogo/a *m/f*

radiology [,reɪdɪ'ɒlədʒɪ] N radiología *f*

radiopager ['reɪdɪəʊ,peɪdʒəʳ] N localizador *m*

radioscopy [,reɪdɪ'ɒskəpɪ] N radioscopia *f*

radiotelephony [,reɪdɪəʊtə'lefənɪ] N radiotelefonía *f*

radiotherapist [,reɪdɪəʊ'θerəpɪst] N

r

radioterapeuta *mf*
radiotherapy [ˌreɪdɪəʊˈθerəpɪ] (N) radioterapia *f*
radish [ˈrædɪʃ] (N) rábano *m*
radium [ˈreɪdɪəm] (N) radio *m*
radius [ˈreɪdɪəs] (N) (PL: **radiuses, radii**) radio *m* • **within a ~ of 50 miles** en un radio de 50 millas
radix [ˈreɪdɪks] (N) (PL: **radixes, radices** [ˈreɪdɪsiːz]) (*Bot, Gram*) raíz *f*; (*Math*) base *f*
radome [ˈreɪdəʊm] (N) (*Tech*) radomo *m*; (*at tip of aircraft*) radomo *m* cónico
radon [ˈreɪdɒn] (N) (*also* **radon gas**) radón *m*
RAF (N ABBR) = **Royal Air Force**
raffia [ˈræfɪə] (N) rafia *f*
raffish [ˈræfɪʃ] (ADJ) disipado, disoluto
raffle [ˈræfl] (N) rifa *f*, sorteo *m*
(VT) [+ *object*] rifar, sortear • **ten bottles will be ~d for charity** se rifarán *or* se sortearán diez botellas con fines benéficos
(CPD) ▸ **raffle ticket** papeleta *f* de rifa
raft [rɑːft] (N) **1** (*Naut*) balsa *f*
2* (= *quantity*) cantidad *f*, montón* *m*; (= *set*) serie *f*
rafter [ˈrɑːftəʳ] (N) viga *f*, cabrio *m* • **the ~s** (*loosely*) el techo
rafting [ˈrɑːftɪŋ] (N) rafting *m*, descenso *m* de ríos de montaña
rag¹ [ræg] (N) **1** (= *piece of cloth*) trapo *m*; **rags** (= *old clothes*) harapos *mpl*, trapos *mpl* viejos • **to be in rags** andar *or* estar en harapos • **dressed in rags** cubierto de harapos • **from rags to riches** de pobre a rico • **to feel like a wet rag*** estar hecho un trapo • IDIOMS: • **to put on one's glad rags** vestirse de domingo • **to chew the rag** (*US**) (= *chat*) charlar, pasar el rato; (= *argue*) discutir • **it's like a red rag to a bull** no hay nada que más le enfurezca • **to lose one's rag** (*Brit‡*) perder los estribos
2* (= *newspaper*) periodicucho* *m*, periódico *m* de mala muerte*
(CPD) ▸ **rag doll** muñeca *f* de trapo ▸ **rag rug** jarapa *f* ▸ **the rag trade*** la industria de la confección
rag² [ræg] (N) (= *practical joke*) broma *f* pesada; (*Univ*) (= *parade*) fiesta *f* benéfica (de estudiantes)
(VT) (= *tease*) tomar el pelo a* • **they were ragging him about his new tie** le estaban tomando el pelo con la corbata nueva*
(VI) guasearse, bromear • **I was only ragging** lo dije en broma, era solo una broma
(CPD) ▸ **rag week** semana *f* de funciones benéficas (estudiantiles)

RAG WEEK
Los universitarios británicos suelen organizar cada año lo que llaman **rag week**. Es costumbre que, durante esa semana, los estudiantes se disfracen y salgan así vestidos a la calle, pidiendo dinero a los transeúntes con el fin de recaudar fondos para fines benéficos.

raga [ˈrɑːgə] (N) (*Mus*) raga *m*
ragamuffin [ˈrægəˌmʌfɪn] (N) granuja *mf*
rag-and-bone man [ˌrægənˈbəʊnmæn] (N) (PL: **rag-and-bone men**) (*Brit*) trapero *m*
ragbag [ˈrægbæg] (N) (= *mixture*) mezcolanza *f*; (*Sew*) bolsa *f* de recortes • **it's a ~ of a book** es un libro muy farragoso, el libro es todo un fárrago
rage [reɪdʒ] (N) **1** (= *anger*) furia *f*, cólera *f*, ira *f* **at** *or* **over sth** (ante algo) • **he attacked her in a drunken ~** la agredió en un ataque de furia *or* cólera *or* ira causado por la bebida • **in a fit of ~** en un ataque de furia *or* cólera *or* ira • **to fly** *or* **go into a ~** montar en cólera, ponerse hecho una furia • **to be in a ~** estar furioso • **she was trembling with ~** temblaba de furia *or* cólera *or* ira • **he was white with ~** estaba blanco de cólera *or* ira; ▹ **road**
2 (= *fashion*) furor *m* • **the ~ for designer jeans** el furor por los vaqueros de diseño exclusivo • **to be all the ~** hacer furor
(VI) [*person*] estar furioso; [*fire*] propagarse con furia; [*epidemic*] propagarse causando estragos; [*battle*] proseguir con furia; [*wind, storm*] bramar; [*sea*] enfurecerse, embravecerse • **she was raging, but she kept her tone cool** estaba furiosa pero conservaba un tono calmado • **outside the storm still ~d** fuera la tempestad seguía bramando • **the battle ~d for three months** la batalla prosiguió con furia durante tres meses • **the debate ~d the whole day long** el airado debate prosiguió el día entero • **to ~ against sth** protestar furiosamente contra algo • **to ~ against sb** estar furioso con algn • **the sound of the sea raging against the rocks** el sonido del mar chocando enfurecido *or* embravecido contra las rocas • **to ~ at sth** estar furioso ante algo • **my mum ~d at the doctor** mi madre se puso como una fiera con el médico • **controversy is raging over her new economic policy** hay una encendida polémica en torno a su nueva política económica • **an infection was raging through her body** una infección se propagaba por su cuerpo causando estragos
(VT) • **"it's none of your business," he ~d** —no es asunto tuyo —dijo enfurecido
-rage (N) (*ending in compounds*) • **air/parking/trolley-rage** conducta *f* agresiva en los aviones/al estacionar/en el supermercado
ragga [ˈrægə] (N) ragga *m*
ragged [ˈrægɪd] (ADJ) **1** (= *in tatters*) [*dress, clothes*] andrajoso, hecho jirones; [*person*] andrajoso, harapiento; [*cuff*] deshilachado • IDIOM: • **to run sb ~*** hacer sudar tinta *or* la gota gorda a algn • **they ran themselves ~** sudaron tinta *or* la gota gorda
2 (= *untidy*) [*beard*] descuidado, desgreñado; [*animal's coat*] desgreñado
3 (= *uneven*) [*edge*] mellado, irregular; [*rock*] recortado; [*hole, line*] irregular; [*coastline*] accidentado, recortado • **~ clouds** jirones *mpl* de nubes
4 (= *disorganized*) [*performance*] desigual, irregular; [*queue*] desordenado; [*line, procession*] confuso, desordenado • **a ~ band of men** un grupo desordenado de hombres • **the orchestra sounded rather ~ in places** la orquesta tocaba de forma algo irregular en algunas partes
5 (*Typ*) • **~ left** margen *m* izquierdo irregular • **~ right** margen derecho irregular
(CPD) ▸ **ragged robin** (*Bot*) flor *f* del cuclillo
raggedly [ˈrægɪdlɪ] (ADV) • **he was ~ dressed** iba vestido con andrajos *or* harapos • **they marched ~ up and down** marchaban arriba y abajo de forma desordenada
raggedy* [ˈrægɪdɪ] (ADJ) [*person*] harapiento; [*clothes*] gastado
raging [ˈreɪdʒɪŋ] (ADJ) **1** (= *fierce*) [*temper*] furioso, rabioso; [*debate*] acalorado; [*nationalist, feminist*] acérrimo, a ultranza; [*nationalism*] enfervorizado • **he was in a ~ temper** estaba muy furioso • **to be ~ mad** estar loco de furia *or* ira
2 (= *violent*) [*storm, thunder, blizzard*] violento, rugiente; [*wind, torrent*] enfurecido, rugiente; [*sea*] embravecido, enfurecido, rugiente; [*fire*] violento
3 (= *intense*) [*temperature, fever, inflation*] altísimo; [*illness, headache, toothache*] atroz; [*thirst*] horroroso • **to be a ~ success** tener un éxito tremendo
(N) [*of person*] furia *f* • **for a few moments he continued his ~** continuó dando rienda suelta a su furia durante un rato • **I couldn't hear her over the ~ of the sea** no podía oírla por el rugir del mar
raglan [ˈræglən] (N) raglán *m*
(CPD) ▸ **raglan sleeve** manga *f* raglán
ragman [ˈrægmæn] (N) (PL: **ragmen**) trapero *m*
ragout [ræˈguː] (N) guisado *m*
ragpicker [ˈrægpɪkəʳ] (N) trapero *m*
rag-tag* [ˈrægˌtæg] (N), **rag-tag and bobtail*** [ˌrægtægənˈbɒbteɪl] (N) chusma *f*
ragtime [ˈrægtaɪm] (N) (*Mus*) ragtime *m* • **in ~** sincopado
ragweed [ˈrægwiːd] (N) ambrosía *f*
ragwort [ˈrægwɜːt] (N) hierba *f* cana, zuzón *m*, hierba *f* de Santiago
raid [reɪd] (N) **1** (*into territory, across border*) incursión *f* (**into** en); (*on specific target*) asalto *m* (**on** a) • **to carry out** *or* **make a ~ on sth** asaltar algo
2 (*by air*) ataque *m* (aéreo) (**on** contra), bombardeo *m* (**on** de) • **only five aircraft returned from the ~** solamente cinco aviones regresaron después del ataque *or* bombardeo; ▹ **air**
3 (*by police*) redada *f* • **a police ~** una redada policial; ▹ **dawn, drug**
4 (*Brit*) (*by criminals*) asalto *m* (**on** a) • **a bank ~** un asalto a un banco • **there was a ~ on the jeweller's last night** anoche fue asaltada la joyería; ▹ **ram, smash-and-grab raid**
(VT) **1** (*by land*) [+ *village*] asaltar; [+ *territory*] invadir, hacer una incursión en
2 (*by air*) atacar, bombardear
3 [*police*] llevar a cabo una redada en
4 (*Brit*) [*criminals*] [+ *bank*] asaltar
5 (*fig*) (*hum*) • **shall we ~ the larder?** ¿asaltamos la despensa? • **the boys ~ed the orchard** los muchachos robaron en el huerto
(VI) hacer incursiones • **they ~ed deep into enemy territory** hicieron incursiones bien adentrados en territorio enemigo
raider [ˈreɪdəʳ] (N) **1** (*across frontier*) invasor(a) *m/f*
2 (*in bank etc*) asaltante *mf*
3 (= *plane*) bombardero *m*
4 (= *ship*) buque *m* corsario
raiding party [ˈreɪdɪŋˌpɑːtɪ] (N) grupo *m* de ataque
rail¹ [reɪl] (N) **1** (= *handrail*) (*on stairs, bridge, balcony*) baranda *f*, barandilla *f*, pasamanos *m inv*; (*for curtains*) riel *m*; (*on ship*) barandilla *f*; (*for feet*) apoyo *m* para los pies; (= *fence*) valla *f*, cerco *m*
2 (*for train*) carril *m*, riel *m*; **rails** vía *fsing* • **to go off** *or* **come off** *or* **leave the ~s** [*train*] descarrilar • **to send sth by ~** enviar algo por ferrocarril • **to travel by ~** viajar por ferrocarril *or* en tren • IDIOM: • **to go off the ~s*** [*person*] descarrilarse
3 rails (*Econ*) acciones *fpl* de sociedades ferroviarias
(CPD) ▸ **rail accident** accidente *m* de ferrocarril, accidente *m* ferroviario ▸ **rail journey** viaje *m* por ferrocarril *or* en tren ▸ **rail link** conexión *f* ferroviaria ▸ **rail strike** huelga *f* de ferroviarios ▸ **rail system** red *f* ferroviaria, sistema *m* ferroviario ▸ **rail traffic** tráfico *m* por ferrocarril ▸ **rail travel** viajes *mpl* por ferrocarril *or* en tren ▸ **rail worker** (*Brit*) ferroviario/a *m/f*, ferrocarrilero/a *m/f* (*Mex*); ▹ **pass**
▸ **rail off** (VT + ADV) [+ *land, pond*] cercar con una barandilla, poner barandilla a
rail²† [reɪl] (VI) (*frm*) • **to ~ against sth** clamar contra algo • **to ~ at sb** recriminar a algn, recriminarle algo a algn, recriminar a algn por hacer algo
rail³ [reɪl] (N) (*Orn*) rascón *m*

r

railcar ['reɪlkɑːʳ] (N) automotor *m*
railcard ['reɪlkɑːd] (N) carnet *m* para obtener descuento en los ferrocarriles • **family ~** carnet *m* de familia (*para viajes en tren*) • **student's ~** carnet *m* de estudiante (*para viajes en tren*)
railhead ['reɪlhed] (N) estación *f* terminal, cabeza *f* de línea
railing ['reɪlɪŋ] (N) baranda *f*, barandilla *f*, pasamanos *m inv* • **~s** verja *fsing*, enrejado *msing*
raillery ['reɪlərɪ] (N) burlas *fpl*, chanzas *fpl*
railroad ['reɪlrəʊd] (N) (US) (= *system*) ferrocarril *m*, ferrocarriles *mpl*; (*as track*) vía *f*, vía *f* férrea
(VT) (*fig*) • **to ~ sb into doing sth** obligar apresuradamente a algn a hacer algo • **to ~ a bill through Parliament** hacer que se apruebe un decreto de ley sin discutirse • **to ~ sth through** llevar algo a cabo muy precipitadamente
(CPD) ▸ **railroad car** (US) vagón *m*, coche *m* ▸ **railroad crossing** paso *m* a nivel ▸ **railroad line** (US) (= *route*) línea *f* ferroviaria *or* de ferrocarril; (= *track*) vía *f* (férrea) ▸ **railroad station** (US) estación *f* (de ferrocarril) ▸ **railroad track** (US) vía *f* (férrea)
railroader ['reɪlrəʊdəʳ] (N) (US) ferroviario *m*, ferrocarrilero *m* (*Mex*)
railway ['reɪlweɪ] (*Brit*) (N) (= *system*) ferrocarril *m*, ferrocarriles *mpl*; (*as track*) vía *f*, vía *f* férrea
(CPD) ▸ **railway bridge** puente *m* de ferrocarril ▸ **railway carriage** vagón *m*, coche *m* (de ferrocarril) ▸ **railway crossing** paso *m* a nivel ▸ **railway engine** máquina *f*, locomotora *f* ▸ **railway line** (= *route*) línea *f* ferroviaria *or* de ferrocarril; (= *track*) vía *f* (férrea) ▸ **railway network** red *f* ferroviaria ▸ **railway porter** mozo *m* ▸ **railway station** estación *f* (de ferrocarril) ▸ **railway timetable** horario *m* de trenes ▸ **railway track** vía *f* (férrea) ▸ **railway worker** ferroviario/a *m/f* ▸ **railway yard** cochera *f*
railwayman ['reɪlweɪmən] (N) (PL: **railwaymen**) (*Brit*) ferroviario *m*, ferrocarrilero *m* (*Mex*)
raiment ['reɪmənt] (N) (= *liter*) vestido *m*, vestimenta *f*
rain [reɪn] (N) (*Met*) lluvia *f* • **in the ~** bajo la lluvia • **a walk in the ~** un paseo bajo la lluvia • **he left his bike out in the ~** dejó la bicicleta bajo la lluvia • **don't go out in the ~** no salgas, que está lloviendo • **if the ~ keeps off** si no llueve • **it looks like ~** parece que va a llover • **come in out of the ~!** ¡entra, que te vas a mojar! • **the ~s** la época de las lluvias • **come ~ or shine** (*lit*) llueva o haga sol; (*fig*) pase lo que pase; ▹ **right**
(VI) **1** (*Met*) llover • **it's ~ing** está lloviendo • **it ~s a lot here** aquí llueve mucho • IDIOM: • **to ~ on sb's parade** (*esp US*) aguar la fiesta a algn • PROVERBS: • **it never ~s but it pours** las desgracias nunca vienen solas • **it ~s on the just as well as on the unjust** la lluvia cae sobre los buenos como sobre los malos
2 (*fig*) • **ash ~ed from the sky** llovía ceniza
(VT) llover • **hereabouts it ~s soot** por aquí llueve hollín • **to ~ blows on sb** llover golpes sobre algn • IDIOM: • **it's ~ing cats and dogs** está lloviendo a cántaros
(CPD) ▸ **rain barrel** (US) tina *f* para recoger el agua de la lluvia ▸ **rain belt** zona *f* de lluvias ▸ **rain check** (US) (*Sport*) *contraseña para usar otro día en caso de cancelación por lluvia* • **I'll take a ~ check*** (*fig*) de momento, paso ▸ **rain cloud** nube *f* de lluvia, nubarrón *m* ▸ **rain forest** (*also* **tropical rain forest**) pluviselva *f*, selva *f* tropical ▸ **rain gauge** pluviómetro *m* ▸ **rain hood** capucha *f* impermeable ▸ **rain shower** chaparrón *m*
▸ **rain down** (VI + ADV) llover • **blows ~ed down on him** llovieron sobre él los golpes
▸ **rain off, rain out** (VT + ADV) (US) • **the match was ~ed off** el partido se canceló por lluvia
rainbow ['reɪnbəʊ] (N) arco *m* iris
(CPD) ▸ **the rainbow coalition** la coalición multicolor ▸ **rainbow trout** trucha *f* arco iris
raincoat ['reɪnkəʊt] (N) gabardina *f*, impermeable *m*
raindrop ['reɪndrɒp] (N) gota *f* de lluvia
rainfall ['reɪnfɔːl] (N) precipitación *f*; (= *quantity*) lluvia *f*, cantidad *f* de lluvia • **the region has three inches of ~ a year** la región recibe tres pulgadas de lluvia al año
raininess ['reɪnɪnɪs] (N) lo lluvioso, pluviosidad *f*
rainless ['reɪnlɪs] (ADJ) sin lluvia, seco
rainmaker* ['reɪnmeɪkəʳ] (N) (= *executive creating new business*) ejecutivo/a *m/f* de éxito
rainout ['reɪnaʊt] (N) (US) (*Sport*) (= *cancellation*) cancelación *f* por lluvia; (= *suspension*) suspensión *f* por lluvia
rainproof ['reɪnpruːf] (ADJ) impermeable
rainstorm ['reɪnstɔːm] (N) aguacero *m*, chaparrón *m*
rainswept ['reɪnswept] (ADJ) barrido con lluvia
raintight ['reɪntaɪt] (ADJ) a prueba de lluvia
rainwater ['reɪnwɔːtəʳ] (N) agua *f* de lluvia
rainwear ['reɪnwɛəʳ] (N) ropa *f* para la lluvia, ropa *f* impermeable
rainy ['reɪnɪ] (ADJ) (COMPAR: **rainier**, SUPERL: **rainiest**) [*climate*] lluvioso; [*day*] de lluvia, lluvioso • **it was so ~ yesterday** llovió tanto ayer • IDIOM: • **to keep** *or* **save sth for a ~ day** [+ *object*] guardar algo para una ocasión más propicia; [+ *money*] ahorrar algo para cuando lleguen tiempos peores
(CPD) ▸ **rainy season** época *f* de las lluvias
raise [reɪz] (VT) **1** (= *lift*) [+ *fallen object, weight, hand*] levantar, alzar; [+ *hat*] levantarse; [+ *blinds, window*] subir; [+ *flag*] izar; [+ *dust*] levantar; [+ *wreck*] sacar a flote; [+ *camp, siege, embargo*] levantar • **to ~ one's eyebrows** (*lit*) arquear las cejas • **her behaviour ~d a lot of eyebrows** (*fig*) su comportamiento escandalizó a mucha gente • **to ~ one's eyes** alzar la vista *or* la mirada, levantar los ojos *or* la vista • **to ~ one's glass to sth/sb** brindar por algo/algn • **he ~d his hands in horror/surrender** levantó *or* alzó las manos horrorizado/rindiéndose • **to ~ o.s.** levantarse, alzarse • **to ~ o.s. into a sitting position** incorporarse; ▹ **curtain, hand, hell, hope, roof, sight, spirit, stake**
2 (= *make higher*) subir • **the rain has ~d the water level in the river** la lluvia ha subido el nivel del agua del río
3 (= *increase*) [+ *prices, salaries, taxes*] aumentar, subir; [+ *temperature*] subir, aumentar, elevar; [+ *standard, level*] subir; [+ *age limit*] extender; [+ *awareness, consciousness*] aumentar • **to ~ standards in education** subir el nivel de la enseñanza • **to ~ the school leaving age** extender la edad de escolarización mínima obligatoria • **we want to ~ the profile of rugby** queremos realzar la imagen del rugby • **don't you ~ your voice to me!** ¡no me levantes *or* alces la voz!
4 [+ *person*] (*in rank*) ascender (**to** a); ▹ **peerage**
5 (= *erect*) [+ *building, statue*] erigir, levantar
6 (= *bring up*) [+ *child, livestock*] criar; [+ *crop*] cultivar • **the house where she was ~d** la casa donde se crió • **I want to settle down, maybe ~ a family** quiero asentarme, y quizá tener una familia
7 (= *produce*) [+ *laugh*] provocar; [+ *doubts, fears*] suscitar; [+ *suspicion*] levantar, despertar; [+ *cry*] dar; [+ *bump*] causar; [+ *blister*] levantar • **his speech ~d a cheer from the crowd** su discurso suscitó una ovación del público • **his forlorn attempts to ~ a few laughs** sus intentos desesperados por provocar unas cuantas risas • **she could barely ~ a smile** apenas pudo sonreír • **to ~ suspicion in sb's mind** levantar *or* despertar las sospechas de algn
8 (= *present, put forward*) [+ *question, point, possibility*] plantear; [+ *subject*] sacar; [+ *complaint*] presentar • **I'll ~ the point with them** se lo mencionaré • **you'll have to ~ that with the director** tendrás que plantearle *or* comentarle eso al director • **to ~ objections to sth** poner objeciones *or* peros a algo • **this ~s the prospect of civil war** esto plantea la posibilidad de una guerra civil • **he gets embarrassed whenever the subject is ~d** se pone violento cada vez que se saca el tema
9 (= *get together*) [+ *funds, money*] recaudar; [+ *capital*] movilizar; [+ *loan*] conseguir, obtener; [+ *army*] reclutar • **they couldn't ~ his bail** no pudieron reunir el dinero de su fianza • **they ~d a loan against the house** consiguieron un préstamo con la casa como garantía • **to ~ money for charity** recaudar dinero con fines benéficos; ▹ **mortgage**
10 (*Cards*) • **I'll ~ you!** ¡subo la apuesta! • **I'll ~ you £10** te subo 10 libras más; ▹ **bid, stake**
11 (= *contact*) (*by phone*) localizar; (*by radio*) contactar con, localizar • **we tried to ~ him on the radio** intentamos contactar con él *or* localizarlo por radio
12 (= *conjure*) [+ *spirits*] evocar • **to ~ sb from the dead** resucitar a algn, levantar a algn de entre los muertos
13 (*Math*) [+ *total*] elevar • **2 ~d to the power 3 is 8** 2 elevado a la tercera potencia es 8
(N) (*esp US*) (*in salary*) aumento *m*, subida *f*; (*in taxes*) subida *f*
▸ **raise up** (VT + ADV) (= *lift*) levantar, alzar • **to ~ o.s. up into a sitting position** incorporarse • **he ~d himself up on one elbow** se apoyó en un codo • **he has ~d himself up from nothing** ha salido de la nada • **to ~ sb up from poverty** sacar a algn de la pobreza, ayudar a algn a salir de la miseria
raised [reɪzd] (ADJ) [*platform*] elevado; [*temperature, blood pressure, level*] alto, elevado; [*voice*] exaltado; (= *in relief*) en relieve • **I could hear ~ voices in the next room** oía voces exaltadas en la habitación de al lado
raisin ['reɪzən] (N) pasa *f*, uva *f* pasa
raison d'être ['reɪzɔːn'deːtr] (N) razón *f* de ser
Raj [rɑːdʒ] (N) • **the British Raj** el imperio británico (en la India)
rajah ['rɑːdʒə] (N) rajá *m*
rake¹ [reɪk] (N) (= *garden rake*) rastrillo *m*
(VT) **1** (*Agr etc*) [+ *sand, leaves, soil*] rastrillar; [+ *fire*] hurgar
2 (= *strafe*) [+ *ship, file of men*] barrer
▸ **rake in** (VT + ADV) **1** [+ *gambling chips*] recoger
2* • **they ~d in a profit of £100** sacaron 100 libras de ganancia • **he ~s in £50 on every deal** se toma una tajada de 50 libras de cada negocio* • **he must be raking it in** está acuñando dinero
▸ **rake off** (VT + ADV) **1** (*lit*) quitar con el rastrillo
2* (*pej*) [+ *share of profits, commission*] sacar
▸ **rake over** (VT + ADV) [+ *flowerbed*] rastrillar; (*fig*) [+ *memories, past*] remover
▸ **rake together** (VT + ADV) reunir *or* recoger con el rastrillo; (*fig*) [+ *money*] reunir • **we managed to ~ a team together** por fin

logramos formar un equipo
▸ **rake up** (VT + ADV) [+ *subject*] sacar a relucir; [+ *memories, the past*] remover • **why did you have to ~ that up?** ¿para qué has vuelto a mencionar eso?
rake² [reɪk] (N) (= *dissolute man*) calavera *m* • **old ~** viejo *m* verde
rake³ [reɪk] (N) (*Archit, Naut*) inclinación *f* (VT) inclinar
rake-off* ['reɪkɒf] (N) comisión *f*, tajada* *f*
rakish ['reɪkɪʃ] (ADJ) **1** (= *dissolute*) [*person*] libertino, disoluto
2 • **at a ~ angle** echado de lado
rakishly ['reɪkɪʃlɪ] (ADV) (*of hat etc*) echado al lado
rally¹ ['rælɪ] (N) **1** (= *mass meeting*) (*gen*) concentración *f*; (*with speeches*) mitin *m* • **there was a ~ in Trafalgar Square** hubo una concentración en Trafalgar Square
2 (*Aut*) (= *competition*) rally *m* • **the Monte Carlo Rally** el Rally de Montecarlo
3 (*Tennis*) intercambio *m* de golpes
4 (*Econ*) (= *revival*) recuperación *f*
5 (*Med*) (= *recovery*) recuperación *f*; (= *improvement*) mejora *f*
6 (*Mil*) repliegue *m*
(VT) **1** (= *gather*) (*Pol*) concentrar; (*Mil*) reunir
2 (= *exhort, unite in spirit*) levantar el ánimo de, fortalecer el espíritu de; (*fig*) [+ *strength, spirits*] recobrar
(VI) **1** (= *gather in support*) • **to ~ to** *or* **behind sb** • **~ to sb's side** *or* **support** solidarizarse con algn • **to ~ to the call** acudir a la llamada
2 (*in demonstration*) concentrarse, reunirse
3 (*Mil*) reorganizarse
4 (*Econ, Med*) (= *recover*) recuperarse; (= *improve*) mejorar
5 (*Aut*) (= *compete*) competir en rallys
(CPD) ▸ **rally car** coche *m* de rally ▸ **rally driver** piloto *m* de rally ▸ **rally driving** rally *m*
▸ **rally round, rally around** (VI + ADV) • **everyone must ~ round** todos tenemos que cooperar • **we all rallied round to help** todos nos juntamos para ayudar
(VI + PREP) • **to ~ round sb** reunirse en torno a algn, solidarizarse con algn
rally² ['rælɪ] (VT) (= *tease*) tomar el pelo a
rallycross ['rælɪkrɒs] (N) *rally sobre un circuito de cross con tramos de asfalto*
rallying ['rælɪɪŋ] (CPD) ▸ **rallying call, rallying cry** llamamiento *m* (*para reanimar la resistencia etc*) ▸ **rallying point** (*Pol, Mil*) punto *m* de reunión
RAM [ræm] (N ABBR) (*Comput*) (= **random access memory**) RAM *f*
(CPD) ▸ **RAM chip** chip *m* de RAM
ram [ræm] (N) **1** (*Zool*) carnero *m*
2 (*Astron*) Aries *m*
3 (*Mil*) ariete *m*
(VT) **1** (= *force*) • **to ram a hat down on one's head** incrustarse el sombrero • **to ram clothes into a case** meter la ropa a la fuerza en una maleta • **to ram a nail into a wall** incrustar un clavo en una pared • **to ram sth into a hole** meter algo a la fuerza en un agujero • **to be rammed up against sth** estar apretado contra algo • **they ram their ideas down your throat** (*fig*) te hacen tragar sus ideas a la fuerza • **we had Campoamor rammed into us at school** tuvimos que darnos un atracón de Campoamor en el colegio
2 (= *collide with*) (*deliberately*) embestir contra; (*Naut*) embestir con el espolón; (*accidentally*) chocar con *or* contra • **the thieves rammed a police car** los ladrones embistieron contra un coche de la policía • **the car rammed the lamppost as it slid off the road** el coche se metió contra la farola al salirse de la carretera
(CPD) ▸ **ram raid*** robo *m* (*rompiendo el escaparate etc con un coche*) ▸ **ram raider*** ladrón/ona *m/f* (*que entra en el establecimiento rompiendo el escaparate etc con un coche*)
Ramadan [ˌræməˈdæn] (N) ramadán *m*
ramble ['ræmbl] (N) paseo *m*, excursión *f* • **to go for a ~** dar un paseo
(VI) **1** (= *walk*) pasear • **we spent a week rambling in the hills** pasamos una semana de excursión en la montaña *or* la sierra
2 (*in speech*) divagar, perder el hilo • **he just ~d on and on** siguió divagando
3 [*river*] formar meandros; [*plant*] trepar, enredarse
rambler ['ræmblə^r] (N) **1** (*Brit*) (= *hiker*) excursionista *mf* (a pie)
2 (*Bot*) trepadora *f*; (= *rose*) = **rambling rose**
rambling ['ræmblɪŋ] (ADJ) **1** (= *straggling*) [*plant*] trepador
2 (= *wandering, incoherent*) [*speech, book*] farragoso, inconexo
3 (= *sprawling*) [*house*] laberíntico
(N) **1** (= *walking*) excursionismo *m* a pie
2 ramblings desvaríos *mpl*, divagaciones *fpl*
(CPD) ▸ **rambling rose** rosal *m* trepador
Rambo* ['ræmbəʊ] (N) machote *m* bravucón*
rambunctious* [ræm'bʌŋkʃəs] (ADJ) (*US*) bullicioso, pendenciero
RAMC (N ABBR) (*Brit*) = **Royal Army Medical Corps**
ramekin ['ræmɪkɪn] (N) (*also* **ramekin dish**) ramequín *m*
ramification [ˌræmɪfɪ'keɪʃən] (N) ramificación *f* • **with numerous ~s** con innumerables ramificaciones • **in all its ~s** en toda su complejidad
ramified ['ræmɪfaɪd] (ADJ) (*lit, fig*) ramificado; (*more intricate*) intricado
ramify ['ræmɪfaɪ] (VI) ramificarse
ramjet ['ræmdʒet] (N) estatorreactor *m*
rammer ['ræmə^r] (N) (*for roadmaking*) pisón *m*; (*for rifle*) baqueta *f*
ramp [ræmp] (N) (= *incline*) rampa *f*; (*on road*) rampa *f*, desnivel *m*
rampage [ræm'peɪdʒ] (N) • **to go on the ~** desbocarse, desmandarse
(VI) desmandarse • **the crowd ~d through the market** la multitud corrió alocada por el mercado
rampancy ['ræmpənsɪ] (N) (= *uncontrolled lust*) desenfreno *m*; (= *aggression*) agresividad *f*; [*of foliage*] exuberancia *f*; [*of disease, inflation, crime*] predominio *m*
rampant ['ræmpənt] (ADJ) **1** (= *uncontrolled*) [*lust*] desenfrenado; [*inflation*] galopante
2 (= *prevailing*) difundido, de uso común • **anarchism is ~ here** aquí el anarquismo está muy extendido
3 (*Bot*) (= *overgrowing*) [*flower, plant*] exuberante
4 (*Heraldry*) • **the lion ~** el león rampante
rampart ['ræmpɑːt] (N) (= *earthwork*) terraplén *m*; (= *city wall*) muralla *f*; (*fig*) (= *bulwark*) baluarte *m*, defensa *f* • **the ~s of York** la muralla de York
ram-raid ['ræmreɪd] (*Brit*) (VI) robar mediante el método del alunizaje
(VT) [+ *shop*] alunizar contra
ram-raiding ['ræmreɪdɪŋ] (N) (robo *m* mediante el método del) alunizaje *m*
ramrod ['ræmrɒd] (N) baqueta *f*
ramshackle ['ræmˌʃækl] (ADJ) (= *tumbledown*) [*house*] destartalado; [*car*] desvencijado
ram's-horn ['ræmzhɔːn] (N) cuerno *m* de carnero
RAN (N ABBR) = **Royal Australian Navy**
ran [ræn] (PT) *of* **run**
ranch [rɑːntʃ] (N) rancho *m*, hacienda *f* (de ganado) (*LAm*), estancia *f* (*S. Cone*)
(CPD) ▸ **ranch hand** peón *m* ▸ **ranch house** casa *f* de rancho
rancher ['rɑːntʃə^r] (N) ganadero/a *m/f*, ranchero/a *m/f*
ranching ['rɑːntʃɪŋ] (N) ganadería *f*
rancid ['rænsɪd] (ADJ) rancio
rancidity [ræn'sɪdɪtɪ] (N), **rancidness** ['rænsɪdnɪs] (N) rancidez *f*, ranciedad *f*
rancor ['ræŋkə^r] (N) (*US*) = **rancour**
rancorous ['ræŋkərəs] (ADJ) rencoroso
rancour, rancor (*US*) ['ræŋkə^r] (N) rencor *m*
rand [rænd] (N) rand *m*
R & B [ˌɑːrən'biː] (N ABBR) = **Rhythm and Blues**
R & D [ˌɑːrən'diː] (N ABBR) (= **research and development**) I. y D., I + D
randiness* ['rændɪnɪs] (N) cachondez* *f*
random ['rændəm] (ADJ) **1** (= *haphazard*) [*arrangement*] hecho al azar • **a ~ selection** una selección hecha al azar • **a wall built of ~ stones** un muro hecho con piedras elegidas al azar
2 (= *capricious, indiscriminate*) caprichoso • **a ~ shot** un disparo hecho sin apuntar, una bala perdida
3 (*Statistics, Maths*) [*sample, distribution*] aleatorio
(N) • **at ~** al azar • **we picked the number at ~** elegimos el número al azar • **to talk at ~** hablar sin pesar las palabras • **to hit out at ~** repartir golpes por todos lados
(CPD) ▸ **random access** (*Comput*) acceso *m* aleatorio ▸ **random access memory** (*Comput*) memoria *f* de acceso aleatorio ▸ **random number** número *m* al azar
randomize ['rændəmaɪz] (VT) aleatorizar
randomly ['rændəmlɪ] (ADV) • **~ chosen** elegido al azar
randomness ['rændəmnɪs] (N) aleatoriedad *f*
R & R (N ABBR) (*US*) (*Mil*) (= **rest and recreation**) descanso *m*
randy* ['rændɪ] (ADJ) (COMPAR: **randier**, SUPERL: **randiest**) (*Brit*) (= *aroused*) caliente‡, cachondo*‡, arrecho (*esp LAm**) • **to feel ~** estar caliente‡, estar cachondo*‡
rang [ræŋ] (PT) *of* **ring²**
range [reɪndʒ] (N) **1** [*of mountains*] cadena *f* • **a ~ of hills** una cadena de colinas • **a ~ of mountains** una cadena montañosa *or* de montañas, una cordillera • **the Absaroka Range** la cordillera Absaroka; ▹ **mountain**
2 (= *extent*) • **there is a wide ~ of ability in the class** los niveles de aptitud en la clase varían mucho • **your weight is within the normal ~** su peso está dentro de lo normal • **all this was beyond her ~ of experience** todo esto estaba fuera de su campo de experiencia • **the full ~ of his work is on view** se expone su obra en todo su ámbito; ▹ **age, price**
3 (*Mus*) [*of instrument, voice*] registro *m*
4 (= *selection, variety*) **a** (*gen*) variedad *f* • **there was a wide ~ of opinions** había gran variedad de opiniones, las opiniones variaban mucho • **a wide ~ of colours** una amplia gama de colores • **they come in a ~ of sizes** vienen en varios *or* diversos tamaños • **she has a wide ~ of interests** tiene muchos y diversos intereses • **there was a whole ~ of options open to us** frente a nosotros se abría un amplio abanico de posibilidades
b (*Comm*) (= *product line*) línea *f*; (= *selection*) gama *f*, selección *f* • **the new autumn ~** la nueva línea de otoño • **we stock a full ~ of wines** tenemos una selección *or* gama completa de vinos; ▹ **product**
5 [*of gun, missile*] alcance *m*; [*of plane, ship*] autonomía *f*, radio *m* de acción; [*of car*]

r

autonomía *f*; [*of transmitter*] radio *m* de acción • **a gun with a ~ of three miles** un cañón con un alcance de tres millas • **within ~ (of sth/sb)** a tiro (de algo/algn) • **to come within ~ (of sth/sb)** ponerse a tiro (de algo/algn) • **out of ~ (of sth/sb)** fuera del alcance (de algo/algn) • **~ of vision** campo *m* visual
6 (= *distance from target*) distancia *f* • **at close ~** de cerca, a corta distancia • **at long ~** de lejos, a larga distancia • **to find the/one's ~** determinar la distancia a la que está el objetivo
7 (*Bot, Zool*) [*of species*] (zona *f* de) distribución *f*
8 (*esp US*) (*Agr*) pradera *f*, pampa *f* (*S. Cone*), llano *m* (*esp Ven*)
9 (*for shooting*) campo *m* de tiro; ▹ **rifle²**
10 (*also* **kitchen range**) fogón *m*
VT **1** (= *line up, place*) (*lit*) alinear • **chairs were ~d against one wall** las sillas estaban alineadas frente a una pared • **~d left/right** [*text*] alineado/a a la izquierda/derecha • **most of the party is ~d against him** la mayoría de los miembros del partido se ha alineado en contra suya
2 (*liter*) (= *rove*) [+ *country*] recorrer • **to ~ the seas** surcar los mares
3 • **to ~ a gun on sth/sb** apuntar un cañón a algo/algn
VI **1** (= *extend*) extenderse • **the search ~d over the whole country** se llevó a cabo la búsqueda por todo el país • **the conversation ~d over many issues** la conversación abarcó muchos temas • **his eye ~d over the horizon** escudriñó el horizonte; ▹ **wide-ranging**
2 (= *vary within limits*) • **prices ~ from £3 to £9** los precios varían de 3 a 9 libras, los precios oscilan entre las 3 y las 9 libras • **the women ~d in age from 14 to 40** la edad de las mujeres iba de los 14 a los 40 años *or* oscilaba entre los 14 y los 40 años
3 (= *wander*) • **hyenas ~ widely in search of carrion** las hienas recorren muchos lugares en busca de carroña • **animals ranging through the jungle** animales vagando por *or* merodeando por la jungla
4 (*Bot*) darse; (*Zool*) distribuirse
5 [*gun*] • **it ~s over 300 miles** tiene un alcance de trescientas millas
▸ **range across** VI + PREP **1** [+ *area*] recorrerse • **helicopters are already ranging across the jungle** los helicópteros ya se están recorriendo la selva
2 (= *cover*) [+ *spectrum*] abarcar • **his skills and tastes ~ across the musical spectrum** sus capacidades y gustos abarcan todo el espectro musical
-range [reɪndʒ] ADJ (*ending in compounds*) • **intermediate-range missile** misil *m* de medio alcance • **short-range missile** misil *m* de corto alcance
rangefinder ['reɪndʒ,faɪndəʳ] N (*Mil, Phot*) telémetro *m*
rangeland ['reɪndʒlænd] N (*US*) ≈ dehesa *f*
ranger ['reɪndʒəʳ] N **1** (= *Girl Guide*) exploradora *f*
2 (= *forest ranger*) guardabosques *mf inv*
Rangoon [ræŋ'gu:n] N Rangún *m*
rangy ['reɪndʒɪ] ADJ alto y delgado
rank¹ [ræŋk] N **1** (= *status*) rango *m*, categoría *f*; (*Mil*) grado *m*, rango *m* • **a writer of the first ~** un escritor de primera categoría • **persons of ~** gente de calidad • **their ~s range from lieutenant to colonel** sus graduaciones van de teniente a coronel • **to attain the ~ of major** ser ascendido a comandante, llegar a(l grado de) comandante • IDIOM: • **to pull ~*** aprovecharse de tener un rango superior
2 (*Mil*) fila *f* • **the ~s** la tropa • **to break ~(s)** romper filas • **to close ~s** (*Mil*) (*also fig*) cerrar filas • **I've joined the ~s of the unemployed** soy un parado más • **to reduce sb to the ~s** degradar a algn a soldado raso • **to rise from the ~s** ascender desde soldado raso
3 (= *row*) fila *f*, hilera *f*, línea *f* • **the ~s of poplars** las hileras de álamos • **in serried ~s** en filas apretadas
4 (*also* **taxi rank**) parada *f* de taxis
VT clasificar • **he's ~ed third in the United States** está clasificado tercero en los Estados Unidos • **I ~ him sixth** yo lo pongo en sexto lugar • **where would you ~ him?** ¿qué posición le darías? • **I ~ her among ...** yo la pongo entre ... • **he was ~ed as (being) ...** se le consideraba ... • **to ~ A with B** igualar A y B, poner A y B en el mismo nivel
VI • **to ~ fourth** ocupar el cuarto lugar • **where does she ~?** ¿qué posición ocupa? • **to ~ above sb** ser superior a *or* sobrepasar a algn • **to ~ among ...** figurar entre ... • **to ~ as** equivaler a • **to ~ high** ocupar una posición privilegiada • **to ~ second to sb** tener el segundo lugar después de algn • **to ~ with** ser igual a
CPD ▸ **rank and file** • **the ~ and file** (*Mil*) los soldados rasos; (*Pol*) la base; ▹ **rank-and-file**
rank² [ræŋk] ADJ **1** (*Bot*) [*plants*] exuberante; [*garden*] muy poblado
2 (= *smelly*) maloliente, apestoso • **to smell ~** oler mal
3 (= *utter*) [*hypocrisy, injustice etc*] manifiesto, absoluto; [*beginner, outsider*] completo, puro • **that's ~ nonsense!** ¡puras tonterías! • **he's a ~ liar** es un mentiroso redomado
rank-and-file ['ræŋkənfaɪl] ADJ [*members, workers*] de base; [*backing, vote*] de la base; [*soldiers, policemen*] de filas • **as a rank and file policeman I must say ...** como policía de filas, debo decir ...; ▹ **rank and file**
ranker ['ræŋkəʳ] N (*Mil*) (= *officer*) oficial *m* patatero*
ranking ['ræŋkɪŋ] ADJ (*esp US*) superior
N **1** ránking *m*; (*Mil*) graduación *f*
2 rankings (*Sport*) clasificación *fsing*, ránking *msing*
-ranking [-'ræŋkɪŋ] SUFFIX • **high-ranking** de alta graduación • **a high-ranking officer** un alto mando • **low-ranking** de baja graduación • **top-ranking** de alta graduación
rankle ['ræŋkl] VI doler • **the fact that he won still ~s with me** todavía me duele *or* me molesta el hecho de que él haya ganado
rankly ['ræŋklɪ] ADV (*Bot*) con exuberancia
rankness ['ræŋknɪs] N **1** (*Bot*) exuberancia *f*
2 (= *bad smell*) mal olor *m*
3 [*of injustice*] enormidad *f*
ransack ['rænsæk] VT **1** (= *search*) registrar de arriba abajo • **they ~ed the house for arms** registraron la casa de arriba abajo buscando armas
2 (= *pillage*) saquear; [+ *house, shop*] desvalijar • **the place had been ~ed** el lugar había sido saqueado
ransom ['rænsəm] N rescate *m* • **to hold sb to ~** pedir un rescate por algn; (*fig*) poner a algn entre la espada y la pared; ▹ **king**
VT rescatar; (*Rel*) redimir
CPD ▸ **ransom demand** petición *f* de rescate ▸ **ransom money** rescate *m*, dinero *m* exigido a cambio del rehén
ransoming ['rænsəmɪŋ] N rescate *m*
ransomware ['rænsəmweəʳ] N (*Comput*) *software que infecta un ordenador y solicita un rescate para que funcione correctamente de nuevo*
rant [rænt] VI (= *declaim*) vociferar • **to ~ at sb** (= *be angry*) despotricar contra algn • **to ~ on about sb** (*angrily*) echar pestes de algn • **he ~ed and raved for hours** despotricó durante varias horas
N diatriba *f*
ranting ['ræntɪŋ] N lenguaje *m* declamatorio • **for all his ~** por mucho que despotrique
ADJ campanudo, declamatorio
rap [ræp] N **1** golpecito *m*, golpe *m* seco • **there was a rap at the door** llamaron (suavemente) a la puerta • **to give sb a rap on** *or* **over the knuckles** (*lit*) dar a algn en los nudillos; (*fig*) echar un rapapolvo a algn
2 (= *blame*) • **to take the rap*** pagar los platos rotos* • **to take the rap for sth** cargar con la culpa de algo
3 (*esp US**) (= *charge*) acusación *f* • **murder rap** acusación *f* de homicidio • **to beat the rap** (lograr) ser absuelto
4 (*Mus*) rap *m*
5 (*esp US**) • **to have a rap with sb** charlar con algn
VT golpetear, dar un golpecito en • **to rap sb's knuckles** • **rap sb on the knuckles** (*lit*) dar a algn en los nudillos; (*fig*) echar un rapapolvo a algn
VI **1** (= *knock*) • **to rap at the door** llamar a la puerta
2 (*US**) (= *chat*) charlar
3 (*Mus*) hacer rap
CPD ▸ **rap artist** rapero/a *m/f* ▸ **rap music** rap *m* ▸ **rap session** (*US**) (= *chat*) charla *f* informal ▸ **rap sheet** (*US**) (= *police record*) antecedentes *mpl* penales
▸ **rap on** VI + PREP [+ *door, window, table*] dar golpecitos en
▸ **rap out** VT + ADV [+ *order*] espetar
rapacious [rə'peɪʃəs] ADJ rapaz
rapaciously [rə'peɪʃəslɪ] ADV con rapacidad
rapacity [rə'pæsɪtɪ] N rapacidad *f*
rape¹ [reɪp] N **1** [*of woman, man*] violación *f*; [*of minor*] estupro *m* (*frm*) • **attempted ~** intento *m* de violación; ▹ **marital**
2 (*fig*) destrucción *f* • **the ~ of Poland** la destrucción de Polonia
VT [+ *man, woman*] violar; [+ *minor*] estuprar (*frm*)
CPD ▸ **rape alarm** alarma *f* personal ▸ **rape crisis centre** centro *m* de ayuda a las víctimas de violaciones
rape² [reɪp] N (*Bot*) colza *f*
CPD ▸ **rape oil** = **rapeseed oil**
rapeseed ['reɪpsi:d] N semilla *f* de colza
CPD ▸ **rapeseed oil** aceite *m* de colza
Raphael ['ræfeɪəl] N Rafael
rapid ['ræpɪd] ADJ rápido
CPD ▸ **rapid fire** fuego *m* rápido ▸ **rapid reaction force** fuerza *f* de intervención inmediata
rapid-fire ['ræpɪd,faɪə] ADJ [*gun*] de fuego racheado; (*fig*) trepidante • **a rapid-fire succession of questions** una sucesión trepidante de preguntas
rapidity [rə'pɪdɪtɪ] N rapidez *f*
rapidly ['ræpɪdlɪ] ADV rápidamente, rápido
rapids ['ræpɪdz] NPL (*in river*) rápidos *mpl*
rapier ['reɪpɪəʳ] N estoque *m*
rapine ['ræpaɪn] N rapiña *f*
rapist ['reɪpɪst] N violador(a) *m/f*
rappel [ræ'pel] VI (*US*) (= *abseil*) descender en rápel • **to ~ down sth** descender en rápel de algo
rapper ['ræpəʳ] N (*Mus*) músico *mf* de rap
rapping ['ræpɪŋ] N **1** (= *knocking*) golpecitos *mpl*, golpes *mpl* secos; (*at door*) llamadas *fpl*, aldabadas *fpl*
2 (*Mus*) rap *m*
rapport [ræ'pɔ:ʳ] N **1** (= *relationship*) relación *f* • **I have a good ~ with him** tengo muy buena relación con él, me entiendo

muy bien con él • **he has established a good ~ with the customers** ha entablado buenas relaciones con los clientes
2 (= *understanding*) • **there was an instant ~ between them** enseguida congeniaron
rapprochement [ræ'prɒʃmɑ̃:ŋ] (N) acercamiento *m*
rapscallion†† [ræp'skæliən] (N) (*also hum*) bribón *m*, golfo *m*
rapt [ræpt] (ADJ) • **they were sitting with ~ attention** estaban sentados prestando mucha atención • **he drew ~ audiences** cautivaba al público, dejaba al público embelesado • **with a ~ expression on his face** con cara de embeleso • **Claud was staring at me, ~** Claud me miraba fijamente, absorto *or* embelesado
raptor ['ræptəʳ] (N) ave *f* raptora
rapture ['ræptʃəʳ] (N) éxtasis *m inv* • **to be in ~s** estar extasiado, extasiarse • **to go into ~s over sth** extasiarse por algo
rapturous ['ræptʃərəs] (ADJ) [*applause*] entusiasta; [*look*] extasiado
rapturously ['ræptʃərəslɪ] (ADV) [*applaud*] con entusiasmo; [*look*] con embeleso
rare [rɛəʳ] (ADJ) (COMPAR: **rarer**, SUPERL: **rarest**) **1** (= *uncommon, infrequent*) [*item, book*] raro; [*plant, animal*] poco común; [*ability, opportunity*] excepcional; [*case, occurrence*] poco frecuente • **it is ~ to find that ...** es raro encontrarse con que ... • **it is ~ for her to come** es raro que venga • **she had a ~ beauty** tenía una belleza singular • **with very ~ exceptions** con muy raras excepciones • **in a moment of ~ generosity** en un momento de inusitada generosidad • **to grow ~(r)** [*animals, plants*] volverse menos común; [*visits*] hacerse más raro • **on the ~ occasions when he spoke** en las poquísimas ocasiones en las que hablaba • **it is a ~ sight** es algo que no se ve frecuentemente • **to have a ~ old time** (*†) pasárselo pipa*; ▹ STRANGE, RARE
2 (= *rarefied*) [*air, atmosphere*] enrarecido
3 (*Culin*) [*steak, meat*] vuelta y vuelta, poco hecho (*Sp*)
(CPD) ▸ **rare earth** tierra *f* rara
rarebit ['rɛəbɪt] (N) • **Welsh ~** pan *m* con queso tostado
rarefaction [ˌrɛərɪ'fækʃən] (N) rarefacción *f*
rarefied ['rɛərɪfaɪd] (ADJ) enrarecido
rarefy ['rɛərɪfaɪ] (VT) enrarecer
(VI) enrarecerse
rarely ['rɛəlɪ] (ADV) casi nunca, rara vez, raramente • **that ~ happens** casi nunca *or* rara vez sucede eso • **that method is ~ satisfactory** ese método no es satisfactorio casi nunca • **it is ~ found here** aquí se encuentra con poca frecuencia
rareness ['rɛənɪs] (N) rareza *f*
raring ['rɛərɪŋ] (ADJ) • **to be ~ to do sth** tener muchas ganas de hacer algo • **to be ~ to go** tener muchas ganas de empezar
rarity ['rɛərɪtɪ] (N) **1** rareza *f*
2 (= *rare thing*) rareza *f*, cosa *f* rara • **it's a ~ here** aquí es una rareza *or* una cosa rara
rascal ['rɑ:skəl] (N) (= *scoundrel*) granuja *mf*; (= *child*) granuja *mf*, pillo *m*
rascally ['rɑ:skəlɪ] (ADJ) granuja, bribón • **a ~ trick** una triquiñuela, una artimaña
rash[1] [ræʃ] (N) **1** (*Med*) sarpullido *m*, erupción *f* (cutánea) • **I've got a ~ on my chest** tengo un sarpullido *or* una erupción en el pecho • **she came out in a ~** le salieron ronchas en la piel
2 (= *spate*) racha *f*, avalancha *f* • **a ~ of complaints** una avalancha *or* una multitud de quejas
rash[2] [ræʃ] (ADJ) [*act, statement*] temerario, precipitado; [*person*] temerario, imprudente • **that was very ~ of you** en eso has sido muy temerario *or* imprudente
rasher ['ræʃəʳ] (N) • **a ~ of bacon** una loncha de beicon
rashly ['ræʃlɪ] (ADV) temerariamente
rashness ['ræʃnɪs] (N) [*of actions*] temeridad *f*, precipitación *f*; [*of person*] temeridad *f*, imprudencia *f*
rasp [rɑ:sp] (N) **1** (= *tool*) escofina *f*, raspador *m*
2 (= *sound*) chirrido *m*; [*of voice*] tono *m* áspero
(VT) **1** (*with file*) raspar, escofinar
2 (= *speak*) (*also* **rasp out**) decir con voz áspera; [+ *order*] espetar
(VI) hacer un sonido desapacible
raspberry ['rɑ:zbərɪ] (N) **1** (= *fruit*) frambuesa *f*
2 • **to blow a ~*** hacer una pedorreta*
(CPD) ▸ **raspberry bush** frambuesero *m*
▸ **raspberry jam** mermelada *f* de frambuesa
▸ **raspberry tart** pastel *m* de frambuesas
rasping ['rɑ:spɪŋ] (ADJ) [*voice*] áspero; [*noise*] chirriante
raspy ['rɑ:spɪ] (ADJ) [*voice*] ronco, áspero; [*tone*] quebrado
Rasta* ['ræstə], **Rastafarian** [ˌræstə'fɛərɪən] (ADJ) rastafario
(N) rastafario/a *m/f*
rasterize ['ræstəraɪz] (VT) rasterizar
rat [ræt] (N) **1** (*Zool*) rata *f* • IDIOM: • **I smell a rat** aquí hay gato encerrado, aquí se está tramando algo • **he could smell a rat** se olió algo sospechoso, le olió a gato encerrado
2 (= *person*) • **you dirty rat!*** ¡canalla!*
3 (*as exclamation*) • **rats!** (*Brit**) ¡narices!*
(VI) **1*** • **to rat on sb** (= *inform on*) chivarse de algn; (= *desert*) abandonar a algn • **to rat on a deal** rajarse de un negocio
2 (= *catch rats*) cazar ratas, matar ratas
(CPD) ▸ **rat pack** (= *journalists*) paparazzi *mpl*
▸ **rat poison** matarratas *m inv* ▸ **the rat race** la lucha por la supervivencia, la competencia • **it's a rat race** es un mundo muy competitivo ▸ **rat run*** (*Brit*) (*Aut*) *calle residencial usada por los conductores para evitar atascos* ▸ **rat trap** trampa *f* para ratas, ratonera *f*
rata ['rɑ:tə] ▹ **pro rata**
ratable ['reɪtəbl] (ADJ) = **rateable**
rat-arsed‡ ['rætɑ:st] (ADJ) (*Brit*) (= *drunk*) pedo‡
rat-a-tat [ˌrætə'tæt], **rat-a-tat-tat** [ˌrætəˌtæt'tæt] (N) (*at door*) golpecitos *mpl*; (*imitating sound*) ¡toc, toc!; [*of machine-gun*] martilleo *m*
ratatouille [ˌrætə'twi:] (N) ≈ pisto *m*
ratbag* ['rætbæg] (N) (*Brit*) borde* *mf*
ratcatcher ['ræt,kætʃəʳ] (N) cazarratas *mf inv*, cazador(a) *m/f* de ratas
ratchet ['rætʃɪt] (N) (*Tech*) trinquete *m*
(CPD) ▸ **ratchet wheel** rueda *f* de trinquete
▸ **ratchet up** (VT + ADV) incrementar
(VI + ADV) incrementarse, sufrir un incremento
rate[1] [reɪt] (N) **1** (= *proportion, ratio*) • **birth ~** índice *m or* tasa *f* de natalidad, natalidad *f* • **death ~** índice *m or* tasa *f* de mortalidad, mortalidad *f* • **the failure/success ~ for this exam is high** el índice de suspensos/ aprobados en este examen es alto • **at a ~ of** a razón de • **it is increasing at a** *or* **the ~ of 5% a year** está aumentando a razón de un 5% al año • **at a** *or* **the ~ of three a minute** a razón de tres por minuto; ▹ **crime, divorce, first-rate, second-rate, third-rate, metabolic, suicide**
2 (= *speed*) (*gen*) velocidad *f*; [*of work*] ritmo *m* • **the population is growing at an alarming ~** la población crece a una velocidad alarmante • **at any ~** (= *at least*) al menos, por lo menos; (= *anyway*) en todo caso • **he is the least appealing, to me at any ~** es el menos atractivo, al menos *or* por lo menos para mí • **I don't know what happened, at any ~ she didn't turn up** no sé lo que pasó, el caso es que *or* en todo caso no se presentó • **~ of climb** (*Aer*) velocidad *f* de subida • **~ of flow** [*of electricity, water*] velocidad *f* de flujo • **at a ~ of knots*** [*of person, vehicle*] a toda pastilla* • **at this ~** a este paso • **if things go on at this ~** si las cosas siguen marchando a este paso • **at the ~ you're going, you'll be dead before long** al paso que vas no vas a durar mucho; ▹ **heart**
3 (= *price*) (*for tickets*) precio *m*; [*of hotel, telephone service*] tarifa *f* • **there is a reduced ~ for children under 12** a los niños menores de 12 años se les hace un descuento, hay una tarifa reducida para niños menores de 12 años • **calls cost 36p per minute cheap ~** el precio de la llamada es de 36 peniques el minuto, dentro de la tarifa barata • **they were paid a ~ of £5 an hour** les pagaban a razón de 5 libras la hora • **the ~ for the job** el sueldo que corresponde al trabajo • **~s of pay** sueldos *mpl*; ▹ **postage, postal, peak, standard**
4 (*Econ*) [*of stocks*] cotización *f* • **bank ~** tipo *m* de interés bancario • **exchange ~** • **~ of exchange** (tipo *m* de) cambio *m* • **growth ~** • **~ of growth** tasa *f* de crecimiento • **inflation ~** • **~ of inflation** tasa *f* de inflación • **interest ~** • **~ of interest** tipo *m or* tasa *f* de interés • **~ of return** tasa *f* de rentabilidad *or* rendimiento; ▹ **basic, fixed-rate, mortgage, tax**
5 rates (*Brit*) (*formerly*) (= *local tax*) contribución *fsing* municipal, impuesto *msing* municipal • **we pay £900 in ~s** pagamos 900 libras de contribuciones; ▹ **water**
(VT) **1** (= *rank*) • **how do you ~ her?** ¿qué opinas de ella? • **how do you ~ his performance on a scale of one to ten?** ¿cuántos puntos le darías a su actuación en una escala del uno al diez? • **she is ~d fifth in the world** ocupa el quinto lugar en la clasificación mundial • **to ~ sth/sb highly**: • **I ~ the book highly** tengo muy buena opinión del libro • **I ~ him highly** lo tengo en muy alta estima • **the most highly ~d player in English football** el jugador mejor considerado del fútbol inglés; ▹ **X-rated, zero-rated**
2 (= *consider, regard*) considerar • **I ~ him among my friends** le considero un amigo • **I ~ him among my best three pupils** lo tengo por uno de mis tres mejores alumnos • **most ~d it a hit** la mayoría de la gente lo consideraba un éxito • **I ~ myself as fairly fit** considero que estoy bastante en forma
3* (= *regard as good*) • **I don't ~ your chances** creo que tienes pocas posibilidades • **he didn't ~ the movie at all** no concedió ningún mérito a la película • **I don't ~ him (as a composer)** no le valoro (como compositor)
4 (= *deserve*) merecer(se) • **I think he ~s a pass (mark)** creo que (se) merece un aprobado • **it didn't ~ a mention** no lo consideraron digno de mención • **in those crowded streets he wouldn't ~ a second glance** en esas calles llenas de gente pasaría desapercibido
5 (*Brit*) (*for local tax*) [+ *property*] tasar, valorar (at en)
(VI) **1** (= *perform, measure up*) • **how did he ~?** ¿qué tal lo hizo?, ¿qué tal se portó?
2 • **to ~ as**: • **it must ~ as one of the most boring films around** debe de estar considerada una de las películas más aburridas del momento
(CPD) ▸ **rate rebate** (*Brit*) (*formerly*)

devolución *f* de contribución municipal
rate² [reɪt] VT (*liter*) (= *scold*) regañar, reñir
-rate [reɪt] ADJ (*ending in compounds*)
▹ **first-rate, second-rate, third-rate**
rateable [ˈreɪtəbl] ADJ (*Brit*) [*property*] susceptible de pagar contribución
CPD ▸ **rateable value** (*Brit*) (*formerly*) valor *m* catastral
rate-capping [ˈreɪtˌkæpɪŋ] N (*Brit*) (*Pol*) (*formerly*) *limitación de la contribución municipal impuesta por el Estado*
ratepayer [ˈreɪtpeɪəʳ] N (*Brit*) (*formerly*) contribuyente *mf*
rather [ˈrɑːðəʳ] ADV **1** (*preference*) • **we decided to camp, ~ than stay at a hotel** decidimos acampar, en lugar de quedarnos en un hotel • **I'll stay ~ than go alone** prefiero quedarme a ir solo • **I'd ~ have this one than that** prefiero este a aquel • **"would you like a sweet?" — "I'd ~ have an apple"** —¿quieres un caramelo? —preferiría una manzana • **would you ~ stay here?** ¿prefieres quedarte? • **I'd ~ stay in tonight** preferiría no salir esta noche • **I'd ~ he didn't come to the party** preferiría que no viniera a la fiesta • **anything ~ than that!** (*hum*) ¡cualquier cosa menos eso! • **play anything ~ than that** toca cualquier cosa que no sea eso • **I'd ~ not** prefiero no hacerlo • **I'd ~ not say** prefiero no decirlo • **"I'm going to have it out with the boss" — "~ you than me!"** —voy a planteárselo al jefe —¡allá tú!
2 (= *somewhat*) algo, un poco • **he looks ~ like his mother** se parece un poco a su madre • **I feel ~ more happy today** hoy me siento algo más contento • **I ~ suspected as much** me lo sospechaba • **I ~ think he won't come** me inclino a creer que no vendrá • **that is ~ too dear** es algo caro (para mí *etc*)
3 (= *quite*) bastante • **it's a ~ difficult task** • **it's ~ a difficult task** es una tarea bastante difícil • **we were ~ tired** estábamos bastante cansados • **I was ~ disappointed** quedé bastante decepcionado • **he did ~ well in the exam** le fue bastante bien en el examen • **"isn't she pretty?" — "yes, she is ~"** —¿es guapa, eh? —sí, bastante • **"are you keen to go?" — "yes, I am ~"** —¿tienes ganas de ir? —sí que quiero • **there's ~ a lot** hay bastante • **£20! that's ~ a lot!** ¡20 libras! ¡es bastante caro! • **I've got ~ a lot of homework to do** tengo muchos deberes que hacer • **it's ~ a pity** es una pena *or* lástima
4 (= *more accurately*) • **~ it is a matter of money** antes es cuestión de dinero, es al contrario *or* más bien cuestión de dinero • **or ~** o mejor dicho, es decir • **a car, or ~ an old banger** un coche, o mejor dicho, un trasto viejo
EXCL † ¡ya lo creo!, ¡cómo no! (*LAm*) • **"would you like some?" — "rather!"** ¿quieres algo de esto? — ¡ya lo creo! *or* ¡por supuesto!
ratification [ˌrætɪfɪˈkeɪʃən] N ratificación *f*
ratify [ˈrætɪfaɪ] VT [+ *treaty, agreement*] ratificar
rat-infested [ˈrætɪnfestɪd] ADJ infestado de ratas
rating¹ [ˈreɪtɪŋ] N **1** (= *ranking*) • **Labour's ~s in the polls are high** las encuestas demuestran que el partido laborista goza de un alto nivel de popularidad • **each wine was given a ~ out of ten** cada vino recibió una puntuación del uno al diez • **jobs which have a low ~ on the social scale** los trabajos que ocupan una posición baja en la escala social; ▹ **credit, poll**
2 ratings (*TV, Rad*) índice *msing* de audiencia • **~s war** *guerra por alcanzar el mayor índice de audiencia*
3 (= *act of valuing*) tasación *f*, valuación *f*
4 (*Brit*) (*Naut*) (= *sailor*) marinero *m*; (*class*) [*of ship*] clase *f* • **a naval ~** un marinero; ▹ **octane**
rating² [ˈreɪtɪŋ] N reprensión *f*
ratio [ˈreɪʃɪəʊ] N razón *f* • **in the ~ of 2 to 1** a razón de 2 a 1 • **in inverse ~** en proporción *or* razón inversa • **in direct ~ to** en proporción *or* razón directa con • **the ~ of wages to raw materials** la relación entre los sueldos y las materias primas
ratiocinate [rætɪˈɒsɪneɪt] VI (*frm*) raciocinar
ratiocination [ˌrætɪɒsɪˈneɪʃən] N (*frm*) raciocinación *f*
ration [ˈræʃən] N (= *portion*) ración *f*, porción *f*; **rations** (*Mil etc*) víveres *mpl*, suministro *msing* • **to be on ~** [*bread, milk*] estar racionado • **to be on short ~s** andar escaso de víveres • **when they put bread on the ~** cuando racionaron el pan • **it's off the ~ now** ya no está racionado • **to draw one's ~s** recibir los víveres
VT (*also* **ration out**) racionar • **they are ~ed to one kilo a day** están racionados a un kilo por día
CPD ▸ **ration book** cartilla *f* de racionamiento ▸ **ration card** tarjeta *f* de racionamiento ▸ **ration coupon** cupón *m* de racionamiento
rational [ˈræʃənl] ADJ **1** (= *logical*) [*argument, explanation*] racional, lógico • **the ~ thing to do would be to ...** lo lógico *or* racional sería ...
2 (= *reasonable*) razonable • **let's be ~ about this** seamos razonables
3 (= *sane*) [*person*] sensato, cuerdo • **he seemed quite ~** parecía estar perfectamente sensato *or* cuerdo
CPD ▸ **rational number** (*Math*) número *m* racional
rationale [ræʃəˈnɑːl] N base *f*, fundamento *m* • **the ~ of** *or* **behind sth** la razón fundamental de algo
rationalism [ˈræʃnəlɪzəm] N racionalismo *m*
rationalist [ˈræʃnəlɪst] ADJ racionalista
N racionalista *mf*
rationalistic [ˌræʃnəˈlɪstɪk] ADJ racionalista
rationality [ˌræʃəˈnælɪtɪ] N racionalidad *f*
rationalization [ˌræʃnəlaɪˈzeɪʃən] N **1** [*of ideas etc*] racionalización *f*
2 (= *reorganization*) reconversión *f*, reorganización *f* • **industrial ~** reconversión *f* industrial, reorganización *f* industrial
rationalize [ˈræʃnəlaɪz] VT **1** [+ *ideas etc*] racionalizar
2 (= *reorganize*) [+ *industry etc*] reconvertir, reorganizar
3 (*Math*) quitar los radicales a, racionalizar
rationally [ˈræʃnəlɪ] ADV racionalmente
rationing [ˈræʃnɪŋ] N racionamiento *m*
ratpack* [ˈrætpæk] N (*Brit*) (*pej*) jauría *f* de periodistas
rats'-tails [ˌrætsˈteɪlz] NPL greñas *fpl*
rattan [rəˈtæn] N rota *f*, junco *m* *or* caña *f* de Indias
rat-tat-tat [ˌrættætˈtæt] N = **rat-a-tat**
ratter [ˈrætəʳ] N cazarratones *m inv*
rattle [ˈrætl] N **1** (= *sound*) [*of cart, train, gunfire*] traqueteo *m*; [*of window, chains, stone in tin*] ruido *m*; [*of hail, rain*] tamborileo *m*; (*in throat*) estertor *m* • **there was an ominous ~ coming from the engine** del motor provenía un ruido que no presagiaba nada bueno • **death ~** estertor *m* de la muerte
2 (= *instrument*) (*child's*) sonajero *m*, sonajas *fpl*; [*of football fan etc*] carraca *f*, matraca *f*
VT **1** (= *shake*) • **the wind ~d the window** el viento hizo vibrar la ventana • **he ~d the tin** agitó la lata (*haciendo sonar lo que tenía dentro*) • **he banged on the table, rattling the cups** golpeó la mesa, haciendo que las tazas tintinearan • **she ~d the door handle** sacudió el picaporte de la puerta • **the monkey was rattling the bars of his cage** el mono estaba sacudiendo los barrotes de la jaula • IDIOM: • **to ~ sb's cage** hacer la Pascua a algn
2* (= *disconcert*) [+ *person*] desconcertar • **to get ~d** ponerse nervioso, perder la calma • **to get sb ~d** poner nervioso a algn, hacer que algn pierda la calma
VI **1** (= *make sound*) [*cart, train*] traquetear; [*window, chains, stone in tin*] sonar, hacer ruido; [*teeth*] castañetear; [*hail, rain*] tamborilear
2* (= *travel*) • **we were rattling along at 50m. p.h.** íbamos traqueteando a 50 millas por hora
▸ **rattle around** VI + ADV • **we're rattling around in this big house** tenemos casa más que de sobra para nosotros
▸ **rattle away*** VI + ADV = **rattle on**
▸ **rattle off** VT + ADV [+ *names, statistics*] recitar de un tirón *or* de una tirada
▸ **rattle on*** VI + ADV parlotear (sin parar) • **I let him ~ on about the virtues of double glazing** le dejé que parloteara ensalzando las virtudes del doble acristalamiento
▸ **rattle through*** VI + PREP • **she ~d through the translation in about ten minutes** hizo la traducción volando en unos diez minutos, se cepilló la traducción en unos diez minutos*
rattled [ˈrætld] ADJ (= *unnerved*) [*person*] trastornado
rattler* [ˈrætləʳ] N (*esp US*) = **rattlesnake**
rattlesnake [ˈrætlsneɪk] N serpiente *f* de cascabel, yarará *f* (*And*)
rattletrap* [ˈrætltræp] ADJ desvencijado
N armatoste *m*
rattling [ˈrætlɪŋ] ADJ • **at a ~ pace** muy rápidamente, a gran velocidad
ADV • **~ good** (*esp Brit**) realmente estupendo*
ratty* [ˈrætɪ] ADJ (COMPAR: **rattier**, SUPERL: **rattiest**) **1** (*Brit*) (= *bad-tempered*) • **to be/get ~** estar/ponerse de malas • **he was pretty ~ about it** se picó mucho por ello
2 (*US*) (= *shabby*) andrajoso
raucous [ˈrɔːkəs] ADJ (= *harsh*) ronco; (= *loud*) chillón, estridente
raucously [ˈrɔːkəslɪ] ADV (= *harshly*) roncamente; (= *loudly*) en tono chillón, estridentemente
raucousness [ˈrɔːkəsnɪs] N (= *harshness*) ronquedad *f*; (= *loudness*) estridencia *f*
raunchy* [ˈrɔːntʃɪ] ADJ (COMPAR: **raunchier**, SUPERL: **raunchiest**) [*story, film, song*] picante, atrevido; [*person*] sexy, provocativo; [*clothing*] atrevido, provocativo
ravage [ˈrævɪdʒ] N **ravages** estragos *mpl* • **the ~s of time** los estragos del tiempo
VT hacer estragos • **the plague ~d the town** la peste hizo estragos en el pueblo • **the region was ~d by floods** las inundaciones causaron estragos en la región, la región fue asolada por las inundaciones • **a body ~d by disease** un cuerpo desfigurado por la enfermedad • **a picture ~d by time** un cuadro muy deteriorado por el tiempo
rave [reɪv] VI **1** (= *be delirious*) delirar, desvariar; (= *talk wildly*) desvariar
2 (= *talk furiously*) despotricar • **to ~ at sb** despotricar contra algn
3 (= *talk enthusiastically*) • **to ~ about sth** entusiasmarse por algo • **they ~d about the film** pusieron la película por las nubes • **to ~ about sb** pirrarse por algn*

r

(N) (*Brit**) fiesta *f* acid*
(CPD) ▸ **rave culture** cultura *f* rave ▸ **rave review** reseña *f* entusiasta • **the play got ~ reviews** los críticos pusieron la obra por las nubes

rave-in* ['reɪvɪn] (N) orgía *f*

ravel ['rævəl] (VT) enredar, enmarañar (*also fig*)

raven ['reɪvn] (N) cuervo *m*
(ADJ) [*hair*] negro

raven-haired [ˌreɪvn'hɛəd] (ADJ) de pelo negro

ravening ['rævnɪŋ] (ADJ) rapaz, salvaje

ravenous ['rævənəs] (ADJ) **1** (= *starving*) hambriento • **I'm ~!** ¡me comería un toro! • **he was ~** tenía un hambre canina
2 (= *voracious*) voraz

ravenously ['rævənəslɪ] (ADV) vorazmente • **to be ~ hungry** tener un hambre canina

raver* ['reɪvəʳ] (N) (*Brit*) juerguista* *mf*, marchoso/a‡ *m/f*

rave-up* ['reɪvʌp] (N) (*Brit*) juerga* *f*

ravine [rə'viːn] (N) barranco *m*, quebrada *f* (*esp LAm*)

raving ['reɪvɪŋ] (ADJ) • **he's a ~ lunatic** está loco de remate
(ADV) • **you must be ~ mad!** ¡tú estás loco de atar!

ravings ['reɪvɪŋz] (NPL) delirio *msing*, desvarío *msing*

ravioli [ˌrævɪ'əʊlɪ] (N) ravioles *mpl*, ravioli *mpl*

ravish ['rævɪʃ] (VT) **1** (= *charm*) encantar, embelesar
2 (*liter*) (= *carry off*) raptar, robar; (= *rape*) violar

ravisher†† ['rævɪʃəʳ] (N) (*liter*) (= *captor*) raptor *m*; (= *rapist*) violador *m*

ravishing ['rævɪʃɪŋ] (ADJ) [*smile*] encantador; [*woman*] bellísimo • **you look ~** estás deslumbrante

ravishingly ['rævɪʃɪŋlɪ] (ADV) encantadoramente • **~ beautiful** enormemente bello

ravishment ['rævɪʃmənt] (N) (*liter*)
1 (= *enchantment*) embeleso *m*, éxtasis *m inv*
2 (*liter*) (= *capture*) rapto *m*, robo *m*; (= *rape*) violación *f*

raw [rɔː] (ADJ) **1** (= *uncooked*) [*meat, vegetable, egg*] crudo
2 (= *unprocessed*) [*sugar*] sin refinar; [*spirit*] puro; [*silk*] crudo, salvaje; [*cotton*] en rama, sin refinar; [*ore*] bruto; [*rubber*] sin tratar, puro; [*sewage*] sin tratar • **raw data** datos *mpl* sin procesar • **raw materials** materias *fpl* primas
3 (= *sore*) [*wound*] abierto • **to be red and raw** estar en carne viva • **his hands were raw from the weather** tenía las manos en carne viva a causa del tiempo • **her throat felt raw** se notaba la garganta muy irritada • **raw flesh** carne *f* viva • **his wife's words touched a raw nerve** las palabras de su mujer le dieron donde más le dolía *or* le dieron en lo más sensible
4 (= *basic*) [*anger, hate, ambition*] puro • **he spoke with raw emotion** habló con verdadero sentimiento • **the raw energy of a teenager** la energía en bruto de un adolescente • **he has raw talent, but it lacks proper direction** tiene el talento en bruto, pero no sabe canalizarlo
5 (= *harsh*) [*wind*] cortante, fuerte; [*weather, night*] crudo
6 (= *inexperienced*) [*person, troops*] novato, inexperto • **they're still very raw** todavía están muy verdes • **a raw recruit** (*Mil*) quinto *m*, soldado *mf* raso; (*fig*) novato/a *m/f*
7* (= *unfair*) • **a raw deal: he got a raw deal** le trataron injustamente • **he's got a raw deal from life** la vida lo ha tratado mal
8 (= *coarse*) [*humour*] crudo
(N) • **it got** *or* **touched him on the raw** (*fig*) lo hirió en lo más vivo, lo hirió donde más le dolía • **life/nature in the raw** la vida/naturaleza tal cual • **in the raw*** (= *naked*) en cueros*, en pelotas‡

Rawalpindi [ˌrɔːl'pɪndɪ] (N) Rawalpindi *f*

rawboned ['rɔː'bəʊnd] (ADJ) huesudo

rawhide ['rɔːhaɪd] (N) (*US*) cuero *m* de vaca
(CPD) de cuero crudo

Rawlplug® ['rɔːlplʌg] (N) taco *m*

rawness ['rɔːnɪs] (N) **1** (= *uncooked state*) crudeza *f*
2 (= *inexperience*) inexperiencia *f*

ray¹ [reɪ] (N) **1** [*of light, heat, sun*] rayo *m*; ▹ **X-ray**
2 (*fig*) (= *trace*) • **a ray of hope** un rayo de esperanza

ray² [reɪ] (N) (= *fish*) raya *f*; ▹ **stingray**

ray³ [reɪ] (N) (*Mus*) re *m*

Ray [reɪ] (N) *familiar form of* **Raymond**

Raymond ['reɪmənd] (N) Raimundo, Ramón

rayon ['reɪɒn] (N) rayón *m*

raze [reɪz] (VT) (*also* **raze to the ground**) arrasar, asolar

razor ['reɪzəʳ] (N) (*open*) navaja *f*, chaveta *f* (*Peru*); (*safety*) maquinilla *f* de afeitar • **electric ~** máquina *f* de afeitar • **it's on a ~'s edge** está en un brete
(CPD) ▸ **razor blade** hoja *f or* cuchilla *f* de afeitar ▸ **razor burn** erosión *f* cutánea ▸ **razor cut** (*Hairdressing*) corte *m* a la navaja ▸ **razor wire** alambrada *f* de seguridad (*con trozos afilados de metal*)

razorback ['reɪzəˌbæk] (N) (= *pig*) *cerdo cimarrón del sureste de Estados Unidos, de lomo angosto y afilado*

razorbill ['reɪzəbɪl] (N) alca *f* común

razor-sharp ['reɪzə'ʃɑːp] (ADJ) [*edge*] muy afilado; [*mind*] agudo, perspicaz

razor-strop ['reɪzəstrɒp] (N) suavizador *m*

razz* [ræz] (VT) (*US*) tomar el pelo a*

razzamatazz [ˌræzəmə'tæz] (N) (*esp Brit*) = **razzmatazz**

razzle* ['ræzl] (N) • **to be/go on the ~** estar/ir de juerga*

razzle-dazzle* [ˌræzl'dæzl] (N) **1** = **razzle**
2 = **razzmatazz**

razzmatazz* [ˌræzmə'tæz] (N) bombo *m* publicitario

RC (ABBR) = **Roman Catholic**

RCAF (N ABBR) = **Royal Canadian Air Force**

RCMP (N ABBR) = **Royal Canadian Mounted Police**

RCN (N ABBR) = **Royal Canadian Navy**

RCP (ABBR) (*Brit*) = **Royal College of Physicians**

RCS (ABBR) (*Brit*) = **Royal College of Surgeons**

RD (ABBR) (*US*) = **rural delivery**

Rd (ABBR) (= **road**) c/, ctra

R/D (ABBR) (= **refer to drawer**) *protestar este cheque por falta de fondos*

RDA (N ABBR) = **recommended daily allowance** *or* **amount**

RDC (N ABBR) **1** = **Rural District Council**
2 = **regional distribution centre**

re¹ [riː] (PREP) (*Comm*) (= *concerning*) relativo a, respecto a • **re my previous account** con referencia a mi cuenta anterior

re² [reɪ] (N) (*Mus*) re *m*

RE (N ABBR) **1** (*Brit*) (*Scol*) (= **religious education**) ed. religiosa
2 (*Brit*) (*Mil*) = **Royal Engineers**

re... [riː] (PREFIX) re...

reabsorb ['riːəb'zɔːb] (VT) reabsorber

reabsorption ['riːəb'zɔːpʃən] (N) reabsorción *f*

reach [riːtʃ] (VT) **1** (= *get as far as*) [+ *place, person, stage, point, age*] llegar a; [+ *speed, level*] alcanzar, llegar a • **to ~ the terrace you have to cross the garden** para llegar a *or* hasta la terraza tienes que cruzar el jardín • **the door is ~ed by a long staircase** se llega a la puerta por una larga escalera • **your letter ~ed me this morning** su carta me llegó esta mañana • **by the time I ~ed her she was dead** cuando llegué a donde estaba, la encontré muerta • **to ~ 40 (years old)** llegar a los 40 • **when you ~ my age** cuando llegues a mi edad • **we hope to ~ a wider audience** esperamos llegar a un público más variado • **not a sound ~ed our ears** ningún sonido llegó a nuestros oídos • **to ~ home** llegar a casa • **I ~ed a point where I was ready to give up** llegué a un punto en el que estaba dispuesto a tirar la toalla • **she ~ed the semi-finals** llegó hasta las semifinales; ▹ **peak, point**
2 (= *achieve*) [+ *goal, target*] lograr; [+ *agreement, compromise*] llegar a; [+ *decision*] tomar • **they failed to ~ agreement** no consiguieron llegar a un acuerdo • **have they ~ed a decision yet?** ¿han tomado ya una decisión? • **to ~ perfection** lograr la perfección
3 (= *extend to*) llegar a • **it doesn't ~ the bottom** no llega al fondo • **her dress ~es the floor** el vestido le llega a *or* hasta el suelo • **the cancer had already ~ed her liver** el cáncer ya le había llegado al hígado • **he ~es her shoulder** le llega al *or* por el hombro; ▹ **far-reaching**
4 (= *stretch to*) alcanzar • **he is tall enough to ~ the top shelf** es lo suficientemente alto como para alcanzar el estante de arriba del todo
5 (= *pass*) alcanzar • **can you ~ me (over) the oil?** ¿me alcanzas el aceite por favor? • **can you ~ me (down) that case?** ¿me alcanzas esa maleta por favor?
6 (= *contact*) [+ *person*] ponerse en contacto con, contactar • **you can ~ me at my hotel** puedes ponerte en contacto conmigo *or* contactarme en el hotel • **you can always ~ me at the office** siempre puedes ponerte en contacto conmigo en la oficina • **to ~ sb by telephone** ponerse en contacto con *or* contactar a algn por teléfono • **the village cannot be ~ed by telephone** no hay comunicación telefónica con el pueblo
7 (*US*) (*Jur*) (= *suborn*) [+ *witness*] sobornar
(VI) **1** (= *stretch out hand*) alargar la mano (**for sth**) para tomar *or* coger algo • **he ~ed across the desk and shook my hand** me tendió la mano por encima del escritorio y estrechó la mía • **she ~ed for the bottle** alargó la mano para tomar *or* coger la botella • **~ for the sky!** (*US**) ¡arriba las manos! • **she ~ed into her bag and pulled out a gun** metió la mano en el bolso y sacó una pistola • **he ~ed up and put the book on the shelf** alargó la mano y puso el libro en el estante • IDIOM: • **to ~ for the stars** apuntar muy alto
2 (= *extend*) [*land*] extenderse; [*clothes, curtains, water level*] llegar; (*fig*) (*in time*) remontarse • **their land ~es to the sea** sus tierras se extienden hasta el mar • **her skirt ~ed down to the ground** la falda le llegaba al *or* hasta el suelo • **the water ~ed up to the windows** el agua llegaba a las ventanas • **it ~es back to 1700** se remonta a 1700 • **it's a tradition that ~es back (for) centuries** es una tradición que se remonta a varios siglos
3 (= *stretch far enough*) [*person*] alcanzar; [*cable, hose*] llegar • **can you ~?** ¿alcanzas? • **it won't ~** no va a llegar
(N) **1** alcance *m* • **beyond (the) ~ of sth/sb: the price is beyond the ~ of ordinary people**

r

el precio está fuera del alcance de la gente corriente • **she was beyond (the) ~ of human help** estaba desahuciada • **this subject is beyond his ~** este tema le viene grande • **beyond the ~ of the law** fuera del alcance de la ley • **to have a long ~** [*boxer, tennis player*] tener brazos largos • **out of ~** fuera del alcance • **the gun lay just out of ~** la pistola estaba justo fuera de su alcance • **keep all medicines out of ~ of children** mantenga todos los medicamentos fuera del alcance de los niños • **within sb's ~** al alcance (de la mano) de algn • **the rope was just within (her) ~** la cuerda estaba justo a su alcance *or* al alcance de su mano • **at last his goal was within ~** por fin el objetivo que tenía estaba a su alcance, por fin tenía su objetivo al alcance de la mano • **cars are within everyone's ~ nowadays** ahora los coches están al alcance (del bolsillo) de cualquiera • **within easy ~** a mano, cerca • **the shops are within easy ~** las tiendas están cerca *or* a mano • **it's within easy ~ by bus** en autobús queda cerca, se puede acceder fácilmente en autobús • **a house within easy ~ of the station** una casa cerca de la estación, una casa bien situada con respecto a la estación • **within ~ of sth** cerca de algo
2 [*of river, canal*] (= *short stretch*) tramo *m* • **the upper/lower ~es of the Amazon** (= *larger area*) la cuenca alta/baja del Amazonas • **the outer ~es of the solar system** los límites exteriores del sistema solar • **the highest ~es of government** los escalafones más altos del gobierno
▸ **reach down** (VI + ADV) **1** (= *extend*) • **to ~ down to** bajar hasta
2 (= *stretching out hand*) bajarse • **bend forward in your chair and ~ down to touch the floor with your hands** inclínese hacia delante en la silla y baje hasta tocar el suelo con las manos
3 (*crouching*) agacharse • **to ~ down to pick sth up** agacharse para recoger algo • **he ~ed down to pick them up** se agachó para recogerlos
(VT + ADV) (= *take from shelf*) [+ *book, bottle*] alcanzar
▸ **reach out** (VI + ADV) **1** (= *stretch out hand*) = **reach**
2 (= *try and get*) • **to ~ out for sth: babies will ~ out for brightly coloured objects** los bebés alargan la mano hacia objetos de colores vivos • **it is important that we can ~ out for help when we need it** es importante que podamos tender la mano en busca de ayuda cuando la necesitemos
3 • **to ~ out to sb** (= *communicate with*) llegar a algn; (= *ask for support*) recurrir *or* acudir a algn • **we need to ~ out to new audiences** tenemos que llegar a nuevos públicos
(VT + ADV) [+ *hand*] alargar, extender
reachable ['ri:tʃəbl] (ADJ) [*place*] accesible; [*object*] asequible; [*goal*] alcanzable, accesible; [*person*] accesible • **she is ~ at ...** se la puede localizar en ...
reach-me-down ['ri:tʃmɪ,daʊn] (ADJ) [*ideas*] común y corriente; [*clothes*] usado, de segunda mano
(NPL) **reach-me-downs** ropa *fsing* usada
react [ri:'ækt] (VI) **1** (*gen*) reaccionar • **to ~ against sth/sb** reaccionar contra algo/algn • **companies have ~ed by increasing their prices** la reacción de las empresas ha sido subir los precios, las empresas han reaccionado subiendo los precios • **to ~ on sth/sb** afectar algo/a algn • **alcohol always ~ed badly on him** el alcohol siempre le afectaba negativamente, siempre tenía una reacción mala con el alcohol • **to ~ to** [+ *news, situation*] reaccionar ante; [+ *foreign substance*] reaccionar a • **to ~ to sb** reaccionar *or* responder ante algn
2 (*Chem, Phys*) reaccionar (**with** con) • **to ~ together** tener una reacción conjunta, reaccionar conjuntamente
reaction [ri:'ækʃən] (N) **1** (= *response*) reacción *f* • **what was his ~ to your suggestion?** ¿cuál fue su reacción a tu sugerencia?, ¿cómo reaccionó frente a tu sugerencia? • **it produced no ~** no surtió efecto • **some foods cause allergic ~s** algunos alimentos provocan reacciones alérgicas
2 reactions (= *reflexes*) reacciones *fpl* • **his ~s were slow because he'd been drinking** tardaba en reaccionar porque había estado bebiendo
3 (*Pol*) (*pej*) reacción *f* • **the forces of ~** las fuerzas de la reacción, las fuerzas reaccionarias
4 (*Chem*) reacción *f*
(CPD) ▸ **reaction time** tiempo *m* de reacción
reactionary [ri:'ækʃənrɪ] (ADJ) reaccionario
(N) reaccionario/a *m/f*
reactivate [ri:'æktɪveɪt] (VT) reactivar
reactivation [ri:,æktɪ'veɪʃən] (N) reactivación *f*
reactive [ri:'æktɪv] (ADJ) reactivo
reactor [ri:'æktə^r] (N) reactor *m* • **nuclear ~** reactor *m* nuclear
read [ri:d] (PT, PP: **read** [red]) (VT) **1** [+ *book, poem, story, music, sign*] leer; [+ *author*] leer a • **can you ~ Russian?** ¿sabes leer en ruso? • **she can't ~ music** no sabe leer música • **I can't ~ your writing** no entiendo tu letra, no puedo leer tu letra • **for "boon" ~ "bone"** en lugar de "boon" léase "bone" • **I ~ "good" as "mood"** al leer confundí "good" con "mood" • **to ~ sth to sb** • **to ~ sb sth** leer algo a algn • **to ~ sth to o.s.** leer algo para sí mismo • **to ~ sb's lips** leer los labios a algn • **~ my lips** (*fig*) fíjate bien en lo que digo • **to ~ the news** leer las noticias • **to ~ sb to sleep** leerle a algn hasta que se quede dormido • **to ~ o.s. to sleep** leer hasta quedarse dormido • IDIOM: • **to take sth as ~** dar algo por sentado • **to take the minutes as ~** (*in meeting*) dar las actas por leídas; ▹ **riot**
2 (*esp Brit*) (*Univ*) (= *study*) • **to ~ chemistry** estudiar química, cursar estudios de química
3 (= *interpret*) [+ *map, meter, thermometer*] leer; [+ *information, remarks, expression, situation*] interpretar; [+ *person*] entender • **the same information can be ~ in different ways** la misma información se puede interpretar de varias formas • **I've never been able to ~ him** nunca he sido capaz de entenderle • **this is how I ~ the situation** así es como yo interpreto *or* veo la situación • **I ~ the disappointment in her face** le noté la decepción en la cara • **to ~ sth as sth** interpretar algo como algo • **to ~ the future** leer *or* adivinar el porvenir • **to ~ sb's hand** *or* **palm** leerle la mano a algn • **to ~ sth into sth**: • **you're ~ing too much into it** le estás dando demasiada importancia • **to ~ into a sentence what is not there** ver en una frase un significado que no tiene • **to ~ sb's mind** *or* **thoughts** leerle el pensamiento a algn, adivinar el pensamiento a algn; ▹ **book**
4 (*Telec*) • **do you ~ me?** ¿me oye? • **I ~ you loud and clear** le oigo perfectamente
5 (= *say, indicate*) [*notice*] decir; [*thermometer, instrument*] indicar, marcar • **it should ~ "friends" not "fiends"** debería decir *or* poner "friends", no "fiends" • **the sign on the bus ~ "private, not in service"** el letrero del autobús decía *or* en el letrero del autobús ponía "privado, fuera de servicio"
6 (*Comput*) leer
(VI) **1** [*person*] leer • **to ~ about sth/sb** leer sobre *or* acerca de algo/algn • **I ~ about it in the papers** lo leí en los periódicos • **I've ~ about him** he leído sobre *or* acerca de él • **I'm ~ing about Napoleon** me estoy documentando sobre Napoleón, estoy leyendo acerca de Napoleón • **to ~ aloud** leer en voz alta • **the ~ing public** el público que lee • **to ~ silently** leer para sí • **to ~ through sth** leer algo de principio a fin • **I've ~ through your letter very carefully** he leído tu carta minuciosamente de principio a fin • **to ~ to sb**: • **he ~ to us from the Bible** nos leyó extractos de la Biblia • **my daughter asked me to ~ to her** mi hija me pidió que le leyera un libro • **I like being ~ to** me gusta que me lean • **to ~ to o.s.** leer para sí • IDIOM: • **to ~ between the lines** leer entre líneas
2 (= *give impression*) • **the book ~s well** el libro está bien escrito • **it would ~ better if you put ...** quedaría mejor si pusieras ... • **it ~s very awkwardly** al leerlo suena muy raro • **his article ~s like an official report** su artículo está escrito como un informe oficial
3 (= *say, indicate*) decir • **the text ~s as follows** el texto dice lo siguiente
4 (= *study*) estudiar • **to ~ for the Bar** estudiar Derecho (para hacerse abogado) • **to ~ for a degree** hacer una carrera, estudiar la licenciatura
(N) lectura *f* • **I like a good ~** me gusta leer un buen libro • **it's a good ~** es un libro que se disfruta leyendo • **I was having a quiet ~ in the garden** leía tranquilamente en el jardín • **can I have a ~ of your paper?** ¿puedo echarle un vistazo a tu periódico?
(CPD) ▸ **read head** (*Comput*) cabezal *m* lector
▸ **read back** (VT + ADV) volver a leer • **can you ~ it back to me?** ¿puedes volvérmelo a leer?
(VI + ADV) • **I was ~ing back over my notes** estaba releyendo *or* repasando mis apuntes
▸ **read off** (VT + ADV) [+ *numbers, items on list*] leer (uno a uno)
▸ **read on** (VI + ADV) seguir leyendo
▸ **read out** (VT + ADV) (*gen*) leer (en voz alta); (*Comput*) leer • **please ~ it out** por favor, léalo en voz alta • **shall I ~ them out?** ¿los leo (en voz alta)?
▸ **read over** (VT + ADV) repasar, volver a leer
▸ **read through** (VT + ADV) leer (entero) • **tell him to ~ it through first** dile que primero lo lea entero • **I have ~ through your letter** he leído tu carta de cabo a rabo
▸ **read up** (VT + ADV) [+ *subject*] estudiar; [+ *notes*] repasar
(VI + ADV) • **to ~ up for an exam** estudiar *or* repasar para un examen • **to ~ up on sth** leer sobre algo, ponerse al tanto de algo
readability [,ri:də'bɪlɪtɪ] (N) legibilidad *f* (*also Comput*); [*of style*] amenidad *f*, interés *m*
readable ['ri:dəbl] (ADJ) [*writing*] legible; [*book etc*] entretenido, que puede leerse
readdress ['ri:ə'dres] (VT) [+ *letter*] cambiar la dirección de
reader ['ri:də^r] (N) **1** (= *person who reads*) lector(a) *m/f*; (*in library*) usuario/a *m/f* • **he's a great ~** lee mucho, es muy aficionado a la lectura • **I'm not much of a ~** leo poco, no me interesan mucho los libros; ▹ **lay³**
2 (*also* **publisher's reader**) lector(a) *m/f*; ▹ **proofreader**
3 (*Univ*) profesor(a) *m/f* adjunto/a
4 (= *schoolbook*) (*to teach reading*) libro *m* de lectura; (= *anthology*) antología *f*
5 (= *machine*) máquina *f* lectora, aparato *m* lector; ▹ **microfiche, optical**
readership ['ri:dəʃɪp] (N) **1** número *m* de lectores

2 (*Brit*) (*Univ*) *puesto de profesor adjunto*

readily ['redɪlɪ] ADV **1** (= *willingly*) [*accept, admit*] de buena gana • **he had ~ agreed to do the job** había accedido de buena gana a hacer el trabajo
2 (= *easily*) [*accessible*] fácilmente • **they are ~ available** se pueden adquirir fácilmente • **I could ~ understand her anxiety** entendía perfectamente su ansiedad • **her confusion was ~ apparent** (*frm*) se advertía su confusión de inmediato

readiness ['redɪnɪs] N **1** (= *willingness*) buena disposición *f* • **his ~ to help us** su buena disposición para ayudarnos
2 (= *preparedness*) • **we laid the tables in ~ for the guests** preparamos las mesas para la llegada de los invitados • **equipment that is kept in ~ for an emergency** material que se mantiene listo *or* preparado para una emergencia • **to hold o.s. in ~ (for sth)** mantenerse listo (para algo)
3 (= *sharpness*) • **~ of wit** viveza *f* de ingenio

reading ['ri:dɪŋ] N **1** (= *activity*) lectura *f* • **suggestions for further ~** sugerencias de lecturas suplementarias • **I only know about it from ~** todo lo que sé sobre ello es a través de lo que he leído
2 (*also* **reading matter**) • **the book is** *or* **makes interesting ~** el libro es *or* resulta interesante • **I'd prefer some light ~** preferiría algo fácil *or* ameno de leer, preferiría algo que no sea muy pesado de leer
3 (= *interpretation*) interpretación *f*; (*Cine, Theat*) [*of part*] lectura *f* • **my ~ of the situation is this** así es como yo interpreto *or* veo la situación
4 (*on thermometer, instrument*) lectura *f* • **to give a true/false ~** [*instrument*] marcar bien/mal • **~s of more than 40°C are common** es normal que los termómetros marquen más de 40°C • **to take a ~ of sth** hacer una lectura de algo, leer algo
5 (= *passage*) lectura *f*
6 (= *recital*) [*of play, poem*] recital *m*; ▸ **play, poetry**
7 (*Parl*) [*of bill*] lectura *f* • **the bill has had its first ~** el proyecto de ley ha pasado por su primera lectura • **to give a bill a second ~** leer un proyecto de ley por segunda vez
8 (*Jur*) [*of will, banns*] lectura *f*
9 (= *knowledge*) • **a person of wide ~** una persona muy leída
ADJ • **the ~ public** el público que lee, el público lector • **he's a great ~ man** es un hombre que lee mucho, es hombre muy aficionado a la lectura
CPD ▸ **reading age** nivel *m* de lectura • **he has a ~ age of eight** tiene el nivel de lectura de un niño de ocho años ▸ **reading book** libro *m* de lectura ▸ **reading comprehension** comprensión *f* lectora ▸ **reading glasses** gafas *fpl* para leer ▸ **reading group** grupo *m* de lectura ▸ **reading knowledge** • **she has a ~ knowledge of Spanish** sabe leer el español ▸ **reading lamp, reading light** lámpara *f* para leer, lámpara *f* portátil ▸ **reading list** lista *f* de lecturas ▸ **reading matter, reading material** material *m* de lectura ▸ **reading room** sala *f* de lectura ▸ **reading speed** velocidad *f* de lectura

readjust ['ri:ə'dʒʌst] VT reajustar
VI reajustarse

readjustment ['ri:ə'dʒʌstmənt] N reajuste *m*

readmit ['ri:əd'mɪt] VT readmitir, volver a admitir

read-only [ˌri:d'əʊnlɪ] ADJ (*Comput*) [*file*] de solo lectura
CPD ▸ **read-only memory** memoria *f* muerta, memoria *f* de sola lectura

read-out ['ri:daʊt] N lectura *f* de salida

read-write [ˌri:d'raɪt] CPD ▸ **read-write head** cabeza *f* de lectura-escritura ▸ **read-write memory** memoria *f* de lectura-escritura ▸ **read-write window** ventana *f* de lectura-escritura

ready ['redɪ] ADJ (COMPAR: **readier**, SUPERL: **readiest**) **1** (= *prepared*) **a** (*physically*) listo • **your glasses will be ~ in a fortnight** sus gafas estarán listas dentro de quince días, tendrá sus gafas listas dentro de quince días • **(are you) ~?** ¿(estás) listo? • **~ when you are!** ¡cuando quieras! • **~, steady, go!** ¡preparados, listos, ya! • **to be ~ to do sth** estar listo para hacer algo • **~ to serve** [*food*] listo para servir • **to be ~ for sth** estar listo para algo • **everything is ~ for the new arrival** todo está listo *or* dispuesto para la llegada del bebé • **~ for use** listo para usar • **the doctor's ~ for you now** el doctor ya puede verlo • **to get (o.s.) ~** prepararse, arreglarse • **to get ~ for school/bed** prepararse para ir al colegio/a la cama • **to get** *or* **make sth ~** preparar algo • **he was getting the children ~ to go out** estaba arreglando a los niños para salir • **I'll have everything ~** lo tendré todo listo • **I had my camera ~** tenía la cámara preparada • **to hold o.s. ~ (for sth)** mantenerse listo (para algo) • **~ and waiting** a punto
b (*mentally, emotionally*) preparado • **I was all ~ with a prepared statement** me había preparado bien con una declaración hecha de antemano • **she wanted a baby but didn't feel ~ yet** quería un bebé, pero todavía no se sentía preparada • **she had her excuses ~** tenía sus excusas preparadas • **to be ~ to do sth** estar preparado para hacer algo • **she's not ~ to take on that kind of responsibility** no está preparada para asumir tanta responsabilidad • **I'm ~ to face him now** ahora me siento con ánimos para enfrentarme a él • **are you ~ to order?** (*in restaurant*) ¿desean pedir ya? • **to be ~ for sth** estar preparado para algo • **to be ~ for anything** estar preparado para lo que sea, estar dispuesto a lo que sea • **I'm ~ for a drink** me muero por beber algo • **I'm ~ for (my) bed** yo ya tengo sueño • **to be ~ with an excuse** tener preparada una excusa • **to be ~ with a joke** tener una broma a punto
2 (= *available*) disponible
3 (= *willing*) dispuesto • **to be ~ to do sth** estar dispuesto a hacer algo • **to be only too ~ to do sth** estar más que dispuesto a hacer algo
4 (= *quick*) [*solution, explanation, smile*] fácil; [*wit*] agudo, vivo; [*market*] muy receptivo • **to have a ~ answer/excuse (for sth)** tener una respuesta/excusa a punto (para algo) • **don't be so ~ to criticize** no te des tanta prisa en criticar • **one advantage of this model is the ~ availability of spare parts** una de las ventajas de este modelo es que se pueden obtener recambios fácilmente • **to ensure a ~ supply of fresh herbs, why not try growing your own?** para contar siempre con una provisión de hierbas ¿por qué no cultivarlas tú mismo?
5 (= *on the point of*) • **to be ~ to do sth** estar a punto de hacer algo • **we were ~ to give up there and then** estábamos a punto de abandonar sin más
N **1** • **at the ~** listo, preparado • **with rifles at the ~** con los fusiles listos *or* preparados para disparar • **pencil at the ~** lápiz en ristre, lápiz en mano • **riot police were at the ~** la policía antidisturbios estaba lista *or* preparada para actuar
2 • **the readies*** (= *cash*) la pasta*, la plata (*LAm**), la lana (*LAm**)
VT (*frm*) (= *prepare*) [+ *object*] disponer, preparar (**for** para) • **to ~ o.s.** (*for news, an event, a struggle*) disponerse, prepararse; (*for a party etc*) arreglarse (**for** para)
CPD ▸ **ready cash, ready money** dinero *m* en efectivo ▸ **ready meal** comida *f* precocinada *or* preparada ▸ **ready reckoner** tabla *f* de equivalencias

ready-cooked ['redɪ'kʊkt] ADJ precocinado, preparado

ready-furnished [ˌredɪ'fɜ:nɪʃt] ADJ (*with everything necessary*) totalmente amueblado; (= *furnished*) ya amueblado

ready-made ['redɪ'meɪd] ADJ [*clothes, curtains*] confeccionado, ya hecho; [*meal, sauce*] precocinado, preparado; [*excuses, ideas*] preparado • **we can't expect to find a ready-made solution for our problems** no podemos esperar que la solución a nuestros problemas nos llegue como caída del cielo • **a ready-made basis for negotiations** una base para las negociaciones muy oportuna • **you can buy your greenhouse ready-made** puede comprar un invernadero ya prefabricado

ready-mix ['redɪmɪks] N (*for cakes etc*) preparado *m* instantáneo
CPD ▸ **ready-mix concrete** cemento *m* premezclado

ready-mixed [ˌredɪ'mɪkst] ADJ [*concrete*] premezclado; [*cake*] de sobre

ready-prepared [ˌredɪprɪ'peəd] ADJ [*meal*] precocinado

ready-to-eat [ˌredɪtə'i:t] ADJ listo para servir

ready-to-serve [ˌredɪtə'sɜ:v] ADJ preparado

ready-to-wear [ˌredɪtə'weəʳ] ADJ [*clothes*] confeccionado, listo para llevar

reaffirm ['ri:ə'fɜ:m] VT [+ *loyalty, affection etc*] reafirmar, reiterar

reaffirmation ['ri:æfə'meɪʃən] N reafirmación *f*, reiteración *f*

reafforest ['ri:ə'fɒrɪst] VT (*Brit*) repoblar de árboles

reafforestation ['ri:əˌfɒrɪs'teɪʃən] N (*Brit*) repoblación *f* forestal

reagent [ri:'eɪdʒənt] N (*Chem*) reactivo *m*

real [rɪəl] ADJ **1** (= *true*) [*reason, surprise, talent, achievement, progress*] verdadero; [*power*] efectivo, verdadero; [*cost, income*] real; [*threat, hardship*] serio, verdadero • **Tina was not their ~ mother** Tina no era su verdadera madre • **you're a ~ friend** eres un verdadero amigo; (*iro*) ¡vaya un amigo estás hecho! • **the only ~ car accident that I've ever had** el único accidente de coche de verdad que he tenido jamás • **we have no ~ reason to suspect him** no tenemos ninguna razón en particular para sospechar de él • **it came as no ~ surprise to him** no le sorprendió en absoluto • **now, that's a ~ paella!** ¡esto sí que es una paella (de verdad)! • **get ~!*** ¡baja de las nubes! • **there was ~ concern that the children were in danger** la gente estaba realmente preocupada por que los niños estuvieran en peligro • **I was never in any ~ danger** nunca estuve realmente en peligro • **the danger was very ~** el peligro era muy real • **there was no ~ evidence that …** no había pruebas contundentes de que … • **my ~ home is in London** mi verdadera casa *or* mi casa de verdad está en Londres • **he showed ~ interest in science** se mostraba verdaderamente interesado por la ciencia • **in ~ life** en la vida real, en la realidad • **~ life just isn't like that** lo que pasa es que la vida real no es así • **a ~ live film star** una estrella

r

de cine en carne y hueso • **a ~ man** un hombre de verdad, todo un hombre • **she's in ~ pain** le duele de verdad • **it's a ~ problem** es un verdadero problema • **in ~ terms** en términos reales • **to be in ~ trouble** estar metido en un buen lío* • **the ~ world** el mundo real

2 (= *not fake*) [*gold*] de ley, auténtico; [*leather, diamond*] auténtico; [*flowers*] de verdad; [*silk*] puro; [*cream*] fresco • **~ coffee** café de cafetera, café de verdad • **it was caviar, the ~ McCoy*** era caviar del auténtico • **this diamond's the ~ thing** *or* **the ~ McCoy*** este diamante es auténtico • **this isn't the ~ thing, it's just a copy** esto no es auténtico *or* genuino, es solo una copia • **this was definitely love, the ~ thing** esto era amor de verdad

3 (= *great*) verdadero • **it's a ~ shame** es una verdadera lástima • **this dessert is a ~ treat** este postre es un verdadero gustazo • **to make ~ money** ganar dinero de verdad

ADV (*US**) (= *really*) muy • **he wrote some ~ good stories** escribió unos relatos muy buenos *or* buenísimos • **we had a ~ good time** lo pasamos realmente bien • **it's ~ heavy** pesa mucho

N • **for ~*** de veras, de verdad • **is this guy for ~?** ¿de qué va este tío?* • **are you for ~?** ¿me estás tomando el pelo?*

CPD ▸ **real ale** cerveza *f* de barril tradicional ▸ **real assets** propiedad *fsing* inmueble, bienes *mpl* raíces ▸ **real estate, real property** (*US*) bienes *mpl* raíces, bienes *mpl* inmuebles ▸ **real time** (*Comput*) tiempo *m* real

real-estate ['rɪəlɪs,teɪt] CPD ▸ **real-estate agency** (*US*) agencia *f* inmobiliaria ▸ **real-estate agent** (*US*) agente *mf* inmobiliario/a ▸ **real-estate office** (*US*) inmobiliaria *f* ▸ **real-estate register** (*US*) catastro *m* inmobiliario

realign [riːə'laɪn] VT [+ *currency*] realinear • **to ~ o.s. with** (*Pol*) realinearse con

realignment [riːə'laɪnmənt] N [*of currency*] (*also Pol*) realineamiento *m*

realism ['rɪəlɪzəm] N realismo *m*

realist ['rɪəlɪst] N realista *mf*

realistic [rɪə'lɪstɪk] ADJ [*person, approach, painting*] realista; [*price*] razonable • **let's be ~** seamos realistas • **we had no ~ chance of winning** no teníamos posibilidades reales de ganar

realistically [rɪə'lɪstɪkəlɪ] ADV [*think, consider, describe*] de manera realista • **~ minded people** la gente que piensa de manera realista • **the best we can ~ expect is ...** lo mejor que podemos esperar, siendo realistas, es ... • **it just isn't ~ possible** siendo realistas, es sencillamente imposible • **her designs are ~ priced** sus diseños tienen un precio razonable • **~, he had little chance of winning** siendo realistas, tenía pocas posibilidades de ganar

reality [riː'ælɪtɪ] N **1** (= *real world*) realidad *f* • **let's get back to ~** volvamos a la realidad

2 (= *fact, truth*) realidad *f* • **the harsh ~ of daily life** la cruda realidad de la vida diaria • **let's stick to realities** atengámonos a la realidad • **to become (a) ~** convertirse en realidad • **in ~** (= *actually*) en realidad

3 (= *trueness to life*) realismo *m*

CPD ▸ **reality check** • **to be a ~ check for sb • provide a ~ check for sb** traer a algn de vuelta a la realidad ▸ **reality show** reality show *m* ▸ **reality TV** telerrealidad *f*

realizable ['rɪəlaɪzəbl] ADJ [*goal, ambition*] alcanzable; [*plan*] realizable, factible

realization [,rɪəlaɪ'zeɪʃən] N

1 (= *comprehension*) comprensión *f*, entendimiento *m* • **she awoke to the ~ that ...** cayó en la cuenta de que ...

2 (= *completion*) realización *f*

realize ['rɪəlaɪz] VT **1** (= *comprehend, become aware of*) darse cuenta de • **he ~d his mistake and went back** se dio cuenta de su error y volvió • **once I ~d how it was done** una vez que caí en la cuenta de cómo se hacía • **then I ~d what had happened** entonces me di cuenta de lo que había pasado, entonces comprendí lo que había pasado • **to ~ that** darse cuenta de que, comprender que • **I began to ~ that it would be impossible** empecé a darme cuenta de que sería imposible, empecé a comprender que sería imposible

2 (= *know*) darse cuenta de • **without realizing it** sin darse cuenta • **I ~ it's difficult, but ...** (ya) sé que es difícil, pero ..., comprendo *or* entiendo que es difícil, pero ... • **yes, I ~ that!** ¡sí, ya me doy cuenta!, ¡sí, ya me hago cargo! • **do you ~ what you've done?** ¿te das cuenta de lo que has hecho?

3 (= *carry out*) [+ *plan*] llevar a cabo • **my worst fears were ~d** mis mayores temores se hicieron realidad • **to ~ one's hopes/ambitions** hacer realidad sus esperanzas/ambiciones • **to ~ one's potential** desarrollar al máximo su potencial

4 (*Comm*) (= *convert into cash*) [+ *assets*] realizar; (= *produce*) [+ *profit*] producir; [+ *savings*] hacer • **the sale of the house ~d £250,000** la venta de la casa generó 250.000 libras

real-life [,rɪəl'laɪf] ADJ de la vida real, auténtico

reallocate [riː'æləˌkeɪt] VT [+ *resources, land, time*] redistribuir

reallocation [,riːælə'keɪʃən] N [*of resources, land, time*] redistribución *f*

really ['rɪəlɪ] ADV **1** (*as intensifier*) (= *very*) • **it's ~ ugly** es feísimo, es feo de verdad • **a ~ good film** una película buenísima *or* verdaderamente buena • **you ~ must see it** no puedes perdértelo • **I ~ ought to go** de verdad que me tengo que ir • **I'm very sorry, I ~ am** lo siento mucho, de veras • **I ~ don't know** de verdad que no lo sé • **this time we're ~ done for*** esta vez sí que la hemos hecho*, esta vez la hemos hecho de verdad*; ▹ **something**

2 (= *genuinely*) • **I don't ~ know** en realidad no lo sé • **what ~ happened?** ¿qué fue lo que pasó en realidad *or* realmente? • **has he ~ gone?** ¿de verdad que *or* es cierto que se ha ido? • **she's quite pretty ~** la verdad es que es bastante guapa • **"would you like to go?" — "not ~"** —¿te gustaría ir? —la verdad es que no mucho

EXCL • **really?: "he left an hour ago" — "really?"** (*expressing doubt*) —se marchó hace una hora —¿de verdad? *or* —¿de veras? • **"I was in Mexico last month" — "really?"** (*expressing interest*) —estuve en Méjico el mes pasado —¿ah sí? • **"she's getting divorced again" — "really!"** (*in surprise, disbelief*) —se va a divorciar otra vez —¡no me digas! • **I'm fine, ~** (*in assurance*) estoy bien, de verdad • **(well) ~!** (*in disapproval*) ¡de verdad! • **(well) ~! it's too bad of him** ¡pero bueno! *or* ¡de verdad!, vaya una forma de comportarse la suya

realm [relm] N (*lit*) (*Jur*) reino *m*; (*fig*) (= *field*) esfera *f*, campo *m* • **in the ~s of fantasy** en el reino de la fantasía • **in the ~ of the possible** dentro de lo posible • **in the ~ of speculation** en la esfera de la especulación

real-time [,riːl'taɪm] ADJ (*Comput*) en tiempo real • **real-time processing** procesamiento *m* en tiempo real

realtor ['rɪəltɔːʳ] N (*US*) corredor(a) *m/f* de bienes raíces

realty ['rɪəltɪ] N bienes *mpl* raíces

ream¹ [riːm] N [*of paper*] resma *f*; **reams*** (*fig*) montones *mpl*

ream² [riːm] VT (*Tech*) (*also* **ream out**) escariar

reamer ['riːməʳ] N escariador *m*

reanimate [riː'ænɪmeɪt] VT reanimar

reap [riːp] VT (*Agr*) (= *cut*) segar; (= *harvest*) cosechar, recoger • **to ~ what one has sown** (*fig*) recoger lo que uno ha sembrado • **who ~s the reward?** ¿quién se lleva los beneficios?

reaper ['riːpəʳ] N **1** (= *person*) segador(a) *m/f*

2 (= *machine*) segadora *f*, agavilladora *f*

reaping ['riːpɪŋ] N siega *f*

CPD ▸ **reaping hook** hoz *f*

reappear ['riːə'pɪəʳ] VI reaparecer, volver a aparecer

reappearance ['riːə'pɪərəns] N reaparición *f*

reapply ['riːə'plaɪ] VI hacer una nueva solicitud, presentar una nueva solicitud • **he reapplied for a transfer** volvió a solicitar traslado, hizo *or* presentó una nueva solicitud de traslado

VT [+ *paint, varnish*] dar otra capa de

reappoint ['riːə'pɔɪnt] VT volver a nombrar

reappointment ['riːə'pɔɪntmənt] N nuevo nombramiento *m*

reapportion ['riːə'pɔːʃən] VT volver a repartir (**among** entre)

reappraisal ['riːə'preɪzəl] N revaluación *f*

reappraise ['riːə'preɪz] VT reevaluar

rear¹ [rɪəʳ] N **1** (= *back part*) parte *f* trasera, parte *f* posterior; (*esp of building*) parte *f* de atrás • **the car behind skidded into his ~** el coche que venía detrás patinó, chocando contra la parte trasera *or* posterior del suyo • **the ~ of the train** la parte trasera *or* posterior del tren, los últimos vagones del tren • **from the ~ he looked just like everybody else** por detrás parecía como todo el mundo

2 [*of procession*] cola *f*, final *m*; [*of battle formation*] retaguardia *f* • **to attack the enemy from the ~** atacar al enemigo por la retaguardia

3* (= *buttocks*) trasero* *m*

4 (*in phrases*) • **at** *or* **in the ~** [*of vehicle*] en la parte trasera; [*of building*] en la parte trasera *or* de atrás; [*of procession*] en la cola, al final • **there is a garden at** *or* (*US*) **in the ~ of the house** detrás de la casa hay un jardín • **he sat in the ~ of the taxi** se sentó en el asiento de atrás del taxi • **to bring up the ~** cerrar la marcha • **to the ~** (*gen*) detrás, en la parte trasera *or* de atrás; (*Mil*) en la retaguardia • **a house with a patio to the ~** una casa con un patio detrás, una casa con un patio en la parte trasera *or* de atrás • **to be well to the ~** quedar muy atrás • **to the ~ of** detrás de • **to the ~ of the house was open countryside** detrás de la casa había campo abierto

ADJ (*gen*) de atrás, trasero

CPD ▸ **rear admiral** contraalmirante *mf* ▸ **rear bumper** paragolpes *m* trasero ▸ **rear door** (*in building, of vehicle*) puerta *f* trasera *or* de atrás ▸ **rear end** [*of vehicle*] parte *f* trasera *or* posterior; (*hum**) (= *buttocks*) trasero* *m* ▸ **rear gunner** artillero *m* de cola ▸ **rear light** piloto *m*, luz *f* trasera, calavera *f* (*Mex*) ▸ **rear seat** asiento *m* trasero *or* de atrás ▸ **rear wheel** rueda *f* trasera *or* de atrás • **~-wheel drive** tracción *f* trasera ▸ **rear window** [*of building*] ventana *f* de atrás; [*of vehicle*] luneta *f* trasera, cristal *m* de atrás

rear² [rɪəʳ] VT **1** (= *raise, bring up*) [+ *children, animals*] criar • **an audience ~ed on a diet of**

pop music un público que ha crecido oyendo música pop; ▹ **hand-rear**
2 (= *raise*) levantar, alzar • **fascism/jealousy ~s its ugly head again** el fascismo/la envidia vuelve a levantar la cabeza
3 (= *build*) erigir
(VI) (*also* **rear up**) 1 (*on hind legs*) [*horse*] empinarse; (*in fright*) encabritarse
2 (= *rise steeply*) [*building, mountain, wave*] alzarse, erguirse • **the mountains ~ed up on each side** las montañas se alzaban *or* se erguían a cada lado

rear-end [ˌrɪər'end] (VT) (*US*) [+ *vehicle*] chocar contra la parte trasera de • **a pick-up truck had rear-ended a car** una camioneta había chocado contra la parte trasera de un coche

rear-engined ['rɪərˌendʒɪnd] (ADJ) con motor trasero

rearguard ['rɪəgɑ:d] (N) (*Mil*) retaguardia *f*
(CPD) ▸ **rearguard action** combate *m* para cubrir una retirada • **to fight a ~ action** (*fig*) resistir en lo posible

rearm ['ri:'ɑ:m] (VT) rearmar
(VI) rearmarse

rearmament ['ri:'ɑ:məmənt] (N) rearme *m*

rearmost ['rɪəməʊst] (ADJ) trasero, último de todos

rear-mounted ['rɪə'maʊntɪd] (ADJ) • **rear-mounted engine** motor *m* trasero *or* posterior

rearrange ['ri:ə'reɪndʒ] (VT) [+ *meeting, appointment*] cambiar de fecha/hora; [+ *furniture*] cambiar de sitio

rearrangement ['ri:ə'reɪndʒmənt] (N) [*of meeting*] cambio *m* de fecha/hora; [*of furniture*] (= *act*) cambio *m* de sitio; (= *effect*) nueva disposición *f*

rear-view mirror [ˌrɪəvju:'mɪrəʳ] (N) (*Aut*) (espejo *m*) retrovisor *m*

rearward ['rɪəwəd] (ADJ) trasero, de atrás, posterior
(ADV) hacia atrás

rearwards ['rɪəwədz] (ADV) = **rearward**

reason ['ri:zn] (N) 1 (= *motive*) razón *f*, motivo *m* • **the only ~ (that) I went was because I was told to** la única razón por la que *or* el único motivo por el que fui fue porque me dijeron que lo hiciera • **who would have a ~ to want to kill her?** ¿quién podría tener motivos para matarla? • **we have ~ to believe that ...** (*frm*) tenemos motivos para creer que ... • **he had every ~ to be upset** estaba disgustado y con razón • **there seems to be no ~ to stay** parece que no hay razón *or* motivo para quedarse • **by ~ of** en virtud de • **the ~ for (doing) sth**: • **the ~ for my going** *or* **my ~ for going** la razón por la que *or* el motivo por el que me marcho • **she is my ~ for living** ella es mi razón de ser • **for ~s best known to himself** por motivos que solo él sabe • **for no ~** sin motivo, sin razón • **for personal/health ~s** por motivos personales/de salud • **for some ~** por la razón *or* el motivo que sea • **for this ~** por esta razón, por eso • **all the more ~ why you should not sell it** razón de más para que no lo vendas • **if he doesn't come I shall want to know the ~ why** si no viene tendrá que explicarme por qué • **I see no ~ why we shouldn't win** no veo razón por la que *or* motivo por el que no debiéramos ganar • **with good ~** con razón • **without ~** sin razón, sin motivo • **not without ~** no sin razón; ▹ **rhyme**
2 (= *faculty*) razón *f* • **only mankind is capable of ~** solo el ser humano es capaz de razonar • **to lose one's ~** perder la razón
3 (= *good sense*) sentido *m* común, sensatez *f* • **the Age of Reason** la Edad de la Razón • **beyond (all) ~**: • **I resented his presence beyond all ~** su presencia me molestaba de una forma inexplicable *or* fuera de toda lógica • **to listen to ~** atender a razones • **to see ~** entrar en razón • **he tried to make her see ~** intentó hacerla entrar en razón • **the voice of ~** la voz de la razón • **within ~** dentro de lo razonable; ▹ **appeal, stand**
(VT) razonar • **I called him, ~ing that I had nothing to lose** me dije que no tenía nada que perder así que lo llamé • **ours (is) not to ~ why** no es responsabilidad nuestra saber el porqué
(VI) razonar, discurrir
▸ **reason out** (VT + ADV) [+ *argument, answer*] razonar; [+ *problem*] resolver razonándolo • **she had felt the same as he did, until ~ing it out** opinaba como él hasta que se paró a pensarlo con un poco de lógica
▸ **reason with** (VI + PREP) • **to ~ with sb** razonar con algn (para convencerle) • **she was in no mood to be ~ed with** no estaba de humor como para que razonaran con ella • **there's no ~ing with him** no hay forma de razonar con él

reasonable ['ri:znəbl] (ADJ) 1 (= *sensible, fair*) [*person, decision, explanation, request*] razonable; [*behaviour*] sensato • **I kept my voice calm and ~** mantuve un tono de voz calmado y de persona razonable • **be ~!** ¡sé razonable! • **it is ~ to suppose that ...** es razonable suponer que ... • **beyond (a** *or* **any) ~ doubt** sin que quede lugar a dudas • **to use ~ force** (*Jur*) hacer uso moderado de la fuerza • **~ grounds** motivos *mpl* fundados • **within a ~ time** dentro de un plazo de tiempo razonable
2 (= *acceptable*) [*amount, distance, price, offer*] razonable; [*standard, results*] aceptable • **there was a ~ chance of finding a peaceful solution** existían bastantes posibilidades de encontrar una solución pacífica • **this suit is very ~** este traje no es nada caro *or* no está nada mal de precio

reasonableness ['ri:znəblnɪs] (N) [*of person, request, offer, behaviour*] lo razonable

reasonably ['ri:znəblɪ] (ADV) 1 (= *sensibly*) [*discuss, expect, suppose*] razonablemente; [*behave*] de manera razonable • **he acted very ~** obró de manera muy razonable • **he argued, quite ~, that ...** argumentó, con toda la razón, que ... • **~ priced clothes** ropa a precios razonables
2 (= *fairly*) [*good, happy, sure, safe*] bastante • **a ~ accurate report** un informe bastante exacto, más o menos • **~ well** bastante bien, dentro de lo que cabe

reasoned ['ri:znd] (ADJ) [*argument*] razonado • **well-reasoned** bien argumentado

reasoning ['ri:znɪŋ] (N) razonamiento *m*, lógica *f* • **I don't see the ~ behind this decision** no veo la lógica *or* el razonamiento que hay detrás de esta decisión • **this line of ~ is supported by recent figures** estos argumentos están respaldados por cifras recientes
(ADJ) racional

reassemble ['ri:ə'sembl] (VT) 1 (*Tech*) montar de nuevo, volver a armar
2 [+ *people*] volver a reunir
(VI) 1 [*people*] volver a reunirse, juntarse de nuevo
2 (*Parl*) volver a celebrar una sesión

reassembly [ˌri:ə'semblɪ] (N) 1 (*Tech*) nuevo montaje *m*
2 (*Parl*) inauguración *f* de la nueva sesión, nueva sesión *f*

reassert ['ri:ə'sɜ:t] (VT) [+ *authority, influence*] reafirmar

reassertion [ˌri:ə'sɜ:ʃən] (N) reafirmación *f*

reassess ['ri:ə'ses] (VT) [+ *situation*] estudiar de nuevo, reestudiar; [+ *tax*] calcular de nuevo • **we shall have to ~ the situation** tendremos que estudiar de nuevo *or* reestudiar la situación

reassessment [ˌri:ə'sesmənt] (N) [*of situation*] nuevo estudio *m*; (*Econ*) revaloración *f*

reassume [ˌri:ə'sju:m] (VT) [+ *work*] volver a empezar; [+ *office*] reasumir

reassurance ['ri:ə'ʃʊərəns] (N) consuelo *m*, confianza *f* • **sometimes we all need ~** hay veces cuando todos necesitamos que se nos anime nuestra confianza

reassure ['ri:ə'ʃʊəʳ] (VT) tranquilizar • **we ~d her that everything was OK** le aseguramos que todo iba bien

reassured [ˌri:ə'ʃʊəd] (ADJ) [*person*] más tranquilo • **to feel ~** sentirse más tranquilo • **she felt ~ in the morning** por la mañana ya se sentía más tranquila

reassuring ['ri:ə'ʃʊərɪŋ] (ADJ) (= *pacifying*) tranquilizador; (= *encouraging*) alentador • **to make ~ noises** (*fig*) hacer comentarios tranquilizadores • **it is ~ to know that ...** (me) tranquiliza saber que ..., es tranquilizador saber que ...

reassuringly ['ri:ə'ʃʊərɪŋlɪ] (ADV) de modo tranquilizador • **he spoke ~** nos tranquilizó con sus palabras • **a ~ strong performance** una actuación cuya fuerza nos alentó • **he was now in ~ familiar surroundings** el entorno era ahora familiar y le hacía sentirse más tranquilo

reawaken ['ri:ə'weɪkən] (VT) volver a despertar
(VI) volver a despertarse, despertarse

reawakening ['ri:ə'weɪknɪŋ] (N) despertar *m*

REB (N ABBR) (= **Revised English Bible**) *versión revisada de la Biblia*

rebadge [ˌri:'bædʒ] (VT) [+ *product*] relanzar con otro nombre

rebarbative [rɪ'bɑ:bətɪv] (ADJ) (*frm*) repugnante, repelente

rebate ['ri:beɪt] (N) 1 (= *discount*) rebaja *f*, descuento *m*
2 (= *money back*) reembolso *m*, devolución *f*

Rebecca [rɪ'bekə] (N) Rebeca

rebel ['rebl] (N) rebelde *mf* • **I was a bit of a ~ at school** era un poco rebelde en el colegio
(VI) [rɪ'bel] (= *rise up*) rebelarse, sublevarse; (= *refuse to conform*) rebelarse • **to ~ against sth/sb** rebelarse contra algo/algn • **at the sight of all that food, his stomach ~led** su estómago se rebeló al ver tanta comida • **I tried to get up but my legs ~led** intenté levantarme pero mis piernas se negaron *or* no me respondieron las piernas
(ADJ) [*forces, soldiers, factions*] rebelde
(CPD) ▸ **rebel leader** cabecilla *mf*

rebellion [rɪ'beljən] (N) rebelión *f*, sublevación *f*

rebellious [rɪ'beljəs] (ADJ) rebelde

rebelliously [rɪ'beljəslɪ] (ADV) [*say*] con rebeldía; [*act*] de manera rebelde

rebelliousness [rɪ'beljəsnɪs] (N) rebeldía *f*

rebind ['ri:'baɪnd] (PT, PP: **rebound**) (VT) 1 (*with string etc*) volver a atar
2 [+ *book, volume*] reencuadernar

rebirth ['ri:'bɜ:θ] (N) (*gen*) renacimiento *m*; (= *re-emergence*) resurgimiento *m*

rebirthing [ˌri:'bɜ:θɪŋ] (N) renacimiento *m*

reboot [ˌri:'bu:t] (VT), (VI) (*Comput*) reinicializar, reiniciar

rebore ['ri:'bɔ:ʳ] (*Tech*) (N) rectificado *m*
(VT) rectificar

reborn ['ri:'bɔ:n] (PP) • **to be ~** renacer

rebound ['ri:baʊnd] (N) • **on the ~** (*Sport*) de rebote • **she hit the ball on the ~** dio al balón

r

de rebote • **she married him on the ~** se casó con él por despecho
VI [rɪ'baʊnd] rebotar
▸ **rebound on** VI + PREP estallar en la cara de
rebrand VT [ˌriː'brænd] [+ *company, product*] relanzar • **to ~ sth as sth** relanzar algo como algo
N ['riːˌbrænd] relanzamiento *m*
rebranding [ˌriː'brændɪŋ] N [*of company, product*] relanzamiento *m*
rebroadcast ['riː'brɔːdkɑːst] N retransmisión *f*
VT retransmitir
rebuff [rɪ'bʌf] N desaire *m*, rechazo *m* • **to meet with a ~** sufrir un desaire *or* rechazo
VT rechazar, desairar
rebuild ['riː'bɪld] (PT, PP: **rebuilt**) VT reconstruir
rebuilding ['riː'bɪldɪŋ] N reconstrucción *f*
rebuilt ['riː'bɪlt] PT, PP *of* **rebuild**
rebuke [rɪ'bjuːk] N reprimenda *f*, reproche *m*
VT reprender, reprochar • **to ~ sb for having done sth** reprender a algn por haber hecho algo, reprochar a algn haber hecho algo
rebus ['riːbəs] N (PL: **rebuses**) jeroglífico *m*
rebut [rɪ'bʌt] VT rebatir, impugnar
rebuttal [rɪ'bʌtl] N refutación *f*, impugnación *f*
recalcitrance [rɪ'kælsɪtrəns] N terquedad *f*, contumacia *f* (*frm*)
recalcitrant [rɪ'kælsɪtrənt] ADJ recalcitrante, contumaz (*frm*)
recall [rɪ'kɔːl] N **1** (= *recollection*) recuerdo *m*; (= *ability to remember*) memoria *f* • **those days are gone beyond ~** aquellos días pasaron al olvido • **he has no ~ of what he did** no recuerda nada de lo que hizo • **to have total ~** tener una memoria infalible
2 (= *calling back*) [*of Parliament*] convocatoria *f* extraordinaria; (*Mil*) [*of troops*] nueva convocatoria *f*
3 (= *withdrawal*) [*of ambassador*] retirada *f*; [*of defective product*] retirada *f* (del mercado); (*US*) [*of elected official*] destitución *f*; (*Mil*) [*of troops*] retirada *f* • **to sound the ~** tocar la retirada, tocar retreta
VT **1** (= *call back*) [+ *Parliament*] convocar en sesión extraordinaria; [+ *ambassador, capital*] retirar; [+ *sports player*] volver a llamar; [+ *library book*] reclamar; [+ *defective product*] retirar (*del mercado*); (*Mil*) (= *call up*) llamar; (*US*) (*Pol*) (= *dismiss*) destituir
2 (= *remember*) recordar • **I can't ~ exactly what we agreed** no recuerdo exactamente en qué quedamos • **I don't ~ saying that** no recuerdo haber dicho eso • **I seem to ~ that …** creo recordar que …
3 (= *bring to mind*) recordar a • **it ~s the time when …** recuerda a aquella ocasión en la que …
4 (*Comput*) volver a llamar
VI recordar • **I'm sorry, I don't ~** lo siento, no recuerdo • **as I ~ …** según recuerdo …, que yo recuerde …
recant [rɪ'kænt] VT retractar, desdecir
VI retractarse, desdecirse
recantation ['riːkæn'teɪʃən] N retractación *f*
recap* ['riːkæp] N recapitulación *f*, resumen *m*
VI (= *sum up*) recapitular, resumir
recapitalization [ˌriːkæpɪtəlaɪ'zeɪʃən] N recapitalización *f*
recapitalize [ˌriː'kæpɪtəlaɪz] VT recapitalizar
recapitulate [ˌriːkə'pɪtjʊleɪt] VT [+ *argument, facts*] recapitular, resumir
VI recapitular, resumir
recapitulation ['riːkəˌpɪtjʊ'leɪʃən] N recapitulación *f*, resumen *m*
recapture ['riː'kæptʃə^r] VT [+ *prisoner*] volver a detener; [+ *town*] reocupar, reconquistar (*Hist*); [+ *memory, scene*] hacer revivir, recordar
N [*of prisoner*] detención *f*; [*of town*] reocupación *f*, reconquista *f* (*Hist*)
recast ['riː'kɑːst] (PT, PP: **recast**) VT **1** (*Theat*) [+ *play*] hacer un nuevo reparto para
2 (*Tech*) refundir
N (*Tech*) refundición *f*
recce* ['rekɪ] (*Brit*) N ABBR (*Mil*) (= **reconnaissance**) reconocimiento *m*
VT (*Mil*) (= **reconnoitre**) reconocer
recd., **rec'd** ABBR (*Comm*) (= **received**) rbdo
recede [rɪ'siːd] VI [*tide, flood*] bajar; [*person etc*] volverse atrás; [*view*] alejarse; [*danger*] disminuir; [*chin*] retroceder • **his hair is receding** tiene entradas
receding [rɪ'siːdɪŋ] ADJ [*prospect*] que va disminuyendo; [*tide*] que va bajando; [*forehead*] huidizo, achatado; [*chin*] (hundida) hacia atrás
CPD ▸ **receding hairline** entradas *fpl*
receipt [rɪ'siːt] N **1** (= *act of receiving*) recepción *f*, recibo *m* • **to acknowledge ~ of** acusar recibo de • **on ~ of** al recibo de, al recibir • **on ~ of these goods** al recibo de *or* al recibir estas mercancías • **I am in ~ of your letter** (*frm*) he recibido su carta, obra su carta en mi poder (*more frm*) • **pay on ~** pago *m* contra entrega *or* al recibo
2 (= *document*) recibo *m* • **please give me a ~** haga el favor de darme un recibo
3 receipts (= *money taken*) recaudación *fsing*
VT [+ *goods*] dar recibo por; [+ *bill*] poner el "recibí" en
CPD ▸ **receipt book** libro *m* talonario
receivable [rɪ'siːvəbl] ADJ (*Comm*) por cobrar, a cobrar
NPL **receivables** cuentas *fpl* por cobrar
receive [rɪ'siːv] VT **1** (= *get*) [+ *letter, gift, money, visit, salary, sacrament*] recibir; [+ *stolen goods*] comerciar con; (*Tennis*) [+ *ball, service*] recibir • **all contributions will be gratefully ~d** todas las contribuciones que nos lleguen serán bien recibidas • **she ~d the Nobel Peace Prize in 1989** le otorgaron el premio Nobel de la Paz en 1989 • **I never ~d her message** nunca llegué a recibir su mensaje, nunca me llegó su mensaje • **she ~d no support from her colleagues** sus colegas no la apoyaron • **he ~d a wound in the leg** resultó herido en la pierna, sufrió una herida en la pierna • **he ~d a blow to the head** recibió un golpe en la cabeza • **a bowl to ~ the liquid that drains off** un cuenco para recoger el líquido que se escurra • **"received with thanks"** (*Comm*) "recibí" • **their plans ~d a setback** sus planes sufrieron un revés • **she is receiving treatment for eczema** está siendo tratada de eczema • **he ~d hospital treatment for cuts to the face** fue tratado en el hospital de unos cortes que tenía en la cara • **he ~d a life sentence** lo sentenciaron a cadena perpetua • **he ~d a suspended sentence** le suspendieron la condena
2 (= *greet*) [+ *visitors*] recibir; [+ *guests*] recibir, acoger; [+ *publication, idea, performance*] acoger • **to be well ~d** [*book, idea*] tener buena acogida • **his suggestion was not well ~d** su sugerencia no tuvo buena acogida • **her book was well ~d** su libro tuvo buena acogida
3 (= *admit*) [+ *new member*] admitir • **to ~ sb into the Church** acoger a algn en el seno de la Iglesia
4 (*Rad, TV*) [+ *transmission*] recibir • **are you receiving me?** ¿me recibe?
VI **1** (= *get*) recibir • PROVERB: • **it is better to give than to ~** más vale dar que recibir
2 (*Jur*) (= *buy and sell stolen goods*) comerciar con artículos robados
3 (*Tennis*) recibir
4 (*frm*) (*socially*) recibir • **the Duchess ~s on Thursdays** la duquesa recibe los jueves
5 (*Rad, TV*) recibir • **whisky two receiving!** ¡aquí whisky two, te recibo!
received [rɪ'siːvd] ADJ [*opinion*] aceptado; [*wisdom*] popular • **the ~ wisdom is that …** la creencia popular es que … • **it came to represent ~ wisdom in classical Marxist theory** llegó a ser parte de lo que se daba por sentado en la teoría marxista clásica
CPD ▸ **Received Pronunciation** pronunciación *f* estándar (*del inglés*); ▷ ENGLISH
receiver [rɪ'siːvə^r] N **1** (= *recipient*) [*of gift, letter*] destinatario/a *m/f*; [*of stolen goods*] comerciante *mf* (*de artículos robados*); (*Psych*) receptor(a) *m/f*
2 (*Telec*) auricular *m* • **to pick up** *or* **lift the ~** coger *or* levantar el auricular • **to put down** *or* **replace the ~** colgar el auricular
3 (*Rad, TV*) receptor *m*
4 (= *liquidator*) (*also* **official receiver**) síndico/a *m/f* • **to call in the ~(s)** entrar en liquidación
5 (*US*) (*Ftbl*) receptor(a) *m/f* • **wide ~** receptor(a) *m/f* abierto/a
receivership [rɪ'siːvəʃɪp] N • **to go into ~** entrar en liquidación
receiving [rɪ'siːvɪŋ] N recepción *f*; [*of stolen goods*] receptación *f*, encubrimiento *m*
ADJ • IDIOM: • **to be on** *or* **at the ~ end (of sth)*** ser el blanco *or* la víctima (de algo)
CPD ▸ **receiving set** receptor *m*, radiorreceptor *m*
recension [rɪ'senʃən] N recensión *f*
recent ['riːsnt] ADJ [*event, survey, trip, photograph, history*] reciente • **his most ~ book** su libro más reciente • **a ~ acquaintance** un conocido de hace poco tiempo • **a ~ arrival** (= *person*) un recién llegado • **~ developments in Biology** los últimos avances en el campo de la biología • **in the ~ past** en los últimos tiempos, en un pasado reciente • **in ~ years** en los últimos años
recently ['riːsntlɪ] ADV **1** (= *not long ago*) recientemente, hace poco, recién (*LAm*) • **until ~** hasta hace poco • **it is only very ~ that I started painting** empecé a pintar hace muy poco *or* apenas nada • **as ~ as 1998 he was living in London** aún en 1998, todavía vivía él en Londres • **it was discovered as ~ as 1903** se descubrió hace apenas nada, en 1903
2 (= *lately*) últimamente, recientemente • **I haven't heard from her ~** últimamente *or* recientemente no he sabido nada de ella • **just ~ he's been acting strangely** últimamente se ha estado comportando de un modo extraño
3 (*before pp*) recién • **~ arrived** recién llegado
receptacle [rɪ'septəkl] N (*frm*) receptáculo *m*, recipiente *m*
reception [rɪ'sepʃən] N **1** (= *act of receiving*) recepción *f*, recibimiento *m*
2 (= *welcome*) acogida *f* • **to get a warm ~** tener buena acogida, ser bien recibido
3 (= *social function*) recepción *f* • **the ~ will be at a big hotel** la recepción tendrá lugar en un gran hotel; ▸ **wedding**
4 (*Rad etc*) recepción *f*
5 (*esp Brit*) (*in hotel*) recepción *f* • **please leave your key at ~** por favor dejen la llave en recepción

6 (*Educ*) clase *f* de primer año
CPD ▸ **reception area** (*in office, hotel*) recepción *f*; (*in hospital*) mostrador *m* de admisión ▸ **reception centre, reception center** (*US*) centro *m* de recepción ▸ **reception class** (*Educ*) clase *f* de primer año ▸ **reception desk** (*esp Brit*) (*in hotel*) mostrador *m* de recepción; (*in hospital*) mostrador *m* de admisión ▸ **reception room** (*esp Brit*) sala *f* de visitas

receptionist [rɪ'sepʃənɪst] N recepcionista *mf*

receptive [rɪ'septɪv] ADJ receptivo

receptiveness [rɪ'septɪvnɪs] N, **receptivity** [rɪsep'tɪvɪtɪ] N receptividad *f*

receptor [rɪ'septəʳ] N (*Physiol, Rad*) receptor *m*

recess [rɪ'ses] N **1** (*Jur, Pol*) (= *cessation of business*) clausura *f*; (*US*) (*Jur*) (= *short break*) descanso *m*; (*esp US*) (*Scol*) recreo *m* • **parliament is in ~** la sesión del parlamento está suspendida
2 (*Archit*) hueco *m*, nicho *m*
3 (= *secret place*) escondrijo *m*; (*fig*) la parte más oculta • **in the ~es of his mind** en los recovecos de su mente, en lo más oculto de su mente
VI (*US*) (*Jur, Parl*) prorrogarse, suspenderse la sesión

recession [rɪ'seʃən] N **1** (*Econ*) recesión *f* • **to be in ~** estar en recesión *or* retroceso
2 (*frm*) (= *receding*) retroceso *m*

recessional [rɪ'seʃənl] N himno *m* de fin de oficio

recessionary [rɪ'seʃənərɪ] ADJ [*factors etc*] recesivo

recessive [rɪ'sesɪv] ADJ recesivo

recharge ['riː'tʃɑːdʒ] VT [+ *battery*] recargar, volver a cargar • **to ~ one's batteries** (*fig*) ponerse las pilas

rechargeable [rɪ'tʃɑːdʒəbl] ADJ recargable

recheck [ˌriː'tʃek] VT volver a revisar

recherché [rə'ʃeəʃeɪ] ADJ rebuscado

rechristen ['riː'krɪsn] VT (*Rel*) rebautizar; (= *rename*) poner nuevo nombre a • **they have ~ed the boat "Gloria"** han puesto al barco el nuevo nombre de "Gloria"

recidivism [rɪ'sɪdɪvɪzəm] N reincidencia *f*

recidivist [rɪ'sɪdɪvɪst] N reincidente *mf*

recipe ['resɪpɪ] N receta *f* (de cocina) • **a ~ for** (*also fig*) una receta para • **it's a ~ for disaster** es una forma segura de buscarse problemas
CPD ▸ **recipe book** libro *m* de cocina, recetario *m*

recipient [rɪ'sɪpɪənt] N [*of letter, gift*] destinatario/a *m/f*

reciprocal [rɪ'sɪprəkəl] ADJ recíproco, mutuo
N (*Math*) recíproca *f*

reciprocally [rɪ'sɪprəkəlɪ] ADV recíprocamente, mutuamente

reciprocate [rɪ'sɪprəkeɪt] VT [+ *good wishes*] intercambiar, devolver • **and this feeling is ~d** y compartimos este sentimiento • **her kindness was not ~d** su amabilidad no fue correspondida
VI **1** (*gen*) corresponder • **but they did not ~** pero ellos no correspondieron a esto • **he ~d with a short speech** pronunció un breve discurso a modo de contestación
2 (*Mech*) oscilar, alternar

reciprocation [rɪˌsɪprə'keɪʃən] N reciprocidad *f*, correspondencia *f* • **there was no ~ of his generosity** su generosidad no fue correspondida

reciprocity [ˌresɪ'prɒsɪtɪ] N reciprocidad *f*

recital [rɪ'saɪtl] N (*Mus*) recital *m*; (= *story*) relato *m*

recitation [ˌresɪ'teɪʃən] N [*of poetry*] recitación *f*; [*of facts*] relación *f*

recitative [ˌresɪtə'tiːv] ADJ recitativo
N recitado *m*

recite [rɪ'saɪt] VT [+ *poetry*] recitar; [+ *story*] relatar; [+ *list*] enumerar • **she ~d her troubles all over again** volvió a detallar todas sus dificultades
VI recitar

reckless ['reklɪs] ADJ [*person*] (= *rash*) temerario; (= *wild*) descabellado; (= *thoughtless*) imprudente; [*speed*] peligroso; [*statement*] inconsiderado • **~ driving** conducción *f* temeraria • **he's a ~ driver** conduce temerariamente

recklessly ['reklɪslɪ] ADV (= *rashly*) temerariamente; (= *thoughtlessly*) imprudentemente • **to drive ~** conducir temerariamente • **to spend ~** derrochar dinero

recklessness ['reklɪsnɪs] N (= *rashness*) temeridad *f*; (= *thoughtlessness*) imprudencia *f* • **the ~ of youth** la temeridad de la juventud • **the ~ of her driving** su modo imprudente de conducir

reckon ['rekən] VT **1** (= *calculate*) calcular • **prices are ~ed to be about 2% up on last year** se calcula que los precios han subido en un 2% comparados con respecto al año pasado
2 (= *consider*) considerar • **he is ~ed to be Spain's top conductor** está considerado como el mejor director de orquesta de España
3* (= *think*) creer • **she'll come, I ~** creo *or* me parece que vendrá, se me hace que vendrá (*Mex*) • **you ~?** ¿tú crees?, ¿te parece a ti? • **I ~ so** eso creo, creo *or* me parece que sí • **I ~ he must be about 40** calculo que debe estar rondando los 40 • **what do you ~ our chances are?** ¿qué posibilidades crees *or* te parece que tenemos?
4 (= *plan, expect*) • **to ~ to do sth** contar con poder hacer algo, esperar poder hacer algo • **they ~ to sell most of them abroad** cuentan con *or* esperan poder vender la mayoría en el extranjero
VI (= *count*) contar • **~ing from today** contando a partir de hoy
▸ **reckon in** VT + ADV tener en cuenta, incluir
▸ **reckon on** VI + PREP contar con • **you can ~ on 30 people** puedes contar con 30 personas • **to ~ on (sth/sb) doing sth: I'd ~ed on doing that tomorrow** había contado con (que iba a) hacer eso mañana • **I hadn't ~ed on the police arriving** no había contado con que llegara la policía
▸ **reckon up** VT + ADV (= *calculate, add up*) calcular
▸ **reckon with** VI + PREP **1** (= *take into account*) contar con, tener en cuenta • **there were factors we had not ~ed with** había factores con los que no habíamos contado, había factores que no habíamos tenido en cuenta • **we hadn't ~ed with having to walk** no habíamos contado con tener que ir a pie; ▹ **force**
2 (= *contend with*) vérselas con • **if you offend him you'll have the whole family to ~ with** si le ofendes tendrás que vértelas con toda la familia
▸ **reckon without** VI + PREP no contar con, no tener en cuenta • **I had ~ed without her brother** no había contado con *or* tenido en cuenta a su hermano

reckoner ['rekənəʳ] ▹ **ready reckoner**

reckoning ['reknɪŋ] N **1** (= *calculation*) cálculo *m* • **according to my ~** según mis cálculos • **to be out in one's ~** errar en el cálculo • **to come into the ~** entrar en los cálculos • **by any ~** a todas luces
2 (= *bill*) cuenta *f* • **to pay the ~** pagar la cuenta
3 • **day of ~** (*fig*) ajuste *m* de cuentas
4 (*Naut*) ▹ **dead**

reclaim [rɪ'kleɪm] VT **1** [+ *throne, title*] reclamar; [+ *language, culture*] recuperar; [+ *inheritance, rights*] reclamar, reivindicar; [+ *baggage*] recoger, reclamar • **she ~ed her British skating title yesterday** ayer reclamó su título británico de patinaje • **you may be eligible to ~ income tax** puede que tenga derecho a que le devuelvan parte de lo que ha pagado del impuesto sobre la renta • **he intended to ~ the money as expenses** tenía pensado cargarlo a la cuenta de la compañía • **the town is gradually being ~ed by the desert** el desierto está reclamando poco a poco el terreno a la ciudad
2 (= *salvage*) [+ *land*] (*gen*) aprovechar; (*from sea*) ganar al mar; [+ *swamp*] sanear; [+ *materials*] recuperar, reciclar
N ▹ **baggage**

reclaimable [rɪ'kleɪməbl] ADJ [*land*] recuperable; [*materials, by-products*] recuperable, reciclable

reclamation [ˌreklə'meɪʃən] N **1** [*of land*] *acción de ganarle terreno al mar o de recuperar tierras pantanosas* • **land ~ scheme/project** un proyecto para ganarle terreno al mar/recuperar tierras pantanosas
2 [*of materials*] recuperación *f*, reciclaje *m*

reclassify [ˌriː'klæsɪfaɪ] VT reclasificar

recline [rɪ'klaɪn] VI recostarse, reclinarse
VT [+ *head*] recostar, reclinar

recliner [rɪ'klaɪnəʳ] N butaca *f* reclinable

reclining [rɪ'klaɪnɪŋ] ADJ [*seat*] reclinable; [*figure, statue*] yacente
CPD ▸ **reclining chair** sillón *m* reclinable; (*Med*) silla *f* de extensión ▸ **reclining seat** asiento *m* reclinable

recluse [rɪ'kluːs] N solitario/a *m/f*

reclusion [rɪ'kluːʒən] N reclusión *f*, soledad *f*

reclusive [rɪ'kluːzɪv] ADJ dado a recluirse, solitario

recognition [ˌrekəg'nɪʃən] N
1 (= *identification, recollection*) reconocimiento *m* • **he gazed blankly at her, then ~ dawned** la miró sin comprender, entonces cayó en la cuenta de quién era • **the bodies were mutilated beyond** *or* **out of (all) ~** los cuerpos estaban tan mutilados que resultaba imposible reconocerlos • **she has changed beyond ~** ha cambiado tanto que está irreconocible; ▹ **optical, speech**
2 (= *acknowledgement*) reconocimiento *m* • **she hasn't got the ~ she deserves** no ha recibido el reconocimiento que se merece • **there is a growing ~ that ...** hay cada vez más gente que admite que ... • **in ~ of** en reconocimiento de • **the awards he won in ~ of his work** los premios que ganó en reconocimiento del trabajo realizado

recognizable ['rekəgnaɪzəbl] ADJ reconocible • **it is ~ as ...** se le reconoce *or* identifica como ...

recognizably [ˌrekəg'naɪzəblɪ] ADV • **it is ~ different/better** *etc* se ve a las claras que es diferente/mejor *etc*

recognizance [rɪ'kɒgnɪzəns] N (*esp US*) (*Jur*) obligación *f* contraída; (= *sum*) fianza *f* • **to enter into ~s to** (+ *infin*) comprometerse legalmente a (+ *infin*)

recognize ['rekəgnaɪz] VT **1** (= *know again*) reconocer • **I hardly ~d myself** apenas me reconocía *or* me conocía a mí mismo • **he was ~d by two policemen** lo reconocieron dos policías
2 (= *acknowledge*) reconocer, admitir • **are**

these qualifications ~d in other European countries? ¿están estos títulos reconocidos en otros países europeos? • **we do not ~ your claim** no reconocemos su derecho a reclamarlo • **they ~ Bosnia as an independent nation** reconocen a Bosnia como nación independiente
3 (*US*) (= *give right to speak*) • **the Chair ~s Mr White** el Sr. White tiene la palabra

recognized ['rekəgnaɪzd] (ADJ)
1 (= *acknowledged*) (*gen*) reconocido, conocido; [*expert*] reconocido • **it is a ~ fact that ...** es un hecho conocido que ...
2 (= *accredited*) [*institution, qualifications*] acreditado

recoil [rɪ'kɔɪl] (VI) [*person*] echarse atrás, retroceder; [*gun*] dar un culatazo • **to ~ from sth** retroceder *or* dar marcha atrás ante algo • **to ~ from doing sth** rehuir hacer algo • **to ~ in fear** retroceder espantado
(N) (*at sight*) retroceso *m*; [*of gun*] culatazo *m*

recoilless [rɪ'kɔɪllɪs] (ADJ) [*gun*] sin retroceso

recollect [,rekə'lekt] (VT) recordar, acordarse de
(VI) recordar, acordarse

recollection [,rekə'lekʃən] (N) recuerdo *m* • **to the best of my ~** que yo recuerde

recommence ['ri:kə'mens] (VT) reanudar, recomenzar, volver a comenzar
(VI) reanudarse, recomenzar, volver a comenzar

recommend [,rekə'mend] (VT) 1 (= *advocate, speak well of*) recomendar • **to ~ sb for a job** recomendar a algn para un trabajo • **she comes highly ~ed (by Anne)** viene muy bien recomendada (por Anne) • **I don't ~ the pizza** no recomiendo la pizza • **the town has much/little to ~ it** el pueblo tiene mucho/poco atractivo
2 (= *advise*) recomendar, aconsejar • **what do you ~ for a sore throat?** ¿qué recomienda para el dolor de garganta? • **this method is not to be ~ed** este método no es nada recomendable *or* aconsejable • **to ~ doing sth** recomendar *or* aconsejar hacer algo • **the doctor ~ed that he (should) stay in bed** el médico le recomendó *or* aconsejó que guardara cama • **to ~ sb to do sth** recomendar *or* aconsejar a algn hacer algo *or* que haga algo • **I would ~ against going on your own** le recomendaría *or* aconsejaría no ir solo *or* que no fuera solo
3 (*frm*) (= *commit*) [+ *person, soul*] encomendar • **I ~ him to your keeping** se lo encomiendo

recommendable [,rekə'mendəbl] (ADJ) recomendable

recommendation [,rekəmen'deɪʃən] (N)
1 (= *endorsement*) recomendación *f*; ▸ **letter**
2 (= *suggestion, proposal*) recomendación *f*, sugerencia *f* • **it is my ~ that it should be destroyed** recomiendo que se destruya • **to make ~s** hacer recomendaciones *or* sugerencias • **to do sth on sb's ~** *or* **on the ~ of sb** hacer algo por recomendación *or* consejo de algn, hacer algo siguiendo la recomendación *or* consejo de algn
3 (= *statement*) recomendación *f*
4 (= *good point*) • **his good looks were his only ~** su buena presencia era lo único que le salvaba *or* su único atractivo

recommendatory [,rekə'mendətərɪ] (ADJ) recomendatorio

recommended [,rekə'mendɪd] (ADJ) 1 [*dose*] recomendado, aconsejado
2 [*book, film*] recomendado • **though ten years old, this book is highly ~** aunque tenga diez años, este libro está muy recomendado
(CPD) ▸ **recommended daily allowance** aporte *m* diario recomendado ▸ **recommended daily intake** consumo *m* diario recomendado, consumo *m* diario aconsejado • **the ~ daily intake is ...** el consumo diario recomendado *or* aconsejado es ... ▸ **recommended reading** lectura *f* recomendada ▸ **recommended retail price** precio *m* de venta al público recomendado

recompense ['rekəmpens] (N) (*gen*) recompensa *f*; (*financial*) indemnización *f*
(VT) (*gen*) recompensar; (*financially*) indemnizar

recompose [,ri:kəm'pəuz] (VT) 1 (= *rewrite*) reescribir
2 (= *calm*) • **to ~ o.s.** recobrar la compostura
3 (*Phot*) recomponer

reconcilable ['rekənsaɪləbl] (ADJ) conciliable, reconciliable

reconcile ['rekənsaɪl] (VT) 1 (= *reunite*) [+ *persons*] reconciliar • **to be ~d (with)** estar reconciliado (con) • **the couple are now ~d** la pareja está ahora reconciliada
2 (= *make compatible*) [+ *theories, ideals*] conciliar • **she ~d the conflicting pressures of motherhood and career** concilió las exigencias contrapuestas de la maternidad y de una profesión
3 (= *settle*) [+ *differences*] resolver • **you must try and ~ your differences** tenéis que intentar resolver vuestras diferencias
4 (= *resign*) • **what ~d him to it was ...** lo que hizo que lo aceptara fue ... • **to become ~d to sth** aceptar algo, resignarse a algo • **to ~ o.s. to sth** resignarse a algo
5 [+ *accounts*] hacer cuadrar, conciliar (*frm*)

reconciliation [,rekənsɪlɪ'eɪʃən] (N)
1 (= *reuniting*) reconciliación *f* • **to bring about a ~** lograr una reconciliación
2 (= *making compatible*) [*of theories, ideals*] conciliación *f*
3 [*of accounts*] conciliación *f*

reconciliatory [,rekən'sɪlɪətərɪ] (ADJ) reconciliatorio, reconciliador

recondite [rɪ'kɒndaɪt] (ADJ) (*frm*) recóndito

recondition ['ri:kən'dɪʃən] (VT) reacondicionar

reconfigure [,ri:kən'fɪgəʳ] (VT) reconfigurar

reconfirm [,ri:kən'fɜ:m] (VT) reconfirmar

reconnaissance [rɪ'kɒnɪsəns] (N) reconocimiento *m* • **to make a ~** reconocer *or* explorar el terreno, hacer un reconocimiento del terreno
(CPD) ▸ **reconnaissance flight** vuelo *m* de reconocimiento

reconnect [,ri:kə'nekt] (VT) [+ *electricity, gas, water supply*] volver a conectar; [+ *customer, house*] devolver la conexión a

reconnection [,ri:kə'nekʃən] (N) [*of supply*] reconexión *f*

reconnoitre, **reconnoiter** (*US*) [,rekə'nɔɪtəʳ] (*Mil*) (VT) reconocer, explorar
(VI) hacer un reconocimiento

reconquer ['ri:'kɒŋkəʳ] (VT) reconquistar

reconquest ['ri:'kɒŋkwest] (N) reconquista *f* • **the Reconquest** [*of Spain*] la Reconquista

reconsider ['ri:kən'sɪdəʳ] (VT) reconsiderar, repensar
(VI) reconsiderar, repensar

reconsideration ['ri:kən,sɪdə'reɪʃən] (N) reconsideración *f* • **on ~** después de volver sobre ello

reconstitute ['ri:'kɒnstɪtju:t] (VT) [+ *events*] (= *piece together*) reconstituir • **~d food** alimentos *mpl* reconstituidos

reconstitution ['ri:,kɒnstɪ'tju:ʃən] (N) reconstitución *f*

reconstruct ['ri:kən'strʌkt] (VT) [+ *building*] reconstruir; [+ *crime, scene of crime*] reconstituir

reconstruction ['ri:kən'strʌkʃən] (N) reconstrucción *f*

reconstructive [,ri:kən'strʌktɪv] (ADJ) [*surgery, treatment*] reparador

reconvene [,ri:kən'vi:n] (VT) reconvocar
(VI) [*committee, jury etc*] reunirse

reconvert ['ri:kən'vɜ:t] (VT) volver a convertir (**to** en)

record ['rekɔ:d] (N) 1 (= *report, account*) (*gen*) documento *m*; (= *note*) nota *f*, apunte *m*; [*of meeting*] acta *f*; [*of attendance*] registro *m*; (*Jur*) [*of case*] acta *f* • **it is the earliest written ~ of this practice** es el documento escrito más antiguo que registra esta costumbre • **there is no ~ of it** no hay constancia de ello, no consta en ningún sitio • **the highest temperatures since ~s began** las temperaturas más altas que se han registrado hasta la fecha • **for the ~:** • **for the ~, I disagree** no estoy de acuerdo, que conste • **will you tell us your full name for the ~, please?** ¿podría decirnos su nombre completo para que quede constancia? • **to keep** *or* **make a ~ of sth** apuntar algo, tomar nota de algo • **it is a matter of (public) ~ that ...** hay constancia de que ... • **off the ~** [*statement, comment*] extraoficial; [*speak, say*] extraoficialmente • **this is strictly off the ~** esto es estrictamente extraoficial • **he told me off the ~** me dijo confidencialmente *or* extraoficialmente • **on ~:** • **there is no similar example on ~** no existe constancia de nada semejante • **the police had kept his name on ~** la policía lo había fichado • **the highest temperatures on ~** las temperaturas más altas que se han registrado hasta la fecha • **to be/have gone on ~ as saying that ...** haber declarado públicamente que ... • **to place** *or* **put sth on ~** hacer constar algo, dejar constancia de algo • **just to put** *or* **set the ~ straight, let me point out that ...** simplemente para que quede claro, permítanme señalar que ...; ▸ **off-the-record**
2 (= *memorial*) testimonio *m* • **the First World War is a ~ of human folly** la primera Guerra Mundial es un testimonio de la locura humana
3 (*Comput*) registro *m*
4 **records** (= *files*) archivos *mpl* • **according to our ~s, you have not paid** según nuestros datos, usted no ha pagado • **public ~s** archivos *mpl* públicos
5 (= *past performance*) **a** (*in work*) • **to have a good ~ at school** tener un buen expediente escolar • **the airline has a good safety ~** la compañía aérea tiene un buen historial en materia de seguridad • **his past ~ is against him** su historial obra en perjuicio suyo • **a country's human rights ~** el historial *or* la trayectoria de un país en materia de derechos humanos • **he left behind a splendid ~ of achievements** ha dejado atrás una magnífica hoja de servicios; ▸ **track**
b (*Med*) historial *m* • **the result will go on your medical ~** el resultado se incluirá en su historial médico
c (*also* **criminal record**) antecedentes *mpl* (penales) • **he's got a clean ~** no tiene antecedentes (penales) • **he's got a ~ as long as my arm** tiene un historial más largo que un día sin pan • **~ of previous convictions** antecedentes penales; ▸ **police**
d (*Mil*) hoja *f* de servicios • **war ~** historial *m* de guerra
6 (*Sport etc*) récord *m* • **the long jump ~** el récord del salto de longitud • **to beat** *or* **break the ~** batir el récord • **the film broke box office ~s** la película batió récords de taquilla • **he won a place in the ~ books** se ganó un lugar en el libro de los récords • **to hold the ~ (for sth)** tener *or* ostentar el récord (de algo) • **to set a ~ (for sth)** establecer un récord (de algo); ▸ **world**

7 (= *disc*) disco *m* • **to cut** *or* **make a ~** grabar un disco • **on ~** en disco; ▹ **long-playing**
ADJ récord, sin precedentes • **in ~ time** en un tiempo récord • **share prices closed at a ~ high** la bolsa cerró con los precios más altos jamás registrados
VT [rɪ'kɔːd] **1** (= *set down*) [+ *facts*] registrar; [+ *events*] (*in journal, diary*) tomar nota de; [+ *protest, disapproval*] hacer constar, dejar constancia de • **the fastest speed ever ~ed** la mayor velocidad jamás registrada • **shares ~ed a 16% fall** las acciones registraron una bajada de un 16% • **it is not ~ed anywhere** no consta en ninguna parte • **her letters ~ the details of diplomatic life in China** sus cartas dejan constancia de los detalles de la vida diplomática en China • **history ~s that ...** la historia cuenta que ...
2 (= *show*) [*instrument*] registrar, marcar
3 [+ *sound, images, data*] grabar
4 (*Comput*) grabar
VI [rɪ'kɔːd] (*on tape, film etc*) grabar • **his voice does not ~ well** su voz no sale bien en las grabaciones • **the ~ button** (*on tape deck, video*) el botón de grabación
CPD ['rekɔːd] ▸ **record book** libro *m* de registro • IDIOM: • **to go into the ~ books** pasar a la historia ▸ **record breaker** (= *woman*) plusmarquista *f*; (= *man*) recordman *m*, plusmarquista *m* ▸ **record card** ficha *f* ▸ **record company** casa *f* discográfica ▸ **record deck** platina *f* grabadora ▸ **record holder** (= *woman*) plusmarquista *f*; (= *man*) recordman *m*, plusmarquista *m* • **she is the world 800 metre ~ holder** tiene *or* ostenta el récord mundial de los 800 metros, es la plusmarquista mundial de los 800 metros ▸ **record keeping** archivación *f* ▸ **record label** sello *m* discográfico ▸ **record library** discoteca *f* ▸ **record player** tocadiscos *m inv* ▸ **record producer** productor(a) *m/f* discográfico/a ▸ **record sleeve** funda *f* de disco ▸ **record store** (*esp US*), **record shop** (*Brit*) tienda *f* de discos ▸ **record token** vale *m* para discos

recordable [rɪ'kɔːdəbl] ADJ [*CD, DVD*] grabable

record-breaking ['rekɔːd,breɪkɪŋ] ADJ [*person, team*] batidor del récord; [*effort, run*] récord

recorded [rɪ'kɔːdɪd] ADJ **1** [*music, programme*] grabado
2 [*history*] escrito, documentado • **it is a ~ fact that ...** hay constancia de que ... • **~ delivery** (*Brit*) (*Post*) servicio *m* de entrega con acuse de recibo
CPD ▸ **recorded message** mensaje *m* grabado

recorder [rɪ'kɔːdəʳ] N **1** (= *tape recorder*) casete *m* (*Sp*), grabadora *f* (*LAm*); (*reel-to-reel*) magnetófono *m*; (= *video recorder*) vídeo *m*, video *m* (*LAm*)
2 (*Jur*) juez *mf* municipal
3 (*Mus*) (= *instrument*) flauta *f* dulce
4 (= *person*) registrador(a) *m/f*, archivero/a *m/f* • **he was a faithful ~ of the facts** registró puntualmente los hechos

recording [rɪ'kɔːdɪŋ] N **1** (= *tape, disc*) grabación *f* • **to make a ~ (of sth)** realizar una grabación (de algo); ▹ **sound, tape, video**
2 (= *act*) [*of sound, images*] grabación *f*; [*of facts*] registro *m*
CPD ▸ **the Recording Angel** *el ángel que registra las acciones buenas o malas de los hombres* ▸ **recording artist** artista *mf* dedicado/a a la grabación ▸ **recording density** densidad *f* de grabación ▸ **recording equipment** equipo *m* de grabación ▸ **the recording industry** la industria discográfica ▸ **recording session** sesión *f* de grabación ▸ **recording studio** estudio *m* de grabación ▸ **recording tape** cinta *f* de grabación, cinta *f* magnetofónica ▸ **recording van** camión *m* de grabación

recordist [rɪ'kɔːdɪst] N (*Cine, TV*) sonista *mf*

recount [rɪ'kaʊnt] VT contar, relatar

re-count ['riːkaʊnt] N [*of votes etc*] recuento *m* • **to have a re-count** someter los votos a un segundo escrutinio
VT [riː'kaʊnt] volver a contar

recoup [rɪ'kuːp] VT recobrar, recuperar

recourse [rɪ'kɔːs] N • **to have ~ to** recurrir a

recover [rɪ'kʌvəʳ] VT **1** (= *regain*) [+ *faculty*] recuperar, recobrar (*frm*) • **he fought to ~ his balance** luchó por recuperar *or* (*frm*) recobrar el equilibrio • **to ~ consciousness** recobrar el conocimiento • **~ing himself with a masterly effort he resumed his narrative** reponiéndose *or* sobreponiéndose con un esfuerzo sobrehumano, terminó su narración; ▹ **composure**
2 (= *retrieve*) [+ *bodies, wreck*] rescatar; [+ *debt*] cobrar; [+ *stolen property, costs, losses, investment*] recuperar; (*Jur*) [+ *money*] recuperar; [+ *property*] reivindicar, recuperar; (*Comput*) [+ *data*] recobrar, recuperar • **to ~ damages from sb** ser indemnizado por daños y perjuicios por algn
3 (= *reclaim*) [+ *materials*] recuperar
VI **1** (*after accident, illness*) reponerse, recuperarse, restablecerse (**from** de); (*after shock, blow*) sobreponerse, reponerse (**from** de) • **he ~ed from being 4-2 down to reach the semi-finals** se recuperó tras ir perdiendo 4-2 y llegó a las semifinales
2 (*Econ*) [*currency*] recuperarse, restablecerse; [*shares, stock market*] volver a subir; [*economy*] reactivarse

re-cover ['riː'kʌvəʳ] VT [+ *chair, sofa*] tapizar de nuevo; [+ *book*] forrar de nuevo

recoverable [rɪ'kʌvərəbl] ADJ recuperable; (*at law*) reivindicable

recovering [rɪ'kʌvərɪŋ] ADJ [*alcoholic, addict*] en vías de rehabilitación

recovery [rɪ'kʌvərɪ] N **1** (*after accident, illness*) recuperación *f*, restablecimiento *m* (*frm*); (*after shock, blow*) recuperación *f*; (*Econ*) [*of currency*] recuperación *f*; (*Econ*) reactivación *f* • **her chances of ~ are not good** no tiene muchas posibilidades de recuperarse • **to be in ~** (*from addiction*) estar en rehabilitación • **to make a ~** recuperarse, restablecerse • **she has made a full ~** se ha recuperado *or* restablecido completamente • **prices made a slow ~** las cotizaciones tardaron en restablecerse • **to be on the road** *or* **way to ~** (*Med*) estar camino de la recuperación; (*Econ*) estar camino de la reactivación
2 (= *retrieval*) [*of bodies, wreck*] rescate *m*; [*of debt*] cobro *m*; [*of stolen property*] recuperación *f*; (*Jur*) [*of money*] recuperación *f*; [*of property*] reivindicación *f*, recuperación *f*; (*Comput*) [*of data*] recuperación *f* • **an action for ~ of damages** una demanda por daños y perjuicios
3 (= *reclaiming*) [*of materials*] recuperación *f*
CPD ▸ **recovery operation** (*after crash, explosion etc*) operación *f* de rescate ▸ **recovery position** (*Med*) posición *f* de decúbito supino • **to put sb in the ~ position** poner a algn en posición de decúbito supino ▸ **recovery room** (*Med*) sala *f* de posoperatorio ▸ **recovery service** (*Aut*) servicio *m* de rescate ▸ **recovery ship, recovery vessel** nave *f* de salvamento ▸ **recovery time** tiempo *m* de recuperación ▸ **recovery vehicle** (*Aut*) grúa *f* ▸ **recovery ward** (*Med*) sala *f* de posoperatorio

recreant†† ['rekrɪənt] N cobarde *mf*
ADJ cobarde

re-create ['riːkrɪ'eɪt] VT (= *create again*) recrear, volver a crear

recreation [,rekrɪ'eɪʃən] N **1** (= *amusement*) (*also Scol*) recreo *m*
2 (= *reconstruction*) reconstrucción *f*; (*Theat*) recreación *f*; (= *representation*) representación *f*
CPD ▸ **recreation area** área *f* recreativa ▸ **recreation centre, recreation center** (*US*) centro *m* de recreo ▸ **recreation ground** campo *m* de deportes ▸ **recreation room** salón *m* de recreo

recreational [,rekrɪ'eɪʃənəl] ADJ recreativo
CPD ▸ **recreational drug** droga *f* recreativa ▸ **recreational facilities** facilidades *fpl* de recreo ▸ **recreational vehicle** (*US*) caravana *f* *or* rulota *f* pequeña

recreative ['rekrɪ,eɪtɪv] ADJ recreativo

recriminate [rɪ'krɪmɪneɪt] VI recriminar

recrimination [rɪ,krɪmɪ'neɪʃən] N recriminación *f*

recross ['riː'krɒs] VT, VI volver a cruzar

recrudesce [,riːkruː'des] VI (*liter*) recrudecer

recrudescence [,riːkruː'desns] N (*liter*) recrudescencia *f*, recrudecimiento *m*

recrudescent [,riːkruː'desnt] ADJ (*liter*) recrudescente

recruit [rɪ'kruːt] N (*Mil*) recluta *mf*; (*to organization*) adquisición *f* • **Janet is our latest ~** (*hum*) Janet es nuestra última adquisición *or* nuestro último fichaje* • **new ~** (*Mil*) nuevo recluta; (*to organization*) nuevo/a *m/f* • **raw ~** (*Mil*) quinto *m*, soldado *mf* raso; (*fig*) novato/a *m/f*
VT **1** (= *enlist*) (*Mil*) reclutar; [+ *staff*] contratar; [+ *new members*] buscar • **he was ~ed into the army at 18** lo reclutaron con 18 años • **they ~ed me to help** me reclutaron para que ayudara
2 (= *obtain, seek out*) [+ *help*] reclutar; [+ *talent*] buscar
VI (*Mil*) alistar reclutas; (*Comm*) reclutar gente • **I am ~ing for staff now** ahora estoy reclutando personal para la plantilla

recruiter [rɪ'kruːtəʳ] N reclutador(a) *m/f*

recruiting [rɪ'kruːtɪŋ] N reclutamiento *m*
CPD ▸ **recruiting office** caja *f* de reclutas ▸ **recruiting officer** oficial *mf* de reclutamiento

recruitment [rɪ'kruːtmənt] N (*Mil*) reclutamiento *m*; [*of staff*] contratación *f*
CPD ▸ **recruitment agency** agencia *f* de colocaciones

rec't ABBR = **receipt**

rectal ['rektəl] ADJ rectal

rectangle ['rek,tæŋgl] N rectángulo *m*

rectangular [rek'tæŋgjʊləʳ] ADJ rectangular

rectifiable ['rektɪfaɪəbl] ADJ rectificable

rectification [,rektɪfɪ'keɪʃən] N rectificación *f*

rectifier ['rektɪfaɪəʳ] N (*Elec, Chem etc*) rectificador *m*; (*Mech*) rectificadora *f*

rectify ['rektɪfaɪ] VT rectificar

rectilinear [,rektɪ'lɪnɪəʳ] ADJ rectilíneo

rectitude ['rektɪtjuːd] N (*frm*) rectitud *f*

rector ['rektəʳ] N (*Rel*) párroco *m*; (*Univ etc*) rector(a) *m/f*

rectorship ['rektəʃɪp] N (*Scot*) (*Scol*) parroquia *f*; (*Univ*) ≈ rectorado *m*

rectory ['rektərɪ] N casa *f* del párroco

rectum ['rektəm] N (PL: **rectums, recta**) (*Anat*) recto *m*

recumbent [rɪ'kʌmbənt] ADJ [*figure, statue*] yacente; [*person*] recostado, acostado

recuperate [rɪ'kuːpəreɪt] VI recuperarse,

reponerse, restablecerse • **to ~ after an illness** recuperarse *or* reponerse de una enfermedad • **to be recuperating from sth** estar convaleciente de algo
(VT) [*+ losses*] recuperar
recuperation [rɪˌkuːpə'reɪʃən] (N) (*Med*) recuperación *f*, restablecimiento *m*; [*of losses*] recuperación *f*
recuperative [rɪ'kuːpərətɪv] (ADJ) [*powers, medicine*] recuperativo
recur [rɪ'kɜːʳ] (VI) (*= happen again*) [*pain, illness*] producirse de nuevo; [*event, mistake, theme*] repetirse; [*difficulty, opportunity*] volver a presentarse • **the idea ~s constantly in his work** la idea se repite constantemente en su obra
recurrence [rɪ'kʌrəns] (N) [*of event, mistake, theme*] repetición *f*; (*Med*) reaparición *f*, recurrencia *f*
recurrent [rɪ'kʌrənt] (ADJ) [*problem, feature*] repetido, constante; (*Anat, Med*) recurrente • **it is a ~ theme** es un tema constante *or* que se repite a menudo
recurring [rɪ'kɜːrɪŋ] (ADJ) (*Math*) • **3.3333 ~** 3,3 periódico puro
(CPD) ▸ **recurring decimal** decimal *m* periódico
recursive [rɪ'kɜːsɪv] (ADJ) recursivo
recursively [rɪ'kɜːsɪvlɪ] (ADV) recursivamente
recusant ['rekjʊzənt] (ADJ) recusante
(N) recusante *mf*
recyclable [ˌriː'saɪkləbl] (ADJ) reciclable
recycle [ˌriː'saɪkl] (VT) reciclar
(CPD) ▸ **recycle bin** (*Comput*) papelera *f* (de reciclaje); (*for bottles, tins, papers*) (*large*) contenedor *m* de reciclaje; (*in kitchen*) cubo *m* de reciclaje (de basuras)
recycling [ˌriː'saɪklɪŋ] (N) reciclado *m*, reciclaje *m*
(CPD) ▸ **recycling bin** (*for bottles, tins, papers*) (*large*) contenedor *m* de reciclaje; (*in kitchen*) cubo *m* de reciclaje (de basuras) ▸ **recycling plant** planta *f* de reciclado *or* reciclaje
red [red] (ADJ) (COMPAR: **redder**, SUPERL: **reddest**) **1** (*gen*) [*apple, sweater, lips, pen*] rojo, colorado; [*flower, sky*] rojo; [*wine*] tinto • **the traffic lights are red** el semáforo está en rojo • **his eyes were red** (*from crying*) tenía los ojos rojos • **the red evening sun** el sol rojizo del atardecer • **bright red** rojo fuerte *or* chillón • **dark red** rojo oscuro • **deep red** rojo intenso • **to have red hair** ser pelirrojo • IDIOMS: • **it's like a red rag to a bull** es lo que más le saca de quicio • **to roll out the red carpet for sb** recibir a algn por todo lo alto *or* a bombo y platillo • **to give sb the red carpet treatment** tratar a algn a cuerpo de rey • **not a red cent** (*US**) ni una gorda* • PROVERB: • **red sky at night, shepherd's delight, red sky in the morning, shepherd's warning** el cielo rojo por la noche es señal de buen tiempo, el cielo rojo por la mañana de mal tiempo; ▹ **paint**
2 (*= flushed*) [*face, cheeks*] (*with shame*) sonrojado; (*with anger*) rojo; (*with embarrassment*) rojo, colorado • **to be red in the face** (*from anger, exertion, heat*) estar rojo, tener la cara encendida (*liter*); (*from embarrassment*) estar rojo *or* colorado, tener la cara encendida (*liter*) • **to go red in the face** (*from anger, exertion, heat*) ponerse rojo *or* colorado; (*with embarrassment*) ponerse colorado; (*with shame*) sonrojarse • IDIOM: • **to go** *or* **turn as red as a beetroot** ponerse como un tomate
3 (*Pol**) (*pej*) rojo • PROVERB: • **better red than dead** más vale el vivir bajo los comunistas que morir luchando contra ellos
(N) **1** (*= colour*) (color *m*) rojo *m* • **to be dressed in red** ir vestido de rojo • **it was underlined in red** estaba subrayado en rojo • IDIOMS: • **to be in the red** [*account, firm*] estar en números rojos • **I'm £100 in the red** tengo un descubierto de 100 libras en el banco • **to go into** *or* **get into the red** contraer deudas • **to get out of the red** liquidar las deudas • **to see red** sulfurarse, salirse de sus casillas • **this makes me see red** esto me saca de quicio
2 (*Pol**) (*pej*) (*= person*) rojo/a *m/f* • IDIOM: • **reds under the bed*** la amenaza comunista
3 (*= red wine*) tinto *m*
(CPD) ▸ **red admiral** vanesa *f* roja ▸ **red alert** alerta *f* roja • **to be on red alert** estar en alerta roja ▸ **the Red Army** el Ejército Rojo ▸ **red blood cell** glóbulo *m* rojo ▸ **red cabbage** col *f* lombarda, lombarda *f* ▸ **red card** (*Ftbl*) tarjeta *f* roja • **to show sb the red card** sacar a algn la tarjeta roja; (*fig*) (*= reprimand*) llamar al orden a algn, amonestar a algn; (*= force to resign*) destituir a algn ▸ **red cedar** cedro *m* rojo ▸ **red cell** glóbulo *m* rojo ▸ **red channel** (*at customs*) canal *m* rojo (*en aduana*) ▸ **Red China** China *f* comunista ▸ **red corpuscle** corpúsculo *m* rojo ▸ **Red Crescent** Media Luna *f* Roja ▸ **Red Cross** Cruz *f* Roja ▸ **red deer** ciervo *m* común ▸ **red ensign** (*Naut*) enseña *f* roja ▸ **red eye** (*Phot*) ojo *m* rojo; ▹ **redeye** ▸ **red flag** (*on beach etc*) bandera *f* roja ▸ **red giant** (*Astron*) gigante *m* rojo ▸ **red heat** calor *m* rojo ▸ **red herring** (*fig*) pista *f* falsa, despiste *m* ▸ **Red Indian** piel roja *mf* ▸ **red lead** minio *m* ▸ **red light** (*Aut*) luz *f* roja • **to go through a red light** saltarse un semáforo en rojo; ▹ **red-light district** ▸ **red meat** carne *f* roja ▸ **red mullet** salmonete *m* ▸ **red pepper** (*= capsicum*) pimiento *m* rojo, pimiento *m* morrón, pimentón *m* rojo (*LAm*); (*= powder*) pimienta *f* de cayena ▸ **Red Riding Hood** (*also* **Little Red Riding Hood**) Caperucita *f* Roja ▸ **red salmon** salmón *m* rojo ▸ **Red Sea** mar *m* Rojo ▸ **red sea bream** besugo *m* (rojo) ▸ **red setter** setter *m* irlandés ▸ **red snapper** pargo *m* ▸ **red spider mite** arador *m* *or* ácaro *m* de la sarna ▸ **Red Square** (*in Moscow*) plaza *f* Roja ▸ **red squirrel** ardilla *f* roja ▸ **red tape** trámites *mpl*, papeleo *m* ▸ **red wine** vino *m* tinto, tinto *m*
redact [rɪ'dækt] (VT) redactar
redaction [rɪ'dækʃən] (N) redacción *f*
red-berried ['red'berɪd] (ADJ) con bayas rojas
red-blooded ['red'blʌdɪd] (ADJ) (*fig*) viril
redbreast ['redbrest] (N) (*= bird*) petirrojo *m* • **robin ~** petirrojo *m*
redbrick ['redbrɪk] (ADJ) [*university*] *construido en el siglo XIX y fuera de Londres*; [*building*] de ladrillo

> **REDBRICK UNIVERSITY**
> El término **redbrick university** se aplica a las universidades británicas construidas en los grandes centros urbanos industriales como Birmingham, Liverpool o Manchester a finales del siglo XIX o principios del XX. Deben su nombre a que sus edificios son normalmente de ladrillo, a diferencia de las universidades tradicionales de Oxford y Cambridge, cuyos edificios suelen ser de piedra.

redcap ['redkæp] (N) **1** (*Brit*) (*Mil**) policía *mf* militar
2 (*US*) (*Rail*) mozo *m* de estación
red-card [red'kɑːd] (VT) (*Sport*) expulsar, mostrar la tarjeta roja a
redcoat ['redkəʊt] (N) (*Hist*) *soldado inglés del siglo XVIII etc*
redcurrant ['red'kʌrənt] (N) (*= fruit*) grosella *f* roja; (*= bush*) grosellero *m* rojo
redden ['redn] (VT) enrojecer, teñir de rojo
(VI) **1** [*sky, leaves*] enrojecerse, ponerse rojo
2 [*person*] (*= blush*) ponerse colorado, ruborizarse; (*with anger*) ponerse rojo *or* colorado
reddish ['redɪʃ] (ADJ) [*colour, hair*] rojizo
redecorate ['riː'dekəreɪt] (VT) [*+ room, house*] redecorar, renovar el decorado de; (*with paint*) pintar de nuevo; (*with wallpaper*) volver a empapelar
redecoration [riːˌdekə'reɪʃən] (N) renovación *f*
redeem [rɪ'diːm] (VT) (*Rel*) [*+ sinner*] redimir; (*= buy back*) [*+ pawned goods*] desempeñar; (*Econ*) [*+ debt, mortgage*] amortizar; (*= fulfil*) [*+ promise, obligation*] cumplir; (*= compensate for*) [*+ fault*] expiar • **to ~ o.s.** redimirse
redeemable [rɪ'diːməbl] (ADJ) (*Comm*) reembolsable; (*Econ*) amortizable
Redeemer [rɪ'diːməʳ] (N) (*Rel*) Redentor *m*
redeeming [rɪ'diːmɪŋ] (ADJ) • **I see no ~ feature in it** no le encuentro ninguna cosa buena *or* ningún punto favorable • **~ virtue** virtud *f* compensadora
redefine [ˌriːdɪ'faɪn] (VT) redefinir
redeliver [ˌriːdɪ'lɪvəʳ] (VT) entregar de nuevo
redemption [rɪ'dempʃən] (N) (*Rel*) redención *f*; (*Econ*) amortización *f* • **to be beyond** *or* **past ~** (*fig*) no tener remedio
(CPD) ▸ **redemption price** precio *m* de retroventa ▸ **redemption value** valor *m* de rescate
redemptive [rɪ'demptɪv] (ADJ) redentor
redeploy ['riːdɪ'plɔɪ] (VT) [*+ troops, forces*] cambiar de destino; [*+ resources*] disponer de otro modo, reorganizar; [*+ workers, staff*] (*at existing location*) redistribuir, adscribir; (*to new location*) cambiar de oficina/sucursal *etc*
redeployment ['riːdɪ'plɔɪmənt] (N) (*= rearrangement*) disposición *f* nueva; (*= redistribution*) redistribución *f*; (*Mil*) cambio *m* de destino
redesign [ˌriːdɪ'zaɪn] (VT) rediseñar
redevelop [ˌriːdɪ'veləp] (VT) [*+ land, site*] reurbanizar; [*+ building, property*] remodelar
redevelopment [ˌriːdɪ'veləpmənt] (N) [*of land, site*] reurbanización *f*; [*of building, property*] remodelación *f*
redeye* ['redˌaɪ] (N) (*esp US*) (*= night flight*) (*also* **redeye flight**) vuelo *m* de noche
red-eyed ['red'aɪd] (ADJ) con los ojos enrojecidos
red-faced ['red'feɪst] (ADJ) (*lit*) con la cara roja; (*fig*) (*= ashamed*) ruborizado, avergonzado; (*with anger*) con la cara encendida *or* colorada *or* roja (*de ira*)
red-haired ['red'hɛəd] (ADJ) pelirrojo
red-handed ['red'hændɪd] (ADJ) • IDIOM: • **to catch sb red-handed** pillar *or* coger *or* (*LAm*) agarrar a algn con las manos en la masa
redhead ['redhed] (N) pelirrojo/a *m/f*
red-headed ['red'hedɪd] (ADJ) pelirrojo
red-hot ['red'hɒt] (ADJ) **1** (*lit*) [*iron, poker*] candente
2* (*fig*) **a** (*= up to the moment*) [*news, information*] de última hora
b (*= very sharp*) [*cardplayer, tennis player etc*] de primera categoría
c (*= very popular*) muy de moda
redial [riː'daɪəl] (VT) volver a marcar
(VI) volver a marcar el número
(N) • **automatic ~** marcación *f* automática
(CPD) ▸ **redial button** tecla *f* de repetición de llamada ▸ **redial facility** función *f* de repetición de llamada
redid [ˌriː'dɪd] (PT) *of* **redo**
redirect ['riːdaɪ'rekt] (VT) [*+ letter*] remitir; [*+ energies*] emplear de otro modo; [*+ traffic*]

desviar, dirigir por otra ruta
rediscover ['ri:dɪs'kʌvəʳ] VT redescubrir, volver a descubrir
rediscovery ['ri:dɪs'kʌvərɪ] N redescubrimiento *m*
redistribute ['ri:dɪs'trɪbju:t] VT distribuir de nuevo, volver a distribuir
redistribution ['ri:ˌdɪstrɪ'bju:ʃən] N redistribución *f*
red-letter ['red'letəʳ] ADJ • **red-letter day** (*fig*) (= *memorable day*) día *m* señalado • **red-letter version** (*of Bible*) *edición de la Biblia con la palabra de Jesucristo impresa en rojo*
red-light district [ˌred'laɪtdɪstrɪkt] N zona *f* de tolerancia, barrio *m* chino (*Sp*)
redlining ['redlaɪnɪŋ] N (*US*) *negativa a conceder préstamos en áreas de alto riesgo*
redneck ['rednek] N (*US*) campesino *m* blanco de los estados del Sur
redness ['rednɪs] N [*of skin, hair*] rojez *f*
redo ['ri:'du:] (PT: **redid**, PP: **redone**) VT rehacer, volver a hacer
redolence ['redəʊləns] N fragancia *f*, perfume *m*
redolent ['redəʊlənt] ADJ • ~ **of** oliente *or* con fragancia a • **to be ~ of** (*fig*) recordar, hacer pensar en
redone [ˌri:'dʌn] PP *of* **redo**
redouble [ri:'dʌbl] VT **1** (= *intensify*) [+ *activity, effort*] redoblar, intensificar
2 (*Bridge*) redoblar
VI **1** (= *intensify*) redoblarse, intensificarse
2 (*Bridge*) redoblar
redoubt [rɪ'daʊt] N reducto *m* • **the last ~ of** el último reducto de
redoubtable [rɪ'daʊtəbl] ADJ temible
redound [rɪ'daʊnd] VI • **to ~ upon sb** repercutir sobre algn • **to ~ to sb's credit** redundar en beneficio de algn
redraft ['ri:'drɑ:ft] VT redactar de nuevo
redraw ['ri:'drɔ:] (PT: **redrew**, PP: **redrawn**) VT [+ *picture*] volver a dibujar; [+ *map, plan*] volver a trazar
redress [rɪ'dres] N (= *compensation*) compensación *f*, indemnización *f*; (*for offence*) reparación *f*; (= *satisfaction*) desagravio *m* • **to seek ~ for** solicitar compensación por • **in such a case you have no ~** en tal caso usted no tiene derecho a compensación
VT (= *compensate for*) reparar, indemnizar; [+ *offence*] reparar; [+ *fault*] remediar • **to ~ the balance** equilibrar la balanza
redshank ['redʃæŋk] N archibebe *m*
redskin*† ['redskɪn] N piel roja *m*
redstart ['redstɑ:t] N colirrojo *m* real
red-top ['redtɒp] N (*Brit*) (= *tabloid newspaper*) tabloide *m*
reduce [rɪ'dju:s] VT **1** (= *decrease*) [+ *number, costs, expenditure, inflation*] reducir; [+ *price*] rebajar; (*Ind*) [+ *output*] reducir, recortar; [+ *speed, heat, visibility*] disminuir; [+ *temperature*] bajar; [+ *stress, tension*] reducir, disminuir; [+ *pain*] aliviar • **it ~s the risk of heart disease (by 20%)** disminuye el riesgo de enfermedades cardíacas (en un 20%) • **"reduce speed now"** "disminuya la velocidad"
2 (= *cut price of*) [+ *goods*] rebajar
3 (= *make smaller*) [+ *drawing*] reducir; (*Med*) [+ *swelling*] bajar; (*Culin*) [+ *sauce*] reducir
4 (= *bring to specified state*) • **to ~ sb to despair** llevar a algn a la desesperación • **to ~ sb to tears** hacer llorar a algn • **to be ~d to penury** estar sumido en la miseria • **to ~ sth to ashes/rubble** reducir algo a cenizas/escombros • **to ~ sb to silence** hacer callar a algn • **we were ~d to begging on the streets** nos vimos obligados a mendigar por las calles; ▷ **minimum**
5 (= *capture, subjugate*) tomar, conquistar
6 (*Mil*) (= *demote*) degradar • **to ~ sb to the ranks** degradar a algn a soldado raso
7 (= *simplify*) reducir • **to ~ an argument to its simplest form** reducir un argumento a su esencia
8 (*Math*) [+ *equation, expression*] reducir
9 (*Chem*) reducir
VI **1** (= *decrease*) reducirse, disminuir
2 (*Culin*) espesarse
3 (= *slim*) adelgazar
reduced [rɪ'dju:st] ADJ **1** (= *lower*) [*numbers, cost, expenditure*] reducido; [*price*] reducido, rebajado • **at a ~ rate** con una tarifa reducida *or* rebajada, con rebaja *or* descuento • **non-smokers have a ~ risk of heart disease** los no fumadores tienen menos riesgo de contraer enfermedades cardíacas • **I had to get used to living on a ~ income** me tuve que acostumbrar a vivir con pocos ingresos • **"reduced to clear"** "rebajas por liquidación"
2 (= *smaller*) [*size*] reducido • **French troops will have a ~ role in the area** las tropas francesas desempeñarán un papel poco importante en la zona • **on a ~ scale** a escala reducida
3 (= *poorer*) • **to be living in ~ circumstances** (*frm, hum*) pasar necesidades *or* estrecheces
reducer [rɪ'dju:səʳ] N (*Phot, Elec*) reductor *m*
reducible [rɪ'dju:səbl] ADJ reducible
reduction [rɪ'dʌkʃən] N **1** (*in size, number, costs, expenditure*) reducción *f* • **a 15% ~ in costs** una reducción del 15% por ciento en los costes • **there has been no ~ in demand** no ha disminuido la demanda • **we have had to make ~s in the budget** hemos tenido que recortar el presupuesto
2 (*in price*) rebaja *f* • **a 50% ~** una rebaja del 50%
3 (*Mil*) (*in rank*) degradación *f*
4 (= *simplification*) reducción *f*
5 (*Phot*) copia *f* reducida
6 (*Math*) reducción *f*
7 (*Chem*) reducción *f*
8 (= *capture, subjugation*) toma *f*, conquista *f*
reductionism [rɪ'dʌkʃənɪzəm] N reduccionismo *m*
reductive [rɪ'dʌktɪv] ADJ reduccionista
redundance [rɪ'dʌndəns] N redundancia *f*
redundancy [rɪ'dʌndənsɪ] (*Brit*) N **1** (= *state of being superfluous*) exceso *m*, superfluidad *f*
2 (*Brit*) [*of worker*] despido *m*; (*among workers*) desempleo *m*; ▸ **compulsory, voluntary**
CPD ▸ **redundancy compensation, redundancy payment** indemnización *f* por desempleo
redundant [rɪ'dʌndənt] ADJ **1** (= *superfluous*) superfluo • **to be ~** estar de más
2 (*Gram*) redundante
3 (*Brit*) [*worker*] sin trabajo, parado • **to be made ~** ser despedido (*por reducción de plantilla*), quedar sin trabajo • **he was made ~ in 1999** lo despidieron en 1999, quedó sin trabajo en 1999 • **automation may make some workers ~** la automatización puede hacer que varios obreros pierdan sus puestos
reduplicate [rɪ'dju:plɪkeɪt] VT reduplicar
reduplication [rɪˌdju:plɪ'keɪʃən] N reduplicación *f*
reduplicative [rɪ'dju:plɪkətɪv] ADJ reduplicativo
redux ['rɪ:dʌks] ADJ [*film, work*] reeditado
redwing ['redwɪŋ] N malvís *m*
redwood ['redwʊd] N (= *tree*) secoya *f*
redye ['ri:'daɪ] VT reteñir, volver a teñir
re-echo ['ri:'ekəʊ] VT repetir, resonar con
VI [*sound*] resonar; (*fig*) repercutirse
reed [ri:d] N **1** (*Bot*) junco *m*, caña *f* • **broken ~** (*fig*) persona *f* quemada
2 (*Mus*) (*in mouthpiece*) lengüeta *f*
3 (= *pipe*) caramillo *m*
CPD ▸ **reed bed** juncal *m*, cañaveral *m* ▸ **reed bunting** verderón *m* común ▸ **reed instrument** instrumento *m* de lengüeta ▸ **reed mace** anea *f*, espadaña *f* ▸ **reed stop** registro *m* de lengüetas ▸ **reed warbler** carricero *m* común
re-edit [ri:'edɪt] VT reeditar
re-educate ['ri:'edjʊkeɪt] VT reeducar
re-education ['ri:ˌedjʊ'keɪʃən] N reeducación *f*
reedy ['ri:dɪ] ADJ (COMPAR: **reedier**, SUPERL: **reediest**) **1** [*place*] lleno de cañas, cubierto de juncos
2 [*voice, tone, instrument*] aflautado
reef¹ [ri:f] N (*Geog*) arrecife *m*
reef² [ri:f] N (= *sail*) rizo *m* • **to let out a ~** largar rizos; (*fig*) aflojar el cinturón • **to take in a ~** tomar rizos; (*fig*) apretarse el cinturón
VT arrizar
CPD ▸ **reef knot** nudo *m* de rizo
reefer¹ ['ri:fəʳ] N (= *jacket*) chaquetón *m*
reefer²* ['ri:fəʳ] N (= *joint*) porro* *m*
reek [ri:k] N tufo *m*, hedor *m* (**of a**)
VI **1** (= *smell*) • **to ~ of sth** apestar a algo • **he comes home simply ~ing** (*of drink*) vuelve a casa que apesta a alcohol • **this ~s of treachery** (*fig*) esto huele a traición • **she ~s with affectation** (*fig*) su afectación es inaguantable
2 (= *smoke*) humear, vahear
reeky ['ri:kɪ] ADJ (= *smelly*) apestoso
reel [ri:l] N **1** (*for cable, hose*) rollo *m*; (*for tape recorder, in fishing*) carrete *m*; (*for thread*) carrete *m*, bobina *f*; (*Phot*) (*for small camera*) carrete *m*, rollo *m*; [*of cine film*] cinta *f*; ▷ **cotton, inertia-reel**
2 (*Mus*) (= *dance*) *baile escocés*
VT (= *wind*) [+ *thread, fishing line, film, tape*] enrollar, devanar
VI **1** (= *sway, stagger*) tambalear(se) • **he was sent ~ing by a blow to the head** un golpe en la cabeza hizo que se tambaleara • **he was ~ing about drunkenly** caminaba tambaleándose, caminaba haciendo eses* • **he lost his balance and ~ed backwards** perdió el equilibrio y se fue para atrás
2 (= *be shaken*) • **our troops were ~ing under the enemy bombardment** nuestras tropas sufrían el impacto del bombardeo enemigo • **I'm still ~ing from the shock** todavía no me he recuperado del susto
3 (= *spin*) [*mind, head, brain*] dar vueltas • **the room ~ed before her eyes** la habitación le daba vueltas
▸ **reel in** VT + ADV [+ *fish*] sacar del agua (enrollando el sedal); [+ *line*] recoger, ir cobrando
▸ **reel off** VT + ADV [+ *statistics, list of names*] recitar de un tirón
re-elect ['ri:ɪ'lekt] VT reelegir
re-election ['ri:ɪ'lekʃən] N reelección *f*
re-eligible ['ri:'elɪdʒəbl] ADJ reelegible
reel-to-reel ['ri:ltə'ri:l] ADJ • **reel-to-reel tape-recorder** grabadora *f* de carrete
re-embark [ˌri:ɪm'bɑ:k] VT, VI reembarcar
re-embarkation ['ri:ˌembɑ:'keɪʃən] N reembarco *m*
re-emerge ['ri:ɪ'mɜ:dʒ] VI volver a salir
re-employ [ˌri:ɪm'plɔɪ] VT volver a emplear
re-enact ['ri:ɪ'nækt] VT **1** (*Parl*) [+ *legislation*] volver a promulgar
2 (*Theat*) volver a representar; [+ *crime, battle*] reconstruir
re-enactment [ˌri:ɪ'næktmənt] N reconstrucción *f*
re-engage ['ri:ɪn'geɪdʒ] VT contratar de nuevo

r

re-enlist [ˈriːɪnˈlɪst] VI reengancharse, alistarse de nuevo
re-enter [ˈriːˈentəʳ] VI **1** volver a entrar
2 • **to re-enter for an exam** volver a presentarse a un examen, presentarse de nuevo a un examen
VT (= *return to*) [+ *room, building, country*] volver a entrar en, entrar de nuevo en; [+ *hospital*] reingresar en, ingresar de nuevo en; [+ *data*] reintroducir en • **to re-enter the Earth's atmosphere** volver a penetrar *or* reentrar en la atmósfera terrestre
re-entry [ˈriːˈentrɪ] N (*to hospital*) reingreso *m*; (*into politics etc*) [*of spacecraft*] reentrada *f* • **the house has been bolted to prevent re-entry** han atrancado la puerta para evitar que se vuelva a entrar en ella
CPD ▸ **re-entry visa** visado *m* de retorno
re-equip [ˈriːɪˈkwɪp] VT equipar de nuevo (**with** con)
re-erect [ˌriːɪˈrekt] VT reerigir
re-establish [ˈriːɪsˈtæblɪʃ] VT restablecer
re-establishment [ˈriːɪsˈtæblɪʃmənt] N restablecimiento *m*
reeve[1] [riːv] VT (*Naut*) [+ *rope, cable*] (= *fasten*) asegurar (con cabo); (= *thread*) pasar por un ojal
reeve[2] [riːv] N (*Hist*) juez *mf* local
re-examination [ˈriːɪgˌzæmɪˈneɪʃən] N reexaminación *f*
re-examine [ˈriːɪgˈzæmɪn] VT [+ *facts, evidence*] reexaminar, repasar; (*Jur*) [+ *witness*] volver a interrogar
re-export [ˈriːˈekspɔːt] VT reexportar
N reexportación *f*
ref[1]* [ref] N (*Sport*) árbitro/a *m/f*
ref[2] PREP ABBR **1** (= **with reference to**) respecto de
2 (*in letter-head*) (= **reference**) ref.
reface [ˈriːˈfeɪs] VT revestir de nuevo (**with** de)
refashion [ˈriːˈfæʃən] VT formar de nuevo, rehacer
refectory [rɪˈfektərɪ] N refectorio *m*
refer [rɪˈfɜːʳ] VT **1** (= *send, direct*) remitir • **to ~ sth to sb** remitir algo a algn • **I have to ~ it to my boss** tengo que remitírselo a mi jefe, tengo que consultarlo con mi jefe • **to ~ a dispute to arbitration** someter *or* remitir una disputa al arbitraje • **the case has been ~red to the Supreme Court** han diferido el caso al Tribunal Supremo • **the decision has been ~red to us** la decisión se ha dejado a nuestro juicio • **to ~ sb to sth/sb: I ~red him to the manager** lo envié a que viera al gerente • **the doctor ~red me to a specialist** el médico me mandó a un especialista • **the reader is ~red to page 15** remito al lector a la página 15 • **"refer to drawer"** (*on cheque*) "devolver al librador"
2 (= *ascribe*) atribuir • **he ~s his mistake to tiredness** el error lo achaca a su cansancio, atribuye el error a su cansancio • **he ~s the painting to the 14th century** atribuye el cuadro al siglo XIV
3 (*Brit*) (*Univ*) [+ *student*] suspender
4 (*Med*) • **~red pain** dolor *m* reflejo
VI • **to ~ to 1** (= *relate to*) referirse a • **this ~s to you all** esto se refiere a todos ustedes, esto va para todos ustedes • **the rules do not ~ to special cases** las normas no son aplicables a los casos especiales
2 (= *allude to*) referirse a • **I am not ~ring to you** no me estoy refiriendo a ti • **I ~ to your letter of 1st May** con relación a su carta con fecha del uno de mayo
3 (= *mention*) mencionar • **he never ~s to that evening** nunca menciona aquella noche
4 (= *consult*) consultar • **she had to ~ to her notes** tuvo que consultar sus apuntes • **please ~ to section three** véase la sección tres
5 (= *describe*) • **he ~red to her as his assistant** cuando se refería a ella la llamaba su ayudante • **this kind of art is often ~red to as "minimal art"** este tipo de arte a menudo se denomina "arte minimalista"
▸ **refer back** VT + ADV [+ *matter, decision*] volver a remitir; [+ *person*] volver a mandar • **the case was ~red back to the Court of Appeal** el caso se volvió a remitir al Tribunal de Apelación • **the pharmacist may ~ you back to your doctor** puede que el farmacéutico te vuelva a mandar al médico de cabecera
VI + ADV • **to ~ back to sth: you should ~ back to your notes** deberías volver a consultar tus apuntes • **~ back to the table in chapter seven** véase de nuevo el recuadro del capítulo siete
referable [rɪˈfɜːrəbl] ADJ • **~ to** (= *related to*) relacionado con; (= *attributable to*) atribuible a; (= *classifiable as*) que se puede clasificar como
referee [ˌrefəˈriː] N **1** (*in dispute, Sport*) árbitro/a *m/f*
2 (*Brit*) (*for application, post*) avalista *mf*, persona *f* que avala • **Pérez has named you as a ~** Pérez dice que usted está dispuesto a avalarle
3 [*of learned paper*] evaluador(a) *m/f*
VT **1** [+ *game*] dirigir, arbitrar en
2 [+ *learned paper*] evaluar
VI arbitrar, hacer de árbitro
refereeing [ˌrefəˈriːɪŋ] N (*Sport*) arbitraje *m* • **~ is his vocation** arbitrar es su vocación
reference [ˈrefrəns] N **1** (= *act of referring*) consulta *f* • **an index is included for ease of ~** *or* **for easy ~** se incluye un índice para facilitar la consulta • **it was agreed without ~ to me** se acordó sin consultarme • **for future ~, please note that …** por si importa en el futuro, obsérvese que … • **I'll keep it for future ~** lo guardo por si hace falta consultarlo en el futuro
2 (= *allusion*) alusión *f*, referencia *f* • **I can't find any ~ to him in the files** no encuentro nada que haga referencia a él en los archivos • **he does this by ~ to the same principles** hace esto tomando como referencia los mismos principios • **without ~ to any particular case** sin referirse a ningún caso (en) concreto • **with particular ~ to …** con referencia especial a … • **he spoke without any ~ to you** habló sin mencionarte para nada • **to make ~ to sth/sb** hacer referencia a algo/algn, hacer alusión a algo/algn; ▹ **passing**
3 (= *identifying source*) (*in text*) referencia *f*, remisión *f*; (= *citation*) referencia *f*; (*Comm*) (*in letter, catalogue*) (*also* **reference number**) número *m* de referencia; (*on map*) indicación *f*; (*Typ*) (*also* **reference mark**) llamada *f* • **"~ XYZ2"** "número de referencia: XYZ2" • **to look up a ~** (*in book*) buscar una referencia; (*on map*) seguir las coordenadas; ▹ **cross-reference, grid**
4 (= *testimonial*) (= *document*) referencia *f*, informe *m*; (= *person*) garante *mf*, fiador(a) *m/f* • **she has good ~s** tiene buenas referencias, tiene buenos informes • **the firm offered to give her a ~** la empresa se ofreció a darle referencias *or* informes • **to take up (sb's) ~s** pedir referencias *or* informes (de algn); ▹ **character, credit**
5 (= *remit*) ▹ **frame, point, term**
VT **1** (= *provide references for*) [+ *book*] dotar de referencias a
2 (= *refer to*) [+ *source*] citar
CPD [*material, tool, room*] de consulta ▸ **reference book** libro *m* de consulta ▸ **reference group** (*Sociol*) grupo *m* de estudio ▸ **reference library** biblioteca *f* de consulta ▸ **reference mark** llamada *f* ▸ **reference number** número *m* de referencia ▸ **reference point** punto *m* de referencia ▸ **reference price** (*Agr*) precio *m* de referencia
referendum [ˌrefəˈrendəm] N (PL: **referendums, referenda** [ˌrefəˈrendə]) referéndum *m* • **to call a ~** convocar un referéndum • **to hold a ~** celebrar un referéndum • **to hold a ~ on sth** someter algo a referéndum
referential [ˌrefəˈrenʃəl] ADJ referencial
referral [rɪˈfɜːrəl] N **1** (*Med, Psych*) • **ask your GP for a ~ to a clinical psychologist** pídale a su médico que le envíe a un psicólogo clínico • **letter of ~** volante *m* médico
2 (*to higher authority*) remisión *f*
3 (*Jur*) [*of case*] remisión *f*
reffing* [ˈrefɪŋ] N = **refereeing**
refill [ˈriːfɪl] N recambio *m*; (*for pencil*) mina *f* • **would you like a ~?** ¿te pongo más vino *etc*?, ¿otro vaso?
VT [ˌriːˈfɪl] [+ *lighter, pen*] recargar; [+ *glass*] volver a llenar
refillable [ˌriːˈfɪləbl] ADJ recargable
refinance [riːˈfaɪnæns] VT refinanciar
refinancing [ˌriːfaɪˈnænsɪŋ] N refinanciación *f*, refinanciamento *m* (*LAm*)
refine [rɪˈfaɪn] VT **1** [+ *sugar, oil*] refinar; [+ *fats*] clarificar; [+ *metal*] refinar, afinar
2 (= *improve*) [+ *design, technique, machine*] perfeccionar; [+ *methods*] refinar; [+ *style*] limar, purificar; [+ *behaviour, style of writing*] pulir, refinar
VI • **to ~ upon sth** (= *improve*) refinar algo, mejorar algo; (= *discuss*) discutir algo con mucha sutileza
refined [rɪˈfaɪnd] ADJ **1** (= *purified*) [*sugar, flour*] refinado
2 (= *sophisticated*) [*clothes, manners, sense of humour*] fino, refinado
3 (= *subtle, polished*) [*style of writing*] elegante, pulido
refinement [rɪˈfaɪnmənt] N **1** [*of person, language*] refinamiento *m*; [*of manners*] educación *f*, finura *f*; [*of style*] elegancia *f*, urbanidad *f* • **a person of some ~** una persona fina
2 (= *improvement*) mejora *f*; (*in machine*) perfeccionamiento *m*
3 (= *subtle detail*) [*of language*] sutileza *f* • **that is a ~ of cruelty** eso es ser más cruel todavía • **with every possible ~ of cruelty** con las formas más refinadas de la crueldad
refiner [rɪˈfaɪnəʳ] N refinador *m*
refinery [rɪˈfaɪnərɪ] N refinería *f*
refit [ˈriːˈfɪt] N (*gen*) reparación *f*, compostura *f*; (*Naut*) reparación *f*
VT (*gen*) reparar, componer; (*Naut*) reparar
VI (*Naut*) repararse
refitment [ˈriːˈfɪtmənt] N (*gen*) reparación *f*, compostura *f*; (*Naut*) reparación *f*
refitting [ˈriːˈfɪtɪŋ] N = **refitment**
reflate [ˌriːˈfleɪt] VT [+ *economy*] reflacionar
reflation [riːˈfleɪʃən] N reflación *f*
reflationary [riːˈfleɪʃnərɪ] ADJ reflacionario
reflect [rɪˈflekt] VT **1** [+ *light, image*] reflejar • **plants ~ed in the water** plantas reflejadas en el agua • **I saw him/myself ~ed in the mirror** lo vi/me vi reflejado en el espejo
2 [+ *situation, emotion, opinion*] reflejar, hacerse eco de • **the difficulties are ~ed in his report** las dificultades se reflejan en su informe, el informe se hace eco de las

dificultades • the speech ~s credit on him el discurso le hace honor • to bask in ~ed glory disfrutar de la gloria ajena
3 (= say) reflexionar • "the war has educated many of us," he ~ed —la guerra nos ha concienciado a muchos —reflexionó • he ~ed that life had not treated him so badly pensándolo bien, la vida no le había tratado tan mal
VI 1 • to ~ off sth [light, heat] reflejarse en algo; [sound] salir rebotado de algo
2 (= think, meditate) reflexionar, pensar • ~ before you act reflexione antes de obrar • if we but ~ a moment sí solo reflexionamos un instante • to ~ on sth reflexionar or meditar sobre algo
3 • to ~ on or upon sth/sb: it ~s on all of us eso tiende a perjudicarnos or desprestigiarnos a todos • it ~s on her reputation eso pone en tela de juicio su reputación • to ~ well on or upon sb hacer honor a algn • to ~ badly on or upon sb decir poco en favor de algn • it will ~ badly on the university eso dará una imagen poco favorable de la universidad

reflection [rɪ'flekʃən] N 1 [of light] (= act) reflexión f; (= image) reflejo m • the ~ of the light in the mirror el reflejo de la luz en el espejo • a pale ~ of former glories un ligero reflejo de glorias pasadas • to see one's ~ in a shop window verse reflejado en un escaparate
2 (= thought) meditación f, reflexión f • on ~ pensándolo bien • without due ~ sin pensarlo lo suficiente • mature ~ suggests that ... una meditación más profunda indica que ...
3 (= aspersion, doubt) tacha f, descrédito m • this is no ~ on your work esto no significa crítica alguna a su trabajo • this is no ~ on your honesty esto no dice nada en contra de su honradez, esto no es ningún reproche a su honradez • to cast ~s on sb reprochar a algn
4 (= idea) pensamiento m, idea f • "Reflections on Ortega" "Meditaciones sobre Ortega"

reflective [rɪ'flektɪv] ADJ 1 [surface] brillante, lustroso
2 (= meditative) pensativo, reflexivo
3 • to be ~ of reflejar

reflectively [rɪ'flektɪvlɪ] ADV pensativamente • he said ~ dijo pensativo • she looked at me ~ me miró pensativa

reflectiveness [rɪ'flektɪvnɪs] N 1 [of surface] brillo m
2 (= thoughtfulness) carácter m pensativo

reflector [rɪ'flektəʳ] N 1 (Aut) (also rear reflector) reflector m inv
2 (= telescope) reflector m

reflex ['riːfleks] ADJ reflejo; (Math) [angle] de reflexión • ~ camera (Phot) cámara f reflex
N reflejo m

reflexion [rɪ'flekʃən] N (Brit) = reflection

reflexive [rɪ'fleksɪv] ADJ (Ling) [verb, pronoun] reflexivo
N (Ling) (= pronoun) pronombre m reflexivo; (= verb) verbo m reflexivo

reflexively [rɪ'fleksɪvlɪ] ADV reflexivamente

reflexologist [ˌriːfleks'ɒlədʒɪst] N reflexólogo/a m/f

reflexology [ˌriːflek'sɒlədʒɪ] N reflexología f, reflejoterapia f

refloat ['riː'fləʊt] VT [+ ship] poner a flote

reflux ['riːflʌks] N reflujo m

reforest ['riː'fɒrɪst] VT repoblar de árboles

reforestation ['riːˌfɒrɪs'teɪʃən] N repoblación f forestal

reform [rɪ'fɔːm] N reforma f; ▷ land
VT [+ law, institution, person] reformar; [+ conduct] corregir
VI [person] reformarse
CPD ▸ Reform Jew judío/a m/f reformista ▸ Reform Judaism judaísmo m reformista ▸ reform law ley f de reforma ▸ reform movement movimiento m de reforma ▸ reform school (US) reformatorio m

re-form ['riː'fɔːm] VT volver a formar, reconstituir
VI [organization, party] volver a formarse, reconstituirse; (Mil) rehacerse

reformat ['riː'fɔːmæt] VT reformatear

reformation [ˌrefə'meɪʃən] N reformación f • the Reformation (Rel) la Reforma

reformatory [rɪ'fɔːmətərɪ] N (Brit) reformatorio m

reformed [rɪ'fɔːmd] ADJ reformado • he's a ~ character these days últimamente se ha reformado

reformer [rɪ'fɔːməʳ] N reformista mf, reformador(a) m/f

reformism [rɪ'fɔːmɪzəm] N reformismo m

reformist [rɪ'fɔːmɪst] ADJ reformista
N reformista mf

refound [ˌriː'faʊnd] VT [+ monastery etc] refundar

refract [rɪ'frækt] VT refractar

refracting [rɪ'fræktɪŋ] ADJ • ~ telescope telescopio m de refracción, telescopio m refractor

refraction [rɪ'frækʃən] N refracción f

refractive [rɪ'fræktɪv] ADJ refractivo

refractor [rɪ'fræktəʳ] N refractor m

refractoriness [rɪ'fræktərɪnɪs] N obstinación f

refractory [rɪ'fræktərɪ] ADJ 1 (= obstinate) obstinado
2 (Tech) refractario

refrain[1] [rɪ'freɪn] N (Mus) estribillo m • his constant ~ is ... siempre está con la misma canción ...

refrain[2] [rɪ'freɪn] VI • to ~ from sth/from doing sth abstenerse de algo/de hacer algo • I couldn't ~ from laughing no pude contener la risa

refresh [rɪ'freʃ] VT 1 [drink, sleep, bath] refrescar • to ~ sb's memory refrescar la memoria a algn • to ~ o.s. refrescarse, tomar un refresco
2 (Comput) [+ screen, page] actualizar

refreshed [rɪ'freʃt] ADJ [person] lleno de energía • to feel ~ sentirse lleno de energía

refresher [rɪ'freʃəʳ] N 1 (= drink) refresco m
2 (Jur) honorarios mpl suplementarios
CPD ▸ refresher course curso m de actualización

refreshing [rɪ'freʃɪŋ] ADJ 1 (lit) [drink] refrescante
2 (fig) • it's ~ to hear some new ideas da gusto escuchar nuevas ideas • it's a ~ change to find this es alentador encontrar esto

refreshingly [rɪ'freʃɪŋlɪ] ADV • she's ~ honest da gusto ver lo honesta que es • his style of writing is ~ different tiene un estilo distinto, lo cual resulta muy grato

refreshment [rɪ'freʃmənt] N (= food) piscolabis m; (= drink) (non-alcoholic) refresco m; (alcoholic) copa f; refreshments refrigerio msing, comida fsing liviana • "~s will be served" "se servirá un refrigerio" • to take some ~ tomar algo, comer or beber etc
CPD ▸ refreshment bar chiringuito m de refrescos ▸ refreshment room (Rail) cantina f, comedor m ▸ refreshment stall, refreshment stand puesto m de refrescos

refried beans [ˌriːfraɪd'biːnz] NPL frijoles mpl refritos

refrigerant [rɪ'frɪdʒərənt] N refrigerante m

refrigerate [rɪ'frɪdʒəreɪt] VT refrigerar

refrigerated [rɪ'frɪdʒəreɪtɪd] ADJ [food, room, storage] refrigerado • ~ display cabinet vitrina f refrigerada
CPD ▸ refrigerated lorry (Brit), refrigerated truck (esp US) camión m refrigerado

refrigeration [rɪˌfrɪdʒə'reɪʃən] N refrigeración f

refrigerator [rɪ'frɪdʒəreɪtəʳ] N frigorífico m, nevera f, refrigeradora f (LAm)
CPD ▸ refrigerator lorry camión m frigorífico ▸ refrigerator ship buque m frigorífico

refuel ['riː'fjʊəl] VI [tank, plane] repostar
VT llenar de combustible; [+ speculation] renovar, volver a despertar

refuelling, **refueling** (US) ['riː'fjʊəlɪŋ] N reabastecimiento m de combustible
CPD ▸ refuelling stop escala f para repostar

refuge ['refjuːdʒ] N (= shelter) refugio m; (= shelter for climbers) albergue m; (= hut) albergue m; (fig) amparo m, abrigo m • God is my ~ Dios es mi amparo • to seek ~ buscar refugio, buscar dónde guarecerse • to take ~ ponerse al abrigo, guarecerse • to take ~ in sth refugiarse en algo; (fig) recurrir a algo

refugee [ˌrefjʊ'dʒiː] N refugiado/a m/f • ~ from justice prófugo/a m/f de la justicia
CPD ▸ refugee camp campamento m para refugiados ▸ refugee status estatus m inv de refugiado

refulgence [rɪ'fʌldʒəns] N refulgencia f

refulgent [rɪ'fʌldʒənt] ADJ refulgente

refund ['riːfʌnd] N (= act) devolución f; (= amount) reembolso m
VT [rɪ'fʌnd] devolver, reembolsar

refundable [rɪ'fʌndəbl] ADJ reembolsable

refurbish ['riː'fɜːbɪʃ] VT [+ building, paintwork] restaurar; [+ literary work] refundir

refurbishment [riː'fɜːbɪʃmənt] N [of building, room] renovación f
CPD [programme, project, work] de renovación

refurnish ['riː'fɜːnɪʃ] VT amueblar de nuevo

refusal [rɪ'fjuːzəl] N 1 negativa f • she brushed aside my ~s hizo caso omiso de mis negativas • he didn't take her ~ seriously no tomó en serio su negativa • he was shot for his ~ to obey orders lo mataron de un tiro por negarse a obedecer órdenes • I'm giving you/you have first ~ (on the house) le daré/tendrá prioridad en la compra (de la casa) • a flat ~ una negativa rotunda • her request met with a flat ~ su solicitud fue rechazada de plano
2 [of application] denegación f
3 (by horse) • the horse had two ~s el caballo se plantó dos veces

refuse[1] [rɪ'fjuːz] VT 1 (= decline) [+ offer, chance] rechazar, rehusar; [+ applicant] rechazar • it was an offer he couldn't ~ era una oferta que no podía rechazar or rehusar • the patient has the right to ~ treatment el paciente tiene derecho a negarse a someterse a tratamiento • he was devastated when she ~d him estaba desolado cuando ella lo rechazó • she ~d their invitation to stay to dinner rechazó or no aceptó su invitación para quedarse a cenar • he never ~s a drink nunca dice que no a una copa • to ~ to do sth [person] negarse a hacer algo • he ~d to comment after the trial se negó a or rehusó hacer comentarios después del juicio • my legs ~d to function mis piernas se negaban a funcionar

r

2 (= *not grant*) [+ *request, permission*] (*gen*) negar; (*officially*) denegar • **the police ~d permission for the march** la policía denegó el permiso *or* les negó el permiso para hacer la marcha • **to ~ sb sth** (*gen*) negar algo a algn; (*officially*) denegar algo a algn • **they were ~d permission to leave** les negaron autorización para salir • **I was ~d entry to Malawi** me denegaron la entrada a Malaui • **they can ~ her nothing** no le pueden negar nada

VI **1** [*person*] negarse • **I don't see how I can ~** no veo cómo puedo negarme

2 [*horse*] plantarse

refuse² ['refju:s] N **1** (= *rubbish*) basura *f*, desperdicios *mpl* • **garden ~** desperdicios *mpl* del jardín • **household ~** basura *f* doméstica, residuos *mpl* domésticos

2 (= *industrial waste*) desechos *mpl*, residuos *mpl*

CPD ▸ **refuse bin** cubo *m or* (*LAm*) bote *m or* tarro *m* de la basura ▸ **refuse chute** rampa *f* de desperdicios, rampa *f* de la basura ▸ **refuse collection** recogida *f* de basura ▸ **refuse collector** basurero *m* ▸ **refuse disposal** eliminación *f* de basuras ▸ **refuse disposal unit** triturador *m* de basura ▸ **refuse dump** = **refuse tip** ▸ **refuse lorry** camión *m* de la basura ▸ **refuse tip** vertedero *m*, basural *m* (*LAm*)

refusenik [rɪ'fju:znɪk] N refusenik *mf*

refutable [rɪ'fju:təbl] ADJ refutable

refutation [ˌrefjʊ'teɪʃən] N refutación *f*

refute [rɪ'fju:t] VT refutar, rebatir

reg. [redʒ] N ABBR (*Brit**) = **registration number**

ADJ ABBR = **registered**

regain [rɪ'geɪn] VT recobrar, recuperar; [+ *breath*] cobrar • **to ~ consciousness** recobrar el conocimiento, volver en sí

regal ['ri:gəl] ADJ regio, real

regale [rɪ'geɪl] VT (= *entertain*) entretener; (= *delight*) divertir • **to ~ sb on oysters** agasajar a algn con ostras • **he ~d the company with a funny story** para entretener a la compañía les contó un chiste • **to ~ o.s. on** *or* **with sth** regalarse con algo, darse el lujo de algo

regalia [rɪ'geɪlɪə] NPL (= *royal trappings*) atributos *mpl*; (*gen*) (= *insignia*) insignias *fpl*

regally ['ri:gəlɪ] ADV regiamente; (*pej*) con pompa regia

regard [rɪ'gɑ:d] N **1** (= *relation*) respecto *m*, aspecto *m* • **in** *or* **with ~ to** con respecto a • **with ~ to your letter of 25 June** con respecto a su carta del 25 de junio • **government policy with ~ to immigration** la política del gobierno con respecto a la inmigración *or* en materia de inmigración • **I was right in one ~** tenía razón en un aspecto • **in this/that ~** en este/ese aspecto, a este/ese respecto

2 (= *esteem*) estima *f*, respeto *m* • **my ~ for him** la estima *or* el respeto que le tengo • **to have a high** *or* **great ~ for sb • hold sb in high ~** tener a algn en gran estima, tener un gran concepto de algn • **out of ~ for** por respeto a; ▹ **self-regard**

3 (= *attention, consideration*) • **it should be done with a proper ~ for safety** debería hacerse prestándole la atención debida a la seguridad • **having ~ to** teniendo en cuenta • **he shows little ~ for their feelings** muestra poca consideración por sus sentimientos • **they have no ~ for human life** no tienen *or* muestran ningún respeto a la vida humana • **without ~ to/for sth: without ~ to race, creed or sex** sin considerar *or* sin tener en cuenta la raza, la religión o el sexo • **without ~ for her own safety** sin reparar en *or* tener en cuenta su propia seguridad

4 regards (*in messages*) recuerdos *mpl*, saludos *mpl* • **(give my) ~s to Yvonne** (dele) recuerdos a Yvonne, salude a Yvonne de mi parte • **(with) kind/best ~s** (*as letter ending*) saludos • **he sends his ~s** os manda recuerdos *or* saludos

5 (*liter*) (= *gaze*) mirada *f*

VT **1** (= *look at*) (*liter*) contemplar, observar; (*fig*) (= *view*) mirar • **to ~ sb with suspicion** mirar a algn con recelo

2 (= *consider*) considerar • **he is ~ed as Britain's foremost composer** se lo considera *or* está considerado el compositor más importante de Gran Bretaña • **we don't ~ it as necessary** no lo consideramos necesario, no nos parece necesario • **would you ~ yourself as a feminist?** ¿se considera usted feminista?

3 (= *esteem*) • **he was a highly ~ed scholar** era un académico muy respetado *or* de mucha reputación

4 (= *concern*) tratar, tocar • **the next item ~s the proposed merger** el siguiente punto trata *or* toca la fusión propuesta • **as ~s** en *or* por lo que respecta a, en *or* por lo que se refiere a, en cuanto a

regardful [rɪ'gɑ:dfʊl] ADJ • **~ of** atento a

regarding [rɪ'gɑ:dɪŋ] PREP con respecto a, en relación con; (*introducing sentence*) en *or* por lo que respecta a, en *or* por lo que se refiere a • **he refused to divulge any information ~ the man's whereabouts** rehusó facilitar cualquier información con respecto a *or* en relación con el paradero del hombre • **and other things ~ money** y otras cosas relativas al dinero

regardless [rɪ'gɑ:dlɪs] ADJ • **~ of** sin reparar en • **buy it ~ of the cost** cómpralo, cueste lo que cueste • **they shot them all ~ of rank** los fusilaron a todos sin miramientos a su graduación • **we did it ~ of the consequences** lo hicimos sin tener en cuenta las consecuencias

ADV a pesar de todo, pase lo que pase • **he went on ~** continuó a pesar de todo • **carry** *or* **press on ~!** ¡a seguir, sin reparar en las consecuencias!

regatta [rɪ'gætə] N regata *f*

regd ADJ ABBR **1** (*Comm*) = **registered**

2 (*Post*) = **registered**

regency ['ri:dʒənsɪ] N regencia *f*

CPD ▸ **Regency furniture** mobiliario *m* Regencia, mobiliario *m* estilo Regencia

regenerate VT [rɪ'dʒenəreɪt] regenerar

ADJ [rɪ'dʒenərɪt] regenerado

regeneration [rɪˌdʒenə'reɪʃən] N regeneración *f*

regenerative [rɪ'dʒenərətɪv] ADJ regenerador

regent ['ri:dʒənt] ADJ • **prince ~** príncipe *m* regente

N regente *mf*

reggae ['regeɪ] N (*Mus*) reggae *m*

regicide ['redʒɪsaɪd] N **1** (= *act*) regicidio *m*

2 (= *person*) regicida *mf*

régime, regime [reɪ'ʒi:m] N **1** (*Pol*) régimen *m* • **the ancien ~** el antiguo régimen • **under the Nazi ~** bajo el régimen de los nazis

2 (= *system, programme*) régimen *m*

CPD ▸ **régime change** cambio *m* de régimen

regimen ['redʒɪmən] N régimen *m*

regiment ['redʒɪmənt] N (*Mil*) regimiento *m*; (*fig*) ejército *m*, batallón *m* • **a whole ~ of mice** todo un ejército *or* batallón de ratones

VT ['redʒɪment] (*fig*) [+ *life*] reglamentar

regimental [ˌredʒɪ'mentl] ADJ (*Mil*) de regimiento; (*fig*) militar • **~ sergeant major** ≈ brigada *m* de regimiento • **with ~ precision** con precisión militar

NPL • **~s** (*Mil*) uniforme *msing*

regimentation [ˌredʒɪmen'teɪʃən] N reglamentación *f*

regimented ['redʒɪmentɪd] ADJ [*system, society, atmosphere*] reglamentado • **trees planted in ~ rows** árboles plantados en hileras perfectamente alineadas

Reginald ['redʒɪnld] N Reinaldo, Reginaldo

region ['ri:dʒən] N **1** [*of country, human body*] región *f*, zona *f* • **the densely populated coastal ~** la región *or* zona costera densamente poblada • **Asia and the Pacific ~** Asia y la región del Pacífico • **the pelvic ~** la región *or* la zona pélvica • **a pain in the ~ of my kidneys** un dolor a la altura de los riñones • **the ~s** (= *provinces*) las provincias

2 (= *field, sphere*) campo *m* • **and here we enter a ~ of moral ambiguity** y aquí entramos en un campo de ambigüedad moral

3 • **in the ~ of** (= *approximately*) aproximadamente, alrededor de • **it will cost in the ~ of £6 million** costará aproximadamente *or* alrededor de 6 millones de libras • **I would say she's in the ~ of 40** yo diría que ronda los 40, yo diría que tiene unos 40 años

regional ['ri:dʒənl] ADJ [*conflicts, autonomy, government, accent*] regional

CPD ▸ **regional authority** autoridad *f* regional ▸ **regional council** (*Scot*) consejo *m* regional ▸ **regional development** (*Brit*) (*Admin*) desarrollo *m* regional ▸ **regional development grant** subsidio *m* para el desarrollo regional ▸ **regional planning** planificación *f* regional

regionalism ['ri:dʒənəlɪzəm] N regionalismo *m*

regionalist ['ri:dʒənəlɪst] ADJ regionalista

N regionalista *mf*

regionalize ['ri:dʒənəlaɪz] VT regionalizar

register ['redʒɪstə^r] N **1** (= *list*) (*in hotel*) registro *m*; (*in school*) lista *f*; [*of members*] lista *f*, registro *m* • **the ~ of births, marriages and deaths** el registro civil • **to call** *or* **take the ~** pasar lista; ▹ **electoral, parish**

2 (*Mus*) [*of instrument, voice*] registro *m*

3 (*Ling*) registro *m* • **there's a difference of** *or* **in ~ between the two terms** existe una diferencia de registro entre los dos términos

4 (*also* **cash register**) caja *f* registradora

5 (*Tech*) (= *gauge of speed, numbers*) indicador *m*

6 (= *air vent*) rejilla *f* de ventilación

7 (*Comput*) registro *m*

VT **1** (= *record*) [+ *fact, figure*] registrar, hacer constar; [+ *birth, marriage, death*] registrar, inscribir; [+ *company, property*] registrar; [+ *car, ship*] matricular, registrar; [+ *letter*] certificar • **are you ~ed with a doctor?** ¿está inscrito en la lista de pacientes de algún médico? • **to be ~ed to vote** estar inscrito en el censo electoral • **to be ~ed blind/disabled** estar registrado como ciego/minusválido

2 (= *show*) [+ *reading*] marcar, indicar; [+ *improvement, reduction*] experimentar • **the petrol gauge was ~ing empty** el indicador de gasolina marcaba *or* indicaba que el depósito estaba vacío • **production has ~ed a big fall** la producción ha experimentado un descenso considerable

3 (= *express*) [+ *emotion*] manifestar, mostrar; [+ *protest, support*] expresar, manifestar; [+ *complaint*] presentar • **he ~ed no surprise** no manifestó *or* mostró sorpresa alguna

VI **1** (= *sign on*) (*with agency, for course or conference*) inscribirse; (*at hotel*) registrarse;

r

(*Univ*) [*student*] matricularse, inscribirse • **to ~ with a doctor** inscribirse en la lista de un médico • **to ~ as unemployed** registrarse como parado • **to ~ with the police** dar parte a la policía • **to ~ to vote** inscribirse *or* registrarse en el censo electoral
2* (= *be understood*) • **it doesn't seem to have ~ed with her** no parece haber hecho mella en ella • **when it finally ~ed** cuando por fin cayó en la cuenta
3 (= *show*) [*reading*] ser detectado; [*emotion*] manifestarse • **surprise ~ed on her face** la sorpresa se manifestó en su cara
CPD ▸ **register office** = registry office

registered [ˈredʒɪstəd] ADJ [*letter*] certificado; [*student, car*] matriculado; [*voter*] inscrito • **to be a ~ Democrat/Republican** (*US*) (*Pol*) estar inscrito como votante demócrata/republicano
CPD ▸ **registered charity** sociedad *f* benéfica legalmente constituida ▸ **registered company** sociedad *f* legalmente constituida ▸ **Registered General Nurse** (*Brit*) ≈ enfermero/a *m/f* titulado/a ▸ **registered mail** = registered post ▸ **registered nurse** (*US*) enfermero/a *m/f* titulado/a ▸ **registered office** domicilio *m* social ▸ **registered post** (*Brit*) servicio *m* de entrega con acuse de recibo ▸ **registered trademark** marca *f* registrada

registrar [ˌredʒɪsˈtrɑː] N **1** [*of births, marriages, deaths*] secretario/a *m/f* del registro civil
2 (*Univ*) secretario/a *m/f* general
3 (*Med*) interno/a *m/f*
4 [*of society*] secretario/a *m/f*
CPD ▸ **registrar's office** (*Brit*) (= *registry office*) registro *m* civil

registration [ˌredʒɪsˈtreɪʃən] N **1** (*for course, conference, of voter*) inscripción *f*; (*Univ*) [*of student*] matriculación *f*, inscripción *f*; [*of company, property, trademark, dog, gun*] registro *m*; [*of car*] matriculación *f*; [*of ship*] matriculación *f*, abanderamiento *m*
2 (= *number*) (*Aut, Naut, Univ*) matrícula *f*
CPD ▸ **registration document** (*Brit*) (*Aut*) documento *m* de matriculación ▸ **registration fee** (*Univ*) matrícula *f*; (*for agency*) cuota *f* de inscripción ▸ **registration form** formulario *m* de inscripción ▸ **registration number** (*Brit*) (*Aut*) matrícula *f* ▸ **registration tag** (*US*) (*Aut*) (placa *f* de) matrícula *f*

registry [ˈredʒɪstrɪ] N registro *m*, archivo *m*; (*Univ*) secretaría *f* general • **servants' ~** agencia *f* de colocaciones
CPD ▸ **registry office** registro *m* civil • **to get married at a ~ office** casarse por lo civil • **it was a ~ office wedding** fue una boda por lo civil

Regius [ˈriːdʒjəs] ADJ (*Brit*) (*Univ*) regio

regress VI [rɪˈgres] retroceder
N [ˈriːgres] regreso *m*

regression [rɪˈgreʃən] N regresión *f*

regressive [rɪˈgresɪv] ADJ regresivo

regret [rɪˈgret] N **1** (= *sorrow*) pena *f*, pesar *m* • **she accepted his resignation with ~** aceptó su dimisión con pena *or* pesar • **the President expressed his ~ for the deaths of civilians** el presidente expresó su pesar *or* dolor por las muertes de los civiles • **my one** *or* **only ~ is that I didn't see her before she died** lo único que siento *or* lamento es no haberla visto antes de que muriera • **I felt no ~ at giving up my work** no sentí dejar el trabajo • **much to my ~** • **to my great ~** con gran pesar mío
2 (= *remorse*) remordimiento(s) *m(pl)* • **I felt a pang of ~** me entraron remordimientos • **I have no ~s** no me arrepiento de nada
3 regrets (= *excuses*) excusas *fpl*, disculpas *fpl* • **to send one's ~s** excusarse *or* mandar sus disculpas (por no poder acudir)
VT **1** (= *apologize for, be sorry for*) [+ *death, inconvenience, error*] lamentar • **we ~ any inconvenience caused by the delay** lamentamos cualquier inconveniente que les pueda haber causado el retraso • **it is to be ~ted that he did not act sooner** lo lamentable es que no actuó antes • **the President ~s (that) he cannot see you today** el presidente lamenta *or* siente no poder verle hoy • **we ~ to inform you that …** lamentamos tener que informarle que … • **her lack of co-operation is nothing new, I ~ to say** lamento decir que su falta de cooperación no es algo nuevo • **we ~ having to do this, but it is necessary** lamentamos *or* sentimos tener que hacer esto, pero es necesario • **he ~ted what had happened** lamentó lo ocurrido
2 (= *rue*) [+ *decision*] arrepentirse de, lamentar • **you won't ~ it!** ¡no te arrepentirás!, ¡no lo lamentarás! • **he ~s saying it** se arrepiente de *or* lamenta haberlo dicho • **he was ~ting that he had asked the question** se arrepentía de *or* lamentaba haber hecho la pregunta • **I don't ~ what I did** no me arrepiento de *or* lamento lo que hice • **to live to ~ sth** arrepentirse de *or* lamentar algo más tarde

regretful [rɪˈgretfʊl] ADJ arrepentido, pesaroso • **to be ~ that …** lamentar que (+ *subjun*) • **he was most ~ about it** lo lamentó profundamente • **we are not ~ about leaving** no nos pesa tener que partir

regretfully [rɪˈgretfəlɪ] ADV (= *sadly*) con pesar • **"I'm sorry that I am unable to go", he said ~** —lamento no poder ir —dijo con pesar • **she spoke ~** habló con sentimiento • **~ I have to tell you that …** siento tener que decirles que …

regrettable [rɪˈgretəbl] ADJ lamentable • **it is ~ that** es lamentable que (+ *subjun*), es de lamentar que (+ *subjun*)

regrettably [rɪˈgretəblɪ] ADV (= *unfortunately*) desgraciadamente, lamentablemente • **there were ~ few replies** fue una lástima que hubiera tan pocas respuestas

regroup [ˈriːˈgruːp] VT reagrupar; (*Mil*) reorganizar
VI reagruparse; (*Mil*) reorganizarse

regrouping [ˈriːˈgruːpɪŋ] N reagrupación *f*

Regt. ABBR (= **Regiment**) regto

regular [ˈregjʊləʳ] ADJ **1** (= *symmetrical*) [*shape, pattern*] (*also Math*) regular • **he has ~ features** es de facciones regulares
2 (= *even*) [*surface, teeth*] uniforme, parejo (*esp LAm*)
3 (= *recurring at even intervals*) [*pulse, flights, breathing, order*] regular • **to take ~ exercise** hacer ejercicio con regularidad • **at ~ intervals** (*in time*) con regularidad; (*in space*) a intervalos regulares • **the doctor examined the baby at ~ intervals** el médico examinaba al bebé con regularidad • **the signs were placed at ~ intervals along the beach** las señales estaban situadas a intervalos regulares a lo largo de la playa • **it's important to eat ~ meals** es importante comer con regularidad • **he placed a ~ order with us** nos hizo un pedido regular • **to make ~ use of sth** usar algo con regularidad • **to be in ~ use** utilizarse de manera regular • IDIOM: • **as ~ as clockwork** como un cronómetro, como un reloj
4 (= *habitual, customary*) [*visitor, customer, reader, listener*] habitual, asiduo; [*doctor, partner*] habitual; [*action, procedure*] acostumbrado, normal • **they are ~ churchgoers** van a misa con regularidad *or* con asiduidad • **our ~ waiter** el camarero que nos sirve normalmente • **it's past his ~ bedtime** ya ha pasado su hora normal de acostarse • **on a ~ basis** con regularidad • **to be in ~ employment** tener un trabajo fijo • **the ~ staff** el personal habitual • **to have a ~ time for doing sth** tener hora fija para hacer algo, hacer algo siempre a la misma hora
5 (= *unvarying*) • **a man of ~ habits** un hombre metódico, un hombre ordenado (en sus costumbres) • **to keep ~ hours** llevar una vida ordenada
6 (= *frequent*) frecuente • **I have to make ~ trips to France** tengo que viajar a Francia con frecuencia, tengo que hacer viajes frecuentes a Francia • **to be in** *or* **to have ~ contact with sb** mantener *or* tener un contacto frecuente con algn • **it's a ~ occurrence** pasa con frecuencia, es algo frecuente
7 (*Mil*) [*soldier, army*] profesional, de carrera
8 (*Ling*) [*verb etc*] regular
9* (*as intensifier*) • **a ~ bore** un auténtico pesado • **a ~ feast** un verdadero banquete • **he's a ~ fool** es un verdadero idiota • **a ~ nuisance** un auténtico pesado
10 (*US*) (= *ordinary, normal*) normal • **I'm just a ~ guy** no soy más que un tío normal (y corriente) • **~ fries** porción *f* mediana de patatas fritas • **~ gasoline** gasolina *f* normal • **~ size** tamaño *m* normal
11* (= *not constipated*) • **to be ~** hacer de vientre con regularidad
12* (*in menstruation*) • **I'm quite ~** mi periodo es bastante regular
N **1** (= *customer*) (*in pub, bar*) cliente *mf* habitual, parroquiano/a *m/f* • **one of the ~s at the club** un asiduo del club • **he's a ~ on the programme** es un invitado habitual del programa
2 (*Mil*) militar *mf* de carrera
3 (*US*) (= *petrol*) gasolina *f* normal

regularity [ˌregjʊˈlærɪtɪ] N regularidad *f*

regularize [ˈregjʊləraɪz] VT (= *standardize*) [+ *activities, procedure*] regularizar, estandarizar; (= *make official*) [+ *situation*] formalizar, regularizar

regularly [ˈregjʊləlɪ] ADV **1** (= *at regular arranged times*) [*exercise, visit*] con regularidad; [*meet, use*] regularmente, con regularidad
2 (= *frequently*) frecuentemente, con frecuencia, a menudo • **the shop is ~ featured in fashion magazines** la tienda aparece frecuentemente *or* con frecuencia *or* a menudo en revistas de moda • **he's ~ late** llega tarde con frecuencia *or* a menudo
3 (= *at evenly spaced intervals*) a intervalos regulares • **beeches were planted ~ along the avenue** había hayas plantadas a intervalos regulares *or* cada cierta distancia a lo largo de la avenida
4 (*Ling*) • **a ~ declined noun** un sustantivo de declinación regular

regulate [ˈregjʊleɪt] VT **1** (= *control*) [+ *expenditure, prices, temperature, level, pressure*] regular • **a well-regulated life** una vida ordenada
2 (= *make rules for*) [+ *industry, products*] regular • **a new body to ~ TV advertising** un nuevo organismo que regula la publicidad que se emite por televisión; ▹ **self-regulating**
3 (*Tech*) [+ *machine, mechanism*] regular

regulation [ˌregjʊˈleɪʃən] N **1** (= *rule*) norma *f* • **fire ~s** normas *fpl* de seguridad contraincendios • **safety ~s** normas *fpl* de seguridad • **it's against (the) ~s** va contra las normas *or* el reglamento; ▹ **rule**
2 (= *control*) (*no pl*) [*of industry, products, prices,*

temperature, level, pressure] regulación *f* • **a body responsible for the ~ of independent television** un organismo regulador responsable de las cadenas de televisión independientes; ▹ **self-regulation**
3 (*Tech*) [*of machine, mechanism*] regulación *f*, reglaje *m*
CPD (= *statutory*) [*dress, size, haircut*] reglamentario ▸ **regulation time** (*Sport*) (= *normal time*) tiempo *m* reglamentario • **at the end of ~ time** al final del tiempo reglamentario

regulative [ˈregjʊlətɪv] ADJ reglamentario

regulator [ˈregjʊleɪtəʳ] N **1** (*Tech*) regulador *m*
2 (= *person, organization*) *persona u organización que regula oficialmente un sector de los negocios o la industria*

regulatory [ˈregjʊˌleɪtərɪ] ADJ regulador

Regulo® [ˈregjʊləʊ] N (*Brit*) *número del mando de temperatura de un horno a gas*

regurgitate [rɪˈgɜːdʒɪteɪt] VT regurgitar; (*fig*) repetir maquinalmente
VI regurgitar

regurgitation [rɪˌgɜːdʒɪˈteɪʃən] N regurgitación *f*; (*fig*) reproducción *f* maquinal

rehab* [ˈriːhæb] N (= **rehabilitation**) rehabilitación *f*
CPD ▸ **rehab centre** (*for drug or alcohol problems*) centro *m* de rehabilitación

rehabilitate [ˌriːəˈbɪlɪteɪt] VT [+ *offenders, drug addicts*] rehabilitar

rehabilitation [ˈriːəˌbɪlɪˈteɪʃən] N rehabilitación *f*
CPD ▸ **rehabilitation centre** centro *m* de rehabilitación

rehash [ˈriːhæʃ] N (*gen*) refrito *m*
VT [ˌriːˈhæʃ] [+ *book, speech*] hacer un refrito de; [+ *food*] recalentar

rehear [ˌriːˈhɪəʳ] VT **1** (= *hear again*) volver a oír
2 (*Jur*) volver a ver

rehearsal [rɪˈhɜːsəl] N (*Mus, Theat*) ensayo *m*; (= *enumeration*) enumeración *f*, repetición *f* • **it was just a ~ for bigger things to come** fue como un ensayo para las empresas mayores que vendrían después

rehearse [rɪˈhɜːs] VT (*Mus, Theat*) ensayar; (= *enumerate*) enumerar, repetir
VI (*Mus, Theat*) ensayar

reheat [ˌriːˈhiːt] VT recalentar

re-home [ˌriːˈhəʊm] VT [+ *animal*] encontrar una nueva casa para • **puppies are always easier to re-home** siempre es más fácil encontrar una nueva casa para los cachorros

re-homing [ˌriːˈhəʊmɪŋ] N [*of animal*] readopción *f*

rehouse [ˈriːˈhaʊz] VT [+ *family*] dar una nueva vivienda a • **200 families have been ~d** 200 familias tienen vivienda nueva ya

reification [ˌriːɪfɪˈkeɪʃən] N cosificación *f*

reify [ˈriːɪˌfaɪ] VT cosificar

reign [reɪn] N [*of king, queen*] reinado *m*; (*fig*) dominio *m* • **in** *or* **under the ~ of Queen Elizabeth II** bajo el reinado de la Reina Isabel II • **~ of terror** régimen *m* de terror • **the ~ of the miniskirt** la moda de la minifalda • **her ~ as champion came to an end** su reino *or* hegemonía como campeona terminó
VI [*king, queen*] reinar; (*fig*) (= *prevail*) predominar • **total silence ~ed** reinaba el silencio más absoluto • PROVERB: • **it is better to ~ in hell than serve in heaven** más vale ser cabeza de ratón que cola de león

reigning [ˈreɪnɪŋ] ADJ [*monarch*] reinante, actual; (*fig*) predominante, que impera • **~ champion** campeón *m* actual

reiki [ˈreɪkɪ] N reiki *m*

reimburse [ˌriːɪmˈbɜːs] VT • **to ~ sb for sth** reembolsar a algn por algo

reimbursement [ˌriːɪmˈbɜːsmənt] N reembolso *m*

reimport [ˌriːɪmˈpɔːt] VT reimportar

reimportation [ˌriːɪmpɔːˈteɪʃən] N reimportación *f*

reimpose [ˈriːɪmˈpəʊz] VT volver a imponer, reimponer

rein [reɪn] N (*usu pl*) rienda *f* • **the ~s of government** (*fig*) las riendas del gobierno • **to draw ~** detenerse, tirar de la rienda (*also fig*) • **to keep a tight ~ on sb** (*fig*) refrenar a algn • **we must keep a tight ~ on expenditure** tenemos que restringir los gastos • **to give sb free ~** (*fig*) dar rienda suelta a algn
▸ **rein back** VT + ADV refrenar
▸ **rein in** VT + ADV refrenar
VI + ADV detenerse

reincarnate [ˌriːɪnˈkɑːneɪt] VT reencarnar • **to be ~d** reencarnar, volver a encarnar

reincarnation [ˈriːɪnkɑːˈneɪʃən] N reencarnación *f*

reindeer [ˈreɪndɪəʳ] N (PL: **reindeer, reindeers**) reno *m*

reinforce [ˌriːɪnˈfɔːs] VT (*gen, fig*) reforzar; [+ *concrete*] armar

reinforced [ˌriːɪnˈfɔːst] ADJ reforzado • **~ concrete** hormigón *m* armado

reinforcement [ˌriːɪnˈfɔːsmənt] N **1** (= *act*) refuerzo *m*
2 (*Mil*) **reinforcements** refuerzos *mpl*

reinsert [ˈriːɪnˈsɜːt] VT volver a insertar *or* introducir

reinstate [ˈriːɪnˈsteɪt] VT [+ *suppressed passage*] reincorporar, incluir de nuevo (**in** a); [+ *dismissed worker*] reincorporar, volver a emplear; [+ *dismissed official*] restituir a su puesto

reinstatement [ˈriːɪnˈsteɪtmənt] N [*of suppressed passage*] reincorporación *f*, restitución *f* (**in** a); [*of dismissed worker*] reincorporación *f* al puesto; [*of dismissed official*] restitución *f* en el puesto

reinsurance [ˈriːɪnˈʃʊərəns] N reaseguro *m*

reinsure [ˈriːɪnˈʃʊəʳ] VT reasegurar

reintegrate [ˈriːˈɪntɪgreɪt] VT reintegrar; (*socially*) reinsertar (**into** en)

reintegration [ˈriːɪntɪˈgreɪʃən] N reintegración *f*; (*socially*) reinserción *f*

reinter [ˈriːɪnˈtɜːʳ] VT enterrar de nuevo

reintroduce [ˌriːɪntrəˈdjuːs] VT [+ *bill, scheme, plant, animal etc*] reintroducir, volver a introducir

reintroduction [ˌriːɪntrəˈdʌkʃən] N reintroducción *f*

reinvent [ˌriːɪnˈvent] VT **1** • IDIOM: • **to ~ the wheel** reinventar la rueda
2 • **to ~ o.s.** reinventarse

reinvention [ˌriːɪnˈvenʃən] N reinvención *f*

reinvest [ˈriːɪnˈvest] VT reinvertir, volver a invertir

reinvestment [ˈriːɪnˈvestmənt] N reinversión *f*

reinvigorate [ˈriːɪnˈvɪgəreɪt] VT vigorizar, infundir nuevo vigor a • **to feel ~d** sentirse con nuevas fuerzas, sentirse vigorizado

reissue [ˈriːˈɪʃjuː] VT [+ *stamp*] volver a emitir; [+ *recording*] reeditar; [+ *film*] reestrenar; [+ *book*] [*publisher*] reimprimir, reeditar; [*library*] renovar
N **1** (= *act*) [*of stamp*] reemisión *f*; [*of recording*] reedición *f*; [*of film*] reestreno *m*; [*of book*] reimpresión *f*, reedición *f*
2 (= *stamp*) nueva emisión *f*; (= *recording*) reedición *f*; (= *film*) reestreno *m*; (= *book*) reimpresión *f*, reedición *f*

reiterate [riːˈɪtəreɪt] VT [+ *statement*] reiterar, repetir • **I must ~ that …** quiero recalcar que …

reiteration [riːɪtəˈreɪʃən] N reiteración *f*, repetición *f*

reiterative [riːˈɪtərətɪv] ADJ reiterativo

reject [rɪˈdʒekt] VT **1** (= *refuse, turn down*) [+ *application*] (*for job*) rechazar; (*for asylum, citizenship*) denegar, rechazar; [+ *candidate, offer, manuscript, sb's advances*] rechazar; [+ *bad coin, damaged goods*] rechazar, no aceptar; [+ *plea*] ignorar, hacer caso omiso de
2 (= *dismiss*) [+ *suggestion, possibility, solution*] descartar, rechazar; [+ *motion, plan, proposal*] rechazar; [+ *argument*] rechazar, no aceptar; [+ *accusation*] negar • **the proposal was ~ed by a narrow margin** la propuesta fue rechazada por un escaso margen • **she ~ed accusations that …** negó las acusaciones de que …
3 (= *disown*) [+ *person*] rechazar • **to feel ~ed** (*emotionally*) sentirse rechazado; (*socially*) sentirse marginado, sentirse rechazado
4 (*Med*) [+ *food, tissue, new organ*] [*body*] rechazar
N [ˈriːdʒekt] **1** (= *person*) • **society's ~s** los marginados de la sociedad
2 (= *unwanted thing*) desecho *m*
3 (*Comm*) (= *product*) artículo *m* defectuoso
CPD [ˈriːdʒekt] (*Comm, Ind*) [*goods*] defectuoso ▸ **reject shop** tienda *f* de objetos con tara

rejection [rɪˈdʒekʃən] N (*gen*) rechazo *m*; [*of help*] denegación *f* • **to meet with a ~** sufrir una repulsa • **the novel has already had three ~s** ya han rechazado la novela tres veces
CPD ▸ **rejection slip** (*Publishing*) nota *f* de rechazo

rejig [riːˈdʒɪg], **rejigger*** [riːˈdʒɪgəʳ] VT [+ *schedule, programme*] reajustar

rejoice [rɪˈdʒɔɪs] VI **1** (= *be happy*) alegrarse, regocijarse (*liter*) (**at, about de**) • **let us not ~ too soon** no echemos las campanas al vuelo demasiado pronto, conviene no alegrarse demasiado pronto
2 (*hum, iro*) • **he ~s in the name of Marmaduke** luce el nombre de Marmaduke
VT alegrar, regocijar (*liter*) • **to ~ that …** alegrarse de que (+ *subjun*)

rejoicing [rɪˈdʒɔɪsɪŋ] N **1** (*general, public*) fiestas *fpl* • **the ~ lasted far into the night** continuaron las fiestas hasta una hora avanzada
2 rejoicings (= *festivities*) regocijo *msing*, júbilo *msing*

rejoin¹ [ˈriːˈdʒɔɪn] VT (= *join again*) reincorporarse a
VI reincorporarse

rejoin² [rɪˈdʒɔɪn] VT (= *retort*) replicar

rejoinder [rɪˈdʒɔɪndəʳ] N (= *retort*) réplica *f* • **as a ~ to …** como contestación a …

rejuvenate [rɪˈdʒuːvɪneɪt] VT rejuvenecer

rejuvenating [rɪˈdʒuːvɪneɪtɪŋ] ADJ [*effect*] rejuvenecedor

rejuvenation [rɪˌdʒuːvɪˈneɪʃən] N rejuvenecimiento *m*

rekindle [ˈriːˈkɪndl] VT **1** [+ *fire*] volver a encender
2 (*fig*) [+ *enthusiasm, hatred*] reanimar, reavivar

relapse [rɪˈlæps] N (*Med*) recaída *f* • **to have** *or* **suffer a ~** sufrir una recaída
VI **1** (*Med*) recaer
2 (= *revert*) • **to ~ into sth: he ~d into his old ways** volvió a las andadas • **he ~d into his usual state of depression** volvió a sumirse en su habitual estado de depresión • **she had ~d into silence** había vuelto a sumirse en el silencio • **he ~d into a coma** volvió a entrar en coma

Relate [rɪ'leɪt] N (*Brit*) *organización benéfica que proporciona un servicio de asesoramiento y ayuda confidencial a parejas*

relate [rɪ'leɪt] VT **1** (= *tell*) [+ *story*] contar, relatar; [+ *conversation*] relatar, referir • **she ~d details of the meeting to her boss** le relató *or* refirió a su jefe detalles de la reunión • **history ~s that he landed here in AD 470** la historia cuenta *or* relata que desembarcó aquí en el año 470 AD • **sad to ~** aunque sea triste decirlo • **strange to ~** aunque parezca mentira, por extraño que parezca
2 (= *establish relation between*) • **to ~ sth to sth** relacionar algo con algo • **they ~ what they read to their own experiences** relacionan lo que leen con sus propias experiencias
VI **1** (= *communicate*) relacionarse, comunicarse • **how you ~ depends on the kind of person you are** cómo te relacionas *or* te comunicas depende del tipo de persona que eres
2 • **to ~ to (sth/sb) a** (= *form a relationship with*) • **to ~ to sb** relacionarse con algn • **he is unable to ~ to other people** no es capaz de relacionarse con otras personas
b (= *understand, identify with*) • **to ~ to sth/sb** identificarse con algo/algn • **I can ~ to that*** yo eso lo entiendo*, yo me identifico con eso • **women ~ more to this than men** las mujeres comprenden esto mejor que los hombres • **it's important for children to have brothers and sisters they can ~ to** es importante que los niños tengan hermanos y hermanas con los que puedan identificarse
c (= *connect with*) • **to ~ to sth** relacionarse con algo • **the way that words in a sentence ~ to each other** la manera en la que las palabras de una frase se relacionan las unas con las otras
d (= *appertain to*) • **to ~ to sth** referirse a algo, estar relacionado con algo, tener que ver con algo • **most of the enquiries ~ to debt** la mayoría de las preguntas se refieren a deudas *or* tienen que ver con deudas • **this ~s to what I said yesterday** esto se refiere a *or* está relacionado con lo que dije ayer;
▹ **relating**

related [rɪ'leɪtɪd] ADJ **1** (= *connected*) [*subject*] relacionado, afín; [*language*] afín; [*issue, problem, offence*] relacionado • **this murder is not ~ to the other** este asesinato no está relacionado con el otro • **pay rises are ~ to performance** los aumentos de sueldo guardan relación con el rendimiento • **the two events are not ~** los dos sucesos no guardan relación
2 (= *attached by family*) **a** [*people*] • **they are ~** son parientes, están emparentados • **are you two ~?** ¿sois familia?, ¿sois parientes? • **we are closely/distantly ~** somos parientes cercanos/lejanos • **are you ~ to the prisoner?** ¿es usted pariente del prisionero? • **the two women aren't ~ to each other** las dos mujeres no están emparentadas • **to be ~ to sb by** *or* **through marriage** ser pariente político de algn
b [*animals, plants*] • **termites are closely ~ to cockroaches** las termitas son de la misma familia que las cucarachas

-related [rɪ'leɪtɪd] ADJ (*ending in compounds*) • **football-related hooliganism** gamberrismo *m* relacionado con el fútbol

relating [rɪ'leɪtɪŋ] VB • **~ to** (*prep*) relativo a, referente a, relacionado con • **documents ~ to nuclear weapons** documentos relativos a *or* referentes a *or* relacionados con las armas nucleares

relation [rɪ'leɪʃən] N **1** (= *relationship*) relación *f* (**to, with** con) • **the ~ between A and B** la relación entre A y B • **to bear little/no ~ to sth** tener poco/no tener nada que ver con algo • **it bears no ~ to the facts** no tiene que ver con los hechos • **to bear a certain ~ to …** guardar cierta relación con … • **to have little/no ~ to sth** tener poco/no tener nada que ver con algo • **the story has little ~ to historical fact** la versión tiene poco que ver con los hechos históricos • **in ~ to** (= *compared to*) en relación con, con relación a; (= *in connection with*) en lo que se refiere a • **Proust in ~ to the French novel** Proust en relación con la novela francesa • **doubts that parents may have in ~ to their children's education** dudas que los padres pudieran tener en lo que se refiere a la educación de sus hijos
2 (= *relative*) pariente *mf*, familiar *mf* • **friends and ~s** amigos *mpl* y familiares *mpl* • **all my ~s came** vinieron todos mis parientes, vino toda mi familia • **close ~** pariente *mf* cercano/a • **this grape is a close ~ to the Gamay** esta uva es de la misma familia que la uva Gamay • **distant ~** pariente *mf* lejano/a • **she's no ~** no es parienta mía • **what ~ is she to you?** ¿qué parentesco tiene contigo?;
▹ **blood, poor**
3 (= *contact*) **relations** relaciones *fpl* • **good ~s** buenas relaciones *fpl* • **~s are rather strained** las relaciones están algo tirantes • **to break off ~s with sb** romper (relaciones) con algn • **we have broken off ~s with Ruritania** hemos roto las relaciones con Ruritania • **we have business ~s with them** tenemos relaciones comerciales con ellos • **diplomatic ~s** relaciones *fpl* diplomáticas • **to enter into ~s with sb** establecer relaciones con algn • **to establish ~s with sb** establecer relaciones con algn • **international ~s** relaciones *fpl* internacionales • **to have sexual ~s with sb** tener relaciones sexuales con algn;
▹ **industrial, public, race²**
4 (= *narration*) relato *m*, relación *f*, narración *f*

relational [rɪ'leɪʃənl] ADJ relacional

relationship [rɪ'leɪʃənʃɪp] N **1** (*between persons*) (*gen*) relación *f*; (*sexual*) relación *f*, relaciones *fpl* • **the mother-child ~** la relación madre-hijo • **our ~ lasted five years** nuestras relaciones continuaron durante cinco años • **they have a beautiful ~** (*US*) tienen una relación de amistad muy bonita • **a business ~** una relación comercial • **to have a ~ with sb** (*gen*) tener relación con algn; (*sexual*) tener relaciones *or* una relación con algn; ▹ **love-hate**
2 (*between things*) relación *f* • **the ~ of A to B** • **the ~ between A and B** la relación entre A y B • **to see a ~ between two events** ver una relación entre dos sucesos
3 (*between countries*) relación *f* • **Britain's special ~ with the USA** la especial relación entre Gran Bretaña y EE. UU.
4 (= *kinship*) parentesco *m* • **what is your ~ to the prisoner?** ¿qué parentesco hay entre usted y el acusado?

relative ['relətɪv] ADJ **1** (= *comparative*) [*safety, peace, comfort, ease*] relativo • **her ~ lack of experience** su relativa falta de experiencia • **he is a ~ newcomer** es relativamente nuevo • **it's all ~** todo es relativo • **in ~ terms** relativamente • **petrol consumption is ~ to speed** el consumo de gasolina está en relación con la velocidad • **there is a shortage of labour ~ to demand** hay escasez de trabajadores en relación con la demanda
2 (= *respective*) • **the ~ merits of the two systems** los méritos de cada uno de los dos sistemas
3 (= *relevant*) • **~ to** relativo a, concerniente a • **the documents ~ to the problem** la documentación relativa *or* concerniente al problema
4 (*Ling*) relativo • **~ clause** oración *f* subordinada relativa, oración *f* (subordinada) de relativo • **~ pronoun** pronombre *m* relativo
5 (*Mus*) relativo
N pariente *mf*, familiar *mf* • **friends and ~s** amigos *mpl* y familiares • **a close/distant ~** un pariente cercano/lejano

relatively ['relətɪvlɪ] ADV [*few, small, slow*] relativamente • **~ speaking** relativamente • **the tests are ~ easy to carry out** las pruebas se pueden llevar a cabo con relativa facilidad

relativism ['relətɪvɪzəm] N relativismo *m*

relativist ['relətɪvɪst] N relativista *mf*

relativistic [,relətɪv'ɪstɪk] ADJ relativista

relativity [,relə'tɪvɪtɪ] N relatividad *f*

relativize ['relətɪvaɪz] VT relativizar

relaunch ['riː'lɔːntʃ] VT [+ *plan, career*] relanzar

relaunching ['riː'lɔːntʃɪŋ] N relanzamiento *m*

relax [rɪ'læks] VT [+ *person, body, part of body*] relajar; [+ *discipline, rules, controls*] relajar; [+ *standards*] dejar que bajen • **to ~ one's muscles** relajar los músculos • **to ~ one's grip** *or* **hold on sth** dejar de agarrarse de *or* a algo tan apretadamente, soltar algo; (*fig*) ejercer menor control sobre algo
VI **1** [*person*] (= *rest, lose inhibitions*) relajarse; (= *calm down*) relajarse, tranquilizarse; (= *amuse oneself*) esparcirse, expansionarse • **I like to ~ with a book** me gusta relajarme leyendo • **~! everything's fine** ¡tranquilízate! todo está bien • **we ~ed in the sun of Majorca** nos relajamos bajo el sol de Mallorca • **I find it difficult to ~ with her** me resulta difícil estar relajado cuando estoy con ella
2 [*person, body, muscles*] relajarse • **his face ~ed into a smile** relajó la cara y sonrió • **we must not ~ in our efforts** es preciso no cejar en nuestros esfuerzos

relaxant [rɪ'læksənt] N (= *drug*) relajante *m*

relaxation [,riːlæk'seɪʃən] N **1** (= *loosening*) [*of discipline*] relajación *f*, relajamiento *m*
2 (= *rest*) descanso *m*, relajación *f* • **to get some ~** esparcirse, expansionarse • **to seek ~ in painting** esparcirse dedicándose a la pintura
3 (= *amusement*) recreo *m*, distracción *f* • **a favourite ~ of the wealthy** un pasatiempo favorito de los ricos

relaxed [rɪ'lækst] ADJ (*gen*) relajado • **in a ~ atmosphere** en un clima de distensión • **he always seems so ~** siempre parece tan sosegado • **try to be more ~** procura ser más tranquilo

relaxing [rɪ'læksɪŋ] ADJ relajante

relay ['riːleɪ] N **1** [*of workmen*] turno *m*; [*of horses*] posta *f* • **to work in ~s** trabajar por turnos, ir relevándose en el trabajo
2 (*Sport*) (*also* **relay race**) carrera *f* de relevos • **the 400 metres ~** los 400 metros relevos
3 (*Tech*) relé *m*
4 (*Rad, TV*) repetidor *m*
VT **1** (*Rad, TV*) [+ *concert, football match*] retransmitir
2 (= *pass on*) transmitir, pasar • **to ~ a message to sb** transmitir *or* pasar un mensaje a algn
CPD ▸ **relay station** (*Elec*) estación *f* repetidora

re-lay ['riː'leɪ] VT [+ *carpet*] volver a colocar; [+ *cable, rail*] volver a tender

release [rɪ'liːs] N **1** (= *liberation*) [*of prisoner, hostage*] liberación *f*, puesta *f* en libertad; [*of*

r

convict] excarcelación *f*, puesta *f* en libertad • **his ~ came through on Monday** se aprobó su excarcelación el lunes, la orden de su puesta en libertad llegó el lunes • **on his ~ from prison he ...** al salir de la cárcel ... • **complications have delayed his ~ from hospital** ciertas complicaciones han impedido que se le dé de alta todavía; ▹ **day**
2 (*fig*) (= *relief*) alivio *m* • **death came as a merciful ~** la muerte fue una bendición *or* un gran alivio
3 (= *issue*) [*of film*] estreno *m*; [*of record, video*] puesta *f* en venta; [*of book*] puesta *f* en venta *or* circulación; [*of news*] publicación *f* • **to be on general ~** exhibirse en todos los cines
4 (= *record, book, film, video*) • **their new ~ is called ...** su nuevo disco se llama ... • **the pick of this month's video ~s** las mejores novedades en vídeo *or* (*LAm*) video de este mes • **new ~s** (= *records*) novedades *fpl* discográficas; (= *films*) nuevas producciones *fpl*; (= *books*) nuevas publicaciones *fpl*; ▹ **press**
5 (= *making available*) [*of documents*] publicación *f*; [*of funds*] cesión *f*
6 (= *emission*) [*of gas, smoke*] escape *m*, emisión *f*; [*of hormones*] secreción *f* • **a sudden ~ of creative energy** un estallido de energía creadora
7 (*Tech, Phot*) (= *catch*) disparador *m*; ▹ **shutter**
8 (*Jur*) [*of right, property*] cesión *f*
VT **1** (= *set free*) [+ *prisoner, hostage*] poner en libertad, liberar; [+ *convict*] excarcelar, poner en libertad; [+ *patient*] dar de alta; [+ *victim*] (*from wreckage*) liberar; [+ *animal*] soltar, dejar en libertad; [+ *person*] (*from obligation*) eximir • **she was ~d from hospital after treatment** le dieron de alta del hospital después de un tratamiento • **they ~d him to go to a new post** permitieron que se fuera a ocupar un nuevo puesto • **to ~ sb from a debt** eximir a algn de una deuda, condonar una deuda a algn (*frm*) • **she ~d him from all his vows** lo eximió de cumplir todas sus promesas • **the bird was ~d into the wild** el pájaro fue devuelto a su hábitat natural; ▹ **bail**
2 (= *issue*) [+ *film*] estrenar; [+ *record, video*] sacar, poner a la venta; [+ *book*] publicar; [+ *news, report, information, statement*] hacer público, dar a conocer • **the police have ~d the names of the victims** la policía ha hecho públicos *or* dado a conocer los nombres de las víctimas
3 (= *make available*) [+ *documents*] facilitar; [+ *funds*] facilitar, ceder
4 (= *emit*) [+ *gas, smoke, heat, energy*] despedir, emitir; [+ *hormones*] secretar, segregar
5 (= *let go*) [+ *sb's hand, arm*] soltar; (*Tech*) [+ *spring, clasp, catch*] soltar; (*Phot*) [+ *shutter*] disparar • **to ~ one's grip** *or* **hold (on sth/sb): he ~d his grip on my arm** me soltó el brazo • **the state has to ~ its hold on the economy** el estado tiene que soltar las riendas de la economía
6 (= *let out, give vent to*) [+ *anger, frustration*] descargar, dar rienda suelta a; [+ *creativity*] sacar a flote; [+ *memories*] desatar, desencadenar; [+ *tension*] relajar • **your book has ~d a flood of memories** tu libro ha desatado *or* desencadenado una lluvia de recuerdos
7 (*Aut*) [+ *brake*] soltar
8 (*Jur*) [+ *right, property*] ceder
CPD ▸ **release date** [*of film*] fecha *f* de estreno; [*of CD*] fecha *f* de salida; [*of prisoner*] fecha *f* de puesta en libertad

relegate [ˈrelɪɡeɪt] VT **1** (= *demote*) [+ *person, old furniture*] relegar • **the news had been ~d to the inside pages** la noticia había sido relegada a las páginas interiores
2 (*Brit*) (*Sport*) [+ *team*] • **they were ~d to the second division** bajaron *or* descendieron a segunda división

relegation [ˌrelɪˈɡeɪʃən] N (= *demotion*) relegación *f*; (*Brit*) (*Sport*) descenso *m*

relent [rɪˈlent] VI **1** (= *show compassion*) ablandarse, aplacarse
2 (= *let up*) [*person*] descansar; (*fig*) [*weather*] mejorar

relentless [rɪˈlentlɪs] ADJ **1** (= *heartless*) [*cruelty*] cruel, despiadado
2 (= *persistent*) [*hard work*] incesante • **with ~ severity** con implacable severidad • **he is quite ~ about it** en esto se muestra totalmente implacable

relentlessly [rɪˈlentlɪslɪ] ADV **1** (= *heartlessly*) cruelmente, despiadadamente
2 (= *persistently*) sin descanso • **he presses on ~** avanza implacable

relet [ˈriːˈlet] (PT, PP: **relet**) VT [+ *flat, house*] realquilar

relevance [ˈreləvəns] N pertinencia *f*, relevancia *f* • **matters of doubtful ~** asuntos de dudosa pertinencia *or* relevancia • **what is the ~ of that?** y eso ¿tiene que ver (con lo que estamos discutiendo)?

relevancy [ˈreləvənsɪ] N = **relevance**

relevant [ˈreləvənt] ADJ [*information, facts, document, page*] pertinente • **they had all the ~ information at their disposal** tenían toda la información pertinente a su disposición • **Shakespeare's plays are still ~ today** las obras de Shakespeare tienen aún trascendencia hoy en día • **he talked to the ~ officials to see what could be done** habló con los oficiales competentes para ver qué se podía hacer • **applicants need a year's ~ experience** los solicitantes necesitan tener un año de experiencia en el campo • **~ to: details ~ to this affair** detalles relacionados con *or* concernientes a este asunto • **information which may be ~ to this case** información que puede ser relevante para este caso • **that's not ~ to the case** eso no viene al caso • **your question is not ~ to the issues we're discussing** tu pregunta no guarda relación con lo que estamos discutiendo

reliability [rɪˌlaɪəˈbɪlɪtɪ] N **1** (= *dependability*) [*of person, firm*] seriedad *f*, formalidad *f*; [*of car, method*] fiabilidad *f* • **they have a reputation for good service and ~** tienen fama de dar un buen servicio y ser formales
2 (= *trustworthiness*) [*of facts*] verosimilitud *f*; [*of information, figures, account*] fiabilidad *f* • **we have doubts about the ~ of the results** dudamos de la fiabilidad de los resultados

reliable [rɪˈlaɪəbl] ADJ **1** (= *dependable*) [*person, firm*] digno de confianza, formal; [*ally*] en el que se puede confiar; [*car*] seguro, fiable; [*method*] de fiar • **she's very ~** puedes confiar completamente en ella, es una persona muy formal • **they provide a cheap and ~ service** proporcionan un servicio barato y fiable
2 (= *trustworthy*) [*information, figures, guide, indicator*] fiable; [*evidence, report, description, account*] fidedigno; [*memory*] de fiar • **~ sources** fuentes *fpl* fidedignas

reliably [rɪˈlaɪəblɪ] ADV • **I am ~ informed that ...** sé de fuentes fidedignas que ... • **equipment that works ~ in most conditions** equipo que funciona sin fallos en la mayoría de las condiciones • **stars whose distances we can ~ measure** estrellas cuyas distancias podemos medir con cierta precisión

reliance [rɪˈlaɪəns] N • **~ on sth** (= *trust*) confianza *f* en algo; (= *dependence*) dependencia *f* de algo • **our excessive ~ on him** nuestra excesiva dependencia con respecto de él, el que dependamos tanto de él • **you can place no ~ on that** no hay que fiarse de eso, no hay que tener confianza en eso

reliant [rɪˈlaɪənt] ADJ • **to be ~ on sth/sb** depender de algo/algn

relic [ˈrelɪk] N (*Rel*) reliquia *f*; (*fig*) vestigio *m*

relict†† [ˈrelɪkt] N viuda *f*

relief [rɪˈliːf] N **1** (*from pain, anxiety*) alivio *m* • **that's a ~!** ¡qué alivio! • **the news came as a great ~ to her parents** la noticia fue un gran alivio para sus padres • **there was a sense of ~ that the war was finally over** todos sintieron un gran alivio cuando se supo que la guerra había terminado por fin • **the ~ of nasal congestion** el alivio de la congestión nasal • **to bring** *or* **give** *or* **provide ~ from sth** aliviar algo • **drugs provide ~ from the pain** las drogas alivian el dolor • **to heave** *or* **breathe a sigh of ~** dar un suspiro de alivio • **to our (great) ~, she accepted** para (gran) alivio nuestro, aceptó • **she almost wept with** *or* **in ~** casi lloró del alivio que sintió
2 (*from monotony*) • **it's a ~ to get out of the office once in a while** es un respiro salir de la oficina de vez en cuando • **by way of light ~** a modo de diversión; ▹ **comic**
3 (= *aid*) auxilio *m*, ayuda *f* • **disaster ~** *auxilio a las víctimas de una catástrofe* • **~ efforts have been hampered by the rains** la lluvia ha dificultado las operaciones de auxilio; ▹ **famine**
4 (= *state welfare*) • **to be on** *or* **get ~** (*US*) recibir prestaciones de la seguridad social • **poor ~** (*Brit*) (*Hist*) socorro *m*, beneficencia *f*
5 (*Mil*) [*of town*] liberación *f*
6 (*Art, Geog*) relieve *m* • **in ~** en relieve • **in high/low ~** en alto/bajo relieve • **to stand out in (bold** *or* **sharp** *or* **stark) ~ against sth** (*lit, fig*) contrastar dramáticamente con algo • **to throw** *or* **bring sth into (sharp) ~** (*fig*) poner algo de relieve, hacer resaltar algo; ▹ **bas-relief**
7 (= *replacement*) relevo *m*, sustituto *m*
8 (= *exemption*) (*from taxation*) desgravación *f*; ▹ **debt**
9 (*Jur*) desagravio *m*
CPD [*train, bus*] de reemplazo; [*typist, secretary*] suplente ▸ **relief agency** organización *f* humanitaria ▸ **relief driver** conductor(a) *m/f* de relevo ▸ **relief fund** fondo *m* de auxilio (a los damnificados) ▸ **relief map** mapa *m* físico *or* de relieve; (*3-D*) mapa *m* en relieve ▸ **relief organization** organización *f* humanitaria ▸ **relief road** carretera *f* de descongestión ▸ **relief supplies** provisiones *fpl* de auxilio ▸ **relief troops** tropas *fpl* de relevo ▸ **relief work** labor *f* humanitaria ▸ **relief worker** trabajador(a) *m/f* humanitario/a • **~ workers** personal *m* de asistencia humanitaria

relieve [rɪˈliːv] VT **1** (= *alleviate*) [+ *sufferings, pain, headache*] aliviar; [+ *burden*] aligerar; [+ *tension, boredom, anxiety*] disipar, aliviar • **to ~ the boredom of the journey** para que el viaje se haga menos aburrido • **the plain is ~d by an occasional hill** de vez en cuando una colina rompe con la monotonía de la llanura
2 (= *ease*) [+ *person's mind*] tranquilizar • **it ~s me to hear it** me tranquiliza saberlo
3 [+ *feelings, anger*] desahogar • **to ~ one's feelings** desahogarse • **I ~d my feelings in a letter** me desahogué escribiendo una carta
4 • **to ~ o.s.** (= *go to lavatory*) ir al baño, hacer pis*
5 (= *release*) • **to ~ sb of a duty** exonerar a algn de un deber • **to ~ sb of a post** destituir a algn • **he was ~d of his command** fue relevado de su mando • **let me ~ you of your**

coat permítame tomarle el abrigo • **to ~ sb of his wallet** (*hum*) quitar la cartera a algn, robar la cartera a algn
6 (*Mil*) [+ *city*] descercar, socorrer; [+ *troops*] relevar • **I'll come and ~ you at six** vengo a las seis a relevarte
7 • **to ~ the poor** (= *help*) socorrer a los pobres
relieved [rɪ'li:vd] (ADJ) aliviado • **to feel ~** sentirse aliviado • **to be ~ (that) ...** estar aliviado por (que) ... • **I'm ~ to hear it** me alivia oír eso
religion [rɪ'lɪdʒən] (N) (= *belief*) religión *f* • **football is like a ~ with him** el fútbol es su religión • **it's against my ~ to do that** hacer eso es contrario a mis creencias religiosas, hacer eso va contra mi religión • **to get ~*** darse a la religión
religiosity [rɪ,lɪdʒɪ'ɒsɪtɪ] (N) religiosidad *f*
religious [rɪ'lɪdʒəs] (ADJ) **1** [*beliefs, leader, service, life*] religioso; [*practice*] de la religión, religioso; [*war*] de religión, religioso • **for ~ reasons** por razones religiosas • **she's deeply ~** es profundamente religiosa • **~ freedom** libertad *f* de culto
2 (*fig*) (= *meticulous*) • **~ attention to detail** una atención minuciosa para los detalles
(N) • **the ~** las personas religiosas, los religiosos
(CPD) ▸ **religious education, religious instruction** enseñanza *f* religiosa
religiously [rɪ'lɪdʒəslɪ] (ADV) **1** (*Rel*) • **a ~ diverse country** un país con diversidad religiosa *or* de religiones • **~ minded people** gente con inclinaciones religiosas • **~ motivated** motivado por la religión
2 (= *meticulously*) religiosamente
religiousness [rɪ'lɪdʒəsnɪs] (N) religiosidad *f*
reline ['ri:'laɪn] (VT) reforrar, poner nuevo forro a
relinquish [rɪ'lɪŋkwɪʃ] (VT) [+ *claim, right*] renunciar a; [+ *control*] ceder; [+ *post*] renunciar a, dimitir de • **to ~ one's grip on sth** (*lit*) soltar algo
relinquishment [rɪ'lɪŋkwɪʃmənt] (N) [*of claim, right*] renuncia *f*; [*of post*] dimisión *f*
reliquary ['relɪkwərɪ] (N) relicario *m*
relish ['relɪʃ] (N) **1** (= *distinctive flavour*) sabor *m*
2 (= *gusto, enthusiasm*) entusiasmo *m* • **to do sth with ~** hacer algo de buena gana • **to eat sth with ~** comer algo con apetito • **hunting has no ~ for me now** ya no disfruto tanto cazando
3 (= *sauce*) salsa *f*
(VT) **1** (= *taste, savour*) [+ *a good meal*] saborear
2 (= *like*) • **I don't ~ the idea of staying up all night** no me hace gracia la idea de estar levantado toda la noche
relive ['ri:'lɪv] (VT) [+ *past*] revivir • **to ~ old memories** rememorar los recuerdos
reload ['ri:'ləʊd] (VT) recargar, volver a cargar
relocate ['ri:ləʊ'keɪt] (VT) [+ *factory, employees*] trasladar, reubicar (*LAm*)
(VI) trasladarse
relocation [,ri:ləʊ'keɪʃən] (N) traslado *m*, nueva ubicación *f*
(CPD) ▸ **relocation expenses** (*paid to employee*) gastos *mpl* de mudanza
▸ **relocation package** prima *f* de traslado
reluctance [rɪ'lʌktəns] (N) reticencia *f*, renuencia *f* (*frm*) • **her ~ to allow it was understandable** era comprensible que se mostrase reacia *or* reticente a permitirlo, su reticencia *or* (*frm*) renuencia a permitirlo era comprensible • **to show ~ (to do sth)** mostrarse reacio *or* reticente *or* (*frm*) renuente (a hacer algo), mostrar reticencia *or* (*frm*) renuencia (a hacer algo) • **with ~** con reticencia, a regañadientes • **to make a show of ~** aparentar reticencia, aparentar estar reticente
reluctant [rɪ'lʌktənt] (ADJ) [*person*] reacio, reticente, renuente (*frm*); [*praise*] a regañadientes • **the case was hampered by ~ witnesses** testigos reacios a colaborar obstaculizaron el caso • **I would make a ~ secretary** yo trabajaría como secretario con desgana *or* a regañadientes • **the ~ dragon** el dragón que no quería • **he indicated his ~ acceptance of the proposals** indicó que aceptaba las propuestas con reservas • **he left with Bernstein's ~ consent** se fue con el consentimiento que Bernstein le había dado a regañadientes *or* muy a su pesar • **he took the ~ decision to stop production** tomó la decisión, muy a su pesar, de parar la producción • **to be ~ to do sth: she was ~ to ask for help** se mostraba reacia a pedir ayuda • **we were ~ to sell the house** éramos reacios a vender la casa, nos resistíamos a vender la casa
reluctantly [rɪ'lʌktəntlɪ] (ADV) [*agree, accept*] de mala gana, a regañadientes • **he ~ accepted their advice** aceptó sus consejos de mala gana *or* a regañadientes
rely [rɪ'laɪ] (VI) • **to ~ (up)on sth/sb** (= *depend on*) depender de algo/algn; (= *count on*) contar con algo/algn; (= *trust*) confiar en algo/algn, fiarse de algo/algn • **he had gradually come to ~ on her** había llegado poco a poco a depender de ella • **can we ~ on your help?** ¿podemos contar con tu ayuda? • **she'll come, you can ~ upon it** vendrá, con eso puedes contar, vendrá, cuenta con ello • **you can't ~ on the trains/the weather** no se puede uno fiar de los trenes/del tiempo • **to ~ (up)on sth/sb for sth** depender de algo/algn para algo • **the island relies on tourism for its income** la isla depende del turismo como fuente de ingresos • **to ~ (up)on sth/sb to do sth: we are ~ing on you to do it** contamos con usted para hacerlo • **you can ~ on him to be late** puedes tener por seguro *or* ten por seguro que va a llegar tarde • **can I ~ on you to behave?** ¿puedo confiar en que te vas a comportar?, ¿puedo fiarme de que te vas a comportar?
REM [rem] (N ABBR) **1** (*Physiol*) (= **rapid eye movement**) movimiento *m* rápido del ojo
2 (*Phys*) = **roentgen equivalent man**
remain [rɪ'meɪn] (VI) **1** (= *be left*) quedar • **little now ~s of the old city** poco queda ya del casco antiguo • **the few pleasures that ~ to me** los pocos placeres que me quedan • **much ~s to be done** queda mucho por hacer • **nothing ~s to be said** no queda nada por decir, no hay nada más que decir • **nothing ~s but to accept** no queda más remedio que aceptar • **it only ~s to thank you** solo queda darle las gracias • **that ~s to be seen** eso está por ver
2 (= *continue to be*) seguir, continuar • **the problem ~s unsolved** el problema sigue *or* continúa sin resolverse • **he ~ed a formidable opponent** siguió *or* continuó siendo un rival formidable • **to ~ seated/standing** permanecer sentado/de pie • **to ~ faithful to sb** seguir *or* permanecer fiel a algn • **they ~ed silent** permanecieron en silencio • **the government ~ed in control** el gobierno mantuvo *or* sostuvo el control • **the two men have ~ed friends** los dos hombres han seguido siendo amigos • **if the weather ~s fine** si el tiempo sigue bueno • **the fact ~s that ...** (*referring to previous statement*) no es menos cierto que ..., sigue siendo un hecho que ...
3 (= *stay*) quedarse • **we ~ed there three weeks** nos quedamos allí tres semanas • **to ~ behind** (*gen*) quedarse; (*after school*) quedarse después de las clases
4 (*in letters*) • **I ~, yours faithfully** le saluda atentamente
remainder [rɪ'meɪndəʳ] (N) **1** (= *part left over*) resto *m* • **the ~ of the debt** el resto de la deuda • **during the ~ of the day** durante el resto del día • **the ~ would not come** los otros *or* los demás no quisieron venir
2 (*Math*) resto *m*
3 remainders (*Comm*) artículos *mpl* no vendidos; (= *books*) restos *mpl* de edición
(VT) [+ *copies of book*] saldar
remaining [rɪ'meɪnɪŋ] (ADJ) • **the three ~ hostages** los tres rehenes restantes *or* que quedaban • **he is her only ~ relative** él es el único pariente que le queda • **the ~ passengers** los otros *or* los demás pasajeros
remains [rɪ'meɪnz] (NPL) [*of building*] restos *mpl*; [*of food*] sobras *fpl*, restos *mpl* • **the ~ of the picnic** los restos *or* las sobras del picnic • **human ~** restos *mpl* humanos • **Roman ~** ruinas *fpl* romanas
remake (VT) [,ri:'meɪk] rehacer, volver a hacer
(N) ['ri:meɪk] (*Cine*) nueva versión *f*
remand [rɪ'mɑ:nd] (*Jur*) (N) • **to be on ~** estar en prisión preventiva
(VT) [+ *case*] remitir • **to ~ sb in custody** poner a algn en prisión preventiva • **to ~ sb on bail** libertar a algn bajo fianza
(CPD) ▸ **remand centre** cárcel *f* transitoria ▸ **remand home** cárcel *f* transitoria para menores ▸ **remand prisoner** recluso/a *m/f* en prisión provisional ▸ **remand wing** galería *f* de prisión preventiva
remark [rɪ'mɑ:k] (N) **1** (= *comment*) comentario *m*, observación *f* • **to let sth pass without ~** dejar pasar algo sin (hacer) comentario • **after some introductory ~s** tras unos comentarios introductorios • **to make a ~** hacer un comentario *or* una observación • **she made the ~ that** observó que • **to make or pass ~s about sb** hacer comentarios sobre algn; ▸ **personal**
2 (= *notice*) • **worthy of ~** digno de mención
(VT) **1** (= *say*) comentar, observar • **to ~ that** comentar que, observar que, decir que • **"it's a pity," she ~ed** —es una lástima —dijo
2 (= *notice*) observar, notar
(VI) (= *comment*) • **to ~ on sth** hacer observaciones sobre algo
remarkable [rɪ'mɑ:kəbl] (ADJ) [*person, success, ability, performance*] extraordinario; [*achievement, recovery, progress*] notable, extraordinario; [*results*] excelente, extraordinario; [*story*] singular • **what's ~ about that?** no sé qué tiene eso de extraordinario • **~ for sth** notable por algo • **his statement was ~ for its clarity** su declaración fue notable por su claridad • **a teacher ~ for her patience** un profesor que destaca por su paciencia • **it's ~ how quickly children grow up** es extraordinario lo rápido que crecen los niños • **he's a most ~ man** es un hombre extraordinario • **we have made ~ progress** hemos realizado notables *or* extraordinarios progresos • **it is ~ that** es sorprendente que (+ *subjun*) • **it was ~ to see how quickly she recovered** fue sorprendente *or* extraordinario lo pronto que se recuperó • **what's ~ to me is that so many people came** lo que me parece sorprendente es que viniera tanta gente
remarkably [rɪ'mɑ:kəblɪ] (ADV) [*similar, beautiful, cheap*] extraordinariamente; [*well, quickly*] increíblemente • **the factory had, ~, escaped the bombing** la fábrica, increíblemente, no resultó dañada en el bombardeo • **~ few people** un número

increíblemente escaso de personas • **there have been ~ few complaints** sorprendentemente, ha habido muy pocas quejas • **the general standard was ~ high** el nivel general era notablemente alto • **he looked ~ like his father** guardaba un parecido extraordinario con su padre • **it tastes ~ good** tiene un sabor extraordinario

remarriage [ˈriːˈmærɪdʒ] N segundo casamiento *m*

remarry [ˈriːˈmærɪ] VI volver a casarse • **she remarried three years ago** se volvió a casar hace tres años

remaster [ˌriːˈmɑːstəʳ] VT [+ *film, recording*] remasterizar

rematch [ˈriːˌmætʃ] N partido *m* de vuelta, revancha *f*

remediable [rɪˈmiːdɪəbl] ADJ remediable

remedial [rɪˈmiːdɪəl] ADJ (*Med*) reparador; (*fig*) correctivo

CPD ▸ **remedial course** curso *m* correctivo ▸ **remedial education** educación *f* especial ▸ **remedial teaching** enseñanza *f* de los niños *etc* con dificultades

remedy [ˈremədɪ] N (*gen*) remedio *m* • **a good ~ for a sore throat** un buen remedio para el dolor de garganta • **to be past ~** (*Med*) (*also fig*) no tener remedio • **there's no ~ for that** eso no tiene remedio • **the best ~ for that is to protest** eso se remedia protestando • **to have no ~ at law** no tener recurso legal

VT (*Med*) [+ *illness*] curar; (*fig*) [+ *situation*] remediar • **that's soon remedied** eso es fácil remediarlo, eso queda arreglado fácilmente

remember [rɪˈmembəʳ] VT **1** (= *recall*) [+ *person, fact, promise*] acordarse de, recordar • **don't you ~ me?** ¿no se acuerda usted de mí?, ¿no me recuerda? • **I can never ~ phone numbers** tengo muy mala memoria para los números de teléfono, soy incapaz de recordar números de teléfono • **I don't ~ a thing about it** no recuerdo ni un solo detalle de ello • **I ~ seeing it** • **I ~ having seen it** me acuerdo de *or* recuerdo haberlo visto, me acuerdo de *or* recuerdo que lo vi • **I seem to ~ (that) you used to do the same** si mal no recuerdo, tú hacías lo mismo • **I don't ~ what he looks like** no me acuerdo de *or* no recuerdo cómo es • **I ~ him as tall and slim** lo recuerdo alto y delgado • **give me something to ~ you by** dame algún recuerdo tuyo • **so I gave him sth to ~ me by** (*fig*) así que le di algo para que no me olvidara *or* para que se acordara de mí • **she will be ~ed for her wonderful sense of humour** se la recordará por su maravilloso sentido del humor • **it was a night to ~** fue una noche memorable *or* inolvidable

2 (= *bear in mind*) recordar, tener presente • **~ that he carries a gun** recuerda *or* ten presente que lleva una pistola • **that's worth ~ing** eso merece la pena recordarlo • **it is worth ~ing that ...** merece la pena recordar que ...

3 (= *not forget*) acordarse de • **have you ~ed your passport?** ¿te has acordado del pasaporte *or* de traer el pasaporte? • **she always ~s the children at Christmas** siempre se acuerda de los niños por Navidad • **to ~ sb in one's prayers** rezar por algn • **to ~ sb in one's will** mencionar a algn en el testamento • **she ~ed to do it** se acordó de hacerlo • **~ to turn out the light** no te olvides de apagar la luz • **~ what happened before** no te olvides *or* acuérdate de lo que pasó antes

4 (= *commemorate*) recordar • **today we ~ those who gave their lives in the war** hoy recordamos a aquellos que dieron sus vidas en la guerra

5 (*with wishes*) • **she asks to be ~ed to you all** manda recuerdos a todos • **~ me to your family** dale recuerdos a tu familia, saluda a tu familia de mi parte

VI **1** (= *recall*) acordarse, recordar • **do you ~?** ¿te acuerdas?, ¿recuerdas? • **try to ~!** ¡haz memoria!, ¡intenta acordarte! • **I don't** *or* **can't ~** no me acuerdo, no recuerdo • **as I ~, you said you would pay** que yo recuerde *or* si mal no recuerdo, tú dijiste que pagarías • **it was a cold day, as you will ~** era un día de frío, como recordarás • **as far as I (can) ~** que yo recuerde • **not as far as I ~** no que yo recuerde • **as far back as** *or* **for as long as I can ~** desde siempre • **if I ~ right(ly)** si mal no recuerdo, si la memoria no me falla

2 (= *not forget*) acordarse • **I asked you to get some stamps, did you ~?** te pedí que compraras sellos, ¿te acordaste? • **I'll try to ~** intentaré acordarme, intentaré no olvidarme *or* que no se me olvide

> **REMEMBER**
>
> **"acordarse de" or "recordar"?**
>
> ▹ *Both* **acordarse de** *and* **recordar** *can be used to translate* **to remember** *(used transitively), provided the object of* **remember** *is not another verb.* **Recordar** *is becoming less common, however, in everyday informal contexts:*
>
> **Do you remember where he lives?**
> ¿Te acuerdas de dónde vive?, ¿Recuerdas dónde vive?
>
> ▹ *Use* **acordarse de** *+ infinitive to translate* **to remember to** *+ verb:*
>
> **Did you remember to close the door?**
> ¿Te acordaste de cerrar la puerta?
>
> *NOTE: Don't use* **recordar** *for* **remembering to do sth.**
>
> ▹ *Use* **recordar** *+ perfect infinitive/clause or* **acordarse de** *+ clause to translate* **to remember** *+ -ing:*
>
> **I remember closing the door**
> Recuerdo haber cerrado *or* Recuerdo que cerré *or* Me acuerdo de que cerré la puerta
>
> **Recordar** *also translates* **remind**:
>
> **I must remind Richard to pay the rent**
> Tengo que recordarle a Richard que pague el alquiler
>
> *For further uses and examples, see main entry.*

remembrance [rɪˈmembrəns] N (= *remembering*) recuerdo *m* • **~s** recuerdos *mpl* • **in ~ of** en conmemoración de • **I have no ~ of it** no lo recuerdo en absoluto

CPD ▸ **Remembrance Day, Remembrance Sunday** (*Brit*) *día en el que se recuerda a los caídos en las dos guerras mundiales;* ▹ POPPY DAY

remind [rɪˈmaɪnd] VT recordar a • **thank you for ~ing me** gracias por recordármelo • **to ~ sb that** recordar a algn que • **customers are ~ed that ...** se recuerda a los clientes que ... • **to ~ sb to do sth** recordar a algn que haga algo • **~ me to fix an appointment** recuérdame que ponga una cita • **you have to keep ~ing him to do it** hay que recordárselo constantemente • **need I ~ you who he is?** ¿tengo que recordarte quién es? • **to ~ sb about sth** recordar algo a algn • **don't forget to ~ her about the party** no te olvides de recordarle lo de la fiesta • **don't ~ me!*** ¡no me lo recuerdes! • **to ~ sb of sth** recordar algo a algn • **that ~s me of last time** eso me recuerda la última vez • **she ~s me of Anne** me recuerda a Anne • **to ~ o.s.:** • **I have to ~ myself to relax** tengo que recordarme a mí mismo que debo relajarme • **he's only a boy, I ~ed myself** no es más que un niño, me recordé • **that ~s me!** ¡a propósito! • **I saw John today, which ~s me ...** hoy vi a John, a propósito ...; ▹ REMEMBER

reminder [rɪˈmaɪndəʳ] N **1** (= *letter etc*) notificación *f*, aviso *m* • **we will send a ~** le enviaremos un recordatorio • **it's a gentle ~** es una advertencia amistosa

2 (= *memento*) recuerdo *m* • **it's a ~ of the good old days** recuerda los buenos tiempos pasados

reminisce [ˌremɪˈnɪs] VI recordar, rememorar

reminiscence [ˌremɪˈnɪsəns] N (= *act*) reminiscencia *f*; (= *individual recollection*) recuerdo *m*

reminiscent [ˌremɪˈnɪsənt] ADJ **1** (= *nostalgic*) nostálgico • **to be in a ~ mood** ponerse nostálgico

2 • **to be ~ of** recordar • **that bit is ~ of Rossini** ese trozo recuerda a *or* tiene reminiscencia de Rossini • **that's ~ of another old joke** eso suena a otro conocido chiste

reminiscently [ˌremɪˈnɪsəntlɪ] ADV • **he spoke ~** habló pensando en el pasado

remiss [rɪˈmɪs] ADJ negligente, descuidado • **I have been very ~ about it** he sido muy negligente *or* descuidado en eso • **it was ~ of me** fue un descuido de mi parte

remission [rɪˈmɪʃən] N **1** (*Rel*) (= *forgiveness*) remisión *f*, perdón *m*; (*gen*) (= *annulment*) exoneración *f* • **~ of sins** remisión *or* perdón de los pecados

2 (*Brit*) (= *shortening of prison sentence*) disminución *f* de pena

3 (*Med*) • **to be in ~** [*sick person*] haberse recuperado (temporalmente); [*disease*] remitir, estar en fase de remisión

remissness [rɪˈmɪsnɪs] N negligencia *f*, descuido *m*

remit [ˈriːmɪt] N (*Brit*) (= *area of responsibility*) competencia *f*; (= *terms of reference*) [*of committee etc*] cometido *m*

VT [rɪˈmɪt] **1** (= *pay by sending*) [+ *amount due*] remitir

2 (= *refer*) [+ *decision*] remitir

3 (*Rel*) (= *forgive*) [+ *sins*] perdonar, remitir

4 (= *let off*) [+ *debt*] remitir • **three months of the sentence were ~ted** se le redujo la pena en tres meses

VI [rɪˈmɪt] disminuir, reducirse

remittal [rɪˈmɪtl] N (*Jur*) remisión *f*

remittance [rɪˈmɪtəns] N (= *payment*) pago *m*, giro *m*

CPD ▸ **remittance advice** aviso *m* de pago

remittee [rɪmɪˈtiː] N consignatario/a *m/f*

remittent [rɪˈmɪtənt] ADJ [*fever etc*] remitente

remitter [rɪˈmɪtəʳ] N remitente *mf*

remix [ˌriːˈmɪks] (*Mus*) N remix *m*

VT [ˌriːˈmɪks] mezclar

remnant [ˈremnənt] N (= *remainder*) resto *m*, remanente *m*; (= *scrap of cloth*) retal *m*

CPD ▸ **remnant day** (*Comm*) día *m* de venta de restos de serie ▸ **remnant sale** venta *f* de restos de serie, liquidación *f* total

remodel [ˈriːˈmɒdl] VT remodelar

remodelling, remodeling (*US*) [ˌriːˈmɒdəlɪŋ] N [*of room, house*] remodelación *f*

remold [ˈriːˈməʊld] N, VT (*US*) = **remould**

remonstrance [rɪˈmɒnstrəns] N (*frm*) (= *complaint, protest*) protesta *f*, queja *f*

remonstrate [ˈremənstreɪt] VI (= *protest*)

protestar, quejarse; (= *argue*) discutir • **to ~ about sth** protestar contra algo, poner reparos a algo • **to ~ with sb** reconvenir a algn

remonstration [ˌremən'streɪʃən] (N) protesta *f*

remorse [rɪ'mɔːs] (N) (= *regret*) remordimiento *m* • **without ~** sin remordimientos • **to feel ~** arrepentirse

remorseful [rɪ'mɔːsfʊl] (ADJ) (= *regretful*) arrepentido

remorsefully [rɪ'mɔːsfəlɪ] (ADV) con remordimiento • **he said ~** dijo arrepentido

remorsefulness [rɪ'mɔːsfʊlnɪs] (N) remordimiento *m*

remorseless [rɪ'mɔːslɪs] (ADJ) **1** (= *merciless*) despiadado
2 (= *relentless*) [*advance, progress*] implacable, inexorable

remorselessly [rɪ'mɔːslɪslɪ] (ADV)
1 (= *mercilessly*) [*pursue, tease*] despiadadamente, de forma despiadada
2 (= *relentlessly*) implacablemente, inexorablemente • **the spread of the virus is continuing ~** el virus continúa propagándose implacablemente, la propagación del virus continúa implacable

remorselessness [rɪ'mɔːslɪsnɪs] (N)
1 (= *mercilessness*) lo despiadado
2 (= *relentlessness*) lo implacable, inexorabilidad *f*

remote [rɪ'məʊt] (ADJ) (COMPAR: **remoter**, SUPERL: **remotest**) **1** (= *distant*) [*village, spot, area*] remoto, apartado; [*star, galaxy*] lejano, remoto; [*relative, ancestor, descendant*] lejano • **in the ~st parts of Africa** en las partes más remotas *or* más apartadas de África • **the ~ past/future** el pasado/futuro remoto • **~ antiquity** la antigüedad remota • **it's ~ from any towns** está muy lejos *or* muy apartado de cualquier ciudad • **events which seem ~ from our daily lives** hechos que parecen muy alejados de nuestras vidas cotidianas • **a village ~ from the world** un pueblo apartado del mundo
2 (= *removed*) lejano, remoto • **villages where the war seemed ~** pueblos donde la guerra parecía algo lejano *or* remoto • **to be ~ from sth** estar alejado de algo • **these events seem ~ from contemporary life** estos sucesos parecen estar alejados de la vida contemporánea • **what he said was rather ~ from the subject in hand** lo que dijo no tenía mucha relación con el tema que se trataba
3 (= *aloof*) [*person, manner, voice*] distante
4 (= *slight*) [*possibility, chance, prospect, hope*] remoto; [*risk, resemblance*] ligero; [*connection*] remoto • **I haven't the ~st idea** no tengo ni la más remota idea
5 (= *remote-controlled*) a distancia
(N) (*also* **remote control**) mando *m* a distancia, telemando *m*
(CPD) ▸ **remote access** (*Comput*) acceso *m* remoto ▸ **remote control** (= *system*) control *m* remoto; (= *device*) mando *m* a distancia, telemando *m* ▸ **remote learning** (*Educ*) educación *f* a distancia ▸ **remote sensing** detección *f* a distancia

remote-controlled [rɪ'məʊtkən'trəʊld] (ADJ) [*toy aircraft etc*] teledirigido

remotely [rɪ'məʊtlɪ] (ADV) **1** (= *distantly*) en un lugar apartado • **they are ~ related** son parientes lejanos • **to be ~ situated** estar situado en un lugar apartado
2 (= *slightly*) [*connected, possible*] remotamente • **it wasn't even ~ amusing** no era ni por asomo divertido • **he isn't even ~ interested in opera** no está ni siquiera remotamente interesado en la ópera • **he failed to say anything ~ interesting** no consiguió decir nada mínimamente interesante • **I've never seen anything ~ like it** nunca he visto nada (ni) remotamente parecido • **it's not even ~ likely** de eso no hay la más remota posibilidad • **he'll eat anything that looks ~ edible** es capaz de comerse cualquier cosa con un mínimo aspecto de comestible • **the struggle to maintain anything ~ resembling decent standards** la lucha por mantener algo que se pareciera aunque fuera de lejos a unos niveles decentes
3 (= *in a detached manner*) [*say, behave*] de forma distante
4 (= *by remote control*) [*control*] a distancia; [*detonate*] por control remoto

remoteness [rɪ'məʊtnɪs] (N) **1** (*in space*) [*of galaxy, village, house*] lo remoto
2 (*in time*) [*of period, age*] lo lejano
3 (= *aloofness*) • **he found her ~ hard to cope with** no llevaba bien que ella fuese tan distante • **her ~ from everyday life** su alejamiento de la vida diaria

remould, remold (US) [ˌriː'məʊld] (VT) recauchutar
(N) ['riːməʊld] neumático *m* recauchutado, llanta *f* recauchutada (*LAm*)

remount ['riː'maʊnt] (VT) (*gen*) montar de nuevo en, volver a montar en
(VI) montar de nuevo, volver a montar
(N) (*Mil etc*) remonta *f*

removable [rɪ'muːvəbl] (ADJ) **1** (= *detachable*) movible; [*collar etc*] de quita y pon
2 (*from job*) amovible

removal [rɪ'muːvəl] (N) (= *transfer*) traslado *m*; [*of word etc*] supresión *f*; (*esp Brit*) (*to new house*) mudanza *f*; (*fig*) (= *murder*) eliminación *f* • **his ~ to a new post** su traslado a un nuevo puesto • **the ~ of this threat** la eliminación de esta amenaza
(CPD) ▸ **removal allowance** (*Brit*) subvención *f* de mudanza ▸ **removal expenses** (*Brit*) gastos *mpl* de traslado de efectos personales ▸ **removal man** mozo *m* de mudanzas ▸ **removal van** (*Brit*) camión *m* de mudanzas

remove [rɪ'muːv] (VT) **1** (= *take away*) [+ *object*] quitar; [+ *documents, evidence*] llevarse • **~ the pan from the heat** quite la cacerola del fuego • **to ~ a child from school** sacar *or* quitar a un niño de la escuela • **the demonstrators were forcibly ~d by police** (*from building*) la policía echó a los manifestantes a la fuerza • **to ~ o.s.** irse, marcharse • **kindly ~ yourself at once** haga el favor de irse *or* marcharse inmediatamente • **to ~ sth/sb to** trasladar *or* llevar algo/a algn a • **her body had been ~d to the mortuary** habían trasladado *or* llevado su cuerpo al tanatorio
2 (= *take off*) quitar; [+ *one's clothing, make-up*] quitarse • **first ~ the lid** primero quite la tapa • **he ~d his jacket** se quitó la chaqueta • **he ~d his hat** se quitó el sombrero, se descubrió • **she had the tattoo ~d from her arm** se fue a que le quitaran *or* se quitó el tatuaje del brazo
3 (= *take out*) [+ *object*] sacar; (*Med*) [+ *organ, tumour*] extirpar, quitar; [+ *bullet*] extraer, quitar • **~ the cake from the oven** saque la tarta del horno
4 (= *delete*) [+ *word, sentence, paragraph*] suprimir, quitar; [+ *name from list*] quitar, tachar (**from** de)
5 (= *get rid of*) [+ *obstacle, threat, waste, problem*] eliminar; [+ *doubt, suspicion*] disipar; [+ *fear*] acabar con; [+ *stain*] quitar • **an agreement on removing trade barriers** un acuerdo sobre la eliminación de las barreras comerciales • **products that ~ unwanted hair** productos que eliminan *or* quitan el vello superfluo
6 (= *dismiss*) [+ *person*] (*from post*) destituir • **to ~ sb from office** destituir a algn de su cargo • **to ~ sb from power** destituir a algn del poder
(VI) (*Brit*) (*frm*) (= *move house*) mudarse, trasladarse, cambiarse (*Mex*) (**to** a)
(N) • **this is but one ~ from disaster** esto raya en la catástrofe, esto está a un paso de la catástrofe • **this is several ~s from our official policy** esto dista *or* se aparta mucho de nuestra política oficial • **it's a far ~ from ...** dista mucho de ... • **at a** *or* **one ~** de lejos • **to experience a foreign culture, albeit at a ~** vivir una cultura extranjera, aunque sea de lejos

removed [rɪ'muːvd] (ADJ) • **to be far ~ from sth** distar *or* apartarse mucho de algo • **his political views are far ~ from theirs** sus ideas políticas distan *or* se apartan mucho de las de ellos • **an indifference not far ~ from contempt** una indiferencia rayana con *or* que rayaba en el desprecio • **first cousin once ~** (= *parent's cousin*) tío/a *m/f* segundo/a; (= *cousin's child*) sobrino/a *m/f* segundo/a, hijo/a *m/f* de primo carnal

remover [rɪ'muːvəʳ] (N) **1** (= *person*) agente *mf* de mudanzas
2 (= *substance*) • **make-up ~** desmaquillador *m*, desmaquillante *m* • **nail polish ~** quitaesmalte *m* • **stain ~** quitamanchas *m inv*

remunerate [rɪ'mjuːnəreɪt] (VT) remunerar

remuneration [rɪˌmjuːnə'reɪʃən] (N) remuneración *f*

remunerative [rɪ'mjuːnərətɪv] (ADJ) remunerativo

Renaissance [rə'neɪsɑːns] (*Art, Hist*) (N) • **the ~** el Renacimiento • **the 12th century ~** el renacimiento del siglo XII
(CPD) renacentista, del Renacimiento

renaissance [rə'neɪsɑːns] (N) renacimiento *m* • **a spiritual ~** un renacimiento *or* despertar espiritual

renal ['riːnl] (ADJ) (*Anat*) renal
(CPD) ▸ **renal failure** insuficiencia *f* renal

rename ['riː'neɪm] (VT) poner nuevo nombre a • **they have ~d it "Mon Repos"** le han puesto el nuevo nombre de "Mon Repos"

renascence [rɪ'næsns] (N) = **renaissance**

renascent [rɪ'næsnt] (ADJ) renaciente, que renace

renationalization ['riːˌnæʃnəlaɪ'zeɪʃən] (N) renacionalización *f*

renationalize ['riː'næʃnəlaɪz] (VT) renacionalizar

rend [rend] (PT, PP: **rent**) (VT) **1** (*poet*) (= *tear*) rasgar, desgarrar; (= *split*) hender • **to ~ sth in twain** partir algo por medio, hender algo • **to ~ one's clothes** rasgar *or* desgarrar su ropa
2 (*fig*) • **a cry rent the air** un grito cortó el aire

render ['rendəʳ] (VT) **1** (*frm*) (= *give*) [+ *honour*] dar, rendir; [+ *service, assistance*] dar, prestar • **to ~ good for evil** devolver bien por mal • **to ~ thanks to sb** dar las gracias a algn • **~ unto Caesar ...** al César lo que es del César (y a Dios lo que es de Dios) • **to ~ an account of one's stewardship** dar cuenta de su gobierno, justificar su conducta durante su mando • **to ~ an account to God** dar cuenta de sí ante Dios
2 (*frm*) (= *make*) dejar, volver • **the accident ~ed him blind** el accidente lo dejó ciego • **to ~ sth useless** inutilizar algo
3 (= *interpret*) [+ *sonata etc*] interpretar; [+ *role, play*] representar, interpretar; (= *translate*) [+ *text*] traducir • **no photograph could adequately ~ the scene** ninguna fotografía

podría reproducir con justicia la escena
4 (*Culin*) (*also* **render down**) derretir
5 (*Constr*) enlucir
6 (*Comm*) • **to ~ an account** pasar factura • **to account ~ed** según factura anterior
▸ **render down** VT + ADV [*fat*] derretir
▸ **render up** VT + ADV [*+ one's/sb's soul*] entregar • **the earth ~s up its treasures** la tierra rinde sus tesoros

rendering ['rendərɪŋ] N (= *translation*) traducción *f*; [*of song, role*] interpretación *f* • **her ~ of the sonata** su interpretación de la sonata • **an elegant ~ of Machado** una elegante versión de Machado

rendezvous ['rɒndɪvu:] N (PL: **rendezvous** ['rɒndɪvu:z]) **1** (= *date*) cita *f*; (= *meeting*) reunión *f* • **to have a ~ with sb** tener una cita con algn • **~ in space** • **space ~** cita espacial • **to make a ~ with another ship at sea** efectuar un enlace con otro buque en el mar
2 (= *meeting-place*) lugar *m* de reunión
VI reunirse, encontrarse; [*spaceship*] tener un encuentro en el espacio (**with** con) • **we will ~ at eight** nos reuniremos a las ocho • **the ships will ~ off Vigo** los buques efectuarán el enlace a la altura de Vigo

rendition [ren'dɪʃən] N **1** (*Mus*) interpretación *f*
2 (*also* **extraordinary rendition**) *práctica de transferir a sospechos de terrorismo de un país a otro para ser interrogados sin ningún tipo de protección legal*
CPD ▸ **rendition flight** (*also* **extraordinary rendition flight**) *vuelo con destino a otro país con presos o sospechosos de terrorismo*

renegade ['renɪgeɪd] ADJ renegado
N renegado/a *m/f*

renege [rɪ'ni:g] VI faltar a su palabra • **to ~ on a promise** no cumplir una promesa

renew [rɪ'nju:] VT **1** (= *restore*) renovar • **skin ~s itself every 28 days** la piel se renueva *or* se regenera cada 28 días
2 (= *resume*) [*+ negotiations, relations*] reanudar • **the storm ~ed itself with a vengeance** la tormenta volvió aún peor, se recrudeció la tormenta • **to ~ the attack** (*Mil*) volver al ataque • **he ~ed his attack on government policy** volvió a arremeter contra la política del gobierno • **to ~ one's efforts (to do sth)** volver a esforzarse (por hacer algo), reanudar sus esfuerzos (por hacer algo) (*frm*); ▹ **acquaintance**
3 (= *extend date of*) [*+ contract, passport, subscription, library book*] renovar; [*+ lease, loan*] renovar, prorrogar
4 (= *reaffirm*) [*+ promise, vow*] renovar
5 (= *replace*) [*+ component*] cambiar; [*+ supplies*] reponer

renewable [rɪ'nju:əbl] ADJ [*contract*] renovable; [*energy, resources*] no perecedero

renewal [rɪ'nju:əl] N **1** (= *reinvigoration*) renacimiento *m* • **there was a ~ of faith in the old values** hubo un renacimiento de la fe en viejos valores • **a spiritual ~** un renacimiento espiritual, una renovación espiritual
2 (= *renovation*) renovación *f* • **a housing ~ programme** un programa de renovación de viviendas • **urban ~** renovación *f* urbanística
3 (= *restarting*) [*of negotiations, relations*] reanudación *f*; [*of attack, hostilities*] recrudecimiento *m*
4 (= *revalidation*) [*of contract, passport, subscription, library book*] renovación *f*; [*of lease, loan*] prórroga *f*, renovación *f* • **his contract is up for ~** le toca que le renueven el contrato

renewed [rɪ'nju:d] ADJ [*enthusiasm*] renovado; [*outbreaks*] nuevo • **with ~ enthusiasm** con renovado entusiasmo • **with ~ strength** con fuerzas renovadas, con nuevas fuerzas • **~ outbreaks of violence** nuevos brotes de violencia • **there have been ~ calls for his resignation** se ha vuelto a pedir su dimisión • **there have been ~ attempts/efforts to reach agreement** se han reanudado los intentos/esfuerzos por llegar a un acuerdo • **there has been a ~ interest in …** se ha renovado el interés por …

rennet ['renɪt] N cuajo *m*

renounce [rɪ'naʊns] VT [*+ right, inheritance, offer etc*] renunciar; [*+ plan, post, the world etc*] renunciar a
VI (*Cards*) renunciar

renouncement [rɪ'naʊnsmənt] N renuncia *f*

renovate ['renəʊveɪt] VT (= *renew*) renovar; (= *restore*) restaurar

renovation [ˌrenəʊ'veɪʃən] N [*of house, building*] restauración *f*

renown [rɪ'naʊn] N renombre *m*, fama *f*

renowned [rɪ'naʊnd] ADJ renombrado, famoso • **it is ~ for …** es famoso por …, es célebre por …

rent[1] [rent] N alquiler *m*, arriendo *m* (*LAm*) • **we pay £350 in ~** pagamos 350 libras de alquiler • **to build flats for ~** construir pisos para alquilarlos • **"for rent"** (*US*) "se alquila"
VT [*+ house, TV, car*] alquilar, arrendar (*LAm*) • **to ~ a flat from sb** alquilar un piso a algn, arrendar un departamento a algn (*LAm*) • **to ~ a house (out) to sb** alquilar una casa a algn • **it is ~ed out at £400 a week** está alquilado a 400 libras por semana
CPD ▸ **rent book** (*for accommodation*) librito *m* del alquiler ▸ **rent boy*** chapero‡ *m* ▸ **rent collector** recaudador(a) *m/f* de alquileres ▸ **rent control** control *m* de alquileres ▸ **rent rebate** devolución *f* de alquiler ▸ **rent roll** lista *f* de alquileres, total *m* de ingresos por alquileres

rent[2] [rent] PT, PP *of* **rend**
N (= *tear*) rasgón *m*, rasgadura *f*; (= *split*) abertura *f*, raja *f*, hendedura *f*; (*fig*) escisión *f*, cisma *m*

rental ['rentl] N [*of car, TV etc*] (= *hire*) alquiler *m*; (*Brit*) (= *cost*) alquiler *m*, arriendo *m* (*LAm*) • **car ~ is included in the price** el alquiler del coche está incluído en el precio
CPD ▸ **rental car** (*US*) coche *m* de alquiler ▸ **rental value** valor *m* de alquiler

rent-a-mob* ['rentəmɒb] N (*Brit*) turba *f* alquilada

rent-controlled ['rentkənˌtrəʊld] ADJ • **a rent-controlled flat** un piso *or* (*LAm*) un departamento de alquiler controlado

rent-free ['rent'fri:] ADJ [*house etc*] exento de alquiler
ADV • **to live rent-free** ocupar una casa sin pagar alquiler

rentier ['rɒntɪeɪ] N rentista *mf*

renting ['rentɪŋ] N arrendamiento *m*

renumber [ˌri:'nʌmbəʳ] VT volver a numerar

renunciation [rɪˌnʌnsɪ'eɪʃən] N renuncia *f*

reoccupy ['ri:'ɒkjʊpaɪ] VT volver a ocupar

reoffend [ˌri:ə'fend] VI reincidir

reopen ['ri:'əʊpən] VT **1** [*+ shop, theatre, border, route*] volver a abrir, reabrir
2 [*+ negotiations, relations, investigation, debate*] reanudar • **to ~ a case** [*police*] reabrir un caso; [*prosecutor, judge*] revisar un proceso • **to ~ old wounds** reabrir viejas heridas
VI [*shop, theatre*] volverse a abrir; [*negotiations*] reanudarse • **school ~s on the 8th** el nuevo curso comienza el día 8

reopening [ˌri:'əʊpnɪŋ] N [*of shop, school, theatre, border, route*] reapertura *f*; [*of investigation, negotiations, debate*] reanudación *f*; (*Jur*) [*of case*] reapertura *f* • **the ~ of old wounds** (*fig*) la reapertura de viejas heridas

reorder ['ri:'ɔ:dəʳ] VT **1** (*Comm*) volver a pedir
2 (= *rearrange*) [*+ objects*] ordenar de nuevo, volver a poner en orden

reorganization [ˈri:ˌɔ:gənaɪ'zeɪʃən] N reorganización *f*

reorganize ['ri:'ɔ:gənaɪz] VT reorganizar
VI reorganizarse

reorientate [ri:'ɔ:rɪenteɪt], **reorient** [ri:'ɔ:rɪent] VT reorientar

reorientation [ri:ɔ:rɪen'teɪʃən] N reorientación *f*

rep[1] [rep] N (= *fabric*) reps *m*

rep[2]* [rep] N (*Comm*) (= **representative**) viajante *mf*, agente *mf*; [*of union etc*] representante *mf*
VI • **to rep for** ser agente de

rep[3]* [rep] N (*Theat*) = **repertory**

Rep. ABBR **1** (= **Republic**) Rep.
2 (*US*) (*Pol*) = **Republican**
3 (*US*) (*Pol*) = **Representative**

repack ['ri:'pæk] VT [*+ object*] reembalar, reenvasar, devolver a su caja *etc*; [*+ suitcase*] volver a hacer

repackage [ˌri:'pækɪdʒ] VT [*+ product*] reempaquetar; [*+ parcel*] reembalar; (*fig*) [*+ proposal, scheme*] reformular

repaid [ri:'peɪd] PT, PP *of* **repay**

repaint ['ri:'peɪnt] VT repintar • **to ~ sth blue** repintar algo de azul

repair[1] [rɪ'pɛəʳ] N **1** (= *act*) reparación *f*, arreglo *m* • **she had taken her car in for ~s** había llevado el coche al taller • **to be beyond ~** (*lit, fig*) no tener arreglo • **the chair is broken beyond ~** la silla no tiene arreglo • **"closed for repairs"** "cerrado por obras", "cerrado por reforma" • **"(shoe) repairs while you wait"** "arreglamos zapatos al momento", "reparaciones de calzado en el acto"; ▹ **road**
2 (= *state*) • **to be in bad** *or* **poor ~** • **be in a bad** *or* **poor state of ~** estar en mal estado • **to be in good ~** • **be in a good state of ~** estar en buen estado
VT **1** (= *mend*) [*+ car, machinery, roof*] arreglar, reparar; [*+ clothes, shoes, road*] arreglar
2 (= *heal*) • **they wish to ~ relations with the West** quieren cerrar la brecha *or* conciliarse con Occidente
3 (= *rectify*) [*+ wrong*] reparar
CPD ▸ **repair job** arreglo *m*, reparación *f* • **they've done a superb ~ job on my car** me han arreglado el coche estupendamente ▸ **repair kit** kit *m* de reparación ▸ **repair shop** taller *m* de reparaciones • **auto ~ shop** (*US*) taller *m* mecánico • **bicycle ~ shop** taller *m* de reparación de bicicletas ▸ **repair work** arreglos *mpl*, reparaciones *fpl*

repair[2] [rɪ'pɛəʳ] VI (*frm*) (= *go*) • **to ~ to** dirigirse a • **we all ~ed to a restaurant** todos nos dirigimos a un restaurante

repairable [rɪ'pɛərəbl] ADJ reparable

repairer [rɪ'pɛərəʳ] N reparador(a) *m/f*

repairman [rɪ'pɛəmæn] N (PL: **repairmen**) (*US*) reparador *m*

repaper ['ri:'peɪpəʳ] VT empapelar de nuevo

reparable ['repərəbl] ADJ = **repairable**

reparation [ˌrepə'reɪʃən] N reparación *f* • **to make ~ to sb for sth** indemnizar a algn por algo

repartee [ˌrepɑ:'ti:] N réplicas *fpl* agudas

repartition [ˌri:pɑ:'tɪʃən] N repartición *f*
VT repartir

repass ['ri:'pɑ:s] VT repasar

repast [rɪ'pɑ:st] N (*liter*) comida *f*

repatriate VT [ri:'pætrɪeɪt] repatriar

(N) [ri:'pætrɪət] repatriado/a *m/f*

repatriation [ri:,pætrɪ'eɪʃən] (N) repatriación *f*

repay [ri:'peɪ] (PT, PP: **repaid**) (VT) [+ *money*] reembolsar, devolver; [+ *debt*] liquidar, pagar; [+ *person*] reembolsar, pagar; [+ *kindness etc*] devolver, corresponder a; [+ *visit*] devolver, pagar • **to ~ sb in full** pagar *or* devolver a algn todo lo que se le debe • **how can I ever ~ you?** ¿podré corresponderle alguna vez? • **I don't know how I can ever ~ you** no sé cómo podré devolverle el favor • **it ~s study** vale la pena estudiarlo • **it ~s a visit** vale la pena visitarlo • **it ~s reading** vale la pena leerlo

repayable [ri:'peɪəbl] (ADJ) reembolsable • **~ on demand** reembolsable a petición • **~ in ten instalments** a pagar en diez cuotas • **£5 deposit not ~** desembolso inicial de 5 libras no reembolsable • **the money is ~ on 5 June** el dinero ha de ser devuelto el 5 de junio

repayment [ri:'peɪmənt] (N) [*of expenses*] reembolso *m* • **now he asks for ~** ahora pide que se le devuelva el dinero • **in six ~s of £8** en seis cuotas de 8 libras cada uno • **mortgage ~s** los pagos de la hipoteca
(CPD) ▸ **repayment mortgage** (*Brit*) hipoteca *f* amortizada (*en la que se va pagando a la vez el capital y los intereses*) ▸ **repayment schedule** plan *m* de amortización

repeal [rɪ'pi:l] (VT) revocar, abrogar
(N) revocación *f*, abrogación *f*

repeat [rɪ'pi:t] (VT) **1** (= *say or do again*) repetir; [+ *thanks*] reiterar, volver a dar; [+ *demand, request, promise*] reiterar; (*Scol*) [+ *year, subject*] repetir • **could you ~ that, please?** ¿podría repetir (eso), por favor? • **this offer cannot be ~ed** esta oferta no se repetirá • **the pattern is ~ed on the collar and cuffs** el dibujo se repite en el cuello y en los puños • **~ after me, I must not steal** repetid conmigo, no debo robar • **could history ~ itself?** ¿se podría repetir la historia? • **to ~ o.s.** repetirse • **at the risk of ~ing myself** con el peligro de repetirme
2 (= *divulge*) contar • **don't ~ this to anybody** no le cuentes esto a nadie
3 (= *recite*) recitar
4 (*esp Brit*) (*TV*) [+ *programme*] repetir; [+ *series*] repetir, reponer • **the programme will be ~ed on Monday** el programa se repetirá el lunes
(VI) **1** (= *say or do again*) repetir • **we are not, I ~, not going to give up** no vamos, repito, no vamos a ceder • **lather the hair, rinse and ~** aplicar al cabello formando espuma, aclarar y repetir la operación
2* [*food*] repetir* • **radishes ~ on me** me repite el rábano*
3 (*Math*) [*number*] repetirse
(N) **1** repetición *f* • **in order to prevent a ~ of the tragedy** para evitar la repetición de la tragedia, para evitar que la tragedia se repita
2 (*esp Brit*) (*TV*) [*of programme*] repetición *f*; [*of series*] repetición *f*, reposición *f* • **it can be seen tonight at eight, with a ~ on Monday** se podrá ver esta noche a las ocho y será repetido el lunes
3 (*Mus*) repetición *f*
(CPD) ▸ **repeat mark(s)** (*Mus*) símbolo(s) *m(pl)* de repetición ▸ **repeat offender** delincuente *mf* reincidente ▸ **repeat order** (*Brit*) (*Comm*) orden *f* repetida ▸ **repeat performance** (*Theat*) (*also fig*) repetición *f* • **he will give a ~ performance on Friday** hará una repetición el viernes, repetirá la función el viernes • **I don't want a ~ performance of your behaviour last time** que no se repita tu comportamiento de la última vez ▸ **repeat prescription** (*Brit*) receta *f* renovada ▸ **repeat sign** (*Mus*) = **repeat mark**

repeated [rɪ'pi:tɪd] (ADJ) [*attacks, warnings, attempts*] repetido; [*requests, demands*] reiterado; [*criticism*] constante • **there have been ~ calls for his resignation** se ha pedido su dimisión reiteradamente *or* repetidas veces

repeatedly [rɪ'pi:tɪdlɪ] (ADV) repetidamente, reiteradamente, repetidas veces • **he has ~ denied the allegations** ha desmentido repetidamente *or* reiteradamente *or* repetidas veces las acusaciones • **they tried ~ to free her** hubo repetidos intentos de liberarla • **he ~ broke the rules** infringía las reglas constantemente

repeater [rɪ'pi:təʳ] (N) **1** (= *watch*) reloj *m* de repetición; (= *rifle*) rifle *m* de repetición
2 (*US*) (*Jur*) reincidente *mf*

repeating [rɪ'pi:tɪŋ] (ADJ) [*clock, rifle*] de repetición; [*pattern*] repetido; (*Math*) periódico

repechage [,repɪ'ʃɑ:ʒ] (N) repesca *f*

repel [rɪ'pel] (VT) **1** (= *force back*) repeler, rechazar
2 (= *disgust*) repugnar, dar asco a • **he ~s me** me da asco, me repugna • **it ~s me to have to** (+ *infin*) me repugna tener que (+ *infin*)
(VI) repelerse mutuamente

repellant [rɪ'pelənt] (N) = **repellent**

repellent [rɪ'pelənt] (ADJ) **1** (= *disgusting*) repugnante, asqueroso
2 • **it is ~ to insects** (= *drives away*) ahuyenta los insectos
(N) (*also* **insect repellent**) repelente *m* contra insectos

repent [rɪ'pent] (VI) arrepentirse (**of** de)
(VT) arrepentirse de

repentance [rɪ'pentəns] (N) arrepentimiento *m*

repentant [rɪ'pentənt] (ADJ) arrepentido

repeople ['ri:'pi:pl] (VT) repoblar

repercussion [,ri:pə'kʌʃən] (N) repercusión *f* • **~s** (*fig*) repercusiones *fpl* • **as for the political ~s** en cuanto a las repercusiones políticas • **it had great ~s in France** tuvo gran resonancia en Francia

repertoire ['repətwɑ:ʳ] (N) [*of songs, jokes*] repertorio *m*

repertory ['repətərɪ] (N) (= *stock*) repertorio *m*
(CPD) ▸ **repertory company** compañía *f* de repertorio ▸ **repertory theatre, repertory theater** (*US*) teatro *m* de repertorio

repetition [,repɪ'tɪʃən] (N) repetición *f*

repetitious [,repɪ'tɪʃəs] (ADJ) = **repetitive**

repetitive [rɪ'petɪtɪv] (ADJ) repetitivo, reiterativo • **the book is a bit ~** el libro tiene sus repeticiones
(CPD) ▸ **repetitive strain injury, repetitive stress injury** *lesión en las muñecas y los brazos sufrida por teclistas*

rephrase [ri:'freɪz] (VT) expresar de otro modo, decir con otras palabras

repine [rɪ'paɪn] (VI) (*liter*) quejarse (**at** de), afligirse (**at** por)

replace [rɪ'pleɪs] (VT) **1** (= *put back*) volver a colocar • **~ the cap after use** vuelva a colocar la tapa después de usarlo • **he ~d the letter in his pocket** se volvió a meter la carta en el bolsillo • **to ~ the receiver** colgar (el auricular)
2 (= *get replacement for*) [+ *object*] reponer; [+ *person*] sustituir, reemplazar • **the body has to ~ lost fluid** el cuerpo tiene que reponer los líquidos perdidos • **we will ~ the broken glasses** repondremos *or* pagaremos los vasos rotos • **they are not going to ~ her when she leaves** cuando se vaya no van sustituirla *or* reemplazarla, no van a poner a nadie en su lugar cuando se vaya
3 (= *put in place of*) • **to ~ sth with sth** sustituir algo por algo • **the airline is replacing its DC10s with Boeing 747s** la compañía aérea está sustituyendo los DC10 por Boeings 747 • **to ~ sb with sth/sb** sustituir a algn por algo/algn, reemplazar a algn por *or* con algo/algn • **many workers are being ~d by machines** están sustituyendo a muchos trabajadores por máquinas, están reemplazando a muchos trabajadores por *or* con máquinas
4 (= *take the place of*) [+ *thing*] sustituir; [+ *person*] sustituir, reemplazar • **chopped chives can ~ the parsley** el perejil se puede sustituir por cebolletas picadas • **he ~d Evans as managing director** sustituyó *or* reemplazó a Evans en el puesto de director gerente • **nobody could ever ~ him in my heart** nadie podrá jamás ocupar su lugar en mi corazón
5 (= *change*) cambiar • **the battery needs replacing** hay que cambiar la pila

replaceable [rɪ'pleɪsəbl] (ADJ) reemplazable, sustituible • **it will not easily be ~** no será fácil encontrar uno igual • **he will not easily be ~** no será fácil encontrar un sustituto

replacement [rɪ'pleɪsmənt] (N) **1** (= *putting back*) reposición *f*; (= *substituting*) sustitución *f* (**by, with** por); ▹ **hormone**
2 (= *substitute*) **a** (= *person*) sustituto/a *m/f*, suplente *mf* (**for** de)
b (= *thing*) • **it took three days to find a ~** tardaron tres días en encontrar un repuesto • **you can get a ~ if the goods are faulty** le damos uno nuevo si el artículo está defectuoso
(CPD) ▸ **replacement cost** costo *m* de sustitución ▸ **replacement engine** motor *m* de repuesto ▸ **replacement part** repuesto *m* ▸ **replacement value** valor *m* de sustitución

replant ['ri:'plɑ:nt] (VT) replantar

replay [,ri:'pleɪ] (*esp Brit*) (VT) (*Sport*) [+ *match*] volver a jugar; (*Mus*) volver a tocar; [+ *tape*] volver a poner
(VI) [,ri:'pleɪ] (*Sport*) volver a jugar
(N) ['ri:pleɪ] [*of match*] repetición *f* de un partido • **there will be a ~ on Friday** el partido se volverá a jugar el viernes; ▹ **action**

replenish [rɪ'plenɪʃ] (VT) [+ *tank etc*] rellenar, llenar de nuevo; [+ *stocks*] reponer

replenishment [rɪ'plenɪʃmənt] (N) [*of tank*] rellenado *m*; [*of stocks*] reposición *f*

replete [rɪ'pli:t] (ADJ) (*liter*) repleto, lleno (**with** de)

repletion [rɪ'pli:ʃən] (N) (*liter*) saciedad *f*, repleción *f* • **to eat to ~** comer realmente bien

replica ['replɪkə] (N) réplica *f*, reproducción *f*

replicate ['replɪ,keɪt] (VT) reproducir exactamente

reply [rɪ'plaɪ] (N) **1** (*spoken, written*) respuesta *f*, contestación *f* • **he has had 12 replies to his ad** han contestado 12 personas a su anuncio • **I sent a ~ to her letter this morning** contesté *or* respondí a su carta esta mañana • **"reply paid"** "no necesita sello", "a franquear en destino" • **~-paid envelope** sobre *m* a franquear en destino • **in ~** en respuesta • **in ~ to your letter** en respuesta a *or* contestando a su carta • **he had nothing to say in ~** no tenía nada que responder *or* contestar • **there's no ~** (*Telec*) no contestan • **to make no ~ (to sth)** no responder (a algo), no contestar (algo) • **she made no ~ except to nod** su única reacción fue asentir con la cabeza

r

2 (*= reaction, response*) reacción *f*, respuesta *f* • **a loud sob was his only ~** un fuerte sollozo fue su única reacción *or* respuesta
3 (*abrupt*) réplica *f*
4 (*Jur*) réplica *f*
VI 1 responder, contestar • **to ~ to sb** contestar *or* responder a algn • **to ~ to sth** responder *or* contestar a algo • **to ~ to a letter** contestar (a) una carta • **the police replied with tear gas** la policía respondió con gas lacrimógeno
2 (*Jur*) replicar
VT 1 (*gen*) responder, contestar • **he replied that this was impossible** respondió *or* contestó que esto era imposible
2 (*abruptly*) replicar
CPD ▸ **reply coupon** cupón *m* de respuesta
repoint [ri:ˈpɔɪnt] VT rejuntar
repointing [ri:ˈpɔɪntɪŋ] N rejuntamiento *m*
repopulate [ˈri:ˈpɒpjʊleɪt] VT repoblar
repopulation [ˈri:ˌpɒpjʊˈleɪʃən] N repoblación *f*
report [rɪˈpɔ:t] N 1 (*= account*) informe *m*; (*Press, Rad, TV*) reportaje *m*, crónica *f*; (*= piece of news*) noticia *f* • **there were no ~s of casualties** no se anunciaron víctimas • **to give** *or* **make** *or* **present a ~ (on sth)** presentar un informe (sobre algo); ▸ **law, progress**
2 (*Brit*) (*also* **school report**) boletín *m or* cartilla *f* de notas; (*US*) (*= assignment*) trabajo *m* • **to get a good/bad ~** sacar buenas/malas notas
3 (*= rumour*) rumor *m* • **according to ~(s)** según se dice
4 (*liter*) (*= reputation*) reputación *f*, fama *f* • **a person of good ~** una persona de buena reputación *or* fama
5 (*= bang*) estallido *m*; (*= shot*) disparo *m*
VT 1 (*= state, make known*) • **it is ~ed from Berlin that ...** comunican *or* se informa desde Berlín que ... • **nothing to ~** sin novedad
2 (*Press, TV, Rad*) [*+ event*] informar acerca de, informar sobre
3 (*= allege*) • **she is ~ed to be in Italy** se dice que está en Italia • **he is ~ed to have said that ...** parece que dijo que ...
4 (*= notify*) [*+ crime*] denunciar, dar parte de; [*+ accident*] dar parte de • **13 people were ~ed killed** hubo informes de que murieron 13 personas • **to ~ sb missing** denunciar la desaparición de algn, declarar a algn desaparecido
5 (*= denounce*) [*+ person*] denunciar • **to ~ sb (to sb) (for sth)** denunciar a algn (a algn) (por algo) • **he ~ed her to the Inland Revenue for not paying her taxes** la denunció a Hacienda por no pagar impuestos
6 • **~ed speech** estilo *m* indirecto
VI 1 (*= make report*) presentar un informe
2 (*Press, TV, Rad*) (*gen*) informar; (*as reporter*) ser reportero/a • **he ~ed for the Daily Echo for 40 years** durante 40 años fue reportero del "Daily Echo" • **this is Jim Dale ~ing from Chicago** aquí Jim Dale (informando) desde Chicago • **to ~ on sth** informar sobre algo
3 (*= present oneself*) presentarse • **when you arrive, ~ to the receptionist** cuando llegue, preséntese en recepción • **he has to ~ to the police every five days** tiene que personarse *or* presentarse en la comisaría cada cinco días • **to ~ for duty** (*Mil*) presentarse para el servicio • **to ~ sick** darse de baja por enfermedad
4 • **to ~ to sb** (*= be responsible to*) estar bajo las órdenes de algn • **he ~s to the marketing director** está bajo las órdenes del director de márketing • **who do you ~ to?** ¿quién es tu superior *or* tu jefe?
CPD ▸ **report card** (*US*) (*Scol*) boletín *m or* cartilla *f* de notas ▸ **report stage** (*Brit*) (*Parl*) • **the bill has reached** *or* **is at the ~ stage** se están debatiendo los informes de las comisiones sobre el proyecto de ley
▸ **report back** VI + ADV 1 (*= give report*) (*gen*) informar; (*officially*) presentar un informe
2 (*= return*) volver (a presentarse) • **~ back at six o'clock** vuelva (a presentarse) a las seis
VT + ADV • **my every move was ~ed back to my superiors** se informaba a mis superiores de todo lo que hacía
reportable [rɪˈpɔ:təbl] ADJ [*event*] denunciable; (*Med*) [*disease*] denunciable, reportable (*LAm*); [*capital gains, income etc*] declarable
reportage [ˌrepɔ:ˈtɑ:ʒ] N (*= news report*) reportaje *m*; (*= technique*) periodismo *m*
reportedly [rɪˈpɔ:tɪdlɪ] ADV según se dice • **he is ~ living in Australia** se dice que está viviendo en Australia
reporter [rɪˈpɔ:təʳ] N (*Press*) periodista *mf*, reportero/a *m/f*; (*TV, Rad*) locutor(a) *m/f*
reporting [rɪˈpɔ:tɪŋ] N (*Press, TV, Rad*) cobertura *f*, reportajes *mpl* • **her ~ of the war in Bosnia** su cobertura *or* sus reportajes de la guerra en Bosnia
CPD ▸ **reporting restrictions** (*Press, TV, Rad*) restricciones *fpl* informativas
repose [rɪˈpəʊz] (*frm*) N (*= rest, sleep*) reposo *m*, descanso *m*; (*= calm*) calma *f*, tranquilidad *f*
VI (*= rest, be buried*) reposar, descansar • **to ~ on** descansar sobre
VT 1 (*= lay*) reposar, descansar
2 (*= put*) • **to ~ confidence in sb** depositar confianza en algn
reposition [ˌri:pəˈzɪʃən] VT reposicionar
repository [rɪˈpɒzɪtərɪ] N depósito *m* • **furniture ~** guardamuebles *m inv*
repossess [ˈri:pəˈzes] VT recobrar • **to ~ o.s. of sth** recobrar algo, volver a tomar algo
repossession [ˌri:pəˈzeʃən] N recuperación *f* (*de un artículo no pagado*)
CPD ▸ **repossession order** orden *m* de recuperación
repot [ri:ˈpɒt] VT poner en nueva maceta, cambiar de maceta
reprehend [ˌreprɪˈhend] VT reprender
reprehensible [ˌreprɪˈhensɪbl] ADJ reprensible, censurable
reprehensibly [ˌreprɪˈhensɪblɪ] ADV censurablemente
reprehension [ˌreprɪˈhenʃən] N reprensión *f*
represent [reprɪˈzent] VT 1 (*= stand for, symbolize*) representar
2 (*= act or speak for*) [*+ client, country*] representar a; [*+ company*] ser agente de; [*+ change, achievement*] representar • **he ~s nobody but himself** no representa a nadie sino a sí mismo • **his early work is well ~ed in the exhibition** sus primeros trabajos están bien representados en la exposición, su primera época está bien representada
3 (*frm*) (*= convey, explain*) presentar, describir • **you ~ed it falsely to us** usted nos lo describió falsamente • **it has been ~ed to us that ...** se ha pretendido que ..., se nos ha dicho que ... • **the goods are not as ~ed** las mercancías no son como nos las describieron
re-present [ˈri:prɪˈzent] VT volver a presentar
representation [ˌreprɪzenˈteɪʃən] N 1 (*also Pol*) representación *f* • **to make false ~s** describir algo falsamente
2 (*= protest*) • **to make ~s to sb** levantar una protesta a algn • **to make ~s about sth** quejarse de algo; ▸ **proportional**
representational [ˌreprɪzenˈteɪʃənəl] ADJ (*Art*) figurativo
representative [ˌreprɪˈzentətɪv] ADJ representativo (**of de**) • **these figures are more ~** estas cifras son más representativas • **~ government** gobierno *m* representativo • **a person not fully ~ of the group** una persona que no representa adecuadamente el grupo
N 1 (*gen*) representante *mf*
2 (*esp Brit*) (*Comm*) viajante *mf*
3 (*US*) (*Pol*) • **Representative** ≈ diputado/a *m/f* • **the House of Representatives** la cámara de Representantes, ≈ el Senado
representativeness [ˌreprɪˈzentətɪvnɪs] N [*of sample, cross-section*] representatividad *f*
repress [rɪˈpres] VT reprimir
repressed [rɪˈprest] ADJ reprimido
repression [rɪˈpreʃən] N (*also Psych*) represión *f*
repressive [rɪˈpresɪv] ADJ represivo
reprieve [rɪˈpri:v] N 1 (*Jur*) indulto *m*; [*of sentence*] conmutación *f* • **to win a last-minute ~** ser indultado a última hora
2 (*= delay*) aplazamiento *m*, alivio *m* temporal • **the building got a ~** se retiró la orden de demoler el edificio
VT 1 (*Jur*) indultar • **to ~ sb from death** suspender la pena de muerte de algn
2 (*fig*) salvar
reprimand [ˈreprɪmɑ:nd] N reprimenda *f*
VT reprender, regañar
reprint [ˈri:prɪnt] N reimpresión *f*, reedición *f*
VT [ˌri:ˈprɪnt] reimprimir
reprisal [rɪˈpraɪzəl] N represalia *f* • **to take ~s** tomar represalias • **as a ~ for** como represalia por • **by way of ~** a modo de represalia
reprise [rɪˈpri:z] N repetición *f*
VT repetir
reprivatize [ˌri:ˈpraɪvətaɪz] VT (*Econ*) reprivatizar
repro* [ˈri:prəʊ] N ABBR = **reprographics, reprography**
ABBR = **reproduction** • **~ furniture** muebles *mpl* de imitación
reproach [rɪˈprəʊtʃ] N reproche *m* • **above** *or* **beyond ~** intachable, irreprochable • **that is a ~ to us all** es un reproche a todos nosotros • **poverty is a ~ to civilization** la pobreza es una vergüenza para la sociedad • **term of ~** término *m* oprobioso
VT • **to ~ sb for sth** reprochar algo a algn • **to ~ o.s. for sth** reprocharse algo • **you have no reason to ~ yourself** no tienes motivos para reprocharte (nada)
reproachful [rɪˈprəʊtʃfʊl] ADJ [*look etc*] de reproche, de acusación
reproachfully [rɪˈprəʊtʃfəlɪ] ADV [*look*] con reproche; [*speak*] en tono acusador
reprobate [ˈreprəʊbeɪt] N réprobo/a *m/f*
reprobation [ˌreprəʊˈbeɪʃən] N reprobación *f*
reprocess [ˌri:ˈprəʊses] VT reprocesar
reprocessing [ˌri:ˈprəʊsesɪŋ] N reprocesamiento *m*
CPD ▸ **reprocessing plant** planta *f* de reprocesamiento
reproduce [ˌri:prəˈdju:s] VT reproducir
VI (*Bio*) reproducirse
reproducible [ˌri:prəˈdju:sɪbl] ADJ reproducible
reproduction [ˌri:prəˈdʌkʃən] N 1 (*= act of reproducing*) reproducción *f*; (*= copy*) copia *f*, reproducción *f*
2 (*Bio*) reproducción *f*
CPD ▸ **reproduction furniture** muebles *mpl* antiguos de imitación

reproductive [ˌri:prəˈdʌktɪv] (ADJ) reproductor

reprographic [ˌri:prəˈgræfɪk] (ADJ) de reprografía • **~s** reprografía

reprography [rɪˈprɒgrəfɪ] (N) reprografía *f*

reproof [ˌri:ˈpru:f] (N) reprobación *f*, regaño *m* • **to administer a ~ to sb** reprender a algn

re-proof [ˌri:ˈpru:f] (VT) [+ *garment*] impermeabilizar de nuevo

reproval [rɪˈpru:vəl] (N) reprobación *f*

reprove [rɪˈpru:v] (VT) • **to ~ sb for sth** reprobar a algn por algo

reproving [rɪˈpru:vɪŋ] (ADJ) reprobador, lleno de reproches

reprovingly [rɪˈpru:vɪŋlɪ] (ADV) [*speak*] en tono reprobador, con reprobación • **she looked at me ~** me miró severa, me reprendió con la mirada

reptile [ˈreptaɪl] (N) reptil *m*
(CPD) ▸ **reptile house** reptilario *m*

reptilian [repˈtɪlɪən] (ADJ) reptil
(N) reptil *m*

Repub. (ABBR) **1** = **Republic**
2 = **Republican**

republic [rɪˈpʌblɪk] (N) república *f*
(CPD) ▸ **Republic of Ireland** • **the Republic of Ireland** la República de Irlanda

republican [rɪˈpʌblɪkən] (ADJ) republicano
(N) republicano/a *m/f*
(CPD) ▸ **Republican Party** (*in US*) Partido *m* Republicano

republicanism [rɪˈpʌblɪkənɪzəm] (N) republicanismo *m*

republication [ˈri:ˌpʌblɪˈkeɪʃən] (N) reedición *f*

republish [ˈri:ˈpʌblɪʃ] (VT) reeditar

repudiate [rɪˈpju:dɪeɪt] (VT) **1** (= *deny*) [+ *charge*] rechazar, negar
2 (= *refuse to recognize*) [+ *debt, treaty*] negarse a reconocer, desconocer; [+ *attitude, values, wife, violence*] repudiar

repudiation [rɪˌpju:dɪˈeɪʃən] (N) **1** (= *denial*) rechazo *m*, negación *f*
2 (= *refusal to recognize*) [*of debt, treaty*] negativa *f* a reconocer, desconocimiento *m*; [*of attitude, values, wife, violence*] repudio *m*

repugnance [rɪˈpʌgnəns] (N) repugnancia *f*

repugnant [rɪˈpʌgnənt] (ADJ) repugnante • **it is ~ to me** me repugna

repulse [rɪˈpʌls] (VT) (*gen*) rechazar
(N) rechazo *m* • **to suffer a ~** ser rechazado

repulsion [rɪˈpʌlʃən] (N) **1** (= *disgust*) repulsión *f*, repugnancia *f*
2 (= *rejection*) rechazo *m*

repulsive [rɪˈpʌlsɪv] (ADJ) repulsivo, repugnante

repulsively [rɪˈpʌlsɪvlɪ] (ADV) de modo repulsivo, de modo repugnante • **~ ugly** tan feo que da/daba *etc* asco

repulsiveness [rɪˈpʌlsɪvnɪs] (N) lo repulsivo, lo repugnante

repurchase [ˈri:ˈpɜ:tʃɪs] (N) readquisición *f*
(VT) readquirir, volver a comprar

reputable [ˈrepjʊtəbl] (ADJ) [*firm, brand*] acreditado, de confianza; [*person*] honroso, formal

reputably [ˈrepjʊtəblɪ] (ADV) seriamente • **he is ~ established in the business world** tiene una seria reputación en el mundo de los negocios

reputation [ˌrepjʊˈteɪʃən] (N) reputación *f*, fama *f* • **to have a bad ~** tener mala fama • **of good ~** de buena fama • **he has a ~ for being awkward** tiene fama de difícil • **the hotel has a ~ for good food** el hotel es célebre por su buena comida • **to live up to one's ~** merecer la reputación • **to ruin a girl's ~** acabar con la buena reputación de una joven

repute [rɪˈpju:t] (N) reputación *f*, renombre *m* • **a firm of ~** una casa acreditada • **a café of ill ~** un café con mala fama • **a house of ill ~** (*euph*) una casa de mala fama • **to hold sb in (high) ~** tener un alto concepto de algn • **his skill was held in high ~** su destreza era muy estimada • **by ~** según la opinión común, según se dice • **to know sb by ~ only** conocer a algn solo por su reputación *or* de oídas nada más
(VT) • **he is ~d to be very fast** se dice que es muy rápido • **she is ~d to be the world's best** tiene fama de ser la mejor del mundo

reputed [rɪˈpju:tɪd] (ADJ) **1** (= *supposed*) supuesto, presunto
2 (= *well known*) renombrado

reputedly [rɪˈpju:tɪdlɪ] (ADV) según dicen

request [rɪˈkwest] (N) (*gen*) solicitud *f*; (= *plea*) petición *f* • **at the ~ of** a petición de • **by ~** a petición • **to play a record by ~** tocar un disco a petición de un oyente • **by popular ~** por petición popular, a petición del público • **a ~ for help** una petición de socorro • **to grant sb's ~** acceder al ruego de algn • **it is much in ~** tiene mucha demanda, está muy solicitado • **to make a ~ for sth** pedir algo • **on ~** a solicitud
(VT) pedir, solicitar • **to ~ sb to do sth** pedir a algn hacer algo • **to ~ sth of sb** pedir algo a algn • **"visitors are requested not to talk"** "se ruega a los visitantes respetar el silencio"
(CPD) ▸ **request (bus) stop** parada *f* discrecional ▸ **request programme** (*Rad*) programa *m* con peticiones de discos

requiem [ˈrekwɪem] (N) réquiem *m*
(CPD) ▸ **requiem mass** misa *f* de réquiem

require [rɪˈkwaɪəʳ] (VT) **1** (= *need*) necesitar • **is there anything you ~?** ¿necesita usted algo? • **this plant ~s watering frequently** esta planta hay que regarla con frecuencia • **we will do all that is ~d** haremos todo lo que haga falta • **as (and when) ~d** cuando haga falta • **I am willing to give evidence if ~d** estoy dispuesto a testificar si se requiere *or* si es necesario
2 (= *call for, take*) [+ *patience, effort*] requerir • **it ~s a lot of patience** requiere mucha paciencia
3 (= *ask, demand*) • **it's not up to the standard I ~** no tiene el nivel que yo exijo • **your presence is ~d** se requiere su presencia • **what qualifications are ~d?** ¿qué títulos se requieren? • **to ~ that: the law ~s that safety belts be worn** la ley exige que se usen los cinturones de seguridad • **to ~ sb to do sth** exigir que algn haga algo • **the course ~s you to be bilingual** el curso exige que seas bilingüe • **as ~d by law** como *or* según exige la ley • **find out what is ~d of you** averigua qué es lo que te piden

required [rɪˈkwaɪəd] (ADJ) **1** (= *necessary*) necesario • **cut the wood to the ~ length** corte la madera del largo que se necesite • **he couldn't raise the ~ amount of money** no pudo recaudar los fondos necesarios • **the qualities ~ for the job** las cualidades que se requieren para el puesto
2 (= *fixed*) establecido • **within the ~ time** dentro del plazo establecido
3 (= *compulsory*) [*reading*] obligatorio

requirement [rɪˈkwaɪəmənt] (N) **1** (= *need*) necesidad *f* • **our ~s are few** nuestras necesidades son pocas, necesitamos poco
2 (= *condition*) requisito *m* • **Latin is a ~ for the course** el latín es un requisito para este curso, para este curso se exige el latín • **it is one of the ~s of the contract** es una de las estipulaciones del contrato • **to meet all the ~s for sth** reunir todos los requisitos para algo

requisite [ˈrekwɪzɪt] (ADJ) = **required**
(N) requisito *m* • **office ~s** material *msing* de oficina • **toilet ~s** artículos *mpl* de tocador

requisition [ˌrekwɪˈzɪʃən] (N) (*Mil*) requisa *f*, requisición *f*; (= *formal request*) solicitud *f*
(VT) (*Mil*) requisar; (= *formally request*) solicitar

requital [rɪˈkwaɪtl] (N) (*frm*) (= *repayment*) compensación *f*; (= *revenge*) desquite *m*

requite [rɪˈkwaɪt] (VT) (*frm*) (= *make return for*) compensar, recompensar • **to ~ sb's love** corresponder al amor de algn • **that love was not ~d** ese amor no fue correspondido

reran [ˌri:ˈræn] (PT) *of* **rerun**

reread [ˌri:ˈri:d] (PT, PP: **reread** [ˌri:ˈred]) (VT) releer, volver a leer

rerecord [ˌri:rɪˈkɔ:d] (VT) regrabar

reredos [ˈrɪədɒs] (N) (PL: **reredoses**) retablo *m*

reroof [ˌri:ˈru:f] (VT) poner un tejado *or* techo nuevo en *or* a

reroute [ˌri:ˈru:t] (VT) desviar • **the train was ~d through Burgos** el tren pasó por Burgos al ser desviado de su ruta habitual

rerun (VB: PT: **reran**, PP: **rerun**) (N) [ˈri:rʌn] repetición *f*; (*Theat*) reestreno *m*, reposición *f*
(VT) [ˌri:ˈrʌn] [+ *race*] correr de nuevo; (*Theat*) reestrenar, reponer

resale [ˌri:ˈseɪl] (N) reventa *f* • **"not for resale"** "prohibida la venta"
(CPD) ▸ **resale price** precio *m* de reventa ▸ **resale price maintenance** mantenimiento *m* del precio de reventa ▸ **resale value** valor *m* de reventa

resat [ˌri:ˈsæt] (PT), (PP) *of* **resit**

reschedule [ˌri:ˈʃedju:l], (*US*) [ˌri:ˈskedju:l] (VT) [+ *meeting, visit, trip, programme*] cambiar la fecha/hora de; [+ *train service etc*] cambiar el horario de; [+ *repayments, debt*] renegociar; [+ *plans, course*] volver a planificar

rescheduling [ˌri:ˈʃedju:lɪŋ], (*US*) [ˌri:ˈskedju:lɪŋ] (N) [*of meeting, visit, trip, programme*] cambio *m* de fecha/hora; [*of debt*] renegociación *f*

rescind [rɪˈsɪnd] (VT) [+ *contract*] rescindir; [+ *order*] anular; (*Jur*) abrogar

rescission [rɪˈsɪʒən] (N) [*of contract*] rescisión *f*; [*of order*] anulación *f*; (*Jur*) abrogación *f*

rescue [ˈreskju:] (N) rescate *m*, salvamento *m* • **the hero of the ~ was ...** el héroe del rescate *or* salvamento fue ... • **to come/go to sb's ~** acudir en auxilio de algn, socorrer a algn • **to the ~!** ¡al socorro! • **Batman to the ~!** ¡Batman acude a la llamada!
(VT) salvar, rescatar • **three men were ~d** se salvaron tres hombres • **they waited three days to be ~d** esperaron tres días hasta ser rescatados • **to ~ sb from death** salvar a algn de la muerte • **the ~d man is in hospital** el hombre rescatado está en el hospital
(CPD) ▸ **rescue attempt** tentativa *f* de salvamento, tentativa *f* de rescate ▸ **rescue dig** excavación *f* de urgencia ▸ **rescue operations** operaciones *fpl* de salvamento, operaciones *fpl* de rescate ▸ **rescue package** (*Pol, Comm*) paquete *m* de medidas urgentes ▸ **rescue party** equipo *m* de salvamento, equipo *m* de rescate ▸ **rescue services** servicios *mpl* de rescate, servicios *mpl* de salvamento ▸ **rescue team** = **rescue party** ▸ **rescue vessel** buque *m* de salvamento ▸ **rescue work** operación *f* de salvamento, operación *f* de rescate ▸ **rescue worker** persona *f* que trabaja en labores de rescate

rescuer [ˈreskjʊəʳ] (N) salvador(a) *m/f*

resealable [ˌri:ˈsi:ləbl] (ADJ) [*container*] que se puede volver a cerrar

research [rɪˈsɜ:tʃ] (N) investigación *f*, investigaciones *fpl* (**in, into** de) • **~ and**

development investigación *f* y desarrollo *m* • **atomic ~** investigaciones *fpl* atómicas • **our ~ shows that ...** nuestras investigaciones demuestran que ... • **a piece of ~** una investigación; ▹ **market**
(VI) hacer investigaciones • **to ~ into sth** investigar algo
(VT) investigar • **to ~ an article** preparar el material para un artículo, reunir datos para escribir un artículo • **a well ~ed book** un libro bien documentado • **a well ~ed study** un estudio bien preparado
(CPD) ▸ **research assistant** ayudante *mf* de investigación ▸ **research establishment** instituto *m* de investigación ▸ **research fellow** investigador(a) *m/f* ▸ **research fellowship** puesto *m* de investigador(a) en la universidad ▸ **research grant** beca *f* de investigación ▸ **research laboratory** laboratorio *m* de investigación ▸ **research scientist** investigador(a) *m/f* científico/a ▸ **research staff** personal *m* investigador ▸ **research student** estudiante *mf* investigador(a) ▸ **research team** equipo *m* de investigación ▸ **research work** trabajo(s) *m(pl)* de investigación ▸ **research worker** investigador(a) *m/f*

researcher [rɪ'sɜ:tʃəʳ] (N) investigador(a) *m/f*

reseat [,ri:'si:t] (VT) [+ *chair*] poner nuevo asiento a

resection [ri:'sekʃən] (N) **1** (*Survey*) triangulación *f*
2 (*Med*) resección *f*

reseed [,ri:'si:d] (VT) [+ *lawn, pitch*] volver a sembrar

reselection [ri:sɪ'lekʃən] (N) (*Pol*) reselección *f*

resell ['ri:'sel] (PT, PP: **resold**) (VT) revender

reseller [,ri:'seləʳ] (N) revendedor(a) *m/f*

resemblance [rɪ'zembləns] (N) semejanza *f*, parecido *m* • **to bear a strong ~ to sb** parecerse mucho a algn, estar clavado a algn • **to bear no ~ to sb** no parecerse en absoluto a algn • **there is no ~ between them** los dos no se parecen en absoluto • **there is hardly any ~ between this version and the one I gave you** apenas existe parecido entre esta versión y la que te di

resemble [rɪ'zembl] (VT) parecerse a • **he doesn't ~ his father** no se parece a su padre • **they do ~ one another** sí se parecen el uno al otro

resent [rɪ'zent] (VT) • **I ~ that!** ¡me molesta *or* me ofende que digas eso! • **he ~s my being here** le molesta que esté aquí • **I ~ your tone** encuentro tu tono ofensivo • **he ~ed my promotion** le molestaba que me hubiesen ascendido • **he ~s having lost his job** no lleva bien lo de haber perdido el trabajo, le amarga haber perdido el trabajo • **he ~ed the fact that I married her** le molestaba que me hubiese casado con ella • **she ~s having to look after her mother** le amarga tener que cuidar de su madre • **I ~ed him because he was her favourite** tenía celos de él porque era su preferido

resentful [rɪ'zentfʊl] (ADJ) [*person*] resentido; [*tone*] resentido, de resentimiento; [*look, air*] de resentimiento • **he watched them, envious and ~** los observaba, con envidia y resentimiento • **to be *or* feel ~ about/at sth** estar resentido por algo • **he felt ~ about his dismissal** estaba resentido porque lo habían despedido • **he was ~ at the way he had been treated** estaba resentido por la forma en que lo habían tratado • **to be *or* feel ~ of sb: she was ~ of her sister, who was cleverer than her** tenía celos de su hermana, que era más inteligente que ella • **to be ~ of sb's success** tener envidia del éxito de algn • **he still felt ~ towards her because she had rejected him** todavía estaba resentido con ella porque lo había rechazado

resentfully [rɪ'zentfəlɪ] (ADV) [*look, behave*] con resentimiento • **he said ~** dijo resentido *or* con resentimiento

resentment [rɪ'zentmənt] (N) resentimiento *m*, rencor *m* (**about** por) • **I feel no ~ towards him** no le guardo rencor, no estoy resentido con él

reservation [,rezə'veɪʃən] (N) **1** (= *booking*) reserva *f*; (= *seat*) plaza *f* reservada; (= *table in restaurant*) mesa *f* reservada • **to make a ~ in a hotel** reservar una habitación en un hotel
2 (= *doubt*) reserva *f*, duda *f* • **I had ~s about it** tenía ciertas dudas sobre ese punto • **with certain ~s** con ciertas reservas • **to accept sth without ~** aceptar algo sin reserva
3 (*in contract*) salvedad *f*; (*in argument*) distingo *m*
4 (= *area of land*) reserva *f*
5 (*on road*) mediana *f*, franja *f* central; ▹ **central**
(CPD) ▸ **reservation desk** (*Brit*) (*in airport, hotels etc*) mostrador *m* de reservas; (*US*) (= *hotel reception desk*) recepción *f*

reserve [rɪ'zɜ:v] (N) **1** [*of money, fuel, minerals*] reserva *f* • **to have sth in ~** tener algo de reserva • **to have a ~ of strength** tener una reserva de fuerzas • **to keep sth in ~** guardar algo en reserva • **there are untapped ~s of energy** hay fuentes de energía sin explotar todavía • **Spain possesses half the world's ~s of pyrites** España posee la mitad de las reservas mundiales de piritas
2 (*Mil*) • **the ~** la reserva
3 (*esp Brit*) (*Sport*) reserva *mf*, suplente *mf* • **to play in *or* with the ~s** jugar en el segundo equipo
4 (= *land*) reserva *f*; (*also* **game reserve**) coto *m* (de caza); (*also* **nature reserve**) reserva *f* natural
5 (= *restriction*) • **without ~** sin reserva
6 (= *hiding one's feelings*) reserva *f* • **without ~** sin reserva
(VT) **1** (= *book, set aside*) reservar • **that's being ~d for me** eso está reservado para mí • **did you ~ the tickets?** ¿has reservado los billetes? • **to ~ the right to do sth** reservarse el derecho de hacer algo • **to ~ one's strength** conservar las fuerzas • **I'm reserving myself for later** me reservo para más tarde
2 (*Jur*) aplazar • **I ~ judgment on this** me reservo el juicio en este asunto • **the judge ~d sentence** el juez difirió la sentencia
(CPD) ▸ **reserve bank** (*US*) banco *m* de reserva ▸ **reserve currency** divisa *f* de reserva ▸ **reserve fund** fondo *m* de reserva ▸ **reserve petrol tank** (*Brit*), **reserve gas tank** (*US*) depósito *m* de gasolina de reserva ▸ **reserve player** suplente *mf* ▸ **reserve price** (*Brit*) precio *m* mínimo (*fijado en una subasta*) ▸ **reserve team** (*Brit*) (*Sport*) equipo *m* de reserva

reserved [rɪ'zɜ:vd] (ADJ) [*person, behaviour, room, table, seat*] reservado • **to be ~ about sth** ser reservado acerca de algo

reservedly [rɪ'zɜ:vɪdlɪ] (ADV) con reserva

reservist [rɪ'zɜ:vɪst] (N) (*Mil*) reservista *mf*

reservoir ['rezəvwɑ:ʳ] (N) **1** (= *lake*) embalse *m*, represa *f* (*LAm*); (= *tank*) depósito *m* • **natural underground ~** depósito *m* subterráneo natural
2 (*fig*) [*of strength, experience*] reserva *f*

reset ['ri:'set] (VB: PT, PP: **reset**) (VT) [+ *machine*] reajustar; [+ *printing press*] recomponer; [+ *computer*] reinicializar; [+ *bone*] volver a encajar; [+ *jewel*] reengastar
(CPD) ▸ **reset switch** conmutador *m* de reajuste

resettle ['ri:'setl] (VT) [+ *persons*] reasentar; [+ *land*] repoblar
(VI) reasentarse

resettlement ['ri:'setlmənt] (N) [*of people*] reasentamiento *m*; [*of land*] nueva colonización *f*, repoblación *f*

reshape ['ri:'ʃeɪp] (VT) [+ *clay, vase*] remodelar; [+ *policy, constitution*] reformar; [+ *organization*] reorganizar

reshaping [,ri:'ʃeɪpɪŋ] (N) [*of policy*] reforma *f*

reshuffle ['ri:'ʃʌfl] (N) (*Pol*) remodelación *f* • **Cabinet ~** remodelación *f* del gabinete
(VT) **1** [+ *cards*] volver a barajar
2 [+ *cabinet, board of directors*] remodelar

reside [rɪ'zaɪd] (VI) (*frm*) residir, vivir • **to ~ in *or* with** (*fig*) residir en • **the problem ~s there** ahí radica el problema

residence ['rezɪdəns] (N) **1** (= *stay*) permanencia *f*, estancia *f* (*LAm*) • **after six months' ~** después de seis meses de permanencia • **to take up ~** (*in house*) instalarse; (*in country*) establecerse • **in ~** residente • **when the students are in ~** cuando están los estudiantes • **there is a doctor in ~** hay un médico interno • **artist in ~** artista *mf* residente • **writer in ~** escritor(a) *m/f* residente
2 (= *home*) residencia *f*, domicilio *m* • **"town and country ~s for sale"** "se venden fincas urbanas y rurales" • **the minister's official ~** la residencia oficial del ministro
3 (*Univ*) (*also* **hall of residence**) residencia *f* universitaria, colegio *m* mayor
(CPD) ▸ **residence hall** (*US*) residencia *f* universitaria, colegio *m* mayor ▸ **residence permit** permiso *m* de residencia

residency ['rezɪdənsɪ] (N) residencia *f*

resident ['rezɪdənt] (ADJ) **1** [*person*] (*also Comput*) residente; [*population*] permanente; [*doctor, servant*] interno; [*bird*] no migratorio • **to be ~ in a town** tener domicilio fijo en una ciudad • **we were ~ there for some years** residimos allí durante varios años
2 (*Comput*) residente
(N) [*of hotel, guesthouse*] huésped *mf*; [*of area, in block of flats*] vecino/a *m/f*; (*in country*) residente *mf* • **~s' association** asociación *f* de vecinos • **the ~s got together to protest** los vecinos se reunieron para protestar

residential [,rezɪ'denʃəl] (ADJ) [*area*] residencial; [*work*] interno
(CPD) ▸ **residential care** atención *f* residencial • **to be in ~ care** [*old person*] estar en una residencia (de ancianos); [*handicapped person*] estar en un centro de atención especial ▸ **residential home** (*for old people*) residencia *f* (de ancianos), hogar *m*; (*for handicapped people*) centro *m* de atención especial ▸ **residential school** internado *m*

residual [rɪ'zɪdjʊəl] (ADJ) residual
(N) **residuals** derechos *mpl* residuales de autor

residuary [rɪ'zɪdjʊərɪ] (ADJ) residual • **~ legatee** legatario/a *m/f* universal

residue ['rezɪdju:] (N) **1** (= *remainder*) resto *m*, residuo *m* • **a ~ of bad feeling** un residuo de rencor, un rencor que queda
2 (*Jur*) bienes *mpl* residuales
3 (*Chem*) residuo *m*

residuum [rɪ'zɪdjʊəm] (N) (PL: **residua**) residuo *m*

resign [rɪ'zaɪn] (VT) [+ *office, post*] dimitir de, renunciar a; [+ *claim, task*] renunciar a • **to ~ a task to others** ceder un cometido a otros • **when he ~ed the leadership** cuando dimitió de *or* renunció a la jefatura • **to ~ o.s. to (doing) sth** resignarse a (hacer) algo • **I ~ed myself to never seeing her again** me

resigné a no volverla a ver nunca más
(VI) 1 dimitir, renunciar • **to ~ in favour of sb** renunciar en favor de algn
2 (*Chess*) abandonar

resignation [,rezɪg'neɪʃən] (N) 1 (= *act*) dimisión *f*, renuncia *f* • **to offer** *or* **send in** *or* **hand in** *or* **submit one's ~** presentar la dimisión
2 (= *state*) resignación *f* (**to** a) • **to await sth with ~** esperar algo resignado, esperar algo con resignación

resigned [rɪ'zaɪnd] (ADJ) resignado (**to** a)

resignedly [rɪ'zaɪnɪdlɪ] (ADV) con resignación

resilience [rɪ'zɪlɪəns] (N) (*Tech*) elasticidad *f*; (*fig*) resistencia *f*

resilient [rɪ'zɪlɪənt] (ADJ) (*Tech*) elástico; (*fig*) resistente

resin ['rezɪn] (N) resina *f*

resinous ['rezɪnəs] (ADJ) resinoso

resist [rɪ'zɪst] (VT) (= *oppose*) resistir(se) a; (= *be unaffected by*) resistir • **to ~ arrest** resistirse a ser detenido, oponer resistencia a la policía • **they ~ed the attack vigorously** resistieron vigorosamente el ataque • **we ~ this change** nos oponemos a este cambio • **to ~ temptation** resistir la tentación • **I couldn't ~ buying it** no me resistí a comprarlo • **I can't ~ saying that ...** no puedo resistir al impulso de decir que ... • **I can't ~ squid** me vuelven loco los calamares • **she can't ~ sweets** no puede resistirse a los dulces
(VI) resistir

resistance [rɪ'zɪstəns] (N) (*gen*) resistencia *f* • **the Resistance** (*Pol*) la Resistencia • **to offer ~** oponer resistencia (**to** a) • **to have good ~ to disease** tener mucha resistencia a la enfermedad • **to take the line of least ~** seguir la ley del mínimo esfuerzo
(CPD) ▸ **resistance fighter** militante *mf* de la Resistencia ▸ **resistance movement** (movimiento *m* de) resistencia *f* ▸ **resistance worker** militante *mf* de la Resistencia

resistant [rɪ'zɪstənt] (ADJ) resistente (**to** a)

resister ['rɪzɪstəʳ] (N) insumiso/a *m/f*

resistible [rɪ'zɪstɪbl] (ADJ) resistible

resistor [rɪ'zɪstəʳ] (N) resistor *m*

resit (VB: PT, PP: **resat**) (*Brit*) (N) ['ri:sɪt] reválida *f*
(VT) ['ri:'sɪt] [+ *exam*] presentarse otra vez a; [+ *subject*] recuperar, examinarse otra vez de
(VI) [,ri:'sɪt] presentarse otra vez, volver a examinarse

resize [,ri:'saɪz] (VT) (*Comput*) [+ *window*] modificar el tamaño de

reskill [,ri:'skɪl] (*Ind*) (VI) reciclarse (*laboralmente*)
(VT) reciclar (*laboralmente*)

resold [,ri:'səʊld] (PT), (PP) *of* **resell**

resole [,ri:'səʊl] (VT) sobresolar, remontar

resolute ['rezəlu:t] (ADJ) [*person*] resuelto, decidido; [*opposition, refusal, faith*] firme • **to take ~ action** actuar con resolución *or* firmeza • **I am ~ in my opposition to these proposals** me opongo firmemente a estas propuestas • **the government is ~ in countering terrorism** el gobierno lucha con firmeza contra el terrorismo

resolutely ['rezəlu:tlɪ] (ADV) [*stride*] resueltamente; [*stare*] con resolución; [*refuse, resist*] firmemente, con firmeza; [*act*] con resolución, con determinación • **to be ~ opposed to sth** • **stand ~ against sth** oponerse firmemente *or* con firmeza a algo

resoluteness ['rezəlu:tnɪs] (N) resolución *f*, determinación *f*

resolution [,rezə'lu:ʃən] (N) 1 (= *determination*) resolución *f*, determinación *f* • **to show ~** mostrarse resuelto *or* determinado
2 (= *solving*) resolución *f*
3 (= *motion*) (*gen*) resolución *f*, proposición *f*; (*Parl*) acuerdo *m* • **to pass a ~** tomar un acuerdo • **to put a ~ to a meeting** someter una moción a votación
4 (= *resolve*) propósito *m* • **good ~s** buenos propósitos *mpl* • **New Year ~s** buenos propósitos *mpl* para el Año Nuevo • **to make a ~ to do sth** resolverse a hacer algo
5 (*Chem*) resolución *f*
6 (*Comput*) definición *f*

resolvable [rɪ'zɒlvəbl] (ADJ) soluble

resolve [rɪ'zɒlv] (N) 1 (= *resoluteness*) resolución *f* • **unshakeable ~** resolución *f* inquebrantable
2 (= *decision*) propósito *m* • **to make a ~ to do sth** resolverse a hacer algo
(VT) 1 (= *find solution to*) resolver, solucionar • **this will ~ your doubts** esto solucionará sus dudas • **the problem is still not ~d** el problema está por resolver
2 (= *decide*) resolver, decidir • **to ~ that ...** acordar que ... • **it was ~d that ...** se acordó que ...
(VI) 1 (= *separate*) resolverse (**into** en) • **the question ~s into four parts** la cuestión se resuelve en cuatro partes
2 (= *decide*) • **to ~ on sth** optar por algo, resolverse por algo • **to ~ on doing sth** acordar hacer algo • **to ~ to do sth** resolverse a hacer algo

resolved [rɪ'zɒlvd] (ADJ) • **to be ~ to do sth** estar resuelto a hacer algo

resonance ['rezənəns] (N) resonancia *f*

resonant ['rezənənt] (ADJ) [*sound*] resonante

resonate ['rezəneɪt] (VI) resonar (**with** de)

resonator ['rezəneɪtəʳ] (N) resonador *m*

resorb [rɪ'sɔ:b] (VT) reabsorber

resorption [rɪ'zɔ:pʃən] (N) resorción *f*

resort [rɪ'zɔ:t] (N) 1 (= *recourse*) recurso *m* • **as a last ~** • **in the last ~** como último recurso • **without ~ to force** sin recurrir a la fuerza
2 (= *place*) lugar *m* de reunión • **holiday ~** (= *area, town*) lugar *m* turístico; (= *complex, hotel*) complejo *m* turístico • **it is a ~ of thieves** es lugar frecuentado por los ladrones, es donde se reúnen los ladrones; ▹ **seaside**
(VI) 1 (= *have recourse to*) recurrir (**to** a) • **to ~ to violence** recurrir a la violencia • **then they ~ed to throwing stones** pasaron luego a tirar piedras • **then you ~ to me for help** así que acudes a mí a pedir ayuda
2 (= *frequent, visit*) • **to ~ to** frecuentar
(CPD) ▸ **resort hotel** hotel *m* (*en un lugar de veraneo*) ▸ **resort town** ciudad *f* de vacaciones

resound [rɪ'zaʊnd] (VI) [*sound*] resonar; [*place*] • **the valley ~ed with shouts** resonaron los gritos por el valle • **the house ~ed with laughter** resonaron las risas por toda la casa

resounding [rɪ'zaʊndɪŋ] (ADJ) [*noise*] sonoro; [*victory, success*] resonante; [*failure*] estrepitoso

resoundingly [rɪ'zaʊndɪŋlɪ] (ADV) • **to defeat sb ~** obtener una victoria resonante sobre algn

resource [rɪ'sɔ:s] (N) 1 (= *expedient*) recurso *m*, expediente *m*
2 resources (= *wealth, goods*) recursos *mpl* • **financial ~s** recursos *mpl* financieros • **natural ~s** recursos *mpl* naturales • **to be at the end of one's ~s** haber agotado sus recursos • **to leave sb to his own ~s** (*fig*) dejar que algn se apañe como pueda • **those ~s are as yet untapped** esos recursos quedan todavía sin explotar
3 (= *resourcefulness*) inventiva *f*
(VT) proveer fondos para • **we are ~d by Pentos** nuestra fuente de fondos es Pentos • **they are generously ~d** son tratados generosamente en cuanto a la provisión de fondos • **an inadequately ~d project** un proyecto insuficientemente financiado

resourced [rɪ'sɔ:st] (ADJ) (*Brit*) • **well-resourced** (*with materials*) bien provisto; (*financially*) con recursos • **under-resourced** (*with materials*) poco provisto; (*financially*) escaso de recursos • **the museum has always been under-resourced in both staff and finances** el museo siempre ha estado escaso de personal y de recursos

resourceful [rɪ'sɔ:sfʊl] (ADJ) ingenioso, con iniciativa

resourcefully [rɪ'sɔ:sfəlɪ] (ADV) ingeniosamente, mostrando tener iniciativa

resourcefulness [rɪ'sɔ:sfʊlnɪs] (N) ingenio *m*, iniciativa *f*

resourcing [rɪ'sɔ:sɪŋ] (N) obtención *f* de recursos

re-sow [,ri:'səʊ] (VT) resembrar, volver a sembrar

re-sowing [,ri:'səʊɪŋ] (N) resembrado *m*

respect [rɪs'pekt] (N) 1 (= *consideration*) respeto *m*, consideración *f* • **she has no ~ for other people's feelings** no respeta los sentimientos de los demás • **out of ~ for sth/sb** por respeto a algo/algn, por consideración hacia algo/algn • **I didn't mention it, out of ~ for Alan** no lo mencioné por respeto a *or* por consideración hacia Alan • **to treat sb with ~** tratar a algn respetuosamente *or* con respeto • **the drink is quite strong so treat it with ~** la bebida es bastante fuerte, así que ten cuidado • **without ~ to the consequences** sin tener en cuenta las consecuencias
2 (= *admiration, esteem*) respeto *m* • **to command ~** imponer respeto, hacerse respetar • **to earn** *or* **gain sb's ~** ganarse el respeto de algn • **we have the greatest ~ for him** le respetamos muchísimo • **she is held in great ~ by her employees** sus empleados le tienen mucho respeto, sus empleados la respetan mucho • **show some ~!** ¡un poco de respeto! • **to win sb's ~** ganarse el respeto de algn • **with (all due) ~** con el debido respeto • **with all due ~, you have no experience in this field** con el debido respeto *or* con todo el respeto del mundo, no tienes experiencia en este campo
3 respects respetos *mpl* (*frm*), recuerdos *mpl*, saludos *mpl* • **give my ~s to everyone** da recuerdos *or* saludos a todos de mi parte • **to pay one's ~s to sb** (*frm*) presentar sus respetos a algn • **to pay one's last ~s to sb** presentar mis/tus/sus *etc* últimos respetos a algn • **John sends his ~s** John os manda recuerdos *or* saludos
4 (= *point, detail*) aspecto *m*, sentido *m* • **in all ~s** en todos los aspectos *or* sentidos • **in certain ~s** hasta cierto punto, en cierta medida, en cierto modo • **in every ~** en todos los aspectos *or* sentidos • **their policies differ in one ~** sus políticas difieren en un aspecto • **in other ~s** por lo demás • **in some/many ~s** en algunos/muchos aspectos *or* sentidos • **in this ~** en este sentido
5 (= *reference, regard*) respecto *m* • **in ~ of** (*frm*) respecto a *or* de • **with ~ to** (*frm*) en lo que respecta a, con respecto a
(VT) 1 (= *esteem*) respetar • **I want him to ~ me as a career woman** quiero que me respete como mujer de carrera • **I ~ him as a musician** lo respeto como músico
2 (= *have consideration for*) [+ *wishes, privacy, opinions*] respetar
3 (= *observe*) [+ *law, treaty*] acatar
4 • **as ~s** por lo que respecta a, en lo

r

concerniente a

respectability [rɪsˌpektəˈbɪlɪtɪ] N respetabilidad *f*

respectable [rɪsˈpektəbl] ADJ **1** (= *deserving respect*) respetable • **for perfectly ~ reasons** por motivos perfectamente legítimos
2 (= *of fair social standing, decent*) respetable, decente • **that's not ~** eso no es respetable *or* decente • **that skirt isn't ~** esa falda no es decente • **a ~ family** una familia respetable • **~ people** gente *f* bien • **in ~ society** en la buena sociedad
3 [*amount*] apreciable • **at a ~ distance** a una distancia prudente • **she lost a ~ sum** perdió una cantidad respetable
4 (= *passable*) • **we made a ~ showing** lo hicimos más o menos bien • **his work is ~ but not brilliant** su obra es aceptable pero no increíble • **my marks were quite ~** mis notas eran bastante decentes

respectably [rɪsˈpektəblɪ] ADV **1** (= *decently*) [*dress, behave*] respetablemente, decentemente
2 (= *quite well*) aceptablemente

respected [rɪsˈpektɪd] ADJ respetado • **a much ~ person** una persona muy respetada

respecter [rɪsˈpektəʳ] N • **to be no ~ of persons** no hacer distinción de personas

respectful [rɪsˈpektfʊl] ADJ respetuoso

respectfully [rɪsˈpektfəlɪ] ADV respetuosamente

respectfulness [rɪsˈpektfʊlnɪs] N respetuosidad *f*, acatamiento *m*

respecting [rɪsˈpektɪŋ] PREP en lo que concierne a, con respecto a

respective [rɪsˈpektɪv] ADJ respectivo

respectively [rɪsˈpektɪvlɪ] ADV respectivamente

respiration [ˌrespɪˈreɪʃən] N respiración *f*

respirator [ˈrespɪreɪtəʳ] N **1** (*Med*) respirador *m*
2 (*Mil*) (= *gas mask*) careta *f* antigás

respiratory [rɪsˈpɪrətərɪ] ADJ respiratorio
CPD ▸ **respiratory failure** insuficiencia *f* respiratoria • **acute ~ failure** insuficiencia respiratoria aguda ▸ **respiratory tract** vías *fpl* respiratorias

respire [rɪsˈpaɪəʳ] VI respirar
VT respirar

respite [ˈrespaɪt] N (*gen*) respiro *m*, tregua *f*; (*Jur*) prórroga *f*, plazo *m* • **without ~** sin descanso • **to get no ~** no tener alivio, no poder descansar • **we got no ~ from the heat** el calor apenas nos dejó respirar • **they gave us no ~** no nos dejaron respirar
CPD ▸ **respite care** *asistencia temporal para cubrir la ausencia de la persona que habitualmente cuida de otra*

resplendence [rɪsˈplendəns] N resplandor *m*, refulgencia *f*

resplendent [rɪsˈplendənt] ADJ resplandeciente, refulgente • **to be ~** resplandecer, refulgir • **she looked ~ in that new dress** estaba espléndida con ese vestido nuevo • **the car is ~ in green** el coche estaba resplandeciente pintado de verde

resplendently [rɪˈsplendəntlɪ] ADV de forma resplandeciente

respond [rɪsˈpɒnd] VI **1** (= *answer*) contestar, responder
2 (= *be responsive*) responder, reaccionar (**to** a) • **it ~s to sunlight** reacciona a la luz solar, es sensible a la luz solar • **to ~ to treatment** responder al tratamiento • **the cat ~s to kindness** el gato es sensible a los buenos tratos

respondent [rɪsˈpɒndənt] N (*Jur*) demandado/a *m/f*; (*to questionnaire*) persona *f* que responde al cuestionario *or* que rellena el cuestionario

responder [rɪsˈpɒndəʳ] N **1** (= *person*) persona *f* que responde • **the ~'s name and address** el remite
2 (*Tech*) respondedor *m*

response [rɪsˈpɒns] N **1** (= *answer*) (*gen*) contestación *f*, respuesta *f*; (*to charity appeal*) acogida *f* • **his only ~ was to yawn** por toda respuesta dio un bostezo • **in ~ to** como respuesta a • **in ~ to many requests ...** accediendo a muchos ruegos ... • **we got a 73% ~** respondió el 73 por ciento • **we had hoped for a bigger ~ from the public** habíamos esperado más correspondencia *or* una mayor respuesta del público • **it found no ~** no encontró eco alguno • **it met with a generous ~** tuvo una generosa acogida
2 (*Rel*) responsorio *m*
3 (= *reaction*) reacción *f* • **the ~ was not favourable** la reacción no fue favorable
CPD ▸ **response time** tiempo *m* de respuesta

responsibility [rɪsˌpɒnsəˈbɪlɪtɪ] N
1 (= *liability*) responsabilidad *f* • **he has accepted** *or* **admitted ~ for the tragedy** ha aceptado ser responsable de la tragedia • **the group which claimed ~ for the attack** el grupo que reivindicó el atentado • **joint ~** responsabilidad *f* conjunta • **to place** *or* **put the ~ for sth on sb** hacer a algn responsable de algo, hacer que la responsabilidad de algo recaiga sobre algn • **shared ~** responsabilidad *f* compartida • **the company takes no ~ for objects left here** la empresa no asume responsabilidad por los objetos que se dejen aquí, la empresa no se responsabiliza de los objetos que se dejen aquí; ▹ **diminished**
2 (= *duty, obligation*) responsabilidad *f* • **that's his ~** eso es responsabilidad suya • **she's not your ~** ella no es responsabilidad tuya, ella no está bajo tu responsabilidad • **it's a big ~ for him** supone una gran responsabilidad para él • **it's my ~ to lock up** cerrar es responsabilidad mía, yo soy el responsable de cerrar • **she didn't want to take on more responsibilities** no quería asumir más responsabilidades • **you have a ~ to your family** tienes una responsabilidad con *or* hacia tu familia
3 (= *authority, accountability*) responsabilidad *f* • **she wants a position with more ~** quiere un puesto de mayor responsabilidad • **to have ~ for sth** ser responsable de algo • **to take on/take over (the) ~ for sth** asumir la responsabilidad de algo, responsabilizarse de algo, hacerse responsable de algo
4 (= *maturity*) responsabilidad *f* • **try to show some ~** a ver si somos más responsables • **he has no sense of ~** no tiene ningún sentido de la responsabilidad

responsible [rɪsˈpɒnsəbl] ADJ
1 (= *accountable*) responsable • **those ~ will be punished** se castigará a los responsables • **who is ~ if anything goes wrong?** ¿quién es el responsable si algo sale mal? • **to be ~ for sth: he is not ~ for his actions** no es responsable de sus actos • **who is ~ for this?** ¿quién es el responsable de esto? • **who was ~ for the delay?** ¿quién tiene la culpa del retraso? • **to hold sb ~ for sth** hacer a algn responsable de algo, responsabilizar a algn de algo • **to be ~ to sb (for sth)** ser responsable ante algn (de algo)
2 (= *in charge of*) • **to be ~ for sth/sb: the children were ~ for tidying their own rooms** los niños tenían la responsabilidad *or* eran responsables de ordenar sus habitaciones • **she is ~ for 40 children** tiene a su cargo 40 niños • **the secretary is ~ for taking the minutes** la secretaria se hace cargo de levantar el acta
3 (= *sensible*) [*person*] serio, responsable; [*behaviour, attitude*] responsable • **to act in a ~ fashion** obrar de forma responsable *or* con responsabilidad • **that wasn't very ~ of you!** ¡eso ha sido una falta de responsabilidad por tu parte!
4 (= *important*) [*post, job*] de responsabilidad

responsibly [rɪsˈpɒnsəblɪ] ADV de forma responsable, responsablemente, con responsabilidad

responsive [rɪsˈpɒnsɪv] ADJ **1** (= *sensitive*) sensible • **to be ~ to sth** ser sensible a algo
2 (= *interested*) (*gen*) interesado; [*audience*] que reacciona con entusiasmo, que reacciona con interés • **he was not very ~** apenas dio muestras de interés

responsiveness [rɪsˈpɒnsɪvnɪs] N
1 (= *sensitivity*) sensibilidad *f* (**to** a)
2 (= *interest*) grado *m* de reacción (**to** a)

respray [ˈriːspreɪ] VT [+ *car*] volver a pintar (a pistola)
N [ˈriːspreɪ] • **the car needs a ~** el coche necesita que lo pinten

rest¹ [rest] N **1** (= *repose*) descanso *m* • **I need a ~** necesito descansar, me hace falta un descanso • **to be at ~** (= *not moving*) estar en reposo; (*euph*) (= *dead*) descansar • **to come to ~** [*ball, vehicle, person*] pararse, detenerse; [*bird, insect, eyes, gaze*] posarse • **her eyes came to ~ on the book** su mirada se posó en el libro • **day of ~** día *m* de descanso • **I need a ~ from gardening** me hace falta descansar de la jardinería • **try to get some ~** intenta descansar • **to give sth a ~** dejar algo (por un tiempo) • **I think you ought to give football a ~** creo que deberías dejar el fútbol por un tiempo • **give it a ~!*** ¡déjalo ya!, ¡vale ya!* • **to have** *or* **take a ~** tomarse un descanso • **why don't you have** *or* **take a ~?** (= *take a break*) ¿por qué no te tomas un descanso?; (= *lie down*) ¿por qué no descansas un rato? • **to have a good night's ~** dormir bien • **to lay sb to ~** enterrar a algn • **to lay** *or* **put sth to ~** [+ *theory*] enterrar algo • **his speech should lay those fears to ~** su discurso debería acabar con *or* enterrar esos temores; ▹ **bed, change, mind, wicked**
2 (*Mus*) silencio *m*
3 (= *support*) apoyo *m*, soporte *m*; (*Billiards*) soporte *m*; (*Telec*) horquilla *f*
VT **1** (= *give rest to*) descansar • **try to ~ the ankle as much as possible** intente descansar el tobillo lo más que pueda • **the horses have to be ~ed** hay que dejar descansar a los caballos • **I feel very ~ed** me siento muy descansado • **to ~ o.s.** descansar • **God ~ his soul!** ¡Dios le acoja en su seno!
2 (= *support*) apoyar (**on** en, sobre, **against** contra) • **~ the ladder against the tree** apoya la escalera contra el árbol • **to ~ one's hand on sb's shoulder** apoyar la mano en el hombro de algn
3 (= *settle*) • **to ~ one's eyes/gaze on sth** posar la mirada en algo
4 (*Jur*) • **to ~ one's case** concluir su alegato • **I ~ my case** concluyo mi alegato; (*fig*) (*hum*) he dicho
VI **1** (= *repose*) descansar • **go back to bed and ~** vuelve a la cama y descansa • **the waves never ~** las olas no descansan nunca • **he won't ~ until he finds out the truth** no descansará hasta que descubra la verdad • **may he ~ in peace** (*euph*) que en paz descanse; ▹ **laurel**
2 (= *lean, be supported*) [*person*] apoyarse (**on** en); [*roof, structure*] estar sostenido (**on** por); (*fig*) [*responsibility*] pesar (**on** sobre) • **he ~ed on his spade for a while** se apoyó en la pala un rato • **his head was ~ing on her shoulder**

tenía la cabeza apoyada en su hombro • **her arm ~ed on my chair** su brazo estaba apoyado en mi silla • **her elbows were ~ing on the table** tenía los codos apoyados en la mesa • **the ladder was ~ing against the wall** la escalera estaba apoyada contra la pared • **a heavy responsibility ~s on him** sobre él pesa una grave responsabilidad
3 (= *alight*) [*eyes, gaze*] posarse • **his eyes ~ed on me** su mirada se posó en mí
4 (= *depend, be based*) [*argument, case*] basarse (**on** en); [*sb's future*] depender (**on** de) • **the future of the country ~s on how we teach our children** el futuro del país depende de la enseñanza que demos a nuestros hijos
5 (= *be, remain*) quedar • **we cannot let the matter ~ there** no podemos permitir que la cosa quede ahí • **the decision ~s with her** • **it ~s with her to decide** la decisión la tiene que tomar ella, ella es la que tiene que decidir, la decisión es suya; ▹ **assure, easy**
6 (*Theat*) (*euph*) • **to be ~ing** no tener trabajo
7 (*Jur*) • **the defence/prosecution ~s** la defensa/el fiscal concluye su alegato
(CPD) ▸ **rest area** (*Aut*) área *f* de descanso ▸ **rest cure** cura *f* de reposo ▸ **rest day** día *m* de descanso ▸ **rest home** residencia *f* de ancianos, asilo *m* (de ancianos) ▸ **rest period** período *m* de descanso ▸ **rest room** (*US*) servicios *mpl*, baño(s) *m(pl)* (*LAm*) ▸ **rest stop** (= *pause*) parada *f* para descansar, parada *f* de descanso; (*Aut*) = **rest area**
▸ **rest up*** (*esp US*) (VI + ADV) descansar

rest² [rest] (N) • **the ~** (= *remainder*) [*of money, food, month*] el resto; [*of people, things*] el resto, los/las demás • **I'm taking the ~ of the week off** me tomaré el resto *or* lo que queda de la semana libre • **the dog ate the ~** el perro se comió el resto *or* lo que sobró • **you go home — I'll do the ~** tú vete a casa, yo hago lo demás *or* lo que queda • **I'll take half of the money — you keep the ~** yo me llevo la mitad del dinero, tú te quedas con el resto • **the ~ of the money** el resto del dinero • **all the ~ of the money** todo lo que sobró del dinero • **they left the ~ of the meal untouched** no tocaron el resto de la comida • **the ~ stayed outside** los demás se quedaron fuera • **the ~ of us will wait here** los demás esperaremos aquí • **the ~ of the boys** los otros chicos, los demás chicos • **he was as drunk as the ~ of them** estaba tan borracho como los demás • **the ~ of them couldn't care less** a los demás *or* a los otros les trae sin cuidado • **what shall we give the ~ of them?** ¿qué les daremos a los otros? • **the ~ of the soldiers** los otros soldados, los demás soldados • **I will take this book and you keep the ~** yo me llevo este libro y tú quédate con los demás • **all the ~ of the books** todos los demás libros, todos los otros libros • **it was just another grave like all the ~** no era más que otra tumba, como todas las demás *or* todas las otras • **and all the ~ (of it)*** etcétera, etcétera* • **he was from a wealthy family, went to Eton, Oxford and all the ~ of it** era de familia rica, estudió en Eton, Oxford etcétera, etcétera* • **she was a deb and all the ~ of it*** era debutante y todo lo demás • **(as) for the ~** por lo demás • **only there did his age show, for the ~, he might have been under seventy** solo en eso se le notaba la edad, por lo demás, podía haber tenido menos de setenta años; ▹ **history**

restage [riːˈsteɪdʒ] (VT) [+ *play etc*] volver a representar, volver a poner en escena; [+ *scene, event*] volver a montar, volver a organizar

restart [ˈriːˈstɑːt] (VT) [+ *book, drawing*] empezar de nuevo, volver a empezar; [+ *negotiations, meeting*] reanudar; [+ *engine*] volver a arrancar
(VI) [*meeting etc*] empezar de nuevo, reanudarse

restate [ˌriːˈsteɪt] (VT) **1** (= *repeat*) [+ *argument*] repetir, reafirmar; [+ *case*] volver a exponer; [+ *problem*] volver a plantear
2 (= *change terms of*) [+ *argument*] modificar

restatement [ˌriːˈsteɪtmənt] (N) [*of argument*] repetición *f*, reafirmación *f*; [*of case*] nueva exposición *f*; [*of problem*] nuevo planteamiento *m*

restaurant [ˈrestərɒŋ] (N) restaurante *m*
(CPD) ▸ **restaurant car** (*Brit*) coche-comedor *m*

restaurateur [ˌrestərəˈtɜːʳ] (N) dueño/a *m/f* de un restaurante, restaurador(a) *m/f*

rested [ˈrestɪd] (ADJ) descansado • **to feel ~** sentirse descansado

restful [ˈrestfʊl] (ADJ) descansado, tranquilo

restfully [ˈrestfəlɪ] (ADV) reposadamente, sosegadamente

resting place [ˈrestɪŋpleɪs] (N) (*also* **last** *or* **final resting place**) última morada *f*

restitution [ˌrestɪˈtjuːʃən] (N) **1** (= *return*) restitución *f* • **to make ~ of sth to sb** restituir algo a algn, devolver algo a algn
2 (= *compensation*) • **to make ~ to sb for sth** indemnizar a algn por algo

restive [ˈrestɪv] (ADJ) [*person, audience, voters*] inquieto; [*horse*] nervioso, inquieto • **to get ~** [*person*] impacientarse; [*horse*] ponerse nervioso *or* inquieto

restiveness [ˈrestɪvnɪs] (N) [*of person*] inquietud *f*, malestar *m*; [*of horse*] nerviosismo *m*, inquietud *f*

restless [ˈrestlɪs] (ADJ) **1** (= *unsettled*) [*person*] inquieto, intranquilo; [*mind*] intranquilo • **he's the ~ sort** es de los inquietos, es de los que no saben quedarse quietos • **to feel ~** sentirse intranquilo • **I had a ~ night** pasé muy mala noche, no dormí bien
2 (= *fidgety*) inquieto • **to become** *or* **get** *or* **grow ~** inquietarse, impacientarse
3 (= *discontented*) [*crowd, mob*] agitado
4 (*liter*) (= *moving*) [*wind, sea, clouds*] agitado
(CPD) ▸ **restless legs syndrome** (*Med*) síndrome *m* de las piernas inquietas

restlessly [ˈrestlɪslɪ] (ADV) nerviosamente • **he paced ~ around the room** se paseaba nerviosamente de un lado a otro de la habitación • **she moved ~ in her sleep** se movió inquieta mientras dormía

restlessness [ˈrestlɪsnɪs] (N) **1** (= *unsettled feeling*) agitación *f*, inquietud *f*
2 (= *fidgety feeling*) agitación *f*
3 (= *discontent*) agitación *f*

restock [ˈriːˈstɒk] (VT) [+ *larder*] reabastecer; [+ *pond*] repoblar (**with** de)
(VI) • **we ~ed with Brand X** renovamos las existencias con la Marca X

restorable [rɪˈstɔːrəbl] (ADJ) restaurable

restoration [ˌrestəˈreɪʃən] (N) **1** [*of money, possession*] devolución *f*, restitución *f* (*frm*)
2 [*of relations, links, order*] restablecimiento *m*; [*of confidence*] devolución *f*; [*of monarchy, democracy*] restauración *f*
3 [*of building, painting, antique*] restauración *f*
4 (*Brit*) (*Hist*) • **the Restoration** la Restauración (*época que comienza con la restauración de Carlos II en el trono británico*)

restorative [rɪsˈtɔːrətɪv] (ADJ) reconstituyente
(N) reconstituyente *m*

restore [rɪsˈtɔːʳ] (VT) **1** (= *give back*) [+ *money, possession*] devolver, restituir (*frm*) • **to ~ sth to sb** devolver algo a algn, restituir algo a algn (*frm*)
2 (= *re-establish, reinstate*) [+ *relations, links, order*] restablecer; [+ *monarch, president, democracy*] restaurar; [+ *confidence, strength*] devolver; [+ *tax, law*] reimplantar, volver a implantar • **order was soon ~d** pronto se restableció el orden • **to ~ sb's sight** devolver la vista a algn • **to ~ sb's strength** devolver las fuerzas a algn • **to ~ sb to health/life** devolver la salud a algn/reanimar a algn • **his supporters want to ~ him to power** sus partidarios quieren conseguir que vuelva al poder • **the investment needed to ~ these depressed areas to life** la inversión que se necesita para reactivar estas zonas deprimidas
3 [+ *building, painting, antique*] restaurar • **to ~ sth to its original state** *or* **condition** restituir *or* devolver algo a su estado original

restorer [rɪsˈtɔːrəʳ] (N) **1** (= *person*) restaurador(a) *m/f*
2 (= *hair restorer*) loción *f* capilar, regenerador *m* del cabello

restrain [rɪsˈtreɪn] (VT) **1** (= *hold back*) refrenar; (= *repress*) reprimir; (= *dissuade*) disuadir; (= *prevent*) impedir; (= *inhibit*) cohibir • **to ~ sb from doing sth** (= *dissuade*) disuadir a algn de hacer algo; (= *physically prevent*) impedir a algn hacer algo • **kindly ~ your friend** haga el favor de refrenar a su amigo
2 (= *contain*) contener; (= *confine*) encerrar • **I managed to ~ my anger** logré contener mi enojo • **to ~ o.s.** contenerse • **to ~ o.s. from doing sth** dominarse para que no haga algo • **but I ~ed myself** pero me contuve, pero me dominé • **please ~ yourself!** ¡por favor, cálmese!

restrained [rɪsˈtreɪnd] (ADJ) [*person*] cohibido; [*style*] reservado • **he was very ~ about it** estuvo muy comedido

restraining order [rɪsˈtreɪnɪŋˌɔːdəʳ] (N) (*Jur*) interdicto *m*

restraint [rɪsˈtreɪnt] (N) **1** (= *check*) restricción *f*; (= *control*) control *m*; (= *check on wages*) moderación *f* • **a ~ on trade** una restricción sobre el comercio • **a ~ on free enterprise** una limitación de la libre empresa • **to be under a ~** estar cohibido • **to fret under a ~** impacientarse por una restricción • **to put sb under a ~** refrenar a algn; (*Jur*) imponer una restricción legal a algn • **without ~** sin restricción
2 (= *constraint*) [*of manner*] reserva *f*; [*of character*] moderación *f*, comedimiento *m*
3 (= *self-control*) autodominio *m*, control *m* de sí mismo • **he showed great ~** mostró poseer un gran autodominio

restrict [rɪsˈtrɪkt] (VT) [+ *visits, price rise*] limitar; [+ *authority, freedom*] restringir, limitar • **the plant is ~ed to Andalusia** la planta está restringida a Andalucía • **his output is ~ed to novels** su producción se limita a las novelas • **to ~ o.s. to sth** limitarse a algo • **I ~ myself to the facts** me limito a exponer los hechos • **nowadays I ~ myself to a litre a day** hoy día me limito a beber un litro diario

restricted [rɪsˈtrɪktɪd] (ADJ) **1** (= *prohibited*) vedado, prohibido • **~ area** (*Mil*) zona *f* prohibida
2 (= *limited*) limitado • **~ area** (*Brit*) (*Aut*) zona *f* de velocidad limitada • **he has rather a ~ outlook** (*fig*) es de miras estrechas
3 (= *kept small*) [*area, circulation*] reducido; [*distribution*] restringido • **~ document** documento *m* de circulación restringida • **~ market** mercado *m* restringido

restriction [rɪsˈtrɪkʃən] (N) restricción *f*, limitación *f* • **without ~ as to ...** sin restricción de ... • **to place ~s on the sale of a drug** poner limitaciones a la venta de una droga • **to place ~s on sb's liberty** restringir

r

la libertad de algn
restrictive [rɪsˈtrɪktɪv] ADJ restringido, limitado • **~ practices** (*Brit*) prácticas *fpl* restrictivas
restring [ˌriːˈstrɪŋ] (PT, PP: **restrung** [ˌriːˈstrʌŋ]) VT [*+ pearls, necklace*] ensartar de nuevo; [*+ violin, racket*] poner nuevas cuerdas a; [*+ bow*] poner una nueva cuerda a
restructure [ˌriːˈstrʌktʃəʳ] VT reestructurar
restructuring [ˌriːˈstrʌktʃərɪŋ] N reestructuración *f*
restrung [ˌriːˈstrʌŋ] PT, PP *of* **restring**
restyle [ˌriːˈstaɪl] VT [*+ car*] remodelar, remozar • **I asked her to ~ my hair** le pedí que me hiciera otro corte de pelo, le pedí que me hiciera un corte de pelo diferente
result [rɪˈzʌlt] N **1** (= *outcome*) resultado *m* • **this oven gives better ~s** este horno da mejores resultados • **he followed his own advice, with disastrous ~s** hizo lo que le pareció, con consecuencias desastrosas *or* resultados desastrosos • **as a ~** por consiguiente • **as a ~ of** como *or* a consecuencia de • **he died as a ~ of his injuries** murió como *or* a consecuencia de las heridas • **to achieve/produce the desired ~** lograr/producir los resultados deseados • **with the ~ that ...** con la consecuencia de que ... • **without ~** sin resultado • IDIOM: • **to get a ~** (*Brit**) (= *succeed*) obtener resultados*; ▹ **end**
2 [*of election, race, match*] resultado *m* • **the election ~s** los resultados de las elecciones • **her exam ~s were excellent** en los exámenes sacó unas notas excelentes • **the football ~s** los resultados de los partidos de fútbol
3 (*Math*) resultado *f*
4 results: **a** (= *favourable outcome*) resultados *mpl* • **to get ~s: if they don't get ~s, heads will begin to roll** como no obtengan resultados, empezarán a cortar cabezas • **if a child sees that crying gets ~s he will take advantage of that** si un niño ve que llorar le da resultado se aprovechará de ello
b (*St Ex*) resultados *mpl* • **half-year ~s** resultados *mpl* semestrales
VI resultar • **a saving in cost would ~** se obtendría como resultado un ahorro en los costos • **the fire had ~ed from carelessness** el incendio fue resultado de un descuido • **to ~ in sth: it ~ed in his death** le acarreó la muerte, tuvo como resultado su muerte • **it ~ed in a large increase** dio como resultado un aumento apreciable • **it didn't ~ in anything useful** no dio ningún resultado útil • **such behaviour may ~ in dismissal** semejante comportamiento puede acarrear el despido
resultant [rɪˈzʌltənt] ADJ resultante
resume [rɪˈzjuːm] VT **1** (= *start again*) [*+ meeting, negotiations, session*] reanudar; [*+ office*] reasumir • **to ~ one's seat** volver al asiento • **to ~ one's work** reanudar el trabajo • **"now then," he ~d** —ahora bien —dijo reanudando la conversación *or* su discurso
2 (= *sum up*) resumir
VI [*class, meeting*] reanudarse
résumé [ˈreɪzjuːmeɪ] N **1** (= *summary*) resumen *m*
2 (*US*) (= *curriculum vitae*) currículum *m* (vitae)
resumption [rɪˈzʌmpʃən] N (*gen*) reanudación *f*; (= *continuation*) continuación *f* • **on the ~ of the sitting** al reanudarse la sesión
resurface [ˈriːˈsɜːfɪs] VT (*gen*) revestir; [*+ road*] rehacer el firme de
VI [*submarine*] volver a la superficie; [*person*] reaparecer
resurgence [rɪˈsɜːdʒəns] N resurgimiento *m*
resurgent [rɪˈsɜːdʒənt] ADJ resurgente, renaciente
resurrect [ˌrezəˈrekt] VT resucitar
resurrection [ˌrezəˈrekʃən] N (*Rel*) Resurrección *f*; (*fig*) resurrección *f*
resuscitate [rɪˈsʌsɪteɪt] VT resucitar
resuscitation [rɪˌsʌsɪˈteɪʃən] N resucitación *f*
resuscitator [rɪˈsʌsɪteɪtəʳ] N resucitador *m*
ret. ABBR = **retired**
retail [ˈriːteɪl] N venta *f* al por menor, venta *f* al detalle
ADV • **to buy/sell sth ~** comprar/vender algo al por menor, comprar/vender algo al detalle
VT **1** (*Comm*) vender al por menor, vender al detalle
2 [*+ gossip*] repetir; [*+ story*] contar
VI (*Comm*) • **to ~ at** tener precio de venta al público de
CPD ▸ **retail business** comercio *m* al por menor, comercio *m* al detalle ▸ **retail dealer** comerciante *mf* al por menor, detallista *mf* ▸ **retail group** grupo *m* minorista ▸ **retail outlet** punto *m* de venta al por menor, punto *m* de venta al detalle ▸ **retail park** *zona de hipermercados* ▸ **retail price** precio *m* de venta al público ▸ **retail price index** índice *m* de precios al consumo ▸ **retail sales** ventas *fpl* al detalle ▸ **retail therapy** (*hum*) (= *shopping*) salir *m* de compras ▸ **retail trade** comercio *m* al por menor, comercio *m* detallista ▸ **retail trader** = **retail dealer**
retailer [ˈriːteɪləʳ] N comerciante *mf* al por menor, detallista *mf*
retailing [ˈriːteɪlɪŋ] N (= *business*) comercio *m* al por menor, comercio *m* detallista
CPD [*industry, business*] al por menor
retain [rɪˈteɪn] VT **1** (= *hold back*) retener; (= *keep in one's possession*) guardar, quedarse con; (= *keep in memory*) recordar, retener
2 (= *sign up*) [*+ lawyer*] contratar
retained [rɪˈteɪnd] ADJ • **~ earnings** beneficios *mpl* retenidos • **~ profit** beneficios *mpl* retenidos
retainer [rɪˈteɪnəʳ] N **1** (= *servant*) criado/a *m/f* • **family ~** • **old ~** viejo criado *m* (*que lleva muchos años sirviendo en la misma familia*)
2 (= *fee*) anticipo *m*; (= *payment on flat, room*) depósito *m*, señal *f* (*para que se guarde el piso etc*)
retaining [rɪˈteɪnɪŋ] ADJ • **~ wall** muro *m* de contención
retake (VB: PT: **retook**, PP: **retaken**) N [ˈriːteɪk] (*Cine*) repetición *f*
VT [ˌriːˈteɪk] **1** (*Mil*) volver a tomar
2 (*Cine*) repetir, volver a tomar
3 [*+ exam*] presentarse segunda vez a; [*+ subject*] examinarse otra vez de
retaliate [rɪˈtælɪeɪt] VI (= *respond*) responder; (*Mil*) tomar represalias • **to ~ against sth/sb** tomar represalias contra algo/algn • **they ~d by bombing Israeli ports** tomaron represalias bombardeando los puertos israelíes • **she ~d by switching the television off** su respuesta fue apagar el televisor, respondió apagando el televisor
retaliation [rɪˌtælɪˈeɪʃən] N (*Mil*) represalias *fpl*; (= *revenge*) represalia *f* • **he sulks as a form of ~** su forma de desquitarse es enfurruñarse • **in** *or* **by way of ~ (for sth): he was executed in ~ for a raid on their headquarters** lo ejecutaron como represalia por el asalto de su sede
retaliatory [rɪˈtælɪətərɪ] ADJ de represalia • **~ raid** ataque *m* de represalia • **to take ~ measures** tomar represalias
retard [rɪˈtɑːd] VT retardar, retrasar
N [ˈriːtɑːd] (*US***) atrasado/a *m/f* mental*
retardant [rɪˈtɑːdənt] N (*Chem*) retardante *m*; ▹ **fire retardant**
retarded** [rɪˈtɑːdɪd] ADJ retardado, retrasado
NPL • **the ~** los retrasados (mentales)
retch [retʃ] VI tener arcadas
retching [ˈretʃɪŋ] N esfuerzo *m* por vomitar
retd ABBR = **retired**
retell [ˈriːˈtel] (PT, PP: **retold**) VT volver a contar
retelling [ˌriːˈtelɪŋ] N [*of story*] (*in a new form*) adaptación *f*
retention [rɪˈtenʃən] N retención *f* (*also Med*)
retentive [rɪˈtentɪv] ADJ retentivo • **a ~ memory** una buena memoria
retentiveness [rɪˈtentɪvnɪs] N retentiva *f*, poder *m* de retención
rethink [ˈriːθɪŋk] (VB: PT, PP: **rethought**) N • **to have a ~** volver a pensarlo
VT reconsiderar
rethought [ˌriːˈθɔːt] PT, PP *of* **rethink**
reticence [ˈretɪsəns] N reticencia *f*, reserva *f*
reticent [ˈretɪsənt] ADJ reticente, reservado • **he has been very ~ about it** ha tratado el asunto con la mayor reserva
reticently [ˈretɪsəntlɪ] ADV con reticencia, con reserva
reticle [ˈretɪkl] N retículo *m*
reticulate [rɪˈtɪkjʊlɪt] ADJ reticular
reticulated [rɪˈtɪkjʊleɪtɪd] ADJ = **reticulate**
reticule [ˈretɪkjuːl] N **1** (*Opt*) retículo *m*
2 (*Hist*) (= *bag*) ridículo *m*
retina [ˈretɪnə] N (PL: **retinas** *or* **retinae** [ˈretɪniː]) (*Anat*) retina *f*
retinue [ˈretɪnjuː] N séquito *m*, comitiva *f*
retire [rɪˈtaɪəʳ] VI **1** (= *give up work*) [*worker*] retirarse; (*at age limit*) jubilarse, retirarse; [*professional sportsperson, military officer*] retirarse • **she is retiring from professional tennis this year** se retira del tenis profesional este año • **she ~d on a good pension** se jubiló *or* se retiró con una buena pensión • **he ~d to the South of France** se jubiló *or* se retiró y se fue a vivir al sur de Francia
2 (*frm*) (= *withdraw*) retirarse • **the jury has ~d to consider its verdict** el jurado se ha retirado a deliberar para dar su veredicto • **to ~ from public life** retirarse de *or* abandonar la vida pública
3 (*frm*) (= *go to bed*) acostarse, retirarse (*frm*) • **to ~ to bed** • **~ for the night** ir a dormir, ir a acostarse
4 (*Sport*) [*competitor*] abandonar, retirarse; [*horse*] retirarse • **he ~d in the fifth lap with engine trouble** abandonó *or* se retiró en la quinta vuelta debido a problemas con el motor
5 (*Mil*) [*troops, army*] retirarse
VT **1** (*from work, service*) [*+ worker*] jubilar; (*Mil*) [*+ officer*] retirar • **he was compulsorily ~d** le dieron la jubilación forzosa, le obligaron a jubilarse
2 (*Horse racing*) [*+ horse*] retirar; (*Baseball*) [*+ batter*] eliminar
3 (*Econ*) [*+ bond*] redimir
4 (*Mil*) [*+ troops, army*] retirar
retired [rɪˈtaɪəd] ADJ (*from work*) (*gen*) jubilado, retirado; (*esp Mil*) retirado • **I've been ~ since 1996** me jubilé en 1996 • **a ~ person** un jubilado/una jubilada • **a lot of ~ people come here** aquí vienen muchos jubilados
retiree [rɪˈtaɪəˌriː] N (*US*) jubilado/a *m/f*
retirement [rɪˈtaɪəmənt] N **1** (= *state of being retired*) retiro *m* • **to live in ~** vivir en el retiro • **to spend one's ~ growing roses** dedicarse a cultivar rosas después de la

jubilación • **how will you spend your ~?** ¿qué piensa hacer cuando se jubile?
2 (= *act of retiring*) (*gen*) jubilación *f*; (*esp Mil*) retiro *m*
3 (*Mil*) (= *withdrawal*) retirada *f*
CPD ▸ **retirement age** edad *f* de jubilación; (*Mil*) edad *f* de retiro ▸ **retirement benefit** prestaciones *fpl* por jubilación ▸ **retirement home** residencia *f* para la tercera edad ▸ **retirement pay, retirement pension** jubilación *f*; (*Mil*) retiro *m*

retiring [rɪˈtaɪərɪŋ] ADJ 1 [*chairman, president*] saliente; [*age*] de jubilación
2 (= *shy*) reservado, retraído

retold [ˌriːˈtəʊld] PT, PP *of* **retell**

retook [ˌriːˈtʊk] PT *of* **retake**

retort [rɪˈtɔːt] N 1 (= *answer*) réplica *f*
2 (*Chem*) retorta *f*
VT replicar • **he ~ed that ...** replicó que ...

retouch [ˈriːˈtʌtʃ] VT retocar

retrace [riːˈtreɪs] VT [+ *path*] desandar; [+ *sb's journey etc*] seguir las huellas de; (*in memory*) recordar, ir recordando, rememorar • **to ~ one's steps** (*lit, fig*) desandar lo andado

retract [rɪˈtrækt] VT 1 [+ *statement*] retractar, retirar
2 (= *draw in*) [+ *claws*] retraer; [+ *head*] meter; (*Tech*) [+ *undercarriage etc*] replegar
VI 1 (= *apologize*) retractarse, desdecirse • **he refuses to ~** se niega a retractarse *or* desdecirse
2 (= *be drawn in*) retraerse, meterse; (*Tech*) replegarse

retractable [rɪˈtræktəbl] ADJ retractable; (*Tech*) replegable, retráctil

retraction [rɪˈtrækʃən] N retractación *f*, retracción *f*

retrain [ˈriːˈtreɪn] VT [+ *workers*] reciclar, recapacitar, reconvertir
VI reciclarse, reconvertirse

retraining [ˈriːˈtreɪnɪŋ] N reciclaje *m*, recapacitación *f*

retransmit [ˈriːtrænzˈmɪt] VT retransmitir

retread [ˈriːtred] N (= *tyre*) neumático *m* recauchutado, llanta *f* recauchutada, llanta *f* reencauchada (*LAm*)
VT [ˌriːˈtred] [+ *tyre*] recauchutar, reencauchar (*CAm*)

re-tread [ˌriːˈtred] VT [+ *path etc*] volver a pisar

retreat [rɪˈtriːt] N 1 (*Mil*) (= *withdrawal*) retirada *f*; (*fig*) vuelta *f* atrás, marcha *f* atrás • **the ~ from Mons** la retirada de Mons • **to beat the ~** dar el toque de retreta • **to beat a ~** retirarse, batirse en retirada; (*fig*) emprender la retirada • **to beat a hasty ~** (*fig*) retirarse en desorden • **the government is in ~ on this issue** en este asunto el gobierno se está echando atrás • **this represents a ~ from his promise** con esto se está volviendo atrás de su promesa • **to be in full ~** retirarse en masa, retirarse en todo el frente
2 (= *place*) (*also Rel*) retiro *m*, refugio *m*; (= *state*) retraimiento *m*, apartamiento *m*
VI 1 (*Mil, Rel*) (= *move back*) retirarse • **they ~ed to Dunkirk** se retiraron a Dunquerque
2 (= *draw back*) retroceder • **the waters are ~ing** las aguas están bajando

retrench [rɪˈtrentʃ] VT reducir, cercenar
VI economizar, hacer economías

retrenchment [rɪˈtrentʃmənt] N 1 (*frm*) (= *cutting back*) racionalización *f* de gastos, recorte *m* de gastos
2 (*Mil*) empalizada *f* interior

retrial [ˈriːˈtraɪəl] N [*of person*] nuevo juicio *m*; [*of case*] revisión *f*

retribution [ˌretrɪˈbjuːʃən] N justo castigo *m*, pena *f* merecida

retributive [rɪˈtrɪbjʊtɪv] ADJ castigador, de castigo

retrievable [rɪˈtriːvəbl] ADJ recuperable; [*error etc*] reparable

retrieval [rɪˈtriːvəl] N 1 (*Comput*) recuperación *f* • **data ~** recuperación *f* de datos
2 (= *recovery*) recuperación *f* • **beyond ~** irrecuperable
3 (*Hunting*) cobra *f*

retrieve [rɪˈtriːv] VT 1 (= *get back*) [+ *object*] recuperar, recobrar; (*Hunting*) cobrar • **to ~ sth from the water** rescatar algo del agua • **she ~d her handkerchief** recogió su pañuelo, volvió a tomar su pañuelo
2 (= *put right*) [+ *error etc*] reparar, subsanar; [+ *fortunes*] reparar
3 (*fig*) (= *rescue*) [+ *situation*] salvar • **we shall ~ nothing from this disaster** no salvaremos nada de esta catástrofe
4 (*Comput, Psych*) [+ *information*] recuperar

retriever [rɪˈtriːvəʳ] N perro *m* cobrador

retro [ˈretrəʊ] ADJ [*fashion, style, music, furniture*] retro (*inv*) • **the ~ look** el look retro
N retro *m* • **~ is in** lo retro está de moda

retro... [ˈretrəʊ] PREFIX retro...

retroactive [ˌretrəʊˈæktɪv] ADJ retroactivo

retroactively [ˌretrəʊˈæktɪvlɪ] ADV (= *retrospectively*) con efectos retroactivos

retrofit [ˈretrəʊfɪt] VT actualizar el diseño de

retroflex [ˈretrəʊfleks] ADJ vuelto hacia atrás

retrograde [ˈretrəʊgreɪd] ADJ (*fig*) [*step, measure*] retrógrado

retrogress [ˌretrəʊˈgres] VI 1 (= *recede*) retroceder
2 (*fig*) (= *degenerate*) empeorar, degenerar, decaer

retrogression [ˌretrəʊˈgreʃən] N retroceso *m*, retrogradación *f*

retrogressive [ˌretrəʊˈgresɪv] ADJ retrógrado

retrorocket [ˈretrəʊˈrɒkɪt] N retrocohete *m*

retrospect [ˈretrəʊspekt] N retrospección *f*, mirada *f* retrospectiva • **in ~** retrospectivamente • **in ~ it seems a happy time** volviendo la vista atrás parece haber sido un período feliz

retrospection [ˌretrəʊˈspekʃən] N retrospección *f*, consideración *f* del pasado

retrospective [ˌretrəʊˈspektɪv] ADJ retrospectivo; [*law etc*] retroactivo, de efecto retroactivo
N (*Art*) (exposición *f*) retrospectiva *f*

retrospectively [ˌretrəʊˈspektɪvlɪ] ADV (*gen*) retrospectivamente; (*Admin, Jur*) de modo retroactivo, con efecto retroactivo

retroussé [rəˈtruːseɪ] ADJ • **~ nose** nariz *f* respingona

retroviral [ˌretrəʊˈvaɪərəl] ADJ [*infection, treatment*] retroviral

retrovirus [ˈretrəʊˌvaɪrəs] N retrovirus *m inv*

retry [ˈriːˈtraɪ] VT (*Jur*) [+ *person*] procesar de nuevo, volver a procesar; [+ *case*] rever

retune [ˌriːˈtjuːn] VT [+ *musical instrument*] afinar de nuevo; [+ *engine*] poner a punto de nuevo; [+ *radio, video recorder*] volver a sintonizar
N [ˈriːtjuːn] [*of engine*] nueva puesta *f* a punto

return [rɪˈtɜːn] N 1 (= *going/coming back*) vuelta *f*, regreso *m* • **the ~ home** la vuelta *or* el regreso a casa • **the ~ to school** la vuelta *or* el regreso al colegio • **he advocates a ~ to Victorian values** aboga por una vuelta *or* un regreso a los valores victorianos • **their ~ to power** su vuelta *or* retorno al poder • **many happy ~s (of the day)!** ¡feliz cumpleaños!, ¡felicidades! • **he has not ruled out the possibility of making a ~ to football** no ha descartado la posibilidad de volver al fútbol • **on my ~** a mi vuelta, a mi regreso • **by ~ (of) post** *or* (*US*) **by ~ mail** a vuelta de correo; ▹ **point**
2 (= *reappearance*) [*of symptoms, pain*] reaparición *f*; [*of doubts, fears*] resurgimiento *m* • **there was no ~ of the symptoms** los síntomas no volvieron a aparecer, los síntomas no reaparecieron
3 (= *giving back*) [*of thing taken away*] devolución *f*, restitución *f* (*frm*); [*of thing borrowed*] devolución *f*; (*Comm*) [*of merchandise*] devolución *f*; [*of money*] reembolso *m*, devolución *f* • **they are demanding the ~ of their lands** exigen la devolución *or* (*frm*) la restitución de sus tierras • **he appealed for the ~ of the hostages** hizo un llamamiento pidiendo la liberación de los rehenes; ▹ **sale**
4 (= *thing returned*) (*Comm*) (= *merchandise*) devolución *f*; (= *theatre, concert ticket*) devolución *f*, entrada *f* devuelta; (= *library book*) libro *m* devuelto • **it's sold out but you might get a ~ on the night** se han agotado las localidades, pero puede que consiga una entrada devuelta *or* una devolución la misma noche de la función
5 (*Econ*) (= *profit*) ganancia *f*; (*from investments, shares*) rendimiento *m* • **he is looking for quick ~s** está buscando rendimiento rápido *or* ganancias rápidas • **they want to get some ~ on their investment** quieren obtener cierto rendimiento de su inversión • **~ on capital** rendimiento del capital; ▹ **diminishing, rate**
6 (= *reward, exchange*) • **in ~** a cambio • **they had nothing to give in ~** no tenían nada que dar a cambio • **in ~ for this service** a cambio de este servicio
7 **returns** (= *figures*) estadísticas *fpl* (**for** de); (= *election results*) resultados *mpl* (del escrutinio) • **early ~s show Dos Santos with 52% of the vote** los primeros resultados del escrutinio muestran que Dos Santos tiene un 52% de los votos; ▹ **tax**
8 (= *answer*) (*in surveys*) respuesta *f*, declaración *f*
9 (*Parl*) [*of member*] (= *election*) elección *f*; (= *reelection*) reelección *f*
10 (*also* **return ticket**) billete *m* de ida y vuelta, billete *m* redondo (*Mex*); ▹ **day**
11 (*Sport*) devolución *f* • **~ of serve** *or* **service** devolución *f* del servicio *or* saque, resto *m*
12 = **return key**
13 = **carriage return**
VT 1 (= *give back*) [+ *item*] devolver, regresar (*LAm*), restituir (*frm*); [+ *favour, sb's visit, telephone call, blow*] devolver; [+ *kindness, love*] corresponder a; [+ *greeting, look, gaze*] devolver, responder a • **they never ~ my calls** nunca me devuelven las llamadas • **to ~ good for evil** devolver bien por mal • **to ~ the compliment** devolver el cumplido • **to ~ fire** (*Mil*) devolver el fuego, responder a los disparos • **"return to sender"** "devuélvase al remitente"
2 (= *put back*) volver a colocar • **we ~ed the books to the shelf** volvimos a colocar los libros en el estante
3 (*Sport*) [+ *ball*] devolver; (*Tennis*) devolver, restar; (*Bridge*) [+ *suit of cards*] devolver
4 (= *declare*) [+ *income, details*] declarar • **to ~ a verdict** emitir *or* pronunciar un veredicto, emitir un fallo • **they ~ed a verdict of guilty/not guilty** lo declararon culpable/inocente
5 (*Pol*) (= *elect*) elegir, votar a; (= *reelect*) reelegir • **to ~ sb to power** reelegir a algn
6 (*Econ*) [+ *profit, income*] reportar, rendir
7 (= *reply*) responder, contestar

r

VI **1** (*= go/come back*) volver, regresar • **he left home, never to ~** se marchó de casa, para no volver *or* regresar jamás • **to ~ home** volver *or* regresar a casa • **to ~ to** [*+ place*] volver *or* regresar a; [*+ activity, state*] volver a • **I ~ed to my hotel** volví *or* regresé a mi hotel • **things have ~ed to normal** las cosas han vuelto a la normalidad • **to ~ to a task** volver a una tarea • **to ~ to a theme** volver sobre un tema • **to ~ to what we were talking about, ...** volviendo al asunto del que estábamos hablando, ...
2 (*= reappear*) [*symptoms*] volver a aparecer, reaparecer; [*doubts, fears, suspicions*] volver a surgir, resurgir • **his good spirits ~ed** renació su alegría
3 (*Jur*) revertir (**to a**) • **on my father's death the farm ~ed to my brother** al morir mi padre, la granja revirtió a mi hermano
CPD ▸ **return address** señas *fpl* del remitente ▸ **return fare** billete *m* de ida y vuelta, billete *m* redondo (*Mex*) ▸ **return flight** (*Brit*) (*= journey back*) (vuelo *m* de) vuelta *f*; (*= two-way journey*) (vuelo *m* de) ida y vuelta *f* ▸ **return game** = **return match** ▸ **return journey** (*Brit*) (*= journey back*) (viaje *m* de) vuelta *f*; (*= two-way journey*) (viaje *m* de) ida y vuelta *f* ▸ **return key** (*Comput*) tecla *f* de retorno ▸ **return match** (*Brit*) (*Sport*) partido *m* de vuelta ▸ **return ticket** (*Brit*) billete *m* de ida y vuelta *or* (*Mex*) redondo ▸ **return trip** (*= journey back*) (viaje *m* de) vuelta *f*; (*= two-way journey*) (viaje *m* de) ida y vuelta *f* ▸ **return visit** (*= repeat visit*) nueva visita *f*

returnable [rɪ'tɜ:nəbl] ADJ restituible; [*deposit*] reintegrable, reembolsable; [*bottle*] retornable; (*Jur*) devolutivo; (*= on approval*) a prueba • **~ empties** envases *mpl* a devolver • **the book is ~ on the 14th** el libro deberá estar de vuelta el 14 • **the deposit is not ~** no se reembolsa el depósito

returnee [rɪtɜ:'ni:] N retornado/a *m/f*

returner [rɪ'tɜ:nəʳ] N (*Brit*) (*Ind*) *persona que regresa al mundo laboral tras un periodo de inactividad*

returning officer [rɪ'tɜ:nɪŋ,ɒfɪsəʳ] N (*Pol*) escrutador(a) *m/f*

retweet [ri:'twi:t] (*Internet*) VT retuitear
N retuit *m*

retype [,ri:'taɪp] VT reescribir (a máquina)

reunification ['ri:,ju:nɪfɪ'keɪʃən] N reunificación *f*

reunify ['ri:'ju:nɪfaɪ] VT reunificar

reunion [ri:'ju:njən] N reencuentro *m*, reunión *f*

reunite ['ri:ju:'naɪt] VT (*often passive*) (volver a) reunir • **eventually the family was ~d** por fin la familia volvió a verse unida • **she was ~d with her husband** volvió a verse al lado de su marido
VI (volver a) reunirse

re-usable [,ri:'ju:zəbl] ADJ reutilizable, que se puede volver a emplear

re-use [,ri:'ju:z] VT volver a usar, reutilizar

rev* [rev] (*Aut etc*) N revolución *f*
VT (*also* **rev up**) [*+ engine*] girar
VI (*also* **rev up**) girar (rápidamente) • **the plane was revving up** se aceleraban los motores del avión
CPD ▸ **rev counter** (*Brit*) cuentarrevoluciones *m inv*

Rev. ABBR (= **Reverend**) R, Rdo, Rvdo • **the ~*** (*Catholic*) el padre, el cura; (*Protestant*) el pastor

revaluation [ri:,væljʊ'eɪʃən] N revaluación *f*, revalorización *f*

revalue ['ri:'vælju:] VT [*+ property, currency*] revaluar, revalorizar

revamp [,ri:'væmp] VT modernizar, renovar
N ['ri:væmp] modernización *f*, renovación *f*

revanchism [rɪ'væntʃɪzəm] N revanchismo *m*

revanchist [rɪ'væntʃɪst] ADJ revanchista
N revanchista *mf*

Revd. ABBR (= **Reverend**) R, Rdo, Rvdo • **the ~*** (*Catholic*) el padre, el cura; (*Protestant*) el pastor

reveal [rɪ'vi:l] VT **1** (*= uncover*) revelar, dejar al descubierto
2 (*= show*) [*survey, test*] poner de manifiesto; (*= make public*) [*person*] revelar; [*+ feelings*] exteriorizar • **I cannot ~ to you what he said** no puedo revelarte *or* contarte lo que dijo • **on that occasion he ~ed great astuteness** en aquella ocasión desplegó gran astucia • **he ~ed himself to be** *or* **as ...** demostró ser ...

revealing [rɪ'vi:lɪŋ] ADJ (*gen*) revelador

revealingly [rɪ'vi:lɪŋlɪ] ADV de modo revelador

reveille [rɪ'vælɪ] N (*Mil*) (toque *m* de) diana *f*

revel ['revl] VI **1** (*= make merry*) ir de juerga *or* de parranda
2 (*= delight*) • **to ~ in sth/doing sth** gozar de algo/haciendo algo
N **revels** (*liter*) jolgorio *msing*, jarana *fsing*; (*organized*) fiestas *fpl*, festividades *fpl* • **let the ~s begin!** ¡que comience la fiesta! • **the ~s lasted for three days** continuaron las fiestas durante tres días

revelation [,revə'leɪʃən] N revelación *f* • **(Book of) Revelation** el Apocalipsis • **it was a ~ to me** fue una revelación para mí

revelatory ['revələtərɪ] ADJ revelador

reveller, **reveler** (*US*) ['revləʳ] N juerguista *mf*, parrandero/a *m/f*; (*= drunk*) borracho/a *m/f*

revelry ['revlrɪ] N juerga *f*, parranda *f*, jarana *f*; (*organized*) fiestas *fpl*, festividades *fpl* • **the spirit of ~** el espíritu de festivo

revenge [rɪ'vendʒ] N venganza *f* • **in ~** para vengarse (**for de**) • **to get one's ~ (for sth)** vengarse (de algo) • **to take ~ on sb for sth** vengarse de algn por algo
VT vengar, vengarse de • **to ~ o.s. on sb** • **be ~d on sb** vengarse de *or* en algn
CPD ▸ **revenge porn** porno *m* vengativo

revengeful [rɪ'vendʒfʊl] ADJ vengativo

revengefully [rɪ'vendʒfəlɪ] ADV vengativamente

revenger [rɪ'vendʒəʳ] N vengador(a) *m/f*

revenue ['revənju:] N (*= profit, income*) ingresos *mpl*, rentas *fpl*; (*on investments*) rédito *m*; [*of country*] rentas *fpl* públicas; ▹ **inland**
CPD ▸ **revenue account** cuenta *f* de ingresos presupuestarios ▸ **revenue expenditure** gasto *m* corriente ▸ **revenue stamp** timbre *m* fiscal ▸ **revenue stream** fuente *f* de ganancias

reverb ['ri:vɜ:b, rɪ'vɜ:b] N reverberación *f*

reverberant [rɪ'vɜ:bərənt] ADJ [*acoustics*] reverberante

reverberate [rɪ'vɜ:bəreɪt] VI **1** [*sound*] resonar, retumbar • **the sound ~d in the distance** el sonido resonaba *or* retumbaba a lo lejos • **the valley ~d with the sound** el ruido resonaba *or* retumbaba por el valle
2 (*fig*) [*news, protests etc*] tener amplia resonancia, tener una fuerte repercusión
3 (*Tech*) [*light*] reverberar

reverberation [rɪ,vɜ:bə'reɪʃən] N **1** [*of sound*] retumbo *m*, eco *m*
2 reverberations (*fig*) [*of news, protests etc*] consecuencias *fpl*
3 [*of light*] reverberación *f*

reverberator [rɪ'vɜ:bəreɪtəʳ] N reverberador *m*

revere [rɪ'vɪəʳ] VT venerar • **a ~d figure** una figura venerada

reverence ['revərəns] N **1** (*= respect*) reverencia *f*
2 (*Rel*) • **Your Reverence** Reverencia
VT (*frm*) (*= revere*) venerar

reverend ['revərənd] ADJ (*in titles*) reverendo • **right** *or* **very ~** reverendísimo • **Reverend Mother** reverenda madre *f*
N* (*Catholic*) padre *m*, cura *m*; (*Protestant*) pastor *m*

reverent ['revərənt] ADJ reverente

reverential [,revə'renʃəl] ADJ reverencial

reverentially [,revə'renʃəlɪ] ADV reverenciosamente

reverently ['revərəntlɪ] ADV reverentemente, con reverencia

reverie ['revərɪ] N ensueño *m* • **to be lost in ~** estar absorto, estar ensimismado

revers [rɪ'vɪəʳ] N (PL: **revers** [rɪ'vɪəz]) solapa *f*

reversal [rɪ'vɜ:səl] N **1** (*= change*) [*of order, roles*] inversión *f*; [*of policy*] cambio *m* de rumbo; [*of decision etc*] revocación *f*
2 (*= setback*) revés *m*, contratiempo *m*

reverse [rɪ'vɜ:s] ADJ **1** [*order*] inverso; [*direction*] contrario, opuesto • **the ~ side** (*of coin, medal*) el reverso; (*of sheet of paper*) el dorso • **in ~ order** en orden inverso
2 (*Aut*) [*gear*] de marcha atrás
N **1** (*= opposite*) • **the ~** lo contrario • **no, quite the ~!** no, ¡todo lo contrario! • **but the ~ is true** pero es al contrario • **it was the ~ of what we had expected** fue todo lo contrario de lo que habíamos esperado • **his remarks were the ~ of flattering** sus observaciones eran poco halagüeñas, todo lo contrario • **it's the same process in ~** es el mismo proceso al revés
2 (*= face*) [*of coin*] reverso *m*; [*of paper etc*] dorso *m*; [*of cloth*] revés *m*
3 (*Aut*) (*also* **reverse gear**) marcha *f* atrás • **to go** *or* **change into ~** dar marcha atrás • **to put a car into ~** dar marcha atrás a un coche • **my luck went into ~** mi suerte dio marcha atrás
4 (*= setback*) revés *m*, contratiempo *m*; (*= defeat*) derrota *f*
VT **1** (*= invert order of*) invertir, invertir el orden de; (*= turn other way*) volver al revés; [*+ arms*] llevar a la funerala • **to ~ A and B** invertir el orden de A y B, anteponer B a A
2 (*= change*) [*+ opinion*] cambiar completamente de; [*+ decision*] revocar, anular, cancelar
3 (*Brit*) (*Telec*) • **to ~ the charges** cobrar al número llamado, llamar a cobro revertido
4 (*esp Brit*) [*+ car, train etc*] dar marcha atrás a • **he ~d the car into the garage** dio marcha atrás para entrar en el garaje • **he ~d the car into a pillarbox** al dar marcha atrás chocó con un buzón
VI (*esp Brit*) (*Aut*) dar marcha atrás • **I ~d into a van** al dar marcha atrás choqué con una furgoneta
CPD ▸ **reverse charge call** (*Brit*) (*Telec*) llamada *f* a cobro revertido ▸ **reverse discrimination** (*US*) discriminación *f* positiva ▸ **reverse turn** (*Aut*) vuelta *f* al revés ▸ **reverse video** (*Comput*) vídeo *m* inverso

reverse-engineer [rɪ,vɜ:senʒɪ'nɪəʳ] VT (*Comput*) aplicar un proceso de retroingeniería a

reversibility [rɪ,vɜ:sɪ'bɪlɪtɪ] N reversibilidad *f*

reversible [rɪ'vɜ:səbl] ADJ reversible

reversing [rɪ'vɜ:sɪŋ] N marcha *f* atrás
CPD ▸ **reversing light** luz *f* de marcha atrás

reversion [rɪ'vɜ:ʃən] N (*also Bio, Jur*) reversión *f* • **~ to type** reversión *f* al tipo, salto *m* atrás

reversionary [rɪˈvɜːʃnərɪ] ADJ reversionario, reversible

revert [rɪˈvɜːt] VI **1** (= *return*) volver • **to ~ to a subject** volver a un tema • **~ing to the matter under discussion …** volviendo al tema de la discusión …
2 (*Jur*) revertir (**to** a)
3 (*Bio*) saltar atrás • **to ~ to type** (*Bio*) saltar atrás en la cadena natural; (*fig*) volver por donde solía, volver a ser el mismo/la misma de antes

revetment [rɪˈvetmənt] N revestimiento *m*

revictual [ˈriːˈvɪtl] VT reabastecer
VI reabastecerse

review [rɪˈvjuː] N **1** (= *survey, taking stock*) examen *m*, análisis *m inv*; [*of research etc*] evaluación *f* • **the annual ~ of expenditure** el examen anual de los gastos • **salaries are under ~** los sueldos están sujetos a revisión • **we shall keep your case under ~** volveremos a considerar su caso
2 (*Mil*) [*of troops*] revista *f* • **the Spithead Review** la revista naval de Spithead • **the general passed the troops in ~** el general pasó revista a las tropas • **the troops passed in ~ before the general** las tropas desfilaron en revista ante el general
3 (*Jur*) (= *revision*) revisión *f* • **when the case comes up for ~** cuando el asunto se someta a revisión • **the sentence is subject to ~ in the high court** la sentencia puede volver a ser vista en el tribunal supremo
4 (= *critique*) crítica *f*, reseña *f* • **the play got good ~s** la obra fue bien recibida por los críticos
5 (= *journal*) revista *f*
6 (*Theat*) revista *f*
VT **1** (= *take stock of*) examinar, analizar; [+ *research etc*] evaluar • **we will ~ the position in a month** volveremos a estudiar la situación dentro de un mes • **we shall have to ~ our policy** tendremos que reconsiderar nuestra política
2 (*Mil*) [+ *troops*] pasar revista a
3 (*Jur*) (= *reconsider*) [+ *case*] revisar
4 (= *write review of*) reseñar, hacer una crítica de
5 (*US*) (*Scol*) repasar
CPD ▸ **review board** comité *m* de evaluación ▸ **review copy** ejemplar *m* para reseñar

reviewer [rɪˈvjuːəʳ] N [*of book, concert*] crítico/a *m/f*

reviewing stand [rɪˈvjuːɪŋˌstænd] N tribuna *f* de autoridades en los desfiles militares

revile [rɪˈvaɪl] VT insultar, injuriar

reviled [rɪˈvaɪld] ADJ vituperado

revise [rɪˈvaɪz] VT **1** (= *alter*) [+ *estimate, figures*] corregir; [+ *offer*] reconsiderar; [+ *schedule*] ajustar • **to ~ one's opinion of sb** cambiar de opinión sobre algn • **to ~ sth upward(s)** ajustar *or* revisar algo al alza
2 (= *amend, update*) [+ *text, dictionary*] revisar; [+ *proofs*] corregir
3 (*Brit*) (*Scol*) [+ *subject, notes*] repasar
VI (*Brit*) (*for exams*) repasar

revised [rɪˈvaɪzd] ADJ [*text, plan, procedure*] revisado; [*version, figure, estimate*] corregido; [*offer*] reconsiderado; [*schedule*] ajustado • **~ edition** edición *f* revisada • **Revised Standard Version** *versión revisada en 1953 de la biblia anglicana* • **Revised Version** (*Brit*) *versión revisada en 1885 de la biblia anglicana*

reviser [rɪˈvaɪzəʳ] N revisor(a) *m/f*, refundidor(a) *m/f*; (*Typ*) corrector(a) *m/f*

revision [rɪˈvɪʒən] N **1** (*for exams*) repaso *m* • **I need two weeks for ~** necesito dos semanas para repasar
2 (= *amendment, updating*) [*of text, dictionary*] revisión *f*; [*of proofs*] corrección *f*
3 (= *alteration*) [*of estimate, figures*] corrección *f*; [*of offer*] reconsideración *f*; [*of schedule*] ajuste *m*
4 (= *revised version*) edición *f* revisada

revisionism [rɪˈvɪʒənɪzəm] N revisionismo *m*

revisionist [rɪˈvɪʒənɪst] ADJ revisionista
N revisionista *mf*

revisit [ˈriːˈvɪzɪt] VT volver a visitar • **"Brideshead Revisited"** "Retorno *m* a Brideshead"

revitalization [riːˌvaɪtəlaɪˈzeɪʃən] N revitalización *f*

revitalize [ˈriːˈvaɪtəlaɪz] VT revitalizar, revivificar

revival [rɪˈvaɪvəl] N **1** (= *bringing back*) [*of custom, usage*] recuperación *f*; [*of old ideas*] resurgimiento *m*
2 (= *coming back*) [*of custom, usage*] vuelta *f*; [*of old ideas*] renacimiento *m* • **the Revival of Learning** (*Hist*) el Renacimiento
3 (*from illness, faint*) reanimación *f*
4 (*Theat*) [*of play*] reposición *f*

revivalism [rɪˈvaɪvəˌlɪzəm] N (*Rel*) evangelismo *m*

revivalist [rɪˈvaɪvəlɪst] N evangelista *mf*; (= *preacher*) predicador(a) *m/f* evangelista
CPD ▸ **revivalist meeting** reunión *f* evangelista

revive [rɪˈvaɪv] VT **1** [+ *person*] (*to life, spirits*) reanimar • **this will ~ you** esto te reanimará
2 [+ *fire*] avivar; [+ *old customs*] restablecer, recuperar; [+ *hopes, suspicions*] despertar; [+ *accusation*] volver a, volver a hacer • **to ~ sb's courage** infundir nuevos ánimos a algn
3 (*Theat*) [+ *play*] reponer
VI **1** [*person*] (*from faint*) reanimarse, volver en sí; (*from tiredness, shock etc*) reponerse, recuperarse; (*from apparent death*) revivir
2 [*hope, emotions*] renacer; [*business, trade*] reactivarse • **interest in Gongora has ~d** ha renacido el interés por Góngora • **the pound has ~d** la libra se ha recuperado • **his courage ~d** recobró su fortaleza de ánimo

reviver [rɪˈvaɪvəʳ] N (= *drink*) bebida *f* que da fuerzas

revivify [riːˈvɪvɪfaɪ] VT revivificar

revocable [ˈrevəkəbl] ADJ revocable

revocation [ˌrevəˈkeɪʃən] N revocación *f*

revoke [rɪˈvəʊk] N (*Cards*) renuncio *m*
VT (*gen*) revocar; [+ *licence*] suspender
VI (*Cards*) renunciar

revolt [rɪˈvəʊlt] N (= *insurrection*) levantamiento *m*, revuelta *f*, sublevación *f*; (= *rejection of authority*) rebelión *f* • **a popular ~** un levantamiento *or* una revuelta popular • **southern cities are in (open) ~ against the regime** las ciudades del sur se han sublevado contra el régimen • **students are in (open) ~ against the new examination system** los estudiantes se han rebelado contra el nuevo sistema de exámenes • **to rise (up) in ~** sublevarse, rebelarse
VT (= *disgust*) dar asco a, repugnar • **I was ~ed by the sight** la escena me dio asco *or* me repugnó
VI (= *rebel*) sublevarse, rebelarse (**against** contra)

revolting [rɪˈvəʊltɪŋ] ADJ (= *disgusting*) [*smell, taste, sight, habit, person*] repugnante, asqueroso; [*behaviour, story*] repugnante; [*place, weather*] asqueroso; [*colour, dress*] horroroso, repelente • **it smells/tastes ~** tiene un olor/sabor repugnante, huele/sabe que da asco

revoltingly [rɪˈvəʊltɪŋlɪ] ADV [*dirty, fat, greasy*] repugnantemente, asquerosamente; [*ugly*] horrorosamente; [*sentimental*] empalagosamente • **they're ~ rich** son tan ricos que da asco, son asquerosamente ricos

revolution [ˌrevəˈluːʃən] N **1** (*Pol*) (*also fig*) revolución *f*
2 (= *turn*) revolución *f*, vuelta *f*; (*Tech*) rotación *f*, giro *m* • **~s per minute** revoluciones por minuto
3 (*Astron*) (= *orbit*) revolución *f*; (*on axis*) rotación *f*

revolutionary [ˌrevəˈluːʃənərɪ] ADJ (*gen*) revolucionario
N (*Pol*) revolucionario/a *m/f*

revolutionize [ˌrevəˈluːʃənaɪz] VT revolucionar

revolve [rɪˈvɒlv] VT girar, hacer girar; (*fig*) (*in the mind*) dar vueltas a, meditar
VI girar, dar vueltas; (*Astron*) revolverse • **to ~ around** (*lit*) girar alrededor de; (*fig*) girar en torno a • **everything ~s round him** todo gira en torno a él • **the discussion ~d around three topics** el debate se centró en tres temas

revolver [rɪˈvɒlvəʳ] N revólver *m*

revolving [rɪˈvɒlvɪŋ] ADJ [*bookcase, stand etc*] giratorio
CPD ▸ **revolving credit** crédito *m* rotativo ▸ **revolving door** puerta *f* giratoria • **the ~ door of the justice system** (*fig*) el círculo vicioso del sistema judicial • **the ~ door of senior executives** (*fig*) los constantes vaivenes laborales de los altos ejecutivos, el baile de nombres constante entre los altos ejecutivos ▸ **revolving presidency** presidencia *f* rotativa ▸ **revolving stage** (*Theat*) escena *f* giratoria

revue [rɪˈvjuː] N (*Theat*) (teatro *m* de) revista *f or* variedades *fpl*

revulsion [rɪˈvʌlʃən] N **1** (= *disgust*) repugnancia *f*, asco *m*; (*Med*) revulsión *f*
2 (= *sudden change*) reacción *f*, cambio *m* repentino

reward [rɪˈwɔːd] N recompensa *f*, premio *m*; (*for finding sth*) gratificación *f* • **as a ~ for** en recompensa de, como premio a • **"£50 reward"** "50 libras de recompensa" • **a ~ will be paid for information about …** se recompensará al que dé alguna información acerca de …
VT recompensar; (*fig*) premiar • **to ~ sb for his services** recompensar a algn por sus servicios • **she ~ed me with a smile** me premió con una sonrisa • **it might ~ your attention** podría valer la pena ir a verlo • **the case would ~ your investigation** le valdría la pena investigar el asunto

rewarding [rɪˈwɔːdɪŋ] ADJ gratificante

rewind [ˈriːˈwaɪnd] VT [+ *cassette, videotape*] rebobinar; [+ *watch*] dar cuerda a; [+ *wool etc*] devanar

rewinding [ˈriːˈwaɪndɪŋ] N [*of cassette, videotape*] rebobinado *m*

rewire [ˈriːˈwaɪəʳ] VT [+ *house*] rehacer la instalación eléctrica de

rewiring [ˌriːˈwaɪərɪŋ] N cableado *m* nuevo

reword [ˈriːˈwɜːd] VT expresar en otras palabras

rework [riːˈwɜːk] VT [+ *novel, piece of writing*] refundir; [+ *idea*] repensar, reelaborar; [+ *song, schedule*] rehacer

reworking [ˌriːˈwɜːkɪŋ] N [*of book, story*] nueva versión *f*

rewound [ˈriːˈwaʊnd] PT, PP *of* **rewind**

rewritable [ˌriːˈraɪtəbl] ADJ [*CD, disk*] reescribible

rewrite [ˌriːˈraɪt] (PT: **rewrote** [ˌriːˈrəʊt]) (PP: **rewritten** [ˌriːˈrɪtn]) VT reescribir; [+ *text*] rehacer, refundir
N [ˈriːraɪt] nueva versión *f*, refundición *f*

Reykjavik [ˈreɪkjəviːk] N Reykjavik *m*

RFD N ABBR (*US*) (*Post*) = **rural free delivery**

RFU N ABBR (*Brit*) (= **Rugby Football Union**)
▹ **RUGBY**
RGN N ABBR = **Registered General Nurse**
Rgt ABBR (= **Regiment**) regto.
Rh N ABBR (= **Rhesus**) Rh
CPD ▸ **Rh factor** factor *m* Rh
r.h. ABBR (= **right hand**) der., der^a^
rhapsodic [ræp'sɒdɪk] ADJ (*Mus*) rapsódico; (*fig*) extático, locamente entusiasmado
rhapsodize ['ræpsədaɪz] VI • **to ~ over sth** extasiarse ante algo, entusiasmarse por algo
rhapsody ['ræpsədɪ] N **1** (*Mus*) rapsodia *f*
2 (*fig*) transporte *m* de admiración • **to be in rhapsodies** estar extasiado • **to go into rhapsodies over** extasiarse por
rhea ['ri:ə] N ñandú *m*
Rhenish ['renɪʃ] ADJ renano
N vino *m* del Rin
rhenium ['ri:nɪəm] N renio *m*
rheostat ['ri:əʊstæt] N reóstato *m*
rhesus ['ri:səs] N **1** (= *monkey*) macaco *m* de la India
2 (*Med*) • **~ negative** Rh negativo, Rhesus negativo • **~ positive** Rh positivo, Rhesus positivo
CPD ▸ **rhesus baby** bebé *m* con factor Rhesus ▸ **rhesus factor** (*Med*) factor *m* Rhesus ▸ **rhesus monkey** macaco *m* de la India
rhetic ['ri:tɪk] ADJ rético
rhetoric ['retərɪk] N retórica *f*
rhetorical [rɪ'tɒrɪkəl] ADJ retórico
• **~ question** pregunta *f* retórica
rhetorically [rɪ'tɒrɪkəlɪ] ADV retóricamente • **I speak ~** hablo en metáfora
rhetorician [,retə'rɪʃən] N retórico/a *m/f*
rheumatic [ru:'mætɪk] ADJ reumático
N (= *person*) reumático/a *m/f*
CPD ▸ **rheumatic fever** fiebre *f* reumática
rheumaticky* [ru:'mætɪkɪ] ADJ reumático
rheumatics* [ru:'mætɪks] NSING reúma *m*, reumatismo *m*
rheumatism ['ru:mətɪzəm] N reumatismo *m*
rheumatoid ['ru:mətɔɪd] ADJ reumatoideo
CPD ▸ **rheumatoid arthritis** reúma *m* articular
rheumatologist [,ru:mə'tɒlədʒɪst] N reumatólogo/a *m/f*
rheumatology [,ru:mə'tɒlədʒɪ] N reumatología *f*
rheumy ['ru:mɪ] ADJ [*eyes*] legañoso, pitañoso
Rhine [raɪn] N • **the ~** el Rin
CPD ▸ **Rhine wine** vino *m* blanco del Rin
Rhineland ['raɪnlənd] N Renania *f*
rhinestone ['raɪn,stəʊn] N diamante *m* de imitación
rhinitis [raɪ'naɪtɪs] N rinitis *f*
rhino ['raɪnəʊ] N (PL: **rhino** *or* **rhinos**) (= *rhinoceros*) rinoceronte *m*
CPD ▸ **rhino horn** cuerno *m* de rinoceronte
rhinoceros [raɪ'nɒsərəs] N (PL: **rhinoceros** *or* **rhinoceroses**) rinoceronte *m*
CPD ▸ **rhinoceros horn** cuerno *m* de rinoceronte
rhinoplasty ['raɪnəʊplæstɪ] N rinoplastia *f*
rhizome ['raɪzəʊm] N rizoma *m*
Rhodes [rəʊdz] N Rodas *f*
Rhodesia [rəʊ'di:ʒə] N (*Hist*) Rodesia *f*
Rhodesian [rəʊ'di:ʒən] (*Hist*) ADJ rodesiano
N rodesiano/a *m/f*
rhodium ['rəʊdɪəm] N rodio *m*
rhododendron [,rəʊdə'dendrən] N rododendro *m*
rhomb [rɒm] N = **rhombus**
rhomboid ['rɒmbɔɪd] ADJ romboidal
N romboide *m*
rhombus ['rɒmbəs] N (PL: **rhombuses** *or* **rhombi**) rombo *m*
Rhone [rəʊn] N • **the ~** el Ródano
rhubarb ['ru:bɑ:b] N **1** (*Bot, Culin*) ruibarbo *m*
2 (*Theat*) *palabra que se repite para representar la conversación callada en escenas de comparsas*
CPD [*jam, pie, tart*] de ruibarbo
rhyme [raɪm] N **1** (= *identical sound*) rima *f*
• IDIOM: • **without ~ or reason** sin ton ni son
2 (= *poem*) poesía *f*, versos *mpl* • **in ~** en verso
VI rimar • **to ~ with sth** rimar con algo
VT rimar
CPD ▸ **rhyme scheme** esquema *m* de la rima, combinación *f* de rimas
rhymed [raɪmd] ADJ rimado
rhymer ['raɪmə^r^] N, **rhymester** ['raɪmstə^r^] N rimador(a) *m/f*
rhyming ['raɪmɪŋ] ADJ [*couplet, verse*] rimado
CPD ▸ **rhyming slang** argot *m* basado en rimas (*p.ej. "apples and pears" = "stairs"*)

RHYMING SLANG
El **rhyming slang (jerga rimada)** es un tipo muy peculiar de jerga que usan los habitantes de un barrio en el este de Londres (los **cockneys**), en la que una palabra o frase determinada se sustituye por otra que rima con ella; por ejemplo, dicen **apples and pears** en vez de **stairs**. Puede resultar muy confuso para las personas que no lo conocen bien, sobre todo porque, además, muchas veces se establece un doble juego de palabras en el que la palabra que rima no se dice; por ejemplo, **butcher's hook** quiere decir **look**, pero a menudo solo se dice **butcher's**, como en la frase **let's have a butcher's**. El uso de algunas de estas expresiones se ha extendido al inglés coloquial habitual, como **use your loaf**, donde **loaf**, que viene de **loaf of bread**, quiere decir **head**.
▹ **COCKNEY**

rhythm ['rɪðəm] N ritmo *m* • **~ and blues** (*Mus*) rhythm and blues *m*
CPD ▸ **rhythm guitar** guitarra *f* rítmica ▸ **rhythm method** [*of contraception*] método *m* de Ogino-Knaus ▸ **rhythm section** (*Mus*) sección *f* rítmica
rhythmic ['rɪðmɪk], **rhythmical** ['rɪðmɪkəl] ADJ rítmico, acompasado
rhythmically ['rɪðmɪkəlɪ] ADV rítmicamente, de forma rítmica
RI N ABBR (*Scol*) (= **religious instruction**) ed. religiosa
ABBR = **Rhode Island**
rib [rɪb] N **1** (*Anat, Culin*) costilla *f*
2 [*of umbrella*] varilla *f*; [*of leaf*] nervio *m*; (*Knitting*) cordoncillo *m*; (*Archit*) nervadura *f*; (*Naut*) costilla *f*, cuaderna *f*
VT* (= *tease*) tomar el pelo a, mofarse de
CPD ▸ **rib cage** tórax *m*
RIBA N ABBR = **Royal Institute of British Architects**
ribald ['rɪbəld] ADJ [*jokes, laughter*] verde, colorado (*LAm*); [*person*] irreverente, procaz
ribaldry ['rɪbəldrɪ] N **1** [*of jokes*] chocarrería *f*; [*of person*] procacidad *f*
2 (= *jokes etc*) cosas *fpl* verdes, cosas *fpl* obscenas
riband†† ['rɪbənd] = **ribbon**
ribbed [rɪbd] ADJ • **~ sweater** jersey *m* de cordoncillo
ribbing ['rɪbɪŋ] N (*in fabric*) cordoncillos *mpl*; (*Archit*) nervaduras *fpl*
ribbon ['rɪbən] N (*gen*) cinta *f*; (*for hair*) moña *f*, cinta *f*; (*Mil*) galón *m* • **to tear sth to ~s** (*lit*) hacer algo trizas; (*fig*) hacer algo pedazos
CPD ▸ **ribbon development** urbanización *f* a lo largo de una carretera
riboflavin [,raɪbəʊ'fleɪvɪn] N riboflavina *f*
ribonucleic [,raɪbəʊnju:'kleɪɪk] ADJ • **~ acid** ácido *m* ribonucleico
rib-tickler* ['rɪb'tɪklə^r^] N (*Brit*) chiste *m* desternillante*
rib-tickling* ['rɪbtɪklɪŋ] ADJ desternillante
ribwort ['rɪbwɜ:t] N llantén *m* menor
rice [raɪs] N arroz *m*
CPD ▸ **rice cake** tortita *f* de arroz ▸ **rice paddy** (*US*) arrozal *m* ▸ **rice paper** papel *m* de arroz ▸ **rice pudding** arroz *m* con leche ▸ **rice wine** vino *m* de arroz
ricefield ['raɪsfi:ld] N arrozal *m*
rice-growing ['raɪs,grəʊɪŋ] ADJ arrocero
ricer ['raɪsə^r^] N (*US*) (*Culin*) pasapurés *m inv*, puretera *f* (*S. Cone*)
rich [rɪtʃ] ADJ (COMPAR: **richer**, SUPERL: **richest**) **1** (= *wealthy*) [*person, country*] rico • **to become** *or* **get** *or* **grow ~(er)** hacerse (más) rico, enriquecerse (más) • **to get ~ quick** hacer fortuna *or* enriquecerse rápidamente
• IDIOMS: • **to be as ~ as Croesus** nadar en la abundancia • **for ~er, for poorer** en la riqueza y en la pobreza; ▹ **get-rich-quick, strike**
2 (= *abundant*) [*variety, source*] grande; [*deposit, harvest*] abundante; [*reward*] generoso
• **seaweed is a ~ source of iodine** las algas son una gran fuente de yodo • **to be ~ in** [+ *flora, fauna*] tener abundancia de, tener gran riqueza de; [+ *natural resources, nutrients, protein*] ser rico en • **the island is ~ in history** la isla tiene mucha historia • **to be ~ in detail** ser rico *or* (*frm*) profuso en detalles
• **the story is ~ in comic and dramatic detail** la historia es rica en *or* abunda en detalles cómicos y dramáticos • **a style ~ in metaphors** un estilo en el que abundan las metáforas; ▹ **pickings**
3 (= *full*) [*life, experience, history*] rico
4 (= *fertile*) [*soil*] rico, fértil
5 (= *heavy, concentrated*) [*food, sauce*] sustancioso (*que contiene mucha grasa, azúcar etc*); (*pej*) pesado, fuerte; [*coffee*] con mucho sabor; [*wine*] generoso • **it's too ~ for me** es muy pesado (*or* dulce *or* grasiento *etc*) para mí • **this chocolate gateau is very ~** esta tarta de chocolate llena mucho, esta tarta de chocolate es muy empalagosa *or* pesada (*pej*)
6 (= *intense*) [*colour*] vivo, cálido; [*sound, smell*] intenso
7 (= *mellow*) [*voice*] sonoro
8 (= *luxurious*) [*tapestries*] lujoso; [*velvet*] exquisito
9* (= *laughable*) • **that's ~!** ¡mira por dónde!*
• **that's ~, coming from her!** ¡ella no es quién para hablar!, ¡tiene gracia que sea ella la que diga eso!
NPL • **the ~** los ricos • **the ~ and famous** los ricos y famosos
CPD ▸ **rich tea biscuit** galleta *f* (*que se toma con una taza de té*)
Richard ['rɪtʃəd] N Ricardo • **~ (the) Lionheart** Ricardo Corazón de León
riches ['rɪtʃɪz] NPL riqueza *fsing*
richly ['rɪtʃlɪ] ADV **1** (= *generously*) [*rewarded*] generosamente; [*illustrated*] profusamente
• **we were ~ rewarded** fuimos generosamente recompensados • **a boy ~ endowed with talent** un chico dotado de un enorme talento • **a ~ endowed library** una biblioteca con abundantes fondos
2 (= *ornately*) [*decorated, furnished*] suntuosamente, lujosamente • **a ~ adorned chair** una silla con exquisitos adornos
• **~ patterned fabrics** telas con ricos estampados

3 (= *strongly*) • **~ coloured fabrics** telas de colores vivos • **a ~ flavoured sauce** una salsa de sabor fuerte • **the flowers are ~ scented** las flores tienen un perfume intenso
4 (= *intensely*) • **the work is ~ rewarding** el trabajo es sumamente *or* enormemente gratificante • **she ~ deserves it** se lo tiene bien merecido • **the success they so ~ deserve** el éxito que tanto merecen

richness ['rɪtʃnɪs] (N) **1** (= *wealth*) [*of person, culture*] riqueza *f*
2 (= *abundance*) [*of variety*] lo enorme; [*of deposits, harvest*] abundancia *f* • **~ in vitamins** riqueza *f* en vitaminas
3 (= *fullness*) [*of life, experience*] riqueza *f*
4 (= *fertility*) [*of soil*] fertilidad *f*
5 (= *heaviness*) [*of food*] lo sustancioso; (*pej*) pesadez *f*
6 (= *intensity*) [*of colour*] viveza *f*; [*of sound, smell*] intensidad *f*
7 (= *mellowness*) [*of voice*] sonoridad *f*

Richter scale ['rɪxtə,skeɪl] (N) (*Geol*) escala *f* Richter

rick[1] [rɪk] (*Agr*) (N) almiar *m*
(VT) almiarar, amontonar

rick[2] [rɪk] (VT) = **wrick**

rickets ['rɪkɪts] (NSING) raquitismo *m*

rickety ['rɪkɪtɪ] (ADJ) **1** (= *wobbly*) tambaleante, inseguro; [*old car*] desvencijado
2 (*Med*) raquítico

rickshaw ['rɪkʃɔː] (N) *carrito de estilo oriental tirado por un hombre*

ricochet ['rɪkəʃeɪ] (N) [*of stone, bullet*] rebote *m*
(VI) rebotar (**off** de)

rictus ['rɪktəs] (N) (PL: **rictus** *or* **rictuses**) rictus *m*

rid [rɪd] (PT, PP: **rid, ridded**) (VT) • **to be rid of sth/sb: she was glad to be rid of him** estaba contenta de haberse librado de él, estaba contenta de habérselo quitado de encima* • **will I never be rid of these debts?** ¿me libraré alguna vez de estas deudas?, ¿me quitaré algún día estas deudas de encima?* • **to be well rid of sb** haber hecho bien en librarse de algn • **to get rid of** [+ *unwanted item*] deshacerse de; [+ *habit*] quitarse; [+ *rats, smell, waste, corruption*] eliminar; (= *sell*) vender, deshacerse de • **he denied helping him get rid of evidence** negó haberle ayudado a deshacerse de las pruebas • **I've been trying to get rid of this headache all day** he estado intentando quitarme esta jaqueca todo el día • **you need to get rid of that excess weight** tienes que eliminar todos esos kilos de más • **to get rid of sb** librarse de algn; [+ *tedious person*] quitarse a algn de encima*; (*euph*) (= *kill*) deshacerse de algn, eliminar a algn • **you won't get rid of me that easily** no te librarás *or* desharás de mí tan fácilmente • **to rid o.s. of sth/sb**: • **I couldn't rid myself of the feeling that I was being watched** no me podía librar de la sensación de que alguien me estaba vigilando • **I can't seem to rid myself of the habit** no me puedo quitar la costumbre • **to rid sth/sb of sth**: • **I couldn't rid my mind of these thoughts** no podía quitarme estos pensamientos de la cabeza • **we want to rid the world of this disease** queremos erradicar esta enfermedad en el mundo, queremos librar a la humanidad de esta enfermedad

riddance ['rɪdəns] (N) • **good ~ (to bad rubbish)!*** (*pej*) ¡vete con viento fresco! • **and good ~ to him!** ¡que se pudra!

ridden ['rɪdn] (VB) (*pp of* **ride**) • **a horse ~ by ...** un caballo montado por ...

riddle[1] ['rɪdl] (N) (= *word puzzle*) acertijo *m*, adivinanza *f*; (= *mystery*) enigma *m*, misterio *m*; (= *person etc*) enigma *m* • **to ask sb a ~** proponer un acertijo a algn • **to speak in ~s** hablar en clave

riddle[2] ['rɪdl] (N) (= *sieve*) criba *f*, criba *f* gruesa; (= *potato sorter etc*) escogedor *m*
(VT) **1** (= *sieve*) cribar; [+ *potatoes etc*] pasar por el escogedor
2 • **to ~ with** [+ *bullets etc*] acribillar a • **the house is ~d with damp** la casa tiene humedad por todas partes • **the organization is ~d with communists** el organismo está plagado de comunistas • **the army is ~d with subversion** el ejército está infectado de elementos subversivos

ride [raɪd] (VB: PT: **rode**, PP: **ridden**) (N)
1 (= *journey*) paseo *m*; (= *car ride*) vuelta *f* en coche; (= *bike ride*) paseo en bicicleta; (= *horse ride*) paseo a caballo; (*esp US*) (= *free ride*) viaje *m* gratuito • **the ~ of the Valkyries** la cabalgata de las valquirias • **it's my first ~ in a Rolls** es la primera vez que viajo en un Rolls • **he gave me a ~ into town** (*in car*) me llevó en coche a la ciudad, me dio aventón hasta la ciudad (*Mex*) • **to get a ~**: • **I got a ~ all the way to Bordeaux** un automovilista me llevó todo hasta Burdeos • **to go for a ~** (*in car, on bike, on horse*) dar una vuelta, pasear • **it was a rough ~** fue un viaje bastante incómodo • **to give sb a rough ~** (*fig*) hacer pasar un mal rato a algn • **to take a ~ in a helicopter** dar un paseo en helicóptero • **to take sb for a ~** (*in car*) dar una vuelta en coche a algn; (= *make fool of**) tomarle el pelo a algn; (= *swindle**) dar gato por liebre a algn; (= *kill*‡) (*US*) mandar a algn al otro barrio‡ • IDIOMS: • **to be taken for a ~*** hacer el primo* • **to come/go along for the ~** apuntarse por gusto
2 (= *distance travelled*) viaje *m*, recorrido *m* • **it's only a short ~** es poco camino • **it's a ten-minute ~ on the bus** son diez minutos en autobús *or* (*Mex*) en camión • **it's a 70p ~ from the station** el viaje desde la estación cuesta 70 peniques
3 (*at fairground*) (= *attraction*) atracción *f*; (= *trip*) viaje *m* • **"50p a ride"** "50 peniques por persona"
4 (= *path*) vereda *f*
(VT) **1** [+ *horse*] montar; [+ *bicycle*] montar en, ir en, andar en • **to ~ an elephant** ir montado en un elefante • **he rode his horse into town** fue a caballo hasta la ciudad • **he rode his horse into the shop** entró a caballo en la tienda • **to ~ a horse hard** castigar mucho a un caballo • **can you ~ a bike?** ¿sabes montar en bicicleta? • **it has never been ridden** hasta ahora nadie ha montado en él • **he rode it in two races** lo corrió en dos carreras
2 [+ *distance*] • **we rode ten km yesterday** recorrimos diez kilómetros ayer
3 • **to ~ a good race** hacer bien una carrera, dar buena cuenta de sí (en una carrera)
4 (*esp US**) • **to ~ sb** tenerla tomada con algn, no dejar en paz a algn • **to ~ sb hard** exigir mucho a algn, darle duro a algn* • **don't ~ him too hard** no seas demasiado severo con él • **to ~ an idea to death** explotar una idea con demasiado entusiasmo, acabar con una idea a fuerza de repetirla demasiado
5 (*Naut*) [+ *waves*] hender, surcar
(VI) **1** (*on horse*) montar • **to ~ on an elephant** ir montado en un elefante • **can you ~?** ¿sabes montar a caballo? • **she ~s every day** monta todos los días • **to ~ ast~** montar a horcajadas • **to ~ like mad** correr como el demonio • **he ~s for a different stable** monta para otra cuadra
2 (*in car*) ir, viajar • **to ~ on a bus/in a car/in a train** viajar en autobús/en coche/en tren • **some rode but I had to walk** algunos fueron en coche pero yo tuve que ir a pie
3 (*with prep, adv*) • **he rode straight at me** arremetió contra mí • **to ~ home on sb's shoulders** ser llevado a casa en los hombros de algn • **to ~ over/through** andar a caballo *etc* por/a través de • **we'll ~ over to see you** vendremos a verte • **to ~ to Jaén** ir (a caballo) a Jaén • **he rode up to me** se me acercó a caballo
4 • **to ~ at anchor** (*Naut*) estar fondeado
5 (*fig*) • **the moon was riding high in the sky** la luna estaba en lo alto del cielo • IDIOMS: • **to be riding high** [*person*] estar alegre, estar en la cumbre de la felicidad • **he's riding high at the moment** por ahora lo va muy bien • **to let things ~** dejar que las cosas sigan su curso
▸ **ride about, ride around** (VI + ADV) pasearse a caballo/en coche/en bicicleta *etc*
▸ **ride away** (VI + ADV) alejarse, irse, partir
▸ **ride back** (VI + ADV) volver (a caballo, en bicicleta *etc*)
▸ **ride behind** (VI + ADV) ir después, caminar a la zaga; (= *in rear seat*) ir en el asiento de atrás; (= *on same horse*) cabalgar a la grupa
▸ **ride by** (VI + ADV) pasar (*a caballo, en bicicleta etc*)
▸ **ride down** (VT + ADV) **1** (= *trample*) atropellar
2 (= *catch up with*) coger, alcanzar
▸ **ride off** (VI + ADV) alejarse, irse, partir • **they rode off in pursuit** se marcharon a caballo en persecución
▸ **ride on** (VI + ADV) seguir adelante
▸ **ride out** (VT + ADV) (*Naut*) [+ *storm*] capear, aguantar; (*fig*) [+ *crisis*] sobrevivir, sobreponerse a
▸ **ride up** (VI + ADV) **1** [*horseman, motorcyclist etc*] llegar, acercarse
2 [*skirt, dress*] subirse

rider ['raɪdə[r]] (N) **1** (= *horserider*) jinete *mf* • **I'm not much of a ~** apenas sé montar • **he's a fine ~** es un jinete destacado
2 (= *cyclist*) ciclista *mf*; (= *motorcyclist*) motociclista *mf*, motorista *mf*; (*US*) (*Aut*) pasajero/a *m/f*, viajero/a *m/f*
3 (= *additional clause*) aditamento *m* • **with the ~ that ...** a condición de que ... • **I must add the ~ that ...** debo añadir que ...

ridge [rɪdʒ] (N) [*of hills, mountains*] cadena *f*; [*of nose*] puente *m*, caballete *m*; [*of roof*] caballete *m*; (*Agr*) caballón *m*; (= *crest of hill*) cumbre *f*, cresta *f*; (*Met*) • **~ of high/low pressure** línea *f* de presión alta/baja
(CPD) ▸ **ridge pole** (*on tent*) caballete *m*, cumbrera *f* ▸ **ridge tent** tienda *f* canadiense ▸ **ridge tile** teja *f* de caballete

ridged ['rɪdʒd] (ADJ) estriado

ridgeway ['rɪdʒweɪ] (N) ruta *f* de las crestas

ridicule ['rɪdɪkjuːl] (N) irrisión *f*, burla *f* • **to expose sb to public ~** exponer a algn a la mofa pública • **to hold sth/sb up to ~** poner algo/a algn en ridículo • **to lay o.s. open to ~** exponerse al ridículo
(VT) dejar *or* poner en ridículo, ridiculizar

ridiculous [rɪ'dɪkjʊləs] (ADJ) [*idea etc*] ridículo, absurdo • **to look ~** [*person*] estar ridículo; [*thing*] ser ridículo • **to make o.s. (look) ~** ponerse en ridículo • **don't be ~!** ¡no seas ridículo!, no digas tonterías *or* chorradas* • **~!** • **how ~!** ¡qué ridículo!, ¡qué estupidez!

ridiculously [rɪ'dɪkjʊləslɪ] (ADV) **1** (= *stupidly*) de forma ridícula
2 (*fig*) (= *disproportionately etc*) absurdamente, ridículamente • **it is ~ easy** es absurdamente *or* ridículamente fácil

ridiculousness [rɪ'dɪkjʊləsnɪs] (N) ridiculez *f*

riding ['raɪdɪŋ] (N) equitación *f* • **I like ~** me gusta montar a caballo
(CPD) ▸ **riding boots** botas *fpl* de montar ▸ **riding breeches** pantalones *mpl* de montar ▸ **riding crop** fusta *f* ▸ **riding habit** amazona *f*, traje *m* de montar ▸ **riding jacket** chaqueta *f* de montar ▸ **riding master** profesor *m* de equitación ▸ **riding school** escuela *f* de equitación ▸ **riding stables** cuadras *fpl* ▸ **riding whip** = **riding crop**

rife [raɪf] (ADJ) • **to be ~** [*problem*] ser muy común; [*rumours, speculation, fears*] abundar, proliferar; [*disease*] hacer estragos; [*unemployment, crime*] abundar, hacer estragos; [*racism, corruption*] estar muy extendido • **smallpox was still ~** la viruela aún hacía estragos • **(to be) ~ with sth: countries ~ with Aids** países plagados de sida, países donde el sida hace estragos • **it is ~ with mistakes** está plagado de errores • **the whole industry is ~ with corruption** la corrupción reina *or* está muy extendida en todo el sector • **the whole town is ~ with rumours** en la ciudad proliferan los rumores • **a region ~ with unemployment** una región donde abunda el paro *or* donde el paro hace estragos • **the media is ~ with speculation about ...** los medios de comunicación no dejan de especular acerca de ..., en los medios de comunicación abundan *or* proliferan las especulaciones acerca de ...

riff [rɪf] (N) (*Mus*) riff *m*, *frase de dos o cuatro compases que se repite continuamente a lo largo de la canción*

riffle ['rɪfəl] (VT) (*also* **riffle through**) hojear • **to ~ (through) a book** hojear (rápidamente) un libro

riff-raff ['rɪfræf] (N) gentuza *f*, chusma *f* • **and all the riff-raff of the neighbourhood** y todos los sinvergüenzas del barrio

rifle¹ ['raɪfl] (VT) (= *search*) desvalijar • **to ~ a case** desvalijar una maleta • **the house had been ~d** habían saqueado la casa • **they ~d the house in search of money** saquearon la casa en busca de dinero • **to ~ sb's pockets** vaciar los bolsillos a algn
▸ **rifle through** (VI + PREP) rebuscar en, revolver

rifle² ['raɪfl] (N) **1** (= *gun*) rifle *m*, fusil *m*
2 the Rifles (= *regiment*) los fusileros, el regimiento de fusileros
(VT) (*Tech*) estriar, rayar
(CPD) ▸ **rifle butt** culata *f* de rifle ▸ **rifle fire** fuego *m* de fusilería ▸ **rifle range** (*Mil*) campo *m* de tiro; (*at fair*) barraca *f* de tiro al blanco ▸ **rifle shot** tiro *m* de fusil • **within ~ shot** a tiro de fusil

rifled ['raɪfld] (ADJ) (*Tech*) estriado, rayado

rifleman ['raɪflmən] (N) (PL: **riflemen**) fusilero *m*

rifling ['raɪflɪŋ] (N) (*Tech*) estría *f*, estriado *m*, rayado *m*

rift [rɪft] (N) **1** (= *fissure*) grieta *f*, fisura *f*; (*in clouds*) claro *m*
2 (*fig*) ruptura *f*, desavenencia *f*; (*in relations etc*) grieta *f*; (*in political party*) escisión *f*, cisma *m*

rig [rɪg] (N) **1** (*Naut*) aparejo *m*
2 (*also* **oil rig**) (*on land*) torre *f* de perforación; (*at sea*) plataforma *f* petrolífera
3†* (= *outfit*) (*also* **rig out**) vestimenta *f*, atuendo *m*
(VT) **1** (*Naut*) [+ *ship*] aparejar, equipar
2 (= *fix dishonestly*) [+ *election, competition*] amañar; [+ *prices*] manipular • **the government had got it all rigged** el gobierno lo había arreglado todo de modo fraudulento • **to rig the market** (*Comm*) manipular la lonja *or* la bolsa • **it was rigged*** hubo tongo*
▸ **rig out** (VT + ADV) **1** (*Naut*) proveer (**with** de), equipar (**with** con)
2* (= *dress*) ataviar, vestir • **to rig sb out in sth** ataviar *or* vestir a algn de algo • **to be rigged out in a new dress** lucir un vestido nuevo
▸ **rig up** (VT + ADV) (= *build*) improvisar; (*fig*) (= *arrange*) organizar, trabar • **we'll see what we can rig up** veremos si podemos arreglar algo

rigger ['rɪgəʳ] (N) (*Naut*) aparejador *m*; (*Aer*) mecánico *m*

rigging ['rɪgɪŋ] (N) (*Naut*) jarcia *f*, aparejo *m*

right [raɪt] (ADJ) **1** (= *morally good, just*) justo • **it is not ~ that he should pay for their mistake** no es justo que él pague por su error • **it is/seems only ~ that she should get the biggest share** es/me parece justo que ella reciba la mayor parte, está/me parece bien que ella reciba la mayor parte • **it doesn't seem ~ that his contribution should not be acknowledged** parece injusto que no se reconozca su aportación • **it's not ~!** ¡no hay derecho! • **I thought it ~ to ask permission first** me pareció conveniente preguntarle antes, pensé que debía preguntarle antes • **would it be ~ for me to ask him?** ¿debería preguntárselo? • **it is only ~ and proper that people should know what is going on** lo suyo es que la gente sepa lo que pasa • **to do the ~ thing** • **do what is ~** hacer lo correcto, actuar correctamente • **to do the ~ thing by sb** portarse como es debido con algn • **doing the ~ thing by a pregnant girlfriend meant marrying her** hacer lo que Dios manda con una novia embarazada significaba casarse con ella
2 (= *suitable*) [*tool, clothes*] apropiado, adecuado; [*time*] oportuno • **to choose the ~ moment for sth/to do sth** elegir el momento oportuno para algo/para hacer algo • **that's the ~ attitude!** ¡haces bien! • **I haven't got the ~ clothes for a formal dinner** no tengo ropa apropiada *or* adecuada para una cena de etiqueta • **you're not using the ~ tool for the job** no estás empleando la herramienta apropiada *or* adecuada para el trabajo • **he's the ~ man for the job** es el hombre más indicado para el cargo • **I don't think he's the ~ sort of person for you** me parece que no es la persona que te conviene • **they holiday in all the ~ places** toman sus vacaciones en todos los sitios que están de moda • **the balance of humour and tragedy is just ~** el equilibrio entre humor y tragedia es perfecto • **she's just ~ for the job** es la persona perfecta para el puesto • **the flat is just ~ for me** el piso es justo lo que necesito • **"is there too much salt in it?" — "no, it's just ~"** —¿tiene demasiada sal? —no, está en su punto justo • **Mr Right** el novio soñado, el marido ideal • **to know the ~ people** tener enchufes *or* (*LAm*) palanca • **he knows all the ~ people** tiene enchufes *or* (*LAm*) palanca en todas partes • **I just happened to be in the ~ place at the ~ time** dio la casualidad de que estaba en el sitio adecuado en el momento adecuado • **if the price is ~** si el precio es razonable • **he's on the ~ side of 40** tiene menos de 40 años • **to say the ~ thing** decir lo que hay que decir, tener las palabras justas • **we'll do it when the time is ~** lo haremos en el momento oportuno *or* a su debido tiempo • **the ~ word** la palabra exacta *or* apropiada
3 (= *correct*) correcto, exacto • **~ first time!** ¡exactamente!, ¡exacto! • **"she's your sister?" — "that's ~!"** —¿es tu hermana? —¡eso es! *or* ¡así es! *or* ¡exacto! • **that's ~! it has to go through that hole** ¡eso es! tiene que pasar por ese agujero • **she said she'd done it, isn't that ~, mother?** dijo que lo había hecho ¿no es así, madre? *or* ¿a que sí, madre? • **you mean he offered to pay? is that ~, Harry?** ¿dices que se ofreció a pagar? ¿es eso cierto, Harry? • **and quite ~ too!** ¡y con razón! • **am I ~ for the station?** ¿por aquí se va a la estación?, ¿voy bien (por aquí) para la estación? • **the ~ answer** la respuesta correcta; (*Math*) (*to problem*) la solución correcta • **~ you are!*** ¡vale!, ¡muy bien! • **I was beginning to wonder whether I had the ~ day** empezaba a preguntarme si me habría equivocado de día • **to get sth ~** (= *guess correctly*) acertar en algo; (= *do properly*) hacer algo bien • **I got the date ~ but not the time** acerté en la fecha pero me equivoqué de hora • **it's vital that we get the timing ~** es esencial que escojamos bien el momento • **you didn't get it ~, so you lose five points** no acertaste *or* te equivocaste, así que pierdes cinco puntos • **let's get it ~ this time!** ¡a ver si esta vez nos sale bien! • **we must get it ~ this time** esta vez tenemos que hacerlo bien *or* nos tiene que salir bien • **is this the ~ house?** ¿es esta la casa? • **he can't even sing the ~ notes** no sabe ni dar las notas bien • **are you sure you've got the ~ number?** (*Telec*) ¿seguro que es ese el número? • **to put sb ~** sacar a algn de su error; (*unpleasantly*) enmendar la plana a algn • **I'm confused, and I wanted you to put me ~** tengo dudas y quisiera que tú me las aclararas • **if you tell the story wrong the child will soon put you ~** si te equivocas al contar la historia, el niño enseguida te corrige *or* te saca de tu error • **to put a clock ~** poner un reloj en hora • **to put a mistake ~** corregir *or* rectificar un error • **is this the ~ road for Segovia?** ¿es este el camino de Segovia?, ¿por aquí se va a Segovia? • **are we on the ~ road?** ¿vamos por buen camino?, ¿vamos bien por esta carretera? • **it's not the ~ shade of green** no es el tono de verde que yo busco • **the ~ side of the fabric** el (lado) derecho de la tela • **is the skirt the ~ size?** ¿va bien la falda de talla? • **it's not the ~ size/length** no vale de talla/de largo • **the ~ time** la hora exacta • **is that the ~ time?** ¿es esa la hora? • **do you have the ~ time?** ¿tienes hora buena?, ¿sabes qué hora es exactamente? • IDIOM: • **to get on the ~ side of sb** (*fig*) congraciarse con algn
4 (= *in the right*) • **to be ~ to do sth** hacer bien en hacer algo • **you were ~ to come to me** has hecho bien en venir a verme • **to be ~** [*person*] tener razón, estar en lo cierto • **you're quite ~** • **you're dead ~*** tienes toda la razón • **how ~ you are!** ¡qué razón tienes! • **to be ~ about sth/sb**: • **you were ~ about there being none left** tenías razón cuando decías que no quedaba ninguno • **you were ~ about Peter, he's totally unreliable** tenías razón en lo de Peter *or* con respecto a Peter: no hay quien se fíe de él • **am I ~ in thinking that we've met before?** si no me equivoco ya nos conocemos ¿no? • **you were ~ in calling the doctor, it was appendicitis** hiciste bien en llamar al médico, era apendicitis
5 (= *in order*) • **I don't feel quite ~** no me siento del todo bien • **I knew something wasn't ~ when she didn't call as usual** supe que algo no iba bien cuando no llamaba como de costumbre • **his leg hasn't been ~ since the accident** tiene la pierna mal desde el accidente • **my stereo still isn't ~** mi equipo sigue sin ir bien • **it will all come ~ in the end** todo se arreglará al final • **she's not quite ~ in the head** no está en sus cabales • **to be in one's ~ mind** en su sano juicio • **to put**

sth/sb ~: • **I hope the garage can put the car ~** espero que me sepan arreglar el coche en el taller • **you've offended her but it's not too late to put things ~** la has ofendido pero aún puedes arreglarlo • **it's nothing a night's sleep won't put ~** no es nada que no se arregle durmiendo toda la noche de un tirón • **a couple of aspirin will put me ~** con un par de aspirinas me pondré bien • **that's soon put ~** eso se arregla fácilmente, eso tiene fácil arreglo • **all's ~ with the world** todo va bien • IDIOM: • **to be/feel as ~ as rain** encontrarse perfectamente • **she'll be as ~ as rain in a few days** en unos pocos días se repondrá completamente de esto
6 (= *not left*) derecho • **I'd give my ~ arm to know** daría cualquier cosa *or* todo el oro del mundo por saberlo • **we are a ~ of centre party** somos un partido de centro derecha • IDIOM: • **it's a case of the ~ hand not knowing what the left hand is doing** es uno de esos casos en que la mano derecha no sabe lo que hace la izquierda
7 (*Math*) [*angle*] recto
8 (*Brit**) (*as intensifier*) (= *complete*) • **he's a ~ idiot** es un auténtico idiota • **I felt a ~ twit** me sentí como un verdadero imbécil • **she made a ~ mess of it** lo hizo fatal*, le salió un buen churro (*Sp**) • **you're a ~ one to talk** (*iro*) mira quién habla; ▷ **Charlie**
9 ▷ **all right**
ADV 1 (= *directly, exactly*) • **~ away** en seguida, ahora mismo, ahorita (mismo) (*Mex, And*) • **it happened ~ before our eyes** ocurrió delante de nuestros propios ojos • **she was standing ~ behind/in front of him** estaba justo detrás/delante de él • **~ here** aquí mismo *or* (*CAm*) mero • **he was standing ~ in the middle of the road** estaba justo en el centro *or* (*CAm*) en el mero centro de la calle • **~ now** (= *immediately*) ahora mismo; (= *at the moment*) (justo) ahora • **I want this done ~ now** quiero que se haga esto ahora mismo • **she's busy ~ now** ahora mismo *or* justo ahora está ocupada • **he could tell ~ off that I was a foreigner** reconoció de inmediato que yo era extranjero • **to go ~ on** seguir todo derecho • **~ on!*†** ¡eso es!, ¡de acuerdo! • **he (just) went ~ on talking** siguió hablando como si nada • **it hit him ~ on the chest** le dio de lleno en el pecho • **she should come ~ out and say so** debería ser clara y decirlo • **it fell ~ on top of me** me cayó justo encima
2 (= *immediately*) justo, inmediatamente • **I'll do it ~ after dinner** lo haré justo *or* inmediatamente después de cenar • **I'll be ~ back** vuelvo en seguida • **come ~ in!** ¡ven aquí dentro! • **I'll be ~ over** voy en seguida • **I had to decide ~ then** tenía que decidirme allí mismo
3 (= *completely*) • **we were sat ~ at the back** estábamos sentados atrás del todo • **we'll have to go ~ back to the beginning now** ahora habrá que volver al principio del todo • **he put his hand in ~ to the bottom** introdujo la mano hasta el mismo fondo • **their house is ~ at the end of the street** su casa está justo al final de la calle • **she was a very active old lady, ~ to the end** fue una anciana muy activa hasta el final • **to go ~ to the end of sth** ir hasta el final de algo • **to push sth ~ in** meter algo hasta el fondo • **there is a fence ~ round the house** hay una valla que rodea la casa por completo • **to read a book ~ through** leer un libro hasta el final • **you could see ~ through her blouse** se le transparentaba la blusa • **he filled it ~ up** lo llenó del todo
4 (= *correctly*) bien, correctamente • **you did ~ to/not to invite them** hiciste bien en invitarlos/en no invitarlos • **to understand sb ~** entender bien a algn • **if I remember ~** si mal no recuerdo, si no me falla la memoria • **it's him, ~ enough!** ¡seguro que es él!
5 (= *fairly*) • **to do ~ by sb** portarse como es debido con algn • **don't worry about the pay, John will see you ~** no te preocupes por el sueldo, John se encargará de que te paguen lo que te corresponde • **to treat sb ~** tratar bien a algn; ▷ **serve**
6 (= *properly, satisfactorily*) bien • **you're not doing it ~** no lo estás haciendo bien • **I felt nothing was going ~ for me** sentía que nada me iba bien • **nothing goes ~ with them** nada les sale bien
7 (= *not left*) a la derecha • **he looked neither left nor ~** no miró a ningún lado • **eyes ~!** (*Mil*) ¡vista a la derecha! • **to turn ~** torcer a la derecha • **~ (about) turn!** ¡media vuelta a la derecha!; ▷ **left²**
8 (*as linker*) • **~, who's next?** a ver, ¿quién va ahora? • **~ then, let's begin!** ¡empecemos, pues!
9 (*in titles*) • **the Right Honourable Edmund Burke** el Excelentísimo Señor Edmund Burke • **the Right Honourable member for Huntingdon** Su Señoría el diputado por Huntingdon • **my Right Honourable friend** mi honorable amigo • **Right Reverend** Reverendísimo
N 1 (= *what is morally right, just*) • **~ and wrong** el bien y el mal • **I don't know the ~s of the matter** no sé quién tiene razón en el asunto • **to know ~ from wrong** saber distinguir el bien del mal • **by ~s the house should go to me** lo suyo *or* lo propio es que la casa me correspondiera a mí • **to be in the ~** tener razón, estar en lo cierto • **to put *or* set sth to ~s** arreglar algo • **this government will put the country to ~s** este gobierno va a arreglar el país • **to set *or* put the world to ~s** arreglar el mundo • **to have ~ on one's side** tener la razón de su parte; ▷ **wrong**
2 (= *prerogative*) derecho *m* • **they have a ~ to privacy** tienen derecho a la *or* su intimidad • **people have the ~ to read any kind of material they wish** la gente tiene derecho a leer lo que desee • **you had no ~ to take it** no tenías (ningún) derecho a llevártelo • **what gives you the ~ *or* what ~ have you got to criticize me?** ¿qué derecho tienes tú a criticarme? • **who gave you the ~ to come in here?** ¿quién te ha dado permiso para entrar aquí? • **as of ~** por derecho propio • **by ~ of** por *or* en razón de • **by what ~ do you make all the decisions?** ¿con qué derecho tomas tú todas las decisiones? • **to own sth in one's own ~** poseer algo por derecho propio • **she's a celebrity in her own ~ now** ahora es una celebridad por méritos propios • **the baby is a person in his own ~** el bebé es una persona de pleno derecho • **~ to reply** derecho *m* de réplica • **~ of way** derecho *m* de paso; (*Aut etc*) (= *precedence*) prioridad *f*; ▷ **abode, assembly, exercise, reserve**
3 **rights** derechos *mpl* • **civil ~s** derechos *mpl* civiles • **film ~s** derechos *mpl* cinematográficos • **human ~s** derechos *mpl* humanos • **insist on your legal ~s** hazte valer tus derechos legales • **they don't have voting ~s** no tienen derecho al voto *or* de voto • **to be (well) within one's ~s** estar en su derecho • **you'd be well within your ~s to refuse to cooperate** estarías en tu derecho a negarte a cooperar • **women's ~s** derechos de la mujer • **"all rights reserved"** "es propiedad", "reservados todos los derechos"
4 (= *not left*) derecha *f* • **reading from ~ to left** leyendo de derecha a izquierda • **to keep to the ~** (*Aut*) circular por la derecha • **"keep to the right"** "manténgase a la derecha" • **our house is the second on the ~** nuestra casa es la segunda a *or* de la derecha • **on *or* to my ~** a mi derecha
5 (*Pol*) • **the ~** la derecha • **to be on *or* to the ~ of sth/sb** (*Pol*) estar a la derecha de algo/algn • **he's further to the ~ than I am** es más de derecha *or* (*Sp*) de derechas que yo
6 (= *right turn*) • **it's the next ~ after the lights** es la próxima a la derecha después del semáforo • **to take *or* make a ~** girar a la derecha
7 (*Boxing*) (= *punch*) derechazo *m*; (= *right hand*) derecha *f*
VT (= *put straight*) [+ *crooked picture*] enderezar; (= *correct*) [+ *mistake*] corregir; [+ *injustice*] reparar; (= *put right way up*) [+ *vehicle, person*] enderezar • **he tried to ~ himself but the leg was broken** intentó ponerse de pie pero tenía la pierna rota • **to ~ itself** [*vehicle*] enderezarse; [*situation*] rectificarse • **to ~ a wrong** deshacer un agravio, reparar un daño
CPD ▸ **right angle** ángulo *m* recto • **to be at ~ angles (to sth)** estar en *or* formar ángulo recto (con algo) ▸ **right back** (*Sport*) (= *player*) lateral *mf* derecho/a; (= *position*) lateral *m* derecho ▸ **right half** (*Sport*) medio *m* (volante) derecho ▸ **rights issue** emisión *f* de acciones ▸ **right to life** derecho *m* a la vida; ▷ **right-to-life** ▸ **right triangle** (*US*) triángulo *m* rectángulo ▸ **right turn** • **to take *or* make a ~ turn** (*Aut*) girar a la derecha; (*Pol*) dar un giro a la derecha ▸ **right wing** (*Pol*) derecha *f*; ▷ **right-wing** (*Sport*) (= *position*) ala *f* derecha

right-angled [ˈraɪtˌæŋɡld] ADJ [*bend, turning*] en ángulo recto; (*Math*) [*triangle*] rectángulo

right-click [ˈraɪtklɪk] VI cliquear con la parte derecha del ratón (**on** en)
VT • **to right-click an icon** cliquear en un icono con la parte derecha del ratón

righteous [ˈraɪtʃəs] ADJ 1 (= *virtuous*) [*person, conduct*] honrado, recto
2 (= *self-righteous*) [*tone, manner*] de superioridad moral • **her ~ manner irritated him** su aire de superioridad moral lo irritaba
3 (= *justified*) [*indignation, anger*] justificado, justo
N • **the ~** (*Bible*) los justos

righteously [ˈraɪtʃəslɪ] ADV 1 (= *virtuously*) honradamente, rectamente
2 (= *self-righteously*) con un aire de superioridad moral; [*say*] con un tono de superioridad moral
3 (= *justifiably*) justamente • **to be ~ indignant/angry** estar justamente indignado/enfadado

righteousness [ˈraɪtʃəsnɪs] N
1 (= *virtuousness*) rectitud *f* • **moral ~** rectitud *f* moral • **to keep to/stray from the path of ~** mantenerse en el/apartarse del camino recto
2 (= *self-righteousness*) aire *m* de superioridad moral

rightful [ˈraɪtfʊl] ADJ [*owner, heir to throne*] legítimo • **~ claimant** derechohabiente *mf*

rightfully [ˈraɪtfəlɪ] ADV legítimamente, por derecho • **she's inherited the money which is ~ hers** ha heredado el dinero que legítimamente *or* por derecho le pertenece • **it's something that's taken very seriously, and ~ so** es algo que se ha tomado muy en serio y con razón

right-hand [ˈraɪthænd] ADJ derecho • **right-hand side** derecha *f* • **right-hand turn** (*Aut*) giro *m* a la derecha
CPD ▸ **right-hand drive** (*Aut*) conducción *f*

por la derecha ▸ **right-hand man** (= *personal aide*) brazo *m* derecho

right-handed ['raɪt'hændɪd] ADJ [*person*] que usa la mano derecha, diestro; [*tool*] para la mano derecha

right-hander [ˌraɪt'hændəʳ] N diestro/a *m/f*

right-ho*, **right-oh*** [ˌraɪt'həʊ] EXCL (*Brit*) ¡vale!, ¡bien!

rightism ['raɪtɪzəm] N (*Pol*) derechismo *m*

rightist ['raɪtɪst] (*Pol*) ADJ, N derechista *mf*

right-justify [ˌraɪt'dʒʌstɪfaɪ] VT [+ *text*] justificar a la derecha

rightly ['raɪtlɪ] ADV **1** (= *correctly*) [*fear, suspect*] con razón; [*assume*] sin equivocarse; [*act, behave*] correctamente, bien • **they ~ feared that she had caught tuberculosis** se temían, y con razón, que había cogido tuberculosis • **the credit for this achievement ~ belongs to her** el mérito por este logro le pertenece a ella con todas las de la ley *or* en justicia le pertenece a ella • **as she ~ points out, more research is needed** como muy bien ella señala, hace falta una mayor investigación • **he ~ points out that these problems are connected** señala con acierto *or* con razón que estos problemas están relacionados • **quite ~** con toda la razón • **if I remember ~** si mal no recuerdo, si no me falla la memoria • **as he (so) ~ said ...** como bien dijo él ...
2 (= *justifiably*) con (toda la) razón • **they are ~ regarded as the best in the world** se les considera, con (toda la) razón, los mejores del mundo • **and ~ so** y con (toda la) razón • **her colleagues were ~ upset by her dismissal** sus colegas estaban disgustados por su dimisión y con razón, sus colegas estaban, con toda justificación, disgustados por su dimisión • **~ or wrongly** con razón o sin ella, justa o injustamente
3 (= *really*) • **I don't ~ know** no sé exactamente • **I can't ~ say** no lo puedo decir con seguridad

right-minded ['raɪt'maɪndɪd] ADJ (= *decent*) honrado; (= *sensible*) prudente

rightness ['raɪtnɪs] N (= *correctness*) exactitud *f*; (= *justice*) justicia *f*

right-of-centre, **right-of-center** (*US*) [ˌraɪtəv'sentəʳ] ADJ (*politically*) (de) centro derecha

right-on [ˌraɪt'ɒn] ADJ [*person, idea*] (= *sound*) todo correcto; (= *politically correct*) políticamente correcto

rightsizing ['raɪtsaɪzɪŋ] N reestructuración *f* (*que conlleva recortes de plantilla*)

right-thinking ['raɪt'θɪŋkɪŋ] ADJ = right-minded

right-to-life [ˌraɪttə'laɪf] ADJ [*movement, group*] pro derecho a la vida

rightward ['raɪtwəd] ADJ [*movement etc*] a *or* hacia la derecha
ADV [*move etc*] a *or* hacia la derecha

rightwards ['raɪtwədz] ADV (*Brit*) = rightward

right-wing ['raɪt'wɪŋ] ADJ (*Pol*) derechista, de derechas; ▹ **right**

right-winger ['raɪt'wɪŋəʳ] N **1** (*Pol*) derechista *mf*
2 (*Sport*) jugador(a) *m/f* de la banda derecha

rigid ['rɪdʒɪd] ADJ **1** (= *stiff*) [*material*] rígido, tieso • **to be ~ with fear** estar paralizado de miedo • IDIOM: • **to be bored ~*** estar aburrido *or* aburrirse como una ostra*
2 (= *strict*) [*rules*] riguroso, estricto
3 (= *inflexible*) [*person, ideas*] inflexible, intransigente • **he is quite ~ about it** es bastante inflexible *or* intransigente sobre ese punto

rigidity [rɪ'dʒɪdɪtɪ] N **1** (= *stiffness*) [*of material*] rigidez *f*
2 (= *strictness*) [*of rules*] rigor *m*
3 (= *inflexibility*) [*of person, ideas*] inflexibilidad *f*, intransigencia *f*

rigidly ['rɪdʒɪdlɪ] ADV **1** (= *stiffly*) rígidamente
2 (= *strictly*) estrictamente
3 (= *inflexibly*) con inflexibilidad, con intransigencia • **he is ~ opposed to it** está totalmente en contra de esto

rigmarole ['rɪgmərəʊl] N (= *process*) galimatías *m inv*, lío *m*; (= *paperwork etc*) trámites *mpl*, papeleo *m*

rigor ['rɪgəʳ] N (*US*) = **rigour**

rigor mortis ['rɪgə'mɔːtɪs] N rigidez *f* cadavérica

rigorous ['rɪgərəs] ADJ riguroso

rigorously ['rɪgərəslɪ] ADV rigurosamente

rigour, **rigor** (*US*) ['rɪgəʳ] N (= *severity*) rigor *m*; [*of climate*] rigores *mpl* • **the full ~ of the law** el máximo rigor de la ley

rig-out* ['rɪgaʊt] N atuendo *m*, atavío *m*

rile* [raɪl] VT sulfurar*, reventar* • **there's nothing that ~s me more** no hay nada que me reviente más* • **it ~s me terribly** me irrita muchísimo

riled ['raɪld] ADJ (= *annoyed*) enfadado, irritado

Riley ['raɪlɪ] N • IDIOM: • **to live the life of ~** (*Brit**) darse buena vida

rill [rɪl] N (= *liter*) arroyo *m*, riachuelo *m*

rim [rɪm] N [*of cup etc*] borde *m*; [*of wheel*] llanta *f*; [*of spectacles*] montura *f*; [*of dirt etc*] cerco *m* • **the rim of the sun** el borde del sol

rime¹ [raɪm] N (*poet*) rima *f*

rime² [raɪm] N (*liter*) (= *frost*) escarcha *f*

rimless ['rɪmlɪs] ADJ [*spectacles*] sin aros

rimmed [rɪmd] ADJ • **~ with ...** con un borde de ... • **glasses ~ with gold** gafas *fpl* con montura dorada

rind [raɪnd] N [*of fruit*] cáscara *f*; [*of cheese, bacon*] corteza *f*

ring¹ [rɪŋ] N **1** (*on finger*) (*plain*) anillo *m*; (*jewelled*) anillo *m*, sortija *f*; (*in nose*) arete *m*, aro *m*; (*on bird's leg, for curtain*) anilla *f*; (*for napkin*) servilletero *m*; (*on stove*) quemador *m*, hornillo *m*; (*for swimmer*) flotador *m*; **rings** (*Gymnastics*) anillas *fpl* • **electric ~** quemador *m* eléctrico, hornillo *m* eléctrico • **gas ~** fuego *m* de gas • **onion ~s** aros *mpl* de cebolla rebozados • **pineapple ~s** rodajas *fpl* de piña; ▹ **diamond, engagement, key, nose, piston, signet, wedding**
2 (= *circle*) [*of people*] círculo *m*; (*in game, dance*) corro *m*; [*of objects*] anillo *m*; (*in water*) onda *f*; (*around planet, on tree, of smoke*) anillo *m*; (*around bathtub*) cerco *m* • **to stand/sit in a ~** ponerse/sentarse en círculo • **a ~ of hills** un anillo de colinas • **he always leaves a dirty ~ round the bath** siempre deja un cerco de suciedad en la bañera • **to have ~s round one's eyes** tener ojeras • **the ~s of Saturn** los anillos de Saturno • IDIOM: • **to run ~s round sb** dar mil vueltas a algn*; ▹ **smoke**
3 (= *group*) [*of criminals, drug dealers*] banda *f*, red *f*; [*of spies*] red *f*; (*Comm*) cartel *m*, cártel *m*; ▹ **drug, spy, vice¹**
4 (= *arena*) (*Boxing*) cuadrilátero *m*, ring *m*; (*at circus*) pista *f*; (= *bullring*) ruedo *m*, plaza *f*; (*at horse race*) cercado *m*, recinto *m*; (*in livestock market*) corral *m* (de exposiciones) • **the ~** (*fig*) el boxeo • IDIOM: • **to throw** *or* **toss one's hat** *or* **cap into the ~** echarse *or* lanzarse al ruedo; ▹ **show**
VT **1** (= *surround*) rodear, cercar • **the building was ~ed by police** la policía rodeaba *or* cercaba el edificio • **the town is ~ed by hills** la ciudad está rodeada de colinas
2 [+ *bird*] anillar
3 (= *mark with ring*) poner un círculo a
CPD ▸ **ring binder** carpeta *f* de anillas *or* (*LAm*) anillos ▸ **ring finger** (dedo *m*) anular *m* ▸ **ring main** (*Elec*) red *f* de suministro *or* abastecimiento ▸ **ring road** (*Brit*) carretera *f* de circunvalación, ronda *f*, periférico *m* (*LAm*) ▸ **ring spanner** llave *f* dentada

ring² [rɪŋ] (VB: PT: **rang**, PP: **rung**) N
1 (= *sound*) [*of bell*] toque *m* de timbre; (*louder, of alarm*) timbrazo *m*; [*of voice*] timbre *m*; (*metallic sound*) sonido *m* metálico • **there was a ~ at the door** llamaron al timbre de la puerta, sonó el timbre de la puerta • **he answered the telephone on the first ~** contestó el teléfono al primer pitido • **the familiar ~ of her voice** el timbre familiar de su voz • **the ~ of sledge runners on the ice** el sonido metálico de los trineos sobre el hielo
2 (*Brit*) (*Telec*) • **to give sb a ~** llamar a algn (por teléfono), dar un telefonazo *or* un toque a algn* • **I'll give you a ~** te llamo, te doy un telefonazo *or* un toque*
3 (= *nuance*) • **the name has a (certain) ~ to it** el nombre tiene algo • **his laugh had a hollow ~ to it** su risa tenía algo de superficial, su risa sonaba (a) superficial • **that has the ~ of truth about it** eso suena a cierto
VT **1** [+ *doorbell, buzzer, handbell, church bell*] tocar • IDIOMS: • **that ~s a bell (with me)** eso me suena • **it doesn't ~ any bells** no me suena • **to ~ the changes:** • **you could ~ the changes by substituting ground almonds** podrías cambiar *or* variar sustituyendo la almendra molida • **he decided to ~ the changes after his side's third consecutive defeat** decidió cambiar de táctica tras la tercera derrota consecutiva de su equipo; ▹ **alarm**
2 (*Brit*) (*Telec*) [+ *house, office, number*] llamar a; [+ *person*] llamar (por teléfono) a • **you must ~ the hospital** tienes que llamar al hospital
VI **1** (= *make sound*) [*doorbell, alarm, telephone*] sonar; [*church bell*] sonar, repicar, tañer (*liter*) • IDIOM: • **to ~ off the hook** (*US*) [*telephone*] sonar constantemente, no parar de sonar
2 (= *use bell*) llamar • **you rang, madam?** ¿me llamó usted, señora? • **to ~ at the door** llamar a la puerta • **to ~ for sth: we'll ~ for some sugar** llamaremos para pedir azúcar • **to ~ for sb** llamar para que venga algn • **"please ring for attention"** "rogamos toque el timbre para que le atiendan"
3 (*Brit*) (= *telephone*) llamar (por teléfono) • **could someone ~ for a taxi?** ¿podría alguien llamar a un taxi?
4 (= *echo*) (*gen*) resonar; [*ears*] zumbar • **the valley rang with cries** los gritos resonaron por el valle • **his words were ~ing in my head** sus palabras resonaban en mi cabeza • **the news set the town ~ing** la noticia causó furor en la ciudad • **the town rang with his praises** por toda la ciudad no se oían más que alabanzas suyas • IDIOM: • **to ~ true/false/hollow** sonar a cierto/falso/hueco • **his suddenly friendly tone rang false** su tono amistoso tan repentino sonaba a falso • **her story just didn't ~ true** la historia no parecía verdad

▸ **ring back** (*Brit*) (*Telec*) VT + ADV (= *ring again*) volver a llamar; (= *return sb's call*) llamar • **could you ask him to ~ me back?** ¿le podría decir que me llame?
VI + ADV (= *ring again*) volver a llamar; (= *return call*) llamar • **can you ~ back later?** ¿puede volver a llamar más tarde?

▸ **ring down** VT + ADV [+ *curtain*] bajar • IDIOM: • **to ~ down the curtain on sth** poner

punto final a algo
▸ **ring in** VT + ADV anunciar • IDIOM: • **to ~ in the New Year** celebrar el año nuevo; ▸ **ring out**
VI + ADV **1** (*Brit*) (*Telec*) llamar (por teléfono) • **I rang in to say I was ill** llamé (por teléfono) para decir que estaba enfermo
2 (*US*) (*Ind*) fichar (al entrar)
▸ **ring off** VI + ADV (*Brit*) (*Telec*) colgar
▸ **ring out** VI + ADV **1** [*bell*] sonar, repicar; [*shot*] oírse, sonar; [*voice*] oírse
2 (*US*) (*Ind*) fichar (al salir)
VT + ADV • **to ~ out the old year** (*lit*) tocar las campanas para señalar el fin del año; (*fig*) despedir el año • **~ out the old, ~ in the new** que suenen las campanas para despedir al año viejo y recibir el nuevo año
▸ **ring round, ring around** VI + ADV (*Brit*) (*Telec*) llamar (por teléfono) • **if you ~ round, you can usually get a good deal** si llamas a varios sitios, generalmente se consiguen gangas
VI + PREP (*Brit*) (*Telec*) • **I'll ~ round my friends** llamaré a mis amigos
▸ **ring up** VI + ADV (*Brit*) (*Telec*) llamar (por teléfono)
VT + ADV **1** (*Brit*) (*Telec*) • **to ~ sb up** llamar a algn (por teléfono)
2 [+ *curtain*] subir, levantar • IDIOM: • **to ~ up the curtain on sth** dar comienzo a algo, iniciar algo
3 (*on cash-register*) [+ *amount, purchase*] registrar; (*fig*) [+ *sales, profits, losses*] registrar

ring-a-ring-a-roses [ˈrɪŋəˈrɪŋəˈrəʊzɪz] N corro *m* • **to play ring-a-ring-a-roses** jugar al corro

ringbolt [ˈrɪŋbəʊlt] N perno *m* con anillo; (*Naut*) cáncamo *m*

ringdove [ˈrɪŋdʌv] N paloma *f* torcaz

ringer [ˈrɪŋəʳ] N **1** (= *bell ringer*) campanero/a *m/f*
2* (*also* **dead ringer**) doble *mf*, viva imagen *f* • **he is a (dead) ~ for the President** se le parece en todo al presidente
3 (*US*) (*Horse racing*) caballo *m* sustituido

ring-fence [ˈrɪŋˈfens] VT blindar

ringing¹ [ˈrɪŋɪŋ] N (*Orn*) anillado *m*, anillamiento *m*

ringing² [ˈrɪŋɪŋ] ADJ **1** (*lit*) [*telephone*] que suena *or* sonaba *etc* • **~ tone** (*Brit*) (*Telec*) señal *f* de llamada
2 (= *resounding*) [*voice*] sonoro, resonante; [*declaration*] grandilocuente; [*endorsement, condemnation*] enérgico • **in ~ tones** en tono enérgico
N [*of large bell*] repique *m*, tañido *m* (*liter*); [*of handbell*] campanilleo *m*; [*of electric bell*] toque *m*; [*of telephone*] timbre *m*, pitidos *mpl*; (*in ears*) zumbido *m*

ringleader [ˈrɪŋ,liːdəʳ] N cabecilla *mf*

ringlet [ˈrɪŋlɪt] N rizo *m*, tirabuzón *m*

ringmaster [ˈrɪŋ,mɑːstəʳ] N maestro *m* de ceremonias

ring-pull [ˈrɪŋpʊl] (*Brit*) N anilla *f*
CPD ▸ **ring-pull can** lata *f* (*de refrescos, cerveza etc*)

ringside [ˈrɪŋsaɪd] N • **to be at the ~** estar junto al cuadrilátero
CPD ▸ **ringside seat** butaca *f* de primera fila • **to have a ~ seat** (*fig*) verlo todo desde muy cerca

ringtone [ˈrɪŋtəʊn] N (*Telec*) tono *f* de llamada

ringway [ˈrɪŋweɪ] N (*US*) = **ring road**

ringworm [ˈrɪŋwɜːm] N tiña *f*

rink [rɪŋk] N (*for ice-skating*) pista *f* de hielo; (*for roller-skating*) pista *f* de patinaje

rinse [rɪns] N **1** [*of clothes*] aclarado *m*; [*of dishes etc*] enjuague *m* • **to give one's stockings a ~** aclarar las medias
2 (= *hair colouring*) reflejo *m* • **to give one's hair a blue ~** dar reflejos azules al pelo
VT **1** [+ *dishes, clothes*] aclarar, enjuagar; [+ *mouth*] lavar, enjuagar • **to ~ one's hands** aclararse *or* enjuagarse las manos
2 (= *colour*) [+ *hair*] dar reflejos a
▸ **rinse out** VT + ADV [+ *dirt*] lavar; [+ *cup*] enjuagar; [+ *one's mouth*] enjuagarse

Rio [ˈriːəʊ] N = **Rio de Janeiro**

Rio de Janeiro [,riːəʊdədʒəˈnɪərəʊ] N Río *m* de Janeiro

riot [ˈraɪət] N **1** (= *uprising*) disturbio *m*, motín *m*; (*in prison*) amotinamiento *m*, sublevación *f* • **there was nearly a ~** hubo casi un motín • **to put down a ~** controlar un disturbio
2 (*fig*) • **a ~ of colour** un derroche de color • IDIOM: • **to run ~** (= *go out of control*) desmandarse; (= *spread*) extenderse por todas partes, cubrirlo todo • **to let one's imagination run ~** dejar volar la imaginación
3* (*fig*) (= *wild success*) exitazo *m* • **it was a ~!** ¡fue divertidísimo!, ¡fue la monda!* • **he's a ~!** ¡es un tipo desternillante!, ¡te mondas de risa con él!
VI amotinarse
CPD ▸ **riot act** • IDIOM: • **to read sb the ~ act*** leerle la cartilla a algn ▸ **riot control** control *m* antidisturbios ▸ **riot gear** uniforme *m* antidisturbios ▸ **riot police** policía *f* antidisturbios ▸ **riot shield** escudo *m* antidisturbios ▸ **riot squad** = **riot police**

riot-control [ˈraɪətkəntrəʊl] CPD [*technique, equipment, team*] antidisturbios (*inv*)

rioter [ˈraɪətəʳ] N amotinado/a *m/f*

rioting [ˈraɪətɪŋ] N disturbios *mpl*

riotous [ˈraɪətəs] ADJ **1** [*person, mob*] amotinado; [*assembly*] desordenado, alborotado
2 (= *wild, exciting*) [*party, living*] desenfrenado, alborotado; (= *very funny*) [*comedy*] divertidísimo • **it was a ~ success** obtuvo un éxito ruidoso • **we had a ~ time** nos divertimos una barbaridad

riotously [ˈraɪətəslɪ] ADV bulliciosamente, ruidosamente • **~ funny** divertidísimo

RIP ABBR (= **requiescat in pace**) (= *may he etc rest in peace*) q.e.p.d., D.E.P., E.P.D.

rip [rɪp] N rasgón *m*, desgarrón *m*
VT rasgar, desgarrar • **to rip open** [+ *envelope, parcel, wound*] abrir desgarrando • **to rip sth to pieces** hacer algo trizas
VI **1** [*cloth*] rasgarse, desgarrarse
2* (*fig*) • **to rip along** volar, ir a todo gas • **to let rip** desenfrenarse • **to let rip at sb** arremeter contra algn • **let her rip!** ¡más rápido!, ¡más gas!*
▸ **rip off** VT + ADV **1** (*lit*) arrancar
2‡ (= *overcharge, cheat*) estafar
3‡ (= *steal*) [+ *object*] pulir‡, birlar*; (= *copy*) [+ *idea, book, film*] calcar, plagiar
▸ **rip out** VT + ADV arrancar
▸ **rip through** VI + PREP • **the fire/explosion ripped through the house** el incendio/la explosión arrasó la casa • **the jet ripped through the sky** el jet surcaba veloz el cielo
▸ **rip up** VT + ADV hacer pedazos • **the train ripped up 100 metres of track** el tren destrozó 100 metros de la vía

riparian [raɪˈpeərɪən] ADJ ribereño
N ribereño/a *m/f*

ripcord [ˈrɪpkɔːd] N (*Aer*) cuerda *f* de apertura

ripe [raɪp] ADJ (COMPAR: **riper**, SUPERL: **ripest**) **1** [*fruit etc*] maduro • **to be ~ for picking** estar bastante maduro para poderse coger • **to grow ~** madurar
2 (*fig*) listo • **to be ~ for sth** [*person*] estar dispuesto a algo; [*situation etc*] estar listo para algo • **the country is ~ for revolution** la revolución está a punto de estallar en el país • **the company is ~ for a takeover** la empresa está en su punto para un cambio de dueño • **to live to a ~ old age** llegar a muy viejo • **until/when the time is ~** hasta/en un momento oportuno
3* [*language*] grosero, verde; [*smell*] fuerte, desagradable • **that's pretty ~!** ¡eso no se puede consentir!

ripen [ˈraɪpən] VT [+ *fruit, cheese, corn*] madurar
VI [*fruit, cheese, corn*] madurar

ripeness [ˈraɪpnɪs] N madurez *f*

rip-off‡ [ˈrɪpɒf] N **1** (= *swindle*) • **it's a rip-off!** ¡es una estafa *or* un robo!
2 (= *copy*) [*of film, song*] plagio *m*, copia *f*

riposte [rɪˈpɒst] N **1** (= *retort*) réplica *f*
2 (*Fencing*) estocada *f*
VI replicar (con agudeza)

ripper [ˈrɪpəʳ] N • **Jack the Ripper** Juanito el Destripador

ripping†* [ˈrɪpɪŋ] ADJ (*Brit*) estupendo*, bárbaro*

ripple [ˈrɪpl] N (= *small wave*) onda *f*, rizo *m*; (= *sound*) murmullo *m* • **a ~ of excitement** un susurro *or* murmullo de emoción • **a ~ of applause** unos cuantos aplausos
VT ondular, rizar
VI rizarse • **the crowd ~d with excitement** el público se estremeció emocionado
CPD ▸ **ripple effect** reacción *f* en cadena, efecto *m* dominó • **to have a ~ effect** provocar una reacción en cadena, tener un efecto dominó

rip-roaring* [ˈrɪp,rɔːrɪŋ] ADJ [*party*] desmadrado*, animadísimo; [*speech*] apasionado, violento; [*success*] clamoroso

riptide [ˈrɪptaɪd] N aguas *fpl* revueltas

RISC N ABBR (*Comput*) **1** = **reduced instruction set computer**
2 = **reduced instruction set computing**

rise [raɪz] (VB: PT: **rose**, PP: **risen**) N
1 (= *upward movement*) subida *f*, ascenso *m*; [*of tide*] subida *f*; [*of river*] crecida *f*; (*in tone, pitch*) subida *f*, elevación *f* • **a rapid ~ in sea level** una rápida subida del nivel del mar • **the gentle ~ and fall of his breathing** el ligero movimiento de su pecho al inspirar y espirar • IDIOMS: • **to get a ~ out of sb*** chinchar a algn* • **to take the ~ out of sb*** tomar el pelo a algn*
2 (= *increase*) (*in number, rate, value*) aumento *m*; (*in price, temperature*) subida *f*, aumento *m*; (*Brit*) (*in salary*) aumento *m* (de sueldo) • **to ask for a ~** pedir un aumento (de sueldo) • **he was given a 30% pay ~** le dieron un aumento de sueldo del 30% • **they got a ~ of 50 dollars** les aumentaron el sueldo en 50 dólares • **a ~ in interest rates** un aumento de los tipos de interés • **prices are on the ~** los precios están subiendo
3 (*fig*) (= *advancement*) ascenso *m*, subida *f*; (= *emergence*) desarrollo *m* • **his meteoric ~ to fame** su ascenso meteórico *or* su subida meteórica a la fama • **Napoleon's ~ to power** el ascenso *or* la subida de Napoleón al poder • **the ~ of the middle class** el desarrollo de la clase media • **the ~ and fall of** [*of organization*] el auge y (la) decadencia de; [*of person*] el ascenso y (la) caída de • **the ~ and fall of the empire** el auge y (la) decadencia del imperio • **nazism was on the ~ in Europe** el nazismo estaba creciendo en Europa
4 (= *small hill*) colina *f*, loma *f*; (= *upward slope*) cuesta *f* (arriba), pendiente *f*; [*of stairs*] subida *f*
5 (= *origin*) [*of river*] nacimiento *m* • **to give ~ to** [+ *innovation*] dar origen a; [+ *problems,*

r

impression] causar; [+ *interest, ideas*] suscitar; [+ *speculation, doubts, suspicion, fear*] suscitar, dar lugar a
(VI) **1** (= *get up*) (*from bed*) levantarse; (= *stand up*) ponerse de pie, levantarse; (= *rear up*) [*building, mountain*] elevarse, alzarse • **to ~ early** madrugar, levantarse temprano • **he rose to greet us** se levantó para recibirnos • **the mountains rose up before him** las montañas se elevaban *or* se alzaban frente a él • **the horse rose on its hind legs** el caballo se alzó sobre sus patas traseras • **to ~ from the dead** resucitar • **to ~ to one's feet** ponerse de pie • **~ and shine!** ¡levántate y espabila! • **to ~ from (the) table** levantarse de la mesa; ▹ **ash²**
2 (= *get higher*) [*sun, moon*] salir; [*smoke, mist, balloon*] subir, ascender, elevarse (*liter*); [*dust, spray, theatre curtain*] levantarse; [*water, tide, level, aircraft, lift*] subir; [*dough, cake*] aumentar, subir; [*river*] crecer; [*hair*] ponerse de punta • **the plane rose to 4,000 metres** el avión subió a 4.000 metros • **his eyebrows rose at the sight of her** al verla se le arquearon las cejas • **her actions caused a few eyebrows to ~** sus acciones causaron cierto escándalo • **her eyes rose to meet mine** alzó la mirada y se encontró con la mía • **the fish are rising well** los peces están picando bien • **to ~ above** (*fig*) [+ *differences, poverty*] superar; [+ *prejudice*] estar por encima de • **to ~ to the bait** (*lit, fig*) picar *or* morder el anzuelo • **to ~ to the surface** (*lit*) salir a la superficie; (*fig*) [*tensions, contradictions*] surgir, aflorar • **it is a time when these tensions may ~ to the surface** es un momento en el que puede que surjan *or* afloren estas tensiones; ▹ **challenge, occasion**
3 (= *increase*) [*price, temperature, pressure*] subir, aumentar; [*number, amount, tension*] aumentar; [*barometer, stocks, shares*] subir; [*wind*] arreciar, levantarse; [*sound*] hacerse más fuerte • **it has ~n 20% in price** su precio ha subido *or* aumentado en un 20% • **new houses are rising in value** las viviendas nuevas se están revalorizando • **unemployment was rising** el paro aumentaba • **the noise rose to almost unbearable levels** el ruido se hizo tan fuerte que era casi insoportable • **her voice rose in anger** levantó *or* alzó la voz enfadada
4 [*ground*] subir (en pendiente)
5 (*in rank*) ascender • **he rose to colonel** ascendió a coronel • **he rose to be president** llegó a ser presidente • **she rose to the top of her profession** llegó a la cumbre de su profesión • **to ~ in sb's estimation** ganar en la estima de algn • **to ~ from nothing** salir de la nada • **to ~ from *or* through the ranks** (*Mil*) ascender de soldado raso; ▹ **prominence**
6 (= *improve*) [*standards*] mejorar • **our spirits rose** nos animamos • **it could cause expectations to ~** podría hacer que las expectativas crecieran
7 (= *come forth*) • **a loud gasp rose from the audience** el público soltó un grito ahogado • **laughter rose from the audience** entre el público estallaron las risas • **from the people, a cheer rose up** la gente empezó a vitorear todos a una • **she could feel a blush rising to her cheeks** sentía que se le subía el color a las mejillas, sentía que se le subían los colores • **tears rose to his eyes** se le saltaron las lágrimas • **a feeling of panic was rising in him** empezó a entrarle una sensación de pánico
8 (= *originate*) [*river*] nacer
9 (= *rebel*) (*also* **rise up**) sublevarse, levantarse (**against** contra) • **the people rose (up) against their oppressors** el pueblo se sublevó *or* levantó contra sus opresores • **to ~ (up) in arms** alzarse en armas • **to ~ (up) in revolt** sublevarse, rebelarse
10 (= *adjourn*) [*parliament, court*] levantar la sesión • **the House rose at 2a.m.** se levantó la sesión parlamentaria a las 2 de la madrugada
▸ **rise above** (VI + PREP) [+ *differences, fears, problems*] superar; [+ *insults*] ignorar

risen ['rɪzn] (PT), (PP) *of* **rise**

riser ['raɪzəʳ] (N) **1** • **to be an early/late ~** ser madrugador(a) /dormilón/ona
2 [*of stair*] contrahuella *f*

risibility [ˌrɪzɪ'bɪlɪtɪ] (N) risibilidad *f*

risible ['rɪzɪbl] (ADJ) risible

rising ['raɪzɪŋ] (ADJ) **1** (= *increasing*) [*number, quantity*] creciente; [*prices etc*] en aumento, en alza; (*Econ*) [*trend*] alcista • **the ~ number of murders** el creciente número de homicidios • **with ~ alarm** con creciente alarma
2 (= *getting higher*) [*sun, moon*] naciente; [*ground*] en pendiente; [*tide*] creciente • **the house stood on ~ ground** la casa estaba construída sobre una pendiente
3 (*fig*) (= *promising*) prometedor • **~ politician** político *m* en alza • **the ~ generation** las nuevas generaciones
(ADV)* (= *almost*) casi • **he's ~ 12** pronto tendrá 12 años
(N) **1** (= *uprising*) rebelión *f*, sublevación *f*
2 [*of river*] nacimiento *m*; [*of sun etc*] salida *f*
3 • **on the ~ of the House** (*Parl*) al suspenderse la sesión
(CPD) ▸ **rising damp** humedad *f* de paredes ▸ **rising star** (*fig*) (= *person*) figura *f* emergente

risk [rɪsk] (N) **1** (*gen*) riesgo *m* • **it's not worth the ~** no merece la pena correr el riesgo • **there is an element of ~** hay un componente de riesgo • **there's too much ~ involved** supone demasiados riesgos • **the benefits outweigh the ~s** los beneficios son mayores que los riesgos • **the building is a fire ~** el edificio es un peligro en caso de un incendio • **a health/security ~** un peligro para la salud/la seguridad • **at ~:** • **the children most at ~** los niños que corren más riesgo *or* peligro • **up to 25,000 jobs are at ~** hay hasta 25.000 trabajos que peligran *or* que están en peligro • **to put sth at ~** poner algo en peligro • **at the ~ of** a riesgo de • **at the ~ of seeming stupid** a riesgo de parecer estúpido • **at the ~ of one's life** con peligro de su vida, arriesgando la vida • **there is no ~ of his coming *or* that he will come** no hay peligro de que venga • **there is little ~ of infection** el riesgo *or* peligro de infección es pequeño • **at one's own ~** por su cuenta y riesgo • **at (the) owner's ~** bajo la responsabilidad del dueño • **you run the ~ of being dismissed** corres el riesgo de que te despidan • **I can't take the ~** no me puedo exponer *or* arriesgar a eso, no puedo correr ese riesgo • **that's a ~ you'll have to take** ese es un riesgo que vas a tener que correr • **you're taking a big ~** te estás arriesgando mucho; ▹ **calculated**
2 (*Econ, Insurance*) riesgo *m* • **insured against all ~s** asegurado contra *or* a todo riesgo • **a bad/good ~:** • **you may be turned down as a bad ~** puede que te rechacen por constituir un riesgo inadmisible • **she is considered a good ~** a sus ojos constituye un riesgo admisible; ▹ **all-risks, high-risk, low-risk**
(VT) **1** (= *put at risk*) arriesgar, poner en peligro • **she ~ed her life for me/to save me** arriesgó su vida por mí/por rescatarme, puso en peligro su vida por mí/por rescatarme • **to ~ everything** arriesgarlo todo • **I'm ~ing my job by saying this** estoy arriesgando *or* poniendo en peligro el puesto al decir esto • **he ~ed all his savings on the project** arriesgó todos sus ahorros en el proyecto; ▹ **life, neck**
2 (= *run the risk of*) correr el riesgo de, arriesgarse a • **I don't want to ~ another accident** no quiero correr el riesgo de *or* arriesgarme a *or* exponerme a otro accidente • **to ~ losing/being caught** correr el riesgo de perder/ser cogido, arriesgarse a perder/ser cogido
3 (= *venture, take a chance on*) arriesgarse a • **shall we ~ it?** ¿nos arriesgamos? • **I'll ~ it** me arriesgo, me voy a arriesgar • **I can't ~ it** no me puedo arriesgar (a eso) • **I ~ed a glance behind me** me arriesgué a mirar hacia atrás • **she won't ~ coming today** no va a arriesgarse a venir hoy
(CPD) ▸ **risk assessment** evaluación *f* de riesgos ▸ **risk aversion** aversión *f* al riesgo ▸ **risk capital** capital *m* riesgo ▸ **risk factor** factor *m* de riesgo • **smoking is a ~ factor for *or* in heart disease** fumar constituye un factor de riesgo en las enfermedades cardíacas ▸ **risk management** gestión *f* de riesgos

risk-averse ['rɪskəvɜːs] (ADJ) averso al riesgo

riskily ['rɪskɪlɪ] (ADV) de forma arriesgada

riskiness ['rɪskɪnɪs] (N) peligro *m*, lo arriesgado, lo riesgoso (*LAm*) • **in view of the ~ of the plan** visto lo peligroso del plan

risk-taking ['rɪskteɪkɪŋ] (N) asunción *f* de riesgos

risky ['rɪskɪ] (ADJ) (COMPAR: **riskier**, SUPERL: **riskiest**) **1** (= *dangerous*) [*venture, plan, investment*] arriesgado, riesgoso (*LAm*) • **investing on the stock market is a ~ business** invertir en bolsa supone muchos riesgos
2 = **risqué**

risotto [rɪ'zɒtəʊ] (N) (*Culin*) risotto *m*, arroz *m* a la italiana

risqué ['riːskeɪ] (ADJ) [*humour, joke*] subido de tono

rissole ['rɪsəʊl] (N) (*Brit*) (*Culin*) ≈ croqueta *f*

rite [raɪt] (N) rito *m*; (= *funeral rites*) exequias *fpl* • **"The Rite of Spring"** "La Consagración de la Primavera"; ▹ **last**
(CPD) ▸ **rite of passage** rito *m* de paso, rito *m* de tránsito; ▹ **rite(s)-of-passage**

rite-of-passage, rites-of-passage [ˌraɪt(s)əv'pæsɪdʒ] (ADJ) • **a rite(s)-of-passage novel** una novela iniciática; ▹ **rite**

ritual ['rɪtjʊəl] (ADJ) **1** [*dancing, murder*] ritual
2 (*fig*) (= *conventional*) consabido • **in the ~ phrase** en la expresión consagrada
(N) **1** (*Rel*) (*Christian*) ritual *m*, ceremonia *f*; (*non-Christian*) rito *m*
2 (*fig*) (= *custom*) rito *m*, ritual *m*

ritualism ['rɪtjʊəlɪzəm] (N) ritualismo *m*

ritualist ['rɪtjʊəlɪst] (N) ritualista *mf*

ritualistic [ˌrɪtjʊə'lɪstɪk] (ADJ) ritualista; (*fig*) consagrado, sacramental

ritualize ['rɪtjʊəˌlaɪz] (VT) • **to ~ sth** hacer de algo un ritual • **it's a highly ~d event** es un acontecimiento de marcado carácter ritualístico

ritually ['rɪtjʊəlɪ] (ADV) ritualmente

ritzy* ['rɪtsɪ] (ADJ) (COMPAR: **ritzier**, SUPERL: **ritziest**) [*car, house*] de lujo

rival ['raɪvəl] (ADJ) [*team, firm*] rival, contrario; [*claim, attraction*] competidor
(N) rival *mf*, contrario/a *m/f* • **to be sb's closest ~** ser el rival más cercano de algn
(VT) competir con, rivalizar con

rivalry ['raɪvəlrɪ] (N) rivalidad *f*, competencia *f* • **to enter into ~ with sb** empezar a competir con algn

rive ['raɪv] VT (PT: **rived**, PP: **riven**) (*liter†*) desgarrar, hendir

riven ['rɪvən] ADJ (*liter*) desgarrado, hendido • **~ by** desgarrado por • **~ by grief** desgarrado por el dolor

river ['rɪvəʳ] N río *m* • **up/down ~** río arriba/abajo • **up ~ from Toledo** aguas arriba de Toledo • IDIOM: • **to sell sb down the ~*** traicionar a algn
CPD ▸ **river basin** cuenca *f* de río ▸ **river fish** pez *m* de río ▸ **river fishing** pesca *f* de río ▸ **river mouth** desembocadura *f* del río ▸ **river police** brigada *f* fluvial ▸ **river traffic** tráfico *m* fluvial

riverbank ['rɪvəbæŋk] N orilla *f*, ribera *f*
ADJ ribereño

riverbed ['rɪvəbed] N lecho *m* (del río)

riverboat ['rɪvəbəʊt] N embarcación *f* fluvial, barcaza *f*

riverfront ['rɪvəfrʌnt] N ribera *f* del río

riverine ['rɪvəraɪn] ADJ fluvial, ribereño

River Plate [ˌrɪvə'pleɪt] N Río *m* de la Plata
ADJ rioplatense

riverside ['rɪvəsaɪd] N orilla *f*, ribera *f*
ADJ ribereño

rivet ['rɪvɪt] N remache *m*
VT **1** (*Tech*) remachar
2 (*fig*) (= *grasp*) [+ *attention*] captar; (= *fasten*) [+ *eyes, attention, gaze*] (*on sth/sb*) fijar • **it ~ed our attention** nos llamó fuertemente la atención, lo miramos fascinados • **to be ~ed to sth** tener los ojos puestos en algo

riveter ['rɪvɪtəʳ] N remachador(a) *m/f*

riveting, rivetting ['rɪvɪtɪŋ] N (*Tech*) remachado *m*
ADJ (= *fascinating*) fascinante, cautivador

Riviera [ˌrɪvɪ'ɛərə] N (*French*) Riviera *f* (francesa), Costa *f* Azul; (*Italian*) Riviera *f* italiana

rivulet ['rɪvjʊlɪt] N riachuelo *m*, arroyuelo *m*

Riyadh [rɪ'jɑːd] N Riyadh *m*

riyal [rɪ'ɑːl] N riyal *m*

RK N ABBR (*Scol*) (= **Religious Knowledge**) ed. religiosa

RL N ABBR = **Rugby League**

Rly ABBR (= **Railway**) ferrocarril, f.c., FC

RM N ABBR (*Brit*) (*Mil*) = **Royal Marines**

rm ABBR = **room**

RMT N ABBR (*Brit*) = **National Union of Rail, Maritime and Transport Workers**

RN N ABBR **1** (*Brit*) (*Mil*) = **Royal Navy**
2 (*US*) = **registered nurse**

RNA N ABBR (= **ribonucleic acid**) ARN *m*

RNAS N ABBR (*Brit*) = **Royal Naval Air Services**

RNLI N ABBR (= **Royal National Lifeboat Institution**) *servicio de lanchas de socorro*

RNR N ABBR (*Brit*) (*Mil*) = **Royal Naval Reserve**

RNVR N ABBR = **Royal Naval Volunteer Reserve**

RNZAF N ABBR = **Royal New Zealand Air Force**

RNZN N ABBR = **Royal New Zealand Navy**

roach [rəʊtʃ] N (PL: **roach** *or* **roaches**)
1 (= *fish*) gobio *m*
2 (*US*) (= *cockroach*) cucaracha *f*
3 (*Drugs‡*) cucaracha‡ *f*

road [rəʊd] N **1** (*residential: Road*) calle *f*; (= *main road*) carretera *f*; (= *route*) camino *m*; (= *surface*) firme *m*; (= *roadway, not pavement*) calzada *f* • **at the 23rd kilometre on the Valencia ~** en el kilómetro 23 de la carretera de Valencia • **"road narrows"** "estrechamiento de la calzada" • **"road up"** "cerrado por obras" • **across the ~** al otro lado de la calle • **she lives across the ~ from us** vive en frente de nosotros • **by ~** por carretera • **to hold the ~** [*car*] agarrar, tener buena adherencia • **to be off the ~** [*car*] estar fuera de circulación • **to be on the ~** (= *be travelling*) estar en camino; (*Comm*) ser viajante de comercio; (*Mus, Theat*) estar de gira • **the dog was wandering on the ~** el perro iba andando por mitad de la calzada • **he shouldn't be allowed on the ~** no deberían permitirle conducir • **my car is on the ~ again** he vuelto a poner mi coche en circulación • **to take the ~** ponerse en camino (**to X** para ir a X) • **to take to the ~** [*tramp*] ponerse en camino • **the ~ to Teruel** el camino de Teruel
2 (*fig*) • **somewhere along the ~** tarde o temprano • **our relationship has reached the end of the ~** nuestras relaciones han llegado al punto final • **to be on the right ~** ir por buen camino • **the ~ to success** el camino del éxito • **he's on the ~ to recovery** se está reponiendo • **we're on the ~ to disaster** vamos camino del desastre • IDIOM: • **one for the ~*** la penúltima • **to have one for the ~*** tomarse la penúltima (copa) • PROVERB: • **the ~ to hell is paved with good intentions** con buenas intenciones no basta; ▹ **Rome**
3‡ (*fig*) (= *way*) • **to get out of the ~** quitarse de en medio
4 roads (*Naut*) (= *roadstead*) rada *fsing*
CPD ▸ **road accident** accidente *m* de tráfico, accidente *m* de circulación, accidente *m* de tránsito (*LAm*) ▸ **road atlas** mapa *m* de carreteras ▸ **road book** libro *m* de mapas e itinerarios ▸ **road bridge** puente *m* de carretera ▸ **road construction** construcción *f* de carreteras ▸ **road haulage** transporte *m* por carretera ▸ **road haulier** (= *company*) compañía *f* de transporte por carretera; (= *person*) transportista *mf* ▸ **road hump** banda *f* sonora, banda *f* de desaceleración ▸ **road junction** empalme *m* ▸ **road manager** (*Mus*) encargado/a *m/f* del transporte del equipo ▸ **road map** (*lit*) mapa *m* de carreteras; (*for future actions*) hoja *f* de ruta • **~ map to peace** hoja *f* de ruta para la paz ▸ **road metal** grava *f*, lastre *m* ▸ **road movie** película *f* de carretera, road movie *f* ▸ **road pricing** (*Brit*) *sistema electrónico que permite el cobro de peaje a conductores en ciertas carreteras* ▸ **road race** carrera *f* en carretera ▸ **road racer** (*Cycling*) ciclista *mf* de fondo en carretera ▸ **road rage*** *conducta agresiva de los conductores* ▸ **road repairs** obras *fpl* en la vía ▸ **road roller** apisonadora *f* ▸ **road safety** seguridad *f* vial ▸ **road sense** conocimiento *m* de la carretera ▸ **road sign** señal *f* de tráfico ▸ **road surface** firme *m* ▸ **road sweeper** (= *person*) barrendero/a *m/f*; (= *vehicle*) máquina *f* barrendera ▸ **road tax** impuesto *m* de rodaje ▸ **road test** prueba *f* en carretera ▸ **road traffic** circulación *f* ▸ **road traffic accident** = **road accident** ▸ **road transport** transportes *mpl* por carretera ▸ **road trial** = **road test** ▸ **road user** usuario/a *m/f* de la vía pública ▸ **road vehicle** vehículo *m* de motor, vehículo *m* de carretera

roadbed ['rəʊdbed] N (*US*) [*of road*] firme *m*; [*of railroad*] capa *f* de balasto

roadblock ['rəʊdblɒk] N control *m*, barricada *f*, retén *m* (*LAm*)

roadhog ['rəʊdhɒg] N loco(a) *m/f* del volante

roadholding ['rəʊdˌhəʊldɪŋ] N agarre *m*

roadhouse ['rəʊdhaʊs] N (PL: **roadhouses** ['rəʊdhaʊzɪz]) (*US*) albergue *m* de carretera, motel *m*

roadie* ['rəʊdɪ] N (*Mus*) *encargado del transporte y montaje del equipo de un grupo de música*

roadkill ['rəʊdkɪl] N animal *m* muerto en la carretera

roadmaking ['rəʊdˌmeɪkɪŋ] N construcción *f* de carreteras

roadman ['rəʊdmæn] (PL: **roadmen**) N peón *m* caminero

roadmender ['rəʊdmendəʳ] N = **roadman**

roadshow ['rəʊdʃəʊ] N (*Theat*) compañía *f* teatral en gira; (*Rad*) programa *m* itinerante

roadside ['rəʊdsaɪd] N borde *m* de la carretera, orilla *f* del camino (*LAm*)
CPD de carretera ▸ **roadside inn** fonda *f* de carretera ▸ **roadside repairs** reparaciones *fpl* al borde de la carretera ▸ **roadside restaurant** (*US*) café-restaurante *m* (de carretera)

roadstead ['rəʊdsted] N (*Naut*) rada *f*

roadster ['rəʊdstəʳ] N (= *car*) coche *m* de turismo; (= *bicycle*) bicicleta *f* de turismo

road-test ['rəʊdtest] VT probar en carretera • **they are road-testing the car tomorrow** están probando el coche en carretera mañana

roadway ['rəʊdweɪ] N calzada *f*

roadworks ['rəʊdwɜːks] NPL obras *fpl* (*en la calzada*)

roadworthiness ['rəʊdˌwɜːðɪnɪs] N [*of car*] condición *f* de apto para circular

roadworthy ['rəʊdˌwɜːðɪ] ADJ [*car etc*] en buen estado (para circular)

roam [rəʊm] VT [+ *streets etc*] rondar, vagar por
VI **1** (= *wander*) [*person etc*] vagar, errar; [*thoughts*] divagar
2 (*Telec*) (*on other network*) hacer roaming
▸ **roam about, roam around** VI + ADV andar sin rumbo fijo

roamer ['rəʊməʳ] N hombre *m* errante, andariego *m*; (= *tramp*) vagabundo *m*

roaming ['rəʊmɪŋ] N **1** (= *wandering*) vagabundeo *m*; (*as tourist etc*) excursiones *fpl*, paseos *mpl*
2 (*Telec*) roaming *m*, itinerancia *f*
CPD ▸ **roaming card** (*Telec*) tarjeta *f* de roaming ▸ **roaming charge** (*Telec*) tarifa *f* de roaming

roan [rəʊn] ADJ ruano
N caballo *m* ruano

roar [rɔːʳ] N **1** [*of animal*] rugido *m*, bramido *m*; [*of person*] rugido *m*; [*of crowd*] clamor *m*; [*of laughter*] carcajada *f* • **with great ~s of laughter** con grandes carcajadas • **he said with a ~** dijo rugiendo
2 (= *loud noise*) estruendo *m*, fragor *m*; [*of fire*] crepitación *f*; [*of river, storm etc*] estruendo *m*
VI **1** [*animal*] rugir, bramar; [*crowd, audience*] clamar • **to ~ (with laughter)** reírse a carcajadas • **this will make you ~** con esto os vais a morir de risa • **to ~ with pain** rugir de dolor
2 [*guns, thunder*] retumbar • **the lorry ~ed past** el camión pasó ruidosamente
VT rugir, decir a gritos • **to ~ one's disapproval** manifestar su disconformidad a gritos • **he ~ed out an order** lanzó una orden a voz en grito • **to ~ o.s. hoarse** ponerse ronco gritando, gritar hasta enronquecerse

roaring ['rɔːrɪŋ] ADJ • **in front of a ~ fire** ante un fuego bien caliente • **it was a ~ success** fue un tremendo éxito • **to do a ~ trade** hacer muy buen negocio
ADV (*Brit**) • **he was ~ drunk** estaba borracho y despotricaba
CPD ▸ **the Roaring Forties** (*Geog*) los cuarenta rugientes

roast [rəʊst] N asado *m*
ADJ asado; [*coffee*] torrefacto, tostado • **~ beef** rosbif *m*
VT **1** [+ *meat*] asar; [+ *coffee*] tostar

r

2 (*fig*) • **the sun which was ~ing the city** el sol que achicharraba la ciudad • **to ~ one's feet by the fire** asarse los pies junto al fuego • **to ~ o.s. in the sun** tostarse al sol
3 • **to ~ sb*** (= *criticize*) criticar a algn, censurar a algn; (= *scold*) desollar vivo a algn
(VI) [*meat*] asarse; (*fig*) [*person*] tostarse • **we ~ed there for a whole month** nos asamos allí durante un mes entero

roaster ['rəʊstəʳ] (N) **1** (= *implement*) asador *m*, tostador *m*
2 (= *bird*) pollo *m* para asar

roasting ['rəʊstɪŋ] (ADJ) **1** [*chicken etc*] para asar
2* (= *hot*) [*day, heat*] abrasador
(N) **1** (*Culin*) asado *m*; [*of coffee*] tostadura *f*, tueste *m*
2 • **to give sb a ~*** (= *criticize*) criticar a algn, censurar a algn; (= *scold*) desollar vivo a algn
(CPD) ▸ **roasting jack, roasting spit** asador *m*

rob [rɒb] (VT) robar; [+ *bank etc*] atracar • **to rob sb of sth** [+ *money etc*] robar algo a algn; (*fig*) [+ *happiness etc*] quitar algo a algn • **I've been robbed!** ¡me han robado! • **we were robbed!** (*Sport**) ¡nos robaron el partido!; ▹ **Peter**

robber ['rɒbəʳ] (N) ladrón/ona *m/f*; (= *bankrobber*) atracador(a) *m/f*; (= *highwayman*) salteador *m* (de caminos); (= *brigand*) bandido *m*
(CPD) ▸ **robber baron** (*pej*) magnate *mf* desaprensivo/a

robbery ['rɒbərɪ] (N) robo *m* • **~ with violence** (*Jur*) robo *m* a mano armada, atraco *m*, asalto *m* • **it's daylight ~!*** ¡es una estafa!, ¡es un robo a mano armada!

robe [rəʊb] (N) (= *ceremonial garment*) traje *m* de ceremonia, túnica *f*; (= *bathrobe*) bata *f*; (= *christening robe*) traje *m* del bautizo; (*lawyer's, academic's etc*) toga *f*; (*monk's*) hábito *m*; (*priest's*) sotana *f*; **robes** traje *msing* de ceremonia, traje *msing* talar
(VT) • **to ~ sb in black** vestir a algn de negro • **to appear ~d in a long dress** aparecer vestido de un traje largo • **to ~ o.s.** vestirse

Robert ['rɒbət] (N) Roberto

robin ['rɒbɪn] (N) (= *bird*) petirrojo *m*

robot ['rəʊbɒt] (N) robot *m*

robotic [rəʊ'bɒtɪk] (ADJ) [*equipment, arm etc*] robótico; (*fig*) de robot, robotizado

robotics [rəʊ'bɒtɪks] (NSING) robótica *f*

robust [rəʊ'bʌst] (ADJ) **1** (= *solid, hardy*) [*person, constitution*] robusto, fuerte; [*plant*] robusto; [*material, design, object*] resistente, sólido; [*economy*] fuerte • **the chair didn't look very ~** la silla no parecía muy sólida • **to have a ~ appetite** tener buen apetito • **to be in ~ health** tener una salud de hierro
2 (= *vigorous*) [*defence*] enérgico, vigoroso; [*sense of humour*] saludable • **to make a ~ defence of sth** defender algo enérgicamente *or* vigorosamente
3 (= *strong*) [*flavour, aroma, wine*] fuerte

robustly [rəʊ'bʌstlɪ] (ADV) **1** (= *solidly*) • **to be ~ built** [*person*] ser de constitución robusta *or* fuerte • **to be ~ built** *or* **made** [*thing*] estar sólidamente construido
2 (= *vigorously*) [*oppose, attack, defend*] enérgicamente, vigorosamente
3 (= *strongly*) • **a ~ flavoured red wine** un vino tinto con un sabor fuerte

robustness [rəʊ'bʌstnɪs] (N) **1** (= *strength*) [*of person, plant*] robustez *f*; [*of material, design, object*] solidez *f*
2 (= *vigour*) [*of defence, attack*] lo enérgico, vigor *m*

rock[1] [rɒk] (N) **1** (= *substance*) roca *f*; (= *crag, rock face*) peñasco *m*, peñón *m*; (= *large stone, boulder*) roca *f*; (*US*) (= *small stone*) piedra *f*; (*in sea*) escollo *m*, roca *f* • **hewn out of solid ~** tallado en la roca viva • **they were drilling into solid ~** estaban perforando rocas vivas • **porous/volcanic ~** roca porosa/volcánica • **the Rock (of Gibraltar)** el Peñón (de Gibraltar) • **an outcrop of ~** un peñasco, un peñón • **"danger: falling rocks"** "desprendimiento de rocas"
2 (*in phrases*) • **to be at ~ bottom** [*person, prices, morale, confidence*] estar por los suelos, haber tocado fondo • **prices are at ~ bottom** los precios están por los suelos *or* han tocado fondo • **morale in the armed forces was at ~ bottom** los ánimos en las fuerzas armadas habían tocado fondo *or* estaban por los suelos • **to hit** *or* **reach ~ bottom** [*person, prices*] tocar fondo • **~ hard** duro como una piedra • **it dries ~ hard in less than an hour** en menos de una hora se seca hasta quedarse duro como una piedra • **he's like a ~, I totally depend on him** es mi pilar *or* puntal, dependo totalmente de él • **whisky on the ~s** whisky con hielo • **to run** *or* **go on(to) the ~s** (*Naut*) chocar contra los escollos, encallar en las rocas • **~ solid** (*lit, fig*) sólido como una roca • **the pound was ~ solid against the mark** la libra permanecía sólida como una roca frente al marco; ▹ **rock-solid** • **he held the gun ~ steady** sujetó la pistola con pulso firme • IDIOMS: • **to be on the ~s*** (= *be broke*) no tener un céntimo, estar sin blanca (*Sp**); (= *fail*) [*marriage*] andar fatal* • **his business went on the ~s last year** su negocio se fue a pique *or* se hundió el año pasado • **to be between** *or* **be caught between a ~ and a hard place** estar entre la espada y la pared; ▹ **hard, solid**
3 (*Brit*) (= *sweet*) palo *m* de caramelo • **a stick of ~** un palo de caramelo
4* (= *diamond*) diamante *m*; **rocks** piedras *fpl*, joyas *fpl*
5* (= *drug*) crack *m*
6 (*esp US*) **rocks**‡ • IDIOM: • **to get one's ~s off** echar un polvo‡
(CPD) ▸ **rock art** arte *m* rupestre ▸ **rock cake, rock bun** *bollito con frutos secos* ▸ **rock candy** (*US*) palo *m* de caramelo ▸ **rock carving** escultura *f* rupestre ▸ **rock climber** escalador(a) *m/f* (de rocas) ▸ **rock climbing** (*Sport*) escalada *f* en rocas • **to go ~ climbing** ir a escalar en roca ▸ **rock crystal** cristal *m* de roca ▸ **rock face** vertiente *f* rocosa, pared *f* de roca ▸ **rock fall** desprendimiento *m* de rocas ▸ **rock formation** formación *f* rocosa ▸ **rock garden** jardín *m* de roca *or* de rocalla ▸ **rock painting** pintura *f* rupestre ▸ **rock plant** planta *f* rupestre *or* de roca ▸ **rock pool** charca *f* (de agua de mar) entre rocas ▸ **rock rose** jara *f*, heliantemo *m* ▸ **rock salmon** (*Brit*) cazón *m* ▸ **rock salt** sal *f* gema *or* mineral *or* sin refinar

rock[2] [rɒk] (VT) **1** (= *swing to and fro*) [+ *child*] acunar; [+ *cradle*] mecer • **she ~ed the child in her arms** acunó al niño en sus brazos • **to ~ o.s. in a chair** mecerse en una silla • **to ~ a child to sleep** arrullar a un niño
2 (= *shake*) (*lit, fig*) sacudir • **his death ~ed the fashion business** su muerte sacudió *or* convulsionó al mundo de la moda; ▹ **boat**
(VI) **1** (*gently*) mecerse, balancearse • **the ship ~ed gently on the waves** el buque se mecía *or* se balanceaba suavemente en las olas • **his body ~ed from side to side with the train** su cuerpo se mecía *or* se balanceaba de un lado a otro con el movimiento del tren • **he ~ed back on his heels** apoyando los talones, se inclinó hacia atrás
2 (*violently*) [*ground, vehicle, building*] sacudirse • **the theatre ~ed with laughter** las risas estremecieron el teatro • **the audience ~ed with laughter** el público se rió a carcajada limpia
3 (= *dance*) bailar rock
(N) (*Mus*) (*also* **rock music**) rock *m*, música *f* rock • **heavy/soft ~** rock *m* duro/blando
(CPD) ▸ **rock and roll** rocanrol *m*, rock and roll *m* • **to do the ~ and roll** bailar el rocanrol *or* el rock and roll; ▹ **rock-and-roll** ▸ **rock band** grupo *m* de rock ▸ **rock chick*** rockera *f* ▸ **rock concert** concierto *m* de rock ▸ **rock festival** festival *m* de rock ▸ **rock group** grupo *m* de rock ▸ **rock music** rock *m*, música *f* rock ▸ **rock musical** musical *m* de rock ▸ **rock musician** músico/a *m/f* de rock ▸ **rock opera** ópera *f* rock ▸ **rock star** estrella *f* de rock

rockabilly [ˌrɒkə'bɪlɪ] (N) rockabilly *m*
(CPD) [*band, style, music*] rockabilly (*inv*)

rock-and-roll [ˌrɒkən'rəʊl] (ADJ) • **a rock-and-roll band/singer** un grupo/cantante de rocanrol *or* rock and roll; ▹ **rock[2]**

rock-bottom [ˌrɒk'bɒtəm] (N) fondo *m*, parte *f* más profunda
(ADJ) • **rock-bottom prices** precios *mpl* mínimos, precios *mpl* tirados

rocker ['rɒkəʳ] (N) **1** [*of cradle etc*] balancín *m*; (*US*) (= *chair*) mecedora *f*, mecedor *m* (*LAm*) • IDIOM: • **to be off one's ~**‡ estar majareta*
2 (*Mus*) (= *person*) rockero/a *m/f*

rockery ['rɒkərɪ] (N) jardín *m* de roca *or* de rocalla

rocket[1] ['rɒkɪt] (N) **1** (*Mil*) cohete *m*; (= *space rocket*) cohete *m* espacial
2 (= *firework*) cohete *m*
3 (*Brit**) (*fig*) • **to get a ~ from sb** recibir una peluca de algn • **to give sb a ~ (for the mistake)** echar un rapapolvo a algn (por el error)
(VI) • **to ~ upwards** subir como un cohete • **to ~ to the moon** ir en cohete a la luna • **to ~ to fame** ascender vertiginosamente a la fama • **prices have ~ed** los precios han subido vertiginosamente
(VT) (*Mil*) atacar con cohetes
(CPD) ▸ **rocket attack** ataque *m* con cohetes ▸ **rocket fuel** propergol *m* ▸ **rocket launcher** lanzacohetes *m inv* ▸ **rocket propulsion** propulsión *f* a cohete ▸ **rocket range** base *f* de lanzamiento de cohetes ▸ **rocket research** investigación *f* de cohetes ▸ **rocket science** astronáutica *f* (de cohetes) • IDIOM: • **this isn't ~ science*** para esto no hay que saber latín ▸ **rocket scientist** ingeniero/a *m/f* astronáutico/a • **it doesn't take a ~ scientist to ...*** no hace falta ser una lumbrera para ...

rocket[2] ['rɒkɪt] (N) (*Bot*) oruga *f*

rocket-propelled ['rɒkɪtprəˌpeld] (ADJ) propulsado por cohete(s)

rocketry ['rɒkɪtrɪ] (N) cohetería *f*

rockfish ['rɒkfɪʃ] (N) (PL: **rockfish** *or* **rockfishes**) pez *m* de roca

rock-hard [ˌrɒk'hɑːd] (ADJ) [*ground*] duro como la roca; [*chair, bed*] duro como una piedra

Rockies ['rɒkɪz] (NPL) = **Rocky Mountains**

rocking ['rɒkɪŋ] (N) balanceo *m*
(CPD) ▸ **rocking chair** mecedora *f*, mecedor *m* (*LAm*) ▸ **rocking horse** caballito *m* de balancín

rock 'n' roll [ˌrɒkən'rəʊl] (N) = **rock and roll**

rock-solid [ˌrɒk'sɒlɪd] (ADJ) sólido

rock-steady ['rɒk'stedɪ] (ADJ) [*hand*] muy firme; [*voice*] firme, muy seguro; [*car*] muy estable; [*camera, gun*] muy preciso

rocky[1] ['rɒkɪ] (ADJ) (COMPAR: **rockier**, SUPERL: **rockiest**) [*substance*] (duro) como la piedra; [*slope etc*] rocoso
(CPD) ▸ **Rocky Mountains** Montañas *fpl* Rocosas

rocky² ['rɒkɪ] ADJ (COMPAR: **rockier**, SUPERL: **rockiest**) (= *shaky, unsteady*) inestable, bamboleante; (*fig*) [*situation*] inseguro, inestable; [*government etc*] débil

rococo [rəʊ'kəʊkəʊ] ADJ rococó
N rococó *m*

Rod [rɒd] N, **Roddy** ['rɒdɪ] N *familiar forms of* **Roderick, Rodney**

rod [rɒd] N **1** [*of wood*] vara *f*; [*of metal*] barra *f*; (= *fishing rod*) caña *f*; (= *curtain rod*) barra *f*; (= *connecting rod*) biela *f*; (*Survey*) jalón *m* • IDIOMS: • **to rule with a rod of iron** gobernar con mano de hierro • **to make a rod for one's own back** hacer algo que después resultará contraproducente • PROVERB: • **spare the rod and spoil the child** quien bien te quiere te hará llorar; ▹ **spare**
2 (= *measure*) *medida de longitud = 5,029 metros*
3 (*US*‡) (= *gun*) pipa‡ *f*, pistola *f*
4 (*US*) (*Aut*‡) = **hotrod**

rode [rəʊd] PT *of* **ride**

rodent ['rəʊdənt] N roedor *m*

rodeo ['rəʊdɪəʊ] N rodeo *m*, charreada *f* (*Mex*)

Roderick ['rɒdərɪk] N Rodrigo • **~, the last of the Goths** Rodrigo el último godo

rodomontade [,rɒdəmɒn'teɪd] N fanfarronada *f*

roe¹ [rəʊ] N (PL: **roe** *or* **roes**) [*of fish*] • **hard roe** hueva *f* • **soft roe** lecha *f*

roe² [rəʊ] N (*also* **roe deer**) (*male*) corzo *m*; (*female*) corza *f*

roebuck ['rəʊbʌk] N (= *male roe deer*) corzo *m*

rogation [rəʊ'geɪʃən] (*Rel*) N **rogations** rogativas *fpl*
CPD ▸ **Rogation Days** Rogativas *fpl* de la Ascensión ▸ **Rogation Sunday** Domingo *m* de la Ascensión

Roger ['rɒdʒəʳ] N Rogelio • **~!** (*Telec etc*) ¡bien!, ¡de acuerdo!

roger‡ ['rɒdʒəʳ] VT joder**

rogue [rəʊg] N **1** (= *thief etc*) pícaro/a *m/f*, pillo/a *m/f*; (*hum*) granuja *mf* • **you ~!** ¡canalla!
2 (*Zool*) animal *m* solitario, animal *m* apartado de la manada
ADJ **1** (*Zool*) [*lion, male*] solitario, apartado de la manada • **~ elephant** elefante *m* solitario (y peligroso)
2 (*Bio, Med*) [*gene*] defectuoso
3 (= *maverick*) [*person*] que va por libre, inconformista; [*company*] sin escrúpulos • **~ cop*** (= *criminal*) policía *mf* corrupto/a
CPD ▸ **rogue's gallery** fichero *m* de delincuentes ▸ **rogue state** estado *m* canalla ▸ **rogue trader** comerciante *mf* sin escrúpulos

roguery ['rəʊgərɪ] N picardía *f*, truhanería *f*; (= *mischief*) travesuras *fpl*, diabluras *fpl* • **they're up to some ~** están haciendo alguna diablura

roguish ['rəʊgɪʃ] ADJ [*child*] travieso; [*look, smile etc*] pícaro

roguishly ['rəʊgɪʃlɪ] ADV [*look, smile etc*] con malicia • **she looked at me ~** me miró picaruela

ROI N ABBR **1** (= **return on investments**) rendimiento *m* de las inversiones
2 = **Republic of Ireland**

roil [rɔɪl] (*esp US*) VI [*water*] enturbiarse
VT (*fig*) agitar • **to ~ the waters** enturbiar *or* agitar las aguas

roister ['rɔɪstəʳ] VI jaranear

roisterer ['rɔɪstərəʳ] N jaranero/a *m/f*, juerguista *mf*

Roland ['rəʊlənd] N Roldán, Rolando

role [rəʊl] N (*Theat*) (*also fig*) papel *m* • **to cast sb in the ~ of** (*Theat, fig*) dar a algn el papel de • **to play a ~** (*Theat*) hacer un papel; (*fig*) desempeñar un papel (**in** en) • **supporting ~** papel *m* secundario
CPD ▸ **role model** modelo *m* a imitar ▸ **role play(ing)** juego *m* de roles ▸ **role playing game** (*also Comput*) juego *m* de rol ▸ **role reversal** inversión *f* de papeles

roll [rəʊl] N **1** [*of paper, cloth, wire, tobacco*] rollo *m*; [*of banknotes*] fajo *m* • **a ~ of film** un carrete *or* un rollo de fotos • **a ~ of wallpaper** un rollo de papel pintado • **~s of fat** (*gen*) rollos *mpl or* pliegues *mpl* de grasa; (*on stomach*) michelines *mpl* (*hum*)
2 [*of bread*] panecillo *m*, bolillo *m* (*Mex*) • **a ~ and butter** un panecillo *or* (*Mex*) bolillo con mantequilla; ▹ **sausage, Swiss**
3 (= *list*) lista *f* • **to have 500 pupils on the ~** tener inscritos a 500 alumnos • **membership ~** • **~ of members** lista *f* de miembros • **to call the ~** pasar lista • **falling ~s** *disminución en el número de alumnos inscritos* • **~ of honour** • **honor ~** (*US*) lista de honor
4 (= *sound*) [*of thunder, cannon*] retumbo *m*; [*of drum*] redoble *m* • **there was a ~ of drums** se oyó un redoble de tambores
5 [*of gait*] contoneo *m*, bamboleo *m*; [*of ship, plane*] balanceo *m*
6 (= *act of rolling*) revolcón *m* • **the horse was having a ~ on the grass** el caballo se estaba revolcando en la hierba • IDIOM: • **a ~ in the hay*** (*euph*) un revolcón* • **to have a ~ in the hay (with sb)*** (*euph*) darse un revolcón *or* revolcarse (con algn)*
7 [*of dice*] tirada *f* • IDIOM: • **to be on a ~** estar en racha, tener una buena racha
VT **1** (= *send rolling*) [+ *ball*] hacer rodar • **to ~ the dice** tirar los dados
2 (= *turn over*) • **~ the meat in the breadcrumbs** rebozar la carne con el pan rallado • **I ~ed her onto her back** la puse boca arriba
3 (= *move*) • **I ~ed the t~ey out of the way** empujé el carro para quitarlo del medio • **to ~ sth between one's fingers** hacer rodar algo entre los dedos • **to ~ one's eyes** poner los ojos en blanco
4 (= *make into roll*) [+ *cigarette*] liar • **he ~ed himself in a blanket** se enrolló en una manta • **she ~ed her sweater into a pillow** hizo una bola con el jersey para usarlo como almohada • **she is trainer and manager ~ed into one** es entrenadora y representante a la vez • **it's a kitchen and dining room ~ed into one** es una cocina comedor • **to ~ one's r's** pronunciar fuertemente las erres • **to ~ one's tongue** enrollar la lengua; ▹ **ball¹**
5 (= *flatten*) [+ *road*] apisonar; [+ *lawn, pitch*] pasar el rodillo por, apisonar; [+ *pastry, dough*] estirar; [+ *metal*] laminar
6 (*US*‡) (= *rob*) atracar
VI **1** (= *go rolling*) ir rodando; (*on ground, in pain*) revolcarse • **the ball ~ed into the net** el balón entró rodando en la red • **the children were ~ing down the slope** los niños iban rodando cuesta abajo • **it ~ed under the chair** desapareció *or* rodó debajo de la silla • **it went ~ing downhill** fue rodando cuesta abajo • **the horse ~ed in the mud** el caballo se revolcó en el barro • IDIOMS: • **to be ~ing in the aisles*** estar muerto de risa • **they're ~ing in money*** • **they're ~ing in it*** están forrados*; ▹ **ball¹, head**
2 (= *move*) • **the bus ~ed to a stop** el autobús se paró • **the tanks ~ed into the city** los tanques entraron en la ciudad • **the convoy ~ed slowly along the road** el convoy avanzaba lentamente por la carretera • **newspapers were ~ing off the presses** los periódicos estaban saliendo de las prensas • **tears ~ed down her cheeks** las lágrimas le corrían *or* caían por la cara • **the waves were ~ing onto the beach** las olas batían contra la playa • **his eyes ~ed wildly** los ojos se le ponían en blanco y parpadeaba descontroladamente; ▹ **tongue**
3 (= *turn over*) [*person, animal*] • **he ~ed off the sofa** se dio la vuelta y se cayó del sofá • **she ~ed onto her back** se puso boca arriba
4 (*fig*) [*land*] ondular • **vast plains ~ed into the distance** las vastas llanuras se perdían en la distancia
5 (= *operate*) [*camera*] rodar; [*machine*] funcionar, estar en marcha • **the presses are ~ing again** las prensas están funcionando *or* en marcha otra vez • **I couldn't think of anything to say to get the conversation ~ing** no se me ocurría nada para empezar la conversación • **his first priority is to get the economy ~ing again** su mayor prioridad es volver a sacar la economía a flote
6 (= *sound*) [*thunder*] retumbar; [*drum*] redoblar
7 (= *sway*) (*in walking*) contonearse, bambolearse; (*Naut*) balancearse
CPD ▸ **roll bar** (*Aut*) barra *f* antivuelco ▸ **roll call** lista *f* • **to take (a) ~ call** pasar lista

▸ **roll about, roll around** VI + ADV [*ball, coin*] rodar de un lado a otro; [*person, dog*] revolcarse; [*ship*] balancearse

▸ **roll around** VI + ADV **1** (*fig*) [*time, event*] llegar • **I was eager for five o'clock to ~ around** tenía muchas ganas de que llegaran las cinco • **by the time the next election ~s around** para cuando sean las próximas elecciones
2 = **roll about**

▸ **roll away** VT + ADV [+ *trolley, bed*] apartar, quitar; [+ *carpet*] enrollar, quitar
VI + ADV **1** [*ball*] alejarse (rodando), irse (rodando); [*person*] apartarse (rodando); [*clouds, mist*] disiparse
2 (*fig*) [*years*] esfumarse; [*landscape*] • **grassland ~ing away to the horizon** praderas que se pierden en el horizonte

▸ **roll back** VT + ADV **1** [+ *carpet*] enrollar; [+ *bedcovers*] echar para atrás
2 (*fig*) [+ *taxes*] reducir, bajar; [+ *enemy*] hacer retroceder • **the government's attempts to ~ back the welfare state** los intentos por parte del gobierno de reducir el estado del bienestar • **to ~ back the years** retroceder en el tiempo, volver atrás en el tiempo
VI + ADV [*clouds, mist*] disiparse; [*eyes*] ponerse en blanco

▸ **roll by** VI + ADV [*vehicle, clouds, time, years*] pasar

▸ **roll down** VT + ADV [+ *sleeve, stockings, car window, shutter*] bajar

▸ **roll in** VI + ADV **1*** [*money, letters*] llover, llegar a raudales; [*person*] aparecer • **offers of help continued to ~ in** seguían lloviendo ofertas de ayuda, seguían llegando ofertas de ayuda a raudales • **he ~ed in at 2a.m.** apareció a las 2 de la mañana
2 [*waves, cloud, mist*] llegar • **the waves came ~ing in** llegaban grandes olas a la playa
VT + ADV [+ *trolley, barrel*] llevar (rodando)

▸ **roll off** VI + ADV caerse (*rodando*)

▸ **roll on** VI + ADV **1** (= *go by*) [*time*] pasar
2 (= *carry on*) [*event*] continuar • **the bombardment of Iraq could ~ on indefinitely** el bombardeo de Iraq podría continuar indefinidamente
3 (*Brit**) (= *arrive quickly*) • **~ on the summer!** ¡que llegue pronto el verano! • **~ on Friday!** ¡que llegue pronto el viernes!

▸ **roll out** VT + ADV **1** [+ *barrel, trolley*] sacar (rodando); (*Comm*) [+ *product*] sacar *or* lanzar (al mercado)

2 [+ *pastry*] extender con el rodillo *or* uslero (*And*); [+ *carpet, map*] desenrollar; [+ *metal*] laminar • **to ~ out the red carpet** sacar la alfombra roja
3 [+ *statistics*] soltar una retahíla de
▸ **roll over** VI + ADV [*object, vehicle*] (180°) volcar, voltearse (*LAm*); (360°) (*once*) dar una vuelta de campana; (*several times*) dar vueltas de campana; [*person, animal*] darse la vuelta • **she ~ed over onto her back** se dio la vuelta poniéndose boca arriba • **the dog ~ed over with his paws in the air** el perro se dio la vuelta quedándose patas arriba • **we ~ed over and over down the slope** rodamos cuesta abajo
VT + ADV 1 [+ *object*] volver; [+ *body*] poner boca arriba
2 [+ *debt*] refinanciar
▸ **roll past** VI + ADV [*cart, procession*] pasar
▸ **roll up** VI + ADV 1 [*vehicle*] llegar, acercarse
2* [*person*] presentarse, aparecer • **you can't ~ up half way through the rehearsal** no puedes presentarte *or* aparecer en mitad del ensayo • **~ up, ~ up!** ¡acérquense!, ¡vengan todos!
3 • **to ~ up in a ball** [*hedgehog*] hacerse un ovillo *or* una bola
VT + ADV 1 (= *close*) [+ *map*] enrollar; [+ *umbrella*] cerrar; [+ *car window*] subir
2 • **to ~ up one's sleeves** remangarse, arremangarse
3 (= *wrap*) enrollar • **to ~ sth up in paper** enrollar algo en un papel, envolver algo en papel • **to ~ o.s. up in a blanket** envolverse en una manta
4 (= *form*) • **to ~ o.s. up into a ball** hacerse un ovillo

rollaway [ˈrəʊləweɪ] N (*US*) (*also* **rollaway bed**) cama *f* desmontable *or* abatible (sobre ruedas)

rollback [ˈrəʊlbæk] N (*US*) 1 (= *reduction*) (*in taxes, prices*) reducción *f*; [*of rights*] restricción *f*
2 (= *reversal*) [*of decision*] revocación *f*

rolled [rəʊld] ADJ [*umbrella*] cerrado • **~ gold** oro *m* chapado • **a ~ gold bracelet** una pulsera chapada en oro • **~ oats** copos *mpl* de avena • **~ r's** (*Ling*) erres *fpl* vibrantes

rolled-up [ˌrəʊldˈʌp] ADJ 1 [*newspaper*] enrollado
2 [*sleeves, trouser legs*] vuelto (hacia arriba)

roller [ˈrəʊləʳ] N 1 (*Agr, Tech*) rodillo *m*; (= *road-roller*) apisonadora *f*; (= *caster*) ruedecilla *f*; (*for hair*) rulo *m*
2 (= *wave*) ola *f* grande
CPD ▸ **roller bandage** venda *f* enrollada ▸ **roller blind** (*Brit*) persiana *f* enrollable ▸ **roller coaster** montaña *f* rusa ▸ **roller skate** patín *m* (de ruedas) ▸ **roller towel** toalla *f* de rodillo *or* sin fin; ▹ **roller-skate, roller-skating**

rollerblade [ˈrəʊləbleɪd] VI patinar en línea

rollerblader [ˈrəʊləbleɪdəʳ] N patinador(a) *m/f* en línea

Rollerblades® [ˈrəʊləbleɪdz] NPL patines *mpl* en línea

rollerblading [ˈrəʊləbleɪdɪŋ] N patinar *m* en línea • **to go ~** ir a patinar en línea

roller-skate [ˈrəʊləˌskeɪt] VI ir en patines de ruedas

roller-skating [ˈrəʊləˌskeɪtɪŋ] N patinaje *m* sobre ruedas

rollick [ˈrɒlɪk] VI (= *play*) jugar; (= *amuse o.s.*) divertirse

rollicking [ˈrɒlɪkɪŋ] ADJ alegre, divertido • **we had a ~ time** nos divertimos una barbaridad • **it was a ~ party** fue una fiesta animadísima • **it's a ~ farce** es una farsa de lo más divertido
N • **to give sb a ~** (*Brit**) poner a algn como un trapo*

rolling [ˈrəʊlɪŋ] ADJ [*waves*] fuerte; [*sea*] agitado; [*ship*] que se balancea; [*countryside, hills*] ondulado • **bring the water to a ~ boil** esperar a que el agua alcance su verdadero punto de ebullición • **to walk with a ~ gait** andar bamboleándose • **a ~ programme of privatization** un programa de privatización escalonado • IDIOM: • **he's a ~ stone** es muy inquieto, es culo de mal asiento* • PROVERB: • **a ~ stone gathers no moss** piedra movediza nunca moho la cobija
ADV • **he was ~ drunk*** estaba tan borracho que se caía, estaba borracho como una cuba*
N (*Naut*) balanceo *m*
CPD ▸ **rolling mill** taller *m* de laminación ▸ **rolling pin** rodillo *m* (de cocina), uslero *m* (*And*) ▸ **rolling stock** material *m* rodante *or* móvil

rollmop [ˈrəʊlmɒp] N arenque *m* adobado

roll-neck [ˈrəʊlnek] N (*Brit*) jersey *m* de cuello vuelto, jersey *m* cuello cisne

roll-necked [ˈrəʊlnekt] ADJ [*sweater*] de cuello vuelto, de cuello cisne

roll-on [ˈrəʊlɒn] N 1 (= *girdle*) faja *f* elástica, tubular *m*
2 (= *deodorant*) = **roll-on deodorant**
CPD ▸ **roll-on deodorant** desodorante *m* roll-on, bola *f* desodorante

roll-on-roll-off [ˌrəʊlɒnrəʊlˈɒf] ADJ • **roll-on-roll-off facility** facilidad *f* para la carga y descarga autopropulsada • **roll-on-roll-off ship** ro-ro *m*

roll-out [ˈrəʊlaʊt] N [*of system, product*] (= *launch*) lanzamiento *m*; (= *development*) desarrollo *m*; [*of new technology*] desarrollo *m*

rollover [ˈrəʊləʊvəʳ] N 1 (*in lottery*) bote *m*
2 [*of loan*] renegociación *f*
3 [*of car, boat*] vuelco *m*

roll-top desk [ˈrəʊltɒpˈdesk] N buró *m*, escritorio *m* de tapa rodadera

roll-up [ˈrəʊlʌp] N (*Brit**) (= *cigarette*) cigarrillo *m* de liar

Rolodex® [ˈrəʊlədeks] N *archivo de fichas giratorio*

roly-poly [ˈrəʊlɪˈpəʊlɪ] N (*Brit*) (*also* **roly-poly pudding**) brazo *m* de gitano
ADJ regordete

ROM [rɒm] N ABBR (= **Read-Only Memory**) ROM *f*

Rom [rɒm] N (PL: **Roma**) (= *man*) romaní *m*

Roma [ˈrəʊmə] N 1 (*also* **Roma gypsy**) romaní *mf*
2 (= *language*) romaní *m*
NPL (= *people*) romanís *mpl*

romaine [rəʊˈmeɪn] N (*US, Canada*) (*also* **romaine lettuce**) lechuga *f* romana, lechuga *f* cos

Roman [ˈrəʊmən] ADJ romano
N (*person*) romano/a *m/f*
CPD ▸ **Roman alphabet** alfabeto *m* romano ▸ **Roman candle** candela *f* romana ▸ **Roman Catholic Church** • **the ~ Catholic Church** la Iglesia católica (apostólica y romana) ▸ **Roman Catholicism** catolicismo *m* ▸ **Roman Empire** • **the ~ Empire** el Imperio romano ▸ **Roman law** derecho *m* romano ▸ **Roman nose** nariz *f* aguileña ▸ **Roman numeral** número *m* romano

roman [ˈrəʊmən] N (*Typ*) tipo *m* romano

Roman Catholic [ˌrəʊmənˈkæθəlɪk] ADJ católico (apostólico y romano)
N católico/a *m/f* (apostólico/a y romano/a)

romance [rəʊˈmæns] N 1 (= *love affair*) romance *m*, idilio *m*, amores *mpl* • **their ~ lasted exactly six months** su romance *or* idilio duró exactamente seis meses, sus amores duraron exactamente seis meses • **a young girl waiting for ~** una joven que espera su primer amor • **I've finished with ~** para mí no más amores
2 (= *romantic character*) lo romántico, lo poético; (= *picturesqueness*) lo pintoresco • **the ~ of travel** lo romántico del viajar • **the ~ of history** lo atractivo *or* lo poético de la historia • **the ~ of the sea** el encanto del mar
3 (= *tale*) novela *f* (sentimental), cuento *m* (de amor); (*medieval*) libro *m* de caballerías, poema *m* caballeresco; (*Mus*) romanza *f*
4 (*Ling*) • **Romance** romance *m*
ADJ [*language*] romance
VI soñar, fantasear

Romanesque [ˌrəʊməˈnesk] ADJ (*Archit*) románico

Romania [rəʊˈmeɪnɪə] N Rumania *f*, Rumanía *f*

Romanian [rəʊˈmeɪnɪən] ADJ rumano
N 1 (= *person*) rumano/a *m/f*
2 (*Ling*) rumano *m*

Romanic [rəʊˈmænɪk] ADJ = **Romanesque**

romanize [ˈrəʊmənaɪz] VT romanizar

Romansch [rəʊˈmænʃ] ADJ rético
N 1 rético/a *m/f*
2 (*Ling*) rético *m*

Romantic [rəʊˈmæntɪk] ADJ [*movement, art, poets*] romántico

romantic [rəʊˈmæntɪk] ADJ romántico
N romántico/a *m/f*
CPD ▸ **romantic involvement** relación *f* amorosa • **they were very good friends but there was no ~ involvement** eran muy buenos amigos, pero no tenían ninguna relación amorosa

romantically [rəʊˈmæntɪkəlɪ] ADV románticamente, de modo romántico

romanticism [rəʊˈmæntɪsɪzəm] N romanticismo *m*

romanticist [rəʊˈmæntɪsɪst] N • **he's a bit of a ~** es un romántico

romanticize [rəʊˈmæntɪsaɪz] VT sentimentalizar
VI fantasear

romanticized [rəʊˈmæntɪsaɪzd] ADJ [*view*] romántico

Romany [ˈrɒmənɪ] ADJ gitano
N 1 gitano/a *m/f*
2 (*Ling*) romaní *m*, lengua *f* gitana; (*in Spain*) caló *m*

Rome [rəʊm] N 1 Roma *f* • PROVERBS: • **all roads lead to ~** todos los caminos llevan a Roma • **~ was not built in a day** no se ganó Zamora en una hora • **when in ~ (do as the Romans do)** donde fueres, haz lo que vieres
2 (*Rel*) la Iglesia, el catolicismo • **Manning turned to ~** Manning se convirtió al catolicismo

Romeo [ˈrəʊmɪəʊ] N Romeo

Romish [ˈrəʊmɪʃ] ADJ (*pej*) católico

romp [rɒmp] N retozo *m* • **to have a ~** retozar • **the play was just a ~** la obra era una farsa alegre nada más • IDIOM: • **to have a ~ in the hay*** darse un revolcón en el pajar *or* en la hierba*
VI retozar; [*lambs etc*] brincar, correr alegremente • **she ~ed through the examination** no tuvo problema alguno para aprobar el examen • **to ~ home** (= *win easily*) ganar fácilmente

rompers [ˈrɒmpəz], **romper suit** [ˈrɒmpəˌsuːt] NPL mono *msing*, pelele *msing*

Romulus [ˈrɒmjʊləs] N Rómulo

rondeau [ˈrɒndəʊ] N (PL: **rondeaux** [ˈrɒndəʊz]) (*Literat*) rondó *m*

rondo [ˈrɒndəʊ] N (*Mus*) rondó *m*

Roneo® [ˈrəʊnɪəʊ] VT reproducir con multicopista

rood [ruːd] N cruz *f*, crucifijo *m*

roodscreen ['ru:dskri:n] N reja *f* entre la nave y el coro

roof [ru:f] N (PL: **roofs**) [*of building*] tejado *m* (*esp Sp*), techo *m* (*esp LAm*); [*of car etc*] techo *m* • **flat ~** azotea *f* • **to have a ~ over one's head** tener dónde cobijarse • **the ~ of heaven** la bóveda celeste • **the ~ of the mouth** el paladar • **to live under the same ~** vivir bajo el mismo techo • **prices are going through the ~** los precios están por las nubes
• IDIOMS: • **he hit the ~*** se subió por las paredes* • **to lift the ~** (*Brit*) • **raise the ~** (= *protest*) poner el grito en el cielo • **when the staff arrived the infant was still raising the ~** cuando el personal llegó, el niño todavía estaba llorando a grito pelado • **the cheers and roars of approval lifted the pavilion ~** el pabellón se vino abajo con los vivas y los gritos de aprobación
VT (*also* **roof in, roof over**) techar, poner techo a • **it is ~ed in wood** tiene techo de madera • **to ~ a hut in** *or* **with wood** poner techo de madera a una caseta
CPD ▸ **roof garden** azotea *f* con flores y plantas ▸ **roof rack** (*esp Brit*) (*Aut*) baca *f*, portamaletas *m inv*, portaequipajes *m inv*, parrilla *f* (*LAm*) ▸ **roof space** desván *m*

roofer ['ru:fəʳ] N instalador(a) *m/f* de tejados

roofing ['ru:fɪŋ] N (= *roof*) techumbre *f*; (= *roofing material*) material *m* para techado
CPD ▸ **roofing felt** fieltro *m* para techar ▸ **roofing material** material *m* para techado

roofless ['ru:flɪs] ADJ sin techo

rooftop ['ru:ftɒp] N techo *m*; (*with flat roof*) azotea *f* • IDIOM: • **we will proclaim it from the ~s** lo proclamaremos a los cuatro vientos
CPD ▸ **rooftop restaurant** restaurante *m* de azotea

rook¹ [rʊk] N (*Orn*) grajo *m*
VT (= *swindle*) estafar, timar • **you've been ~ed** te han estafado *or* timado

rook² [rʊk] N (*Chess*) torre *f*

rookery ['rʊkərɪ] N colonia *f* de grajos

rookie ['rʊkɪ] (*US*) N **1** (*Mil**) novato/a *m/f*, bisoño/a *m/f*
2 (*Sport*) debutante *mf* (*en la temporada*)

room [rʊm] N **1** (*in house, hotel*) habitación *f*, cuarto *m*, pieza *f* (*esp LAm*), recámara *f* (*Mex*), ambiente *m* (*Arg*); (*large, public*) sala *f* • **in ~ 504** (*hotel*) en la habitación número 504 • **double ~** habitación *f etc* doble • **furnished ~** cuarto *m* amueblado • **ladies' ~** servicios *mpl* de señoras • **this is my ~** esta es mi habitación • **single ~** habitación *f* individual
2 rooms (= *lodging*) alojamiento *msing* • **they've always lived in ~s** siempre han vivido de alquiler • **he has ~s in college** tiene un cuarto en el colegio
3 (= *space*) sitio *m*, espacio *m*, campo *m* (*And*) • **is there ~?** ¿hay sitio? • **there's plenty of ~** hay sitio de sobra • **is there ~ for this?** ¿cabe esto?, ¿hay cabida para esto? • **is there ~ for me?** ¿quepo yo?, ¿hay sitio para mí? • **to make ~ for sb** hacer sitio a algn • **make ~!** ¡abran paso! • **there's no ~ for anything else** no cabe más • **standing ~ only!** no queda asiento
4 (*fig*) • **there is no ~ for doubt** no hay lugar a dudas • **to leave ~ for imponderables** dar cabida a un margen de imponderables • **there is ~ for improvement** esto se puede mejorar todavía
VI (*US*) • **to ~ with three other students** estar en una pensión con otros tres estudiantes, compartir un piso *or* (*LAm*) un departamento con otros tres estudiantes • **to ~ with a landlady** alojarse en casa de una señora
CPD ▸ **room clerk** (*US*) recepcionista *mf* (de hotel) ▸ **room divider** (= *screen*) biombo *m*; (= *wall*) tabique *m* ▸ **room service** (*in hotel*) servicio *m* de habitaciones ▸ **room temperature** temperatura *f* ambiente

-roomed [rʊmd] ADJ (*ending in compounds*) de ... piezas • **seven-roomed** de siete piezas

roomer ['rʊməʳ] N (*US*) inquilino/a *m/f*

roomette [ru:'met] N (*US*) departamento *m* de coche-cama

roomful ['rʊmfʊl] N • **a ~ of priests** un cuarto lleno de curas • **they have Picassos by the ~** tienen salas enteras llenas de cuadros de Picasso

roominess ['rʊmɪnɪs] N espaciosidad *f*, amplitud *f*; [*of garment*] holgura *f*

rooming house ['rʊmɪŋhaʊs] N (PL: **rooming houses** ['rʊmɪŋ,haʊzɪz]) (*US*) pensión *f*

roommate ['rʊmmeɪt] N compañero/a *m/f* de cuarto

roomy ['rʊmɪ] ADJ (COMPAR: **roomier**, SUPERL: **roomiest**) (*flat, cupboard etc*) amplio, espacioso; (*garment*) holgado

roost [ru:st] N (*gen*) percha *f*; (= *hen roost*) gallinero *m* • IDIOM: • **to rule the ~** llevar la batuta
VI **1** (*lit*) dormir posado
2 (*fig*) • IDIOMS: • **to come home to ~: now his policies have come home to ~** ahora su política produce su fruto amargo, ahora se están viendo los malos resultados de su política • **these measures only camouflaged the real problem, now the chickens are coming home to ~** estas medidas no eran más que una manera de camuflar el problema y ahora se vuelven contra nosotros, estas medidas solo camuflaban el problema y ahora se ve que fueron pan para hoy y hambre para mañana

rooster ['ru:stəʳ] N (*esp US*) gallo *m*

root [ru:t] N **1** (*Bot*) raíz *f* • **the plant's ~ system** las raíces de la planta • **to pull sth up by the ~s** arrancar algo de raíz • **to take ~** echar raíces, arraigar • IDIOM: • **~ and branch** completamente, del todo • **they aimed to eliminate Marxism ~ and branch** su objetivo era erradicar el marxismo, su objetivo era acabar con el marxismo de raíz • **a ~ and branch overhaul of the benefits system** una revisión completa *or* de cabo a rabo del sistema de prestaciones
2 (*Bio*) [*of hair, tooth*] raíz *f*
3 (= *origin*) [*of problem, word*] raíz *f* • **the ~ of the problem is that ...** la raíz del problema es que ... • **her ~s are in Manchester** tiene sus raíces en Manchester • **she has no ~s** no tiene raíces • **to pull up one's ~s** levantar raíces • **to put down ~s in a country** echar raíces en un país • **to take ~** [*idea*] arraigarse; ▹ **money**
4 (*Math*) • **square ~** raíz *f* cuadrada
5 (*Ling*) raíz *f*, radical *m*
VT **1** (*Bot*) [+ *plant*] hacer arraigar
2 (*fig*) ▹ **rooted**
VI **1** (*Bot*) [*plant*] echar raíces, arraigar
2 (= *search*) [*animal*] hozar, hocicar • **I was ~ing through some old photos the other day** el otro día estaba husmeando entre viejas fotos
CPD ▸ **root beer** (*US*) *bebida refrescante elaborada a base de raíces* ▸ **root canal treatment** tratamiento *m* de endodoncia ▸ **root cause** causa *f* primordial ▸ **root crops** cultivos *mpl* de tubérculos ▸ **root ginger** raíz *f* de jengibre ▸ **root vegetable** tubérculo *m* comestible ▸ **root word** (*Ling*) palabra *f* que es raíz *or* radical de otras
▸ **root about, root around** VI + ADV [*pig*] hozar, hocicar; [*person*] (= *search*) andar buscando por todas partes; (= *investigate*) investigar • **to ~ around for sth** andar buscando algo
▸ **root for*** VI + PREP [+ *team*] animar (*con gritos y pancartas*); [+ *cause*] hacer propaganda por, apoyar a
▸ **root out** VT + ADV [+ *plant*] arrancar (de raíz), desarraigar; (= *find*) desenterrar, encontrar; (= *do away with*) acabar con, arrancar de raíz, extirpar
▸ **root through** VI + PREP **1** [*pig*] hocicar
2 (*fig*) examinar, explorar
▸ **root up** VT + ADV [+ *plant, tree*] arrancar (de raíz), desarraigar

rooted ['ru:tɪd] ADJ **1** • **~ in sth** [+ *tradition, religion, faith*] enraizado en algo • **to be ~ in** [*music, ideas, attitudes, problems*] tener sus raíces en
2 • **deeply ~** [*opinions, feelings, prejudice*] muy arraigado • **a deeply ~ prejudice** un prejuicio muy arraigado
3 • **to be ~ to the spot** quedar paralizado

rooter* ['ru:təʳ] N (*esp US*) (*Sport*) hincha *mf*, seguidor(a) *m/f*

rootless ['ru:tlɪs] ADJ [*person etc*] desarraigado

rootlessness ['ru:tləsnɪs] N falta *f* de raíces

rootstock ['ru:tstɒk] N rizoma *m*

rope [rəʊp] N cuerda *f*, soga *f*, mecate *m* (*Mex*); (*Naut*) (= *hawser*) maroma *f*, cable *m*; (*in rigging*) cabo *m*; (*hangman's*) dogal *m*; [*of pearls*] collar *m*; [*of onions etc*] ristra *f* • **the ~s** (*Boxing*) las cuerdas • **to jump** *or* **skip ~** (*US*) saltar a la comba • **there were three of us on the ~** (*Mountaineering*) éramos tres los encordados
• IDIOMS: • **to give sb more ~** dar a algn mayor libertad de acción • **if you give him enough ~ he'll hang himself** déjale actuar y él se condenará a sí mismo • **to know/learn the ~s** estar/ponerse al tanto • **to be on the ~s** estar en las cuerdas • **I'll show you the ~s** te voy a mostrar cómo funciona todo • **to be at the end of one's ~** (*esp US*) no poder soportarlo más, no aguantar más
VT atar *or* (*LAm*) amarrar con (una) cuerda; (*US*) [+ *animal*] coger *or* (*LAm*) agarrar con lazo • **to ~ two things together** atar dos cosas con una cuerda • **they ~d themselves together** (*Mountaineering*) se encordaron • **there were four climbers ~d together** había cuatro escaladores que formaban una cordada *or* iban encordados
CPD ▸ **rope burn** quemadura *f* por fricción ▸ **rope ladder** escala *f* de cuerda ▸ **rope trick** truco *m* de la cuerda
▸ **rope in*** VT + ADV • **they managed to ~ in their friends** consiguieron arrastrar a sus amigos • **to ~ sb in (to do sth)** enganchar a algn (para que haga algo)
▸ **rope off** VT + ADV acordonar • **to ~ off an area** acordonar un espacio, cercar un espacio con cuerdas
▸ **rope up** VI + ADV [*climbers*] encordarse, formar una cordada

ropemaker ['rəʊp,meɪkəʳ] N cordelero/a *m/f*

ropewalker ['rəʊp,wɔ:kəʳ] N funámbulo/a *m/f*, volatinero/a *m/f*

ropy*, **ropey*** ['rəʊpɪ] (*Brit*) ADJ (COMPAR: **ropier**, SUPERL: **ropiest**) (= *off colour*) pachucho*, chungo*; (= *weak*) [*plan, argument etc*] nada convincente, flojo; (= *sinewy*) [*muscles, arms*] fibroso • **I feel a bit ropey** me siento un poco chungo*, no me siento del todo bien • **this car looks a bit ropey** este coche parece una auténtica tartana*

RORO, RO/RO ['rəʊrəʊ] ABBR = **roll-on-roll-off**

rosary ['rəʊzərɪ] N (*Rel*) rosario *m* • **to say**

the/one's ~ rezar el rosario
rose¹ [rəʊz] N **1** (*Bot*) (= *flower*) rosa *f*; (= *bush, tree*) rosal *m* • **the Wars of the Roses** (*Brit*) (*Hist*) la Guerra de las Dos Rosas • **wild ~** rosal silvestre • IDIOMS: • **all ~s***: • **it's all ~s among them by the end of the film** al final de la película todo es maravilloso entre ellos • **life isn't all ~s** la vida no es un lecho de rosas • **to come up ~s** salir a pedir de boca • **the fresh air will soon put the ~s back in your cheeks** el aire fresco te devolverá rápidamente el color a las mejillas • **an English ~** una belleza típicamente inglesa • **an English ~ complexion** un cutis de porcelana • PROVERB: • **there's no ~ without a thorn** no hay rosa sin espina; ▹ **bed, Christmas, damask, tea**
2 (= *colour*) rosa *m*
3 (*on shower*) alcachofa *f*; (*on watering can*) alcachofa *f*, roseta *f*
4 (*Archit*) (*also* **ceiling rose**) roseta *f*, rosetón *m*
ADJ (= *rose-coloured*) (de color de) rosa (*inv*), rosado • ~ **pink** rosado, rosa • ~ **red** rojo de rosa
CPD ▸ **rose bush** rosal *m* ▸ **rose garden** rosaleda *f* ▸ **rose grower** cultivador(a) *m/f* de rosas ▸ **rose petal** pétalo *m* de rosa ▸ **rose quartz** cuarzo *m* rosa ▸ **rose tree** rosal *m* ▸ **rose window** (*Archit*) rosetón *m*
rose² [rəʊz] PT *of* **rise**
Rose [rəʊz] N Rosa
rosé ['rəʊzeɪ] ADJ rosado
N rosado *m*
roseate ['rəʊzɪɪt] ADJ róseo, rosado
rosebay ['rəʊzbeɪ] N adelfa *f*
rosebed ['rəʊzbed] N rosaleda *f*
rosebowl ['rəʊzbəʊl] N jarrón *m or* florero *m* para rosas
rosebud ['rəʊzbʌd] N capullo *m or* botón *m* de rosa
rose-coloured, rose-colored (*US*) ['rəʊz,kʌləd] ADJ = **rose-tinted**
rosehip ['rəʊzhɪp] N escaramujo *m*
CPD ▸ **rosehip syrup** jarabe *m* de escaramujo
rosemary ['rəʊzmərɪ] N (= *herb*) romero *m*
rose-pink [,rəʊz'pɪŋk] ADJ rosado, rosa
rose-red [,rəʊz'red] ADJ color rojo de rosa
rose-tinted ['rəʊztɪntɪd] ADJ color de rosa • **to look at sb/sth through rose-tinted glasses** *or* (*Brit*) **spectacles** ver solo la parte buena de algn/algo • **to see life through rose-tinted glasses** *or* **spectacles** ver la vida de color de rosa
rosette [rəʊ'zet] N (*Archit*) rosetón *m*; (= *emblem*) escarapela *f*; (= *prize*) premio *m*
rosewater ['rəʊz,wɔːtəʳ] N agua *f* de rosas
rosewood ['rəʊzwʊd] N palo *m* de rosa, palisandro *m*
Rosicrucian [,rəʊzɪ'kruːʃən] N rosacruz *mf*
ADJ rosacruz
rosin ['rɒzɪn] N colofonia *f*
ROSPA ['rɒspə] N ABBR = **Royal Society for the Prevention of Accidents**
roster ['rɒstəʳ] N lista *f* • **duty ~** lista *f* de turnos
VT distribuir tareas entre • **to be ~ed for sth/to do sth** tener asignado algo/hacer algo
rostrum ['rɒstrəm] N (PL: **rostrums** *or* **rostra** ['rɒstrə])
N tribuna *f*
CPD ▸ **rostrum cameraman** (*TV*) cámara-truca *m*
rosy ['rəʊzɪ] ADJ (COMPAR: **rosier**, SUPERL: **rosiest**) **1** [*cheeks*] sonrosado; [*colour*] rosáceo
2 (*fig*) [*future, prospect*] prometedor, halagüeño
rot [rɒt] N **1** (= *process*) putrefacción *f*; (= *substance*) podredumbre *f* • IDIOMS: • **the rot set in** la decadencia comenzó, todo empezó a decaer • **to stop the rot** cortar el problema de raíz, cortar por lo sano
2 (*esp Brit**) (= *nonsense*) tonterías *fpl*, babosadas *fpl* (*LAm*) • **oh rot!** • **what rot!** ¡qué tonterías! • **don't talk rot!** ¡no digas bobadas!
VT pudrir, descomponer
VI pudrirse, descomponerse • **to rot in jail** pudrirse en la cárcel • **you can rot for all I care!** ¡que te pudras!
▸ **rot away** VI + ADV pudrirse, descomponerse • **it had rotted away with the passage of time** con el tiempo se había pudrido *or* descompuesto • **it had quite rotted away** se había pudrido *or* descompuesto del todo
rota ['rəʊtə] N (*esp Brit*) lista *f* (de tareas)
Rotarian [rəʊ'tɛərɪən] ADJ rotario
N rotario/a *m/f*
rotary ['rəʊtərɪ] ADJ [*movement*] giratorio; [*blade*] rotativo, giratorio
CPD ▸ **Rotary Club** Sociedad *f* Rotaria
▸ **rotary press** prensa *f* rotativa
rotate [rəʊ'teɪt] VT hacer girar, dar vueltas a; [+ *crops*] alternar, cultivar en rotación; [+ *staff*] alternar; (*Comput*) [+ *graphics*] rotar, girar • **to ~ A and B** alternar A con B
VI girar, dar vueltas; [*staff*] alternarse
rotating [rəʊ'teɪtɪŋ] ADJ [*blade*] rotativo, giratorio; [*presidency*] rotatorio
rotation [rəʊ'teɪʃən] N rotación *f* • ~ **of crops** rotación de cultivos • **in ~** por turnos • **orders are dealt with in strict ~** los pedidos se sirven por riguroso orden
rotational [rəʊ'teɪʃənəl] ADJ rotacional
rotatory [rəʊ'teɪtərɪ] ADJ rotativo
rotavate ['rəʊtəveɪt] VT trabajar con motocultor
Rotavator® ['rəʊtəveɪtəʳ] N (*Brit*) motocultor *m*
rote [rəʊt] N • **by ~** de memoria • **to learn sth by ~** aprender algo a fuerza de repetirlo
CPD ▸ **rote learning** • ~ **learning was the fashion** era costumbre aprender las cosas a fuerza de repetirlas
rotgut‡ ['rɒtgʌt] N (*pej*) matarratas *m inv*
rotisserie [rəʊ'tɪsərɪ] N rotisserie *f*
rotor ['rəʊtəʳ] N rotor *m*
CPD ▸ **rotor arm** (*Aut*) rotor *m* ▸ **rotor blade** paleta *f* de rotor
Rototiller® ['rəʊtəʊtɪləʳ] N (*US*) motocultor *m*
Rotovator® ['rəʊtəveɪtəʳ] N (*Brit*) motocultor *m*
rotproof ['rɒtpruːf] ADJ a prueba de putrefacción, imputrescible
rotten ['rɒtn] ADJ **1** (*gen*) podrido; [*food*] pasado; [*tooth*] cariado, podrido; [*wood*] carcomido, podrido • **to smell ~** oler a podrido; ▹ **apple**
2 (*fig*) [*system, government*] corrompido; (= *of bad quality**) pésimo, fatal* • **it's a ~ novel** es una novela pésima *or* malísima • **his English is ~** tiene un inglés fatal* • **how ~ for you!** ¡cuánto te compadezco!, ¡lo que habrás sufrido! • **he's ~ at chess** para el ajedrez es un desastre • **I feel ~** (= *ill*) me encuentro fatal*; (= *mean*) me siento culpable • **they made me suffer something ~*** me hicieron pasarlas negras • **what a ~ thing to do!** ¡qué maldad! • **what a ~ thing to happen!** ¡qué mala suerte! • **to be ~ to sb*** portarse como un canalla con algn • **what ~ weather!** ¡qué tiempo de perros! • **he's ~ with money** está podrido de dinero*
ADV‡ malísimamente, fatal* • **they played real ~** jugaron fatal*
rottenly* ['rɒtnlɪ] ADV • **to behave ~ to sb** portarse como un canalla con algn
rottenness ['rɒtnnɪs] N podredumbre *f*; (*fig*) corrupción *f*
rotter†* ['rɒtəʳ] N (*Brit*) caradura* *mf*, sinvergüenza *mf* • **you ~!** ¡canalla!
rotting ['rɒtɪŋ] ADJ podrido, que se está pudriendo
Rottweiler ['rɒt,vaɪləʳ] N Rottweiler *m*
rotund [rəʊ'tʌnd] ADJ [*person*] corpulento, rotundo
rotunda [rəʊ'tʌndə] N rotonda *f*
rotundity [rəʊ'tʌndɪtɪ] N corpulencia *f*
rouble, ruble (*US*) ['ruːbl] N rublo *m*
roué ['ruːeɪ] N libertino *m*
Rouen ['ruːɑ̃ːŋ] N Ruán *m*
rouge [ruːʒ] N colorete *m*, carmín *m*
VT • **to ~ one's cheeks** ponerse colorete
rough [rʌf] ADJ (COMPAR: **rougher**, SUPERL: **roughest**) **1** (= *coarse*) [*surface, texture*] áspero, rugoso; [*skin*] áspero; [*cloth*] basto; [*hand*] calloso • IDIOM: • **to give sb the ~ edge** *or* **side of one's tongue*** echar una buena bronca a algn
2 (= *uneven*) [*terrain*] accidentado, escabroso; [*road*] desigual, lleno de baches; [*track, ground*] desigual; [*edge*] irregular • **he'll be a good salesman once we knock off the ~ edges** será un buen vendedor una vez que lo hayamos pulido un poco
3 (= *harsh, unpleasant*) [*voice, sound*] ronco; [*wine*] áspero; [*life*] difícil, duro; [*climate, winter*] duro, severo
4 (= *not gentle*) [*behaviour, person, voice, manner*] brusco; [*words, tone*] severo, áspero; [*play, sport, game*] violento; [*neighbourhood, area*] malo, peligroso • **you're too ~** eres demasiado bruto • **he's a ~ customer** es un tipo peligroso • **to get ~** [*person*] ponerse bruto; [*game*] volverse violento • **children's toys must be able to withstand a lot of ~ handling** los juguetes de niños tienen que ser resistentes porque con frecuencia los tratan sin ningún cuidado • **he got ~ justice** recibió un castigo duro pero apropiado • ~ **stuff*** violencia *f* • **there were complaints of ~ treatment at the hands of the police** hubo quejas de malos tratos a manos de la policía • **he came in for some ~ treatment in the press** fue objeto de duras críticas por parte de la prensa • **to be ~ with sb** ser brusco con algn • **to be ~ with sth** ser brusco con algo
5 (= *stormy*) [*sea*] agitado, encrespado; [*wind*] violento; [*weather*] tormentoso, tempestuoso • **we had a ~ crossing** el barco se movió mucho durante la travesía • **to get ~** [*sea*] embravecerse
6 (= *unpolished, crude*) [*person*] tosco, rudo; [*manners, speech*] tosco; [*shelter, table, tunic*] tosco, basto; [*gemstone*] en bruto • IDIOM: • **he's a ~ diamond** es un diamante en bruto
7* (= *hard, tough*) duro • **things are ~ now, but they will get better** las cosas están un poco difíciles ahora pero mejorarán • **to be ~ on sb** [*situation*] ser duro para algn; [*person*] ser duro con algn • **parents' divorce can be really ~ on children** el divorcio de los padres puede ser muy duro para los niños • **don't be so ~ on him, it's not his fault** no seas tan duro con él, no es culpa suya • **it's a bit ~ on him to have to do all the housework** no es muy justo que él tenga que hacer todo el trabajo de la casa • **to give sb a ~ ride** *or* **a ~ time** hacérselo pasar mal a algn • **to have a ~ time (of it)** pasarlo mal • IDIOM: • **when the going gets ~** cuando las cosas se ponen feas
8 (*Brit**) (= *ill*) • **"how are you?" — "a bit ~"** —¿cómo estás? —no muy bien • **to feel ~** encontrarse mal • **to look ~** tener muy mal aspecto *or* muy mala cara
9 (= *approximate*) [*calculation, estimate,*

description, outline] aproximado; [translation] hecho a grandes rasgos, aproximado • **I would say 50 at a ~ guess** diría que 50 aproximadamente • **as a ~ guide, it should take about ten minutes** llevará unos diez minutos más o menos, llevará aproximadamente diez minutos • **can you give me a ~ idea of how long it will take?** ¿puedes darme una idea aproximada *or* más o menos una idea de cuánto tiempo llevará?
10 (= *preparatory*) [*work*] de preparación, preliminar • **~ book** cuaderno *m* de borrador • **~ copy** • **~ draft** borrador *m* • **~ paper** papel *m* de borrador • **~ plan** • **~ sketch** bosquejo *m*, boceto *m*
(ADV) • **to live ~** vivir sin las comodidades más básicas • **to play ~** jugar duro • **to sleep ~** dormir a la intemperie • IDIOM: • **to cut up ~***: • **she cut up ~ when she discovered what had been going on** se puso hecha una furia cuando descubrió lo que había estado pasando
(N) **1** (= *person*) matón *m*, tipo *m* duro
2 (= *draft*) borrador *m* • **we'll do it in ~ first** lo haremos primero en borrador
3 • IDIOM: • **to take the ~ with the smooth** tomar las duras con las maduras
4 (*Golf*) rough *m*, zona *f* de matojos
(VT) • **to ~ it** vivir sin comodidades
(CPD) ▸ **rough puff pastry** hojaldre *m*
▸ **rough work** (= *draft*) borrador *m*
▸ **rough in** (VT + ADV) [+ *shape, figure, outline*] esbozar, bosquejar
▸ **rough out** (VT + ADV) [+ *plan*] esbozar, bosquejar
▸ **rough up** (VT + ADV) **1** [+ *hair*] despeinar
2* • **to ~ sb up** dar una paliza a algn
roughage ['rʌfɪdʒ] (N) (*for animals*) forraje *m*; (*for people*) alimentos *mpl* ricos en fibra
rough-and-ready ['rʌfən'redɪ] (ADJ) [*person*] tosco, burdo, basto; [*structure*] tosco, basto; [*accommodation*] humilde, sencillo; [*method*] improvisado
rough-and-tumble ['rʌfən'tʌmbl] (N) • **the rough-and-tumble play of young boys** las peleíllas *or* riñas de los chavales • **the rough-and-tumble of life** los vaivenes de la vida • **the rough-and-tumble of politics** los avatares *or* los altibajos de la política
roughcast ['rʌfkɑːst] (N) mezcla *f* gruesa
roughen ['rʌfn] (VT) [+ *skin*] poner áspero, dejar áspero; [+ *surface*] raspar; (*Carpentry*) desbastar
(VI) [*skin*] ponerse áspero; [*sea*] embravecerse; [*voice*] volverse ronco, enronquecer
rough-hewn ['rʌf'hjuːn] (ADJ) toscamente labrado; (*fig*) tosco, inculto
roughhouse* ['rʌfhaʊs] (N) (PL: **roughhouses** ['rʌfhaʊzɪz]) trifulca* *f*, riña *f* general, reyerta *f*
roughing ['rʌfɪŋ] (N) (*Ice hockey*) empujones *mpl*
roughly ['rʌflɪ] (ADV) **1** (= *approximately*) [*equal*] aproximadamente, más o menos • **he was ~ the same age/height as me** tenía aproximadamente *or* más o menos la misma edad/altura que yo • **~ similar** más o menos parecido • **~ translated** traducido a grandes rasgos *or* de forma aproximada
2 (= *generally*) [*describe, outline*] en líneas generales, más o menos • **they fall ~ into two categories** en términos generales se dividen en dos categorías • **~ speaking, it means an increase of 10%** en líneas generales, supone un incremento del 10% • **~ speaking, it acts as a transformer** viene a actuar más o menos como un transformador • **~ speaking, his job is that of an administrator** su trabajo es, por así decirlo, de administrador
3 (= *not gently*) [*push*] bruscamente; [*play*] de forma violenta; [*speak, order*] con brusquedad • **to treat sth/sb ~** tratar mal algo/tratar a algn con brusquedad
4 (= *crudely*) [*constructed, built, carved*] toscamente • **to sketch sth ~** hacer un bosquejo de algo
5 (*Culin*) [*chop*] en trozos grandes; [*slice*] en rodajas grandes
roughneck* ['rʌfnek] (N) (*US*) duro *m*, matón *m*
roughness ['rʌfnɪs] (N) [*of hands, surface*] aspereza *f*; [*of sea*] agitación *f*, encrespamiento *m*; [*of road*] desigualdad *f*; [*of person*] (= *brusqueness*) brusquedad *f*; (= *crudeness*) tosquedad *f*; (= *violence*) violencia *f*
roughrider ['rʌf,raɪdəʳ] (N) domador(a) *m/f* de caballos
roughshod ['rʌfʃɒd] (ADV) • **to ride ~ over sth/sb** pisotear algo/a algn • **he thinks he can ride ~ over the wishes of the majority** se cree que puede saltarse a la torera *or* pisotear la voluntad de la mayoría
rough-spoken ['rʌf'spəʊkən] (ADJ) malhablado
roulette [ruː'let] (N) ruleta *f*
Roumania *etc* [ruː'meɪnɪə] = **Romania** *etc*
round [raʊnd]

> *When* **round** *is an element in a phrasal verb, eg* **ask round, call round, rally round**, *look up the verb.*

(ADJ) (COMPAR: **rounder**, SUPERL: **roundest**) (*gen*) redondo; [*sum, number*] redondo • **a ~ dozen** una docena redonda • **in ~ figures** *or* **numbers** en números redondos
(ADV) • **the park is eight miles ~** el parque tiene un perímetro de ocho millas • **there is a fence all ~** está rodeado por un cercado • **it would be better all ~ if we didn't go** (*in every respect*) sería mejor en todos los sentidos que no fuéramos; (*for all concerned*) sería mejor para todos que no fuéramos • **all year ~** (durante) todo el año • **drinks all ~!** ¡pago la ronda para todos! • **we shook hands all ~** todos nos dimos la mano • **to ask sb ~** invitar a algn a casa *or* a pasar (por casa) • **we were ~ at my sister's** estábamos en casa de mi hermana • **we'll be ~ at the pub** estaremos en el bar • **the wheels go ~** las ruedas giran *or* dan vuelta • **it flew round and round** voló dando vueltas • **the long way ~** el camino más largo • **it's a long way ~** es mucho rodeo • **the other/wrong way ~** al revés
(PREP) **1** (*of place etc*) alrededor de • **we were sitting ~ the table/fire** estábamos sentados alrededor de la mesa/en torno a la chimenea • **the wall ~ the garden** el muro que rodea el jardín • **a walk ~ the town** un paseo por la ciudad • **all the people ~ about** toda la gente alrededor • **all ~ the house** (*inside*) por toda la casa; (*outside*) alrededor de toda la casa • **she's 36 inches ~ the bust** tiene 90 de busto *or* de pecho • **~ the clock** (= *at any time*) a todas horas, a cualquier hora; (= *non-stop*) permanentemente, día y noche, las 24 horas del día • **~ the corner** a la vuelta de la esquina • **are you from ~ here?** ¿eres de por aquí? • **to look ~ the shop** echar una mirada por la tienda • **wear it ~ your neck** llévalo en el cuello • **he sells them ~ the pubs** los vende de bar en bar • **when you're ~ this way** cuando pases por aquí • **a trip ~ the world** un viaje alrededor del mundo
2 (*esp Brit*) (= *approximately*) (*also* **round about**) alrededor de, más o menos • **~ four o'clock** a eso de las cuatro • **~ about £50** alrededor de 50 libras, 50 libras más o menos • **somewhere ~ Derby** cerca de Derby • **somewhere ~ that sum** esa cantidad más o menos
3 (= *using as theme*) • **it's written ~ the Suez episode** tiene por tema principal el episodio de Suez
(N) **1** (= *circle*) círculo *m*; (= *slice*) tajada *f*, rodaja *f* • **a ~ of sandwiches** (*Brit*) un sandwich • **a ~ of toast** una tostada
2 [*of postman, milkman etc*] recorrido *m*; [*of watchman*] ronda *f* • **the watchman was doing his ~** el vigilante estaba de ronda • **the story is going the ~s that ...** se dice *or* se rumorea que ... • **she did** *or* **went** *or* **made the ~s of the agencies** visitó *or* recorrió todas las agencias • **the story went the ~s of the club** el chiste se contó en todos los corrillos del club • **the doctor's on his ~s** el médico está haciendo sus visitas
3 (*Boxing*) asalto *m*, round *m*; (*Golf*) partido *m*, recorrido *m*, vuelta *f*; (*Showjumping*) recorrido *m*; (*Cards*) (= *game*) partida *f*; (*in tournament*) vuelta *f* • **to have a clear ~** hacer un recorrido sin penalizaciones • **the first ~ of the elections** la primera vuelta de las elecciones
4 [*of drinks*] ronda *f* • **whose ~ is it?** ¿a quién le toca (pagar)? • **it's my ~** yo invito, me toca a mí • **~ of ammunition** cartucho *m*, bala *f*, tiro *m* • **~ of applause** salva *f* de aplausos • **let's have a ~ of applause for ...** demos un fuerte aplauso a ... • **~ of shots** descarga *f*
5 (= *series*) • **the first ~ of negotiations** la primera ronda de negociaciones • **life was one long ~ of parties** la vida consistía en una sucesión constante de fiestas
6 (= *routine*) • **the daily ~** la rutina cotidiana
7 • **in the ~** (*Theat*) circular, en redondo
8 (*Mus*) canon *m*
(VT) **1** (= *make round*) [+ *lips, edges*] redondear
2 (= *go round*) [+ *corner*] doblar, dar la vuelta a; (*Naut*) doblar • **the ship ~ed the headland** el buque dobló el promontorio
(CPD) ▸ **round arch** arco *m* de medio punto
▸ **round dance** baile *m* en corro ▸ **round robin** (= *request*) petición *f* firmada en rueda; (= *protest*) protesta *f* firmada en rueda
▸ **Round Table** (*Hist*) Mesa *f* Redonda
▸ **round table** (= *conference*) mesa *f* redonda
▸ **round trip** viaje *m* de ida y vuelta • **~ trip ticket** (*US*) billete *m* de ida y vuelta
▸ **round down** (VT + ADV) [+ *price etc*] redondear (rebajando)
▸ **round off** (VT + ADV) acabar, rematar • **to ~ off the evening** dar el remate a la fiesta
▸ **round on, round upon** (VI + PREP) volverse en contra de
▸ **round up** (VT + ADV) [+ *cattle*] acorralar, rodear; [+ *friends*] reunir; [+ *criminals*] coger, agarrar (*LAm*); [+ *figures*] redondear por arriba
roundabout ['raʊndəbaʊt] (ADJ) indirecto • **by a ~ way** dando un rodeo, por una ruta alternativa • **to speak in a ~ way** ir con rodeos, hablar con circunloquios
(N) **1** (*Brit*) (*at fair*) tiovivo *m*; (*in playground*) carrusel *m*, *plataforma giratoria que se instala en parques infantiles para que los niños la empujen y se monten*
2 (*Brit*) (*Aut*) cruce *m* giratorio, glorieta *f*, rotonda *f* (*S. Cone*), redoma *f* (*Carib*)
rounded ['raʊndɪd] (ADJ) **1** (= *curved*) [*shape, hills, hips, shoulders*] redondeado; [*face*] redondo, relleno; [*handwriting*] redondo
2 (= *complete, mature*) [*style, film, book*] pulido, maduro; [*individual*] maduro, equilibrado; [*character*] (*in novel etc*) bien desarrollado; [*education*] completo; [*flavour*] equilibrado

3 (= *resonant*) [*vowel*] redondeado • **the beautifully ~ tone of the clarinet** el tono profundo y lleno de belleza del clarinete
4 (*Culin*) [*tablespoon, dessertspoon*] casi colmado
roundelay [ˈraʊndɪleɪ] N (= *song*) canción *f* que se canta en rueda; (= *dance*) baile *m* en círculo
rounder [ˈraʊndəʳ] N (*Brit*) (*Sport*) • **to score a ~** marcar una carrera
rounders [ˈraʊndəz] NSING (*Brit*) *juego similar al béisbol*
round-eyed [ˈraʊndˈaɪd] ADJ, ADV • **to look at sb round-eyed** mirar a algn con los ojos desorbitados
round-faced [ˈraʊndˈfeɪst] ADJ de cara redonda
Roundhead [ˈraʊndhed] N (*Brit*) (*Hist*) cabeza *f* pelada
roundhouse [ˈraʊndhaʊs] N (PL: **roundhouses** [ˈraʊndhaʊzɪz]) **1** (*Rail*) cocherón *m* circular, rotonda *f* para locomotoras
2 (*Naut††*) chupeta *f*
roundly [ˈraʊndlɪ] ADV [*condemn, criticize*] duramente; [*reject, deny*] categóricamente, rotundamente • **he was ~ defeated in the election** sufrió una derrota aplastante en las elecciones
round-necked [ˈraʊndˌnekt] ADJ • **round-necked pullover** jersey *m* de cuello cerrado *or* redondo
roundness [ˈraʊndnɪs] N redondez *f*, rotundidad *f*
round-shouldered [ˈraʊndˈʃəʊldəd] ADJ cargado de espaldas
roundsman [ˈraʊndzmən] N (PL: **roundsmen**) (*Brit*) repartidor *m or* proveedor *m* casero
round-table discussion [ˌraʊndˌteɪbldɪsˈkʌʃən] N mesa *f* redonda
round-the-clock [ˈraʊndðəˈklɒk] ADJ (*surveillance etc*) de veinticuatro horas
round-up [ˈraʊndʌp] N (*Agr*) rodeo *m*; [*of suspects etc*] detención *f*; (*by police*) redada *f* • **a round-up of the latest news** un resumen de las últimas noticias
roundworm [ˈraʊndwɜːm] N lombriz *f* intestinal
rouse [raʊz] VT [*+ person*] despertar; [*+ interest*] despertar, suscitar; [*+ anger*] provocar • **to ~ sb from sleep** despertar a algn • **it ~d the whole house** despertó a todo el mundo • **to ~ sb to action** mover a algn a actuar • **to ~ sb to fury** enfurecer a algn • **to ~ o.s.** despertarse • **to ~ o.s. to do sth** animarse a hacer algo • **he ~d himself from his lazy contemplation of the scene** salió del ensimismamiento indiferente con el que contemplaba la escena
VI despertar, despertarse
rousing [ˈraʊzɪŋ] ADJ [*applause*] caluroso; [*song*] vivo, lleno de vigor; [*speech*] conmovedor; [*welcome*] emocionado, entusiasta
Roussillon [rusijɔ̃] N Rosellón *m*
roust [raʊst] VT (*US*) (*also* **roust out**) hacer salir bruscamente
roustabout* [ˈraʊstəbaʊt] N (*US*) peón *m*
rout¹ [raʊt] N (= *defeat*) derrota *f* aplastante; (= *flight*) desbandada *f*, fuga *f* desordenada
VT aplastar, derrotar aplastantemente • **the enemy was ~ed** (= *defeated*) el enemigo fue aplastado; (= *put to flight*) el enemigo salió en desbandada
rout² [raʊt] VI (*also* **rout about**) (= *search*) hurgar
▸ **rout out** VT + ADV **1** (= *force out*) • **to ~ sb out** hacer salir a algn • **to ~ sb out of bed** sacar a algn de la cama
2 (= *search for*) buscar; (= *discover*) desenterrar
route [ruːt] N **1** (*gen*) ruta *f*, camino *m*; [*of bus*] recorrido *m*; [*of ship*] rumbo *m*, derrota *f*; (= *itinerary*) itinerario *m*; (= *direction*) rumbo *m* • **Route 31** (*US*) Ruta 31 • **the ~ to the coast** el camino de la costa • **to go by a new ~** seguir una ruta nueva • **shipping ~** vía *f* marítima • **air ~** ruta *f* aérea
2 (*US*) [ruːt, raʊt] (= *delivery round*) recorrido *m*
VT fijar el itinerario de; (*Comput*) encaminar • **the train is now ~d through Derby** ahora el tren pasa por Derby
CPD ▸ **route map** mapa *m* de carreteras ▸ **route march** marcha *f* de entrenamiento
router [ˈruːtəʳ] N (*Comput*) router *m*, enrutador *m*, encaminador *m*
routine [ruːˈtiːn] N **1** (= *normal procedure*) rutina *f* • **the daily ~** la rutina diaria • **the school ~** la rutina escolar • **she went through the ~ of introducing everyone** hizo las presentaciones de rigor • **as a matter of ~** como parte de la rutina • **people entering the country are asked certain questions as a matter of ~** como parte de la rutina a la gente que entra en el país se le hacen ciertas preguntas • **schoolchildren were tested for tuberculosis as a matter of ~** de forma rutinaria *or* rutinariamente se les hacía a los alumnos la prueba de la tuberculosis
2 (*esp Theat*) número *m* • **dance ~** número *m* de baile • **exercise ~** tabla *f* de ejercicios
3 (= *spiel*) • **he gave me the old ~ about his wife not understanding him*** me vino con la historia de siempre de que su mujer no le entendía • **he went through his sales ~** metió el típico rollo de vendedor
4 (*Comput*) rutina *f*
ADJ [*test, check-up, maintenance, inspection*] de rutina; [*matter, problem*] rutinario; [*work*] habitual, de rutina • **to make ~ enquiries** hacer averiguaciones rutinarias *or* de rutina • **it's just ~** es cosa de rutina • **reports of thefts had become almost ~** las denuncias de robos se habían convertido en algo casi habitual • **on a ~ basis** de forma rutinaria
routinely [ruːˈtiːnlɪ] ADV [*use, check*] de forma rutinaria, rutinariamente • **the drug is ~ used to treat depression** el fármaco es utilizado rutinariamente para el tratamiento de la depresión • **she ~ works a 60-hour week** trabajar 60 horas por semana forma parte de su rutina
routing [ˈruːtɪŋ] N (*Comput*) encaminamiento *m*
rove [rəʊv] VT vagar *or* errar por, recorrer
VI vagar, errar • **his eye ~d over the room** recorrió la habitación con la vista
▸ **rove about, rove around** VI + PREP [*+ place*] [*person*] vagar por; [*eyes*] recorrer
rover [ˈrəʊvəʳ] N vagabundo/a *m/f*
roving [ˈrəʊvɪŋ] ADJ (= *wandering*) errante; [*salesman*] ambulante; [*ambassador*] itinerante; [*disposition*] andariego • **to have a ~ commission** (*fig*) tener vía libre para investigar donde sea necesario • **he has a ~ eye** se le van los ojos tras las faldas
CPD ▸ **roving reporter** enviado/a *m/f* especial
row¹ [rəʊ] N (= *line*) fila *f*, hilera *f*; (*Theat etc*) fila *f*; [*of books, houses etc*] hilera *f*, fila *f*; (*in knitting*) pasada *f*, vuelta *f* • **in a row** en fila • **in the front row** en primera fila, en la fila uno • **in the fourth row** en la cuarta fila, en la fila cuatro • **he killed four in a row** mató cuatro seguidos, mató cuatro uno tras otro • **for five days in a row** durante cinco días seguidos
CPD ▸ **row house** (*US*) casa *f* adosada
row² [rəʊ] N (= *trip*) paseo *m* en bote de remos • **to go for a row** pasearse *or* hacer una excursión en bote • **it was a hard row to the shore** nos costó llegar a la playa remando
VT [*+ boat*] remar; [*+ person*] llevar en bote • **you rowed a good race** habéis remado muy bien • **he rowed the Atlantic** cruzó el Atlántico a remo • **to row sb across a river** llevar a algn en bote al otro lado de un río • **can you row me out to the yacht?** ¿me lleva en bote al yate?
VI remar • **to row hard** esforzarse remando, hacer fuerza de remos • **he rowed for Oxford** remó en el bote de Oxford • **to row against sb** competir con algn en una regata a remo • **we rowed for the shore** remamos hacia la playa, nos dirigimos remando hacia la playa • **to row across a river** cruzar un río a remo • **to row round an island** dar la vuelta a una isla remando *or* a remo
row³ [raʊ] (*esp Brit*) N **1** (= *noise*) ruido *m*, bulla* *f* • **the row from the engine** el ruido del motor • **it makes a devil of a row** hace un ruido de todos los demonios • **hold your row!** • **stop your row!** ¡cállate!
2 (= *dispute*) bronca *f*, pelea *f* • **to have a row** reñir, pelearse (*LAm*) • **now don't let's start a row** no riñamos • **the row about wages** la disputa acerca de los salarios
3 (= *fuss, disturbance, incident*) jaleo *m*, escándalo *m*, lío *m*, follón *m* (*Sp*), bronca *f* (*esp LAm*) • **what's the row about?** ¿a qué se debe el lío? • **to kick up** *or* **make a row*** armar un lío; (= *protest*) poner el grito en el cielo
4 (= *scolding*) regaño *m*, regañina *f* • **to get into a row** ganarse una regañina (**for** por) • **you'll get into a row** te van a regañar
VI reñir, pelear (*LAm*) • **they're always rowing** siempre están riñendo • **to row with sb** reñir *or* pelearse con algn
rowan [ˈraʊən] N (*also* **rowan tree**) serbal *m*; (= *berry*) serba *f*
rowboat [ˈrəʊbəʊt] N (*US*) = **rowing boat**
rowdiness [ˈraʊdɪnɪs] N escándalo *m*, alboroto *m*
rowdy [ˈraʊdɪ] ADJ (COMPAR: **rowdier**, SUPERL: **rowdiest**) [*person*] (= *loud*) escandaloso; (= *quarrelsome*) pendenciero; [*meeting etc*] alborotado, agitado
N (= *person*) (= *loud*) escandaloso/a *m/f*; (= *quarrelsome*) pendenciero/a *m/f*
rowdyism [ˈraʊdɪɪzəm] N disturbios *mpl*
rower [ˈrəʊəʳ] N remero/a *m/f*
rowing [ˈrəʊɪŋ] N remo *m*
CPD ▸ **rowing boat** (*Brit*) barca *f* de remos, bote *m* de remos ▸ **rowing club** club *m* de remo ▸ **rowing machine** máquina *f* de remo
rowlock [ˈrɒlək] N (*esp Brit*) tolete *m*, escálamo *m*, chumacera *f*
royal [ˈrɔɪəl] ADJ **1** real • **His/Her Royal Highness** Su Alteza Real • **the ~ "we"** el plural mayestático
2* (= *splendid*) magnífico, espléndido, regio • **to have a right ~ time** pasarlo en grande
N* personaje *m* real, miembro *mf* de la familia real • **the ~s*** la realeza
CPD ▸ **the Royal Academy (of Arts)** (*Brit*) la Real Academia (de Bellas Artes); ▹ RA - ROYAL ACADEMY OF ARTS ▸ **the Royal Air Force** las Fuerzas Aéreas Británicas ▸ **royal blue** azul *m* marino intenso; ▹ **royal-blue** ▸ **Royal Commission** (*Brit*) Comisión *f* Real ▸ **royal enclosure** (*at race course*) palco *m* de honor (*para la Familia Real*) ▸ **the Royal Engineers** (*Brit*) el Cuerpo de Ingenieros ▸ **the royal family** la familia real ▸ **the royal household** la casa real ▸ **royal jelly** jalea *f* real ▸ **royal line** familia *f* real, casa *f* real ▸ **Royal Mail** (*Brit*) • **the Royal Mail** *servicio de Correos en el Reino Unido* ▸ **Royal Marines** (*Brit*)

• **the Royal Marines** la infantería *fsing* de marina ▸ **the Royal Navy** la Marina Británica ▸ **Royal Shakespeare Company** (*Brit*) • **the Royal Shakespeare Company** *grupo de teatro especializado en el repertorio de Shakespeare* ▸ **Royal Society** (*Brit*) ≈ Real Academia *f* de Ciencias ▸ **Royal Ulster Constabulary** (*Brit*) (*formerly*) • **the Royal Ulster Constabulary** *la policía de Irlanda del Norte*

royal-blue [ˌrɔɪəl'bluː] ADJ azul marino intenso; ▹ **royal**

royalism ['rɔɪəlɪzəm] N sentimiento *m* monárquico, monarquismo *m*

royalist ['rɔɪəlɪst] ADJ monárquico N monárquico/a *m/f*

royally ['rɔɪəlɪ] ADV (*fig*) magníficamente, espléndidamente

royalty ['rɔɪəltɪ] N **1** realeza *f*, familia *f* real • **in the presence of ~** estando presente un miembro de la familia real, en presencia de la realeza • **a shop patronized by ~** una tienda que visita la familia real, una tienda donde la familia real hace compras
2 (= *payment*) (*also* **royalties**) (*on books*) derechos *mpl* de autor; (*gen*) regalías *fpl*, royalti(e)s *mpl* (*LAm*)

rozzer‡ ['rɒzəʳ] N (*Brit*) poli* *mf*, guindilla *mf* (*Sp*‡), cana *mf* (*S. Cone*‡), tira *mf* (*Mex*‡)

RP N ABBR (*Brit*) (*Ling*) (= **Received Pronunciation**) *pronunciación estándar del inglés*; ▹ ENGLISH, HOME COUNTIES
ABBR (*Post*) (= **reply paid**) CP

RPG ABBR (*Mil*) = **rocket-propelled grenade**

RPI N ABBR (= **Retail Price Index**) IPC *m*

RPM N ABBR = **resale price maintenance**

rpm N ABBR (= **revolutions per minute**) r.p.m.

RR ABBR (*US*) (= **Railroad**) FC, f.c.

RRP N ABBR (= **recommended retail price**) PVP *m*

RSA N ABBR **1** = **Republic of South Africa**
2 (*Brit*) = **Royal Society of Arts**
3 = **Royal Scottish Academy**

RSC N ABBR (*Brit*) = **Royal Shakespeare Company**

RSC - ROYAL SHAKESPEARE COMPANY
La **Royal Shakespeare Company** o **RSC** es una compañía de teatro británica fundada en 1960 en Stratford-Upon-Avon, el lugar de nacimiento de William Shakespeare. Además de esta sede, la compañía cuenta en la actualidad con otro teatro en el complejo Barbican de Londres y, aunque están especializados en la representación de obras de Shakespeare, también ponen en escena obras de otros dramaturgos clásicos y contemporáneos. En los últimos años la **RSC** ha dedicado la mitad del año a hacer giras por todo el Reino Unido, lo que ha acrecentado aún más su popularidad, con la que ya contaba dada la fama internacional que han alcanzado sus representaciones.

RSI N ABBR = **repetitive strain injury**

RSM N ABBR = **Regimental Sergeant Major**

RSPB N ABBR (*Brit*) = **Royal Society for the Protection of Birds**

RSPCA N ABBR (*Brit*) = **Royal Society for the Prevention of Cruelty to Animals**

RSS N ABBR (= **Rich Site Summary** *or* **Really Simple Syndication**) RSS *m*
CPD ▸ **RSS newsfeed** feed *m* de noticias en RSS

RSV N ABBR = **Revised Standard Version**

RSVP ABBR (= **répondez s'il vous plaît**) (= *please reply*) S.R.C.

rt ABBR = **right**

RTA N ABBR = **road traffic accident**

RTC N ABBR (= **road traffic collision**) accidente *m* de tráfico

RTE N ABBR (*Irl*) (= **Raidió Teilifís Éireann**) *Radio y Televisión Nacional Irlandesa*

RTF ABBR (= **rich text format**) RTF *m*, formato *m* de texto enriquecido

Rt Hon. ABBR (*Brit*) (= **Right Honourable**) *título honorífico de diputado*

Rt Rev. ABBR (= **Right Reverend**) Rmo.

RU N ABBR = **Rugby Union**

rub [rʌb] N **1** (*gen*) • **to give sth a rub** frotar algo • **to give one's shoes a rub (up)** limpiar los zapatos • **to give the silver a rub** sacar brillo a la plata • **to give sb's back a rub** frotar la espalda de algn
2 (*fig*) • **there's the rub** ahí está el problema, esa es la dificultad • **the rub is that ...** el problema es que ...
VT (= *apply friction*) frotar; (*hard*) restregar, estregar; (*Med etc*) friccionar; (*to clean*) limpiar frotando; (= *polish*) sacar brillo a • **to rub one's hands together** frotarse las manos • **to rub sth dry** secar algo frotándolo • **to rub a surface bare** alisar una superficie a fuerza de frotarla • **to rub a cream into the skin** frotar la piel con una crema
VI • **to rub against/on sth** rozar algo
▸ **rub along*** VI + ADV (*Brit*) ir tirando • **I can rub along in Arabic** me defiendo en árabe • **to rub along with sb** llevarse *or* entenderse bastante bien con algn
▸ **rub away** VT + ADV (= *wipe away*) quitar frotando; (= *wear off*) desgastar
▸ **rub down** VT + ADV **1** [+ *body*] secar frotando; [+ *horse*] almohazar
2 [+ *door, wall etc*] lijar
VI + ADV [*person*] secarse frotándose con una toalla
▸ **rub in** VT + ADV **1** [+ *ointment, cream*] aplicar frotando
2* • **don't rub it in!** ¡no me lo refriegues por las narices!
VT + PREP • IDIOM: • **to rub sb's nose in it** *or* **in the dirt** restregarle algo a algn por las narices
▸ **rub off** VI + ADV [*dirt*] quitarse (frotando); [*writing, pattern*] borrarse; [*paint*] quitarse • **to rub off on sb** (*fig*) pegarse a algn • **some of their ideas have rubbed off on him** se le han pegado algunas de sus ideas, ha hecho suyas algunas de sus ideas
VT + ADV [+ *writing, pattern*] borrar; [+ *dirt etc*] quitar (frotando); [+ *paint*] quitar
▸ **rub out** VT + ADV **1** (= *erase*) borrar
2‡ (= *kill*) • **to rub sb out** cargarse a algn*
VI + ADV borrarse • **it rubs out easily** es fácil de quitar, se borra fácilmente
▸ **rub up** VT + ADV pulir, sacar brillo a
• IDIOM: • **to rub sb up the wrong way** buscar las cosquillas a algn

rub-a-dub ['rʌbə'dʌb] N rataplán *m*

rubber¹ ['rʌbəʳ] N **1** (= *material*) goma *f*, caucho *m*, hule *m* (*LAm*), jebe *m* (*Col, Peru*)
2 (*Brit*) (= *eraser*) goma *f* de borrar
3 (*esp US*‡) (= *condom*) condón *m*, goma *f*
4 (*Mech etc*) paño *m* de pulir
CPD [*ball, dinghy, gloves, boots*] de goma *etc* ▸ **rubber band** goma *f*, gomita *f* ▸ **rubber boots** (*US*) botas *fpl* de agua, botas *fpl* altas de goma ▸ **rubber bullet** bala *f* de goma ▸ **rubber cement** adhesivo *m* de goma ▸ **rubber cheque*** (*Brit*) cheque *m* sin fondos ▸ **rubber dinghy** lancha *f* neumática ▸ **rubber gloves** guantes *mpl* de goma ▸ **rubber goods** artículos *mpl* de goma ▸ **rubber industry** industria *f* del caucho, industria *f* cauchera ▸ **rubber plant** ficus *m inv* ▸ **rubber plantation** cauchal *m* ▸ **rubber raft** balsa *f* neumática ▸ **rubber ring** (*for swimming*) flotador *m* ▸ **rubber solution** disolución *f* de goma ▸ **rubber stamp** estampilla *f* de goma; ▹ **rubber-stamp** ▸ **rubber tree** árbol *m* gomero *or* de caucho

rubber² ['rʌbəʳ] N (*Cards*) partida *f*

rubberize ['rʌbəraɪz] VT engomar, cauchutar

rubberized ['rʌbəraɪzd] ADJ engomado, cauchutado, cubierto de goma

rubberneck* ['rʌbənek] (*US*) N mirón/ona *m/f*
VI curiosear

rubbernecker ['rʌbənekəʳ] N mirón/ona *m/f* descarado/a

rubber-stamp [ˌrʌbə'stæmp] VT (*officially*) aprobar con carácter oficial; (*fig*) (= *without questioning*) aprobar maquinalmente; ▹ **rubber**

rubbery ['rʌbərɪ] ADJ gomoso, parecido a la goma

rubbing ['rʌbɪŋ] N **1** (= *act*) frotamiento *m*
2 (= *brass rubbing*) calco *m*
CPD ▸ **rubbing alcohol** (*US*) alcohol *m*

rubbish ['rʌbɪʃ] N **1** basura *f*
2* (*fig*) (= *goods, film etc*) basura *f*, birria *f*, porquería *f*; (*spoken, written*) tonterías *fpl*, disparates *mpl* • **he talks a lot of ~** no dice más que tonterías • **the book is ~** la novela es una basura
ADJ • **to be ~ at sth** (*Brit**) (= *useless*) no tener ni idea de algo*, ser un negado* *or* (*Sp**) un manta en algo
VT* poner por los suelos
CPD ▸ **rubbish bag** bolsa *f* de basura ▸ **rubbish bin** (*Brit*) cubo *m* de la basura, basurero *m* ▸ **rubbish chute** rampa *f* de la basura ▸ **rubbish collection** recogida *f* de basuras, recolección *f* de la basura ▸ **rubbish dump, rubbish heap, rubbish tip** basurero *m*, vertedero *m*, basural *m* (*LAm*)

rubbishy* ['rʌbɪʃɪ] ADJ (*esp Brit*) [*goods*] de pacotilla; [*film, novel etc*] que no vale para nada, malísimo

rubble ['rʌbl] N escombros *mpl* • **the town was reduced to ~** el pueblo quedó reducido a escombros

rub-down ['rʌbdaʊn] N (*gen*) masaje *m*, friega *f*; (*drying*) secada *f* con toalla • **to give o.s. a rub-down** secarse frotándose con una toalla

rube‡ [ruːb] N (*US*) patán *m*, palurdo *m*

rubella [rʊ'belə] N rubéola *f*

Rubicon ['ruːbɪkən] N Rubicón *m* • **to cross the ~** pasar el Rubicón

rubicund ['ruːbɪkənd] ADJ rubicundo

rubidium [ruː'bɪdɪəm] N rubidio *m*

ruble ['ruːbl] N (*US*) = **rouble**

rubric ['ruːbrɪk] N rúbrica *f*

ruby ['ruːbɪ] N rubí *m*
ADJ (*in colour*) color rubí
CPD [*necklace, ring*] de rubí(es) ▸ **ruby wedding** bodas *fpl* de rubí

ruby-red [ˌruːbi'red] ADJ rubí (*inv*)

RUC N ABBR (= **Royal Ulster Constabulary**) *Policía de Irlanda del Norte*

ruched [ruːʃt] ADJ fruncido

ruck¹ [rʌk] N (*Racing*) grueso *m* del pelotón; (*Rugby*) melé *f*; (*fig*) gente *f*, común personas *fpl* corrientes • **to get out of the ~** empezar a destacar, adelantarse a los demás

ruck² [rʌk] N (*in clothing etc*) arruga *f*
VT (*also* **ruck up**) arrugar
VI arrugarse

ruckle ['rʌkl] N, VT, VI = **ruck²**

rucksack ['rʌksæk] N (*esp Brit*) mochila *f*

ruckus* ['rʌkəs] N (PL: **ruckuses**) (*US*) = **ructions**

ructions* ['rʌkʃənz] NPL jaleo *msing*, follón *msing*, tensiones *fpl* • **there'll be ~ if you do that** se va a armar la gorda si haces eso

rudder ['rʌdə^r^] (N) (*Naut, Aer*) timón *m*
rudderless ['rʌdəlɪs] (ADJ) sin timón
ruddiness ['rʌdɪnɪs] (N) [*of complexion*] rubicundez *f*; [*of sky*] lo rojizo
ruddy ['rʌdɪ] (ADJ) (COMPAR: **ruddier**, SUPERL: **ruddiest**) **1** [*complexion*] rubicundo, coloradote; [*sky*] rojizo
2 (*Brit*‡) (*euph*) maldito, condenado*
rude [ru:d] (ADJ) (COMPAR: **ruder**, SUPERL: **rudest**) **1** (= *impolite*) [*person*] grosero, maleducado; [*remark*] grosero • **to be ~ to sb** ser grosero con algn • **it's ~ to stare** mirar fijamente es de mala educación • **it was ~ of you to ignore him** ignorarlo fue una grosería por tu parte • **he was ~ about her new dress** hizo comentarios poco halagüeños respecto a su vestido nuevo • **how ~!** ¡qué poca educación!, ¡qué grosero!
2 (= *indecent*) [*gesture*] grosero, obsceno; [*joke, song*] verde, colorado (*LAm*) • **a ~ word** una grosería, una mala palabra
3 (*liter*) (= *primitive*) [*shelter, table*] tosco, rudimentario; [*tool, device, implement*] burdo, rudimentario
4 (*liter*) (= *unexpected and unpleasant*) • **a ~ awakening** una sorpresa muy desagradable • **a ~ shock** un golpe inesperado
5 (*liter*) (= *vigorous*) • **to be in ~ health** gozar de muy buena salud, estar más sano que un roble
rudely ['ru:dlɪ] (ADV) **1** (= *impolitely*) [*say, interrupt, stare*] groseramente; [*push*] bruscamente • **before I was so ~ interrupted** antes de que me interrumpieran tan groseramente *or* de forma tan grosera
2 (= *crudely*) [*carved, shaped*] toscamente, de forma rudimentaria
3 (= *unexpectedly*) bruscamente • **she was ~ awakened** la despertaron bruscamente; (*fig*) le dieron una sorpresa muy desagradable
rudeness ['ru:dnɪs] (N) **1** (= *impoliteness*) [*of person, behaviour*] grosería *f*, falta *f* de educación; [*of reply, remark*] falta *f* de educación
2 (= *obscenity*) grosería *f*
3 (= *primitiveness*) [*of shelter, table*] tosquedad *f*, lo rudimentario; [*of tool, device, implement*] lo burdo, lo rudimentario
rudiment ['ru:dɪmənt] (N) (*Bio*) rudimento *m*; **rudiments** rudimentos *mpl*, primeras nociones *fpl*
rudimentary [ˌru:dɪ'mentərɪ] (ADJ) (*gen*) rudimentario; (*Bio*) rudimental • **he has ~ Latin** tiene las primeras nociones de latín, sabe un poquito de latín
rue¹ [ru:] (VT) arrepentirse de, lamentar • **you shall rue it** te arrepentirás de haberlo hecho • **I rue the day when I did it** ojalá no lo hubiera hecho nunca • **he lived to rue it** vivió para arrepentirse
rue² [ru:] (N) (*Bot*) ruda *f*
rueful ['ru:fʊl] (ADJ) (= *sorrowful*) triste; (= *repentant*) arrepentido
ruefully ['ru:fəlɪ] (ADV) (= *sorrowfully*) tristemente; (= *with repentance*) con arrepentimiento
ruefulness ['ru:fʊlnɪs] (N) (= *sorrowfulness*) tristeza *f*; (= *repentance*) arrepentimiento *m*
ruff¹ [rʌf] (N) **1** (*Dress*) gorguera *f*, gola *f*
2 (*Orn, Zool*) collarín *m*
ruff² [rʌf] (*Cards*) (N) **1** (= *game*) *viejo juego de cartas similar al whist*
2 (= *act of trumping*) fallo *m*
(VT) fallar
ruffian ['rʌfɪən] (N) rufián *m*
ruffianly ['rʌfɪənlɪ] (ADJ) brutal
ruffle ['rʌfl] (N) arruga *f*; (*Sew*) volante *m* fruncido; (= *ripple*) rizo *m*
(VT) [+ *surface of water*] agitar, rizar; [+ *hair*] despeinar; [+ *feathers*] erizar; [+ *fabric*] fruncir; [+ *bedclothes*] arrugar • **nothing ~s him** no se altera por nada • **she wasn't at all ~d** no se perturbó en lo más mínimo
• IDIOMS: • **to ~ sb's feathers** herir las susceptibilidades de algn • **to smooth sb's ~d feathers** alisar las plumas erizadas de algn
rug [rʌg] (N) **1** (= *floor-mat*) alfombrilla *f*, tapete *m* • IDIOM: • **to pull the rug from under sb** *or* **sb's feet** mover la silla para que algn se caiga
2 (*esp Brit*) (= *wrap*) manta *f* • **travel(ling) rug** manta *f* de viaje
3‡ (*hum*) (= *wig*) peluquín *m*
rugby ['rʌgbɪ] (N) (*also* **rugby football**) rugby *m*
(CPD) [*player, match*] de rugby ▸ **rugby league** rugby *m* a trece ▸ **rugby player** jugador(a) *m/f* de rugby ▸ **rugby tackle** placaje *m*; ▹ **rugby-tackle** ▸ **rugby union** *tipo de rugby en que los equipos tienen quince jugadores*

RUGBY
Se cree que el rugby comenzó a jugarse en el colegio **Rugby** de Inglaterra en 1823. Sin embargo, cuando la **Rugby Football Union** estableció las reglas de este deporte, el juego profesional quedó prohibido, por lo que un grupo decidió formar el **Rugby League**, lo que dio origen a dos tipos distintos de rugby. El **Rugby League** se juega con 13 jugadores por equipo, tiene sus propias reglas y sistema de tanteo y sus jugadores pueden ser profesionales. Se juega sobre todo en el norte de Inglaterra y Australia.
Por su parte, el **Rugby Union** se juega con equipos compuestos por 15 jugadores y es un deporte muy popular en todo el mundo. El carácter amateur de esta versión del rugby se mantuvo hasta 1995, año en que la Federación Internacional de este deporte (**International Rugby Board**) decidió permitir que los jugadores y directivos pudiesen cobrar. Como deporte escolar en el Reino Unido, el rugby es frecuente en los colegios privados, mientras que, en los colegios públicos, el fútbol es el deporte más extendido.

rugby-tackle ['rʌgbɪˌtækl] (VT) placar; ▹ **rugby tackle**
rugged ['rʌgɪd] (ADJ) **1** (= *rough*) [*terrain, landscape*] accidentado, escabroso; [*coastline, mountains*] escarpado • **the ~ beauty of the island** la belleza violenta de la isla
2 (= *strongly built, angular*) [*features*] duro; [*man*] de rasgos duros
3 (= *tough*) [*personality, character*] duro, áspero; [*conditions*] duro; [*individualism*] fuerte; [*determination*] inquebrantable • **hill farmers are a ~ breed** los ganaderos de las montañas son una raza dura de pelar
4 (= *unrefined*) [*manners, character*] tosco, rudo
5 (= *durable*) [*machine, clothing*] resistente; [*construction*] fuerte, resistente
ruggedized ['rʌgɪdaɪzd] (ADJ) (*esp US*) [*product*] resistente, reforzado • **~ laptop** ordenador *m* portátil de máxima resistencia (*Sp*), computador *m* *or* computadora *f* portátil de máxima resistencia (*LAm*)
ruggedness ['rʌgɪdnɪs] (N) [*of terrain*] lo accidentado, lo escabroso; [*of coastline*] lo escarpado; [*of features*] dureza *f*; [*of character*] (= *toughness*) aspereza *f*; (= *lack of refinement*) tosquedad *f*, rudeza *f*; [*of conditions*] dureza *f*; [*of machine, clothing, construction*] resistencia *f*
rugger* ['rʌgə^r^] (N) (*Brit*) = **rugby**
ruin ['ru:ɪn] (N) **1** (= *building*) ruina *f* • **the ~s of a castle** las ruinas *or* los restos de un castillo • **to fall into ~** convertirse en ruinas • **the town lay** *or* **was in ~s** la ciudad estaba en ruinas
2 (*fig*) ruina *f*, perdición *f* • **he faced the prospect of financial ~** se enfrentaba a la posibilidad de la ruina económica *or* de acabar en la bancarrota • **her hopes were in ~s** sus esperanzas estaban destruidas • **my life/career is in ~s** mi vida/carrera está destruida *or* arruinada • **drink will be his ~** *or* **the ~ of him** el alcohol será su ruina *or* su perdición • **the country has gone to ~** el país se ha arruinado; ▹ **rack²**
(VT) **1** (= *destroy*) [+ *reputation, career, life*] arruinar, destruir; [+ *hopes*] destruir, echar por tierra; [+ *plans*] estropear, echar por tierra • **it ~ed his chances of playing in the final** dio al traste con sus posibilidades de jugar en la final
2 (= *spoil*) [+ *clothes, car*] estropear, destrozar; [+ *meal, event, eyesight*] estropear • **look at my dress, it's ~ed!** mira mi vestido, ¡está destrozado! • **don't eat that now, you'll ~ your appetite** no te comas eso ahora, se te quitarán las ganas de comer • **their chatter ~ed my enjoyment of the concert** su charla no me dejó disfrutar del concierto
3 [+ *person*] (*financially*) arruinar; (*morally*) perder • **what ~ed him was gambling** lo que le perdió fue el juego, el juego fue su ruina
ruination [ˌru:ɪ'neɪʃən] (N) ruina *f*, perdición *f*
ruined ['ru:ɪnd] (ADJ) [*building*] en ruinas; [*reputation, career, life*] arruinado; [*hopes*] defraudado; [*plans*] frustrado
ruinous ['ru:ɪnəs] (ADJ) ruinoso
ruinously ['ru:ɪnəslɪ] (ADV) ruinosamente • **~ expensive** carísimo, de lo más caro
rule [ru:l] (N) **1** (= *regulation*) regla *f*, norma *f*; **rules** [*of competition*] bases *fpl* • **it's the ~s** son las reglas, esa es la norma • **the ~s of the game** las reglas del juego • **the ~s of chess** las reglas del ajedrez • **school ~s** reglamento *msing* escolar • **it's a ~ that all guests must vacate their rooms by 10a.m.** por norma los clientes tienen que dejar la habitación antes de las 10 de la mañana • **running is against the ~s** • **it's against the ~s to run** está prohibido correr • **to break the ~s** infringir las reglas *or* las normas *or* el reglamento • **to make the ~s** dictar las normas • **in my job I'm allowed to make my own ~s** en mi trabajo se me permite decidir cómo se hacen las cosas • **to play by the ~s** (*fig*) obedecer las reglas *or* las normas • **I couldn't stand a life governed by ~s and regulations** no soportaría una vida llena de reglas y normas • **~s of the road** normas *fpl* *or* reglamento *msing* de tráfico; ▹ **bend, golden, ground, work**
2 (= *guiding principle*) regla *f* • **~ of three** (*Math*) regla *f* de tres • **~ of thumb** regla *f* general • **as a ~ of thumb, a bottle of wine holds six glasses** por regla general, una botella de vino da para seis vasos • **I just do it by ~ of thumb** lo hago simplemente siguiendo mi criterio
3 (= *habit, custom*) norma *f* • **short haircuts became the ~** el pelo corto se convirtió en la norma • **as a (general) ~** por regla general, en general, normalmente • **he makes it a ~ to get up early** tiene por norma *or* por sistema levantarse temprano; ▹ **exception**
4 (= *government*) gobierno *m*; (= *reign*) reinado *m* • **military/one-party ~** gobierno *m* militar/unipartidista • **the ~ of law** el imperio de la ley • **under British ~** bajo el dominio británico • **under the ~ of Louis XV** bajo el reinado de Luis XV
5 (*for measuring*) regla *f*

VT **1** (= *govern*) gobernar • IDIOM: • **to ~ the roost** llevar la batuta
2 (= *dominate, control*) controlar, dominar • **you shouldn't let work ~ your life** no deberías permitir que el trabajo controlara *or* dominara tu vida • **Mars ~s Aries** Aries está bajo la influencia de Marte; ▹ **heart**
3 (*esp Jur*) (= *declare*) dictaminar • **the court has ~d the strike to be illegal** el tribunal ha dictaminado que la huelga es ilegal • **the motion was ~d out of order** se decidió que la moción no procedía
4 (= *draw*) [+ *line*] trazar; (= *draw lines on*) [+ *paper*] reglar; ▹ **ruled**
VI **1** (= *govern*) gobernar; [*monarch*] reinar • **to ~ over sth/sb** gobernar algo/a algn • **the king ~d over his subjects wisely** el rey gobernaba a sus súbditos con sabiduría • **the British ~d over a vast empire** los británicos poseyeron un vasto imperio • **the ancient dynasties that ~d over China** las viejas dinastías que reinaban en China • **one god who ~s over all mankind** un dios que tiene poder sobre toda la humanidad; ▹ **rod**
2 (= *prevail*) reinar • **United ~s OK** (*in graffiti*) ¡aúpa United!, ¡arriba United!
3 (= *decide*) [*chairman, president*] decidir, resolver; [*judge, jury*] fallar • **to ~ against sth/sb** fallar *or* resolver en contra de algo/algn • **to ~ in favour of sth/sb** fallar en *or* a favor de algo/algn, resolver en *or* a favor de algo/algn • **to ~ on sth** fallar *or* resolver *or* decidir en algo
CPD ▸ **rule book** reglamento *m* • **we'll do it by** *or* **go by the ~ book** lo haremos de acuerdo con las normas ▸ **rule of law** • **the ~ of law** el estado de derecho
▸ **rule in** VT + ADV confirmar • **I cannot ~ anything out and I cannot ~ anything in** no puedo ni descartar ni confirmar nada
▸ **rule off** VT + ADV **1** (*with ruler*) separar con una línea
2 (*Comm*) [+ *account*] cerrar
▸ **rule out** VT + ADV **1** (= *exclude*) [+ *action, possibility*] descartar, excluir; [+ *candidate*] excluir • **military intervention has not been ~d out** no se ha descartado una intervención militar • **a back injury has ~d him out of the match** una lesión en la espalda lo ha excluido del partido • **the age limit ~s him out** el límite de edad lo excluye, queda excluido por el límite de edad
2 (= *make impossible*) hacer imposible, imposibilitar • **the TV was on, effectively ruling out conversation** la televisión estaba puesta, lo que de hecho hacía imposible *or* imposibilitaba toda conversación

RULE BRITANNIA
Rule Britannia es una canción patriótica que data de 1740. La letra, escrita por el poeta escocés James Thomson, celebra el control marítimo del que Gran Bretaña disfrutaba en aquella época. Aunque algunos critican el tono excesivamente chovinista de la canción, **Rule Britannia** aún se canta en algunas celebraciones de carácter patriótico, como la **Last Night of the Proms**. El estribillo reza así: **Rule Britannia, Britannia rule the waves, Britons never never never shall be slaves.**
▹ PROM

ruled [ruːld] ADJ [*paper*] de rayas, pautado
ruler [ˈruːləʳ] N **1** (= *person*) gobernante *mf*; (= *monarch*) soberano/a *m/f*
2 (*for measuring*) regla *f*
ruling [ˈruːlɪŋ] ADJ **1** (= *governing*) [*class, body*] dirigente; [*party*] en el poder; [*monarch*] reinante • **~ planet** (*Astrol*) planeta *m* dominante
2 (= *predominant*) [*passion, factor*] dominante
3 (*Econ*) [*price*] que rige, vigente
N (*Jur*) fallo *m*, resolución *f*; (*Admin, Sport*) decisión *f* • **to give a ~ on a dispute** fallar en una disputa
rum¹ [rʌm] N (= *drink*) ron *m*
CPD ▸ **rum toddy** *ron con agua caliente y azúcar*
rum²*† [rʌm] ADJ (*Brit*) raro
Rumania *etc* [ruːˈmeɪnɪə] = **Romania** *etc*
rumba [ˈrʌmbə] N rumba *f*
rumble¹ [ˈrʌmbl] N [*of traffic etc*] ruido *m* sordo, retumbo *m*, rumor *m*; [*of thunder etc*] estruendo *m*; [*of tank, heavy vehicle*] estruendo *m* • **~s of discontent** murmullos *mpl* de descontento
VI [*thunder*] retumbar; [*guns*] hacer un ruido sordo; [*stomach*] sonar, hacer ruidos • **the train ~d past** el tren pasó con estruendo
CPD ▸ **rumble seat** (*US*) (*Aut*) asiento *m* trasero exterior ▸ **rumble strip** banda *f* sonora
▸ **rumble on** VI + ADV (*Brit*) [*argument, scandal*] colear, seguir coleando • **he ~d on another half-hour*** se enrolló media hora más*
rumble²* [ˈrʌmbl] VT (*Brit*) calar, pillar • **we've been ~d** nos han calado *or* pillado • **I soon ~d what was going on** pronto me olí lo que estaban haciendo
rumbling [ˈrʌmblɪŋ] N = **rumble¹**
rumbustious* [rʌmˈbʌstʃəs] ADJ (*Brit*) bullicioso, ruidoso
ruminant [ˈruːmɪnənt] ADJ rumiante
N rumiante *m*
ruminate [ˈruːmɪneɪt] VI (*lit, fig*) rumiar • **to ~ on sth** rumiar algo
VT (*lit, fig*) rumiar
rumination [ˌruːmɪˈneɪʃən] N (= *act*) rumia *f*; (= *thought*) meditación *f*, reflexión *f*
ruminative [ˈruːmɪnətɪv] ADJ **1** (*Bio*) rumiante
2 (*fig*) pensativo, meditabundo
ruminatively [ˈruːmɪnətɪvlɪ] ADV pensativamente • **"I hope so", he said ~** —espero que sí —dijo pensativo
rummage [ˈrʌmɪdʒ] VI hurgar • **he ~d in his pocket and produced a key** hurgando en el bolsillo sacó una llave • **to ~ about** revolverlo todo, buscar revolviéndolo todo • **to ~ about in a drawer** hurgar *or* revolver en un cajón
N (*US*) (= *clothes*) ropa *f* usada; (= *bric-à-brac*) objetos *mpl* usados
CPD ▸ **rummage sale** (*US*) venta *f* de objetos usados (*con fines benéficos*)
rummy¹* [ˈrʌmɪ] ADJ (*Brit*) = **rum²**
N (*US**) (= *drunk*) borracho/a *m/f*
rummy² [ˈrʌmɪ] N (*Cards*) rummy *m*
rumour, **rumor** (*US*) [ˈruːməʳ] N rumor *m* • **~ has it that …** se rumorea que …, corre la voz de que …
VT • **it is ~ed that …** se rumorea que …, corre la voz de que … • **he is ~ed to be rich** se rumorea que es rico
CPD ▸ **rumour mill** (*Brit*), **rumor mill** (*US*) (= *source of rumours*) rumorología *f*
rumour-monger, **rumor-monger** (*US*) [ˈruːməmʌŋgəʳ] N *persona que difunde rumores*
rump [rʌmp] N **1** (*Anat*) [*of horse etc*] ancas *fpl*, grupa *f*; [*of bird*] rabadilla *f*; [*of person**] trasero *m*; (*Culin*) cuarto *m* trasero, cadera *f*
2 (*esp Brit*) [*of party etc*] parte *f* que queda • **there's just a ~ left** quedan solamente unos pocos
CPD ▸ **rump steak** filete *m* de lomo de vaca *or* (*LAm*) de res
rumple [ˈrʌmpl] VT arrugar; [+ *hair*] despeinar
rumpled [ˈrʌmpld] ADJ **1** [*clothes, sheets*] arrugado
2 [*person, hair*] despeinado
rumpus* [ˈrʌmpəs] N (PL: **rumpuses**) lío* *m*, jaleo *m* • **to kick up a ~** armar un lío* *or* un jaleo
CPD ▸ **rumpus room** (*US*) cuarto *m* de los niños, cuarto *m* de juegos
rumpy-pumpy* [ˈrʌmpɪpʌmpɪ] N (*Brit*) (*hum*) chiquichín *m*, ñaka-ñaka *m*
run [rʌn] (VB: PT: **ran**, PP: **run**) N **1** (= *act of running*) carrera *f* • **at a run** corriendo, a la carrera • **to go at a steady run** correr a un paso regular • **to break into a run** echar a correr, empezar a correr • **to go for/have a run before breakfast** (salir a) correr antes del desayuno • **to make a run for it** (= *escape*) darse a la fuga, huir; (= *move quickly*) echarse a correr • **we shall have to make a run for it** tendremos que correr • **to be on the run** (*from police*) estar huido de la justicia, ser fugitivo • **a prisoner on the run** un preso fugado • **he's on the run from prison** (se) escapó *or* se fugó de la cárcel • **he's on the run from his creditors** se está escapando de sus acreedores • **to keep sb on the run** mantener a algn en constante actividad • **we've got them on the run** (*Mil etc*) los hemos puesto en fuga; (*fig*) están casi vencidos • IDIOM: • **to give sb a run for their money** hacer sudar a algn • **he's had a good run (for his money)*** (*on sb's death*) ha tenido una vida larga y bien aprovechada
2 (= *outing in car etc*) vuelta *f*, paseo *m*, excursión *f* • **let's go for a run down to the coast** vamos a dar una vuelta por la costa
3 (= *journey*) viaje *m*; (*Aer, Rail etc*) (= *route*) ruta *f*, línea *f* • **it's a short run in the car** es un breve viaje en coche • **it's a 30-minute run by bus** en autobús se tarda 30 minutos • **the Calais run** la ruta de Calais • **the Plymouth-Santander run** la línea Plymouth-Santander, el servicio de Plymouth a Santander • **the boat no longer does that run** el barco ya no hace esa ruta
4 (= *sequence*) serie *f* • **in the long run** a la larga • **a run of luck** una racha de suerte • **a run of bad luck** una racha *or* temporada de mala suerte • **in the short run** a plazo corto • **a run of five wins** una racha de cinco victorias
5 (*Theat, TV*) temporada *f* • **the play had a long run** la obra se mantuvo mucho tiempo en cartelera • **when the London run was over** al terminarse la serie de representaciones en Londres
6 (= *generality*) • **the common run** lo común y corriente • **it stands out from the general run of books** destaca de la generalidad de los libros
7 (= *trend*) • **the run of the market** la tendencia del mercado • **they scored against the run of play** marcaron un gol cuando menos se podía esperar
8 (*Comm, Econ*) (= *increased demand*) gran demanda *f* • **there was a run on sugar** el azúcar tenía mucha demanda • **a run on the banks** una gran demanda de fondos en los bancos • **a run on sterling** una gran demanda de libras esterlinas
9 (*for animals*) corral *m* • **ski run** pista *f* de esquí
10 (*Cards*) escalera *f*
11 (*Cricket, Baseball*) carrera *f* • **to make** *or* **score a run** hacer *or* anotar(se) una carrera; ▹ CRICKET
12 (*Publishing*) • **a run of 5,000 copies** una tirada de 5.000 ejemplares
13 (*in tights*) carrera *f*

14 (*Mus*) carrerilla *f*
15 (*Aer etc*) (= *raid*) ataque *m* • **a bombing run** un bombardeo
16 (*US*) (*Pol*) (= *bid for leadership*) carrera *f*, campaña *f*
17 (= *access, use*) • **they gave us the run of their garden** nos dejaron usar su jardín • **to have the run of sb's house** tener el libre uso de la casa de algn
18 • **to have the runs*** andar muy suelto*, tener cagalera‡
(VT) **1** (*gen*) correr • **she ran 20km** corrió 20km • **to run the 100 metres** participar en *or* correr los 100 metros lisos • **let things run their course** (*fig*) deja que las cosas sigan su curso • **to run errands** hacer recados • **to run a horse** correr un caballo • **to run a race** participar en una carrera • **the race is run over four km** la carrera se hace sobre una distancia de cuatro km • **you ran a good race** corriste muy bien • IDIOMS: • **to run sb close** casi alcanzar a algn, ir pisando los talones a algn • **to run it close** *or* **fine** dejarse muy poco tiempo • **to be run off one's feet** estar ocupadísimo; ▹ **mile**
2 (= *take, drive*) • **to run a boat ashore** varar una embarcación • **this will run you into debt** esto te endeudará • **I'll run you home** te llevo a casa • **to run a car into a lamppost** estrellar un coche contra un farol • **to run sb into town** llevar a algn (en coche) a la ciudad • **the sheriff ran him out of town** el sheriff lo echó del pueblo
3 (= *put, move*) • **to run a comb through one's hair** peinarse rápidamente • **to run one's eye over a letter** echar un vistazo a una carta • **to run a fence round a field** poner una valla alrededor de un campo • **to run one's fingers through sb's hair** pasar los dedos por el pelo de algn • **let me run this idea past you** (*US*) a ver qué piensas de esta idea • **to run a pipe through a wall** pasar un tubo por una pared • **to run water into a bath** hacer correr agua en un baño, llenar un baño de agua • **to run one's words together** comerse las palabras, hablar atropelladamente
4 (= *organize etc*) [+ *business, hotel etc*] dirigir, llevar; [+ *country*] gobernar; [+ *campaign, competition*] organizar • **she's the one who really runs everything** la que en realidad lo dirige todo es ella • **the school runs courses for foreign students** la escuela organiza cursos para estudiantes extranjeros • **to run the house for sb** llevar la casa a algn • **a house which is easy to run** una casa de fácil manejo • **he wants to run my life** quiere organizarme la vida • **they ran a series of tests on the product** llevaron a cabo *or* efectuaron una serie de pruebas con el producto
5 (*esp Brit*) (= *operate, use*) [+ *car*] tener; [+ *machine*] hacer funcionar, hacer andar; [+ *train*] poner; (*Comput*) [+ *programme*] ejecutar • **to run a new bus service** poner en funcionamiento un nuevo servicio de autobuses • **we don't run a car** no tenemos coche • **he runs two cars** tiene dos coches • **the car is very cheap to run** el coche gasta muy poco *or* tiene muy pocos gastos de mantenimiento • **you can run this machine on gas** puedes hacer funcionar esta máquina a gas • **you can run it on** *or* **off the mains** funciona con corriente de la red • **they ran an extra train** pusieron un tren suplementario
6 (= *enter in contest*) • **the liberals are not running anybody this time** esta vez los liberales no tienen candidato • **to run a candidate** presentar (un) candidato • **to run a horse** correr un caballo
7 (= *publish*) [+ *report, story*] publicar, imprimir
8 (= *smuggle*) [+ *guns, whisky*] pasar de contrabando
9 (= *not stop for*) • **to run a blockade** saltarse un bloqueo, burlar un bloqueo • **to run a stoplight** (*US*) saltarse un semáforo en rojo; ▹ **gauntlet, risk, temperature**
(VI) **1** (*gen*) correr; (*in race*) competir, correr, tomar parte; (= *flee*) huir • **to run across the road** cruzar la calle corriendo • **to run down the garden** correr por el jardín • **to run downstairs** bajar la escalera corriendo • **to run for a bus** correr tras el autobús • **we shall have to run for it** (= *move quickly*) tendremos que correr; (= *escape*) habrá que darse a la fuga • **to run for all one is worth** • **run like the devil** correr a todo correr • **run for your lives!** ¡sálvese el que pueda! • **to run to help sb** correr al auxilio de algn • **to run to meet sb** correr al encuentro de algn • **he ran up to me** se me acercó corriendo • **he ran up the stairs** subió la escalera corriendo • IDIOM: • **he's trying to run before he can walk** (*Brit*) quiere empezar la casa por el tejado
2 (*of bus service etc*) • **the train runs between Glasgow and Edinburgh** el tren circula entre Glasgow y Edimburgo • **the bus runs every 20 minutes** hay un autobús cada 20 minutos • **there are no trains running to Toboso** no hay servicio de trenes a Toboso • **steamers run daily between the two ports** hay servicio diario de vapores entre los dos puertos • **that train does not run on Sundays** ese tren no circula los domingos
3 (*Naut*) • **to run aground** encallar • **to run before the wind** navegar con viento a popa
4 (= *function*) funcionar • **the car is not running well** el coche no funciona bien • **you mustn't leave the engine running** no se debe dejar el motor en marcha • **the lift isn't running** el ascensor no funciona • **it runs off the mains** funciona con corriente de la red • **it runs on petrol** funciona con gasolina, tiene motor de gasolina • **things did not run smoothly for them** (*fig*) las cosas no les fueron bien
5 (= *extend*) **a** (*in time*) • **the contract has two years left to run** al contrato le quedan dos años de duración • **the contract ran for seven years** el contrato duró siete años • **it runs in the family** [*characteristic*] viene de familia; [*disease*] es algo genético • **the play ran for two years** la obra estuvo dos años en cartelera • **the play ran for 200 performances** la obra tuvo 200 representaciones seguidas • **the programme ran for an extra ten minutes** el programa se prolongó diez minutos, el programa duró diez minutos de más • **the sentences will run concurrently** las condenas se cumplirán al mismo tiempo • **it runs through the whole history of art** afecta toda la historia del arte, se observa en toda la historia del arte
b (*in space*) • **he has a scar running across his chest** tiene una cicatriz que le atraviesa el pecho • **the road runs along the river** la carretera va a lo largo del río • **a fence runs along that side** hay una cerca por ese lado • **the road runs by our house** la carretera pasa delante de nuestra casa • **the path runs from our house to the station** el sendero va de nuestra casa a la estación • **this street runs into the square** esta calle desemboca en la plaza • **a balcony runs round the hall** una galería se extiende a lo largo del perímetro de la sala • **the city has walls running right round it** la ciudad está completamente rodeada por una muralla • **the ivy runs up the wall** la hiedra trepa por la pared
6 (= *flow*) correr; (*Med*) [*sore*] supurar • **your bath is running** tienes el baño llenándose • **blood ran from the wound** la sangre manaba de la herida, la herida manaba sangre • **to run dry** [*river, well*] secarse; [*resources*] agotarse • **the milk ran all over the floor** la leche se derramó por todo el suelo • **money simply runs through his fingers** es un manirroto • **his nose was running** le moqueaba la nariz • **my pen runs** mi pluma gotea • **the river runs for 300 miles** el río corre 300 millas • **the river runs into the sea** el río desemboca en el mar • **you left the tap running** dejaste abierto el grifo *or* (*LAm*) abierta la llave • **the tears ran down her cheeks** las lágrimas le corrían por las mejillas • **when the tide is running strongly** cuando sube la marea rápidamente • **the streets were running with water** el agua corría por las calles • **we were running with sweat** chorreábamos (de) sudor
7 [*colour*] correrse, desteñirse • **the colours have run** los colores se han corrido *or* desteñido • **colours that will not run** colores que no (se) destiñen *or* que no se corren
8 (= *melt*) derretirse • **my ice cream is running** mi helado se está derritiendo
9 (= *go*) • **a rumour ran through the town** corrió la voz por la ciudad • **a ripple of excitement ran through the crowd** una ola de entusiasmo hizo vibrar *or* estremeció a la multitud • **that tune keeps running through my head** esa melodía la tengo metida en la cabeza • **the thought ran through my head that ...** se me ocurrió pensar que ...; ▹ **seed, wild**
10 (= *be*) • **the train is running late** el tren lleva retraso • **I'm running a bit late** se me está haciendo un poco tarde • **the service usually runs on time** el servicio generalmente es puntual; ▹ **high, low¹**
11 (*Pol*) (= *stand for election*) presentarse como candidato/a • **are you running?** ¿vas a presentar tu candidatura? • **to run against sb** medirse con algn, enfrentarse a algn • **to run for office** presentarse como candidato a un cargo
12 (= *say*) • **so the story runs** así dice el cuento • **the text runs like this** el texto dice así, el texto reza así
13 [*stocking*] hacerse una carrera
14 (*Comput*) ejecutarse
(CPD) ▸ **run time** tiempo *m* de ejecución
▸ **run about** (VI + ADV) = run around
▸ **run across** (VI + PREP) (= *encounter*) [+ *person*] tropezar con, encontrarse con; [+ *object*] encontrar, topar(se) con
▸ **run after** (VI + PREP) (= *to catch up*) correr tras; (= *chase*) perseguir; (*fig*) [+ *women, men*] correr detrás de, perseguir
▸ **run along** (VI + ADV) • **run along now!** (*to child*) ¡hala, vete!; (*to children*) ¡idos ya!
▸ **run around** (VI + ADV) ir corriendo de aquí para allá • **I've been running around all day trying to get everything ready** llevo todo el día corriendo de aquí para allá para que todo esté listo • **to run around with** (*fig*) [+ *person*] salir con; [+ *group*] andar con, juntarse con
▸ **run at** (VI + PREP) lanzarse sobre, precipitarse sobre
▸ **run away** (VI + ADV) **1** [*prisoner*] escaparse, fugarse • **don't run away, I need your advice** no te escapes, que necesito que me des tu opinión • **to run away from home** huir de casa • **to run away from one's responsibilities** evadir sus

responsabilidades
2 [water] correr
▸ **run away with** (VI + PREP) **1** [+ money, jewels etc] llevarse; [+ person] fugarse con • **don't run away with the idea that ...** (fig) no te vayas a imaginar que ...
2 (= control) • **he let his imagination run away with him** se dejó llevar por su imaginación • **don't let your feelings run away with you** no te dejes dominar por las emociones
3 (= win easily) • **to run away with a race** ganar fácilmente una carrera
4 (= use up) [+ funds, resources] comerse • **it simply runs away with the money** es que se come todo el dinero
▸ **run back** (VT + ADV) **1** [+ film, tape] rebobinar
2 (= drive) [+ person] llevar (a su casa etc) en coche
(VI + ADV) volver corriendo
▸ **run down** (VT + ADV) **1** (Aut) (= knock down) atropellar; (Naut) hundir
2 (esp Brit) (= reduce) [+ production] ir reduciendo; [+ supplies] agotar
3 (= find) localizar, encontrar; (= catch up with) alcanzar; (= capture) coger, cazar
4 (= disparage) menospreciar
(VI + ADV) [battery] acabarse, gastarse, agotarse; [car battery] descargarse; [supplies] agotarse • **the spring has run down** se ha acabado la cuerda
▸ **run in** (VT + ADV) **1** (Brit) [+ new machine] rodar, hacer funcionar; (Aut) • **"running in"** "en rodaje"
2* (= arrest) detener
▸ **run into** (VI + PREP) **1** (= encounter) [+ person] tropezar con, encontrarse con; [+ problems] tropezar con • **to run into debt** contraer deudas, endeudarse • **the negotiations have run into difficulties** ha habido dificultades que han entorpecido or obstaculizado las negociaciones
2 (= collide with) • **the car ran into the lamppost** el coche chocó contra el farol • **the two cars ran into each other** chocaron los dos coches
3 (= merge) • **the colours have run into each other** se han mezclado or desteñido los colores
4 (= amount to) elevarse a, ascender a • **the cost will run into millions** el coste se elevará a or ascenderá a varios millones
▸ **run off** (VI + ADV) **1** [prisoner] escaparse, fugarse • **don't run off, I need your advice** no te escapes, que necesito que me des tu opinión
2 (= drain away) [water] correr
(VT + ADV) **1** (= print) [+ copies] tirar; [+ photocopies] hacer, sacar; (= recite) enumerar rápidamente • **he ran off the opera in six weeks** (music) compuso toda la ópera en solo seis semanas; (lyrics) escribió el libreto de la ópera en solo seis semanas
2 (= drain away) [+ water etc] vaciar, dejar salir
▸ **run off with** (VI + PREP) = **run away with**
▸ **run on** (VI + ADV) **1** (= continue) prolongarse • **the film ran on too long** la película duraba or se prolongaba demasiado • **the list ran on and on** la lista era interminable
2* (= talk) seguir hablando
3 (Typ) continuar sin dejar espacio
(VT + ADV) (Typ) unir al párrafo anterior
(VI + PREP) • **the conversation ran on wine** el tema de la conversación era el vino • **my thoughts ran on Mary†** mi pensamiento se concentró en Mary
▸ **run out** (VI + ADV) **1** [person etc] salir corriendo; [liquid] irse
2 (= come to an end) [time, food, money] acabarse; [contract] vencer; [supplies] agotarse • **when the money runs out** cuando se acabe el dinero • **my patience is running out** se me está agotando la paciencia, estoy perdiendo la paciencia • **their luck ran out** se les acabó la suerte
(VT + ADV) [+ rope] soltar, ir dando
▸ **run out of** (VI + PREP) [+ food, money] quedarse sin • **I've run out of petrol** me he quedado sin gasolina, se me acabó la gasolina • **I'm afraid we've run out of time** me temo que no nos queda más tiempo or que se nos ha acabado el tiempo • **I ran out of patience** se me acabó la paciencia
▸ **run out on** (VI + PREP) (= abandon) abandonar • **she ran out on her husband** abandonó a su marido • **you're not going to run out on us now?** ¿no nos irás a dejar tirados?
▸ **run over** (VI + ADV) **1** (= overflow) [liquid] rebosar, derramarse; [cup, saucepan etc] rebosar(se), desbordarse
2 (in time) durar más de la cuenta, pasarse del tiempo • **the show ran over by five minutes** la función duró cinco minutos más de la cuenta • **this text runs over by 200 words** este texto tiene 200 palabras más de lo permitido
(VI + PREP) (= read quickly) leer (por encima), echar un vistazo a; (= go through again) repasar; (= rehearse) volver a hacer, volver a ensayar • **I'll run over your part with you** repasaremos juntos tu papel
(VT + ADV) (Aut) atropellar
▸ **run through** (VI + PREP) **1** (= use up) (gen) consumir; [+ money] gastar
2 (= read quickly) leer (por encima), echar un vistazo a
3 (= rehearse) [+ play] ensayar; (= recapitulate) repasar • **let's run through the chorus bit again** ensayemos otra vez la parte del coro • **let's just run through that again** vamos a repasarlo otra vez
(VT + ADV) (with sword etc) traspasar, atravesar
▸ **run to** (VI + PREP) **1** (= extend to) • **the talk ran to two hours** la charla se extendió a dos horas • **the book has run to 20 editions** el libro ha alcanzado 20 ediciones • **the book will run to 700 pages** el libro tendrá 700 páginas en total
2 (= amount to) elevarse a, ascender a • **the cost ran to hundreds of pounds** el coste se elevó a or ascendió a cientos de libras
3 (= be enough for) alcanzar para • **my salary won't run to a car** mi sueldo no alcanza para un coche
4 (= afford) permitirse • **I can't run to a second holiday** no me puedo permitir (el lujo de) otras vacaciones • **we can't possibly run to a grand piano** no podemos permitirnos or nos es imposible comprar un piano de cola
▸ **run up** (VT + ADV) **1** [+ debt] contraer; [+ account] crear, hacerse • **she had run up a huge bill at the hairdresser's** tenía acumulada una factura enorme de peluquería
2 [+ dress etc] hacer rápidamente
3 [+ flag] izar
(VI + ADV) ▸ **run**
(VI + PREP) ▸ **run**
▸ **run up against** (VI + PREP) [+ problem etc] tropezar con • **to run up against sb** tener que habérselas con algn
runabout ['rʌnəbaʊt] (N) **1** (Aut) coche m pequeño
2 (Rail etc) billete m kilométrico
runaround ['rʌnəraʊnd] (N) • IDIOM: • **to give sb the ~*** traer a algn al retortero
runaway ['rʌnəweɪ] (ADJ) [prisoner, slave] fugitivo; [soldier] desertor; [horse] desbocado; [lorry] sin frenos, fuera de control; [inflation] galopante, desenfrenado; [success] arrollador; [victory] aplastante, abrumador; [marriage] clandestino, fugitivo
(N) (= person) fugitivo/a m/f; (= horse) caballo m desbocado
rundown ['rʌndaʊn] (N) **1** (= slowing down, reduction) [of industry etc] cierre m gradual; [of activity, production] disminución f, reducción f
2 (= résumé) resumen m (**on** de) • **to give sb a ~** poner a algn al tanto
run-down ['rʌn'daʊn] (ADJ) [battery] agotado, gastado; [car battery] descargado; [building] destartalado, ruinoso; [organization] en decadencia; [health] debilitado • **to be run-down** [person] estar pachucho*, no encontrarse bien
rune [ruːn] (N) runa f
rung¹ [rʌŋ] (N) escalón m, peldaño m
rung² [rʌŋ] (PP) of **ring²**
runic ['ruːnɪk] (ADJ) rúnico
run-in ['rʌnɪn] (N) **1** (= approach) etapa f previa
2* (= argument) altercado m
3 (in contest, election) desempate m
4 (= rehearsal) ensayo m
5 (Typ) palabras fpl insertadas en un párrafo
runlet ['rʌnlɪt] (N), **runnel** ['rʌnl] (N) arroyuelo m
runner ['rʌnəʳ] (N) **1** (= athlete) corredor(a) m/f; (= horse) (in race) caballo m; (= messenger) mensajero/a m/f; (Mil) ordenanza mf; (Econ) corredor(a) m/f
2 (= wheel) ruedecilla f; [of sledge, aircraft] patín m; [of skate] cuchilla f
3 (= carpet) alfombra f de pasillo; (= table runner) tapete m
4 (Bot) tallo m rastrero, estolón m
5 • IDIOM: • **to do a ~*** largarse* (sin pagar)
(CPD) ▸ **runner bean** (Brit) judía f (escarlata), habichuela f
runner-up ['rʌnər'ʌp] (N) (PL: **runners-up**) subcampeón/ona m/f, segundo/a m/f
running ['rʌnɪŋ] (ADJ) **1** (= flowing) [water] corriente; [tap] abierto; [stream] de agua corriente • **hot and cold ~ water** agua corriente caliente y fría
2 (= continuous) continuo • **a ~ battle** (lit) continuos enfrentamientos mpl; (fig) una lucha continua • **a ~ commentary (on sth)** (TV, Rad) un comentario en directo (sobre algo) • **we can do without a ~ commentary on the plot, thank you!** (iro) ¡podemos pasar perfectamente sin que nos cuentes el argumento de la película a cada paso! • **a ~ joke** una broma continua; ▹ **long-running**
3 (Med) [nose] que moquea; [sore] que supura
(ADV) • **for five days ~** durante cinco días seguidos or consecutivos • **for the third year ~, the weather was awful** por tercer año consecutivo el tiempo era horroroso
(N) **1** (= management) [of business, organization, school] gestión f, dirección f; [of country] gestión f
2 (= operation) [of machine, car] funcionamiento m, marcha f • **to be in ~ order** [vehicle] estar en buen estado
3 (= activity, sport) • **~ is not allowed in the school corridors** no está permitido correr por los pasillos del colegio • **his hobby is ~** le gusta correr • **~ gear** ropa f de correr • **he started professional ~ eight years ago** empezó a correr profesionalmente hace ocho años
4 (fig) • **to be in the ~ for sth**: • **she's in the ~ for promotion** tiene posibilidades de que la asciendan • **to make the ~** (esp Brit) (Sport) ir a la cabeza; (fig) tomar la iniciativa • **to be out of the ~** (lit, fig) estar fuera de combate • **his illness put him out of the ~ for the**

presidency su enfermedad lo ha dejado fuera de combate en lo que respecta a la presidencia, su enfermedad ha acabado con sus posibilidades de conseguir la presidencia • **he's out of the ~ for the job now** ahora no tiene posibilidades de conseguir el trabajo
(CPD) ▸ **running board** (*Aut*) estribo *m* ▸ **running costs, running expenses** (*esp Brit*) [*of business*] gastos *mpl* corrientes; [*of car*] gastos *mpl* de mantenimiento ▸ **running head** (*Typ, Comput*) título *m* de página ▸ **running in** (*Aut*) rodaje *m* ▸ **running jump** (*Sport*) salto *m* con carrerilla • **to take a ~ jump** (*lit*) saltar tomando carrerilla • IDIOM: • **he can (go) take a ~ jump!*** ¡puede irse a la porra!* ▸ **running mate** (*US*) (*Pol*) [*of presidential candidate*] candidato/a *m/f* a la vicepresidencia ▸ **running repairs** reparaciones *fpl* provisionales ▸ **running shoe** zapatilla *f* de correr *or* de deporte ▸ **running stitch** (*countable*) puntada *f* de bastilla; (*uncountable*) bastilla *f* ▸ **running time** [*of film*] duración *f* ▸ **running total** suma *f* parcial • **to keep a ~ total (of sth)** llevar la cuenta del total (de algo) ▸ **running track** pista *f* (de atletismo)

runny ['rʌnɪ] (ADJ) (COMPAR: **runnier**, SUPERL: **runniest**) [*substance*] líquido; [*eyes*] lloroso • **I don't like my boiled egg to be ~** no me gustan los huevos cocidos poco hechos • **I've got a ~ nose** no paro de moquear

run-off ['rʌnɒf] (N) **1** (*Sport*) carrera *f* de desempate; (*Pol*) desempate *m*, segunda vuelta *f*
2 (*Agr*) escorrentía *f*
(CPD) ▸ **run-off water** aguas *fpl* de escorrentía

run-of-the-mill ['rʌnəvðə'mɪl] (ADJ) (= *ordinary*) común y corriente, corriente y moliente; (= *mediocre*) mediocre

runproof ['rʌnpru:f] (ADJ) [*mascara*] que no se corre; [*tights*] indesmallable

runt [rʌnt] (N) (*also fig*) redrojo *m*, enano *m* • **you little ~!** ¡canalla!

run-through ['rʌnθru:] (N) ensayo *m*

run-up ['rʌnʌp] (N) **1** (*Brit*) (*to election etc*) período *m* previo (**to** a)
2 (*Sport*) carrerilla *f*

runway ['rʌnweɪ] (N) **1** (*Aer*) pista *f* (de aterrizaje)
2 (*US*) (*Theat etc*) pasarela *f*
(CPD) ▸ **runway lights** balizas *fpl*

rupee [ru:'pi:] (N) rupia *f*

rupture ['rʌptʃə^r] (N) (*Med*) hernia *f*; (*fig*) ruptura *f*
(VT) **1** causar una hernia en, quebrarse • **to ~ o.s.** causarse una hernia, herniarse; (*fig*) (*hum*) herniarse
2 (*fig*) romper, destruir

ruptured ['rʌptʃəd] (ADJ) [*tank, pipe*] roto; (*Med*) [*organ, tendon*] desgarrado; [*blood vessel*] reventado

rural ['rʊərəl] (ADJ) rural • **~ development** desarrollo *m* rural • **~ planning** planificación *f* rural

ruse [ru:z] (N) ardid *m*, treta *f*, estratagema *f*

rush¹ [rʌʃ] (N) (*Bot*) junco *m*
(CPD) ▸ **rush basket** cesto *m* de mimbre ▸ **rush light** vela *f* de junco ▸ **rush mat** estera *f* ▸ **rush matting** estera *f*, esterilla *f*

rush² [rʌʃ] (N) **1** (= *act of rushing*) • **there was a ~ for the door** se precipitaron todos hacia la puerta • **the gold ~** la fiebre del oro • **two were injured in the ~** hubo dos heridos en el tumulto • **the annual ~ to the beaches** la desbandada de todos los años hacia las playas
2 (= *hurry*) prisa *f*, apuro *m* (*LAm*) • **what's all the ~ about?** ¿por qué tanta prisa? • **we had a ~ to get it ready** tuvimos que darnos prisa *or* (*LAm*) apurarnos para tenerlo listo • **is there any ~ for this?** ¿corre prisa esto? • **it got lost in the ~** con el ajetreo se perdió • **I'm in a ~** tengo prisa *or* (*LAm*) apuro • **I did it in a ~** lo hice deprisa, lo hice muy apurada (*LAm*) • **it all happened in a ~** todo pasó deprisa y corriendo • **he's in no ~** no tiene prisa alguna *or* (*LAm*) apuro ninguno
3 (= *current, torrent*) • **a ~ of warm air** una ráfaga de aire caliente • **a ~ of water** un torrente de agua • **a ~ of words** un torrente de palabras • **the words came out in a ~** las palabras salieron a borbotones
4 (*Comm*) demanda *f* • **we've had a ~ of orders** ha habido una enorme demanda de pedidos • **the Christmas ~** la actividad frenética de las Navidades • **a ~ for tickets** una enorme demanda de entradas • **there has been a ~ on suntan lotion** ha habido una enorme demanda de crema bronceadora
5 (*US*) (*Ftbl*) carga *f*
6 rushes (*Cine*) primeras pruebas *fpl*
(VT) **1** [+ *person*] meter prisa a, apurar (*LAm*) • **don't ~ me!** ¡no me metas prisa!, ¡no me apures! (*LAm*) • **I hate being ~ed** no aguanto que me metan prisa, no aguanto que me apuren (*LAm*) • **to ~ sb into (doing) sth**: • **she knew he was trying to ~ her into a decision** sabía que trataba de meterle prisa *or* (*LAm*) apurarla para que se decidiera • **don't be ~ed into signing anything** no dejes que te hagan firmar deprisa y corriendo, no dejes que te metan prisa *or* (*LAm*) que te apuren para firmar • **we were ~ed off our feet** estábamos hasta arriba de trabajo*
2 [+ *work, job*] hacer con mucha prisa *or* a la carrera • **I ~ed my lunch** comí el almuerzo a toda prisa *or* a todo correr *or* a la carrera • **I'm not going to ~ things** no voy a precipitarme
3 (= *carry, take*) • **reinforcements were ~ed to the scene** mandaron rápidamente refuerzos al lugar del incidente • **he was ~ed (off) to hospital** lo llevaron al hospital con la mayor urgencia • **please ~ me my free copy** por favor, mándenme la copia gratuita tan pronto como puedan
4 (= *attack*) [+ *building, enemy positions*] asaltar, atacar; [+ *opponent, barrier, stage*] abalanzarse sobre
5* (= *charge*) soplar*, clavar‡
(VI) **1** (= *run*) • **to ~ downstairs** bajar la escalera corriendo *or* a toda prisa • **to ~ past** *or* **by** pasar a toda velocidad • **everyone ~ed to the windows** todos corrieron *or* se precipitaron hacia las ventanas • **neighbours ~ed to his aid** los vecinos corrieron en su ayuda • **I ~ed to her side** corrí a su lado • **to ~ upstairs** subir la escalera corriendo *or* a toda prisa
2 (= *hurry*) • **I must ~** me voy corriendo • **don't ~!** ¡con calma! • **I was ~ing to finish it** me daba prisa *or* (*LAm*) me estaba apurando por terminarlo • **people are ~ing to buy the book** la gente corre a comprar el libro • **the blood ~ed to her cheeks** *or* **face** enrojeció violentamente • **to ~ to conclusions** sacar conclusiones precipitadas • **the train went ~ing into the tunnel** el tren entró en el túnel a toda velocidad • **he will not ~ into any decisions** no tomará ninguna decisión precipitada • **the sound of ~ing water** el sonido de agua corriendo con fuerza; ▹ **headlong**
(CPD) ▸ **rush hour** hora *f* punta, hora *f* pico (*LAm*) • **~ hour traffic** tráfico *m* de hora punta *or* (*LAm*) de hora pico ▸ **rush job** (= *urgent*) trabajo *m* urgente; (= *too hurried*) trabajo *m* hecho deprisa y corriendo ▸ **rush order** pedido *m* urgente

▸ **rush about, rush around** (VI + ADV) correr de un lado a otro, correr de acá para allá
▸ **rush at** (VI + PREP) **1** (= *run towards*) [+ *door, exit*] precipitarse hacia; [+ *person*] abalanzarse sobre
2 (= *hurry*) • **you tend to ~ at things** sueles precipitarte al hacer las cosas
▸ **rush away** (VI + ADV) irse corriendo, largarse a toda prisa* • **don't go ~ing away!** ¡no te vayas tan deprisa!
▸ **rush in** (VI + ADV) (*lit*) entrar corriendo, entrar a toda prisa; (*fig*) precipitarse • **before you ~ in, get some advice** no te precipites, pide consejo; ▹ **fool**
▸ **rush off** (VI + ADV) irse corriendo, largarse a toda prisa* • **don't ~ off!** ¡no te vayas tan deprisa! • **don't ~ off and buy the first one you see** no vayas corriendo y compres el primero que veas
▸ **rush out** (VT + ADV) [+ *book*] publicar a toda prisa; [+ *statement*] hacer público a toda prisa
(VI + ADV) salir corriendo
▸ **rush over** (VI + ADV) ir/venir corriendo
▸ **rush through** (VI + PREP) [+ *meal*] comer a toda prisa *or* a todo correr; [+ *work, job*] hacer a toda prisa *or* a todo correr *or* a la carrera; [+ *place*] pasar a toda velocidad • **we ~ed through dinner** cenamos a toda prisa *or* a todo correr *or* a la carrera • **the orchestra ~ed through the Mozart** la orquesta impuso un ritmo demasiado rápido a la pieza de Mozart
(VT + ADV) [+ *legislation*] aprobar a toda prisa; (*Comm*) [+ *order, supplies*] despachar rápidamente
▸ **rush up** (VI + ADV) = **rush over**

rushed [rʌʃt] (ADJ) • **I didn't feel ~ or under pressure** no sentí que me estuvieran metiendo prisa *or* presionando, no me sentí presionado *or* (*LAm*) apurado • **breakfast had been a ~ affair** habíamos desayunado a toda prisa *or* a todo correr *or* a la carrera

rushy ['rʌʃɪ] (ADJ) juncoso

rusk [rʌsk] (N) (*esp Brit*) (*esp for babies*) galleta *f*, bizcocho *m* tostado

russet ['rʌsɪt] (N) (= *colour*) color *m* rojizo *or* bermejo
(ADJ) (*in colour*) rojizo, bermejo

Russia ['rʌʃə] (N) Rusia *f*

Russian ['rʌʃən] (ADJ) ruso
(N) **1** (= *person*) ruso/a *m/f*
2 (*Ling*) ruso *m*
(CPD) ▸ **Russian doll** muñeca *f* rusa ▸ **the Russian Federation** la Federación Rusa ▸ **Russian Orthodox Church** Iglesia *f* Ortodoxa Rusa ▸ **Russian roulette** ruleta *f* rusa ▸ **Russian salad** ensaladilla *f* (rusa), ensalada *f* rusa

Russki*, Russky* ['rʌskɪ] (ADJ), (N) (*esp US*) (*pej, hum*) = **Russian**

rust [rʌst] (N) (= *action*) oxidación *f*; (= *substance*) orín *m*, herrumbre *f*, óxido *m*; (= *colour*) color *m* herrumbre *or* de orín; (*Agr*) roya *f*
(VI) oxidarse, aherrumbrarse
(VT) oxidar, aherrumbrar
(CPD) ▸ **the Rust Belt** (*US*) el cinturón industrial; ▹ SUNBELT ▸ **rust bucket*** (= *car, boat*) montón *m* de chatarra*

rust-coloured, rust-colored (*US*) ['rʌst,kʌləd] (ADJ) de color herrumbre *or* de orín

rusted ['rʌstɪd] (ADJ) oxidado, aherrumbrado

rustic ['rʌstɪk] (ADJ) [*pursuits*] rústico, del campo; [*restaurant, cottage*] rústico, de campo; [*style*] rústico; [*setting, atmosphere*] rústico, campestre
(N) aldeano/a *m/f*

rusticate ['rʌstɪkeɪt] (VT) (*Brit*) (*Univ*) suspender temporalmente
(VI) rusticar
rustication [,rʌstɪ'keɪʃən] (N) (*Brit*) (*Univ*) suspensión *f* temporal
rusticity [rʌs'tɪsɪtɪ] (N) rusticidad *f*
rustiness ['rʌstɪnɪs] (N) **1** herrumbre *f*, lo aherrumbrado
2 (*fig*) falta *f* de práctica
rustle¹ ['rʌsl] (N) [*of leaves, wind*] susurro *m*; [*of paper*] crujido *m*; [*of silk, dress*] frufrú *m*, crujido *m*
(VT) [+ *leaves*] hacer susurrar; [+ *paper*] mover ligeramente, hacer crujir
(VI) [*leaves*] susurrar; [*paper*] crujir; [*silk, dress*] hacer frufrú
rustle² ['rʌsl] (VT) (= *steal*) robar, abigear (*Mex*)
▸ **rustle up*** (VT + ADV) (= *find*) encontrar, dar con; (= *obtain*) conseguir, (lograr) reunir; (= *make*) [+ *meal*] improvisar, preparar • **I'll see what I can ~ up** veré lo que hay • **can you ~ up some coffee?** ¿podrías hacernos un café?
rustler ['rʌsləʳ] (N) ladrón/ona *m/f* de ganado, abigeo/a *m/f* (*Mex*)
rustless ['rʌstlɪs] (ADJ) inoxidable

rustling¹ ['rʌslɪŋ] (N) = **rustle¹**
rustling² ['rʌslɪŋ] (N) (*US*) (*also* **cattle rustling**) robo *m* de ganado, abigeato *m* (*Mex*)
rustproof ['rʌstpru:f] (ADJ) inoxidable
(VT) tratar contra la corrosión
rustproofing ['rʌst,pru:fɪŋ] (N) tratamiento *m* anticorrosión
rust-resistant ['rʌstrɪ,zɪstənt] (ADJ) anticorrosivo, antioxidante
rusty ['rʌstɪ] (ADJ) (COMPAR: **rustier**, SUPERL: **rustiest**) **1** oxidado, herrumbrado, herrumbroso; [*colour*] de orín
2 (*fig*) • **my Greek is pretty ~** me falta práctica en griego, tengo el griego muy olvidado
rut¹ [rʌt] (N) surco *m*, rodera *f*, rodada *f*
• IDIOMS: • **to be in/get into a rut** ser/hacerse esclavo de la rutina • **I need to change jobs, I'm in a rut here** necesito cambiar de trabajo, aquí me estoy anquilosando *or* estancando • **to get out of the rut** salir de la rutina
rut² [rʌt] (N) (*Bio*) celo *m* • **to be in rut** estar en celo
(VI) (= *be in rut*) estar en celo; (= *begin to rut*) caer en celo

rutabaga [,ru:tə'beɪgə] (N) (*US*) nabo *m* sueco, naba *f*
ruthenium [ru:'θi:nɪəm] (N) rutenio *m*
ruthless ['ru:θlɪs] (ADJ) [*person, act*] despiadado, cruel; [*efficiency, determination*] inquebrantable, implacable; [*opponent, enemy*] implacable
ruthlessly ['ru:θlɪslɪ] (ADV) [*exploit, suppress, kill*] despiadadamente; [*hunt down*] implacablemente, inexorablemente
ruthlessness ['ru:θlɪsnɪs] (N) crueldad *f*
rutted ['rʌtɪd] (ADJ) lleno de baches
rutting ['rʌtɪŋ] (ADJ) (*Bio*) en celo
(CPD) ▸ **rutting season** época *f* de celo
rutty ['rʌtɪ] (ADJ) lleno de baches
RV (N ABBR) **1** (*Bible*) (= **Revised Version**) *versión revisada de la Biblia*
2 (*US*) = **recreational vehicle**
Rwanda [rʊ'ændə] (N) Ruanda *f*
Rwandan [rʊ'ændən] (ADJ) ruandés
(N) ruandés/esa *m/f*
rye [raɪ] (N) (= *grain, grass*) centeno *m*
(CPD) ▸ **rye bread** pan *m* de centeno ▸ **rye (whisky)** whisky *m* de centeno
ryegrass ['raɪgrɑ:s] (N) ballico *m*, césped *m* inglés

r

Ss

S¹, s¹ [es] (N) (*letter*) S, s *f* • **S for sugar** S de Soria • **S-bend** curva *f* en S

S² (ABBR) **1** (= **south**) S
2 (= **Saint**) Sto., Sta., S.
3 (*US*) (*Scol*) (= **satisfactory**) suficiente

s² (ABBR) **1** = **second**
2 = **son**
3 (*Brit*) (*Econ*†) = **shilling(s)**

SA (N ABBR) **1** = **South Africa**
2 = **South America**
3 = **South Australia**

Saar [zɑːʳ] (N) Sarre *m*

sab* [sæb] (N) (*Brit*) *persona que se opone activamente a deportes que, como la caza, impliquen el sacrificio de animales*

sabbatarian [ˌsæbəˈtɛərɪən] (ADJ) sabatario
(N) sabatario/a *m/f*, *partidario/a de guardar estrictamente el domingo*

Sabbath [ˈsæbəθ] (N) (*Jewish*) sábado *m*; (*Christian*) domingo *m*; ▹ **keep**

sabbatical [səˈbætɪkəl] (ADJ) (*Rel*) sabático
(N) (*also* **sabbatical year**) año *m* sabático

sabbing* [ˈsæbɪŋ] (N) (*Brit*) sabotaje *m* (*de una caza de zorros*)

saber [ˈseɪbəʳ] (N) (*US*) = **sabre**

saber-rattler [ˈseɪbəˌrætləʳ] (N) (*US*) = **sabre-rattler**

saber-rattling [ˈseɪbəˌrætlɪŋ] (N) (*US*) = **sabre-rattling**

sable [ˈseɪbl] (N) (= *fur*) marta *f* cibelina *or* cebellina; (= *colour*) negro *m*
(ADJ) negro

sabot [ˈsæbəʊ] (N) zueco *m*

sabotage [ˈsæbətɑːʒ] (N) sabotaje *m* • **an act of ~** un acto de sabotaje
(VT) (*also fig*) sabotear

saboteur [ˌsæbəˈtɜːʳ] (N) saboteador(a) *m/f*

sabre, saber (*US*) [ˈseɪbəʳ] (N) sable *m*

sabre-rattler, saber-rattler (*US*) [ˈseɪbəˌrætləʳ] (N) *alguien que hace alarde de un poder militar que generalmente no tiene*

sabre-rattling, saber-rattling (*US*) [ˈseɪbəˌrætlɪŋ] (N) *alarde de un poder militar que generalmente no se tiene*

sac [sæk] (N) (*Anat, Bio*) saco *m*

saccharin, saccharine [ˈsækərɪn] (N) sacarina *f*
(ADJ) sacarino; (*fig*) (= *sentimental*) azucarado, empalagoso

sacerdotal [ˌsæsəˈdəʊtl] (ADJ) sacerdotal

sachet [ˈsæʃeɪ] (N) [*of shampoo, ketchup, sugar, coffee*] sobrecito *m*, bolsita *f*

sack¹ [sæk] (N) **1** (= *bag*) **a** (*Brit*) (*for coal, grain*) saco *m* • **a ~ of potatoes** un saco de patatas • IDIOM: • **to look like a ~ of potatoes** parecer un saco de patatas
b (*US*) (*for shopping*) bolsa *f* de papel
2* (*from job*) • **to get the ~** ser despedido • **he got the ~** lo despidieron • **to give sb the ~** despedir *or* echar a algn
3 (*esp US‡*) (= *bed*) • **the ~** la cama, el sobre* • **to hit the ~** echarse a dormir
(VT) **1** (= *put into sacks*) ensacar, meter en sacos
2* (= *dismiss*) despedir • **he was ~ed** lo despidieron • **to be ~ed for doing sth** ser despedido por hacer algo
(CPD) ▸ **sack dress** vestido *m* tipo saco ▸ **sack race** carrera *f* de sacos

sack² [sæk] (*liter*) (N) (= *plundering*) saqueo *m*
(VT) (= *lay waste*) saquear

sackbut [ˈsækbʌt] (N) (*Mus*) sacabuche *m*

sackcloth [ˈsækklɒθ] (N) arpillera *f* • **to wear ~ and ashes** ponerse el hábito de penitencia, ponerse cenizas en la cabeza

sackful [ˈsækfʊl] (N) saco *m*, contenido *m* de un saco

sacking¹ [ˈsækɪŋ] (N) **1** (= *cloth*) arpillera *f*
2* (= *dismissal*) despido *m*

sacking² [ˈsækɪŋ] (N) (*Mil*) (= *plundering*) saqueo *m*

sacra [ˈsækrə] (NPL) *of* **sacrum**

sacral [ˈseɪkrəl] (ADJ) sacral

sacrament [ˈsækrəmənt] (N) (*Rel*) sacramento *m* • **to receive the Holy Sacrament** comulgar

sacramental [ˌsækrəˈmentl] (ADJ) sacramental

sacred [ˈseɪkrɪd] (ADJ) (= *holy*) [*shrine, object*] sagrado • **~ places** lugares *mpl* sagrados • **~ music** música *f* sacra • **~ to the memory of ...** consagrado a la memoria de ... • **a ~ promise** (*fig*) una promesa solemne • **is nothing ~?** ¿ya no se respeta nada? • **~ cow** (*lit, fig*) vaca *f* sagrada • **the Sacred Heart** el Sagrado Corazón

sacredness [ˈseɪkrɪdnɪs] (N) lo sagrado

sacrifice [ˈsækrɪfaɪs] (N) (*lit, fig*) sacrificio *m* • **to offer sth in ~** ofrecer algo como sacrificio • **no ~ was too great** todo sacrificio merecía la pena • **to make ~s (for sb)** hacer sacrificios (por algn), sacrificarse (por algn) • **the ~ of the mass** el sacrificio de la misa • **to sell sth at a ~** vender algo con pérdida
(VT) (*lit, fig*) sacrificar; (*Comm*) vender con pérdida • **she ~d everything for me** lo ha sacrificado todo por mí • **to ~ o.s. (for sb/sth)** sacrificarse (por algn/algo) • **accuracy should never be ~d to speed** nunca debería sacrificarse la exactitud por la rapidez

sacrificial [ˌsækrɪˈfɪʃəl] (ADJ) sacrificatorio • **~ lamb** chivo *m* expiatorio

sacrilege [ˈsækrɪlɪdʒ] (N) (*lit, fig*) sacrilegio *m*

sacrilegious [ˌsækrɪˈlɪdʒəs] (ADJ) sacrílego

sacrist [ˈsækrɪst] (N) = **sacristan**

sacristan [ˈsækrɪstən] (N) sacristán *m*

sacristy [ˈsækrɪstɪ] (N) sacristía *f*

sacrosanct [ˈsækrəʊsæŋkt] (ADJ) (*lit, fig*) sacrosanto

sacrum [ˈsækrəm] (N) (PL: **sacra**) (*Anat*) sacro *m*

SAD [sæd] (N ABBR) = **seasonal affective disorder**

sad [sæd] (ADJ) (COMPAR: **sadder**, SUPERL: **saddest**) **1** (= *unhappy*) [*person, eyes, smile*] triste • **I'm sad that I won't be able to play football any more** estoy triste porque no voy a poder volver a jugar al fútbol, me entristece no poder volver a jugar al fútbol • **we were sad about** *or* **at the news of her illness** nos entristeció *or* nos apenó enterarnos de su enfermedad • **to become sad** entristecerse, ponerse triste • **to feel sad** sentirse triste, estar triste • **to grow sad** entristecerse, ponerse triste • **to be sad at heart** estar profundamente triste, tener el corazón oprimido • **to make sb sad** entristecer *or* poner triste a algn • **he left a sadder and a wiser man** cuando se marchó era un hombre escarmentado
2 (= *distressing*) [*story, occasion, loss*] triste; [*news*] malo, triste • **it is my sad duty to inform you that ...** tengo el penoso deber de informarle de que ... • **the sad fact** *or* **truth is that ...** la triste realidad es que ... • **how sad!** ¡qué triste!, ¡qué pena! • **it is sad to see such expertise wasted** es lamentable *or* da pena ver tanta pericia echada a perder • **it was a sad sight** era una triste escena
3 (= *deplorable*) [*situation, state of affairs*] lamentable, penoso • **it's a sad business** es un asunto lamentable • **a sad mistake** un error lamentable • **sad to say** lamentablemente
4* (= *pathetic*) [*performance, attempt, joke*] penoso • **what sad people they must be if they have to complain about a little innocent fun** si se quejan de que la gente lo pase bien un rato es realmente como para tenerles pena
(CPD) ▸ **sad case*** (= *socially inadequate person*) • **he's a real sad case** es un tipo patético* *or* penoso ▸ **sad sack*** (*US*) inútil* *mf*

> **SAD**
>
> **Position of "triste"**
>
> *You should generally put* **triste** *after the noun when translating* **sad** *in the sense of "unhappy", and before the noun in the sense of "distressing":*
>
> **He always seemed a sad little boy**
> Siempre pareció un niño triste
> **... the sad reality ...**
> ... la triste realidad ...
>
> *For further uses and examples, see main entry.*

sadden [ˈsædn] (VT) entristecer • **it ~s me** me entristece mucho, me da (mucha) pena

saddening [ˈsædənɪŋ] (ADJ) triste

saddle [ˈsædl] (N) **1** [*of bicycle*] silla *f*; [*of horse*] silla *f* de montar • **Red Rum won with Stack in the ~** ganó Red Rum montado por Stack • **to be in the ~** (*fig*) estar en el poder
2 (*Culin*) • **~ of lamb** cuarto *m* (trasero) de cordero
3 [*of hill*] collado *m*
(VT) **1** (*also* **saddle up**) [+ *horse*] ensillar
2* (= *lumber*) • **to ~ sb with sth** cargar a algn

con algo • **now we're ~d with it** ahora tenemos que cargar con ello • **to get ~d with sth** tener que cargar con algo • **to ~ o.s. with sth** cargar con algo
saddle-backed ['sædlbækt] (ADJ) (*Zool*) ensillado
saddlebag ['sædlbæg] (N) alforja *f*
saddlebow ['sædlbəʊ] (N) arzón *m* delantero
saddlecloth ['sædlklɒθ] (N) sudadero *m*
saddler ['sædləʳ] (N) talabartero/a *m/f*, guarnicionero/a *m/f*
saddlery ['sædlərɪ] (N) talabartería *f*, guarnicionería *f*
saddle-sore ['sædl,sɔːʳ] (ADJ) • **he was saddle-sore** le dolían las posaderas de tanto montar
saddo* ['sædəʊ] (PL: **saddos** or **saddoes**) (*Brit*) (ADJ) penoso, patético (N) mamarracho/a* *m/f*
sadism ['seɪdɪzəm] (N) sadismo *m*
sadist ['seɪdɪst] (N) sadista *mf*
sadistic [sə'dɪstɪk] (ADJ) sádico
sadistically [sə'dɪstɪklɪ] (ADV) con sadismo
sadly ['sædlɪ] (ADV) **1** (= *sorrowfully*) [*say, smile*] con tristeza, tristemente
2 (= *regrettably*) desgraciadamente, lamentablemente • **~, we don't have much chance of winning** desgraciadamente *or* lamentablemente, no tenemos muchas posibilidades de ganar • **his uncle, who ~ died** su tío, que tristemente *or* desgraciadamente falleció • **it is a ~ familiar pattern** es un hecho por desgracia familiar • **~ for him** lamentablemente *or* desgraciadamente para él
3 (= *severely*) • **their education has been ~ neglected** han descuidado su educación de forma lamentable • **to be ~ lacking in sth** ser muy deficiente en algo • **he will be ~ missed** se le echará mucho de menos • **you are ~ mistaken** estás muy equivocado • **to be ~ in need of sth** necesitar imperiosamente algo
sadness ['sædnɪs] (N) tristeza *f*
sadomasochism [,seɪdəʊ'mæsə,kɪzəm] (N) sadomasoquismo *m*
sadomasochist [,seɪdəʊ'mæsəkɪst] (N) sadomasoquista *mf*
sadomasochistic [,seɪdəʊ,mæsə'kɪstɪk] (ADJ) sadomasoquista
s.a.e. (N ABBR) **1** (= **stamped addressed envelope**) *sobre con las propias señas de uno y con sello*
2 = **self-addressed envelope**
safari [sə'fɑːrɪ] (N) safari *m* • **to be on ~** estar de safari
(CPD) ▸ **safari jacket** chaqueta *f* de safari, sahariana *f* ▸ **safari park** (*Brit*) safari park *m* ▸ **safari suit** traje *m* de safari
safe [seɪf] (ADJ) (COMPAR: **safer**, SUPERL: **safest**) **1** (= *not in danger*) [*person*] a salvo, seguro; [*object*] seguro • **you'll be ~ here** aquí no correrás peligro, aquí estarás a salvo • **your pearls will be quite ~ in the bank** tus perlas estarán totalmente seguras en el banco • **to feel ~** sentirse seguro • **to be ~ from** [+ *attack, predator, sarcasm*] estar a salvo de; [+ *contamination*] estar libre de • **to keep sth ~** guardar algo (en lugar seguro) • **I'll keep it ~ for you** yo te lo guardo • **where can I put this to keep it ~?** ¿dónde puedo poner esto para que esté seguro? • **the secret is ~ with me** guardaré el secreto • **the documents are ~ with him** cuidará bien de los documentos, con él los documentos están en buenas manos • IDIOMS: • **~ and sound** sano y salvo • **as ~ as houses** completamente seguro • PROVERB: • **better ~ than sorry** más vale prevenir que curar
2 (= *not dangerous*) [*ladder, load, vehicle, option*] seguro; [*method, handling*] seguro, fiable; [*structure, bridge*] sólido; [*investment*] seguro, sin riesgo; [*level*] que no entraña riesgo • **the ~ disposal of hazardous wastes** la eliminación sin riesgos de residuos peligrosos • **is nuclear power ~?** ¿es segura la energía nuclear? • **these stairs are not very ~** esta escalera no es muy segura • **don't walk on the ice, it isn't ~** no andes por el hielo, es peligroso • **keep your alcohol consumption within ~ limits** mantén tu consumo de alcohol dentro de los límites de seguridad • **it's not ~ to go out after dark** es peligroso salir de noche • **it's ~ to eat** se puede comer sin peligro • **it's ~ to say that …** se puede decir sin miedo a equivocarse que … • **it's ~ to assume that …** cabe suponer con bastante seguridad que … • **it might be ~r to wait** puede que sea mejor esperar • **it is a ~ assumption that she was very disappointed** a buen seguro que estaba muy decepcionada • **it's a ~ bet!** ¡es cosa segura! • **to keep a ~ distance from sth** mantenerse a una distancia prudencial de algo; (*when driving*) mantener la distancia de seguridad con algo • **to follow sb at a ~ distance** seguir a algn manteniendo cierta distancia • **to be a ~ driver** conducir con prudencia *or* con cuidado • **a team of experts made the building ~** un equipo de expertos se ocupó de que el edificio no constituyese un peligro • **a ~ margin** un margen de seguridad • **just to be on the ~ side** para mayor seguridad, por si acaso • **the ~st thing is to …** lo más seguro es (+ *infin*) • **he's ~ with children** [*man*] es de fiar con los niños; [*dog*] no es un peligro para los niños
3 (= *secure*) [*environment, neighbourhood, harbour*] seguro • **to be in ~ hands** estar a salvo, estar en buenas manos • **to keep sth in a ~ place** guardar algo en un lugar seguro • IDIOM: • **a ~ pair of hands** (*Brit*) una persona competente
4 (= *trouble-free*) [*arrival, delivery*] sin problemas; [*landing*] sin riesgo, sin peligro • **~ journey!** ¡buen viaje! • **have a ~ journey home!** ¡que llegues bien (a casa)! • **~ passage** paso *m* franco, libre tránsito *m* • **the ~ return of the hostages** la vuelta de los rehenes sanos y salvos
(N) (*for valuables*) caja *f* fuerte; (*for meat*) fresquera *f*
(ADV) • **to play (it) ~** ir a lo seguro, no arriesgarse
(CPD) ▸ **safe area** [*of country*] zona *f* de seguridad ▸ **safe breaker** ladrón/ona *m/f* de cajas fuertes ▸ **safe deposit** (= *vault*) cámara *f* acorazada; (= *box*) (*also* **safe deposit box**) caja *f* fuerte, caja *f* de seguridad ▸ **safe haven** refugio *m* seguro ▸ **safe house** piso *m* franco ▸ **the safe period*** (*Med*) el periodo de infertilidad ▸ **safe seat** (*esp Brit*) (*Pol*) • **it was a ~ Conservative seat** era un escaño prácticamente seguro para los conservadores, el escaño estaba prácticamente asegurado para los conservadores ▸ **safe sex** sexo *m* seguro *or* sin riesgo
safe-blower ['seɪf,bləʊəʳ] (N), **safe-breaker** ['seɪf,breɪkəʳ] (N) ladrón/ona *m/f* de cajas fuertes
safe-conduct ['seɪf'kɒndəkt] (N) salvoconducto *m*
safe-cracker ['seɪf,krækəʳ] (N) (*US*) ladrón/ona *m/f* de cajas fuertes
safeguard ['seɪfgɑːd] (N) resguardo *m* • **as a ~ against …** como defensa contra …
(VT) proteger, resguardar
safe-keeping [,seɪf'kiːpɪŋ] (N) custodia *f* • **in his safe-keeping** bajo su custodia • **to put into safe-keeping** poner a buen recaudo *or* bajo custodia
safelight ['seɪflaɪt] (N) (*Phot*) luz *f* de seguridad
safely ['seɪflɪ] (ADV) **1** (= *without danger*) • **it can ~ be frozen for months** se puede congelar sin ningún problema *or* sin peligro durante varios meses • **you can walk about quite ~ in this town** no se corre peligro andando por esta ciudad, no es peligroso andar por esta ciudad • **drive ~** conduce con prudencia *or* cuidado • **I can ~ say that …** puedo afirmar con toda seguridad *or* sin miedo a equivocarme que …
2 (= *without incident*) [*land, return*] (*gen*) sin ningún percance; (*in the midst of danger*) sano y salvo • **to arrive ~** llegar bien, llegar sin ningún percance
3 (= *securely*) • **all the doors were ~ shut** todas las puertas estaban bien cerradas • **to put sth away ~** guardar algo en un lugar seguro • **she was ~ tucked up in bed** estaba bien metidita en la cama • **the dogs were ~ locked in the van** los perros estaban encerrados en la furgoneta, donde no podían hacer daño • **he's ~ through to the semi-final** ya se ha asegurado el paso a las semifinales • **now that the exams are ~ out of the way we can relax a bit** ahora que no tenemos la preocupación de los exámenes podemos relajarnos un poco
safeness ['seɪfnɪs] (N) seguridad *f*
safety ['seɪftɪ] (N) seguridad *f* • **our primary concern is ~** nuestra principal preocupación es la seguridad • **for his (own) ~** por su seguridad • **people worry about the ~ of nuclear energy** a la gente le preocupa que la energía nuclear no sea segura • **they helped the survivors to ~** ayudaron a los sobrevivientes a ponerse a salvo • **he sought ~ in flight** intentó ponerse a salvo huyendo • **to ensure sb's ~** garantizar la seguridad de algn • **~ first!** ¡lo primero es la seguridad! • **there's ~ in numbers** cuantos más, menos peligro • **in a place of ~** en un lugar seguro • **to reach ~** ponerse a salvo • **for ~'s sake** para mayor seguridad • **with complete ~** con la mayor seguridad; ▹ **road**
(CPD) ▸ **safety belt** cinturón *m* de seguridad ▸ **safety catch** (*on gun*) seguro *m*; (*on bracelet*) cierre *m* de seguridad ▸ **safety chain** (*on bracelet*) cadena *f* de seguridad ▸ **safety curtain** (*in theatre*) telón *m* de seguridad ▸ **safety deposit box** caja *f* fuerte, caja *f* de seguridad ▸ **safety device** dispositivo *m* de seguridad ▸ **safety factor** factor *m* de seguridad ▸ **safety glass** vidrio *m* inastillable *or* de seguridad ▸ **safety harness** arnés *m* de seguridad ▸ **safety helmet** casco *m* de protección ▸ **safety inspection** inspección *f* de seguridad ▸ **safety inspector** (*at workplace*) inspector(a) *m/f* de seguridad en el trabajo ▸ **safety island** (*US*) isleta *f* ▸ **safety lamp** [*of miner*] lámpara *f* de seguridad ▸ **safety lock** seguro *m*, cerradura *f* de seguridad ▸ **safety margin** margen *m* de seguridad ▸ **safety match** fósforo *m* or (*Sp*) cerilla *f* de seguridad ▸ **safety measure** medida *f* de seguridad *or* de precaución ▸ **safety mechanism** (*lit, fig*) mecanismo *m* de seguridad ▸ **safety net** (*in circus*) red *f* de seguridad; (*fig*) protección *f* ▸ **safety officer** encargado/a *m/f* de seguridad ▸ **safety pin** imperdible *m* (*Sp*), seguro *m* (*CAm, Mex*) ▸ **safety precaution** medida *f* de seguridad *or* de precaución ▸ **safety rail** barandilla *f* ▸ **safety razor** maquinilla *f* de afeitar ▸ **safety regulations** normas *fpl* de seguridad ▸ **safety valve** válvula *f* de seguridad *or* de escape; (*fig*)

válvula *f* de escape, desahogo *m* ▸ **safety zone** (*US*) refugio *m*
safety-conscious ['seɪftɪkɒnʃəs] ADJ precavido, preocupado por la seguridad
saffron ['sæfrən] N (= *powder*) azafrán *m*; (= *colour*) color *m* azafrán
ADJ (*also* **saffron yellow**) de color azafrán, amarillo azafrán (*inv*)
CPD ▸ **saffron rice** arroz *m* amarillo (*con azafrán*)
saffron yellow [ˌsæfrən'jeləʊ] ADJ de color azafrán, amarillo azafrán (*inv*)
N color *m* azafrán, amarillo *m* azafrán
sag [sæg] VI [*roof, awning etc*] combarse; [*bed*] hundirse; [*shoulders*] encorvarse; [*rope*] aflojarse; [*prices*] bajar • **his spirits sagged** le flaquearon los ánimos, se desanimó
N (*in roof, ceiling*) combadura *f*
saga ['sɑːgə] N (*Hist*) saga *f*; (= *novel*) serie *f* (de novelas); (*fig*) epopeya *f* • **he told me the whole ~ of what had happened** me contó toda la odisea *or* historia de lo ocurrido
sagacious [sə'geɪʃəs] ADJ (*frm*) [*person, remark*] sagaz
sagaciously [sə'geɪʃəslɪ] ADV (*frm*) sagazmente
sagacity [sə'gæsɪtɪ] N (*frm*) sagacidad *f*
sage¹ [seɪdʒ] ADJ (= *wise*) sabio; (= *sensible*) cuerdo
N sabio/a *m/f*
sage² [seɪdʒ] N (= *herb*) salvia *f*
CPD ▸ **sage and onion stuffing** relleno *m* de cebolla con salvia
sagebrush ['seɪdʒbrʌʃ] N (*US*) artemisa *f* • **the Sagebrush State** Nevada
sage green ['seɪdʒgriːn] ADJ verde salvia
N (*inv*) verde *m* salvia
sagely ['seɪdʒlɪ] ADV (= *wisely*) sabiamente; (= *sensibly*) con cordura
sagging ['sægɪŋ] ADJ [*ground*] hundido; [*beam*] combado; [*cheek*] fofo; [*rope*] flojo; [*gate, hemline, breasts*] caído; [*shoulders*] encorvado
saggy* ['sægɪ] ADJ [*mattress, sofa,*] deformado, hundido; [*garment*] deformado, dado de sí, colgón; [*bottom, breasts*] colgón, caído
Sagittarian [ˌsædʒɪ'tɛəriən] N sagitario *mf* • **to be (a) ~** ser sagitario
Sagittarius [ˌsædʒɪ'tɛəriəs] N **1** (= *sign, constellation*) Sagitario *m*
2 (= *person*) sagitario *mf* • **she's (a) ~** es sagitario
sago ['seɪgəʊ] N sagú *m*
CPD ▸ **sago palm** palmera *f* sagú ▸ **sago pudding** pudín *m* de sagú
Sahara [sə'hɑːrə] N Sáhara *m* • **the ~ Desert** el (desierto del) Sáhara
Sahel [sɑː'hel] N Sahel *m*
sahib ['sɑːhɪb] N (*India*) **1** señor *m* • **Smith Sahib** (el) señor Smith
2 (*hum*) caballero *m* • **pukka ~** caballero *m* de verdad
said [sed] PT, PP *of* **say**
ADJ dicho • **the ~ animals** dichos animales • **the ~ general** dicho general
Saigon [saɪ'gɒn] N Saigón *m*
sail [seɪl] N **1** (*Naut*) (= *cloth*) vela *f* • **the age of ~** la época de la navegación a vela • **in** *or* **under full ~** a toda vela, a vela llena • **to lower the ~s** arriar las velas • **to set ~** [*ship, person*] hacerse a la vela, zarpar • **we set ~ from Portsmouth** nos hicimos a la vela en Portsmouth • **to set ~ for Liverpool** zarpar hacia Liverpool, hacerse a la vela con rumbo a Liverpool • **to take in the ~s** amainar las velas • **under ~** a vela • IDIOM: • **to take the wind out of sb's ~s** bajarle los humos a algn
2 (*Naut*) (= *trip*) paseo *m* en barco • **it's three days' ~ from here** desde aquí se tarda tres días en barco • **to go for a ~** dar una vuelta en barco
3 (*Naut*) (= *boat*) (PL: **sail**) barco *m* de vela, velero *m* • **20 ~** 20 veleros
4 [*of windmill*] aspa *f*
VT [+ *boat, ship*] gobernar • **to ~ the Atlantic** cruzar el Atlántico • **he ~s his own boat** tiene barco propio • **they ~ed the ship to Cadiz** fueron con el barco a Cádiz • IDIOM: • **to ~ the (seven) seas** navegar (en alta mar)
VI **1** (*Naut*) [*boat, ship, person*] navegar • **to ~ at 12 knots** navegar a 12 nudos, ir a 12 nudos • **we ~ed into harbour** entramos a puerto • **we ~ed into Lisbon** llegamos a Lisboa • **to ~ round the world** dar la vuelta al mundo en barco • **to ~ round a headland** doblar un cabo • **to ~ up the Tagus** navegar por el Tajo, subir el Tajo • IDIOM: • **to ~ close to the wind** pisar terreno peligroso
2 (*Naut*) (= *leave*) zarpar, salir • **the boat ~s at eight o'clock** el barco zarpa *or* sale a las ocho • **we ~ for Australia soon** pronto zarpamos *or* salimos hacia Australia • **she ~s on Monday** zarpa *or* sale el lunes
3 (*fig*) • **she ~ed into the room** entró majestuosamente en la sala • **the plate ~ed over my head** el plato voló por encima de mi cabeza
▸ **sail into*** VI + PREP • **to ~ into sb** (= *scold*) poner a algn como un trapo*; (= *attack*) arremeter contra algn, atacar a algn
▸ **sail through** VI + PREP [+ *life, situation*] pasar sin esfuerzo por; [+ *exam, driving test*] no tener problemas para aprobar • **don't worry, you'll ~ through it** no te preocupes, todo te resultará facilísimo
sailable ['seɪləbl] ADJ (*Naut*) [*canal, river, boat*] navegable
sailboard ['seɪlbɔːd] N plancha *f* de windsurf
sailboarder ['seɪlbɔːdəʳ] N windsurfista *mf*
sailboarding ['seɪlbɔːdɪŋ] N windsurf *m*, surf *m* a vela
sailboat ['seɪlbəʊt] N (*US*) = **sailing boat**
sailcloth ['seɪlklɒθ] N lona *f*
sailfish ['seɪlfɪʃ] N aguja *f* de mar, pez *m* vela
sailing ['seɪlɪŋ] N **1** (*Sport*) vela *f*, navegación *f* a vela • **to go ~** hacer vela • IDIOM: • **to be plain ~**: • **now it's all plain ~** ahora es coser y cantar • **it's not exactly plain ~** no es muy sencillo que digamos
2 (*Naut*) (= *departure*) salida *f*
CPD ▸ **sailing boat** velero *m*, barco *m* de vela ▸ **sailing date** fecha *f* de salida (*de un barco*) ▸ **sailing dinghy** barca *f* a vela ▸ **sailing orders** últimas instrucciones *fpl* (*dadas al capitán de un buque*) ▸ **sailing ship** velero *m*, buque *m* de vela ▸ **sailing time** hora *f* de salida (*de un barco*)
sailmaker ['seɪlˌmeɪkəʳ] N velero *m*
sailor ['seɪləʳ] N marinero *m* • **to be a bad ~** marearse fácilmente • **to be a good ~** no marearse
CPD ▸ **sailor hat** sombrero *m* de marinero ▸ **sailor suit** traje *m* de marinero (*de niño*)
sailplane ['seɪlpleɪn] N planeador *m*
sainfoin ['sænfɔɪn] N pipirigallo *m*
saint [seɪnt] N **1** santo/a *m/f* • **~'s day** fiesta *f* (de santo) • **All Saints' Day** día *m* de Todos los Santos (*1 noviembre*) • **my mother was a ~** (*fig*) mi madre era una santa • **she's no ~** (*iro*) ella no es una santa, que digamos
2 (*in names*) • **Saint John** San Juan • **Saint Bernard** (= *dog*) perro *m* de San Bernardo • **Saint Elmo's fire** fuego *m* de Santelmo • **Saint Kitts** (*in West Indies*) San Cristóbal • **Saint Patrick's Day** el día *or* la fiesta de San Patricio • **Saint Theresa** Santa Teresa • **Saint Vitus' dance** baile *m* de San Vito; ▹ **valentine**
3 (*as name of church*) • **they were married at Saint Mark's** se casaron en la iglesia de San Marcos
CPD ▸ **Saint Lawrence (River)** • **the Saint Lawrence (River)** el (río) San Lorenzo
sainted ['seɪntɪd] ADJ [*martyr*] canonizado; [*wife, mother*] santo, bendito; (*of dead*) que en gloria esté • **my ~ aunt!** (*†) (*hum*) ¡caray!*
sainthood ['seɪnthʊd] N santidad *f*
saint-like ['seɪntlaɪk] ADJ = **saintly**
saintliness ['seɪntlɪnɪs] N santidad *f*
saintly ['seɪntlɪ] ADJ (COMPAR: **saintlier**, SUPERL: **saintliest**) (*gen*) santo; (= *pious*) pío; (*pej*) santurrón
sake¹ [seɪk] N • **for the ~ of sb/sth** por algn/algo • **for the ~ of the children** por (el bien de) los niños • **(just) for the ~ of it** (solo) porque sí • **he was talking just for the ~ of it** estaba hablando por hablar • **a film with a lot of violence thrown in just for the ~ of it** una película con mucha violencia añadida que no venía a cuento • **for the ~ of argument** digamos, pongamos por caso • **art for art's ~** el arte por el arte • **for goodness ~!** ¡por el amor de Dios! • **for God's ~!** • **for heaven's ~!** ¡por Dios! • **for my ~** por mí • **for old times' ~** por los viejos tiempos • **for your own ~** por tu propio bien • **she likes this kind of music for its own ~** le gusta este tipo de música por sí misma • **for the ~ of peace** para garantizar la paz • **to talk for the ~ of talking** hablar por hablar; ▹ **Pete, safety**
sake² ['sɑːkɪ] N sake *m*, saki *m*
sal [sæl] N sal *f*
CPD ▸ **sal ammoniac** sal *f* amoníaca ▸ **sal volatile** sal *f* volátil
salaam [sə'lɑːm] N zalema *f*
VI hacer zalemas
salability [ˌseɪlə'bɪlɪtɪ] N (*US*) = **saleability**
salable ['seɪləbl] ADJ (*US*) = **saleable**
salacious [sə'leɪʃəs] ADJ (*frm*) salaz
salaciousness [sə'leɪʃəsnɪs] N, **salacity** [sə'læsɪtɪ] N (*frm*) salacidad *f*
salad ['sæləd] N ensalada *f* • **fruit ~** ensalada *f* de frutas, macedonia *f* de frutas (*Sp*) • **Russian ~** ensaladilla *f* (rusa), ensalada *f* rusa
CPD ▸ **salad bar** (*in restaurant, canteen*) buffet *m* de ensaladas ▸ **salad bowl** ensaladera *f* ▸ **salad cream** (*Brit*) mayonesa *f* ▸ **salad days** juventud *fsing* ▸ **salad dish** ensaladera *f* ▸ **salad dressing** aliño *m* ▸ **salad oil** aceite *m* para ensaladas ▸ **salad servers** palas *fpl* para ensalada ▸ **salad shaker** mezclador *m* para ensaladas ▸ **salad spinner** centrifugadora *f* de verduras
salamander ['sæləˌmændəʳ] N salamandra *f*
salami [sə'lɑːmɪ] N salami *m*, salame *m* (*S. Cone*)
salaried ['sælərɪd] ADJ [*person*] asalariado; [*position*] retribuido, con sueldo
salary ['sælərɪ] N salario *m*, sueldo *m* • **"~ negotiable"** "salario *or* sueldo a convenir"
CPD ▸ **salary bracket** categoría *f* salarial ▸ **salary earner** asalariado/a *m/f* ▸ **salary package** paquete *m* salarial ▸ **salary range** gama *f* de salarios ▸ **salary review** revisión *f* de sueldos ▸ **salary scale** escala *f* salarial ▸ **salary structure** estructuración *f* salarial
sale [seɪl] N **1** [*of item, object, house*] venta *f* • **newspaper ~s have fallen** ha descendido la venta de periódicos • **~ and lease back** venta y arrendamiento al vendedor • **is it for ~?** ¿está en venta? • **the house is for ~** la casa está en venta, esta casa se vende • **it's not for ~** no está en venta • **to put a house up for ~** poner una casa en venta • **"for sale"** "se vende" • **to be on ~** (*Brit*) estar a la venta;

(*US*) estar rebajado • **on ~ at all fishmongers** de venta en todas las pescaderías • **it's going cheap for a quick ~** se ofrece a bajo precio porque se tiene prisa en venderlo • **it found a ready ~** se vendió pronto • **on a ~ or return basis** en depósito
2 (= *event*) rebajas *fpl* • **there's a ~ on at Harrods** en Harrods están de rebajas • **"sale"** (*in shop window*) "rebajas" • **clearance ~** liquidación *f* (total) • **he bought a leather jacket in a ~** compró una chaqueta de cuero en unas rebajas • **the January ~s** las rebajas de enero • **the ~s are on** hay rebajas
3 (= *auction*) subasta *f*; ▹ **jumble**
CPD ▸ **sale goods** artículos *mpl* rebajados ▸ **sale item** artículo *m* rebajado ▸ **sale price** (= *cost*) precio *m* de venta; (= *reduced cost*) precio *m* rebajado, precio *m* de rebaja ▸ **sales agent** agente *mf* de ventas ▸ **sales assistant** (*Brit*) dependiente/a *m/f* ▸ **sales brochure** folleto *m* publicitario ▸ **sales budget** presupuesto *m* de ventas ▸ **sales call** visita *f* de un representante ▸ **sales campaign** campaña *f* de promoción y venta ▸ **sales check** (*US*) hoja *f* de venta ▸ **sales clerk** (*US*) dependiente/a *m/f* ▸ **sales conference** conferencia *f* de ventas ▸ **sales department** sección *f* de ventas ▸ **sales director** director(a) *m/f* de ventas ▸ **sales drive** promoción *f* de ventas ▸ **sales executive** ejecutivo/a *m/f* de ventas ▸ **sales figures** cifras *fpl* de ventas ▸ **sales force** personal *m* de ventas ▸ **sales forecast** previsión *f* de ventas ▸ **sales invoice** factura *f* de ventas ▸ **sales leaflet** folleto *m* publicitario ▸ **sales ledger** libro *m* de ventas ▸ **sales literature** folletos *mpl* de venta ▸ **sales manager** jefe/a *m/f* de ventas ▸ **sales meeting** reunión *f* de ventas ▸ **sales office** oficina *f* de ventas ▸ **sales pitch*** rollo *m* publicitario* ▸ **sales promotion** campaña *f* de promoción de ventas ▸ **sales rep, sales representative** representante *mf*, agente *mf* comercial ▸ **sales resistance** resistencia *f* a comprar ▸ **sales revenue** beneficios *mpl* de las ventas ▸ **sales slip** (*US*) (= *receipt*) hoja *f* de venta ▸ **sales talk** jerga *f* de vendedor ▸ **sales target** objetivo *m* de ventas ▸ **sales tax** (*US*) impuesto *m* sobre las ventas ▸ **sales volume** volumen *m* de ventas ▸ **sale value** valor *m* comercial, valor *m* en el mercado

saleability [ˌseɪlə'bɪlɪtɪ] N vendibilidad *f*

saleable, salable (*US*) ['seɪləbl] ADJ vendible

saleroom ['seɪlrʊm] N (*Brit*) sala *f* de subastas

salesgirl ['seɪlzgɜːl] N dependienta *f*, vendedora *f*

salesman ['seɪlzmən] N (PL: **salesmen**) (*in shop*) dependiente *m*, vendedor *m*; (= *traveller*) viajante *m*, representante *m* • **a car ~** un vendedor de coches • **an insurance ~** un representante de seguros • **"Death of a Salesman"** "La muerte de un viajante"

salesmanship ['seɪlzmənʃɪp] N arte *m* de vender

salespeople ['seɪlzˌpiːpl] NPL vendedores/as *mpl/fpl*, dependientes/as *mpl/fpl*

salesperson ['seɪlzˌpɜːsn] N (*esp US*) vendedor(a) *m/f*, dependiente/a *m/f*

salesroom ['seɪlzrʊm] N (*US*) = **saleroom**

saleswoman ['seɪlzwʊmən] N (PL: **saleswomen**) (*in shop*) dependienta *f*, vendedora *f*; (= *traveller*) viajante *f* • **an insurance ~** una representante de seguros

salient ['seɪlɪənt] ADJ 1 [*angle*] saliente
2 (*fig*) sobresaliente • **the most ~ feature** el aspecto más notable • **~ points** puntos *mpl* principales
N saliente *m*

salina [sə'liːnə] N 1 (= *marsh etc, saltworks*) salina *f*
2 (= *mine*) mina *f* de sal, salina *f*

saline ['seɪlaɪn] ADJ salino • **~ drip** gota-a-gota *m* salino

salinity [sə'lɪnɪtɪ] N salinidad *f*

saliva [sə'laɪvə] N saliva *f*

salivary gland ['sælɪvərɪˌglænd] N glándula *f* salival

salivate ['sælɪveɪt] VI salivar

salivation [ˌsælɪ'veɪʃən] N salivación *f*

sallow¹ ['sæləʊ] ADJ amarillento, cetrino

sallow² ['sæləʊ] N (*Bot*) sauce *m* cabruno

sallowness ['sæləʊnɪs] N lo amarillo, lo cetrino

Sallust ['sæləst] N Salustio

Sally ['sælɪ] N *familiar form of* **Sarah**

sally ['sælɪ] VI • **to ~ forth** *or* **out** salir airado
N salida *f* • **to make a ~** hacer una salida

Sally Army* [ˌsælɪ'ɑːmɪ] N (*Brit*) = **Salvation Army**

salmon ['sæmən] N (PL: **salmons** *or* **salmon**) 1 (= *fish*) salmón *m*
2 (= *colour*) color *m* salmón
ADJ color salmón (*inv*), asalmonado
CPD ▸ **salmon farm** piscifactoría *f* de salmónidos ▸ **salmon fishing** pesca *f* del salmón ▸ **salmon pink** color *m* salmón, color *m* asalmonado ▸ **salmon river** río *m* salmonero ▸ **salmon steak** filete *m* de salmón ▸ **salmon trout** trucha *f* asalmonada

salmonella [ˌsælmə'nelə] N (PL: **salmonellae** [ˌsælmə'neliː]) (= *bacterium*) salmonela *f*; (= *illness*) salmonelosis *f*
CPD ▸ **salmonella poisoning** salmonelosis *f*

salmonellosis [ˌsælməne'ləʊsɪs] N salmonelosis *f*

Salome [sə'ləʊmɪ] N Salomé

salon ['sælɒn] N salón *m* • **hair ~** salón *m* de peluquería • **beauty ~** salón *m* de belleza

saloon [sə'luːn] N 1 (*Brit*) (= *car*) turismo *m*
2 (= *room*) • **billiard/dancing ~** sala *f* *or* salón *m* de billar/de baile
3 (*US*) (= *bar*) taberna *f*, bar *m*, cantina *f* (*esp Mex*)
4 (*on ship*) salón *m*
CPD ▸ **saloon car** (*Brit*) turismo *m*

salopettes [ˌsælə'pets] NPL peto *msing* de esquiar

salsa ['sælsə] N 1 (= *sauce*) salsa *f* brava
2 (= *music*) salsa *f*

salsify ['sælsɪfɪ] N (*Bot*) salsifí *m*

SALT [sɔːlt] N ABBR = **Strategic Arms Limitation Talks**

salt [sɔːlt] N 1 (*Culin*) sal *f* • IDIOMS: • **the ~ of the earth** la sal de la tierra • **to take sth with a pinch** *or* **grain of ~** no tomarse algo al pie de la letra • **to rub ~ into the wound** poner sal en la llaga • **he's worth his ~** es una persona que vale
2 (*Med*) **salts** sales *fpl* • IDIOM: • **like a dose of ~s*** en un santiamén*, en menos que canta un gallo*
VT (= *flavour*) salar; (= *preserve*) conservar en sal; [+ *road*] poner sal en, tratar con sal
ADJ [*meat, water, taste*] salado • **it's very ~** está muy salado
CPD ▸ **salt beef** carne *f* de vaca salada ▸ **salt cod** bacalao *m* salado ▸ **salt fish** pescado *m* salado, pescado *m* en salazón ▸ **salt flats** salinas *fpl* ▸ **salt lake** lago *m* de agua salada ▸ **salt marsh** saladar *m*, salina *f* ▸ **salt mine** mina *f* de sal ▸ **salt pan** salina *f* ▸ **salt pork** cerdo *m* en salazón ▸ **salt shaker** salero *m* ▸ **salt spoon** cucharita *f* de sal ▸ **salt water** agua *f* salada; ▹ **saltwater**
▸ **salt away** VT + ADV ahorrar, ocultar para uso futuro
▸ **salt down** VT + ADV conservar en sal, salar

saltcellar ['sɔːltˌseləʳ] N salero *m*

salted ['sɔːltɪd] ADJ salado, con sal

salt-free ['sɔːltfriː] ADJ sin sal

saltine [sɔː'tiːn] N (*US*) galleta *f* salada, cracker *m*

saltiness ['sɔːltɪnɪs] N 1 (= *salty flavour*) sabor *m* a sal, salobridad *f*
2 (= *salinity*) salinidad *f*

saltings ['sɔːltɪŋz] NPL saladar *msing*

saltpetre, saltpeter (*US*) ['sɔːltˌpiːtəʳ] N salitre *m*

saltwater ['sɔːltˌwɔːtəʳ] ADJ [*fish etc*] de agua salada

saltworks ['sɔːltwɜːks] N salinas *fpl*

salty ['sɔːltɪ] ADJ (COMPAR: **saltier**, SUPERL: **saltiest**) [*taste*] salado

salubrious [sə'luːbrɪəs] ADJ (*frm*) (= *healthy*) saludable, salubre; (*fig*) (= *desirable, pleasant*) [*district etc*] salubre

salubrity [sə'luːbrɪtɪ] N salubridad *f*

salutary ['sæljʊtərɪ] ADJ (= *healthy*) saludable; (= *beneficial*) conveniente

salutation [ˌsæljʊ'teɪʃən] N salutación *f*, saludo *m*

salute [sə'luːt] N (*Mil*) (*with hand*) saludo *m*; (*with guns*) salva *f* • **to take the ~** responder al saludo (*en un desfile militar*) • **to fire a ~ of 21 guns for sb** saludar a algn con una salva de 21 cañonazos
VT 1 (*Mil etc*) saludar, hacer un saludo
2 (*fig*) (= *acclaim*) aclamar
VI saludar, hacer un saludo

Salvadoran [ˌsælvə'dɔːrən], **Salvadorean, Salvadorian** [ˌsælvə'dɔːrɪən] ADJ salvadoreño
N salvadoreño/a *m/f*

salvage ['sælvɪdʒ] N 1 (= *rescue*) [*of ship etc*] salvamento *m*
2 (= *things rescued*) objetos *mpl* salvados; (*for re-use*) material *m* reutilizable
3 (= *fee*) derechos *mpl* de salvamento
VT 1 (= *save*) salvar • **to ~ sth from the wreckage** salvar algo de las ruinas
2 (*fig*) [+ *sth from theory, policy etc*] rescatar; [+ *pride, reputation*] (= *manage to keep*) conservar; (= *regain*) recuperar, salvar
CPD ▸ **salvage fee** derechos *mpl* de salvamento ▸ **salvage operation** operación *f* de rescate, operación *f* de salvamento ▸ **salvage value** valor *m* de desecho ▸ **salvage vessel** buque *m* de salvamento

salvageable ['sælvɪdʒəbəl] ADJ [*object*] recuperable; [*event*] que se puede salvar

salvation [sæl'veɪʃən] N salvación *f*
CPD ▸ **Salvation Army** Ejército *m* de Salvación

salvationist [sæl'veɪʃnɪst] N miembro *mf* del Ejército de Salvación

salve¹ [sælv] VT (= *soothe*) • **to ~ one's conscience** descargar la conciencia
N (*lit*) pomada *f* bálsamica; (*fig*) bálsamo *m*

salve² [sælv] VT (*Naut etc*) (= *salvage*) salvar

salver ['sælvəʳ] N bandeja *f*

salvia ['sælvɪə] N salvia *f*

salvo¹ ['sælvəʊ] N (PL: **salvos** *or* **salvoes**) (*Mil*) salva *f* • **a ~ of applause** una salva de aplausos

salvo² ['sælvəʊ] N (PL: **salvos**) (*Jur*) salvedad *f*, reserva *f*

Salzburg ['sæltsbɜːg] N Salzburgo *m*

SAM [sæm] N ABBR = **surface-to-air missile**

Sam [sæm] N (*familiar form of* **Samuel**) • **Sam Browne (belt)** correaje *m* de oficial

Samaritan [sə'mærɪtn] N • **the Good ~** el buen samaritano • **to call the ~s** (*organization*) llamar al teléfono de la

esperanza
(ADJ) samaritano
samarium [sə'mɛərɪəm] (N) samario *m*
samba ['sæmbə] (N) samba *f*
sambo** ['sæmbəʊ] (N) *(pej)* negro/a *m/f*
same [seɪm] (ADJ) mismo • **two different photographs of the ~ man** dos fotografías diferentes del mismo hombre • **he and Tom were exactly the ~ age** Tom y él tenían exactamente la misma edad • **he will never be the ~ again** nunca volverá a ser el mismo • **the two houses are the ~** las dos casas son iguales • **it's always the ~** siempre pasa lo mismo • **it's not the ~ at all** no es en absoluto lo mismo • **for the ~ reason** por la misma razón • **if it's all the ~ to you*** si a ti te da igual *or* lo mismo • **we sat at the ~ table as usual** nos sentamos en la (misma) mesa de siempre • **the carpet was the ~ colour as the wall** la moqueta era del mismo color que la pared • **the price is the ~ as last year** el precio es el mismo que el año pasado • **their house is almost the ~ as ours** su casa es casi igual a *or* que la nuestra • **"how's Derek?" — "~ as usual/ever"** —¿qué tal está Derek? —como siempre • **the ~ day** el mismo día • **~ day delivery** entrega *f* en el mismo día • **~ difference*** lo mismo da* • **they are much the ~** son más o menos iguales • **they ask the ~ old questions** siempre hacen las mismas preguntas, siempre hacen las mismas preguntas de siempre • **the ~ one** el mismo • **the ~ ones** los mismos • **one and the ~ person** la misma persona • **it comes to the ~ thing** viene a ser lo mismo • **at the ~ time** (= *at once*) al mismo tiempo, a la vez; (= *on the other hand*) por otro lado • **the very ~ day/person** justo ese mismo día/esa misma persona • **in the ~ way** de la misma manera *or* forma • **do you still feel the ~ way about me?** ¿aún sientes lo mismo por mí? • **do you still feel the ~ way about it?** ¿sigues pensando lo mismo?, ¿lo sigues viendo de la misma forma? • **to go the ~ way as sth/sb** *(fig) (pej)* seguir el mismo camino que algo/algn; ▸ **boat, breath, language, mind, story, tar, token, wavelength**
(PRON) **1** • **the ~** lo mismo • **I'd do the ~ again** volvería a hacer lo mismo, haría lo mismo otra vez • **I don't feel the ~ about it as I did** ya no lo veo de la misma forma • **I still feel the ~ about you** sigo sintiendo lo mismo por ti • **the ~ again!** *(in bar etc)* ¡otra de lo mismo! • **the ~ is true of the arts** lo mismo se puede decir de las artes • **all** *or* **just the ~** *(as adverb)* (= *even so*) de todas formas *or* maneras • **no, but thanks all the ~** no, pero de todas formas, gracias • **I want the best for him, the ~ as you** quiero lo mejor para él, igual que tú • **the ~ goes for you** eso también va por ti • **~ here!*** ¡yo también! • **one and the ~** el mismo/la misma • **(and the) ~ to you!*** *(returning insult)* ¡lo mismo digo!; *(returning good wishes)* ¡igualmente! • **"Mr. Smith?" — "the very ~!"** —¿el Sr. Smith? —¡el mismo!
2 *(Comm)* • **for repair of door and repainting of ~** reparación de la puerta y pintar la misma
same-day ['seɪm,deɪ] (ADJ) *[delivery]* en el mismo día
sameness ['seɪmnɪs] (N) (= *similarity*) igualdad *f*, identidad *f*; (= *monotony*) monotonía *f*, uniformidad *f*
same-sex [seɪm,seks] (ADJ) **1** (= *gay*) *[relationship, couple]* homosexual; *[family]* homoparental
2 (= *friend*) del mismo sexo
(CPD) ▸ **same -sex marriage** matrimonio *m* entre personas del mismo sexo
samey* ['seɪmɪ] (ADJ) *(pej) [song]* machacón*
• **I find her books very ~** me parece que sus libros son todos iguales
samizdat [səmiz'dat] (N) samizdat *m*
Samoa [sə'məʊə] (N) Samoa *f*
Samoan [sə'məʊən] (ADJ) samoano
(N) samoano/a *m/f*
samosa [sə'məʊsə] (N) (PL: **samosas** *or* **samosa**) samosa *f*
samovar [,sæməʊ'vɑːʳ] (N) samovar *m*
sampan ['sæmpæn] (N) sampán *m*
sample ['sɑːmpl] (N) **1** (= *example*) muestra *f* • **send in a ~ of your artwork** envíe una muestra de sus ilustraciones
2 *(Med, Bot, Zool) [of substance]* muestra *f* • **a blood/urine ~** una muestra de sangre/orina • **to take a ~** tomar una muestra
3 *(Comm) [of product]* muestra *f* • **free ~** muestra *f* gratuita
(VT) **1** (= *try out*) *[+ food, drink]* probar • **the chance to ~ a different way of life** la oportunidad de probar un modo de vida distinto
2 (= *take samples*) tomar muestras de
3 *(Statistics)* muestrear
(CPD) ▸ **sample book** muestrario *m* ▸ **sample pack** paquete *m* de muestra ▸ **sample survey** estudio *m* de muestras
sampler ['sɑːmpləʳ] (N) **1** (= *person*) catador(a) *m/f*
2 *(Sew)* dechado *m*
sampling ['sɑːmplɪŋ] (N) muestreo *m*
Samson ['sæmsn] (N) Sansón
Samuel ['sæmjʊəl] (N) Samuel
samurai ['sæmʊ,raɪ] (**samurai** *or* **samurais**)
(N) (= *warrior*) samurái *m*
(ADJ) samurái *(inv)*
(CPD) ▸ **samurai sword** espada *f* samurái ▸ **samurai warrior** guerrero *m* samurái
San Andreas Fault [,sænæn,dreɪəs'fɔːlt] (N) falla *f* de San Andrés
sanatorium [,sænə'tɔːrɪəm] (N) (PL: **sanatoriums** *or* **sanatoria** [,sænə'tɔːrɪə]) sanatorio *m*
sanctification [,sæŋktɪfɪ'keɪʃən] (N) santificación *f*
sanctify ['sæŋktɪfaɪ] (VT) santificar
sanctimonious [,sæŋktɪ'məʊnɪəs] (ADJ) mojigato, santurrón
sanctimoniously [,sæŋktɪ'məʊnɪəslɪ] (ADV) con mojigatería, con santurronería • **she said ~** dijo con mojigatería *or* santurronería
sanctimoniousness [,sæŋktɪ'məʊnɪəsnɪs] (N) mojigatería *f*, santurronería *f*
sanction ['sæŋkʃən] (N) **1** (= *approval*) permiso *m*, autorización *f*
2 (= *penalty*) sanción *f*; *(esp Pol)*; **sanctions** sanciones *fpl* • **to impose economic ~s on** *or* **against** imponer sanciones económicas a *or* contra
(VT) **1** (= *approve*) sancionar, autorizar
2 (= *penalize*) sancionar
(CPD) ▸ **sanction busting, sanctions busting** ruptura *f* de sanciones
sanctity ['sæŋktɪtɪ] (N) (= *sacredness*) lo sagrado; (= *inviolability*) inviolabilidad *f*
sanctuary ['sæŋktjʊərɪ] (N) *(Rel)* santuario *m*; *(fig)* (= *refuge*) asilo *m*; *(for wildlife)* reserva *f* • **to seek ~** acogerse a sagrado • **to seek ~ in** refugiarse en • **to seek ~ with** acogerse a
sanctum ['sæŋktəm] (N) (PL: **sanctums** *or* **sancta**) lugar *m* sagrado; *(fig)* sanctasanctórum *m*; ▸ **inner**
sand [sænd] (N) **1** (= *substance*) arena *f* • **grains of ~** granos *mpl* de arena • IDIOM: • **the ~s are running out** queda poco tiempo
2 sands (= *beach*) playa *fsing*; *[of desert]* arenas *fpl*
(VT) **1** *[+ road]* echar arena a
2 *(also* **sand down***)* *[+ wood etc]* lijar; *[+ floor]* pulir
(CPD) ▸ **sand bar** barra *f* de arena, banco *m* de arena ▸ **sand dune** duna *f* ▸ **sand flea** pulga *f* de mar ▸ **sand fly** jején *m*, mosquito *m* ▸ **sand martin** avión *m* zapador ▸ **sand trap** *(US) (Golf)* búnker *m* ▸ **sand yacht** triciclo *m* a vela
sandal ['sændl] (N) sandalia *f*, guarache *m or* huarache *m (Mex)* • **a pair of ~s** unas sandalias
sandalwood ['sændlwʊd] (N) sándalo *m*
sandbag ['sændbæg] (N) saco *m* de arena
(VT) proteger con sacos de arena
sandbank ['sændbæŋk] (N) banco *m* de arena
sandblast ['sændblɑːst] (VT) *[+ building]* limpiar con chorro de arena
sandblasting ['sænd,blɑːstɪŋ] (N) limpieza *f* con chorro de arena
sandbox ['sændbɒks] (N) *(US)* cajón *m* de arena
sandboy ['sændbɔɪ] (N) • IDIOM: • **to be as happy as a ~** estar como unas pascuas
sandcastle ['sænd,kɑːsl] (N) castillo *m* de arena
sander ['sændəʳ] (N) (= *tool*) *(gen)* lijadora *f*; *(for floor)* pulidora *f*
sandglass ['sændglɑːs] (N) reloj *m* de arena
sanding ['sændɪŋ] (N) *[of road]* enarenamiento *m*; *[of floor]* pulimiento *m*; (= *sandpapering*) lijamiento *m*
S & L (N ABBR) *(US) (Econ)* = **savings and loan association**
sandlot ['sændlɒt] *(US)* (N) *terreno en una ciudad que se usa para el béisbol etc*
(ADJ) *(Sport)* de barrio, de vecindad • **~ baseball** béisbol *m* de barrio
S & M (N ABBR) = **sadomasochism**
(ADJ) (= **sadomasochistic**) sadomasoca*
sandman ['sændmæn] (N) (PL: **sandmen**) *ser imaginario que hace que los niños se duerman trayéndoles sueño*
sandpaper ['sænd,peɪpəʳ] (N) papel *m* de lija
(VT) lijar
sandpiper ['sænd,paɪpəʳ] (N) andarríos *m*, lavandera *f*
sandpit ['sændpɪt] (N) *(esp Brit) recinto de arena para juegos infantiles*
sandshoes ['sændʃuːz] (NPL) playeras *fpl*, tenis *mpl*
sandstone ['sændstəʊn] (N) arenisca *f*
sandstorm ['sændstɔːm] (N) tempestad *f* de arena
sandwich ['sænwɪdʒ] (N) *(with French bread)* bocadillo *m (Sp)*, sandwich *m (esp LAm)*, emparedado *m (esp LAm)*; *(with sliced bread)* sandwich *m*
(VT) *(also* **sandwich in***)* *[+ person, appointment etc]* intercalar • **to ~ sth between two things** hacer un hueco para algo entre dos cosas
(CPD) ▸ **sandwich bar** bar *m* de bocadillos, bocadillería *f* ▸ **sandwich board** cartelón *m (que lleva el hombre-anuncio)* ▸ **sandwich cake** *(Brit) tarta hecha con dos capas de bizcocho y relleno de mermelada, chocolate o crema* ▸ **sandwich course** *(Univ etc) programa que intercala periodos de estudio con prácticas profesionales* ▸ **sandwich loaf** pan *m* de molde ▸ **sandwich man** (PL: **sandwich men**) hombre-anuncio *m*
sandworm ['sændwɜːm] (N) gusano *m* de arena
sandy ['sændɪ] (ADJ) (COMPAR: **sandier**, SUPERL: **sandiest**) **1** *[beach]* arenoso
2 *(in colour) [hair]* rubio
sand-yachting ['sænd,jɒtɪŋ] (N) • **to go sand-yachting** ir con triciclo a vela
sane [seɪn] (ADJ) (COMPAR: **saner**, SUPERL: **sanest**) *[person]* cuerdo; *[judgment etc]* sabio, sensato
sanely ['seɪnlɪ] (ADV) sensatamente

Sanforized® ['sænfəraɪzd] ADJ sanforizado®
sang [sæŋ] PT *of* sing
sangfroid ['sɑ̃frwɑ] N sangre *f* fría
sangria [sæŋ'gri:ə] N sangría *f*
sanguinary ['sæŋgwɪnərɪ] ADJ (*frm*)
1 (= *bloodthirsty*) sanguinario
2 (= *bloody*) [*battle*] sangriento
sanguine ['sæŋgwɪn] ADJ (*fig*) optimista
sanguineous [sæŋ'gwɪnɪəs] ADJ sanguíneo
sanguinity [sæŋ'gwɪnɪtɪ] N sanguineidad *f*
sanitarium [ˌsænɪ'tɛərɪəm] N (PL: **sanitariums** *or* **sanitaria** [ˌsænɪ'tɛərɪə]) (*esp US*) = **sanatorium**
sanitary ['sænɪtərɪ] ADJ (= *clean*) higiénico; (= *for health protection*) de sanidad
CPD ▸ **sanitary engineer** ingeniero/a *m/f* sanitario/a ▸ **sanitary inspector** inspector(a) *m/f* de sanidad ▸ **sanitary napkin** (*US*) compresa *f*, paño *m* higiénico ▸ **sanitary protection** (= *tampons, sanitary towels*) protección *f* higiénica ▸ **sanitary towel** (*Brit*) compresa *f*, paño *m* higiénico
sanitation [ˌsænɪ'teɪʃən] N (= *science*) higiene *f*; (= *plumbing*) instalación *f* sanitaria
CPD ▸ **sanitation department** (*US*) departamento *m* de limpieza y recogida de basuras ▸ **sanitation man** (*US*) basurero *m*
sanitize ['sænɪtaɪz] VT sanear • **to ~ the image of war** dar una imagen aséptica de la guerra
sanitized ['sænɪtaɪzd] ADJ saneado
sanity ['sænɪtɪ] N [*of person*] cordura *f*, juicio *m*; [*of judgment*] sensatez *f* • **to lose one's ~** perder el juicio *or* la razón • **to be restored to ~** • **return to ~** recobrar el juicio *or* la razón • **fortunately ~ prevailed** afortunadamente prevaleció el sentido común
sank [sæŋk] PT *of* **sink**¹
San Marino [ˌsænmə'ri:nəʊ] N San Marino *m*
Sanskrit ['sænskrɪt] ADJ sánscrito
N sánscrito *m*
sans serif [ˌsæn'serɪf] N grotesca *f*
Santa Claus [ˌsæntə'klɔ:z] N Papá Noel *m*, San Nicolás *m*
Santiago [ˌsæntɪ'ɑ:gəʊ] N (*in Chile*) Santiago *m* (de Chile); (*in Spain*) • **~ de Compostela** Santiago *m* (de Compostela)
sap¹ [sæp] N (*Bot*) savia *f*
sap² [sæp] N (*Mil*) (= *trench*) zapa *f*
VT (= *undermine*) minar; (= *weaken*) debilitar; (= *exhaust*) agotar (las fuerzas de)
sap³‡ [sæp] N (= *fool*) bobo/a *m/f* • **you sap!** ¡bobo!
sapling ['sæplɪŋ] N árbol *m* joven
sapper ['sæpəʳ] N (*Brit*) (*Mil*) zapador *m*
Sapphic ['sæfɪk] ADJ sáfico
sapphic ['sæfɪk] ADJ (= *lesbian*) sáfico
sapphire ['sæfaɪəʳ] N zafiro *m*
CPD [*ring, necklace*] de zafiro ▸ **sapphire blue** azul *m* zafiro ▸ **sapphire (blue) sky** cielo *m* azul zafiro
sappiness ['sæpɪnɪs] N jugosidad *f*
sappy¹ ['sæpɪ] ADJ (*Bot*) lleno de savia, jugoso
sappy²‡ ['sæpɪ] ADJ (= *foolish*) bobo
SAR N ABBR = **Search and Rescue**
saraband ['særəbænd] N zarabanda *f*
Saracen ['særəsn] ADJ sarraceno
N sarraceno/a *m/f*
Saragossa [ˌsærə'gɒsə] N Zaragoza *f*
Sarah ['sɛərə] N Sara
Saranwrap® [sə'rænræp] N (*US*) film *m* adherente (*para envolver alimentos*)
sarcasm ['sɑ:kæzəm] N sarcasmo *m*
sarcastic [sɑ:'kæstɪk] ADJ [*person, remark*] sarcástico
sarcastically [sɑ:'kæstɪkəlɪ] ADV con sarcasmo, sarcásticamente
sarcoma [sɑ:'kəʊmə] N (PL: **sarcomas** *or* **sarcomata** [sɑ:'kəʊmətə]) sarcoma *m*
sarcophagus [sɑ:'kɒfəgəs] N (PL: **sarcophaguses** *or* **sarcophagi** [sɑ:'kɒfəgaɪ]) sarcófago *m*
sardine [sɑ:'di:n] N (PL: **sardine** *or* **sardines**) sardina *f* • **packed in like ~s** como sardinas en lata
Sardinia [sɑ:'dɪnɪə] N Cerdeña *f*
Sardinian [sɑ:'dɪnɪən] ADJ sardo
N sardo/a *m/f*
sardonic [sɑ:'dɒnɪk] ADJ [*humour, laugh*] sardónico; [*person*] sarcástico, burlón; [*tone*] burlón • **she gave a ~ smile** sonrió con sarcasmo *or* con aire burlón
sardonically [sɑ:'dɒnɪkəlɪ] ADV [*smile*] con sarcasmo, con aire burlón; [*say*] con sarcasmo
sarge* [sɑ:dʒ] N = **sergeant** • **yes, ~** sí, mi sargento
sari ['sɑ:rɪ] N sari *m*
sarin ['sɑ:rɪn] N sarín *m*
sarky*‡ ['sɑ:kɪ] ADJ = **sarcastic**
sarnie* ['sɑ:nɪ] N (*Brit*) bocata* *f*
sarong [sə'rɒŋ] N sarong *m*
SARS [sɑ:z] N ABBR (= **severe acute respiratory syndrome**) neumonía *f* asiática, SARS *m*
sarsaparilla [ˌsɑ:səpə'rɪlə] N zarzaparrilla *f*
sartorial [sɑ:'tɔ:rɪəl] ADJ relativo al vestido • **~ elegance** elegancia *f* en el vestido • **~ taste** gusto *m* en vestidos
sartorially [sɑ:'tɔ:rɪəlɪ] ADV [*dressed*] elegantemente; (= *regarding dress*) en cuanto a la ropa
SAS N ABBR (*Brit*) (*Mil*) = **Special Air Service**
SASE, s.a.s.e. N ABBR (*US*) (= **self-addressed stamped envelope**) *sobre con las propias señas de uno y con sello*
sash¹ [sæʃ] N [*of dress etc*] faja *f*
sash² [sæʃ] N (= *window sash*) bastidor *m* de ventana, marco *m* de ventana
CPD ▸ **sash cord** cuerda *f* de ventana (de guillotina) ▸ **sash window** ventana *f* de guillotina
sashay* [sæ'ʃeɪ] VI pasearse • **to ~ off** largarse*
Sask. ABBR (*Canada*) = **Saskatchewan**
sass* [sæs] (*US*) N réplicas *fpl*, descoco *m*
VT • **to ~ sb** replicar a algn
sassafras ['sæsəfræs] N sasafrás *m*
Sassenach ['sæsənæx] N (*Scot*) (*esp pej*) inglés/esa *m/f*
sassy* ['sæsɪ] ADJ (COMPAR: **sassier**, SUPERL: **sassiest**) (*US*) fresco, descarado
SAT N ABBR (*US*) (*Educ*) = **Scholastic Aptitude Test**
sat [sæt] PT, PP *of* **sit**
Sat. N ABBR (= **Saturday**) sáb.
Satan ['seɪtn] N Satanás *m*
satanic [sə'tænɪk] ADJ satánico
Satanism ['seɪtənɪzəm] N satanismo *m*
Satanist ['seɪtənɪst] N satanista *mf*
ADJ = **satanic**
satay ['sæteɪ] N *brochetas de carne de pollo o ternera acompañadas de una salsa picante de cacahuete*
satchel ['sætʃəl] N cartera *f*, mochila *f* (*S. Cone*)
sate [seɪt] VT saciar, hartar
sated ['seɪtɪd] ADJ saciado • **to be ~ with sth** estar saciado de algo
sateen [sæ'ti:n] N satén *m*
satellite ['sætəlaɪt] N **1** (*artificial*) satélite *m* • **by** *or* **via ~** vía satélite
2 (*natural*) satélite *m* • **the ~s of Jupiter** los satélites de Júpiter
3 (*Pol*) (= *country, organisation*) satélite *m* • **Russia and its former ~s** Rusia y sus antiguos estados satélite
CPD ▸ **satellite broadcast** retransmisión *f* vía satélite ▸ **satellite broadcasting** retransmisión *f* vía satélite ▸ **satellite channel** canal *m* de retransmisión por vía satélite ▸ **satellite country** país *m* satélite ▸ **satellite dish** antena *f* parabólica para TV por satélite ▸ **satellite link** conexión *f* vía satélite ▸ **satellite navigation system** sistema *m* de navegación por satélite ▸ **satellite technology** tecnología *f* de retransmisiones vía satélite ▸ **satellite television** televisión *f* vía satélite ▸ **satellite town** ciudad *f* satélite ▸ **satellite transmission** retransmisión *f* vía satélite ▸ **satellite TV** TV *f* vía satélite
satiate ['seɪʃɪeɪt] VT (*with food*) hartar; (*with pleasures*) saciar
satiated ['seɪʃɪeɪtɪd] ADJ (*with food*) harto; (*with pleasures*) saciado
satiation [ˌseɪʃɪ'eɪʃən] N, **satiety** [sə'taɪətɪ] N (*with food*) hartura *f*; (*with pleasures*) saciedad *f*
satin ['sætɪn] N satén *m*, raso *m*
ADJ [*dress, blouse etc*] de satén; [*paper, finish*] satinado
satin-smooth [ˌsætɪn'smu:ð] ADJ [*skin*] de seda
satinwood ['sætɪnwʊd] N madera *f* satinada de las Indias, doradillo *m*, satín *m*
satiny ['sætɪnɪ] ADJ satinado
satire ['sætaɪəʳ] N sátira *f* (**on** contra)
satiric [sə'tɪrɪk] ADJ satírico
satirical [sə'tɪrɪkəl] ADJ satírico
satirically [sə'tɪrɪkəlɪ] ADV satíricamente
satirist ['sætərɪst] N (= *writer*) escritor(a) *m/f* satírico/a; (= *cartoonist*) caricaturista *mf*
satirize ['sætəraɪz] VT satirizar
satisfaction [ˌsætɪs'fækʃən] N
1 (= *contentment*) satisfacción *f* • **has it been done to your ~?** ¿se ha hecho a su gusto? • **it gives me every ~ …** es para mí una gran satisfacción … • **to demand ~** pedir satisfacción • **to express one's ~ at a result** expresar su satisfacción con un resultado, declararse satisfecho con un resultado
2 [*of debt*] pago *m*, liquidación *f*
satisfactorily [ˌsætɪs'fæktərɪlɪ] ADV de modo satisfactorio
satisfactory [ˌsætɪs'fæktərɪ] ADJ (= *pleasing*) satisfactorio; (= *sufficient*) adecuado
satisfied ['sætɪsfaɪd] ADJ [*person, customer*] satisfecho • **a ~ customer** un cliente satisfecho • **he's never ~** no está nunca contento *or* satisfecho • **to be ~ with sth** estar satisfecho con algo • **we are very ~ with it** estamos muy satisfechos con ello • **you'll have to be ~ with that** tendrás que contentarte con eso • **I am not ~ that …** (= *convinced*) no estoy convencido de que … (+ *subjun*)
satisfy ['sætɪsfaɪ] VT **1** (= *make content*) satisfacer, dejar satisfecho • **it completely satisfies me** me satisface del todo, me ha dejado totalmente satisfecho, nos satisface en grado sumo • **to ~ o.s. with sth** contentarse con algo
2 (= *convince*) convencer • **to ~ sb that …** convencer a algn de que … • **to ~ o.s. that …** convencerse de que …
3 (= *fulfil*) satisfacer, cumplir • **to ~ the examiners** recibir la aprobación del tribunal examinador • **to ~ the requirements** cumplir los requisitos
4 (= *pay off*) [+ *debt*] pagar, liquidar
satisfying ['sætɪsfaɪɪŋ] ADJ [*result etc*] satisfactorio; [*food, meal*] que satisface, que llena

satnav* ['sætnæv] N (= **satellite navigation**) (= *system*) GPS *m*; (*also* **satnav unit**) navegador *m* (GPS)
satsuma [,sæt'su:mə] N satsuma *f*
saturate ['sætʃəreɪt] VT empapar, saturar (**with** de) • **to be ~d with** (*fig*) estar empapado de • **to ~ o.s. in** (*fig*) empaparse en
saturated ['sætʃəreɪtɪd] ADJ (= *soaking wet*) empapado • **~ fat** grasa *f* saturada
saturation [,sætʃə'reɪʃən] N saturación *f*
CPD ▸ **saturation bombing** bombardeo *m* por saturación ▸ **saturation coverage** cobertura *f* mediática exhaustiva ▸ **saturation diving** buceo *m* de saturación ▸ **saturation point** • **to reach ~ point** (*Chem*) (*also fig*) alcanzar el punto de saturación
Saturday ['sætədɪ] N sábado *m*; ▹ **Tuesday**
CPD ▸ **Saturday job** • **I've got a ~ job** tengo un trabajo los sábados
Saturn ['sætən] N Saturno *m*
Saturnalia [,sætə'neɪlɪə] NPL (PL: **Saturnalia** *or* **Saturnalias**) saturnales *fpl*
saturnine ['sætənaɪn] ADJ saturnino
satyr ['sætəʳ] N sátiro *m*
sauce [sɔ:s] N **1** (*savoury*) salsa *f*; (*sweet*) crema *f* • **tomato ~** salsa *f* de tomate; (= *ketchup*) salsa *f* de tomate, ketchup *m* • **chocolate ~** crema *f* de chocolate • PROVERB: • **what's ~ for the goose is ~ for the gander** lo que es bueno para uno es bueno para el otro; ▹ **apple, cheese, cranberry, mint², orange, soya, white**
2†* (= *impudence*) frescura *f*, descaro *m* • **what ~!** ¡qué frescura! • **none of your ~!** ¡eres un fresco!*
3 (*US*‡) (= *drink*) • **the ~** la bebida, la priva (*Sp*‡) • **to hit the ~** • **to be on the ~** empinar el codo*, darle a la bebida, darle a la priva (*Sp*‡)
CPD ▸ **sauce boat** salsera *f*
saucepan ['sɔ:spən] N cacerola *f*, cazo *m*, olla *f* (*esp LAm*)
saucer ['sɔ:səʳ] N platillo *m*
saucily ['sɔ:sɪlɪ] ADV [*reply etc*] con frescura, con descaro
sauciness ['sɔ:sɪnɪs] N frescura *f*, descaro *m*
saucy* ['sɔ:sɪ] ADJ (COMPAR: **saucier**, SUPERL: **sauciest**) **1** (= *cheeky*) [*person*] fresco, descarado • **don't be ~!** ¡qué fresco!
2 (*esp Brit*) [*joke, humour, postcard, photo*] picante; [*clothes*] provocativo
Saudi ['saʊdɪ] ADJ saudí, saudita
N saudí *mf*, saudita *mf*
Saudi Arabia ['saʊdɪə'reɪbɪə] N Arabia *f* Saudí, Arabia *f* Saudita
Saudi Arabian ['saʊdɪə'reɪbɪən] ADJ, N = Saudi
sauerkraut ['saʊəkraʊt] N chucrut *m*, chucrú *m*
Saul [sɔ:l] N Saúl
sauna ['sɔ:nə] N sauna *f* (*m in Cono Sur*)
saunter ['sɔ:ntəʳ] N paseo *m* tranquilo • **to go for a ~ around the park** pasearse *or* (*LAm*) caminar por el parque
VI pasearse, deambular (*LAm*) • **to ~ in/out** entrar/salir sin prisa • **to ~ up and down** pasearse para arriba y para abajo • **he ~ed up to me** se acercó a mí con mucha calma
saurian ['sɔ:rɪən] N saurio *m*
sausage ['sɒsɪdʒ] N (*to be cooked*) salchicha *f*; (= *salami, mortadella etc*) embutido *m*, fiambre *m* • **not a ~** (*Brit**) ¡ni un botón!*, ¡nada de nada!
CPD ▸ **sausage dog*** perro *m* salchicha* ▸ **sausage machine** máquina *f* de hacer salchichas ▸ **sausage meat** carne *f* de salchicha ▸ **sausage roll** (*esp Brit*) *masa de hojaldre con una salchicha en su interior*
sauté ['səʊteɪ] ADJ salteado • **~ potatoes** patatas *fpl* salteadas
VT saltear

savable ['seɪvəbl] ADJ (*gen*) salvable; [*goal*] evitable
savage ['sævɪdʒ] ADJ **1** (= *ferocious*) [*animal, attack*] feroz, salvaje; [*person*] salvaje; [*blow*] violento; [*war, criticism, remark*] despiadado • **to have a ~ temper** tener un carácter muy violento
2 (= *primitive*) [*custom, tribe*] salvaje, primitivo
3 (= *drastic*) [*cuts, reductions*] drástico, radical
N salvaje *mf*; ▹ **noble**
VT **1** (= *injure*) atacar salvajemente • **two children have been ~d by an alsatian** dos niños fueron salvajemente atacados por un pastor alemán
2 (= *criticize*) atacar ferozmente *or* despiadadamente • **she was ~d by the press** la prensa la atacó ferozmente *or* despiadadamente, la prensa se ensañó con ella
savagely ['sævɪdʒlɪ] ADV **1** (= *ferociously*) [*beat, attack*] salvajemente, violentamente; [*fight*] violentamente; [*say*] con crueldad, despiadadamente • **a ~ funny film** una película brutalmente divertida • **the ~ beautiful scenery** el paisaje de belleza salvaje
2 (= *severely*) [*criticize, attack*] despiadadamente
3 (= *drastically*) [*cut, edit*] drásticamente, radicalmente
savageness ['sævɪdʒnɪs] N = **savagery**
savagery ['sævɪdʒrɪ] N **1** (= *violence*) [*of attack, blow*] ferocidad *f*, violencia *f*; [*of criticism*] saña *f*, ferocidad *f* • **the sheer ~ of war** el puro salvajismo *or* la pura brutalidad de la guerra
2 (= *primitiveness*) salvajismo *m*, estado *m* salvaje
3 (= *drastic nature*) [*of cuts, reductions*] radicalidad *f*, carácter *m* drástico
savannah [sə'vænə] N sabana *f*, pampa *f* (*S. Cone*), llanos *mpl* (*Ven*)
savant ['sævənt] N (*frm*) sabio/a *m/f*, erudito/a *m/f*
save¹ [seɪv] VT **1** (= *rescue*) [+ *person in danger*] rescatar, salvar; [+ *lives, jobs*] salvar; (*Rel*) [+ *soul*] salvar • **she wants to ~ the world** quiere salvar el mundo • **firefighters were unable to ~ the children** los bomberos no pudieron rescatar *or* salvar a los niños • **they accepted a pay cut to ~ their jobs** han aceptado una reducción de sueldo para salvar sus puestos de trabajo • **to ~ the day** *or* **the situation**: • **reinforcements sent by the Allies ~d the day** los refuerzos que enviaron los Aliados los sacaron del apuro • **to ~ face** guardar las apariencias • **to ~ sth/sb from sth/doing sth**: • **he ~d the company from bankruptcy** salvó a la empresa de la bancarrota • **he ~d me from falling/drowning** me salvó de caerme/de morir ahogado, impidió que me cayera/que muriera ahogado • **you have to ~ these people from themselves** tienes que salvar a esta gente del daño de sus propias acciones • **to ~ sb's life** salvar la vida a algn • **I can't sing to ~ my life** soy una negada para cantar* • **I put out a hand to ~ myself** estiré el brazo y me agarré con la mano para salvarme de una caída • IDIOMS: • **to ~ one's bacon** *or* **one's (own) skin*** salvar el pellejo* • **all he's bothered about is saving his own skin** lo único que le importa es salvar el pellejo* • **to ~ sb's ass** *or* **butt** (*esp US***) salvar el pellejo a algn*
2 (= *preserve, conserve*) • **to ~ a building for posterity** conservar un edificio para la posteridad • **I'm saving my voice for the concert** estoy reservando la voz para el concierto • **to ~ o.s. for sth** reservarse para algo • **God ~ the Queen!** ¡Dios salve *or* guarde a la Reina! • **to ~ one's strength (for sth)** conservar *or* reservar (las) fuerzas (para algo)
3 (= *keep, put aside*) (*gen*) guardar; [+ *money*] (*also* **save up**) ahorrar • **to ~ sb sth** • **to ~ sth for sb** guardar algo a algn • **we've ~d you a piece of cake** te hemos guardado un pedazo de tarta • **to ~ sth till last** guardar algo para el final • **he ~d the best till last, scoring two goals in the final ten minutes** guardó lo mejor para el final, marcando dos goles en los últimos diez minutos • **~ me a seat** guárdame un asiento • **if you ~ six tokens you get a free book** si junta *or* reúne seis vales, recibirá un libro gratis
4 (= *not spend*) [+ *time*] ahorrar, ganar; [+ *money*] ahorrar; [+ *trouble*] evitar, ahorrar • **we did it to ~ time** lo hicimos para ahorrar *or* ganar tiempo • **it ~d us a lot of trouble** nos evitó *or* ahorró muchas molestias • **it will ~ me an hour** ganaré una hora • **that way you ~ £10** así (te) ahorras 10 libras • **it ~s fuel** economiza *or* ahorra combustible • **to ~ sb (from) sth/doing sth: it ~s me (from) having to make a decision** me ahorra *or* evita tener que tomar una decisión • **I'll take him, it'll ~ you the journey** yo lo llevaré, así te ahorras *or* evitas el viaje • IDIOM: • **~ your breath** no gastes saliva (en balde)
5 (*Sport*) [+ *penalty, shot*] parar • **to ~ a goal** hacer una parada, parar un disparo a gol
6 (*Comput*) archivar, guardar
VI **1** (*also* **save up**) ahorrar • **he's saving for a new bike** está ahorrando (dinero) para (comprarse) una bici nueva
2 (= *economize*) • **to ~ on sth**: • **to ~ on petrol** ahorrar gasolina • **the new system ~s on staff time** el nuevo sistema economiza el tiempo del personal • **appliances that ~ on housework** aparatos que aligeran las tareas domésticas
3 (*US*) (= *keep*) [*food*] conservarse, aguantar*
N (*Sport*) parada *f* • **to make a ~** hacer una parada

SAVE THE CHILDREN
Save the Children es una organización benéfica fundada en el Reino Unido en 1919 para ayudar a los niños que sufrieron las secuelas de la Revolución Rusa y de la Segunda Guerra Mundial. Hoy en día se dedica a ofrecer ayuda de emergencia a los niños de todo el mundo que sufren de inanición o son víctimas de los efectos de guerras y desastres naturales y desarrolla proyectos a largo plazo para mejorar la higiene, la nutrición y la educación, además de luchar para que los gobiernos den prioridad a los derechos de los niños.

save² [seɪv] PREP (*liter*) salvo • **all ~ one** todos excepto *or* menos uno • **~ for** excepto • **~ that ...** excepto que ...
saveloy ['sævəlɔɪ] N frankfurt *m*
saver ['seɪvəʳ] N **1** (= *person*) (*having account*) ahorrador(a) *m/f*; (*by nature*) persona *f* ahorrativa, persona *f* ahorradora
2 (= *ticket*) billete-abono *m*
Savile Row ['sævɪl'rəʊ] N (*Brit*) *calle londinense donde están las mejores sastrerías*
saving ['seɪvɪŋ] N **1** (= *putting aside*) ahorro *m* • **a policy to encourage ~ and investment** una política para fomentar el ahorro y la inversión • **regular ~ is the best provision for the future** ahorrar con regularidad es la mejor manera de hacer previsiones para el futuro
2 (= *economy*) ahorro *m* • **this price represents a ~ of £100** este precio supone un ahorro de

100 libras • **we must make ~s** tenemos que economizar *or* hacer economías • **this ticket enables you to make a ~ on standard rail fares** este billete le supondrá un ahorro con respecto a las tarifas de tren normales
3 savings ahorros *mpl* • **she has ~s of £3,000** sus ahorros suman 3.000 libras, tiene ahorradas 3.000 libras • **life ~s** los ahorros de toda una vida
(ADJ) • **~ grace: his only ~ grace was that ...** lo único que lo salvaba era que ...
(PREP) (= *apart from*) salvo, excepto
(CPD) ▸ **savings account** cuenta *f* de ahorros ▸ **savings and loan association** (*US*) sociedad *f* de ahorro y préstamo ▸ **savings bank** caja *f* de ahorros ▸ **savings bond** bono *m* de ahorros ▸ **savings book** cartilla *f* *or* libreta *f* de ahorros ▸ **savings certificate** bono *m* de ahorros ▸ **savings stamp** sello *m* de ahorros

saviour, savior (*US*) ['seɪvjəʳ] (N) salvador(a) *m/f* • **Saviour** Salvador *m*

savoir-faire ['sævwɑː'fɛəʳ] (N) desparpajo *m*

savor *etc* ['seɪvəʳ] (*US*) = **savour** *etc*

savory[1] ['seɪvərɪ] (N) (*Bot*) tomillo *m* salsero

savory[2] ['seɪvərɪ] (*US*) = **savoury**

savour, savor (*US*) ['seɪvəʳ] (N) sabor *m*, gusto *m* • **to add ~ to sth** dar sabor a algo • **it has lost its ~** ha perdido su sabor
(VT) saborear

savouriness, savoriness (*US*) ['seɪvərɪnɪs] (N) lo sabroso, buen sabor *m*

savourless, savorless (*US*) ['seɪvəlɪs] (ADJ) soso, insípido

savoury, savory (*US*) ['seɪvərɪ] (ADJ)
1 (= *appetizing*) sabroso
2 (= *not sweet*) salado
3 (*fig*) • **it's not a very ~ district** no es un barrio muy respetable • **it's not a very ~ subject** no es un tema muy apto
(N) entremés *m* salado

Savoy [sə'vɔɪ] (N) Saboya *f*

savoy [sə'vɔɪ] (N) berza *f* de Saboya

savvy* ['sævɪ] (N) inteligencia *f*
(VT) comprender • **~?** ¿comprende?

-savvy [sævɪ] (SUFFIX) • **computer-savvy** con conocimientos de informática • **how computer-savvy are you?** ¿cuánto sabes de informática? • **media-savvy** con conocimientos de los medios de comunicación

saw[1] [sɔː] (VB: PT: **sawed**, PP: **sawed** *or* **sawn**)
(N) (= *tool*) sierra *f*
(VT) serrar
(VI) • **to saw through** cortar con (una) sierra
(CPD) ▸ **saw edge** filo *m* dentado *or* de sierra
▸ **saw away** (VT + ADV) quitar con la sierra
(VI + ADV) • **she was sawing away at the violin** iba rascando el violín
▸ **saw off** (VT + ADV) cortar con la sierra
▸ **saw up** (VT + ADV) cortar con la sierra

saw[2] [sɔː] (PT) *of* **see[1]**

saw[3] [sɔː] (N) (= *saying*) refrán *m*, dicho *m*

sawbench ['sɔːbentʃ] (N) (*US*) caballete *m* para serrar

sawbones†* ['sɔːbəʊnz] (N) (*pej*) matasanos *m inv*

sawbuck ['sɔːbʌk] (N) (*US*) caballete *m* para serrar

sawdust ['sɔːdʌst] (N) serrín *m*, aserrín *m*

sawed-off shotgun [,sɔːdɒf'ʃɒtgʌn] (N) (*US*) = **sawn-off shotgun**

sawfish ['sɔːfɪʃ] (N) (PL: **sawfish** *or* **sawfishes**) pez *m* sierra

sawhorse ['sɔːhɔːs] (N) caballete *m*

sawmill ['sɔːmɪl] (N) aserradero *m*

sawn [sɔːn] (PP) *of* **saw[1]**

sawn-off shotgun [,sɔːnɒf'ʃɒtgʌn] (N) (*Brit*) escopeta *f* de cañones recortados

sawtooth ['sɔːtuːθ] (N) diente *m* de sierra

sawyer ['sɔːjəʳ] (N) aserrador *m*

sax* [sæks] (N) saxo* *m*

saxhorn ['sækshɔːn] (N) bombardino *m*

saxifrage ['sæksɪfrɪdʒ] (N) saxífraga *f*

Saxon ['sæksn] (ADJ) sajón
(N) **1** (= *person*) sajón/ona *m/f*
2 (*Ling*) sajón *m*

Saxony ['sæksənɪ] (N) Sajonia *f*

saxophone [,sæksəfəʊn] (N) saxofón *m*, saxófono *m*

saxophonist [,sæk'sɒfənɪst] (N) saxofonista *mf*, saxofón *mf*

say [seɪ] (VB: PT, PP: **said**) (VT), (VI) **1** [*person*] (= *speak, tell*) decir • **"hello," he said** —hola —dijo • **what did you say?** ¿qué dijiste? • **he said to me that ...** me dijo que ... • **to say to o.s.** decir para sí • **he said (that) he'd do it** dijo que él lo haría • **she said (that) I was to give you this** me pidió que te diera esto • **I say (that) we should go** yo digo que nos vayamos • **say after me** repite lo que digo yo • **to say sth again** repetir algo • **to say goodbye to sb** despedirse de algn • **to say good morning/goodnight to sb** dar los buenos días/las buenas noches a algn • **to say mass** decir misa • **I've nothing more to say** se acabó • **let's say no more about it** se acabó el asunto • **I must say (that) I disapprove of the idea** la verdad es que no me parece bien la idea • **I must say she's very pretty** tengo que *or* debo reconocer que es muy guapa • **it's difficult, I must say** es difícil, lo confieso • **to say no** decir que no • **to say no to a proposal** rechazar una propuesta • **I wouldn't say no** (*Brit**) me encantaría • **to say a prayer** rezar • **that's what I say** eso digo yo, lo mismo digo yo • **I will say this about him, he's bright** reconozco (a pesar de todo) que es listo • **to say yes** decir que sí • **to say yes to a proposal** aceptar una propuesta
2 (= *show on dial*) marcar; (= *show in print*) poner, decir • **my watch says three o'clock** mi reloj marca las tres • **it says 30 degrees** marca 30 grados • **it says here that it was built in 1066** aquí pone *or* dice que se construyó en 1066 • **the rules say that ...** según las reglas ..., en las reglas pone ...
3 (*in phrases*) • **when all is said and done** al fin y al cabo, a fin de cuentas • **she has nothing to say for herself** no tiene conversación, nunca abre la boca • **what have you got to say for yourself?** ¿y tú, qué dices? • **he never has much to say for himself** habla poco • **that doesn't say much for him** eso no es una gran recomendación para él • **it says much for his courage that he stayed** el que permaneciera allí demuestra su valor • **it's not for me to say** no me toca a mí decir • **to say the least** para no decir más • **say what you like about her hat, she's charming** dígase lo que se quiera acerca de su sombrero, es encantadora • **that's saying a lot** y eso es algo • **his suit says a lot about him** su traje dice mucho de él • **though I say it** *or* **so myself** aunque soy yo el que lo dice • **there's no saying what he'll do** quién sabe lo que hará • **I'd rather not say** prefiero no decir (nada) • **it's an original, not to say revolutionary, idea** la idea es original y hasta revolucionaria • **to say nothing of the rest** sin hablar de lo demás • **would you really say so?** ¿lo crees de veras? • **that is to say** o sea, es decir • **what do** *or* **would you say to a walk?** ¿le apetece *or* se le antoja un paseo? • **what would you say to that?** ¿qué contestas a eso? • **it goes without saying that ...** ni que decir tiene que ..., huelga decir que ... • **that goes without saying** eso cae de su peso • IDIOM: • **what he says goes** aquí manda él
4 (*impersonal use*) • **it is said that ...** • **they say that ...** se dice que ..., dicen que ... • **he is said to have been the first** dicen que fue el primero • **it's easier said than done** del dicho al hecho hay gran trecho • **there's a lot to be said for it/for doing it** hay mucho que decir a su favor/a favor de hacerlo • **it must be said that ...** hay que decir *or* reconocer que ... • **there's something to be said for it/for doing it** hay algo que decir a su favor/a favor de hacerlo • **there's something to be said on both sides** hay algo que decir en pro y en contra • **no sooner said than done** dicho y hecho
5 (*in exclamations*) • **say!** (*esp US*) • **I'll say!*** • **I should say so!*** • **you can say that again!*** ¡ya lo creo!, ¡exacto! • **you don't say!*** (*often hum*) ¡no me digas! • **enough said!** ¡basta! • **I say!** (*Brit*) (*calling attention*) ¡oiga!; (*in surprise, appreciation*) ¡vaya!, ¡anda! • **say no more!** ¡basta!, ¡ni una palabra más! • **so you say!** ¡eso es lo que tú dices! • **well said!** ¡muy bien dicho! • **you've said it!*** ¡exacto!, ¡tú lo dijiste!
6 (= *suppose*) suponer, decir, poner • **(let's) say it's worth £20** supongamos *or* digamos *or* pon que vale 20 libras • **I should say it's worth about £100** yo diría que vale unas cien libras • **shall we say Tuesday?** ¿quedamos en el martes? • **shall we say £5?** ¿convenimos en 5 libras? • **we sell it at say £25** pongamos que lo vendemos por 25 libras • **we were going at say 80kph** íbamos a 80kph más o menos
(N) • **to have one's say** dar su opinión • **I've had my say** yo he dado mi opinión *or* he dicho lo que pensaba • **to have a say in the matter** tener voz y voto • **if I had had a say in it** si hubieran pedido mi parecer *or* opinión • **to have no say in the matter** no tener voz en capítulo • **let him have his say!** ¡que hable él!

SAYE (ABBR) = **save as you earn**

saying ['seɪɪŋ] (N) dicho *m*, refrán *m* • **it's just a ~** es un refrán, es un dicho • **as the ~ goes** como dice el refrán

say-so* ['seɪsəʊ] (N) (= *authority*) • **on whose say-so?** ¿autorizado por quién?, ¿con permiso de quién? • **it depends on his say-so** tiene que darle el visto bueno

SBA (N ABBR) (*US*) = **Small Business Administration**

SBU (N ABBR) = **strategic business unit**

SC (ABBR) (*US*) **1** = **Supreme Court**
2 = **South Carolina**

s/c, s.c. (ABBR) = **self-contained**

scab [skæb] (N) **1** (*Med*) costra *f*
2 (*Vet*) roña *f*
3* (*pej*) (= *strikebreaker*) esquirol *mf*, rompehuelgas *mf inv*

scabbard ['skæbəd] (N) vaina *f*, funda *f*

scabby ['skæbɪ] (ADJ) **1** [*skin, knee etc*] lleno de costras
2 (*Vet*) roñoso

scabies ['skeɪbiːz] (NSING) sarna *f*

scabious[1] ['skeɪbɪəs] (ADJ) (*Med*) sarnoso

scabious[2] ['skeɪbɪəs] (N) (*Bot*) escabiosa *f*

scabrous ['skeɪbrəs] (ADJ) escabroso

scads* [skædz] (NPL) montones* *mpl* • **we have ~ of it** lo tenemos a montones*, tenemos montones de eso*

scaffold ['skæfəld] (N) **1** (*Constr*) (*also* **scaffolding**) andamio *m*, andamiaje *m*
2 (*for execution*) patíbulo *m*, cadalso *m*

scaffolder ['skæfəldəʳ] (N) andamista *mf*, trabajador(a) *m/f* de andamio

scaffolding ['skæfəldɪŋ] (N) andamio *m*, andamiaje *m*

scag‡ [skæg] (N) (= *heroin*) caballo‡ *m*

s

scalable ['skeɪləbl] ADJ (*Comput*) [*network, technology, computing*] escalable • **~ font** fuente *f* escalable

scalawag* ['skæləwæg] N (*US*) = **scallywag**

scald [skɔːld] N escaldadura *f*
VT (*gen*) escaldar; [+ *milk*] calentar • IDIOM: • **to run like a ~ed cat** (*Brit**) correr como gato escaldado, correr como alma que lleva el diablo*

scalding ['skɔːldɪŋ] ADJ • **it's ~ (hot)** está hirviendo *or* (*LAm*) que arde • **the soup is ~** la sopa está muy caliente

scale[1] [skeɪl] N [*of fish, reptile etc*] escama *f*; (= *flake*) [*of rust, chalk*] hojuela *f*; [*of skin*] escama *f*; (*inside kettle, boiler*) costra *f*; (*on teeth*) sarro *m*
VT [+ *fish*] quitar las escamas a, escamar; (*Tech*) raspar; [+ *teeth*] quitar el sarro a
VI (*also* **scale off**) [*skin*] descamarse

scale[2] [skeɪl] N **1** (= *weighing device*) (*often pl*) balanza *f*; (*for heavy weights*) báscula *f* • **bathroom ~(s)** báscula *f* (de baño) • **a kitchen ~** • **a pair of kitchen ~s** una balanza de cocina • **he tips the ~s at 70 kilos** pesa 70 kilos • **to turn** *or* **tip the ~s (in sb's favour/against sb)** inclinar la balanza (a favor de algn/en contra de algn)
2 [*of balance*] platillo *m*

scale[3] [skeɪl] N **1** (= *size, extent*) (*gen*) escala *f*; [*of problem, disaster*] magnitud *f*, escala *f* • **he likes to do things on a grand ~** le gusta hacer las cosas a gran escala *or* por todo lo alto *or* a lo grande • **on a large ~** a gran escala • **they were engaged in fraud on a massive ~** estaban realizando un fraude a gran escala *or* de gran envergadura • **on a national ~** a escala nacional • **on a small ~** a pequeña escala • **borrowing on this ~ will bankrupt the country** el país va a caer en la bancarrota si sigue aceptando préstamos de esta magnitud
2 (= *graduated system*) (*gen, for salaries*) escala *f* • **~ of charges** (lista *f* de) tarifas *fpl* • **the Richter ~** la escala de Richter • **the social ~** la escala *or* jerarquía social; ▹ **pay, sliding**
3 (= *ratio, proportion*) [*of map, model*] escala *f* • **on a ~ of 1cm to 5km** con una escala de 1cm a 5km • **to be out of ~ (with sth)** no guardar proporción (con algo) • **the drawing is not to ~** el dibujo no está a escala • **to draw sth to ~** dibujar algo a escala
4 (*Mus*) escala *f*
VT [+ *wall*] trepar a, escalar; [+ *tree*] trepar a; [+ *mountain*] escalar
CPD ▸ **scale drawing** dibujo *m* a escala
▸ **scale model** modelo *m* a escala
▸ **scale back** VT + ADV (= *reduce*) [+ *production, operations, demands, plan*] recortar
▸ **scale down** VT + ADV **1** (= *make proportionately smaller*) reducir a escala
2 (= *reduce*) = **scale back**
▸ **scale up** VT + ADV **1** (= *make proportionately bigger*) aumentar a escala
2 (= *increase*) [+ *operations*] ampliar

scaled-down ['skeɪld,daʊn] ADJ [*numbers, costs, quantities*] a escala reducida • **it is a scaled down replica of the real building** es una réplica del edificio a escala reducida, es una maqueta del edificio

scalene ['skeɪliːn] ADJ [*triangle, cone*] escaleno

scaliness ['skeɪlɪnɪs] N escamosidad *f*

scallion ['skæljən] N cebolleta *f* (para ensalada), cebollita *f* (*LAm*)

scallop ['skɒləp] N **1** (*Zool*) venera *f*
2 (*Sew*) festón *m*, onda *f*
VT **1** (*Culin*) guisar en conchas
2 (*Sew*) festonear
CPD ▸ **scallop shell** venera *f*

scalloped ['skæləpt] ['skɒləpt] ADJ [*edge, neckline*] festoneado

scallywag* ['skælɪwæg] N (= *child*) diablillo *m*, travieso/a *m/f*; (= *rogue*) pillín/ina *m/f* • **you little ~!** ¡ay pillín!

scalp [skælp] N cuero *m* cabelludo; (*as trophy*) cabellera *f* • **to demand sb's ~** (*fig*) exigir la cabeza de algn
VT **1** (*lit*) arrancar la cabellera de • **he'll ~ you if he finds out!*** ¡si se entera, te arranca la cabellera!
2 (*US**) [+ *tickets*] revender
VI (*US**) revender

scalpel ['skælpəl] N escalpelo *m*

scalper* ['skælpəʳ] N (*US*) revendedor(a) *m/f*

scalping* ['skælpɪŋ] N (*US*) reventa *f*

scaly ['skeɪlɪ] ADJ (COMPAR: **scalier**, SUPERL: **scaliest**) escamoso

scam* [skæm] N estafa *f*, timo *m*

scamp[1]* [skæmp] N = **scallywag**

scamp[2] [skæmp] VT [+ *one's work etc*] chapucear, frangollar

scamper ['skæmpəʳ] VI escabullirse • **to ~ in/out** entrar/salir corriendo • **to ~ along** ir corriendo
▸ **scamper about** VI + ADV corretear
▸ **scamper away, scamper off** VI + ADV escabullirse

scampi ['skæmpɪ] N gambas *fpl* rebozadas

scan [skæn] VT **1** (= *inspect closely*) escudriñar; [+ *horizon etc*] otear; (*Comput*) examinar, explorar
2 (= *glance at*) echar un vistazo a
3 (*Tech*) explorar, registrar
4 (*Poetry*) [+ *verse*] medir, escandir
VI [*poetry*] estar bien medido • **it does not ~** no está bien medido
N (*Med*) exploración *f* con un escáner • **to go for a ~** • **have a ~** hacerse un escáner

scandal ['skændl] N **1** (= *public furore*) escándalo *m* • **it caused** *or* **created a ~** causó escándalo • **he was involved in a sex/drugs ~** estuvo involucrado en un escándalo sexual/de drogas
2 (= *disgraceful state of affairs*) vergüenza *f* • **it's a ~!** • **what a ~!** ¡qué vergüenza!
3 (= *gossip*) chismes *mpl* • **it's just ~** no son más que habladurías *or* chismes • **she reads all the ~ in the tabloid press** se lee todos los chismes de los periódicos sensacionalistas • **there's a lot of ~ going round about her** circulan muchos chismes sobre ella • **the local ~** los chismes del pueblo *or* del barrio *etc* • **the latest ~** lo último en cotilleo • **to talk ~** murmurar, contar chismes
CPD ▸ **scandal sheet** (*US*) (= *newspaper*) periódico *m* sensacionalista • **the ~ sheets** la prensa sensacionalista

scandalize ['skændəlaɪz] VT escandalizar • **she was ~d** se escandalizó

scandalmonger ['skændl,mʌŋgəʳ] N chismoso/a *m/f*

scandalous ['skændələs] ADJ [*behaviour, story, price*] escandaloso • **to reach ~ proportions** alcanzar proporciones escandalosas • **it's simply ~!** ¡es un escándalo! • **it's ~ that …** es vergonzoso que … • **~ talk** habladurías *fpl*, chismes *mpl*

scandalously ['skændələslɪ] ADV escandalosamente

Scandinavia [,skændɪ'neɪvɪə] N Escandinavia *f*

Scandinavian [,skændɪ'neɪvɪən] ADJ escandinavo
N escandinavo/a *m/f*

scandium ['skændɪəm] N escandio *m*

scanner ['skænəʳ] N **1** (*Med*) escáner *m*, scanner *m*; (*also* **ultra-sound scanner**) ecógrafo *m*
2 (*Comput*) (*in airports*) escáner *m*
3 (*Tech*) antena *f* direccional

scanning ['skænɪŋ] N (*Med*) visualización *f* radiográfica
CPD ▸ **scanning device** detector *m*

scansion ['skænʃən] N [*of poetry*] escansión *f*

scant [skænt] ADJ (COMPAR: **scanter**, SUPERL: **scantest**) escaso • **it measures a ~ 2cm** mide dos centímetros escasos • **to pay ~ attention to sth** prestar escasa atención a algo • **a ~ tablespoon of sugar** una cucharada rasa de azúcar

scantily ['skæntɪlɪ] ADV insuficientemente • **~ clad** *or* **dressed** ligero de ropa • **~ provided with …** con escasa cantidad de …

scantiness ['skæntɪnɪs] N escasez *f*, insuficiencia *f*

scanty ['skæntɪ] ADJ (COMPAR: **scantier**, SUPERL: **scantiest**) [*meal etc*] insuficiente; [*clothing*] ligero; [*evidence*] insuficiente; [*information*] insuficiente, escaso

scapegoat ['skeɪpgəʊt] N cabeza *f* de turco, chivo *m* expiatorio • **to be a ~ for** pagar el pato por, pagar los cristales rotos por

scapegrace† ['skeɪpgreɪs] N pícaro *m*, bribón *m*

scapula ['skæpjʊlə] N (PL: **scapulas** *or* **scapulae** ['skæpjʊliː]) escápula *f*

scapular ['skæpjʊləʳ] ADJ, N escapulario *m*

scar[1] [skɑːʳ] N (*Med*) cicatriz *f*; (*fig*) (*on building, landscape etc*) huella *f* • **it left a deep ~ on his mind** dejó una huella profunda en su ánimo
VT dejar una cicatriz en; (*fig*) marcar, rayar • **he was ~red with many wounds** tenía cicatrices de muchas heridas • **he was ~red for life** quedó marcado para toda la vida • **the walls are ~red with bullets** las balas han dejado marca en las paredes
VI (= *leave a scar*) cicatrizar; (*also* **scar over**) (= *heal*) cicatrizarse
CPD ▸ **scar tissue** tejido *m* cicatricial

scar[2] [skɑːʳ] N (*Geog*) (= *crag*) paraje *m* rocoso, pendiente *f* rocosa

scarab ['skærəb] N escarabajo *m*

scarce [skɛəs] ADJ (COMPAR: **scarcer**, SUPERL: **scarcest**) [*reserves, resources*] escaso • **to be ~** [*doctors, food, resources*] escasear; [*money*] escasear, faltar • **jobs were very ~ in those days** en aquella época escaseaban los puestos de trabajo • **paintings of this quality are ~** no abundan los cuadros de esta calidad • **to grow** *or* **become ~** volverse escaso, escasear • **to make o.s. ~*** largarse*, esfumarse*
ADV† = **scarcely**

scarcely ['skɛəslɪ] ADV (= *barely*) apenas • **~ anybody** casi nadie • **I can ~ believe it** apenas puedo creerlo, casi no puedo creerlo • **~ ever** casi nunca • **I ~ know what to say** no sé qué puedo decir • **he was ~ more than a boy** era apenas un niño • **we could ~ refuse** ¿cómo podíamos negarnos?, difícilmente podíamos negarnos • **it is ~ surprising that …** no es ni mucho menos sorprendente que … • **he's ~ what you'd call a cordon bleu chef** (*iro*) no es precisamente un maestro de la cocina • **the car had ~ drawn to a halt when …** apenas se había parado el coche cuando …

scarceness ['skɛəsnɪs] N ▹ **scarcity**

scarcity ['skɛəsɪtɪ] N (= *shortage*) [*of money, food, resources*] escasez *f*, carestía *f*; [*of doctors, teachers*] escasez *f*
CPD ▸ **scarcity value** • **it has ~ value** tiene valor por lo escaso que es

scare [skɛəʳ] N **1** (= *fright*) susto *m* • **to cause a ~** sembrar el pánico • **to give sb a ~** dar un susto *or* asustar a algn • **what a ~ you gave**

me! ¡qué susto me diste! • **we got a bit of a ~** nos pegamos un susto, tuvimos un sobresalto
2 (= *panic, threat*) • **bomb ~** amenaza *f* de bomba • **the invasion ~** (= *panic*) el pánico de la invasión; (= *rumours*) los rumores alarmistas de una invasión
VT **1** (= *frighten*) asustar • **you ~d me!** ¡me has asustado! • **to ~ sb to death*** darle un susto de muerte a algn • **to ~ the hell** *or* **life out of sb*** darle un susto de muerte a algn • **to ~ sb stiff*** darle un susto de muerte a algn
2 • **to be ~d** (= *frightened*) tener miedo, estar asustado • **don't be ~d** no tengas miedo, no te asustes • **we were really ~d** teníamos mucho miedo, estábamos muy asustados • **to be ~d to do sth** tener miedo de hacer algo • **she was too ~d to talk** estaba demasiado asustada para poder hablar, no podía hablar del susto • **to be ~d to death*** estar muerto de miedo • **to be ~d of sb/sth**: • **he's ~d of women** tiene miedo a las mujeres • **are you ~d of him?** ¿le tienes miedo? • **I'm ~d of spiders** les tengo miedo a *or* me dan miedo las arañas • **to be ~d of doing sth** tener miedo de hacer algo • **to be ~d stiff*** estar muerto de miedo • **to be ~d out of one's wits*** estar muerto de miedo
VI • **he doesn't ~ easily** no se asusta fácilmente
CPD ▸ **scare campaign** campaña *f* alarmista, campaña *f* de intimidación ▸ **scare story** • **it's only a ~ story** se trata de un reportaje alarmista ▸ **scare tactics** tácticas *fpl* alarmistas
▸ **scare away, scare off** VT + ADV espantar, ahuyentar
scarecrow ['skɛəkrəʊ] N espantapájaros *m inv*, espantajo *m*
scared ['skɛəd] ADJ ▸ scare
scaredy-cat* ['skɛədɪ,kæt] N miedica* *mf*
scarehead* ['skɛəhed] N (*US*) (*Press*) titulares *mpl* sensacionales
scaremonger ['skɛəmʌŋgəʳ] N alarmista *mf*
scaremongering ['skɛə,mʌŋgərɪŋ] N alarmismo *m*
scarf [skɑːf] N (PL: **scarfs** *or* **scarves**) (*woollen, for neck*) bufanda *f*; (= *headscarf*) pañuelo *m*
scarface ['skɑːfeɪs] N (*as nickname*) caracortada *mf*
scarify ['skɛərɪfaɪ] VT (*Med, Agr*) escarificar; (*fig*) despellejar, desollar, criticar severamente
scarifying ['skɛərɪfaɪɪŋ] ADJ [*attack etc*] mordaz, severo
scarlatina [,skɑːlə'tiːnə] N escarlatina *f*
scarlet ['skɑːlɪt] N escarlata *f*
ADJ color escarlata, colorado (*LAm*)
• **~ fever** escarlatina *f* • **~ pimpernel** (*Bot*) pimpinela *f* • **~ runner** judía *f* escarlata • **to blush ~** • **turn ~** enrojecer, ponerse colorado • **he was ~ with rage** se puso rojo de furia
scarp [skɑːp] N escarpa *f*, declive *m*
scarper‡ ['skɑːpəʳ] VI (*Brit*) largarse*
scarves [skɑːvz] NPL *of* **scarf**
scary* ['skɛərɪ] ADJ (COMPAR: **scarier**, SUPERL: **scariest**) [*face, house, person, monster*] que da miedo; [*moment*] espeluznante • **it was really ~** daba verdadero miedo • **a ~ film** una película de miedo • **that's a ~ thought** esa es una idea espeluznante
scat[1]* [skæt] EXCL ¡zape!, ¡fuera de aquí!
scat[2] [skæt] N (*Mus*) *modalidad de jazz en la que el cantante emite sonidos inconexos en lugar de palabras enteras*
scathing ['skeɪðɪŋ] ADJ [*criticism, article, remark*] mordaz; [*look*] feroz • **he was ~ about our trains** hizo comentarios mordaces sobre nuestros trenes • **he was pretty ~** dijo cosas bastante duras • **to make a ~ attack on sb/sth** atacar mordazmente a algn/algo
scathingly ['skeɪðɪŋlɪ] ADV mordazmente • **he spoke ~ of ...** habló mordazmente *or* con mordacidad de ...
scatological [,skætə'lɒdʒɪkəl] ADJ escatológico
scatology [skæ'tɒlədʒɪ] N escatología *f*
scatter ['skætəʳ] VT **1** (= *strew around*) [+ *crumbs, papers etc*] esparcir, desparramar; [+ *seeds*] sembrar a voleo, esparcir • **the flowers were ~ed about on the floor** las flores estaban desparramadas por el suelo • **the floor was ~ed with flowers** en el suelo había flores desparramadas
2 (= *disperse*) [+ *clouds*] dispersar; [+ *crowd*] dispersar • **her relatives are ~ed about the world** sus familiares se encuentran dispersos por el mundo
VI [*crowd*] dispersarse • **the family ~ed to distant parts** la familia se dispersó por lugares alejados
N (*Math, Tech*) dispersión *f* • **a ~ of houses** unas casas dispersas • **a ~ of raindrops** unas gotas dispersas de lluvia
CPD ▸ **scatter cushions** almohadones *mpl*
scatterbrain ['skætəbreɪn] N cabeza *mf* de chorlito
scatterbrained* ['skætəbreɪnd] ADJ (= *scatty*) atolondrado, ligero de cascos
scattered ['skætəd] ADJ disperso • **the village is very ~** las casas del pueblo son muy dispersas • **~ showers** chubascos *mpl* dispersos
scattering ['skætərɪŋ] N • **a ~ of books** unos cuantos libros aquí y allá
scattershot ['skætəʃɒt] ADJ • **the money has been spent in ~ fashion** el dinero se ha gastado sin ton ni son • **the message is somewhat ~** el mensaje es muy poco consistente
scattiness* ['skætɪnɪs] N (*Brit*) ligereza *f* de cascos, atolondramiento *m*
scatty* ['skætɪ] ADJ (COMPAR: **scattier**, SUPERL: **scattiest**) (*Brit*) ligero de cascos, atolondrado • **to drive sb ~** volver majareta a algn*
scavenge ['skævɪndʒ] VT [+ *streets*] limpiar las calles de, recoger la basura de
VI remover basuras, pepenar (*Mex*) • **to ~ for food** andar buscando comida (entre la basura)
scavenger ['skævɪndʒəʳ] N **1** (= *person*) persona *f* que rebusca en las basuras, pepenador(a) *m/f* (*Mex*)
2 (*Zool*) (= *animal*) animal *m* carroñero; (= *bird*) ave *f* de carroña; (= *insect*) insecto *m* de carroña
Sc.D. N ABBR = **Doctor of Science**
SCE N ABBR = **Scottish Certificate of Education**
scenario [sɪ'nɑːrɪəʊ] N **1** (*Theat*) argumento *m*; (*Cine*) guión *m*
2 (*fig*) escenario *m*
scenarist ['siːnərɪst] N guionista *mf*
scene [siːn] N **1** (*Theat, Cine, TV, Literat*) escena *f* • **Act I, Scene 1** acto I, escena 1 • **a bedroom ~** una escena de dormitorio • **behind the ~s** (*lit, fig*) entre bastidores • **the big ~ in the film** la principal escena de la película • **indoor ~** interior *m* • **love ~s** escenas *fpl* de amor • **outdoor ~** exterior *m* • **the ~ is set in a castle** la escena tiene lugar en un castillo • **to set the ~ for a love affair** crear el ambiente para una aventura sentimental • **now let our reporter set the ~ for you** ahora permitan que nuestro reportero les describa la escena
2 (= *sight*) escena *f* • **it was an amazing ~** era una escena asombrosa • **it was a ~ of utter destruction** la escena *or* el panorama era de destrucción total • **there were ~s of violence** hubo escenas de violencia
3 (= *view*) vista *f*, panorama *m*; (= *landscape*) paisaje *m* • **the ~ from the top is marvellous** desde la cumbre la vista es maravillosa *or* el panorama es maravilloso • **the ~ spread out before you** el panorama que tienes delante • **it is a lonely ~** es un paisaje solitario
4 (= *place*) escenario *m*, lugar *m* • **the ~s of one's early life** los lugares frecuentados por uno en su juventud • **to appear** *or* **come on the ~** llegar • **when I came on the ~** cuando llegué • **he appeared unexpectedly on the ~** se presentó inesperadamente • **I need a change of ~** necesito un cambio de aires • **the ~ of the crime** el lugar *or* escenario del crimen • **to disappear from the ~** desaparecer (de escena) • **the ~ of the disaster** el lugar de la catástrofe • **the police were soon on the ~** la policía no tardó en acudir al lugar de los hechos; (*Mil*) • **the ~ of operations** el teatro de operaciones
5 (= *sphere of activity*) • **to be part of the Madrid ~** formar parte de la movida madrileña* • **the music ~** la escena musical • **it's not my ~*** no me interesa *or* llama la atención • **the political ~ in Spain** el panorama político español • **to disappear from the political ~** desaparecer de la escena política • **the pop ~** el mundo del pop
6 (= *painting, drawing*) escena *f* • **country ~s** escenas *fpl* campestres
7* (= *fuss*) escena *f*, escándalo *m*, bronca *f* (*esp LAm*) • **try to avoid a ~** procura que no se monte una escena *or* el número* • **I hate ~s** detesto las escenas *or* los escándalos • **to make a ~** hacer *or* montar una escena, montar un número* • **she had a ~ with her husband** riñó con su marido
8 (= *display of emotion*) • **there were emotional ~s as the hostages appeared** hubo escenas de emoción cuando aparecieron los rehenes • **their argument ended in an ugly ~** su discusión acabó mal • **there were unhappy ~s at the meeting** en la reunión pasaron cosas nada agradables
CPD ▸ **scene change** (*Theat*) cambio *m* de escena ▸ **scene painter** (= *designer*) escenógrafo/a *m/f*; (= *workman*) pintor(a) *m/f* (de paredes) ▸ **scene shift** cambio *m* de escena ▸ **scene shifter** tramoyista *mf*
scenery ['siːnərɪ] N **1** (= *landscape*) paisaje *m*
2 (*Theat*) decorado *m*
scenic ['siːnɪk] ADJ **1** (*gen*) pintoresco • **an area of ~ beauty** una región de bellos paisajes • **~ railway** (= *miniature railway*) *tren pequeño que hace recorridos turísticos por un recinto*; (*Brit*) (= *roller coaster*) montaña *f* rusa • **~ road** carretera *f* que recorre lugares pintorescos
2 (*Theat*) escénico, dramático
scenography [siː'nɒgrəfɪ] N escenografía *f*
scent [sent] N **1** (= *smell*) [*of flowers, perfume*] perfume *m*, fragancia *f*; [*of food*] aroma *m*
2 (*esp Brit*) (= *perfume, toilet water*) perfume *m*, fragancia *f*
3 (*Hunting etc*) rastro *m*, pista *f* • **to be on the ~** (*also fig*) seguir el rastro *or* la pista • **to pick up/lose the ~** (*also fig*) encontrar/perder el rastro *or* la pista • **to put** *or* **throw sb off the ~** (*fig*) despistar a algn
VT **1** (= *make sth smell nice*) perfumar (**with** de)
2 (= *smell*) olfatear; (*fig*) [+ *danger, trouble etc*] presentir, sentir • **to ~ sth out** olfatear *or* husmear algo
CPD ▸ **scent bottle** (*esp Brit*) frasco *m* de perfume ▸ **scent spray** atomizador *m* (de

S

perfume), pulverizador *m* (de perfume)
scented ['sentɪd] ADJ perfumado
scentless ['sentlɪs] ADJ inodoro
scepter ['septəʳ] N (*US*) = sceptre
sceptic, skeptic (*US*) ['skeptɪk] N escéptico/a *m/f*
sceptical, skeptical (*US*) ['skeptɪkəl] ADJ escéptico (**of, about** acerca de) • **he was ~ about it** se mostró escéptico acerca de ello, tenía dudas sobre ello
sceptically, skeptically (*US*) ['skeptɪkəlɪ] ADV con escepticismo
scepticism, skepticism (*US*) ['skeptɪsɪzəm] N escepticismo *m*
sceptre, scepter (*US*) ['septəʳ] N cetro *m*
schadenfreude, Schadenfreude ['ʃɑ:dənfrɔɪdə] N alegría *f* maligna (*suscitada por el mal de los otros*)
schedule ['ʃedju:l, (*US*) 'skedju:l] N
1 (= *timetable*) [*of work, visits, events*] programa *m*, calendario *m*; [*of trains, buses*] horario *m*; (*TV, Rad*) (*often pl*) programación *f* • **a busy/punishing ~** un programa *or* calendario apretado/agotador, una agenda apretada/agotadora • **we are working to a very tight ~** tenemos un programa *or* calendario de trabajo muy apretado • **the strike could threaten Christmas ~s** la huelga podría afectar a la programación de Navidad • **everything went according to ~** todo sucedió según se había previsto • **the work is behind/ahead of ~** el trabajo lleva retraso/va adelantado (con respecto al programa *or* calendario) • **I was running one hour behind ~** llevaba una hora de retraso con respecto a mi agenda • **the train arrived on/ahead of ~** el tren llegó a la hora prevista/antes de lo previsto
2 (= *list*) [*of contents, goods, charges*] lista *f*
3 (*Jur*) inventario *m*
VT (= *programme, timetable*) [+ *meeting*] programar, fijar; [+ *TV programmes*] programar; [+ *trains, planes*] programar el horario de • **the meeting is ~d for seven o'clock** *or* **to begin at seven o'clock** la reunión está programada *or* fijada para las siete • **the plane is ~d for two o'clock** *or* **to land at two o'clock** la hora de llegada prevista del avión es a las dos • **an election was ~d for last December** se habían programado *or* planeado unas elecciones para el pasado mes de diciembre • **you are ~d to speak for 20 minutes** según el programa hablarás durante 20 minutos • **I have nothing ~d for Friday** no tengo nada programado *or* planeado para el viernes • **I've ~d an appointment with the doctor** he pedido hora con el médico • **a second attempt to ~ a presidential debate has failed** ha fracasado un segundo intento de fijar una fecha para el debate presidencial • **this building is ~d for demolition** se ha previsto la demolición de este edificio • **as ~d** según lo previsto, de acuerdo con lo previsto
scheduled ['ʃedju:ld, (*US*) 'skedju:ld] ADJ [*date, time*] previsto, programado; [*meeting, visit*] programado • **at the ~ time** a la hora prevista *or* programada • **a week before the ~ date** una semana antes de lo previsto *or* programado
CPD ▸ **scheduled building** edificio *m* protegido ▸ **scheduled flight** vuelo *m* regular ▸ **scheduled stop** parada *f* programada; (*Aer*) escala *f* programada
scheduling ['ʃedju:lɪŋ, (*US*) 'skedju:lɪŋ] N [*of event, visit, meeting*] organización *f*; [*of TV programmes*] programación *f*; (*Comput*) planificación *f* • **the ~ of classes** la programación del horario de clases

Scheldt [ʃelt] N Escalda *m*
schema ['ski:mə] N (PL: **schemata** ['ski:mətə]) esquema *m*
schematic [skɪ'mætɪk] ADJ esquemático
schematically [skɪ'mætɪkəlɪ] ADV esquemáticamente
scheme [ski:m] N **1** (= *project*) plan *m*, proyecto *m*; (= *plan*) plan *m* • **a road-widening ~** un plan de ensanchamiento de calzadas
2 (= *idea*) idea *f* • **it's not a bad ~*** no es mala idea • **it's some crazy ~ of his** es otro de sus proyectos alocados
3 (= *programme*) programa *m* • **a ~ of work** un programa de trabajo
4 (= *structure*) esquema *m* • **colour ~** combinación *f* de colores • **pension ~** sistema *m* de pensión • **man's place in the ~ of things** el puesto del hombre en el diseño divino • **in the government's ~ of things there is no place for protest** la política del gobierno no deja espacio para la protesta
5 (= *conspiracy*) intriga *f*; (*crafty*) ardid *m* • **it's a ~ to get him out of the way** es una jugada para quitarle de en medio
VI intrigar (**to do** para hacer) • **they're scheming to get me out** están intrigando para expulsarme • **their opponents were scheming against them** sus adversarios estaban conspirando contra ellos
VT proyectar; (*pej*) tramar, urdir
schemer ['ski:məʳ] N (*pej*) intrigante *mf*
scheming ['ski:mɪŋ] ADJ (*pej*) maquinador, intrigante
N conspiración *f*, maquinación *f*
scherzo ['skɜ:tsəʊ] N (PL: **scherzos** *or* **scherzi** ['skɜ:tsi:]) scherzo *m*
schilling ['ʃɪlɪŋ] N chelín *m* austríaco
schism ['sɪzəm, 'skɪzəm] N cisma *m*
schismatic [sɪz'mætɪk, skɪz'mætɪk] ADJ cismático
N cismático/a *m/f*
schismatical [sɪz'mætɪkəl, skɪz'mætɪkəl] ADJ cismático
schist [ʃɪst] N esquisto *m*
schizo‡ ['skɪtsəʊ] N esquizo/a* *m/f*
schizoid‡ ['skɪtsɔɪd] ADJ esquizoide
N esquizoide *mf*
schizophrenia [,skɪtsəʊ'fri:nɪə] N esquizofrenia *f*
schizophrenic [,skɪtsəʊ'frenɪk] ADJ esquizofrénico
N esquizofrénico/a *m/f*
schlemiel‡, schlemihl‡ [ʃlə'mi:l] N (*US*) (= *clumsy person*) persona *f* desmañada; (= *unlucky person*) persona *f* desgraciada
schlep*, schlepp* [ʃlep] (*US*) VT (= *lug*) arrastrar
VI (= *traipse*) andar con trabajo • **to ~ through the traffic** abrirse camino entre el tráfico
N **1** (= *strenuous journey*) viaje *m* penoso; (*on foot*) paseo *m* dificultoso
2 = schlepper
schlepper* ['ʃlepəʳ] N petardo/a *m/f*
schlock‡ [ʃlɒk] N (*US*) porquería *f* • **I think he writes ~** me parece que lo que escribe es una porquería
ADJ de pacotilla
schlocky‡ ['ʃlɒkɪ] ADJ (*US*) de pacotilla
schlong‡ [ʃlɒŋ] N (*US*) verga *f***, pollón** *m*
schmaltz* [ʃmɔ:lts] N sentimentalismo *m*, sensiblería *f*
schmaltzy* ['ʃmɔ:ltsɪ] ADJ sentimental, sensiblero
schmo* [ʃməʊ] N (PL: **schmoes**) (*US*) chiquilicuatro* *mf*
schmooze* [ʃmu:z] VI (*US*) cascar*, estar de cháchara*
schmuck‡ [ʃmʌk] N (*US*) imbécil *mf*
schnapps [ʃnæps] N schnapps *m*

schnitzel ['ʃnɪtsəl] N escalope *m*; ▸ **wiener schnitzel**
schnozzle‡ ['ʃnɒzəl] N (*esp US*) napia‡ *f*, nariz *f*
scholar ['skɒləʳ] N **1** (= *learned person*) sabio/a *m/f*; (= *expert*) estudioso/a *m/f*, experto/a *m/f* • **a famous Dickens ~** un conocido especialista en Dickens • **I'm no ~** yo apenas sé nada, yo no soy nada intelectual
2† (= *pupil*) alumno/a *m/f*; (= *scholarship holder*) becario/a *m/f* • **he's never been much of a ~** nunca fue muy aficionado a los libros • **~'s list** (*US*) (*Univ*) *lista de honor académica*; ▸ **DEAN'S LIST**
scholarly ['skɒləlɪ] ADJ (= *studious*) erudito, estudioso; (= *pedantic*) pedante
scholarship ['skɒləʃɪp] N **1** (= *learning*) erudición *f*
2 (= *money award*) beca *f*
CPD ▸ **scholarship holder** becario/a *m/f*
scholastic [skə'læstɪk] ADJ **1** (= *educational*) escolar • **~ books** libros *mpl* escolares • **the ~ year** el año escolar • **the ~ profession** el magisterio • **Scholastic Aptitude Test** (*US*) examen *m* de acceso a la universidad
2 (= *relative to scholasticism*) escolástico
N escolástico *m*
scholasticism [skə'læstɪsɪzəm] N escolasticismo *m*
school¹ [sku:l] N **1** (*for children*) **a** (= *institution*) escuela *f*, colegio *m* • **what did you learn at ~ today?** ¿qué has aprendido hoy en el colegio? • **to be at ~** asistir a la escuela • **which ~ were you at?** ¿a qué colegio fue? • **we have to be at ~ by nine** tenemos que estar en el colegio a las nueve • **you weren't at ~ yesterday** ayer faltaste a la clase • **to go to ~** ir a la escuela • **which ~ did you go to?** ¿a qué colegio fue? • **to leave ~** terminar el colegio; ▸ **primary, secondary, high**
b (= *lessons*) clase *f* • **after ~** después de clase • **there's no ~ today** hoy no hay clase • **~ starts again in September** las clases empiezan de nuevo en septiembre
2 (*Univ*) **a** (= *faculty*) facultad *f* • **art ~** Facultad *f* de bellas artes • **School of Languages** departamento *m* de lenguas modernas • **law ~** Facultad *f* de derecho • **medical ~** Facultad *f* de medicina
b (*US*) (= *university*) universidad *f* • **I went back to ~ at 35** a los 35 años volví a la universidad
3 (= *group of artists, writers, thinkers*) escuela *f* • **the Dutch ~** la escuela holandesa • **Plato and his ~** Platón y su escuela, Platón y sus discípulos
4 (*specialist*) escuela *f* • **~ of art** escuela *f* de bellas artes • **~ of dancing** escuela *f* de baile • **~ of motoring** autoescuela *f*, escuela *f* de manejo (*LAm*) • **~ of music** academia *f* de música, conservatorio *m*; ▸ **ballet, driving, riding**
5 (*in expressions*) • **I am not of that ~** yo no soy de esa opinión, yo no pertenezco a esa escuela • **I am not of the ~ that ...** yo no soy de los que ... • **of the old ~** (*fig*) de la vieja escuela • **~ of thought** (*fig*) corriente *f* de opinión
VT [+ *horse*] amaestrar; [+ *person*] educar, instruir; [+ *reaction, voice etc*] dominar • **he has been well ~ed** ha recibido una buena educación • **to ~ sb in sth** educar *or* instruir a algn en algo • **to ~ sb to do sth** preparar a algn para hacer algo • **to ~ o.s. in patience** aprender a tener paciencia
CPD ▸ **school age** edad *f* escolar • **~-age child** niño *m* en edad escolar ▸ **school attendance** asistencia *f* a la escuela

• ~ **attendance officer** *inspector de educación encargado de problemas relacionados con la falta de asistencia o el bajo rendimiento de los alumnos*
▸ **school board** (US) (= *board of governors*) consejo *m* escolar; (= *board of education*) *consejo supervisor del sistema educativo local* ▸ **school bus** autobús *m* escolar ▸ **school counsellor** (US) consejero/a *m/f* escolar ▸ **school dinner** comida *f* escolar, comida *f* de colegio
▸ **school district** (US) distrito *m* escolar
▸ **school doctor** médico *mf* de escuela
▸ **school fees** matrícula *fsing* (escolar)
▸ **school friend** amigo/a *m/f* de clase
▸ **school holidays** vacaciones *fpl* escolares
▸ **school hours** • **during ~ hours** durante las horas de clase ▸ **school inspector** inspector(a) *m/f* de enseñanza ▸ **school kid*** niño/a *m/f* en edad escolar ▸ **school leaver** persona *f* que termina la escuela ▸ **school library** biblioteca *f* escolar ▸ **school life** vida *f* escolar ▸ **school lunch** comida *f* escolar, comida *f* de colegio • **to take ~ lunches** comer *or* almorzar en la escuela ▸ **school meal** comida *f* provista por la escuela
▸ **school night** *noche anterior a un día de colegio*
▸ **school outing** • **to go on a ~ outing to the zoo** ir de visita al zoo con el colegio ▸ **school playground** (*Brit*) patio *m* (de recreo)
▸ **school record** expediente *m* académico
▸ **school report** boletín *m* escolar ▸ **school run** • **to do the ~ run** llevar a los niños al colegio en coche ▸ **school superintendent** (US) superintendente *mf* escolar ▸ **school time** = **school hours** ▸ **school trip** = **school outing** ▸ **school uniform** uniforme *m* escolar
▸ **school yard** (US) = **school playground**
▸ **school year** año *m* escolar

school² [sku:l] (N) [*of fish, dolphins, whales*] banco *m*

schoolbag ['sku:lbæg] (N) bolso *m*, cabás *m*

schoolbook ['sku:lbʊk] (N) libro *m* de texto (escolar)

schoolboy ['sku:lbɔɪ] (N) colegial *m*
(CPD) ▸ **schoolboy slang** jerga *f* de colegial

schoolchild ['sku:ltʃaɪld] (N) (PL: **schoolchildren**) colegial(a) *m/f*

schooldays ['sku:ldeɪz] (NPL) años *mpl* del colegio

schoolfellow ['sku:l,feləʊ] (N) compañero/a *m/f* de clase

schoolgirl ['sku:lgɜ:l] (N) colegiala *f*
(CPD) ▸ **schoolgirl complexion** cutis *m* de colegiala ▸ **schoolgirl crush*** enamoramiento *m* de colegiala

schoolhouse ['sku:lhaʊs] (N) (US) (PL: **schoolhouses**) escuela *f*

schooling ['sku:lɪŋ] (N) (= *education*) instrucción *f*, enseñanza *f*; (= *studies*) estudios *mpl* • **compulsory ~** escolaridad *f* obligatoria • **he had little formal ~** apenas asistió a la escuela

schoolkid ['sku:lkɪd] (N) colegial(a) *m/f*

school-leaving age [,sku:l'li:vɪŋ,eɪdʒ] (N) edad *f* en que se termina la escuela • **to raise the school-leaving age** aumentar la edad de escolaridad obligatoria

schoolman ['sku:lmən] (N) (PL: **schoolmen**) (*Philos*) escolástico *m*

schoolmarm* ['sku:lmɑ:m] (N) (*pej*) institutriz *f*

schoolmaster ['sku:l,mɑ:stəʳ] (N) maestro *m* (de escuela), profesor *m* (de escuela)

schoolmate ['sku:lmeɪt] (N) compañero/a *m/f* de clase

schoolmistress ['sku:l,mɪstrɪs] (N) maestra *f* (de escuela), profesora *f* (de escuela)

schoolroom ['sku:lrʊm] (N) aula *f*, sala *f* de clase

schoolteacher ['sku:l,ti:tʃəʳ] (N) (*gen*) maestro/a *m/f* (de escuela), profesor(a) *m/f* (de escuela)

schoolteaching ['sku:l,ti:tʃɪŋ] (N) enseñanza *f*

schoolwork ['sku:lwɜ:k] (N) trabajo *m* de clase

schooner ['sku:nəʳ] (N) **1** (*Naut*) goleta *f*
2 (*for sherry*) copa *f* grande

schtick* [ʃtɪk] (N) (US) (= *routine, act*) rutina *f*; (= *favourite line*) frase *f* favorita

schwa, schwah [ʃwɑ:] (N) vocal *f* neutra

sciatic [saɪ'ætɪk] (ADJ) ciático

sciatica [saɪ'ætɪkə] (N) (*Med*) ciática *f*

science ['saɪəns] (N) ciencia *f* • **the natural/social ~s** las ciencias naturales/sociales • **the ~s** las ciencias • **it's a real ~*** es una verdadera ciencia • **to blind sb with ~** impresionar *or* deslumbrar a algn citándole muchos datos científicos
(CPD) de ciencias ▸ **science fiction** ciencia-ficción *f* ▸ **science park** zona *f* de ciencias ▸ **science teacher** profesor(a) *m/f* de ciencias

scientific [,saɪən'tɪfɪk] (ADJ) científico

scientifically [,saɪən'tɪfɪkəlɪ] (ADV) científicamente

scientist ['saɪəntɪst] (N) científico/a *m/f*

scientologist [,saɪən'tɒlədʒɪst] (N) cientólogo/a *m/f*

scientology [,saɪən'tɒlədʒɪ] (N) cienciología *f*, cientología *f*

sci-fi* ['saɪfaɪ] (N ABBR) = **science-fiction**

Scillies ['sɪlɪz] (NPL), **Scilly Isles** ['sɪlɪ,aɪlz] (NPL) islas *fpl* Sorlinga

scimitar ['sɪmɪtəʳ] (N) cimitarra *f*

scintillate ['sɪntɪleɪt] (VI) centellear, chispear; (*fig*) brillar

scintillating ['sɪntɪleɪtɪŋ] (ADJ) [*wit, conversation, company*] chispeante, brillante; [*jewels, chandelier*] relumbrante

scintillatingly ['sɪntɪleɪtɪŋlɪ] (ADV) • **~ witty** de un ingenio brillante • **~ clever** de una inteligencia brillante

scion ['saɪən] (N) (*Bot*) (*also fig*) vástago *m* • **~ of a noble family** vástago *m* de una familia noble

Scipio ['skɪpɪəʊ] (N) Escipión

scissors ['sɪzəz] (NPL) tijeras *fpl* • **a pair of ~** unas tijeras
(CPD) ▸ **scissors jump** tijera *f* ▸ **scissors kick** chilena *f*, tijereta *f*

scissors-and-paste [,sɪzəzən'peɪst] (ADJ) (*Brit*) • **a scissors-and-paste job** un refrito

sclerosis [sklɪ'rəʊsɪs] (N) (PL: **scleroses** [sklɪ'rəʊsi:z]) (*Med*) esclerosis *f*; ▹ **multiple**

sclerotic [sklə'rɒtɪk] (ADJ) (*lit, fig*) esclerótico

SCM (N ABBR) (*Brit*) = **State-Certified Midwife**

scoff [skɒf] (VI) mofarse, burlarse (**at sb/sth** de algn/algo) • **my friends ~ed at the idea** mis amigos se mofaron *or* se burlaron de la idea
(VT)* (= *eat*) zamparse*, papearse‡ • **she ~ed the lot** se lo zampó todo • **my brother ~ed all the sandwiches** mi hermano se zampó todos los bocadillos

scoffer ['skɒfəʳ] (N) mofador(a) *m/f*

scoffing ['skɒfɪŋ] (N) mofas *fpl*, burlas *fpl*

scold [skəʊld] (VT) reñir, regañar (**for** por)
(N) (= *woman*) virago *f*

scolding ['skəʊldɪŋ] (N) reprimenda *f*, regañina *f*

scoliosis [,skəʊlɪ'əʊsɪs] (N) escoliosis *f*

scollop ['skɒləp] = **scallop**

sconce [skɒns] (N) candelabro *m* de pared

scone [skɒn] (N) bollo *m* (inglés)

scoop [sku:p] (N) **1** (*for flour*) pala *f*; (*for ice cream, water*) cucharón *m*; (= *quantity scooped*) palada *f*, cucharada *f*
2 (*by newspaper*) exclusiva *f*; (*Comm**) golpe *m* financiero, pelotazo* *m* • **to make a ~** (*Press*) dar una exclusiva; (*Comm*) ganar un dineral de golpe y porrazo*, dar el pelotazo* • **it was a ~ for the paper** fue un gran éxito para el periódico • **we brought off the ~** logramos un triunfo con la exclusiva
(VT) **1** (= *pick up*) recoger
2 (*Comm*) [+ *profit*] sacar; (*Comm, Press*) [+ *competitors*] adelantarse a; (*Press*) [+ *exclusive story*] publicar en exclusiva • **we ~ed the other papers** quedamos por encima de los demás periódicos con nuestra exclusiva
3 [+ *prize, award*] hacerse con, obtener
(CPD) ▸ **scoop neck** cuello *m* en forma de U
▸ **scoop neck top** blusa *f* con el cuello en forma de U
▸ **scoop out** (VT + ADV) (*with scoop*) sacar con pala; (*with spoon*) sacar con cuchara; [+ *water*] achicar; [+ *hollow*] excavar, ahuecar
▸ **scoop up** (VT + ADV) recoger

scoot* [sku:t] (VI) (*also* **scoot away, scoot off**) largarse*, rajarse (*LAm*) • **~!** ¡lárgate!* • **I must ~** tengo que marcharme

scooter ['sku:təʳ] (N) (*child's*) patinete *m*; (*adult's*) moto *f*, escúter *m*, motoneta *f* (*LAm*)

scope [skəʊp] (N) (= *opportunity*) (*for action etc*) libertad *f*, oportunidades *fpl*; (= *range*) [*of law, activity*] ámbito *m*; [*of responsibilities*] ámbito *m*; (= *capacity*) [*of person, mind*] alcance *m*; (= *room*) (*for manoeuvre etc*) esfera *f* de acción, campo *m* de acción • **a programme of considerable ~** un programa de gran alcance • **the ~ of the new measures must be defined** conviene delimitar el campo de aplicación de las nuevas medidas • **it is beyond her ~** está fuera de su alcance • **it is beyond the ~ of this book** está fuera del ámbito del presente libro • **to extend the ~ of one's activities** ampliar su campo de actividades • **there is plenty of ~ for** hay bastante campo para • **this should give you plenty of ~ for your talents** esto ha de darte grandes posibilidades para explotar tus talentos • **to give sb full ~** dar carta blanca a algn • **I'm looking for a job with more ~** busco un puesto que ofrezca más posibilidades • **it is outside my ~** eso está fuera de mi alcance • **it is within her ~** está a su alcance • **it is within the ~ of this book** está dentro del ámbito del presente libro
▸ **scope out** (VT) investigar

scorbutic [skɔ:'bju:tɪk] (ADJ) escorbútico

scorch [skɔ:tʃ] (N) (*also* **scorch mark**) quemadura *f*
(VT) (= *burn*) quemar; [*sun*] abrasar; (= *singe*) chamuscar; [+ *plants, grass*] quemar, secar
• **~ed earth policy** política *f* de tierra quemada
(VI) **1** [*linen*] chamuscarse; [*grass*] agostarse, secarse
2 • **to ~ along** (*Brit**) ir volando, correr a gran velocidad

scorcher* ['skɔ:tʃəʳ] (N) (= *hot day*) día *m* abrasador

scorching ['skɔ:tʃɪŋ] (ADJ) (*also* **scorching hot**) [*heat, day, sun*] abrasador; [*sand*] que quema • **it's a ~ day** hoy hace un día abrasador • **it's ~ hot** hace un calor tremendo • **a few ~ remarks** algunas observaciones mordaces

score [skɔ:ʳ] (N) **1** (*in game, match*) (= *result*) resultado *m*; (= *goal*) gol *m*, tanto *m*; (*at cards, in test, competition*) puntuación *f*, puntaje *m* (*LAm*) • **there's no ~ yet** están a cero; (*in commentary*) no se ha abierto el marcador todavía • **there was no ~ at half-time** en el primer tiempo no hubo goles • **what's the ~?** ¿cómo van?, ¿cómo va el marcador? • **the final ~ was 4-1** el resultado final fue 4 a 1 • **we give each entry a ~ out of ten** damos

una puntuación *or* (*LAm*) un puntaje de uno a diez a cada participante • **he missed a chance to make the ~ 1-1** perdió la oportunidad de empatar a 1 *or* de igualar el marcador a 1 • **with the ~ at 40-0 she has three match points** con 40-0 a su favor, tiene tres bolas de partido • **to keep (the) ~** (*Sport*) llevar la cuenta; (*Cards*) sumar los puntos
2 • **the ~*** (= *situation*): • **what's the ~?** ¿qué pasa?, ¿qué hubo? (*Mex, Chile*) • **you know the ~** ya estás al cabo de la calle *or* de lo que pasa*, ya estás al tanto
3 (= *subject*) • **you've got no worries on that ~** en ese sentido *or* aspecto no tienes por qué preocuparte
4 (= *dispute*) • **to have a ~ to settle with sb** tener cuentas pendientes con algn • **to settle** *or* **pay off old ~s (with sb)** saldar las cuentas pendientes (con algn)
5 (*Mus*) partitura *f*; [*of show, play*] música *f*; [*of film*] banda *f* sonora (original) • **film ~** banda *f* sonora (original) • **piano ~** partitura para piano • **vocal ~** partitura para voz
6 (= *line*) (*on card*) raya *f*, línea *f*; (= *scratch*) (*on wood*) marca *f*, muesca *f*
7 (= *twenty*) veintena *f* • **three ~ years and ten** (*liter*) 70 años • **~s of people** montones de gente*, muchísima gente • **bombs were falling by the ~** caían bombas a mansalva
(VT) **1** (*Sport*) [+ *points*] conseguir, anotarse (*LAm*), apuntarse (*LAm*); [+ *runs*] hacer; [+ *goal, try*] marcar • **they went five games without scoring a point** en cinco partidos no consiguieron *or* no se anotaron un solo punto • **to ~ a hit** (*Shooting*) dar en el blanco • **to ~ a run** (*Baseball*) hacer una carrera
2 (*in exam, test, competition*) [+ *marks, points*] sacar • **to ~ 75% in an exam** sacar 75 sobre 100 en un examen • **she ~d well in the test** sacó *or* obtuvo buena nota en el test • **if you answered yes, ~ five points** si contestó "sí", saca *or* suma cinco puntos
3 [+ *success, victory*] conseguir • **he's certainly ~d a hit with the voters/with his latest novel** no cabe la menor duda de que ha impresionado a los votantes/ha tenido mucho éxito con su última novela • **to ~ points off sb** aventajarse con respecto a algn
4 (*Mus*) [+ *piece*] instrumentar, orquestar
5 (= *cut*) [+ *meat*] hacer unos pequeños cortes en; (= *mark*) [+ *line*] marcar • **her face was weathered, ~d with lines** su rostro estaba curtido y surcado de arrugas
6‡ [+ *drugs*] conseguir, comprar, pillar (*Sp‡*)
(VI) **1** (*Sport*) marcar • **no one has ~d yet** aún no ha marcado nadie; (*in commentary*) aún no se ha abierto el marcador • **he has failed to ~ this season** no ha marcado esta temporada • **that's where he ~s (over the others)** (*fig*) en eso es en lo que tiene más ventaja (sobre los demás)
2 (= *keep score*) (*Sport*) llevar la cuenta; (*Cards*) sumar los puntos
3‡ (= *buy drugs*) conseguir drogas, pillar (*Sp‡*) • **to ~ with sb** (= *have sex*) acostarse con algn; (= *get off with*) ligarse a algn
(CPD) ▸ **score draw** (*Ftbl*) empate *m* • **no-score draw** empate *m* a cero
▸ **score off, score out, score through** (VT + ADV) [+ *text*] tachar

scoreboard ['skɔ:bɔ:d] (N) marcador *m*

scorebook ['skɔ:bʊk] (N) cuaderno *m* de tanteo

scorecard ['skɔ:kɑ:d] (N) (*Golf*) tarjeta *f* donde se apuntan los resultados

scorekeeper ['skɔ:,ki:pəʳ] (N) tanteador(a) *m/f*

scoreless ['skɔ:lɪs] (ADJ) • **~ draw** empate *m* a cero

scoreline ['skɔ:laɪn] (N) (*Sport*) marcador *m*

scorer ['skɔ:rəʳ] (N) (= *person keeping score*) persona *f* que va apuntando los resultados; (= *player*) (*also* **goal scorer**) él/la *m/f* que marca un gol *etc* • **he is top ~ in the league** es el principal goleador en la liga, ha marcado más goles que ningún otro en la liga • **the ~s were Juan and Pablo** marcaron los goles Juan y Pablo

scoresheet ['skɔ:ʃi:t] (N) acta *f* de tanteo

scoring ['skɔ:rɪŋ] (N) **1** (*Sport*) (= *keeping score*) tanteo *m*
2 (= *act of scoring*) • **Evans opened the ~ in the third minute** Evans abrió el marcador en el tercer minuto • **he has a good ~ record** marca muchos goles *or* tantos
3 (*Mus*) orquestación *f*

scorn [skɔ:n] (N) desprecio *m*, menosprecio *m* • **to pour ~ on sth** • **laugh sth to ~** ridiculizar algo
(VT) despreciar, menospreciar • **to ~ to do sth** no dignarse a hacer algo

scornful ['skɔ:nfʊl] (ADJ) desdeñoso, despreciativo • **to be ~ about sth** desdeñar algo

scornfully ['skɔ:nfəlɪ] (ADV) desdeñosamente, con desprecio

Scorpio ['skɔ:pɪəʊ] (N) **1** (= *sign, constellation*) Escorpión *m*
2 (= *person*) escorpión *mf* • **I'm (a) ~** soy escorpión

scorpion ['skɔ:pɪən] (N) alacrán *m*, escorpión *m*

Scot [skɒt] (N) escocés/esa *m/f*

Scotch [skɒtʃ] (ADJ) • **~ broth** sopa *f* de verduras • **~ egg** (*esp Brit*) huevo *m* cocido rodeado de carne de salchicha y rebozado • **~ mist** llovizna *f* • **~ tape** ® (*esp US*) cinta *f* adhesiva, scotch *m* (*LAm*), durex *m* (*Mex*) • **~ terrier** terrier *m* escocés • **~ whisky** whisky *m* escocés, scotch *m*
(N) (= *whisky*) whisky *m* escocés, scotch *m*

scotch [skɒtʃ] (VT) [+ *attempt, plan*] frustrar; [+ *rumour, claim*] acallar
(N) (= *wedge*) calza *f*, cuña *f*

scot-free ['skɒt'fri:] (ADJ) • **to get off scot-free** (= *unpunished*) salir impune; (= *unhurt*) salir ileso

Scotland ['skɒtlənd] (N) Escocia *f*
(CPD) ▸ **Scotland Yard** *oficina central de la policía de Londres*

Scots [skɒts] (ADJ) escocés • **a ~ accent** un acento escocés • **~ pine** pino *m* escocés
(N) (*Ling*) escocés *m*

Scotsman ['skɒtsmən] (N) (PL: **Scotsmen**) escocés *m*

Scotswoman ['skɒts,wʊmən] (N) (PL: **Scotswomen**) escocesa *f*

Scotticism ['skɒtɪsɪzəm] (N) giro *m* escocés, escocesismo *m*

Scottie ['skɒtɪ] (N) (= *dog*) terrier *m* escocés

Scottish ['skɒtɪʃ] (ADJ) escocés • **a ~ accent** un acento escocés • **the ~ Parliament** el Parlamento Escocés
(CPD) ▸ **Scottish Office** Ministerio *m* de Asuntos Escoceses ▸ **Scottish Secretary** Ministro/a *m/f* para Escocia, Secretario/a *m/f* (Parlamentario/a) para Escocia

scoundrel ['skaʊndrəl] (N) sinvergüenza *mf*

scoundrelly† ['skaʊndrəlɪ] (ADJ) canallesco, vil

scour ['skaʊəʳ] (VT) **1** [+ *pan, floor*] fregar, restregar (*esp LAm*); [+ *channel*] limpiar
2 (= *search*) registrar • **we ~ed the countryside for him** hicimos una batida por el campo buscándole
(VI) • **to ~ about for sth** buscar algo por todas partes
▸ **scour out** (VT + ADV) [+ *pan etc*] fregar, restregar (*esp LAm*); [+ *channel*] limpiar • **the river had ~ed out part of the bank** el río se había llevado una parte de la orilla

scourer ['skaʊərəʳ] (N) (= *pad*) estropajo *m*; (= *powder*) limpiador *m*, quitagrasas *m inv*

scourge [skɜ:dʒ] (N) (*lit, fig*) azote *m* • **the ~ of malaria** el azote del paludismo • **the ~ of war** el azote de la guerra • **it is the ~ of our times** es la plaga de nuestros tiempos • **God sent it as a ~** Dios lo envió como castigo
(VT) (*lit*) azotar, flagelar; (*fig*) hostigar

scouring pad ['skaʊrɪŋpæd] (N) estropajo *m*

scouring powder ['skaʊrɪŋpaʊdəʳ] (N) limpiador *m* (en polvos), quitagrasas *m inv* (en polvo)

Scouse* [skaʊs] (ADJ) de Liverpool
(N) **1** nativo/a *m/f* de Liverpool, habitante *mf* de Liverpool
2 (*Ling*) dialecto *m* de Liverpool

scout [skaʊt] (N) **1** (= *person*) (*Mil*) explorador(a) *m/f*; (*also* **boy scout**) muchacho *m* explorador • **(talent) ~** (*Sport, Cine, Theat*) cazatalentos *mf inv*
2* (= *reconnaissance*) reconocimiento *m*; (= *search*) búsqueda *f* • **to have a ~ round** reconocer *or* explorar el terreno • **we'll have a ~ (round) for it** (*fig*) lo buscaremos
(VI) (= *explore*) explorar; (*Mil*) reconocer el terreno • **to ~ for sth** buscar algo
(CPD) ▸ **scout car** (*Mil*) vehículo *m* de reconocimiento
▸ **scout about, scout around, scout round** (VI + ADV) (*Mil*) ir de reconocimiento, reconocer el terreno • **to ~ around for sth** (*Mil*) hacer un reconocimiento *or* explorar buscando algo; (*fig*) buscar algo

scouting ['skaʊtɪŋ] (N) actividades *fpl* de los exploradores

scoutmaster ['skaʊt,mɑ:stəʳ] (N) jefe *m* de exploradores

scow [skaʊ] (N) gabarra *f*

scowl [skaʊl] (N) ceño *m* fruncido • **he said with a ~** dijo con el ceño fruncido
(VI) fruncir el ceño, fruncir el entrecejo • **to ~ at sb** mirar a algn con el ceño fruncido, mirar a algn frunciendo el ceño *or* el entrecejo

scowling ['skaʊlɪŋ] (ADJ) ceñudo

SCR (N ABBR) (*Brit*) (*Univ*) = **senior common room**

scrabble ['skræbl] (VI) • **to ~ about** *or* **around for sth** revolver todo buscando algo • **she was scrabbling about in the coal** andaba rebuscando por entre el carbón
(N) • **Scrabble** ® (*game*) Scrabble® *m*

scrag [skræg] (N) pescuezo *m*
(VT) [+ *animal*] torcer el pescuezo a; [+ *person**] dar una paliza a

scragginess ['skrægɪnɪs] (N) flaqueza *f*

scraggly ['skræglɪ] (ADJ) (*US*) [*beard*] descuidado; [*hair*] revuelto; [*plant*] asalvajado, de aspecto salvaje

scraggy ['skrægɪ] (ADJ) (COMPAR: **scraggier**, SUPERL: **scraggiest**) flacucho

scram* [skræm] (VI) largarse*, rajarse (*LAm*) • **~!** ¡lárgate!*

scramble ['skræmbl] (VI) **1** • **to ~ up/down** subir gateando/bajar con dificultad • **to ~ out** salir con dificultad • **we ~d through the hedge** nos abrimos paso con dificultad a través del seto • **to ~ for** [+ *coins, seats*] luchar entre sí por, pelearse por; (*fig*) [+ *jobs*] pelearse por
2 (*Sport*) • **to go scrambling** hacer motocross
(VT) **1** (*Culin*) revolver • **~d eggs** huevos *mpl* revueltos
2 (*Telec*) [+ *message*] cifrar; (*TV*) codificar
3 [+ *aircraft*] hacer despegar con urgencia (*por alarma*)
(N) **1** (= *rush*) lucha *f*, pelea *f* (**for por**)
2 (*Sport*) (= *motorcycle meeting*) carrera *f* de

motocross
3 (= *climb*) subida *f*; (= *outing*) excursión *f* de montaña (*por terreno escabroso etc*)

scrambler ['skræmblə^r] (N) **1** (*Telec*) emisor *m* de interferencias
2 (= *motorcyclist*) motociclista *mf* de motocross

scrambling ['skræmblɪŋ] (N) **1** (*Sport*) motocross *m* campo a través
2 (*TV*) codificación *f*

scran‡ [skræn] (N) (*Brit*) comida *f*

scrap¹ [skræp] (N) **1** (= *small piece*) pedacito *m*; [*of newspaper*] recorte *m*; [*of material*] retal *m*, retazo *m*; (*fig*) pizca *f* • **it's a ~ of comfort** es una migaja de consolación • **a ~ of conversation** un fragmento de conversación • **a few ~s of news** unos fragmentos de noticias • **there is not a ~ of truth in it** no hay ni un ápice de verdad en eso, no tiene nada de cierto • **not a ~ of proof** ni la más mínima prueba • **not a ~ of use** sin utilidad alguna • **not a ~!** ¡ni pizca!, ¡en absoluto! • **a ~ of paper** un trocito de papel
2 scraps (= *leftovers*) restos *mpl*, sobras *fpl* • **the dog feeds on ~s** el perro come de las sobras de la mesa
3 (*also* **scrap metal**) chatarra *f*, desecho *m* de hierro • **what is it worth as ~?** ¿cuánto vale como chatarra? • **to sell a ship for ~** vender un barco como chatarra
(VT) [+ *car, ship etc*] chatarrear, convertir en chatarra; [+ *old equipment etc*] tirar; [+ *idea, plan etc*] desechar, descartar • **we had to ~ that idea** tuvimos que descartar *or* desechar esa idea • **in the end the plan was ~ped** al final se desechó *or* se descartó el plan
(CPD) ▸ **scrap dealer** chatarrero/a *m/f* ▸ **scrap heap** montón *m* de desechos • **this is for the ~ heap** esto es para tirar • **to throw sth on the ~ heap** (*fig*) desechar *or* descartar algo • **I was thrown on the ~ heap at the age of 50** me dieron la patada cuando tenía 50 años • **workers are being thrown on the ~ heap** los obreros van al basurero • **to be on the ~ heap** [*person*] no tener nada a que agarrarse • **he ended up on the ~ heap** se quedó sin nada a que agarrarse ▸ **scrap iron** chatarra *f*, hierro *m* viejo ▸ **scrap merchant** chatarrero/a *m/f* ▸ **scrap metal** chatarra *f* ▸ **scrap paper** pedazos *mpl* de papel suelto (*que se utilizan para borrador*) ▸ **scrap value** valor *m* como chatarra • **its ~ value is £30** como chatarra vale 30 libras ▸ **scrap yard** chatarrería *f*; (*for cars*) cementerio *m* de coches

scrap²* [skræp] (N) (= *fight*) riña *f*, pelea *f* • **there was a ~ outside the pub** hubo una riña *or* pelea a la salida del pub • **to get into** *or* **have a ~ with sb** reñir *or* pelearse con algn
(VI) reñir, pelearse (**with sb** con algn) • **they were ~ping in the street** se estaban peleando en la calle

scrapbook ['skræpbʊk] (N) álbum *m* de recortes

scrape [skreɪp] (N) **1** (= *act*) raspado *m*, raspadura *f*; (= *sound*) chirrido *m*; (= *mark*) arañazo *m*, rasguño *m* • **to give sth a ~** raspar algo, limpiar algo raspándolo • **to give one's knee a ~** rasguñarse la rodilla
2 (*fig*) lío *m*, aprieto *m* • **to get into/out of a ~** meterse en/salir de un lío *or* aprieto • **to get sb out of a ~** sacar a algn de un lío *or* aprieto
(VT) [+ *knee, elbow*] arañarse, rasguñarse; (= *clean*) [+ *vegetables*] raspar, limpiar; [+ *walls, woodwork*] raspar • **to ~ on/along/against sth** arrastrar en/a lo largo de/contra algo • **the lorry ~d the wall** el camión rozó el muro • **to ~ one's boots** limpiarse las botas • **to ~ one's plate clean** dejar completamente limpio el plato • **to ~ a living** sacar lo justo para vivir • **the ship ~d the bottom** el barco rozó el fondo • **to ~ one's feet across the floor** arrastrar los pies por el suelo • IDIOM: • **to ~ the bottom of the barrel** tocar fondo
(VI) (= *make sound*) chirriar; (= *rub*) • **to ~ (against)** pasar rozando • **to ~ past** pasar rozando • **we just managed to ~ through the gap** nos costó pasar por la abertura sin tocar las paredes
▸ **scrape along*** (VI + ADV) (*financially*) sacar lo justo para vivir; (= *live*) ir tirando • **I can ~ along in Arabic** me defiendo en árabe
▸ **scrape away** (VT + ADV) raspar, quitar raspando
(VI + ADV) • **to ~ away at the violin** ir rascando el violín
▸ **scrape back** (VT + ADV) [+ *hair*] peinar para atrás
▸ **scrape by** (VI + ADV) arreglárselas, ir tirando
▸ **scrape off** (VT + ADV) raspar, quitar raspando
(VT + PREP) raspar de
▸ **scrape out** (VT + ADV) [+ *contents*] remover raspando
▸ **scrape through** (VI + ADV) (= *succeed*) lograr hacer algo por los pelos • **I just ~d through** aprobé por los pelos
(VI + PREP) [+ *narrow gap*] pasar muy justo por • **to ~ through an exam** aprobar un examen por los pelos
▸ **scrape together** (VT + ADV) (*fig*) reunir poco a poco • **we managed to ~ enough money together** logramos reunir suficiente dinero
▸ **scrape up** (VT + ADV) (*fig*) reunir poco a poco • **to ~ up an acquaintance with sb** trabar amistad con algn

scraper ['skreɪpə^r] (N) (= *tool*) raspador *m*, rascador *m*; (*on doorstep*) limpiabarros *m inv*

scraperboard ['skreɪpəbɔːd] (N) *cartulina entintada sobre la cual se realiza un dibujo rascando la capa de tinta*

scrapie ['skreɪpɪ] (N) scrapie *m*

scraping ['skreɪpɪŋ] (N) **1** (= *sound*) sonido *m* áspero • **the ~ of chairs** el ruido de arrastrar sillas
2 (= *thin layer*) [*of butter, margarine, jam*] capa *f* fina
3 (= *sample*) [*of skin, cells, tissue*] raspado *m*
(ADJ) • **a ~ noise** un sonido áspero

scrapings ['skreɪpɪŋz] (NPL) raspaduras *fpl* • **~ of the gutter** (*fig*) hez *fsing* de la sociedad

scrappy ['skræpɪ] (ADJ) (COMPAR: **scrappier**, SUPERL: **scrappiest**) [*essay etc*] deshilvanado; [*knowledge, education*] incompleto; [*meal*] hecho con sobras

scratch ['skrætʃ] (N) **1** (= *mark*) (*on skin*) arañazo *m*, rasguño *m*; (*on surface, record*) raya *f* • **it's just a ~** es solo un rasguño, nada más • **the cat gave her a ~** el gato la arañó • **he hadn't a ~ on him** no tenía ni un arañazo • **to have a good ~** rascarse con ganas
2 (= *noise*) chirrido *m*
3 • **to start from ~** (*fig*) partir de *or* empezar desde cero • **we shall have to start from ~ again** tendremos que partir nuevamente de cero, tendremos que comenzar desde el principio otra vez • **to be** *or* **come up to ~** cumplir con los requisitos • **to bring/keep sth up to ~** poner/mantener algo en buenas condiciones
(VT) **1** (*with claw, nail etc*) rasguñar, arañar; (*making sound*) rascar, raspar; [+ *surface, record*] rayar; (= *scramble, dig*) escarbar • **you'll ~ the worktop with that knife** vas a rayar la encimera con ese cuchillo • **the glass of this watch cannot be ~ed** el cristal de este reloj no se raya • **he ~ed his hand on a rose bush** se arañó la mano en un rosal • **the lovers ~ed their names on the tree** los amantes grabaron sus nombres en el árbol; ▹ **surface**
2 (*to relieve itch*) rascarse • **he ~ed his head** se rascó la cabeza • **she ~ed the dog's ear** le rascó la oreja al perro • IDIOM: • **you ~ my back and I'll ~ yours** un favor con favor se paga
3 (= *cancel*) [+ *meeting, game*] cancelar; (= *cross off list*) [+ *horse, competitor*] tachar, borrar • **to ~ sb off a list** tachar a algn de una lista
4 (*Comput*) borrar
(VI) [*person, dog etc*] rascarse; [*hens*] escarbar; [*pen*] rascar; [*clothing*] rascar, picar • **stop ~ing!** ¡deja de rascarte! • **the dog ~ed at the door** el perro arañó la puerta
(CPD) [*competitor*] sin ventaja ▸ **scratch card** tarjeta *f* de "rasque y gane" ▸ **scratch file** (*Comput*) fichero *m* de trabajo ▸ **scratch meal** comida *f* improvisada ▸ **scratch pad** (*US*) (= *notepad*) bloc *m* (*para apuntes o para borrador*); (*Comput*) bloc *m* de notas ▸ **scratch pad memory** (*Comput*) memoria *f* del bloc de notas ▸ **scratch paper** (*US*) papel *m* de borrador ▸ **scratch score** (*Golf*) puntuación *f* par ▸ **scratch tape** cinta *f* reutilizable ▸ **scratch team** equipo *m* improvisado
▸ **scratch out** (VT + ADV) (*from list*) borrar, tachar • **to ~ sb's eyes out** sacarle los ojos a algn

scratchpad ['skrætʃpæd] (N) (*US*) bloc *m* (*para apuntes o para borrador*)

scratchy ['skrætʃɪ] (ADJ) (COMPAR: **scratchier**, SUPERL: **scratchiest**) [*fabric*] que rasca *or* pica; [*pen*] que rasca; [*writing*] flojo, irregular

scrawl [skrɔːl] (N) garabatos *mpl* • **I can't read her ~** no puedo leer sus garabatos • **the word finished in a ~** la palabra terminaba en un garabato
(VT) garabatear • **to ~ a note to sb** garabatear una nota a algn • **a wall ~ed all over with rude words** una pared llena de palabrotas
(VI) garabatear, hacer garabatos

scrawny ['skrɔːnɪ] (ADJ) (COMPAR: **scrawnier**, SUPERL: **scrawniest**) [*neck, limb*] flaco; [*animal*] escuálido, descarnado

scream [skriːm] (N) **1** (= *yell*) grito *m*; (*high-pitched*) chillido *m*; (*stronger*) alarido *m* • **a ~ of agony** un grito *or* alarido de dolor • **a ~ of delight** un grito de alegría • **the ~ of the eagle** el chillido del águila • **to let out** *or* **give a ~** pegar un grito, soltar un grito • **a ~ of joy** un grito de alegría • **there were ~s of laughter** hubo sonoras carcajadas • **his voice rose to a ~** levantó la voz y empezó a gritar • **a ~ of terror** un grito *or* alarido de terror
2 [*of machinery, brakes*] chirrido *m*
3* (*fig*) • **it was a ~** fue la monda*, fue para morirse de la risa • **he's a ~** es graciosísimo, es de lo más chistoso, es la monda*
(VT) **1** [+ *abuse, orders*] gritar • **they started ~ing abuse at us** nos empezaron a insultar a voz en grito, nos empezaron a gritar insultos • IDIOM: • **to ~ blue murder** (= *protest*) poner el grito en el cielo
2 [*headlines*] • **"650 dead," ~ed the headlines** 650 muertos rezaban los enormes titulares
(VI) [*person*] chillar, gritar; [*baby*] berrear • **if I hear one more joke about my hair, I shall ~** una palabra más acerca de mi pelo y me pongo a gritar • **they dragged him ~ing out of the shop** lo tuvieron que sacar de la tienda a rastras • **I was kept awake by a ~ing baby** me tenía despierto un niño que no hacía más que berrear • **to ~ at sb** gritar a algn • **to ~ for help** pedir ayuda a gritos • **to ~**

in *or* **with pain** pegar *or* soltar un grito de dolor, gritar de dolor • **I must have ~ed out in my sleep** debí de chillar *or* gritar entre sueños • **the headline ~ed out from the page** el titular saltaba a la vista • **to ~ with laughter** reírse a carcajada limpia

screamer* ['skri:məʳ] (N) (*US*) **1** (= *headline*) titular *m* muy grande
2 (= *joke*) chiste *m* desternillante • **he's a ~‡** es la monda*
3 (*Sport*) (= *shot*) trallazo *m*

screamingly* ['skri:mɪŋlɪ] (ADV) • **a ~ funny joke** un chiste de lo más divertido • **it was ~ funny** fue para morirse de risa*

scree ['skri:] (N) pedregal *m* (*en una ladera*)

screech [skri:tʃ] (N) [*of brakes, tyres*] chirrido *m*; [*of person*] grito *m*; [*of animal*] chillido *m*
(VI) [*brakes, tyres*] chirriar; [*person*] gritar, chillar; [*animal*] chillar

screech-owl ['skri:tʃaʊl] (N) lechuza *f*

screed* [skri:d] (NPL) rollo *m* • **to write ~s** estar venga a escribir, escribir hojas y hojas

screen [skri:n] (N) **1** (= *physical barrier*) (*in room*) biombo *m*; (*on window, door*) (*to keep out mosquitos*) mosquitera *f*; (*for fire*) pantalla *f*; (*in front of VDU*) filtro *m*
2 (*Cine, TV, Tech, Comput*) [*of television, computer, in cinema, for slides*] pantalla *f* • **radar ~** pantalla *f* de radar • **she was the ideal mother, both on and off ~** era la madre ideal, tanto dentro como fuera de la pantalla • **to write for the ~** escribir para el cine • **stars of the ~** estrellas *fpl* de la pantalla, estrellas *fpl* de cine • **the big/small ~** la pantalla grande/pequeña
3 (*fig*) • **a ~ of trees** una pantalla de árboles • **a ~ of smoke** una cortina de humo
4 (*Mil*) cortina *f*
(VT) **1** • **to ~ (from)** (= *hide*) (*from view, sight*) ocultar *or* tapar (de); (= *protect*) proteger (de) • **the house is ~ed (from view) by trees** la casa queda oculta detrás de los árboles • **he ~ed his eyes with his hand** se puso la mano sobre los ojos a modo de pantalla • **in order to ~ our movements from the enemy** para impedir que el enemigo pudiera ver nuestros movimientos
2 (= *show*) [+ *film*] proyectar; [+ *TV programme*] emitir; (*for the first time*) estrenar; [+ *novel etc*] adaptar para el cine, hacer una versión cinematográfica de
3 (= *sieve*) [+ *coal*] tamizar
4 (*for security*) [+ *suspect, applicant*] investigar • **he was ~ed by Security** Seguridad le investigó, estuvo sometido a investigaciones de Seguridad
5 (*Med*) • **to ~ sb for sth** hacer una exploración a algn buscando algo
6 [+ *telephone calls*] filtrar
(CPD) ▸ **screen actor** actor *m* de cine ▸ **screen actress** actriz *f* de cine ▸ **screen display** (*Comput*) visualización *f* en pantalla ▸ **screen door** puerta *f* con mosquitera ▸ **screen dump** (*Comput*) pantallazo *m*, captura *f* de pantalla ▸ **screen editing** (*Comput*) corrección *f* en pantalla ▸ **screen goddess** diosa *f* de la gran pantalla ▸ **screen legend** leyenda *f* de la gran pantalla ▸ **screen memory** (*Comput*) memoria *f* de la pantalla ▸ **screen name** [*of actor*] nombre *m* artístico; (*on the internet*) nick *m* ▸ **screen print** serigrafía *f* ▸ **screen printing** serigrafiado *m*, serigrafía *f* ▸ **screen rights** derechos *mpl* cinematográficos ▸ **screen saver** salvapantallas *m inv* ▸ **screen test** prueba *f* cinematográfica ▸ **screen writer** guionista *mf*

▸ **screen off** (VT + ADV) tapar

▸ **screen out** (VT + ADV) [+ *light, noise*] eliminar, filtrar

screencast ['skri:nka:st] (N) screencast *m*

screenful ['skri:nfʊl] (N) pantalla *f*

screening ['skri:nɪŋ] (N) **1** [*of film*] proyección *f*; [*of TV programme*] emisión *f*; (*for the first time*) estreno *m*
2 (*for security*) investigación *f*
3 (*Med*) [*of person*] exploración *f*

screenplay ['skri:npleɪ] (N) guión *m*

screen-printed ['skri:n,prɪntɪd] (ADJ) [*design, T-shirt*] serigrafiado

screenshot ['skri:nʃɒt] (N) pantallazo *m*, captura *f* de pantalla

screenwriter ['skri:n,raɪtəʳ] (N) guionista *mf*

screenwriting ['skri:n,raɪtɪŋ] (N) escritura *f* de guiones

screw [skru:] (N) **1** tornillo *m* • IDIOMS: • **he's got a ~ loose*** le falta un tornillo • **to put the ~s on sb*** apretar las clavijas a algn, presionar a algn
2 (*Aer, Naut*) hélice *f*
3‡ (= *prison officer*) carcelero/a *m/f*
4** (= *sexual intercourse*) polvo** *m*
(VT) **1** [+ *screw*] atornillar; [+ *nut*] apretar; [+ *lid*] dar vueltas a, enroscar • **to ~ sth down** fijar algo con tornillos • **to ~ sth to the wall** fijar algo a la pared con tornillos • **to ~ sth (in) tight** atornillar algo bien fuerte • **to ~ money out of sb*** sacarle dinero a algn • **to ~ the truth out of sb*** arrancarle la verdad a algn
2** (= *have sex with*) joder** • **~ the cost, it's got to be done!** (*fig*) ¡a la porra el gasto, tiene que hacerse!
3* (= *defraud*) timar, estafar
(VI)** joder**, echar un polvo**, coger (*LAm***), chingar (*Mex***)
(CPD) ▸ **screw cap, screw top** tapón *m* de rosca; ▹ **screw-top**

▸ **screw around**** (VI + ADV) ligar*

▸ **screw down** (VT + ADV) **1** (= *fix with screws*) [+ *floorboards etc*] atornillar
2 (= *fasten by twisting*) [+ *lid, top*] enroscar • **~ the lid down tightly** enrosque la tapa con fuerza
(VI + ADV) [*lid, top*] enroscarse

▸ **screw off** (VT + ADV) desenroscar
(VI + ADV) desenroscarse • **the lid ~s off** la tapadera se desenrosca

▸ **screw on** (VT + ADV) **1** (*with screws*) • **to ~ sth on to a board** fijar algo en un tablón con tornillos • **he's got his head ~ed on** sabe cuántas son cinco
2 (*by twisting*) • **to ~ on a lid** enroscar una tapa • **~ the lid on tightly** enrosca *or* mete bien la tapa
(VI + ADV) **1** (*with screws*) • **it ~s on here** se fija aquí con tornillos
2 (*by twisting*) • **the lid ~s on** la tapa se cierra a rosca *or* enroscándose

▸ **screw together** (VI + ADV) juntarse con tornillos
(VT + ADV) armar (con tornillos)

▸ **screw up** (VT + ADV) **1** [+ *paper, material*] arrugar • **to ~ up one's eyes** arrugar el entrecejo • **to ~ up one's face** torcer la cara • **to ~ up one's courage** (*fig*) armarse de valor • **to ~ o.s. up to do sth** armarse de valor para hacer algo
2 [+ *screw*] atornillar; [+ *nut*] apretar • **to ~ sth up tight** atornillar algo bien fuerte
3* (= *ruin*) fastidiar, joder**, fregar (*LAm*), chingar (*Mex***) • **the experience really ~ed him up** la experiencia lo dejó completamente hecho polvo
(VI + ADV) **1** (*by turning*) • **it will ~ up tighter than that** se puede apretar todavía más
2 (*US**) • **he really ~ed up this time** esta vez sí que lo fastidió *or* (*LAm*) fregó

screwball* ['skru:bɔ:l] (*esp US*) (ADJ) excéntrico, estrafalario
(N) chiflado/a* *m/f*, chalado/a* *m/f*, tarado/a *m/f* (*esp LAm**)

screwdriver ['skru:,draɪvəʳ] (N) **1** (= *tool*) destornillador *m*, desarmador *m* (*Mex*)
2 (= *drink*) destornillador *m*

screwed‡ [skru:d] (ADJ) (*Brit*) (= *drunk*) pedo‡, borracho

screwed-up* [,skru:d'ʌp] (ADJ) (*psychologically*) tarado • **to be screwed-up** estar tarado • **to be screwed-up about sth** estar chiflado por algo

screw-in ['skru:ɪn] (ADJ) de rosca

screw-on ['skru:ɒn] (ADJ) [*cap, top*] enroscable

screw-top ['skru:tɒp] (ADJ), **screw-topped** ['skru:tɒpt] (ADJ) [*bottle, jar*] de rosca; ▹ **screw**

screw-up‡ ['skru:ʌp] (N) lío* *m*, embrollo *m*, cacao* *m*

screwy* ['skru:ɪ] (ADJ) (COMPAR: **screwier**, SUPERL: **screwiest**) (= *mad*) chiflado, tarado (*LAm*)

scribble ['skrɪbl] (N) garabatos *mpl* • **I can't read his ~** no consigo leer sus garabatos • **a wall covered in ~s** una pared llena de garabatos
(VT) garabatear • **to ~ sth down** garabatear algo • **to ~ one's signature** garabatear la firma, firmar a toda prisa • **a word ~d on a wall** una palabra garabateada en una pared • **a sheet of paper ~d (over) with notes** una hoja de papel emborronada de notas
(VI) garabatear

scribbler ['skrɪbləʳ] (N) escritorzuelo/a *m/f*

scribbling ['skrɪblɪŋ] (N) garabato *m*
(CPD) ▸ **scribbling pad** bloc *m* (*para apuntes o para borrador*)

scribe [skraɪb] (N) [*of manuscript*] escribiente/a *m/f*; (*Bible*) escriba *m*

scrimmage ['skrɪmɪdʒ] (N) **1** (= *fight*) escaramuza *f*
2 (*US*) (*Sport*) = **scrum**

scrimp [skrɪmp] (VI) • **to ~ and save** hacer economías, apretarse el cinturón

scrimpy ['skrɪmpɪ] (ADJ) [*person*] tacaño; [*supply etc*] escaso

scrimshank* ['skrɪmʃæŋk] (VI) (*Brit*) (*Mil*) racanear*, hacer el rácano*

scrimshanker* ['skrɪm,ʃæŋkəʳ] (N) (*Brit*) (*Mil*) rácano* *m*

scrip [skrɪp] (N) (*Econ*) vale *m*, abonaré *m*

script [skrɪpt] (N) **1** (*Cine*) guión *m* • **film ~** guión *m*; (*Theat, TV, Rad*) argumento *m*
2 (= *system of writing*) escritura *f*; (= *handwriting*) letra *f*; (= *typeface*) fuente *f*, tipo *m* de letra • **Arabic/Gothic ~** escritura *f* árabe/gótica
3 (*in exam*) escrito *m*
(VT) [+ *film*] escribir el guión de; [+ *play*] escribir el argumento de • **the film was not well ~ed** la película no tenía un buen guión
(CPD) ▸ **script editor** (*Cine, TV*) revisor(a) *m/f* de guión ▸ **script girl** (*Cine*) script *f*, anotadora *f*

scripted ['skrɪptɪd] (ADJ) (*Rad, TV*) escrito

scriptural ['skrɪptʃərəl] (ADJ) escriturario, bíblico

Scripture ['skrɪptʃəʳ] (N) **1** (*also* **Holy Scripture**) Sagrada Escritura *f*
2 (*Scol*) (= *subject, lesson*) Historia *f* Sagrada

scriptwriter ['skrɪpt,raɪtəʳ] (N) guionista *mf*

scrivener ['skrɪvənəʳ] (N) (*Hist*) escribano *m*

scrofula ['skrɒfjʊlə] (N) escrófula *f*

scrofulous ['skrɒfjʊləs] (ADJ) escrofuloso

scroll [skrəʊl] (N) **1** (= *roll of parchment*) rollo *m*; (= *ancient manuscript*) manuscrito *m* • **the Dead Sea ~s** los manuscritos del Mar Muerto • **~ of fame** lista *f* de la fama
2 (*Archit*) voluta *f*

(VT) (*Comput*) desplazar
(CPD) ▸ **scroll bar** (*Comput*) barra *f* de desplazamiento ▸ **scroll key** (*Comput*) tecla *f* de desplazamiento
▸ **scroll down** (VT + ADV) desplazar hacia abajo
(VI + ADV) desplazarse hacia abajo
▸ **scroll up** (VT + ADV) desplazar hacia arriba
(VI + ADV) desplazarse hacia arriba
scrollable ['skrəʊləbl] (ADJ) (*Comput*) desplazable
scrolling ['skrəʊlɪŋ] (N) (*Comput*) desplazamiento *m*
Scrooge [skru:dʒ] (N) el avariento típico (*personaje del "Christmas Carol" de Dickens*)
scrotum ['skrəʊtəm] (N) (PL: **scrotums** *or* **scrota** ['skrəʊtə]) escroto *m*
scrounge* [skraʊndʒ] (N) • **to be on the ~ (for sth)** ir sacando (algo) de gorra • **to have a ~ round for sth** ir por ahí pidiendo algo
(VT) gorronear*, gorrear* • **I ~d a ticket** gorroneé una entrada • **to ~ sth from sb** gorronear algo a algn • **can I ~ a drink from you?** ¿me invitas a un trago?*
(VI) • **to ~ on** *or* **off sb** vivir a costa de algn • **to ~ around for sth** ir por ahí pidiendo algo
scrounger* ['skraʊndʒəʳ] (N) gorrón/ona *m/f*, sablista *mf*
scrub[1] [skrʌb] (N) (*Bot*) (= *undergrowth*) monte *m* bajo, maleza *f*; (= *bushes*) matas *fpl*, matorrales *mpl*
(CPD) ▸ **scrub fire** incendio *m* de monte bajo
scrub[2] [skrʌb] (N) fregado *m*, restregado *m* (*esp LAm*) • **to give sth a (good) ~** fregar *or* restregar algo (bien) • **it needs a hard ~** hay que fregarlo *or* restregarlo con fuerza
(VT) **1** (= *clean*) [+ *floor, hands etc*] fregar • **to ~ sth clean** fregar *or* restregar algo hasta que quede limpio
2* (= *cancel*) cancelar, anular • **let's ~ it** bueno, lo borramos
(CPD) ▸ **scrub brush** (*US*) cepillo *m* de fregar
▸ **scrub away** (VT + ADV) [+ *dirt*] quitar restregando; [+ *stain*] quitar frotando
▸ **scrub down** (VT + ADV) [+ *room, wall*] fregar • **to ~ o.s. down** fregarse
▸ **scrub off** (VT + ADV) [+ *mark, stain*] quitar cepillando; [+ *name*] tachar
(VT + PREP) quitar de
▸ **scrub out** (VT + ADV) [+ *stain*] limpiar restregando; [+ *pan*] fregar; [+ *name*] tachar
▸ **scrub up** (VI + ADV) [*doctor, surgeon*] lavarse
scrubber[1] ['skrʌbəʳ] (N) (*also* **pan scrubber**) estropajo *m*
scrubber[2]‡ ['skrʌbəʳ] (N) (*Brit*) (= *whore*) putilla‡ *f*
scrubbing brush ['skrʌbɪŋˌbrʌʃ] (N) cepillo *m* de fregar
scrubby ['skrʌbɪ] (ADJ) **1** [*person*] achaparrado, enano
2 [*land*] cubierto de maleza
scrubland ['skrʌblænd] (N) monte *m* bajo, maleza *f*
scrubwoman ['skrʌbˌwʊmən] (N) (PL: **scrubwomen**) (*US*) fregona *f*
scruff [skrʌf] (N) **1** • **by the ~ of the neck** del cogote
2* (= *untidy person*) dejado/a *m/f*
scruffily ['skrʌfɪlɪ] (ADV) • **~ dressed** mal vestido, vestido con desaliño
scruffiness ['skrʌfɪnɪs] (N) (= *untidiness*) desaliño *m*; (= *dirtiness*) suciedad *f*
scruffy ['skrʌfɪ] (ADJ) (COMPAR: **scruffier**, SUPERL: **scruffiest**) [*person, appearance*] desaliñado, dejado; [*clothes*] desaliñado; [*building*] destartalado • **he looks ~** tiene aspecto descuidado
scrum [skrʌm] (N) (*Rugby*) melé *f* • **loose ~** melé *f* abierta *or* espontánea • **set ~** melé *f* cerrada *or* ordenada
(CPD) ▸ **scrum half** medio *m* de melé
▸ **scrum down** (VI + ADV) formar la melé (cerrada *or* ordenada)
scrummage ['skrʌmɪdʒ] (N) = **scrum**
scrummy* ['skrʌmɪ] (ADJ) [*food, taste*] riquísimo, sabrosísimo
scrumptious* ['skrʌmpʃəs] (ADJ) riquísimo, sabrosísimo
scrumpy ['skrʌmpɪ] (N) (*Brit*) sidra *f* muy seca
scrunch [skrʌntʃ] (VT) (*also* **scrunch up**) ronzar
scrunchie ['skrʌntʃɪ] (N) (*for hair*) scrunchie *m*
scruple ['skru:pl] (N) escrúpulo *m* • **a person of no ~s** una persona sin escrúpulos • **he is entirely without ~s** no tiene conciencia • **to have no ~s about ...** no tener escrúpulos acerca de ... • **to make no ~ to do sth** no tener escrúpulos para hacer algo
(VI) (*frm*) • **not to ~ to do sth** no vacilar en hacer algo
scrupulous ['skru:pjʊləs] (ADJ) escrupuloso (**about** en cuanto a)
scrupulously ['skru:pjʊləslɪ] (ADV) escrupulosamente • **~ honest/clean** sumamente honrado/limpio
scrupulousness ['skru:pjʊləsnɪs] (N) escrupulosidad *f*
scrutineer [ˌskru:tɪ'nɪəʳ] (N) escrutador(a) *m/f*
scrutinize ['skru:tɪnaɪz] (VT) [+ *work etc*] escudriñar; [+ *votes*] efectuar el escrutinio de
scrutiny ['skru:tɪnɪ] (N) (= *examination*) examen *m* detallado; (*Pol*) [*of votes*] escrutinio *m*, recuento *m* • **under the ~ of sb** bajo la mirada de algn • **under his ~ she felt nervous** bajo su mirada se sintió nerviosa • **to keep sb under close ~** vigilar a algn de cerca • **to submit sth to a close ~** someter algo a un detallado *or* cuidadoso examen • **it does not stand up to ~** no resiste un examen
SCSI ['skʌzɪ] (N ABBR) (*Comput*) (= **small computer systems interface**) SCSI *m or f*, *controlador de dispositivos de entrada y salida de alta velocidad de transferencia*
scuba ['sku:bə] (CPD) ▸ **scuba diver** buceador(a) *m/f*, submarinista *mf* ▸ **scuba diving** buceo *m*, submarinismo *m* • **to go ~ diving** hacer buceo *or* submarinismo
▸ **scuba suit** traje *m* de submarinismo
scuba-dive (VI) hacer buceo *or* submarinismo
scud [skʌd] (VI) • **to ~ along** correr (llevado por el viento), deslizarse rápidamente • **the clouds were ~ding across the sky** las nubes pasaban rápidamente a través del cielo • **the ship ~ded before the wind** el barco iba viento en popa
scuff [skʌf] (VT) [+ *shoes, floor*] rayar, marcar; [+ *feet*] arrastrar
(VI) andar arrastrando los pies
(CPD) ▸ **scuff marks** rozaduras *fpl*
scuffed [skʌft] (ADJ) arañado
scuffle ['skʌfl] (N) refriega *f*
(VI) tener una refriega (**with sb** con algn) • **to ~ with the police** tener una refriega con la policía
scuffling ['skʌflɪŋ] (ADJ) [*noise, sound*] *de algo moviéndose casi en silencio*
scull [skʌl] (N) espadilla *f*
(VT) remar (*con espadilla*)
(VI) remar (*con espadilla*)
scullery ['skʌlərɪ] (N) (*esp Brit*) trascocina *f*, fregadero *m*
(CPD) ▸ **scullery maid** fregona *f*
sculpt [skʌlpt] (VT) esculpir
(VI) esculpir
sculptor ['skʌlptəʳ] (N) escultor(a) *m/f*
sculptress ['skʌlptrɪs] (N) escultora *f*
sculptural ['skʌlptʃərəl] (ADJ) escultural
sculpture ['skʌlptʃəʳ] (N) escultura *f*
(VT) = **sculpt**
(VI) = **sculpt**
(CPD) ▸ **sculpture garden**, **sculpture park** jardín *m* de esculturas
sculptured ['skʌlptʃəd] (ADJ) esculpido
scum [skʌm] (N) **1** (*on liquid*) espuma *f*; (*on pond*) verdín *m*
2 (*pej*) (= *people*) escoria *f* • **the ~ of the earth** la escoria de la tierra
3** (*pej*) = **scumbag**
scumbag** ['skʌmˌbæg] (N) cabronazo* *m*, borde‡ *mf*
scummy ['skʌmɪ] (ADJ) **1** [*liquid*] lleno de espuma; [*pond*] cubierto de verdín
2‡ (*pej*) canallesco, vil
scunner‡ ['skʌnəʳ] (N) (*esp N Engl, Scot*) • **to take a ~ to sb/sth** tomarla con algn/algo*, tenerle ojeriza a algn/algo*
scupper ['skʌpəʳ] (N) (*Naut*) imbornal *m*
(VT) **1** (*Naut*) abrir los imbornales de, barrenar
2 (*Brit**) [+ *plan*] echar por tierra
scurf [skɜ:f] (N) caspa *f*
scurfy ['skɜ:fɪ] (ADJ) casposo
scurrility [skʌ'rɪlɪtɪ] (N) lo difamatorio, lo calumnioso
scurrilous ['skʌrɪləs] (ADJ) [*gossip, allegations, article*] difamatorio, calumnioso; [*publication*] calumnioso • **to make a ~ attack on sb** calumniar a algn, difamar a algn
scurrilously ['skʌrɪləslɪ] (ADV) con calumnias
scurry ['skʌrɪ] (VI) (= *run*) ir corriendo; (= *hurry*) apresurarse, apurarse (*LAm*) • **to ~ along** ir corriendo • **to ~ for shelter** correr para ponerse al abrigo • **to ~ away** *or* **off** escabullirse
scurvy ['skɜ:vɪ] (ADJ) vil, canallesco
(N) escorbuto *m*
scut [skʌt] (N) rabito *m* (*esp de conejo*)
scutcheon ['skʌtʃən] (N) = **escutcheon**
scutter* ['skʌtəʳ] (VI) (*Brit*) = **scurry**
scuttle[1] ['skʌtl] (VT) **1** [+ *ship*] barrenar
2 (*fig*) [+ *hopes, plans*] dar al traste con, echar por tierra
scuttle[2] ['skʌtl] (VI) (= *run*) echar a correr • **to ~ away** *or* **off** escabullirse • **to ~ along** correr, ir a toda prisa • **we must ~** tenemos que marcharnos
scuttle[3] ['skʌtl] (N) (*for coal*) cubo *m*, carbonera *f*
scuzzy‡ ['skʌzɪ] (ADJ) (*esp US*) cutre*
Scylla ['sɪlə] (N) • **~ and Charybdis** Escila y Caribdis
scythe [saɪð] (N) guadaña *f*
(VT) guadañar, segar
SD (ABBR) (*US*) = **South Dakota**
S.Dak. (ABBR) (*US*) = **South Dakota**
SDI (N ABBR) (= **Strategic Defense Initiative**) IDE *f*
SDLP (N ABBR) (*in Northern Ireland*) (*Pol*) = **Social Democratic and Labour Party**
SDP (N ABBR) (*Brit*) (*Pol*) (*formerly*) = **Social Democratic Party**
SDR (N ABBR) (= **special drawing rights**) DEG *mpl*
SE (ABBR) (= **southeast**) SE
sea [si:] (N) **1** (= *not land*) mar *m* (*or f in some phrases*) • **(out) at sea** en alta mar • **to spend three years at sea** pasar tres años navegando • **to remain two months at sea** estar navegando durante dos meses, pasar dos meses en el mar • **beside the sea** a la orilla del mar, junto al mar • **beyond the seas** más allá de los mares • **from beyond the seas** desde más allá de los mares • **to go by sea** ir por mar • **a house by the sea** una

casa junto al mar *or* a la orilla del mar • **heavy sea(s)** mar agitado *or* picado • **to ship a heavy sea** ser inundado por una ola grande • **on the high seas** en alta mar • **on the sea** *(boat)* en alta mar • **rough sea(s)** mar agitado *or* picado • **to sail the seas** navegar los mares • **the seven seas** todos los mares del mundo • **in Spanish seas** en aguas españolas • **the little boat was swept out to sea** la barquita fue arrastrada mar adentro • **to go to sea** *[person]* hacerse marinero • **to put (out) to sea** *[sailor, boat]* hacerse a la mar, zarpar • **to stand out to sea** apartarse de la costa • IDIOM: • **to be all at sea (about** *or* **with sth)** estar en un lío (por algo) • PROVERB: • **worse things happen at sea** cosas peores ocurren por ahí; ▹ north

2 *(fig)* • **a sea of blood** un río *or* mar de sangre • **a sea of corn** un mar de espigas • **a sea of faces** un mar de caras • **a sea of flame** un mar de llamas • **a sea of troubles** un mar de penas

CPD ▸ **sea air** aire *m* de mar ▸ **sea anemone** anémona *f* de mar ▸ **sea bass** corvina *f* ▸ **sea bathing** baño *m* en el mar ▸ **sea battle** batalla *f* naval ▸ **sea bed** fondo *m* del mar, lecho *m* marino *(frm)* ▸ **sea bird** ave *f* marina ▸ **sea boot** bota *f* de marinero ▸ **sea bream** besugo *m* ▸ **sea breeze** brisa *f* marina ▸ **sea captain** capitán *m* de barco ▸ **sea change** *(fig)* viraje *m*, cambio *m* radical ▸ **sea chest**† cofre *m* ▸ **sea coast** litoral *m*, costa *f* marítima ▸ **sea cow** manatí *m* ▸ **sea crossing** travesía *f* ▸ **sea defences** estructuras *fpl* de defensa (contra el mar) ▸ **sea dog** *(lit, fig)* lobo *m* de mar ▸ **sea fight** combate *m* naval ▸ **sea fish** pez *m* marino ▸ **sea floor** fondo *m* del mar ▸ **sea front** paseo *m* marítimo ▸ **sea grass** hierbas *fpl* marinas ▸ **sea green** verde mar *m*; ▹ sea-green ▸ **sea horse** caballito *m* de mar, hipocampo *m* ▸ **sea kale** col *f* marina ▸ **sea lamprey** lamprea *f* marina ▸ **sea lane** ruta *f* marítima ▸ **sea legs** • **to find one's sea legs** mantener el equilibrio (en barco) ▸ **sea level** nivel *m* del mar • **800 metres above sea level** 800 metros sobre el nivel del mar ▸ **sea lion** león *m* marino ▸ **sea mist** bruma *f* marina ▸ **sea perch** perca *f* de mar ▸ **sea power** potencia *f* naval ▸ **sea room** espacio *m* para maniobrar ▸ **sea route** ruta *f* marítima ▸ **sea salt** sal *f* marina ▸ **sea scout** scout *m/f* marino/a ▸ **sea serpent** serpiente *f* de mar ▸ **sea shanty** saloma *f* ▸ **sea transport** transporte *m* por mar, transporte *m* marítimo ▸ **sea trip** viaje *m* por mar ▸ **sea trout** trucha *f* marina, reo *m* ▸ **sea turtle** *(US)* tortuga *f* de mar, tortuga *f* marina ▸ **sea urchin** erizo *m* de mar ▸ **sea view** *(Brit)* vistas *fpl* al mar ▸ **sea wall** malecón *m*, rompeolas *m inv* ▸ **sea water** agua *f* de mar ▸ **sea wrack** algas *fpl* (en la playa)

seaboard ['si:bɔ:d] N *(US)* litoral *m*

seaborne ['si:bɔ:n] ADJ transportado por mar

seafarer ['si:ˌfɛərəʳ] N marinero *m*

seafaring ['si:ˌfɛərɪŋ] ADJ *[community]* marinero; *[life]* de marinero • **~ man** marinero *m*

N *(also* **seafaring life***)* vida *f* de marinero

seafood ['si:fu:d] N marisco *m*, mariscos *mpl*

CPD ▸ **seafood cocktail** cóctel *m* de marisco(s) ▸ **seafood platter** fuente *f* de marisco, mariscada *f* ▸ **seafood restaurant** marisquería *f*

seagirt ['si:gɜ:t] ADJ *(liter)* rodeado por el mar

seagoing ['si:ˌgəʊɪŋ] ADJ marítimo

sea-green ['si:gri:n] ADJ verdemar

seagull ['si:gʌl] N gaviota *f*

seahorse ['si:hɔ:s] N caballito *m* de mar, hipocampo *m*

seal¹ [si:l] N *(Zool)* foca *f*

VI • **to go ~ing** ir a cazar focas

CPD ▸ **seal cull, seal culling** matanza *f* (selectiva) de focas

seal² [si:l] N **1** (= *official stamp*) sello *m* • **the papal/presidential ~** el sello papal/ presidencial • **they have given their ~ of approval to the proposed reforms** han dado el visto bueno a *or* han aprobado las reformas que se planean • **it has the Royal Academy's ~ of approval** cuenta con la aprobación *or* el visto bueno de la Real Academia • **~ of quality** sello *or* marchamo *m* de calidad • **this set the ~ on their friendship/on her humiliation** esto selló su amistad/remató su humillación • **under my hand and ~** *(frm)* firmado y sellado por mí

2 *[of envelope, parcel, exterior of bottle, jar]* precinto *m*; *(inside lid of jar)* aro *m* de goma; *(on fridge door)* cierre *m* de goma; *(on door, window)* burlete *m* • **the ~ on the windows is not very good** estas ventanas no cierran bien

3 *(Rel)* • **the ~ of the confessional** el secreto de confesión

VT **1** (= *close*) *[+ envelope]* cerrar; *[+ package, coffin]* precintar; *[+ border]* cerrar • **a ~ed envelope** un sobre cerrado; ▹ lip, sign

2 (= *stop up, make airtight*) *[+ container]* tapar *or* cerrar herméticamente; *[+ surface]* sellar • **the wood is ~ed with several coats of varnish** la madera se sella con varias capas de barniz

3 (= *enclose*) • **to ~ sth in sth**: • **~ the letter in a blank envelope** mete la carta en un sobre en blanco y ciérralo • **~ in airtight containers** guárdelos en recipientes herméticos

4 *(fig)* (= *confirm*) *[+ bargain, deal]* sellar; *[+ victory]* decidir; *[+ sb's fate]* decidir, determinar • **that goal ~ed the match** ese gol decidió *or* determinó el resultado del partido

5 *(Culin)* *[+ meat]* sofreír a fuego vivo *(para que no pierda el jugo)*

▸ **seal in** VT + ADV conservar • **this ~s in the flavour** esto conserva el sabor

▸ **seal off** VT + ADV *[+ building, room]* cerrar; *[+ area, road]* acordonar

▸ **seal up** VT + ADV *[+ letter, parcel, building, tunnel]* precintar; *[+ window, door]* condenar, precintar; *[+ hole]* rellenar, tapar

sealant ['si:lənt] N (= *device*) sellador *m*, tapador *m*; (= *substance*) silicona *f* selladora

sealer ['si:ləʳ] N (= *person*) cazador(a) *m/f* de focas; (= *boat*) barco *m* para la caza de focas

sealing ['si:lɪŋ] N caza *f* de focas

sealing wax ['si:lɪŋwæks] N lacre *m*

sealskin ['si:lskɪn] N piel *f* de foca

seam [si:m] N **1** *(Sew)* costura *f* • **to fall** *or* **come apart at the ~s** descoserse • **to be bursting at the ~s** *[dress etc]* estar a punto de reventar por las costuras; *(fig*)* *[room etc]* estar a rebosar

2 *(Welding)* juntura *f*

3 *(Geol)* filón *m*, veta *f*

VT *(Sew)* coser; *(Tech)* juntar

seaman ['si:mən] N (PL: **seamen**) marinero *m*, marino *m*

seamanlike ['si:mənlaɪk] ADJ de buen marinero

seamanship ['si:mənʃɪp] N náutica *f*

seamless ['si:mlɪs] ADJ *(Sew)* sin costura; *(Tech)* sin soldadura

seamlessly ['si:mləslɪ] ADV de forma impecable, sin que se note • **he has moved ~ from theory to practice** ha pasado de la teoría a la práctica sin que se note

seamstress ['semstrɪs] N costurera *f*

seamy* ['si:mɪ] ADJ (COMPAR: **seamier**, SUPERL: **seamiest**) sórdido, insalubre • **the ~ side** *(fig)* el revés de la medalla

seance, séance ['seɪɑ:ns] N sesión *f* de espiritismo

seapiece ['si:pi:s] N *(Art)* marina *f*

seaplane ['si:pleɪn] N hidroavión *m*

seaport ['si:pɔ:t] N puerto *m* de mar

SEAQ ['si:ˌæk] N ABBR = **Stock Exchange Automated Quotations**

sear [sɪəʳ] VT (= *wither*) secar, marchitar; *(Med)* cauterizar; *[pain etc]* punzar; (= *scorch*) chamuscar, quemar • **it was ~ed into my memory** me quedó grabado en la memoria

▸ **sear through** VI + PREP *[+ walls, metal]* penetrar a través de

search [sɜ:tʃ] N **1** (= *hunt*) búsqueda *f* **(for** de) • **after a long ~ I found the key** después de mucho buscar, encontré la llave • **police launched a massive ~ for the killer** la policía ha emprendido una enorme operación de búsqueda para encontrar al asesino • **the ~ for peace** la búsqueda de la paz • **in ~ of** en busca de • **they come to the city in ~ of work** vienen a la ciudad en busca de trabajo • **we went in ~ of a restaurant** fuimos a buscar un restaurante • **to make** *or* **conduct a ~** llevar a cabo una búsqueda • **~ and rescue** búsqueda y rescate

2 (= *inspection*) *[of building, place]* registro *m*; *[of records]* inspección *f* • **she had to submit to a body ~** tuvo que dejar que la registraran *or* cachearan • **police made a thorough ~ of the premises** la policía registró todo el local

3 *(Comput)* búsqueda *f*

4 *(Brit)* *(Jur)* *comprobación de datos de un inmueble en el registro de la propiedad* • **to get a (local authority) ~ done** ≈ sacar una nota simple en el registro de la propiedad *(Sp)*

VT **1** *[+ building, luggage, pockets]* registrar, catear *(Mex)*; *[+ person]* registrar, cachear, catear *(Mex)* • **to ~ sth/sb (for sth/sb)**: • **he ~ed his pockets for change** se miró los bolsillos en busca de monedas • **she ~ed the kitchen drawers for her keys** buscó las llaves en los cajones de la cocina • **I ~ed the whole house for food** he revuelto toda la casa en busca de comida • **we ~ed the entire office but the file didn't turn up** registramos la oficina de arriba abajo pero no encontramos el archivo • **they were ~ed for weapons as they left** los registraron *or* cachearon *or* *(Mex)* catearon a la salida para ver si llevaban armas • **to ~ high and low (for sth/sb)** remover el cielo y la tierra (en busca de algo/algn) • **~ me!*** ¡yo qué sé!, ¡ni idea!

2 (= *scan*) *[+ documents, records]* examinar • **his eyes ~ed the sky for the approaching helicopter** escudriñó el cielo en busca del helicóptero que se acercaba • **his eyes ~ed my face for any sign of guilt** sus ojos escudriñaban mi rostro en busca de algún rastro de culpabilidad • **to ~ one's conscience** examinar (uno) su conciencia • **to ~ one's memory** hacer memoria

3 *(Comput)* buscar en

VI buscar • **to ~ after truth/happiness** buscar la verdad/la felicidad • **to ~ for sth/sb** buscar algo/a algn • **we ~ed everywhere for the missing keys** buscamos las llaves que faltaban en todas partes • **they are ~ing for a solution to the crisis** están buscando una solución a la crisis • **to ~ through sth (for sth)**: • **rescuers ~ed through the rubble for survivors** los del equipo de rescate buscaron supervivientes entre los escombros • **he ~ed through our passports** examinó nuestros pasaportes

CPD ▸ **search algorithm** = search engine algorithm ▸ **search engine** (*Internet*) buscador *m*, motor *m* de búsqueda ▸ **search engine algorithm** algoritmo *m* de motor de búsqueda ▸ **search engine marketing** márketing *m* de motor de búsqueda ▸ **search engine optimization** optimización *f* para buscadores, posicionamiento *m* en buscadores ▸ **search party** pelotón *m* de búsqueda ▸ **search warrant** orden *f* de registro

▸ **search about, search around** VI + ADV buscar por todas partes

▸ **search out** VT + ADV • **I ~ed him out in the coffee break** fui a buscarlo durante la pausa para el café • **if you can ~ out a copy, it is worth reading** si encuentras un ejemplar, merece la pena que lo leas • **~ out the less well-known wines** trate de descubrir los vinos menos conocidos

searcher ['sɜːtʃəʳ] N buscador(a) *m/f*

searching ['sɜːtʃɪŋ] ADJ [*look, glance*] inquisitivo; [*eyes*] penetrante; [*question, mind*] perspicaz; [*examination*] exhaustivo; [*test*] duro • **you need to ask yourself some ~ questions** te hace falta hacerte de verdad ciertas preguntas

searchingly ['sɜːtʃɪŋlɪ] ADV [*look, ask*] inquisitivamente

searchlight ['sɜːtʃlaɪt] N reflector *m*, proyector *m*

searing ['sɪərɪŋ] ADJ [*heat*] ardiente; [*pain*] agudo; [*criticism*] mordaz, acerbo

seascape ['siːskeɪp] N (*Art*) paisaje *m* marino

seashell ['siːʃel] N concha *f* marina

seashore ['siːʃɔːʳ] N (= *beach*) playa *f*; (*gen*) orilla *f* del mar • **by** *or* **on the ~** en la playa, a la orilla del mar

seasick ['siːsɪk] ADJ mareado • **to get** *or* **be ~** marearse (*en barco*)

seasickness ['siːsɪknɪs] N mareo *m* (*al estar en una embarcación*)

seaside ['siːsaɪd] N (= *beach*) playa *f*; (= *shore*) orilla *f* del mar • **we want to go to the ~** queremos ir a la playa • **to take the family to the ~ for a day** llevar a la familia a pasar un día a la playa • **at the ~** en la playa
CPD [*hotel*] de playa, en la playa; [*town*] costero, costeño ▸ **seaside holidays** • **we like ~ holidays** nos gusta pasar las vacaciones en la playa *or* costa, nos gusta veranear junto al mar ▸ **seaside resort** *lugar de veraneo en la playa*

season ['siːzn] N **1** (= *period of the year*) estación *f* • **the four ~s** las cuatro estaciones • **what's your favourite ~?** ¿cuál es tu estación preferida? • **at this ~** en esta época del año • **the dry/rainy ~** la temporada de secas/de lluvias
2 (*for specific activity*) temporada *f* • **for a ~** durante una temporada • **we did a ~ at La Scala** (*Theat*) representamos en la Scala durante una temporada • **did you have a good ~?** ¿qué tal la temporada? • **"Season's Greetings"** "Felices Pascuas" • **the busy ~** la temporada alta • **the Christmas ~** las navidades • **the closed ~** (*Hunting*) la veda • **the fishing/football ~** la temporada de pesca/de fútbol • **at the height of the ~** en plena temporada • **during the holiday ~** en la temporada de vacaciones • **to be in ~** [*fruit*] estar en sazón; [*animal*] estar en celo • **the London ~** la temporada social de Londres • **the open ~** (*Hunting*) la temporada de caza *or* de pesca • **to be out of ~** estar fuera de temporada
3 (*liter*) (= *appropriate time*) • **for everything there is a ~** todo tiene su momento • **in due ~** a su tiempo • **it was not the ~ for jokes** no era el momento oportuno para chistes • **a word in ~** una palabra a propósito • **in ~ and out of ~** a tiempo y a destiempo
VT **1** (*Culin*) sazonar, condimentar (**with** con) • **~ to taste** sazonar a gusto • **a speech ~ed with wit** un discurso salpicado de agudezas
2 [+ *wood, timber*] curar
CPD ▸ **season ticket** (*Theat, Rail, Sport*) abono *m* ▸ **season ticket holder** abonado/a *m/f*

seasonable ['siːznəbl] ADJ [*weather*] propio de la estación

seasonal ['siːzənl] ADJ [*work, labour, migration*] de temporada, estacional; [*changes, variations*] estacional; [*fruit, vegetable*] del tiempo, de temporada; [*migrant*] temporal • **the tourism business is ~** el negocio del turismo es de temporada
CPD ▸ **seasonal adjustment** (*Econ, Pol*) ajuste *m* estacional, desestacionalización *f* • **prices rose 0.2% in July, after ~ adjustments** tras eliminar las fluctuaciones estacionales se vio que los precios subieron un 0,2% en julio, las cifras desestacionalizadas demostraron una subida de los precios del 0,2% en julio ▸ **seasonal affective disorder** trastorno *m* afectivo estacional ▸ **seasonal worker** temporero/a *m/f*

seasonally ['siːzənəlɪ] ADV • **~ adjusted figures** cifras *fpl* desestacionalizadas

seasoned ['siːznd] ADJ **1** (*Culin*) [*food*] sazonado, condimentado
2 (= *matured*) [*wood, timber*] curado; [*wine*] maduro
3 (*fig*) [*soldier*] aguerrido, veterano; [*worker, actor*] experimentado; [*player*] experimentado, curtido; [*traveller*] curtido, con muchos kilómetros a sus espaldas • **she's a ~ campaigner** es una veterana de las campañas, está curtida en mil y una campañas

seasong ['siːsɒŋ] N canción *f* de marineros; (= *shanty*) saloma *f*

seasoning ['siːznɪŋ] N **1** (*for food*) aliño *m*, condimentos *mpl* • **with a ~ of jokes** con un aliño de chistes
2 [*of wood, timber*] cura *f*

seat [siːt] N **1** (= *place to sit*) asiento *m*; (*in cinema, theatre*) butaca *f*, asiento *m*; (*in car, plane, train, bus*) asiento *m*; (*on cycle*) sillín *m*, asiento *m* • **is this ~ free?** ¿está libre este asiento? • **the back ~ of the car** el asiento trasero del coche • **save me a ~** guárdame un sitio *or* asiento • **he used the log as a ~** usaba el tronco de silla • **do have** *or* **take a ~** siéntese por favor, tome asiento por favor (*frm*) • **to take one's ~** sentarse, tomar asiento • **please take your ~s for supper** la cena está servida • IDIOM: • **to take a back ~** mantenerse al margen • **his private life takes a back ~ to the problems of the company** su vida privada ocupa un segundo lugar después de los problemas de la compañía; ▹ **driving, hot**
2 [*of chair, toilet*] asiento *m*
3 (= *ticket*) (*Theat, Cine, Sport*) localidad *f*, entrada *f*; (*for plane, train, bus*) plaza *f* • **we need two ~s on the first available flight** necesitamos dos plazas en el primer vuelo disponible • **are there any ~s left?** (*Theat, Cine, Sport*) ¿quedan localidades *or* entradas?; (*on plane*) ¿quedan plazas?
4 (*Pol*) (*in parliament*) escaño *m*, curul *f* (*Col*); (= *constituency*) circunscripción *f* electoral • **she kept/lost her ~ in the election** retuvo/perdió su escaño en las elecciones; ▹ **safe**
5 (*on board, committee*) puesto *m* • **to have a ~ on the board** ser miembro de la junta directiva
6 [*of trousers*] fondillos *mpl* • IDIOM: • **to do sth by the ~ of one's pants** hacer algo guiado por el instinto
7 (= *centre*) [*of government*] sede *f*; [*of family*] residencia *f*, casa *f* solariega • **family ~** casa *f* solariega • **~ of learning** (*liter*) centro *m* de estudios, templo *m* del saber (*liter*)
8 (= *source*) [*of infection, problem*] foco *m*
9 (= *buttocks*) (*euph*) trasero* *m*, posaderas* *fpl*
10 [*of rider*] • **to have a good ~** montar bien • **to keep one's ~** mantenerse sobre el caballo • **to lose one's ~** caer del caballo
VT **1** [+ *person*] [+ *child, invalid*] sentar • **they ~ guests at a different table every day** todos los días ponen a los invitados en mesas diferentes • **please remain ~ed** por favor permanezcan sentados (*frm*) • **please be ~ed** tome asiento por favor (*frm*) • **to ~ o.s.** sentarse, tomar asiento (*frm*)
2 (= *hold*) [*hall, vehicle*] tener cabida para • **the bus ~s 53 people** el autobús tiene cabida para 53 personas (sentadas), el autobús tiene 53 plazas *or* asientos • **the car ~s five** caben cinco personas en el coche, el coche tiene cabida para cinco personas • **the theatre ~s 900** el teatro tiene un aforo de 900 localidades, el teatro tiene cabida para 900 personas • **the table can ~ 20 comfortably** en la mesa caben 20 personas cómodamente
3 (*Mech*) [+ *valve, bearing*] asentar, ajustar
4 (*fig*) • **deeply ~ed attitudes** actitudes *fpl* muy arraigadas
CPD ▸ **seat back** respaldo *m* del asiento ▸ **seat belt** cinturón *m* de seguridad • **he wasn't wearing a ~ belt** no llevaba puesto el cinturón de seguridad • **fasten your ~ belts** (*Aer*) abróchense el cinturón de seguridad • **put your ~ belt on** (*Aut*) póngase el cinturón de seguridad ▸ **seat cover** funda *f* de asiento

-seater ['siːtəʳ] (*ending in compounds*) N • **a two-seater** (= *car etc*) un coche *etc* de dos asientos
ADJ • **a ten-seater plane** un avión de diez plazas, un avión con capacidad para diez personas

seating ['siːtɪŋ] N asientos *mpl*
CPD ▸ **seating accommodation** plazas *fpl*, asientos *mpl* ▸ **seating arrangements** = seating plan ▸ **seating capacity** número *m* de asientos, cabida *f* ▸ **seating plan** disposición *f* de los asientos

seatmate ['siːtmeɪt] N compañero/a *m/f* de asiento

SEATO ['siːtəʊ] N ABBR (= **Southeast Asia Treaty Organization**) OTASE *f*

seaward ['siːwəd] ADJ de hacia el mar, de la parte del mar • **on the ~ side** en el lado del mar
ADV hacia el mar • **to ~** en la dirección del mar

seawards ['siːwədz] ADV (*esp Brit*) = **seaward**

seaway ['siːweɪ] N vía *f* marítima

seaweed ['siːwiːd] N alga *f*

seaworthiness ['siːˌwɜːðɪnɪs] N navegabilidad *f*

seaworthy ['siːˌwɜːðɪ] ADJ en condiciones de navegar

sebaceous [sɪ'beɪʃəs] ADJ sebáceo

seborrhoea, seborrhea (*US*) [ˌsebə'rɪə] N seborrea *f*

sebum ['siːbəm] N sebo *m*

SEC N ABBR (*US*) = **Securities and Exchange Commission**

sec* [sek] N ABBR = **second**

Sec. ABBR (= **Secretary**) Sec., Srio., Sria.

S

SECAM ['si:kæm] (N ABBR) (*TV*) (= **séquentiel à mémoire**) SECAM *m*
secant ['si:kənt] (N) secante *f*
secateurs [,sekə'tɜ:z] (NPL) podadera *fsing*
secede [sɪ'si:d] (VI) separarse, escindirse (**from** de)
secession [sɪ'seʃən] (N) secesión *f*, separación *f* (**from** de)
secessionism [sɪ'seʃənɪzəm] (N) secesionismo *m*
secessionist [sɪ'seʃnɪst] (ADJ) secesionista, separatista
(N) secesionista *mf*, separatista *mf*
secluded [sɪ'klu:dɪd] (ADJ) retirado, apartado
seclusion [sɪ'klu:ʒən] (N) aislamiento *m* • **to live in ~** vivir aislado
second¹ ['sekənd] (ADJ) **1** (*gen*) segundo • **they have a ~ home in Oxford** tienen otra casa en Oxford, en Oxford tienen una segunda vivienda • **will you have a ~ cup?** ¿quieres otra taza? • **give him a ~ chance** dale otra oportunidad • **you won't get a ~ chance** no tendrás otra oportunidad • **in ~ gear** (*Aut*) en segunda (velocidad) • **it's ~ nature to her** lo hace sin pensar • **for some of us swimming is not ~ nature** para muchos de nosotros nadar no es algo que nos salga hacer de forma natural • **violence was ~ nature to him** la violencia era parte de su naturaleza • **he had practised until it had become ~ nature** había practicado hasta que le salía con naturalidad • **to ask for a ~ opinion** pedir una segunda opinión • **to be/lie in ~ place** estar/encontrarse en segundo lugar *or* segunda posición • **to have ~ sight** tener clarividencia, ser clarividente • **Charles the Second** (*spoken form*) Carlos Segundo; (*written form*) Carlos II • **without a** *or* **with hardly a ~ thought** sin pensarlo dos veces • **I didn't give it a ~ thought** no volví a pensar en ello • **to have ~ thoughts (about sth/about doing sth)** tener sus dudas (sobre algo/si hacer algo) • **I'm having ~ thoughts about hiring him** tengo mis dudas sobre si contratarle • **on ~ thoughts ...** pensándolo bien ... • **for the ~ time** por segunda vez • **fatherhood ~ time around has not been easy for him** volver a ser padre no le ha resultado fácil • **to be ~ to none** no tener rival, ser inigualable • **Bath is ~ only to Glasgow as a tourist attraction** Bath es la atracción turística más popular aparte de Glasgow, solo Glasgow gana en popularidad a Bath como atracción turística • **to get one's ~ wind** conseguir recobrar fuerzas; ▹ **floor**
2 (*Mus*) segundo • **I played ~ clarinet** era segundo clarinete; ▹ **fiddle**
(ADV) **1** (*in race, competition, election*) en segundo lugar • **to come/finish ~** quedar/llegar en segundo lugar *or* segunda posición • **in popularity polls he came ~ only to Nelson Mandela** en los sondeos era el segundo más popular por detrás de Nelson Mandela
2 (= *secondly*) segundo, en segundo lugar
3 (*before superl adj*) • **the ~ tallest building in the world** el segundo edificio más alto del mundo • **the ~ largest fish** el segundo pez en tamaño, el segundo mayor pez • **this is the ~ largest city in Spain** ocupa la segunda posición entre las ciudades más grandes de España
(N) **1** (*in race, competition*) • **he came a good/poor ~** quedó segundo a poca/gran distancia del vencedor • **studying for his exams comes a poor ~ to playing football** prepararse los exámenes no tiene ni de lejos la importancia que tiene jugar al fútbol • **I feel I come a poor ~ in my husband's affections to our baby daughter** tengo la sensación de que mi marido vuelca todo su cariño en la pequeña y a mí me tiene olvidada; ▹ **close**
2 (*Aut*) segunda velocidad *f* • **in ~** en segunda (velocidad)
3 (= *assistant*) (*in boxing*) segundo *m*, cuidador *m*; (*in duel*) padrino *m* • **~s out!** ¡segundos fuera!
4 (*Brit*) (*Univ*) • **Lower/Upper Second** *calificación que ocupa el tercer/segundo lugar en la escala de las que se otorgan con un título universitario*; ▹ DEGREE
5 seconds: **a** (*Comm*) artículos *mpl* con defecto de fábrica • **these dresses are slight ~s** estos vestidos tienen pequeños defectos de fábrica
b (*Culin*) • **will you have ~s?** ¿quieres más? • **I went back for ~s** volví a repetir
(VT) **1** [+ *motion, speaker, nomination*] apoyar, secundar • **I'll ~ that*** lo mismo digo yo, estoy completamente de acuerdo
2 [sɪ'kɒnd] [+ *employee*] trasladar temporalmente; [+ *civil servant*] enviar en comisión de servicios (*Sp*)
(CPD) ▸ **second chamber** [*of parliament*] cámara *f* alta ▸ **second childhood** segunda infancia *f* • **he's in his ~ childhood** está en su segunda infancia ▸ **the Second Coming** (*Rel*) el segundo Advenimiento ▸ **second cousin** primo/a segundo/a *m/f* ▸ **second fiddle** ▹ **fiddle** ▸ **second form** *curso de secundaria para alumnos de entre 12 y 13 años* ▸ **second gear** segunda *f* ▸ **second generation** segunda generación *f* ▸ **second half** (*Sport*) segundo tiempo *m*, segunda parte *f*; (*Econ*) segundo semestre *m* (*del año económico*) ▸ **second house** (*Theat*) segunda función *f* ▸ **second language** segunda lengua *f* • **English as a ~ language** inglés como segunda lengua ▸ **second lieutenant** (*in army*) alférez *mf*, subteniente *mf* ▸ **second mate, second officer** (*in Merchant Navy*) segundo *m* de a bordo ▸ **second mortgage** segunda hipoteca *f* ▸ **second name** apellido *m* ▸ **second person** (*Gram*) segunda persona *f* • **the ~ person singular/plural** la segunda persona del singular/plural ▸ **second sight** • **to have ~ sight** ser clarividente ▸ **second string** (*esp US*) (*Sport*) (= *player*) suplente *mf*; (= *team*) equipo *m* de reserva ▸ **the Second World War** la Segunda Guerra Mundial
second² ['sekənd] (N) (*in time, Geog, Math*) segundo *m* • **just a ~!** • **half a ~!*** ¡un momento!, ¡momentito! (*esp LAm*) • **I'll be with you in (just) a ~** un momento y estoy contigo • **in a split ~** en un instante, en un abrir y cerrar de ojos • **the operation is timed to a split ~** la operación está concebida con la mayor precisión en cuanto al tiempo • **it won't take a ~** es cosa de un segundo, es un segundo nada más • **at that very ~** en ese mismo instante
(CPD) ▸ **second hand** [*of clock*] segundero *m*
secondarily ['sekəndərɪlɪ] (ADV) en segundo lugar
secondary ['sekəndərɪ] (ADJ) **1** (= *less important*) [*character, role, effect, source*] secundario • **of ~ importance** de importancia secundaria, de segundo orden • **the cost is a ~ consideration** el coste es un factor secundario *or* de interés secundario • **my desire to have children was always ~ to my career** el deseo de tener hijos siempre se vio supeditado a mi carrera, el deseo de tener hijos siempre ocupó un lugar secundario en relación con mi carrera
2 (*Educ*) [*education*] secundario; [*schooling, student, teacher*] de enseñanza secundaria • **after five years of ~ education** tras cinco años de educación *or* enseñanza secundaria • **subjects taught at ~ level** materias impartidas en los ciclos de educación *or* enseñanza secundaria
(N) **1** (*Univ etc*) (= *minor subject*) asignatura *f* menor
2 (*also* **secondary school**) centro *m or* instituto *m* de enseñanza secundaria; ▹ COMPREHENSIVE SCHOOLS
3 (*Med*) (*also* **secondary tumour**) tumor *m* secundario
(CPD) ▸ **secondary action** (*Pol*) movilizaciones *fpl* de apoyo ▸ **secondary cancer** (*Med*) metástasis *f inv* ▸ **secondary colour** color *m* secundario ▸ **secondary education** educación *f or* enseñanza *f* secundaria, segunda enseñanza *f* ▸ **secondary era** (*Geol*) era *f* secundaria ▸ **secondary explosion** explosión *f* por simpatía ▸ **secondary infection** (*Med*) infección *f* secundaria ▸ **secondary modern (school)** (*Brit*) (*formerly*) *instituto de enseñanza secundaria que centraba su actividad docente más en conocimientos prácticos y tecnológicos que en la formación académica* ▸ **secondary picket(ing)** piquete *m* secundario (*en centros relacionados con el sector o fábrica en huelga*) ▸ **secondary production** producción *f* secundaria ▸ **secondary road** carretera *f* secundaria ▸ **secondary school** centro *m or* instituto *m* de enseñanza secundaria; ▹ COMPREHENSIVE SCHOOLS ▸ **secondary school teacher** profesor(a) *m/f* de secundaria ▸ **secondary storage** almacenamiento *m* secundario ▸ **secondary stress** (*Ling*) acento *m* secundario ▸ **secondary tumour** tumor *m* secundario
second-best ['sekənd'best] (N) segundo *m*
(ADV) • **to come off second-best** quedar en segundo lugar
(ADJ) segundo • **our second-best car** nuestro coche número dos
second-class ['sekənd'klɑ:s] (ADJ) [*compartment, carriage*] de segunda clase • **second-class citizen** ciudadano/a *m/f* de segunda clase • **second-class degree** (*Univ*) licenciatura *f* con media de notable • **second-class hotel** hotel *m* de segunda • **second-class mail** • **second-class post** correo *m* de segunda clase • **a second-class return to London** (*Rail*) un billete de ida y vuelta a Londres en segunda • **second-class seat** (*Rail*) asiento *m* de *or* en segunda • **second-class stamp** sello *m* para correo ordinario • **second-class ticket** billete *m* de segunda clase
(ADV) • **to send sth second-class** enviar algo por segunda clase • **to travel second-class** viajar en segunda
second-degree [,sekənddɪ'gri:] (ADJ) **1** (*esp US*) [*murder, assault*] en segundo grado
2 [*burn*] de segundo grado
seconder ['sekəndəʳ] (N) *el/la que apoya una moción*
second-grader [,sekənd'greɪdəʳ] (N) (*US*) alumno/a *m/f* de segundo de primaria (*de entre 7 y 8 años*)
second-guess* [,sekənd'ges] (VT) [+ *sb's reaction*] anticiparse a • **they're still trying to second-guess his motives** todavía están intentando anticiparse a sus motivos
second-half ['sekənd,hɑ:f] (ADJ) (*Sport*) [*goal, try, substitution*] en el segundo tiempo *or* la segunda parte
second-hand ['sekənd'hænd] (ADJ) (*gen*) de segunda mano; [*car*] usado, de segunda mano • **second-hand bookseller** librero/a *m/f* de viejo • **second-hand bookshop** librería *f* de viejo • **second-hand clothes**

ropa *f* usada *or* de segunda mano • **second-hand information** información *f* de segunda mano • **second-hand shop** tienda *f* de segunda mano, bazar *m* (*Mex*), cambalache *m* (*S. Cone*)
ADV • **to buy sth second-hand** comprar algo de segunda mano • **I heard it only second-hand** yo lo supe solamente por otro • **she heard it second-hand from her friend** se enteró por su amiga

second-in-command ['sekəndɪnkə'mɑ:nd] N segundo/a *m/f* de a bordo

secondly ['sekəndlɪ] ADV en segundo lugar

secondment [sɪ'kɒndmənt] N traslado *m* • **on ~** trasladado, destacado • **she is on ~ to section B** ha sido trasladada temporalmente a la sección B, está destacada en la sección B

second-rate ['sekənd'reɪt] ADJ de segunda fila • **some second-rate writer** algún escritor de segunda fila

second-string [ˌsekənd'strɪŋ] ADJ (*esp US*) (*Sport*) [*team, goalkeeper, horse etc*] reserva (*inv*)
CPD ▸ **second-string player** suplente *mf*; ▹ **second string**

second-tier ['sekənd,tɪə^r] ADJ (= *second-rate*) [*player, writer, actor, film*] de segunda fila

secrecy ['si:krəsɪ] N secreto *m* • **in ~** en secreto, a escondidas • **in the strictest ~** de manera totalmente confidencial, en el más absoluto secreto • **I was told in the strictest ~** se me dijo de manera totalmente confidencial • **to swear sb to ~** hacer que algn jure no revelar algo • **there's no ~ about it** no es ningún secreto • **there was an air of ~ about her** la rodeaba un halo de misterio; ▹ **shroud, veil**

secret ['si:krɪt] ADJ [*plan, ingredient, admirer, mission*] secreto; [*information, document*] secreto, confidencial; [*drinker, drug addict*] a escondidas • **it's all highly ~** todo es de lo más secreto • **to keep sth ~** mantener algo en secreto • **to keep sth ~ from sb** ocultar algo a algn • **they held a ~ meeting** mantuvieron una reunión en secreto
N secreto *m* • **the ~s of nature** los misterios de la naturaleza • **to do sth in ~** hacer algo en secreto *or* a escondidas • **to be in on the ~** estar en el secreto, estar al corriente • **to keep a ~** guardar un secreto • **to keep sth a ~ from sb** ocultar algo a algn • **to let sb into a/the ~** contar *or* revelar a algn un/el secreto • **it's no ~ that ...** no es ningún secreto que ... • **there's no ~ about it** esto no tiene nada de secreto • **to have no ~s from sb** no tener secretos para algn • **to make no ~ of sth** no ocultar algo • **to remain a ~** seguir siendo un secreto • **to tell sb a ~** contar un secreto a algn • **the ~:** • **the ~ is to** (+ *infin*) el secreto consiste en (+ *infin*) • **the ~ of success** el secreto del éxito; ▹ **open, state**
CPD ▸ **secret agent** agente *mf* secreto/a, espía *mf* ▸ **secret drawer** cajón *m* secreto *or* oculto ▸ **secret police** policía *f* secreta ▸ **secret service** servicio *m* secreto ▸ **secret society** sociedad *f* secreta ▸ **secret weapon** (*lit, fig*) arma *f* secreta

secretaire [ˌsekrɪ'tɛə^r] N (*Brit*) escritorio *m* secretaire

secretarial [ˌsekrə'tɛərɪəl] ADJ • **~ college** colegio *m* de secretariado • **~ course** curso *m* de secretariado • **~ school** colegio *m* de secretariado • **~ services** servicios *mpl* de secretaría • **~ skills** técnicas *fpl* de secretaría • **~ work** trabajo *m* de secretario

secretariat [ˌsekrə'tɛərɪət] N secretaría *f*, secretariado *m*

secretary ['sekrətrɪ] N **1** (= *profession*) secretario/a *m/f*
2 (*Pol*) ministro/a *m/f* • **Secretary of State** (*Brit*) Ministro/a *m/f* (**for** de); (*US*) Ministro/a *m/f* de Asuntos Exteriores
CPD ▸ **secretary pool** (*US*) servicio *m* de mecanógrafos

secretary-general ['sekrətrɪ'dʒenərəl] N (PL: **secretaries-general**) secretario-general/secretaria-general *m/f*

secretaryship ['sekrətrɪʃɪp] N secretaría *f*, secretariado *m*

secrete [sɪ'kri:t] VT **1** (*Med*) secretar, segregar
2 (= *hide*) ocultar, esconder

secretion [sɪ'kri:ʃən] N **1** (*Med*) secreción *f*
2 (= *hiding*) ocultación *f*

secretive ['si:krətɪv] ADJ [*person*] reservado, callado; [*behaviour*] reservado; [*organization*] hermético • **to be ~ about sth** ser reservado con respecto a algo

secretively ['si:krətɪvlɪ] ADV **1** (= *furtively*) [*behave, smile*] con mucho secreto
2 (= *in secret*) a escondidas

secretiveness ['si:krətɪvnɪs] N • **she knew that something was up because of the children's ~** supo que pasaba algo porque los niños actuaban con mucho secreto

secretly ['si:krɪtlɪ] ADV [*meet, plan, film*] en secreto, a escondidas; [*marry*] en secreto; [*hope, want*] en el fondo • **she was ~ relieved/pleased** en su fuero interno sintió alivio/estaba contenta

secretory [sɪ'kri:tərɪ] ADJ [*gland etc*] secretorio

sect [sekt] N secta *f*

sectarian [sek'tɛərɪən] ADJ sectario
N sectario/a *m/f*

sectarianism [sek'tɛərɪənɪzəm] N sectarismo *m*

section ['sekʃən] N **1** (= *part*) [*of pipeline, road*] tramo *m*; [*of self-assembly item*] pieza *f*, parte *f*; [*of orange etc*] gajo *m*; [*of book, text*] parte *f*; [*of code, law*] artículo *m*; [*of document, report*] apartado *m*, punto *m*; [*of orchestra*] sección *f*; [*of country*] región *f*; [*of community, opinion*] sector *m*; [*of town*] (*Brit*) sector *m*, zona *f*; (*US*) (= *district*) barrio *m* • **the ship was transported in ~s** el barco fue trasladado por partes • **the bookcase comes in ~s** la estantería viene desmontada (en piezas *or* partes) • **the first-class ~ of the train** los vagones de primera clase del tren • **passports ~** sección *f* de pasaportes • **the sports/finance ~** [*of newspaper*] la sección de deportes/economía • **in all ~s of the public** en todos los sectores del público; ▹ **brass, string, percussion, woodwind**
2 (= *cut*) (*in diagram, dissection*) sección *f*, corte *m* • **cross ~** (*lit*) sección *f* transversal • **the research was compiled using a cross ~ of the British population** el estudió se realizó utilizando un sector representativo de la población británica
3 (*Med*) (*also* **Caesarean section**) ▹ **Caesarean**
VT **1** (= *divide*) partir, trocear
2 [+ *mentally ill person*] internar en un psiquiátrico
CPD ▸ **section mark** párrafo *m*
▸ **section off** VT + ADV cortar, seccionar

sectional ['sekʃənl] ADJ **1** [*bookcase etc*] desmontable
2 [*interests*] particular
3 [*diagram*] en corte

sectionalism ['sekʃənəlɪzəm] N faccionalismo *m*

sector ['sektə^r] N **1** (*Econ, Ind*) sector *m* • **the public ~** el sector público; ▹ **voluntary**
2 (*Mil*) sector *m*
3 (*Geom*) sector *m*

sectoral ['sektərəl] ADJ (*Econ*) sectorial

secular ['sekjʊlə^r] ADJ [*authority*] laico; [*writings, music*] profano; [*priest*] secular, seglar • **~ school** escuela *f* laica

secularism ['sekjʊlərɪzəm] N laicismo *m*

secularist ['sekjʊlərɪst] N laico/a *m/f*

secularization [ˌsekjʊləraɪ'zeɪʃən] N secularización *f*

secularize ['sekjʊləraɪz] VT secularizar

secularized ['sekjʊləraɪzd] ADJ secularizado

secure [sɪ'kjʊə^r] ADJ **1** (= *firm, solid*) [*knot, rope, hold*] seguro; [*door, window, lock, bolt*] bien cerrado; [*structure, foothold*] firme; [*ladder*] bien sujeto; [*base, foundation*] sólido • **to have a ~ foothold in a market** tener un punto de apoyo firme en un mercado
2 (= *safe*) [*job, place, building*] seguro; [*position*] garantizado; [*career, future*] asegurado • **to be financially ~** tener seguridad económica • **to be ~ from** *or* **against sth** estar protegido contra algo • **I want to make my home ~ against burglars** quiero proteger mi casa contra los ladrones • **to make an area ~** hacer de una zona un lugar seguro
3 (*emotionally*) [*person*] seguro; [*relationship, environment*] estable • **children need a ~ home life** los niños necesitan un ambiente estable en el hogar • **to be emotionally ~** tener estabilidad emocional • **to feel ~ (about sth)** sentirse seguro (con respecto a algo) • **to make sb feel ~** hacer a algn sentirse seguro • **~ in the knowledge that** seguro de que, confiado de que
VT **1** (= *make fast*) [+ *rope*] sujetar bien; (*to floor etc*) afianzar; [+ *load*] asegurar; [+ *door, window*] cerrar bien; (= *tie up*) [+ *person, animal*] atar, amarrar (*LAm*) • **a shawl ~d at the neck by a broch** un chal sujeto a la altura del cuello con un broche
2 (= *make safe*) [+ *home, building*] proteger (**against** de, contra, **from** de, contra); [+ *career, future*] asegurar
3 (*frm*) (= *obtain*) [+ *job, peace, freedom, support*] conseguir, obtener • **they have not got enough evidence to ~ a conviction** no tienen suficientes pruebas para conseguir que lo condenen • **a win that ~d them a place in the final** una victoria que les aseguró un puesto en la final • **to ~ victory** conseguir la victoria
4 (*Econ*) [+ *loan, debt*] garantizar • **you can ~ the loan against your home** puedes poner la casa como garantía *or* aval del préstamo • **~d creditor** acreedor(a) *m/f* con garantía • **~d debt** deuda *f* garantizada • **~d loan** préstamo *m* con garantía
5 (*Mil*) (= *capture*) tomar, capturar
CPD ▸ **secure accommodation** (*Brit*) (*Jur*) *centro de prevención contra la delincuencia*
▸ **secure unit** (*Brit*) (*for young offenders, mental patients*) unidad *f* de seguridad

securely [sɪ'kjʊəlɪ] ADV **1** (= *firmly*) [*fasten, lock, fix, tie*] bien • **it is ~ fastened** está bien abrochado
2 (= *safely*) firmemente • **he remains ~ in power** permanece firmemente afincado en el poder • **~ established** firmemente establecido

security [sɪ'kjʊərɪtɪ] N **1** (= *precautions*) seguridad *f* • **for ~ reasons** • **for reasons of ~** por razones de seguridad • **the Queen's visit has been marked by tight ~** la visita de la reina se ha visto caracterizada por estrechas medidas de seguridad; ▹ **maximum**
2 (= *safety*) **a** (*from harm or loss*) seguridad *f* • **the ~ of the passengers on the aircraft** la seguridad de los pasajeros a bordo del avión • **~ of tenure** (*in one's job*) seguridad *f* en el cargo; [*of tenant*] derecho *m* de ocupación (*de un inmueble*); ▹ **job, national**
b (*from worry*) seguridad *f*, estabilidad *f*

• **emotional/financial ~** estabilidad *f* emocional/económica, seguridad *f* en el plano emocional/económico; ▹ **false**
3 (= *guarantee*) garantía *f*, aval *m* • **to lend money on ~** prestar dinero con un aval *or* bajo fianza • **to stand** *or* **go ~ for sb** salir garante *or* avalista de algn, avalar a algn
4 securities valores *mpl*, títulos *mpl* • **government securities** bonos *mpl* del Estado
(CPD) ▸ **securities dealer** corredor(a) *m/f* de Bolsa ▸ **securities firm** sociedad *f* de valores ▸ **security agreement** (*Econ*) acuerdo *m* de garantía ▸ **securities market** (*Econ*) mercado *m* bursátil ▸ **securities portfolio** cartera *f* de valores ▸ **security alarm** alarma *f* de seguridad ▸ **security blanket** (*Psych*) manta *f* de seguridad ▸ **security camera** cámara *f* de seguridad ▸ **security check** control *m* de seguridad ▸ **security clearance** certificado *m* de seguridad ▸ **Security Council** Consejo *m* de Seguridad • **the Security Council of the United Nations** el Consejo de Seguridad de las Naciones Unidas ▸ **security firm** empresa *f* de seguridad ▸ **security forces** fuerzas *fpl* de seguridad ▸ **security guard** guarda *mf* jurado ▸ **security leak** filtración *f* de información secreta ▸ **security measures** medidas *fpl* de seguridad ▸ **security officer** (*Mil, Naut*) oficial *mf* de las fuerzas de seguridad; (*Comm, Ind*) encargado/a *m/f* de seguridad ▸ **security police** policía *f* de seguridad ▸ **security precaution** precaución *f* ▸ **security risk** riesgo *m* para la seguridad ▸ **security system** sistema *m* de seguridad ▸ **security van** furgón *m* blindado ▸ **security vetting** acreditación *f* por la Seguridad ▸ **security video** vídeo *m* de seguridad (*Sp*), video *m* de seguridad (*LAm*)

secy, Secy. (ABBR) (= **secretary**) sec., srio. *m*, sria. *f*

sedan [sɪˈdæn] (N) **1** (*also* **sedan chair**) silla *f* de manos
2 (*US*) (*Aut*) sedán *m*

sedate [sɪˈdeɪt] (ADJ) serio, formal
(VT) (*Med*) sedar

sedated [sɪˈdeɪtɪd] (ADJ) [*patient*] sedado • **lightly ~** con sedación ligera • **heavily ~** con sedación profunda

sedately [sɪˈdeɪtlɪ] (ADV) seriamente, formalmente

sedateness [sɪˈdeɪtnɪs] (N) seriedad *f*

sedation [sɪˈdeɪʃən] (N) sedación *f* • **under ~** bajo sedación

sedative [ˈsedətɪv] (ADJ) sedante
(N) sedante *m*

sedentariness [ˈsedntərɪnɪs] (N) **1** [*of work, life, animal*] sedentariedad *f*
2 [*of previously nomadic tribe*] sedentarismo *m*

sedentary [ˈsedntrɪ] (ADJ) sedentario

sedge [sedʒ] (N) junco *m*, juncia *f*

sedgy [ˈsedʒɪ] (ADJ) **1** (*growing with sedge*) lleno de juncos
2 (= *resembling sedge*) que parecen juncos

sediment [ˈsedɪmənt] (N) (*in liquids, boiler*) sedimento *m*, poso *m*; (*Geol*) sedimento *m*

sedimentary [ˌsedɪˈmentərɪ] (ADJ) sedimentario

sedimentation [ˌsedmenˈteɪʃən] (N) sedimentación *f*

sedition [səˈdɪʃən] (N) sedición *f*

seditious [səˈdɪʃəs] (ADJ) sedicioso

seduce [sɪˈdjuːs] (VT) (*sexually*) seducir • **to ~ sb into doing sth** (*fig*) engatusar *or* convencer a algn para que haga algo • **to ~ sb from his duty** apartar a algn de su deber

seducer [sɪˈdjuːsəʳ] (N) seductor(a) *m/f*

seduction [sɪˈdʌkʃən] (N) (= *act*) seducción *f*; (= *attraction*) tentación *f*

seductive [sɪˈdʌktɪv] (ADJ) [*person, voice, clothes, perfume*] seductor; [*smile*] seductor, provocativo; [*offer*] tentador, atractivo

seductively [sɪˈdʌktɪvlɪ] (ADV) [*smile, behave, look at, dress*] de modo seductor, de manera seductora; [*say*] en tono seductor

seductiveness [sɪˈdʌktɪvnɪs] (N) [*of person, look, clothes, smile*] seducción *f*; [*of offer*] atractivo *m*

seductress [sɪˈdʌktrɪs] (N) seductora *f*

sedulous [ˈsedjʊləs] (ADJ) asiduo, diligente

sedulously [ˈsedjʊləslɪ] (ADV) asiduamente, diligentemente

see[1] [siː] (PT: **saw**, PP: **seen**) (VT), (VI) **1** (*gen*) ver • **I saw him yesterday** lo vi ayer • **I can't see** no veo nada • **to see sb do** *or* **doing sth** ver a algn hacer algo • **I saw him coming** lo vi venir • **(go and) see who's at the door** ve a ver quién llama (a la puerta) • **he was seen to fall** se le vio caer • **I saw it done in 1988** lo vi hacer en 1988 • **"see page eight"** "véase la página ocho" • **did you see that Queen Anne is dead?** ¿has oído que ha muerto la reina Ana? • **he's seen it all** está de vuelta de todo • **there was nobody to be seen** no se veía ni nadie • **there was not a house to be seen** no se veía ni una sola casa • **as you can see** como ves • **as far as the eye can see** hasta donde alcanza la vista • **from here you can see for miles** desde aquí se ve muy lejos • **I'll see him damned first** antes le veré colgado • **I never thought I'd see the day when …** nunca pensé ver el día en que … • **this car has seen better days** este coche ha conocido mejores tiempos • **this dress isn't fit to be seen** este vestido no se puede ver • **he's not fit to be seen in public** no se le puede presentar a los ojos del público • **see for yourself** velo tú • **I'll go and see** voy a ver • **now see here!** (*in anger*) ¡mira!, ¡oiga!, ¡escuche! • **I see nothing wrong in it** no le encuentro nada malo • **I don't know what she sees in him** no sé lo que encuentra en él • **I see in the paper that …** sale en el periódico que … • **let me see** • **let's see** (= *show me/us*) a ver; (= *let me/us think*) vamos a ver • **she's certainly seeing life** es seguro que está viendo muchas cosas • **we'll not see his like again** no veremos otro como él • **he's seen a lot of the world** ha visto mucho mundo • **so I see** ya lo veo • **I must be seeing things*** estoy viendo visiones • **I can't see to read** no veo lo suficiente para leer • **can you see your way to helping us?** (*fig*) ¿nos hace el favor de ayudarnos? • **we'll see** ya veremos, a ver • **I'll see what I can do** veré si puedo hacer algo • **she won't see 40 again** los 40 ya no los cumple
2 (= *visit, meet*) ver, visitar; (= *have an interview with*) tener una entrevista con, entrevistarse con • **the minister saw the Queen yesterday** el ministro se entrevistó *or* tuvo una entrevista con la Reina ayer • **I'm afraid I can't see you tomorrow** lamento no poder verle mañana • **I want to see you about my daughter** quiero hablar con usted acerca de mi hija • **what did he want to see you about?** ¿qué asunto quería discutir contigo?, ¿qué motivo tuvo su visita? • **we'll be seeing them for dinner** vamos a cenar con ellos • **to see the doctor** ir a ver al médico, consultar al médico • **you need to see a doctor** tienes que ir a ver *or* consultar a un médico • **to go and see sb** ir a ver a algn; (*a friend*) visitar a algn • **we don't see much of them nowadays** ahora les vemos bastante poco • **see you!*** chau* • **see you on Sunday!** ¡hasta el domingo! • **see you tomorrow!** ¡hasta mañana! • **see you later!** ¡hasta luego! • **see you soon!** ¡hasta pronto!
3 (= *understand, perceive*) entender • **I see** lo veo • **I see!** ya entiendo • **this is how I see it** este es mi modo de entenderlo, yo lo entiendo así • **I saw only too clearly that …** percibí claramente que … • **it's all over, see?*** se acabó, ¿entiendes? • **I can't** *or* **don't see why/how** *etc* … no veo *or* entiendo por qué/cómo *etc* … • **I don't see it, myself** yo no creo que sea posible • **he's dead, don't you see?** está muerto, ¿me entiendes? • **the Russians see it differently** los rusos lo miran desde otro punto de vista, el criterio de los rusos es distinto • **I fail to see how** no comprendo *or* entiendo cómo • **as far as I can see** por lo visto, por lo que yo veo • **the way I see it** a mi parecer
4 (= *accompany*) acompañar • **he was so drunk we had to see him to bed** estaba tan borracho que tuvimos que llevarle a la cama • **to see sb to the door** acompañar a algn a la puerta • **to see sb home** acompañar a algn a casa • **may I see you home?** ¿puedo acompañarte a casa?
5 (= *try*) procurar • **see if …** ve a ver si …, mira a ver si …
6 (= *imagine*) imaginarse • **I can just see him as a teacher** me lo imagino de profesor • **I don't see her as a minister** no la veo *or* no me la imagino de ministra • **I can't see myself doing that** no me imagino con capacidad para hacer eso • **I can't really see myself being elected** en realidad no creo que me vayan a elegir • **I can't see him winning** me parece imposible que gane
7 (= *ensure*) • **to see (to it) that** procurar que (+ *subjun*) • **see that he has all he needs** procura que tenga todo lo que necesita • **to see that sth is done** procurar que algo se haga • **see that you have it ready for Monday** procura tenerlo listo para el lunes • **see that it does not happen again** y que no vuelva a ocurrir

▸ **see about** (VI + PREP) **1** (= *deal with*) ocuparse de • **I'll see about it** yo me ocupo *or* me encargo de eso • **he came to see about our TV** vino a ver nuestra televisión
2 (= *consider*) pensar • **I'll see about it** lo veré, lo pensaré • **we'll see about that!** ¡eso está por ver! • **we must see about getting a new car** tenemos que pensar en comprar un nuevo coche

▸ **see in** (VT + ADV) [+ *person*] hacer entrar, hacer pasar • **to see the New Year in** celebrar *or* festejar el Año Nuevo
(VI + ADV) • **he was trying to see in** se esforzaba por ver el interior

▸ **see into** (VI + PREP) (= *study, examine*) investigar, examinar

▸ **see off** (VT + ADV) **1** (= *say goodbye to*) despedir, despedirse de • **we went to see him off at the station** fuimos a despedirnos de él *or* a despedirlo a la estación
2* (= *defeat*) vencer; (= *destroy*) acabar con
3* (= *send away*) • **the policeman saw them off** el policía les dijo que se fueran

▸ **see out** (VT + ADV) **1** (= *survive*) sobrevivir a • **we wondered if he would see the month out** nos preguntábamos si viviría hasta el fin del mes • **to see a film out** quedarse hasta el final de una película
2 (= *take to the door*) acompañar hasta la puerta • **I'll see myself out*** no hace falta que me acompañe hasta la puerta
(VI + ADV) • **we shan't be able to see out** no podremos ver el exterior

▸ **see over** (VI + PREP) recorrer

▸ **see through** (VI + PREP) [+ *person, behaviour*] calar • **I can see right through him** lo tengo calado • **I saw through him at once** lo calé enseguida, enseguida lo vi venir • **to see**

through a mystery penetrar un misterio
(VT + ADV) [+ project, deal] llevar a cabo • **don't worry, we'll see it through** no te preocupes, nosotros lo llevaremos a cabo • **we'll see him through** nosotros le ayudaremos • **£100 should see you through** tendrás bastante con 100 libras
(VT + PREP) • **this money should see you through your stay in Egypt** este dinero te bastará para tu estancia en Egipto
▸ **see to** (VI + PREP) (= *deal with*) atender a; (= *take care of*) ocuparse de, encargase de • **the shower isn't working, can you see to it please?** la ducha se ha estropeado ¿podrías ocuparte *or* encargarte de eso? • **please see to it that ...** por favor procura que ... • **the rats saw to that** las ratas se encargaron de eso

see² [siː] (N) (*Rel*) sede *f*; [*of archbishop*] arzobispado *m*; [*of bishop*] obispado *m* • **the Holy See** la Santa Sede

seed [siːd] (N) **1** (*Bot*) [*of plant*] semilla *f*, simiente *f*; (*inside fruit*) pepita *f*; [*of grain*] grano *m* • **poppy ~s** semillas *fpl* de amapola • **to go** *or* **run to ~** (*lit*) granar, dar en grana; (*fig*) ir a menos • **he's really gone to ~** se ha echado a perder, ha ido cada vez a peor; ▹ **sesame, sunflower**
2 (*Sport*) (= *player, team*) cabeza *mf* de serie • **she's the number one ~** es cabeza de serie número uno • **she's the first ~** es la primera cabeza de serie
3 (*fig*) [*of idea etc*] germen *m* • **to sow ~s of doubt in sb's mind** sembrar la duda en la mente de algn
4 (*euph*) (= *semen*) simiente *f*; (= *offspring*) descendencia *f*
(VT) **1** (= *plant with seeds*) sembrar (**with** de)
2 (= *remove seed of*) [+ *fruits*] despepitar
3 (*Sport*) clasificar como cabeza de serie • **the US are ~ed number one** Estados Unidos parte como cabeza de serie número uno
(VI) (*Bot*) (= *form seeds*) granar, dar en grana; (= *shed seeds*) dejar caer semillas
(CPD) ▸ **seed box** caja *f* de simientes, semillero *m* ▸ **seed corn** (*lit*) trigo *m* de siembra ▸ **seed drill** sembradora *f* ▸ **seed merchant** vendedor(a) *m/f* de semillas ▸ **seed money** (*Comm*) capital *m* inicial ▸ **seed pearl** aljófar *m* ▸ **seed pod** vaina *f* ▸ **seed potato** patata *f* *or* (*LAm*) papa *f* de siembra ▸ **seed time** siembra *f* ▸ **seed tray** = **seed box**

seedbed ['siːdbed] (N) semillero *m*

seedcake ['siːdkeɪk] (N) torta *f* de alcaravea

seeded ['siːdɪd] (ADJ) (*Sport*) • **a ~ player** un cabeza de serie • **to be ~ second** ser cabeza de serie número dos

seedily ['siːdɪlɪ] (ADV) [*dress*] andrajosamente, desastradamente

seediness ['siːdɪnɪs] (N) (= *shabbiness*) [*of hotel, nightclub*] sordidez *f*, cutrez *f* (*Sp**); [*of clothes*] lo raído, cutrez *f* (*Sp**); [*of person*] pinta *f* desastrada

seedless ['siːdlɪs] (ADJ) sin semillas

seedling ['siːdlɪŋ] (N) planta *f* de semillero

seedsman ['siːdzmən] (N) (PL: **seedsmen**) = **seed merchant**

seedy ['siːdɪ] (ADJ) (COMPAR: **seedier**, SUPERL: **seediest**) **1** (= *shabby*) [*hotel, nightclub*] sórdido, de mala muerte*, cutre (*Sp**); [*clothes*] raído, cutre (*Sp**); [*person*] de pinta desastrada • **a ~-looking bar** un bar sórdido, un bar de mala muerte*, un bar cutre (*Sp**)
2 (= *unwell*) • **I'm feeling ~** tengo un poco de mal cuerpo • **he looks a bit ~** tiene mala cara

seeing ['siːɪŋ] (CONJ) • **~ (that)** visto que, en vista de que
(N) • PROVERB: • **~ is believing** ver para creer

seeing-eye dog [ˌsiːɪŋ'aɪdɒg] (N) (*US*) perro *m* guía

seek [siːk] (PT, PP: **sought**) (VT) **1** (= *look for*) [+ *work, refuge*] buscar; [+ *candidate*] solicitar; [+ *honour*] ambicionar • **he has been sought in many countries** se le ha buscado en muchos países • **it is much sought after** está muy cotizado • **to ~ death** buscar la muerte • **the reason is not far to ~** no es difícil indicar la causa • **to ~ shelter (from)** buscar abrigo (de)
2 (= *ask for*) pedir, solicitar • **to ~ advice from sb** pedir consejo a algn • **the couple sought a second opinion** la pareja quiso tener una segunda opinión
3 (*frm*) (= *attempt*) • **to ~ to do sth** tratar de *or* procurar hacer algo
(VI) (*frm*) • **to ~ after** *or* **for** buscar
▸ **seek out** (VT + ADV) buscar

seeker ['siːkəʳ] (N) buscador(a) *m/f*

seem [siːm] (VI) parecer • **he ~s capable** parece capaz • **he ~ed absorbed in ...** parecía estar absorto en ... • **he ~ed to be in difficulty** parecía tener dificultades • **the shop ~ed to be closed** parecía que la tienda estaba cerrada • **she ~s not to want to go** parece que no quiere ir • **what ~s to be the trouble?** ¿qué pasa? • **I ~ to have heard that before** me parece que ya me contaron eso antes • **it ~s that ...** parece que ... • **it ~s you have no alternative** parece que no te queda otra alternativa • **it ~s she's getting married** por lo visto se casa • **I can't ~ to do it** me parece imposible hacerlo • **that ~s like a good idea** parece una buena idea • **it ~s not** parece que no • **it ~s so** parece que sí • **so it ~s** así parece • **there ~s to be a problem** parece que hay un problema • **there ~s to be a mistake** parece que hay un error • **it ~s to me/him that ...** me/le parece que ... • **how did he ~ to you?** ¿qué te pareció?

seeming ['siːmɪŋ] (ADJ) aparente
(N) apariencia *f*

seemingly ['siːmɪŋlɪ] (ADV) según parece, aparentemente • **it is ~ finished** según parece *or* aparentemente está terminado • **there has ~ been a rise in inflation** parece que ha habido un aumento de la inflación • **"he's left then?" — "seemingly"** —¿o sea que se ha ido? —eso parece

seemliness ['siːmlɪnɪs] (N) (*frm*) decoro *m*, decencia *f*

seemly ['siːmlɪ] (ADJ) (COMPAR: **seemlier**, SUPERL: **seemliest**) (*frm*) [*behaviour, language, dress*] decoroso, decente

seen [siːn] (PP) *of* **see¹**

seep [siːp] (VI) filtrarse • **to ~ through/into/from** filtrarse *or* colarse por/en/de
▸ **seep away** (VI + ADV) escurrirse
▸ **seep in** (VI + ADV) filtrarse
▸ **seep out** (VI + ADV) escurrirse

seepage ['siːpɪdʒ] (N) filtración *f*

seer [sɪəʳ] (N) vidente *mf*

seersucker ['sɪəˌsʌkəʳ] (N) sirsaca *f*

seesaw ['siːsɔː] (N) (= *apparatus, game*) subibaja *m*, balancín *m*
(ADJ) [*movement*] oscilante, de vaivén • **~ motion** movimiento *m* oscilante *or* de vaivén
(VI) columpiarse; (*fig*) vacilar

seethe [siːð] (VI) **1** (*lit*) borbotear, hervir
2 (*fig*) • **he's seething** está furioso • **to ~ with anger** estar furioso

see-through ['siːθruː] (ADJ) transparente

segment (N) ['segmənt] (*gen*) segmento *m*; [*of citrus fruit*] gajo *m*; (*Geom*) [*of circle*] segmento *m*
(VT) [seg'ment] [+ *circle, society, journey, market*] segmentar; [+ *citrus fruit*] desgajar, separar en gajos
(VI) [seg'ment] segmentarse

segmentation [ˌsegmən'teɪʃən] (N) segmentación *f*

segregate ['segrɪgeɪt] (VT) segregar, separar (**from** de) • **to be ~d from** estar separado de

segregated ['segrɪgeɪtɪd] (ADJ) segregado, separado

segregation [ˌsegrɪ'geɪʃən] (N) segregación *f*, separación *f* • **racial ~** la segregación racial

segregationism [ˌsegrɪ'geɪʃənɪsm] (N) segregacionismo *m*

segregationist [ˌsegrɪ'geɪʃənɪst] (N) segregacionista *mf*

Seine [seɪn] (N) Sena *m*

seine [seɪn] (N) jábega *f*

seismic ['saɪzmɪk] (ADJ) (*lit*) sísmico; (*fig*) [*shift, change*] radical

seismograph ['saɪzməgrɑːf] (N) sismógrafo *m*

seismography [saɪz'mɒgrəfɪ] (N) sismografía *f*

seismological [ˌsaɪzmə'lɒdʒɪkəl] (ADJ) sismológico

seismologist [saɪz'mɒlədʒɪst] (N) sismólogo/a *m/f*

seismology [saɪz'mɒlədʒɪ] (N) sismología *f*

seize [siːz] (VT) **1** (= *physically take hold of*) coger, agarrar • **to ~ hold of sth/sb** coger *or* agarrar algo/a algn • **to ~ sb by the arm** coger *or* agarrar a algn por el brazo
2 (= *capture*) [+ *person*] detener; [+ *territory*] apoderarse de; [+ *power*] tomar, hacerse con
3 (*Jur*) (= *confiscate*) [+ *property*] incautar, embargar
4 (= *kidnap*) secuestrar
5 (*fig*) [+ *opportunity*] aprovechar • **to be ~d with fear/rage** estar sobrecogido por el miedo/la cólera • **he was ~d with a desire to leave** el deseo de marcharse se apoderó de él
(VI) ▹ **seize up**
▸ **seize on** (VI + PREP) = **seize upon**
▸ **seize up** (VI + ADV) [*machine, limbs*] agarrotarse
▸ **seize upon** (VI + PREP) [+ *chance*] aprovechar; [+ *idea*] fijarse en

seizure ['siːʒəʳ] (N) **1** [*of goods*] embargo *m*, incautación *f*; [*of person*] secuestro *m*; [*of land, city, ship*] toma *f*
2 (*Med*) ataque *m* • **to have a ~** sufrir un ataque

seldom ['seldəm] (ADV) rara vez, pocas veces, casi nunca • **it ~ rains here** aquí rara vez llueve, aquí llueve pocas veces, aquí no llueve casi nunca • **~, if ever** rara vez *or* pocas veces, si es que alguna

select [sɪ'lekt] (VT) [+ *team, candidate*] seleccionar; [+ *book, gift etc*] escoger, elegir • **~ed works** obras *fpl* escogidas
(ADJ) [*school, restaurant, club*] selecto, exclusivo; [*tobacco, wine, audience*] selecto • **a ~ group of people** un grupo selecto de personas • **a very ~ neighbourhood** un barrio de muy buen tono • **a ~ few** una minoría privilegiada
(CPD) ▸ **select committee** comité *m* de investigación

selection [sɪ'lekʃən] (N) **1** (= *act of choosing*) elección *f*
2 (= *person/thing chosen*) elección *f*, selección *f* • **~s from** (*Mus, Literat*) selecciones de
3 (= *range, assortment*) surtido *m*, selección *f* • **the widest ~ on the market** el más amplio surtido *or* la más amplia selección del mercado
(CPD) ▸ **selection committee** (*esp Pol*) comisión *f* de nombramiento ▸ **selection procedure, selection process** proceso *m* de selección ▸ **selection test** prueba *f* de selección

selective [sɪ'lektɪv] (ADJ) selectivo • **one has**

to be ~ hay que escoger
CPD ▸ **selective breeding** cría *f* selectiva
▸ **selective memory** memoria *f* selectiva
selectively [sɪ'lektɪvlɪ] ADV selectivamente
selectivity [sɪlek'tɪvɪtɪ] N selectividad *f*
selector [sɪ'lektəʳ] N (= *person*) seleccionador(a) *m/f*; (*Tech*) selector *m*
selenium [sɪ'li:nɪəm] N selenio *m*
self [self] N (PL: **selves**) uno/a mismo/a *m/f* • **the ~** el yo • **my better ~** mi lado bueno • **my former ~** el que era • **my true ~** mi verdadero yo • **he's quite his old ~ again** vuelve a ser el que era • **if your good ~ could possibly ...**† (*also hum*) si usted tuviera la suprema amabilidad de ... • **he thinks of nothing but ~** no piensa más que en sí mismo
CPD ▸ **self worth** autoestima *f*
self- [self] PREFIX auto..., ... de sí mismo
self-abasement [,selfə'beɪsmənt] N rebajamiento *m* de sí mismo, autodegradación *f*
self-absorbed [,selfəb'zɔ:bd] ADJ ensimismado
self-abuse† [,selfə'bju:s] N (*euph*) masturbación *f*
self-acting [,self'æktɪŋ] ADJ automático
self-addressed [,selfə'drest] ADJ • **self-addressed envelope** (*Brit*) • **self-addressed stamped envelope** (*US*) sobre *m* con dirección propia
self-adhesive [,selfəd'hi:zɪv] ADJ [*envelope, label, tape*] autoadhesivo, autoadherente
self-advertisement [,selfəd'vɜ:tɪsmənt] N autobombo *m*
self-aggrandizement [,selfə'grændɪzmənt] N autobombo *m*
self-analysis [,selfə'næləsɪs] N autoanálisis *m*
self-apparent [,selfə'pærənt] ADJ evidente, patente
self-appointed [,selfə'pɔɪntɪd] ADJ que se ha nombrado a sí mismo
self-appraisal [,selfə'preɪzl] N autovaloración *f*
self-assembly [,selfə'semblɪ] ADJ [*furniture etc*] automontable
self-assertion [,selfə'sɜ:ʃən] N asertividad *f*
self-assertive [,selfə'sɜ:tɪv] ADJ asertivo
self-assertiveness [,selfə'sɜ:tɪvnɪs] N asertividad *f*
self-assessment [,selfə'sesmənt] N **1** autoevaluación *f* **2** (*Brit*) (*Tax*) autoliquidación *f*
self-assurance [,selfə'ʃʊərəns] N confianza *f* en sí mismo
self-assured [,selfə'ʃʊəd] ADJ seguro de sí mismo
self-aware [,selfə'wɛəʳ] ADJ • **to be self-aware** conocerse bien • **studying has increased my confidence and I am much more self-aware** estudiar ha aumentado mi confianza y me conozco mucho mejor
self-awareness [,selfə'wɛənɪs] N conocimiento *m or* conciencia *f* de sí mismo
self-belief [,selfbɪ'li:f] N (= *self-confidence*) confianza *f* en sí mismo
self-build N [,self'bɪld] autoconstrucción *f* ADJ ['self,bɪld] [*home, housing*] construido por uno mismo
self-catering [,self'keɪtərɪŋ] ADJ • **self-catering apartment** apartamento *m* con acceso a cocina (*p.ej. en unas vacaciones organizadas*) • **self-catering holiday** vacaciones *fpl* en piso *or* chalet *or* casita con cocina propia
self-centred, **self-centered** (*US*) [,self'sentəd] ADJ egocéntrico
self-cleaning [,self'kli:nɪŋ] ADJ [*oven etc*] autolimpiable
self-closing [,self'kləʊzɪŋ] ADJ de cierre automático
self-coloured, **self-colored** (*US*) [,self'kʌləd] ADJ de color uniforme, unicolor
self-command [,selfkə'mɑ:nd] N dominio *m* sobre sí mismo, autodominio *m*
self-complacent [,selfkəm'pleɪsənt] ADJ satisfecho de sí mismo
self-composed [,selfkəm'pəʊzd] ADJ sereno, dueño de sí mismo
self-composure [,selfkəm'pəʊʒəʳ] N serenidad *f*, dominio *m* de sí mismo
self-conceit [,selfkən'si:t] N presunción *f*, vanidad *f*, engreimiento *m*
self-conceited [,selfkən'si:tɪd] ADJ presumido, vanidoso, engreído
self-confessed [,selfkən'fest] ADJ confeso
self-confidence [,self'kɒnfɪdəns] N confianza *f* en sí mismo • **I lost all my self-confidence** perdí toda la confianza en mí mismo
self-confident [,self'kɒnfɪdənt] ADJ seguro de sí mismo, lleno de confianza en sí mismo
self-congratulation [,selfkən,grætjʊ'leɪʃən] N • **he had little cause for self-congratulation** no tenía muchas razones para estar satisfecho consigo mismo • **MPs sensed that this was not the time for self-congratulation** los diputados se dieron cuenta de que no era el momento de comenzar a felicitarse a sí mismos • **the mood was one of self-congratulation** había un ambiente de satisfacción con uno mismo
self-congratulatory [,selfkəngrætjʊ'leɪtərɪ] ADJ satisfecho con sí mismo • **to be self-congratulatory** estar satisfecho con sí mismo • **officials were self-congratulatory about how well the day had gone** los oficiales estaban satisfechos consigo mismos por lo bien que les había ido el día
self-conscious [,self'kɒnʃəs] ADJ cohibido, tímido • **she was really self-conscious at first** al principio estaba muy cohibida • **she was self-conscious about her height** estaba acomplejada por su estatura
self-consciously [,self'kɒnʃəslɪ] ADV cohibidamente, tímidamente
self-consciousness [,self'kɒnʃəsnɪs] N timidez *f*, inseguridad *f*
self-contained [,selfkən'teɪnd] ADJ [*flat*] con entrada propia, independiente; [*person*] autónomo, autosuficiente
self-contradiction [,selfkɒntrə'dɪkʃən] N contradicción *f* en sí
self-contradictory [,selfkɒntrə'dɪktərɪ] ADJ que se contradice a sí mismo, que lleva implícita una contradicción
self-control [,selfkən'trəʊl] N dominio *m* de sí mismo, autocontrol *m* • **to exercise one's self-control** contenerse, dominarse • **to lose one's self-control** no poder contenerse *or* dominarse
self-controlled [,selfkən'trəʊld] ADJ sereno • **she's very self-controlled** tiene mucho autocontrol
self-correcting [,selfkə'rektɪŋ] ADJ autocorrector
self-critical [,self'krɪtɪkl] ADJ autocrítico
self-criticism [,self'krɪtɪsɪzəm] N autocrítica *f*
self-deception [,selfdɪ'sepʃən] N engaño *m* de sí mismo • **this is mere self-deception** esto es engañarse a sí mismo
self-declared [,selfdɪ'klɛəd] ADJ [*leader, president*] autoproclamado; [*liar*] impenitente; [*racist*] declarado
self-defeating [,selfdɪ'fi:tɪŋ] ADJ contraproducente
self-defence, **self-defense** (*US*) [,selfdɪ'fens] N autodefensa *f*, defensa *f* propia • **she killed him in self-defence** lo mató en defensa propia • **to act in self-defence** obrar en defensa propia
CPD ▸ **self-defence classes** clases *fpl* de defensa personal
self-delusion [,selfdɪ'lu:ʒən] N autoengaño *m*
self-denial [,selfdɪ'naɪəl] N abnegación *f*
self-denying [,selfdɪ'naɪɪŋ] ADJ abnegado • **self-denying ordinance** resolución *f* abnegada
self-deprecating [,self'deprɪkeɪtɪŋ] ADJ autodesaprobatorio • **she tells the story of that night with self-deprecating humour** cuenta la historia de esa noche con un humor autodesaprobatorio
self-destruct [,selfdɪs'trʌkt] VI autodestruirse
self-destruction [,selfdɪs'trʌkʃən] N suicidio *m*; [*of weapon*] autodestrucción *f*
self-destructive [,selfdɪs'trʌktɪv] ADJ autodestructivo
self-determination [,selfdɪ,tɜ:mɪ'neɪʃən] N autodeterminación *f*
self-determined [,selfdɪ'tɜ:mɪnd] ADJ autodeterminado
self-discipline [,self'dɪsɪplɪn] N autodisciplina *f*
self-disciplined [,self'dɪsɪplɪnd] ADJ autodisciplinado
self-doubt [,self'daʊt] N desconfianza *f* de sí mismo
self-drive ['self,draɪv] (*Brit*) ADJ **1** [*car, van*] sin conductor **2** [*holiday*] con su propio vehículo
CPD ▸ **self-drive hire** (*Brit*) (*Aut*) alquiler *m* sin conductor
self-educated [,self'edjʊkeɪtɪd] ADJ autodidacta
self-effacement [,selfɪ'feɪsmənt] N modestia *f*, humildad *f*
self-effacing [,selfɪ'feɪsɪŋ] ADJ modesto, humilde
self-employed [,selfɪm'plɔɪd] ADJ autónomo, que trabaja por cuenta propia • **to be self-employed** ser autónomo, trabajar por cuenta propia • **the self-employed** los trabajadores autónomos, los que trabajan por cuenta propia
self-employment [,selfɪm'plɔɪmənt] N trabajo *m* autónomo, trabajo *m* por cuenta propia
self-esteem [,selfɪs'ti:m] N amor *m* propio
self-evident [,self'evɪdənt] ADJ manifiesto, patente
self-examination [,selfɪg,zæmɪ'neɪʃən] N autoexamen *m*; (*Rel*) examen *m* de conciencia
self-explanatory [,selfɪks'plænɪtərɪ] ADJ que se explica por sí mismo *or* solo
self-expression [,selfɪks'preʃən] N autoexpresión *f*
self-filling [,self'fɪlɪŋ] ADJ de relleno automático
self-financing [,selffaɪ'nænsɪŋ] N autofinanciación *f*, autofinanciamiento *m* ADJ autofinanciado
self-fulfilling [,selffʊl'fɪlɪŋ] ADJ • **self-fulfilling prophecy** profecía *f* que por su propia naturaleza contribuye a cumplirse
self-fulfilment, **self-fulfillment** (*US*) [,selffʊl'fɪlmənt] N realización *f* de los más íntimos deseos de uno, realización *f* completa de la potencialidad de uno
self-governing [,self'gʌvənɪŋ] ADJ autónomo

self-government [ˌselfˈɡʌvəmənt] N autonomía *f*, autogobierno *m*
self-harm [ˌselfˈhɑːm] VI automutilarse
N automutilación *f*
self-harming [ˌselfˈhɑːmɪŋ] N (= *self-mutilation*) automutilación *f*
self-hatred [ˌselfˈheɪtrɪd] N odio *m* a sí mismo
self-help [ˌselfˈhelp] N autosuficiencia *f*
CPD [*book, method*] de autoayada
▸ **self-help group** grupo *m* de apoyo mutuo
selfie* [ˈselfɪ] N selfie *m or f*, selfi *m or f*
CPD ▸ **selfie stick** palo *m* de selfi(e)
self-image [ˌselfˈɪmɪdʒ] N autoimagen *f*, imagen *f* de sí mismo
self-importance [ˌselfɪmˈpɔːtəns] N prepotencia *f*
self-important [ˌselfɪmˈpɔːtənt] ADJ prepotente
self-imposed [ˌselfɪmˈpəʊzd] ADJ [*punishment etc*] autoimpuesto, voluntario
self-improvement [ˌselfɪmˈpruːvmənt] N autosuperación *f*
self-induced [ˌselfɪnˈdjuːst] ADJ autoinducido
self-indulgence [ˌselfɪnˈdʌldʒəns] N excesos *mpl*, falta *f* de moderación
self-indulgent [ˌselfɪnˈdʌldʒənt] ADJ que se permite excesos
self-inflicted [ˌselfɪnˈflɪktɪd] ADJ [*wound*] autoinfligido, infligido a sí mismo
self-injure [ˌselfˈɪndʒəʳ] VI automutilarse
self-injury [ˌselfˈɪndʒərɪ] N automutilación *f*
self-interest [ˌselfˈɪntrɪst] N interés *m* propio
self-interested [ˌselfˈɪntrɪstɪd] ADJ que actúa en interés propio, egoísta
selfish [ˈselfɪʃ] ADJ egoísta
selfishly [ˈselfɪʃlɪ] ADV con egoísmo, de modo egoísta
selfishness [ˈselfɪʃnɪs] N egoísmo *m*
self-justification [ˌselfˌdʒʌstɪfɪˈkeɪʃən] N autojustificación *f*
self-knowledge [ˌselfˈnɒlɪdʒ] N conocimiento *m* de sí mismo
selfless [ˈselflɪs] ADJ desinteresado
selflessly [ˈselflɪslɪ] ADV desinteresadamente
selflessness [ˈselflɪsnɪs] N desinterés *m*
self-loading [ˌselfˈləʊdɪŋ] ADJ autocargador, de autocarga
self-loathing [ˌselfˈləʊðɪŋ] N desprecio *m* por sí mismo
self-locking [ˌselfˈlɒkɪŋ] ADJ de cierre automático
self-love [ˌselfˈlʌv] N egoísmo *m*, narcisismo *m*
self-made [ˌselfˈmeɪd] ADJ • **self-made man** hombre *m* que ha llegado a su posición actual por sus propios esfuerzos, hijo *m* de sus propias obras
self-management [ˌselfˈmænɪdʒmənt] N autogestión *f*
self-mockery [ˌselfˈmɒkərɪ] N burla *f* de sí mismo
self-neglect [ˌselfnɪˈɡlekt] N abandono *m* de sí mismo
self-opinionated [ˌselfəˈpɪnjəneɪtɪd] ADJ terco
self-parody [ˌselfˈpærədɪ] N parodia *f* de sí mismo
self-perpetuating [ˌselfpəˈpetjʊeɪtɪŋ] ADJ que se autoperpetúa
self-pity [ˌselfˈpɪtɪ] N autocompasión *f*
self-pitying [ˌselfˈpɪtɪɪŋ] ADJ autocompasivo
self-pollination [ˌselfpɒlɪˈneɪʃən] N autopolinización *f*
self-portrait [ˌselfˈpɔːtrɪt] N autorretrato *m*
self-possessed [ˌselfpəˈzest] ADJ sereno, dueño de sí mismo
self-possession [ˌselfpəˈzeʃən] N serenidad *f*, autodominio *m*
self-praise [ˌselfˈpreɪz] N autobombo *m*
self-preservation [ˌselfprezəˈveɪʃən] N autopreservación *f*, propia conservación *f*
self-proclaimed [ˌselfprəˈkleɪmd] ADJ autoproclamado
self-promotion [ˌselfprəˈməʊʃən] N autopromoción *f*
self-propelled [ˌselfprəˈpeld] ADJ autopropulsado, automotor (*fem: automotriz*)
self-protection [ˌselfprəˈtekʃən] N autoprotección *f* • **what I did was simple self-protection** lo que hice fue por autoprotección • **out of self-protection** en defensa propia
self-raising flour [ˈselfˌreɪzɪŋˈflaʊəʳ] N (*Brit*) harina *f* con levadura *or* (*And, S. Cone*) leudante
self-referential [ˌselfrefəˈrenʃəl] ADJ autorreferencial • **a self-referential film** una película llena de referencias personales
self-regard [ˌselfrɪˈɡɑːd] N amor *m* propio; (*pej*) egoísmo *m*
self-regulating [ˌselfˈreɡjʊleɪtɪŋ] ADJ de regulación automática
self-regulation [ˌselfreɡjʊˈleɪʃən] N autorregulación *f*
self-regulatory [ˌselfˈreɡjʊlətərɪ] ADJ autorregulado
self-reliance [ˌselfrɪˈlaɪəns] N independencia *f*, autosuficiencia *f*
self-reliant [ˌselfrɪˈlaɪənt] ADJ independiente, autosuficiente
self-reproach [ˌselfrɪˈprəʊtʃ] N remordimiento *m*
self-respect [ˌselfrɪsˈpekt] N amor *m* propio
self-respecting [ˌselfrɪsˈpektɪŋ] ADJ que tiene amor propio
self-restraint [ˌselfrɪsˈtreɪnt] N = **self-control**
self-righteous [ˌselfˈraɪtʃəs] ADJ santurrón, farisaico, creído (*LAm*)
self-righteousness [ˌselfˈraɪtʃəsnɪs] N santurronería *f*, farisaísmo *m*
self-rising flour [ˈselfˌraɪzɪŋˈflaʊəʳ] N (*US*) = **self-raising flour**
self-rule [ˌselfˈruːl] N autonomía *f*
self-sacrifice [ˌselfˈsækrɪfaɪs] N abnegación *f*
self-sacrificing [ˌselfˈsækrɪfaɪsɪŋ] ADJ abnegado
self-same [ˈselfseɪm] ADJ mismo, mismísimo
self-satisfaction [ˌselfsætɪsˈfækʃən] N satisfacción *f* de sí mismo
self-satisfied [ˌselfˈsætɪsfaɪd] ADJ satisfecho de sí mismo
self-sealing [ˌselfˈsiːlɪŋ] ADJ [*envelope*] autoadhesivo, autopegado
self-seeking [ˌselfˈsiːkɪŋ] ADJ egoísta
N egoísmo *m*
self-service [ˌselfˈsɜːvɪs], **self-serve** [ˌselfˈsɜːv] (*esp US*) ADJ de autoservicio
CPD ▸ **self-service laundry** lavandería *f* de autoservicio ▸ **self-service restaurant** autoservicio *m*, self-service *m*
self-serving [ˌselfˈsɜːvɪŋ] ADJ egoísta, interesado
self-starter [ˌselfˈstɑːtəʳ] N **1** (*Aut*) arranque *m* automático
2 (*Comm etc*) persona *f* dinámica
self-study [selfˈstʌdɪ] N autoaprendizaje *m*, autoestudio *m*
CPD ▸ **self-study course** curso *m* de autoaprendizaje *or* autoestudio
self-styled [ˌselfˈstaɪld] ADJ supuesto, sedicente
self-sufficiency [ˌselfsəˈfɪʃənsɪ] N [*of person*] independencia *f*, confianza *f* en sí mismo; (*economic*) autosuficiencia *f*
self-sufficient [ˌselfsəˈfɪʃənt] ADJ [*person*] independiente, seguro de sí mismo; (*economically*) autosuficiente
self-supporting [ˌselfsəˈpɔːtɪŋ] ADJ económicamente independiente
self-tanning [ˌselfˈtænɪŋ] ADJ [*cream, lotion*] autobronceador
self-taught [ˌselfˈtɔːt] ADJ autodidacta
self-test [ˌselfˈtest] N (*Comput*)
N autocomprobación *f*
VI autocomprobarse
self-timer [ˌselfˈtaɪməʳ] N (*on camera*) disparador *m* automático
self-will [ˌselfˈwɪl] N voluntad *f*, terquedad *f* • **she had a lot of self-will** ella tenía mucha voluntad
self-willed [ˌselfˈwɪld] ADJ terco, voluntarioso
self-winding watch [ˈselfˌwaɪndɪŋˈwɒtʃ] N reloj *m* de cuerda automática
self-worth [ˌselfˈwɜːθ] N autoestima *f*
sell [sel] (PT, PP: **sold**) VT vender • **do you ~ flowers?** ¿vende flores? • **to ~ sth to sb** vender algo a algn • **he sold it to me** me lo vendió • **I was sold this in London** me vendieron esto en Londres • **you've been sold*** (*fig*) te han dado gato por liebre • **to ~ sth for £1** vender algo por una libra • **he doesn't ~ himself very well** no es capaz de causar buena impresión, no convence mucho • **to ~ sb an idea** (*fig*) convencer a algn de una idea • **to be sold on sth/sb*** estar cautivado por algo/algn • **I'm not exactly sold on the idea** no me entusiasma la idea, para mí la idea deja mucho que desear • **to ~ sb into slavery** vender a algn como esclavo • IDIOM: • **to ~ sb down the river** traicionar a algn
VI **1** [*merchandise*] venderse • **these ~ at 15p** estos se venden a 15 peniques • **this line just isn't ~ing** esta línea no tiene demanda • **it ~s well** se vende bien • **the idea didn't ~** (*fig*) la idea no convenció
2 (= *person*) • **the owner seemed a bit reluctant to ~** parecía que el dueño estaba un poco reacio a vender
N (*Comm*) ▹ **hard, soft**
▸ **sell back** VT + ADV • **to ~ sth back to sb** revender algo a algn
▸ **sell off** VT + ADV [+ *stocks and shares*] vender; [+ *goods*] liquidar
▸ **sell on** VT + ADV revender
▸ **sell out** VI + ADV **1** [*tickets, goods*] agotarse • **the tickets sold out in three hours** las entradas se agotaron en tres horas • **football matches often ~ out in advance** en los partidos de fútbol a menudo se venden todas las entradas antes del partido • **"could I buy some sun cream?" — "sorry, we've sold out"** —¿me puede dar bronceador? —lo siento, no nos queda • **to ~ out of sth** vender todas las existencias de algo • **we've sold out of bananas** no nos quedan plátanos, hemos agotado las existencias de plátanos
2 (*fig*) claudicar, venderse, transar (*LAm*)
3 (*US*) = **sell up**
VT + ADV **1** [+ *goods*] agotar las existencias de, venderlo todo • **the tickets are all sold out** los billetes están agotados • **stocks of umbrellas are sold out** las existencias de paraguas están agotadas • **we are sold out of bread** se terminó el pan, no nos queda pan
2 [+ *person*] traicionar; [+ *compromise*] transigir, transar (*LAm*)
▸ **sell up** VI + ADV (*esp Brit*) liquidarse,

venderlo todo
VT + ADV vender

sell-by date ['selbaɪ,deɪt] N fecha *f* de caducidad

seller ['seləʳ] N **1** (= *person who sells*) vendedor(a) *m/f*; (= *dealer*) comerciante *mf* (of en) • **~'s market** mercado *m* favorable al vendedor
2 (= *item*) • **a good ~** un artículo que se vende bien

selling ['selɪŋ] N venta *f*, el vender • **a career in ~** una carrera en ventas
CPD ▸ **selling point** punto *m* fuerte ▸ **selling price** precio *m* de venta *or* (*LAm*) de menudeo ▸ **selling rate** (*Econ*) precio *m* de venta medio

selloff ['selɒf] N (*Econ*) liquidación *f*, venta *f*; [*of public company*] privatización *f*

Sellotape® ['seləʊteɪp] N cinta *f* adhesiva, celo *m*, Scotch® *m* (*esp LAm*), Durex® *m* (*LAm*)
VT pegar con cinta adhesiva *etc*

sellout ['selaʊt] N **1** (*Theat*) lleno *m*, éxito *m* de taquilla
2 (= *betrayal*) claudicación *f*, traición *f*

seltzer water ['seltsə,wɔːtəʳ] N agua *f* de seltz

selvage, selvedge ['selvɪdʒ] N (*Sew*) orillo *m*, bordo *m*

selves [selvz] NPL *of* **self**

semantic [sɪ'mæntɪk] ADJ semántico

semantically [sɪ'mæntɪkəlɪ] ADV semánticamente

semanticist [sɪ'mæntɪsɪst] N semasiólogo/a *m/f*, semantista *mf*

semantics [sɪ'mæntɪks] NSING semántica *f*

semaphore ['seməfɔːʳ] N semáforo *m*
VT comunicar por semáforo

semblance ['sembləns] N apariencia *f* • **when they have restored the country to some ~ of order** cuando hayan devuelto al país cierta apariencia de normalidad • **without a ~ of regret** sin mostrar ningún remordimiento • **without a ~ of fear** sin dar señal alguna de miedo • **to put on a ~ of sorrow** procurar mostrarse *or* parecer triste

seme [siːm] N sema *m*

semen ['siːmən] N semen *m*

semester [sɪ'mestəʳ] N (*esp US*) semestre *m*

semi* ['semɪ] N **1** (*Brit*) (*also* **semi-detached house**) casa *f* con una pared medianera
2 = semi-final
3 (*US*) (*also* **semi-trailer**) trailer *m*

semi... ['semɪ] PREFIX semi..., medio...

semi-annual [,semɪ'ænjʊəl] ADJ (*US*) (= *biannual*) semestral

semi-automatic [,semɪ,ɔːtə'mætɪk] ADJ semiautomático
N arma *f* semiautomática

semi-basement ['semɪ'beɪsmənt] N semisótano *m*

semibreve ['semɪbriːv] N (*Brit*) semibreve *f*

semicircle ['semɪ,sɜːkl] N semicírculo *m*

semicircular ['semɪ'sɜːkjʊləʳ] ADJ semicircular

semi-colon ['semɪ'kəʊlən] N punto y coma *m*

semiconductor [,semɪkən'dʌktəʳ] N semiconductor *m*

semi-conscious ['semɪ'kɒnʃəs] ADJ semiconsciente

semi-consonant ['semɪ'kɒnsənənt] N semiconsonante *f*

semi-darkness ['semɪ'dɑːknɪs] N • **in the semidarkness** en la casi oscuridad

semi-detached ['semɪdɪ'tætʃt] ADJ • **semi-detached house** (*Brit*) casa *f* con una pared medianera
N = **semi-detached house**

semi-final ['semɪ'faɪnl] N semifinal *f* • **they went out in the semi-finals** los eliminaron en las semifinales

semi-finalist ['semɪ'faɪnəlɪst] N semifinalista *mf*

semi-finished [,semɪ'fɪnɪʃt] ADJ [*product*] semiacabado, semielaborado

semi-literate [,semɪ'lɪtərɪt] ADJ semialfabetizado

seminal ['semɪnl] ADJ **1** (*Physiol*) [*fluid, liquid*] seminal
2 (*fig*) [*idea, work, event, study*] seminal

seminar ['semɪnɑːʳ] N (*Univ*) (= *class*) clase *f*, seminario *m*; (= *conference*) congreso *m*

seminarian [,semɪ'nɛərɪən] N, **seminarist** ['semɪnərɪst] N seminarista *m*

seminary ['semɪnərɪ] N seminario *m*

semi-official ['semɪə'fɪʃəl] ADJ semioficial

semiology [,semɪ'ɒlədʒɪ] N semiología *f*

semiotic [,semɪ'ɒtɪk] ADJ semiótico

semiotics [,semɪ'ɒtɪks] NSING semiótica *f*

semi-precious ['semɪ,preʃəs] ADJ semiprecioso • **semi-precious stone** piedra *f* semipreciosa

semipro* ['semɪ,prəʊ] N = **semi-professional**

semi-professional [,semɪprə'feʃənl] N semiprofesional *mf*
ADJ semiprofesional

semi-quaver ['semɪ,kweɪvəʳ] N (*Brit*) semicorchea *f*

semi-skilled ['semɪ'skɪld] ADJ semicalificado, semicualificado (*Sp*); [*work*] para persona semicalificada *or* (*Sp*) semicualificada

semi-skimmed milk [,semɪskɪmd'mɪlk] N leche *f* semidesnatada, leche *f* semidescremada (*LAm*)

semisolid [,semɪ'sɒlɪd] ADJ semisólido
N semisólido *m*

Semite ['siːmaɪt] N semita *mf*

Semitic [sɪ'mɪtɪk] ADJ semítico

semitone ['semɪtəʊn] N semitono *m*

semi-trailer ['semɪ'treɪləʳ] N (*US*) trailer *m*

semi-vowel ['semɪ'vaʊəl] N semivocal *f*

semolina [,semə'liːnə] N sémola *f*

sempiternal [,sempɪ'tɜːnl] ADJ sempiterno

sempstress ['sempstrɪs] N costurera *f*

SEN N ABBR (*Brit*) (*formerly*) = **State-Enrolled Nurse**

Sen. ABBR **1** = **Senior**
2 (*US*) (*Pol*) = **Senator**
3 (*US*) (*Pol*) = **Senate**

sen. ABBR = **senior**

senate ['senɪt] N **1** (*Pol*) senado *m* • **the Senate** (*US*) el Senado; ▹ CABINET, CONGRESS
2 (*Univ*) consejo *m* universitario
CPD ▸ **senate bill** proyecto *m* de ley del Senado ▸ **senate committee** comisión *f* del Senado

senator ['senɪtəʳ] N (*Pol*) senador(a) *m/f*; ▹ CONGRESS

senatorial [,senə'tɔːrɪəl] ADJ senatorial

send [send] (PT, PP: **sent**) VT **1** (= *dispatch*) [+ *letter, parcel, money, telegram*] mandar, enviar • **please ~ me further details** ruego me mande *or* me envíe más detalles • **I wrote the letter but didn't ~ it** escribí la carta pero no la eché al correo • **Jan ~s her apologies** Jan pide que la disculpen *or* excusen • **I had some flowers sent to her** le mandé *or* envié unas flores • **to ~ sb one's love** mandar recuerdos a algn • **he sent word that he wished to discuss peace** avisó *or* (*LAm*) mandó (a) decir que quería hablar de hacer las paces • PROVERB: • **these things are sent to try us** esto es que Dios *or* el Señor nos pone a prueba
2 (= *cause to go*) [+ *person*] mandar; [+ *troops*] mandar, enviar • **they sent him here to help** lo mandaron para que nos ayudara, lo mandaron a ayudarnos • **to ~ a child to bed/to school** mandar a un niño a la cama/a la escuela • **to ~ sb for sth: I sent her for some bread** la mandé a comprar pan *or* (*Sp*) a por pan • **they sent me for an X-ray** me mandaron a hacerme una radiografía • **to ~ sb home** mandar a algn a casa; (*from abroad*) repatriar a algn • **to ~ sb to prison** mandar a algn a la cárcel • **he was sent to prison for seven years** fue condenado a siete años de cárcel • IDIOMS: • **to ~ sb to Coventry** hacer el vacío a algn • **to ~ sb packing** mandar a algn a freír espárragos*
3 (= *convey*) [+ *signal*] enviar, mandar
4 (= *propel*) • **he sent the ball into the back of the net** lanzó *or* mandó el balón al fondo de la red • **the blow sent him sprawling** el golpe lo tumbó • **it has sent prices through the roof** ha hecho que los precios se pongan por las nubes *or* se disparen • **to ~ sth/sb flying** mandar algo/a algn volando por los aires; ▹ **shiver¹**
5 (= *drive*) • **their music sent the fans wild** su música volvía locos a los fans • **my attempt sent him into fits of laughter** le entró un ataque de risa al ver cómo lo intentaba • **the rain sent us indoors** la lluvia nos obligó a meternos en casa • **the sight sent her running to her mother** lo que vio la hizo ir corriendo a su madre • **his lessons used to ~ me to sleep** me solía quedar dormido en sus clases
6* (= *enthral*) • **that tune ~s me** esa melodía me chifla* • **he ~s me** me vuelve loca
VI • **she sent to say that ...** mandó *or* envió un recado diciendo que ..., mandó (a) decir que ... (*LAm*) • **we shall have to ~ to France for reinforcements** tendremos que pedir *or* (*LAm*) mandar a pedir refuerzos a Francia

▸ **send away** VI + ADV • **to ~ away for sth** escribir pidiendo algo, pedir algo por correo
VT + ADV **1** [+ *person*] (= *dismiss*) despachar; (= *send to another place*) mandar • **I ordered the servants to ~ him away** ordené a los criados que lo despacharan • **I was sent away to boarding school at 13** me mandaron a un internado a los 13 años • **please don't ~ me away again** por favor no me vuelvas a pedir que me vaya; ▹ **flea**
2 [+ *goods*] mandar, enviar • **it will have to be sent away to be repaired** habrá que mandarlo *or* enviarlo a que lo arreglen

▸ **send back** VT + ADV [+ *person*] hacer volver, hacer regresar; [+ *goods*] mandar de vuelta, devolver; [+ *ball*] devolver

▸ **send down** VT + ADV **1** (= *cause to go down*) [+ *prices*] provocar la bajada de, hacer bajar; [+ *diver*] mandar, enviar
2 (*Brit*) (*Univ*) (= *expel*) expulsar
3* (= *imprison*) meter en la cárcel • **he was sent down for two years** lo condenaron a dos años de cárcel

▸ **send for** VI + PREP **1** [+ *person*] mandar a buscar, mandar llamar • **the manager sent for me** el jefe mandó a buscarme *or* me mandó llamar
2 [+ *catalogue, information*] escribir pidiendo, pedir por correo

▸ **send forth** VT + ADV (*liter*) [+ *smoke etc*] emitir, arrojar; [+ *sparks*] lanzar • **to ~ sb forth into the world** enviar a algn a vivir en el mundo

▸ **send in** VT + ADV [+ *report, application, competition entry*] mandar, enviar; [+ *resignation*] presentar; [+ *troops, reinforcements*] enviar, mandar; [+ *visitor*] hacer pasar • **~ him in!** ¡que pase!

▸ **send off** VI + ADV = **send away**
VT + ADV **1** [+ *letter, parcel*] mandar, enviar; [+ *goods*] despachar, expedir
2 [+ *person*] mandar; (= *say goodbye to*)

despedir • **they sent the children off to play** mandaron a los niños a jugar
3 (*Sport*) [+ *player*] expulsar • **he got sent off for swearing** lo expulsaron por decir palabrotas
▸ **send on** (VT + ADV) **1** [+ *letter*] remitir, reexpedir; [+ *luggage, document, report*] remitir; [+ *person*] mandar • **an advance guard was sent on ahead with the news** mandaron a una avanzadilla por delante con la noticia
2 (*Sport*) [+ *substitute*] mandar a jugar
▸ **send out** (VI + ADV) • **to ~ out for sth: we sent out for sandwiches** mandamos a alguien a traer *or* (*Sp*) a por unos sándwiches
(VT + ADV) **1** (= *dispatch*) [+ *invitations, circulars, scout, envoy*] mandar, enviar; [+ *person*] (*on errand*) mandar • **I sent him out to get a paper** lo mandé a comprar un periódico
2 (= *dismiss*) echar • **she was sent out for talking** la echaron (de clase) por hablar
3 (= *emit*) [+ *smoke*] despedir; [+ *signal*] emitir; (*Bot*) [+ *shoot*] echar
▸ **send round** (VT + ADV) (= *dispatch*) [+ *item*] mandar, enviar; [+ *person*] mandar • **can you ~ someone round to fix it?** ¿puede mandar a alguien a arreglarlo *or* para que lo arregle? • **we'll ~ a car round to pick you up** mandaremos un coche a recogerlo • **I'll have it sent round to you** haré que te lo manden *or* envíen
▸ **send up** (VT + ADV) **1** (= *cause to rise*) [+ *rocket, balloon,*] lanzar; [+ *smoke, dust, spray*] despedir; [+ *prices*] provocar la subida de, hacer subir
2 (= *dispatch*) • **~ him up!** ¡que suba! • **I'll have some coffee sent up** mandaré *or* pediré que me suban café
3 (*Brit**) (= *parody*) burlarse de, parodiar
4 (= *blow up*) volar
sender [ˈsendəʳ] (N) **1** (*Post*) remitente *mf*
2 (*Elec*) transmisor *m*
sending-off [ˌsendɪŋˈɒf] (N) (*Sport*) expulsión *f*
send-off [ˈsendɒf] (N) despedida *f* • **they gave him a rousing send-off** le hicieron una gran despedida
send-up* [ˈsendʌp] (N) (*Brit*) parodia *f*
Seneca [ˈsenɪkə] (N) Séneca
Senegal [ˌsenɪˈgɔːl] (N) el Senegal
Senegalese [ˈsenɪgəˈliːz] (ADJ) senegalés
(N) senegalés/esa *m/f*
senescence [sɪˈnesns] (N) (*frm*) senescencia *f*
senescent [sɪˈnesnt] (ADJ) (*frm*) senescente
senile [ˈsiːnaɪl] (ADJ) senil • **to go ~** empezar a chochear • **to have gone ~** padecer debilidad senil
(CPD) ▸ **senile dementia** demencia *f* senil
senility [sɪˈnɪlɪtɪ] (N) senilidad *f*
senior [ˈsiːnɪəʳ] (ADJ) **1** (*in age*) mayor • **he is ~ to me by five years** (*frm*) es cinco años mayor que yo, tiene cinco años más que yo • **Douglas Fairbanks Senior** Douglas Fairbanks padre • **~ pupils** los alumnos de los cursos más avanzados
2 (*in rank*) [*position, rank*] superior; [*partner, executive, officer*] mayoritario; (*in length of service*) de más antigüedad • **he is ~ to me in the firm** es mi superior en la compañía • **~ management** los altos directivos
(N) **1** (*in age*) mayor *mf* • **he is my ~** es mayor que yo • **he's my ~ by two years** es dos años mayor que yo, tiene dos años más que yo
2 (*in rank*) superior *mf*, socio/a *m/f* más antiguo/a • **he's my ~** es mi superior
3 (*Scol*) alumno/a *m/f* de los cursos más avanzados; (*US*) estudiante *mf* del último año; ▷ **GRADE**
4 (*US*) = **senior citizen**
(CPD) ▸ **senior citizen** jubilado/a *m/f*, persona *f* de la tercera edad ▸ **senior common room** (*Brit*) (*in university*) (= *room*) sala *f* de profesores (titulares); (= *lecturing staff collectively*) claustro *m* de profesores (titulares) ▸ **senior executive** alto/a ejecutivo/a *m/f* ▸ **senior high school** (*US*) ≈ instituto *m* de enseñanza superior (*Sp*), ≈ preparatoria *f* (*Mex*) ▸ **senior partner** socio/a *m/f* mayoritario/a ▸ **senior school** instituto *m* de enseñanza secundaria ▸ **the Senior Service** (*Brit*) la marina ▸ **senior prom** (*US*) baile *m* del último año *or* curso ▸ **senior year** (*US*) (*at school*) último año *m*, último curso *m*
seniority [ˌsiːnɪˈɒrɪtɪ] (N) antigüedad *f*
senna [ˈsenə] (N) sena *f*
sensation [senˈseɪʃən] (N) **1** (= *feeling*) sensación *f* • **to have a dizzy ~** tener (una) sensación de mareo • **to lose all ~ in one's arm** perder la sensibilidad en el brazo
2 (= *impression*) sensación *f* • **to have the ~ of doing sth** tener la sensación de estar haciendo algo • **I had the ~ that I was being watched** tenía la sensación de que me estaban observando
3 (= *excitement, success*) sensación *f* • **to be a ~** ser un éxito • **it was a ~ in New York** en Nueva York causó sensación • **to cause** *or* **create a ~** causar sensación
sensational [senˈseɪʃənl] (ADJ) **1** [*event*] sensacional; [*fashion*] que causa sensación • **~ murder** espectacular asesinato *m*
2 [*film, novel, newspaper*] sensacionalista • **he gave a ~ account of the accident** hizo un relato sensacionalista del accidente
3* (= *marvellous*) sensacional, fantástico
sensationalism [senˈseɪʃnəlɪzəm] (N) sensacionalismo *m*
sensationalist [senˈseɪʃnəlɪst] (ADJ) sensacionalista
(N) sensacionalista *mf*
sensationalize [senˈseɪʃnəlaɪz] (VT) sensacionalizar, presentar en términos sensacionales
sensationally [senˈseɪʃnəlɪ] (ADV) [*report, describe*] sensacionalmente • **it was ~ successful** tuvo un éxito sensacional • **it was ~ popular** era increíblemente popular
sense [sens] (N) **1** (*bodily*) sentido *m* • **~ of hearing/smell/taste/touch** sentido *m* del oído/olfato/gusto/tacto • **~ of sight** sentido *m* de la vista • **to have a keen ~ of smell** tener un (sentido del) olfato muy agudo • **sixth ~** sexto sentido
2 (= *feeling*) sensación *f* • **I was overcome by a ~ of failure** me invadió una sensación de fracaso • **I felt a terrible ~ of guilt** me invadió un tremendo sentimiento de culpa *or* culpabilidad • **I felt a terrible ~ of loss** sentí un tremendo vacío • **have you no ~ of shame?** ¿es que no tienes vergüenza? • **there is a ~ of space in his paintings** sus cuadros transmiten una sensación de espacio • **I lost all ~ of time** perdí la noción del tiempo
3 (= *good judgement*) sentido *m* común • **she has more ~ than to go out on her own** tiene el suficiente sentido común como para no salir sola • **I thought you would have had more ~** pensé que eras más sensato *or* tenías más sentido común • **he has more money than ~** le sobra dinero pero le falta sentido común • **he had the ~ to call the doctor** tuvo bastante sentido común como para llamar al médico • **to make sb see ~** hacer que algn entre en razón • **to talk ~** hablar con sentido común, hablar con juicio
4 • **to make ~** (= *be advisable*) ser conveniente; (= *be comprehensible, logical*) tener sentido • **it makes ~ to eat a balanced diet** es conveniente llevar una dieta equilibrada • **it makes ~ to me** a mí me parece lógico • **it doesn't make ~** *or* **it makes no ~** no tiene sentido • **to make ~ of sth:** • **I could make no ~ of what he was saying** no entendía nada de lo que decía, no podía sacar nada en claro de lo que decía
5 (= *point, use*) sentido *m* • **what's the ~ of having another meeting?** ¿qué sentido tiene celebrar otra reunión? • **there's no ~ in making people unhappy** no tiene sentido disgustar a la gente
6 senses (= *sanity*) • **I hope this warning will bring him to his ~s** espero que esta advertencia le haga entrar en razón • **to come to one's ~s** entrar en razón • **no-one in his right ~s would do that** nadie (que esté) en su sano juicio haría eso • **have you taken leave of your ~s?** ¿has perdido el juicio?
7 (= *meaning*) (*gen*) sentido *m*; (*in dictionary*) acepción *f*, significado *m* • **it has several ~s** tiene varias acepciones *or* varios significados • **in what ~ are you using the word?** ¿qué significado le das a la palabra? • **in a ~** en cierto modo • **in every ~ (of the word)** en todos los sentidos (de la palabra) • **in the full ~ of that word** en toda la extensión de la palabra • **in no ~ can it be said that …** de ninguna manera se puede decir que … • **in one ~** en cierto modo • **in the strict/true ~ of the word** en el sentido estricto/en el verdadero sentido de la palabra
8 (= *awareness*) sentido *m* • **she has very good business ~** tiene muy buen ojo para los negocios • **~ of direction** sentido *m* de la orientación • **she has a strong ~ of duty** tiene un arraigado sentido del deber • **~ of humour** sentido *m* del humor • **they have an exaggerated ~ of their own importance** se creen bastante más importantes de lo que son • **where's your ~ of occasion?** tienes que estar a la altura de las circunstancias *or* la ocasión • **we must keep a ~ of proportion about this** no debemos darle a esto más importancia de la que tiene • **one must have some ~ of right and wrong** uno tiene que tener cierta noción de lo que está bien y lo que está mal • **~ of self** (señas *fpl* de) identidad *f* • **he has no ~ of timing** es de lo más inoportuno • **she needs to regain a ~ of her own worth** necesita recuperar la confianza en sí misma
9 (= *opinion*) opinión *f* • **what is your ~ of the mood of the electorate?** ¿qué opinión le merece el clima que se respira entre el electorado?
(VT) **1** (= *suspect, intuit*) presentir • **he looked about him, sensing danger** miró a su alrededor, presintiendo peligro • **to ~ that** notar que • **he ~d that he wasn't wanted** notó que estaba de más
2 (= *be conscious of*) percibir • **the horse can ~ your fear** el caballo percibe si tienes miedo
3 (= *realize*) darse cuenta de
(CPD) ▸ **sense organ** órgano *m* sensorial
senseless [ˈsenslɪs] (ADJ) **1** [*waste, violence etc*] sin sentido • **it is ~ to protest** no tiene sentido protestar
2 (= *unconscious*) sin sentido, inconsciente • **he was lying ~ on the floor** yacía sin sentido *or* inconsciente en el suelo • **to knock sb ~** derribar a algn y dejarle sin sentido • **he fell ~ to the floor** cayó al suelo sin sentido
senselessly [ˈsenslɪslɪ] (ADV) sin sentido
senselessness [ˈsenslɪsnɪs] (N) falta *f* de sentido
sensibility [ˌsensɪˈbɪlɪtɪ] (N) **1** sensibilidad *f* (to a)

2 **sensibilities** susceptibilidad *fsing*

sensible ['sensəbl] ADJ **1** (= *having good sense*) sensato • **she's a very ~ girl** es una chica muy sensata • **be ~!** ¡sé sensato! • **it would be ~ to check first** lo más sensato sería comprobarlo antes
2 (= *reasonable*) [*act*] prudente; [*decision, choice*] lógico; [*clothing, shoes*] práctico • **that is very ~ of you** en eso haces muy bien, me parece muy lógico • **try to be ~ about it** procura ser razonable
3† (= *appreciable*) apreciable, perceptible
4† (= *aware*) • **to be ~ of** ser consciente de, darse cuenta de • **I am ~ of the honour you do me** soy consciente del honor que se me hace

sensibleness ['sensəblnɪs] N **1** (= *good sense*) sensatez *f*
2 (= *reasonableness*) [*of actions*] prudencia *f*; [*of decision, choice*] lógica *f*; [*of clothing*] lo práctico

sensibly ['sensəblɪ] ADV (= *carefully*) con sensatez; (= *wisely*) prudentemente • **she acted very ~** obró muy prudentemente • **he ~ answered that ...** contestó con tino que ... • **try to behave ~** intenta comportarte como es debido

sensitive ['sensɪtɪv] ADJ **1** (= *emotionally aware, responsive*) [*person*] sensible; [*story, novel, film*] lleno de sensibilidad • **to be ~ to sth** ser sensible a algo, ser consciente de algo
2 (= *touchy*) [*person*] susceptible • **to be ~ about sth: young people are very ~ about their appearance** a los jóvenes les preocupa mucho su aspecto • **he is deeply ~ to criticism** es muy susceptible a las críticas
3 (= *delicate*) [*issue, subject*] delicado; [*region, area*] conflictivo • **this is politically very ~** esto es muy conflictivo *or* muy delicado desde el punto de vista político
4 (= *confidential*) [*document, report, information*] confidencial
5 (= *easily affected*) [*skin*] delicado, sensible; [*teeth*] sensible
6 (= *highly responsive*) [*instrument*] sensible; (*Phot*) [*paper, film*] sensible; (*Econ*) [*market*] volátil • **to be ~ to light/heat** ser sensible a la luz/al calor

sensitively ['sensɪtɪvlɪ] ADV (= *sympathetically*) con sensibilidad

sensitiveness ['sensɪtɪvnɪs] N ▸ **sensitivity**

sensitivity [,sensɪ'tɪvɪtɪ] N **1** (= *emotional awareness*) sensibilidad *f* (**to a**)
2 (= *touchiness*) susceptibilidad *f* (**to a**)
3 (= *delicate nature*) [*of issue, subject*] lo delicado
4 (= *confidentiality*) [*of document, information*] carácter *m* confidencial, confidencialidad *f*
5 [*of skin, teeth*] sensibilidad *f* (**to a**)
6 (= *responsiveness*) [*of instrument, film*] sensibilidad *f*

sensitize ['sensɪtaɪz] VT sensibilizar

sensitized ['sensɪtaɪzd] ADJ sensibilizado

sensor ['sensəʳ] N sensor *m*

sensorimotor [,sensərɪ'məʊtəʳ] ADJ sensorimotor

sensory ['sensərɪ] ADJ sensorial, sensorio
CPD ▸ **sensory deprivation** aislamiento *m* sensorial

sensual ['sensjʊəl] ADJ sensual

sensualism ['sensjʊəlɪzəm] N sensualismo *m*

sensualist ['sensjʊəlɪst] N sensualista *mf*

sensuality [,sensjʊ'ælɪtɪ] N sensualidad *f*

sensually ['sensjʊəlɪ] ADV sensualmente

sensuous ['sensjʊəs] ADJ sensual, sensorio

sensuously ['sensjʊəslɪ] ADV sensualmente, con sensualidad

sensuousness ['sensjʊəsnɪs] N sensualidad *f*

sent [sent] PT, PP *of* **send**

sentence ['sentəns] N **1** (*Ling*) frase *f*, oración *f* • **he writes very long ~s** escribe frases *or* oraciones larguísimas • **what does this ~ mean?** ¿qué significa esta frase *or* oración?
2 (*Jur*) sentencia *f*, fallo *m* • **a ~ of ten years** una condena de diez años • **the judge gave him a six-month ~** el juez le condenó a seis meses de prisión • **the death ~** la pena de muerte • **under ~ of death** condenado a la pena de muerte • **he got a life ~** fue condenado a cadena perpetua • **a long ~** una larga condena • **to pass ~ on sb** (*lit, fig*) condenar a algn (a una pena) • **he got a five-year prison ~** se le condenó a cinco años de prisión • **to serve one's ~** cumplir su condena
VT condenar (**to a**) • **to ~ sb to life imprisonment** condenar a algn a cadena perpetua • **to ~ sb to death** condenar a muerte a algn
CPD ▸ **sentence adverb** (*Gram*) adverbio *m* oracional ▸ **sentence structure** estructura *f* de la frase

sententious [sen'tenʃəs] ADJ sentencioso

sententiously [sen'tenʃəslɪ] ADV sentenciosamente

sententiousness [sen'tenʃəsnɪs] N sentenciosidad *f*, estilo *m* sentencioso

sentience ['senʃəns] N sensitividad *f*, sensibilidad *f*

sentient ['senʃənt] ADJ sensitivo, sensible

sentiment ['sentɪmənt] N **1** (= *feeling*) sentimiento *m*
2 (= *opinion, thought*) opinión *f*, juicio *m* • **those are my ~s too** ese es mi criterio también, así lo pienso yo también
3 (= *sentimentality*) sentimentalismo *m*, sensiblería *f* • **to wallow in ~** nadar en el sentimentalismo *or* la sensiblería

sentimental [,sentɪ'mentl] ADJ sentimental; (*pej*) sentimental, sensiblero • **to have ~ value** tener un valor sentimental

sentimentalism [,sentɪ'mentəlɪzəm] N sentimentalismo *m*

sentimentalist [,sentɪ'mentəlɪst] N persona *f* sentimental

sentimentality [,sentɪmen'tælɪtɪ] N sentimentalismo *m*, sensiblería *f*

sentimentalize [,sentɪ'mentəlaɪz] VT sentimentalizar, imbuir de sentimiento
VI dejarse llevar por el sentimentalismo

sentimentally [,sentɪ'mentəlɪ] ADV de modo sentimental; [*say*] en tono sentimental

sentinel ['sentɪnl] N centinela *mf*

sentry ['sentrɪ] N centinela *mf*, guardia *mf*
CPD ▸ **sentry box** garita *f* de centinela ▸ **sentry duty** • **to be on ~ duty** estar de guardia ▸ **sentry go** turno *m* de centinela • **to be on ~ go** estar de guardia

SEO N ABBR (*Internet*) = **search engine optimization**

Seoul [səʊl] N Seúl *m*

sep ABBR = **separate**

sepal ['sepəl] N sépalo *m*

separability [,sepərə'bɪlɪtɪ] N separabilidad *f*

separable ['sepərəbl] ADJ separable

separate ['seprɪt] ADJ (= *apart*) separado; (= *different*) distinto, diferente; (= *distant*) apartado, retirado • **"with separate toilet"** "con inodoro separado" • **could we have ~ bills?** queremos cuentas individuales, ¿podemos pagar por separado? • **under ~ cover** por separado • **~ from** (= *apart from*) separado de; (= *different from*) distinto de • **that's a ~ issue** esa es una cuestión aparte • **they live very ~ lives** viven independientes uno de otro • **it was discussed at a ~ meeting** se trató en otra reunión *or* reunión aparte • **on ~ occasions** en diversas ocasiones • **the children have ~ rooms** los niños tienen cada uno su habitación • **they sleep in ~ rooms** duermen en habitaciones distintas • **I wrote it on a ~ sheet** lo escribí en una hoja aparte • **we sat at ~ tables** nos sentamos en mesas distintas • **they went their ~ ways** fueron cada uno por su lado
N **separates** (= *clothes*) coordinados *mpl*
VT ['sepəreɪt] (= *keep apart*) separar; (= *set aside*) apartar; (= *divide*) dividir, partir; (= *distinguish*) distinguir • **police moved in to ~ the two groups** la policía intervino para separar a los dos grupos • **to ~ truth from error** separar lo falso de lo verdadero, distinguir entre lo falso y lo verdadero
VI ['sepəreɪt] separarse • **her parents ~d last year** sus padres se separaron el año pasado
▸ **separate off** VT + ADV separar
▸ **separate out** VT + ADV (= *set apart*) apartar

separated ['sepəreɪtɪd] ADJ **1** (= *not living with wife, husband*) separado • **he is ~ from his wife** está separado de su mujer
2 (= *away from sb*) separado, distanciado

separately ['seprɪtlɪ] ADV por separado

separateness ['seprɪtnɪs] N estado *m* de separación

separation [,sepə'reɪʃən] N separación *f*
CPD ▸ **separation anxiety** ansiedad *f* por separación

separatism ['sepərətɪzəm] N separatismo *m*

separatist ['sepərətɪst] ADJ separatista
N separatista *mf*

separator ['sepəreɪtəʳ] N separador *m*

Sephardi [se'fɑːdɪ] N (PL: **Sephardim** [se'fɑːdɪm]) sefardí *mf*, sefardita *mf*

Sephardic [se'fɑːdɪk] ADJ sefardí, sefardita

sepia ['siːpɪə] N (= *colour, ink*) sepia *f*
CPD color sepia

sepoy ['siːpɔɪ] N cipayo *m*

sepsis ['sepsɪs] N sepsis *f*

Sept ABBR (= **September**) sep., set.

September [sep'tembəʳ] N setiembre *m*, septiembre *m*; ▸ **July**

septet [sep'tet] N septeto *m*

septic ['septɪk] ADJ séptico • **to become** *or* **go** *or* **turn ~** infectarse
CPD ▸ **septic poisoning** septicemia *f* ▸ **septic tank** fosa *f* séptica, pozo *m* séptico

septicaemia, **septicemia** (US) [,septɪ'siːmɪə] N septicemia *f*

septuagenarian [,septjʊədʒɪ'neərɪən] ADJ septuagenario
N septuagenario/a *m/f*

Septuagesima [,septjʊə'dʒesɪmə] N Septuagésima *f*

Septuagint ['septjʊədʒɪnt] N versión *f* de los setenta

septuplet [sep'tjʊplɪt] N septillizo/a *m/f*

sepulchral [sɪ'pʌlkrəl] ADJ sepulcral (*also fig*)

sepulchre, **sepulcher** (US) ['sepəlkəʳ] N (*poet*) sepulcro *m* • **whited ~** sepulcro *m* blanqueado

sequel ['siːkwəl] N **1** (= *film, book*) continuación *f*
2 (= *consequence*) consecuencia *f*, resultado *m* • **it had a tragic ~** tuvo un resultado trágico

sequence ['siːkwəns] N **1** (= *order*) orden *m* • **in ~** en orden • **in historical ~** en orden cronológico • **logical ~** secuencia *f* lógica • **to arrange things in ~** ordenar cosas secuencialmente
2 (= *series*) serie *f* • **a ~ of events** una serie de

acontecimientos
3 (*Cine*) secuencia *f* • **the best ~ in the film** la mejor secuencia de la película
4 (*Cards*) escalera *f*
sequencer [ˈsiːkwənsəʳ] (N) (= *electronic instrument*) secuenciador *m*
sequencing [ˈsiːkwənsɪŋ] (N) secuenciado *m*; ▹ **gene sequencing**
sequential [sɪˈkwenʃəl] (ADJ) secuencial
(CPD) ▸ **sequential access** (*Comput*) acceso *m* en serie
sequester [sɪˈkwestəʳ] (VT) **1** (= *isolate, shut up*) aislar
2 (*Jur*) [+ *property*] secuestrar, confiscar
sequestered [sɪˈkwestəd] (ADJ) **1** (= *isolated*) aislado, remoto
2 [*property*] secuestrado, confiscado
sequestrate [sɪˈkwestreɪt] (VT) secuestrar
sequestration [ˌsiːkwesˈtreɪʃən] (N) secuestración *f*
sequin [ˈsiːkwɪn] (N) lentejuela *f*
sequinned, **sequined** [ˈsiːkwɪnd] (ADJ) con lentejuelas, cubierto de lentejuelas
sequoia [sɪˈkwɔɪə] (N) secoya *f*
sera [ˈsɪərə] (NPL) *of* **serum**
seraglio [seˈrɑːlɪəʊ] (N) serallo *m*
seraph [ˈserəf] (N) (PL: **seraphs** *or* **seraphim** [ˈserəfɪm]) serafín *m*
seraphic [səˈræfɪk] (ADJ) seráfico
Serb [sɜːb] (N) serbio/a *m/f*
Serbia [ˈsɜːbɪə] (N) Serbia *f*
Serbian [ˈsɜːbɪən] (ADJ) serbio
(N) serbio/a *m/f*
Serbo-Croat [ˈsɜːbəʊˈkrəʊæt], **Serbo-Croatian** [ˈsɜːbəʊkrəʊˈeɪʃən] (ADJ) serbocroata
(N) **1** (= *person*) serbocroata *mf*
2 (*Ling*) serbocroata *m*
SERC (N ABBR) (*Brit*) = **Science and Engineering Research Council**
sere [sɪəʳ] (ADJ) seco, marchito
serenade [ˌserəˈneɪd] (N) serenata *f*, mañanitas *fpl* (*Mex*)
(VT) dar una serenata a, cantar las mañanitas a (*Mex*)
serendipitous [ˌserənˈdɪpɪtəs] (ADJ) [*discovery, event*] serendípico
serendipity [ˌserənˈdɪpɪtɪ] (N) serendipia *f*
serene [səˈriːn] (ADJ) sereno
serenely [səˈriːnlɪ] (ADV) con serenidad, con calma • **"no," he said ~** —no —dijo con serenidad *or* calma • **~ indifferent to the noise** sin molestarse en lo más mínimo por el ruido
serenity [sɪˈrenɪtɪ] (N) serenidad *f*
serf [sɜːf] (N) siervo/a *m/f* (*de la gleba*)
serfdom [ˈsɜːfdəm] (N) servidumbre *f* (*de la gleba*); (*fig*) servidumbre *f*
serge [sɜːdʒ] (N) sarga *f*
sergeant [ˈsɑːdʒənt] (N) **1** (*Mil*) sargento *mf* • **yes, ~** sí, mi sargento
2 (*Pol*) oficial *mf* de policía
(CPD) ▸ **sergeant major** sargento *mf* mayor
serial [ˈsɪərɪəl] (N) (*in magazine*) novela *f* por entregas; (*on TV, radio*) serial *m* (*f in Cono Sur*), serie *f*; (= *soap opera*) (*on TV*) telenovela *f*; (*on radio*) radio-novela *f*
(CPD) ▸ **serial access** acceso *m* en serie ▸ **serial interface** interface *m* (*sometimes f*) en serie ▸ **serial killer** asesino/a *m/f* (*que comete crímenes en serie*) ▸ **serial killing** asesinatos *mpl* en serie, cadena *f* de asesinatos ▸ **serial monogamy** monogamia *f* en serie ▸ **serial number** [*of goods, machinery, banknotes etc*] número *m* de serie ▸ **serial port** (*Comput*) puerto *m* en serie ▸ **serial printer** impresora *f* en serie ▸ **serial rights** derechos *mpl* de publicación por entregas
serialization [ˌsɪərɪəlaɪˈzeɪʃən] (N) [*of novel etc*] (*on TV*) serialización *f*; (*in magazine*) publicación *f* por entregas
serialize [ˈsɪərɪəlaɪz] (VT) (= *publish*) publicar por entregas; (= *show on TV*) televisar por entregas • **it has been ~d in the papers** ha aparecido en una serie de entregas en los periódicos
serially [ˈsɪərɪəlɪ] (ADV) en serie
seriatim [ˌsɪərɪˈeɪtɪm] (ADV) (*frm*) en serie
sericulture [ˌserɪˈkʌltʃəʳ] (N) sericultura *f*
series [ˈsɪərɪz] (N) (PL: **series**) **1** (*gen, TV*) serie *f*; [*of lectures, films*] ciclo *m* • **a ~ of events** una serie de acontecimientos
2 (*Math*) serie *f*, progresión *f*
3 (*Elec*) • **to connect in ~** conectar en serie
(CPD) ▸ **series producer** (*TV*) productor(a) *m/f* de la serie
series-wound [ˈsɪərɪzˈwaʊnd] (ADJ) arrollado en serie
serif [ˈserɪf] (N) serifa *f*
(ADJ) [*font*] serifo
serious [ˈsɪərɪəs] (ADJ) **1** (= *in earnest, not frivolous*) [*person*] serio, formal; [*expression, discussion, newspaper, music*] serio • **a rather ~ girl** una chica bastante seria *or* formal • **are you ~?** ¿lo dices en serio? • **you can't be ~!** no lo dices en serio, ¿verdad? • **gentlemen, let's be ~** señores, un poco de formalidad • **to be ~ about sth/sb:** • **she's ~ about her studies** se toma sus estudios en serio • **are you ~ about giving up the job?** ¿hablas en serio de dejar el trabajo? • **he is ~ about this threat** sus amenazas van en serio • **he's ~ about leaving home** está decidido a irse de casa • **is she ~ about him?** ¿va ella en serio con él? • **they haven't made a ~ attempt to solve the problem** no han intentado realmente resolver el problema • **the ~ business of running the country** la importante tarea de gobernar el país • **eating shellfish is a ~ business in France** comer marisco no es algo que se tome a la ligera en Francia • **to give ~ consideration to sth** considerar algo seriamente • **to take a ~ interest in sth** interesarse seriamente por algo • **don't look so ~!** ¡no te pongas tan serio! • **on a more ~ note** pasando a un tema más serio • **all ~ offers considered** cualquier oferta (que sea) seria se tendrá en cuenta • **to give ~ thought to sth** considerar algo seriamente; ▹ **deadly**
2 (= *grave*) [*problem, consequences, situation*] grave, serio; [*danger, illness, injury, mistake*] grave • **the patient's condition is ~** el paciente está grave • **to have ~ doubts about sth** tener serias dudas sobre algo • **to get ~** [*shortage, epidemic, drought*] convertirse en un serio *or* grave problema • **things are getting ~** la situación se está poniendo seria • **she is in ~ trouble** está en serios apuros
3* • **she's earning ~ money** no está ganando ninguna tontería*
3* (= *really*) • **a hotel like the Grand is ~ expensive** un hotel como el Grand es caro de verdad* • **he's ~ into body-building** está metido a tope en el culturismo*
seriously [ˈsɪərɪəslɪ] (ADV) **1** (= *in earnest*) [*think, consider*] seriamente; [*speak*] seriamente, en serio • **yes, but ~ ...** sí, pero en serio ... • **we are ~ considering emigrating** estamos considerando seriamente la posibilidad de emigrar • **do you ~ expect me to believe that?** ¿esperas en serio que me lo crea?, ¿de verdad esperas que me lo crea? • **~?** ¿en serio?, ¿de verdad? • **to take sth/sb ~** tomar algo/a algn en serio • **to take o.s. too ~** tomarse a sí mismo demasiado en serio
2 (= *badly*) [*damage, affect*] seriamente, gravemente; [*injured, wounded*] gravemente • **no-one was ~ hurt** nadie resultó gravemente herido • **he is ~ ill** está grave, está gravemente enfermo • **the pilot realized that something was ~ wrong** el piloto se dio cuenta de que algo iba realmente mal *or* de que pasaba algo muy grave
seriousness [ˈsɪərɪəsnɪs] (N) **1** (= *earnestness*) [*of suggestion, publication, occasion, voice*] seriedad *f*; [*of report, information, account*] fiabilidad *f* • **in all ~** hablando en serio
2 (= *gravity*) [*of situation, problem, threat, damage*] gravedad *f*, seriedad *f*; [*of illness, injury, mistake*] gravedad *f*
sermon [ˈsɜːmən] (N) sermón *m* • **the Sermon on the Mount** el Sermón de la Montaña • **to give sb a ~** (*fig*) (*pej*) sermonear a algn, echar un sermón a algn
sermonize [ˈsɜːmənaɪz] (VT) sermonear
(VI) sermonear
serology [sɪˈrɒlədʒɪ] (N) serología *f*
seropositive [ˌsɪərəʊˈpɒzɪtɪv] (ADJ) seropositivo
serotonin [ˌserəʊˈtəʊnɪn] (N) serotonina *f*
serous [ˈsɪərəs] (ADJ) seroso
serpent [ˈsɜːpənt] (N) (*poet*) serpiente *f*, sierpe *f* (*liter*)
serpentine [ˈsɜːpəntaɪn] (ADJ) serpentino
(N) (*Min*) serpentina *f*
SERPS [sɜːps] (N ABBR) (*Brit*) = **state earnings-related pension scheme**
serrated [seˈreɪtɪd] (ADJ) serrado, dentellado
serration [seˈreɪʃən] (N) borde *m* dentado
serried [ˈserɪd] (ADJ) apretado • **in ~ ranks** en filas apretadas
serum [ˈsɪərəm] (N) (PL: **serums** *or* **sera**) suero *m* • **blood ~** suero *m* sanguíneo
servant [ˈsɜːvənt] (N) **1** (*domestic*) criado/a *m/f*, sirviente/a *m/f*, muchacho/a *m/f*, mucamo/a *m/f* (*S. Cone*) • **the ~s** (*collectively*) la servidumbre
2 (*fig*) servidor(a) *m/f* • **your devoted ~** • **your humble ~** un servidor, servidor de usted • **your obedient ~** (*in letters*) suyo afmo., atento y seguro servidor; ▹ **civil**
(CPD) ▸ **servant girl** criada *f*
serve [sɜːv] (VT) **1** (= *work for*) [+ *employer, God, country*] servir a • **he ~d his country well** sirvió dignamente a la patria, prestó valiosos servicios a la patria
2 (= *be used for, be useful as*) servir • **that ~s to explain ...** eso sirve para explicar ... • **it ~s its/my purpose** viene al caso • **it ~s you right** te lo mereces, te lo tienes merecido, te está bien empleado • **it ~d him right for being so greedy** se lo mereció por ser tan glotón, le está bien empleado por glotón • **if my memory ~s me right** si la memoria no me falla
3 (*in shop, restaurant*) [+ *customer*] servir, atender; [+ *food, meal*] servir • **to ~ sb with hors d'oeuvres** servir los entremeses a algn • **are you being ~d, madam?** ¿le están atendiendo, señora? • **dinner is ~d** la cena está servida • **they ~d cod as halibut** hicieron pasar bacalao por halibut • **main courses are ~d with vegetables or salad** el plato principal se sirve acompañado de verduras o ensalada
4 (= *complete*) cumplir, hacer • **to ~ an apprenticeship** hacer el aprendizaje • **to ~ ten years in the army** servir diez años en el ejército • **to ~ a prison sentence** • **~ time (in prison)** cumplir una condena *or* una pena de cárcel
5 (*Jur*) [+ *writ, summons*] entregar • **to ~ a summons on sb** entregar una citación a algn
6 (*Travel*) • **in towns ~d by this line** en las ciudades por donde pasa esta línea • **these villages used to be ~d by buses** antes en estos pueblos había servicio de autobuses
7 (*Culin*) (= *be enough for*) • **this recipe ~s six**

esta receta es (suficiente) para seis personas
8 (*Tennis etc*) • **to ~ the ball** servir (la bola), sacar • **he ~d 17 double faults** hizo 17 dobles faltas
VI 1 [*servant, soldier*] servir • **he is not willing to ~** no está dispuesto a ofrecer sus servicios • **to ~ on a committee/jury** ser miembro de una comisión/un jurado • **to ~ on the council** ser concejal • **to ~ in parliament** ser diputado
2 (*at mealtime*) servir • **shall I ~?** ¿sirvo? • **to ~ at table** servir en la mesa
3 (*in shop*) atender
4 (= *be useful*) • **to ~ for** *or* **as** servir de • **it will ~** servirá para el caso • **it ~s to show that ...** sirve para demostrar que ...
5 (*Tennis*) sacar
N (*Tennis etc*) servicio *m*, saque *m* • **whose ~ is it?** ¿quién saca?, ¿de quién es el servicio? • **he has a strong ~** tiene un servicio *or* saque muy fuerte
▸ **serve out** VT + ADV 1 (= *complete*) [+ *term of office, sentence*] cumplir
2 (= *dish up*) [+ *food*] servir
▸ **serve up** VT + ADV 1 [+ *food, drink*] servir
2 (*fig*) • **he ~d that up as an excuse*** eso lo ofreció como excusa

server ['sɜːvə^{r}] N 1 (*Rel*) monaguillo *m*
2 (*Tennis*) jugador(a) *m/f* que tiene el saque *or* servicio
3 [*of food*] camarero/a *m/f*, mesero/a *m/f* (*LAm*), mero/a *m/f* (*Mex*)
4 (*Comput*) servidor *m*
5 (= *cutlery*) cubierto *m* de servir; (= *tray*) bandeja *f*, charola *f* (*Mex*)
CPD ▸ **server farm** (*Comput*) granja *f* de servidores

service ['sɜːvɪs] N 1 (= *work*) **a** (= *period of work*) trabajo *m* • **he retired after 50 years' ~** se jubiló después de 50 años de trabajo • **a middle manager with over 20 years ~** un mando medio con más de 20 años de antigüedad (en la empresa) • **he saw ~ in Egypt** combatió en Egipto • **he never saw active ~** nunca estuvo en servicio activo
b (= *work provided*) servicio *m* • **the company has a reputation for good ~** la empresa tiene fama de dar un buen servicio (a los clientes) • **they offered their ~s free of charge** ofrecieron sus servicios gratuitamente • **they provide a 24-hour ~** proporcionan un servicio de 24 horas
c (*domestic*) • **to be in ~** ser criado/a, servir • **she was in ~ at Lord Olton's** era criada *or* servía en casa de Lord Olton • **to go into ~ (with sb)** entrar a servir (en casa de algn)
2 (= *organization, system*) servicio *m* • **the diplomatic ~** el servicio diplomático • **they are attempting to maintain essential ~s** están intentando mantener en funcionamiento los servicios mínimos • **the postal ~** el servicio postal • **rail ~s were disrupted by the strike** el servicio ferroviario se vio afectado por la huelga • **the train ~ to Pamplona** el servicio de trenes a Pamplona; ▹ **secret, social**
3 (= *help, use*) servicio *m* • **he was knighted for his ~s to industry** le concedieron el título de Sir por sus servicios a la industria • **he died in the ~ of his country** murió en acto de servicio a su patria • **this machine will give years of ~** esta máquina durará años • **Tristram Shandy, at your ~!** ¡Tristram Shandy, para servirle *or* a sus órdenes! • **I am at your ~** estoy a su disposición • **to be of ~** ayudar, servir • **how can I be of ~?** ¿en qué puedo ayudar *or* servir? • **the new buses were brought into ~ in 1995** los autobuses nuevos entraron en servicio en 1995 • **to come into ~** [*vehicle, weapon*] entrar en servicio • **to do sth/sb a ~:** • **you have done me a great ~** me ha hecho un gran favor, me ha sido de muchísima ayuda • **they do their country/profession no ~** no hacen ningún favor a su patria/profesión • **to be out of ~** (*Mech*) no funcionar, estar fuera de servicio; ▹ **community**
4 (*in hotel, restaurant, shop*) servicio *m* • **"service not included"** "servicio no incluido"; ▹ **room**
5 **services** (*Econ*) (= *tertiary sector*) sector *m* terciario *or* (de) servicios; (*on motorway*) área *f* de servicio
6 (*Mil*) • **~ life didn't suit him** la vida militar no le pegaba • **the Services** las fuerzas armadas; ▹ **military, national**
7 (*Rel*) (= *mass*) misa *f*; (*other*) oficio *m* (religioso) • **I usually go to morning ~** normalmente voy a la misa *or* al oficio matinal; ▹ **funeral, wedding**
8 (*Aut, Mech*) revisión *f* • **the car is in for a ~** están revisando el coche, están haciendo una revisión al coche • **to send one's car in for a ~** mandar el coche a revisar
9 (= *set of crockery*) vajilla *f* • **dinner ~** vajilla *f* • **tea ~** juego *m or* servicio *m* de té
10 (*Tennis*) servicio *m*, saque *m* • **a break of ~** una ruptura de servicio • **to break sb's ~** romper el servicio a *or* de algn • **to hold/lose one's ~** ganar/perder el servicio
VT 1 [+ *car*] revisar, hacer la revisión a; [+ *appliance*] realizar el mantenimiento de
2 [+ *organization, committee, customers*] dar servicio a, proveer de servicios a
3 [+ *debt*] pagar el interés de
CPD ▸ **service area** (*on motorway*) área *f* de servicio ▸ **service charge** (*in restaurant*) servicio *m*; [*of flat*] gastos *mpl* de comunidad *or* de escalera (*Sp*), gastos *mpl* comunes (*LAm*) ▸ **service department** (= *repair shop*) taller *m* de reparaciones ▸ **service economy** economía *f* de servicios ▸ **service elevator** (*US*) = **service lift** ▸ **service engineer** técnico/a *m/f* (de mantenimiento) ▸ **service families** familias *fpl* de miembros de las fuerzas armadas ▸ **service flat** (*Brit*) *piso o apartamento con servicio de criada y conserje* ▸ **service hatch** ventanilla *f* de servicio ▸ **service history** [*of car*] historial *m* de reparaciones • **the car has a full ~ history** el coche tiene un completo historial de reparaciones ▸ **service industry** (= *company*) empresa *f* de servicios • **the ~ industry** *or* **industries** el sector terciario *or* (de) servicios ▸ **service lift** montacargas *m inv* ▸ **service line** (*Tennis*) línea *f* de servicio *or* saque ▸ **service provider** (*Internet*) proveedor *m* de (acceso a) Internet, proveedor *m* de servicios ▸ **service road** vía *f* de acceso *or* de servicio ▸ **service sector** (*Econ*) sector *m* terciario *or* (de) servicios ▸ **service station** gasolinera *f*, estación *f* de servicio, bencinera *f* (*Chile*), grifo *m* (*Peru*) ▸ **service tree** serbal *m* ▸ **service wife** esposa *f* de un miembro de las fuerzas armadas

serviceable ['sɜːvɪsəbl] ADJ (= *practical*) [*clothes etc*] práctico; (= *lasting*) duradero; (= *usable, working*) utilizable

serviceman ['sɜːvɪsmən] N (PL: **servicemen**) militar *m*

servicewoman ['sɜːvɪs,wʊmən] N (PL: **servicewomen**) (mujer) militar *f*

servicing ['sɜːvɪsɪŋ] N [*of car*] revisión *f*; [*of appliance*] mantenimiento *m*; [*of debt*] pago *m* del interés de

serviette [,sɜːvɪ'et] N servilleta *f*
CPD ▸ **serviette ring** servilletero *m*

servile ['sɜːvaɪl] ADJ servil

servility [sɜː'vɪlɪtɪ] N servilismo *m*

serving ['sɜːvɪŋ] ADJ [*officer*] en activo
N [*of meal*] servicio *m*
CPD ▸ **serving cart** (*US*) ▸ **serving spoon** cuchara *f* de servir ▸ **serving trolley** (*Brit*) carrito *m* ▸ **serving dish** plato *m* de servir

servitude ['sɜːvɪtjuːd] N servidumbre *f*

servo ['sɜːvəʊ] N servo *m*

servoassisted ['sɜːvəʊə'sɪstɪd] ADJ servoasistido

sesame ['sesəmɪ] N 1 (*Bot*) sésamo *m*
2 (*Literat*) • **open ~!** ¡ábrete sésamo!
CPD ▸ **sesame oil** aceite *m* de sésamo ▸ **sesame seeds** semillas *fpl* de sésamo

sesquipedalian [,seskwɪpɪ'deɪlɪən] ADJ sesquipedal, polisilábico • **~ word** palabra *f* kilométrica

sessile ['sesaɪl] ADJ sésil

session ['seʃən] N 1 (= *meeting, sitting*) (*Comput*) sesión *f* • **I had a long ~ with her** tuve una larga entrevista con ella; ▹ **jam, photo, recording**
2 (*Scol, Univ*) (= *year*) año *m* académico, curso *m*
3 (*Pol, Jur*) sesión *f* • **to be in ~** estar en sesión, estar reunido • **to go into secret ~** celebrar una sesión secreta
CPD ▸ **session musician** músico/a *m/f* de estudio, músico/a *m/f* de sesión

sessional ['seʃənl] ADJ [*exam*] de fin de curso

sestet [ses'tet] N sexteto *m*

set [set] (VB: PT, PP: **set**) N 1 (= *matching series*) [*of golf clubs, pens, keys*] juego *m*; [*of books, works*] colección *f*; [*of tools*] equipo *m*, estuche *m*; [*of gears*] tren *m*; [*of stamps*] serie *f*; (*Math*) conjunto *m* • **the sofa and chairs are only sold as a set** el sofá y los sillones no se venden por separado • **a chess set** un ajedrez • **I need one more to make up the complete set** me falta uno para completar la serie • **a complete set of Jane Austen's novels** una colección completa de las novelas de Jane Austen • **a set of crockery** una vajilla • **a set of cutlery** una cubertería • **they are sold in sets** se venden en juegos completos • **a set of kitchen utensils** una batería de cocina • **it makes a set with those over there** hace juego con los que ves allá • **set of teeth** dentadura *f* • **a train set** un tren eléctrico
2 (*Tennis*) set *m* • **she was leading 5-1 in the first set** iba ganando 5 a 1 en el primer set
3 (*Elec*) aparato *m*; (*Rad*) aparato *m* de radio; (*TV*) televisor *m*, televisión *f*
4 (*Theat*) decorado *m*; (*Cine*) plató *m* • **to be on the set** estar en plató
5 (*Hairdressing*) • **to have a shampoo and set** hacerse lavar y marcar el pelo
6 (*esp pej*) (= *group*) grupo *m*, pandilla *f*; (= *clique*) camarilla *f* • **we're not in their set** no formamos parte de su grupo • **they're a set of thieves** son unos ladrones • **they form a set by themselves** forman un grupo aparte • **the fast set** la gente de vida airada • **the literary set** los literatos, la gente literaria • **the smart set** el mundo elegante, los elegantes; ▹ **jet**^{2}
7 (*Brit*) (*Scol*) clase *f* • **the mathematics set** la clase de matemáticas
8 • IDIOM: • **to make a dead set at sb** (= *pick on*) emprenderla resueltamente con algn, escoger a algn como víctima; (*amorously*) proponerse conquistar a algn
9 (= *disposition*) [*of tide, wind*] dirección *f*; [*of fabric*] caída *f*; [*of dress*] corte *m*, ajuste *m*; [*of head*] porte *m*, manera *f* de llevar; [*of saw*] triscamiento *m*; ▹ **mind-set**
10 (*Hort*) planta *f* de transplantar • **onion sets** cebollitas *fpl* de transplantar
ADJ 1 (= *fixed*) [*price, purpose*] fijo; [*smile*]

forzado; [*opinions*] inflexible, rígido; [*talk*] preparado de antemano; [*expression*] hecho; [*date, time*] señalado; (*Scol*) [*books, subjects*] obligatorio; [*task*] asignado • **to be set in one's ways/opinions** tener costumbres/ opiniones profundamente arraigadas • **set books** (*Scol, Univ*) lecturas *mpl* obligatorias • **with no set limits** sin límites determinados • **set menu** menú *m*, comida *f* corrida (*Mex*) • **a set phrase** una frase hecha • **set piece** (*Art*) grupo *m*; (= *fireworks*) cuadro *m*; (*Literat etc*) escena *f* importante; (*Sport*) jugada *f* ensayada, jugada *f* de pizarra • **he gave us a set speech** pronunció un discurso preparado de antemano • **he has a set speech for these occasions** para estas ocasiones tiene un discurso estereotipado • **at a set time** a una hora señalada • **there is no set time for it** para eso no hay hora fija • **there's no set way to do it** no hay una forma establecida *or* determinada de hacerlo
2 (= *determined*) resuelto, decidido • **to be (dead) set against (doing) sth** estar (completamente) opuesto a (hacer) algo • **to be set in one's purpose** tener un propósito firme, mantenerse firme en su propósito • **to be (dead) set on (doing) sth** estar (completamente) decidido a *or* empeñado en (hacer) algo • **since you are so set on it** puesto que te empeñas en ello, puesto que estás decidido a hacerlo
3 (= *ready*) listo • **to be all set to do sth** estar listo para hacer algo • **to be all set for** estar listo para • **all set?** ¿(estás) listo? • **the scene was set for ...** (*fig*) todo estaba listo para ...
4 (*Culin*) • **the fruit is set** el fruto está formado • **the jelly is set** la gelatina está cuajada
5 (= *disposed*) • **the tide is set in our favour** la marea fluye para llevarnos adelante; (*fig*) la tendencia actual nos favorece, llevamos el viento en popa • **the wind is set strong from the north** el viento sopla recio del norte
VT **1** (= *place, put*) poner • **set the chairs by the window** pon las sillas junto a la ventana • **she set the dish before me** puso el plato delante de mí • **to set a plan before a committee** exponer un plan ante una comisión • **the film/scene is set in Rome** la película/escena se desarrolla *or* está ambientada en Roma • **to set fire to sth** • **set sth on fire** prender fuego a algo • **a novel set in Madrid** una novela ambientada en Madrid • **to set places for 14** poner cubiertos para 14 personas • **to set a poem to music** poner música a un poema • **what value do you set on it?** ¿en cuánto lo valoras?; (*fig*) ¿qué valor tiene para ti?
2 (= *arrange*) poner, colocar; (= *adjust*) [+ *clock*] poner en hora; [+ *mechanism*] ajustar; [+ *hair*] marcar, fijar; [+ *trap*] armar • **bricks set in mortar** ladrillos puestos en argamasa • **the alarm clock is set for seven** el despertador está puesto para las siete • **I set the alarm for seven o'clock** puse el despertador a las siete • **I'll set your room** (*US*) voy a limpiar y arreglar su habitación • **to set the table** poner la mesa • **he sets his watch by Big Ben** pone su reloj en hora por el Big Ben; ▹ **sail**
3 (= *mount*) [+ *gem*] engastar, montar
4 (*Med*) [+ *broken bone*] encajar, reducir
5 (*Typ*) [+ *type*] componer
6 (= *fix, establish*) [+ *date, limit*] fijar, señalar; [+ *record*] establecer; [+ *fashion*] imponer; [+ *dye, colour*] fijar • **to set a course for** salir rumbo a • **to set one's heart on sth** tener algo como máximo deseo • **to set limits to sth** señalar límites a algo • **the meeting is set for Tuesday** (*US*) la reunión se celebrará el martes • **to set a period of three months** señalar un plazo de tres meses • **to set a record of ten seconds** establecer un récord de diez segundos • **the world record was set last year** el récord mundial se estableció el año pasado • **to set a time for a meeting** fijar una hora para una reunión; ▹ **example**
7 (= *assign*) [+ *task*] dar • **to set Lorca for 2001** poner una obra de Lorca en el programa de estudios para 2001 • **Cela is not set this year** este año Cela no figura en el programa • **to set an exam in French** preparar un examen de francés • **to set sb a problem** dar a algn un problema que resolver • **to set sb a task** dar a algn una tarea que hacer
8 (= *cause to start*) • **the noise set the dogs barking** el ruido hizo ladrar a los perros • **to set a fire** (*US*) provocar un incendio • **to set sth going** poner algo en marcha • **to set sb laughing** hacer reír a algn • **to set everyone talking** dar que hablar a todos • **it set me thinking** me puso a pensar • **to set sb to work** poner a algn a trabajar
9 (= *cause to pursue*) • **to set a dog on sb** azuzar un perro contra algn • **I was set on by three dogs** me atacaron tres perros • **we set the police on to him** le denunciamos a la policía • **what set the police on the trail?** ¿qué puso a la policía sobre la pista?
10 (= *make solid*) [+ *cement*] solidificar, endurecer; [+ *jelly*] cuajar
VI **1** (= *go down*) [*sun, moon*] ponerse • **the sun was setting** se estaba poniendo el sol
2 (= *go hard*) [*concrete, glue*] endurecerse; (*fig*) [*face*] congelarse
3 (*Med*) [*broken bone, limb*] componerse
4 (*Culin*) [*jelly, jam*] cuajarse
5 (= *begin*) • **to set to work** ponerse a trabajar
CPD ▸ **set designer** (*Theat*) director(a) *m/f* de arte, decorador(a) *m/f* ▸ **set point** (*Tennis*) punto *m* de set ▸ **set square** escuadra *f*; (*with 2 equal sides*) cartabón *m*
▸ **set about** VI + PREP **1** (= *begin*) [+ *task*] empezar • **to set about doing sth** ponerse a hacer algo
2 (= *attack*) atacar, agredir
▸ **set against** VT + PREP **1** (= *turn against*) • **to set sb against sb** enemistar a algn contra algn • **to set sb against sth** hacer que algn coja aversión por algo • **he is very set against it** se opone rotundamente a ello
2 (= *balance against*) comparar con
▸ **set apart** VT + ADV (*lit*) separar (**from** de) • **his genius set him apart from his contemporaries** destacó de entre sus contemporáneos a causa de su genialidad
▸ **set aside** VT + ADV **1** (= *separate*) [+ *book, work*] poner aparte, apartar
2 (= *save*) [+ *money, time*] reservar, guardar
3 (= *put to one side*) [+ *differences, quarrels*] dejar de lado
4 (= *reject*) [+ *proposal*] rechazar; [+ *petition*] desestimar; [+ *law, sentence, will*] anular
5 (= *put away*) poner a un lado
▸ **set back** VT + ADV **1** (= *retard*) [+ *project, process*] retrasar; [+ *clocks*] atrasar • **this has set us back some years** esto nos ha retrasado varios años
2 (= *place apart*) apartar • **a house set back from the road** una casa apartada de la carretera
3* (= *cost*) costar • **the dinner set me back £40** la cena me costó 40 libras
4 (= *replace*) devolver a su lugar
▸ **set by** VT + ADV (= *save*) reservar, guardar
▸ **set down** VT + ADV **1** (= *put down*) [+ *object*] dejar; [+ *passenger*] bajar, dejar • **to set sth down on the table** poner algo sobre la mesa
2 (= *record*) poner por escrito • **to set sth down in writing** *or* **on paper** poner algo por escrito
▸ **set forth** VT + ADV (= *expound*) [+ *theory*] exponer, explicar; (= *display*) mostrar
VI + ADV = **set out**
▸ **set in** VI + ADV [*bad weather*] establecerse; [*winter, rain, snow*] empezar; [*night*] caer • **the rain has set in for the night** la lluvia continuará toda la noche • **the rain has really set in now** ahora está lloviendo de verdad • **the reaction set in after the war** la reacción se afianzó después de la guerra
▸ **set off** VI + ADV (= *leave*) salir, partir (*esp LAm*) • **we set off for London at nine o'clock** salimos para Londres a las nueve • **to set off on a journey** salir de viaje
VT + ADV **1** (= *start*) provocar, desencadenar • **that was what set off the riot** eso fue lo que provocó *or* desencadenó el motín • **to set sb off** (*laughing*) hacer reír a algn; (*talking*) hacer que algn se ponga a hablar • **that really set him off** (*angrily*) aquello le puso furioso • **that set him off (all over) again** (*angrily*) eso le provocó de nuevo
2 (= *trigger off*) [+ *burglar alarm*] hacer sonar; [+ *bomb*] hacer estallar, explotar; [+ *mechanism*] hacer funcionar
3 (= *enhance*) hacer resaltar • **the black sets off the red** el negro hace resaltar *or* pone de relieve el rojo • **her dress sets off her figure** el vestido le realza la figura
4 (= *balance*) contraponer • **to set off profits against losses** contraponer las ganancias a las pérdidas • **these expenses are set off against tax** estos gastos son desgravables
▸ **set on** VI + PREP (= *attack*) (*physically, verbally*) agredir, atacar • **he was set on by four of them** fue agredido *or* atacado por cuatro de ellos
▸ **set out** VI + ADV salir, partir (*esp LAm*) (**for** para, **from** de) • **we set out for London at nine o'clock** salimos para Londres a las nueve • **to set out in search of sth/sb** salir en busca de algo/algn • **to set out to do sth** proponerse hacer algo • **what are you setting out to do?** ¿qué os proponéis?, ¿cuál es vuestro objetivo? • **we did not set out to do that** no teníamos esa intención al principio
VT + ADV **1** (= *display*) [+ *goods*] exponer
2 (= *present*) [+ *reasons, ideas*] presentar, exponer
▸ **set to** VI + ADV **1** (= *start*) empezar; (= *start working*) ponerse (resueltamente) a trabajar; (= *start eating*) empezar a comer (con buen apetito) • **to set to and do sth** ponerse a trabajar para hacer algo • **set to!** ¡a ello!
2 • **they set to with their fists** empezaron a pegarse, se liaron a golpes
▸ **set up** VI + ADV • **to set up in business** establecerse en un negocio • **to set up (in business) as a baker** establecerse de panadero
VT + ADV **1** (= *place in position*) [+ *chairs, tables etc*] disponer, colocar; [+ *statue, monument*] levantar, erigir; [+ *fence*] construir, poner • **to set up camp** acampar
2 (= *start*) [+ *school, business, company*] establecer, fundar; [+ *committee*] poner en marcha; [+ *inquiry*] constituir; [+ *fund*] crear; [+ *government*] establecer, instaurar; [+ *record*] establecer; [+ *precedent*] sentar; [+ *infection*] causar, producir • **to set up house** establecerse, poner casa • **to set up shop** (*Comm*) poner (un) negocio • **to set sb up in business** poner un negocio a algn, establecer a algn • **he set her up in a flat** la instaló en un piso *or* (*LAm*) departamento • **now he's set up for life** ahora tiene el porvenir asegurado
3 (= *pose*) • **to set o.s. up as sth** presumir de

algo, hacérselas de algo
4* (= *frame*) tender una trampa a
5* (= *lure into a trap*) engañar, llevar al huerto a*
6* (= *fix, rig*) [+ *fight*] amañar, apañar
7 (= *equip*) equipar, proveer (**with** de) • **to be well set up for** estar bien provisto de, tener buena provisión de
8 (*Typ*) componer
9 (= *raise*) [+ *cry*] levantar, lanzar, dar; [+ *protest*] levantar, formular
▸ **set upon** (VI + PREP) = set on

set-aside ['setəsaɪd] (N) (*Agr*) retirada *f* de tierras, abandono *m* de tierras • **set-aside land** tierra *f* en barbecho

setback ['setbæk] (N) revés *m* • **to suffer a ~** sufrir un revés

setscrew ['setskru:] (N) tornillo *m* de presión

sett [set] (N) madriguera *f* (*de tejón*)

settee [se'ti:] (N) sofá *m*
(CPD) ▸ **settee bed** sofá-cama *m*

setter ['setəʳ] (N) **1** (= *dog*) setter *m*, perro *m* de muestra
2 [*of puzzle etc*] autor(a) *m/f*
3 (= *person*) [*of gems*] engastador(a) *m/f*
4 = **typesetter**

setting ['setɪŋ] (N) **1** [*of novel etc*] escenario *m*; (= *scenery*) marco *m*; [*of jewels*] engaste *m*, montura *f*
2 (*Mus*) arreglo *m*
3 [*of controls*] ajuste *m*
4 [*of sun*] puesta *f*
5 [*of bone*] encaje *m*, reducción *f*
6 (*Typ*) composición *f*
(CPD) ▸ **setting lotion** fijador *m* (para el pelo)

setting-up ['setɪŋ'ʌp] (N) **1** (= *erection*) [*of monument*] erección *f*
2 (= *foundation*) [*of institution, company*] fundación *f*, establecimiento *m*
3 (*Typ*) composición *f*

settle¹ ['setl] (VT) **1** (= *resolve*) [+ *dispute, problem*] resolver • **several points remain to be ~d** quedan varios puntos por resolver • **the result was ~d in the first half** el resultado se decidió en el primer tiempo • **to ~ a case** *or* **claim out of court** llegar a un acuerdo sin recurrir a los tribunales • **the terms were ~d by negotiation** se acordaron las condiciones mediante una negociación • **~ it among yourselves!** ¡arregladlo entre vosotros! • **so that's ~d then** así que ya está decidido • **it's all ~d — we're going in June** ya está decidido — nos vamos en junio • **that ~s it! — you're not going** ¡no hay más que hablar! *or* ¡pues ya está! — tú te quedas • **the couple have ~d their differences** la pareja ha resuelto sus diferencias
2 (= *make comfortable*) [+ *person*] poner cómodo, acomodar • **to ~ an invalid for the night** poner cómodo *or* acomodar a un enfermo para que duerma (por la noche) • **to get (sb) ~d: I'd just got the baby ~d when ...** acababa de acostar al bebé cuando ... • **it took a long time to get ~d in our new home** nos costó mucho instalarnos en la nueva casa • **to ~ o.s.** ponerse cómodo, acomodarse • **she ~d herself at the desk** se puso cómoda *or* se acomodó delante de la mesa
3 (= *place*) [+ *object*] colocar; [+ *gaze*] posar
4 (= *colonize*) [+ *land*] colonizar
5 (= *calm*) [+ *nerves*] calmar, sosegar; [+ *doubts*] disipar, desvanecer; [+ *stomach*] asentar
6 (= *pay*) [+ *bill*] pagar; [+ *debt*] saldar, liquidar
7 (= *put in order*) [+ *affairs*] poner en orden • **to ~ one's affairs** poner en orden sus asuntos
8* (= *deal with*) [+ *person*] • **I'll soon ~ him** ya me encargaré de ponerlo en su sitio* • **that ~d him** con eso se le acabó la tontería*
9 (*Jur*) asignar • **to ~ sth on sb** asignar algo a algn
(VI) **1** (= *establish o.s.*) (*in a house*) instalarse; (*in a country*) establecerse; [*first settlers*] establecerse • **she visited Paris in 1974 and eventually ~d there** visitó París en 1974 y finalmente decidió establecerse allí
2 (= *come to rest*) [*bird, insect*] posarse; [*dust*] asentarse; [*snow*] cuajar • **a deep gloom had ~d on the party** un profundo pesimismo se había apoderado del grupo • **my eyes ~d on her immediately** al momento mi mirada se fijó en ella
3 (= *sink*) [*sediment*] depositarse; [*building*] asentarse • **the boat slowly ~d in the mud** poco a poco el bote se hundió en el barro
4 (= *separate*) [*liquid*] reposar
5 (= *get comfortable*) (*in chair*) arrellanarse; (*in new job, routine*) adaptarse, establecerse • **he ~d deeper into the cushions** se arrellanó entre los cojines • **I couldn't ~ to anything** no me podía concentrar en nada, no lograba ponerme a hacer nada
6 (= *calm down*) [*weather*] estabilizarse, asentarse; [*conditions, situation*] volver a la normalidad, normalizarse; [*nerves*] calmarse; ▸ **dust**
7 (= *reach an agreement*) llegar a un acuerdo *or* arreglo • **they ~d with us for £12,000** lo arreglamos extrajudicialmente y nos pagaron 12.000 libras
8 (= *pay*) • **I'll ~ with you on Friday** te pagaré el viernes, ajustaremos cuentas el viernes
▸ **settle down** (VI + ADV) **1** (= *get comfortable*) ponerse cómodo, acomodarse • **I ~d down in my favourite chair** me puse cómodo *or* me acomodé *or* me arrellané en mi silla preferida • **they ~d down to wait** se prepararon para la espera
2 (= *apply o.s.*) • **to ~ down to sth: after dinner, he ~d down to a video** después de cenar se puso a ver un vídeo • **I couldn't get the children to ~ down to work** no conseguía que los niños se pusieran a trabajar
3 (= *calm down*) calmarse, tranquilizarse
4 (= *adopt a stable life*) echar raíces • **I'm not ready to ~ down yet** aún no estoy listo para echar raíces • **why don't you ~ down and get married?** ¿por qué no sientas cabeza y te casas?*
5 (= *get back to normal*) [*situation*] volver a la normalidad, normalizarse • **things are beginning to ~ down** las cosas empiezan a volver a la normalidad
(VT + ADV) **1** (= *make comfortable*) poner cómodo, acomodar • **he ~d the children down for the night** acostó a los niños • **why don't you help Philippa unpack and ~ her down?** ¿por qué no le ayudas a Philippa a deshacer las maletas e instalarse?
2 (= *calm down*) calmar, tranquilizar • **I turned on the TV to ~ them down** encendí la tele para calmarlos *or* tranquilizarlos
▸ **settle for** (VI + PREP) **1** (= *accept*) conformarse con • **don't ~ for second best** confórmate solo con lo mejor • **I won't ~ for less** no me conformo con menos • **to ~ for £250** convenir en aceptar 250 libras
2 (= *choose*) decidirse por, escoger
▸ **settle in** (VI + ADV) (*in new home, hotel*) instalarse; (*in new job, school*) adaptarse • **he's settling in well at his new school** se está adaptando bien a la nueva escuela • **are you all ~d in?** ¿ya estás instalado?
▸ **settle on** (VI + PREP) (= *choose*) decidirse por, escoger
▸ **settle up** (VI + ADV) ajustar cuentas (**with sb** con algn) • **I'll pay for everything and we can ~ up later** yo pagaré todo y ya ajustaremos cuentas después

settle² ['setl] (N) banco *m*, escaño *m* (*a veces con baúl debajo*)

settled ['setld] (ADJ) **1** (= *fixed, established*) [*ideas, opinions*] fijo; [*order, rhythm*] estable; [*team*] fijo, estable • **a ~ social order** un orden social estable • **the first ~ civilization** la primera civilización estable • **to feel ~** (*in a place, job*) sentirse adaptado • **to get ~** adaptarse, amoldarse
2 (= *colonized*) • **the eastern ~ regions of the country** los poblados *or* asentamientos permanentes de las regiones del este del país
3 [*weather*] estable, asentado

settlement ['setlmənt] (N) **1** (= *payment*) [*of claim, bill, debt*] liquidación *f*; (= *dowry*) dote *f* • **please find enclosed my cheque in full ~ of ...** adjunto le remito el talón a cuenta de la total liquidación de ...
2 (= *agreement*) acuerdo *m* • **to reach a ~** llegar a un acuerdo • **to secure a peace ~** alcanzar un acuerdo de paz
3 (= *colony, village*) colonia *f*, poblado *m*; (= *archaeological site*) asentamiento *m*
4 (= *act of settling persons*) establecimiento *m*; [*of land*] colonización *f*
5 (*Jur*) (= *sum of money*) • **she accepted an out-of-court ~ of £4000** aceptó una compensación de 4000 libras a cambio de no seguir adelante con el juicio

settler ['setləʳ] (N) colonizador(a) *m/f*

set-to* ['set'tu:] (N) (= *fight*) pelea *f*; (= *quarrel*) agarrada* *f*, bronca* *f*

set-top box ['settɒp'bɒks] (N) descodificador *m* de televisión digital

setup* ['setʌp] (N) **1** (= *way sth is organised*) sistema *m* • **it's an odd ~ here** aquí todo es en un plan raro • **you have to know the ~** hay que conocer el tinglado • **what's the ~?** ¿cuál es el sistema?, ¿cómo está organizado? • **he's joining our ~** formará parte de nuestro equipo
2* (= *trick, trap*) trampa *f*, montaje* *m*
(CPD) ▸ **setup file** (*Comput*) archivo *m* de configuración

seven ['sevn] (ADJ), (PRON) siete • **the ~ wonders of the world** las siete maravillas del mundo • **the ~ deadly sins** los siete pecados capitales • **the ~-year itch*** *sensación de monotonía y aburrimiento a los siete años de estar con la misma pareja*
(N) (= *numeral*) siete *m*; ▸ **five**

sevenfold ['sevnfəʊld] (ADJ) séptuplo
(ADV) siete veces

seventeen ['sevn'ti:n] (ADJ), (PRON) diecisiete
(N) (= *numeral*) diecisiete *m*; ▸ **five**

seventeenth ['sevn'ti:nθ] (ADJ) decimoséptimo • **the ~ century** el siglo diecisiete
(N) (*in series*) decimoséptimo/a *m/f*; (= *fraction*) decimoséptima parte *f*; ▸ **fifth**

seventh ['sevnθ] (ADJ) séptimo • **Seventh Cavalry** (US) Séptimo *m* de Caballería
(N) **1** (*in series*) séptimo/a *m/f*; (= *fraction*) séptima parte *f*; ▸ **fifth**
2 (*Mus*) (= *interval*) séptima *f*

seventh-grader [ˌsevnθ'greɪdəʳ] (N) (US) alumno/a *m/f* de séptimo curso (*de entre 12 y 13 años*)

seventieth ['sevntɪɪθ] (ADJ) septuagésimo
(N) (*in series*) septuagésimo/a *m/f*; (= *fraction*) septuagésima parte *f*; ▸ **fifth**

seventy ['sevntɪ] (ADJ), (PRON) setenta
(N) (= *numeral*) setenta *m*; ▸ **fifty**

sever ['sevəʳ] (VT) cortar; (*fig*) [+ *relations, communications*] romper
(VI) [*rope etc*] cortarse

several ['sevrəl] (ADJ) **1** (*in number*) varios

• ~ **times** varias veces • ~ **hundred people** varios cientos de personas
2 (*frm*) (= *separate*) diverso • **their ~ occupations** sus diversas ocupaciones • **they went their ~ ways** tomaron cada uno su camino
PRON varios • ~ **of them wore hats** varios (de ellos) llevaban sombrero
severally ['sevrəlɪ] ADV (*frm*) **1** (= *separately, individually*) por separado, individualmente
2 (= *respectively*) respectivamente
severance ['sevərəns] N ruptura *f*; (*Ind*) despido *m*
CPD ▸ **severance package, severance pay** indemnización *f* por despido
severe [sɪ'vɪəʳ] ADJ (COMPAR: **severer**, SUPERL: **severest**) **1** (= *serious*) [*problem, consequence, damage*] grave, serio; [*injury, illness*] grave; [*defeat, setback, shortage*] serio; [*blow, reprimand*] fuerte, duro; [*pain, headache*] fuerte • **I suffered from ~ bouts of depression** padecía profundas *or* serias depresiones • **many families suffered ~ hardship as a consequence** muchas familias sufrieron enormes penurias a consecuencia de ello • **we have been under ~ pressure to cut costs** nos han presionado mucho para reducir gastos • **to suffer a ~ loss of blood** sufrir gran pérdida de sangre • ~ **losses** (*Econ*) enormes *or* cuantiosas pérdidas *fpl*
2 (= *harsh*) [*weather, conditions, winter*] duro, riguroso; [*cold*] extremo; [*storm, flooding, frost*] fuerte
3 (= *strict*) [*person, penalty*] severo; [*discipline*] estricto • **I was his severest critic** yo era su crítico más severo • **to be ~ with sb** ser severo con algn
4 (= *austere*) [*person, appearance, expression*] severo, adusto; [*clothes, style*] austero; [*hairstyle*] (de corte) serio; [*architecture*] sobrio
severely [sɪ'vɪəlɪ] ADV **1** (= *seriously*) **a** (*with verb*) [*damage, disrupt, hamper*] seriamente; [*limit, restrict*] severamente; [*injure, affect*] gravemente • **the competitors were ~ tested by the conditions** las condiciones meteorológicas habían supuesto una dura prueba para los participantes
b (*with adj*) [*ill, disabled*] gravemente; [*depressed, disturbed*] profundamente
2 (= *harshly*) [*punish, criticize*] duramente, con severidad; [*look*] con severidad
3 (= *austerely*) [*dress*] austeramente
severity [sɪ'verɪtɪ] N **1** (= *seriousness*) [*of illness*] gravedad *f*, seriedad *f*; [*of pain*] intensidad *f*; [*of attack*] dureza *f*
2 (= *strictness*) [*of character, criticism*] severidad *f*
3 (= *harshness*) [*of conditions, winter*] rigor *m*
Seville [sə'vɪl] N Sevilla *f*
CPD ▸ **Seville orange** naranja *f* amarga ▸ **Seville orange tree** (*Brit*) naranjo *m* amargo
Sevillian [sə'vɪlɪən] ADJ sevillano
N sevillano/a *m/f*
sew [səʊ] (PT: **sewed**, PP: **sewn, sewed**) VT • **to sew a button on** *or* **onto sth** coser un botón en algo
VI coser
▸ **sew on** VT + ADV coser • **do you know how to sew on a button?** ¿sabes coser un botón?
▸ **sew up** VT + ADV (*gen*) coser; (*mend*) remendar • **it's all sewn up*** (*fig*) está todo arreglado
sewage ['sju:ɪdʒ] N aguas *fpl* residuales *or* cloacales
CPD ▸ **sewage disposal** depuración *f* de aguas residuales *or* cloacales ▸ **sewage farm, sewage works** estación *f* depuradora ▸ **sewage system** alcantarillado *m*
sewer ['sjʊəʳ] N alcantarilla *f*, albañal *m*, cloaca *f* • **to have a mind like a ~** tener la mente podrida
sewerage ['sjʊərɪdʒ] N alcantarillado *m*; (*as service on estate etc*) saneamiento *m*
sewing ['səʊɪŋ] N (*activity, object*) costura *f*
CPD ▸ **sewing basket** cesta *f* de costura ▸ **sewing machine** máquina *f* de coser ▸ **sewing pattern** patrón *m* (de costura) ▸ **sewing silk** torzal *m*, seda *f* de coser
sewn [səʊn] PP *of* **sew**
sex [seks] N **1** (= *gender*) sexo *m* • **inequalities between the sexes** desigualdades entre los sexos • **the fair** *or* **gentle sex** (*euph*) el sexo débil, el bello sexo • **the opposite sex** el sexo opuesto • **the weaker sex** (*euph*) (*pej*) el sexo débil
2 (= *sexual activities*) sexo *m*; (= *sexual intercourse*) relaciones *fpl* sexuales • **the film contains no sex or violence** la película no contiene escenas eróticas *or* de sexo o de violencia • **to have sex** tener relaciones sexuales (**with** con)
3 (= *sex organ*) sexo *m*, genitales *mpl*
VT [+ *animal, bird*] sexar, determinar el sexo de
CPD ▸ **sex abuse** abuso *m* sexual ▸ **sex abuser** autor(a) *m/f* de abusos sexuales ▸ **the sex act** el acto sexual, el acto ▸ **sex addict** adicto/a *m/f* al sexo ▸ **sex addiction** adicción *f* al sexo ▸ **sex aid** juguete *m* erótico ▸ **sex appeal** atractivo *m* sexual, sex-appeal *m* ▸ **sex buddy*** follamigo/a* *m/f* ▸ **sex change** cambio *m* de sexo ▸ **sex change operation** operación *f* de cambio de sexo ▸ **sex crime** (= *criminality*) delitos *mpl* sexuales, delitos *mpl* contra la honestidad (*Jur*), delitos *mpl* contra la libertad sexual (*Jur*); (= *single crime*) delito *m* (de naturaleza) sexual, delito *m* contra la honestidad (*Jur*), delito *m* contra la libertad sexual (*Jur*) ▸ **sex discrimination** discriminación *f* por cuestión de sexo ▸ **sex drive** libido *f*, líbido *f*, apetito *m* sexual • **to have a high/low sex drive** tener la libido *or* líbido alta/baja, tener mucho/poco apetito sexual ▸ **sex education** educación *f* sexual ▸ **sex game** juego *m* erótico ▸ **sex god** sex symbol *m* ▸ **sex goddess** sex symbol *f* ▸ **sex hormone** hormona *f* sexual ▸ **sex life** vida *f* sexual ▸ **sex machine** (*hum*) máquina *f* de hacer el amor, bestia *mf* en la cama ▸ **sex maniac** maníaco/a *m/f* sexual ▸ **sex object** objeto *m* sexual ▸ **sex offender** delincuente *mf* sexual ▸ **sex organ** órgano *m* sexual ▸ **sex partner** compañero/a *m/f* (de cama), pareja *f* ▸ **sex scene** escena *f* erótica, escena *f* de sexo ▸ **sex selection** elección *f* del sexo ▸ **sex shop** sex-shop *m* ▸ **sex symbol** sex símbol *mf* ▸ **sex therapist** sexólogo/a *m/f*, terapeuta *mf* sexual ▸ **sex therapy** terapia *f* sexual ▸ **sex tourism** turismo *m* sexual ▸ **sex toy** juguete *m* erótico ▸ **sex worker** trabajador(a) *m/f* del sexo
▸ **sex up*** VT + ADV hacer más atractivo
sexagenarian [,seksədʒɪ'nɛərɪən] ADJ sexagenario
N sexagenario/a *m/f*
Sexagesima [,seksə'dʒesɪmə] N Sexagésima *f*
sex-crazed ['sekskreɪzd] ADJ obsesionado por el sexo
sexed [sekst] ADJ • **to be highly ~** tener un apetito sexual muy alto
sexily ['seksɪlɪ] ADV de forma sexy • **to dress ~** vestirse sexy
sexiness ['seksɪnɪs] N **1** (= *sexual attractiveness*) [*of person, voice, eyes, underwear*] erotismo *m*, atractivo *m* sexual
2 (= *interest in sex*) excitación *f* sexual, libido *f* alta
3 (= *eroticism*) [*of film, scene, book*] erotismo *m*
4* (= *excitement*) gancho* *m*, interés *m*
sexism ['seksɪzəm] N sexismo *m*
sexist ['seksɪst] ADJ sexista
N sexista *mf*
sexless ['sekslɪs] ADJ (= *not interested in sex*) asexuado, desprovisto de instinto sexual; (= *not sexually attractive*) desprovisto de atractivo sexual; (*Bio*) sin sexo, asexual • **a ~ marriage** un matrimonio sin sexo
sex-linked ['seks'lɪŋkt] ADJ (*Bio*) ligado al sexo
sex-mad* [,seks'mæd] ADJ obsesionado por el sexo
sexologist [sek'sɒlədʒɪst] N sexólogo/a *m/f*
sexology [sek'sɒlədʒɪ] N sexología *f*
sexpert* ['seksp3:t] N (*hum*) experto/a *m/f* en sexo
sexploitation [,seksplɔɪ'teɪʃən] N explotación *f* sexual
sexpot* ['sekspɒt] N (*hum*) cachonda *f*
sex-starved ['sekssta:vd] ADJ sexualmente frustrado
sext* [sekst] VT • **to ~ sb** sextear a algn*, *enviar un mensaje de texto con contenido sexual a algn*
VI sextear*, *enviar mensajes de texto con contenido sexual*
CPD ▸ **sext message** mensaje *m* de texto con contenido sexual
sextant ['sekstənt] N sextante *m*
sextet, sextette [seks'tet] N (*Mus*) (= *players, composition*) sexteto *m*
sexting* ['sekstɪŋ] N sexteo* *m*, *envío de mensajes de texto con contenido sexual*
sexton ['sekstən] N sacristán *m*
sextuplet ['sekstjʊplɪt] N sextillizo/a *m/f*
sexual ['seksjʊəl] ADJ sexual • **she's very ~** es muy sensual
CPD ▸ **sexual abuse** abuso *m* sexual ▸ **sexual assault** atentado *m* contra el pudor ▸ **sexual discrimination** discriminación *f* a base de sexo ▸ **sexual equality** igualdad *f* entre los sexos ▸ **sexual harassment** acoso *m* sexual ▸ **sexual intercourse** relaciones *fpl* sexuales • **to have ~ intercourse (with sb)** tener relaciones sexuales (con algn) ▸ **sexual orientation** orientación *f* sexual ▸ **sexual partner** pareja *f* sexual ▸ **sexual politics** política *fsing* sexual ▸ **sexual preference** preferencia *f* sexual ▸ **the sexual revolution** la revolución sexual ▸ **sexual stereotyping** categorización *f* en estereotipos sexuales
sexuality [,seksjʊ'ælɪtɪ] N sexualidad *f*
sexualize ['seksjʊəlaɪz] VT sexualizar
sexually ['seksjʊəlɪ] ADV sexualmente • **to be ~ abused** ser víctima de abusos sexuales • **to be ~ active** ser sexualmente activo • **to become** *or* **get ~ aroused** excitarse sexualmente • **to be ~ assaulted** ser víctima de una agresión sexual • **to be ~ explicit** contener imágenes de sexo explícito • **to be ~ harassed** sufrir acoso sexual • **to be ~ involved with sb** mantener relaciones sexuales con algn • **~ mature** sexualmente maduro • **~ transmitted disease** enfermedad *f* de transmisión sexual
sexy ['seksɪ] ADJ (COMPAR: **sexier**, SUPERL: **sexiest**) **1** (= *sexually attractive*) sexy • **you look very ~ in that dress** estás muy sexy con ese vestido
2 (= *interested in sex*) sensual • **to make sb feel ~** excitar a algn, hacer que algn se excite
3 (= *erotic*) [*film, scene, book*] erótico
4* (= *exciting*) [*issue, subject, object*] excitante
Seychelles [seɪ'ʃelz] NPL Seychelles *fpl*
sez‡ [sez] = **says** • **sez you!** ¡lo dices tú!
SF N ABBR **1** = **science fiction**
2 (*Pol*) = **Sinn Féin**

S

SFA (N ABBR) **1** (= **Scottish Football Association**) ≈ AFE *f*
2‡ = **sweet Fanny Adams**
SFO (N ABBR) (*Brit*) = **Serious Fraud Office**
sfx (ABBR) = **special effects**
SG (N ABBR) (*US*) (= **Surgeon General**) jefe *mf* del servicio federal de sanidad
sgd (ABBR) = **signed**
SGML (N) SGML *m* • **in ~** en SGML
sgraffito [sgræ'fi:təʊ] (N) esgrafiado *m*
Sgt (ABBR) = **Sergeant**
sh [ʃ] (EXCL) ¡chitón!, ¡chist!
shabbily ['ʃæbɪlɪ] (ADV) **1** [*dress*] desaliñadamente, pobremente
2 [*treat*] fatal, vilmente
shabbiness ['ʃæbɪnɪs] (N) **1** [*of dress, person*] desaliño *m*, pobreza *f*
2 [*of treatment*] injusticia *f*, vileza *f*
shabby ['ʃæbɪ] (ADJ) (COMPAR: **shabbier**, SUPERL: **shabbiest**) **1** [*building*] desvencijado; [*clothes*] andrajoso; (*also* **shabby-looking**) [*person*] andrajoso, desaliñado
2 [*treatment*] injusto, vil; [*behaviour*] poco honrado; [*excuse*] poco convincente • **a ~ trick** una mala jugada
shabby-looking ['ʃæbɪ,lʊkɪŋ] (ADJ) [*person*] andrajoso, desaliñado; [*hotel, room*] desvencijado
shack [ʃæk] (N) choza *f*, jacal *m* (*CAm, Mex*)
▸ **shack up**‡ (VI + ADV) • **to ~ up with sb** arrejuntarse con algn* • **to ~ up together** arrejuntarse*, vivir arrejuntados*
shackle ['ʃækl] (VT) [+ *prisoner*] poner grilletes a, poner grillos a; (= *obstruct*) echar trabas a
(NPL) **shackles** (= *chains*) grilletes *mpl*, grillos *mpl*; (*fig*) (= *obstruction*) trabas *fpl*
shad [ʃæd] (N) (PL: **shad** *or* **shads**) sábalo *m*
shade [ʃeɪd] (N) **1** (= *area of darkness*) sombra *f* • **in the ~** a la sombra • **35 degrees in the ~** 35 grados a la sombra • **to put sb in the ~** (*fig*) hacer sombra a algn • **to put sth in the ~** (*fig*) dejar algo en la sombra
2 [*of colour*] tono *m*, matiz *m*; (*fig*) [*of meaning, opinion*] matiz *m* • **all ~s of opinion are represented** está representada la gama entera de opiniones
3 (*Art*) sombra *f*
4 shades* (= *sunglasses*) gafas *fpl* de sol
5 (= *lampshade*) pantalla *f*; (= *eye-shade*) visera *f*; (*US*) (= *blind*) persiana *f*
6 (= *small quantity*) poquito *m*, tantito *m* (*LAm*) • **just a ~ more** un poquito más
7 (*liter*) (= *ghost*) fantasma *m*
8 (= *reminder*) • **~s of Professor Dodd!** ¡eso recuerda al profesor Dodd!
(VT) **1** (= *protect from light*) dar sombra a • **the beaches are ~d by palm trees** las palmeras dan sombra a las playas • **she put up her hand to ~ her eyes (from the sun)** levantó la mano para protegerse los ojos (del sol)
2 (*Art*) (= *shade in*) sombrear
▸ **shade away** (VI + ADV) = **shade off**
▸ **shade in** (VT + ADV) sombrear
▸ **shade off** (VT + ADV) (*Art*) [+ *colours*] degradar
(VI + ADV) cambiar poco a poco (**into** hasta hacerse), transformarse gradualmente (**into** en) • **blue that ~s off into black** azul que se transforma *or* se funde gradualmente en negro
shaded ['ʃeɪdɪd] (ADJ) **1** (= *shady*) [*spot, patio*] con sombra
2 (*Art*) [*area*] sombreado
shadeless ['ʃeɪdlɪs] (ADJ) sin sombra, privado de sombra
shadiness ['ʃeɪdɪnɪs] (N) **1** (= *shade*) sombra *f*, lo umbroso
2* (= *dubiousness*) [*of person*] dudosa honradez *f*; [*of deal*] lo turbio, carácter *m* turbio

shading ['ʃeɪdɪŋ] (N) **1** [*of colour*] sombreado *m*
2 (*fig*) [*of meaning*] matiz *m*
shadow ['ʃædəʊ] (N) **1** (= *dark shape*) sombra *f*; (= *darkness*) oscuridad *f*, tinieblas *fpl* • **in the ~** a la sombra • **five o'clock ~** barba *f* de ocho horas • **doctors have discovered a ~ on his lung** los médicos le han detectado una sombra *or* mancha en el pulmón • **to cast a ~ over sth** (*fig*) ensombrecer algo • **to live in the ~ of sth/sb** vivir eclipsado por algo/algn
2* (= *tail*) perseguidor(a) *m/f* • **to put a ~ on sb** hacer seguir a algn
3 (*fig*) (= *faithful companion*) sombra *f*
4 (*Pol*) *miembro de la oposición con un cargo análogo al de ministro* • **Clarke flung at his ~ the accusation that he was a "tabloid politician"** Clarke lanzó a su homólogo en la oposición la acusación de ser un "político sensacionalista"
5 (*fig*) (= *small amount*) [*of doubt, suspicion*] atisbo *m*, asomo *m*, sombra *f* • **I never had a** *or* **the ~ of a doubt that he was right** jamás tuve el menor asomo *or* atisbo *or* la menor sombra de duda de que tenía razón • **without a ~ of a doubt** sin (la menor) sombra de duda
6 (= *vestige*) sombra *f* • **he is a ~ of the man he used to be** no es ni sombra de lo que era • **a ~ of his former self** la sombra de lo que fue
(VT) **1** (= *follow*) seguir y vigilar • **I was ~ed all the way home** me siguieron hasta mi casa
2 (= *darken*) ensombrecer, oscurecer • **the hood ~ed her face** la capucha ensombrecía *or* oscurecía su rostro
(CPD) ▸ **shadow cabinet** (*Brit*) (*Pol*) consejo *m* de ministros de la oposición • **the ~ Foreign Secretary** el portavoz parlamentario de la oposición en materia de asuntos extranjeros ▸ **shadow Chancellor** (*Brit*) (*Pol*) responsable *mf or* portavoz *mf* de Economía y Hacienda de la oposición ▸ **shadow minister** (*Brit*) portavoz *mf* de la oposición, ministro/a *m/f* en la sombra • **the Shadow Minister for Sport** el responsable *or* portavoz de Deportes de la oposición
shadow-box ['ʃædəʊbɒks] (VI) boxear con un adversario imaginario; (*fig*) disputar con un adversario imaginario
shadow-boxing ['ʃædəʊ,bɒksɪŋ] (N) boxeo *m* con un adversario imaginario; (*fig*) disputa *f* con un adversario imaginario
shadowy ['ʃædəʊɪ] (ADJ) **1** (= *ill-lit*) oscuro, tenebroso; (= *blurred*) indistinto, vago, indefinido • **a ~ form** un bulto, una sombra
2 (= *mysterious*) oscuro, misterioso • **the ~ world of espionage** el oscuro *or* misterioso mundo del espionaje
shady ['ʃeɪdɪ] (ADJ) (COMPAR: **shadier**, SUPERL: **shadiest**) **1** (= *shaded*) [*place*] sombreado • **it's ~ here** aquí hay sombra • **under a ~ tree** a la sombra de un árbol frondoso
2* (= *dubious*) [*person*] dudoso; [*deal*] turbio, chueco (*Mex**)
shaft [ʃɑ:ft] (N) **1** (= *stem, handle*) [*of arrow, spear*] astil *m*; [*of tool, golf club etc*] mango *m*; [*of cart etc*] vara *f* • **a ~ of light** un rayo de luz • **drive ~** (*Tech*) árbol *m* motor
2 [*of mine, lift etc*] pozo *m*
(VT)**‡ (= *have sex with*) joder**‡ • **we'll be ~ed if that happens** como pase eso estamos jodidos**‡
shag[1] [ʃæg] (N) tabaco *m* picado
shag[2] [ʃæg] (N) (*Orn*) cormorán *m* moñudo
shag[3]**‡ [ʃæg] (*Brit*) (N) polvo**‡ *m* • **to have a ~**‡ echar un polvo**‡
(VT) joder**‡
(VI) joder**‡
shag[4] [ʃæg] (N) (= *carpet*) tripe *m*
shagged‡ [ʃægd] (ADJ) (*also* **shagged out**) hecho polvo*

shaggy ['ʃægɪ] (ADJ) (COMPAR: **shaggier**, SUPERL: **shaggiest**) [*hair, beard, mane*] greñudo; [*fur, eyebrows, animal*] peludo; [*carpet, rug*] de mucho pelo; [*person*] melenudo, greñudo • **~ dog story** chiste *m* largo y pesado
shagreen [ʃæ'gri:n] (N) chagrín *m*, zapa *f*
Shah [ʃɑ:] (N) cha *m*
shake [ʃeɪk] (VB: PT: **shook**, PP: **shaken**) (N)
1 (= *act of shaking*) sacudida *f* • **to give sth/sb a ~**: • **she gave the tin a ~** agitó la lata • **I gave the boy a good ~** zarandeé *or* sacudí bien al chico • **she declined the drink with a ~ of her head** rechazó la copa moviendo la cabeza *or* con un movimiento de la cabeza • **he gave a puzzled ~ of his head** movió la cabeza confundido • IDIOMS: • **in two ~s*** • **in a brace of ~s*** en un santiamén*, en un abrir y cerrar de ojos* • **no great ~s***: • **he's no great ~s as a swimmer** *or* **at swimming*** no es nada del otro mundo *or* del otro jueves nadando*
2 the shakes el tembleque*, la tembladera* • **to get the ~s**: • **I got a bad case of the ~s** me entró un tembleque* *or* una tembladera* muy fuerte • **to have the ~s** tener el tembleque* *or* la tembladera*
3 (*also* **milkshake**) batido *m*
4 (= *small amount*) [*of liquid*] chorro *m*; [*of salt, sugar*] pizca *f*
(VT) **1** (= *agitate*) [+ *bottle, tin, dice, cocktail*] agitar; [+ *towel, duster*] sacudir; [+ *head*] mover; [+ *building*] hacer temblar, sacudir; [+ *person*] zarandear, sacudir • **"shake well before use"** "agítese bien antes de usar" • **a fit of coughing that shook his entire body** un ataque de tos que le sacudió *or* le estremeció todo el cuerpo • **high winds shook the trees** fuertes vientos sacudieron los árboles • **to ~ hands** estrecharse la mano • **to ~ hands with sb** estrechar la mano a algn • **to ~ one's head** (*in refusal*) negar con la cabeza; (*in disbelief*) mover la cabeza con gesto incrédulo; (*in dismay*) mover la cabeza con gesto de disgusto • **I shook the snow off my coat** me sacudí la nieve del abrigo • **to ~ o.s.**: • **the dog shook itself** el perro se sacudió • **she tried to hug him but he shook himself free** intentó abrazarlo pero él se la sacudió de encima • **she shook some change out of her purse** sacudió el monedero para sacar calderilla • IDIOM: • **~ a leg!*** ¡ponte las pilas!*, ¡muévete!*
2 (= *wave*) [+ *stick, paper*] blandir, agitar • **to ~ one's finger at sb** señalar a algn agitando el dedo • **to ~ one's fist at sb** amenazar a algn con el puño
3 (*fig*) (= *weaken*) [+ *faith*] debilitar; [+ *resolve*] afectar; (= *impair, upset, shock*) afectar; (= *disconcert*) desconcertar • **the firm's reputation has been badly ~n** la reputación de la empresa se ha visto muy afectada • **he was ~n by the news of her death** la noticia de su muerte lo afectó mucho *or* lo conmocionó • **he needs to be ~n out of his smugness** necesita que se le bajen esos humos • **it shook me rigid** me dejó pasmado *or* helado • **seven days that shook the world** siete días que conmocionaron al mundo
(VI) **1** (= *tremble*) [*ground, building*] temblar, estremecerse; [*person, animal, voice*] temblar • **I was shaking all over** me temblaba todo el cuerpo • **he was shaking with rage/fear/cold** estaba temblando de rabia/miedo/frío • **her voice shook with rage** la voz le temblaba de rabia • **to ~ with laughter** caerse de risa • IDIOM: • **to ~ like a leaf** temblar como un flan *or* una hoja
2 • **to ~ on sth**: • **the two men shook on it** los

dos hombres cerraron el trato con un apretón de manos • **let's ~ on it** venga esa mano

▸ **shake down** (VT + ADV) **1** [+ *fruit, snow*] hacer caer, sacudir; [+ *thermometer*] agitar (*para bajar la temperatura*)
2 (*US‡*) • **to ~ sb down** (= *rob*) sacar dinero a algn, estafar *or* timar a algn • **they shook him down for 5,000 dollars** le sacaron 5.000 dólares; (= *search*) • **to ~ sb down for weapons** cachear a algn en busca de armas
(VI + ADV)* **1** (= *settle for sleep*) acostarse, echarse a dormir
2 (= *settle in*) adaptarse • **I'll give them a few weeks to see how they ~ down** les daré unas semanas para ver cómo se adaptan

▸ **shake off** (VT + ADV) **1** (*lit*) [+ *water, snow, dust*] sacudir • **he grabbed my arm, I shook him off** me agarró por el brazo, yo me lo sacudí de encima
2 (*fig*) [+ *pursuer*] zafarse de, dar esquinazo a; [+ *illness*] deshacerse de, librarse de; [+ *cold, habit*] quitarse (de encima); [+ *depression*] salir de

▸ **shake out** (VT + ADV) [+ *tablecloth, bedding, rug*] sacudir • **I took off my boot and shook out a stone** me quité la bota y la sacudí para sacar una piedra • **she pulled her hat off and shook out her hair** se quitó el sombrero y se soltó el pelo

▸ **shake up** (VT + ADV) **1** [+ *bottle*] agitar; [+ *pillow*] sacudir
2 (= *upset*) conmocionar • **she was badly ~n up** estaba muy conmocionada *or* afectada • **he was ~n up but not hurt** estaba en estado de shock, pero ileso
3 (= *rouse, stir*) [+ *person*] espabilar, despabilar
4 (= *reform*) [+ *company*] reorganizar, reestructurar; [+ *system*] reformar • **you need to ~ up your ideas a bit!** ¡tienes que replantearte las ideas!

shakedown [ˈʃeɪkdaʊn] (N) **1** (= *shaking*) sacudida *f*
2 (*Brit*) (= *bed*) camastro *m*, cama *f* improvisada
3* (*before noun*) • **a ~ cruise/flight** una travesía/un vuelo de prueba
4 (*US**) (= *swindle*) estafa *f*, timo *m*; (= *search*) • **to give sth a ~** registrar algo

shaken [ˈʃeɪkən] (PP) *of* **shake**

shake-out [ˈʃeɪkaʊt] (N) [*of company*] reorganización *f*, reestructuración *f*; [*of workforce*] reducción *f*

shaker [ˈʃeɪkəʳ] (N) (= *cocktail shaker*) coctelera *f*

Shakespeare [ˈʃeɪkspɪəʳ] (N) Shakespeare, Chéspir

Shakespearean, Shakespearian [ʃeɪksˈpɪərɪən] (ADJ) shakespeariano

shake-up [ˈʃeɪkʌp] (N) [*of company, system*] reorganización *f*, reestructuración *f* • **today a cabinet shake-up was announced** hoy se anunció una reestructuración *or* remodelación del gabinete ministerial

shakily [ˈʃeɪkɪlɪ] (ADV) [*speak*] con voz temblorosa; [*walk*] con paso vacilante; [*write*] con mano temblorosa • **the play started ~** el principio de la obra fue flojo

shakiness [ˈʃeɪkɪnɪs] (N) **1** (= *trembling*) [*of person, legs*] temblor *m*
2 (= *wobbliness*) [*of table, chair*] inestabilidad *f*
3 (= *weakness*) [*of person*] debilidad *f*
4 (*fig*) (= *uncertainty*) [*of health, memory*] fragilidad *f*, precariedad *f*; [*of finances*] precariedad *f*; [*of knowledge*] deficiencia *f*

shaking [ˈʃeɪkɪŋ] (N) **1** (= *trembling*) temblor *m*
2 (= *jolting*) • **to give sb a good ~** zarandear bien a algn, sacudir violentamente a algn

shako [ˈʃækəʊ] (N) (PL: **shakos** *or* **shakoes**) chacó *m*

shaky [ˈʃeɪkɪ] (ADJ) (COMPAR: **shakier**, SUPERL: **shakiest**) **1** (= *trembling*) [*person, legs*] tembloroso
2 (= *wobbly*) inestable, poco firme
3 (= *weak*) [*person*] débil
4 (*fig*) (= *uncertain*) [*health, memory*] frágil, precario; [*finances*] precario; [*knowledge*] deficiente, flojo • **my Spanish is rather ~** mi español es bastante flojo

shale [ʃeɪl] (N) esquisto *m*
(CPD) ▸ **shale gas** gas *m* de esquisto ▸ **shale oil** petróleo *m* de esquisto

shall [ʃæl] (MODAL VB) **1** (*used to form 1st person in future tense and questions*) • **I ~ go** yo iré • **no I ~ not (come)** • **no I shan't (come)** no, yo no (vendré *or* voy a venir) • **~ I go now?** ¿me voy ahora? • **let's go in, ~ we?** ¿entramos? • **~ we let him?** ¿se lo permitimos? • **~ we hear from you soon?** ¿te pondrás en contacto pronto?
2 (*in commands, emphatic*) • **you ~ pay for this!** ¡me las vas a pagar! • **"but I wanted to see him" — "and so you ~"** —pero quería verle —y le vas a ver

shallot [ʃəˈlɒt] (N) chalote *m*

shallow [ˈʃæləʊ] (ADJ) (COMPAR: **shallower**, SUPERL: **shallowest**) **1** (*gen*) poco profundo, playo (*S. Cone*); [*dish etc*] llano • **the ~ end** (*of swimming pool*) la parte poco profunda
2 [*breathing*] superficial
3 [*person, mind, character*] superficial; [*argument, novel, film*] superficial, trivial
(NPL) **shallows** bajío *msing*, bajos *mpl*

shallowly [ˈʃæləʊlɪ] (ADV) • **to breathe ~** respirar superficialmente

shallowness [ˈʃæləʊnɪs] (N) **1** [*of water, pool*] poca profundidad *f*
2 [*of breathing*] superficialidad *f*
3 [*of person*] superficialidad *f*

shalom [ʃæˈlɒm] (EXCL) *palabra hebrea que se utiliza como saludo*

shalt†† [ʃælt] (VB) *2nd pers sing of* **shall**

sham [ʃæm] (ADJ) falso, fingido
(N) **1** (= *imposture*) farsa *f* • **it was all a ~** fue una farsa, fue pura pantalla (*Mex*)
2 (= *person*) impostor(a) *m/f*
(VT) fingir, simular • **to ~ illness** fingirse enfermo
(VI) fingir, fingirse • **he's just ~ming** lo está fingiendo

shaman [ˈʃæmən] (N) chamán *m*

shamanism [ˈʃæməˌnɪzəm] (N) chamanismo *m*

shamateur* [ˈʃæmətəʳ] (N) amateur *mf* fingido/a

shamble [ˈʃæmbl] (VI) (*also* **shamble along**) andar arrastrando los pies • **he ~d across to the window** fue arrastrando los pies a la ventana

shambles [ˈʃæmblz] (NSING) (= *scene of confusion*) desorden *m*, confusión *f* • **this room is a ~!** ¡esta habitación está hecha un desastre! • **the place was a ~** el lugar quedó hecho pedazos • **the game was a ~** el partido fue desastroso

shambolic* [ʃæmˈbɒlɪk] (ADJ) caótico

shame [ʃeɪm] (N) **1** (= *guilt*) vergüenza *f*, pena *f* (*LAm*) • **she has no sense of ~** no tiene vergüenza ninguna • **to put sb to ~** (*fig*) poner a algn en evidencia • **to put sth to ~** (*fig*) dejar algo en la sombra • **the ~ of it!** ¡qué vergüenza! • **~ (on you)!** ¡qué vergüenza!, ¡vergüenza debería darte!
2 (= *loss of respect*) deshonra *f* • **to bring ~ upon sb** deshonrar a algn
3 (= *pity*) lástima *f*, pena *f* • **it's a ~ that …** es una lástima *or* pena que (+ *subjun*) • **what a ~!** ¡qué lástima!, ¡qué pena!
(VT) **1** (= *cause to feel shame*) avergonzar • **to ~ sb into/out of doing sth** hacer avergonzarse a algn para que haga/no haga algo
2 (= *cause loss of respect for*) deshonrar

shamefaced [ˈʃeɪmfeɪst] (ADJ) avergonzado, apenado (*LAm*)

shamefacedly [ˈʃeɪmfeɪsɪdlɪ] (ADV) con vergüenza, apenadamente (*LAm*)

shamefacedness [ˈʃeɪmfeɪstnɪs] (N) vergüenza *f*, pena *f* (*LAm*)

shameful [ˈʃeɪmfʊl] (ADJ) vergonzoso • **how ~!** ¡qué vergüenza!

shamefully [ˈʃeɪmfəlɪ] (ADV) vergonzosamente • **~ ignorant** tan ignorante que da/daba *etc* vergüenza • **they are ~ underpaid** se les paga terriblemente mal, tienen un sueldo de vergüenza

shamefulness [ˈʃeɪmfʊlnɪs] (N) vergüenza *f*, lo vergonzoso

shameless [ˈʃeɪmlɪs] (ADJ) descarado, desvergonzado

shamelessly [ˈʃeɪmlɪslɪ] (ADV) descaradamente, desvergonzadamente

shamelessness [ˈʃeɪmlɪsnɪs] (N) descaro *m*, desvergüenza *f*

shaming [ˈʃeɪmɪŋ] (ADJ) vergonzoso • **this is too ~!** ¡qué vergüenza!

shammy* [ˈʃæmɪ] (N) gamuza *f*

shampoo [ʃæmˈpuː] (N) champú *m* • **a ~ and set** un lavado y marcado
(VT) [+ *carpet*] lavar con champú • **I ~ my hair twice a week** me lavo el pelo dos veces por semana

shamrock [ˈʃæmrɒk] (N) trébol *m*

shandy [ˈʃændɪ] (N) cerveza *f* con gaseosa, clara *f* (*Sp*)

shandygaff [ˈʃændɪˌgæf] (N) (*US*) = **shandy**

Shanghai [ʃæŋˈhaɪ] (N) Shanghai *m*

shanghai* [ʃæŋˈhaɪ] (VT) • **to ~ sb** (*Naut††*) narcotizar *or* emborrachar a algn y llevarle como marinero; (*fig*) secuestrar a algn

Shangri-la [ˈʃæŋrɪˈlɑː] (N) jauja *f*, paraíso *m* terrestre

shank [ʃæŋk] (N) (= *part of leg*) caña *f*; (= *bird's leg*) zanca *f*; (*Bot*) tallo *m*; (= *handle*) mango *m*; **shanks*** piernas *fpl* • IDIOM: • **to go on** *or* **by Shanks's pony** (*hum*) ir en el coche de San Francisco, ir a golpe de calcetín

shan't [ʃɑːnt] = **shall not**

shantung [ʃænˈtʌŋ] (N) shantung *m*

shanty¹ [ˈʃæntɪ] (N) (*Brit*) (*also* **sea shanty**) saloma *f*

shanty² [ˈʃæntɪ] (N) chabola *f*, jacal *m* (*Mex*), bohío *m* (*CAm*), callampa *f* (*Chile*)

shantytown [ˈʃæntɪˌtaʊn] (N) chabolas *fpl* (*Sp*), villa *f* miseria (*Mex*), (población *f*) callampa *f* (*Chile*), ciudad *f* perdida (*Mex*), colonia *f* proletaria (*Mex*), pueblo *m* joven (*Peru*), cantegriles *mpl* (*Uru*), ranchitos *mpl* (*Ven*)

SHAPE [ʃeɪp] (N ABBR) (= **Supreme Headquarters Allied Powers Europe**) *cuartel general de las fuerzas aliadas en Europa*

shape [ʃeɪp] (N) **1** (= *outline*) forma *f*, figura *f*; (= *figure*) [*of person*] silueta *f*, figura *f* • **what ~ is it?** ¿de qué forma es? • **all ~s and sizes** todas las formas • **universities come in all ~s and sizes** (*fig*) hay universidades de todo tipo • **it is rectangular in ~** es de forma rectangular • **in the ~ of …** (*fig*) en forma de … • **to bend** *or* **twist sth into ~** dar forma a algo doblándolo • **to hammer sth into ~** dar forma a algo a martillazos • **to lose its ~** [*sweater etc*] perder la forma • **to bend** *or* **twist sth out of ~** deformar algo doblándolo • **to take ~** cobrar forma • **to take the ~ of sth** cobrar *or* tomar la forma de algo
2 (= *undefined object*) forma *f*, bulto *m*; (= *striking object*) figura *f* • **a ~ loomed up out of the fog/darkness** una forma *or* un bulto surgió de la niebla/la oscuridad • **the great grey ~ of a tank rolled out of the village** la imponente figura gris de un tanque salió

S

del pueblo
3 (= *nature, appearance*) estructura *f*, configuración *f* • **the future ~ of industry** la futura estructura *or* configuración de la industria • **I can't bear gardening in any ~ or form** no aguanto la jardinería bajo ningún concepto • **the ~ of things to come** lo que nos depara el mañana • **to take ~** tomar forma
4 (= *mould*) molde *m* • **use star ~s to cut out the biscuits** utilice moldes en forma de estrella para cortar las galletas
5 (= *condition*) forma *f* (física), estado *m* físico • **to be in bad ~** [*person*] estar en mala forma (física); [*object*] estar en mal estado • **to be in good ~** [*person*] estar en buena forma (física); [*object*] estar en buen estado • **to be in ~** [*person*] estar en buena forma • **to get o.s. into ~** ponerse en forma • **to keep in ~** mantenerse en forma • **to knock** *or* **lick** *or* **whip sth/sb into ~** (*fig*) poner algo/a algn a punto • **to be out of ~** [*person*] estar en mala forma
VT **1** (*lit*) (= *mould*) dar forma a, formar
2 (*fig*) (= *influence, determine*) conformar, determinar • **the forces that have ~d the 20th century** los elementos que han conformado *or* configurado el siglo XX • **democracy is shaping the future of Western Europe** la democracia está determinando el futuro de Europa Occidental
3 (= *prepare*) [+ *plan*] trazar • **to ~ a plan of action** trazar un plan de acción
▸ **shape up** VI + ADV **1** (= *progress*) [*person*] ir, marchar; [*campaign, plan*] desarrollarse • **how are the new staff shaping up?** ¿cómo va *or* marcha el personal nuevo? • **to ~ up well** ir bien, marchar bien • **it's shaping up as one of the most intensive sales campaigns ever** se perfila *or* se está desarrollando como una de las campañas de ventas más agresiva de la historia • **it's shaping up to be a terrible winter** (*esp US*) promete ser un invierno muy crudo, ya se perfila como un invierno muy crudo
2 (= *improve*) (*esp US*) espabilarse, enmendarse • **you'd better ~ up or you won't have a job!** ¡más vale que te espabiles o no tendrás trabajo! • IDIOM: • **~ up or ship out!** (*esp US**) ¡o te pones las pilas o te largas!*
3 (= *get fit*) (*esp US*) ponerse en forma
shaped [ˈʃeɪpt] ADJ • **oddly ~** con forma rara • **~ like sth** en forma de algo
-shaped [ˈʃeɪpt] ADJ (*ending in compounds*) en forma de ... • **heart-shaped** en forma de corazón; ▹ **pear-shaped**
shapeless [ˈʃeɪplɪs] ADJ sin forma definida, informe (*frm*)
shapelessness [ˈʃeɪplɪsnɪs] N falta *f* de forma definida, lo informe (*frm*)
shapeliness [ˈʃeɪplɪnɪs] N [*of object*] proporción *f*; [*of woman*] figura *f* bonita, buen cuerpo *m*
shapely [ˈʃeɪplɪ] ADJ [*object*] proporcionado, bien formado; [*woman*] con una bonita figura, de buen cuerpo • **~ legs** piernas torneadas
shard [ʃɑːd] N tiesto *m*, casco *m*, fragmento *m*
share¹ [ʃɛəʳ] N **1** (= *portion*) parte *f*, porción *f* • **a ~ of** *or* **in the profits** una proporción de las ganancias • **how much will my ~ be?** ¿cuánto me corresponderá a mí? • **your ~ is £5** te tocan 5 libras • **to do one's (fair) ~ (of sth)** hacer lo que a uno le toca *or* corresponde (de algo) • **he doesn't do his ~** no hace todo lo que debiera, no hace todo lo que le toca *or* corresponde • **to have a ~ in sth** participar en algo • **we've had our ~ of misfortunes** hemos sufrido bastante infortunio, hemos sufrido lo nuestro • **market ~** cuota *f* del mercado • **to take a ~ in doing sth** hacer su parte en algo • IDIOM: • **the lion's ~** la parte del león
2 (*Econ*) acción *f*
VT **1** (= *split, divide*) [+ *resource, benefit*] repartir, dividir, partir • **would you like to ~ the bottle with me?** ¿quieres compartir la botella conmigo? • **a ~d room** una habitación compartida
2 (= *accept equally*) [+ *duty, responsibility, task*] compartir, corresponsabilizarse de • **to ~ the blame** [*one person*] aceptar su parte de culpa; [*more than one person*] corresponsabilizarse de la culpa
3 (= *have in common*) [+ *characteristic, quality*] compartir, tener en común; [+ *experience, opinion*] compartir • **two nations who ~ a common language** dos naciones que tienen en común *or* comparten la misma lengua • **I do not ~ that view** no comparto ese criterio
4 (= *tell, relate*) [+ *piece of news, thought*] contar, compartir, hacer partícipe de (*frm*) (**with** a) • **it can be beneficial to ~ your feelings with someone you trust** puede resultar beneficioso compartir *or* contar tus sentimientos a alguien de confianza
VI compartir (**with** con) • **I ~ with three other women** (*room, flat etc*) vivo con otras tres mujeres • **to ~ in sth** participar en algo • IDIOM: • **~ and ~ alike** todos por igual
CPD ▸ **share capital** capital *m* social en acciones ▸ **share certificate** (certificado *m or* título *m* de una) acción *f* ▸ **share earnings** dividendos *mpl* ▸ **share index** índice *m* de la Bolsa ▸ **share issue** emisión *f* de acciones ▸ **share offer** oferta *f* de acciones ▸ **share option** stock option *f*, opción *f* sobre acciones ▸ **share ownership** propiedad *f* de acciones ▸ **share premium** prima *f* de emisión ▸ **share price** precio *m* de las acciones
▸ **share out** VT + ADV repartir, distribuir
share² [ʃɛəʳ] N (*Agr*) (= *ploughshare*) reja *f*
sharecropper [ˈʃɛəˌkrɒpəʳ] N (*esp US*) aparcero/a *m/f*, mediero/a *m/f* (*Mex*)
sharecropping [ˈʃɛəˌkrɒpɪŋ] N (*esp US*) aparcería *f*
shared [ʃɛəd] ADJ (*gen*) compartido; [*facilities etc*] comunitario
shareholder [ˈʃɛəˌhəʊldəʳ] N accionista *mf*
shareholding [ˈʃɛəˌhəʊldɪŋ] N accionariado *m*
share-out [ˈʃɛəraʊt] N reparto *m*
shareware [ˈʃɛəʳˌwɛəʳ] N (*Comput*) shareware *m*
Sharia, sharia [ʃəˈriːə] N charia *f*
ADJ [*law, court*] de la charia
shark [ʃɑːk] N **1** (= *fish*) tiburón *m*
2* (= *swindler*) estafador(a) *m/f*
shark-infested [ʃɑːkɪnˈfestɪd] ADJ infestado de tiburones
sharkskin [ˈʃɑːkskɪn] N zapa *f*
sharon [ˈʃærən] N (*also* **sharon fruit**) sharon *m*
sharp [ʃɑːp] ADJ (COMPAR: **sharper**, SUPERL: **sharpest**) **1** (= *not blunt*) [*edge*] afilado; [*needle*] puntiagudo • **to have a ~ point** ser muy puntiagudo • **the stick ended in a ~ point** el palo acababa en una punta afilada • IDIOM: • **to be at the ~ end*** estar en primera línea de fuego • **they are living at the ~ end of the recession** son los que se llevan la peor parte de la recesión, son los más afectados por la recesión
2 (= *abrupt, acute*) [*bend, angle*] cerrado; [*rise, drop, turn by car*] brusco • **he made a ~ turn to the left** giró bruscamente a la izquierda
3 (*of person*) (= *alert*) avispado, perspicaz; (= *unscrupulous*) listo, vivo; [*mind*] agudo, perspicaz • **you'll have to be ~er than that** tendrás que espabilarte • **he's as ~ as they come** es de lo más listo *or* vivo • **his ~ eyes spotted a free seat** sus ojos de lince vieron un asiento libre • **I have to keep a ~ eye on him** con él tengo que estar ojo avizor • **~ practice** artimañas *fpl* • IDIOM: • **to be as ~ as a needle** ser más listo que el hambre
4 (= *brusque*) [*retort*] seco, cortante; [*rebuke, tone*] áspero, severo; [*tongue*] afilada, mordaz • **to have a ~ tongue** tener la lengua afilada, tener una lengua viperina • **to be ~ with sb** ser seco *or* cortante con algn
5 (= *strong*) [*taste*] ácido; [*smell, cheese*] fuerte
6 (= *clear, well-defined*) [*outline, image*] nítido; [*contrast*] claro, marcado; [*sound*] claro; [*features*] marcado, anguloso • **these issues have been brought into ~ focus by the economic crisis** la crisis económica ha situado estos temas en primer plano
7 (= *intense*) [*pain*] agudo; [*cold, wind*] cortante; [*frost*] fuerte • **a ~ blow to the head** un fuerte golpe en la cabeza • **with a ~ cry she jumped back** soltando un grito agudo retrocedió de un salto
8* (= *stylish*) [*suit*] elegante • **he was a ~ dresser** vestía con mucha elegancia
9 (*Mus*) (= *raised a semitone*) sostenido; (= *too high*) demasiado alto • **C ~** do *m* sostenido
ADV **1** (= *quickly, abruptly*) • **and be** *or* **look ~ about it!** ¡y date prisa! • **look ~!** ¡rápido!, ¡apúrate! (*LAm*) • **to pull up ~** parar en seco • **you turn ~ left at the lights** al llegar al semáforo se tuerce muy cerrado a la izquierda
2 (= *precisely*) en punto • **at five o'clock ~** a las cinco en punto
3 (*Mus*) demasiado alto • **she was singing/ playing ~** cantaba/tocaba demasiado alto
N **1** (*Mus*) sostenido *m*
2 (= *con artist*) estafador(a) *m/f*; (= *card-sharp*) fullero/a *m/f*, tramposo/a *m/f*
sharp-edged [ˈʃɑːpˈedʒd] ADJ afilado, de filo cortante
sharpen [ˈʃɑːpən] VT **1** (= *make sharp*) [+ *tool, blade*] afilar; [+ *pencil*] sacar punta a, afilar • **to ~ sth to a point** afilar algo hasta sacarle punta
2 (= *intensify, increase*) [+ *reactions*] agudizar; [+ *resolve*] aumentar; [+ *contrast*] marcar; [+ *appetite*] abrir; [+ *skills*] mejorar • **this will ~ awareness of other people's needs** esto hará que se tome más conciencia de las necesidades de los demás • **to ~ one's wits** espabilarse
3 (= *make clearer*) [+ *image*] definir, hacer más nítido
VI [*voice*] volverse más agudo; [*desire*] avivarse; [*pain*] agudizarse
▸ **sharpen up** VT + ADV [+ *person*] espabilar • **to ~ up one's act** enmendarse
VI + ADV [*person*] espabilarse
sharpener [ˈʃɑːpnəʳ] N (*for pencil*) sacapuntas *m inv*; (*for knife*) afilador *m*
sharper [ˈʃɑːpəʳ] N (= *con artist*) estafador(a) *m/f*; (= *card-sharp*) fullero/a *m/f*, tramposo/a *m/f*
sharp-eyed [ˈʃɑːpˈaɪd] ADJ de vista aguda
sharp-faced [ˈʃɑːpˈfeɪst] ADJ, **sharp-featured** [ˈʃɑːpˈfiːtʃəd] ADJ de facciones angulosas
sharpish* [ˈʃɑːpɪʃ] ADV (= *quickly*) rapidito* • **it needs to be ready ~** hay que hacerlo rapidito
sharply [ˈʃɑːplɪ] ADV **1** (= *abruptly*) [*fall, rise, turn, brake*] bruscamente • **the road turned ~ left** la carretera giraba bruscamente hacia la izquierda • **he drew in his breath ~** inspiró

S

bruscamente
2 (= *clearly*) marcadamente, claramente • **this attitude contrasts ~ with his caring image** esta actitud contrasta marcadamente *or* claramente con su imagen de hombre humanitario • **the party is ~ divided over this issue** el partido está claramente dividido con respecto a este asunto
3 (= *brusquely*) con aspereza • **he spoke to me quite ~** me habló con bastante aspereza
4 (= *severely*) [*criticize*] severamente, con dureza
5 (= *hard*) fuertemente • **the ball struck him ~ on the head** la pelota le golpeó fuertemente en la cabeza

sharpness ['ʃɑːpnɪs] N **1** [*of knife, point*] lo afilado; [*of edge*] lo afilado, lo cortante
2 (= *abruptness*) [*of bend*] lo cerrado; [*of turn*] brusquedad *f*
3 (= *clarity*) [*of outline, image*] nitidez *f*, definición *f*; [*of contrast*] lo marcado
4 (= *keenness*) [*of mind*] perspicacia *f*, agudeza *f*; [*of reflexes*] rapidez *f* • **his eyes hadn't lost any of their ~** sus ojos no habían perdido nada de su agudeza
5 (= *severity*) [*of pain*] agudeza *f*, intensidad *f*; [*of remark, tone*] aspereza *f*; [*of tongue*] mordacidad *f* • **there was a note of ~ in his voice** se notaba cierta aspereza en su tono • **there is a ~ in the air** empieza a notarse el frío
6 [*of taste*] acidez *f*

sharpshooter ['ʃɑːpʃuːtə^r] N (*esp US*) tirador(a) *m/f* de primera

sharp-sighted ['ʃɑːp'saɪtɪd] ADJ = sharp-eyed

sharp-tempered [ʃɑːp'tempəd] ADJ de genio arisco

sharp-tongued ['ʃɑːp'tʌŋd] ADJ de lengua mordaz

sharp-witted ['ʃɑːp'wɪtɪd] ADJ perspicaz, despabilado

shat** [ʃæt] PT, PP *of* shit

shatter ['ʃætə^r] VT **1** (= *break*) romper en pedazos *or* añicos, hacer pedazos *or* añicos
2 (*fig*) • **to ~ sb's health/hopes** quebrantar la salud/frustrar las esperanzas de algn • **I was ~ed to hear it** al saberlo quedé estupefacto • **she was ~ed by his death** su muerte la dejó destrozada
VI **1** (= *break*) hacerse pedazos, hacerse añicos
2 (*fig*) [*health*] quebrantarse; [*hopes*] frustrarse

shattered ['ʃætəd] ADJ **1*** (= *exhausted*) hecho polvo*
2 (= *grief-stricken*) trastornado, destrozado; (= *aghast, overwhelmed*) abrumado, confundido

shattering ['ʃætərɪŋ] ADJ [*attack, defeat*] aplastante; [*experience, news*] pasmoso • **it was a ~ blow to his hopes** deshizo sus esperanzas

shatterproof ['ʃætəpruːf] ADJ inastillable

shave [ʃeɪv] (VB: PT: **shaved**, PP: **shaved**, **shaven**) N • **to have a ~** afeitarse, rasurarse (*esp LAm*) • **to have a close** *or* **narrow ~** (*fig*) salvarse de milagro *or* por los pelos • **that was a close ~!** ¡qué poco le ha faltado!, ¡(ha sido) por los pelos!
VT [+ *person, face*] afeitar, rasurar (*esp LAm*); [+ *wood*] cepillar; (*fig*) (= *skim, graze*) pasar rozando • **to ~ (off) one's beard** afeitarse la barba • **to ~ one's legs** afeitarse las piernas
VI [*person*] afeitarse, rasurarse (*esp LAm*)
▸ **shave off** VT + ADV • **to ~ off one's beard** afeitarse la barba

shaven ['ʃeɪvn] PP *of* shave
ADJ afeitado

shaver ['ʃeɪvə^r] N **1** (*electric*) máquina *f* de afeitar, rasuradora *f* eléctrica (*Mex*)
2 • **young ~** (*†) muchachuelo *m*, rapaz *m*, chaval* *m*
CPD ▸ **shaver outlet** (*US*), **shaver point** enchufe *m* para la máquina de afeitar, enchufe *m* para la rasuradora (*Mex*)

Shavian ['ʃeɪvɪən] ADJ shaviano, típico de G. B. Shaw

shaving ['ʃeɪvɪŋ] N **1** (= *act of shaving*) afeitado *m* • **~ is a nuisance** afeitarse es una lata
2 (= *piece of wood, metal etc*) viruta *f*
CPD ▸ **shaving brush** brocha *f* de afeitar ▸ **shaving cream** crema *f* de afeitar ▸ **shaving foam** espuma *f* de afeitar ▸ **shaving gel** gel *m* de afeitar ▸ **shaving lotion** loción *f* para el afeitado ▸ **shaving mirror** espejo *m* de tocador (de aumento) ▸ **shaving point** enchufe *m* para máquinas de afeitar ▸ **shaving soap** jabón *m* de afeitar ▸ **shaving stick** barra *f* de jabón de afeitar

shawl [ʃɔːl] N chal *m*, rebozo *m* (*LAm*)

shawm [ʃɔːm] N chirimía *f*

she [ʃiː] PERS PRON **1** (*emphatic, to avoid ambiguity*) ella • **we went to the cinema but she didn't** nosotros fuimos al cine pero ella no • **it's she who ...** es ella quien ... • **you've got more money than she has** tienes más dinero que ella

Don't translate the subject pronoun when not emphasizing or clarifying:

• **she's very nice** es muy maja • **she's a teacher** es profesora
2 (*frm*) • **she who wishes to ...** quien desee ..., la que desee ...
N • **it's a she** (= *animal*) es hembra; (= *baby*) es una niña
CPD ▸ **she-bear** osa *f* ▸ **she-cat** gata *f*

s/he PRON (= *he or she*) él o ella

sheaf [ʃiːf] N (PL: **sheaves**) (*Agr*) gavilla *f*; [*of arrows*] haz *m*; [*of papers*] fajo *m*, manojo *m*

shear [ʃɪə^r] (PT: **sheared**, PP: **sheared**, **shorn**) VT [+ *sheep*] esquilar • **to be shorn of sth** (*fig*) quedar pelado de algo, quedar sin algo
VI (= *give way*) partirse, romperse
▸ **shear off** VT + ADV cortar • **the machine ~ed off two fingers** la máquina le cortó *or* (*frm*) cercenó dos dedos
VI + ADV (= *break off*) partirse, romperse
▸ **shear through** VI + PREP cortar

shearer ['ʃɪərə^r] N esquilador(a) *m/f*

shearing ['ʃɪərɪŋ] N esquileo *m*; **shearings** lana *fsing* esquilada
CPD ▸ **shearing machine** esquiladora *f*

shears [ʃɪəz] NPL (*for sheep*) tijeras *fpl* de esquilar; (*for hedges*) tijeras *fpl* de podar; (*for metals*) cizalla *fsing*

shearwater ['ʃɪə,wɔːtə^r] N pardela *f*

sheath [ʃiːθ] N (PL: **sheaths** [ʃiːðz]) **1** (*for sword*) vaina *f*, funda *f*
2 (*around cable*) cubierta *f*
3 (*Bio*) vaina *f*
4 (= *contraceptive*) preservativo *m*
CPD ▸ **sheath dress** vestido *m* tubo ▸ **sheath knife** cuchillo *m* de monte

sheathe [ʃiːð] VT envainar, enfundar (in en)

sheathing ['ʃiːðɪŋ] N revestimiento *m*, cubierta *f*

sheaves [ʃiːvz] NPL *of* sheaf

Sheba ['ʃiːbə] N Sabá • **Queen of ~** reina *f* de Sabá

shebang‡ [ʃə'bæŋ] N • **the whole ~** (= *the whole thing*) todo el tinglado*

shebeen [ʃɪ'biːn] N (*Irl, South Africa*) bar *m* clandestino

shed¹ [ʃed] (PT, PP: **shed**) VT **1** (= *get rid of*) [+ *clothes, fur, leaves, skin*] despojarse de; [+ *jobs*] suprimir, recortar • **our dog ~s hair all over the carpet** nuestro perro va soltando pelo por toda la moqueta • **to ~ one's clothes** desvestirse, quitarse la ropa, despojarse de la ropa (*frm*) • **the roof is built to ~ water** el techo está construido para que el agua no quede en él • **the lorry ~ its load** la carga cayó del camión • **to ~ one's inhibitions** desinhibirse
2 [+ *tears, blood*] derramar • **the ~ding of innocent blood** el derramamiento de sangre inocente • **those heroes that ~ their blood in the cause of freedom** aquellos héroes que entregaron sus vidas en pro de la libertad
3 (= *send out*) [+ *warmth*] dar; [+ *light*] echar • IDIOM: • **to ~ light on sth** (*fig*) arrojar luz sobre algo

shed² [ʃed] N (*in garden*) cobertizo *m*, galpón *m* (*S. Cone*); (*for cattle*) establo *m*; (*Ind, Rail*) nave *f*

she'd [ʃiːd] = she would, she had

sheen [ʃiːn] N brillo *m*, lustre *m*

sheeny ['ʃiːnɪ] ADJ brillante, lustroso

sheep [ʃiːp] N (*pl inv*) oveja *f* • IDIOMS: • **to be the black ~ of the family** ser la oveja negra de la familia • **to make ~'s eyes at sb** mirar a algn con ojos de cordero • **we must sort out** *or* **separate the ~ from the goats** tenemos que apartar *or* separar el grano de la paja
CPD ▸ **sheep dip** (baño *m*) desinfectante *m* para ovejas ▸ **sheep farm** granja *f* de ovejas, granja *f* ovina, granja *f* de ganado lanar ▸ **sheep farmer** criador(a) *m/f* de ganado lanar, ganadero/a *m/f* de ovejas ▸ **sheep farming** ganadería *f* ovina *or* lanar, cría *f* de ganado ovino *or* lanar ▸ **sheep run** pasto *m* de ovejas, dehesa *f* de ovejas ▸ **sheep station** granja *f* de ovejas ▸ **sheep track** cañada *f* (de pastoreo) ▸ **sheep worrying** acoso *m* de ovejas

sheepdog ['ʃiːpdɒg] N perro *m* pastor

sheepfold ['ʃiːpfəʊld] N redil *m*, aprisco *m*

sheepish ['ʃiːpɪʃ] ADJ avergonzado

sheepishly ['ʃiːpɪʃlɪ] ADV avergonzadamente

sheepishness ['ʃiːpɪʃnɪs] N vergüenza *f*

sheepmeat ['ʃiːpmiːt] N carne *f* de oveja

sheepshearer ['ʃiːp,ʃɪərə^r] N **1** (= *person*) esquilador(a) *m/f*
2 (= *machine*) esquiladora *f*

sheepskin ['ʃiːpskɪn] N zamarra *f*, piel *f* de carnero
CPD ▸ **sheepskin jacket** zamarra *f*

sheepwalk ['ʃiːpwɔːk] N = sheep run

sheer¹ [ʃɪə^r] ADJ (COMPAR: **sheerer**, SUPERL: **sheerest**) **1** (= *absolute*) puro, absoluto • **by ~ accident** • **by ~ chance** de pura casualidad • **in ~ desperation** en último extremo • **by ~ hard work** gracias simplemente al trabajo • **the ~ impossibility of ...** la total imposibilidad de ...; ▷ PURE
2 (= *transparent*) transparente, fino
3 (= *precipitous*) escarpado
ADV • **it falls ~ to the sea** baja sin obstáculo alguno hasta el mar • **it rises ~ for 100 metres** se levanta verticalmente unos 100 metros

sheer² [ʃɪə^r] VI • **to ~ away from a topic** desviarse de un tema, evitar hablar de un tema
▸ **sheer off** VI + ADV (*Naut*) [*ship*] desviarse; (*fig*) largarse

sheet [ʃiːt] N **1** (*also* **bedsheet**) sábana *f*
2 [*of metal, glass, plastic*] lámina *f*
3 [*of paper*] hoja *f*; [*of labels, stamps, stickers*] pliego *m*, hoja *f* • **an information ~** una hoja informativa • IDIOM: • **to start again with a clean ~** hacer borrón y cuenta nueva
4 [*of ice, water*] capa *f* • **a ~ of flame** una

cortina de fuego • **the rain was coming down in ~s** estaba cayendo una cortina de agua *or* lluvia, llovía a mares
5 (*Naut*) escota *f*
6 (*Press*) periódico *m*
7 • IDIOM: • **to keep a clean ~** (*Brit*) (*Ftbl*) mantener la portería imbatida, no encajar ningún gol
CPD ▸ **sheet anchor** (*Naut*) ancla *f* de la esperanza ▸ **sheet bend** nudo *m* de escota, vuelta *f* de escota ▸ **sheet feed** alimentador *m* de papel ▸ **sheet ice** capa *f* de hielo ▸ **sheet lightning** fucilazo *m* ▸ **sheet metal** metal *m* en lámina ▸ **sheet music** hojas *fpl* de partitura

sheeting ['ʃi:tɪŋ] N (= *cloth*) lencería *f* para sábanas; (= *metal*) laminado *m* metálico, chapa *f* metálica

sheik, sheikh [ʃeɪk] N jeque *m*

sheikdom, sheikhdom ['ʃeɪkdəm] N reino *m or* territorio *m* de un jeque

sheila* ['ʃi:lə] N (*Australia*) piva* *f*

shekel ['ʃekl] N (*Hist, Bible etc*) siclo *m*; **shekels*** pasta* *fsing*, parné‡ *msing*

sheldrake ['ʃeldreɪk] N, **shelduck** ['ʃeldʌk] N tadorna *f*

shelf [ʃelf] N (PL: **shelves**) **1** (*fixed to wall, in shop*) estante *m*, balda *f*; (*in cupboard*) tabla *f*, anaquel *m*; (*in oven*) parrilla *f* • **to buy a product off the ~** comprar un producto ya hecho • IDIOM: • **to be (left) on the ~** [*proposal etc*] quedar arrinconado; [*woman**] quedarse para vestir santos
2 (= *edge*) (*in rock face*) saliente *m*; (*underwater*) plataforma *f*
CPD ▸ **shelf life** (*Comm*) tiempo *m* de durabilidad antes de la venta • IDIOM: • **most pop stars have a very short ~ life** la mayoría de las estrellas del pop son flor de un día *or* tienen una carrera efímera ▸ **shelf mark** (*in library*) código *m* ▸ **shelf space** cantidad *f* de estanterías (*para exponer la mercancía*)

she'll [ʃi:l] = **she will, she shall**

shell [ʃel] N **1** [*of egg, nut*] cáscara *f*; [*of tortoise, turtle*] caparazón *m*, carapacho *m*; [*of snail, shellfish*] concha *f*, caracol *m* (*LAm*); [*of pea*] vaina *f*; [*of coconut*] cáscara *f* leñosa • IDIOMS: • **to come out of one's ~** (*fig*) salir del caparazón *or* (*LAm*) carapacho • **to crawl** *or* **go into one's ~** (*fig*) encerrarse *or* meterse en su concha, encerrarse *or* meterse en su caparazón
2 [*of building, vehicle, ship*] armazón *m or f*, casco *m*
3 (= *artillery round*) obús *m*, proyectil *m*; (*US*) [*of shotgun*] cartucho *m*
4 (*Culin*) [*of pie, flan*] masa *f*
VT **1** [+ *peas*] pelar, desvainar; [+ *nuts*] pelar, descascarar; [+ *mussels, cockles*] quitar la concha a; [+ *prawns*] pelar; [+ *eggs*] quitar la cáscara a • **~ed prawns** gambas *fpl* peladas • IDIOM: • **it's like** *or* **as easy as ~ing peas** es pan comido, es coser y cantar
2 (*Mil*) bombardear
CPD ▸ **shell game** (*US*) (*lit*) (= *trick*) *juego consistente en adivinar en cuál de tres cubiletes se esconde un objeto*, triles‡ *fpl*; (*fig*) (= *fraud*) artimaña *f* ▸ **shell hole** *hoyo que forma un obús al explotar* ▸ **shell shock** neurosis *f inv* de guerra ▸ **shell suit** *tipo de chandal*
▸ **shell out*** VI + ADV (= *pay*) soltar el dinero
VT + ADV [+ *money*] desembolsar • **to ~ out for sth** desembolsar para pagar algo

shellac [ʃə'læk] N goma *f* (laca *f*)

shelled [ʃeld] ADJ • **~ nuts** nueces *fpl* sin cáscara

shellfire ['ʃelfaɪəʳ] N = **shelling**

shellfish ['ʃelfɪʃ] N (PL: **shellfish**) (*Zool*) crustáceo *m*; (*as food*) marisco(s) *m(pl)*

shelling ['ʃelɪŋ] N bombardeo *m*

shellproof ['ʃelpru:f] ADJ a prueba de bombas

shell-shocked ['ʃelʃɒkt] ADJ que padece neurosis de guerra

shelter ['ʃeltəʳ] N **1** (= *protection*) protección *f*, refugio *m* • **there was no ~ from the rain/sun** no había dónde protegerse de la lluvia/del sol • **to seek ~ (from)** (*rain, sun*) buscar dónde protegerse (de); (*persecution*) buscar dónde refugiarse (de) • **to take ~** refugiarse, guarecerse • **we took ~ from the storm in a cave** nos refugiamos *or* nos cobijamos de la tormenta en una cueva
2 (= *accommodation*) alojamiento *m* • **to seek ~ for the night** buscar dónde pasar la noche
3 (= *construction*) (*on mountain*) refugio *m*, albergue *m*; (*for homeless people, battered women*) refugio *m*, centro *m* de acogida • **bus ~** marquesina *f* de autobús • **air-raid ~** refugio *m* antiaéreo
VT **1** (= *protect*) proteger (**from** de) • **a spot ~ed from the wind** un sitio protegido *or* al abrigo del viento
2 (*fig*) proteger (**from** de) • **you can't ~ your children from the outside world forever** no se puede proteger a nuestros hijos del mundo exterior eternamente
3 (= *hide*) [+ *fugitive, criminal*] esconder, ocultar, dar asilo a
VI refugiarse, guarecerse (**from** de) • **to ~ from the rain** refugiarse *or* guarecerse de la lluvia • **to ~ behind sth** (*fig*) escudarse en *or* tras algo, ampararse en algo

sheltered ['ʃeltəd] ADJ [*harbour, valley, garden*] protegido; [*industry*] protegido (contra la competencia extranjera) • **a ~ environment** (*fig*) un ambiente protegido • **she has led a very ~ life** ha tenido una vida muy protegida
CPD ▸ **sheltered accommodation, sheltered housing** alojamiento *m* vigilado • **she lives in ~ accommodation** *or* **housing** vive en alojamiento vigilado

shelve [ʃelv] VT (= *postpone*) dar carpetazo a
VI (= *slope away*) formar declive

shelves [ʃelvz] NPL *of* **shelf**

shelving ['ʃelvɪŋ] N estantería *f*

shemozzle* [ʃə'mɒzl] N (*Brit*) (= *confusion*) lío* *m*; (= *dispute*) bronca *f*, follón* *m*

shenanigans* [ʃə'nænɪgənz] NPL (= *trickery*) chanchullos* *mpl*; (= *mischief*) correrías* *fpl*, travesuras *fpl*; (= *rowdy fun*) bromas *fpl*

shepherd ['ʃepəd] N **1** pastor *m* • **the Good Shepherd** el Buen Pastor
2 (*also* **shepherd dog**) perro *m* pastor
VT • **to ~ children across a road** llevar niños a través de una calle, cruzar a los niños la calle • **to ~ sb in/out** acompañar a algn al entrar/salir • **to ~ sb around** hacer de guía para algn
CPD ▸ **shepherd boy** zagal *m* ▸ **shepherd's pie** pastel *m* de carne con patatas

shepherdess ['ʃepədɪs] N pastora *f*, zagala *f*

sherbert ['ʃɜ:bɜ:t] N = **sherbet**

sherbet ['ʃɜ:bət] N **1** (*Brit*) (= *powder*) polvos *mpl* azucarados
2 (*US*) (= *water ice*) sorbete *m*

sherd [ʃɜ:d] N = **shard**

sheriff ['ʃerɪf] N (*in US*) alguacil *m*, sheriff *m*; (*in England*) gobernador *m* civil; (*in Scotland*) juez *mf*
CPD ▸ **sheriff court** (*Scot*) tribunal *m* de distrito

Sherpa ['ʃɜ:pə] N (PL: **Sherpas** *or* **Sherpa**) sherpa *mf*

sherry ['ʃerɪ] N jerez *m*

she's [ʃi:z] = **she is, she has**

Shetland ['ʃetlənd] N las islas Shetland
CPD ▸ **the Shetland Islands, the Shetland Isles** las islas Shetland ▸ **Shetland pony** pony *m* de (las) Shetland ▸ **Shetland wool** lana *f* de las Shetland

shew†† [ʃəʊ] VT, VI = **show**

shewn†† [ʃəʊn] PP *of* **show**

shhh [ʃ:] EXCL ¡chitón!

Shia, Shiah ['ʃi:ə] N **1** (= *doctrine*) chiísmo *m*
2 (= *follower*) (*also* **Shia Muslim**) chiíta *mf*
ADJ chiíta

shiatsu [ʃi:'ætsu:] N shiatsu *m*, digitopuntura *f*

shibboleth ['ʃɪbəleθ] N (*Bible*) lema *m*, santo *m* y seña; (*fig*) dogma *m* hoy desacreditado, doctrina *f* que ha quedado anticuada

shield [ʃi:ld] N **1** (*armour*) (*also Her*) escudo *m*; (*Tech*) (*on machine etc*) blindaje *m*, capa *f* protectora
2 (*US*) (= *badge*) [*of policeman*] placa *f*
VT proteger • **to ~ sb from sth** proteger a algn de algo • **to ~ one's eyes** taparse los ojos

shieling ['ʃi:lɪŋ] N (*Scot*) (= *pasture*) pasto *m*, prado *m*; (= *hut*) choza *f*, cabaña *f*

shift [ʃɪft] N **1** (= *change*) cambio *m* • **there has been a ~ in attitudes on the part of consumers** ha habido un cambio de actitud por parte de los consumidores • **a ~ in weather patterns** un cambio en el comportamiento del tiempo • **there was a ~ in the wind** el viento cambió de dirección, se produjo un cambio de dirección del viento • **the ~ to a market economy** la transición hacia una economía de mercado • **some have problems making the ~ from one culture to another** algunos tienen problemas al hacer el cambio de una cultura a otra • IDIOM: • **to make ~ with/without sth** arreglárselas con/sin algo
2 (= *period of work*) turno *m*; (= *group of workers*) tanda *f* • **day/night ~** turno *m* de día/noche • **to work (in) ~s** trabajar por turnos • **I work an eight-hour ~** trabajo *or* hago turnos de ocho horas
3 (*US*) (*Aut*) (= *gear shift*) palanca *f* de cambio
4 (= *dress*) vestido *m* suelto; (= *undergarment*) combinación *f*, viso *m*
5 (*Geol*) desplazamiento *m*
VT **1** (= *change*) [+ *opinion, tactics, policy*] cambiar • **the result ~ed the balance of power in their favour** el resultado cambió el equilibrio político *or* inclinó la balanza del poder a su favor • **to ~ one's ground** cambiar de opinión *or* parecer • **to ~ one's position** cambiar de postura
2 (= *transfer*) • **she ~ed her weight to the other leg** cambió el peso a la otra pierna, volcó su peso sobre la otra pierna • **voters ~ed their allegiance** los votantes trasladaron su lealtad a otro partido • **to ~ the blame onto sb else** cargar a otro con la culpa, echar la culpa a otro • **they're trying to ~ the blame** intentan cargar a otro con la culpa, intentan echar *or* pasar la culpa a otro • **he ~ed his gaze to me** pasó a fijarse en mí
3 (= *move*) mover • **he ~ed the chair closer to the bed** movió la silla acercándola a la cama • **to ~ scenery** (*Theat*) cambiar el decorado • **~ yourself!*** ¡quítate del medio *or* de en medio!, ¡muévete!
4 (= *sell*) [+ *stock*] deshacerse de, vender
5 (= *get rid of*) [+ *cold*] quitarse (de encima); [+ *stain*] quitar
6 (*US*) (*Aut*) [+ *gear*] cambiar de
VI **1** (= *move*) [*person*] moverse; [*load, cargo*] correrse • **he ~ed uncomfortably in his seat** se removía incómodo en la silla • **she ~ed from one foot to the other** cambiaba de un pie a otro

2 (= *change, transfer*) [*wind*] cambiar de dirección; [*attitudes, mood*] cambiar • **world attention has ~ed away from China** el foco de atención mundial se ha alejado de China • **the emphasis now has ~ed to preventive medicine** ahora se hace más hincapié en la medicina preventiva • **the scene ~s to Burgos** la escena se traslada a Burgos • **we couldn't get him to ~** no logramos hacerle cambiar de actitud
3* (= *move quickly*) volar • **that car was really ~ing** ¡ese coche corría que volaba *or* que se las pelaba!*
4 (*US*) (*Aut*) • **to ~ into high/low gear** cambiar a una velocidad más alta/baja • **the presidential campaign has ~ed into high gear** la campaña por la presidencia se ha acelerado
5 • **to ~ for o.s.** arreglárselas solo
CPD ▸ **shift key** tecla *f* de mayúsculas ▸ **shift lock** tecla *f* de bloqueo de mayúsculas (*Sp*), tecla *f* fijamayúsculas (*LAm*) ▸ **shift system** [*of work*] sistema *m* de turnos ▸ **shift register** registro *m* de desplazamiento ▸ **shift work** trabajo *m* por turnos ▸ **shift worker** trabajador(a) *m/f* por turnos
▸ **shift along** VI + ADV = shift over
▸ **shift around, shift about** VI + ADV • **his men ~ed around nervously** sus hombres se movían nerviosos de un lado para otro
VT + ADV [+ *objects*] mover, cambiar de sitio
▸ **shift down** VI + ADV (*US*) (*Aut*) cambiar a una velocidad *or* marcha inferior
▸ **shift over*** VI + ADV correrse • **can you ~ over a bit?** ¿puedes correrte un poco a ese lado?
▸ **shift up** = shift over

shiftily [ˈʃɪftɪlɪ] ADV furtivamente, sospechosamente
shiftiness [ˈʃɪftɪnɪs] N [*of person, behaviour*] lo sospechoso; [*of look*] lo furtivo
shifting [ˈʃɪftɪŋ] ADJ [*sand*] movedizo; [*winds*] cambiante; [*values, attitudes*] cambiante • **his constantly ~ moods** sus cambios de humor constantes
shiftless [ˈʃɪftlɪs] ADJ holgazán, perezoso, flojo (*esp LAm*)
shiftlessness [ˈʃɪftlɪsnɪs] N holgazanería *f*, pereza *f*, flojera (*esp LAm*) *f*
shifty [ˈʃɪftɪ] ADJ (COMPAR: **shiftier**, SUPERL: **shiftiest**) [*look*] furtivo; [*person, behaviour*] sospechoso
shifty-eyed [ˈʃɪftɪˈaɪd] ADJ de mirada furtiva
shiitake [ʃɪˈtɑːkɪ] N (PL: **shiitake**) (*Bot*) shiitake *m*
Shiite, Shi'ite [ˈʃiːaɪt] N chiíta *mf*
ADJ chiíta
shillelagh [ʃəˈleɪlə, ʃəˈleɪlɪ] N (*Irl*) cachiporra *f*
shilling [ˈʃɪlɪŋ] N (*Brit*) chelín *m*
shilly-shally [ˈʃɪlɪˌʃælɪ] VI vacilar, titubear
shilly-shallying [ˈʃɪlɪˌʃælɪɪŋ] N vacilación *f*, titubeos *mpl*
shimmer [ˈʃɪməʳ] N luz *f* trémula, brillo *m*
VI rielar, relucir
shimmering [ˈʃɪmərɪŋ] ADJ, **shimmery** [ˈʃɪmərɪ] ADJ reluciente
shimmy [ˈʃɪmɪ] N **1** (= *dance*) shimmy *m*
2 (*Aut*) (= *vibration*) vibraciones *fpl*
3 (= *chemise*) camisa *f* (*de mujer*)
shin [ʃɪn] N espinilla *f*; (*Brit*) [*of meat*] jarrete *m*
VI • **to ~ up/down a tree** trepar a/bajar de un árbol
CPD ▸ **shin guard, shin pad** espinillera *f*
shinbone [ˈʃɪnbəʊn] N tibia *f*
shindig‡ [ˈʃɪndɪg] N juerga* *f*, guateque *m*
shindy‡ [ˈʃɪndɪ] N (= *noise*) conmoción *f*, escándalo *m*; (= *brawl*) jaleo *m*, bronca *f*
• IDIOM: • **to kick up a ~** armar un jaleo *or* una bronca
shine [ʃaɪn] (VB: PT, PP: **shone**) N (= *brilliance*) brillo *m*, lustre *m* • **to give sth a ~** sacar brillo a algo • **to take the ~ off sth** (*lit*) deslustrar algo; (*fig*) deslucir algo, quitar a algo su encanto • IDIOMS: • **come rain or ~** haga el tiempo que haga • **to take a ~ to sb*** tomar simpatía por algn
VT **1** (PT, PP: **shined**) (= *polish*) sacar brillo a, pulir
2 • **to ~ a light on sth** echar luz sobre algo
VI **1** [*sun, light etc*] brillar; [*metal*] relucir • **the sun is shining** brilla el sol • **the metal shone in the sun** el metal relucía al sol • **her face shone with happiness** su cara irradiaba felicidad
2 (*fig*) [*student etc*] destacar, sobresalir • **to ~ at English** destacar *or* sobresalir en inglés
▸ **shine down** VI + ADV [*sun, moon, stars*] brillar
shiner* [ˈʃaɪnəʳ] N (= *black eye*) ojo *m* a la funerala
shingle [ˈʃɪŋgl] N **1** (*on beach*) guijarros *mpl*
2 (*on roof*) tablilla *f*
3 (*US*) (= *signboard*) placa *f* • **to hang out one's ~** (*fig*) montar *or* abrir la oficina
4† (= *hairstyle*) corte *m* a lo garçon
CPD ▸ **shingle beach** playa *f* de piedras ▸ **shingle roof** tejado *m* de tablillas
shingles [ˈʃɪŋglz] N (*Med*) herpes *m* (zoster)
shingly [ˈʃɪŋglɪ] ADJ guijarroso
shinguard [ˈʃɪngɑːd] N espinillera *f*
shininess [ˈʃaɪnɪnɪs] N brillo *m*
shining [ˈʃaɪnɪŋ] ADJ [*surface, light*] brillante; [*face*] radiante; [*hair*] brillante, lustroso; [*eyes*] brillante, chispeante • IDIOM: • **a ~ example** un ejemplo perfecto
shinpad [ˈʃɪnpæd] N espinillera *f*
Shinto [ˈʃɪntəʊ] N shinto *m*
Shintoism [ˈʃɪntəʊɪzəm] N sintoísmo *m*
Shintoist [ˈʃɪntəʊɪst] ADJ, N sintoísta *mf*
shinty [ˈʃɪntɪ] N (*Scot*) *especie de hockey*
shiny [ˈʃaɪnɪ] ADJ (COMPAR: **shinier**, SUPERL: **shiniest**) brillante
ship [ʃɪp] N **1** (= *sea-going vessel*) (*gen*) barco *m*; (*for carrying cargo*) (*also Mil*) buque *m*, navío *m* • **Her or His Majesty's Ship Victory** el buque *or* navío Victory de la Marina Real Británica • **to abandon ~** abandonar el barco • **on board ~** a bordo • **by ~** en barco, por barco • **the good ~ Beagle** el buque Beagle, el Beagle • **to jump ~** abandonar el barco, desertar • **to take ~ for** embarcarse para • IDIOMS: • **when my ~ comes in** (*fig*) cuando lleguen las vacas gordas • **~s that pass in the night** personas que pasan por la vida y desaparecen • **the ~ of the desert** (= *the camel*) el camello
2 (= *aircraft, spacecraft*) nave *f*
VT **1** (= *transport*) enviar, consignar • **to ~ sth/sb in** traer algo/a algn • **to ~ sth/sb off** (*lit*) enviar algo/a algn • **he ~ped all his sons off to boarding school*** (*fig*) mandó a todos sus hijos a un internado • **to ~ sth/sb out** enviar algo/a algn • **a new engine had to be ~ped out to them** hubo que enviarles un nuevo motor
2 (*Naut*) • **we are ~ping water** estamos haciendo agua, nos está entrando agua
3 [+ *oars*] desarmar
CPD ▸ **ship broker** agente *mf* marítimo/a ▸ **ship canal** canal *m* de navegación ▸ **ship chandler, ship's chandler** proveedor *m* de efectos navales, abastecedor *m* de buques ▸ **ship's company** tripulación *f* ▸ **ship's doctor** médico *m* de a bordo ▸ **ship's manifest** manifiesto *m* del buque ▸ **ship-to-shore radio** radio *f* de barco a costa
shipboard [ˈʃɪpbɔːd] N • **on ~** a bordo
shipbreaker [ˈʃɪpˌbreɪkəʳ] N desguazador *m*
shipbuilder [ˈʃɪpˌbɪldəʳ] N constructor(a) *m/f* de buques
shipbuilding [ˈʃɪpˌbɪldɪŋ] N construcción *f* marina
shipload [ˈʃɪpləʊd] N cargamento *m*
shipmate [ˈʃɪpmeɪt] N compañero/a *m/f* de tripulación
shipment [ˈʃɪpmənt] N (= *act*) transporte *m*, embarque *m*; (= *load*) consignación *f*; (= *quantity*) cargamento *m*, remesa *f*
shipowner [ˈʃɪpˌəʊnəʳ] N naviero/a *m/f*, armador(a) *m/f*
shipper [ˈʃɪpəʳ] N (= *company*) empresa *f* naviera
shipping [ˈʃɪpɪŋ] N **1** (= *ships*) barcos *mpl*, buques *mpl*; (= *fleet*) flota *f* • **a danger to ~** un peligro para la navegación
2 (= *transporting*) transporte *m* (en barco), embarque *m*; (= *sending*) envío *m*
CPD ▸ **shipping agent** agente *mf* marítimo/a ▸ **shipping channel** canal *m* de navegación ▸ **shipping clerk** expedidor(a) *m/f* ▸ **shipping company, shipping line** compañía *f* naviera ▸ **shipping container** contenedor *m* marítimo ▸ **shipping forecast** • **the ~ forecast** el pronóstico del tiempo en la mar, el estado de la mar ▸ **shipping industry** industria *f* de transporte marítimo ▸ **shipping instructions** instrucciones *fpl* de embarque ▸ **shipping lane** ruta *f* de navegación
shipshape [ˈʃɪpʃeɪp] ADJ en buen orden • **all ~ and Bristol fashion** (*Brit*) todo limpio y en su sitio
shipwreck [ˈʃɪprek] N (= *event*) naufragio *m*; (= *wrecked ship*) buque *m* naufragado, nave *f* or embarcación *f* naufragada
VT • **to be ~ed** naufragar • **~ed on a desert island** [*vessel*] naufragado en una isla desierta; [*person*] náufrago en una isla desierta • **a ~ed person** un náufrago • **a ~ed sailor** un marinero náufrago • **a ~ed vessel** un buque naufragado
shipwright [ˈʃɪpraɪt] N carpintero *m* de navío
shipyard [ˈʃɪpjɑːd] N astillero *m*
shire [ˈʃaɪəʳ] N (*Brit*) condado *m*
CPD ▸ **shire horse** ≈ percherón/ona *m/f*
shirk [ʃɜːk] VT [+ *duty*] esquivar, zafarse de
VI gandulear
shirker [ˈʃɜːkəʳ] N gandul(a) *m/f*, flojo/a *m/f* (*LAm*)
shirr [ʃɜːʳ] VT **1** (*Sew*) fruncir
2 (*US*) • **~ed eggs** huevos *mpl* al plato
shirring [ˈʃɜːrɪŋ] N (*Sew*) frunce *m*
shirt [ʃɜːt] N camisa *f* • IDIOMS: • **to put one's ~ on a horse** (*fig*) (*Betting*) apostarlo todo a un caballo • **keep your ~ on!*** (*fig*) ¡no te sulfures!*, ¡cálmate!
CPD ▸ **shirt button** botón *m* de la camisa ▸ **shirt collar** cuello *m* de camisa ▸ **shirt front** pechera *f* ▸ **shirt pocket** bolsillo *m* de la camisa ▸ **shirt sleeves** • **to be in (one's) ~ sleeves** estar en mangas de camisa ▸ **shirt tail** faldón *m* (de camisa)
shirtdress [ˈʃɜːtdres] N camisa *f* vestido
shirtless [ˈʃɜːtlɪs] ADJ sin camisa, descamisado
shirtwaist [ˈʃɜːtweɪst] N (*US*) blusa *f* (de mujer)
shirty [ˈʃɜːtɪ] ADJ (COMPAR: **shirtier**, SUPERL: **shirtiest**) • **he was pretty ~ about it*** no le gustó nada, no le cayó en gracia
shish kebab [ˈʃiːʃkəˈbæb] N = **kebab**
shit** [ʃɪt] (VB: PT, PP: **shit** *or* **shat**) N
1 (= *excrement*) mierda** *f* • **to have** *or* **take a ~** cagar** • **to have the ~s** tener el vientre descompuesto • **~!** ¡mierda!**, ¡joder!**,

¡carajo! (*esp LAm***) • **tough ~!** ¡mala suerte! • IDIOM: • **to beat the ~ out of sb** darle hostias a algn‡, hostiar a algn‡; ▸ **fan**
2 (= *trouble*) • **to be in the ~** estar bien jodido(s)** • **he landed us in the ~** nos dejó bien jodidos**
3 (= *nonsense*) gilipolleces** *fpl* • IDIOM: • **no ~?** (= *seriously?*) ¡no (me) jodas!**, ¿de verdad?
4 (= *stuff*) mierdas** *fpl*, historias‡ *fpl*, cosas *fpl*
5 (= *person*) mierda** *mf*
VI cagar**
VT cagar** • **to ~ o.s.** cagarse** • IDIOM: • **to ~ bricks** (*from fear*) cagarse de miedo**

shite** [ʃaɪt] N (*Brit*) = **shit**

shitfaced** [ˈʃɪtfeɪst] ADJ (*with alcohol*) pedo** (*inv*); (*with drugs*) colocado**

shithead** [ˈʃɪthed] N gilipollas** *mf*

shithouse** [ˈʃɪthaʊs] N (= *lavatory*) cagadero** *m* • **this ~ of a country** este país de mierda**

shitless** [ˈʃɪtlɪs] ADJ • **to be scared ~** estar acojonado** • **to be bored ~** estar más harto que la hostia**

shitlist** [ˈʃɪtlɪst] N lista *f* negra

shitload‡ [ˈʃɪtləʊd] N • **a ~ of sth** • **~s of sth** (= *lots*) un mogollón de algo* • **a ~ of trouble** un mogollón de problemas*

shitty** [ˈʃɪtɪ] ADJ (COMPAR: **shittier**, SUPERL: **shittiest**) **1** (*lit*) lleno de mierda**
2 (*fig*) (= *crappy*) de mierda**

shiver[1] [ˈʃɪvəʳ] N (*with cold*) tiritón *m*; [*of horror etc*] escalofrío *m* • **it sent ~s down my spine** me dio escalofríos • **it gives me the ~s** (*fear*) me da horror • **to get the ~s** (*fear*) aterrorizarse, sentir escalofríos de miedo
VI (*with cold*) tiritar; (*with emotion*) temblar, estremecerse

shiver[2] [ˈʃɪvəʳ] VT (= *break*) romper, hacer añicos
VI romperse, hacerse añicos

shivery [ˈʃɪvərɪ] ADJ (= *feverish*) destemplado; (= *shaking*) estremecido; (= *sensitive to cold*) friolero, friolento (*LAm*)

shmuck* [ʃmʌk] N (*US*) = **schmuck**

shoal[1] [ʃəʊl] N [*of fish*] banco *m*

shoal[2] [ʃəʊl] N (= *sandbank etc*) banco *m* de arena, bajío *m*, bajo *m*

shock[1] [ʃɒk] N **1** (*emotional*) conmoción *f*, golpe *m*, impresión *f*; (= *start*) susto *m* • **the ~ killed him** la impresión le mató • **the ~ was too much for him** la impresión fue demasiado para él • **to come as a ~** resultar sorprendente *or* asombroso, causar estupefacción • **it comes as a ~ to hear that …** resulta sorprendente *or* asombroso saber que …, causa estupefacción saber que … • **frankly, this has all come as a bit of a ~** con toda franqueza, para mí esto ha sido un duro golpe • **to get a ~** llevarse *or* pegarse un susto • **to give sb a ~** dar un susto a algn • **what a ~ you gave me!** ¡qué susto me diste!, ¡me has asustado! • **pale with ~** lívido del susto
2 (*lit*) (= *impact*) sacudida *f*; (*fig*) (= *shakeup*) choque *m*, sacudida *f* • **the ~ of the explosion was felt five miles away** la sacudida de la explosión se sintió a una distancia de cinco millas • **~ resistant** antichoque • **it was a ~ to the establishment** sacudió el sistema, fue un serio golpe para el sistema
3 (*Elec*) descarga *f* • **she got a ~ from the refrigerator** la nevera le dio una descarga *or* un calambre
4 (*Med*) shock *m*, postración *f* nerviosa • **to be suffering from ~** • **be in (a state of) ~** estar en estado de shock, padecer una postración nerviosa
5 **shocks*** (*Aut*) (*also* **shock absorbers**) amortiguadores *mpl*
VT **1** (= *startle*) sobresaltar, asustar • **to ~ sb into doing sth** dar una sacudida a algn para animarle a hacer algo
2 (= *affect emotionally*) (= *upset*) conmover, chocar; (= *offend*) escandalizar • **it ~s me that people are so narrow-minded** me choca que la gente sea tan cerrada • **easily ~ed** que se escandaliza por nada
VI causar escándalo, chocar • **this film is not intended to ~** esta película no pretende escandalizar a nadie
CPD ▸ **shock absorber** (*Aut*) amortiguador *m* ▸ **shock jock*** (*esp US*) *presentador(a) polémico/a de coloquios radiofónicos abiertos al público* ▸ **shock tactics** (*lit*) (*Mil*) táctica *fsing* de choque; (*fig*) provocación *f* • **to use ~ tactics** (*fig*) recurrir a la provocación, provocar ▸ **shock therapy**, **shock treatment** (*Med*) (*also* **electric shock treatment**) tratamiento *m* por electrochoque ▸ **shock troops** guardias *mpl* de asalto ▸ **shock wave** onda *f* de choque

shock[2] [ʃɒk] N (*also* **shock of hair**) mata *f* de pelo

shock[3] [ʃɒk] (*Agr*) N tresnal *m*, garbera *f*
VT poner en tresnales

shockable [ˈʃɒkəbl] ADJ • **she's very ~** se escandaliza por poca *or* por cualquier cosa

shocked [ʃɒkt] ADJ **1** (= *horrified*) espantado; (= *surprised*) estupefacto • **I was ~ at the verdict** el veredicto me dejó espantado • **don't look so ~!** ¡no pongas esa cara de sorpresa! • **there was a ~ silence** hubo un silencio de estupefacción • **the jury listened to the tape in ~ silence** el jurado escuchaba la cinta enmudecido por el espanto
2 (= *outraged, offended*) escandalizado • **~ listeners/viewers rang up in their thousands** miles de oyentes/espectadores llamaron escandalizados

shocker* [ˈʃɒkəʳ] N **1** • **it's a ~** es horrible, es un desastre • **he's a ~** es un sinvergüenza
2 (*Literat*) (= *cheap book*) novelucha *f*

shock-headed [ˈʃɒkˈhedɪd] ADJ melenudo

shock-horror*, **shock horror*** [ʃɒkˈhɒrəʳ] ADJ (= *sensational*) [*story*] sensacional; [*headlines*] sensacionalista
EXCL (*hum*) ¡qué horror!

shocking [ˈʃɒkɪŋ] ADJ **1** (= *extremely bad*) [*weather, performance, handwriting*] pésimo, espantoso • **she has ~ taste** tiene un pésimo gusto • **to be in a ~ state** estar en un pésimo estado, estar en un estado penoso
2 (= *appalling*) [*news, sight, murder*] espeluznante, espantoso • **the ~ truth** la sobrecogedora verdad
3 (= *outrageous*) [*book, film, act*] escandaloso • **it was ~ how badly paid these young girls were** era de escándalo *or* era escandaloso lo mal que se pagaba a estas chicas • **it's ~ to think that …** escandaliza pensar que …
CPD ▸ **shocking pink** rosa *m* estridente, rosa *m* fosforito

shockingly [ˈʃɒkɪŋlɪ] ADV **1** (*with adj*) [*bad, expensive*] terriblemente
2 (*with verb*) [*behave*] terriblemente mal, fatal; [*age, change*] de manera espantosa

shockproof [ˈʃɒkpruːf] ADJ [*watch*] antichoque; (*fig**) [*person*] que no se escandaliza por nada

shock-resistant [ˈʃɒkrɪˌzɪstənt] ADJ resistente a los golpes

shod [ʃɒd] PT, PP *of* **shoe**

shoddily [ˈʃɒdɪlɪ] ADV • **~ made** chapucero, hecho chapuceramente • **~ built** mal hecho, mal construido • **she was very ~ treated by him** él la trató fatal

shoddiness [ˈʃɒdɪnɪs] N [*of merchandise, product*] baja calidad *f*; [*of work, service*] chapucería *f*

shoddy [ˈʃɒdɪ] ADJ (COMPAR: **shoddier**, SUPERL: **shoddiest**) [*merchandise, product*] de baja calidad, de pacotilla; [*work, service*] chapucero
N (= *cloth*) paño *m* burdo de lana; (= *wool*) lana *f* regenerada; (*as waste, fertilizer*) desechos *mpl* de lana

shoe [ʃuː] (VB: PT, PP: **shod**) N **1** (= *footwear*) zapato *m*; (*for horse*) herradura *f* • **to put on one's ~s** ponerse los zapatos, calzarse (*frm*) • **to take off one's ~s** quitarse los zapatos, descalzarse (*frm*) • IDIOMS: • **I wouldn't like to be in his ~s** no quisiera estar en su lugar *or* pellejo • **if I were in your ~s** si yo estuviese en tu lugar, yo que tú • **to step into sb's ~s** pasar a ocupar el puesto de algn • **to be waiting for dead men's ~s** *esperar a que muera algn (para pasar luego a ocupar su puesto)*
2 (*Aut*) (*also* **brake shoe**) zapata *f*
VT [+ *horse*] herrar
CPD ▸ **shoe box** caja *f* de zapatos ▸ **shoe brush** cepillo *m* para zapatos ▸ **shoe cream** crema *f* de zapatos, crema *f* para el calzado ▸ **shoe leather** cuero *m* para zapatos • IDIOM: • **to wear out one's ~ leather** gastarse el calzado • **I wore out a lot of ~ leather** • **it cost me a lot in ~ leather** tuve que andar lo mío, tuve que recorrer mucho camino ▸ **shoe polish** betún *m*, lustre *m* (*LAm*) ▸ **shoe repairer** zapatero/a *m/f* remendón/ona ▸ **shoe repairs** reparación *fsing* de zapatos, reparación *fsing* de calzado ▸ **shoe shop** (*esp Brit*), **shoe store** (*US*) zapatería *f*

shoeblack† [ˈʃuːblæk] N limpiabotas *mf inv*, lustrabotas *mf inv* (*LAm*)

shoeblacking [ˈʃuːˌblækɪŋ] N betún *m*, lustre *m* (*LAm*)

shoehorn [ˈʃuːhɔːn] N calzador *m*

shoelace [ˈʃuːleɪs] N cordón *m*, pasador *m* (*And*)

shoeless [ˈʃuːlɪs] ADJ descalzo

shoemaker [ˈʃuːˌmeɪkəʳ] N zapatero/a *m/f*

shoeshine [ˈʃuːʃaɪn] N • **to have a ~** hacerse limpiar los zapatos
CPD ▸ **shoeshine boy**, **shoeshine man** limpiabotas *m inv*, lustrabotas *m inv* (*LAm*), bolero *m* (*Mex*), embolador *m* (*Col*)

shoestring [ˈʃuːstrɪŋ] N (*US*) cordón *m*, lazo *m* • IDIOM: • **to do sth on a ~** hacer algo con muy poco dinero • **to live on a ~** vivir muy justo
CPD ▸ **shoestring budget** presupuesto *m* muy limitado

shoetree [ˈʃuːtriː] N horma *f*

shone [ʃɒn] PT, PP *of* **shine**

shoo [ʃuː] EXCL ¡fuera!, ¡zape!, ¡ándale! (*Mex*)
VT (*also* **shoo away, shoo off**) ahuyentar, espantar

shoo-in* [ˈʃuːɪn] N (*US*) • **it's a shoo-in** es cosa de coser y cantar • **he's a shoo-in for the presidency** es el favorito para hacerse con la presidencia, es el más firme candidato a la presidencia

shook [ʃʊk] PT *of* **shake**

shook-up* [ʃʊkˈʌp] ADJ • **to be shook-up about sth** estar conmocionado por algo

shoot [ʃuːt] (VB: PT, PP: **shot**) N **1** (*Bot*) brote *m*, retoño *m*
2 (*Cine*) rodaje *m*; (*Phot*) sesión *f* fotográfica
3 (= *shooting party*) cacería *f*, partida *f* de caza; (= *preserve*) coto *m* de caza, vedado *m* de caza; (= *competition*) concurso *m* de tiro al blanco, certamen *m* de tiro al blanco
VT **1** (= *wound*) pegar un tiro a; (= *kill*) matar de un tiro; (*more brutally*) matar a tiros; (= *execute*) fusilar; (= *hunt*) cazar • **she shot her husband** pegó un tiro a su marido • **you'll get me shot!*** ¡me van a asesinar *or* matar por tu culpa!* • **he was shot as a spy**

lo fusilaron por espía • **to ~ sb dead** matar a algn de un tiro *or* a tiros • **we often go ~ing rabbits at the weekend** solemos ir a cazar conejos los fines de semana • **he was shot in the leg** una bala le hirió en la pierna • **he had been shot through the heart** la bala le había atravesado el corazón • IDIOM: • **to ~ o.s. in the foot** cavar su propia fosa sin darse cuenta
2 (= *launch*) [+ *bullet, gun, arrow*] disparar; [+ *missile*] lanzar
3 (= *propel*) [+ *object*] lanzar (**at** hacia) • **the impact shot them forward** el impacto hizo que salieran despedidos hacia delante • **the volcano shot lava high into the air** el volcán despidió *or* arrojó lava por los aires
4 (*fig*) [+ *glance, look*] lanzar; [+ *smile*] dedicar; [+ *ray of light*] arrojar, lanzar • **she shot me a sideways glance** me lanzó una mirada de reojo, me miró de reojo • **he began ~ing questions at her** empezó a acribillarla a preguntas • IDIOMS: • **to ~ the breeze** *or* **bull** (*US‡*) darle a la lengua* • **to ~ a line** (*Brit**) marcarse un farol* • **to ~ one's mouth off*** irse de la lengua*, hablar más de la cuenta*; ▹ **bolt**
5 (*Cine*) rodar, filmar; (*Phot*) [+ *subject of picture*] tomar, sacar
6 (= *speed through*) • **to ~ the lights** (*Aut**) saltarse un semáforo en rojo • **to ~ the rapids** sortear *or* salvar los rápidos
7 (= *close*) [+ *bolt*] correr
8 (= *play*) • **to ~ dice/pool** (*US*) jugar a los dados/al billar
9* (= *inject*) [+ *drugs*] inyectarse, chutarse*, pincharse*
(VI) **1** (*with gun*) disparar, tirar; (= *hunt*) cazar • **to ~ at sth/sb** disparar a algo/algn • **to go ~ing** ir de caza • **to ~ to kill** disparar a matar, tirar a matar • **~-to-kill policy** programa *m* de tirar a matar
2 (*in ball games*) (*gen*) tirar; (*Ftbl*) disparar, chutar • **to ~ at goal** tirar a gol, chutar • **to ~ wide** fallar el tiro, errar el tiro
3 (= *move rapidly*) • **she shot ahead to take first place** se adelantó rápidamente para ponerse en primer puesto • **the car shot forward** el coche salió disparado hacia delante • **flames shot 100ft into the air** las llamas saltaron por los aires a 100 pies de altura • **he shot out of his chair/out of bed** salió disparado de la silla/de la cama • **to ~ past** *or* **by** pasar como un rayo • **the car shot past** *or* **by us** el coche pasó como un rayo *or* una bala • **to ~ to fame/stardom** lanzarse a la fama/al estrellato • **the pain went ~ing up his arm** un dolor punzante le subía por el brazo
4 (*Bot*) (= *produce buds*) brotar; (= *germinate*) germinar
5 (*Cine*) rodar, filmar; (*Phot*) sacar la foto, disparar
6 (*US**) (*in conversation*) • **shoot!** ¡adelante!, ¡dispara!
(EXCL)* (*euph*) • **oh ~!** ¡caracoles!*, ¡mecachis! (*Sp**)
▸ **shoot away** (VT + ADV) = **shoot off**
(VI + ADV) **1** (*Mil*) seguir tirando
2 (= *move*) partir como una bala, salir disparado
▸ **shoot back** (VT + ADV) devolver rápidamente, devolver en el acto
(VI + ADV) **1** (*Mil*) devolver el tiro, responder con disparos
2 (= *move*) volver como una bala (**to** a)
▸ **shoot down** (VT + ADV) [+ *aeroplane*] derribar; [+ *person*] matar a tiros, balear (*LAm*); (*fig*) [+ *argument*] echar por tierra
▸ **shoot off** (VT + ADV) **1** [+ *gun*] disparar; ▹ **mouth**
2 • **he had a leg shot off** un disparo le cercenó una pierna
(VI + ADV) = **shoot away**
▸ **shoot out** (VT + ADV) **1** (= *eject*) [+ *sparks*] arrojar, soltar
2 (= *move rapidly*) [+ *hand*] sacar rápidamente
3 (*with gun*) [+ *lights*] apagar a tiros; [+ *windows, tyres*] coser a tiros • **to ~ it out** (*lit, fig*) resolverlo a tiros
(VI + ADV) (= *come out suddenly*) [*person, animal*] salir disparado • **his hand shot out and grabbed a cake** alargó la mano rápidamente y agarró un pastel
▸ **shoot up** (VI + ADV) **1** (= *move upwards rapidly*) [*prices, value, temperature*] dispararse; [*hand, head*] alzarse de repente; [*eyebrows*] arquearse de repente; [*smoke, flames, water*] salir disparado • **every hand in the classroom shot up** todas las manos de la clase se alzaron de repente, todo el mundo en la clase alzó la mano de repente
2 (= *grow quickly*) [*plant*] crecer rápidamente • **your son's shot up over the last few months** tu hijo ha dado un estirón en estos últimos meses*
3* [*drug user*] chutarse*, pincharse*
(VT + ADV) **1** [+ *town, district*] barrer a tiros *or* balazos; [+ *vehicle*] coser a tiros *or* balazos • **he's pretty badly shot up, but he'll live** ha recibido bastantes tiros, pero sobrevivirá
2* [+ *drugs*] chutarse*, pincharse*
shoot-em-up* [ˈʃuːtəmʌp] (ADJ) [*film*] de tiros; (*Comput*) [*game*] de acción
shooter [ˈʃuːtəʳ] (N) **1‡** (= *gun*) arma *f* (de fuego)
2 (*also* **target shooter**) tirador(a) *m/f*
shooting [ˈʃuːtɪŋ] (N) **1** (= *shots*) tiros *mpl*, disparos *mpl*; (= *continuous shooting*) tiroteo *m*, balacera *f* (*LAm*)
2 (= *murder*) asesinato *m*; (= *execution*) fusilamiento *m*
3 [*of film*] rodaje *m*, filmación *f*
4 (*esp Brit*) (= *hunting*) caza *f* • **good ~!** (*said as congratulation*) ¡buen tiro!; (*said before hunt*) ¡buena caza!
5 (*Sport*) tiro *m* al blanco
(ADJ) [*pain*] punzante
(CPD) ▸ **shooting box** pabellón *m* de caza ▸ **shooting brake†** (*Brit*) (*Aut*) (= *estate car*) furgoneta *f*, rubia *f*, camioneta *f* ▸ **shooting gallery** barraca *f* de tiro al blanco ▸ **shooting incident** tiroteo *m*, balacera *f* (*LAm*) ▸ **shooting iron†** (*US*) arma *f* (de fuego) ▸ **shooting jacket** chaquetón *m* ▸ **shooting lodge** = **shooting box** ▸ **shooting match** concurso *m* de tiro al blanco, certamen *m* de tiro al blanco • **the whole ~ match*** (= *the whole thing*) todo el tinglado* ▸ **shooting party** partida *f* de caza, cacería *f* ▸ **shooting practice** prácticas *fpl* de tiro ▸ **shooting range** campo *m* de tiro ▸ **shooting spree** • **to go on a ~ spree** ir por ahí disparando a la gente ▸ **shooting star** estrella *f* fugaz ▸ **shooting stick** bastón *m* taburete ▸ **shooting war** guerra *f* a tiros
shoot-out [ˈʃuːtaʊt] (N) **1** tiroteo *m*, balacera *f* (*LAm*)
2 (*Sport*) ▹ **penalty**
shop [ʃɒp] (N) **1** (*Comm*) (= *store*) tienda *f*; (= *workshop*) taller *m* • **the ~s** las tiendas, los comercios • **he's just gone (round) to the ~s** acaba de salir a comprar • **it's not available in the ~s** no se encuentra *or* se comercializa en las tiendas • **shop!†** ¿quién despacha? • **butcher's ~** carnicería *f* • **a repair ~** un taller de reparaciones • **to set up ~** montar un negocio, establecerse • **to shut up ~** cerrar • **to talk ~*** hablar de trabajo, hablar de negocios • IDIOM: • **all over the ~‡** en *or* por todas partes; ▹ **barber, betting, flower, sweet, video**
2 (*Brit**) (= *act of shopping*) compra *f* • **the weekly ~** la compra de la semana
(VI) comprar, hacer las compras • **I hate ~ping in supermarkets** odio hacer (las) compras en los supermercados • **to go ~ping** ir de compras *or* de tiendas
(VT)‡ (= *inform on*) delatar
(CPD) ▸ **shop assistant** (*Brit*) dependiente/a *m/f*, empleado/a *m/f* de una tienda ▸ **shop floor** (*lit*) taller *m*; (*bigger*) planta *f* de producción • **to work on the ~ floor** trabajar en la producción, ser obrero/a de la producción • **the ~ floor (workers)** los obreros ▸ **shop front** fachada *f* de la tienda ▸ **shop steward** (*Ind*) enlace *mf* sindical ▸ **shop talk*** charla *f* sobre el trabajo ▸ **shop window** escaparate *m*, vitrina *f*, vidriera *f* (*S. Cone*)
▸ **shop around** (VI + ADV) (*lit*) comparar precios; (*fig*) andar a la caza y captura • **she was ~ping around for the perfect partner** andaba a la caza y captura del novio ideal
shopaholic* [ʃɒpəˈhɒlɪk] (N) comprador(a) *m/f* obsesivo/a, adicto/a *m/f* a las compras
shopbot [ˈʃɒpbɒt] (N) robot *m* de compras
shopfitter [ˈʃɒpˌfɪtəʳ] (N) (*esp Brit*) instalador(a) *m/f* comercial
shopgirl [ˈʃɒpgɜːl] (N) (*Brit*) dependienta *f*, empleada *f* (*de una tienda*) (*LAm*)
shopkeeper [ˈʃɒpˌkiːpəʳ] (N) tendero/a *m/f*
shoplift [ˈʃɒplɪft] (VI) hurtar en tiendas
(VT) robar en una tienda, hurtar en una tienda
shoplifter [ˈʃɒpˌlɪftəʳ] (N) ratero/a *m/f*, ladrón/a *m/f* (de tiendas)
shoplifting [ˈʃɒpˌlɪftɪŋ] (N) ratería *f*
shopper [ˈʃɒpəʳ] (N) **1** (= *person*) comprador(a) *m/f*; (= *customer*) cliente *mf*
2 (= *bag*) bolsa *f* de compras; (*on wheels*) carrito *m* de la compra
shopping [ˈʃɒpɪŋ] (N) (= *act of buying*) compra *f*; (= *goods bought*) compras *fpl* • **I like ~** me gusta ir de tiendas • **to do the ~** hacer la compra • **to go ~** ir de tiendas *or* de compras
(CPD) ▸ **shopping arcade** centro *m* comercial ▸ **shopping bag** bolsa *f* de compras ▸ **shopping basket** cesta *f*, canasta *f* (*LAm*) ▸ **shopping cart** (*US*) = **shopping trolley** ▸ **shopping centre, shopping center** (*US, Brit*) centro *m* comercial ▸ **shopping channel** canal *m* de televentas ▸ **shopping complex** centro *m* comercial ▸ **shopping facilities** tiendas *fpl*, comercios *mpl* ▸ **shopping hours** horario *m* comercial ▸ **shopping list** lista *f* de compras ▸ **shopping mall** (*esp US*) centro *m* comercial ▸ **shopping precinct** (*Brit*) centro *m* comercial ▸ **shopping spree** • **to go on a ~ spree** salir de compras (*gastando mucho dinero*) ▸ **shopping trip** viaje *m* de compras ▸ **shopping trolley** (*Brit*) carrito *m* de la compra ▸ **shopping village** gran centro *m* comercial
shop-soiled [ˈʃɒpsɔɪld] (ADJ) deteriorado
shopwalker [ˈʃɒpˌwɔːkəʳ] (N) (*Brit*) vigilante/a *m/f*
shopworn [ˈʃɒpwɔːn] (ADJ) (*US*) = **shop-soiled**
shore¹ [ʃɔːʳ] (N) **1** [*of sea, lake*] orilla *f* • **the eastern ~s of Lake Tanganyika** la orilla oriental del lago Tanganika • **we were now a few hundred yards from ~** ahora nos hallábamos a unos cientos de yardas de la orilla *or* de la costa • **on ~** en tierra
2 shores [*of country*] (*liter*) tierras *fpl* • **he will soon be leaving these ~s** pronto abandonará estas tierras
(CPD) ▸ **shore bird** ave *f* zancuda ▸ **shore**

S

leave permiso *m* para bajar a tierra ▸ **shore patrol** (*US*) patrulla *f* costera
shore² [ʃɔːʳ] VT • **to ~ up** (*lit*) apuntalar; (*fig*) apoyar, reforzar, sostener
N (= *prop*) puntal *m*
shoreline [ˈʃɔːlaɪn] N línea *f* de la costa
shoreward [ˈʃɔːwəd] ADV hacia la costa, hacia la playa
shorewards [ˈʃɔːwədz] ADV (*esp Brit*) = **shoreward**
shorn [ʃɔːn] VB *pp of* **shear**
short [ʃɔːt] ADJ (COMPAR: **shorter**, SUPERL: **shortest**) **1** (*in length, distance, duration*) [*message, journey, hair, skirt*] corto; [*person*] bajo, chaparro (*CAm, Mex*); [*vowel, syllable*] breve; [*memory*] malo, flaco • **the ~est route** la ruta más corta • **February is a ~ month** febrero es un mes corto • **it was a great holiday, but too ~** fueron unas vacaciones estupendas, pero demasiado cortas • **she's quite ~** es bastante baja • **the ~ answer is that ...** en pocas palabras la razón es que ... • **to have a ~ back and sides** llevar el pelo corto por detrás y por los lados • **a ~ break** un pequeño descanso • **the days are getting ~er** los días se vuelven más cortos • **time is getting ~er** nos queda poco tiempo • **to win by a ~ head** (*Racing*) ganar por una cabeza escasa • **to be ~ in the leg** [*person*] tener las piernas cortas • **these trousers are a bit ~ in the leg** estos pantalones tienen la pierna algo pequeña • **at ~ notice** con poco tiempo de antelación • **in ~ order** en breve, en seguida • **to take ~ steps** dar pequeños pasos • **in the ~ term** a corto plazo • **a ~ time ago** hace poco • **to work ~ time** • **be on ~ time** (*Ind*) trabajar una jornada reducida • **to take a ~ walk** dar un paseo corto • **a ~ way off** a poca distancia, no muy lejos • **a few ~ words** algunas palabritas • IDIOMS: • **that was ~ and sweet** eso fue corto y bueno • **to make ~ work of sth** despachar algo
2 (= *insufficient*) escaso • **I'm £3 ~** me faltan 3 libras • **it's two kilos ~** faltan dos kilos • **bananas are very ~** escasean los plátanos, casi no hay plátanos • **I'm a bit ~ at the moment*** en este momento ando un poco corto *or* escaso de dinero • **to be ~ of sth** andar falto *or* escaso de algo • **we're ~ of petrol** andamos escasos de gasolina • **we're not ~ of volunteers** se han ofrecido muchos voluntarios, no andamos escasos de voluntarios • **to be ~ of breath** estar sin aliento • **to give sb ~ change** no darle el cambio completo a algn • **to give ~ measure to sb** dar de menos a algn • **gold is in ~ supply** escasea el oro, hay escasez de oro • **~ ton** (*US*) (= *2,000lb*) tonelada *f* corta • **to give ~ weight to sb** dar de menos a algn; ▹ **supply**
3 • **~ of** (= *less than*): • **~ of blowing it up** a menos que lo volemos, a no ser que lo volemos • **~ of murder I'll do anything** lo haré todo menos matar • **not far ~ of £100** poco menos de 100 libras • **it's little ~ of madness** dista poco de la locura • **nothing ~ of total surrender** nada menos que la rendición incondicional • **it's nothing ~ of robbery** es nada menos que un robo • **nothing ~ of a bomb would stop him** fuera de una bomba nada le impediría • **nothing ~ of a miracle can save him** solo un milagro le puede salvar, se necesitaría un milagro para salvarle
4 (= *concise*) corto, breve • **~ and to the point** corto y bueno • **"Pat" is ~ for "Patricia"** "Patricia" se abrevia en "Pat" • **Rosemary is called "Rose" for ~** a Rosemary le dicen "Rose" para abreviar • **"TV" is ~ for "television"** "TV" es abreviatura de "televisión" • **in ~** en pocas palabras, en resumen • **in ~, the answer is no** en una palabra, la respuesta es no; ▹ **long¹**
5 (= *curt*) [*reply, manner*] brusco, seco • **to have a ~ temper** ser de mal genio, tener mal genio *or* mal carácter *or* corto de genio • **to be ~ with sb** tratar a algn con sequedad
6 [*pastry*] quebradizo
ADV **1** (= *suddenly, abruptly*) en seco • **to stop ~** • **pull up ~** pararse en seco
2 (*insufficiency*) • **to come ~ of** no alcanzar • **to cut sth ~** suspender algo • **they had to cut ~ their holiday** tuvieron que interrumpir sus vacaciones • **to fall ~ of** no alcanzar • **to fall ~ of the target** no alcanzar el blanco, no llegar al blanco • **to fall ~ of expectations** no cumplir las esperanzas • **it falls far ~ of what we require** dista mucho de satisfacer nuestras exigencias • **production has fallen ~ by 100 tons** la producción arroja un déficit de 100 toneladas • **to go ~ of** pasarse sin • **no one goes ~ in this house** en esta casa nadie padece hambre • **we never went ~ (of anything) as children** no nos faltó nada de niños • **we're running ~ of bread** tenemos poco pan, se nos acaba el pan (*LAm*) • **we ran ~ of petrol** se nos acabó la gasolina, quedamos sin gasolina • **to sell ~** vender al descubierto • **to sell sb ~** (*lit*) engañar a algn en un negocio; (*fig*) menospreciar a algn • **to stop ~ of** (*lit*) detenerse antes de llegar a • **I'd stop ~ of murder** (*fig*) menos matar, haría lo que fuera • **to be taken ~** necesitar urgentemente ir al wáter
3 (= *except*) • **~ of apologizing ...** fuera de pedirle perdón ...
N **1** (*Elec*) = **short-circuit**
2 (*Brit**) (= *drink*) bebida *f* corta
3 (*Cine*) cortometraje *m*; ▹ **shorts**
VT, VI (*Elec*) = **short-circuit**
CPD ▸ **short cut** atajo *m* ▸ **short list** lista *f* de candidatos preseleccionados ▸ **short message service, short message system** SMS *m* ▸ **short sight** miopía *f* • **to have ~ sight** ser miope, ser corto de vista ▸ **short story** cuento *m* • **~ story writer** escritor(a) *m/f* de cuentos ▸ **short wave** (*Rad*) onda *f* corta
shortage [ˈʃɔːtɪdʒ] N **1** (= *lack*) escasez *f*, falta *f* • **a water ~** escasez *or* falta de agua • **~ of staff** escasez *or* falta de personal • **the housing ~** la crisis de la vivienda • **there is no ~ of advice** no es que falten consejos, no faltan los consejos
2 (= *state of deficiency*) escasez *f* • **in times of ~** en las épocas de escasez
shortbread [ˈʃɔːtbred] N *especie de mantecada*
shortcake [ˈʃɔːtkeɪk] N **1** (*Brit*) *especie de mantecada*
2 (*US*) torta *f* de frutas
short-change [ˈʃɔːtˈtʃeɪndʒ] VT • **to short-change sb** no dar el cambio completo a algn; (*fig*) defraudar a algn • **to do this is to short-change the project** (*esp US*) hacer esto es tratar inadecuadamente el proyecto
short-circuit [ˈʃɔːtˈsɜːkɪt] (*Elec*) N cortocircuito *m*
VT **1** (*Elec*) provocar un cortocircuito en
2 (*fig*) (= *bypass*) evitar (la necesidad de pasar por)
VI hacer un cortocircuito
shortcomings [ˈʃɔːtkʌmɪŋz] NPL defectos *mpl*
shortcrust pastry [ˈʃɔːtkrʌstˈpeɪstrɪ] N (*Brit*) pasta *f* quebradiza
short-dated [ˈʃɔːtˈdeɪtɪd] ADJ (*Econ*) a corto plazo
shorten [ˈʃɔːtn] VT (*gen*) acortar; [+ *journey etc*] acortar, abreviar; [+ *rations etc*] reducir
VI (*gen*) acortarse, reducirse • **the days are ~ing** los días se están acortando • **the odds have ~ed** los puntos de ventaja se han reducido
shortening [ˈʃɔːtnɪŋ] N **1** (= *making shorter*) (*gen*) acortamiento *m*; [*of rations etc*] reducción *f*
2 (*esp US*) (*Culin*) manteca *f*, grasa *f*
shortfall [ˈʃɔːtfɔːl] N (*in profits*) déficit *m* (**in** en); (*in payments, savings*) disminución *f* (**in** de); (*in numbers*) insuficiencia *f* (**in de**) • **~ in earnings** ingresos *mpl* insuficientes • **there is a ~ of £5,000** faltan 5.000 libras • **the ~ of £5,000** las 5.000 libras que faltan • **there is a ~ of 200 in the registrations for this course** hay 200 matriculaciones menos para este curso
short-haired [ˈʃɔːtˈhɛəd] ADJ pelicorto
shorthand [ˈʃɔːthænd] N taquigrafía *f* • **to take ~** escribir en taquigrafía • **to take sth down in ~** escribir algo taquigráficamente
CPD ▸ **shorthand note** nota *f* taquigráfica ▸ **shorthand notebook** cuaderno *m* de taquigrafía ▸ **shorthand speed** palabras *fpl* por minuto (en taquigrafía) ▸ **shorthand typing** taquimecanografía *f* ▸ **shorthand typist** taquimecanógrafo/a *m/f* ▸ **shorthand writer** taquígrafo/a *m/f*
short-handed [ˈʃɔːtˈhændɪd] ADJ falto de mano de obra/personal
short-haul [ˈʃɔːthɔːl] ADJ de corto recorrido
shortie* [ˈʃɔːtɪ] N = **shorty**
shortish [ˈʃɔːtɪʃ] ADJ [*person*] más bien bajo, bajito; [*novel, play, film*] más bien corto
short-list [ˈʃɔːtˈlɪst] VT • **to short-list sb** preseleccionar a algn, poner a algn en la lista de candidatos a entrevistar
short-lived [ˈʃɔːtˈlɪvd] ADJ [*of happiness*] efímero
shortly [ˈʃɔːtlɪ] ADV **1** (= *soon*) dentro de poco, en breve (*frm*), ahorita (*Mex*) • **she's going to London ~** irá a Londres dentro de poco • **details will be released ~** los detalles se comunicarán en breve • **we'll be along ~** iremos enseguida • **~ before/after** poco antes/después • **~ before two** poco antes de las dos
2 (= *curtly*) bruscamente, secamente
shortness [ˈʃɔːtnɪs] N **1** (*in length, distance*) lo corto; [*of message etc*] brevedad *f*; [*of person*] baja estatura *f* • **because of the ~ of my memory** debido a mi mala memoria • **~ of sight** miopía *f* • **~ of breath** falta *f* de aliento, respiración *f* difícil
2 (= *curtness*) brusquedad *f*, sequedad *f*
short-order cook [ʃɔːtɔːdəˈkʊk] N (*esp US*) cocinero/a *m/f* de comida rápida
short-range [ˈʃɔːtˈreɪndʒ] ADJ [*gun*] de corto alcance; [*aircraft*] de autonomía limitada, de corto radio en acción
short-run [ˈʃɔːtrʌn] ADJ breve, de alcance limitado
shorts [ʃɔːts] NPL pantalones *mpl* cortos • **a pair of ~** un pantalón corto, unos pantalones cortos
short-sighted [ˈʃɔːtˈsaɪtɪd] ADJ **1** (*lit*) miope, corto de vista
2 (*fig*) [*person*] miope, con poca visión (de futuro); [*measure etc*] con poca visión (de futuro)
short-sightedly [ˈʃɔːtˈsaɪtɪdlɪ] ADV **1** (*lit*) con ojos de miope
2 (*fig*) con poca visión (de futuro)
short-sightedness [ˈʃɔːtˈsaɪtɪdnɪs] N **1** (*lit*) miopía *f*
2 (*fig*) falta *f* de visión (de futuro)
short-sleeved [ˈʃɔːtsliːvd] ADJ de manga corta
short-staffed [ʃɔːtˈstɑːft] ADJ falto de personal
short-stay [ˈʃɔːtsteɪ] ADJ [*ward*] de hospitalización breve; [*visitor, student*] de

estancia limitada
CPD ▸ **short-stay car park** aparcamiento *m* de corta duración, aparcamiento *m* de tiempo limitado

shortstop [ˈʃɔːtstɒp] N (*Baseball*) shortstop *m*

short-tempered [ˈʃɔːtˈtempəd] ADJ irritable

short-term [ˈʃɔːttɜːm] ADJ a corto plazo • **a short-term loan** un préstamo a plazo corto • **short-term car park** zona *f* de estacionamiento limitado
CPD ▸ **short-term memory** memoria *f* a corto plazo

short-termism [ˌʃɔːtˈtɜːmɪzəm] N política *f* del corto plazo

short-time [ˈʃɔːtˈtaɪm] ADJ • **short-time working** trabajo *m* de horario reducido • **to be on short-time working** trabajar jornadas reducidas *or* de horarios reducidos
ADV • **to work short-time** trabajar jornadas reducidas *or* de horarios reducidos

short-wave [ˈʃɔːtˌweɪv] ADJ (*Rad*) de onda corta

short-winded [ˈʃɔːtˈwɪndɪd] ADJ corto de resuello

shorty* [ˈʃɔːtɪ] N persona *f* bajita

shot [ʃɒt] PT, PP *of* **shoot**
N **1** (= *act of shooting*) tiro *m*; (*causing wound*) balazo *m*; (= *sound*) tiro *m*, disparo *m* • **his ~ missed** erró el tiro • **he received a ~ in the leg** recibió un balazo en la pierna • **two ~s rang out** se oyeron dos tiros *or* disparos • **a ~ across the bows** (*lit, fig*) un cañonazo de advertencia • **there was an exchange of ~s** hubo un tiroteo • **to fire a ~ at sth/sb** disparar a algo/disparar a *or* sobre algn • **he fired two ~s into her head** le disparó dos tiros a la cabeza • **they surrendered without a ~ being fired** se rindieron sin ofrecer resistencia • **he was off like a ~** salió disparado *or* como un rayo • **I'd do it like a ~ if I had the chance** no dudaría en hacerlo si se me presentara la oportunidad • **I was over there like a ~** en un segundo me presenté allí • **to take a ~ at sth/sb** (*lit*) pegar un tiro a algo/algn; (*fig*) atacar algo/a algn; ▹ **long[1], parting**
2 (= *missile*) bala *f*, proyectil *m*; (= *shotgun pellets*) perdigones *mpl*; (*Athletics*) peso *m* • **to put the ~** lanzar el peso
3 (= *person*) tirador(a) *m/f* • **he's a bad/good ~** es un mal/buen tirador; ▹ **big, hotshot**
4 (*Ftbl*) tiro *m*; (*Golf, Tennis*) golpe *m*; (*Snooker*) golpe *m*, jugada *f*; (= *throw*) tirada *f*, echada *f* • **he missed two ~s at goal** falló dos tiros a puerta • **good ~!** ¡buen tiro! • IDIOM: • **to call the ~s** mandar, llevar la voz cantante
5 (= *attempt*) tentativa *f*, intento *m* • **just give it your best ~** limítate a hacerlo lo mejor que puedas • **to have a ~ at sth** intentar algo • **I don't think there's much chance of persuading her but I'll have a ~ at it** no creo que haya muchas posibilidades de convencerla pero probaré *or* lo intentaré • **do you want another ~ at it?** ¿quieres volver a intentarlo?, ¿quieres volver a probar? • IDIOM: • **a ~ in the dark** un palo de ciego, una tentativa a ciegas
6 (= *turn to play*) • **it's your ~** te toca (a ti)
7 (= *injection*) inyección *f*; (= *dose*) dosis *f inv*; [*of alcohol*] trago *m*; [*of drug**] pico* *m*, chute* *m* • **a ~ of rum** un trago de ron • IDIOM: • **a ~ in the arm***: • **it's a ~ in the arm for the peace process** es una importante ayuda para el proceso de paz • **the economy needs a ~ in the arm** la economía necesita estímulo
8 (*Phot*) foto *f*; (*Cine*) toma *f*, plano *m*
ADJ **1** (= *suffused*) • **~ silk** seda *f* tornasolada • **his story is ~ through with inconsistencies** su narración está plagada de incongruencias • **black marble ~ through with red veins** mármol negro con vetas rojas
2* (= *rid*) • IDIOM: • **to get ~ of sth/sb** deshacerse *or* librarse de algo/algn
3* (= *exhausted*) [*person, nerves*] deshecho, hecho polvo* • **what little confidence he had is ~ to pieces** la poca seguridad que tenía en sí mismo se ha ido al traste
CPD ▸ **shot glass** copa *f* de chupito ▸ **shot put** (*Sport*) lanzamiento *m* de pesos ▸ **shot putter** lanzador(a) *m/f* de pesos ▸ **shot silk** seda *f* tornasolada

shotgun [ˈʃɒtgʌn] N escopeta *f*
CPD ▸ **shotgun marriage, shotgun wedding** casamiento *m* a la fuerza • **to have a ~ wedding** casarse a la fuerza, casarse de penalty*

should [ʃʊd] MODAL VB **1** (*used to form conditional tense*) • **I ~ go if they sent for me** iría si me llamasen • **I ~ be out at the time • if I ~ be out at the time** si estoy fuera en ese momento • **I ~n't be surprised if ...** no me sorprendería si ... • **I ~ have liked to ...** me hubiera gustado ..., quisiera haber ... • **thanks, I ~ like to** gracias, me gustaría • **I ~n't like to say** prefiero no decirlo • **I ~ think so** supongo que sí • **I ~ be so lucky!** ¡ojalá!
2 (*duty, advisability, desirability*) deber • **all cars ~ carry a first-aid kit** todos los coches deberían llevar un botiquín • **you ~ take more exercise** deberías hacer más ejercicio • **I ~ have been a doctor** yo debería haber sido médico • **you ~n't do that** no deberías hacerlo, más vale no hacer eso • **I ~n't if I were you** yo que tú no lo haría • **he ~ know that ...** debiera *or* debería saber que ... • **all is as it ~ be** todo está en regla • **..., which is as it ~ be ...**, como es razonable, ..., que es como tiene que ser • **why ~ I?** ¿por qué lo voy a hacer?, ¿por qué tengo que hacerlo? • **why ~ he (have done it)?** ¿por qué lo iba a hacer?, ¿por qué tenía que hacerlo? • **why ~ you want to know?** ¿por qué has de saberlo tú?
3 (*statements of probability*) deber de • **he ~ pass his exams** debería de aprobar los exámenes • **they ~ have arrived by now** deben (de) haber llegado ya • **he ~ be there by now** ya debería estar allí • **they ~ arrive tomorrow** deberán *or* deben (de) llegar mañana • **that ~n't be too hard** eso no debería ser muy difícil • **I ~ have told you before** tendría que *or* debería habértelo dicho antes • **this ~ be good** esto promete ser bueno
4 (*subjunctive uses*) • **... and who ~ I bump into but Mike?** ... ¿y con quién crees que me encuentro? ¡pues con Mike! • **he ordered that it ~ be done** mandó que se hiciera

shoulder [ˈʃəʊldə^r] N **1** (*Anat*) hombro *m* • **to have broad ~s** (*lit*) ser ancho de espaldas; (*fig*) tener mucho aguante • **they carried him ~ high** le llevaron a hombros • **he was carried out on their ~s** le sacaron a hombros • **all the responsibilities fell on his ~s** tuvo que cargar con todas las responsabilidades • **to look over one's ~** mirar por encima del hombro • **to look over sb's ~** (*lit*) mirar por encima del hombro de algn; (*fig*) vigilar a algn • **to carry sth over one's ~** llevar algo en hombros • **to stand ~ to ~** estar hombro con hombro • IDIOMS: • **to give sb the cold ~** dar de lado a algn • **to cry on sb's ~** desahogarse con algn • **to put one's ~ to the wheel** arrimar el hombro • **to rub ~s with sb** codearse con algn • **to give sb sth straight from the ~** decir algo a algn sin rodeos; ▹ **round-shouldered**
2 [*of coat etc*] hombro *m* • **padded ~s** hombreras *fpl*
3 [*of meat*] lomo *m*
4 [*of hill, mountain*] lomo *m*
5 [*of road*] arcén *m*
VT **1** (= *carry*) llevar al hombro; (*pick up*) poner al hombro • **~ arms!** ¡armas al hombro!
2 (*fig*) [+ *burden, responsibility*] cargar con • **to ~ the blame** cargar con la culpa
3 (= *push*) • **to ~ sb aside** apartar a algn a un lado de un empujón • **to ~ one's way through** abrirse paso a empujones
CPD ▸ **shoulder bag** bolso *m* de bandolera ▸ **shoulder blade** omóplato *m* ▸ **shoulder flash** (*Mil*) charretera *f* ▸ **shoulder holster** pistolera *f* ▸ **shoulder joint** articulación *f* del hombro ▸ **shoulder pad** hombrera *f* ▸ **shoulder patch** = **shoulder flash** ▸ **shoulder strap** tirante *m*; [*of satchel*] bandolera *f*; (*Mil*) dragona *f*

shoulder-high [ʃəʊldəˈhaɪ] ADJ a la altura de los hombros

shoulderknot [ˈʃəʊldənɒt] N dragona *f*, charretera *f*

shoulder-length [ˈʃəʊldəˌleŋθ] ADJ que llega hasta los hombros

shouldn't [ˈʃʊdnt] = **should not**

should've [ˈʃʊdv] = **should have**

shout [ʃaʊt] N **1** (= *loud cry*) grito *m* • **a ~ of anger** un grito de ira • **there were ~s of applause** hubo grandes aplausos • **to give sb a ~** pegar un grito a algn*, avisar a algn • **give me a ~ when you've finished** pégame un grito* *or* avísame cuando hayas terminado • **a ~ of joy** un grito de alegría • **there were ~s of laughter** hubo grandes carcajadas • **a ~ of pain** un grito de dolor • **a ~ of protest** un grito de protesta • IDIOM: • **he's still in with a ~*** todavía tiene una posibilidad de ganar
2 (*Brit**) (= *round of drinks*) ronda *f* • **it's my ~ — what are you drinking?** me toca pagar esta ronda — ¿qué tomáis?
VT gritar • **to ~ abuse at sb** insultar a algn a gritos • **to ~ o.s. hoarse** gritar hasta quedarse ronco • **he ~ed a warning** pegó un grito de advertencia
VI (= *cry out*) gritar • **I had to ~ to make myself heard** tenía que gritar para que se me oyese • **his goal gave the fans something to ~ about** su gol les dio motivo a los hinchas para que gritaran • **to ~ at sb** gritar a algn • **his parents were ~ing at each other** sus padres estaban discutiendo a gritos • **to ~ for sth/sb** pedir algo a gritos/llamar a algn a gritos • **I ~ed for help** pedí socorro a gritos • **she ~ed for Jane to come** llamó a Jane a gritos para que viniera • **to ~ with glee/joy** gritar de alegría • **to ~ with laughter** reírse a carcajadas
▸ **shout down** VT + ADV [+ *person*] abuchear, hacer callar a gritos
▸ **shout out** VT + ADV gritar, decir a voz en grito • **we ~ed out our thanks** gritamos las gracias, dimos las gracias a gritos • **they ~ed out greetings** gritaron los saludos, nos saludaron a gritos
VI + ADV gritar, dar un grito, pegar un grito*

shouting [ˈʃaʊtɪŋ] N gritos *mpl*, vocerío *m* • **within ~ distance (of sth)** a tiro de piedra (de algo) • IDIOM: • **it's all over bar the ~** ya es asunto concluido
CPD ▸ **shouting match** pelea *f or* riña *f* de gallos • **the TV debate turned into a ~ match** el debate televisado se convirtió en una pelea *or* riña de gallos

shove [ʃʌv] N empujón *m* • **to give sth/sb a ~** dar un empujón a algo/algn • **give it a good ~** dale un buen empujón

(VT) **1** (= *push*) empujar • **he ~d everyone aside** apartó a un lado a todo el mundo a empujones • **she ~d her plate away** apartó su plato de un empujón • **~ the table back against the wall** empuja la mesa contra la pared • **his friends ~d him forward** sus amigos le empujaron hacia adelante • **to ~ sth/sb in** meter a algo/algn a empujones • **they ~d the car over the cliff** fueron empujando el coche hasta que cayó por el acantilado
2* (= *put*) poner, meter • **~ it here** ponlo aquí • **~ another record on** pon otro disco • **~ it over to me** trae pa'acá*
(VI) empujar, dar empujones • **stop shoving!*** ¡deja de empujar!
▸ **shove about, shove around** (VT + ADV) **1** (*lit*) [+ *object, person*] empujar de un lado a otro
2* (= *bully*) tiranizar
▸ **shove off** (VI + ADV) **1** (*Naut*) alejarse del muelle *etc*
2* (= *leave*) largarse, marcharse • **~ off!** ¡lárgate!*
(VT + ADV) • **to ~ a boat off** echar afuera un bote
▸ **shove out** (VT + ADV) • **to ~ a boat out** echar afuera un bote
▸ **shove over, shove up** (VI + ADV) correrse • **~ over!** ¡córrete!
shovel ['ʃʌvl] (N) pala *f* • **mechanical ~** pala *f* mecánica, excavadora *f*
(VT) mover con pala • **to ~ earth into a pile** amontonar tierra con una pala • **to ~ coal on to a fire** añadir carbón a la lumbre con pala • **they were ~ling out the mud** estaban sacando el lodo con palas • **he was ~ling food into his mouth*** se zampaba la comida
▸ **shovel up** (VT + ADV) [+ *coal etc*] levantar con una pala; [+ *snow*] quitar con pala
shovelboard ['ʃʌvlbɔːd] (N) juego *m* de tejo
shoveler ['ʃʌvləʳ] (N) **1** (*Orn*) espátula *f* común, pato *m* cuchareta
2 (= *tool*) paleador *m*
shovelful ['ʃʌvlfʊl] (N) paletada *f*
show [ʃəʊ] (VB: PT: **showed**, PP: **shown**) (N)
1 (= *showing*) demostración *f*, manifestación *f* • **~ of hands** votación *f* a mano alzada • **an impressive ~ of power** una impresionante exhibición de poder • **a ~ of strength** una demostración de fuerza
2 (= *exhibition*) exposición *f*; [*of trade*] feria *f* • **agricultural ~** feria *f* agrícola • **fashion ~** pase *m* de modelos • **motor ~** salón *m* del automóvil • **to be on ~** estar expuesto;
▹ **flower, horse, Lord Mayor**
3 (= *sight*) • **the garden is a splendid ~** el jardín es un espectáculo • **the dahlias make a fine ~** las dalias están espléndidas
4 (*Theat*) **a** (= *performance*) espectáculo *m*, función *f* • **to go to a ~** ir al teatro • **the last ~ starts at 11** la última función empieza a las 11 • **there is no ~ on Sundays** el domingo no hay función • **to stage a ~** montar un espectáculo
b (*fig*) • **bad ~!** ¡malo! • **good ~!*** ¡muy bien hecho! • **to put up a good ~*** dar buena cuenta de sí, hacer un buen papel • **on with the ~!** • **the ~ must go on!** ¡que siga el espectáculo! • **to put up a poor ~*** no dar buena cuenta de sí, hacer un mal papel • **it's a poor ~*** es una vergüenza • IDIOMS: • **to give the ~ away** (*deliberately*) tirar de la manta; (*involuntarily*) clarearse • **let's get this ~ on the road** echémosnos a la carretera • **to steal the ~** acaparar toda la atención
5 (*Rad, TV*) programa *m* • **a radio ~** un programa de radio
6 (= *outward appearance*) apariencia *f* • **it's all ~ with him** en su caso todo es apariencia, todo lo hace para impresionar • **to do sth for ~** hacer algo para impresionar • **it's just for ~** (*behaviour*) es para impresionar nada más; (*object*) (= *for decoration*) es solo un adorno; (= *not real*) es de adorno • **the party made a ~ of unity at its conference** el partido presentó una fachada de gran unidad en su congreso • **to make a ~ of resistance** fingir resistencia
7 (= *affected display*) alarde *m* • **to make a great ~ of sympathy** hacer un gran alarde de compasión
8* (= *organization*) • **who's in charge of this ~?** ¿quién manda aquí? • **this is my ~** aquí mando yo • **he runs the ~** manda él, él es el amo
(VT) **1** (*gen*) enseñar, mostrar • **to ~ sb sth** • **~ sth to sb** enseñar *or* mostrar algo a algn • **have I ~n you my hat?** ¿te he enseñado *or* mostrado ya mi sombrero? • **he ~ed me his new car** me enseñó *or* mostró su nuevo coche • **to ~ o.s.: she won't ~ herself here again** no volverá a dejarse ver por aquí • **come on, ~ yourself!** vamos, ¡sal de ahí! • **it ~s itself in his speech** se revela en su forma de hablar, se le nota en el habla • **to ~ one's cards** *or* **one's hand** (*lit*) poner las cartas boca arriba; (*fig*) descubrir el juego • **don't ~ your face here again** no te vuelvas a dejar ver por aquí • **she likes to ~ her legs** le gusta enseñar *or* (*frm*) hacer exhibición de sus piernas • **he had nothing to ~ for his trouble** no vió recompensado su esfuerzo, no le lució nada el esfuerzo • **to ~ one's passport** mostrar *or* presentar su pasaporte
2 (= *exhibit*) [+ *paintings*] exhibir; [+ *goods*] exponer; [+ *film*] proyectar, pasar; [+ *slides*] proyectar; (*Theat*) representar, dar* • **to ~ a picture at the Academy** exhibir un cuadro en la Academia • **to ~ a film at Cannes** proyectar una película en Cannes • **the film was first ~n in 1968** la película se estrenó en 1968
3 (= *indicate*) [*dial, gauge, instrument*] marcar • **the speedometer ~s a speed of ...** el velocímetro marca ... • **it ~s 200 degrees** marca *or* indica 200 grados • **the motorways are ~n in black** las autopistas están marcadas en negro • **the clock ~s two o'clock** el reloj marca las dos • **the figures ~ a rise** las cifras arrojan un aumento • **as ~n in the illustration** como se ve en el grabado • **to ~ a loss/profit** (*Comm*) arrojar un saldo negativo/positivo
4 (= *demonstrate*) demostrar • **to ~ that ...** demostrar que ..., hacer ver que ... • **it just goes to ~ (that) ...** queda demostrado (que) ... • **I ~ed him that this could not be true** le hice ver *or* demostré que esto no podía ser cierto • **this ~s him to be a coward** esto deja manifiesto lo cobarde que es, esto demuestra que es un cobarde • **I'll ~ him!*** ¡ya va a ver!, ¡ese se va a enterar! • **to ~ what one is made of** demostrar de lo que uno es capaz
5 (= *express, manifest*) demostrar • **to ~ one's affection** demostrar su cariño • **she ~ed great courage** demostró gran valentía • **to ~ his disagreement, he ...** para mostrar su disconformidad, él ... • **he ~ed no fear** no demostró tener miedo, no mostró ningún miedo • **her face ~ed her happiness** se le veía la felicidad en la cara • **she ~ed great intelligence** demostró ser muy inteligente, mostró gran inteligencia • **she ~ed no reaction** no acusó reacción alguna • **the choice of dishes ~s excellent taste** la selección de platos demuestra *or* muestra un gusto muy fino
6 (= *reveal*) • **she's beginning to ~ her age** ya empieza a aparentar su edad • **white shoes soon ~ the dirt** los zapatos blancos pronto dejan ver la suciedad • **to ~ o.s. incompetent** descubrir su incompetencia, mostrarse incompetente
7 (= *direct, conduct*) • **to ~ sb to the door** acompañar a algn a la puerta • **to ~ sb the door** (*fig*) echar a algn con cajas destempladas • **to ~ sb into a room** hacer que pase algn, hacer entrar a algn en un cuarto • **I was ~n into a large hall** me hicieron pasar a un vestíbulo grande • **to ~ sb over** *or* **round a house** enseñar a algn una casa • **they ~ed us round the garden** nos mostraron *or* enseñaron el jardín • **who is going to ~ us round?** ¿quién actuará de guía?, ¿quién será nuestro guía? • **to ~ sb to his seat** acompañar a algn a su asiento • **to ~ sb the way** señalar el camino a algn
(VI) **1** [*stain, emotion, underskirt*] notarse, verse • **it doesn't ~** no se ve, no se nota • **your slip's ~ing** se te ve la combinación • **fear ~ed on her face** se le notaba *or* (*frm*) manifestaba el miedo en la cara • **don't worry, it won't ~** no te preocupes, no se notará • **"I've never been riding before" — "it ~s"** —nunca había montado a caballo antes —se nota • **the tulips are beginning to ~** empiezan a brotar los tulipanes
2 [*film*] • **there's a horror film ~ing at the Odeon** están pasando *or* (*LAm*) dando una película de horror en el Odeón
3 (= *demonstrate*) • **it just goes to ~ that ...!** ¡hay que ver que ...!
4 (*esp US*) (*also* **show up**) (= *arrive*) venir, aparecer
(CPD) ▸ **show apartment** (*Brit*) apartamento *m* modelo, piso *m* piloto (*Sp*), departamento *m* piloto *or* modelo (*LAm*) ▸ **show bill** cartel *m* ▸ **show biz***, **show business** el mundo del espectáculo; ▹ **showbiz column, showbiz reporter** ▸ **show flat** (*Brit*) apartamento *m* modelo, piso *m* piloto (*Sp*), departamento *m* piloto *or* modelo (*LAm*) ▸ **show home, show house** (*Brit*) casa *f* modelo, casa *f* piloto ▸ **show jumper** participante *mf* en concursos de saltos *or* de hípica ▸ **show jumping** concursos *mpl* de saltos *or* de hípica ▸ **show ring** pista *f* de exhibición ▸ **show trial** proceso *m* organizado con fines propagandísticos ▸ **show window** escaparate *m*
▸ **show around** (VT + ADV) enseñar • **would you ~ me around?** ¿me lo vas a enseñar todo?
(VT + PREP) enseñar • **he ~ed me around the house** me enseñó la casa
▸ **show in** (VT + ADV) hacer pasar • **~ him in!** ¡que pase!
▸ **show off** (VI + ADV) presumir, darse tono • **to ~ off in front of one's friends** presumir *or* darse tono delante de las amistades • **stop ~ing off!** ¡no presumas!
(VT + ADV) **1** [+ *beauty etc*] hacer resaltar, destacar
2 (*pej*) (= *display*) hacer alarde de, ostentar
▸ **show out** (VT + ADV) acompañar a la puerta
▸ **show round** (VT + ADV), (VT + PREP) (*Brit*) = show around
▸ **show through** (VI + ADV) verse
▸ **show up** (VI + ADV) **1** (= *be visible*) verse, notarse
2* (= *arrive*) venir, aparecer • **he ~ed up late as usual** vino *or* apareció tarde, como de costumbre
(VT + ADV) **1** [+ *visitor etc*] hacer subir • **~ him up!** ¡hazle subir!
2 (= *reveal*) [+ *defect*] poner de manifiesto • **he was ~n up as an imposter** se demostró que era un impostor • **the bright lighting ~ed up**

S

her scars el alumbrado hizo resaltar sus cicatrices
3 (= *embarrass*) dejar en ridículo, poner en evidencia • **please don't ~ me up!** por favor, no me hagas quedar en ridículo *or* no me pongas en evidencia
showbiz column (N) columna *f* de prensa rosa; ▹ show biz
showbiz reporter (N) *periodista especializado en prensa rosa*; ▹ show biz
showboat [ˈʃəʊbəʊt] (N) barco-teatro *m*
(VI)* alardear, fardar (*Sp**), vacilar (*Sp**)
showcase [ˈʃəʊkeɪs] (N) (*in shop, museum*) vitrina *f*
(VT) (*fig*) (= *exhibit, display*) exhibir, mostrar • **the festival ~s an impressive line-up of previously banned work** el festival exhibe *or* muestra una impresionante selección de obras anteriormente prohibidas • **an album which also ~s her strong singing voice** un disco que también sirve de escaparate a *or* para su portentosa voz
(CPD) ▸ **showcase project** proyecto *m* modelo
showdown [ˈʃəʊdaʊn] (N) enfrentamiento *m* (final) • **to have a ~ with sb** enfrentarse con algn • **if it comes to a ~** si llega a producirse un conflicto • **the Suez ~** la crisis de Suez
shower [ˈʃaʊəʳ] (N) **1** [*of rain*] chubasco *m*, chaparrón *m* • **scattered ~s** chubascos dispersos
2 (*fig*) [*of arrows, stones, blows etc*] lluvia *f*
3 (*in bathroom*) ducha *f*, regadera *f* (*Mex*) • **to have** *or* **take a ~** ducharse, tomar una ducha
4 (*Brit**) (*pej*) (= *people*) • **what a ~!** ¡que montón de inútiles!
5 (*US*) (= *party*) fiesta *f* de obsequio; ▹ baby
(VT) (*fig*) • **they ~ed gifts (up)on the queen** colmaron a la reina de regalos • **he was ~ed with invitations** le llovieron invitaciones • **to ~ sb with honours** • **~ honours on sb** colmar a algn de honores
(VI) **1** (= *rain*) caer un chaparrón *or* chubasco
2 (= *take a shower*) ducharse, tomar una ducha
(CPD) ▸ **shower attachment** (*to put on taps*) conexión *f* de ducha (*para los grifos de la bañera*) ▸ **shower cap** gorro *m* de baño ▸ **shower cubicle** cabina *f* de ducha ▸ **shower curtain** cortina *f* de ducha ▸ **shower gel** gel *m* de baño ▸ **shower head** alcachofa *f* de la ducha ▸ **shower room** baño *m* con ducha ▸ **shower stall** cabina *f* de ducha ▸ **shower tray** plato *m* de la ducha ▸ **shower unit** ducha *f*
showerbath† [ˈʃaʊəbɑːθ] (N) (PL: **showerbaths** [ˈʃaʊəbɑːðz]) ducha *f* • **to take a ~** ducharse, tomar una ducha
showerproof [ˈʃaʊəpruːf] (ADJ) impermeable
showery [ˈʃaʊərɪ] (ADJ) [*weather*] lluvioso; [*day*] lluvioso, de lluvia • **it will be ~ tomorrow** mañana habrá chubascos *or* chaparrones*
showgirl [ˈʃəʊgɜːl] (N) corista *f*
showground [ˈʃəʊgraʊnd] (N) recinto *m* ferial, real *m* de la feria
showily [ˈʃəʊɪlɪ] (ADV) ostentosamente
showiness [ˈʃəʊɪnɪs] (N) ostentación *f*
showing [ˈʃəʊɪŋ] (N) **1** [*of film*] proyección *f*, pase *m*; [*of paintings etc*] exposición *f* • **a private ~** [*of film*] un pase privado; [*of paintings*] una exposición a puertas cerradas • **a second ~ of "The Blue Angel"** un reestreno de "El Ángel Azul"
2 (= *performance*) actuación *f* • **the poor ~ of the team** la pobre actuación del equipo
showing-off [ˌʃəʊɪŋˈɒf] (N) **1** (= *displaying*) lucimiento *m*
2 (*pej*) presunción *f*
showman [ˈʃəʊmən] (N) (PL: **showmen**) (*at fair, circus*) empresario *m* • **he's a real ~!** (*fig*) ¡es todo un número *or* espectáculo!
showmanship [ˈʃəʊmənʃɪp] (N) (*fig*) espectacularidad *f*, teatralidad *f*
shown [ʃəʊn] (PP) *of* show
show-off* [ˈʃəʊɒf] (N) presumido/a *m/f*, fantasmón/ona *m/f* (*Sp**)
showpiece [ˈʃəʊpiːs] (N) (= *centrepiece*) joya *f*, lo mejor • **the ~ of the exhibition is …** la joya *or* lo mejor de la exposición es … • **this vase is a real ~** este florero es realmente excepcional
showplace [ˈʃəʊpleɪs] (N) lugar *m* de interés turístico • **Granada is a ~** Granada es un lugar de interés turístico, Granada es ciudad monumental
showroom [ˈʃəʊrʊm] (N) (*Comm*) sala *f* de muestras; (*Art*) sala *f* de exposición, galería *f* de arte • **in ~ condition** en excelentes condiciones, como nuevo
show-stopper* [ˈʃəʊˌstɒpəʳ] (N) sensación *f* • **to be a show-stopper** quitar el hipo*, causar sensación
show-stopping* [ʃəʊˈstɒpɪŋ] (ADJ) [*performance*] sensacional, impresionante; [*product*] sensacional
showtime [ˈʃəʊtaɪm] (N) (*Theat, TV*) comienzo *m* del espectáculo
showy [ˈʃəʊɪ] (ADJ) (COMPAR: **showier**, SUPERL: **showiest**) ostentoso
shpt (ABBR) (*Comm*) (= **shipment**) e/
shrank [ʃræŋk] (PT) *of* shrink
shrapnel [ˈʃræpnl] (N) metralla *f*
shred [ʃred] (N) [*of cloth*] jirón *m*; [*of paper*] tira *f* • **without a ~ of clothing on** sin nada de ropa encima • **if you had a ~ of decency** si usted tuviese un mínimo de honradez • **you haven't got a ~ of evidence** no tienes la más mínima prueba • **in ~s** (*lit, fig*) hecho jirones *or* trizas • **her dress hung in ~s** su vestido estaba hecho jirones *or* trizas • **to tear sth to ~s** (*lit, fig*) hacer algo trizas • **to tear an argument to ~s** hacer pedazos *or* trizas un argumento • **the crowd will tear him to ~s** la gente le hará pedazos • **there isn't a ~ of truth in it** eso no tiene ni pizca *or* chispa de verdad
(VT) [+ *paper*] hacer trizas, triturar; [+ *food*] despedazar
shredder [ˈʃredəʳ] (N) (*for documents, papers*) trituradora *f*; (*for vegetables*) picadora *f*
shrew [ʃruː] (N) **1** (*Zool*) musaraña *f*
2 (*fig*) (*pej*) (= *woman*) arpía *f*, fiera *f* • **"The Taming of the Shrew"** "La fierecilla domada"
shrewd [ʃruːd] (ADJ) (COMPAR: **shrewder**, SUPERL: **shrewdest**) [*person, politician, businessperson*] astuto, sagaz; [*observer, glance, look*] perspicaz; [*remark, observation*] sagaz, perspicaz; [*eyes*] perspicaz, inteligente; [*assessment*] muy acertado; [*investment*] inteligente • **it was seen as a ~ political move** se vio como una hábil *or* astuta maniobra política • **I can make a ~ guess at how many people were there** estoy casi seguro de acertar si digo cuánta gente había allí • **she had a ~ idea** *or* **suspicion (that) …** estaba casi segura de que … • **I've got a pretty ~ idea of what's going on here** ya me puedo imaginar lo que está pasando aquí • **she's very ~ in matters of money** es un lince para cuestiones de dinero • **to be a ~ judge of character** tener buen ojo para juzgar a la gente • **that was very ~ of you** en eso has sido muy perspicaz
shrewdly [ˈʃruːdlɪ] (ADV) [*say, ask, point out*] sagazmente; [*reason*] con perspicacia, con sagacidad; [*act*] hábilmente, con astucia; [*invest*] inteligentemente • **she had ~ guessed the reason for his absence** había adivinado astutamente la razón de su ausencia, se había dado cuenta hábilmente de la razón de su ausencia
shrewdness [ˈʃruːdnɪs] (N) [*of person*] astucia *f*, sagacidad *f*; [*of assessment, reasoning*] lo acertado; [*of remark, observation*] sagacidad *f*, perspicacia *f*; [*of plan*] lo inteligente
shrewish [ˈʃruːɪʃ] (ADJ) regañón, de mal genio
shriek [ʃriːk] (N) chillido *m*, grito *m* agudo • **a ~ of pain** un grito de dolor • **with ~s of laughter** con grandes carcajadas
(VI) chillar • **to ~ with laughter/pain** chillar de risa/dolor • **the colour just ~s at you** es un color de lo más chillón
(VT) gritar • **"I hate you!" she ~ed** —¡te odio! —gritó • **to ~ abuse at sb** lanzar improperios contra algn
shrieking [ˈʃriːkɪŋ] (ADJ) [*child*] chillón
(N) chillidos *mpl*, gritos *mpl*
shrift [ʃrɪft] (N) • **to give sb short ~** despachar a algn sin rodeos • **he gave that idea short ~** mostró su completa disconformidad con tal idea • **he got short ~ from the boss** el jefe se mostró poco compasivo con él • **he'll get short ~ from me!** ¡que no venga a mí a pedir compasión!
shrike [ʃraɪk] (N) alcaudón *m*
shrill [ʃrɪl] (ADJ) (COMPAR: **shriller**, SUPERL: **shrillest**) [*voice*] chillón, agudo; [*sound*] estridente, agudo
(VT) gritar (con voz estridente)
(VI) chillar
shrillness [ˈʃrɪlnɪs] (N) [*of voice*] lo chillón, lo agudo; [*of sound*] estridencia *f*, lo agudo
shrilly [ˈʃrɪlɪ] (ADV) de modo estridente
shrimp [ʃrɪmp] (N) **1** (*Zool*) camarón *m*
2 (*fig*) enano/a *m/f*
(VI) • **to go ~ing** pescar camarones
(CPD) ▸ **shrimp cocktail** cóctel *m* de camarones ▸ **shrimp sauce** salsa *f* de camarones
shrine [ʃraɪn] (N) (*Rel*) (= *tomb*) sepulcro *m*; (= *sacred place*) lugar *m* sagrado
shrink [ʃrɪŋk] (PT: **shrank**, PP: **shrunk**) (VI) **1** (= *get smaller*) encogerse • **to ~ in the wash** encogerse al lavar • **"will not shrink"** "no se encoge", "inencogible" • **to ~ away to nothing** reducirse a nada, desaparecer
2 (*also* **shrink away, shrink back**) retroceder, echar marcha atrás • **I ~ from doing it** no me atrevo a hacerlo • **he did not ~ from touching it** no vaciló en tocarlo
(VT) encoger • **to ~ a part on** (*Tech*) montar una pieza en caliente
(N)* (= *psychiatrist*) psiquiatra *mf*
(CPD) ▸ **shrink wrap** = **shrink-wrap**
shrinkage [ˈʃrɪŋkɪdʒ] (N) (*gen*) encogimiento *m*; (*Tech*) (= *contraction*) contracción *f*; (*Comm*) (*in shops*) pérdidas *fpl*
shrinking [ˈʃrɪŋkɪŋ] (ADJ) [*clothes*] que encoge(n); [*resources etc*] que escasea(n)
(CPD) ▸ **shrinking violet** (*fig*) tímido/a *m/f*, vergonzoso/a *m/f*
shrink-wrap [ˈʃrɪŋkræp] (VT) empaquetar *or* envasar al calor
(N) plástico *m* adherente
shrink-wrapped [ˈʃrɪŋkræpt] (ADJ) empaquetado *or* envasado al calor
shrink-wrapping [ˈʃrɪŋkræpɪŋ] (N) envasado *m* al calor
shrivel [ˈʃrɪvl] (*also* **shrivel up**) (VT) [+ *plant etc*] marchitar, secar; [+ *skin*] arrugar
(VI) [*plant etc*] marchitarse, secarse; [*skin etc*] arrugarse
shrivelled, shriveled (*US*) [ˈʃrɪvld] (ADJ) [*plant etc*] marchito, seco; [*skin*] arrugado, apergaminado • **to have a ~ skin** tener la

S

piel arrugada

shroud [ʃraʊd] (N) **1** (*around corpse*) sudario *m*, mortaja *f* • **the Shroud of Turin** la Sábana Santa de Turín, el Santo Sudario de Turín
2 (*fig*) • **a ~ of mystery** un velo *or* halo de misterio
3 shrouds (*Naut*) obenques *mpl*
(VT) **1** [+ *corpse*] amortajar
2 (*fig*) velar, cubrir • **the castle was ~ed in mist** el castillo estaba envuelto en niebla • **the whole thing is ~ed in mystery** el asunto está envuelto en un halo de misterio • **the whole affair is ~ed in secrecy** el asunto se mantiene en secreto

Shrovetide [ˈʃrəʊvtaɪd] (N) carnestolendas *fpl*

Shrove Tuesday [ˈʃrəʊvˈtjuːzdɪ] (N) martes *m inv* de Carnaval (*en que en Inglaterra se sirven hojuelas*)

shrub [ʃrʌb] (N) arbusto *m*

shrubbery [ˈʃrʌbərɪ] (N) arbustos *mpl*

shrubby [ˈʃrʌbɪ] (ADJ) [*tree*] con forma de arbusto; [*area*] con muchos matojos

shrug [ʃrʌg] (N) encogimiento *m* de hombros • **he said with a ~** dijo encogiéndose de hombros
(VT) • **to ~ one's shoulders** encogerse de hombros
(VI) encogerse de hombros
▸ **shrug off** (VT + ADV) no hacer caso de • **he just ~ged it off** se encogió de hombros y no hizo caso • **you can't just ~ that off** no puedes negarle la importancia que tiene

shrunk [ʃrʌŋk] (PP) *of* **shrink**

shrunken [ˈʃrʌŋkən] (ADJ) encogido

shtick* [ʃtɪk] (N) (*US*) (= *routine, act*) rutina *f*; (= *favourite line*) frase *f* favorita

shtoom‡ [ʃtʊm] (ADJ) • **to keep ~ (about sth)** no decir ni mu (de algo)*, no decir esta boca es mía (sobre algo)*

shuck [ʃʌk] (N) **1** (= *husk*) vaina *f*, hollejo *m*
2 (*US*) [*of shellfish*] concha *f* (de marisco)
3 • **~s!** ¡cáscaras!
(VT) **1** [+ *peas etc*] desenvainar
2 (*US*) [+ *shellfish*] desbullar

shudder [ˈʃʌdəʳ] (VI) [*person*] estremecerse (**with** de); [*machinery*] vibrar • **the car ~ed to a halt** el coche paró a sacudidas • **I ~ to think** (*fig*) solo pensarlo me da horror
(N) [*of person*] estremecimiento *m*, escalofrío *m*; [*of machinery*] vibración *f*, sacudida *f* • **it gave a ~** dio una sacudida • **a ~ ran through her** se estremeció • **she realized with a ~ that ...** se estremeció al darse cuenta de que ... • **it gives me the ~s** me da escalofríos

shuffle [ˈʃʌfl] (N) **1** • **to walk with a ~** caminar arrastrando los pies
2 (*Cards*) • **to give the cards a ~** barajar (las cartas) • **whose ~ is it?** ¿a quién le toca barajar?
(VT) **1** [+ *feet*] arrastrar
2 (= *mix up*) [+ *papers*] revolver, traspapelar; [+ *cards*] barajar
3 (= *move*) • **to ~ sb aside** apartar a algn, relegar a algn a un puesto menos importante
(VI) **1** (= *walk*) arrastrar los pies • **to ~ about** moverse de un lado para otro • **to ~ in/out** entrar/salir arrastrando los pies
2 (*Cards*) barajar
▸ **shuffle off** (VI + ADV) marcharse arrastrando los pies
(VT + ADV) [+ *garment*] despojarse de; (*fig*) [+ *responsibility*] rechazar • **to ~ sth off** deshacerse de algo

shuffleboard [ˈʃʌflbɔːd] (N) juego *m* de tejo

shuffling [ˈʃʌflɪŋ] (ADJ) [*walk, steps, sound*] arrastrado • **the ~ movement of a badger** el movimiento arrastrado de un tejón

shufti, shufty‡ [ˈʃʊftɪ] (N) (*Brit*) ojeada *f* • **let's have a ~** a ver, déjame ver • **we went to take a ~** fuimos a echar un vistazo

shun [ʃʌn] (VT) **1** (= *reject*) [+ *person*] rechazar • **to feel ~ned by the world** sentirse rechazado por la gente
2 (= *avoid*) [+ *work*] evitar; [+ *publicity*] rehuir • **to ~ doing sth** evitar hacer algo

shunt [ʃʌnt] (VT) **1** (*Rail*) cambiar de vía, shuntar
2 (*fig*) • **to ~ sb about** enviar a algn de acá para allá • **the form was ~ed about between different departments** la solicitud fue enviada de departamento a departamento (sin que nadie la atendiese) • **we were ~ed about all day** nos tuvieron dando vueltas todo el día • **to ~ sb aside** apartar a algn, relegar a algn a un puesto menos importante • **he was ~ed into retirement** lograron con maña que se jubilase
(VI) • **to ~ to and fro** trajinar de acá para allá

shunter [ˈʃʌntəʳ] (N) (*Brit*) guardagujas *mf inv*

shunting [ˈʃʌntɪŋ] (N) cambio *m* de vía
(CPD) ▸ **shunting engine** locomotora *f* de maniobra ▸ **shunting yard** estación *f* de maniobras

shush [ʃʊʃ] (EXCL) ¡chis!, ¡chitón!
(VT)* callar, hacer callar

shut [ʃʌt] (PT, PP: **shut**) (VT) cerrar • **~ the door/window please** cierra la puerta/ventana por favor • **to find the door ~** encontrar que la puerta está cerrada • **they ~ the door in his face** le dieron con la puerta en las narices • **to ~ one's fingers in the door** pillarse los dedos en la puerta
(VI) cerrarse • **what time do the shops ~?** ¿a qué hora cierran las tiendas? • **we ~ at five** cerramos a las cinco • **the lid doesn't ~** la tapa no cierra (bien)
▸ **shut away** (VT + ADV) encerrar • **to ~ o.s. away** encerrarse • **he ~s himself away all day in his room** permanece encerrado todo el día en su habitación
▸ **shut down** (VI + ADV) cerrarse • **the cinema ~ down last year** el cine cerró el año pasado
(VT + ADV) [+ *lid, business, factory*] cerrar; [+ *machine*] apagar; (*by law*) clausurar
▸ **shut in** (VT + ADV) (= *enclose*) encerrar; (= *surround*) cercar, rodear • **to feel ~ in** sentirse encerrado • **the runner was ~ in** el atleta se encontró tapado, al atleta se le cerró el paso
▸ **shut off** (VT + ADV) **1** (= *stop*) [+ *water, power*] cortar, cerrar; [+ *engine, machine*] apagar
2 (= *isolate*) aislar (**from** de) • **to be ~ off from** estar aislado de
▸ **shut out** (VT + ADV) (= *leave outside*) dejar fuera; (= *put outside*) sacar; (= *close door on*) cerrar la puerta a; (= *keep out*) excluir; (= *block*) tapar
▸ **shut to** (VT + ADV) cerrar
(VI + ADV) cerrarse
▸ **shut up** (VI + ADV)* (= *be quiet*) callarse • **~ up!** ¡cállate! • IDIOM: • **to ~ up like a clam** callarse como un muerto
(VT + ADV) **1** (= *close*) cerrar
2 (= *enclose*) encerrar
3* (= *silence*) callar, hacer callar

shutdown [ˈʃʌtdaʊn] (N) **1** [*of factory, shop, business*] cierre *m*
2 (*Ftbl*) (*also* **winter shutdown**) *suspensión temporal de la actividad futbolística durante las semanas más inclementes del invierno*

shut-eye* [ˈʃʌtaɪ] (N) sueño *m* • **to get some shut-eye** echar un sueñecito*

shut-in [ˈʃʌtɪn] (ADJ) encerrado

shutoff [ˈʃʌtɒf] (N) interruptor *m*

shutout [ˈʃʌtaʊt] (N) **1** (*US*) (= *lockout*) cierre *m* patronal
2 (*Brit*) (*Sport*) • **the goalkeeper had ten successive ~s** el portero salió imbatido en diez partidos sucesivos
(CPD) ▸ **shutout bid** declaración *f* aplastante ▸ **shutout record** récord *m* de imbatibilidad

shutter [ˈʃʌtəʳ] (N) **1** (*on window*) contraventana *f*, postigo *m* • **to put up the ~s** [*shop*] cerrar del todo; (*fig*) abandonar; (*Sport**) no arriesgar
2 (*Phot*) obturador *m*
(CPD) ▸ **shutter release** (*Phot*) disparador *m* ▸ **shutter speed** velocidad *f* de obturación

shuttered [ˈʃʌtəd] (ADJ) [*house, window*] (= *fitted with shutters*) con contraventanas; (= *with shutters closed*) con las contraventanas cerradas • **the windows were ~** (= *had shutters*) las ventanas tenían contraventana(s); (= *had shutters closed*) las ventanas tenían las contraventanas cerradas

shuttle [ˈʃʌtl] (N) **1** (*for weaving, sewing*) lanzadera *f*
2 (*Aer*) puente *m* aéreo; (= *plane, train etc*) servicio *m* regular de enlace • **air ~** puente *m* aéreo
3 (*Space*) (*also* **space shuttle**) lanzadera *f or* transbordador *m* espacial
4* (*in badminton*) (= *shuttlecock*) volante *m*
(VI) [*person*] (= *go regularly*) ir y venir (**between** entre)
(VT) (= *transport*) transportar, trasladar
(CPD) ▸ **shuttle bus** autobús *m* lanzadera ▸ **shuttle flight** vuelo *m* de puente aéreo ▸ **shuttle diplomacy** viajes *mpl* diplomáticos ▸ **shuttle service** servicio *m* regular de enlace

shuttlecock [ˈʃʌtlkɒk] (N) (*Badminton*) volante *m*

shy[1] [ʃaɪ] (ADJ) (COMPAR: **shyer**, SUPERL: **shyest**) **1** (= *nervous*) [*person*] vergonzoso, tímido; [*smile*] tímido; [*animal*] asustadizo, huraño • **he was too shy to talk to anyone** era demasiado tímido para hablar con nadie • **come on, don't be shy!** ¡venga, no seas tímido *or* no tengas vergüenza! • **she went all shy when asked to give her opinion** le dio vergüenza cuando le preguntaron su opinión, le dio corte cuando le preguntaron su opinión (*Sp**) • **they may feel shy about talking to her** puede que les dé vergüenza hablar con ella, puede que les dé corte hablar con ella (*Sp**) • **she's shy of cameras** se siente cohibida delante de las cámaras • **don't be shy of telling them what you think** no tengas miedo decirles lo que piensas • **to be shy with people** ser tímido con la gente, sentirse cohibido con la gente; ▹ **bite, camera-shy, fight, gun-shy**
2 • **shy of** (*esp US*) (= *short of*): • **we're $65,000 shy of the $1 million that's needed** nos faltan 65.000 dólares para el millón de dólares que se necesitan • **he's two months shy of 70** le faltan dos meses para cumplir 70 años • **he passed away two days shy of his 95th birthday** murió a dos días de cumplir los 95 años
(VI) [*horse*] asustarse, espantarse (**at** de)
▸ **shy away** (VI + ADV) **1** (*lit*) [*horse*] asustarse, espantarse; [*person*] asustarse
2 (*fig*) • **to shy away from sth** huir *or* rehuir de algo • **to shy away from doing sth** tener miedo a hacer algo

shy[2] [ʃaɪ] (*Brit*) (N) (= *throw*) tirada *f* • **50 pence a shy** 50 peniques la tirada • **to have a shy at sth** intentar dar a algo

-shy [-ʃaɪ] (SUFFIX) ▹ **publicity-shy, camera-shy**

shyly [ˈʃaɪlɪ] (ADV) tímidamente, con timidez

shyness [ˈʃaɪnɪs] (N) [*of person, smile*] timidez *f*; [*of animal*] lo asustadizo

shyster* ['ʃaɪstəʳ] (N) (esp US) tramposo/a m/f, estafador(a) m/f; (= lawyer) picapleitos mf inv sin escrúpulos*
SI (N ABBR) (= **Système International (d'unités)**) (= system of metric units) sistema m métrico internacional
Siam [saɪ'æm] (N) (formerly) Siam m
Siamese [,saɪə'mi:z] (N) **1** (= person) siamés/esa m/f
2 (Ling) siamés m
3 (= cat) gato m siamés
(ADJ) siamés
(CPD) ▸ **Siamese cat** gato m siamés
▸ **Siamese twins** hermanos/as mpl/fpl siameses/esas
SIB (N ABBR) (Brit) = **Securities and Investments Board**
Siberia [saɪ'bɪərɪə] (N) Siberia f
Siberian [saɪ'bɪərɪən] (ADJ) siberiano
(N) siberiano/a m/f
sibilant ['sɪbɪlənt] (ADJ) sibilante
(N) sibilante f
sibling ['sɪblɪŋ] (N) hermano/a m/f
(CPD) ▸ **sibling rivalry** rivalidad f entre hermanos
Sibyl ['sɪbɪl] (N) Sibila
sibyl ['sɪbɪl] (N) sibila f
sibylline ['sɪbɪlaɪn] (ADJ) sibilino
sic [sɪk] (ADV) sic
Sicilian [sɪ'sɪlɪən] (ADJ) siciliano
(N) **1** (= person) siciliano/a m/f
2 (Ling) siciliano m
Sicily ['sɪsɪlɪ] (N) Sicilia f
sick [sɪk] (ADJ) (COMPAR: **sicker**, SUPERL: **sickest**) **1** (= ill) [person] enfermo; [animal] malo, enfermo • **your uncle is very ~** tu tío está muy enfermo • **to fall ~**† enfermar, caer enfermo • **to go ~** faltar por estar enfermo (al colegio, trabajo etc); (with a medical certificate) estar de baja • **to make sb look ~** (US) (fig) (= appear inferior) hacer parecer poca cosa a algn • **the Romanians made our team look ~** los rumanos dejaron a nuestro equipo muy atrás, el equipo rumano era como para darle complejo a nuestro equipo* • **to be off ~** faltar por estar enfermo (al colegio, trabajo etc); (with a medical certificate) estar de baja • **she phoned** or **called in ~** llamó para decir que estaba enferma • IDIOM: • **to be ~ at heart**† (also liter) (= despondent) estar angustiado; ▹ **worried, worry**
2 • **to be ~** (Brit) (= vomit) devolver, vomitar • **to feel ~** (Brit) (= nauseous) tener ganas de devolver or de vomitar, tener náuseas • **flying makes me feel ~** ir en avión me produce mareo or náuseas • **to make sb ~** (lit) hacer devolver or vomitar a algn • **to make o.s. ~** (deliberately) hacerse vomitar or devolver • **you'll make yourself ~ if you eat all those sweets** te vas a poner malo si comes todos esos caramelos • IDIOM: • **to be as ~ as a dog*** echar las tripas‡, echar la primera papilla‡; ▹ **airsick, seasick, travel-sick**
3 (= fed up) • **to be ~ of (doing) sth** estar harto de (hacer) algo* • **to be ~ and tired** or **~ to death of (doing) sth** estar hasta la coronilla de (hacer) algo*, estar más que harto de (hacer) algo* • **to be ~ of the sight of sb** estar más que harto de algn* • IDIOM: • **to be as ~ as a parrot** (Brit*) sentirse fatal
4 (= disgusted) • **I feel ~ about the way she was treated** me asquea la forma en que la trataron • **it makes me ~ the way they waste our money** me pone enferma ver la manera en que malgastan nuestro dinero • **she's never without a boyfriend, makes you ~, doesn't it?*** siempre tiene algún novio, da rabia ¿no?* • **it's enough to make you ~** es como para sacarle a uno de quicio, es como para desesperarse • **you make me ~!** ¡me das asco! • **it makes me ~ to my stomach** me revienta, me da ganas de vomitar
5 (pej) (= morbid) [joke, act] de mal gusto; [person, mind, sense of humour] morboso
(N) **1** • **the ~** los enfermos
2 (Brit) (= vomit) vómito m, devuelto m
(CPD) ▸ **sick bag** bolsa f para el mareo ▸ **sick building syndrome** síndrome m del edificio enfermo ▸ **sick leave** • **to be on ~ leave** tener permiso or (Sp) baja por enfermedad ▸ **sick list** lista f de enfermos • **to be on the ~ list** estar de permiso or (Sp) de baja por enfermedad ▸ **sick note** justificante m por enfermedad ▸ **sick pay** pago que se percibe mientras se está con permiso por enfermedad, baja f (Sp)
▸ **sick up*** (VT + ADV) (Brit) vomitar, devolver
sickbay ['sɪkbeɪ] (N) enfermería f
sickbed ['sɪkbed] (N) lecho m de enfermo
sicken ['sɪkn] (VT) **1** (= make ill) poner enfermo
2 (fig) (= revolt) dar asco • **it ~s me** me da asco • **it ~s me to think I missed the party** me enferma pensar que me perdí la fiesta
(VI) caer enfermo, enfermarse • **to be ~ing for** (= show signs of) mostrar síntomas de; (= miss) echar de menos, echar a faltar • **I ~ at the sight of blood** (el) ver sangre me da náuseas
sickening ['sɪknɪŋ] **1** (= disgusting) [sight, smell] nauseabundo, asqueroso; [cruelty, crime] espeluznante, repugnante; [waste] indignante, escandaloso • **a ~ feeling of failure** una asqueante or insoportable sensación de fracaso • **a ~ feeling of panic** un sensación de pánico atenazadora
2* (= annoying) [person, behaviour, situation] odioso, exasperante
3 (= unpleasant) [blow, crunch] tremendo • **with a ~ thud** con un golpetazo tremendo
sickeningly ['sɪknɪŋlɪ] (ADV) [familiar] tremendamente • **~ violent/polite** asquerosamente violento/cortés • **it is ~ sweet** es realmente empalagoso • **he made it all look ~ easy** él hacía que todo pareciera tremendamente fácil • **he seems ~ happy** parece tan feliz que da asco • **he stood at the top of a ~ steep gully** estaba subido en la cima de un barranco empinadísimo • **the ship was rolling ~** el barco daba tumbos de acá para allá
sickie* ['sɪkɪ] (N) • **he took a ~** llamó diciendo que estaba enfermo
sickle ['sɪkl] (N) hoz f
sickle-cell anaemia, sickle-cell anemia (US) ['sɪkl,selə'ni:mɪə] (N) anemia f de células falciformes, drepanocitosis f
sickliness ['sɪklɪnɪs] (N) **1** (= ill health, feebleness) lo enfermizo; (= paleness) palidez f; (= weakness) debilidad f
2 (= sweetness) lo empalagoso
sickly ['sɪklɪ] (ADJ) (COMPAR: **sicklier**, SUPERL: **sickliest**) **1** [person] (= unwell, feeble) enfermizo, enclenque; (= pale) pálido; [smile] forzado; [plant] débil
2 (= cloying) [taste, smell] empalagoso • **~ sweet** dulzón
sick-making* ['sɪkmeɪkɪŋ] (ADJ) asqueroso
sickness ['sɪknɪs] (N) **1** (= illness) enfermedad f • **after several months of ~ he was able to return to work** después de varios meses de enfermedad pudo regresar al trabajo • **in ~ and in health** en la salud y en la enfermedad
2 (= feeling of nausea) náuseas fpl; (= vomiting) vómitos mpl; ▹ **altitude, mountain, travel**
(CPD) ▸ **sickness benefit** subsidio m de enfermedad • **to be on ~ benefit** recibir el subsidio de enfermedad
sicko* ['sɪkəʊ] (esp US) (N) psicópata mf
(ADJ) [person, group] psicópata
sick-out ['sɪkaʊt] (N) (US) (Ind) baja colectiva por enfermedad como forma de protesta
sickroom ['sɪkrʊm] (N) cuarto m del enfermo
side [saɪd] (N) **1** [of person] lado m, costado m • **at** or **by sb's ~** (lit) al lado de algn; (fig) en apoyo a algn • **the assistant was at** or **by his ~** el ayudante estaba a su lado • **he had the telephone by his ~** tenía el teléfono a su lado • **by the ~ of** al lado de • **to sit by sb's ~** estar sentado al lado de algn • **~ by ~** uno al lado del otro • **we sat ~ by ~** nos sentamos uno al lado del otro • **to sit ~ by ~ with sb** estar sentado al lado de algn • **to sleep on one's ~** dormir de costado • **to split one's ~s** desternillarse de risa
2 [of animal] ijar m, ijada f • **~ of bacon/beef** (Culin) lonja f de tocino/vaca or (LAm) res
3 (= edge) [of box, square, building etc] lado m; [of boat, vehicle] costado m; [of hill] ladera f, falda f; [of lake] orilla f; [of road, pond] borde m • **a house on the ~ of a mountain** una casa en la ladera de una montaña • **by the ~ of the lake** a la orilla del lago • **the car was abandoned at the ~ of the road** el coche estaba abandonado al borde de la carretera • **on the other ~ of the road** al otro lado de la calle • **he was driving on the wrong ~ of the road** iba por el lado contrario de la carretera
4 (= face, surface) [of box, solid figure, paper, record etc] cara f • **please write on both ~s of the paper** escribir en ambas caras del papel • **play ~ A** pon la cara A • **what's on the other ~?** [of record] ¿qué hay a la vuelta? • **right ~ up** boca arriba • **wrong ~ up** boca abajo • **to be wrong ~ out** estar al revés • IDIOMS: • **let's look at the other ~ of the coin** veamos el revés de la medalla • **these are two ~s of the same coin** son dos caras de la misma moneda • **the other ~ of the picture** el reverso de la medalla
5 (= aspect) lado m, aspecto m • **to see only one ~ of the question** ver solo un lado or aspecto de la cuestión • **to hear both ~s of the question** escuchar los argumentos en pro y en contra • **on one ~ ..., on the other ...** por una parte ..., por otra ...
6 (= part) lado m • **from all ~s** de todas partes, de todos lados • **on all ~s** por todas partes, por todos lados • **on both ~s** por ambos lados • **to look on the bright ~** ser optimista • **from every ~** de todas partes, de todos lados • **the left-hand ~** el lado izquierdo • **on the mother's ~** por parte de la madre • **to make a bit (of money) on the ~*** ganar algún dinero extra, hacer chapuzas (Sp) • **to move to one ~** apartarse, ponerse de lado • **to take sb on** or **to one ~** apartar a algn • **to put sth to** or **on one ~ (for sb)** guardar algo (para algn) • **leaving that to one ~ for the moment, ...** dejando eso a un lado por ahora, ... • **it's the other ~ of Illescas** está más allá de Illescas • **to be on the right ~ of 30** no haber cumplido los 30 años • **to be on the right ~ of sb** caerle bien a algn • **to get on the right ~ of sb** procurar congraciarse con algn • **to keep on the right ~ of sb** congraciarse or quedar bien con algn • **the right-hand ~** el lado derecho • **it's on the right-hand ~** está a mano derecha • **to be on the safe ~ ...** para estar seguro ..., por si acaso ... • **let's be on the safe ~** atengámonos a lo más seguro • **it's this ~ of Segovia** está más acá de Segovia • **it won't happen this ~ of Christmas** no será antes de Navidades • **from ~ to ~** de un lado a otro • **to be on the wrong ~ of 30** haber cumplido los 30 años • IDIOMS: • **to be on the wrong ~ of sb** caerle

S

mal a algn • **to get on the wrong ~ of sb** ponerse a malas con algn • **to get out of bed on the wrong ~** levantarse con el pie izquierdo
7 (*fig*) • **the weather's on the cold ~** el tiempo es algo frío • **it's a bit on the large ~** es algo *or* (*LAm*) tantito grande • **the results are on the poor ~** los resultados son más bien mediocres
8 (= *team*) (*Sport*) equipo *m* • **to change ~s** pasar al otro bando; (*opinion*) cambiar de opinión • **to choose ~s** seleccionar el equipo • **to let the ~ down** (*Sport*) dejar caer a los suyos; (*fig*) decepcionar • **he's on our ~** (*fig*) es de los nuestros • **whose ~ are you on?** ¿a quiénes apoyas? • **I'm on your ~** yo estoy de tu parte • **with a few concessions on the government ~** con algunas concesiones por parte del gobierno • **to be on the ~ of sth/sb** ser partidario de algo/algn • **to have age/justice on one's ~** tener la juventud/la justicia de su lado • **our ~ won** ganaron los nuestros • **to pick ~s** seleccionar el equipo • **to take ~s (with sb)** tomar partido (con algn) • **to take sb's ~** ponerse de parte de algn
9 (*Pol*) (= *party*) partido *m*
10 (*Brit**) (= *conceit, superiority*) tono *m*, postín* *m* • **there's no ~ about** *or* **to him** • **he's got no ~** no presume, no se da aires de superioridad • **to put on ~** darse tono
(VI) (*in argument*) • **to ~ against sb** tomar el partido contrario a algn, alinearse con los que se oponen a algn • **to ~ with sb** ponerse de parte de algn • **I'm siding with nobody** yo no tomo partido
(CPD) ▸ **side arms** armas *fpl* de cinto ▸ **side dish** plato *m* adicional (servido con el principal) ▸ **side door** puerta *f* de al lado ▸ **side drum** tamboril *m* ▸ **side effect** efecto *m* secundario ▸ **side entrance** entrada *f* lateral ▸ **side glance** mirada *f* de soslayo ▸ **side issue** cuestión *f* secundaria ▸ **side order** plato *m* de acompañamiento • **served with a ~ order of potato salad** servido con acompañamiento *or* guarnición de ensaladilla de patatas ▸ **side plate** platito *m* (*para el pan, ensalada etc*) ▸ **side road** carretera *f* secundaria ▸ **side saddle** silla *f* de amazona; ▸ **side-saddle** ▸ **side street** calle *f* lateral ▸ **side table** trinchero *m* ▸ **side view** perfil *m* ▸ **side whiskers** patillas *fpl*
sidebar ['saɪdbɑːʳ] (N) (*on web page*) barra *f* lateral
sideboard ['saɪdbɔːd] (N) aparador *m*
sideboards ['saɪdbɔːdz] (NPL) (*Brit*), **sideburns** ['saɪdbɜːnz] (NPL) patillas *fpl*
sidecar ['saɪdkɑːʳ] (N) sidecar *m*
-sided ['saɪdɪd] (ADJ) (*ending in compounds*) de … caras, de … aspectos • **three-sided** de tres caras • **many-sided** de muchos aspectos
side-face ['saɪdfeɪs] (ADJ), (ADV) de perfil
side-foot ['saɪdfʊt] (VT) [+ *ball, shot*] lanzar con el interior del pie
side-impact protection [,saɪdɪmpæktprə'tekʃən] (N) (*Aut*) protección *f* contra impactos laterales
sidekick* ['saɪdkɪk] (N) secuaz* *mf*
sidelight ['saɪdlaɪt] (N) **1** (*Aut*) luz *f* lateral
2 (*fig*) detalle *m* incidental, información *f* incidental (**on** relativo a)
sideline ['saɪdlaɪn] (N) **1** (*Ftbl, Tennis etc*) línea *f* de banda • **to be on the ~s** (*Sport*) estar fuera del terreno de juego, estar en la banda; (*fig*) estar al margen
2 (*Rail*) apartadero *m*, vía *f* secundaria
3 (*Comm*) actividad *f* suplementaria • **it's just a ~** (*fig*) es un pasatiempo, nada más
(VT) (*esp US*) marginar • **we won't be ~d** no permitimos que se nos margine • **he was ~d by injury the whole season** quedó fuera del equipo durante toda la temporada debido a una lesión
sidelong ['saɪdlɒŋ] (ADV) de costado
(ADJ) [*glance*] de soslayo, de reojo
side-on [,saɪd'ɒn] (ADJ) [*collision, view*] lateral
sidereal [saɪ'dɪːrɪəl] (ADJ) sidéreo
side-saddle ['saɪd,sædl] (ADV) • **to ride side-saddle** montar a la amazona
sideshow ['saɪdʃəʊ] (N) (*at fair*) atracción *f* secundaria
sideslip ['saɪdslɪp] (N) (*Aer*) deslizamiento *m* lateral
side-slipping ['saɪd,slɪpɪŋ] (N) (*Ski*) derrapaje *m*
sidesman ['saɪdzmən] (N) (PL: **sidesmen**) (*Brit*) (*Rel*) acólito *m*
side-splitting* ['saɪd,splɪtɪŋ] (ADJ) para reírse a carcajadas, para morirse de risa
sidestep ['saɪdstep] (VT) [+ *problem, question*] eludir, esquivar • **he neatly ~ped the question** eludió *or* esquivó hábilmente la pregunta
(VI) (*Boxing etc*) dar un quiebro, fintar, dar una finta (*LAm*)
(N) **1** (= *step*) paso *m* hacia un lado
2 (= *dodge*) esquivada *f*
sidestroke ['saɪdstrəʊk] (N) natación *f* de costado
sideswipe ['saɪdswaɪp] (N) (*also fig*) golpe *m* de refilón
sidetrack ['saɪdtræk] (VT) [+ *person*] despistar; [+ *discussion*] conducir por cuestiones de poca importancia • **I got ~ed** me despisté
(N) (*Rail*) apartadero *m*, vía *f* muerta; (*fig*) cuestión *f* secundaria
sidewalk ['saɪdwɔːk] (N) (*US*) (= *pavement*) acera *f*, vereda *f* (*LAm*), andén *m* (*CAm, Col*), banqueta *f* (*Mex*)
(CPD) ▸ **sidewalk artist** (*US*) (*creating and selling pictures*) pintor(a) *m/f* callejero/a; (*chalking on ground*) *artista que dibuja con tiza sobre la acera* ▸ **sidewalk café** (*US*) café *m* con terraza
sidewall ['saɪdwɔːl] (N) pared *f* lateral
sidewards ['saɪdwədz] (ADV) = **sideways**
sideways ['saɪd,weɪz] (ADJ) (*gen*) de lado, lateral; [*look*] de reojo, de soslayo
(ADV) • **to step ~** hacerse a un lado • **to walk/move ~** andar/moverse de lado • **to look ~** mirar de reojo, mirar de soslayo • **it goes** *or* **fits in ~** se mete de lado *or* de costado • **~ on** de perfil
sidewind ['saɪdwɪnd] (N) viento *m* lateral
siding ['saɪdɪŋ] (N) (*Rail*) apartadero *m*, vía *f* muerta
sidle ['saɪdl] (VI) • **to ~ up (to sb)** acercarse furtivamente (a algn) • **to ~ in/out** entrar/salir furtivamente
Sidon ['saɪdən] (N) Sidón *m*
SIDS (N ABBR) (*Med*) = **sudden infant death syndrome**
siege [siːdʒ] (N) cerco *m*, sitio *m* • **to lay ~ to** cercar, sitiar • **to raise the ~** levantar el cerco
(CPD) ▸ **siege economy** economía *f* de sitio ▸ **siege mentality** • **to have a ~ mentality** tener manía persecutoria ▸ **siege warfare** guerra *f* de sitio *or* asedio
sienna [sɪ'enə] (N) siena *f*
Sierra Leone [sɪ'eərəlɪ'əʊn] (N) Sierra *f* Leona
Sierra Leonean [sɪ'eərəlɪ'əʊnɪən] (ADJ) sierraleonés
(N) sierraleonés/esa *m/f*
siesta [sɪ'estə] (N) siesta *f* • **to have** *or* **take a ~** dormir la siesta
sieve [sɪv] (N) (*for liquids*) colador *m*; (*for solids*) criba *f*, tamiz *m*
(VT) [+ *liquid*] colar; [+ *flour, soil*] cribar, tamizar
sift [sɪft] (VT) [+ *flour, soil*] cerner, tamizar
(VI) • **to ~ through** (*fig*) examinar cuidadosamente
sigh [saɪ] (N) [*of person*] suspiro *m*; [*of wind*] susurro *m*, gemido *m* • **to give** *or* **heave a ~** dar un suspiro • **to breathe a ~ of relief** suspirar aliviado, dar un suspiro de alivio
(VI) [*person*] suspirar; [*wind*] susurrar • **to ~ for** suspirar por
sighing ['saɪɪŋ] (N) [*of person*] suspiros *mpl*; [*of wind*] susurro *m*
sight [saɪt] (N) **1** (= *eyesight*) vista *f* • **to have good ~** tener buena vista • **I'm losing my ~** estoy perdiendo la vista • **to have poor ~** tener mala vista • **to regain one's ~** recobrar la vista
2 (= *act of seeing*) vista *f* • **I can't bear the ~ of blood** no aguanto la vista de la sangre • **I can't stand the ~ of him** no le puedo ver • **at ~** a la vista • **at first ~** a primera vista • **it was love at first ~** fue un flechazo • **I know her by ~** la conozco de vista • **it came into ~** apareció • **to catch ~ of sth/sb** divisar algo/a algn • **to be in ~** estar a la vista (**of** de) • **to keep sth in ~** no perder de vista algo • **our goal is in ~** ya vemos la meta • **we are in ~ of victory** estamos a las puertas de la victoria • **to find favour in sb's ~** [*plan etc*] ser aceptable a algn; [*person*] merecerse la aprobación de algn • **to lose ~ of sth/sb** perder algo/a algn de vista • **to lose ~ of sb** (*fig*) perder contacto con algn • **to lose ~ of the fact that …** no tener presente el hecho de que … • **to be lost to ~** desaparecer, perderse de vista • **to shoot on ~** disparar sin previo aviso • **to be out of ~** no estar a la vista • **keep out of ~!** ¡que no te vean! • **not to let sb out of one's ~** no perder a algn de vista • **to drop out of ~** desaparecer • **out of ~** (*US**) fabuloso* • **to buy sth ~ unseen** comprar algo sin verlo • **to be within ~** estar a la vista (**of** de) • **to have sth within ~** tener algo a la vista • **we were within ~ of the coast** teníamos la costa a la vista • PROVERB: • **out of ~, out of mind** ojos que no ven, corazón que no siente
3 (= *spectacle*) espectáculo *m* • **it was an amazing ~** era un espectáculo asombroso • **his face was a ~!** ¡había que ver su cara!; (*after injury etc*) ¡había que ver el estado en que quedaba su cara! • **I must look a ~** debo parecer horroroso, ¿no? • **doesn't she look a ~ in that hat!** ¡con ese sombrero parece un espantajo! • **what a ~ you are!** ¡qué adefesio! • **the ~s** los lugares de interés turístico • **to see** *or* **visit the ~s of Madrid** visitar los lugares de interés turístico de Madrid, hacer turismo por Madrid • **it's not a pretty ~** no es precisamente bonito • **it's a sad ~** es una cosa triste • IDIOM: • **it's a ~ for sore eyes** da gusto verlo
4 (*on gun*) (*often pl*) mira *f*, alza *f* • **in one's ~s** en la línea de tiro • IDIOMS: • **to lower one's ~s** renunciar a algunas de sus aspiraciones • **to raise one's ~s** volverse más ambicioso, apuntar más alto • **to set one's ~s on sth/doing sth** aspirar a *or* ambicionar algo/hacer algo • **to set one's ~s too high** ser demasiado ambicioso
5* (= *a great deal*) • **this is a ~ better than the other one** este no tiene comparación con el otro • **he's a ~ too clever** es demasiado listo • **it's a ~ dearer** es mucho más caro
(VT) **1** (*Naut*) [+ *land*] ver, divisar; [+ *bird, rare animal*] observar, ver; [+ *person*] ver
2 (= *aim*) • **to ~ a gun** apuntar un cañón (**at, on** a)
(CPD) ▸ **sight draft** letra *f* a la vista ▸ **sight translation** traducción *f* oral *or* a libro abierto

sighted ['saɪtɪd] ADJ vidente
NPL • **the ~** los que pueden ver, las personas videntes
-sighted ['saɪtɪd] ADJ (*ending in compounds*) • **short-sighted** corto de vista, miope • **long-sighted** hipermétrope
sighting ['saɪtɪŋ] N observación *f* • **further ~s of the missing girl have been reported** se sabe que la chica desaparecida ha sido vista en más ocasiones
sightless ['saɪtlɪs] ADJ ciego, invidente
sightly ['saɪtlɪ] ADJ • **not very ~** no muy agradable para la vista
sight-read ['saɪtri:d] (PT, PP: **sight-read**) (*Mus*) VT repentizar
VI repentizar
sight-reading ['saɪt,ri:dɪŋ] N (*Mus*) repentización *f*, acción *f* de repentizar
sightseeing ['saɪt,si:ɪŋ] N turismo *m* • **to go ~** • **do some ~** hacer turismo
sightseer ['saɪt,si:əʳ] N turista *mf*, excursionista *mf*
sight-singing ['saɪt,sɪŋɪŋ] N ejecución *f* a la primera lectura
sign [saɪn] N **1** (= *indication*) señal *f*, indicio *m*; (*Med*) síntoma *m* • **it's a ~ of rain** es señal *or* indicio de lluvia • **he searched for a ~ of recognition on her face** buscó en su rostro una señal *or* muestra de reconocimiento • **there was no ~ of him anywhere** no había ni rastro de él • **there was no ~ of life** no había señales *or* rastro de vida • **it was seen as a ~ of weakness** se interpretaba como una muestra *or* señal de flaqueza • **at the first ~ of a cold, take vitamin C** al primer indicio de un resfriado, tome vitamina C • **it's a good/bad ~** es buena/mala señal • **to show ~s of sth/doing sth** dar muestras *or* señales de algo/de hacer algo • **the economy is beginning to show ~s of recovery** la economía está dando muestras *or* señales de recuperarse • **the storm showed no ~ of abating** la tormenta no daba muestras *or* señales de calmarse • **that's a sure ~ he's feeling better** es una señal inconfundible de que se encuentra mejor • **it's a ~ of the times** es señal de los tiempos que vivimos
2 (= *gesture*) seña *f* • **to communicate by ~s** hablar *or* comunicarse por señas • **he gave the victory ~** hizo la seña de victoria • **to make a ~ to sb** hacer una seña a algn • **he made a ~ for them to leave** les hizo una seña para que se marcharan • **to make the ~ of the Cross** hacerse la señal de la cruz, santiguarse • **to make the ~ of the Cross over sth** bendecir algo
3 (= *notice*) letrero *m*; (= *road sign*) señal *f* (de tráfico); (= *direction indicator*) indicador *m*; (= *shop sign*) letrero *m*, rótulo *m*; (*US*) (*carried in demonstration*) pancarta *f* • **exit ~** letrero *m* de salida • **a no-entry ~** una señal de prohibición de entrada • **a give way ~** una señal de ceda el paso
4 (= *written symbol*) símbolo *m*; (*Math, Mus, Astrol*) signo *m* • **the text was full of strange ~s and symbols** el texto estaba lleno de símbolos extraños • **what ~ are you?** ¿de qué signo eres? • **plus/minus ~** signo de más/menos
VT **1** [+ *contract, agreement, treaty*] firmar • **she ~s herself B. Smith** firma con el nombre B. Smith • **Sue Townsend will be ~ing her new book** Sue Townsend firmará autógrafos en su nuevo libro • **to ~ one's name** firmar • **~ed and sealed** firmado y lacrado, firmado y sellado
2 (= *recruit*) [+ *player*] fichar, contratar; [+ *actor, band*] contratar
3 (= *use sign language*) • **the programme is ~ed for the hearing-impaired** el programa incluye traducción simultánea al lenguaje de signos para aquellos con discapacidades auditivas
VI **1** (*with signature*) firmar • **~ here please** firme aquí, por favor; ▸ **dotted line**
2 (= *be recruited*) (*Sport*) firmar un contrato • **he has ~ed for *or* with Arsenal** ha firmado un contrato con el Arsenal, ha fichado por el Arsenal (*Sp*)
3 (= *signal*) hacer señas • **to ~ to sb to do sth** hacer señas a algn para que haga algo • **he ~ed to me to wait** me hizo señas para que esperara
4 (= *use sign language*) hablar con señas
CPD ▸ **sign language** lenguaje *m* por señas • **to talk in ~ language** hablar por señas ▸ **sign painter, sign writer** rotulista *mf*
▸ **sign away** VT + ADV [+ *rights*] ceder • **he ~ed away his soul to the devil** entregó su alma al diablo
▸ **sign for** VI + PREP [+ *item*] firmar el recibo de
▸ **sign in** VI + ADV (*at hotel*) firmar el registro (al entrar), registrarse; (*at work*) firmar la entrada
VT + ADV (*at club*) [+ *visitor*] firmar por
▸ **sign off** VI + ADV **1** (*ending activity*) terminar; (*ending letter*) despedirse; (*Rad, TV*) cerrar el programa, despedirse
2 (*Brit*) (*as unemployed*) darse de baja en el paro, quitarse del paro
▸ **sign on** VI + ADV (*Brit*) (*as unemployed*) registrarse como desempleado; (*as employee*) firmar un contrato; (*Mil*) (= *enlist*) alistarse
VT + ADV [+ *employee*] contratar; (*Sport*) [+ *player*] fichar, contratar; (*Mil*) [+ *soldier*] reclutar
▸ **sign out** VI + ADV [*hotel guest*] firmar el registro (al marcharse); [*employee, visitor*] firmar la salida
VT + ADV [+ *item*] • **you must ~ all books out** tiene que firmar al retirar cualquier libro
▸ **sign over** VT + ADV [+ *property, rights*] ceder • **she ~ed the house over to her son** cedió la casa a su hijo, puso la casa a nombre de su hijo
▸ **sign up** VI + ADV (= *be recruited*) (*as employee*) firmar un contrato; (= *register*) registrarse; (*Sport*) [*player*] fichar (**with, for** por); (*Mil*) alistarse • **to ~ up for a course** inscribirse en un curso
VT + ADV [+ *employee*] contratar; (*Sport*) [+ *player*] fichar, contratar; (*Mil*) [+ *soldier*] reclutar • **the party desperately needed to ~ up new members** el partido necesitaba conseguir urgentemente nuevos afiliados
signage ['saɪnɪdʒ] N señalización *f*
signal ['sɪgnl] N señal *f*; (*Telec*) señal *f*, tono *m*; (*TV, Rad*) sintonía *f* • **it was the ~ for revolt** fue la señal para la sublevación • **I can't get a ~** (*Telec*) no hay cobertura • **to give the ~ for** dar la señal de *or* para • **to make a ~ to sb** hacer una señal a algn • **railway ~s** semáforos *mpl* de ferrocarril • **traffic ~s** semáforo *msing*
VT **1** [+ *message*] comunicar por señales • **to ~ sb to do sth** hacer señas a algn para que haga algo • **to ~ that ...** comunicar por señas que ... • **to ~ one's approval** hacer una seña de aprobación • **to ~ sb on/through** dar a algn la señal de pasar • **to ~ a train** anunciar por señales la llegada de un tren • **the train is ~led** la señal indica la llegada del tren • **to ~ a left-/right-hand turn** (*Aut*) indicar un giro a la izquierda/derecha
2 (= *signify*) señalar
VI (*gen*) dar una señal; (*with hands*) hacer señas • **to ~ to sb to do sth** hacer señas a algn para que haga algo • **to ~ to sb that ...** comunicar a algn por señas que ... • **to ~ before stopping** hacer una señal antes de parar
ADJ (*frm*) notable, señalado, insigne
CPD ▸ **signal book** (*Naut*) código *m* de señales ▸ **signal box** (*Rail*) garita *f* de señales ▸ **signal flag** bandera *f* de señales ▸ **signal lamp** reflector *m* or lámpara *f* de señales
signalize ['sɪgnəlaɪz] VT distinguir, señalar
signaller, signaler (*US*) ['sɪgnələʳ] N (*Mil*) señalizador(a) *m/f*
signally ['sɪgnəlɪ] ADV notablemente, señaladamente • **he has ~ failed to do it** ha sufrido un notable fracaso al tratar de hacerlo
signalman ['sɪgnlmən] N (PL: **signalmen**) (*Rail*) guardavía *mf*
signatory ['sɪgnətərɪ] ADJ firmante, signatario • **the ~ powers to an agreement** las potencias firmantes *or* signatarias de un acuerdo
N firmante *mf*, signatario/a *m/f*
signature ['sɪgnətʃəʳ] N **1** [*of person*] firma *f* • **to put one's ~ to sth** firmar algo
2 (*Mus*) armadura *f*
CPD ▸ **signature tune** (*Brit*) sintonía *f* de apertura (*de un programa*)
signboard ['saɪnbɔ:d] N (*small*) letrero *m*; (*large*) cartelera *f*; (*for adverts*) valla *f* publicitaria
signer ['saɪnəʳ] N firmante *mf*
signet ['sɪgnɪt] N sello *m*
CPD ▸ **signet ring** sello *m*
significance [sɪg'nɪfɪkəns] N **1** (= *meaning*) • **she gave him a look full of ~** le dirigió una mirada muy significativa *or* elocuente
2 (= *importance*) importancia *f* • **can we attach any ~ to this promise?** ¿podemos darle importancia a esta promesa? • **to be of some ~** ser importante • **to be of no ~** no tener ninguna importancia
significant [sɪg'nɪfɪkənt] ADJ **1** (= *important*) [*number, event, achievement, part, development*] importante; [*effect, amount, improvement, sum of money, victory*] considerable; [*contribution, reduction, increase*] significativo, considerable; [*difference*] significativo; [*change*] importante, considerable; [*factor, impact, step*] significativo, importante • **it is ~ that ...** es significativo que ... • **Japan has made ~ progress in reducing pollution** Japón ha dado un gran paso adelante en la reducción de la contaminación • **~ other** (= *partner*) pareja *f*
2 (= *meaningful*) [*look, gesture, tone of voice*] significativo, elocuente • **could this be ~ of a change of heart?** ¿podría esto suponer un cambio de idea?
significantly [sɪg'nɪfɪkəntlɪ] ADV
1 (= *considerably*) (*with adj*) [*higher, lower, better, reduced*] considerablemente; (*with verb*) [*change, improve, reduce, increase*] de forma significativa, considerablemente
2 (= *notably*) • **~, most of them are Scottish** es significativo que la mayoría sean escoceses • **they have ~ different ideas** sus ideas son notablemente distintas
3 (= *meaningfully*) • **she looked at me ~** me lanzó una mirada significativa *or* elocuente
signify ['sɪgnɪfaɪ] VT **1** (= *mean*) querer decir, significar • **what does it ~?** ¿qué quiere decir?, ¿qué significa?
2 (= *make known*) indicar • **to ~ one's approval** indicar su aprobación
VI • **it does not ~** no importa • **in the wider context it does not ~** en el contexto más amplio no tiene importancia
signing ['saɪnɪŋ] N **1** [*of letter, contract, treaty*

S

etc] firma *f*
2 (*Sport*) fichaje *m*
3 (= *sign language*) lenguaje *m* por señas
signpost ['saɪnpəʊst] (N) poste *m* indicador
(VT) indicar • **the road is well ~ed** la carretera tiene buena señalización, la carretera está bien señalizada
signposting ['saɪnpəʊstɪŋ] (N) señalización *f*
Sikh [si:k] (ADJ) sij
(N) sij *mf*
Sikhism ['si:kɪzəm] (N) sijismo *m*
silage ['saɪlɪdʒ] (N) ensilaje *m*
silence ['saɪləns] (N) **1** (= *absence of speech*) silencio *m* • **a two minutes' ~** dos minutos de silencio • **~!** ¡silencio! • **they stood in ~** permanecieron en silencio • **in dead** *or* **complete ~** en silencio absoluto • **there was ~ on the matter** no se hizo comentario alguno sobre la cuestión • **to pass over sth in ~** silenciar algo • **to reduce sb to ~** dejar a algn sin argumentos • PROVERBS: • **~ is golden** en boca cerrada no entran moscas • **~ gives** *or* **means** *or* **lends consent** quien calla otorga
2 (= *absence of sound*) silencio *m* • **a sudden shot broke the ~** un disparo repentino rompió el silencio
3 (= *unwillingness to communicate*) silencio *m* • **he broke his ~ for the first time yesterday** rompió su silencio ayer por primera vez
(VT) **1** (= *quieten*) [+ *person, crowd*] hacer callar, acallar; [+ *bells, guns, cries*] silenciar, acallar • **to ~ one's conscience** acallar la conciencia
2 (= *put a stop to*) [+ *criticism, fears, doubts*] acallar, silenciar • **he ~d his critics** silenció a sus críticos
3 (= *kill*) eliminar
silencer ['saɪlənsəʳ] (N) (*Aut*) (*on gun*) silenciador *m*
silent ['saɪlənt] (ADJ) **1** (= *noiseless, soundless*) • **to be ~** [*person*] quedarse callado; [*place, room, street*] estar en silencio • **the law is ~ on this point** la ley no se pronuncia a este respecto • **to fall ~** [*person*] quedarse callado; [*room*] quedar en silencio • **the guns have fallen ~** el tiroteo ha cesado, las armas han quedado en silencio (*liter*) • **to lie ~** [*factory, machine*] permanecer parado • **the ~ majority** la mayoría silenciosa • **~ partner** (*US*) socio/a *m/f* comanditario/a • **I've remained ~ for too long on this issue** he guardado silencio sobre este asunto por demasiado tiempo • **you have the right to remain ~** tiene derecho a permanecer callado, no está obligado a responder • **to give sb the ~ treatment** hacer el vacío a algn • **to bear ~ witness to sth** ser mudo testigo de algo • IDIOM: • **to be as ~ as the grave** *or* **tomb** estar silencioso como una tumba
2 (= *wordless*) [*prayer, march, vigil*] silencioso; [*contempt, protest*] mudo • **she looked at him in ~ contempt** le miró con mudo desprecio • **~ tears ran down her cheeks** las lágrimas le corrían silenciosas por la cara • **to pay ~ tribute to sb** homenajear en silencio a algn
3 (*Cine*) [*film, movie*] mudo • **the ~ screen** el cine mudo
4 (*Ling*) [*letter*] mudo • **the "k" in knee is ~** la "k" en "knee" es muda *or* no se pronuncia
(N) • **the ~s** (*Cine*) las películas mudas; (*as genre*) el cine mudo
silently ['saɪləntlɪ] (ADV) **1** (= *without speaking*) en silencio • **she ~ cursed her bad luck** maldijo calladamente su mala suerte • **I vowed ~ never to mention it again** juré para mis adentros no volver a mencionarlo
2 (= *without making noise*) silenciosamente
silhouette [,sɪlu:'et] (N) silueta *f* • **in ~** en silueta

S

(VT) • **to be ~d against sth** destacarse *or* perfilarse en *or* contra algo
silica ['sɪlɪkə] (N) sílice *f*
(CPD) ▸ **silica gel** gel *m* de sílice
silicate ['sɪlɪkɪt] (N) silicato *m*
siliceous [sɪ'lɪʃəs] (ADJ) silíceo
silicon ['sɪlɪkən] (N) silicio *m*
(CPD) ▸ **Silicon Alley** Silicon Alley *m* (*distrito donde se concentran muchas empresas de informática*) ▸ **silicon carbide** carburo *m* de silicio ▸ **silicon chip** chip *m or* plaqueta *f* de silicio ▸ **Silicon Valley** Silicon Valley *m*
silicone ['sɪlɪkəʊn] (N) silicona *f*
(CPD) ▸ **silicone breast implant** implante *m* mamario de silicona ▸ **silicone implant** implante *m* de silicona
silicosis [,sɪlɪ'kəʊsɪs] (N) silicosis *f*
silk [sɪlk] (N) **1** seda *f*
2 (*Brit*) (*Jur*) (= *barrister*) abogado/a *m/f* superior • **to take ~** (*Brit*) ser ascendido a la abogacía superior; ▷ QC/KC
(NPL) **silks** (*Racing*) colores *mpl*
(CPD) [*blouse, scarf*] de seda • IDIOM: • **you can't make a ~ purse out of a sow's ear** aunque la mona se vista de seda, mona se queda ▸ **silk finish** • **with a ~ finish** (*cloth, paintwork*) satinado ▸ **silk hat** sombrero *m* de copa ▸ **silk industry** industria *f* sedera ▸ **silk route** • **the ~ route** la ruta de la seda ▸ **silk thread** hilo *m* de seda
silken ['sɪlkən] (ADJ) **1** (= *of silk*) de seda; (= *like silk*) sedoso, sedeño
2 (= *suave*) [*manner, voice*] suave, mimoso
silkiness ['sɪlkɪnɪs] (N) **1** [*of fabric*] sedosidad *f*, lo sedoso
2 [*of manner, voice*] suavidad *f*, lo mimoso
silkmoth ['sɪlkmɒθ] (N) mariposa *f* de seda
silk-raising ['sɪlk,reɪzɪŋ] (N) sericultura *f*
silk-screen print ['sɪlkskri:n,prɪnt] (N) serigrafía *f*
silk-screen printing [,sɪlkskri:n'prɪntɪŋ] (N) serigrafía *f*
silkworm ['sɪlkwɜ:m] (N) gusano *m* de seda
silky ['sɪlkɪ] (ADJ) (COMPAR: **silkier**, SUPERL: **silkiest**) **1** [*material*] sedoso; [*sound, voice*] suave • **a ~ sheen** un brillo sedoso • **~ smooth** *or* **soft** suave como la seda
2 (*fig*) [*skills*] fino, depurado • **a ~ gear change** un suave cambio de marchas
sill [sɪl] (N) **1** (= *windowsill*) alféizar *m*
2 (*Aut*) umbral *m*
silliness ['sɪlɪnɪs] (N) (= *quality*) estupidez *f*; (= *act*) tontería *f*
silly ['sɪlɪ] (ADJ) (COMPAR: **sillier**, SUPERL: **silliest**) (= *stupid*) [*person*] tonto, bobo, sonso *or* zonzo (*LAm*); [*act, idea*] absurdo; (= *ridiculous*) ridículo • **how ~ of me!** • **~ me!** ¡qué tonto *or* bobo soy! • **that was ~ of you** • **that was a ~ thing to do** eso que hiciste fue muy tonto *or* bobo, fue una tontería *or* estupidez por tu parte • **don't be ~** no seas tonto *or* bobo • **I feel ~ in this hat** me siento ridículo con este sombrero • **to knock sb ~*** dar una paliza a algn • **the blow knocked him ~** el golpe le dejó tonto *or* sin sentido • **to laugh o.s. ~*** desternillarse de risa* • **you look ~ carrying that fish** pareces tonto llevando ese pez • **to make sb look ~** poner a algn en ridículo • **~ season** temporada *f* boba, canícula *f* • **I've done a ~ thing** he hecho una tontería, he sido un tonto
silo ['saɪləʊ] (N) (PL: **silos**) (*gen*) silo *m*
silt [sɪlt] (N) sedimento *m*, aluvión *m*
▸ **silt up** (VI + ADV) obstruirse (con sedimentos)
(VT + ADV) obstruir (con sedimentos)
silting [sɪltɪŋ] (N) (*also* **silting up**) obstrucción *f* con sedimentos
silver ['sɪlvəʳ] (N) **1** (= *metal*) plata *f*; (= *silverware, silver cutlery*) plata *f*, vajilla *f* de plata
2 (= *money*) monedas *fpl* de plata, monedas *fpl* plateadas • **"have you got any ~?" — "sorry, only notes and coppers"** ¿tienes monedas de plata? — no, solo billetes y monedas de cobre • **£2 in ~** 2 libras en monedas de plata
(ADJ) **1** (= *made of silver*) [*ring, cutlery*] de plata
2 (*in colour*) plateado; [*car*] gris plata (*inv*); ▷ **spoon, cloud**
(VT) [+ *metal*] platear; [+ *mirror*] azogar; [+ *hair*] blanquear
(VI) [*hair*] blanquear
(CPD) ▸ **silver beet** (*US*) acelga *f* ▸ **silver birch** abedul *m* plateado ▸ **silver coin** moneda *f* de plata ▸ **silver fir** abeto *m* blanco, pinabete *m* ▸ **silver foil** papel *m* de aluminio *or* plata ▸ **silver fox** zorro *m* plateado ▸ **silver gilt** plata *f* dorada ▸ **silver jubilee** vigésimo quinto aniversario *m* ▸ **silver lining** (*fig*) resquicio *m* de esperanza ▸ **silver medal** medalla *f* de plata ▸ **silver medallist** medallero/a *m/f* de plata ▸ **silver paper** papel *m* de plata ▸ **silver plate** (= *material*) plateado *m*; (= *objects*) vajilla *f* plateada; ▷ **silver-plate** ▸ **silver polish** producto *m* para limpiar la plata ▸ **the silver screen** la pantalla cinematográfica ▸ **silver surfer** (= *older internet user*) internauta *mf* de la tercera edad ▸ **silver tongue** • **to have a ~ tongue** (*fig*) tener un pico de oro ▸ **the Silver State** (*US*) Nevada *f* ▸ **silver wedding** bodas *fpl* de plata
silverfish ['sɪlvəfɪʃ] (N) (PL: **silverfish**) lepisma *f*
silver-grey ['sɪlvə'greɪ] (ADJ) gris perla
silver-haired ['sɪlvə'hɛəd] (ADJ) de pelo entrecano
silver-plate [,sɪlvə'pleɪt] (VT) platear
silver-plated [,sɪlvə'pleɪtɪd] (ADJ) plateado
silverside ['sɪlvəsaɪd] (N) (*Culin*) *corte del lomo posterior de la ternera*
silversmith ['sɪlvəsmɪθ] (N) platero/a *m/f* • **~'s (shop)** platería *f*
silver-tongued ['sɪlvə'tʌŋd] (ADJ) elocuente, con pico de oro
silverware ['sɪlvəwɛəʳ] (N) plata *f*, vajilla *f* de plata; (= *trophies**) trofeos *mpl*
silvery ['sɪlvərɪ] (ADJ) [*colour*] plateado; [*sound, voice*] argentino
silviculture ['sɪlvɪ,kʌltʃəʳ] (N) silvicultura *f*
sim ['sɪm] (N) (*Comput*) simulación *f*
SIM card ['sɪm,kɑ:d] (N) (= **Subscriber Identity Module card**) tarjeta *f* SIM
simian ['sɪmɪən] (ADJ) símico
similar ['sɪmɪləʳ] (ADJ) **1** parecido, similar, semejante • **they are of a ~ colour** son de un color parecido *or* similar • **they were of a ~ age** eran más o menos de la misma edad • **to be ~ in shape/size** tener una forma parecida *or* similar, tener un tamaño parecido *or* similar, parecerse en la forma *or* el tamaño • **to be ~ to** parecerse a, ser parecido *or* similar *or* semejante a
2 (*Geom*) semejante
similarity [,sɪmɪ'lærɪtɪ] (N) **1** (*uncountable*) (= *resemblance*) parecido *m*, semejanza *f* • **there is no ~ between them** no existe ningún parecido *or* ninguna semejanza entre ellos • **any ~ is purely coincidental** cualquier parecido es pura coincidencia • **the ~ ends there** el parecido no va más allá
2 (*countable*) (= *feature in common*) semejanza *f*, rasgo *m* común, similitud *f*
similarly ['sɪmɪləlɪ] (ADV) (= *equally*) igualmente; (= *in a like manner*) de modo parecido, de manera parecida, de modo *or* manera similar • **and ~, …** y del mismo modo, …, y asimismo, …
simile ['sɪmɪlɪ] (N) símil *m*
similitude [sɪ'mɪlɪtju:d] (N) similitud *f*,

semejanza *f*
simmer ['sɪməʳ] (VT) cocer a fuego lento
(VI) hervir a fuego lento; (*fig*) estar a punto de estallar
(N) • **to be/keep on the ~** hervir a fuego lento
▸ **simmer down*** (VI + ADV) (*fig*) calmarse, tranquilizarse • **~ down!** ¡cálmate!
Simon ['saɪmən] (N) Simón
simony ['saɪmənɪ] (N) simonía *f*
simp* [sɪmp] (N) (*US*) bobo/a *m/f*
simper ['sɪmpəʳ] (N) sonrisa *f* afectada
(VI) sonreír con afectación
(VT) • **"yes," she ~ed** —sí —dijo sonriendo afectada
simpering ['sɪmpərɪŋ] (ADJ) (= *affected*) afectado; (= *foolish*) atontado
simperingly ['sɪmpərɪŋlɪ] (ADV) (= *affectedly*) afectadamente; (= *foolishly*) tontamente
simple ['sɪmpl] (ADJ) (COMPAR: **simpler**, SUPERL: **simplest**) **1** (= *uncomplicated*) [*problem, idea, task*] sencillo, simple • **there is no ~ answer** no existe una respuesta sencilla • **nothing could be ~r** no hay nada más simple • **it's as ~ as that** la cosa es así de sencilla • **it's not as ~ as you think** no es tan sencillo como piensas • **it should be a ~ enough job** no debería ser un trabajo difícil • **keep it ~** no lo compliques • **in ~ terms** en lenguaje sencillo • **the ~st thing would be to phone** lo más sencillo sería llamar por teléfono • **to be ~ to make/use** ser sencillo de hacer/usar
2 (= *mere*) simple • **a ~ phone call could win you a week's holiday in Florida** con una simple llamada de teléfono podría ganar una semana de vacaciones en Florida • **by the ~ fact that ...** por el simple hecho de que ... • **to be a ~ matter of doing sth** ser simplemente una cuestión de hacer algo
3 (= *elementary*) simple • **a ~ act of kindness** un simple acto de bondad • **the ~ fact is ...** la pura realidad es ... • **for the ~ reason that ...** por la simple razón de que ... • **the ~ truth** la pura verdad; ▸ **pure**
4 (= *not fussy*) [*dress, style, food*] sencillo
5 (= *unsophisticated*) [*person, life, pleasures, pursuits*] sencillo • **these are ~ people** son gente sencilla • **the ~ things in** *or* **of life** las cosas sencillas de la vida
6* (= *mentally retarded*) simple
7 (*Chem, Bio, Bot, Med*) simple
8 (*Gram*) [*sentence, tense*] simple
(CPD) ▸ **simple division** división *f* simple ▸ **simple equation** ecuación *f* de primer grado ▸ **simple fraction** fracción *f* simple ▸ **simple interest** interés *m* simple ▸ **simple majority** (*Pol*) mayoría *f* simple ▸ **Simple Simon** tontorrón *m*, simplón *m*, alma *m* de cántaro (*Sp*) ▸ **simple tense** (*Gram*) tiempo *m* simple
simple-hearted ['sɪmpl'hɑːtɪd] (ADJ) candoroso, ingenuo
simple-minded ['sɪmpl'maɪndɪd] (ADJ) ingenuo, simple • **I'm not so simple-minded** no soy tan ingenuo • **in their simple-minded way** a su modo ingenuo
simple-mindedness ['sɪmpl'maɪndɪdnɪs] (N) ingenuidad *f*, simpleza *f*
simpleton ['sɪmpltən] (N) inocentón/ona *m/f*, simplón/ona *m/f*
simplicity [sɪm'plɪsɪtɪ] (N) **1** (= *uncomplicated nature*) [*of solution, idea, plan*] sencillez *f*, simplicidad *f* • **it's ~ itself** es la sencillez personificada
2 (= *unpretentiousness*) [*of dress, style, food*] sencillez *f*
3 (= *ingenuousness*) [*of person, way of life*] simpleza *f*
simplifiable ['sɪmplɪfaɪəbl] (ADJ) simplificable
simplification [ˌsɪmplɪfɪ'keɪʃən] (N) simplificación *f*
simplified ['sɪmplɪfaɪd] (ADJ) [*version, account*] simplificado
simplify ['sɪmplɪfaɪ] (VT) simplificar
simplistic [sɪm'plɪstɪk] (ADJ) simplista
simplistically [sɪm'plɪstɪkəlɪ] (ADV) de manera simplista
simply ['sɪmplɪ] (ADV) **1** (= *in a simple way*) [*dress, furnish*] sencillamente; [*speak, explain*] en términos sencillos • **to put it ~ ...** hablando claro ...
2 (= *merely, just*) simplemente • **~ add hot water and stir** simplemente, añada agua caliente y remueva • **I ~ said that ...** solo dije que ...
3 (*emphatic*) (= *absolutely*) simplemente • **he ~ refused to listen to me** se negó simplemente a escucharme • **it ~ isn't possible** sencillamente no es posible • **that is ~ not true** eso sencillamente, no es verdad • **she's quite ~ the best** sin ninguna duda es la mejor • **I thought her performance was ~ marvellous/awful** su actuación me pareció francamente maravillosa/terrible • **you ~ must come!** ¡no dejes de venir!
simulacrum [ˌsɪmjʊ'leɪkrəm] (N) (PL: **simulacra** [ˌsɪmjʊ'leɪkrə]) simulacro *m*
simulate ['sɪmjʊleɪt] (VT) simular
simulated ['sɪmjʊˌleɪtɪd] (ADJ) [*surprise, shock*] fingido, simulado • **~ attack** simulacro *m* de ataque • **~ leather** cuero *m* de imitación
simulation [ˌsɪmjʊ'leɪʃən] (N) simulación *f*
simulator ['sɪmjʊleɪtəʳ] (N) simulador *m*
simulcast ['sɪməlˌkɑːst] (N) emisión *f* simultánea por radio y televisión
(VT) emitir simultáneamente por radio y televisión
simultaneity [ˌsɪməltə'niːətɪ] (N) simultaneidad *f*
simultaneous [ˌsɪməl'teɪnɪəs] (ADJ) simultáneo
(CPD) [*interpreting, translation, processing*] simultáneo ▸ **simultaneous equation** ecuación *f* simultánea
simultaneously [ˌsɪməl'teɪnɪəslɪ] (ADV) simultáneamente, a la vez
sin [sɪn] (N) pecado *m* • **sins of omission/commission** pecados *mpl* por omisión/acción • **mortal sin** pecado *m* mortal • **for my sins** por mis pecados • **it would be a sin to do that** (*Rel*) sería un pecado hacer eso; (*fig*) sería un crimen hacer eso • **to fall into sin** caer en el pecado • **to live in sin†** (*unmarried*) vivir amancebados, vivir en el pecado; ▸ **ugly**
(VI) pecar • **he was more sinned against than sinning** era más bien el ofendido que (no) el ofensor
(CPD) ▸ **sin bin*** (*Sport*) banquillo *m* de los expulsados ▸ **sin tax*** (*US*) impuesto *m* sobre el tabaco y/o el alcohol
Sinai ['saɪnɪaɪ] (N) Sinaí *m* • **Mount ~** el monte Sinaí
(CPD) ▸ **the Sinai Desert** el desierto del Sinaí
Sinbad ['sɪnbæd] (N) Simbad • **~ the Sailor** Simbad el marino
since [sɪns] (ADV) desde entonces • **I haven't seen him ~** desde entonces no lo he vuelto a ver • **ever ~** desde entonces • **not long ~** • **a short time ~** hace poco • **a long time ~** hace mucho (tiempo) • **her parents have long ~ died** sus padres hace tiempo que fallecieron, sus padres fallecieron tiempo ha (*frm*) • **the time for talking has long ~ passed** la hora de hablar ya pasó hace tiempo
(PREP) desde • **~ Monday** desde el lunes • **~ Christmas** desde Navidad • **~ then** desde entonces • **I've been waiting ~ ten** espero desde las diez • **ever ~ then ...** desde entonces ... • **ever ~ that ...** desde aquello ...

SINCE

Time

▸ *When* **since** *is followed by a noun or noun phrase, you can usually translate it as* **desde**:

Spain has changed a lot since Franco's death
España ha cambiado mucho desde la muerte de Franco

▸ *When* **since** *is followed by a verb phrase, use* **desde que** *instead:*

Since I saw you a fortnight ago a lot of things have happened
Desde que te vi hace quince días han pasado muchas cosas

NOTE: Use the present tense in Spanish to describe a situation that started in the past and has continued up to now (present perfect or present perfect continuous in English):

I have been here since this morning
Estoy aquí *or* Llevo aquí desde esta mañana
They've been waiting since nine o'clock
Están esperando *or* Llevan esperando desde las nueve
He has been taking more exercise since he talked to his doctor
Hace más ejercicio desde que habló con el médico

But the perfect tense is used in Spanish when the verb is in the negative:

I haven't seen her since she left
No la he visto desde que se fue

▸ *Translate* **since then** *or* **ever since** *using* **desde entonces**:

She came home at five and has been studying ever since
Llegó a casa a las cinco y está estudiando desde entonces

▸ *Translate* **long since** *using* **hace tiempo** *(+* **que** *+ past tense) or* **hacía tiempo** *(+* **que** *+ past/past perfect) as relevant:*

His wife has long since died
Hace tiempo que murió su mujer, Su mujer murió hace tiempo

Meaning "as", "because"

▸ *In formal contexts you can usually translate* **since** *using* **ya que** *or* **puesto que**. *In more everyday Spanish, use* **como**, *which must go at the beginning of the sentence:*

They could not afford the house since they were not earning enough
No podían pagar la casa puesto que *or* ya que no ganaban bastante
Since I hadn't heard from you, I decided to give you a call
Como no sabía nada de ti, decidí llamarte

For further uses and examples, see main entry.

• **~ that day he has been a changed man** desde *or* a partir de ese día es un hombre nuevo • **how long is it ~ the accident?** ¿cuánto tiempo ha pasado desde el accidente? • **~ arriving** desde que llegué, desde mi llegada
(CONJ) **1** (= *from the time that*) desde que • **~ I arrived** desde que llegué • **I haven't seen her ~ she left** no la he visto desde que se fue • **I've been wearing glasses ~ I was three** llevo gafas desde los tres años • **it's a week ~ he left** hace una semana que se fue, se fue hace una semana • **it's a few years ~ I've seen them** hace varios años que no los veo • **ever ~ I've been here** desde que estoy aquí
2 (= *as, because*) ya que, puesto que, como • **~ you can't come** ya que no puedes venir, como no puedes venir, puesto que no puedes venir • **~ you're tired, let's stay at home** ya que *or* puesto que *or* como estás cansado vamos a quedarnos en casa • **~ he is Spanish** ya que *or* como *or* puesto que es español, siendo él español (*frm*)

sincere [sɪnˈsɪəʳ] (ADJ) sincero (**about sth** sobre algo, con respecto a algo) • **my ~ good wishes** mi más sincera enhorabuena • **it is my ~ belief that ...** creo sinceramente que ... • **to be ~ in one's desire to do sth** *or* **in wanting to do sth** desear *or* querer sinceramente hacer algo

sincerely [sɪnˈsɪəlɪ] (ADV) **1** (= *genuinely*) [*hope, believe, regret, say*] sinceramente • **his ~ held religious beliefs** sus sinceras creencias religiosas
2 (*in letters*) • **Yours ~** (*Brit*) • **Sincerely yours** (*US*) (le saluda) atentamente

sincerity [sɪnˈserɪtɪ] (N) sinceridad *f* • **in all ~** con toda sinceridad

sine [saɪn] (N) (*Math*) seno *m*

sinecure [ˈsaɪnɪkjʊəʳ] (N) sinecura *f*

sine qua non [ˈsaɪnɪkweɪˈnɒn] (N) sine qua non *m*

sinew [ˈsɪnjuː] (N) **1** (= *tendon*) tendón *m*; (*fig*) (= *strength*) nervio *m*, vigor *m*
2 sinews (= *muscles*) músculos *mpl*

sinewy [ˈsɪnjuːɪ] (ADJ) **1** (= *muscular*) [*person*] musculoso, fibroso; [*body, arms, muscles*] nervudo, fibroso
2 (*Culin*) [*of meat*] fibroso, con mucho nervio
3 (= *vigorous*) [*music, performance, writing, style*] brioso, vigoroso

sinfonietta [ˌsɪnfənˈjetə] (N) sinfonieta *f*

sinful [ˈsɪnfʊl] (ADJ) [*act, thought*] pecaminoso; [*person*] pecador; [*town etc*] inmoral, depravado; (*fig*) (= *disgraceful*) escandaloso

sinfully [ˈsɪnfəlɪ] (ADV) de modo pecaminoso

sinfulness [ˈsɪnfʊlnɪs] (N) [*of behaviour, way of life*] pecaminosidad *f*

sing [sɪŋ] (PT: **sang**, PP: **sung**) (VT) [+ *song, words*] cantar; (*fig*) (= *intone*) entonar • **~ us a song!** ¡cántanos una canción! • **the words are sung to the tune of ...** la letra se canta con la melodía de ... • **she ~s alto** canta contralto • **to ~ a child to sleep** arrullar a un niño, adormecer a un niño cantando
• IDIOMS: • **to ~ sb's praises** cantar las alabanzas de algn • **to ~ a different tune** ver las cosas de otro color; ▷ **heart**
(VI) **1** [*person, bird*] cantar • **"what do you do for a living?" — "I ~"** —¿a qué te dedicas? —canto *or* —soy cantante • **to ~ to/for sb** cantar a algn • **to ~ to o.s.** cantar solo • **they sang to the accompaniment of the piano** cantaban acompañados del piano
2 [*wind, kettle*] silbar; [*ears*] zumbar
3 (*US**) (*fig*) (= *act as informer*) cantar*; (= *confess*) confesar

▸ **sing along** (VI + ADV) • **he invited the audience to ~ along** invitó al publico a cantar (a coro) con él • **I like records that get people ~ing along** me gustan los discos en que la gente corea las canciones • **to ~ along with** *or* **to a song** corear una canción • **to ~ along with** *or* **to a record/the radio** cantar con un disco/la radio • **the audience was ~ing along to his latest hit** el público cantaba a coro *or* coreaba su último éxito

▸ **sing out** (VI + ADV) (*lit*) cantar con voz fuerte; (*fig*) pegar un grito* • **if you want anything, just ~ out** si quieres algo no tienes más que pegarme un grito*
(VT + ADV) vocear • **"hello! I'm back," he sang out cheerfully** —¡hola! estoy de vuelta —voceó alegre

▸ **sing up** (VI + ADV) cantar más fuerte • **~ up!** ¡más fuerte!

sing. (ABBR) = **singular**

Singapore [ˌsɪŋgəˈpɔːʳ] (N) Singapur *m*

Singaporean [ˌsɪŋgəˈpɔːrɪən] (ADJ) de Singapur
(N) nativo/a *m/f or* habitante *mf* de Singapur

singe [sɪndʒ] (VT) (*gen*) chamuscar, quemar; [+ *hair*] quemar las puntas de
(N) (*also* **singe mark**) quemadura *f*

singer [ˈsɪŋəʳ] (N) cantante *mf*

singer-songwriter [ˌsɪŋəʳˈsɒŋraɪtəʳ] (N) cantautor(a) *m/f*

Singhalese [ˌsɪŋgəˈliːz] (ADJ) cingalés
(N) **1** (= *person*) cingalés/esa *m/f*
2 (*Ling*) cingalés *m*

singing [ˈsɪŋɪŋ] (N) **1** (= *act of singing*) canto *m* • **she is studying ~** estudia canto • **the ~ stopped** dejaron de cantar • **his ~ was atrocious** cantaba pésimamente, cantaba fatal* • **they stood for the ~ of the Internationale** se pusieron de pie para cantar la Internacional
2 [*of kettle*] silbido *m*; (*in ears*) zumbido *m*
(CPD) ▸ **singing lesson** lección *f* de canto ▸ **singing teacher** profesor(a) *m/f* de canto ▸ **singing telegram** telegrama *m* cantado ▸ **singing voice** • **to have a good ~ voice** tener una buena voz para cantar

single [ˈsɪŋgl] (ADJ) **1** (*before noun*) (= *one only*) solo • **in a ~ day** en un solo día • **we heard a ~ shot** oímos un solo disparo • **our team won by a ~ point** nuestro equipo ganó por un solo punto
2 (*before noun*) (*emphatic*) • **we didn't see a ~ car that afternoon** no vimos ni un solo coche esa tarde • **not a ~ one was left** no quedó ni uno • **it rained every ~ day** no dejó de llover ni un solo día, llovió todos los días sin excepción • **I did not doubt her sincerity for a ~ moment** no dudé de su sinceridad ni por un momento • **not a** *or* **one ~ person came to her aid** ni una sola persona fue a ayudarla • **the ~ biggest problem** el problema más grande • **the US is the ~ biggest producer of carbon dioxide** los EEUU son los mayores productores de carbón • **I couldn't think of a ~ thing to say** no se me ocurría nada que decir
3 (*before noun*) (= *individual*) • **he gave her a ~ rose** le dio una rosa • **a ~ diamond** un solitario
4 (*before noun*) (= *not double*) [*bed, sheet, room*] individual; [*garage*] para un solo coche; [*whisky, gin etc*] sencillo; [*bloom*] simple • **a ~ knot** un nudo sencillo; ▷ **figure**
5 (= *unmarried*) [*person*] soltero; [*mother, father*] sin pareja; [*life*] de soltero; ▷ **single-parent**
6 (*before noun*) (*Brit*) (= *one-way*) [*ticket, fare*] de ida
(N) **1** (*in hotel*) (*also* **single room**) habitación *f* individual
2 (*Brit*) (*also* **single ticket**) billete *m* de ida
3 (= *record*) sencillo *m*, single *m*
4 (*Cricket*) (= *one run*) tanto *m*
5 (*Brit*) (= *pound coin or note*) billete *m or* moneda *f* de una libra; (*US*) (= *dollar note*) billete *m* de un dólar
6 singles: **a** (*Tennis etc*) individuales *mpl* • **the men's ~s** los individuales masculinos
b (= *unmarried people*) solteros *mpl*
(CPD) ▸ **single combat** combate *m* singular • **in ~ combat** en combate singular ▸ **single cream** (*Brit*) crema *f* de leche líquida, nata *f* líquida (*Sp*) ▸ **single currency** moneda *f* única ▸ **single density disk** disco *m* de densidad sencilla ▸ **single European currency** moneda *f* europea ▸ **Single European Market** • **the Single European Market** el Mercado Único Europeo ▸ **single father** padre *m* soltero, padre *m* sin pareja ▸ **single file** • **in ~ file** en fila india ▸ **single honours** *licenciatura universitaria en la que se estudia una sola especialidad* ▸ **single lens reflex (camera)** cámara *f* réflex de una lente ▸ **single malt (whisky)** whisky *m* de malta ▸ **single market** mercado *m* único ▸ **single mother** madre *f* soltera, madre *f* sin pareja ▸ **single parent** (= *woman*) madre *f* soltera, madre *f* sin pareja; (= *man*) padre *m* soltero, padre *m* sin pareja ▸ **single parent benefit** *ayuda del Estado por ser padre soltero o madre soltera* ▸ **singles bar** bar *m* para solteros ▸ **singles chart** lista *f* de los singles más vendidos ▸ **single spacing** (*Typ*) interlineado *m* simple • **in ~ spacing** a espacio sencillo ▸ **single supplement, single person supplement, single room supplement** (*in hotel*) recargo *m* por reserva individual ▸ **single transferable vote** (*Pol*) • **~ transferable vote system** sistema *m* del voto único transferible

▸ **single out** (VT + ADV) (= *choose*) elegir; (= *distinguish*) hacer resaltar • **he was ~d out to lead the team** fue elegido para ser capitán del equipo • **to ~ out plants** entresacar plantas

single-barrelled [ˌsɪŋglˈbærəld] (ADJ) [*gun*] de cañón único

single-breasted [ˌsɪŋglˈbrestɪd] (ADJ) recto

single-cell [ˌsɪŋglˈsel] (ADJ) unicelular

single-celled [ˌsɪŋglˈseld] (ADJ) = **single-cell**

single-chamber [ˌsɪŋglˈtʃeɪmbəʳ] (ADJ) unicameral

single-decker [ˌsɪŋglˈdekəʳ] (N) autobús *m* de un solo piso

singledom* [ˈsɪŋgldəm] (N) soltería *f*

single-engined [ˌsɪŋglˈendʒɪnd] (ADJ) monomotor

single-entry [ˌsɪŋglˈentrɪ] (N) partida *f* simple
(CPD) ▸ **single-entry book-keeping** contabilidad *f* por partida simple

single-family [ˌsɪŋglˈfæmlɪ] (ADJ) unifamiliar

single-figure [ˌsɪŋglˈfɪgəʳ] (ADJ) • **single-figure inflation** inflación *f* por debajo del 10%

single-handed [ˌsɪŋglˈhændɪd] (ADJ), (ADV) sin ayuda

single-handedly [ˌsɪŋglˈhændɪdlɪ] (ADV) sin ayuda • **she single-handedly turned gymnastics into a major event** convirtió ella sola la gimnasia en una de las pruebas principales

single-hearted [ˌsɪŋglˈhɑːtɪd] (ADJ) **1** (= *loyal*) sincero, leal
2 (= *single-minded*) resuelto, firme

single-masted [ˌsɪŋglˈmɑːstɪd] (ADJ) de palo único

single-minded [ˌsɪŋglˈmaɪndɪd] (ADJ) resuelto, firme

single-mindedly [ˌsɪŋglˈmaɪndɪdlɪ] (ADV) resueltamente, firmemente

single-mindedness [ˌsɪŋglˈmaɪndɪdnɪs] (N) resolución *f*, firmeza *f*

singleness ['sɪŋglnɪs] N • **~ of purpose** resolución *f*, firmeza *f*
single-parent ['sɪŋgl,peərənt] ADJ • **single-parent family** familia *f* monoparental • **single-parent household** hogar *m* sin pareja, familia *f* monoparental
single-party [,sɪŋgl'pɑːtɪ] ADJ [*state etc*] de partido único
single-seater [,sɪŋgl'siːtəʳ] ADJ • **single-seater aeroplane** monoplaza *m*
N monoplaza *m*
single-sex [,sɪŋgl'seks] ADJ [*education, class*] no mixto
CPD ▸ **single-sex school** (*for boys*) colegio *m* de niños; (*for girls*) colegio *m* de niñas
single-sided disk [,sɪŋgsaɪdɪd'dɪsk] N disco *m* de una cara
single-space ['sɪŋgl'speɪs] VT [+ *text*] mecanografiar a espacio sencillo
singlet ['sɪŋglɪt] N camiseta *f* sin mangas, camiseta *f* de tirantes, playera *f* (*LAm*)
singleton ['sɪŋgltən] N (*Bridge*) semifallo *m* (in a)
single-track ['sɪŋgl'træk] ADJ [*railway*] de vía única
CPD ▸ **single-track road** carretera *f* de un solo carril (*con espacios para que los vehículos se puedan cruzar*)
single-use [,sɪŋgl'juːs] ADJ [*camera*] de usar y tirar, de un solo uso; [*medical instrument, syringe*] desechable
singly ['sɪŋglɪ] ADV (= *separately*) por separado; (= *one at a time*) uno por uno
singsong ['sɪŋ,sɒŋ] ADJ [*voice, tone*] cantarín
N (*Brit*) (= *songs*) concierto *m* improvisado; (= *sound*) sonsonete *m* • **to get together for a ~** reunirse para cantar (*canciones populares, folklóricas etc*)
singular ['sɪŋgjʊləʳ] ADJ **1** (*Ling*) singular • **a ~ noun** un sustantivo en singular
2 (= *extraordinary*) singular, excepcional • **a most ~ occurrence** un suceso de lo más singular *or* excepcional • **how very ~!** ¡qué raro!
N singular *m* • **in the ~** en singular
singularity [,sɪŋgjʊ'lærɪtɪ] N (= *extraordinariness*) singularidad *f*, lo excepcional
singularize ['sɪŋgjʊlə,raɪz] VT singularizar
singularly ['sɪŋgjʊləlɪ] ADV (= *extraordinarily*) extraordinariamente, singularmente • **he was ~ unhelpful** no se mostró dispuesto a ayudar en absoluto • **a ~ inappropriate remark** una observación de lo más inoportuna
Sinhalese [,sɪŋə'liːz] = **Singhalese**
sinister ['sɪnɪstəʳ] ADJ siniestro • **a ~-looking man** un hombre de apariencia siniestra
sinisterly ['sɪnɪstəlɪ] ADV siniestramente
sink¹ [sɪŋk] (PT: **sank**, PP: **sunk**) VT
1 (= *submerge*) [+ *ship*] hundir; (*fig*) (= *destroy*) [+ *person*] hundir; [+ *project*] acabar con, dar al traste con; [+ *theory*] destruir, acabar con • **to be sunk*** estar perdido
2 (= *open up*) [+ *mineshaft*] abrir, excavar; [+ *hole*] hacer, excavar; [+ *well*] perforar, abrir
3 (= *bury, lay*) **a** [+ *pipe*] enterrar; [+ *foundations*] echar • **to ~ a post two metres into the ground** fijar un poste dos metros bajo tierra • **she sunk her face into her hands** hundió la cara en las manos • **his eyes were sunk deep into their sockets** tenía los ojos hundidos
b (*fig*) • **to be sunk in thought** estar absorto en mis *etc* pensamientos, estar ensimismado • **to be sunk in depression** estar sumido en la depresión
4 (= *forget*) [+ *feelings*] ahogar • IDIOM: • **let's ~ our differences** hagamos las paces, olvidemos nuestras diferencias
5 (= *dig in*) [+ *knife*] hundir, clavar; [+ *teeth*] hincar • **I sank my knife into the cheese** hundí *or* clavé el cuchillo en el queso • **he sank his teeth into my arm** me hincó los dientes en el brazo
6 (= *invest*) • **to ~ money in** *or* **into sth** invertir dinero en algo
7 (*Brit**) [+ *drink*] tragarse*
8 (*Sport*) [+ *ball, putt*] embocar
VI **1** [*ship, object*] hundirse • **the body sank to the bottom of the lake** el cadáver se hundió en el fondo del lago • **the yeast ~s to the bottom in beer** la levadura se deposita en el fondo de la cerveza • **to ~ out of sight** desaparecer • **to ~ without trace** (*fig*) desaparecer sin dejar rastro • IDIOM: • **to leave sb to ~ or swim** abandonar a algn a su suerte • **we're all in the same boat and we ~ or swim together** todos estamos en la misma situación, y una de dos: o nos hundimos o salimos a flote juntos
2 (= *subside*) [*building, land*] hundirse; [*flood waters*] bajar de nivel; [*sun*] ponerse
3 (= *slump*) [*person*] • **to ~ into a chair** arrellanarse en una silla, dejarse caer en una silla • **to ~ to one's knees** caer de rodillas • **I sank into a deep sleep** caí en un sueño profundo • **she would sometimes ~ into depression** a veces se sumía en la depresión • **he sank deeper into debt** se hundió más y más en las deudas • **to ~ into poverty** hundirse *or* caer en la miseria • **my heart sank** se me cayó el alma a los pies • **her spirits sank lower and lower** tenía la moral cada vez más baja
4 (= *deteriorate*) [*sick person*] • **he's ~ing fast** está cada vez peor
5 (= *fall*) (*in amount, value*) • **the shares have sunk to three dollars** las acciones han bajado a tres dólares • **he has sunk in my estimation** ha bajado en mi estima • **his voice sank to a whisper** su voz se redujo a un susurro
CPD ▸ **sink estate** *urbanización en una zona deprimida y con graves problemas sociales y de orden público*
▸ **sink back** VI + ADV (= *slump*) (*into chair*) arrellanarse, ponerse cómodo • **I sank back onto the pillows** me puse cómodo en las almohadas
▸ **sink down** VI + ADV [*building*] ceder, hundirse; [*post*] hundirse, clavarse • **to ~ down into a chair** apoltronarse *or* arrellanarse en un sillón • **to ~ down on one's knees** caer de rodillas, arrodillarse • **he sank down (out of sight) behind the bush** se agachó detrás del matorral
▸ **sink in** VI + ADV **1** (= *penetrate*) penetrar • **in time the water ~s in** con el tiempo el agua va penetrando
2* (*fig*) • **she paused to let the news ~ in** hizo una pausa para que pudieran asimilar la noticia • **it hasn't sunk in that he's gone forever** aún no ha asimilado *or* asumido el hecho de que se ha ido para siempre
sink² [sɪŋk] N (*in kitchen*) fregadero *m*, pila *f*; (*in bathroom*) lavabo *m*
ADJ [*estate*] degradado, deprimido; [*school*] con un nivel muy bajo
CPD ▸ **sink tidy** *recipiente para lavavajillas, jabón y estropajos* ▸ **sink unit** fregadero *m*
sinker ['sɪŋkəʳ] N **1** (*Fishing*) (= *lead*) plomo *m*
2 (*US**) (= *doughnut*) donut *m*
sinking ['sɪŋkɪŋ] N (= *shipwreck*) hundimiento *m*
ADJ **1** (= *foundering*) • **a ~ ship** (*lit*) un barco que se hunde; (*fig*) (= *cause*) una causa en declive *or* que va a pique; (= *organization*) una organización en declive *or* que va a pique
2 • **with a ~ feeling she picked the phone up** con una sensación de ansiedad contestó el teléfono • **that ~ feeling** esa sensación de ansiedad *or* desazón • **with a ~ heart** entristecido
3 (*Econ*) • **a ~ pound/dollar** una libra/un dólar cayendo en picado
CPD ▸ **sinking fund** (*Econ*) fondo *m* de amortización
sinless ['sɪnlɪs] ADJ libre de pecado, inmaculado
sinner ['sɪnəʳ] N pecador(a) *m/f*
Sinn Féin [ʃɪn'feɪn] N Sinn Féin *m* (*partido político de Irlanda del Norte*)
Sino... ['saɪnəʊ] PREFIX sino..., chino...
Sinologist [,saɪ'nɒlədʒɪst] N sinólogo/a *m/f*
Sinology [,saɪ'nɒlədʒɪ] N sinología *f*
sinuosity [,sɪnjʊ'ɒsɪtɪ] N sinuosidad *f*
sinuous ['sɪnjʊəs] ADJ (*gen*) sinuoso; [*road*] serpenteante, con muchos rodeos
sinuously ['sɪnjʊəslɪ] ADV sinuosamente
sinus ['saɪnəs] N (PL: **sinuses**) (*Anat*) seno *m*
sinusitis [,saɪnə'saɪtɪs] N sinusitis *f*
sip [sɪp] N sorbo *m*
VT sorber, beber a sorbos
VI (*also* **sip at**) sorber, beber a sorbitos
siphon ['saɪfən] N sifón *m*
VT (*also* **siphon off, siphon out**) sacar con sifón; (*fig*) [+ *traffic, funds*] desviar
SIPS [sɪps] N ABBR (= **side-impact protection system**) sistema *m* de protección contra impactos laterales
sir [sɜːʳ] N señor *m* • **Sirs** (*US*) muy señores nuestros • **yes, sir** sí, señor • **Dear Sir** (*in letter*) muy señor mío, estimado señor • **Sir Winston Churchill** Sir Winston Churchill
sire ['saɪəʳ] N (*Zool*) padre *m* • **Sire**†† (*to monarch*) Señor *m*
VT ser el padre de • **he ~d 49 children** tuvo 49 hijos
siree* [sɪ'riː] N (*US*) (*emphatic*) • **yes/no ~!** ¡sí/no señor!
siren ['saɪərən] N (*all senses*) sirena *f*
CPD ▸ **siren call, siren song** canto *m* de sirenas
Sirius ['sɪrɪəs] N Sirio
sirloin ['sɜːlɔɪn] N solomillo *m*
CPD ▸ **sirloin steak** filete *m* de solomillo
sirocco [sɪ'rɒkəʊ] N siroco *m*
sirup ['sɪrəp] N (*US*) = **syrup**
sis* [sɪs] N = **sister**
sisal ['saɪsəl] N (= *material*) sisal *m*, henequén *m* (*LAm*); (= *fibre*) pita *f*, sisal *m*
sissy‡ ['sɪsɪ] N **1** (= *effeminate*) marica‡ *m*, mariquita‡ *m* • **the last one's a ~!** ¡maricón el último!‡
2 (= *coward*) gallina* *f*
sister ['sɪstəʳ] N **1** (= *relation*) hermana *f* • **my little ~** mi hermana pequeña • **my brothers and ~s** mis hermanos
2 (*Brit*) (*Med*) (*also* **nursing sister**) enfermera *f* jefe
3 (*Rel*) hermana *f*; (*before name*) sor *f* • **the Sisters of Charity** las Hermanas de la Caridad
4 (*US*) • **listen ~!‡** ¡mira, hermana!, ¡mira, tía *or* colega! (*Sp‡*)
CPD ▸ **sister city** (*US*) ciudad *f* gemela ▸ **sister college** colegio *m* hermano ▸ **sister company** empresa *f* hermana, empresa *f* asociada ▸ **sister nation** nación *f* hermana ▸ **sister organization** organización *f* hermana ▸ **sister ship** barco *m* gemelo
sisterhood ['sɪstəhʊd] N hermandad *f*
sister-in-law ['sɪstərɪnlɔː] N (PL: **sisters-in-law**) cuñada *f*
sisterly ['sɪstəlɪ] ADJ de hermana
Sistine ['sɪstiːn] ADJ • **the ~ Chapel** la Capilla Sixtina
Sisyphus ['sɪsɪfəs] N Sísifo

sit [sɪt] (PT, PP: **sat**) (VI) **1** (= *be seated*) [*person*] estar sentado; [*bird*] estar posado; [*hen*] (*on eggs*) empollar • **she was sitting at her desk** estaba sentada delante de su mesa • **don't just sit there, do something!** ¡no te quedes ahí sentado, haz algo! • **are you sitting comfortably?** ¿estás cómodo (en la silla)? • **that's where I sit** ese es mi sitio • **to sit at home all day** pasar todo el día en casa (sin hacer nada) • **they were sitting in a traffic jam for two hours** estuvieron dos horas metidos en un atasco sin moverse • **we're sitting on a fortune here** estamos ante una mina de oro • **he sat over his books all night** pasó toda la noche con sus libros • **to sit still/straight** estarse *or* (*LAm*) quedarse quieto/ponerse derecho (en la silla) • **will you sit still!** ¡te quieres estar *or* quedar quieto (en la silla)! • **to sit and wait** esperar sentado • IDIOMS: • **to be sitting pretty*** estar bien colocado *or* situado • **to sit tight**: • **"sit tight, I'll be right back"** —no te muevas, ahora vuelvo • **we'll just have to sit tight till we hear from him** tendremos que esperar sin hacer nada hasta recibir noticias suyas; ▸ **fence**
2 (= *sit down*) sentarse; (= *alight*) [*bird*] posarse • **sit by me** siéntate a mi lado, siéntate conmigo • **sit!** (*to dog*) ¡quieto!
3 (*Art, Phot*) (= *pose*) • **to sit for a painter/a portrait** posar para un pintor/un retrato
4 (*Educ*) • **to sit for an examination** presentarse a un examen
5 (*Brit*) (*Pol*) • **to sit for Bury** representar a Bury, ser diputado de *or* por Bury • **to sit in Parliament** ser diputado, ser miembro del Parlamento; ▸ **sit on**
6 (= *be in session*) [*assembly*] reunirse, celebrar sesión • **the House sat all night** la sesión de la Cámara duró toda la noche; ▸ **judg(e)ment**
7 (= *be situated*) [*object*] estar colocado; [*building*] estar situado • **the house sits next to a stream** la casa está situada junto a un arroyo • **the hat sat awkwardly on her head** llevaba el sombrero mal puesto • **the car sat in the garage for over a year** el coche estuvo aparcado en el garaje más de un año
8 (= *weigh*) • **that pie sits heavy on the stomach** esa empanada es muy indigesta • **it sat heavy on his conscience** le pesaba en la conciencia, le producía remordimientos de conciencia • **her years sit lightly on her** los años apenas han dejado huella en ella
9 (= *be compatible*) • **his authoritarian style did not sit well with their progressive educational policies** su estilo autoritario era poco compatible con la política educativa activa de ellos
10 (= *to fit*) [*clothing*] sentar • **to sit well/badly (on sb)** sentar bien/mal (a algn)
11 (= *babysit*) cuidar a los niños
(VT) **1** [+ *person*] sentar; [+ *object*] colocar • **she sat the vase on the windowsill** colocó el jarrón sobre la repisa de la ventana • **to sit a child on one's knee** sentar a un niño sobre las rodillas • **he sat himself on the edge of the bed** se sentó en el borde de la cama
2 (= *have capacity for*) • **this table sits 12 (people)** en esta mesa caben 12 (personas) • **the concert hall sits 2,000 (people)** el auditorio tiene cabida *or* capacidad para 2.000 personas
3 [+ *exam, test*] presentarse a • **to sit an examination in French** presentarse a un examen de francés, examinarse de francés
▸ **sit around** (VI + ADV) • **we can't have you sitting around wasting your life** no podemos dejar que desperdicies tu vida sin hacer nada • **I'm tired of sitting around waiting for him** estoy aburrida de esperar sentada a que venga • **we sat around talking** pasamos el tiempo charlando
▸ **sit back** (VI + ADV) **1** (*in seat*) recostarse • **just sit back and enjoy the show** póngase cómodo y disfrute del espectáculo • **she sat back on her heels** se sentó en cuclillas
2 (*fig*) • **we can't just sit back and do nothing** no podemos quedarnos cruzados de brazos sin hacer nada • **to sit back and take stock** hacer una pausa y reflexionar
▸ **sit down** (VI + ADV) (= *take a seat*) sentarse • **do sit down!** ¡siéntese por favor! • **we sat down to a huge meal** nos sentamos a darnos un auténtico banquete • **to be sitting down** estar sentado
(VT + ADV) [+ *person*] sentar • **I sat him down and gave him a drink** lo senté y le di de beber • **sit yourself down and tell me all about it** siéntate y cuéntamelo todo
▸ **sit in** (VI + ADV) **1** (= *observe*) estar presente • **they said I could sit in on the meeting/the discussions** me dijeron que podía asistir a la reunión/a los debates (como observador)
2 (= *substitute*) sustituir • **to sit in for sb** sustituir a algn
3 [*students, workers*] hacer una sentada, ocupar las aulas/la fábrica *etc*
▸ **sit on** (VI + PREP) **1** (= *be member of*) [+ *jury, committee*] ser miembro de, formar parte de
2* (= *keep secret*) [+ *news, information*] ocultar, callar; (= *delay taking action on*) [+ *document, application, plan*] no dar trámite a, dar carpetazo a*
3* (= *silence*) [+ *person*] hacer callar; (= *oppress*) [+ *opponents, dissent*] reprimir a, silenciar • **he won't be sat on** no quiere callar, no da su brazo a torcer
▸ **sit out** (VT + ADV) **1** (= *not take part in*) [+ *dance*] no bailar; (*Sport*) [+ *game, event*] no participar en • **let's sit this dance out** no bailemos esta vez
2 (= *endure*) aguantar • **he decided to sit the war out in Brussels** decidió aguantar en Bruselas hasta que terminara la guerra • **to sit it out** aguantarse
▸ **sit through** (VI + PREP) • **I wouldn't want to have to sit through that film again** no me gustaría tener que volver a ver esa película otra vez • **it was the most boring speech he'd ever had to sit through** fue el discurso más aburrido que jamás tuvo que escuchar *or* aguantar
▸ **sit up** (VI + ADV) **1** (= *straighten o.s.*) ponerse derecho, enderezarse; (*after lying*) incorporarse • **sit up straight!** ¡ponte derecho!, ¡enderézate! • **when someone was killed they finally began to sit up and take notice of the situation** tuvo que morir alguien para que finalmente decidieran tomar cartas en la situación • **he knew the offer of money would make them sit up and take notice** sabía que la oferta de dinero conseguiría hacerles prestar atención • **a defeat like that makes you sit up and think** una derrota como esa te da en qué pensar
2 (= *stay up late*) • **they often sit up late, talking** a menudo trasnochan, hablando • **I sat up all night trying to work it out** me quedé toda la noche levantado intentando descifrarlo • **I'll be late back so don't sit up for me** volveré tarde así que no me esperes levantado • **to sit up with a child** pasar la noche en vela con un niño • **I sat up with her for most of the night** estuve con ella casi toda la noche, haciéndole compañía
(VT + ADV) [+ *doll, baby*] sentar; [+ *patient, invalid*] incorporar
▸ **sit upon*** (VI + PREP) = **sit on**

sitar [sɪ'tɑːʳ] (N) sitar *m*

sitcom* ['sɪtkɒm] (N) (*Rad, TV*) (*also* **situation comedy**) comedia *f* de situación

sit-down ['sɪtdaʊn] (ADJ) [*meal*] servido en la mesa • **they gave us a sit-down lunch** nos ofrecieron un almuerzo servido en la mesa • **sit-down protest** sentada *f* • **sit-down strike** huelga *f* de brazos caídos, sentada *f*
(N) • **I must have a sit-down*** tengo que sentarme a descansar un rato

site [saɪt] (N) **1** (= *place*) sitio *m*, lugar *m*; (= *location*) situación *f*; (= *scene*) escenario *m*; (*for building*) solar *m*, terreno *m*; (*archaeological*) yacimiento *m* • **the ~ of the accident** el lugar del accidente • **the ~ of the battle** el escenario de la batalla • **a late Roman ~** un emplazamiento romano tardío • **building ~** obra *f* • **burial ~** necrópolis *f inv* • **camp ~** camping *m*
2 (*Internet*) = **website**
(VT) situar, ubicar (*esp LAm*) • **a badly ~d building** un edificio mal situado

sit-in ['sɪtɪn] (N) (= *protest, demonstration*) encierro *m*, ocupación *f*; (= *strike*) huelga *f* de brazos caídos, sentada *f*

siting ['saɪtɪŋ] (N) (= *position*) situación *f*; (= *placement*) emplazamiento *m* • **the ~ of new industries** la localización de las nuevas industrias

Sits Vac. [,sɪts'væk] (N ABBR) = **Situations Vacant**

sitter ['sɪtəʳ] (N) **1** (*Art*) modelo *mf*
2 (= *babysitter*) babysitter *mf*, canguro *mf* (*Sp*)
3* cosa *f* fácil • **it was a ~** (*Sport**) fue un gol que se canta* • **you missed a ~*** erraste un tiro de lo más fácil

sitting ['sɪtɪŋ] (N) **1** (= *session*) (*Pol, Art etc*) sesión *f*; (*in canteen*) turno *m* • **second ~ for lunch** segundo turno de comedor • **to eat it all at one ~** comérselo todo de una sentada • **to read a book in one ~** leer un libro de un tirón
2 (*Zool*) [*of eggs*] nidada *f*
(ADJ) (*also* **sitting down**) sentado • **a ~ bird** una ave que está posada *or* inmóvil • **a ~ hen** una gallina clueca
(CPD) ▸ **sitting duck*** (*fig*) blanco *m* facilísimo ▸ **sitting member** miembro *mf* actual *or* en funciones ▸ **sitting room** (= *living room*) sala *f*, cuarto *m* de estar, salón *m*, living *m* (*LAm*); (= *space*) • **~ and standing room** sitio *m* para sentarse y para estar de pie ▸ **sitting target** objetivo *m* fácil ▸ **sitting tenant** inquilino/a *m/f* en posesión

situ ['sɪtjuː] (*frm*) ▸ **in situ**

situate ['sɪtjʊeɪt] (VT) situar, ubicar (*esp LAm*) • **a pleasantly ~d house** una casa bien situada *or* ubicada • **the bank is ~d in the high street** el banco está situado *or* ubicado *or* se encuentra en la calle principal • **how are you ~d for money?** (*fig*) ¿cómo vas *or* andas de dinero?

situation [,sɪtjʊ'eɪʃən] (N) **1** (= *position*) situación *f*, ubicación *f* (*esp LAm*)
2 (= *circumstances*) situación *f* • **to save the ~** salvar la situación
3 (= *job*) empleo *m*, vacante *f* • **"situations vacant"** "ofertas de empleo" • **"situations wanted"** "demandas de empleo"
(CPD) ▸ **situation comedy** (*TV, Rad*) comedia *f* de situación

situational [,sɪtjʊ'eɪʃənl] (ADJ) situacional

Situationism [sɪtjʊ'eɪʃənɪzəm] (N) (*Philos*) situacionismo *m*

Situationist [sɪtjʊ'eɪʃənɪst] (*Philos*) (ADJ) situacionista
(N) situacionista *mf*

sit-up ['sɪtʌp] (N) abdominal *m*

six [sɪks] (ADJ), (PRON) seis
(N) **1** (= *numeral*) seis *m* • IDIOMS: • **to be (all) at sixes and sevens** [*person*] estar confuso;

[*things*] estar en desorden • **it's six of one and half a dozen of the other*** • **it's six and half a dozen*** da lo mismo, da igual • **six of the best** (*Brit*) seis azotes *mpl* (*castigo escolar*)
2 (*Cricket*) seis *m*, *golpe de bate que lanza la bola sin botar fuera del terreno y sirve para anotarse seis carreras* • **to hit a six** batear un seis, hacer seis carreras de un golpe • **he hit three sixes** bateó tres seises • IDIOM: • **to knock sb for six*** dejar pasmado a algn; ▹ **five**
CPD ▸ **Six Nations** (*rugby tournament*) • **the Six Nations** el torneo de las Seis Naciones
six-eight time [ˌsɪkseɪt'taɪm] N • **in six-eight time** en un compás de seis por ocho
sixfold ['sɪksfəʊld] ADJ séxtuplo
ADV seis veces
six-footer ['sɪks'fʊtəʳ] N hombre *m or* mujer *f* que mide seis pies
six-pack ['sɪkspæk] N paquete *m* de seis
sixpence ['sɪkspəns] N (*Brit*) (*formerly*) seis peniques *mpl*
sixpenny† ['sɪkspənɪ] ADJ (*Brit*) de seis peniques; (*pej*) insignificante, inútil
six-shooter ['sɪks'ʃuːtəʳ] N revólver *m* de seis tiros
sixteen ['sɪks'tiːn] ADJ, PRON dieciséis • **she was sweet ~** tenía dieciséis años y estaba en la flor de la vida
N (= *numeral*) dieciséis *m*; ▹ **five**
sixteenth ['sɪks'tiːnθ] ADJ decimosexto
N (*in series*) decimosexto/a *m/f*; (= *fraction*) dieciseisavo *m*, decimosexta parte *f*; ▹ **fifth**
sixth [sɪksθ] ADJ sexto
N (*in series*) sexto/a *m/f*; (= *fraction*) sexto *m*, sexta parte *f*; ▹ **fifth**
CPD ▸ **sixth form** clase *f* de alumnos del sexto año (*de 16 a 18 años de edad*) ▸ **sixth former** alumno/a *m/f* de 16 a 18 años ▸ **sixth grade** (*US*) (*in schools*) • **the ~ grade** ≈ el sexto curso (*para niños de 11 años*) ▸ **sixth sense** sexto sentido *m*
sixth-form college [ˌsɪksθfɔːm'kɒlɪdʒ] N instituto *m* para alumnos de 16 a 18 años
sixth-grader [ˌsɪksθ'greɪdəʳ] N (*US*) alumno/a *m/f* de sexto curso (*de entre 11 y 12 años*)
sixtieth ['sɪkstɪɪθ] ADJ sexagésimo
N (*in series*) sexagésimo/a *m/f*; (= *fraction*) sexagésima parte *f*, sesentavo *m* • **the ~ anniversary** el sesenta aniversario; ▹ **fifth**
sixty ['sɪkstɪ] ADJ, PRON sesenta
N (= *numeral*) sesenta *m* • **to be in one's sixties** tener sesenta y tantos años, ser sesentón; ▹ **fifty**
sixty-four thousand dollar question* [ˌsɪkstɪfɔːʳˌθaʊzəndˌdɒləʳ'kwestʃən] N • **that's the sixty-four thousand dollar question** es la pregunta del millón
sixtyish ['sɪkstɪɪʃ] ADJ de unos sesenta años • **she must be ~** debe andar por los sesenta
six-yard box [sɪks'jɑːdbɒks] N • **the six-yard box** el área pequeña (*de seis metros*) • **alone in the six-yard box** solo en el área pequeña
sizable ['saɪzəbl] = **sizeable**
sizably ['saɪzəblɪ] = **sizeably**
size¹ [saɪz] N [*of object, place*] tamaño *m*; [*of person*] talla *f*, estatura *f*; [*of garments*] talla *f*, medida *f*; [*of shoes, gloves*] número *m*; (= *scope*) [*of problem*] magnitud *f*, envergadura *f* • **plates of various ~s** platos de varios tamaños • **it's the ~ of a brick** es del tamaño de un ladrillo • **the skirt is two ~s too big** la falda es dos tallas grande • **a hall of immense ~** una sala de vastas dimensiones • **try this (on) for ~** prueba esto a ver si te conviene • **they're all of a ~** tienen todos el mismo tamaño • **it's quite a ~** es bastante grande • **I take ~ nine** (*shoes*) uso *or* tengo el número nueve • **I take ~ 14** (*blouse etc*) uso *or* tengo la talla 14 • **to cut sth to ~** cortar algo al tamaño que se necesita • **what ~ is the room?** ¿de qué tamaño *or* (*LAm*) qué tan grande es el cuarto? • **what ~ are you?** ¿qué talla usas *or* tienes?, ¿de qué talla eres? • **what ~ shoes do you take?** ¿qué número (de zapato) calzas *or* gastas? • **what ~ shirt do you take?** ¿qué talla de camisa tiene *or* es la de usted? • **he's about your ~** tiene más o menos tu talla • IDIOMS: • **that's about the ~ of it** eso es lo que puedo decirle acerca del asunto, es más o menos eso • **to cut sb down to ~*** bajar los humos a algn
VT clasificar según el tamaño
▸ **size up** VT + ADV [+ *problem, situation*] evaluar, apreciar; [+ *person*] • **they looked at each other, sizing each other up** se miraban el uno al otro, intentando formarse *or* hacerse un juicio; (*for a fight*) se miraban el uno al otro, tratando de medir sus fuerzas • **I've got her all ~d up** la tengo calada • **I can't quite ~ him up** no consigo hacerme una idea clara de cómo es
size² [saɪz] N (*for plaster, paper*) cola *f*; (*for cloth*) apresto *m*
VT [+ *plaster, paper*] encolar; [+ *cloth*] aprestar
sizeable ['saɪzəbl] ADJ [*sum of money etc*] considerable, importante; [*object*] bastante grande • **it's quite a ~ house** es una casa bastante grande • **a ~ sum** una cantidad importante
sizeably ['saɪzəblɪ] ADV considerablemente
-sized [saɪzd] ADJ (*ending in compounds*) de tamaño …
sizzle ['sɪzl] VI chisporrotear; (*in frying*) crepitar (al freírse)
sizzler* ['sɪzləʳ] N día *f* de calor sofocante
sizzling ['sɪzlɪŋ] ADJ [*heat*] sofocante; [*shot etc*] fulminante
N chisporroteo *m*, crepitación *f*
S.J. ABBR (= **Society of Jesus**) C. de J.
SK ABBR (*Canada*) = **Saskatchewan**
skag‡ [skæg] N (= *heroin*) caballo‡ *m*
skate¹ [skeɪt] N (= *fish*) raya *f*
skate² [skeɪt] N patín *m* • IDIOM: • **get your ~s on!*** ¡date prisa!
VI patinar • **it went skating across the floor** se deslizó velozmente sobre el suelo
CPD ▸ **skate park** parque *m* de patinaje
▸ **skate around, skate over, skate round** VI + PREP [+ *problem, issue*] pasar por alto de, pasar por encima de
skateboard ['skeɪtbɔːd] N monopatín *m*
CPD ▸ **skateboard park** = **skate park**
skateboarder ['skeɪtbɔːdəʳ] N monopatinador(a) *m/f*
skateboarding ['skeɪtbɔːdɪŋ] N monopatinaje *m* • **to go ~** montar en monopatín
skater ['skeɪtəʳ] N patinador(a) *m/f*
skating ['skeɪtɪŋ] N patinaje *m* • **do you like ~?** ¿te gusta patinar? • **to go ~** ir a patinar
CPD ▸ **skating championship** campeonato *m* de patinaje ▸ **skating rink** (*for ice skating*) pista *f* de hielo; (*for roller skating*) pista *f* de patinaje
skean dhu ['skiːən'duː] N (*Scot*) puñal *m* (*que se lleva en el calcetín del traje típico escocés*)
skedaddle* [skɪ'dædl] VI escabullirse, salir pitando* • **they ~d in all directions** huyeron por todos lados
skein [skeɪn] N madeja *f* • **a tangled ~** (*fig*) un asunto enmarañado
skeletal ['skelɪtl] ADJ **1** (*Anat*) [*structure, development*] óseo, del esqueleto; [*remains*] de huesos • **~ structure** *or* **system** esqueleto *m*, sistema *m* óseo
2 (= *emaciated*) [*person, body*] esquelético; [*face*] enjuto
3 (= *schematic*) [*timetable*] reducido
skeleton ['skelɪtn] N [*of person*] esqueleto *m*; [*of building*] armazón *f*, armadura *f*; (= *structure*) estructura *f*; [*of novel, report*] esquema *m*, bosquejo *m* • IDIOM: • **~ in the cupboard** secreto *m* de familia
CPD [*service*] mínimo; [*outline*] esquemático ▸ **skeleton draft** esquema *m* del borrador ▸ **skeleton key** llave *f* maestra ▸ **skeleton staff** • **with a ~ staff** con un personal mínimo
skeptic *etc* ['skeptɪk] (*US*) = **sceptic** *etc*
sketch [sketʃ] N **1** (= *drawing*) dibujo *m*; (= *preliminary drawing*) esbozo *m*, bosquejo *m*; (= *rough drawing*) croquis *m inv*; (= *plan*) borrador *m*, esquema *m*
2 (*Theat*) sketch *m*
VT (*gen*) (= *draw*) dibujar; [+ *preliminary drawing, plan etc*] bosquejar, esbozar
VI hacer bosquejos
CPD ▸ **sketch map** croquis *m inv* ▸ **sketch pad** bloc *m* de dibujos ▸ **sketch show** programa *m* de sketches ▸ **sketch writer** escritor(a) *m/f* de sketches
▸ **sketch in** VT + ADV [+ *details*] explicar • **he ~ed in the details for me** me explicó los detalles
▸ **sketch out** VT + ADV (= *outline*) [+ *situation*] hacer un esquema de; [+ *incident, plan*] describir
sketchbook ['sketʃbʊk] N bloc *m* de dibujos
sketchily ['sketʃɪlɪ] ADV incompletamente
sketching ['sketʃɪŋ] N dibujo *m*, arte *m* de dibujar
CPD ▸ **sketching pad** bloc *m* de dibujos
sketchy ['sketʃɪ] ADJ (COMPAR: **sketchier**, SUPERL: **sketchiest**) incompleto, sin detalles
skew [skjuː] N • **to be on the ~** estar desviado, estar sesgado
ADJ sesgado, oblicuo, torcido
VT sesgar, desviar
VI (*also* **skew round**) desviarse, ponerse al sesgo, torcerse
skewbald ['skjuːbɔːld] ADJ pintado, con pintas
N pinto *m*
skewed ['skjuːd] ADJ sesgado, torcido (*also fig*)
skewer ['skjʊəʳ] N pincho *m*, broqueta *f*, brocheta *f*
VT ensartar, espetar
skew-whiff* [ˌskjuː'wɪf] ADJ (*Brit*) (= *twisted*) torcido, chueco (*LAm*)
ski [skiː] N (PL: **skis** *or* **ski**) esquí *m* • **a pair of skis** unos esquís
VI esquiar • **to go skiing** practicar el esquí, (ir a) esquiar • **to ski down** bajar esquiando
CPD ▸ **ski binding** sujeción *f* a la bota ▸ **ski boot** bota *f* de esquí ▸ **ski instructor** instructor(a) *m/f* de esquí, monitor(a) *m/f* de esquí ▸ **ski jump** (= *action*) salto *m* con esquís; (= *course*) pista *f* de salto ▸ **ski jumper** saltador(a) *m/f* de esquí ▸ **ski jumping** salto *m* de esquí ▸ **ski lift** telesquí *m*, telesilla *m or f* ▸ **ski mask** (*US*) pasamontaña(s) *m inv* ▸ **ski pants** pantalones *mpl* de esquí ▸ **ski pass** forfait *m* ▸ **ski pole** bastón *m* ▸ **ski rack** baca *f* portaesquís ▸ **ski resort** estación *f* de esquí ▸ **ski run** pista *f* de esquí ▸ **ski slope** pista *f* de esquí ▸ **ski stick** bastón *m* ▸ **ski suit** traje *m* de esquiar ▸ **ski tow** telearrastre *m* ▸ **ski trousers** pantalones *mpl* de esquí
skid [skɪd] N **1** (*Aut etc*) patinazo *m*, resbalón *m*
2 (*Aer*) patín *m* • IDIOMS: • **to grease the ~s** (*US**) engrasar el mecanismo • **to put the ~s under sb** deshacerse de algn con maña • **her marriage/career is on the ~s** su

matrimonio/carrera se está yendo al garete, su matrimonio/carrera está cayendo en picado
VI (*Aut*) patinar; [*person, object*] deslizarse, resbalarse • **it went ~ding across the floor** se deslizó velozmente sobre el suelo • **to ~ into** dar con *or* contra • **I ~ded into a tree** patiné y di contra un árbol, de un patinazo di contra un árbol • **the car ~ded to a halt** el coche patinó y paró
CPD ▸ **skid mark** (*on road*) marca *f* de frenazo; (*in underpants*) palomino* *m* ▸ **skid row*** (*US*) *calles donde se refugian los borrachos, drogadictos etc*

skiddoo* [skɪ'du:] VI (*US*) largarse*

skidlid* ['skɪdlɪd] N casco *m* protector (de motorista)

skidmark ['skɪdmɑ:k] N = **skid mark**

Ski-Doo® [skɪ'du:] N motonieve *f*

skidproof ['skɪdpru:f] ADJ a prueba de patinazos

skier ['ski:əʳ] N esquiador(a) *m/f*

skiff [skɪf] N esquife *m*

skiffle ['skɪfl] N *estilo de música popular de los años cincuenta de guitarra y percusión*

skiing ['ski:ɪŋ] N esquí *m* • **do you like ~?** ¿te gusta esquiar? • **to go ~** ir a esquiar
CPD ▸ **skiing holiday** vacaciones *fpl* de esquí • **to go on a ~ holiday** irse de vacaciones a esquiar ▸ **skiing instructor** monitor(a) *m/f* de esquí ▸ **skiing resort** estación *f* de esquí

skilful, skillful (*US*) ['skɪlfʊl] ADJ hábil, diestro (**at, in en**)

skilfully, skillfully (*US*) ['skɪlfəlɪ] ADV hábilmente, con destreza

skilfulness, skillfulness (*US*) ['skɪlfʊlnɪs] N habilidad *f*, destreza *f*

skill [skɪl] N **1** (= *ability*) (*gen*) habilidad *f*; (*technical*) destreza *f* • **diamond-cutting requires considerable ~** tallar diamantes requiere mucha destreza • **his ~ in battle** su destreza en el campo de la batalla • **his ~ as a fundraiser came in useful** su habilidad para recaudar fondos resultó útil • **a job that matches her ~s** un trabajo que se ajusta a sus aptitudes • **his lack of ~ in dealing with people** su inaptitud *or* falta de capacidad para tratar con la gente • **a game of ~** un juego de habilidad • **we need someone with proven management ~s** necesitamos a alguien con probadas dotes directivas • **technical ~(s)** conocimientos *mpl* técnicos
2 (= *technique*) técnica *f* • **to learn new ~s** aprender nuevas técnicas • **the basic ~s of reading and writing** los conocimientos básicos de lectura y escritura • **communication ~s** habilidad *f or* aptitud *f* para comunicarse • **language ~s** (*with foreign languages*) habilidad *f* para hablar idiomas • **he seemed to lack the most basic social ~s** carecía totalmente de don de gentes

skilled [skɪld] ADJ **1** [*person*] (= *specialized*) especializado; (= *skilful*) experto, hábil, diestro • **she is a ~ negotiator** es una negociadora muy experta *or* hábil *or* diestra • **~ craftsmen are employed in the restoration work** el trabajo de restauración lo realizan artesanos especializados • **he is ~ at** *or* **in dealing with children** tiene muy buena mano con los niños
2 [*worker*] cualificado (*esp Sp*), calificado (*esp LAm*), especializado • **~ labour** *or* (*US*) **labor** mano *f* de obra cualificada (*esp Sp*), mano *f* de obra calificada (*esp LAm*), mano *f* de obra especializada
3 [*job, work*] especializado

skillet ['skɪlɪt] N sartén *f* pequeña, sartén *m* pequeño (*LAm*)

skillful *etc* ['skɪlfʊl] ADJ (*US*) = **skilful** *etc*

skim [skɪm] VT **1** [+ *milk*] desnatar, descremar; [+ *soup, liquid*] espumar • **to ~ the cream off the milk** quitar la nata a la leche, desnatar la leche • **~med milk** leche *f* descremada *or* desnatada
2 (= *graze*) [+ *surface*] rozar • **to ~ the ground** [*plane, bird etc*] volar a ras de la tierra
3 [+ *stone*] hacer cabrillas con, hacer el salto de la rana con
4 (*fig*) [+ *subject*] tratar superficialmente
VI • **to ~ along the ground** pasar rozando la tierra • **to ~ through a book** (*fig*) echar una ojeada *or* hojear a un libro
▸ **skim across** VI + PREP (= *glide over*) deslizarse a través de
▸ **skim off** VT + ADV [+ *cream, grease*] desnatar • **they ~med off the brightest pupils** separaron a la flor y nata de los alumnos
▸ **skim through** VI + PREP (= *read quickly*) hojear

skimmer ['skɪməʳ] N (*Orn*) picotijera *m*, rayador *m*

skimp [skɪmp] VT [+ *material etc*] escatimar; [+ *work*] chapucear; [+ *praise*] ser tacaño en *or* con
VI economizar • **to ~ on fabric/work/food** escatimar tela/trabajo/alimento

skimpily ['skɪmpɪlɪ] ADV [*serve, provide*] escasamente; [*live*] mezquinamente

skimpy ['skɪmpɪ] ADJ (COMPAR: **skimpier**, SUPERL: **skimpiest**) [*skirt etc*] breve; [*allowance, meal*] escaso, mezquino

skin [skɪn] N **1** [*of person*] piel *f*; [*of face*] cutis *m*; (= *complexion*) tez *f* • **to wear wool next to one's ~** llevar prenda de lana sobre la piel • IDIOMS: • **to be ~ and bone** estar en los huesos • **he's nothing but ~ and bone** está en los huesos • **to jump out of one's ~** llevarse un tremendo susto • **it's no ~ off my nose*** a mí ni me va ni me viene, me da igual *or* lo mismo • **to save one's ~** salvar el pellejo • **by the ~ of one's teeth** por los pelos • **to have a thick/thin ~** ser poco sensible/ muy susceptible • **to get under sb's ~** (= *annoy*) irritar *or* molestar a algn • **I've got you under my ~*** no puedo dejar de pensar en ti
2 [*of animal*] piel *f*, pellejo *m*; (*as hide*) piel *f*, cuero *m*
3 [*of fruit, vegetable*] piel *f*, cáscara *f*; (*discarded*) mondaduras *fpl*
4 (= *crust*) (*on paint, milk pudding*) nata *f*
5 (*for wine*) odre *m*
6 (*Aer, Naut*) revestimiento *m*
7* = **skinhead**
8 (*Drugs*‡) (= *cigarette paper*) papelillo* *m*, papel *m* de fumar
VT **1** [+ *animal*] despellejar, desollar • **I'll ~ him alive!** (*fig*) ¡lo voy a matar!*, ¡lo voy a desollar vivo! • IDIOMS: • **to keep one's eyes ~ned for sth*** andar ojo alerta por algo • **there's more than one way to ~ a cat** cada uno tiene su manera de hacer las cosas, cada maestrillo tiene su librillo
2 [+ *fruit*] pelar, quitar la piel a; [+ *tree*] descortezar
3 (= *graze*) • **to ~ one's knee/elbow** desollarse la rodilla/el codo
4‡ (= *steal from*) despellejar, esquilmar
CPD ▸ **skin cancer** cáncer *m* de piel ▸ **skin care** cuidado *m* de la piel ▸ **skin colour** (= *colour of one's skin*) color *m* de la piel; (= *shade*) color *m* natural ▸ **skin disease** enfermedad *f* de la piel ▸ **skin diver** buceador(a) *m/f*, buzo *mf*, submarinista *mf* ▸ **skin diving** buceo *m*, submarinismo *m* ▸ **skin flick*** película *f* porno* ▸ **skin freshener** tónico *m* para la piel ▸ **skin game*** (*US*) estafa *f* ▸ **skin graft(ing)** injerto *m* de piel ▸ **skin test** prueba *f* de piel ▸ **skin trade*** publicación *f* de revistas porno ▸ **skin wound** herida *f* superficial
▸ **skin up**‡ VI + ADV liar (*un porro*)

skincare ['skɪnkɛəʳ] N cuidado *m* de la piel
ADJ [*product, line, range, routine*] para el cuidado de la piel

skin-deep ['skɪn'di:p] ADJ superficial; ▹ **beauty**

skinflick‡ ['skɪnflɪk] N película *f* porno*

skinflint ['skɪnflɪnt] N tacaño/a *m/f*, roñoso/a *m/f*

skinful* ['skɪnfʊl] N • **to have had a ~** estar borracho/a *or* (*LAm*) tomado/a

skinhead ['skɪnhed] N cabeza *mf* rapada

skinless ['skɪnlɪs] ADJ [*chicken, sausages*] sin piel

-skinned [skɪnd] ADJ (*ending in compounds*) de piel ... • **dark-skinned** de piel morena • **rough-skinned** de piel áspera

skinny* ['skɪnɪ] ADJ (COMPAR: **skinnier**, SUPERL: **skinniest**) flaco

skinny-dipping* ['skɪnɪdɪpɪŋ] N • **to go skinny-dipping** bañarse en bolas*

skinny-rib sweater* [ˌskɪnɪrɪb'swetəʳ] N blusa *f* ajustada

skint [skɪnt] ADJ • **to be ~*** estar sin cuartos, estar pelado

skin-tight ['skɪntaɪt] ADJ muy ajustado

skip¹ [skɪp] N salto *m*, brinco *m*
VI **1** (= *jump*) brincar, saltar • **to ~ with joy** dar brincos *or* saltos de alegría, brincar *or* saltar de alegría • **to ~ in/out** entrar/salir dando brincos • **he ~ped out of the way** se apartó de un salto • **to ~ off** (*fig*) largarse, rajarse (*LAm*)
2 (*with a rope*) saltar a la comba
3 (*fig*) • **to ~ over sth** pasar algo por alto, saltarse algo • **to ~ from one thing to another** saltar de un tema a otro • **the book ~s about a lot** el libro da muchos saltos
VT (*fig*) [+ *meal, lesson, page*] saltarse • **to ~ lunch** saltarse el almuerzo, no almorzar • **you should never ~ breakfast** no debes saltarte nunca el desayuno • **to ~ school** hacer novillos, hacer la rabona • **let's ~ it!*** ¡basta de eso!
CPD ▸ **skip rope** (*US*) = **skipping rope**

skip² [skɪp] N (*Brit*) (= *container*) contenedor *m* de basuras

skipper ['skɪpəʳ] N (*Sport*) capitán/ana *m/f*; (*Naut*) capitán/ana *m/f*, patrón/a *m/f* • **well, you're the ~** bueno, tú eres el jefe
VT [+ *boat*] capitanear, patronear; [+ *team*] capitanear

skipping ['skɪpɪŋ] N comba *f*
CPD ▸ **skipping rope** (*Brit*) cuerda *f*, comba *f*

skirl [skɜ:l] N (*Scot*) • **the ~ of the pipes** el son *or* la música de la gaita

skirmish ['skɜ:mɪʃ] N escaramuza *f*, refriega *f*; (*fig*) roce *m* • **to have a ~ with** (*fig*) tener un roce con
VI pelear

skirmisher ['skɜ:mɪʃəʳ] N escaramuzador(a) *m/f*

skirt [skɜ:t] N falda *f*, pollera *f* (*LAm*); [*of coat etc*] faldón *m* • **flared/split/straight ~** falda *f* acampanada/pantalón/estrecha *or* recta
VT (*also* **skirt around**) rodear, dar la vuelta a; (*fig*) (= *avoid*) esquivar • **we ~ed Seville to the north** pasamos al norte de Sevilla
CPD ▸ **skirt length** tela *f* suficiente para una falda
▸ **skirt around** VI + PREP = **skirt**, ▹ VT

skirting ['skɜ:tɪŋ] N, **skirting board** ['skɜ:tɪŋ,bɔ:d] N zócalo *m*, cenefa *f*

skit [skɪt] N (*Theat*) sátira *f* (**on de**)

skitter ['skɪtəʳ] VI • **to ~ across the water/along the ground** [*bird*] volar rozando el agua/el suelo; [*stone*] saltar por encima

del agua/por el suelo
skittish ['skɪtɪʃ] ADJ (= *capricious*) caprichoso, delicado; (= *nervous*) [*horse etc*] nervioso, asustadizo; (= *playful*) juguetón
skittishly ['skɪtɪʃlɪ] ADV (= *capriciously*) caprichosamente; (= *nervously*) nerviosamente; (= *playfully*) de modo juguetón
skittishness ['skɪtɪʃnɪs] N (= *playfulness*) juego *m*; (= *flirtatiousness*) flirteo *m*; (= *nervousness*) [*of horse*] nerviosismo *m*
skittle ['skɪtl] N bolo *m* • **~s** el juego de bolos • **to play ~s** jugar a los bolos
CPD ▸ **skittle alley** bolera *f*
skive‡ [skaɪv] (*Brit*) VI (= *not work*) gandulear*, haraganear*; (= *disappear*) escabullirse, escaquearse*, rajarse (*LAm**)
N • **to be on the ~** • **have a good ~** gandulear, no hacer nada
▸ **skive off**‡ VI + ADV (*Brit*) (= *not work*) gandulear*, haraganear*; (= *disappear*) escabullirse, escaquearse*, rajarse (*LAm**)
VI + PREP • **to ~ off school** hacer novillos, hacer la rabona
skiver‡ ['skaɪvəʳ] N (*Brit*) gandul(a) *m/f*
skivvy* ['skɪvɪ] N (*pej*) esclava *f* del hogar
skua ['skju:ə] N págalo *m*
skulduggery (*†) [skʌl'dʌgərɪ] N trampas *fpl*, embustes *mpl* • **a piece of ~** una trampa, un embuste
skulk [skʌlk] VI esconderse • **to ~ about** esconderse
skull [skʌl] N calavera *f*; (*Med*) cráneo *m* • **~ and crossbones** (= *flag*) la bandera pirata • **I can't get it into his (thick) ~ that ...** no hay quien le meta en la cabeza que ...
skullcap ['skʌlkæp] N (*gen*) gorro *m*; [*of priest*] solideo *m*
skunk [skʌŋk] N (PL: **skunk** *or* **skunks**) (*Zool*) mofeta *f*, zorrillo *m* (*LAm**) • **you ~!** (*fig*) ¡canalla!
sky [skaɪ] N cielo *m* • **under blue skies** bajo un cielo azul • **the skies over England** el cielo en Inglaterra • **to praise sb to the skies** poner a algn por las nubes • **the sky's the limit*** (*fig*) no hay límite • **out of a clear blue sky** (*fig*) de repente, inesperadamente
CPD ▸ **sky marshal** agente *mf* de seguridad (*en vuelos comerciales*)
sky-blue ['skaɪ'blu:] ADJ celeste, azul celeste
N azul *m* celeste
skydive ['skaɪdaɪv] N caída *f* libre
VI saltar en caída libre
skydiver ['skaɪdaɪvəʳ] N paracaidista *mf* de caída libre, paracaidista *mf* acrobático/a
skydiving ['skaɪdaɪvɪŋ] N caída *f* libre, paracaidismo *m* acrobático
sky-high ['skaɪ'haɪ] ADV por las nubes • **prices have gone sky-high** los precios están por las nubes • **he hit the ball sky-high** mandó el balón por los aires; ▹ **blow²**
skyjack* ['skaɪdʒæk] VT atracar, piratear
skyjacking* ['skaɪdʒækɪŋ] N atraco *m* aéreo, piratería *f* aérea
skylab ['skaɪlæb] N skylab *m*, laboratorio *m* espacial
skylark ['skaɪlɑ:k] N (= *bird*) alondra *f*
VI (*fig**) hacer travesuras
skylight ['skaɪlaɪt] N tragaluz *m*, claraboya *f*
skyline ['skaɪlaɪn] N (= *horizon*) horizonte *m*; [*of city*] contorno *m*, perfil *m*
Skype® [skaɪp] N Skype® *m*
VT llamar por Skype®
VI hablar por Skype®
skyrocket ['skaɪˌrɒkɪt] N cohete *m*
VI subir (como un cohete); (*fig*) [*prices etc*] ponerse por las nubes, dispararse
skyscraper ['skaɪˌskreɪpəʳ] N rascacielos *m inv*
sky-surfing ['skaɪsɜ:fɪŋ] N surf *m* aéreo
skytrain ['skaɪtreɪn] N puente *m* aéreo
skyward ['skaɪwəd] ADV hacia el cielo
skywards ['skaɪwədz] ADV (*esp Brit*) = skyward
skyway ['skaɪweɪ] N ruta *f* aérea
skywriting ['skaɪˌraɪtɪŋ] N publicidad *f* aérea
SL N ABBR = **source language**
slab [slæb] N **1** [*of stone*] losa *f*
2 (*in mortuary*) plancha *f* de mármol, tabla *f* de mármol
3 [*of chocolate*] tableta *f*; [*of cake etc*] trozo *m*, tajada *f*; [*of meat*] tajada *f* (gruesa)
slack [slæk] ADJ (COMPAR: **slacker**, SUPERL: **slackest**) **1** (= *not tight or firm*) flojo
2 (= *lax*) descuidado, negligente; (= *lazy*) perezoso, vago, flojo • **to be ~ about one's work** desatender su trabajo, ser negligente en su trabajo • **to be ~ about** *or* **in doing sth** dejar de hacer algo por desidia
3 (*Comm*) [*market*] flojo, encalmado; [*period*] de inactividad; [*season*] muerto • **business is ~** hay poco movimiento *or* poca actividad en el negocio • **demand was ~** hubo poca demanda
N **1** (= *part of rope etc*) comba *f* • **to take up the ~** tensar una cuerda • **to take up the ~ in the economy** utilizar toda la capacidad productiva de la economía
2 (= *coal*) cisco *m*
3 (*Comm*) (= *period*) período *m* de inactividad; (= *season*) estación *f* muerta; ▹ **slacks**
VI* gandulear, holgazanear • **he's been ~ing** ha sido muy gandul
VT = **slacken**
▸ **slack off** VI + ADV, VT + ADV = **slacken off**
slacken ['slækn] VT [+ *reins*] aflojar; (*fig*) [+ *policy*] aflojar • **he ~ed his grip on her wrist** dejó de apretarle tan fuerte la muñeca • **to ~ one's pace** aflojar el paso • **to ~ speed** [*person*] aflojar el paso; [*vehicle*] disminuir la velocidad
VI **1** (= *loosen*) [*rope*] aflojarse; [*muscle*] ponerse flácido
2 (= *reduce*) [*activity, demand*] disminuir, bajar; [*trade*] decaer; [*wind, rain*] amainar • **business tends to ~ in summer** el comercio tiende a decaer en verano
▸ **slacken off** (*esp Brit*) VI + ADV **1** (= *be less active*) [*person*] aflojar el ritmo (de trabajo, de juego *etc*) • **their game ~ed off in the second half** su juego perdió ímpetu en la segunda mitad
2 (= *reduce*) [*demand*] disminuir, bajar
VT + ADV [+ *rope*] aflojar
▸ **slacken up** VI + ADV = **slacken off**
slackening ['slæknɪŋ] N **1** (= *loosening*) [*of rope*] aflojamiento *m*; [*of muscles*] pérdida *f* de tensión
2 (= *reduction in amount, intensity*) disminución *f* • **there must be no ~ of vigilance/discipline** no debe bajarse la guardia/relajarse la disciplina
slacker* ['slækəʳ] N holgazán/ana *m/f*, vago/a *m/f*, gandul(a) *m/f*
slack-jawed [ˌslæk'dʒɔ:d] ADJ (= *open-mouthed*) con la boca abierta
slackly ['slæklɪ] ADV **1** (*lit*) [*hang*] flojamente
2 (*fig*) [*work*] sin poner cuidado, negligentemente
slackness ['slæknɪs] N **1** [*of rope etc*] flojedad *f*, lo flojo
2 [*of person*] (= *laxity*) descuido *m*, negligencia *f*; (= *laziness*) pereza *f*, vaguedad *f*
3 (*Comm*) flojedad *f*, inactividad *f*
slacks [slæks] NPL pantalones *mpl*
slag¹ [slæg] N (*Min*) escoria *f*
CPD ▸ **slag heap** escorial *m*
slag²‡ [slæg] N (*Brit*) (*pej*) (= *slut*) puta* *f*, ramera *f*
▸ **slag off**‡ VT + ADV (*esp Brit*) (= *criticize*) poner como un trapo*
slain [sleɪn] PP *of* **slay**
NPL • **the ~** los caídos *mpl*
slake [sleɪk] VT **1** [+ *thirst*] apagar, aplacar
2 (*Chem*) [+ *lime*] apagar • **~d lime** cal *f* muerta
slalom ['slɑ:ləm] N eslálom *m*, slalom *m*
CPD ▸ **slalom racer** corredor(a) *m/f* de eslálom
slam [slæm] N **1** [*of door*] portazo *m* • **to close the door with a ~** dar un portazo, cerrar la puerta de un portazo
2 (*Bridge*) slam *m* • **grand ~** gran slam *m* • **small ~** pequeño slam *m*
VT **1** (= *strike*) • **to ~ the door** dar un portazo, cerrar (la puerta) de un portazo • **to ~ sth shut** cerrar algo de golpe • **to ~ sth (down) on the table** dejar de golpe algo sobre la mesa, estampar algo sobre la mesa • **to ~ on the brakes** dar un frenazo • **he ~med the ball into the net** disparó la pelota a la red
2* (= *criticize*) vapulear, criticar severamente
3* (= *defeat*) cascar*, dar una paliza a*
4‡ • **to get ~med** agarrarse una buena curda *or* melopea*
VI **1** [*door*] cerrarse de golpe, cerrarse de un portazo • **the door ~med shut** *or* **to** la puerta se cerró de golpe *or* de un portazo
2 • **to ~ into/against sth** estrellarse contra algo
▸ **slam down** VT + ADV • **to ~ sth down on the table** dejar de golpe algo sobre la mesa, estampar algo sobre la mesa
slam-dunk [ˌslæm'dʌŋk] (*Basketball*) N mate *m*
VT [+ *ball*] dar un mate con
VI hacer un mate
slammer‡ ['slæməʳ] N trena‡ *f*, talego‡ *m*
slander ['slɑ:ndəʳ] N (*gen*) calumnia *f*; (*Jur*) difamación *f* • **they have been spreading ~s about the company** han estado levantando calumnias sobre la empresa • **to sue sb for ~** demandar a algn por difamación
VT (*gen*) calumniar; (*Jur*) difamar • **they have ~ed my name/reputation** han deshonrado mi nombre/han manchado mi reputación
slanderer ['slɑ:ndərəʳ] N calumniador(a) *m/f*, difamador(a) *m/f*
slanderous ['slɑ:ndərəs] ADJ calumnioso, difamatorio
slanderously ['slɑ:ndərəslɪ] ADV calumniosamente
slang [slæŋ] N (*gen*) argot *m*, jerga *f*; [*of a group, trade etc*] jerga *f* • **to talk ~** hablar en argot *or* jerga • **that word is ~** esa palabra es del argot
ADJ argótico, jergal • **~ word** palabra *f* del argot, palabra *f* argótica *or* jergal
VT* (= *insult, criticize*) poner verde a, injuriar • **a ~ing match** una disputa a voces
slangily* ['slæŋɪlɪ] ADV • **to talk ~** hablar con mucho argot *or* mucha jerga
slangy* ['slæŋɪ] ADJ (COMPAR: **slangier**, SUPERL: **slangiest**) [*person*] que usa mucho argot, que usa mucha jerga; [*style etc*] argótico, jergal
slant [slɑ:nt] N **1** (*gen*) inclinación *f*, sesgo *m*; (= *slope*) pendiente *f*, cuesta *f* • **to be on the ~** estar inclinado, estar sesgado
2 (*fig*) (= *point of view*) punto *m* de vista, interpretación *f* • **what is your ~ on this?** ¿cuál es su punto de vista sobre esto?, ¿cómo interpreta usted esto? • **to get a ~ on a topic** pedir pareceres sobre un asunto • **the situation is taking on a new ~** la situación está tomando un nuevo giro
VT inclinar, sesgar • **to ~ a report** (*fig*)

S

enfocar una cuestión de manera parcial
VI inclinarse, sesgarse • **the light ~ed in at the window** la luz entraba oblicuamente por la ventana

slant-eyed ['slɑːnt'aɪd] ADJ de ojos almendrados

slanting ['slɑːntɪŋ] ADJ inclinado, sesgado

slantwise ['slɑːntwaɪz] ADJ oblicuamente, al sesgo

slap [slæp] N palmada *f*, manotada *f* • **a ~ on the back** un espaldarazo • **to give sb a ~ on the back** (*fig*) felicitar a algn • **a ~ in the face** una bofetada, un bofetón; (*fig*) un desaire • **they were having a bit of the old ~ and tickle*** los dos se estaban sobando • **to give sb a ~ on the wrist** (*fig*) dar un tirón de orejas a algn
ADV* de lleno • **he ran ~ into a tree** dio de lleno contra un árbol • **it fell ~ in the middle** cayó justo en el medio
VT 1 (= *strike*) dar manotadas a; (*once*) dar una manotada a; (*in the face*) abofetear, dar una bofetada a • **to ~ sb's face** • **~ sb in the face** dar una bofetada a algn, abofetear a algn • **she ~ped the little boy's leg** • **she ~ped the little boy on the leg** le dio al niño un cachete en la pierna • **to ~ sb on the back** dar a algn una palmada en la espalda • **to ~ sb down** (*fig*) bajarle los humos a algn • **to ~ one's knees** palmotearse las rodillas • **to ~ one's thighs** darse palmadas en los muslos • **to ~ sb's wrist** (*fig*) dar un tirón de orejas a algn
2 (= *put*) • **he ~ped the book on the table** tiró *or* arrojó el libro sobre la mesa • **the judge ~ped £100 on the fine** el juez aumentó la multa en 100 libras • **they've ~ped another storey on the house** han añadido un piso a la casa (como si tal cosa) • **she ~ped on some make-up** se maquilló a la carrera • **to ~ paint on sth** pintar algo a brochazos
EXCL ¡zas!

slap-bang* ['slæp'bæŋ] ADV (*Brit*) justo, exactamente

slapdash ['slæpdæʃ] ADJ, **slap-happy** ['slæphæpɪ] ADJ descuidado, chapucero

slaphead* ['slæphed] N (*Brit*) (= *bald person*) calvo/a *m/f*, bola *f* de billar*

slapper‡ ['slæpəʳ] N (*Brit*) putilla‡ *f*

slapstick ['slæpstɪk] N (*also* **slapstick comedy**) bufonada *f*

slap-up* ['slæpʌp] ADJ (*Brit*) • **slap-up meal** banquete *m*, comilona *f*

slash [slæʃ] N 1 (*gen*) tajo *m*; (*with knife*) cuchillada *f*; (*with machete*) machetazo *m*; (*with razor*) navajazo *m*
2 (*Typ*) barra *f* oblicua
3 (*esp Brit‡*) • **to go for a ~** • **have a ~** cambiar el agua al canario‡
VT 1 (= *cut*) (*with knife etc*) acuchillar; (*with razor*) hacer un tajo a; [+ *tyre*] rajar • **to ~ one's wrists** cortarse las venas (*de la muñeca*)
2 (= *cut down*) [+ *trees*] talar • **~ and burn agriculture** agricultura *f* de rozas y quema
3 (= *reduce*) [+ *price*] reducir, rebajar; [+ *estimate etc*] reducir radicalmente; [+ *text*] cortar • **"prices slashed"** "grandes rebajas"
4* (= *condemn*) atacar, criticar severamente
VI • **to ~ at sb** tirar tajos a algn, tratar de acuchillar a algn
CPD ▸ **slash and burn, slash-and-burn** (= *method of farming*) agricultura *f* de rozas y quema

slasher film* ['slæʃəfɪlm], **slasher movie*** ['slæʃə,muːvɪ] N película *f* de casquería* (*con muchos degüellos*)

slashing ['slæʃɪŋ] ADJ [*attack etc*] fulminante

slat [slæt] N 1 (*wooden*) tablilla *f*, listón *m*
2 [*of blind*] lama *f*

slate [sleɪt] N 1 (= *substance*) pizarra *f*; (= *tile*) teja *f* de pizarra • **put it on the ~** (*Brit**) apúntalo en mi cuenta • **to wipe the ~ clean** (*fig*) hacer borrón y cuenta nueva
2 (*US*) (*Pol*) lista *f* de candidatos
ADJ (= *made of slate*) de pizarra; (*in colour*) color pizarra
VT 1 [+ *roof*] empizarrar
2* (= *criticize*) vapulear, criticar duro
3 (*US*) (*Pol*) [+ *candidate*] nombrar
4 (*US*) anunciar • **it is ~d to start at nine** según el programa comienza a las nueve, deberá comenzar a las nueve
CPD ▸ **slate pencil** pizarrín *m* ▸ **slate quarry** pizarral *m* ▸ **slate roof** empizarrado *m*

slate-blue ['sleɪt'bluː] ADJ de color azul pizarra

slate-coloured, slate-colored (*US*) ['sleɪt,kʌləd] ADJ color pizarra

slate-grey [,sleɪt'greɪ] ADJ de color gris pizarra
N gris *m* pizarra

slater ['sleɪtəʳ] N pizarrero/a *m/f*

slating* ['sleɪtɪŋ] N (*Brit*) varapalo *m* • **to give sb a ~** dar a algn un varapalo • **to get a ~** [*person*] sufrir un varapalo; [*play, performance etc*] ser vapuleado

slatted ['slætɪd] ADJ de tablillas, hecho de listones
CPD ▸ **slatted floor** suelo *m* de tablillas *or* listones

slattern ['slætən] N mujer *f* dejada, mujer *f* sucia, pazpuerca *f*

slatternly ['slætənlɪ] ADJ sucio, puerco, desaseado

slaty ['sleɪtɪ] ADJ (*in appearance, texture etc*) parecido a pizarra, pizarroso; (*in colour*) color pizarra

slaughter ['slɔːtəʳ] N [*of animals*] matanza *f*, sacrificio *m*; [*of persons*] matanza *f*, carnicería *f* • **the ~ on the roads** el gran número de muertes en las carreteras • **the Slaughter of the Innocents** la Degollación de los Inocentes • **like a lamb to the ~** como borrego al matadero • **there was great ~** hubo gran mortandad
VT 1 (= *kill*) [+ *animals*] matar, sacrificar; [+ *person, people*] matar brutalmente
2 (*Sport etc**) (= *beat*) dar una paliza a*

slaughterer ['slɔːtərəʳ] N jifero/a *m/f*, matarife *mf*

slaughterhouse ['slɔːtəhaʊs] N (PL: **slaughterhouses**) matadero *m*

slaughterman ['slɔːtəmən] N (PL: **slaughtermen**) jifero *m*, matarife *m*

Slav [slɑːv] ADJ eslavo
N eslavo/a *m/f*

slave [sleɪv] N esclavo/a *m/f* • **to be a ~ to sth** (*fig*) ser esclavo de algo • **to be a ~ to tobacco** ser esclavo del tabaco • **to be a ~ to duty** ser esclavo del deber
VI • **to ~ (away) at sth/at doing sth** trabajar como un negro en algo/haciendo algo
CPD ▸ **slave driver** negrero/a *m/f*; (*fig*) tirano/a *m/f* ▸ **slave labour** (= *work*) trabajo *m* de esclavos; (= *persons*) esclavos *mpl* ▸ **slave ship** barco *m* de esclavos ▸ **slave trade** trata *f* de esclavos, comercio *m* de esclavos, tráfico *m* de esclavos ▸ **slave trader** traficante *mf* en esclavos

slaver¹ ['slævəʳ] N baba *f*
VI babear

slaver² ['sleɪvəʳ] N (= *ship*) barco *m* negrero; (= *person*) traficante *mf* en esclavos

slavery ['sleɪvərɪ] N esclavitud *f*

slavey* ['sleɪvɪ] N fregona *f*

Slavic ['slɑːvɪk] ADJ eslavo
N (*Ling*) eslavo *m*

slavish ['sleɪvɪʃ] ADJ servil, de esclavo

slavishly ['sleɪvɪʃlɪ] ADV servilmente

slavishness ['sleɪvɪʃnɪs] N servilismo *m*

Slavonic [slə'vɒnɪk] ADJ eslavo
N eslavo *m*

slaw [slɔː] N (*US*) ensalada *f* de col

slay [sleɪ] (PT: **slew**, PP: **slain**) VT 1 (*poet*) (= *kill*) matar
2* hacer morir de risa* • **this will ~ you** esto os hará morir de risa* • **you ~ me!** (*iro*) ¡qué divertido!

slayer ['sleɪəʳ] N asesino/a *m/f*

slaying ['sleɪɪŋ] N 1 (= *killing*) [*of animal, dragon etc*] matanza *f*
2 (*esp US*) (= *murder*) asesinato *m*

SLD N ABBR (*Brit*) (*Pol*) = **Social and Liberal Democrats**

sleaze* ['sliːz] N, **sleaziness*** ['sliːzɪnɪs] N 1 (= *sordidness*) sordidez *f*, asco *m*; (= *filth*) desaseo *m*, desaliño *m*
2 (*Pol*) (= *corruption*) corrupción *f*

sleazebag‡ ['sliːzbæg], **sleazeball‡** ['sliːzbɔːl] N depravado/a *m/f*

sleazy ['sliːzɪ] ADJ (COMPAR: **sleazier**, SUPERL: **sleaziest**) (= *sordid*) [*place*] sórdido, asqueroso; (= *filthy*) [*person*] desaseado, desaliñado; (= *corrupt*) [*deal etc*] poco limpio, sucio

sled [sled] N, VI, VT = **sledge²**

sledge¹ [sledʒ] N = **sledgehammer**

sledge² [sledʒ] N trineo *m*
VI ir en trineo
VT transportar por trineo, llevar en trineo

sledgehammer ['sledʒ,hæməʳ] N almádena *f*

sleek [sliːk] ADJ (COMPAR: **sleeker**, SUPERL: **sleekest**) [*hair, fur*] lustroso; [*person*] (*of general appearance*) impecable; (*in manner*) zalamero, meloso; [*boat, car*] de líneas puras; [*animal*] gordo y de buen aspecto
VT • **to ~ one's hair down** alisarse el pelo

sleekly ['sliːklɪ] ADV [*smile, reply*] zalameramente

sleekness ['sliːknɪs] N [*of hair, fur, animal*] lustre *m*; [*of person's appearance*] pulcritud *f*; [*of car*] pureza *f* de líneas

sleep [sliːp] (VB: PT, PP: **slept**) N 1 (= *rest*) sueño *m* • **lack of ~** falta *f* de sueño • **I need some ~** necesito dormir • **to drop off to ~** quedarse dormido • **he fell into a deep ~** se quedó profundamente dormido • **I couldn't get to ~** no podía dormirme *or* conciliar el sueño • **to go to ~** [*person*] dormirse, quedarse dormido; (= *limb*) dormirse • **to have a ~** dormir • **to have a good night's ~** dormir bien (durante) toda la noche • **to have a little ~** dormir un rato, descabezar un sueño • **I shan't lose any ~ over it** eso no me va a quitar el sueño • **to put sb to ~** [+ *patient*] dormir a algn • **to put an animal to ~** (*euph*) (= *kill*) sacrificar un animal • **to send sb to ~** (= *bore*) dormir a algn • **to talk in one's ~** hablar en sueños • **to walk in one's ~** pasearse dormido; (*habitually*) ser sonámbulo • **she walked downstairs in her ~** estando dormida bajó la escalera • **I didn't get a wink of ~ all night** no pegué ojo en toda la noche • IDIOM: • **to ~ the ~ of the just** dormir a pierna suelta
2* (*in eyes*) legañas *fpl*
VT 1 (= *accommodate*) • **we can ~ four** hay cama para cuatro • **can you ~ all of us?** ¿hay cama(s) para todos nosotros?
2 (= *rest*) dormir • **I only slept a couple of hours** solo dormí un par de horas • **to ~ the hours away** pasar las horas durmiendo
VI dormir • **I couldn't ~ last night** anoche no pude dormir • **to ~ deeply** dormir profundamente *or* a pierna suelta • **to ~ heavily** (*habitually*) tener el sueño pesado;

(*on particular occasion*) dormir profundamente • **to ~ lightly** (*habitually*) tener el sueño ligero • **she was ~ing lightly** no estaba profundamente dormida • **to ~ on sth** (*fig*) consultar algo con la almohada • **to ~ out** (= *not at home*) dormir fuera de casa; (= *in open air*) dormir al aire libre, pasar la noche al raso • **to ~ soundly** dormir profundamente *or* a pierna suelta • **he was ~ing soundly** estaba profundamente dormido • **he slept through the alarm clock** no oyó el despertador • **I slept through till the afternoon** dormí hasta la tarde • **~ tight!** ¡que duermas bien!, ¡que descanses! • **to ~ with sb** (*euph*) (= *have sex*) acostarse con algn • IDIOM: • **to ~ like a log** *or* **top** *or* **baby** dormir como un tronco; ▸ rough
CPD ▸ **sleep deprivation** falta *f* de sueño
▸ **sleep around*** VI + ADV irse a la cama con cualquiera
▸ **sleep away** VT + ADV • **to ~ the morning away** pasarse la mañana durmiendo
▸ **sleep in** VI + ADV (*deliberately*) dormir hasta tarde; (*accidentally*) quedarse dormido
▸ **sleep off** VT + ADV • **to ~ off a big dinner** dormir hasta que baje una cena grande • **she's ~ing off the effects of the drug** duerme hasta que desaparezcan los efectos de la droga • **to ~ it off*** • **~ off a hangover** dormir la mona*, dormir la curda*
▸ **sleep over** VI + ADV pasar la noche
▸ **sleep together** VI + ADV **1** (= *share a room or bed*) dormir juntos
2 (= *have sex*) acostarse juntos
sleeper ['sli:pəʳ] N **1** (= *person*) durmiente *mf*
2 (*fig*) (= *spy*) *espía emplazado en un objetivo, pero sin misión concreta o que aún no es operativo* • **to be a heavy/light ~** tener el sueño pesado/ligero • **to be a good/poor ~** dormir bien/mal
3 (*Brit*) (*Rail*) (*on track*) traviesa *f*, durmiente *m*; (= *berth*) litera *f*; (= *compartment*) camarín *m*, alcoba *f*; (= *coach*) coche-cama *m*
4 (*esp Brit*) (= *earring*) arete *m*
5 (*US*) (*for baby*) pijama *m* de niño
sleepily ['sli:pɪlɪ] ADV soñolientamente • **"yes," she said ~** —sí —dijo adormilado *or* soñoliento
sleepiness ['sli:pɪnɪs] N **1** [*of person*] somnolencia *f*
2 [*of town, village*] tranquilidad *f*; (*pej*) sopor *m* (*pej*)
sleeping ['sli:pɪŋ] ADJ dormido • **Sleeping Beauty** la bella durmiente • PROVERB: • **let ~ dogs lie** más vale no meneallo
N sueño *m*, el dormir • **between ~ and waking** a duermevela
CPD ▸ **sleeping bag** (*camper's*) saco *m* de dormir; (*baby's*) pelele *m* ▸ **sleeping car** (*Rail*) coche-cama *m* ▸ **sleeping draught** soporífero *m* ▸ **sleeping giant** • **to be a ~ giant** (= *have unrealized potential*) ser un gigante en potencia ▸ **sleeping partner** socio/a *m/f* comanditario/a ▸ **sleeping pill** somnífero *m* ▸ **sleeping policeman** (*Aut*) banda *f* sonora ▸ **sleeping quarters** dormitorio *msing* ▸ **sleeping sickness** encefalitis *f* letárgica ▸ **sleeping tablet** = **sleeping pill**
sleepless ['sli:plɪs] ADJ [*person*] insomne • **many ~ nights** muchas noches en blanco *or* sin dormir • **to have a ~ night** pasar la noche en blanco *or* sin dormir
sleeplessness ['sli:plɪsnɪs] N insomnio *m*
sleepover ['sli:pəʊvəʳ] N • **we're having a ~ at Fiona's** pasamos la noche en casa de Fiona • **can I have a ~ on Friday?** ¿puedo invitar a mis amigos a pasar la noche el viernes?
sleep-talk ['sli:ptɔ:k] VI (*US*) hablar estando dormido
sleepwalk ['sli:p,wɔ:k] VI ser sonámbulo, pasearse dormido
sleepwalker ['sli:p,wɔ:kəʳ] N sonámbulo/a *m/f*
sleepwalking ['sli:p,wɔ:kɪŋ] N sonambulismo *m*
sleepwear ['sli:pwɛəʳ] N ropa *f* de dormir
sleepy ['sli:pɪ] ADJ (COMPAR: **sleepier**, SUPERL: **sleepiest**) **1** (= *drowsy*) [*person, voice*] soñoliento • **to be** *or* **feel ~** tener sueño • **I began to feel ~** me empezó a entrar sueño, me entró sueño • **she came in looking very ~** entró con cara de sueño
2 (= *quiet*) [*place*] tranquilo; (*pej*) soporífero • **a ~ little village** un pueblecito tranquilo • **a ~ summer's afternoon** una soporífera tarde de verano
sleepyhead ['sli:pɪhed] N dormilón/ona *m/f*
sleet [sli:t] N aguanieve *f*, cellisca *f*
VI • **it was ~ing** caía aguanieve *or* cellisca
sleeve [sli:v] N **1** [*of garment*] manga *f* • **to roll up one's ~s** arremangarse • IDIOMS: • **to have sth up one's ~** tener algo en reserva • **to laugh up one's ~** reírse para su capote
2 [*of record*] funda *f*
3 (*Mech*) manguito *m*, enchufe *m*
CPD ▸ **sleeve notes** (*Brit*) (*Mus*) *texto de la carátula de un disco*
sleeved [sli:vd] ADJ con mangas
-sleeved [sli:vd] ADJ (*ending in compounds*) con mangas … • **long-sleeved** con mangas largas
sleeveless ['sli:vlɪs] ADJ sin mangas
sleigh [sleɪ] N trineo *m*
VI, VT = **sledge²**
CPD ▸ **sleigh bell** cascabel *m* ▸ **sleigh ride** • **to go for a ~ ride** ir a pasear en trineo
sleight [slaɪt] N • **~ of hand** prestidigitación *f*, juegos *mpl* de manos
slender ['slendəʳ] ADJ **1** [*person*] (= *thin*) delgado, fino; (= *slim and graceful*) esbelto; [*waist, neck, hand*] delgado
2 (*fig*) [*resources*] escaso; [*hope etc*] lejano, remoto • **by a ~ majority** por escasa mayoría
slenderize ['slendəraɪz] VT (*US*) adelgazar
slenderly ['slendəlɪ] ADV • **she is ~ built** es delgada *or* esbelta • **~ made** de construcción delicada
slenderness ['slendənɪs] N **1** [*of person, waist, hand*] delgadez *f*
2 [*of resources*] escasez *f*; [*of hope etc*] lo lejano, lo remoto
slept [slept] PT, PP *of* **sleep**
sleuth (*†) [slu:θ] N (*hum*) detective *mf*, sabueso *mf*
slew¹ [slu:] (*also* **slew round**) VT torcer • **to ~ sth to the left** torcer algo a la izquierda • **to be ~ed‡** tener una buena curda *or* melopea*
VI torcerse
slew² [slu:] PT *of* **slay**
slew³ [slu:] N (*esp US*) (= *range*) montón* *m*
slice [slaɪs] N **1** [*of bread*] rebanada *f*; [*of salami, sausage*] loncha *f*, raja *f*; [*of cheese, ham*] loncha *f*; [*of beef, lamb etc*] tajada *f*; [*of lemon, cucumber, pineapple*] rodaja *f*; [*of cake, pie*] trozo *m*
2 (*fig*) (= *portion*) parte *f* • **it affects a large ~ of the population** afecta a buena parte *or* a un amplio sector de la población • **a ~ of life** un trozo de la vida tal como es • **a ~ of the profits** una participación (en los beneficios)
3 (= *utensil*) pala *f*
4 (*Sport*) pelota *f* cortada; (*Golf*) golpe *m* con efecto a la derecha
VT **1** (= *cut into slices*) [+ *bread*] rebanar; [+ *salami, sausage, ham, cheese*] cortar en lonchas; [+ *beef, lamb*] cortar en tajadas; [+ *lemon, cucumber, pineapple*] cortar en rodajas; [+ *cake, pie*] partir en trozos
2 (= *cut*) cortar • **to ~ sth in two** cortar algo en dos • **to ~ sth open** abrir algo de un tajo
3 (*Sport*) [+ *ball*] dar efecto a, cortar; (*Golf*) golpear oblicuamente (a derecha)
▸ **slice off** VT + ADV cortar
▸ **slice through** VI + PREP cortar, partir
▸ **slice up** VT + ADV cortar (*en rebanadas etc*)
sliced [slaɪst] ADJ [*bread*] rebanado, en rebanadas; [*lemon*] en rodajas • **it's the best thing since ~ bread*** (*hum*) es la octava maravilla (del mundo)
slicer ['slaɪsəʳ] N máquina *f* de cortar
slick [slɪk] ADJ (COMPAR: **slicker**, SUPERL: **slickest**) **1** (*pej*) (= *superficial, glib*) hábil • **he's too ~ for me** es demasiado hábil para mi gusto
2 (= *polished, skilful*) impecable • **a ~ performance** una actuación impecable • **be ~ about it!** ¡date prisa!
N • **oil ~** (*large*) marea *f* negra; (*small*) mancha *f* de petróleo, capa *f* de petróleo (en el agua)
VT alisar • **to ~ down one's hair** alisarse el pelo • **to ~ o.s. up** acicalarse
slicker ['slɪkəʳ] N **1** (= *person*) embaucador(a) *m/f*, tramposo/a *m/f* • **city ~*** capitalino/a* *m/f*
2 (*US*) (= *coat*) chubasquero *m*, impermeable *m*
slickly ['slɪklɪ] ADV **1** (*pej*) (= *superficially, glibly*) hábilmente
2 (= *skilfully*) impecablemente
slickness ['slɪknɪs] N **1** (*pej*) (= *superficiality, glibness*) habilidad *f*, maña *f*
2 (= *skill, efficiency*) habilidad *f*, destreza *f*
slid [slɪd] PT, PP *of* **slide**
slide [slaɪd] (VB: PT, PP: **slid**) N **1** (*in playground, swimming pool*) tobogán *m*
2 (= *act of sliding*) deslizamiento *m*; (*by accident*) resbalón *m*
3 (= *landslide*) corrimiento *m* de tierras, desprendimiento *m*
4 (= *fall*) (*in share prices*) baja *f*, bajón* *m* • **the ~ into chaos/debt** la caída en el caos/en la deuda
5 (*in microscope*) portaobjetos *m inv*, platina *f*
6 (*Phot*) (= *transparency*) diapositiva *f*, filmina *f*
7 (*also* **hair slide**) (*Brit*) pasador *m*
8 (*Mus*) [*of trombone*] vara *f*; (*for guitar*) cuello *m* de botella, slide *m*
VI **1** (= *glide*) deslizarse; (= *slip*) resbalar • **they were sliding across the floor/down the banisters** se deslizaban por el suelo/por la barandilla • **the drawer ~s in and out easily** el cajón se abre y se cierra suavemente • **the lift doors slid open** las puertas del ascensor se abrieron • **I slid into/out of bed** me metí en/me levanté de la cama sigilosamente • **she slid into her seat** se dejó deslizar en su asiento • **a tear slid down his cheek** una lágrima se deslizó por su mejilla • **the book slid off my knee** el libro se me resbaló de la rodilla • IDIOM: • **to let things ~** dejar que las cosas se vengan abajo • **these last few months he's let everything ~** estos últimos meses se ha desentendido de todo
2 (= *decline*) • **the economy is sliding into recession** la economía está cayendo en la recesión • **the shares slid 12 points** las acciones bajaron 12 puntos
VT • **he slid his hands into his pockets** metió las manos en los bolsillos • **she slid a hand along his arm** le deslizó una mano por el brazo • **he slid the plate across the table** hizo deslizar el plato al otro lado de la mesa • **she slid the door open** corrió la puerta para

abrirla • **she slid the key into the keyhole** deslizó la llave en el ojo de la cerradura
(CPD) ▸ **slide guitar** guitarra *f* con cuello de botella, guitarra *f* con slide ▸ **slide-magazine** (*Phot*) cartucho *m or* guía *f* para diapositivas ▸ **slide projector** (*Phot*) proyector *m* de diapositivas ▸ **slide rule** regla *f* de cálculo ▸ **slide show** (*Phot*) exposición *f* de diapositivas

slideholder ['slaɪd,həʊldəʳ] (N) portadiapositiva *m*

slider ['slaɪdəʳ] (N) (*Comput*) (*in dialog box*) slider *m*

sliding ['slaɪdɪŋ] (ADJ) [*part*] corredizo; [*door, seat*] corredero • **~ roof** techo *m* corredizo, techo *m* de corredera • **~ scale** escala *f* móvil

slight [slaɪt] (ADJ) (COMPAR: **slighter**, SUPERL: **slightest**) **1** (= *small, minor*) **a** [*difference, change, increase, improvement*] ligero, pequeño; [*injury, problem, exaggeration*] pequeño; [*accent, movement*] ligero; [*breeze*] suave; [*smile, pain*] leve • **after a ~ hesitation, he agreed** después de vacilar ligeramente, accedió • **the chances of him winning are very ~** tiene muy pocas posibilidades de ganar • **the wall is at a ~ angle** la pared está ligeramente inclinada • **to have a ~ cold** tener un pequeño resfriado, estar un poco resfriado • **to walk with a ~ limp** cojear ligeramente • **to have a ~ temperature** tener un poco de fiebre; ▹ **second**
b • **the ~est: it doesn't make the ~est bit of difference** no importa en lo más mínimo • **without the ~est hesitation** sin dudarlo ni un momento • **I haven't the ~est idea** no tengo ni la más remota idea • **not in the ~est** en absoluto • **nobody showed the ~est interest** nadie mostró el menor interés • **he takes offence at the ~est thing** se ofende por la menor cosa *or* por cualquier nimiedad
2 (= *slim*) [*figure, person*] delgado, menudo • **to be of ~ build** ser de constitución delgada *or* menuda
3 (*frm*) (= *insignificant*) [*book, piece of music*] de poca envergadura • **a book of very ~ scholarship** un libro de poca erudición
(N) (*frm*) desaire *m* • **this is a ~ on all of us** es un desaire para todos nosotros
(VT) (*frm*) [+ *person*] desairar a, hacer un desaire a; [+ *work, efforts*] menospreciar, despreciar • **he felt that he had been ~ed** sintió que le habían desairado, sintió que le habían hecho un desaire

slighting ['slaɪtɪŋ] (ADJ) despreciativo, menospreciativo

slightingly ['slaɪtɪŋlɪ] (ADV) con desprecio

slightly ['slaɪtlɪ] (ADV) **1** (= *a little*) [*different, uneasy, deaf, damp, damaged*] ligeramente, un poco; [*rise, fall, improve*] ligeramente, levemente, un poco; [*change, cool, rain*] ligeramente, un poco • **~ better** algo mejor, un poco mejor • **he hesitated ever so ~** vaciló apenas un poco • **she was ~ injured** resultó levemente herida • **~ less** un poco menos • **he looks ~ like James Dean** guarda un ligero parecido con James Dean, se parece un poco a James Dean • **~ more** un poco más • **"do you know him?" — "only ~"** —¿lo conoces? —solo un poco • **it smells ~ of vanilla** huele un poco a vainilla, tiene un ligero olor a vainilla
2 (= *slenderly*) • **~ built** delgado, menudo, de constitución delgada *or* menuda

slightness ['slaɪtnɪs] (N) **1** [*of difference, change, improvement, increase*] insignificancia *f*; [*of injury, problem*] levedad *f*, poca importancia *f*; [*of accent*] lo poco marcado; [*of movement*] lo leve
2 (= *slimness*) delgadez *f*, lo menudo

slim [slɪm] (ADJ) (COMPAR: **slimmer**, SUPERL: **slimmest**) **1** [*figure, person*] (= *slender*) delgado, fino; (= *elegant*) esbelto; [*waist, neck, hand*] delgado • **to get ~** adelgazar
2 (*fig*) [*resources*] escaso; [*evidence*] insuficiente; [*hope etc*] lejano • **his chances are pretty ~** sus posibilidades son bastante limitadas • **by a ~ majority** por escasa mayoría
3 (= *thin*) [*book, volume, wallet*] fino, delgado
(VI) adelgazar • **I'm trying to ~** estoy intentando adelgazar • **I'm ~ming** estoy haciendo régimen, estoy a régimen
(VT) adelgazar
▸ **slim down** (VT + ADV) **1** (= *make slender*) adelgazar
2 (*fig*) • **~med down** [+ *business, industry*] reconvertido, saneado
(VI + ADV) bajar de peso, adelgazar

slime [slaɪm] (N) (*in pond*) cieno *m*, fango *m*; [*of snail*] baba *f*

sliminess ['slaɪmɪnɪs] (N) **1** [*of substance*] viscosidad *f*; [*of snail*] lo baboso
2 [*of person*] zalamería *f*

slimline ['slɪm,laɪn] (ADJ) **1** [*drink*] light (*inv*); [*food*] reductivo, que no engorda
2 [*body, person*] esbelto, delgadísimo; [*screen, calculator*] extraplano; [*fridge, washing machine*] de diseño estrecho; [*book, diary*] finísimo

slimmer ['slɪməʳ] (N) persona *f* que está a dieta

slimming ['slɪmɪŋ] (ADJ) [*dress, skirt etc*] que adelgaza • **~ diet** régimen *m* (para adelgazar) • **to be on a ~ diet** seguir un régimen para adelgazar, estar a dieta • **to eat only ~ foods** comer solamente cosas que no engordan
(N) adelgazamiento *m*
(CPD) ▸ **slimming aid** (= *food*) (producto *m*) adelgazante *m*

slimness ['slɪmnɪs] (N) delgadez *f*

slimy ['slaɪmɪ] (ADJ) (COMPAR: **slimier**, SUPERL: **slimiest**) limoso **1** [*substance*] viscoso; [*snail*] baboso
2 (*Brit*) (*fig*) [*person*] adulón, zalamero

sling [slɪŋ] (VB: PT, PP: **slung**) (N) **1** (= *weapon*) honda *f*
2 (*Med*) cabestrillo *m* • **to have one's arm in a ~** llevar el brazo en cabestrillo • IDIOM: • **to have one's ass in a ~** (*esp US***) estar con el culo a rastras*, tener la soga al cuello*
3 (*Naut*) eslinga *f*
4 (*for rifle etc*) portafusil *m*
(VT) **1** (= *throw*) arrojar, lanzar, echar • **to ~ sth over** *or* **across one's shoulder** lanzar algo al hombro • **with a rifle slung across his shoulder** con un fusil en bandolera • **to ~ sth over to sb** tirar algo a algn
2 (= *throw away*) tirar, botar (*LAm*)
3 (= *hang*) colgar, suspender
4 (*Naut*) eslingar
▸ **sling away*** (VT + ADV) (= *throw away*) echar, tirar, botar (*LAm*)
▸ **sling out*** (VT + ADV) **1** (= *throw away*) [+ *rubbish*] echar, tirar, botar (*LAm*)
2 (= *throw out*) [+ *person*] echar, poner de patitas en la calle*

slingback ['slɪŋbæk] (ADJ) • **~ shoes** zapatos *mpl* destalonados (*con tira*); (= *sandals*) sandalias *fpl* de talón (*con tira*)
(N) **slingbacks** zapatos *mpl* destalonados

slingshot ['slɪŋʃɒt] (N) **1** (= *weapon*) honda *f*; (= *shot*) hondazo *m*
2 (*US*) (= *catapult*) tirador *m*, tirachinas *m inv*

slink [slɪŋk] (PT, PP: **slunk**) (VI) • **to ~ away** • **~ off** escabullirse, zafarse

slinky* ['slɪŋkɪ] (ADJ) (COMPAR: **slinkier**, SUPERL: **slinkiest**) [*clothes*] ajustado, pegado al cuerpo; [*movement*] sensual; [*walk*] sinuoso, ondulante

slip [slɪp] (N) **1** (= *slide*) resbalón *m* • IDIOM: • **to give sb the ~** escabullirse *or* zafarse de algn, dar esquinazo a algn
2 (= *mistake*) error *m*, equivocación *f* • **I must have made a ~ somewhere** debo de haberme equivocado en algo, debo de haber cometido un error en algún sitio • **a ~ of the pen/tongue** un lapsus calami/linguae • PROVERB: • **there's many a ~ 'twixt cup and lip** de la mano a la boca desaparece la sopa, del dicho al hecho va mucho trecho; ▹ **Freudian**
3 (= *fall*) bajada *f*
4 (= *undergarment*) combinación *f*, enagua† *f*; (*full length*) viso *m*; (= *pillowcase*) funda *f*
5 (= *receipt*) (*in filing system*) ficha *f* • **I wrote the number on a ~ of paper** escribí el número en un papelito *or* un trocito de papel; ▹ **betting, deposit, pay, paying-in slip**
6 (= *landslide*) corrimiento *m* de tierras, desprendimiento *m*
7 (*Cricket*) (*usu pl*) *la posición posterior derecha del receptor (si el bateador es diestro) ocupada por los defensores de campo en un partido de críquet*
8 slips (*Theat*) • **the ~s** la galería
9 [*of person*] • **a ~ of a boy/girl** un chiquillo/una chiquilla
10 (*in pottery*) *arcilla que se ha mezclado con agua hasta estar cremosa*
11 (*Bot*) esqueje *m*
12 (*Naut*) grada *f*
(VI) **1** (= *slide, shift*) resbalar • **she ~ped and broke her ankle** (se) resbaló y se rompió el tobillo • **my foot ~ped** se me fue el pie • **the knife ~ped and I cut my hand** se me fue el cuchillo y me hice un corte en la mano • **the glass ~ped from her hand** el vaso se le fue *or* se le resbaló de la mano • **the clutch ~s** el embrague patina • **the knot has ~ped** el nudo se ha corrido • **we let the game ~ through our fingers** dejamos que el partido se nos escapara *or* se nos fuera de las manos
2 (= *move quickly*) • **to ~ into bed** meterse en la cama • **he ~ped into his bathrobe** se puso el albornoz • **to ~ out of a dress** quitarse un vestido • **I soon ~ped back into the routine** enseguida volví a adaptarme a la rutina • **I ~ped downstairs to fetch it** bajé a traerlo rápidamente
3 (= *move imperceptibly*) pasar desapercibido • **he managed to ~ through the enemy lines** consiguió pasar desapercibido por las líneas enemigas • **he ~ped out of the room while my back was turned** salió sigilosamente de la habitación mientras estaba de espaldas; ▹ **net¹**
4 (= *decline*) [*shares, currency*] bajar • **shares ~ped to 63p** las acciones bajaron a 63 peniques • **to ~ into a coma** caer en coma • **you're ~ping** (*hum*) estás decayendo • **he soon ~ped back into his old ways** al poco tiempo volvió a las andadas
5 (= *become known*) • **he let (it) ~ that he was a Democrat** dejó escapar que era demócrata • **she let ~ the names of the people involved** dejó escapar los nombres de las personas involucradas
(VT) **1** (= *move quickly and smoothly*) pasar, deslizar • **he ~ped an arm around her waist** le pasó *or* deslizó el brazo por la cintura • **~ a knife round the edges of the tin** pasar un cuchillo por el borde del molde • **I ~ped a note under his door** deslicé *or* le pasé una nota por debajo de la puerta • **to ~ a coin into a slot** introducir una moneda en una ranura
2 (= *move imperceptibly*) • **he ~ped his hand into her bag** le metió disimuladamente la mano en el bolso • **to ~ sth to sb** pasarle disimuladamente algo a algn • **he ~ped the waiter a fiver** le pasó disimuladamente un

billete de cinco libras al camarero
3 (= *escape from*) • **the dog ~ped its collar** el perro se soltó del collar • **to ~ anchor** levar anclas • **one or two facts may have ~ped my memory** puede que algún que otro dato se me haya olvidado • **I meant to do it but it ~ped my mind** lo quise hacer pero se me olvidó *or* se me pasó • **the ship could ~ its moorings** al barco podrían soltársele las amarras
4 (*Med*) • **he's ~ped a disc** tiene una hernia de disco
5 (*Aut*) [+ *clutch*] soltar
6 (*Knitting*) [+ *stitch*] pasar (sin hacer)
(CPD) ▸ **slip road** (*on motorway*) vía *f* de acceso
▸ **slip stitch** (*Knitting*) punto *m* sin hacer
▸ **slip away** (VI + ADV) **1** (*also* **slip off**) [*person*] escabullirse, escurrirse
2 (= *fade*) • **he felt his strength ~ping away** sentía que las fuerzas se le iban *or* se le escapaban
3 (= *pass by*) [*time, opportunity*] = **slip by**
▸ **slip by** (VI + ADV) [*time*] pasar • **to let an opportunity ~ by** dejar pasar *or* escapar una oportunidad
▸ **slip down** (VI + ADV) **1** [*food, drink*] • **this wine ~s down a treat** este vino sienta de maravilla
2 (= *go quickly*) • **I'll just ~ down and get it** bajo un momento y lo traigo
3 (= *fall*) [*object*] caerse • **she had ~ped down in her chair** se había dejado caer en su silla
▸ **slip in** (VT + ADV) [+ *comment, word*] incluir
(VI + ADV) (= *sneak in*) entrar desapercibido; (= *enter quickly*) entrar deprisa *or* rápidamente
▸ **slip off** (VT + ADV) [+ *clothes, shoes, ring*] quitarse
(VI + ADV) = **slip away**
▸ **slip on** (VT + ADV) [+ *clothes, shoes, ring*] ponerse
▸ **slip out** (VI + ADV) [*person*] salir un momento • **to ~ out (to the shops)** salir un momento (a las tiendas); [*remark, secret*] • **I didn't mean to say it — it just ~ped out** no quería decirlo, pero se me escapó
▸ **slip past** (VI + ADV) = **slip by**
▸ **slip up** (VI + ADV) (= *make a mistake*) equivocarse; (= *commit a faux pas*) cometer un desliz, meter la pata*
slipcase ['slɪpkeɪs] (N) estuche *m*
slipcovers ['slɪp,kʌvəz] (NPL) (*US*) fundas *fpl* que se pueden quitar
slipknot ['slɪpnɒt] (N) nudo *m* corredizo
slip-ons ['slɪpɒnz], **slip-on shoes** [,slɪpɒn'ʃu:z] (NPL) zapatos *mpl* sin cordones
slipover ['slɪpəʊvəʳ] (N) pullover *m* sin mangas
slippage ['slɪpɪdʒ] (N) (= *slip*) deslizamiento *m*; (= *loss*) pérdida *f*; (= *shortage*) déficit *m*; (= *delay*) retraso *m*
slipped [slɪpt] (ADJ) • **~ disc** hernia *f* discal, vértebra *f* dislocada
slipper ['slɪpəʳ] (N) **1** (*for foot*) zapatilla *f*, pantufla *f* (*esp LAm*) • **a pair of ~s** unas zapatillas
2 (*Tech*) zapata *f*, patín *m*
slippery ['slɪpərɪ] (ADJ) **1** (*lit*) [*mud, ground, surface*] resbaladizo, escurridizo; [*hands, skin*] resbaladizo; [*object, fish*] escurridizo • IDIOM: • **to be on a ~ slope** estar en terreno resbaladizo
2 (*fig*) (*pej*) [*person*] (= *evasive*) escurridizo; (= *unreliable*) poco de fiar • IDIOM: • **he's as ~ as they come** *or* **as an eel** tiene más conchas que un galápago
slippy* ['slɪpɪ] (ADV) (*Brit*) • **to be ~** • **look ~ about it** darse prisa, menearse • **look ~!** ¡menearse! • **we shall have to look ~** tendremos que darnos prisa
slipshod ['slɪpʃɒd] (ADJ) descuidado, chapucero
slipstream ['slɪpstri:m] (N) estela *f*
slip-up ['slɪpʌp] (N) (= *mistake*) error *m*, desliz *m*, metedura *f* de pata*
slipway ['slɪpweɪ] (N) gradas *fpl*
slit [slɪt] (VB: PT, PP: **slit**) (N) **1** (= *opening*) abertura *f*, hendidura *f*; (= *cut*) corte *m* • **to make a ~ in sth** hacer un corte en algo
2 (*in dress etc*) raja *f*
3** (= *vagina*) coño** *m*
(VT) cortar, abrir • **to ~ a sack open** abrir un saco con un cuchillo • **to ~ sb's throat** cortarle el pescuezo a algn
slit-eyed [,slɪt'aɪd] (ADJ) de ojos rasgados
slither ['slɪðəʳ] (VI) deslizarse • **to ~ down a rope** deslizarse por una cuerda • **to ~ down a slope** ir rodando por una pendiente • **to ~ about on ice** ir resbalando sobre el hielo
sliver ['slɪvəʳ] (N) lonja *f*, tajada *f*; [*of wood*] astilla *f*
Sloane Ranger* [,sləʊn'reɪndʒəʳ] (N) niño/a *m/f* bien (londinense)*

> **SLOANE RANGER**
> El término **Sloane Ranger** o **Sloane** se usa para referirse a los jóvenes de clase alta que viven en las zonas más refinadas de Londres, como por ejemplo Chelsea o Kensington, y que visten ropa muy cara de estilo campero. Los **Sloane** hablan con un acento típico de su clase, tienen, en general, ideas conservadoras y le dan mucha importancia al rango social y a la apariencia. Este término fue acuñado por un escritor de moda en los años 70 y se usa en la actualidad con un tono despectivo para referirse a las personas con valores superficiales. La expresión proviene de un juego de palabras hecho con **Lone Ranger** (el Llanero Solitario) y el nombre de una zona elegante del centro de Londres, **Sloane Square**.

slob* [slɒb] (N) vago/a *m/f*, dejado/a *m/f*
▸ **slob out*** (VI + ADV) holgazanear, zanganear, haraganear
slobber ['slɒbəʳ] (VI) babear • **to ~ over** besuquear; (*fig*) caerse la baba por
(N) baba *f*
slobbery ['slɒbərɪ] (ADJ) [*kiss*] mojado, baboso; [*person*] sensiblero, tontamente sentimental
sloe [sləʊ] (N) (= *fruit*) endrina *f*; (= *tree*) endrino *m*
(CPD) ▸ **sloe gin** licor *m* de endrinas
slog [slɒg] (N) • **it was a ~** me costó trabajo • **it's a hard ~ to the top** cuesta trabajo llegar a la cumbre
(VI) **1** (= *work*) afanarse, sudar tinta • **to ~ away at sth** afanarse por hacer algo
2 (= *walk etc*) caminar trabajosamente, avanzar trabajosamente • **we ~ged on for eight kilometres** seguimos la marcha otros ocho kilómetros más
(VT) [+ *ball, opponent*] golpear
▸ **slog out** (VT + ADV) • **to ~ it out** (*fighting*) luchar hasta el fin, seguir luchando; (*arguing*) discutir sin ceder terreno; (*working*) aguantarlo todo, no cejar
slogan ['sləʊgən] (N) slogan *m*, lema *m*
sloganeering [,sləʊgə'nɪərɪŋ] (N) abuso *m* de eslóganes
slogger ['slɒgəʳ] (N) trabajador(a) *m/f*
sloop [slu:p] (N) balandra *f*
slop [slɒp] (VI) (*also* **slop over**) [*water, tea etc*] derramarse, verterse • **the water was ~ping about in the bucket** el agua se agitaba en el cubo • **to ~ about in the mud** chapotear en el lodo
(VT) (= *spill*) derramar, verter; (= *tip carelessly*) derramar, tirar • **you've ~ped paint all over the floor** has salpicado todo el suelo de pintura, has puesto el suelo perdido de pintura
(NPL) **slops** (= *food*) gachas *fpl*; (= *liquid waste*) agua *f sing* sucia, lavazas *fpl*; [*of tea*] posos *mpl* de té; [*of wine*] heces *fpl*
(CPD) ▸ **slop basin** recipiente *m* para agua sucia; (*at table*) taza *f* para los posos del té
▸ **slop pail** cubeta *f* para agua sucia
▸ **slop out** (VI + ADV) (*Brit*) *vaciar los cubos usados como retretes por los prisioneros en sus celdas*
slope [sləʊp] (N) (*up*) cuesta *f*, pendiente *f*; (*down*) declive *m*, bajada *f*; [*of hill*] falda *f*, ladera *f* • **the street was on a ~** la calle era en cuesta • **the car got stuck on a ~** el coche se atascó en una cuesta • **there is a ~ down to the town** la ciudad está bajando una cuesta *or* ladera • **on the eastern ~** en la vertiente este • **a ~ of ten degrees** una pendiente del diez por ciento
(VI) inclinarse • **to ~ forwards** estar inclinado hacia delante • **to ~ up/away** *or* **down** subir/bajar en pendiente • **the garden ~s down to the stream** el jardín baja hacia el arroyo
▸ **slope off*** (VI + ADV) escabullirse, largarse, rajarse (*LAm*)
sloping ['sləʊpɪŋ] (ADJ) inclinado, al sesgo
sloppily ['slɒpɪlɪ] (ADV) **1** (= *carelessly*) en forma descuidada • **to dress ~** vestirse sin atención
2 (= *sentimentally*) en forma sentimentaloide *or* ñoña
sloppiness ['slɒpɪnɪs] (N) **1** (= *carelessness*) [*of work*] descuido *m*, lo descuidado; [*of dress, appearance*] desaliño *m*, desaseo *m*
2 (= *sentimentality*) sentimentalismo *m*, sensiblería *f*
slopping out [,slɒpɪŋ'aʊt] (N) (*Brit*) *vaciado de los cubos usados como retretes por los prisioneros en sus celdas*
sloppy ['slɒpɪ] (ADJ) (COMPAR: **sloppier**, SUPERL: **sloppiest**) **1** (= *runny*) [*food*] aguado
2 (= *careless*) [*work etc*] descuidado; [*appearance, dress*] desaliñado, desaseado; [*thinking*] poco riguroso
3 (= *sentimental*) sentimentaloide, ñoño
4 (= *wet*) mojado • **a big ~ kiss** un besazo con todas las babas
(CPD) ▸ **sloppy Joe** (= *sweater*) jersey *m* suelto; (*US*) (= *sandwich*) *bocadillo de carne picada con cebolla y tomate en pan de hamburguesa*
slops [slɒps] (NPL) ▸ **slop**
slop shop* ['slɒpʃɒp] (N) (*US*) bazar *m* de ropa barata, tienda *f* de pacotilla
slosh* [slɒʃ] (VT) **1** (= *splash*) [+ *liquid*] • **to ~ some water over sth** echar agua sobre algo
2 (= *hit*) [+ *person*] pegar
(VI) • **to ~ about in the puddles** chapotear en los charcos • **the water was ~ing about in the pail** el agua chapoteaba en el cubo
sloshed* [slɒʃt] (ADJ) • **to be ~** tener una buena curda *or* melopea* • **to get ~** agarrarse una buena curda *or* melopea*
slot [slɒt] (N) **1** (= *hole*) (*in machine etc*) ranura *f*; (= *groove*) muesca *f* • **to put a coin in the ~** meter una moneda en la ranura
2 (= *space*) (*in timetable, programme etc*) hueco *m*; (= *advertising slot*) cuña *f* (publicitaria); (= *job slot*) vacante *f*
(VT) • **to ~ in(to)** [+ *object*] introducir *or* meter en; (*fig*) [+ *activity, speech*] incluir (en) • **to ~ a part into another part** encajar una pieza en (la ranura de) otra pieza • **to ~ sth into place** colocar algo en su lugar • **we can ~ you into the programme** te podemos dar un espacio en el programa, te podemos incluir en el programa
(VI) introducirse • **it doesn't ~ in with the**

S

rest no encaja con los demás • **it ~s in here** entra en esta ranura, encaja aquí
CPD ▸ **slot machine** (*at funfair*) tragaperras *f inv*; (*= vending machine*) máquina *f* expendedora ▸ **slot meter** contador *m*

sloth [sləʊθ] N **1** (*= idleness*) pereza *f*, indolencia *f*
2 (*Zool*) oso *m* perezoso

slothful ['sləʊθfʊl] ADJ perezoso, vago, flojo

slotted spoon ['slɒtɪd'spuːn] N cucharón *m* perforado

slouch [slaʊtʃ] N **1** • **to walk with a ~** andar con un aire gacho
2* • **he's no ~** (*in skill*) no es ningún principiante; (*at work*) no es ningún vago • **he's no ~ in the kitchen** tiene buena mano para cocina
VI (*walking*) andar desgarbado • **to ~ in a chair** repantigarse en un sillón • **he was ~ed over his desk** estaba inclinado sobre su mesa de trabajo en postura desgarbada
CPD ▸ **slouch hat** sombrero *m* flexible
▸ **slouch about, slouch around** VI + ADV **1** andar desgarbado; (*aimlessly*) andar de un lado para otro (sin saber qué hacer)
2 (*fig*) (*= laze around*) gandulear, golfear
▸ **slouch along** VI + ADV andar desgarbado; (*aimlessly*) andar de un lado para otro (sin saber qué hacer)
▸ **slouch off** VI + ADV irse cabizbajo, alejarse con un aire gacho

slough[1] [slʌf] N **1** (*Zool*) camisa *f*, piel *f* vieja (*que muda la serpiente*)
2 (*Med*) escara *f*
VT mudar, echar de sí; (*fig*) deshacerse de, desechar
VI desprenderse, caerse
▸ **slough off** VT + ADV mudar, echar de sí; (*fig*) deshacerse de, desechar
VI + ADV desprenderse, caerse

slough[2] [slaʊ] N (*= swamp*) fangal *m*, cenagal *m*; (*fig*) abismo *m* • **the ~ of despond** el abatimiento más profundo, el abismo de la desesperación

Slovak ['sləʊvæk] ADJ eslovaco
N eslovaco/a *m/f*
CPD ▸ **the Slovak Republic** la República Eslovaca

Slovakia [sləʊ'vækɪə] N Eslovaquia *f*

Slovakian [sləʊ'vækɪən] ADJ eslovaco

sloven ['slʌvn] N (*in appearance*) persona *f* desgarbada, persona *f* desaseada; (*at work*) vago/a *m/f*

Slovene ['sləʊviːn] ADJ esloveno
N esloveno/a *m/f*

Slovenia [sləʊ'viːnɪə] N Eslovenia *f*

Slovenian [sləʊ'viːnɪən] ADJ esloveno
N **1** esloveno/a *m/f*
2 (*Ling*) esloveno *m*

slovenliness ['slʌvnlɪnɪs] N [*of appearance*] desaseo *m*; [*of work*] chapucería *f*, descuido *m*

slovenly ['slʌvnlɪ] ADJ [*person*] descuidado; [*appearance*] desaliñado, desaseado; [*work*] chapucero, descuidado

slow [sləʊ] (COMPAR: **slower**, SUPERL: **slowest**) ADJ **1** (*= not speedy*) [*vehicle, music, progress, death, pulse*] lento • **putting them all in order is ~ work** es un trabajo lento ponerlos todos en orden • **this car is ~er than my old one** este coche corre menos que el que tenía antes • **he's a ~ eater** come despacio • **to be ~ in doing sth** tardar *or* (*LAm*) demorar en hacer algo • **she wasn't ~ in taking up their offer** no tardó en aceptar su ofrecimiento • **extra lessons for ~ learners** clases extra para alumnos con problemas de aprendizaje • **it has a ~ puncture** está perdiendo aire poco a poco • **he's a ~ reader** lee despacio • **after a ~ start, he managed to end up in third place** después de un comienzo flojo, consiguió llegar en tercer puesto • **to be ~ to do sth** tardar *or* (*LAm*) demorar en hacer algo • **they were ~ to act** tardaron en actuar • **he's ~ to learn** aprende lentamente, tarda mucho en aprender • **to be ~ to anger** tener mucho aguante; ▹ **going, mark**[2], **uptake**
2 [*clock, watch*] atrasado • **my watch is 20 minutes ~** mi reloj está 20 minutos atrasado
3 (*= mentally sluggish*) torpe, lento • **he's a bit ~ at maths** es algo torpe para las matemáticas
4 (*= boring, dull*) [*match, game, film, plot*] lento, pesado; [*party, evening*] pesado, aburrido • **business is ~** hay poco movimiento (en el negocio) • **life here is ~** aquí se vive a un ritmo lento *or* pausado
5 (*Culin*) • **cook over a ~ heat** cocinar a fuego lento • **bake for two hours in a ~ oven** cocer dos horas en el horno a fuego lento
6 (*Sport*) [*pitch, track, surface*] lento
7 (*Phot*) [*film*] lento
ADV despacio, lentamente, lento • **I began to walk ~er and ~er** empecé a andar cada vez más despacio *or* lentamente *or* lento • **how ~ would you like me to play?** ¿cómo de lento le gustaría que tocara? • **to go ~** [*driver*] conducir despacio; (*in industrial dispute*) trabajar a ritmo lento, hacer huelga de celo (*Sp*)
VT (*also* **slow down, slow up**) [+ *person*] retrasar; [+ *progress*] retrasar, disminuir el ritmo de; [+ *engine, machine*] reducir la marcha de; [+ *reactions*] entorpecer; [+ *economy*] ralentizar; [+ *development*] retardar • **he ~ed his car before turning in at the gate** redujo la marcha del coche antes de entrar por el portón • **they want to ~ the pace of reform** quieren reducir el ritmo de la reforma • **as she approached, she ~ed her pace** a medida que se acercaba, fue aminorando la marcha *or* fue aflojando el paso • **we ~ed our speed to 30 miles an hour** redujimos la velocidad a 30 millas por hora • **that car is ~ing (up *or* down) the traffic** aquel coche está entorpeciendo la circulación
VI [*vehicle, runner*] reducir la marcha; [*driver*] reducir la velocidad *or* la marcha; [*growth*] disminuir; [*breathing*] hacerse más lento • **production has ~ed to almost nothing** la producción ha bajado casi a cero • **he ~ed to a walk** aflojó la marcha y se puso a caminar • **the car ~ed to a stop** el coche redujo la marcha hasta detenerse • **the flow of refugees has ~ed to a trickle** el flujo de refugiados se ha reducido a un goteo
CPD ▸ **slow burn*** (*US*) • **he did a ~ burn** fue poniéndose cada vez más furioso ▸ **slow cooker** olla *f* eléctrica de cocción lenta ▸ **slow cooking** cocción *f* a fuego lento ▸ **slow fuse** espoleta *f* retardada ▸ **slow handclap** (*Brit*) (*by audience*) palmadas *fpl* lentas • **he was given a ~ handclap** recibió palmadas lentas ▸ **slow lane** (*Brit*) (*Aut*) carril *m* de la izquierda; (*most countries*) carril *m* de la derecha ▸ **slow motion** (*Cine*) • **in ~ motion** a *or* (*LAm*) en cámara lenta; ▹ **slow-motion** ▸ **slow puncture** pinchazo *m* lento ▸ **slow train** (*Brit*) *tren que para en todas las estaciones*
▸ **slow down** VI + ADV **1** (*= go slower*) [*engine, vehicle, runner*] reducir la marcha; [*driver*] reducir la velocidad *or* la marcha • **~ down, I can't keep up with you** (*to sb running*) no corras tanto, no puedo seguirte; (*to sb speaking*) no hables tan rápido, que no te sigo
2 (*= work less*) • **you must ~ down or you'll make yourself ill** tienes que aflojar el ritmo de vida o te pondrás enfermo
VT + ADV **1** (*= reduce speed of*) [+ *vehicle*] reducir la velocidad de • **his injury ~ed him down** su lesión le restaba rapidez
2 (*= cause delay to*) retrasar • **all these interruptions have ~ed us down** todas estas interrupciones nos han retrasado
▸ **slow off** VI + ADV = **slow**
▸ **slow up** VI + ADV, VT + ADV = **slow down**

slow-acting ['sləʊ,æktɪŋ] ADJ de efecto retardado

slow-burning ['sləʊ'bɜːnɪŋ] ADJ que se quema lentamente • **slow-burning fuse** espoleta *f* retardada

slowcoach* ['sləʊkəʊtʃ] N (*Brit*) (*= dawdler*) tortuga *f*

slow-cooked [,sləʊ'kʊkt] ADJ cocido a fuego lento

slowdown ['sləʊdaʊn] N **1** (*= reduction*) [*of productivity, growth*] disminución *f* del ritmo; [*of economy*] ralentización *f*
2 (*US*) (*= go-slow*) huelga *f* de manos caídas, huelga *f* de celo (*Sp*)

slowing-down ['sləʊɪŋ'daʊn] N [*of productivity, growth*] disminución *f* del ritmo; [*of economy*] ralentización *f*

slowly ['sləʊlɪ] ADV **1** (*= not quickly*) [*move*] lentamente, despacio; [*drive*] despacio; [*walk*] lentamente, despacio, con paso lento; [*say*] pausadamente, lentamente; [*nod*] lentamente
2 (*= gradually*) poco a poco • **~ but surely he was killing himself** lenta pero inexorablemente estaba acabando con su vida • **she is recovering ~ but surely** se está recuperando de manera lenta pero positivamente

slow-mo*, **slomo*** ['sləʊməʊ] ADJ, N = **slow-motion**

slow-motion ['sləʊ'məʊʃən] ADJ • **slow-motion film** película *f* a cámara lenta
N • **to show a film in slow-motion** pasar una película a cámara lenta, pasar una película ralentizada

slow-moving [,sləʊ'muːvɪŋ] ADJ [*film, play*] lento, de acción lenta; [*animal, person, vehicle*] lento

slowness ['sləʊnɪs] N **1** (*= lack of speed*) lentitud *f* • **he was criticized for his ~ to act** *or* **in acting** le criticaron por la lentitud con la que actuó
2 (*= mental sluggishness*) torpeza *f*
3 (*= dullness*) [*of plot, film, book, match*] lentitud *f*, pesadez *f*

slowpoke* ['sləʊ,pəʊk] N (*US*) = **slowcoach**

slow-witted ['sləʊ'wɪtɪd] ADJ torpe, lento

slowworm ['sləʊwɜːm] N lución *m*

SLR N ABBR (*Phot*) = **single lens reflex (camera)**

sludge [slʌdʒ] N (*= mud*) fango *m*, lodo *m*; (*= sediment*) residuos *mpl*; (*= sewage*) aguas *fpl* residuales

slue [sluː] VT, VI (*US*) = **slew**[1]

slug [slʌg] N **1** (*Zool*) babosa *f*
2 (*= bullet*) posta *f*
3‡ (*= blow*) porrazo *m*; (*with fist*) puñetazo *m* • **a ~ of whisky** un trago de whisk(e)y
VT ‡ pegar, aporrear
▸ **slug out** VT + ADV • **to ~ it out (with sb)** (*= fight*) pegarse (con algn), aporrearse (con algn); (*= end argument*) resolver un asunto con los puños (con algn)

sluggard ['slʌgəd] N haragán/ana *m/f*

slugger ['slʌgəʳ] N (*Baseball*) *bateador que golpea la bola muy fuerte*

sluggish ['slʌgɪʃ] ADJ **1** (*= indolent*) perezoso, flojo
2 (*= slow moving*) [*river, engine, car*] lento; [*business, market, sales*] inactivo; [*liver*] perezoso

sluggishly ['slʌgɪʃlɪ] ADV **1** (*= indolently*)

perezosamente
2 (= *slowly*) lentamente
sluggishness [ˈslʌɡɪʃnɪs] N **1** (= *indolence*) pereza *f*
2 (= *slowness*) lentitud *f*
sluice [sluːs] N (= *gate*) esclusa *f*, compuerta *f*; (= *waterway*) canal *m*, conducto *m*; (= *barrier*) dique *m* de contención • **to give sth a ~ down** regar algo, echar agua sobre algo (para lavarlo)
VT • **to ~ sth down** *or* **out** regar algo, echar agua sobre algo (para lavarlo)
sluicegate [ˈsluːsɡeɪt] N esclusa *f*, compuerta *f*
sluiceway [ˈsluːsweɪ] N canal *m*, conducto *m*
slum [slʌm] N (= *area*) barrio *m* bajo, suburbio *m*, colonia *f* proletaria (*Mex*), barriada *f* (*Peru*); (= *house*) casucha *f*, tugurio *m*, chabola *f* (*Sp*) • **the ~s** los barrios bajos, los suburbios • **they live in a ~** viven en una casucha *or* en un tugurio • **this house will be a ~ in ten years** dentro de diez años esta casa será una ruina • **they've made their house a ~** su casa es un desastre
VT • **to ~ it** (*esp Brit**) vivir como pobres; (= *live cheaply*) vivir muy barato
VI • **to ~** • **go ~ming** visitar los barrios bajos
CPD ▸ **slum area** barrio *m* bajo ▸ **slum clearance** deschabolización *f* ▸ **slum clearance programme** programa *m* de deschabolización ▸ **slum dweller** barriobajero/a *m/f* ▸ **slum dwelling** tugurio *m*
slumber [ˈslʌmbəʳ] N (= *sleep*) sueño *m*; (= *deep sleep*) sopor *m*; **slumbers** sueño *msing* • **my ~s were rudely interrupted** mis sueños fueron bruscamente interrumpidos
VI dormir
CPD ▸ **slumber party** (*US*) *fiesta en la que los invitados se quedan a dormir en la casa del anfitrión* ▸ **slumber wear** (*Comm*) ropa *f* de dormir
slumberous, slumbrous [ˈslʌmbərəs] ADJ soñoliento; (*fig*) inactivo, inerte
slummy* [ˈslʌmɪ] ADJ muy pobre, sórdido
slump [slʌmp] N (*gen*) baja *f* (repentina), bajón *m*; (*in production, sales*) caída *f*, baja *f*; (*economic*) depresión *f* • **the Slump** el crac • **the 1929 ~** la depresión de 1929, la crisis económica de 1929 • **~ in prices** hundimiento *m* de los precios • **the ~ in the price of copper** la baja repentina del precio del cobre • **~ in morale** bajón *m* de moral
VI **1** [*price etc*] hundirse; [*production, sales*] bajar, caer; (*fig*) [*morale etc*] desplomarse
2 • **to ~ into a chair** hundirse en una silla • **he ~ed to the floor** se desplomó al suelo • **he was ~ed over the wheel** se había caído encima del volante
slung [slʌŋ] PT, PP *of* **sling**
slunk [slʌŋk] PT, PP *of* **slink**
slur [slɜːʳ] N **1** (= *stigma*) mancha *f*, calumnia *f* • **to cast a ~ on sb** manchar la reputación de algn • **it is no ~ on him to say that ...** no es hacer un reparo a él decir que ..., no es baldonarle decir que ...
2 (*Mus*) ligado *m*
VT **1** [+ *word etc*] pronunciar mal, tragar
2 (*Mus*) ligar
▸ **slur over** VI + PREP pasar por alto de, omitir, suprimir
slurp [slɜːp] VT sorber ruidosamente
VI sorber ruidosamente
slurred [slɜːd] ADJ [*pronunciation*] mal articulado, borroso
slurry [ˈslʌrɪ] N lodo *m* líquido; (*Agr*) estiércol *m* líquido
slush [slʌʃ] N **1** (= *melting snow*) aguanieve *f*, nieve *f* medio derretida
2 (= *mud*) fango *m*, lodo *m*
3* (= *bad poetry etc*) sentimentalismo *m*
CPD ▸ **slush fund** fondos *mpl* para sobornar
slushy [slʌʃɪ] ADJ (COMPAR: **slushier**, SUPERL: **slushiest**) **1** [*snow*] medio derretido
2* [*poetry etc*] sentimentaloide, sensiblero
slut‡ [slʌt] N (*immoral*) puta* *f*; (*dirty, untidy*) marrana *f*, guarra *f*
sluttish [ˈslʌtɪʃ] ADJ (= *dirty, untidy*) guarro, puerco
slutty [ˈslʌtɪ] ADJ guarro, puerco
sly [slaɪ] ADJ (COMPAR: **slyer**, SUPERL: **slyest**)
1 (= *wily*) [*person*] astuto, taimado • **he's a sly one!** ¡es un zorro!
2 (= *mischievous*) [*person*] pícaro, travieso; [*look, smile*] pícaro, malicioso
N • **on the sly*** a hurtadillas, a escondidas
slyboots [ˈslaɪˌbuːts] NSING taimado/a *m/f*
slyly [ˈslaɪlɪ] ADV **1** (= *cunningly*) con astucia, astutamente
2 (= *mischievously*) [*smile, say*] pícaramente
slyness [ˈslaɪnɪs] N **1** (= *wiliness*) astucia *f*, lo taimado
2 (= *mischievousness*) picardía *f*; (*pej*) malicia *f*
smack¹ [smæk] VI • **to ~ of** (= *taste of*) saber a, tener un saborcillo a; (*fig*) oler a • **the whole thing ~s of bribery** todo este asunto huele a corrupción • **it ~s of treachery to me** me huele *or* suena a traición
N (= *taste*) sabor *m*, saborcillo *m*, dejo *m* (of a)
smack² [smæk] N **1** (= *slap*) bofetada *f*, tortazo *m* • **to give a child a ~** dar una bofetada a *or* abofetear a un niño • **stop it or you'll get a ~** déjalo o te pego • IDIOM: • **it was a ~ in the eye for them** (*esp Brit**) fue un golpe duro para ellos
2 (= *sound*) sonido *m* de una bofetada *or* de un tortazo • **it hit the wall with a great ~** chocó contra la pared con un fuerte ruido
3* (= *kiss*) besazo *m*, besucón *m*
VT (= *slap*) dar una bofetada a, abofetear • **she ~ed the child's bottom** le pegó al niño en el trasero *or* culo • **to ~ one's lips** relamerse, chuparse los labios • **he ~ed it on to the table** lo dejó en la mesa con un fuerte ruido, lo estampó encima de la mesa
ADV • **it fell ~ in the middle*** cayó justo en medio • **she ran ~ into the door** chocó contra la puerta, dio de lleno con la puerta
EXCL ¡zas!
smack³ [smæk] N (*Naut*) barca *f* de pesca
smack⁴‡ [smæk] N heroína *f*
smacker* [ˈsmækəʳ] N **1** (= *kiss*) besazo *m*, besucón *m*
2 (= *blow*) golpe *m* ruidoso
3 (*Brit*) (= *pound*) libra *f*; (*US*) (= *dollar*) dólar *m*
smackhead* [ˈsmækhed] N (= *heroin addict*) adicto/a *m/f* a la heroína
smacking [ˈsmækɪŋ] ADJ • **at a ~ pace** a gran velocidad, muy rápidamente
N zurra *f*, paliza *f* • **to give sb a ~** dar una paliza a algn
small [smɔːl] ADJ (COMPAR: **smaller**, SUPERL: **smallest**) **1** (= *not big*) [*object, building, room, animal, group*] pequeño, chico (*LAm*); (*in height*) bajo, pequeño, chaparro (*LAm*); [*family, population*] pequeño, poco numeroso; [*audience*] reducido, poco numeroso; [*stock, supply*] reducido, escaso; [*waist*] estrecho; [*clothes*] de talla pequeña; [*meal*] ligero; [*coal*] menudo • **the dress is too ~ for her** el vestido le viene pequeño *or* chico • **the ~er of the two** el menor (de los dos) • **with a ~ "e"** con "e" minúscula • **to have a ~ appetite** no ser de mucho comer, comer poco • **to become** *or* **get** *or* **grow ~er** [*income, difficulties, supply, population, amount*] disminuir, reducirse; [*object*] hacerse más pequeño • **mobile phones are getting ~er** los teléfonos móviles son cada vez más pequeños • **to break/cut sth up ~** romper algo en trozos pequeños/cortar algo en trocitos • **to get** *or* **grow ~er** • **until the ~ hours** hasta altas horas de la noche • **to be ~ in size** [*country*] ser pequeño; [*animal, object*] ser de pequeño tamaño; [*room*] ser de dimensiones reducidas • **in ~ letters** en minúsculas • **this house makes the other one look ~** esta casa hace que la otra se quede pequeña • **to make o.s. ~** achicarse • **to make sth ~er** [+ *income, difficulties, supply, population, amount*] reducir algo; [+ *object, garment*] reducir algo de tamaño, hacer algo más pequeño • **the ~est room** (*euph*) (*hum*) el excusado • IDIOM: • **to be ~ beer** *or* (*US*) **~ potatoes** ser poca cosa • **it was ~ beer compared to the money he was getting before** no era nada *or* era poca cosa comparado con lo que ganaba antes;
▹ **world, wee¹**
2 (= *minor*) [*problem, mistake, job, task*] pequeño, de poca importancia; [*contribution*] pequeño; [*difference, change, increase, improvement*] pequeño, ligero • **to start in a ~ way** empezar desde abajo
3 (= *inconsequential*) • **to feel ~** sentirse insignificante • **to make sb look ~** rebajar a algn • **she said in a ~ voice** dijo con un hilo de voz
4 (= *young*) [*child, baby*] pequeño, chico (*esp LAm*) • **when we were ~** cuando éramos pequeños *or* chicos
5 (*frm*) (= *slight, scant*) poco • **to be ~ comfort** *or* **consolation (to sb)** servir de poco consuelo (a algn) • **to be of ~ concern (to sb)** importar poco (a algn) • **to have ~ hope of success** tener pocas esperanzas de éxito • **a matter of ~ importance** un asunto de poca importancia; ▹ **measure, wonder**
N **1** • **the ~ of the back** la región lumbar
2 smalls (*Brit**) (= *underwear*) ropa *fsing* interior *or* (*esp LAm*) íntima
ADV • **don't think too ~** piensa más a lo grande • **try not to write so ~** intenta no escribir con una letra tan pequeña
CPD ▸ **small ad** (*Brit*) anuncio *m* por palabras ▸ **small arms** armas *fpl* ligeras de bajo calibre ▸ **small business** pequeña empresa *f* ▸ **the small businessman** el pequeño empresario ▸ **small capitals** (*Typ*) (*also* **small caps**) versalitas *fpl* ▸ **small**

SMALL

Position of "pequeño"

▹ **Pequeño** *usually follows the noun when making implicit or explicit comparison with something bigger:*
He picked out a small melon
Escogió un melón pequeño
At that time, Madrid was a small city
En aquella época Madrid era una ciudad pequeña

▹ *When used more subjectively with no attempt at comparison,* **pequeño** *usually precedes the noun:*
But there's one small problem ...
Pero existe un pequeño problema ...
She lives in the little village of La Granada
Vive en el pequeño pueblo de La Granada

For further uses and examples, see main entry.

S

change suelto *m*, cambio *m*, calderilla *f*, sencillo *m* (*LAm*), feria *f* (*Mex**) ▸ **small claims court** tribunal *m* de instancia (*que se ocupa de asuntos menores*) ▸ **small end** (*Aut*) pie *m* de biela ▸ **small fry*** • **to be ~ fry** ser de poca monta ▸ **small intestine** intestino *m* delgado ▸ **small investor** pequeño/a inversionista *mf* ▸ **small print** letra *f* menuda ▸ **small screen** pequeña pantalla *f*, pantalla *f* chica (*LAm*) ▸ **small talk** charla *f*, charloteo* *m* • **to make ~ talk** charlar, charlotear* ▸ **small town** (*US*) ciudad *f* pequeña

small-boned [ˌsmɔːlˈbəʊnd] ADJ de huesos pequeños

small-bore [ˈsmɔːlbɔːʳ] ADJ de bajo calibre

smallholder [ˈsmɔːlˌhəʊldəʳ] N (*Brit*) cultivador(a) *m/f* de una granja pequeña, minifundista *mf*

smallholding [ˈsmɔːlˌhəʊldɪŋ] N parcela *f*, minifundio *m*, chacra *f* (*S. Cone*)

smallish [ˈsmɔːlɪʃ] ADJ más bien pequeño, más bien chico

small-minded [ˈsmɔːlˈmaɪndɪd] ADJ mezquino, de miras estrechas

small-mindedness [ˈsmɔːlˈmaɪndɪdnɪs] N mezquindad *f*, estrechez *f* de miras

smallness [ˈsmɔːlnɪs] N **1** [*of object, animal, room*] pequeñez *f*, lo chico (*LAm*); [*of income, sum, contribution*] lo pequeño; (*in height*) [*of person*] lo bajo, lo chaparro (*LAm*); [*of problem*] insignificancia *f*; [*of waist*] estrechez *f*; [*of group, population*] lo poco numeroso; [*of stock, supply*] lo reducido; [*of print, writing*] pequeñez *f*, lo pequeño, lo menudo
2 (= *small-mindedness*) estrechez *f* de miras

smallpox [ˈsmɔːlpɒks] N (*Med*) viruela *f*

small-scale [ˈsmɔːlˈskeɪl] ADJ (*gen*) en pequeña escala

small-size [ˈsmɔːlsaɪz], **small-sized** [ˈsmɔːlsaɪzd] ADJ pequeño

small-time* [ˈsmɔːlˈtaɪm] ADJ de poca categoría, de poca monta • **a small-time criminal** un delincuente menor

small-town [ˈsmɔːlˈtaʊn] ADJ (*esp US*) provinciano, pueblerino

> **SMALL TOWN**
>
> EL término **small town** (ciudad pequeña) se usa en Estados Unidos para referirse a las localidades de menos de 10.000 habitantes. La palabra **village** (pueblo) no se suele usar por tener connotaciones del Viejo Continente o del Tercer Mundo. Los valores de estas ciudades pequeñas, que se ven como algo positivo, representan sobre todo la amabilidad, la honradez, la ayuda entre vecinos y el patriotismo, aunque a veces la expresión se usa en un sentido negativo, como por ejemplo cuando se habla de **small-town attitudes** (actitudes provincianas), haciendo referencia a las mentes estrechas o con prejuicios.

smarm* [smɑːm] (*Brit*) VT • **to ~ one's hair down** alisarse y fijarse el pelo
VI dar coba*, hacer la pelota*
N coba* *f*, zalamería *f*

smarmy* [ˈsmɑːmɪ] ADJ (COMPAR: **smarmier**, SUPERL: **smarmiest**) (*Brit*) zalamero

smart [smɑːt] ADJ (COMPAR: **smarter**, SUPERL: **smartest**) **1** (= *elegant*) [*person, appearance, clothes, car, decor*] elegante; [*garden*] bien arreglado; [*house*] bien puesto • **to look ~** [*person*] estar elegante; [*restaurant, hotel*] ser elegante; [*home*] estar muy bien puesto
2 (= *chic*) [*suburb, party, restaurant*] elegante; [*society*] de buen tono, fino • **the ~ set** la buena sociedad, la gente de buen tono
3 (= *clever*) [*person*] listo, inteligente; [*idea*] inteligente, bueno; [*computer, bombs, missiles*] inteligente • **that was pretty ~ of you** ¡qué listo *or* astuto! • **that wasn't very ~** no ha sido una idea muy buena • **he was too ~ for me** era muy listo y me ganó la batalla • **~ work by the police led to an arrest** la inteligente labor de la policía condujo a un arresto • **the ~ money is on the French** la gente que entiende apuesta por los franceses
4 (*pej*) (= *cocky*) • **don't get ~ with me!** ¡no te las des de listo conmigo! • **she's too ~ for her own good** se pasa de lista • **she's got a ~ answer to everything** tiene respuesta para todo
5 (= *brisk*) [*pace, action*] rápido • **look ~ about it!** ¡date prisa!, ¡apúrate! (*LAm*) • **give the nail a ~ tap** dale un golpe seco al clavo
VI **1** (= *sting*) [*wound, eyes*] escocer, picar, arder (*esp LAm*); [*iodine etc*] escocer • **my eyes are ~ing** me escuecen *or* me pican los ojos • **the smoke made his throat ~** el humo le irritó la garganta
2 (*fig*) dolerse • **she's still ~ing from his remarks** todavía se duele *or* se resiente de sus comentarios • **to ~ under an insult** sentirse dolido por una injuria
N **smarts** (*US**) (= *brains*) cerebro *msing* • **to have the ~s to do sth** ser lo suficientemente inteligente como para hacer algo
CPD ▸ **smart Alec***, **smart Aleck*** sabelotodo* *mf inv*, sabihondo/a* *m/f* ▸ **smart bomb** bomba *f* con mecanismo inteligente ▸ **smart card** tarjeta *f* electrónica, tarjeta *f* inteligente

smart-arse* [ˈsmɑːtɑːs], **smart-ass*** [ˈsmɑːtæs] N sabelotodo* *mf*, sabihondo/a* *m/f* • **smart-arse comments** comentarios *mpl* de sabelotodo

smarten [ˈsmɑːtn] VT = **smarten up**
▸ **smarten up** VT + ADV arreglar • **to ~ o.s. up** arreglarse, adecentarse • **I must go and ~ myself up** tengo que ir a arreglarme *or* adecentarme un poco • **she has ~ed herself up a lot in the last year** durante el año pasado ha mejorado mucho de aspecto *or* se ha arreglado mucho • **to ~ up one's ideas** espabilarse
VI + ADV [*person*] arreglarse, adecentarse; [*town*] mejorar de aspecto

smartly [ˈsmɑːtlɪ] ADV **1** (= *elegantly*) [*dressed, furnished*] con elegancia, elegantemente • **a ~ tailored suit** un traje de corte elegante
2 (= *cleverly*) inteligentemente
3 (= *briskly*) rápidamente • **we left pretty ~** salimos a toda prisa • **they marched him ~ off to the police station** lo llevaron sin más a la comisaría • **to tap sth ~** dar un golpe seco a algo

smartness [ˈsmɑːtnɪs] N **1** [*of appearance*] (= *elegance*) elegancia *f*; (= *neatness*) lo bien arreglado • **~ is very important when you are going to an interview** la buena presencia es muy importante cuando se va a una entrevista
2 (= *cleverness*) inteligencia *f*, agudeza *f*
3 (= *briskness*) rapidez *f*

smartphone [ˈsmɑːtfəʊn] N (*Telec*) teléfono *m* inteligente, smartphone *m*

smartwatch [ˈsmɑːtwɒtʃ] N reloj *m* inteligente

smarty* [ˈsmɑːtɪ] N (*also* **smarty-pants**) sabelotodo* *mf*

smash [smæʃ] N **1** (= *breakage*) rotura *f*, quiebra *f* (*LAm*); (= *sound of breaking*) estruendo *m* • **the cup fell with a ~** la taza cayó con gran estruendo
2 (≠ *collision*) choque *m* • **he died in a car ~** murió en un accidente de coche • **the 1969 rail ~** el accidente de ferrocarril de 1969
3 (*Tennis, Badminton etc*) smash *m*, remate *m*, remache *m*
4 (*Econ*) (= *bankruptcy*) quiebra *f*; (= *crisis*) crisis *f inv* económica • **the 1929 ~** la crisis de 1929
5* (= *success*) exitazo *m*
VT **1** (= *break*) romper, quebrar (*esp LAm*); (= *shatter*) hacer pedazos, hacer trizas • **they ~ed windows** rompieron ventanas • **I've ~ed my watch** he estropeado mi reloj • **when they ~ed the atom*** cuando desintegraron el átomo • **to ~ sth to pieces** *or* **bits** hacer pedazos *or* añicos algo • **he ~ed it against the wall** lo estrelló contra la pared • **the waves ~ed the boat on the rocks** las olas estrellaron el barco contra las rocas • **he ~ed his way out of the building** se escapó del edificio a base de golpes • **he ~ed his fist into Paul's face** le dio *or* pegó un fuerte puñetazo en la cara a Paul
2 (= *wreck*) dar al traste con; (= *ruin*) arruinar, minar • **we will ~ this crime ring** acabaremos con esta banda de delincuentes
3 (= *beat*) [+ *team, enemy, opponent*] aplastar; [+ *record etc*] pulverizar, batir
4 (*Tennis, Badminton etc*) [+ *ball*] rematar, remachar
VI **1** (= *break*) romperse, hacerse pedazos, quebrarse (*esp LAm*) • **the glass ~ed into tiny pieces** el vaso se rompió en pedazos
2 (= *crash*) • **the car ~ed into the wall** el coche se estrelló contra la pared
3 (*Econ*) quebrar
ADV • **to go ~ into sth** dar de lleno contra algo, dar violentamente contra algo
CPD ▸ **smash hit** exitazo *m*
▸ **smash down** VT + ADV [+ *door*] echar abajo
▸ **smash in** VT + ADV [+ *door, window*] forzar • **to ~ sb's face in*** romperle la cara a algn
▸ **smash up*** VT + ADV [+ *car, person, place*] pulverizar, hacer pedazos • **he was all ~ed up in the accident** salió destrozado del accidente

smash-and-grab* [ˈsmæʃənˈgræb], **smash-and-grab raid*** [ˈsmæʃənˈgræbˌreɪd] N robo *m* relámpago (*con rotura de escaparate*)

smashed‡ [smæʃt] ADJ (= *drunk*) como una cuba*; (= *drugged*) flipado‡, colocado‡

smasher‡ [ˈsmæʃəʳ] N (*esp Brit*) cosa *f* estupenda; (= *esp girl*) bombón* *m*, guayabo* *m* • **she's a ~** está como un tren* • **it's a ~!** ¡es estupendo!

smashing* [ˈsmæʃɪŋ] ADJ estupendo (*Sp*), bárbaro, macanudo (*LAm*) • **that's a ~ idea** me parece una idea estupenda • **we had a ~ time** lo pasamos estupendamente *or* de maravilla *or* (*S. Cone*) regio • **isn't it ~?** ¿es estupendo, no?

smash-up [ˈsmæʃʌp] N violenta colisión *f*, grave accidente *m* de tráfico

smattering [ˈsmætərɪŋ] N • **to have a ~ of** tener cierta idea *or* algunas nociones de • **I have a ~ of Catalan** tengo cierta idea *or* algunas nociones de catalán

SME N ABBR (= **small and medium(-sized) enterprise**) PyME *f*

smear [smɪəʳ] N **1** (= *mark*) mancha *f*
2 (*fig*) (= *libel*) calumnia *f*
3 (*Med*) frotis *m*
VT **1** untar • **to ~ one's face with blood** untarse la cara de sangre • **to ~ wet paint** manchar la pintura fresca
2 [+ *print, lettering etc*] borrar
3 (*fig*) (= *libel*) calumniar, difamar • **to ~ sb as a traitor** tachar a algn de traidor • **to ~ sb because of his past** tachar a algn por su pasado

4 (US‡) (= *defeat*) derrotar sin esfuerzo
(VI) [*paint, ink etc*] correrse
(CPD) ▸ **smear campaign** campaña *f* de difamación ▸ **smear tactics** tácticas *fpl* de difamación ▸ **smear test** (*Med*) frotis *m*, citología *f*

smell [smel] (VB: PT, PP: **smelled, smelt**) (N)
1 (= *sense*) olfato *m* • **to have a keen sense of ~** tener buen olfato, tener un buen sentido del olfato
2 (= *odour*) olor *m* • **it has a nice ~** tiene un olor agradable, huele bien • **there's a ~ of gas/of burning** huele a gas/a quemado • **there was an unpleasant ~** había un olor desagradable • **it eliminates cooking ~s** elimina los olores de la cocina • **the sweet ~ of success** la seducción del éxito
3 (= *sniff*) • **let's have a ~** déjame olerlo, déjame que lo huela • **here, have a ~** huele esto
(VT) **1** (= *perceive odour*) oler • **I can ~ gas/burning** huele a gas/a quemado, hay olor a gas/a quemado • **I could ~ cigarettes on his breath** el aliento le olía a tabaco • **dogs can ~ fear** los perros pueden olfatear *or* oler el miedo
2 (= *sniff*) [*person*] oler; [*animal*] olfatear, oler
3 (*fig*) • **he ~ed trouble** se olió problemas • **to ~ danger** olfatear el peligro • **the press ~ed a good story here** la prensa se olió que aquí había noticia; ▹ **rat**
(VI) **1** (= *emit odour*) oler • **it ~s good** huele bien • **that flower doesn't ~** esa flor no tiene olor • **it ~s damp in here** aquí huele a humedad • **to ~ like sth** oler a algo • **what does it ~ like?** ¿a qué huele? • **to ~ of sth** (*lit, fig*) oler a algo • **it ~s of garlic** huele a ajo • **it's beginning to ~ of a cover-up** está empezando a oler a encubrimiento • **if food ~s off, throw it away** si la comida huele mal *or* a pasada, tírela
2 (= *smell bad*) oler • **that man ~s** ese hombre huele • **your feet ~** te huelen los pies • **her breath ~s** le huele el aliento
3 (= *have sense of smell*) • **since the operation she can't ~** desde que se operó ha perdido el sentido del olfato
4 (= *sniff*) [*person*] olisquear; [*animal*] olfatear

▸ **smell out** (VT + ADV) **1** (= *find by scent*) [*dog*] olfatear
2 (= *detect*) • **she can always ~ out a bargain** siempre sabe oler *or* olfatear una ganga
3 (= *cause to smell*) hacer oler mal; (*stronger*) apestar • **it's ~ing the room out** está haciendo oler mal el cuarto, está apestando el cuarto

smelliness ['smelɪnɪs] (N) peste *f*, hediondez *f*

smelling bottle ['smelɪŋ,bɒtl] (N) frasco *m* de sales

smelling salts ['smelɪŋsɔːlts] (NPL) sales *fpl* aromáticas

smelly* ['smelɪ] (ADJ) (COMPAR: **smellier**, SUPERL: **smelliest**) maloliente, apestoso • **the pub was dirty and ~** el pub era sucio y maloliente *or* apestoso • **it's ~ in here** aquí dentro huele mal *or* apesta • **he's got ~ feet** le huelen los pies

smelt¹ [smelt] (PT), (PP) *of* **smell**

smelt² [smelt] (VT) fundir

smelt³ [smelt] (N) (= *fish*) eperlano *m*

smelter ['smeltəʳ] (N) horno *m* de fundición

smelting ['smeltɪŋ] (N) fundición *f*
(CPD) ▸ **smelting furnace** horno *m* de fundición

smidgen, smidgin ['smɪdʒən] (N) • **a ~ of*** un poquito de, un poquitín de

smile [smaɪl] (N) sonrisa *f* • **... she said with a ~** ... dijo con una sonrisa, ... dijo sonriente *or* sonriendo • **to be all ~s** ser todo sonrisas • **her story brought a ~ to my face** su historia me alegró la cara • **to force a ~** forzar una sonrisa • **to give sb a ~** sonreír a algn • **he gave me a big ~** me sonrió de oreja a oreja • **come on, give me a ~!** ¡vamos, una sonrisa! • **she gave a wry ~** sonrió irónicamente • **with a ~ on one's lips** con una sonrisa en los labios • **he managed a ~** sonrió a duras penas • **his jokes failed to raise a ~** sus chistes no hicieron reír a nadie • **to wipe the ~ off sb's face** quitar a algn las ganas de reír
(VI) sonreír • **"yes" I said, smiling** —sí, dije sonriente *or* sonriendo • **to ~ at sb** sonreír a algn • **to ~ at sth** reírse de algo • **what are you smiling at?** ¿de qué te ríes? • **she's had her problems but she always comes up smiling** ha tenido sus problemas, pero siempre se la ve sonriente • **to keep smiling** seguir con la sonrisa en los labios • **keep smiling!** ¡ánimo! • **fortune ~d on him** le sonrió la fortuna • **to ~ to o.s.** reírse por dentro *or* para sus adentros
(VT) • **"of course!" she ~d** —por supuesto —dijo sonriente *or* sonriendo • **she ~d a faint smile** sonrió débilmente • **he ~d his thanks** dio las gracias sonriente *or* sonriendo

smiley ['smaɪlɪ] (ADJ) **1*** [*face, eyes*] sonriente, risueño; [*person*] sonriente, jovial
2 [*badge, symbol, email*] smiley
(N) (*in email etc*) smiley *m*

smiling ['smaɪlɪŋ] (ADJ) sonriente

smilingly ['smaɪlɪŋlɪ] (ADV) con una sonrisa

smirch [smɜːtʃ] (VT) (*liter*) mancillar, desdorar

smirk [smɜːk] (N) sonrisa *f* de satisfacción
(VI) sonreír de satisfacción

smirkingly ['smɜːkɪŋlɪ] (ADV) con una sonrisa de satisfacción

smishing, SMiShing ['smɪʃɪŋ] (N) estafa *f* por SMS
(CPD) ▸ **smishing attack** SMS *m* con intenciones fraudulentas

smite [smaɪt] (PT: **smote**, PP: **smitten**) (VT) †† (*liter*) (= *strike*) golpear; (= *punish*) castigar • **my conscience smote me** me remordió la conciencia; ▹ **smitten**

smith [smɪθ] (N) herrero/a *m/f*

smithereens [,smɪðə'riːnz] (NPL) • **to smash sth to ~** hacer añicos *or* trizas algo • **it was in ~** estaba hecho añicos *or* trizas

> **SMITHSONIAN INSTITUTION**
> La **Smithsonian Institution**, en Washington DC, es el complejo de museos más grande del mundo. Fue fundado por el Congreso en 1846 gracias a fondos donados por el científico inglés James Smithson (de ahí su nombre) y en la actualidad está patrocinado por el gobierno estadounidense como centro para la ciencia y el arte. Posee alrededor de cien millones de piezas y catorce museos, que incluyen el **National Museum of American History**, la **National Gallery of Art** y el **National Portrait Gallery**. También cuenta con un zoológico y lleva a cabo labores de investigación. A esta institución se la conoce como **the nation's attic** (la buhardilla de la nación).

smithy ['smɪðɪ] (N) herrería *f*, fragua *f*

smitten ['smɪtn] (PP) *of* **smite**
(ADJ) • **to be ~ (with sb)** estar locamente enamorado (de algn) • **to be ~ with an idea** entusiasmarse por una idea • **to be ~ with flu** estar aquejado de gripe • **to be ~ with the plague** sufrir el azote de la peste, ser afligido por la peste • **to be ~ with remorse** remorderle a algn la conciencia • **I was ~ by the urge to run out of the house** me daban unas ganas tremendas de salir corriendo de la casa

smock [smɒk] (N) (*for artist*) bata *f*, guardapolvo *m*; (*for expectant mother*) bata *f* corta, tontón *m*
(VT) fruncir, adornar con frunces

smocked ['smɒkt] (ADJ) [*dress, blouse*] fruncido

smocking ['smɒkɪŋ] (N) adorno *m* de frunces

smog [smɒg] (N) smog *m*, niebla *f* mezclada con humo

smoggy ['smɒgɪ] (ADJ) [*city*] envuelto de niebla tóxica; [*sky*] cubierto de niebla tóxica; [*air*] cargado con niebla tóxica

smoke [sməʊk] (N) **1** humo *m* • **cigarette ~** humo *m* de cigarrillos • **~ blue** azul *m* grisáceo • **~ grey** gris *m* humo • **to go up in ~** [*building*] quemarse (totalmente); [*plans*] quedar en agua de borrajas; [*hopes, money*] esfumarse; [*future*] malograrse • **the (Big) Smoke** (*Brit**) Londres • IDIOM: • **~ and mirrors** (*esp US*) artificios *mpl* • PROVERBS: • **there's no ~ without fire** • **where there's ~ there's fire** cuando el río suena, piedras *or* agua lleva
2* (= *cigarette*) pitillo* *m*, cigarrillo *m*, cigarro *m* • **I'm dying for a ~** tengo unas ganas locas de fumarme un pitillo* *or* un cigarrillo *or* un cigarro • **to have a ~** fumar(se) un pitillo* *or* un cigarrillo *or* un cigarro
3* (= *drugs*) hierba* *f*, maría* *f*
(VT) **1** [+ *cigarette, cigar, pipe*] fumar • **she ~d 60 a day** (se) fumaba 60 al día • **she wouldn't let him ~ his pipe** (*in general*) no le dejaba fumar en pipa; (*on one occasion*) no le dejaba fumarse su pipa
2 (*Culin*) [+ *bacon, fish, cheese*] ahumar
(VI) **1** (= *emit smoke*) echar humo • **the chimney always ~d** la chimenea siempre estaba echando humo • **the chimney was smoking, so someone was home** salía humo de la chimenea, así que había alguien en casa
2 [*person*] fumar • **do you ~?** ¿fumas? • **do you mind if I ~?** ¿le importa que fume? • **to ~ like a chimney*** fumar como un carretero *or* como una chimenea*
(CPD) ▸ **smoke alarm** detector *m* de humo, alarma *f* contra incendios ▸ **smoke bomb** bomba *f or* granada *f* de humo ▸ **smoke detector** detector *m* de humo ▸ **smoke inhalation** inhalación *f* de humo ▸ **smoke ring** anillo *m or* aro *m* de humo • **to blow ~ rings** hacer anillos *or* aros de humo ▸ **smoke shop** (*US*) estanco *m* ▸ **smoke signal** señal *f* de humo

▸ **smoke out** (VT + ADV) (*lit*) [+ *animal, demonstrators*] hacer salir con humo; (*fig*) (= *expose*) poner al descubierto

smoked [sməʊkt] (ADJ) [*Culin*] ahumado • **~ glass** cristal *m or* (*LAm*) vidrio *m* ahumado
(CPD) ▸ **smoked haddock** ≈ bacalao *m* ahumado, eglefino *m* ahumado ▸ **smoked salmon** salmón *m* ahumado

smoke-dried ['sməʊkdraɪd] (ADJ) ahumado, curado al humo

smoke-filled ['sməʊkfɪld] (ADJ) lleno de humo

smoke-free [,sməʊk'friː] (ADJ) [*area, environment, workplace*] libre de humo

smokeless ['sməʊklɪs] (ADJ) • **~ fuel** combustible *m* sin humo • **~ zone** zona *f* libre de humos

smoker ['sməʊkəʳ] (N) **1** (= *person*) fumador(a) *m/f* • **~'s cough** tos *f* de fumador • **I'm not a ~** no fumo • **to be a heavy ~** fumar mucho
2 (= *railway carriage*) coche *m* de fumar,

S

vagón *m* de fumar
smokescreen ['sməʊkskri:n] (N) (*lit, fig*) cortina *f* de humo • **to put up a ~** (*fig*) entenebrecer un asunto, enmarañar un asunto (*para despistar a la gente*)
smokestack ['sməʊkstæk] (N) chimenea *f*
(CPD) ▸ **smokestack industries** industrias *fpl* con chimeneas
smokey ['sməʊkɪ] = **smoky**
smoking ['sməʊkɪŋ] (N) • **~ is bad for you** el fumar te perjudica • **~ or non-smoking?** ¿fumador o no fumador? • **to give up ~** dejar de fumar • **"no smoking"** "prohibido fumar" • **no ~ area** zona *f* de no fumadores
(CPD) ▸ **smoking area** zona *f* de fumadores ▸ **smoking ban** prohibición *f* de fumar ▸ **smoking car** (*US*) coche *m* de fumadores ▸ **smoking compartment** compartimento *m* de fumadores ▸ **smoking gun*** prueba *f* tangible ▸ **smoking jacket** batín *m* corto ▸ **smoking room** sala *f* de fumadores
smoking-related [ˌsməʊkɪŋrɪ'leɪtɪd] (ADJ) [*disease, illness*] relacionado con el tabaco
smoky ['sməʊkɪ] (ADJ) (COMPAR: **smokier**, SUPERL: **smokiest**) [*chimney, fire*] humeante, que humea; [*room, atmosphere*] lleno de humo; [*flavour, surface etc*] ahumado • **it's ~ in here** aquí hay mucho humo
smolder ['sməʊldə^r] (VI) (*US*) = **smoulder**
smoldering ['sməʊldərɪŋ] (ADJ) (*US*) = **smouldering**
smooch* [smu:tʃ] (VI) besuquearse
smoochy* ['smu:tʃɪ] (ADJ) [*record, song etc*] sentimental
smooth [smu:ð] (ADJ) (COMPAR: **smoother**, SUPERL: **smoothest**) **1** (= *not rough*) [*surface, stone*] liso; [*skin*] suave, terso; [*hair*] suave; [*road*] llano, parejo (*esp LAm*); [*sea, lake*] tranquilo, en calma • **the flagstones had been worn ~ by centuries of use** las losas estaban lisas por siglos de uso • **for a ~er shave, use Gillinson** para un afeitado apurado, use Gillinson • IDIOMS: • **as ~ as a baby's bottom** suave como la piel de un bebé • **to be as ~ as silk** *or* **satin** ser suave como la seda • **the sea was as ~ as glass** la mar estaba lisa como un espejo
2 (= *not lumpy*) [*paste, sauce*] sin grumos
3 (= *not jerky*) [*running of engine, take-off, landing, motion*] suave, parejo (*esp LAm*); [*crossing, flight*] bueno; [*breathing*] regular • **extra roads to ensure the ~ flow of traffic** más carreteras para asegurar un tráfico fluido • **he lit his pipe without interrupting the ~ flow of his speech** encendió su pipa sin interrumpir el hilo de su narración • **this car gives a very ~ ride** en este coche se viaja muy cómodo
4 (= *trouble-free*) [*transition, takeover*] sin problemas, poco conflictivo; [*journey*] sin problemas, sin complicaciones • **the ~ passage of a bill through Parliament** la sosegada discusión de un proyecto de ley en el parlamento • **the ~ running of a company** la fluida gestión de una empresa
5 (= *mellow*) [*flavour, whisky, cigar, voice, sound*] suave
6 (= *polished*) [*style*] fluido, suave; [*performance*] fluido
7 (*pej*) (= *slick*) [*person*] zalamero; [*manner*] experimentado • **beneath the ~ exterior, he's rather insecure** bajo ese aire experimentado, es bastante inseguro • **the ~ talk of the salesman** la labia del vendedor • **to be a ~ talker** tener pico de oro; ▹ **operator**
(VT) **1** (= *flatten*) (*also* **smooth down**) [+ *hair, clothes, sheets, piece of paper*] alisar • **she ~ed her skirt** se alisó la falda • **to ~ one's hair back from one's forehead** alisarse el pelo retirándolo de la frente; ▹ **flat**
2 (= *polish*) (*also* **smooth down**) [+ *wood, surface*] lijar, pulir
3 (= *soften*) [+ *skin*] suavizar • **to ~ away wrinkles** hacer desaparecer las arrugas, eliminar las arrugas
4 (= *make easy*) [+ *transition*] facilitar; [+ *process*] suavizar • **to ~ the path** *or* **way for sth/sb** allanar el camino para algo/a algn • **to ~ relations** limar asperezas
5 (= *rub*) • **to ~ cream into one's skin** untarse crema en la piel
(N) ▹ **rough**
▸ **smooth down** (VT + ADV) **1** (= *flatten*) [+ *hair, sheet, covers, clothes*] alisar; [+ *surface, road*] allanar, igualar
2 (= *polish*) [+ *wood, surface*] lijar, pulir
3 (= *pacify*) [+ *person*] aplacar
▸ **smooth out** (VT + ADV) **1** (= *flatten*) [+ *fabric, creases, dress*] alisar; [+ *road surface*] aplanar, allanar
2 (*fig*) [+ *problem*] solucionar, resolver; [+ *difficulties*] allanar; [+ *anxieties*] disipar • **to ~ things out** limar las asperezas
▸ **smooth over** (VT + ADV) **1** (*lit*) [+ *soil*] allanar; [+ *wood*] lijar, pulir
2 (*fig*) [+ *difficulties*] allanar; [+ *differences*] resolver • **to ~ things over** limar las asperezas
smooth-faced ['smu:ð'feɪst] (ADJ) [*man*] (*after shaving*) bien afeitado; [*boy*] (*too young to shave*) imberbe, barbilampiño
smoothie ['smu:ðɪ] (N) **1‡** (= *person*) zalamero/a *m/f*
2 (= *drink*) batido *m* de yogur con frutas
smoothing-iron ['smu:ðɪŋˌaɪən] (N) plancha *f*
smoothly ['smu:ðlɪ] (ADV) **1** (= *not jerkily*) [*drive, move, land, glide*] suavemente
2 (= *with no trouble*) • **everything went ~** todo fue muy bien, todo fue sobre ruedas • **the move to the new house went off ~** la mudanza a la otra casa transcurrió sin contratiempos, todo fue sobre ruedas cuando nos mudamos a la otra casa • **to run ~** [*engine*] funcionar muy bien; [*event*] transcurrir sin contratiempos *or* complicaciones *or* problemas; [*business, talks*] ir muy bien, marchar sobre ruedas*
3 (*pej*) (= *slickly*) [*speak, talk*] con mucha labia
smoothness ['smu:ðnɪs] (N) **1** [*of hair*] suavidad *f*; [*of skin*] suavidad *f*, tersura *f*
2 [*of road, surface*] lo llano; [*of stone*] lisura *f*
3 [*of sea, lake*] tranquilidad *f*, calma *f*
4 [*of paste, sauce*] homogeneidad *f*
5 [*of landing*] la suavidad, lo suave; [*of flight, crossing, journey*] lo poco accidentado
6 (= *ease*) [*of transition, takeover*] lo poco conflictivo
7 [*of flavour, whisky, cigar, voice, sound*] suavidad *f*
8 [*of style, prose*] fluidez *f*
9 (*pej*) [*of person, manners*] zalamería *f*
smooth-running ['smu:ð'rʌnɪŋ] (ADJ) [*engine etc*] suave, parejo (*esp LAm*)
smooth-shaven ['smu:ð'ʃeɪvn] (ADJ) bien afeitado
smooth-spoken ['smu:ð'spəʊkən] (ADJ), **smooth-talking** ['smu:ð'tɔ:kɪŋ] (ADJ) afable; (*pej*) zalamero, meloso
smooth-tongued ['smu:ð'tʌŋd] (ADJ) zalamero, meloso
smoothy‡ ['smu:ðɪ] (N) = **smoothie**
smorgasbord ['smɔ:gəsˌbɔ:d] (N) (*Culin*) smorgasbord *m*
smote [sməʊt] (PT) *of* **smite**
smother ['smʌðə^r] (VT) **1** (= *stifle*) [+ *person*] ahogar, asfixiar; [+ *fire*] apagar; [+ *yawn, sob, laughter*] contener
2 (= *cover*) cubrir • **fruit ~ed in cream** fruta *f* cubierta de crema • **a book ~ed in dust** un libro cubierto de polvo • **the child was ~ed in dirt** el niño estaba todo sucio • **they ~ed him with kisses** le colmaron *or* abrumaron de besos
(VI) (= *asphyxiate*) asfixiarse, ahogarse
smoulder, smolder (*US*) ['sməʊldə^r] (VI) [*fire*] arder sin llama; (*fig*) [*passion etc*] arder
smouldering, smoldering (*US*) ['sməʊldərɪŋ] (ADJ) que arde lentamente; (*fig*) latente • **she gave me a ~ look** me miró provocativa
SMP [ˌesem'pi:] (N ABBR) (*Brit*) = **Statutory Maternity Pay**
SMS (N ABBR) (= **Short Message Service**) SMS *m*
smudge [smʌdʒ] (N) borrón *m*
(VT) manchar
(VI) correrse
smudgy ['smʌdʒɪ] (ADJ) [*photo*] movido, borroso; [*page*] emborronado, lleno de borrones; [*writing etc*] borroso
smug [smʌg] (ADJ) (COMPAR: **smugger**, SUPERL: **smuggest**) creído, engreído • **he said with ~ satisfaction** dijo muy pagado de sí, dijo con engreimiento • **don't be so ~!** ¡no presumas!
smuggle ['smʌgl] (VT) (= *bring or take secretly*) pasar de contrabando • **~d goods** mercancías *fpl* de contrabando • **to ~ goods in/out** meter/sacar mercancías de contrabando • **to ~ sth past** *or* **through Customs** pasar algo de contrabando por la aduana • **to ~ sb out in disguise** pasar a algn disfrazado
(VI) hacer contrabando, dedicarse al contrabando
smuggler ['smʌglə^r] (N) contrabandista *mf*
smuggling ['smʌglɪŋ] (N) contrabando *m*
(CPD) ▸ **smuggling ring** red *f* de contrabando, red *f* de contrabandistas
smugly ['smʌglɪ] (ADV) con engreimiento, con suficiencia
smugness ['smʌgnɪs] (N) engreimiento *m*, suficiencia *f*
smut [smʌt] (N) **1** (= *grain of soot*) carbonilla *f*, hollín *m*
2 (= *crudity*) obscenidades *fpl* • **to talk ~** decir obscenidades
3 (*Bot*) tizón *m*
smuttiness ['smʌtɪnɪs] (N) (= *crudity*) obscenidad *f*
smutty ['smʌtɪ] (ADJ) (COMPAR: **smuttier**, SUPERL: **smuttiest**) **1** (= *dirty*) manchado
2 (= *crude*) obsceno, verde, colorado (*LAm*) • **a lot of ~ talk** muchas indecencias • **~ jokes** chistes *mpl* verdes
3 (*Bot*) atizonado
Smyrna ['smɜ:nə] (N) Esmirna *f*
snack [snæk] (N) tentempié *m* • **to have a ~** tomar un tentempié, picar algo
(VI) tomar un tentempié, picar algo
(CPD) ▸ **snack bar** cafetería *f*, lonchería *f* (*LAm*)
snaffle¹ ['snæfl] (N) (*also* **snaffle bit**) bridón *m*
snaffle²* ['snæfl] (VT) (*Brit*) (= *steal*) afanar*, birlar*
snafu‡ [snæ'fu:] (*US*) (N) jodienda** *f*
(VT) joder**
snag [snæg] (N) **1** (= *difficulty*) inconveniente *m*, problema *m* • **there's a ~** hay un inconveniente *or* problema • **what's the ~?** ¿cuál es el problema?, ¿qué pega hay? (*Sp*) • **the ~ is that ...** la dificultad es que ... • **that's the ~** ahí está el problema • **to run into** *or* **hit a ~** encontrar inconvenientes, dar con un obstáculo
2 [*of tooth*] raigón *m*
3 [*of tree*] tocón *m*; (*in wood*) nudo *m*
4 (*in fabric*) enganchón *m*

S

VT enganchar, coger (on en)
VI engancharse, quedar cogido (on en)

snail [sneɪl] N caracol *m* • IDIOM: • **at a ~'s pace** a paso de tortuga
CPD ▸ **snail mail*** (*hum*) correo *m* normal
▸ **snail shell** concha *f* de caracol

snake [sneɪk] N serpiente *f*; (*harmless*) culebra *f* • **a ~ in the grass** (*fig*) un traidor
VI • **a hand ~d out of the curtain** una mano apareció por detrás de la cortina • **the road ~d down the mountain** la carretera serpenteaba montaña abajo
CPD ▸ **snake charmer** encantador(a) *m/f* de serpientes ▸ **snakes and ladders** ≈ juego *m* de la oca ▸ **snake pit** nido *m* de serpientes
▸ **snake about, snake along** VI + ADV serpentear

snakebite ['sneɪkbaɪt] N mordedura *f* de serpiente, picadura *f* de serpiente

snakeskin ['sneɪkskɪn] N piel *f* de serpiente

snaky ['sneɪkɪ] ADJ serpentino, tortuoso

snap [snæp] N **1** (= *sound*) golpe *m*, ruido *m* seco; [*of sth breaking, of whip, of fingers*] chasquido *m* • **it shut with a ~** se cerró de golpe, se cerró con un ruido seco
2 (= *photograph*) foto *f* • **to take a ~ of sb** sacar una foto de algn • **these are our holiday ~s** estas son las fotos de nuestras vacaciones
3 (= *short period*) • **a cold ~** una ola de frío
4 (= *attempt to bite*) • **the dog made a ~ at the biscuit** el perro se lanzó sobre la galleta
5* (= *energy*) vigor *m*, energía *f* • **put some ~ into it!** ¡menearse!
6 • **it's a ~** (*US**) (= *easy*) eso está tirado*, es muy fácil
ADJ (= *sudden*) repentino, sin aviso
• **~ decision** decisión *f* instantánea
• **~ answer** respuesta *f* sin pensar, respuesta *f* instantánea • **~ judgement** juicio *m* instantáneo
VT **1** (= *break*) partir, quebrar (*esp LAm*)
2 (= *click*) chasquear • **to ~ one's fingers** chasquear los dedos • **to ~ one's fingers at sb/sth** (*fig*) burlarse de algn/algo • **to ~ a box shut** cerrar una caja de golpe • **to ~ sth into place** colocar algo con un golpe seco
3 • **"be quiet!" she ~ped** —¡cállate! —espetó ella enojada
4 (*Phot*) sacar una foto de
VI **1** (= *break*) [*elastic*] romperse • **the branch ~ped** la rama se partió
2 (= *make sound*) [*whip*] chasquear • **it ~ped shut** se cerró de golpe • **to ~ into place** meterse de golpe
3 • **to ~ at sb** [*person*] regañar a algn; [*dog*] intentar morder a algn • **don't ~ at me!** ¡a mí no me hables en ese tono!
4 (= *move energetically*) • **she ~ped into action** echó a trabajar *etc* en seguida
ADV • **snap!** ¡crac! • **to go ~** hacer crac
EXCL ¡lo mismo!; (= *me too*) ¡yo también!
CPD ▸ **snap bean** (*US*) judía *f* verde, ejote *m* (*Mex*), poroto *m* verde (*And, S. Cone*), chaucha *f* (*Arg*) ▸ **snap fastener** (*US*) cierre *m* (automático) ▸ **snap pea** tirabeque *m*, arveja *f* china
▸ **snap back** VI + ADV • **to ~ back at sb** contestar *or* hablar *etc* bruscamente a algn
▸ **snap off** VT + ADV separar, quebrar • **to ~ sb's head off** (*fig*) regañarle a algn, echarle un rapapolvo a algn
VI + ADV • **it ~ped off** se desprendió, se partió
▸ **snap out** VI + ADV* • **to ~ out of sth** [+ *gloom, lethargy*] sacudirse algo; [+ *self-pity*] dejarse de algo; [+ *bad temper*] quitarse algo de encima • **~ out of it!** [+ *gloom etc*] ¡anímate!; [+ *bad temper*] ¡alegra esa cara!
VT + ADV [+ *question, order etc*] soltar, espetar (*con brusquedad*)
▸ **snap up** VT + ADV • **to ~ up a bargain** (*fig*) agarrar una ganga • **our stock was ~ped up at once** nuestras existencias quedaron agotadas al instante

snapdragon ['snæp,drægən] N (*Bot*) dragón *m*

snap-on ['snæpɒn] ADJ [*hood, lining*] de quita y pon (*con botones de presión*)

snapper ['snæpəʳ] N (PL: **snapper** *or* **snappers**) (*Zool, Culin*) pargo *m*

snappish ['snæpɪʃ] ADJ (= *irritable*) [*person*] irritable, gruñón; [*reply, tone*] brusco, seco; [*dog*] con mal genio

snappishness ['snæpɪʃnɪs] N [*of person*] irritabilidad *f*; [*of reply*] brusquedad *f*, sequedad *f*

snappy* ['snæpɪ] ADJ (COMPAR: **snappier**, SUPERL: **snappiest**) **1** (= *quick*) rápido; (= *energetic*) enérgico, vigoroso • **make it ~!** ¡date prisa!, ¡apúrate! (*esp LAm*) • **to be ~ about sth** hacer algo con toda rapidez • **and be ~ about it!** ¡y date prisa!, ¡y apúrate! (*esp LAm*)
2 (= *smart*) elegante • **he's a ~ dresser** se viste con elegancia
3 (= *punchy*) [*slogan*] conciso
4 = **snappish**

snapshot ['snæpʃɒt] N (*Phot*) foto *f*

snare [snɛəʳ] N lazo *m*; (*fig*) trampa *f*
VT coger *or* (*LAm*) agarrar con lazo; (*fig*) atrapar
CPD ▸ **snare drum** tambor *m* militar pequeño

snarf‡ [snɑːf] VT **1** (= *wolf down*) tragarse, engullir
2 (= *steal*) [+ *property*] afanar

snarl¹ [snɑːl] N (= *noise*) gruñido *m* • **he said with a ~** dijo gruñendo
VI [*dog, lion*] gruñir • **to ~ at sb** [*person, dog*] gruñir a algn
VT gruñir, decir gruñendo • **"no!" he ~ed** —¡no! —gruñó él

snarl² [snɑːl] N **1** (*in wool etc*) maraña *f*, enredo *m*
2 (*in traffic*) atasco *m*, embotellamiento *m*
VT (*also* **snarl up**) [+ *wool*] enmarañar; [+ *plans*] confundir, enredar; [+ *traffic*] atascar • **the traffic was all ~ed up** había un gran atasco, el tráfico estaba atascado
VI (*also* **snarl up**) enmarañarse, enredarse

snarl-up ['snɑːlʌp] N **1** (*Aut etc*) atasco *m*, embotellamiento *m*
2 (*in plans etc*) enredo *m*, maraña *f*

snatch [snætʃ] N **1** (= *act of snatching*) arrebatamiento *m* • **to make a ~ at sth** intentar arrebatar *or* agarrar algo
2* (= *theft*) robo *m*, hurto *m*; (= *kidnapping*) secuestro *m* • **jewellery ~** robo *m or* hurto *m* de joyas
3 (= *snippet*) trocito *m* • **to whistle ~es of Mozart** silbar trocitos de Mozart • **~es of conversation** fragmentos *mpl* de conversación • **to sleep in ~es** dormir a ratos
4** (= *vagina*) coño** *m*
VT **1** (= *grab*) arrebatar • **to ~ sth from sb** arrebatar algo a algn • **he ~ed the keys from my hand** me arrebató las llaves de la mano • **to ~ a knife out of sb's hand** arrebatarle *or* arrancarle un cuchillo a algn de las manos • **to ~ a meal** comer a la carrera • **to ~ some sleep** buscar tiempo para dormir • **to ~ an opportunity** asir una ocasión • **to ~ an hour of happiness** procurarse (a pesar de todo) una hora de felicidad
2 (= *steal*) robar; (= *kidnap*) secuestrar • **my bag was ~ed** me robaron el bolso
VI • **don't ~!** ¡no me lo quites! • **to ~ at sth** (*lit, fig*) intentar agarrar algo
CPD ▸ **snatch squad** unidad *f* de arresto
▸ **snatch away, snatch off** VT + ADV • **to ~ sth away from** *or* **off sb** arrebatar algo a algn
▸ **snatch up** VT + ADV agarrar (*rápidamente*) • **to ~ up a knife** agarrar un cuchillo • **to ~ up a child** agarrar a un niño en brazos

snatchy* ['snætʃɪ] ADJ [*work*] irregular, intermitente; [*conversation*] intermitente, inconexo

snazzy* ['snæzɪ] ADJ (COMPAR: **snazzier**, SUPERL: **snazziest**) • **a ~ dress** un vestido vistoso

sneak [sniːk] VT • **to ~ sth out of a place** sacar algo furtivamente de un lugar • **I managed to ~ one in** logré meter uno sin ser visto • **to ~ a look at sth** mirar algo de reojo *or* soslayo
VI **1** • **to ~ about** ir a hurtadillas, moverse furtivamente • **to ~ in/out** entrar/salir a hurtadillas • **to ~ away** *or* **off** escabullirse • **to ~ off with sth** llevarse algo furtivamente • **to ~ up on sb** acercarse sigilosamente a algn
2 • **to ~ on sb*** delatar a algn, dar el soplo sobre algn*, chivarse de algn (*Sp**) • **to ~ to the teacher** ir con el cuento *or* (*Sp*) chivarse al profesor*
N* (= *tale-teller*) chivato/a *m/f*, soplón/ona *m/f*
CPD ▸ **sneak preview** [*of film*] preestreno *m*; (*gen*) anticipo *m* no autorizado ▸ **sneak thief** ratero/a *m/f* ▸ **sneak visit** visita *f* furtiva

sneakers ['sniːkəz] NPL (*esp US*) zapatos *mpl* de lona, zapatillas *fpl*

sneaking ['sniːkɪŋ] ADJ ligero • **to have a ~ dislike of sb** sentir antipatía hacia algn • **I have a ~ feeling that ...** tengo la sensación de que ... • **to have a ~ regard for sb** respetar a algn a pesar de todo, respetar a algn sin querer confesarlo abiertamente

sneaky* ['sniːkɪ] ADJ (COMPAR: **sneakier**, SUPERL: **sneakiest**) soplón

sneer [snɪəʳ] N (= *expression*) cara *f* de desprecio; (= *remark*) comentario *m* desdeñoso • **he said with a ~** dijo con desprecio • **the book is full of ~s about ...** el libro se mofa constantemente de ...
VI hablar con desprecio, hablar con desdén • **to ~ at sb/sth** (= *laugh*) mofarse de algn/algo; (= *scorn*) despreciar a algn/algo

sneerer ['snɪərəʳ] N mofador(a) *m/f*

sneering ['snɪərɪŋ] ADJ [*tone etc*] burlador y despreciativo, lleno de desprecio

sneeringly ['snɪərɪŋlɪ] ADV [*say*] en tono burlador y despreciativo; [*smile*] con una mueca de desprecio

sneeze [sniːz] N estornudo *m*
VI estornudar • **an offer not to be ~d at** (*fig*) una oferta que no es de despreciar

snick [snɪk] N **1** (= *cut*) corte *m*, tijeretada *f*
2 (*Sport*) toque *m* ligero
VT **1** (= *cut*) cortar (un poco), tijeretear • **to ~ sth off** cortar algo con un movimiento rápido
2 (*Sport*) [+ *ball*] desviar ligeramente

snicker ['snɪkəʳ] N, VI = **snigger**

snide* [snaɪd] ADJ bajo, sarcástico

sniff [snɪf] N **1** (= *act*) sorbo *m* (por la nariz); (*by dog*) husmeo *m* • **one ~ of that would kill you** una inhalación de eso te mataría • **to go out for a ~ of air** salir a tomar el fresco • **we never got a ~ of the vodka*** no llegamos siquiera a oler el vodka
2 (= *faint smell*) olorcito *m*
VT [+ *snuff etc*] sorber (por la nariz), aspirar; [+ *smell*] oler; [*dog etc*] olfatear, husmear • **just ~ these flowers** huele un poco estas flores • **the dog ~ed my hand** el perro me olfateó *or* me husmeó la mano • **you can ~ the sea air here** aquí se huele ese aire de mar • **~ the gas deeply** aspire profundamente el gas • **to ~ glue** esnifar *or*

S

inhalar pegamento
VI [*person*] aspirar por la nariz, sorber, sorberse la nariz; [*dog etc*] oler, husmear, olfatear • **stop ~ing!** ¡deja de sorberte la nariz! • **to ~ at sth** (*lit*) oler algo; (*fig*) despreciar algo, desdeñar algo • **an offer not to be ~ed at** una oferta que no es de despreciar *or* desdeñar • **the dog ~ed at my shoes** el perro olió mis zapatos
▸ **sniff out** VT + ADV (= *discover*) encontrar husmeando; (= *pry*) fisgar, fisgonear; (*fig*) (= *dig out*) desenterrar

sniffer dog [ˈsnɪfədɒɡ] N perro *m* rastreador; (*for drugs*) perro *m* antidroga; (*for explosives*) perro *m* antiexplosivos

sniffle [ˈsnɪfl] N • **to have the ~s** estar resfriado *or* constipado
VI sorber con ruido

sniffy* [ˈsnɪfɪ] ADJ (= *disdainful*) estirado, desdeñoso • **he was pretty ~ about it** trató el asunto con bastante desdén

snifter* [ˈsnɪftəʳ] N **1** (= *drink*) copa *f*, trago *m*
2 (*US*) (= *glass*) copita *f* para coñac

snigger [ˈsnɪɡəʳ] N risilla *f*, risita *f*
VI reír disimuladamente • **to ~ at sth** reírse tontamente de algo

sniggering [ˈsnɪɡərɪŋ] N risillas *fpl*, risitas *fpl*
ADJ que se ríe tontamente

snip [snɪp] N **1** (= *cut*) tijeretada *f*; (= *action, noise*) tijereteo *m* • **to have the ~*** esterilizarse
2 (= *small piece*) recorte *m*
3 (*Brit**) (= *bargain*) ganga *f*
VT tijeretear • **to ~ sth off** cortar algo con tijeras

snipe [snaɪp] N (= *bird*) agachadiza *f*
VI • **to ~ at sb** (*lit*) disparar a algn desde un escondite • **to ~ at one's critics** responder ante las críticas • **he was really sniping at the Minister** en realidad sus ataques iban dirigidos contra el Ministro

sniper [ˈsnaɪpəʳ] N francotirador(a) *m/f*

snippet [ˈsnɪpɪt] N [*of cloth, paper*] pedacito *m*, recorte *m*; [*of information, conversation etc*] retazo *m*, fragmento *m* • **"Snippets"** (= *heading in press etc*) "Breves", "Noticias Breves"

snippy* [ˈsnɪpɪ] ADJ (*US*) [*person, tone*] brusco, cortante • **to be in a ~ mood** estar con el ánimo que echa chispas

snitch‡ [snɪtʃ] VI • **to ~ on sb** chivarse *or* soplar a algn
VT (= *steal*) birlar*
N **1** (= *nose*) napias‡ *fpl*
2 (= *informer*) soplón/ona* *m/f*

snivel [ˈsnɪvl] VI lloriquear

sniveller, sniveler (*US*) [ˈsnɪvləʳ] N quejica* *mf*

snivelling, sniveling (*US*) [ˈsnɪvlɪŋ] ADJ llorón
N lloriqueo *m*

snob [snɒb] N snob *mf*, esnob *mf* • **he's an intellectual ~** presume de intelectual

snobbery [ˈsnɒbərɪ] N snobismo *m*, esnobismo *m*

snobbish [ˈsnɒbɪʃ] ADJ snob, esnob

snobbishness [ˈsnɒbɪʃnɪs] N snobismo *m*, esnobismo *m*

snobby* [ˈsnɒbɪ] ADJ (COMPAR: **snobbier**, SUPERL: **snobbiest**) snob, esnob

snog‡ [snɒɡ] N • **to have a ~** besuquearse*
VI besuquearse*

snood [snuːd] N (= *band*) cintillo *m*; (= *net*) redecilla *f*

snook* [snuːk] N • **to cock a ~ at sb** (*fig*) hacer un palmo de narices a algn, hacer burlas a algn

snooker [ˈsnuːkəʳ] N snooker *m*, billar *m* inglés
VT • **to be properly ~ed*** (*fig*) estar en un aprieto serio

snoop [snuːp] N **1** (= *person*) fisgón/ona *m/f*
2 (= *act*) • **to have a ~ round** fisgar, fisgonear • **I had a ~ round the kitchen** estuve fisgando *or* fisgoneando *or* husmeando por la cocina
VI (*also* **snoop about, snoop around**) (= *pry*) fisgar, fisgonear; (= *interfere*) entrometerse • **if he comes ~ing around here ...** si viene fisgando *or* fisgoneando por aquí ...

snooper [ˈsnuːpəʳ] N fisgón/ona *m/f*

snooty* [ˈsnuːtɪ] ADJ (COMPAR: **snootier**, SUPERL: **snootiest**) presumido • **the people round here are very ~** la gente de por aquí es muy presumida, por aquí la gente se da mucho tono *or* muchos aires • **there's no need to be ~ about it** no hace falta andar presumiendo de ello

snooze [snuːz] N cabezada *f*; (*in the afternoon*) siestecita *f* • **to have a ~** dar *or* echar una cabezada *or* cabezadita; (*in the afternoon*) echar una siestecita
VI dormitar
CPD ▸ **snooze button** botón *m* de repetición de alarma (*de un despertador*)

snore [snɔːʳ] N ronquido *m*
VI roncar

snorer [ˈsnɔːrəʳ] N persona *f* que ronca mucho

snoring [ˈsnɔːrɪŋ] N ronquidos *mpl*

snorkel [ˈsnɔːkl] N [*of swimmer*] tubo *m* de respiración; [*of submarine*] snorquel *m*, esnorquel *m*
VI bucear con tubo respiratorio

snorkelling, snorkeling (*US*) [ˈsnɔːkəlɪŋ] N esnórquel *m* • **to go ~** hacer esnórquel

snort [snɔːt] N **1** [*of horse, person*] resoplido *m*, bufido *m* • **with a ~ of rage** con un bufido (de enojo)
2‡ [*of whisky etc*] trago *m*; [*of cocaine etc*] esnife* *m*
VI **1** [*horse, person*] resoplar, bufar • **he ~ed with anger** bufó enojado • **he ~ed with impatience** resopló impaciente
2 (*Drugs**) esnifar*
VT **1** (= *say*) bufar • **"no!" he ~ed** —¡no! —bufó él
2 (*Drugs**) [+ *cocaine etc*] inhalar, esnifar*

snorter* [ˈsnɔːtəʳ] N **1** • **a real ~ of a problem** un problemón • **a ~ of a question** una pregunta dificilísima • **it was a ~ of a game** fue un partido maravilloso
2 (= *drink*) trago *m*, copa *f*

snot* [snɒt] N **1** (= *mucus*) mocos *mpl*, mocarro *m*
2 (= *person*) mocoso/a *m/f* insolente*

snotty* [ˈsnɒtɪ] ADJ (COMPAR: **snottier**, SUPERL: **snottiest**) **1** [*nose, handkerchief*] lleno de mocos
2 (*Brit*) (= *snooty*) presumido

snotty-faced* [ˈsnɒtɪˌfeɪst] ADJ mocoso

snotty-nosed* [ˈsnɒtɪˌnəʊzd] ADJ **1** (*lit*) mocoso
2 (*fig*) presumido

snout [snaʊt] N **1** (= *nose*) [*of animal*] hocico *m*, morro *m*; [*of person‡*] napias‡ *fpl*
2‡ (= *tobacco*) tabaco *m*, cigarrillos *mpl*

snow [snəʊ] N **1** (*Met*) nieve *f* • IDIOM: • **white as ~** blanco como la nieve
2 (*on TV screen*) lluvia *f*, nieve *f*
3‡ (= *cocaine*) nieve‡ *f*, cocaína *f*
VT **1** (*Met*) • **to be ~ed in** *or* **up** quedar aislado por la nieve
2 (*fig*) • **to be ~ed under with work** estar agobiado de trabajo
3 (*US**) (= *charm glibly*) • **to ~ sb** camelar a algn*
VI nevar • **it's ~ing** está nevando
CPD ▸ **snow bank** banco *m* de nieve ▸ **snow blindness** (*Med*) ceguera *f* de nieve ▸ **snow cap** casquete *m* de nieve, corona *f* de nieve ▸ **snow goose** ánsar *m* nival ▸ **snow leopard** onza *f* ▸ **snow line** límite *m* de las nieves perpetuas ▸ **snow machine** cañón *m* de nieve artificial ▸ **snow pea** (*US, Australia*) tirabeque *m*, arveja *f* china ▸ **Snow Queen** Reina *f* de las nieves ▸ **snow report** (*Met*) informe *m* sobre el estado de la nieve ▸ **snow tyre, snow tire** (*US*) neumático *m* antideslizante ▸ **Snow White** Blancanieves *f* • **"Snow White and the Seven Dwarfs"** "Blancanieves y los siete enanitos";
▹ **snow-white**

snowball [ˈsnəʊbɔːl] N bola *f* de nieve
VT lanzar bolas de nieve a
VI (*fig*) aumentar progresivamente, ir aumentándose
CPD ▸ **snowball fight** batalla *f* de bolas de nieve

snow-blind [ˈsnəʊˌblaɪnd] ADJ cegado por la nieve

snowboard [ˈsnəʊbɔːd] N tabla *f* de snowboard

snowboarder [ˈsnəʊbɔːdəʳ] N snowboarder *mf*, *persona que practica el snowboard*

snowboarding [ˈsnəʊbɔːdɪŋ] N snowboard *m* • **to go ~** hacer snowboard

snow-boot [ˈsnəʊbuːt] N bota *f* de nieve

snow-bound [ˈsnəʊbaʊnd] ADJ aislado por la nieve, bloqueado por la nieve

snow-capped [ˈsnəʊkæpt] ADJ cubierto de nieve, nevado

snow-covered [ˈsnəʊˈkʌvəd] ADJ cubierto de nieve, nevado

snowdrift [ˈsnəʊdrɪft] N ventisca *f*, ventisquero *m*

snowdrop [ˈsnəʊdrɒp] N campanilla *f* de invierno

snowfall [ˈsnəʊfɔːl] N nevada *f*

snowfence [ˈsnəʊfens] N valla *f* paranieves

snowfield [ˈsnəʊfiːld] N campo *m* de nieve

snowflake [ˈsnəʊfleɪk] N copo *m* de nieve

snowman [ˈsnəʊmæn] N (PL: **snowmen**) muñeco *m* de nieve • **to build a ~** hacer un muñeco de nieve • **the abominable ~** el abominable hombre de las nieves

snowmobile [ˈsnəʊməˌbiːl] N motonieve *f*

snowplough, snowplow (*US*) [ˈsnəʊplaʊ] N quitanieves *m inv*

snowshoe [ˈsnəʊʃuː] N raqueta *f* (de nieve)

snowslide [ˈsnəʊslaɪd] N (*US*) alud *m* (de nieve), avalancha *f*

snowstorm [ˈsnəʊstɔːm] N temporal *m* de nieve, ventisca *f*, nevasca *f*

snowsuit [ˈsnəʊsuːt] N mono *m* acolchado de nieve

snow-white [ˈsnəʊˈwaɪt] ADJ blanco como la nieve

snowy [ˈsnəʊɪ] ADJ (COMPAR: **snowier**, SUPERL: **snowiest**) **1** (*Met*) [*climate, region*] de mucha nieve; [*day etc*] de nieve; [*countryside etc*] cubierto de nieve • **~ season** estación *f* de las nieves • **it was very ~ yesterday** ayer nevó mucho, ayer cayó mucha nieve
2 (= *white as snow*) blanco como la nieve

SNP N ABBR (*Brit*) (*Pol*) = **Scottish National Party**

Snr ABBR = **Senior**

snub¹ [snʌb] N desaire *m*
VT [+ *person*] desairar, volver la espalda a; [+ *offer*] rechazar

snub² [snʌb] ADJ • **~ nose** nariz *f* respingona

snub-nosed [ˈsnʌbˈnəʊzd] ADJ chato, ñato (*LAm*)

snuck [snʌk] PT, PP *of* **sneak**

snuff¹ [snʌf] N rapé *m* • **to take ~** tomar rapé

snuff² [snʌf] (VT) apagar • **to ~ it*** estirar la pata*, liar el petate*
(CPD) ▸ **snuff film, snuff movie*** película *f* porno en que muere realmente uno de los participantes
▸ **snuff out** (VT + ADV) [+ *candle*] apagar; (*fig*) extinguir
snuffbox [ˈsnʌfbɒks] (N) caja *f* de rapé, tabaquera *f*
snuffer [ˈsnʌfəʳ] (N) matacandelas *m inv*; **snuffers** • **pair of ~s** (= *scissors*) apagaderas *fpl*
snuffle [ˈsnʌfl] (N), (VI) = **sniffle**
snug [snʌg] (ADJ) (COMPAR: **snugger**, SUPERL: **snuggest**) **1** (= *cosy*) [*house, room*] acogedor; [*bed*] confortable • **it's nice and ~ here** aquí se está bien • **to be/feel ~** estar/sentirse cómodo • **to be ~ in bed** estar calentito y a gusto en la cama, estar arrebujado en la cama • IDIOM: • **to be as ~ as a bug in a rug*** estar bien tapadito*
2 (= *close-fitting*) ajustado, ceñido, justo (*esp LAm*); (= *too tight*) apretado • **it's a ~ fit** [*garment*] ciñe bien; [*object*] cabe justito
(N) (*Brit*) (*in pub*) salón *m* pequeño
snuggle [ˈsnʌgl] (VI) • **to ~ down in bed** acurrucarse en la cama • **to ~ up to sb** arrimarse a algn • **I like to ~ up with a book** me gusta ponerme cómodo a leer
snugly [ˈsnʌglɪ] (ADV) **1** (= *cosily*) • **wrap your baby ~ in a blanket** abrigue bien a su bebé con una manta • **the children were ~ tucked up in bed** los niños estaban bien abrigados en la cama, los niños estaban bien tapaditos en la cama*
2 (= *tightly*) • **make sure the doors close ~** asegúrate de que las puertas encajan bien al cerrarlas • **it fits ~** [*jacket*] (= *well*) queda bien ajustado *or* ceñido *or* (*esp LAm*) justo; [*one object in another*] encaja perfectamente
so¹ [səʊ] (ADV) **1** (= *to such an extent*) **a** (*with adj/adv*) tan • **I'm so worried** estoy tan preocupado • **it is so big that ...** es tan grande que ... • **he was talking so fast I couldn't understand** hablaba tan rápido que no lo entendía • **I wish you weren't so clumsy** ¡ojalá no fueras tan patoso! • **it was so heavy!** ¡pesaba tanto! • **"how's your father?" — "not so good"** —¿cómo está tu padre? —no muy bien • **it's about so high/long** es más o menos así de alto/largo • **she's not so clever as him** no es tan lista como él • **he's not so silly as to do that** no es bastante tonto para hacer eso, no es tan tonto como para hacer eso • **so many** tantos/as • **we don't need so many** no necesitamos tantos • **I haven't got so many pairs of shoes as you** no tengo tantos pares de zapatos como tú • **so much** tanto/a • **we spent so much** gastamos tanto • **I haven't got so much energy as you** no tengo tanta energía como tú • **I've got so much to do** tengo tantísimo que hacer • **thank you so much** muchísimas gracias, muy agradecido • **it's not so very difficult** no es tan difícil; ▹ **kind, sure** *etc*
b (*with vb*) tanto • **I love you so** te quiero tanto • **he who so loved Spain** (*liter*) él que amó tanto a España
2 (= *thus, in this way, likewise*) así, de esta manera, de este modo • **so it was that ...** así fue que ..., de esta manera *or* de este modo fue como ... • **it is so** es así • **we so arranged things that ...** lo arreglamos de modo que ... • **so it is! • so it does!** ¡es verdad!, ¡es cierto!, ¡correcto! • **is that so?** ¿de veras? • **isn't that so?** ¿no es así? • **that's so** eso es • **that's not so** no es así • **so be it** así sea • **and he did so** y lo hizo • **do so then!** ¡hazlo, pues! • **by so doing** haciéndolo así • **I expect so** supongo que sí, a lo mejor • **so far** hasta aquí *or* ahora • **and so forth** y así sucesivamente, etcétera • **it so happens that ...** resulta que ..., el caso es que ... • **I hope so** eso espero yo, espero que sí • **how so?** ¿cómo es eso? • **if so** en este caso, en cuyo caso • **just so!** ¡eso!, ¡eso es! • **he likes things just so** le gusta que todo esté en su lugar • **you do it like so*** se hace así, se hace de esta manera • **only more so** pero en mayor grado • **so much so that ...** hasta tal punto *or* grado que ..., tanto es así que ... • **not so!** ¡nada de eso! • **and so on** y así sucesivamente, etcétera • **so saying he walked away** dicho eso, se marchó • **so he says** eso dice él • **so to speak** por decirlo así • **I think so** creo que sí • **I thought so** me lo figuraba *or* suponía • **I told you so** ya te lo dije • **why so?** ¿por qué?, ¿cómo?
3 (= *also*) • **he's wrong and so are you** se equivocan tanto usted como él • **so do I** (y) yo también • **"I work a lot" — "so do I"** —trabajo mucho —(y) yo también • **"I love horses" — "so do I"** —me encantan los caballos —a mí también • **"I've been waiting for ages!" — "so have we"** —¡llevo esperando un siglo! —(y) nosotros también • **so would I** yo también
4 (*phrases*) • **so long!*** ¡adiós!, ¡hasta luego! • **so much the better/worse** tanto mejor/peor • **she didn't so much as send me a birthday card** no me mandó ni una tarjeta siquiera para mi cumpleaños • **I haven't so much as a penny** no tengo ni un peso • **she gave me back the book without so much as an apology** me devolvió el libro sin pedirme siquiera una disculpa • **so much for her promises!** ¡eso valen sus promesas! • **ten or so** unos diez, diez más o menos • **ten or so people** unas diez personas, diez personas o así *or* más o menos • **at five o'clock or so** a las cinco o así *or* o por ahí *or* más o menos
(CONJ) **1** (*expressing purpose*) para • **he took her upstairs so they wouldn't be overheard** la subió al piso de arriba para que nadie los oyera • **so as to do sth** para hacer algo, a fin de hacer algo • **we hurried so as not to be late** nos dimos prisa para no llegar tarde *or* a fin de no llegar tarde • **so that** para que (+ *subjun*), a fin de que (+ *subjun*) • **I bought it so that you should see it** lo compré para que *or* a fin de que lo vieras
2 (*expressing result*) así que, de manera que • **he hadn't studied, so he found the exam difficult** no había estudiado, así que *or* de manera que el examen le resultó difícil • **it rained and so we could not go out** llovió, así que no pudimos salir, llovió y no pudimos salir • **so that** de modo que, de manera que • **he stood so that he faced west** se puso de tal modo que *or* de manera que miraba al oeste, se puso mirando al oeste
3 (= *therefore*) así que • **the shop was closed, so I went home** la tienda estaba cerrada, así que me fui a casa • **so you see ...** por lo cual, entenderás ...
4 (*in questions, exclamations*) entonces, así que • **so you're Spanish?** entonces *or* así que ¿eres español? • **so?*** ¿y?, ¿y qué? • **so that's the reason!** ¡por eso es! • **so that's why he stayed home** de allí que se quedó en casa • **so there you are!** ¡ahí estás! • **so what?*** ¿y?, ¿y qué?; ▹ **there**
so² [səʊ] (N) (*Mus*) = **soh**
SO, S/O (ABBR) = **standing order**
soak [səʊk] (VT) **1** (= *immerse*) poner en remojo • **~ the beans for two hours** ponga las judías en remojo dos horas • **to ~ sth in a liquid** remojar algo en un líquido
2 (= *make wet*) empapar • **water had ~ed his jacket** el agua le había empapado la chaqueta • **you've ~ed yourself!** ¡te has empapado entero!, ¡te has puesto perdido de agua!
3* • **to ~ sb** (= *take money from*) desplumar a algn*, clavar a algn* • **to ~ the rich** clavarles a los ricos • **to ~ sb for a loan** pedir prestado dinero a algn
(VI) remojarse • **to leave sth to ~** dejar algo en *or* al remojo
(N) **1** (= *rain*) diluvio *m* • **to have a good ~ in the bath** darse un buen baño • **give your shirt a ~ overnight** deja la camisa en remojo toda la noche
2* (= *drunkard*) borracho/a *m/f*
▸ **soak in** (VI + ADV) penetrar
▸ **soak through** (VT + ADV) • **to be ~ed through** [*person*] estar calado hasta los huesos, estar empapado
(VI + PREP) calar, penetrar
▸ **soak up** (VT + ADV) absorber
soaked [səʊkt] (ADJ) empapado • **by the time we got back we were ~** cuando volvimos estábamos empapados • **to get ~ to the skin** calarse hasta los huesos
soaking [ˈsəʊkɪŋ] (ADJ) (*also* **soaking wet**) [*person*] calado hasta los huesos, empapado; [*object*] empapado, calado • **by the time we got back we were ~** cuando regresamos estábamos calados hasta los huesos *or* empapados • **your shoes are ~ wet** tienes los zapatos empapados *or* calados • **a ~ wet day** un día de muchísima lluvia
(N) (*in liquid*) remojo *m*; [*of rain*] diluvio *m* • **to get a ~** calarse hasta los huesos, empaparse
so-and-so [ˈsəʊənsəʊ] (N) (PL: **so-and-sos**) **1** (= *somebody*) fulano/a *m/f* • **Mr so-and-so** don Fulano (de Tal) • **any so-and-so could steal it** cualquiera podría robarlo
2 (*pej*) • **he's a so-and-so** es un tal, es un hijo de su madre* • **you old so-and-so!** (*hum*) ¡sinvergüenza!
soap [səʊp] (N) **1** (*for washing*) jabón *m* • **soft ~*** coba *f*
2* = **soap opera**
(VT) jabonar
(CPD) ▸ **soap dish** jabonera *f* ▸ **soap flakes** jabón *msing* en escamas ▸ **soap opera** (*TV*) telenovela *f*; (*Rad*) radionovela *f* ▸ **soap powder** polvos *mpl* de jabón, detergente *m* en polvo
▸ **soap up** (VT + ADV) • **to ~ sb up*** dar coba a algn*
soapbox [ˈsəʊpbɒks] (N) tribuna *f* improvisada
(CPD) ▸ **soapbox orator** orador(a) *m/f* callejero/a
soapstone [ˈsəʊpstəʊn] (N) esteatita *f*
soapsuds [ˈsəʊpsʌdz] (NPL) jabonaduras *fpl*, espuma *fsing*
soapy [ˈsəʊpɪ] (ADJ) (COMPAR: **soapier**, SUPERL: **soapiest**) **1** (= *covered in soap*) cubierto de jabón; (= *like soap*) parecido a jabón, jabonoso • **it tastes ~** sabe a jabón
2* (= *flattering*) zalamero, cobista*
soar [sɔːʳ] (VI) **1** (= *rise*) [*birds etc*] remontar el vuelo
2 (*fig*) [*tower etc*] elevarse; [*price etc*] subir vertiginosamente, ponerse por las nubes; [*ambition, hopes*] aumentar; [*morale, spirits*] renacer, reanimarse • **the new tower ~s over the city** la nueva torre se eleva sobre la ciudad • **our spirits ~ed** renació nuestra esperanza
soaraway* [ˈsɔːrəweɪ] (ADJ) [*success, career*] fulminante • **~ sales** ventas que se disparan
soaring [ˈsɔːrɪŋ] (ADJ) [*flight*] planeador, que vuela; [*building*] altísimo; [*prices*] en alza, en aumento; [*hopes, imagination*] expansivo; [*ambition*] inmenso
sob [sɒb] (N) sollozo *m* • **she said with a sob** dijo sollozando, dijo entre sollozos

S

(VI) sollozar
(VT) • "no," she sobbed —no —dijo sollozando, —no —dijo entre sollozos • to sob o.s. to sleep dormirse sollozando • to sob one's heart out llorar a lágrima viva • she sobbed out her troubles contó sus penas llorando *or* entre sollozos
(CPD) ▸ sob story* tragedia *f* ▸ sob stuff* sentimentalismo *m*, sensiblería *f*
S.O.B., s.o.b.‡ (N ABBR) (US) (= son of a bitch) hijo *m* de puta‡
sobbing ['sɒbɪŋ] (N) sollozos *mpl*
sober ['səʊbəʳ] (ADJ) **1** (= *not drunk*) sobrio • to stay ~ mantenerse sobrio • IDIOMS: • to be as ~ as a judge • be stone-cold ~* estar perfectamente sobrio
2 (= *serious, calm*) [*person*] serio, formal; [*expression*] grave; [*attitude, assessment*] serio, sobrio; [*fact*] cruel; [*reality*] crudo, duro • after ~ reflection después de una seria reflexión
3 (= *dull, subdued*) [*clothes, suit, style, decor*] sobrio, discreto; [*colour*] discreto
(VT) **1** (*also* sober up) (= *stop being drunk*) despejar, quitar la borrachera a
2 (= *make more serious*) volver más serio
(VI) **1** (*also* sober up) (= *stop being drunk*) despejarse, pasársele la borrachera
2 (= *become more serious*) volverse más serio
▸ **sober up** (VT + ADV) **1** (= *stop being drunk*) despejar, quitar la borrachera a
2 (= *make more serious*) volver más serio a
(VI + ADV) **1** (= *stop being drunk*) • when she had ~ed up cuando se hubo despejado, cuando se le hubo pasado la borrachera
2 (= *become serious*) volverse más serio
sober-headed ['səʊbə'hedɪd] (ADJ) [*person*] sensato, sobrio; [*decision*] sensato
sobering ['səʊbərɪŋ] (ADJ) • it had a ~ effect on me fue aleccionador • it's a ~ thought da que pensar
soberly ['səʊbəlɪ] (ADV) **1** (= *not drunkenly*) sobriamente
2 (= *seriously*) [*say, look*] con seriedad, sobriamente
3 (= *plainly*) [*decorated, dressed*] sobriamente, discretamente • he was ~ dressed in a dark suit vestía un traje oscuro y sobrio *or* discreto
sober-minded ['səʊbə'maɪndɪd] (ADJ) serio
soberness ['səʊbənɪs] (N) = sobriety
sobersides* ['səʊbəsaɪdz] (NSING) persona *f* muy reservada
sobriety [səʊ'braɪətɪ] (N) **1** (= *not being drunk*) • ~ test (US) prueba *f* de alcoholemia
2 (= *seriousness*) seriedad *f*, sobriedad *f*
3 (= *subdued nature*) sobriedad *f*, discreción *f*
sobriquet ['səʊbrɪkeɪ] (N) apodo *m*, mote *m*
Soc (ABBR) **1** = society
2 = Socialist
soc. (ABBR) = society
so-called ['səʊ'kɔ:ld] (ADJ) supuesto, presunto • all these so-called journalists todos estos supuestos *or* presuntos *or* así llamados periodistas • in the so-called rush hours en las llamadas horas punta
soccer ['sɒkəʳ] (N) fútbol *m* • to play ~ jugar al fútbol
(CPD) ▸ soccer pitch campo *m* de fútbol ▸ soccer player futbolista *mf* ▸ soccer season temporada *f* de fútbol
sociability [ˌsəʊʃə'bɪlɪtɪ] (N) sociabilidad *f*
sociable ['səʊʃəbl] (ADJ) [*person*] sociable, tratable; [*occasion*] social • I don't feel very ~ no estoy para hacer vida social • I'll have one drink, just to be ~ para hacerles compañía, tomaré una copa
sociably ['səʊʃəblɪ] (ADV) sociablemente • to live ~ together vivir juntos amistosamente
social ['səʊʃəl] (ADJ) **1** (= *relating to society*) [*customs, problems, reforms*] social • the ~ order el orden social; ▸ conscience
2 (= *in society*) [*engagements, life etc*] social • her ~ acquaintances sus conocidos • ~ circle círculo *m* de amistades • he has little ~ contact with his business colleagues apenas trata con sus colegas fuera del trabajo • I'm a ~ drinker only solo bebo cuando estoy con gente • she does not regard me as her ~ equal no me trata como a alguien de su misma clase • to have a good ~ life hacer buena vida social • clothes for ~ occasions ropa para la vida social • this isn't a ~ visit *or* call esta no es una visita de cortesía
3 (= *interactive*) [*person, animal, behaviour*] social • man is a ~ animal el hombre es social por naturaleza • I don't feel very ~ just now no me apetece estar con gente ahora mismo • he has poor ~ skills no tiene aptitud para el trato social, no tiene mucho don de gentes
(N) reunión *f* (social)
(CPD) ▸ social administration gestión *f* social ▸ social anthropologist antropólogo/a *m/f* social ▸ social anthropology antropología *f* social ▸ social benefits prestaciones *fpl* sociales ▸ the Social Charter [*of EU*] la Carta Social ▸ social class clase *f* social ▸ social climber arribista *mf* ▸ social climbing arribismo *m* (social) ▸ social club club *m* social ▸ social column (*Press*) ecos *mpl* de sociedad, notas *fpl* sociales (*LAm*) ▸ the social contract (*Brit*) (*Ind*) el convenio social ▸ social democracy socialdemocracia *f*, democracia *f* social ▸ Social Democrat socialdemócrata *mf* • the Social Democratic Party el Partido Socialdemócrata ▸ social disease (*euph*) enfermedad *f* venérea; (*relating to society*) enfermedad *f* social ▸ social exclusion exclusión *f* social ▸ social gaming juegos *mpl* sociales ▸ social gathering encuentro *m* social ▸ social housing (*Brit*) viviendas *fpl* sociales ▸ social inclusion integración *f* social ▸ social insurance (US) seguro *m* social ▸ social intelligence inteligencia *f* social ▸ social media redes *fpl* sociales ▸ social mobility mobilidad *f* social ▸ social network red *f* social ▸ social networking site sitio *m* de redes sociales ▸ social order orden *m* social ▸ social outcast marginado/a *m/f* social ▸ social science ciencias *fpl* sociales ▸ social scientist sociólogo/a *m/f* ▸ social secretary secretario/a *m/f* para asuntos sociales ▸ social security seguridad *f* social • to be on ~ security vivir de la seguridad social ▸ Social Security Administration (US) *organismo estatal encargado de la Seguridad Social y de gestionar las ayudas económicas y sanitarias a los ciudadanos* ▸ social security benefits prestaciones *fpl* sociales ▸ social security card (US) ≈ tarjeta *f* de la Seguridad Social ▸ social security number (US) número *m* de la Seguridad Social ▸ social security payment pago *m* de la Seguridad Social ▸ the social services los servicios sociales ▸ social standing estatus *m* social • she had the wealth and ~ standing to command respect tenía el dinero y el estatus social para infundir respeto ▸ social studies estudios *mpl* sociales ▸ social welfare asistencia *f* social ▸ social work asistencia *f* social ▸ social worker asistente/a *m/f* social, trabajador(a) *m/f* social (*Mex*), visitador(a) *m/f* social (*Chile*)
socialism ['səʊʃəlɪzəm] (N) socialismo *m*
socialist ['səʊʃəlɪst] (ADJ) socialista
(N) socialista *mf*
socialistic [ˌsəʊʃə'lɪstɪk] (ADJ) socialista
socialite ['səʊʃəlaɪt] (N) famosillo/a* *m/f* (*pej*), vividor(a) *m/f*
socialization [ˌsəʊʃəlaɪ'zeɪʃən] (N) socialización *f*
socialize ['səʊʃəlaɪz] (VT) socializar
(VI) alternar, salir • you should ~ more deberías alternar *or* salir más • we don't ~ much these days últimamente no alternamos *or* salimos mucho
socializing ['səʊʃəlaɪzɪŋ] (N) • he doesn't like ~ no le gusta hacer vida social
socially ['səʊʃəlɪ] (ADV) [*develop, integrate, interact*] socialmente; [*inferior, necessary*] socialmente, desde el punto de vista social • ~ acceptable aceptado por la sociedad • ~ aware con conciencia social • to be ~ aware tener conciencia social • the ~ correct way of doing sth la manera socialmente correcta de hacer algo • ~ excluded excluido (*socialmente*) • the ~ excluded los excluidos (*de la sociedad*) • to be ~ inadequate no tener aptitud para el trato social, no saber tratar con la gente • I didn't really get to know him ~ apenas tuve trato con él • I don't really mix with him ~ no suelo alternar con él • to be ~ unacceptable ser mal visto
societal [sə'saɪətəl] (ADJ) societal
society [sə'saɪətɪ] (N) **1** (= *social community*) sociedad *f* • he was a danger to ~ era un peligro para la sociedad • a multi-cultural ~ una sociedad pluricultural
2 (= *company*) compañía *f* • I enjoyed his ~ me encantó su compañía • in the ~ of en compañía de, acompañado por • in polite ~ entre gente educada
3 (= *high society*) alta sociedad *f* • to go into ~ [*girl*] ponerse de largo • to move in ~ frecuentar la alta sociedad
4 (= *club*) asociación *f*, sociedad *f* • a drama ~ una asociación *or* sociedad de amigos del teatro • learned ~ sociedad *f* científica, academia *f* • the Society of Friends los cuáqueros
(CPD) ▸ society column ecos *mpl* de sociedad, notas *fpl* sociales (*LAm*) ▸ society news notas *fpl* de sociedad ▸ society party fiesta *f* de sociedad ▸ society wedding boda *f* de sociedad ▸ society woman mujer *f* conocida en la alta sociedad
socio... ['səʊsɪəʊ] (PREFIX) socio...
sociobiology [ˌsəʊsɪəʊbaɪ'ɒlədʒɪ] (N) sociobiología *f*
sociocultural [ˌsəʊsɪəʊ'kʌltʃərəl] (ADJ) sociocultural
socioeconomic ['səʊsɪəʊˌi:kə'nɒmɪk] (ADJ) socioeconómico
sociolect ['səʊsɪəʊˌlekt] (N) sociolecto *m*
sociolinguistic [ˌsəʊsɪəʊlɪŋ'gwɪstɪk] (ADJ) sociolingüístico
sociolinguistics [ˌsəʊsɪəʊlɪŋ'gwɪstɪks] (NSING) sociolingüística *f*
sociological [ˌsəʊsɪə'lɒdʒɪkəl] (ADJ) sociológico
sociologically [ˌsəʊsɪə'lɒdʒɪkəlɪ] (ADV) sociológicamente
sociologist [ˌsəʊsɪ'ɒlədʒɪst] (N) sociólogo/a *m/f*
sociology [ˌsəʊsɪ'ɒlədʒɪ] (N) sociología *f*
sociopath ['səʊsɪəʊpæθ] (N) sociópata *mf*, inadaptado/a *m/f* social
sociopathic [ˌsəʊsɪəʊ'pæθɪk] (ADJ) sociopático, anti-social
sociopolitical [ˌsəʊsɪəʊpə'lɪtɪkəl] (ADJ) sociopolítico
sock¹ [sɒk] (N) **1** calcetín *m*, media *f* (*LAm*) • IDIOMS: • to pull one's ~s up hacer esfuerzos, despabilarse • put a ~ in it!* ¡a callar!, ¡cállate! • this will knock your ~s off* esto es para quitarse el sombrero
2 (= *windsock*) manga *f* (de viento)
sock²* [sɒk] (N) (= *blow*) puñetazo *m* • to give sb a ~ on the jaw pegar a algn en la cara

(VT) pegar • **~ him one!** ¡pégale!

socket ['sɒkɪt] (N) **1** (*Anat*) [*of eye*] cuenca *f*; [*of joint*] glena *f*; [*of tooth*] alvéolo *m*
2 (*Elec*) enchufe *m*, toma *f* de corriente, tomacorriente *m* (*LAm*)
3 (*Mech*) encaje *m*, cubo *m*
(CPD) ▸ **socket joint** (*Carpentry*) machihembrado *m*; (*Anat*) articulación *f* esférica

socko* ['sɒkəʊ] (ADJ) (*US*) estupendo*, extraordinario

Socrates ['sɒkrəti:z] (N) Sócrates

Socratic [sɒ'krætɪk] (ADJ) socrático

sod[1] [sɒd] (N) [*of earth*] terrón *m*, tepe *m*, césped *m*

sod[2]** [sɒd] (*Brit*) (N) cabrón/ona** *m/f* • **you sod!** ¡cabrón!** • **he's a real sod** es un auténtico cabrón** • **you lazy sod!** ¡vago! • **some poor sod** algún pobre diablo • **this job is a real sod** este trabajo es la monda* • **the lid is a sod to get off** quitar la tapa hace sudar la gota gorda • **sod's law** (*Brit*) ley *f* de la indefectible mala voluntad de los objetos inanimados
(VT) • **sod it!** ¡mierda!** • **sod him!** ¡que se joda!**
▸ **sod off**** (VI + ADV) • **sod off!** ¡vete a la porra!*

soda ['səʊdə] (N) **1** (*Chem*) sosa *f*; (*Culin*) bicarbonato *m* (sódico)
2 (= *drink*) soda *f* • **whisky and ~** whisky-soda *m* • **do you like ~ with it?** ¿te echo un poco de sifón?, ¿con soda?
3 (*US*) (= *pop*) gaseosa *f*, refresco *m*
(CPD) ▸ **soda ash** sosa *f* comercial, ceniza *f* de soda ▸ **soda biscuit** (*US*) galleta *f* salada ▸ **soda bread** *pan hecho con levadura de bicarbonato* ▸ **soda cracker** (*US*) galleta *f* salada ▸ **soda fountain** café-bar *m* ▸ **soda pop** (*US*) refresco *m* (*con gas*) ▸ **soda siphon** sifón *m* ▸ **soda water** soda *f*

sodality [səʊ'dælɪtɪ] (N) hermandad *f*, cofradía *f*

sod-all** ['sɒdɔ:l] (*Brit*) = **damn-all**

sodden ['sɒdn] (ADJ) empapado

sodding** ['sɒdɪŋ] (*Brit*) (ADJ) jodido**, puñetero‡ • **her ~ dog** su jodido perro**, su puñetero perro‡ • **shut the ~ door!** ¡cierra la jodida puerta!** • **it's a ~ disgrace!** ¡no hay derecho, joder!** • **~ hell!** ¡joder!**, ¡me cago en la leche!**
(ADV) • **it's ~ difficult** es muy jodido**, es puñeteramente complicado‡ • **he's ~ crazy!** ¡está como una puta cabra!**

sodium ['səʊdɪəm] (N) sodio *m*
(CPD) ▸ **sodium bicarbonate** bicarbonato *m* sódico ▸ **sodium carbonate** carbonato *m* sódico ▸ **sodium chloride** cloruro *m* sódico, cloruro *m* de sodio ▸ **sodium lamp** lámpara *f* de vapor de sodio ▸ **sodium nitrate** nitrato *m* sódico ▸ **sodium sulphate** sulfato *m* sódico

Sodom ['sɒdəm] (N) Sodoma *f*

sodomite ['sɒdəmaɪt] (N) sodomita *mf*

sodomize ['sɒdəmaɪz] (VT) sodomizar

sodomy ['sɒdəmɪ] (N) sodomía *f*

sofa ['səʊfə] (N) sofá *m*
(CPD) ▸ **sofa bed** sofá-cama *m*

Sofia ['səʊfɪə] (N) Sofía *f*

soft [sɒft] (ADJ) (COMPAR: **softer**, SUPERL: **softest**) **1** (= *not hard*) [*ground, water, cheese, pencil, contact lens*] blando; [*bed, mattress, pillow*] blando, mullido; [*metal*] maleable, dúctil; (*pej*) [*muscles, flesh*] blando • **to go ~** [*biscuits etc*] ablandarse • **his muscles have gone ~** sus músculos han perdido su fuerza, se le han ablandado los músculos
2 (= *smooth*) [*skin, hair, fur, fabric, texture*] suave • **to make ~** [+ *skin, clothes*] suavizar; [+ *leather*] ablandar
3 (= *gentle, not harsh*) [*breeze, landing*] suave; [*accent*] ligero, leve; [*music*] suave; [*light*] tenue; [*colour*] delicado; [*line*] difuminado • **in ~ focus** desenfocado • **~ lighting** luz *f* tenue
4 (= *quiet*) [*whisper, laugh, step*] suave; [*whistle*] flojo; [*voice*] suave, tenue • **his voice was so ~ she scarcely heard it** hablaba tan bajito que apenas le oía • **the music is too ~** esta música está demasiado baja
5 (= *kind*) [*smile, person*] dulce; [*words*] tierno, dulce • **to have a ~ heart** ser todo corazón
6 (= *lenient, weak*) blando • **the ~ left** (*Pol*) la izquierda moderada, el centro-izquierda • **to take a ~ line against sth** adoptar una línea suave en contra de algo • **to be (too) ~ on/with sth/sb** ser (demasiado) blando *or* indulgente con algo/algn
7 (= *easy*) fácil • **~ job** chollo *m* (*Sp**), trabajo *m* fácil • **~ option** camino *m* fácil • **~ target** blanco *m* fácil; ▹ **touch**
8* (= *foolish*) bobo*, tonto • **you must be ~!** ¡tú eres tonto!, ¡has perdido el juicio! • **to be ~ in the head** ser un poco bobo*
9 (= *fond*) • **to be ~ on sb** sentir afecto por algn • **to have a ~ spot for sb** tener debilidad por algn
10 (*Ling*) débil
11 (*Econ*) [*prices, economy*] débil; [*sales, market, growth*] flojo
(CPD) [*currency, drug, fruit*] blando ▸ **soft brown sugar** azúcar *f* morena blanda, azúcar *m* moreno blando ▸ **soft centre** relleno *m* blando ▸ **soft commodities** (*Econ*) bienes *mpl* perecederos, bienes *mpl* no durables ▸ **soft copy** (*Comput*) copia *f* transitoria ▸ **soft drink** bebida *f* refrescante, refresco *m* ▸ **soft fruit** (*Brit*) bayas *fpl* ▸ **soft furnishings** textiles *mpl* ▸ **soft goods** (*Comm*) géneros *mpl* textiles, tejidos *mpl* ▸ **soft landing** aterrizaje *m* suave ▸ **soft margarine** margarina *f* (*fácil de untar*) ▸ **soft money** (*US*) papel *m* moneda ▸ **soft palate** (*Anat*) velo *m* del paladar ▸ **soft pedal** (*Mus*) pedal *m* suave; ▹ **soft-pedal** ▸ **soft phone** (*Comput*) teléfono *m* de software ▸ **soft porn, soft pornography** pornografía *f* blanda ▸ **soft sell** venta *f* por persuasión ▸ **soft shoulder** (*US*) arcén *m* de tierra (*para frenazos de emergencia*) ▸ **soft skills** habilidades *fpl* interpersonales ▸ **soft soap*** coba** *f* • **to give sb ~ soap** dar coba a algn*; ▹ **soft-soap** ▸ **soft top** (*esp US*) descapotable *m* ▸ **soft toy** juguete *m* de peluche

softback ['sɒftbæk] (ADJ) en rústica
(N) (*also* **softback book**) libro *m* en rústica

softball ['sɒftbɔ:l] (N) (*US*) *especie de béisbol sobre un terreno más pequeño que el normal, con pelota grande y blanda*

soft-boiled ['sɒft,bɔɪld] (ADJ) [*egg*] pasado (por agua)

soft-bound ['sɒftbaʊnd] (ADJ) • **soft-bound book** libro *m* en rústica

soft-centred [,sɒft'sentəd] (ADJ) (*Brit*) [*chocolate, boiled sweet*] con relleno blando

soft-core [,sɒft'kɔ:ʳ] (ADJ) [*pornography*] blando

softcover ['sɒftkʌvəʳ] (*US*) (ADJ) en rústica
(N) (*also* **softcover book**) libro *m* en rústica

soften ['sɒfn] (VT) **1** (= *make less hard*) [+ *butter, ground, metal, leather, water*] ablandar
2 (= *make smooth*) [+ *fabric, skin, hair*] suavizar
3 (= *make gentle*) [+ *sound, outline*] suavizar; [+ *lights, lighting*] hacer más tenue; [+ *person*] ablandar
4 (= *mitigate*) [+ *effect, reaction*] mitigar, atenuar • **to ~ the blow** (*fig*) amortiguar el golpe
(VI) **1** (= *become less hard*) [*butter, ground, metal*] ablandarse
2 (= *become smooth*) [*fabric, skin, hair*] suavizarse
3 (= *become gentle*) [*voice, outline*] suavizarse; [*lighting*] hacerse más tenue; [*person*] ablandarse • **her heart ~ed** se le ablandó el corazón
4 (= *become moderate*) [*effect*] mitigarse, atenuarse; [*attitude*] suavizarse, moderarse
▸ **soften up** (VT + ADV) [+ *resistance*] debilitar
(VI + ADV) • **to ~ up on sb** volverse menos severo con algn • **we must not ~ up on communism** debemos seguir tan opuestos como siempre al comunismo

softener ['sɒfnəʳ] (N) (= *water softener*) descalcificador *m*, decalcificador *m*; (= *fabric softener*) suavizante *m*

softening ['sɒfnɪŋ] (N) [*of ground, metal, leather*] reblandecimiento *m*; (*Econ*) [*of economy, market*] debilitamiento *m* • **~ of the brain** reblandecimiento *m* cerebral • **there has been a ~ of his attitude/position** ha suavizado *or* moderado su actitud/posición

soft-headed ['sɒft'hedɪd] (ADJ) bobo, tonto

soft-hearted ['sɒft'hɑ:tɪd] (ADJ) compasivo, bondadoso

soft-heartedness ['sɒft'hɑ:tɪdnɪs] (N) compasión *f*, bondad *f*

softie* ['sɒftɪ] (N) = **softy**

soft-liner [,sɒft'laɪnəʳ] (N) blando/a *m/f*

softly ['sɒftlɪ] (ADV) **1** (= *quietly*) [*walk, move*] silenciosamente, sin hacer ruido; [*say*] bajito, en voz baja; [*whistle*] bajito • **he closed the door ~** cerró la puerta silenciosamente • **he swore ~** dijo una palabrota en voz baja, susurró una palabrota • **the radio was playing ~ in the kitchen** la radio sonaba bajito en la cocina • **a ~ spoken young man** un joven de voz suave
2 (= *gently*) [*touch, tap, kiss*] suavemente; [*smile*] con ternura, dulcemente; [*say*] dulcemente
3 (= *not brightly*) [*glow, gleam, shine*] tenuemente • **~ lit** iluminado con luz tenue

softly-softly [,sɒftlɪ'sɒftlɪ] (ADJ) • **to adopt a softly-softly approach** adoptar una política cautelosa

softness ['sɒftnɪs] (N) **1** [*of ground, bread*] blandura *f*, lo blando; [*of pencil, water, butter*] lo blando; [*of bed, pillow*] lo mullido; [*of muscles, flesh*] blandura *f*
2 [*of skin, hair, fabric*] suavidad *f*
3 [*of breeze, touch, voice, light, colour*] suavidad *f*; [*of light*] lo tenue
4 [*of sound, laugh*] suavidad *f*
5 (= *kindness*) ternura *f*
6 (= *leniency*) [*of person, approach*] indulgencia *f*, blandura *f*
7 (= *weakness*) debilidad *f*
8 (= *stupidity*) estupidez *f*

soft-pedal ['sɒft'pedl] (VT) (*esp US*) (*fig*) minimizar la importancia de

soft-soap* [,sɒft'səʊp] (VT) dar coba a*

soft-spoken ['sɒft'spəʊkən] (ADJ) de voz suave

software ['sɒftwɛəʳ] (N) (*Comput*) software *m*
(CPD) ▸ **software engineer** ingeniero/a *m/f* de software ▸ **software engineering** ingeniería *f* de software ▸ **software house** compañía *f* especializada en programación ▸ **software library** biblioteca *f* de software ▸ **software package** paquete *m* de programas ▸ **software program** programa *m* de software

softwood ['sɒftwʊd] (N) madera *f* blanda

softy* ['sɒftɪ] (N) blandengue* *mf*; (= *too tender-hearted*) blandengue* *mf*, buenazo/a* *m/f*; (= *no stamina etc*) blandengue* *mf*; (= *coward*) gallina* *mf*, cobardica* *mf* • **you big ~, stop crying!** ¡no seas llorón *or* llorica!*

soggy ['sɒgɪ] (ADJ) (COMPAR: **soggier**, SUPERL:

soggiest) [*paper*] mojado; [*clothes, ground*] empapado; [*bread, biscuits*] revenido; [*salad, vegetables*] pasado

soh [səʊ] N (*Mus*) sol *m*

soi-disant ['swɑ:'di:zɔ:ŋ] ADJ supuesto, presunto, sedicente

soigné ['swɑ:njeɪ] ADJ pulcro, acicalado

soil¹ [sɔɪl] N (= *earth*) tierra *f* • **his native ~** su tierra natal, su patria • **on British ~** en suelo británico • **the ~** (= *farmland*) la tierra

soil² [sɔɪl] VT **1** (= *dirty*) ensuciar; (= *stain*) manchar • **to ~ o.s.** ensuciarse
2 (*fig*) [+ *reputation, honour etc*] manchar • **I would not ~ myself by contact with ...** no me rebajaría a tener contacto con ...
VI ensuciarse

soiled [sɔɪld] ADJ (= *dirty*) sucio; (= *stained*) manchado

soilpipe ['sɔɪlpaɪp] N tubo *m* de desagüe sanitario

soirée ['swɑ:reɪ] N velada *f*

sojourn ['sɒdʒɜ:n] N permanencia *f*, estancia *f*
VI permanecer, residir, morar; (*for short time*) pasar una temporada

solace ['sɒlɪs] N consuelo *m* • **to seek ~ with ...** procurar consolarse con ..., buscar consuelo en
VT consolar • **to ~ o.s.** consolarse (**with** con)

solar ['səʊlə^r] ADJ solar
CPD ▸ **solar battery** pila *f* solar ▸ **solar calculator** calculadora *f* solar ▸ **solar calendar** calendario *m* solar ▸ **solar cell** célula *f* solar ▸ **solar eclipse** eclipse *m* solar ▸ **solar energy** energía *f* solar ▸ **solar flare** erupción *f* solar ▸ **solar heat** calor *m* solar ▸ **solar heating** calefacción *f* solar ▸ **solar panel** panel *m* solar ▸ **solar plexus** (*Anat*) plexo *m* solar ▸ **solar power** energía *f* solar ▸ **solar system** sistema *m* solar ▸ **solar wind** viento *m* solar ▸ **solar year** año *m* solar

solarium [səʊ'lɛərɪəm] N (PL: **solariums** *or* **solaria** [səʊ'lɛərɪə]) solárium *m*, solario *m*

solar-powered ['səʊlə'paʊəd] ADJ de energía solar

sold [səʊld] PT, PP *of* **sell**

solder ['səʊldə^r] N soldadura *f*
VT soldar

soldering-iron ['səʊldərɪŋ,aɪən] N soldador *m*

soldier ['səʊldʒə^r] N **1** (*Mil*) soldado *mf*, militar *mf* • **common ~** soldado *mf* raso • **~ of fortune** aventurero/a *m/f* militar • **an old ~** un veterano *or* excombatiente • **to come the old ~ with sb*** tratar de imponerse a algn (por más experimentado) • **to play at ~s** jugar a los soldados • **a woman ~** una soldado, una mujer soldado
2 (*Brit**) (= *strip of bread or toast*) *tira de pan (tostada) para mojar en los huevos pasados por agua*
3 (*Zool*) (= *ant*) hormiga *f* soldado, soldado *m*
VI ser soldado • **he ~ed for ten years in the East** sirvió durante diez años en el Oriente
CPD ▸ **soldier ant** hormiga *f* soldado, soldado *m*
▸ **soldier on** VI + ADV seguir adelante

soldierly ['səʊldʒəlɪ] ADJ militar

soldiery ['səʊldʒərɪ] N soldadesca *f* • **a brutal and licentious ~** la soldadesca indisciplinada

sold out [səʊld'aʊt] ADJ (*Comm*) agotado

sole¹ [səʊl] N **1** (*Anat*) planta *f*
2 [*of shoe*] suela *f* • **half ~** media suela *f* • **inner ~** plantilla *f*
VT poner suela a

sole² [səʊl] N (PL: **sole** *or* **soles**) (= *fish*) lenguado *m*

sole³ [səʊl] ADJ (= *only*) único; (= *exclusive*) exclusivo, en exclusividad • **the ~ reason is that ...** la única razón es que ... • **to be ~ agent for** tener la representación exclusiva de
CPD ▸ **sole owner, sole proprietor** propietario/a *m/f* único/a ▸ **sole trader** empresario/a *m/f* individual

solecism ['sɒləsɪzəm] N solecismo *m*

solely ['səʊllɪ] ADV (= *only*) únicamente, solamente, solo, sólo; (= *exclusively*) exclusivamente

In the past the standard spelling for **solo** *as an adverb was with an accent* (**sólo**). *Nowadays the* **Real Academia Española** *advises that the accented form is only required where there might otherwise be confusion with the adjective* **solo**.

solemn ['sɒləm] ADJ [*person, face*] serio, adusto; [*warning*] serio; [*occasion, promise*] solemne • **he looked ~** estaba muy serio, tenía un aspecto adusto

solemnity [sə'lemnɪtɪ] N [*of occasion, promise*] solemnidad *f*; [*of person's expression*] seriedad *f*, adustez *f*; [*of warning*] seriedad *f*

solemnization [,sɒləmnaɪ'zeɪʃən] N solemnización *f*

solemnize ['sɒləmnaɪz] VT solemnizar

solemnly ['sɒləmlɪ] ADV [*nod, look*] seriamente, con gesto adusto; [*say*] con seriedad, con tono solemne; [*promise, declare, swear*] solemnemente

solenoid ['səʊlənɔɪd] N solenoide *m*

sol-fa ['sɒl'fɑ:] N (*Mus*) solfeo *m*

solicit [sə'lɪsɪt] VT (= *request*) solicitar; (= *demand*) exigir; (= *beg for*) pedir • **to ~ sb for sth** • **~ sth of sb** solicitar algo a algn
VI [*prostitute*] ejercer la prostitución abordando a clientes

solicitation [sə,lɪsɪ'teɪʃən] N (*esp US*) solicitación *f*

soliciting [sə'lɪsɪtɪŋ] N abordamiento *m*; (*by prostitute*) ejercicio *m* de la prostitución (*abordando a los clientes*)

solicitor [sə'lɪsɪtə^r] N **1** (*Brit*) (*Jur*) (= *lawyer*) procurador(a) *m/f*, abogado/a *m/f*; (*for wills*) notario/a *m/f*; ▸ LAWYERS
2 (*US*) (= *officer*) representante *mf*, agente *mf*; (*Jur*) abogado/a *m/f* asesor(a) adscrito/a a un municipio
CPD ▸ **Solicitor General** (*Brit*) subfiscal *mf* de la corona; (*US*) Procurador(a) *m/f* general del Estado

solicitous [sə'lɪsɪtəs] ADJ • **~ (about** *or* **for)** (= *anxious*) atento (a) • **~ to please** deseoso de agradar *or* quedar bien

solicitude [sə'lɪsɪtju:d] N (*frm*) (= *consideration*) solicitud *f*; (= *concern*) preocupación *f*; (= *anxiety*) ansiedad *f*; (= *attention*) atención *f*

solid ['sɒlɪd] ADJ **1** (= *not liquid*) sólido • **to become ~** solidificarse • **~ food** alimentos *mpl* sólidos • **to freeze ~** congelarse por completo • **to be frozen ~** estar completamente congelado • **to go ~** solidificarse
2 (= *firm*) [*masonry, building, understanding, basis*] sólido; [*argument*] sólido, bien fundamentado; [*relationship*] sólido, firme • **get a good ~ grip on the handle** agarra bien el mango • **~ ground** tierra *f* firme • **to have ~ grounds for thinking that ...** tener bases sólidas para creer que ... • IDIOM: • **as ~ as a rock** [*structure, relationship*] sólido como una roca; [*substance*] duro como una piedra; [*person*] digno de confianza
3 (= *not hollow*) [*rock*] sólido; [*wood, steel*] macizo, puro; [*tyre, ball, block*] macizo • **~ gold** oro *m* puro
4 (= *compact, dense*) [*layer, crowd*] compacto • **flights to Israel are booked ~** los vuelos a Israel están completamente llenos • **a man of ~ build** un hombre fornido *or* de constitución robusta • **a ~ mass of colour** una masa sólida de color • **a ~ mass of people** una masa compacta de gente • **he's six feet of ~ muscle** mide uno ochenta y es todo músculo • **the streets were packed ~ with people** las calles estaban abarrotadas de gente • **the bolts have rusted ~** los tornillos están tan oxidados que es imposible girarlos • **the traffic was ~ going into town** había una caravana tremenda en dirección a la ciudad*
5 (= *continuous*) [*line, rain*] ininterrumpido • **we waited two ~ hours** esperamos dos horas enteras • **I've been working on this for eight hours ~** he estado trabajando sobre esto durante ocho horas ininterrumpidas, llevo trabajando sobre esto ocho horas sin parar
6 (= *reliable*) [*person, relationship*] serio; [*evidence, reason, values*] sólido; [*information*] fiable; [*work*] concienzudo; [*citizen*] responsable; [*advice*] útil • **he's a good ~ worker** es un trabajador responsable
7 (= *substantial*) • **a ~ meal** una comida sustanciosa
8 (= *unanimous*) • **~ support** un apoyo unánime
9 (*Geom*) [*figure*] tridimensional
N **1** (*Phys, Chem*) sólido *m*
2 (*Geom*) sólido *m*
3 solids (= *solid food*) (alimentos *mpl*) sólidos *mpl* • **is he on ~s yet?** ¿come ya alimentos sólidos?
CPD ▸ **solid angle** (*Geom*) ángulo *m* sólido ▸ **solid compound** (*Ling*) *compuesto que se escribe como una sola palabra* ▸ **solid fuel** combustible *m* sólido ▸ **solid geometry** geometría *f* de los cuerpos sólidos

solidarity [,sɒlɪ'dærɪtɪ] N solidaridad *f* • **out of ~ with the workers** por solidaridad con los obreros
CPD ▸ **solidarity strike** huelga *f* por solidaridad

solidification [sə,lɪdɪfɪ'keɪʃən] N solidificación *f*

solidify [sə'lɪdɪfaɪ] VI **1** (= *become solid*) solidificarse
2 (*fig*) (= *become strong, united etc*) unirse
VT solidificar

solidity [sə'lɪdɪtɪ] N solidez *f*

solidly ['sɒlɪdlɪ] ADV **1** (= *firmly*) con firmeza • **he placed his hands ~ on the desk** colocó sus manos con firmeza sobre la mesa • **it was ~ under Communist rule** estaba firmemente sometida a la ley comunista • **a ~ based theory** una teoría bien fundamentada, una teoría de una base sólida
2 (= *sturdily*) • **~ made** sólidamente construido, de construcción sólida • **~ built** *or* **constructed** de construcción sólida • **a solidly-built man** un hombre fornido *or* de constitución robusta
3 (= *without pause*) ininterrumpidamente, sin parar • **we drove/it rained ~ for two days** condujimos/llovió ininterrumpidamente durante dos días, condujimos/llovió dos días sin parar • **to work ~** trabajar sin descanso *or* sin parar
4 (= *unanimously*) unánimemente • **to vote ~ for sb** votar unánimemente por algn • **to be ~ behind sth/sb** apoyar algo/a algn unánimemente
5 (= *thoroughly*) • **a ~ reasoned argument** un argumento sólidamente razonado • **a ~ middle-class neighbourhood** un barrio totalmente de clase media

solid-state physics [,sɒlɪdsteɪt'fɪzɪks]

S

(NSING) física *f* del estado sólido
solidus ['sɒlɪdəs] (N) (*Typ*) barra *f*
soliloquize [sə'lɪləkwaɪz] (VI) decir un soliloquio, monologar
(VT) • **"perhaps," he ~d** —quizás —dijo para sí
soliloquy [sə'lɪləkwɪ] (N) soliloquio *m*
solipsism ['səʊlɪpsɪzəm] (N) solipsismo *m*
solipsist ['sɒlɪpsɪst] (N) solipsista *mf*
solipsistic [,sɒlɪp'sɪstɪk] (ADJ) solipsístico
solitaire [,sɒlɪ'tɛəʳ] (N) **1** (= *gem*) solitario *m*
2 (= *board game*) solitario *m*
3 (*esp US*) (*Cards*) solitario *m* • **to play ~** hacer un solitario
solitariness ['sɒlɪtərɪnɪs] (N) [*of task*] lo solitario; [*of life, person*] soledad *f*
solitary ['sɒlɪtərɪ] (ADJ) **1** (= *lonely, lone*) [*person, life, childhood*] solitario • **to take a ~ walk** dar un paseo solo, pasearse sin compañía • **to feel rather ~** sentirse solo, sentirse aislado
2 (= *secluded*) retirado
3 (= *sole*) solo, único • **not a ~ one** ni uno (solo) • **there has been one ~ case** ha habido un caso único • **there has not been one ~ case** no ha habido ni un solo caso
(N) **1** (= *person*) solitario/a *m/f*
2* = **solitary confinement**
(CPD) ▸ **solitary confinement** • **to be in ~ confinement** estar incomunicado, estar en pelota‡
solitude ['sɒlɪtju:d] (N) soledad *f*
solo ['səʊləʊ] (N) (PL: **solos**) **1** (*Mus*) solo *m* • **a tenor ~** un solo para tenor • **a guitar ~** un solo de guitarra
2 (*Cards*) solo *m*
(ADJ) • **~ flight** vuelo *m* a solas • **passage for ~ violin** pasaje *m* para violín solo • **~ trip round the world** vuelta *f* al mundo en solitario
(ADV) solo, a solas • **to fly ~** volar a solas • **to sing ~** cantar solo
soloist ['səʊləʊɪst] (N) solista *mf*
Solomon ['sɒləmən] (N) Salomón
(CPD) ▸ **Solomon Islands** islas *fpl* Salomón
solstice ['sɒlstɪs] (N) solsticio *m* • **summer ~** solsticio *m* de verano • **winter ~** solsticio *m* de invierno
solubility [,sɒljʊ'bɪlɪtɪ] (N) solubilidad *f*
soluble ['sɒljʊbl] (ADJ) soluble • **~ in water** soluble en agua
solution [sə'lu:ʃən] (N) **1** (= *answer*) solución *f* • **the ~ to a problem** la solución de *or* a un problema
2 (*Chem*) solución *f* • **in ~** en solución
solvable ['sɒlvəbl] (ADJ) soluble, que se puede resolver
solve [sɒlv] (VT) [+ *problem, puzzle*] resolver, solucionar; [+ *mystery, crime*] resolver, esclarecer • **to ~ a riddle** resolver una adivinanza, adivinar *or* resolver un acertijo • **that question remains to be ~d** aún queda por resolver esa cuestión
solvency ['sɒlvənsɪ] (N) (*Econ*) solvencia *f*
solvent ['sɒlvənt] (ADJ) (*Chem, Econ*) solvente
(N) (*Chem*) disolvente *m*
(CPD) ▸ **solvent abuse** abuso *m* de los disolventes ▸ **solvent liquid** líquido *m* disolvente
solver ['sɒlvəʳ] (N) solucionista *mf*
Som. (ABBR) (*Brit*) = **Somerset**
Somali [səʊ'mɑ:lɪ] (ADJ) somalí
(N) somalí *mf*
Somalia [səʊ'mɑ:lɪə] (N) Somalia *f*
Somalian [səʊ'mɑ:lɪən] (ADJ) somalí
(N) somalí *mf*
Somaliland [səʊ'mɑ:lɪlænd] (N) Somalia *f*
somatic [səʊ'mætɪk] (ADJ) somático
sombre, somber (*US*) ['sɒmbəʳ] (ADJ)
1 (= *sober*) sombrío • **a ~ prospect** una perspectiva sombría • **in ~ hues** en colores sombríos
2 (= *pessimistic*) pesimista • **he was ~ about our chances** se mostró pesimista acerca de nuestras posibilidades
3 (= *melancholy*) melancólico
sombrely, somberly (*US*) ['sɒmbəlɪ] (ADV)
1 (= *soberly*) sombríamente
2 (= *pessimistically*) con pesimismo, en tono pesimista
sombreness, somberness (*US*) ['sɒmbənɪs] (N) **1** (= *soberness*) lo sombrío
2 (= *pessimism*) pesimismo *m*
sombrero [sɒm'breərəʊ] (N) sombrero *m* mejicano

some [sʌm]

ADJECTIVE
PRONOUN
ADVERB

ADJECTIVE

1 (= *an amount of*)

When **some** *refers to something you can't count, it usually isn't translated:*

• **will you have ~ tea?** ¿quieres té? • **have ~ more cake** toma *or* sírvete más pastel • **you've got ~ money, haven't you?** tienes dinero, ¿no? • **let's have ~ breakfast** vamos a desayunar • **we gave them ~ food** les dimos comida *or* algo de comida • **there's ~ great acting in this film** hay algunas actuaciones muy buenas en esta película
2 (= *a little*) algo de, un poco de • **all I have left is ~ chocolate** solamente me queda algo de *or* un poco de chocolate • **she has ~ experience with children** tiene algo de *or* un poco de experiencia con niños • **the book was ~ help, but not much** el libro ayudó algo *or* un poco, pero no mucho, el libro fue de alguna ayuda, pero no mucha • **I did ~ writing this morning** he escrito un poco esta mañana • **she went out for ~ fresh air** salió para tomar un poco de aire fresco
3 (= *a number of*) unos • **~ boys were shouting at him** unos chicos le estaban gritando • **I have ~ wonderful memories** tengo unos recuerdos maravillosos • **would you like ~ sweets/grapes?** ¿quieres caramelos/uvas? • **we've got ~ biscuits, haven't we?** tenemos galletas, ¿no? • **you need ~ new trousers/glasses** necesitas unos pantalones nuevos/unas gafas nuevas • **surely she has ~ friends?** debe de tener por lo menos algún amigo
4 (= *certain*) • **~ people say that …** algunos dicen que …, algunas personas dicen que …, hay gente que dice que … • **~ people hate fish** algunas personas odian el pescado, hay gente que odia el pescado • **~ people just don't care** hay gente que no se preocupa en lo más mínimo • **~ people have all the luck!** ¡los hay que tienen suerte!, ¡algunos parece que nacen de pie!* • **in ~ ways he's right** en cierto modo *or* sentido, tiene razón • **I paid for mine, unlike ~ people I could mention** yo pagué el mío, no como ciertas personas *or* algunos a los que no quiero nombrar • **~ mushrooms are poisonous** ciertos tipos de setas son venenosas • **I like ~ jazz music** me gusta cierto tipo de jazz
5 (*indefinite*) algún (+ *masc noun*), alguna (+ *fem noun*) • **~ day** algún día • **~ day next week** algún día de la semana que viene • **~ idiot of a driver** algún imbécil de conductor • **I read it in ~ book (or other)** lo he leído en algún libro • **for ~ reason (or other)** por alguna razón, por una u otra razón • **there must be ~ solution** alguna solución tiene que haber • **~ man was asking for you** un hombre estuvo preguntando por ti • **this will give you ~ idea of …** esto te dará una idea de … • **let's make it ~ other time** hagámoslo otro día
6 (= *a considerable amount of*) bastante • **it took ~ courage to do that** hacer eso exigió bastante valor • **it's a matter of ~ importance** es un asunto de bastante importancia • **she is ~ few years younger than him** es bastantes años más joven que él • **I haven't seen him for ~ time** hace bastante (tiempo) que no lo veo; ▸ **length**
7 (= *a considerable number of*) • **I haven't seen him for ~ years** hace bastantes años que no lo veo • **I posted it ~ days ago (now)** lo mandé por correo hace (ya) varios días
8* (*emphatic*) **a** (*admiring*) • **that's ~ fish!** ¡eso sí que es un pez!, ¡eso es lo que se llama un pez!, ¡vaya pez! • **that's ~ woman** ¡qué mujer! • **it was ~ party** ¡vaya fiesta!, ¡menuda fiesta!
b (*iro*) • **"he says he's my friend" — "~ friend!"** —dice que es mi amigo —¡menudo amigo! • **you're ~ help, you are!** ¡vaya ayuda das!, ¡menuda ayuda eres tú! • **~ expert!** ¡valiente experto!
c (*in annoyance*) • **~ people!** ¡qué gente!

PRONOUN

1 (= *a certain amount, a little*) un poco • **have ~!** ¡toma un poco! • **could I have ~ of that cheese?** ¿me das un poco de ese queso? • **I only want ~ of it** solo quiero un poco • **thanks, I've got ~** gracias, ya tengo • **"I haven't got any paper" — "I'll give you ~"** —no tengo nada de papel —yo te doy • **it would cost twice that much and then ~*** costaría el doble de eso y algo más de propina*
2 (= *a part*) una parte • **I've read ~ of the book** he leído (una) parte del libro • **~ of what he said was true** parte de lo que dijo era cierto • **~ (of it) has been eaten** se han comido un poco *or* una parte • **give me ~!** ¡dame un poco!
3 (= *a number*) algunos/as *mpl/fpl* • **~ (of them) have been sold** algunos (de ellos) se han vendido • **~ of my friends came** vinieron algunos de mis amigos • **I don't want them all, but I'd like ~** no los quiero todos, pero sí unos pocos *or* cuantos, no los quiero todos, pero sí algunos • **would you like ~?** ¿quieres unos pocos *or* cuantos?, ¿quieres algunos?
4 (= *certain people*) algunos, algunas personas • **~ believe that …** algunos creen que …, algunas personas creen que …, hay gente que cree que …

ADVERB

1 (= *about*) • **~ 20 people** unas 20 personas, una veintena de personas • **~ £30** unas 30 libras
2 (*esp US*)* **a** (= *a lot*) mucho • **we laughed ~** nos reímos mucho • **Edinburgh to London in five hours, that's going ~!** de Edimburgo a Londres en cinco horas, ¡eso sí que es rapidez!
b (= *a little*) • **you'll feel better when you've slept ~** te sentirás mejor cuando hayas dormido un poco

somebody ['sʌmbədɪ] (PRON) alguien • **there's ~ coming** viene alguien • **~ knocked at the door** alguien llamó a la puerta • **~ speak to me!** ¡que alguien me diga algo! • **I need ~ to help me** necesito que alguien me ayude, necesito a alguien que me ayude • **~ Italian** un italiano • **~ from the audience**

S

alguien del público • **we need ~ strong for that** necesitamos a alguien fuerte para eso • **you must have seen ~!** ¡a alguien tienes que haber visto! • **let ~ else try** deja que otro *or* otra persona *or* alguien más lo intente • **~ or other** alguien • IDIOM: • **~ up there loves/hates me** tengo una buena/mala racha
(N) • **to be ~** ser un personaje, ser alguien • **he really thinks he's ~ doesn't he?** realmente se cree alguien, ¿verdad?

someday ['sʌmdeɪ] (ADV) algún día

somehow ['sʌmhaʊ] (ADV) **1** (*= by some means*) de algún modo, de alguna manera • **I'll do it ~** de algún modo *or* de alguna manera lo haré • **it has to be done ~ or other** de un modo u otro *or* de una manera u otra tiene que hacerse
2 (*= for some reason*) por alguna razón • **~ I didn't get on with her** por alguna razón *or* no sé porqué, no me llevaba bien con ella • **~ I don't think he believed me** no sé porqué, pero me parece que no me creyó • **~ or other I never liked him** por alguna razón u otra nunca me cayó bien • **it seems odd, ~** • **it seems ~ odd** no sé porqué pero me parece extraño

someone ['sʌmwʌn] (PRON) = **somebody**

someplace ['sʌmpleɪs] (ADV) (*US*) = **somewhere**

somersault ['sʌməsɔːlt] (N) (*by person*) voltereta *f*, salto *m* mortal; (*by car etc*) vuelco *m*, vuelta *f* de campana • **to turn** *or* **do a ~** dar una voltereta, dar un salto mortal
(VI) [*person*] dar una voltereta, dar un salto mortal; [*car etc*] dar una vuelta de campana

something ['sʌmθɪŋ] (PRON) **1** algo • **cook ~ nice** haz algo que esté rico • **wear ~ warm** ponte algo que abrigue • **there's ~ about him I don't like** hay algo que no me gusta de él • **let me ask you ~** déjame hacerte una pregunta, deja que te pregunte algo • **it's come to ~ when you get the sack for that** ¡a lo que hemos llegado! ¡que te echen por eso! • **that has ~ to do with accountancy** eso tiene que ver *or* está relacionado con la contabilidad • **he's got ~ to do with it** está metido *or* involucrado en eso • **~ else** otra cosa • **here's ~ for your trouble**† aquí tiene, por la molestia • **I think you may have ~ there** puede que tengas razón, puede que estés en lo cierto • **there's ~ in what you say** hay algo de verdad en lo que dices • **he's ~ in the City** trabaja de algo *or* de no sé qué en la City • **the music spoke to ~ in me** la música inspiró algo en mí • **~ of the kind** algo por el estilo • **do you want to make ~ of it?** ¿quieres hacer un problema de esto? • **there's ~ the matter** pasa algo • **it's not ~ I approve of** no es algo que yo apruebe • **you can't get ~ for nothing** las cosas no las regalan • **there's ~ odd here** aquí hay *or* pasa algo (raro) • **it's ~ of a problem** es de algún modo *or* en cierto modo un problema, en cierto sentido representa un problema • **he's ~ of a musician** tiene algo de músico, tiene cierto talento para la música • **he's getting ~ of a reputation around here** se está ganando cierta fama por aquí • **the play proved to be ~ of a letdown** la obra resultó ser un tanto decepcionante • **I hope to see ~ of you** espero que nos seguiremos viendo, nos estaremos viendo, espero (*LAm*) • **did you say ~?** ¿dijiste algo? • **well, that's ~** eso ya es algo • **will you have ~ to drink?** ¿quieres tomar algo? • **I need ~ to eat** necesito comer algo • **it gives her ~ to live for** le da un motivo para vivir
2* (*= something special or unusual*) • **he thinks he's ~*** se cree alguien • **their win was quite ~** su victoria fue extraordinaria • **that's really ~!** ¡eso sí que es fenomenal *or* estupendo!
3 (*in guesses, approximations*) • **he's called John ~** se llama John no sé qué, se llama John algo • **there were 30 ~** había 30 y algunos más • **the four ~ train** el tren de las cuatro y pico • **are you mad or ~?** ¿estás loco o qué?, ¿estás loco o algo así? • **her name is Camilla or ~** se llama Camilla o algo así, se llama algo así como Camilla, se llama Camilla o algo por el estilo • **he's got flu or ~** tiene gripe o algo parecido • **~ or other** algo, alguna cosa
(ADV) **1** (*= a little, somewhat*) **a** • **there were ~ like 80 people there** había algo así como 80 personas allí, había como unas 80 personas allí • **it's ~ like ten o'clock** son algo así como las diez, son las diez más o menos • **it cost £100, or ~ like that** costó 100 libras, o algo así • **he looks ~ like me** se parece algo *or* un poco a mí • **he talks ~ like his father** tiene algo de su padre cuando habla • **now that's ~ like a rose!** ¡eso es lo que se llama una rosa! • **now that's ~ like it!** ¡así es como debe ser!
b • **~ over 200** algo más de 200, un poco más de 200
2* • **they pull her leg ~ chronic** le toman el pelo una barbaridad*, le toman el pelo que es una cosa mala* • **it hurts ~ awful** duele un montón* • **she loves him ~ awful** le quiere una barbaridad*
(N) • **she has a certain ~** tiene un algo, tiene un no sé qué • **that certain ~ that makes all the difference** ese no sé qué que importa tanto • **it's just a little ~ I picked up in a sale** es una tontería que compré en las rebajas • **would you like a little ~ before dinner?** ¿quieres tomar *or* picar algo antes de la cena?

sometime ['sʌmtaɪm] (ADV) **1** (*in future*) algún día • **you must come and see us ~** tienes que venir a vernos algún día • **I'll finish it ~** lo voy a terminar un día de estos • **~ soon** un día de estos, antes de que pase mucho tiempo • **~ before tomorrow** antes de mañana • **~ next year** en algún momento el año que viene, el año que viene, no sé cuándo exactamente • **~ or other it will have to be done** tarde o temprano tendrá que hacerse
2 (*in past*) • **~ last month** (en algún momento) el mes pasado, el mes pasado, no sé cuándo exactamente • **the victim died ~ during the last 24 hours** la víctima murió durante las últimas 24 horas, no se sabe el momento preciso • **~ last century** en el siglo pasado, durante el siglo pasado
(ADJ) **1** (*= former*) ex ..., antiguo
2 (*US*) (*= occasional*) intermitente

sometimes ['sʌmtaɪmz] (ADV) a veces • **I ~ drink beer** a veces bebo cerveza • **~ I lose interest** hay veces que pierdo el interés

someway ['sʌmweɪ] (ADV) (*US*) de algún modo

somewhat ['sʌmwɒt] (ADV) algo, un tanto • **he was ~ puzzled** se quedó algo *or* un tanto perplejo • **we are ~ worried** estamos algo inquietos • **it was done ~ hastily** se hizo con demasiada prisa

somewhere ['sʌmweəʳ] (ADV) **1** (*location*) en alguna parte, en algún lugar, en algún sitio; (*direction*) a alguna parte, a algún lugar *or* sitio • **I left my keys ~** me he dejado las llaves en alguna parte *or* en algún sitio • **let's go ~ private** vamos a algún sitio *or* lugar donde podamos estar solos • **I'd like to go on holiday ~ exotic** me gustaría irme de vacaciones a algún sitio *or* lugar exótico • **he's ~ around** anda por ahí • **~ else** (*location*) en otra parte; (*direction*) a otra parte, a otro sitio • **the bar was full so we decided to go ~ else** el bar estaba lleno, así es que decidimos ir a otra parte *or* a otro sitio • **she lives ~ in Wales** vive en algún lugar *or* en alguna parte de Gales • **~ in the back of my mind** en algún lugar de mi mente • **~ near Huesca** cerca de Huesca, en algún lugar *or* sitio cerca de Huesca • **I left it ~ or other** lo dejé en alguna parte *or* en algún sitio, lo dejé por ahí • IDIOMS: • **~ along the line**: • **~ along the line they changed the title** en algún momento cambiaron el título • **to get ~*** (*= make progress*) hacer progresos, conseguir algo • **now we're getting ~** ahora sí que estamos haciendo progresos, ahora sí que estamos consiguiendo algo
2 (*= approximately*) • **~ around three o'clock** alrededor de las tres, a eso de las tres • **he's been given ~ between three and six months to live** le han dado entre tres y seis meses de vida • **he's ~ in his fifties** tiene cincuenta y tantos años • **he paid ~ in the region of £1000** pagó alrededor de 1000 libras
(PRON) algún lugar, algún sitio • **you'll have to find ~ else to live** tendrás que buscarte otro sitio *or* lugar para vivir • **we decided to hire ~ for the party** decidimos alquilar un lugar para la fiesta • **they broadcast from ~ in Europe** emiten desde algún lugar de Europa

Somme [sɒm] (N) Somme *m* • **the Battle of the ~** la batalla del Somme

somnambulism [sɒm'næmbjʊlɪzəm] (N) sonambulismo *m*

somnambulist [sɒm'næmbjʊlɪst] (N) sonámbulo/a *m/f*

somniferous [sɒm'nɪfərəs] (ADJ) somnífero

somnolence ['sɒmnələns] (N) somnolencia *f*

somnolent ['sɒmnələnt] (ADJ) (*= sleepy*) soñoliento

son [sʌn] (N) hijo *m* • **the youngest/eldest son** el hijo menor/mayor • **the Son of God** el Hijo de Dios • **the Son of Man** el Hijo del Hombre • **come here, son*** ven, hijo • **son of a bitch**** hijo *m* de puta**, hijo *m* de la chingada (*Mex***)

sonar ['səʊnɑːʳ] (N) sonar *m*

sonata [sə'nɑːtə] (N) sonata *f*

son et lumière [ˌsɔ̃eɪluːm'jeəʳ] (N) luz *f* y sonido *m*

song [sɒŋ] (N) **1** (*= ballad etc*) canción *f* • **to sing a ~** cantar una canción • **give us a ~!** ¡cántanos algo! • **festival of Spanish ~** festival *m* de la canción española • **to burst into ~** romper a cantar • IDIOMS: • **to make a ~ and dance about sth** hacer aspavientos por algo • **there's no need to make a ~ and dance about it** no es para tanto • **I got it for a ~** lo compré regalado • **to be on ~** (*Brit*) [*footballer etc*] estar entonado, estar inspirado • **to sing another ~** bajar el tono, desdecirse
2 [*of birds*] canto *m*
(CPD) ▸ **song and dance routine** número *m* de canción y baile ▸ **song book** cancionero *m* ▸ **song cycle** ciclo *m* de canciones ▸ **song hit** canción *f* de moda, canción *f* popular del momento ▸ **Song of Solomon, Song of Songs** Cantar *m* de los Cantares ▸ **song sheet** letra *f* de las canciones ▸ **song thrush** tordo *m* cantor, tordo *m* melodioso

songbird ['sɒŋbɜːd] (N) pájaro *m* cantor

songfest ['sɒŋfest] (N) festival *m* de canciones

songsheet ['sɒŋʃiːt] letra *f* de las canciones

songster ['sɒŋstəʳ] (N) (*= singer*) cantante *m*; (*= bird*) pájaro *m* cantor

songstress ['sɒŋstrɪs] (N) cantante *f*

songwriter ['sɒŋˌraɪtəʳ] (N) compositor(a)

m/f (de canciones)
sonic ['sɒnɪk] ADJ sónico
CPD ▸ **sonic boom** estampido *m* sónico
sonics ['sɒnɪks] NSING sónica *f*
son-in-law ['sʌnɪnlɔː] N (PL: **sons-in-law**) yerno *m*, hijo *m* político
sonnet ['sɒnɪt] N soneto *m*
sonny* ['sʌnɪ] N hijo *m*
son-of-a-gun‡ [ˌsʌnəvə'gʌn] N hijo *m* de su madre*
sonority [sə'nɒrɪtɪ] N sonoridad *f*
sonorous ['sɒnərəs] ADJ (*gen*) sonoro
sonorously ['sɒnərəslɪ] ADV sonoramente
sonorousness ['sɒnərəsnɪs] N sonoridad *f*
soon [suːn] ADV **1** (= *before long*) pronto, dentro de poco • **they'll be here ~** pronto llegarán, llegarán dentro de poco • **it will ~ be summer** pronto llegará el verano, falta poco para que llegue el verano • **~ afterwards** poco después • **come back ~** vuelve pronto
2 (= *early, quickly*) pronto, temprano • **how ~ can you be ready?** ¿cuánto tardas en prepararte? • **how ~ can you come?** ¿cuándo puedes venir? • **Friday is too ~** el viernes es muy pronto • **we got there too ~** llegamos demasiado pronto *or* temprano • **it's too ~ to tell** es demasiado pronto para saber • **we were none too ~** no llegamos antes de tiempo, llegamos justo • **all too ~ it was over** terminó demasiado pronto • **not a minute** *or* **moment too ~** ya era hora
3 • **as ~ as** en cuanto, tan pronto como • **I'll do it as ~ as I can** lo haré en cuanto pueda, lo haré tan pronto como pueda • **as ~ as you see her** en cuanto la veas, tan pronto como la veas • **as ~ as it was finished** en cuanto se terminó • **as ~ as possible** cuanto antes, lo antes posible, lo más pronto posible
4 (*expressing preference*) • **I would (just) as ~ not go** preferiría no ir • **I would (just) as ~ he didn't know** preferiría que él no lo supiera • **she'd marry him as ~ as not** se casaría con él y tan contenta; ▸ **sooner**

AS SOON AS

▸ *As with other time conjunctions,* **en cuanto** *and* **tan pronto como** *are used with the subjunctive if the action which follows hasn't happened yet or hadn't happened at the time of speaking:*

As soon as *or* **The moment we finish, I've got to write an editorial**
En cuanto terminemos *or* Tan pronto como terminemos, tengo que escribir un editorial

As soon as I know the dates, I'll let you know
En cuanto sepa *or* Tan pronto como sepa las fechas, te lo diré

▸ **En cuanto** *and* **tan pronto como** *are used with the indicative when the action in the time clause has already taken place:*

He left the podium as soon as *or* **the moment he received his prize**
Se bajó del podio en cuanto recibió *or* tan pronto como recibió el premio

▸ **En cuanto** *and* **tan pronto como** *are also used with the indicative when describing habitual actions:*

As soon as any faxes arrive, they're put in a special box
En cuanto llegan *or* Tan pronto como llegan los faxes, se guardan en una caja especial

For further uses and examples, see main entry.

sooner ['suːnəʳ] ADV **1** (*of time*) antes, más temprano • **can't you come a bit ~?** ¿no puedes venir un poco antes *or* un poco más temprano? • **we got there ~** nosotros llegamos antes • **the ~ we start the ~ we finish** cuanto antes empecemos, antes acabaremos • **the ~ the better** cuanto antes mejor • **~ or later** tarde o temprano • **no ~ had we left than they arrived** apenas nos habíamos marchado cuando llegaron
• IDIOM: • **no ~ said than done** dicho y hecho
2 (*of preference*) • **I'd** *or* **I would ~ not do it** preferiría no hacerlo • **I'd ~ die!*** ¡antes morir! • **~ you than me!*** ¡allá tú, yo no!
soot [sʊt] N hollín *m*
sooth†† [suːθ] N • **in ~** en realidad
soothe [suːð] VT [+ *person, baby*] calmar, tranquilizar; [+ *nerves*] calmar; [+ *mind*] relajar; [+ *anger*] aplacar; [+ *doubts*] acallar; [+ *pain, cough*] aliviar • **to ~ sb's fears** disipar los temores de algn, tranquilizar a algn • **to ~ sb's vanity** halagar la vanidad a algn
VI aliviar
soothing ['suːðɪŋ] ADJ [*ointment, lotion*] balsámico, calmante; [*massage, bath, music*] relajante; [*tone, words, voice, manner*] tranquilizador • **it has a ~ effect** [*massage, bath, music*] tiene un efecto relajante; [*ointment*] tiene un efecto balsámico; [*cough mixture, herbal tea*] tiene un efecto calmante; [*words, voice*] tiene un efecto tranquilizador
soothingly ['suːðɪŋlɪ] ADV [*speak, say, whisper, murmur*] en tono tranquilizador • **the old house was ~ familiar** la familiaridad de la vieja casa tenía un efecto relajante
soothsayer ['suːθˌseɪəʳ] N adivino/a *m/f*
soothsaying ['suːθˌseɪɪŋ] N adivinación *f*
sooty ['sʊtɪ] ADJ (COMPAR: **sootier**, SUPERL: **sootiest**) hollinoso; (*fig*) negro como el hollín
SOP N ABBR = **standard operating procedure**
sop [sɒp] N **1** (*fig*) (= *pacifier*) compensación *f* • **as a sop to his pride** para que su orgullo no quedara/quede herido
2 sops (= *food*) sopa *fsing*
3* (= *person*) bobo/a *m/f*
▸ **sop up** VT + ADV absorber
Sophia [səʊ'faɪə] N Sofía
sophism ['sɒfɪzəm] N sofisma *m*
sophist ['sɒfɪst] N sofista *mf*
sophistical [sə'fɪstɪkəl] ADJ sofístico
sophisticate [sə'fɪstɪkeɪt] N persona *f* sofisticada
sophisticated [sə'fɪstɪkeɪtɪd] ADJ
1 (= *refined*) [*person, lifestyle, tastes, clothes*] sofisticado
2 (= *complex*) [*idea*] sofisticado; [*equipment*] sofisticado, complejo, altamente desarrollado; [*technique*] sofisticado, muy elaborado, complejo; [*play, film, book*] muy elaborado, complejo • **a ~ approach to planning** un modo sofisticado de enfocar la planificación
sophistication [səˌfɪstɪ'keɪʃən] N (= *refinement*) sofisticación *f*; (= *complexity*) complejidad *f*
sophistry ['sɒfɪstrɪ] N sofistería *f* • **a ~** un sofisma
Sophocles ['sɒfəkliːz] N Sófocles
sophomore ['sɒfəmɔːʳ] N (*US*) estudiante *mf* de segundo año; ▸ **GRADE**
soporific [ˌsɒpə'rɪfɪk] ADJ soporífero
sopping ['sɒpɪŋ] ADJ • **it's ~ (wet)** está empapado • **he was ~ wet** estaba hecho una sopa, estaba calado *or* empapado hasta los huesos
soppy* ['sɒpɪ] ADJ (COMPAR: **soppier**, SUPERL: **soppiest**) **1** (= *mushy*) sentimentaloide
2 (= *foolish*) bobo, tonto

soprano [sə'prɑːnəʊ] N (PL: **sopranos** *or* **soprani** [sə'prɑːniː]) (*Mus*) (*female*) soprano *f*; (*male*) tiple *m*; (= *voice, part*) soprano *m*
ADJ [*part*] de soprano, para soprano; [*voice*] de soprano
ADV • **to sing ~** cantar soprano
sorb [sɔːb] N (= *tree*) serbal *m*; (= *fruit*) serba *f*
sorbet ['sɔːbeɪ] N sorbete *m* • **lemon ~** sorbete *m* de limón
sorbic acid [ˌsɔːbɪk'æsɪd] N ácido *m* sórbico
sorbitol ['sɔːbɪtɒl] N sorbitol *m*
sorcerer ['sɔːsərəʳ] N hechicero *m*, brujo *m* • **the ~'s apprentice** el aprendiz de brujo
sorceress ['sɔːsəres] N hechicera *f*, bruja *f*
sorcery ['sɔːsərɪ] N hechicería *f*, brujería *f*
sordid ['sɔːdɪd] ADJ [*place, room etc*] miserable, sórdido; [*deal, motive etc*] mezquino • **it's a pretty ~ business** es un asunto de lo más desagradable
sordidly ['sɔːdɪdlɪ] ADV sórdidamente
sordidness ['sɔːdɪdnɪs] N sordidez *f*, lo miserable
sore [sɔːʳ] ADJ (COMPAR: **sorer**, SUPERL: **sorest**) **1** (*Med*) (= *aching*) [*part of body*] dolorido; (= *painful*) [*cut, graze*] doloroso • **it's ~** me duele • **my eyes are ~** • **I have ~ eyes** me duelen los ojos • **I'm ~ all over** me duele todo el cuerpo • **I have a ~ throat** me duele la garganta • IDIOM: • **to be ~ at heart** (*liter*): • **he was ~ at heart** le dolía el corazón
2 (= *angry, upset*) • **to be ~ about sth** estar resentido por algo • **what are you so ~ about?** ¿por qué estás tan resentido? • **to be ~ at sb** estar enfadado *or* (*LAm*) enojado con algn • **don't get ~!*** ¡no te vayas a ofender!, ¡no te enojes! (*LAm*) • **it's a ~ point** es un tema delicado *or* espinoso • **to be ~ with sb** estar enfadado *or* (*LAm*) enojado con algn
3 (*liter*) (= *very great*) • **there is a ~ need of ...** hay gran necesidad de ... • **it was a ~ temptation** era una fuerte tentación
N (*Med*) llaga *f*, úlcera *f* • IDIOM: • **to open up old ~s** abrir viejas heridas
sorehead* ['sɔːhed] N (*US*) persona *f* resentida
sorely ['sɔːlɪ] ADV (= *very*) muy; (= *much*) mucho; (= *deeply*) profundamente; (= *seriously*) seriamente • **I am ~ tempted** estoy muy tentado • **I am ~ tempted to dismiss him** casi estoy por despedirlo • **he has been ~ tried** ha tenido que aguantar muchísimo
soreness ['sɔːnɪs] N (*Med*) dolor *m*
sorghum ['sɔːgəm] N sorgo *m*
sorority [sə'rɒrɪtɪ] N (*US*) (*Univ*) hermandad *f* de mujeres

SORORITY/FRATERNITY

Muchas universidades estadounidenses poseen dentro del campus hermandades conocidas como **fraternities** o **frats** (de hombres) o **sororities** (de mujeres). Estas hermandades, a las que solo se puede ingresar mediante invitación, organizan fiestas, recogen fondos con fines benéficos e intentan hacer que su hermandad sobresalga entre las demás. Suelen tener nombres compuestos de letras del alfabeto griego, como por ejemplo **Kappa Kappa Gamma**. Existe división de opiniones en cuanto a los beneficios o ventajas de estas hermandades; para los miembros es una buena manera de hacer amigos, pero la mayoría de los estudiantes piensan que son elitistas y discriminatorias. Durante las ceremonias secretas de iniciación, que incluyen varias pruebas físicas y novatadas que se denominan **hazing**, se ha producido la muerte de varios estudiantes, lo cual ha aumentado la polémica.

S

sorrel[1] ['sɒrəl] N (Bot) acedera f

sorrel[2] ['sɒrəl] ADJ alazán
N (= horse) alazán m, caballo m alazán

sorrow ['sɒrəʊ] N (= grieving) pena f, pesar m, dolor m • to my ~ con or para gran pesar mío • her ~ at the death of her son su pena por la muerte de su hijo • more in ~ than in anger con más pesar que enojo • this was a great ~ to me esto me causó mucha pena • IDIOM: • to drown one's ~s ahogar las penas (en alcohol)
VI apenarse, afligirse (at, for, over de)

sorrowful ['sɒrəfʊl] ADJ afligido, triste, apenado

sorrowfully ['sɒrəflɪ] ADV con pena, tristemente

sorrowing ['sɒrəʊɪŋ] ADJ afligido

sorry ['sɒrɪ] ADJ (COMPAR: **sorrier**, SUPERL: **sorriest**) 1 (= apologetic) • I'm so ~! ¡lo siento mucho!, ¡perdón! • sorry! ¡perdón!, ¡perdone!, ¡disculpe! (esp LAm) • ~ I'm late! ¡siento llegar tarde! • I'm ~ to bother you but ... siento or (frm) lamento molestarle, pero ... • to be ~ about/for sth sentir algo, lamentar algo (frm) • I'm ~ about what I said last night siento lo que dije anoche • we are ~ for any inconvenience caused lamentamos cualquier molestia ocasionada • to say ~ (to sb) (for sth) pedir perdón or (esp LAm) disculpas (a algn) (por algo) • go and say ~! ¡anda ve y pide perdón or disculpas! • I've said I'm ~, what more do you want? ya he dicho que lo siento, ¿qué más quieres?
2 (= repentant) arrepentido • he wasn't in the least bit ~ no estaba arrepentido en lo más mínimo • you'll be ~ for this! ¡me las pagarás!, ¡te arrepentirás (de esto)!
3 (= regretful, sad) • I'm ~, she's busy at the moment lo siento, en este momento está ocupada • I can't say I'm ~ no puedo decir que lo sienta • to be ~ about sth/sb: • I'm ~ about your mother/about what happened siento or (frm) lamento lo de tu madre/lo sucedido • I can't tell you how ~ I am no te puedes hacer una idea de cuánto lo siento • to be ~ that ... sentir or (frm) lamentar que (+ subjun) • I'm ~ he didn't get the job siento que no consiguiera el trabajo • I'm ~ to hear that you're leaving me da pena saber que te vas • we are ~ to have to tell you that ... lamentamos tener que decirle que ... • I was ~ to hear of your accident siento or lamento lo de tu accidente • it was a failure, I'm ~ to say me duele reconocerlo, pero fue un fracaso • no one seemed very ~ to see him go nadie parecía sentir or lamentar mucho que se fuera
4 (= pitying) • to be or feel ~ for sb: • I'm ~ for him lo compadezco • I feel ~ for the child el niño me da lástima or pena • it's no good feeling ~ for yourself no sirve de mucho lamentarte de tu suerte • to look ~ for o.s. tener un aspecto triste
5 (= pitiful) • the garden was a ~ sight el jardín estaba en un estado lamentable, el jardín estaba hecho una pena* • to be in a ~ state encontrarse en un estado lamentable • he poured out his ~ tale to his mother le contó su triste historia a su madre
6 (when sb has not heard) • ~, I didn't catch what you said perdón, no entendí lo que dijiste
7 (when correcting o.s.) • it's the third, sorry, the fourth on the left es la tercera, perdón, la cuarta a la izquierda
8 (when disagreeing) • I'm ~, I can't agree with you lo siento or perdona, pero no puedo darte la razón

sort [sɔ:t] N 1 (= kind) clase f, tipo m • a new ~ of car una nueva clase or un nuevo tipo de coche • the ~ you gave me last time de la misma clase or del mismo tipo que me dio la última vez • books of all ~s • all ~s of books libros de toda clase or de todo tipo, toda clase or todo tipo de libros • I know his/her ~ conozco el paño, conozco a esa clase de gente • he's a painter of a ~ or of ~s se puede decir que es pintor • it's tea of a ~ es té, pero de bastante mala calidad • something of the ~ algo por el estilo • nothing of the ~! ¡nada de eso! • I shall do nothing of the ~ no lo haré bajo ningún concepto, ni se me ocurriría hacerlo • but not that ~ pero no de ese tipo, pero no así • he's the ~ who will cheat you es de esa clase or de ese tipo de personas que te engañará, es de esos que or de los que te engañan • what ~ do you want? (= make) ¿qué marca quieres?; (= type) ¿de qué tipo lo quieres? • PROVERB: • it takes all ~s (to make a world) de todo hay en la viña del Señor
2 • ~ of a (= type of) • it's a ~ of dance es una especie de baile • he's a ~ of agent es algo así como un agente • he's not the ~ of man to say that no es de los que dicen eso • an odd ~ of novel una novela rara, un tipo extraño de novela • he's some ~ of painter es pintor de algún tipo • that's the ~ of person I am así soy yo • he's not that ~ of person no es capaz de hacer eso, no es ese tipo de persona • I'm not that ~ of girl yo no soy de esas • that's the ~ of thing I need eso es lo que me hace falta • that's just the ~ of thing I mean eso es precisamente lo que quiero decir • and all that ~ of thing y otras cosas por el estilo • this ~ of house una casa de este estilo • what ~ of car? ¿qué tipo de coche? • what ~ of man is he? ¿qué clase de hombre es?
b* • it's ~ of awkward es bastante or (LAm) medio difícil • it's ~ of blue es más bien azul • I'm ~ of lost estoy como perdido • it's ~ of finished está más o menos terminado • I have a ~ of idea that ... tengo cierta idea de que ... • I ~ of thought that ... quedé con la idea de que ... • I ~ of feel that ... en cierto modo creo que ... • it ~ of made me laugh no sé por qué pero me hizo reír • "aren't you pleased?" — "~ of" —¿no te alegras? —en cierto sentido
3 (= person) • he's a good ~ es buena persona or (esp LAm) buena gente • he's an odd ~ es un tipo raro • your ~ never did any good las personas como usted nunca hicieron nada bueno
4 • IDIOM: • to be out of ~s (= unwell) estar indispuesto, no estar del todo bien; (= in bad mood) estar de mal humor, estar de malas
5 (Comput) ordenación f
VT 1 (= classify, arrange) clasificar • to ~ the good apples from the bad ones separar las manzanas malas de las buenas; ▹ sheep
2 (Comput) ordenar
3* (= resolve, settle) arreglar • we've got it ~ed now ya se arregló
CPD ▸ sort code [of bank] número m de agencia

▸ **sort out** VT + ADV 1 (= organize) ordenar, organizar • ~ out all your books ordena todos tus libros • to ~ out the bad ones separar or quitar los malos; ▹ sheep
2 (= resolve) [+ problem, situation etc] arreglar, solucionar • they've ~ed out their problems han arreglado or solucionado sus problemas
3 • to ~ sb out* ajustar cuentas con algn • I'll come down there and ~ you out!* ¡si bajo, te pego una paliza!
4 (= explain) • to ~ sth out for sb explicar or aclarar algo a algn • can you ~ this out for me? ¿puede explicarme or aclararme esto?

▸ **sort through** VI + ADV revisar

sorta* ['sɔ:tə] ADV = sort of ▹ sort

sorter ['sɔ:təʳ] N clasificador(a) m/f

sortie ['sɔ:tɪ] N (Aer, Mil) salida f • to make a ~ hacer una salida • a ~ into town una escapada a la ciudad

sorting ['sɔ:tɪŋ] N clasificación f; (Comput) ordenación f
CPD ▸ sorting office (Post) sala f de batalla

sort-out* ['sɔ:taʊt] N • to have a sort-out (= clean-up) hacer limpieza; (= tidy-up) ordenar las cosas

SOS N (= signal) SOS m; (fig) llamada f de socorro

so-so ['səʊ'səʊ] ADV regular, así así • "how are you feeling?" — "so-so" —¿cómo te encuentras? —regular or —así así

sot [sɒt] N borrachín/ina* m/f

sottish ['sɒtɪʃ] ADJ embrutecido (por el alcohol)

sotto voce ['sɒtəʊ'vəʊtʃɪ] ADV en voz baja

soubriquet ['səʊbrɪkeɪ] N ▹ sobriquet

Soudan [su'dɑ:n] = Sudan

soufflé ['su:fleɪ] N soufflé m, suflé m
CPD ▸ soufflé dish fuente f de soufflé

sough [saʊ] N susurro m
VI susurrar

sought [sɔ:t] PT, PP of seek

sought-after ['sɔ:t,ɑ:ftəʳ] ADJ [person] solicitado; [object] codiciado • this much sought-after title este codiciado título

souk [su:k] N zoco m

soul [səʊl] N 1 (Rel) alma f • with all one's ~ con todo el alma • All Souls' Day (el día de) Todos los Santos • (God) bless my ~!† ¡que Dios me ampare! • God rest his ~ que Dios lo acoja en su seno • upon my ~!† ¡cielo santo! • IDIOMS: • like a lost ~ como alma en pena • to sell one's ~ to the devil vender el alma al diablo; ▹ possess
2 (= feeling) • you have no ~! ¡no tienes sentimientos! • the music lacks ~ a la música le falta sentimiento • these places have no ~ estos sitios no tienen vida
3 (= essence) [of people, nation] espíritu m; ▹ bare, body, heart, life
4 (fig) (= person) alma f • 3,000 ~s 3.000 almas • there was not a (living) ~ in sight no se veía (ni) un alma • a few brave ~s ventured out unos cuantos valientes se aventuraron a salir • the poor ~ had nowhere to sleep el pobre no tenía dónde dormir • poor ~! ¡pobrecito! • I won't tell a ~ no se lo diré a nadie
5 (= embodiment) • to be the ~ of discretion ser la discreción personificada or en persona; ▹ brevity
6 (Mus) (also soul music) música f soul
CPD ▸ soul food cocina negra del Sur de EE.UU. ▸ soul music música f soul ▸ soul singer cantante mf de soul

soul-destroying ['səʊldɪs'trɔɪɪŋ] ADJ (fig) de lo más aburrido

soulful ['səʊlfʊl] ADJ [gaze, look, eyes] conmovedor; [music] lleno de sentimiento

soulfully ['səʊlfəlɪ] ADV [gaze, look] de forma conmovedora

soulless ['səʊllɪs] ADJ [person] sin alma, desalmado; [work] mecánico, monótono

soulmate ['səʊlmeɪt] N compañero/a m/f del alma, alma f gemela

soul-searching ['səʊl,sɜ:tʃɪŋ] N • after a lot of soul-searching después de revolverlo muchas veces

soul-stirring ['səʊl,stɜ:rɪŋ] ADJ conmovedor, emocionante, inspirador

sound[1] [saʊnd] N 1 (Phys) sonido m • the speed of ~ la velocidad del sonido
2 (= noise) ruido m • the ~ of footsteps el ruido de pasos • the ~ of breaking glass el ruido de cristales que se rompen/rompían

• **consonant ~s** consonantes *fpl*, sonidos *mpl* consonánticos • **I didn't hear a ~** no oí ni un ruido • **don't make a ~!** ¡no hagas el menor ruido! • **not a ~ was to be heard** no se oía *or* (*esp LAm*) sentía ruido alguno • **to the ~ of the national anthem** al son del himno nacional • **they were within ~ of the camp** el campamento estaba al alcance del oído • **he opened the door without a ~** abrió la puerta sin hacer nada de ruido
3 (= *volume*) volumen *m* • **can I turn the ~ down?** ¿puedo bajar el volumen?
4 (= *musical style*) • **the Glenn Miller ~** la música de Glenn Miller
5 (*fig*) (= *impression*) • **by the ~ of it** según parece • **I don't like the ~ of it** (*film etc*) por lo que he oído, no me gusta nada; (*situation*) me preocupa, me da mala espina
(VT) **1** [+ *horn, trumpet*] tocar, hacer sonar; [+ *bell*] tocar; [+ *alarm, warning*] dar; [+ *praises*] cantar, entonar • **to ~ the charge** (*Mil*) tocar la carga • **~ your horn!** (*Aut*) ¡toca el claxon! • **to ~ a note of warning** (*fig*) dar la señal de alarma • **to ~ the retreat** (*Mil*) tocar la retirada
2 (= *pronounce*) pronunciar • **~ your "r"s more** pronuncia más claro la "r" • **to ~ the "d" in "hablado"** pronunciar la "d" en "hablado"
(VI) **1** (= *emit sound*) sonar • **the bell ~ed** sonó el timbre • **a cannon ~ed a long way off** se oyó un cañón a lo lejos, sonó *or* resonó un cañón a lo lejos
2 (= *appear to be*) **a** (*from aural clues*) sonar • **it ~s hollow** suena a hueco • **he ~s Italian to me** por la voz, diría que es italiano • **he ~ed angry** parecía enfadado • **it ~s like French** suena a francés • **that ~s like them arriving now** parece que llegan ahora
b (*from available information*) sonar, parecer • **it ~s very odd** suena muy raro • **that ~s interesting** eso suena interesante • **it ~s as if** *or* **as though she won't be coming** parece que no va a venir • **how does it ~ to you?** ¿qué te parece? • **that ~s like a good idea** eso parece buena idea • **she ~s like a nice girl** parece una chica simpática
(CPD) ▸ **sound archive** archivo *m* de sonido ▸ **sound barrier** barrera *f* del sonido ▸ **sound bite** cita *f* jugosa ▸ **sound card** (*Comput*) tarjeta *f* de sonido ▸ **sound effect** efecto *m* sonoro ▸ **sound engineer** ingeniero/a *m/f* de sonido ▸ **sound file** (*Comput*) fichero *m* de sonido ▸ **sound law** ley *f* fonética ▸ **sound library** fonoteca *f* ▸ **sound mixer** (= *engineer*) ingeniero/a *m/f* de sonido ▸ **sound recording** grabación *f* sonora ▸ **sound recordist** (*TV*) registrador(a) *m/f* de sonido ▸ **sound shift** cambio *m* de pronunciación ▸ **sound system** (*Ling*) sistema *m* fonológico; (= *hi-fi*) cadena *f* de sonido ▸ **sound truck** (*US*) furgón *m* publicitario ▸ **sound wave** (*Phys*) onda *f* sonora
▸ **sound off*** (VI + ADV) discursear* (**about** sobre)

sound[2] [saʊnd] (VT) **1** (*Naut*) sondar
2 (*Med*) [+ *chest*] auscultar; [+ *cavity, passage*] sondar • **to ~ sb's chest** auscultar el pecho a algn
▸ **sound out** (VT + ADV) [+ *intentions, person*] sondear, tantear • **to ~ sb out about sth** sondear *or* tantear a algn sobre algo, tratar de averiguar lo que piensa algn sobre algo

sound[3] [saʊnd] (ADJ) (COMPAR: **sounder**, SUPERL: **soundest**) **1** (= *in good condition*) sano; [*constitution*] robusto; [*structure*] sólido, firme • **to be ~ in mind and body** ser sano de cuerpo y de espíritu • **in ~ condition** en buenas condiciones • **to be of ~ mind** estar en su cabal juicio • IDIOM: • **to be as ~ as a bell** [*person*] gozar de perfecta salud; [*thing*] estar en perfectas condiciones; ▹ **safe**
2 (= *well-founded*) [*argument*] bien fundado, sólido; [*ideas, opinions*] válido, razonable; [*investment*] bueno, seguro; [*training*] sólido; [*decision, choice*] acertado • **his reasoning is perfectly ~** su argumentación es perfectamente válida • **she gave me some ~ advice** me dio un buen consejo • **he's ~ enough on the theory** tiene una preparación sólida en cuanto a la teoría
3 (= *dependable*) [*person*] formal, digno de confianza • **he's a very ~ man** es un hombre formal *or* digno de confianza • **he's a ~ worker** es buen trabajador, trabaja con seriedad
4 (= *thorough*) • **to give sb a ~ beating** dar a algn una buena paliza
5 (= *deep, untroubled*) [*sleep*] profundo
(ADV) • **to be ~ asleep** estar profundamente dormido • **I shall sleep the ~er for it** por eso dormiré más tranquilamente

sound[4] [saʊnd] (N) (*Geog*) estrecho *m*, brazo *m* de mar

soundboard ['saʊndbɔːd] (N) **1** (*Comput*) consola *f* de sonido
2 = **sounding board**

soundbox ['saʊndbɒks] (N) (*Mus*) caja *f* de resonancia

sounding[1] ['saʊndɪŋ] (N) **1** (*Naut*) sondeo *m*
2 soundings (*for oil etc*) sondeos *mpl* • **to take ~s** (*lit*) hacer sondeos; (*fig*) sondear la opinión
3 (*Med*) sondeo *m*
(CPD) ▸ **sounding board** (*lit, fig*) caja *f* de resonancia

sounding[2] ['saʊndɪŋ] (N) [*of trumpet, bell etc*] sonido *m*, son *m* • **the ~ of the retreat/the alarm** el toque de retirada/de generala

soundless ['saʊndlɪs] (ADJ) silencioso, mudo

soundlessly ['saʊndlɪslɪ] (ADV) silenciosamente, sin ruido

soundly ['saʊndlɪ] (ADV) [*built*] sólidamente; [*argued*] lógicamente; [*invested*] con cordura, con prudencia • **to beat sb ~** dar a algn una buena paliza • **to sleep ~** dormir profundamente

soundness ['saʊndnɪs] (N) (= *good condition*) [*of structure*] firmeza *f*, solidez *f*; (= *validity*) [*of ideas, opinions*] validez *f*; [*of argument*] solidez *f*; (= *prudence*) [*of investment*] prudencia *f*; (= *solvency*) [*of business*] solvencia *f*

soundproof ['saʊndpruːf] (ADJ) insonorizado, a prueba de ruidos
(VT) insonorizar

soundproofing ['saʊndpruːfɪŋ] (N) insonorización *f*

soundscape ['saʊndskeɪp] (N) paisaje *m* sonoro

soundtrack ['saʊndtræk] (N) banda *f* sonora

soup [suːp] (N) (*thin*) caldo *m*, consomé *m*; (*thick*) sopa *f* • **vegetable ~** sopa *f* de verduras • IDIOM: • **to be in the ~*** estar en apuros
(CPD) ▸ **soup bowl** plato *m* sopero ▸ **soup course** plato *m* de cuchara ▸ **soup kitchen** comedor *m* popular, olla *f* común ▸ **soup plate** plato *m* sopero ▸ **soup spoon** cuchara *f* sopera ▸ **soup tureen** sopera *f*

soupçon ['suːpsɔ̃] (N) (*Culin*) pizca *f* • **with a ~ of ginger** con una pizca de jengibre • **with a ~ of cream** con un chorrito de nata *or* (*LAm*) crema

souped-up* ['suːpt,ʌp] (ADJ) [*car*] trucado

soupy ['suːpɪ] (ADJ) [*liquid*] espeso, turbio; [*atmosphere*] pesado, espeso

sour ['saʊəʳ] (ADJ) (COMPAR: **sourer**, SUPERL: **sourest**) **1** (= *not sweet*) [*fruit, flavour*] agrio, ácido; [*smell*] acre • **whisky ~** whisky *m* sour • IDIOM: • **~ grapes** envidia *f* • **that's just ~ grapes** eso es simplemente envidia • **it was clearly ~ grapes on his part** estaba claro que tenía envidia
2 (*Agr*) [*soil*] ácido, yermo
3 (= *bad*) [*milk*] cortado, agrio; [*wine*] agrio • **to go** *or* **turn ~** [*milk*] cortarse; [*wine*] agriarse; [*plan*] venirse abajo • **their marriage turned ~** su matrimonio empezó a deteriorarse • **their dream of equality for all turned ~** su sueño de igualdad para todos se tornó amargo • **does this milk taste ~ to you?** ¿te sabe esta leche a cortada?, ¿te sabe esta leche agria?
4 (*fig*) [*person*] avinagrado; [*expression, look, mood, comment*] avinagrado, agrio
(VT) **1** (*lit*) agriar
2 (*fig*) [+ *person*] agriar, amargar; [+ *relationship*] deteriorar; [+ *atmosphere*] agriar; [+ *outlook, success*] empañar
(VI) **1** (*lit*) [*wine*] agriarse, volverse agrio; [*milk*] agriarse, cortarse
2 (*fig*) [*mood, attitude*] avinagrarse, agriarse; [*relationship*] deteriorarse • **the atmosphere in the office had ~ed** el ambiente en la oficina se había vuelto rancio • **his financial partners ~ed on the deal** (*US*) sus socios financieros se volvieron en contra del acuerdo
(CPD) ▸ **sour cream** nata *f* or (*LAm*) crema *f* agria

source [sɔːs] (N) **1** (= *origin*) fuente *f*; [*of gossip etc*] procedencia *f* • **coal was their only ~ of heat** el carbón era su única fuente de calor • **we have other ~s of supply** tenemos otras fuentes de suministro • **I have it from a reliable ~ that …** sé de fuente fidedigna que … • **what is the ~ of this information?** ¿de dónde proceden estos informes? • **his antics were a ~ of much amusement** sus gracias fueron motivo de diversión • **at ~** en su origen
2 [*of river*] nacimiento *m*
(CPD) ▸ **source file** archivo *m* fuente ▸ **source language** (*Ling*) lengua *f* de partida; (*Comput*) lenguaje *m* origen ▸ **source materials** materiales *mpl* de referencia ▸ **source program** programa *m* fuente

sourdine [sʊə'diːn] (N) sordina *f*

sourdough bread [,saʊədəʊ'bred] (N) (*esp US*) pan *m* de masa fermentada

sour-faced ['saʊəfeɪst] (ADJ) con cara de pocos amigos, con cara avinagrada

sourish ['saʊərɪʃ] (ADJ) agrete

sourly ['saʊəlɪ] (ADV) **1** (= *disagreeably*) [*say, complain, look*] agriamente; [*think*] con amargura
2 • **to smell ~ (of sth)** despedir un olor agrio (a algo)

sourness ['saʊənɪs] (N) **1** (*lit*) [*of fruit, wine, soil*] acidez *f*; [*of milk*] sabor *m* agrio, sabor *m* a cortado
2 (*fig*) [*of person, expression, mood, tone*] amargura *f*

sourpuss* ['saʊəpʊs] (N) amargado/a *m/f*

sousaphone ['suːzə,fəʊn] (N) sousáfono *m*

souse [saʊs] (VT) **1** (*Culin*) (= *pickle*) escabechar, adobar (*LAm*)
2 (= *plunge*) zambullir; (= *soak*) mojar • **he ~d himself with water** se empapó de agua
3 • IDIOM: • **to be ~d‡** estar mamado*, estar tomado (*LAm*) • **to get ~d** coger una trompa (*Sp**), agarrarse una borrachera (*LAm*)
(N) (*US‡*) borracho/a *m/f*

soutane [suː'tɑːn] (N) sotana *f*

south [saʊθ] (N) (= *direction*) sur *m*; (= *region*) sur *m*, mediodía *m* • **the South of France** el sur de Francia, el mediodía francés, la Francia meridional • **in the ~ of England** al sur *or* en el sur de Inglaterra • **to live in the ~** vivir en el sur • **to the ~ of** al sur de • **the**

wind is from the *or* **in the ~** el viento sopla *or* viene del sur • **in the ~ of the country** al sur *or* en el sur del país
(ADJ) del sur, sureño, meridional
(ADV) (= *southward*) hacia el sur; (= *in the south*) al sur, en el sur • **to travel ~** viajar hacia el sur • **this house faces ~** esta casa mira al sur *or* tiene vista hacia el sur • **my window faces ~** mi ventana da al sur • **~ of the border** al sur de la frontera • **it's ~ of London** está al sur de Londres • **to sail due ~** (*Naut*) ir proa al sur, navegar rumbo al sur
(CPD) ▸ **South Africa** Suráfrica *f*, Sudáfrica *f*; ▹ **South African** ▸ **South America** América *f* del Sur, Sudamérica *f*; ▹ **South American** ▸ **South Atlantic** Atlántico *m* Sur ▸ **South Australia** Australia *f* del Sur ▸ **South Carolina** Carolina *f* del Sur ▸ **South Dakota** Dakota *f* del Sur ▸ **South Georgia** Georgia *f* del Sur ▸ **South Korea** Corea *f* del Sur; ▹ **South Korean** ▸ **South Pacific** Pacífico *m* Sur ▸ **the South Pole** el Polo sur ▸ **the South Sea Islands** las islas de los mares del Sur ▸ **the South Seas** los mares del Sur, el mar austral ▸ **South Vietnam** Vietnam *m* del Sur; ▹ **South Vietnamese** ▸ **South Wales** Gales *m* del Sur ▸ **South West Africa** África *f* del Suroeste

South African [saʊθ'æfrɪkən] (ADJ) sudafricano
(N) sudafricano/a *m/f*

South American [,saʊθə'merɪkən] (ADJ) sudamericano
(N) sudamericano/a *m/f*

southbound ['saʊθbaʊnd] (ADJ) [*traffic*] en dirección sur; [*carriageway*] de dirección sur, en dirección sur

southeast [saʊθ'i:st] (N) sudeste *m*, sureste *m*
(ADJ) [*point, direction*] sudeste, sureste; [*wind*] del sudeste, del sureste
(ADV) (= *southeastward*) hacia el sudeste *or* sureste; (= *in the southeast*) al sudeste *or* sureste, en el sudeste *or* sureste
(CPD) ▸ **Southeast Asia** el sudeste de Asia, el sudeste asiático

southeasterly [saʊθ'i:stəlɪ] (ADJ) [*wind*] del sudeste, del sureste • **in a ~ direction** hacia el sudeste *or* sureste, rumbo al sudeste *or* sureste, en dirección sudeste *or* sureste
(N) viento *m* del sudeste *or* sureste

southeastern [saʊθ'i:stən] (ADJ) sudeste, sureste • **the ~ part of the island** la parte sudeste *or* sureste de la isla • **in ~ Spain** al sudeste *or* sureste de España • **the ~ coast** la costa sudoriental *or* suroriental

southeastward [saʊθ'i:stwəd] (ADJ) [*movement, migration*] hacia el sudeste *or* sureste, en dirección sudeste *or* sureste
(ADV) hacia el sudeste *or* sureste, en dirección sudeste *or* sureste

southeastwards [saʊθ'i:stwədz] (ADV) (*esp Brit*) = **southeastward**

southerly ['sʌðəlɪ] (ADJ) [*wind*] del sur • **we were headed in a ~ direction** íbamos hacia el sur *or* rumbo al sur *or* en dirección sur • **the most ~ point in Europe** el punto más meridional *or* más al sur de Europa
(N) (= *wind*) viento *m* del sur

southern ['sʌðən] (ADJ) del sur, sureño, meridional • **in ~ Spain** al sur *or* en el sur de España, en la España meridional • **the ~ part of the island** la parte sur *or* meridional de la isla • **the ~ coast** la costa meridional *or* (del) sur • **~ cuisine** la cocina sureña
(CPD) ▸ **Southern Cone** Cono *m* Sur ▸ **Southern Cross** Cruz *f* del Sur ▸ **Southern Europe** Europa *f* meridional, Europa del Sur ▸ **the southern hemisphere** el hemisferio sur, el hemisferio austral

southerner ['sʌðənəʳ] (N) habitante *mf* del sur, sureño/a *m/f* (*esp LAm*) • **she's a ~** es del sur

southernmost ['sʌðənməʊst] (ADJ) más meridional, más al sur • **the ~ town in Europe** la ciudad más meridional *or* más al sur de Europa

south-facing ['saʊθ,feɪsɪŋ] (ADJ) con cara al sur, orientado hacia el sur • **south-facing slope** vertiente *f* sur

South Korean ['saʊθkə'rɪən] (ADJ) surcoreano
(N) surcoreano/a *m/f*

southpaw ['saʊθpɔ:] (N) (*esp US*) zurdo *m*

south-southeast [,saʊθsaʊθ'i:st] (N) sudsudeste *m*, sursureste *m*
(ADJ) sudsudeste, sursureste
(ADV) (= *toward south-southeast*) hacia el sudsudeste *or* sursureste; [*situated*] al sudsudeste *or* sursureste, en el sudsudeste *or* sursureste

south-southwest [,saʊθsaʊθ'west] (N) sudsudoeste *m*, sursuroeste *m*
(ADJ) sudsudoeste, sursuroeste
(ADV) (= *toward south-southwest*) hacia el sudsudoeste *or* sursuroeste; [*situated*] al sudsudoeste *or* sursuroeste, en el sudsudoeste *or* sursuroeste

South Vietnamese ['saʊθ,vjetnə'mi:z] (ADJ) survietnamita
(N) survietnamita *mf*

southward ['saʊθwəd] (ADJ) [*movement, migration*] hacia el sur, en dirección sur
(ADV) hacia el sur, en dirección sur

southwards ['saʊθwədz] (ADV) (*esp Brit*) = **southward**

southwest [saʊθ'west] (N) sudoeste *m*, suroeste *m*
(ADJ) [*point, direction*] sudoeste, suroeste; [*wind*] del sudoeste, del suroeste
(ADV) (= *toward southwest*) hacia el sudoeste, hacia el suroeste; (= *in the southwest*) al sudoeste, en el sudoeste

southwester [saʊθ'westəʳ] (N) (= *wind*) sudoeste *m*, suroeste *m*

southwesterly [saʊθ'westəlɪ] (ADJ) [*wind*] del sudoeste, del suroeste • **in a ~ direction** hacia el sudoeste *or* suroeste, rumbo al sudoeste *or* suroeste, en dirección sudoeste *or* suroeste
(N) (= *wind*) viento *m* del sudoeste *or* suroeste

southwestern [saʊθ'westən] (ADJ) sudoeste, suroeste, del sudoeste, del suroeste • **the ~ part of the island** la parte sudoeste *or* suroeste de la isla • **in ~ Spain** en el sudoeste *or* suroeste de España, al sudoeste *or* suroeste de España • **the ~ coast** la costa sudoeste *or* suroeste *or* suroccidental

southwestward [saʊθ'westwəd] (ADJ) [*movement, migration*] hacia el sudoeste *or* suroeste, en dirección sudoeste *or* suroeste
(ADV) hacia el sudoeste *or* suroeste, en dirección sudoeste *or* suroeste

southwestwards [saʊθ'westwədz] (ADV) (*esp Brit*) = **southwestward**

souvenir [,su:və'nɪəʳ] (N) recuerdo *m*, souvenir *m*
(CPD) ▸ **souvenir shop** tienda *f* de recuerdos

sou'wester [saʊ'westəʳ] (N) sueste *m*

sovereign ['sɒvrɪn] (ADJ) **1** (= *supreme*) soberano • **with ~ contempt** con soberano desprecio
2 (= *self-governing*) soberano • **~ state** estado *m* soberano
(N) **1** (= *monarch*) soberano/a *m/f*
2 (*Hist*) (= *coin*) soberano *m*

sovereignty ['sɒvrəntɪ] (N) soberanía *f*

soviet ['səʊvɪət] (*Pol*) (*formerly*) (N) soviet *m* • **the Soviets** (= *people*) los soviéticos
(ADJ) soviético • **Soviet Russia** Rusia *f* Soviética • **the Soviet Union** la Unión Soviética

Sovietologist [,səʊvɪə'tɒlədʒɪst] (N) sovietólogo/a *m/f*

sow[1] [səʊ] (PT: **sowed**, PP: **sown**) (VT) [+ *seed*] sembrar • **to sow doubt in sb's mind** sembrar dudas en algn • **to sow mines in a strait** • **sow a strait with mines** sembrar un estrecho de minas, colocar minas en un estrecho

sow[2] [saʊ] (N) (*Zool*) puerca *f*, marrana *f*

sower ['səʊəʳ] (N) sembrador(a) *m/f*

sowing ['səʊɪŋ] (N) siembra *f*
(CPD) ▸ **sowing machine** sembradora *f* ▸ **sowing time** época *f* de la siembra, sementera *f*

sown [səʊn] (PP) *of* **sow**[1]

sow-thistle ['saʊθɪsl] (N) cerraja *f*

sox* [sɒks] (NPL) (*US*) (*Comm*) = **socks**

soy [sɔɪ] (N) (*esp US*) = **soya**

soya ['sɔɪə] (N) soja *f*
(CPD) ▸ **soya bean** semilla *f* de soja ▸ **soya flour** harina *f* de soja ▸ **soya milk** leche *f* de soja ▸ **soya oil** aceite *m* de soja ▸ **soya sauce** salsa *f* de soja

sozzled‡ ['sɒzld] (ADJ) • **to be ~** estar mamado*, estar tomado (*LAm*) • **to get ~** coger una trompa*, agarrarse una borrachera (*LAm*)

SP (N ABBR) (*Brit*) = **starting price 1** (*Racing*) precio *m* de salida
2* (= *information*) • **what's the SP on him?** ¿qué sabemos acerca de él? • **to give sb the SP on sb/sth** dar a algn los datos de algn/algo

spa [spɑ:] (N) balneario *m*
(CPD) ▸ **spa bath** bañera *f* de hidromasaje ▸ **spa treatment** hidroterapia *f*

space [speɪs] (N) **1** (*Phys, Astron*) espacio *m* • **in ~** en el espacio • **the rocket vanished into ~** el cohete desapareció en el espacio • **to stare into ~** (*fig*) mirar al vacío • **outer ~** el espacio exterior
2 (= *room*) espacio *m*, sitio *m* • **there isn't enough ~** no hay espacio *or* sitio suficiente • **to buy ~ in a newspaper** comprar espacio en un periódico • **to clear a ~ for sth** • **make ~ for sth** hacer espacio *or* sitio *or* lugar para algo • **to take up a lot of ~** ocupar mucho sitio *or* espacio
3 (= *gap, empty area*) espacio *m* • **blank ~** espacio *m* en blanco • **in a confined ~** en un espacio restringido • **to leave a ~ for sth** dejar sitio *or* lugar para algo • **wide open ~s** campo *m* abierto • **we couldn't find a parking ~** no pudimos encontrar aparcamiento, no pudimos encontrar un sitio para aparcar *or* (*LAm*) estacionar • **answer in the ~ provided** conteste en el espacio indicado
4 [*of time*] espacio *m*, lapso *m* • **after a ~ of two hours** después de un lapso de dos horas • **for a ~** durante cierto tiempo • **for the ~ of a fortnight** durante un período de quince días • **in the ~ of one hour** en el espacio de una hora • **in the ~ of three generations** en el espacio de tres generaciones • **in a short ~ of time** en un corto espacio *or* lapso de tiempo
5 (*fig*) (= *personal space*) espacio *m*
(VT) **1** (*also* **space out**) espaciar, separar • **well ~d out** bastante espaciados
2 • **to be ~d out*** estar ido*
(CPD) ▸ **space age** era *f* espacial ▸ **space bar** (*on keyboard*) espaciador *m*, barra *f* espaciadora ▸ **space capsule** cápsula *f* espacial ▸ **space centre, space center** (*US*) centro *m* espacial ▸ **space exploration** exploración *f* espacial ▸ **space flight** vuelo *m* espacial ▸ **space heater** calefactor *m* ▸ **space helmet** casco *m* espacial ▸ **Space Invaders**

S

(= *game*) Marcianitos *mpl* ▸ **space junk** basura *f* espacial ▸ **space lab** laboratorio *m* espacial ▸ **space platform** plataforma *f* espacial ▸ **space probe** sonda *f* espacial ▸ **space programme, space program** (*US*) programa *m* de investigaciones espaciales ▸ **space race** carrera *f* espacial ▸ **space research** investigaciones *fpl* espaciales ▸ **space shot** (= *vehicle*) vehículo *m* espacial; (= *launch*) lanzamiento *m* de un vehículo espacial ▸ **space shuttle** transbordador *m* espacial, lanzadera *f* espacial ▸ **space sickness** enfermedad *f* espacial ▸ **space station** estación *f* espacial ▸ **space tourism** turismo *m* espacial ▸ **space travel** viajes *mpl* espaciales ▸ **space vehicle** vehículo *m* espacial ▸ **space walk** paseo *m* por el espacio

space-age ['speɪseɪdʒ] ADJ futurista, de la era espacial

spacecraft ['speɪskrɑ:ft] N (*pl inv*) nave *f* espacial, astronave *f*

spaced-out* [,speɪst'aʊt] ADJ [*person*] • **to be spaced-out** estar ido* • **he's got this spaced-out look** parece que está ido*

spaceman ['speɪsmæn] N (PL: **spacemen**) astronauta *m*, cosmonauta *m*

spaceport ['speɪspɔ:t] N centro *m* espacial

spacer ['speɪsəʳ] N (*on keyboard*) espaciador *m*, barra *f* espaciadora

space-saving ['speɪs,seɪvɪŋ] ADJ que economiza espacio, que ahorra espacio

spaceship ['speɪsʃɪp] N nave *f* espacial, astronave *f*

spacesuit ['speɪssu:t] N traje *m* espacial

space-time continuum [,speɪs,taɪmkən'tɪnjʊəm] N continuo *m* espacio-tiempo

spacewalk ['speɪswɔ:k] N paseo *m* por el espacio
VI pasear por el espacio

spacewoman ['speɪs,wʊmən] N (PL: **spacewomen**) astronauta *f*, cosmonauta *f*

spacey* ['speɪsɪ] ADJ [*music*] psicodélico, sideral; [*person*] ausente, en babia

spacing ['speɪsɪŋ] N espaciamiento *m*; (*Typ*) espaciado *m* • **in** *or* **with double ~** a doble espacio • **in** *or* **with single ~** a un solo espacio
CPD ▸ **spacing bar** espaciador *m*, barra *f* espaciadora

spacious ['speɪʃəs] ADJ espacioso, amplio

spaciousness ['speɪʃəsnɪs] N espaciosidad *f*, amplitud *f*

spade [speɪd] N **1** (= *tool*) pala *f* • IDIOM: • **to call a ~ a ~** llamar al pan pan y al vino vino
2 spades (*Cards*) picas *fpl*, picos *mpl*; (*in Spanish pack*) espadas *fpl* • **the three of ~s** el tres de espadas • **to play ~s** jugar espadas • **to play a ~** jugar una espada
3 (*pej***) negro/a *m/f*

spadeful ['speɪdfʊl] N pala *f* • **by the ~** (*fig*) en grandes cantidades

spadework ['speɪdwɜ:k] N (*fig*) trabajo *m* preliminar

spaghetti [spə'getɪ] N (*gen*) espaguetis *mpl*; (*thin*) fideos *mpl*
CPD ▸ **spaghetti bolognese** espaguetis *mpl* a la boloñesa ▸ **spaghetti junction*** scalextric *m* ▸ **spaghetti western** película *f* de vaqueros hecha por un director italiano

Spain [speɪn] N España *f*

spake†† [speɪk] PT *of* **speak**

Spam® [spæm] N carne *f* de cerdo en conserva

spam [spæm] (*Internet*) N correo *m* basura, spam *m*
VT enviar spam *or* correo basura por Internet a

spammer ['spæməʳ] N (*Internet*) spammer *mf*

spamming ['spæmɪŋ] N (*Internet*) spamming *m*

span¹ [spæn] N **1** [*of hand*] palmo *m*; [*of wing*] envergadura *f*
2 [*of road etc*] tramo *m*; [*of bridge, arch*] luz *f*; [*of roof*] vano *m* • **a ~ of 50 metres** (= *bridge*) una luz de 50 metros • **a bridge with seven ~s** un puente de siete arcadas *or* ojos • **the longest single-span bridge in the world** el puente de una sola arcada más largo del mundo
3 [*of time*] lapso *m*, espacio *m* • **for a brief ~** durante un breve lapso • **the average ~ of life** la duración promedia de la vida
4 (*fig*) • **the whole ~ of world affairs** toda la extensión de los asuntos mundiales, los asuntos mundiales en toda su amplitud
5† (= *measure*) palmo *m*
6 (= *yoke*) [*of oxen*] yunta *f*; [*of horses*] pareja *f*
VT **1** [*bridge*] extenderse sobre, cruzar
2 (*in time*) abarcar • **his life ~ned four reigns** su vida abarcó cuatro reinados
3 (= *measure*) medir a palmos

span² [spæn] PT *of* **spin**

spangle ['spæŋgl] N lentejuela *f*
VT adornar con lentejuelas • **~d with** (*fig*) sembrado de; ▹ **star-spangled**

Spanglish ['spæŋglɪʃ] N (*hum*) espanglish *m*

spangly ['spæŋglɪ] ADJ cubierto con lentejuelas, de lentejuelas

Spaniard ['spænjəd] N español(a) *m/f*

spaniel ['spænjəl] N spaniel *m*

Spanish ['spænɪʃ] ADJ español
N **1** • **the ~** (= *people*) los españoles
2 (*Ling*) español *m*, castellano *m* (*esp LAm*)
CPD ▸ **Spanish America** Hispanoamérica *f*; ▹ **Spanish American** ▸ **the Spanish Armada** la Armada invencible ▸ **Spanish chestnut** castaña *f* dulce ▸ **the Spanish Civil War** la Guerra Civil Española ▸ **Spanish fly** cantárida *f* ▸ **Spanish guitar** guitarra *f* española ▸ **Spanish omelette** tortilla *f* de patatas ▸ **Spanish speaker** hispanohablante *mf*, hispanoparlante *mf*

Spanish American ['spænɪʃə'merɪkən] ADJ hispanoamericano
N hispanoamericano/a *m/f*

Spanishness ['spænɪʃnɪs] N carácter *m* español, cualidad *f* española

Spanish-speaking ['spænɪʃspi:kɪŋ] ADJ hispanohablante, de habla española

spank [spæŋk] N azote *m*, manotazo *m* (en las nalgas) • **to give sb a ~** dar un azote a algn (en las nalgas)
VT zurrar*
VI† • **to be** *or* **go ~ing along** correr, ir volando

spanking ['spæŋkɪŋ] N zurra *f* • **to give sb a ~** zurrar a algn*
ADJ [*pace*] rápido; [*breeze*] fuerte
ADV† • **in his ~ new uniform/car** con su nuevo y flamante uniforme/coche • **the kitchen was ~ clean** la cocina estaba reluciente

spanner ['spænəʳ] N (*gen*) llave *f* de tuercas, llave *f* de tubo; (*adjustable*) llave *f* inglesa • IDIOM: • **to throw** *or* **put a ~ in the works** meter un palo en la rueda

spar¹ [spɑ:ʳ] N (*Naut*) palo *m*, verga *f*

spar² [spɑ:ʳ] VI **1** (*Boxing*) entrenarse en el boxeo • **~ring match** combate *m* con spárring • **~ring partner** sparring *m*
2 (= *argue*) discutir • **to ~ with sb about sth** discutir algo amistosamente con algn

spar³ [spɑ:ʳ] N (*Min*) espato *m*

spare [speəʳ] ADJ **1** (= *extra*) de más, de sobra; (= *reserve*) de reserva; (= *free*) libre • **there's a ~ blanket if you're cold** hay una manta de más *or* de sobra si tienes frío • **take a ~ pair of socks** llévate otro par de calcetines • **I keep a ~ pair of glasses** guardo unas gafas de reserva • **I leave a ~ key with the neighbours** dejo una llave de reserva en casa de los vecinos • **I always keep a bit of ~ cash for emergencies** siempre guardo un poco de dinero extra para emergencias • **is there a seat ~?** ¿queda algún asiento libre? • **is there any milk ~?** ¿queda leche? • **have you got a ~ jacket I could borrow?** ¿tienes otra chaqueta para prestarme? • **I do it whenever I get a ~ moment** lo hago cuando tengo un momento libre • **~ time** tiempo *m* libre • **to go ~*** (= *be available*) sobrar, quedar; (*Brit*) (= *get angry*) ponerse como loco* • **there are two tickets going ~** quedan *or* sobran dos entradas • **the boss will go ~ when he finds out** el jefe se pondrá como loco cuando se entere*
2 (= *lean*) [*body, build*] enjuto (*liter*)
3 (= *sparse*) (*liter*) austero, sobrio
N **1** (*gen*) • **always carry a ~ in case you have a puncture** lleve siempre una rueda de recambio *or* repuesto por si tiene un pinchazo • **I've lost my toothbrush and I don't have a ~** he perdido el cepillo de dientes y no tengo otro
2 (*also* **spare part**) (pieza *f* de) recambio *m*, (pieza *f* de) repuesto *m*, refacción *f* (*Mex*)
VT **1** (= *make available*) • **can you ~ the time?** ¿dispones del tiempo?, ¿tienes tiempo? • **it's good of you to ~ the time** es muy amable de su parte dedicarme (este) tiempo • **I can ~ you five minutes** le puedo conceder *or* dedicar cinco minutos • **to ~ a thought for sb** pensar un momento en algn
2 (= *do without*) • **can you ~ this for a moment?** ¿me puedo llevar esto un momento? • **if you can ~ it** si no lo vas a necesitar • **we can't ~ him now** ahora no podemos prescindir de él • **we completed the job with three days to ~** terminamos el trabajo con tres días de antelación • **I arrived at the station with two minutes/time to ~** llegué a la estación con dos minutos de antelación/con tiempo de sobra • **there's enough and to ~** basta y sobra, hay más que suficiente para todos
3 (= *be grudging with*) • **she ~d no effort in helping me** no escatimó esfuerzos para ayudarme • **they ~d no expense in refurbishing the house** no repararon en *or* escatimaron gastos a la hora de renovar la casa • PROVERB: • **~ the rod, spoil the child** la letra con sangre entra
4 (= *show mercy to*) perdonar • **the fire ~d nothing** el incendio no perdonó nada • **to ~ sb's feelings** no herir los sentimientos de algn • **to ~ sb's life** perdonar la vida a algn
5 (= *save*) ahorrar, evitar • **I'll ~ you the gory details** me ahorraré los detalles escabrosos, te evitaré los detalles escabrosos • **to ~ sb the trouble of doing sth** ahorrar *or* evitar a algn la molestia de hacer algo • **I could have ~d myself the trouble** podía haberme ahorrado *or* evitado la molestia; ▹ **blush**
CPD ▸ **spare bedroom** cuarto *m* de invitados, habitación *f* de invitados ▸ **spare part** (pieza *f* de) repuesto *m*, (pieza *f* de) recambio *m*, refacción *f* (*Mex*) ▸ **spare room** cuarto *m* de invitados, cuarto *m* para las visitas ▸ **spare tyre, spare tire** (*US*) (*Aut*) neumático *m* de recambio, llanta *f* de recambio (*LAm*); (*Brit*) (*hum*) michelín *m* ▸ **spare wheel** (*Aut*) rueda *f* de repuesto *or* recambio

sparely ['speəlɪ] ADV • **~ built** poco fortachón

spare-part surgery* [,speəpɑ:t'sɜ:dʒərɪ] N cirugía *f* de trasplantes

sparerib [ˌspɛəˈrɪb] (N) (*Culin*) costilla *f* de cerdo

sparing [ˈspɛərɪŋ] (ADJ) **1** (= *economical*) • **his ~ use of colour** su parquedad *or* moderación en el uso del color • **to be ~ in one's use of sth** usar algo con moderación • **to be ~ with** *or* (*frm*) **of sth: he was ~ with the wine** no fue muy generoso con el vino • **I've not been ~ with the garlic** he sido generoso con el ajo • **to be ~ of praise** escatimar los elogios, ser parco en elogios
2 (= *merciful*) piadoso, compasivo

sparingly [ˈspɛərɪŋlɪ] (ADV) [*use, apply*] con moderación, en pequeñas cantidades; [*eat*] frugalmente, con moderación • **he spends his money ~** es cuidadoso con el dinero, mira mucho lo que gasta • **we used water ~** tuvimos cuidado de no gastar mucha agua • **he uses colour ~** es parco en el uso de los colores

spark [spɑːk] (N) **1** (*from fire, Elec*) chispa *f*
• IDIOMS: • **to make the ~s fly** provocar una bronca • **they struck ~s off each other** por efecto mutuo hacían chispear el ingenio; ▹ **bright**
2 (= *trace, hint*) pizca *f* • **the book hasn't a ~ of interest** el libro no tiene ni pizca de interés • **there's not a ~ of life about it** no tiene ni un átomo de vida
3 sparks* (*Naut*) telegrafista *mf*; (*Cine, TV*) iluminista *mf*; (*Elec*) electricista *mf*
(VT) (*also* **spark off**) provocar
(VI) chispear, echar chispas
(CPD) ▸ **spark gap** entrehierro *m* ▸ **spark plug** (*Aut*) bujía *f*

sparking plug [ˈspɑːkɪŋplʌg] (N) = **spark plug**

sparkle [ˈspɑːkl] (N) centelleo *m*, destello *m*; (*fig*) chispa *f*, viveza *f* • **a person without ~** una persona sin chispa *or* viveza
(VI) (= *flash*) centellear, echar chispas; (= *shine*) brillar; (= *stand out*) relucir • **the conversation ~d** la conversación fue animadísima • **she doesn't exactly ~** no tiene mucha alegría que digamos

sparkler [ˈspɑːkləʳ] (N) **1** (= *firework*) bengala *f*
2* (= *diamond*) diamante *m*
3* (= *sparkling wine*) vino *m* espumoso

sparkling [ˈspɑːklɪŋ] (ADJ) **1** (= *bright*) [*glass etc*] centelleante; [*eyes*] chispeante
2 (= *fizzy*) [*wine*] espumoso • **a ~ drink** una bebida espumosa • **~ water** agua con gas
3 (= *scintillating*) [*person, wit, conversation*] chispeante

sparkly* [ˈspɑːklɪ] (ADJ) [*necklace, eyes*] brillante, centelleante

sparky [ˈspɑːkɪ] (ADJ) vivaracho, marchoso*

sparrow [ˈspærəʊ] (N) gorrión *m*

sparrowhawk [ˈspærəʊhɔːk] (N) gavilán *m*

sparse [spɑːs] (ADJ) (COMPAR: **sparser**, SUPERL: **sparsest**) (= *thin*) escaso; (= *dispersed*) disperso, esparcido; [*hair*] ralo • **~ furnishings** muebles *mpl* escasos • **~ population** poca densidad *f* de población

sparsely [ˈspɑːslɪ] (ADV) (= *thinly*) escasamente; (= *in scattered way*) en forma dispersa • **~ populated** escasamente poblado • **a ~ furnished room** un cuarto con pocos muebles

sparseness [ˈspɑːsnɪs] (N) escasez *f*

Sparta [ˈspɑːtə] (N) Esparta *f*

Spartacus [ˈspɑːtəkəs] (N) Espartaco

Spartan [ˈspɑːtən] (ADJ) espartano
(N) espartano/a *m/f*

spartan [ˈspɑːtən] (ADJ) (*fig*) espartano

spasm [ˈspæzəm] (N) **1** (*Med*) espasmo *m*
2 (= *fit*) ataque *m*, acceso *m* • **a ~ of coughing** un ataque *or* acceso de tos • **in a ~ of fear** en un arrebato de miedo • **a sudden ~ of activity** un arranque *or* arrebato de actividad • **to work in ~s** trabajar a rachas

spasmodic [spæzˈmɒdɪk] (ADJ) **1** (*Med*) espasmódico
2 (= *intermittent*) irregular, intermitente

spasmodically [spæzˈmɒdɪkəlɪ] (ADV) **1** (*Med*) de forma espasmódica
2 (= *intermittently*) de forma irregular, de forma intermitente

spastic** [ˈspæstɪk] (ADJ) espástico
(N) espástico/a *m/f*

spasticity [spæsˈtɪsɪtɪ] (N) espasticidad *f*

spat¹ [spæt] (PT), (PP) *of* **spit¹**

spat² [spæt] (N) (= *overshoe*) polaina *f*

spat³* [spæt] (US) (N) riña *f*, disputa *f* (sin trascendencia)
(VI) reñir

spat⁴ [spæt] (N) (= *oyster*) freza *f*; [*of oysters*] hueva *f* de ostras

spate [speɪt] (N) **1** (*fig*) torrente *m*, avalancha *f*; [*of burglaries*] serie *f*
2 • **to be in (full) ~** [*river*] estar (muy) crecido

spatial [ˈspeɪʃəl] (ADJ) espacial

spatio-temporal, spatiotemporal [ˌspeɪʃɪəʊˈtempərəl] (ADJ) espaciotemporal

spatter [ˈspætəʳ] (VT) salpicar (**with** de) • **a dress ~ed with mud** un vestido salpicado de lodo • **a wall ~ed with blood** una pared salpicada de sangre

spatula [ˈspætjʊlə] (N) espátula *f*

spavin [ˈspævɪn] (N) esparaván *m*

spawn [spɔːn] (N) **1** [*of fish, frogs*] freza *f*, huevas *fpl*; [*of mushrooms*] semillas *fpl*
2 (*pej*) (= *offspring*) prole *f*
(VI) frezar
(VT) (*pej*) engendrar, producir

spawning [ˈspɔːnɪŋ] (N) desove *m*, freza *f*

spay [speɪ] (VT) [+ *animal*] sacar los ovarios a

SPCA (N ABBR) (US) = **Society for the Prevention of Cruelty to Animals**

SPCC (N ABBR) (US) = **Society for the Prevention of Cruelty to Children**

speak [spiːk] (PT: **spoke**, PP: **spoken**) (VI)
1 hablar • **to ~ to sb** hablar con algn • **have you spoken to him?** ¿has hablado con él? • **she never spoke to me again** no volvió a dirigirme la palabra • **since they quarrelled they don't ~ to each other** desde que riñeron no se hablan • **I don't know him to ~ to** no lo conozco bastante como para hablar con él • **I know him to ~ to** lo conozco bastante bien para cambiar algunas palabras con él • **did you ~?** ¿dijiste algo? • **technically/biologically ~ing** en términos técnicos/biológicos, desde el punto de vista técnico/biológico • **I'll ~ to him about it** (= *discuss it with him*) lo hablaré con él; (= *point it out to him*) se lo diré • **~ing as a student myself** hablando desde mi experiencia como estudiante • **we're not ~ing** no nos hablamos • **~ now or forever hold your peace** hable ahora o guarde para siempre silencio • **he's very well spoken of** tiene buen nombre *or* buena fama • **~ing of holidays …** a propósito de las vacaciones … • **it's nothing to ~ of** no tiene importancia • **he has no money to ~ of** no tiene dinero que digamos • **everything spoke of hatred** en todo había un odio latente • **everything spoke of luxury** todo reflejaba el lujo • **~ing personally …** en cuanto a mí …, yo por mi parte … • **roughly ~ing** en términos generales • **so to ~** por decirlo así, por así decir • **to ~ well of sb** hablar bien de algn • **to ~ in a whisper** hablar bajo
2 (= *make a speech, give one's opinion*) hablar • **he spoke on Greek myths** habló sobre los mitos griegos • **when the minister had spoken …** cuando terminó de hablar el ministro … • **the member rose to ~** el diputado se levantó para tomar la palabra • **the chairman asked Mr Wright to ~** el presidente le concedió la palabra al Sr. Wright • **are you ~ing in the debate?** ¿interviene usted en el debate?
3 (*Telec*) • **~ing!** ¡al habla! • **"could I ~ to Alison?" — "~ing!"** —¿podría hablar con Alison? —¡al habla! *or* —¡soy yo! *or* (*esp LAm*) —¡con ella! • **this is Peter ~ing** ¡soy Peter!, ¡habla Peter! • **may I ~ to Mr Jones?** ¿me pone con el Sr. Jones, por favor? • **who is that ~ing?** ¿con quién hablo?, ¿quién es?; (*taking message*) ¿de parte (de quién)?
4 (*fig*) [*gun*] oírse, sonar
(VT) **1** (= *talk*) [+ *language*] hablar • **he ~s Italian** habla italiano • **do you ~ English?** ¿hablas inglés? • **he can ~ seven languages** habla siete idiomas • **"English spoken here"** "se habla inglés"
2 (= *utter*) decir • **to ~ one's mind** hablar claro *or* con franqueza • **to ~ the truth** decir la verdad • **nobody spoke a word** nadie habló, nadie dijo palabra

▸ **speak for** (VI + PREP) **1** • **to ~ for sb** (*as representative*) hablar por algn, hablar en nombre de algn; (*as defender*) interceder por algn • **he ~s for the miners** habla por los mineros, representa a los mineros • **~ing for myself** en cuanto a mí, yo por mi parte • **~ for yourself!** ¡eso lo dirás tú! • **let her ~ for herself** déjala que hable
2 • **it ~s for itself** es evidente, habla por sí mismo • **the facts ~ for themselves** los datos hablan por sí solos
3 • **to be spoken for: that's already been spoken for** eso ya está reservado *or* apartado • **she's already spoken for*** ya está comprometida

▸ **speak out** (VI + ADV) • **he's not afraid to ~ out** no tiene miedo a decir lo que piensa • **to ~ out against sth** denunciar algo • **to ~ out for** *or* **on behalf of sb** defender a algn

▸ **speak up** (VI + ADV) **1** (= *raise voice*) hablar más fuerte *or* alto • **~ up!** ¡más fuerte!
2 (= *give one's opinion*) decir lo que se piensa • **don't be afraid to ~ up** no tengas miedo de decir lo que piensas • **to ~ up for sb** defender a algn

-speak [spiːk] (N) (*ending in compounds*) (*pej*) • **computer-speak** lenguaje *m* de los ordenadores, jerga *f* informática

speakeasy* [ˈspiːkˌiːzɪ] (N) (US) taberna *f* clandestina

speaker [ˈspiːkəʳ] (N) **1** (*gen*) el/la *m/f* que habla; (*in public*) orador(a) *m/f*; (*at conference*) ponente *mf*, orador(a) *m/f*; (= *lecturer*) conferenciante *mf* • **as the last ~ said …** como dijo el señor/la señora que acaba de hablar … • **he's a good ~** es buen orador, habla bien
2 [*of language*] hablante *mf* • **French ~s** los hablantes de francés, los francoparlantes • **he's a French ~** habla francés • **all ~s of Spanish** todos los que hablan español, todos los hispanohablantes • **Catalan has several million ~s** el catalán es hablado por varios millones • **are you a Welsh ~?** ¿habla usted galés?
3 (= *loud-speaker*) altavoz *m*, altoparlante *m* (*LAm*); **speakers** [*of hi-fi system*] bafles *mpl*, parlantes *mpl*
4 (*Pol*) • **the Speaker** (*Brit*) el Presidente/la Presidenta de la Cámara de los Comunes; (*US*) el Presidente/la Presidenta de la Cámara de los Representantes; ▹ SPEAKER, FRONT BENCH

SPEAKER

En el sistema parlamentario británico el **Speaker** es la máxima autoridad de la Cámara de los Comunes (**House of Commons**) y su misión es presidirla y hacer que se guarde el orden y que se acaten las normas establecidas. Es elegido al comienzo de la legislatura por parlamentarios (**MPs**) de todos los partidos y puede pertenecer a cualquiera de ellos. Una vez que toma posesión de su cargo, el **Speaker** no vota ni toma la palabra (excepto a nivel oficial) y ha de ser totalmente imparcial. Los parlamentarios suelen comenzar sus discursos dirigiéndose al **Speaker** en vez de a toda la Cámara, como por ejemplo en: **Mister/Madam Speaker, I feel very strongly about this.**

En Estados Unidos, el **Speaker** es el encargado de presidir la Cámara de los Representantes (**House of Representatives**) y es también el dirigente del partido mayoritario, además de miembro de la Cámara. Es elegido por los miembros de su partido y se encarga de las actas de las sesiones de la Cámara y de actuar como portavoz de su partido. Es uno de los puestos más influyentes del gobierno federal, además de ser el que sigue al Vicepresidente (**Vice-President**) en la sucesión a la presidencia.

speaking ['spi:kɪŋ] ADJ **1** (= *talking*) [*doll, computer*] que habla, parlante
2 (= *eloquent, striking*) • **~ likeness** vivo retrato *m*
N (= *skill*) oratoria *f*
CPD ▸ **speaking clock** servicio *f* telefónico de información horaria ▸ **speaking distance** • **to be within ~ distance** estar al alcance de la voz ▸ **speaking part** papel *m* hablado ▸ **speaking terms** • **to be on ~ terms with sb** hablarse con algn • **we're not on ~ terms** no nos hablamos ▸ **speaking trumpet** bocina *f* ▸ **speaking tube** tubo *m* acústico ▸ **speaking voice** • **a pleasant ~ voice** una voz agradable

-speaking ['spi:kɪŋ] ADJ (*ending in compounds*) • **English-speaking** de habla inglesa, anglohablante • **French-speaking** de habla francés, francoparlante • **Spanish-speaking people** los hispanohablantes, los de habla española *or* (*esp LAm*) castellana

spear [spɪəʳ] N (*gen*) lanza *f*; (= *harpoon*) arpón *m*
VT **1** (*with spear*) alancear, herir con lanza; (*with harpoon*) arponear
2 (*fig*) atravesar, pinchar • **he ~ed a potato with his fork** atravesó *or* pinchó una patata con el tenedor

speargun ['spɪəgʌn] N harpón *m* submarino

spearhead ['spɪəhed] N (*Mil*) (*also fig*) punta *f* de lanza
VT encabezar

spearmint ['spɪəmɪnt] N (*Bot etc*) menta *f* verde, hierbabuena *f*
CPD ▸ **spearmint chewing gum** chicle *m* de menta

spec* [spek] N • **to buy sth on ~** comprar algo como especulación • **to go along on ~** ir a ver lo que sale • **to turn up on ~** presentarse por si acaso

special ['speʃəl] ADJ **1** (= *important, exceptional*) [*occasion, day, permission, price, attention, diet*] especial • **my ~ chair** mi silla preferida • **what's so ~ about that?** y eso ¿qué tiene de especial? • **is there anyone ~ in your life?** ¿hay alguien especial en tu vida? • **~ arrangements will be made for disabled people** se tomarán medidas especiales para las personas discapacitadas • **to take ~ care of sth** cuidar especialmente de algo • **in ~ cases** en casos especiales *or* extraordinarios • **to make a ~ effort to do sth** esforzarse especialmente *or* hacer un esfuerzo extra para hacer algo • **you're extra ~** tú eres lo mejor de lo mejor • **to make sb feel ~** hacer que algn se sienta especial • **my ~ friend** mi amigo del alma • **his ~ interest was always music** siempre tuvo especial interés por la música • **there's nothing ~ about being a journalist** ser periodista no tiene nada de especial • **it's nothing ~*** no es nada especial, no es nada del otro mundo • **~ powers** (*Pol*) poderes *mpl* extraordinarios • **I've cooked something ~ for dinner** he preparado algo especial para cenar • **she's very ~ to us** la apreciamos mucho • **~ to that country** exclusivo de ese país • **as a ~ treat** como algo especial • **to expect ~ treatment** esperar un trato especial
2 (= *specific*) especial • **a ~ tool for working leather** una herramienta especial para trabajar el cuero • **have you any ~ date in mind?** ¿tienes en mente alguna fecha concreta *or* en particular *or* en especial? • **is there anything ~ you would like?** ¿hay algo que quieras en especial? • **I had no ~ reason for suspecting him** no tenía ningún motivo en especial para sospechar de él • **"why do you say that?" — "oh, no ~ reason"** —¿por qué dices eso? —por nada en especial • **I've no-one ~ in mind** no tengo en mente a nadie en concreto *or* en especial • **"what are you doing this weekend?" — "nothing ~"** —¿qué haces este fin de semana? —nada (en) especial *or* nada en particular • **Britain has its own ~ problems** Gran Bretaña tiene sus propios problemas particulares
3 (*Brit*) (*iro*) (= *strange*) • **to be a bit ~** [*person*] ser un poco especial
N **1** (= *train*) tren *m* especial; (*TV, Rad*) programa *m* especial; (= *newspaper*) número *m* extraordinario • **the chef's ~** • **today's ~** la especialidad del día
2 (*US**) (= *special offer*) oferta *f* especial • **to be on ~** estar de oferta
3 (*Brit**) (= *special constable*) *ciudadano que en determinadas ocasiones realiza funciones de policía*
CPD ▸ **special adviser** consejero/a *m/f* de asuntos extraordinarios ▸ **special agent** agente *mf* especial ▸ **Special Air Service** (*Brit*) *regimiento del ejército británico que se especializa en operaciones clandestinas* ▸ **Special Branch** (*Brit*) Servicio *m* de Seguridad del Estado ▸ **special constable** (*Brit*) *ciudadano que en ciertas ocasiones realiza funciones de policía* ▸ **special correspondent** corresponsal *mf* especial ▸ **special delivery** correo *m* exprés ▸ **special edition** edición *f* especial ▸ **special education** educación *f* especial ▸ **special educational needs** necesidades *fpl* educativas especiales ▸ **special effects** efectos *mpl* especiales ▸ **special interest group** grupo *m* de presión que persigue un tema específico ▸ **special investigator** investigador(a) *m/f* especial ▸ **special jury** jurado *m* especial ▸ **special licence** (*Brit*) (*Jur*) *permiso especial para contraer matrimonio sin cumplir los requisitos legales normalmente necesarios* ▸ **special needs** • **children with ~ needs** • **~ needs children** niños que requieren una atención diferenciada ▸ **special offer** (*Comm*) oferta *f* especial, oferta *f* de ocasión ▸ **special school** colegio *m* de educación especial ▸ **special student** (*US*) (*at university*) oyente *mf* libre ▸ **special subject** (*at school, university*) optativa *f*; (*advanced*) asignatura *f* especializada

specialism ['speʃəˌlɪzəm] N especialidad *f*

specialist ['speʃəlɪst] N especialista *mf* • **heart ~** (*Med*) especialista *mf* del corazón
ADJ especializado • **that's ~ work** eso es trabajo especializado • **~ knowledge** conocimientos *mpl* especializados

speciality [ˌspeʃɪ'ælɪtɪ], **specialty** (*US*) ['speʃəltɪ] N especialidad *f* • **to make a ~ of sth** especializarse en algo • **it's a ~ of the house** es una especialidad de la casa, es un plato especial de la casa

specialization [ˌspeʃəlaɪ'zeɪʃən] N (= *act*) especialización *f*; (= *subject*) especialidad *f*

specialize ['speʃəlaɪz] VI especializarse (**in** en) • **she ~d in Russian** se especializó en ruso • **we ~ in skiing equipment** estamos especializados en material de esquí

specialized ['speʃəlaɪzd] ADJ • **~ knowledge** conocimientos *mpl* especializados

specially ['speʃəlɪ] ADV **1** (= *specifically*) [*designed, made, adapted, trained, selected*] especialmente, expresamente • **a lotion ~ formulated for children** una loción formulada especialmente *or* expresamente para niños • **we asked for it ~** lo pedimos a propósito
2 (= *particularly*) especialmente, en especial, en particular • **we would ~ like to see the orchard** nos gustaría especialmente *or* en especial ver el huerto, nos gustaría ver el huerto en particular • **~ the yellow ones** especialmente *or* sobre todo los amarillos
3 (= *exceptionally*) especialmente, particularmente • **her job is not ~ important to her** su trabajo no es especialmente *or* particularmente importante para ella • **the food was ~ good** la comida era excepcional *or* excepcionalmente buena

specialty ['speʃəltɪ] N (*US*) = **speciality**

specie ['spi:ʃi:] N metálico *m*, efectivo *m* • **in ~** en metálico

species ['spi:ʃi:z] N (*pl inv*) especie *f*

specific [spə'sɪfɪk] ADJ **1** (= *definite, particular*) [*need, plan*] específico; [*issue, area, problem*] específico, concreto; [*question, reason, example*] concreto • **for ~ political ends** con fines políticos concretos • **with the ~ aim of achieving sth** con el propósito expreso de lograr algo • **problems which are ~ to a particular group of people** problemas que son específicos *or* propios de un grupo particular de personas
2 (= *precise*) [*description, instructions*] preciso; [*meaning*] exacto • **can you be more ~?** ¿puedes ser más concreto?, ¿puedes puntualizar? • **it was a tooth, a shark's tooth, to be more ~** era un diente: un diente de un tiburón para ser más preciso • **you will be asked to be ~ about what the problem is** te pedirán que especifiques con exactitud el problema, te pedirán que seas preciso a la hora de identificar el problema
3 (*Bio, Phys, Chem, Med*) específico
N **1** (*Med*) (= *drug*) específico *m*
2 specifics (= *particulars*) aspectos *mpl* concretos, detalles *mpl* • **we have yet to work out the ~s of the plan** todavía tenemos que elaborar los aspectos concretos *or* los detalles del plan • **to get down to ~s** ir a los aspectos concretos *or* los detalles
CPD ▸ **specific gravity** peso *m* específico

specifically [spə'sɪfɪkəlɪ] ADV **1** (= *especially*) [*design, aim*] específicamente, expresamente; [*relate to*] específicamente • **projects ~ designed to strengthen British industries** proyectos diseñados específicamente *or* expresamente para fortalecer las industrias británicas
2 (= *more precisely*) en concreto,

concretamente • **fear was the main factor, ~ a fear of pregnancy** el temor era el factor principal, en concreto *or* concretamente, el temor a quedarse embarazada
3 (= *explicitly*) [*mention, refer to*] explícitamente; [*ask, authorize*] expresamente, explícitamente • **he ~ asked us not to mention the fact** nos pidió expresamente *or* explícitamente que no mencionáramos ese hecho • **they will take no further action unless ~ instructed to** no van a tomar más medidas salvo que se les instruya de manera expresa
4 (= *uniquely*) específicamente • **it isn't a ~ medical problem** no es un problema específicamente médico

specification [ˌspesɪfɪˈkeɪʃən] (N) **1** (= *act of specifying*) especificación *f*
2 (= *requirement*) especificación *f* • **the computers are customized to your ~(s)** los ordenadores *or* (*LAm*) computadores se diseñan de acuerdo con sus especificaciones
3 specifications (= *plan*) presupuesto *m*, plan *m* detallado

specified [ˈspesɪfaɪd] (ADJ) (= *particular*) [*amount, number*] especificado; [*period, price*] indicado • **at a ~ time** en un momento indicado • **~ risk material** material de riesgo indicado

specify [ˈspesɪfaɪ] (VT) especificar • **in the order specified** en el orden especificado
(VI) precisar • **he did not ~** no precisó • **unless otherwise specified** salvo indicaciones en sentido contrario

specimen [ˈspesɪmɪn] (N) **1** (= *sample*) [*of blood, urine, tissue, rock*] muestra *f*
2 (= *example*) [*of species, genus etc*] ejemplar *m*, espécimen *m* • **that trout is a fine ~** esa trucha es un magnífico ejemplar
3* (= *person*) • **he's an odd ~** es un bicho raro* • **you're a pretty poor ~** no vales para mucho
(CPD) ▸ **specimen copy** ejemplar *m* de muestra ▸ **specimen page** página *f* que sirve de muestra ▸ **specimen signature** muestra *f* de firma

specious [ˈspiːʃəs] (ADJ) especioso

speciousness [ˈspiːʃəsnɪs] (N) lo especioso

speck [spek] (N) **1** (= *small stain*) pequeña mancha *f*
2 (= *particle*) [*of dust*] mota *f*
3 (= *dot, point*) punto *m* • **it's just a ~ on the horizon** es un punto en el horizonte nada más
4 (= *small portion*) pizca *f* • **there's not a ~ of truth in it** no tiene ni pizca de verdad • **just a ~, thanks** un poquitín, gracias
(VT) = **speckle**

speckle [ˈspekl] (N) punto *m*, mota *f*
(VT) salpicar, motear (**with** de)

speckled [ˈspekld] (ADJ) moteado, con puntos

specs[1]* [speks] (NPL) gafas *fpl*, anteojos *mpl* (*LAm*), lentes *mpl* (*LAm*)

specs[2]* [speks] (NPL ABBR) = **specifications**

spectacle [ˈspektəkl] (N) **1** espectáculo *m* • **a sad ~** un triste espectáculo • **to make a ~ of o.s.** hacer el ridículo, ponerse en ridículo
2 spectacles gafas *fpl*, lentes *mpl* (*LAm*), anteojos *mpl* (*LAm*) • **a pair of ~s** unas gafas
• IDIOM: • **to see everything through rose-coloured** *or* **rose-tinted ~s** verlo todo color de rosa
(CPD) ▸ **spectacle case** estuche *m* de gafas

spectacled [ˈspektəkld] (ADJ) con gafas

spectacular [spekˈtækjʊləʳ] (ADJ) [*results, display, view, scenery, increase, improvement*] espectacular, impresionante; [*success*] impresionante; [*failure, fall, defeat*] espectacular, estrepitoso
(N) (*TV, Cine*) show *m* espectacular

spectacularly [spekˈtækjʊləlɪ] (ADV) [*increase, grow, improve*] de modo *or* manera espectacular, espectacularmente; [*crash, fail*] de modo espectacular, estrepitosamente; [*good*] verdaderamente, realmente; [*bad*] terriblemente • **~ beautiful** de una belleza impresionante • **the campaign has proved ~ successful** la campaña ha sido todo un éxito *or* ha sido un éxito impresionante • **everything went ~ wrong** todo salió terriblemente mal

spectate [spekˈteɪt] (VI) mirar • **they come to ~** vienen de espectadores

spectator [spekˈteɪtəʳ] (N) espectador(a) *m/f*; **spectators** público *msing*
(CPD) ▸ **spectator sport** deporte *m* espectáculo

specter [ˈspektəʳ] (N) (*US*) = **spectre**

spectral [ˈspektrəl] (ADJ) espectral

spectre, specter (*US*) [ˈspektəʳ] (N) espectro *m*, fantasma *m*

spectrogram [ˈspektrəʊgræm] (N) espectrograma *m*

spectrograph [ˈspektrəʊgrɑːf] (N) espectrógrafo *m*

spectrometer [spekˈtrɒmɪtəʳ] (N) espectrómetro *m*

spectrometry [spekˈtrɒmɪtrɪ] (N) espectrometría *f*

spectroscope [ˈspektrəskəʊp] (N) espectroscopio *m*

spectroscopic [spektrəˈskɒpɪk] (ADJ) espectroscópico

spectroscopy [spekˈtrɒskəpɪ] (N) espectroscopia *f*

spectrum [ˈspektrəm] (N) (PL: **spectra** [ˈspektrə]) **1** (= *range*) espectro *m*, gama *f* • **we went through the whole ~ of emotions** experimentamos todo el espectro *or* toda la gama de emociones posibles • **a wide ~ of opinions** un amplio espectro *or* abanico de opiniones, una amplia gama de opiniones • **the political ~** el espectro político
2 (*Phys*) espectro *m*
(CPD) ▸ **spectrum analysis** análisis *m inv* espectral

specula [ˈspekjʊlə] (NPL) *of* **speculum**

speculate [ˈspekjʊleɪt] (VI) **1** (= *conjecture*) especular • **to ~ about/on** especular sobre, hacer conjeturas acerca de
2 (*Econ*) especular (**on** en)

speculation [ˌspekjʊˈleɪʃən] (N)
1 (= *conjecture*) especulación *f* • **it is pure ~** es pura especulación • **it is the subject of much ~** se está especulando mucho sobre el tema, es un tema sobre el que se está especulando mucho
2 (*Econ*) especulación *f* • **to buy sth as a ~** comprar algo con fines especulativas • **it's a good ~** vale como especulación

speculative [ˈspekjʊlətɪv] (ADJ) especulativo

speculator [ˈspekjʊleɪtəʳ] (N) especulador(a) *m/f*

speculum [ˈspekjʊləm] (N) (PL: **speculums, specula**) espéculo *m*

sped [sped] (PT), (PP) *of* **speed**

speech [spiːtʃ] (N) **1** (= *faculty*) habla *f*; (= *words*) palabras *fpl*; (= *language*) lenguaje *m*; (= *manner of speaking*) lenguaje *m*, forma *f* de hablar • **to lose the power of ~** perder el habla • **to recover one's ~** recobrar el habla, recobrar la palabra • **his ~ was slurred** arrastraba las palabras, farfullaba al hablar • **he expresses himself better in ~ than in writing** se expresa mejor hablando *or* de palabra que por escrito • **children's ~** el lenguaje de los niños • **freedom of ~** libertad *f* de expresión • **to be slow of ~** hablar lentamente, ser torpe de palabra
2 (= *address*) discurso *m* • **to make a ~** pronunciar un discurso • **speech, speech!** ¡que hable! ¡que hable!
3 (*Brit*) (*Gram*) • **direct/indirect ~** estilo *m* directo/indirecto; ▹ **part**
(CPD) ▸ **speech act** acto *m* de habla ▸ **speech analysis** análisis *m* de la voz ▸ **speech bubble** bocadillo *m* (*de historieta*) ▸ **speech command** comando *m* vocal ▸ **speech community** comunidad *f* lingüística ▸ **speech day** (*Brit*) reparto *m* de premios ▸ **speech defect, speech impediment** defecto *m* del habla ▸ **speech organ** órgano *m* del habla ▸ **speech recognition** (*Comput*) reconocimiento *m* de voz ▸ **speech synthesizer** sintetizador *m* de la voz humana ▸ **speech therapist** logopeda *mf* ▸ **speech therapy** terapia *f* de la palabra ▸ **speech training** lecciones *fpl* de elocución ▸ **speech writer** escritor(a) *m/f* de discursos, redactor(a) *m/f* de discursos

speechify [ˈspiːtʃɪfaɪ] (VI) (*pej*) disertar prolijamente, perorar

speechifying [ˈspiːtʃɪfaɪɪŋ] (N) (*pej*) disertaciones *fpl*, prolijas peroratas *fpl*

speechless [ˈspiːtʃlɪs] (ADJ) (= *dumbstruck*) estupefacto, sin habla • **everybody was ~ at this** con esto todos quedaron estupefactos *or* sin habla • **I'm ~!** no sé qué decir, estoy estupefacto • **to be ~ with rage** enmudecer de rabia

speechmaking [ˈspiːtʃˌmeɪkɪŋ] (N)
1 (= *making of speeches*) pronunciación *f* de discursos
2 (= *speeches collectively*) discursos *mpl*
3 (*pej*) = **speechifying**

speed [spiːd] (VB: PT, PP: **sped** *or* **speeded**) (N)
1 (= *rate of movement*) velocidad *f*, rapidez *f*; (= *rapidity, haste*) rapidez *f*, prisa *f* • **shorthand/typing ~** velocidad *f* en taquigrafía/mecanografía • **my typing ~ is 60 words per minute** mecanografío 60 palabras por minuto • **at ~** a gran velocidad • **at a ~ of 70km/h** a una velocidad de 70km por hora • **what ~ were you doing?** (*Aut*) ¿a qué velocidad ibas? • **at full ~** a toda velocidad, a máxima velocidad • **full ~ ahead!** ¡avante toda!* • **to gather ~** acelerar, cobrar velocidad • **the ~ of light** la velocidad de la luz • **the maximum ~ is 120km/h** la velocidad máxima es de 120km por hora • **to pick up ~** acelerar, cobrar velocidad • **the ~ of sound** la velocidad del sonido • **at top ~** a toda velocidad, a máxima velocidad
• IDIOMS: • **to be up to ~** (= *well-informed*) estar al día, estar al corriente; (= *functioning properly*) estar a punto, funcionar a pleno rendimiento • **to bring sb up to ~** poner a algn al día *or* al corriente • **to bring sth up to ~** poner algo a punto; ▹ **full**
2 (*Aut, Tech*) (= *gear*) velocidad *f* • **a three-speed bike** una bicicleta de tres marchas *or* velocidades • **a five-speed gearbox** una caja de cambios de cinco velocidades
3 (*Phot*) velocidad *f*
4 (*Drugs‡*) speed *m*, anfetamina *f*
(VI) **1** (PT, PP: **sped**) (= *go fast*) correr a toda prisa; (= *hurry*) darse prisa, apresurarse • **he sped down the street** corrió a toda prisa por la calle • **to ~ along** ir a gran velocidad • **the years sped by** pasaron los años volando • **to ~ off** marcharse a toda prisa
2 (PT, PP: **speeded**) (*Aut*) (= *exceed speed limit*) conducir *or* (*LAm*) manejar por encima del límite de velocidad permitido
(VT) (PT, PP: **speeded**) • **to ~ sb on his way** despedir a algn, desear un feliz viaje a algn
(CPD) ▸ **speed bump** banda *f* sonora ▸ **speed camera** cámara *f* de control de velocidad, radar *m* ▸ **speed cop*** policía *m* de tráfico,

policía *m* de tránsito ▸ **speed dating** speed dating *m*, citas *fpl* rápidas (*para buscar pareja*) ▸ **speed dial** (= *facility*) marcación *f* rápida; ▹ **speed-dial** ▸ **speed limit** velocidad *f* máxima, límite *m* de velocidad • **a 50km/h ~ limit** velocidad máxima (permitida) de 50km por hora • **to exceed the ~ limit** exceder la velocidad permitida *or* el límite de velocidad ▸ **speed limiter** (*Aut*) limitador *m* de velocidad ▸ **speed merchant*** corredor(a) *m/f* ▸ **speed restriction** limitación *f* de velocidad ▸ **speed skater** patinador(a) *m/f* de velocidad ▸ **speed skating** patinaje *m* de velocidad ▸ **speed trap** (*Aut*) *sistema policial para detectar infracciones de velocidad*

▸ **speed up** (PT, PP: **speeded up**) (VI + ADV) [*person*] apresurarse, apurarse (*LAm*); [*process*] acelerarse
(VT + ADV) [+ *object*] acelerar; [+ *person*] apresurar, apurar (*LAm*)

speedball ['spi:dbɔ:l] (N) **1** (= *game*) speedball *m*
2 (= *drugs*) chute *m* de cocaína con heroína‡

speedboat ['spi:d,bəʊt] (N) lancha *f* motora

speed-dial ['spi:ddaɪəl] (VT) [+ *person*] llamar mediante marcación rápida
(VI) utilizar la marcación rápida

speeder ['spi:dəʳ] (N) (= *fast driver*) automovilista *mf* que conduce a gran velocidad; (*convicted*) infractor(a) *m/f* de los límites de velocidad

speedily ['spi:dɪlɪ] (ADV) (= *quickly*) rápidamente, con la mayor prontitud; (= *promptly*) prontamente, en seguida

speediness ['spi:dɪnɪs] (N) (= *speed*) velocidad *f*, rapidez *f*; (= *promptness*) prontitud *f*

speeding ['spi:dɪŋ] (N) (*Aut*) exceso *m* de velocidad • **he was fined for ~** le pusieron una multa por exceso de velocidad

speedo* ['spi:dəʊ] (N) (*Brit*) = **speedometer**

speedometer [spɪ'dɒmɪtəʳ] (N) velocímetro *m*, cuentakilómetros *m inv*

speed-up ['spi:dʌp] (N) aceleración *f*, agilización *f*

speedway ['spi:dweɪ] (N) **1** (= *sport*) carreras *fpl* de motos
2 (= *track*) pista *f* de carreras
3 (*US*) autopista *f*

speedwell ['spi:dwel] (N) (*Bot*) verónica *f*

speedy ['spi:dɪ] (ADJ) (COMPAR: **speedier**, SUPERL: **speediest**) veloz, rápido; [*answer*] pronto

speleologist [,spi:lɪ'ɒlədʒɪst] (N) espeleólogo/a *m/f*

speleology [,spi:lɪ'ɒlədʒɪ] (N) espeleología *f*

spell¹ [spel] (N) encanto *m*, hechizo *m* • **to be under a ~** estar hechizado • **to be under sb's ~** estar hechizado por algn • **to break the ~** romper el hechizo *or* encanto • **to cast a ~ over** *or* **on sb** • **put sb under a ~** hechizar a algn • **Seville casts its ~ over the tourists** Sevilla embruja a los turistas

spell² [spel] (PT, PP: **spelled** *or* **spelt**) (VT) **1** (= *write*) escribir; (*letter by letter*) deletrear • **how do you ~ your name?** ¿cómo se escribe tu nombre? • **can you ~ that please?** ¿me lo deletrea, por favor? • **c-a-t ~s "cat"** "cat" se deletrea c-a-t • **what do these letters ~?** ¿qué palabra se forma con estas letras?
2 (= *denote*) significar, representar • **it ~s ruin** significa *or* representa la ruina • **it ~s disaster for us** significa *or* representa un desastre para nosotros
(VI) (= *write correctly*) escribir correctamente • **she can't ~** no sabe escribir correctamente, sabe poco de ortografía

▸ **spell out** (VT + ADV) **1** (= *read letter by letter*) deletrear
2 (= *explain*) • **to ~ sth out for sb** explicar algo a algn en detalle

spell³ [spel] (N) **1** (= *period*) racha *f* • **a prolonged ~ of bad weather** una larga racha de mal tiempo • **a cold ~** una racha de frío • **they're going through a bad ~** están pasando por una mala racha
2 (= *shift, turn*) turno *m* • **we each took a ~ at the wheel** nos turnamos al volante • **a ~ of duty** una temporada • **I did a ~ as a commercial traveller** durante cierto tiempo trabajé como viajante

spellbinder ['spel,baɪndəʳ] (N) (= *speaker*) orador(a) *m/f* que fascina; (= *book*) obra *f* que fascina

spellbinding ['spel,baɪndɪŋ] (ADJ) cautivador, fascinante

spellbound ['spelbaʊnd] (ADJ) embelesado, hechizado • **to hold sb ~** tener a algn embelesado

spellcheck ['spel,tʃek] (VT) pasar el corrector (ortográfico) a
(N) • **to do a ~ (on sth)** pasar el corrector (ortográfico) (a algo)

spellchecker ['spel,tʃekəʳ] (N) corrector *m* ortográfico

speller ['speləʳ] (N) • **to be a bad ~** cometer muchas faltas de ortografía, tener mala ortografía

spelling ['spelɪŋ] (N) ortografía *f* • **the correct ~ is ...** la ortografía correcta es ... • **my ~ is terrible** cometo muchas faltas de ortografía
(CPD) ▸ **spelling bee** certamen *m* de ortografía ▸ **spelling checker** corrector *m* ortográfico ▸ **spelling error, spelling mistake** falta *f* de ortografía ▸ **spelling pronunciation** pronunciación *f* ortográfica

spelt¹ [spelt] (*esp Brit*) (PT), (PP) *of* **spell²**

spelt² [spelt] (N) (*Bot*) espelta *f*

spelunker [spɪ'lʌŋkəʳ] (N) (*US*) espeleólogo/a *m/f*

spelunking [spɪ'lʌŋkɪŋ] (N) (*US*) espeleología *f*

spend [spend] (PT, PP: **spent**) (VT) **1** (= *pay out*) [+ *money*] gastar • **to ~ sth on sth/sb** gastar algo en algo/algn • **she ~s too much money on clothes** gasta demasiado dinero en ropa • **they've spent a fortune on the house** (se) han gastado un dineral en la casa • **the buildings need a lot ~ing on them** a los edificios les hace falta una buena inyección de dinero • **it's money well spent** es dinero bien empleado • IDIOM: • **to ~ a penny** (*Brit*) (*euph*) cambiar de agua al canario
2 (= *devote*) [+ *effort, time*] dedicar • **we ~ time, money and effort training these people** dedicamos tiempo, dinero y trabajo a formar a estas personas
3 (= *pass*) [+ *period of time*] pasar • **where are you ~ing your holiday?** ¿dónde vas a pasar las vacaciones? • **he spent eight years learning his trade** pasó ocho años aprendiendo los gajes del oficio • **he ~s all his time sleeping** se pasa la vida durmiendo; ▹ **night**
4 (= *use up*) [+ *force, ammunition, provisions*] (*liter*) agotar • **the storm has spent its fury** la tempestad ha agotado *or* perdido su fuerza • **I ~ all my energy just getting to work** nada más que en llegar al trabajo se me van todas las energías • **the bullets spent themselves among the trees** las balas se desperdiciaron en los árboles
(VI) gastar

spender ['spendəʳ] (N) gastador(a) *m/f* • **big ~** persona *f* generosa; (*pej*) derrochador(a) *m/f* • **to be a free ~** gastar libremente su dinero; (*pej*) ser derrochador

spending ['spendɪŋ] (N) gastos *mpl* • **to keep one's ~ down** mantener los gastos bajos • **the latest figures for consumer ~** las últimas cifras correspondientes a los gastos del consumidor • **to reduce government** *or* **public ~** reducir el gasto público • **military/ defence ~** gastos *mpl* militares/de defensa • **they pledged to increase ~ on education** prometieron incrementar el presupuesto de educación
(CPD) ▸ **spending cuts** recortes *mpl* presupuestarios ▸ **spending limit** límite *m* de gastos ▸ **spending money** (*for holiday*) dinero *m* para gastar; (= *allowance*) dinero *m* para gastos (personales) ▸ **spending power** poder *m* de compra, poder *m* adquisitivo ▸ **spending spree** derroche *m* de dinero • **we went on a ~ spree** salimos a gastar dinero

spendthrift ['spendθrɪft] (ADJ) derrochador, pródigo
(N) derrochador(a) *m/f*, pródigo/a *m/f*

spent [spent] (PT), (PP) *of* **spend**
(ADJ) [*match, light bulb, battery*] gastado; [*bullet, cartridge, ammunition*] usado • **he's a ~ force** ya no es lo que era

sperm [spɜ:m] (N) (*Bio*) esperma *m or f*
(CPD) ▸ **sperm bank** banco *m* de esperma ▸ **sperm count** recuento *m* de espermas ▸ **sperm whale** cachalote *m*

spermaceti [,spɜ:mə'setɪ] (N) esperma *m or f* de ballena

spermatozoon [,spɜ:mətəʊ'zəʊɒn] (N) (PL: **spermatozoa** [,spɜ:mətəʊ'zəʊə]) espermatozoo *m*

spermicidal [,spɜ:mɪ'saɪdl] (ADJ) espermicida

spermicide ['spɜ:mɪsaɪd] (N) espermicida *m*

spew [spju:] (VT) (*also* **spew up**) vomitar; (*fig*) arrojar, vomitar
(VI) vomitar • **it makes me want to ~*** (*fig*) me da asco

▸ **spew out** (VT + ADV) **1** [+ *smoke, flames, gas, lava*] expulsar
2* [+ *dinner, food*] potar*
(VI + ADV) (= *vomit*) potar*

SPF (N ABBR) (= **sun protection factor**) factor *m* de protección, FP *m* • **SPF 15** FP 15

SPG (N ABBR) (*Brit*) (*Police*) = **Special Patrol Group**

sphagnum ['sfægnəm] (N) esfagno *m*

sphere [sfɪəʳ] (N) **1** (*Astron, Math etc*) esfera *f*
2 (*fig*) esfera *f* • **in the social ~** en la esfera social • **~ of influence** esfera *f* de influencia • **~ of activity** campo *m* de actividad, esfera *f* de actividad • **his ~ of interest** el ámbito de sus intereses • **in the ~ of politics** en el mundo de la política • **that's outside my ~** eso no es de mi competencia

spherical ['sferɪkəl] (ADJ) esférico

spheroid ['sfɪərɔɪd] (N) esferoide *m*

sphincter ['sfɪŋktəʳ] (N) esfínter *m*

sphinx [sfɪŋks] (N) (PL: **sphinxes**) esfinge *f*

spice [spaɪs] (N) **1** (*Culin*) especia *f* • **mixed ~(s)** especias *fpl* mixtas • PROVERB: • **variety is the ~ of life** en la variedad está el gusto
2 (*fig*) lo picante • **the papers like stories with some ~** a los periódicos les gustan los reportajes con algo de picante • **the details add ~ to the story** los detalles dan sabor a la historia
(VT) **1** (*Culin*) condimentar, sazonar
2 (*fig*) • **a highly ~d account** un relato de mucho picante • **gossip ~d with scandal** cotilleos con el sabor picante que da el escándalo
(CPD) ▸ **spice rack** especiero *m*

▸ **spice up** (VT + ADV) **1** (= *season*) condimentar, dar más sabor a • **use it to ~ up rice dishes and stews** úselo para condimentar *or* dar mas sabor a los platos de arroz y estofados

S

2 (= *enliven*) • **it could help ~ up your sex life** podría ayudar a estimular su vida sexual

spiced ['spaɪst] (ADJ) [*dish, sauce*] condimentado, sazonado • **~ with sth** condimentado con algo, sazonado con algo

spiciness ['spaɪsɪnɪs] (N) **1** [*of food*] lo picante
2 [*of story*] lo picante

Spick** [spɪk] (N) (*US*) (*pej*) hispano/a *m/f*

spick-and-span ['spɪkən'spæn] (ADJ) [*house, room*] impecable, como los chorros del oro*; [*person*] acicalado • **they left the cottage spick-and-span** dejaron el chalet impecable, dejaron el chalet como los chorros del oro* • **everything must be kept spick-and-span** todo tiene que estar impecable

spicy ['spaɪsɪ] (ADJ) (COMPAR: **spicier**, SUPERL: **spiciest**) **1** (*Culin*) (*gen*) muy condimentado, muy sazonado; (= *hot*) picante, picoso (*LAm*)
2 (*fig*) [*joke etc*] picante, colorado (*LAm*)

spider ['spaɪdəʳ] (N) araña *f* • **~'s web** telaraña *f*
(CPD) ▸ **spider crab** centollo *m*, centolla *f* ▸ **spider monkey** mono *m* araña ▸ **spider plant** cinta *f*

spiderman ['spaɪdəmæn] (N) (PL: **spidermen**) (*Constr*) *obrero que trabaja en la construcción de edificios altos*

spiderweb ['spaɪdəweb] (N) (*US*) telaraña *f*

spidery ['spaɪdərɪ] (ADJ) delgado; [*writing*] de patas de araña

spiel* [spiːl] (N) (= *speech*) arenga *f*, discurso *m*; [*of salesman etc*] rollo* *m*, material *m* publicitario • **it's just his usual ~** es el mismo cuento de siempre

spiffing†* ['spɪfɪŋ] (ADJ) fetén†*, estupendo*, fenomenal*

spigot ['spɪgət] (N) espita *f*, bitoque *m*

spike [spaɪk] (N) **1** (= *point*) punta *f*; (= *metal rod*) pincho *m*; (= *stake*) estaca *f*; (= *tool*) escarpia *f*; (*on railing*) barrote *m*; (*on sports shoes*) clavo *m*
2 (*Zool*) [*of hedgehog etc*] púa *f*
3 (*Elec*) pico *m* parásito
4 (*Bot*) espiga *f*
5 **spikes** (*Sport*) zapatillas *fpl* con clavos
(VT) **1** (= *fix*) clavar; (= *impale*) atravesar
2 (= *stop*) [+ *rumour*] acabar con; (= *thwart*) [+ *plan etc*] frustrar • IDIOM: • **to ~ sb's guns** poner trabas a los planes de algn
3 • **a ~d drink*** (*with added alcohol*) una bebida con alcohol añadido de extranjis; (*drugged*) *una bebida a la que le han echado algo, como un somnífero, droga etc.*
(CPD) ▸ **spike heel** (*US*) tacón *m* de aguja

spiked [spaɪkt] (ADJ) [*shoe*] con clavos

spikenard ['spaɪknɑːd] (N) nardo *m*

spiky ['spaɪkɪ] (ADJ) (COMPAR: **spikier**, SUPERL: **spikiest**) **1** (= *sharp, pointed*) puntiagudo; (= *thorny*) cubierto de púas; (*Zool*) erizado; [*hair*] de punta
2 (*Brit**) (= *irritable*) [*person*] quisquilloso, susceptible

spill¹ [spɪl] (PT, PP: **spilled** *or* **spilt**) (VT)
1 [+ *water, salt*] derramar, verter • **you're ~ing the milk** estás derramando la leche • **you've ~ed** *or* **spilt coffee on your shirt** te ha caído café en la camisa • **she ~ed** *or* **spilt wine all over the table** derramó el vino por toda la mesa • IDIOM: • **to ~ the beans*** descubrir el pastel*, contarlo todo; ▹ **cry**
2 [+ *rider*] hacer caer, desarzonar
(VI) derramarse, verterse
(N) **1** (= *fall*) caída *f* • **to have a ~** sufrir una caída, tener un accidente
2 (= *spillage*) vertido *m*

▸ **spill out** (VI + ADV) [*liquid*] derramarse; [*contents, objects*] desparramarse; [*people*] salir en avalancha • **the crowd ~ed out into the streets** la gente salió a la calle en avalancha • **the audience ~ed out of the cinema** el público salió en masa del cine
(VT + ADV) volcar; (*fig*) soltar

▸ **spill over** (VI + ADV) [*liquid*] derramarse; [*cup, pan*] desbordarse • **these problems ~ed over into his private life** estos problemas llegaron a afectar su vida privada

spill² [spɪl] (N) (*for lighting fire*) pajuela *f*

spillage ['spɪlɪdʒ] (N) vertido *m*

spillover ['spɪləʊvəʳ] (N) **1** (= *act of spilling*) derrame *m*; (= *quantity spilt*) cantidad *f* derramada
2 (*fig*) (= *excess part*) excedente *m*
3 (*Econ*) (= *effect*) incidencia *f* indirecta en el gasto público

spillway ['spɪlweɪ] (N) (*US*) derramadero *m*, aliviadero *m*

spilt [spɪlt] (*esp Brit*) (PT), (PP) *of* **spill**

spin [spɪn] (VB: PT, PP: **spun**) (N) **1** (= *rotating motion*) vuelta *f*, revolución *f* • **to give a wheel a ~** hacer girar una rueda • IDIOM: • **to be in a (flat) ~** (*Brit**) [*person*] andar muy confundido • **the news sent the stock market into a flat ~** la noticia creó un estado de gran confusión en la bolsa
2 (*in washing machine*) • **give the towels another ~** vuelve a centrifugar las toallas (en la lavadora) • **long/short ~** centrifugado *m* largo/corto
3 (*Sport*) (*on ball*) efecto *m* • **to put (a) ~ on a ball** dar efecto a una pelota
4 (= *loss of control*) (*Aer*) barrena *f*; (*Aut*) trompo *m* • **to go into a ~** (*Aer*) entrar en barrena; (*Aut*) hacer un trompo • **to pull** *or* **come out of a ~** (*Aer*) salir de barrena
5 (*Brit**) (= *short ride*) vuelta *f*, paseo *m*, garbeo *m* (*Sp**) • **to go for a ~** dar una vuelta *or* un paseo (en coche/moto etc), darse un garbeo (en coche/moto etc) (*Sp**)
6* (= *interpretation*) interpretación *f* • **to put a positive ~ on sth** interpretar positivamente algo, dar un sesgo positivo a algo
(VT) **1** (= *rotate*) (*gen*) hacer girar; [+ *top*] hacer bailar • **to ~ a coin** hacer girar una moneda; (*to decide sth*) echar una moneda a cara o cruz
2 (= *spin-dry*) [+ *clothes*] centrifugar
3 (= *turn suddenly*) girar • **he spun the steering wheel sharply to the right** giró el volante bruscamente hacia la derecha • **to ~ sth/sb round** dar la vuelta a algo/algn
4 (*Sport*) [+ *ball*] dar efecto a
5 [+ *thread*] hilar; [+ *web*] tejer; [+ *cocoon*] devanar, hacer • IDIOMS: • **to ~ a web of lies** hilar una sarta de mentiras • **to ~ a yarn*** (*in order to deceive*) inventar una historia
(VI) **1** (= *rotate*) girar, dar vueltas • **his wheels began to ~ as he tried to get off the grass** las ruedas empezaron a dar vueltas cuando intentó salir de la hierba • **she spun around** *or* **round to face him** se dio la vuelta para tenerlo de frente • **my head is ~ning** me da vueltas la cabeza • **it makes my head ~** me marea
2 (= *move quickly*) • **to ~ along** correr a gran velocidad • **the car spun out of control** el coche se descontroló y empezó a dar vueltas • **to send sth/sb ~ning: the blow sent him ~ning** el golpe le hizo rodar por el suelo • **she sent the plate ~ning through the air** lanzó el plato a rodar por los aires
3 [*washing machine*] centrifugar
4 (*with spinning wheel*) hilar
(CPD) ▸ **Spin® class** clase *f* de Spinning® ▸ **spin doctor*** (*Pol*) asesor(a) *m/f* político(a)

▸ **spin out*** (VT + ADV) [+ *process, story*] alargar, prolongar; [+ *money, drink*] estirar

▸ **spin round** (VT + ADV) (= *spin round and round*) [+ *wheel, display stand*] girar; [+ *person*] hacer girar
(VI + ADV) **1** (= *spin round and round*) [*wheel, display stand, skater, dancer*] dar vueltas (sobre sí mismo)
2 (= *turn round quickly once*) [*person*] volverse rápidamente

spina bifida [ˌspaɪnə'bɪfɪdə] (N) espina *f* bífida

spinach ['spɪnɪdʒ] (N) **1** (*Culin*) espinacas *fpl*
2 (= *plant*) espinaca *f*

spinal ['spaɪnl] (ADJ) espinal, vertebral
(CPD) ▸ **spinal column** columna *f* vertebral ▸ **spinal cord** médula *f* espinal

spindle ['spɪndl] (N) **1** (*for spinning*) huso *m*
2 (*Tech*) eje *m*

spindleshanks* ['spɪndlʃæŋks] (N) zanquivano/a *m/f*

spindly ['spɪndlɪ] (ADJ) (COMPAR: **spindlier**, SUPERL: **spindliest**) [*person*] alto y delgado, larguirucho*; [*legs*] largo y delgado, largo y delgaducho*; [*plant, tree*] alto y delgado, alto y delgaducho*

spin-drier ['spɪn'draɪəʳ] (N) = **spin-dryer**

spindrift ['spɪndrɪft] (N) rocío *m* del mar, espuma *f*

spin-dry [ˌspɪn'draɪ] (VT) centrifugar

spin-dryer ['spɪn'draɪəʳ] (N) secadora-centrifugadora *f*

spine [spaɪn] (N) **1** (*Anat*) (= *backbone*) columna *f* (vertebral), espina *f* dorsal
2 (*Zool*) (= *spike*) púa *f*, pincho *m*; (*Bot*) espina *f*, pincho *m*
3 [*of book*] lomo *m*
4 [*of mountain range*] espinazo *m*

spine-chiller ['spaɪnˌtʃɪləʳ] (N) (= *film*) película *f* de terror; (= *book*) libro *m* de terror

spine-chilling ['spaɪnˌtʃɪlɪŋ] (ADJ) escalofriante

spineless ['spaɪnlɪs] (ADJ) (*fig*) débil

spinelessly ['spaɪnlɪslɪ] (ADV) débilmente

spinet [spɪ'net] (N) espineta *f*

spine-tingling ['spaɪnˌtɪŋglɪŋ] (ADJ) (= *frightening*) inquietante; (= *moving*) emocionante

spinnaker ['spɪnəkəʳ] (N) balón *m*, espinaquer *m*

spinner ['spɪnəʳ] (N) **1** [*of cloth*] hilandero/a *m/f*
2 (*Cricket, Baseball*) el/la que da efecto a la pelota
3 (*Fishing*) cebo *m* artificial de cuchara
4* (= *spin-dryer*) secadora-centrifugadora *f*

spinneret [ˌspɪnə'ret] (N) pezón *m* hilador

spinney ['spɪnɪ] (N) bosquecillo *m*

spinning ['spɪnɪŋ] (N) (= *act*) hilado *m*; (= *art*) hilandería *f*, arte *m* de hilar
(CPD) ▸ **spinning jenny** máquina *f* de hilar de husos múltiples ▸ **spinning mill** hilandería *f* ▸ **spinning top** peonza *f*, trompo *m* ▸ **spinning wheel** rueca *f* *or* torno *m* de hilar

spin-off ['spɪnɒf] (N) (*Comm*) (= *product*) derivado *m*, producto *m* secundario; (= *secondary effect*) consecuencia *f* indirecta; (= *incidental benefit*) beneficio *m* incidental, beneficio *m* indirecto

spinster ['spɪnstəʳ] (N) soltera *f*; (*pej*) solterona *f*

spinsterhood† ['spɪnstəhʊd] (N) soltería *f* • **she preferred ~** prefería la soltería

spiny ['spaɪnɪ] (ADJ) (COMPAR: **spinier**, SUPERL: **spiniest**) **1** [*rose*] espinoso; [*animal*] con púas
2 [*problem*] espinoso

spiracle ['spɪrəkl] (N) espiráculo *m*

spiraea [spaɪ'rɪə] (N) espirea *f*

spiral ['spaɪərəl] (ADJ) espiral, en espiral • **a ~ staircase** una escalera de caracol
(N) espiral *f*, hélice *f* • **the inflationary ~** la espiral inflacionista
(VI) • **to ~ up/down** subir/bajar en espiral • **the plane ~led down** el avión bajó en

espiral • **the smoke ~led up** • **the smoke went ~ling up** el humo subió formando una espiral • **prices have ~led up** los precios han subido vertiginosamente

spirally ['spaɪərəlɪ] ADV en espiral

spire ['spaɪəʳ] N aguja *f*

spirea [spaɪ'rɪə] N (*US*) = **spiraea**

spirit ['spɪrɪt] N **1** (= *soul, inner force*) espíritu *m* • **I'll be with you in ~** estaré contigo en espíritu • **young in ~** joven de espíritu • **the ~ is willing but the flesh is weak** las intenciones son buenas pero la carne es débil
2 (= *ghost, supernatural being*) espíritu *m* • **evil ~** espíritu *m* maligno • **the ~ world** el mundo de los espíritus
3 (= *courage*) espíritu *m*; (= *liveliness*) ímpetu *m*, energía *f* • **to break sb's ~** quebrantar el espíritu a algn • **they lack ~** les falta espíritu • **a woman of ~** una mujer con espíritu *or* brío • **show some ~!** ¡anímate! • **the team soon began to show their ~** el equipo pronto empezó a animarse • **to do sth with ~** hacer algo con energía • **to sing with ~** cantar con brío
4 (= *attitude, mood*) espíritu *m* • **a ~ of adventure** un espíritu aventurero • **community ~** civismo *m* • **they wish to solve their problems in a ~ of cooperation** quieren resolver sus problemas con espíritu de cooperación • **he refused to enter into the ~ of things** se negó a entrar en ambiente • **festive ~** espíritu *m* festivo • **in a ~ of friendship** con espíritu de amistad • **generosity of ~** bondad *f* de espíritu • **a ~ of optimism** un espíritu optimista • **public ~** civismo *m* • **to take sth in the right/wrong ~** interpretar bien/mal algo • **that's the ~!** ¡así me gusta!, ¡ánimo!; ▹ **fighting, team**
5 (= *essence*) [*of agreement, law*] espíritu *m* • **the ~ of the age/the times** el espíritu de la época/de los tiempos • **the ~ of the law** el espíritu de la ley
6 (= *person*) alma *f* • **the leading** *or* **moving ~ in the party** el alma del partido, la figura más destacada del partido • **she was a free ~** era una persona sin convencionalismos; ▹ **kindred**
7 spirits: **a** (= *state of mind*) • **to be in good ~s** tener la moral alta • **to be in high ~s** estar animadísimo, estar muy alegre • **it was just a case of youthful high ~s** no fue más que una demostración típica del comportamiento impetuoso de la juventud • **I tried to keep his ~s up** intenté animarlo *or* darle ánimos • **we kept our ~s up by singing** mantuvimos la moral alta cantando • **to lift** *or* **raise sb's ~s** levantar el ánimo *or* la moral a algn • **to be in low ~s** tener la moral baja, estar bajo de moral • **my ~s rose somewhat** se me levantó un poco el ánimo *or* la moral
b (= *alcohol*) licores *mpl* • **I keep off ~s** no bebo licores • **a measure of ~s** un (vasito de) licor • **~s of wine** espíritu *m* de vino
8 (*Chem*) alcohol *m*
VT (= *take*) • **to ~ sth away** llevarse algo como por arte de magia, hacer desaparecer algo • **he was ~ed out of the country** lo sacaron del país clandestinamente *or* de forma clandestina
CPD ▸ **spirit duplicator** copiadora *f* al alcohol ▸ **spirit gum** cola *f* de maquillaje ▸ **spirit lamp** lamparilla *f* de alcohol ▸ **spirit level** nivel *m* de burbuja ▸ **spirit stove** infernillo *m* de alcohol

spirited ['spɪrɪtɪd] ADJ (= *lively*) [*person*] animado, lleno de vida; [*horse*] fogoso; [*debate, discussion*] animado, enérgico; [*attack*] enérgico • **he made a ~ defence of his position** defendió su postura con vehemencia • **he gave a ~ performance** (*Mus*) tocó con brío • **they put up a ~ resistance** organizaron una enérgica resistencia, resistieron enérgicamente

spiritedly ['spɪrɪtɪdlɪ] ADV [*talk*] con entusiasmo, con energía

spiritedness ['spɪrɪtɪdnɪs] N animación *f*; [*of horse*] fogosidad *f*; [*of performance*] energía *f*; (= *courage*) [*of person, reply, attempt etc*] fuerza *f*

spiritless ['spɪrɪtlɪs] ADJ apocado, sin ánimo

spiritual ['spɪrɪtjʊəl] ADJ espiritual
N (*Mus*) canción *f* religiosa

spiritualism ['spɪrɪtjʊəlɪzəm] N espiritismo *m*

spiritualist ['spɪrɪtjʊəlɪst] N espiritista *mf*

spirituality [,spɪrɪtjʊ'ælɪtɪ] N espiritualidad *f*

spiritually ['spɪrɪtjʊəlɪ] ADV espiritualmente

spirituous ['spɪrɪtjʊəs] ADJ espirituoso

spirt [spɜːt] ▹ **spurt**

spit¹ [spɪt] (VB: PT, PP: **spat**) N saliva *f*, esputo *m* • **a few ~s of rain** unas gotas de lluvia • IDIOMS: • **~ and polish*** limpieza *f* • **that table needs a bit of ~ and polish*** esa mesa hay que limpiarla • **to be the dead ~ of sb*** ser la viva imagen *or* el vivo retrato de algn
VT **1** (*lit*) [+ *blood, crumb*] escupir
2 (= *exclaim*) espetar, soltar • **"traitor!" he spat** —¡traidor! —espetó *or* soltó él • **he spat the words** escupió las palabras
VI **1** [*person*] escupir (**at** a, **on** en); [*cat*] bufar • **to ~ in sb's face** escupir a la cara a algn • **it's ~ting with rain** (*Brit*) están cayendo algunas gotas
2 [*fat, fire*] chisporrotear • **the fish is ~ting in the pan** chisporrotea el pescado en la sartén
▸ **spit forth** VT + ADV = **spit out**
▸ **spit out** VT + ADV **1** [+ *pip, pill*] escupir • **I spat it out** lo escupí
2 (*fig*) • **~ it out!*** ¡dilo!, ¡habla! • **he spat out the words** escupió las palabras
▸ **spit up** VT + ADV [+ *blood*] soltar un esputo de

spit² [spɪt] N **1** (*Culin*) asador *m*, espetón *m*
2 (*Geog*) [*of land*] lengua *f*; (= *sandbank*) banco *m* de arena
VT espetar
CPD ▸ **spit roast** asado *m*; ▹ **spitroast**

spit³ [spɪt] N (*Agr*) azadada *f* • **to dig three ~s deep** excavar a una profundidad de tres azadadas

spite [spaɪt] N **1** (= *ill will*) rencor *m*, ojeriza *f* • **to do sth out of** *or* **from ~** hacer algo por inquina • **to have a ~ against sb*** tener rencor a *or* hacia algn
2 • **in ~ of** (= *despite*) a pesar de, pese a • **in ~ of the fact that** a pesar de que, pese a que • **in ~ of herself** a pesar de sí misma • **in ~ of all he says** a pesar de todo lo que dice
VT herir, dañar • **she just does it to ~ me** lo hace solamente para causarme pena

spiteful ['spaɪtfʊl] ADJ [*person*] (= *resentful*) rencoroso; (= *malicious*) malicioso; [*action*] malintencionado • **to be ~ to sb** tratar a algn con rencor, ser rencoroso con algn

spitefully ['spaɪtfəlɪ] ADV (= *out of resentment*) por despecho • **she said ~** dijo, con malicia

spitefulness ['spaɪtfʊlnɪs] N (= *resentment*) rencor *m*; (= *malice*) malicia *f*

spitfire ['spɪt,faɪəʳ] N fierabrás *mf*

spitroast ['spɪtrəʊst] VT rostizar

spitting ['spɪtɪŋ] N • **"spitting prohibited"** • **"no spitting"** "se prohíbe escupir"
ADJ • **it's within ~ distance*** está muy cerca • IDIOM: • **to be the ~ image of sb** ser la viva imagen *or* el vivo retrato de algn

spittle ['spɪtl] N saliva *f*, baba *f*

spittoon [spɪ'tuːn] N escupidera *f*

spiv* [spɪv] N (*Brit*) chanchullero* *m*, caballero *m* de industria; (= *slacker*) gandul *m*; (= *black marketeer*) estraperlista *mf*

splash [splæʃ] N **1** (= *spray*) salpicadura *f*; (= *splashing noise*) chapoteo *m* • **I heard a ~** oí un chapoteo • **it fell with a great ~ into the water** hizo mucho ruido al caer al agua • **whisky with a ~ of water** whisky *m* con un poquitín de agua
2 (= *patch, spot*) [*of light*] mancha *f* • **a ~ of colour** una mancha de color
3 (*fig*) • **with a great ~ of publicity*** con mucho bombo publicitario* • IDIOM: • **to make a ~*** causar sensación
VT **1** (*gen*) salpicar • **to ~ sb with water** salpicar a algn de agua • **don't ~ me!** ¡no me salpiques! • **he ~ed water on his face** se echó agua en la cara
2 (= *stain*) manchar • **to ~ paint on the floor** manchar el suelo de pintura
3 (*fig*) • **the story was ~ed across the front page*** el reportaje apareció con grandes titulares en primera plana
VI **1** [*liquid, mud etc*] • **mud ~ed all over his trousers** el barro le salpicó los pantalones
2 [*person, animal*] (*in water*) chapotear • **to ~ across a stream** cruzar un arroyo chapoteando
▸ **splash about** VT + ADV • **to ~ water about** desparramar (el) agua • **to ~ one's money about** derrochar su dinero por todas partes
VI + ADV chapotear • **to ~ about in the water** chapotear en el agua
▸ **splash down** VI + ADV amarar, amerizar
▸ **splash out*** VI + ADV (*Brit*) derrochar dinero • **so we ~ed out and bought it** decidimos echar la casa por la ventana y comprarlo
▸ **splash up** VT + ADV salpicar
VI + ADV salpicar

splashback ['splæʃbæk] N salpicadero *m*

splashboard ['splæʃbɔːd] N guardabarros *m inv*

splashdown ['splæʃdaʊn] N amaraje *m*, amerizaje *m*

splashy* ['splæʃɪ] ADJ (*US*) (COMPAR: **splashier**, SUPERL: **splashiest**) (= *showy*) ostentoso

splat [splæt] N • **with a ~** con un plaf
EXCL ¡plaf!

splatter ['splætəʳ] = **spatter**

splay [spleɪ] VT **1** [+ *feet, legs*] abrir, extender
2 (*Tech*) biselar, achaflanar

spleen [spliːn] N **1** (*Anat*) bazo *m*
2 • **to vent one's ~** (*fig*) descargar la bilis

splendid ['splendɪd] ADJ (= *magnificent*) espléndido, magnífico; (= *excellent*) estupendo, magnífico • **he has done ~ work** ha hecho una magnífica labor • **splendid!** ¡magnífico!, ¡estupendo! • **in ~ isolation** en total *or* absoluto aislamiento

splendidly ['splendɪdlɪ] ADV (= *magnificently*) espléndidamente, magníficamente; (= *wonderfully*) estupendamente • **everything went ~** todo fue de maravilla • **we get along ~** nos llevamos muy bien • **you did ~** hiciste muy bien • **a ~ dressed man** un hombre muy bien vestido

splendiferous* [splen'dɪfərəs] ADJ (*hum*) = **splendid**

splendour, splendor (*US*) ['splendəʳ] N esplendor *m*

splenetic [splɪ'netɪk] ADJ **1** (*Anat*) esplénico
2 (*frm*) (= *short-tempered*) enojadizo, de genio vivo; (= *bad-tempered*) malhumorado

splice [splaɪs] VT **1** [+ *rope, tape etc*]

empalmar, juntar • IDIOM: • **to get ~d*** casarse
2 (*Naut*) ayustar
N empalme *m*, junta *f*

splicer ['splaɪsəʳ] N (*for film*) máquina *f* de montaje

spliff‡ [splɪf] N (*Drugs*) porro *m*, canuto *m*

splint [splɪnt] N (*Med*) tablilla *f* • **to put sb's arm in ~s** entablillar el brazo a algn • **to be in ~s** estar entablillado
VT entablillar

splinter ['splɪntəʳ] N [*of wood, metal*] astilla *f*; [*of glass*] fragmento *m*; [*of bone*] esquirla *f*, fragmento *m* • **I've got a ~ in my finger** tengo una astilla en el dedo
VI astillarse, hacerse astillas; (*fig*) [*party*] escindirse • **to ~ off from** escindirse *or* separarse de
VT 1 (*lit*) astillar, hacer astillas
2 (*fig*) [+ *party*] dividir
CPD ▸ **splinter group** grupo *m* disidente, facción *f* ▸ **splinter party** partido *m* nuevo (*formado a raíz de la escisión de otro*)

splinterbone ['splɪntəbəʊn] N peroné *m*

splinterless ['splɪntəlɪs] ADJ inastillable

splinterproof ['splɪntəpru:f] ADJ • **~ glass** cristal *m* inastillable

split [splɪt] (VB: PT, PP: **split**) N 1 (= *crack*) (*in wood, rock*) hendidura *f*, grieta *f*
2 (= *rift*) ruptura *f*, escisión *f* • **there are threats of a ~ in the progressive party** se oyen voces *or* hay amenazas de escisión en el partido progresista
3 (= *division*) división *f* • **the ~ between the rich and the poor** la división entre ricos y pobres • **a three-way ~** una división en tres partes
4 • **to do the ~s** (*Gymnastics*) hacer el spagat; (*accidentally*) abrirse completamente de piernas, espatarrarse*
5 (*Culin*) • **jam ~** pastel *m* de mermelada • **banana ~** (banana) split *m*
6 (*Sew*) (*in skirt*) abertura *f*
ADJ 1 (= *cracked*) [*wood, rock*] partido, hendido • **he had a ~ lip** tenía un labio partido
2 (= *divided*) dividido • **the government is ~ on this question** el gobierno está dividido en este asunto • **it was a ~ decision** la decisión no fue unánime • **the party was ~** el partido estaba escindido *or* dividido • **the votes are ~ 15-13** los votos están repartidos 15 a 13 • **the party is ~ three ways** el partido está escindido *or* dividido en tres grupos
VT 1 (= *break*) partir • **the sea had ~ the ship in two** el mar había partido el barco en dos • **he ~ the wood with an axe** partió la madera con un hacha • **to ~ the atom** desintegrar el átomo • **to ~ sth open** abrir algo • **he ~ his head open** se abrió la cabeza de un golpe • IDIOMS: • **to ~ hairs** hilar muy fino *or* delgado, buscarle tres pies al gato, buscarle mangas al chaleco (*LAm*) • **to ~ one's sides laughing** partirse de risa, morirse de (la) risa
2 (= *divide, share*) repartir • **let's ~ the money between us** repartámonos el dinero • **to ~ the difference** repartir la diferencia (a partes iguales) • **to ~ sth into three parts** dividir algo en tres partes • **the children were ~ into two groups** dividieron a los niños en dos grupos • **to ~ the vote** (*Pol*) repartirse los votos • **to ~ the profit five ways** repartir las ganancias entre cinco
3 (*fig*) [+ *government, group*] dividir; [+ *party*] escindir, dividir • **the dispute ~ the party** la disputa escindió *or* dividió el partido
VI 1 (= *come apart*) [*stone etc*] henderse, rajarse • **the jeans ~ the first time she wore them** los vaqueros se le abrieron por las costuras la primera vez que se los puso • **to ~ open** abrirse • **the ship hit a rock and ~ in two** el barco chocó con una roca y se partió en dos • IDIOM: • **my head is ~ting** me va a estallar la cabeza
2 (*fig*) [*government, group*] dividirse; [*party*] escindirse, dividirse
3* (= *tell tales*) chivatear‡, soplar* • **to ~ on sb** chivatear contra algn‡, soplar contra algn* • **don't ~ on me** de esto no digas ni pío
4 (*esp US**) (= *leave*) largarse‡, irse
CPD ▸ **split ends** puntas *fpl* abiertas ▸ **split infinitive** *infinitivo en el que un adverbio o una frase se intercala entre "to" y el verbo* ▸ **split pea** guisante *m* majado ▸ **split personality** personalidad *f* desdoblada ▸ **split pin** (*Brit*) chaveta *f*, pasador *m* ▸ **split screen** pantalla *f* partida; ▹ **split-screen** ▸ **split second** fracción *f* de segundo • **in a ~ second** en un instante, en un abrir y cerrar de ojos; ▹ **split-second** ▸ **split shift** jornada *f* partida ▸ **split ticket** (*US*) • **to vote a ~ ticket** dar el voto fraccionado, *votar a candidatos de diferentes partidos en la misma papeleta*

▸ **split off** VI + ADV separarse
VT + ADV separar

▸ **split up** VI + ADV 1 (= *break up*) estrellarse
2 (= *separate*) [*partners*] separarse; [*meeting, crowd*] dispersarse • **they were married 14 years but then they ~ up** estuvieron casados durante 14 años pero luego se separaron • **let's ~ up for safety** separémonos para mayor seguridad • **we ~ up into two groups** nos dividimos en dos grupos
VT + ADV 1 (= *break up*) partir
2 (= *divide up*) repartir; [+ *estate*] parcelar • **we'll ~ the work up among us** nos repartiremos *or* dividiremos el trabajo
3 (= *separate*) dividir • **~ the children up into small groups** divide a los niños en grupos pequeños

split-level ['splɪt,levl] ADJ [*room*] a desnivel; [*house*] dúplex; [*cooker*] en dos niveles

split-off ['splɪtɒf] N separación *f*; (*Pol*) escisión *f*

split-screen [splɪt'skri:n] CPD ▸ **split-screen facility** capacidad *f* de pantalla partida

split-second ['splɪt,sekənd] ADJ [*timing*] de una fracción de segundo

splitting ['splɪtɪŋ] ADJ [*headache*] terrible
N • **~ of the atom** desintegración *f* del átomo

split-up ['splɪtʌp] N ruptura *f*; [*of couple*] separación *f*

splodge [splɒdʒ], **splotch** [splɒtʃ] N mancha *f*, borrón *m*

splurge* [splɜ:dʒ] N (= *excess*) derroche *m*
VI • **to ~ on sth** derrochar dinero comprando algo

splutter ['splʌtəʳ] N 1 [*of fat etc*] chisporroteo *m*
2 [*of speech*] farfulla *f*
VI 1 [*person*] (= *spit*) escupir, echar saliva; (= *stutter*) farfullar, balbucear • **to ~ with indignation** farfullar indignado
2 [*fire, fat*] chisporrotear; [*engine*] renquear
VT farfullar, balbucear • **"yes", he ~ed** —sí —farfulló *or* balbuceó

spoil [spɔɪl] (VB: PT, PP: **spoiled** *or* **spoilt**) VT 1 (= *ruin*) estropear, arruinar; (= *harm*) dañar; (= *invalidate*) [+ *voting paper*] invalidar • **the coast has been ~ed by development** la costa ha sido arruinada por las urbanizaciones • **it ~ed our holiday** nos estropeó las vacaciones • **and there were 20 ~ed papers** y hubo 20 votos nulos • **it will ~ your appetite** te quitará el apetito • **to ~ sb's fun** aguar la fiesta a algn • **to get ~ed** echarse a perder, estropearse
2 (= *pamper*) mimar, consentir (*LAm*) • **grandparents like to ~ their grandchildren** a los abuelos les encanta mimar a los nietos
VI 1 [*food*] estropearse, echarse a perder • **if we leave it here it will ~** si lo dejamos aquí se estropeará *or* se echará a perder
2 • **to be ~ing for a fight** estar con ganas de luchar *or* (*LAm*) pelear

spoilage ['spɔɪlɪdʒ] N (= *process*) deterioro *m*; (= *thing, amount spoilt*) desperdicio *m*

spoiled [spɔɪld] = **spoilt**

spoiler ['spɔɪləʳ] N 1 (*Aut, Aer*) alerón *m*, spoiler *m*
2 (*Press*) • **a rival paper brought out a ~** un periódico rival publicó otra exclusiva para quitarles parte de las ventas
3* (= *person etc*) aguafiestas *mf inv*

spoils [spɔɪlz] NPL botín *msing* • **the ~ of war** el botín de la guerra

spoilsport* ['spɔɪlspɔ:t] N aguafiestas *mf inv*

spoilt [spɔɪlt] PT, PP *of* **spoil**
ADJ 1 (= *ruined*) [*meal etc*] estropeado, echado a perder; [*vote*] nulo
2 (= *pampered*) [*child*] mimado, consentido
3 (*US*) (= *gone off*) [*food*] pasado, malo; [*milk*] cortado

spoke¹ [spəʊk] N [*of wheel*] rayo *m*, radio *m* • IDIOM: • **to put a ~ in sb's wheel** ponerle trabas a algn

spoke² [spəʊk] PT *of* **speak**

spoken ['spəʊkən] PP *of* **speak**
ADJ hablado • **the ~ language** la lengua hablada; ▹ **well-spoken**

spokeshave ['spəʊkʃeɪv] N raedera *f*

spokesman ['spəʊksmən] N (PL: **spokesmen**) portavoz *mf*, vocero *mf* (*LAm*) • **to act as ~ for** hablar en nombre de • **they made him ~** lo eligieron para hablar en su nombre

spokesperson ['spəʊkspɜ:sn] N (PL: **spokespeople**) portavoz *mf*, vocero *mf* (*LAm*)

spokeswoman ['spəʊkswʊmən] N (PL: **spokeswomen**) portavoz *f*, vocero *f* (*LAm*)

spoliation [,spəʊlɪ'eɪʃən] N despojo *m*

spondee ['spɒndi:] N espondeo *m*

spondylosis [,spɒndɪ'ləʊsɪs] N espondilosis *f* • **cervical ~** espondilosis cervical

sponge [spʌndʒ] N 1 (*for washing*) esponja *f* • IDIOM: • **to throw in the ~** darse por vencido, tirar la toalla
2 (*Culin*) (*also* **sponge cake**) bizcocho *m*, queque *m*, pastel *m* (*LAm*)
3 (*Zool*) esponja *f*
VT 1 (= *wash*) lavar con esponja, limpiar con esponja
2* (= *scrounge*) • **he ~d £15 off me** me sacó 15 libras de gorra*
VI* (= *scrounge*) dar sablazos*, vivir de gorra* • **to ~ off** *or* **on sb** (= *depend on*) vivir de algn; (*on occasion*) dar sablazos a algn*
CPD ▸ **sponge bag** esponjera *f* ▸ **sponge cake** bizcocho *m*, queque *m*, pastelito *m* (*LAm*) ▸ **sponge pudding** pudín *m* de bizcocho ▸ **sponge rubber** gomaespuma *f*

▸ **sponge down** VT + ADV limpiar con esponja, lavar con esponja

▸ **sponge off** VT + ADV quitar con esponja • **to ~ a stain off** quitar una mancha con esponja
VI + ADV quitarse con (una) esponja
VI + PREP ▹ **sponge**

▸ **sponge up** VT + ADV absorber

sponger* ['spʌndʒəʳ] N gorrón/ona* *m/f*, sablista* *mf*

sponginess ['spʌndʒɪnɪs] N esponjosidad *f*

sponging* ['spʌndʒɪŋ] N gorronería* *f*

spongy ['spʌndʒɪ] ADJ (COMPAR: **spongier**,

SUPERL: **spongiest**) esponjoso

sponsor ['spɒnsəʳ] (N) **1** (= *provider of funds*) (*Sport, Rad, TV*) patrocinador(a) *m/f*, sponsor *mf*
2 (*for participant in charity event*) patrocinador(a) *m/f*
3 (*for loan*) fiador(a) *m/f*, avalista *mf*
4 [*of membership*] • **your application must be signed by two ~s** su solicitud tiene que estar firmada por dos socios
5 (= *godparent*) (*male*) padrino *m*; (*female*) madrina *f*
6 [*of bill, motion*] proponente *mf*
(VT) **1** (= *fund*) [+ *event*] patrocinar, auspiciar; [+ *studies, research*] financiar; [+ *participant in charity event*] *respaldar or avalar mediante un donativo a favor de una obra benéfica* • **~ed walk/swim** *marcha/prueba de natación emprendida a cambio de donaciones a una obra benéfica*
2 (= *support*) respaldar, apoyar • **they have been accused of ~ing terrorism** se los ha acusado de respaldar *or* apoyar al terrorismo
3 [+ *bill, motion*] proponer
4 [+ *loan*] fiar, avalar

sponsorship ['spɒnsəʃɪp] (N) **1** (= *funding*) [*of event*] patrocinio *m*, auspicio *m*; [*of studies, research*] financiación *f* • **corporate ~ of the arts** patrocinio de las artes por parte de empresas • **a £10m ~ deal** un contrato de patrocinio de 10 millones de libras • **under the ~ of** [*event*] bajo los auspicios de, patrocinado por
2 (= *support*) respaldo *m*, apoyo *m*
3 (= *guaranteeing*) fianza *f*, aval *m*

spontaneity [ˌspɒntə'neɪɪtɪ] (N) espontaneidad *f*

spontaneous [spɒn'teɪnɪəs] (ADJ) espontáneo • **~ combustion** combustión *f* espontánea

spontaneously [spɒn'teɪnɪəslɪ] (ADV) espontáneamente

spoof* [spu:f] (N) (= *parody*) burla *f*, parodia *f*; (= *hoax*) trampa *f*, truco *m*
(ADJ) • **~ letter** carta *f* paródica
(VT) (= *parody*) parodiar; (= *trick*) engañar
(VI) bromear

spook* [spu:k] (N) **1*** (*hum*) (= *ghost*) espectro *m*, aparición *f*
2 (*US‡*) (= *secret agent*) espía *mf*, agente *mf* secreto/a
(VT) (*US*) **1** (= *haunt*) aparecerse en, rondar
2 (= *frighten*) asustar, pegar un susto a

spooky* ['spu:kɪ] (ADJ) (COMPAR: **spookier**, SUPERL: **spookiest**) espeluznante, horripilante • **the house is really ~ at night** la casa te pone los pelos de punta de noche

SPOOL [spu:l] (N ABBR) = **simultaneous peripherical operation on-line**

spool [spu:l] (N) (*Phot*) (*for thread*) carrete *m*; (*for film etc*) bobina *f*; (*on fishing line*) cucharilla *f*; (*on sewing machine*) canilla *f*

spoon [spu:n] (N) **1** (*gen*) cuchara *f*; (= *teaspoon*) cucharita *f* • IDIOM: • **to be born with a silver ~ in one's mouth** nacer de pie, nacer con un pan debajo del brazo
2 (= *spoonful*) cucharada *f*
(VT) (*also* **spoon out**) • **to ~ sth onto a plate** echar cucharadas de algo en un plato
(VI) †* acariciarse amorosamente, besuquearse*
▸ **spoon off** (VT + ADV) [+ *fat, cream etc*] quitar con la cuchara
▸ **spoon out** (VT + ADV) = **spoon**
▸ **spoon up** (VT + ADV) recoger con cuchara

spoonbill ['spu:nbɪl] (N) espátula *f*

spoonerism ['spu:nərɪzəm] (N) trastrueque *m* verbal, trastrueque *m* de palabras

spoon-fed ['spu:nfed] (ADJ) malacostumbrado, que siempre lo tiene todo hecho

spoon-feed ['spu:nfi:d] (PT, PP: **spoon-fed**) (VT) **1** (*lit*) dar de comer con cuchara a
2 (*fig*) dar todo hecho a, poner todo en bandeja a, malacostumbrar • **it isn't good to spoon-feed children** no es bueno dárselo todo hecho *or* ponérselo todo en bandeja *or* malacostumbrar a los niños

spoonful ['spu:nfʊl] (N) cucharada *f*

spoor [spʊəʳ] (N) pista *f*, rastro *m*

sporadic [spə'rædɪk] (ADJ) esporádico • **~ gunfire** tiroteo *m* intermitente *or* esporádico

sporadically [spə'rædɪkəlɪ] (ADV) esporádicamente

spore [spɔ:ʳ] (N) espora *f*

sporran ['spɒrən] (N) escarcela *f*

sport [spɔ:t] (N) **1** (= *game*) deporte *m* • **he is good at several ~s** se le dan bien varios deportes • **the ~ of kings** el deporte de los reyes, la hípica
2 (= *games in general*) deporte(s) *m(pl)* • **I love ~** me encantan los deportes *or* el deporte • **to be good at ~** ser buen deportista
3 sports (= *athletics meeting*) juegos *mpl* deportivos
4 (= *hunting*) caza *f* • **to have some good ~** tener éxito en la caza, lograr unas cuantas piezas hermosas • **the trout here give good ~** aquí las truchas no se rinden fácilmente
5 (= *fun*) juego *m*, diversión *f* • **to say sth in ~** decir algo en broma • **to make ~ of sb** burlarse de algn
6* (= *person*) persona *f* amable • **she's a good ~** es buena persona, es buena gente (*esp LAm*) • **he's a real ~** es una persona realmente buena • **be a ~!** ¡no seas malo!
7 (*liter*) (= *plaything*) víctima *f*, juguete *m*
8 (*Bio*) mutación *f*
(VI) (*liter*) divertirse
(VT) lucir, ostentar
(CPD) ▸ **sport jacket** (*US*) = **sports jacket** ▸ **sports bag** bolsa *m* de deportes ▸ **sports car** coche *m* deportivo ▸ **sports centre, sports complex** polideportivo *m* ▸ **sports day** (*Brit*) día *m* de competiciones deportivas (de un colegio) ▸ **sports desk** sección *f* de deportes ▸ **sports drink** bebida *f* isotónica ▸ **sports editor** jefe *mf* de la sección de deportes ▸ **sports facilities** instalaciones *fpl* deportivas ▸ **sports ground** campo *m* deportivo, centro *m* deportivo ▸ **sports hall** = sports centre ▸ **sports injury** lesión *f* deportiva ▸ **sports jacket** chaqueta *f* sport, saco *m* sport (*LAm*) ▸ **sports page** página *f* de deportes ▸ **sports shop** tienda *f* de deportes ▸ **sports stadium** estadio *m* deportivo ▸ **sport(s) utility vehicle** deportivo *m* utilitario, SUV *m* ▸ **sports writer** cronista *mf* deportivo/a

sportiness ['spɔ:tɪnɪs] (N) deportividad *f*

sporting ['spɔ:tɪŋ] (ADJ) **1** [*activity, career*] deportivo
2 (= *fair*) [*conduct, spirit etc*] deportivo, caballeroso • **that's very ~ of you** eres muy amable, es muy amable de su parte • **there's a ~ chance that ...** existe la posibilidad de que ...

sportingly ['spɔ:tɪŋlɪ] (ADV) **1** (*lit*) de modo deportivo
2 (*fig*) muy amablemente • **she ~ agreed to help** ella muy amablemente accedió a prestar ayuda

sportive ['spɔ:tɪv] (ADJ) juguetón

sportscast ['spɔ:tskɑ:st] (N) (*esp US*) programa *m* deportivo

sportscaster ['spɔ:tskɑ:stəʳ] (N) (*esp US*) comentarista *mf* deportivo/a

sportsman ['spɔ:tsmən] (N) (PL: **sportsmen**) deportista *m* • **the ~ of the year** el deportista del año

sportsmanlike ['spɔ:tsmənlaɪk] (ADJ) caballeroso

sportsmanship ['spɔ:tsmənʃɪp] (N) espíritu *m* deportivo

sportsperson ['spɔ:tspɜ:sn] (N) deportista *mf*

sportswear ['spɔ:tswɛəʳ] (N) ropa *f* deportiva

sportswoman ['spɔ:tswʊmən] (N) (PL: **sportswomen**) deportista *f*

sporty* ['spɔ:tɪ] (ADJ) (COMPAR: **sportier**, SUPERL: **sportiest**) deportivo, aficionado a los deportes

spot [spɒt] (N) **1** (= *dot*) lunar *m* • **a red dress with white ~s** un vestido rojo con lunares blancos • **to have ~s before one's eyes** tener la vista nublada • IDIOM: • **to knock ~s off sb*** dar ciento y raya a algn, vencer fácilmente a algn • **this can knock ~s off yours any time*** este le da ciento y raya al tuyo en cualquier momento
2 (= *stain, mark*) mancha *f* • **~s of blood/grease** manchas de sangre/grasa • **it made a ~ on the table** hizo una mancha en la mesa • **there's a ~ on your shirt** tienes una mancha en la camisa
3 (*Med*) (= *pimple*) grano *m*, granito *m* • **she broke out** *or* **came out in ~s** (= *pimples*) le salieron granos en la piel; (= *rash*) le salió un sarpullido, le salieron granos en la piel • **he's covered in ~s** (= *pimples*) está lleno de granos; (= *rash*) le ha salido un sarpullido por todo el cuerpo, está lleno de granos • **measles ~s** manchas *fpl* de sarampión; ▹ **beauty**
4 (= *place*) sitio *m*, lugar *m*; (= *scene*) escena *f*, escenario *m* • **it's a lovely ~ for a picnic** es un sitio *or* lugar precioso para un picnic • **a tender ~ on the arm** un punto *or* lugar sensible en el brazo • **an accident black ~** un punto negro para los accidentes • **night ~** centro *m* nocturno • **on the ~** (= *immediately*) en el acto; (= *there*) en el mismo sitio • **they gave her the job on the ~** le dieron el trabajo en el acto • **luckily they were able to mend the car on the ~** afortunadamente consiguieron arreglar el coche allí mismo • **the reporter was on the ~** el reportero estaba presente • **the firemen were on the ~ in three minutes** los bomberos acudieron *or* llegaron en tres minutos • **I always have to be on the ~** estoy de servicio siempre • **our man on the ~** nuestro hombre sobre el terreno • **to run on the ~** correr en parada • **to pay cash on the ~** (*US*) pagar al contado • **his soft ~** su debilidad, su punto flaco, su lado flaco (*LAm*) • **to have a soft ~ for sb** tener debilidad por algn • **his weak ~** su debilidad, su punto flaco, su lado flaco (*LAm*) • **to know sb's weak ~s** conocer las debilidades de algn, saber de qué pie cojea algn* • IDIOM: • **to touch a sore ~** tocar la fibra sensible, poner el dedo en la llaga
5 (*Brit**) (= *small quantity*) poquito *m*, pizca *f* • **just a ~, thanks** un poquitín, gracias • **a ~ of bother** un pequeño disgusto • **he had a ~ of bother with the police** se metió en un lío con la policía* • **we had a ~ of rain yesterday** ayer se sintieron gotas de lluvia • **we're in a ~ of trouble** estamos en un pequeño apuro
6 (= *difficulty*) apuro *m*, aprieto *m* • **to be in a (tight) ~** estar en un apuro *or* aprieto • **now I'm really on the ~** ahora me veo de verdad entre la espada y la pared • **to put sb on the ~** (= *put in difficulty*) poner a algn en un apuro *or* aprieto; (= *compromise*) comprometer a algn
7 (*Rad, Theat, TV*) (*in show*) espacio *m*; (*Rad, TV*)

(= *advertisement*) espacio *m* publicitario
8* (= *spotlight*) foco *m*
VT **1** (*with mud etc*) salpicar, manchar (**with** de)
2 (= *notice*) darse cuenta de, notar; (= *see*) observar, darse cuenta de; (= *recognize*) reconocer; (= *catch out*) coger, pillar • **I ~ted a mistake** descubrí un error • **I ~ted him at once** lo reconocí en seguida • **to ~ the winner** elegir al ganador
VI • **to ~ with rain** chispear
CPD ▸ **spot cash** dinero *m* contante ▸ **spot check** comprobación *f* en el acto, reconocimiento *m* rápido; ▹ **spot-check** ▸ **spot fine** multa *f* que se paga en el acto ▸ **spot market** mercado *m* al contado ▸ **spot price** precio *m* de entrega inmediata ▸ **spot remover** quitamanchas *m inv* ▸ **spot survey** inspección *f* sorpresa
spot-check [ˈspɒtˌtʃek] VT revisar en el acto; ▹ **spot**
spotless [ˈspɒtlɪs] ADJ **1** (= *clean*) inmaculado, sin mancha; (= *tidy, neat*) [*appearance*] impecable, pulcro; [*house*] limpísimo
2 (= *flawless*) [*reputation*] impecable, intachable
spotlessly [ˈspɒtlɪslɪ] ADV • **~ clean** limpísimo
spotlessness [ˈspɒtlɪsnɪs] N perfecta limpieza *f*
spotlight [ˈspɒtlaɪt] N (= *beam, lamp*) foco *m*, reflector *m*; (*Theat*) proyector *m*; (*Aut*) faro *m* auxiliar orientable • **he doesn't like being in the ~** no le gusta ser el centro de atención • IDIOM: • **to turn the ~ on sth/sb** exponer algo/a algn a la luz pública
VT **1** (*lit*) iluminar
2 (*fig*) destacar, subrayar
spotlit [ˈspɒtlɪt] ADJ iluminado
spot-on* [ˌspɒtˈɒn] ADJ • **what he said was spot-on** dio en el clavo con lo que dijo
ADV • **she guessed spot-on** lo adivinó exactamente
spotted [ˈspɒtɪd] ADJ con motas, con puntos; (*with dirt*) salpicado, manchado • **a dress ~ with mud** un vestido salpicado *or* manchado de lodo
spotter [ˈspɒtəʳ] N (*Aer etc*) observador(a) *m/f*; (*Brit*) (*Rail*) (= *trainspotter*) coleccionista *mf* de números de locomotoras
CPD ▸ **spotter plane** avión *m* de observación
spotting [ˈspɒtɪŋ] N ▹ **trainspotting**
spotty* [ˈspɒtɪ] ADJ (COMPAR: **spottier**, SUPERL: **spottiest**) **1** (= *pimply*) con granos
2* (= *patterned*) [*dress, material*] de lunares, con motas; [*dog*] con manchas
spot-weld [ˈspɒtˌweld] VT soldar por puntos
spousal [ˈspaʊzəl] ADJ (*esp US*) conyugal
spouse [spaʊs] N cónyuge *mf*
spout [spaʊt] N [*of jar*] pico *m*; [*of teapot etc*] pitón *m*, pitorro *m*; [*of guttering*] canalón *m*; (= *jet of water*) surtidor *m*, chorro *m* • **to be up the ~** (*Brit**) [*person*] (= *in a jam*) estar en un apuro; (= *pregnant*) estar en estado • **my holiday's up the ~*** mis vacaciones se han ido al garete*
VT **1** [+ *water*] arrojar en chorro
2* [+ *poetry etc*] declamar
VI **1** [*water*] brotar, salir en chorros
2* (= *declaim*) hablar incansablemente
sprain [spreɪn] N torcedura *f*
VT torcer • **to ~ one's wrist/ankle** hacerse un esguince en la muñeca/el tobillo
sprained [spreɪnd] ADJ • **to have a ~ wrist/ankle** tener un esguince de muñeca/tobillo
sprang [spræŋ] PT *of* **spring**

sprat [spræt] N espadín *m*, sardineta *f*
sprawl [sprɔːl] VI **1** [*person*] (= *sit down, lie down*) tumbarse, echarse; (*untidily*) despatarrarse; (= *fall down*) derrumbarse • **he was ~ing in a chair** estaba despatarrado en un sillón • **to send sb ~ing** (*with a blow*) derribar a algn por el suelo • **the jolt sent him ~ing** la sacudida le hizo ir rodando por el suelo
2 [*plant, town*] extenderse
N **1** [*of body*] postura *f* desgarbada
2 [*of town etc*] extensión *f* • **an endless ~ of suburbs** una interminable extensión de barrios exteriores • **urban ~** crecimiento *m* urbano descontrolado
▸ **sprawl out** VI + ADV [*person*] despatarrarse
sprawled [sprɔːld] ADJ [*person*] despatarrado • **he was ~ in a chair** estaba despatarrado en un sillón • **the body was ~ on the floor** el cadáver estaba tumbado en el suelo
sprawling [ˈsprɔːlɪŋ] ADJ [*person*] despatarrado, tumbado; [*city, town*] en crecimiento rápido; [*handwriting*] desgarbado
spray¹ [spreɪ] N **1** (= *liquid*) rociada *f*; [*of sea*] espuma *f*; (*from atomizer, aerosol*) pulverización *f*
2 (= *aerosol, atomizer*) atomizador *m*, spray *m*; (*Med*) rociador *m* • **paint ~** pistola *f* (rociadora) de pintura • **to paint with a ~** pintar con pistola
VT [+ *water etc*] rociar • **she ~ed perfume on my hand** me roció perfume en la mano • **to ~ sth/sb with water/bullets** rociar algo/a algn de agua/balas • **to ~ the roses with insecticide** rociar las rosas de insecticida • **to ~ paint on to a car** pintar un coche con una pistola rociadora • **there was graffiti ~ed on the wall** había pintadas de spray en la pared
CPD ▸ **spray can** espray *m*, pulverizador *m* ▸ **spray gun** pistola *f* rociadora, pulverizador *m* ▸ **spray paint** pintura *f* spray
▸ **spray out** VI + ADV [*liquid etc*] salir a chorro • **water ~ed out all over them** el agua les caló
spray² [spreɪ] N (*Bot*) ramita *f*, ramo *m*
sprayer [ˈspreɪəʳ] N = **spray¹**
spray-on [ˈspreɪɒn] ADJ **1** (*lit*) en aerosol, en spray
2* (*hum*) [*jeans, dress etc*] apretadísimo • **he was wearing spray-on jeans** llevaba unos vaqueros apretadísimos *or* que le iban a reventar
spread [spred] (VB: PT, PP: **spread**) N
1 (= *propagation*) [*of infection, disease, fire*] propagación *f*; [*of idea, information*] difusión *f*, divulgación *f*; [*of crime*] aumento *m*, proliferación *f*; [*of education*] extensión *f*, generalización *f*; [*of nuclear weapons*] proliferación *f*
2 (= *extent*) (*gen*) extensión *f*; [*of wings, sails*] envergadura *f* • **middle-age ~** gordura *f* de la mediana edad
3 (= *range*) • **there is a broad ~ of interest and opinion represented on the committee** hay una gran diversidad de intereses y opiniones representados en el comité
4* (= *meal*) comilona* *f*, banquetazo* *m* • **they laid on a huge ~** ofrecieron una espléndida comilona *or* un banquetazo espléndido*
5 (= *cover*) (*for bed*) cubrecama *m*, sobrecama *m or f*
6 (*Culin*) (*for bread*) pasta *f* para untar • **cheese ~** queso *m* para untar
7 (*Press, Typ*) • **a full-page ~** una plana entera • **a two-page** *or* **double-page ~** una página doble, una doble plana
8 (*Econ*) diferencial *m*
9 (*US**) (= *ranch*) finca *f*, hacienda *f* (*LAm*), estancia *f* (*Arg, Uru*), fundo *m* (*Chile*)
VT **1** (*also* **spread out**) (= *lay or open out*) [+ *tablecloth, blanket*] extender, tender; [+ *map*] extender, desplegar; [+ *arms, fingers, legs*] extender; [+ *banner, sails, wings*] desplegar; [+ *net*] tender • **she lay ~ out on the floor** estaba tendida en el suelo • **the peacock ~ its tail** el pavo real hizo la rueda • **he ~ his hands in a gesture of resignation/helplessness** extendió los brazos en ademán de resignación/impotencia • **I like to be able to ~ myself** me gusta tener mucho espacio • **to ~ one's wings** (*lit, fig*) desplegar las alas
2 (= *scatter*) esparcir, desparramar • **her clothes were ~ all over the floor** su ropa estaba esparcida *or* desparramada por todo el suelo
3 (= *apply*) [+ *butter*] untar • **to ~ butter on one's bread** untar mantequilla en el pan, untar el pan con mantequilla • **to ~ cream on one's face** untarse *or* ponerse crema en la cara
4 (= *cover*) • **tables ~ with food** mesas llenas *or* repletas de comida • **she ~ her bread with honey** puso miel en el pan, untó el pan con miel • **the floors are ~ with sand** los suelos están cubiertos de arena
5 (= *distribute*) distribuir • **you are advised to ~ the workload** le aconsejamos que se distribuya el trabajo • **repayments will be ~ over 18 months** los pagos se efectuarán a lo largo de 18 meses • IDIOM: • **don't ~ yourself too thin** no intentes abarcar más de la cuenta
6 (= *disseminate*) [+ *news, information*] divulgar, difundir; [+ *rumour*] hacer correr, difundir; [+ *disease*] propagar; [+ *panic, fear*] sembrar • **he loves ~ing gossip** le encanta difundir *or* divulgar cotilleos; ▹ **word**
VI **1** (= *extend, advance*) [*fire*] propagarse, extenderse; [*stain*] extenderse; [*disease*] propagarse; [*panic, fear*] cundir; [*information, news, ideas*] difundirse • **general alarm ~ through the population** cundió la alarma por toda la población • **the cancer had ~ to his lungs** el cáncer se había extendido a los pulmones • **the troops ~ south** las tropas se desplegaron hacia el sur • **a smile ~ over** *or* **across his face** sonrió de oreja a oreja • IDIOM: • **to ~ like wildfire**: • **the rumours ~ like wildfire** los rumores corrieron como la pólvora
2 (= *stretch*) (*in space*) extenderse • **the city ~s several miles to the north** la ciudad se extiende varias millas hacia el norte • **a process ~ing over several months** un proceso que abarca varios meses
3 [*butter*] untarse
CPD ▸ **spread betting** ≈ apuesta *f* múltiple, *modalidad de apuesta en la que se juega sobre una variedad de resultados en lugar de uno en concreto*
▸ **spread out** VI + ADV (= *disperse*) [*people*] dispersarse; (= *extend*) [*city, liquid*] extenderse; (= *widen*) [*river*] ensancharse
VT + ADV ▹ **spread**
spreadable [ˈspredəbl] ADJ fácil de untar
spread-eagle [spredˈiːgl] VT extender (completamente), despatarrar
spread-eagled [spredˈiːgld] ADJ a pata tendida
spreader [ˈspredəʳ] N **1** (*for butter etc*) cuchillo *m* para esparcir; (*for glue etc*) paleta *f*
2 (*Agr*) esparcidor *m*
spreadsheet [ˈspredʃiːt] N hoja *f* electrónica, hoja *f* de cálculo
spree* [spriː] N juerga *f*, parranda *f*, farra *f* (*esp S. Cone*) • **to go on a ~** ir de juerga *or* parranda *or* (*esp S. Cone*) farra • **to go on a killing ~** matar a una serie de personas; ▹ **spending**

S

sprig [sprɪg] (N) **1** [*of heather etc*] espiga *f*
2 (*Tech*) puntilla *f*
sprightliness ['spraɪtlɪnɪs] (N) energía *f*
sprightly ['spraɪtlɪ] (ADJ) (COMPAR: **sprightlier**, SUPERL: **sprightliest**) enérgico
spring [sprɪŋ] (VB: PT: **sprang**, PP: **sprung**)
(N) **1** (*also* **Spring**) (= *season*) primavera *f* • **in ~** en primavera • **in early/late ~** a principios/a finales de la primavera • **I like to go walking in (the) ~** me gusta salir a pasear en primavera • **in the ~ of 1956** en la primavera de 1956 • **one ~ morning** una mañana de primavera • **~ is in the air** se siente la llegada de la primavera
2 (*in watch*) muelle *m*, resorte *m*; (*in mattress, sofa*) muelle *m*; **springs** (*Aut*) ballestas *fpl*
3 [*of water*] fuente *f*, manantial *m* • **a mountain ~** un manantial • **hot ~s** fuentes *fpl* termales
4 (= *leap*) salto *m*, brinco *m* • **in one ~** de un salto *or* brinco • **to walk with a ~ in one's step** caminar con brío
5 (= *elasticity*) elasticidad *f*
6 (*liter*) (*usu pl*) (= *origin, source*) origen *m*
(VT) **1** (= *present suddenly*) • **to ~ sth on sb** soltar algo a algn (de buenas a primeras)* • **the redundancies were sprung on the staff without warning** soltaron la noticia de los despidos a la plantilla sin previo aviso • **to ~ a surprise on sb** dar una sorpresa a algn • **to ~ a leak** [*boat*] empezar a hacer agua • **the fuel tank sprang a leak** el depósito del combustible empezó a perder
2 (= *release*) [+ *trap*] hacer saltar; [+ *lock*] soltar • **to ~ sb from jail*** ayudar a algn a fugarse de la cárcel
3 (= *leap over*) saltar, saltar por encima de
(VI) **1** (= *leap*) saltar • **to ~ aside** hacerse rápidamente a un lado • **to ~ at sb** abalanzarse sobre algn • **the cat sprang at my face** el gato se me tiró *or* se me abalanzó a la cara • **to ~ back** [*person, animal*] saltar para atrás • **the branch sprang back** la rama volvió hacia atrás como un látigo • **where did you ~ from?*** ¿de dónde diablos has salido?* • **to ~ into action** entrar en acción • **to ~ into the air** dar un salto en el aire • **the engine finally sprang into life** por fin el motor arrancó • **the cat sprang onto the roof** el gato dio un salto y se puso en el tejado • **to ~ open** abrirse de golpe • **her name sprang out at me from the page** al mirar la página su nombre me saltó a la vista • **to ~ out of bed** saltar de la cama • **she sprang over the fence** saltó por encima de la valla • **to ~ shut** cerrarse de golpe • **to ~ to sb's aid** *or* **help** correr a ayudar a algn • **to ~ to attention** ponerse en posición de firme • **to ~ to one's feet** levantarse de un salto • **a number of examples ~ to mind** se me vienen a la mente *or* se me ocurren varios ejemplos
2 (= *originate*) [*stream*] brotar, nacer; [*river*] nacer; [*buds, shoots*] brotar • **to ~ from sth: the idea sprang from a TV programme he saw** la idea surgió de un programa de televisión que vio • **his anger sprang from his suffering** la furia le venía del sufrimiento
3 (*liter*) (= *be born*) [*person*] nacer • **to ~ into existence** surgir de la noche a la mañana, aparecer repentinamente
(CPD) [*flowers, rain, sunshine, weather*] primaveral, de primavera ▸ **spring balance** peso *m* de muelle ▸ **spring binder** (= *file*) carpeta *f* de muelles ▸ **spring bolt** pestillo *m* de golpe ▸ **spring break** (*US*) (*Educ*) vacaciones *fpl* de Semana Santa ▸ **spring chicken** polluelo *m* • **she's no ~ chicken*** no es ninguna niña ▸ **spring equinox** equinoccio *m* de primavera, equinoccio *m* primaveral ▸ **spring fever** fiebre *f* primaveral ▸ **spring greens** (*Brit*) verduras *fpl* de primavera ▸ **spring gun** trampa *f* de alambre y escopeta ▸ **spring lock** candado *m* ▸ **spring mattress** colchón *m* de muelles, somier *m* ▸ **spring onion** cebolleta *f*, cebollino *m* ▸ **spring roll** rollito *m* de primavera ▸ **spring tide** marea *f* viva ▸ **spring water** agua *f* de manantial
▸ **spring up** (VI + ADV) **1** [*building, settlement, organization*] surgir; [*plant, weeds*] brotar; [*wind, storm*] levantarse; [*doubt, rumour, friendship*] surgir, nacer
2 [*person*] (*from chair*) levantarse de un salto
springboard ['sprɪŋbɔ:d] (N) trampolín *m*; (*fig*) plataforma *f* de lanzamiento
(CPD) ▸ **springboard dive** salto *m* de trampolín
springbok ['sprɪŋbɒk] (N) (PL: **springbok, springboks**) gacela *f* (*del sur de África*)
spring-clean [,sprɪŋ'kli:n] (VT) limpiar completamente
(VI) limpiarlo todo, limpiar toda la casa
spring-cleaning [,sprɪŋ'kli:nɪŋ] (N) limpieza *f* general • **to do the spring-cleaning** limpiar toda la casa
springform ['sprɪŋfɔ:m] (N) (*also* **springform pan**) (*Culin*) molde *m* de resorte
springiness ['sprɪŋɪnɪs] (N) elasticidad *f*; [*of step*] ligereza *f*
spring-like ['sprɪŋlaɪk] (ADJ) [*day, weather*] primaveral
spring-loaded ['sprɪŋ,ləʊdɪd] (ADJ) con resorte
springtime ['sprɪŋtaɪm] (N) primavera *f*
springy ['sprɪŋɪ] (ADJ) (COMPAR: **springier**, SUPERL: **springiest**) [*mattress, carpet, turf*] mullido; [*floor, rubber*] elástico; [*step*] ligero
sprinkle ['sprɪŋkl] (N) rociada *f*, salpicadura *f* • **a ~ of salt** un poquito de sal • **a ~ of rain** unas gotitas de lluvia
(VT) rociar (**with** de) • **to ~ water on a plant** • **~ a plant with water** rociar una planta de agua • **to ~ sugar over a cake** • **~ a cake with sugar** espolvorear un bizcocho con azúcar • **a rose ~d with dew** una rosa cubierta de rocío • **a lawn ~d with daisies** una extensión de césped salpicada de margaritas • **they are ~d about here and there** están esparcidos aquí y allá
(VI) (*with rain*) lloviznar
sprinkler ['sprɪŋklə^r] (N) **1** (*for lawn*) aspersor *m*; (*Agr*) rociadera *f*, aparato *m* de lluvia artificial; [*of watering can etc*] regadera *f*
2 (*for sugar*) espolvoreador *m* de azúcar
3 (= *fire safety device*) aparato *m* de rociadura automática
(CPD) ▸ **sprinkler system** (*Agr*) sistema *m* de regadío por aspersión
sprinkling ['sprɪŋklɪŋ] (N) **1** (*with water*) rociada *f* • **a ~ of rain** unas gotitas de lluvia
2 (= *small quantity*) • **there was a ~ of young people** había unos cuantos jóvenes • **a ~ of knowledge** unos pocos conocimientos
sprint [sprɪnt] (N) (*in race*) sprint *m*, esprint *m*; (= *dash*) carrera *f* sprint • **the women's 100 metres ~** los 100 metros lisos femeninos
(VI) (*in race*) sprintar, esprintar; (= *dash*) correr a toda velocidad; (= *rush*) precipitarse • **he ~ed for the bus** corrió tras el autobús • **we'll have to ~** tendremos que correr
(CPD) ▸ **sprint finish** (*Sport*) final *m* al sprint
sprinter ['sprɪntə^r] (N) (*Sport*) velocista *mf*, (e)sprínter *mf*
sprit [sprɪt] (N) botavara *f*, verga *f* de abanico
sprite [spraɪt] (N) elfo *m*, duende *m*
spritsail ['sprɪtseɪl], (*Naut*) ['sprɪtsl] (N) cebadera *f*, vela *f* de abanico
spritzer ['sprɪtsə^r] (N) vino *m* blanco con soda
sprocket ['sprɒkɪt] (N) rueda *f* de espigas
(CPD) ▸ **sprocket feed** avance *m* por rueda de espigas ▸ **sprocket wheel** rueda *f* de cadena
sprog‡ [sprɒg] (N) (*Brit*) (*pej or hum*) (= *child*) rorro* *m*, bebé *m*
sprout [spraʊt] (N) **1** (*from bulb, seeds*) brote *m*, retoño *m*
2 (*also* **Brussels sprout**) col *f* de Bruselas
(VT) echar, hacerse • **to ~ new leaves** echar hojas nuevas • **the calf is ~ing horns** le salen los cuernos al ternero • **the town is ~ing new buildings** en la ciudad se levantan edificios nuevos
(VI) (= *bud*) brotar, retoñar, echar retoños; (= *grow quickly*) crecer rápidamente • **skyscrapers are ~ing up** se están levantando rascacielos por todos lados
spruce¹ [spru:s] (N) (*Bot*) pícea *f*
spruce² [spru:s] (ADJ) (= *neat*) pulcro
▸ **spruce up** (VT + ADV) arreglar • **to ~ o.s. up** arreglarse • **all ~d up** muy acicalado
sprucely ['spru:slɪ] (ADV) • **~ dressed** elegantemente vestido, vestido de punta en blanco
spruceness ['spru:snɪs] (N) pulcritud *f*
sprung [sprʌŋ] (PP) *of* **spring**
(ADJ) • **interior ~ mattress** colchón *m* de muelles • **~ bed** cama *f* de muelles • **~ seat** asiento *m* de ballesta
spry [spraɪ] (ADJ) ágil, activo
SPUC [spʌk] (N ABBR) = **Society for the Protection of Unborn Children**
spud [spʌd] (N) **1*** (= *potato*) patata *f*, papa *f* (*LAm*)
2 (*Agr*) (= *tool*) escarda *f*
(VT) (*Agr*) escardar
spume [spju:m] (N) (*liter*) espuma *f*
spun [spʌn] (PT), (PP) *of* **spin**
(ADJ) • **~ glass** lana *f* de vidrio • **~ silk** seda *f* hilada • **~ yarn** meollar *m*
spunk [spʌŋk] (N) **1**‡ (= *spirit*) ánimo *m*, valor *m*, agallas* *fpl*
2 (*Brit***) (*sperm*) leche** *f*
spunky‡ ['spʌŋkɪ] (ADJ) (COMPAR: **spunkier**, SUPERL: **spunkiest**) **1** (= *spirited*) valiente, arrojado
2 (*esp Australia*) (= *hunky*) guaperas* (*inv*)
spur [spɜ:^r] (N) **1** (*for horse riding*) espuela *f* • IDIOM: • **to win one's ~s** pasar pruebas
2 [*of cock*] espolón *m*
3 (*fig*) estímulo *m*, aguijón *m* • **the ~ of hunger** el aguijón del hambre • **it will be a ~ to further progress** servirá de estímulo *or* acicate al progreso • IDIOM: • **on the ~ of the moment** sin pensar • **it was a ~ of the moment decision** fue una decisión tomada al instante
4 (*Geog*) [*of mountain, hill*] espolón *m*
5 (*Rail*) ramal *m* corto
(VT) (*also* **spur on**) [+ *horse*] espolear, picar con las espuelas; (*fig*) • **to ~ sb (on) to do sth** incitar a algn a hacer algo • **this ~red him on to greater efforts** esto lo animó a hacer mayores esfuerzos • **~red on by greed** bajo el aguijón de la codicia
(CPD) ▸ **spur gear** rueda *f* dentada recta ▸ **spur wheel** engranaje *m* cilíndrico
spurge [spɜ:dʒ] (N) euforbio *m*
spurge laurel ['spɜ:dʒ,lɒrəl] (N) lauréola *f*, torvisco *m*
spurious ['spjʊərɪəs] (ADJ) falso, espurio
spuriously ['spjʊərɪəslɪ] (ADV) falsamente
spuriousness ['spjʊərɪəsnɪs] (N) falsedad *f*
spurn [spɜ:n] (VT) desdeñar, rechazar
spurt [spɜ:t] (N) **1** [*of water, blood*] chorro *m*, borbotón *m*
2 [*of energy*] • **to put in** *or* **on a ~** hacer un gran

esfuerzo • **final ~** esfuerzo *m* final (*para ganar una carrera*)
VI (= *gush*) (*also* **spurt out**) salir a chorros, borbotar, chorrear
VT hacer salir a chorros, arrojar un chorro de
sputnik ['spʊtnɪk] N satélite *m* artificial
sputter ['spʌtəʳ] = **splutter**
sputum ['spjuːtəm] N (PL: **sputa**) esputo *m*
spy [spaɪ] N espía *mf*
VT (= *catch sight of*) divisar • **finally I spied him coming** por fin pude verlo viniendo • **to play I spy** jugar al veo-veo • **I spy, with my little eye, something beginning with A** veo, veo una cosa que empieza con A
VI espiar, ser espía • **to spy on sb** espiar a algn, observar a algn clandestinamente • **he spied for the USA** fue espía al servicio de los EE.UU.
CPD ▸ **spy plane** avión *m* espía ▸ **spy ring** red *f* de espionaje ▸ **spy satellite** satélite *m* espía ▸ **spy ship** buque *m* espía ▸ **spy story** novela *f* de espionaje
▸ **spy out** VT + ADV hacer un reconocimiento de • **to spy out the land** reconocer el terreno
spycam ['spaɪkæm] N cámara *f* oculta
spycatcher ['spaɪkætʃəʳ] N agente *mf* de contraespionaje
spyglass ['spaɪglɑːs] N catalejo *m*
spyhole ['spaɪhəʊl] N mirilla *f*
spying ['spaɪɪŋ] N espionaje *m*
CPD ▸ **spying charge** acusación *f* de espionaje
spy-in-the-sky* [,spaɪɪnðə'skaɪ] N (= *satellite*) satélite *m* espía
spymaster ['spaɪmæstəʳ] N jefe/a *m/f* de espías
spyware ['spaɪweəʳ] N (*Comput*) software *m* espía
Sq ABBR (*in address*) = **square**
sq. ABBR (*Math*) = **square**
sq.ft. ABBR = **square foot/feet**
squab [skwɒb] N (PL: **squabs, squab**) (*Orn*) (= *young pigeon*) pichón *m*; (= *chick*) pollito *m*, polluelo *m*
squabble ['skwɒbl] N riña *f*, pelea *f*, pleito *m* (*esp LAm*)
VI reñir, pelearse (**over, about** por, sobre) • **stop squabbling!** ¡vale ya de pelearse *or* reñir!
squabbler ['skwɒbləʳ] N pendenciero/a *m/f*
squabbling ['skwɒblɪŋ] N riñas *fpl*, peleas *fpl*, pleitos *mpl* (*esp LAm*)
squad [skwɒd] N **1** (*Mil*) pelotón *m*
2 [*of police*] brigada *f* • **flying ~** brigada *f* móvil
3 [*of workmen etc*] cuadrilla *f*
4 (*Sport*) [*of players*] equipo *m*
CPD ▸ **squad car** (*Police*) coche-patrulla *m*
squaddie* ['skwɒdɪ] N recluta *m*
squadron ['skwɒdrən] N (*Mil*) escuadrón *m*; (*Aer*) escuadrilla *f*, escuadrón *m*; (*Naut*) escuadra *f*
CPD ▸ **squadron leader** (*Brit*) comandante *m* (de aviación)
squalid ['skwɒlɪd] ADJ **1** (= *dirty*) miserable, vil
2 (= *base*) [*affair*] asqueroso; [*motive*] vil
squall¹ [skwɔːl] N **1** (= *wind*) ráfaga *f*; (= *rain*) chubasco *m*
2 (*fig*) tempestad *f* • **there are ~s ahead** el futuro se anuncia no muy tranquilo
squall² [skwɔːl] N (= *cry*) chillido *m*, grito *m*, berrido *m*
VI chillar, gritar, berrear
squalling ['skwɔːlɪŋ] ADJ [*child*] chillón, berreador
squally ['skwɔːlɪ] ADJ **1** [*wind*] que viene a ráfagas; [*day*] de chubascos
2 (*fig*) turbulento, lleno de dificultades

squalor ['skwɒləʳ] N miseria *f*, vileza *f* • **to live in ~** vivir en la miseria, vivir en la sordidez
squander ['skwɒndəʳ] VT [+ *money*] derrochar, despilfarrar; [+ *opportunity*] desperdiciar; [+ *time, resources*] emplear mal
square [skwɛəʳ] N **1** (= *shape*) cuadrado *m*, cuadro *m*; (*on graph paper, chessboard, crossword*) casilla *f*; (= *piece*) [*of material, paper, chocolate etc*] cuadrado *m*; (= *scarf*) pañuelo *m* • **to cut into ~s** cortar en cuadros *or* cuadrados • IDIOM: • **to go back to ~ one*** volver a empezar desde cero
2 (*in town*) plaza *f* • **the town ~** la plaza del pueblo
3 (*US*) (= *block of houses*) manzana *f*, cuadra *f* (*LAm*)
4 (*Math*) cuadrado *m* • **16 is the ~ of 4** 16 es el cuadrado de 4
5 (= *drawing instrument*) escuadra *f*
6* (= *old-fashioned person*) • **he's a real ~** es un carca *or* un carroza *or* (*Chile*) un momio*
ADJ **1** (*in shape*) cuadrado • IDIOM: • **to be a ~ peg in a round hole** estar como un pulpo en un garaje
2 (*forming right angle*) en ángulo recto, en escuadra • **to be ~ with sth** estar en ángulo recto *or* en escuadra con algo • **ensure that the frame is ~** asegúrese de que el marco forme ángulos rectos
3 [*face, jaw, shoulder*] cuadrado
4 (*Math*) cuadrado • **a ~ foot/kilometre** un pie/kilómetro cuadrado • **a kilometre ~** un kilómetro por un kilómetro
5 (= *substantial*) [*meal*] decente, como Dios manda • **it's three days since I had a ~ meal** hace tres días que no como decentemente *or* como Dios manda
6 (= *fair, honest*) justo, equitativo • **to give sb a ~ deal** ser justo con algn • **he didn't get a ~ deal** lo trataron injustamente • **I'll be ~ with you** seré justo contigo
7 (= *even*) • **now we're all ~** (*Sport*) ahora vamos iguales *or* (*LAm*) parejos, ahora estamos empatados; (*financially*) ahora estamos en paz • **if you pay me a pound we'll call it ~** dame una libra y me quedo conforme • **to get ~ with sb** ajustar las cuentas con algn
8* (= *conventional*) anticuado*, carca*, carroza (*Sp**) • **he's so ~** es un carca *or* un carroza *or* (*Chile*) un momio*
ADV • **~ in the middle** justo en el centro, justo en el medio • **to look sb ~ in the eye** mirar a algn directamente a los ojos • **the blow caught him ~ on the chin** el golpe le dio en plena barbilla *or* de lleno en la barbilla • **he turned to face me ~ on** se volvió para tenerme de cara; ▸ **fair¹**
VT **1** (= *make square*) cuadrar • **to ~ one's shoulders** ponerse derecho • IDIOM: • **to try to ~ the circle** intentar lograr la cuadratura del círculo
2 (= *settle, reconcile*) [+ *accounts*] ajustar; [+ *debts*] pagar • **can you ~ it with your conscience?** ¿te lo va a permitir tu conciencia? • **I'll ~ it with him*** yo lo arreglo con él
3 (*Math*) elevar al cuadrado • **two ~d is four** dos al cuadrado es cuatro
VI cuadrar (**with** con) • **it doesn't ~ with what you said before** esto no cuadra con lo que dijiste antes
CPD ▸ **square brackets** corchetes *mpl* ▸ **square dance** cuadrilla *f* (*baile*) ▸ **Square Mile** • **the Square Mile** (*in London*) la City ▸ **square rigger** buque *m* de vela con aparejo de cruz ▸ **square root** raíz *f* cuadrada
▸ **square off** VT + ADV cuadrar
▸ **square up** VI + ADV **1** [*boxers, fighters*] ponerse en guardia • **to ~ up to sb** enfrentarse con algn
2 (= *settle*) • **to ~ up with sb** ajustar cuentas con algn

SQUARE DANCE

Se llama **square dance** a un baile folklórico tradicional de origen francés en el que cuatro parejas de bailarines se colocan formando un cuadrado. Es un baile muy popular en Estados Unidos y Canadá y a veces se enseña en la escuela. En algunas ocasiones alguien se encarga de explicar los pasos que se han de seguir, de modo que los que no los conocen bien puedan participar. El instrumento musical más utilizado en ellos es el violín, aunque también se usan a veces la guitarra, el banjo o el acordeón.

squarebashing* ['skwɛə,bæʃɪŋ] N (*Brit*) instrucción *f*
squared [skwɛəd] ADJ [*paper*] cuadriculado
square-faced [,skwɛə'feɪst] ADJ de cara cuadrada
squarely ['skwɛəlɪ] ADV **1** (= *directly*) directamente • **responsibility for that failure rests ~ with the President** la responsabilidad de ese fracaso cae directamente sobre el presidente • **to look sb ~ in the eye** mirar a algn directamente a los ojos • **~ in the middle** justo en el centro, justo en el medio • **the blow caught him ~ on the chin** el golpe le dio en plena barbilla *or* de lleno en la barbilla
2 (= *honestly, fairly*) justamente • **to deal ~ with sb** tratar justamente a algn; ▸ **fairly**
square-rigged ['skwɛəʳrɪgd] ADJ con aparejo de cruz
square-toed [,skwɛə'təʊd] ADJ [*shoes*] de punta cuadrada
squarial ['skwɛərɪəl] N antena *f* cuadrada
squash¹ [skwɒʃ] N (PL: **squashes, squash**) **1** (= *drink*) • **orange ~** naranjada *f* (*sin burbujas*) • **lemon ~** limonada *f* (*sin burbujas*)
2 (= *crowd*) apiñamiento *m*, agolpamiento *m* • **there was such a ~ in the doorway** había tantísima gente apiñada en la puerta, se apiñaba tanto la gente en la puerta
VT **1** (= *flatten*) aplastar • **you're ~ing me** me estás aplastando • **to ~ sth in** meter algo a la fuerza • **can you ~ my shoes in?** ¿caben dentro mis zapatos? • **can you ~ two more in the car?** ¿caben dos más en el coche? • **to be ~ed together** ir apretujados
2 (*fig*) [+ *argument*] dar al traste con; [+ *person*] apabullar
VI • **to ~ in** entrar con dificultad • **we all ~ed in** entramos todos aunque con dificultad • **to ~ up** arrimarse
squash² [skwɒʃ] N (= *vegetable*) calabaza *f*
squash³ [skwɒʃ] N (= *sport*) squash *m*
CPD ▸ **squash court** cancha *f* de squash ▸ **squash racket** raqueta *f* de squash
squashy ['skwɒʃɪ] ADJ (COMPAR: **squashier**, SUPERL: **squashiest**) blando y algo líquido, muelle y húmedo
squat [skwɒt] ADJ [*person*] rechoncho, achaparrado; [*building, shape etc*] desproporcionadamente bajo
VI **1** (*also* **squat down**) agacharse, sentarse en cuclillas
2 (*on property*) ocupar un inmueble ilegalmente
N *piso etc ocupado ilegalmente*
squatter ['skwɒtəʳ] N ocupa *mf*, okupa *mf*
squatting ['skwɒtɪŋ] N *ocupación ilegal de un inmueble*
squaw*!* [skwɔː] N india *f*, piel roja *f*
squawk [skwɔːk] N graznido *m*, chillido *m*
VI graznar, chillar

squeak [skwi:k] (N) **1** [*of hinge, wheel*] chirrido *m*; [*of mouse, person*] chillido *m*; [*of shoe*] crujido *m*; [*of pen*] raspeo *m*
2 (*fig*) • **I don't want to hear another ~ out of you** y no vuelvas a abrir la boca, y sin rechistar • **"have you heard anything from him?" — "not a ~"** (*sleeping child*) —¿le has oído? —ni el menor ruido; (*absent friend*) —¿sabes algo de él? —ni una palabra
• IDIOM: • **to have a narrow ~** escaparse por los pelos • **they won, but it was a narrow ~** ganaron, pero por los pelos
(VI) [*hinge, wheel*] chirriar, rechinar; [*mouse*] chillar; [*shoes*] crujir; [*pen*] raspear • **the door ~ed open** la puerta chirrió *or* rechinó al abrirse, la puerta se abrió con un chirrido
(VT) chillar
▸ **squeak by*** (VI + ADV) **1** (*also* **squeak through**) (= *win by a narrow margin*) pasar muy justo, pasar raspando*
2 (= *subsist, manage*) subsistir • **to ~ by on sth** arreglárselas con algo
squeaker ['skwi:kəʳ] (N) (*in toy etc*) chirriador *m*
squeaky ['skwi:kɪ] (ADJ) (COMPAR: **squeakier**, SUPERL: **squeakiest**) [*hinge, door*] chirriante; [*voice*] chillón; [*shoes*] crujiente • **~ clean** (= *clean*) relimpio; (*fig*) perfectamente honrado
squeal [skwi:l] (N) chillido *m* • **with a ~ of pain** con un chillido de dolor • **a ~ of tyres** un chillido de ruedas
(VI) **1** (= *make noise*) [*person, animal*] chillar; [*brakes, tyres*] chirriar
2‡ (= *inform*) cantar, soplar
3* (= *complain*) quejarse • **don't come ~ing to me** no vengas a quejarte a mí
(VT) • **"yes", he ~ed** —sí —dijo chillando
squeamish ['skwi:mɪʃ] (ADJ) • **it's no good being ~ if you're a surgeon** si eres cirujano no puedes ser aprensivo • **I'm ~ about having needles stuck in me** me da aprensión que me claven agujas • **I felt ~ about touching a live snake** me daba repugnancia tocar una serpiente viva • **I'm not ~** no soy muy delicado • **don't be so ~** no seas tan delicado *or* tiquismiquis
squeamishness ['skwi:mɪʃnɪs] (N) (= *fear*) aprensión *f*; (= *fussiness*) remilgos *mpl* • **to feel a certain ~** sentir cierta aprensión *or* repugnancia
squeegee ['skwi:'dʒi:] (N) enjugador *m*
(CPD) ▸ **squeegee merchant*** limpiador(a) *m/f* ambulante de parabrisas
squeeze [skwi:z] (N) **1** (*act of squeezing*) (= *handclasp*) apretón *m*; (= *hug*) estrujón *m* • **he put his arm round her and gave her a quick ~** le pasó el brazo por encima y le dio un estrujoncito* *or* un apretón • **to give sth a ~** apretar algo • **to give sb's hand a ~** dar a algn un apretón de manos, apretar la mano a algn
2 (= *crush*) • **it was a tight ~ in the bus** íbamos muy apretados en el autobús • **it was a tight ~ to get through** había muy poco espacio para pasar
3 (= *restriction*) restricciones *fpl* • **small businesses are feeling the ~** las restricciones están afectando sobre todo a la pequeña empresa • **a ~ on profits** un recorte de beneficios • IDIOM: • **to put the ~ on sb*** apretar las tuercas *or* los tornillos a algn*; ▷ **credit**
4 (= *small amount*) [*of liquid*] chorrito *m*; [*of toothpaste*] poquito *m*, pizca *f* • **a ~ of lemon (juice)** un chorrito de zumo de limón, unas gotas de limón
5* (= *difficult situation*) aprieto *m* • **to be in a (tight) ~** encontrarse en un aprieto
6 (*Brit**) (= *boyfriend, girlfriend*) noviete/a* *m/f*, novio/a *m/f*
(VT) **1** (= *press firmly*) [+ *pimple, tube, trigger*] apretar; [+ *citrus fruit*] exprimir • **I ~d her tightly** la estreché entre mis brazos • **to ~ one's eyes shut** cerrar los ojos apretándolos • **to ~ sb's hand** apretar la mano a algn
2 (= *cram, fit*) meter • **to ~ clothes into a suitcase** meter ropa en una maleta a la fuerza • **can you ~ two more in?** ¿puedes hacer hueco para dos más?, ¿puedes meter a dos más? • **I could ~ you in on Thursday** le podría hacer un hueco para el jueves • **she ~d herself into the dress** se enfundó el vestido • **I ~d my way through the crowd** me abrí camino entre la multitud
3 (= *extract*) sacar • **to ~ money/a confession/information out of sb** sacar dinero/una confesión/información a algn • **rich city dwellers are squeezing the locals out** la gente acomodada de la ciudad está echando poco a poco a la población local • **freshly ~d orange juice** zumo *m* de naranjas recién exprimidas
4 (= *reduce*) recortar • **wage increases are squeezing profit margins** los aumentos salariales están recortando los márgenes de beneficios
(VI) • **they all ~d into the car** se metieron todos apretujados en el coche • **could I just ~ past?** ¿me deja pasar? • **he ~d past me** me pasó rozando • **to ~ through a hole** pasar por un agujero con dificultad
(CPD) ▸ **squeeze box** concertina *f*
▸ **squeeze in** (VT + PREP) [+ *person*] (= *find time for*) buscar un hueco para • **I can ~ you in at two o'clock** te he encontrado un hueco a las dos
(VI + ADV) • **it was a tiny car, but we managed to ~ in** era un coche pequeñísimo, pero nos las apañamos para caber
squeezer ['skwi:zəʳ] (N) exprimidor *m* • **lemon ~** exprimelimones *m inv*, exprimidor *m*
squeezy ['skwi:zɪ] (ADJ) [*object, bottle, tube*] blando
squelch [skweltʃ] (VI) chapotear • **to ~ through the mud** ir chapoteando por el lodo
(VT) aplastar, despachurrar
squib [skwɪb] (N) (= *firework*) buscapiés *m inv*; ▷ **damp**
squid [skwɪd] (N) (PL: **squid** *or* **squids**) calamar *m*, sepia *f*
squidgy* ['skwɪdʒɪ] (ADJ) (*Brit*) blanducho
squiffy* ['skwɪfɪ] (ADJ) (*Brit*) • **to be ~** estar achispado*
squiggle ['skwɪgl] (N) garabato *m*
squiggly ['skwɪglɪ] (ADJ) [*line*] garrapatoso
squint [skwɪnt] (N) **1** (*Med*) estrabismo *m* • **to have a ~** tener estrabismo, ser bizco • **he has a terrible ~** se le nota mucho que es bizco
2 (= *sidelong look*) mirada *f* de soslayo, mirada *f* de reojo • **let's have a ~*** déjame ver • **have a ~ at this*** mírame esto
(VI) **1** (*Med*) bizquear, ser bizco
2 • **to ~ at sth** (*quickly*) echar un vistazo a algo; (*with half-closed eyes*) mirar algo con los ojos entrecerrados • **he ~ed in the sunlight** entrecerró los ojos por el sol
squint-eyed ['skwɪnt'aɪd] (ADJ) bizco
squire ['skwaɪəʳ] (N) † (= *landowner*) terrateniente *m*, hacendado *m* (*LAm*), estanciero *m* (*LAm*); (*Hist*) (= *knight's attendant*) escudero *m*; (= *lady's escort*) galán *m*, acompañante *m* • **the ~** (*in relation to villagers etc*) el señor • **the ~ of Ambridge** el señor de Ambridge, el mayor terrateniente de Ambridge • **yes, ~!** (*Brit**) ¡sí, jefe! • **which way, ~?*** ¿por dónde, caballero?
(VT) [+ *lady*] acompañar
squirearchy ['skwaɪərɑ:kɪ] (N) aristocracia *f* rural, terratenientes *mpl*
squirm [skwɜ:m] (VI) retorcerse • **I'll make him ~** yo lo haré sufrir • **to ~ with embarrassment** estar violento, avergonzarse mucho
squirrel ['skwɪrəl] (N) (PL: **squirrels** *or* **squirrel**) ardilla *f*
▸ **squirrel away** (VT + ADV) [+ *nuts etc*] almacenar
squirt [skwɜ:t] (N) **1** (= *jet, spray*) chorro *m*
2* (= *child*) mequetrefe *mf*, chiquitajo/a* *m/f*, escuincle *mf* (*Mex*); (= *person*) farolero/a *m/f*, presumido/a *m/f*
(VT) [+ *liquid*] lanzar; [+ *person, car*] mojar • **to ~ water at sb** lanzar un chorro de agua hacia algn
(VI) • **to ~ out/in** salir/entrar a chorros • **the water ~ed into my eyes** salió un chorro de agua que me dio en los ojos
(CPD) ▸ **squirt gun** (*US*) pistola *f* de agua
squirter ['skwɜ:təʳ] (N) atomizador *m*
squish* ['skwɪʃ] (VT) (= *crush*) despachurrar
squishy ['skwɪʃɪ] (ADJ) [*fruit*] blando • **~ wet fields** campos como barrizales
Sr (ABBR) = **Senior**
Sr. (ABBR) (= **Sister**) Hna.
SRC (N ABBR) (*Brit*) **1** = **Science Research Council**
2 = **Students' Representative Council**
Sri Lanka [ˌsri:'læŋkə] (N) Sri Lanka *m*
Sri Lankan [ˌsri:'læŋkən] (ADJ) de Sri Lanka
(N) nativo/a *m/f* de Sri Lanka, habitante *mf* de Sri Lanka
SRM (ABBR) = **specified risk material**
SRN (N ABBR) (*Brit*) (*formerly*) = **State Registered Nurse**
SRO (ABBR) (*US*) = **standing room only**
Srs. (ABBR) (= **Sisters**) Hnas.
SRU (*Scot*) (N ABBR) = **Scottish Rugby Union**
SS (ABBR) **1** (*Brit*) = **steamship**
2 (= **Saints**) SS.
SSA (N ABBR) (*US*) = **Social Security Administration**
SSE (ABBR) (= **south-southeast**) SSE
SSI (N ABBR) = **small-scale integration**
SSP (N ABBR) (*Brit*) (= **statutory sick pay**) subsidio *m* obligatorio por enfermedad
SSSI (N ABBR) = **Site of Special Scientific Interest**
SST (N ABBR) (*US*) = **supersonic transport**
SSW (ABBR) (= **south-southwest**) SSO
St (ABBR) **1** (*Rel*) (= **Saint**) Sto., Sta., S.
2 (*Geog*) = **Strait**
3 (= **Street**) c/
4 (= **stone**) = 14 *libras*, = 6,348*kg*
5 = **summer time**
(CPD) ▸ **St John Ambulance, St John Ambulance Brigade** (*Brit*) *asociación benéfica de voluntarios*
St. (ABBR) = **Station**
stab [stæb] (N) **1** (*with knife etc*) puñalada *f*, navajazo *m* • IDIOM: • **~ in the back** puñalada *f* por la espalda, puñalada *f* encubierta
2 [*of pain*] punzada *f*
3 • IDIOM: • **to have a ~ at sth** intentar hacer algo
(VT) apuñalar, dar una puñalada a • **to ~ sb with a knife** apuñalar a algn con un cuchillo • **to ~ sb in the back** (*lit*) apuñalar a algn por la espalda; (*fig*) clavar a algn un puñal por la espalda • **to ~ sb to death** matar a algn a puñaladas
(VI) • **to ~ at sb** tratar de apuñalar a algn • **he ~bed at the picture with his finger** señaló el cuadro con un movimiento brusco del dedo
(CPD) ▸ **stab wound** puñalada *f*
stabbing ['stæbɪŋ] (N) (= *incident*) apuñalamiento *m*

S

(ADJ) [*pain, ache*] punzante
stability [stəˈbɪlɪtɪ] (N) estabilidad *f*
stabilization [ˌsteɪbəlaɪˈzeɪʃən] (N) estabilización *f*
stabilize [ˈsteɪbəlaɪz] (VT) [+ *boat*] estabilizar
(VI) [*currency, economy*] estabilizarse
stabilizer [ˈsteɪbəlaɪzəʳ] (N) **1** (*usu pl*) (*Naut*) (*also on bike*) estabilizador *m*
2 (*Culin*) estabilizante *m*
stable¹ [ˈsteɪbl] (ADJ) (COMPAR: **stabler**, SUPERL: **stablest**) [*relationship, country, situation, substance*] estable; [*job*] estable, permanente; (*Med*) [*condition*] estacionario; [*blood pressure, weight*] estable, estacionario; (*Psych*) [*person, character*] equilibrado
• **sterling has remained ~ against the franc** la libra se ha mantenido estable frente al franco • **the weight of the machine makes it very ~** el peso de la máquina le da estabilidad • **that ladder's not very ~** esa escalera no está muy firme
stable² [ˈsteɪbl] (N) (= *building*) cuadra *f*, caballeriza *f*; (= *establishment*) cuadra *f*
(VT) (= *keep in stable*) guardar en una cuadra; (= *put in stable*) poner en una cuadra
(CPD) ▸ **stable door** • **IDIOM:** • **to shut** *or* **close the ~ door after the horse has bolted** a buenas horas, mangas verdes ▸ **stable lad** = **stableboy**
stableboy [ˈsteɪblbɔɪ] (N) mozo *m* de cuadra
stableman [ˈsteɪblmən] (N) (PL: **stablemen**) mozo *m* de cuadra
stablemate [ˈsteɪblmeɪt] (N) (= *horse*) caballo *m* de la misma cuadra; (*fig*) (= *person*) camarada *mf*
staccato [stəˈkɑːtəʊ] (ADV) staccato
(ADJ) staccato
stack [stæk] (N) **1*** (= *pile*) montón *m*, pila *f*
• **there were ~s of books on the table** había montones *or* pilas de libros sobre la mesa
2 stacks* (= *lots*) • **I have ~s of work to do** tengo un montón* *or* una gran cantidad de trabajo • **they've got ~s of money** tienen cantidad de dinero • **we have ~s of time** nos sobra tiempo
3 (= *section in library*) estantería *f*; (= *book stack*) estantería *f* de libros
4 (*Agr*) almiar *m*, hacina *f*
5 (*Mil*) pabellón *m* de fusiles
6 [*of chimney*] cañón *m* de chimenea, fuste *m* de chimenea
(VT) **1** (= *pile up*) amontonar, apilar • **IDIOM:** • **the cards are ~ed against us** todo va en contra nuestra
2 • **(well) ~ed** (*US‡*) [*woman*] bien formada, muy buena*
stacker [ˈstækəʳ] (N) (*Comput*) apiladora *f*
stadium [ˈsteɪdɪəm] (N) (PL: **stadiums** *or* **stadia** [ˈsteɪdɪə]) estadio *m*
staff¹ [stɑːf] (N) **1** (= *personnel*) personal *m*, empleados *mpl* • **the administrative ~** (el personal de) la administración • **the teaching ~** el cuerpo docente, el profesorado • **to be on the ~** ser de plantilla • **to join the ~** entrar en la plantilla • **to leave the ~** dimitir
2 (*Mil*) estado *m* mayor
3† (= *stick*) bastón *m*, vara *f*; (*pilgrim's*) bordón *m*; (= *symbol of authority*) bastón *m* de mando; (*bishop's*) báculo *m*; [*of flag, lance etc*] asta *f*
(VT) proveer de personal • **to be well ~ed** (*fully staffed*) tener la plantilla completa; (*with good workers*) tener un buen personal
• **the centre is ~ed by qualified lawyers** el centro cuenta con abogados titulados en plantilla
(CPD) ▸ **staff association** asociación *f* del personal ▸ **staff canteen** comedor *m* de personal ▸ **staff college** escuela *f* militar superior ▸ **staff discount** descuento *m* para el personal ▸ **staff meeting** reunión *f* de personal ▸ **staff nurse** enfermero/a *m/f* titulado/a ▸ **staff officer** oficial *m* del Estado Mayor ▸ **staff room** sala *f* de profesores
▸ **staff-student ratio** proporción *f* alumnos-profesor ▸ **staff training** formación *f* de personal
staff² [stɑːf] (N) (PL: **staves, staff**) (*Mus*) pentagrama *m*
staffer [ˈstɑːfəʳ] (N) (*esp US*) miembro *mf* del personal, empleado/a *m/f* de plantilla
staffing [ˈstɑːfɪŋ] (N) (= *employment*) empleo *m* de personal; (= *number of employees*) dotación *f* de personal, plantilla *f* • **~ is inadequate** la dotación de personal *or* la plantilla es insuficiente
(CPD) ▸ **staffing ratio** proporción *f* alumnos-profesor
Staffs (ABBR) (*Brit*) = **Staffordshire**
stag [stæg] (N) **1** (*Zool*) ciervo *m*, venado *m*
2 (*Econ*) especulador(a) *m/f* con nuevas emisiones
(CPD) ▸ **stag beetle** ciervo *m* volante ▸ **stag night** despedida *f* de soltero ▸ **stag party** fiesta *f* de despedida de soltero
stage [steɪdʒ] (N) **1** (= *platform*) tablado *m*; (*in conference hall*) estrado *m*
2 (*Theat*) escenario *m* • **I get nervous on ~** me pongo nervioso en el escenario • **to put a play on the ~** poner una obra en escena • **to go on ~** salir a escena *or* al escenario • **you're on ~ in two minutes** sales (a escena) en dos minutos • **~ left/right** *la parte del escenario a la izquierda/derecha del actor (de cara al público)* • **the ~** (*as profession*) el teatro • **he writes for the ~** escribe para el teatro • **to go on the ~** hacerse actor/actriz • **IDIOM:** • **to set the ~ for sth** crear el marco idóneo para algo • **the ~ was set for a political showdown** se había creado el marco idóneo para una confrontación política
3 (*fig*) (= *scene*) escena *f* • **he occupies the centre of the political ~** ocupa el centro de la escena política
4 (= *step*) (*in process*) etapa *f*, fase *f* • **at this ~ in the negotiations** en esta etapa *or* a estas alturas de las negociaciones • **we can't cancel at this late ~** no podemos cancelarlo a estas alturas • **problems could arise at a later ~** podrían surgir problemas más adelante • **he's bound to find out at some ~** seguro que se entera tarde o temprano • **the project is still in its early ~s** el proyecto se encuentra todavía en su fase *or* etapa inicial
• **the war was in its final ~s** la guerra estaba en sus últimas etapas • **to go through a difficult ~** pasar por una etapa difícil • **it's just a ~ he's going through** no es más que una fase que está atravesando • **in ~s** por etapas • **in** *or* **by easy ~s** en etapas *or* fases cortas; ▹ **committee**
5 [*of rocket*] fase *f*; [*of pipeline*] tramo *m*
• **a four-stage rocket** un cohete de cuatro fases
6 (= *stagecoach*) diligencia *f*
(VT) **1** (*Theat*) [+ *play*] representar, poner en escena
2 (= *organize*) [+ *concert, festival*] organizar, montar
3 (= *carry out*) [+ *protest*] organizar; [+ *demonstration, strike*] hacer; [+ *attack*] lanzar • **the sixties rock legend is staging a comeback** la leyenda rockera de los sesenta prepara una vuelta a escena • **sterling has ~d a recovery on foreign exchange markets** la libra esterlina ha experimentado una mejora en los mercados de divisas extranjeros
4 (*pej*) (= *orchestrate*) montar, organizar • **that was no accident, it was ~d** eso no fue ningún accidente, estaba montado *or* organizado
(CPD) ▸ **stage adaptation** adaptación *f* teatral ▸ **stage designer** escenógrafo/a *m/f*
▸ **stage direction** acotación *f* ▸ **stage director** = **stage manager** ▸ **stage door** entrada *f* de artistas ▸ **stage fright** miedo *m* a las tablas *or* al escenario, miedo *m* escénico • **to get ~ fright** ponerse nervioso al salir a las tablas *or* al escenario ▸ **stage manager** director(a) *m/f* de escena ▸ **stage name** nombre *m* artístico ▸ **stage presence** presencia *f* en el escenario ▸ **stage set** decorado *m* ▸ **stage show** espectáculo *m*
▸ **stage whisper** aparte *m*
stagecoach [ˈsteɪdʒkəʊtʃ] (N) diligencia *f*
stagecraft [ˈsteɪdʒkrɑːft] (N) arte *m* teatral, escenotecnia *f*
stagehand [ˈsteɪdʒhænd] (N) tramoyista *mf*, sacasillas *m*
stage-manage [ˈsteɪdʒˌmænɪdʒ] (VT) [+ *play, production*] dirigir; (*fig*) [+ *event, confrontation etc*] orquestar
stager [ˈsteɪdʒəʳ] (N) • **old ~** veterano/a *m/f*
stagestruck [ˈsteɪdʒstrʌk] (ADJ) enamorado del teatro, fascinado por el teatro
stagey [ˈsteɪdʒɪ] (ADJ) = **stagy**
stagflation [stægˈfleɪʃən] (N) (*Econ*) (e)stagflación *f*, estanflación *f*
stagger [ˈstægəʳ] (N) **1** tambaleo *m*
2 staggers (*Vet*) modorra *f*
(VI) tambalear • **he ~ed to the door** fue tambaleándose hasta la puerta • **he was ~ing about** iba tambaleándose
(VT) **1** (= *amaze*) dejar anonadado, dejar pasmado • **we were ~ed by the number of letters we received** nos dejó anonadados *or* pasmados la cantidad de cartas que recibimos
2 [+ *hours, holidays, payments, spokes*] escalonar
staggered [ˈstægəd] (ADJ) **1** (= *amazed*) anonadado, pasmado • **I was ~ to learn I'd won first prize** me quedé anonadado *or* pasmado al enterarme de que había ganado el primer premio • **I was ~ to hear that ...** (= *dismayed*) me consterné al saber que ...
2 [*hours, junction*] escalonado
staggering [ˈstægərɪŋ] (ADJ) (= *astonishing*) asombroso, pasmoso
staggeringly [ˈstægərɪŋlɪ] (ADV) (= *astonishingly*) asombrosamente, pasmosamente
staghound [ˈstæghaʊnd] (N) perro *m* de caza, sabueso *m*
staghunt [ˈstæghʌnt] (N) cacería *f* de venado
staghunting [ˈstægˌhʌntɪŋ] (N) caza *f* de venado
staging [ˈsteɪdʒɪŋ] (N) **1** (= *scaffolding*) andamiaje *m*
2 (*Theat*) escenificación *f*, puesta *f* en escena
3 (*Space*) desprendimiento *m* (de una sección de un cohete)
(CPD) ▸ **staging post** (*Mil*) (*also gen*) escala *f*
stagnancy [ˈstægnənsɪ] (N) estancamiento *m*
stagnant [ˈstægnənt] (ADJ) **1** [*water*] estancado
2 (*fig*) [*economy, industry*] estancado, paralizado; [*market*] inactivo, estancado; [*society*] anquilosado
stagnate [stægˈneɪt] (VI) **1** [*water*] estancarse
2 (*fig*) [*economy, market, industry*] estancarse; [*society, person*] estancarse, anquilosarse
stagnation [stægˈneɪʃən] (N) **1** [*of water*] estancamiento *m*
2 (*fig*) [*of economy, industry*] estancamiento *m*, paralización *f*; [*of market*] inactividad *f*, estancamiento *m*; [*of society, person*] anquilosamiento *m*, estancamiento *m*
stagy [ˈsteɪdʒɪ] (ADJ) (COMPAR: **stagier**,

SUPERL: **stagiest**) *(pej)* teatral, histriónico
staid [steɪd] ADJ *[person]* serio; *[clothes]* sobrio, serio
staidness ['steɪdnɪs] N *[of person]* seriedad *f*; *[of clothes]* sobriedad *f*
stain [steɪn] N **1** *(= mark)* mancha *f*; *(= dye)* tinte *m*, tintura *f*; *(= paint)* pintura *f*
2 *(fig)* mancha *f* • **without a ~ on one's character** sin una sola mancha en la reputación
VT *(= mark)* manchar; *(= dye)* teñir, colorar; *(= paint)* pintar
VI manchar
CPD ▸ **stain remover** quitamanchas *m inv*
stained [steɪnd] ADJ *(= dirty)* manchado • **to be ~ with sth** estar manchado de algo • **her hands were ~ with blood** sus manos estaban manchadas de sangre, tenía las manos manchadas de sangre
-stained [-steɪnd] SUFFIX • **ink-stained** manchado de tinta
stained glass [ˌsteɪnd'glɑːs] N vidrio *m* de color
stained-glass [ˌsteɪnd'glɑːs] ADJ • **stained-glass window** vidriera *f* (de colores)
stainless ['steɪnlɪs] ADJ inmaculado
CPD ▸ **stainless steel** acero *m* inoxidable
stair [stɛəʳ] N **1** *(= single step)* escalón *m*, peldaño *m*; *(= stairway)* escalera *f*
2 stairs escalera *f* • **a flight of ~s** un tramo de escalera • **life below ~s** la vida de los criados • **gossip below ~s** habladurías *fpl* de la servidumbre
CPD ▸ **stair carpet** alfombra *f* de escalera ▸ **stair lift** (plataforma *f*) salvaescaleras *m inv*, elevador *m* de escaleras ▸ **stair rod** varilla *f* (para sujetar la alfombra de la escalera)
staircase ['stɛəkeɪs] N escalera *f*; ▹ **spiral**
stairway ['stɛəweɪ] N = **staircase**
stairwell ['stɛəwel] N hueco *m* or caja *f* de la escalera
stake [steɪk] N **1** *(= bet)* apuesta *f* • **the average ~ is just 80p** la apuesta media es de solo 80 peniques • **to be at ~** estar en juego • **the company's reputation is at ~** la reputación de la empresa está en juego • **there's a lot at ~ in this** es mucho lo que está en juego, hay mucho en juego • **he has got a lot at ~** • **there is a lot at ~ for him** es mucho lo que se está jugando • **the issue at ~** el asunto en cuestión, el asunto de que se trata • **the ~s are high** *(lit)* se apuesta fuerte, las apuestas son muy elevadas; *(fig)* es mucho lo que está en juego, hay mucho en juego • **to play for high ~s** *(lit)* apostar fuerte; *(fig)* tener mucho en juego • **to raise the ~s** *(Gambling)* subir la apuesta • **developments that raised the ~s in the elections** acontecimientos que hicieron más aventuradas las elecciones
2 *(= interest)* **a** *(Econ)* participación *f* • **he bought a 12 per cent ~ in the company** compró un 12 por ciento de participación en la compañía
b *(fig)* • **every employee has a ~ in the success of the firm** a todos los empleados les interesa que la empresa sea un éxito • **through your children you have a ~ in the future** tus hijos son tu participación en el futuro
3 stakes: **a** *(= race) carrera de caballos en la que el dinero del premio lo han puesto los propietarios de los caballos*; *(= prize money)* bote *m*
b *(fig)* • **he is still in front in the popularity ~s** sigue siendo el más popular de todos • **the President is riding high in the popularity ~s** el presidente goza de mucha popularidad
4 *(= post)* poste *m*; *(for plant)* rodrigón *m*; *(for execution)* hoguera *f* • **to be burned at the ~** • **die at the ~** morir en la hoguera
VT **1** *(= bet)* [+ *money, jewels*] jugarse, apostar; *(fig)* [+ *one's reputation, life*] jugarse • **to ~ one's reputation on sth** jugarse la reputación en algo • **I'd ~ my life on it** me jugaría la vida a que es así
2 *(with posts)* **a** *(= delimit)* [+ *area, path, line*] marcar con estacas, señalar con estacas • IDIOM: • **to ~ a** or **one's claim to** [+ *piece of land*] reivindicar, reclamar • **with this win he has ~d his claim for a place in the final** con esta victoria se ha asegurado un puesto en la final
b *(also* **stake up***)* *(= support with stakes)* [+ *fence*] apuntalar; [+ *plants*] arrodrigar
▸ **stake off** VT + ADV = **stake out**
▸ **stake out** VT + ADV **1** *(with posts)* [+ *piece of land, path, line*] marcar con estacas, señalar con estacas
2 *(= reserve, lay claim to)* • **you have to ~ out your place on the beach early** tienes que asegurarte un lugar en la playa bien temprano • **he has ~d out his position on social policy** ha afianzado su postura en lo referente a política social
3 *(= watch)* [+ *property etc*] *[journalist, criminal]* vigilar; *[police]* poner bajo vigilancia, mantener vigilado
stakeholder ['steɪkˌhəʊldəʳ] N **1** *(in gambling) persona que guarda las apuestas*
2 *(Econ)* accionista *mf*
3 *(fig)* interesado/a *m/f*
CPD ▸ **stakeholder pension** *(Brit) plan de pensiones complementario regulado por el gobierno británico* ▸ **stakeholder society** *(Brit) (Pol)* sociedad *f* participativa
stakeout ['steɪkaʊt] N operación *f* de vigilancia
stalactite ['stæləktaɪt] N estalactita *f*
stalagmite ['stæləgmaɪt] N estalagmita *f*
stale [steɪl] ADJ (COMPAR: **staler**, SUPERL: **stalest**) **1** *(= not fresh)* *[cheese, butter, sweat, cigarette smoke]* rancio; *[breath]* maloliente; *[air]* viciado; *[biscuit, beer]* pasado; *[cake]* seco; *[bread]* correoso; *(= hard)* duro • **to go ~** *[biscuit, beer]* pasarse; *[cake]* secarse; *[bread]* ponerse correoso; *(= become hard)* ponerse duro • **to have gone ~** *(lit)* estar pasado • **to smell ~** oler a viejo
2 *(fig)* *[news, joke]* viejo; *[idea]* marchito • **he felt tired and ~** se sentía cansado y hastiado • **their relationship had become ~** la relación se había estancado or anquilosado • **to get** or **become ~** *[person]* estancarse, anquilosarse • **I'm getting ~** me estoy estancando or anquilosando • **the show's got a little ~** el espectáculo está ya un poco gastado • **if they rehearse too much they'll become ~** si ensayan demasiado se van a quemar
VI *(liter)* *[relationship, author, writing]* quedarse estancado or anquilosado; *[pleasures]* perder la frescura *(liter)*
stalemate ['steɪlmeɪt] N **1** *(Chess)* ahogado *m*
2 *(fig)* punto *m* muerto • **there is ~ between the two powers** las relaciones entre las dos potencias están en un punto muerto or en un impasse • **the ~ is complete** la paralización es completa • **to reach ~** estancarse
VT *(Chess)* ahogar, dar tablas por ahogado a; *(fig)* paralizar
stalemated ['steɪlmeɪtɪd] ADJ *(fig)* *[discussions]* estancado, en un punto muerto; *[project]* en un punto muerto; *[person]* en tablas
staleness ['steɪlnɪs] N **1** *(= lack of freshness)* *[of cheese, butter, sweat, cigarette smoke]* lo rancio; *[of air]* lo viciado; *[of biscuit, beer]* lo pasado; *[of cake]* sequedad *f*, lo seco; *[of bread]* lo correoso; *(= hardness)* dureza *f*
2 *(fig)* *[of news, joke]* lo viejo; *[of person, relationship]* estancamiento *m*, anquilosamiento *m*
Stalin ['stɑːlɪn] N Stalin
Stalinism ['stɑːlɪnɪzəm] N estalinismo *m*
Stalinist ['stɑːlɪnɪst] ADJ estalinista
N estalinista *mf*
stalk¹ [stɔːk] VT [+ *animal*] *[hunter]* cazar al acecho; *[animal]* acechar; [+ *person*] seguir los pasos de
VI *(= walk)* • **to ~ away** or **off** irse con paso airado • **she ~ed out of the room** salió airada del cuarto
stalk² [stɔːk] N **1** *(Bot)* tallo *m*, caña *f*; *(= cabbage stalk)* troncho *m*
2 *[of glass]* pie *m*
3 *(Aut)* *(= control stalk)* palanca *f*
stalker ['stɔːkəʳ] N *persona que está obsesionada con otra y la acosa constantemente con llamadas telefónicas o siguiéndola a todas partes*
stalk-eyed ['stɔːkaɪd] ADJ *(Zool)* de ojos pedunculares
stalking ['stɔːkɪŋ] N *(Jur) acoso cometido por un "stalker" y que constituye un delito*
CPD ▸ **stalking horse** pretexto *m*; *(Pol) candidato que en unas elecciones desafía a un líder de su propio partido, con el propósito de medir la fuerza de la oposición*
stall [stɔːl] N **1** *(Agr)* *(= stable)* establo *m*; *(= manger)* pesebre *m*; *(for single horse etc)* casilla *f*
2 *(in market etc)* puesto *m*; *(in fair)* caseta *f*, casilla *f*; *(= newspaper stall)* quiosco *m*, puesto *m* *(esp LAm)* • IDIOM: • **to set out one's ~** exponer lo que se ofrece (a la venta)
3 *(Brit) (Theat)* • **the ~s** el patio de butacas
4 *(in church)* silla *f* de coro
5 *(US) (in car park)* emplazamiento *m*
VT **1** [+ *car, plane*] parar, calar • **the talks are ~ed** las negociaciones están en un callejón sin salida
2 [+ *person*] entretener
VI **1** *[car]* pararse; *[plane]* perder velocidad • **we ~ed on a steep hill** quedamos parados en una cuesta abrupta, se nos atascó el motor en una cuesta abrupta • **the talks have ~ed** las negociaciones están en un callejón sin salida
2 *(fig)* *(= delay)* andar con rodeos, esquivar • **stop ~ing!** ¡déjate de evasivas! • **the minister ~ed for 20 minutes** durante 20 minutos el ministro evitó contestar directamente
stall-fed ['stɔːlfed] ADJ engordado en establo
stallholder ['stɔːlˌhəʊldəʳ] N dueño/a *m/f* de un puesto, puestero/a *m/f* *(LAm)*
stallion ['stæliən] N semental *m*, padrillo *m* *(LAm)*
stalwart ['stɔːlwət] ADJ *[person]* *(in spirit)* fuerte, robusto; *(in build)* fornido, robusto; *[supporter, opponent]* leal, fiel; *[belief]* empedernido
N partidario/a *m/f* incondicional
stamen ['steɪmen] N (PL: **stamens** or **stamina** ['stæmɪnə]) estambre *m*
stamina ['stæmɪnə] N resistencia *f*, aguante *m* • **has he enough ~ for the job?** ¿tiene bastante resistencia para el puesto? • **you need ~** hace falta tener nervio • **intellectual ~** vigor *m* intelectual
stammer ['stæməʳ] N tartamudeo *m* • **he has a bad ~** tartamudea terriblemente
VI tartamudear
VT *(also* **stammer out***)* decir tartamudeando
stammerer ['stæmərəʳ] N tartamudo/a *m/f*
stammering ['stæmərɪŋ] ADJ tartamudo
N tartamudeo *m*

S

stammeringly ['stæmərɪŋlɪ] (ADV) • **he said ~** dijo tartamudeando

stamp [stæmp] (N) **1** (= *postage stamp*) sello *m*, estampilla *f* (*LAm*); (= *fiscal stamp, revenue stamp*) timbre *m*, póliza *f*; (*for free food etc*) bono *m*, vale *m*
2 (= *rubber stamp*) estampilla *f*; (*for metal*) cuño *m*
3 (*fig*) (= *mark*) sello *m* • **it bears the ~ of genius** tiene el sello del genio • **to leave** *or* **put one's ~ on sth** poner *or* dejar su sello en algo • **a man of his ~** un hombre de su temple; (*pej*) un hombre de esa calaña
4 (*with foot*) taconazo *m* • **with a ~ of her foot** dando un taconazo
(VT) **1** • **to ~ one's foot** patear, patalear; (*in dancing*) zapatear • **to ~ the ground** [*person*] dar patadas en el suelo; [*horse*] piafar
2 [+ *letter*] sellar, poner el sello a • **the letter is insufficiently ~ed** la carta no tiene suficientes sellos
3 (= *mark with rubber stamp*) marcar con sello; (= *mark with fiscal stamp*) timbrar; (= *emboss*) grabar; [+ *passport*] sellar • **they ~ed my passport at the frontier** sellaron mi pasaporte en la frontera
4 (= *impress mark etc on*) estampar, imprimir; [+ *coin, design*] estampar • **paper ~ed with one's name** papel *m* con el nombre de uno impreso, papel *m* con membrete
5 (*fig*) marcar, señalar • **to ~ sth on one's memory** grabar algo en la memoria de uno • **his manners ~ him as a gentleman** sus modales lo señalan como caballero • **to ~ o.s. on sth** poner *or* dejar su sello en algo
(VI) **1** (*single movement*) patear, patalear • **to ~ on sth** pisotear algo, hollar algo • **ouch, you ~ed on my foot!** ¡ay, me has pisado el pie!
2 (= *walk*) • **to ~ in/out** entrar/salir dando fuertes zancadas • **he ~s about the house** anda por la casa pisando muy fuerte
(CPD) ▸ **stamp album** álbum *m* de sellos ▸ **stamp book** (= *collection*) álbum *m* de sellos; (*for posting*) libro *m* de sellos ▸ **stamp collecting** filatelia *f* ▸ **stamp collection** colección *f* de sellos ▸ **stamp collector** filatelista *mf* ▸ **stamp dealer** comerciante *mf* en sellos (de correo) ▸ **stamp duty** (*Econ*) impuesto *m* *or* derecho *m* del timbre ▸ **stamp machine** expendedor *m* automático de sellos (de correo)
▸ **stamp down** (VT + ADV) • **to ~ sth down** apisonar algo, comprimir algo con los pies
▸ **stamp out** (VT + ADV) **1** • **they ~ed out the rhythm** marcaron el ritmo con los pies
2 (= *extinguish*) [+ *fire, cigarette*] apagar con el pie
3 (= *eliminate*) [+ *crime, corruption, activity*] erradicar, acabar con; [+ *rebellion*] sofocar • **we must ~ out this abuse** tenemos que acabar con esta injusticia • **the doctors ~ed out the epidemic** los médicos erradicaron la epidemia

stamped [stæmpt] (ADJ) [*envelope*] con sello, que lleva sello; [*paper*] sellado, timbrado • **~ addressed envelope** sobre *m* sellado con las señas propias

stampede [stæm'pi:d] (N) (*lit*) estampida *f*, desbandada *f*; (*fig*) desbandada *f* • **there was a sudden ~ for the door** todo el mundo corrió en estampida hacia la puerta • **the exodus turned into a ~** el éxodo se transformó en una fuga precipitada
(VT) [+ *cattle*] provocar la desbandada de • **to ~ sb into doing sth** presionar fuerte a algn para que haga algo • **let's not be ~d** no obremos precipitadamente
(VI) (*lit*) ir en desbandada; (*fig*) precipitarse

stamping-ground* ['stæmpɪŋ,graʊnd] (N) territorio *m* • **this is his private stamping-ground** este es terreno particular suyo, este es coto cerrado de su propiedad • **to keep off sb's stamping-ground** no invadir el territorio de algn

Stan [stæn] (N) *familiar form of* **Stanley**

stance [stæns] (N) **1** (*lit*) postura *f*
2 (*fig*) actitud *f* • **to take up a ~** adoptar una actitud
3 (*Scot*) (= *taxi rank*) parada *f* (de taxis)

stanch [stɑ:ntʃ] (VT) [+ *blood*] restañar

stanchion ['stɑ:nʃən] (N) puntal *m*, montante *m*

stand [stænd] (VB: PT, PP: **stood**) (N)
1 (= *position*) posición *f*, puesto *m* • **to take up a ~ near the door** colocarse cerca de la puerta
2 (*fig*) (= *stance*) actitud *f*, postura *f* • **to take a ~ on an issue** adoptar una actitud hacia una cuestión • **to take a firm ~** adoptar una actitud firme
3 (*Mil*) • **the ~ of the Australians at Tobruk** la resistencia de los australianos en Tobruk • **Custer's last ~** la última batalla del General Custer • IDIOM: • **to make a ~** hacer parada, plantarse • **to make** *or* **take a ~ against sth** oponer resistencia a algo; ▹ **one-night stand**
4 (*for taxis*) parada *f* (de taxis)
5 (= *lamp stand*) pie *m*; (= *music stand*) atril *m*; (= *hallstand*) perchero *m*
6 (= *newspaper stand*) quiosco *m*, puesto *m* (*esp LAm*); (= *market stall*) puesto *m*; (*in shop*) estante *m*, puesto *m*; (*at exhibition*) caseta *f*, stand *m*; (= *bandstand*) quiosco *m*
7 (*Sport*) (= *grandstand*) tribuna *f*
8 (*Jur*) estrado *m* • **to take the ~** (*esp US*) (= *go into witness box*) subir a la tribuna de los testigos; (= *give evidence*) prestar declaración
9 [*of trees*] hilera *f*, grupo *m*
10** (= *erection*) empalme** *m*
11 = **standstill**
(VT) **1** (= *place*) poner, colocar • **to ~ sth against the wall** apoyar algo en la pared • **to ~ a vase on a table** poner un florero sobre una mesa
2 (= *withstand*) resistir • **it won't ~ serious examination** no resistirá un examen detallado • **it won't ~ the cold** no resiste el *or* al frío • **his heart couldn't ~ the shock** su corazón no resistió el *or* al choque • IDIOMS: • **to ~ one's ground** mantenerse firme, plantarse • **if you can't ~ the heat, get out of the kitchen** si no puedes lidiar el toro, quítate de en medio
3 (= *tolerate*) aguantar • **I can ~ anything but that** lo aguanto todo menos eso • **I can't ~ it any longer!** ¡no aguanto más! • **I can't ~ Debussy** no aguanto a Debussy • **I can't ~ (the sight of) him** no lo aguanto, no lo puedo tragar • **I can't ~ waiting for people** no aguanto *or* soporto que me hagan esperar; ▹ **chance**
4* (= *pay for*) • **to ~ sb a drink/meal** invitar a algn a una copa/a comer • **he stood me lunch** me pagó la comida • **the company will have to ~ the loss** la compañía tendrá que encargarse de las pérdidas
(VI) **1** (= *be upright*) estar de pie *or* derecho, estar parado (*LAm*) • **he could hardly ~** hasta tenía problemas para ponerse de pie • **the house is still ~ing** la casa sigue en pie • **we must ~ together** (*fig*) debemos unirnos *or* ser solidarios • IDIOMS: • **to ~ on one's own two feet** valerse por sí mismo, defenderse solo (*LAm*) • **to ~ tall** pisar fuerte; ▹ **ease**
2 (= *get up*) levantarse, pararse (*LAm*) • **all ~!** ¡levántense!
3 (= *stay, stand still*) • **they were ~ing at the bar** estaban juntos al bar • **to ~ in the doorway** estar en la puerta • **don't just ~ there, do something!** ¡no te quedes ahí parado, haz algo! • **they stood patiently in the rain** se quedaron esperando pacientemente bajo la lluvia • **to ~ talking** seguir hablando, quedarse a hablar • **we stood chatting for half an hour** charlamos durante media hora, pasamos media hora charlando • **~ and deliver!** ¡la bolsa o la vida! • IDIOM: • **he left the others ~ing** dejó a todos atrás *or* (*LAm*) parados
4 (= *tread*) • **to ~ on sth** pisar algo • **you're ~ing on my foot** me estás pisando • **he stood on the beetle** pisó el escarabajo • **he stood on the brakes** (*Aut**) pisó el freno a fondo
5 (= *measure*) medir • **he ~s a good six feet** mide seis pies largos • **the tower ~s 50m high** la torre tiene 50m de alta • **the mountain ~s 3,000m high** la montaña tiene una altura de 3.000m
6 (= *have reached*) • **the thermometer ~s at 40°** el termómetro marca 40 grados • **the record ~s at ten minutes** el record está en diez minutos, el tiempo récord sigue siendo de diez minutos • **sales are currently ~ing at two million** las ventas ya han alcanzado los dos millones • **sales ~ at five per cent more than last year** las ventas han aumentado en un cinco por cien en relación con el año pasado
7 (= *be situated*) encontrarse, ubicarse (*LAm*) • **it ~s beside the town hall** está junto al ayuntamiento
8 (= *be mounted, based*) apoyarse
9 (= *remain valid*) [*offer, argument, decision*] seguir en pie *or* vigente • **my objection still ~s** mis reservas siguen en pie • **the contract ~s** el contrato sigue en vigor • **the theory ~s or falls on this** de allí depende la teoría entera • **it has stood for 200 years** ha durado 200 años ya, lleva ya 200 años de vida
10 (*fig*) (= *be placed*) estar, encontrarse • **as things ~** • **as it ~s** tal como están las cosas • **I'd like to know where I ~** quisiera saber a qué atenerme • **how do we ~?** ¿cómo estamos? • **where do you ~ with him?** ¿cuáles son tus relaciones con él? • **nothing ~s between us** nada nos separa • **nothing ~s between you and success** no tienes ningún obstáculo en el camino al éxito
11 (= *be in a position*) • **to ~ to do sth** arriesgar hacer algo • **he ~s to gain a great deal** tiene la posibilidad de ganar mucho • **what do we ~ to gain by it?** ¿qué posibilidades hay para nosotros de ganar algo?, ¿qué ventaja nos daría esto? • **we ~ to lose a lot** para nosotros supondría una pérdida importante, estamos en peligro de perder bastante
12 (= *be*) • **she ~s in need of a friend** lo que necesita es un amigo • **to ~ accused of murder** estar acusado de asesinato • **he ~s alone in this matter** no tiene ningún apoyo en este caso • **to ~ (as) security for sb** (*Econ*) salir fiador de algn; (*fig*) salir por algn • **it ~s to reason that …** es evidente que …, no cabe duda de que …; ▹ **clear, correct**
13 (= *remain undisturbed*) estar • **to allow a liquid to ~** dejar estar un líquido • **let it ~ for three days** déjelo reposar durante tres días • **don't let the tea ~** no dejes que se pase el té • **to let sth ~ in the sun** poner algo al sol, dejar algo al sol • **the car has been ~ing in the sun** el coche ha estado expuesto al sol
14 (*Brit*) (*Pol*) presentarse (como candidato) • **to ~ against sb in an election** presentarse como oponente a algn en unas elecciones • **to ~ as a candidate** presentarse como candidato • **to ~ for Parliament** presentarse como candidato a diputado • **to ~ for president** presentarse como candidato a la

presidencia • **he stood for Castroforte** fue uno de los candidatos en Castroforte • **he stood for Labour** fue candidato laborista
15 (*Econ*) • **there is £50 ~ing to your credit** usted tiene 50 libras en el haber

▸ **stand about, stand around** (VI + ADV) estar, esperar, seguir en un sitio sin propósito fijo • **they just ~ about all day** pasan todo el día por ahí sin hacer nada • **they kept us ~ing about for ages** nos hicieron esperar mucho tiempo

▸ **stand aside** (VI + ADV) apartarse, mantenerse al margen • **~ aside, please!** ¡apártense, por favor! • **we cannot ~ aside and do nothing** no podemos quedarnos sin hacer nada • **he stood aside when he could have helped** se mantuvo al margen en vez de ayudar • **to ~ aside from sth** (*fig*) mantenerse al margen de algo

▸ **stand back** (VI + ADV) **1** [*person*] retirarse; (*fig*) tomar una posición más objetiva • **~ back, please!** ¡más atrás, por favor!
2 [*building*] (= *be placed further back*) estar apartado (**from** de)

▸ **stand by** (VI + ADV) **1** (= *do nothing*) mantenerse aparte
2 (= *be ready*) estar preparado *or* listo • **~ by for further news** seguirán más noticias • **~ by for take-off!** ¡listos para despegar! • **the Navy is ~ing by to help** unidades de la Flota están listas para prestar ayuda
(VI + PREP) [+ *person*] apoyar *or* respaldar a; [+ *promise*] cumplir con • **we ~ by what we said** nos atenemos a lo dicho • **the Minister stood by his decision** el Ministro mantuvo su decisión

▸ **stand down** (VI + ADV) **1** (= *resign*) [*official, chairman*] dimitir; (= *withdraw*) [*candidate*] retirarse • **the candidate is ~ing down in favour of a younger person** el candidato se retira a favor de una persona más joven
2 (*Jur*) [*witness*] retirarse • **you may ~ down** usted puede retirarse
3 (*Mil*) • **the troops have stood down** ha terminado el estado de alerta (militar)

▸ **stand for** (VI + PREP) **1** (= *represent*) [*abbreviation*] significar • **MP ~s for Member of Parliament** MP significa Miembro del Parlamento • **A ~s for apple** M es de manzana • **here a dash ~s for a word** aquí una raya representa una palabra
2 (= *support*) [+ *principle, honesty*] representar
3 (= *permit*) permitir; (= *tolerate*) admitir • **I won't ~ for that** eso no lo admito • **I'll not ~ for your whims any longer** no aguanto tus caprichos un momento más
4 ▹ **stand**

▸ **stand in** (VI + ADV) sustituir • **to ~ in for sb** sustituir a algn

▸ **stand off** (VT + ADV) (*Brit*) [+ *workers*] despedir (*temporalmente, por falta de trabajo*), suspender
(VI + ADV) apartarse, guardar las distancias; (*Naut*) apartarse

▸ **stand out** (VI + ADV) **1** (= *project*) [*ledge, buttress, vein*] sobresalir, salir
2 (= *be conspicuous, clear*) destacar (**against** contra) • **to ~ out in relief** resaltar • IDIOM: • **it ~s out a mile*** se ve a la legua
3 (= *be outstanding*) destacarse
4 (= *be firm, hold out*) mantenerse firme, aferrarse • **to ~ out against sth** oponerse a algo • **to ~ out for sth** insistir en algo

▸ **stand over** (VI + PREP) • **he stood over me while I did it** me vigiló mientras lo hacía
(VI + ADV) [*items for discussion*] quedar en suspenso • **to let an item ~ over** dejar un asunto para la próxima vez

▸ **stand to** (VI + ADV) (*Mil*) estar alerta, estar sobre las armas

▸ **stand up** (VI + ADV) **1** (= *rise*) levantarse, ponerse de pie; (= *be standing*) estar de pie • **she had nothing but the clothes she was ~ing up in** no tenía más que lo que llevaba puesto • IDIOM: • **we must ~ up and be counted** tenemos que declararnos abiertamente
2 [*argument etc*] ser sólido, ser lógico, convencer • **the case did not ~ up in court** la acusación no se mantuvo en el tribunal
3 • **to ~ up for sb** (*fig*) respaldar a algn • **to ~ up for sth** defender algo • **to ~ up for o.s.** defenderse solo
4 • **to ~ up to sb** hacer frente a algn • **it ~s up to hard wear** es muy resistente • **to ~ up to a test** salir bien de una prueba • **it won't ~ up to close examination** no resistirá un examen minucioso
(VT + ADV) **1** (= *place upright*) colocar de pie • IDIOM: • **a soup so thick that you could ~ a spoon up in it** una sopa tan espesa que una cuchara se quedaría de pie en él
2* [+ *girlfriend, boyfriend*] dejar plantado*, dar plantón a*

stand-alone [ˈstændələʊn] (ADJ) [*computer system etc*] autónomo

standard [ˈstændəd] (N) **1** (= *measure*) estándar *m* • **his ~s are high/low** sus estándares son altos/bajos, los niveles que requiere son altos/bajos • **by any ~ the work was good** el trabajo era bueno desde cualquier punto de vista • **the food was awful even by my (undemanding) ~s** la comida era espantosa incluso para mí (que soy poco exigente); ▹ **double**
2 (= *norm*) • **to be below ~** no tener la suficiente calidad • **~s of conduct** normas *fpl* de conducta • **the gold ~** (*Econ*) el patrón oro • **to set a ~**: • **the society sets ~s for judging different breeds of dog** la asociación establece ciertos patrones *or* ciertas normas para juzgar las distintas razas de perros • **society sets impossible ~s for feminine beauty** la sociedad impone unos patrones de belleza femenina imposibles • **to set a good ~** imponer un nivel alto • **her work has set a ~ for excellence which it will be hard to equal** su labor ha establecido unos niveles de excelencia que serán muy difíciles de igualar • **this film sets a new ~** esta película establece nuevos niveles de calidad cinematográfica, esta película supera los niveles cinematográficos anteriores • **her work/performance was not up to ~** su trabajo/actuación no estaba a la altura (requerida) • **the product is not up to ~** el producto no tiene la calidad requerida
3 (= *level*) nivel *m*; (= *quality*) calidad *f* • **she has French to first-year university ~** su francés es de un nivel de primer año de carrera • **the ~ of service** el nivel de servicio • **their ~ of hygiene leaves much to be desired** los niveles de higiene que tienen dejan mucho que desear • **the ~ of medical care** la calidad de atención médica • **of (a) high/low ~** de alto/bajo nivel • **high ~s of conduct are expected of students** a los alumnos se les exige un nivel de comportamiento muy elevado
4 standards valores *mpl* morales • **she has no ~s** carece de valores morales *or* principios • **there has been a corruption of moral ~s** han decaído los valores morales
5 (= *flag*) estandarte *m*, bandera *f*
6 (= *pole*) (*for flag*) poste *m*; (*for lamp*) pie *m*
7 (*Bot*) *árbol o arbusto de tronco erecto y desprovisto de ramas*
8 (= *song*) tema *m* clásico, clásico *m*
(ADJ) **1** (= *normal*) [*design, length*] estándar (*adj inv*); [*amount, size*] normal; [*feature*] normal, corriente; [*charge*] fijo; [*procedure*] habitual • **electric windows come as ~ on this car** las ventanillas eléctricas son de serie en este coche • **the ~ treatment is an injection of glucose** el tratamiento habitual es una inyección de glucosa • **to become ~** [*practice, procedure*] imponerse como norma • **it has become ~ practice for many surgeons** se ha convertido en una norma entre muchos cirujanos
2 (= *officially approved*) [*spelling, pronunciation*] estándar (*adj inv*); [*grammar*] normativa; [*measure*] legal
3 (= *classic, recommended*) • **it's a ~ text** es un texto clásico
(CPD) ▸ **standard bearer** (*lit*) abanderado/a *m/f*; (*fig*) abanderado/a *m/f*, adalid *mf* ▸ **standard class** clase *f* turista ▸ **standard deviation** (*Statistics*) desviación *f* estándar *or* típica ▸ **standard English** inglés *m* estándar *or* normativo ▸ **standard error** (*Statistics*) error *m* estándar *or* típico ▸ **standard gauge** (*Rail*) vía *f* normal ▸ **Standard Grade** (*Scot*) (*Scol*) *certificado obtenido tras aprobar los exámenes al final de la educación secundaria obligatoria*; ▹ GCSE ▸ **standard lamp** lámpara *f* de pie ▸ **standard model** modelo *m* estándar ▸ **standard of living** nivel *m* de vida ▸ **standard price** precio *m* oficial ▸ **standard quality** calidad *f* normal ▸ **standard rate** (*Econ*) tipo *m* de interés vigente ▸ **standard time** hora *f* oficial ▸ **standard unit** (*Elec, Gas*) paso *m* (de contador) ▸ **standard weight** peso *m* legal

standard-issue [ˌstændədˈɪʃuː] (ADJ) • **a standard-issue shirt** una camisa de uniforme

standardization [ˌstændədaɪˈzeɪʃən] (N) normalización *f*, estandar(d)ización *f*

standardize [ˈstændədaɪz] (VT) normalizar, estandar(d)izar

stand-by [ˈstændbaɪ] (N) **1** (*in case of need*) (= *person*) suplente *mf*; (= *spare*) repuesto *m*; (= *loan*) crédito *m* contingente, stand-by *m*
2 (= *alert, readiness*) • **to be on stand-by** [*troops*] (= *ready for attack*) estar preparado para el ataque; [*doctor*] estar listo para acudir; [*passenger*] estar en lista de espera • **to be on 24-hour stand-by** (= *ready to leave*) estar listo para partir dentro de 24 horas
3 (= *stand-by ticket*) billete *m* de lista de espera, billete *m* de stand-by
(CPD) ▸ **stand-by aircraft** avión *m* de reserva ▸ **stand-by arrangements** (*Econ*) acuerdo *m* de reserva ▸ **stand-by credit** crédito *m* disponible, crédito *m* stand-by ▸ **stand-by facility** stand-by *m*, lista *f* de reserva ▸ **stand-by generator** generador *m* de reserva ▸ **stand-by passenger** (*Aer*) pasajero/a *m/f* de la lista de espera ▸ **stand-by ticket** billete *m* stand-by

standee* [stænˈdiː] (N) (*US*) espectador(a) *m/f* que asiste de pie

stand-in [ˈstændɪn] (N) sustituto/a *m/f* (**for** por); (*Cine*) doble *mf*

standing [ˈstændɪŋ] (ADJ) **1** (= *not sitting*) de pie, parado (*LAm*); (= *upright*) [*stone, corn*] derecho, recto; [*water*] estancado, encharcado
2 (= *permanent*) [*army, committee, rule etc*] permanente; [*custom*] arraigado; [*grievance, joke*] constante, eterno
(N) **1** (= *social position*) rango *m*, estatus *m inv*; (= *reputation*) reputación *f*, fama *f* • **what is his ~ locally?** ¿cómo se le considera en círculos locales? • **financial ~** solvencia *f* • **to be in good ~** tener buena reputación; (*Econ*) gozar de buen crédito • **of high ~** de categoría • **the restaurant has a high ~** el restaurante tiene una buena reputación

• **he has no ~ in this matter** no tiene voz ni voto en este asunto • **the relative ~ of these problems** la importancia relativa de estos problemas • **social ~** posición *f* social • **a man of some ~** un hombre de cierta categoría
2 (= *duration*) duración *f*; (= *seniority*) antigüedad *f* • **of six months' ~** que lleva seis meses • **a captain of only a month's ~** un capitán que lleva solamente un mes en el puesto *or* en tal graduación • **of long ~** de mucho tiempo (acá), viejo
3 (*US*) (*Aut*) • **"no standing"** "prohibido estacionar"
(CPD) ▸ **standing order** (*Econ*) giro *m or* pedido *m* regular; (*Comm*) pedido *m* permanente, pedido *m* regular ▸ **standing orders** [*of meeting*] reglamento *m*, estatuto *m* ▸ **standing ovation** ovación *f* en pie • **he got a ~ ovation** todos se pusieron en pie para ovacionarlo ▸ **standing room** sitio *m* para estar de pie • **~ room only** ya no quedan asientos ▸ **standing start** (*Sport*) salida *f* desde posición de paro

stand-off ['stændɒf] (N) (= *deadlock*) punto *m* muerto, callejón *m* sin salida; (*Sport*) (= *stalemate*) empate *m*
(CPD) ▸ **stand-off half** (*Rugby*) medio *m* de apertura

stand-offish [ˌstænd'ɒfɪʃ] (ADJ) distante, reservado

stand-offishly [ˌstænd'ɒfɪʃlɪ] (ADV) fríamente

stand-offishness [ˌstænd'ɒfɪʃnɪs] (N) frialdad *f*, reserva *f*

stand-pat* ['stændpæt] (ADJ) (*US*) inmovilista

standpipe ['stændpaɪp] (N) **1** (*Tech*) columna *f* de alimentación
2 (*in street*) fuente *f* provisional

standpoint ['stændpɔɪnt] (N) punto *m* de vista • **from the ~ of …** desde el punto de vista de …

standstill ['stændstɪl] (N) parada *f* • **to be at a ~** [*vehicle*] estar parado; [*industry etc*] estar paralizado • **negotiations are at a ~** las negociaciones están paralizadas • **to bring a car to a ~** parar un coche • **to bring an industry to a ~** paralizar una industria • **to bring traffic to a ~** paralizar el tráfico, parar totalmente el tráfico • **to come to a ~** [*person*] pararse, hacer un alto; [*vehicle*] pararse; [*industry etc*] estancarse

stand-to [ˌstænd'tuː] (N) alerta *f*

stand-up ['stændʌp] (ADJ) • **stand-up buffet** comida *f* tomada de pie • **stand-up collar** cuello *m* alto • **stand-up fight** (*lit*) pelea *f* violenta; (*fig*) altercado *m* violento
(N) (*also* **stand-up comedian, stand-up comic**) cómico/a *m/f*; (*also* **stand-up comedy**) comedia *f*

stank [stæŋk] (PT) *of* **stink**

Stanley knife® ['stænlɪˌnaɪf] (N) cuchilla *f* para moqueta

stannic ['stænɪk] (ADJ) estánnico

stanza ['stænzə] (N) estrofa *f*, estancia *f*

stapes ['steɪpiːz] (N) (PL: **stapes** *or* **stapedes** [stæ'piːdiːz]) (*Anat*) estribo *m*

staphylococcus [ˌstæfɪlə'kɒkəs] (N) (PL: **staphylococci** [ˌstæfɪlə'kɒkaɪ]) estafilococo *m*

staple¹ ['steɪpl] (N) (= *fastener*) grapa *f*, corchete *m* (*S. Cone*)
(VT) sujetar con grapa
(CPD) ▸ **staple gun** grapadora *f*

staple² ['steɪpl] (ADJ) [*product*] de primera necesidad; [*topic of conversation*] clásico • **their ~ food** *or* **diet** su comida cotidiana, su alimento de primera necesidad
(N) (= *chief product*) artículo *m* de primera necesidad; (= *food*) alimento *m* de primera necesidad; (= *raw material*) materia *f* prima; [*of wool*] fibra *f* (textil); [*of conversation*] asunto *m* principal, elemento *m* esencial

stapler ['steɪpləʳ], **stapling machine** ['steɪplɪŋməʃiːn] (N) grapadora *f*

star [stɑːʳ] (N) **1** (*Astron*) estrella *f*, astro *m* • **the Stars and Stripes** (*US*) las barras y las estrellas • **the Stars and Bars** (*US*) (*Hist*) la bandera de los estados confederados
• IDIOMS: • **to have ~s in one's eyes** estar ilusionado • **to see ~s** ver (las) estrellas • **it's written in the ~s** está escrito (en las estrellas) • **to be born under a lucky ~** nacer con estrella • **to believe in one's lucky ~** creer en su buena estrella • **you can thank your lucky ~s that …** da gracias que …
2 (= *film star, sports star etc*) estrella *f* • **the ~ of the team was Green** la figura más destacada del equipo fue Green
3 (*Typ*) asterisco *m*
4 stars (= *horoscope*) horóscopo *m*
(VT) **1** (= *adorn with stars*) estrellar, adornar con estrellas, sembrar de estrellas; (= *mark with star*) señalar con asterisco
2 (*Cine etc*) presentar como estrella • **a film ~ring Greta Garbo** una película con Greta Garbo en el papel principal
(VI) (*Cine etc*) tener el papel principal • **the three films in which James Dean ~red** las tres películas que protagonizó James Dean
(CPD) estrella, estelar ▸ **star anise** anís *m* estrellado ▸ **star attraction** atracción *f* principal ▸ **star grass** azucena *f* ▸ **star of Bethlehem** (*Bot*) leche *f* de gallina, matacandiles *m* ▸ **Star of David** estrella *f* de David ▸ **star player** estrella *f* ▸ **star prize** gran premio *m*, primer premio *m* ▸ **star rating** [*of hotel, restaurant*] categoría *f* ▸ **star role** papel *m* estelar ▸ **star screwdriver** destornillador *m* de estrella ▸ **star shell** cohete *m* luminoso, bengala *f* ▸ **star sign** signo *m* del Zodíaco ▸ **star system** (*Astron*) sistema *m* estelar; (*Cine*) star-system *m* ▸ **star turn** = **star attraction** ▸ **"star wars"** (*Mil*) "guerra *f* de las galaxias"

-star [stɑːʳ] (ADJ) (*ending in compounds*) • **four- star hotel** hotel *m* de cuatro estrellas • **4-star (petrol)** gasolina *f* extra, súper *f*

starboard ['stɑːbɔːd] (N) estribor *m* • **the sea to ~** la mar a estribor • **land to ~!** ¡tierra a estribor!
(ADJ) [*lights*] de estribor • **on the ~ side** a estribor
(VT) • **to ~ the helm** poner el timón a estribor, virar a estribor

starburst ['stɑːˌbɜːst] (N) (*liter*) explosión *f* de color

starch [stɑːtʃ] (N) (*for clothes etc*) almidón *m*; (*in food*) fécula *f*
(VT) almidonar

star-chamber ['stɑːˌtʃeɪmbəʳ] (ADJ) (*fig*) secreto y arbitrario

starched [stɑːtʃt] (ADJ) almidonado

starch-reduced ['stɑːtʃrɪˌdjuːst] (ADJ) [*bread etc*] de régimen, con menos fécula

starchy ['stɑːtʃɪ] (ADJ) (COMPAR: **starchier**, SUPERL: **starchiest**) **1** [*food*] con fécula
2 (*fig*) [*person*] rígido, estirado

star-crossed ['stɑːˌkrɒst] (ADJ) malhadado, desventurado

stardom ['stɑːdəm] (N) estrellato *m* • **to rise to** *or* **achieve ~** alcanzar el estrellato

stardust ['stɑːdʌst] (N) (*fig*) encanto *m*, embeleso *m*

stare [stɛəʳ] (N) mirada *f* fija • **to give sb a ~** mirar fijamente a algn
(VT) • **to ~ sb out** *or* **down** mirar a algn fijamente hasta que aparte la vista • IDIOM: • **it's staring you in the face** salta a la vista
(VI) mirar fijamente • **he wouldn't stop staring** no paraba de mirar fijamente • **don't ~!** ¡no mires tan fijo! • **to ~ at sth/sb** mirar algo/a algn fijamente, mirar algo/a algn de hito en hito • **it's rude to ~ at people** está mal visto fijar la mirada en la gente • **to ~ into the distance** • **~ into space** estar con la mirada perdida *or* mirando a las nubes

starfish ['stɑːfɪʃ] (N) (PL: **starfish, starfishes**) estrella *f* de mar

stargaze ['stɑːgeɪz] (VI) mirar las estrellas; (*fig*) distraerse, mirar las telarañas

stargazer ['stɑːˌgeɪzəʳ] (N) astrónomo/a *m/f*

stargazing ['stɑːˌgeɪzɪŋ] (N) **1** (= *astronomy*) astronomía *f*
2 (= *astrology*) astrología *f*
3 (*fig*) distracción *f*

staring ['stɛərɪŋ] (ADJ) que mira fijamente, curioso; [*eyes*] saltón; (*in fear*) lleno de espanto

stark [stɑːk] (ADJ) (COMPAR: **starker**, SUPERL: **starkest**) **1** (= *austere*) [*simplicity, colour, beauty, décor, outline*] austero; [*conditions*] severo, duro; [*landscape*] inhóspito; [*description*] escueto, sucinto
2 (= *harsh*) [*reality, poverty*] crudo, sin adornos; [*choice, warning, reminder*] duro • **those are the ~ facts of the matter** esa es la cruda realidad del asunto
3 (= *absolute*) [*terror, folly*] absoluto • **to be in ~ contrast to sth** contrastar brutalmente con algo
(ADV) • **~ staring** *or* **raving mad*** loco de remate* • **~ naked*** en cueros*, en pelotas‡, encuerado (*LAm**), pilucho (*Chile**), calato (*Peru, Bol**)

starkers‡ ['stɑːkəz] (ADJ) • **to be ~** (*Brit*) estar en cueros*, estar en pelotas‡, estar encuerado (*LAm**), estar pilucho (*Chile**), estar calato (*Peru, Bol**)

starkly ['stɑːklɪ] (ADV) **1** (= *austerely*) [*furnished*] austeramente; [*describe*] escuetamente, sucintamente • **~ beautiful** de una belleza austera
2 (= *clearly*) [*illustrate*] crudamente; [*outline*] claramente; [*stand out*] con claridad; [*different, apparent, evident*] completamente • **to contrast ~ with sth** contrastar brutalmente con algo • **to be ~ exposed** quedar completamente al descubierto • **he put the choice ~** expuso la alternativa sin ambages, nos ofreció la alternativa y nada más

starkness ['stɑːknɪs] (N) **1** (= *austerity*) [*of landscape, desert*] lo inhóspito; [*of conditions*] severidad *f*; [*of simplicity, contrast, décor, outline*] austeridad *f*; [*of colour, beauty*] sobriedad *f*; [*of description*] lo escueto, lo sucinto
2 (= *harshness*) [*of reality, poverty*] crudeza *f*; [*of choice, warning, reminder*] lo duro

starless ['stɑːlɪs] (ADJ) sin estrellas

starlet ['stɑːlɪt] (N) (*Cine*) joven aspirante *f* a estrella

starlight ['stɑːlaɪt] (N) luz *f* de las estrellas • **by ~** a la luz de las estrellas

starling ['stɑːlɪŋ] (N) estornino *m*

starlit ['stɑːlɪt] (ADJ) iluminado por las estrellas

starring role [ˌstɑːrɪŋ'rəʊl] (N) papel *m* principal

starry ['steɪnd] (ADJ) (COMPAR: **starrier**, SUPERL: **starriest**) sembrado de estrellas

starry-eyed ['stɑːrɪ'aɪd] (ADJ) (= *idealistic*) idealista, ingenuo; (= *in love*) sentimentaloide

star-spangled ['stɑːˌspæŋgld] (ADJ) estrellado • **the Star-spangled Banner** (*US*) la Bandera Estrellada

starstruck ['stɑːstrʌk] (ADJ) chiflado por los

ídolos • **a ~ teenager** un adolescente chiflado por los ídolos

star-studded ['stɑːˌstʌdɪd] (ADJ) [*sky*] estrellado • **a star-studded cast** (*Cine, Theat*) un elenco *m* estelar

START [stɑːt] (N ABBR) = **Strategic Arms Reduction Talks**

start [stɑːt] (N) **1** (= *beginning*) principio *m*, comienzo *m* • **at the ~** al principio, en un principio • **at the very ~** muy al principio, en los mismos comienzos • **at the ~ of the century** a principios del siglo • **we are at the ~ of something big** estamos en los comienzos de algo grandioso • **for a ~** en primer lugar, para empezar • **from the ~** desde el principio • **from ~ to finish** desde el principio hasta el fin • **to get a good ~ in life** disfrutar de una infancia privilegiada • **to get off to a good/bad/slow ~** empezar bien/mal/lentamente • **to give sb a (good) ~ in life** ayudar a algn a situarse en la vida • **to make a ~** empezar • **to make a ~ on the painting** empezar a pintar • **to make an early ~** (*on journey*) ponerse en camino temprano; (*with job*) empezar temprano • **to make a fresh** *or* **new ~ in life** hacer vida nueva
2 (= *departure*) salida *f* (*also Sport*); (= *starting line*) línea *f* de salida
3 (= *advantage*) ventaja *f* • **to give sb five minutes'** *or* **a five-minute ~** dar a algn cinco minutos de ventaja • **to have a ~ on sb** tener ventaja sobre algn
4 (= *fright etc*) susto *m*, sobresalto *m* • **to give sb a ~** asustar *or* dar un susto a algn • **to give a sudden ~** sobresaltarse • **what a ~ you gave me!** ¡qué susto me diste! • **to wake with a ~** despertarse sobresaltado
(VT) **1** (= *begin*) empezar, comenzar; [+ *discussion etc*] abrir, iniciar; [+ *bottle*] abrir; [+ *quarrel, argument*] empezar; [+ *journey*] iniciar • **to ~ a new cheque book/page** comenzar *or* empezar un talonario nuevo/una página nueva • **don't ~ that again!** ¡no vuelvas a eso! • **to ~ doing sth** *or* **to do sth** empezar a hacer algo • **~ moving!** ¡menearse! • **~ talking!** ¡desembucha! • **to ~ sth again** *or* **afresh** comenzar *or* empezar algo de nuevo • **to ~ the day right** empezar bien el día • **he always ~s the day with a glass of milk** lo primero que toma cada mañana es un vaso de leche • **he ~ed life as a labourer** empezó de *or* como peón • **to ~ a new life** comenzar una vida nueva • **to ~ negotiations** iniciar *or* entablar las pláticas • **to ~ a novel** empezar a escribir (*or* leer) una novela • **to ~ school** empezar a ir al colegio • **he ~ed work yesterday** entró a trabajar ayer
2 (= *cause to begin or happen*) [+ *fire*] provocar; [+ *war*] [*person, country*] empezar, iniciar; [*incident, act*] desencadenar; [+ *fashion*] empezar, iniciar; [+ *rumour, tradition*] iniciar, dar comienzo a • **it ~ed the collapse of the empire** provocó el derrumbamiento del imperio • **you ~ed it!** ¡tú diste el primer golpe! • **to ~ a family** (empezar a) tener hijos • **to ~ a race** (= *give signal for*) dar la señal de salida para una carrera
3 • **to get ~ed** empezar, ponerse en marcha • **let's get ~ed** empecemos • **to get sth ~ed** [+ *engine, car*] poner algo en marcha, arrancar algo; [+ *project*] poner algo en marcha • **to get sb ~ed** (*on activity*) poner a algn en marcha; (*in career*) iniciar a algn en su carrera • **to get ~ed on (doing) sth** empezar a hacer algo • **to get sb ~ed on (doing) sth** poner a algn a hacer algo
4 (= *found*) (*also* **start up**) [+ *business*] montar, poner; [+ *newspaper*] fundar, establecer
5 (*also* **start up**) [+ *car, engine*] arrancar, poner en marcha; [+ *clock*] poner en marcha
6 (*with personal object*) • **don't ~ him (off) on that!** ¡no le des cuerda! • **to ~ sb (off) reminiscing** hacer que algn empiece a contar sus recuerdos • **that ~ed him (off) sneezing** eso le hizo empezar a estornudar • **to ~ sb (off) on a career** ayudar a algn a emprender una carrera • **they ~ed her (off) in the sales department** la emplearon primero en la sección de ventas
7 (= *disturb*) • **to ~ (up) a partridge** levantar una perdiz
(VI) **1** (= *begin*) empezar, comenzar; [*conversation, discussion*] iniciarse; [*quarrel, argument*] producirse; [*fashion*] empezar, iniciar; [*war*] estallar, empezar; [*rumour, tradition*] originarse; [*fire*] empezar, iniciarse; [*music*] empezar • **classes ~ on Monday** las clases comienzan *or* empiezan el lunes • **that's when the trouble ~ed** entonces fue cuando empezaron los problemas • **it all ~ed when he refused to pay** todo empezó cuando se negó a pagar • **it ~ed (off) rather well/badly** [*film, match*] empezó bastante bien/mal • **to ~ again** *or* **afresh** volver a empezar, comenzar de nuevo • **he ~ed (off** *or* **out) as a postman** empezó como *or* de cartero • **he ~ed (off** *or* **out) as a Marxist** empezó como marxista • **to ~ at the beginning** empezar desde el principio • **he ~ed (off) by saying …** empezó por decir *or* diciendo … • **the route ~s from here** la ruta sale de aquí • **~ing from Tuesday** a partir del martes • **to ~ (out** *or* **up) in business** montar *or* poner un negocio • **to ~ (off) with …** (= *firstly*) en primer lugar …, para empezar …; (= *at the beginning*) al principio …, en un principio … • **what shall we ~ (off) with?** ¿con qué empezamos? • **to ~ (off) with a prayer** empezar con una oración • **he ~ed (off** *or* **out) with the intention of writing a thesis** empezó con la intención de escribir una tesis
2 (= *embark*) • **to ~ on a task** emprender una tarea • **to ~ on something new** emprender algo nuevo • **to ~ on a book** (= *begin reading*) empezar a leer un libro; (= *begin writing*) empezar a escribir un libro • **to ~ on a course of study** empezar un curso • **they ~ed on another bottle** abrieron *or* empezaron otra botella
3 (*also* **start off, start out**) (*on journey*) [*person*] partir, ponerse en camino; [*bus, train, runner*] salir • **to ~ (off** *or* **out) from London/for Madrid** salir de Londres/partir con rumbo a *or* para Madrid • **he ~ed (off) down the street** empezó a caminar calle abajo
4 (*also* **start up**) [*car, engine*] arrancar, ponerse en marcha; [*washing machine*] ponerse en marcha
5 (= *jump nervously*) asustarse, sobresaltarse (**at** a) • **to ~ from one's chair** levantarse asustado de su silla • **tears ~ed to her eyes** se le llenaron los ojos de lágrimas • IDIOM: • **his eyes were ~ing out of his head** se le saltaban los ojos de la cara
6 [*timber etc*] combarse, torcerse; [*rivets etc*] soltarse

▸ **start after** (VI + PREP) • **to ~ after sb** salir en busca de algn

▸ **start back** (VI + ADV) **1** (= *return*) emprender el viaje de regreso (**for** a) • **it's time we ~ed back** es hora de volvernos
2 (= *recoil*) retroceder • **to ~ back in horror** retroceder horrorizado

▸ **start in** (VI + ADV) empezar, poner manos a la obra, empezar a trabajar (*etc*) • **then she ~ed in** luego ella metió su cuchara*

▸ **start off** (VI + ADV) ▹ **start**
(VT + ADV) ▹ **start**

▸ **start on*** (VI + PREP) (= *scold*) regañar; ▹ **start**

▸ **start out** (VI + ADV) ▹ **start**

▸ **start over** (*esp US*) (VI + ADV) volver a empezar
(VT + ADV) comenzar *or* empezar de nuevo

▸ **start up** (VI + ADV) ▹ **start**
(VT + ADV) ▹ **start**

starter ['stɑːtəʳ] (N) **1** (*Sport*) (= *judge*) juez *mf* de salida; (= *competitor*) corredor(a) *m/f* • **to be under ~'s orders** (*Horse racing*) estar listos para la salida
2 (= *button*) botón *m* de arranque; (*Aut*) (= *motor*) motor *m* de arranque
3 (*Brit*) (*Culin*) (= *first course*) entrada *f* • **for ~s*** (*fig*) en primer lugar
(CPD) ▸ **starter flat** (*Brit*) primera vivienda *f* ▸ **starter home** primera vivienda *f* ▸ **starter motor** (*Aut*) motor *m* de arranque ▸ **starter pack** pack *m* inicial

starting ['stɑːtɪŋ] (CPD) ▸ **starting block** (*Athletics*) taco *m* de salida ▸ **starting gate** (*US*) (*Horse racing*) cajón *m* de salida, parrilla *f* de salida ▸ **starting grid** (*Motor racing*) parrilla *f* de arranque ▸ **starting handle** (*Brit*) (*Aut*) manivela *f* de arranque ▸ **starting line** (*Athletics*) línea *f* de salida ▸ **starting pistol** (= *object*) pistola *f* para dar la salida; (= *sound signalling start*) pistoletazo *m* de salida ▸ **starting point** (*fig*) punto *m* de partida ▸ **starting post** (*Sport*) poste *m* de salida ▸ **starting price** (*St Ex*) cotización *f* ▸ **starting salary** sueldo *m* inicial ▸ **starting stalls** (*Brit*) (*Horse racing*) cajones *mpl* de salida

startle ['stɑːtl] (VT) asustar, sobresaltar • **you quite ~d me!** ¡vaya susto que me has dado! • **it ~d him out of his serenity** le hizo perder su serenidad

startled ['stɑːtld] (ADJ) [*animal*] asustado, espantado; [*person*] sorprendido; [*expression, voice*] de sobresalto, sobresaltado

startling ['stɑːtlɪŋ] (ADJ) [*news*] alarmante; [*discovery*] inesperado; [*appearance*] llamativo

startlingly ['stɑːtlɪŋlɪ] (ADV) • **he was ~ handsome** era de una belleza alucinante

start-up ['stɑːtʌp] (ADJ) [*costs, loan*] de puesta en marcha
(CPD) ▸ **start-up capital** capital *m* inicial ▸ **start-up company, start-up firm** start-up *f*, nueva empresa *f*

starvation [stɑː'veɪʃən] (N) hambre *f*, inanición *f*, hambruna *f* (*LAm*); (*fig*) privación *f* • **to die of ~** morir de hambre • **they are threatened with ~** les amenaza el hambre • **fuel ~** (*Tech*) agotamiento *m* del combustible
(CPD) ▸ **starvation diet** régimen *m* de hambre ▸ **starvation wages** sueldo *m* de hambre

starve [stɑːv] (VT) **1** (= *deprive of food*) privar de comida • **to ~ sb to death** hacer que algn muera de hambre • **to ~ a town into surrender** impedir la entrada de alimentos a una ciudad hasta que se rinda
2 (= *deprive*) • **to ~ sb of sth** privar a algn de algo • **to be ~d of affection** estar privado de afecto
(VI) (= *lack food*) pasar hambre, padecer hambre; (= *die*) morir(se) de hambre • **to ~ to death** morirse de hambre • **I'm starving!*** estoy muerto de hambre

▸ **starve out** (VT + ADV) • **to ~ a garrison out** hacer que una guarnición se rinda por hambre

starving ['stɑːvɪŋ] (ADJ) hambriento

stash* [stæʃ] (N) escondite *m*, alijo *m*
(VT) (*also* **stash away**) (= *hide*) esconder;

(= *save up, store away*) guardar

stasis ['steɪsɪs] N estasis *f*

state [steɪt] N **1** (= *condition*) estado *m* • **the current ~ of the housing market** el estado actual del mercado inmobiliario • **if this ~ of affairs continues** si las cosas siguen así • **it is a sorry ~ of affairs when ...** es una situación lamentable cuando ... • **~ of alert** estado *m* de alerta • **~ of grace** estado *m* de gracia • **~ of health** (estado *m* de) salud *f* • **to be in a bad** *or* **poor ~** estar en mal estado • **to be in a good ~** estar en buenas condiciones • **it wasn't in a fit ~ to be used** no estaba en condiciones de ser usado • **he's not in a fit ~ to do it** no está en condiciones para hacerlo • **he arrived home in a shocking ~** llegó a casa hecho una pena • **she was in no ~ to talk** no estaba en condiciones para hablar • **~ of mind** estado *m* de ánimo • **he was in an odd ~ of mind** estaba raro • **the ~ of the nation** el estado de la nación • **~ of play** (*Sport*) situación *f* del juego • **what's the ~ of play?** (*fig*) ¿cuál es la situación? • **~ of repair** estado *m* • **~ of siege** estado *m* de sitio • **~ of war** estado *m* de guerra • **~ of weightlessness** estado *m* de ingravidez

2* (= *poor condition*) • **you should have seen the ~ the car was in** tenías que haber visto cómo estaba el coche • **just look at the ~ of this room!** ¡mira cómo está esta habitación! • **the flat was in a right ~ after the party** el piso estaba hecho un asco después de la fiesta*

3* (= *agitated condition*) • **to be in a ~** estar nervioso • **his wife is in a terrible ~** su mujer está nerviosísima • **to get into a ~** ponerse nervioso • **now don't get into a ~ about it** no te pongas nervioso

4 (= *region, country*) estado *m* • **the State of Washington** el estado de Washington • **the State of Israel** el estado de Israel • **the States*** (= *USA*) los Estados Unidos • **a ~ within a ~** un estado dentro de un estado

5 (= *government*) • **the State** el Estado • **affairs of ~** asuntos *mpl* de estado • **Secretary of State** (*US*) Secretario/a *m/f* de Asuntos Exteriores • **Secretary of State for Education** (*Brit*) Secretario/a *m/f* de Educación

6 (= *rank*) rango *m*; (= *office*) cargo *m* • **the ~ of bishop** la dignidad de obispo

7 (= *pomp*) • **to dine in ~** cenar con mucha ceremonia • **to lie in ~** estar de cuerpo presente • **to live in ~** vivir lujosamente • **robes of ~** ropas *fpl* de investidura

VT **1** (*frm*) (= *say, show*) • **~ your address and telephone number** (*on form*) escriba su dirección y número de teléfono; (*orally*) diga su dirección y número de teléfono • **as ~d above** como se indica más arriba • **to ~ that ...** [*rules, law*] estipular que ... • **it is nowhere ~d that ...** no se dice en ninguna parte que ... • **the article ~d that she had been interviewed by the police** el artículo afirmaba que la policía la había interrogado • **it must be ~d in the records that ...** tiene que hacerse constar en los archivos que ...

2 (= *declare, affirm*) declarar • **he has ~d his intention to run for President** ha declarado su intención de presentarse como candidato a la presidencia • **he has publicly ~d that ...** ha declarado públicamente que ...

3 (= *expound on, set out*) [+ *views*] dar, expresar; [+ *facts, case, problem*] exponer • **he was asked to ~ his views on the subject** se le pidió que diera *or* expresara su opinión sobre el asunto • **I'm simply stating the facts** simplemente estoy exponiendo los hechos • **to ~ the case for the prosecution** exponer los argumentos de la acusación

CPD (*Pol*) [*policy, documents, security*] del estado; [*capitalism, socialism, visit, funeral, business*] de estado ▸ **state aid** ayuda *f* estatal ▸ **state apartments** *apartamentos destinados a visitas de mandatarios* ▸ **state bank** (*US*) banco *m* estatal *or* del estado ▸ **state banquet** banquete *m* de gala ▸ **state benefit** subsidios *mpl* del estado, subsidios *mpl* estatales • **those receiving** *or* **on ~ benefit** aquellos que cobran subsidios del estado *or* estatales ▸ **State Capitol** (*US*) *edificio donde tiene su sede el poder legislativo de un estado* ▸ **state control** control *m* público *or* estatal • **to be/come under ~ control** pasar a manos del Estado ▸ **State Department** (*US*) Ministerio *m* de Asuntos Exteriores ▸ **state education** enseñanza *f* pública ▸ **State Enrolled Nurse** (*Brit*) (*formerly*) enfermero/a *m/f* diplomado/a (*con dos años de estudios*) ▸ **state fair** (*US*) feria *f* estatal ▸ **state funding** financiación *f* pública ▸ **state highway** (*US*) carretera *f* nacional ▸ **state legislature** (*US*) poder *m* legislativo del estado ▸ **state line** (*US*) frontera *f* de estado ▸ **state militia** (*US*) [*of specific state*] milicia *f* del estado ▸ **state occasion** acontecimiento *m* solemne ▸ **state of emergency** estado *m* de emergencia ▸ **State of the Union Address** (*US*) discurso *m* sobre el estado de la nación; ▹ STATE OF THE UNION ADDRESS ▸ **state ownership** • **they believe in state ownership of the means of production** creen que los medios de producción deberían estar en manos del Estado, son partidarios de que los medios de producción estén en manos del Estado ▸ **state pension** pensión *f* del Estado, pensión *f* estatal ▸ **state police** [*of country*] policía *f* nacional; (*US*) [*of specific state*] policía *f* del estado ▸ **state prison** (*US*) cárcel *f* estatal, prisión *f* estatal ▸ **State Registered Nurse** (*Brit*) (*formerly*) enfermero/a *m/f* diplomado/a (*con tres años de estudios*) ▸ **State Representative** (*US*) (*Pol*) representante *mf* del estado ▸ **State's attorney** (*US*) procurador(a) *m/f* del Estado ▸ **state school** (*Brit*) colegio *m* público, escuela *f* pública ▸ **state secret** (*lit, fig*) secreto *m* de estado ▸ **state sector** sector *m* estatal ▸ **State Senator** (*US*) senador(a) *m/f* del estado ▸ **States' rights** (*US*) derechos *mpl* de los estados ▸ **state subsidy** subvención *f* estatal ▸ **state tax** (*US*) [*of specific state*] impuesto *m* del estado ▸ **state trooper** (*US*) [*of specific state*] policía *mf* del estado ▸ **state university** (*US*) universidad *f* pública

STATE OF THE UNION ADDRESS

Se denomina **State of the Union Address** al discurso que el presidente de Estados Unidos dirige cada mes de enero al Congreso y al pueblo estadounidense, en que muestra su visión de la nación y la economía y explica sus planes para el futuro. Como el discurso recibe una amplia cobertura informativa, el mensaje del presidente va dirigido no solo a los parlamentarios sino a todo el país. Esta tradición de dirigirse al Congreso tras las vacaciones de Navidad se debe a que es un requisito de la Constitución que el presidente informe al Congreso de vez en cuando sobre **the State of the Union**.

STATES' RIGHTS

En EE.UU., **States' rights** son los derechos de los estados (como por ejemplo la recaudación de impuestos, la aprobación de leyes o el control sobre la educación pública) frente a los del gobierno federal. En la Décima Enmienda de la Constitución se dice que los poderes que la Constitución no concede a los Estados Unidos "se reservan a cada estado particular o al pueblo" y este polémico principio sirvió para justificar la secesión de los estados sureños antes de la Guerra Civil y se convirtió en una consigna contra la integración racial en el sur durante los años 50. Debido a la actual falta de confianza en el gobierno federal, que acapara cada vez más poderes a costa de un aumento del gasto, este principio tiene cada vez más seguidores.

state-controlled ['steɪtkən'trəʊld] ADJ controlado por el Estado, estatal

statecraft ['steɪtkrɑːft] N arte *m* de gobernar

stated ['steɪtɪd] ADJ **1** (= *indicated*) indicado, señalado • **on the ~ date** en la fecha indicada *or* señalada • **do not exceed the ~ dose** no exceda la dosis indicada *or* señalada • **the sum ~** la cantidad establecida

2 (= *declared*) [*aim, purpose*] expresado • **the organization's ~ aim is to improve communications** la intención expresada por la organización es la de mejorar las comunicaciones

3 (= *fixed*) [*limit*] establecido • **within ~ limits** dentro de límites establecidos • **at the ~ time** a la hora señalada • **within the ~ time** dentro del plazo fijado *or* señalado

state-funded [ˌsteɪt'fʌndɪd] ADJ [*schools, education*] estatal; [*services, projects*] realizado con fondos públicos

statehood ['steɪthʊd] N (= *independence*) independencia *f*; (*as federal state*) categoría *f* de estado

statehouse ['steɪthaʊs] N (*New Zealand*) vivienda *f* de alquiler (*que pertenece al estado*)

stateless ['steɪtlɪs] ADJ desnacionalizado, apátrida

statelet ['steɪtlət] N (*Pol*) pequeño estado *m*

stateliness ['steɪtlɪnɪs] N majestad *f*, majestuosidad *f*

stately ['steɪtlɪ] ADJ (COMPAR: **statelier**, SUPERL: **stateliest**) [*person, manner*] imponente; [*pace, music*] majestuoso

CPD ▸ **stately home** casa *f* solariega

state-maintained [ˌsteɪtmeɪn'teɪnd] ADJ (*Brit*) [*school*] público

statement ['steɪtmənt] N **1** (= *declaration*) (*also Jur*) declaración *f* • **a written ~ of terms and conditions** una declaración escrita de los términos y las condiciones • **to make a ~** (*Jur*) prestar declaración • **he made a ~ to the press** hizo una declaración a la prensa • **in an official ~, the government said ...** en un comunicado oficial, el gobierno dijo ... • **to issue a press ~** emitir un comunicado de prensa • **a signed and sworn ~** una declaración firmada bajo juramento; ▹ **policy**

2 (= *exposition*) [*of views, facts, problem, theory*] exposición *f* • **a ~ of fact** una exposición de los hechos • **he gave a detailed ~ of his party's position** hizo una exposición detallada de la postura de su partido

3 (*fig*) (= *critique*) alegato *m*, proclama *f* • **the film is a powerful anti-war ~** la película es un poderoso alegato contra la guerra • **the paintings are intended to make a ~ about contemporary society** lo que se pretende con los cuadros es expresar una opinión acerca de la sociedad contemporánea

4 (*Econ*) (*also* **statement of account**) estado *m* de cuenta; (*also* **bank statement**) extracto *m* de cuenta; ▹ **financial**

5 (*Ling*) afirmación *f*

6 (*Comput*) instrucción *f*, sentencia *f*

state-of-the-art [ˌsteɪtəvðɪˈɑːt] (ADJ) [*equipment*] de lo más moderno *or* reciente; [*technology*] de vanguardia
state-owned [ˌsteɪtˈəʊnd] (ADJ) nacional, estatal
stateroom [ˈsteɪtrʊm] (N) (*Naut*) camarote *m*; (*esp Brit*) (*in palace etc*) salón *m* de gala
state-run [ˌsteɪtˈrʌn] (ADJ) del Estado
stateside* [ˈsteɪtsaɪd] (ADV) (*esp US*) [*be*] en Estados Unidos; [*go*] a Estados Unidos, hacia Estados Unidos
statesman [ˈsteɪtsmən] (N) (PL: **statesmen**) estadista *m*, hombre *m* de estado
statesmanlike [ˈsteɪtsmənlaɪk] (ADJ) (digno) de estadista
statesmanship [ˈsteɪtsmənʃɪp] (N) habilidad *f* política, capacidad *f* para gobernar • **that showed true ~** eso demostró su verdadera capacidad de estadista • **~ alone will not solve the problem** la habilidad de los estadistas no resolverá el problema por sí sola
state-subsidized [ˌsteɪtˈsʌbsɪdaɪzd] (ADJ) subvencionado por el Estado
stateswoman [ˈsteɪtsˌwʊmən] (N) (PL: **stateswomen**) mujer *f* de estado
state-trading countries [ˈsteɪtˌtreɪdɪŋˈkʌntrɪz] (NPL) países *mpl* de comercio estatal
statewide, state-wide [ˌsteɪtˈwaɪd] (ADJ) [*elections, event*] de todo el estado
(ADV) en todo el estado
static [ˈstætɪk] (ADJ) (*gen*) estático, inmóvil; (*Phys*) estático
(N) **1** (*Rad etc*) (= *noise*) parásitos *mpl*
2 (*Phys*) (*also* **statics**) estática *f*
(CPD) ▸ **static electricity** estática *f*
station [ˈsteɪʃən] (N) **1** (*Rail*) estación *f* (de ferrocarril); (= *police station*) comisaría *f*; (*US*) (= *gas station*) gasolinera *f*, fuente *f*, grifo *m* (*Peru*); ▹ **bus, fire**
2 (*esp Mil*) (= *post*) puesto *m* • **to take up one's ~** colocarse, ir a su puesto • **from my ~ by the window** desde el sitio donde estaba junto a la ventana • **Roman ~** sitio *m* ocupado por los romanos • **Stations of the Cross** (*Rel*) Vía *f* Crucis
3 (*Rad*) emisora *f*
4 (= *social position*) rango *m* • **to have ideas above one's ~** darse aires de superioridad • **to marry below one's ~** casarse con un hombre/una mujer de posición social inferior • **of humble ~** de baja posición social, de condición humilde • **a man of exalted ~** un hombre de rango elevado
(VT) **1** (*Mil*) estacionar, apostar; [+ *missile etc*] emplazar
2 (*fig*) colocar, situar • **to ~ o.s.** colocarse, situarse
(CPD) ▸ **station break** (*US*) *pausa para publicidad de la propia cadena* ▸ **station house** (*US*) (*Rail*) estación *f* de ferrocarril; (*US*) (*Police*) comisaría *f* ▸ **station master** (*Rail*) jefe *m* de estación ▸ **station wag(g)on** (*esp US*) (*Aut*) furgoneta *f*, camioneta *f*
stationary [ˈsteɪʃənərɪ] (ADJ) inmóvil; (= *not movable*) parado, estacionario • **to remain ~** quedarse inmóvil
stationer [ˈsteɪʃənəʳ] (N) papelero/a *m/f* • **~'s (shop)** papelería *f*
stationery [ˈsteɪʃənərɪ] (N) artículos *mpl* de papelería *or* de escritorio
(CPD) ▸ **stationery cupboard** armario *m* de artículos de papelería ▸ **Stationery Office** (*Brit*) Imprenta *f* Nacional
statist [ˈsteɪtɪst] (ADJ) (*Pol*) controlado por el estado
statistic [stəˈtɪstɪk] (N) estadística *f*, número *m*; ▹ **statistics**

statistical [stəˈtɪstɪkəl] (ADJ) estadístico • **~ package** paquete *m* estadístico
statistically [stəˈtɪstɪkəlɪ] (ADV) según las estadísticas • **to prove sth ~** probar algo por medios estadísticos • **~, that may be true** según las estadísticas *or* estadísticamente, puede ser cierto
statistician [ˌstætɪsˈtɪʃən] (N) estadístico/a *m/f*
statistics [stəˈtɪstɪks] (NSING) (= *subject*) estadística *f*
(NPL) (= *numbers*) estadísticas *fpl*; ▹ **vital**
stative [ˈsteɪtɪv] (ADJ) (*Gram*) • **~ verb** verbo *m* de estado
stator [ˈsteɪtəʳ] (N) estator *m*
stats* [stæts] (NPL ABBR) = **statistics**
statuary [ˈstætjʊərɪ] (ADJ) estatuario
(N) (= *art*) estatuaria *f*; (= *statues*) estatuas *fpl*
statue [ˈstætjuː] (N) estatua *f* • **the Statue of Liberty** la estatua de la libertad
statuesque [ˌstætjʊˈesk] (ADJ) escultural
statuette [ˌstætjʊˈet] (N) figurilla *f*, estatuilla *f*
stature [ˈstætʃəʳ] (N) **1** (= *size*) estatura *f*, talla *f* • **to be of short ~** ser de baja estatura
2 (*fig*) rango *m*, estatus *m inv* • **to have sufficient ~ for a post** estar a la altura de un cargo • **he lacks moral ~** le falta carácter
status [ˈsteɪtəs] (N) (PL: **statuses**) **1** [*of person*] (*legal*) estado *m*; [*of agreement*] situación *f* • **marital ~** estado *m* civil • **social ~** posición *f* social, estatus *m inv* • **the ~ of the Black population** la posición social de la población negra
2 (= *rank, prestige*) • **what is his ~ in the profession?** ¿qué rango ocupa en la profesión?, ¿cómo se le considera en la profesión?
(CPD) ▸ **status inquiry** comprobación *f* de valoración crediticia ▸ **status line** (*Comput*) línea *f* de situación ▸ **status quo** (e)statu quo *m* ▸ **status report** informe *m* situacional ▸ **status symbol** símbolo *m* de rango
statute [ˈstætjuːt] (N) ley *f*, estatuto *m* • **by ~** según la ley, de acuerdo con la ley
(CPD) ▸ **statute book** (*esp Brit*) código *m* de leyes • **in** *or* **on the ~ book** en el código de leyes ▸ **statute law** derecho *m* escrito ▸ **statute of limitations** (*US*) estatuto *m* de prescripción legal
statutorily [ˈstætjʊtərɪlɪ] (ADV) (= *legally*) • **broadcasting needs to be regulated ~** las transmisiones tienen que regularse según los estatutos • **refugee families are ~ homeless** las familias de refugiados no tienen hogar por ley
statutory [ˈstætjʊtərɪ] (ADJ) **1** reglamentario, estatutario; [*holiday, right etc*] legal • **~ meeting** junta *f* ordinaria
2 (*pej*) (= *token*) • **I was the ~ woman on the committee** yo tan solo estaba en el comité porque la ley exigía que hubiese una mujer
3 (= *expected, predictable*) consabido
(CPD) ▸ **statutory rape** (*US*) (*Jur*) *relaciones sexuales con un(a) menor*
staunch¹ [stɔːntʃ] (ADJ) (COMPAR: **stauncher**, SUPERL: **staunchest**) leal, firme
staunch² [stɔːntʃ] (VT) [+ *bleeding*] restañar
staunchly [ˈstɔːntʃlɪ] (ADV) lealmente, firmemente
staunchness [ˈstɔːntʃnɪs] (N) lealtad *f*, firmeza *f*
stave [steɪv] (N) **1** [*of barrel*] duela *f*; [*of ladder*] peldaño *m*
2 (*Mus*) pentagrama *m*
3 (*Literat*) estrofa *f*
▸ **stave in** (VT + ADV) (PT, PP: **stove in**) desfondar
▸ **stave off** (VT + ADV) (PT, PP: **staved off**) [+ *attack, crisis, illness*] evitar; [+ *threat etc*] evitar, conjurar; (*temporarily*) aplazar, posponer
staves [steɪvz] (NPL) *of* **staff¹**
stay¹ [steɪ] (VI) **1** (*in place*) **a** (= *remain*) quedarse, permanecer (*more frm*) • **she came for a weekend and ~ed three years** vino a pasar el fin de semana y se quedó tres años • **you ~ right there** no te muevas de ahí, quédate ahí • **to ~ at home** quedarse en casa • **video recorders are here to ~** los vídeos no son una simple moda pasajera • **to ~ in bed** guardar cama • **to ~ put** (*on spot*) no moverse; (*in same house, city, job*) quedarse • **did you ~ till the end of the speeches?** ¿te quedaste hasta el final de los discursos? • **can you ~ to dinner?** ¿puedes quedarte a cenar?
b (*as guest*) (*with friends, relatives*) quedarse, alojarse; (*in hotel*) alojarse, hospedarse • **to ~ with friends** quedarse *or* hospedarse *or* alojarse en casa de unos amigos • **I'm ~ing with my aunt for a few days** estoy pasando unos días en casa de mi tía • **he's ~ing at my house** está *or* se aloja en mi casa • **where are you ~ing?** ¿dónde te alojas *or* hospedas? • **I'm ~ing at the Europa Hotel** estoy *or* me alojo *or* me hospedo en el Hotel Europa • **where do you ~ when you go to London?** ¿dónde te sueles alojar *or* hospedar cuando vas a Londres? • **did he ~ the night?** ¿se quedó a pasar la noche?, ¿se quedó a dormir?
c (*Scot*) (= *live*) vivir • **where do you ~?** ¿dónde vives?
2 (*in current state*) seguir, quedarse • **it ~s motionless for hours** se queda *or* se mantiene inmóvil durante horas • **I just hope the public ~ loyal to us** solo espero que el público siga (siendo) fiel *or* se mantenga fiel a nosotros • **if only we could ~ this young for ever** ojalá pudiéramos quedarnos así de jóvenes para siempre • **she didn't ~ a teacher for long** no siguió mucho tiempo de profesora • **she didn't ~ a spinster for long** no se quedó soltera mucho tiempo • **to ~ ahead of the competition** mantenerse a la cabeza de la competencia • **to ~ awake** quedarse despierto • **the unemployment rate ~ed below four per cent** el índice de paro continuó *or* siguió por debajo de un cuatro por ciento • **I tried to ~ calm** intenté mantener la calma • **he ~ed faithful to his wife** se mantuvo fiel a su mujer • **if it ~s fine** si continúa el buen tiempo, si el tiempo sigue siendo bueno • **I hope we can ~ friends** espero que podamos seguir siendo amigos • **to ~ healthy** mantenerse en buen estado de salud • **things can't be allowed to ~ like this** no podemos permitir que las cosas sigan así • **pubs should be allowed to ~ open until one a.m.** debería permitirse que los bares estuvieran abiertos hasta la una de la mañana • **while prices rise, our pensions ~ the same** aunque los precios suben, nuestras pensiones siguen igual • **to ~ together** seguir juntos • **they are unbeaten and look likely to ~ that way** nadie los ha vencido y parece que nadie va a hacerlo • **~ with it!*** ¡sigue adelante!, ¡no te desanimes!
(VT) **1** (*Jur*) (= *delay*) [+ *execution, proceedings*] suspender
2 (= *last out*) [+ *distance*] aguantar, resistir; [+ *race*] terminar • **to ~ the course** terminar la carrera; (*fig*) aguantar hasta el final • **to ~ the pace** (*lit, fig*) aguantar el ritmo
3 (= *check*) [+ *epidemic*] tener a raya; [+ *hunger*] matar, engañar • IDIOM: • **to ~ one's hand** contenerse
(N) **1** (= *short period*) estancia *f*, estadía *f* (*LAm*) • **this will involve a short ~ in hospital** esto supondrá una corta estancia en el hospital

• **during our ~ in London** durante nuestra estancia en Londres • **he is in Rome for a short ~** está en Roma para una estancia corta • **our second ~ in Murcia** nuestra segunda visita a Murcia • **come for a longer ~ next year** el año que viene vente más tiempo
2 (*Jur*) suspensión *f*, prórroga *f* • **~ of execution** aplazamiento *m* de la sentencia
▸ **stay away** (VI + ADV) **1** (= *keep at a distance*) (*from person, building*) no acercarse (**from** a) • **~ away from my daughter!** ¡no te acerques a mi hija! • **~ away from that machine** no te acerques a esa máquina • **~ away from here** no vuelvas por aquí • **tourists were warned to ~ away from the beaches** se aconsejó a los turistas que no fueran a las playas • **~ away from chocolate** el chocolate ni lo pruebes
2 (= *not attend, be absent*) (*from event*) no acudir (**from** a) • **they decided to ~ away from the Olympics** decidieron no acudir a las Olimpiadas • **not all employees ~ed away from work during the strike** durante la huelga, no todos los empleados se abstuvieron de ir a trabajar
▸ **stay behind** (VI + ADV) (*after work, school*) quedarse • **they made him ~ behind after school** le hicieron quedarse en la escuela después de las clases • **he usually ~s behind until the last lap** (*Sport*) generalmente se queda atrás hasta la última vuelta
▸ **stay down** (VI + ADV) **1** (= *not increase*) mantenerse al mismo nivel, no subir • **we have to ensure inflation ~s down** tenemos que asegurarnos de que la inflación se mantiene al mismo nivel *or* no sube
2 (= *not get up*) no levantarse; (= *remain lying*) permanecer tendido • **~ down!** ¡no te levantes! • **when he ~ed down and didn't move we realized there was a problem** cuando vimos que permanecía tendido sin moverse nos dimos cuenta que le pasaba algo
3 (= *remain under water*) permanecer bajo el agua
4 (*Scol*) (*in lower class*) repetir el curso
5 (*Sport*) (*in lower division*) • **the team will have to ~ down again next year** el año que viene el equipo tendrá que seguir en la división a la que había descendido
6 [*food*] • **nothing he eats will ~ down** no retiene nada de lo que come, vomita todo lo que come • **rice was the only thing that would ~ down** el arroz era lo único que no vomitaba *or* que retenía
▸ **stay in** (VI + ADV) **1** (*at home*) quedarse en casa, no salir
2 (*after school*) quedarse (después de las clases) • **I was made to ~ in (after school)** me hicieron quedarme después de las clases
3 (*in place*) • **the filling only ~ed in for a week** el empaste duró solo una semana • **the nail doesn't seem to want to ~ in** parece que el clavo no quiere quedarse en su sitio • **this paragraph must ~ in** hay que dejar este párrafo
▸ **stay off** (VT + ADV) • **to ~ off school/work** no ir al colegio/trabajo • **to ~ off drink/drugs** (= *stop taking*) dejar de beber/drogarse; (= *avoid taking*) no beber/drogar • **I have ~ed off the booze for more than a year now** llevo más de un año sin probar la bebida
▸ **stay on** (VI + ADV) **1** [*person*] (*in job, at school*) seguir, quedarse; (*after party*) quedarse • **he ~ed on as manager** siguió *or* se quedó en la empresa de gerente • **fewer teenagers are ~ing on at school** cada vez menos adolescentes siguen *or* se quedan en la escuela
2 [*lid, top*] quedarse en su sitio • **her wig wouldn't ~ on** no había forma de que la peluca se quedara en su sitio
▸ **stay out** (VI + ADV) **1** (= *not come home*) • **she ~ed out all night** pasó *or* estuvo toda la noche fuera, no volvió a casa en toda la noche • **get out and ~ out!** ¡vete y no vuelvas!
2 (= *remain outside*) quedarse fuera • **let's ~ out in the sun** quedémosnos fuera al sol
3 (*on strike*) seguir en huelga
4 • **to ~ out of** [+ *trouble, discussion*] no meterse en • **she warned her son to ~ out of trouble** advirtió a su hijo que no se metiera en líos* • **~ out of this!** ¡no te metas! • **try to ~ out of sight while he's around** procura pasar desapercibido mientras él está por aquí • **~ out of my sight!** ¡no te quiero ni ver! • **to ~ out of the sun** quedarse a la sombra
▸ **stay over** (VI + ADV) pasar la noche, quedarse a dormir
▸ **stay up** (VI + ADV) **1** (= *not fall*) [*tent*] mantenerse de pie; [*trousers*] no caerse • **my trousers won't ~ up** los pantalones se me caen • **my zip won't ~ up** la cremallera se me cae • **the tent wouldn't ~ up** no había forma de que la tienda se mantuviera de pie
2 (= *not go to bed*) quedarse levantado • **I'd rather not ~ up too late** preferiría no quedarme levantado hasta muy tarde • **we ~ed up late to see a film** nos quedamos levantados hasta tarde para ver una película • **he ~ed up all night working** se quedó toda la noche trabajando • **don't ~ up for me** no te quedes levantado esperándome
3 (*Sport*) (*in higher division*) • **the team ~s up** el equipo no desciende, el equipo mantiene la categoría

stay² [steɪ] (N) **1** (*Mech*) sostén *m*, soporte *m*, puntal *m*
2 (*Naut*) estay *m*
3 (= *guy rope*) viento *m*
4 stays (= *corset*) corsé *m*
5 (*fig*) sostén *m*, apoyo *m* • **the ~ of one's old age** el sostén de su vejez
(VT) (*frm*) sostener, apoyar, apuntalar • **this will ~ you till lunchtime** con esto te mantendrás hasta la comida, esto engañará el hambre hasta la comida

stay-at-home ['steɪəthəʊm] (ADJ) casero, hogareño
(N) persona *f* hogareña, persona *f* casera

staycation* [steɪ'keɪʃən] (N) vacaciones *fpl* en casa

stayer ['steɪə^r] (N) (*Horse racing*) *caballo de mucha resistencia, apto para carreras de distancia*; (*fig*) persona *f* de mucho aguante *or* resistencia

staying power ['steɪɪŋ,paʊə^r] (N) aguante *m*, resistencia *f*

staysail ['steɪseɪl, (*Naut*) 'steɪsl] (N) vela *f* de estay

STD (N ABBR) **1** (*Brit*) (*Telec*) = **Subscriber Trunk Dialling**
2 (= **sexually transmitted disease**) ETS *f*
(CPD) ▸ **STD code** prefijo *m* para conferencias interurbanas (automáticas)

stead [sted] (N) • **in sb's ~** en lugar de algn • **to stand sb in good ~** ser muy útil a algn

steadfast ['stedfəst] (ADJ) [*person*] firme, resuelto; [*gaze*] fijo • **~ in adversity** firme en el infortunio • **~ in danger** impertérrito • **~ in love** constante en el amor

steadfastly ['stedfəstlɪ] (ADV) firmemente, resueltamente

steadfastness ['stedfəstnɪs] (N) (= *determination*) firmeza *f*, resolución *f*; (= *loyalty*) constancia *f*; (= *tenacity*) [*of resistance*] tenacidad *f*

steadicam® ['stedɪkæm] (N) *cámara con estabilizador óptico de imagen*

steadily ['stedɪlɪ] (ADV) **1** (= *continuously*) [*improve, grow, move, advance*] a un ritmo constante, de manera *or* forma continuada, de manera *or* forma constante; [*increase, rise*] a un ritmo constante; [*work*] a un ritmo constante; (*without stopping*) sin parar; [*rain*] ininterrumpidamente • **it gets ~ worse** se pone cada vez peor • **a ~ increasing number of people** un número cada vez mayor de gente
2 (= *regularly*) [*breathe, beat*] regularmente
3 (= *calmly*) [*speak*] con firmeza; [*gaze, look*] fijamente, sin pestañear
4 (= *firmly*) [*walk*] con paso seguro; [*hold, grasp*] firmemente

steadiness ['stedɪnɪs] (N) **1** (= *regularity*) [*of demand, supply, rain, temperature*] lo constante; [*of decline, increase, improvement, flow*] lo continuo; [*of pace, breathing*] regularidad *f*; [*of currency, prices, economy*] estabilidad *f*
2 (= *calmness*) [*of voice*] firmeza *f*; [*of gaze*] lo fijo; [*of nerves*] lo templado
3 (= *firmness*) [*of chair, table, ladder*] lo firme; [*of boat*] lo estable • **it requires ~ of hand** se necesita buen pulso
4 (= *reliability*) [*of person*] formalidad *f*, seriedad *f*

steady ['stedɪ] (ADJ) (COMPAR: **steadier**, SUPERL: **steadiest**) **1** (= *continuous*) [*decline, increase, improvement, flow*] continuo; [*demand, wind, supply*] constante; [*rain*] constante, ininterrumpido; [*breathing, beat*] regular; [*temperature*] constante, uniforme • **we were going at a ~ 70kph** íbamos a una velocidad constante de 70kph • **there was a ~ downpour for three hours** llovió durante tres horas ininterrumpidamente *or* sin parar • **he plays a very ~ game** juega sin altibajos • **to hold** *or* **keep sth ~** [+ *prices, demand*] mantener algo estable • **he doesn't have a ~ income** no tiene ingresos regulares *or* estables • **a ~ job** un empleo fijo • **at a ~ pace** a paso regular *or* constante • **we have been making ~ progress** hemos ido mejorando de forma continuada *or* constante • **we have a ~ stream of visitors** tenemos un flujo constante de visitantes
2 (= *calm*) [*voice*] firme; [*gaze*] fijo; [*nerves*] templado
3 (= *firm*) [*chair, table*] firme, seguro; [*boat*] estable • **a ~ hand** un pulso firme • **hold the camera ~** no muevas la cámara • **the unemployment rate is holding ~ at 7.3%** el índice de paro se mantiene estable a un 7,3% • **to be ~ on one's feet** caminar con paso seguro • **the car is not very ~ on corners** el coche no es muy estable en las curvas
4 (= *reliable*) [*person*] formal, serio
5 (= *regular*) [*boyfriend, girlfriend*] formal; [*relationship*] estable
(ADV) **1** (*in exclamations*) • **~! you're rocking the boat** ¡quieto! estás haciendo que se balancee la barca • **~ as she goes!** (*Naut*) ¡mantenga el rumbo! • **~ on! there's no need to lose your temper** ¡tranquilo! no hay necesidad de perder los estribos
2* • **to go ~ with sb** ser novio formal de algn • **they're going ~** son novios formales
(VT) **1** (= *stabilize*) [+ *wobbling object*] estabilizar; [+ *chair, table*] (*with hands*) sujetar para que no se mueva; (*with wedge*) poner un calzo a (para que no cojee) • **two men steadied the ladder** dos hombres sujetaron la escalera para que no se moviese • **to ~ o.s.** equilibrarse • **to ~ o.s. against** *or* **on sth** recobrar el equilibrio apoyándose en algo
2 (= *compose*) [+ *nervous person*] calmar, tranquilizar; [+ *wild person*] apaciguar; [+ *horse*] tranquilizar • **to ~ o.s.** calmarse,

tranquilizarse • **she smokes to ~ her nerves** fuma para calmar los nervios • **she breathed in to ~ her voice** aspiró para hacer que su voz sonase tranquila
(VI) **1** (*= stop moving*) dejar de moverse • **the shadows from the lamp steadied** las sombras que hacía la lámpara dejaron de moverse
2 (*= grow calm*) [*voice*] calmarse; [*prices, market*] estabilizarse, hacerse más estable • **to have a ~ing influence on sb** ejercer una buena influencia sobre algn

steak [steɪk] (N) (*= one piece*) filete *m or* bistec *m* de vaca, filete *m or* bistec *m* de res (*LAm*), bife *m* (*And, S. Cone*); (*for stewing etc*) carne *f* de vaca *or* res; (*= barbecued steak*) churrasco *m* (*And, S. Cone*)
(CPD) ▸ **steak and kidney pie** pastel *m* de carne y riñones ▸ **steak and kidney pudding** pastel *m* relleno de ternera y riñones en salsa ▸ **steak house** asador *m* ▸ **steak knife** cuchillo *m* para la carne

steal [sti:l] (PT: **stole**, PP: **stolen**) (VT)
1 (*= take*) [*+ object*] robar, hurtar (*frm*); [*+ idea*] robar • **to ~ sth from sb** robar algo a algn • **he stole it from school** lo robó del colegio • **she used to ~ money from her parents** solía robar dinero a sus padres • **she stole her best friend's boyfriend (from her)** (le) robó el novio a su mejor amiga • IDIOMS: • **to ~ sb's heart** robar el corazón a algn • **to ~ a march on sb*** adelantarse a algn • **to ~ the show** llevarse todos los aplausos, acaparar la atención de todos • **to ~ sb's thunder** eclipsar a algn
2 (*liter*) (*= sneak*) • **to ~ a glance at sb** mirar a algn de soslayo, echar una mirada de soslayo a algn • **to ~ a kiss from sb** robar un beso a algn
(VI) **1** (*= take things*) robar • **to ~ from sb** robar a algn
2 (*= creep*) **a** • **to ~ into a room** entrar sigilosamente en una habitación, entrar en una habitación a hurtadillas • **to ~ out of a room** salir sigilosamente de una habitación, salir de una habitación a hurtadillas • **to ~ up/down the stairs** subir/bajar sigilosamente las escaleras, subir/bajar las escaleras a hurtadillas • **to ~ up on sb** acercarse a algn sigilosamente
b (*fig*) • **a smile stole across her lips** una sonrisa se escapó de sus labios • **a tear stole down her cheek** una lágrima se deslizó por su mejilla • **the light was ~ing through the shutters** la luz se filtraba por las contraventanas
(N)* (*= bargain*) • **it's a ~** es una ganga* *or* un regalo*
▸ **steal away** (VI + ADV) escabullirse, irse furtivamente • **the intruders stole away into the night** los intrusos se escabulleron en la noche

stealing ['sti:lɪŋ] (N) robo *m*, hurto *m* (*frm*) • **there have been cases of ~** ha habido casos de robo *or* (*frm*) hurto • **~ is wrong** robar *or* (*frm*) hurtar está mal

stealth [stelθ] (N) sigilo *m* • **by ~** a hurtadillas, sigilosamente
(CPD) ▸ **stealth bomber** bombardero *m* invisible ▸ **stealth tax** impuesto *m* invisible

stealthily ['stelθɪlɪ] (ADV) a hurtadillas, sigilosamente

stealthiness ['stelθɪnɪs] (N) sigilo *m*

stealthy ['stelθɪ] (ADJ) (COMPAR: **stealthier**, SUPERL: **stealthiest**) cauteloso, sigiloso

steam [sti:m] (N) vapor *m* • **to get up** *or* **pick up ~** dar presión • **full ~ ahead!** (*Naut*) ¡a todo vapor! • **the ship went on under its own ~** el buque siguió adelante con sus propios motores • IDIOMS: • **to go full ~ ahead with sth** avanzar a toda marcha con algo • **to let off ~** desahogarse • **under one's own ~** por sus propios medios *or* propias fuerzas • **to run out of ~** quedar sin fuerza
(VT) **1** (*Culin*) cocer al vapor
2 • **to ~ open an envelope** abrir un sobre con vapor • **to ~ a stamp off** despegar un sello con vapor
(VI) **1** (*= give off steam*) echar vapor • **the bowl was ~ing on the table** la cacerola humeaba encima de la mesa
2 (*= move*) • **we were ~ing at 12 knots** íbamos a 12 nudos, navegábamos a 12 nudos • **to ~ ahead** (*lit*) avanzar; (*fig*) adelantarse mucho • **to ~ along** avanzar (echando vapor) • **the ship ~ed into harbour** el buque entró al puerto echando vapor • **the train ~ed out** salió el tren
(CPD) ▸ **steam bath** baño *m* de vapor ▸ **steam engine** máquina *f* de vapor ▸ **steam hammer** martillo *m* pilón ▸ **steam heat** calor *m* por vapor ▸ **steam iron** plancha *f* de vapor ▸ **steam organ** órgano *m* de vapor ▸ **steam room** sauna *f* finlandesa, sala *f* de vapor ▸ **steam shovel** (*US*) pala *f* mecánica de vapor, excavadora *f* ▸ **steam train** tren *m* de vapor ▸ **steam turbine** turbina *f* de vapor
▸ **steam up** (VI + ADV) [*window*] empañarse (VT + ADV) [*+ window*] empañar • **the windows quickly get ~ed up** las ventanas se empañan enseguida • IDIOM: • **to get ~ed up about sth*** (*= angry*) ponerse negro por algo; (*= worried*) preocuparse por algo • **don't get ~ed up!*** ¡no te exaltes!, ¡cálmate!

steamboat ['sti:mbəʊt] (N) vapor *m*, buque *m* de vapor

steam-driven ['sti:m,drɪvn] (ADJ) impulsado por vapor, a vapor

steamer ['sti:məʳ] (N) **1** (*Culin*) olla *f* de estofar
2 (*Naut*) vapor *m*, buque *m* de vapor

steaming ['sti:mɪŋ] (ADJ) **1** [*kettle, plate*] humeante
2* (*= angry*) negro*, furioso
3 (*Scot‡*) (*= drunk*) mamado*

steamroller ['sti:m,rəʊləʳ] (N) apisonadora *f*
(VT) **1** (*lit*) allanar con apisonadora
2 (*fig*) aplastar, arrollar • **to ~ a bill through Parliament** hacer aprobar un proyecto de ley por mayoría aplastante *or* arrolladora

steamship ['sti:mʃɪp] (N) vapor *m*, buque *m* de vapor
(CPD) ▸ **steamship company, steamship line** compañía *f* naviera

steamy ['sti:mɪ] (ADJ) (COMPAR: **steamier**, SUPERL: **steamiest**) **1** [*room etc*] lleno de vapor; [*atmosphere*] húmedo y caluroso; [*window*] empañado
2* [*film, novel*] erótico; [*relationship*] apasionado

steed [sti:d] (N) (*liter*) corcel *m*

steel [sti:l] (N) **1** (*= metal*) acero *m* • **nerves of ~** nervios *mpl* de acero • IDIOM: • **to fight with cold ~** luchar con armas blancas
2 (*= sharpener*) chaira *f*, eslabón *m*; (*for striking spark*) eslabón *m*
(VT) • **to ~ one's heart** endurecer el corazón • **to ~ o.s.** fortalecerse (**against** contra) • **to ~ o.s. for sth** cobrar ánimo para algo • **to ~ o.s. to do sth** cobrar ánimo para hacer algo
(CPD) de acero ▸ **steel band** (*Mus*) *banda de percusión del Caribe* ▸ **steel guitar** guitarra *f* de cordaje metálico ▸ **steel helmet** casco *m* (de acero) ▸ **steel industry** industria *f* siderúrgica ▸ **steel maker, steel manufacturer** fabricante *mf* de acero ▸ **steel mill** fundición *f*, fundidora *f* (*LAm*) ▸ **steel tape** cinta *f* métrica de acero ▸ **steel wool** estropajo *m* de aluminio

steel-clad ['sti:lklæd] (ADJ) revestido de acero, acorazado

steel-grey [,sti:l'greɪ] (ADJ) gris metálico

steel-plated [,sti:l'pleɪtɪd] (ADJ) chapado en acero

steelworker ['sti:l,wɜ:kəʳ] (N) trabajador(a) *m/f* siderúrgico/a

steelworks ['sti:lwɜ:ks] (NSING) fundición *f*, fundidora *f* (*LAm*)

steely ['sti:lɪ] (ADJ) (COMPAR: **steelier**, SUPERL: **steeliest**) acerado; (*fig*) [*determination*] inflexible; [*gaze*] duro, de acero • **~ blue** azul metálico

steelyard ['sti:ljɑ:d] (N) romana *f*

steely-eyed [,sti:lɪ'aɪd] (ADJ) de mirada penetrante

steep¹ [sti:p] (ADJ) (COMPAR: **steeper**, SUPERL: **steepest**) **1** [*hill, cliff*] empinado, escarpado; [*stairs, slope, climb*] empinado • **it's too ~ for the tractor** está demasiado pendiente para el tractor, la pendiente es demasiado empinada para el tractor • **it's a ~ climb to the top** hay una subida empinada hasta la cumbre
2 (*= sharp*) [*drop*] abrupto, brusco; [*increase*] pronunciado
3* [*price, demands*] excesivo
4 (*Brit**) (*= unreasonable*) • **that's pretty ~!** ¡eso es demasiado!, ¡no hay derecho! • **it's a bit ~ that you've got to do it yourself** no es justo que lo tengas que hacer tú solo

steep² [sti:p] (VT) **1** [*+ washing*] remojar, poner a *or* en remojo (**in** en)
2 • **~ed in** (*fig*) impregnado de • **a town ~ed in history** una ciudad cargada *or* impregnada de historia • **she is ~ed in the Celtic tradition** ella está empapada de la tradición celta • **a ceremony which is ~ed in ancient tradition** una ceremonia que hunde sus raíces en la más antigua tradición • **he was ~ed in the religion and laws of Judaism** estaba imbuido de la religión y las leyes judaicas
(VI) • **to leave sth to ~** dejar algo a *or* en remojo

steeple ['sti:pl] (N) aguja *f*, chapitel *m*

steeplechase ['sti:pl,tʃeɪs] (N) carrera *f* de obstáculos

steeplechasing ['sti:pl,tʃeɪsɪŋ] (N) deporte *m* de las carreras de obstáculos

steeplejack ['sti:pldʒæk] (N) *reparador de chimeneas, torres etc*

steeply ['sti:plɪ] (ADV) • **the mountain rises ~** la montaña está cortada a pico • **the road climbs ~** la carretera sube muy empinada • **prices have risen ~** los precios han subido muchísimo

steepness ['sti:pnɪs] (N) [*of hill, cliff*] lo empinado, lo escarpado; [*of stairs, climb*] lo empinado; [*of drop*] lo abrupto, brusquedad *f*; [*of increase*] lo pronunciado

steer¹ [stɪəʳ] (VT) **1** [*+ car, van*] conducir, manejar (*LAm*); [*+ trolley*] llevar, conducir; [*+ ship*] gobernar • **he ~ed the wheelbarrow along the garden path** llevó la carretilla por la senda del jardín • **to ~ one's way through a crowd** abrirse paso por entre una multitud • **you nearly ~ed us into that rock** por poco nos llevas contra aquella roca
2 (*= lead*) [*+ person*] dirigir, llevar; [*+ conversation etc*] llevar • **I ~ed her across to the bar** la dirigí hacia el bar • **he ~ed me into a good job*** me enchufó para un buen trabajo*
(VI) [*car*] conducir, manejar (*LAm*); [*ship*] gobernar • **who's going to ~?** (*in car*) ¿quién manejará el volante?; (*in boat*) ¿quién manejará el timón? • **you ~ and I'll push** tú ponte al volante y yo empujo • **can you ~?** ¿sabes gobernar el barco *etc*? • **to ~ for sth** dirigirse hacia algo • IDIOM: • **to ~ clear of sb/sth** esquivar a algn/evadir algo

N (*US**) (= *tip, advice*) • **to sell sb a bum ~** dar información falsa a algn

steer² [stɪəʳ] N (= *bull*) novillo *m*

steerage [ˈstɪərɪdʒ] N (*Naut*) entrepuente *m* • **to go ~** viajar en tercera clase

steering [ˈstɪərɪŋ] N (*Aut etc*) dirección *f*, conducción *f*; (*Naut*) gobierno *m*
CPD ▸ **steering arm** brazo *m* de dirección ▸ **steering column** columna *f* de dirección ▸ **steering committee** comité *m* de dirección ▸ **steering lock** (*Aut*) (= *anti-theft device*) dispositivo *m* antirrobo; (= *turning circle*) capacidad *f* de giro ▸ **steering wheel** volante *m*, manubrio *m* (*LAm*)

steersman [ˈstɪəzmən] N (PL: **steersmen**) (*Naut*) timonero *m*

stele [stiːl] N (*Archeol*) estela *f*

stellar [ˈsteləʳ] ADJ estelar

stem¹ [stem] N **1** [*of plant*] tallo *m*; [*of tree*] tronco *m*; [*of leaf*] pedúnculo *m*; [*of glass*] pie *m*; [*of pipe*] tubo *m*, cañón *m*; (*Mech*) vástago *m*; [*of word*] tema *m*
2 (*Naut*) roda *f*, tajamar *m* • **from ~ to stern** de proa a popa
VI • **to ~ from sth** ser el resultado de algo
CPD ▸ **stem cell** célula *f* madre ▸ **stem cell research** investigación *f* con células madre

stem² [stem] VT (= *check, stop*) [+ *blood*] restañar; [+ *attack, flood*] detener • **to ~ the tide of events** detener el curso de los acontecimientos

stench [stentʃ] N hedor *m*

stencil [ˈstensl] N (*for lettering etc*) plantilla *f*; (*for typing*) cliché *m*, clisé *m*
VT estarcir; (*in typing*) hacer un cliché de

Sten gun [ˈstengʌn] N metralleta *f* Sten

steno* [ˈstenəʊ] N (*US*) = **stenographer, stenography**

stenographer [steˈnɒgrəfəʳ] N (*US*) taquígrafo/a *m/f*, estenógrafo/a *m/f*

stenography [steˈnɒgrəfɪ] N (*US*) taquigrafía *f*, estenografía *f*

stent [stent] N (*Med*) estent *m*, cánula *f*

stentorian [stenˈtɔːrɪən] ADJ (*liter*) estentóreo

STEP [step] N ABBR = **Science and Technology for Environmental Protection**

step [step] N **1** (= *movement*) (*lit, fig*) paso *m*; (= *sound*) paso *m*, pisada *f* • **with slow ~s** con pasos lentos • **he heard ~s outside** oyó pasos *or* pisadas fuera • **to take a ~ back** dar un paso atrás • **it's a big ~ for him** es un gran paso *or* salto para él • **~ by ~** (*lit, fig*) poco a poco • **to be a ~ closer to doing sth** estar más cerca de hacer algo • **at every ~** (*lit, fig*) a cada paso • **we'll keep you informed every ~ of the way** le mantendremos informado en todo momento • **I'll fight this decision every ~ of the way** voy a oponerme a esta decisión hasta el final • **the first ~ is to decide ...** el primer paso es decidir ... • **to follow in sb's ~s** seguir los pasos de algn • **it's a great ~ forward** es un gran paso *or* salto adelante • **to take a ~ forward** dar un paso adelante • **I would go one ~ further and make all guns illegal** yo iría aún más lejos y prohibiría todo tipo de armas de fuego • **what's the next ~?** ¿cuál es el siguiente paso? • **it's a ~ in the right direction** es un paso adelante • **a ~ towards peace** un paso hacia la paz • **to turn one's ~s towards sth** dirigir los pasos hacia algo • **it's a ~ up in his career** es un ascenso en su carrera profesional • **it's a bit of a ~ up from the house where I was born** es mucho mejor que la casa en la que nací • **to watch one's ~** (*lit, fig*) ir con cuidado
• IDIOMS: • **to be one ~ ahead of sb** llevar ventaja a *or* sobre algn • **to keep one ~ ahead (of)** mantenerse en una posición de ventaja (con respecto a) • **it's a case of one ~ forward, two ~s back** es un caso típico de un paso adelante y dos hacia atrás; ▹ **false, spring**
2 (*in dancing, marching*) paso *m* • **to break ~** romper el paso • **he quickly fell into ~ beside me** no tardó en ajustar su paso al mío • **to be in ~ with sb** (*lit*) llevar el paso de algn • **the party is in ~ with the country** el partido está en sintonía con el país • **to be in ~ with public opinion** sintonizar con la opinión pública • **the bright colours are perfectly in ~ with the current mood** los colores vivos reflejan perfectamente el clima actual • **to be/keep in ~ (with)** (*in marching*) llevar el paso (de); (*in dance*) llevar el compás *or* ritmo (de) • **to be out of ~** (*in marching*) no llevar el paso; (*in dance*) no llevar el compás *or* el ritmo • **to get out of ~** (*in march*) perder el paso; (*in dance*) perder el ritmo *or* compás
• IDIOMS: • **to be out of ~ with sth/sb** no estar sintonizado con algo/algn • **to fall** *or* **get out of ~ with sth/sb** desconectarse de algo/algn
3 (= *distance*) paso *m* • **I'm just a ~ away if you need me** si me necesitas, solo estoy a un paso • **the beach is just a ~ away (from the hotel)** la playa está a un paso (del hotel) • **it's a good ~** *or* **quite a ~ to the village*** el pueblo queda bastante lejos
4 (= *footprint*) huella *f*
5 (= *measure*) medida *f* • **to take ~s** tomar medidas • **we must take ~s to improve things** tenemos que tomar medidas para mejorar la situación
6 (= *stair*) peldaño *m*, escalón *m*; (*on bus*) peldaño *m*, estribo *m*; (*also* **doorstep**) escalón *m* de la puerta • **"mind the step"** "cuidado con el escalón" • **I'll meet you on the library ~s** quedamos en los escalones *or* la escalinata de la biblioteca • **a flight of stone ~s** un tramo de escalera *or* de escalones de piedra
7 steps (= *stepladder*) escalera *f* (de mano/de tijera)
8 (*in scale*) peldaño *m*, grado *m* • **to get onto the next ~ in the salary scale** ascender un peldaño *or* subir de grado en la escala salarial
9 (*also* **step aerobics**) step *m*
10 (*US*) (*Mus*) tono *m*
VI **1** (= *walk*) • **to ~ on board** subir a bordo • **won't you ~ inside?** ¿no quiere pasar? • **he ~ped into the room** entró en la habitación • **he ~ped into his slippers/trousers** se puso las zapatillas/los pantalones • **to ~ off a bus/plane/train** bajarse de un autobús/avión/tren • **as he ~ped onto the pavement ...** al poner el pie en la acera ... • **as she ~ped out of the car** al bajar del coche • **she looked as if she had ~ped out of a fairytale** parecía recién salida de un cuento de hadas • **she ~ped out of her dress** se quitó el vestido (por abajo) • **I had to ~ outside for a breath of fresh air** tuve que salir fuera a tomar el aire • **to ~ over sth** pasar por encima de algo • **~ this way** haga el favor de pasar por aquí
• IDIOM: • **to ~ out of line** desobedecer, romper las reglas; ▹ **shoe**
2 (= *tread*) • **to ~ in/on sth** pisar algo • **don't ~ in that puddle** no te metas en ese charco • **~ on it!*** (= *hurry up*) ¡date prisa!, ¡ponte las pilas!*, ¡apúrate! (*LAm*); (*Aut*) ¡acelera! • **to ~ on the accelerator** (*Brit*) • **~ on the gas** (*US*) pisar el acelerador; ▹ **toe**
CPD ▸ **step aerobics** step *m* ▸ **step change** cambio *m* radical

▸ **step aside** VI + ADV (*lit*) hacerse a un lado, apartarse • **many would prefer to see him ~ aside in favour of a younger man** muchos preferirían que renunciase *or* dimitiese en favor de alguien más joven

▸ **step back** VI + ADV **1** (*lit*) dar un paso hacia atrás, retroceder • **it's like ~ping back in time** es como viajar hacia atrás *or* retroceder en el tiempo
2 (= *detach o.s.*) distanciarse un poco • **I needed to ~ back from the situation** necesitaba distanciarme un poco de la situación

▸ **step down** VI + ADV **1** (*lit*) bajar (**from** de)
2 (*fig*) (= *resign*) renunciar, dimitir • **to ~ down in favour of sb** renunciar *or* dimitir en favor de algn

▸ **step forward** VI + ADV **1** (*lit*) dar un paso hacia adelante
2 (*fig*) (= *volunteer*) ofrecerse

▸ **step in** VI + ADV **1** (*lit*) entrar
2 (*fig*) (= *intervene*) intervenir; (= *volunteer*) ofrecerse • **the government must ~ in and sort out this situation** el gobierno debe intervenir para solucionar esta situación • **Mrs White has kindly ~ped in to help us out** la Sra. White se ha ofrecido amablemente a ayudarnos

▸ **step out** VI + ADV **1** (= *go outside*) salir
2 (= *present o.s.*) presentarse, aparecer • **she likes to ~ out in designer clothes** le gusta presentarse *or* aparecer llevando ropa exclusiva
3† (*romantically*) salir • **Jake is ~ping out with my niece** Jake sale con mi sobrina
4 (= *walk briskly*) apretar el paso
5 (*US**) • **to ~ out on sb** ser infiel a algn
VT + ADV (= *measure*) [+ *distance*] medir a pasos

▸ **step up** VI + ADV • **to ~ up to sth/sb** acercarse a algo/algn
VT + ADV **1** (= *increase*) [+ *production, sales*] aumentar; [+ *campaign*] intensificar; [+ *attacks, attempts, efforts*] intensificar, redoblar
2 (*Elec*) [+ *current*] aumentar

stepbrother [ˈstepˌbrʌðəʳ] N hermanastro *m*

step-by-step [ˌstepbaɪˈstep] ADJ • **step-by-step instructions** instrucciones *fpl* paso a paso

stepchild [ˈsteptʃaɪld] N (PL: **stepchildren**) hijastro/a *m/f*

stepdad* [ˈstepˌdæd] N padrastro *m*

stepdaughter [ˈstepˌdɔːtəʳ] N hijastra *f*

stepfather [ˈstepˌfɑːðəʳ] N padrastro *m*

Stephen [ˈstiːvn] N Esteban

stepladder [ˈstepˌlædəʳ] N escalera *f* de mano, escalera *f* de tijera

stepmother [ˈstepˌmʌðəʳ], **stepmum*** [ˈstepˌmum] N madrastra *f*

step-parent [ˈstepˌpeərənt] N (= *father*) padrastro *m*; (= *mother*) madrastra *f*

steppe [step] N (*also* **steppes**) estepa *f*

stepping stone [ˈstepɪŋstəʊn] N **1** (*lit*) pasadera *f*
2 (*fig*) trampolín *m* (**to** para llegar a)

stepsister [ˈstepˌsɪstəʳ] N hermanastra *f*

stepson [ˈstepsʌn] N hijastro *m*

step-up [ˈstepʌp] N (= *increase*) (*in production, sales*) aumento *m*; (*in campaign, attempts, efforts*) intensificación *f*

stepwise [ˈstepwaɪz] ADJ, ADV (= *step-by-step*) paso a paso

ster. ABBR = **sterling**

stereo [ˈsterɪəʊ] N (= *hi-fi equipment*) equipo *m* estereofónico; (= *sound*) estéreo *m* • **in ~** en estéreo
ADJ estereofónico

stereo... [ˈsterɪəʊ] PREFIX estereo...

stereogram [ˈsterɪəgræm] N, **stereograph** [ˈsterɪəgræf] N estereografía *f*

stereophonic [ˌsterɪəˈfɒnɪk] ADJ estereofónico

stereophony [sterɪ'ɒfənɪ] (N) estereofonía *f*
stereoscope ['sterɪəskəʊp] (N) estereoscopio *m*
stereoscopic [ˌsterɪəs'kɒpɪk] (ADJ) estereoscópico; [*film*] tridimensional, en relieve
stereotype ['sterɪətaɪp] (N) estereotipo *m* (VT) (*Typ*) clisar, estereotipar; (*fig*) estereotipar
stereotyped ['sterɪətaɪpt] (ADJ) estereotipado
stereotypical [ˌstɪərɪə'tɪpɪkl] (ADJ) estereotípico
sterile ['steraɪl] (ADJ) **1** (= *germ-free*) esterilizado
2 (= *infertile*) estéril
sterility [ste'rɪlɪtɪ] (N) esterilidad *f*
sterilization [ˌsterɪlaɪ'zeɪʃən] (N) esterilización *f*
sterilize ['sterɪlaɪz] (VT) esterilizar
sterilizer ['sterɪlaɪzəʳ] (N) (*for instruments*) esterilizador *m*
sterling ['stɜːlɪŋ] (ADJ) **1** (*Econ*) • **pound ~** libra *f* esterlina • **~ traveller's cheques** cheques *mpl* de viaje en libras esterlinas
2 [*quality etc*] destacado • **a ~ character** una persona de toda confianza • **a person of ~ worth** una persona de grandes méritos
(N) (= *currency*) (libras *fpl*) esterlinas *fpl*
(CPD) ▸ **sterling area** zona *f* de la libra esterlina ▸ **sterling balances** balances *mpl* de libras esterlinas ▸ **sterling silver** plata *f* de ley
stern¹ [stɜːn] (ADJ) (COMPAR: **sterner**, SUPERL: **sternest**) [*person, look*] severo; [*reprimand*] duro • **a ~ glance** una mirada severa • **a ~ warning** un serio aviso • **he was very ~ with me** fue muy duro conmigo • **but he was made of ~er stuff** pero él tenía más carácter
stern² [stɜːn] (N) (*Naut*) popa *f*
sternly ['stɜːnlɪ] (ADV) [*look*] severamente; [*reprimand*] severamente, con dureza; [*warn*] con seriedad
sternness ['stɜːnnɪs] (N) [*of person, look*] severidad *f*; [*of reprimand*] severidad *f*, dureza *f*
sternum ['stɜːnəm] (N) (PL: **sternums** *or* **sterna**) esternón *m*
steroid ['stɪərɔɪd] (N) esteroide *m*
stertorous ['stɜːtərəs] (ADJ) (*frm*) estertoroso
stet [stet] (VI) (*Typ*) vale, deje como está
stethoscope ['steθəskəʊp] (N) estetoscopio *m*
Stetson® ['stetsən] (N) sombrero *m* tejano
Steve [stiːv] (N) *familiar form of* **Stephen, Steven**
stevedore ['stiːvɪdɔːʳ] (N) estibador *m*
Steven ['stiːvn] (N) Esteban
stew [stjuː] (N) **1** (*Culin*) estofado *m*, guisado *m* (*esp LAm*)
2* • **IDIOM:** • **to be in a ~** sudar la gota gorda*
(VT) [+ *meat*] estofar, guisar (*esp LAm*); [+ *fruit*] cocer, hacer una compota de; [+ *tea*] dejar que se repose • **~ed apples** compota *f* de manzanas
(VI) [*tea*] quedarse reposando demasiado • **IDIOM:** • **to let sb ~ in his/her own juice** dejar a algn que cueza en su propia salsa
(CPD) ▸ **stew meat** (US) carne *f* de vaca ▸ **stew pan, stew pot** cazuela *f*, cacerola *f*, puchero *m*
steward ['stjuːəd] (N) (*on estate*) administrador(a) *m/f*, mayordomo *m*; (= *butler*) mayordomo *m*; (*Aer*) auxiliar *m* de vuelo, auxiliar *m* de cabina, aeromozo *m* (*LAm*), sobrecargo *m* (*Mex*), cabinero *m* (*Col*); (*Naut*) camarero *m*; (= *bouncer*) portero *m*, encargado/a *m/f* del servicio de orden y entrada; ▹ **shop**
stewardess ['stjʊədes] (N) (*Aer*) azafata *f*, auxiliar *f* de vuelo *or* de cabina, aeromoza *f* (*LAm*), sobrecargo *f* (*Mex*), cabinera *f* (*Col*); (*Naut*) camarera *f*
stewardship ['stjʊədʃɪp] (N) administración *f*, gobierno *m*
stewing steak ['stjuːɪŋˌsteɪk] (N) (*Brit*) carne *f* de vaca *or* (*LAm*) res para estofar
St. Ex., St. Exch. (ABBR) = **Stock Exchange**
Stg, stg (ABBR) (= **sterling**) ester.
STI (N ABBR) (= **sexually transmitted infection**) ETS *f*
stick¹ [stɪk] (N) **1** (= *length of wood*) (trozo *m* de) madera *f*; (*shaped*) palo *m*, vara *f*; (*as weapon*) palo *m*, porra *f*; (= *walking stick*) bastón *m*; (*Aer*) (= *joystick*) palanca *f* de mando; (*Hockey, Ice hockey etc*) palo *m*; (= *drumstick*) palillo *m*; (*Mus**) (= *baton*) batuta *f* • **~ of furniture** mueble *m* • **to give sb the ~** • **take the ~ to sb** dar palo a algn • **IDIOMS:** • **to use** *or* **wield the big ~** amenazar con el garrote • **policy of the big ~** política *f* de la mano dura • **policy of the ~ and carrot** política *f* de incentivos y amenazas • **a ~ to beat sb with** un arma con la que atacar a algn; ▹ **cleft, end**
2 [*of wax, gum, shaving soap*] barra *f*; [*of celery*] rama *f*; [*of dynamite*] cartucho *m*; [*of bombs*] grupo *m*
3 (*esp Brit**) (= *criticism*) • **the critics gave him a lot of ~** los críticos le dieron una buena paliza* • **to get** *or* **take a lot of ~** recibir una buena paliza*, tener que aguantar mucho
4 • **old ~** (*Brit†**) tío* *m* • **he's a funny old ~** es un tío raro *or* divertido*
5 sticks: **a** (*for the fire*) astillas *fpl*, leña *f*
b (*Horse racing**) (= *hurdles*) obstáculos *mpl*
c • **IDIOMS:** • **to live in the ~s*** vivir en el quinto pino *or* infierno • **to up ~s*** recoger los bártulos*
(CPD) ▸ **stick insect** insecto *m* palo ▸ **stick shift** (US) (*Aut*) palanca *f* de marchas
stick² [stɪk] (VB: PT, PP: **stuck**) (VT) **1** (*with glue etc*) pegar, encolar • **he was ~ing stamps into his album** pegaba sellos en su álbum • **to ~ a poster on the wall** pegar un póster a la pared • **"stick no bills"** "prohibido fijar carteles" • **he tried to ~ the crime on his brother*** trató de colgar el crimen a su hermano*
2 (= *thrust, poke*) meter; (= *stab*) [+ *sth pointed*] clavar, hincar • **he stuck his hand in his pocket** metió la mano en el bolsillo • **to ~ a knife into a table** clavar un cuchillo en una mesa • **I've stuck the needle into my finger** me he clavado la aguja en el dedo; ▹ **nose**
3 (= *pierce*) picar • **to ~ sb with a bayonet** herir a algn con bayoneta, clavar la bayoneta a algn • **IDIOM:** • **to squeal like a stuck pig** chillar como un cerdo
4* (= *place, put*) poner; (= *insert*) meter • **~ it on the shelf** ponlo en el estante • **~ it in your case** mételo en la maleta • **we'll ~ an advert in the paper** pondremos un anuncio en el periódico • **they stuck him on the committee** lo metieron en el comité • **IDIOM:** • **you know where you can ~ that!‡** ¡que te jodas!** • **she told him he could ~ his job‡** le dijo que se metiera el trabajo donde le cupiera‡
5 (*esp Brit**) (= *tolerate*) aguantar • **I can't ~ him** no lo aguanto • **I can't ~ it any longer** no aguanto más
6 • **to be stuck a** (= *jammed*) estar atascado, estar atorado (*esp LAm*); (*in mud etc*) estar atascado; [*sth pointed*] estar clavado • **the mechanism was stuck** el mecanismo estaba atascado *or* bloqueado • **the window is stuck** se ha atrancado la ventana • **the lift is stuck at the ninth floor** el ascensor se ha quedado parado *or* colgado *or* atrancado en el piso nueve • **to be stuck fast** (= *jammed*) estar totalmente atascado *or* atorado; (*in mud etc*) estar totalmente atascado; [*sth pointed*] estar bien clavado
b (= *trapped*) • **to be stuck in the lift** quedarse atrapado en el ascensor • **the car was stuck between two trucks** el coche estaba atrapado entre dos camiones • **the train was stuck at the station** el tren se quedó parado en la estación • **I'm stuck at home all day** estoy metida en casa todo el día • **we're stuck here for the night** tendremos que pasar aquí la noche • **he's stuck in France** sigue en Francia sin poder moverse • **he's stuck in a boring job** tiene un trabajo muy aburrido (y no puede buscarse otro)
c* (= *have a problem*) estar en un apuro *or* aprieto • **I'm stuck** (*in crossword puzzle, guessing game, essay etc*) estoy atascado • **he's never stuck for an answer** no le falta nunca una respuesta • **the problem had them all stuck** el problema los tenía a todos perplejos
d • **to be stuck with sth/sb*** tener que aguantar algo/a algn • **I was stuck with him for two hours*** tuve que soportar su compañía durante dos horas • **and now we're stuck with it*** y ahora no lo podemos quitar de encima, y ahora no hay manera de deshacernos de eso
e • **to be stuck on sb*** estar enamorado de algn
7 • **to get stuck a** • **to get stuck in the snow** quedar sin poderse mover en la nieve • **a bone got stuck in my throat** se me había clavado una espina en la garganta • **to get stuck fast** (= *jammed*) atascarse totalmente, atorarse totalmente (*esp LAm*); (*in mud etc*) atascarse totalmente; [*sth pointed*] clavarse bien
b • **we got stuck with this problem*** nos quedamos con este problema
(VI) **1** (= *adhere*) [*glue, sticky object etc*] pegarse • **this stamp won't ~** este sello no se pega • **it stuck to the wall** quedó pegado a la pared • **the name seems to have stuck** el apodo se le pegó • **the charge seems to have stuck** la acusación no ha sido olvidada nunca • **to make a charge ~** hacer que una acusación tenga efecto
2 (= *get jammed*) atascarse, atorarse (*esp LAm*); (*in mud etc*) atascarse; [*sth pointed*] quedar clavado, clavarse • **to ~ fast in the mud** quedar clavado en el barro • **the door ~s in wet weather** en tiempo de lluvia la puerta se pega • **the bidding stuck at £100** la puja no subió de las 100 libras • **IDIOM:** • **that really ~s in my throat** eso me indigna • **the word "thanks" seems to ~ in her throat** la palabra "gracias" no le sale de la boca
3 (= *extend, protrude*) • **the nail was ~ing through the plank** el clavo sobresalía del tablón
4 (= *be embedded*) • **he had a knife ~ing into his back** tenía una navaja clavada en la espalda
5 (*fig*) (*with prep or adv*) • **just ~ at it and I'm sure you'll manage it** no te amedrentes y al fin llegarás • **we'll all ~ by you** (= *support you*) te apoyaremos todos; (= *stay with you*) no te abandonaremos • **to ~ close to sb** pegarse a algn, no separarse de algn • **it stuck in my mind** se me quedó grabado • **to ~ to one's principles** seguir fiel a sus principios, aferrarse a sus principios • **to ~ to a promise** cumplir una promesa • **she stuck to her decision** se plantó en su decisión • **decide what you're going to do, then ~ to it** ¡decídete y no te dejes desviar! • **he stuck to his story** se mantuvo firme en su versión de los hechos • **let's ~ to the matter in hand** ciñámonos al asunto, no perdamos de vista

S

el tema principal • **I'd better ~ to fruit juice** creo que seguiré con el zumo de frutas • **if I ~ to a saltless diet, I'm fine** mientras siga una dieta sin sal voy bien • **let's ~ to the main roads** vamos a seguir por carreteras principales • **~ with us and you'll be all right** quédate con nosotros y todo saldrá bien • **I'll ~ with the job for another few months** seguiré con el trabajo unos meses más • **you'll have to ~ with it** tendrás que seguir del mismo modo • IDIOM: • **to ~ to sb like a limpet** *or* **leech** pegarse a algn como una lapa; ▸ **gun**
6 (= *balk*) • **she will ~ at nothing to get what she wants** no se para en barras para conseguir lo que quiere • **he wouldn't ~ at murder** hasta cometería un asesinato, no se arredraría ante el homicidio • **that's where I ~** yo de ahí no paso
7 (*Cards*) • **I ~** • **I'm ~ing** me planto
▸ **stick around*** (VI + ADV) quedarse
▸ **stick back** (VT + ADV) **1*** (= *replace*) volver a su lugar
2 (*with glue etc*) volver a pegar
▸ **stick down** (VT + ADV) **1** (*with glue etc*) pegar • **she stuck the envelope down** pegó el sobre
2* (= *put down*) poner, dejar
3* (= *write down*) apuntar (rápidamente)
▸ **stick in** (VT + ADV) **1** (= *thrust in*) [+ *knife, fork etc*] clavar, hincar; [+ *one's hand*] meter, introducir;* (= *add, insert*) introducir, añadir
2* • **get stuck in!** (= *work*) ¡manos a la obra!; (= *eat*) ¡atacar! • **let's get stuck in!** (= *work*) ¡(pongamos) manos a la obra!; (= *eat*) ¡atacar! • **to get stuck into sth** meterse de lleno en algo
▸ **stick on** (VT + ADV) **1** [+ *stamp, label*] pegar
2* [+ *hat*] ponerse, calarse; [+ *coat etc*] ponerse; [+ *tape, CD*] meter, poner
3* [+ *extra cost*] añadir • **they've stuck ten pence on a litre** han subido el precio del litro diez peniques
(VI + ADV) [*label, stamp*] adherirse, pegarse
▸ **stick out** (VI + ADV) **1** (= *protrude*) [*balcony*] sobresalir; [*nail*] sobresalir • **her feet stuck out over the end of the bed** sus pies asomaban por la punta de la cama • **his teeth ~ out** tiene los dientes salidos • **his ears ~ out** tiene las orejas de soplillo
2 (= *be noticeable*) destacarse, resaltar • IDIOMS: • **it ~s out a mile** salta a la vista • **to ~ out like a sore thumb** llamar la atención
3 (= *insist, persevere*) • **to ~ out for sth** empeñarse en conseguir algo • **they're ~ing out for more money** porfían en reclamar más dinero, se empeñan en pedir más dinero
(VT + ADV) **1** (= *extend*) [+ *tongue*] asomar, sacar; [+ *leg*] extender; [+ *chest*] sacar; [+ *head*] asomar
2* (= *tolerate, endure*) aguantar • **to ~ it out** aguantar
▸ **stick to** (VI + PREP) ▸ **stick²**
▸ **stick together** (VT + ADV) (*with glue etc*) pegar, unir con cola *etc* • **to ~ two things together** pegar dos cosas
(VI + ADV) **1** (= *adhere*) pegarse, quedar pegados
2 [*people*] mantenerse unidos, no separarse; (*fig*) cerrar las filas
▸ **stick up** (VT + ADV) **1** (= *raise*) [+ *notice etc*] fijar, pegar; [+ *hand etc*] levantar • **~ 'em up!*** ¡arriba las manos!
2‡ (= *rob*) [+ *person*] atracar, encañonar‡; [+ *bank*] asaltar
(VI + ADV) **1** (= *protrude*) sobresalir; [*hair*] ponerse de punta, pararse (*LAm*)
2* • **to ~ up for sb** defender a algn • **to ~ up for o.s.** hacerse valer • **to ~ up for one's rights** hacer valer sus derechos, defender sus derechos

sticker [ˈstɪkəʳ] (N) **1** (= *label*) etiqueta *f*; (*with slogan*) pegatina *f*
2* (= *person*) persona *f* aplicada, persona *f* perseverante
(CPD) ▸ **sticker price** (*US*) (*in car sales*) ≈ precio *m* de catálogo
stickiness [ˈstɪkɪnɪs] (N) **1** (= *gooiness*) [*of substance, object*] lo pegajoso • **to remove ~ from your hands, use a damp cloth** para que los dedos dejen de estar pegajosos, usar un trapo húmedo
2 (= *adhesiveness*) adherencia *f* • **the tape has lost its ~** la cinta ya no pega
3 (= *mugginess*) [*of weather, day*] lo bochornoso; [*of climate, heat*] lo húmedo
4 (= *sweatiness*) [*of person, palms*] lo húmedo
5* (= *awkwardness*) [*of situation*] lo difícil, lo delicado; [*of problem, moment*] lo difícil
sticking plaster [ˈstɪkɪŋˌplɑːstəʳ] (N) (*Brit*) esparadrapo *m*, tirita *f*, curita *f* (*LAm*)
sticking point [ˈstɪkɪŋˌpɔɪnt] (N) (*fig*) punto *m* de fricción
stick-in-the-mud* [ˈstɪkɪnðəmʌd] (N) (*Brit*) *persona rutinaria y poco aventurera*
stickleback [ˈstɪklbæk] (N) espinoso *m*
stickler [ˈstɪkləʳ] (N) • **to be a ~ for** insistir mucho en • **he's a real ~ for correct spelling** insiste mucho en la correcta ortografía
stick-on [ˈstɪkɒn] (ADJ) adhesivo • **stick-on label** etiqueta *f* adhesiva
stickpin [ˈstɪkpɪn] (N) (*US*) alfiler *m* de corbata
stick-up‡ [ˈstɪkʌp] (N) atraco *m*, asalto *m*
sticky [ˈstɪkɪ] (ADJ) (COMPAR: **stickier**, SUPERL: **stickiest**) **1** (= *gooey*) [*substance, object*] pegajoso; [*fingers*] pegajoso, pringoso • **to have ~ eyes** tener los ojos legañosos; (*Med*) tener los ojos pegados por la conjuntivitis • IDIOMS: • **to have ~ fingers*** tener la mano larga* • **to be** *or* **bat on a ~ wicket*** estar en un aprieto
2 (= *adhesive*) [*label*] engomado, adhesivo
3 (= *muggy*) [*weather, day*] bochornoso; [*climate*] húmedo (y caluroso); [*heat*] húmedo
4 (= *sweaty*) sudado • **to feel hot and ~** sudar y pasar calor
5* (= *awkward*) [*situation*] difícil, delicado; [*problem, moment, start*] difícil • **to be ~ about doing sth** ser reticente a hacer algo, poner muchas pegas para hacer algo • **to go through a ~ patch** pasar por una mala racha • IDIOM: • **to come to a ~ end** acabar mal
(CPD) ▸ **sticky bun** *bollo, a menudo de frutas o especias, cubierto con una capa de azúcar* ▸ **sticky tape** cinta *f* adhesiva
stiff [stɪf] (ADJ) (COMPAR: **stiffer**, SUPERL: **stiffest**) **1** (= *rigid*) [*card, paper, chair*] rígido, duro; [*collar, fabric*] duro, tieso; [*brush, boots*] duro; [*corpse*] rígido
2 (= *firm*) [*paste, mixture*] compacto, consistente • **beat the egg whites until ~** bata las claras de huevo a punto de nieve
3 (*Physiol*) [*joints, limbs, muscles*] entumecido, agarrotado; [*fingers*] rígido, agarrotado; [*movement*] rígido • **inactivity can make your joints ~** sus articulaciones se pueden entumecer *or* agarrotar por la inactividad • **to become** *or* **get ~** [*joints, limbs, muscles*] entumecerse, agarrotarse • **to feel ~** (*because of cold, injury etc*) sentirse agarrotado; (*after exercise*) tener agujetas • **I feel ~ all over** (*after exercise*) tengo agujetas por todo el cuerpo • **to have a ~ neck** tener tortícolis • **to be ~ with cold** estar aterido, estar entumecido de frío • IDIOMS: • **to be (as) ~ as a board** *or* **poker** estar más tieso que un palo* • **to keep a ~ upper lip** mantener el tipo, poner a mal tiempo buena cara
4 (= *unresponsive*) [*door, drawer, lock*] duro, que no abre bien, atorado (*esp LAm*) • **the lock was ~** costaba abrir el cerrojo, el cerrojo no abría bien
5 (= *cold, formal*) [*smile, bow*] frío; [*person, manner*] estirado, frío; [*atmosphere*] estirado, frío • **he gave a ~ bow** se inclinó con frialdad *or* con formalidad • **~ and formal** [*person, manner, atmosphere*] estirado y formal
6 (= *tough*) [*climb, test*] difícil, duro; [*penalty, sentence, fine*] severo; [*resistance*] tenaz; [*challenge*] difícil; [*opposition, competition*] duro
7 (= *high*) [*price*] excesivo, exorbitante; [*price rise*] fuerte
8 (= *strong*) [*breeze*] fuerte; [*drink*] cargado • **she poured herself a ~ whisky** se sirvió un vaso grande de whisky • **that's a bit ~!*** ¡eso es mucho *or* demasiado!, ¡se han pasado!*
(ADV) • **to be bored ~** aburrirse como una ostra • **to be frozen ~** estar muerto de frío • **to be scared ~** estar muerto de miedo • **to be worried ~** estar muy preocupado, estar preocupadísimo
(N)‡ **1** (= *corpse*) cadáver *m*, fiambre* *m* (*hum*)
2 (*US*) (= *tramp*) vagabundo/a *m/f*; (= *drunk*) borracho/a *m/f*
stiffen [ˈstɪfn] (VT) **1** [+ *card, fabric etc*] reforzar; (*with starch*) almidonar
2 (*also* **stiffen up**) [+ *limb, muscle*] contraer, poner tieso; [+ *joint*] agarrotar
3 (*fig*) [+ *morale, resistance etc*] fortalecer
(VI) **1** [*card, fabric*] hacerse más rígido, atiesarse
2 (*also* **stiffen up**) [*limb, muscle*] contraerse, ponerse tieso; [*joint*] agarrotarse
3 (*fig*) [*person, manner*] endurecerse • **the breeze ~ed** refrescó el viento • **resistance to the idea seems to have ~ed** la oposición a esta idea parece haberse hecho más tenaz aún
stiffener [ˈstɪfənəʳ] (N) **1** (= *starch etc*) apresto *m*
2 (= *plastic strip*) lengüeta *f*
3* (= *drink*) trago* *m*
stiffening [ˈstɪfnɪŋ] (N) [*of muscles*] contracción *f*; [*of joints*] agarrotamiento *m*
stiffly [ˈstɪflɪ] (ADV) **1** (= *firmly*) • **the napkins were ~ starched** las servilletas estaban almidonadas y tiesas
2 (= *uncomfortably*) [*walk, move, bend*] con rigidez • **she stood up ~** se levantó tieso
3 (= *coldly, formally*) [*smile, greet*] con formalidad; [*say*] con frialdad, fríamente; [*nod, bow*] fríamente, con formalidad • **they sat ~ on the edges of their chairs** estaban sentados tiesos en el borde de las sillas
stiff-necked [ˈstɪfˈnekt] (ADJ) (*fig*) porfiado, terco
stiffness [ˈstɪfnɪs] (N) **1** (= *rigidness*) [*of card, paper, chair, collar, fabric*] rigidez *f*, dureza *f*; [*of boots, brush*] dureza *f*
2 (= *firmness*) [*of paste, mixture*] lo compacto, consistencia *f*
3 (*Physiol*) [*of joints, muscles, limbs*] entumecimiento *m*, agarrotamiento *m*; [*of fingers*] agarrotamiento *m* • **~ in** *or* **of the neck** tortícolis *f* (*sometimes m*) • **the ~ you feel after exercise** las agujetas que sientes después de hacer ejercicio
4 (= *unresponsiveness*) [*of door, drawer, lock*] dificultad *f* en abrirse
5 (= *coldness, formality*) [*of smile, bow, atmosphere, person, manner*] frialdad *f*
6 (= *toughness*) [*of climb, test*] dificultad *f*; [*of penalty, sentence, fine*] severidad *f*; [*of resistance*] tenacidad *f*; [*of opposition, competition*] dureza *f*
7 (= *strength*) [*of breeze*] fuerza *f*
stifle [ˈstaɪfl] (VT) **1** [+ *person*] ahogar, sofocar
2 (*fig*) suprimir • **to ~ a yawn** contener un

bostezo • **to ~ opposition** reprimir a la oposición
(VI) ahogarse, sofocarse
stifling ['staɪflɪŋ] (ADJ) (*lit, fig*) agobiante • **it's ~ in here** ¡hace un calor agobiante *or* sofocante aquí dentro! • **the atmosphere in the company is ~** en la compañía hay una atmósfera agobiante
stigma ['stɪgmə] (N) (PL: **stigmas** *or* **stigmata** [stɪg'mɑːtə]) (*Rel*) estigma *m*; (= *moral stain*) estigma *m*, tacha *f*, baldón *m*
stigmata [stɪg'mɑːtə] (NPL) estigmas *mpl*
stigmatic [stɪg'mætɪk] (*Rel*) (ADJ) estigmatizado
(N) estigmatizado/a *m/f*
stigmatize ['stɪgmətaɪz] (VT) estigmatizar • **to ~ sb as** calificar a algn de, tachar a algn de
stile [staɪl] (N) escalones *mpl* para saltar una cerca
stiletto [stɪ'letəʊ] (N) (PL: **stilettos** *or* **stilettoes**) **1** (= *knife*) estilete *m*; (= *tool*) pinzón *m*
2 (*Brit*) (= *shoe*) zapato *m* con tacón de aguja
(CPD) ▸ **stiletto heel** (*Brit*) tacón *m* de aguja
still¹ [stɪl] (ADJ) (COMPAR: **stiller**, SUPERL: **stillest**) **1** (= *motionless*) [*person, hands*] inmóvil, quieto; [*air*] en calma, manso; [*water*] quieto, manso • **try to hold it ~** intenta que no se te mueva • **to keep ~** quedarse quieto • **keep ~!** ¡no te muevas!, ¡quédate quieto! • **to lie ~**: • **she lay ~** estaba tendida sin moverse • **to sit/stand ~** (*lit*) estarse quieto • **sit/stand ~!** ¡estáte quieto!, ¡quieto! • **time stood ~** el tiempo se detuvo • **her heart stood ~** se le paró el corazón • PROVERB: • **~ waters run deep** las apariencias engañan, es más inteligente de lo que parece
2 (= *quiet, calm*) [*place, night*] tranquilo, silencioso • **all was ~** todo estaba en calma • **a ~, small voice** una voz queda
3 (= *not fizzy*) [*orange drink, mineral water*] sin gas
(N) **1** (= *quiet*) • **in the ~ of the night** en el silencio de la noche
2 (*Cine*) fotograma *m*
(VT) **1** (*liter*) (= *silence*) [+ *protest, voice*] acallar; (= *calm*) [+ *waves*] calmar; [+ *storm*] calmar, apaciguar • **he wanted to ~ the gossiping tongues** quería acallar los rumores
2 (= *allay*) [+ *doubt, fear*] disipar; [+ *anger*] aplacar
(VI) apagarse • **the roar of the crowd ~ed to an expectant murmur** el rugido de la multitud se apagó hasta convertirse en un murmullo de expectación
(CPD) ▸ **still life** (*Art*) naturaleza *f* muerta, bodegón *m*; ▹ **still-life**
still² [stɪl] (ADV) **1** (= *up to this/that time*) todavía, aún • **she ~ lives in London** todavía *or* aún vive en Londres, sigue viviendo en Londres • **I ~ don't understand** sigo sin entender, todavía *or* aún no lo entiendo • **you could ~ change your mind** todavía *or* aún puedes cambiar de idea • **I was very angry, I ~ am** estaba muy enfadado, todavía *or* aún lo estoy • **I've ~ got three left** todavía *or* aún me quedan tres • **there are ~ two more** quedan dos más, todavía *or* aún quedan dos
2 (= *nevertheless, all the same*) aun así, de todas formas • **I didn't win, still, it's been a good experience** no he ganado, pero aun así *or* de todas formas *or* con todo, ha sido una buena experiencia • **I'm ~ going, even if it rains** iré de todas formas, incluso si llueve • **his mother was Canadian, Irish-Canadian, but ~ Canadian** su madre era canadiense, irlandesa y canadiense, pero con todo *or* aun así canadiense • **~, it was worth it** pero en fin, valió la pena • **whatever they have done, they are ~ your parents** a pesar de todo lo que han hecho, siguen siendo tus padres
3 (= *besides, in addition*) todavía, aún • **the next day there were ~ more problems** al día siguiente había todavía *or* aún más problemas • **the hall was full and there were ~ more people waiting outside** el vestíbulo estaba lleno y había todavía *or* aún más gente esperando fuera • **~ another possibility would be to …** e incluso otra posibilidad sería …
4 (*with compar*) (= *even*) todavía, aún • **more serious ~** • **~ more serious** aún *or* todavía más grave, más grave aún *or* todavía • **you need a rest, better ~, have a holiday** necesitas un descanso, mejor todavía *or* aún, tómate unas vacaciones • **worse ~, the disease seems to be spreading** (lo que es) peor todavía *or* aún, la enfermedad parece propagarse

STILL

▹ *Translate* **still** *relating to time using* **todavía** *or* **aún** *(with an accent):*
They are still working for the same company
Todavía *or* Aún están trabajando en la misma empresa

Both **todavía** *and* **aún** *normally come before the verb group in this meaning.*

▹ *Alternatively, use* **seguir** *+ gerund (with or without* **todavía/aún***):*
Siguen *or* Todavía siguen *or* Aún siguen trabajando en la misma empresa

▹ **Still** *with* **more, less** *and other comparatives is normally translated by* **todavía** *or* **aún** *(with an accent):*
More important still are the peace talks
Todavía *or* Aún más importantes son las negociaciones de paz
He lowered his voice still further
Bajó la voz todavía *or* aún más
Within a couple of weeks matters got still worse
Al cabo de dos semanas los problemas empeoraron todavía *or* aún más

NOTE: Whenever it is synonymous with **todavía, aún** *carries an accent.*

For further uses and examples, see main entry.

still³ [stɪl] (N) (*for alcohol*) alambique *m*
stillbirth ['stɪl,bɜːθ] (N) mortinato *m*
stillborn ['stɪl,bɔːn] (ADJ) **1** (*Med*) nacido muerto • **the child was ~** el niño nació muerto
2 (*fig*) fracasado, malogrado
still-life [,stɪl'laɪf] (CPD) ▸ **still-life painter** pintor(a) *m/f* de bodegones ▸ **still-life painting** bodegón *m*
stillness ['stɪlnɪs] (N) **1** (= *motionlessness*) [*of person, hands, air, water*] quietud *f*
2 (= *quiet, calm*) tranquilidad *f*, calma *f*
stilt [stɪlt] (N) zanco *m*; (*Archit*) pilar *m*, soporte *m*
stilted ['stɪltɪd] (ADJ) [*person*] afectado; [*conversation, style, manner*] forzado, poco natural • **her English is rather ~** (*non-native speaker*) su inglés no suena muy natural; (*native speaker*) tiene un inglés bastante rebuscado *or* afectado
stimulant ['stɪmjʊlənt] (ADJ) estimulante
(N) (= *drug, coffee, cigarettes*) estimulante *m*, excitante *m*; (*fig*) acicate *m* (**to** para)
stimulate ['stɪmjʊleɪt] (VT) estimular; [+ *growth etc*] favorecer; [+ *demand*] estimular • **to ~ sb to do sth** alentar a algn a que haga algo
stimulating ['stɪmjʊleɪtɪŋ] (ADJ) (*Med etc*) estimulador, estimulante; [*experience, book etc*] estimulante, inspirador
stimulation [,stɪmjʊ'leɪʃən] (N) (= *stimulus*) estímulo *m*; (= *act*) estimulación *f*; (= *state*) excitación *f*
stimulative ['stɪmjʊlətɪv] (ADJ) [*effect*] estimulador; [*measure, policy*] alentador
stimulus ['stɪmjʊləs] (N) (PL: **stimuli** ['stɪmjʊlaɪ]) estímulo *m*, incentivo *m*
sting [stɪŋ] (VB: PT, PP: **stung**) (N) **1** (*Zool, Bot*) (= *organ*) aguijón *m* • IDIOM: • **but there's a ~ in the tail** pero viene algo no tan agradable al final
2 (= *act, wound*) [*of insect, nettle*] picadura *f*; (= *sharp pain*) punzada *f* • **a ~ of remorse** el gusanillo de la conciencia • **the ~ of the rain in one's face** el azote de la lluvia en la cara • **I felt the ~ of his irony** su ironía me hirió en lo vivo • IDIOM: • **to take the ~ out of sth** restar fuerza a algo
3 (*esp US**) (= *confidence trick*) timo *m*
(VT) **1** [*insect, nettle*] picar; (= *make smart*) escocer, picar, arder (*esp LAm*); [*hail*] azotar
2 (*fig*) [*conscience*] remorder; [*remark, criticism*] herir • **my conscience stung me** me remordió la conciencia • **the reply stung him to the quick** la respuesta lo hirió en lo vivo • **he was clearly stung by this remark** era evidente que este comentario hizo mella en él
3 (= *provoke*) • **he was stung into action** lo provocaron a actuar
4‡ • **they stung me for four pounds** me clavaron cuatro libras* • **how much did they ~ you for?** ¿cuánto te clavaron?*
(VI) **1** [*insect etc*] picar • **moths don't ~** las mariposas no pican
2 • **my eyes ~** me pican los ojos • **that blow really stung** ese golpe me dolió de verdad
stinger ['stɪŋəʳ] (N) **1** (= *cocktail*) stinger *m*, *cóctel de crema de menta y coñac*
2 (*US*) (= *insect*) *insecto que pica*
3 (*Australia*) (= *jellyfish*) medusa *f* (*que pica*)
4 (*US**) (= *remark*) pulla *f*
stingily ['stɪndʒɪlɪ] (ADV) con tacañería
stinginess ['stɪndʒɪnɪs] (N) tacañería *f*
stinging ['stɪŋɪŋ] (ADJ) **1** [*insect etc*] que pica, que tiene aguijón; [*pain*] punzante
2 [*remark etc*] mordaz
(N) (= *sensation*) escozor *m*
(CPD) ▸ **stinging nettle** ortiga *f*
stingray ['stɪŋreɪ] (N) pastinaca *f*
stingy ['stɪndʒɪ] (ADJ) (COMPAR: **stingier**, SUPERL: **stingiest**) [*person*] tacaño; [*meal*] parco, escaso • **to be ~ with sth** ser tacaño con algo
stink [stɪŋk] (VB: PT: **stank**, PP: **stunk**) (N) **1** (= *smell*) peste *f*, hedor *m* • **a ~ of …** un hedor a … • **the ~ of corruption** el olor a corrupción
2* (*fig*) (= *row, trouble*) lío* *m*, follón *m* (*Sp**) • **there was a tremendous ~ about it** se armó un tremendo lío* • **to kick up** *or* **raise** *or* **make a ~** armar un escándalo
(VI) **1** • **to ~ (of)** apestar (a), heder (a) • **it ~s in here** aquí apesta
2‡ (= *be very bad*) • **the idea ~s** es una pésima idea • **I think the plan ~s** creo que es un proyecto abominable • **as a headmaster he ~s** como director es fatal*
(VT) • **to ~ the place out*** infestar el lugar de olor
(CPD) ▸ **stink bomb** bomba *f* fétida

stinker‡ [ˈstɪŋkəʳ] (N) (= *person*) mal bicho* *m*, canalla* *mf* • **you ~!** ¡bestia!* • **this problem is a ~** es un problema peliagudo

stinking [ˈstɪŋkɪŋ] (ADJ) **1** (*lit*) hediondo, fétido
2* horrible, bestial, asqueroso
(ADV) • **they are ~ rich*** son unos ricachos*

stinky* [ˈstɪŋkɪ] (ADJ) apestoso, maloliente

stint [stɪnt] (N) **1** (= *amount of work*) • **to do a** *or* **one's ~ (at)** hacer su parte (de) • **I've done my ~** he hecho lo que me corresponde
2 (= *period*) periodo *m*, período *m* • **she did a two-year ~ on the committee** fue miembro del comité durante un periodo *or* período de dos años • **after a brief ~ in a law firm he went to Hong Kong** tras una breve temporada trabajando en un bufete de abogados, se fue a Hong-Kong
3 • **without ~** libremente, generosamente
(VT) limitar, restringir • **he did not ~ his praises** no escatimó elogios • **to ~ sb of sth** privar a algn de algo, dar a algn menor cantidad de algo de la que pide *or* necesita • **to ~ o.s.** estrecharse, privarse de cosas • **don't ~ yourself!** ¡no te prives de nada! • **to ~ o.s. of sth** privarse de algo, negarse algo, no permitirse algo
(VI) • **he did not ~ on praise** no escatimó elogios

stipend [ˈstaɪpend] (N) salario *m*, estipendio *m*

stipendiary [staɪˈpendɪərɪ] (ADJ) estipendiario
(N) estipendiario *m*

stipple [ˈstɪpl] (VT) puntear

stipulate [ˈstɪpjʊleɪt] (VT) estipular, poner como condición, especificar
(VI) • **to ~ for sth** estipular algo, poner algo como condición

stipulation [ˌstɪpjʊˈleɪʃən] (N) estipulación *f*, condición *f*

stir¹ [stɜːʳ] (N) **1** • **to give sth a ~** remover algo
2 (= *disturbance, ado*) conmoción *f* • **to cause a ~** causar conmoción • **there was a great ~ in parliament** hubo una gran conmoción en el parlamento • **it didn't make much of a ~** apenas despertó interés alguno
(VT) **1** [+ *liquid etc*] remover, revolver; [+ *fire*] atizar, hurgar • **to ~ sugar into coffee** añadir azúcar al café removiéndolo • **"stir before using"** "agítese antes de usar"
2 (= *move*) mover • **a breeze ~red the leaves** una brisa agitó las hojas • **nothing could ~ him from his chair** no había nada que lo levantara de la silla • **come on, ~ yourself** *or* **your stumps*** ¡venga, muévete!, ¡anda, muévete!
3 (*fig*) [+ *interest*] despertar; [+ *emotions*] provocar, excitar; [+ *imagination*] estimular, avivar • **to ~ sb to pity** causar compasión a algn • **to feel deeply ~red** conmoverse profundamente, estar muy emocionado • **we were all ~red by the speech** el discurso nos conmovió a todos • **to ~ sb to do sth** incitar a algn a hacer algo
(VI) **1** (= *move*) moverse • **she hasn't ~red all day** no se ha movido en todo el día • **don't you ~ from here** no te muevas de aquí • **he never ~red from the spot** no se apartó del lugar ni un momento • **nobody is ~ring yet** están todavía en la cama
2* (= *make trouble*) acizañar, meter cizaña

▸ **stir up** (VT + ADV) **1** [+ *liquid etc*] remover, agitar, revolver; [+ *dust*] levantar
2 (*fig*) [+ *memories*] traer a la memoria; [+ *passions*] provocar, despertar; [+ *revolt*] fomentar; [+ *trouble*] provocar • **to ~ up the past** remover el pasado • **he's always trying to ~ things up** siempre anda provocando

stir²‡ [stɜːʳ] (N) (*esp US*) (= *prison*) chirona‡ *f*

stir-fry [ˈstɜːfraɪ] (VT) sofreír
(N) sofrito *m* (chino)

stirrer* [ˈstɜːrəʳ] (N) (*Brit*) (= *troublemaker*) liante/a *m/f*

stirring [ˈstɜːrɪŋ] (ADJ) [*speech, music*] emocionante, conmovedor
(N) • **I sense no ~ of interest** no creo que esté despertando ningún interés • **there were ~s of protest** la gente empezó a protestar

stirrup [ˈstɪrəp] (N) (*on saddle*) estribo *m*
(CPD) ▸ **stirrup cup** copa *f* del estribo ▸ **stirrup pump** bomba *f* de mano

stitch [stɪtʃ] (N) **1** (*Sew*) puntada *f*, punto *m* • IDIOM: • **she hadn't a ~ on** andaba en cueros *or* (*LAm*) encuerada* • PROVERB: • **a ~ in time saves nine** más vale prevenir que lamentar, una puntada a tiempo ahorra ciento
2 (*Med*) punto *m* de sutura • **to put ~es in a wound** suturar una herida
3 (= *pain*) punto *m*, punzada *f* • **to have a ~** tener flato • IDIOMS: • **we were in ~es*** nos moríamos *or* (*LAm*) partíamos de (la) risa • **she had us all in ~es*** nos hizo partirnos de risa
(VT) **1** (*Sew*) coser • **to ~ (up) a hem** coser un dobladillo
2 (*Med*) suturar • **to ~ (up) a wound** suturar una herida
(VI) (*Sew*) coser

▸ **stitch up** (VT + ADV) **1** (*lit*) ▹ stitch
2* (= *arrange, finalize*) [+ *agreement, deal*] concertar
3‡ (= *frame*) vender*, incriminar dolosamente

stitching [ˈstɪtʃɪŋ] (N) (*Sew*) puntadas *fpl*; (*Med*) puntos *mpl*

stitch-up* [ˈstɪtʃʌp] (N) (*Brit*) montaje* *m*

stoat [stəʊt] (N) armiño *m*

stock [stɒk] (N) **1** (*Comm*) existencias *fpl* • **"offer valid while stocks last"** "oferta válida hasta que se agoten las existencias" • **he sold his father's entire ~ of cloth** vendió todas las existencias de telas que tenía su padre • **to have sth in ~** tener algo en existencia • **check that your size is in ~** compruebe que tengan su talla • **to be out of ~** estar agotado • **camping-gas stoves are out of ~** se han agotado las cocinillas de gas • **to take ~** (= *make inventory*) hacer el inventario; (*fig*) evaluar la situación • **to take ~ of** [+ *situation, prospects*] evaluar; [+ *person*] formarse una opinión sobre
2 (= *supply*) reserva *f* • **~s of ammunition** reservas de municiones • **fish/coal ~s are low** las reservas de peces/carbón escasean • **~s of food were running low** se estaban agotando las provisiones de alimentos • **to get in** *or* **lay in a ~ of sth** abastecerse de algo • **I always keep a ~ of tinned food** siempre estoy bien abastecido de latas de comida; ▹ housing
3 (= *selection*) surtido *m* • **luckily he had a good ~ of books** por suerte tenía un buen surtido de libros • **we have a large ~ of sportswear** tenemos un amplio surtido de ropa deportiva
4 (*Theat*) • **~ of plays** repertorio *m* de obras
5 (*Econ*) (= *capital*) capital *m* social, capital *m* en acciones; (= *shares*) acciones *fpl*; (= *government securities*) bonos *mpl* del estado • **~s and shares** acciones *fpl*
6 (= *status*) prestigio *m* • **his ~ has gone up** *or* **risen (with the public)** ha ganado prestigio (entre el público); ▹ laughing
7 (*Agr*) (= *livestock*) ganado *m* • **breeding ~** ganado de cría
8 (= *descent*) • **people of Mediterranean ~** gentes *fpl* de ascendencia mediterránea • **to be of peasant ~** ser de ascendencia campesina • **to be** *or* **come of good ~** ser de buena cepa
9 (*Culin*) caldo *m* • **beef/chicken ~** caldo de vaca/pollo
10 (*Rail*) (*also* **rolling stock**) material *m* rodante
11 (= *handle*) (*gen*) mango *m*; [*of gun, rifle*] culata *f*
12 (*Bot*) **a** (= *flower*) alhelí *m*
b (= *stem, trunk*) [*of tree*] tronco *m*; [*of vine*] cepa *f*; (= *source of cuttings*) planta *f* madre; (= *plant grafted onto*) patrón *m*
13 stocks: **a** • **the ~s** (*Hist*) el cepo
b (*Naut*) astillero *m*, grada *f* de construcción • **to be on the ~s** [*ship*] estar en vías de construcción; (*fig*) [*piece of work*] estar en preparación • **he has three plays on the ~s** tiene tres obras entre manos
14 (= *tie*) fular *m*
(VT) **1** (= *sell*) [+ *goods*] vender • **do you ~ light bulbs?** ¿vende usted bombillas? • **we don't ~ that brand** no vendemos esa marca • **we ~ a wide range of bicycles** tenemos un gran surtido de bicicletas
2 (= *fill*) [+ *shop*] surtir, abastecer (**with** de); [+ *shelves*] reponer; [+ *library*] surtir, abastecer (**with** de); [+ *farm*] abastecer (**with** con); [+ *freezer, cupboard*] llenar (**with** de); [+ *lake, river*] poblar (**with** de) • **a well ~ed shop/library** una tienda/biblioteca bien surtida • **the lake is ~ed with trout** han poblado el lago de truchas
(ADJ) **1** (*Comm*) [*goods, model*] de serie, estándar • **~ line** línea *f* estándar • **~ size** tamaño *m* estándar
2 (= *standard, hackneyed*) [*argument, joke, response*] típico • **"mind your own business" is her ~ response to such questions** —no es asunto tuyo, es la respuesta típica que da a esas preguntas • **a ~ phrase** una frase hecha
3 (*Theat*) [*play*] de repertorio
4 (*Agr*) (*for breeding*) de cría • **~ mare** yegua *f* de cría
(CPD) ▸ **stock book** libro *m* de almacén, libro *m* existencias ▸ **stock car** (*US*) (*Rail*) vagón *m* para el ganado; (*Aut, Sport*) stock-car *m*; ▹ **stock-car racing** ▸ **stock certificate** certificado *m or* título *m* de acciones ▸ **stock company** sociedad *f* anónima, sociedad *f* de acciones ▸ **stock control** control *m* de existencias ▸ **stock cube** (*Culin*) pastilla *f or* cubito *m* de caldo ▸ **stock dividend** dividendo *m* en acciones ▸ **Stock Exchange** (*Econ*) Bolsa *f* • **to be on the Stock Exchange** [*listed company*] ser cotizado en bolsa • **prices on the Stock Exchange** • **Stock Exchange prices** cotizaciones *fpl* en bolsa ▸ **stock farm** granja *f* para la cría de ganado ▸ **stock farmer** ganadero/a *m/f* ▸ **stock index** índice *m* bursátil ▸ **stock list** (*Econ*) lista *f* de valores y acciones; (*Comm*) lista *f or* inventario *m* de existencias ▸ **stock management** gestión *f* de existencias ▸ **stock market** (*Econ*) bolsa *f*, mercado *m* bursátil • **~ market activity** actividad *f* bursátil ▸ **stock option** (*US*) stock option *f*, opción *f* sobre acciones ▸ **stock option plan** *plan que permite que los ejecutivos de una empresa compren acciones de la misma a un precio especial* ▸ **stock raising** ganadería *f*; ▹ **joint**

▸ **stock up** (VI + ADV) [*shopkeeper*] proveerse de existencias; [*private individual*] abastecerse • **to ~ up on** *or* **with sth** [*shopkeeper*] proveerse de algo; [*private individual*] abastecerse de algo
(VT + ADV) (= *fill*) [+ *larder, cupboard, freezer*] llenar (**with** de); [+ *shelves*] reponer (**with** con)

stockade [stɒˈkeɪd] (N) **1** (= *fencing*) estacada *f*

2 (*US*) (*Mil*) prisión *f* militar
stockbreeder ['stɒkˌbriːdə^r] N ganadero/a *m/f*
stockbreeding ['stɒkˌbriːdɪŋ] N ganadería *f*
stockbroker ['stɒkˌbrəʊkə^r] N corredor(a) *m/f* de Bolsa, bolsista *mf*
CPD ▸ **stockbroker belt** (*Brit*) zona *f* residencial de los bolsistas
stockbroking ['stɒkˌbrəʊkɪŋ] N correduría *f* de bolsa
stock-car racing ['stɒkkɑːˌreɪsɪŋ] N carreras *fpl* de stock-car, carreras *fpl* de choque
stockfish ['stɒkfɪʃ] N pescado *m* de seco
stockholder ['stɒkˌhəʊldə^r] N accionista *mf*
stockholding ['stɒkhəʊldɪŋ] N **1** (*Econ*) tenencia *f* de acciones
2 (*Comm*) (= *storage*) almacenamiento *m*; (= *stock stored*) existencias *fpl*
Stockholm ['stɒkhəʊm] N Estocolmo *m*
stockily ['stɒkɪlɪ] ADV • **~ built** de complexión robusta
stockiness ['stɒkɪnɪs] N robustez *f*
stockinet [ˌstɒkɪ'net] N tela *f* de punto
stocking ['stɒkɪŋ] N media *f*; (*knee-length*) calceta *f* • **a pair of ~s** unas medias, un par de medias
CPD ▸ **stocking(ed) feet** • **in one's ~(ed) feet** sin zapatos ▸ **stocking filler, stocking stuffer** (*US*) pequeño regalo *m* de Navidad
stock-in-trade ['stɒkɪn'treɪd] N (= *tools etc*) existencias *fpl*; (*fig*) repertorio *m* • **that joke is part of his stock-in-trade** es un chiste de su repertorio
stockist ['stɒkɪst] N (*Brit*) distribuidor(a) *m/f*, proveedor(a) *m/f*
stockjobber ['stɒkˌdʒɒbə^r] N (*Brit*) agiotista *mf*
stockjobbing ['stɒkˌdʒɒbɪŋ] N (*Brit*) agiotaje *m*
stockkeeper ['stɒk'kiːpə^r] N almacenero/a *m/f*
stockman ['stɒkmən] N (PL: **stockmen**) (*Agr*) ganadero *m*
stockpile ['stɒkpaɪl] N reservas *fpl*
VT (= *accumulate*) acumular; (= *store*) almacenar
stockpiling ['stɒkˌpaɪlɪŋ] N (= *accumulation*) acumulación *f*; (= *storing*) almacenamiento *m*
stockroom ['stɒkrʊm] N almacén *m*, depósito *m*
stock-still ['stɒk'stɪl] ADV • **to be** *or* **stand stock-still** mantenerse *or* quedarse inmóvil
stocktaking ['stɒkˌteɪkɪŋ] N (*Brit*) inventario *m*, balance *m* • **to do the ~** hacer el inventario
CPD ▸ **stocktaking sale** venta *f* postbalance
stocky ['stɒkɪ] ADJ (COMPAR: **stockier**, SUPERL: **stockiest**) fornido
stockyard ['stɒkjɑːd] N (= *pens etc*) corral *m* de ganado; (*US*) (= *abattoir*) matadero *m*
stodge* [stɒdʒ] N (*Brit*) comida *f* indigesta
stodgy ['stɒdʒɪ] ADJ (COMPAR: **stodgier**, SUPERL: **stodgiest**) **1** [*food*] indigesto
2 (*fig*) [*book, style, person*] pesado
stogie*, stogy* ['stəʊgɪ] N (*US*) cigarro *m*, puro *m*
stoic ['stəʊɪk] ADJ estoico
N estoico *m*
stoical ['stəʊɪkəl] ADJ estoico
stoically ['stəʊɪklɪ] ADV estoicamente, impasiblemente
stoicism ['stəʊɪsɪzəm] N estoicismo *m*
stoke [stəʊk] VT (*also* **stoke up**) **1** [+ *fire, furnace*] atizar
2 (*fig*) [+ *fears, hopes*] cebar
▸ **stoke up** VI + ADV (*lit*) cebar el hogar, echar carbón a la lumbre; (*hum**) (= *eat*) atiborrarse
VT + ADV = **stoke**
stokehold ['stəʊkhəʊld] N cuarto *m* de calderas
stokehole ['stəʊkhəʊl] N boca *f* del horno
stoker ['stəʊkə^r] N fogonero *m*
STOL [stɒl] N ABBR = **short take-off and landing**
stole[1] [stəʊl] N (= *garment*) estola *f*
stole[2] [stəʊl] PT *of* **steal**
stolen ['stəʊlən] PP *of* **steal**
ADJ **1** (*lit*) robado • **~ goods** artículos *mpl* robados • **~ property** bienes *mpl* robados
2 (*fig*) [*moment, pleasures, kisses*] robado
stolid ['stɒlɪd] ADJ impasible, imperturbable; (*pej*) terco
stolidity [stɒ'lɪdɪtɪ] N impasibilidad *f*, imperturbabilidad *f*; (*pej*) terquedad *f*
stolidly ['stɒlɪdlɪ] ADV impasiblemente, imperturbablemente
stomach ['stʌmək] N **1** (= *organ*) estómago *m* • **I've got a pain in my ~** me duele el estómago, tengo dolor de estómago • **it turns my ~** (*lit, fig*) me revuelve el estómago • **he had an upset ~** tenía el estómago revuelto • IDIOM: • **to have no ~ for sth**: • **he had no ~ for another argument with them** no se sentía con ánimos para tener otra discusión con ellos • **they have no ~ for the fight** no tienen agallas para luchar • PROVERB: • **an army marches on its ~** la marcha de un ejército depende del contenido de los estómagos de sus soldados; ▹ **empty, full, sick**
2 (= *belly*) barriga *f* • **to hold one's ~ in** meter estómago • **to lie on one's ~** estar tumbado boca abajo • **I always sleep on my ~** siempre duermo boca abajo
VT **1** (*lit*) [+ *food*] tolerar
2* (*fig*) aguantar, soportar • **I can't ~ the thought of him cheating on her** no aguanto *or* soporto la idea de que la esté engañando • **it was more than I could ~** era inaguantable *or* insoportable
CPD ▸ **stomach ache** dolor *m* de estómago, dolor *m* de barriga ▸ **stomach cramps** retortijones *mpl* de barriga ▸ **stomach disorder** trastorno *m* estomacal ▸ **stomach lining** membrana *f* que recubre las paredes del estómago ▸ **stomach muscle** músculo *m* del abdomen ▸ **stomach pump** bomba *f* gástrica ▸ **stomach stapling** grapado *m* de estómago ▸ **stomach ulcer** úlcera *f* gástrica ▸ **stomach upset** trastorno *m* estomacal • **to have a ~ upset** tener un trastorno estomacal ▸ **stomach wall** pared *f* del estómago ▸ **stomach wound** herida *f* estomacal
stomach-churning ['stʌmək,tʃɜːnɪŋ] ADJ de revolver el estómago
stomach-stapling surgery [ˌstʌmək'steɪplɪŋˌsɜːdʒərɪ] N grapado *m* de estómago
stomp [stɒmp] VI dar patadas • **to ~ in/out** entrar/salir dando fuertes pisotones
VT (*US*) = **stamp**
stone [stəʊn] N **1** (*gen*) piedra *f*; (= *gravestone*) lápida *f*; (= *gemstone*) piedra *f*, gema *f* • IDIOMS: • **a ~'s throw away** • **within a ~'s throw** a un tiro de piedra • **to cast the first ~** lanzar la primera piedra • **which of you shall cast the first ~?** ¿cuál de vosotros se atreve a lanzar la primera piedra? • **to leave no ~ unturned** no dejar piedra por mover • **it isn't cast** *or* **set in ~** no es inamovible, no es para toda la vida
2 (*Brit*) [*of fruit*] hueso *m*
3 (*Med*) cálculo *m*, piedra *f*; (*as complaint*) mal *m* de piedra
4 (*Brit*) (= *weight*) 6.350kg • **he weighs 12 ~(s)** pesa 76 kilos; ▹ IMPERIAL SYSTEM
VT **1** [+ *person*] apedrear, lapidar • IDIOMS: • **~ me!‡** • **~ the crows!*** ¡caray!*
2 [+ *fruit*] deshuesar
CPD de piedra ▸ **the Stone Age** la Edad de Piedra ▸ **stone circle** (*Brit*) círculo *m* de piedra, crómlech *m* ▸ **stone pit, stone quarry** cantera *f*
stone-blind ['stəʊn'blaɪnd] ADJ completamente ciego
stone-broke* ['stəʊn'brəʊk] ADJ (*US*) = **stony-broke**
stonechat ['stəʊntʃæt] N culiblanco *m*
stone-cold [ˌstəʊn'kəʊld] ADJ como un témpano • **to be stone-cold sober*** estar completamente sobrio
stonecrop ['stəʊnkrɒp] N uva *f* de gato
stonecutter ['stəʊnˌkʌtə^r] N = **stonemason**
stoned‡ [stəʊnd] ADJ (*on drugs*) colocado*; (= *drunk*) borracho
stone-dead ['stəʊn'ded] ADJ tieso • **it killed the idea stone-dead** dio completamente al traste con la idea
stone-deaf ['stəʊn'def] ADJ sordo como una tapia, sordo del todo
stoneground ['stəʊnˌgraʊnd] ADJ [*flour*] molido por piedras
stonemason ['stəʊnˌmeɪsn] N albañil *mf*; (*in quarry*) cantero *m*
stoner‡ ['stəʊnə^r] N porrero/a *m/f*
stonewall ['stəʊn'wɔːl] VI **1** (*Sport*) jugar a la defensiva
2 (*in answering questions*) negarse a contestar
stonewalling ['stəʊn'wɔːlɪŋ] N táctica *f* de cerrojo
stoneware ['stəʊnwɛə^r] N gres *m*
ADJ de gres
stonewashed ['stəʊnˌwɒʃt] ADJ [*jeans*] lavado a la piedra
stonework ['stəʊnwɜːk] N cantería *f*
stonily ['stəʊnɪlɪ] ADV (*fig*) glacialmente, fríamente
stoning ['stəʊnɪŋ] N lapidación *f*
stonking‡ ['stɒŋkɪŋ] ADJ (*Brit*) cojonudo‡, de puta madre‡
stony ['stəʊnɪ] ADJ (COMPAR: **stonier**, SUPERL: **stoniest**) **1** [*ground, beach*] pedregoso; [*material*] pétreo
2 (*fig*) [*glance, silence*] glacial, frío; [*heart*] empedernido; [*stare*] duro
stony-broke* ['stəʊnɪ'brəʊk] ADJ • **to be stony-broke** (*Brit*) estar sin un duro*, estar pelado*, estar sin un peso (*LAm**)
stony-faced [ˌstəʊnɪ'feɪst] ADJ de expresión pétrea
stony-hearted ['stəʊnɪ'hɑːtɪd] ADJ de corazón empedernido
stood [stʊd] PT, PP *of* **stand**
stooge [stuːdʒ] N [*of comedian*] compañero/a *m/f*; (= *lackey**) secuaz *mf*, siervo/a *m/f*
VI • **to ~ for sb*** servir humildemente a algn
▸ **stooge about*, stooge around*** VI + ADV estar por ahí
stook [stuːk] N tresnal *m*, garbera *f*
VT poner en tresnales
stool [stuːl] N **1** (= *seat*) taburete *m*, escabel *m*; (*folding*) silla *f* de tijera • IDIOM: • **to fall between two ~s** quedarse sin lo uno y sin lo otro, quedarse nadando entre dos aguas y no llegar a ningún lado
2 (*Med*) (= *faeces*) deposición *f*
3 (*Bot*) planta *f* madre
CPD ▸ **stool pigeon*** (= *informer*) chivato/a* *m/f*, soplón/ona* *m/f*; (= *decoy*) señuelo *m*
stoop[1] [stuːp] N • **to have a ~** ser un poco encorvado • **to walk with a ~** andar encorvado
VI **1** (= *bend*) (*also* **stoop down**) inclinarse,

S

agacharse; (*permanently, as defect*) andar encorvado • **to ~ to pick sth up** inclinarse para recoger algo
2 (*fig*) • **to ~ to sth/doing sth** rebajarse a algo/hacer algo • **I wouldn't ~ so low!** ¡a eso no llegaría!, ¡no me rebajaría tanto!

stoop² [stu:p] N (*US*) (= *verandah*) pórtico *m*, pequeña veranda *f*

stooping ['stu:pɪŋ] ADJ encorvado

stop [stɒp] N **1** (= *halt*) parada *f*, alto *m* • **to be at a ~** [+ *vehicle*] estar parado; [+ *production, process*] quedar paralizado • **to bring to a ~** [+ *vehicle*] parar, detener; [+ *production, process*] paralizar, interrumpir • **to come to a ~** [*vehicle*] parar(se), detenerse; [*production, progress*] interrumpirse • **to come to a dead** *or* **sudden ~** pararse en seco, detenerse repentinamente • **to come to a full ~** [*negotiations, discussions*] paralizarse, quedar detenido en un punto muerto • **to put a ~ to sth** poner fin *or* término a algo, acabar con algo
2 (= *break, pause*) descanso *m*, pausa *f*; (*overnight*) estancia *f*, estadía *f* (*LAm*), estada *f* (*LAm*); (*for refuelling*) escala *f* • **a ~ for coffee** un descanso para tomar café • **to make a ~ at Bordeaux** hacer escala en Burdeos • **a ~ of a few days** una estancia de unos días • **without a ~** sin parar
3 (= *stopping place*) (*for bus etc*) parada *f*; (*Aer, Naut*) escala *f*
4 (*Typ*) (*also* **full stop**) punto *m*
5 (*Mus*) (*on organ*) registro *m*; [*of guitar*] traste *m*; [*of other instrument*] llave *f* • IDIOM: • **to pull out all the ~s** tocar todos los registros
6 (*Mech*) tope *m*, retén *m*
7 (*Phon*) (*also* **stop consonant**) (consonante *f*) oclusiva *f*
VT **1** (= *block*) [+ *hole*] tapar; [+ *leak, flow of blood*] restañar; [+ *tooth*] empastar • **to ~ one's ears** taparse los oídos • **to ~ a gap** tapar un agujero; (*fig*) llenar un vacío • **the curtains ~ the light** las cortinas impiden la entrada de la luz • **the walls ~ some of the noise** las paredes absorben parte del ruido
2 (= *arrest movement of*) [+ *runaway engine, car*] detener, parar; [+ *blow, punch*] parar • IDIOM: • **to ~ a bullet*** (= *be shot*) ser disparado *or* (*LAm*) baleado
3 (= *put an end to*) [+ *rumour, abuse, activity, injustice*] poner fin a, poner término a, acabar con; [+ *conversation*] interrumpir, suspender; [+ *aggression*] rechazar, contener; [+ *production*] (*permanently*) terminar; (*temporarily*) interrumpir
4 (= *prevent*) evitar; (= *forbid*) prohibir, poner fin a • **this should ~ any further trouble** esto debería evitar cualquier dificultad en el futuro • **to ~ sth (from) happening** evitar que algo ocurra • **to ~ sb (from) doing sth** (= *prevent*) impedir a algn hacer algo, impedir que algn haga algo; (= *forbid*) prohibir a algn hacer algo, prohibir a algn que haga algo • **can't you ~ him?** ¿no le puedes impedir que lo haga? • **there is nothing to ~ him** y no hay nada que se lo impida • **to ~ o.s. (from doing sth)** abstenerse (de hacer algo) • **I can't seem to ~ myself doing it** parece que no puedo dejar de hacerlo • **I ~ped myself in time** me detuve a tiempo
5 (= *cease*) • **to ~ doing sth** dejar de hacer algo • **~ it!** ¡basta ya! • **I just can't ~ it** (= *help it*) ¡qué remedio!, ¡qué le vamos a hacer! • **~ that noise!** ¡basta ya de ruido! • **~ that nonsense!** ¡déjate de tonterías! • **it has ~ped raining** ha dejado de llover, ya no llueve • **I'm trying to ~ smoking** estoy intentando dejar de fumar • **she never ~s talking** habla sin parar • **to ~ work** dejar de trabajar
6 (= *suspend*) [+ *payments, wages, subscription*] suspender; [+ *cheque*] invalidar; [+ *supply*] cortar, interrumpir • **to ~ sb's electricity** cortar la electricidad a algn • **all leave is ~ped** han sido cancelados todos los permisos • **to ~ the milk for a fortnight** (*Brit*) pedir al lechero que no traiga leche durante quince días • **to ~ sb's wages** suspender el pago del sueldo de algn • **to ~ ten pounds from sb's wages** retener diez libras del sueldo de algn
VI **1** (= *stop moving*) [*person, vehicle*] pararse, detenerse; [*clock, watch*] pararse • **the car ~ped** se paró el coche • **where does the bus ~?** ¿dónde para el autobús? • **the clock has ~ped** el reloj se ha parado • **stop!** ¡pare! • **~, thief!** ¡al ladrón!
2 (= *pause, take a break*) parar, hacer alto • **to ~ to do sth** detenerse a hacer algo • **without ~ping** sin parar
3 (= *cease, come to an end*) terminar, acabar(se); [*supply etc*] cortarse, interrumpirse; [*process, rain etc*] terminar, cesar • **payments have ~ped** (*temporarily*) se han suspendido los pagos; (*permanently*) han terminado los pagos • **when the programme ~s** cuando termine el programa • **the rain has ~ped** ha dejado de llover • **he seems not to know when to ~** parece no saber cuándo conviene hacer alto • IDIOM: • **to ~ at nothing (to do sth)** no detenerse ante nada (para hacer algo)
4* (= *stay*) • **to ~ (at/with)** hospedarse *or* alojarse (con) • **she's ~ping with her aunt** se hospeda en casa de su tía • **I'm not ~ping** no me quedo • **did you ~ till the end?** ¿te quedaste hasta el final?
CPD ▸ **stop button** botón *m* de parada ▸ **stop press** noticias *fpl* de última hora • **"stop press"** (*as heading*) "al cierre de la edición" ▸ **stop sign** (*Aut*) stop *m*, señal *f* de stop

▸ **stop away*** VI + ADV ausentarse (from de), no asistir (from a)

▸ **stop behind*** VI + ADV quedarse • **they made him ~ behind after school** le hicieron quedar en la escuela después de las clases

▸ **stop by*** VI + ADV detenerse brevemente • **I'll ~ by on the way to school** me asomaré de paso al colegio
VI + PREP • **I'll ~ by your place later** pasaré por tu casa más tarde

▸ **stop in*** VI + ADV quedarse en casa, no salir • **don't ~ in for me** no te quedes esperándome en casa

▸ **stop off** VI + ADV interrumpir el viaje • **to ~ off at** (= *drop by*) pasar por; (= *stop at*) parar en

▸ **stop out*** VI + ADV (= *remain outside*) quedarse fuera; (= *not come home*) no volver a casa

▸ **stop over** VI + ADV (= *stay the night*) pasar la noche; (*Aer*) (*for refuelling etc*) hacer escala

▸ **stop up** VT + ADV [+ *hole*] tapar
VI + ADV (*Brit**) velar, no acostarse, seguir sin acostarse • **don't ~ up for me** no os quedéis esperándome hasta muy tarde

stop-and-go ['stɒpən'gəʊ] N (*US*) = **stop-go**

stopcock ['stɒpkɒk] N llave *f* de paso

stopgap ['stɒpgæp] N (= *thing*) recurso *m* provisional, expediente *m*; (= *person*) sustituto/a *m/f*
CPD ▸ **stopgap measure** medida *f* provisional

stop-go ['stɒp'gəʊ] N (*Brit*) • **period of stop-go** periodo *m* cuando una política de expansión económica alterna con otra de restricción

stoplight ['stɒplaɪt] N **1** (= *brakelight*) luz *f* de freno
2 (*esp US*) (= *traffic light*) semáforo *m* rojo

stop-off ['stɒpɒf] N = **stopover**

stopover ['stɒpəʊvəʳ] N (*Aer*) escala *f*

stoppage ['stɒpɪdʒ] N **1** [*of work*] paro *m*, suspensión *f*; (= *strike*) huelga *f*
2 [*of pay*] suspensión *f*; (*from wages*) deducción *f*
3 (*Sport*) detención *f*
4 (*in pipe etc*) obstrucción *f*
CPD ▸ **stoppage time** (*Sport*) tiempo *m* de descuento

stopper ['stɒpəʳ] N tapón *m*; (*Tech*) taco *m*, tarugo *m*
VT tapar, taponar

stopping ['stɒpɪŋ] N **1** (= *halting*) [*of activity, progress, process*] suspensión *f*, interrupción *f*; [*of vehicle*] detención *f*, parada *f*; [*of cheque, wages*] bloqueo *m*, retención *f*; [*of match, game, payment*] suspensión *f*; [*of allowance, leave, privileges*] retirada *f*
2 (= *filling*) [*of tooth*] empaste *m*
3 (= *blocking*) [*of hole, pipe, leak*] relleno *m*, sellado *m*
CPD ▸ **stopping place** paradero *m*; [*of bus*] parada *f* ▸ **stopping train** tren *m* correo, tren *m* ómnibus

stopwatch ['stɒpwɒtʃ] N cronómetro *m*

storage ['stɔ:rɪdʒ] N almacenaje *m*, almacenamiento *m*; (*Comput*) almacenamiento *m* • **to put sth into ~** (*in a warehouse*) almacenar algo; (*furniture*) llevar algo a un guardamuebles
CPD ▸ **storage battery** acumulador *m* ▸ **storage capacity** capacidad *f* de almacenaje ▸ **storage charges** derechos *mpl* de almacenaje ▸ **storage heater** acumulador *m* ▸ **storage room** (*US*) trastero *m* ▸ **storage space** lugar *m* para los trastos ▸ **storage tank** (*for oil etc*) tanque *m* de almacenamiento; (*for rainwater*) tanque *m* de reserva ▸ **storage unit** (= *furniture*) armario *m*

store [stɔ:ʳ] N **1** (= *supply, stock*) **a** [*of food, candles, paper*] reserva *f* • **to have** *or* **keep sth in ~** tener algo en reserva • **to keep a ~ of sth** tener una reserva de algo • **to lay in a ~ of sth** hacer una reserva de algo, proveerse de algo
b (*fig*) [*of jokes, stories*] repertorio *m*; [*of information*] cúmulo *m* • **he has a vast ~ of dirty jokes** tiene un repertorio enorme de chistes verdes • **he possessed a vast ~ of knowledge** tenía una cultura muy amplia • **the company has a great ~ of expertise** la compañía cuenta con una multitud de gente competente • **to be in ~ for sb** (*fig*) aguardar a algn • **you never know what's in ~ (for you)** nunca se sabe lo que le aguarda a uno • **little did I know what the future had in ~** qué poco sabía lo que nos deparaba el futuro • **there's a surprise in ~ for you!** ¡te espera una sorpresa! • **to set great/little ~ by sth** tener algo en mucho/poco, dar mucho/poco valor a algo • **I wouldn't set much ~ by that** yo no le daría mucho valor
2 (= *depository*) almacén *m*, depósito *m* • **to put sth in(to) ~** (*in a warehouse*) almacenar algo; (*in a furniture store*) llevar algo a un guardamuebles • **to be in ~** (*in a warehouse*) estar en un almacén; (*in a furniture store*) estar en un guardamuebles • **furniture ~** guardamuebles *m inv*
3 stores (= *provisions*) provisiones *fpl*, existencias *fpl*; (*esp Mil*) (= *equipment*) pertrechos *mpl*
4 (= *shop*) **a** (*esp US*) [*of any size*] tienda *f* • **record ~** tienda *f* de discos • **book ~** librería *f* • **hardware ~** ferretería *f* • IDIOM: • **to mind the ~** (*US**) cuidar de los asuntos;

▸ **grocery, village**
b (*also* **department store**) grandes almacenes *mpl* • **he owns a ~ in Oxford Street** es propietario de unos grandes almacenes en Oxford Street; ▸ **chain, department**
VT **1** (= *keep, collect*) **a** (*gen*) [+ *food*] conservar, guardar; [+ *water, fuel, electricity*] almacenar; [+ *heat*] acumular; [+ *documents*] archivar • **~ in an airtight tin** consérvense en un frasco hermético • **avoid storing food for too long** evite tener la comida guardada durante mucho tiempo
b (*Comput*) [+ *information*] almacenar, guardar; (*Physiol*) [+ *fat, energy*] almacenar, acumular • **where in the brain do we ~ information about colours?** ¿en qué parte del cerebro almacenamos *or* guardamos información sobre los colores?
2 (= *put away*) guardar • **I've got the camping things ~d (away) till we need them** tengo las cosas de acampar guardadas hasta que las necesitemos
3 (= *put in depository*) [+ *furniture*] depositar en un guardamuebles; [+ *goods, crop, waste*] almacenar
VI conservarse • **fruits which won't ~ (well)** fruta que no se conserva (bien)
CPD ▸ **store card** tarjeta *f* de compra ▸ **store clerk** (*US*) dependiente/a *m/f* ▸ **store cupboard** despensa *f* ▸ **store detective** vigilante *mf* jurado (*de paisano en grandes almacenes*) ▸ **store manager** gerente *mf* de tienda (*de grandes almacenes*) ▸ **store window** (*US*) escaparate *m*, vitrina *f*, vidriera *f* (*S. Cone*)
▸ **store away** VT + ADV (*in bulk*) almacenar; [+ *individual items*] guardar
▸ **store up** VT + ADV [+ *fat, energy*] almacenar, acumular; [+ *feelings, bitterness, memories*] acumular, ir acumulando • **a hatred ~d up over centuries** un odio acumulado durante siglos • **to ~ up trouble** *or* **problems for the future** ir acumulando problemas para el futuro
store-bought [ˈstɔːbɔːt] ADJ (*US*) de confección, de serie
storefront [ˈstɔːfrʌnt] N (*US*) escaparate *m*
storehouse [ˈstɔːhaʊs] N (PL: **storehouses** [ˈstɔːhaʊzɪz]) almacén *m*, depósito *m*; (*fig*) mina *f*, tesoro *m*
storekeeper [ˈstɔːˌkiːpəʳ] N
1 (= *warehouseman*) almacenero *m*
2 (*US*) (= *shopkeeper*) tendero/a *m/f*
3 (*Naut*) pañolero *m*
storeroom [ˈstɔːrʊm] N despensa *f*; (*Naut*) pañol *m*
storey, story (*US*) [ˈstɔːrɪ] N piso *m*
-storey, -story (*US*) [ˈstɔːrɪ] ADJ (*ending in compounds*) • **a nine-storey building** un edificio de nueve pisos *or* plantas
-storeyed, -storied (*US*) [ˈstɔːrɪd] ADJ (*ending in compounds*) • **an eight-storeyed building** un edificio de ocho pisos
stork [stɔːk] N cigüeña *f*
storm [stɔːm] N **1** (*gen*) tormenta *f*, tempestad *f*; (= *gale*) vendaval *m*; (= *hurricane*) huracán *m*; (*Naut*) borrasca *f*, tormenta *f*
• IDIOMS: • **to brave the ~** aguantar la tempestad • **to ride out a ~** capear un temporal, hacer frente a un temporal
2 (= *uproar*) escándalo *m*, bronca *f* • **there was a political ~** hubo un gran revuelo político • **it caused an international ~** levantó una polvareda internacional • **a ~ of abuse** un torrente de injurias • **a ~ of applause** una salva de aplausos • **a ~ of criticism** un aluvión *or* vendaval de críticas • IDIOM: • **a ~ in a teacup** (*Brit*) una tormenta *or* tempestad en un vaso de agua
3 • **to take by ~: to take a town by ~** (*Mil*) tomar una ciudad por asalto • **the play took Paris by ~** la obra cautivó a todo París
VT (*Mil*) asaltar, tomar por asalto • **angry ratepayers ~ed the town hall** los contribuyentes enfurecidos asaltaron *or* invadieron el ayuntamiento
VI **1** (= *move angrily*) • **he came ~ing into my office** entró en mi despacho echando pestes • **he ~ed out of the meeting** salió de la reunión como un huracán
2 (= *speak angrily*) bramar, vociferar • **"you're fired!" he ~ed** —¡quedá despedido! —bramó *or* vociferó • **to ~ at sb** tronar contra algn, enfurecerse con algn • **he ~ed on for an hour about the government** pasó una hora lanzando improperios contra el gobierno
CPD ▸ **storm centre, storm center** (*US*) centro *m* de la tempestad; (*fig*) foco *m* de los disturbios, centro *m* de la agitación ▸ **storm cloud** nubarrón *m* ▸ **storm damage** daños *mpl* causados por temporales ▸ **storm door** contrapuerta *f* ▸ **storm signal** señal *f* de temporal ▸ **storm trooper** (*Mil*) guardia *mf* de asalto ▸ **storm troops** (*Mil*) tropas *fpl* de asalto, guardia *fsing* de asalto ▸ **storm window** contraventana *f*
stormbound [ˈstɔːmbaʊnd] ADJ inmovilizado por el mal tiempo
storminess [ˈstɔːmɪnɪs] N [*of relationship*] lo tormentoso; [*of reaction, temper*] lo violento • **the ~ of the weather** lo tormentoso del tiempo • **the ~ of his reception** la tempestuosidad de tu recibimiento
storming [ˈstɔːmɪŋ] (= *impressive*) arrollador, arrasador N (*Mil etc*) asalto *m* (**of a**)
stormproof [ˈstɔːmpruːf] ADJ a prueba de tormentas
storm-tossed [ˈstɔːmtɒst] ADJ sacudido por la tempestad
stormwater [ˈstɔːmˌwɔːtəʳ] N agua *f* de lluvia
stormy [ˈstɔːmɪ] ADJ (COMPAR: **stormier**, SUPERL: **stormiest**) **1** (*lit*) [*weather, night, skies*] tormentoso • **it's ~** hay tormenta
2 (*fig*) (= *turbulent*) [*meeting, scene*] tumultuoso, turbulento; [*relationship*] tormentoso
CPD ▸ **stormy petrel** (*Orn*) petrel *m* de la tempestad; (*fig*) persona *f* pendenciera, persona *f* de vida borrascosa
story¹ [ˈstɔːrɪ] N **1** (= *account*) historia *f*; (= *tale*) cuento *m*, relato *m*; (= *joke*) chiste *m* • **his ~ is that …** según él dice …, según lo que él cuenta … • **but that's another ~** pero eso es otro cantar • **a children's ~** un cuento infantil • **the ~ goes that …** se dice *or* se cuenta que … • **the ~ of her life** la historia de su vida • **that's the ~ of my life!*** ¡siempre me pasa lo mismo! • **it's a long ~** es/sería largo de contar • **to cut a long ~ short** en resumidas cuentas, en pocas palabras • **it's the same old ~** es la historia de siempre • **to tell a ~** (*fictional*) contar un cuento; (= *recount what happened*) contar *or* narrar una historia • **the marks tell their own ~** las señales hablan por sí solas, las señales no necesitan interpretación • **the full ~ has still to be told** todavía no se ha hecho pública toda la historia • **what a ~ this house could tell!** ¡cuántas cosas nos diría esta casa! • **the ~ of their travels** la relación de sus viajes • **that's not the whole ~** eso no es todo
2 (= *plot*) argumento *m*, trama *f*
3 (*Press*) artículo *m*, reportaje *m*
4 (*euph*) (= *lie*) mentira *f*, cuento *m* • **a likely ~!** ¡puro cuento! • **to tell stories** (*lies*) contar embustes
CPD ▸ **story writer** narrador(a) *m/f*
story² [ˈstɔːrɪ] N (*US*) = **storey**
storyboard [ˈstɔːrɪˌbɔːd] (*Cine*) N story board *m*, desarrollo *m* secuencial en viñetas
VT hacer el story board de, hacer el desarrollo secuencial en viñetas de
storybook [ˈstɔːrɪbʊk] N libro *m* de cuentos
ADJ • **a ~ ending** un final como el de una novela
storyline [ˈstɔːrɪlaɪn] N argumento *m*
storyteller [ˈstɔːrɪˌteləʳ] N **1** (*gen*) cuentista *mf*
2* (= *liar*) cuentista *mf*, embustero/a *m/f*
storytelling [ˈstɔːrɪˌtelɪŋ] N (*spoken*) cuentacuentos *m*; (*written*) historias *fpl*
stoup [stuːp] N copa *f*, frasco *m*; (*Rel*) pila *f*
stout [staʊt] ADJ (COMPAR: **stouter**, SUPERL: **stoutest**) **1** (= *sturdy*) [*stick, shoes etc*] fuerte, sólido
2 (= *fat*) [*person*] gordo, robusto
3 (= *determined*) [*supporter, resistance*] resuelto, empedernido • **~ fellow!**† ¡muy bien! • **he's a ~ fellow**† es un buen chico • **with ~ hearts** resueltamente
N (*Brit*) (= *beer*) cerveza *f* negra
stout-hearted [ˈstaʊtˈhɑːtɪd] ADJ valiente, resuelto
stoutly [ˈstaʊtlɪ] ADV **1** • **~ built** de construcción sólida, fuerte
2 [*deny*] categóricamente, rotundamente; [*resist*] tenazmente • **he ~ maintains that …** sostiene resueltamente que …
stoutness [ˈstaʊtnɪs] N gordura *f*, corpulencia *f*
stove¹ [stəʊv] N (*for heating*) estufa *f*; (*for cooking*) cocina *f*, horno *m* (*LAm*)
stove² [stəʊv] ▸ **stave in**
stovepipe [ˈstəʊvpaɪp] N tubo *m* de estufa
CPD ▸ **stovepipe hat** chistera *f*
stow [stəʊ] VT **1** (*Naut*) [+ *cargo*] estibar, arrumar
2 (= *put away*) guardar • **where can I ~ this?** ¿esto dónde lo pongo? • **~ it!‡** ¡déjate de eso!, ¡cállate!, ¡basta ya!
▸ **stow away** VT + ADV (= *put away*) guardar; (= *hide*) esconder • **to ~ food away*** (*fig*) despachar rápidamente una comida, zamparse una comida
VI + ADV (*on ship, plane*) viajar de polizón
stowage [ˈstəʊɪdʒ] N (= *act*) estiba *f*, arrumaje *m*; (= *place*) bodega *f*
stowaway [ˈstəʊəweɪ] N polizón *m*, llovido *m*
strabismus [strəˈbɪzməs] N estrabismo *m*
Strabo [ˈstreɪbəʊ] N Estrabón
straddle [ˈstrædl] VT [+ *horse*] montar a horcajadas, ponerse a horcajadas sobre; [+ *target*] horquillar; [*town*] [+ *river etc*] hacer puente sobre
strafe [strɑːf] VT ametrallar, abalear (*LAm*)
strafing [ˈstrɑːfɪŋ] N ametrallamiento *m*
straggle [ˈstrægl] VI **1** (= *lag behind*) rezagarse • **the guests ~d out into the night** los invitados salieron poco a poco y desaparecieron en la noche • **as the last runners ~d over the finishing line …** a medida que iban cruzando la meta los últimos corredores …
2 (= *spread untidily*) (*Bot*) lozanear; [*hair*] caer lacio • **the village ~s on for miles** el pueblo se extiende varios kilómetros (sin tener un plano fijo) • **her hair ~s over her face** el pelo le cae lacio delante de la cara
▸ **straggle away, straggle off** VI + ADV dispersarse
straggler [ˈstrægləʳ] N rezagado/a *m/f*
straggling [ˈstræglɪŋ], **straggly** [ˈstræglɪ] ADJ [*town*] disperso; [*plants*] extendido; [*hair*] despeinado, desordenado
straight [streɪt] ADJ (COMPAR: **straighter**, SUPERL: **straightest**) **1** (= *not bent or curved*) [*line, road, nose, skirt*] recto; [*trousers*] de

S

perneras estrechas, de pata estrecha*; [*hair*] lacio, liso; [*shoulders*] erguido, recto • **he couldn't even walk in a ~ line** ni siquiera podía caminar en línea recta • **she was keeping the boat on a ~ course** mantenía el barco navegando en línea recta • **to have a ~ back** tener la espalda erguida *or* recta • **I couldn't keep a ~ face** • **I couldn't keep my face ~** no podía mantener la cara seria • **she said it with a completely ~ face** lo dijo con la cara totalmente seria
2 (= *not askew*) [*picture, rug, hat, hem*] derecho • **the picture isn't ~** el cuadro está torcido *or* (*LAm*) chueco • **your tie isn't ~** tienes la corbata torcida, tu corbata no está bien • **to put** *or* **set ~** [+ *picture, hat, tie, rug*] poner derecho
3 (= *honest, direct*) [*answer*] franco, directo; [*question*] directo; [*refusal, denial*] categórico, rotundo • **all I want is a ~ answer to a ~ question** lo único que pido es que respondas con franqueza a una pregunta directa • **it's time for some ~ talking** es hora de hablar con franqueza *or* claramente • **to be ~ with sb** ser franco con algn, hablar a algn con toda franqueza • IDIOM: • **as ~ as a die** honrado a carta cabal
4 (= *unambiguous*) claro • **is that ~?** ¿está claro? • **to get sth ~**: • **let's get that ~ right from the start** vamos a dejar eso claro desde el principio • **there are a couple of things we'd better get ~** hay un par de cosas que debemos dejar claras • **have you got that ~?** ¿lo has entendido?, ¿está claro? • **he had to get things ~ in his mind** tenía que aclararse las ideas • **he hasn't got his facts ~** no tiene la información correcta • **to put** *or* **set sth ~** aclarar algo • **to put** *or* **set things** *or* **matters ~** aclarar las cosas • **to put** *or* **set the record ~** aclarar las cosas • **he soon put** *or* **set me ~** enseguida me aclaró las cosas
5 (= *tidy, in order*) [*house, room*] arreglado, ordenado; [*books, affairs, accounts*] en orden • **I like to keep my house ~** me gusta tener la casa arreglada *or* ordenada • **the paperwork still isn't ~** los papeles no están todavía en orden • **to get** *or* **put sth ~** arreglar algo
6 (= *clear-cut, simple*) [*choice, swap*] simple • **her latest novel is ~ autobiography** su última novela es una simple autobiografía • **we made £50 ~ profit on the deal** sacamos 50 libras limpias del negocio • **a ~ cash offer** una oferta de dinero en mano
7 (= *consecutive*) [*victories, defeats, games*] consecutivo • **this is the fifth ~ year that she has won** este es el quinto año consecutivo en el que ha ganado • **to get ~ As** sacar sobresaliente en todo • **a ~ flush** (*in poker*) una escalera real • **she lost in ~ sets to Pat Hay** (*in tennis*) perdió contra Pat Hay sin ganar ningún set • **we had ten ~ wins** ganamos diez veces seguidas, tuvimos diez victorias consecutivas
8 (= *neat*) [*whisky, vodka*] solo
9 (*Theat*) (= *not comic*) [*part, play, theatre, actor*] dramático, serio
10* (= *conventional*) [*person*] de cabeza cuadrada* • **she's a nice person, but very ~** es maja pero tiene la cabeza demasiado cuadrada*
11* (= *not owed or owing money*) • **if I give you a fiver, then we'll be ~** si te doy cinco libras, estamos en paz
12* (= *heterosexual*) heterosexual, hetero*
13* (= *not criminal*) [*person*] • **he's been ~ for two years** ha llevado una vida honrada durante dos años
14‡ (= *not using drugs*) • **I've been ~ for 13 years** hace 13 años que dejé las drogas, llevo 13 años desenganchado de las drogas
(ADV) **1** (= *in a straight line*) [*walk, shoot, fly*] en línea recta; [*grow*] recto • **they can't even shoot ~** ni siquiera saben disparar en línea recta • **he was sitting up very ~** estaba sentado muy derecho *or* erguido • **stand up ~!** ¡ponte derecho *or* erguido! • **~ above us** directamente encima de nosotros • **it's ~ across the road from us** está justo al otro lado de la calle • **to go ~ ahead** ir todo recto, ir todo derecho • **to look ~ ahead** mirar al frente, mirar hacia adelante • **~ ahead of us** justo en frente de nosotros • **to look ~ at sb** mirar derecho hacia algn • **he came ~ at me** vino derecho hacia mí • **to hold o.s. ~** mantenerse derecho • **to look sb ~ in the eye** mirar directamente a los ojos de algn • **to look sb ~ in the face** mirar a algn directamente a la cara • **to go ~ on** ir todo recto, ir todo derecho • **the bullet went ~ through his chest** la bala le atravesó limpiamente el pecho • **I saw a car coming ~ towards me** vi un coche que venía derecho hacia mí • **to look ~ up** mirar hacia arriba • **the cork shot ~ up in the air** el corcho salió disparado hacia arriba
2 (= *level*) • **to hang ~** [*picture*] estar derecho • **the picture isn't hanging ~** el cuadro está torcido *or* (*LAm*) chueco
3 (= *directly*) directamente; (= *immediately*) inmediatamente • **youngsters who move ~ from school onto the dole queue** jóvenes que pasan directamente del colegio a la cola del paro • **I went ~ home/to bed** fui derecho a casa/a la cama • **come ~ back** vuelve directamente aquí • **to come ~ to the point** ir al grano • **to drink ~ from the bottle** beber de la botella • **~ after this** inmediatamente después de esto • **~ away** inmediatamente, en seguida, al tiro (*Chile*) • **~ off** (= *without hesitation*) sin vacilar; (= *immediately*) inmediatamente; (= *directly*) directamente, sin rodeos • **she just went ~ off** se marchó sin detenerse • IDIOM: • **I heard it ~ from the horse's mouth** se lo oí decir a él mismo (*or* a ella misma)
4 (= *frankly*) francamente, con franqueza • **just give it to me** *or* **tell me ~** dímelo francamente *or* con franqueza • **to tell sb sth ~ out** decir algo a algn sin rodeos *or* directamente • **~ up** (*Brit**) en serio • IDIOM: • **~ from the shoulder**: • **I let him have it ~ from the shoulder** se lo dije sin rodeos
5 (= *neat*) [*drink*] solo • **I prefer to drink whisky ~** prefiero tomar el whisky solo
6 (= *clearly*) [*think*] con claridad • **he was so frightened that he couldn't think ~** tenía tanto miedo que no podía pensar con claridad • **I was so drunk I couldn't see ~** estaba tan borracho que no veía
7* • **to go ~** (= *reform*) [*criminal*] enmendarse; [*drug addict*] dejar de tomar drogas, desengancharse • **he's been going ~ for a year now** [*ex-criminal*] hace ahora un año que lleva una vida honrada; [*ex-addict*] hace un año que dejó las drogas, lleva un año desenganchado de las drogas
8 (*Theat*) • **he played the role ~** interpretó el papel de manera clásica
9 (= *consecutively*) • **we worked on the harvest for three days ~** hicimos la cosecha durante tres días seguidos
(N) **1** (= *straight line*) • **to cut sth on the ~** cortar algo derecho • IDIOM: • **the ~ and narrow** el buen camino • **to keep to the ~ and narrow** ir por buen camino • **to keep sb on the ~ and narrow** mantener a algn por el buen camino • **to depart from the ~ and narrow** apartarse del buen camino
2 (*Brit*) (*on racecourse*) • **the ~** la recta • **as the cars entered the final ~ Hill was in the lead** cuando los coches entraron en la recta final Hill iba a la cabeza
3 (*Cards*) runfla *f*, escalera *f*
4* (= *heterosexual*) heterosexual *mf*
(CPD) ▸ **straight angle** ángulo *m* llano ▸ **straight arrow*** (*US*) estrecho/a *m/f* de miras ▸ **straight man** actor *m* que da pie al cómico • **I was the ~ man and he was the comic** yo era el actor que daba pie a sus chistes y él era el cómico ▸ **straight razor** (*US*) navaja *f* de barbero ▸ **straight sex** (= *not homosexual*) sexo *m* entre heterosexuales; (= *conventional*) relaciones *fpl* sexuales convencionales, sexo *m* sin florituras* ▸ **straight ticket** (*US*) (*Pol*) • **to vote a ~ ticket** votar a candidatos del mismo partido para todos los cargos

straightaway [ˈstreɪtəˈweɪ] (ADV) inmediatamente, en seguida, al tiro (*Chile*)

straightedge [ˈstreɪtedʒ] (N) regla *f* de borde recto

straighten [ˈstreɪtn] (VT) [+ *wire, nail*] (*also* **straighten out**) enderezar; [+ *picture, tie, hat*] poner derecho, enderezar; [+ *tablecloth*] (= *arrange*) poner bien; (= *smooth out*) alisar; [+ *hair*] alisar; [+ *hem*] igualar; (*also* **straighten up**) [+ *room, house*] ordenar, arreglar; [+ *papers*] ordenar • **to have one's teeth ~ed** ponerse bien los dientes • **to ~ one's shoulders** poner la espalda erguida *or* recta *or* derecha • **to ~ one's back** ponerse derecho *or* erguido • **to ~ o.s. (up)** arreglarse
(VI) = **straighten out**
▸ **straighten out** (VT + ADV) **1** [+ *wire, nail*] enderezar
2 (= *resolve*) [+ *problem*] resolver
3* [+ *person*] • **I soon ~ed him out on that point** enseguida le aclaré las cosas a ese respecto • **they sent me to a psychoanalyst to try and ~ me out** me mandaron a un psicoanalista para ver si resolvía mis problemas • **if you don't behave I'll send your father in to ~ you out** si no te comportas llamaré a tu padre para que te ajuste las cuentas
(VI + ADV) **1** [*road*] • **after the crossroads the road ~s out** tras el cruce ya no hay más curvas • **the road hardly ~s out at all from here to Bangor** son todo curvas de aquí a Bangor
2‡ (= *give up drugs*) desengancharse*

straight-faced [ˈstreɪtˈfeɪst] (ADJ) serio • **a straight-faced newsreader** un locutor de expresión seria
(ADV) con cara seria • **"whatever gives you that idea?" she asked straight-faced** —¿qué te hace pensar eso? —preguntó con cara seria

straightforward [ˌstreɪtˈfɔːwəd] (ADJ)
1 (= *honest*) honrado; (= *sincere*) sincero
2 (= *simple*) sencillo; [*answer*] claro, franco

straightforwardly [ˌstreɪtˈfɔːwədlɪ] (ADV) (= *honestly*) honradamente; (= *frankly*) francamente; (= *simply*) sencillamente

straightforwardness [ˌstreɪtˈfɔːwədnɪs] (N) (= *honesty*) honradez *f*; (= *frankness*) franqueza *f*; (= *simplicity*) sencillez *f*; [*of answer*] claridad *f*

straight-laced [ˌstreɪtˈleɪst] (ADJ) = **strait-laced**

straightness [ˈstreɪtnɪs] (N) **1** (*lit*) [*of road, arm leg*] lo recto; [*of hair*] lo liso; [*of back*] lo recto, lo erguido
2 (*fig*) (= *honesty*) honestidad *f*; (= *frankness*) franqueza *f*

straight-out* [ˈstreɪtaʊt] (ADJ) [*answer*] sincero, franco; [*refusal*] tajante, rotundo; [*supporter, enthusiast, thief*] cien por cien; ▷ **straight**

strain¹ [streɪn] (N) **1** (= *physical pressure*) (*on*

rope, cable) tensión *f*; (*on beam, bridge, structure*) presión *f* • **the ~ on a rope** la tensión de una cuerda • **this puts a ~ on the cable** esto tensa el cable • **that puts a great ~ on the beam** esto pone mucha presión sobre la viga • **to take the ~** (*lit*) aguantar el peso • **to take the ~ off** [+ *rope, cable*] disminuir la tensión de; [+ *beam, bridge, structure*] disminuir la presión sobre • **to break under the ~** [*rope, cable*] romperse debido a la tensión • **to collapse under the ~** [*bridge, ceiling*] venirse abajo debido a la presión
2 (*fig*) (= *burden*) carga *f*; (= *pressure*) presión *f*; (= *stress*) tensión *f* • **I found it a ~ being totally responsible for the child** me suponía una carga llevar toda la responsabilidad del niño yo solo • **it was a ~ on the economy/his purse** suponía una carga para la economía/su bolsillo • **the ~s on the economy** las presiones sobre la economía • **the ~s of modern life** las tensiones de la vida moderna • **mental ~** cansancio *m* mental • **to put a ~ on** [+ *resources*] suponer una carga para; [+ *system*] forzar al límite; [+ *relationship*] crear tirantez *or* tensiones en • **it put a great ~ on their friendship** creó mucha tirantez en su amistad • **his illness has put a terrible ~ on the family** su enfermedad ha creado mucha tensión *or* estrés para la familia • **he has been under a great deal of ~** ha estado sometido a mucha presión; ▹ **stress**
3 (= *effort*) esfuerzo *m* • **the ~ of climbing the stairs** el esfuerzo de subir las escaleras
4 (*Physiol*) **a** (= *injury*) (*from pull*) esguince *m*; (*involving twist*) esguince *m*, torcedura *f* • **back ~** torcedura de espalda • **muscle ~** esguince muscular
b (= *wear*) (*on eyes, heart*) esfuerzo *m* • **he knew tennis put a ~ on his heart** sabía que el tenis le sometía el corazón a un esfuerzo *or* le forzaba el corazón; ▹ **eyestrain, repetitive**
5 strains (*liter*) (= *sound*) compases *mpl* • **we could hear the gentle ~s of a Haydn quartet** oíamos los suaves compases de un cuarteto de Haydn • **the bride came in to the ~s of the wedding march** la novia entró al son *or* a los compases de la marcha nupcial
VT **1** (= *stretch*) (*beyond reasonable limits*) [+ *system*] forzar al límite; [+ *friendship, relationship, marriage*] crear tensiones en, crear tirantez en; [+ *resources, budget*] suponer una carga para; [+ *patience*] poner a prueba • **the demands of the welfare state are ~ing public finances to the limit** las exigencias del estado de bienestar están resultando una carga excesiva para las arcas públicas • **to ~ relations with sb** tensar las relaciones con algn
2 (= *damage, tire*) [+ *back*] dañar(se), hacerse daño en; [+ *eyes*] cansar • **to ~ a muscle** hacerse un esguince • **to ~ o.s.: you shouldn't ~ yourself** no deberías hacer mucha fuerza • **he ~ed himself lifting something** se hizo daño levantando algo • **don't ~ yourself!** (*iro*) ¡no te vayas a quebrar *or* herniar!
3 (= *make an effort with*) [+ *voice, eyes*] forzar • **to ~ one's ears to hear sth** aguzar el oído para oír algo • **to ~ every nerve** *or* **sinew to do sth** esforzarse mucho por hacer algo, hacer grandes esfuerzos por hacer algo
4 (= *filter*) (*Chem*) filtrar; (*Culin*) [+ *gravy, soup, custard*] colar; [+ *vegetables*] escurrir • **to ~ sth into a bowl** colar algo en un cuenco • **the mixture through a sieve** pase la mezcla por un tamiz
VI (= *make an effort*) • **to ~ to do sth** esforzarse por hacer algo • **he ~ed to hear what she was saying** se esforzaba por oír lo que decía • **he ~ed against the bonds that held him** (*liter*) hacía esfuerzos para soltarse de las cadenas que lo retenían • **to ~ at sth** tirar de algo • **to ~ at the leash** [*dog*] tirar de la correa; (*fig*) saltar de impaciencia • **to ~ under a weight** ir agobiado por un peso
▸ **strain off** VT + ADV [+ *liquid*] escurrir
VT + PREP • **to ~ the water off sth** escurrir el agua a algo

strain² [streɪn] N **1** (= *breed*) (*of animal*) raza *f*; (*of plant*) variedad *f*; (*of virus*) tipo *m* • **every year new ~s of flu develop** cada año aparecen nuevos tipos de gripe
2 (= *streak, element*) vena *f* • **there is a ~ of madness in the family** tienen vena de locos en la familia • **there is a ~ of cynicism in her writing** hay cierta vena de cinismo en sus escritos

strained [streɪnd] ADJ **1** (= *tense*) [*person*] tenso; [*face*] crispado; [*voice, laugh, jollity, politeness*] forzado; [*atmosphere, relations, silence*] tirante, tenso • **she gave a ~ laugh** forzó una risa, se rió con una risa forzada
2 [*wrist, ankle*] torcido; [*eyes*] cansado; [*voice*] cansado • **a ~ muscle** un esguince • **he has a ~ shoulder/back** tiene una lesión en un hombro/en la espalda
3 (= *overtaxed*) [*economy*] debilitado
4 (*Culin*) [*baby food*] pasado por el pasapurés *or* el tamiz; [*soup, gravy*] colado; [*yoghurt*] espeso

strainer ['streɪnəʳ] N (*Culin*) colador *m*; (*Tech*) filtro *m*, coladero *m*

strait [streɪt] N **1** (*Geog*) (*also* **straits**) estrecho *m* • **the Straits of Dover** el estrecho de Dover
2 straits (*fig*) situación *f* apurada, apuro *m* • **to be in dire ~s** estar en un gran apuro • **the economic ~s we are in** el apuro económico en que nos encontramos

straitened ['streɪtnd] ADJ (*frm*) • **in ~ circumstances** en condiciones difíciles, en condiciones de apuro

straitjacket ['streɪt,dʒækɪt] N camisa *f* de fuerza; (*fig*) corsé *m*

strait-laced ['streɪt'leɪst] ADJ puritano

strand¹ [strænd] N **1** [*of thread*] hebra *f*, hilo *m*; [*of hair*] pelo *m*; [*of rope*] ramal *m*; [*of plant*] brizna *f*
2 (*fig*) [*of plan, theory*] aspecto *m*, faceta *f*; [*of story*] hilo *m* argumental

strand² [strænd] N (*liter*) (= *beach, shore*) playa *f*
VT [+ *ship*] varar, encallar • **to be (left) ~ed** [*ship, fish*] quedar varado; (*fig*) [*person*] (*without money*) quedar desamparado; (*without transport*) quedar tirado • IDIOM: • **to leave sb ~ed** (*in the lurch*) dejar a algn plantado

strange [streɪndʒ] ADJ (COMPAR: **stranger**, SUPERL: **strangest**) **1** (= *odd*) [*person, event, behaviour, feeling*] extraño, raro; [*experience, place, noise*] extraño; [*coincidence, story*] extraño, curioso • **it is ~ that ...** es extraño *or* raro que (+ *subjun*) • **it's ~ that he should come today of all days** es extraño *or* raro que venga precisamente hoy • **there's something ~ about him** hay algo extraño *or* raro en él • **what's so ~ about that?** ¿qué tiene eso de extraño *or* raro? • **I felt rather ~ at first** al principio me sentía bastante raro • **I find her attitude rather ~** encuentro su actitud un tanto extraña *or* rara • **I find it ~ that we never heard anything about this** me parece raro *or* me extraña que nunca hayamos oído hablar de esto • **how ~!** ¡qué raro!, ¡qué extraño! • **for some ~ reason** por alguna razón inexplicable • **~ as it may seem** • **~ to say** por extraño que parezca, aunque parezca mentira • **the ~ thing is that he didn't even know us** lo extraño *or* lo curioso es que ni nos conocía • **children come out with the ~st things** a los niños se les ocurren las cosas más extrañas • **the family would think it ~ if we didn't go** la familia se extrañaría si no fuésemos; ▹ **bedfellow, truth**
2 (= *unknown, unfamiliar*) [*person, house, car, country*] desconocido; [*language*] desconocido, extranjero • **I never sleep well in a ~ bed** nunca duermo bien en una cama que no sea la mía • **don't talk to any ~ men** no hables con ningún desconocido • **I was ~ to this part of town** esta parte de la ciudad me era desconocida • **this man I loved was suddenly ~ to me** este hombre al que amaba era de pronto un desconocido para mí *or* un extraño

> **STRANGE, RARE**
>
> **Position of "raro"**
>
> *You should generally put* **raro** *after the noun when you mean* **strange** *or* **odd** *and before the noun when you mean* **rare**:
>
> **He has a strange name**
> Tiene un nombre raro
> **... a rare congenital syndrome ...**
> ... un raro síndrome congénito ...
>
> *For further uses and examples, see main entry.*

strangely ['streɪndʒlɪ] ADV [*act, behave*] de una forma extraña *or* rara • **the room was ~ quiet** en la habitación había un silencio extraño • **her voice sounded ~ familiar** su voz me resultaba extrañamente familiar • **the ~ named death's head moth** la extrañamente denominada mariposa de calavera • **~ (enough), ...** por extraño que parezca, ..., aunque resulte extraño, ...

strangeness ['streɪndʒnɪs] N **1** (= *oddness*) lo extraño, rareza *f*
2 (= *unfamiliarity*) novedad *f*

stranger ['streɪndʒəʳ] N (= *unknown person*) desconocido/a *m/f*, extraño/a *m/f*; (*from another area etc*) forastero/a *m/f* • **he's a ~ to me** es un desconocido para mí • **I'm a ~ here** yo soy nuevo aquí • **hello, ~!** ¡cuánto tiempo sin vernos! • **you're quite a ~!** ¡apenas te dejas ver! • **he is no ~ to vice** conoce bien los vicios

strangle ['stræŋgl] VT estrangular; (*fig*) [+ *sob*] ahogar

strangled ['stræŋgld] ADJ [*voice*] entrecortado • **a ~ cry** un grito entrecortado

stranglehold ['stræŋglhəʊld] N **1** (*Sport*) collar *m* de fuerza
2 (*fig*) dominio *m* completo • **to have a ~ on sb/sth** tener dominio completo sobre algn/monopolizar algo

strangler ['stræŋgləʳ] N estrangulador(a) *m/f*

strangling ['stræŋglɪŋ] N estrangulación *f*, estrangulamiento *m*

strangulate ['stræŋgjʊ,leɪt] VT (*Med*) estrangular

strangulated ['stræŋgjʊleɪtɪd] ADJ estrangulado • **~ hernia** hernia *f* estrangulada

strangulation [,stræŋgjʊ'leɪʃən] N estrangulación *f*

strap [stræp] N correa *f*, tira *f*; (= *shoulder strap*) tirante *m*, bretel *m* (*LAm*); (= *safety strap*) cinturón *m* • **to give sb the ~** (= *punish*) azotar a algn con la correa, dar a algn con la correa
VT **1** (= *fasten*) atar con correa • **to ~ sth on/down** sujetar algo con correa • **to ~ sb/o.s. in** (*with seatbelt*) poner a algn/ponerse el

S

cinturón de seguridad • **he isn't properly ~ped in** no está bien atado
2 (*Med*) (*also* **strap up**) vendar
3 • **to ~ sb** (*as punishment*) azotar a algn con la correa, dar a algn con la correa

strap-hang* ['stræphæŋ] VI viajar de pie (*agarrado a la correa*)

strap-hanger* ['stræphæŋəʳ] N pasajero/a *m/f* que va de pie (*agarrado a la correa*)

strap-hanging* ['stræp,hæŋɪŋ] N viajar *m* de pie

strapless ['stræplɪs] ADJ [*dress, bra*] sin tirantes

strapline ['stræp,laɪn] N (*Press*) titular *m*

strapped* [stræpt] ADJ • **to be ~ for cash** andar escaso de dinero

strapping ['stræpɪŋ] ADJ [*person*] fornido, robusto

strappy ['stræpɪ] ADJ **1** [*dress*] de tirantes
2 [*sandals*] de tiras

Strasbourg ['stræzbɜːg] N Estrasburgo *m*

strata ['strɑːtə] NPL *of* **stratum**

stratagem ['strætɪdʒəm] N estratagema *f*

strategic [strə'tiːdʒɪk] ADJ estratégico
CPD ▸ **strategic fit** (*Comm*) adecuación *f* estratégica

strategical [strə'tiːdʒɪkəl] ADJ = **strategic**

strategically [strə'tiːdʒɪkəlɪ] ADV [*act, think*] con una estrategia, estratégicamente; [*important, positioned*] estratégicamente

strategist ['strætɪdʒɪst] N estratega *mf*

strategy ['strætɪdʒɪ] N estrategia *f*

stratification [,strætɪfɪ'keɪʃən] N estratificación *f*

stratified ['strætɪfaɪd] ADJ estratificado

stratify ['strætɪfaɪ] VT estratificar
VI estratificarse

stratigraphic [,strætɪ'græfɪk] ADJ estratigráfico

stratigraphy [strə'tɪgrəfɪ] N estratigrafía *f*

stratocumulus [,streɪtəʊ'kjuːmjʊləs] N (PL: **stratocumuli** [,streɪtəʊ'kjuːmjʊlaɪ]) estratocúmulo *m*

stratosphere ['strætəʊsfɪəʳ] N estratosfera *f*

stratospheric [,strætəʊs'ferɪk] ADJ estratosférico

stratum ['strɑːtəm] N (PL: **stratums** *or* **strata**) **1** (*lit*) estrato *m*
2 (*fig*) estrato *m*, capa *f*

stratus ['streɪtəs] N (PL: **strati** ['streɪtaɪ]) estrato *m*

straw [strɔː] N **1** (*Agr*) paja *f* • IDIOMS: • **the ~ that breaks the camel's back** la gota que colma el vaso • **to clutch** *or* **grasp at ~s** agarrarse a un clavo ardiendo • **to draw** *or* **get the short ~** ser elegido para hacer algo desagradable • **I always draw the short ~** siempre me toca a mí la china* • **it's the last ~!** ¡es el colmo!, ¡solo faltaba eso! • **it's a ~ in the wind** sirve de indicio
2 (= *drinking straw*) pajita *f*, caña *f*, popote *m* (*Mex*) • **to drink through a ~** beber con pajita
ADJ (= *made of straw*) de paja; (= *colour*) pajizo, color paja
CPD ▸ **straw hat** sombrero *m* de paja ▸ **straw man** hombre *m* de paja ▸ **straw poll, straw vote** votación *f* de tanteo

strawberry ['strɔːbərɪ] N (= *fruit, plant*) fresa *f*, frutilla *f* (*LAm*); (*large, cultivated*) fresón *m*
CPD [*jam, ice cream, tart*] de fresa ▸ **strawberry bed** fresal *m* ▸ **strawberry blonde** rubia *f* fresa; ▹ **strawberry-blonde** ▸ **strawberry mark** (*on skin*) mancha *f* de nacimiento

strawberry-blonde [,strɔːbərɪ'blɒnd] ADJ bermejo

straw-coloured, straw-colored (*US*) ['strɔːkʌləd] ADJ pajizo, (de) color de paja

strawloft ['strɔːlɒft] N pajar *m*, pajera *f*

stray [streɪ] ADJ **1** (= *errant*) [*bullet*] perdido; [*sheep*] descarriado; [*cow, dog*] extraviado • **a ~ cat** (= *lost*) un gato extraviado; (= *alley cat*) un gato callejero
2 (= *isolated, occasional*) aislado • **in a few ~ cases** en algunos casos aislados • **a few ~ cars** algún que otro coche • **a few ~ thoughts** unos cuantos pensamientos inconexos
N **1** (= *animal*) animal *m* extraviado; (= *child*) niño/a *m/f* sin hogar, niño/a *m/f* desamparado/a
2 strays (*Rad*) parásitos *mpl*
VI **1** [*animal*] (= *roam*) extraviarse; (= *get lost*) perderse, extraviarse • **if the gate is left open the cattle ~** si se deja abierta la puerta las vacas se escapan
2 (= *wander*) [*person*] vagar, ir sin rumbo fijo; [*speaker, thoughts*] desvariar • **to ~ from** (*also fig*) apartarse de • **we had ~ed two kilometres from the path** nos habíamos desviado dos kilómetros del camino • **they ~ed into the enemy camp** erraron el camino y se encontraron en el campamento enemigo • **my thoughts ~ed to the holidays** empecé a pensar en las vacaciones

streak [striːk] N **1** (*line*) raya *f*; [*of mineral*] veta *f*, vena *f* • **to have ~s in one's hair** tener mechas en el pelo • IDIOM: • **like a ~ of lightning** como un rayo
2 (*fig*) (*of madness etc*) vena *f*; [*of luck*] racha *f* • **he had a cruel ~ (in him)** tenía un rasgo cruel • **there is a ~ of Spanish blood in her** tiene una pequeña parte de sangre española • **he had a yellow ~** era un tanto cobarde
VT rayar (**with** de)
VI **1** (= *rush*) • **to ~ along** correr a gran velocidad • **to ~ in/out/past** entrar/salir/pasar como un rayo
2* (= *run naked*) correr desnudo

streaker* ['striːkəʳ] N corredor(a) *m/f* desnudo/a

streaking* ['striːkɪŋ] N carrera *f* desnudista

streaky ['striːkɪ] ADJ rayado, listado; [*rock etc*] veteado
CPD ▸ **streaky bacon** (*Brit*) tocino *m* con grasa, bacon *m*, beicon *m*

stream [striːm] N **1** (= *brook*) arroyo *m*, riachuelo *m*
2 (= *current*) corriente *f* • **to go with/against the ~** (*lit, fig*) ir con/contra la corriente
3 (= *jet, gush*) [*of liquid*] chorro *m*; [*of light*] raudal *m*; [*of air*] chorro *m*, corriente *f*; [*of lava*] río *m*; [*of insults, abuse*] sarta *f*; [*of letters, questions, complaints*] lluvia *f* • **a thin ~ of water** un chorrito de agua • **she exhaled a thin ~ of smoke** lanzó *or* exhaló un chorrillo de humo • **a steady ~ of cars** un flujo constante *or* ininterrumpido de coches • **people were coming out of the cinema in a steady ~** había una continua hilera de gente que iba saliendo del cine • **we had a constant ~ of visitors** recibíamos visitas continuamente *or* sin parar • **he let out a ~ of insults** soltó una sarta de insultos • **~ of consciousness** monólogo *m* interior
4 (*Brit*) (*Scol*) *grupo de alumnos de la misma edad y aptitud académica* • **the top/middle/bottom ~** la clase de nivel superior/medio/inferior
5 (*Ind*) • **to be on/off ~** [*machinery, production line*] estar/no estar en funcionamiento; [*oil well*] estar/no estar en producción • **to come on ~** [*machinery, production line*] entrar en funcionamiento; [*oil well*] entrar en producción
VI **1** (= *pour*) **a** (*lit*) • **tears were ~ing down her face** le corrían las lágrimas por la cara • **rain ~ed down the windows** la lluvia chorreaba por las ventanas • **blood ~ed from a cut on his knee** le chorreaba sangre de un corte en la rodilla • **water ~ed from a cracked pipe** salía agua a chorros de una cañería rota • **his head was ~ing with blood** la cabeza le chorreaba sangre
b (*fig*) • **people ~ed into the hall** la gente entró en tropel a la sala • **bright sunlight ~ed in through the window/into the room** la fuerte luz del sol entraba a raudales por la ventana/en la habitación • **people came ~ing out** la gente salía en tropel • **as holiday traffic ~s out of the cities ...** a medida que las caravanas de las vacaciones van saliendo de las ciudades ... • **the cars kept ~ing past** los coches pasaban ininterrumpidamente *or* sin parar
2 (= *water, run*) • **her eyes were ~ing** le lloraban los ojos • **my nose was ~ing** me moqueaba la nariz
3 (= *flutter*) [*flag, hair, scarf*] ondear • **flags ~ed in the wind** las banderas ondeaban al viento
VT **1** • **his face ~ed blood** la sangre le corría *or* chorreaba por la cara
2 (*Brit*) (*Scol*) [+ *pupils*] agrupar, clasificar (*según su aptitud académica*)
CPD ▸ **stream feed** (*on photocopier, printer*) alimentación *f* continua

streamer ['striːməʳ] N **1** [*of paper, at parties etc*] serpentina *f*
2 (*Naut*) gallardete *m*

streaming ['striːmɪŋ] ADJ • **to have a ~ cold** tener un resfriado muy fuerte • **I had a ~ nose** me moqueaba la nariz • **to have ~ eyes** tener los ojos llorosos
N (*Scol*) división *f* de alumnos por grupos (*según su aptitud académica*)

streamline ['striːmlaɪn] VT (*lit*) aerodinamizar; (*fig*) racionalizar

streamlined ['striːmlaɪnd] ADJ [*air*] aerodinámico; (*fig*) racionalizado

street [striːt] N calle *f*, jirón *m* (*Peru*) • **he lives in** *or* **on the High Street** vive en la Calle Mayor • **to be on the ~s** (= *homeless*) estar sin vivienda; (*euph*) (*as prostitute*) hacer la calle • IDIOMS: • **to be ~s ahead of sb** (*Brit**) adelantarle por mucho a algn • **we are ~s ahead of them in design** les damos ciento y raya en el diseño • **they're ~s apart** (*Brit**) los separa un abismo • **they're not in the same ~ as us** (*Brit**) no están a nuestra altura, no admiten comparación con nosotros • **it's right up my ~** (*Brit**) esto es lo que me va, esto es lo mío
CPD ▸ **street arab**† golfo *m*, chicuelo *m* de la calle ▸ **street child** niño/a *m/f* de la calle ▸ **street cleaner** barrendero/a *m/f* ▸ **street corner** esquina *f* (de la calle) ▸ **street cred***, **street credibility** dominio *m* de la contracultura urbana ▸ **street crime** delitos *mpl* cometidos en la vía pública ▸ **street directory** callejero *m* ▸ **street door** puerta *f* principal, puerta *f* de la calle ▸ **street fight** pelea *f* callejera ▸ **street fighting** peleas *fpl* callejeras ▸ **street food** comida *f* callejera ▸ **street guide** callejero *m* ▸ **street lamp** farola *f*, faro *m* (*LAm*) ▸ **street level** • **at ~ level** en el nivel de la calle ▸ **street light** = **street lamp** ▸ **street lighting** alumbrado *m* público ▸ **street map** plano *m* (de la ciudad) ▸ **street market** mercado *m* callejero, tianguis *m* (*Mex*), feria *f* (*LAm*) ▸ **street musician** músico *m* ambulante ▸ **street people** (*homeless*) los sin techo, gente *f* que vive en la calle ▸ **street photographer** fotógrafo *m* callejero ▸ **street plan** plano *m*, callejero *m* ▸ **street sweeper** barrendero/a *m/f* ▸ **street theatre** teatro *m* en la calle, teatro *m* de calle ▸ **street urchin** golfo *m*, chicuelo *m* de la calle ▸ **street value** valor *m*

en la calle ▸ **street vendor** (*US*) vendedor(a) *mf* callejero/a
streetcar ['stri:tkɑ:ʳ] (N) (*US*) tranvía *m*, tren *m*
streetsmart ['stri:tsmɑ:t] (ADJ) (*US*) = streetwise
streetwalker ['stri:t,wɔ:kəʳ] (N) (= *prostitute*) mujer *f* de la vida
streetwise ['stri:twaɪz] (ADJ) despabilado
strength [streŋθ] (N) **1** (= *might, energy*) (*for particular task*) fuerzas *fpl*; (= *general attribute*) fuerza *f* • **he hadn't the ~ to lift it** no tenía fuerzas para levantarlo • **his ~ failed him** le fallaron las fuerzas • **she swims to build up the ~ in her muscles** nada para fortalecer los músculos *or* coger fuerza en los músculos • **you don't know your own ~** no controlas tu propia fuerza • **you'll soon get your ~ back** pronto recobrarás las fuerzas *or* te repondrás • **to save one's ~** ahorrar las energías • **with all my ~** con todas mis fuerzas
2 (= *fortitude*) fortaleza *f*, fuerzas *fpl*; (= *firmness*) [*of belief, conviction*] firmeza *f* • **his help gives me the ~ to carry on** su ayuda me da fortaleza *or* fuerzas para seguir adelante • **~ of character** fortaleza *f or* firmeza *f* de carácter • **to draw ~ from sth** sacar fuerzas de algo • **the independence movement is gathering ~** el movimiento independiente está cobrando fuerza • **give me ~!*** ¡Dios dame paciencia!* • **inner ~** fuerza interior • **~ of purpose** determinación *f*; ▹ **gather, tower**
3 (= *sturdiness*) [*of material, structure, frame*] resistencia *f*
4 (= *power*) [*of argument*] lo convincente, solidez *f*; [*of claim, case, evidence*] peso *m*; [*of protests*] lo enérgico; [*of magnet, lens, drug*] potencia *f*; [*of wind*] fuerza *f*; [*of alcohol*] graduación *f* • **on the ~ of that success she applied for promotion** en base a ese éxito, solicitó un ascenso • **he was recruited on the ~ of his communication skills** lo contrataron en virtud de *or* debido a su aptitud para comunicarse
5 (= *intensity*) [*of emotion*] intensidad *f*, fuerza *f*; [*of sound*] potencia *f*; [*of colour*] intensidad *f* • **he warned the government not to underestimate the ~ of feeling among voters** advirtió al gobierno que no subestimara la intensidad *or* fuerza de los sentimientos de los votantes
6 [*of currency*] (= *value*) valor *m*; (= *high value*) solidez *f*, fuerza *f* • **our decision will depend on the ~ of the pound** nuestra decisión dependerá del valor de la libra • **exports fell owing to the ~ of the pound** las exportaciones bajaron debido a la solidez *or* la fuerza de la libra
7 (= *good point, asset*) punto *m* fuerte • **their chief ~ is technology** su punto fuerte es la tecnología • IDIOM: • **to go from ~ to ~**: • **his movie career is going from ~ to ~** su carrera cinematográfica marcha viento en popa • **the company has gone from ~ to ~** la empresa ha ido teniendo un éxito tras otro
8 (*in number*) número *m*; (*Mil, Police*) efectivos *mpl* • **he has promised to increase the ~ of the police force** ha prometido incrementar los efectivos de la policía • **to be at full ~** [*army*] disponer de todos sus efectivos; (*Sport*) [*team*] contar con todos sus jugadores; [*office*] contar con todo el personal • **his supporters were there in ~** *or* **had come in ~** sus partidarios habían acudido en masa • **to be on the ~** (*gen*) formar parte de la plantilla; (*Mil*) formar parte del regimiento • **to take sb on to the ~** admitir a algn en la plantilla; (*Mil*) admitir a algn en el regimiento • **to be under** *or* **below ~**: • **the team was under** *or* **below ~ due to injuries** el equipo contaba con pocos jugadores debido a las lesiones • **two people are off sick so we're a bit under** *or* **below ~** dos de los empleados se encuentran enfermos y estamos un poco cortos de personal • **his army was seriously under** *or* **below ~** su ejército contaba con poquísimos efectivos
strengthen ['streŋθən] (VT) **1** (*lit*) [+ *wall, roof, building*] reforzar; [+ *back, muscle*] fortalecer • **he does exercises to ~ his legs** hace ejercicios para fortalecer las piernas
2 (*fig*) [+ *currency, economy, bond, relationship, character*] fortalecer, consolidar; [+ *government*] consolidar; [+ *case, argument, law*] reforzar; [+ *power*] consolidar, afianzar; [+ *resolve, belief, impression*] reafirmar; [+ *person*] (*morally*) fortalecer • **this served to ~ opposition to the strike** esto sirvió para afianzar la oposición a la huelga • **her rejection only ~ed his resolve** el rechazo de ella solo sirvió para hacer más firme su propósito de conquistarla • **to ~ sb's position** • **~ sb's hand** afianzar la posición de algn
(VI) **1** (*lit*) [*muscle, arm, back*] fortalecerse; [*wind, storm*] hacerse más fuerte
2 (*fig*) [*currency, economy*] fortalecerse, consolidarse; [*prices*] afianzarse; [*desire, determination*] redoblarse, intensificarse
strengthening ['streŋθənɪŋ] (ADJ) (*physically*) fortificante, tonificante • **~ exercises** ejercicios *mpl* fortificantes *or* tonificantes • **this may have a ~ effect on the economy** puede que esto tenga un efecto fortificante en la economía
(N) **1** [*of arm, back, muscles*] fortalecimiento *m*
2 (*fig*) [*of currency, stock market*] fortalecimiento *m*, consolidación *f*; [*of prices*] afianzamiento *m*
strenuous ['strenjʊəs] (ADJ) **1** (= *physically demanding*) [*efforts*] intenso, arduo; [*work*] agotador, arduo; [*exercise, walk*] agotador, fatigoso
2 (= *vigorous*) [*objections, protest, opposition*] enérgico; [*denial*] enérgico, rotundo • **to make ~ efforts to do sth** esforzarse afanosamente *or* hacer intensos esfuerzos por hacer algo
strenuously ['strenjʊəslɪ] (ADV) [*deny*] enérgicamente, rotundamente; [*object, protest, oppose*] enérgicamente; [*resist*] tenazmente, con tenacidad; [*exercise*] con intensidad • **he has ~ denied the allegations** ha rechazado enérgicamente *or* rotundamente las acusaciones • **to try ~ to do sth** esforzarse afanosamente por hacer algo, procurar por todos los medios hacer algo
strep throat* [,strep'θrəʊt] (N) infección *f* de garganta (*por estreptococos*)
streptococcus [,streptəʊ'kɒkəs] (N) (PL: **streptococci** [,streptəʊ'kɒkaɪ]) estreptococo *m*
streptomycin [,streptəʊ'maɪsɪn] (N) estreptomicina *f*
stress [stres] (N) **1** (*Tech*) tensión *f*, carga *f*
2 (*psychological etc*) (= *strain*) estrés *m*, tensión *f* (nerviosa) • **in times of ~** en épocas de estrés *or* tensión • **to subject sb to great ~** someter a algn a grandes tensiones • **the ~es and strains of modern life** las presiones de la vida moderna • **to be under ~** estar estresado, tener estrés
3 (= *emphasis*) hincapié *m*, énfasis *m* • **to lay great ~ on sth** recalcar algo
4 (*Ling, Poetry*) acento *m* • **the ~ is on the second syllable** el acento tónico cae en la segunda sílaba
(VT) **1** (= *emphasize*) subrayar, insistir en • **I must ~ that ...** tengo que subrayar que ...
2 (*Ling, Poetry*) acentuar
(CPD) ▸ **stress fracture** [*of bone*] fractura *f* por fatiga; [*of rock*] fractura *f* por tensión ▸ **stress mark** (*Ling*) tilde *f* ▸ **stress pattern** patrón *m* acentual ▸ **stress system** (*Ling*) sistema *m* de acentos, acentuación *f*
▸ **stress out*** (VT + ADV) estresar, agobiar
stressed [strest] (ADJ) **1** (= *tense*) [*person*] estresado, agobiado
2 (*Ling, Poetry*) [*syllable*] acentuado
stressed out* [,strest'aʊt] (ADJ) estresado, agobiado • **to be ~** estar estresado *or* agobiado
stressful ['stresfʊl] (ADJ) [*job*] estresante, que produce tensión nerviosa
stressor ['stresəʳ] (N) (= *stress factor*) factor *m* estrés
stress-related ['stresrɪ,leɪtɪd] (ADJ) [*illness*] relacionado con el estrés
stretch [stretʃ] (N) **1** (= *elasticity*) elasticidad *f*
2 (= *act of stretching*) • **to have a ~** [*person*] estirarse • **to be at full ~** [*person*] (*physically*) estirarse al máximo; (*at work*) estar trabajando a toda mecha* • **with arms at full ~** con los brazos completamente extendidos • **when the engine is at full ~** cuando el motor está a la máxima potencia, cuando el motor rinde su potencia máxima • **by a ~ of the imagination** con un esfuerzo de imaginación • **by no ~ of the imagination** bajo ningún concepto
3 (= *distance*) trecho *m* • **for a long ~ it runs between mountains** corre entre montañas durante un buen trecho
4 (= *expanse*) extensión *f*; [*of road etc*] tramo *m*; [*of rope*] trozo *m*; [*of time*] periodo *m*, tiempo *m* • **in that ~ of the river** en aquella parte del río • **a splendid ~ of countryside** un magnífico paisaje • **for a long ~ of time** durante mucho tiempo • **for hours at a ~** durante horas enteras • **for three days at a ~** tres días de un tirón *or* (*LAm*) jalón • **he read the lot at one ~** se los leyó todos de un tirón *or* (*LAm*) jalón
5‡ (*in prison*) • **a five-year ~** una condena de cinco años • **he's doing a ~** está en chirona‡
(VT) **1** (= *pull out*) [+ *elastic*] estirar; [+ *rope etc*] tender (**between** entre)
2 (= *make larger*) [+ *pullover, shoes*] ensanchar; (= *make longer*) alargar; (= *spread on ground etc*) extender • **the blow ~ed him (out) cold on the floor** el golpe lo tumbó sin sentido en el suelo
3 (= *exercise*) • **to ~ one's legs** estirar las piernas; (*after stiffness*) desentumecerse las piernas; (*fig*) (= *go for a walk*) dar un paseíto • **to ~ o.s.** (*after sleep etc*) desperezarse
4 [+ *money, resources, meal*] hacer que llegue *or* alcance • **our resources are fully ~ed** nuestros recursos están aprovechados al máximo
5 [+ *meaning, law, truth*] forzar, violentar • **that's ~ing it too far** eso va demasiado lejos • **to ~ a point** hacer una excepción • **to ~ the rules for sb** ajustar las reglas a beneficio de algn
6 [+ *athlete, student etc*] exigir el máximo esfuerzo a • **the course does not ~ the students enough** el curso no exige bastante esfuerzo a los estudiantes • **to be fully ~ed** llegar a sus límites • **to ~ o.s.** esforzarse • **he doesn't ~ himself** no se esfuerza bastante, puede dar más de sí • **to ~ sb to the limits** sacar el máximo provecho de algn
(VI) **1** (= *be elastic*) estirar(se), dar (de sí) • **this cloth won't ~** esta tela no se estira, esta tela no da de sí
2 (= *become larger*) [*clothes, shoes*] ensancharse
3 (= *stretch one's limbs, reach out*) estirarse;

S

(after sleep etc) desperezarse
4 (= *reach, extend*) [*rope, area of land*] llegar (**to** a); [*power, influence*] permitir (**to** que) • **will it ~?** ¿llega? • **it ~es for miles along the river** se extiende varios kilómetros a lo largo del río
5 (= *be enough*) [*money, food*] alcanzar (**to** para)
CPD ▸ **stretch fabric** tela *f* elástica
▸ **stretch limo*** limusina *f* extralarga
▸ **stretch marks** (*Med*) estrías *fpl*
▸ **stretch out** VT + ADV **1** [+ *arm*] extender; [+ *hand*] tender, alargar; [+ *leg*] estirar
2 (= *lengthen*) [+ *essay, discussion*] alargar
VI + ADV **1** [*person*] estirarse; (= *lie down*) tumbarse, tenderse • **he ~ed out on the ground** se tumbó *or* se tendió en el suelo • **to ~ out to take sth** alargar el brazo para tomar algo
2 [*space, time*] extenderse
▸ **stretch up** VI + ADV • **to ~ up to take sth** alargar el brazo para tomar algo
stretcher ['stretʃəʳ] N **1** (*Med*) camilla *f*
2 (*Tech*) (*for gloves etc*) ensanchador *m*; (*for canvas*) bastidor *m*
3 (*Archit*) soga *f*
VT (*Med*) llevar en camilla
CPD ▸ **stretcher bearer** camillero/a *m/f*
▸ **stretcher case** *enfermo o herido que tiene que ser llevado en camilla* ▸ **stretcher party** equipo *m* de camilleros
▸ **stretcher away** VT + ADV retirar en camilla, llevarse en camilla
▸ **stretcher off** VT + ADV retirar en camilla
stretchy ['stretʃɪ] ADJ elástico
strew [stru:] (PT: **strewed**, PP: **strewed**, **strewn** [stru:n]) VT **1** (= *scatter*) regar, esparcir • **there were fragments ~n about everywhere** había fragmentos esparcidos por todas partes • **to ~ sand on the floor** cubrir el suelo de arena, esparcir arena sobre el suelo • **to ~ one's belongings about the room** desparramar las cosas por el cuarto
2 (= *cover*) cubrir, tapizar (**with** de) • **the floors are ~n with rushes** los suelos están cubiertos de juncos
striated [straɪ'eɪtɪd] ADJ estriado
striation [straɪ'eɪʃən] N (*frm*) estriación *f*
stricken ['strɪkən] PP *of* **strike**
ADJ **1** (= *distressed, upset*) afligido, acongojado • **to be ~ with** estar afligido por • **to be ~ with grief** estar agobiado por el dolor • **she was ~ with remorse** le remordía la conciencia
2 (= *damaged*) [*ship etc*] destrozado, dañado; (= *wounded*) herido; (= *ill*) enfermo; (= *suffering*) afligido; (= *doomed*) condenado • **the ~ families** las familias afligidas • **the ~ city** la ciudad condenada, la ciudad destrozada
-stricken ['strɪkən] ADJ (*ending in compounds*) • **drought-stricken** aquejado de sequía, afectado por la sequía
strict [strɪkt] ADJ (COMPAR: **stricter**, SUPERL: **strictest**) **1** (= *stern, severe*) [*person, discipline*] estricto, severo • **her ~ upbringing** la educación estricta *or* rigurosa que recibió • **to be ~ with sb** ser estricto *or* severo con algn
2 (= *stringent*) [*rules*] estricto; [*control*] estricto, riguroso; [*limit*] riguroso; [*security measures*] riguroso, estricto; [*orders*] tajante, terminante, estricto • **to be under ~ orders (not) to do sth** tener órdenes estrictas de (no) hacer algo
3 (= *precise*) [*meaning*] estricto • **in ~ order of precedence** por riguroso *or* estricto orden de precedencia • **in the ~ sense of the word** en el sentido estricto de la palabra
4 (= *absolute*) [*secrecy*] absoluto • **I told you that in ~ confidence** te lo dije con la más absoluta reserva • **all your replies will be treated in the ~est confidence** todas las respuestas serán tratadas con la reserva más absoluta • **~ liability** (*Jur*) responsabilidad *f* absoluta
5 (= *rigorous*) [*Methodist*] estricto; [*vegetarian, diet*] estricto, riguroso; [*hygiene*] absoluto • **I'm a ~ teetotaller** soy estrictamente *or* rigurosamente abstemio
strictly ['strɪktlɪ] ADV **1** (= *sternly, severely*) severamente • **she was ~ brought up** recibió una educación muy estricta *or* rigurosa
2 (= *stringently*) [*control, adhere to*] estrictamente, rigurosamente; [*limit*] rigurosamente
3 (= *absolutely*) [*forbidden*] terminantemente; [*necessary*] absolutamente; [*confidential*] estrictamente • **it is not ~ accurate to say that ...** no es del todo preciso decir que ... • **"strictly private"** (*on fence, gate*) "prohibido el paso", "propiedad privada"; (*on letter*) "estrictamente confidencial" • **~ speaking** en (el) sentido estricto (de la palabra) • **that's not ~ true** eso no es del todo cierto, eso no es rigurosamente cierto
4 (= *exclusively*) exclusivamente • **this is ~ business** esto es exclusivamente una cuestión de trabajo • **the car park is ~ for the use of residents** el aparcamiento es para uso exclusivo de los residentes • **everything he said was ~ to the point** todo lo que decía iba directamente al grano
strictness ['strɪktnɪs] N **1** (= *severity*) [*of person*] severidad *f*; [*of discipline*] lo estricto, severidad *f*
2 (= *stringency*) [*of rules, control, security*] lo riguroso
stricture ['strɪktʃəʳ] N **1** (*usu pl*) (= *criticism*) censura *f*, crítica *f* • **to pass ~s on sb** censurar a algn, poner reparos a algn
2 (*Med*) constricción *f*
stridden ['strɪdn] PP *of* **stride**
stride [straɪd] (VB: PT: **strode**, PP: **stridden**) N zancada *f*, tranco *m*; (*in measuring*) paso *m* • **to make great ~s** (*fig*) hacer grandes progresos • IDIOMS: • **to get into** *or* **hit one's ~** coger *or* (*LAm*) agarrar el ritmo • **to take things in one's ~** *or* (*US*) **in ~** tomar las cosas con calma • **to put sb off their ~** (*Brit*) hacer perder los papeles a algn
VI (*also* **stride along**) andar a zancadas
VT **1**† [+ *horse*] montar a horcajadas sobre
2 (= *cross*) [+ *deck, yard etc*] cruzar de un tranco
▸ **stride away, stride off** VI + ADV alejarse a grandes zancadas
▸ **stride up** VI + ADV • **to ~ up to sb** acercarse resueltamente a algn • **to ~ up and down** andar de aquí para allá a pasos largos
stridency ['straɪdənsɪ] N [*of voice, colour, person*] estridencia *f*; [*of protests*] fuerza *f*, lo ruidoso
strident ['straɪdənt] ADJ [*voice, sound*] estridente; [*colour, person*] chillón, estridente; [*protest*] fuerte, ruidoso
stridently ['straɪdəntlɪ] ADV [*hoot, sound, whistle*] con estridencia, de modo estridente; [*demand, declare*] con estridencia, con grandes alharacas; [*protest*] ruidosamente
strife [straɪf] N conflictos *mpl* • **domestic ~** riñas *fpl* domésticas • **internal ~** conflictos *mpl* internos • **to cease from ~** (*frm*) deponer las armas
strife-ridden ['straɪf,rɪdn] ADJ conflictivo
strike [straɪk] (VB: PT, PP: **struck**) N **1** (*by workers*) huelga *f*, paro *m* • **to be on ~** estar en huelga • **to come out** *or* **go on ~** declarar la huelga; ▹ **hunger**
2 (= *discovery*) [*of oil, gold*] descubrimiento *m* • **a big oil ~** un descubrimiento de petróleo en gran cantidad • **to make a ~** hacer un descubrimiento
3 (*Baseball*) golpe *m*; (*Bowling*) strike *m* • **you have two ~s against you** (*esp US*) (*fig*) tienes dos cosas en contra • **three ~s and you're out** (*US*) (*Jur*) *pena de cadena perpetua tras el tercer delito grave*
4 (*Mil*) ataque *m*; (= *air strike*) ataque *m* aéreo, bombardeo *m*
VT **1** (= *hit*) golpear; (*with fist etc*) pegar, dar una bofetada a; (*with bullet etc*) alcanzar; [+ *ball*] golpear; [+ *chord, note*] tocar; [+ *instrument*] herir, pulsar • **never ~ a woman** no pegar nunca a una mujer • **the president was struck by two bullets** dos balas alcanzaron al presidente • **to ~ sb a blow** • **~ a blow at sb** pegar *or* dar un golpe a algn, pegar a algn • **to ~ one's fist on the table** • **~ the table with one's fist** golpear la mesa con el puño • **the clock struck the hour** el reloj dio la hora • **to be struck by lightning** ser alcanzado por un rayo • **the tower was struck by lightning** la torre fue alcanzada por un rayo, cayó un rayo en la torre • IDIOMS: • **to ~ a blow for sth** romper una lanza a favor de algo • **to ~ a blow against sth** socavar algo • **that ~s a chord!** ¡eso me suena!
2 (= *collide with*) [+ *rocks, landmine etc*] chocar con, chocar contra; [+ *difficulty, obstacle*] encontrar, dar con, tropezar con • **the ship struck an iceberg** el buque chocó con *or* contra un iceberg • **his head struck the beam** • **he struck his head on the beam** dio con la cabeza contra *or* en la viga • **the light ~s the window** la luz hiere la ventana • **disaster struck us** el desastre nos vino encima • **a sound struck my ear** (*liter*) un ruido hirió mi oído • **what ~s the eye is the poverty** lo que más llama la atención es la pobreza • **a ghastly sight struck our eyes** se nos presentó un panorama horroroso
3 (= *produce, make*) [+ *coin, medal*] acuñar; [+ *a light, match*] encender, prender (*LAm*) • **to ~ root** (*Bot*) echar raíces, arraigar • **to ~ sparks from sth** hacer que algo eche chispas • **to ~ terror into sb's heart** infundir terror a algn
4 (= *appear to, occur to*) • **it ~s me as being most unlikely** me parece poco factible, se me hace poco probable (*LAm*) • **how did it ~ you?** ¿qué te pareció?, ¿qué impresión te causó? • **at least that's how it ~s me** por lo menos eso es lo que pienso yo • **it ~s me that ...** • **the thought ~s me that ...** se me ocurre que ... • **has it ever struck you that ...?** ¿has pensado alguna vez que ...?
5 (= *impress*) • **I was much struck by his sincerity** su sinceridad me impresionó mucho • **I'm not much struck (with him)** no me llama la atención, no me impresiona mucho
6 (= *find*) [+ *gold, oil*] descubrir • IDIOMS: • **to ~ gold** triunfar • **to ~ it lucky** tener suerte • **he struck it rich** le salió el gordo
7 (= *arrive at, achieve*) [+ *agreement*] alcanzar, llegar a • **to ~ an average** sacar el promedio • **to ~ a balance** encontrar el equilibrio • **to ~ a bargain** cerrar un trato • **to ~ a deal** alcanzar un acuerdo, llegar a un acuerdo; (*Comm*) cerrar un trato
8 (= *assume, adopt*) • **to ~ an attitude** adoptar una actitud
9 (= *cause to become*) • **to ~ sb blind** cegar a algn • **to ~ sb dead** matar a algn • **may I be struck dead if ...** que me maten si ... • **to be struck dumb** quedarse sin habla
10 (= *take down*) • **to ~ camp** levantar el campamento • **to ~ the flag** arriar la bandera
11 (= *remove, cross out*) suprimir (**from** de)
VI **1** (*Mil etc*) (= *attack*) atacar; [*disaster*]

sobrevenir; [*disease*] golpear; [*snake etc*] morder, atacar • **now is the time to ~** este es el momento en que conviene atacar • **when panic ~s** cuando cunde el pánico, cuando se extiende el pánico • **to ~ against sth** dar con algo, dar contra algo, chocar contra algo • **to ~ at sb** (*with fist*) tratar de golpear a algn; (*Mil*) atacar a algn • **we must ~ at the root of this evil** debemos atacar la raíz de este mal, debemos cortar este mal de raíz • **this ~s at our very existence** esto amenaza nuestra existencia misma • **to be within striking distance of** [+ *place*] estar a poca distancia *or* a un paso de • **he had come within striking distance of the presidency** estuvo muy cerca de ocupar la presidencia; ▷ **home, iron**
2 [*workers*] declarar la huelga, declararse en huelga • **to ~ for higher wages** hacer una huelga para conseguir un aumento de los sueldos
3 [*clock*] dar la hora • **the clock has struck** ha dado la hora ya
4 [*match*] encenderse
5 • IDIOM: • **to ~ lucky** tener suerte
6 (= *move, go*) • **to ~ across country** ir a campo traviesa • **to ~ into the woods** ir por el bosque, penetrar en el bosque
7 (*Naut*) (= *run aground*) encallar, embarrancar
8 (*esp Naut*) (= *surrender*) arriar la bandera
9 (*Bot*) echar raíces, arraigar
CPD ▸ **strike ballot** votación *f* a huelga ▸ **strike committee** comité *m* de huelga ▸ **strike force** fuerza *f* de asalto, fuerza *f* de choque ▸ **strike fund** fondo *m* de huelga ▸ **strike pay** subsidio *m* de huelga ▸ **strike vote** = strike ballot
▸ **strike back** VI + ADV (*gen*) devolver el golpe (**at** a); (*Mil*) contraatacar
▸ **strike down** VT + ADV [*illness*] (= *incapacitate*) fulminar; (= *kill*) matar • **he was struck down by paralysis** tuvo una parálisis • **he was struck down in his prime** se lo llevó la muerte en la flor de la vida
▸ **strike off** VT + ADV **1** (= *cut off*) [+ *branch*] cortar • **to ~ off sb's head** decapitar a algn, cortar la cabeza a algn, cercenar la cabeza a algn
2 [+ *name from list*] tachar; [+ *doctor*] suspender
3 (*Typ*) tirar, imprimir
VI + ADV (= *change direction*) • **the road ~s off to the right** el camino se desvía para la derecha
▸ **strike on** VI + PREP • **to ~ on an idea: he struck on an idea** se le ocurrió una idea
▸ **strike out** VT + ADV (= *cross out*) tachar
VI + ADV **1** (= *hit out*) arremeter (**at** contra) • **to ~ out wildly** dar golpes sin mirar a quien
2 (= *set out*) dirigirse • **to ~ out for the shore** (empezar a) nadar (resueltamente) hacia la playa • **to ~ out on one's own** (*in business*) volar con sus propias alas
▸ **strike through** VI + PREP **1** (= *delete*) [+ *word, name*] tachar
2 • **the sun ~s through the mist** el sol penetra por entre la niebla
▸ **strike up** VT + ADV **1** [+ *friendship, conversation*] entablar, empezar
2 [+ *tune*] atacar
VI + ADV [*band*] empezar a tocar
▸ **strike upon** VI + PREP = **strike on**
strike-bound ['straɪkbaʊnd] ADJ paralizado por la huelga
strikebreaker ['straɪk,breɪkəʳ] N esquirol(a) *m/f*, rompehuelgas *mf inv*
striker ['straɪkəʳ] N **1** (*in industry*) huelguista *mf*
2 (*Sport*) delantero/a *m/f*, ariete *m*
striking ['straɪkɪŋ] ADJ **1** (= *remarkable, arresting*) [*picture, clothes, colour*] llamativo; [*contrast*] notable; [*similarity, difference*] sorprendente; [*beauty*] imponente, impresionante; [*woman*] imponente • **her ~ good looks** su imponente *or* impresionante belleza • **to bear a ~ resemblance to sb** parecerse muchísimo a algn • **the most ~ feature of the house** el detalle que más llama la atención de la casa • **her thesis has several ~ features** su tesis contiene varios aspectos sobresalientes • **it is ~ that ...** es impresionante que ...
2 • **a ~ clock** un reloj que marca las horas
3 (*Ind*) • **the ~ workers** los obreros en huelga
strikingly ['straɪkɪŋlɪ] ADV [*similar, different, bold*] sorprendentemente; [*attractive*] extraordinariamente • **a ~ attractive woman** una mujer extraordinariamente atractiva, una mujer imponente • **to contrast ~ with sth** contrastar notablemente con algo
Strimmer® ['strɪməʳ] N desbrozadora *f*
string [strɪŋ] (VB: PT, PP: **strung**) N **1** (= *cord*) cuerda *f*, cordel *m*, cabuya *f* (*LAm*), mecate *m* (*Mex*); (= *lace etc*) cordón *m* • IDIOMS: • **to have sb on a ~** dominar a algn completamente, tener a algn en un puño • **to pull ~s** mover palancas • **to have two ~s to one's bow** tener dos cuerdas en su arco
2 (= *row*) [*of onions, garlic*] ristra *f*; [*of beads*] hilo *m*, sarta *f*; [*of vehicles*] caravana *f*, fila *f*; [*of people*] hilera *f*, desfile *m*; [*of horses etc*] reata *f*; [*of excuses, lies*] sarta *f*, serie *f*; [*of curses*] retahíla *f* • **a whole ~ of errors** toda una serie de errores
3 (*on musical instrument, racket*) cuerda *f* • **the ~s** (= *instruments*) los instrumentos de cuerda
4 (*fig*) condición *f* • **without ~s** sin condiciones • **there are no ~s attached** esto es sin compromiso alguno • **with no ~s attached** sin compromiso
5 (*Comput*) cadena *f*
6 (*Bot*) fibra *f*, nervio *m*
VT **1** [+ *pearls etc*] ensartar • **he can't even ~ two sentences together** ni sabe conectar dos frases seguidas • **they are just stray thoughts strung together** son pensamientos aislados que se han ensartado sin propósito
2 [+ *violin, tennis racket, bow*] encordar
3 [+ *beans etc*] desfibrar
CPD ▸ **string bag** bolsa *f* de red ▸ **string bean** (*US*) judía *f* verde, ejote *m* (*Mex*), poroto *m* verde (*S. Cone*) ▸ **string instrument** instrumento *m* de cuerda ▸ **string orchestra** orquesta *f* de cuerdas ▸ **string quartet** cuarteto *m* de cuerda(s) ▸ **string section** (*Mus*) sección *f* de cuerda(s), cuerda(s) *f(pl)* ▸ **string vest** camiseta *f* de malla
▸ **string along*** VT + ADV (= *give false hope to*) dar falsas esperanzas a; (= *con*) embaucar
VI + ADV ir también, venir también • **to ~ along with sb** acompañar a algn, pegarse a algn (*pej*)
▸ **string out** VT + ADV **1** (= *space out*) • **to be strung out behind sb** seguir a algn en fila • **to be strung out along sth** hacer fila a lo largo de algo • **the posts are strung out across the desert** hay una serie de puestos aislados a través del desierto • **his plays were strung out over 40 years** aparecieron sus obras cada cierto tiempo durante 40 años
2 (*Drugs‡*) • **to be strung out** (= *addicted*) estar enganchado (**on** a); (= *under influence*) estar colgado* *or* flipado‡ *or* colocado‡ (**on** de); (= *suffering withdrawal symptoms*) estar con el mono*
▸ **string up** VT + ADV **1** [+ *onions etc*] colgar (con cuerda); [+ *nets*] extender
2* (= *hang*) ahorcar; (= *lynch*) linchar
3 (*Brit**) • **to be all strung up** estar muy tenso, estar muy nervioso
4 • **to ~ o.s. up to do sth** resolverse a hacer algo, cobrar ánimo para hacer algo
stringed [strɪŋd] ADJ [*instrument*] de cuerdas • **four-stringed** de cuatro cuerdas
stringency ['strɪndʒənsɪ] N **1** [*of regulations, controls, standards*] rigor *m*, severidad *f*
2 (*Econ*) tirantez *f*, dificultad *f* • **economic ~** situación *f* económica apurada, estrechez *f*
stringent ['strɪndʒənt] ADJ **1** [*controls, standards*] riguroso, severo, estricto • **~ rules** reglas *fpl* estrictas
2 (*Econ*) tirante, difícil
stringently ['strɪndʒəntlɪ] ADV severamente, rigurosamente
stringer ['strɪŋəʳ] N (= *journalist*) corresponsal *mf* local (*a tiempo parcial*)
string-pulling* ['strɪŋ,pʊlɪŋ] N enchufismo* *m*
stringy ['strɪŋɪ] ADJ (COMPAR: **stringier**, SUPERL: **stringiest**) fibroso, lleno de fibras
strip [strɪp] N **1** [*of paper etc*] tira *f*; [*of metal*] fleje *m* • IDIOMS: • **to tear sb off a ~*** • **tear a ~ off sb*** echar una bronca a algn*
2 [*of land*] franja *f*, faja *f*; (*Aer*) (= *landing strip*) pista *f*
3 (*Brit*) (*Ftbl etc*) (= *clothes*) uniforme *m*; (= *colours*) colores *mpl*
4* (= *striptease*) striptease *m*, despelote* *m* • **to do a ~** desnudarse, hacer un striptease, despelotarse*
5 (= *strip cartoon*) tira *f*
VT **1** [+ *person*] desnudar • **to ~ sb naked** desnudar a algn completamente, dejar a algn en cueros* • **to ~ sb to the skin** dejar a algn en cueros*
2 [+ *bed*] quitar la ropa de; [+ *wall*] desempapelar; [+ *wallpaper*] quitar • **to ~ the bark off sth** descortezar algo
3 (= *deprive*) • **to ~ sb of sth** despojar a algn de algo • **to ~ a house of its furniture** dejar una casa sin muebles • **to ~ a company of its assets** despojar a una empresa de su activo • **~ped of all the verbiage, this means ...** sin toda la palabrería, esto quiere decir ...
4 (*Tech*) **a** (*also* **strip down**) [+ *engine*] desmontar
b (= *damage*) [+ *gears*] estropear
VI **1** (= *undress*) desnudarse • **to ~ naked** *or* **to the skin** quitarse toda la ropa • **to ~ to the waist** desnudarse hasta la cintura
2 (= *do striptease*) hacer striptease
CPD ▸ **strip cartoon** (*Brit*) tira *f* cómica, historieta *f*, caricatura *f* (*LAm*) ▸ **strip club** club *m* de striptease ▸ **strip joint*** (*esp US*) = **strip club** ▸ **strip light** lámpara *f* fluorescente ▸ **strip lighting** (*Brit*) alumbrado *m* fluorescente, alumbrado *m* de tubos ▸ **strip mine** (*US*) mina *f* a cielo abierto ▸ **strip mining** (*US*) minería *f* a cielo abierto ▸ **strip poker** strip póker *m* ▸ **strip search** registro *m* integral; ▷ **strip-search** ▸ **strip show** espectáculo *m* de striptease ▸ **strip wash** lavado *m* por completo; ▷ **strip-wash**
▸ **strip down** VT + ADV = **strip**
▸ **strip off** VT + ADV **1** [+ *paint etc*] quitar; (*violently*) arrancar • **the wind ~ped the leaves off the trees** el viento arrancó las hojas de los árboles
2 • **to ~ off one's clothes** quitarse (rápidamente) la ropa
VI + ADV **1** [*person*] desnudarse
2 [*paint etc*] desprenderse
stripe [straɪp] N **1** (= *line*) raya *f*, lista *f*; (*on flag etc*) franja *f*
2 (*Mil*) galón *m*
3† (= *lash*) azote *m*; (= *weal*) cardenal *m*
4 (*esp US*) (= *kind, sort*) • **of the worst ~** de la peor calaña

S

(VT) rayar, listar (**with** de)
striped [straɪpt] (ADJ) [*clothes, trousers*] de rayas, a rayas; [*pattern, wallpaper*] rayado, listado, de rayas
stripling ['strɪplɪŋ] (N) mozuelo *m*, joven *m* imberbe
stripped pine [ˌstrɪpt'paɪn] (N) pino *m* natural, pino *m* desnudo
stripper ['strɪpəʳ] (N) stripper *mf*, *persona que hace striptease*
strip-search ['strɪpsɜːtʃ] (VT) • **he was strip-searched at the airport** lo desnudaron para registrarlo en el aeropuerto
striptease ['strɪptiːz] (N) striptease *m*
strip-wash ['strɪpwɒʃ] (VT) lavar por completo
stripy ['straɪpɪ] (ADJ) [*clothes, trousers*] de rayas, a rayas; [*pattern, wallpaper*] rayado, listado, de rayas
strive [straɪv] (PT: **strove**, PP: **striven**) (VI) esforzarse, procurar • **to ~ after** *or* **for sth** esforzarse por conseguir algo • **to ~ against sth** luchar contra algo • **to ~ to do sth** esforzarse por hacer algo
striven ['strɪvn] (PP) *of* **strive**
striving ['straɪvɪŋ] (N) esfuerzos *mpl*, el esforzarse
strobe [strəʊb] (ADJ) [*lights*] estroboscópico
(N) **1** (*also* **strobe light**) luz *f* estroboscópica; (*also* **strobe lighting**) luces *fpl* estroboscópicas
2 = **stroboscope**
stroboscope ['strəʊbəskəʊp] (N) estroboscopio *m*
strode [strəʊd] (PT) *of* **stride**
stroke [strəʊk] (N) **1** (= *blow*) golpe *m* • **ten ~s of the lash** diez azotes • **with one ~ of his knife** de un solo navajazo • **at a** *or* **one ~** de un solo golpe • **~ of lightning** rayo *m*
2 (*fig*) • **his greatest ~ was to ...** su golpe maestro fue ... • **a ~ of diplomacy** un éxito diplomático • **he hasn't done a ~ (of work)** no ha dado golpe • **a ~ of genius** una ocurrencia genial • **the idea was a ~ of genius** la idea ha sido genial • **a ~ of luck** un golpe de suerte • **by a ~ of luck** por suerte • **then we had a ~ of luck** luego nos favoreció la suerte
3 (= *caress*) caricia *f* • **she gave the cat a ~** acarició el gato • **with a light ~ of the hand** con un suave movimiento de la mano
4 [*of pen*] trazo *m*, plumada *f*; [*of brush*] pincelada *f*; (*Typ*) barra *f* oblicua • **with a thick ~ of the pen** con un trazo grueso de la pluma • **at a ~ of the pen** • **with one ~ of the pen** de un plumazo
5 (*Cricket, Golf*) golpe *m*, jugada *f*; (*Billiards*) tacada *f* • **good ~!** ¡buen golpe!, ¡muy bien! • **to put sb off his/her ~** (= *distract*) hacer perder la concentración a algn, distraer a algn • **he tried to put me off my ~** (*Sport*) trató de hacerme errar el golpe • IDIOM: • **different ~s for different folks** (*esp US*) cada cual tiene sus gustos, hay gustos como colores
6 (*Swimming*) (= *single movement*) brazada *f*; (= *type of stroke*) estilo *m* • **he went ahead at every ~** se adelantaba con cada brazada
7 (*Rowing*) remada *f*; (= *person*) primer(a) remero/a *m/f* • **they are rowing a fast ~** reman a ritmo rápido • **to row ~** ser el primer remero, remar en el primer puesto
8 [*of bell, clock*] campanada *f*, toque *m* • **on the ~ of 12** al dar las 12
9 [*of piston*] carrera *f*
10 (*Med*) derrame *m* cerebral, apoplejía *f* • **to have a ~** tener un derrame cerebral, tener un ataque de apoplejía
(VT) **1** [+ *cat, sb's hair*] acariciar; [+ *chin*] pasar la mano sobre, pasar la mano por
2 (*Rowing*) • **to ~ a boat** ser el primero remero • **to ~ a boat to victory** ser el primero remero del bote vencedor
stroll [strəʊl] (N) paseo *m*, vuelta *f* • **to go for a ~** • **have** *or* **take a ~** dar un paseo, dar una vuelta
(VI) dar un paseo, pasear, dar una vuelta • **to ~ up and down** pasearse de acá para allá • **to ~ up to sb** acercarse tranquilamente a algn
stroller ['strəʊləʳ] (N) **1** (= *person*) paseante *mf*
2 (*esp US*) (= *pushchair*) cochecito *m*, sillita *f* de paseo
strong [strɒŋ] (ADJ) (COMPAR: **stronger**, SUPERL: **strongest**) **1** (= *physically tough*) fuerte • **I'm not ~ enough to carry him** no soy lo suficientemente fuerte para cargar con él • **to have ~ nerves** tener nervios de acero • **to have a ~ stomach** (*lit, fig*) tener un buen estómago • IDIOM: • **to be as ~ as an ox** ser fuerte como un toro; ▷ **arm¹**
2 (= *healthy*) [*teeth, bones*] sano; [*heart*] fuerte, sano • **she has never been very ~** nunca ha tenido una constitución fuerte • **he's getting ~er every day** (*after operation*) se va reponiendo poco a poco
3 (= *sturdy*) [*material, structure, frame*] fuerte
4 (= *powerful*) [*drug, wine, cheese, wind, voice*] fuerte; [*coffee*] fuerte, cargado; [*argument, evidence*] sólido, de peso; [*currency*] fuerte; [*magnet, lens*] potente; [*impression, influence*] grande • **music with a ~ beat** música *f* con mucho ritmo • **we have a ~ case (against them)** las razones que nosotros exponemos son muy sólidas (en contraposición a las de ellos)
5 (= *firm*) [*opinion, belief, supporter*] firme • **a man of ~ principles** un hombre de principios firmes • **Delhi developed ~ ties with Moscow** Delhi desarrolló vínculos muy estrechos con Moscú • **I am a ~ believer in tolerance** creo firmemente en *or* soy gran partidario de la tolerancia
6 (= *mentally*) fuerte • **he has a ~ personality** tiene un carácter *or* una personalidad fuerte • **he tries to be ~ for the sake of his children** intenta mostrarse fuerte por el bien de sus hijos • **he is a ~ leader** es un líder fuerte *or* sólido • **he's the ~ silent type** es de los muy reservados
7 (= *intense*) [*emotion, colour, smell*] fuerte, intenso; [*light*] potente, intenso • **there was a ~ smell of petrol** había un fuerte *or* intenso olor a gasolina
8 (= *good*) [*team*] fuerte; [*candidate*] bueno, firme; [*marriage, relationship*] sólido • **he is a ~ swimmer/runner** es un buen nadador/corredor • **the show has a ~ cast** el espectáculo tiene un buen reparto *or* un reparto muy sólido • **a ~ performance from Philippa Lilly in the title role** una actuación sólida *or* convincente por parte de Philippa Lilly en el papel de protagonista • **she is ~ in maths** las matemáticas se le dan muy bien • **he's not very ~ on grammar** no está muy fuerte en gramática • **discretion is not Jane's ~ point** la discreción no es el fuerte de Jane • **geography was never my ~ point** la geografía nunca fue mi fuerte • **to be in a ~ position** encontrarse en una buena posición • **there is a ~ possibility that ...** hay muchas posibilidades de que ...; ▷ **suit**
9 (= *severe, vehement*) [*words*] subido de tono, fuerte; [*denial*] tajante • **there has been ~ criticism of the military regime** se ha criticado duramente el régimen militar • **he has written a very ~ letter of protest to his MP** ha escrito una carta de protesta muy enérgica a su diputado • **~ language** (= *swearing*) lenguaje *m* fuerte; (= *frank*) lenguaje *m* muy directo • **in the ~est possible terms** enérgicamente
10 (= *noticeable*) [*resemblance*] marcado; [*presence*] fuerte • **he had a ~ German accent** tenía un fuerte *or* marcado acento alemán • **there is a ~ element of truth in this** hay gran parte de verdad en esto
11 [*features*] pronunciado, marcado
12 (*in number*) • **they are 20 ~** son 20 en total • **a group 20 ~** un grupo de 20 (miembros *etc*) • **a 1000-strong crowd** una multitud de 1000 personas
13 (*Ling*) [*verb*] irregular
(ADV) **1** • **to come on ~** (= *be harsh*) ser duro, mostrarse demasiado severo • **don't you think you came on a bit ~ there?** ¿no crees que fuiste un poco duro?, ¿no crees que te mostraste un poco severo? • **she was coming on ~** (= *showing attraction*) se veía que él le gustaba
2 • **to be going ~:** • **the firm is still going ~** la empresa se mantiene próspera • **their marriage is still going ~ after 50 years** después de 50 años su matrimonio sigue viento en popa • **he was still going ~ at 90** a sus 90 años todavía se conservaba en forma
strong-arm ['strɒŋɑːm] (ADJ) [*tactics, methods*] represivo
strong-armed ['strɒŋ'ɑːmd] (ADJ) de brazos fuertes
strongbox ['strɒŋbɒks] (N) caja *f* fuerte
stronghold ['strɒŋhəʊld] (N) fortaleza *f*, plaza *f* fuerte; (*fig*) baluarte *m*, centro *m* • **the last ~ of ...** el último baluarte de ...
strongly ['strɒŋlɪ] (ADV) **1** (= *sturdily*) • **~ built** [*person*] de constitución fuerte *or* robusta • **~ constructed** *or* **made** *or* **built** [*furniture, structure*] de construcción sólida
2 (= *firmly*) [*recommend, advise*] encarecidamente; [*believe, suspect*] firmemente • **I would ~ urge you to reconsider** le ruego encarecidamente que recapacite • **I feel very ~ that ...** creo firmemente que ... • **I ~ disagree with the decision** estoy totalmente en desacuerdo con la decisión • **he is a man with ~ held views** es un hombre de convicciones firmes • **~ recommended** [*book, film*] muy recomendado
3 (= *vehemently*) **a** (*with verb*) [*criticize*] duramente; [*oppose, support, protest, react*] enérgicamente; [*deny*] tajantemente, rotundamente; [*defend, argue*] firmemente • **a ~ worded letter** una carta subida de tono
b (*with adj, prep*) • **the mood here is still very ~ anti-British** el clima aquí continúa siendo profundamente antibritánico • **to be ~ against** *or* **opposed to sth** estar totalmente en contra de algo, oponerse enérgicamente a algo • **to be ~ critical of sth/sb** criticar duramente algo/a algn • **to be ~ in favour of sth** estar totalmente a favor de algo
4 (= *powerfully*) [*indicate*] claramente • **she was ~ attracted to him** sentía una fuerte atracción hacia él, se sentía fuertemente atraída hacia él • **if you feel ~ about this issue ...** si este tema te parece que es importante ... • **his early works were ~ influenced by jazz** sus primeras obras estaban muy influenciadas por el jazz • **he reminds me ~ of his uncle** me recuerda mucho a su tío • **to smell/taste ~ of sth** tener un fuerte olor/sabor a algo, oler/saber mucho a algo • **I'm ~ tempted to accompany you** me siento muy tentado a acompañarte • **she is ~ tipped to become party leader** es una de las favoritas para convertirse en líder del partido
5 (= *prominently*) • **to feature** *or* **figure ~ in sth** ocupar un lugar destacado *or* prominente

en algo • **two stories feature ~ in today's papers** hay dos noticias que ocupan un lugar destacado *or* prominente en los periódicos de hoy • **fish features ~ in the Japanese diet** el pescado ocupa un lugar destacado *or* prominente en la dieta japonesa

strongman ['strɒŋmæn] (N) (PL: **strongmen**) (*Circus*) forzudo *m*, hércules *m*; (*Pol etc*) hombre *m* fuerte

strong-minded ['strɒŋ'maɪndɪd] (ADJ) resuelto, decidido

strong-mindedly [ˌstrɒŋ'maɪndɪdlɪ] (ADV) resueltamente

strong-mindedness ['strɒŋ'maɪndɪdnɪs] (N) resolución *f*

strongpoint ['strɒŋpɔɪnt] (N) fuerte *m*, puesto *m* fortificado

strongroom ['strɒŋrʊm] (N) cámara *f* acorazada

strong-willed ['strɒŋ'wɪld] (ADJ) resuelto, decidido; (*pej*) obstinado

strontium ['strɒntɪəm] (N) estroncio *m* • **~ 90** estroncio *m* 90

strop [strɒp] (N) suavizador *m*
(VT) suavizar

strophe ['strəʊfɪ] (N) estrofa *f*

stroppiness* ['strɒpɪnɪs] (N) (*Brit*) [*of answer, children*] bordería *f*; [*of bouncer etc*] lo borde; [*of official*] mala educación *f*

stroppy* ['strɒpɪ] (ADJ) (*Brit*) borde‡ • **to get ~** ponerse borde‡

strove [strəʊv] (PT) *of* **strive**

struck [strʌk] (PT), (PP) *of* **strike**

structural ['strʌktʃərəl] (ADJ) estructural
(CPD) ▸ **structural engineer** ingeniero/a *m/f* de estructuras

structuralism ['strʌktʃərəlɪzəm] (N) estructuralismo *m*

structuralist ['strʌktʃərəlɪst] (ADJ) estructuralista
(N) estructuralista *mf*

structurally ['strʌktʃərəlɪ] (ADV) estructuralmente, desde el punto de vista de la estructura • **~ sound** de estructura sólida

structure ['strʌktʃəʳ] (N) **1** (= *organization, make-up*) estructura *f*
2 (= *thing constructed*) construcción *f*
(VT) [+ *essay, argument*] estructurar

structured ['strʌktʃəd] (ADJ) estructurado • **~ activity** actividad *f* estructurada

strudel ['ʃtru:dəl] (N) (*esp US*) strudel *m*

struggle ['strʌgl] (N) **1** (*lit*) pelea *f*, forcejeo *m* • **there were signs of a ~** había señales de haberse producido una pelea *or* un forcejeo • **two men went up to him and a ~ broke out** dos hombres se acercaron a él y se desencadenó una pelea • **he lost his glasses in the ~** perdió las gafas en la pelea *or* refriega • **to put up a ~** oponer resistencia, forcejear • **he handed over his wallet without a ~** entregó su billetera sin oponer resistencia
2 (*fig*) lucha *f* (**for** por) • **her ~ to feed her children** su lucha por poder dar de comer a sus hijos • **I had a ~ to persuade her** me costó trabajo persuadirla • **he finally lost his ~ against cancer** finalmente perdió su lucha contra el cáncer • **the ~ for survival** la lucha por la supervivencia • **there is a fierce power ~ going on behind the scenes** hay una intensa lucha por el poder entre bastidores • **local shopkeepers are not giving up without a ~** los tenderos del barrio no van a rendirse sin luchar; ▹ **class, uphill**
(VI) **1** (= *scuffle*) forcejear • **stop struggling!** ¡deja de forcejear! • **he ~d to get free from the ropes** forcejeó para soltarse de las cuerdas • **we were struggling for the gun when it went off** forcejeábamos para hacernos con la pistola cuando se disparó • **to ~ with sb** forcejear con algn
2 (= *move with difficulty*) • **to ~ free** lograr soltarse con dificultad • **I ~d into my costume** logré ponerme el disfraz como pude • **we ~d through the crowd** nos abrimos paso a duras penas entre la multitud • **she ~d to her feet** logró ponerse de pie • **the bus was struggling up the hill** el autobús subía con dificultad la cuesta • **he was struggling with his luggage** cargaba con su equipaje con gran esfuerzo
3 (= *fight against odds*) luchar • **to ~ to do sth** luchar por hacer algo, esforzarse por hacer algo • **to ~ against sth** luchar contra algo • **he ~d against the disease for 20 years** luchó contra la enfermedad durante 20 años • **we could see she was struggling for breath** veíamos como respiraba con dificultad • **to ~ in vain** luchar en vano
4 (= *have difficulties*) tener problemas • **they were struggling to pay their bills** tenían problemas *or* iban apurados para pagar las facturas • **the economy is struggling** la economía está en apuros • **he's struggling in his present class** se ve apurado en la clase en la que está ahora • **I ~d through the book** me costó terminar de leer el libro, tuve problemas para terminar de leer el libro • **she has ~d with her weight for years** ha tenido problemas con su peso durante años

▸ **struggle along** (VI + ADV) **1** (*lit*) avanzar con dificultad *or* penosamente
2 (*fig*) (*financially*) ir apurado

▸ **struggle on** (VI + ADV) **1** (= *keep moving*) • **we ~d on for another kilometre** conseguimos avanzar otro kilómetro a duras penas
2 (*fig*) seguir bregando • **many old people choose to ~ on alone** muchas personas mayores prefieren seguir bregando solas

▸ **struggle through** (VI + ADV) • **we'll ~ through somehow** saldremos adelante de algún modo

struggling ['strʌglɪŋ] (ADJ) [*artist, writer, actor*] que lucha por abrirse camino; [*business, team*] en apuros

strum [strʌm] (VT) [+ *guitar etc*] rasguear
(VI) cencerrear

strumpet† ['strʌmpɪt] (N) ramera *f*

strung [strʌŋ] ▹ **string, highly**

strut¹ [strʌt] (VI) (*also* **strut about, strut along**) pavonearse, contonearse • **to ~ into a room** entrar dándose aires *or* pavoneándose en una habitación • **to ~ past sb** pasar delante de algn pavoneándose
(VT) • IDIOM: • **to ~ one's stuff*** pavonearse, darse pisto*

strut² [strʌt] (N) (= *beam*) puntal *m*, riostra *f*

strychnine ['strɪkni:n] (N) estricnina *f*

Stuart ['stju:ət] (N) Estuardo

stub [stʌb] (N) [*of cigarette*] colilla *f*, pitillo *m*; [*of candle, pencil etc*] cabo *m*; [*of cheque, receipt*] talón *m*; [*of tree*] tocón *m*
(VT) • **to ~ one's toe (on sth)** dar con el dedo del pie (contra algo)

▸ **stub out** (VT + ADV) [+ *cigarette*] apagar

▸ **stub up** (VT + ADV) [+ *tree trunks*] desarraigar, quitar, arrancar

stubble ['stʌbl] (N) **1** (*Agr*) rastrojo *m*
2 (*on chin*) barba *f* (incipiente)

stubblefield ['stʌblfi:ld] (N) rastrojera *f*

stubbly ['stʌblɪ] (ADJ) [*chin*] sin afeitar; [*beard*] de tres días; [*person*] con barba de tres días

stubborn ['stʌbən] (ADJ) **1** (= *obstinate*) [*person*] testarudo, terco, tozudo; [*animal*] terco; [*nature, attitude, silence, refusal*] obstinado; [*resistance, insistence, determination*] obstinado, pertinaz • **she has a very ~ streak** puede ser muy testaruda *or* terca *or* tozuda • IDIOM: • **as ~ as a mule** terco como una mula
2 (= *hard to deal with*) [*problem*] pertinaz; [*stain, lock*] difícil, resistente • **he had a ~ cold** tenía un resfriado persistente

stubbornly ['stʌbənlɪ] (ADV) [*insist, say*] obstinadamente, tercamente; [*refuse, continue, oppose*] obstinadamente; [*resist, cling*] (= *steadfastly*) tenazmente; (= *pig-headedly*) obstinadamente • **he was ~ determined/persistent** su resolución era obstinada/su insistencia era tenaz • **interest rates have remained ~ high** perduran los tipos altos de interés

stubbornness ['stʌbənnɪs] (N) [*of person*] testarudez *f*, terquedad *f*, tozudez *f*; [*of animal*] terquedad *f*; [*of cough, cold*] lo persistente

stubby ['stʌbɪ] (ADJ) (COMPAR: **stubbier**, SUPERL: **stubbiest**) achaparrado

STUC (N ABBR) = **Scottish Trades Union Congress**

stucco ['stʌkəʊ] (N) (PL: **stuccoes** *or* **stuccos**) estuco *m*
(ADJ) de estuco
(VT) estucar

stuck [stʌk] (PT), (PP) *of* **stick**

stuck-up* ['stʌk'ʌp] (ADJ) presumido, engreído • **to be very stuck-up about sth** presumir mucho a causa de algo

stud¹ [stʌd] (N) (*in road*) clavo *m*, tope *m* (*Mex*); (*decorative*) tachón *m*, tachuela *f*, clavo *m* (de adorno); (*on boots*) taco *m*; (= *collar stud, shirt stud*) corchete *m*
(VT) [+ *boots, jacket, shield, door*] tachonar

stud² [stʌd] (N) **1** (*also* **stud farm**) caballeriza *f*, cuadra *f*; (*also* **stud horse**) caballo *m* semental
2‡ (= *man*) semental* *m*
(CPD) ▸ **stud book** registro *m* genealógico de caballos ▸ **stud mare** yegua *f* de cría

studded ['stʌdɪd] (ADJ) **1** (= *decorated with studs*) [*jacket, leather belt*] con tachuelas • **~ with sth** (= *decorated*) (*with diamonds, precious stones*) incrustado de algo
2 • **~ with sth** (= *full of*) lleno de algo; ▹ **star-studded**

student ['stju:dənt] (N) (*Scol*) alumno/a *m/f*; (*Univ*) estudiante *mf*, universitario/a *m/f*; (= *researcher*) investigador(a) *m/f* • **a law/medical ~** un(a) estudiante de derecho/medicina • **French ~** (*by nationality*) estudiante *mf* francés/esa; (*by subject*) estudiante *mf* de francés • **he is a ~ of bird life** es un estudioso de las aves
(CPD) [*life, unrest, attitude*] estudiantil ▸ **student body** [*of school*] alumnado *m*; [*of university*] estudiantado *m* ▸ **student council** comité *m* de delegados de clase ▸ **student driver** (*US*) *persona que está sacando el carnet de conducir* ▸ **student file** (*US*) archivo *m* escolar ▸ **student grant** beca *f* ▸ **student ID card** (*US*) carnet *m* de estudiante ▸ **student loan** crédito *m* personal para estudiantes ▸ **student nurse** estudiante *mf* de enfermería ▸ **student teacher** (*studying*) (*at college*) estudiante *mf* de magisterio; (*doing teaching practice*) (*in secondary school*) profesor(a) *m/f* en prácticas; (*in primary school*) maestro/a *m/f* en prácticas ▸ **student(s') union** (= *building*) centro *m* estudiantil; (*Brit*) (= *association*) federación *f* de estudiantes

studentship ['stju:dəntʃɪp] (N) beca *f*

studied ['stʌdɪd] (ADJ) (*gen*) estudiado, pensado; [*calm, insult*] calculado, premeditado; [*pose, style*] estudiado, afectado

studio ['stju:dɪəʊ] (N) (*TV, Mus*) estudio *m*; [*of*

S

artist] estudio *m*, taller *m*
CPD ▸ **studio apartment** estudio *m* ▸ **studio audience** público *m* de estudio ▸ **studio complex, studio lot** (*for making films*) complejo *m* de estudios ▸ **studio couch** sofá-cama *m* ▸ **studio director** director(a) *m/f* de interiores ▸ **studio flat** (*Brit*) estudio *m* ▸ **studio theatre** teatro *m* de ensayo

studious ['stju:dɪəs] ADJ **1** (= *devoted to study*) estudioso
2 (= *thoughtful*) atento; [*effort*] asiduo; [*politeness*] calculado, esmerado

studiously ['stju:dɪəslɪ] ADV con aplicación • **he ~ avoided mentioning the matter** evitó cuidadosamente aludir al asunto, se guardó muy bien de aludir al asunto

studiousness ['stju:dɪəsnɪs] N aplicación *f*

study ['stʌdɪ] N **1** (*gen*) estudio *m*; [*of text, evidence etc*] investigación *f*, estudio *m* • **my studies show that ...** mis estudios demuestran que ... • **to make a ~ of sth** realizar una investigación de algo • IDIOM: • **his face was a ~** (*hum*) ¡si le hubieras visto la cara!; ▹ **brown**
2 (= *room*) biblioteca *f*, despacho *m*
VT **1** (*gen*) estudiar; (*as student*) estudiar, cursar
2 (= *examine*) [+ *evidence, painting*] examinar, investigar
VI estudiar • **to ~ to be an agronomist** estudiar para agrónomo • **to ~ under sb** estudiar con algn, trabajar bajo la dirección de algn • **to ~ for an exam** estudiar *or* preparar un examen
CPD ▸ **study group** grupo *m* de estudio ▸ **study hall** (*US*) (= *hour for study*) hora *f* de estudio; (*longer*) periodo *m* de estudios; (= *room*) sala *f* de estudios ▸ **study leave** *permiso en el trabajo para realizar estudios* ▸ **study period** (*Brit*) (= *hour for study*) hora *f* de estudio; (*longer*) periodo *m* de estudios; (= *observation time for research*) periodo *m* del estudio ▸ **study tour** viaje *m* de estudios

stuff [stʌf] N **1*** (= *substance, material*) **a** (*lit*) • **what's that ~ in the bucket?** ¿qué es eso que hay en el cubo? • **"do you want some beetroot?" — "no, I hate the ~"** —¿quieres remolacha? —no, la detesto • **"would you like some wine?" — " no, thanks, I never touch the ~"** —¿quieres un poco de vino? —no gracias, nunca lo pruebo • **have you got any more of that varnish ~?** ¿tienes más barniz de ese? • **do you call this ~ beer?** ¿a esto lo llamas cerveza? • **radioactive waste is dangerous ~** los residuos radiactivos son cosa peligrosa
b (*fig*) • **there is some good ~ in that book** ese libro tiene cosas buenas • **I can't read his ~** no puedo con sus libros • **he was made of less heroic ~** no tenía tanta madera de héroe • **to be made of sterner ~** no ser tan blandengue* • **show him what kind of ~ you are made of** demuéstrale de qué tienes madera • **that's the ~!** ¡muy bien!, ¡así se hace!
2* (= *belongings*) cosas *fpl*, bártulos* *mpl*, chismes *mpl* (*Sp**) • **where have you put my ~?** ¿dónde has puesto mis cosas?, ¿dónde has puesto mis bártulos *or* (*Sp*) chismes?* • **quite a lot of ~ had been stolen** habían robado bastantes cosas • **can I put my ~ in your room?** ¿puedo poner mis cosas en tu cuarto? • **he brought back a lot of ~ from China** trajo muchas cosas de China
3* (= *nonsense*) historias *fpl* • **all that ~ about how he wants to help us** todas esas historias *or* todo el cuento ese de que quiere ayudarnos • **don't give me that ~! I know what you're been up to!** ¡no me vengas con esas historias *or* ese cuento! ¡sé lo que pretendes! • **~ and nonsense!**†* ¡tonterías!, ¡puro cuento!
4* • IDIOMS: • **to do one's ~**: • **go on, Jim, do your ~! let's see a goal!** ¡venga Jim! ¡muéstranos lo que vales, mete ese gol! • **we'll have to wait for the lawyers to do their ~** tendremos que esperar a que los abogados hagan su parte • **to know one's ~** ser un experto; ▹ **strut'**
5* • **and ~** y tal* • **he was busy writing letters and ~** estaba ocupado escribiendo cartas y tal* • **I haven't got time for boyfriends, the cinema and ~ like that** *or* **and all that ~** no tengo tiempo para novios, el cine y rollos por el estilo*
6 (= *essence*) • **the (very) ~ of sth: the pleasures and pains that are the ~ of human relationships** las alegrías y las penas que constituyen la esencia de las relaciones humanas • **he's hardly the ~ of romantic dreams** no es precisamente el ideal de los sueños románticos • **his feats on the tennis court are the ~ of legend** sus proezas en la cancha de tenis son legendarias
7‡ • **I couldn't give a ~ what he thinks** me importa un comino lo que piense*
8 (*Brit‡*) (= *girl, woman*) • **she's a nice bit of ~** está bien buena‡; ▹ **hot**
9 (*Drugs‡*) mercancía‡ *f*
10†† (= *fabric*) género *m*, tela *f*
VT **1** (= *fill, pack*) [+ *chicken, peppers, cushion, toy*] rellenar (**with** con); [+ *sack, box, pockets*] llenar (**with** de); [+ *hole, leak*] tapar; (*in taxidermy*) [+ *animal*] disecar, embalsamar • **he had to ~ his ears with cotton wool** tuvo que llenarse las orejas de algodón • **they ~ed him with morphine*** lo atiborraron de morfina* • **to ~ one's head with useless facts*** llenarse la cabeza de información que no vale para nada • **her head is ~ed with formulae*** tiene la cabeza llena de fórmulas • **to ~ a ballot box** (*US*) (*Pol*) *llenar una urna de votos fraudulentos* • **to ~ one's face*** • **~ o.s. (with food)*** atracarse *or* atiborrarse de comida*, darse un atracón*
2* (= *put*) • **to ~ sth in** *or* **into sth** meter algo en algo • **he ~ed his hands in his pockets** se metió las manos en los bolsillos • **he ~ed it into his pocket** se lo metió de prisa en el bolsillo • **can we ~ any more in?** ¿caben más? • **~ your books on the table** pon tus libros en la mesa • IDIOM: • **to ~ sth down sb's throat** meter a algn algo por la fuerza* • **I'm sick of having ideology ~ed down my throat** estoy harto de que me metan la ideología a la fuerza*
3 (*Brit‡*) (*in exclamations*) • **~ you!** ¡vete a tomar por culo! (*Sp***), ¡vete al carajo! (*LAm***) • **oh, ~ it! I've had enough for today** ¡a la mierda! ¡por hoy ya vale!‡ • **if you don't like it, you can ~ it** si no te gusta te jodes** • **(you know where) you can ~ that!** ¡ya sabes por dónde te lo puedes meter!‡ • **~ the government!** ¡que se joda el gobierno!** • **get ~ed!** ¡vete a tomar por culo! (*Sp***), ¡vete al carajo! (*LAm***)
4‡ (= *defeat*) dar un palizón a*, machacar*
VI* (= *guzzle*) atracarse de comida*, atiborrarse de comida*, darse un atracón*

▸ **stuff up** VT + ADV • **to be ~ed up** [*person*] estar constipado • **my nose is ~ed up** tengo la nariz taponada *or* atascada • **to get ~ed up** [*pipe*] atascarse

stuffed [stʌft] ADJ **1** (*in taxidermy*) [*animal*] disecado, embalsamado
2 (*Culin*) • **~ peppers/tomatoes** pimientos *mpl*/tomates *mpl* rellenos
3* (= *full*) • **I'm ~** estoy hasta arriba*
CPD ▸ **stuffed animal** (*following taxidermy*) animal *m* disecado, animal *m* embalsamado; (*US*) (= *toy*) muñeco *m* de peluche ▸ **stuffed shirt*** (*fig*) • **he's a bit of a ~ shirt** es un poco estirado* ▸ **stuffed toy** (*US*) muñeco *m* de peluche

stuffily ['stʌfɪlɪ] ADV [*say*] en tono de desaprobación, con desaprobación

stuffiness ['stʌfɪnɪs] N **1** (*in room*) mala ventilación *f*, falta *f* de aire
2 (*fig*) (= *narrow-mindedness*) estrechez *f* de miras, remilgos *mpl*; (= *starchiness*) lo estirado; (= *prudishness*) remilgos *mpl*; (= *dullness*) pesadez *f*

stuffing ['stʌfɪŋ] N [*of furniture, stuffed animal*] relleno *m*, borra *f*; (*Culin*) relleno *m* • IDIOMS: • **he's got no ~*** no tiene carácter, no tiene agallas • **to knock the ~ out of sb*** dejar a algn para el arrastre • **he had the ~ knocked out of him by the blow*** el golpe lo dejó sin fuerzas ni ánimo

stuffy ['stʌfɪ] ADJ (COMPAR: **stuffier**, SUPERL: **stuffiest**) **1** [*room*] mal ventilado; [*atmosphere*] cargado, sofocante • **it's ~ in here** aquí huele a cerrado, el ambiente está un poco cargado aquí
2 [*person*] (= *narrow-minded*) remilgado, de miras estrechas; (= *prudish*) remilgado; (= *stiff, starchy*) tieso; (= *dull, boring*) pesado, poco interesante
3 (= *congested*) [*nose*] taponado, atascado • **I've got a ~ nose** tengo la nariz taponada *or* atascada

stultify ['stʌltɪfaɪ] VT anular, aniquilar

stultifying ['stʌltɪfaɪɪŋ] ADJ [*work, regime, routine*] embrutecedor; [*atmosphere*] sofocante, agobiante

stumble ['stʌmbl] N tropezón *m*, traspié *m*
VI tropezar, dar un traspié • **to ~ against sth** tropezar contra algo • **to ~ on** • **to go stumbling on** (= *keep walking*) avanzar dando traspiés • **to ~ over sth** tropezar en algo • **to ~ through a speech** pronunciar un discurso de cualquier manera, pronunciar un discurso atracándose • **to ~ (up)on** *or* **across sth** (*fig*) tropezar con algo

stumbling block ['stʌmblɪŋblɒk] N (*fig*) tropiezo *m*, escollo *m*

stump [stʌmp] N **1** (*gen*) cabo *m*; [*of limb*] muñón *m*; [*of tree*] tocón *m*; [*of tooth*] raigón *m* • IDIOM: • **to find o.s. up a ~** (*US**) quedarse de piedra, estar perplejo
2 (*Cricket*) palo *m*
3 (*Art*) difumino *m*, esfumino *m*
4 • **to be** *or* **go on the ~** (*US*) (*Pol*) hacer campaña electoral
5‡ (= *leg*) pierna *f*; ▹ **stir**
VT **1*** (= *perplex*) dejar perplejo *or* confuso • **I'm completely ~ed** estoy totalmente perplejo • **to be ~ed for an answer** no tener respuesta
2 (*Cricket*) eliminar
3 • **to ~ the country** (*US*) (*Pol*) *recorrer el país pronunciando discursos*
VI (= *hobble, limp*) renquear, cojear
CPD ▸ **stump speech** (*US*) (*Pol*) discurso *m* de campaña

▸ **stump up*** (*Brit*) VT + ADV • **to ~ up five pounds** apoquinar cinco libras, desembolsar cinco libras (**for sth**) para comprar algo *or* por algo
VI + ADV apoquinar, soltar la guita* (**for sth** para pagar algo)

stumpy ['stʌmpɪ] ADJ [*person etc*] achaparrado; [*pencil etc*] corto, reducido a casi nada, muy gastado

stun [stʌn] VT **1** (= *render unconscious*) dejar sin sentido
2 (= *daze*) aturdir, atontar • **he was ~ned by the blow** el golpe lo aturdió *or* atontó, el golpe lo dejó aturdido *or* atontado
3 (= *amaze*) dejar pasmado

S

4 (= *shock*) dejar anonadado • **the news ~ned everybody** la noticia dejó anonadados a todos • **the family were ~ned by his death** la familia quedó anonadada a raíz de su muerte

CPD ▸ **stun grenade** granada *f* detonadora, granada *f* de estampida ▸ **stun gun** *arma para inmovilizar a animales o a personas temporalmente*

stung [stʌŋ] PT, PP *of* **sting**

stunk [stʌŋk] PP *of* **stink**

stunned [stʌnd] ADJ **1** (= *unconscious*) sin sentido

2 (= *dazed*) aturdido, atontado

3 (= *amazed*) pasmado • **I was absolutely ~ when I realized I had won** me quedé pasmado cuando me di cuenta de que había ganado, me quedé alucinado cuando me di cuenta de que había ganado* • **~ passers-by could not believe what was happening** los transeúntes, estupefactos, no podían creer lo que estaba sucediendo

4 (= *shocked*) anonadado • **I was too ~ to reply** me quedé tan anonadado que no pude contestar • **he had a ~ expression on his face** tenía una expresión de asombro en el rostro • **I sat in ~ silence** me senté en silencio, anonadado • **people reacted to the news with ~ disbelief** al enterarse de la noticia la gente se quedó anonadada, sin dar crédito a lo que oía

stunner* ['stʌnəʳ] N (= *person*) persona *f* maravillosa; (= *thing*) cosa *f* estupenda* • **she's a real ~** está buenísima *or* como un tren*, es una mujer despampanante* • **the picture is a ~** el cuadro es maravilloso

stunning ['stʌnɪŋ] ADJ **1** (= *fabulous*) [*dress, girl*] imponente, deslumbrante, despampanante*; [*film, performance*] impresionante, sensacional • **a ~ blonde** una rubia imponente, una rubia despampanante* • **you look absolutely ~** estás deslumbrante • **the effect is ~** el efecto es impresionante

2 (= *startling*) [*news*] asombroso; [*success*] increíble; [*defeat*] aplastante • **his death came as a ~ blow** su muerte fue un golpe tremendo

3 (= *violent*) • **he dealt me a ~ blow on the jaw** me dio un golpe en la mandíbula que me dejó aturdido *or* atontado

stunningly ['stʌnɪŋlɪ] ADV [*dressed, painted*] maravillosamente; [*original*] increíblemente • **she was ~ beautiful** tenía una belleza deslumbrante, era de una belleza imponente • **she looked ~ beautiful** estaba deslumbrante *or* imponente • **~ beautiful scenery** paisajes de una belleza impresionante • **a ~ simple design** un diseño de una sencillez asombrosa

stunt¹ [stʌnt] VT [+ *tree, growth*] impedir (el crecimiento de), atrofiar

stunt² [stʌnt] N **1** (= *feat*) proeza *f*, hazaña *f*; (*for film*) escena *f* peligrosa, toma *f* peligrosa; (*Aer*) vuelo *m* acrobático, ejercicio *m* acrobático • **to pull a ~** hacer algo peligroso (y tonto)

2 (= *publicity stunt*) truco *m* publicitario • **it's just a ~ to get your money** es solo un truco para sacarte dinero

VI (*Aer*) hacer vuelos acrobáticos

CPD ▸ **stunt flier** aviador(a) *m/f* acrobático/a ▸ **stunt kite** cometa *f* acrobática

stunted ['stʌntɪd] ADJ enano, mal desarrollado

stuntman ['stʌntmæn] N (PL: **stuntmen**) doble *m* (*especializado en escenas peligrosas*)

stuntwoman ['stʌntwʊmən] N (PL: **stuntwomen**) doble *f* (*especializada en escenas peligrosas*)

stupefaction [ˌstju:pɪ'fækʃən] N estupefacción *f*

stupefy ['stju:pɪfaɪ] VT **1** (*through tiredness, alcohol*) atontar • **stupefied by drink** en estado de estupor después de haber bebido; (*permanently*) embrutecido por el alcohol

2 (= *astound*) dejar estupefacto *or* pasmado

stupefying ['stju:pɪfaɪɪŋ] ADJ (*fig*) pasmoso

stupendous* [stju:'pendəs] ADJ (= *wonderful*) estupendo; (= *extraordinary*) extraordinario

stupendously* [stju:'pendəslɪ] ADV (= *wonderfully*) estupendamente; (= *extraordinarily*) extraordinariamente

stupid ['stju:pɪd] ADJ **1** (= *unintelligent*) [*person*] estúpido, tonto, imbécil; [*question, remark, idea*] estúpido, tonto; [*mistake, game*] tonto, bobo • **don't be (so) ~** no seas tonto • **I'll never do anything so ~ again** nunca volveré a cometer semejante estupidez • **don't do anything ~, will you?** no vayas a hacer alguna tontería ¿eh? • **it's ~ to leave money lying around** es una estupidez *or* es de tontos dejar el dinero a la vista de todos • **to act ~*** (= *pretend to be stupid*) hacerse el tonto; (= *behave stupidly*) hacer el tonto • **she looks ~ in that hat** • **that hat looks ~ on her** está ridícula con ese sombrero • **it looks ~** se ve ridículo, queda ridículo • **to make sb look ~** dejar a algn en ridículo • **it was ~ of you** fue una tontería por tu parte, ¡qué tonto *or* imbécil fuiste! • **it was ~ of me to say that** fui tonto al decir eso, cometí una estupidez al decir eso • **it was a ~ thing to do** fue una tontería *or* una estupidez • **that's the ~est thing I ever heard** jamás he oído semejante tontería *or* estupidez; ▹ **plain**

2* (= *insensible, dazed*) atontado • **to bore sb ~** matar a algn de aburrimiento • **to drink o.s. ~** pillarse una trompa de miedo* • **to knock sb ~** dejar a algn atontado *or* aturdido de un golpe, dejar a algn tonto *or* lelo de un golpe* • **to laugh o.s. ~** partirse de risa*

3* (= *pesky*) maldito*, condenado* • **I hate these ~ shoes** odio estos malditos *or* condenados zapatos* • **you ~ idiot!** ¡idiota!, ¡imbécil! • **she gets annoyed by ~ little things** se molesta por cualquier tontería, se molesta por cualquier chorrada (*Sp**)

N* (*as excl*) • **don't do that, ~!** ¡no hagas eso, imbécil!* • **come on, ~!** (*said affectionately*) ¡venga bobo!*

ADV* • **don't talk ~!** ¡no digas tonterías *or* estupideces!*

stupidity [stju:'pɪdɪtɪ] N **1** (= *quality*) estupidez *f* • **he laughed at their ~** se reía de su estupidez • **an act of ~** una acción estúpida

2 (= *stupid thing*) estupidez *f*, tontería *f*

stupidly ['stju:pɪdlɪ] ADV [*behave, act*] como un idiota; [*stare, grin*] como un bobo, como un tonto • **~, I said I would help her** como un tonto, dije que la ayudaría, cometí la estupidez de decir que la ayudaría • **~, he'd not anticipated that this might happen** había sido una estupidez por su parte, pero no había previsto que esto pudiera ocurrir • **somebody had ~ left the door open** alguien había cometido la estupidez de dejar la puerta abierta

stupidness ['stju:pɪdnɪs] N = **stupidity**

stupor ['stju:pəʳ] N estupor *m*

sturdily ['stɜ:dɪlɪ] ADV **1** • **~ built** [*house*] de construcción sólida; [*person*] robusto; [*furniture*] sólido

2 (= *stoically*) [*say*] firmemente, enérgicamente; [*oppose*] enérgicamente, tenazmente

sturdiness ['stɜ:dɪnɪs] N **1** [*of person, tree*] robustez *f*, fuerza *f*; [*of boats, material*] fuerza *f*; [*of furniture*] solidez *f*

2 (*fig*) [*of supporter, refusal*] energía *f*, firmeza *f*

sturdy ['stɜ:dɪ] ADJ (COMPAR: **sturdier**, SUPERL: **sturdiest**) **1** [*person, tree*] robusto, fuerte; [*boat, material*] fuerte; [*table, furniture*] sólido

2 (*fig*) [*supporter, refusal*] enérgico, firme; [*resistance*] tenaz • **~ independence** espíritu *m* fuerte de independencia

sturgeon ['stɜ:dʒən] N esturión *m*

stutter ['stʌtəʳ] N tartamudeo *m* • **he has a bad ~** tartamudea terriblemente • **to say sth with a ~** decir algo tartamudeando

VI tartamudear

VT (*also* **stutter out**) decir tartamudeando

stutterer ['stʌtərəʳ] N tartamudo/a *m/f*

stuttering ['stʌtərɪŋ] ADJ tartamudo

N tartamudeo *m*

stutteringly ['stʌtərɪŋlɪ] ADV • **he said ~** dijo tartamudeando

STV N ABBR **1** (*Pol*) = **Single Transferable Vote**

2 = **Scottish Television**

sty¹ [staɪ] N **1** [*of pigs*] pocilga *f*, chiquero *m* (*S. Cone*)

2‡ (*fig*) pocilga* *f*, leonera* *f*

sty², stye [staɪ] N (*Med*) orzuelo *m*

Stygian ['stɪdʒɪən] ADJ estigio

style [staɪl] N **1** (*Mus, Art, Literat*) estilo *m* • **in the ~ of Mozart** al estilo de Mozart • **a building in the neoclassical ~** un edificio de estilo neoclásico

2 (= *design, model*) estilo *m* • **I want something in that ~** quiero algo de ese estilo

3 (= *mode*) estilo *m* • **we must change our ~ of play** debemos cambiar nuestro estilo de juego • **the present ~ of leadership** el estilo actual de liderazgo • **management ~** estilo *m* administrativo • **~ of living** estilo *m* de vida • **in the Italian ~** al estilo italiano, a la italiana • **that's the ~!** ¡así se hace!, ¡muy bien! • **this is a lesson in economics, nineties ~** esta es una lección de economía al estilo de los noventa • **6 March, old/new ~** 6 de marzo, según el calendario juliano/gregoriano; ▹ **house**

4 (= *elegance*) estilo *m* • **there's no ~ about him** no tiene nada de estilo • **to have ~** tener estilo • **to do sth in ~** hacer algo por todo lo alto *or* a lo grande • **they celebrated in ~** lo celebraron por todo lo alto *or* a lo grande • **to live in ~** vivir por todo lo alto *or* rodeado de lujo • **to travel in ~** viajar por todo lo alto • **he won in fine ~** ganó de manera impecable

5 (= *fashion*) moda *f* • **to go out of ~** [*mode of dress*] pasar de moda • **they spent money like it was going out of ~*** (*hum*) gastaban dinero a troche y moche *or* como si fuera agua • **she was drinking vodka like it was going out of ~** bebía vodka como si se estuviera acabando el mundo

6* (= *way of behaving*) estilo *m* • **I like your ~** me gusta tu estilo • **that's not her ~** eso no es su estilo; ▹ **cramp¹**

7 (*also* **hairstyle**) peinado *m*

8 (= *form of address*) título *m*

VT **1** (*frm*) (= *call, designate*) • **the headmaster is ~d "rector"** al director se le llama "rector" • **he ~s himself "Doctor"** se hace llamar "Doctor"; ▹ **self-styled**

2 (= *design*) [+ *clothes, car, model*] diseñar • **to ~ sb's hair** peinar a algn • **Jackie's hair was ~d by …** Jackie ha sido peinada por … • **her hair is ~d in a bob** lleva una melena corta

3 (*Typ*) [+ *manuscript*] editar (*siguiendo el estilo de la editorial*)

CPD ▸ **style book** (*Typ*) libro *m* de estilo ▸ **style guru*** gurú *mf* de la moda ▸ **style sheet** (*Comput*) hoja *f* de estilo

style-conscious ['staɪlkɒnʃəs] ADJ • **the**

style-conscious teenager el/la adolescente que se preocupa por la moda

styli ['staɪlaɪ] NPL *of* **stylus**

styling ['staɪlɪŋ] N estilización *f*
CPD ▸ **styling brush** (cepillo *m*) rizador *m*

stylisation [,staɪlaɪ'zeɪʃən], **stylization** N estilización *f*

stylish ['staɪlɪʃ] ADJ [*performance*] elegante; [*clothes, car, décor, area*] (= *elegant*) elegante; (= *modern*) moderno • **she's a ~ dresser** (= *elegant*) viste con elegancia *or* con estilo; (= *fashionable*) siempre va vestida muy a la moda

stylishly ['staɪlɪʃlɪ] ADV [*perform*] con estilo, con elegancia; [*dress*] (= *elegantly*) con estilo, con elegancia; (= *fashionably*) a la moda; [*write*] con elegancia

stylishness ['staɪlɪʃnɪs] N [*of area, resort, performance*] elegancia *f*; [*of clothes, car, décor, person*] estilo *m*, elegancia *f*

stylist ['staɪlɪst] N **1** (*also* **hair stylist**) peluquero/a *m/f*
2 (*Literat*) estilista *mf*

stylistic [staɪ'lɪstɪk] ADJ [*device*] estilístico; [*improvement*] del estilo

stylistically [staɪ'lɪstɪklɪ] ADV estilísticamente

stylistics [staɪ'lɪstɪks] NSING estilística *f*

stylized ['staɪlaɪzd] ADJ estilizado

stylus ['staɪləs] N (PL: **styluses** *or* **styli**) (= *pen*) estilo *m*; [*of record-player*] aguja *f*

stymie* ['staɪmɪ] VT • **to ~ sb** bloquear a algn, poner obstáculos infranqueables delante de algn • **now we're really ~d!** ¡la hemos pringado de verdad!*, ¡la hemos liado!*

styptic ['stɪptɪk] ADJ astringente
N estíptico *m*
CPD ▸ **styptic pencil** lapicero *m* hemostático

Styrofoam® ['staɪrə,fəʊm] N (*US*) poliestireno *m*
CPD [*cup*] de poliestireno

Styx [stɪks] N Estigio *m*, Laguna *f* Estigia

suasion ['sweɪʒən] N (= *liter*) persuasión *f*

suave [swɑːv] ADJ fino; (*pej*) hábil

suavely ['swɑːvlɪ] ADV (*pej*) [*say, smile*] hábilmente

suavity ['swɑːvɪtɪ] N finura *f*; (*pej*) habilidad *f*

sub¹ [sʌb] N ABBR **1** = **subaltern**
2 = **subeditor**
3 = **submarine**
4 = **subscription**
5 = **substitute**
VT ABBR = **sub-edit**

sub² [sʌb] VI • **to sub for sb** hacer las veces de algn

sub³* [sʌb] N (= *advance on wages*) avance *m*, anticipo *m*
VT anticipar dinero a

sub... [sʌb] PREFIX sub...

subalpine ['sʌb'ælpaɪn] ADJ subalpino

subaltern ['sʌbltən] N (*Brit*) (*Mil*) alférez *mf*

subaqua [,sʌb'ækwə] ADJ subacuático, de submarinismo

subarctic ['sʌb'ɑːktɪk] ADJ subártico

subatomic [,sʌbə'tɒmɪk] ADJ subatómico

sub-basement ['sʌb,beɪsmənt] N subsótano *m*

sub-branch ['sʌbbrɑːntʃ] N subdelegación *f*

subcategory ['sʌb,kætɪgərɪ] N subcategoría *f*

subclass ['sʌbklɑːs] N subclase *f*

subcommittee ['sʌbkə,mɪtɪ] N subcomisión *f*, subcomité *m*

subcompact ['sʌbkɒmpækt] N (*US*) (*Aut*) subcompacto *m*

subconscious ['sʌb'kɒnʃəs] ADJ subconsciente
N • **the ~** el subconsciente • **in one's ~** en el subconsciente

subconsciously ['sʌb'kɒnʃəslɪ] ADV subconscientemente

subcontinent ['sʌb'kɒntɪnənt] N • **the (Indian) ~** el subcontinente (de la India)

subcontract N [,sʌb'kɒntrækt] subcontrato *m*
VT [,sʌbkən'trækt] subcontratar

subcontracting ['sʌbkɒn'træktɪŋ] ADJ subcontratado
N subcontratación *f*

subcontractor [,sʌbkən'træktəʳ] N subcontratista *mf*

subculture ['sʌb,kʌltʃəʳ] N subcultura *f*

subcutaneous ['sʌbkjʊ'teɪnɪəs] ADJ subcutáneo

subdirectory ['sʌbdɪ,rektərɪ] N (*Comput*) subdirectorio *m*

subdivide ['sʌbdɪ'vaɪd] VT subdividir
VI subdividirse

subdivision ['sʌbdɪ,vɪʒən] N subdivisión *f*

subdominant [sʌb'dɒmɪnənt] N subdominante *f*
ADJ subdominante • **~ chord** acorde subdominante

subdue [səb'djuː] VT [+ *enemy*] someter, sojuzgar; [+ *children, revellers*] calmar, tranquilizar; [+ *animal*] amansar, domar; [+ *noise*] bajar; [+ *passions*] dominar

subdued [səb'djuːd] ADJ [*colours, light, lighting*] tenue, suave; [*voice*] suave; [*mood*] apagado; [*person*] (= *quiet*) apagado; (= *passive*) sumiso, manso; (= *depressed*) deprimido • **you were very ~ last night** anoche se te veía muy apagado

sub-edit ['sʌb'edɪt] VT (*Brit*) [+ *article*] corregir, preparar para la prensa

subeditor [sʌb'edɪtəʳ] N (*esp Brit*) (= *copy editor*) redactor(a) *m/f*

sub-entry ['sʌbentrɪ] N (*Book-keeping*) subasiento *m*, subapunte *m*

subfamily ['sʌb,fæmɪlɪ] N (*esp Bio*) subfamilia *f*

subfolder ['sʌbfəʊldəʳ] N (*Comput*) subcarpeta *f*

sub-frame ['sʌbfreɪm] N (*Aut*) subchasis *m*

subgenre ['sʌbʒɑ̃ːnr] N subgénero *m*

subgrade ['sʌbgreɪd] N [*of road etc*] subgrado *m*

subgroup ['sʌbgruːp] N subgrupo *m*

subhead ['sʌb,hed], **subheading** ['sʌb,hedɪŋ] N subtítulo *m*

subhuman ['sʌb'hjuːmən] ADJ infrahumano

subject N ['sʌbdʒɪkt] **1** (= *topic, theme*) tema *m*; (= *plot*) argumento *m*, asunto *m* • **to change the ~** cambiar de tema • **let's change the ~** cambiemos de tema • **changing the ~** … hablando de otra cosa …, cambiando de tema … • **it's a delicate ~** es un asunto delicado • **on the ~ of …** a propósito de … • **(while we're) on the ~ of money** … ya que de dinero se trata … • **this raises the whole ~ of money** esto plantea el problema general del dinero
2 (*Scol, Univ*) asignatura *f*
3 (*Gram*) sujeto *m*
4 (*Med*) caso *m* • **he's a nervous ~** es un caso nervioso
5 (*Sci*) • **guinea pigs make excellent ~s** los conejillos son materia excelente (*para los experimentos etc*)
6 (*esp Brit*) (*Pol*) súbdito/a *m/f* • **British ~** súbdito/a *m/f* británico/a • **liberty of the ~** libertad *f* del ciudadano
ADJ ['sʌbdʒɪkt] **1** [*people, nation*] dominado, subyugado
2 • **subject to** (= *liable to*) [+ *law, tax, delays*] sujeto a; [+ *disease*] propenso a; [+ *flooding*] expuesto a; (= *conditional on*) [+ *approval etc*] sujeto a • **these prices are ~ to change without notice** estos precios están sujetos a cambio sin previo aviso • **~ to correction** bajo corrección • **~ to confirmation in writing** sujeto a confirmación por escrito
VT [səb'dʒekt] • **to ~ sb to sth** someter a algn a algo • **to ~ a book to criticism** someter un libro a la crítica • **to be ~ed to inquiry** ser sometido a una investigación • **I will not be ~ed to this questioning** no tolero este interrogatorio *or* esta interrogación • **she was ~ed to much indignity** tuvo que aguantar muchas afrentas
CPD ['sʌbdʒɪkt] ▸ **subject heading** título *m* de materia ▸ **subject index** (*in book*) índice *m* de materias; (*in library*) catálogo *m* de materias ▸ **subject matter** (= *topic*) tema *m*, asunto *m*; [*of letter*] contenido *m* ▸ **subject pronoun** pronombre *m* (de) sujeto

subjection [səb'dʒekʃən] N sometimiento *m* (**to** a) • **to be in ~ to sb** estar sometido a algn • **to bring a people into ~** subyugar a un pueblo • **to hold a people in ~** tener subyugado a un pueblo

subjective [səb'dʒektɪv] ADJ subjetivo

subjectively [səb'dʒektɪvlɪ] ADV subjetivamente

subjectivism [səb'dʒektɪvɪzəm] N subjetivismo *m*

subjectivity [,sʌbdʒek'tɪvɪtɪ] N subjetividad *f*

subjoin ['sʌb'dʒɔɪn] VT adjuntar

sub judice [sʌb'djuːdɪsɪ] ADJ (*Jur*) • **the matter is ~** el asunto está en manos del tribunal

subjugate ['sʌbdʒʊgeɪt] VT subyugar, sojuzgar

subjugation [,sʌbdʒʊ'geɪʃən] N subyugación *f* • **to live in ~** vivir subyugado

subjunctive [səb'dʒʌŋktɪv] ADJ subjuntivo • **~ mood** modo *m* subjuntivo
N subjuntivo *m* • **the verb is in the ~** el verbo está en subjuntivo

sublease VT ['sʌb'liːs] subarrendar
N ['sʌb,liːs] subarriendo *m*

sublessee [,sʌble'siː] N subarrendatario/a *m/f*

sublessor [,sʌble'sɔːʳ] N subarrendador(a) *m/f*

sublet ['sʌb'let] (PT, PP: **sublet**) VT subarrendar
VI • **they were considering ~ting** estaban pensando en subarrendar el piso (*or* la casa *etc*)

sub-librarian ['sʌblaɪ'breərɪən] N subdirector(a) *m/f* de biblioteca

sub-lieutenant, **sublieutenant** ['sʌblef'tenənt] N (*Naut*) alférez *mf* de fragata; (*Mil*) subteniente *mf*, alférez *mf*

sublimate VT ['sʌblɪmeɪt] (*all senses*) sublimar
N ['sʌblɪmɪt] sublimado *m*

sublimation [,sʌblɪ'meɪʃən] N sublimación *f*

sublime [sə'blaɪm] ADJ sublime; (*iro*) [*indifference, contempt*] supremo, total
N • **the ~** lo sublime • **to go from the ~ to the ridiculous** pasar de lo sublime a lo ridículo

sublimely [sə'blaɪmlɪ] ADV maravillosamente • **he played ~** tocó maravillosamente • **~ funny** terriblemente graciosa • **~ beautiful** de una belleza sublime • **~ unaware of …** completamente *or* absolutamente inconsciente de …

subliminal [sʌb'lɪmɪnl] ADJ subliminal • **~ advertising** publicidad *f* subliminal

subliminally [sʌb'lɪmɪnəlɪ] ADV subliminalmente

sublimity [sə'blɪmɪtɪ] N sublimidad *f*
submachine gun ['sʌbmə'ʃi:ngʌn] N ametralladora *f*, pistola *f* ametralladora, metralleta *f*
submarginal [sʌb'mɑ:dʒɪnl] ADJ (*Agr*) [*land*] submarginal
submarine [ˌsʌbmə'ri:n] N **1** (= *vessel*) submarino *m*
2 (*US**) *sándwich mixto de tamaño grande*
ADJ submarino
CPD ▸ **submarine chaser** cazasubmarinos *m inv*
submariner [sʌb'mærɪnəʳ] N submarinista *mf*
submenu, sub-menu ['sʌbˌmenju:] N (*Comput*) submenú *m*
submerge [səb'mɜ:dʒ] VT **1** (= *plunge*) hundir (**in** en)
2 (= *flood*) inundar
VI [*submarine, person*] sumergirse
submerged [səb'mɜ:dʒd] ADJ sumergido
submergence [səb'mɜ:dʒəns] N sumersión *f*, sumergimiento *m*, hundimiento *m*
submersible [səb'mɜ:səbl] ADJ sumergible
submersion [səb'mɜ:ʃən] N sumersión *f*
submicroscopic ['sʌbˌmaɪkrəs'kɒpɪk] ADJ submicroscópico
submission [səb'mɪʃən] N
1 (= *submissiveness*) sumisión *f* • **to beat sb into ~** (*lit*) someter a algn a base de golpes; (*fig*) someter a algn, subyugar a algn
2 (= *handing in*) [*of evidence, plan*] presentación *f*; [*of proposal, application*] presentación *f*, entrega *f*
3 (*Jur etc*) alegato *m*
4 (*to committee etc*) (= *plan, proposal*) propuesta *f* • **a written ~ is required** se requiere una propuesta por escrito • **~s are judged by a panel of authors** un panel de autores juzga las obras
submissive [səb'mɪsɪv] ADJ sumiso
submissively [səb'mɪsɪvlɪ] ADV sumisamente
submissiveness [səb'mɪsɪvnɪs] N sumisión *f*
submit [səb'mɪt] VT **1** (= *put forward*) [+ *proposal, claim, report*] presentar; [+ *evidence*] presentar, aducir; [+ *account*] rendir • **to ~ that ...** proponer que ..., sugerir que ... • **I ~ that ...** me permito sugerir que ... • **to ~ a play to the censor** someter una obra a la censura • **to ~ a dispute to arbitration** someter una disputa a arbitraje
2 (= *subject*) someter • **to ~ o.s. to sth** someterse a algo • **to ~ o.s. to sb** someterse a algn
VI (= *give in*) rendirse, someterse • **to ~ to sth** someterse a algo • **he refused to ~ to drugs tests** se negó a someterse a la prueba del doping • **to ~ to authority** someterse a la autoridad • **to ~ to pressure** ceder ante la presión • **he had to ~ to this indignity** tuvo que aguantar esta afrenta
subnormal ['sʌb'nɔ:məl] ADJ subnormal
NPL • **the ~** los subnormales
suborbital ['sʌb'ɔ:bɪtəl] ADJ suborbital
subordinate N [sə'bɔ:dnɪt] subordinado/a *m/f*
ADJ [sə'bɔ:dnɪt] [*officer, member of staff, group*] subordinado; [*role*] subordinado, secundario • **to be ~ to sb** (*in rank*) ser subordinado de algn • **to be ~ to sth** (= *secondary*) estar subordinado a algo • **~ clause** oración *f* subordinada
VT [sə'bɔ:dɪneɪt] subordinar • **to ~ sth to sth** subordinar algo a algo • **subordinating conjunction** conjunción *f* de subordinación
subordination [səˌbɔ:dɪ'neɪʃən] N subordinación *f*

suborn [sʌ'bɔ:n] VT (*frm*) sobornar
subparagraph [sʌb'pærəˌgrɑ:f] N subpárrafo *m*
subplot ['sʌbˌplɒt] N intriga *f* secundaria
subpoena [səb'pi:nə] (*Jur*) N citación *f* • **to serve sb with a ~** • **serve a ~ on sb** enviar una citación a algn
VT [+ *witness*] citar; [+ *document*] reclamar como pruebas • **to ~ sb to do sth** citar a algn para hacer algo
subpopulation ['sʌbˌpɒpjʊ'leɪʃən] N subgrupo *m* de población
sub post-office [ˌsʌb'pəʊstˌɒfɪs] N subdelegación *f* de correos
subprime ['sʌbpraɪm] CPD ▸ **subprime lender** prestamista *mf* subprime ▸ **subprime lending** crédito *m* subprime ▸ **subprime loan** préstamo *m* subprime ▸ **subprime market** mercado *m* subprime ▸ **subprime mortgage** hipoteca *f* subprime ▸ **subprime mortgage market** • **the ~ mortgage market** el mercado de las hipotecas subprime
subrogate ['sʌbrəgɪt] ADJ subrogado, sustituido • **~ language** lenguaje *m* subrogado
sub rosa ['sʌb'rəʊzə] ADJ secreto, de confianza
ADV en secreto, en confianza
subroutine [ˌsʌbru:'ti:n] N subrutina *f*
sub-Saharan ['sʌbsə'hɑ:rən] ADJ subsahariano
subscribe [səb'skraɪb] VI **1** • **to ~ to a** (= *buy, pay for*) [+ *magazine, newspaper*] su(b)scribirse *or* abonarse a; [+ *email list*] su(b)scribirse a • **he ~s to a pay TV channel** está abonado a un canal de televisión de pago
b (= *contribute to*) [+ *charity, good cause*] contribuir con
c (= *share*) • **I've personally never ~d to that view** yo personalmente nunca he sido de esa opinión • **I don't ~ to the idea that money should be given to people like that** yo no soy partidario de que se dé dinero a gente como esa
2 • **to ~ for** [+ *stocks, shares*] su(b)scribir • **~d capital** (*Comm*) capital *m* su(b)scrito
VT **1** (= *contribute*) [+ *money*] donar
2 (= *apply for*) • **the share issue was heavily ~d** la oferta de venta de acciones ha tenido mucha demanda • **the language courses are all fully ~d** la matrícula de los cursos de idiomas está completa
3 (*frm*) [+ *signature*] poner; [+ *document*] su(b)scribir
subscriber [səb'skraɪbəʳ] N **1** (*to magazine, newspaper*) su(b)scriptor(a) *m/f*, abonado/a *m/f*; (*to pay TV, telephone, concert series*) abonado/a *m/f*; (*to email*) su(b)scriptor(a) *m/f*; (*to charity*) donante *mf*; (*to campaign*) partidario/a *m/f*, seguidor(a) *m/f*
2 (*St Ex*) su(b)scriptor(a) *m/f*
subscript ['sʌbskrɪpt] N subíndice *m*
subscription [səb'skrɪpʃən] N **1** (= *act of subscribing*) (*to magazine, newspaper*) su(b)scripción *f*; (*to club, telephone service, pay TV*) abono *m*; (*to email provider*) conexión *f*
2 (= *fee*) (*to magazine, newspaper, pay TV, email provider*) su(b)scripción *f*, tarifa *f* de su(b)scripción; (*to club*) cuota *f* • **to pay one's ~** (*monthly, annually etc*) (*to magazine, newspaper*) pagar la su(b)scripción; (*to pay TV*) pagar el abono *or* la cuota de abono; (*to club*) pagar la cuota • **annual** *or* **yearly ~** (*to magazine, journal*) su(b)scripción *f* anual; (*to club*) cuota *f* anual • **by public ~** con donativos (de particulares) • **to take out a ~ to sth** (*to club, pay TV, telephone service*) abonarse a algo; (*to magazine, newspaper*) su(b)scribirse a algo
CPD ▸ **subscription fee** (*for magazine, email, pay TV*) tarifa *f* de su(b)scripción; (*for club membership, telephone service*) cuota *f* ▸ **subscription form** hoja *f* de su(b)scripción ▸ **subscription rate** tarifa *f* de su(b)scripción ▸ **subscription reminder card** tarjeta *f* recordatoria de renovación de suscripción
subsection ['sʌbˌsekʃən] N subsección *f*, subdivisión *f*
subsequent ['sʌbsɪkwənt] ADJ posterior, subsiguiente (*more frm*) • **on a ~ visit** en una visita posterior • **in ~ years** en años posteriores • **all ~ studies confirmed that finding** todos los estudios subsiguientes *or* posteriores confirmaron esa conclusión • **~ to** con posterioridad a • **~ to that** posteriormente
subsequently ['sʌbsɪkwəntlɪ] ADV posteriormente
subserve [səb'sɜ:v] VT ayudar, favorecer
subservience [səb'sɜ:vɪəns] N **1** [*of person*] (= *submissiveness*) sumisión *f*; (= *servility*) servilismo *m* • **a life of ~ and drudgery** una vida de sumisión y monotonía • **~ to sb** sumisión a algn
2 (= *secondary position*) subordinación *f* (**to a**)
subservient [səb'sɜ:vɪənt] ADJ **1** [*person*] (= *submissive*) sumiso; (*pej*) (= *servile*) servil • **to be ~ to sb** someterse a algn
2 (= *secondary*) subordinado (**to a**)
subset ['sʌbˌset] N subconjunto *m*
subside [səb'saɪd] VI [*floods*] bajar, descender; [*road, land, house*] hundirse; [*wind*] amainar; [*anger, laughter, excitement*] apagarse; [*threat*] disminuir, alejarse; [*violence, pain*] disminuir • **to ~ into a chair** dejarse caer en una silla
subsidence [səb'saɪdəns] N [*of road, land, house*] hundimiento *m*; [*of floods*] bajada *f*, descenso *m* • **"road liable to subsidence"** "firme en mal estado"
subsidiarity [sʌbsɪdɪ'ærɪtɪ] N (*Pol*) subsidiariedad *f*
subsidiary [səb'sɪdɪərɪ] ADJ **1** (= *secondary*) [*interest, importance, role, question*] secundario
2 (*Comm*) [*company, bank*] filial
3 (*Univ*) [*subject, course*] complementario • **I want to do ~ Spanish** quiero hacer español como asignatura complementaria
N **1** (*Comm*) (= *company*) filial *f*; (= *bank*) sucursal *f*, filial *f*
2 (*Univ*) asignatura *f* complementaria
subsidization [ˌsʌbsɪdaɪ'zeɪʃən] N subvenciones *fpl*
subsidize ['sʌbsɪdaɪz] VT subvencionar • **rice is imported at ~d prices** el arroz se importa subvencionado
subsidized ['sʌbsɪdaɪzd] ADJ [*prices, food, exports*] subvencionado; [*housing*] de promoción oficial
subsidizing ['sʌbsɪdaɪzɪŋ] N subvenciones *fpl*
subsidy ['sʌbsɪdɪ] N subvención *f* • **government ~** subvención *f* estatal, subvención *f* del gobierno • **state ~** subvención *f* estatal
subsist [səb'sɪst] VI subsistir • **to ~ on sth** subsistir a base de algo
subsistence [səb'sɪstəns] N (= *nourishment*) sustento *m*, subsistencia *f*; (= *existence*) existencia *f* • **means of ~** medios *mpl* de subsistencia
CPD ▸ **subsistence allowance** dietas *fpl* ▸ **subsistence economy** economía *f* de subsistencia ▸ **subsistence farmer** *campesino que se dedica a la agricultura de subsistencia* ▸ **subsistence farming** agricultura *f* de subsistencia ▸ **subsistence level** nivel *m* mínimo de subsistencia • **to live at ~ level** vivir muy justo, poderse sustentar apenas ▸ **subsistence wage** salario *m* de

S

subsistencia

subsoil ['sʌbsɔɪl] (N) subsuelo *m*

subsonic ['sʌb'sɒnɪk] (ADJ) subsónico

subspecies ['sʌb'spiːʃiːz] (N) (*pl inv*) subespecie *f*

substance ['sʌbstəns] (N) **1** (*physical*) **a** (= *solution, chemical*) sustancia *f* • **a sticky ~** una sustancia pegajosa; ▸ **illegal** **b** (= *solidity*) corporeidad *f*; [*of fabric*] cuerpo *m* • **line the fabric to give it more ~** ponle un forro a la tela para darle más cuerpo **2** (*fig*) **a** (= *basis*) (*to allegation*) base *f*, fundamento *m* • **the rumours are completely without ~** los rumores no tienen ninguna base *or* ningún fundamento **b** (= *profundity*) (*to book, plot, argument*) enjundia *f*, sustancia *f* • **there wasn't much ~ in** *or* **to his lectures** sus conferencias no tenían mucha enjundia *or* sustancia • **issues of ~** asuntos fundamentales *or* de importancia **c** (= *gist, essence*) [*of speech, writing*] esencia *f* • **the ~ of his talk** la esencia de su charla • **I agree with the ~ of his proposals** estoy de acuerdo en lo esencial de sus propuestas • **the dispute was about style not ~** la discusión fue sobre forma, no sobre fondo • **what he is saying in ~ is that ...** en esencia, lo que está diciendo es que ... • **the Court agreed in ~ with this argument** el tribunal estuvo de acuerdo con este argumento en lo esencial **d** • **a man/woman of ~** (= *wealthy person*) un hombre/una mujer de fortuna (CPD) ▸ **substance abuse** abuso *m* de estupefacientes, toxicomanía *f* ▸ **substance abuser** toxicómano/a *m/f*

substandard ['sʌb'stændəd] (ADJ) **1** (= *inferior*) [*products, material*] de calidad inferior; [*service, work, performance*] poco satisfactorio • **~ housing** viviendas que no reúnen condiciones de habitabilidad **2** (*Ling*) (= *nonstandard*) no estándar

substantial [səb'stænʃəl] (ADJ) **1** (= *significant*) [*amount, progress, improvement, damage*] considerable, importante; [*difference*] importante, sustancial • **there has been ~ agreement on this question** ha habido un alto *or* considerable grado de acuerdo sobre esta cuestión • **to win by a ~ majority** ganar por una mayoría considerable • **a ~ majority of families** una mayoría considerable de familias **2** (= *weighty*) [*evidence*] sustancial, de peso; [*document, book*] sustancioso **3** (= *solid*) [*building*] sólido **4** (= *filling*) [*meal, dish*] sustancioso

S

substantially [səb'stænʃəlɪ] (ADV) **1** (= *significantly*) [*increase, change, contribute*] sustancialmente, considerablemente • **a ~ different approach** un enfoque sustancialmente *or* considerablemente distinto • **~ higher/lower** bastante más alto/bajo **2** (= *largely*) [*correct, true*] básicamente • **Webster's thesis is ~ correct** la tesis de Webster es básicamente correcta

substantiate [səb'stænʃɪeɪt] (VT) [+ *claims, allegations, evidence*] confirmar, corroborar

substantiation [səb,stænʃɪ'eɪʃən] (N) comprobación *f*, justificación *f*

substantival [,sʌbstən'taɪvəl] (ADJ) (*Ling*) sustantivo

substantive ['sʌbstəntɪv] (ADJ) **1** (= *significant*) [*role*] fundamental; [*talks, progress, difference*] sustancial; [*reason*] de peso • **the two sides remain divided on several ~ issues** las dos partes permanecen divididas en varios puntos fundamentales *or* de importancia **2** (*Mil*) [*captain, lieutenant*] sustantivo (N) (*Gram*) sustantivo *m* (CPD) ▸ **substantive law** derecho *m* sustantivo ▸ **substantive motion** moción *f* de fondo

substation ['sʌb,steɪʃən] (N) (*Elec*) subestación *f*

substitute ['sʌbstɪtjuːt] (N) **1** (= *thing, artificial product*) sucedáneo *m* • **it may replace saccharin as a sugar ~** puede reemplazar a la sacarina como sucedáneo del azúcar • **he uses honey as a ~ for sugar** usa miel como sustituto del azúcar • **a correspondence course is a poor** *or* **no ~ for personal tuition** un curso por correspondencia no puede sustituir a la enseñanza cara a cara • **there's no ~ for being informed** no hay nada como estar informado **2** (= *person*) sustituto/a *m/f*, suplente *mf*; (*Sport*) suplente *mf* • **to be a poor** *or* **no ~ for sb** no poder sustituir a algn • **friends are no ~ for parents** los amigos no pueden sustituir a los padres • **he seems to be looking for a mother ~** parece que está buscando a alguien que reemplace a su madre • **to come on as (a) ~** (*Sport*) entrar como suplente (VT) (*gen, Sport*) sustituir • **the striker was ~d by Johnston** Johnston sustituyó al delantero • **to ~ margarine for butter** • **~ butter with margarine** sustituir la mantequilla por margarina (VI) • **to ~ for sth/sb** (*gen, Sport*) sustituir a algo/algn (CPD) ▸ **substitute goalkeeper** portero/a *m/f* suplente ▸ **substitute teacher** (*US*) profesor(a) *m/f* suplente

substitution [,sʌbstɪ'tjuːʃən] (N) **1** sustitución *f* • **a simple ~ of cocoa for chocolate** una simple sustitución de chocolate por cacao **2** (*Sport*) (= *action*) suplencia *f*, sustitución *f*; (= *person*) suplente *mf* • **to make a ~** hacer una suplencia *or* sustitución

substrate ['sʌbstreɪt] (N) (*Chem*) sustrato *m*

substratum ['sʌb'strɑːtəm] (N) (PL: **substrata** ['sʌb'strɑːtə]) sustrato *m*

substructure ['sʌb,strʌktʃəʳ] (N) infraestructura *f*

subsume [səb'sjuːm] (VT) (*frm*) subsumir

subsystem ['sʌb,sɪstəm] (N) subsistema *m*

subteen* [,sʌb'tiːn] (N) preadolescente *mf*, menor *mf* de 13 años

subtenancy ['sʌb'tenənsɪ] (N) subarriendo *m*

subtenant ['sʌb'tenənt] (N) subarrendatario/a *m/f*

subterfuge ['sʌbtəfjuːdʒ] (N) subterfugio *m*

subterranean [,sʌbtə'reɪnɪən] (ADJ) (*lit, fig*) subterráneo

subtext ['sʌbtekst] (N) subtexto *m*

subtilize ['sʌtɪlaɪz] (VT) sutilizar (VI) sutilizar

subtitle ['sʌb,taɪtl] (N) [*of book, play etc*] subtítulo *m* • **~s** (*Cine, TV*) subtítulos *mpl* (VT) **1** (*Cine, TV*) subtitular **2** [+ *book, play*] subtitular

subtitled ['sʌbtaɪtld] (ADJ) [*film*] subtitulado, con subtítulos

subtitling ['sʌb,taɪtlɪŋ] (N) subtitulado *m*

subtle ['sʌtl] (ADJ) (COMPAR: **subtler**, SUPERL: **subtlest**) **1** (= *delicate, fine*) [*perfume, flavour*] suave, sutil; [*colour*] tenue; [*charm, beauty, nuance, reminder, person*] sutil; [*humour, irony*] sutil, fino • **the ~ fragrance of the violet** la suave fragancia *or* la fragancia sutil de la violeta • **a ~ hint of pink** un ligero toque de rosa • **there's a ~ difference between these two words** hay una diferencia sutil entre estas dos palabras • **she was never very ~** nunca fue muy sutil • **it was a ~ form of racism** era una forma sutil de racismo **2** (= *perceptive*) [*person*] perspicaz, agudo; [*mind*] sutil, agudo; [*analysis*] ingenioso

subtlety ['sʌtltɪ] (N) **1** (= *delicacy, refinement*) [*of colour, book, humour, person*] sutileza *f* • **his performance lacked ~** su actuación carecía de matices • **he has all the ~ of a herd of rhinoceroses** es más bruto que un arao • **the subtleties of English** los matices del inglés **2** (= *perceptiveness*) perspicacia *f*, agudeza *f* • **he analyses the situation with great ~** analiza la situación con gran perspicacia *or* agudeza

subtly ['sʌtlɪ] (ADV) **1** (= *delicately*) [*imply, remind, suggest*] sutilmente, de manera sutil • **~ flavoured dishes** platos ligeramente sazonados • **~ coloured garments** prendas de colores tenues • **~ erotic images** imágenes de un sutil erotismo **2** (= *slightly*) [*change*] ligeramente, levemente; [*enhance*] sutilmente, de manera sutil • **~ different** ligeramente distinto

subtopia [,sʌb'təʊpɪə] (N) (*hum*) (vida *f* de los) barrios *mpl* exteriores

subtotal ['sʌb,təʊtl] (N) subtotal *m* • **to do a ~ (of)** calcular el subtotal (de) (VT) calcular el subtotal de

subtract [səb'trækt] (VT) (*gen*) restar; (*fig*) sustraer • **to ~ five from nine** restar cinco de nueve (VI) restar • **it doesn't ~ from her beauty** no le resta belleza

subtraction [səb'trækʃən] (N) resta *f*

subtropical ['sʌb'trɒpɪkəl] (ADJ) subtropical

subtropics [sʌb'trɒpɪks] (NPL) zona *fsing* subtropical

subtype ['sʌbtaɪp] (N) (*Bio*) subtipo *m*

suburb ['sʌbɜːb] (N) **1** (*affluent*) • **a London ~** una zona residencial de las afueras de Londres • **I live in the ~s** vivo en una zona residencial de las afueras (de la ciudad) • **new ~** barrio *m* nuevo, ensanche *m* **2** (*poor*) suburbio *m* • **one of the city's poorer ~s** uno de los suburbios más pobres de la ciudad

suburban [sə'bɜːbən] (ADJ) **1** (*lit*) • **people who live in ~ areas** la gente que vive en las zonas residenciales de las afueras de una ciudad • **he was born in ~ London** nació en una zona residencial de las afueras de Londres • **~ train** tren *m* de cercanías **2** (= *middle-class*) [*lifestyle, values, housewife, family*] de clase media

suburbanite [sə'bɜːbənaɪt] (N) *habitante de una zona residencial de las afueras de una ciudad*

suburbia [sə'bɜːbɪə] (N) *zonas residenciales de las afueras de las ciudades*

subvention [səb'venʃən] (N) (*frm*) subvención *f*

subversion [səb'vɜːʃən] (N) subversión *f* • **she was arrested on charges of ~** fue arrestada y acusada de subversión

subversive [səb'vɜːsɪv] (ADJ) [*activity, literature, idea, group*] subversivo • **the court found him guilty of ~ activities** el tribunal lo declaró culpable de llevar a cabo actividades subversivas (N) elemento *m* subversivo

subvert [sʌb'vɜːt] (VT) (*frm*) subvertir, trastornar

subway ['sʌbweɪ] (N) **1** (= *underpass*) paso *m* subterráneo **2** (*US*) (*Rail*) metro *m*, subterráneo *m* (*Arg*), subte *m* (*Arg**) • **to go by ~** ir en metro • **to ride** *or* **take the ~** coger *or* tomar el metro (CPD) ▸ **subway station** (*US*) estación *f* de metro ▸ **subway train** (*US*) metro *m*

sub-zero, subzero ['sʌb'zɪərəʊ] (ADJ)

[*temperature*] bajo cero • **sub-zero temperatures** temperaturas *fpl* bajo cero

succeed [sək'si:d] (VI) **1** [*person*] **a** (*in business, career*) tener éxito, triunfar (**in** en) • **he ~ed in business** tuvo éxito *or* triunfó en los negocios • **a burning desire to ~** un deseo ardiente de triunfar • **to ~ in life** triunfar en la vida
b (*in task, aim*) • **she tried to smile but did not ~** intentó sonreír pero no lo consiguió *or* no lo logró • **to ~ in doing sth** conseguir hacer algo, lograr hacer algo • **they ~ed in finishing the job** consiguieron *or* lograron terminar el trabajo • **he only ~ed in making it worse** lo único que consiguió *or* logró fue empeorar las cosas • **I finally ~ed in getting him out of the room** por fin conseguí *or* logré que saliera de la habitación • **I ~ed in getting the job** conseguí el empleo • PROVERB: • **if at first you don't ~, try, try again** si no lo consigues a la primera, sigue intentándolo
c (= *take over*) • **if she dies, who will ~?** si muere, ¿quién la sucederá? • **to ~ to the throne** subir al trono • **to ~ to a title** heredar un título
2 [*thing*] **a** (= *work*) [*plan, strategy, experiment*] dar resultado, salir bien • **had the plan ~ed, our lives might have been very different** si el plan hubiera dado resultado *or* salido bien, nuestras vidas podrían haber sido muy distintas
b (= *do well*) [*business*] prosperar; [*film*] tener éxito • **to ~ at the box office** ser un éxito de taquilla • IDIOM: • **nothing ~s like success** el éxito llama al éxito
(VT) (= *follow*) suceder a • **the dry weather was ~ed by a month of rain** un mes de lluvia sucedió al tiempo seco • **on his death, his eldest son ~ed him** a su muerte, su hijo mayor lo sucedió • **he ~ed Lewis as Olympic champion** sucedió a Lewis como campeón olímpico

succeeding [sək'si:dɪŋ] (ADJ) sucesivo • **each ~ year brought further tribulations** cada año sucesivo trajo más tribulaciones • **in ~ chapters** en capítulos sucesivos • **on two/three ~ Saturdays** dos/tres sábados seguidos • **~ generations** generaciones sucesivas

success [sək'ses] (N) **1** (*at task*) éxito *m* (**at, in** en) • **the ~ or failure of the strategy** el éxito o el fracaso de la estrategia • **~ never went to his head** el éxito nunca se le subió a la cabeza • **congratulations on your ~!** ¡enhorabuena, lo has conseguido! • **the key to ~ at school** la clave del éxito escolar • **his ~ at the Olympics** sus logros en las Olimpiadas • **we have had some ~ in reducing the national debt** hemos conseguido *or* logrado reducir en parte la deuda pública • **to make a ~ of sth**: • **would you say he's made a ~ of his life?** ¿dirías que ha triunfado en la vida? • **we have made a ~ of the venture** hemos conseguido *or* logrado que la operación sea un éxito • **to meet with ~** tener éxito • **to wish sb every ~** desear a algn todo lo mejor • **she tried without ~ to get a loan from the bank** intentó, sin éxito, obtener un préstamo del banco • **I tried to distract him but without ~** intenté distraerlo pero no lo conseguí *or* logré
2 (= *sensation, hit*) éxito *m* • **to be a ~** [*product, event*] ser un éxito; [*person*] tener éxito • **he was a great ~** tuvo un gran éxito • **he was a ~ at last** por fin consiguió el éxito • **a commercial ~** un éxito comercial
(CPD) ▸ **success rate** • **the ~ rate of organ transplants** el índice de transplantes de órganos que salen bien, el número de transplantes de órganos realizados con éxito (*frm*) • **the police ~ rate in tracking down murderers** el número de asesinos que la policía logra atrapar ▸ **success story** éxito *m*

successful [sək'sesfʊl] (ADJ) **1** • **to be ~ a** [*campaign, scheme, attempt, book*] tener éxito; [*plan, strategy, experiment*] salir bien • **the campaign was very ~** la campaña tuvo mucho éxito • **their mission was ~** llevaron la misión a buen término • **the company has been very ~ over the past five years** a la empresa le ha ido muy bien en los últimos cinco años • **the film was very ~ at the box office** la película fue muy taquillera *or* fue todo un éxito de taquilla • **the film is ~ at capturing the atmosphere of the time** la película consigue *or* logra captar el ambiente de la época
b [*person*] (= *do well*) tener éxito; (= *reach the top*) triunfar • **the secret of being ~ with men** el secreto para tener éxito *or* triunfar con los hombres • **they are ambitious and want to be ~** son ambiciosos y quieren triunfar • **we have been ~ at achieving our objectives** hemos conseguido *or* logrado alcanzar nuestros objetivos • **we have not been very ~ at** *or* **in attracting new contracts** no hemos tenido mucho éxito a la hora de atraer nuevos contratos
2 (*before noun*) **a** (= *winning*) [*product, film, novelist*] de éxito • **one of the most ~ movies of all time** una de las películas de más éxito de todos los tiempos • **a ~ range of giftware** una gama de artículos de regalo que ha tenido mucho éxito • **a commercially ~ work** una obra de éxito comercial
b (= *prosperous*) [*company, businessperson*] próspero
c (= *effective*) [*treatment, remedy*] eficaz • **a generally ~ attempt to adapt this novel** una adaptación, en general lograda, de esta novela • **he had a ~ operation for an eye problem** lo operaron con éxito de un problema en el ojo
d (= *satisfactory*) [*conclusion*] satisfactorio; [*deal*] favorable • **it was a ~ end to an excellent campaign** fue un final satisfactorio para una campaña excelente • **to bring sth to a ~ conclusion** llevar algo a buen término • **there is little hope of a ~ outcome to the meeting** hay pocas esperanzas de que la reunión dé resultados satisfactorios • **we've had a very ~ day** nos han salido muy bien las cosas hoy
e [*applicant*] • **the ~ candidate will be notified by post** se notificará al candidato elegido por correo

successfully [sək'sesfəlɪ] (ADV) **1** (= *effectively*) con éxito • **he ~ defended his title** defendió con éxito su título • **our main objective has been ~ accomplished** hemos conseguido *or* logrado nuestro objetivo principal • **Pattie ~ evaded the police** Pattie consiguió *or* logró evadir a la policía
2 (= *satisfactorily*) satisfactoriamente • **the problem has been ~ resolved** el problema se ha resuelto satisfactoriamente

succession [sək'seʃən] (N) **1** (= *series*) sucesión *f*, serie *f* • **after a ~ of disasters** después de una sucesión *or* serie de catástrofes • **they each went in ~ to the headmaster** fueron todos a ver al director uno detrás de otro • **she has won three games in ~** ha ganado tres partidos seguidos *or* sucesivos *or* consecutivos • **he was my tutor two years in ~** fue mi tutor dos años seguidos *or* consecutivos • **for the third day/year in ~** por tercer día/año consecutivo • **in close** *or* **quick** *or* **rapid ~** uno tras de otro, en rápida sucesión • **four times in ~** cuatro veces seguidas
2 (*to a post*) sucesión *f* • **in ~ to sb** sucediendo a algn • **Princess Rebecca is seventh in (line of) ~ to the throne** la princesa Rebeca ocupa el séptimo puesto en la línea de sucesión a la corona
3 (= *descendants*) descendencia *f*
(CPD) ▸ **succession duty** derechos *mpl* de sucesión

successive [sək'sesɪv] (ADJ) [*governments, generations, owners*] sucesivo; [*nights, days*] seguido, consecutivo • **~ governments have failed to resolve the problem** sucesivos gobiernos no han logrado resolver el problema • **on four/five ~ nights** cuatro/cinco noches seguidas *or* consecutivas • **for the third/fourth ~ time** por tercera/cuarta vez consecutiva • **the percentage of female students increased with each ~ year** el porcentaje de estudiantes del sexo femenino aumentaba año tras año

successively [sək'sesɪvlɪ] (ADV) sucesivamente • **they lived ~ in Denmark, Sweden and Finland** vivieron en Dinamarca, Suecia y Finlandia sucesivamente • **~ higher levels of unemployment** niveles de desempleo cada vez más altos

successor [sək'sesəʳ] (N) (*in office*) sucesor(a) *m/f*

succinct [sək'sɪŋkt] (ADJ) [*comment, account, person*] sucinto, conciso

succinctly [sək'sɪŋktlɪ] (ADV) [*express, reply, sum up*] sucintamente, de manera sucinta, concisamente • **to put sth ~** decir algo en pocas palabras • **or, to put it ~, ...** o, en pocas palabras, ...

succinctness [sək'sɪŋktnɪs] (N) concisión *f*

succour, succor (US) ['sʌkəʳ] (*frm*) (N) socorro *m*
(VT) socorrer

succubus ['sʌkjʊbəs] (N) (PL: **succubi**) súcubo *m*

succulence ['sʌkjʊləns] (N) suculencia *f*

succulent ['sʌkjʊlənt] (ADJ) **1** [*meat, fruit, vegetable*] suculento
2 (*Bot*) [*plant, leaves*] carnoso
(N) (*Bot*) planta *f* carnosa

succumb [sə'kʌm] (VI) sucumbir (**to** a)

such [sʌtʃ] (ADJ) (= *of that kind*) tal; (= *so much*) tanto • **~ a book** tal libro • **~ books** tales libros • **books ~ as these** semejantes libros • **did you ever see ~ a thing?** ¿has visto alguna vez cosa semejante?, ¿se vio jamás tal cosa? • **I was in ~ a hurry** tenía tanta prisa • **it caused ~ trouble that ...** dio lugar a tantos disgustos que ... • **~ an honour!** ¡tanto honor! • **it made ~ a stir as had not been known before** tuvo una repercusión como no se había conocido hasta entonces • **in ~ cases** en tales casos, en semejantes casos • **we had ~ a case last year** tuvimos un caso parecido el año pasado • **~ is not the case** (*frm*) la cosa no es así • **on just ~ a day in June** justo en un día parecido de junio • **~ a plan is most unwise** un proyecto así es poco aconsejable, un proyecto de ese tipo no es aconsejable • **writers ~ as Updike** • **~ writers as Updike** autores como Updike • **~ a man as Ganivet** un hombre tal como Ganivet • **~ a man as you** un hombre como tú • **~ money as I have** el dinero que tengo • **~ stories as I know** las historias que conozco • **this is my car ~ as it is** aunque valga poco, es mi coche • **he read the documents ~ as they were** leyó los documentos que había • **~ as?** ¿por ejemplo? • **~ is life** así es la vida • **there's no ~ thing** no existe tal cosa • **there's no ~ thing as a unicorn** el unicornio no existe • **the Gautier case was ~ a one** el caso Gautier era

S

de ese tipo • **some ~ idea** algo por el estilo
(ADV) tan • **~ good food** comida tan buena • **~ a clever girl** una muchacha tan inteligente • **it's ~ a long time now** hace tanto tiempo
(PRON) los que, las que • **we took ~ as we wanted** tomamos los que queríamos • **I will send you ~ as I receive** te mandaré los que reciba • **may all ~ perish!** ¡mueran cuantos hay como él! • **rabbits and hares and ~** conejos y liebres y tal • **as ~**: • **and as ~ he was promoted** y así fue ascendido • **there are no trees as ~** no hay árboles propiamente dichos, no hay árboles que digamos • **we know of none ~** no tenemos noticias de ninguno así

such-and-such ['sʌtʃənsʌtʃ] (ADJ) tal o cual • **she lives in such-and-such a street** vive en tal o cual calle • **on such-and-such a day in May** a tantos de mayo • **he wanted the report completed by such-and-such a date** quería el informe terminado en tal o cual fecha

suchlike ['sʌtʃlaɪk] (ADJ) semejante • **pots, pans and ~ things** cazuelas, sartenes y cosas semejantes *or* cosas por el estilo
(PRON) • **media people and ~** gente de los medios de comunicación y personas por el estilo • **buses, lorries and ~** autobuses, camiones y vehículos por el estilo

suck [sʌk] (VT) *[person]* sorber; *[machine]* aspirar • **to ~ one's thumb/fingers** chuparse el dedo/los dedos • **we were ~ed into the controversy** nos vimos envueltos en la polémica • IDIOMS: • **to ~ sb dry (of sth)** exprimir (algo) a algn • **to ~ it and see** *(Brit)* probar a ver
(VI) **1** *(gen)* chupar; *[baby]* *(at breast)* mamar • **to ~ on/at sth** chupar algo • **to ~ at one's mother's breast** mamar del pecho de su madre
2 *(esp US)* • **this ~s‡** es una mierda‡

▸ **suck down** (VT + ADV) *[current, mud]* tragar
▸ **suck in** (VT + ADV) **1** *(lit)* **a** *[machine]* *[+ dust, air]* aspirar
b *[black hole]* *[+ matter]* tragar, aspirar
c *[person]* *[+ air]* tomar • **he heard her ~ in her breath sharply** le oyó aspirar sobresaltada • **to ~ one's cheeks in** hundir los carrillos • **to ~ one's stomach in** meter el estómago
2 *(fig)* • **to get ~ed in** *(to war, argument)* verse envuelto
▸ **suck off**** (VT + ADV) *(sexually)* mamar**
▸ **suck out** (VT + ADV) succionar
▸ **suck up** (VT + ADV) *[+ dust, liquid]* aspirar
(VI + ADV) • **to ~ up to sb*** dar coba a algn

sucker ['sʌkəʳ] (N) **1** *(Zool, Tech)* ventosa *f*; *(Bot)* serpollo *m*, mamón *m*
2 *(US)* (= *lollipop*) pirulí *m*, chupete *m* *(LAm)*
3* (= *gullible person*) primo/a *m/f*, bobo/a *m/f* • **there's a ~ born every minute** nace un primo *or* un bobo cada minuto • **he's a ~ for a pretty girl*** no puede resistirse a una chica guapa
(VT) *(US‡)* • **to ~ sb into doing sth** embaucar a algn para que haga algo • **they ~ed him out of six grand** le estafaron *or* timaron 6.000 dólares
(CPD) ▸ **sucker pad** ventosa *f* ▸ **sucker punch** *(Boxing)* *(also fig)* golpe *m* a traición

sucking pig ['sʌkɪŋpɪg] (N) lechón *m*, lechoncillo *m*, cochinillo *m*

suckle ['sʌkl] (VT) amamantar, dar de mamar
(VI) mamar • **to ~ at one's mother's breast** mamar del pecho de su madre

suckling ['sʌklɪŋ] (N) mamón/ona *m/f* • **~ pig** lechón *m*, lechoncillo *m*, cochinillo *m*

sucks-boo* ['sʌks'bu:] (EXCL) ¡narices!*

sucrose ['su:krəʊz] (N) sucrosa *f*

suction ['sʌkʃən] (N) succión *f*, aspiración *f* • **by ~** por succión *or* aspiración
(CPD) ▸ **suction cup** ventosa *f* ▸ **suction disc, suction pad** ventosa *f* ▸ **suction pump** bomba *f* de aspiración, bomba *f* de succión ▸ **suction valve** válvula *f* de aspiración

Sudan [sʊ'dɑ:n] (N) Sudán *m*

Sudanese [,su:də'ni:z] (ADJ) sudanés
(N) *(pl inv)* sudanés(esa) *m/f*

sudden ['sʌdn] (ADJ) **1** (= *hasty, swift*) repentino; (= *unexpected*) inesperado • **a ~ drop in temperature** un descenso repentino de la temperatura • **a ~ increase in unemployment** un aumento repentino del número de parados • **with ~ enthusiasm** con un entusiasmo repentino • **this is all so ~!** ¡todo esto es tan repentino! • **his death was ~** su muerte ocurrió de repente, su muerte fue inesperada • **she looked startled by his ~ appearance** parecía asustada cuando él apareció de repente • **when the soldiers came it was very ~** la llegada de los soldados ocurrió de improviso • **all of a ~** de pronto, de repente
2 (= *abrupt*) *[movement]* brusco
(CPD) ▸ **sudden death** *(Tennis)* muerte *f* súbita • **they had to go to ~ death** *(Tennis)* tuvieron que recurrir a la muerte súbita; *(Ftbl)* *(penalty shoot-out)* tuvieron que recurrir a los goles; *(extra time)* tuvieron que recurrir a la prórroga de desempate ▸ **sudden death extra time** prórroga *f* de desempate ▸ **sudden death goal** gol *m* de desempate ▸ **sudden death play-off** desempate *m* instantáneo ▸ **sudden infant death syndrome** *(Med)* síndrome *m* de la muerte súbita infantil

suddenly ['sʌdnlɪ] (ADV) **1** (= *all at once*) de repente, de pronto • **I ~ felt faint** de repente *or* de pronto sentí que me mareaba • **he resigned ~ in June** de repente en junio dimitió • **~, the door opened** de repente *or* de pronto se abrió la puerta
2 (= *abruptly*) *[cease, die]* repentinamente, de repente; *[move]* bruscamente • **the rain stopped as ~ as it had begun** la lluvia paró tan repentinamente *or* de repente como había empezado • **the taxi stopped ~ in front of the hotel** el taxi paró bruscamente delante del hotel

suddenness ['sʌdnnɪs] (N) **1** (= *speed*) lo repentino • **I do wonder at the ~ of his decision** me sorprende lo repentino *or* lo súbito de su decisión • **it had all happened with terrifying ~** todo había ocurrido con una rapidez espantosa • **having started suddenly, the pain stops with equal ~** habiendo empezado repentinamente, el dolor cesa con la misma rapidez
2 (= *unexpectedness*) lo inesperado • **the ~ of his resignation** lo inesperado *or* imprevisto de su dimisión
3 (= *abruptness*) brusquedad *f* • **the car came to a halt with a ~ that sent her jerking forward** el coche se paró con tal brusquedad que la lanzó hacia adelante

sudoku [sʊ'dəʊku:] (N) sudoku *m*

suds [sʌdz] (NPL) **1** espuma *fsing* de jabón
2 *(US‡)* cerveza *fsing*

Sue [su:] (N) *familiar form of* **Susan**

sue [su:] (VT) demandar (**for** por) • **to sue sb for damages** demandar *or* poner pleito a algn por daños y perjuicios • **he was sued for libel** lo demandaron por difamación
(VI) *(Jur)* presentar una demanda • **to sue for divorce** solicitar el divorcio • **to sue for peace** pedir la paz

suede, suède [sweɪd] (N) ante *m*
(CPD) de ante ▸ **suede gloves** guantes *mpl* de ante ▸ **suede shoes** zapatos *mpl* de ante

suet [sʊɪt] (N) sebo *m* • **~ pudding** pudín *m* a base de sebo

Suetonius [swi:'təʊnɪəs] (N) Suetonio

suety ['sʊɪtɪ] (ADJ) seboso

Suez ['su:ɪz] (CPD) ▸ **Suez Canal** Canal *m* de Suez

Suff (ABBR) *(Brit)* = **Suffolk**

suffer ['sʌfəʳ] (VT) **1** (= *experience*) *[+ pain, hardship]* sufrir, padecer; *[+ loss, decline, setback]* sufrir, experimentar • **to ~ a heart attack** sufrir un infarto • **the peace process has ~ed a serious blow** el proceso de paz ha sufrido *or* experimentado un serio contratiempo • **to ~ the same fate as** sufrir la misma suerte que • **to ~ the consequences** sufrir las consecuencias
2 (= *tolerate*) *[+ opposition, rudeness]* soportar, aguantar • **I can't ~ it a moment longer** no lo soporto *or* aguanto un minuto más • **to ~ sb to do sth** *(Literat)* permitir que algn haga algo • IDIOM: • **he/she doesn't ~ fools gladly** no soporta a los imbéciles
(VI) **1** (= *experience pain*) sufrir • **to ~ for sth** sufrir las consecuencias de algo • **you'll ~ for this!** ¡me las pagarás! • **I'll make him ~ for it!** ¡me las pagará! • **to ~ for one's sins** expiar sus pecados • **to make sb ~** hacer sufrir a algn • **to ~ in silence** sufrir en silencio
2 • **to ~ from sth** (= *experience*): • **the house is ~ing from neglect** la casa está en un cierto estado de abandono • **Madrid ~s from overcrowding** Madrid adolece de superpoblación • **to ~ from an illness** padecer una enfermedad • **they were ~ing from shock** se encontraban en estado de shock • **to ~ from the effects of alcohol** sufrir los efectos del alcohol • **to ~ from the effects of a fall** resentirse de una caída
3 (= *worsen*) *[studies, business, eyesight, health]* verse afectado, resentirse • **sales have ~ed badly** las ventas se han visto afectadas seriamente

sufferance ['sʌfərəns] (N) • **on ~** a disgusto, a regañadientes • **she made it clear that he was only here on ~** dejó claro que él solo estaba aquí a disgusto *or* a regañadientes • **the civilian authorities are only there on ~ of the military** las autoridades civiles están allí solo porque los militares las toleran

sufferer ['sʌfərəʳ] (N) *(Med)* enfermo/a *m/f* (**from** de) • **~s from diabetes** los enfermos de diabetes, los diabéticos • **asthma ~s** las personas que sufren de asma, los asmáticos

suffering ['sʌfərɪŋ] (ADJ) que sufre; *(Med)* doliente, enfermo
(N) sufrimiento *m*, padecimiento *m* • **the ~s of the soldiers** los sufrimientos *or* padecimientos de los soldados • **after months of ~** después de sufrir durante meses, después de meses de sufrimiento

suffice [sə'faɪs] *(frm)* (VI) ser suficiente, bastar • **a short letter will ~** una carta breve será suficiente *or* bastará • **military initiatives alone will not ~** por sí solas las iniciativas militares no serán suficientes *or* bastarán
(VT) • **~ it to say** basta con decir

sufficiency [sə'fɪʃənsɪ] (N) (PL: **sufficiencies**) (= *state*) suficiencia *f*; (= *quantity*) cantidad *f* suficiente

sufficient [sə'fɪʃənt] (ADJ) **1** *(before noun)* suficiente • **given ~ time** con suficiente tiempo • **if the matter is of ~ importance** si el asunto es lo bastante importante *or* lo suficientemente importante
2 • **to be ~** bastar, ser suficiente • **ten minutes is quite ~** con diez minutos basta *or* es suficiente • **it is ~ to say that ...** basta decir *or* es suficiente decir que ... • PROVERB: • **~ unto the day (is the evil thereof)** ya nos

preocuparemos de eso cuando llegue el momento
sufficiently [səˈfɪʃəntlɪ] (ADV) **1** (*before adjective, adverb*) (lo) suficientemente, (lo) bastante • **~ large/high to do sth** (lo) suficientemente *or* (lo) bastante grande/alto (como) para hacer algo
2 (*after verb*) lo suficiente • **I think he has been punished ~** creo que ya lo han castigado lo suficiente • **he had recovered ~ to get out of bed** se había recuperado lo suficiente como para levantarse de la cama
suffix [ˈsʌfɪks] (N) sufijo *m*
(VT) añadir como sufijo (**to** a)
suffocate [ˈsʌfəkeɪt] (VT) asfixiar, ahogar
(VI) asfixiarse, ahogarse
suffocating [ˈsʌfəkeɪtɪŋ] (ADJ) **1** (= *choking*) [*heat*] sofocante, agobiante; [*fumes, smell*] asfixiante • **the ~ heat of the day** el calor sofocante *or* agobiante del día • **it's ~ in here** hace un calor sofocante *or* agobiante aquí dentro
2 (= *oppressive*) [*atmosphere, life, relationship*] agobiante; [*regime*] opresivo • **the ~ atmosphere of life in the country** el ambiente agobiante de la vida en el campo
suffocation [ˌsʌfəˈkeɪʃən] (N) asfixia *f*, ahogo *m*
suffragan [ˈsʌfrəgən] (ADJ) sufragáneo
(N) obispo *m* sufragáneo
suffrage [ˈsʌfrɪdʒ] (N) **1** (= *franchise*) sufragio *m* • **universal ~** sufragio *m* universal
2 (*frm*) (= *vote*) sufragio *m*, voto *m*
suffragette [ˌsʌfrəˈdʒet] (N) sufragista *f*
(CPD) ▸ **suffragette movement** movimiento *m* sufragista
suffuse [səˈfjuːz] (VT) [*light*] bañar; [*colour, flush*] teñir; [*delight, relief*] inundar • **~d with light** bañado de luz • **eyes ~d with tears** ojos bañados de lágrimas • **this book is ~d with the author's Irish humour** este libro está impregnado del humor irlandés del autor
suffusion [səˈfjuːʒən] (N) difusión *f*
sugar [ˈʃʊgəʳ] (N) **1** azúcar *m or f* • **to put ~ in sth** echar azúcar en algo • **how many ~s do you take?** (*in general*) ¿cuánta *or* cuánto azúcar tomas?; (*offering tea, coffee*) ¿cuánta *or* cuánto azúcar quieres?, ¿cuántos terrones quieres?
2 (*US**) • **hi, ~!** ¡oye, preciosidad!*
3* (*euph*) • **oh ~!** ¡mecachis!*
(VT) [+ *tea etc*] azucarar, echar azúcar a; ▹ **pill**
(CPD) ▸ **sugar basin** (*Brit*) azucarero *m* ▸ **sugar beet** remolacha *f* azucarera ▸ **sugar bowl** azucarero *m* ▸ **sugar candy** azúcar *m* candi ▸ **sugar cane** caña *f* de azúcar ▸ **sugar cube** terrón *m* de azúcar ▸ **sugar daddy*** *viejo adinerado amante o protector de una joven* ▸ **sugar factory** refinería *f* de azúcar ▸ **sugar loaf** pan *m* de azúcar ▸ **sugar lump** terrón *m* de azúcar ▸ **sugar mill** ingenio *m* azucarero ▸ **sugar pea** tirabeque *m*, arveja *f* china ▸ **sugar plantation** plantación *f* azucarera ▸ **sugar refinery** ingenio *m* azucarero ▸ **sugar snap pea** tirabeque *m*, arveja *f* china ▸ **sugar tongs** tenacillas *fpl* para azúcar
sugar-coated [ˈʃʊgəˈkəʊtɪd] (ADJ) azucarado
sugared [ˈʃʊgəd] (ADJ) • **~ almonds** almendras *fpl* garrapiñadas
sugar-free [ʃʊgəˈfriː], **sugarless** [ˈʃʊgəlɪs] (ADJ) sin azúcar
sugarplum [ˈʃʊgəplʌm] (N) confite *m*
sugary [ˈʃʊgərɪ] (ADJ) **1** (= *sweet*) [*food*] dulce; (*more technical*) con alto contenido en azúcar; [*drink*] azucarado, dulce; [*taste*] dulce
2 (*pej*) (= *sentimental*) [*film, smile, words*] empalagoso; [*voice*] meloso
suggest [səˈdʒest] (VT) **1** (= *propose, put forward*) [+ *plan, candidate, idea etc*] sugerir, proponer • **to ~ sth to sb** sugerir algo a algn, proponer algo a algn • **I ~ed to him that we go out for a drink** le sugerí *or* propuse ir a tomar algo • **I ~ed taking her out to dinner** propuse llevarla a cenar • **could you ~ someone to advise me?** ¿se te ocurre alguien que me pueda aconsejar? • **an idea ~ed itself (to me)** se me ocurrió una idea • **nothing ~s itself** no se me ocurre nada
2 (= *advise*) aconsejar • **we ~ you contact him** le aconsejamos que contacte con él • **he ~ed that they (should) go** *or* **that they went to London** les aconsejó que fueran a Londres • **to ~ doing sth** aconsejar que se haga algo
3 (= *imply*) insinuar • **what are you trying to ~?** ¿qué insinúas? • **I'm not ~ing that the accident was your fault** no estoy insinuando que el accidente fuera culpa tuya • **it has been ~ed that ...** se ha insinuado que ...
4 (= *evoke*) sugerir, hacer pensar en • **what does that smell ~ to you?** ¿qué te sugiere ese olor?, ¿en qué te hace pensar ese olor?
5 (= *indicate*) parecer indicar • **this ~s that ...** esto hace pensar que ... • **the coins ~ a Roman settlement** las monedas parecen indicar *or* nos hacen pensar que era una colonia romana • **it doesn't exactly ~ a careful man** no parece indicar que sea un hombre cauteloso
suggestibility [səˌdʒestɪˈbɪlɪtɪ] (N) sugestionabilidad *f*
suggestible [səˈdʒestɪbl] (ADJ) sugestionable
suggestion [səˈdʒestʃən] (N) **1** (= *proposal, recommendation*) sugerencia *f* • **have you any ~s?** ¿tienes alguna sugerencia?, ¿se te ocurre algo? • **if I may make** *or* **offer a ~** si se me permite proponer algo • **to be open to ~s** estar abierto a cualquier sugerencia • **my ~ is that we ignore her** yo propongo que no la hagamos caso • **my ~ to you would be to take the job** yo te aconsejaría que aceptaras el trabajo • **I am writing at the ~ of Hugh Smith** le escribo siguiendo la indicación de Hugh Smith
2 (= *implication*) insinuación *f* • **we reject any ~ that the law needs amending** rechazamos cualquier insinuación de que la ley necesite una modificación
3 (= *indication*) indicio *m* • **there is no ~ that the two sides are any closer** no hay indicios de que ambas partes se hayan acercado • **there are ~s that he might be supported by the socialists** hay indicios de que le puedan apoyar los socialistas, se comenta que quizá le apoyen los socialistas
4 (= *trace*) [*of doubt*] sombra *f* • **he replied with the ~ of a smile** contestó esbozando una sonrisa • **with just a ~ of garlic** con una pizca de ajo
5 (*Psych*) sugestión *f* • **the power of ~** el poder de la sugestión
(CPD) ▸ **suggestion box** buzón *m* de sugerencias
suggestive [səˈdʒestɪv] (ADJ) **1** (= *improper*) [*remark, look, clothing*] provocativo, insinuante • **sexually ~** provocativo
2 (= *indicative*) • **to be ~ of sth: symptoms which were ~ of heart failure** síntomas que sugerían que pod(r)ía tratarse de un fallo cardíaco, síntomas que parecían indicar que se trataba de un fallo cardíaco • **his behaviour was ~ of a cultured man** su comportamiento parecía indicar que era un hombre culto • **the atmosphere was ~ of a jazz session** (= *evocative of*) el ambiente evocaba el de una sesión de jazz
3 (= *thought-provoking*) sugerente
suggestively [səˈdʒestɪvlɪ] (ADV) [*dance, move, leer*] de manera provocativa, de manera insinuante • **"like to see my etchings?" he asked ~** —¿quieres ver mi colección de sellos? —preguntó de manera insinuante *or* provocativa
suggestiveness [səˈdʒestɪvnɪs] (N) • **~ and titillation are the main ingredients of these films** la insinuación y la excitación son los principales ingredientes de estas películas • **the ~ of the phrase** lo insinuante de la frase
suicidal [ˌsuːɪˈsaɪdl] (ADJ) **1** (= *depressed*) [*feeling, tendency*] suicida • **~ prisoners** prisioneros suicidas • **to be ~** estar al borde del suicidio • **he has often felt ~** a menudo ha tenido ganas de suicidarse
2 (*fig*) • **such a policy is ~** una política semejante es suicida • **an act of ~ bravery** un acto de valentía suicida • **it would be ~ to do that** sería suicida hacer eso
suicide [ˈsuːɪsaɪd] (N) **1** (= *act*) suicidio *m* • **to commit ~** suicidarse • **it would be ~ to do that** (*lit, fig*) sería suicida hacer eso • **it would be political ~ to agree to this** consentir esto supondría el suicidio político • **a case of attempted ~** un caso de intento de suicidio
2 (= *person*) suicida *mf*
(CPD) ▸ **suicide attack** atentado *m* suicida ▸ **suicide attempt** intento *m* de suicidio ▸ **suicide bomber** terrorista *mf* suicida ▸ **suicide bombing** bombardeo *m* suicida ▸ **suicide mission** misión *f* suicida ▸ **suicide note** *carta en que se explica el motivo del suicidio* ▸ **suicide pact** pacto *m* suicida ▸ **suicide rate** índice *m* de suicidios ▸ **suicide squad** comando *m* suicida
suit [suːt] (N) **1** (= *clothing*) (*for man*) traje *m*, terno *m* (*LAm*); (*for woman*) traje *m* (de chaqueta) • **three-piece/two-piece ~** traje *or* (*LAm*) terno de tres/dos piezas • **a rubber ~** un traje de goma • **~ of armour** armadura *f* • **~ of clothes** conjunto *m*; ▹ **bathing, birthday**
2 (*also* **lawsuit**) pleito *m* • **to bring** *or* **file a ~ (against sb)** entablar un pleito (contra algn) • **civil ~** pleito *m* civil
3 (*Cards*) palo *m* • **to follow ~** (*in cards*) jugar una carta del mismo palo; (*fig*) seguir el ejemplo • IDIOM: • **modesty is not his strong** *or* (*esp US*) **long ~** la modestia no es su fuerte
4 (*frm*) (= *petition*) petición *f*; (*liter*) (*for marriage*) petición *f* de mano • **her parents gave me permission to plead** *or* **press my ~** sus padres me dieron permiso para pedir su mano
5* (= *business executive*) ejecutivo/a *m/f*
(VT) **1** (= *look good on*) [*clothes, shoes, hairstyle*] quedar bien a, sentar bien a • **the coat ~s you** el abrigo te queda *or* te sienta bien • **choose earrings which ~ the shape of your face** elige pendientes que vayan bien con la forma de tu cara
2 (= *be acceptable to, please*) a [*date, time, arrangement*] venir bien a, convenir • **when would ~ you?** ¿cuándo te viene bien *or* te conviene? • **I'll do it when it ~s me** lo haré cuando me venga bien *or* cuando me convenga • **I don't think a sedentary life would ~ me** no creo que la vida sedentaria sea para mí • **it ~s him to work nights** le viene *or* le va bien trabajar de noche • **choose the method which ~s you best** elige el método que te vaya mejor *or* que más te convenga • **it would ~ us better to come back tomorrow** nos vendría mejor *or* nos convendría más volver mañana • **he found a life that ~ed him better** encontró una forma de vida más apropiada para él • **that ~s me fine** eso me va bien *or* me conviene • **the climate ~s me fine** el clima me sienta bien

• **to ~ sth to sth/sb** (*frm*) adaptar algo a algo/algn • IDIOM: • **to ~ sb down to the ground** [*plan, situation*] venir de perlas a algn; [*house, job*] ser perfecto para algn; ▹ **book**
b (*reflexive*) • **I can come and go to ~ myself** puedo ir y venir como me convenga *or* plazca • **he has already arranged his life to ~ himself** ya ha organizado su vida como le conviene *or* place • **~ yourself!** ¡como quieras! • **~ yourself whether you do it or not** hazlo o no según te parezca
(VI) (= *be convenient*) • **will tomorrow ~?** ¿te viene bien mañana? • **come whenever it ~s** ven cuando más te convenga

suitability [ˌsu:təˈbɪlɪtɪ] (N) **1** (= *adequacy*) [*of person, tool*] idoneidad *f* • **criteria for judging an applicant's ~ for a job** criterios para juzgar la idoneidad de un candidato para un trabajo • **there is some doubt about the ~ of this house for disabled occupants** existen dudas de que esta casa sea adecuada para personas discapacitadas, existen dudas sobre la idoneidad de esta casa para personas discapacitadas
2 (= *fitness*) [*of clothes*] lo apropiado • **I'd question the ~ of wearing low-cut blouses to work** pondría en duda lo apropiado de llevar blusas escotadas al trabajo

suitable [ˈsu:təbl] (ADJ) **1** (= *satisfactory*) adecuado, apropiado • **the shortage of ~ housing** la escasez de viviendas adecuadas *or* apropiadas • **his qualifications weren't considered ~** consideraron que no tenía la formación adecuada *or* apropiada
2 (= *valid, apt*) apropiado • **both courses are ~ for beginners** ambos cursos son apropiados para principiantes • **the products are ~ for all skin types** los productos son apropiados para todo tipo de pieles • **the garden is not ~ for wheelchairs** el jardín no está adaptado para sillas de ruedas • **dishes that are ~ for freezing** platos preparados que se pueden congelar • **"suitable for children"** "apto para niños" • **eminently ~** idóneo • **to make sth ~ for sth** (= *adapt*) adaptar algo para algo
3 (= *fitting*) apropiado • **a ~ reply** una respuesta apropiada • **a ~ dress for the occasion** un vestido apropiado para la ocasión • **the committee met to consider ~ action** el comité se reunió para considerar las medidas oportunas *or* convenientes *or* apropiadas • **choose a ~ moment to talk** escoja un momento oportuno *or* apropiado para hablar
4 (= *recommendable*) adecuado • **a more ~ diet** una dieta más adecuada • **the most ~ man for the job** el hombre más indicado *or* adecuado para el puesto

suitably [ˈsu:təblɪ] (ADV) [*dressed*] apropiadamente, adecuadamente; [*equipped*] adecuadamente • **~ qualified staff** personal con la formación adecuada *or* apropiada • **I heard their album, and was ~ impressed** escuché su disco y como era de esperar me causó muy buena impresión • **Andy tried to look ~ impressed** Andy intentó parecer todo lo impresionado que la ocasión requería • **he tried to adopt a ~ grave tone** intentó adoptar un tono serio acorde con *or* apropiado para la ocasión

suitcase [ˈsu:tkeɪs] (N) maleta *f*, valija *f* (*LAm*), veliz *m* (*Mex*)

suite [swi:t] (N) **1** (*Mus*) suite *f*
2 (= *rooms*) suite *f* • **a ~ of rooms** habitaciones *fpl* • **bridal ~** suite *f* nupcial • **honeymoon ~** suite *f* nupcial • **a ~ of offices** un grupo de oficinas
3 [*of furniture*] juego *m* • **we're going to buy a new ~ this year** vamos a comprar un nuevo juego de sofá y sillones este año • **bathroom ~** conjunto *m or* muebles *mpl* de baño • **bedroom ~** (juego *m* de) dormitorio *m* • **dining-room ~** comedor *m* • **a ~ of furniture** un juego de muebles • **three-piece ~** tresillo *m*
4 (= *entourage*) séquito *m*
5 (*Comput*) • **a ~ of programs** una serie *f* de programas

suited [ˈsu:tɪd] (ADJ) **1** • **to be ~ to a** [+ *environment, user*] [*thing*] ser apropiado para • **these crops are more ~ to monsoon lands than to deserts** estos cultivos son más apropiados para las tierras de monzón que para el desierto • **goats are well ~ to the terrain** las cabras están bien adaptadas al terreno
b [+ *task*] [*person, thing*] servir para, estar hecho para • **many people are not ~ to this work** mucha gente no sirve para *or* no está hecha para este trabajo • **some people are not ~ to parenthood** algunas personas no están hechas para ser padres • **women are better ~ to computing than men** las mujeres están más capacitadas para la informática que los hombres • **a camera which is well ~ to all types of photography** una cámara que sirve para *or* que se adapta bien a todo tipo de fotografía
2 • **to be well ~** [*couple*] hacer buena pareja

suiting [ˈsu:tɪŋ] (N) (*Textiles*) tela *f* para trajes

suitor [ˈsu:təʳ] (N) **1** (= *lover*) pretendiente *m*
2 (*Jur*) demandante *mf*

sulfa drug [ˈsʌlfədrʌg] (N) (*US*) sulfamida *f*

sulfate [ˈsʌlfeɪt] (N) (*US*) = **sulphate**

sulfide [ˈsʌlfaɪd] (N) (*US*) = **sulphide**

sulfite [ˈsʌlfaɪt] (N) (*US*) = **sulphite**

sulfonamide [sʌlˈfɒnəmaɪd] (N) (*US*) = **sulphonamide**

sulfur [ˈsʌlfəʳ] (N) (*US*) = **sulphur**

sulfureous [sʌlˈfjʊərɪəs] (ADJ) (*US*) = **sulphureous**

sulfuric [sʌlˈfjʊərɪk] (ADJ) (*US*) = **sulphuric**

sulfurous [ˈsʌlfərəs] (ADJ) (*US*) = **sulphurous**

sulk [sʌlk] (VI) (= *get sulky*) enfurruñarse; (= *be sulky*) estar enfurruñado
(N) • **to get the ~s** enfurruñarse • **to have (a fit of) the ~s** enfurruñarse • **to go off in a ~** irse enfurruñado

sulkily [ˈsʌlkɪlɪ] (ADV) de mal humor • **"I don't like it," he said ~** —no me gusta —dijo enfurruñado *or* de mal humor

sulkiness [ˈsʌlkɪnɪs] (N) mal humor *m*, enfurruñamiento *m*

sulky [ˈsʌlkɪ] (ADJ) (COMPAR: **sulkier**, SUPERL: **sulkiest**) [*person, voice*] malhumorado, enfurruñado; [*expression*] ceñudo, malhumorado • **to be ~ about sth** estar malhumorado *or* enfurruñado por algo, estar de mal humor por algo

sullen [ˈsʌlən] (ADJ) **1** (= *moody*) [*person, expression, voice*] hosco, huraño • **the men lapsed into a ~ silence** los hombres se sumieron en un hosco silencio
2 (= *leaden*) [*sky, landscape*] plomizo, triste

sullenly [ˈsʌlənlɪ] (ADV) hoscamente • **they stared ~ at him** le miraron hoscamente, con fijeza • **the ~ resentful expression on her face** la expresión huraña y de resentimiento de su rostro

sullenness [ˈsʌlənnɪs] (N) hosquedad *f*

sully [ˈsʌlɪ] (VT) (*poet*) [+ *name, reputation*] manchar, mancillar

sulpha drug [ˈsʊlfədrʌg] = **sulfa drug**

sulphate [ˈsʌlfeɪt] (N) sulfato *m* • **copper ~** sulfato *m* de cobre

sulphide [ˈsʌlfaɪd] (N) sulfuro *m*

sulphite [ˈsʌlfaɪt] (N) sulfito *m*

sulphonamide [sʌlˈfɒnəmaɪd] (N) sulfamida *f*

sulphur [ˈsʌlfəʳ] (N) azufre *m*
(CPD) ▸ **sulphur dioxide** dióxido *m* de azufre

sulphureous [sʌlˈfjʊərɪəs] (ADJ) sulfúrico

sulphuric [sʌlˈfjʊərɪk] (ADJ) • **~ acid** ácido *m* sulfúrico

sulphurous [ˈsʌlfərəs] (ADJ) sulfuroso, sulfúreo

sultan [ˈsʌltən] (N) sultán *m*

sultana [sʌlˈtɑ:nə] (N) **1** (*esp Brit*) pasa *f* sultana
2 (= *person*) sultana *f*

sultanate [ˈsʌltənɪt] (N) sultanato *m*

sultriness [ˈsʌltrɪnɪs] (N) **1** (= *mugginess*) bochorno *m*, calor *m* sofocante
2 (= *seductiveness*) sensualidad *f*

sultry [ˈsʌltrɪ] (ADJ) **1** (= *muggy*) [*day, weather*] bochornoso, sofocante; [*heat, air*] sofocante, agobiante • **it was hot and ~** hacía bochorno, hacía un calor sofocante
2 (= *seductive*) [*woman*] seductor, sensual • **she gave him a ~ look** lo miró seductora, lo miró de forma sensual

sum [sʌm] (N) **1** (= *piece of arithmetic*) suma *f*, adición *f* • **I was very bad at sums** era muy malo en aritmética • **to do one's sums** hacer cuentas • **to do sums in one's head** hacer un cálculo mental
2 (= *total*) suma *f*, total *m*; (= *amount of money*) suma *f*, importe *m* • **in sum** en suma, en resumen • **more/greater than the sum of its parts** más que la suma de las partes • **sum total** total *m* (completo) • **the sum total of my ambitions is ...** la meta de mis ambiciones es ..., lo único que ambiciono es ... • **that was the sum (total) of his achievements** y de allí no pasó; ▹ **lump**

▸ **sum up** (VI + ADV) (= *summarize*) resumir; [*judge*] recapitular • **to sum up, I would say** en resumidas cuentas, yo diría
(VT + ADV) **1** (= *summarize*) [+ *speech, facts, argument*] resumir • **you could sum up what he said in a couple of words** se podría resumir lo que dijo en dos palabras • **to sum up an argument** resumir un argumento
2 (= *encapsulate*) resumir • **that picture summed up the situation for me** esa fotografía resumió la situación para mí *or* captaba la situación en un solo trazo
3 (= *assess*) [+ *person*] calar; [+ *situation*] evaluar • **they had summed him up and liked what they found** lo habían calado y les había agradado lo que descubrieron • **he summed up the situation quickly** se dio cuenta rápidamente de la situación

sumac, sumach [ˈsu:mæk] (N) zumaque *m*

Sumatra [sʊˈmɑ:trə] (N) Sumatra *f*

Sumatran [sʊˈmɑ:trən] (ADJ) sumatreño, de Sumatra
(N) sumatreño/a *m/f*

Sumerian [su:ˈmɪərɪən] (ADJ) sumerio
(N) **1** (= *person*) sumerio/a *m/f*
2 (*Ling*) sumerio *m*

summarily [ˈsʌmərɪlɪ] (ADV) [*execute, dismiss, shoot*] sumariamente

summarize [ˈsʌməraɪz] (VT) resumir
(VI) resumir • **to ~, ...** en resumen, ...

summary [ˈsʌmərɪ] (N) resumen *m* • **in ~** en resumen
(ADJ) [*trial, execution, justice*] sumario

summat‡ [ˈsʌmət] (*dialect*) = **something**

summation [sʌˈmeɪʃən] (N) (= *act*) adición *f*; (= *summary*) recapitulación *f*, resumen *m*; (= *total*) suma *f*, total *m*

summer [ˈsʌməʳ] (N) verano *m*, estío *m* (*liter, poet*) • **to go away for the ~** irse fuera todo el verano • **a ~'s day** un día de verano • **in ~** en verano • **I like to go walking in (the) ~** me gusta ir a la playa en verano • **in the ~ of 1987** en el verano de 1987 • **to spend the ~ in Spain** veranear en España, pasar el verano en

España • IDIOM: • **a girl of 17 ~s** (*liter*) una chica de 17 primaveras *or* abriles
(VI) [*birds*] pasar el verano • **we ~ed in Maine** veraneamos *or* pasamos el verano en Maine
(CPD) [*clothing, residence, holiday*] de verano; [*weather, heat*] veraniego ▸ **summer camp** colonia *f or* campamento *m* de vacaciones ▸ **summer holidays** vacaciones *fpl* de verano, veraneo *msing* ▸ **summer job** trabajo *m* de verano ▸ **summer school** escuela *f* de verano ▸ **summer season** temporada *f* veraniega, temporada *f* estival, temporada *f* de verano ▸ **summer term** tercer trimestre *m* ▸ **summer time** (*Brit*) (*daylight saving*) hora *f* de verano; ▹ **summertime**

summerhouse ['sʌməhaʊs] (N) (PL: **summerhouses** ['sʌməhaʊzız]) cenador *m*, glorieta *f*

summersault ['sʌməsɔ:lt] (N), (VI) = somersault

summertime ['sʌmətaım] (N) (= *season*) verano *m*

summery ['sʌmərı] (ADJ) [*day*] veraniego; [*clothes, colour*] veraniego, de verano; [*weather*] estival

summing-up ['sʌmıŋ'ʌp] (N) (*Jur*) resumen *m*

summit ['sʌmıt] (N) **1** [*of mountain*] cima *f*, cumbre *f* • **did anyone reach the ~?** ¿alcanzó alguien la cima *or* la cumbre?
2 (*fig*) cima *f*, cumbre *f* • **a man at the ~ of his career** un hombre en la cima *or* la cumbre de su trayectoria profesional
3 (*Pol*) (*also* **summit conference**) cumbre *f*, conferencia *f* al más alto nivel
(CPD) ▸ **summit conference** cumbre *f*, conferencia *f* al más alto nivel ▸ **summit meeting** cumbre *f*

summiteer [,sʌmı'tıəʳ] (N) participante *mf* en una cumbre

summitry ['sʌmıtrı] (N) (*esp US*) (*hum*) práctica *f* de celebrar conferencias cumbre

summon ['sʌmən] (VT) [+ *servant, doctor etc*] llamar; [+ *meeting*] convocar; [+ *aid*] pedir; (*Jur*) citar, emplazar • **to be ~ed to sb's presence** ser llamado a la presencia de algn • **they ~ed me to advise them** me llamaron para que les aconsejara • **to ~ a town to surrender** hacer una llamada a una ciudad para que se rinda
▸ **summon up** (VT + ADV) [+ *courage*] armarse de, cobrar; [+ *memory*] evocar

summons ['sʌmənz] (N) (PL: **summonses**) (*Jur*) citación *f* judicial, emplazamiento *m*; (*fig*) llamada *f* • **he got a ~ for drink driving** recibió una citación por conducir borracho • **she received a ~ to appear in court** recibió una citación para presentarse en el juzgado • **to serve a ~ on sb** entregar una citación a algn • **to take out a ~ against sb** entablar demanda contra algn, citar a algn (para estrados)
(VT) citar, emplazar • **she has been ~ed to appear in court** ha sido citada *or* emplazada a presentarse en el juzgado

sumo ['su:məʊ] (N) **1** (*Sport*) (*also* **sumo wrestling**) sumo *m*
2 (*also* **sumo wrestler**) luchador *m* de sumo

sump [sʌmp] (N) (*Aut*) cárter *m*; (*Min*) sumidero *m*; (= *cesspool*) letrina *f*

sumptuary ['sʌmptjʊərı] (ADJ) suntuario

sumptuous ['sʌmptjʊəs] (ADJ) [*feast, fabrics, silk*] suntuoso

sumptuously ['sʌmptjʊəslı] (ADV) suntuosamente

sumptuousness ['sʌmptjʊəsnıs] (N) suntuosidad *f*

sun [sʌn] (N) sol *m* • **the sun is shining** brilla el sol, hace sol • **the sun is in my eyes** me da el sol en los ojos • **he rises with the sun** se levanta con el sol • **to catch the sun: you've caught the sun** te ha cogido el sol • **to be (out) in the sun** estar al sol • IDIOM: • **under the sun:** • **they have everything under the sun** no les falta de nada • **they would do anything under the sun to stay in power** serían capaces de hacer cualquier cosa para seguir en el poder • **he called me all the names under the sun** me llamó de todo • PROVERB: • **there is nothing new under the sun** no hay nada nuevo bajo el sol
(VT) • **to sun o.s.** tomar el sol, asolearse (*LAm*), tomar sol (*S. Cone*)
(CPD) ▸ **sun cream** crema *f* solar ▸ **sun dress** vestido *m* de playa ▸ **sun god** dios *m* del sol, divinidad *f* solar ▸ **sun hat** pamela *f*, sombrero *m* de ala ancha ▸ **sun index** índice *m* solar ▸ **sun lamp** lámpara *f* solar ultravioleta ▸ **sun lotion** bronceador *m* ▸ **sun lounge** solana *f* ▸ **sun lounger** tumbona *f* ▸ **sun oil** aceite *m* solar ▸ **sun parlour, sun parlor** (*US*) solana *f* ▸ **sun umbrella** sombrilla *f* ▸ **sun visor** (*for eyes*) visor *m*; (*on car*) visera *f*, quitasol *m*

Sun. (ABBR) (= **Sunday**) dom.º

sunbaked ['sʌnbeıkt] (ADJ) endurecido al sol

sunbathe (VI) tomar el sol, asolearse (*LAm*), tomar sol (*S. Cone*)

sunbather ['sʌnbeıðəʳ] (N) persona *f* que toma el sol

sunbathing ['sʌnbeıðıŋ] (N) baños *mpl* de sol • **I like ~ in the garden** me gusta tomar el sol *or* (*LAm*) asolearme *or* (*S. Cone*) tomar sol en el jardín

sunbeam ['sʌnbi:m] (N) rayo *m* de sol

sunbed ['sʌnbed] (N) cama *f* solar

sunbelt ['sʌnbelt] (N) (*US*) *franja del sur de Estados Unidos caracterizada por su clima cálido*

> **SUNBELT**
> A los estados del sur de EE.UU. que van desde Carolina del Norte hasta California se les denomina **sunbelt** (cinturón del sol) por su clima cálido. Este nombre también se asocia con el reciente desarrollo económico de la zona, lo cual ha dado lugar a un aumento de población (por el movimiento demográfico de norte a sur) y a un mayor poder político. Por oposición a este término, a los estados del norte se les llama a veces **frostbelt** (cinturón de escarcha) o **rustbelt** (cinturón de óxido), por el número de fábricas ya en declive que hay en la zona.

sunblind ['sʌnblaınd] (N) toldo *m*

sunblock ['sʌnblɒk] (N) filtro *m* solar

sunbonnet ['sʌn,bɒnıt] (N) gorro *m* de sol

sunburn ['sʌnbɜ:n] (N) quemaduras *fpl* del sol

sunburned ['sʌnbɜ:nd], **sunburnt** ['sʌnbɜ:nt] (ADJ) (*painfully*) quemado por el sol; (= *tanned*) bronceado • **a badly ~ back** una espalda muy quemada por el sol • **to get ~** (*painfully*) quemarse

sunburst ['sʌnbɜ:st] (N) explosión *f* de sol

sundae ['sʌndeı] (N) helado *m* con frutas y nueces

Sunday ['sʌndı] (N) domingo *m*; ▹ **Tuesday**
(CPD) ▸ **Sunday best** • **in one's ~ best** en traje de domingo, endomingado ▸ **Sunday newspaper** periódico *m* del domingo, (periódico *m*) dominical *m* ▸ **Sunday opening** = **Sunday trading** ▸ **Sunday paper** periódico *m* del domingo, (periódico *m*) dominical *m* ▸ **Sunday school** escuela *f* dominical, catequesis *f* ▸ **Sunday school teacher** profesor(a) *m/f* de escuela dominical ▸ **Sunday supplement** suplemento *m* dominical ▸ **Sunday trading** apertura *f* en domingo ▸ **Sunday trading laws** leyes *fpl* reguladoras de la apertura en domingo

> **SUNDAY PAPERS**
> Los periódicos dominicales (**Sunday papers**) juegan un papel importante en el Reino Unido. Algunos de ellos, como **The Observer** o **News of the World** solo se publican ese día, mientras que otros, como **The Sunday Times, The Sunday Telegraph, The Independent on Sunday, The Sunday Express** o **The Sunday Mirror**, son ediciones especiales de periódicos diarios. Los dominicales suelen tener distintas secciones, con espacios para cultura, viajes, deportes o negocios, además de incluir muchos de ellos una revista en color.
> En Estados Unidos se suelen comprar más los periódicos locales que los de tirada nacional. De estos, el principal es el **New York Times**. Al igual que en el Reino Unido, los periódicos dominicales tienen más secciones de lo habitual, con artículos más extensos y venden más ejemplares. Pero a diferencia de los británicos, los estadounidenses suelen comprar un solo periódico los domingos.

sundeck ['sʌndek] (N) cubierta *f* superior

sunder ['sʌndəʳ] (VT) (*liter*) romper, dividir, hender

sundew ['sʌndju:] (N) rocío *m* de sol

sundial ['sʌndaıəl] (N) reloj *m* de sol

sundown ['sʌndaʊn] (N) (*US*) anochecer *m* • **at ~** al anochecer • **before ~** antes del anochecer

sundowner* ['sʌndaʊnəʳ] (N) trago *m* de licor que se toma al anochecer

sun-drenched ['sʌndrentʃt] (ADJ) bañado de sol

sun-dried ['sʌndraıd] (ADJ) secado al sol

sundry ['sʌndrı] (ADJ) diversos, varios • **all and ~** todos sin excepción
(N) **sundries** (*Comm*) artículos *mpl* diversos; (= *expenses*) gastos *mpl* diversos

sun-filled ['sʌnfıld] (ADJ) soleado

sunfish ['sʌnfıʃ] (N) peje-sol *m*

sunflower ['sʌn,flaʊəʳ] (N) girasol *m*
(CPD) ▸ **sunflower oil** aceite *m* de girasol ▸ **sunflower seeds** pipas *fpl*

sung [sʌŋ] (PP) *of* sing

sunglasses ['sʌn,glɑ:sız] (NPL) gafas *fpl* de sol, anteojos *mpl* de sol (*LAm*)

sunk [sʌŋk] (PP) *of* sink

sunken ['sʌŋkən] (ADJ) **1** (*liter*) (= *submerged*) [*ship, treasure*] hundido
2 (= *hollow*) [*cheeks, eyes*] hundido
3 (= *low*) [*garden, road, bath*] que está a un nivel inferior *or* más bajo

sun-kissed ['sʌnkıst] (ADJ) soleado

sunless ['sʌnlıs] (ADJ) sin sol

sunlight ['sʌnlaıt] (N) sol *m*, luz *f* del sol • **those plants must be kept out of direct ~** a esas plantas no las debe dar el sol directamente • **hours of ~** (*Met*) horas *fpl* de sol • **in the ~** al sol

sunlit ['sʌnlıt] (ADJ) iluminado por el sol

Sunni ['sʌnı] (ADJ) sunita, suní
(N) sunita *mf*, suní *mf*

sunnily ['sʌnılı] (ADV) [*smile, say*] con alegría

sunny ['sʌnı] (ADJ) (COMPAR: **sunnier**, SUPERL: **sunniest**) **1** (= *bright*) [*weather, climate, morning, place*] soleado • **it was a ~ spring morning** era una soleada mañana de primavera • **on ~ days** los días soleados *or* en que hace sol • **it's a lovely ~ day** hace un día de sol precioso • **the sunniest place in Alaska** el lugar de Alaska donde hace más sol, el lugar más soleado de Alaska • **~ intervals**

S

(*Met*) intervalos *mpl* soleados • **it's ~** hace sol • **the outlook is ~** el pronóstico es soleado • IDIOM: • **I'd like my egg ~ side up** (*Culin*) quiero que mi huevo esté frito solo por un lado
2 (= *cheery*) [*person*] risueño, alegre; [*smile, disposition*] alegre • **to have a ~ disposition** *or* **temperament** ser de temperamento alegre

sunray ['sʌnreɪ] (ADJ) • **~ lamp** lámpara *f* ultravioleta • **~ treatment** helioterapia *f*, tratamiento *m* con lámpara ultravioleta

sunrise ['sʌnraɪz] (N) salida *f* del sol • **at ~** al amanecer • **from ~ to sunset** de sol a sol
(CPD) ▸ **sunrise industries** industrias *fpl* del porvenir, industrias *fpl* de alta tecnología

sunroof ['sʌnru:f] (N) (*on building*) azotea *f*, terraza *f*; (*Aut*) techo *m* solar

sunscreen ['sʌnskri:n] (N) bronceador *m* con filtro solar

sunset ['sʌnset] (N) puesta *f* del sol • **at ~** al atardecer, al ponerse el sol

sunshade ['sʌnʃeɪd] (N) (*portable*) sombrilla *f*; (= *awning*) toldo *m*

sunshine ['sʌnʃaɪn] (N) 1 sol *m*, luz *f* del sol • **in the ~** al sol • **hours of ~** (*Met*) horas *fpl* de sol • **daily average ~** media *f* de horas de sol diarias
2* • **hello, ~!** (*to little girl*) ¡hola, nena!* • **now look here, ~** (*iro*) mira, macho*
(CPD) ▸ **sunshine law** (*US*) *ley que obliga a mantener informado al público* ▸ **sunshine roof** (*Aut*) techo *m* solar

sunspot ['sʌnspɒt] (N) 1 (= *resort*) *centro turístico muy soleado*
2 (*Astron*) mancha *f* solar

sunstroke ['sʌnstrəʊk] (N) insolación *f* • **to get** *or* **catch ~** coger *or* agarrar una insolación • **to have ~** tener una insolación

sunsuit ['sʌnsu:t] (N) traje *m* de playa

suntan ['sʌntæn] (N) bronceado *m*, moreno *m* (*Sp*) • **to get a ~** broncearse, ponerse moreno (*Sp*)
(CPD) ▸ **suntan lotion** bronceador *m* ▸ **suntan oil** aceite *m* solar

suntanned ['sʌntænd] (ADJ) bronceado, moreno (*Sp*)

suntrap ['sʌntræp] (N) *lugar muy soleado y protegido*

sunup ['sʌnʌp] (N) (*US*) salida *f* del sol

sunworshipper ['sʌnwɜ:ʃɪpəʳ] (N) fanático/a *m/f* del sol

sup [sʌp] (VI) cenar • **to sup off sth** • **sup on sth** cenar algo
(VT) (*also* **sup up**) sorber, beber a sorbos

super* ['su:pəʳ] (ADJ) (*esp Brit*) bárbaro, estupendo (*Sp*), tremendo, macanudo (*LAm*), regio (*S. Cone**), chévere (*Ven*) • **we had a ~ time** lo pasamos la mar de bien *or* (*S. Cone*) regio* • **that's a ~ idea** es una idea estupenda • **that would be ~** sería estupendo
(CPD) ▸ **Super Bowl** (*US*) Super Bowl *f*, *Liga Nacional de Fútbol Americano* ▸ **super volcano** supervolcán *m*

super... ['su:pəʳ] (PREFIX) (= *more than the norm*) super..., sobre...

superabound [ˌsu:pərə'baʊnd] (VI) sobreabundar (**in, with** en)

superabundance [ˌsu:pərə'bʌndəns] (N) superabundancia *f*, sobreabundancia *f*

superabundant [ˌsu:pərə'bʌndənt] (ADJ) sobreabundante, superabundante

superannuate [ˌsu:pə'rænjʊeɪt] (VT) jubilar

superannuated [ˌsu:pə'rænjʊeɪtɪd] (ADJ) jubilado; (*fig*) anticuado

superannuation [ˌsu:pəˌrænjʊ'eɪʃən] (*Brit*) (N) (= *pension*) jubilación *f*, pensión *f*
(CPD) ▸ **superannuation contribution** cuota *f* de jubilación ▸ **superannuation scheme** plan *m* de jubilación

superb [su:'pɜ:b] (ADJ) estupendo, magnífico

superblock ['su:pəblɒk] (N) (*US*) *manzana de viviendas de tamaño mucho más grande de lo habitual*

superbly [su:'pɜ:blɪ] (ADV) [*play, perform*] estupendamente; [*crafted, decorated, equipped*] magníficamente • **the strategy worked ~** la estrategia funcionó estupendamente • **a ~ fit man** un hombre en estupendo estado físico • **some ~ elegant curtains** unas cortinas sumamente elegantes

superbug* ['su:pəbʌg] (N) bacteria *f* asesina

supercargo ['su:pəˌkɑ:gəʊ] (N) sobrecargo *m*

supercharged ['su:pətʃɑ:dʒd] (ADJ) 1 (*Aut*) sobrealimentado
2 [*atmosphere, environment*] sobrecargado

supercharger ['su:pətʃɑ:dʒəʳ] (N) compresor *m* de sobrealimentación

supercilious [ˌsu:pə'sɪlɪəs] (ADJ) desdeñoso, altanero

superciliously [ˌsu:pə'sɪlɪəslɪ] (ADV) (*pej*) con desdén, desdeñosamente

superciliousness [ˌsu:pə'sɪlɪəsnɪs] (N) desdén *m*, altanería *f*

supercomputer ['su:pəkəm'pju:təʳ] (N) superordenador *m*

superconductive [ˌsu:pəkən'dʌktɪv] (ADJ) superconductor

superconductivity [ˌsu:pəˌkɒndʌk'tɪvɪtɪ] (N) superconductividad *f*

superconductor [ˌsu:pəkən'dʌktəʳ] (N) superconductor *m*

supercool* [ˌsu:pə'ku:l] (ADJ) superguay*

super-duper* [ˌsu:pə'du:pəʳ] (ADJ) estupendo, magnífico

superego ['su:pərˌi:gəʊ] (N) superego *m*

supererogation [ˌsu:pərˌerə'geɪʃən] (N) supererogación *f*

superficial [ˌsu:pə'fɪʃəl] (ADJ) 1 (= *not deep*) superficial • **she was treated for ~ cuts and bruises** le curaron algunos cortes superficiales y moratones • **most of the buildings had sustained only ~ damage** la mayoría de los edificios solo habían sufrido daños superficiales • **I suddenly realized how ~ she was** de repente me di cuenta de lo superficial que era
2 (*in measurements*) [*area*] de superficie

superficiality [ˌsu:pəˌfɪʃɪ'ælɪtɪ] (N) superficialidad *f*

superficially [ˌsu:pə'fɪʃəlɪ] (ADV) 1 (= *in a shallow way*) [*deal with, treat, know, discuss*] superficialmente, de manera superficial, por encima
2 (= *at first glance*) • **~, the plane looked more or less conventional, but actually ...** en apariencia era un avión convencional pero de hecho ... • **although this explanation seems ~ attractive ...** aunque superficialmente *or* a primera vista esta explicación parece interesante ...
3 (*Tech, Med*) • **the incision is made ~** la incisión se hace en la superficie

superfine ['su:pəfaɪn] (ADJ) extrafino

superfluity [ˌsu:pə'flʊɪtɪ] (N) superfluidad *f* • **there is a ~ of** hay exceso de

superfluous [sʊ'pɜ:flʊəs] (ADJ) superfluo • **~ details** detalles superfluos • **to be ~** [*comment, detail, explanation*] ser superfluo, sobrar; [*object, person*] sobrar • **further comment was ~** todo otro comentario era superfluo, sobraba decir nada más • **maps were ~ with Eddie around** cuando estaba Eddie, sobraban los mapas • **my presence was ~** mi presencia estaba de más • **he felt rather ~** se sentía bastante de más

superfluously [sʊ'pɜ:flʊəslɪ] (ADV) innecesariamente • **... he added ~** ... añadió sin necesidad

superfood ['su:pəˌfu:d] (N) superalimento *m*

superglue ['su:pəˌglu:] (N) supercola *f*

supergrass* ['su:pəgrɑ:s] (N) (*Brit*) soplón/ona *m/f*

supergroup ['su:pəgru:p] (N) grupo *m* estrella, superbanda *f*

superheat [ˌsu:pə'hi:t] (VT) sobrecalentar

superheavyweight [ˌsu:pə'hevɪˌweɪt] (*Boxing*) (N) 1 (= *weight category*) peso *m* superpesado
2 (= *boxer*) peso *mf* superpesado
(ADJ) superpesado

superhero ['su:pəˌhɪərəʊ] (N) superhéroe *m*

superhighway ['su:pə'haɪweɪ] (N) (*US*) autopista *f* (de varios carriles); ▹ **information**

superhuman [ˌsu:pə'hju:mən] (ADJ) [*strength, efforts, powers*] sobrehumano

superimpose ['su:pərɪm'pəʊz] (VT) sobreponer (**on** en)

superinduce ['su:pərɪn'dju:s] (VT) sobreañadir, inducir por añadidura

superintend [ˌsu:pərɪn'tend] (VT) supervisar

superintendence [ˌsu:pərɪn'tendəns] (N) supervisión *f* • **under the ~ of** bajo la supervisión *or* dirección de

superintendent [ˌsu:pərɪn'tendənt] (N) [*of institution, orphanage*] director(a) *m/f*; (*in swimming pool*) vigilante *mf*; (*US*) (= *porter*) conserje *mf* • **police ~** (*Brit*) subjefe *mf* de policía; (*US*) superintendente *mf*

superior [sʊ'pɪərɪəʳ] (ADJ) 1 (= *better*) superior • **to be ~ to sth/sb** ser superior a algo/algn • **to be ~ to sth/sb in sth** superar *or* ser superior a algo/algn en algo
2 (= *good*) [*product*] de primera calidad • **it's a very ~ model** es un modelo de primerísima calidad, es un modelo muy superior • **thanks to its ~ design** gracias a la supremacía del diseño • **a ~ being** un ser superior
3 (= *senior*) (*in hierarchy, rank*) superior • **to be ~ to sb** ser superior a algn • **his ~ officer** (*Mil*) su superior
4 (*numerically*) • **the enemy's ~ numbers** la superioridad numérica del enemigo • **the enemy were ~ to them in number** el enemigo los superaba *or* era superior a ellos en número
5 (= *smug*) [*person*] altanero, desdeñoso; [*tone, expression, smile*] de superioridad, de suficiencia • **"you don't understand," Clarissa said in a ~ way** —tú no lo entiendes —dijo Clarissa con aire de superioridad *or* de suficiencia
6 (*Tech*) (= *upper*) superior
(N) 1 (*in rank, organization*) superior *m* • **people he perceives as his social ~s** personas que él considera de un nivel social superior
2 (*in ability*) • **to be sb's ~ in sth** superar a algn en algo
3 (*Rel*) superior *m* • **Mother Superior** madre *f* superiora
(CPD) ▸ **superior court** tribunal *m* superior

superiority [sʊˌpɪərɪ'ɒrɪtɪ] (N) 1 (*in quality, amount*) superioridad *f*
2 (= *smugness*) superioridad *f*, altanería *f*
(CPD) ▸ **superiority complex** complejo *m* de superioridad

superjumbo ['su:pəˌdʒʌmbəʊ] (N) superjumbo *m*

superlative [sʊ'pɜ:lətɪv] (ADJ) 1 (= *outstanding*) excepcional • **~ wines** vinos de excepcional calidad
2 (*Gram*) superlativo *m*
(N) 1 (*Gram*) superlativo *m* • **in the ~** en el superlativo
2 (*fig*) • **the critics were reaching for ~s** los críticos se deshacían en elogios • **he tends to talk in ~s** tiende a hablar en términos muy elogiosos de todo

superlatively [sʊ'pɜːlətɪvlɪ] (ADV) [perform, sing] excepcionalmente, de manera excepcional • **a ~ nice man** un hombre extremadamente or excepcionalmente agradable • **~ fit** en una forma física excepcional • **his ability to get things ~ right** su habilidad para hacer las cosas excepcionalmente or extraordinariamente bien • **he knew his job ~ well** conocía su trabajo a la perfección, conocía su trabajo excepcionalmente or extraordinariamente bien

superman ['suːpəmæn] (N) (PL: **supermen**) superhombre m

supermarket ['suːpə,mɑːkɪt] (N) supermercado m

supermodel ['suːpəmɒdəl] (N) top model mf

supernatural [,suːpə'nætʃərəl] (ADJ) sobrenatural
(N) • **the ~** lo sobrenatural

supernormal [,suːpə'nɔːməl] (ADJ) superior a lo normal

supernova [,suːpə'nəʊvə] (N) (PL: **supernovae** [,suːpə'nəʊviː]) (Astron) supernova f

supernumerary [,suːpə'njuːmərərɪ] (ADJ) (Admin, Bio etc) supernumerario
(N) (Admin etc) supernumerario/a m/f; (Theat, Cine) figurante/a m/f, comparsa mf

superordinate [,suːpər'ɔːdənɪt] (ADJ) superior
(N) (Ling) término m genérico, archilexema m

superphosphate [,suːpə'fɒsfeɪt] (N) superfosfato m

superpose ['suːpəpəʊz] (VT) sobreponer, superponer

superposition ['suːpəpəzɪʃən] (N) superposición f

superpower ['suːpə,paʊə^r] (N) superpotencia f

supersaver ['suːpə,seɪvə^r] (N) **1** (= special offer) superdescuento m, superahorro m
2 (also **supersaver ticket**) (for bus, train) billete m con superdescuento (esp Sp), boleto m con superdescuento (LAm); (for plane) pasaje m con superdescuento, billete m con superdescuento (esp Sp)

superscript [,suːpə'skrɪpt] (N) superíndice m

superscription [,suːpə'skrɪpʃən] (N) sobrescrito m

supersede [,suːpə'siːd] (VT) desbancar, suplantar

supersensitive ['suːpə'sensɪtɪv] (ADJ) extremadamente sensible (to a)

supersize ['suːpəsaɪz], **supersized** ['suːpəsaɪzd] (ADJ) [portion, order] gigante

supersonic ['suːpə'sɒnɪk] (ADJ) [aircraft, speed, flight] supersónico

supersonically ['suːpə'sɒnɪkəlɪ] (ADV) [fly] a velocidad supersónica

superstar ['suːpəstɑː^r] (N) superestrella f

superstardom [,suːpə'stɑːdəm] (N) superestrellato m

superstate ['suːpəsteɪt] (N) superestado m

superstition [,suːpə'stɪʃən] (N) superstición f

superstitious [,suːpə'stɪʃəs] (ADJ) supersticioso • **to be ~ about sth** ser supersticioso con respecto a algo

superstitiously [,suːpə'stɪʃəslɪ] (ADV) supersticiosamente

superstore ['suːpəstɔː^r] (N) (Brit) hipermercado m

superstratum [,suːpə'strɑːtəm] (N) (PL: **superstratums** or **superstrata** [,suːpə'strɑːtə]) superstrato m

superstructure ['suːpə,strʌktʃə^r] (N) superestructura f

supertanker ['suːpə,tæŋkə^r] (N) superpetrolero m

supertax ['suːpətæks] (N) sobretasa f, sobreimpuesto m

supervene [,suːpə'viːn] (VI) sobrevenir

supervise ['suːpəvaɪz] (VT) **1** [+ work, people] supervisar
2 (Univ) [+ thesis] dirigir

supervision [,suːpə'vɪʒən] (N) supervisión f • **to work under the ~ of** trabajar bajo la supervisión de

supervisor ['suːpəvaɪzə^r] (N) **1** (gen) supervisor(a) m/f
2 (Univ) [of thesis] director(a) m/f

supervisory ['suːpəvaɪzərɪ] (ADJ) [body, staff, powers] de supervisión; [role] de supervisor • **he stayed on in a ~ capacity** se quedó en calidad de supervisor • **~ board** (Comm, Ind) junta f de supervisión

superwoman ['suːpə,wʊmən] (N) (PL: **superwomen**) supermujer f

supine ['suːpaɪn] (ADJ) (frm) **1** (= prostrate) [person, position] de espaldas, sobre el dorso, supino (more frm) • **he lay ~ on the couch** estaba tendido sobre el dorso or (more frm) en posición supina en el sofá
2 (fig) (= passive) abúlico • **the government's ~ response to the rise in petrol prices** la reacción abúlica del gobierno ante la subida de los precios de la gasolina
(N) supino m

supper ['sʌpə^r] (N) (= evening meal) cena f • **what's for ~ tonight?** ¿qué hay de cena hoy? • **to stay to ~** quedarse a cenar • **to have ~** cenar • **the Last Supper** (Rel) La Ultima Cena • IDIOM: • **to sing for one's ~** trabajárselo
(CPD) ▸ **supper club** (US) restaurante pequeño en el que se incluye baile y espectáculo

suppertime ['sʌpətaɪm] (N) hora f de cenar

supplant [sə'plɑːnt] (VT) suplantar, reemplazar

supple ['sʌpl] (ADJ) [body, leather] flexible; [joint, limb] ágil; [skin] suave • **this will keep your skin ~** esto mantendrá tu piel suave • **to keep o.s. ~** mantenerse flexible

supplement (N) ['sʌplɪmənt] (gen) suplemento m
(VT) [sʌplɪ'ment] complementar • **to ~ sth with sth** complementar algo con algo • **I ~ my diet with vitamin pills** complemento mi dieta con vitaminas • **to ~ one's income by writing** aumentar sus ingresos escribiendo

supplemental [,sʌplɪ'mentəl] (ADJ) (esp US) suplementario

supplementary [,sʌplɪ'mentərɪ] (ADJ) suplementario
(CPD) ▸ **supplementary benefit** (Brit) prestación f complementaria (de ayuda social)

suppleness ['sʌplnɪs] (N) [of body, leather] flexibilidad f; [of joint, limb] agilidad f; [of skin] suavidad f

suppliant ['sʌplɪənt] (frm) (ADJ) suplicante
(N) suplicante mf

supplicant ['sʌplɪkənt] (N) suplicante mf

supplicate ['sʌplɪkeɪt] (VT), (VI) suplicar

supplication [,sʌplɪ'keɪʃən] (N) súplica f

supplier [sə'plaɪə^r] (N) (Comm) (= distributor) distribuidor(a) m/f; (= provider) abastecedor(a) m/f, proveedor(a) m/f • **from your usual ~** de su proveedor habitual

supply [sə'plaɪ] (N) **1** (= stock, amount) [of oil, coal, water] reservas fpl, existencias fpl; [of goods, merchandise] existencias fpl • **America has a 300-year ~ of coal** América tiene reservas or existencias de carbón para 300 años • **oil supplies are running low** las reservas de petróleo se están agotando • **he must have used up his ~ of drugs by now** ahora ya debe haber agotado todas sus reservas or existencias de medicamentos • **he had only a small ~ of gin left** solo le quedaba una pequeña cantidad de ginebra • **a three-month ~ of drugs** medicinas suficientes para tres meses • **an adequate ~ of food** suficientes víveres or provisiones • **we need a fresh ~ of coffee** nos hace falta proveernos de café • **they seem to have an inexhaustible ~ of ammunition** parece que tengan una reserva inagotable de municiones • **to lay in a ~ of sth** proveerse de algo, hacer provisión de algo • **a limited ~ of fine wines** existencias limitadas de buenos vinos • **there is a plentiful ~ of fish in the river** en el río hay peces en abundancia • **to be in short ~** escasear • **vegetables are in short ~** hay escasez de verduras, escasean las verduras
2 supplies (= provisions) provisiones fpl, víveres mpl; (Mil) pertrechos mpl • **supplies are still being flown into the capital** aún se están llevando provisiones or víveres a la capital por aire • **emergency supplies** provisiones fpl de emergencia • **food supplies** víveres mpl, provisiones fpl • **medical supplies** suministros mpl médicos • **office supplies** materiales mpl or artículos mpl de oficina
3 (= provision) suministro m • **the ~ of fuel to the engine** el suministro de combustible al motor • **electricity/gas ~** suministro de electricidad/gas • **blood ~** (Physiol) riego m sanguíneo
4 (Econ) oferta f • **~ and demand** la oferta y la demanda
5 (Parl) provisión f financiera • **to vote supplies** votar créditos
(VT) **1** (= provide) **a** [+ merchandise, goods, materials, food] suministrar, proporcionar; [+ information] facilitar, proporcionar • **Japan will ~ the materials** Japón suministrará or proporcionará los materiales • **he accused the company of ~ing arms to terrorists** acusó a la empresa de suministrar or proporcionar armas a grupos terroristas • **~ the missing word and win a prize** adivine la palabra que falta y gane un premio • **she supplied the vital clue** ella nos dio la pista esencial • **I supplied the feminine intuition** yo aportaba la intuición femenina • **the arteries that ~ blood to the heart** las arterias que llevan la sangre al corazón, las arterias que irrigan el corazón
b • **to ~ sb with** [+ merchandise, equipment] suministrar algo a algn, proporcionar algo a algn; [+ services] proveer a algn de algo; [+ information] facilitar algo a algn • **they kept us supplied with milk/vegetables** nos fueron abasteciendo de leche/verduras
2 (frm) (= satisfy) [+ need] satisfacer; [+ want] suplir
(CPD) ▸ **supply chain** (Comm) cadena f de abastecimiento ▸ **supply dump** (Mil) intendencia f ▸ **supply line** línea f de abastecimiento ▸ **supply route** ruta f de abastecimiento ▸ **supply ship** buque m de abastecimiento ▸ **supply teacher** (Brit) profesor(a) m/f suplente, profesor(a) m/f sustituto/a ▸ **supply teaching** (Brit) suplencias fpl ▸ **supply truck** camión m de abastecimiento

supply-side [sə'plaɪ,saɪd] (ADJ) • **supply-side economics** economía f de oferta

support [sə'pɔːt] (N) **1** (for weight) **a** (= object) soporte m • **use the stool as a ~ for your feet** usa el taburete como soporte para los pies • **steel ~s** soportes mpl de acero
b (= capacity to support) soporte m • **a good bed should provide adequate ~ for your back** una buena cama debe ofrecerle un soporte

S

adecuado para su espalda • **to lean on sb for ~** apoyarse en algn
c (*Med*) soporte *m* • **back ~** espaldera *f*
2 (*fig*) **a** (= *help*) apoyo *m* • **I've had a lot of ~ from my family** mi familia me ha apoyado mucho *or* me ha dado mucho apoyo • **she was a real ~ to her mother** fue un verdadero apoyo para su madre • **to give sb ~** dar apoyo a algn, apoyar a algn • **moral ~** apoyo moral
b (= *backing*) apoyo *m* • **he has given his ~ to the reform programme** ha apoyado *or* respaldado el programa de reforma, ha dado su apoyo *or* respaldo al programa de reforma • **do I have I your ~ in this?** ¿puedo contar con tu apoyo para esto? • **our ~ comes from the workers** los que nos apoyan son los obreros • **their capacity to act in ~ of their political objectives** su capacidad de actuar en pos de sus objetivos políticos • **a campaign in ~ of these aims** una campaña en apoyo de estos objetivos • **he spoke in ~ of the motion** habló en apoyo de la moción • **popular ~** apoyo *m* popular
c (*financial*) ayuda *f*, respaldo *m* • **financial ~** ayuda *f* económica, respaldo *m* económico • **they depend on him for financial ~** económicamente dependen de él • **with Government ~** con la ayuda del Gobierno, respaldado por el Gobierno • **a man with no visible means of ~** un hombre sin una fuente de ingresos aparente
d (*esp Comm*) (= *backup*) servicio *m* de asistencia (al cliente) • **after-sales ~** servicio *m* posventa, asistencia *f* posventa • **technical ~** servicio *m* de asistencia técnica
e (*Mil*) apoyo *m* • **military ~** apoyo militar
f (= *evidence*) • **history offers some ~ for this view** la historia respalda en cierta medida esta opinión • **scholars have found little ~ for this interpretation** los académicos han encontrado pocas pruebas que apoyen *or* respalden esta interpretación • **in ~ of this argument he states that ...** para apoyar *or* respaldar este argumento aduce que ... • **evidence in ~ of a particular theory** pruebas que confirman una determinada teoría
(VT) **1** (= *hold up*) sostener • **his knees wouldn't ~ him any more** sus rodillas ya no lo sostenían • **that chair won't ~ your weight** esa silla no resistirá *or* aguantará tu peso • **raise your upper body off the ground, ~ing your weight on your arms** apoyándose en los brazos levante el tronco del suelo • **to ~ o.s.** (*physically*) apoyarse (**on** en)
2 (= *help*) **a** (*emotionally*) apoyar
b (*financially*) [+ *person*] mantener; [+ *organization, project*] financiar • **he has a wife and three children to ~** tiene una mujer y tres hijos que mantener • **to ~ o.s.** (*financially*) ganarse la vida
3 (= *back*) [+ *proposal, project, person*] apoyar • **his colleagues refused to ~ him** sus colegas se negaron a apoyarlo
4 (*Sport*) [+ *team*] • **who do you ~?** ¿de qué equipo eres (hincha)? • **Tim ~s Manchester United** Tim es hincha de Manchester United • **come and ~ your team!** ¡ven a animar a tu equipo!
5 (= *corroborate*) [+ *theory, view*] respaldar, confirmar
6 (= *sustain*) • **an environment capable of ~ing human life** un medio en que existen las condiciones necesarias para que se desarrolle la vida humana • **land so poor that it cannot ~ a small family** un terreno tan poco fértil que no puede sustentar a una familia pequeña
7 (*frm*) (= *tolerate*) tolerar
8 (*Mus*) [+ *band*] actuar de telonero/teloneros de • **a good band ~ed by an exciting new group** un buen grupo con unos teloneros nuevos muy interesantes
9 (*Cine, Theat*) [+ *principal actor*] secundar • **he is ~ed by a wonderful cast** está secundado por un estupendo reparto
(CPD) ▸ **support band** (*Mus*) teloneros *mpl* ▸ **support group** grupo *m* de apoyo • **a ~ group for victims of crime** un grupo de apoyo *or* una asociación de ayuda a las víctimas de la delincuencia ▸ **support hose** medias *fpl* de compresión graduada ▸ **support network** red *f* de apoyo ▸ **support ship** barco *m* de apoyo ▸ **support stocking** media *f* de compresión graduada ▸ **support tights** medias *fpl* de compresión (graduada) ▸ **support troops** tropas *fpl* de apoyo

supportable [sə'pɔːtəbl] (ADJ) soportable

supporter [sə'pɔːtəʳ] (N) **1** [*of proposal, party etc*] partidario/a *m/f*; (*Sport*) hincha *mf* • **I'm a United ~** soy del United, soy hincha del United; **supporters** la afición • **the ~s really got behind the team last night** la afición apoyó totalmente al equipo ayer • **~s' club** peña *f* deportiva • **football ~s** hinchas *mpl* de fútbol
2 (*Tech*) soporte *m*, sostén *m*; (*Heraldry*) tenante *m*, soporte *m*

supporting [sə'pɔːtɪŋ] (ADJ) **1** [*documents*] acreditativo • **there is no ~ evidence for this theory** no hay pruebas que confirmen esta teoría
2 (*Theat*) [*role, cast*] secundario; [*actor*] secundario, de reparto
(CPD) ▸ **supporting actor** actor *m* secundario, actor *m* de reparto • **best ~ actor** mejor actor de reparto ▸ **supporting actress** actriz *f* secundaria, actriz *f* de reparto • **best ~ actress** mejor actriz de reparto ▸ **supporting feature** (*Cine*) cortometraje *m* ▸ **supporting role, supporting rôle** (*in film*) papel *m* secundario, papel *m* de reparto ▸ **supporting wall** pared *f* maestra

supportive [sə'pɔːtɪv] (ADJ) [*role*] de apoyo • **a ~ role** un papel de apoyo • **I have a very ~ family** tengo una familia que me apoya mucho • **to be ~: her boss was very ~ and gave her time off work** su jefe la apoyó mucho y le dio unos días libres • **to be ~ of sb** apoyar a algn

supportively [sə'pɔːtɪvlɪ] (ADV) [*act, behave*] con actitud de apoyo

supportiveness [sə'pɔːtɪvnɪs] (N) sustentación *f*

suppose [sə'pəʊz] (VT) **1** (= *assume*) suponer • **let us ~ that** supongamos que, pongamos por caso que • **but just ~ he's right** y ¿si tiene razón? • **supposing it rains, what shall we do?** pongamos que llueve, entonces ¿qué hacemos? • **always supposing he comes** siempre y cuando venga • **even supposing that were true** aun en el caso de que fuera verdad
2 (= *assume, believe*) suponer, creer • **I ~ she'll come** supongo que vendrá • **I don't ~ she'll come** no creo que venga • **you'll accept, I ~?** aceptarás, supongo, ¿no? • **who do you ~ was there?** ¿quién crees tú que estaba allí? • **you don't ~ they'd start without us, do you?** no empezarán sin nosotros, ¿verdad? • **I ~ so/not** supongo que sí/no
3 • **to be ~d to do sth: you're ~d to be in bed by ten** tendrías que estar acostado a las diez • **you're not ~d to do that** no deberías hacer eso • **you're ~d to be my friend!** ¡yo creía que eras mi amigo! • **what am I ~d to have done wrong now?** ¿qué se supone que he hecho mal ahora? • **what's that ~d to mean?** ¿qué quieres decir con eso? • **he's ~d to be an expert** se le supone un experto
4 (*in requests, suggestions*) • **do you ~ we could take a lunch break now?** ¿podríamos hacer un descanso para almorzar ahora? • **do you ~ you could wrap this up for me?** ¿podrías envolverme esto? • **I don't ~ you could lend me ten pounds** ¿no podrías prestarme diez libras? • **~ we talk about something else now** ¿y si hablamos sobre algo distinto ahora?
5 (= *presuppose*) suponer, presuponer

supposed [sə'pəʊzd] (ADJ) [*ally, benefit, threat*] supuesto

supposedly [sə'pəʊzɪdlɪ] (ADV) supuestamente • **he had ~ gone to Scotland** según se suponía había ido a Escocia, supuestamente había ido a Escocia • **the ~ brave James Bond** el James Bond que se suponía tan valiente

supposing [sə'pəʊzɪŋ] (CONJ) si, en el caso de que; ▹ **suppose**

supposition [ˌsʌpə'zɪʃən] (N) suposición *f* • **that is pure ~** eso es una suposición *or* hipótesis nada más • **the report was based on ~** el informe estaba basado en suposiciones • **it's based on the ~ that ...** se basa en la hipótesis de que ...

suppositional [ˌsʌpə'zɪʃənəl], **suppositious** [ˌsʌpə'zɪʃəs] (ADJ) hipotético

supposititious [səˌpɒzɪ'tɪʃəs] (ADJ) espurio, supositicio

suppository [sə'pɒzɪtərɪ] (N) supositorio *m*

suppress [sə'pres] (VT) [+ *symptoms, dissent, opposition, publication*] suprimir; [+ *feelings*] reprimir; [+ *emotion*] contener, dominar; [+ *yawn, smile*] contener; [+ *news, the truth*] callar, ocultar; [+ *scandal*] acallar, ocultar; [+ *revolt, uprising*] sofocar, reprimir • **with ~ed emotion** con emoción contenida • **a half ~ed laugh** una risa mal disimulada

suppressant [sə'presnt] (N) inhibidor *m* • **appetite ~** inhibidor *m* del apetito

suppression [sə'preʃən] (N) [*of symptoms, dissent, opposition, publication*] supresión *f*; [*of feelings*] represión *f*; [*of news, scandal, the truth*] ocultación *f*; [*of revolt*] represión *f*

suppressive [sə'presɪv] (ADJ) supresor

suppressor [sə'presəʳ] (N) supresor *m*

suppurate ['sʌpjʊəreɪt] (VI) supurar

suppuration [ˌsʌpjʊə'reɪʃən] (N) supuración *f*

supra ... ['suːprə] (PREFIX) supra ... • **supranormal** supranormal • **suprarenal** suprarrenal

supranational ['suːprə'næʃənl] (ADJ) supranacional

suprasegmental [ˌsuːprəseg'mentl] (ADJ) suprasegmental

supremacist [sʊ'preməsɪst] (N) *partidario o defensor de la supremacía de un grupo, raza etc* • **male ~** machista *mf* • **white ~** racista *mf* (blanco/a)

supremacy [sʊ'preməsɪ] (N) supremacía *f* • **naval/political ~** supremacía *f* naval/política • **the struggle for ~** la lucha por la supremacía

supreme [sʊ'priːm] (ADJ) [*effort*] supremo; [*heroism, confidence*] sumo; [*achievement*] mayor • **it is of ~ importance** es de suma importancia • **with ~ indifference** con suma indiferencia • **it was a ~ irony that ...** la mayor ironía fue que ... • **the ~ sacrifice** el sacrificio supremo • **to reign ~** (*fig*) [*team, individual, city*] no tener rival, gozar del dominio absoluto; [*ideology, tradition*] predominar por encima de todo
(CPD) ▸ **the Supreme Being** el Ser Supremo ▸ **supreme champion** campeón/ona *m/f* absoluto/a ▸ **Supreme Commander** comandante *mf* en jefe, comandante *mf* supremo/a ▸ **Supreme Court** Tribunal *m*

Supremo, Corte *f* Suprema (*LAm*)
supremely [sʊˈpriːmlɪ] (ADV) [*confident, important, elegant*] sumamente • **she does her job ~ well** hace su trabajo a la perfección *or* sumamente bien • **he is a ~ gifted musician** es un músico de extraordinario talento
supremo [sʊˈpriːməʊ] (N) jefe *m*
Supt (ABBR) (*Brit*) = **Superintendent**
sura [ˈsʊərə] (N) sura *m*
surcharge [ˈsɜːtʃɑːdʒ] (N) recargo *m* • **to introduce/impose a ~ on sth** introducir/imponer un recargo en algo • **import ~** sobretasa *f* de importación
(VT) [+ *person*] cobrar un recargo a
surd [sɜːd] (N) número *m* sordo
sure [ʃʊəʳ] (ADJ) (COMPAR: **surer**, SUPERL: **surest**)
(ADJ) **1** (= *certain*) **a** seguro • **"do you want to see that film?" — "I'm not ~"** —¿quieres ver esa película? —no sé *or* no estoy seguro • **she seemed honest enough but I had to be ~** parecía bastante sincera, pero tenía que asegurarme *or* estar seguro • **"I know my duty" — "I'm ~ you do"** —sé cuál es mi deber —de eso estoy seguro • **to be ~ that** estar seguro de que • **I'm ~ that she's right** estoy seguro de que tiene razón • **I'm not ~ that I can help you** no estoy seguro de que te pueda ayudar, no estoy seguro de poder ayudarte • **are you ~ you won't have another drink?** ¿seguro que no quieres tomarte otra copa? • **I'm quite ~ her decision was right** estoy convencido de que *or* estoy completamente seguro de que su decisión fue correcta • **to be ~ about sth** estar seguro de algo • **I'm not ~ about the date yet** todavía no estoy seguro de la fecha • **I like the colour but I'm not ~ about the shape** me gusta el color pero la forma no acaba de convencerme • **to be ~ what/who** estar seguro de qué/quién • **Jane wasn't ~ (in her mind) what she thought about abortion** Jane no tenía muy claras las ideas sobre el aborto • **I'm not ~ whether ...** no estoy seguro (de) si ...
b • **to be ~ of sth** estar seguro de algo • **you can be ~ of our support** puedes estar seguro de nuestro apoyo • **Cameroon is ~ of a place in the second round** Camerún tiene una plaza asegurada *or* segura en la segunda ronda • **book now to be ~ of a place on the course** haga la reserva ahora para tener la plaza en el curso asegurada *or* segura • **we can't be ~ of winning** no podemos estar seguros de que vayamos a ganar • **to be ~ of one's facts** estar seguro de lo que se dice
c • **to be ~ of sb: I've always felt very ~ of John** siempre he confiado mucho en John • **he was not quite ~ of Flora** tenía sus dudas acerca de Flora • **to be ~ of o.s.** estar seguro de sí mismo • **to be ~ of sb** confiar en algn
d (+ *infin*) • **it is ~ to rain** seguro que llueve, seguramente lloverá • **she is ~ to agree** seguro que está de acuerdo, seguramente estará de acuerdo • **be ~ to** *or* **be ~ and close the window** asegúrate de que cierras la ventana • **be ~ to** *or* **be ~ and tell me** que no se te olvide contármelo • **be ~ not to take any weapons** no se te ocurra ir armado
e • **to make ~ (that)** asegurarse (de que) • **I knocked on his door to make ~ that he was all right** llamé a su puerta para asegurarme de que estaba bien • **make ~ it doesn't happen again** asegúrate de que no vuelva a ocurrir • **her friends made ~ that she was never alone** sus amigos se encargaron de que no estuviera nunca sola • **please make ~ that your children get to school on time** consiga de la forma que sea que sus hijos lleguen a la escuela a tiempo • **better get a ticket beforehand, just to make ~** mejor compre el billete de antemano, más que nada para ir sobre seguro *or* para tener esa seguridad • **to make ~ to do sth** asegurarse de hacer algo
2 (= *reliable*) [*sign*] claro; [*way*] seguro • **one ~ way to lose is ...** una forma segura de perder es ... • **she had a ~ grasp of the subject** tenía un gran dominio del tema • **to do sth in the ~ knowledge that** hacer algo sabiendo bien que *or* con la seguridad de que
3 (*in phrases*) • **it's a ~ bet that he'll come** segurísimo que viene • **for ~*** seguro* • **you'll get it tomorrow for ~** lo recibirás mañana seguro • **nobody** *or* **no one knows for ~** nadie lo sabe con seguridad • **I can't say for ~** no puedo decirlo con seguridad • **that's for ~** • **one thing's for ~** una cosa está clara
• **~ thing**: • **a month ago, a yes-vote seemed a ~ thing** hace un mes, el voto a favor parecía algo seguro • **he's a ~ thing for president** no cabe la menor duda de que llegará a presidente; (*esp US*) • **"I'd like to hire a car" — "~ thing"** —quiero alquilar un coche —sí, claro • **"can I go with you?" — "~ thing"** —¿puedo ir contigo? —claro que sí *or* por supuesto • **"did you like it?" — "~ thing"** —¿te ha gustado? —ya lo creo • **this is a plausible interpretation, to be sure, but ...** desde luego que *or* claro que esta es una interpretación muy verosímil pero ... • **well, that's bad luck to be ~!** vaya, ¡eso sí que es tener mala suerte!
(ADV) **1** (*US**) (= *certainly*) (*emphatic*) • **he ~ is cute** no veas si es guapo* • **I ~ am bored** no veas si estoy aburrido* • **"know what I mean?" — "~ do"** —sabes, ¿no? —claro que sí *or* claro que lo sé • **(as) ~ as**: • **I'm ~ as hell not going to help him** yo sí que no le voy a ayudar • IDIOM: • **as ~ as eggs is eggs, he did it*** lo hizo él, como que me llamo Elena/Juan *etc*
2 (*esp US*) (= *of course*) claro • **"did you tell your uncle about her?" — "oh, sure"** —¿le hablaste a tu tío de ella? —¡claro! *or* (*LAm*) —¡cómo no! • **"can I go with you?" — "sure"** —¿puedo ir contigo? —¡por supuesto! *or* —¡claro que sí! • **"is that OK?" — "sure!"** —¿está bien así? —¡claro que sí! *or* (*LAm*) —¡cómo no!
3 (= *true*) claro • **~, it's never been done before** claro que no se ha hecho antes
4 • **~ enough** efectivamente, en efecto • **he said he'd be here, and ~ enough, there he is** dijo que estaría aquí y efectivamente *or* en efecto, aquí está
sure-fire* [ˈʃʊəˈfaɪəʳ] (ADJ) [*way*] seguro; [*method*] infalible • **a sure-fire success** un éxito seguro • **he's a sure-fire winner** tiene el éxito asegurado
sure-footed [ˈʃʊəˈfʊtɪd] (ADJ) (*lit*) de pie firme; (*fig*) [*leadership*] firme • **to be sure-footed** (*lit, fig*) conocer el terreno que se pisa
surely [ˈʃʊəlɪ] (ADV) **1** (*emphatic*) **a** (*in questions*) • **~ there must be something we can do?** algo habrá que podemos hacer, ¿no?
b (*expressing opinion*) • **there must ~ be a more effective way of punishing such people** tiene que haber una forma más eficaz de castigar a esa clase de gente, digo *or* creo yo • **~ it is better to steal than to starve** mejor será robar que pasar hambre, digo *or* creo yo • **it is ~ no coincidence that ...** digo *or* creo yo que no es una coincidencia que ...
c (*expressing surprise*) • **~ you are not suggesting she did it on purpose?** no estarás insinuando que lo hizo a propósito ¿verdad? • **~ it's obvious?** pero si es obvio, ¿no? • **~ the logical thing would have been to change banks?** lo más lógico habría sido cambiar de banco, ¿no? • **you ~ don't think it was me!** ¡no pensarás que fui yo! • **~ not** no puede ser • **~ to God‡** • **~ to goodness***: • **~ to God that's what everyone wants‡** está claro que es eso lo que quiere todo el mundo ¿no? • **~ to goodness that itself is reason enough to call the police*** seguro que eso en sí mismo es motivo suficiente para llamar a la policía, ¿no?
2 (= *undoubtedly*) sin duda • **she was ~ one of the greatest sopranos of all time** sin duda fue una de las sopranos más destacadas de todos los tiempos • **justice will ~ prevail** sin duda la justicia prevalecerá • **he is an artist, just as ~ as Rembrandt** es pintor, tan seguro como que lo era Rembrandt • **his time will ~ come** no cabe duda de que le llegará su momento
3 (*US*) (= *of course*) por supuesto, ¡cómo no! (*LAm*) • **"will you excuse me just a second?" — "surely"** —¿me permite un momento? —¡por supuesto! *or* (*LAm*) —¡cómo no!
4 (= *safely, confidently*) con seguridad • **he handles the issue ~ but with sensitivity** maneja el asunto con seguridad y sensibilidad a la vez • **slowly but ~** lento pero seguro
sureness [ˈʃʊənɪs] (N) [*of aim, footing*] firmeza *f*; (= *certainty*) seguridad *f* • **the ~ of his touch** su pulso firme
surety [ˈʃʊərətɪ] (N) (= *sum*) garantía *f*, fianza *f*, caución *f*; (= *person*) fiador(a) *m/f*, garante *mf* • **on his own ~ of £500** bajo su propia fianza de 500 libras • **to go** *or* **stand ~ for sb** ser fiador de algn, salir garante de algn • **to take sth as ~** usar algo como fianza
surf [sɜːf] (N) (= *waves*) olas *fpl*, rompientes *mpl*; (= *foam*) espuma *f*; (= *swell*) oleaje *m*; (= *current*) resaca *f*
(VI) hacer surf
(VT) **1** (*lit*) hacer surf en
2 (*Internet*) • **to ~ the Net** navegar por Internet
surface [ˈsɜːfɪs] (N) **1** [*of table, skin, lake, sun*] superficie *f*; [*of road*] firme *m* • **beneath** *or* **below** *or* **under the ~**: • **the box was buried two metres beneath** *or* **below the ~** la caja estaba enterrada a dos metros por debajo de la superficie • **the tensions that simmer beneath** *or* **below the ~ in our society** las tensiones que bullen por debajo de la superficie en nuestra sociedad • **she appeared calm, but beneath** *or* **below the ~ she was seething with rage** parecía estar tranquila pero en el fondo *or* por dentro hervía de rabia • **to break the ~** romper la superficie • **to be close to the ~** (*lit*) estar cerca de la superficie • **her grief was still close to the ~** su dolor estaba todavía a flor de piel • **ethnic tensions are never far from the ~** las tensiones étnicas siempre parece que están a punto de estallar • **on the ~ it seems that ...** a primera vista parece que ... • **outer ~** capa *f* exterior *or* externa • **to come** *or* **rise to the ~** (*lit*) salir a la superficie; (*fig*) aflorar (a la superficie) • **these feelings may come** *or* **rise to the ~** estos sentimientos pueden aflorar (a la superficie) • **upper ~** superficie *f* de la parte superior • IDIOM: • **to scratch or touch the ~ (of sth)** arañar la superficie (de algo) • **this book only scratches the ~ of philosophical thought** este libro aborda el pensamiento filosófico solo por encima, este libro solo araña la superficie del pensamiento filosófico;
▷ **work**
2 (*Math, Geom*) **a** (*also* **surface area**) superficie *f*
b (= *side*) [*of solid*] cara *f*
(VT) [+ *road*] revestir, asfaltar

S

VI **1** (*lit*) [*swimmer, diver, whale*] salir a la superficie; [*submarine*] emerger
2 (*fig*) [*information, news*] salir a la luz; [*feeling*] salir, aflorar; [*issue*] salir a relucir; [*problem*] presentarse, surgir; [*person*] (*in place*) dejarse ver; (*hum*) (= *get up*) salir de la cama • **what time did you ~?** ¿a qué hora saliste de la cama?
CPD ▸ **surface area** área *f* (de la superficie) ▸ **surface fleet** flota *f* de superficie ▸ **surface force** (*Mil*) fuerza *f* de superficie ▸ **surface mail** • **by ~ mail** por vía terrestre ▸ **surface temperature** temperatura *f* en la superficie ▸ **surface tension** (*Phys*) tensión *f* superficial ▸ **surface water** agua *f* de la superficie

surface-air ['sɜːfɪs'ɛəʳ], **surface-to-air** ['sɜːfɪstʊ'ɛəʳ] ADJ • **surface-(to-)air missile** misil *m* tierra-aire

surface-to-surface ['sɜːfɪstə'sɜːfɪs] ADJ tierra-tierra

surfactant [sɜː'fæktənt] N (*Chem*) surfactante *m*

surfboard ['sɜːfbɔːd] N plancha *f* de surf, tabla *f* de surf

surfboarder ['sɜːf,bɔːdəʳ] N surfista *mf*, tablista *mf* de surf

surfboarding ['sɜːf,bɔːdɪŋ] N surf *m*

surfeit ['sɜːfɪt] N exceso *m* • **there is a ~ of** hay exceso de
VT hartar, saciar (**on, with** de) • **to ~ o.s.** hartarse, saciarse (**on, with** de)

surfer ['sɜːfəʳ] N surfista *mf*, tablista *mf* de surf

surfing ['sɜːfɪŋ], **surfriding** ['sɜːf,raɪdɪŋ] N surf *m*

surge [sɜːdʒ] N [*of sea*] oleaje *m*, oleada *f* • **a ~ of people** una oleada de gente • **a ~ of sympathy** una oleada de compasión • **a power ~** (*Elec*) una subida de tensión
VI [*water*] levantarse, hincharse; [*people*] • **to ~ in/out** entrar/salir en tropel • **the crowd ~d into the building** la multitud entró en tropel en el edificio • **people ~d down the street** una oleada de gente avanzó por la calle • **they ~d round him** se apiñaban en torno suyo • **the blood ~d to her cheeks** se le subió la sangre a las mejillas

surgeon ['sɜːdʒən] N cirujano/a *m/f*; (*Mil, Naut*) médico *m*, oficial *m* médico; ▹ **veterinary**
CPD ▸ **Surgeon General** (*US*) *jefe del servicio federal de sanidad*

surgery ['sɜːdʒərɪ] N **1** (*Med*) (= *branch of medicine, operation*) cirugía *f* • **brain ~** neurocirugía *f* • **heart ~** cardiocirugía *f* • **he was admitted for ~ on his knee** lo ingresaron para operarlo de la rodilla • **to have ~** ser operado, someterse a una operación (quirúrgica); ▹ **plastic**
2 (*Brit*) (= *consulting room*) (*doctor's, vet's*) consultorio *m*
3 (*Brit*) (= *consultation*) **a** (*with doctor, vet*) consulta *f* • **she has a Wednesday afternoon ~** tiene *or* pasa consulta los miércoles por la tarde
b (*with MP*) *sesión de consulta y atención de reclamaciones de un diputado con los electores de su circunscripción* • **he holds a ~ for his constituents every Saturday** todos los sábados atiende las reclamaciones de los electores de su circunscripción
4 (*US*) (= *operating theatre*) quirófano *m*, sala *f* de operaciones
CPD ▸ **surgery hours** (*Med*) horas *fpl* de consulta

surgical ['sɜːdʒɪkəl] ADJ quirúrgico
CPD ▸ **surgical dressing** vendaje *m* quirúrgico ▸ **surgical spirit** alcohol *m* de 90°

surgically ['sɜːdʒɪklɪ] ADV quirúrgicamente

Surinam [,sʊərɪ'næm] N Surinam *m*

Surinamese [,sʊərɪnæ'miːz] ADJ surinamés
N surinamés/esa *m/f*

surliness ['sɜːlɪnɪs] N hosquedad *f*, mal humor *m*

surly ['sɜːlɪ] ADJ (COMPAR: **surlier**, SUPERL: **surliest**) hosco, malhumorado • **he gave me a ~ answer** contestó malhumorado

surmise [sɜː'maɪz] N conjetura *f*, suposición *f*
VT conjeturar, suponer • **I ~d as much** ya me lo suponía *or* imaginaba

surmount [sɜː'maʊnt] VT **1** [+ *difficulty*] superar, vencer
2 • **~ed by** (*Archit*) coronado de

surmountable [sɜː'maʊntəbl] ADJ superable

surname ['sɜːneɪm] N apellido *m*
VT apellidar

surpass [sɜː'pɑːs] VT (= *go above*) [+ *amount, level, record*] superar, sobrepasar; (= *go beyond*) [+ *expectations*] rebasar, superar • **he has never been ~ed in his mastery of the violin** su maestría al violín nunca ha sido superada • **to ~ o.s.** (*lit*) superarse a sí mismo; (*iro*) pasarse (de la raya) • **I know you're tactless, but this time you've ~ed yourself!** sabía que no eras muy discreto, pero esta vez sí que te has pasado

surpassing [sɜː'pɑːsɪŋ] ADJ (*liter*) incomparable, sin par • **of ~ beauty** de hermosura sin par

surplice ['sɜːpləs] N sobrepelliz *f*

surplus ['sɜːpləs] N (PL: **surpluses**)
1 (= *excess*) exceso *m*; (*Comm, Agr*) (*from overproduction*) excedente *m* • **a ~ of teachers** un exceso de profesores • **the 1995 wheat ~** el excedente *or* los excedentes de trigo de 1995 • **a pair of army ~ boots** un par de botas provenientes de excedentes militares
2 (*Econ, Econ*) superávit *m* • **budget ~** superávit *m* presupuestario • **trade ~** balanza *f* comercial favorable, superávit *m* (en balanza) comercial
ADJ sobrante; (*Comm, Agr*) (*from overproduction*) excedentario, excedente • **~ energy** energía *f* sobrante • **to be ~ to requirements** no ser ya necesario, sobrar • **stocks ~ to requirements** existencias *fpl* que exceden de las necesidades • **I was made to feel ~ to requirements** (*iro*) hicieron que me sintiera (como que estaba) de más
CPD ▸ **surplus stock** saldos *mpl* • **sale of ~ stock** liquidación *f* de saldos ▸ **surplus store** tienda *f* de excedentes

surprise [sə'praɪz] N **1** (= *astonishment*) sorpresa *f* • **imagine my ~ when I found a cheque for £5,000** puedes imaginarte la sorpresa que me llevé al encontrar *or* cuando encontré un cheque de 5.000 libras • **"what?" George asked in ~** —¿qué? —preguntó George sorprendido • **he saw my look of ~** me vio la cara de sorpresa • **there was a look of ~ on his face** tenía cara de sorpresa • **surprise, surprise!** (*iro*) ¡menuda sorpresa! (*iro*) • **to my/his ~** para mi/su sorpresa • **much to my ~, he agreed** para gran sorpresa mía, accedió
2 (*as tactic*) sorpresa *f* • **the element of ~** el elemento sorpresa • **to catch** *or* **take sb by ~** coger *or* (*LAm*) tomar a algn por sorpresa
3 (= *unexpected thing*) sorpresa *f* • **I have a ~ for you** tengo una sorpresa para ti • **what a lovely ~!** ¡qué sorpresa más *or* tan agradable! • **all this comes as something of a ~** todo esto es en cierto modo una sorpresa • **it may come as a ~ to some people** puede que algunos se lleven una sorpresa • **it came as a ~ to me to learn that ...** me llevé una sorpresa al enterarme de que ... • **life is full of ~s** la vida está llena de sorpresas • **to give sb a ~** dar una sorpresa a algn
ADJ [*party, present*] sorpresa (*inv*); [*announcement, defeat, decision*] inesperado • **a ~ visit** una visita sorpresa *or* inesperada • **a ~ attack** un ataque por sorpresa
VT **1** (= *astonish*) sorprender • **he may ~ us all one day** puede que algún día nos sorprenda a todos • **go on, ~ me!** (*iro*) ¡venga, sorpréndeme! (*iro*) • **you ~ me** (*also iro*) me sorprende usted • **it ~d her to hear John sounding so angry** le sorprendió oír a John hablar tan enfadado • **no one will be ~d by her appointment** a nadie le extrañará *or* sorprenderá su nombramiento • **it wouldn't ~ me if he ended up in jail** no me extrañaría *or* sorprendería que terminara en la cárcel • **it ~s me that ...** me sorprende que (+ *subjun*) • **to ~ o.s.** sorprenderse (a sí mismo)
2 (= *catch unawares*) coger por sorpresa, tomar por sorpresa (*LAm*) • **to ~ sb in the act** sorprender a algn in fraganti, coger a algn in fraganti

surprised [sə'praɪzd] ADJ [*look, expression, smile*] de sorpresa • **he was ~ to hear that ...** se sorprendió *or* quedó sorprendido al enterarse de que ... • **I was rather ~ to see Martin there** me sorprendió bastante ver a Martin allí, me quedé bastante sorprendido al ver a Martin allí • **they were ~ that she hadn't told them about her new job** se sorprendieron de que no les hubiera dicho nada de su nuevo trabajo • **I was ~ at his ignorance** me sorprendió su ignorancia, me quedé sorprendido de lo ignorante que era • **I'm ~ at you!** ¡me sorprendes! • **he was ~ how good the food tasted** se sorprendió de lo buena que estaba la comida, se quedó sorprendido de lo buena que estaba la comida • **you'd be ~ how many people have difficulty reading** te sorprenderías de la cantidad de gente que tiene problemas para leer, te quedarías sorprendido si supieras la cantidad de gente que tiene problemas para leer • **don't be ~ if he doesn't recognize you** no te sorprendas si no te reconoce • **I wouldn't be ~ if he won** no me sorprendería que ganara; ▹ **surprise**

surprising [sə'praɪzɪŋ] ADJ sorprendente • **he won the match with ~ ease** ganó el partido con una facilidad sorprendente • **it is ~ how many people eat chips every day** es sorprendente la cantidad de gente que come patatas fritas todos los días • **it is ~ that no one has thought of it before** es sorprendente que no se le haya ocurrido a nadie antes • **it is not** *or* **hardly ~ that some teachers are leaving the profession** no es de extrañar que algunos profesores estén dejando la profesión • **it would be ~ if errors did not occur from time to time** sería extraño que no se cometieran errores de vez en cuando

surprisingly [sə'praɪzɪŋlɪ] ADV [*good, large, easy*] sorprendentemente • **~, it's been a great success** lo sorprendente es que ha sido todo un éxito • **~ enough this is her first film** esta es su primera película, lo cual es bastante sorprendente • **~ few people are interested** lo sorprendente es que muy poca gente está interesada, muy poca gente está interesada, lo cual es sorprendente • **~ little information is available** es sorprendente la poca información que existe • **not ~ he didn't come** como era de esperar, no vino • **the referee, rather ~, awarded a penalty** el árbitro, para sorpresa de todos, señaló penalty • **they are coping ~ well** es sorprendente lo bien que se las están arreglando, se las están arreglando sorprendentemente bien

surreal [sə'rɪəl] ADJ surrealista

surrealism [sə'rɪəlɪzəm] N surrealismo *m*

surrealist [sə'rɪəlɪst] ADJ surrealista
N surrealista *mf*

surrealistic [sə,rɪə'lɪstɪk] ADJ surrealista

surrender [sə'rendəʳ] N **1** (= *capitulation*) (*Mil*) rendición *f*; (*fig*) claudicación *f* • **no ~!** ¡no nos rendimos nunca!
2 (= *handover*) [*of weapons*] entrega *f*
3 (*Jur*) [*of lease, property*] cesión *f*
4 (*Insurance*) [*of policy*] rescate *m* (previo al vencimiento)
VI (*Mil*) rendirse • **I ~!** ¡me rindo! • **to ~ to the police** entregarse a la policía • **to ~ to despair** abandonarse *or* entregarse a la desesperación
VT **1** (*Mil*) [+ *weapons*] rendir, entregar; [+ *territory, city*] entregar • **to ~ o.s.** (*Mil*) rendirse; (*to police*) entregarse • **to ~ o.s. to despair** abandonarse *or* entregarse a la desesperación • **I ~ed myself to his charms** me rendí a *or* ante sus encantos
2 (= *renounce, give up*) [+ *claim, right*] renunciar a; [+ *lease, ownership*] ceder; (*liter*) [+ *hope*] abandonar
3 (= *hand over*) [+ *passport, ticket*] entregar, hacer entrega de (*more frm*)
4 (= *redeem*) [+ *insurance policy*] rescatar (antes del vencimiento)
CPD ▸ **surrender value** valor *m* de rescate

surreptitious [,sʌrəp'tɪʃəs] ADJ subrepticio • **she took a ~ look at her watch** miró furtivamente su reloj

surreptitiously [,sʌrəp'tɪʃəslɪ] ADV [*glance, signal*] subrepticiamente • **he was ~ stuffing himself with chocolate** se estaba atiborrando de chocolate a escondidas

surrogacy ['sʌrəgəsɪ] N (*in child-bearing*) alquiler *m* de úteros

surrogate ['sʌrəgeɪt] N sustituto *m*; (= *substance, material*) sucedáneo *m*; (*Brit*) (*Rel*) vicario *m*
ADJ [*substance, material*] sucedáneo • **the army became his ~ family** el ejército se convirtió en su segunda familia
CPD ▸ **surrogate mother** madre *f* de alquiler ▸ **surrogate motherhood** alquiler *m* de úteros

surround [sə'raʊnd] VT **1** (= *encircle*) rodear • **a town ~ed by hills** una ciudad rodeada de montes • **the house was ~ed by a high wall** la casa estaba rodeada por un muro muy alto • **she was ~ed by children** estaba rodeada de niños • **the uncertainty ~ing the future of the project** la incertidumbre que envuelve *or* rodea al proyecto
2 (*Mil, Pol*) [*troops, police*] [+ *enemy, town, building*] rodear, cercar • **you are ~ed!** ¡estáis rodeados!
N (= *border*) marco *m*, borde *m*; [*of fireplace*] marco *m* • **the bath/swimming pool had a tiled ~** el baño/la piscina tenía un borde alicatado
CPD ▸ **surround sound** sonido *m* (de efecto) surround

surrounding [sə'raʊndɪŋ] ADJ [*countryside*] circundante; [*hills*] circundante, de alrededor • **they disappeared into the ~ darkness** desaparecieron en la oscuridad (que los envolvía)

surroundings [sə'raʊndɪŋz] NPL [*of town, city*] alrededores *mpl*, cercanías *fpl*; (= *environment*) ambiente *msing*; (= *setting*) entorno *msing* • **he'll soon get used to his new ~** pronto se acostumbrará al nuevo ambiente *or* entorno que le rodea • **a hotel set in peaceful ~** un hotel situado en un apacible entorno • **he looked around at his ~** miró a su alrededor, miró en torno suyo

surtax ['sɜːtæks] N sobreimpuesto *m*; (= *rate*) sobretasa *f*

surtitle ['sɜːtaɪtl] N sobretítulo *m*

surveil [sə'veɪl] VT (*US*) vigilar

surveillance [sɜː'veɪləns] N • **to be under ~** estar vigilado, estar bajo vigilancia • **to keep sb under ~** vigilar a algn, tener vigilado a algn

survey ['sɜːveɪ] N **1** (= *study*) estudio *m* • **to make a ~ of housing in a town** estudiar la situación de la vivienda en una ciudad
2 (= *poll*) encuesta *f* • **to carry out** *or* **conduct a ~** realizar una encuesta • **they did a ~ of a thousand students** hicieron una encuesta a mil estudiantes
3 (*esp Brit*) [*of land*] inspección *f*, reconocimiento *m*; (*in topography*) medición *f*; [*of building, property*] tasación *f*, peritaje *m*; (= *report to purchaser*) informe *m* de tasación, informe *m* de peritaje • **to have a ~ done** (*of property*) mandar hacer una tasación
4 (= *general view*) visión *f* global, vista *f* de conjunto • **he gave a general ~ of the situation** dio una visión global *or* de conjunto de la situación
VT [sɜː'veɪ] **1** (= *contemplate*) contemplar, mirar • **he ~ed the desolate scene** miró detenidamente la triste escena • **he was master of all he ~ed** era dueño de todo cuanto alcanzaba a dominar con la vista
2 (= *study*) estudiar, hacer un estudio de • **the report ~s housing in Glasgow** el informe estudia la situación de la vivienda en Glasgow
3 (= *poll*) [+ *person, group*] encuestar; [+ *town*] hacer una encuesta en, pulsar la opinión de; [+ *reactions*] sondear • **95% of those ~ed believed that ...** el 95% de los encuestados creía que ...
4 (= *inspect*) [+ *building*] inspeccionar; [+ *land*] hacer un reconocimiento de; (*in topography*) medir; (= *map*) [+ *town*] levantar el plano de
5 (= *take general view of*) pasar revista a • **the book ~s events up to 1972** el libro pasa revista a los sucesos acaecidos hasta 1972

surveying [sɜː'veɪɪŋ] N agrimensura *f*, topografía *f*

surveyor [sə'veɪəʳ] N (*Brit*) [*of land*] agrimensor(a) *m/f*, topógrafo/a *m/f*; [*of property*] tasador(a) *m/f* (de la propiedad), perito *mf* tasador(a)

survival [sə'vaɪvəl] N **1** (= *act*) supervivencia *f* • **the ~ of the fittest** la ley del más fuerte
2 (= *relic*) vestigio *m*, reliquia *f* • **this practice is a ~ from Victorian times** esta costumbre es un vestigio *or* una reliquia de la época victoriana
CPD ▸ **survival bag** saco *m* de supervivencia ▸ **survival course** curso *m* de supervivencia ▸ **survival kit** equipo *m* de emergencia ▸ **survival mechanism** mecanismo *m* de supervivencia ▸ **survival rate** tasa *f* de supervivencia ▸ **survival skills** técnicas *fpl* de supervivencia

survivalist [sə'vaɪvəlɪst] N (*US*) *persona obsesionada por las catástrofes*

survive [sə'vaɪv] VI **1** (= *remain alive, in existence*) [*person, species*] sobrevivir; [*painting, building, manuscript*] conservarse; [*custom*] pervivir • **not one of the passengers ~d** no sobrevivió ninguno de los pasajeros • **he ~d on nuts for several weeks** logró sobrevivir durante varias semanas comiendo nueces • **he ~d to the age of 83** vivió hasta los 83 años • **only two of his paintings ~** solo se conservan dos de sus cuadros
2 (= *cope*) sobrevivir • **people struggling to ~ without jobs** gente luchando para sobrevivir sin trabajo • **I'll ~!** ¡de esta no me muero!, ¡sobreviviré! • **Jim ~s on £65 a fortnight** Jim se las arregla para vivir con 65 libras a la quincena
VT **1** (= *outlive*) [+ *person*] sobrevivir a • **she will probably ~ me by many years** probablemente me sobreviva por muchos años, probablemente viva muchos más años que yo • **he is ~d by a wife and two sons** deja una mujer y dos hijos
2 (= *not die in*) [+ *accident, illness, war*] sobrevivir a • **he ~d a heart attack** sobrevivió a un ataque al corazón • **he ~d being struck by lightning** sobrevivió tras haberle caído un rayo
3 (= *cope with*) aguantar, sobrellevar • **I couldn't ~ the day without breakfast** no podría aguantar *or* sobrellevar el día sin desayunar

surviving [sə'vaɪvɪŋ] ADJ (= *living*) vivo; (*after catastrophe, also Jur*) sobreviviente • **the last ~ member of the band** el último miembro vivo del grupo • **he had no ~ siblings** no dejó hermanos vivos • **the ~ wife is entitled to a widow's pension** la esposa sobreviviente tiene derecho a una pensión de viudedad • **~ company** (*after merger*) compañía *f* resultante, empresa *f* resultante

survivor [sə'vaɪvəʳ] N (*lit, fig*) superviviente *mf*, sobreviviente *mf* • **the sole ~ of the 1979 cabinet** el único superviviente *or* sobreviviente del consejo de ministros de 1979 • **I'm a ~, I'll get by** soy de los que no se hunden, me las arreglaré
CPD ▸ **survivor benefits** (*US*) *ayuda que el Estado presta a la familia de una persona fallecida*

sus‡ [sʌs] N (= *suspicion*) • **he was picked up on sus** la policía le detuvo por sospechoso

Susan ['suːzn] N Susana

susceptibility [sə,septə'bɪlɪtɪ] N (*to attack*) susceptibilidad *f*; (*Med*) (*to illness, infection*) propensión *f* (**to** a); (*to persuasion, flattery*) sensibilidad *f* (**to** a) • **to offend sb's susceptibilities** herir la sensibilidad de algn

susceptible [sə'septəbl] ADJ (*to attack*) susceptible (**to** a); (*Med*) (*to illness, infection*) propenso (**to** a); (*to persuasion, flattery*) sensible (**to** a); (= *easily moved*) impresionable • **to be ~ of** admitir, ser susceptible de • **it is ~ of several interpretations** admite diversas interpretaciones, es susceptible de (recibir) diversas interpretaciones

sushi ['suːʃɪ] N sushi *m*
CPD ▸ **sushi bar** bar *m* de sushi ▸ **sushi restaurant** restaurante *m* de sushi

Susie ['suːzɪ] N *familiar form of* **Susan**

suspect ['sʌspekt] ADJ [*person, package*] sospechoso; [*motives*] dudoso, sospechoso; [*testimony*] dudoso • **his credentials are ~** su historial deja lugar a muchas dudas
N sospechoso/a *m/f* • **the prime** *or* **chief ~ is the butler** el principal sospechoso es el mayordomo • **is she a ~?** ¿está ella bajo sospecha? • **the usual ~s** (*fig*) los de siempre, los habituales
VT [səs'pekt] **1** (= *have suspicions about*) [+ *person*] sospechar de; [+ *plot*] sospechar la existencia de • **he never ~ed her** él nunca sospechó de ella • **to ~ sb of a crime** sospechar que algn ha cometido un crimen • **I ~ her of having stolen it** sospecho que ella lo ha robado • **he ~s nothing** no sospecha nada
2 (= *believe*) • **I ~ it's not paid for** sospecho que *or* me temo que no está remunerado • **I ~ it may be true** tengo la sospecha de que puede ser verdad, sospecho que *or* me temo que puede ser verdad • **foul play is not ~ed** no se advierten indicios de juego sucio • **I ~ed you**

S

weren't listening me figuraba *or* me imaginaba que no estabas escuchando • **I ~ed as much** ya me lo figuraba *or* imaginaba

suspected [səs'pektɪd] ADJ [*thief, murderer, crime*] presunto • **she was taken to hospital with ~ appendicitis** la llevaron al hospital pensando que podía tener apendicitis • **she collapsed yesterday with a ~ heart attack** ayer sufrió un colapso y se sospecha que la causa fue un ataque al corazón

suspend [səs'pend] VT **1** (= *hang*) suspender, colgar
2 (= *remove*) (*from job*) suspender (**from** de); (*from school*) expulsar temporalmente (**from** de); (*from team*) excluir (**from** de) • **to ~ sb from office** relevar a algn de su cargo (provisionalmente)
3 (= *discontinue*) [+ *hostilities, aid, flights*] suspender; [+ *licence*] retirar • **his licence was ~ed for six months** (*Aut*) le retiraron el carnet durante seis meses
4 (= *withhold, defer*) [+ *judgement, decision*] aplazar, posponer; (*Jur*) [+ *sentence*] suspender provisionalmente, dejar en suspenso • **he was given a two-year ~ed sentence** fue condenado a dos años en libertad condicional • **to ~ disbelief** creer lo inverosímil
5 • **~ed animation** constantes *fpl* vitales mínimas • **in a state of ~ed animation** (*lit*) con las constantes vitales al mínimo • **the audience was in a state of ~ed animation** el público tenía el alma en vilo *or* el corazón en un puño

suspender [səs'pendəʳ] N (*for stocking, sock*) liga *f* • **~s** (*US*) (= *braces*) tirantes *mpl*, tiradores *mpl* (*S. Cone*)
CPD ▸ **suspender belt** portaligas *m inv*, liguero *m*

suspense [səs'pens] N incertidumbre *f*; (*Theat, Cine*) intriga *f*, suspense *m* • **to keep sb in ~** mantener a algn en vilo • **don't keep me in ~!** ¡no me tengas en vilo! • **the ~ became unbearable** la tensión se hizo inaguantable • **the ~ is killing me!** ¡no puedo con tanta emoción!
CPD ▸ **suspense account** cuenta *f* en suspenso, cuenta *f* transitoria

suspenseful ['səspensfʊl] ADJ [*story, situation*] de suspense

suspension [səs'penʃən] N **1** (*from job*) suspensión *f*; (*from school*) expulsión *f* temporal; (*from team*) exclusión *f* • **~ of payments** suspensión *f* de pagos
2 (*Aut, Chem*) suspensión *f*
CPD ▸ **suspension bridge** puente *m* colgante ▸ **suspension file** archivador *m* colgante ▸ **suspension points** puntos *mpl* suspensivos

suspensory [səs'pensərɪ] ADJ suspensorio
N (*also* **suspensory bandage**) suspensorio *m*

suspicion [səs'pɪʃən] N **1** (= *belief*) sospecha *f* • **my ~ is that ...** tengo la sospecha de que ... • **my ~ is that they are acting on their own** tengo la sospecha de que actúan solos • **there is a ~ that ...** se sospecha que ... • **to be above ~** estar por encima de toda sospecha • **to have one's ~s (about sth)** tener sus sospechas (acerca de algo) • **she had her ~s** ella tenía sus sospechas • **I have a sneaking ~ that ...** tengo la leve sospecha de que ... • **I had no ~ that ...** no sospechaba que ... • **he was arrested on ~ of spying** fue arrestado bajo sospecha de espionaje, fue arrestado como sospechoso de espionaje • **to lay o.s. open to ~** hacerse sospechoso • **to be shielded from ~** estar a salvo de sospechas • **to be under ~** estar bajo sospecha
2 (= *mistrust*) desconfianza *f*, recelo *m* • **to arouse sb's ~s** despertar los recelos de algn • **to regard sb/sth with ~** desconfiar de algn/algo
3 (= *trace*) rastro *m* • **with just a ~ of lemon/garlic** con apenas un ligero sabor a limón/ajo, con apenas un rastro de sabor a limón/ajo • **"good morning," he said without a ~ of a smile** —buenos días —dijo sin la más leve insinuación de una sonrisa

suspicious [səs'pɪʃəs] ADJ **1** (= *mistrustful*) [*person, nature*] desconfiado; [*glance*] receloso • **Paul was a ~ man** Paul era un hombre desconfiado • **many people are ~ that the government will reduce benefits further** mucha gente tiene la sospecha de que el gobierno va a reducir aún más los subsidios • **to be ~ about sth** desconfiar de algo • **to become** *or* **grow ~ (of sth/sb)** empezar a desconfiar (de algo/algn) • **that made him ~** eso le hizo sospechar • **to have a ~ mind** tener una mente desconfiada *or* recelosa • **he is ~ of visitors** se muestra receloso ante las visitas
2 (= *causing suspicion*) [*person, behaviour, package*] sospechoso • **did you see anything ~?** ¿viste algo sospechoso? • **it looks very ~ to me** me parece muy sospechoso • **is there anything ~ about the crash?** ¿hay algo sospechoso acerca del choque? • **in ~ circumstances** en circunstancias sospechosas

suspiciously [səs'pɪʃəslɪ] ADV
1 (= *mistrustfully*) [*look, ask*] con recelo, con desconfianza
2 (= *causing suspicion*) [*behave, act*] de modo sospechoso • **their essays were ~ similar** sus trabajos se parecían sospechosamente • **he arrived ~ early** llegó sospechosamente pronto • **to look ~ like sth** tener todo el aspecto de ser algo • **the stain looked ~ like blood** la mancha tenía todo el aspecto de ser de sangre • **a man who looked ~ like her husband** un hombre que se parecía sospechosamente a su marido • **it looks ~ like measles to me** para mí que *or* (*LAm*) se me hace que es sarampión

suspiciousness [səs'pɪʃəsnɪs] N
1 (= *mistrust*) desconfianza *f*, recelo *m*
2 (= *questionable nature*) [*of circumstances etc*] lo sospechoso

suss* [sʌs] VT (*Brit*) (*also* **suss out**)
1 (= *realize*) percatarse de, coscarse de* • **they never ~ed what was going on** no llegaron a percatarse *or* coscarse* de lo que pasaba
2 (= *understand*) [+ *person*] calar* • **I ~ed him out at once** lo calé en seguida* • **she's got you ~ed** te tiene calado* • **we couldn't ~ it out at all** no logramos sacar nada en claro
3 (= *investigate*) investigar, echar un ojo a • **I'll have to ~ out the job market** tendré que ver cómo está la cosa de trabajo
4 (= *find out*) averiguar • **I've ~ed out the best restaurants** he averiguado cuáles son los mejores restaurantes

sussed* ['sʌst] ADJ (*Brit*) (= *smart*) entendido

sustain [səs'teɪn] VT **1** (= *keep going*) [+ *interest, relationship, marriage*] mantener; [+ *effort*] sostener, continuar; [+ *life*] sustentar; (*Mus*) [+ *note*] sostener • **the economy was not able to ~ a long war** la economía no podía soportar una guerra larga
2 (*frm*) (= *suffer*) [+ *attack*] sufrir (y rechazar); [+ *damage, loss*] sufrir; [+ *injury*] recibir, sufrir; [+ *defeat*] padecer • **both ships ~ed minor damage** ambos buques sufrieron daños de menor consideración
3 (= *support*) (*lit*) [+ *weight*] sostener, apoyar; (*fig*) [+ *theory*] confirmar, corroborar • **it is his belief in God that ~s him** su fe en Dios es lo que lo sostiene *or* mantiene
4 (*Jur*) (= *uphold*) [+ *objection*] admitir; [+ *claim*] corroborar, respaldar; [+ *charge*] confirmar, corroborar • **objection ~ed** la objeción está admitida

sustainability [sə,steɪnə'bɪlətɪ] N **1** [*of rate, growth*] durabilidad *f*
2 (*Ecol*) [*of agriculture, development, resource*] sostenibilidad *f*

sustainable [səs'teɪnəbl] ADJ [*growth, development, agriculture*] sostenible; [*charge*] sustentable

sustainably [sə'steɪnəblɪ] ADV sosteniblemente • **~ managed** gestionado de forma sostenible

sustained [səs'teɪnd] ADJ [*effort*] constante, ininterrumpido; [*note*] sostenido; [*applause*] prolongado • **a period of ~ economic growth** un periodo de crecimiento económico sostenido

sustaining [səs'teɪnɪŋ] ADJ [*food*] nutritivo
CPD ▸ **sustaining pedal** pedal *m* de apoyo, pedal *m* derecho

sustenance ['sʌstɪnəns] N sustento *m* • **they depend for their ~ on** • **they get their ~ from** se sustentan *or* alimentan de

suture ['su:tʃəʳ] N sutura *f*
VT suturar, coser

SUV N ABBR (= **sport(s) utility vehicle**) deportivo *m* utilitario, SUV *m*

suzerain ['su:zəreɪn] N (= *state*) estado *m* protector; (= *sovereign*) monarca *mf* protector(a)

suzerainty ['su:zəreɪntɪ] N protectorado *m*

svelte [svelt] ADJ esbelto

SVGA N ABBR (*Comput*) = **super video graphics array**

SVQ N ABBR (= **Scottish Vocational Qualification**) ▸ **NVQ**

SW ABBR **1** (= **southwest**) SO
2 (*Rad*) (= **short wave**) OC *f*

swab [swɒb] N **1** (= *cloth, mop*) estropajo *m*, trapo *m*
2 (*Naut*) lampazo *m*
3 (*Med*) (*for cleaning wound*) algodón *m*, tampón *m*; (*for specimen*) frotis *m*
VT **1** (*Naut*) (*also* **swab down**) limpiar, fregar
2 (*Med*) [+ *wound*] limpiar (con algodón)

swaddle ['swɒdl] VT envolver (**in** en)

swaddling clothes ['swɒdlɪŋkləʊðz] NPL (*Literat*) pañales *mpl*

swag* [swæg] N botín *m*

swagger ['swægəʳ] N **1** (*in walk*) paso *m* decidido y arrogante, pavoneo *m* al caminar • **to walk with a ~** andar con paso decidido y arrogante, pavonearse al caminar
2 (= *bravado*) fanfarronería *f*, pavoneo *m*
VI (*also* **swagger about, swagger along**) pavonearse, andar pavoneándose • **he ~ed over to our table** se acercó a nuestra mesa dándoselas de algo, se acercó a nuestra mesa con aire fanfarrón • **with that he ~ed out** dijo eso y salió con paso firme y arrogante
CPD ▸ **swagger stick** bastón *m* de mando

swaggering ['swægərɪŋ] ADJ [*person*] fanfarrón, jactancioso; [*gait*] importante, jactancioso

Swahili [swɑː'hiːlɪ] N swahili *m*, suajili *m*

swain [sweɪn] N (*liter*) (= *lad*) zagal *m*; (= *suitor*) pretendiente *m*, amante *m*

swallow¹ ['swɒləʊ] N trago *m* • **in** *or* **with one ~** de un trago
VT **1** [+ *food, drink*] tragar; [+ *pill*] tomar • IDIOM: • **to ~ the bait** (*fig*) tragar el anzuelo
2 (*fig*) [+ *insult*] tragarse • **he ~ed the story** se tragó el cuento • **he ~ed the lot** se lo tragó todo • **to ~ one's words** desdecirse,

retractarse • IDIOM: • **to ~ one's pride** tragarse el orgullo
VI tragar • **to ~ hard** (*fig*) tragar saliva
▸ **swallow down** VT + ADV tragar
▸ **swallow up** VT + ADV [+ *savings*] agotar, consumir; [*sea*] tragar • **the mist ~ed them up** la niebla los envolvió • **they were soon ~ed up in the darkness** al poco desaparecieron en la oscuridad *or* se los tragó la oscuridad • **I wish the ground would open and ~ me up!** ¡trágame tierra!

swallow[2] ['swɒləʊ] N (= *bird*) golondrina *f*
• PROVERB: • **one ~ doesn't make a summer** una golondrina no hace primavera
CPD ▸ **swallow dive** salto *m* del ángel

swallowtail ['swɒləʊteɪl] N (= *butterfly*) macaón *m*

swam [swæm] PT *of* swim

swamp [swɒmp] N pantano *m*, ciénaga *f*, marisma *f*
VT **1** [+ *land*] inundar; [+ *boat*] hundir
2 (*fig*) abrumar (**with** con), agobiar (**with** de) • **they have been ~ed with applications** se han visto abrumados *or* desbordados por las solicitudes • **we're ~ed with work** estamos agobiados de trabajo
CPD ▸ **swamp fever** paludismo *m*

swampland ['swɒmplænd] N ciénaga *f*, pantano *m*, marisma *f*

swampy ['swɒmpɪ] ADJ pantanoso, cenagoso

swan [swɒn] N cisne *m* • **Swan Lake** El Lago de los Cisnes
VI* • **to ~ around** pavonearse • **to ~ off to New York** escaparse a Nueva York
CPD ▸ **swan dive** (*US*) = **swallow dive**
▸ **swan song** canto *m* del cisne

swank* [swæŋk] N **1** (= *vanity, boastfulness*) fanfarronada* *f* • **he does it for ~** lo hace para darse tono *or* lucirse
2 (= *person*) fanfarrón/ona *m/f*
VI fanfarronear* • **to ~ around** pavonearse

swanky* ['swæŋkɪ] ADJ (COMPAR: **swankier**, SUPERL: **swankiest**) [*person*] fanfarrón*, presumido; [*car*] despampanante; [*restaurant, hotel*] de postín

swannery ['swɒnərɪ] N colonia *f* de cisnes

swansdown ['swɒnzdaʊn] N (= *feathers*) plumón *m* de cisne; (*Textiles*) fustán *m*, muletón *m*

swap [swɒp] N (= *exchange*) trueque *m*, canje *m* • **~s** (*when collecting*) duplicados *mpl* • **it's a fair ~** es un trato equitativo
VT [+ *cars, stamps*] trocar, canjear, intercambiar • **will you ~ your hat for my jacket?** ¿quieres cambiar tu sombrero por mi chaqueta? • **we sat ~ping reminiscences** estábamos contando nuestros recuerdos • **to ~ stories (with sb)** contarse chascarrillos *or* historietas (con algn) • **to ~ places (with sb)** (*lit*) cambiar(se) de sitio con algn • **I wouldn't mind ~ping places with him!** (*fig*) ¡ya me gustaría a mí estar en su pellejo!
VI hacer un intercambio • **I asked her but she wouldn't ~** se lo pedí pero no quería cambiarse • **I wouldn't ~ with anyone** no me cambiaría por nadie • **do you want to ~?** ¿quieres que cambiemos?
▸ **swap around, swap over, swap round** VT + ADV cambiar de sitio • **I like to ~ the furniture around** me gusta cambiar los muebles de sitio
VI + ADV cambiar de sitio

SWAPO ['swɑːpəʊ] N ABBR = **South-West Africa People's Organization**

sward [swɔːd] N (*liter*) césped *m*

swarm[1] [swɔːm] N [*of bees, mosquitoes*] enjambre *m*; [*of people*] multitud *f* • **there were ~s of people** había (una) multitud de gente • **they came in ~s** vinieron en tropel
VI [*bees*] enjambrar • **Stratford is ~ing with tourists** Stratford está plagado de turistas • **journalists ~ed around her** los periodistas se arremolinaban alrededor de ella • **children ~ed all over the car** había niños pululando alrededor del coche

swarm[2] [swɔːm] VI • **to ~ up a tree/rope** trepar rápidamente por un árbol/una cuerda

swarthiness ['swɔːðɪnɪs] N tez *f* morena, color *m* moreno

swarthy ['swɔːðɪ] ADJ (COMPAR: **swarthier**, SUPERL: **swarthiest**) moreno

swashbuckler ['swɒʃ,bʌkləʳ] N (*Hist*) espadachín *m*; (= *adventurer*) intrépido *m*

swashbuckling ['swɒʃ,bʌklɪŋ] ADJ [*hero*] de historia de aventuras, bravucón; [*film*] de aventuras, de capa y espada

swastika ['swɒstɪkə] N esvástica *f*, cruz *f* gamada

SWAT [swɒt] ABBR (*esp US*) = **Special Weapons and Tactics** • **~ team** *un cuerpo especial de intervención de la policía*

swat [swɒt] VT [+ *fly*] aplastar, matar
VI • **to ~ at a fly** tratar de aplastar *or* matar una mosca
N • **to give sth/sb a ~** dar un zurriagazo a algo/algn • **to take a ~ at sth/sb** intentar darle un zurriagazo a algo/algn

swatch [swɒtʃ] N (*Textiles*) muestra *f*

swath [swɔːθ] N (PL: **swaths**), **swathe[1]** [sweɪð] N [*of hay*] ringlera *f* • **to cut corn in ~s** segar el trigo y dejarlo en ringleras • **to cut a ~ through sth** avanzar por algo a guadañadas

swathe[2] [sweɪð] VT (= *wrap*) envolver; (= *bandage*) vendar • **~d in sheets** envuelto en sábanas

swatter ['swɒtəʳ] N palmeta *f* matamoscas

sway [sweɪ] N **1** (*also* **swaying**) (= *movement*) balanceo *m*, oscilación *f*; [*of train, bus, boat*] vaivén *m*, balanceo *m*; (= *violent swaying*) bamboleo *m*; (= *violent jerk*) sacudimiento *m*; (= *totter*) tambaleo *m*
2 (= *rule*) dominio *m*; (= *influence*) influencia *f*; (= *power*) poder *m* • **his ~ over the party** su influencia en el partido, su dominio del partido • **to bring a people under one's ~** sojuzgar un pueblo • **to hold ~ over a nation** gobernar *or* dominar una nación • **to hold ~ over sb** mantener el dominio sobre algn • **this theory held ~ during the 1970s** esta teoría se impuso durante la década de los setenta
VI (= *swing*) balancearse, oscilar; (*gently*) mecerse; (*violently*) bambolearse; (= *totter*) tambalearse • **the train ~ed from side to side** el tren se balanceaba *or* bamboleaba de un lado para otro • **she ~s as she walks** se cimbrea al andar
VT **1** (= *move*) balancear; (*gently*) mecer; [+ *hips*] menear, cimbrear
2 (= *influence*) mover, influir en • **he is not ~ed by any such considerations** tales cosas no influyen en él en absoluto • **I allowed myself to be ~ed** me dejé influir • **these factors finally ~ed me** estos factores terminaron de *or* por convencerme

Swazi ['swɑːzɪ] ADJ swazilandés, suazilandés
N swazilandés/esa *m/f*, suazilandés/esa *m/f*

Swaziland ['swɑːzɪlænd] N Swazilandia *f*, Suazilandia *f*

swear [swɛəʳ] (PT: **swore**, PP: **sworn**) VT jurar • **I ~ it!** ¡lo juro! • **I ~ (that) I did not steal it** juro que no lo robé • **to ~ to do sth** jurar hacer algo • **I could have sworn that it was Janet** juraría que fue Janet • **to ~ sb to secrecy** hacer que algn jure guardar el secreto • **to ~ allegiance to** jurar lealtad a • **they swore an oath of allegiance to him** le prestaron juramento de fidelidad • **they swore an oath not to fight again** juraron no volver a pelear
VI **1** (*solemnly*) jurar • **to ~ on the Bible** jurar sobre la Biblia • **I could ~ to it** juraría que fue así • **I can't ~ to it** no lo juraría
2 (= *use swearwords*) decir palabrotas, soltar tacos; (*blasphemously*) blasfemar • **don't ~ in front of the children** no digas palabrotas estando los niños delante • **to ~ at sb** insultar a algn, mentar la madre a algn (*Mex*) • IDIOM: • **to ~ like a trooper** jurar como un carretero
▸ **swear by*** VI + PREP tener plena confianza en, creer ciegamente en
▸ **swear in** VT + ADV [+ *witness, president*] tomar juramento a, juramentar a • **to be sworn in** prestar juramento
▸ **swear off** VI + PREP • **to ~ off alcohol** (jurar) renunciar al alcohol

swearing ['swɛərɪŋ] N (= *bad language*) palabrotas *fpl*

swearword ['swɛəwɜːd] N palabrota *f*, taco *m*

sweat [swet] N **1** sudor *m* • **to be in a ~** estar sudando, estar todo sudoroso; (*fig**) estar en un apuro • **to be in a ~ about sth*** estar muy preocupado por algo • **to get into a ~** empezar a sudar • **to get into a ~ about sth*** apurarse por algo • IDIOM: • **by the ~ of one's brow** con el sudor de su frente; ▹ **cold**
2* (= *piece of work*) trabajo *m* difícil, trabajo *m* pesado • **what a ~ that was!** eso ¡cómo nos hizo sudar! • **we had such a ~ to do it** nos costó hacerlo • **no ~!** ¡ningún problema!
3 • **old ~*** veterano *m*
4 sweats (*US**) = **sweatsuit, sweatpants**
VI sudar, transpirar; (= *work hard**) sudar la gota gorda (**over sth** por algo) • **they will lose everything they have ~ed for** van a perder todo lo que tanto sudor les ha costado conseguir • IDIOM: • **he was ~ing buckets** *or* **like a pig*** estaba sudando tinta *or* como un pollo
VT **1** (*Anat*) sudar • IDIOM: • **to ~ blood** sudar tinta
2 (*Culin*) [+ *vegetables*] rehogar
CPD ▸ **sweat gland** glándula *f* sudorípara
▸ **sweat off** VT + ADV • **I ~ed off half a kilo** me quité medio kilo sudando
▸ **sweat out** VT + ADV • **to ~ a cold/fever out** quitarse un resfriado/la fiebre sudando • IDIOM: • **to ~ it out*** aguantar, aguantarse • **we'll let him ~ it out for a couple of weeks** lo vamos a dejar que sufra un par de semanas, vamos a dejarlo sufrir un par de semanas • **they left him to ~ it out** no hicieron nada para ayudarlo

sweatband ['swetbænd] N **1** (*Sport*) (*round forehead*) banda *f* elástica; (*round wrist*) muñequera *f*
2 (*on hat*) badana *f*

sweated ['swetɪd] ADJ • **~ labour** trabajo *m* muy mal pagado

sweater ['swetəʳ] N suéter *m*, jersey *m*, chompa *f* (*Peru*)

sweating ['swetɪŋ] ADJ sudoroso
N transpiración *f*

sweatpants ['swetpænts] NPL (*US*) pantalón *m* de chándal

sweatshirt ['swetʃɜːt] N sudadera *f*

sweatshop ['swetʃɒp] N *fábrica donde se explota al obrero*

sweatsuit ['swetsuːt] N (*US*) chandal *m*, buzo *m* (*Chile, Bol, Peru*)

sweaty ['swetɪ] ADJ (COMPAR: **sweatier**, SUPERL: **sweatiest**) [*face, hands, person, horse*] sudoroso; [*clothes*] sudado • **to be all ~** estar todo sudoroso

Swede [swi:d] N sueco/a *m/f*

swede [swi:d] N (*= vegetable*) nabo *m* sueco

Sweden ['swi:dn] N Suecia *f*

Swedish ['swi:dɪʃ] ADJ sueco
N **1** (*= people*) • **the ~** los suecos
2 (*Ling*) sueco *m*

sweep [swi:p] (VB: PT, PP: **swept**) VT
1 [*+ place, area*] **a** (*= clean*) [*+ floor, room, street*] barrer; [*+ chimney*] deshollinar • **have you had your chimney swept lately?** ¿te han deshollinado la chimenea recientemente? • **the floor had been swept clean** el suelo estaba limpio porque lo habían barrido
b (*= touch*) rozar • **her long dress swept the ground as she walked** su vestido largo rozaba el suelo al caminar
c (*= spread through*) [*disease, idea, craze*] arrasar; [*rumours*] correr por, extenderse por • **the cycling craze ~ing the nation** la locura del ciclismo que está arrasando el país
d (*= lash*) [*storm, rain, waves*] azotar, barrer • **torrential storms swept the country** tormentas torrenciales azotaron *or* barrieron el país • **the beach was swept by great waves** olas gigantescas azotaron *or* barrieron la playa
e (*= scan*) [*searchlight, eyes*] recorrer • **he swept the horizon with his binoculars** recorrió el horizonte con sus prismáticos
f (*= search*) peinar • **to ~ the sea for mines** dragar el mar en busca de minas
2 (*= move*) **a** (*with brush*) • **she was ~ing crumbs into a dustpan** estaba recogiendo las migas con una escoba y un recogedor • **she swept the snow into a heap** barrió la nieve y la amontonó • **he swept the leaves off the path** barrió las hojas del camino • IDIOMS: • **to ~ sth under the carpet** (*Brit*) • **~ sth under the rug** (*US*) ocultar algo
b (*with hand, arm*) • **she swept her hair back with a flick of her wrist** se echó el pelo hacia atrás con un movimiento rápido de muñeca • **her hair was swept back in a ponytail** tenía el pelo peinado hacia atrás en una cola de caballo • **the curtains were swept back in an elegant fashion** las cortinas estaban recogidas con elegancia • **he swept the stamps into a box** recogió los sellos en una caja • **to ~ sb into one's arms** coger *or* tomar a algn en brazos • **I swept the rainwater off the bench with my hand** quité el agua de la lluvia del banco con la mano
c (*forcefully*) • **she was swept along by the crowd** • **the crowd swept her along** la multitud la arrastró • **to be swept along by** *or* **on a wave of sth** (*fig*) dejarse llevar por una ola de algo • **landslides that swept cars into the sea** corrimientos de tierra que arrastraron coches hasta el mar • **the election which swept Labour into office** *or* **power** las elecciones en la que los laboristas arrasaron haciéndose con el poder • **the water swept him off his feet** la fuerza del agua lo derribó • **he swept her off her feet** la conquistó totalmente • **they swept him off to lunch** se lo llevaron a comer apresuradamente • **a wave swept him overboard** una ola lo arrastró por encima de la borda • IDIOM: • **to ~ all before one** arrasar con todo
3 (*= win decisively*) [*+ election*] arrasar en • IDIOM: • **to ~ the board** (*= win prizes*) arrasar con todo • **the socialists swept the board at the election** los socialistas arrasaron en las elecciones
VI **1** (*= clean*) barrer
2 (*= spread*) **a** [*violence, disease, storm*] • **the violence which swept across Punjab** la violencia que arrasó el Punjab • **the storm which swept over the country** la tormenta que arrasó el país • **plague swept through the country** la peste arrasó el país
b [*fire, smoke*] • **the fire swept rapidly through the forest** el fuego se propagó *or* extendió rápidamente por el bosque • **thick smoke swept through their home** una densa humareda se propagó *or* extendió por la casa
c [*emotion*] • **a great wave of anger swept over me** me invadió una gran oleada de ira • **panic swept through the city** en la ciudad cundió el pánico
3 (*= move*) **a** [*crowd, procession*] • **an angry crowd swept along the main thoroughfare** una multitud airada avanzaba por la calle principal
b (*majestically*) [*person, car*] • **to ~ past/in/out** pasar/entrar/salir majestuosamente • **to ~ into** *or* **out of a place** entrar/salir de un sitio majestuosamente
c (*quickly*) [*vehicle, convoy*] • **the convoy swept along the road** la caravana pasó por la carretera a toda velocidad • IDIOM: • **to ~ into power** arrasar haciéndose con el poder
4 (*= stretch*) [*land, water*] • **the bay ~s away to the south** la bahía se extiende (majestuosamente) hacia el sur • **the hills/woods ~ down to the sea** las colinas/los bosques bajan (majestuosamente) hacia el mar; ▷ **sweep up**
N **1** (*with broom, brush*) barrido *m*, barrida *f* • **the floor/the kitchen could do with a ~** al suelo/a la cocina le hace falta un barrido *or* una barrida • **to give sth a ~** darle un barrido *or* una barrida a algo
2 (*Brit*) (*also* **chimney sweep**) deshollinador(a) *m/f*
3 (*= movement*) [*of pendulum*] movimiento *m*; [*of scythe*] golpe *m*; [*of beam*] trayectoria *f*; (*fig*) [*of events, progress, history*] marcha *f* • **with a ~ of his arm** con un amplio movimiento del brazo • **with one ~ of his scythe, he cleared all the nettles** con un golpe de guadaña hizo desaparecer todas las ortigas • **with a ~ of her hand she indicated the desk** extendió la mano indicando el pupitre con un gesto amplio
4 (*= search*) (*for criminals, drugs*) batida *f*, rastreo *m* • **to make a ~: they made a ~ for hidden arms** dieron una batida *or* hicieron un rastreo buscando armas ocultas • **to make a ~ of sth** (*with binoculars, torch*) hacer una pasada por algo; (*with team of people*) rastrear algo • **the police began making a ~ of the premises** la policía comenzó a rastrear el lugar • **his eyes made a ~ of the audience** paseó la mirada por el público
5 • **clean ~ a** (*= change*) • **to make a clean ~** hacer tabla rasa • **there will be a clean ~ of all those involved in this cover-up** se hará tabla rasa con todos los que estén involucrados en esta tapadera
b (*in competition, series of competitions*) • **to make a clean ~** arrasar ganándolo todo; (*Cards*) ganar todas las bazas • **it was the first club to make a clean ~ of all three trophies** fue el primer club que arrasó llevándose *or* ganando el total de los tres trofeos
6 (*= curve, line*) [*of coastline, river*] curva *f*; [*of land*] extensión *f*; [*of staircase*] trazado *m*; [*of long skirt, curtains*] vuelo *m*; [*of wings*] envergadura *f* • **a wide ~ of meadowland** una gran extensión de pradera
7 (*= range*) **a** (*lit*) [*of telescope, gun, lighthouse, radar*] alcance *m* • **with a ~ of 180°** con un alcance de 180°
b (*fig*) [*of views, ideas*] espectro *m* • **representatives from a broad ~ of left-wing opinion** representantes de un amplio espectro de la izquierda
8 (*= wave*) [*of emotion*] ola *f*
9 = **sweepstake**

▸ **sweep aside** VT + ADV **1** (*lit*) [*+ object*] apartar bruscamente
2 (*fig*) [*+ objections protest, suggestion*] desechar, descartar; [*+ obstacle*] pasar por alto; [*+ difficulty*] sortear • **accusations that customers' interests were being swept aside** acusaciones de que se estaban pasando por alto los intereses de los clientes

▸ **sweep away** VI + ADV ▷ **sweep**
VT + ADV **1** (*= remove with brush*) barrer
2 (*= wash away*) [*river, storm*] [*+ building, car, person*] llevarse por delante • **he was swept away by strong currents** fuertes corrientes se lo llevaron por delante
3 (*= rush away*) llevar a (toda) prisa (**to a**) • **his aides swept him away** sus ayudantes se lo llevaron a (toda) prisa
4 (*fig*) (*= throw out*) eliminar; (*= put an end to*) barrer, poner fin a • **scripture and traditional values were swept away in our determination to accept the feminist challenge** la religión y los valores tradicionales fueron barridos cuando resolvimos aceptar el reto feminista, pusimos fin a la religión y los valores tradicionales al resolvernos a aceptar el reto feminista
5 (*= overwhelm*) • **she was swept away by his charm** su encanto la conquistó, se dejó llevar por su encanto • **he let himself be swept away by emotion** se dejó llevar por la emoción

▸ **sweep up** VI + ADV **1** (*with broom, brush*) barrer
2 • **to ~ up to sth: the car swept up to the house** (*majestically*) el coche subió majestuosamente hasta la casa; (*fast*) el coche subió a toda velocidad hasta la casa • **the lawn swept up to the woods** el césped llegaba *or* se extendía hasta el bosque • **the drive ~s up to the house** el camino de entrada se alza majestuoso hasta la casa
VT + ADV **1** (*= clean up*) (*with brush*) recoger con un cepillo; (*with broom*) recoger con una escoba
2 (*= seize, pick up*) [*person*] coger, agarrar (*LAm*); [*storm*] arrastrar • **I swept her up in my arms** la levanté en mis brazos
3 (*= arrange*) recoger • **her hair was swept up in a bun** tenía el pelo recogido en un moño
4 (*fig*) (*= carry along*) • **she had been swept up in an exciting relationship** se había dejado arrastrar por una relación apasionante • **they became so swept up with excitement that ...** se dejaron llevar tanto por el entusiasmo que ...

sweepback ['swi:pbæk] N [*of aircraft wing*] ángulo *m* de flecha

sweeper ['swi:pə^r] N **1** (*= cleaner*) barrendero/a *m/f*; (*= machine*) (*for streets*) barredora *f*; (*also* **carpet sweeper**) cepillo *m* mecánico
2 (*Ftbl*) líbero *m*

sweeping ['swi:pɪŋ] ADJ [*gesture, movement*] amplio; [*generalization*] excesivo; [*curve*] abierto; [*view*] magnífico; [*skirt*] de vuelo amplio; [*change*] radical; [*victory*] arrollador, aplastante • **a large house with ~ lawns** una gran casa con amplias extensiones de césped • **that's rather a ~ statement** eso es generalizar demasiado
N **1** (*= action*) barrido *m*, barrida *f* • **we gave it a ~** le dimos un barrido *or* una barrida, lo barrimos
2 sweepings basura *f* (*tras un barrido*); (*fig*) [*of*

society etc] desechos *mpl*, escoria *f*
sweepingly ['swi:pɪŋlɪ] ADV [*gesture*] exageradamente; [*speak*] de forma indiscriminada; [*condemn*] totalmente
sweepstake ['swi:psteɪk] N, **sweepstakes** (*US*) N (= *lottery*) lotería *f* (*esp de carreras de caballos*); (= *race*) *carrera de caballos en que el ganador recibe el dinero de las apuestas del resto de los participantes*
sweet [swi:t] ADJ (COMPAR: **sweeter**, SUPERL: **sweetest**) **1** (= *sugary*) [*taste, drink, food*] dulce • **this coffee is too ~** este café está demasiado dulce • **a glass of ~ white wine** una copa de vino blanco dulce • **I love ~ things** me encanta lo dulce, me encantan las cosas dulces • **are those pies ~ or savoury?** esos pasteles, ¿son dulces o salados? • **~ and sour** agridulce • **to taste ~** tener un sabor dulce • **the beer was ~ to the taste** la cerveza tenía un gusto dulce
2 (= *agreeable*) [*smell, perfume*] agradable; [*sound*] melodioso, dulce • **~ dreams!** (*Brit*) (*gen*) que duermas bien; (*to child*) ¡que sueñes con los angelitos! • **to smell ~** tener un olor fragante *or* aromático • **the ~ smell of success** las mieles del éxito • **the ~ taste of victory** el dulce sabor de la victoria • IDIOMS: • **the news was ~ music to my ears** la noticia fue música celestial para mis oídos • **to whisper ~ nothings in sb's ear/to sb** decirle cariñitos a algn al oído • PROVERB: • **revenge is ~!** ¡la dulce venganza!
3 (= *gentle, kind*) [*nature, smile*] dulce; [*face*] dulce, lindo (*esp LAm*) • **she is a very ~ person** es un verdadero encanto, es una persona muy linda (*LAm*) • **that's very ~ of you** es muy amable de tu parte, ¡qué amable! • **how ~ of you to think of me!** ¡qué detalle acordarte de mí! • **to keep sb ~*** tener a algn contento • **~ Jesus!**‡* ¡Dios Bendito!‡ • **to be ~ to sb** ser bueno con algn • IDIOM: • **to do ~ Fanny Adams** *or* **~ F.A.**: • **politicians do ~ Fanny Adams** *or* **~ F.A.** (*Brit*‡) los políticos no hacen más que tocarse las narices‡
4 (= *enchanting*) [*child, animal, house, hat*] mono, lindo (*esp LAm*) • **he was a ~ little boy** ¡era un niñito tan mono! • **what a ~ little puppy!** ¡qué perrito más *or* tan mono! • **the cottage was really ~** la casita era monísima *or* una monada *or* (*esp LAm*) lindísima
5 (= *fresh*) [*water*] dulce; [*air*] fresco; [*breath*] sano • **~ milk** leche fresca
6 (*iro*) • **to do sth in one's own ~ time** hacer algo a su aire, hacer algo cuando le parece a uno • **to go one's own ~ way** ir a su aire • **he carried on in his own ~ way** siguió a su aire
7 • IDIOM: • **to be ~ on sb**†* estar colado por algn*
N **1** (*esp Brit*) (= *piece of confectionery*) [*of any sort*] golosina *f*; (= *boiled sweet, toffee*) caramelo *m*
2 (*Brit*) (= *dessert*) postre *m*
3 • **my ~**†* mi cielo*
4 (*fig*) • **the ~s of success** las mieles del éxito • **the ~s of solitude** el encanto de la soledad
CPD ▸ **sweet basil** albahaca *f* ▸ **sweet bay** laurel *m* ▸ **sweet cherry** cereza *f* dulce ▸ **sweet chestnut** castaño *m* dulce ▸ **sweet pea** guisante *m* de olor, clarín *m* (*Chile*) ▸ **sweet pepper** pimiento *m* (dulce) ▸ **sweet potato** batata *f*, boniato *m*, camote *m* (*LAm*) ▸ **sweet shop** (*Brit*) tienda *f* de chucherías, dulcería *f* (*esp LAm*) ▸ **sweet talk*** zalamerías *fpl*; ▹ **sweet-talk** ▸ **sweet tooth** • **to have a ~ tooth** ser goloso ▸ **sweet trolley** carrito *m* de los postres ▸ **sweet william** minutisa *f*
sweet-and-sour [ˌswi:tən'saʊəʳ] ADJ agridulce
N plato *m* agridulce (*especialmente en la comida china*) • **is sweet-and-sour all right for you?** ¿te parece bien un plato agridulce?
sweetbreads ['swi:tbredz] NPL mollejas *fpl*, lechecillas *fpl* (*Sp*)
sweetbriar, **sweetbrier** ['swi:tbraɪəʳ] N eglantina *f*, escaramujo *m* oloroso
sweetcorn ['swi:tkɔ:n] N maíz *m* dulce (*Sp*), maíz *m* tierno (*esp LAm*), elote *m* (*Mex*), choclo *m* (*And, S. Cone*)
sweeten ['swi:tn] VT **1** [+ *tea, coffee, dish*] endulzar • **~ to taste** endulzar al gusto • **~ with honey if desired** endulzar con miel si se desea
2 (= *freshen*) [+ *breath*] refrescar; [+ *room*] ambientar
3 (*fig*) **a** (= *placate, soften*) [+ *temper*] aplacar, calmar; [+ *process, reforms*] suavizar, facilitar; (*also* **sweeten up**) [+ *person*] ablandar; ▹ **pill**
b (*with financial incentives*) [+ *deal*] hacer más atractivo; [+ *person*] (= *bribe*) sobornar; (= *win over*) ganarse a
VI [*person*] volverse (más) dulce
sweetener ['swi:tnəʳ] N **1** (*Culin*) dulcificante *m*; (*artificial*) edulcorante *m*
2* (= *incentive*) incentivo *m*
sweetening ['swi:tnɪŋ] N (*Culin*) dulcificante *m*
sweetheart ['swi:thɑ:t] N novio/a *m/f*, amor *mf* • **he was her childhood ~** era su amor de infancia • **yes, ~** sí, mi amor
sweetie* ['swi:tɪ] N **1** (*also* **sweetie-pie**) • **he's/she's a ~** es un cielo* • **yes, ~** sí, cielo*
2 (*esp Scot*) (= *sweet*) [*of any sort*] golosina *f*; (= *boiled sweet, toffee*) caramelo *m*
sweetish ['swi:tɪʃ] ADJ algo dulce
sweetly ['swi:tlɪ] ADV [*sing*] dulcemente; [*smile, answer, act*] con dulzura; (= *kindly*) (muy) amablemente • **she ~ offered to bring some refreshments** se ofreció (muy) amablemente a traer algo para comer y beber
sweetmeats ['swi:tmi:ts] NPL dulces *mpl*, confites *mpl*
sweet-natured [ˌswi:t'neɪtʃəd] ADJ dulce, amable
sweetness ['swi:tnɪs] N **1** [*of food*] sabor *m* dulce, dulzor *m*
2 (*fig*) [*of smell*] fragancia *f*, buen olor *m*; [*of sound*] suavidad *f*; [*of person, character*] dulzura *f*; [*of appearance*] encanto *m*; (= *kindness*) simpatía *f* • IDIOM: • **now all is ~ and light** reina ahora la más perfecta armonía • **he was all ~ and light yesterday** ayer estuvo la mar de amable
sweet-scented ['swi:tˌsentɪd] ADJ fragante, de aroma agradable
sweet-smelling ['swi:tˌsmelɪŋ] ADJ fragante, de olor agradable
sweet-talk* ['swi:ttɔ:k] VT engatusar*, camelar* • **to sweet-talk sb into doing sth** engatusar *or* camelar a algn para que haga algo*
sweet-talking* ['swi:ttɔ:kɪŋ] ADJ zalamero
sweet-tempered [ˌswi:t'tempəd] ADJ de carácter dulce, amable • **she's always sweet-tempered** es siempre amable, no se altera nunca
sweet-toothed [ˌswi:t'tu:θt] ADJ goloso
swell [swel] (VB: PT: **swelled**, PP: **swollen**) N
1 (*Naut*) (= *movement*) oleaje *m*; (= *large wave*) marejada *f*
2 (= *bulge*) • **the gentle ~ of her hips** la suave turgencia de sus caderas
3 (= *surge*) [*of anger*] arrebato *m*, arranque *m*; [*of sympathy, emotion*] oleada *f*
4 (*Mus*) crescendo *m*; (*on organ*) regulador *m* de volumen
5†* (= *stylish man*) majo *m*; (= *important man*) encopetado *m* • **the ~s** la gente bien, la gente de buen tono
ADJ (*US**) (= *fine, good*) fenomenal*, bárbaro* • **we had a ~ time** lo pasamos en grande* • **it's a ~ place** es un sitio estupendo*
VI **1** (*physically*) [*ankle, eye etc*] (*also* **swell up**) hincharse; [*sails*] (*also* **swell out**) inflarse, hincharse; [*river*] crecer • **her arm ~ed up** se le hinchó el brazo • **to ~ with pride** hincharse de orgullo
2 (*in size, number*) aumentar, crecer • **numbers have swollen greatly** el número ha aumentado muchísimo • **the little group soon ~ed into a crowd** el pequeño grupo se transformó pronto en multitud • **the cheers ~ed to a roar** los vítores fueron creciendo hasta convertirse en un estruendo
VT **1** (*physically*) hinchar • **to have a swollen hand** tener la mano hinchada • **my ankle is very swollen** tengo el tobillo muy hinchado • **her eyes were swollen with tears** tenía los ojos hinchados de lágrimas • **the rains had swollen the river** las lluvias habían hecho crecer el río • **the river is swollen** el río está crecido • IDIOM: • **you'll give him a swollen head** le vas a hacer que se lo crea
2 [+ *numbers, sales*] aumentar • **all they are doing is ~ing the ranks of the unemployed** lo único que hacen es engrosar las cifras de desempleados
swellhead* ['swelhed] N (*US*) engreído/a *m/f*
swell-headed* ['swel'hedɪd] ADJ engreído, presumido, presuntuoso
swelling ['swelɪŋ] N (*Med*) hinchazón *f*
swelter ['sweltəʳ] VI abrasarse, sofocarse de calor • **we ~ed in 40°** nos sofocábamos a una temperatura de 40 grados
sweltering ['sweltərɪŋ] ADJ [*day*] de calor sofocante, de muchísimo calor; [*heat*] sofocante, abrasador • **it's ~ in here** hace un calor sofocante aquí • **I'm ~** me ahogo de calor
swept [swept] PT, PP *of* **sweep**
sweptback ['swept'bæk] ADJ [*wing*] en flecha; [*aircraft*] con alas en flecha
swerve [swɜ:v] N (*by car, driver*) viraje *m* brusco; (*by boxer, runner*) finta *f*, regate *m* • **to put a ~ on a ball** darle con efecto a la pelota
VI **1** (*lit*) [*boxer, fighter*] hurtar el cuerpo; [*ball*] ir con efecto; (*on hitting obstacle*) desviarse; [*vehicle, driver*] virar bruscamente • **I was forced to ~ violently to avoid him** me vi obligado a virar bruscamente para esquivarlo • **the car ~d away from the lorry** el coche viró bruscamente para esquivar el camión • **the car ~d in and out of traffic** el coche zigzagueaba bruscamente por entre el tráfico • **to ~ to the right** [*vehicle, driver*] virar bruscamente a *or* hacia la derecha
2 (*frm*) (*fig*) desviarse, apartarse (**from** de) • **we shall not ~ from our duty** no nos apartaremos del cumplimiento de nuestro deber
VT [+ *boat, horse, car*] hacer virar bruscamente; [+ *ball*] dar efecto a, sesgar
swift [swɪft] ADJ (COMPAR: **swifter**, SUPERL: **swiftest**) [*runner, animal, vehicle, current*] rápido, veloz; [*reaction*] pronto, rápido; [*decision, response, journey, victory*] rápido; [*river*] de corriente rápida • **we must be ~ to act** tenemos que obrar con prontitud • **to wish sb a ~ recovery** desear a algn una pronta mejoría • **~ of foot** de pies ligeros • **to be ~ to anger** ser propenso a enfadarse
N (= *bird*) vencejo *m*
swift-flowing ['swɪft'fləʊɪŋ] ADJ [*current*] rápido; [*river*] de corriente rápida
swift-footed ['swɪft'fʊtɪd] ADJ veloz, de pies ligeros
swiftly ['swɪftlɪ] ADV [*run*] rápidamente,

velozmente; [*react, act*] con prontitud, rápidamente; [*become, walk*] rápidamente; [*spread, rise, flow*] con rapidez • **events have moved ~** los acontecimientos se han desencadenado con rapidez • **the company has moved** *or* **acted ~ to deny the rumours** la empresa ha actuado con prontitud para desmentir los rumores • **for most of them, death came ~** para casi todos, la muerte llegó repentinamente • **a ~ flowing river** un río de corriente rápida

swiftness ['swɪftnɪs] (N) [*of runner*] rapidez *f*, velocidad *f*; [*of reaction*] prontitud *f*, rapidez *f*

swig* [swɪg] (VT) beber (a tragos)
(N) trago *m* • **have a ~ of this** bébete un poco de esto • **he took a ~ from his flask** se echó un trago de la botella

swill [swɪl] (N) **1** (= *food for pigs*) comida *f* para los cerdos; (= *revolting food, drink*) bazofia *f*, basura *f* • **how can you drink this ~?** ¿cómo te es posible beber esta basura?
2 (= *wash*) • **to give sth a ~ (out)** limpiar algo con agua
3 (= *swallow, draught*) • **he took a ~ from the bottle** echó *or* dio un trago de la botella
(VT) **1** (= *clean*) (*also* **swill out**) lavar, limpiar con agua
2 (= *drink*) [+ *beer*] beber a tragos
▸ **swill around** (VT + ADV) [+ *liquid*] dar vueltas • **she ~ed the whisky around in her glass** le dio vueltas al whisky en su vaso
(VI + ADV) [*liquid*] remover

swim [swɪm] (VB: PT: **swam**, PP: **swum**) (N) • **to have a ~** darse un baño, nadar • **I had a lovely ~ this morning** me di un baño estupendo esta mañana • **after a two-kilometre ~** después de nadar dos kilómetros • **it's a long ~ back to the shore** hay un buen trecho a nado hasta la playa • **that was a long ~ for a child** eso fue mucho nadar para un niño • **to go for a ~** ir a nadar *or* a bañarse • IDIOMS: • **to be in the ~**† estar al corriente *or* al tanto • **to keep in the ~**† mantenerse al día
(VT) **1** [+ *stretch of water*] pasar a nado, cruzar a nado • **he was the first man to ~ the English channel** fue el primer hombre que cruzó a nado el Canal de la Mancha
2 [+ *length, race*] nadar • **he can ~ two lengths** puede nadar dos largos • **she swam ten lengths of the pool** se hizo diez largos en la piscina • **to ~ (the) crawl** nadar a crol • **before I had swum ten strokes** antes de haber dado diez brazadas • **she can't ~ a stroke** no sabe nadar en absoluto • **she swam the 400 metres medley** nadó los 400 metros a cuatro estilos
(VI) **1** [*person, fish*] nadar • **I can't ~** no sé nadar • **to ~ across a river** pasar *or* cruzar un río a nado • **we managed to ~ ashore** logramos llegar nadando hasta la orilla • **then we swam back** luego volvimos (nadando) • **we shall have to ~ for it*** tendremos que echarnos al agua, tendremos que salvarnos nadando • **to go ~ming** ir a nadar *or* bañarse • **to learn to ~** aprender a nadar • **to ~ out to sea** alejarse nadando de la playa • **to ~ under water** nadar debajo del agua, bucear • IDIOMS: • **to ~ against the stream** *or* **tide** nadar contra corriente • **to ~ with the stream** *or* **tide** dejarse llevar por la corriente
2 (= *float*) flotar • **the meat was ~ming in gravy** la carne flotaba *or* nadaba en la salsa • **her eyes were ~ming with tears** tenía los ojos inundados de lágrimas • IDIOM: • **to be ~ming in money** nadar en la abundancia
3 (*dizzily*) (= *reel*) [*room, head*] dar vueltas • **my head is ~ming** me estoy mareando, me da vueltas la cabeza • **everything swam before my eyes** todo parecía que daba vueltas ante mis ojos

swimmer ['swɪməʳ] (N) nadador(a) *m/f*

swimming ['swɪmɪŋ] (N) natación *f* • **do you like ~?** ¿te gusta nadar?
(CPD) ▸ **swimming bath(s)** = swimming pool ▸ **swimming cap** gorro *m* de baño ▸ **swimming costume** traje *m* de baño, bañador *m* (*Sp*) ▸ **swimming gala** festival *m* de natación ▸ **swimming instructor** monitor(a) *m/f* de natación ▸ **swimming lesson** clase *f* de natación ▸ **swimming pool** piscina *fsing*, alberca *fsing* (*Mex*), pileta *fsing* (de natación) (*S. Cone*) ▸ **swimming trunks** bañador *msing* (*Sp*)

swimmingly ['swɪmɪŋlɪ] (ADV) • **to go ~** ir a las mil maravillas

swimsuit ['swɪmsu:t] (N) traje *m* de baño, bañador *m* (*Sp*)

swimwear ['swɪmwɛəʳ] (N) trajes *mpl* de baño

swindle ['swɪndl] (N) estafa *f*, timo *m* • **it's a ~!** ¡nos han estafado *or* timado!
(VT) estafar, timar • **to ~ sb out of sth** estafar algo a algn, quitar algo a algn estafándolo

swindler ['swɪndləʳ] (N) estafador(a) *m/f*, timador(a) *m/f*

swine [swaɪn] (N) **1** (*Zool*) (*pl inv*) cerdo *m*, puerco *m*
2 (*fig**) (= *person*) canalla *mf*, cochino/a *m/f*, marrano/a *m/f* • **you ~!** ¡canalla! • **what a ~ he is!** ¡es un canalla!
(CPD) ▸ **swine fever** fiebre *f* porcina

swineherd†† ['swaɪnhɜ:d] (N) porquero *m*

swing [swɪŋ] (VB: PT, PP: **swung**) (N) **1** (= *movement*) [*of needle, pointer, boom*] movimiento *m*; [*of pick, axe*] movimiento *m* (amplio); [*of pendulum*] oscilación *f*, movimiento *m*; (*Boxing, Cricket, Golf*) (= *technique*) swing *m* • **with a quick ~ of his axe he felled the young tree** con un amplio y rápido movimiento del hacha taló el arbolito • **he was out on the course practising his ~** estaba en el campo de golf practicando su swing • **to take a ~ at sb*** (*with fist*) intentar darle un puñetazo a algn; (*with weapon*) intentar darle un golpe a algn • **the golfer took a ~ at the ball** el golfista intentó darle a la pelota
2 (= *change*) (*in opinion*) cambio *m*; (*in vote*) desplazamiento *m* • **a sudden ~ in opinion** un cambio repentino de opinión • **they need a ~ of 5% to win** necesitan un desplazamiento de los votos de un 5% para ganar • **the ~s of the market** las fluctuaciones del mercado • **a ~ to the left** un viraje *or* desplazamiento hacia la izquierda
3 (= *rhythm*) (*in dance etc*) ritmo *m* • **to walk with a ~ (in one's step)** andar rítmicamente • **music/poetry with a ~ to it** *or* **that goes with a ~** música/poesía con ritmo *or* que tiene ritmo • IDIOMS: • **to go with a ~** [*evening, party*] estar muy animado; [*business*] ir a las mil maravillas • **to be in full ~** [*party, election, campaign*] estar en pleno apogeo; [*business*] estar en pleno desarrollo • **to get into the ~ of things** coger el tranquillo a algo, captar el ritmo de las cosas (*LAm*)
4 (*also* **swing music**) swing *m*, música *f* swing
5 (= *scope, freedom*) • **he was given full ~ to make decisions** le dieron carta blanca para que tomara decisiones • **he gave his imagination full ~** dio rienda suelta a su imaginación
6 (= *garden swing*) columpio *m* • **to have a ~** columpiarse • IDIOMS: • **it's ~s and roundabouts • what you lose on the ~s you gain on the roundabouts** lo que se pierde aquí, se gana allá
(VI) **1** (= *move to and fro*) [*hanging object, hammock*] balancearse; [*pendulum, pointer*] oscilar; [*person*] (*on swing, hammock*) columpiarse • **it ~s in the wind** se balancea al viento • **he was sitting on the end of the table, his legs ~ing** estaba sentado en el borde de la mesa, columpiando las piernas • **her handbag swung back and forth** *or* **to and fro as she walked** su bolso se balanceaba (de un lado al otro) al andar • **the pendulum swung back and forth** *or* **to and fro** el péndulo oscilaba *or* se movía de un lado para otro • **a revolver swung from his belt** un revólver colgaba de su cinturón • **he was ~ing from a trapeze** se columpiaba colgado de un trapecio
2 (= *pivot*) girar • **the door ~s on its hinges** la puerta gira sobre sus goznes • **he was hit by the car door as it swung back** la puerta del coche le golpeó al volver a cerrarse • **to ~ open/shut** abrirse/cerrarse • **the bar swung round and hit him in the jaw** la barra giró y le dio en la mandíbula • IDIOM: • **now the pendulum has swung back the other way** ahora se ha dado la vuelta la tortilla
3 • **to ~ at sb (with one's fist)** intentar dar un puñetazo a algn • **he swung at me with an axe** intentó darme (un golpe) con un hacha • **he swung at the ball** intentó dar a la pelota
4 (= *turn*) • **the car swung into the square** el coche viró *or* dio un viraje y entró en la plaza • **he swung out to overtake** viró *or* dio un viraje para adelantar; ▸ **swing round**
5 (= *jump*) • **he swung across the river on a rope** cruzó el río colgado de una cuerda • **I swung down from my bunk** salté de mi litera • **the orang-utang swung from tree to tree** el orangután se columpiaba de árbol en árbol • IDIOM: • **to ~ into action** ponerse en marcha
6 (= *move rhythmically*) • **a group of schoolchildren were ~ing along up the road** un grupo de colegiales subían por la calle, andando al compás • **as the military band went ~ing along up the road ...** a medida que la banda militar marchaba siguiendo el compás calle arriba ... • **music that really ~s** música que tiene mucho ritmo
7* (= *be hanged*) • **he'll ~ for it** le colgarán por eso
8 (= *change*) • **local opinion could ~ against the company** la opinión local podría cambiar y ponerse en contra de la empresa • **the balance of power is ~ing away from him** la balanza del poder se está inclinando hacia el lado contrario al suyo • **the currency should ~ back to its previous level** es de esperar que las divisas vuelvan a su nivel anterior • **to ~ to the left/right** dar un viraje hacia la izquierda *or* derecha
9 (*Psych*) [*mood*] cambiar • **his mood ~s wildly** le cambia el humor de forma descontrolada
10* (= *be lively*) [*entertainment, party*] ambientarse; [*place*] tener ambiente • **the party's beginning to ~** la fiesta está empezando a ambientarse
11‡ (*sexually*) • **everyone seemed to be ~ing in those days** en aquellos tiempos parecía que a todo el mundo le iba la marcha‡ • IDIOM: • **to ~ both ways** ser bisexual
(VT) **1** (= *move to and fro*) [+ *bag, arms, legs*] columpiar, balancear • **he was ~ing his bag back and forth** *or* **to and fro** columpiaba *or* balanceaba la bolsa de un lado al otro • **to ~ one's hips** andar contoneándose • IDIOMS: • **there isn't enough room in here to ~ a cat*** aquí no caben ni cuatro gatos • **to ~ the lead**†* hacerse el remolón*

2 (= *pivot*) [+ *door*] • **he swung the door open/closed** abrió/cerró la puerta de un golpe
3 (= *move*) **a** [+ *weapon*] blandir • **he swung his sword above his head** blandió la espada por encima de la cabeza • **he swung his axe at the tree** blandió el hacha con intención de darle al árbol • **he swung his racket at the ball** intentó darle a la pelota con la raqueta • **he swung his case down from the rack** bajó su maleta de la rejilla portaequipajes con un rápido movimiento del brazo • **Roy swung his legs off the couch** Roy quitó rápidamente las piernas del sofá • **he swung the box up onto the roof of the car** con un amplio movimiento de brazos, puso la caja en el techo del coche • **he swung the case up onto his shoulder** se echó la maleta a los hombros
b (*reflexive*) • **he swung himself across the stream** cruzó el arroyo de un salto • **to ~ o.s. (up) into the saddle** subirse a la silla de montar de un salto • **he swung himself over the wall** saltó la tapia apoyándose en un brazo
4 (= *turn*) • **he swung the car off the road** viró con el coche y se salió de la carretera
5 (= *influence*) [+ *opinion, decision, vote, voters*] decidir; [+ *outcome*] determinar, decidir • **his speech swung the decision against us** su discurso dio un giro a la decisión desfavorable para nosotros • **the promised tax cuts could ~ the vote in our favour** los recortes prometidos en los impuestos podrían hacer cambiar el voto a nuestro favor • **she managed to ~ it so that we could all go** consiguió arreglarlo para que todos pudiéramos ir • **what swung it for me was ...** lo que me decidió fue ... • **it could ~ the election his way** podría decidir el resultado de las elecciones a su favor
6 (*Mus*) [+ *tune*] tocar con swing
(CPD) ▸ **swing band** (*Mus*) banda *f* de música swing ▸ **swing bin** cubo *m* de la basura (con tapa oscilante) ▸ **swing bridge** puente *m* giratorio ▸ **swing door** puerta *f* de batiente, puerta *f* de vaivén ▸ **swing music** música *f* swing ▸ **swing vote** (*esp US*) voto *m* de los indecisos ▸ **swing voter** (*esp US*) indeciso/a *m/f*
▸ **swing by*** (VI) (*US*) pasar por casa, dejarse caer por casa
▸ **swing round, swing around** (VI + ADV)
1 (*lit*) [*person*] girar sobre sus talones, girar en redondo; [*car, plane, procession*] girar en redondo
2 (*fig*) [*voters*] cambiar de opinión; [*opinion*] cambiar
(VT + ADV) [+ *object on rope etc*] hacer girar; [+ *sword, axe*] blandir; [+ *car, ship, procession, horse*] hacer girar en redondo
▸ **swing to** (VI + ADV) [*door*] cerrarse

swingeing [ˈswɪndʒɪŋ] (ADJ) (*Brit*) [*increase*] vertiginoso; [*cut*] fulminante, drástico; [*fine*] severísimo; [*majority*] abrumador

swinger [ˈswɪŋəʳ] (N) • **he's a ~†*** (*gen*) es muy marchoso, le va la marcha; (*sexually*) le va la marcha

swinging [ˈswɪŋɪŋ] (ADJ) **1** (*lit*) • **the rhythmic ~ motion of his axe against the wood** el rítmico vaivén *or* balanceo de su hacha al golpear la madera • **she walked along with a ~ gait** andaba con garbo
2†* (= *lively*) [*city, party*] con mucha marcha* • **~ London** el Londres marchoso *or* de la marcha* • **the Swinging Sixties** los marchosos años sesenta*
3 [*music, rhythm*] con swing
(N) vaivén *m*, oscilación *f*
(CPD) ▸ **swinging door** (*US*) puerta *f* de vaivén, puerta *f* de batiente

swing-wing [ˈswɪŋwɪŋ] (ADJ) [*aircraft*] con alas de geometría variable

swinish* [ˈswaɪnɪʃ] (ADJ) (*fig*) cochino, canallesco

swipe [swaɪp] (N) • **to take a ~ at sb** asestar un golpe a algn
(VT) **1** (= *hit*) golpear, pegar
2* (= *steal*) birlar*, afanar*
3 (*Comput*) [+ *card*] pasar (*por un lector de tarjetas*)
(VI) • **to ~ at sth/sb** asestar un golpe a algo/algn
(CPD) ▸ **swipe card** tarjeta *f* de banda magnética

swirl [swɜːl] (N) (= *movement*) remolino *m*, torbellino *m* • **it disappeared in a ~ of water** desapareció en un remolino de agua • **the ~ of the dancers' skirts** el girar *or* el movimiento de las faldas de las bailadoras
(VI) [*water, dust, mist*] arremolinarse; [*person*] dar vueltas, girar

swish [swɪʃ] (N) [*of cane*] silbido *m*; [*of skirt*] frufrú *m*; [*of water*] susurro *m*
(ADJ)* (= *smart*) muy elegante
(VT) [+ *cane*] agitar, blandir (*produciendo un silbido*); [+ *skirt*] hacer frufrú con; [+ *tail*] agitar, menear
(VI) [*skirts*] hacer frufrú; [*long grass*] silbar; [*water*] susurrar • **a car ~ed past** pasó un coche deslizándose por el asfalto mojado

Swiss [swɪs] (ADJ) suizo
(N) suizo/a *m/f*
(CPD) ▸ **Swiss army knife** navaja *f* multiuso(s), navaja *f* suiza ▸ **Swiss chard** acelga *f* ▸ **Swiss cheese** queso *m* suizo ▸ **Swiss cheese plant** costilla *f* de Adán ▸ **Swiss Guard** (= *corps*) Guardia *f* Suiza; (= *person*) guardia *m* suizo ▸ **Swiss roll** (*Brit*) (*Culin*) brazo *m* de gitano ▸ **Swiss steak** (*US*) *filete rebozado con cebollas y tomates a la brasa*

Swiss-French [swɪsˈfrentʃ] (N) (*Ling*) el francés de Suiza

Swiss-German [swɪsˈdʒɜːmən] (N) • **Swiss-German** (*Ling*) el alemán de Suiza

switch [swɪtʃ] (N) **1** (*Elec*) interruptor *m*, suich(e) *m* (*LAm*), switch *m* (*LAm*) • **the ~ was on/off** el interruptor estaba encendido/apagado • **at the flick of a ~** con solo darle a un interruptor • **to flick a ~ on/off** encender/apagar un interruptor • **light ~** interruptor *m* de la luz • **the on-off ~** el interruptor de encendido y apagado • **he threw the ~ on the tape recorder** dio al interruptor del magnetofón
2 (= *change*) cambio *m* (**from** de, **to** a) • **this represents a dramatic ~ in US policy** esto representa un cambio dramático en la política estadounidense • **to make the ~ from X to Y** pasar de X a Y • **he had made the ~ from writing screenplays to novels** había pasado de escribir guiones a escribir novelas • **they have made the ~ from dictatorship to democracy** han hecho la transición de la dictadura a la democracia
3 (= *swap, substitution*) cambio *m* • **to make a ~** hacer un cambio • **that's not my necklace, there has been a ~** esa no es mi gargantilla, me la han cambiado *or* me han hecho un cambio, esa no es mi gargantilla, me han dado un cambiazo*
4† (= *stick*) vara *f*; (*for riding*) fusta *f*
5 [*of hair*] postizo *m*
6 (*US*) (*Rail*) (= *points*) agujas *fpl*; (= *siding*) vía *f* muerta
(VT) **1** (= *change*) [+ *tactics*] cambiar de • **if you ~ allegiance from one party to another ...** si cambias de bando y vas de un partido a otro ... • **how quickly people ~ allegiances!** ¡hay que ver con qué rapidez se cambia de chaqueta la gente! • **50 per cent of car buyers are prepared to ~ brands** un 50 por ciento de los compradores de coche están dispuestos a pasarse a una nueva marca
2 (= *move*) [+ *production*] trasladar (**from** de, **to** a) • **she quickly ~ed the conversation to another topic** rápidamente desvió la conversación hacia otro tema
3 (= *swap, exchange*) (*honestly*) cambiar; (*dishonestly*) cambiar, dar el cambiazo a* • **we had to ~ taxis when the first broke down** tuvimos que cambiar de taxi cuando el primero tuvo una avería • **the ballot boxes have been ~ed** han cambiado las urnas, han dado el cambiazo a las urnas* • **to ~ sth for sth** cambiar algo por algo • **he ~ed the real painting with the fake one** cambió el cuadro verdadero por el falso
4 (*Elec*) • **he ~ed the heater to "low"** puso el calentador en "bajo"
5 (*esp US*) (*Rail*) • **to ~ a train to another line** cambiar un tren a otra vía
6 (= *lash*) [+ *tail*] mover, agitar • **to ~ the grass with one's cane** agitar la hierba con la vara
(VI) **1** (= *change*) cambiar (**from** de, **to** a) • **he ~ed to another topic** cambió de tema • **I've ~ed to a cheaper brand of washing powder** (me) he cambiado a una marca de detergente más barata
2 (= *swap round*) hacer un cambio, cambiarse (**with** con) • **he had ~ed with another driver** había hecho un cambio con otro conductor, se había cambiado con otro conductor
3 (= *move*) [*production*] trasladarse (**to** a) • **production will ~ to the Glasgow plant next week** la producción se trasladará a la planta de Glasgow la semana que viene • **you can ~ between windows using the mouse** puedes cambiar de una ventana a otra utilizando el ratón
▸ **switch back** (VI + ADV) (*to original plan, product, allegiance*) volver a cambiarse • **to ~ back to sth** volver a (cambiar a) algo • **let's ~ back to the other programme** volvamos (a cambiar) al otro programa
(VT + ADV) • **she ~ed the heater back to high/low** volvió a cambiar el calentador a la posición alta/baja • **to ~ the light back on** volver a encender la luz • **to ~ the heater/oven back on** volver a poner *or* encender el calentador/horno
▸ **switch off** (VT + ADV) [+ *light, television, gas*] apagar; (*Aut*) [+ *ignition, engine*] parar • **he ~ed the radio off** apagó la radio • **the oven ~es itself off** el horno se apaga solo • **to ~ off the electricity** apagar la corriente *or* la luz
(VI + ADV) **1** (*Elec*) [*washing-machine, light, heating*] apagarse • **the dryer ~es on and off automatically** la secadora se enciende y apaga automáticamente
2* (= *stop listening*) desconectar(se)
▸ **switch on** (VT + ADV) **1** (*Elec, Aut*) [+ *light, television, gas, electricity*] encender, prender (*LAm*); [+ *alarm clock, burglar alarm*] poner • **he ~ed on the light** encendió la luz • **to leave the television ~ed on** dejar la televisión puesta *or* encendida; ▹ **ignition**
2 (*fig*) **a** (= *use*) • **to ~ on the charm** ponerse encantador
b (= *excite*) • **his music ~es me on‡** su música me pone a tono‡
(VI + ADV) (*Elec*) [*washing-machine, light, heating*] encenderse; [*viewer*] encender la televisión, poner la televisión, prender la televisión (*LAm*); [*listener*] encender la radio, poner la radio, prender la radio (*LAm*); [*driver*] arrancar • **the light ~es on automatically** las luces se encienden automáticamente
▸ **switch over** (VT + ADV) • **to ~ over A and B** cambiar A por B • **to ~ the programme over** cambiar de cadena

S

VI + PREP • **to ~ over** (*TV, Rad*) cambiar de canal • **to ~ over to another station** cambiar a otra emisora • **we've ~ed over to gas** (nos) hemos cambiado *or* pasado a gas
▸ **switch round, switch around** VT + ADV 1 (= *swap round*) cambiar
2 (= *move*) [+ *furniture*] cambiar de sitio
VI + ADV cambiarse

switchback ['swɪtʃbæk] N (*Brit*) (*at fair*) montaña *f* rusa; (= *road*) camino *m* de fuertes altibajos

switchblade ['swɪtʃ,bleɪd] N (*US*) navaja *f* de muelle *or* de resorte

switchboard ['swɪtʃbɔ:d] N (*Telec*) (*at exchange*) central *f*; (*in offices*) centralita *f*, conmutador *m* (*LAm*)
CPD ▸ **switchboard operator** telefonista *mf*

switchgear ['swɪtʃ,gɪə^r] N (*Elec*) cuadro *m* eléctrico

switch-hit [,swɪtʃ'hɪt] (*US*) VI ser ambidextro en el bateo

switch-hitter [,swɪtʃ'hɪtə^r] N 1 (*Baseball*) bateador *m* ambidextro
2 (*US‡*) (= *bisexual*) bisexual *mf*

switchman ['swɪtʃmən] N (PL: **switchmen**) (*US*) guardagujas *m inv*

switch-over ['swɪtʃəʊvə^r] N cambio *m* (**from** de, **to** a)

switchtower ['swɪtʃ,taʊə^r] N (*US*) (*Rail*) garita *f* de señales

switchyard ['swɪtʃjɑ:d] N (*US*) (*Rail*) patio *m* de maniobras, estación *f* clasificadora

Switzerland ['swɪtsələnd] N Suiza *f*

swivel ['swɪvl] N eslabón *m* giratorio
VI (*also* **swivel round**) girar; [*person*] volverse, girar sobre los talones
VT (*also* **swivel round**) girar
CPD ▸ **swivel chair** silla *f* giratoria

swivelling ['swɪvəlɪŋ] ADJ giratorio

swizz* [swɪz] N, **swizzle** ['swɪzl] N (*Brit*) camelo* *m*

swizzle-stick ['swɪzlstɪk] N paletilla *f* para cóctel

swollen ['swəʊlən] PP *of* **swell**

swollen-headed ['swəʊlən'hedɪd] ADJ engreído, presumido, presuntuoso

swoon [swu:n] N desmayo *m*, desvanecimiento *m* • **to fall in a ~** desmayarse, desvanecerse
VI desmayarse, desvanecerse

swoop [swu:p] N [*of bird*] descenso *m* súbito; (*by police*) redada *f* (**on** de) • IDIOM: • **at one fell ~** de un solo golpe
VI [*bird*] (*also* **swoop down**) abatirse, lanzarse en picado (**on** sobre); [*police*] hacer una redada (**on** en) • **the plane ~ed low over the village** el avión se lanzó en picado y pasó en vuelo rasante sobre el pueblo • **the police ~ed on the club and arrested eight suspects** la policía hizo una redada en el club y detuvo a ocho sospechosos • **he ~ed on this mistake** se lanzó sobre este error

swoosh [swʊ(:)ʃ] = **swish**

swop [swɒp] = **swap**

sword [sɔ:d] N espada *f* • **to put sb to the ~** pasar a algn a cuchillo • IDIOMS: • **to cross ~s with sb** habérselas con algn • **to be a double-edged ~** ser un arma de doble filo • PROVERB: • **those that live by the ~ die by the ~** el que a hierro mata a hierro muere
CPD ▸ **sword dance** danza *f* de espadas
▸ **sword fight** combate *m* con espada
▸ **Sword of Damocles** (*liter*) espada *f* de Damocles • IDIOM: • **to have the Sword of Damocles hanging over one's head** tener la espada de Damocles pendiendo sobre su cabeza

swordfish ['sɔ:dfɪʃ] (PL: **swordfish, swordfishes**) N pez *m* espada

swordplay ['sɔ:dpleɪ] N manejo *m* de la espada

swordsman ['sɔ:dzmən] N (PL: **swordsmen**) espada *f*, espadachín *m* • **a good ~** una buena espada

swordsmanship ['sɔ:dzmənʃɪp] N manejo *m* de la espada

swordstick ['sɔ:dstɪk] N bastón *m* de estoque

sword-swallower ['sɔ:d,swɒləʊə^r] N tragasables *mf inv*

sword-thrust ['sɔ:dθrʌst] N estocada *f*

swore [swɔ:^r] PT *of* **swear**

sworn [swɔ:n] PP *of* **swear**
ADJ [*enemy*] declarado; [*testimony*] dado bajo juramento, jurado

swot* [swɒt] N empollón/ona *m/f*
VT, VI • **to ~ up (on) sth** empollar algo* • **to ~ for an exam** empollar para un examen*

swotting* ['swɒtɪŋ] N • **to do some ~** empollar*

swum [swʌm] PP *of* **swim**

swung [swʌŋ] PT, PP *of* **swing**

sybarite ['sɪbəraɪt] N sibarita *mf*

sybaritic [,sɪbə'rɪtɪk] ADJ sibarita, sibarítico

sycamore ['sɪkəmɔ:^r] N (*also* **sycamore tree**) sicomoro *m*, sicómoro *m*

sycophancy ['sɪkəfənsɪ] N adulación *f*, servilismo *m*

sycophant ['sɪkəfənt] N adulador(a) *m/f*

sycophantic [,sɪkə'fæntɪk] ADJ [*person*] servil, sobón; [*speech*] adulatorio; [*manner*] servil

Sydney ['sɪdnɪ] N Sidney *m*

syllabary ['sɪləbərɪ] N silabario *m*

syllabi ['sɪlə,baɪ] NPL *of* **syllabus**

syllabic [sɪ'læbɪk] ADJ silábico

syllabication [sɪ,læbɪ'keɪʃən] N, **syllabification** [sɪ,læbɪfɪ'keɪʃən] N silabeo *m*, división *f* en sílabas

syllabify [sɪ'læbɪfaɪ] VT dividir en sílabas

syllable ['sɪləbl] N sílaba *f* • **I will explain it in words of one ~** te lo explico como a un niño

syllabub ['sɪləbʌb] N *dulce frío hecho con nata o leche, licor y zumo de limón*

syllabus ['sɪləbəs] N (PL: **syllabuses** *or* **syllabi**) (*Scol, Univ*) (*gen*) plan *m* de estudios; (*specific*) programa *m* (de estudios)

syllogism ['sɪlədʒɪzəm] N silogismo *m*

syllogistic [,sɪlə'dʒɪstɪk] ADJ silogístico

syllogize ['sɪlədʒaɪz] VI silogizar

sylph [sɪlf] N (*Myth*) (*male*) silfo *m*, sílfide *f*; (*female*) sílfide *f*

sylphlike ['sɪlflaɪk] ADJ de sílfide

sylvan ['sɪlvən] ADJ silvestre

Sylvia ['sɪlvɪə] N Silvia

symbiosis [,sɪmbɪ'əʊsɪs] N simbiosis *f*

symbiotic [,sɪmbɪ'ɒtɪk] ADJ simbiótico

symbol ['sɪmbəl] N 1 (= *representation*) símbolo *m* • **she became a ~ of hope to the downtrodden** se convirtió en un símbolo de esperanza para los oprimidos
2 (*Chem*) símbolo *m*; (*Math*) signo *m* • **the chemical ~ for mercury** el símbolo químico del mercurio

symbolic [sɪm'bɒlɪk] ADJ simbólico (**of** de)
CPD ▸ **symbolic logic** lógica *f* simbólica

symbolical [sɪm'bɒlɪkəl] ADJ simbólico

symbolically [sɪm'bɒlɪkəlɪ] ADV simbólicamente

symbolism ['sɪmbəlɪzəm] N simbolismo *m*

symbolist ['sɪmbəlɪst] ADJ simbolista
N simbolista *mf*

symbolize ['sɪmbəlaɪz] VT simbolizar

symmetrical [sɪ'metrɪkəl] ADJ simétrico

symmetrically [sɪ'metrɪkəlɪ] ADV simétricamente

symmetry ['sɪmɪtrɪ] N simetría *f*

sympathetic [,sɪmpə'θetɪk] ADJ 1 (= *showing pity*) compasivo (**to** con); (= *kind, understanding*) comprensivo • **they were ~ but could not help** estaban de nuestra parte pero no podían ayudarnos • **we found a ~ policeman who helped us** encontramos a un policía que amablemente nos ayudó • **he wasn't in the least ~** no mostró compasión alguna • **they are ~ to actors** están dispuestos a escuchar a los actores • **to be ~ to a cause** (= *well-disposed*) solidarizarse con *or* apoyar una causa
2 [*ink, nerve, pain etc*] simpático

sympathetically [,sɪmpə'θetɪkəlɪ] ADV (= *showing pity*) con compasión; (= *with understanding*) con comprensión • **she looked at me ~** me miró compasiva • **the book has been ~ adapted for the screen** el libro ha sido llevado a la pantalla con gran esmero

sympathize ['sɪmpəθaɪz] VI (= *feel pity*) compadecerse; (= *understand*) comprender • **to ~ with sb** compadecerse de algn, compadecer a algn • **I ~ with what you say, but ...** comprendo tu punto de vista, pero ... • **those who ~ with our demands** los que apoyan nuestras reclamaciones • **to ~ with sb in his bereavement** acompañar a algn en el sentimiento • **they wrote to ~** escribieron para dar el pésame

sympathizer ['sɪmpəθaɪzə^r] N simpatizante *mf*, partidario/a *m/f* (**with** de)

sympathy ['sɪmpəθɪ] N 1 (= *compassion*) compasión *f* • **have you no ~?** ¿no tiene compasión? • **his ~ for the underdog** su compasión por los desvalidos • **you have my deepest ~** te compadezco • **you won't get any ~ from me!** ¡no me das ninguna pena! • **a letter of ~** un pésame • **I have no ~ for him** no siento ninguna compasión *or* pena por él • **to express one's ~ (on the death of)** dar el pésame (por la muerte de)
2 (= *agreement*) solidaridad *f* • **they came out in ~ with their colleagues** se declararon en huelga por solidaridad con sus colegas • **I have some ~ with this point of view** comparto en parte este punto de vista • **the sympathies of the crowd were with him** la multitud estaba de su lado *or* lo apoyaba • **the sky clouded over, in ~ with her mood** el cielo se nubló, poniéndose así a tono con su estado de ánimo
3 **sympathies** (*Pol*) simpatías *fpl* • **she has expressed Republican sympathies** ha expresado sus simpatías por los republicanos
4 (= *affinity*) comprensión *f*, afinidad *f* (**between** entre)
CPD ▸ **sympathy strike** huelga *f* de solidaridad ▸ **sympathy vote** voto *m* de solidaridad

symphonic [sɪm'fɒnɪk] ADJ sinfónico

symphony ['sɪmfənɪ] N sinfonía *f*
CPD ▸ **symphony orchestra** orquesta *f* sinfónica

symposium [sɪm'pəʊzɪəm] N (PL: **symposiums** *or* **symposia** [sɪm'pəʊzɪə]) simposio *m*

symptom ['sɪmptəm] N 1 (*Med*) síntoma *m*
2 (*fig*) (= *indication*) síntoma *m*, indicio *m*

symptomatic [,sɪmptə'mætɪk] ADJ sintomático (**of** de)

synaesthesia, synesthesia (*US*) [,sɪnəs'θi:zɪə] N sinestesia *f*

synagogue ['sɪnəgɒg] N sinagoga *f*

synapse ['saɪnæps] N sinapsis *f*

sync*, **synch*** [sɪŋk] N ABBR (= **synchronization**) • **in ~** en sincronización • **they are in ~** (*fig*) están sincronizados • **out of ~** (*fig*) desincronizado

synchro* ['sɪŋkrəʊ] (*Aut*) (= **synchromesh**)
N ABBR = **synchromesh**
CPD ▸ **synchro gearbox** caja *f* de cambios sincronizada

synchromesh ['sɪŋkrəʊ'meʃ] N (*also* **synchromesh gear**) cambio *m* sincronizado de velocidades

synchronic [sɪŋ'krɒnɪk] ADJ sincrónico

synchronism ['sɪŋkrənɪzəm] N sincronismo *m*

synchronization [ˌsɪŋkrənaɪ'zeɪʃən] N sincronización *f*

synchronize ['sɪŋkrənaɪz] VT sincronizar (**with** con) • **~d swimming** natación *f* sincronizada
VI sincronizarse, ser sincrónico (**with** con)

synchronous ['sɪŋkrənəs] ADJ sincrónico, síncrono

synchrotron ['sɪŋkrəˌtrɒn] N sincrotrón *m*

syncopate ['sɪŋkəpeɪt] VT sincopar

syncopated ['sɪŋkəpeɪtɪd] ADJ sincopado

syncopation [ˌsɪŋkə'peɪʃən] N síncopa *f*

syncope ['sɪŋkəpɪ] N **1** (*Med*) síncope *m*
2 (*Ling, Mus*) síncopa *f*

syncretism ['sɪŋkrətɪzəm] N sincretismo *m*

syndic ['sɪndɪk] N síndico *m*

syndicalism ['sɪndɪkəlɪzəm] N sindicalismo *m*

syndicalist ['sɪndɪkəlɪst] ADJ sindicalista
N sindicalista *mf*

syndicate N ['sɪndɪkɪt] **1** (*Comm*) sindicato *m*, corporación *f*
2 (*esp US*) (= *news agency*) agencia *f* de prensa; (= *chain of papers*) cadena *f* de periódicos
3* (= *criminals*) • **crime ~** banda *f* de malhechores, cuadrilla *f* de bandidos
VT ['sɪndɪkeɪt] **1** (*esp US*) (*Press*) [+ *article, interview etc*] sindicar
2 (*Econ*) • **~d loan** préstamo *m* sindicado

syndicated ['sɪndɪkeɪtɪd] ADJ (*Press*) [*articles*] de agencia

syndrome ['sɪndrəʊm] N síndrome *m*

synecdoche [sɪ'nekdəkɪ] N sinécdoque *f*

synergistic [ˌsɪnə'dʒɪstɪk] ADJ sinergístico
• **~ effect** efecto *m* sinergístico

synergy ['sɪnədʒɪ] N sinergia *f*

synesthesia [ˌsɪnəs'θi:zɪə] N (*US*) = **synaesthesia**

synod ['sɪnəd] N sínodo *m*

synonym ['sɪnənɪm] N sinónimo *m*

synonymous [sɪ'nɒnɪməs] ADJ sinónimo (**with** con)

synonymy [sɪ'nɒnəmɪ] N sinonimia *f*

synopsis [sɪ'nɒpsɪs] N (PL: **synopses** [sɪ'nɒpsi:z]) sinopsis *f inv*

synoptic [sɪ'nɒptɪk] ADJ sinóptico

synoptical [sɪ'nɒptɪkəl] ADJ = **synoptic**

synovial [saɪ'nəʊvɪəl] ADJ sinovial

syntactic [sɪn'tæktɪk], **syntactical** [sɪn'tæktɪkəl] ADJ sintáctico

syntagm ['sɪntæm] N (PL: **syntagms**), **syntagma** [sɪn'tægmə] N (PL: **syntagmata** [sɪn'tægmətə]) sintagma *m*

syntagmatic [ˌsɪntæg'mætɪk] ADJ sintagmático

syntax ['sɪntæks] N sintaxis *f*
CPD ▸ **syntax error** error *m* sintáctico

synth* [sɪnθ] ADJ, N (*Mus*) = **synthesizer**

synthesis ['sɪnθəsɪs] N (PL: **syntheses** ['sɪnθəsi:z]) síntesis *f inv*

synthesize ['sɪnθəsaɪz] VT sintetizar

synthesized ['sɪnθəsaɪzd] ADJ [*voice, speech, music, sound*] sintetizado

synthesizer ['sɪnθəsaɪzəʳ] N sintetizador *m*

synthetic [sɪn'θetɪk] ADJ **1** (= *man-made*) [*material, chemical, drug*] sintético
2 (*pej*) (= *false*) [*person, behaviour, emotion, taste*] artificial
N fibra *f* sintética • **~s** fibras *fpl* sintéticas
CPD ▸ **synthetic fibre, synthetic fiber** (*US*) fibra *f* sintética ▸ **synthetic rubber** caucho *m* artificial

synthetically [sɪn'θetɪkəlɪ] ADV sintéticamente

syphilis ['sɪfɪlɪs] N sífilis *f*

syphilitic [ˌsɪfɪ'lɪtɪk] ADJ sifilítico
N sifilítico/a *m/f*

syphon ['saɪfən] = **siphon**

Syracuse ['saɪərəkju:z] N Siracusa *f*

Syria ['sɪrɪə] N Siria *f*

Syrian ['sɪrɪən] ADJ sirio
N sirio/a *m/f*

syringe [sɪ'rɪndʒ] N jeringa *f*, jeringuilla *f*
VT jeringar

syrup ['sɪrəp] N (*Culin*) almíbar *m*, jarabe *m*; (*Med*) jarabe *m*

syrupy ['sɪrəpɪ] ADJ **1** parecido a jarabe, espeso como jarabe
2 (*fig*) sensiblero, almibarado

system ['sɪstəm] N **1** (= *method*) sistema *m*
• **new teaching ~s** nuevos sistemas *or* métodos de enseñanza
2 (*Pol, Sociol*) (= *organization*) sistema *m*
• **a political/economic/social ~** un sistema político/económico/social
3 (*Math, Sci*) (= *principles*) sistema *m* • **binary/decimal/metric ~** sistema *m* binario/decimal/métrico
4 (*Elec, Comput, Mech*) sistema *m* • **the ~'s down again** el sistema no funciona otra vez
5 (= *network*) sistema *m*, red *f* • **transport ~** sistema *m or* red *f* de transportes
6 (= *order*) método *m* • **he lacks ~** carece de método
7 (*Med*) (= *organism*) organismo *m*, cuerpo *m*
• **the nervous/immune ~** el sistema nervioso/inmunitario • **the digestive ~** el aparato digestivo • **it was quite a shock to the ~** (*fig*) fue un buen golpe para el organismo • IDIOM: • **to get sth out of one's ~** quitarse algo de encima
8 • **the ~** (= *the establishment*) el sistema • **to beat the ~** burlar el sistema
9 (= *classification*) sistema *m* • **a chronological ~** un sistema cronológico
10 (*Astron*) sistema *m* • **solar ~** sistema *m* solar
CPD ▸ **system disk** disco *m* del sistema ▸ **system operator** (*Comput*) operador(a) *m/f* de sistemas ▸ **system requirements** requisitos *mpl* de configuración ▸ **systems analysis** análisis *m inv* de sistemas ▸ **systems analyst** (*Comput*) analista *mf* de sistemas ▸ **systems engineer** (*Comput*) ingeniero/a *m/f* de sistemas ▸ **systems engineering** ingeniería *f* de sistemas ▸ **systems integrator** (= *business*) integrador *m* de sistemas; (= *person*) integrador(a) *m/f* de sistemas ▸ **systems programmer** programador(a) *m/f* de sistemas ▸ **systems software** software *m* del sistema

systematic [ˌsɪstə'mætɪk] ADJ sistemático, metódico

systematically [ˌsɪstə'mætɪkəlɪ] ADV sistemáticamente, metódicamente

systematization ['sɪstəmətaɪ'zeɪʃən] N sistematización *f*

systematize ['sɪstəmətaɪz] VT sistematizar

systemic [sɪ'stemɪk] ADJ **1** sistémico
2 [*chemicals, drugs*] sistémico

systole ['sɪstəlɪ] N (*Med*) sístole *f*

systolic [sɪ'stɒlɪk] ADJ • **~ pressure** presión *f* sistólica

Tt

T, t [tiː] (N) (= *letter*) T, t *f* • **T for Tommy** T de Tommy • **the buildings were arranged in a T** los edificios estaban situados en forma de T • IDIOM: • **to a T**: • **it fits you to a T** te sienta que ni pintado • **it suits you to a T** te viene de perlas • **he described the house to a T** describió la casa hasta el último detalle • **that's it to a T** es eso exactamente

TA (N ABBR) **1** (*Brit*) (*Mil*) (= **Territorial Army**) ▸ TERRITORIAL ARMY
2 (*US*) (*Univ*) = **teaching assistant**

ta* [tɑː] (EXCL) (*Brit*) gracias • **ta very much!** ¡muchas gracias!

tab [tæb] (N) **1** (*on garment*) (= *flap*) oreja *f*, lengüeta *f*; (= *loop*) presilla *f*; (= *label*) etiqueta *f*; (= *marker*) (*on file*) ceja *f*; [*of cheque*] resguardo *m* • IDIOMS: • **to keep tabs on sb*** vigilar a algn • **to keep tabs on** [+ *situation*] seguir de cerca
2 (*US*) cuenta *f* • IDIOM: • **to pick up the tab*** pagar la cuenta; (*fig*) asumir la responsabilidad
3 (*also* **tabulator**) tabulador *m*
(CPD) ▸ **tab key** tecla *f* de tabulación

tabard ['tæbəd] (N) tabardo *m*

Tabasco® [tə'bæskəʊ] (N) salsa *f* tabasco, tabasco *m*

tabbed [tæbd] (ADJ) (*Comput*) [*window, dialogue box etc*] con pestañas

tabby ['tæbɪ] (ADJ) atigrado
(N) (*also* **tabby cat**) gato/a *m/f* atigrado/a

tabernacle ['tæbənækl] (N) (*in Judaism*) tabernáculo *m*; (= *church*) templo *m*, santuario *m*; (*in church*) sagrario *m*

table ['teɪbl] (N) **1** (= *piece of furniture*) mesa *f* • **I'd like a ~ for two, please** (quiero) una mesa para dos, por favor • **kitchen ~** mesa *f* de cocina • **they were at ~ when we arrived** (*frm*) estaban sentados a la mesa cuando llegamos • **don't read at the ~** no leas en la mesa • **you will join us at our ~, won't you?** se sentará (a la mesa) con nosotros ¿verdad? • **to clear the ~** quitar *or* recoger *or* levantar la mesa • **to lay the ~** poner la mesa • **why isn't dinner on the ~?** ¿por qué no está servida la cena? • **to set the ~** poner la mesa • **to sit down to ~** sentarse a la mesa • IDIOMS: • **under the ~**: • **I'll be under the ~ if I have any more wine** si bebo más vino me voy a caer redondo *or* no voy a tenerme en pie • **he was accepting money under the ~*** aceptaba dinero bajo cuerda *or* bajo mano • **to get one's feet under the ~*** hacerse un hueco* • **to turn the ~s** dar la vuelta a la tortilla • **to turn the ~s on sb** volver las tornas a *or* contra algn; ▸ **card[1], drink, high, wait**
2 (= *people at table*) mesa *f*
3 (*frm*) (= *food*) mesa *f* • **to keep a good ~** tener buena mesa
4 (*for discussion*) mesa *f* de negociaciones • **he managed to get all the parties around the ~** consiguió que todos los interesados se sentaran a la mesa de negociaciones • **to put sth on the ~** (*Brit*) poner algo sobre el tapete • **there are two proposals on the ~** hay dos propuestas sobre el tapete • **they're willing to put 12 million dollars on the ~ to get this company** están dispuestos a pagar 12 millones de dólares para conseguir esta empresa • **round ~** mesa *f* redonda
5 (= *chart*) tabla *f*, cuadro *m* • **a ~ of the top 12 best and worst performers** una tabla *or* un cuadro de los 12 mejores y los 12 peores • **~ of contents** índice *m* de materias; ▸ **periodic**
6 (*Math*) (*also* **multiplication table**) tabla *f* de multiplicar • **the eleven-times ~** la tabla (de multiplicar) del once
7 (*Sport*) (*also* **league table**) liga *f*, clasificación *f*
8 (*Geog*) (*also* **water table**) capa *f* freática; (*also* **tableland**) meseta *f*, altiplano *m* (*LAm*)
(VT) **1** (*Brit*) (*frm*) (= *propose*) [+ *motion, amendment*] presentar
2 (*US*) (= *postpone*) aplazar, posponer
(CPD) ▸ **table dancing** striptease *m* en pasarela *or* en barra ▸ **table football** futbolín *m* ▸ **table lamp** lámpara *f* de mesa ▸ **table leg** pata *f* de mesa ▸ **table linen** mantelería *f* ▸ **table manners** comportamiento *msing* en la mesa, modales *mpl* en la mesa ▸ **Table Mountain** Montaña *f* de la Tabla ▸ **table napkin** servilleta *f* ▸ **table runner** tapete *m* ▸ **table salt** sal *f* de mesa ▸ **table saw** sierra *f* circular ▸ **table setting** cubierto *m*, servicio *m* ▸ **table talk** sobremesa *f*, conversación *f* de sobremesa ▸ **table tennis** ping-pong *m*, pimpón *m*, tenis *m* de mesa ▸ **table wine** vino *m* de mesa

tableau ['tæbləʊ] (N) (PL: **tableaux** *or* **tableaus** ['tæbləʊz]) (*Art, Theat*) cuadro *m* (vivo)

tablecloth ['teɪblklɒθ] (N) mantel *m*

table d'hôte ['tɑːbl'dəʊt] (N) menú *m*, comida *f* (corrida) (*Mex*)

tableland ['teɪbllænd] (N) meseta *f*, altiplano *m* (*LAm*)

tablemat ['teɪblmæt] (N) salvamanteles *m inv*

tablespoon ['teɪblspuːn] (N) (= *spoon*) cuchara *f* grande, cuchara *f* de servir; (= *quantity*) cucharada *f* grande

tablespoonful ['teɪbl,spuːnfʊl] (N) cucharada *f* grande

tablet ['tæblɪt] (N) **1** (*Med*) (*gen*) pastilla *f*; (= *round pill*) comprimido *m*
2 [*of soap, chocolate*] pastilla *f*
3 (= *writing tablet*) bloc *m*, taco *m* (de papel)
4 (= *inscribed stone*) lápida *f*
5 (*Comput*) tableta *f*, tablet *f*

table-tennis player [,teɪbl'tenɪspleɪəʳ] (N) jugador(a) *m/f* de tenis de mesa, jugador(a) *m/f* de ping-pong

tabletop ['teɪbltɒp] (N) tablero *m* de la mesa
(CPD) ▸ **tabletop games** juegos *mpl* de mesa

tableware ['teɪblweəʳ] (N) vajilla *f*, servicio *m* de mesa

tabloid ['tæblɔɪd] (N) (= *newspaper*) tabloide *m*, periódico *m* popular • **the ~s** (*pej*) la prensa amarilla; ▸ BROADSHEETS AND TABLOIDS

taboo, tabu [tə'buː] (ADJ) (*socially*) tabú; (*religiously*) sagrado • **the subject is ~** el asunto es tema tabú
(N) (*social*) tabú *m*
(VT) declarar tabú, prohibir

tabular ['tæbjʊləʳ] (ADJ) tabular

tabulate ['tæbjʊleɪt] (VT) exponer en forma de tabla; (*Comput*) tabular

tabulation [,tæbjʊ'leɪʃən] (N) [*of information, results*] exposición *f* en forma de tabla; (= *table*) tabla *f*

tabulator ['tæbjʊleɪtəʳ] (N) tabulador *m*

tache* [tæʃ] (N) (= **moustache**) bigote *m*

tachograph ['tækəgrɑːf] (N) (*Brit*) tacógrafo *m*

tachometer [tæ'kɒmɪtəʳ] (N) taquímetro *m*

tachycardia [,tækɪ'kɑːdɪə] (N) taquicardia *f*

tachymeter [tæ'kɪmɪtəʳ] (N) taquímetro *m*

tacit ['tæsɪt] (ADJ) tácito

tacitly ['tæsɪtlɪ] (ADV) tácitamente

taciturn ['tæsɪtɜːn] (ADJ) taciturno

taciturnity [,tæsɪ'tɜːnɪtɪ] (N) taciturnidad *f*

Tacitus ['tæsɪtəs] (N) Tácito

tack [tæk] (N) **1** (= *nail*) tachuela *f*; (*US*) (*also* **thumbtack**) chincheta *f*, chinche *m or f*
2 (*Naut*) (= *course*) bordada *f*; (= *turn*) virada *f*
3 (*fig*) rumbo *m*, dirección *f* • IDIOMS: • **to change ~** cambiar de rumbo *or* sentido • **to try a different ~** abordar un problema desde otro punto de partida • **to be on the right ~** ir por buen camino • **to be on the wrong ~** estar equivocado
4 (*Sew*) hilván *m*
5 (*for horse*) arreos *mpl*
6* (= *cheap shoddy objects*) baratijas *fpl*, chucherías *fpl*, horteradas *fpl* (*Sp**)
(VT) **1** (= *nail*) clavar con tachuelas
2 (*Sew*) (*also* **tack up**) hilvanar
(VI) (*Naut*) dar bordadas; (= *change course*) virar, cambiar de bordada
▸ **tack down** (VT + ADV) (*Carpentry etc*) • **to ~ sth down** afirmar algo con tachuelas, sujetar algo con tachuelas
▸ **tack on** (VT + ADV) • **to ~ sth on to a letter** añadir algo a una carta • **somehow it got ~ed on** de algún modo u otro llegó a ser añadido a la parte principal

tackiness ['tækɪnɪs] (N) **1*** [*of area, bar*] chabacanería *f*; (= *tastelessness*) [*of clothes, food, colour scheme*] mal gusto *m*
2 (= *stickiness*) [*of paint etc*] carácter *m* pegajoso

tackle ['tækl] (N) **1** (= *lifting gear*) aparejo *m*, polea *f*; (= *ropes*) jarcia *f*, cordaje *m*

2 (= *equipment*) equipo *m*, avíos *mpl*; (*fig*) (= *bits and pieces*) cosas *fpl*, trastos *mpl*; (*also* **fishing tackle**) equipo *m* de pesca
3 (*Ftbl*) entrada *f*; (*Rugby*) placaje *m* • **flying ~** placaje *m* en el aire
VT 1 (= *attempt to deal with*) [+ *problem*] abordar, enfrentar; [+ *task*] enfrentar, emprender • **firemen ~d the blaze** los bomberos lucharon contra las llamas • **can you ~ another helping?** ¿quieres comerte otra porción? • **he ~d Greek on his own** emprendió el estudio del griego sin ayuda de nadie
2 (= *grapple with*) [+ *thief, intruder*] enfrentarse con; (*fig*) (= *confront*) encararse con • **I'll have to ~ him about that money he owes me** voy a tener que encararme con él y plantearle lo del dinero que me debe
3 (*Ftbl*) entrar a; (*Rugby*) placar, taclear
VI (*Sport*) placar, taclear

tacky ['tækɪ] ADJ (COMPAR: **tackier**, SUPERL: **tackiest**) 1* (= *cheap-looking*) [*furniture*] chabacano, hortera (*Sp**); [*restaurant, hotel*] destartalado; (= *tasteless*) [*behaviour, remark*] de mal gusto, vulgar
2 (= *sticky*) pegajoso

taco ['tɑːkəʊ] N *tortilla rellena hecha con harina de maíz*

tact [tækt] N tacto *m*

tactful ['tæktfʊl] ADJ [*person, behaviour, remark, question*] diplomático, discreto • **she's very ~** • **she's a very ~ person** tiene mucho tacto, es muy diplomática *or* discreta • **the ~ thing would have been to say nothing** lo diplomático hubiese sido no decir nada • **that wasn't a very ~ question** no fue una pregunta muy diplomática *or* discreta • **he maintained a ~ silence** mantuvo un discreto silencio

tactfully ['tæktfəlɪ] ADV [*suggest, point out*] con mucho tacto, discretamente • **as ~ as possible** con el mayor tacto posible, lo más diplomáticamente posible

tactfulness ['tæktfʊlnɪs] N tacto *m*, discreción *f*

tactic ['tæktɪk] N táctica *f*

tactical ['tæktɪkəl] ADJ táctico • **~ voting** votación *f* táctica

tactically ['tæktɪkəlɪ] ADV tácticamente

tactician [tæk'tɪʃən] N táctico/a *m/f*

tactics ['tæktɪks] NPL (*gen*) (*Mil*) táctica *fsing* • **to change ~** cambiar de táctica • **delaying ~** tácticas *fpl* dilatorias • **scare ~** tácticas *fpl* para infundir miedo

tactile ['tæktaɪl] ADJ táctil

tactless ['tæktlɪs] ADJ [*person*] falto de tacto, poco diplomático; [*comment, behaviour*] indiscreto, poco diplomático • **it was a ~ remark** fue un comentario poco diplomático *or* bastante indiscreto • **how could you be so ~?** ¿cómo puedes haber tenido tan poco tacto?, ¿cómo puedes haber sido tan poco diplomático?

tactlessly ['tæktlɪslɪ] ADV con poco tacto

tactlessness ['tæktlɪsnɪs] N falta *f* de tacto

tad* [tæd] N • **a tad big/small** un poco grande/pequeño

Tadjikistan [tɑ,dʒɪkɪ'stɑːn] = **Tadzhikistan**

tadpole ['tædpəʊl] N renacuajo *m*

Tadzhikistan [tɑ,dʒɪkɪ'stɑːn] N Tayikistán *m*

taffeta ['tæfɪtə] N tafetán *m*

taffrail ['tæfreɪl] N (*Naut*) (= *part of stern*) coronamiento *m*; (= *rail*) pasamano *m* de la borda

Taffy* ['tæfɪ] N (*pej*) galés *m*

taffy ['tæfɪ] N (*US*) (= *toffee*) melcocha *f*

tag [tæg] N 1 (= *label*) etiqueta *f*, marbete *m*; (*on shoelace*) herrete *m*; (*for identification*) chapa *f*; (= *surveillance device*) etiqueta *f* personal de control • **name tag** etiqueta *f* de identificación; ▹ **price**
2 (= *game*) • **to play tag** jugar al cogecoge *or* (*LAm*) a la pega
3 (= *cliché*) tópico *m*, dicho *m*, lugar *m* común; (= *catchword*) muletilla *f*; (= *quotation*) cita *f* trillada; (= *proverb*) refrán *m*
4 (*Ling*) (*also* **tag question**) cláusula *f* final interrogativa
VT 1 (= *follow*) seguirle la pista a
2 (= *describe*) [+ *person*] poner una etiqueta a
3 [+ *criminal*] controlar electrónicamente
VI • **to tag after sb** seguir a algn
CPD ▸ **tag line** [*of joke, film, advertisement*] muletilla *f*
▸ **tag along** VI + ADV • **we don't want your brother tagging along** no queremos que tu hermano se nos pegue • **there was another boat tagging along behind us** había otro barco que nos seguía
▸ **tag on** VT + ADV añadir
VI + ADV • **to tag on to sb** pegarse a algn

Tagalog [tə'gɑːlɒg] N (= *language*) tagalo *m*

tagger ['tægəʳ] N (*Comput*) generador *m* de etiquetas

tagliatelle [,tæljə'telɪ, ,tæglɪə'telɪ] N tagliatelle *mpl*

tagline ['tæglaɪn] = **tag line**

tagmeme ['tægmiːm] N tagmema *m*

tagmemics [tæg'miːmɪks] N tagmética *f*

Tagus ['teɪgəs] N Tajo *m*

tahini [tə'hiːnɪ] N *pasta hecha con semillas de sésamo*

Tahiti [tɑː'hiːtɪ] N Tahití *m*

Tahitian [tə'hiːʃɪən] ADJ tahitiano
N 1 tahitiano/a *m/f*
2 (*Ling*) tahitiano *m*

t'ai chi, tai chi [,taɪ'tʃiː] N tai chi *m*

taiga ['taɪgə] N taiga *f*

tail [teɪl] N 1 [*of bird, horse, fish, plane*] cola *f*; [*of dog, bull, ox*] cola *f*, rabo *m*; [*of comet*] cabellera *f*, cola *f*; [*of shirt*] faldón *m*; [*of procession*] cola *f*, tramo *m* final; (= *loose end*) cabo *m*; [*of hair*] mechón *m* • IDIOMS: • **to turn ~ (and flee)** huir • **he went off with his ~ between his legs** se fue con el rabo entre las piernas • **it's a case of the ~ wagging the dog** es el mundo al revés
2 **tails** (= *coat*) frac *msing*; [*of coin*] cruz *fsing* • **heads or ~s** cara o cruz • **~s you lose** si sale cruz pierdes
3‡ (= *buttocks*) trasero *m* • **to work one's ~ off** sudar tinta*
4 (= *person following*) sombra *f* • **to put a ~ on sb** hacer seguir a algn
5 (*US***) (= *girls*) tipas* *fpl*, tías *fpl* (*Sp**) • **a piece of ~** una tipa*, una tía (*Sp**)
VT (= *follow*) seguirle la pista a; ▹ **top¹**
CPD ▸ **tail end** [*of procession, queue*] cola *f*, tramo *m* final; (*fig*) [*of party, storm*] final *m* • **at the ~ end of the summer** en los últimos días del verano ▸ **tail section** [*of aeroplane*] sección *f* de cola
▸ **tail away** VI + ADV [*sound*] ir apagándose • **his voice ~ed away** su voz se fue desvaneciendo *or* apagando • **after that the book ~s away** después de eso el libro pierde interés
▸ **tail back** VI + ADV • **the traffic ~ed back to the bridge** la cola de coches se extendía atrás hasta el puente
▸ **tail off** VI + ADV 1 [*production, demand*] disminuir • **business has ~ed off lately** el negocio ha decaído *or* empeorado últimamente; ▹ **tail-off**
2 [*voice, sound*] ir apagándose • **his voice ~ed off** su voz se fue desvaneciendo *or* apagando

tailback ['teɪlbæk] N caravana *f*, cola *f*

tailboard ['teɪlbɔːd] = **tailgate**

tailcoat ['teɪlkəʊt] N frac *m*

-tailed [teɪld] ADJ (*ending in compounds*) con rabo ... • **long-tailed** con rabo largo, rabilargo

tailgate ['teɪlgeɪt] N (*Aut*) puerta *f* trasera
VT ir a rebufo de
VI ir a rebufo

tailgating ['teɪlgeɪtɪŋ] N • **~ is extremely dangerous** conducir a rebufo del coche de delante es muy peligroso

tail-gunner ['teɪl,gʌnəʳ] N artillero *m* de cola

tail-lamp ['teɪllæmp] = **tail-light**

tailless ['teɪllɪs] ADJ sin rabo

tail-light ['teɪllaɪt] N (*US*) piloto *m*, luz *f* trasera, calavera *f* (*Mex*)

tail-off ['teɪlɒf] N disminución *f* (paulatina)

tailor ['teɪləʳ] N sastre *m* • **~'s (shop)** sastrería *f*
VT [+ *suit*] confeccionar, hacer; (*fig*) adaptar • **a well-tailored suit** un traje bien hecho, un traje que entalla bien
CPD ▸ **tailor's chalk** jabón *m* de sastre ▸ **tailor's dummy** maniquí *m*

tailored ['teɪləd] ADJ (= *fitted*) [*shirt, jacket*] entallado; (= *tailor-made*) [*suit*] hecho a (la) medida

tailoring ['teɪlərɪŋ] N (= *craft*) sastrería *f*; (= *cut*) corte *m*, hechura *f*

tailor-made ['teɪləmeɪd] ADJ 1 [*suit*] hecho a (la) medida
2 (*fig*) (= *customized*) [*computer program*] hecho según los requisitos del usuario • **it's tailor-made for you** te viene al pelo • **the part could have been tailor-made for her** (*Theat*) parece que el papel se ha escrito para ella

tailor-make ['teɪlə'meɪk] VT diseñar a medida

tailpiece ['teɪlpiːs] N [*of violin*] cordal *m*; (= *addition*) apéndice *m*, añadidura *f*

tailpipe ['teɪlpaɪp] N (*US*) tubo *m* de escape

tailplane ['teɪlpleɪn] N (*Aer*) plano *m* de cola

tailskid ['teɪlskɪd] N patín *m* de cola

tailspin ['teɪlspɪn] N (*Aer*) barrena *f* • **the market went into a ~** (*St Ex*) el mercado cayó en picado *or* (*LAm*) picada

tailwheel ['teɪl'wiːl] N rueda *f* de cola

tailwind ['teɪlwɪnd] N viento *m* de cola

taint [teɪnt] N (*liter*) mancha *f*, mácula *f* (*liter*) • **the ~ of sin** la mancha del pecado
VT 1 (= *spoil*) [+ *food, medicine*] contaminar
2 (*fig*) [+ *reputation*] mancillar • **the elections have been ~ed by corruption** las elecciones se han visto empañadas *or* salpicadas por la corrupción

tainted ['teɪntɪd] ADJ 1 (= *contaminated*) [*food, air, blood, medicine*] contaminado • **her breath was ~ with alcohol** su aliento estaba corrompido por el alcohol
2 (= *tarnished*) [*reputation*] mancillado • **the issue is ~ with racism** el tema está contaminado de racismo

Taiwan [,taɪ'wɑːn] N Taiwán *m*

Taiwanese [,taɪwə'niːz] ADJ taiwanés
N taiwanés/esa *m/f*

Tajikistan [tɑːdʒɪkɪs'tɑːn] N Tayikistán *m*

take [teɪk] (VB: PT: **took**, PP: **taken**) VT
1 (= *remove*) llevarse; (= *steal*) robar, llevarse

• **who took my beer?** ¿quién se ha llevado mi cerveza? • **someone's ~n my handbag** alguien se ha llevado mi bolso, alguien me ha robado el bolso • **I picked up the letter but he took it from me** cogí la carta pero él me la quitó • **to ~ a book from a shelf** sacar un libro de un estante • **to ~ a passage from an author** tomar un pasaje de un autor • **~ 37 from 121** resta 37 de 121
2 (= *take hold of, seize*) tomar, coger, agarrar (*LAm*) • **she took the spade and started digging** cogió la pala y empezó a excavar • **I took him by the scruff of the neck** le cogí por el pescuezo • **let me ~ your case/coat** permíteme tu maleta/abrigo • **I'll ~ the blue one, please** me llevaré el azul • **to ~ sb's arm** tomar del brazo a algn • **to ~ sb in one's arms** abrazar a algn • **the devil ~ it!** ¡maldición!† • **~ five!*** ¡hagan una pausa!, ¡descansen un rato! • **~ your partners for a waltz** saquen a su pareja a bailar un vals • **to ~ sb into partnership** tomar a algn como socio • **please ~ a seat** tome asiento, por favor • **is this seat ~n?** ¿está ocupado este asiento? • **it took me by surprise** me cogió desprevenido, me pilló *or* agarró desprevenido (*LAm*) • **~ ten!** (*US**) ¡hagan una pausa!, ¡descansen un rato! • **to ~ a wife**† casarse, contraer matrimonio
3 (= *lead, transport*) llevar • **to ~ sth to sb** llevar algo a algn • **I took her some flowers** le llevé unas flores • **her work took her to Bonn** su trabajó la destinó *or* llevó a Bonn • **we took her to the doctor** la llevamos al médico • **he took me home in his car** me llevó a casa en su coche • **they took me over the factory** me mostraron la fábrica, me acompañaron en una visita a la fábrica • **he took his suitcase upstairs** subió su maleta • **to ~ sb for a walk** llevar a algn de paseo • **it took us out of our way** nos hizo desviarnos
4 [+ *bus, taxi*] (= *travel by*) ir en; (*at specified time*) coger, tomar (*esp LAm*); [+ *road, short cut*] ir por • **I took a taxi because I was late** fui en taxi porque llegaba tarde • **we decided to ~ the train** decidimos ir en tren • **we took the five o'clock train** cogimos *or* tomamos el tren de las cinco • **~ the first on the right** vaya por *or* tome la primera calle a la derecha • **we took the wrong road** nos equivocamos de camino
5 (= *capture*) [+ *person*] coger, agarrar (*LAm*); [+ *town, city*] tomar; (*Chess*) comer • **to ~ sb hostage** tomar *or* (*LAm*) agarrar a algn como rehén • **to ~ sb prisoner** tomar preso a algn
6 (= *obtain, win*) [+ *prize*] ganar, llevarse; [+ *1st place*] conseguir, obtener; [+ *trick*] ganar, hacer • **we took £500 today** (*Brit*) (*Comm*) hoy hemos ganado 500 libras
7 (= *accept, receive*) [+ *money*] aceptar; [+ *advice*] seguir; [+ *news, blow*] tomar, recibir; [+ *responsibility*] asumir; [+ *bet*] aceptar, hacer • **~ my advice, tell her the truth** sigue mi consejo *or* hazme caso y dile la verdad • **he took the ball full in the chest** el balón le dio de lleno en el pecho • **what will you ~ for it?** ¿cuál es tu mejor precio? • **he took it badly** le afectó mucho • **London took a battering in 1941** Londres recibió una paliza en 1941, Londres sufrió terriblemente en 1941 • **will you ~ a cheque?** ¿aceptaría un cheque? • **he can certainly ~ his drink** tiene buen aguante para la bebida • **you must ~ us as you find us** nos vas a tener que aceptar tal cual • **~ it from me!** ¡escucha lo que te digo! • **you can ~ it from me that …** puedes tener la seguridad de que … • **losing is hard to ~** es difícil aceptar la derrota • **it's £50, ~ it or leave it!** son 50 libras, lo toma o lo deja • **whisky? I can ~ it or leave it** ¿el whisky? ni me va ni me viene • **I won't ~ no for an answer** no hay pero que valga • **I ~ your point** entiendo lo que dices • **he took a lot of punishment** (*fig*) le dieron muy duro • **~ that!** ¡toma!
8 (= *rent*) alquilar, tomar; (= *buy regularly*) [+ *newspaper*] comprar, leer • **we shall ~ a house for the summer** alquilaremos una casa para el verano
9 (= *have room or capacity for*) tener cabida para; (= *support weight of*) aguantar • **a car that ~s five passengers** un coche con cabida para *or* donde caben cinco personas • **can you ~ two more?** ¿puedes llevar dos más?, ¿caben otros dos? • **it won't ~ any more** no cabe(n) más • **it ~s weights up to eight tons** soporta pesos hasta de ocho toneladas
10 (= *wear*) [+ *clothes size*] gastar, usar (*LAm*); [+ *shoe size*] calzar • **what size do you ~?** (*clothes*) ¿qué talla usas?; (*shoes*) ¿qué número calzas?
11 (= *call for, require*) necesitar, requerir • **it took three policemen to hold him down** se necesitaron tres policías para sujetarlo • **it ~s a lot of courage** exige *or* requiere gran valor • **it ~s a brave man to do that** hace falta que un hombre tenga mucho valor para hacer eso • **that will ~ some explaining** a ver cómo explicas eso • **it ~s two to make a quarrel** uno solo no puede reñir • **she's got what it ~s** tiene lo que hace falta
12 (*of time*) • **it ~s an hour to get there** se tarda una hora en llegar • **a letter ~s four days to get there** una carta tarda cuatro días en llegar allá • **it will only ~ me five minutes** solo tardo cinco minutos • **the job will ~ a week** el trabajo llevará una semana • **I'll just iron this, it won't ~ long** voy a planchar esto, no tardaré *or* no me llevará mucho tiempo • **however long it ~s** el tiempo que sea • **it ~s time** lleva tiempo • **~ your time!** ¡despacio!
13 (= *conduct*) [+ *meeting, church service*] presidir; (= *teach*) [+ *course, class*] enseñar; [+ *pupils*] tomar; (= *study*) [+ *course*] hacer; [+ *subject*] dar, estudiar; (= *undergo*) [+ *exam, test*] presentarse a, pasar • **what are you taking next year?** ¿qué vas a hacer *or* estudiar el año que viene? • **the teacher who took us for economics** el profesor que nos daba clase de económicas • **he is not taking any more pupils at the moment** en este momento no está cogiendo a más estudiantes • **to ~ a degree in** licenciarse en • **to ~ (holy) orders** ordenarse de sacerdote
14 (= *record*) [+ *sb's name, address*] anotar, apuntar; [+ *measurements*] tomar • **to ~ notes** tomar apuntes
15 (= *understand, assume*) • **I ~ it that …** supongo que …, me imagino que … • **am I to ~ it that you refused?** ¿he de suponer que te negaste? • **I ~ her to be about 30** supongo que tiene unos 30 años • **how old do you ~ him to be?** ¿cuántos años le das? • **I took him for a doctor** lo tenía por médico, creí que era médico • **what do you ~ me for?** ¿por quién me has tomado? • **I don't quite know how to ~ that** no sé muy bien cómo tomarme eso
16 (= *consider*) [+ *case, example*] tomar • **now ~ Ireland, for example** tomemos, por ejemplo, el caso de Irlanda, pongamos como ejemplo Irlanda • **let us ~ the example of a family with three children** tomemos el ejemplo de una familia con tres hijos • **~ John, he never complains** por ejemplo John, él nunca se queja • **taking one thing with another …** considerándolo todo junto …, considerándolo en conjunto …
17 (= *put up with, endure*) [+ *treatment, climate*] aguantar, soportar • **we can ~ it** lo aguantamos *or* soportamos todo • **I can't ~ any more!** ¡no aguanto más!, ¡no soporto más! • **I won't ~ any nonsense!** ¡no quiero oír más tonterías!
18 (= *eat*) comer; (= *drink*) tomar • **will you ~ sth before you go?** ¿quieres tomar algo antes de irte? • **"to be taken three times a day"** "a tomar tres veces al día" • **"not to be taken (internally)"** "para uso externo" • **to ~ drugs** (*narcotics*) tomar drogas • **he took no food for four days** estuvo cuatro días sin comer • **don't forget to ~ your medicine** no te olvides de tomar la medicina • **he ~s sugar in his tea** toma *or* pone azúcar en el té • **to ~ a tablet** tomar una pastilla • **to ~ tea (with sb)**† tomar té (con algn)
19 (= *negotiate*) [+ *bend*] tomar; [+ *fence*] saltar, saltar por encima de
20 (= *acquire*) • **to ~ against sb** • **~ a dislike to sb** tomar antipatía a algn • **to ~ fright** asustarse (**at** de) • **to be ~n ill** ponerse enfermo, enfermar • **he took great pleasure in teasing her** se regodeaba tomándole el pelo • **I do not ~ any satisfaction in knowing that …** no experimento satisfacción alguna sabiendo que …
21 (*Ling*) [+ *case*] regir • **that verb ~s the dative** ese verbo rige el dativo
22 • **to be ~n with sth/sb** (= *attracted*): • **he's very ~n with her** le gusta mucho • **I'm not at all ~n with the idea** la idea no me gusta nada *or* no me hace gracia
23† (*liter*) (= *have sexual intercourse with*) tener relaciones sexuales con
24 (*as function verb*) [+ *decision, holiday*] tomar; [+ *step, walk*] dar; [+ *trip*] hacer; [+ *opportunity*] aprovechar • **to ~ a bath** bañarse • **to ~ a photograph** sacar una fotografía
(VI) **1** (= *be effective*) [*dye*] coger, agarrar (*LAm*); [*vaccination, fire*] prender; [*glue*] pegar
2 (*Bot*) [*cutting*] arraigar
3 (= *receive*) • **she's all ~, ~, ~** ella mucho dame, dame, pero luego no da nada;
▹ **give**
(N) **1** (*Cine*) toma *f*
2 (= *takings*) ingresos *mpl*; (= *proceeds*) recaudación *f*; (*US*) (*Comm*) caja *f*, ventas *fpl* del día
3 • IDIOM: • **to be on the ~** (*US**) estar dispuesto a dejarse sobornar
4 (= *share*) parte *f*; (= *commission*) comisión *f*, tajada* *f*
5* (= *opinion*) opinión *f* • **what's your ~ on the new government?** ¿qué piensas de *or* qué opinión te merece el nuevo gobierno?
▸ **take aback** (VT + ADV) ▹ **aback**
▸ **take after** (VI + PREP) (*in looks*) parecerse a, salir a
▸ **take along** (VT + ADV) [+ *person, thing*] llevar (consigo)
▸ **take apart** (VT + ADV) **1** (= *dismantle*) [+ *clock, machine*] desmontar, desarmar
2* (= *destroy*) [+ *room, premises*] destrozar; (= *defeat*) [+ *opponent, team*] dar una paliza a* • **I'll ~ him apart!*** ¡le rompo la cara!
3 (= *search*) • **the police took the place apart** la policía registró el local de arriba abajo
(VI + ADV) • **it ~s apart easily** se desmonta fácilmente
▸ **take aside** (VT + ADV) llevar aparte, llevar a un lado
▸ **take away** (VT + ADV) **1** (= *remove*) [+ *person, thing*] llevarse; [+ *privilege*] quitar; (= *carry away, transport*) llevar • **she took her children**

away from the school sacó a los niños del colegio • **"not to be taken away"** (*on book*) "para consulta en sala"
2 (= *subtract*) restar • **~ 9 away from 12** reste 9 de 12 • **7 ~ away 4 is 3** 7 menos 4 son 3
(VI + ADV) • **to ~ away from sth: this does not ~ away from their achievement** esto no quita mérito *or* resta valor a su éxito • **the argument took away from the joy of the occasion** la discusión aguó la ocasión • **putting butter on it ~s away from the taste of the bread itself** añadiendo mantequilla se estropea lo que es el sabor del pan
▸ **take back** (VT + ADV) **1** (= *return*) [+ *book, goods*] devolver; [+ *person*] llevar (de vuelta) • **can you ~ him back home?** ¿le puedes acompañar a su casa?
2 (= *accept back*) [+ *purchase, gift*] aceptar la devolución de; [+ *one's wife, husband*] aceptar que vuelva • **the company took him back** la compañía volvió a emplearlo *or* lo restituyó a su puesto
3 (= *retract*) [+ *statement, words*] retirar • **she took back everything she had said about him** retiró todo lo que había dicho de él • **I ~ it all back!** ¡retiro lo dicho! • **to ~ back one's promise** retirar su promesa
4 (= *get back, reclaim*) [+ *territory*] retomar
5 (*fig*) (= *transport*) • **it ~s me back to my childhood** me recuerda a mi niñez • **it ~s you back, doesn't it?** ¡cuántos recuerdos (de los buenos tiempos)!
▸ **take down** (VT + ADV) **1** (*off shelf etc*) bajar; [+ *decorations, curtains*] quitar; [+ *picture*] descolgar, bajar; [+ *poster*] despegar; [+ *trousers*] bajar; ▹ **peg**
2 (= *dismantle*) [+ *scaffolding*] desmantelar, desmontar; [+ *building*] derribar
3 (= *write down*) apuntar
▸ **take from** (VT + PREP) = **take away from** ▹ **take away**
▸ **take in** (VT + ADV) **1** (= *bring in*) [+ *person*] hacer entrar; [+ *chairs, toys*] recoger, meter para dentro; [+ *harvest*] recoger; [+ *sail*] desmontar
2 (= *give home to*) [+ *orphan, stray dog*] acoger, recoger • **to ~ in lodgers** alquilar habitaciones
3 (= *receive*) [+ *laundry, sewing*] coger para hacer en casa
4 [+ *skirt, dress, waistband*] achicar
5 (= *include, cover*) [+ *possibilities, cases*] abarcar, incluir • **we took in Florence on the way** pasamos por Florencia en el camino • **to ~ in a movie*** ir al cine
6 (= *grasp, understand*) [+ *situation*] comprender; [+ *impressions*] asimilar; (*visually*) [+ *surroundings*] captar • **that child ~s everything in** a esa criatura no se le escapa nada • **it's so incredible you can't quite ~ it in** es tan increíble que es difícil de asimilar • **he took the situation in at a glance** comprendió la situación con una sola mirada
7 (= *deceive, cheat*) engañar • **to be ~n in by appearances** dejarse engañar por las apariencias
▸ **take off** (VT + ADV) **1** (= *remove*) [+ *lid, wrapping, label, stain*] quitar; [+ *clothes*] quitarse, sacarse (*LAm*); [+ *limb*] amputar; [+ *train*] cancelar; [+ *item from menu*] quitar • **the five o'clock train has been ~n off** han cancelado el tren de las cinco
2 (= *deduct*) (*from bill, price*) descontar • **she took 50p off** descontó *or* hizo un descuento de 50 peniques
3 (= *lead away*) [+ *person, object*] llevarse • **they took him off to lunch** se lo llevaron a comer • **she was ~n off to hospital** la llevaron al hospital • **to ~ o.s. off** irse, largarse*
4 (= *not work*) • **he took the day off work** se tomó el día libre • **I'm going to ~ two weeks off at Christmas** me voy a tomar dos semanas de vacaciones en Navidad • **he has to work weekends but ~s time off in lieu** tiene que trabajar los fines de semana pero le dan días libres a cambio
5 (= *imitate*) imitar
(VI + ADV) **1** [*plane, passengers*] despegar, decolar (*LAm*) (**for** con rumbo a); [*high jumper*] saltar
2 (= *succeed*) empezar a tener éxito • **the idea never really took off** la idea no llegó a cuajar • **the style really took off among young people** el estilo se puso muy de moda entre los jóvenes
(VT + PREP) **1** (= *remove*) quitar, sacar (*LAm*) • **they took two names off the list** quitaron *or* tacharon dos nombres de la lista • **she's been ~n off the case** le han hecho dejar el caso • **to ~ sth off sb*** quitar algo a algn • **~ your hands off me!** ¡no me toques! • **her new hairstyle ~s ten years off her** ese peinado nuevo le quita diez años de encima
2 (= *deduct*) (*from bill, price*) descontar • **he took £5 off the price** descontó 5 libras del precio
▸ **take on** (VT + ADV) **1** [+ *work*] aceptar, encargarse de; [+ *responsibility, risk*] asumir; [+ *bet, challenge*] aceptar; [+ *challenger*] enfrentarse a, aceptar el reto de • **when she invited Hayley to come and stay for a week she took on more than she bargained for** cuando invitó a Hayley a quedarse una semana, no sabía lo que le esperaba • **I felt I could ~ on the whole world** sentía que me podía comer el mundo
2 [+ *worker*] contratar; [+ *passengers*] recoger; [+ *cargo*] cargar
3 (= *assume*) [+ *form, qualities*] asumir • **her face took on a wistful expression** quedó cariacontecida
(VI + ADV) **1**†* (= *become upset*) • **don't ~ on so!** ¡no te pongas así!, ¡no te agites!
2 (= *become popular*) [*fashion*] hacerse muy popular; [*song*] hacerse muy popular, ponerse de moda
▸ **take out** (VT + ADV) **1** (= *bring, carry out*) sacar • **he took the dog out for a walk** sacó el perro a pasear • **can I ~ you out to lunch/the cinema?** ¿le puedo invitar a almorzar/al cine?
2 (= *remove*) (*gen*) sacar; [+ *tooth*] extraer, sacar; [+ *stain*] quitar, limpiar; (*Mil*) [+ *target, enemy position*] eliminar
3 (= *procure*) [+ *patent, licence*] obtener; [+ *insurance policy*] sacar • **to ~ out insurance** hacerse un seguro
4 • **to ~ it out on sb: when he got the sack he took it out on his wife** cuando le despidieron del trabajo, se desquitó con su mujer • **don't ~ it out on me!** ¡no te desquites conmigo!
5 • **to ~ out of: seeing that film took me out of myself** esa película me hizo olvidar mis propios problemas • **it ~s it out of you** te deja hecho pedazos*
▸ **take over** (VT + ADV) **1** (= *assume*) [+ *responsibility*] asumir; (= *become responsible for*) [+ *job*] encargarse de • **he took over the business from his father** se hizo cargo del negocio cuando lo dejó su padre • **to ~ over sb's job** sustituir a algn
2 (= *take control of*) [+ *building, country*] tomar; (*Econ*) [+ *company*] adquirir • **the tourists have ~n over the beaches** los turistas han invadido *or* acaparado las playas
(VI + ADV) **1** (= *take charge*) [*new president, official*] entrar en funciones; (*Aut*) [*driver*] tomar el volante; (*Aer*) [*pilot*] tomar los mandos • **when the new government ~s over** cuando el nuevo gobierno entre en poder • **to ~ over from sb** (*in job*) (*temporarily*) hacer de suplente para algn; (*permanently*) reemplazar a algn • **they want me to ~ over as editor when Evans leaves** quieren que reemplace a Evans como editor cuando este marche • **can you ~ over for a few minutes, while I go to the Post Office?** ¿puedes cubrirme unos minutos mientras voy a Correos?
2 (= *seize control*) [*dictator, political party*] tomar el poder
3 (= *become more important*) • **then panic took over** luego cundió el pánico • **cars gradually took over from horses** poco a poco el automóvil fue sustituyendo al caballo
▸ **take to** (VI + PREP) **1** (= *form liking for*) [+ *person*] tomar cariño a algn, encariñarse con algn; [+ *sport*] aficionarse a; [+ *surroundings, idea*] hacerse a • **she didn't ~ kindly to the idea** no le gustó *or* no le hizo gracia la idea • **they took to one another on the spot** se congeniaron al instante • **I didn't much ~ to him** no me resultó simpático
2 (= *form habit of*) • **to ~ to doing sth: she took to inviting them round every Sunday** empezó a invitarles a casa todos los domingos • **she took to telling everyone that ...** le dio por contar a todos que ...
3 (= *escape to*) • **to ~ to one's bed** guardar cama • **to ~ to drink** darse a la bebida; ▹ **heel[1], hill, wood**
▸ **take up** (VT + ADV) **1** (= *raise, lift*) [+ *object from ground*] levantar, recoger; [+ *carpet, floorboards*] quitar; [+ *road*] levantar; [+ *dress, hem*] acortar; ▹ **arm[2], slack**
2 (= *lead, carry upstairs*) subir
3 (= *pick up*) [+ *pen, one's work*] coger, agarrar (*LAm*); [+ *passengers*] recoger
4 (= *continue*) [+ *story*] continuar con
5 (= *occupy*) [+ *time, attention*] ocupar; [+ *space*] llenar, ocupar • **it ~s up a lot of his time** le dedica mucho tiempo • **he's very ~n up with his work** está absorto en el trabajo • **he's very ~n up with her** está ocupado con ella; ▹ **post[3], residence**
6 (= *absorb*) [+ *liquid*] absorber
7 (= *raise question of*) [+ *matter, point*] retomar, volver sobre • **I shall ~ the matter up with the manager** hablaré del asunto con el gerente
8 (= *take issue with*) • **I feel I must ~ you up on that** siento que debo contestar a lo que has dicho
9 (= *start*) [+ *hobby, sport*] dedicarse a; [+ *career*] emprender
10 (= *accept*) [+ *offer, challenge*] aceptar • **I'll ~ you up on your offer** te acepto la oferta • **I'll ~ you up on that some day** algún día recordaré lo que has dicho
11 (= *adopt*) [+ *cause*] apoyar; [+ *case*] ocuparse de; [+ *person*] adoptar
(VI + ADV) • **to ~ up with sb** (*as friend*) hacerse amigo de algn; (*romantically*) juntarse con algn • **he took up with a woman half his wife's age** se juntó con una mujer que tenía la mitad de la edad de su mujer
▸ **take upon** (VT + PREP) • **to ~ sth upon o.s.** tomar algo sobre sí • **to ~ it upon o.s. to do sth** atreverse a hacer algo

t

TAKE

Both **tardar** *and* **llevar** *can be used to translate* **take** *with time.*

▹ *Use* **tardar** *(***en** *+ infinitive) to describe how long someone or something will take to do something. The subject of* **tardar** *is the person or thing that has to complete the activity or undergo the process:*

How long do letters take to get to Spain?
¿Cuánto (tiempo) tardan las cartas en llegar a España?
How much longer will it take you to do it?
¿Cuánto más vas a tardar en hacerlo?
It'll take us three hours to get to Douglas if we walk
Tardaremos tres horas en llegar a Douglas si vamos andando

▹ *Use* **llevar** *to describe how long an activity, task or process takes to complete. The subject of* **llevar** *is the activity or task:*

The tests will take at least a month
Las pruebas llevarán por lo menos un mes
How long will it take?
¿Cuánto tiempo llevará?

▹ *Compare the different focus in the alternative translations of the following example:*

It'll take me two more days to finish this job
Me llevará dos días más terminar este trabajo, Tardaré dos días más en terminar este trabajo

For further uses and examples, see main entry.

takeaway ['teɪkəweɪ] (N) **1** (= *restaurant*) tienda *f* de comida para llevar
2 (= *meal*) comida *f* para llevar • **we decided to order a Chinese ~** decidimos pedir una comida china para llevar
(ADJ) [*food*] para llevar

take-home pay [ˌteɪkhəʊm'peɪ] (N) sueldo *m* neto, sueldo *m* líquido

taken ['teɪkən] (PP) *of* **take**

takeoff ['teɪkɒf] (N) **1** (*Aer, Econ*) despegue *m*
2 (= *imitation*) imitación *f*, parodia *f*
3 (*Mech*) • **power ~** toma *f* de fuerza

takeout ['teɪkaʊt] (US) (N) **1** (= *restaurant*) tienda *f* de comida para llevar
2 (= *meal*) comida *f* para llevar
(ADJ) [*food, meal*] para llevar

takeover ['teɪkˌəʊvəʳ] (N) **1** (*Comm*) [*of company*] adquisición *f*, compra *f*
2 (*Pol*) [*of new government*] toma *f* de posesión; [*of new premier*] entrada *f* en funciones
3 (*Mil*) (= *coup*) toma *f* del poder • **military ~** golpe *m* de estado
(CPD) ▸ **takeover bid** oferta *f* pública de adquisición (de acciones), OPA *f*

taker ['teɪkəʳ] (N) • **at £5 there were no ~s** a un precio de 5 libras nadie se ofreció a comprarlo • **the challenge found no ~s** no hubo nadie que quisiera aceptar el desafío

take-up ['teɪkʌp] (N) (*Brit*) • **this benefit has a low take-up rate** muy poca gente reclama esta prestación • **there was an enthusiastic public take-up of shares in privatized companies** hubo muchísima demanda para comprar acciones en las empresas privatizadas

taking ['teɪkɪŋ] (ADJ) (= *attractive*) atractivo
(N) (*Mil*) [*of town*] toma *f*, conquista *f*; [*of hostages*] toma *f* • **the job's yours for the ~** el trabajo es tuyo si lo quieres • **the match was theirs for the ~** tenían el partido prácticamente ganado

takings ['teɪkɪŋz] (*Brit*) (NPL) (*Comm*) recaudación *fsing*; (*at show*) taquilla *fsing*, entrada *fsing* • **this year's ~ were only half last year's** la recaudación de este año ha sido solo la mitad que la del año pasado

talc [tælk] (N) talco *m*

talcum powder ['tælkəmˌpaʊdəʳ] (N) polvos *mpl* de talco, talco *m*

tale [teɪl] (N) **1** (= *story*) cuento *m*, historia *f* • **he told us the ~ of his adventures** nos contó sus aventuras • **he had quite a ~ to tell** vaya historia que tenía para contar • **it tells its own ~** habla por sí solo • **"Tales of King Arthur"** "Leyendas *fpl* del Rey Arturo" • **sound the alarm, or we shan't live to tell the ~** toca el timbre, o no salimos vivos de esto, toca el timbre, o no lo contamos • **few people get caught in an avalanche and live to tell the ~** muy poca gente sobrevive una avalancha; ▹ **fairy, hang, woe**
2 (= *fabrication*) cuento *m*, patraña *f* • IDIOM: • **to tell ~s (out of school)** (= *inform*) chivarse, chismear; (= *fib*) contar cuentos; ▹ **old**

Taleban ['tælɪbæn] (NPL), (ADJ) = **Taliban**

talebearer ['teɪlˌbɛərəʳ] (N) soplón/ona *m/f*, chismoso/a *m/f*

talent ['tælənt] (N) **1** (= *natural ability*) talento *m* (**for** para) • **a writer of great ~** un escritor de muchísimo talento • **to have a ~ for sth: he's got a real ~ for languages** tiene verdadera facilidad para los idiomas • **she had a ~ for making people laugh** tenía el don de saber hacer reír a la gente
2 (= *talented people*) gente *f* capaz, gente *f* de talento; (= *talented person*) talento *m* • **he encourages young ~** promociona a los jóvenes talentos • **he watches for ~ at away matches** busca jugadores de talento en los partidos fuera de casa
3* (= *opposite sex*) tíos/as *mpl/fpl* buenos/as*, material* • **there's not much ~ here tonight** aquí no hay mucho donde escoger esta noche, aquí no hay material* • **to eye up the ~** pasar revista a lo que se ofrece*, comprobar el material*
4 (*Hist*) (= *coin, weight*) talento *m*
(CPD) ▸ **talent contest** concurso *m* de talentos ▸ **talent scout, talent spotter** cazatalentos *mf inv* ▸ **talent show** concurso *m* de talentos • **he began his musical career in ~ shows** comenzó su carrera musical en concursos de talentos

talented ['tæləntɪd] (ADJ) talentoso, de talento

talentless ['tæləntləs] (ADJ) sin talento

taletelling ['teɪlˌtelɪŋ] (N) chismorreo *m*

Taliban ['tælɪbæn] (NPL) • **the ~** los talibanes
(ADJ) talibán/ana

talisman ['tælɪzmən] (N) (PL: **talismans**) talismán *m*

talismanic [ˌtælɪz'mænɪk] (ADJ) (*lit, fig*) talismánico • **without their ~ leader they seemed destined to play badly** sin su líder y talismán, parecían condenados a jugar mal

talk [tɔːk] (N) **1** (= *conversation*) conversación *f*, charla *f*, plática *f* (*Mex*) • **I enjoyed our (little) ~** disfruté de nuestra (pequeña) conversación *or* charla • **to have a ~ (with sb)** hablar (con algn), tener una conversación (con algn) • **I think it's time we had a ~** creo que es hora de que hablemos (seriamente) • **we had a long ~ over supper** hablamos largo y tendido durante la cena
2 (= *lecture*) charla *f* • **to give a ~ (on sth)** dar una charla (sobre algo)
3 talks (= *negotiations*) (*gen*) conversaciones *fpl*, pláticas *fpl* (*Mex*); (*with defined aim*) negociaciones *fpl* • **the foreign secretary will be holding ~s with his French counterpart** el ministro de asuntos exteriores mantendrá conversaciones con su homólogo francés
4 (= *rumours*) rumores *mpl* • **there is some ~ of his resigning** se habla de *or* corren rumores sobre su posible dimisión • **there's been a lot of ~ about you two** se ha hablado mucho de vosotros dos, están circulando muchos rumores acerca de vosotros dos • **any ~ of divorce is just wild speculation** cualquier rumor acerca de un divorcio no es más que pura especulación • IDIOM: • **to be the ~ of the town** ser la comidilla de la ciudad, estar en boca de todos
5 (= *remarks*) • **that's the kind of ~ we could do without** esos comentarios sobran • **careless ~ costs lives** las palabras dichas a la ligera cuestan vidas; ▹ **small**
6 (= *speech, language*) lenguaje *m* • **children's ~** lenguaje *m* infantil *or* de niños
7 (= *hot air*) (*pej*) palabrería *f*, cuento *m* • **it's just ~** es pura palabrería, es todo cuento • **he'll never give up smoking, he's all ~** nunca va a dejar de fumar, mucho hablar pero luego nada *or* no es más que un cuentista • **he's all ~ and no action** ¿ése? ¡mucho ruido y pocas nueces!, habla mucho pero no hace nada
(VI) **1** (= *speak*) hablar • **she can't ~ yet** aún no sabe hablar • **can you ~ a little more slowly?** ¿podría hablar un poquito más despacio? • **a doll that can ~** una muñeca que habla • **it's easy for you to ~** para ti es fácil hablar • **he ~s too much** habla demasiado • **she never stops ~ing** no deja *or* para de hablar • **I wasn't ~ing about you** no hablaba de ti • **he doesn't know what he's ~ing about** no sabe de qué habla • **everyone's ~ing about him** anda en boca de todos • **it's the most ~ed-about film this year** es la película más comentada del año • **we're ~ing about a potentially enormous loss here** estamos hablando de una pérdida potencialmente enorme • **~ about rich! he's absolutely loaded*** ¡vaya que si es rico! ¡está forrado!* • **~ about a stroke of luck!*** ¡qué suerte! • **to ~ big** (*fig*) darse importancia, fanfarronear • **"and she's so untidy around the house" — "you can ~!** *or* **look who's ~ing!"** —y además, es tan desordenada en casa —¡mira quién habla! *or* —¡mira quién fue a hablar! • **now you're ~ing!** ¡así se habla! • **~ing of films, have you seen ...?** hablando de películas, ¿has visto ...? • **don't ~ to your mother like that!** ¡no le hables así a tu madre! • **I'm not ~ing to him any more** ya no me hablo con él • **the way you ~ you'd think this was all my fault!** ¡oyéndote hablar cualquiera diría que toda la culpa es mía! • IDIOMS: • **money ~s** poderoso caballero es don dinero, el dinero todo lo puede • **~ of the devil!** ¡hablando del rey de Roma...! • **to ~ through one's hat** decir tonterías; ▹ **dirty**
2 (= *converse*) hablar, platicar (*Mex*) (**to** con) • **we ~ed all night** nos pasamos toda la noche hablando • **I was only ~ing to her last week** si justo estuve hablando con ella la semana pasada • **stop ~ing!** ¡callaos!, ¡dejad de hablar! • **she had no one to ~ to** no tenía con quién hablar • **who were you ~ing to on the phone just now?** ¿con quién hablabas (por teléfono) ahora mismo? • **were you ~ing to me?** ¿me hablas a mí? • **to ~ to o.s.** hablar solo • **to ~ about sth/sb** hablar de algo/algn • **they ~ed about old times** hablaron de los viejos tiempos • **I don't want to ~ about it** no quiero hablar de ello • **the sort of person who ~s at you rather than to you** el tipo de persona que habla mucho pero no escucha nada • **to get ~ing**

t

ponerse a hablar, entablar conversación • **to keep sb ~ing** dar charla a algn para entretenerlo, entretener a algn hablando • **it was easy to ~ with her** era fácil hablar con ella
3 (= *have discussion*) hablar, hablar seriamente • **we really need to ~** tenemos que hablar (seriamente) • **the two sides need to sit down and ~** las dos partes necesitan reunirse para hablar (seriamente) • **GA and Fox Ltd might be ~ing** puede que GA y Fox Ltd estén manteniendo negociaciones • **to ~ (to sb) about sth** discutir algo (con algn) • **the two companies are ~ing about a possible merger** las dos empresas están discutiendo *or* negociando una posible fusión
4 (= *gossip*) hablar (**about** de) • **people will ~** la gente hablará *or* murmurará
5 (= *lecture*) dar una charla, hablar (**about, on** de, sobre) • **he'll be ~ing on his life in India** dará una charla sobre su vida en la India, hablará de *or* sobre su vida en la India
6 (= *reveal information*) hablar • **we have ways of making you ~** sabemos cómo hacerle hablar
(VT) **1** (= *speak*) hablar • **they were ~ing Arabic** hablaban (en) árabe • **we're ~ing big money here*** estamos hablando de mucho dinero • **she ~ed herself hoarse** habló tanto que se quedó afónica • **to ~ nonsense** • **~ rubbish** decir tonterías • **to ~ sense** hablar con juicio *or* sensatez • IDIOM: • **to ~ the hind legs off a donkey** hablar por los codos*
2 (= *discuss*) hablar de • **we were ~ing politics/business** hablábamos de política/negocios • IDIOM: • **to ~ shop** hablar del trabajo
3 (= *persuade*) • **to ~ sb into doing sth** convencer a algn de que haga algo • **I was a fool to have let her ~ me into it** fui idiota por dejarle convencerme • **ok! you've ~ed me into it** ¡vale! me has convencido • **I ~ed myself into believing it** yo solo me terminé convenciendo de que era cierto • **to ~ sb out of doing sth** convencer a algn de que no haga algo, disuadir a algn de que haga algo • **we managed to ~ him out of it** conseguimos convencerle de que no lo hiciera, conseguimos disuadirle de que lo hiciera • **he performed so badly in the interview he ~ed himself out of the job** habló tan mal en la entrevista que consiguió que no le dieran el puesto • **he managed to ~ his way out of a prison sentence** habló de tal manera que no le condenaron a pena de cárcel
(CPD) ▸ **talk radio** radio *f* hablada ▸ **talk show** (*Rad, TV*) programa *m* de entrevistas ▸ **talk time** (*on mobile phone*) tiempo *m* de conversación
▸ **talk around** (VT + ADV) (= *persuade*) convencer • **he went to the house to try to ~ her around** fue a la casa para intentar convencerla
▸ **talk back** (VI + ADV) (*gen*) replicar • **this is where voters get the chance to ~ back** ahora es cuando los votantes tienen la oportunidad de replicar; (*rudely*) • **how dare you ~ back to me?** ¿cómo te atreves a replicarme *or* llevarme la contraria? • **he's very good - he never ~s back** es muy bueno - no es nada respondón
▸ **talk down** (VI + ADV) • **to ~ down to sb** hablar con aires de superioridad a algn
(VT + ADV) **1** (= *help to land*) [+ *pilot*] dirigir por radio el aterrizaje a
2 (= *dissuade from jumping*) [+ *suicidal person*] disuadir (*para que no salte*)
3 (*esp Brit*) (*Econ*) [+ *currency, shares*] hacer bajar; (*in deal*) • **I ~ed him down another thousand** hice que rebajara el precio otras mil libras
4 (= *denigrate*) menospreciar
5 (= *interrupt remorselessly*) hacer callar
▸ **talk on** (VI + ADV) no parar de hablar
▸ **talk out** (VT + ADV) **1** (= *discuss thoroughly*) • **to ~ it/things out** hablar detenidamente de ello/la situación
2 (*Parl*) • **to ~ out a bill** *alargar el debate para que no dé tiempo a votar un proyecto de ley*
▸ **talk over** (VT + ADV) (= *discuss*) hablar, discutir • **let's ~ it/things over** vamos a hablarlo *or* discutirlo • **to ~ sth over with sb** consultar algo con algn
▸ **talk round** (VT + ADV) (*esp Brit*) (= *persuade*) convencer • **he went to the house to try to ~ her round** fue a la casa para intentar convencerla
▸ **talk through** (VT + ADV) (= *discuss*) [+ *plan, problem*] discutir detenidamente
(VT + PREP) (= *explain*) • **to ~ sb through sth** explicar algo a algn
▸ **talk up** (VI + ADV) (*US*) (= *speak frankly*) hablar claro *or* sin rodeos
(VT + ADV) **1** (= *exaggerate*) exagerar
2 (*Econ*) [+ *economy*] inflar; [+ *shares*] inflar la cotización de, inflar el valor de
3 (*esp Brit*) (*in deal*) • **to ~ sb up** hacer que algn mejore la oferta • **try to ~ him up to 50,000** intenta que mejore su oferta a 50.000

talkative [ˈtɔːkətɪv] (ADJ) hablador, platicón (*Mex*) • **he became quite ~** habló mucho • **she wasn't very ~ at breakfast** estuvo bastante callada durante el desayuno
talkativeness [ˈtɔːkətɪvnɪs] (N) locuacidad *f*
talkboard [ˈtɔːkbɔːd] (N) foro *m* de discusión
talked-of [ˈtɔːktɒv] (ADJ) • **a much talked-of event** un suceso muy comentado
talker [ˈtɔːkəʳ] (N) hablador(a) *m/f* • **to be a good ~** hablar con soltura, tener una conversación amena • **I'm not much of a ~** no soy buen conversador • **he's just a ~** se le va la fuerza por la boca
talkfest* [ˈtɔːkfest] (N) (*US*) cháchara* *f*
talkie [ˈtɔːkɪ] (N) película *f* sonora • **the ~s** el cine sonoro
talking [ˈtɔːkɪŋ] (ADJ) [*bird, doll*] que habla
(N) • **we could hear ~ downstairs** oíamos a algn hablando abajo • **she does all the ~** ella es quien habla siempre • **I'll do the ~** yo seré el que hable • **no ~, please!** ¡silencio, por favor!
(CPD) ▸ **talking book** audiolibro *m* ▸ **talking head** (*TV*) busto *m* parlante* ▸ **talking newspaper** periódico *m* grabado (en cinta) ▸ **talking picture** película *f* sonora ▸ **talking point** tema *m* de conversación ▸ **talking shop** (*esp Brit*) reunión *f* donde se habla mucho pero no se hace nada
talking-to [ˈtɔːkɪŋtuː] (N) • **I gave him a good talking-to** le llamé al orden, le leí la cartilla • **that boy needs a good talking-to** a ese chico le hace falta que le lean la cartilla
tall [tɔːl] (ADJ) (COMPAR: **taller**, SUPERL: **tallest**) alto • **he's very ~ for his age** es *or* está muy alto para su edad • **a six-foot ~ man** ≈ un hombre de uno ochenta • **how ~ are you?** ¿cuánto mides?, ¿qué altura tienes? • **I'm 1.6 metres ~** mido 1,60m (de alto) • **he's not as ~ as me** no es tan alto como yo • **she's ~er than me** es más alta que yo, mide más que yo • **she's 5cm ~er than me** • **she's ~er than me by 5cm** es cinco centímetros más alta que yo, mide cinco centímetros más que yo, me saca cinco centímetros • **it's the ~est building in Europe** es el edificio más alto *or* de más altura de Europa • **to get** *or* **grow ~er** crecer, ponerse más alto; ▷ **stand, walk**
(CPD) ▸ **tall order*** • **it's a bit of a ~ order, but we'll try** no es fácil, pero lo intentaremos • **it was a ~ order to expect us to finish in three days** esperar que terminásemos en tres días era mucho pedir* ▸ **tall ship** gran velero *m* ▸ **tall story*** cuento *m* chino*
tallboy [ˈtɔːlbɔɪ] (N) (*Brit*) cómoda *f* alta
tallish [ˈtɔːlɪʃ] (ADJ) [*person, building*] bastante alto
tallness [ˈtɔːlnɪs] (N) altura *f*
tallow [ˈtæləʊ] (N) sebo *m*
tallowy [ˈtæləʊɪ] (ADJ) seboso
tally [ˈtælɪ] (N) **1** (= *running total, score*) cuenta *f*, total *m* • **to keep a ~ of** llevar la cuenta de
2 (= *stick*) tarja *f*
(VI) [*stories, accounts*] concordar, coincidir (**with** con)
(VT) (*also* **tally up**) contar, hacer recuento de
(CPD) ▸ **tally clerk** medidor(a) *m/f*
tallyho [ˈtælɪˈhəʊ] (EXCL) ¡hala! (*grito del cazador de zorras*)
Talmud [ˈtælmʊd] (N) Talmud *m*
Talmudic [tælˈmʊdɪk] (ADJ) talmúdico
talon [ˈtælən] (N) garra *f*
tamable [ˈteɪməbl] (ADJ) domable, domesticable
tamale [təˈmɑːlɪ] (N) tamal *m*
tamarind [ˈtæmərɪnd] (N) tamarindo *m*
tamarisk [ˈtæmərɪsk] (N) tamarisco *m*
tambour [ˈtæmbʊəʳ] (N) tambor *m*
tambourine [ˌtæmbəˈriːn] (N) pandereta *f*
Tamburlaine [ˈtæmbəˌleɪn] (N) Tamerlán
tame [teɪm] (ADJ) (COMPAR: **tamer**, SUPERL: **tamest**) **1** (= *no longer wild*) [*lion, tiger*] domesticado, manso; [*hedgehog, fox*] dócil, manso • **do you know of a ~ plumber who can fix it?** (*hum*) ¿sabes de un fontanero fiable que lo pueda arreglar?
2 (= *boring*) [*book, film, match, performance*] soso, insulso • **the report was pretty ~ stuff** el informe era bastante anodino • **these films are ~ by today's standards** estas películas resultan poco atrevidas para los tiempos que corren
(VT) [+ *lion, tiger*] domar, amansar; [+ *passion*] dominar • **no man could ~ her** no había hombre que pudiese domarla
tamely [ˈteɪmlɪ] (ADV) dócilmente
tameness [ˈteɪmnɪs] (N) **1** [*of lion, tiger*] mansedumbre *f*; [*of hedgehog, fox*] docilidad *f*, mansedumbre *f*
2 [*of person*] sosería *f*; [*of book, film*] (= *lacking excitement*) sosería *f*; (= *lacking sex, violence*) falta *f* de atrevimiento
tamer [ˈteɪməʳ] (N) domador(a) *m/f*
Tamil [ˈtæmɪl] (ADJ) tamil
(N) tamil *mf*
taming [ˈteɪmɪŋ] (N) domadura *f* • **"the Taming of the Shrew"** "la fierecilla domada"
tam o' shanter [ˌtæməˈʃæntəʳ] (N) boina *f* escocesa
tamp [tæmp] (VT) (*also* **tamp down, tamp in**) apisonar; (*Min*) (*in blasting*) atacar
Tampax® [ˈtæmpæks] (N) tampax® *m*, támpax *m*
tamper [ˈtæmpəʳ] (VI) • **to ~ with** (= *interfere with*) [+ *machinery, brakes etc*] manipular; [+ *lock*] tratar de forzar; (= *alter*) [+ *papers, evidence*] falsificar; (= *attempt to influence*) [+ *witness, jury*] sobornar; (= *handle*) manosear • **my car had been ~ed with** algo se había hecho a mi coche
tamper-proof [ˈtæmpəpruːf] (ADJ) inviolable
tampon [ˈtæmpən] (N) tampón *m*
tan [tæn] (N) **1** (= *suntan*) bronceado *m* • **to get a tan** broncearse
2 (= *colour*) canela *f*, café *m* claro (*esp LAm*)

3 (= *bark*) (*also* **tanbark**) casca *f*
ADJ color canela, color café claro (*esp LAm*); [*shoes*] marrón
VI [*person*] broncearse, ponerse moreno, tostarse
VT **1** [+ *person, skin*] broncear, poner moreno (*esp Sp*), quemar (*LAm*)
2 [+ *leather*] curtir • IDIOM: • **to tan sb's hide*** curtir a algn a palos*, zurrarle la badana a algn (*Sp**)

tandem ['tændəm] N (= *bicycle*) tándem *m*
ADV • **in ~** [*work, function*] conjuntamente • **the two systems will run in ~** los dos sistemas funcionarán conjuntamente *or* en tándem • **the two plays were written in ~** las dos obras fueron escritas simultáneamente • **in ~ with** conjuntamente con • **to ride ~** montar en un tándem

tandoori [ˌtæn'dʊərɪ] N tandoori *m*, *horno de la cocina hindú en el que se cocinan muchos platos tradicionales* • **a chicken ~** un pollo tandoori
ADJ tandoori • **a ~ oven** un horno *m* tandoori • **a ~ chicken** un pollo tandoori

tang [tæŋ] N **1** (= *taste*) sabor *m* fuerte y picante; (= *smell*) olor *m* acre • **the salt ~ of the sea air** el olor salobre de la brisa marina
2 [*of knife*] espiga *f*

tanga ['tæŋgə] N (= *bikini bottoms, briefs*) tanga *m*

tangent ['tændʒənt] N (*Geom*) tangente *f* • IDIOM: • **to go** *or* **fly off at a ~** salirse por la tangente

tangential [tæn'dʒenʃəl] ADJ tangencial

tangentially [tæn'dʒenʃəlɪ] ADV (= *indirectly*) tangencialmente • **the question was only touched on ~** el asunto solo fue abordado tangencialmente

tangerine [ˌtændʒə'ri:n] N mandarina *f*, tangerina *f*

tangibility [ˌtændʒɪ'bɪlɪtɪ] N tangibilidad *f*

tangible ['tændʒəbl] ADJ [*object*] tangible; [*difference, proof, evidence*] tangible, palpable • **~ assets** bienes *mpl* tangibles, inmovilizado *msing* material

tangibly ['tændʒəblɪ] ADV [*demonstrate, show*] de modo palpable • **it is ~ different** la diferencia es tangible *or* palpable

Tangier [tæn'dʒɪəʳ], **Tangiers** [tæn'dʒɪəz] N Tánger *m*

tangle ['tæŋgl] N (*in hair*) enredo *m*, maraña *f*; [*of streets*] laberinto *m*; (*fig*) (= *muddle*) enredo *m*, lío *m* • **a ~ of weeds** una maraña de malas hierbas • **a ~ of wool** una maraña de lana • **to be in a ~** [*hair, thread*] estar enredado • **the sheets were in a ~** las sábanas estaban hechas una maraña • **I'm in a ~ with the accounts** me he hecho un lío con las cuentas* • **to get into a ~** [*hair, thread*] enredarse • **I got into a ~ with the police** me metí en un lío con la policía
VT (*also* **tangle up**) enredar, enmarañar
VI (*also* **tangle up**) enredarse, enmarañarse • **to ~ with sth/sb*** (*fig*) meterse en algo/con algn

tangled ['tæŋgld] ADJ [*hair, wool*] enredado, enmarañado; (*fig*) enmarañado, complicado

tango ['tæŋgəʊ] N (PL: **tangos**) tango *m*
VI bailar el tango • IDIOM: • **it takes two to ~*** es cosa de dos

tangy ['tæŋɪ] ADJ fuerte y picante

tank [tæŋk] N **1** (= *container*) (*for liquid*) tanque *m*, depósito *m*; (*large*) cisterna *f*; (*Aut*) depósito *m* (*Sp*), tanque *m* (*esp LAm*) • **fuel ~** depósito *m* (de combustible) • **fish ~** acuario *m* • **petrol** *or* (*US*) **gas ~** depósito *m* (de gasolina) • **water ~** (*for village, in house*) depósito *m* de agua; (*on lorry*) cisterna *f*; ▹ **septic, think**
2 (*also* **tankful**) (= *quantity*) depósito *m*
3 (*Mil*) tanque *m*, carro *m* (de combate)
4 (*Phot*) (*also* **developing tank**) cubeta *f* de revelado
5 (*also* **swimming tank**) (*US*) piscina *f*, alberca *f* (*Mex*), pileta *f* (de natación) (*S. Cone*)
6 (*US‡*) (= *jail*) cárcel *f*, chirona *f* (*Sp**)
CPD ▸ **tank car** (*US*) vagón *m* cisterna ▸ **tank engine** locomotora *f* ténder ▸ **tank top** chaleco *m* cerrado ▸ **tank truck** (*US*) camión *m* cisterna ▸ **tank wagon** (*Rail*) vagón *m* cisterna; (*Aut*) camión *m* cisterna
▸ **tank along*** VI + ADV ir a toda pastilla*
▸ **tank up** VI + ADV (*with fuel*) llenar el tanque (**with** de); (*with alcohol**) emborracharse (**on** bebiendo)

tankard ['tæŋkəd] N bock *m*, pichel *m*

tanked* [tæŋkt] ADJ (*Brit*) • **to be ~** estar borracho

tanked up* [ˌtæŋkt'ʌp] ADJ (*Brit*) • **to be ~ (on sth)** estar borracho (de algo) • **to get ~ (on sth)** emborracharse (de algo)

tanker ['tæŋkəʳ] N (= *ship*) buque-cisterna *m*; (*carrying oil*) petrolero *m*; (= *lorry*) camión *m* cisterna • **an oil ~** un petrolero • **a petrol ~** un camión cisterna

tankful ['tæŋkfʊl] N tanque *m* • **to get a ~ of petrol** llenar el depósito de gasolina • **a ~ is 25 litres** la capacidad del depósito es de 25 litros

tanned [tænd] ADJ moreno, bronceado

tanner¹ ['tænəʳ] N curtidor(a) *m/f*

tanner²* ['tænəʳ] N (*Brit*) (*formerly*) *moneda de seis peniques (antiguos)*

tannery ['tænərɪ] N curtiduría *f*, tenería *f*

tannic ['tænɪk] ADJ [*wine*] con mucho tanino
CPD ▸ **tannic acid** ácido *m* tánico

tannin ['tænɪn] N tanino *m*

tanning ['tænɪŋ] N **1** [*of leather*] curtido *m*
2* zurra* *f* • **to give sb a ~*** zurrar a algn*
CPD ▸ **tanning cream, tanning lotion** bronceador *m* ▸ **tanning salon** centro *m* de bronceado

tannoy® ['tænɔɪ] N sistema *m* de anuncios por altavoces • **on** *or* **over the ~** por los altavoces

tansy ['tænzɪ] N tanaceto *m*, atanasia *f*

tantalize ['tæntəlaɪz] VT **1** (= *excite*) tentar • **he was ~d by her perfume** su perfume le resultaba incitante
2 (= *torment*) • **to ~ sb (with sth)** atormentar a algn (con algo)

tantalizing ['tæntəlaɪzɪŋ] ADJ [*aroma, sight, offer*] tentador; [*perfume*] incitante

tantalizingly ['tæntəlaɪzɪŋlɪ] ADV • **the chocolate biscuits beckoned ~** las galletas de chocolate se ofrecían tentadoras, las galletas de chocolate estaban diciendo "cómeme" • **we came ~ close to victory** tuvimos la victoria casi en nuestras manos

tantamount ['tæntəmaʊnt] ADJ • **~ to** equivalente a • **this is ~ to a refusal** esto equivale a una negativa

tantrum ['tæntrəm] N rabieta* *f*, berrinche* *m* • **she had** *or* **threw a ~** le dio una rabieta *or* un berrinche*

Tanzania [ˌtænzə'ni:ə] N Tanzania *f*

Tanzanian [ˌtænzə'nɪən] ADJ tanzano
N tanzano/a *m/f*

Tao [taʊ] N Tao *m*

Taoiseach ['ti:ʃək] N ≈ primer(a) ministro/a *m/f* (*de la República de Irlanda*)

Taoism ['taʊɪzəm] N taoísmo *m*

Taoist ['tɑ:əʊɪst] ADJ taoísta
N taoísta *mf*

tap¹ [tæp] N **1** (*Brit*) (= *water tap*) grifo *m*, canilla *f* (*S. Cone*); (= *gas tap*) llave *f* • **cold/hot water tap** grifo *m* de agua fría/caliente • **you've left the tap running** has dejado el grifo abierto • **to turn the tap on/off** abrir/cerrar el grifo
2 (= *stopper*) [*of barrel*] espita *f*, canilla *f* • **on tap: beer on tap** cerveza *f* de barril • **to have sth on tap** disponer de algo • **he seems to have unlimited money on tap** parece disponer de un caudal de dinero ilimitado
3 (*Telec*) micrófono *m* • **to put a tap on sb's phone** intervenir *or* pinchar el teléfono de algn*
4 (*Med*) punción *f* • **spinal tap** punción *f* lumbar
VT **1** (= *use*) [+ *resource, situation*] explotar • **to tap sb for information*** tratar de (son)sacar información a algn • **he tried to tap me for £5** intentó sonsacarme cinco libras
2 [+ *barrel*] espitar
3 (*Telec*) [+ *telephone*] intervenir, pinchar*; [+ *conversation*] interceptar • **my phone is tapped** mi teléfono está intervenido *or* pinchado*
4 (= *cut into*) [+ *tree*] sangrar • **to tap the rubber from a tree** sangrar un árbol para extraer el caucho
5 (*Elec*) [+ *electricity, current*] derivar; [+ *wire*] hacer una derivación en
6 (*Med*) [+ *spine*] hacer una punción en
VI ▹ **tap into**
CPD ▸ **tap water** agua *f* corriente, agua *f* del grifo (*Sp*)

tap² [tæp] N **1** (= *knock*) (*on door*) toque *m*; (*on back, shoulder*) golpecito *m*, toque *m* • **I felt a tap on my shoulder** sentí un golpecito *or* toque en el hombro • **there was a tap at** *or* **on the door** llamaron *or* tocaron suavemente a la puerta • **I gave him a gentle tap on the back** le di un golpecito en la espalda
2 (*also* **tap dancing**) claqué *m*
3 (*on dancing shoe*) lámina *f* de metal, tapa *f* de metal
VT (= *hit lightly*) [+ *table, surface*] golpear suavemente; [+ *typewriter keys*] pulsar • **he was tapping his fingers on the steering wheel** estaba repiqueteando *or* tamborileando sobre el volante con los dedos • **to tap one's foot** (*impatiently*) taconear (impacientemente) • **they were tapping their feet in time to the music** seguían el compás de la música con el pie • **to tap sb on the back/shoulder** dar un golpecito *or* toque a algn en la espalda/el hombro • **she tapped a rhythm on the table** golpeó la mesa marcando un ritmo, repiqueteó un ritmo en la mesa
VI dar golpecitos • **please, stop tapping!** ¡haz el favor de dejar de dar golpecitos! • **she tapped at the door** llamó suavemente a la puerta • **she tapped at the window** dio unos golpecitos en la ventana • **he was tapping away at his word processor** estaba (tecleando) dale que te pego en su procesador de textos • **I could hear sth tapping on the window** oía que algo daba golpecitos en la ventana
CPD ▸ **tap dance** claqué *m*; ▹ **tap-dance** ▸ **tap dancer** bailarín/ina *m/f* de claqué ▸ **tap dancing** claqué *m* ▸ **tap shoes** zapatos *mpl* de claqué
▸ **tap in** VT + ADV **1** (*on computer*) [+ *number, code*] teclear
2 • **to tap in a nail** hacer que entre un clavo golpeándolo suavemente
▸ **tap into** VI + PREP • **to tap into a computer** acceder ilegalmente a un ordenador (*Sp*) *or* (*LAm*) una computadora • **they are trying to tap into the youth market** están intentando introducirse en el mercado juvenil • **to tap into sb's ideas** aprovechar las ideas de algn • **to tap into one's potential** aprovechar al máximo su capacidad

▸ **tap out** VT + ADV **1** • **to tap out a message in morse** enviar un mensaje en Morse
2 • **to tap out one's pipe** vaciar la pipa golpeándola suavemente
tapas ['tæpəs] NPL tapas *fpl*
tap-dance ['tæpdɑːns] VI bailar claqué
tape [teɪp] N **1** *(made of cloth)* cinta *f*; (= *adhesive tape*) cinta *f* adhesiva, Scotch® *m*; *(Sport)* meta *f*; *(ceremonial)* cinta *f* simbólica; *(also* **tape measure**) cinta *f* métrica, metro *m*; ▹ **name**
2 *(for recording)* (= *magnetic strip*) cinta *f* (magnetofónica); (= *cassette, recording*) cinta *f* • **I'll do you a ~ of it** te lo grabaré (en cinta) • **a blank ~** una cinta virgen • **on ~** grabado (en cinta); ▹ **cassette**
VT **1** (= *record*) grabar (en cinta)
2 (= *seal*) *(also* **tape up**) cerrar con cinta, poner una cinta a
3 (= *fasten*) • **to ~ sth to sth** pegar algo a algo con cinta adhesiva
4 • IDIOM: • **to have sth/sb ~d*** • **I've got him ~d** ya le tengo calado* • **I've got it ~d** ya le he cogido el tranquillo* • **we've got it all ~d** lo tenemos todo organizado, todo funciona perfectamente
CPD ▸ **tape deck** pletina *f*, unidad *f* de cinta ▸ **tape drive** *(Comput)* accionador *m* de cinta ▸ **tape machine** casete *m*, magnetofón *m* ▸ **tape measure** cinta *f* métrica, metro *m* ▸ **tape recorder** casete *m* *(Sp)*, grabadora *f (esp LAm)*; *(reel-to-reel)* magnetofón *m*, magnetófono *m* ▸ **tape recording** grabación *f* (en cinta) ▸ **tape streamer** *(Comput)* dispositivo *m* de copia de seguridad
taper ['teɪpəʳ] N (= *spill*) astilla *f*; (= *candle*) vela *f*
VI afilarse, estrecharse • **to ~ to a point** rematar en punta
VT afilar, estrechar
▸ **taper off, taper away** VI + ADV
1 (= *narrow*) ▹ **taper**
2 (= *reduce*) *[spending, fighting, violence]* ir disminuyendo; *[storm, snowfall]* ir amainando • **his popularity is ~ing off** su popularidad está decayendo
tape-record ['teɪprɪˌkɔːd] VT grabar (en cinta)
tapered ['teɪpəd], **tapering** ['teɪpərɪŋ] ADJ *[shape]* ahusado, que termina en punta; *[finger]* afilado; *[table leg]* que se va estrechando; *(Mech)* cónico
tapestry ['tæpɪstrɪ] N (= *object*) tapiz *m*; (= *art*) tapicería *f*
tapeworm ['teɪpwɜːm] N tenia *f*, solitaria *f*
tapioca [ˌtæpɪ'əʊkə] N tapioca *f*
CPD ▸ **tapioca pudding** postre *m* de tapioca
tapir ['teɪpəʳ] N tapir *m*
tapper ['tæpəʳ] N *(Elec, Telec)* manipulador *m*
tappet ['tæpɪt] N empujador *m*, empujaválvula *m*
taproom ['tæprʊm] N *(Brit)* bar *m*
taproot ['tæpruːt] N raíz *f* central
tar [tɑːʳ] N **1** (= *substance*) alquitrán *m*, brea *f*, chapopote *m (Mex)* • **low/middle tar cigarettes** cigarrillos con contenido bajo/medio de alquitrán
2 *(also* **Jack Tar**†) marinero *m*
VT *[+ road, surface]* alquitranar • **to tar and feather sb** emplumar a algn • IDIOM: • **to be tarred with the same brush** *(fig)* estar cortado por el mismo patrón
taramasalata [ˌtærəməsə'lɑːtə] N taramasalata *f*, *aperitivo griego a base de huevas de pescado ahumadas*
tarantella [ˌtærən'telə] N tarantela *f*
tarantula [tə'ræntjʊlə] N (PL: **tarantulas** *or* **tarantulae** [tə'ræntjʊliː]) tarántula *f*
tardily ['tɑːdɪlɪ] ADV *(frm)* (= *belatedly*) tardíamente; (= *slowly*) lentamente
tardiness ['tɑːdɪnɪs] N *(frm)* (= *lateness*) tardanza *f*; (= *slowness*) lentitud *f*
tardy ['tɑːdɪ] ADJ (COMPAR: **tardier**, SUPERL: **tardiest**) *(frm)* (= *late*) tardío; (= *slow*) lento
CPD ▸ **tardy slip** *(US) (at school) papel que reciben los alumnos que llegan tarde*
tare [teəʳ] N *(Bot) (also* **tares**) arveja *f*; *(Bible)* cizaña *f*; *(Comm)* tara *f*
target ['tɑːgɪt] N **1** *(Sport)* blanco *m*, diana *f*; *(Mil)* objetivo *m* • **he missed the ~** no dio en el blanco *or* la diana • **they deliberately attacked civilian ~s** atacaron objetivos civiles deliberadamente • **an easy ~** *(lit, fig)* un blanco fácil • **a fixed ~** un blanco fijo • **a moving ~** un blanco móvil • **the shot was off ~** *(Ftbl, Hockey etc)* el tiro iba desviado a gol • **the bombs were way off ~** las bombas cayeron muy lejos del objetivo • **the shot was on ~** *(Ftbl, Hockey etc)* el tiro iba directo a gol • **a soft ~** *(lit, fig)* un blanco fácil
2 (= *person on receiving end*) *[of criticism, remark]* blanco *m*; *[of advertising]* objetivo *m* • **he has been the ~ of criticism over his handling of the affair** ha sido el blanco de las críticas por su manejo del asunto • **this made him a prime ~ for blackmail** esto le convirtió en un blanco perfecto para el chantaje
3 (= *objective*) objetivo *m*, meta *f* • **production ~s for 1980** los objetivos *or* las metas de producción para 1980 • **the project is on ~ for completion** el proyecto lleva camino de terminarse dentro del plazo previsto • **to set a ~ for sth** fijar un objetivo para algo • **to set o.s. a ~** fijarse un objetivo
VT **1** *(Mil)* fijar como objetivo
2 (= *select, single out*) • **cigarette companies seem to be ~ing children intentionally** las tabacaleras parecen estar dirigiendo su publicidad a los niños deliberadamente • **a mugger who ~ed elderly women** un atracador que asaltaba en particular a ancianas • **to ~ sth/sb for sth**: • **the government will ~ high earners for tax increases** el gobierno hará recaer la subida de los impuestos particularmente sobre aquellos con sueldos elevados • **the factory is ~ed for closure** se propone cerrar la fábrica
3 *(fig)* (= *aim*) • **to ~ sth at sb/sth**: • **products ~ed at children** productos dirigidos a los niños • **programs ~ed at reducing infant deaths** programas que tienen como objetivo reducir el número de muertes infantiles • **to ~ aid at the people who need it** concentrar la ayuda en las personas que la necesitan
CPD ▸ **target area** *(Mil)* zona *f* objetivo ▸ **target audience** público *m* objetivo ▸ **target date** fecha *f* límite ▸ **target group** grupo *m* objetivo, grupo *m* destinatario ▸ **target language** lengua *f* de destino ▸ **target market** mercado *m* objetivo ▸ **target practice** tiro *m* al blanco, prácticas *fpl* de tiro ▸ **target price** precio *m* indicativo ▸ **target weight** peso *m* ideal
targetable ['tɑːgɪtəbl] ADJ dirigible
tariff ['tærɪf] N **1** (= *tax*) tarifa *f*, arancel *m*
2 (= *schedule of prices*) tarifa *f*
CPD ▸ **tariff agreement** acuerdo *m* arancelario ▸ **tariff barrier** barrera *f* arancelaria ▸ **tariff reform** reforma *f* arancelaria ▸ **tariff wall** = **tariff barrier**
Tarmac®, tarmac ['tɑːmæk] (VB: PT, PP: **tarmacked**) *(esp Brit)* N (= *substance*) asfalto *m*, alquitranado *m* • **the ~** *(Aer)* (= *runway*) la pista de despegue; *(Aut)* (= *road*) el asfalto
VT asfaltar, alquitranar
tarn [tɑːn] N lago *m* pequeño de montaña
tarnation†* [tɑː'neɪʃən] N *(US) (dialect)* ¡diablos!
tarnish ['tɑːnɪʃ] VT *(lit)* deslustrar, quitar el brillo a; *(fig)* manchar, empañar
VI *[metal]* deslustrarse, perder el brillo
tarnished ['tɑːnɪʃt] ADJ *[metal]* deslustrado, sin brillo; *[reputation]* manchado, empañado
taro ['tɑːrəʊ] N (PL: **taros**) taro *m*
tarot ['tærəʊ] N tarot *m*
CPD ▸ **tarot card** carta *f* de tarot
tarp* [tɑːp] N *(US)* = **tarpaulin**
tarpaulin [tɑː'pɔːlɪn] N lona *f* alquitranada
tarpon ['tɑːpɒn] N tarpón *m*
tarragon ['tærəgən] N *(Bot)* estragón *m*
tarring ['tɑːrɪŋ] N asfaltado *m*
tarry[1] ['tærɪ] VI *(liter)* (= *stay*) quedarse; (= *dally*) entretenerse, quedarse atrás; (= *be late*) tardar (en venir), demorarse
tarry[2] ['tɑːrɪ] ADJ *[substance]* alquitranado, embreado; (= *covered with tar*) cubierto de alquitrán; (= *stained with tar*) manchado de alquitrán • **to taste ~** saber a alquitrán
tarsus ['tɑːsəs] N (PL: **tarsi** ['tɑːsaɪ]) tarso *m*
tart[1] [tɑːt] ADJ **1** (= *sour*) *[flavour, fruit]* ácido, agrio
2 *(fig) [expression, remark]* áspero
tart[2] [tɑːt] N **1** *(Culin) (large)* tarta *f*; *(small)* pastelillo *m* • **jam ~** tarta *f* de mermelada
2‡ (= *prostitute*) puta*‡ *f*, furcia *f (Sp‡)*; *(pej)* (= *promiscuous woman*) fulana* *f*
▸ **tart up*** VT + ADV *(Brit) [+ house]* pintar, remodelar, renovar • **to ~ o.s. up** vestirse y pintarse
tartan ['tɑːtən] N tartán *m*, tela *f* a cuadros escoceses • **a ~ scarf** una bufanda escocesa
CPD ▸ **Tartan Army*** *apodo de los hinchas de la sección nacional escocesa de fútbol*
Tartar ['tɑːtəʳ] ADJ tártaro
N tártaro/a *m/f*
tartar ['tɑːtəʳ] N **1** *(on teeth)* sarro *m*, tártaro *m*
2 *(Chem)* tártaro *m*
3 *(also* **cream of tartar**) crémor *m* tartárico
4 (= *woman*) *(fig)* fiera *f*
CPD ▹ **tartare**
tartare, tartar ['tɑːtəʳ] CPD ▸ **tartar(e) sauce** salsa *f* tártara ▸ **tartar(e) steak** *biftec crudo, picado y condimentado con sal, pimiento, cebolla etc*
tartaric acid [tɑːˌtærɪk'æsɪd] N ácido *m* tartárico
Tartary ['tɑːtərɪ] N Tartaria *f*
tartlet ['tɑːtlɪt] N *(Brit)* tartaleta *f*, tartita *f*
tartly ['tɑːtlɪ] ADV *(fig)* ásperamente
tartness ['tɑːtnɪs] N **1** *[of flavour, fruit]* acidez *f*
2 *(fig)* aspereza *f*
tarty* ['tɑːtɪ] ADJ putesco*
Tarzan ['tɑːzən] N Tarzán
Taser® ['teɪzəʳ] N pistola *f* Taser®, Taser® *m*
VT **to ~ sb** disparar a algn con una pistola Taser®
tash* [tæʃ] N *(Brit)* = **tache**
task [tɑːsk] N **1** (= *job*) tarea *f* • **I had to keep the children amused, which was no easy ~** tenía que entretener a los niños, lo cual no era tarea fácil • **to give** *or* **set sb the ~ of doing sth** pedir a algn que haga algo • IDIOM: • **to take sb to ~ (for sth)** reprender *or* regañar a algn (por algo), llamar a algn a capítulo (por algo) *(frm)*
2 (= *function, aim*) cometido *m* • **it was the ~ of the army to maintain order** mantener el orden era el cometido del ejército
3 *(Comput)* tarea *f*
VT • **to ~ sb with sth** hacer que algn se encargue de algo
CPD ▸ **task force** *(Mil)* destacamento *m*

especial; (*Naut*) fuerza *f* expedicionaria; (= *working group*) grupo *m* de trabajo
taskmaster ['tɑːsk,mɑːstə^r] N • **he's a hard ~** es muy exigente, es un tirano
Tasmania [tæz'meɪnɪə] N Tasmania *f*
Tasmanian [tæz'meɪnɪən] ADJ tasmanio
N tasmanio/a *m/f*
CPD ▸ **Tasmanian devil** (*Zool*) demonio *m* de Tasmania, diablo *m* de Tasmania
tassel ['tæsəl] N borla *f*
tasselled ['tæsəld] ADJ con borlas
taste [teɪst] N **1** (= *sense*) gusto *m* • **a keen sense of ~** un agudo sentido del gusto • **it's quite sweet to the ~** tiene un gusto bastante dulce al paladar
2 (= *flavour*) sabor *m*, gusto *m* • **it has an odd ~** tiene un sabor *or* gusto raro • **to leave a bad** *or* **nasty ~ in the mouth** (*fig*) dejar mal sabor de boca • **his jokes leave a bad** *or* **nasty ~ in the mouth** sus chistes te dejan mal sabor de boca • **it has no ~** no sabe a nada, no tiene sabor
3 (= *small amount*) • **"more wine?" — "just a ~"** —¿más vino? —solo un poco *or* un poquito • **would you like a ~?** ¿quieres probarlo? • **may I have a ~?** ¿puedo probarlo? • IDIOMS: • **to give sb a ~ of their own medicine** pagar a algn con la misma moneda • **to get a ~ of one's own medicine** recibir el mismo (mal) trato que uno da a los demás
4 (= *experience*) experiencia *f*; (= *sample*) muestra *f* • **it was her first ~ of freedom** fue su primera experiencia de la libertad *or* su primer contacto con la libertad • **we got a ~ of his anger** nos ofreció una muestra de su enfado • **now that she has had a ~ of stardom, she won't ever be content with ordinariness again** ahora que ha probado las mieles del estrellato *or* saboreado el estrellato, nunca más se conformará con lo normal y corriente • **he's had a ~ of prison** ha conocido *or* probado la cárcel • **to give sb a ~ of sth** dar una idea de algo a algn • **it gave him a ~ of military life** le dio una idea de lo que era la vida militar • **it was a ~ of things to come** era una muestra de lo que estaba por venir
5 (= *liking*) gusto *m* • **~s differ** los gustos cambian • **he was a man of catholic ~s** era un hombre de gustos variados • **a ~ for sth**: • **to acquire** *or* **develop a ~ for sth** tomarle gusto a algo • **it gave him a ~ for reading** esto hizo que le tomara gusto a la lectura • **she has a ~ for adventure** le gusta la aventura • **we have the same ~s in music** tenemos el mismo gusto para la música • **he has expensive ~s in cars** en cuanto a coches, tiene gustos caros • **season to ~** (*Culin*) sazonar al gusto • **it's not to my ~** no es de mi gusto • **is it to your ~?** ¿le gusta?, ¿es de su gusto? • IDIOM: • **there's no accounting for ~** sobre gustos no hay nada escrito; ▸ **acquired**
6 (= *discernment*) gusto *m* • **people of ~** la gente con gusto • **to be in bad ~** ser de mal gusto • **it would be in bad ~ to meet without him** sería de mal gusto reunirnos sin él, reunirnos sin él sería hacerle un desprecio *or* un feo • **she has very good ~** tiene muy buen gusto • **his ~ in clothes is extremely good** viste con muchísimo gusto • **I don't think that remark was in very good ~** no me pareció un comentario de muy buen gusto • **to have ~** [*person*] tener gusto • **to have no ~** [*person*] no tener gusto • **the house is furnished in impeccable ~** la casa está amueblada con muchísimo gusto *or* con un gusto exquisito • **to be in poor ~** ser de mal gusto
VT **1** (= *sample*) [+ *food, drink*] probar; (*at tasting*) degustar, catar • **just ~ this** pruebe esto; ▸ **wine**
2 (= *perceive flavour of*) • **I can't ~ the rum in this** no noto el sabor del ron en esto, esto apenas me sabe a ron • **I can't ~ anything when I have a cold** la comida no me sabe a nada cuando estoy resfriado
3 (= *eat*) comer, probar • **I haven't ~d salmon for years** hace años que no como salmón *or* pruebo el salmón • **he had not ~d food for a week** llevaba una semana sin probar bocado
4 (= *experience*) [+ *success, power*] saborear; [+ *poverty, loneliness*] conocer
VI (= *have flavour*) saber • **the brandy ~d bitter** el brandy sabía amargo, el brandy tenía un sabor *or* un gusto amargo • **it ~s good** está rico *or* bueno • **it ~s all right to me** a mí me sabe bien • **it ~s horrible** tiene un sabor horrible, sabe horrible *or* a rayos* • **to ~ like sth** saber a algo • **the meat ~d like chicken** la carne sabía a pollo • **to ~ of sth** saber a algo • **what does it ~ of?** ¿a qué sabe?
CPD ▸ **taste bud** papila *f* gustativa
tasteful ['teɪstfʊl] ADJ de buen gusto
tastefully ['teɪstfəlɪ] ADV con buen gusto • **the sex scenes are very ~ done** las escenas sexuales están hechas con buen gusto
tastefulness ['teɪstfʊlnɪs] N buen gusto *m*
tasteless ['teɪstlɪs] ADJ **1** (= *without flavour*) **a** (*by nature*) [*substance*] insípido • **sodium is ~** el sodio es insípido *or* no tiene sabor
b (*pej*) (*through cooking*) [*food, meal*] soso, insípido • **the fish was ~** el pescado estaba soso *or* no sabía a nada
2 (= *vulgar*) [*ornament, decor*] de mal gusto, ordinario
3 (= *offensive*) [*remark, joke*] de mal gusto
tastelessly ['teɪstlɪslɪ] ADV con mal gusto
tastelessness ['teɪstlɪsnɪs] N **1** (= *lack of flavour*) [*of food, substance*] insipidez *f*
2 (= *bad taste*) [*of ornament, joke, remark*] mal gusto *m*
taster ['teɪstə^r] N **1** (= *person*) catador(a) *m/f*, degustador(a) *m/f*
2 (*Brit*) (*fig*) muestra *f* • **that is just a ~ of things to come** esto es un anticipo de lo que nos espera
tastiness ['teɪstɪnɪs] N lo sabroso, lo apetitoso
tasting ['teɪstɪŋ] N degustación *f*
tasty ['teɪstɪ] ADJ (COMPAR: **tastier**, SUPERL: **tastiest**) **1** (= *well-flavoured*) [*food, dish*] sabroso, apetitoso • **this is very ~** esto sabe muy rico
2* (= *salacious*) • **a ~ piece of gossip** un cotilleo sustancioso • **a ~ piece of news** una noticia jugosa
3‡ (= *sexy*) • **he/she's very ~!** ¡está buenísimo/buenísima!*, ¡está más bueno/buena que el pan!‡
tat¹ [tæt] VI (*Sew*) hacer encaje
tat²* [tæt] N (*Brit*) basura* *f*
ta-ta* ['tæ'tɑː] EXCL (*Brit*) adiós, adiosito*
Tatar ['tɑːtə^r] = **Tartar**
tattered ['tætəd] ADJ [*clothes, flag*] en jirones; [*book*] destrozado; [*person*] andrajoso, harapiento; (*fig*) [*reputation*] hecho trizas
tatters ['tætəz] NPL (= *rags*) andrajos *mpl*, harapos *mpl*; (= *shreds*) jirones *mpl* • **to be in ~** [*clothes*] estar hecho jirones; (*fig*) [*reputation*] estar hecho trizas; [*marriage*] andar muy mal • **the coalition is in ~** la coalición anda muy mal
tatting ['tætɪŋ] N trabajo *m* de encaje, encaje *m*
tattle ['tætl] N (= *chat*) charla *f*; (= *gossip*) chismes *mpl*, habladurías *fpl*
VI (= *chat*) charlar, parlotear; (= *gossip*) chismear, contar chismes
tattler ['tætlə^r] N (= *chatterbox*) charlatán/ana *m/f*; (= *gossip*) chismoso/a *m/f*
tattletale* ['tætlteɪl] N (*US*) (= *person*) soplón/ona *m/f*, acusica *mf* (*Sp**); (= *talk*) cotilleo *m*, chismes *mpl* y cuentos *mpl*
tattoo¹ [tə'tuː] N (*on body*) tatuaje *m*
VT (PT, PP: **tattooed**) tatuar
tattoo² [tə'tuː] N (*Mil*) (= *signal*) retreta *f*; (*Brit*) (= *pageant*) gran espectáculo *m* militar, exhibición *f* del arte militar • **the Edinburgh ~** el espectáculo militar de Edimburgo • **to beat a ~ with one's fingers** tamborilear con los dedos; ▸ EDINBURGH FESTIVAL
tattooist [tə'tuːɪst] N tatuador(a) *m/f*
tatty* ['tætɪ] ADJ (COMPAR: **tattier**, SUPERL: **tattiest**) (= *shabby*) [*clothes*] raído, deshilachado; [*furniture*] estropeado
taught [tɔːt] PT, PP *of* **teach**
taunt [tɔːnt] N (= *jeer*) pulla *f*, mofa *f*; (= *insult*) insulto *m*
VT (= *jeer at*) mofarse de; (= *insult*) insultar • **to ~ sb (with sth)** mofarse de algn (por algo)
taunting ['tɔːntɪŋ] ADJ (= *jeering*) mofador, burlón; (= *insulting*) insultante
tauntingly ['tɔːntɪŋlɪ] ADV burlonamente, en son de burla
taupe [təʊp] ADJ de color marrón topo
N marrón *m* topo
Taurean [,tɔː'riːən] N • **to be a ~** ser tauro
tauromachy ['tɔːrəmækɪ] N tauromaquia *f*
Taurus ['tɔːrəs] N **1** (= *sign, constellation*) Tauro *m*
2 (= *person*) tauro *mf* • **she's (a) ~** es tauro
taut [tɔːt] ADJ **1** (= *tight*) [*rope*] tirante, tenso; [*skin*] tirante • **the rope is held ~ by weights** la cuerda se mantiene tirante *or* tensa mediante unos pesos • **to pull sth ~** tensar algo • **to stretch sth ~** estirar algo hasta que quede tirante
2 (= *tense*) [*person, face, voice*] tenso • **their faces were ~ with fear** tenían el rostro tenso por el miedo
3 (= *firm*) [*body, legs*] firme, de carnes prietas; [*muscles*] firme
4 (= *tightly written*) [*novel, film*] compacto
tauten ['tɔːtn] VT [+ *muscles, body, rope, cable*] tensar; [+ *skin*] estirar; (*Naut*) tesar
VI [*muscles, body, rope, cable*] tensarse; [*skin*] ponerse tirante
tautly ['tɔːtlɪ] ADV (*lit*) [*stretch*] con tersura; (*fig*) [*say*] con voz tensa, con voz crispada
tautness ['tɔːtnɪs] N **1** [*of rope*] tensión *f*; [*of skin*] tirantez *f*
2 [*of face, expression*] tensión *f*
3 [*of body, muscles*] firmeza *f*
4 [*of writing*] lo compacto
tautological [,tɔːtə'lɒdʒɪkəl] ADJ tautológico
tautology [tɔː'tɒlədʒɪ] N tautología *f*
tavern†† ['tævən] N taberna *f*
tawdriness ['tɔːdrɪnɪs] N [*of place, town*] chabacanería *f*
tawdry ['tɔːdrɪ] ADJ (COMPAR: **tawdrier**, SUPERL: **tawdriest**) [*jewellery*] de oropel, de relumbrón; [*clothes*] chabacano, hortera (*Sp**); [*decor*] charro, hortera (*Sp**); [*place, town*] chabacano; (= *sordid*) [*affair, business*] sórdido
tawny ['tɔːnɪ] (COMPAR: **tawnier**, SUPERL: **tawniest**) ADJ leonado; (*wine parlance*) ámbar oscuro, tostado
CPD ▸ **tawny owl** cárabo *m* ▸ **tawny port** puerto *m* seco
tax [tæks] N **1** (*Econ*) (= *contribution*) impuesto *m*, tributo *m* (*frm*) • **half of it goes in tax** la mitad se me va en impuestos • **petrol tax** • **tax on petrol** impuesto *m* sobre

la gasolina • **profits after tax** beneficios después de impuestos • **profits before tax** beneficios antes de impuestos • **free of tax** exento *or* libre de impuestos • **to impose** *or* **levy** *or* **put a tax on sth** gravar algo con un impuesto • **to pay tax on sth** pagar impuestos por algo • **to pay one's taxes** pagar los impuestos • **how much tax do you pay?** ¿cuánto paga de impuestos? • **I paid £3,000 in tax last year** el año pasado pagué 3.000 libras de impuestos • **for tax purposes** a efectos fiscales; ▹ **capital, council, income, value-added tax**
2 (*= strain*) • **the extra administrative work was a tax on the resources of schools** el trabajo adicional de administración supuso una carga pesada para los recursos de las escuelas • **it was a tax on his strength/patience** puso a prueba sus fuerzas/su paciencia
(VT) **1** (*Econ*) [*+ income, profit*] gravar; [*+ person*] cobrar impuestos a, imponer cargas fiscales a • **household goods are taxed at the rate of 15%** los artículos del hogar se gravan con el 15% *or* llevan un impuesto del 15% • **the wife is separately taxed** la esposa paga impuestos por separado
2 (*Brit*) (*Aut*) • **I haven't got my car taxed yet** aún no he pagado el impuesto de circulación
3 (*= place a burden on*) poner a prueba • **these dilemmas would tax the best of statesmen** estos dilemas pondrían a prueba al mejor de los estadistas
4 (*frm*) (*= accuse*) • **to tax sb with sth** acusar a algn de algo
5 (*Jur*) [*+ costs*] tasar
(CPD) ▸ **tax allowance** desgravación *f* fiscal ▸ **tax avoidance** evasión *f* legal de impuestos ▸ **tax base** base *f* imponible ▸ **tax bracket** grupo *m* impositivo ▸ **tax break** ventaja *f* fiscal ▸ **tax code, tax coding** código *m* impositivo ▸ **tax collecting** recaudación *f* de impuestos ▸ **tax collector** recaudador(a) *m/f* de impuestos ▸ **tax credit** crédito *m* fiscal ▸ **tax cuts** reducciones *fpl* en los impuestos ▸ **tax disc** (*Brit*) pegatina *f* del impuesto de circulación ▸ **tax dodge*** evasión *f* de impuestos ▸ **tax evasion** evasión *f* fiscal ▸ **tax exemption** exención *f* de impuestos, exención *f* tributaria ▸ **tax exile** (*= person*) *persona autoexiliada para evitar los impuestos*; (*= state*) exilio *m* voluntario para evitar los impuestos ▸ **tax form** impreso *m* para la declaración de la renta ▸ **tax haven** paraíso *m* fiscal ▸ **tax incentive** aliciente *m* fiscal ▸ **tax inspector** inspector(a) *m/f* fiscal, inspector(a) *m/f* de Hacienda ▸ **tax law** derecho *m* tributario ▸ **tax liability** obligación *f* fiscal, obligación *f* tributaria ▸ **tax purposes** • **for tax purposes** a efectos fiscales ▸ **tax rate** tasa *f* impositiva ▸ **tax rebate** devolución *f* de impuestos ▸ **tax relief** desgravación *f* fiscal ▸ **tax return** declaración *f* fiscal *or* de la renta • **to fill in** *or* **out one's tax return** hacer la declaración fiscal *or* de la renta ▸ **tax revenue** ingresos *mpl* tributarios ▸ **tax shelter** refugio *m* fiscal ▸ **tax system** sistema *m* tributario, sistema *m* fiscal ▸ **tax year** año *m* fiscal, ejercicio *m* fiscal

taxability [ˌtæksəˈbɪlɪtɪ] (N) carácter *m* gravable

taxable [ˈtæksəbl] (ADJ) gravable, imponible
(CPD) ▸ **taxable income** renta *f* gravable, renta *f* imponible

taxation [tækˈseɪʃən] (N) (*= taxes*) impuestos *mpl*, contribuciones *fpl*; (*= system*) sistema *m* tributario
(CPD) ▸ **taxation system** sistema *m* tributario, tributación *f*

tax-deductible [ˈtæksdɪˈdʌktəbl] (ADJ) desgravable

taxeme [ˈtæksiːm] (N) taxema *m*

tax-exempt [ˌtæksɪɡˈzempt] (ADJ) (*US*) exento de impuestos, libre de impuestos

tax-free [ˈtæksˈfriː] (*Brit*) (ADJ) exento de impuestos, libre de impuestos
(ADV) • **to live tax-free** vivir sin pagar impuestos

taxi [ˈtæksɪ] (N) (PL: **taxis** *or* **taxies**) (*= cab*) taxi *m*; (*= collective taxi*) colectivo *m* (*LAm*), pesero *m* (*Mex*)
(VI) **1** (*Aer*) rodar por la pista
2 (*= go by taxi*) ir en taxi
(CPD) ▸ **taxi driver** taxista *mf* ▸ **taxi fare** tarifa *f* de taxi • **I'll pay the ~ fare** yo pagaré el taxi ▸ **taxi rank** (*Brit*), **taxi stance** (*Scot*), **taxi stand** (*US*) parada *f* de taxis

taxicab [ˈtæksɪkæb] (N) (*esp US*) taxi *m*

taxidermist [ˈtæksɪdɜːmɪst] (N) taxidermista *mf*

taxidermy [ˈtæksɪdɜːmɪ] (N) taxidermia *f*

taxi-man [ˈtæksɪmæn] (N) (PL: **taxi-men**) taxista *m*

taximeter [ˈtæksɪˌmiːtəʳ] (N) taxímetro *m*

taxing [ˈtæksɪŋ] (ADJ) **1** (*mentally*) [*problem, task*] dificilísimo; [*period, time*] muy duro • **his job was mentally ~** su trabajo requería muchísima concentración mental
2 (*physically*) [*task, journey*] agotador, duro • **physically ~** agotador

taxiway [ˈtæksɪweɪ] (N) (*Aer*) pista *f* de rodaje

taxman* [ˈtæksmæn] (N) (PL: **taxmen**) recaudador *m* de impuestos; (*euph*) (*= tax authorities*) • **the ~** Hacienda *f*

taxonomist [tækˈsɒnəmɪst] (N) taxonomista *mf*

taxonomy [tækˈsɒnəmɪ] (N) taxonomía *f*

taxpayer [ˈtæksˌpeɪəʳ] (N) contribuyente *mf*

TB (N ABBR) = **tuberculosis**

tba (ABBR) = **to be arranged** *or* **to be announced**

T-bar [ˈtiːbɑːʳ] (N) hierro *m* en T; (*also* **T-bar lift**) (*Ski*) telesquí *m*

tbc (ABBR) = **to be confirmed**

T-bone [ˈtiːbəʊn], **T-bone steak** (N) chuleta *f* en forma de T

tbs (PL: **tbs**), **tbsp** (PL: **tbsp** *or* **tbsps**), **tblsp** (PL: **tblsp** *or* **tblsps**) (ABBR) = **tablespoonful**

T-cell [ˈtiːˌsel] (N) célula *f* T, linfocito *m* T

TD (N ABBR) **1** (*American Ftbl*) = **touchdown**
2 (*US*) = **Treasury Department**
3 (*Irl*) (= **Teachta Dála**) *miembro del parlamento irlandés*
4 (*Brit*) = **Territorial Decoration**

te [tiː] (N) (*Mus*) si *m*

tea [tiː] (N) **1** (*= drink, plant*) té *m* • **would you like some tea?** ¿te apetece un té? • **a cup of tea** una taza de té • **I'm making another pot of tea** voy a hacer otra tetera • **tea with lemon** • **lemon tea** té con limón • **camomile tea** manzanilla *f* • **herbal/mint tea** té *m* de hierbas/menta • **iced tea** te *m* helado • IDIOMS: • **not for all the tea in China** por nada del mundo • **tea and sympathy** (*euph*) té y sonrisas; ▹ **cup**
2 (*= cup of tea*) té *m* • **three teas and a coffee please** tres tés y un café por favor
3 (*= meal*) (*afternoon*) té *m*, merienda *f*; (*evening*) (*Brit*) cena *f* • **an invitation to tea** una invitación a tomar el té *or* merendar • **high tea** merienda-cena *f* (*que se toma con té*) • **to have tea** tomar el té, merendar
(CPD) ▸ **tea bag** bolsita *f* de té ▸ **tea boy** *chico que prepara y sirve el té en una fábrica u oficina* ▸ **tea break** descanso *m* para el té ▸ **tea caddy** bote *m* para té ▸ **tea cart** (*US*) = **tea trolley** ▸ **tea chest** caja *f* grande de madera ▸ **tea cloth** (*for trolley, tray*) mantelito *m*, pañito *m*; (*for dishes*) = **tea towel** ▸ **tea cosy, tea cozy** (*US*) cubretetera *m* ▸ **tea dance** té *m* bailable, té-baile *m* ▸ **tea garden** (*= café*) café *m* al aire libre; (*Agr*) plantación *f* de té ▸ **tea lady** (*Brit*) *señora que prepara y sirve el té en una fábrica u oficina* ▸ **tea leaf** hoja *f* de té ▸ **tea party** té *m*, merienda *f* ▸ **tea plate** plato *m* llano (*pequeño*) ▸ **tea rose** rosa *f* de té ▸ **tea service, tea set** servicio *m* de té, juego *m* de té ▸ **tea strainer** colador *m* de té ▸ **tea table** mesita *f* de té ▸ **tea things** servicio *m* del té ▸ **tea towel** paño *m* de cocina, trapo *m* de cocina (*LAm*) ▸ **tea tray** bandeja *f* del té ▸ **tea trolley** (*Brit*) carrito *m* del té ▸ **tea urn** tetera *f* grande ▸ **tea wagon** (*US*) carrito *m* del té

teacake [ˈtiːkeɪk] (N) *bollo con pasas que generalmente se come tostado y untado con mantequilla*

teach [tiːtʃ] (PT, PP: **taught**) (VT) **1** (*in class*) [*+ subject*] dar clases de, enseñar; [*+ group*] dar clases a • **Miss Hardy taught us needlework** la Srta. Hardy nos daba clases de *or* nos enseñaba costura • **he ~es primary-school children** es maestro de escuela (primaria), da clases a niños de primaria • **to ~ school** (*US*) (*primary*) dar clases en un colegio de enseñanza primaria; (*secondary*) dar clases en un colegio de enseñanza secundaria • **she taught English to Japanese businessmen** enseñaba inglés *or* daba clases de inglés a ejecutivos japoneses
2 (*not in class*) enseñar • **to ~ sb to do sth** enseñar a algn a hacer algo • **his parents taught him never to lie** sus padres le enseñaron a no mentir nunca • **he taught himself Arabic** aprendió árabe por su cuenta • **I'll ~ you to speak to me like that!** ¡ya te enseñaré yo a hablarme así! • **you can't ~ him anything about cars** no le puedes enseñar nada sobre coches • **my mother taught me how to cook** mi madre me enseñó a cocinar • **history ~es us a valuable lesson** la historia nos enseña una valiosa lección • **that'll ~ you!** ¡eso te servirá de lección!, ¡te está bien empleado! • **that will ~ you to mind your own business!** ¡eso te enseñará a no meterte en lo que no te importa! • IDIOMS: • **don't ~ your grandmother to suck eggs** a tu padre no le puedes enseñar a ser hijo • **to ~ sb a lesson*** darle una lección a algn • **you can't ~ an old dog new tricks** perro viejo no aprende gracias
(VI) (*= give classes*) dar clases • **his wife ~es at our school** su esposa da clases *or* es profesora en nuestro colegio • **he has always wanted to ~** siempre ha querido ser profesor *or* dedicarse a la enseñanza

teachability [ˌtiːtʃəˈbɪlɪtɪ] (N) (*esp US*) educabilidad *f*

teachable [ˈtiːtʃəbl] (ADJ) (*esp US*) educable

teacher [ˈtiːtʃəʳ] (N) (*in secondary school*) profesor(a) *m/f*; (*in primary school*) maestro/a *m/f* • **French ~** profesor(a) *m/f* de francés
(CPD) ▸ **teacher certification** (*US*) certificación *f* de docentes ▸ **teacher evaluation** (*US*) (*= assessment of teaching*) evaluación *f* docente ▸ **teacher training** (*Brit*) formación *f* pedagógica ▸ **teacher training college** (*for primary schools*) escuela *f* normal; (*for secondary schools*) ≈ Instituto *m* de Ciencias de la Educación, ICE *m*; ▹ **pet**

teacher-pupil ratio [ˌtiːtʃəˌpjuːplˈreɪʃɪəʊ] (N) proporción *f* profesor-alumnos

teach-in [ˈtiːtʃˌɪn] (N) reunión *f* de autoenseñanza colectiva

teaching [ˈtiːtʃɪŋ] (N) **1** (*= profession*) enseñanza *f*, docencia *f* (*more frm*) • **have you**

considered a career in ~? ¿has pensado en dedicarte a la enseñanza? • **her son's gone into ~** su hijo se ha metido a profesor
2 (= *activity*) enseñanza *f* • **our aim is to improve the ~ in our schools** nuestra meta es mejorar (el nivel de) la enseñanza en los colegios • **he's got 16 hours ~ a week** da 16 horas de clase a la semana • **I like ~** me gusta dar clases *or* enseñar • **the Teaching of English as a Foreign Language** la enseñanza del inglés c
3 (*esp pl*) [*of philosopher, prophet*] enseñanzas *fpl* • **according to the ~(s) of Socrates** según las enseñanzas de Sócrates • **the church's ~ on birth control** las enseñanzas *or* la doctrina de la Iglesia con respecto al control de la natalidad
(CPD) ▸ **teaching aid** artículo *m* didáctico, artículo *m* de enseñanza ▸ **teaching aids** material *m* didáctico, material *m* de enseñanza ▸ **teaching assistant** (*US*) profesor(a) *m/f* auxiliar ▸ **teaching certificate** (*US*) ≈ certificado *m* de aptitud pedagógica, ≈ CAP *m* (*Sp*) ▸ **teaching hospital** (*Brit*) hospital *m* clínico ▸ **teaching job** trabajo *m* de docente ▸ **teaching material** material *m* didáctico, material *m* de enseñanza ▸ **teaching post** puesto *m* de profesor, puesto *m* docente ▸ **teaching practice** (*Brit*) prácticas *fpl* de enseñanza ▸ **the teaching profession** la profesión docente, la docencia ▸ **the teaching staff** el profesorado, el cuerpo docente

teacup ['tiːkʌp] (N) taza *f* para el té

teahouse ['tiːhaʊs] (N) (PL: **teahouses** ['tiːhaʊzɪz]) salón *m* de té

teak [tiːk] (N) teca *f*, madera *f* de teca

teakettle ['tiːketl] (N) (*US*) tetera *f*

teal [tiːl] (N) (PL: **teal** *or* **teals**) cerceta *f*

team [tiːm] (N) (*gen*) equipo *m*; (= *group*) grupo *m*, equipo *m*; [*of horses*] tiro *m*; [*of oxen*] yunta *f* • **the national ~** la selección nacional • **home/away ~** equipo *m* de casa/visitante
(VT) • **to ~ sth with sth** [+ *clothes*] combinar algo con algo • **to ~ sb with sb** asociar a algn con algn
(VI) • **to ~ with sth** [*items of clothing*] combinar con algo
(CPD) ▸ **team championship** campeonato *m* por equipos ▸ **team game** juego *m* de equipo ▸ **team leader** líder *mf* del equipo ▸ **team member** miembro *mf* del equipo ▸ **team player** persona *f* que trabaja bien en equipo ▸ **team spirit** espíritu *m* de equipo, compañerismo *m* ▸ **team sport** deporte *m* de equipo
▸ **team up** (VI + ADV) juntarse, asociarse (**with** con); (*Sport*) formar un equipo (**with** con)

team-mate ['tiːmmeɪt] (N) compañero/a *m/f* de equipo

teamster ['tiːmstəʳ] (N) (*US*) camionero *m*, camionista *m*

teamwork ['tiːmwɜːk] (N) labor *f* de equipo, trabajo *m* en *or* de equipo

teapot ['tiːpɒt] (N) tetera *f*

tear¹ [tɛəʳ] (VB: PT: **tore**, PP: **torn**) (N) **1** (= *rip*) (*in fabric, paper*) roto *m*, rasgón *m*, desgarrón *m* • **your shirt has a ~ in it** llevas la camisa rota, tu camisa está rota, tienes un roto *or* rasgón *or* desgarrón en la camisa; ▹ **wear**
2 (*Med*) (= *injury*) (*in muscle*) desgarro *m*; (*in ligament*) rotura *f*; [*of tissue*] (*in childbirth*) desgarro *m*
(VT) **1** (= *rip*) [+ *fabric, paper*] romper, rasgar • **you've torn your trousers** te has roto *or* rasgado el pantalón • **Jane tore my dress** Jane me rompió *or* rasgó el vestido • **to ~ a hole in sth** hacer un agujero en algo • **she tore open the envelope** abrió el sobre rápidamente • **to ~ sth to pieces** *or* **bits** (*lit*) [+ *letter, photograph*] hacer pedazos algo, destrozar algo; [+ *animal*] descuartizar algo; (*fig*) [+ *argument, essay, idea*] echar algo por tierra • **the antelope was torn to pieces by the lions** los leones descuartizaron el antílope • **to ~ sb to pieces** *or* **bits** (*lit*) descuartizar a algn; (*fig*) poner a algn por los suelos • IDIOM: • **that's torn it!*** ¡ya la hemos fastidiado!*, ¡buena la hemos hecho!*; ▹ **hair, limb**
2 (= *injure*) [+ *muscle*] desgarrarse; [+ *ligament*] romperse • **he tore a muscle in his thigh** se desgarró un músculo del muslo • **torn ligaments** rotura *f* de ligamentos
3 (= *pull, remove*) • **he tore the shelf away from the wall with his bare hands** arrancó el estante de la pared con sus propias manos • **to ~ o.s. free** *or* **loose** soltarse • **to ~ sth from/off sth** arrancar algo de algo • **he tore a page from** *or* **out of his notebook** arrancó una hoja del bloc de notas • **she tried to ~ the book from my hands** intentó arrancarme el libro de las manos • **the wind tore the roof off a building** el viento arrancó (de cuajo) el tejado de un edificio • IDIOM: • **to ~ sb off a strip** (*Brit**) poner a algn de vuelta y media*
4 (*fig*) • **having to make a decision like that can ~ you in two** tomar una decisión así puede ser una experiencia desgarradora • **he was torn by his emotions** estaba desgarrado por las emociones • **a country torn by war** un país desgarrado por la guerra • **she is torn between her job and her family** se debate entre su trabajo y su familia • **she was torn between the two men in her life** no se decidía entre los dos hombres que formaban parte de su vida; ▹ **tear apart**
(VI) **1** (= *get torn*) [*fabric, paper*] rasgarse, romperse; (*Med*) [*muscle, tissue*] desgarrarse; [*ligament*] romperse
2 (= *pull*) • **~ along the dotted line** rasgar por la línea de puntos • **to ~ at sth**: • **he tore at the wrapping paper** tiró del papel de regalo • **the eagles tore at its flesh with their beaks** las águilas le arrancaban la carne con los picos • **the brambles tore at his face** las zarzas le arañaron la cara • **she managed to ~ free** *or* **loose** logró soltarse
3 (= *rush*) • **to ~ along/out/down** *etc* ir/salir/bajar *etc* embalado, ir/salir/bajar *etc* a toda velocidad • **she tore out of the room/up the stairs** salió de la habitación/subió las escaleras embalada, salió de la habitación/subió las escaleras a toda velocidad • **we were ~ing along the motorway** íbamos embalados por la autopista, íbamos por la autopista a toda velocidad *or* a toda pastilla* • **to ~ past** pasar como un rayo • **an explosion tore through the building** una explosión sacudió el edificio
(CPD) ▸ **tear sheet** hoja *f* separable, página *f* recortable
▸ **tear along** (VI + ADV) (= *run*) correr precipitadamente, precipitarse, ir a máxima velocidad
(VI + PREP) = **tear¹**
▸ **tear apart** (VT + ADV) **1** (= *rip to pieces*) [+ *object*] hacer pedazos, hacer trizas; [+ *prey*] descuartizar
2 (*in search*) [+ *room, house*] destrozar • **they tore the room apart, searching for drugs** destrozaron la habitación en busca de drogas
3 (= *damage*) [+ *family, organization, person*] desgarrar • **the family had been torn apart by the divorce** el divorcio había desgarrado a la familia • **it ~s me apart to know you're unhappy** me desgarra el corazón saber que no eres feliz
4 (= *criticize*) [+ *idea, theory*] echar por tierra
▸ **tear away** (VT + ADV) (*fig*) • **the exhibition was so interesting I could hardly ~ myself away** era una exposición tan interesante que me costaba horrores marcharme • **eventually we tore him away from the party** por fin conseguimos arrancarlo de la fiesta, por fin conseguimos que se marchara de la fiesta • **I couldn't ~ my eyes away from him** no le podía quitar los ojos de encima • **if you can ~ yourself away from that book/the television** si puedes dejar ese libro/despegarte del televisor un momento
(VI + ADV) (*at speed*) salir embalado, salir a toda velocidad
▸ **tear down** (VT + ADV) [+ *building, statue*] derribar; [+ *poster, flag*] arrancar
▸ **tear off** (VT + ADV) **1** (= *remove*) [+ *sheet of paper, label, wrapping*] arrancar • **he tore off his clothes and fell into bed** se quitó la ropa a tirones y cayó sobre la cama • **he tried to ~ off her burning dress** intentó quitarle a tirones el vestido en llamas • **the hurricane/explosion tore off the roof** el huracán/la explosión arrancó el techo de cuajo
2* (= *write hurriedly*) [+ *letter*] escribir deprisa y corriendo, garrapatear
(VI + ADV) **1** (*at speed*) salir embalado, salir a toda velocidad • **she tore off on her motorbike** salió embalada *or* a toda velocidad en la moto
2 (= *be removable*) • **the label ~s off** la etiqueta se puede arrancar
(VT + PREP) ▹ **tear¹**
▸ **tear out** (VT + ADV) [+ *cheque, page*] arrancar; [+ *plant, stake, tree*] arrancar, arrancar de cuajo • **to ~ sb's eyes out** sacar los ojos a algn • **to ~ one's hair (out)** (*lit*) arrancarse el pelo a manojos; (*in exasperation, worry*) tirarse de los pelos
(VI + ADV) (= *rush*) ▹ **tear¹**
▸ **tear up** (VT + ADV) **1** (= *rip to pieces*) (*lit*) [+ *letter, photo*] romper, hacer pedazos; (*fig*) [+ *contract, agreement*] romper, anular
2 (= *pull up*) [+ *plant, stake, tree*] arrancar, arrancar de cuajo; [+ *forest, woodland*] talar, despoblar; [+ *road*] levantar
3 (= *damage*) [+ *pitch, surface*] destrozar

tear² [tɪəʳ] (N) lágrima *f* • **to burst into ~s** echarse a llorar • **she was close to ~s** estaba a punto de llorar • **to dissolve into ~s** deshacerse en lágrimas • **to be in ~s** estar llorando • **to end in ~s: it'll end in ~s!** (*lit*) ¡luego vendrán los llantos!, ¡al final acabaráis llorando!; (*fig*) acabará mal • **it was a marriage destined to end in ~s** era un matrimonio que estaba condenado a acabar mal • **to be moved to ~s** llorar de la emoción • **I was moved to ~s by their generosity** lloré de la emoción por la generosidad que mostraron • **to reduce sb to ~s** hacerle llorar a algn • **she didn't shed a single ~** no derramó ni una sola lágrima • **nobody is going to shed a ~ over that** nadie se va a disgustar por eso • **to wipe away one's ~s** secarse las lágrimas • IDIOM: • **to bore sb to ~s** aburrir soberanamente a algn • **I was bored to ~s** me aburrí soberanamente *or* como una ostra*
(CPD) ▸ **tear duct** conducto *m* lacrimal ▸ **tear gas** gas *m* lacrimógeno ▸ **tear gas bomb** bomba *f* lacrimógena ▸ **tear gas canister** bote *m* de gas lacrimógeno ▸ **tear gas grenade** granada *f* lacrimógena

tearaway* ['tɛərəweɪ] (N) (*Brit*) gamberro/a

t

m/f, alborotador(a) *m/f*
teardrop ['tɪədrɒp] (N) lágrima *f*
tearful ['tɪəfʊl] (ADJ) [*eyes, voice*] lloroso; [*farewell, reunion*] emotivo • **she was surrounded by ~ children** estaba rodeada de niños que lloraban • **she felt a bit ~** se le saltaron las lágrimas • **to become** *or* **get ~** ponerse a llorar
tearfully ['tɪəfəlɪ] (ADV) [*say, reply, smile*] con lágrimas en los ojos, llorando
tearing ['tɛərɪŋ] (ADJ) **1** • **with a ~ noise** con un ruido de tela que se rasga
2 (*fig*) • **at a ~ pace** a un paso vertiginoso • **to be in a ~ hurry** estar muy de prisa
tear-jerker* ['tɪə,dʒɜːkəʳ] (N) (= *film*) película *f* lacrimógena; (= *play*) dramón *m* muy sentimental*, obra *f* lacrimógena
tear-jerking* ['tɪə,dʒɜːkɪŋ] (ADJ) lacrimógeno, muy sentimental
tearless ['tɪəlɪs] (ADJ) sin lágrimas
tearlessly ['tɪəlɪslɪ] (ADV) sin llanto, sin llorar
tear-off ['tɛərɒf] (ADJ) [*tab, ticket*] con trepado, con taladrado
(CPD) ▸ **tear-off calendar** calendario *m* de taco ▸ **tear-off notebook** bloc *m* de notas
tearoom ['tiːrʊm] (N) salón *m* de té
tear-stained ['tɪəsteɪnd] (ADJ) manchado de lágrimas
teary ['tɪərɪ] (ADJ) [*eyes, voice*] lloroso; [*farewell, reunion*] emotivo • **to get ~** ponerse a llorar
tease [tiːz] (N) **1** (= *person*) (= *leg-puller*) bromista *mf*, guasón/ona* *m/f* • **he's a dreadful ~** es muy bromista, es muy guasón*
2 (= *flirt*) • **he's a dreadful ~** le gusta mucho flirtear
3 (= *joke*) • **to do sth for a ~** hacer algo para divertirse
(VT) **1** [+ *person*] (= *make fun of*) tomar el pelo a, mofarse de; (= *annoy*) fastidiar, molestar; (*cruelly*) atormentar; (*sexually*) coquetear con • **they ~ her about her hair** la molestan con chistes acerca de su pelo • **I don't like being ~d** no me gusta que se me tome el pelo
2 [+ *animal*] provocar
3 (*Tech*) [+ *fibres*] cardar
▸ **tease out** (VT + ADV) [+ *tangles*] desenredar, separar; (*fig*) [+ *information*] sonsacar, ir sacando
teasel ['tiːzl] (N) **1** (*Bot*) cardencha *f*
2 (*Tech*) carda *f*
teaser ['tiːzəʳ] (N) **1** (= *person*) = **tease**
2* (= *problem*) rompecabezas *m inv*
teashop ['tiːʃɒp] (N) (*Brit*) café *m*, cafetería *f*; (*strictly*) salón *m* de té
teasing ['tiːzɪŋ] (ADJ) burlón, guasón*
(N) burlas *fpl*, guasa* *f*
teasingly ['tiːzɪŋlɪ] (ADV) **1** (= *jokingly*) [*say*] de manera burlona, de cachondeo (*Sp**)
2 (= *flirtatiously*) [*smile*] coquetamente
Teasmade, **Teasmaid®** ['tiːzmeɪd] (N) tetera *f* automática (*que funciona al sonar el despertador*)
teaspoon ['tiːspuːn] (N) (= *spoon*) cucharilla *f*, cucharita *f* (de postre); (= *quantity*) cucharadita *f*
teaspoonful ['tiːspʊnfʊl] (N) cucharadita *f*
teat [tiːt] (N) [*of bottle*] tetina *f*; [*of animal*] teta *f*
teatime ['tiːtaɪm] (N) (*esp Brit*) **1** (= *time for drinking tea*) hora *f* del té • **at ~** a la hora del té
2 (= *time of evening meal*) hora *f* de cenar
TEC (N ABBR) (*Brit*) = **Training and Enterprise Council**
'tec* [tek] (N) = **detective**
tech [tek] (N ABBR) **1** = **technology**
2 = **technical college**
techie* ['tekɪ] (N) tecnologuillo/a *m/f*
technetium [tek'niːʃɪəm] (N) tecnetio *m*
technical ['teknɪkəl] (ADJ) técnico • **this is getting too ~** esto se está poniendo muy técnico • **a ~ hitch** un fallo técnico • **a ~ offence** (*Jur*) un delito de carácter técnico, un cuasidelito • **a ~ point** un detalle técnico • **for ~ reasons** por motivos técnicos • **the government has scored a ~ victory** teóricamente, el gobierno ha logrado una victoria
(CPD) ▸ **technical college** (*Brit*) (*Scol*) ≈ escuela *f* politécnica, ≈ instituto *m* de formación profesional (*Sp*) ▸ **technical drawing** dibujo *m* técnico ▸ **technical institute** (*US*) instituto *m* tecnológico ▸ **technical knockout** (*Boxing*) K.O. *m* técnico ▸ **technical support** (*Comput*) (servicio *m* de) asistencia *f* técnica
technicality [,teknɪ'kælɪtɪ] (N) **1** (= *technical detail*) detalle *m* (técnico); (= *word*) tecnicismo *m* • **I don't understand all the technicalities** no entiendo todos los detalles (técnicos) • **it failed because of a ~** fracasó debido a una dificultad técnica
2 (= *nature*) tecnicidad *f*, carácter *m* técnico
technically ['teknɪkəlɪ] (ADV)
1 (= *technologically*) [*advanced*] técnicamente; [*superior, feasible*] técnicamente, desde el punto de vista técnico
2 (= *strictly*) [*illegal, correct*] técnicamente • **~, they aren't eligible for a grant** técnicamente *or* en teoría, no tienen derecho a una ayuda • **~ speaking** hablando en sentido estricto, en puridad (*frm*)
3 (= *regarding technique*) [*proficient, demanding*] desde el punto de vista técnico, técnicamente
technician [tek'nɪʃən] (N) técnico/a *m/f*; ▹ **dental**, **laboratory**
Technicolor® ['teknɪ,kʌləʳ] (N) tecnicolor® *m* • **in ~** en tecnicolor
(ADJ) en tecnicolor, de tecnicolor
technique [tek'niːk] (N) (*gen*) técnica *f*
techno ['teknəʊ] (*Mus*) (N) tecno *m*
(ADJ) [*music, scene*] tecno (*inv*)
techno... ['teknəʊ] (PREFIX) tecno...
techno-babble ['teknəʊbæbl] (N) jerga *f* técnica
technocracy [tek'nɒkrəsɪ] (N) tecnocracia *f*
technocrat ['teknəʊkræt] (N) tecnócrata *mf*
technocratic [,teknə'krætɪk] (ADJ) tecnocrático
technological [,teknə'lɒdʒɪkəl] (ADJ) tecnológico
technologically [,teknə'lɒdʒɪkəlɪ] (ADV) tecnológicamente
technologist [tek'nɒlədʒɪst] (N) tecnólogo/a *m/f*
technology [tek'nɒlədʒɪ] (N) tecnología *f*
technophobe [,teknəʊ'fəʊb] (N) tecnófobo/a *m/f*
technophobia [,teknəʊ'fəʊbɪə] (N) tecnofobia *f*
technophobic [,teknəʊ'fəʊbɪk] (ADJ) tecnofóbico
techy ['tetʃɪ] (ADJ) = **tetchy**
tectonic [tek'tɒnɪk] (ADJ) tectónico • **~ movement** movimiento *m* tectónico • **~ plate** placa *f* tectónica
tectonics [tek'tɒnɪks] (N) tectónica *f*
Ted [ted] (N) *familiar form of* **Edward**
tedder ['tedəʳ] (N) heneador *m*
Teddy ['tedɪ] (N) *familiar form of* **Edward**
teddy ['tedɪ] (N) (*also* **teddy bear**) osito *m* (de peluche)
(CPD) ▸ **teddy boy** (*Brit*) *hombre vestido a la moda de los rockeros de los años 50 y considerado a menudo una persona violenta*
tedious ['tiːdɪəs] (ADJ) pesado, aburrido
tediously ['tiːdɪəslɪ] (ADV) • **~ dull** mortalmente aburrido • **his speech was ~ long** su discurso fue largo y pesado *or* aburrido
tediousness ['tiːdɪəsnɪs], **tedium** ['tiːdɪəm] (N) pesadez *f*, lo aburrido
tee [tiː] (N) **1** (*Golf*) (= *object*) tee *m*; (= *area*) punto *m* de salida • **the third tee** el punto de salida del tercer hoyo
2, ▹ **T**
▸ **tee off** (VI + ADV) dar el primer golpe
▸ **tee up** (VT + ADV) (*Golf*) [+ *ball*] colocar en el tee; (*Ftbl*) preparar
(VI + ADV) colocar la pelota en el tee
tee-hee ['tiː'hiː] (N) risita *f* (tonta)
(EXCL) ¡ji!, ¡ji!, ¡je!, ¡je!
(VI) reírse con una risita tonta, reírse un poquito
teem [tiːm] (VI) **1** • **to ~ (with)** [+ *insects, fish*] abundar (en) • **a lake ~ing with fish** un lago que abunda en peces, un lago repleto de peces • **through streets ~ing with people** por calles atestadas de gente
2 • **it's ~ing (with rain)** está lloviendo a mares *or* a cántaros
▸ **teem down** (VI + ADV) (= *rain hard*) llover a mares, llover a cántaros • **it's ~ing down** está lloviendo a mares *or* a cántaros
teeming ['tiːmɪŋ] (ADJ) numerosísimo; [*rain*] torrencial • **the ~ millions** los muchos millones
teen* [tiːn] (ADJ) = **teenage**
teenage ['tiːneɪdʒ] (ADJ) [*fashion*] para adolescentes, juvenil • **a ~ boy/girl** un/una adolescente • **memories of her ~ years** recuerdos *mpl* de sus años de adolescencia • **to reduce the number of ~ pregnancies** reducir el número de embarazos entre las jóvenes adolescentes
teenaged ['tiːneɪdʒd] (ADJ) • **~ boy** adolescente *m* • **~ girl** adolescente *f*
teenager ['tiːn,eɪdʒəʳ] (N) adolescente *mf* • **a club for ~s** un club para jóvenes
teens [tiːnz] (NPL) adolescencia *fsing* • **to be in one's ~** ser adolescente • **he is still in his ~** es adolescente todavía, no ha cumplido aún los 20
teensy* ['tiːnzɪ], **teensy-weensy*** ['tiːnzɪ'wiːnzɪ] (ADJ) = **teeny**
teeny* ['tiːnɪ], **teeny-weeny*** ['tiːnɪ'wiːnɪ] (ADJ) chiquito, chiquitín
teenybopper ['tiːnɪ'bɒpəʳ] (N) quinceañero/a *m/f*
teepee ['tiːpiː] = **tepee**
tee-shirt ['tiːʃɜːt] (N) = **T-shirt**
teeter ['tiːtəʳ] (VI) bambolearse, tambalearse; (*fig*) vacilar, titubear • **to ~ on the edge of a nervous breakdown** estar al borde de un ataque nervioso
(CPD) ▸ **teeter totter** (*US*) subibaja *m*, balancín *m*
teeth [tiːθ] (NPL) *of* **tooth**
teethe [tiːð] (VI) echar los dientes • **he's teething** le están saliendo los dientes, está echando los dientes
teething ['tiːðɪŋ] (N) dentición *f*
(CPD) ▸ **teething ring** chupador *m*, mordedor *m* ▸ **teething troubles**, **teething problems** (*Brit*) (*fig*) problemas *mpl* iniciales
teetotal ['tiː'təʊtl] (ADJ) [*person*] abstemio • **the Methodist church used to be ~** los metodistas eran abstemios
teetotalism ['tiː'təʊtəlɪzəm] (N) abstinencia *f* (de bebidas alcohólicas)
teetotaller, **teetotaler** (*US*) ['tiː'təʊtləʳ] (N) (= *person*) abstemio/a *m/f*
TEFL ['tefl] (N ABBR) = **Teaching of English as a Foreign Language**

t

TEFL/EFL, TESL/ESL, ELT, TESOL/ESOL

Los términos **TEFL (Teaching (of) English as a Foreign Language**: enseñanza del inglés como lengua extranjera) y **EFL (English as a Foreign Language**: inglés para extranjeros) se usan para hablar de la enseñanza del inglés a personas que no viven en un país de habla inglesa.

TESL (Teaching (of) English as a Second Language: enseñanza del inglés como segunda lengua) y **ESL (English as a Second Language**: inglés como segunda lengua) se refieren a la enseñanza del inglés a personas que viven en un país de habla inglesa pero tienen otra lengua materna, por ejemplo, los miembros de las minorías étnicas. Este tipo de enseñanza intenta integrar el entorno cultural del alumno y aprovechar el conocimiento de su lengua materna en el proceso de aprendizaje.

ELT (English Language Teaching: enseñanza del inglés) es el término que se aplica a la enseñanza del inglés en general y, por tanto, engloba a los ya mencionados.

TESOL (Teaching (of) English to Speakers of Other Languages) es el término de inglés americano que equivale a **TEFL** y a **TESL**. **ESOL (English for Speakers of Other Languages)** es el equivalente a **EFL** y **ESL**.

Teflon® ['teflɒn] (N) teflón® *m*

tegument ['tegjʊmənt] (N) tegumento *m*

Teheran, Tehran [tɛə'rɑːn] (N) Teherán *m*

tel. (ABBR) (= **telephone**) tel, tfno, Tfno

Tel Aviv [ˌteləˈviːv] (N) Tel Aviv *m*

tele... ['telɪ] (PREFIX) tele...

telebanking ['telɪˌbæŋkɪŋ] (N) telebanco *m*, telebanca *f*

telecamera ['telɪˌkæmərə] (N) telecámara *f*

telecast ['telɪkɑːst] (US) (N) programa *m* de televisión
(VT), (VI) transmitir (por televisión)

telecommunications ['telɪkəˌmjuːnɪ'keɪʃənz] (N) (= *area of study*) telecomunicaciones *fpl*
(CPD) [*company, equipment*] de telecomunicaciones ▸ **the telecommunications industry** el sector de telecomunicaciones, la industria de telecomunicaciones ▸ **telecommunications satellite** satélite *m* de telecomunicaciones

telecommute ['telɪkə'mjuːt] (VI) teletrabajar, trabajar a distancia

telecommuter ['telɪkə'mjuːtəʳ] (N) teletrabajador(a) *m/f*, trabajador(a) *m/f* a distancia

telecommuting ['telɪkə'mjuːtɪŋ] (N) teletrabajo *m*, trabajo *m* a distancia

telecoms* ['telɪkɒmz] (NPL) telecomunicaciones *fpl*
(ADJ) [*analyst, business, company, equipment*] de telecomunicaciones; [*giant, industry*] de las telecomunicaciones

teleconference ['telɪkɒnfərəns] (N) teleconferencia *f*

teleconferencing ['telɪkɒnfərənsɪŋ] (N) teleconferencias *fpl*

Telecopier® ['telɪˌkɒpɪəʳ] (N) telecopiadora *m*

telecopy ['telɪˌkɒpɪ] (N) telecopia *f*

telefax ['telɪfæks] (N) telefax *m*

telefilm ['telɪfɪlm] (N) telefilm(e) *m*

telegenic [ˌtelɪ'dʒenɪk] (ADJ) televisivo, telegénico

telegram ['telɪgræm] (N) telegrama *m*

telegraph ['telɪgrɑːf] (N) (= *message*) telegrama *m*; (= *apparatus*) aparato *m* telegráfico
(VT), (VI) telegrafiar
(CPD) ▸ **telegraph pole, telegraph post** poste *m* telegráfico ▸ **telegraph wire** hilo *m* telegráfico

telegraphese ['telɪgrɑː'fiːz] (N) estilo *m* telegráfico

telegraphic [ˌtelɪ'græfɪk] (ADJ) telegráfico

telegraphically [ˌtelɪ'græfɪkəlɪ] (ADV) telegráficamente

telegraphist [tɪ'legrəfɪst] (N) telegrafista *mf*

telegraphy [tɪ'legrəfɪ] (N) telegrafía *f*

telekinesis [ˌtelɪkɪ'niːsɪs] (N) telequinesia *f*

telekinetic [ˌtelɪkɪ'netɪk] (ADJ) telequinético

telemarketer ['telɪmɑːkɪtəʳ] (N) (= *person*) especialista *mf* en telemárketing; (= *company*) empresa *f* de telemárketing

telemarketing ['telɪmɑːkɪtɪŋ] (N) (*Comm*) telemárketing *m*

telematic [ˌtelɪ'mætɪk] (ADJ) telemático

telemessage ['telɪmesɪdʒ] (N) (*Brit*) telegrama *m*

telemetric [ˌtelɪ'metrɪk] (ADJ) telemétrico

telemetry [tɪ'lemɪtrɪ] (N) telemetría *f*

teleological [ˌtelɪə'lɒdʒɪkl] (ADJ) teleológico

teleology [ˌtelɪ'ɒlədʒɪ] (N) teleología *f*

teleordering ['telɪˌɔːdərɪŋ] (N) pedido *m* telefónico

telepath ['telɪpæθ] (N) telépata *mf*

telepathic [ˌtelɪ'pæθɪk] (ADJ) telepático

telepathically [ˌtelɪ'pæθɪklɪ] (ADV) telepáticamente, por telepatía

telepathist [tɪ'lepəθɪst] (N) telepatista *mf*

telepathy [tɪ'lepəθɪ] (N) telepatía *f*

telephone ['telɪfəʊn] (N) teléfono *m* • **to be on the ~** (= *be connected*) tener teléfono; (= *be speaking*) estar hablando por teléfono • **you're wanted on the ~** le llaman al teléfono
(VI) telefonear • **I'll ~ for an ambulance** llamaré a una ambulancia
(VT) llamar por teléfono, telefonear
(CPD) ▸ **telephone answering machine** contestador *m* automático ▸ **telephone book** = **telephone directory** ▸ **telephone booth** (*US*), **telephone box** (*Brit*) cabina *f* telefónica ▸ **telephone call** llamada *f* (telefónica) ▸ **telephone directory** guía *f* telefónica ▸ **telephone exchange** central *f* (telefónica); (*private*) centralita *f* (*Sp*), conmutador *m* (*LAm*) ▸ **telephone kiosk** = **telephone box** ▸ **telephone number** número *m* de teléfono, fono *m* (*Chile*) • **he's paid in ~ numbers*** le pagan un dineral* ▸ **telephone operator** telefonista *mf* ▸ **telephone pole** (*US*) poste *m* telegráfico ▸ **telephone sex** teléfono *m* erótico ▸ **telephone subscriber** abonado/a *m/f* telefónico/a ▸ **telephone tapping** intervención *f* telefónica ▸ **telephone warning** aviso *m* telefónico ▸ **telephone wires** hilos *mpl* telefónicos

telephonic [ˌtelɪ'fɒnɪk] (ADJ) telefónico

telephonist [tɪ'lefənɪst] (N) telefonista *mf*

telephony [tɪ'lefənɪ] (N) telefonía *f*

telephotography [ˌtelɪfə'tɒgrəfɪ] (N) telefotografía *f*

telephoto lens ['telɪˌfəʊtəʊ'lenz] (N) teleobjetivo *m*

teleport ['telɪpɔːt] (VT) teletransportar

teleprint ['telɪˌprɪnt] (VT) (*Brit*) transmitir por teletipo

teleprinter ['telɪˌprɪntəʳ] (N) teletipo *m*

teleprocessing [ˌtelɪ'prəʊsesɪŋ] (N) teleproceso *m*

teleprompter® ['telɪˌprɒmptəʳ] (N) teleprompter *m*

telesales ['telɪˌseɪlz] (NPL) televenta(s) *f(pl)*
(CPD) ▸ **telesales person** televendedor(a) *m/f*

telescope ['telɪskəʊp] (N) telescopio *m*
(VI) [*aerial, umbrella*] plegarse
(VT) abatir, plegar • **to ~ A into B** meter A dentro de B

telescopic [ˌtelɪs'kɒpɪk] (ADJ) telescópico
(CPD) ▸ **telescopic lens** teleobjetivo *m* ▸ **telescopic sight** mira *f* telescópica, visor *m* telescópico ▸ **telescopic umbrella** paraguas *m* plegable

teleshopping ['telɪˌʃɒpɪŋ] (N) (*US*) telecompra(s) *f(pl)*

teletex ['telәteks] (N) teletexto *m*

teletext ['telɪtekst] (N) teletex(to) *m*

telethon ['teləθɒn] (N) (*TV*) telemaratón *m* (con fines benéficos)

Teletype® ['telɪˌtaɪp] (N) teletipo *m*

teletypewriter [ˌtelɪ'taɪpraɪtəʳ] (*US*) (N) = **teleprinter**

televangelist [ˌtelɪ'vændʒəlɪst] (N) evangelista *mf* de la tele

teleview ['teləvjuː] (VI) (*US*) ver la televisión

televiewer ['telɪˌvjuːəʳ] (N) televidente *mf*, telespectador(a) *m/f*

televise ['telɪvaɪz] (VT) transmitir (por televisión), televisar

television ['telɪˌvɪʒən] (N) (= *broadcast, broadcasting industry*) televisión *f*; (*also* **television set**) televisor *m*, aparato *m* de televisión • **to be on ~** [*person*] salir por la televisión • **to watch ~** ver *or* mirar la televisión • **to speak on ~** hablar por televisión
(CPD) [*broadcast, play, report, serial*] televisivo; [*camera*] de televisión; [*personality*] de la televisión ▸ **television aerial** antena *f* de televisión ▸ **television announcer** locutor(a) *m/f* de televisión ▸ **television broadcast** emisión *f* televisiva ▸ **television licence** (*Brit*) *licencia que se paga por el uso del televisor, destinada a financiar la BBC* ▸ **television licence fee** (*Brit*) *impuesto que se paga por el uso del televisor, destinado a financiar la BBC* ▸ **television lounge** sala *f* de televisión ▸ **television network** cadena *f* de televisión, red *f* de televisión ▸ **television programme** programa *m* de televisión ▸ **television room** sala *f* de televisión ▸ **television screen** pantalla *f* de televisión ▸ **television set** televisor *m*, aparato *m* de televisión ▸ **television studio** estudio *m* de televisión ▸ **television tube** tubo *m* de rayos catódicos, cinescopio *m*

televisual [telɪ'vɪzjʊəl] (ADJ) (*Brit*) televisivo

telework ['telɪwɜːk] (VI) teletrabajar

teleworker ['telɪwɜːkəʳ] (N) teletrabajador(a) *m/f*

teleworking ['telɪwɜːkɪŋ] (N) teletrabajo *m*

telex ['teleks] (N) (*gen*) télex *m inv*
(VT), (VI) enviar un télex (a)

tell [tel] (PT, PP: **told**) (VT) **1** [+ *story, experiences*] contar; [+ *truth*] decir; [+ *secret*] contar, divulgar (*frm*); (*formally*) comunicar, informar • **to ~ sb sth** decir algo a algn • **to ~ sb whether/how/why** *etc* decir a algn si/cómo/por qué *etc* • **to ~ sb that ...** decir a algn que ... • **I have been told that ...** me han dicho que ..., se me ha dicho que ... (*frm*) • **I am pleased to ~ you that ...** (*frm*) me complace comunicarle que ..., me es grato comunicarle que ... • **I ~ you it isn't!** ¡te digo que no! • **let me ~ you, I didn't enjoy it** si te digo la verdad, no me gustó nada • **there were three, I ~ you, three** había tres, ¿me oyes?, tres • **I ~ myself it can't be true** digo para mí que no puede ser verdad • **I told him about the missing money** le dije lo del dinero que faltaba, le informé acerca del dinero que faltaba (*frm*) • **~ me all about it**

cuéntame todo • **I'll ~ you all about it** te (lo) diré todo • **~ me another!*** ¡cuéntaselo a tu abuela!* • **he's no saint, I can ~ you!** ¡no es ningún santo, te lo aseguro! • **so much happened that I can't begin to ~ you** pasaron tantas cosas no sé por dónde empezar a contarte • **I cannot ~ you how pleased I am** no encuentro palabras para expresarle lo contento que estoy • **I could ~ you a thing or two about him** hay cosas de él que yo me sé • **don't ~ me you can't do it!** ¡no me vayas a decir *or* no me digas que no lo puedes hacer! • **to ~ sb's fortune** • **~ sb the future** decir a algn la buenaventura • **to ~ a lie** mentir • **you're ~ing me!*** ¡a quién se lo cuentas!, ¡a mí no me lo vas a contar! • **I told you so!** ¡ya lo decía yo! • **didn't I ~ you so?** ¿no te lo dije ya? • **(I) ~ you what, let's go now** sabes qué, vámonos ya • **I ~ you what!** ¡se me ocurre una idea!; ▹ **marine**

2 (= *order*) • **to ~ sb to do sth** decir a algn que haga algo, mandar a algn a hacer algo • **do as you are told!** ¡haz lo que te digo! • **he won't be told** no acepta consejos de nadie, no quiere hacer caso de nadie • **I told you not to** te dije que no lo hicieras

3 (= *indicate*) [*sign, dial, clock*] indicar • **to ~ sb sth** indicar algo a algn • **there was a sign ~ing us which way to go** una señal nos indicaba el camino • **the clock ~s the quarter hours** el reloj da los cuartos de hora

4 (= *distinguish*) distinguir • **I couldn't ~ them apart** no sabía distinguirlos • **to ~ the difference between A and B** distinguir entre A y B • **I can't ~ the difference** no veo la diferencia • **to ~ right from wrong** distinguir el bien del mal; ▹ **time**

5 (= *know, be certain*) saber • **you can ~ he's a German** se (le) nota que es alemán • **you can ~ a horse's age by its teeth** la edad de un caballo se sabe por los dientes • **how can I ~ what she will do?** ¿cómo voy a saber lo que ella hará? • **you can't ~ much from his letter** su carta nos dice bien poco • **I couldn't ~ how it was done** no sabía cómo se hizo • **there is no ~ing what he will do** es imposible saber qué va a hacer

6 (= *count*) • **to ~ one's beads** rezar el rosario • **400 all told** 400 en total

(VI) **1** (= *speak*) • **to ~ (of)** hablar de • **the ruins told of a sad history** las ruinas hablaban de una triste historia • **"did you love her?" — "more than words can ~"** —¿la amabas? —más de lo que pueda expresar con palabras • **it hurt more than words can ~** dolió una barbaridad, dolió lo indecible • **I hear ~ that …** dicen que … • **I hear ~ of a disaster** he oído que ha ocurrido una catástrofe • **I have never heard ~ of it** no he oído nunca hablar de eso

2* (= *sneak, tell secrets*) • **please don't ~!** ¡no vayas contándolo *or* soplándolo* por ahí! • **he told on me to my parents** se chivó de mí a mis padres (*Sp**) • **that would be ~ing!** ¡es un secreto!

3 (= *know, be certain*) saber • **how can I ~?** ¿cómo lo voy a saber?, ¿yo qué sé? • **I can't ~** (me) es imposible saberlo, no le puedo decir, no sabría decirle • **who can ~?** ¿quién sabe? • **there is no ~ing** no se puede saber • **you never can ~** nunca se sabe; ▹ **time**

4 (= *have an effect*) • **every blow told** cada golpe tuvo su efecto • **stamina ~s in the long run** a la larga importa *or* vale más la resistencia • **blood will ~** la sangre cuenta • **to ~ against sb** obrar en contra de algn • **the strain is beginning to ~ on him** la tensión está empezando a afectarle

▸ **tell off** (VT + ADV) **1** (= *order*) ordenar, mandar

2* • **to ~ sb off (for sth/for doing sth)** regañar a algn (por algo/por haber hecho algo)

teller ['teləʳ] (N) **1** [*of story*] narrador(a) *m/f*
2 (*US, Scot*) (*in bank*) cajero/a *m/f*; (*at election*) escrutador(a) *m/f*

telling ['telɪŋ] (ADJ) (= *effective*) [*blow*] certero; [*argument*] contundente, eficaz; (= *significant*) [*figures, remark*] revelador
(N) narración *f* • **the story did not lose in the ~** la historia no perdió nada al ser narrada

telling-off [ˌtelɪŋ'ɒf] (N) bronca *f*, reprimenda *f* • **to give sb a telling-off** echar una bronca *or* regañar a algn

telltale ['telteɪl] (ADJ) [*sign*] revelador, indicador
(N) **1** (= *person*) soplón/ona *m/f*
2 (*Naut*) catavientos *m inv*

tellurium [te'lʊərɪəm] (N) telurio *m*

telly* ['telɪ] (*Brit*) (N) tele* *f*
(CPD) ▸ **telly addict*** teleadicto/a *m/f*

temazepam [tɪ'mæzɪˌpæm] (N) temazepam *m*

temblor ['tembləʳ] (N) (*US*) temblor *m* de tierra

temerity [tɪ'merɪtɪ] (N) temeridad *f* • **to have the ~ to** (+ *infin*) atreverse a (+ *infin*) • **and you have the ~ to say that …!** ¡y usted se atreve a decir que …!, ¡y usted me dice tan fresco que …!

temp* [temp] (N ABBR) (= **temporary**) empleado/a *m/f* eventual, temporero/a *m/f*
(VI) trabajar como empleado/a eventual, trabajar de temporero

temp. (ABBR) = **temperature**

temper ['tempəʳ] (N) **1** (= *nature*) carácter *m*, genio *m*; (= *mood*) humor *m* • **to be in a ~** estar furioso • **to be in a good/bad ~** estar de buen/mal humor • **to keep one's ~** no perder la calma, contenerse • **to lose one's ~** perder los estribos • **to have a quick ~** tener genio • **in a fit of ~** en un acceso de furia *or* ira • **to fly into a ~** ponerse furioso, montar en cólera • **mind your ~!** • **temper, temper!** ¡contrólate *or* controla ese genio!
2 [*of metal*] temple *m*
(VT) **1** (= *moderate*) [+ *remarks*] suavizar, atenuar; [+ *energy, enthusiasm*] atemperar • **to ~ justice with mercy** templar la justicia con la compasión
2 (= *soften*) [+ *metal*] templar
(CPD) ▸ **temper tantrum** rabieta *f* • **to have a ~ tantrum** coger una rabieta

tempera ['tempərə] (N) pintura *f* al temple

temperament ['tempərəmənt] (N)
1 (= *disposition*) temperamento *m*, disposición *f*
2 (= *moodiness, difficult temperament*) genio *m* • **he has a ~** tiene genio

temperamental [ˌtempərə'mentl] (ADJ)
1 (= *moody*) [*person, machine*] caprichoso
2 (= *caused by one's nature*) temperamental, por temperamento

temperamentally [ˌtempərə'mentəlɪ] (ADV) (*by nature*) • **he's ~ suited/unsuited to this job** por naturaleza sirve/no sirve para hacer este trabajo • **~, he is more like …** en cuanto a temperamento, se parece más a …

temperance ['tempərəns] (N) **1** (= *moderation*) templanza *f* (*frm*), moderación *f*
2 (= *teetotalism*) abstinencia *f* de bebidas alcohólicas
(CPD) ▸ **temperance hotel** hotel *m* donde no se sirven bebidas alcohólicas ▸ **temperance movement** campaña *f* antialcohólica

temperate ['tempərɪt] (ADJ) [*climate, zone*] templado; [*person*] moderado; (*in drinking*) abstemio • **to be ~ in one's demands** ser moderado en sus exigencias

temperature ['temprɪtʃəʳ] (N) **1** (*Met*) temperatura *f*
2 (*Med*) (= *high temperature*) calentura *f*, fiebre *f* • **to have *or* run a ~** tener fiebre *or* calentura • **she has a ~ of 103°** ≈ tiene 39° de fiebre • **to take sb's ~** tomar la temperatura a algn
(CPD) ▸ **temperature chart** gráfico *m* de temperaturas ▸ **temperature gauge** indicador *m* de temperatura

tempered ['tempəd] (ADJ) templado

-tempered ['tempəd] (ADJ) (*ending in compounds*) de … humor

tempest ['tempɪst] (N) (*poet*) tempestad *f* • IDIOM: • **a ~ in a teapot** (*US*) una tormenta *or* tempestad en un vaso de agua

tempestuous [tem'pestjʊəs] (ADJ) [*relationship, meeting*] tempestuoso

tempi ['tempi:] (NPL) *of* **tempo**

Templar ['templəʳ] (N) templario *m*

template, templet (*US*) ['templɪt] (N) plantilla *f*

temple ['templ] (N) **1** (*Rel*) templo *m*
2 (*Anat*) sien *f*
3 • **the Temple** (*in London*) el Colegio de Abogados

templet ['templɪt] (N) (*US*) = **template**

tempo ['tempəʊ] (N) (PL: **tempos,** (*Mus*) **tempi** ['tempi:]) (*Mus*) tempo *m*; (*fig*) ritmo *m*

temporal ['tempərəl] (ADJ) (*Ling*) [*conjunction, clause*] temporal

temporarily ['tempərərɪlɪ] (ADV) temporalmente

temporary ['tempərərɪ] (ADJ) [*accommodation, solution, licence*] temporal, provisional; [*secretary, job, staff*] temporal, eventual; [*problem*] pasajero, temporal • **this is just a ~ measure** esto es solo una medida temporal *or* provisional • **orthodox treatment gave only ~ relief** el tratamiento ortodoxo proporcionó solo un alivio temporal *or* pasajero • **~ workers** trabajadores *mpl* temporales; (*agricultural*) temporeros *mpl* • **"temporary road surface"** "asfalto provisional"

temporize ['tempəraɪz] (VI) tratar de ganar tiempo

tempt [tempt] (VT) **1** (*gen*) tentar • **to ~ sb to do sth** tentar a algn a hacer algo • **I'm ~ed to do it** estoy tentado de hacerlo • **they've offered me a job in France and I must say I'm ~ed** me han ofrecido un trabajo en Francia y la verdad es que me tienta mucho • **can I ~ you to another cake?** ¿le apetece otro pastelito?
2 (*Rel*) tentar, poner a prueba • **you shouldn't ~ fate *or* providence** no hay que tentar a la suerte

temptation [temp'teɪʃən] (N) tentación *f* • **there is always a ~ to …** existe siempre la tentación de … • **to resist ~** resistir (a) la tentación • **I couldn't resist the ~ to tell him *or* of telling him** no pude resistir la tentación de decírselo • **to give way *or* yield to ~** ceder a la tentación • **to put ~ in sb's way** exponer a algn a la tentación • **lead us not into ~** (*Bible*) no nos dejes caer en la tentación

tempter ['temptəʳ] (N) tentador *m*

tempting ['temptɪŋ] (ADJ) [*food*] apetitoso; [*offer, idea*] tentador • **it would be ~ to agree** uno se siente tentado a pensar lo mismo

temptingly ['temptɪŋlɪ] (ADV) [*displayed, arrayed*] de modo tentador • **their strawberry gateau is ~ fruity** su pastel de fresa lleno de fruta resulta de lo más apetitoso • **it is ~ easy to …** lo más fácil sería …, uno se siente tentado a …

temptress ['temptrɪs] (N) tentadora *f*

ten [ten] (ADJ), (PRON) diez
(N) (= *numeral*) diez *m* • **tens of thousands** decenas de miles • **ten to one he'll be late*** te

apuesto que llega tarde • IDIOM: • **they're ten a penny*** se encuentran en todas partes; ▹ **five**

tenable ['tenəbl] ADJ [*argument*] sostenible, defendible; [*proposal*] válido

tenacious [tɪ'neɪʃəs] ADJ [*person*] tenaz; [*belief, idea*] firme

tenaciously [tɪ'neɪʃəslɪ] ADV tenazmente, con tenacidad

tenacity [tɪ'næsɪtɪ] N tenacidad *f*

tenancy ['tenənsɪ] N (= *possession, period*) tenencia *f*, inquilinato *m*; (= *lease*) arriendo *m*, alquiler *m* • **joint/multiple ~** arriendo *m* or alquiler *m* conjunto/múltiple

CPD ▸ **tenancy agreement** contrato *m* de alquiler

tenant ['tenənt] N inquilino/a *m/f*, arrendatario/a *m/f*

CPD ▸ **tenant farmer** agricultor(a) *m/f* arrendatario/a

tenantry ['tenəntrɪ] N inquilinos *mpl*; (*Agr*) agricultores *mpl* arrendatarios

tench [tentʃ] N (*pl inv*) tenca *f*

tend[1] [tend] VI **1** • **to ~ to do sth** tender a hacer algo, soler hacer algo • **men ~ to die younger than women** los hombres tienden a or suelen morir más jóvenes que las mujeres • **this type of material ~s to shrink** este tipo de tela tiene tendencia a or tiende a or suele encoger • **that ~s to be the case** tiende a ser así, suele ser así • **I ~ to agree** me inclino a pensar lo mismo

2 • **to ~ towards** tender a • **her stories ~ towards the melodramatic** sus historias tienden a ser melodramáticas • **he ~s towards conservatism** es de tendencias conservadoras

tend[2] [tend] VT **1** (= *care for*) [+ *patient, invalid*] cuidar, atender; [+ *sheep, cattle, horses*] cuidar, ocuparse de; [+ *garden*] ocuparse de; [+ *grave*] cuidar de; [+ *fire*] atender, ocuparse de

2 • **to ~ bar** (*US*) servir en el bar

VI • **to ~ to** [+ *patient, invalid*] atender a, cuidar; [+ *sheep, cattle, horses*] cuidar, ocuparse de; [+ *fire*] atender, ocuparse de; [+ *housework, wounds, needs*] ocuparse de

tendency ['tendənsɪ] N **1** (*gen*) tendencia *f* • **to have a ~ to do sth** [*person*] tener tendencia a hacer algo; (*Med*) tener propensión or ser propenso a hacer algo • **he has a ~ to exaggerate** tiene tendencia a exagerar • **there is a ~ for companies to recruit fewer staff** existe tendencia por parte de las empresas a emplear a menos trabajadores • **there is a ~ for prices to rise** los precios tienen tendencia a subir • **she has a ~ to or towards depression** tiene propensión or es propensa a la depresión

2 (= *leaning*) • **left-wing/right-wing tendencies** tendencias *fpl* izquierdistas/derechistas • **suicidal tendencies** tendencias *fpl* or inclinaciones *fpl* suicidas

tendentious [ten'denʃəs] ADJ tendencioso

tendentiously [ten'denʃəslɪ] ADV de modo tendencioso

tendentiousness [ten'denʃəsnɪs] N tendenciosidad *f*

tender[1] ['tendəʳ] N **1** (*Comm*) oferta *f* • **call for ~** propuesta *f* para licitación de obras • **to put in or make a ~ (for)** presentarse a concurso or a una licitación (para) • **to put sth out to ~** sacar algo a concurso or a licitación

2 [*of currency*] • **legal ~** moneda *f* corriente or de curso legal

VT (*frm*) (= *proffer*) [+ *money*] ofrecer; [+ *thanks*] dar • **he ~ed his resignation** presentó su dimisión

VI (*Comm*) • **to ~ (for)** presentarse a concurso or a una licitación (para)

CPD ▸ **tender documents** pliegos *mpl* de propuesta

tender[2] ['tendəʳ] N **1** (*Rail*) ténder *m*

2 (*Naut*) gabarra *f*, embarcación *f* auxiliar

tender[3] ['tendəʳ] ADJ **1** (= *gentle, affectionate*) [*person, expression, kiss, word*] tierno; [*voice*] lleno de ternura • **he gave her a ~ smile** le sonrió tiernamente or con ternura • **a child needs ~ loving care** un niño necesita que le den cariño y que lo cuiden • **to bid sb a ~ farewell** (*liter*) despedirse de algn con ternura, dar a algn una cariñosa despedida

2 (*esp hum*) (= *young*) tierno • **at the ~ age of seven** a la tierna edad de siete años • **in spite of his ~ years** a pesar de su tierna edad

3 (= *sensitive, sore*) sensible, dolorido • **the skin will be ~ for a while** la piel te dolerá durante algún tiempo • **~ to the touch** sensible al tacto

4 (*Culin*) [*meat, vegetables*] tierno • **cook the vegetables until ~** cocer las verduras hasta que estén or se pongan tiernas

5 (*Bot*) [*plant*] delicado; [*shoot*] tierno

tenderfoot ['tendəfʊt] N (PL: **tenderfoots**) (*esp US*) principiante *m*, novato *m*

tender-hearted ['tendə'hɑːtɪd] ADJ compasivo, bondadoso, tierno de corazón

tender-heartedness ['tendə'hɑːtɪdnɪs] N compasión *f*, bondad *f*, ternura *f*

tenderize ['tendəraɪz] VT ablandar

tenderizer ['tendəraɪzəʳ] N ablandador *m*

tenderloin ['tendəlɔɪn] N **1** (= *meat*) lomo *m*, filete *m*

2 (*US**) *barrio de vicio y corrupción reconocidos*

tenderly ['tendəlɪ] ADV (= *affectionately*) [*kiss, say, smile*] tiernamente, con ternura

tenderness ['tendənɪs] N **1** (= *gentleness*) [*of person, kiss, smile*] ternura *f*

2 (= *sensitivity, soreness*) dolor *m* • **breast ~** dolor *m* en el pecho • **some ~ around the area is to be expected** es de esperar que la zona duela un poco

3 (*Culin*) [*of meat, vegetables*] lo tierno

4 (*Bot*) fragilidad *f*

tendon ['tendən] N tendón *m*

tendril ['tendrɪl] N zarcillo *m*

tenement ['tenɪmənt] N vivienda *f*; (*Scot*) (= *flat*) piso *m* (*Sp*), departamento *m* (*LAm*)

CPD ▸ **tenement block** bloque *m* de pisos (*Sp*), bloque *m* de departamentos (*LAm*) ▸ **tenement house** casa *f* de vecinos, casa *f* de vecindad

Tenerife [,tenə'riːf] N Tenerife *m*

tenet ['tenət] N principio *m*

tenfold ['tenfəʊld] ADJ • **there has been a ~ increase in accidents** se ha multiplicado por diez el número de accidentes, el número de accidentes es diez veces mayor

ADV diez veces

ten-gallon hat [,tengælən'hæt] N sombrero *m* tejano

Tenn. ABBR (*US*) = **Tennessee**

tenner* ['tenəʳ] N (*Brit*) (= *£10*) diez libras; (= *£10 note*) billete *m* de diez libras; (*US*) (= *$10*) diez dólares; (= *$10 note*) billete *m* de diez dólares

tennis ['tenɪs] N tenis *m*

CPD ▸ **tennis ball** pelota *f* de tenis ▸ **tennis camp** (*US*) • **to go to ~ camp** ir a un campamento de verano con tenis ▸ **tennis club** club *m* de tenis ▸ **tennis court** pista *f* de tenis (*Sp*), cancha *f* de tenis (*LAm*) ▸ **tennis elbow** (*Med*) sinovitis *f* del codo, codo *m* de tenista ▸ **tennis match** partido *m* de tenis ▸ **tennis player** tenista *mf* ▸ **tennis racquet** raqueta *f* de tenis ▸ **tennis shoe** zapatilla *f* de tenis

tenon ['tenən] N espaldón *m*

tenor ['tenəʳ] ADJ [*instrument, part, voice*] de tenor; [*aria*] para tenor

N **1** (*Mus*) tenor *m*

2 (= *purport*) [*of speech*] tenor *m*

tenpin bowling [,tenpɪn'bəʊlɪŋ] N, **tenpins** ['tenpɪnz] NPL bolos *mpl*, bolera *f*

tense[1] [tens] N (*Ling*) tiempo *m* • **in the present ~** en presente

tense[2] [tens] ADJ (COMPAR: **tenser**, SUPERL: **tensest**) **1** (= *nervous*) [*person, expression*] tenso • **her voice was ~** se le notaba la tensión en la voz • **to feel ~** sentirse tenso • **to get or grow ~** ponerse tenso

2 (= *stiff*) [*body, muscles, neck*] tenso, en tensión • **my shoulders are ~** tengo los hombros tensos or en tensión

3 (= *strained*) [*atmosphere, silence*] tenso; [*relations*] tenso, tirante; [*period, moment*] de tensión • **the ~ situation in the Persian Gulf** la situación de tensión en el golfo Pérsico

4 (= *taut*) [*rope, wire*] tenso, tirante

VI (*also* **tense up**) [*person*] ponerse tenso; [*muscle, body*] ponerse tenso, ponerse en tensión

VT (*also* **tense up**) tensar, poner tenso • **she ~d her muscles** tensó or puso tensos los músculos

▸ **tense up** VI + ADV ▹ **tense**[2]

VT + ADV ▹ **tense**[2]

tensely ['tenslɪ] ADV [*say, wait*] tensamente

tenseness ['tensnɪs] N tensión *f*

tensile ['tensaɪl] ADJ (= *relating to tension*) de tensión, relativo a la tensión; (= *stretchable*) extensible • **~ strength** resistencia *f* a la tensión

tension ['tenʃən] N **1** (= *unease*) (*in atmosphere, situation*) tensión *f*; (*in relations*) tensión *f*, tirantez *f* • **there is a lot of ~ between them** entre ellos existe mucha tirantez

2 (= *stiffness*) [*of person, in shoulders*] tensión *f*

3 (= *tightness*) [*of rope, wire*] tensión *f*, tirantez *f*

tent [tent] N tienda *f* de campaña, carpa *f* (*LAm*)

CPD ▸ **tent city** gran campamento *m* ▸ **tent peg** (*Brit*) estaca *f* de tienda, estaquilla *f* ▸ **tent pole, tent stake** palo *m*

tentacle ['tentəkl] N tentáculo *m*

tentative ['tentətɪv] ADJ **1** (= *provisional*) [*agreement, plan, arrangement*] provisional, provisorio (*LAm*); [*conclusion*] provisional, no definitiva

2 (= *hesitant*) [*gesture*] vacilante, tímido; [*smile, attempt*] tímido • **the first ~ steps toward democracy** los primeros pasos vacilantes hacia la democracia • **he made a ~ suggestion that ...** sugirió tímidamente que ...

tentatively ['tentətɪvlɪ] ADV **1** (= *provisionally*) [*agree, arrange, plan*] provisionalmente, provisoriamente (*LAm*)

2 (= *hesitantly*) [*smile*] tímidamente; [*say*] tímidamente, con vacilación • **he touched one of the boxes ~** tocó una de las cajas con cuidado

tenterhooks ['tentəhʊks] NPL • IDIOMS: • **to be on ~** estar sobre ascuas, tener el alma en vilo • **to keep sb on ~** tener a algn sobre ascuas

tenth [tenθ] ADJ décimo

N (*in series*) décimo *m*; (= *fraction*) décimo *m*, décima parte *f*; ▹ **fifth**

tenth-grader [,tenθ'greɪdəʳ] N (*US*) alumno/a *m/f* de décimo curso (*de entre 15 y 16 años*)

tenuity [te'njuːɪtɪ] N tenuidad *f*

tenuous ['tenjʊəs] ADJ [*connection, link*] vago, ligero; [*argument*] flojo, endeble; [*evidence*] poco sólido; [*alliance, peace*] frágil, endeble • **he has only a ~ grasp of reality** solo tiene una escasa conciencia de la realidad • **to have a ~ hold on sth** tener (un) escaso control sobre algo

tenuously ['tenjʊəslɪ] ADV [*linked, connected*] vagamente

tenuousness ['tenjʊəsnɪs] N [*of link, connection*] lo vago; [*of argument*] endeblez *f*, falta *f* de fundamento; [*of evidence*] falta *f* de solidez

tenure ['tenjʊəʳ] N **1** [*of land*] posesión *f*, tenencia *f*, ocupación *f*; [*of office*] ocupación *f*, ejercicio *m*
2 (= *guaranteed employment*) puesto *m* asegurado, permanencia *f* • **teacher with ~** profesor(a) *m/f* de número, profesor(a) *m/f* numerario/a • **teacher without ~** profesor(a) *m/f* no numerario/a
CPD • **~ track position** (US) puesto *m* con posibilidad de obtener la permanencia

tepee ['ti:pi:] N (US) tipi *m*

tepid ['tepɪd] ADJ (*lit*) tibio; (*fig*) [*reception, welcome*] poco entusiasta, poco caluroso

tepidity [te'pɪdɪtɪ], **tepidness** ['tepɪdnɪs] N tibieza *f*

tequila [tɪ'ki:lə] N tequila *m*

Ter. ABBR = **Terrace**

terabyte ['terəbaɪt] N (*Comput*) terabyte *m*

terbium ['tɜ:bɪəm] N terbio *m*

tercentenary [,tɜ:sen'ti:nərɪ] N tricentenario *m*

tercet ['tɜ:sɪt] N terceto *m*

Terence ['terəns] N Terencio

term [tɜ:m] N **1** (= *period*) periodo *m*, período *m*; (*as President, governor, mayor*) mandato *m* • **in the long ~** a largo plazo • **in the longer ~** a un plazo más largo • **in the medium ~** a medio plazo • **during his ~ of office** bajo su mandato • **we have been elected for a three-year ~ (of office)** hemos sido elegidos para un periodo legislativo de tres años • **he will not seek a third ~ (of office) as mayor** no irá a por un tercer mandato de alcalde, no renovará por tercera vez su candidatura como alcalde • **he is currently serving a seven-year prison ~** actualmente está cumpliendo una condena de siete años • **he served two ~s as governor** ocupó el cargo de gobernador durante dos periodos de mandato • **in the short ~** a corto plazo • **despite problems, she carried the baby to ~** a pesar de los problemas llevó el embarazo a término
2 (*Educ*) trimestre *m* • **in the autumn** *or* (US) **fall/spring/summer ~** en el primer/segundo/tercer trimestre • **they don't like you to take holidays during ~** no les gusta que se tomen vacaciones durante el trimestre *or* en época de clases
3 (*Comm, Jur, Econ*) (= *period of validity*) plazo *m* • **the policy is near the end of its ~** el plazo de la póliza está a punto de vencer • **interest rates change over the ~ of the loan** los tipos de interés cambian a lo largo del plazo del préstamo
4 (= *word*) término *m* • **what do you understand by the ~ "radical"?** ¿qué entiende usted por (el término) "radical"? • **explain it in ~s a child might understand** explícalo de manera que un niño lo pueda entender • **legal/medical ~s** términos *mpl* legales/médicos • **a ~ of abuse** un término ofensivo, un insulto • **a ~ of endearment** un apelativo cariñoso • **he spoke of it only in general ~s** solo habló de ello en términos generales • **he spoke of her in glowing ~s** habló de ella en términos muy elogiosos • **in simple ~s** de forma sencilla • **she condemned the attacks in the strongest ~s** condenó los ataques de la forma más enérgica • **technical ~** tecnicismo *m*, término *m* técnico; ▹ **contradiction**, uncertain
5 (*Math, Logic*) término *m*
6 terms: a (= *conditions*) condiciones *fpl*, términos *mpl* • **according to the ~s of the contract** según las condiciones *or* los términos del contrato • **to dictate ~s (to sb)** poner condiciones (a algn) • **we offer easy ~s** ofrecemos facilidades de pago • **~s of employment** condiciones *fpl* de empleo • **to compete on equal ~s** competir en igualdad de condiciones *or* en pie de igualdad • **they accepted him on his own ~s** lo aceptaron con las condiciones que él había puesto • **~s of reference** (= *brief*) [*of committee, inquiry*] cometido *m*, instrucciones *fpl*; [*of study*] ámbito *m*; (= *area of responsibility*) responsabilidades *fpl*, competencia *f*; (= *common understanding*) puntos *mpl* de referencia • **~s of sale** condiciones *fpl* de venta • **~s of trade** condiciones *fpl* de transacción • IDIOM: • **to come to ~s with sth** asumir *or* asimilar algo
b (= *relations*) • **to be on bad ~s with sb** llevarse mal con algn, no tener buenas relaciones con algn • **we're on first name ~s with all the staff** nos tuteamos con todos los empleados • **she is still on friendly ~s with him** todavía mantiene una relación amistosa con él • **to be on good ~s with sb** llevarse bien con algn, tener buenas relaciones con algn • **they have managed to remain on good ~s** se las arreglaron para quedar bien • **we're not on speaking ~s at the moment** actualmente no nos hablamos
c (= *sense*) • **in ~s of: in ~s of production we are doing well** en cuanto a la producción vamos bien, por lo que se refiere *or* por lo que respecta a la producción vamos bien • **he never describes women in ~s of their personalities** nunca describe a las mujeres refiriéndose a su personalidad • **he was talking in ~s of buying it** hablaba como si fuera a comprarlo • **in economic/political ~s** desde el punto de vista económico/político, en términos económicos/políticos • **in practical ~s this means that ...** en la práctica esto significa que ... • **in real ~s incomes have fallen** en términos reales los ingresos han bajado • **seen in ~s of its environmental impact, the project is a disaster** desde el punto de vista de su impacto en el medio ambiente, el proyecto es un desastre • **we were thinking more in ~s of an au pair** nuestra idea era más una au pair, teníamos en mente a una au pair
VT (= *designate*) calificar de • **he was ~ed a thief** lo calificaron de ladrón • **he ~ed the war a humanitarian nightmare** calificó la guerra de pesadilla humanitaria • **I was what you might ~ a gangster** yo era lo que se podría llamar un gángster • **the problems of what is now ~ed "the mixed economy"** los problemas de lo que ahora se da en llamar "la economía mixta"
CPD ▸ **term insurance** seguro *m* temporal ▸ **term loan** préstamo *m* a plazo fijo ▸ **term paper** (US) trabajo *m* escrito trimestral

termagant ['tɜ:məgənt] N arpía *f*, fiera *f*

terminal ['tɜ:mɪnl] ADJ **1** (= *incurable*) [*cancer, patient, case*] terminal, en fase terminal • **the government's problems may be ~** los problemas del gobierno pueden no tener solución • **to be in (a state of) ~ decline** estar en un estado de declive irreversible
2* (= *utter*) [*boredom*] mortal*; [*adolescent*] incorregible, impenitente • **an act of ~ stupidity** un acto de una estupidez supina*
N **1** (*Elec*) borne *m*, polo *m*; (*Comput*) terminal *m*
2 [*of bus, train*] terminal *f* • **~ building** edificio *m* de la terminal

terminally ['tɜ:mɪnəlɪ] ADV **1** (= *incurably*) • **to be ~ ill** estar en fase terminal • **he was ~ ill with lung cancer** sufría un cáncer de pulmón en fase terminal
2* (= *utterly*) [*boring, dull*] mortalmente*; [*stupid*] irremediablemente

terminate ['tɜ:mɪneɪt] VT [+ *meeting*] concluir; [+ *conversation, relationship*] poner fin a; [+ *contract*] finalizar; [+ *pregnancy*] interrumpir
VI [*contract*] finalizarse, concluir; [*train, bus*] terminar • **this train ~s here** este tren termina aquí su recorrido, este tren muere aquí

termination [,tɜ:mɪ'neɪʃən] N [*of contract*] terminación *f*; [*of pregnancy*] interrupción *f* • **~ of employment** baja *f*, cese *m*

termini ['tɜ:mɪnaɪ] NPL *of* **terminus**

terminological [,tɜ:mɪnə'lɒdʒɪkəl] ADJ terminológico

terminologist [,tɜ:mɪ'nɒlədʒɪst] N terminólogo/a *m/f*

terminology [,tɜ:mɪ'nɒlədʒɪ] N terminología *f*

terminus ['tɜ:mɪnəs] N (PL: **terminuses, termini** ['tɜ:mɪnaɪ]) **1** (*Rail*) estación *f* terminal
2 [*of buses*] (= *last stop*) última parada *f*, final *f* del recorrido; (= *building*) terminal *f*

termite ['tɜ:maɪt] N termita *f*, comején *m*

termtime ['tɜ:mtaɪm] N • **in ~** durante el trimestre • **they don't like you to take holidays during ~** no les gusta que se tomen vacaciones durante el trimestre *or* en época de clases

tern [tɜ:n] N golondrina *f* de mar • **common ~** charrán *m* común

ternary ['tɜ:nərɪ] ADJ ternario

Terpsichorean [,tɜ:psɪ'kɔ:rɪən] ADJ (*frm, hum*) [*skill etc*] de la danza • **~ art** arte de Terpsícore

Terr. ABBR = **Terrace**

terrace ['terəs] N **1** (= *patio, verandah*) terraza *f*; (= *roof*) azotea *f*
2 (= *raised bank*) terraplén *m*
3 [*of houses*] hilera *f* de casas (adosadas); (= *name of street*) calle *f*
4 (*Agr*) terraza *f*
5 (*Sport*) • **the ~s** las gradas *fpl*, el graderío
VT [+ *hillside, garden*] construir terrazas en, terraplenar

terraced ['terəst] ADJ (= *layered*) [*hillside, garden*] en terrazas, terraplenado; (= *in a row*) [*house, cottage*] adosado • **~ gardens** jardines *mpl* formando terrazas, jardines *mpl* colgantes

terracotta ['terə'kɒtə] N terracota *f*
ADJ terracota

terra firma [,terə'fɜ:mə] N tierra *f* firme

terrain [te'reɪn] N terreno *m*

terrapin ['terəpɪn] N tortuga *f* de agua dulce

terrarium [te'rɛərɪəm] N terrario *m*

terrazzo [te'rætsəʊ] N terrazo *m*

terrestrial [tɪ'restrɪəl] ADJ **1** [*life, animal, plant*] terrestre
2 (*esp Brit*) (*TV*) [*broadcasting, channel*] de transmisión (por) vía terrestre

terrible ['terəbl] ADJ **1** (= *very unpleasant*) [*experience, accident, disease*] terrible, espantoso • **it was a ~ thing to have happened** era terrible que hubiese sucedido algo así • **it was a ~ thing to see** era horrible verlo • **the ~ thing is that I've lost it** lo peor de todo es que lo he perdido
2* (= *very bad*) [*weather, food*] horrible, espantoso • **her French is ~** habla fatal el francés, habla un francés espantoso • **"what was it like?" — "terrible!"** —¿qué tal fue?

t

—¡espantoso! • **I'm ~ at cooking** se me da fatal la cocina* • **I'm ~ at remembering names** se me da fatal recordar (los) nombres, soy malísimo para recordar (los) nombres • **I've got a ~ cold** tengo un resfriado espantoso • **I've had a ~ day at the office** he tenido un día malísimo *or* horrible en la oficina • **to feel ~** (= *guilty, ill*) sentirse fatal *or* muy mal • **to look ~** (= *ill*) tener muy mal aspecto • **she looked ~ in that trouser suit** ese traje pantalón le quedaba fatal • **I've got a ~ memory** tengo una memoria malísima • **I've made a ~ mistake** he cometido un terrible error • **you sound ~, is something wrong?** ¡vaya tono!, ¿pasa algo? • **we had a ~ time** lo pasamos fatal
3* (*as intensifier*) (= *great*) [*pity, shame*] verdadero • **I've been a ~ fool** he sido un verdadero imbécil • **the garden is in a ~ mess** el jardín está hecho un verdadero desastre • **it was** *or* **it came as a ~ shock** fue un golpe terrible • **he's having ~ trouble with his homework** le está costando horrores *or* un montón hacer los deberes*

terribly ['terəblɪ] ADV **1** (= *extremely*) [*worried, difficult, important*] terriblemente, tremendamente • **it's ~ good/bad** es buenísimo/malísimo • **it's ~ hard for me to make a decision** me resulta dificilísimo *or* terriblemente difícil tomar una decisión • **he's been ~ ill** ha estado terriblemente enfermo, ha estado fatal • **I'm ~ sorry** lo siento muchísimo • **we aren't doing ~ well at the moment** ahora no nos va muy bien que digamos • **he plays the piano a little, not ~ well** toca un poco el piano, no excesivamente bien • **there's something ~ wrong here** aquí hay algo que va realmente mal • **a practical joke which had gone ~ wrong** una broma que había tenido unos resultados terribles
2* (= *very much*) • **I miss him ~** le echo muchísimo de menos • **to suffer ~** sufrir horrores*, pasarlo fatal*
3 (= *very poorly*) [*play, perform, behave*] muy mal, fatal

terrier ['terɪəʳ] N terrier *m*

terrific [tə'rɪfɪk] ADJ **1** (= *very great*) [*explosion, problem, disappointment*] tremendo, enorme; [*pain, noise, heat*] terrible, tremendo • **a ~ amount of money** una enorme cantidad de dinero
2* (= *excellent*) [*idea, news, person*] genial*, estupendo • **terrific!** ¡genial!, ¡estupendo! • **we had ~ fun** nos lo pasamos estupendamente *or* fenomenal* • **to do a ~ job** hacer un trabajo estupendo *or* fantástico* • **you look ~!** ¡estás guapísimo/a! • **she looked ~ in a leotard** estaba sensacional en mallas • **~ stuff!** ¡estupendo!, ¡fenomenal! • **to have a ~ time** pasárselo estupendamente *or* fenomenal*

terrifically [tə'rɪfɪkəlɪ] ADV **1** (= *extremely*) terriblemente • **it's a ~ funny book** es un libro graciosísimo *or* terriblemente gracioso • **it was ~ hot** hacía un calor terrible *or* tremendo • **house prices have gone up ~** las casas han subido terriblemente de precio • **we get on ~ well** nos llevamos estupendamente bien • **they did ~ well to reach the final** fue un tremendo logro que llegasen a la final
2* (= *very well*) [*play, perform*] fenomenal*, genial*

terrified ['terɪfaɪd] ADJ • **to be ~** estar aterrorizado, estar aterrado • **to be ~ of sth/sb** tener terror *or* pavor a algo/algn • **he was ~ of catching Aids** le aterrorizaba *or* le daba terror (la idea de) coger el sida • **I was ~ of her meeting another man** me daba terror que conociera a otro hombre • **she was ~ that they'd lose their home** le aterrorizaba *or* le daba terror el pensar que pudieran perder su casa • **I was ~ that he might follow me** le tenía terror de que pudiera seguirme

terrify ['terɪfaɪ] VT (= *terrorize*) [*animal, violent person etc*] aterrorizar; (= *horrify*) aterrar • **it terrifies me to think that I might lose her** me aterra pensar que podría perderla • **to ~ sb out of his wits** dar un susto mortal a algn

terrifying ['terɪfaɪɪŋ] ADJ [*experience, sound, sight*] espantoso, aterrador; [*person*] aterrador • **it was ~!** ¡fue espantoso *or* aterrador! • **what a ~ thought!** ¡qué idea más aterradora!, ¡qué espanto! • **I still find it ~ to walk along that street** todavía me da muchísimo miedo caminar por esa calle

terrifyingly ['terɪfaɪɪŋlɪ] ADV espantosamente, aterradoramente

terrine [te'ri:n] N terrina *f*

territorial [ˌterɪ'tɔ:rɪəl] ADJ territorial
• **Territorial Army** ejército *m* de reserva
• **~ waters** aguas *fpl* jurisdiccionales *or* territoriales
N (*Brit*) reservista *m*

TERRITORIAL ARMY
La organización británica **Territorial Army** o **TA** es un ejército de reserva formado exclusivamente por voluntarios civiles que reciben entrenamiento militar en su tiempo libre y están disponibles para ayudar al ejército profesional en tiempos de guerra o crisis. Como compensación por sus servicios, los voluntarios reciben una paga. En Estados Unidos el equivalente es la llamada **National Guard**.

territoriality [ˌterɪˌtɔ:rɪ'ælɪtɪ] N territorialidad *f*

territory ['terɪtərɪ] N territorio *m*; [*of salesman*] zona *f*, sector *m*; (*Sport*) campo *m*, terreno *m* • **mandated ~** territorio *m* bajo mandato • IDIOM: • **it comes** *or* **goes with the ~** es parte del juego, es un gaje del oficio

terror ['terəʳ] N **1** (= *fear*) terror *m* • **to live in ~** vivir en el terror • **to live in ~ of sth** vivir aterrorizado por algo • **he went** *or* **was in ~ of his life** temía por su vida, temía ser asesinado • **I have a ~ of bats** tengo horror a los murciélagos • **he had a ~ of flying** le daba miedo volar • **the headmistress holds no ~s for me** la directora no me infunde miedo a mí • **to sow ~ everywhere** sembrar el terror por todas partes
2* (= *person, child*) • **she's a ~ on the roads** es un peligro conduciendo • **you little ~!** ¡eres un diablillo!*
CPD ▸ **terror attack** atentado *m* (terrorista) ▸ **terror campaign** campaña *f* de terror

terrorism ['terərɪzəm] N terrorismo *m*

terrorist ['terərɪst] ADJ, N terrorista *mf*

terrorize ['terəraɪz] VT (= *terrify*) aterrorizar; (= *threaten, coerce*) atemorizar • **they ~d the population into submission** hicieron que la población se sometiera a base de atemorizarlos

terror-stricken ['terəˌstrɪkən], **terror-struck** ['terəˌstrʌk] ADJ aterrorizado

Terry ['terɪ] N *familiar form of* **Terence**, **Theresa**

terry ['terɪ] N (*US*) (*also* **terry towelling, terry cloth**) (*Brit*) felpa *f*, toalla *f*

terse [tɜ:s] ADJ (COMPAR: **terser**, SUPERL: **tersest**) [*reply, tone, person*] lacónico, seco; [*statement*] escueto

tersely ['tɜ:slɪ] ADV lacónicamente, secamente

terseness ['tɜ:snɪs] N laconismo *m*, sequedad *f*

tertiary ['tɜ:ʃərɪ] ADJ **1** (*Econ*) [*sector*] terciario
2 (*Geol*) [*rocks, deposits*] terciario • **the Tertiary period** la época terciaria
CPD ▸ **tertiary college** (*Brit*) *centro de enseñanza que prepara estudiantes para la universidad y las carreras profesionales* ▸ **tertiary education** enseñanza *f* superior ▸ **tertiary sector** • **the ~ sector** el sector terciario

Tertullian [tɜ:'tʌlɪən] N Tertuliano

Terylene® ['terəli:n] N (*Brit*) terylene® *m*

TESL ['tes(ə)l] N ABBR (= **Teaching (of) English as a Second Language**) ▹ **TEFL/EFL, TESL/ESL, ELT, TESOL/ESOL**

TESOL ['tesɒl] N ABBR (= **Teaching of English to Speakers of Other Languages**) ▹ **TEFL/EFL, TESL/ESL, ELT, TESOL/ESOL**

Tess [tes], **Tessa** ['tesə] N *familiar forms of* **Teresa**

TESSA ['tesə] N ABBR (*Brit*) (= **Tax Exempt Special Savings Account**) *antigua cuenta de ahorros con exenciones fiscales*

tesselated, tessellated ['tesɪleɪtɪd] ADJ de mosaico, formado con teselas • **tessel(l)ated pavement** mosaico *m*

tesselation, tessellation [ˌtesɪ'leɪʃən] N mosaico *m*

test [test] N **1** (*Scol, Univ*) examen *m*; (*multiple-choice*) test *m*; (*esp for job*) prueba *f* • **we've got a maths ~ tomorrow** mañana tenemos (un) examen de matemáticas • **to do a ~** (*Scol, Univ*) hacer un examen; (*multiple choice*) hacer un test; (*for job*) hacer una prueba • **to fail a ~** (*Scol, Univ*) suspender un examen; (*multiple choice*) suspender un test; (*for job*) no pasar una prueba • **to give sb a ~ (in sth)** examinar a algn (de algo), poner a algn un examen (de algo) • **an oral ~** un examen oral • **to pass a ~** (*Scol, Univ*) aprobar un examen; (*multiple choice*) aprobar un test; (*for job*) pasar una prueba • **to take a ~** (*Scol, Univ*) hacer un examen; (*multiple choice*) hacer un test; (*for job*) hacer una prueba • **a written ~** un examen oral/escrito; ▹ **aptitude, intelligence**
2 (*Aut*) (*also* **driving test**) examen *m* de conducir • **to fail one's ~** suspender el examen de conducir • **to pass one's ~** aprobar el examen de conducir • **to take one's ~** hacer el examen de conducir
3 (*Med*) [*of organs, functioning*] prueba *f*; [*of sample, substance*] análisis *m inv* • **AIDS ~** prueba *f* del sida • **blood ~** análisis *m inv* de sangre • **eye ~** revisión *f* de la vista • **it was sent to the laboratory for ~s** lo mandaron al laboratorio para que lo analizaran • **hearing ~** revisión *f* del oído • **medical ~** examen *m* médico • **pregnancy ~** prueba *f* del embarazo • **urine ~** análisis *m inv* de orina; ▹ **breath, fitness, litmus, smear**
4 (= *trial*) [*of aircraft, new product, drug*] prueba *f* • **nuclear ~** prueba *f* nuclear • **they want to ban cosmetics ~s on animals** quieren prohibir las pruebas de cosméticos en animales; ▹ **flight¹, screen**
5 (*fig*) prueba *f* • **he now faces the toughest ~ of his leadership** ahora se enfrenta a la prueba más difícil durante su periodo como líder • **holidays are a major ~ of any relationship** irse de vacaciones es una de las pruebas más difíciles a la que se somete cualquier relación • **to put sth to the ~** poner *or* someter algo a prueba • **to stand the ~ of time** resistir el paso del tiempo; ▹ **acid, endurance**
6 (*Cricket, Rugby*) (*also* **test match**) partido *m* internacional
VT **1** [+ *student, pupil*] examinar; [+ *candidate*] (*for job*) hacer una prueba a; [+ *knowledge*]

evaluar; [+ *understanding*] poner a prueba • **to ~ sb on sth** (*Scol, Univ*) examinar a algn de algo; (*esp for job*) hacer una prueba de algo a algn; (*for revision*) hacer preguntas de algo a algn (para repasar) • **she was ~ed on her computer skills** le hicieron una prueba de informática • **can you ~ me on my French/spelling?** ¿me haces preguntas de francés/ortografía?
2 (*Med*) [+ *blood, urine, sample*] analizar • **to have one's eyes ~ed** hacerse una revisión de la vista • **to ~ sb/sth for sth:** • **to ~ sb for AIDS** hacer la prueba del SIDA a algn • **to ~ sb for drugs** (*gen*) realizar pruebas a algn para comprobar si ha consumido drogas; [+ *athlete, sportsperson*] realizar el control antidoping a algn • **my doctor wants me to be ~ed for diabetes** mi médico quiere que me haga un análisis para ver *or* (*frm*) determinar si tengo diabetes • **the urine is ~ed for protein** se hace un análisis de orina para determinar el contenido de proteínas
3 (= *conduct trials on*) [+ *aircraft, weapon, new product, drug*] probar • **the drug was ~ed in clinical trials** se sometió el medicamento a pruebas clínicas • **all our products are ~ed for quality** probamos la calidad de todos nuestros productos • **to ~ sth on sth/sb** probar algo con *or* en algo/algn • **none of our products are ~ed on animals** ninguno de nuestros productos se prueba con *or* en animales • **~ the cream on an unaffected area of skin** pruebe la crema sobre una zona cutánea no afectada
4 (= *check*) probar • **~ the water temperature with your elbow** pruebe la temperatura del agua con el codo • **he ~ed the ice with a stick** usó un palo para comprobar la solidez del hielo • IDIOM: • **to ~ the water(s)** tantear el terreno
5 (*fig*) (= *put to the test*) [+ *person, courage*] poner a prueba • **his resolve will be ~ed to the limits this week** su resolución se pondrá a prueba al máximo esta semana • **to ~ sb's patience** poner a prueba la paciencia de algn
(VI) (= *conduct a test*) • **testing, testing ...** (*Telec*) probando, probando ... • **it is a method used to ~ for allergies** es un método utilizado en pruebas de alergia • **just ~ing!** (*hum*) ¡por si acaso pregunto! • **to ~ negative/positive (for sth)** dar negativo/positivo (en la prueba de algo)
(CPD) ▸ **(nuclear) test ban** prohibición *f* de pruebas nucleares ▸ **test ban treaty** (*also* **nuclear test ban treaty**) tratado *m* de prohibición de pruebas nucleares ▸ **test bed** banco *m* de pruebas ▸ **test card** (*TV*) carta *f* de ajuste ▸ **test case** (*Jur*) juicio *m* que sienta jurisprudencia ▸ **test cricket** críquet *m* a nivel internacional ▸ **test data** resultados *mpl* de prueba ▸ **test drive** (*by potential buyer*) prueba *f* en carretera; (*by mechanic, technician*) prueba *f* de rodaje • **to take sth for a ~ drive** probar algo en carretera; ▹ **test-drive** ▸ **test flight** vuelo *m* de prueba, vuelo *m* de ensayo ▸ **test marketing** *pruebas de un producto nuevo en el mercado* • **~ marketing has already shown the product to be a great success** las pruebas realizadas en el mercado ya han mostrado que el producto tiene un éxito tremendo ▸ **test match** (*Cricket, Rugby*) partido *m* internacional ▸ **test paper** (*Scol, Univ*) examen *m*; (*multiple-choice*) test *m*; (*Chem*) papel *m* reactivo ▸ **test pattern** (*US*) (*TV*) = **test card** ▸ **test piece** (*Mus*) pieza *f* elegida para un certamen de piano ▸ **test pilot** piloto *mf* de pruebas ▸ **test run** (*lit*) vuelta *f* de prueba, prueba *f*; (*fig*) puesta *f* a prueba ▸ **test tube** probeta *f*, tubo *m* de ensayo ▸ **test tube baby** bebé *mf* probeta
▸ **test out** (VT + ADV) probar
testament ['testəmənt] (N) **1** (= *will*) testamento *m*; ▹ **will²**
2 (*Bible*) • **the Old/New Testament** el Antiguo/Nuevo Testamento
3 (= *proof*) testimonio *m* • **the building is a ~ to his skills as an architect** el edificio es testimonio de su competencia como arquitecto
testamentary [ˌtestəˈmentərɪ] (ADJ) testamentario
testator [tesˈteɪtəʳ] (N) testador *m*
testatrix [tesˈteɪtrɪks] (N) testadora *f*
test-drill [ˈtestˌdrɪl] (VI) sondear
test-drive [ˈtestˌdraɪv] (VB: PT: **test-drove**, PP: **test-driven**) (VT) [+ *car*] [*prospective buyer*] probar en carretera; [*mechanic, technician*] hacer la prueba de rodaje a; ▹ **test**
tester¹ [ˈtestəʳ] (N) (= *person*) ensayador(a) *m/f*; (= *sample, trial product*) muestra *f*, artículo *m* de muestra
tester²† [ˈtestəʳ] (N) baldaquín *m*
testes [ˈtestiːz] (NPL) testes *mpl*
testicle [ˈtestɪkl] (N) testículo *m*
testicular [tesˈtɪkjʊləʳ] (ADJ) testicular • **~ cancer** cáncer *m* de testículo, cáncer *m* testicular
testify [ˈtestɪfaɪ] (VI) **1** (*Jur*) prestar declaración, declarar
2 • **to ~ to sth** (*Jur*) declarar algo, testificar algo; (= *be sign of*) atestiguar algo, dar fe de algo
(VT) declarar, testificar • **to ~ that ...** declarar *or* testificar que ...
testily [ˈtestɪlɪ] (ADV) con irritación, malhumoradamente
testimonial [ˌtestɪˈməʊnɪəl] (N)
1 (= *certificate*) certificado *m*; (= *reference*) carta *f* de recomendación, recomendación *f*
2 (= *gift*) obsequio *m*
3 (*Sport*) (*also* **testimonial match**) partido *m* homenaje
testimony [ˈtestɪmənɪ] (N) (*Jur*) (= *statement in court*) testimonio *m*, declaración *f*; (*fig*) (= *indication of sth*) muestra *f*, señal *f* • **in ~ whereof ...** (*frm*) en fe de lo cual ... • **to bear ~ to sth** atestiguar algo, dar fe de algo
testiness [ˈtestɪnɪs] (N) irritabilidad *f*
testing [ˈtestɪŋ] (ADJ) (= *difficult*) duro • **it was a ~ experience for her** fue una experiencia muy dura para ella • **it was a ~ time** fue un período difícil
(N) pruebas *fpl*
(CPD) ▸ **testing ground** zona *f* de pruebas, terreno *m* de pruebas ▸ **testing kit** • **pregnancy ~ kit** kit *m* de embarazo • **drug ~ kit** kit *m* de presencia de droga • **HIV ~ kit** test *m* de VIH
testis [ˈtestɪs] (N) (PL: **testes** [ˈtestiːz]) testículo *m*, teste *m*
testosterone [teˈstɒstərəʊn] (N) testosterona *f*
testy [ˈtestɪ] (ADJ) (COMPAR: **testier**, SUPERL: **testiest**) [*person*] irritable; [*reply*] irritado
tetanus [ˈtetənəs] (N) tétanos *m*
(CPD) [*injection*] del tétanos, contra el tétanos; [*vaccine*] contra el tétanos, antitetánica
tetchily [ˈtetʃɪlɪ] (ADV) con irritación, malhumoradamente
tetchiness [ˈtetʃɪnɪs] (N) irritabilidad *f*
tetchy [ˈtetʃɪ] (ADJ) (COMPAR: **tetchier**, SUPERL: **tetchiest**) [*person*] irritable, picajoso*; [*mood*] irritable
tête-à-tête [ˈteɪtɑːˈteɪt] (N) (PL: **tête-à-tête**, **tête-à-têtes**) conversación *f* íntima
tether [ˈteðəʳ] (N) ronzal *m*, soga *f* • IDIOM: • **to be at the end of one's ~** no aguantar más, no poder más
(VT) [+ *animal*] atar (con una cuerda) (**to** a)
tetrachloride [ˌtetrəˈklɔːraɪd] (N) tetracloruro *m*
tetragon [ˈtetrəgən] (N) tetrágono *m*
tetrahedron [ˈtetrəˈhiːdrən] (N) (PL: **tetrahedrons, tetrahedra** [ˌtetrəˈhiːdrə]) tetraedro *m*
tetrameter [teˈtræmɪtəʳ] (N) tetrámetro *m*
tetraplegic [ˌtetrəˈpliːdʒɪk] (ADJ) tetrapléjico
(N) tetrapléjico/a *m/f*
tetrapod [ˈtetrəˌpɒd] (N) tetrápodo *m*
tetrathlon [teˈtræθlən] (N) tetratlón *m*
Teuton [ˈtjuːtən] (N) teutón/ona *m/f*
Teutonic [tjʊˈtɒnɪk] (ADJ) teutónico
Tex. (ABBR) (*US*) = **Texas**
Texan [ˈteksən] (ADJ) tejano
(N) tejano/a *m/f*
Texas [ˈteksəs] (N) Tejas *m*
Texican [ˈteksɪkən] (N) (*esp hum*) **1** (= *person*) texano/a *m/f* mexicano/a
2 (= *language*) *lengua mixta angloespañola de los estados del suroeste de EE.UU.*
Tex-Mex [ˌteksˈmeks] (ADJ) [*food, cuisine, restaurant, music*] tex-mex (*inv*)
(N) (= *language*) *lengua mixta angloespañola de los estados del suroeste de EE.UU.*
text [tekst] (N) **1** (= *written or printed matter*) texto *m*; (= *book*) libro *m* de texto; (= *subject*) tema *m*; (*Rel*) pasaje *m* • **to stick to one's ~** no apartarse de su tema
2 (*also* **text message**) mensaje *m* (de texto), SMS *m*
(VT) • **to ~ sb*** enviar un mensaje (de móvil) *o* un SMS a algn
(CPD) ▸ **text editor** (*Comput*) editor *m* de texto ▸ **text file** (*Comput*) archivo *m* de texto ▸ **text message** mensaje *m* de texto ▸ **text messaging** (envío *m* de) mensajes *mpl* de texto ▸ **text processing** proceso *m* de textos, tratamiento *m* de textos ▸ **text processor** procesador *m* de textos
textbook [ˈtekstbʊk] (N) libro *m* de texto • **a ~ case of ...** un caso clásico de ...
textile [ˈtekstaɪl] (ADJ) textil
(N) textil *m*, tejido *m*
(CPD) ▸ **textile industry** industria *f* textil ▸ **textile worker** obrero/a *m/f* (del ramo) textil
texting [ˈtekstɪŋ] (N) = **text messaging**
textual [ˈtekstjʊəl] (ADJ) **1** (= *of, relating to text*) [*criticism*] de textos; [*alterations*] textual • **~ notes** notas *fpl* al pie de página
2 (= *literal*) textual
textually [ˈtekstjʊəlɪ] (ADV) textualmente
texture [ˈtekstʃəʳ] (N) textura *f*
textured [ˈtekstʃəd] (ADJ) (= *not smooth*) texturizado
TGIF* (ABBR) (*hum*) = **Thank God it's Friday**
TGWU (N ABBR) (*Brit*) = **Transport and General Workers' Union**
Thai [taɪ] (ADJ) tailandés
(N) **1** (= *person*) tailandés/esa *m/f*
2 (*Ling*) tailandés *m*
Thailand [ˈtaɪlænd] (N) Tailandia *f*
thalamus [ˈθæləməs] (N) tálamo *m*
thalassaemia [ˌθæləˈsiːmɪə] (N) anemia *f* de Cooley
thalidomide® [θəˈlɪdəʊmaɪd] (N) talidomida *f*
(CPD) ▸ **thalidomide baby** bebé *m* víctima de la talidomida
thallium [ˈθælɪəm] (N) talio *m*
Thames [temz] (N) • **the ~** el Támesis
than [ðæn] (CONJ) **1** (*in comparisons*) que • **I have more ~ you** tengo más que usted • **nobody is more sorry ~ I (am)** nadie lo siente más que yo • **more often ~ not** en la mayoría de los casos • **they have more**

t

money ~ we have tienen más dinero que nosotros • **the car went faster ~ we had expected** el coche alcanzó una velocidad mayor de lo que habíamos esperado • **it is better to phone ~ to write** más vale llamar por teléfono que escribir
2 (*with numerals*) de • **more/less ~ 90** más/menos de 90 • **more ~ once** más de una vez
3 (*stating preference*) antes que • **rather you ~ me** tú antes que yo

thank [θæŋk] (VT) **1** • **to ~ sb** dar las gracias *or* agradecer a algn • **I cannot ~ you enough!** ¡cuánto te lo agradezco! • **to ~ sb for sth** agradecer algo a algn, dar las gracias a algn por algo • **did you ~ him for the flowers?** ¿le diste las gracias por las flores? • **he has only himself to ~ for that** él mismo tiene la culpa de eso • **I have John to ~ for that** eso se lo tengo que agradecer a Juan; (*iro*) Juan tiene la culpa de eso • **he won't ~ you for telling her** no te agradecerá de que se lo hayas dicho • **I'll ~ you not to interfere!** ¡agradecería que no te metieras! • **~ heavens/goodness/God (for that)!** ¡gracias a Dios!, ¡menos mal!
2 • **~ you** (*as excl*) ¡gracias! • **~ you very much** muchas gracias • **~ you for the present** muchas gracias por el regalo • **no ~ you** no, gracias • **¡no ~ you!** (*iro*) ¡ni hablar!, ¡no faltaba más! • **did you say ~ you?** ¿has dado las gracias?; ▷ **thanks, thank-you**
(CPD) ▸ **thank offering** prueba *f* de gratitud

thankful [ˈθæŋkfʊl] (ADJ) agradecido • **to be ~ for sth** estar agradecido por algo • **I've got so much to be ~ for** tengo tantas cosas por las que estar agradecido • **let's be ~ that it's over** demos gracias que haya terminado • **she was ~ to be alive** daba gracias por estar viva • IDIOM: • **to be ~ for small mercies** dar gracias por que la cosa no sea peor

thankfully [ˈθæŋkfəlɪ] (ADV) **1** (= *fortunately*) gracias a Dios, afortunadamente • **~, someone had called the police** menos mal que alguien había llamado a la policía, gracias a Dios *or* afortunadamente, alguien había llamado a la policía • **~ for my family, I wasn't hurt** afortunadamente *or* por suerte para mi familia, no resulté herido
2 (= *gratefully*) • **he accepted the drink ~** aceptó la bebida agradecido

thankfulness [ˈθæŋkfʊlnɪs] (N) gratitud *f*, agradecimiento *m*

thankless [ˈθæŋklɪs] (ADJ) (= *unrewarding, ungrateful*) ingrato

thanks [θæŋks] (NPL) **1** (= *gratitude*) agradecimiento *msing*, gratitud *fsing* • **they deserve our ~** merecen nuestro agradecimiento *or* nuestra gratitud • **in his speech of ~** en su discurso de agradecimiento • **that's all the ~ I get!** ¡y así se me agradece! • **she murmured her ~** dio las gracias murmurando • **to give ~** dar las gracias (**for** por) • **~ be to God** (*Rel*) alabado sea Dios
2 • **~ to:** • **~ to you ...** gracias a ti ...; (*iro*) por culpa tuya ... • **small/no ~ to you** no fue gracias a ti • **I got the job ~ to him** conseguí el trabajo a *or* por mediación suya • **~ to the rain the game was abandoned** debido a la lluvia el partido fue anulado
(EXCL)* • **thanks!** ¡gracias! • **many ~!** • **~ very much!** • **~ a lot!** ¡muchas gracias!, ¡muchísimas gracias! • **you went and told her? ~ a lot!** (*iro*) ¡y se lo dijiste!, ¡gracias, hombre! (*iro*); ▷ **bunch**

thanksgiving [ˈθæŋks,gɪvɪŋ] (N) acción *f* de gracias, voto *m* de gracias
(CPD) ▸ **Thanksgiving Day** (*US*) día *m* de Acción de Gracias

> **THANKSGIVING**
> Desde 1621, el cuarto jueves de noviembre se celebra en Estados Unidos el Día de Acción de Gracias (**Thanksgiving** o **Thanksgiving Day**) para conmemorar la fecha en que los primeros colonos norteamericanos (**Pilgrim Fathers**) celebraron un acto de acción de gracias por el éxito de su primera cosecha en suelo americano. La celebración suele reunir a toda la familia alrededor de la comida típica del Día de Acción de Gracias (**Thanksgiving meal**), que consiste en pavo asado y pastel de calabaza.
> En Canadá se celebra una fiesta semejante el segundo lunes de octubre, aunque no está relacionada con dicha fecha histórica.
> ▷ PILGRIM FATHERS, MACY'S THANKSGIVING PARADE

thank-you, thankyou [ˈθæŋkjʊ] (N) • **to say a special thank-you to sb** agradecer a algn especialmente • **she said her thank-yous and goodbyes and left** dio las gracias, se despidió y se marchó • **now a big thank-you to John** ahora, nuestras gracias más sinceras para John • **without so much as a thank-you** sin la menor señal de agradecimiento

that

DEMONSTRATIVE ADJECTIVE
DEMONSTRATIVE PRONOUN
RELATIVE PRONOUN
ADVERB
CONJUNCTION

(*strong form*) [ðæt], (*weak form*) [ðət]
(PL: **those**)

> *Those is treated as a separate entry.*

DEMONSTRATIVE ADJECTIVE

1 (+ *objects/people*)

> *You can generally use **ese** etc when pointing to something near the person you are speaking to. Use **aquel** etc for something which is distant from both of you:*

(*nearer*) ese *m*, esa *f*; (*more remote*) aquel *m*, aquella *f* • **~ book** ese libro • **~ hill over there** aquella colina de allí • **~ car is much better value than ~ sports model at the end** ese coche está mejor de precio que aquel modelo deportivo que hay al final • **~ lad of yours** ese chico tuyo • **~ wretched dog!** ¡ese maldito perro! • **what about ~ cheque?** ¿y el cheque ese? • **I only met her ~ once** la vi solamente aquella vez • **~ one** ese/a, ése/a; (*more remote*) aquel(la), aquél(la)

> *In the past the standard spelling for **ese/esa** and **aquel/aquella** used as pronouns (as when they are used to translate **that one**) was with an accent (**ése/ésa** and **aquél/aquélla**). Nowadays the **Real Academia Española** advises that the accented forms are only required where there might otherwise be confusion with the adjectives **este/esta** and **aquel/aquella**.*

• **there's little to choose between this model and ~ one** no hay mucho que elegir entre este modelo y aquel

2 (+ *event, year, month*)

> ***Aquel** is used to refer to a time in the distant past. Use **ese** if you mention a concrete date, month, year etc:*

• **do you remember ~ holiday we had in Holland?** ¿te acuerdas de aquellas vacaciones que pasamos en Holanda? • **1992? I can't remember where we holidayed ~ year** ¿1992? no recuerdo dónde pasamos las vacaciones ese año • **May? we can't come ~ month because we'll be moving house** ¿en mayo? no podemos venir ese mes porque nos estaremos mudando de casa

DEMONSTRATIVE PRONOUN

> *The pronoun **that (one)** is translated by **ese** and **aquel** (masc), **esa** and **aquella** (fem) and **eso** and **aquello** (neuter). You can generally use **ese** etc when pointing to something near the person you are speaking to. Use **aquel** etc for something which is distant from both of you. Note that in the past the standard spelling for the masculine and feminine pronouns was with an accent (**ése/ésa** and **aquél/aquélla**). Nowadays the **Real Academia Española** advises that the accented forms are only required where there might otherwise be confusion with the adjectives **ese/esa** and **aquel/aquella**. Neuter pronouns never carry an accent.*

(*nearer*) ese *m*, esa *f*, ése *m*, ésa *f*, eso (*neuter*); (*more remote*) aquel(la) *m/f*, aquél(la) *m/f*, aquello (*neuter*) • **who's ~?** ¿quién es ese? • **what is ~?** ¿qué es eso?, ¿eso qué es? • **~'s my French teacher over there** aquel es mi profesor de francés • **~'s my sister over by the window** aquella de la ventana es mi hermana • **~'s Joe** es Joe • **is ~ you, Paul?** ¿eres tú, Paul? • **£5? it must have cost more than ~** ¿5 libras? debe haber costado más (que eso) • **~'s true** eso es verdad, es cierto (*esp LAm*) • **~'s odd!** ¡qué raro!, ¡qué cosa más rara! • **1988? ~ was the year you graduated, wasn't it?** ¿1988? ese fue el año en que acabaste la carrera, ¿no es así? • **"will he come?" — "~ he will!"** †—¿vendrá? —¡ya lo creo! • **after ~** después de eso • **bees and wasps and all ~** abejas, avispas y cosas así • **~'s all I can tell you** eso es todo lo que puedo decirte • **is ~ all?** ¿eso es todo?, ¿nada más? • **she's not as stupid as (all) ~** no es tan estúpida como para eso • **and it was broken at ~** y además estaba roto • **I realized he meant to speak to me and at ~ I panicked** me di cuenta de que quería hablar conmigo y entonces me entró el pánico • **what do you mean by ~?** ¿qué quieres decir con eso? • **if it comes to ~** en tal caso, si llegamos a eso • **it will cost 20 dollars, if ~** costará 20 dólares, si es que llega • **~ is** (= *ie*) es decir ... • **~'s it, we've finished** ya está, hemos terminado • **they get their wages and ~'s it** tienen un sueldo y eso es todo • **~'s it! she can find her own gardener!** ¡se acabó! ¡que se busque un jardinero por su cuenta! • **~ of** el/la de • **a hurricane like ~ of 1987** un huracán como el de 1987 • **a recession like ~ of 1973-74** una recesión como la de 1973-1974 • **~ is to say** es decir ... • **why worry about ~ which may never happen?** (*frm*) ¿por qué preocuparse por aquello que *or* por lo que puede que nunca vaya a pasar? • **with ~** con eso • IDIOMS: • **that's that: you can't go and that's that** no puedes irte sin más, no puedes ir y no hay más qué decir, no puedes ir y sanseacabó • **so ~ was ~** y no había más que hacer, y ahí terminó la cosa

RELATIVE PRONOUN

*Unlike **that**, the Spanish relative cannot be omitted.*

1 que • **the man ~ came in** el hombre que entró • **the book ~ I read** el libro que leí • **the houses ~ I painted** las casas que pinté • **the girl ~ he met on holiday and later married** la chica que conoció durante las vacaciones y con la que después se casó • **all ~ I have** todo lo que tengo • **fool ~ I am!** ¡tonto que soy!

2 *(with preposition)*

*If the **that** clause ends in a preposition, you can either translate **that** as **que** (usually preceded by the definite article) or as article + **cual/cuales**. Use the second option particularly in formal language or after long prepositions or prepositional phrases:*

• **the actor ~ I was telling you about** el actor del que te hablaba • **the car ~ she got into** el coche al que se subió • **the film ~ I read about in the papers** la película sobre la que leí en el periódico • **the box ~ I put it in** la caja donde lo puse, la caja en la que *or* en la cual lo puse • **a planet ~ satellites go round** un planeta alrededor del cual giran satélites

3 *(in expressions of time)* • **the evening ~ we went to the theatre** la tarde (en) que fuimos al teatro • **the summer ~ it was so hot** el verano que hizo tanto calor

ADVERB

1 *(= so)* tan • **~ far** tan lejos • **he can't be ~ clever** no puede ser tan inteligente • **I didn't know he was ~ ill** no sabía que estuviera tan enfermo • **it's about ~ big** *(with gesture)* es más o menos así de grande • **cheer up! it isn't ~ bad** ¡ánimo! ¡no es para tanto! • **~ many frogs** tantas ranas • **~ much money** tanto dinero

2* *(= so very)* tan • **he was ~ wild** estaba tan furioso • **it was ~ cold!** ¡hacía tanto frío!

CONJUNCTION

*Unlike **that**, **que** cannot be omitted.*

1 *(after verb)* que • **he said ~ …** dijo que … • **he said ~ he was going to London and would be back in the evening** dijo que se iba a Londres y (que) volvería por la tarde • **I believe ~ he exists** creo que existe

2 *(after noun)*

*Translate as **de que** in phrases like **the idea/belief/hope that**:*

• **any hope ~ they might have survived was fading** toda esperanza de que hubiesen sobrevivido se estaba desvaneciendo • **the idea ~ we can profit from their labour** la idea de que podemos aprovecharnos de su trabajo • **…, not ~ I want to, of course** …, no es que yo quiera, por supuesto • **oh ~ we could!** ¡ojalá pudiéramos!, ¡ojalá!

3 *('that' clause as subject)*

*If the **that** clause is the subject of another verb it is usual to translate **that** as **el que** rather than **que** especially if it starts the sentence:*

• **~ he did not know surprised me** (el) que no lo supiera me extrañó, me extrañó (el) que no lo supiera

In these cases the verb which follows will be in the subjunctive:

• **~ he refuses is natural** (el) que rehúse es natural • **~ he should behave like this is incredible** (el) que se comporte así es increíble, es increíble que se comporte así; ▹ **would**

4 *(= in order that)* para que (+ *subjun*) • **it was done (so) ~ he might sleep** se hizo para que pudiera dormir • **those who fought and died ~ we might live** los que lucharon y murieron para que nosotros pudiésemos vivir

5 • **in ~** en el sentido de que • **it's an attractive investment in ~ it is tax-free** es una inversión atractiva en el sentido de que está exenta de impuestos

---

thatch [θætʃ] N (= *straw*) paja *f*; (= *roof*) techo *m* de paja
VT cubrir con paja, poner techo de paja a

thatched [θætʃt] ADJ • **~ cottage** casita *f* con techo de paja • **~ roof** techo *m* de paja

thatcher [ˈθætʃəʳ] N empajador(a) *m/f* de tejados

Thatcherism [ˈθætʃərɪzəm] N thatcherismo *m*

Thatcherite [ˈθætʃəraɪt] ADJ thatcheriano N thatcheriano/a *m/f*

thatching [ˈθætʃɪŋ] N (= *material*) paja *f* (para techar); (= *activity*) empajado *m* de tejados

that'd [ˈðætəd] = **that would, that had**

that'll [ˈðætəl] = **that will**

that's [ˈðæts] = **that is, that has**

thaw [θɔː] N **1** *(gen)* deshielo *m*; [*of snow*] derretimiento *m* • **a ~ had set in** había empezado el deshielo
2 *(fig)* (= *easing up*) descongelación *f* • **the ~ in East-West relations** la distensión en las relaciones Este-Oeste
VT *(also* **thaw out***)* [+ *frozen food*] descongelar
VI **1** *(Met)* [*snow*] derretirse; [*ice*] deshelarse • **it is ~ing** está deshelando
2 *(also* **thaw out***)* [*frozen food, cold toes*] descongelarse; *(fig)* [*relations*] distenderse • **I sat by the fire to ~ out** me senté junto al fuego para entrar en calor • **after a couple of glasses of wine he soon began to ~** tras tomar un par de vasos de vino empezó a relajarse *or* perder su reserva inicial

the *(strong form)* [ðiː], *(weak form)* [ðə] DEF ART
1 *(singular)* el/la; *(plural)* los/las • **the boy** el niño • **the woman** la mujer • **the cars** los coches • **the chairs** las sillas • **do you know the Smiths?** ¿conoce a los Smith? • **how's the leg?** ¿cómo va la pierna? • **all the …** todo el …/toda la …, todos los …/todas las … • **I'll meet you at the bank/station** quedamos en el banco/la estación • **the cheek of it!** ¡qué frescura! • **he's the man for the job** es el más indicado para el puesto • **from the** del/de la, de los/las • **it's ten miles from the house/village** está a diez millas de la casa/del pueblo • **I haven't the money** no tengo dinero • **of the** del/de la, de los/las • **the soup of the day** la sopa del día • **it was the year of the student riots** fue el año de los disturbios estudiantiles • **oh, the pain!** ¡ay qué dolor! • **he hasn't the sense to understand** no tiene bastante inteligencia para comprender • **I haven't the time** no tengo tiempo • **to the** al/a la, a los/las • **we went to the theatre** fuimos al teatro
2 (+ *adjective*) **a** *(denoting plural)* los/las • **the rich and the poor** los ricos y los pobres
b *(denoting sing)* lo • **within the realms of the possible** dentro de lo posible • **the good and the beautiful** lo bueno y lo bello
3 (+ *noun*) *(denoting whole class)* el/la • **to play the piano/flute** tocar el piano/la flauta • **in this age of the computer …** en esta época del ordenador …
4 (+ *comparative*) el/la • **she was the elder** era la mayor
5 *(distributive)* • **50 pence the pound** 50 peniques la libra • **eggs are usually sold by the dozen** los huevos se venden normalmente por docena • **paid by the hour** pagado por hora • **25 miles to the gallon** 25 millas por galón • **700 lire to the dollar** 700 liras por dólar
6 *(emphatic)* • **you don't mean the professor Bloggs?** ¿quieres decir el profesor Bloggs del que tanto se habla? • **it was the colour of 1995** fue el color que estaba tan de moda en 1995
7 *(in titles)* • **Richard the Second** Ricardo Segundo • **Ivan the Terrible** Iván el Terrible
ADV • **she looks all the better for it** se la ve mucho mejor por eso • **it will be all the better** será tanto mejor • **the more he works the more he earns** cuanto más trabaja más gana • **(all) the more so because …** tanto más cuanto que … • **the more … the less** mientras más … menos … • **the sooner the better** cuanto antes mejor

theatre, theater (US) [ˈθɪətəʳ] N
1 (= *building*) teatro *m* • **to go to the ~** ir al teatro • **lecture ~** aula *f* • **operating ~** sala *f* de operaciones
2 (= *profession*) teatro *m* • **she's been working in the ~ for 20 years** lleva trabajando el teatro 20 años
3 (= *drama*) teatro *m* • **~ of the absurd** teatro *m* del absurdo
4 *(fig)* teatro *m*, escenario *m*
CPD ▸ **theatre company** compañía *f* de teatro ▸ **theatre of war** escenario *m* de guerra

theatre-goer, theater-goer (US) [ˈθɪətəˌɡəʊəʳ] N aficionado/a *m/f* al teatro • **I'm not a keen theatre-goer** no soy un gran aficionado al teatro

theatre-in-the-round [ˈθɪətərɪnðəˈraʊnd] N (PL: **theatres-in-the-round**) teatro *m* de escenario central

theatreland [ˈθɪətəlænd] N teatrolandia *f*

theatrical [θɪˈætrɪkəl] ADJ **1** (= *of the theatre*) [*production, performance, tradition*] teatral • **the ~ world** el mundo del teatro *or* de las tablas • **she comes from a ~ background** viene de un ambiente de teatro
2 *(fig)* [*person, gesture, manner*] teatral, histriónico, teatrero* • **there was something very ~ about him** tenía un aire muy teatral • **don't be so ~!** ¡no seas tan teatral *or* teatrero*!, ¡no hagas tanto teatro!
NPL **theatricals** funciones *fpl* teatrales

theatricality [θɪˌætrɪˈkælɪtɪ] N teatralidad *f*

theatrically [θɪˈætrɪkəlɪ] ADV **1** *(Theat)* [*accomplished, effective*] desde el punto de vista teatral
2 (= *exaggeratedly*) de manera teatral • **he groaned ~** soltó un gemido teatral, gimió de manera teatral

theatrics [θ ɪˈæ trɪks] NPL *(fig) (pej)* teatro *msing*

Thebes [θiːbz] N Tebas *f*

thee†† [ðiː] PRON te; *(after prep)* ti • **with ~** contigo

theft [θeft] N *(gen)* robo *m*

their [ðɛəʳ] POSS ADJ *(with singular noun)* su; *(with plural noun)* sus • **~ father** su padre

t

• ~ **house** su casa • ~ **parents** sus padres • ~ **sisters** sus hermanas • **they took off ~ coats** se quitaron los abrigos • **after washing ~ hands** después de lavarse las manos • **someone stole ~ car** alguien les robó el coche

theirs [ðɛəz] (POSS PRON) (*referring to singular possession*) (el/la) suyo/a; (*referring to plural possession*) (los/las) suyos/as • **it's not our car, it's ~** no es nuestro coche, es suyo *or* es de ellos • **the suitcase is ~** la maleta es suya *or* es de ellos • **"whose is this?" — "it's ~"** —¿de quién es esto? —es suyo *or* de ellos • ~ **is a happy home** el suyo es un hogar feliz • **Isobel is a friend of ~** Isobel es amiga suya • **"is this their house?" — "no, ~ is white"** —¿es esta su casa? —no, la suya *or* la de ellos es blanca • **my parents and ~** mis padres y los suyos

theism ['θiːɪzəm] (N) teísmo *m*

theist ['θiːɪst] (N) teísta *mf*

theistic [θiː'ɪstɪk] (ADJ) teísta

them [ðem, ðəm] (PRON) **1** (*direct object*) los/las • **I didn't know ~** no los conocía • **look at ~!** ¡míralos! • **I had to give ~ to her** tuve que dárselos

2 (*indirect object*) les; (*combined with direct object pron*) se • **I gave ~ some brochures** les di unos folletos • **you must tell ~ the truth** tienes que decirles la verdad • **yes, of course I gave ~ the book** sí, claro que les di el libro • **yes, of course I gave it to ~** sí, claro que se lo di • **I gave the money to ~, not their parents** les di el dinero a ellos, no a sus padres • **I'm giving it to ~ not you** se lo doy a ellos, no a ti • **give it to ~ when you go to Liverpool** dáselo cuando vayas a Liverpool • **give it to ~, not me** dáselo a ellos, no a mí

3 (*after prepositions, in comparisons, with verb "to be"*) ellos/ellas • **it's for ~** es para ellos • **my sisters didn't go, my mother stayed with ~** mis hermanas no fueron, mi madre se quedó con ellas • **we are older than ~** somos mayores que ellos • **it must be ~** deben de ser ellos • **that's ~, they're coming now** son ellos, ya vienen • **they were carrying ~ on ~** los llevaban consigo

4 (*referring back to "someone", "anyone" etc: direct object*) lo *or* (*Sp*) le/la; (*indirect object*) le • **if anyone tries to talk to you, ignore ~** si alguien trata de hablar contigo, no le hagas caso

thematic [θɪ'mætɪk] (ADJ) temático

theme [θiːm] (N) (*gen*) tema *m*
(CPD) ▸ **theme music** = theme tune ▸ **theme park** parque *m* temático ▸ **theme pub** (*esp Brit*) bar *m* temático ▸ **theme song** tema *m* musical ▸ **theme tune** • **he was humming the ~ tune to James Bond** tarareaba la música de James Bond

themed [θiːmd] (ADJ) (*esp Brit*) [*place, event*] temático

themselves [ðəm'selvz] (PRON) **1** (*reflexive*) se • **did they hurt ~?** ¿se hicieron daño?

2 (*for emphasis*) ellos mismos/ellas mismas • **they built it ~** lo construyeron ellos mismos

3 (*after prep*) sí (mismos/as) • **they talked mainly about ~** hablaron principalmente de sí mismos

4 (*phrases*) • **by ~** solos/as • **she left the children at home by ~** dejó a los niños solos en casa • **don't leave the two of them alone by ~** no se te ocurra dejar a estos dos solos • **the girls did it all by ~** las chicas lo hicieron todo por sí mismas

then [ðen] (ADV) **1** (= *at that time*) entonces; (= *on that occasion*) en aquel momento, en aquella ocasión; (= *at that period in time*) en aquel entonces, en aquella época, a la sazón (*frm*) • **it was ~ that** ... fue entonces cuando ... • **it was ~ eight o'clock** eran las ocho • ~ **he used to go out, but now he never does** entonces *or* en aquella época salía, pero ahora no sale nunca • **before ~:** • **she couldn't remember anything that had happened before ~** no podía recordar nada de lo que había ocurrido hasta entonces *or* hasta ese momento • **you should have told me before ~** me lo tenías que haber dicho antes • **by ~** para entonces • **even ~:** • **they existed even ~, in 1953** existían incluso entonces, en 1953 • **even ~ it didn't work** aún así, no funcionaba • **from ~ on** desde aquel momento, desde entonces, a partir de entonces • **just ~:** • **just ~ he came in** entró justo entonces • **I wasn't doing anything just ~** justo en ese momento no estaba haciendo nada • **(every) now and ~** de vez en cuando • **since ~** desde entonces • **he wanted it done ~ and there** quería que lo hicieran en el acto *or* en ese mismo momento • **until ~** hasta entonces

2 (= *afterwards, next*) después, luego • ~ **we went to Jaca** después *or* luego fuimos a Jaca • **what happened ~?** ¿qué pasó después *or* luego? • **I chop the onions and ~ what?** pico las cebollas, ¿y luego qué?; ▸ **now**

3 (= *in that case*) entonces • **what do you want me to do ~?** ¿entonces, qué quieres que haga? • **"but I don't want a new one" — "what do you want ~?"** —pero yo no quiero uno nuevo —¿pues, qué es lo que quieres entonces? • ~ **you don't want it?** ¿así que no lo quieres? • **can't you hear me ~?** ¿es que no me oyes?, ¿pues *or* entonces no me oyes? • **but ~ we shall lose money** pero en ese caso perderemos dinero • **that's settled ~** entonces quedamos en eso • **"it doesn't work" — "well ~, we'll buy another one"** —no funciona —bueno, pues entonces compraremos otro

4 (= *furthermore*) además • **it would be awkward at work, and ~ there's the family** en el trabajo habría problemas, y además tengo que pensar en la familia

5 (*in summarizing*) • **this, ~, was the situation at the beginning of his reign** esta era, pues, *or* esta era, por (lo) tanto, la situación al principio de su reinado

6 (= *having said that*) • **and** *or* **but ~ again** por otra parte • **I like it, but ~ I'm biased** a mí sí me gusta, pero yo no soy objetivo • **but ~, you never can tell** pero vamos, nunca se sabe
(ADJ) entonces, de entonces • **the ~ Labour government** el gobierno laborista de entonces, el entonces gobierno, que era laborista • **the ~ king** el entonces rey

THEN

Time

▹ *When* **then** *means "at that time", translate using* **entonces**:

It was then that she heard Gwen cry out
Fue entonces cuando oyó gritar a Gwen
I hadn't heard about it till then
Hasta entonces no había oído hablar de ello

▹ *Alternatively, use expressions like* **en aquella época** *to refer to a particular period or* **en ese momento** *to refer to a particular moment:*

... my sister, who was then about 17 ...
... mi hermana, que en aquella época tenía unos 17 años ... *or* que tenía entonces unos 17 años ...

▹ *When* **then** *is used in the sense of "next", translate using* **luego** *or* **después**:

At first he refused but then he changed his mind
Primero se negó, pero luego *or* después cambió de opinión
He went to Julián's house and then to the chemist's
Fue a casa de Julián y luego *or* después a la farmacia

Reason

▹ *When* **then** *means "so" or "in that case", translate using* **entonces** *(placed at the beginning of the sentence):*

"I have a headache" - "So you won't be coming to the theatre, then?"
"Me duele la cabeza" - "¿Entonces no vienes al teatro?"
Then you'll already know about the bomb
Entonces ya sabrás lo de la bomba

▹ *Alternatively, use* **pues entonces**:

Pues entonces ya sabrás lo de la bomba

▹ *In more formal and written language, use* **por (lo) tanto** *or alternatively,* **pues**, *particularly when you are introducing a summary or a conclusion. These often appear between commas:*

Their decision, then, was based on a detailed analysis of the situation
Su decisión, pues, *or* Su decisión, por (lo) tanto, estaba basada en un análisis detallado de la situación

For further uses and examples, see main entry.

thence [ðens] (ADV) (*frm*) (*liter*) **1** (= *from that place*) de allí, desde allí

2 (= *consequently*) por lo tanto, por eso, por consiguiente • ~ **the fact that** de ahí que

3 (= *from that time*) = **thenceforth**

thenceforth ['ðens'fɔːθ], **thenceforward** [,ðens'fɔːwəd] (ADV) (*frm*) (*liter*) desde entonces, de allí en adelante, a partir de entonces

theocracy [θɪ'ɒkrəsɪ] (N) teocracia *f*

theocratic [θɪə'krætɪk] (ADJ) teocrático

theodolite [θɪ'ɒdəlaɪt] (N) teodolito *m*

theologian [θɪə'ləʊdʒɪən] (N) teólogo/a *m/f*

theological [θɪə'lɒdʒɪkəl] (ADJ) teológico
(CPD) ▸ **theological college** seminario *m*

theologist [θɪ'ɒlədʒɪst] (N) teólogo/a *m/f*

theology [θɪ'ɒlədʒɪ] (N) teología *f*

theorem ['θɪərəm] (N) (*Math*) teorema *m*

theoretic [θɪə'retɪk] (ADJ) = **theoretical**

theoretical [θɪə'retɪkəl] (ADJ) (*gen*) teórico

theoretically [θɪə'retɪkəlɪ] (ADV) (*gen*) teóricamente, en teoría

theoretician [,θɪərə'tɪʃən], **theorist** ['θɪərɪst] (N) teórico/a *m/f*

theorize ['θɪəraɪz] (VI) • **to ~ (about/on)** teorizar (acerca de/sobre)

theorizer ['θɪəraɪzəʳ] (N) teorizante *mf*

theory ['θɪərɪ] (N) (= *statement, hypothesis*) teoría *f* • **in ~** en teoría, teóricamente • **it's my ~** *or* **my ~ is that** ... tengo la teoría de que ..., mi teoría es que ...

theosophical [θɪə'sɒfɪkəl] (ADJ) teosófico

theosophist [θɪ'ɒsəfɪst] (N) teósofo/a *m/f*

theosophy [θɪ'ɒsəfɪ] (N) teosofía *f*

therapeutic [,θerə'pjuːtɪk] (ADJ) terapéutico

therapeutical [,θerə'pjuːtɪkl] (ADJ) terapéutico

therapeutics [,θerə'pjuːtɪks] (N) terapéutica *f*

t

therapist ['θerəpɪst] (N) terapeuta *mf*
therapy ['θerəpɪ] (N) terapia *f*
there (ADV) [ðɛəʳ] **1** (*place*) (= *there near you*) ahí; (*less precisely*) allí; (*further away*) allá • **put it ~, on the table** ponlo ahí, en la mesa • **when we left ~** cuando partimos de allí • **I don't know how to get ~** no sé cómo llegar allí • **~ he is!** ¡allí está! • **~'s the bus** ahí viene el autobús, ya viene el autobús • **~ we were, stuck** así que nos encontramos allí sin podernos mover • **to go ~ and back** ir y volver • **12 kilometres ~ and back** 12 kilómetros ida y vuelta • **we left him back ~ at the crossroads** lo dejamos allí atrás, en el cruce • **to be ~ for sb** (= *supportive*) estar al lado de algn, apoyar a algn • **down ~ on the floor** ahí en el suelo • **let's go down ~ by the river** vamos allí por el río • **I'm going to London, my sister's already down ~** voy a Londres, mi hermana ya está allí • **it's in ~** está ahí dentro • **it's on ~** está ahí encima • **it's over ~ by the TV** está allí, junto al televisor • **~ and then** en el acto, en seguida • **they're through ~ in the dining room** están por esa puerta *or* por ahí, en el comedor • **what's the cat doing up ~?** ¿qué hace el gato ahí arriba? • IDIOM: • **he's not all ~*** le falta un tornillo*
2 (*as addition to phrase*) • **hurry up ~!** ¡menearse! • **mind out ~!** ¡cuidado ahí! • **move along ~!** (*on street*) ¡retírense!; (*in bus, train*) ¡muévanse!, ¡no se paren, sigan para atrás! • **you ~!** ¡oye, tú!, ¡eh, usted! (*more frm*)
3 (= *in existence, available*) • **if the demand is ~, the product will appear** si existe la demanda, aparecerá el producto • **it's no good asking because the money just isn't ~** no sirve de nada pedir dinero, sencillamente porque no hay • **the old church is still ~ today** la vieja iglesia todavía está en pie *or* existe hoy • **is John ~, please?** (*on phone*) ¿está John?
4 (= *on that point*) en eso • **~ we differ** en eso discrepamos *or* no estamos de acuerdo • **you're right ~** en eso tienes razón • **I agree with you ~** en eso estoy de acuerdo contigo • **~ you are wrong** ahí se equivoca, en eso te equivocas
5 (= *at that point*) • **we'll leave it ~ for today** lo dejaremos aquí por hoy • **could I just stop you ~ and say something?** ¿puedo interrumpirte para decir algo al respecto?
6 (*emphasizing, pointing out*) • **~, now look what you've done!** desde luego, ¡mira lo que has hecho! • **~ again** por otra parte • **~ you are, what did I tell you!** ¿ves? es lo que te dije • **"~ you are," — he said, handing the book over** —ahí lo tienes —dijo, entregando el libro • **~ you go again, upsetting the children** ¿vuelta a las andadas, molestando a los niños?, ¿ya estamos otra vez molestando a los niños? • **it wasn't what I wanted, but ~ you go*** no era lo que buscaba, pero ¿qué le vamos a hacer? • **I'm not going, so ~!*** pues no voy, y fastídiate*
(PRON) • **~ is** • **~ are** hay • **~ will be** habrá • **~ were ten bottles** había *or* (*esp LAm*) habían diez botellas • **how many are ~?** ¿cuántos hay? • **~ will be eight people for dinner tonight** seremos ocho para cenar esta noche • **~ was laughter at this** en esto hubo risas • **~ was singing and dancing** se cantó y se bailó • **~ has been an accident** ha habido un accidente • **are ~ any bananas?** ¿hay plátanos? • **is ~ any coffee?** ¿hay café? • **~ is no wine left** no queda vino • **~ might be time/room** puede que haya tiempo/sitio • **~ is a pound missing** falta una libra
(EXCL) • **~, drink this** bebe esto • **there, there** (*comforting*) no te preocupes, no pasa nada • **but ~, what's the use?** pero ¡vamos!, es inútil

> **THERE IS, THERE ARE**
>
> ▸ *Unlike* **there is/are** *etc,* **hay, hubo, había, ha habido** *etc do not change to reflect number:*
> **There were two kidnappings and a murder**
> Hubo dos secuestros y un asesinato
> **Will there be many students at the party?**
> ¿Habrá muchos estudiantes en la fiesta?
>
> ▸ *To translate* **there must be, there may be** *etc, you can use* **tiene que haber, debe (de) haber, puede haber** *etc although other constructions will also be possible:*
> **There may be a strike**
> Puede haber *or* Puede que haya huelga
> **There must be all sorts of things we could do**
> Tiene que haber muchas cosas que podamos hacer
>
> ▸ *If* **there is/there are** *is followed by* **the,** *you should normally not use* **hay** *etc. Use* **estar** *instead:*
> **And then there are the neighbours to consider**
> Están también los vecinos, a los que hay que tener en cuenta
> **There is also the question of the money transfer**
> Está también la cuestión de la transferencia del dinero
>
> ▸ **Hay** *etc should only be used to talk about existence and occurrence. Don't use it to talk about location. Use* **estar** *instead to say where things are:*
> **After the shop there's the bus station**
> Después de la tienda está la estación de autobuses
>
> ▸ *Don't use* **hay** *etc to translate phrases like* **there are four of us, there will be six of them.** *Instead, use* **ser** *in the relevant person:*
> **There are four of us**
> Somos cuatro
> **There will be six of them**
> Serán seis
>
> ▸ *Remember to use* **que** *in the construction* **hay algo que hacer (there is sth to do)**:
> **There is a lot to do**
> Hay mucho que hacer
> **What is there to do?**
> ¿Qué hay que hacer?
>
> *For further uses and examples, see* **there**

thereabouts ['ðɛərəbaʊts] (ADV) **1** (*place*) por ahí, allí cerca
2 (*number*) • **12 or ~** 12 más o menos, alrededor de 12 • **£5 or ~** cinco libras o así
thereafter [ðɛər'ɑːftəʳ] (ADV) (*frm*) después de eso, de allí en adelante, a partir de entonces
thereat [ðɛər'æt] (ADV) (*frm*) (= *thereupon*) con eso, acto seguido; (= *for that reason*) por eso, por esa razón
thereby ['ðɛə'baɪ] (ADV) así, de ese modo • **~ hangs a tale** eso tiene su cuento
therefore ['ðɛəfɔːʳ] (ADV) por tanto, por lo tanto • **he wanted to become the richest, and ~ the happiest, man in the world** quería convertirse en el hombre más rico, y por (lo) tanto más feliz, del mundo • **I think, ~ I am** pienso, luego existo • **therefore X = 4** luego X es igual a 4 (*Math*)
therefrom [ðɛə'frɒm] (ADV) (*frm*) de ahí, de allí
therein [ðɛər'ɪn] (ADV) (*frm*) **1** (= *inside*) allí dentro
2 (= *in this regard*) en eso, en esto • **~ lies the danger** ahí está el peligro, en eso consiste el peligro
thereof [ðɛər'ɒv] (ADV) (*frm*) de eso, de esto, de lo mismo
thereon [ðɛər'ɒn] (ADV) (*frm*) • **the land and the buildings ~** la tierra y los edificios que se asientan sobre ella • **the symbol of the Lion is embroidered ~** el símbolo del león aparece bordado sobre ello
there's [ðɛəz] = **there is, there has**
Theresa [tɪ'riːzə] (N) Teresa
thereto [ðɛə'tuː] (ADV) (*frm*) a eso, a ello
thereunder [,ðɛər'ʌndəʳ] (ADV) (*frm*) allí expuesto
thereupon ['ðɛərə'pɒn] (ADV) (*frm*) **1** (= *at that point*) acto seguido, en eso, con eso
2 (= *on that subject*) sobre eso
therewith [ðɛə'wɪθ] (ADV) (*frm*) con eso, con lo mismo
therm [θɜːm] (N) termia *f*
thermal ['θɜːməl] (ADJ) [*current*] termal; [*underwear, blanket*] térmico
(N) **1** (*Met*) térmica *f*, corriente *f* térmica
2 thermals (= *underwear*) ropa *f* interior térmica
(CPD) ▸ **thermal baths** = **thermal springs** ▸ **thermal imaging camera** cámara *f* de imágenes térmicas ▸ **thermal printer** termoimpresora *f* ▸ **thermal reactor** reactor *m* térmico ▸ **thermal springs** termas *fpl*, fuentes *fpl* termales
thermic ['θɜːmɪk] (ADJ) térmico
thermionic [,θɜːmɪ'ɒnɪk] (ADJ) termiónico
(CPD) ▸ **thermionic valve** lámpara *f* termiónica
thermistor [θɜː'mɪstəʳ] (N) (*Tech*) termistor *m*
thermo... ['θɜːməʊ] (PREFIX) termo...
thermocouple ['θɜːməʊ,kʌpl] (N) termopar *m*, par *m* térmico
thermodynamic ['θɜːməʊdaɪ'næmɪk] (ADJ) termodinámico
thermodynamics ['θɜːməʊdaɪ'næmɪks] (NSING) termodinámica *f*
thermoelectric ['θɜːməʊɪ'lektrɪk] (ADJ) termoeléctrico
(CPD) ▸ **thermoelectric couple** par *m* termoeléctrico
thermoelectricity [,θɜːməʊɪlek'trɪsɪtɪ] (N) termoelectricidad *f*
thermometer [θə'mɒmɪtəʳ] (N) termómetro *m*
thermonuclear ['θɜːməʊ'njuːklɪəʳ] (ADJ) termonuclear
thermopile ['θɜːməʊpaɪl] (N) termopila *f*
thermoplastic [,θɜːməʊ'plæstɪk] (N) termoplástico *m*
Thermopylae [θɜː'mɒpɪliː] (N) Termópilas *fpl*
Thermos® ['θɜːməs] (N) (*also* **Thermos flask** *or* **bottle**) termo *m*
thermosetting [,θɜːməʊ'setɪŋ] (ADJ) • **~ plastics** plásticos *mpl* termoestables
thermostat ['θɜːməstæt] (N) termostato *m*
thermostatic [,θɜːməs'tætɪk] (ADJ) termostático
thermotherapy [,θɜːməʊ'θerəpɪ] (N) (*Med*) termoterapia *f*
thesaurus [θɪ'sɔːrəs] (N) (PL: **thesauruses, thesauri** [θɪ'sɔːraɪ]) tesauro *m*
these [ðiːz] (DEM ADJ) estos/estas • **it's not ~ chocolates but those ones I like** no son estos

t

bombones los que me gustan sino aquellos • **~ ones over here** estos/estas de aquí, estos/estas que están aquí • **how are you getting on ~ days?** ¿cómo le va últimamente?

(DEM PRON) estos/estas, éstos/éstas

In the past the standard spelling for ***estos/estas*** *as pronouns was with an accent* ***(éstos/éstas)****. Nowadays the* ***Real Academia Española*** *advises that the accented forms are only required where there might otherwise be confusion with the adjectives* ***estos/estas****.*

• **I'm looking for some sandals, can I try ~?** quiero unas sandalias, ¿puedo probarme estas? • **what are ~?** ¿qué son estos? • **~ are my friends/my books** estos son mis amigos/mis libros • **I prefer ~ to those** prefiero estos a aquellos

Theseus ['θiːsjuːs] (N) Teseo

thesis ['θiːsɪs] (N) (PL: **theses** ['θiːsiːz]) tesis *f inv*

Thespian ['θespɪən] (ADJ) **1** (= *of Thespis*) de Tespis

2 (*fig*) dramático, trágico

(N) actor *m*, actriz *f*

Thespis ['θespɪs] (N) Tespis

Thessalonians [ˌθesə'ləʊnɪənz] (NPL) tesalonios *mpl*

Thessaly ['θesəlɪ] (N) Tesalia *f*

Thetis ['θiːtɪs] (N) Tetis

they [ðeɪ] (PRON) **1** (*referring to particular people, things*) **a** (*emphatic, to avoid ambiguity*) ellos/ellas • **we went to the cinema but ~ didn't** nosotros fuimos al cine pero ellos no • **I spoke to my sisters and ~ agreed with me** hablé con mis hermanas y ellas estaban de acuerdo conmigo • **it's ~ who ...** son ellos quienes ... • **we work harder than ~ do** trabajamos más que ellos

b

Don't translate the subject pronoun when not emphasizing or clarifying:

• **~'re fine, thank you** están bien, gracias • **~'re yellow** son amarillos

c (*frm*) • **~ who ...** los que ..., quienes ...

2 (*referring to "someone", "anyone"*) • **if anyone tells you otherwise, ~'re mistaken** si alguien te dice lo contrario, no tiene razón

3 (*generalizing*) • **~ say that ...** se dice que ..., dicen que ... • **as ~ say** como dicen, según dicen • **~ are making it illegal** lo van a hacer ilegal

they'd [ðeɪd] = **they would, they had**

they'll [ðeɪl] = **they will, they shall**

they're [ðeəʳ] = **they are**

they've [ðeɪv] = **they have**

thiamine ['θaɪəmiːn] (N) tiamina *f*

thick [θɪk] (ADJ) (COMPAR: **thicker**, SUPERL: **thickest**) **1** (= *not thin*) [*wall, line, slice, neck*] grueso; [*lips*] grueso, carnoso; [*waist*] ancho; [*sweater*] gordo; [*spectacles*] de lente gruesa • **a ~ layer of snow/dust** una espesa capa de nieve/polvo • **a ~ layer of potatoes/butter** una capa gruesa de patatas/mantequilla • **a tree root as ~ as a man's arm** una raíz de árbol tan gruesa *or* gorda como el brazo de un hombre • **it's 2 metres ~** tiene 2 metros de grosor • **a 5 centimetres ~ door** una puerta de 5 centímetros de grosor • **to give sb a ~ ear*** dar un sopapo a algn* • **how ~ is it?** ¿qué grosor tiene?, ¿cómo es de grueso? • **it's** *or* **that's a bit ~*** (= *unreasonable*) eso ya pasa de castaño oscuro*

2 (= *dense*) [*beard, eyebrows*] poblado; [*carpet, fur*] tupido; [*forest*] tupido, poblado; [*vegetation, dust*] espeso; [*air, atmosphere*] cargado, denso; [*smoke, clouds, night*] denso; [*fog*] espeso, denso • **to have ~ hair** tener mucho pelo, tener una melena tupida • **to be ~ with** (*gen*) estar lleno de • **the pavements were ~ with people** las aceras estaban abarrotadas *or* llenas de gente • **the air was ~ with smoke** el aire estaba cargado *or* lleno de humo • **the air was ~ with rumours** (*fig*) corrían *or* circulaban muchos rumores • IDIOM: • **to be ~ on the ground***: • **cameramen and interviewers were ~ on the ground** había cámaras y entrevistadores a patadas*

3 (= *not runny*) [*yoghurt, sauce*] espeso • **if the soup becomes too ~, add more water** si la sopa se pone muy espesa, añada más agua • **whisk until ~** bátase hasta que se ponga espeso

4‡ (= *stupid*) corto*, burro* • **he's a bit ~** es un poco corto *or* burro* • **I finally got it into** *or* **through his ~ head** por fin conseguí que le entrase en esa cabeza hueca* • IDIOMS: • **to be as ~ as a brick** *or* **two short planks** ser más burro *or* bruto que un arado* • **as ~ as (pig)shit**** más burro *or* bruto que la hostia**

5 (= *strong*) [*accent*] fuerte, marcado

6 (*from drink, illness, tiredness*) [*voice*] pastoso • **his voice was ~ with emotion** su voz estaba empañada por la emoción *or* cargada de emoción • **his voice was ~ with sarcasm** su tono iba cargado de sarcasmo

7* (= *very friendly*) • **to be ~ (with sb)** ser uña y carne (con algn)* • IDIOM: • **to be (as) ~ as thieves** ser uña y carne*

8 (= *groggy*) • **I woke up with a ~ head** me desperté con la cabeza embotada

(ADV) (= *in a thick layer*) • **the fog hung ~ over the city** una capa espesa de niebla pendía sobre la ciudad • **the dust/snow lay ~** había una capa espesa de polvo/nieve • **slice the bread nice and ~** corte el pan en rebanadas bien gruesas • **he spread the butter on ~** untó una capa gruesa de mantequilla • IDIOMS: • **to come/follow ~ and fast** llegar/sucederse con rapidez • **the jokes came ~ and fast** los chistes iban surgiendo uno detrás de otro con rapidez • **distress calls were coming in ~ and fast** llovían las llamadas de auxilio • **the snow was falling ~ and fast** nevaba copiosamente *or* sin parar • **to lay it on ~*** (= *exaggerate*) cargar *or* recargar las tintas*

(N) • **to be in the ~ of sth: he likes to be in the ~ of it** *or* **things** *or* **the action** le gusta estar metido en el meollo del asunto *or* en el ajo • **he was in the ~ of the fighting** estaba en lo más intenso de la lucha • IDIOM: • **through ~ and thin** en las duras y en las maduras

thicken ['θɪkən] (VT) espesar, hacer más espeso

(VI) **1** (*Culin*) [*mixture, sauce*] espesarse

2 [*darkness*] aumentar; [*clouds, wood, jungle*] hacerse más denso • **her voice ~ed with emotion** se le empañó la voz de emoción *or* por la emoción • IDIOM: • **the plot ~s** la cosa se complica

thickener ['θɪkənəʳ] (N) espesador *m*

thicket ['θɪkɪt] (N) matorral *m*

thickhead* ['θɪkhed] (N) bruto/a *m/f*

thickheaded* [ˌθɪk'hedɪd] (ADJ) **1** (= *stupid*) bruto, estúpido

2 (= *obstinate*) terco, cabezón

3 (= *groggy*) grogui

thickheadedness* [ˌθɪk'hedɪdnɪs] (N)

1 (= *stupidness*) estupidez *f*

2 (= *obstinacy*) terquedad *f*

thickie‡ ['θɪkɪ] (N) bobo/a *m/f*

thick-lipped [ˌθɪk'lɪpt] (ADJ) de labios gruesos, bezudo

thickly ['θɪklɪ] (ADV) **1** (= *densely*) • **a ~ populated area** una zona densamente poblada • **the snow was falling ~** la nieve caía con fuerza *or* copiosamente • **the trees grew ~ along the river** los árboles crecían en abundancia a orillas del río • **~ wooded** densamente poblado de árboles

2 (= *in a thick layer*) • **she spread the butter ~ on the toast** untó una gruesa capa de mantequilla en la tostada • **dust/snow lay ~** había una espesa capa de polvo/nieve • **the ~ carpeted dining room** el comedor con el suelo cubierto por una tupida moqueta • **the ground was ~ carpeted with pine needles** el suelo estaba cubierto de una gruesa capa de agujas de pino

3 (= *in thick pieces*) • **to cut/slice sth ~** cortar algo en rodajas gruesas

4 (= *unclearly*) [*say, reply*] (*from drink, tiredness*) con voz pastosa; (*with emotion*) con voz emocionada

thickness ['θɪknɪs] (N) **1** (= *denseness*) [*of wall, door, layer*] grosor *m*, espesor *m*; [*of line, slice, fabric, lens*] grosor *m*; [*of hair*] abundancia *f*; [*of fur, carpet*] lo tupido; [*of smoke*] densidad *f*; [*of cream, sauce*] lo espeso • **it is 4mm in ~** tiene 4 milímetros de grosor

2 (= *layer*) capa *f* • **three ~es of material** tres capas de tela

thicko‡ ['θɪkəʊ] (N) = **thickie**

thickset [ˌθɪk'set] (ADJ) [*person*] robusto, fornido; [*features*] grueso, gordo

thick-skinned [ˌθɪk'skɪnd] (ADJ) **1** [*orange*] de piel gruesa

2 (= *insensitive*) [*person*] insensible, duro

thief [θiːf] (N) (PL: **thieves** [θiːvz]) ladrón/ona *m/f* • **stop ~!** ¡al ladrón! • IDIOM: • **you have to set a ~ to catch a ~** no hay como un ladrón para atrapar a otro; ▷ **thick**

thieve [θiːv] (VT), (VI) robar, hurtar

thievery ['θiːvərɪ] (N) robo *m*, hurto *m*

thieving ['θiːvɪŋ] (ADJ) ladrón

(N) robo *m*, hurto *m*

thievish ['θiːvɪʃ] (ADJ) ladrón • **to have ~ tendencies** ser largo de uñas

thievishness ['θiːvɪʃnɪs] (N) propensión *f* a robar

thigh [θaɪ] (N) muslo *m*

(CPD) ▸ **thigh bone** fémur *m*

thimble ['θɪmbl] (N) **1** (*Sew*) dedal *m*

2 (*Naut*) guardacabo *m*

thimbleful ['θɪmblfʊl] (N) dedada *f* • **just a ~** unas gotas nada más

thin [θɪn] (ADJ) (COMPAR: **thinner**, SUPERL: **thinnest**) **1** (= *not fat*) [*person, legs, arms*] delgado, flaco (*pej*); [*waist*] delgado, estrecho; [*face*] delgado; [*nose*] delgado, afilado; [*lips*] fino; [*animal*] flaco • **to get** *or* **grow ~** adelgazar • **I want to get nice and ~ for the holidays** quiero adelgazar bien para estas vacaciones • **you're getting ~, aren't you eating enough?** te estás quedando muy delgado, ¿comes lo suficiente? • **she was painfully ~** estaba tan flaca que daba pena verla • IDIOM: • **to be as ~ as a rake*** estar en los huesos*

2 (= *not thick*) [*layer, sheet*] fino, delgado; [*wall*] delgado; [*slice, line, fabric*] fino • **a ~ layer of paint** una capa fina de pintura • **a ~ volume of poetry** un delgado tomo de poesía • **to wear ~** [*fabric, clothing*] desgastarse • **his trousers had worn ~ at the knee** el pantalón se le había desgastado por las rodillas • **the joke had begun to wear very ~** (*fig*) la broma ya empezaba a resultar muy pesada • **my patience is wearing ~** (*fig*) se me está agotando *or* acabando la paciencia • IDIOMS: • **it's the ~ end of the wedge** es el principio de algo que puede tener terribles

consecuencias • to be *or* skate *or* walk on ~ ice estar pisando terreno resbaladizo *or* peligroso • to have a ~ skin ofenderse por nada, tomárselo todo a mal; ▸ line
3 (= *watery*) [*custard, sauce, paint*] poco espeso
4 (= *not dense*) [*smoke, fog, rain*] fino
5 (= *sparse*) [*beard, hair*] ralo, escaso; [*eyebrows*] fino, delgado; [*crowd*] escaso, poco numeroso • IDIOMS: • to be ~ on the ground (*esp Brit*) escasear • to be ~ on top estar casi calvo, tener poco pelo (en la cabeza)
6 (= *unconvincing*) [*excuse*] pobre, poco convincente; [*evidence*] poco concluyente; [*argument, essay, script*] pobre, flojo • a ~ majority una mayoría escasa • a ~ smile una débil sonrisa
7 (= *weak*) [*voice*] aflautado
8 (*Econ*) [*profit*] escaso • trading was ~ on the stock market hubo poca actividad en la bolsa
9 (= *lacking oxygen*) [*air, atmosphere*] enrarecido, rarificado • IDIOM: • out of/into ~ air: • to appear out of ~ air aparecer como por arte de magia • to produce sth out of ~ air sacar algo de la nada • I can't conjure up the money out of ~ air no puedo sacar el dinero de la nada • he disappeared *or* vanished into ~ air despareció como por arte de magia, se lo tragó la tierra
(ADV) (= *thinly*) • slice the potatoes very ~ corta las patatas en rodajas muy finas • don't slice the bread too ~ no cortes el pan demasiado fino • spread the butter very ~ untar una capa muy fina de mantequilla; ▸ spread
(VT) 1 (*also* **thin out**) (= *reduce in number*) [+ *population, group*] mermar; [+ *seedlings*] entresacar
2 (*also* **thin down**) (= *dilute*) [+ *sauce, soup*] aclarar; [+ *paint*] diluir • aspirin ~s the blood la aspirina hace que la sangre sea menos espesa • greenhouse gases are ~ning the ozone layer los gases que causan el efecto invernadero están haciendo que la capa de ozono sea cada vez menos espesa
(VI) (*also* **thin out**) (= *lessen*) [*fog*] aclararse; [*ozone layer*] hacerse menos espeso; [*crowd*] disminuir; [*population*] mermar, reducirse • his hair is ~ning slightly está empezando a perder pelo
▸ **thin down** (VT + ADV) (= *dilute*) [+ *sauce, gravy, custard*] aclarar; [+ *paint*] diluir
(VI + ADV) (= *become slim*) adelgazar
▸ **thin out** (VT + ADV) (= *reduce in number*) [+ *population, group*] mermar; [+ *seedlings*] entresacar
(VI + ADV) (= *lessen*) [*fog*] aclararse; [*ozone layer*] hacerse menos denso; [*crowd*] disminuir; [*population*] mermar, reducirse • his hair is ~ning out está empezando a perder pelo

thine†† [ðaɪn] (POSS PRON) (*sing*) (el) tuyo, (la) tuya; (*pl*) (los) tuyos, (las) tuyas • for thee and ~ para ti y los tuyos • what is mine is ~ lo que es mío es tuyo
(ADJ) (*sing*) tu; (*pl*) tus

thing [θɪŋ] (N) 1 (*concrete*) (= *object*) cosa *f* • they were selling all sorts of ~s vendían todo tipo de cosas • what's that ~ called? ¿cómo se llama eso? • get that ~ off the sofa! ¡quita esa cosa del sofá! • dogs? I can't stand the ~s ¿perros? no puedo con ellos • a ~ of beauty una belleza, un objeto bello • ~s of value objetos *mpl* de valor • IDIOM: • you must be seeing ~s estás viendo visiones
2 (*non-concrete*) (= *matter, circumstance, action*) cosa *f*, asunto *m*, cuestión *f* • as ~s are • with ~s as they are tal como están las cosas • that's how ~s are así están las cosas • how are ~s? ¿qué tal? • how are ~s with you? ¿qué tal te va?, ¿cómo andas? • ~s are going badly las cosas van *or* marchan mal • ~s aren't what they used to be las cosas ya no son como antes *or* ya no son lo que eran • the ~ is ... lo que pasa es que ..., el caso es que ... • the ~ is to sell your car first conviene vender primero tu coche • what a ~ to say! ¡qué dices!, ¡cómo se te ocurre! • I haven't done a ~ about it no he hecho nada de nada al respecto • I don't know a ~ about cars no sé nada en absoluto de coches • I didn't know a ~ for that exam para ese examen no sabía nada de nada, para ese examen yo estaba pez (*Sp**) • above all ~s ante todo, sobre todo • all ~s considered bien mirado • all ~s being equal si las cosas siguen como ahora • the system cannot be all ~s to all people el sistema no puede contentar a todo el mundo • a gentleman in all ~s un caballero en todos los aspectos • and for another ~ ... y además ..., y por otra parte ... • the best ~ would be to wait lo mejor sería esperar • the next best ~ lo mejor después de eso • we had hoped for better ~s habíamos esperado algo mejor • it was a close *or* near ~ [*race*] fue una carrera muy reñida; [*accident*] por poco chocamos, casi chocamos; [*escape*] escapamos por un pelo • it's not the done ~ eso no se hace • the first ~ to do is ... lo primero que hay que hacer es ... • first ~ (in the morning) a primera hora (de la mañana) • you don't know the first ~ about it no sabes nada en absoluto de esto • first ~s first! ¡lo primero es lo primero! • it's a good ~ he didn't see you menos mal que no te vio • the good ~ about it is that ... lo bueno es que ... • it's finished and a good ~ too se acabó y me alegro de ello • she knows a good ~ when she sees it sabe obrar de acuerdo con su propio interés • this is too much of a good ~ esto es demasiado • it's just the ~! ¡es justo lo que me faltaba! • that's the last ~ we want eso es lo último que queremos • last ~ (at night) antes de acostarse • the main ~ lo más importante, lo principal • to make a mess of ~s estropearlo todo • (the) next ~ I knew, he'd gone cuando me di cuenta, ya se había ido • not a ~ nada • for one ~ en primer lugar • what with one ~ and another entre una(s) cosa(s) y otra(s) • it's one ~ to buy it, quite another to make it work es fácil comprarlo, pero no es tan fácil hacerlo funcionar • if it's not one ~ it's the other si no es una cosa es otra • neither one ~ nor the other ni lo uno ni lo otro • the only ~ is to paint it la única cosa que se puede hacer es pintarlo • I showed him the copy and he thought it was the real ~ le enseñé la copia y pensó que era el auténtico • this time I'm in love, it's the real ~ esta vez estoy enamorada de verdad • to do the right ~ obrar bien, obrar honradamente • you did the right ~ hiciste bien • I've done a silly ~ he hecho algo tonto • did you ever see such a ~? ¿se vio jamás tal cosa? • there's no such ~! ¡no hay tal! • the play's the ~ lo que importa es la representación • it's just one of those ~s son cosas que pasan, son cosas de la vida • he knows a ~ or two sabe de qué va • I could tell you a ~ or two about her podría decirte unas cuantas cosas sobre ella • it's the very ~! ¡es justo lo que me faltaba! • IDIOMS: • to try to be all ~s to all men tratar de serlo todo para todos • to be on to a good ~*: • he knew he was on to a good ~ when the orders started flowing in supo que había dado con chollo cuando empezaron a llover los pedidos* • to make a (big) ~ (out) of sth*: • he made a big ~ out of the accident exageró mucho el accidente • she made a big ~ of introducing him to me me lo presentó con mucho aparato • don't make a ~ of it! ¡no es para tanto!
3 things (= *belongings*) cosas *fpl*; (= *clothes*) ropa *fsing*; (= *luggage*) equipaje *msing* • where shall I put my ~s? ¿dónde pongo mis cosas? • to pack up one's ~s hacer las maletas • she had brought her painting ~s with her se había traído sus utensilios de pintura • to wash up/clear away the supper ~s lavar los platos/quitar la mesa de la cena • to take off one's ~s quitarse la ropa, desnudarse
4* (= *person*) • you mean ~! ¡mira que eres tacaño! • you nasty ~! ¡mira que eres desagradable! • you poor (old) ~! • poor ~! ¡pobrecito! • the stupid ~ went and sold it el muy estúpido fue y lo vendió • she's a sweet little ~, isn't she? es monísima, ¿verdad?
5 (= *fashion*) • the latest ~ in hats lo último en sombreros • it's quite the ~ está muy de moda
6* (= *activity, preference*) • his ~ is fast cars lo suyo son los coches rápidos • it's not my ~ no es lo mío • IDIOM: • to do one's own ~* ir a su aire • you know her, she likes to do her own ~ ya la conoces, le gusta ir a su aire
7* (= *obsession*) obsesión *f* • he has a ~ about cleanliness está obsesionado con la limpieza, tiene obsesión *or* manía con la limpieza • he has a ~ about steam engines está obsesionado por las locomotoras a vapor, le obsesionan las locomotoras a vapor • I have a ~ about punctuality soy un maniático de la puntualidad • he's got a ~ for her* está colado por ella*
8* (= *phobia*) fobia *f* • she has a ~ about snakes le tiene fobia a las serpientes
9* (= *relationship, affair*) • he's got a ~ going with her se entiende con ella • he had a ~ with her two years ago se lió con ella hace dos años*

thingumabob* ['θɪŋəmɪbɒb], **thingamajig** ['θɪŋəmɪdʒɪg], **thingummy** ['θɪŋəmɪ], **thingy** ['θɪŋɪ] (N) (= *object*) chisme *m*, cosa *f*; (= *person*) fulano/a *m/f* • old ~ with the specs fulano el de las gafas

think [θɪŋk] (VB: PT, PP: **thought**) (VI)
1 (= *exercise mind*) pensar; (= *ponder*) reflexionar • I ~, therefore I am pienso, luego existo • give me time to ~ dame tiempo para reflexionar • to act without ~ing actuar sin pensar • ~ before you reply piénselo antes de contestar • I'm sorry, I wasn't ~ing lo siento, estaba distraído • now let me ~, where did I last see it? a ver, déjame pensar, ¿cuándo lo vi por última vez? • to ~ about sth (= *occupy one's thoughts with*) pensar en algo; (= *consider*) pensar algo • what are you ~ing about? ¿en qué estás pensando? • you've given us a lot to ~ about nos ha dado mucho en que pensar • I'll ~ about it lo voy a pensar • it's worth ~ing about vale la pena de pensarlo • you ~ too much about money le das demasiada importancia al dinero • what he said made me ~ again lo que dijo hizo que me lo volviera a pensar • did you ~ I was going to give you the money? well, ~ again! ¿creíste que iba a darte el dinero? ¡vamos, piensa un poco! • to ~ aloud pensar en voz alta • ~ carefully before you reply piénsalo bien antes de responder • to ~ for o.s. pensar por sí mismo • to ~ (long and) hard pensar mucho • I ~ of you always • I am always ~ing of you pienso constantemente en ti • I'll be ~ing of you me acordaré de ti • ~ of me tomorrow in the exam acuérdate de mí mañana, haciendo el examen • to ~ straight concentrarse • to ~ twice before doing sth pensar algo dos veces antes de hacerlo • we didn't ~ twice about it no vacilamos un instante

2 (= *imagine*) imaginarse • **just ~!** ¡fíjate!, ¡imagínate!, ¡te das cuenta! • **~ of the expense** imagínate lo que costaría • **~ of what might have happened!** ¡piensa en lo que podía haber ocurrido! • **and to ~ of her going there alone!** ¡y pensar que ella fue allí sola!
3 (= *remember*) • **you can't ~ of everything** no se puede estar en todo • **now I come to ~ of it …** ahora que lo pienso … • **I couldn't ~ of the right word** no pude acordarme de la palabra exacta
4 (= *have opinion*) • **see what you ~ about it and let me know** piénsalo y dime luego tu opinión • **I didn't ~ much of the play** la obra no me convenció, la obra no me gustó mucho • **we don't ~ much of him** tenemos un concepto más bien bajo de él • **what do you ~ of it?** ¿qué te parece? • **what do you ~ of him?** ¿qué opinas de él?, ¿qué te parece (él)? • **to ~ highly of sb** tener muy buena opinión de algn, tener a algn en muy buen concepto • **I told him what I thought of him** le dije lo que pensaba de él; ▹ **well²**
5 (= *consider, take into account*) • **to ~ of other people's feelings** pensar en *or* tener en cuenta los sentimientos de los demás • **one has to ~ of the expense** hay que pensar en lo que se gasta • **there are the children to ~ about** hay que pensar en los niños • **he ~s of nobody but himself** no piensa más que en sí mismo
6 • **to ~ of** (= *wonder about, dream up*) • **I thought of going to Spain** pensé en ir a España • **have you ever thought of going to Cuba?** ¿has pensado alguna vez en ir a Cuba? • **don't you ever ~ of washing?** ¿no se te ocurre alguna vez lavarte? • **whatever were you ~ing of?** ¿cómo se te ocurrió hacer eso? • **I was the one who thought of it first** fui yo quien tuve la idea primero • **whatever will he ~ of next?** ¡a ver qué es lo que se le ocurre ahora!
7 (= *choose*) • **~ of a number** piensa en un número
VT 1 (= *cogitate*) pensar • **to ~ great thoughts** pensar cosas profundas, tener pensamientos profundos • **to ~ evil thoughts** tener malos pensamientos • **~ what you've done** piense en lo que hizo
2 (= *believe*) creer • **I ~ (that) it is true** creo que es verdad • **I don't ~ it can be done** no creo que se pueda hacer • **you must ~ me very rude** va a creer que soy muy descortés • **we all thought him a fool** lo teníamos todos por idiota • **he ~s himself very clever** se cree muy listo • **I don't ~ it likely** lo creo *or* me parece muy poco probable • **I ~ (that) you're wrong** me parece que estás equivocado • **she's very pretty, don't you ~?** es muy guapa, ¿no crees? • **he'll be back, I don't ~!*** ¿que volverá? ¡no creo! • **I ~ not** creo que no • **I ~ so** creo que sí, me parece que sí • **I don't ~ so** creo que no • **now I don't know what to ~** ahora estoy en duda • **what do you ~ I should do?** ¿qué crees que debo hacer? • **what do you ~ you're doing?** ¿se puede saber lo que estás haciendo? • **who do you ~ you are?** ¿quién te crees que eres? • **who do you ~ you are to come marching in here?** y tú ¿qué derecho crees tener para entrar aquí tan fresco? • **anyone would ~ she was dying** cualquiera diría que se estaba muriendo • **I would have thought that …** hubiera creído que … • **that's what you ~!** ¡(que) te crees tú eso!
3 (= *imagine*) imaginar(se) • **~ what we could do with that house!** ¡imagina lo que podríamos hacer con esa casa! • **to ~ she once slept here!** ¡pensar que ella durmió aquí una vez! • **I can't ~ what he can want** no me puedo imaginar qué quiere • **I can't ~ what you mean** no llego a entender lo que quieres decir • **I thought as much** ya me lo figuraba, ya lo sabía • **I never thought that …** nunca pensé *or* imaginé que … • **who'd have thought it?** ¿quién lo diría? • **who'd have thought it possible?** ¿quién se lo hubiera imaginado?
4 (= *remember*) recordar • **try to ~ where you last saw it** intenta recordar dónde lo viste por última vez
5 (= *be of opinion*) opinar • **this is my new dress, what do you ~?** este es mi vestido nuevo, ¿qué te parece? *or* ¿qué opinas? • **I ~ we should wait, what do you ~?** creo que deberíamos esperar, ¿qué opinas?
6 (= *envisage, have idea*) • **I was ~ing that …** estaba pensando que … • **did you ~ to bring a corkscrew?** ¿te acordaste de traer un sacacorchos? • **I didn't ~ to tell him** no se me ocurrió decírselo • **I thought/I'd thought I might go swimming** pensé/había pensado en ir a nadar
7 (= *expect*) pensar, esperar • **I didn't ~ to see you here** no pensaba *or* esperaba verte aquí • **I came here ~ing to get some answers** vine aquí pensando que obtendría *or* esperando recibir algunas respuestas • **I never thought to hear that from you** nunca pensé que te oiría decir eso, nunca esperé oírte decir eso • **we little thought that …** estábamos lejos de pensar que … • **"is she going?" — "I should/shouldn't ~ so"** —¿va a ir? —yo diría que sí/no • **"I paid him for it" — "I should ~ so too!"** —se lo he pagado —¡faltaría más!
N • **to have a ~** • **I'll have a ~ about it** lo pensaré • **I was just having a quiet ~** meditaba tranquilamente • IDIOM: • **if you ~ that, you've got another ~ coming*** si crees eso, te equivocas
CPD ▸ **think piece** (*Press*) artículo *m* de opinión ▸ **think tank** grupo *m* de expertos; (*in government*) gabinete *m* de estrategia
▸ **think back** VI + ADV recordar • **try to ~ back** trata de recordar • **I ~ back to that moment when …** recuerdo ese momento cuando … • **when I ~ back over my life** cuando hago un repaso de mi vida
▸ **think out** VT + ADV [+ *plan*] elaborar; [+ *problem*] meditar a fondo; [+ *solution, response*] encontrar • **I need to ~ out what I'm going to do** tengo que planear bien lo que voy a hacer • **his ideas are well thought out** tiene ideas muy elaboradas • **a well thought out answer** una respuesta muy elaborada • **he ~s things out for himself** razona por sí mismo
▸ **think over** VT + ADV [+ *offer, suggestion*] pensar, considerar • **I'll ~ it over** lo pensaré • **~ it over!** ¡piénsatelo!, ¡piénsalo! • **I've thought it over very carefully** lo he pensado muy bien
▸ **think through** VT + ADV [+ *plan*] planear detenidamente, planear cuidadosamente; [+ *objectives*] pensar detenidamente en, pensar cuidadosamente en • **this plan has not been properly thought through** este proyecto no ha sido planeado con el debido cuidado • **we need to ~ through the implications of this proposal** tenemos que considerar *or* examinar detenidamente las implicaciones de esta propuesta
▸ **think up** VT + ADV [+ *plan*] idear; [+ *idea*] tener; [+ *solution*] idear, inventar • **who thought this one up?** ¿quién ideó esto?, ¿a quién se le ocurrió esto?

thinkable [ˈθɪŋkəbl] ADJ concebible • **it isn't ~ that …** es inconcebible *or* impensable que …
thinker [ˈθɪŋkəʳ] N pensador(a) *m/f*
thinking [ˈθɪŋkɪŋ] N 1 (= *ideas, opinions*) pensamiento *m*, ideas *fpl* • **the new direction of Tyler's ~** el nuevo enfoque en el pensamiento *or* las ideas de Tyler • **we are so alike in our ~** pensamos de una forma tan parecida • **he hoped we would come round to his way of ~** esperaba que al final terminaríamos pensando como él • **to my way of ~** en mi opinión, bajo mi punto de vista • **good ~!** ¡buena idea! • **the ~ behind the campaign** la línea de pensamiento en la que se basa la campaña
2 (= *activity*) • **I've done some ~** he estado pensando • **I'll have to do some serious ~** voy a tener que pensar *or* reflexionar seriamente; ▹ **lateral, wishful**
3 (= *ability to think*) pensamiento *m*
ADJ [*person, machine*] inteligente • **it is obvious to any ~ person** resulta obvio para cualquier persona inteligente • **the ~ mind** la mente racional • IDIOM: • **to put on one's ~ cap** estrujarse el cerebro*
CPD ▸ **thinking patterns** (*Psych*) modelos *mpl* de pensamiento ▸ **thinking process** proceso *m* mental ▸ **thinking time** tiempo *m* para pensar
thin-lipped [ˈθɪnˈlɪpt] ADJ de labios apretados
thinly [ˈθɪnlɪ] ADV 1 (= *in thin pieces*) • **~ cut/sliced** [*vegetable, fruit*] cortado en rodajas finas; [*bread*] cortado en rebanadas finas; [*ham, bacon*] cortado en lonchas finas
2 (= *in a thin layer*) • **roll out the pastry very ~** estirar la masa hasta que quede muy fina • **~ clad** ligero de ropa • **~ disguised** poco *or* apenas disimulado • **spread the butter ~** untar una capa fina de mantequilla • **the troops were ~ spread** las tropas se hallaban muy diseminadas *or* dispersas • **our resources are too ~ spread** nuestros recursos están distribuidos por un área demasiado grande • **a ~ veiled threat/warning** una amenaza/advertencia mal disimulada
3 (= *sparsely*) • **the island is ~ populated** la isla tiene poca densidad de población *or* está escasamente poblada • **there were a few ~ scattered houses** había unas cuantas casas dispersas • **the seed is ~ sown** las semillas se siembran bien esparcidas • **a ~ wooded area** un área con pocos árboles
4 (= *without humour*) [*smile*] fríamente
thinner [ˈθɪnəʳ] N disolvente *m*
thinness [ˈθɪnnɪs] N 1 [*of person, arms, face*] delgadez *f*; [*of animal*] flacura *f*
2 [*of layer, sheet, wall*] delgadez *f*; [*of slice, line*] lo fino; [*of fabric*] finura *f*
3 [*of liquid, sauce, paint*] poco espesor *m*
4 [*of excuse, argument*] pobreza *f*
5 [*of air, atmosphere*] lo enrarecido
thin-skinned [ˈθɪnˈskɪnd] ADJ (*fig*) [*person*] sensible, susceptible
third [θɜːd] ADJ tercero; (*before m sing noun*) tercer • **~ time lucky!** ¡a la tercera va la vencida!
N 1 (*in series*) tercero/a *m/f*
2 (= *fraction*) tercio *m*, tercera parte *f* • **two ~s of the votes** dos tercios de los votos • **two ~s of those present** las dos terceras partes de los asistentes
3 (*Mus*) tercera *f*
4 (*Brit*) (*Univ*) tercera clase *f*
5 (*Aut*) tercera *f* velocidad, tercera *f* • **in ~** en tercera; ▹ **fifth**
ADV en tercer lugar • **to finish ~** (*in race*) llegar en tercer lugar • **to travel ~** viajar en

tercera clase
(CPD) ▸ **third degree** ▹ degree, third-degree ▸ **third estate** estado *m* llano ▸ **third form** *curso de secundaria para alumnos de entre 13 y 14 años* ▸ **third party** tercero *m*, tercera persona *f* ▸ **third party, fire and theft** seguro *m* a terceros con robo e incendio ▸ **third party insurance** seguro *m* a terceros ▸ **third person** (*Ling*) tercera persona *f* ▸ **third way** (*Pol*) tercera vía *f* ▸ **Third World** Tercer Mundo *m*; ▹ third-world

third-class [ˌθɜːdˈklɑːs] (ADJ) de tercera clase; (*pej*) de tercera
(ADV) • **to travel third-class** viajar en tercera
(N) (*US*) (*Post*) tarifa *f* de impreso

third-degree [ˌθɜːdɪˈgriː] (ADJ) [*burns*] de tercer grado

third-grader [ˈθɜːdˈɡreɪdə^{r}] (N) (*US*) alumno/a *m/f* de tercer curso (*de entre 8 y 9 años*)

thirdly [ˈθɜːdlɪ] (ADV) en tercer lugar

third-rate [ˌθɜːdˈreɪt] (ADJ) (*pej*) de tercera

third-world [ˈθɜːdwɜːld] (ADJ) tercermundista

thirst [θɜːst] (N) sed *f* • **to have a ~ for sth** (*fig*) tener sed *or* ansias de algo • **the ~ for knowledge** la sed *or* el afán de saber • **I've got a real ~ (on me)*** ¡me muero de sed!*
(VI) • **to ~ after** *or* **for sth** (*fig*) tener sed *or* ansias de algo, estar sediento de algo (*liter*)

thirstily [ˈθɜːstɪlɪ] (ADV) • **he drank it ~** lo bebió con avidez • **young Emlyn read ~ anything he could get hold of** el joven Emlyn leía con avidez todo lo que caía en sus manos

thirsty [ˈθɜːstɪ] (ADJ) (COMPAR: **thirstier**, SUPERL: **thirstiest**) **1** (*lit*) [*person, animal*] que tiene sed, sediento (*liter*) • **to be ~** tener sed • **I suddenly felt very ~** de pronto me entró mucha sed • **to be ~ for sth** (*fig*) tener sed *or* ansias de algo, estar sediento de algo (*liter*) • **I'm getting ~** me está entrando *or* dando sed • **all this work is making me ~** todo este trabajo me está dando sed • **gardening is ~ work** (*hum*) trabajar en el jardín da sed
2 (*fig*) [*land, fields*] sediento; [*car*] que consume mucha gasolina

thirteen [ˈθɜːˈtiːn] (ADJ), (PRON) trece
(N) (= *numeral*) trece *m*; ▹ five

thirteenth [ˈθɜːˈtiːnθ] (ADJ) decimotercero
(N) (*in series*) decimotercero/a *m/f*; (= *fraction*) decimotercio *m*; ▹ fifth

thirtieth [ˈθɜːtɪɪθ] (ADJ) trigésimo • **the ~ anniversary** el treinta aniversario
(N) (*in series*) trigésimo/a *m/f*; (= *fraction*) treintavo *m*; ▹ fifth

thirty [ˈθɜːtɪ] (ADJ), (PRON) treinta
(N) (= *numeral*) treinta *m* • **the thirties** (1930s) los años treinta • **to be in one's thirties** tener treinta y tantos años; ▹ fifty

thirtyish [ˈθɜːtɪɪʃ] (ADJ) treintañero, de unos treinta años • **he must be ~** debe andar por los treinta

thirty-second [ˈθɜːtɪˈsekənd] (ADJ)
• **thirty-second note** (*US*) fusa *f*

this [ðɪs] (DEM ADJ) (PL: **these**) este/a
• **~ man/book** este hombre/libro • **~ woman** esta mujer • **~ evening** esta tarde • **~ one here** este/esta que está aquí, este/esta de aquí • **it's not that picture but ~ one I like** no es ese cuadro el que me gusta sino este • **~ time** esta vez • **~ time next week** de hoy en una semana • **~ time last year** hoy hace un año • **~ way** por aquí • **~ week** esta semana • **~ coming week** esta semana que viene; ▹ these
(DEM PRON) (PL: **these**) este/a, éste/a; (*neuter*) esto

> *The pronoun **this (one)** is translated by **este** (masc), **esta** (fem) and **esto** (neuter). Note that in the past the standard spelling for the masculine and feminine pronouns was with an accent (**éste/ésta**). Nowadays the **Real Academia Española** advises that the accented forms are only required where there might otherwise be confusion with the adjectives **este/esta**. The neuter pronoun never carries an accent.*

• **~ is the house I was telling you about** esta es la casa de la que te hablaba • **who is ~?** ¿quién es? • **what is ~?** ¿qué es esto? • **~ is new** esto es nuevo • **~ is Mr Brown** (*in introductions*) le presento al señor Brown; (*in photo*) este es el señor Brown; (*on phone*) soy *or* habla el señor Brown • **I prefer ~ to that** prefiero esto a aquello • **but ~ is April** pero estamos en abril • **~ is Friday** hoy es viernes • **where did you find ~?** ¿dónde encontraste esto? • **~ is where I live** aquí vivo • **"but he's nearly bald" — "~ is it"** —pero está casi calvo —ahí está la dificultad • **what's all ~?** ¿qué pasa? • **what's all ~ I hear about you leaving?** ¿qué es eso de que te vas? • **do it like ~** hágalo así • **it was like ~** … te diré lo que pasó … • **what with ~, that and the other I was busy all week** entre una cosa y otra estuve ocupado toda la semana • **they sat talking of ~ and that** sentados, hablaban de esto y lo otro; ▹ these
(DEM ADV) • **I didn't know it was ~ far** no sabía que estaba tan lejos • **I've never been ~ far before** nunca había llegado hasta aquí • **the wall is ~ high** la pared es así de alta • **he is ~ high** es así de alto • **I've never seen ~ much money** nunca había visto tanto dinero junto • **I can tell you ~ much** … lo que sí te puedo decir es …

thistle [ˈθɪsl] (N) cardo *m*

thistledown [ˈθɪsldaʊn] (N) vilano *m* (de cardo)

thistly [ˈθɪslɪ] (ADJ) **1** (= *prickly*) espinoso; (= *full of thistles*) lleno de cardos
2 [*problem*] espinoso, erizado de dificultades

thither† [ˈðɪðə^{r}] (ADV) allá

tho'* [ðəʊ] (CONJ) = though

thole [θəʊl] (N) escálamo *m*

Thomas [ˈtɒməs] (N) Tomás • **Saint ~** Santo Tomás • **~ More** Tomás Moro

Thomism [ˈtɒmɪzəm] (N) tomismo *m*

Thomist [ˈtɒmɪst] (ADJ) tomista
(N) tomista *mf*

thong [θɒŋ] (N) **1** (= *strap*) correa *f*
2 (= *sandal*) chancleta *f*

Thor [θɔː^{r}] (N) Tor *m*

thoracic [θɔːˈræsɪk] (ADJ) torácico

thorax [ˈθɔːræks] (N) (PL: **thoraxes**, **thoraces** [ˈθɔːrəsiːz]) tórax *m*

thorium [ˈθɔːrɪəm] (N) torio *m*

thorn [θɔːn] (N) **1** (= *prickle*) espina *f* • IDIOM: • **to be a ~ in sb's side** *or* **flesh** ser una espina para algn
2 (= *bush, tree*) espino *m*
(CPD) ▸ **thorn bush, thorn tree** espino *m*

thornless [ˈθɔːnlɪs] (ADJ) sin espinas

thorny [ˈθɔːnɪ] (ADJ) (COMPAR: **thornier**, SUPERL: **thorniest**) (*lit, fig*) espinoso

thorough [ˈθʌrə] (ADJ) **1** (= *complete*) [*examination, search, investigation*] riguroso, minucioso; [*training*] riguroso, a fondo; [*knowledge, understanding*] profundo, sólido • **to give sth a ~ clean/wash** limpiar/lavar algo bien *or* a fondo • **the room needed a ~ clean** la habitación necesitaba una buena limpieza *or* una limpieza a fondo • **to have a ~ grounding in sth** tener una base sólida en algo
2 (= *meticulous*) [*person, teacher*] concienzudo, meticuloso • **to be ~ in doing sth** hacer algo a conciencia, ser meticuloso a la hora de hacer algo
3 (*as intensifier*) (= *complete, total*) • **it was a ~ waste of time** era una pérdida de tiempo absoluta *or* total • **to make a ~ nuisance of o.s.** dar la lata a base de bien* • **he made a ~ fool of himself** hizo un ridículo espantoso • **he gave them a ~ walloping** les dio una buena zurra* • **it's a ~ disgrace** es un verdadero escándalo

thoroughbred [ˈθʌrəbred] (ADJ) [*horse*] de pura sangre
(N) pura sangre *mf*

thoroughfare [ˈθʌrəfɛə^{r}] (N) (= *public highway*) vía *f* pública, carretera *f*; (= *street*) calle *f* • **"no thoroughfare"** "callejón sin salida"; (= *no entry*) "prohibido el paso"

thoroughgoing [ˈθʌrəˌɡəʊɪŋ] (ADJ) [*analysis*] minucioso; [*restructuring*] concienzudo, a fondo; [*conservative, revolutionary*] convencido, auténtico

thoroughly [ˈθʌrəlɪ] (ADV) **1** (= *meticulously*) [*clean, rinse*] a fondo, a conciencia; [*search, check*] a fondo; [*research*] minuciosamente, meticulosamente; [*mix*] bien • **they examined me ~** (*Med*) me hicieron un reconocimiento a fondo *or* a conciencia • **to know sth ~** conocer algo a fondo
2 (= *utterly*) **a** (*with verb*) [*understand*] plenamente, a la perfección; [*deserve*] totalmente; [*discredit*] totalmente, por completo • **he ~ enjoyed himself** se divirtió muchísimo, se lo pasó en grande*
b (*with adj*) [*enjoyable, unpleasant, miserable*] realmente, verdaderamente; [*modern*] totalmente • **a ~ bad influence** una influencia realmente mala • **that was a ~ stupid thing to do** hacer eso fue una completa estupidez

thoroughness [ˈθʌrənɪs] (N) [*of examination, search, research*] rigurosidad *f*, minuciosidad *f*; [*of person*] meticulosidad *f*

those [ðəʊz] (DEM ADJ) esos/esas; (*further away*) aquellos/aquellas • **ask ~ children** pregúntales a esos niños • **~ ones over there** aquellos de allí, aquellos que están allí • **it's not these chocolates but ~ ones I like** no son estos bombones los que me gustan sino aquellos
(DEM PRON) esos/esas, ésos/ésas; (*further away*) aquellos/aquellas, aquéllos/aquéllas

> *In the past the standard spelling for **esos/esas** and **aquellos/aquellas** as pronouns was with an accent (**ésos/ésas** and **aquéllos/aquéllas**). Nowadays the **Real Academia Española** advises that the accented forms are only required where there might otherwise be confusion with the adjectives **esos/esas** and **aquellos/aquellas**.*

• **~ which** los que, las que • **~ who** los que, las que, quienes • **~ of you/us who** … los/las que … • **I prefer these to ~** prefiero estos a aquellos; ▹ that

thou[1]†† [ðaʊ] (PRON) tú, vos††

thou[2]* [θaʊ] (N ABBR) (PL: **thou** *or* **thous**) = **thousand, thousandth**

though [ðəʊ] (CONJ) aunque • **~ it was raining** aunque llovía • **~ small, it's good** aunque (es) pequeño, es bueno, si bien es pequeño, es bueno • **as ~** como si (+ *subjun*) • **even ~ he doesn't want to** aunque no quiera • **strange ~ it may appear** aunque parezca extraño, por muy extraño que

parezca • **young ~ she is** aunque es joven, por muy joven que sea; ▹ **as**
ADV sin embargo, aun así • **it's not so easy, ~** sin embargo *or* pero no es tan fácil • **it's difficult, ~, to put into practice** pero es difícil llevarlo a la práctica • **did he ~?** ¿de veras?

thought [θɔːt] PT, PP *of* **think**
N **1** (= *mental activity*) pensamiento *m*; ▹ **line, train**
2 (= *philosophy*) pensamiento *m* • **Western ~** el pensamiento occidental; ▹ **school¹**
3 (= *cogitation*) pensamiento *m* • **you need to free your mind of negative ~s** tienes que despejar los malos pensamientos de tu mente • **to collect one's ~s** ordenar sus pensamientos *or* ideas • **to be deep in ~** estar ensimismado, estar absorto en sus pensamientos • **my ~s were elsewhere** estaba pensando en otra cosa • **to gather one's ~s** ordenar sus pensamientos *or* ideas • **he was always in her ~s** lo tenía *or* llevaba siempre en el pensamiento • **to be lost in ~** estar ensimismado, estar absorto en sus pensamientos • **he pushed the ~ from his mind** se obligó a dejar de pensar en ello, borró la idea de su mente; ▹ **penny, read**
4 (= *consideration*) • **after much ~** después de mucho pensarlo *or* pensarlo mucho • **a lot of ~ went into the work** se dedicó mucho tiempo a pensar en el trabajo • **I'll give it some ~ over the next few days** lo pensaré durante los próximos días • **I've given it a lot of ~** lo he pensado mucho • **I didn't give it another ~** no volví a pensar en ello • **don't give it another ~** no te preocupes, no lo pienses más • **spare a ~ for the homeless at Christmas** acuérdese de la gente sin hogar en Navidad; ▹ **food, pause, second**
5 (= *concern*) • **his first ~ was always for other people** siempre pensaba primero en los demás • **with no ~ for o.s.** sin pensar en sí mismo • **with no ~ of reward** sin pensar en una recompensa
6 (= *intention*) intención *f* • **they had no ~ of surrender** no tenían ninguna intención de rendirse • **he gave up all ~(s) of marrying her** renunció a la idea de casarse con ella
• IDIOM: • **it's the ~ that counts** la intención es lo que cuenta
7 (= *idea*) idea *f* • **what a frightening ~!** ¡qué idea más aterradora! • **what a lovely ~!** ¡qué detalle! • **the ~ crossed my mind that …** se me ocurrió que … • **the ~ had crossed my mind** la idea se me llegó a pasar por la cabeza • **to have a ~**: • **I've just had a ~** se me acaba de ocurrir una idea • **he hasn't a ~ in his head** no tiene ni idea de nada • **never mind, it was just a ~** no importa, no era más que una idea • **that's a ~!** ¡no es mala idea!, ¡qué buena idea! • **"she might still be there" — "that's a ~"** —puede que todavía esté allí —es una posibilidad • **the very** *or* **mere ~ of him made her nervous** se ponía nerviosa solo de pensar en él
8 thoughts (= *opinion*) • **do you have any ~s on that?** ¿tiene alguna opinión al respecto? • **he keeps his ~s to himself** se reserva su opinión
9 (= *little*) • **it is a ~ too large** es un poquito grande • **that was a ~ unwise, wasn't it?** eso fue un tanto imprudente, ¿no?
CPD ▸ **thought police** policía *f* política ▸ **thought process** proceso *m* mental ▸ **thought reader** adivino/a *m/f* • **I'm not a ~ reader** no soy adivino, no leo el pensamiento ▸ **thought reading** adivinación *f* de pensamientos ▸ **thought transference** transmisión *f* de pensamientos

thoughtful ['θɔːtfʊl] ADJ **1** (= *pensive*) [*expression, look*] pensativo, meditabundo • **he looked ~** estaba pensativo *or* meditabundo
2 (= *considerate*) [*person*] atento, considerado; [*gesture*] amable, atento • **these items make ~ gifts** como regalos, estos artículos son un detalle • **to be ~ of others** pensar en los demás, tener en cuenta a los demás • **it was very ~ of you** fue muy amable de tu parte • **how ~ of him to invite me!** ¡qué detalle tuvo al invitarme!, ¡qué detalle por su parte el invitarme!
3 (= *mindful*) • **he was very ~ of the family reputation** siempre tenía muy en cuenta la reputación de la familia
4 (= *serious*) [*book, film, person*] serio, sesudo

thoughtfully ['θɔːtfəlɪ] ADV **1** (= *pensively*) [*look, nod, smile*] pensativamente, con aire pensativo • **"I see," said Holmes ~** —ya veo —dijo Holmes (con aire) pensativo
2 (= *considerately*) • **she very ~ left out some food for us** tuvo el detalle de dejarnos algo de comida • **land mines which the enemy had ~ left behind** (*iro*) minas terrestres que el enemigo había ido plantando con todo el cariño a su paso (*iro*)
3 (= *intelligently*) [*designed, constructed, produced*] cuidadosamente, con esmero

thoughtfulness ['θɔːtfʊlnɪs] N
1 (= *pensiveness*) • **her face was a picture of ~** su rostro tenía un aire muy pensativo
2 (= *consideration*) amabilidad *f* • **I appreciate your ~** te agradezco la amabilidad *or* que seas tan amable
3 (= *serious thought*) seriedad *f* • **it is a work of great ~** es un trabajo muy serio *or* meditado, es un trabajo de mucha seriedad

thoughtless ['θɔːtlɪs] ADJ **1** (= *inconsiderate*) [*person*] poco considerado, desconsiderado; [*remark*] desconsiderado • **how ~ of you!** ¡qué desconsiderado *or* poco considerado por tu parte!, ¡qué falta de consideración por tu parte! • **it was ~ of him to say that** fue una falta de consideración por su parte decir eso
2 (= *unthinking*) irreflexivo, inconsciente

thoughtlessly ['θɔːtlɪslɪ] ADV
1 (= *inconsiderately*) desconsideradamente
2 (= *unthinkingly*) sin pensar, inconscientemente

thoughtlessness ['θɔːtlɪsnɪs] N **1** (= *lack of consideration*) falta *f* de consideración, desconsideración *f*
2 (= *carelessness*) irreflexión *f*, inconsciencia *f*

thought-out [ˌθɔːt'aʊt] ADJ (bien) pensado

thought-provoking ['θɔːtprəˌvəʊkɪŋ] ADJ que hace reflexionar

thousand ['θaʊzənd] ADJ, PRON mil
N (= *numeral*) mil *m* • **a ~** • **one ~** mil • **two/five ~** dos/cinco mil • **a ~ and one/two** mil uno/dos • **I've got a ~ and one things to do** tengo la mar de cosas que hacer* • **they sell them by the ~** los venden a millares • **in their ~s** a millares • **~s of …** miles de … • **I've told you a ~ times** *or* **~s of times** te lo he dicho mil veces

thousandfold ['θaʊzəndfəʊld] ADJ multiplicado por mil, de mil veces
ADV mil veces

thousandth ['θaʊzəntθ] ADJ milésimo
N (*in classification*) número mil *m*; (= *fraction*) milésimo *m*

thraldom ['θrɔːldəm] N (*liter*) esclavitud *f*

thrall [θrɔːl] N (*liter*) (= *person*) esclavo/a *m/f*; (= *state*) esclavitud *f* • **to be in ~ to** ser esclavo de • **to hold sb in ~** retener a algn en la esclavitud

thrash [θræʃ] VT **1** (= *beat*) golpear; [+ *person*] apalear, dar una paliza a; (*as punishment*) azotar
2* (= *defeat*) dar una paliza a*, cascar*
3 (*also* **thrash about, thrash around**) [+ *legs, arms*] agitar mucho
VI (*also* **thrash about, thrash around**) revolverse; (*in water*) revolcarse • **he ~ed about with his stick** daba golpes por todos lados con su bastón • **they were ~ing about in the water** se estaban revolcando en el agua
N (*Brit‡*) juerga *f*, fiesta *f*
▸ **thrash out** VT + ADV [+ *problem, difficulty*] discutir a fondo; [+ *plan*] idear; [+ *deal*] alcanzar • **to ~ out an agreement** llegar a un acuerdo

thrashing ['θræʃɪŋ] N zurra *f*, paliza *f* • **to give sb a ~** (*lit*) (= *beat*) zurrar a algn, dar una paliza a algn; (*Sport*) (= *defeat*) dar una paliza a algn*, cascar a algn*

thread [θred] N **1** (*Sew*) hilo *m* • **a needle and ~** una aguja e hilo • **cotton/nylon ~** hilo *m* de algodón/nylon • IDIOM: • **to hang by a ~** pender de un hilo
2 [*of silkworm, spider*] hebra *f*
3 (= *drift, theme*) hilo *m* • **to lose the ~ (of what sb is saying)** perder el hilo (de lo que algn está diciendo) • **to pick up the ~(s) again** [*of conversation, thought*] retomar el hilo; [*of process, problem*] volver a tomar las riendas • **she picked up the ~s of her life/career again** tomó de nuevo las riendas de su vida/carrera
4 [*of screw*] rosca *f*, filete *m*
VT [+ *needle*] enhebrar; [+ *beads*] ensartar • **he ~ed the string through the hole** ensartó la cuerda por el agujero • **to ~ one's way through a crowd** colarse entre *or* abrirse paso por una multitud • **the river ~s its way through the valley** el río se abre paso a través del valle

threadbare ['θredbɛəʳ] ADJ [*coat, blanket, carpet*] raído, gastado; (*fig*) [*argument*] trillado

threadworm ['θredwɜːm] N lombriz *f* intestinal

threat [θret] N amenaza *f* • **to be a ~ to sth/sb** ser una amenaza para algo/algn • **their lives are constantly under ~** sus vidas se ven constantemente amenazadas • **agricultural land is under ~ from urban development** las tierras de cultivo se ven amenazadas por el crecimiento de las ciudades • **the factory is under ~ of closure** existe el peligro de que cierren la fábrica

threaten ['θretn] VT **1** (= *menace verbally*) amenazar • **to ~ to do sth** amenazar con hacer algo • **she ~ed to kill him** amenazó con matarlo • **to ~ sb with sth** amenazar a algn con algo • **they were ~ed with the sack** los amenazaron con el despido, amenazaron con despedirlos
2 (= *pose a threat to*) [+ *environment, community, way of life*] amenazar • **some schools have been ~ed with closure** la amenaza de cierre se cierne sobre algunos colegios • **to be ~ed with extinction** estar amenazado de extinción
3 (= *promise*) [+ *rain, bad weather*] amenazar • **it's ~ing to rain** amenaza lluvia, amenaza (con) llover • **it's ~ing to turn into a full-scale war** amenaza (con) convertirse en una guerra declarada
VI [*sky, clouds*] amenazar

threatened ['θretnd] ADJ • **to feel ~** sentirse amenazado

threatening ['θretnɪŋ] ADJ **1** (= *menacing*) [*letter, gesture, phone call*] amenazador, de amenaza; [*manner, voice*] amenazador • **some men find her ~** algunos hombres se sienten intimidados por ella • **~ behaviour**

comportamiento *m* intimidatorio, conducta *f* intimidatoria *or* amenazadora
2 (= *unpromising*) [*clouds, sky*] amenazador
• **the weather looked ~** amenazaba temporal

threateningly ['θretnɪŋlɪ] ADV [*behave*] de modo amenazador; [*say*] en tono amenazador

three [θriː] ADJ, PRON tres • **~ cheers!** ¡tres hurras! • **the best of ~** (*Sport*) hasta tres sets *or* partidos
N (= *numeral*) tres *m*; ▹ **five, two**

THREE RS
La expresión **the three Rs** hace referencia a los tres aspectos que se consideran fundamentales en educación: **reading, writing, and arithmetic** (lectura, escritura y aritmética). La expresión, que tiene su origen en la forma humorística en la que se escribe a veces la frase: **reading, 'riting, and 'rithmetic**, se menciona a menudo cuando se habla de la necesidad de mejorar la calidad de la enseñanza.

three-act ['θriː'ækt] ADJ [*play*] de *or* en tres actos

three-colour, **three-color** (*US*) ['θriː'kʌləʳ], **three-coloured**, **three-colored** (*US*) ['θriː'kʌləd] ADJ de tres colores, tricolor

three-cornered ['θriː'kɔːnəd] ADJ triangular • **three-cornered hat** tricornio *m*, sombrero *m* de tres picos

three-D, **3-D** ['θriː'diː] (*also* **three-dimensional**) ADJ tridimensional
N • **in three-D** en tres dimensiones

three-day eventing [ˌθriːdeɪ'ventɪŋ] N *concurso hípico que dura tres días y consta de tres pruebas distintas*

three-decker ['θriː'dekəʳ] N **1** (*Naut*) barco *m* de tres cubiertas
2 (*Literat*) novela *f* de tres tomos
3 (*Culin*) sándwich *m* de tres pisos

three-dimensional ['θriːdɪ'menʃənl] ADJ tridimensional

three-door ['θriː,dɔːʳ] N (= *car*) tres puertas *m inv*

threefold ['θriːfəʊld] ADJ triple
ADV tres veces

three-fourths [ˌθriː'fɔːθs] N (*US*) tres cuartos *mpl*

three-legged ['θriː'legɪd] ADJ de tres patas, de tres pies

threepence ['θrepəns] N (*Brit*) tres peniques *mpl*

threepenny ['θrepənɪ] ADJ (*Brit*) de tres peniques; (*fig*) de poca monta, despreciable • **~ bit** • **~ piece** moneda *f* de tres peniques
• **Threepenny Opera** Ópera *f* de perra gorda

three-phase ['θriːfeɪz] ADJ (*Elec*) trifásico

three-piece ['θriːpiːs] ADJ • **three-piece band** trío *m* • **three-piece suit** terno *m*, traje *m* de tres piezas • **three-piece suite** tresillo *m*, juego *m* de living (*LAm*)

three-ply ['θriːplaɪ] ADJ [*wool*] triple, de tres hebras, de tres cabos; [*wood, tissue paper*] de tres capas

three-point turn [ˌθriːpɔɪnt'tɜːn] N (*Aut*) cambio *m* de sentido haciendo tres maniobras

three-quarter [ˌθriː'kwɔːtəʳ] ADJ
• **three-quarter-length sleeves** mangas *fpl* tres cuartos

three-quarters [ˌθriː'kwɔːtəz] N tres cuartos *mpl*, tres cuartas partes *fpl*
• **three-quarters of the people** las tres cuartas partes de la gente • **in three-quarters of an hour** en tres cuartos de hora
ADV • **the tank is three-quarters full** el depósito está lleno en sus tres cuartas partes

threescore ['θriːskɔːʳ] N (*liter*) sesenta • **~ years and ten** setenta años

three-sided ['θriː'saɪdɪd] ADJ trilátero

threesome ['θriːsəm] N (= *group of 3 people*) grupo *m* de tres, trío *m*

three-way ['θriːweɪ] ADJ [*conversation*] entre tres personas; [*race, competition, debate*] *entre tres personas, grupos etc*; (*Comm*) entre tres compañías; [*mirror*] de tres lunas
• **three-way split** división *f* en tercios

three-wheeler ['θriː'wiːləʳ] N (= *car*) coche *m* de tres ruedas; (= *tricycle*) triciclo *m*

threnody ['θrenədɪ] N lamento *m*; (*for the dead*) canto *m* fúnebre

thresh [θreʃ] VT [+ *corn*] trillar
VI trillar

thresher ['θreʃəʳ] N (= *person*) trillador(a) *m/f*; (= *machine*) trilladora *f*

threshing ['θreʃɪŋ] N trilla *f*
CPD ▸ **threshing floor** era *f* ▸ **threshing machine** trilladora *f*

threshold ['θreʃhəʊld] N **1** (= *doorway*) umbral *m*
2 (*fig*) umbral *m*, puertas *fpl* • **to be on the ~ of** estar en el umbral *or* a las puertas de
• **pain ~** umbral *m* de dolor • **sound ~** umbral *m* sonoro • **to have a low pain ~** tener poca tolerancia del dolor
CPD ▸ **threshold agreement** convenio *m* de nivel crítico ▸ **threshold price** precio *m* umbral, precio *m* mínimo

threw [θruː] PT *of* **throw**

thrice†† [θraɪs] ADV tres veces

thrift [θrɪft], **thriftiness** ['θrɪftɪnɪs] N economía *f*, frugalidad *f*
CPD ▸ **thrift store** (*US*) *tienda de artículos de segunda mano que dedica su recaudación a causas benéficas*

thriftily ['θrɪftɪlɪ] ADV con frugalidad

thriftless ['θrɪftlɪs] ADJ malgastador, pródigo

thriftlessness ['θrɪftlɪsnɪs] N prodigalidad *f*

thrifty ['θrɪftɪ] ADJ (COMPAR: **thriftier**, SUPERL: **thriftiest**) [*person*] ahorrativo, frugal • **~ habits** hábitos *mpl* de ahorro

thrill [θrɪl] N emoción *f* • **all the ~s of the circus** todas las emociones del circo • **she felt a ~ (of joy)** se estremeció (de alegría) • **it gives him a cheap ~ to spy on her in the bathroom** le da morbo espiarla en el baño
• **it was a great ~ to meet her** me hizo muchísima ilusión conocerla • **he gets a real ~ out of parachuting** hacer paracaidismo le resulta muy emocionante *or* excitante • **the film is full of ~s and spills** la película está llena de emoción • **what a ~!** ¡qué emoción!
VT [+ *person, audience*] emocionar, excitar
• **I'm not exactly ~ed by the idea** la idea no es que me entusiasme precisamente
VI • **she ~ed at** *or* **to his touch** se estremeció cuando él la tocó

thrilled [θrɪld] ADJ • **to be ~ (to bits** *or* **pieces)** estar contentísimo • **"how did he react?" — "oh, he was ~!"** —¿cómo reaccionó? —¡huy! se puso contentísimo *or* le hizo muchísima ilusión • **to be ~ with/at sth** estar contentísimo con algo • **I was ~ to meet him** me hizo mucha ilusión conocerlo

thriller ['θrɪləʳ] N (= *novel*) novela *f* de suspense *or* (*LAm*) de suspenso, novela *f* de misterio; (= *film*) película *f* de suspense *or* (*LAm*) de suspenso, thriller *m*

thrilling ['θrɪlɪŋ] ADJ [*experience, match, climax*] emocionante; [*performance*] apasionante • **it was one of the most ~ moments of my life** fue uno de los momentos más emocionantes de mi vida
• **you've actually met her? how ~!** ¿llegaste a conocerla? ¡qué emoción!

thrillingly ['θrɪlɪŋlɪ] ADV apasionantemente • **~ new** apasionantemente nuevo

thrive [θraɪv] (PT: **throve** *or* **thrived**, PP: **thrived** *or* **thriven**) VI (= *do well*) [*company, economy*] prosperar; (= *grow*) [*plant*] crecer muy bien, prosperar; [*animal, child*] desarrollarse; (*fig*) prosperar, medrar • **the plant ~s here** la planta crece muy bien *or* prospera aquí • **business is thriving** el negocio prospera • **to ~ on sth: children ~ on milk** la leche contribuye al desarrollo de los niños • **she seems to ~ on adversity** parece que se crece en la adversidad

thriven ['θrɪvn] PP *of* **thrive**

thriving ['θraɪvɪŋ] ADJ [*industry, business*] próspero, floreciente

throat [θrəʊt] N **1** (*interior*) garganta *f* • **to clear one's ~** aclararse la voz, carraspear • **to have a sore ~** tener dolor de garganta
• IDIOMS: • **to jump down sb's ~** arremeter contra algn sin más (*fig*) • **to ram sth down sb's ~** meter algo a algn por las narices
• **there's no need to ram it down my ~** no hace falta que me lo metas por las narices
2 (*from exterior*) cuello *m* • **they are at each other's ~s all the time** se atacan uno a otro todo el tiempo • **to cut** *or* **slit sb's ~** cortar el cuello a algn • **to cut** *or* **slit one's ~** cortarse la garganta, cortarse el cuello • **he's cutting his own ~** (*fig*) está actuando en perjuicio propio, se está haciendo daño a sí mismo
CPD ▸ **throat infection** infección *f* de garganta

throaty ['θrəʊtɪ] ADJ (COMPAR: **throatier**, SUPERL: **throatiest**) [*person, voice*] ronco, afónico; [*laugh*] gutural; [*roar of engine*] ronco

throb [θrɒb] N [*of heart etc*] latido *m*, pulso *m*; [*of engine*] vibración *f*
VI [*heart*] latir, palpitar; [*engine*] vibrar; [*wound, sore finger*] dar punzadas • **my head was ~bing** la cabeza estaba a punto de estallarme de dolor • **Berlin is ~bing with life** Berlín está rebosante de vida

throbbing ['θrɒbɪŋ] ADJ [*heart*] palpitante; [*engine*] vibrante; [*pain*] punzante; [*rhythm*] palpitante, vibrante
N [*of heart*] latido *m*; [*of sore finger, head*] punzadas *fpl*; [*of engine, music*] vibración *f*

throes [θrəʊz] NPL [*of death*] agonía *f* • **to be in the ~ of sth/doing sth: she was in the ~ of an unpleasant divorce** estaba en medio de los trámites de un divorcio nada agradable
• **I was still in the first ~ of grief** eran solo los primeros ramalazos de una profunda pena
• **we're in the ~ of a major restructuring at work** en el trabajo estamos en plena reestructuración • **to be in the ~ of childbirth** estar en medio de los dolores del parto
• **while he was in the ~ of writing his book** mientras estaba inmerso en la redacción de su libro • **while we were in the ~ of deciding what to do** mientras nos debatíamos sobre qué decisión tomar; ▹ **death**

thrombosis [θrɒm'bəʊsɪs] N (PL: **thromboses** [θrɒm'bəʊsiːz]) trombosis *f*
• **coronary ~** trombosis *f* coronaria

thrombus ['θrɒmbəs] N trombo *m*

throne [θrəʊn] N trono *m* • **to ascend the ~** • **come to the ~** subir al trono • **to succeed to the ~** suceder en el trono • **the heir to the ~** el/la heredero/a del trono • **the ~ of France** • **the French ~** el trono de Francia, el trono francés
CPD ▸ **throne room** sala *f* del trono

throng [θrɒŋ] N multitud *f*, muchedumbre *f* • **great ~s of tourists** multitudes *fpl* de turistas

t

VT atestar • **the streets are ~ed with tourists** las calles están atestadas de turistas

VI • **the schoolchildren came ~ing in** los escolares entraron en tropel • **to ~ round sb** apiñarse en torno a algn • **to ~ to hear sb** venir en tropel *or* en masa a escuchar a algn

thronging ['θrɒŋɪŋ] ADJ [*crowd etc*] grande, apretado, nutrido

throttle ['θrɒtl] N (*Mech*) regulador *m*, válvula *f* reguladora, estrangulador *m*; (*Aut*) (= *accelerator*) acelerador *m* • **the engine was at full ~** el motor estaba funcionando a toda marcha • **to give an engine full ~** acelerar un motor al máximo

VT (= *strangle*) ahogar, estrangular

▸ **throttle back, throttle down** (*Mech*)

VT + ADV • **to ~ back** *or* **~ down the engine** moderar la marcha

VI + ADV moderar la marcha

through [θruː]

*When **through** is an element in a phrasal verb, eg **break through, fall through**, look up the verb.*

PREP **1** (*place*) por • **to look ~ a telescope** mirar por un telescopio • **to walk ~ the woods** pasear por el bosque • **he shot her ~ the head** le pegó un tiro en la cabeza • **I saw him ~ the crowd** lo vi entre la multitud • **to go ~ sth**: • **to go ~ a tunnel** atravesar un túnel • **the bullet went ~ three layers** la bala penetró tres capas • **it went right ~ the wall** atravesó por toda la pared • **to go ~ sb's pockets/belongings/papers** hurgar en los bolsillos/entre las cosas/entre los papeles de algn • **to post a letter ~ the letterbox** echar una carta al buzón

2 (*time, process*) • **we're staying ~ till Tuesday** nos quedamos hasta el martes • **(from) Monday ~ Friday** (*US*) de lunes a viernes • **to go ~ a bad/good period** pasar una mala/buena racha • **we've been ~ a lot together** hemos pasado mucho juntos • **to be halfway ~ a book** ir por la mitad de un libro • **halfway ~ the film** a la mitad de la película • **all** *or* **right ~ the night** durante toda la noche • **right ~ the year** durante el año entero *or* todo el año

3 (*means*) por • **~ lack of resources** por falta de recursos • **~ him I found out that ...** por *or* a través de él supe que ... • **it was ~ you that we were late** fue por tu culpa que llegamos tarde • **to act ~ fear** obrar movido por el miedo • **he got the job ~ friends** consiguió el trabajo por mediación de *or* a través de unos amigos

4 (*having completed*) • **he's ~ the exam** ha aprobado el examen

ADV **1** (*place*) • **it's frozen (right) ~** está completamente helado • **does this train go ~ to London?** ¿este tren va directamente a Londres? • **he went straight ~ to the dining room** pasó directamente al comedor • **the nail went right ~** el clavo penetró de parte a parte • **can you put me ~ to sales, please?** (*Telec*) ¿puede ponerme *or* pasarme con el departamento de ventas, por favor? • **the wood has rotted ~** la madera se ha podrido completamente • **the window was dirty and I couldn't see ~** la ventana estaba sucia y no podía ver nada • **wet ~** [*person*] mojado hasta los huesos, empapado; [*object*] empapado

2 (*time, process*) • **I read the book right ~** leí el libro entero • **to sleep the whole night ~** dormir la noche entera • **did you stay right ~ to the end?** ¿te quedaste hasta el final? • **we're staying ~ till Tuesday** nos quedamos hasta el martes • **he is ~ to the finals of the competition** pasó a la final del concurso

3 • **~ and ~** [*be something*] hasta la médula, completamente; [*know something*] de pe a pa

ADJ **1** [*road, train*] directo; [*traffic*] de paso • **"no through road"** "calle sin salida"

2 (= *finished*) terminado • **we'll be ~ at seven** terminaremos a las siete • **you're ~!** ¡se acabó (para ti)! • **are you ~ criticizing?** ¿has terminado *or* acabado de criticarme? • **she told him they were ~** ella le dijo que todo había acabado entre ellos • **I'm ~ with my girlfriend** he roto *or* terminado con mi novia • **are you ~ with that book?** ¿has terminado de leer ese libro? • **I'm ~ with bridge** renuncio al bridge, ya no vuelvo a jugar al bridge • **I'm not ~ with you yet** todavía no he terminado contigo • **when I'm ~ with him** cuando haya terminado con él

3 (*Telec*) • **you're ~!** ¡ya puede hablar!, ¡hable!

throughout [θrʊ'aʊt] PREP **1** (*place*) por todo • **we have branches ~ the country** tenemos sucursales por todo el país • **there were flowers ~ the house** había flores por toda la casa • **the company is known ~ the world** la compañía es conocida en todo el mundo

2 (*time, process*) durante todo • **~ last winter** durante todo el invierno pasado • **he was a socialist ~ his life** fue un socialista durante toda su vida

ADV **1** (= *fully*) completamente; (= *everywhere*) en todas partes, por todas partes • **the house is carpeted ~** la casa está completamente alfombrada

2 (*time, process*) de principio a fin • **on this project, the emphasis has been on teamwork ~** en este proyecto, se ha hecho hincapié en el trabajo en equipo de principio a fin • **the film was boring ~** la película fue aburrida de principio a fin • **the weather was good ~** hizo buen tiempo todos los días

throughput ['θruːpʊt] N (= *production*) producción *f*; (= *total quantity*) [*of applicants, patients*] movimiento *m*, número *m*; (*Comput*) capacidad *f* de procesamiento • **to increase the volume of ~** incrementar el volumen de producción • **patient ~ has not been affected by hospital closures** el movimiento de pacientes *or* el número de pacientes tratados no se ha visto afectado por el cierre de hospitales

throughway ['θruːweɪ] N (*US*) autopista *f* (*de peaje*)

throve [θrəʊv] PT *of* **thrive**

throw [θrəʊ] (VB: PT: **threw**, PP: **thrown**) VT

1 (= *toss*) [+ *ball, stone*] tirar, echar; (*violently*) tirar, arrojar, lanzar; [+ *dice*] echar, tirar; [+ *javelin, discus, grenade*] lanzar • **the crowd began ~ing stones** la multitud empezó a tirar *or* arrojar *or* lanzar piedras • **he threw a double six** sacó dos seises • **to ~ sb sth** • **~ sth to sb** tirar *or* echar algo a algn • **he threw Brian a rope** le tiró *or* echó una cuerda a Brian • **to ~ sth at sb** tirar *or* arrojar algo a algn • **on one occasion he threw a radio at this mother** en una ocasión le tiró *or* arrojó una radio a su madre • **they think they can solve problems by ~ing money at them** (*fig*) piensan que metiendo dinero pueden solucionar cualquier problema • **she threw the letters in the bin** tiró *or* echó las cartas a la basura • **he threw a glass of water over her head** le echó *or* vació un vaso de agua en la cabeza • IDIOM: • **to ~ one's hat** *or* **cap into the ring** echarse *or* lanzarse al ruedo; ▹ **book, caution, cold, glass, spanner**

2 (= *hurl to the ground*) [+ *person*] (*in fight, wrestling*) derribar; [*horse*] desmontar

3 (= *send, hurl*) • **the blast threw her across the room** la explosión la lanzó *or* arrojó al otro lado de la sala • **to ~ o.s. at sb** (*lit*) abalanzarse sobre algn, echarse encima de algn; (*fig*) (= *flirt*) insinuarse descaradamente a algn, tirar los tejos a algn* • **to ~ o.s. at sb's feet** echarse a los pies de algn • **he was ~n clear of the car** salió despedido del coche • **she threw herself into the river** se tiró al río • **the kidnap threw the family into panic** el secuestro infundió pánico *or* hizo que cundiera el pánico en la familia • **the country was ~n into turmoil** el país se sumió en el caos • **to ~ sb into jail** *or* **prison** meter a algn en la cárcel • **he threw himself into his work** se metió de lleno en el trabajo • **to ~ o.s. on sb's mercy** ponerse a merced de algn • **she threw herself onto the bed** se tiró en la cama • **she was ~n out of her seat** salió despedida de su asiento • **the recession has ~n millions out of work** la recesión ha dejado a millones de personas sin trabajo • **he threw me to the ground** me arrojó al suelo; ▹ **scent, track**

4 (= *direct*) [+ *light, shadow*] proyectar; [+ *look, smile*] lanzar • **this new information ~s doubt on their choice** esta nueva información pone en duda su elección • **this question has been ~n at me many times** me han hecho esta pregunta *or* me han preguntado esto muchas veces • **he was ~ing random suggestions at her** le estaba sugiriendo cosas al azar • **she didn't attempt to ~ any suspicion on you** no intentó hacer que las sospechas recayeran sobre ti • **to ~ one's voice** [*actor, public speaker*] proyectar la voz; ▹ **light¹, punch¹**

5 (= *disconcert*) desconcertar • **this answer seemed to ~ him** esta respuesta pareció desconcertarle • **he was ~n by her question** su pregunta lo desconcertó *or* lo dejó desconcertado

6 (= *put*) • **she threw her arms around his neck** le echó los brazos al cuello, le abrazó por el cuello • **to ~ a coat round one's shoulders** echarse un abrigo por los hombros • **a police cordon was ~n around the area** la policía acordonó la zona, se cercó la zona con un cordón policial • **to ~ open** [+ *doors, windows*] abrir de par en par; [+ *house, gardens*] abrir al público; [+ *competition, race*] abrir a todos

7 (= *have*) • **she threw a fit (of hysterics)** le dio un ataque (de histeria) • **to ~ a party** dar *or* hacer una fiesta • **she threw a tantrum** le dio una rabieta *or* un berrinche*

8 (= *move*) [+ *lever, switch*] dar a

9 (*Pottery*) • **to ~ a pot** tornear un tiesto, hacer un tiesto con el torno

10* (= *lose on purpose*) [+ *contest, game*] perder a posta

11 (*Zool*) (= *give birth to*) parir

N **1** (*lit*) [*of ball, stone*] tiro *m*; [*of javelin, discus*] lanzamiento *m*; [*of dice*] tirada *f*; (*in judo, wrestling*) derribo *m* • **it's your ~** te toca tirar (a ti) • **I needed a ~ of four to win** necesitaba sacar un cuatro para ganar; ▹ **stone**

2* (= *each one*) • **"how much are they?" — "50 quid a ~"** —¿cuánto cuestan? —50 libras cada uno

3 (= *cover*) (*for sofa*) cubresofá *m*; (*for bed*) cubrecama *m*, colcha *f*

▸ **throw about, throw around** VT + ADV

1 (*lit*) • **they were ~ing a ball about** jugaban con una pelota • **don't ~ it about or it might break** no lo manosees para arriba y para abajo, que se puede romper • **they were ~n about in the back of the lorry** se zarandeaban de un lado para otro en la parte trasera del camión

2 (*fig*) [+ *ideas*] intercambiar • **let's have a meeting and ~ a few ideas about** vamos a reunirnos para intercambiar ideas • **occasionally he ~s fancy words about** de vez en cuando se deja caer con alguna palabreja *or* suelta alguna palabreja • **his name is ~n about a lot** su nombre no para de sonar por ahí • **to ~ one's arms about** agitar mucho los brazos • **to ~ (one's) money about** derrochar *or* despilfarrar el dinero, tirar el dinero; ▹ **weight**

▸ **throw aside** (VT + ADV) (*lit*) [+ *object*] echar a un lado; (*fig*) dejar • **I've been ~n aside for a younger woman** me han dejado por una mujer más joven

▸ **throw away** (VT + ADV) **1** (= *discard*) [+ *rubbish*] tirar, botar (*LAm*); (*Cards*) echar
2 (= *waste*) [+ *chance, opportunity*] desperdiciar; [+ *one's life, health, happiness*] echar a perder; [+ *money*] tirar, derrochar, despilfarrar • **don't ~ your money away on that** no malgastes el dinero en eso • **we should have won — we just threw it away** deberíamos haber ganado, y no hicimos más que echarlo (todo) a perder
3 (= *say casually*) [+ *line, remark*] soltar

▸ **throw back** (VT + ADV) **1** (*lit*) (= *return*) [+ *ball*] devolver; [+ *fish*] devolver al agua; (= *move backwards*) [+ *head, shoulders, hair*] echar para atrás, echar hacia atrás
2 (*fig*) (= *reject*) [+ *offer, suggestion*] rechazar (*con desprecio*); (= *drive back*) [+ *enemy*] rechazar, repeler • **they threw his generosity back in his face** le devolvieron su generosidad con una patada • **I should never have told you that, I knew you'd ~ it back at me** nunca debería habértelo dicho, sabía que me lo echarías en cara • **he was ~n back on his own resources** tuvo que depender de sus propios recursos

▸ **throw down** (VT + ADV) [+ *object*] tirar; [+ *challenge*] lanzar

▸ **throw in** (VT + ADV) **1** (*Sport*) [+ *ball*] sacar • IDIOM: • **to ~ in the towel** (*lit, fig*) tirar la toalla; ▹ **deep, lot**
2 (= *include*) incluir • **a cruise round the Caribbean with Cuba ~n in for good measure** un crucero por el Caribe en el que además se incluye Cuba para que no falte de nada • **pay for extra prints and they ~ in a photo album** pague copias extra y le regalan un álbum de fotos
3 (= *interpose*) [+ *remark, question*] soltar • **"she's done this before," Joan threw in** —esto ya lo ha hecho antes —añadió Joan

▸ **throw off** (VT + ADV) **1** (= *remove*) [+ *clothes, shoes, disguise*] quitarse a toda prisa
2 (= *get rid of*) [+ *depression*] salir de; [+ *cold, infection, habit*] quitarse; [+ *burden, yoke*] librarse de, quitarse de encima • **I can't seem to ~ off this cold** no consigo quitarme este resfriado
3 (= *escape*) [+ *pursuers*] zafarse de, dar esquinazo a
4 (= *make wrong*) [+ *calculations, timing*] desbaratar, dar al traste con
5 (= *emit*) [+ *heat*] despedir, emitir; [+ *sparks*] echar
6* (= *write quickly*) [+ *poem, composition*] improvisar

▸ **throw on** (VT + ADV) **1** (*lit*) [+ *coal, fuel*] echar
2 (*fig*) (= *put on quickly*) [+ *clothes, make-up*] ponerse a toda prisa • **he threw his clothes on** se puso la ropa a toda prisa

▸ **throw out** (VT + ADV) **1** (= *throw away*) [+ *rubbish, old clothes*] tirar, botar (*LAm*); ▹ **baby**
2 (= *expel*) [+ *person*] (*from organization, team*) echar; (*from country*) expulsar, echar • **he was ~n out of the team** lo echaron del equipo
3 (= *reject*) [+ *proposal*] rechazar; (*Jur*) [+ *case, claim*] desestimar, rechazar; (*Parl*) [+ *bill*] rechazar
4 (= *make*) [+ *idea, suggestion, remark*] soltar
5 (= *emit*) [+ *heat*] despedir, emitir; [+ *smoke, lava*] arrojar
6 (= *disconcert*) [+ *person*] desconcertar, dejar totalmente confundido
7 (= *make wrong*) [+ *calculation, prediction*] desbaratar, dar al traste con
8 • **to ~ out one's chest** sacar pecho

▸ **throw over** (VT + ADV) [+ *friend, lover*] dejar, abandonar

▸ **throw together** (VT + ADV) **1** (= *make hastily*) [+ *costume, plan, essay*] hacer a la carrera, pergeñar; [+ *meal*] preparar a la carrera, improvisar
2 (= *gather together*) [+ *clothes*] juntar rápidamente; [+ *people*] juntar • **he threw a few things together and dashed out of the house** juntó rápidamente unas cuantas cosas y salió disparado de la casa • **fate had ~n them together** el destino les había juntado • **people whom circumstances have ~n together** personas a las que han juntado *or* unido las circunstancias • **we were ~n together a good deal, working in the same office** como trabajábamos en la misma oficina nos veíamos mucho

▸ **throw up** (VI + ADV)* (= *vomit*) devolver*, vomitar • **it makes me want to ~ up** (*lit*) me da ganas de devolver*; (*fig*) me da asco
(VT + ADV) **1** (*lit*) [+ *object*] lanzar *or* echar al aire; [+ *dust*] levantar; [+ *sparks*] echar • **to ~ up one's hands in horror** llevarse las manos a la cabeza horrorizado
2 (*esp Brit*) (= *produce, bring to light*) [+ *result*] dar, producir; [+ *idea, dilemma*] producir; [+ *problem*] crear
3* (= *give up*) [+ *job, task, studies*] dejar
4 (= *make quickly*) [+ *building*] construir rápidamente
5* (= *vomit*) devolver*, vomitar

throwaway ['θrəʊəweɪ] (ADJ) **1** (= *disposable*) [*bottle, container*] desechable, para tirar
2 (= *casual*) [*remark*] hecho de paso
(CPD) ▸ **throwaway society** • **the ~ society** la sociedad del usar y tirar

throwback ['θrəʊbæk] (N) (*gen*) salto *m* atrás • **it's like a ~ to the old days** es como un salto atrás a los viejos tiempos • **the film is a ~ to early Minelli movies** la película supone una vuelta a las primeras películas de Minelli

thrower ['θrəʊə^r] (N) lanzador(a) *m/f*

throw-in ['θrəʊɪn] (N) (*Ftbl*) saque *m* (de banda)

throwing ['θrəʊɪŋ] (N) (*Sport*) lanzamiento *m*

thrown [θrəʊn] (PP) *of* **throw**

throw-out ['θrəʊaʊt] (N) cosa *f* desechada • **his flat is furnished with other people's throw-outs** tiene amueblado el piso con lo que otra gente no quería

thru [θru:] (*US*) = **through**

thrum [θrʌm] (VT) [+ *guitar*] rasguear, rasguear las cuerdas de
(VI) [*wings of bird*] producir un aleteo vibrante; [*machine, engine*] producir un sonido vibrante

thrush¹ [θrʌʃ] (N) (= *bird*) zorzal *m*, tordo *m*

thrush² [θrʌʃ] (N) (*Med*) afta *f*

thrust [θrʌst] (VB: PT, PP: **thrust**) (N) **1** (= *push*) empujón *m*; [*of dagger*] puñalada *f*; [*of knife*] cuchillada *f*; [*of sword*] estocada *f*; (*Mil*) (= *offensive*) ofensiva *f*; (= *advance*) avance *m*
2 (*Mech*) empuje *m*; (*Aer, Naut*) propulsión *f* • **forward/reverse ~** empuje *m* de avance/de marcha atrás
3 (= *basic meaning*) [*of speech*] idea *f* clave
4 (= *dynamism*) empuje *m*, dinamismo *m*
(VT) (= *push*) empujar; (= *insert*) introducir, meter (**into** en); (= *insert piercingly*) clavar, hincar (**into** en) • **to ~ one's hands into one's pockets** meter las manos en los bolsillos • **he ~ a book into my hands** me metió un libro entre las manos • **to ~ a dagger into sb's back** clavar un puñal a algn en la espalda • **to ~ a stick into the ground** clavar *or* hincar un palo en el suelo • **she ~ her head out of the window** asomó *or* sacó la cabeza por la ventana • **she found herself suddenly ~ into the limelight** de pronto, sin comerlo ni beberlo, se vio convertida en el centro de atención • **he ~ out his lower lip** sacó hacia fuera el labio inferior • **to ~ sth on** *or* **upon sb** imponer algo a algn, obligar a algn a aceptar algo • **they ~ the job on me** me cargaron el trabajo • **Spain had greatness ~ upon her** España recibió su grandeza sin buscarla, se le impuso la grandeza a España sin quererlo ella • **to ~ o.s. (up)on sb** (*fig*) pegarse a algn • **to ~ sb through with a sword** atravesar a algn (de parte a parte) con una espada • **I ~ my way through the crowd/to the front** me abrí paso entre la multitud/hacia adelante
(VI) • **to ~ at sb: he ~ at me with a sword/knife** me asestó una estocada/cuchillada • **to ~ past sb** apartar de un empujón a algn para pasar • **he ~ past me into the room** me apartó bruscamente para entrar en la habitación • **to ~ through** abrirse paso a la fuerza

▸ **thrust aside** (VT + ADV) [+ *person*] apartar bruscamente; (*fig*) dar de lado; [+ *objections*] ignorar; [+ *plan, proposal*] rechazar

▸ **thrust forward** (VT + ADV) [+ *head, chin*] sacar hacia adelante
(VI + ADV) (*Mil*) avanzar

thrustful ['θrʌstfʊl], **thrusting** ['θrʌstɪŋ] (ADJ) emprendedor, vigoroso, dinámico; (*pej*) agresivo

thrustfulness ['θrʌstfʊlnɪs] (N) empuje *m*, pujanza *f*, dinamismo *m*; (*pej*) agresividad *f*

thruway ['θru:weɪ] (N) (*US*) autopista *f* de peaje

Thucydides [θju:'sɪdɪdi:z] (N) Tucídides

thud [θʌd] (N) ruido *m* sordo, golpe *m* sordo • **he landed on the floor with a dull ~** cayó al suelo con un ruido sordo
(VI) hacer un ruido sordo • **to ~ to the ground** caer al suelo con un ruido sordo • **a shell ~ded into the hillside** una granada estalló en el monte • **he was ~ding about upstairs all night** pasó la noche andando con pasos pesados por el piso de arriba

thudding ['θʌdɪŋ] (N) [*of heart, feet, bombs*] ruido *m* sordo

thug [θʌg] (N) matón/ona *m/f*; (*fig*) (*as term of abuse*) bruto *m*, bestia *f*

thuggery ['θʌgərɪ] (N) matonismo *m*, brutalidad *f*

thuggish ['θʌgɪʃ] (ADJ) [*person*] desalmado; [*behaviour*] propio de un matón, desalmado, canallesco

thulium ['θju:lɪəm] (N) tulio *m*

thumb [θʌm] (N) pulgar *m* • **he gave me a ~s-up sign** me indicó con el pulgar que todo iba bien • IDIOMS: • **to be all ~s**: • **I'm all ~s today** hoy soy un manazas • **to twiddle one's ~s** estar mano sobre mano, estar sin hacer nada • **to be under sb's ~** estar dominado por algn • **she's got him under her ~** le tiene metido en un puño • **they gave it the ~s down** lo rechazaron, lo desaprobaron • **they gave it the ~s up** lo aprobaron • **the voters have given him the ~s up/down** el electorado votó a favor de/en contra de él; ▹ **rule**
(VT) **1** [+ *book*] manosear • **a well-thumbed book** un libro muy manoseado
2 • **to ~ a lift** *or* **a ride** hacer autostop, hacer

dedo, pedir aventón (*LAm*) • **to ~ a lift to London** viajar en autostop a Londres
3 • **to ~ one's nose at sth/sb** (*lit*) hacer burla a algo/algn (*agitando la mano con el pulgar sobre la nariz*); (*fig*) burlarse de algo/algn
VI • **to ~ through a book/magazine** hojear un libro/una revista
CPD ▸ **thumb index** índice *m* recortado
▸ **thumb through** VI + PREP (*book*) hojear
thumbnail [ˈθʌmneɪl] N uña *f* del pulgar
CPD ▸ **thumbnail sketch** pequeño *m* esbozo
thumbprint [ˈθʌmprɪnt] N impresión *f* del pulgar
thumbscrew [ˈθʌmskruː] N empulgueras *fpl*
thumbstall [ˈθʌmstɔːl] N dedil *m*
thumbtack [ˈθʌmtæk] N (*US*) chincheta *f*, chinche *m or f* (*LAm*)
thump [θʌmp] N (= *blow*) golpetazo *m*, porrazo *m*; (= *noise of fall etc*) golpetazo *m* • **it came down with a ~** cayó dando un golpetazo
VT (= *hit hard*) golpear; (*accidentally*) [+ *head etc*] dar *or* topar con; (= *put down heavily*) poner *or* (*frm*) deponer violentamente • **to ~ sb** pegar un puñetazo a algn • **to ~ the table** golpear la mesa, dar golpes en la mesa • **he ~ed me on the back** me dio un golpetazo en la espalda • **to ~ out a tune on the piano** tocar una melodía aporreando el piano
VI **1** [*person*] (*on door, table*) dar golpes, aporrear; [*heart*] (= *pound*) latir con fuerza; [*machine*] vibrar con violencia • **someone was ~ing on the door** había alguien dando golpes a *or* aporreando la puerta
2 (= *move heavily*) • **he ~ed upstairs** subió pesadamente las escaleras
thumping* [ˈθʌmpɪŋ] (*Brit*) ADJ enorme, descomunal • **the company has suffered a ~ loss this year** este año la compañía ha sufrido unas pérdidas enormes *or* descomunales • **a ~ headache** una jaqueca terrible
ADV • **a ~ great book** un tocho de libro*
thunder [ˈθʌndəʳ] N (*Met*) truenos *mpl*; [*of traffic, applause*] estruendo *m*; [*of hooves*] estampido *m* • **a clap of ~** un trueno • **there is ~ in the air** amenaza tronar • **with a face like** *or* **as black as ~** con cara de furia, con cara de pocos amigos • IDIOM: • **to steal sb's ~** robar el éxito a algn
VI (*Met*) tronar; [*waterfall, waves*] bramar • **the guns ~ed in the distance** los cañones tronaban a lo lejos • **the train ~ed by** el tren pasó con gran estruendo • **to ~ at sb** (= *shout*) gritar muy fuerte a algn
VT • **to ~ out an order** dar una orden a gritos • **"yes!", he ~ed** —¡sí! —rugió
thunderbolt [ˈθʌndəbəʊlt] N rayo *m*; (*fig*) rayo *m*, bomba *f*
thunderclap [ˈθʌndəklæp] N trueno *m*
thundercloud [ˈθʌndəklaʊd] N nube *f* tormentosa, nubarrón *m*
thunderer [ˈθʌndərəʳ] N • **the Thunderer** (*Myth*) Perkunas *m*
thunderflash [ˈθʌndəflæʃ] N petardo *m*
thundering* [ˈθʌndərɪŋ] ADJ • **it's a ~ disgrace** es un escándalo • **it was a ~ success** obtuvo un tremendo éxito
ADV • **a ~ great row** un ruido de todos los demonios • **it's a ~ good film** es una película la mar de buena*
thunderous [ˈθʌndərəs] ADJ [*applause*] estruendoso, atronador
thunderstorm [ˈθʌndəstɔːm] N tormenta *f*
thunderstruck [ˈθʌndəstrʌk] ADJ (*fig*) atónito, pasmado, estupefacto • **he was ~ by what he discovered** lo que descubrió lo dejó atónito *or* pasmado *or* estupefacto
thundery [ˈθʌndərɪ] ADJ [*weather, shower, sky*] tormentoso
thurible [ˈθjʊərɪbl] N incensario *m*
thurifer [ˈθjʊərɪfəʳ] N monaguillo *m* que lleva el incensario
Thuringia [θjʊəˈrɪndʒɪə] N Turingia *f*
Thurs. ABBR (= **Thursday**) juev.
Thursday [ˈθɜːzdɪ] N jueves *m inv*; ▹ **Tuesday**
thus [ðʌs] ADV (= *in this way*) así, de este modo; (= *as a result*) por eso, así que, de modo que • **he withdrew from the competition, ~ allowing his rival to win** se retiró de la competición, así que *or* de modo que ganó su rival • **~ it is that …** así es que …, es por eso que … • **~, when he got home …** así que, cuando llegó a casa … • **~ far** hasta ahora *or* aquí
thwack [θwæk] = **whack**
thwart¹ [θwɔːt] VT [+ *plan*] frustrar, desbaratar; [+ *attempt, efforts*] frustrar • **to be ~ed at every turn** verse frustrado en todo • **there's no knowing what she'll do if she's ~ed** quién sabe qué hará si alguien se interpone en su camino • **he was trying to commit suicide but had been ~ed** intentaba suicidarse pero alguien interrumpió su propósito • **their takeover bid was ~ed** su intento de adquirir la compañía fue frustrada
thwart² [θwɔːt] N (*Naut*) bancada *f*
thx, thxs ABBR (*Internet etc*) = **thanks**
thy†† [ðaɪ] POSS ADJ (*sing*) tu; (*pl*) tus
thyme [taɪm] N tomillo *m*
thymus [ˈθaɪməs] N (PL: **thymuses, thymi** [ˈθaɪmaɪ]) timo *m*
thyroid [ˈθaɪrɔɪd] N (*also* **thyroid gland**) tiroides *m or f inv*
ADJ tiroideo
thyself†† [ðaɪˈself] PRON (*acc, dative*) te; (*after prep*) ti (mismo/a) • **know ~** conócete a ti mismo
ti [tiː] N (*Mus*) si *m*
tiara [tɪˈɑːrə] N (*royal*) diadema *f*; (*pope's*) tiara *f*
Tiber [ˈtaɪbəʳ] N Tíber *m*
Tiberius [taɪˈbɪərɪəs] N Tiberio
Tibet [tɪˈbet] N el Tibet
Tibetan [tɪˈbetən] ADJ tibetano
N **1** (= *person*) tibetano/a *m/f*
2 (*Ling*) tibetano *m*
tibia [ˈtɪbɪə] N (PL: **tibias, tibiae** [ˈtɪbɪiː]) tibia *f*
tic [tɪk] N (*Med*) tic *m* • **a nervous tic** un tic nervioso
tich* [tɪtʃ] N = **titch**
tichy* [ˈtɪtʃɪ] ADJ = **titchy**
tick¹ [tɪk] N **1** [*of clock*] tictac *m*
2 (*Brit**) (= *moment*) momentito *m*, segundito *m* • **half a ~!** • **just a ~!** ¡un momentito *or* segundito! • **I shan't be a ~** en seguida voy, no tardo, ahorita voy (*LAm*) • **it won't take two ~s** será solo un momentito *or* segundito
3 (*esp Brit*) (= *mark*) señal *f*, visto *m* • **to put a ~ against sth** poner una señal *or* un visto a algo • **place a ~ in the appropriate box** marque la casilla correspondiente
VT (*esp Brit*) [+ *right answer*] marcar; (*also* **tick off**) [+ *name, item on list*] marcar, poner una señal contra • **to ~ boxes** marcar casillas • **this model ~s all the boxes** este modelo marca todas las casillas
VI [*clock*] hacer tictac • **I can't understand what makes him ~** no comprendo su forma de ser
▸ **tick away, tick by** VI + ADV • **time is ~ing away** *or* **by** el tiempo pasa
▸ **tick off** VT + ADV **1** (= *mark with tick*) [+ *name, item on list*] marcar, poner una señal contra
2 (= *count*) contar en los dedos
3 (*Brit**) (= *reprimand*) • **to ~ sb off** echar una bronca a algn, regañar *or* reñir a algn • **he was ~ed off for being late** le regañaron *or* riñeron por llegar tarde
4 (*US**) (= *annoy*) fastidiar, dar la lata a*
▸ **tick over** VI + ADV (*Brit*) (*Aut, Mech*) marchar al ralentí; (*fig*) [*business*] ir tirando • **she's keeping things ~ing over until the new boss arrives** hace que las cosas sigan funcionando hasta que llegue el nuevo jefe
tick² [tɪk] N (*Zool*) garrapata *f*
tick³ [tɪk] N (= *cover*) funda *f*
tick⁴* [tɪk] N (= *credit*) • IDIOM: • **to buy sth on ~** comprar algo de fiado
ticker [ˈtɪkəʳ] N* (= *watch*) reloj *m*; (= *heart*) corazón *m*
CPD ▸ **ticker tape** cinta *f* de teletipo
ticket [ˈtɪkɪt] N **1** (*for bus, train*) billete *m*, boleto *m* (*LAm*); (*for plane*) pasaje *m*, billete *m* (*esp Sp*); (*for concert, film, play*) entrada *f*, boleto *m* (*LAm*), boleta *f* (*LAm*); (*for library membership*) carné *m*, carnet *m*; (*Comm*) (= *label*) etiqueta *f*; (= *counterfoil*) talón *m*; (*at dry-cleaner's etc*) resguardo *m*; (*in lottery*) boleto *m* • **return ~** • **round-trip ~** (*US*) billete *m* de ida y vuelta, billete *m* redondo (*Mex*) • **hold it there, that's the ~!** ¡sujétalo ahí! ¡eso es! • **that holiday was just the ~** esas vacaciones eran justo lo que necesitaba
2 (*for parking offence*) multa *f* (por estacionamiento indebido) • **to get a (parking) ~** ser multado por aparcar mal* *or* por estacionamiento indebido
3 (*US*) (*Pol*) (= *candidates*) lista *f* (de candidatos), candidatura *f*, planilla *f* (*LAm*); (= *programme*) programa *m* político, programa *m* electoral • **to run on a republican ~** presentarse como candidato republicano
VT **1** (*Aut*) (= *fine*) [+ *person*] multar; [+ *vehicle*] dejar la papeleta de una multa en
2 (*US*) [+ *passenger*] expedir un billete a
CPD ▸ **ticket agency** (*Rail etc*) agencia *f* de viajes; (*Theat*) agencia *f* de localidades, boletería *f* (*LAm*) ▸ **ticket barrier** (*Brit*) (*Rail*) *barrera más allá de la cual se necesita billete*
▸ **ticket booth** taquilla *f*, despacho *m* de billetes ▸ **ticket collector, ticket inspector** revisor(a) *m/f*, controlador(a) *m/f* de boletos (*LAm*) ▸ **ticket counter, ticket desk** taquilla *f*, despacho *m* de billetes ▸ **ticket holder** poseedor(a) *m/f* de billete; (= *season-ticket holder*) (*Theat*) abonado/a *m/f*; (*Ftbl*) socio/a *m/f*; (*of travelcard etc*) titular *mf*
▸ **ticket machine** máquina *f* de billetes
▸ **ticket office** (*Rail*) despacho *m* de billetes, despacho *m* de boletos (*LAm*); (*Theat, Cine*) taquilla *f*, boletería *f* (*LAm*) ▸ **ticket of leave**† (*Brit*) cédula *f* de libertad condicional
▸ **ticket tout** revendedor *m* (de entradas)
▸ **ticket window** ventanilla *f*; (*Rail etc*) despacho *m* de billetes; (*Theat etc*) taquilla *f*
ticketing [ˈtɪkɪtɪŋ] N emisión *f* de billetes
ticking [ˈtɪkɪŋ] N **1** [*of clock*] tictac *m*
2 (= *material*) cutí *m*, terliz *m*
ticking-off* [ˈtɪkɪŋˈɒf] N bronca *f* • **to give sb a ticking-off** echar una bronca a algn, regañar *or* reñir a algn
tickle [ˈtɪkl] VT **1** [+ *person*] hacer cosquillas a; [+ *cat, dog*] acariciar • **she enjoyed tickling the baby** le gustaba hacer cosquillas al niño
2* (= *amuse*) divertir, hacer gracia a • **it ~d us no end** nos divirtió mucho, nos hizo mucha gracia
3* (= *please*) • **we were ~d to death at being invited** fue una sorpresa maravillosa que nos invitaran • **it ~d his fancy** se le antojó • IDIOM: • **to be ~d pink*** estar encantado *or*

t

como unas castañuelas
(VI) • **my ear ~s** siento cosquillas *or* hormiguillo en la oreja • **it ~s** [*material*] pica • **don't, it ~s!** ¡no, que me hace cosquillas!
(N) • **to give sb a ~** hacer cosquillas a algn • **to have a ~ in one's throat** tener picor de garganta • **he never got a ~ all day** (*Fishing*) no picó ni un pez en todo el día • **at £5 he never got a ~*** a cinco libras nadie le echó un tiento*
tickler* ['tɪkləʳ] (N) (*Brit*) problema *m* difícil
tickling ['tɪklɪŋ] (N) cosquillas *fpl*
ticklish ['tɪklɪʃ], **tickly** ['tɪklɪ] (ADJ) **1** (*lit*) (= *sensitive to tickling*) [*person*] cosquilloso; (= *which tickles*) [*blanket*] que pica; [*cough*] irritante • **to be ~** [*person*] tener cosquillas, ser cosquilloso
2 (*fig*) (= *touchy*) [*person*] picajoso, delicado; (= *delicate*) [*situation, problem*] peliagudo, delicado • **it's a ~ business** es un asunto delicado
tick-over ['tɪkəʊvəʳ] (N) (*Brit*) [*of engine*] ralentí *m*
ticktack ['tɪktæk] (N) (*Racing*) *lenguaje de signos utilizado por los corredores de apuestas en las carreras de caballos*
tick-tock ['tɪk'tɒk] (N) tictac *m*
tic-tac-toe [,tɪktæk'təʊ] (N) (*US*) tres *m* en raya
tidal ['taɪdl] (ADJ) de (la) marea • **the river is ~ up to here** la marea sube hasta aquí • **the Mediterranean is not ~** en el Mediterráneo no hay mareas
(CPD) ▸ **tidal basin** dique *m* de marea ▸ **tidal energy** energía *f* de las mareas, energía *f* mareomotriz ▸ **tidal wave** maremoto *m*; (*fig*) ola *f* gigantesca
tidbit ['tɪdbɪt] (N) (*US*) = **titbit**
tiddler ['tɪdləʳ] (N) **1** (= *small fish*) pececillo *m*; (= *stickleback*) espinoso *m*
2* (= *child*) nene/a *m/f*, renacuajo* *m*
tiddly* ['tɪdlɪ] (ADJ) (COMPAR: **tiddlier**, SUPERL: **tiddliest**) (*Brit*) **1** (= *drunk*) alegre, achispado, tomado (*LAm**)
2 (= *tiny*) pequeñito, pequeñín
tiddlywink ['tɪdlɪwɪŋk] (N) pulga *f*; **tiddlywinks** (= *game*) juego *m* de las pulgas
tide [taɪd] (N) **1** [*of sea*] marea *f* • **high ~** marea *f* alta, pleamar *f* • **we sailed at high ~** *or* **with the high ~** zarpamos cuando la marea estaba alta • **low ~** marea *f* baja, bajamar *f* • **it is possible to walk across at low ~** es posible cruzar cuando la marea está baja • **the ~ has turned** ha cambiado la marea
2 (*fig*) corriente *f*; [*of emotion*] ola *f* • **the rising ~ of public indignation** la creciente indignación pública • **the ~ of events** la marcha de los sucesos • **the ~ has turned** han cambiado las cosas • **the ~ of battle turned** cambió la suerte de la batalla
• IDIOMS: • **to go against the ~** ir contra la corriente • **to go with the ~** seguir la corriente
(CPD) ▸ **tide table** tabla *f* de mareas
▸ **tide over** (VT + ADV) • **can you lend me some money to ~ me over till the end of the month?** ¿puedes dejarme algo de dinero para que pueda llegar a final de mes *or* para sacarme de apuros hasta final de mes?
(VT + PREP) • **he got a loan to ~ him over the first three months** consiguió un préstamo para salir adelante los tres primeros meses • **to ~ sb over a difficult period** ayudar a algn a salir de un apuro
tideless ['taɪdlɪs] (ADJ) sin mareas
tideline ['taɪdlaɪn] (N) línea *f* de la marea alta
tidemark ['taɪdmɑːk] (N) **1** (= *tideline*) línea *f* de la marea alta
2 (*hum*) (*in bath, on neck*) cerco *m* (de suciedad)
tiderace ['taɪdreɪs] (N) aguaje *m*, marejada *f*
tidewater ['taɪd,wɔːtəʳ] (*Brit*) (N) agua *f* de marea
(CPD) [*land, area*] drenado por las mareas, costero
tideway ['taɪdweɪ] (N) canal *m* de marea
tidily ['taɪdɪlɪ] (ADV) [*arranged, piled, stacked*] ordenadamente; [*dressed*] bien, perfectamente
tidiness ['taɪdɪnɪs] (N) [*of room, house, desk*] orden *m*; [*of person's appearance*] pulcritud *f*
tidings ['taɪdɪŋz] (NPL) (*liter*) noticias *fpl*
tidy ['taɪdɪ] (ADJ) (COMPAR: **tidier**, SUPERL: **tidiest**) **1** (= *neat, orderly*) **a** (*in appearance*) [*house, room*] ordenado, arreglado; [*garden*] cuidado; [*cupboard, desk, pile*] ordenado; [*appearance*] aseado, pulcro; [*hair*] arreglado; [*schoolwork*] limpio • **he likes to keep the house ~** le gusta tener la casa ordenada *or* arreglada • **to look ~** [*person*] tener un aspecto aseado *or* pulcro; [*room*] tener un aspecto ordenado
b (*in character*) [*person, child*] ordenado • **she's not very ~** no es muy ordenada • **I'm an obsessively ~ person** soy un obseso del orden
2* (= *sizeable*) [*sum*] bonito*; [*income, profit*] bueno • **he'll make a ~ sum out of it** sacará de ello un buen dinero *or* una bonita cantidad*
(VT) (*also* **tidy up**) [+ *room, house*] ordenar, arreglar; [+ *drawer, cupboard, desk*] ordenar
(N) **1** (= *container for desk, kitchen etc*) *recipiente para poner utensilios de escritorio, cubiertos etc*
2 (= *act*) • **I gave the lounge a quick ~ (up)** arreglé un poco el salón
▸ **tidy away** (VT + ADV) (*Brit*) [+ *toys, books, papers*] guardar, poner en su sitio • **to ~ the dishes away** guardar los platos, poner los platos en su sitio
▸ **tidy out** (VT + ADV) limpiar, ordenar
▸ **tidy up** (VI + ADV) ordenar
(VT + ADV) **1** = **tidy**
2 • **to ~ o.s. up** arreglarse
tidy-out ['taɪdɪ'aʊt] (N), **tidy-up** ['taɪdɪ'ʌp] (N) • **to have a tidy-out** ordenar (la casa, la habitación *etc*)
tie [taɪ] (N) **1** (= *necktie*) corbata *f*; ▹ **black, bow, white**
2 (= *fastening*) (*for plastic bags*) atadura *f*; (*on garment*) lazo *m*
3 (= *bond*) lazo *m*, vínculo *m* • **the ties of friendship** los lazos *or* vínculos de la amistad • **the ties that bind us** los lazos que nos unen • **he wants to maintain close ties with the US** quiere mantener unos vínculos *or* lazos estrechos con Estados Unidos • **diplomatic ties** relaciones *fpl* diplomáticas • **family ties** lazos *mpl* familiares
4 (= *hindrance, obligation*) atadura *f* • **pets are as much of a tie as children** las mascotas te atan tanto como los niños, las mascotas son una atadura tan grande como los niños • **I have no ties here** no tengo nada que me retenga aquí *or* que me impida irme de aquí • **I can't go because of family ties** no puedo ir debido a obligaciones familiares
5 (*esp Sport*) (= *draw*) empate *m* • **the match ended in a tie** el partido terminó en empate *or* con (un) empate
6 (*Brit*) (*Sport*) (*also* **cup tie**) partido *m* (de copa), eliminatoria *f* (de copa)
7 (*Archit*) (= *support*) tirante *m*
8 (*Mus*) ligadura *f*
9 (*US*) (*Rail*) traviesa *f*
(VT) **1** (= *fasten*) [+ *one's shoelaces*] atarse, amarrarse (*LAm*); [+ *sb's shoelaces*] atar, amarrar (*LAm*); [+ *one's necktie*] hacerse el nudo de; [+ *sb's necktie*] hacer el nudo de; [+ *parcel*] atar, amarrar (*LAm*) • **she tied a ribbon around the kitten's neck** ató un lazo al cuello del gatito • **he tied the rope around his waist** se ató la cuerda a la cintura • **her hands were tied behind her back** tenía las manos atadas a la espalda • **to tie sth in a bow** hacer un lazo con algo • **to tie a knot in sth** hacer un nudo en *or* con algo • **he tied the dog to a lamppost** ató el perro a una farola • **he tied the ends of the cord together** ató los extremos de la cuerda • **he tied her hands together** le ató las manos • IDIOM: • **we'd like to help, but our hands are tied** nos gustaría ayudar pero tenemos atadas las manos; ▹ **knot**
2 (= *link*) relacionar (**to** con) • **rates are tied to property values** las contribuciones urbanas están relacionadas con el valor *or* van ligadas al valor del inmueble
3 (= *restrict*) atar • **I'm tied to the house/my desk all day** me paso todo el día atada a la casa/la mesa de trabajo • **are we tied to this plan?** ¿estamos atados *or* restringidos a este plan? • **she didn't want to be tied to a long-term contract** no quería atarse a un contrato a largo plazo
4 (*Sport*) [+ *game, match*] empatar
(VI) **1** (= *fasten*) atarse • **the overall ties at the back** el delantal se ata a la espalda
2 (= *draw*) (*in match, competition, election*) empatar
(CPD) ▸ **tie clip, tie clasp** pinza *f* de corbata ▸ **tie rack** corbatero *m* ▸ **tie tack** (*US*) = **tiepin**
▸ **tie back** (VT + ADV) [+ *curtains*] recoger • **to tie one's hair back** recogerse el pelo • **her hair was tied back with a ribbon** llevaba el pelo recogido con un lazo
▸ **tie down** (VT + ADV) **1** (*with rope*) [+ *object, person, animal*] sujetar, amarrar (*LAm*)
2 (= *restrict*) atar • **having a pet ties you down** tener una mascota te ata • **he felt tied down by the relationship** se sentía atado por la relación • **we didn't want to tie ourselves down to a mortgage** no queríamos atarnos a una hipoteca
3 (= *commit*) • **to tie sb down** hacer que algn se comprometa • **we can't tie him down to a date** no conseguimos que se comprometa a una fecha concreta
▸ **tie in** (VI + ADV) • **to tie in with sth** (= *tally*) (*with facts*) concordar *or* cuadrar con algo; (= *fit in*) (*with arrangements*) coincidir con algo • **it doesn't tie in with what he told us** no concuerda *or* cuadra con lo que nos dijo • **the wedding was arranged to tie in with David's leave** la boda se planeó de modo que coincidiera con el permiso de David
(VT + ADV) • **to tie sth in with sth** (= *link*) relacionar algo con algo; (= *fit in*) [+ *meeting, visit*] hacer coincidir algo con algo • **you can't tie me in with any of the killings** no puedes relacionarme con *or* vincularme a ninguno de los asesinatos
▸ **tie on** (VT + ADV) atar
▸ **tie up** (VT + ADV) **1** (= *fasten, secure*) [+ *parcel, person, horse, sb's shoelaces*] atar, amarrar (*LAm*); [+ *one's shoelaces*] atarse, amarrarse (*LAm*); [+ *boat*] amarrar; ▹ **loose**
2 (= *make inaccessible*) [+ *money, capital*] inmovilizar • **he has a fortune tied up in property** tiene una fortuna inmovilizada *or* invertida en bienes inmuebles • **how much money have you got tied up in the product?** ¿cuánto dinero tienes invertido *or* metido en el producto?
3 (= *conclude*) [+ *business deal*] concluir, cerrar
4 (= *link*) • **to be tied up with sth** estar relacionado con algo, estar vinculado a algo • **I'm sure her disappearance is tied up with the robbery** estoy seguro de que su

t

desaparición está relacionada con el robo *or* vinculada al robo • **don't get tied up with people like him** no te mezcles con gente como él
5 (= *occupy*) • **to be tied up (with sth/sb)** estar ocupado (con algo/algn) • **he's tied up with the manager just now** ahora está ocupado *or* tratando un asunto con el jefe • **I'm tied up tomorrow** mañana estoy ocupado • **sorry I'm late, I got tied up** siento llegar tarde, me entretuvieron
6 (*esp US*) (= *obstruct, hinder*) [+ *traffic*] paralizar, inmovilizar; [+ *production*] paralizar; [+ *programme*] interrumpir
(VI + ADV) **1** (= *be linked*) • **to tie up with sth** estar relacionado con algo, estar vinculado a algo
2 (*Naut*) atracar, amarrar

tie-break ['taɪbreɪk], **tie-breaker** ['taɪbreɪkəʳ] (N) (*Sport*) muerte *f* rápida, desempate *m*

tied [taɪd] (ADJ) **1** (*Sport*) empatado • **the match was ~ at 2-2** el partido estaba empatado a dos
2 (*Mus*) [*note*] ligado
3 (*Brit*) • **~ cottage** *casa de campo cedida o alquilada a un empleado, generalmente a un trabajador del campo* • **~ house** (= *pub*) *bar que está obligado a vender una marca de cerveza en exclusiva*

tie-in ['taɪɪn] (N) (= *link*) vinculación *f*, relación *f* • **police are looking for a tie-in to connect the two cases** la policía busca una vinculación *or* relación entre ambos casos • **guides on cooking and gardening with a TV tie-in** libros de cocina y jardinería relacionados *or* vinculados con un programa de TV

tieless ['taɪlɪs] (ADJ) sin corbata

tie-on ['taɪɒn] (ADJ) [*label*] para atar

tiepin ['taɪpɪn] (N) alfiler *m* de corbata

tier [tɪəʳ] (N) **1** (*in stadium, amphitheatre*) (= *row of seats*) grada *f*; [*of cake*] piso *m* • **to arrange in ~s** disponer en gradas *or* pisos
2 (*fig*) (*in management, system*) nivel *m* • **a two-tier health service** un sistema sanitario que hace distinciones entre dos grupos

tiered ['tɪəd] (ADJ) con gradas, en una serie de gradas • **steeply ~** con gradas en fuerte pendiente • **a three-tiered cake** un pastel de tres pisos

Tierra del Fuego [tɪ,ɛərədel'fweɪgəʊ] (N) Tierra *f* del Fuego

tie-up ['taɪʌp] (N) **1** (= *connection*) enlace *m*, vínculo *m*; (*Comm*) (*between companies*) acuerdo *m* (*para llevar a cabo un proyecto*)
2 (*US*) [*of traffic*] embotellamiento *m*

tiff* [tɪf] (N) pelea *f*, riña *f* (sin trascendencia) • **a lover's ~** una pelea de amantes

tiffin† ['tɪfɪn] (N) almuerzo *m*

tig [tɪg] (N) • **to play tig** jugar al marro

tiger ['taɪgəʳ] (N) tigre *m*
(CPD) ▸ **tiger economy** economía *f* emergente ▸ **tiger lily** tigridia *f* ▸ **tiger moth** mariposa *f* tigre ▸ **tiger mother*** madre *f* estricta y exigente ▸ **tiger's eye** (*Min*) ojo *m* de gato

tigerish ['taɪgərɪʃ] (ADJ) (*fig*) salvaje, feroz

tight [taɪt] (ADJ) (COMPAR: **tighter**, SUPERL: **tightest**) **1** [*clothes, jeans*] (= *close-fitting*) ajustado, ceñido; (= *uncomfortably tight*) apretado, estrecho • **my shoes are too ~** me aprietan los zapatos • **the hat was a ~ fit** el sombrero quedaba muy apretado *or* muy justo
2 (= *stretched out*) [*rope, skin*] tirante • **my skin feels ~** tengo la piel tirante, me tira la piel • **to pull sth ~** tensar algo • IDIOMS: • **as ~ as a drum** [*surface, material*] tenso como la piel de un tambor • **she has a body as ~ as a drum** tiene el cuerpo firme como una piedra • **to keep a ~ rein on sth/sb** mantener un control estricto sobre algo/algn; ▹ **skin-tight**
3 (= *not loose*) [*screw, knot, curl*] apretado; [*seal*] hermético; [*embrace, grip*] fuerte • **his fingers were ~ on Thomas's arm** le apretaba el brazo a Thomas fuertemente con los dedos • **the insect curled up in a ~ ball** el insecto se enroscó formando una pequeña bola • **to have a ~ grip on** [+ *power, economy*] ejercer un firme control sobre • **to keep a ~ grip on** [+ *finances, discipline*] mantener un firme control de • **to have a ~ hold of sth** tener algo bien agarrado • **to keep a ~ hold of sth** agarrar algo con fuerza • **it was a ~ squeeze in the lift** íbamos muy apretados *or* apiñados en el ascensor • IDIOM: • **to keep a ~ lid on sth** controlar bien algo, mantener algo bajo control
4 (= *tense*) [*voice, throat, smile*] tenso; [*muscle*] tenso, tirante • **my chest feels ~** siento una opresión en el pecho
5 (= *strict*) [*schedule*] apretado; [*budget*] ajustado, limitado; [*control*] estricto • **security will be ~** habrá fuertes medidas de seguridad
6 (= *close-knit*) [*group, community*] muy unido
7 (= *sharp*) [*bend*] cerrado • **to make a ~ turn** girar bruscamente, dar un giro brusco
8* (= *scarce*) [*space, resources*] limitado, escaso • **things were ~ during the war** el dinero era escaso durante la guerra • **when we first got married money was ~** al principio de casarnos estábamos bastante escasos de dinero
9* (= *difficult*) [*situation*] apurado, difícil • IDIOM: • **to be in a ~ corner** *or* **spot*** estar en una situación apurada *or* comprometida
10 (= *close*) [*competition, match*] reñido
11* (= *drunk*) mamado*, tomado (*LAm**) • **to get ~** agarrarse una moña*, cogérsela*
12* (= *tight-fisted*) agarrado*
(ADV) [*hold, grip*] bien, con fuerza; [*squeeze*] con fuerza; [*shut, seal, tie*] bien • **hold (on) ~!** ¡agárrate *or* sujétate bien!, ¡agárrate *or* sujétate fuerte! • **to be packed ~ (with sth)** estar lleno hasta arriba (de algo)*, estar abarrotado (de algo)* • IDIOMS: • **to sit ~** • **do we just sit ~ while thousands of people are dying?** ¿vamos a quedarnos cruzados de brazos *or* sin hacer nada mientras mueren miles de personas? • **sleep ~!** ¡que duermas bien!, ¡que descanses!
(CPD) ▸ **tight end** (*US*) tight end *m* (*en fútbol americano*)

tightarsed‡ ['taɪtɑːst] (ADJ) (= *inhibited*) [*person, behaviour*] estrecho*; (= *miserly*) roñoso*

tighten ['taɪtn] (VT) (*also* **tighten up**) [+ *rope*] estirar, tensar; [+ *nut, belt, shoes*] apretar; [+ *regulations*] hacer más severo; [+ *restrictions, discipline, security*] reforzar
(VI) (*also* **tighten up**) [*rope, knot*] estirarse; [*skin*] ponerse tirante; [*grasp*] apretarse
▸ **tighten up** (VT + ADV) **1** = **tighten**
2 • **to ~ up on sth** ser más estricto con algo • **they have decided to ~ up on this type of import** han decidido controlar más este tipo de importaciones
(VI + ADV) = **tighten**

tightening ['taɪtnɪŋ] (N) [*of rope*] tensamiento *m*; [*of controls, security*] refuerzo *m*; [*of skin*] tirantez *f*

tight-fisted ['taɪt'fɪstɪd] (ADJ) (= *mean*) [*person*] tacaño, agarrado*

tight-fitting ['taɪt'fɪtɪŋ] (ADJ) muy ajustado, muy ceñido

tightknit, tight-knit ['taɪt'nɪt] (ADJ) [*family, group, community*] muy unido; [*community*] muy integrado

tight-lipped ['taɪt'lɪpt] (ADJ) **1** (= *secretive*) hermético • **to be/remain tight-lipped about sth** mantener la boca cerrada respecto a algo • **tight-lipped silence** silencio *m* hermético
2 (= *angry*) [*person*] mudo de rabia; [*expression*] de rabia contenida

tightly ['taɪtlɪ] (ADV) **1** (= *firmly*) [*hold*] bien, con fuerza; [*close, tie, wrap*] bien; [*bind*] firmemente • **the prisoners were ~ bound** los prisioneros estaban firmemente atados • **the bandages need to be ~ bound** hay que apretar bien los vendajes • **they hold on ~ to their religious traditions** se aferran firmemente a sus tradiciones religiosas
2 (= *closely*) • **the shelves were packed ~ with books** las estanterías estaban abarrotadas de libros • **~ fitting clothes** ropa ceñida *or* ajustada
3 (= *strictly*) [*controlled, enforced*] estrictamente

tightness ['taɪtnɪs] (N) **1** [*of clothes*] (*comfortable*) lo ceñido, lo ajustado; (*uncomfortable*) estrechez *f*; [*of shoes*] estrechez *f*; [*of lid, screw*] lo apretado
2 [*of muscle, throat*] tensión *f* • **I can feel a ~ in my chest** siento una opresión en el pecho
3 [*of budget, schedule*] lo ajustado, lo limitado; [*of discipline, regulations*] severidad *f*
4 [*of bend, corner*] lo cerrado

tightrope ['taɪtrəʊp] (N) cuerda *f* floja • IDIOMS: • **to be on a ~** • **be walking a ~** andar en la cuerda floja
(CPD) ▸ **tightrope walker** equilibrista *mf*, funámbulo/a *m/f*

tights [taɪts] (*Brit*) (NPL) (= *clothes*) pantis *mpl*, medias *fpl*; (*for sport, ballet*) leotardos *mpl*

tightwad* ['taɪtwɒd] (N) (*US*) cicatero/a* *m/f*, agarrado/a* *m/f*

tigress ['taɪgrɪs] (N) tigresa *f*

Tigris ['taɪgrɪs] (N) Tigris *m*

tilapia [tɪ'læpɪə] (N) tilapia *f*

tilde ['tɪldɪ] (N) tilde *f*

tile [taɪl] (N) (= *roof tile*) teja *f*; (= *floor tile*) baldosa *f*; (= *wall tile, decorative tile*) azulejo *m* • IDIOM: • **a night on the ~s*** una noche de juerga *or* parranda*
(VT) [+ *floor*] embaldosar; [+ *wall*] revestir de azulejos, alicatar (*Sp*); [+ *ceiling*] tejar

tiled [taɪld] (ADJ) [*floor*] embaldosado; [*wall*] revestido de azulejos, alicatado (*Sp*); [*ceiling*] tejado de tejas • **~ roof** tejado *m*

tiling ['taɪlɪŋ] (N) (*on roof*) tejas *fpl*, tejado *m*; (*on floor*) baldosas *fpl*, embaldosado *m*; (*on wall*) azulejos *mpl*

till[1] [tɪl] (VT) (*Agr*) [+ *land, soil*] cultivar, labrar

till[2] [tɪl] (PREP), (CONJ) = **until**

till[3] [tɪl] (N) (*for money*) (= *drawer*) cajón *m*; (= *machine*) caja *f*, caja *f* registradora • **they caught him with his hand** *or* **fingers in the ~** lo cogieron robando (dentro de la empresa *etc*)
(CPD) ▸ **till receipt** tíquet *m* de compra

tillage ['tɪlɪdʒ] (N) cultivo *m*, labranza *f*

tiller ['tɪləʳ] (N) (*Naut*) caña *f* del timón, timón *m*

tilt [tɪlt] (N) **1** (= *slant*) inclinación *f* • **the ~ of the earth's axis** la inclinación del eje de la Tierra • **the ~ of his head when he listened** la inclinación *or* el ladeo de su cabeza cuando escuchaba • **a ~ in the balance of power** un cambio en el equilibrio del poder • **to give sth a ~** inclinar algo, ladear algo • **on/at a ~** inclinado, ladeado
2 (*Hist*) torneo *m*, justa *f* • **(at) full ~** a toda velocidad *or* carrera • **to run full ~ into a wall** dar de lleno contra una pared • **to have a ~ at** arremeter contra
(VT) inclinar, ladear • **~ it this way/the other way** inclínalo hacia este/el otro lado

t

• **he ~ed his chair back** inclinó la silla hacia atrás
(VI) **1** (= *lean*) inclinarse, ladearse • **to ~ to one side** inclinarse hacia un lado • **he ~ed back in his chair** se recostó en la silla • **to ~ over** (= *lean*) inclinarse; (= *fall*) volcarse, caer • **a lorry that ~s up** un camión basculante *or* que bascula
2 (*Hist*) justar • **to ~ against** arremeter contra

tilth [tɪlθ] (N) (= *act*) cultivo *m*, labranza *f*; (= *state*) condición *f* (cultivable) de la tierra

tilting [ˈtɪltɪŋ] (ADJ) inclinado
(CPD) ▸ **tilting train** tren *m* pendular

Tim [tɪm] (N) *familiar form of* **Timothy**

timber [ˈtɪmbəʳ] (N) (= *wood*) madera *f*; (= *growing trees*) árboles *mpl* (productores de madera); (= *beam*) viga *f*, madero *m*; (*Naut*) cuaderna *f* • **timber!** ¡tronco va!
(CPD) ▸ **timber merchant** (*Brit*) maderero *m* ▸ **timber wolf** lobo *m* gris norteamericano ▸ **timber yard** (*Brit*) almacén *m* de madera

timbered [ˈtɪmbəd] (ADJ) [*house*] (= *made of wood*) de madera; (= *with individual timbers*) con vigas de madera; [*land*] arbolado • **the land is well ~** el terreno tiene mucho bosque

timber-framed [ˈtɪmbəfreɪmd] (ADJ) con entramado de madera

timbering [ˈtɪmbərɪŋ] (N) maderamen *m*

timberland [ˈtɪmbəlænd] (N) (*US*) tierras *fpl* maderables

timberline [ˈtɪmbəlaɪn] (N) límite *m* forestal

timbre [ˈtæmbrə] (N) (*Mus*) [*of instrument, voice*] timbre *m*

timbrel [ˈtɪmbrəl] (N) pandereta *f*

Timbuktu [ˌtɪmbʌkˈtuː] (N) Timbuktú *m* • **he could be in ~ for all I know** podría estar en la conchinchina

time [taɪm] (N) **1** (*gen*) tiempo *m* • **as ~ goes on** *or* **by** con el (paso del) tiempo, a medida que pasa/pasaba el tiempo • **race against ~** carrera *f* contra (el) reloj • **for all ~** para siempre • **one of the best of all ~** uno de los mejores de todos los tiempos • **Father Time** el Tiempo • **to find (the) ~ for sth** encontrar tiempo para algo • **I can't find the ~ for reading** no encuentro tiempo para leer • **~ flies** el tiempo vuela • **how ~ flies!** ¡cómo pasa el tiempo! • **to gain ~** ganar tiempo • **half the ~ he's drunk** la mayor parte del tiempo está borracho • **to have (the) ~ (to do sth)** tener tiempo (para hacer algo) • **we have plenty of ~** tenemos tiempo de sobra • **to make ~** (*US**) ganar tiempo, apresurarse • **to make up for lost ~** recuperar el tiempo perdido • **it's only a matter** *or* **question of ~ before it falls** solo es cuestión de tiempo antes de que caiga • **I've no ~ for him** (*too busy*) no tengo tiempo para él; (*contemptuous*) no le aguanto • **I've no ~ for sport** odio los deportes • **there is no ~ to lose** no hay tiempo que perder • **he lost no ~ in doing it** no tardó en hacerlo • **my ~ is my own** yo dispongo de mi tiempo • **~ presses** el tiempo apremia • **~ is on our side** el tiempo obra a nuestro favor • **~ and space** el tiempo y el espacio • **to take ~**: • **it takes ~** requiere tiempo, lleva su tiempo • **it'll take ~ to get over the loss of her family** le llevará tiempo superar la pérdida de su familia • **it took him all his ~ to find it** solo encontrarlo le ocupó bastante tiempo • **to take one's ~** hacer las cosas con calma • **take your ~!** tómate el tiempo que necesites, ¡no hay prisa! • **you certainly took your ~!** (*iro*) ¡no es precisamente que te mataras corriendo! • **(only) ~ will tell** el tiempo lo dirá • IDIOMS: • **to have ~ on one's hands**: • **she has too much ~ on her hands** dispone de demasiado tiempo libre • **once you retire you'll have ~ on your hands** cuando te hayas jubilado, tendrás todo el tiempo del mundo • **to kill ~** entretener el tiempo, pasar el rato, matar el tiempo • **to pass the ~ of day with sb** detenerse a charlar un rato con algn • **to play for ~** tratar de ganar tiempo • **to be pressed for ~** andar escaso de tiempo • PROVERB: • **~ is money** el tiempo es oro; ▹ **spare, waste**
2 (= *period of time*) tiempo *m*, período *m*; (*relatively short*) rato *m* • **have you been here all this ~?** ¿has estado aquí todo este tiempo? • **for the ~ being** por ahora, de momento • **for a ~** durante un rato; (*longer*) durante una temporada • **a long ~** mucho tiempo • **to take a long ~ to do sth** tardar mucho en hacer algo • **a long ~ ago** hace mucho (tiempo), hace tiempo • **he hasn't been seen for a long ~** hace mucho tiempo que no se le ve • **she'll be in a wheelchair for a long ~ to come** le queda mucho tiempo de estar en silla de ruedas por delante • **in no ~ at all** en un abrir y cerrar de ojos • **it will last our ~** durará lo que nosotros • **a short ~** poco tiempo, un rato • **a short ~ ago** hace poco • **a short ~ after** poco (tiempo) después, al poco tiempo • **in a short ~ they were all gone** muy pronto habían desaparecido todos • **for some ~ past** de algún tiempo a esta parte • **after some ~ she looked up at me/wrote to me** después de cierto tiempo levantó la vista hacia mí/me escribió, pasado algún tiempo levantó la vista hacia mí/me escribió • **in a week's ~** dentro de una semana • **in two weeks' ~** en dos semanas, al cabo de dos semanas • IDIOM: • **to do ~*** cumplir una condena; ▹ **serve**
3 (*at work*) • **on Saturdays they pay ~ and a half** los sábados pagan lo normal más la mitad • **he did it in his own ~** lo hizo en su tiempo libre *or* fuera de (las) horas de trabajo • **to be on short ~** • **work short ~** trabajar en jornadas reducidas; ▹ **full-time, part-time, short-time**
4 (= *moment, point of time*) momento *m* • **I was watching TV at the ~** en ese momento estaba viendo la televisión • **from ~ to ~** de vez en cuando • **about ~ too!** ¡ya era hora! • **it's about ~ you had a haircut** ya es hora de que te cortes el pelo • **come (at) any ~ (you like)** ven cuando quieras • **it might happen (at) any ~** podría ocurrir en un momento a otro *or* en cualquier momento • **any ~ now** de un momento a otro • **at ~s** a veces, a ratos • **at all ~s** siempre, en todo momento • **to die before one's ~** morir temprano • **not before ~!** ¡ya era hora! • **between ~s** en los intervalos • **by the ~ he arrived** para cuando él llegó • **by the ~ we got there he'd left** cuando llegamos allí ya se había ido • **by this ~** ya, antes de esto • **(by) this ~ next year** el año que viene por estas fechas • **to choose one's ~ carefully** elegir con cuidado el momento más propicio • **the ~ has come to leave** ha llegado el momento de irse • **when the ~ comes** cuando llegue el momento • **at a convenient ~** en un momento oportuno • **at any given ~** en cualquier momento dado • **her ~ was drawing near** (*to give birth*) se acercaba el momento de dar a luz; (*to die*) estaba llegando al final de su vida • **it's high ~ you got a job** ya va siendo hora de que consigas un trabajo • **at my ~ of life** a mi edad, con los años que yo tengo • **at no ~ did I mention it** no lo mencioné en ningún momento • **this is no ~ for jokes** este no es momento para bromas • **now is the ~ to go** ahora es el momento de irse • **now is the ~ to plant roses** esta es la época para plantar las rosas • **at odd ~s** (= *occasionally*) de vez en cuando • **he calls at some odd ~s** llama a las horas más intempestivas • **from that ~ on** a partir de entonces, desde entonces • **at one ~** en cierto momento, en cierta época • **this is neither the ~ nor the place to discuss it** este no es ni el momento ni el lugar oportuno para hablar de eso • **there's a ~ and a place for everything** todo tiene su momento y su lugar • **at the present ~** actualmente, en la actualidad • **at the proper ~** en el momento oportuno • **at the same ~** (= *simultaneously*) al mismo tiempo, a la vez; (= *even so*) al mismo tiempo, por otro lado • **until such ~ as he agrees** hasta que consienta • **at that ~** por entonces, en aquel entonces, en aquella época • **at this particular ~** en este preciso momento • **at this ~ of the year** en esta época del año • **it's a lovely ~ of year** es una estación encantadora; ▹ **bide**
5 (*by clock*) hora *f* • **what's the ~?** ¿qué hora es? • **the ~ is 2.30** son las dos y media • **it's ~ to go** es hora de irse • **"~ gentlemen please!"** "¡se cierra!" • **to arrive ahead of ~** llegar temprano • **to be 30 minutes ahead of ~** llevar 30 minutos de adelanto • **at any ~ of the day or night** en cualquier momento *or* a cualquier hora del día o de la noche • **to be 30 minutes behind ~** llevar 30 minutos de retraso • **it's coffee ~** es la hora del café • **at this ~ of day** a esta hora • **it's ~ for the news** es (la) hora de las noticias • **it's ~ for lunch** es (la) hora de comer • **let me know in good ~** avíseme con anticipación • **make sure you get there in good ~** asegúrate de que llegas allí con tiempo • **he'll come in his own good ~** vendrá cuando le parezca conveniente • **all in good ~** todo a su (debido) tiempo • **to start in good ~** partir a tiempo, partir pronto • **have you got the (right) ~?** ¿tiene la hora (exacta)? • **Greenwich mean ~** hora *f* de Greenwich • **we were just in ~ to see it** llegamos justo a tiempo para verlo • **a watch that keeps good ~** un reloj muy exacto • **just look at the ~!** ¡fíjate qué hora es ya!, ¡mira qué tarde es! • **what ~ do you make it?** • **what do you make the ~?** ¿qué hora es *or* tiene? • **we made good ~ on the journey** el viaje ha sido rápido • **to be on ~** [*person*] ser puntual, llegar puntualmente; [*train, plane*] llegar puntual • **to tell the ~** [*clock*] dar la hora; [*child*] saber decir la hora • IDIOM: • **I wouldn't give him the ~ of day** a mí él me tiene sin cuidado; ▹ **closing, opening**
6 (= *era, period*) tiempo *m*, época *f* • **in Elizabethan ~s** en tiempos isabelinos, en la época isabelina • **in our own ~(s)** en nuestra época • **in my ~(s)** en mis tiempos • **what ~s they were!** • **what ~s we had!** ¡qué tiempos aquellos! • **one of the greatest footballers of our ~** uno de los mejores futbolistas de nuestros tiempos • **to be ahead of one's ~** adelantarse a su época • **that was all before my ~** todo eso fue antes de mis tiempos • **to be behind the ~s** [*person*] estar atrasado de noticias; [*thing, idea*] estar fuera de moda, haber quedado anticuado • **how ~s change!** ¡cómo cambian las cosas! • **in ~s to come** en tiempos venideros • **~s were hard** fueron tiempos duros • **~s are hard** atravesamos un período bastante difícil • **they fell on hard ~s** entraron en un periodo de vacas flacas • **to keep abreast of** *or* **up with the ~s** ir con los tiempos, mantenerse al día • **the ~s we live in** los tiempos en que vivimos • **in modern ~s** en tiempos modernos • **to move with the ~s** ir con los tiempos, mantenerse al día • **in olden ~s** • **in ~s past** en otro tiempo, antiguamente • **~ was when …** hubo un

tiempo en que ...; ▹ **sign**

7 (= *experience*) • **to have a bad** *or* **rough** *or* **thin ~ (of it)** pasarlo mal, pasarlas negras • **to have a good ~** pasarlo bien, divertirse • **all they want to do is have a good ~** no quieren más que divertirse • **to give sb a good ~** hacer que algn lo pase bien • **she's out for a good ~** se propone divertirse • **we had a high old ~*** lo hemos pasado en grande* • **we have a lovely ~** lo pasamos la mar de bien* • **have a nice ~!** ¡que lo pases/paséis *etc* bien! • IDIOM: • **the big ~*** el estrellato, el éxito • **to make the big ~** alcanzar el éxito, triunfar; ▹ **big-time**

8 (= *occasion*) vez *f* • **three ~s** tres veces • **I remember the ~ he came here** recuerdo la ocasión en que vino por aquí, me acuerdo de cuando vino por aquí • **~ after ~** • **~ and again** repetidas veces, una y otra vez • **to carry three boxes at a ~** llevar tres cajas a la vez • **he ran upstairs three at a ~** subió la escalera de tres en tres escalones • **for weeks at a ~** durante semanas enteras *or* seguidas • **each ~** • **every ~** cada vez • **he won every ~** ganó todas las veces • **it's the best, every ~!** ¡es el mejor, no hay duda! • **give me beer every ~!** ¡para mí, siempre cerveza! • **the first ~ I did it** la primera vez que lo hice • **for the first ~** por primera vez • **last ~** la última vez • **the last ~ I did it** la última vez que lo hice • **for the last ~** por última vez • **many ~s** muchas veces • **many's the ~ ...** no una vez, sino muchas ... • **next ~** la próxima vez, a la próxima (*esp LAm*) • **the second ~ round** (= *second marriage*) la segunda intentona de matrimonio • **several ~s** varias veces • **this ~** esta vez • **at various ~s in the past** en determinados momentos del pasado • IDIOMS: • **nine ~s out of ten** • **ninety-nine ~s out of a hundred** (*fig*) casi siempre • **third ~ lucky!** ¡a la tercera va la vencida!

9 (*Mus*) compás *m* • **in 3/4 ~** al compás de 3 por 4 • **to beat ~** marcar el compás • **in ~ to the music** al compás de la música • **to keep ~** llevar el compás • **to get out of ~** perder el compás; ▹ **beat, mark^2**

10 (*Math*) • **4 ~s 3 is 12** 4 por 3 son 12 • **it's five ~s faster than** *or* **as fast as yours** es cinco veces más rápido que el tuyo

11 (*Mech*) • **the ignition is out of ~** el encendido está fuera de fase

VT 1 (= *schedule*) planear, calcular; (= *choose time of*) [+ *remark, request*] elegir el momento para • **the race is ~d for 8.30** el comienzo de la carrera está previsto para las 8.30 • **you ~d that perfectly** elegiste a la perfección el momento para hacerlo • **the bomb was ~d to explode five minutes later** la bomba estaba sincronizada para explotar cinco minutos más tarde • **the strike was carefully ~d to cause maximum disruption** se había escogido el momento de la huelga para ocasionar el mayor trastorno posible • **the decision to sell was badly ~d** se decidió vender en un mal momento; ▹ **ill-timed, well-timed**

2 (= *reckon time of*) [+ *call, journey*] calcular la duración de; (*with stopwatch*) cronometrar • **to ~ o.s.** cronometrarse • **I ~d him doing the washing-up** le cronometré mientras lavaba los platos

CPD ▸ **time and motion study** estudio *m* de tiempos y movimientos ▸ **time bomb** bomba *f* de relojería ▸ **time capsule** cápsula *f* del tiempo ▸ **time card** tarjeta *f* de registro horario ▸ **time check** (*Sport*) control *m* de tiempos • **can I have a ~ check, please?** ¿qué hora es ahora, por favor? ▸ **time clock** reloj *m* registrador, reloj *m* de control de asistencia ▸ **time deposit** (*US*) depósito *m* a plazo ▸ **time difference** diferencia *f* horaria ▸ **time exposure** (*Phot*) exposición *f* ▸ **time frame** margen *m* de tiempo • **to set a ~ frame for sth** poner fecha a algo ▸ **time fuse** temporizador *m*, espoleta *f* graduada, espoleta *f* de tiempo ▸ **time lag** (= *delay*) retraso *m*; (= *lack of synchronization*) desfase *m* ▸ **time limit** plazo *m*, límite *m* de tiempo; (= *closing date*) fecha *f* tope • **to set a ~ limit (for sth)** fijar un plazo (para algo) ▸ **time loan** (*US*) préstamo *m* a plazo fijo ▸ **time lock** cerradura *f* de tiempo ▸ **time machine** máquina *f* de transporte a través del tiempo ▸ **time management** gestión *f* del tiempo ▸ **time management consultant** consultor(a) *m/f* de gestión del tiempo ▸ **time management course** curso *m* de gestión del tiempo ▸ **time management skills** técnicas *fpl* de gestión del tiempo ▸ **time management training** formación *f* en gestión del tiempo ▸ **time off** (= *free time*) tiempo *m* libre • **to take ~ off from work** tomarse tiempo libre • **you'll have to take some ~ off when your wife has her operation** tendrás que tomarte unos días de vacaciones cuando operen a tu mujer ▸ **time out** (*esp US*) (*Sport*) (*also fig*) tiempo *m* muerto • **to take ~ out (from sth/from doing sth)** descansar (de algo/de hacer algo) ▸ **time payment** (*US*) pago *m* a plazos ▸ **time saver** • **it is a great ~ saver** ahorra mucho tiempo ▸ **time sheet** = **time card** ▸ **time signal** señal *f* horaria ▸ **time signature** (*Mus*) compás *m*, signatura *f* de compás ▸ **time slice** fracción *f* de tiempo ▸ **time slot** franja *f* horaria ▸ **time span** periodo *m* de tiempo ▸ **time switch** interruptor *m* horario ▸ **time trial** (*Cycling*) prueba *f* contra reloj, contrarreloj *f* ▸ **time warp** salto *m* en el tiempo, túnel *m* del tiempo ▸ **time zone** huso *m* horario

time-consuming ['taɪmkən,sjuːmɪŋ] ADJ que requiere mucho tiempo

time-honoured, time-honored (*US*) ['taɪm,ɒnəd] ADJ consagrado

timekeeper ['taɪm,kiːpəʳ] N 1 (= *watch*) reloj *m*, cronómetro *m*
2 (= *official*) cronometrador(a) *m/f*
3 • **to be a good ~** (= *punctual*) ser puntual • **to be a poor ~** (= *not punctual*) no ser nada puntual

timekeeping ['taɪm,kiːpɪŋ] N (*gen*) cronometraje *m*; (*in factory etc*) control *m* • **her ~ has always been very good** siempre ha sido muy puntual

time-lapse photography ['taɪmlæpsfə'tɒgrəfɪ] N fotografía *f* de lapso de tiempo

timeless ['taɪmlɪs] ADJ [*book, experience*] intemporal

timelessly ['taɪmlɪslɪ] ADV • **a ~ beautiful building** un edificio de una belleza intemporal • **a ~ elegant restaurant** un restaurante de una elegancia intemporal

timelessness ['taɪmlɪsnɪs] N intemporalidad *f*, atemporalidad *f*

time-limited ['taɪm,lɪmɪtɪd] ADJ temporal

timeline ['taɪmlaɪn] N 1 (= *time frame*) calendario *m*
2 (= *historical diagram*) línea *f* del tiempo

timeliness ['taɪmlɪnɪs] N oportunidad *f*

timely ['taɪmlɪ] ADJ oportuno

timepiece ['taɪmpiːs] N reloj *m*

time-poor [,taɪm'pʊəʳ] ADJ (= *lacking in time*) sin tiempo • **people are becoming increasingly time-poor** la gente tiene cada vez menos tiempo

timer ['taɪməʳ] N 1 (= *egg timer*) reloj *m* de arena
2 (*Aut*) distribuidor *m*; (*Tech*) reloj *m* automático; (= *regulator*) temporizador *m*

time-saving ['taɪm,seɪvɪŋ] ADJ que ahorra tiempo

timescale ['taɪmskeɪl] N escala *f* de tiempo

time-server ['taɪm,sɜːvəʳ] N (*pej*) contemporizador *m*

time-share ['taɪmʃɛəʳ] N 1 (*for holiday*) multipropiedad *f*
2 (*Comput*) tiempo *m* compartido
VT (*Comput*) utilizar colectivamente, utilizar en sistema de tiempo compartido
CPD ▸ **time-share apartment** piso *m* en multipropiedad

time-sharing ['taɪm,ʃɛərɪŋ] N 1 (*for holiday*) multipropiedad *f*
2 (*Comput*) tiempo *m* compartido

timetable ['taɪm,teɪbl] N (*for trains, buses*) horario *m*; (= *programme of events etc*) programa *m*, agenda *f*; [*of negotiations*] calendario *m*; (*Scol*) horario *m*; (*as booklet*) guía *f*, horario *m*
VT (*Brit*) programar

timetabling ['taɪmteɪblɪŋ] N programación *f*

time-waster ['taɪm,weɪstəʳ] N (= *activity*) pérdida *f* de tiempo • **to be a time-waster** (= *person*) ser de los que pierden el tiempo

time-wasting ['taɪmweɪstɪŋ] ADJ que hace perder tiempo

time-worn ['taɪmwɔːn] ADJ [*building*] deteriorado por el tiempo; [*custom, method*] añejo; [*anecdote, phrase*] gastado

timid ['tɪmɪd] ADJ [*person*] tímido; [*animal*] huraño, asustadizo

timidity [tɪ'mɪdɪtɪ] N timidez *f*

timidly ['tɪmɪdlɪ] ADV tímidamente

timidness ['tɪmɪdnɪs] N timidez *f*

timing ['taɪmɪŋ] N 1 (= *time chosen*) • **the ~ of the meeting was inconvenient** la hora fijada para la reunión no era muy conveniente • **the ~ of this is important** es importante hacer esto en el momento exacto • **it's all a matter of ~** todo es cuestión de elegir el momento oportuno • **that was good/bad ~** (= *opportunity*) lo hiciste en buen/mal momento; (= *on time*) lo hiciste a tiempo/destiempo
2 (*Sport*) cronometraje *m*
3 (= *rhythm*) ritmo *m*, cadencia *f*, compás *m*
CPD (*Mech, Aut*) de distribución, de encendido ▸ **timing device** [*of bomb*] temporizador *m* ▸ **timing gear** engranaje *m* de distribución ▸ **timing mechanism** dispositivo *m* para medir el tiempo

Timor ['tiːmɔː] N Timor *m*

Timorese ['tɪməriːz] ADJ timorés
N timorés/esa *m/f*

timorous ['tɪmərəs] ADJ (*liter*) [*person*] temeroso, tímido; [*animal*] huraño, asustadizo

Timothy ['tɪməθɪ] N Timoteo

timpani ['tɪmpənɪ] NPL (*Mus*) tímpanos *mpl*, timbales *mpl*

timpanist ['tɪmpənɪst] N timbalero/a *m/f*

tin [tɪn] N 1 (= *ore*) estaño *m*; (= *metal*) hojalata *f*
2 (*Brit*) (= *container*) lata *f*, bote *m* • **meat in tins** carne *f* en lata *or* enlatada
VT 1 (*Brit*) [+ *food*] enlatar
2 (= *coat with tin*) estañar
CPD [*roof, tray, trunk*] de hojalata ▸ **tin can** lata *f*, bote *m* ▸ **tin ear** (*Mus*) • **he has a tin ear** tiene mal oído ▸ **tin god** (*fig*) héroe *m* de cartón ▸ **tin hat** casco *m* de acero ▸ **tin lizzie*** (*Aut*) genoveva *f*, viejo trasto *m* ▸ **tin mine** mina *f* de estaño ▸ **tin miner** minero/a *m/f* de estaño ▸ **tin opener** (*Brit*) abrelatas *m inv* ▸ **Tin Pan Alley** (*Mus*) industria *f* de la música pop ▸ **tin plate** hojalata *f* ▸ **tin**

soldier soldadito *m* de plomo ▸ **tin tack** (*Brit*) tachuela *f* ▸ **tin whistle** (*Mus*) pito *m*

tincture ['tɪŋktʃəʳ] N tintura *f*
VT tinturar, teñir (**with** de)

tinder ['tɪndəʳ] N (*lit, fig*) yesca *f* • IDIOM: • **to burn like ~** arder como la yesca

tinderbox ['tɪndəbɒks] N yescas *fpl*; (*fig*) polvorín *m*

tinder-dry [ˌtɪndə'draɪ] ADJ muy seco, reseco

tine [taɪn] N [*of fork*] diente *m*; [*of pitchfork*] púa *f*

tinfoil ['tɪnfɔɪl] N papel *m* de estaño

ting [tɪŋ] = **tinkle**

ting-a-ling ['tɪŋə'lɪŋ] N tilín *m* • **to go ting-a-ling** hacer tilín

tinge [tɪndʒ] N **1** [*of colour*] tinte *m*, matiz *m*
2 (*fig*) [*of irony, sadness*] deje *m*, matiz *m* • **a ~ of nostalgia** cierta nostalgia • **not without a ~ of regret** no sin cierto arrepentimiento
VT **1** (*lit*) teñir, matizar (**with** de)
2 (*fig*) matizar (**with** de) • **pleasure ~d with sadness** placer *m* matizado *or* no exento de tristeza

tingle ['tɪŋgl] N [*of skin*] hormigueo *m*; (= *thrill*) estremecimiento *m*
VI [*ears*] zumbar • **her cheeks were tingling after a walk in the snow** después de pasear por la nieve le ardían las mejillas • **your skin will ~ a bit when you apply the cream** te escocerá un poco la piel al aplicar la crema • **to ~ with excitement** estremecerse de emoción

tingling ['tɪŋglɪŋ] N hormigueo *m*
ADJ • **a ~ sensation** una sensación de hormigueo

tingly ['tɪŋglɪ] ADJ • **a ~ feeling** una sensación de hormigueo • **my arm feels ~** siento hormigueo en el brazo • **I feel ~ all over** se me estremece todo el cuerpo

tinker ['tɪŋkəʳ] N (*esp Brit*) **1** (= *mender*) calderero *m*; (*pej*) (= *gipsy*) gitano *m*
2 (*Brit*†*) (= *child*) pícaro/a *m/f*, tunante/a *m/f* • **you little ~!** ¡tunante!
VI (*also* **tinker about**) • **to ~ with** toquetear, jugar con • **he's been ~ing with the car all day** ha pasado todo el día tratando de reparar el coche • **they're only ~ing with the problem** no se esfuerzan seriamente por resolver el problema

tinkle ['tɪŋkl] N **1** [*of bell etc*] tintín *m*, tintineo *m*
2 (*Brit*) (*Telec**) llamada *f* • **give me a ~ some time** llámame *or* pégame un telefonazo algún día
VI tintinear
VT hacer tintinear

tinkling ['tɪŋklɪŋ] ADJ que hace tilín • **a ~ sound** un tilín • **a ~ stream** un arroyo cantarín
N tintineo *m*, tilín *m*

tinned [tɪnd] ADJ (*Brit*) en *or* de lata, enlatado • **~ peaches** melocotones *mpl* en lata *or* en conserva

tinnitus [tɪ'naɪtəs] N tinnitus *m*, zumbido *m*

tinny ['tɪnɪ] ADJ (COMPAR: **tinnier**, SUPERL: **tinniest**) **1** (= *metallic*) [*sound*] metálico; [*taste*] que sabe a lata
2 (*pej*) [*car, machine*] poco sólido, de pacotilla

tinpot* ['tɪnpɒt] ADJ de pacotilla, de poca monta

tinsel ['tɪnsəl] N (*lit, fig*) oropel *m*; (= *cloth*) lama *f* de oro/plata
ADJ de oropel; (*fig*) de oropel, de relumbrón

Tinseltown ['tɪnsəltaʊn] N (*gen pej*) Hollywood *m*

tinsmith ['tɪnsmɪθ] N hojalatero/a *m/f*

tint [tɪnt] N (*gen*) tono *m*, matiz *m*; (*for hair*) tinte *m*
VT teñir, matizar • **to ~ sth blue** teñir *or* matizar algo de azul • **it's yellow ~ed with red** es amarillo matizado de rojo • **to ~ one's hair** teñirse el pelo

tinted ['tɪntɪd] ADJ [*glass, windscreen*] tintado; [*spectacles*] ahumado; [*hair*] teñido

-tinted ['tɪntɪd] SUFFIX • **he wore green-tinted glasses** llevaba gafas ahumadas de color verde

tintinnabulation ['tɪntɪˌnæbjʊ'leɪʃən] N (*liter*) campanilleo *m*

tiny ['taɪnɪ] ADJ (COMPAR: **tinier**, SUPERL: **tiniest**) diminuto, minúsculo

tip¹ [tɪp] N **1** (= *end*) [*of knife, paintbrush, finger, nose*] punta *f*; [*of shoe, boot*] puntera *f* • **he stood on the tips of his toes** se puso de puntillas • **he touched it with the tip of his toe** lo tocó con la punta del pie • **from tip to toe** de pies a cabeza • **the southern tip of Florida** el extremo sur de Florida • IDIOMS: • **it's only the tip of the iceberg** no es más que la punta del iceberg • **I had it** *or* **it was on the tip of my tongue** lo tenía en la punta de la lengua; ▹ **asparagus**
2 (= *protective piece*) [*of umbrella*] contera *f*
3 (= *filter*) [*of cigarette*] filtro *m*

tip² [tɪp] N **1** (= *gratuity*) propina *f* • **to give sb a tip** dar una propina a algn • **to leave (sb) a tip** dejar propina (a algn)
2 (= *hint*) consejo *m*; (*Racing, Gambling*) pronóstico *m* • **to give sb a tip** dar un consejo a algn • **let me give you a tip** déjame que te dé un consejo • **take a tip from an old friend and leave well alone** acepta un consejo de un viejo amigo y mantente bien alejado • **a hot tip*** (*Racing, Gambling*) un pronóstico fiable
VT **1** [+ *driver, waiter*] dar una propina a • **she tipped the barman ten dollars** le dio diez dólares de propina *or* una propina de diez dólares al barman • **I never know how much to tip** nunca sé cuánto dar de propina
2 (*Racing, Gambling*) • **to tip the winner** pronosticar quién va a ganar • **her horse was tipped to win** se pronosticaba que su caballo sería el ganador • **they are tipped to win the next election** son los favoritos para ganar las próximas elecciones • **he is already being tipped as a future prime minister** ya se habla de él como de un futuro primer ministro
VI (= *give gratuity*) dar propina

▸ **tip off** VT + ADV (= *forewarn*) (*gen*) avisar; [+ *police*] dar el soplo a*, dar el chivatazo a (*Sp**) • **the police had been tipped off** a la policía le habían dado el soplo *or* el chivatazo*, la policía había recibido un soplo*

tip³ [tɪp] N **1** (= *rubbish dump*) vertedero *m*, basurero *m*, basural *m* (*LAm*), tiradero(s) *m(pl)* (*Mex*)
2 (*Brit**) (= *mess*) • **this room is a tip** este cuarto es una pocilga*
VT **1** (= *tilt*) inclinar • **he tipped the soup bowl towards him** inclinó el cuenco de sopa hacia sí • **to tip sb off their seat** quitar a algn de su asiento (inclinándolo) • **tip the cat off the chair** inclina un poco la silla para que se baje el gato • **to tip one's hat to sb** saludar a algn con el sombrero *or* ladeando el sombrero • IDIOMS: • **to tip the balance** *or* **scales (in sb's favour/against sb)** inclinar la balanza (a favor de algn/en contra de algn) • **to tip sb over the edge** (*into insanity*) sumir algn en la locura; ▹ **scales²**
2 (= *pour*) • **to tip sth into sth: tip the vegetables into a bowl** eche las verduras en un cuenco • **they tip the rubbish into the river** vierten *or* tiran la basura en el río • **he tipped some sweets into her hand** le echó unos caramelos en la mano • **she tipped her things out of the suitcase** volcó la maleta y sacó sus cosas
VI **1** (= *incline*) inclinarse, ladearse; (= *topple*) (*also* **tip over**) volcarse, voltearse (*LAm*)
2 (= *dump rubbish*) tirar *or* (*LAm*) botar basura • **"no tipping"** "prohibido arrojar basura"
3 • IDIOM: • **it's tipping (down)*** está diluviando*

▸ **tip away** VT + ADV tirar, botar (*LAm*)

▸ **tip back** VT + ADV [+ *chair*] inclinar hacia atrás; [+ *one's head*] echar hacia atrás
VI + ADV [*chair*] inclinarse hacia atrás

▸ **tip forward, tip forwards** VT + ADV inclinar hacia delante
VI + ADV [*seat*] inclinarse hacia delante

▸ **tip out** VT + ADV [+ *contents*] verter; [+ *container*] vaciar

▸ **tip over** VI + ADV [*chair, vehicle*] volcar, volcarse, voltearse (*LAm*)
VT + ADV volcar

▸ **tip up** VI + ADV [*seat*] levantarse; [*lorry*] bascular
VT + ADV [+ *chair*] levantar, alzar; [+ *container*] volcar • **she tipped up her chin defiantly** alzó la barbilla con gesto desafiante

tip⁴ [tɪp] N (= *tap*) golpecito *m*
VT (= *tap, touch*) tocar ligeramente

tip-off ['tɪpɒf] N (= *warning*) información *f*, advertencia *f*; (*to police*) soplo* *m*, chivatazo *m* (*Sp**)

tipped [tɪpt] ADJ [*cigarette*] con filtro • **the end of the walking stick was ~ with metal** la contera del bastón era de metal • **they use arrows which are ~ with poison** utilizan flechas con las puntas envenenadas • **the parrots' wings were ~ with red** los loros tenían los extremos de las alas de color rojo

-tipped [tɪpt] ADJ (*ending in compounds*) • **a gold-tipped cane** un bastón con la contera de oro • **the black-tipped wings of the albatross** las alas de puntas negras *or* negras en los extremos de los albatros

tipper ['tɪpəʳ] N **1** (= *vehicle*) volquete *m*
2 (= *person*) • **he is a good** *or* **big ~** es de los que dejan buenas propinas
CPD ▸ **tipper truck** volquete *m*

tippet ['tɪpɪt] N esclavina *f*

Tipp-Ex® ['tɪpeks] N Tippex® *m*, corrector *m*
VT (*also* **Tipp-Ex out, Tipp-Ex over**) corregir con Tippex

tipping ['tɪpɪŋ] N **1** (= *leaving a gratuity*) • **~ is customary here** aquí dar propina es habitual • **he doesn't believe in ~** no cree en las propinas • **a 10 percent service charge is added in lieu of ~** se añade un 10% en lugar de la propina
2 (= *dumping rubbish*) vertido *m* de residuos

tipple* ['tɪpl] (*Brit*) N • **his ~ is Cointreau** él bebe Cointreau • **what's your ~?** ¿qué quieres tomar?
VI empinar el codo

tippler* ['tɪpləʳ] N (*Brit*) amante *mf* de la bebida • **he's a bit of a ~** le gusta tomar un trago de vez en cuando

tippy-toe ['tɪpɪtəʊ] (*US*) = **tiptoe**

tipsily ['tɪpsɪlɪ] ADV como borracho • **to walk ~** andar con pasos de borracho

tipster ['tɪpstəʳ] N pronosticador(a) *m/f*

tipsy ['tɪpsɪ] ADJ (COMPAR: **tipsier**, SUPERL: **tipsiest**) achispado, piripi (*Sp**), tomado (*LAm**)

tiptoe ['tɪptəʊ] N • **to walk on ~** andar *or* (*LAm*) caminar de puntillas • **to stand on ~** ponerse de puntillas
VI ir de puntillas • **to ~ to the window** ir de puntillas a la ventana • **to ~ across the floor** cruzar el cuarto de puntillas • **to ~ in/out** entrar/salir de puntillas

t

tiptop ['tɪp'tɒp] (ADJ) de primera, excelente • **in ~ condition** [*car*] en excelentes condiciones; [*person*] en plena forma • **a ~ show** un espectáculo de primerísima calidad
tip-truck ['tɪptrʌk] (N) volquete *m*
tip-up ['tɪpʌp] (ADJ) [*truck*] con volquete; [*seat*] abatible
tirade [taɪ'reɪd] (N) diatriba *f*
tire[1] ['taɪəʳ] (VT) cansar
(VI) cansarse • **he ~s easily** se cansa fácilmente • **to ~ of sb/sth** cansarse *or* aburrirse de algn/algo
▸ **tire out** (VT + ADV) agotar, dejar rendido
tire[2] ['taɪəʳ] (N) (*US*) = **tyre**
tired ['taɪəd] (ADJ) **1** [*person, eyes*] cansado; [*voice*] cansino • **to be/feel ~** estar/sentirse cansado • **my legs/eyes are ~** tengo las piernas cansadas/los ojos cansados • **to get ~** cansarse • **to look ~** tener cara de cansancio • **to be ~ of sb/sth** estar cansado *or* aburrido de algn/algo • **to get** *or* **grow ~ of (doing) sth** cansarse *or* aburrirse de (hacer) algo • **to be ~ out** estar agotado *or* rendido; ▹ **sick**
2 (*fig*) (= *worn-out*) [*coat*] raído, gastado; [*car, chair*] cascado; [*cliché, ritual, excuse*] manido, trillado • **a ~ lettuce leaf** una hoja de lechuga mustia • **it's a ~ old cliché** es un tópico muy manido *or* trillado
tiredly ['taɪədlɪ] (ADV) [*smile, get up*] con aire cansado; [*say, reply*] con voz cansina
tiredness ['taɪədnɪs] (N) cansancio *m*
tireless ['taɪəlɪs] (ADJ) [*person, work*] incansable, infatigable
tirelessly ['taɪəlɪslɪ] (ADV) incansablemente, infatigablemente
tiresome ['taɪəsəm] (ADJ) [*job, situation, person*] pesado, aburrido
tiring ['taɪərɪŋ] (ADJ) cansado, cansador (*S. Cone*) • **it's very ~** es muy cansado
tiro ['taɪərəʊ] (N) = **tyro**
Tirol [tɪ'rəʊl] = **Tyrol**
tisane [tɪ'zæn] (N) tisana *f*
tissue ['tɪʃuː] (N) **1** (= *thin paper*) (*for wrapping, decoration*) papel *m* de seda; (= *paper handkerchief*) pañuelo *m* de papel, klínex *m inv*
2 (*Anat*) tejido *m*
3 (*fig*) • **a ~ of lies** una sarta de mentiras
(CPD) ▸ **tissue paper** (*for wrapping, decoration*) papel *m* de seda; (= *paper handkerchief*) pañuelo *m* de papel, klínex® *m inv*
tit[1] [tɪt] (N) (= *bird*) paro *m*, herrerillo *m* • **blue tit** herrerillo *m* común, alionín *m* • **coal tit** carbonero *m* garrapinos • **long-tailed tit** mito *m*
tit[2] [tɪt] (N) • IDIOM: • **tit for tat** ojo por ojo • **so that was tit for tat** así que ajustamos cuentas, así que le pagué en la misma moneda • **tit-for-tat killing** asesinato *m* en represalia, (asesinato *m* por) ajuste *m* de cuentas
tit[3]*‡ [tɪt] (N) **1** (= *breast*) teta* *f* • IDIOM: • **to get on sb's tits***‡ sacar de quicio a algn, cabrear a algn*
2 (= *person*) gilipollas‡ *m*
Titan ['taɪtən] (N) titán *m*
titanic [taɪ'tænɪk] (ADJ) [*struggle*] titánico; [*scale, proportions*] inmenso, gigantesco
titanium [tɪ'teɪnɪəm] (N) titanio *m*
titbit ['tɪtbɪt], **tidbit** ['tɪdbɪt] (*US*) (N) [*of food*] golosina *f*; [*of gossip*] cotilleo *m*
titch* [tɪtʃ] (N) enano/a* *m/f*, renacuajo* *m*
titchy* ['tɪtʃɪ] (ADJ) pequeñito*, chiquitito*
titfer†‡ ['tɪtfəʳ] (N) (*Brit*) sombrero *m*
tithe [taɪð] (N) diezmo *m*
Titian ['tɪʃɪən] (N) Ticiano
titillate ['tɪtɪleɪt] (VT) [+ *audience, reader*] despertar el interés de; (*sexually*) excitar
titillating ['tɪtɪleɪtɪŋ] (ADJ) (= *stimulating*) estimulante; (*sexually*) excitante
titillation [,tɪtɪ'leɪʃən] (N) [*of audience, reader*] estimulación *f*; (*sexual*) excitación *f*
titivate ['tɪtɪveɪt] (VT) emperejilar, arreglar • **to ~ o.s.** emperejilarse, arreglarse
(VI) emperejilarse, arreglarse
title ['taɪtl] (N) **1** [*of book, chapter*] título *m*; (= *headline*) titular *m*, cabecera *f* • **what ~ are you giving the book?** ¿qué título vas a dar al libro?, ¿cómo vas a titular el libro?
2 (= *form of address*) fórmula *f* de tratamiento, tratamiento *m*; [*of nobility etc*] título *m* • **what ~ should I give him?** ¿qué tratamiento debo darle? • **noble ~** • **~ of nobility** título *m* de nobleza • **George V gave him a ~** Jorge V le dio un título de nobleza *or* le ennobleció • **what's your job ~?** ¿cómo se llama *or* qué nombre recibe tu puesto?
3 (*Sport*) título *m* • **to hold a ~** ser campeón/ona *m/f*, tener un título
4 (*Publishing*) (= *book, periodical*) título *m*, publicación *f*
5 (*Jur*) (= *right*) derecho *m* • **his ~ to the property** su derecho a la propiedad
6 titles (*Cine, TV*) créditos *mpl* • **the opening/closing ~s** créditos *mpl* iniciales/finales
(VT) titular, intitular (*frm*)
(CPD) ▸ **title deed** (*Jur*) título *m* de propiedad ▸ **title fight** combate *m* por el título ▸ **title holder** (*Sport*) campeón/ona *m/f* ▸ **title page** portada *f* ▸ **title role** (*Theat, Cine*) papel *m* principal ▸ **title track** (*Mus*) corte *m* que da nombre al álbum
titled ['taɪtld] (ADJ) [*person*] con título de nobleza
-titled [-,taɪtld] (SUFFIX) • **an oddly-titled book** un libro con un título extraño
titmouse ['tɪtmaʊs] (N) (PL: **titmice** ['tɪtmaɪs]) paro *m*
titrate ['taɪtreɪt] (VT) valorar
titration [taɪ'treɪʃən] (N) valoración *f*
titter ['tɪtəʳ] (N) (= *snigger*) risa *f* tonta
(VI) reírse tontamente
tittering ['tɪtərɪŋ] (N) risitas *fpl* tontas
tittle ['tɪtl] (N) pizca *f*, ápice *m* • **there's not a ~ of truth in it** eso no tiene ni pizca de verdad
tittle-tattle* ['tɪtl,tætl] (N) chismes *mpl*
(VI) chismear
titty‡ ['tɪtɪ] (N) teta* *f* • IDIOM: • **that's tough ~!** ¡mala suerte!
titular ['tɪtjʊləʳ] (ADJ) titular; (= *in name only*) nominal
tiz* [tɪz] (N) = **tizzy**
tizzy* ['tɪzɪ] (N) • **to be in/get into a ~ (about sth)** (= *nervous*) estar/ponerse nervioso (por algo); (= *hassled*) estar hecho/hacerse un lío (por algo)
T-junction ['tiː,dʒʌŋkʃən] (N) (*Aut*) cruce *m* en T
TLC (N ABBR) = **tender loving care**
TLS (N ABBR) (*Brit*) (= **Times Literary Supplement**) *revista literaria*
TM (N ABBR) **1** = **transcendental meditation**
2 (*Comm*) = **trademark**
TN (ABBR) (*US*) = **Tennessee**
TNT (N ABBR) (= **trinitrotoluene**) TNT *m*

to [tʊ, tuː, tə]

PREPOSITION
INFINITIVE PARTICLE
ADVERB

PREPOSITION

When **to** *is the second element in a phrasal verb, eg* **set to, heave to**, *look up the phrasal verb.*

When **to** *is part of a set combination, eg* **nice to, to my mind, to all appearances, appeal to**, *look up the other word.*

1 (*destination*) a

Note: **a + el = al**

• **it's 90 kilometres to Lima** de aquí a Lima hay 90 kilómetros, hay 90 kilómetros a Lima • **a letter to his wife** una carta a su mujer • **he fell to the floor** cayó al suelo • **to go to Paris/Spain** ir a París/España • **to go to Peru** ir al Perú • **to go to school/university** ir al colegio/a la Universidad • **to go to the doctor's** ir al médico • **I liked the exhibition, I went to it twice** me gustó la exposición, fui a verla dos veces • **we're going to John's/my parents' for Christmas** vamos a casa de John/mis padres por Navidad • **have you ever been to India?** ¿has estado alguna vez en la India? • **flights to Heathrow** vuelos a *or* con destino a Heathrow • **the road to Edinburgh** la carretera de Edimburgo; ▹ **church**
2 (= *towards*) hacia • **he walked slowly to the door** caminó despacio hacia la puerta • **he turned to me** se giró hacia mí • **move it to the left/right** muévelo hacia la izquierda/derecha
3 (= *as far as*) hasta • **from here to London** de aquí a *or* hasta Londres • **I'll see you to the door** te acompaño hasta la puerta
4 (= *up to*) hasta • **to count to ten** contar hasta diez • **it's accurate to (within) a millimetre** es exacto hasta el milímetro • **to some extent** hasta cierto punto, en cierta medida • **we are expecting 40 to 50 people** esperamos entre 40 y 50 personas • **to this day I still don't know what he meant** aún hoy no sé lo que quiso decir • **eight years ago to the day** hoy hace exactamente ocho años • **he didn't stay to the end** no se quedó hasta el final • **from Monday to Friday** de lunes a viernes • **from morning to night** de la mañana a la noche, desde la mañana hasta la noche • **funds to the value of ...** fondos por valor de ...; ▹ **decimal**
5 (= *located at*) a • **the door is to the left (of the window)** la puerta está a la izquierda (de la ventana) • **the airport is to the west of the city** el aeropuerto está al oeste de la ciudad
6 (= *against*) contra • **he stood with his back to the wall** estaba con la espalda contra la pared • **he clasped her to him** la estrechó contra sí • **to turn a picture to the wall** volver un cuadro mirando a la pared
7 (*when telling time*) • **it's a quarter to three** son las tres menos cuarto, es *or* (*LAm*) falta un cuarto para las tres • **at eight minutes to ten** a las diez menos ocho
8 (*introducing indirect object*) a • **to give sth to sb** dar algo a algn • **I gave it to my friend** se lo di a mi amigo • **the man I sold it to** *or* (*frm*) **to whom I sold it** el hombre a quien se lo vendí • **it belongs to me** me pertenece (a mí), es mío • **they were kind to me** fueron amables conmigo • **it's new to me** es nuevo para mí • **what is that to me?** ¿y a mí qué me importa eso? • **"that's strange," I said to myself** —es raro —me dije para mis adentros
9 (*in dedications, greetings*) • **greetings to all our friends!** ¡saludos a todos los amigos! • **welcome to you all!** ¡bienvenidos todos! • **"to P.R. Lilly"** (*in book*) "para P.R. Lilly" • **here's to you!** ¡va por ti!, ¡por ti! • **a monument to the fallen** un monumento a los caídos, un monumento en honor a los caídos

10 (*in ratios, proportions*) por • **there were three men to a cell** había tres hombres por celda • **it does 30 miles to the gallon** hace 30 millas por galón • **eight apples to the kilo** ocho manzanas por kilo • **there are about five pesos to the dollar** son unos cinco pesos por dólar • **a scale of 1 centimetre to 1 kilometre** una escala de 1 centímetro por kilómetro • **200 people to the square mile** 200 personas por milla cuadrada • **the odds are 8 to 1** las probabilidades son de 8 a 1 • **the odds against it happening are a million to one** las probabilidades de que eso ocurra son una entre un millón • **by a majority of 12 to 10** por una mayoría de 12 a 10 • **they won by four goals to two** ganaron por cuatro goles a dos • **three to the fourth** • **three to the power of four** (*Math*) tres a la cuarta potencia

11 (*in comparisons*) a • **superior to the others** superior a los demás • **A is to B as C is to D** A es a B como C es a D • **that's nothing to what is to come** eso no es nada en comparación con lo que está por venir

12 (*= about, concerning*) • **what do you say to that?** ¿qué te parece (eso)? • **what would you say to a beer?** ¿te parece que tomemos una cerveza? • **"to repairing pipes: ..."** (*on bill*) "reparación de las cañerías: ..."

13 (*= according to*) según • **to my way of thinking** a mi modo de ver, según mi modo de pensar

14 (*= to the accompaniment of*) • **we danced to the music of the band** bailamos con la música de la orquesta • **they came out to the strains of the national anthem** salieron a los compases del himno nacional • **it is sung to the tune of "Tipperary"** se canta con la melodía de "Tipperary"

15 (*= of, for*) de • **the key to the front door** la llave de la puerta principal • **assistant to the manager** asistente del gerente • **he was a good father to the children** fue un buen padre para sus hijos • **it offers a solution to your problem** te ofrece una solución para el problema • **we've found the solution to the problem** hemos encontrado solución al problema • **the British ambassador to Moscow** el embajador británico en Moscú • **he has been a good friend to us** ha sido un buen amigo para nosotros

16 (*with gerund/noun*) • **to look forward to doing sth** tener muchas ganas de hacer algo • **I'm really looking forward to the holidays** estoy deseando que lleguen las vacaciones • **to prefer painting to drawing** preferir pintar a dibujar • **to be used to (doing) sth** estar acostumbrado a (hacer) algo

17 (*in set expressions*) • **to this end** a *or* con este fin • **to my enormous shame I did nothing** para gran vergüenza mía, no hice nada • **to my great surprise** con gran sorpresa por mi parte, para gran sorpresa mía

(INFINITIVE PARTICLE)

1 (*infinitive*) • **to come** venir • **to sing** cantar • **to work** trabajar

2 (*following another verb*) **a**

A preposition may be required with the Spanish infinitive, depending on what precedes it: look up the verb.

• **she refused to listen** se negó a escuchar • **to start to cry** empezar *or* ponerse a llorar • **to try to do sth** tratar de hacer algo, intentar hacer algo • **to want to do sth** querer hacer algo

b (*object as subject of following infinitive*) • **I'd advise you to think this over** te aconsejaría que te pensaras bien esto • **he'd like me to give up work** le gustaría que dejase de trabajar • **we'd prefer him to go to university** preferiríamos que fuese a la universidad • **I want you to do it** quiero que lo hagas

c • **I have things to do** tengo cosas que hacer • **he has a lot to lose** tiene mucho que perder • **there was no one for me to ask** • **there wasn't anyone for me to ask** no había nadie a quien yo pudiese preguntar • **he's not the sort** *or* **type to do that** no es de los que hacen eso • **that book is still to be written** ese libro está todavía por escribir • **now is the time to do it** ahora es el momento de hacerlo • **and who is he to criticize?** ¿y quién es él para criticar?

3 (*purpose, result*) para • **he did it to help you** lo hizo para ayudarte • **I have done nothing to deserve this** no he hecho nada para merecer esto • **it disappeared, never to be seen again** desapareció para siempre • **I arrived to find she had gone** cuando llegué me encontré con que se había ido • **he came to see you** vino a verte • **he's gone to get the paper** ha ido a por el periódico

4 (*standing in for verb*)

*The particle **to** is not translated when it stands for the infinitive:*

• **we didn't want to sell it but we had to** no queríamos venderlo pero tuvimos que hacerlo *or* no hubo más remedio • **"would you like to come to dinner?" — "I'd love to!"** —¿te gustaría venir a cenar? —¡me encantaría! • **you may not want to do it but you ought to for the sake of your education** tal vez no quieres hacerlo pero deberías en aras de tu educación • **I don't want to** no quiero • **I forgot to** se me olvidó

5 (*after adjective*)

*For combinations like **difficult/easy/foolish/ready/slow to** etc, look up the adjective.*

• **it is very expensive to live in London** resulta muy caro vivir en Londres • **it's hard to describe the feeling** es difícil describir la sensación • **these dogs are hard to control** estos perros son difíciles de controlar • **the first/last to go** el primero/último en irse • **he's young to be a grandfather** es joven para ser abuelo; ▹ EASY, DIFFICULT, IMPOSSIBLE

6 (*in exclamations*) • **and then to be let down like that!** ¡y para que luego te decepcionen así! • **and to think he didn't mean a word of it!** ¡y pensar que nada de lo que dijo era de verdad!

7 • **to see him now one would never think that ...** al verlo *or* viéndolo ahora nadie creería que ...

(ADVERB)

• **to pull the door to** tirar de la puerta para cerrarla, cerrar la puerta tirando • **to push the door to** empujar la puerta para cerrarla, cerrar la puerta empujando

toad [təʊd] (N) sapo *m*

toadflax [ˈtəʊdflæks] (N) linaria *f*

toad-in-the-hole [ˌtəʊdɪnðəˈhəʊl] (N) (*Brit*) (*Culin*) salchichas *fpl* en pasta

toadstool [ˈtəʊdstuːl] (N) hongo *m* venenoso

toady [ˈtəʊdɪ] (*pej*) (N) adulador(a) *m/f*, pelotilla* *mf inv*, pelota* *mf*
(VI) • **to ~ to sb** adular *or* hacer la pelotilla a algn*, dar coba a algn*

toadying [ˈtəʊdɪɪŋ], **toadyism** [ˈtəʊdɪɪzəm] (N) adulación *f* servil, coba* *f*

toast [təʊst] (N) **1** (*= bread*) pan *m* tostado, tostada *f* • **a piece of ~** una tostada
2 (*= drink*) brindis *m inv* (**to** por) • **to drink a ~ to sb** brindar por algn • **here's a ~ to all who ...** brindemos por todos los que ... • **to propose a ~ to sb** proponer un brindis por algn • IDIOM: • **to be the ~ of the town** ser el niño bonito de la ciudad
(VT) **1** [+ *bread*] tostar • **~ed sandwich** sándwich *m* tostado • **to ~ one's toes by the fire** calentar los pies cerca del fuego
2 (*= drink to*) brindar por • **we ~ed the newlyweds** brindamos por los recién casados • **we ~ed the victory in champagne** celebramos la victoria con champán
(CPD) ▸ **toast list** lista *f* de brindis ▸ **toast rack** rejilla *f* para tostadas

toaster [ˈtəʊstəʳ] (N) tostadora *f*

toasting fork [ˈtəʊstɪŋfɔːk] (N) tostadera *f*

toastmaster [ˈtəʊstˌmɑːstəʳ] (N) *persona que propone los brindis y presenta a los oradores*

toasty [ˈtəʊstɪ] (N) sándwich *m* tostado
(ADJ)* (*= warm*) calentito

tobacco [təˈbækəʊ] (N) (PL: **tobaccos, tobaccoes**) tabaco *m*; ▹ **pipe**
(CPD) ▸ **tobacco industry** industria *f* tabacalera ▸ **tobacco jar** tabaquera *f* ▸ **tobacco leaf** hoja *f* de tabaco ▸ **tobacco plant** planta *f* de tabaco ▸ **tobacco plantation** tabacal *m* ▸ **tobacco pouch** petaca *f*

tobacconist [təˈbækənɪst] (N) (*Brit*) estanquero/a *m/f*, tabaquero/a *m/f* • **~'s (shop)** estanco *m*, tabaquería *f*

Tobago [təˈbeɪgəʊ] (N) Tobago *f*

-to-be [təˈbiː] (ADJ) (*ending in compounds*) futuro • **mothers-to-be** futuras madres

toboggan [təˈbɒgən] (N) tobogán *m*
(VI) ir en tobogán, deslizarse en tobogán
(CPD) ▸ **toboggan run** pista *f* de tobogán

toby jug [ˈtəʊbɪdʒʌg] (N) *bock de cerveza en forma de hombre*

toccata [təˈkɑːtə] (N) tocata *f*

tocsin [ˈtɒksɪn] (N) **1** (*= alarm*) campana *f* de alarma, rebato *m*
2 (*fig*) voz *f* de alarma • **to sound the ~** dar la voz de alarma, tocar a rebato

tod‡ [tɒd] (N) (*Brit*) • **on one's tod** a solas

today [təˈdeɪ] (ADV) **1** (*= the present day*) hoy • **from ~** desde hoy, a partir de hoy • **early ~** hoy temprano • **all day ~** todo el día de hoy • **what day is it ~?** ¿qué día es hoy?, ¿a cuántos estamos? • **what date is it ~?** ¿a qué fecha estamos? • **~ week** • **a week ~** de hoy en ocho días, dentro de una semana • **a fortnight ~** de hoy en quince días, dentro de dos semanas • **a year ago ~** hoy hace un año • IDIOM: • **here ~ and gone tomorrow** se cambia constantemente
2 (*= these days*) hoy (en) día • **young people ~ have it easy** la gente joven lo tiene muy fácil hoy en día
(N) **1** (*= the present day*) hoy *m* • **~ is Monday** hoy es lunes • **~ is 4 March** *or* **the 4th of March** hoy es el cuatro de marzo • **~'s paper** el periódico de hoy
2 (*= these days*) hoy *m*, el presente • **the writers of ~** los escritores de hoy

toddle [ˈtɒdl] (VI) **1** (*= begin to walk*) empezar a andar, dar los primeros pasos; (*= walk unsteadily*) caminar sin seguridad
2* (*= go*) marcharse; (*= stroll*) dar un paseo; (*= depart*) (*also* **toddle off**) irse, marcharse • **he ~d off** se marchó • **we must be toddling** es hora de irnos • **so I ~d round to see him** así que fui a visitarle

toddler [ˈtɒdləʳ] (N) (*= small child*) niño/a *m/f* pequeño/a (que empieza a caminar *or* en edad de aprender a andar)

toddy ['tɒdɪ] (N) • **hot ~** ponche *m*
todger** ['tɒdʒəʳ] (N) (*Brit*) chorra** *f*
to-do* [tə'du:] (N) (PL: **to-dos**) (= *fuss*) lío *m*, follón *m* (*Sp**) • **there was a great to-do** hubo un tremendo lío • **what's all the to-do about?** ¿a qué tanto jaleo? • **she made a great to-do** armó un lío imponente*
toe [təʊ] (N) (*Anat*) dedo *m* del pie; [*of shoe*] puntera *f*; [*of sock*] punta *f* • **big/little toe** dedo *m* gordo/pequeño del pie • **to tread** *or* **step on sb's toes** (*lit*) pisar el pie a algn; (*fig*) meterse con algn • IDIOMS: • **to keep sb on his toes** mantener a algn sobre ascuas • **to keep on one's toes** estar alerta, mantenerse bien despierto • **you have to keep on your toes** hay que estar alerta, hay que mantenerse bien despierto • **to turn up one's toes*** estirar la pata*
(VT) tocar con la punta del pie • IDIOM: • **to toe the line** (= *conform*) conformarse
(CPD) ▸ **toe clip** (*for cycling*) rastral *m*, calapiés *m* ▸ **toe piece** espátula *f*, punta *f*
toecap ['təʊkæp] (N) puntera *f*
toe-curling* ['təʊ,kɜ:lɪŋ] (ADJ) sonrojante, bochornoso
-toed [təʊd] (ADJ) (*ending in compounds*) de ... dedos del pie • **four-toed** de cuatro dedos del pie
TOEFL ['təʊfəl] (N ABBR) = **Test of English as a Foreign Language**
toehold ['təʊhəʊld] (N) punto *m* de apoyo (para el pie); (*fig*) espacio *m*
toenail ['təʊneɪl] (N) uña *f* del dedo del pie
toerag‡ ['təʊræg] (N) (*Brit*) mequetrefe* *m*
toe-to-toe [,təʊtə'təʊ] (ADV) • **to go toe-to-toe** (= *face each other*) ponerse frente a frente; (*in combat*) enfrentarse • **to go toe-to-toe with sb** (= *face*) ponerse frente a algn; (*in combat*) enfrentarse a algn
toey‡ ['təʊɪ] (ADJ) (*Australia*) (= *nervous*) inquieto, intranquilo
toff* [tɒf] (N) (*Brit*) encopetado/a *m/f*
toffee ['tɒfɪ] (N) caramelo *m*, dulce *m* de leche • IDIOM: • **he/she can't do it for ~*** no tiene ni idea de cómo hacerlo
(CPD) ▸ **toffee apple** manzana *f* de caramelo
toffee-nosed* ['tɒfɪ'nəʊzd] (ADJ) presumido, engreído
tofu ['təʊ,fu:] (N) tofu *m*, tofú *m*
tog [tɒg] (VT)* • **to tog sb up** ataviar a algn (in de) • **to tog o.s. up** ataviarse, vestirse (in de), emperejilarse • **to get togged up** ataviarse, vestirse
(N) **1** (*Brit*) (= *measure*) tog *m* calorífico, *unidad que sirve para medir lo que abrigan los tejidos, prendas de ropa, edredones etc.*
2 togs* (= *clothes*) ropa *fsing*
toga ['təʊgə] (N) toga *f*
together [tə'geðəʳ]

When ***together*** *is an element in a phrasal verb, eg* ***bring together, get together, sleep together****, look up the verb.*

(ADV) **1** (= *in company*) [*live, work, be*] juntos/as • **now we're ~** ahora estamos juntos • **they work ~** trabajan juntos • **~ they managed it** entre los dos lo lograron • **all ~** todos/as juntos/as, todos/as en conjunto • **they were all ~ in the bar** todos estaban reunidos en el bar • **they belong ~** [*couple*] están hechos el uno para el otro; [*socks*] esos van juntos • **let's get it ~*** (*fig*) organicémonos, pongamos manos a la obra • **we're in this ~** estamos metidos todos por igual • **they were all in it ~** (*pej*) todos estaban metidos en el asunto • **to put a meal ~** preparar una comida • **to put a show ~** montar un show • **~ with** junto con • **~ with his colleagues, he accepted responsibility** él, junto con sus colegas, admitió ser responsable
2 (= *simultaneously*) a la vez • **you can't all get in ~** no podéis entrar todos a la vez • **don't all talk ~** no habléis todos a la vez • **all ~ now!** (*singing*) ¡todos en coro!; (*pulling*) ¡todos a la vez! • **we'll do parts A and B ~** haremos juntamente las partes A y B
3 (= *continuously*) seguidos/as • **for weeks ~** durante semanas seguidas
(ADJ)* (= *well-adjusted*) equilibrado, cabal
togetherness [tə'geðənɪs] (N) compañerismo *m*
toggle ['tɒgl] (N) (*on coat*) botón *m* alargado de madera
(CPD) ▸ **toggle key** (*Comput*) tecla *f* de conmutación binaria ▸ **toggle switch** (*Elec*) conmutador *m* de palanca
Togo ['təʊgəʊ] (N) Togo *m*
Togolese [,təʊgəʊ'li:z] (ADJ) togolés
(N) togolés/esa *m/f*
toil [tɔɪl] (*liter*) (N) trabajo *m*, esfuerzo *m* • **after months of ~** después de meses de trabajo (agotador)
(VI) **1** (= *work hard*) trabajar duro • **to ~ away at sth** darle duro a algo • **to ~ to do sth** esforzarse *or* afanarse por hacer algo • **they ~ed on into the night** siguieron trabajando hasta muy entrada la noche
2 (= *move with difficulty*) • **to ~ along** caminar con dificultad, avanzar penosamente • **to ~ up a hill** subir trabajosamente una cuesta • **the engine is beginning to ~** el motor empieza a funcionar con dificultad
toilet ['tɔɪlɪt] (N) **1** (= *lavatory*) **a** (= *room*) servicio *m*, wáter *m*, lavabo *m*, baño *m* (*esp LAm*) • **"Toilets"** "Servicios", "Baño" • **to go to the ~** ir al servicio *or* al baño • **she's in the ~** está en el servicio *or* el baño
b (= *installation*) wáter *m*, retrete *m*, inodoro *m* (*euph, frm*) • **the ~ is blocked** se ha atascado el wáter *or* retrete • **to throw sth down the ~** tirar algo al wáter *or* retrete
2 (= *dressing, washing etc*) aseo *m*
(CPD) ▸ **toilet articles** artículos *mpl* de tocador ▸ **toilet bag** neceser *m* ▸ **toilet bowl** taza *f* (de retrete) ▸ **toilet case** = **toilet bag** ▸ **toilet cubicle** cubículo *m* de baño ▸ **toilet pan** = **toilet bowl** ▸ **toilet paper** papel *m* higiénico ▸ **toilet requisites** = **toilet articles** ▸ **toilet roll** rollo *m* de papel higiénico ▸ **toilet seat** asiento *m* de retrete ▸ **toilet set** juego *m* de tocador ▸ **toilet soap** jabón *m* de tocador ▸ **toilet tissue** = **toilet paper** ▸ **toilet training** • **~ training can be difficult** acostumbrar a un niño a ir solo al baño puede resultar difícil ▸ **toilet water** agua *f* de colonia, colonia *f*
toiletries ['tɔɪlɪtrɪz] (NPL) artículos *mpl* de tocador
toilette [twɑ:'let] (N) = **toilet**
toilet-train ['tɔɪlɪttreɪn] (VT) • **to toilet-train a child** acostumbrar a un niño a ir solo al baño
toils [tɔɪlz] (NPL) (*liter*) (= *snares, nets*) redes *fpl*, lazos *mpl*
toilsome ['tɔɪlsəm] (ADJ) (*liter*) penoso, laborioso, arduo
toilworn ['tɔɪlwɔ:n] (ADJ) (*liter*) completamente cansado
toing, to-ing ['tu:ɪŋ] (N) • **~ and froing** *or* **fro-ing** ir y venir *m*, idas y vueltas *fpl*
Tokay [təʊ'keɪ] (N) (= *wine*) Tokay *m*, muscadelle *f*
toke‡ [təʊk] (*Drugs*) (N) calada* *f*
(VI) dar una calada*
token ['təʊkən] (N) **1** (= *voucher*) vale *m*; (= *metal disc*) ficha *f*
2 (= *sign, symbol*) muestra *f*, señal *f*; (= *remembrance*) prenda *f*, recuerdo *m*; [*of one's appreciation etc*] detalle *m* • **love ~** prenda *f* de amor • **as a ~ of friendship** como prueba de amistad • **this is just a small ~ of our appreciation** esto no es más que un detalle en señal de (nuestro) agradecimiento • **by the same ~** por la misma razón
(ADJ) [*payment, resistance, gesture*] simbólico; [*strike*] nominal, simbólico • **the ~ black** el negro simbólico • **~ woman** mujer-muestra *f*, representación *f* femenina
tokenism ['təʊkənɪzəm] (N) (= *tokenistic act*) acción *f* simbólica • **his nomination was pure ~ on the part of the administration** su nombramiento fue una acción puramente simbólica por parte de la administración • **he rejected charges of ~** negó las acusaciones de estar llevando a cabo acciones simbólicas
tokenistic [,təʊkə'nɪstɪk] (ADJ) simbólico
Tokyo ['təʊkjəʊ] (N) Tokio *m*, Tokío *m*
told [təʊld] (PT), (PP) *of* **tell**
tolerable ['tɒlərəbl] (ADJ) **1** (= *bearable*) [*pain, heat*] soportable, tolerable
2 (= *not too bad*) [*film, food*] pasable
tolerably ['tɒlərəblɪ] (ADV) (= *moderately*) [*good, comfortable*] medianamente • **a ~ good player** un jugador pasable • **it is ~ certain that ...** es casi seguro que ...
tolerance ['tɒlərəns] (N) tolerancia *f* • **she had shown great ~** había mostrado una gran tolerancia • **he had built up a ~ to his medication** (= *receptiveness*) cada vez toleraba mejor la medicación; (= *resistance*) la medicación ya no le surtía efecto
tolerant ['tɒlərənt] (ADJ) **1** (= *open-minded*) [*person, society, attitude*] tolerante • **to be ~ of sb/sth** ser tolerante con algn/algo
2 (*Med*) • **to be ~ to sth** tolerar algo • **his body is becoming ~ to the drugs** (= *receptive*) su cuerpo tolera cada vez mejor los medicamentos; (= *resistant*) los medicamentos ya no le surten efecto
tolerantly ['tɒlərəntlɪ] (ADV) con tolerancia
tolerate ['tɒləreɪt] (VT) [+ *heat, pain*] aguantar, soportar; [+ *person*] tolerar, soportar • **I can't ~ any more** no aguanto más • **are we to ~ this?** ¿hemos de soportar esto? • **it is not to be ~d** es intolerable, es insoportable
toleration [,tɒlə'reɪʃən] (N) tolerancia *f* • **religious ~** tolerancia *f* religiosa
toll¹ [təʊl] (N) **1** (*on road, bridge*) peaje *m*, cuota *f* (*Mex*) • **to pay ~** pagar el peaje
2 (= *losses, casualties*) número *m* de víctimas, mortandad *f* • **the death ~ on the roads** el número de víctimas de accidentes de tráfico • **there is a heavy ~** hay muchas víctimas, son muchos los muertos • **the disease takes a heavy ~ each year** cada año la enfermedad se lleva a muchas víctimas *or* causa gran número de muertes • **the effort took its ~ on all of us** el esfuerzo tuvo un grave efecto en todos nosotros • **the severe weather has taken its ~ on the crops** el mal tiempo ha ocasionado pérdidas en la cosecha
(CPD) ▸ **toll bar** barrera *f* de peaje ▸ **toll booth** cabina *f* de peaje ▸ **toll bridge** puente *m* de peaje *or* (*Mex*) de cuota ▸ **toll call** (*US*) (*Telec*) conferencia *f* ▸ **toll charge** peaje *m* ▸ **toll gate** barrera *f* de peaje ▸ **toll motorway** (*Brit*) autopista *f* de peaje ▸ **toll road** carretera *f* de peaje
toll² [təʊl] (VT) [+ *bell*] tañer, tocar • **to ~ the hour** dar la hora
(VI) [*bell*] tañer, doblar • **the bells were ~ing in mourning for ...** doblaron las campanas en señal de duelo por ... • **"for whom the bell ~s"** "por quién doblan las campanas"
(N) [*of bell*] tañido *m*, doblar *m*
toll-free [,təʊl'fri:] (ADV) (*US*) (*Telec*) • **to call**

toll-free llamar gratuitamente

tolling [ˈtəʊlɪŋ] N tañido *m*, doblar *m*

tollkeeper [ˈtəʊl,kiːpəʳ] N peajero *m*, portazguero *m*

tollway [ˈtəʊlweɪ] N (*US*) autopista *f* de peaje *or* (*Mex*) cuota

toluene [ˈtɒljʊiːn] N (*Chem*) tolueno *m*

Tom [tɒm] N (*familiar form of* **Thomas**) • **IDIOM:** • **any Tom, Dick or Harry** un fulano cualquiera
CPD ▸ **Tom Thumb** Pulgarcito

tom [tɒm] N (*also* **tom cat**) gato *m* (macho)

tomahawk [ˈtɒməhɔːk] N tomahawk *m* • **IDIOM:** • **to bury the ~** (*US*) echar pelillos a la mar, envainar la espada

tomato [təˈmɑːtəʊ], (*US*) [təˈmeɪtəʊ] N (PL: **tomatoes**) (= *fruit*) tomate *m*, jitomate *m* (*Mex*); (= *plant*) tomatera *f*
CPD ▸ **tomato juice** jugo *m* de tomate ▸ **tomato ketchup** salsa *f* de tomate, ketchup *m* ▸ **tomato paste** = **tomato purée** ▸ **tomato plant** tomatera *f* ▸ **tomato purée** puré *m* de tomate, concentrado *m* de tomate ▸ **tomato sauce** salsa *f* de tomate; (*Brit*) (*in bottle, sachet*) = **tomato ketchup** ▸ **tomato soup** sopa *f* de tomate

tomb [tuːm] N tumba *f*, sepulcro *m*

tombola [tɒmˈbəʊlə] N (*Brit*) tómbola *f*

tomboy [ˈtɒmbɔɪ] N marimacho *m*

tomboyish [ˈtɒmbɔɪɪʃ] ADJ marimacho

tombstone [ˈtuːmstəʊn] N lápida *f* (sepulcral)

tombstoning* [ˈtuːmstəʊnɪŋ] N (*Brit*) tirarse de pie al mar desde gran altura

tomcat [ˈtɒmkæt] N **1** (= *cat*) gato *m* (macho)
2 (*US*‡) (= *womanizer*) mujeriego *m*, calavera *m*

tome [təʊm] N (*hum*) mamotreto* *m* • **a weighty ~** un pesado mamotreto*

tomfool [ˈtɒmˈfuːl] ADJ tonto, estúpido
N tonto/a *m/f*, imbécil *mf*

tomfoolery [tɒmˈfuːlərɪ] N payasadas *fpl*, tonterías *fpl*

Tommy [ˈtɒmɪ] N **1** *familiar form of* **Thomas**
2 (*Brit*) (*Mil**) (*also* **tommy**) soldado *m* raso inglés
CPD ▸ **Tommy gun** pistola *f* ametralladora, ametralladora *f*, metralleta *f*

tommyrot* [ˈtɒmɪrɒt] N tonterías *fpl*

tomography [təˈmɒgrəfɪ] N tomografía *f*

tomorrow [təˈmɒrəʊ] ADV **1** mañana • **~ evening** mañana por la tarde • **~ morning** mañana por la mañana • **a week ~** de mañana en ocho días
2 (= *in the future*) en el mañana, en el futuro
N **1** mañana *f* • **~ is Sunday** mañana es domingo • **the day after ~** pasado mañana • **will ~ do?** (*for piece of work*) ¿lo puedo dejar para mañana?; (*for appointment*) ¿te conviene mañana? • **~'s paper** el periódico de mañana • **IDIOMS:** • **~ is another day** mañana sera otro día • **like there's no ~: he drank like there was no ~*** bebió como si le fuera la vida en ello
2 (= *the future*) mañana *m*, porvenir *m* • **the writers of ~** los escritores del mañana

tom-tit [ˈtɒmtɪt] N paro *m*, carbonero *m* común

tom-tom [ˈtɒmtɒm] N (= *drum*) tantán *m*

ton [tʌn] N **1** (= *weight*) tonelada *f* (*Brit* = *1016.06kg; Can, US etc.* = *907.20kg*) • **metric ton** tonelada *f* métrica (= *1.000kg*) • **this cargo weighs 1,000 tons** esta carga pesa 1.000 toneladas • **a three-ton lorry** un camión de tres toneladas • **IDIOMS:** • **to weigh a ton*** pesar un quintal* • **this suitcase weighs a ton*** esta maleta pesa un quintal* • **to come down on sb like a ton of bricks** echar una bronca descomunal a algn
2* • **tons of sth** montones *mpl* de algo* • **we have tons of it at home** en casa lo tenemos a montones* • **we have tons of time** nos sobra tiempo, tenemos tiempo de sobra
3 (*Aut*‡) (= *100mph*) velocidad *f* de 100 millas por hora • **to do a ton** ir a 100 millas por hora
4 (*Cricket**) (= *100 runs*) cien carreras *fpl*

tonal [ˈtəʊnl] ADJ tonal

tonality [təʊˈnælɪtɪ] N tonalidad *f*

tone [təʊn] N **1** (*Mus*) tono *m*
2 [*of voice*] tono *m* • **in an angry ~** en tono de enojo • **in low ~s** en tono bajo • **they were whispering in low ~s** cuchicheaban • **~ of voice** tono *m* de voz • **IDIOM:** • **to praise sb in ringing ~s** poner a algn por las nubes
3 (*Telec*) señal *f* • **dialling ~** señal *f* para marcar • **please speak after the ~** (*Telec*) por favor, hable después de oír la señal
4 (= *shade of colour*) tono *m*, matiz *m* • **two-tone colour scheme** combinación *f* de dos tonalidades
5 (= *tendency*) tono *m*, nota *f*; [*of speech, article*] tono *m*, cariz *m* • **the ~ of the market** (*Econ*) la nota dominante del mercado, el tono del mercado
6 (= *character, dignity*) buen tono *m*, elegancia *f* • **the place has ~** el sitio tiene buen tono, es un sitio elegante • **the clientèle gives the restaurant ~** la clientela da distinción al restaurante • **to raise/lower the ~ of sth** levantar/bajar el nivel de algo
7 [*of muscles etc*] • **muscle ~** tono *m* muscular
VI (*Brit*) (*also* **tone in**) [*colours*] armonizar, combinar
VT **1** (*Mus*) entonar
2 (*Phot*) virar
3 [+ *body, muscles*] (*also* **tone up**) tonificar, fortalecer
CPD ▸ **tone colour, tone color** (*US*) (*Mus*) timbre *m* ▸ **tone control** control *m* de tonalidad ▸ **tone language** lengua *f* tonal ▸ **tone poem** poema *m* sinfónico
▸ **tone down** VT + ADV (= *moderate*) [+ *colour*] atenuar, suavizar; [+ *noise*] reducir, disminuir; (*fig*) [+ *language, criticism etc*] moderar
▸ **tone up** VT + ADV [+ *muscles*] tonificar, fortalecer

-toned [təʊnd] ADJ (*ending in compounds*) • **sepia-toned** en tono sepia • **high-toned** en tono altisonante

tone-deaf [ˈtəʊnˈdef] ADJ que no tiene oído musical

toneless [ˈtəʊnlɪs] ADJ [*voice*] monótono, apagado, inexpresivo; [*muscle tissue*] flojo

tonelessly [ˈtəʊnlɪslɪ] ADV monótonamente

toner [ˈtəʊnəʳ] N (*for photocopier*) tóner *m*; (*Phot*) virador *m*; (*for skin*) tonificante *m*

toney* [ˈtəʊnɪ] ADJ (*US*) = tony

Tonga [ˈtɒŋə] N Tonga *f*

tongs [tɒŋz] NPL (*for coal etc*) tenazas *fpl*; (= *curling tongs*) tenacillas *fpl* • **a pair of ~** unas tenazas, unas tenacillas

tongue [tʌŋ] N **1** (*Anat, Culin*) lengua *f* • **to put** *or* **stick one's ~ out (at sb)** sacar la lengua (a algn) • **she has a quick/nasty ~** (*fig*) tiene mucha labia/una lengua viperina • **IDIOMS:** • **with (one's) ~ in (one's) cheek** irónicamente, burla burlando • **to say sth ~ in cheek** decir algo en tono de burla • **to keep a civil ~ in one's head** moderar las palabras *or* el lenguaje • **to get one's ~ around sth:** • **I can't get my ~ round these Latin names** estos nombres latinos resultan impronunciables • **to find one's ~:** • **so you've found your ~?** ¿así que estás dispuesto por fin a hablar? • **to give ~** [*hounds*] empezar a ladrar • **to hold one's ~** callarse • **hold your ~!** ¡cállate la boca! • **to loosen sb's ~** hacer hablar a algn • **wine loosens the ~** el vino suelta la lengua • **to lose one's ~:** • **have you lost your ~?** ¿te has tragado la lengua? • **to trip or roll off the ~:** • **the formula came tripping** *or* **rolling off his/her ~** pronunció la fórmula con la mayor facilidad • **it doesn't exactly trip off the ~** no se puede decir que sea fácil de pronunciar
2 [*of shoe*] lengüeta *f*; [*of bell*] badajo *m*; (*fig*) [*of flame, land*] lengua *f*
3 (= *language*) lengua *f*, idioma *m* • **in the German ~** en alemán, en la lengua alemana • **to speak in ~s** (*Rel*) hablar en lenguas desconocidas
CPD ▸ **tongue twister** trabalenguas *m inv*

tongue-and-groove [,tʌŋənˈgruːv] N machihembrado *m*

tongue-in-cheek [ˈtʌŋɪnˈtʃiːk] ADJ irónico

tongue-lashing* [ˈtʌŋ,læʃɪŋ] N latigazo *m*, reprensión *f* • **to give sb a tongue-lashing** poner a algn como un trapo

tongue-tied [ˈtʌŋtaɪd] ADJ con la lengua trabada; (*fig*) tímido, cortado, premioso (*frm*)

tonic [ˈtɒnɪk] N **1** (*Med*) (*also fig*) tónico *m* • **this news will be a ~ for the market** esta noticia será un tónico para la bolsa
2 (*also* **tonic water**) agua *f* tónica, tónica *f*
3 (*Mus*) tónica *f*
ADJ (*all senses*) tónico
CPD ▸ **tonic accent** (*Mus*) acento *m* tónico

tonicity [tɒˈnɪsɪtɪ] N tonicidad *f*

tonight [təˈnaɪt] ADV esta noche • **I'll see you ~** nos vemos esta noche
N • **~'s TV programmes** los programas de TV de esta noche

tonnage [ˈtʌnɪdʒ] N (= *weight*) tonelaje *m*

tonne [tʌn] N tonelada *f* (métrica) (*1.000kg*)

-tonner [ˈtʌnəʳ] N (*ending in compounds*) de ... toneladas • **a 1,000-tonner** un barco de 1.000 toneladas

tonometer [təʊˈnɒmɪtəʳ] N tonómetro *m*

tonsil [ˈtɒnsl] N amígdala *f*, angina *f* (*Mex*) • **to have one's ~s out** quitarse las amígdalas

tonsillectomy [,tɒnsɪˈlektəmɪ] N tonsilectomía *f*, amigdalotomía *f*

tonsillitis [,tɒnsɪˈlaɪtɪs] N amigdalitis *f*

tonsorial [tɒnˈsɔːrɪəl] ADJ (*esp hum*) [*look, style*] barberil; [*matters*] relativo a la barba

tonsure [ˈtɒnʃəʳ] (*frm*) N tonsura *f*
VT tonsurar

Tony [ˈtəʊnɪ] N *familiar form of* **Anthony**

tony* [ˈtəʊnɪ] ADJ (*US*) de buen tono, elegante

too [tuː] ADV **1** (= *excessively*) demasiado • **it's too easy** es demasiado fácil • **it's too sweet** está demasiado *or* muy dulce • **it's too heavy for me to lift** es demasiado pesado para que yo lo levante • **it's too hot to drink** está demasiado caliente para beberlo • **it's not too difficult** no es muy difícil • **too bad!** ¡mala suerte!, ¡qué le vamos a hacer!, ¡ni modo! (*Mex*) • **it's too early for that** es (muy) temprano para eso • **it's too good to be true** no puede ser • **I'm not too keen on the idea** la idea no me hace gracia que digamos • **too many** demasiados • **too many difficulties** demasiadas dificultades • **too much** demasiado • **too much jam** demasiada mermelada *f* • **he talks too much** habla demasiado • **you gave me a dollar too much** me dio un dólar de más • **that's too much by half** de eso sobra la mitad • **don't make too much of it** no le des mucha importancia • **it was all too much for her** [*emotion*] era demasiado para ella, era más de lo que pudo soportar; [*work*] estaba agobiada por tanto trabajo • **it's too much for me to cope with** yo no puedo con tanto • **his rudeness is too**

much su descortesía es intolerable • **it's too much!*** (= *fantastic*) ¡qué demasiado!*, ¡esto es demasiado!; (= *excessive*) esto pasa de la raya, esto pasa de castaño oscuro • **too often** con demasiada frecuencia, muy a menudo • **too right!*** • **too true!** ¡muy bien dicho!, ¡y cómo!
2 (= *also*) también; (= *moreover*) además • **I went too** yo fui también • **I speak French and Japanese too** hablo francés y también japonés • **not only that, he's blind too!** no solo eso, ¡además es ciego! • **she is, too!** ¡y tanto que lo es!

took [tʊk] (PT) *of* take

tool [tu:l] (N) **1** (*carpenter's, mechanic's etc*) herramienta *f*; (*gardener's*) útil *m*, utensilio *m* • **a set of ~s** un juego de herramientas • **the ~s of his trade** las herramientas de su trabajo • **give us the ~s and we will finish the job** (*fig*) dadnos las herramientas y nosotros terminaremos la obra; ▹ **down¹**
2 (*fig*) (= *person, book etc*) instrumento *m* • **he was a mere ~ in their hands** fue instrumento en sus manos, nada más • **the book is an essential ~** el libro es indispensable, el libro es instrumento imprescindible
(VT) [+ *wood, metal*] labrar con herramienta; [+ *book, leather*] estampar en seco
(CPD) ▸ **tool bag** estuche *m* de herramientas ▸ **tool box, tool chest** caja *f* de herramientas ▸ **tool kit** juego *m* de herramientas, estuche *m* de herramientas ▸ **tool room** departamento *m* de herramientas ▸ **tool shed** cobertizo *m* para herramientas

toolbar ['tu:lbɑ:ʳ] (N) barra *f* de herramientas

tooled-up‡ ['tu:ld'ʌp] (ADJ) armado

tooling ['tu:lɪŋ] (N) (*on book*) estampación *f* en seco

toolmaker ['tu:l,meɪkəʳ] (N) tallador *m* de herramientas

toolmaking ['tu:l,meɪkɪŋ] (N) talladura *f* de herramientas

toot [tu:t] (N) toque *m*, bocinazo *m* • **he went off with a ~ on the horn** partió con un breve toque de bocina
(VT) [+ *horn*] tocar, hacer sonar
(VI) [*person*] tocar la bocina, dar un bocinazo

tooth [tu:θ] (N) (PL: **teeth**) **1** (*Anat*) diente *m*; (*esp molar*) muela *f* • **to clean one's teeth** lavarse los dientes • **to cut a ~** echar un diente • **she's cutting her first ~** le está saliendo el primer diente, está echando el primer diente • **to have a ~ out** sacarse una muela • **to show one's teeth** (*smiling or aggressive*) enseñar los dientes • IDIOMS: • **to cut one's teeth on sth** foguearse con *or* en algo, dar los primeros pasos con algo • **to be fed up to the (back) teeth with sth/sb*** estar hasta la coronilla de algo/algn • **to get one's teeth into sth** hincarle el diente a algo, meterse de lleno en algo • **in the teeth of the wind** contra un viento violento • **in the teeth of great opposition** haciendo frente a una gran resistencia • **to lie through one's teeth** mentir descaradamente • **long in the ~*** con muchos años a cuestas • **to fight ~ and nail** luchar a brazo partido • **it sets my/his teeth on edge** me/le da dentera • **by the skin of one's teeth** por un pelo • **to have a sweet ~** ser goloso; ▹ **armed, false, grit, wisdom**
2 [*of saw, wheel*] diente *m*; [*of comb*] púa *f*
3 (*fig*) • **the Commission must be given more teeth** hay que dar poderes efectivos a la Comisión
(CPD) ▸ **tooth decay** caries *f* ▸ **tooth fairy** ratoncito *m* Pérez ▸ **tooth glass** vaso *m* para los cepillos de dientes ▸ **tooth powder** polvos *mpl* dentífricos ▸ **tooth rot*** caries *f* ▸ **tooth socket** alvéolo *m* dental

toothache ['tu:θeɪk] (N) dolor *m* de muelas • **to have ~** tener dolor de muelas

toothbrush ['tu:θbrʌʃ] (N) cepillo *m* de dientes
(CPD) ▸ **toothbrush holder** porta *m inv* cepillo de dientes ▸ **toothbrush moustache** bigote *m* de cepillo

toothed [tu:θt] (ADJ) [*wheel*] dentado • **big-toothed** de dientes grandes

toothless ['tu:θlɪs] (ADJ) desdentado, sin dientes; (*fig*) sin poder efectivo, ineficaz

toothpaste ['tu:θpeɪst] (N) pasta *f* de dientes, dentífrico *m*

toothpick ['tu:θpɪk] (N) palillo *m* (de dientes)

toothsome ['tu:θsəm] (ADJ) (*liter*) sabroso

toothy* ['tʊθɪ] (ADJ) (COMPAR: **toothier**, SUPERL: **toothiest**) dentudo • **to give sb a ~ smile** sonreír a algn enseñando mucho los dientes

tootle ['tu:tl] (N) (*Mus*) sonido *m* breve (de flauta, trompeta *etc*)
(VT) [+ *flute etc*] tocar
(VI) **1** (*Mus*) tocar la flauta *etc*
2 (*Aut**) • **we ~d down to Brighton** hicimos una escapada a Brighton, fuimos de excursión a Brighton • **we were tootling along at 60** íbamos a 60

tootsie‡, tootsy‡ ['tʊtsɪ] (N) **1** (= *toe*) dedo *m* del pie; (= *foot*) pie *m*
2 (*US*) (= *girl*) chica *f*, gachí‡ *f* • **hey ~!** ¡oye, guapa!

top¹ [tɒp] (N) **1** (= *highest point, peak*) cumbre *f*, cima *f*; [*of hill*] cumbre *f*; [*of tree*] copa *f*; [*of head*] coronilla *f*; [*of building*] remate *m*; [*of wall*] coronamiento *m*; [*of wave*] cresta *f*; [*of stairs, ladder*] lo alto; [*of page*] cabeza *f*; [*of list, table, classification*] cabeza *f*, primer puesto *m*, primera posición *f* • **at the top of the hill** en la cumbre de la colina • **to reach the top** • **make it to the top** [*of career etc*] alcanzar la cumbre (del éxito) • **the men at the top** (*fig*) los que mandan • **executives who are at the top of their careers** ejecutivos que están en la cumbre de sus carreras • **top of the charts** (*Mus*) el número uno • **to be at the top of the class** (*Scol*) ser el/la mejor de la clase • **Liverpool are at the top of the league** Liverpool encabeza la liga • **at the top of the page** a la cabeza de la página • **top of the range** (*Comm*) lo mejor de la gama • **at the top of the stairs** en lo alto de la escalera • **at the top of the tree** (*lit*) en lo alto del árbol; (*Brit*) (*fig*) en la cima, en lo más alto • IDIOM: • **at the top of the pile** *or* **heap*** en la cima, en lo más alto; ▹ **blow²**
2 (= *upper part*) parte *f* superior, parte *f* de arriba; [*of bus*] piso *m* superior; [*of turnip, carrot, radish*] rabillo *m*, hojas *fpl* • **he lives at the top of the house** ocupa el piso más alto de la casa • **the top of the milk** la nata • **at the top of the street** al final de la calle • **he sits at the top of the table** se sienta a la cabecera de la mesa
3 (= *surface*) superficie *f* • **oil comes** *or* **floats** *or* **rises to the top** el aceite sube a la superficie • **the top of the table needs wiping** hay que pasar una bayeta por la mesa
4 (= *lid*) [*of pen, bottle, jar*] tapa *f*, cubierta *f*, tapón *m*
5 (= *blouse*) blusa *f* • **pyjama top** parte *f* de arriba del pijama • **I want a top to go with this skirt** quiero algo para arriba que me vaya con esta falda
6 (*Brit*) (*Aut*) = **top gear**
7 (*US*) (*Aut*) capota *f*
8 (*Naut*) cofa *f*
9 • **on top** encima, arriba • **to be on top** estar encima; (*fig*) (= *winning etc*) llevar ventaja, estar ganando • **seats on top!** (*on bus*) ¡hay sitio arriba! • **let's go up on top** (*Naut*) vamos a (subir a) cubierta • **thin on top*** con poco pelo, medio calvo • **on top of** sobre, encima de • **it floats on top of the water** flota sobre el agua • **the next second the lorry was on top of us** al instante el camión se nos echó encima • **the flat is so small we live on top of each other** el piso es tan pequeño que vivimos amontonados • **on top of (all) that** (= *in addition to that*) y encima *or* además de (todo) eso • **on top of which** y para colmo, más encima • **it's just one thing on top of another** es una cosa tras otra • **to be/get on top of things** estar/ponerse a la altura de las cosas • **I'm on top of my work now** ahora puedo con el trabajo • **things are getting on top of me** ya no puedo más • IDIOMS: • **to come out on top** salir ganando *or* con éxito • **to be/feel on top of the world** estar/sentirse en el paraíso *or* en el séptimo cielo
10 • **tops: it's (the) tops*** es tremendo*, es fabuloso* • **she's (the) tops** es la reoca*
11 (*in phrases*) • **from top to bottom** de arriba abajo • **the system is rotten from top to bottom** el sistema entero está podrido • **to be at the top of one's form** estar en plena forma • **the top of the morning to you!** (*Irl*) ¡buenos días! • **over the top** (*Brit**) (= *excessive*) excesivo, desmesurado • **this proposal is really over the top** (*Brit*) esta propuesta pasa de la raya • **to go over the top** (*Mil*) lanzarse al ataque (saliendo de las trincheras); (*Brit**) (*fig*) pasarse (de lo razonable), desbordarse • **he doesn't have much up top*** (= *stupid*) no es muy listo que digamos; (= *balding*) tiene poco pelo, se le ven las ideas* • **she doesn't have much up top*** (= *flat-chested*) está lisa (basilisa)* • **at the top of one's voice** a voz en grito • IDIOM: • **he said it off the top of his head*** lo dijo sin pensar • **speaking off the top of my head, I would say ...** hablando así sin pensarlo, yo diría que ...
(ADJ) **1** (= *highest*) [*drawer, shelf*] de arriba, más alto; [*edge, side, corner*] superior, de arriba; [*floor, step, storey*] último • **at the top end of the scale** en el extremo superior de la escala • **at the top end of the range** (*Comm*) en el escalón más alto de la gama • **top note** (*Mus*) nota *f* más alta
2 (= *maximum*) [*price*] máximo • **top priority** principal prioridad *f*, asunto *m* primordial • **at top speed** a máxima velocidad, a toda carrera
3 (*in rank etc*) más importante • **the top class at school** (= *final year*) el último año en la escuela • **a top executive** un(a) alto/a ejecutivo/a • **a top job** un puesto de importancia • **top management** alta gerencia *f* • **top people** gente *f* bien • **the top people in the party** la dirección del partido • **top stream** (*Scol*) clase *f* del nivel más avanzado
4 (= *best, leading*) mejor • **a top surgeon** uno de los mejores cirujanos • **the top 10/20/30** (*Mus*) los 10/20/30 mejores éxitos, el hit parade de los 10/20/30 mejores • **to come top** ganar, ganar el primer puesto • **to come top of the class** ser el primero de la clase • **he came top in maths** sacó la mejor nota de la clase en matemáticas • **to be on top form** estar en plena forma • **to get top marks** sacar la mejor nota • **top scorer** máximo/a goleador(a) *m/f*, pichichi *mf* (*Sp**) • **top team** equipo *m* líder
5 (= *final*) [*coat of paint*] último • **the top layer of skin** la epidermis
6 (= *farthest*) superior • **the top right-hand**

t

corner la esquina superior derecha • **the top end of the field** el extremo superior del campo
(ADV) • **tops*** (= *maximum, at most*) como mucho
(VT) **1** (= *form top of*) [+ *building*] coronar; [+ *cake*] cubrir, recubrir • **a cake topped with whipped cream** una tarta cubierta *or* recubierta de nata *or* (*LAm*) crema • **a church topped by a steeple** una iglesia coronada por un campanario • **the wall is topped with stone** el muro tiene un coronamiento de piedras
2 (= *be at top of*) [+ *class, list*] encabezar, estar a la cabeza de • **to top the bill** (*Theat*) encabezar el reparto • **to top the charts** (*Mus*) ser el número uno de las listas de éxitos *or* de los superventas • **the team topped the league all season** el equipo iba en cabeza de la liga toda la temporada
3 (= *exceed, surpass*) exceder, superar • **profits topped £50,000 last year** las ganancias excedieron (las) 50.000 libras el año pasado • **sales topped the million mark** las ventas rebasaron el millón • **we have topped last year's takings by £200** hemos recaudado 200 libras más que el año pasado, los ingresos exceden a los del año pasado en 200 libras • **and to top it all ...** y para colmo ..., como remate ..., y para rematar las cosas ... • **how are you going to top that?** (*joke, story etc*) ¿cómo vas a superar eso?, te han puesto el listón muy alto
4 [+ *vegetables, fruit, plant*] descabezar; [+ *tree*] desmochar • **to top and tail fruit** (*Brit*) quitar los extremos de la fruta
5 (= *reach summit of*) llegar a la cumbre de
6‡ (= *kill*) colgar • **to top o.s.** suicidarse
(CPD) ▸ **top banana*** (*US*) pez *m* gordo* ▸ **top boots** botas *fpl* de campaña ▸ **top brass*** jefazos* *mpl* ▸ **top copy** original *m* ▸ **top dog*** • **she's top dog at work** ella es mandamás en el trabajo ▸ **top dollar*** (*esp US*) • **to pay top dollar for sth** pagar algo a precio de oro ▸ **the top drawer** (*fig*) la alta sociedad, la crema; ▹ **top-drawer** ▸ **top dressing** (*Hort, Agr*) abono *m* (aplicado a la superficie) ▸ **top floor** último piso *m* ▸ **top gear** (*Brit*) (*Aut*) directa *f* • **in top gear** (*four-speed box*) en cuarta, en la directa; (*five-speed box*) en quinta, en la directa ▸ **top hat** sombrero *m* de copa, chistera *f* ▸ **top spin** (*Tennis*) efecto *m* alto, efecto *m* liftado ▸ **top ten** (= *songs*) • **the top ten** el top diez, los diez primeros ▸ **top thirty** • **the top thirty** el top treinta, los treinta primeros
▸ **top off** (VT + ADV) (= *complete*) coronar, rematar • **he topped this off by saying that ...** esto lo remató diciendo que ... • **he topped off the fourth course with a cup of coffee** para completar el cuarto plato se bebió una taza de café
▸ **top up** (*Brit*) (VT + ADV) [+ *cup, glass*] llenar; [+ *mobile phone*] recargar • **to top sb's glass up** rellenar el vaso de algn • **shall I top you up?** ¿te doy más? • **to top up a battery** (= *refill it*) llenar a nivel una batería • **her parents topped up her grant** sus padres le añadieron un complemento *or* suplemento a la beca
(VI + ADV) • **to top up with oil** poner aceite • **we topped up with a couple of beers*** como remate nos bebimos un par de cervezas

top² [tɒp] (N) **1** (= *spinning top*) peonza *f*, peón *m*; (= *humming top, musical top*) trompa *f*; ▹ **sleep**
2 (*Circus*) ▹ **big**

topaz ['təʊpæz] (N) topacio *m*

top-class [,tɒp'klɑːs] (ADJ) [*restaurant, hotel*] de primera categoría; [*athlete, player*] de primera

topcoat ['tɒpkəʊt] (N) (= *overcoat*) abrigo *m*, sobretodo *m*

top-down [,tɒp'daʊn] (ADJ) [*approach, theory, leadership*] verticalista

top-drawer [,tɒp'drɔː'] (ADJ) (*fig*) de alta sociedad; ▹ **top**

tope† [təʊp] (VI) beber (más de la cuenta), emborracharse

topee ['təʊpiː] (N) salacot *m*

top-end ['tɒpend] (ADJ) de gama alta

toper† ['təʊpə'] (N) borrachín/ina *m/f*

top-flight ['tɒpflaɪt] (ADJ) de primera (categoría)

topgallant [tɒp'gælənt], (*Naut*) [tə'gælənt] (N) (*also* **topgallant sail**) juanete *m*

top-hatted ['tɒp'hætɪd] (ADJ) en chistera, enchisterado

top-heaviness ['tɒp'hevɪnɪs] (N) (*fig*) (*in organization*) exceso *m* de altos cargos

top-heavy [,tɒp'hevɪ] (ADJ) (*lit*) demasiado pesado en la parte superior; (*fig*) • **the army was top-heavy with officers** el ejército tenía demasiados oficiales

topi ['təʊpɪ] (N) = **topee**

topiary ['təʊpɪərɪ] (N) arte *m* de recortar los arbustos en formas de animales *etc*

topic ['tɒpɪk] (N) tema *m*, asunto *m*

topical ['tɒpɪkəl] (ADJ) **1** (= *current and relevant*) de interés actual, de actualidad • **a highly ~ question** un tema de gran actualidad • **~ talk** charla *f* sobre cuestiones del día
2 (*US*) local

topicality [,tɒpɪ'kælɪtɪ] (N) **1** (= *current interest, importance*) actualidad *f*, interés *m* actual, importancia *f* actual
2 (*US*) localidad *f*

topically ['tɒpɪkəlɪ] (ADV) **1** (*Med*) tópicamente
2 (= *relevantly*) con gran actualidad

topknot ['tɒpnɒt] (N) **1** (*on head*) moño *m*
2 (*Orn*) moño *m*

topless ['tɒplɪs] (ADJ) topless
(ADV) • **to go ~** ir en topless
(CPD) ▸ **topless bar** bar *m* topless ▸ **topless swimsuit** monoquini *m*

top-level [,tɒp'levl] (ADJ) del más alto nivel • **top-level conference** conferencia *f* de alto nivel

top-loader [,tɒp'ləʊdə'] (N) (= *washing machine*) lavadora *f* de carga superior

topmast ['tɒpmɑːst] (N) mastelero *m*

topmost ['tɒpməʊst] (ADJ) más alto

top-notch* [,tɒp'nɒtʃ] (ADJ) de primerísima categoría

top-of-the-range [,tɒpəvðə'reɪndʒ], **top-of-the-line** [,tɒpəvðə'laɪn] (ADJ) más alto de la gama

topographer [tə'pɒgrəfə'] (N) topógrafo/a *m/f*

topographic [,tɒpə'græfɪk] (ADJ) = **topographical**

topographical [,tɒpə'græfɪkl] (ADJ) topográfico

topography [tə'pɒgrəfɪ] (N) topografía *f*

topological [,tɒpə'lɒdʒɪkəl] (ADJ) topológico

topology [tə'pɒlədʒɪ] (N) topología *f*

toponym ['tɒpənɪm] (N) topónimo *m*

topper* ['tɒpə'] (N) **1** (= *hat*) sombrero *m* de copa, chistera *f*
2 (*US*) • **the ~ was that ...** para colmo ..., para acabar de rematar ...*

topping ['tɒpɪŋ] (N) (*Culin*) cubierta *f*
(ADJ) (*Brit†*) bárbaro*, pistonudo*

topple ['tɒpl] (VT) **1** (*also* **topple over**) (= *knock over*) volcar; (= *cause to fall*) hacer caer
2 (= *overthrow*) derribar, derrocar
(VI) **1** (*also* **topple down**) caerse, venirse abajo; (*also* **topple over**) volcarse; (= *lose balance*) perder el equilibrio • **he ~d over a cliff** cayó por un precipicio • **after the crash the bus ~d over** después del choque el autobús se volcó
2 (*fig*) [*government etc*] venirse abajo, caer

top-quality [,tɒp'kwɒlɪtɪ] (ADJ) de la mejor calidad

top-ranked ['tɒp'ræŋkt] (ADJ) [*player, team*] primero en el ránking

top-ranking [,tɒp'ræŋkɪŋ] (ADJ) de alto rango; [*officer*] de alta graduación

top-rated ['tɒp'reɪtɪd] (ADJ) [*TV series*] de más audiencia; [*hotel, school*] más prestigioso

topsail ['tɒpsl] (N) gavia *f*

top-secret [,tɒp'siːkrɪt] (ADJ) de alto secreto

top-security [,tɒpsɪ'kjʊərɪtɪ] (ADJ) [*prison, hospital*] de alta seguridad, de máxima seguridad
(CPD) ▸ **top-security wing** ala *f* de máxima seguridad

top-selling [,tɒp'selɪŋ] (ADJ) = **best-selling**

top-shelf [,tɒp'ʃelf] (ADJ) (*Brit*) [*magazine, material*] para adultos

topside ['tɒpsaɪd] (N) **1** (= *uppermost side*) lado *m* superior, superficie *f* superior
2 (*Culin*) tapa *f* y tajo redondo

topsoil ['tɒpsɔɪl] (N) capa *f* superficial del suelo

topsy-turvy [,tɒpsɪ'tɜːvɪ] (ADJ) en desorden, revuelto
(ADV) patas arriba, al revés • **everything is topsy-turvy** todo está patas arriba

top-to-toe [,tɒptə'təʊ] (ADJ) [*beauty treatment*] de la cabeza a los pies

top-up ['tɒpʌp] (N) (*Brit**) (= *refill*) • **can I give you a top-up?** ¿te sirvo un poco más?
(CPD) ▸ **top-up card** (*for mobile phone*) tarjeta *f* de recarga ▸ **top-up loan** (*Brit*) préstamo *m* gubernamental a estudiantes

toque [təʊk] (N) gorro *m* de cocinero

tor [tɔː'] (N) colina *f* abrupta y rocosa, pico *m* pequeño (*esp en el suroeste de Inglaterra*)

Torah ['tɔːrə] (N) • **the ~** la Torá

torc [tɔːk] (N) = **torque**

torch [tɔːtʃ] (N) **1** (*flaming*) antorcha *f*, tea *f* • **to carry the ~ of democracy/progress** (*fig*) mantener viva la llama de la democracia/del progreso • IDIOM: • **to carry a ~ for sb** estar enamorado de algn
2 (*Brit*) (*electric*) linterna *f*
3 (*Tech*) (*also* **blow torch**) soplete *m*
(VT) (= *set fire to*) [+ *building, vehicle*] prender fuego a, incendiar

torchbearer ['tɔːtʃ,beərə'] (N) persona *f* que lleva una antorcha

torchlight ['tɔːtʃlaɪt] (N) (*flaming*) luz *f* de antorcha; (*electric*) luz *f* de linterna
(CPD) ▸ **torchlight procession** desfile *m* con antorchas

torch song ['tɔːtʃsɒŋ] (N) canción *f* de amor

tore [tɔː'] (PT) *of* **tear**

toreador ['tɒrɪədɔː'] (N) torero *m*

torment (N) ['tɔːment] tormento *m* • **the ~s of jealousy** los tormentos de los celos • **to be in ~** estar atormentado
(VT) [tɔː'ment] (= *hurt*) atormentar, torturar; (= *annoy*) fastidiar, molestar; (= *torture*) (*fig*) atormentar • **she was ~ed by doubts** la atormentaban las dudas • **we were ~ed by thirst** nos moríamos de sed • **don't ~ the cat** no le des guerra al gato

tormentor [tɔː'mentə'] (N) atormentador(a) *m/f*

torn [tɔːn] (PP) *of* **tear**

tornado [tɔː'neɪdəʊ] (N) (PL: **tornados, tornadoes**) tornado *m*

torpedo [tɔː'piːdəʊ] (N) (PL: **torpedoes**) torpedo *m*
(VT) (*lit, fig*) torpedear
(CPD) ▸ **torpedo boat** torpedero *m*, lancha *f* torpedera ▸ **torpedo tube** tubo *m* lanzatorpedos, lanzatorpedos *m inv*

t

torpid ['tɔ:pɪd] ADJ aletargado
torpidity [tɔ:'pɪdɪtɪ] N letargo *m*
torpor ['tɔ:pəʳ] N letargo *m*
torque [tɔ:k] N **1** (*also* **torc**) (= *jewellery*) torques *f inv*
2 (*Mech*) par *m* de torsión
CPD ▸ **torque wrench** llave *f* dinamométrica
torrent ['tɒrənt] N (*lit, fig*) torrente *m* • **it rained in ~s** llovía a cántaros • **a ~ of abuse** un torrente de insultos, una sarta de injurias
torrential [tɒ'renʃəl] ADJ torrencial
torrid ['tɒrɪd] ADJ **1** (= *hot and dry*) [*climate, heat, sun*] tórrido
2 (= *passionate*) [*love affair, romance*] tórrido, apasionado
3 (= *very difficult*) • **to have a ~ time** (*Brit*) pasar las de Caín, sufrir lo indecible
torsion ['tɔ:ʃən] N torsión *f*
torso ['tɔ:səʊ] N (PL: **torsos,** (*rare*) **torsi**)
1 (*Anat*) torso *m*
2 (= *sculpture*) torso *m*
tort [tɔ:t] N (*Jur*) agravio *m*, tuerto *m*
tortilla [tɔ:'ti:ə] N tortilla *f*
CPD ▸ **tortilla chips** chips *fpl* de tortilla
tortoise ['tɔ:təs] N tortuga *f*
tortoiseshell ['tɔ:təsʃel] N **1** (= *shell*) carey *m*, concha *f*
2 (= *cat*) gato *m* pardo
3 (= *butterfly*) ortiguera *f*
CPD [*box, ornament*] de carey, de concha
▸ **tortoiseshell glasses** gafas *fpl* de carey
tortuous ['tɔ:tjʊəs] ADJ **1** (= *winding*) [*path, road, process*] tortuoso
2 (= *convoluted*) [*sentence, essay, logic*] enrevesado
torture ['tɔ:tʃəʳ] N **1** (*lit*) tortura *f* • **to put sb to (the) ~** torturar a algn
2 (*fig*) tormento *m* • **it was sheer ~!** ¡era una verdadera tortura!
VT **1** (*lit*) torturar
2 (= *torment*) atormentar • **to be ~d by doubts** ser atormentado por las dudas
CPD ▸ **torture chamber** cámara *f* de tortura
torturer ['tɔ:tʃərəʳ] N torturador(a) *m/f*
torturing ['tɔ:tʃərɪŋ] ADJ torturador, atormentador
torturous ['tɔ:tʃərəs] ADJ muy doloroso
Tory ['tɔ:rɪ] (*Brit*) ADJ conservador • **the ~ Party** el Partido Conservador
N conservador(a) *m/f*
Toryism ['tɔ:rɪɪzəm] N (*Brit*) conservatismo *m*, conservadurismo *m*
tosh* [tɒʃ] N tonterías *fpl*
toss [tɒs] N **1** (= *shake*) [*of head*] sacudida *f* • **a ~ of the head** una sacudida de cabeza
• IDIOM: • **I don't give a ~** (*Brit‡*) me importa un bledo*
2 (= *throw*) echada *f*, tirada *f*; (*by bull*) cogida *f* • **the ball came to him full ~** la pelota llegó a sus manos sin tocar la tierra • **to take a ~** (*from horse*) caerse del caballo
3 [*of coin*] tirada *f*, echada *f* (*esp LAm*) • **to win/lose the ~** ganar/perder (a cara o cruz)
• IDIOM: • **to argue the ~*** machacar el asunto*
VT **1** (= *shake*) sacudir • **the boat was ~ed by the waves** las olas sacudían el barco • **the horse ~ed its head** el caballo sacudió la cabeza
2 (= *throw*) tirar, lanzar, echar, aventar (*Mex*); [*bull*] coger (y lanzar al aire) • **to ~ sth to sb** tirar *or* lanzar algo a algn • **to ~ sb in a blanket** mantear a algn • **to ~ the caber** (*Scot*) lanzar troncos • **to ~ a coin** echar a cara o cruz • **I'll ~ you for it** lo echamos a cara o cruz • **to ~ a pancake** dar la vuelta a *or* voltear una tortita • **to ~ a salad** mezclar una ensalada; ▹ HIGHLAND GAMES
VI **1** (*also* **toss about, toss around**) sacudirse, agitarse; [*boat*] (*gently*) balancearse sobre las ondas; (*violently*) ser sacudido por las ondas • **to ~ (in one's sleep)** • **~ and turn** dar vueltas *or* revolverse (en la cama)
2 (*also* **toss up**) echar a cara o cruz; (*Sport*) sortear (**for sth** algo) • **we ~ed (up) for the last piece of cake** nos jugamos *or* echamos a cara o cruz el último trozo de pastel • **we'll ~ (up) to see who does it** echaremos a cara o cruz quién lo hace
▸ **toss about, toss around** VT + ADV lanzar acá y allá • **the currents ~ed the boat about** las corrientes zarandeaban el barco
VI + ADV = toss
▸ **toss aside** VT + ADV [+ *object*] echar a un lado, apartar bruscamente; [+ *person*] abandonar; [+ *objection*] desechar, desestimar
▸ **toss away** VT + ADV echar, tirar
▸ **toss off** VT + ADV **1*** [+ *poem etc*] escribir rapidísimamente • **to ~ off a drink** beberse algo de un trago
2** (= *masturbate*) hacer una paja a**
VI + ADV** (= *masturbate*) hacerse una paja**
▸ **toss over** VT + ADV • **to ~ a book over to sb** tirar un libro a algn • **~ it over!** ¡dámelo!
▸ **toss up** VT + ADV [+ *coin*] echar a cara o cruz
VI + ADV = toss
tosser** ['tɒsəʳ], **tosspot**** ['tɒspɒt] N (*Brit*) mamón‡ *m*, gilipollas‡ *m*
toss-up ['tɒsʌp] N • **we'll settle it by a toss-up** nos lo jugaremos *or* lo echaremos a cara o cruz • **it was a toss-up between me and him** la cosa estaba entre él y yo (al cincuenta por ciento) • **it's a toss-up whether I go or stay** no me decido si irme o quedarme
tot¹ [tɒt] N **1** (= *child*) nene/a *m/f*, chiquillo/a *m/f*, niñito/a *m/f*
2 (*esp Brit*) (= *drink*) trago *m*, traguito *m* • **a tot of rum** un dedo de ron
tot² [tɒt] (*esp Brit*) VT • **to tot up** sumar, hacer la cuenta de
VI • **it tots up to £5** suma cinco libras, viene a ser cinco libras • **what does it tot up to?** ¿cuánto suma?
total ['təʊtl] ADJ **1** (= *complete, utter*) [*lack, commitment*] total, absoluto; [*ban*] total; [*failure*] rotundo, absoluto • **his attempt to try to resolve the dispute was a ~ failure** su intento de resolver la disputa fue un fracaso rotundo *or* absoluto • **he felt like a ~ failure** se sentía un completo fracasado • **a ~ stranger** un completo desconocido • **the car was a ~ write-off** el coche quedó totalmente destrozado; ▹ eclipse, recall
2 (= *overall*) [*amount, number, cost*] total; [*effect, policy*] global • **a ~ population of 650,000** una población total de 650.000 habitantes • **~ sales/assets** el total de ventas/activo • **~ losses amount to £100,000** las pérdidas ascienden a (un total de) 100.000 libras, el total de pérdidas asciende a 100.000 libras
N total *m* • **the jobless ~ was three million** el total de parados fue de tres millones • **in ~** en total • **a ~ of** un total de; ▹ grand, sum
VT **1** (= *add up*) [+ *figures*] sacar el total de, sumar el total de
2 (= *amount to*) ascender a • **that ~s £20** el total asciende a 20 libras • **the class now ~s 20 students** en la clase hay ahora un total de 20 alumnos • **prizes ~ling £300** premios por un (valor) total de 300 libras
3 (*esp US**) (= *wreck*) destrozar, hacer fosfatina* • **the car was completely ~led** el coche quedó hecho fosfatina*, el coche quedó para el arrastre*
totalitarian [ˌtəʊtælɪ'teərɪən] ADJ totalitario
totalitarianism [ˌtəʊtælɪ'teərɪənɪzəm] N totalitarismo *m*
totality [təʊ'tælɪtɪ] N totalidad *f* • **in its ~** en su totalidad
totalizator ['təʊtəlaɪzeɪtəʳ] N totalizador *m*
totalize ['təʊtəlaɪz] VT totalizar
totalizer ['təʊtəlaɪzəʳ] = totalizator
totally ['təʊtəlɪ] ADV totalmente • **such a compromise would be ~ unacceptable** un compromiso así sería totalmente *or* completamente *or* del todo inaceptable • **he's not ~ without principle** no carece totalmente de principios • **I'm still not ~ convinced** aún no estoy del todo convencido • **a view which has been almost ~ ignored** una postura que ha sido ignorada casi por completo
Tote ['təʊt] N (*Brit*) • **the ~** ≈ la quiniela hípica
tote [təʊt] VT* (= *carry*) cargar con • **I ~d it around all day** cargué con él todo el día • **to ~ a gun** llevar pistola • **gun-toting policemen** policías *mpl* pistoleros
CPD ▸ **tote bag** bolsa *f*, bolso *m*
totem ['təʊtəm] N tótem *m*
CPD ▸ **totem pole** tótem *m*
totemic [təʊ'temɪk] ADJ totémico
totemism ['təʊtəmɪzəm] N totemismo *m*
totter ['tɒtəʳ] VI (= *stagger*) bambolearse, tambalearse; (= *be about to fall*) tambalearse, estar para desplomarse
tottering ['tɒtərɪŋ] ADJ [*step*] tambaleante, inseguro, vacilante; [*economy, government*] inestable
tottery ['tɒtərɪ] ADJ [*elderly person*] de paso tambaleante, de paso nada seguro • **he's getting ~** empieza a andar con poca seguridad
totty‡ ['tɒtɪ] N (*Brit*) nenas* *fpl*, tías‡ *fpl*, titis‡ *fpl* • **a nice piece of ~** una tía buenísima‡
toucan ['tu:kən] N tucán *m*
touch [tʌtʃ] N **1** (= *sense, feel*) tacto *m* • **sense of ~** sentido *m* del tacto, tacto *m*
2 (= *pressure*) • **he felt the ~ of a hand on his shoulder** sintió el tacto *or* el roce de una mano en su hombro • **the merest ~ might break it** el más mínimo roce podría romperlo • **at the ~ of a button** con solo dar a un botón • **it's soft to the ~** es blando al tacto • **she responded to his ~** reaccionaba a sus caricias • IDIOM: • **to be an easy** *or* **a soft ~*** ser fácil de convencer
3 (= *technique, manner*) • **to have the common ~** saber tratar *or* sintonizar con el pueblo • **to have a light ~** [*pianist*] tocar con delicadeza *or* suavidad • **you need a light ~ to make good pastry** necesitas manos de seda para conseguir una buena masa • **to lose one's ~** perder facultades • **he had lost his scoring ~** había perdido habilidad *or* eficacia de cara al gol • **the director handles these scenes with a sure ~** el director trata estas escenas con mucha seguridad *or* gran pericia; ▹ common
4 (= *stamp, mark*) toque *m* • **the final ~** • **the finishing ~** el último toque, el toque final • **to put the finishing ~es to sth** dar los últimos toques *or* los toques finales a algo • **it has a ~ of genius** tiene un toque de genialidad • **the human ~** el calor humano • **the personal ~** el toque personal • **the house needs a woman's ~** la casa necesita un toque femenino
5 (= *detail*) detalle *m* • **that was a nice ~** eso fue un bonito detalle

6 (= *small quantity*) **a • a ~ of** [*of milk, water*] un chorrito de; [*of salt, pepper*] una pizca de; [*of irony, sarcasm*] un toque *or* un dejo de • **to have a ~ of flu** estar algo griposo • **there was a ~ of frost this morning** había algo de *or* un poco de escarcha esta mañana • **it needs a ~ of paint** le hace falta un poquito de pintura • **he got a ~ of the sun** le dio el sol un poquito

b (*with adjective, adverb*) • **it's a ~ (too) expensive** es algo *or* un poquito caro • **move it just a ~ to the left** muévelo un poquito a *or* hacia la izquierda

7 (= *contact*) • **to be in ~ (with sb)** estar en contacto (con algn) • **we are still in ~** todavía estamos en contacto • **I'll be in ~** (*writing*) te escribiré; (*phoning*) te llamaré • **to get in ~ (with sb)** ponerse en contacto (con algn) • **get in ~ with your emotions** conecte con sus emociones • **to keep in ~ (with sb)** mantener el contacto (con algn) • **well, keep in ~!** ¡bueno, no pierdas contacto!, ¡bueno, no dejes de llamar o escribir! • **to lose ~ (with sth/sb)** perder el contacto (con algo/algn) • **I lost ~ with her after she moved to London** perdí el contacto con ella después de que se mudara a Londres • **the party has lost ~ with the voters** el partido está desconectado de los votantes • **to be out of ~** no estar al corriente • **the Prime Minister was completely out of ~** el Primer Ministro no estaba al corriente de nada • **I'm out of ~ with the latest political developments** no estoy al corriente de los últimos acontecimientos políticos • **to put sb in ~ with sb** poner a algn en contacto con algn

8 (*Rugby*) • **to kick the ball into ~** poner el balón fuera de juego • **he had a foot in ~** tenía un pie fuera del terreno de juego *or* más allá de la línea de banda

(VT) 1 (*with hand*) tocar • **she ~ed his arm** le tocó el brazo • **they can't ~ you** (*fig*) no te pueden hacer nada • **to ~ one's toes** tocarse los dedos de los pies • **~ wood!** ¡toca madera!; ▹ **raw**

2 (= *come into contact with*) tocar; (= *brush against*) rozar • **I just ~ed the car in front** no hice más que rozar el coche que tenía delante • **I can ~ the bottom** (*in swimming pool*) puedo tocar el fondo; (*in sea*) hago pie • **my feet haven't ~ed the ground since I started this job** desde que empecé en este trabajo no he parado; ▹ **barge, base**

3 (= *harm, disturb*) tocar • **don't ~ anything!** ¡no toques nada! • **I never ~ed him!** ¡ni le toqué! • **if you ~ him I'll kill you!** ¡como le pongas la mano encima *or* si le tocas te mato!

4 (= *try*) [+ *food, drink*] probar • **I never ~ gin** no pruebo la ginebra • **you haven't ~ed your dinner** no has probado bocado, no has tocado la cena • **I haven't ~ed a typewriter in ages** hace siglos que no toco una máquina de escribir

5 (= *affect*) afectar • **it ~es all our lives** nos afecta a todos

6 (= *move*) • **her faith ~ed me** su fe me conmovió *or* me llegó al alma • **she was ~ed by his gift** el regalo la emocionó mucho

7 (= *compare with*) igualar • **no artist in the country can ~ him** no hay artista en todo el país que (se) le iguale • **nobody can ~ him as a pianist** como pianista es inigualable

8 (*esp Brit*) (= *reach*) • **he was ~ing 290mph** alcanzaba las 290 millas por hora • **his hair ~es his shoulders** tiene una melena que le llega por los hombros

9 (*Brit**) • **to ~ sb for money** dar un sablazo a algn*, pedir dinero prestado a algn

10 • **to be ~ed with sth: clouds ~ed with pink** nubes con un toque rosa • **his hair was ~ed with grey** tenía algunas canas en el pelo

(VI) 1 (*with hand*) • **don't ~!** (*to child*) ¡no se toca! • **"please do not touch"** "se ruega no tocar"

2 (= *come into contact*) [*hands*] encontrarse; [*lips*] rozarse; [*wires*] hacer contacto • **our hands ~ed** nuestras manos se encontraron

(CPD) ▸ **touch judge** (*Rugby*) juez *mf* de línea, juez *mf* de banda ▸ **touch screen** pantalla *f* táctil; ▹ **touchscreen**

▸ **touch at** (VI + PREP) tocar en, hacer escala en

▸ **touch down** (VI + ADV) 1 (*Aer, Space*) (*on land*) aterrizar; (*on sea*) amerizar; (*on water*) acuatizar; (*on moon*) alunizar; ▹ **touchdown**

2 (*Rugby*) marcar un ensayo; (*American Ftbl*) (= *score*) hacer un touchdown; (*behind one's own goal line*) poner balón en tierra; ▹ **touchdown**

(VT + ADV) (*Rugby*) • **he ~ed the ball down** (= *scored a try*) marcó un ensayo; (*behind his own goal line*) puso el balón en tierra

▸ **touch off** (VT + ADV) [+ *argument, violence, riot, fire*] provocar; [+ *explosive*] hacer estallar

▸ **touch on, touch upon** (VI + PREP) [+ *subject*] [*speaker, film, book*] tocar; [+ *fact*] [*speaker*] mencionar (de pasada)

▸ **touch up** (VT + ADV) 1 (= *improve*) [+ *photograph, painting, make-up*] retocar

2* (*sexually*) meter mano a*, sobar*

touch-and-go [ˈtʌtʃənˈgəʊ] (N) • **it's touch-and-go whether he'll survive** no se sabe si sobrevivirá • **it was touch-and-go whether we'd arrive before we ran out of petrol** no estaba nada seguro de que la gasolina nos fuera a dar para llegar • **we made it, but it was touch-and-go** lo conseguimos, pero por los pelos*

(ADJ) [*decision*] difícil, dudoso

touchdown [ˈtʌtʃdaʊn] (N) 1 (*Aer, Space*) (*on land*) aterrizaje *m*; (*on sea*) amerizaje *m*; (*on water*) acuatizaje *m*; (*on moon*) alunizaje *m*

2 (*Rugby*) ensayo *m*; (*American Ftbl*) touchdown *m*

touché [tuːˈʃeɪ] (EXCL) ¡dices bien!

touched* [tʌtʃt] (ADJ) (= *crazy*) tocado*, majara* • **he must be ~ in the head!** ¡tiene que estar tocado del ala!*

touchiness [ˈtʌtʃɪnɪs] (N) susceptibilidad *f*

touching [ˈtʌtʃɪŋ] (ADJ) conmovedor, patético

(PREP) tocante a

touchingly [ˈtʌtʃɪŋlɪ] (ADV) de modo conmovedor, patéticamente

touchline [ˈtʌtʃlaɪn] (N) (*Brit*) (*Sport*) línea *f* de banda

touchpad [ˈtʌtʃpæd] (N) (*Comput*) ratón *m* táctil, touchpad *m*

touchpaper [ˈtʌtʃpeɪpəʳ] (N) mecha *f*

touchscreen [ˈtʌtʃskriːn] (N) (*Comput*) pantalla *f* táctil

touch-sensitive [ˈtʌtʃsensɪtɪv] (ADJ) sensible al tacto

touchstone [ˈtʌtʃstəʊn] (N) (*lit, fig*) piedra *f* de toque

touch-tone [ˈtʌtʃtəʊn] (ADJ) (*Telec*) digital, por tonos

touch-type [ˈtʌtʃtaɪp] (VI) mecanografiar al tacto

touch-typing [ˈtʌtʃˌtaɪpɪŋ] (N) mecanografía *f* al tacto

touch-typist [ˈtʌtʃˌtaɪpɪst] (N) mecanógrafo/a *m/f* al tacto

touchy [ˈtʌtʃɪ] (ADJ) (COMPAR: **touchier**, SUPERL: **touchiest**) 1 (= *sensitive*) [*person*] susceptible; [*subject*] delicado • **to be ~** ofenderse por poca cosa, ser (muy) susceptible • **he's ~ about his weight** su peso es un tema delicado • **that's a ~ subject with him** es delicado mencionarle ese asunto

2* (= *tactile*) [*person*] sobón

touchy-feely* [ˈtʌtʃifiːlɪ] (ADJ) [*person*] sobón; [*talk, session*] íntimo

tough [tʌf] (ADJ) (COMPAR: **tougher**, SUPERL: **toughest**) 1 (= *robust*) fuerte • **granny may be old, but she's ~** puede que la abuela sea vieja, pero es fuerte • IDIOM: • **to be (as) ~ as old boots*** (*hum*) [*person*] ser fuerte como un roble*

2 (= *hard, uncompromising*) [*person*] duro; [*neighbourhood, school*] peligroso • **~ customer*** tío/a *m/f* duro/a* • **~ guy*** tipo *m* duro • **~ nut*** tío/a *m/f* duro/a* • **to do some ~ talking** hablar sin rodeos

3 (= *resistant*) [*substance, material*] fuerte, resistente; [*skin*] duro

4 (= *not tender*) [*meat*] duro • **the steak was as ~ as old boots*** el filete estaba duro como la suela de un zapato*

5 (= *harsh*) [*policies*] duro, de mano dura; [*measures*] duro; [*teacher, parent*] severo • **to take a ~ line on sth** adoptar una línea dura con respecto a algo • **to take a ~ line with sb** ponerse duro con algn • **to be ~ on sb** ser duro con algn

6 (= *difficult*) [*way of life, situation, day*] duro, difícil; [*choice, question*] difícil; [*competition*] fuerte • **it's a ~ job being Prime Minister** es duro ser primer ministro • **it's a ~ job, but somebody has to do it** es un trabajo duro, pero alguien tiene que hacerlo • **it's ~ when you have kids** es difícil cuando tienes niños • **it will be ~ to finish it in time** va a ser difícil acabarlo a tiempo • **his team will be ~ to beat** su equipo será difícil de vencer, va a ser difícil vencer a su equipo • **it was ~ trying to raise the cash** fue difícil conseguir el dinero • **he has found it ~ going this year** este año se le ha hecho muy cuesta arriba, este año le ha resultado muy difícil • **when the going gets ~** cuando las cosas se ponen difíciles • **to have a ~ time (of it)** pasarlo mal *or* fatal*, pasar las de Caín* • IDIOM: • **when the going gets ~, the ~ get going** la gente con arrestos se crece ante las adversidades

7 (*set expressions*) • **tough! • ~ luck!*** ¡mala suerte! • **that's your ~ luck!** ¡te fastidias! • **~ shit**** te jodes**

(N)* (= *thug*) matón *m*, macarra* *m*

(VT)* • **to ~ it out** aguantar el tipo*

(ADV)* 1 • **to act/talk ~** hacerse el duro*

2 (*US*) • **to hang ~** mantenerse firme

(CPD) ▸ **tough love** amor *m* exigente

toughen [ˈtʌfn] (*also* **toughen up**) (VT) [+ *material*] endurecer; [+ *person*] fortalecer, hacer más fuerte; (*fig*) [+ *position*] endurecer

(VI) endurecerse

toughened [ˈtʌfnd] (ADJ) [*material*] endurecido

toughie* [ˈtʌfɪ] (N) (= *difficult question*) pregunta *f* peliaguda; (= *person*) bravucón/ona *m/f*

tough-minded [ˈtʌfˈmaɪndɪd] (ADJ) duro, nada sentimental

toughness [ˈtʌfnɪs] (N) 1 [*of person*] dureza *f* • **she has a reputation for ~** tiene fama de dura

2 [*of substance, material*] dureza *f*, resistencia *f*

3 [*of meat*] dureza *f*

4 [*of policy, measure*] dureza *f*

Toulon [tuːˈlɔ̃ːŋ] (N) Tolón *m*

Toulouse [tuːˈluːz] (N) Tolosa *f* (*de Francia*)

toupée [ˈtuːpeɪ] (N) peluca *f*, postizo *m*

tour [ˈtʊəʳ] (N) 1 (*by tourist*) [*of country*] gira *f*, viaje *m*; [*of city*] recorrido *m*; [*of building, exhibition*] visita *f* • **a ~ around Europe** una gira *or* un viaje por Europa • **to go on a ~ of sth:** • **they went on a ~ of the Lake District**

hicieron una excursión *or* un viaje por la Región de los Lagos • **to go on a walking/ cycling ~** hacer una excursión a pie/en bicicleta • **we went on a ~ around London** hicimos un recorrido por Londres • **guided ~** [*of famous building*] visita *f* guiada *or* con guía; [*of city*] recorrido *m* turístico (con guía); ▹ **coach, conducted, grand, mystery**
2 (*by musician, team, statesman*) gira *f* • **concert ~** gira *f* de conciertos • **he is currently on a lecture ~ in the States** actualmente está dando una serie de conferencias por Estados Unidos • **they gave us a ~ of the factory** nos enseñaron la fábrica • **~ of inspection** recorrido *m or* ronda *f* de inspección • **he made a ~ of the villages threatened by the volcano** visitó *or* recorrió los pueblos amenazados por el volcán • **to be/go on ~** estar/ir de gira • **to take a play on ~** hacer una gira con una obra de teatro • **world ~** gira *f* mundial; ▹ **whistle-stop**
3 (*Mil*) • **~ of duty** periodo *m* de servicio
4 (*US*) (*Golf*) • **the ~** la temporada
VT **1** (*as tourist*) [+ *country, region*] recorrer, viajar por; [+ *town*] recorrer • **they are ~ing France** están recorriendo Francia, están viajando por Francia
2 (*officially*) ir de gira por • **the band ~ed Europe last year** el año pasado el grupo se fue de gira por Europa • **the Royal Opera is currently ~ing Japan** actualmente la Royal Opera está de gira por Japón • **the play is ~ing the provinces** están de gira con la obra por provincias • **the England team will be ~ing South Africa this winter** el equipo inglés hará una gira por Sudáfrica este invierno • **the Prince ~ed the factory** el Príncipe visitó la fábrica
VI **1** [*tourist*] viajar • **they went ~ing in Italy** se fueron de viaje por Italia
2 (*officially*) [*musician, team*] ir de gira • **he's currently ~ing in the States** actualmente está de gira por Estados Unidos
CPD ▸ **tour bus** autobús *m* de la gira ▸ **tour company** touroperador *m* ▸ **tour director** (*US*) guía *mf* turístico/a ▸ **tour guide** guía *mf* turístico/a ▸ **tour manager** (*Sport, Mus*) encargado/a *m/f* de gira ▸ **tour operator** touroperador(a) *m/f* ▸ **tour rep** (*Brit*) guía *mf* (*del touroperador*)

Touraine [tʊ'reɪn] N Turena *f*
tour de force ['tʊədə'fɔːs] N (PL: **tours de force**) proeza *f*, hazaña *f*
tourer ['tʊərəʳ] N coche *m* de turismo, turismo *m*
Tourette syndrome [tʊə'ret,sɪndrəʊm], **Tourette's syndrome** [tʊə'rets,sɪndrəʊm] N síndrome *m* de Tourette
touring ['tʊərɪŋ] N **1** (*by tourist*) turismo *m* • **I'd like to do some ~ in a camper van** me gustaría hacer un poco de turismo en una autocaravana
2 (*by band, statesman etc*) giras *fpl* • **the company has done more ~ this year** la compañía ha realizado más giras este año
CPD ▸ **touring bicycle** bicicleta *f* de paseo ▸ **touring company** (*Theat*) compañía *f* (de teatro) ambulante ▸ **touring exhibition** exposición *f* itinerante ▸ **touring holiday** viaje *m* turístico ▸ **touring map** mapa *m* turístico ▸ **touring production** montaje *m* itinerante ▸ **touring team** equipo *m* en gira
tourism ['tʊərɪzəm] N turismo *m*
tourist ['tʊərɪst] N **1** (*on holiday*) turista *mf*
2 (*Sport*) (= *visiting team*) • **the ~s** el equipo visitante
CPD [*attraction, season*] turístico ▸ **tourist agency** agencia *f* de turismo ▸ **tourist bureau** = **tourist information centre** ▸ **tourist class** clase *f* turista ▸ **tourist industry** industria *f* del turismo ▸ **tourist information** (= *office*) oficina *f* de turismo; (= *facts*) información *f* turística ▸ **tourist information centre, tourist office** oficina *f* de turismo, oficina *f* de información turística ▸ **tourist season** temporada *f* del turismo ▸ **the tourist trade** el turismo ▸ **tourist trap** sitio *m* para turistas ▸ **tourist visa** visado *m* turístico, visa *f* turística (*LAm*)
touristy* ['tʊərɪstɪ] ADJ (demasiado) turístico, turistizado
tournament ['tʊənəmənt] N torneo *m* • **tennis ~** torneo *m* de tenis
tournedos ['tʊənə'dəʊ] N turnedó *m*, tournedós *m*
tourney ['tʊənɪ] N (*Hist*) torneo *m*
tourniquet ['tʊənɪkeɪ] N (*Med*) torniquete *m*
touse* [taʊz] VT (*lit, fig*) dar una paliza a
tousing* ['taʊzɪŋ] N (*lit, fig*) paliza *f*
tousle ['taʊzl] VT ajar, desarreglar; [+ *hair*] despeinar
tousled ['taʊzld] ADJ [*appearance, style*] desaliñado, desarreglado; [*hair*] despeinado
tout [taʊt] N (*for hotels etc*) gancho/a *m/f*; (*Racing*) pronosticador(a) *m/f*; (*Brit*) (= *ticket tout*) revendedor(a) *m/f*
VI (*Brit*) • **to ~ for business** *or* **custom** tratar de captar clientes
VT [+ *wares*] ofrecer, pregonar; (*Brit*) [+ *tickets*] revender
tout court ['tuː'kʊəʳ] ADV • **his name is Rodríguez ~** se llama Rodríguez a secas
tow[1] [təʊ] N **1** (*Aut*) (= *act*) remolque *m*; (= *rope*) remolque *m*, cable *m* de remolque; (= *thing towed*) vehículo *m* remolcado • **to give sb a tow** dar remolque *or* remolcar a algn • **on tow** (*Brit*) • **in tow** (*US*) a remolque • **to have a car in tow** llevar un coche de remolque • **to take in tow** dar remolque a
2 (*fig**) • **he arrived with a friend in tow** llegó acompañado de un amigo; (*unwillingly*) llegó con un amigo a rastras *or* a remolque
VT **1** [+ *car, caravan, boat*] remolcar; [+ *barge*] (*on canal*) sirgar
2 (*fig*) • **to tow sth about** llevar algo consigo
CPD ▸ **tow bar** barra *f* de remolque ▸ **tow car** (*US*) grúa *f*, coche *m* de remolque ▸ **tow line** (*Naut*) (*at sea*) maroma *f* de remolque; (*on canal*) sirga *f*; (*Aut*) remolque *m*, cable *m* de remolque ▸ **tow truck** (*esp US*) camión *m* grúa, grúa *f*, coche *m* de remolque
▸ **tow away** VT + ADV remolcar, quitar remolcando • **to tow a car away** llevar un coche a la comisaría
tow[2] [təʊ] N (*Textiles*) estopa *f*
towage ['təʊɪdʒ] N (= *act*) remolque *m*; (= *fee*) derechos *mpl* de remolque
toward [tə'wɔːd] PREP **1** (*direction*) hacia • **we walked ~ the sea** caminamos hacia el mar *or* rumbo al mar • **the government is moving ~ disaster** el gobierno se encamina hacia el desastre
2 (*time*) alrededor de, a eso de • **~ noon** alrededor de mediodía • **~ six o'clock** hacia las seis, a eso de las seis
3 (*attitude*) para con, con respecto a, hacia • **his attitude ~ the church** su actitud para con *or* con respecto a *or* hacia la iglesia • **to feel friendly ~ sb** sentir simpatía hacia *or* por algn
4 (*purpose*) para • **we're saving ~ our holiday** ahorramos dinero para nuestras vacaciones • **it helps ~ a solution** contribuye a la solución, ayuda en el esfuerzo por encontrar una solución • **half my salary goes ~ paying the rent** la mitad de mi sueldo se va en el alquiler
towards [tə'wɔːdz] PREP (*esp Brit*) = **toward**
towaway zone ['təʊəweɪ,zəʊn] N (*US*) (*Aut*) *zona de aparcamiento prohibido donde la grúa procede a retirar los vehículos*
towboat ['təʊbəʊt] N (*US*) remolcador *m*
towel ['taʊəl] N (*for body*) toalla *f*; (*for hands*) paño *m*, toalla *f* • IDIOM: • **to throw in the ~** darse por vencido
VT frotar con toalla • **to ~ sth/sb dry** secar algo/a algn con toalla
CPD ▸ **towel rack, towel rail** toallero *m*
towelette [,taʊə'let] N toallita *f*
towelling, toweling (*US*) ['taʊəlɪŋ] N felpa *f*
tower ['taʊəʳ] N **1** [*of castle*] torre *f* • **the Tower of London** la Torre de Londres • **a ~ of strength** (*fig*) una gran ayuda
2 (*also* **bell tower**) campanario *m*
VI elevarse • **it ~s to over 300 metres** se eleva a más de 300 metros • **to ~ above** *or* **over sth** dominar algo • **to ~ above** *or* **over sb** destacar *or* descollar sobre algn • **he ~s above** *or* **over his contemporaries** (*fig*) destaca *or* descuella claramente entre sus coetáneos
CPD ▸ **tower block** (*Brit*) bloque *m* de pisos, torre *f* de pisos
towering ['taʊərɪŋ] ADJ [*peak, mountain*] elevado, imponente; [*building*] muy alto, imponente por su altura; [*figure*] (*in stature*) imponente, altísimo; (*in literature, arts etc*) destacado, sobresaliente • **in a ~ rage** con una rabia terrible
tow-headed [,təʊ'hedɪd] ADJ rubio, rubiacho
towing rope ['təʊɪŋ,rəʊp] N cuerda *f* de remolque
towing truck ['təʊɪŋ,trʌk] N grúa *f*
town [taʊn] N ciudad *f*; (*smaller*) pueblo *m*, población *f* • **~ and gown** (*Univ*) ciudadanos *mpl* y universitarios, ciudad *f* y universidad • **to live in a ~** vivir en una ciudad • **Jake's back in ~!** ¡ha vuelto Jake! • **to be out of ~** [*place*] estar fuera de la ciudad; [*person*] estar de viaje • **he's from out of ~** (*US*) es forastero, no es de aquí • **to go into ~** ir al centro • IDIOMS: • **to go out on the ~*** salir de juerga *or* de parranda* • **to go to ~ (on sth)*** dedicarse con entusiasmo (a algo), no cortarse nada (con algo); (*spending*) no reparar en gastos (con algo); ▹ **paint**
CPD ▸ **town centre, town center** (*US*) centro *m* urbano ▸ **town clerk** secretario/a *m/f* del ayuntamiento ▸ **town council** ayuntamiento *m* ▸ **town councillor** concejal(a) *m/f* ▸ **town crier** pregonero *m* público ▸ **town dweller** habitante *mf* de la ciudad ▸ **town hall** ayuntamiento *m*, municipalidad *f* ▸ **town house** casa *f* adosada; (= *not country*) residencia *f* urbana ▸ **town meeting** (*US*) pleno *m* municipal ▸ **town plan** plan *m* de desarrollo urbano ▸ **town planner** (*Brit*) urbanista *mf* ▸ **town planning** (*Brit*) urbanismo *m*
townee [taʊ'niː], **townie** ['taʊnɪ] N habitante *mf* de la ciudad
townscape ['taʊnskeɪp] N paisaje *m* urbano
townsfolk ['taʊnzfəʊk] NPL ciudadanos *mpl*
township ['taʊnʃɪp] N (= *small town*) pueblo *m*; (*US*) municipio *m*; (*South Africa*) *asentamiento urbano creado en tiempos del apartheid para gente de raza negra en Sudáfrica*
townsman ['taʊnzmən] N (PL: **townsmen**) ciudadano *m*; (*as opposed to country-dweller*) hombre *m* de la ciudad, habitante *m* de la ciudad
townspeople ['taʊnz,piːpl] NPL ciudadanos *mpl*
townswoman ['taʊnzwʊmən] N (PL: **townswomen**) ciudadana *f*; (*as opposed to*

countrywoman) habitante *f* de la ciudad

towpath ['təʊpɑ:θ] (N) camino *m* de sirga

towrope ['təʊrəʊp] (N) remolque *m*, cable *m* de remolque; (*on canal*) sirga *f*

toxaemia, **toxemia** (US) [tɒk'si:mɪə] (N) toximia *f*

toxic ['tɒksɪk] (ADJ) **1** [*substance, alga*] tóxico
2 (*Fin*) [*loan, investment*] tóxico
(N) tóxico *m*
(CPD) ▸ **toxic waste** desechos *mpl* tóxicos

toxicity [ˌtɒk'sɪsɪtɪ] (N) toxicidad *f*

toxicological [ˌtɒksɪkə'lɒdʒɪkəl] (ADJ) toxicológico

toxicologist [ˌtɒksɪ'kɒlədʒɪst] (N) toxicólogo/a *m/f*

toxicology [ˌtɒksɪ'kɒlədʒɪ] (N) toxicología *f*

toxin ['tɒksɪn] (N) toxina *f*

toy [tɔɪ] (N) juguete *m*
(VI) • **to toy with** [+ *object, sb's affections*] jugar con, juguetear con; [+ *food*] comiscar; [+ *idea*] acariciar
(CPD) ▸ **toy car** coche *m* de juguete ▸ **toy dog** (= *small breed of dog*) perrito *m*, perro *m* faldero ▸ **toy gun** arma *f* de juguete ▸ **the toy industry** la industria juguetera ▸ **toy maker** (= *person*) fabricante *mf* de juguetes; (= *company*) empresa *f* de juguetes ▸ **toy poodle** (= *small breed of poodle*) caniche *mf* enano/a ▸ **toy soldier** soldadito *m* de juguete ▸ **toy theatre** teatro *m* de títeres ▸ **toy train** tren *m* de juguete

toybox ['tɔɪbɒks] (N) caja *f* de juguetes

toyboy ['tɔɪbɔɪ] (N) (*Brit*) amante *m* (de una mujer mayor)

toyshop ['tɔɪʃɒp] (N) juguetería *f*

toytown ['tɔɪtaʊn] (ADJ) **1** (= *not serious*) [*politician, police, institution*] de pacotilla • **he's a ~ revolutionary** es un revolucionario de pacotilla
2 (= *toy*) [*money, building, uniform*] de juguete

tpi (N ABBR) (*Comput*) = **tracks per inch**

TQM (N) (= **total quality management**) TQM *f*, gestión *f* de calidad total

trace [treɪs] (N) **1** (= *sign*) rastro *m*, señal *f* • **the search for ~s of life on Mars** la búsqueda de señales *or* indicios de vida en Marte • **she wanted to remove all ~ of him from the flat** quería deshacerse de todo rastro de él en el piso • **I've lost all ~ of my relations** perdí todo contacto con mis familiares, les perdí la pista *or* el rastro a mis familiares • **there was no ~ of him having been there** no había ningún indicio *or* rastro de que hubiera estado allí • **she had no ~ of an accent** no tenía ni pizca de acento • **he showed no ~ of shyness** no dio muestras de timidez, no mostró señales de timidez • **to disappear** *or* **vanish without (a) ~** desaparecer sin dejar huella *or* rastro • **the group had a few hits then sank without ~** el grupo tuvo unos cuantos éxitos y luego desapareció sin dejar huella *or* rastro
2 (= *remains*) vestigio *m* • **they found ~s of an ancient settlement** encontraron vestigios de un antiguo poblado
3 (= *small amount*) rastro *m* • **the blood test revealed ~s of poison** el análisis de sangre reveló rastros de veneno • **there was a ~ of a smile on her face** tenía el esbozo de una sonrisa en la cara • **rinse well and remove all ~s of soap** enjuague bien y elimine cualquier rastro *or* resto de jabón • **she said it without a ~ of irony** lo dijo sin (ningún) asomo de ironía
4 (*Tech*) (= *line*) traza *f*
5 (= *strap on harness*) tirante *m*, correa *f* • IDIOM: • **to kick over the ~s** rebelarse, sacar los pies del plato *or* tiesto*
(VT) **1** (= *find*) [+ *missing document, fault*] localizar, encontrar; [+ *missing person, suspect*] averiguar el paradero de, localizar, ubicar (*LAm*) • **we have been unable to ~ your letter** no hemos podido localizar *or* encontrar su carta • **I cannot ~ any reference to it** no encuentro ninguna referencia a eso
2 (= *follow trail of*) [+ *person*] seguir la pista a • **she was finally ~d to a house in Soho** le siguieron la pista hasta dar con ella en una casa del Soho • **they ~d the van to a car rental agency** averiguaron que la furgoneta era de una agencia de alquiler de automóviles
3 (= *find source of*) [+ *phone call*] averiguar el origen de • **I can ~ my family back to Elizabethan times** las raíces de mi familia se remontan a la época isabelina • **to ~ a rumour back to its source** averiguar dónde se originó un rumor, seguir la pista de un rumor hasta llegar a su punto de partida
(CPD) ▸ **trace element** oligoelemento *m*

traceability [ˌtreɪsə'bɪlɪtɪ] (N) rastreabilidad *f*

traceable ['treɪsəbl] (ADJ) [*data*] rastreable • **a person not now ~** una persona cuyo paradero actual es imposible de encontrar • **an easily ~ reference** una referencia fácil de encontrar

tracer ['treɪsə^r] (N) (*Chem, Med*) indicador *m*, trazador *m*
(CPD) ▸ **tracer bullet** bala *f* trazadora ▸ **tracer element** elemento *m* trazador

tracery ['treɪsərɪ] (N) tracería *f*

trachea [trə'kɪə] (N) (PL: **tracheas, tracheae** [trə'kɪi:]) (*Anat*) tráquea *f*

tracheotomy [ˌtrækɪ'ɒtəmɪ] (N) traqueotomía *f*

trachoma [træ'kəʊmə] (N) tracoma *m*

tracing ['treɪsɪŋ] (N) **1** (*with tracing paper*) calco *m*
2 (*electronically*) traza *f*
3 [*of phone call*] seguimiento *m*
(CPD) ▸ **tracing paper** papel *m* de calco

track [træk] (N) **1** (= *trail*) [*of animal, person*] rastro *m*, pista *f*; [*of vehicle*] rastro *m*; [*of wheel*] huellas *fpl*, rodada *f* • **to cover one's ~s** borrar las huellas • **to keep ~ of sth/sb**: • **they prefer him to live at home where they can keep ~ of him** prefieren que viva en casa donde le pueden seguir la pista • **do you find it hard to keep ~ of all your bills?** ¿le resulta difícil mantenerse al corriente de todas sus facturas? • **start keeping ~ of how much you spend** empiece a tomar nota de cuánto gasta • **to lose ~ of sth/sb**: • **I lost all ~ of time** perdí la noción del tiempo por completo • **to lose ~ of what sb is saying** perder el hilo de lo que está diciendo algn • **to make ~s*** (*fig*) irse marchando, empezar a irse • **it's time we were making ~s** es hora de irse marchando *or* de que empecemos a irnos • **to be on sb's ~** seguirle la pista *or* el rastro a algn • **to stop (dead) in one's ~s** pararse en seco • **the sound stopped him in his ~s** el sonido le hizo pararse en seco • **to throw sb off the ~** (*fig*) despistar a algn
2 (= *course*) [*of missile, bullet, satellite*] trayectoria *f*; [*of storm*] curso *m* • **it will take time to get the economy back on ~** se tardará un tiempo en volver a encarrilar la economía • **to be on the right ~** ir por buen camino • **to be on the wrong ~** ir por mal camino; ▹ **one-track**
3 (= *path*) camino *m*, sendero *m*
4 (*Sport*) pista *f* • **~ and field** atletismo *m* • **~ and field events** pruebas *fpl* de atletismo • **race ~** (*for horses*) hipódromo *m*; (*for bicycles*) velódromo *m*; (*for cars*) autódromo *m*, pista *f* *or* circuito *m* de automovilismo • **running ~** pista *f* de atletismo • IDIOMS: • **to be on a fast ~ to sth** ir rápidamente camino de algo • **to have the inside ~** (*esp US*) estar en una posición de ventaja
5 (*Rail*) vía *f* • **double ~** vía *f* doble • **to jump the ~s** descarrilar • **single ~** vía *f* única • IDIOM: • **the wrong side of the ~s** (*esp US**) los barrios bajos • **she was born on the wrong side of the ~s** nació en los barrios bajos • **she's from the wrong side of the ~s** proviene de los barrios bajos
6 (*Aut*) (*on tank, tractor*) oruga *f*; (*between wheels*) ancho *m* de vía (*Tech*) (*distancia entre los puntos de contacto con el suelo de dos ruedas paralelas*)
7 (*Audio*) pista *f* • **four/eight ~ recording system** equipo *m* de grabación de cuatro/ocho pistas
8 (*Comput*) pista *f*
9 (= *song, piece*) tema *m* • **title ~** tema *m* que da título *or* nombre al álbum
10 (*for curtains*) riel *m*
11 (*US*) (*Educ*) (= *stream*) *agrupamiento de alumnos según su capacidad*
(VT) **1** (= *follow*) [+ *animal*] seguir las huellas de, seguir el rastro de; [+ *person, vehicle*] seguir la pista a; [+ *satellite, missile*] seguir la trayectoria de, rastrear • **the camera was ~ing his movements** la cámara seguía sus movimientos
2 (= *deposit*) ir dejando • **she was ~ing dirt all over the carpet** iba dejando suciedad por toda la moqueta
(VI) [*stylus*] seguir el surco
(CPD) ▸ **track events** (*Sport*) pruebas *fpl* en pista ▸ **track maintenance** (*Rail*) mantenimiento *m* de la vía ▸ **track meet** (*US*) concurso *m* de atletismo ▸ **track race** carrera *f* en pista ▸ **track racing** carreras *fpl* en pista, ciclismo *m* en pista ▸ **track record** historial *m* • **he had a good ~ record** su historial era bueno • **it's a company with a poor ~ record** es una empresa con un historial no muy bueno (en materia de ganancias) ▸ **track shoes** zapatillas *fpl* para pista de atletismo (claveteadas)

▸ **track down** (VT + ADV) (= *locate*) [+ *suspect, document, information*] localizar, ubicar (*LAm*); [+ *missing person*] averiguar el paradero de, localizar • **we eventually ~ed him down in the library** finalmente lo localizamos *or* dimos con él en la biblioteca • **scientists have ~ed down the bacteria that causes the infection** los científicos han localizado la bacteria que causa la infección • **eventually I ~ed down a copy of the novel** finalmente localicé un ejemplar de la novela

trackball ['trækbɔ:l] (N) (*Comput*) bola *f* rastreadora, trackball *m*

tracked [trækt] (ADJ) • **~ vehicle** vehículo *m* de oruga

tracker ['trækə^r] (N) rastreador *m*
(CPD) ▸ **tracker dog** perro *m* rastreador ▸ **tracker fund** = **index-tracking fund**

tracking ['trækɪŋ] (N) rastreo *m*
(CPD) ▸ **tracking device** dispositivo *m* de localización ▸ **tracking shot** (*Cine, TV*) travelling *m* ▸ **tracking station** estación *f* de seguimiento

trackless ['træklɪs] (ADJ) sin caminos, impenetrable

trackman ['trækmən] (N) (PL: **trackmen**) (*US*) obrero *m* de ferrocarril

trackpad ['trækpæd] (N) ratón *m* táctil, trackpad *m*

tracksuit ['træksu:t] (N) (*Brit*) chándal *m*

tract[1] [trækt] (N) **1** (= *area of land, sea*) extensión *f*
2 (*Anat*) tracto *m* • **respiratory ~** vías *fpl* respiratorias, aparato *m* respiratorio
(CPD) ▸ **tract house** (*US*) casa *f* unifamiliar (*idéntica a las demás*)

t

tract² [trækt] (N) (= *pamphlet*) folleto *m*, panfleto *m*; (= *treatise*) tratado *m*
tractable ['træktəbl] (ADJ) [*person*] tratable; [*problem*] soluble; [*material*] dúctil, maleable
traction ['trækʃən] (N) tracción *f*
(CPD) ▸ **traction engine** locomotora *f* de tracción
tractive ['træktɪv] (ADJ) tractivo
tractor ['træktəʳ] (N) tractor *m*
(CPD) ▸ **tractor drive** tractor *m* ▸ **tractor driver** tractorista *mf* ▸ **tractor feed** arrastre *m* de papel por tracción
tractor-drawn ['træktədrɔːn] (ADJ) arrastrado por tractor
tractor-trailer [ˌtræktə'treɪləʳ] (N) (*US*) camión *m* articulado
trad* [træd] (ADJ ABBR) (*esp Brit*) (*Mus*) = traditional
trade [treɪd] (N) **1** (= *buying and selling*) comercio *m* • **domestic/foreign/world ~** comercio *m* interior/exterior/internacional • **to do ~ with sb** comerciar con algn • **to do a good** *or* **brisk** *or* **roaring ~ (in sth)** (*Brit*) hacer (un) buen negocio (con algo) • **all ~ in ivory is banned** el comercio de todo tipo de *or* con marfil está prohibido • **to be in ~**† ser comerciante
2 (= *industry*) industria *f* • **the building ~** la industria de la construcción • **the antiques ~** la compraventa de antigüedades • **the arms ~** el tráfico de armas • **the tourist ~** el turismo, el sector turístico
3 (= *profession, occupation*) oficio *m* • **he's a butcher by ~** es carnicero de oficio • **known in the ~ as ...** conocido en el gremio como ... • **as we/they say in the ~** como decimos/dicen en el oficio; ▹ **tool, trick**
4 (= *people in trade*) • **to sell to the ~** vender al por mayor *or* (*LAm*) al mayoreo • **"no trade"** "solo particulares" • **"trade only"** "solo mayoristas"
5 (= *clientele*) clientela *f* • **passing ~** clientela *f* de paso • **he hires boats out for the tourist ~** alquila barcas a los turistas
6 (*esp US*) (= *exchange*) cambio *m* • **it was fair ~** fue un cambio justo • **I'm willing to do** *or* **make a ~ with you** estoy dispuesto a hacerte un cambio *or* a hacer un cambio contigo
(VT) (*esp US*) (= *exchange*) [+ *goods*] cambiar; [+ *blows, insults, jokes*] intercambiar • **to ~ sth for sth** cambiar algo por algo • **to ~ sth with sb** intercambiar algo con algn • **I wouldn't ~ places with her for anything** no quisiera estar en su lugar por nada del mundo • **managers ~d places with cleaners for a day** los gerentes y el personal de limpieza se cambiaron los trabajos por un día
(VI) **1** (= *do business*) comerciar • **we are trading at a loss** estamos comerciando con pérdida • **to cease trading** cerrar • **to ~ in sth** comerciar con algo • **to ~ in ivory/hardware** comerciar con marfil/artículos de ferretería • **he ~s in antique dolls** se dedica a la compraventa de muñecas antiguas • **he ~s under a business name** opera con un nombre comercial • **to ~ with sb** comerciar con algn
2 (= *exchange*) (*esp US*) hacer un cambio
3 (= *sell*) [*currency, shares*] cotizarse (**at** a)
(CPD) ▸ **trade agreement** acuerdo *m* comercial, convenio *m* comercial ▸ **trade association** asociación *f* gremial, asociación *f* mercantil ▸ **trade balance** balanza *f* comercial ▸ **trade barriers** barreras *fpl* arancelarias ▸ **trade deficit** déficit *m* comercial ▸ **Trade Descriptions Act** (*Brit*) ley *f* de protección al consumidor ▸ **trade discount** descuento *m* comercial ▸ **trade embargo** embargo *m* comercial ▸ **trade fair** feria *f* de muestras, feria *f* comercial ▸ **trade figures** estadísticas *fpl* comerciales ▸ **trade gap** déficit *m* comercial ▸ **trade journal** revista *f* especializada ▸ **trade magazine** = **trade journal** ▸ **trade name** nombre *m* comercial ▸ **trade price** precio *m* al por mayor, precio *m* de mayoreo (*LAm*) ▸ **trade restrictions** restricciones *fpl* comerciales ▸ **trade route** ruta *f* comercial ▸ **trade sanctions** sanciones *fpl* comerciales ▸ **trade secret** secreto *m* comercial; (*fig*) secreto *m* profesional ▸ **trades union** = **trade union** ▸ **Trades Union Congress** (*Brit*) Federación *f* de los Sindicatos ▸ **trade surplus** balanza *f* comercial favorable, superávit *m* (en balanza) comercial ▸ **trade talks** negociaciones *fpl* comerciales ▸ **trade union** sindicato *m* ▸ **trade unionism** sindicalismo *m* ▸ **trade unionist** sindicalista *mf*, miembro *mf* de un sindicato ▸ **trade union leader** líder *mf* sindicalista ▸ **trade union movement** movimiento *m* sindical, movimiento *m* sindicalista ▸ **trade union official** representante *mf* sindical ▸ **trade war** guerra *f* comercial ▸ **trade winds** vientos *mpl* alisios
▸ **trade in** (VT + ADV) (= *exchange*) cambiar; (= *give as deposit*) [+ *car, appliance*] ofrecer como parte del pago
▸ **trade off** (VT + ADV) • **to ~ off manpower costs against computer costs** compensar los costes de personal con los costes de informatización • **he ~d off information for a reduced sentence** pasó información a cambio de una reducción de la condena
▸ **trade on** (VI + PREP) explotar, aprovecharse de • **he ~s shamelessly on his good looks** explota su atractivo sin vergüenza ninguna, se aprovecha de su atractivo sin avergonzarse en absoluto
▸ **trade up** (VI + ADV) • **they buy a house and then ~ up as their income rises** compran una casa y luego, cuando aumentan sus ingresos, la venden para comprar otra mejor
trade-in ['treɪdɪn] (N) *sistema de devolver un artículo usado al comprar uno nuevo* • **it proved difficult to negotiate a trade-in on a new property** resultó difícil negociar un cambio como parte del pago de una propiedad nueva • **the company operates a trade-in policy** la empresa acepta la entrega de artículos usados como parte del pago
(CPD) ▸ **trade-in price, trade-in value** *valor de un artículo usado que se descuenta del precio de otro nuevo*
trademark ['treɪdmɑːk] (N) (*Comm*) marca *f* de fábrica, marca *f* comercial; (*fig*) marca *f* personal; ▹ **registered**
trade-off ['treɪdɒf] (N) • **there is always a trade-off between risk and return** siempre existe un elemento de compensación entre el riesgo y las ganancias
trader ['treɪdəʳ] (N) comerciante *mf*, negociante *mf*; (= *street trader*) vendedor(a) *m/f* ambulante; (*Hist*) mercader *m*
tradescantia [ˌtrædəs'kæntɪə] (N) tradescantia *f*
tradesman ['treɪdzmən] (N) (PL: **tradesmen**) (= *shopkeeper*) tendero *m*; (= *roundsman*) repartidor *m*, proveedor *m*; (= *artisan*) artesano *m* • **~'s entrance** entrada *f* de servicio
tradespeople ['treɪdzˌpiːpl] (NPL) tenderos *mpl*
tradeswoman ['treɪdzˌwʊmən] (N) (PL: **tradeswomen**) (= *shopkeeper*) tendera *f*; (= *roundswoman*) repartidora *f*, proveedora *f*; (= *artisan*) artesana *f*
trading ['treɪdɪŋ] (N) **1** (*Comm*) comercio *m*, actividad *f* comercial • **the laws on Sunday ~** las leyes con respecto al comercio los domingos
2 (*St Ex*) operaciones *fpl* bursátiles • **to stop** *or* **suspend ~** suspender las operaciones bursátiles
(CPD) ▸ **trading account** (*St Ex*) cuenta *f* de explotación ▸ **trading centre** centro *m* de comercio ▸ **trading company** empresa *f* mercantil ▸ **trading estate** (*Brit*) zona *f* industrial, polígono *m* industrial (*Sp*) ▸ **trading floor** parqué *m*, patio *m* de operaciones ▸ **trading links** vínculos *mpl* comerciales ▸ **trading loss** pérdidas *fpl* comerciales, pérdidas *fpl* de explotación ▸ **trading partner** socio/a *m/f* comercial ▸ **trading post** factoría *f* ▸ **trading profits** beneficios *mpl* comerciales, beneficios *mpl* de explotación ▸ **trading stamp** cupón *m* ▸ **trading standards office** *organismo que regula la actividad comercial*
tradition [trə'dɪʃən] (N) tradición *f* • **according to ~** de acuerdo con la tradición • **~ has it that ...** según la tradición ... • **in the (best) ~ of** a la mejor usanza de • **it is a ~ that ...** es tradición que ...
traditional [trə'dɪʃənl] (ADJ) tradicional • **the clothes which are ~ to his country** la ropa tradicional de su país
traditionalism [trə'dɪʃnəlɪzəm] (N) tradicionalismo *m*
traditionalist [trə'dɪʃnəlɪst] (ADJ) tradicionalista
(N) tradicionalista *mf*
traditionality [trəˌdɪʃə'nælətɪ] (N) tradicionalidad *f*
traditionally [trə'dɪʃnəlɪ] (ADV) **1** (= *according to custom*) tradicionalmente • **~, election campaigns start on Labor Day** tradicionalmente *or* por tradición, las campañas electorales comienzan el Día del Trabajo
2 (= *in the traditional way*) [*produced, made*] de forma tradicional, a la manera tradicional
traduce [trə'djuːs] (VT) (*frm*) calumniar, denigrar
traffic ['træfɪk] (VB: PT, PP: **trafficked**) (N) **1** (*Aut, Aer, Naut, Rail*) tráfico *m*, circulación *f*, tránsito *m* (*esp LAm*) • **the ~ is heavy during the rush hour** hay mucho tráfico durante las horas punta • **~ was quite light** había poco tráfico • **~ was blocked for some hours** la circulación quedó interrumpida durante varias horas • **closed to heavy ~** cerrado a los vehículos pesados • **air ~** tráfico *m* aéreo
2 (= *trade*) tráfico *m*, comercio *m* (**in** en) • **drug ~** narcotráfico *m*, tráfico *m* de drogas
(VI) • **to ~ (in)** traficar (en)
(CPD) (*Aut*) [*regulations*] de circulación, de tránsito (*esp LAm*) ▸ **traffic accident** accidente *m* de tráfico, accidente *m* de circulación, accidente *m* de tránsito (*LAm*) ▸ **traffic calming** *medidas para reducir la velocidad del tráfico* ▸ **traffic circle** (*US*) rotunda *f*, glorieta *f* ▸ **traffic cone** cono *m* señalizador ▸ **traffic control** (= *act*) control *m* del tráfico; (= *lights*) semáforo *m* ▸ **traffic control tower** torre *f* de control ▸ **traffic cop*** policía *mf* de tráfico ▸ **traffic court** (*US*) *tribunal en el que se juzgan las infracciones de tráfico* ▸ **traffic duty** • **to be on ~ duty** estar en tráfico ▸ **traffic flow** flujo *m* de tráfico ▸ **traffic island** refugio *m* ▸ **traffic jam** embotellamiento *m*, atasco *m* • **a five-mile ~ jam** un atasco de cinco millas ▸ **traffic light** semáforo *msing* ▸ **traffic lights** semáforo *msing* ▸ **traffic offence** (*Brit*) infracción *f* de tráfico ▸ **traffic police** policía *f* de tráfico, policía *f* de tránsito ▸ **traffic sign** señal *f* de tráfico ▸ **traffic violation** (*US*) = **traffic offence** ▸ **traffic warden** guardia *mf* de

tráfico *or* tránsito; ▹ **road**
trafficator ['træfɪkeɪtəʳ] (N) (*Brit*) indicador *m* de dirección, flecha *f* de dirección
trafficker ['træfɪkəʳ] (N) traficante *mf* (**in** en)
trafficking ['træfɪkɪŋ] (N) tráfico *m* • **drug ~** tráfico de drogas, narcotráfico
tragedian [trə'dʒiːdɪən] (N) trágico *m*
tragedienne [trədʒiːdɪ'en] (N) trágica *f*, actriz *f* trágica
tragedy ['trædʒɪdɪ] (N) (*gen*) (*Theat*) tragedia *f* • **it is a ~ that ...** es una tragedia que ... • **the ~ of it is that ...** lo trágico del asunto es que ... • **a personal ~** una tragedia personal
tragic ['trædʒɪk] (ADJ) (*gen*) (*Theat*) trágico
tragically ['trædʒɪkəlɪ] (ADV) trágicamente • **her career ended ~ at the age of 19** su carrera se vio truncada trágicamente a la edad de 19 años • **~, she never lived to see her grandson** desgraciadamente, jamás llegó a ver a su nieto • **he died ~ young** murió terriblemente joven • **the operation went ~ wrong** la operación tuvo consecuencias trágicas
tragicomedy ['trædʒɪ'kɒmɪdɪ] (N) tragicomedia *f*
tragicomic ['trædʒɪ'kɒmɪk] (ADJ) tragicómico
trail [treɪl] (N) **1** (= *wake*) [*of dust, smoke*] estela *f*; [*of blood*] reguero *m*; [*of comet, meteor*] cola *f* • **the hurricane left a ~ of destruction** el huracán dejó una estela de estragos • **the murderer left a ~ of clues** el asesino dejó un reguero de pistas • **he left a ~ of wet footprints all through the house** dejó pisadas húmedas por toda la casa
2 (= *track*) (*left by animal, person*) rastro *m*, pista *f* • **to be on sb's ~** seguir la pista a algn • **the police are hard** *or* **hot on his ~** la policía le sigue de cerca *or* está sobre su pista • **to pick up sb's ~** dar con algn • **we managed to throw** *or* **put them off our ~** conseguimos despistarlos
3 (= *path*) camino *m*, sendero *m* • **tourist ~** ruta *f* turística; (*fig*) ▹ **blaze²**, **nature**
(VT) **1** (= *drag*) arrastrar • **he was ~ing his schoolbag behind him** iba arrastrando la cartera (de la escuela) • **the jeep ~ed clouds of dust behind it** el jeep iba dejando nubes de polvo a su paso • **to ~ one's fingers in** *or* **through the water** hacer surcos en el agua con los dedos
2 (= *deposit*) • **the children ~ed dirt all over the carpet** los niños iban dejando suciedad por toda la moqueta
3 (= *track*) [+ *animal, person*] seguir la pista a, seguir el rastro a; [+ *suspect*] seguir de cerca • **two detectives were ~ing him** dos detectives le seguían de cerca
4 (= *lag behind*) ir rezagado con respecto a, ir a la zaga de • **the President ~s his opponent in opinion polls** el Presidente va rezagado con respecto a *or* va a la zaga de su adversario en las encuestas de opinión • **they are ~ing the leaders by just two points** los líderes solo les llevan *or* sacan dos puntos de ventaja
(VI) **1** (= *drag*) arrastrarse • **your coat is ~ing in the mud** se te está arrastrando *or* vas arrastrando el abrigo por el barro • **she walked with her skirt ~ing on the ground** andaba arrastrando la falda por el suelo
2 (= *dangle, spread*) • **plants ~ from balconies** las plantas cuelgan de los balcones • **wires ~ing across the floor are dangerous** los cables sueltos por el suelo son peligrosos
3 (= *trudge*) • **I spent the afternoon ~ing around the shops** pasé la tarde pateándome las tiendas • **we ~ed home again in the rain** a duras penas y lloviendo nos hicimos el camino de vuelta a casa • **her husband ~ed along behind** su marido iba detrás arrastrando los pies
4 (= *lag behind*) ir rezagado, ir a la zaga • **to ~ (far) behind sb** quedar (muy) a la zaga de algn, ir (muy) rezagado con respecto a algn • **he's ~ing in the polls** va por detrás *or* a la zaga en las encuestas • **they were ~ing 2-0 at half-time** en el descanso iban perdiendo dos a cero
(CPD) ▸ **trail bike** moto *f* de motocross, moto *f* de trial ▸ **trail mix** revuelto *m* de frutos secos
▸ **trail away**, **trail off** (VI + ADV) [*sound*] irse apagando • **the last note ~s away to nothing** la última nota se va apagando hasta dejar de oírse • **her voice ~ed off** *or* **away** se le fue la voz • **he let the sentence ~ off meaningfully** dejó la frase en puntos suspensivos de forma significativa
trailblazer ['treɪlbleɪzəʳ] (N) pionero/a *m/f*
trailblazing ['treɪlbleɪzɪŋ] (ADJ) pionero (N) *trabajo o viaje etc pionero*
trailer ['treɪləʳ] (N) **1** (*Aut*) remolque *m*; (*of truck*) tráiler *m*, remolque *m*; (*US*) (= *caravan*) caravana *f*, rulot *f*
2 (*Cine*) tráiler *m*, avance *m*
(CPD) ▸ **trailer park** (*US*) (*for caravans*) camping *m* para caravanas *or* rulots; (*for trailers*) camping *m* para remolques ▸ **trailer tent** tienda *f* de campaña (*que se monta acoplada a un vehículo*) ▸ **trailer trash*** (*US*) (*pej*) *personas de pocos ingresos que viven en caravanas* ▸ **trailer truck** (*US*) camión *m* articulado
trailing ['treɪlɪŋ] (ADJ) [*plant*] trepador; [*branches*] colgante • **she wore a long ~ scarf** llevaba un pañuelo largo que le colgaba • **~ edge** (*Aer*) borde *m* de salida, borde *m* posterior
train [treɪn] (N) **1** (*Rail*) tren *m* • **diesel/electric ~** tren *m* diesel/eléctrico • **express/fast/slow ~** tren *m* expreso/rápido/ordinario • **high-speed ~** tren *m* de alta velocidad • **steam ~** tren *m* de vapor • **connecting ~** tren *m* de enlace • **through ~** (tren *m*) directo *m* • **to catch a ~ (to)** coger *or* (*LAm*) tomar un tren (a) • **I've got a ~ to catch** tengo que coger *or* (*LAm*) tomar un tren • **to change ~s** cambiar de tren, hacer tra(n)sbordo • **to go by ~** ir en tren • **to send sth by ~** mandar algo por ferrocarril • **to take the ~** coger *or* (*LAm*) tomar el tren • **to travel by ~** viajar en tren; ▹ **gravy**
2 (= *line*) [*of people, vehicles*] fila *f*; [*of mules, camels*] recua *f*, reata *f* • **a ~ of reporters followed her everywhere** una cohorte de reporteros la seguía a todos sitios
3 (= *sequence*) serie *f* • **a ~ of disasters/events** una serie de catástrofes/acontecimientos • **the earthquake brought great suffering in its ~** el terremoto trajo consigo gran sufrimiento • **the next stage of the operation was well in ~** la siguiente fase de la operación ya estaba en marcha • **to put sth in ~** • **set sth in ~** poner algo en marcha • **~ of thought**: • **to lose one's ~ of thought** perder el hilo • **you're interrupting my ~ of thought** me cortas el hilo de mis pensamientos • **they were both silent, each following her own ~ of thought** estaban las dos calladas, cada una pensando en lo suyo
4 (= *entourage*) séquito *m*, comitiva *f*
5 [*of dress*] cola *f* • **to carry sb's ~** llevar la cola del vestido de algn
6 (*Mech*) [*of gears*] tren *m*
(VT) **1** (= *instruct*) [+ *staff*] formar; [+ *worker*] (*in new technique*) capacitar; [+ *soldier, pilot*] adiestrar; [+ *athlete, team*] entrenar; [+ *animal*] (*for task*) adiestrar; (*to do tricks*) amaestrar; [+ *racehorse*] entrenar, preparar • **our staff are ~ed to the highest standards** el nivel de formación de nuestros empleados es del más alto nivel • **you've got him well ~ed!** (*hum*) ¡le tienes bien enseñado! (*hum*) • **he was ~ed in Salamanca** (*for qualification*) estudió en Salamanca; (*for job*) recibió su formación profesional en Salamanca • **to ~ sb to do sth: his troops are ~ed to kill** a sus tropas se les enseña a matar • **professional counsellors are ~ed to be objective** los consejeros profesionales están capacitados *or* adiestrados para ser objetivos • **he had ~ed himself to write left-handed** aprendió por su cuenta a escribir con la izquierda • **~ yourself to think positively** habitúate a pensar de manera positiva • **the dogs were ~ed to attack intruders** se adiestraba a los perros para que atacaran a los intrusos • **to ~ sb for sth**: • **the programme ~s young people for jobs in computing** el programa forma a la gente joven para realizar trabajos en informática • **nobody ~s you for the job of being a parent** nadie te enseña a ser padre • **to ~ sb in sth**: • **officers ~ed in the use of firearms** oficiales entrenados *or* adiestrados en el uso de armas de fuego • **they are ~ing women in non-traditional female jobs** están formando a mujeres en trabajos que tradicionalmente no realizan las mujeres
2 (= *develop*) [+ *voice, mind*] educar
3 (= *direct*) [+ *gun*] apuntar (**on** a); [+ *camera, telescope*] enfocar (**on** a) • **his gun was ~ed on Jo** apuntaba a Jo con la pistola • **the camera was ~ed on me** la cámara me estaba enfocando
4 (= *guide*) [+ *plant*] guiar (**up, along** por)
(VI) **1** (= *learn a skill*) estudiar • **where did you ~?** (*for qualification*) ¿dónde estudió?; (*for job*) ¿dónde se formó? • **he ~ed to be a lawyer** estudió derecho • **she was ~ing to be a teacher** estudiaba para (ser) maestra, estudiaba magisterio • **she ~ed as a hairdresser** estudió peluquería, aprendió el oficio de peluquera • **he's ~ing for the priesthood** estudia para meterse en el sacerdocio
2 (*Sport*) entrenar, entrenarse • **I ~ for six hours a day** (me) entreno seis horas diarias • **to ~ for sth** entrenar(se) para algo
(CPD) ▸ **train attendant** (*US*) empleado/a *m/f* de a bordo de un tren ▸ **train crash** accidente *m* ferroviario ▸ **train driver** maquinista *mf* ▸ **train fare** • **I gave him the money for the ~ fare** le di dinero para el billete de tren ▸ **train journey** viaje *m* en tren ▸ **train service** servicio *m* de trenes ▸ **train set** tren *m* de juguete (*con vías, estaciones etc*) ▸ **train station** estación *f* de ferrocarril, estación *f* de tren
▸ **train up*** (VT + ADV) (*Brit*) [+ *new staff*] empezar a formar a partir de cero
trained [treɪnd] (ADJ) **1** [*teacher, nurse*] titulado; [*worker, staff*] cualificado; [*animal*] (*for task*) adiestrado; (*to do tricks*) amaestrado • **there was a lack of ~ men and equipment** faltaban hombres entrenados y equipo • **she is a ~ singer** ha recibido formación de cantante, ha estudiado canto • **we have counsellors ~ to deal with these sorts of problems** tenemos asesores capacitados para llevar este tipo de problemas • **they have a highly-trained workforce** tienen una mano de obra altamente cualificada • **a well-trained army** un ejército disciplinado, un ejército bien entrenado
2 [*eye, ear, voice*] educado
trainee [treɪ'niː] (N) aprendiz(a) *m/f*; (*US*) (*Mil*) recluta *mf* en período de aprendizaje

• **management ~** aprendiz(a) *m/f* de administración
CPD ▸ **trainee manager** aprendiz(a) *m/f* de administración ▸ **trainee teacher** estudiante *mf* de magisterio

trainer ['treɪnəʳ] N **1** (*Sport*) [*of athletes, gymnasts, footballers*] entrenador(a) *m/f*; [*of horses*] preparador(a) *m/f*; [*of circus animals*] domador(a) *m/f*
2 (= *plane*) entrenador *m*
3 trainers (= *shoes*) zapatillas *fpl* de deporte

training ['treɪnɪŋ] N **1** (*for job*) formación *f*; (*Mil*) instrucción *f*; [*of animals*] (*for task*) adiestramiento *m*; (*to do tricks*) amaestramiento *m*; (= *teaching*) enseñanza *f*, instrucción *f*; (= *period of training*) aprendizaje *m*, periodo *m* de formación • **~ will be provided** se ofrece formación • **she has no ~ or experience with children** no tiene formación o experiencia con niños • **she has no ~ as a nurse** no tiene (el) título de enfermera • **staff ~** formación *f* de empleados; ▹ **assertiveness, teacher**
2 (*Sport*) entrenamiento *m* • **he injured a knee during** *or* **in ~** se lesionó una rodilla durante el entrenamiento • **to be in ~ for sth** estar entrenando *or* entrenándose para algo • **to be out of ~** estar desentrenado *or* bajo de forma; ▹ **weight**
CPD ▸ **training camp** (*Mil*) campo *m* de instrucción, campo *m* de entrenamiento; (*Sport*) lugar *m* de concentración ▸ **training centre, training center** (*US*) centro *m* de formación, centro *m* de capacitación ▸ **training college** escuela *f* de formación profesional; (*for teachers*) escuela *f* normal ▸ **training course** curso *m* de formación, curso *m* de capacitación ▸ **training flight** vuelo *m* de instrucción ▸ **training ground** (*Mil*) campo *m* de pruebas; (*Sport*) campo *m* de entrenamiento; (*fig*) • **the band was a ~ ground for future jazz giants** la banda era como una especie de escuela para las futuras estrellas del jazz ▸ **training instructor** formador(a) *m/f* ▸ **training manual** manual *m* de instrucción ▸ **training scheme** plan *m* de formación profesional ▸ **training ship** buque *m* escuela ▸ **training shoes** zapatillas *fpl* de deporte

trainman ['treɪnmæn] N (PL: **trainmen**) (*US*) (*Rail*) ferroviario *m*

trainspotter ['treɪnspɒtəʳ] N (*Brit*) **1** *persona cuyo hobby es apuntar los números de serie de los trenes que pasan*
2 (*Brit**) (*pej*) pelmazo/a* *m/f*, petardo/a* *m/f*

trainspotting ['treɪnspɒtɪŋ] N (*Brit*) • **to go train-spotting** *ir a apuntar el número de serie de los trenes que pasan*

traipse [treɪps] VI* andar penosamente • **to ~ in/out** entrar/salir penosamente • **we ~d about all morning** pasamos toda la mañana yendo de acá para allá • **I had to ~ over to see him** tuve que tomarme la molestia de ir a verle
N caminata *f*

trait [treɪt] N rasgo *m*

traitor ['treɪtəʳ] N traidor(a) *m/f* • **to be a ~ to one's country** traicionar a la patria • **to turn ~** volverse traidor

traitorous ['treɪtərəs] ADJ [*person*] traidor; [*attempt, intention*] traicionero

traitorously ['treɪtərəslɪ] ADV traidoramente, a traición

traitress ['treɪtrɪs] N traidora *f*

Trajan ['treɪdʒən] N Trajano

trajectory [trə'dʒektərɪ] N trayectoria *f*, curso *m*

tram [træm] N **1** (*Brit*) tranvía *m*
2 (*in mine*) vagoneta *f*

tramcar ['træmkɑːʳ] N = **tram**

tramlines ['træmlaɪnz] NPL (*Brit*) **1** (*for tram*) rieles *mpl* de tranvía
2 (*Tennis*) líneas *f* laterales

trammel ['træməl] VT poner trabas a
NPL **trammels** trabas *fpl*

tramp [træmp] N **1** (= *sound of feet*) ruido *m* de pasos
2 (= *long walk*) caminata *f* • **to go for a ~ in the hills** ir de paseo por la montaña • **it's a long ~** es mucho camino
3 (= *homeless person*) vagabundo/a *m/f*
4 (*esp US**) (*pej*) (= *loose woman*) • **she's a ~** es una zorra*, es una golfa*
5 (*Naut*) (*also* **tramp steamer**) vapor *m* volandero
VT **1** (= *stamp on*) pisar con fuerza
2 (= *walk across*) recorrer a pie, hacer una excursión por • **to ~ the streets** andar por las calles, callejear
VI • **to ~ (along)** caminar (con pasos pesados) • **the soldiers ~ed past** los soldados pasaron marchando • **to ~ up and down** andar de acá para allá • **he ~ed up to the door** se acercó con pasos pesados a la puerta

trample ['træmpl] VT (*also* **trample underfoot**) pisar, pisotear
VI (*also* **trample about, trample along**) pisar fuerte, andar con pasos pesados • **to ~ on sth** pisar algo, pisotear algo • **to ~ on sb** (*fig*) tratar a algn sin miramientos • **to ~ on sb's feelings** herir los sentimientos de algn

trampoline ['træmpəlɪn] N cama *f* elástica

trampolining ['træmpəliːnɪŋ] N salto *m* sobre cama elástica

tramway ['træmweɪ] N (*Brit*) tranvía *m*

trance [trɑːns] N trance *m* • **to go into a ~** (*lit, fig*) entrar en trance

tranche [trɑːnʃ] N parte *f*, tajada *f*

trannie, tranny ['trænɪ] N (PL: **trannies**)
1* = **transistor radio**
2 (*Phot**) = **transparency**
3‡ (= *transvestite*) travesti‡ *mf*

tranquil ['træŋkwɪl] ADJ tranquilo, calmo

tranquillity, tranquility (*US*) [træŋ'kwɪlɪtɪ] N tranquilidad *f*, calma *f*

tranquillize, tranquilize (*US*) ['træŋkwɪlaɪz] VT tranquilizar

tranquillizer, tranquilizer (*US*) ['træŋkwɪlaɪzəʳ] N (*Med*) tranquilizante *m*

tranquilly ['træŋkwɪlɪ] ADV tranquilamente

trans ABBR **1** = **translation**
2 (= **translated**) trad.
3 = **translator**
4 = **transitive**
5 = **transport(ation)**
6 = **transferred**

trans... [trænz] PREFIX trans...

transact [træn'zækt] VT negociar, tramitar

transaction [træn'zækʃən] N **1** (= *deal*) operación *f*, transacción *f* • **cash ~s** operaciones *fpl* al contado
2 (= *paperwork*) tramitación *f*
3 transactions (= *records*) [*of society*] actas *fpl*, memorias *fpl*

transactional [træn'zækʃənl] ADJ transaccional • **~ analysis** análisis *m* transaccional

transalpine ['trænz'ælpaɪn] ADJ transalpino

transatlantic ['trænzət'læntɪk] ADJ
1 [*flight, crossing, phone call, liner*] transatlántico
2 (*Brit*) (= *American*) norteamericano

transceiver [træn'siːvəʳ] N transceptor *m*, transmisor-receptor *m*

transcend [træn'send] VT sobrepasar, rebasar

transcendence [træn'sendəns] N
1 (= *superiority*) lo sobresaliente
2 (*Philos*) trascendencia *f*

transcendency [træn'sendənsɪ] N = **transcendence**

transcendent [træn'sendənt] ADJ
1 (= *outstanding*) sobresaliente
2 (*Philos*) transcendente

transcendental [ˌtrænsen'dentl] ADJ (*Philos*) trascendental
CPD ▸ **transcendental meditation** meditación *f* trascendental

transcendentalism ['trænsen'dentlɪzəm] N trascendentalismo *m*

transcontinental ['trænzˌkɒntɪ'nentl] ADJ transcontinental

transcribe [træn'skraɪb] VT transcribir, copiar

transcript ['trænskrɪpt] N **1** (= *copy*) transcripción *f*
2 (*US*) (*Scol*) expediente *m*

transcription [træn'skrɪpʃən] N (*gen*) transcripción *f* • **phonetic ~** pronunciación *f* fonética

transculturation [ˌtrænzkʌltʃʊ'reɪʃən] N transculturación *f*

transducer [trænz'djuːsəʳ] N transductor *m*

transect [træn'sekt] N transecto *m*

transept ['trænsept] N crucero *m*

transfer ['trænsfəʳ] N **1** (= *conveyance*) traslado *m* • **we will arrange the ~ of your medical records** nos encargaremos del traslado de su historial médico • **technology ~** transferencia *f* de tecnología
2 (= *change*) [*of job*] traslado *m*; [*of power*] traspaso *m*; [*of vehicle*] transbordo *m* • **I've applied for a ~ to head office** he solicitado el traslado a la oficina central
3 (*Jur, Econ*) [*of property*] transmisión *f*, traspaso *m*; [*of funds*] transferencia *f* • **bank ~** transferencia *f* bancaria • **direct ~** abono *m* en cuenta • **~ of ownership** traspaso *m* de propiedad
4 (*Sport*) traspaso *m* • **to ask for a ~** pedir el traspaso
5 (= *picture*) calcomanía *f*
VT **1** (= *convey*) [+ *object, person*] trasladar (**from** de, **to** a) • **~ the chops to a serving dish** pase las chuletas a una fuente • **the train broke down and passengers were ~red to a bus** el tren se averió y los pasajeros tuvieron que pasarse a un autobús • **the disease can be ~red to humans** la enfermedad puede transmitirse *or* contagiarse a seres humanos
2 (= *relocate*) [+ *person*] trasladar (**from** de, **to** a); [+ *power*] traspasar; [+ *allegiance*] mudar • **the company ~red her to another department** la empresa la trasladó a otro departamento • **to ~ one's affections to another** dar su amor a otro
3 (*Jur, Econ*) [+ *property*] traspasar, transmitir; [+ *funds*] transferir • **she ~red the house to her son's name** puso la casa a nombre de su hijo • **to ~ money from one account to another** transferir dinero de una cuenta a otra
4 (*Sport*) [+ *player*] traspasar
5 (= *copy*) [+ *design*] pasar, trasladar • **the documents were ~red to microfilm** los documentos se pasaron *or* se trasladaron a microfilm
6 (*Telec*) [+ *call*] pasar • **please hold while I ~ you** no cuelgue, que ahora mismo le paso • **can you ~ me back to the switchboard?** ¿puede volverme a pasar con la centralita?
VI **1** (= *change*) (*from course, job*) trasladarse; (*from vehicle*) hacer transbordo • **he has ~red to another department** se ha trasladado a otro departamento • **I've ~red to a new**

pension scheme/course/school me he pasado a otro plan de pensiones/curso/colegio • **she ~red from French to Spanish** se cambió *or* se trasladó del curso de francés al de español • **passengers ~red from a train to a bus** los pasajeros hicieron transbordo del tren al autobús • **we had to ~ to another coach** tuvimos que pasarnos a otro autobús
2 (*Sport*) [*player*] ser traspasado, traspasarse
CPD ▸ **transfer desk** mostrador *m* de conexiones ▸ **transfer fee** traspaso *m* ▸ **transfer list** lista *f* de posibles traspasos ▸ **transfer student** (*US*) estudiante *mf* procedente de otra universidad ▸ **transfer window** (*Ftbl*) periodo *m* de traspasos

transferable [træns'fɜːrəbl] ADJ transferible • **not ~** no transferible

transference ['trænsfərəns] N
1 (= *relocation*) [*of information*] transferencia *f*, transmisión *f*; [*of affection*] cambio *m*; [*of power*] traspaso *m* • **the ~ of the papal seat to Avignon** el traslado de la sede pontificia a Aviñón
2 (*Psych*) transferencia *f* • **thought ~** transmisión *f* de pensamientos

transfiguration [ˌtrænsfɪgə'reɪʃən] N transfiguración *f*

transfigure [træns'fɪgəʳ] VT transfigurar, transformar (**into** en)

transfix [træns'fɪks] VT traspasar, paralizar • **he stood ~ed with fear** se quedó paralizado por el miedo

transform [træns'fɔːm] VT transformar (**into** en)

transformation [ˌtrænsfə'meɪʃən] N transformación *f*

transformational [ˌtrænsfə'meɪʃənl] ADJ transformacional

transformer [træns'fɔːməʳ] N (*Elec*) transformador *m*
CPD ▸ **transformer station** estación *f* transformadora

transfuse [træns'fjuːz] VT transfundir; [+ *blood*] hacer una transfusión de

transfusion [træns'fjuːʒən] N transfusión *f* • **to give sb a blood ~** hacer a algn una transfusión de sangre

transgender [ˌtrænz'dʒendəʳ] ADJ [*person*] transgénero (*inv*)
N transgénero *mf inv*

transgenic [trænz'dʒenɪk] ADJ transgénico

transgress [træns'gres] VT **1** (= *go beyond*) traspasar
2 (= *violate*) violar, infringir
3 (= *sin against*) pecar contra
VI pecar, cometer una transgresión

transgression [træns'greʃən] N transgresión *f*, infracción *f*; (*Rel*) pecado *m*

transgressive [trænz'gresɪv] ADJ (*frm*) [*behaviour, act*] transgresor

transgressor [træns'gresəʳ] N transgresor(a) *m/f*, infractor(a) *m/f*; (*Rel*) pecador(a) *m/f*

tranship [træn'ʃɪp] VT = **transship**

transhipment [træn'ʃɪpmənt] N = **transshipment**

transience ['trænziəns] N lo pasajero, transitoriedad *f*

transient ['trænziənt] ADJ transitorio, pasajero
N (*US*) transeúnte *mf*

transistor [træn'zɪstəʳ] N (*Elec*) transistor *m*; (*also* **transistor set**) transistor *m*
CPD ▸ **transistor radio** radio *f* de transistores

transistorized [træn'zɪstəraɪzd] ADJ [*circuit*] transistorizado

transit ['trænzɪt] N tránsito *m* • **in ~** en tránsito
CPD ▸ **transit camp** campo *m* de tránsito ▸ **transit lounge** (*Brit*) sala *f* de tránsito ▸ **transit system** (*US*) transportes *fpl* ▸ **Transit van®** furgoneta *f* ▸ **transit visa** visado *m or* (*LAm*) visa *f* de tránsito

transition [træn'zɪʃən] N transición *f*
CPD ▸ **transition period** período *m* de transición

transitional [træn'zɪʃənəl] ADJ transicional, de transición

transitive ['trænzɪtɪv] ADJ transitivo • **~ verb** verbo *m* transitivo

transitively ['trænzɪtɪvlɪ] ADV transitivamente

transitivity [ˌtrænsɪ'tɪvɪtɪ] N transitividad *f*

transitory ['trænzɪtərɪ] ADJ transitorio

translatable [trænz'leɪtəbl] ADJ traducible

translate [trænz'leɪt] VT **1** (*Ling*) traducir (**from** de, **into** a) • **~ this text into Spanish** traduzca este texto al español • **how do you ~ "posh"?** ¿cómo se traduce "posh"?
2 (= *convert*) • **to ~ centigrade into Fahrenheit** convertir grados centígrados en Fahrenheit • **to ~ words into deeds** convertir palabras en acción
3 (= *transfer*) (*esp Rel*) trasladar (**from** de, **to** a)
VI [*person*] traducir; [*word, expression*] traducirse • **poetry does not ~ easily** la poesía no es fácil de traducir

translation [trænz'leɪʃən] N **1** (*Ling*) traducción *f*
2 (= *transfer*) (*esp Rel*) traslado *m*

translator [trænz'leɪtəʳ] N traductor(a) *m/f*

transliterate [trænz'lɪtəreɪt] VT transcribir

transliteration [ˌtrænzlɪtə'reɪʃən] N transliteración *f*, transcripción *f*

translucence [trænz'luːsns] N translucidez *f*

translucent [trænz'luːsnt] ADJ translúcido

transmigrate ['trænzmaɪ'greɪt] VI transmigrar

transmigration [ˌtrænzmaɪ'greɪʃən] N transmigración *f*

transmissible [trænz'mɪsəbl] ADJ transmisible

transmission [trænz'mɪʃən] N (*Rad, TV, Aut*) transmisión *f*
CPD ▸ **transmission shaft** (*Aut*) eje *m* de transmisión

transmit [trænz'mɪt] VT [+ *illness, programme, message*] transmitir (**to** a)

transmitter [trænz'mɪtəʳ] N (*Rad, TV, Telec*) emisora *f*

transmogrify [trænz'mɒgrɪfaɪ] VT transformar (como por encanto) (**into** en), metamorfosear (extrañamente) (**into** en)

transmutable [trænz'mjuːtəbl] ADJ transmutable

transmutation [ˌtrænzmjuː'teɪʃən] N transmutación *f*

transmute [trænz'mjuːt] VT • **to ~ (into)** transmutar (en)

transnational [trænz'næʃənəl] ADJ transnacional
N transnacional *f*

transoceanic ['trænzˌəʊʃɪ'ænɪk] ADJ [*travel, migration*] transoceánico; [*countries*] del otro lado del océano

transom ['trænsəm] N (*Archit*) (*across window*) travesaño *m*; (*US*) (= *window*) montante *m* de abanico, abanico *m*

transpacific [ˌtrænzpə'sɪfɪk] ADJ (= *crossing the Pacific*) a través del Pacífico; [*countries*] del otro lado del Pacífico

transparency [træns'pærənsɪ] N **1** [*of object, material, substance*] transparencia *f*
2 [*of statement*] claridad *f*
3 (*Phot*) (*for overhead projector*) transparencia *f*; (= *slide*) diapositiva *f*

transparent [træns'pærənt] ADJ
1 (= *see-through*) [*object, material, substance*] transparente
2 (= *easy to understand*) [*situation, system, operation*] claro, transparente • **I like his ~ honesty** me gusta el que sea de una honestidad tan clara • **he's so ~** se le ve venir, es una persona sin tapujos* • **it is ~ that ...** está claro que ..., se ve claramente que ...
3 (= *blatant*) [*lie*] obvio; [*attempt, device*] claro

transparently [træns'pærəntlɪ] ADV claramente • **a ~ one-sided examination of the pros and cons of nuclear power** un examen claramente sesgado de los pros y los contras de la energía nuclear • **it is ~ clear** *or* **obvious that ...** está meridianamente claro que ... • **the reason is ~ obvious** la razón está clarísima, la razón está más clara que el agua • **he had been ~ honest with her** había sido claro y sincero con ella

transpiration [ˌtrænspɪ'reɪʃən] N transpiración *f*

transpire [træns'paɪəʳ] VI **1** (*Bot, Anat*) transpirar
2 (= *become known*) • **it finally ~d that ...** al final se supo que ...
3 (= *happen*) ocurrir, suceder • **his report on what ~d** su informe acerca de lo que pasó
VT transpirar

transplant VT [træns'plɑːnt] (*Bot, Med*) trasplantar
N ['trænsplɑːnt] (*Med*) trasplante *m* • **she had a heart ~** le hicieron un trasplante de corazón

transplantation [ˌtrænsplɑː'nteɪʃən] N (*Bot, Med*) trasplante *m*

transponder [træn'spɒndəʳ] N transpondedor *m*

transport ['trænspɔːt] N **1** (= *conveying, movement*) transporte *m* • **air ~** transporte *m* aéreo • **Department of Transport** (*Brit*) Ministerio *m* de Transporte(s) • **means of ~** medio *m* de transporte • **I was stranded with no means of ~** me quedé colgado sin medio de transporte • **rail ~** transporte *m* ferroviario • **road ~** transporte *m* por carretera • **sea ~** transporte *m* marítimo; ▹ **public**
2 (= *vehicle*) transporte *m* • **I haven't got any ~** no tengo transporte • **own ~ required** se requiere vehículo propio
3 (= *ship*) buque *m* de transporte
4 (= *plane*) avión *m* de transporte
5 (*fig*) (*liter*) • **it sent her into ~s of delight** la dejó extasiada • **to be in a ~ of rage** estar fuera de sí (de rabia)
VT **1** (= *move*) [+ *goods, people*] transportar
2 (*Hist*) (= *deport*) [+ *criminal*] deportar
3 (*fig*) transportar • **the musical ~s the audience to the days of 1950s America** el musical transporta *or* traslada al público a la América de los años 50 • **I felt as though I'd been ~ed back in time** me sentí como si me hubiera remontado en el tiempo • **to be ~ed with joy** (*liter*) quedarse embelesado *or* (*liter*) arrobado, estar extasiado
CPD ▸ **transport café** cafetería *f* de carretera ▸ **transport costs** gastos *mpl* de transporte ▸ **transport plane** avión *m* de transporte ▸ **transport police** policía *f* de tráfico ▸ **transport policy** política *f* de transportes ▸ **transport ship** buque *m* de transporte ▸ **transport system** sistema *m* de transportes, red *f* de transportes

transportable [træns'pɔːtəbl] ADJ transportable

transportation [ˌtrænspɔːˈteɪʃən] (N) **1** (*esp US*) (= *transport*) transporte *m* • **mass ~** (*US*) transporte *m* público
2 (*Hist*) [*of criminal*] deportación *f*
transporter [trænsˈpɔːtəʳ] (N) transportador *m*
transpose [trænsˈpəʊz] (VT) **1** [+ *words*] transponer
2 (*Mus*) transportar
3 (= *transfer*) trasladar
transposition [ˌtrænspəˈzɪʃən] (N) **1** [*of words*] transposición *f*
2 (*Mus*) transporte *m*
3 (= *transfer*) traslado *m*
transputer [trænsˈpjuːtəʳ] (N) (*Comput*) transputor *m*
trans-Pyrenean [trænzˌpɪrəˈniːən] (ADJ) transpirenaico
transsexual [trænzˈseksjʊəl] (ADJ) transexual
(N) transexual *mf*
transsexualism [trænzˈseksjʊəlɪzəm] (N) transexualismo *m*
transsexuality [trænzseksjʊˈælɪtɪ] (N) transexualidad *f*
tranship [trænsˈʃɪp] (VT) transbordar
transshipment [trænsˈʃɪpmənt] (N) transbordo *m*
trans-Siberian [trænzsaɪˈbɪərɪən] (ADJ) transiberiano
transubstantiate [ˌtrænsəbˈstænʃɪeɪt] (VT) transubstanciar
transubstantiation [ˈtrænsəbˌstænʃɪˈeɪʃən] (N) transubstanciación *f*
Transvaal [ˈtrænzvɑːl] (N) Transvaal *m*
transversal [trænzˈvɜːsəl] (ADJ) transversal
transversally [trænzˈvɜːsəlɪ] (ADV) transversalmente
transverse [ˈtrænzvɜːs] (ADJ) transverso, transversal
transversely [trænzˈvɜːslɪ] (ADV) transversalmente
transvestism [ˈtrænzˌvestɪzəm] (N) travestismo *m*
transvestite [trænzˈvestaɪt] (ADJ) travestido, travesti
(N) travesti *mf*, travestido/a *m/f*
Transylvania [trænsəlˈveɪnɪə] (N) Transilvania *f*
trap [træp] (N) **1** (*lit, fig*) trampa *f* • **it's a ~!** ¡es una trampa! • **he was caught in his own ~** cayó en su propia trampa • **we were caught like rats in a ~** estábamos atrapados como en una ratonera • **that car is a death ~** ese coche es una bomba *or* tiene mucho peligro • **curtains are a natural dust ~** en las cortinas se suele acumular mucho el polvo • **to fall into a ~** caer en una trampa • **to lay a ~ (for sb)** tender una trampa (a algn) • **to lure sb into a ~** hacer que algn caiga en una trampa • **to set a ~ (for sb)** tender una trampa (a algn) • **they walked straight into our ~** cayeron de lleno en nuestra trampa; ▹ **poverty, speed, tourist**
2‡ (= *mouth*) boca *f* • **shut your ~!** ¡cierra el pico!*, ¡cállate la boca!* • **to keep one's ~ shut** cerrar el pico*, callar la boca* • **you keep your ~ shut about this** de esto no digas ni pío*
3 (= *carriage*) *coche ligero de dos ruedas*
4 (*in greyhound racing*) caseta *f* de salida
5 (*for clay pigeon shooting*) lanzaplatos *m inv*
6 (*Golf*) búnker *m*
7 (*Tech*) sifón *m*, bombillo *m*
8 (*also* **trapdoor**) trampilla *f*; (*Theat*) escotillón *m*
(VT) **1** (= *snare*) [+ *animal*] atrapar, cazar con trampa; [+ *criminal*] atrapar, coger, agarrar (*LAm*)
2 (= *dupe*) hacer caer en la trampa, engañar • **you're not going to ~ me like that** con esas no me vas a hacer caer en la trampa, con esas no me vas a engañar • **to ~ sb into sth** tender una trampa a algn para que haga algo • **he felt he had been ~ped into marriage** le parecía que le habían cazado al casarse, le parecía que le habían tendido una trampa para que se casara • **they ~ped her into confessing** le tendieron una trampa y confesó
3 (= *hold fast, confine*) atrapar • **survivors are ~ped in the rubble** los supervivientes están enterrados *or* atrapados bajo los escombros • **the miners are ~ped underground** los mineros están atrapados bajo tierra • **heavy snowfalls had ~ped us in the village** las fuertes nevadas nos habían dejado incomunicados *or* aislados en el pueblo • **they tied a rope around his body, ~ping his arms** le ataron una cuerda alrededor del cuerpo, inmovilizándole los brazos • **to ~ one's finger in sth** pillarse *or* cogerse *or* (*LAm*) atraparse el dedo con algo • **to ~ a nerve** pillar *or* (*Sp*) coger un nervio
4 (= *retain*) [+ *heat, gas, water*] retener
5 (*Sport*) [+ *ball*] parar (con el pie)
(CPD) ▸ **trap door** trampilla *f*; (*Theat*) escotillón *m*
trapes [treɪps] (VI) = **traipse**
trapeze [trəˈpiːz] (N) trapecio *m*
(CPD) ▸ **trapeze artist** trapecista *mf*
trapezium [trəˈpiːzɪəm] (N) (PL: **trapeziums, trapezia** [trəˈpiːzɪə]) (*Math*) trapecio *m*
trapezoid [ˈtræpɪzɔɪd] (N) (*Math*) trapezoide *m*
trapper [ˈtræpəʳ] (N) trampero *m*, cazador *m*
trappings [ˈtræpɪŋz] (NPL) **1** [*of horse*] arreos *mpl*, jaeces *mpl*
2 (*fig*) adornos *mpl* • **shorn of all its ~** sin ninguno de sus adornos, desprovisto de adorno • **that statement, shorn of its ~ …** esa declaración, en términos escuetos … • **with all the ~ of kingship** con todo el boato de la monarquía
Trappist [ˈtræpɪst] (ADJ) trapense
(N) trapense *m*
(CPD) ▸ **Trappist monk** monje *m* trapense
trapse [treɪps] (VI) = **traipse**
trash [træʃ] (US) (N) **1** (= *rubbish*) basura *f*, desperdicios *mpl*
2 (*fig*) tonterías *fpl*, babosadas *fpl* (*LAm*) • **the book is ~** el libro es una basura • **he talks a lot of ~** no dice más que tonterías • **trash!** ¡tonterías!
3 (*pej*) (= *people*) • **(human) ~** gente *f* inútil, gentuza *f*; ▹ **white**
(VT)* **1** (= *wreck*) hacer polvo*, destrozar
2 (= *criticize*) [+ *person*] poner verde*; [+ *ideas*] poner por los suelos
(CPD) ▸ **trash bag** bolsa *f* de basura ▸ **trash can** cubo *m* de la basura, bote *m* de la basura, tarro *m* de la basura (*LAm*) ▸ **trash heap** basurero *m*
trashy [ˈtræʃɪ] (ADJ) malo, barato
trattoria [ˌtrætəˈrɪə] (N) trattoria *f*
trauma [ˈtrɔːmə] (N) (PL: **traumas, traumata** [ˈtrɔːmətə]) **1** (*Psych*) trauma *m*
2 (*Med*) traumatismo *m*, trauma *m*
(CPD) ▸ **trauma centre, trauma center** (*US*) departamento *m* (hospitalario) de urgencias
traumatic [trɔːˈmætɪk] (ADJ) traumatizante, traumático
traumatism [ˈtrɔːmætɪzəm] (N) traumatismo *m*
traumatize [ˈtrɔːmətaɪz] (VT) traumatizar
traumatized [ˈtrɔːmətaɪzd] (ADJ) traumatizado
traumatology [ˌtrɔːməˈtɒlədʒɪ] (N) traumatología *f*
travail [ˈtræveɪl] (N) (*liter*) esfuerzo *m* penoso; (*Med*) dolores *mpl* del parto • **to be in ~** afanarse, azacanarse††; (*Med*) estar de parto
travel [ˈtrævl] (N) **1** (= *travelling*) viajes *mpl* • **the job involves frequent ~** el trabajo requiere viajes frecuentes • **she is returning after two years' ~ in Africa** vuelve tras dos años de viajes por África, vuelve después de viajar dos años por África • **students can get cheap ~** los estudiantes pueden viajar a precios reducidos • **~ broadens the mind** viajar te abre más la mente *or* te da más amplitud de miras • **air ~** viajes *mpl* en avión • **I have made my own ~ arrangements** he hecho mis propios planes para el viaje • **foreign ~** viajes *mpl* por el extranjero
2 travels viajes *mpl* • **she told us about her ~s in Africa** nos habló de sus viajes por África • **to set off on one's ~s** emprender el viaje • **you'll never guess who I met on my ~s today!** ¡no te vas a imaginar *or* a que no sabes con quién me he topado en la calle hoy!
3 (= *movement*) • **direction/line of ~** dirección *f*/línea *f* de desplazamiento
4 (*Tech*) [*of lever, pedal*] desplazamiento *m*
(VI) **1** (= *make a journey*) viajar • **she'd always wanted to ~** siempre había querido viajar • **she ~s into the centre to work** se desplaza *or* va al centro a trabajar • **to ~ abroad**: • **she spent six months ~ling abroad** pasó seis meses viajando por el extranjero • **he was forbidden to ~ abroad** le prohibieron que viajara al extranjero • **to ~ by sth**: • **to ~ by air/plane** viajar en avión • **to ~ by car/train/bus** (*short journeys*) ir en coche/tren/autobús; (*longer journeys*) viajar en coche/tren/autobús • **I ~ to work by train** voy al trabajo en tren • **to ~ light** viajar con poco equipaje • **we'll be ~ling round Italy** recorreremos Italia • **we'll be ~ling through France** viajaremos *or* pasaremos por Francia • **he's ~ling to Helsinki tomorrow** mañana viaja a Helsinki • **he has ~led widely** ha viajado mucho
2 (= *move*) ir • **we were ~ling at 30mph** íbamos a 30 millas por hora • **light/sound ~s at a speed of …** la luz/el sonido viaja *or* se desplaza a una velocidad de … • **the current ~s along this wire** la corriente va *or* pasa por este alambre • **news ~s fast** las noticias vuelan • **his eyes ~led swiftly around the room** recorrió rápidamente la habitación con la mirada
3* (= *move quickly*) • **he was really ~ling!** ¡iba a toda pastilla *or* a toda mecha!* • **that car certainly ~s** ese coche sí que corre
4 (= *react to travelling*) • **this wine ~s well** este vino no se estropea con los viajes • **British dance music does not ~ well** la música de baile británica no se recibe bien en otros países
5 (*Comm*) ser viajante (de comercio) • **he ~s in soap** es representante de jabones
6 (*Basketball*) dar pasos, hacer pasos
(VT) [+ *country*] viajar por, recorrer; [+ *road*] recorrer; [+ *distance*] recorrer, hacer • **he has ~led the world** ha viajado por *or* ha recorrido todo el mundo
(CPD) ▸ **travel agency** agencia *f* de viajes ▸ **travel agent** agente *mf* de viajes ▸ **travel alarm** despertador *m* de viaje ▸ **travel bag** bolso *m* de viaje ▸ **travel book** libro *m* de viajes ▸ **travel brochure** folleto *m* turístico ▸ **travel bureau** agencia *f* de viajes ▸ **travel company** empresa *f* de viajes ▸ **travel documents** documentos *mpl* de viaje ▸ **travel expenses** gastos *mpl* de viaje, gastos *mpl* de desplazamiento ▸ **travel insurance** seguro *m* de viaje ▸ **travel news**

t

información *f* sobre viajes y transporte
▸ **travel rep** (*Brit*) guía *mf* (*del touroperador*)
▸ **travel sickness** mareo *m* (*por el viaje*)
▸ **travel writer** *escritor o periodista que escribe libros o artículos sobre viajes*

travelator ['trævəleɪtə^r] (N) (*US*) cinta *f* transbordadora, pasillo *m* móvil

traveler ['trævlə^r] (N) (*US*) ▹ **traveller**

travelled, traveled (*US*) ['trævld] (ADJ) • **it is a little-travelled route** es una ruta (que ha sido) poco transitada • **she is much** *or* **well** *or* **widely ~** ha viajado mucho, ha visto mucho mundo • **he was carrying a much-travelled suitcase** llevaba una maleta muy usada

traveller, traveler (*US*) ['trævlə^r] (N) (*gen*) viajero/a *m/f*; (*Comm*) (*also* **commercial traveller**) viajante *mf* • **a ~ in soap** un viajante en jabones
(CPD) ▸ **traveller's cheque, traveler's check** (*US*) cheque *m* de viajero ▸ **traveller's joy** (*Bot*) clemátide *f*

travelling, traveling (*US*) ['trævlɪŋ] (ADJ) [*circus*] ambulante; [*exhibition*] itinerante
(N) • **I've always loved ~** siempre me ha encantado viajar, siempre me han encantado los viajes • **he had done a bit of ~ in Europe** había viajado un poco por Europa
(CPD) ▸ **travelling bag** bolso *m* de viaje
▸ **travelling companion** compañero/a *m/f* de viaje ▸ **travelling expenses** gastos *mpl* de viaje, gastos *mpl* de desplazamiento
▸ **travelling salesman** viajante *mf* (de comercio), representante *mf*

travelogue, travelog (*US*) ['trævəlɒg] (N) (= *brochure*) folleto *m* de viajes; (= *lecture*) charla *f* sobre viajes; (= *film*) película *f* de viajes; (= *documentary*) documental *m* de viajes

travel-sick ['trævəlsɪk] (ADJ) mareado (*por el viaje*) • **to get travel-sick** marearse al viajar

travel-sickness pill ['trævəl,sɪknɪs,pɪl] (N) pastilla *f* antimareo

travel-weary ['trævlwɪərɪ] (ADJ) fatigado por el viaje

travel-worn ['trævlwɔ:n] (ADJ) fatigado por el viaje, rendido después de tanto viajar

traverse ['trævəs] (N) **1** (*Tech*) travesaño *m*
2 (*Mil*) través *m*
3 (*Mountaineering*) escalada *f* oblicua, camino *m* oblicuo
(VT) (*frm*) atravesar • **we are traversing a difficult period** atravesamos un período difícil
(VI) (*Mountaineering*) hacer una escalada oblicua

travesty ['trævɪstɪ] (N) parodia *f*, farsa *f*
(VT) parodiar

trawl [trɔ:l] (N) **1** (= *net*) red *f* barredera, red *f* de arrastre
2 (= *act*) rastreo *m* • **a ~ through police files** un rastreo de los archivos policiales
(VT) [+ *area*] rastrear; [+ *river, lake*] dragar • **to ~ up** pescar, sacar a la superficie
(VI) **1** (= *fish*) pescar al arrastre, rastrear • **to ~ (for sth)** rastrear (algo)
2 (= *search*) • **to ~ through the files** rastrear los archivos • **to ~ for evidence** rastrear buscando pruebas

trawler ['trɔ:lə^r] (N) trainera *f*, barco *m* pesquero de arrastre

trawling ['trɔ:lɪŋ] (N) pesca *f* a la rastra

tray [treɪ] (N) (*for food, dishes*) bandeja *f*, charola *f* (*Mex*); (= *tea tray*) bandeja *f* del té; (= *filing tray*) cesta *f*; [*of balance*] platillo *m*; (= *drawer*) cajón *m*, batea *f*; (*Phot, Tech*) cubeta *f*
(CPD) ▸ **tray cloth** cubrebandeja *m*

treacherous ['tretʃərəs] (ADJ) **1** (= *disloyal*) [*person*] traidor; [*attempt, intention*] traicionero • **a ~ act** *or* **action** una traición
2 (= *dangerous*) [*road, bend*] peligroso; [*tide, current*] traicionero • **~ road** *or* **driving conditions** condiciones peligrosas para la conducción

treacherously ['tretʃərəslɪ] (ADV)
1 (= *disloyally*) traidoramente, a traición
2 (= *dangerously*) • **the roads are ~ icy** el hielo que cubre las carreteras hace peligrosa la conducción

treachery ['tretʃərɪ] (N) traición *f* • **an act of ~** una traición

treacle ['tri:kl] (N) melaza *f*
(CPD) ▸ **treacle tart** tarta *f* de melaza

treacly ['tri:klɪ] (ADJ) (= *like treacle*) parecido a melaza; (= *covered in treacle*) cubierto de melaza

tread [tred] (VB: PT: **trod**, PP: **trodden**) (N)
1 (= *footsteps*) paso *m*; (= *gait*) andar *m*, modo *m* de andar • **with (a) heavy ~** con paso pesado • **with measured ~** con pasos rítmicos
2 [*of stair*] huella *f*; [*of shoe*] suela *f*; [*of tyre*] rodadura *f*, banda *f* rodante (*LAm*)
(VT) [+ *ground, grapes*] pisar; [+ *path*] (= *make*) marcar; (= *follow*) seguir • **to ~ water** flotar en el agua en posición vertical • **a place never trodden by human feet** un sitio no hollado por pie humano • **he trod his cigarette end into the mud** apagó la colilla pisándola en el barro
(VI) (= *walk*) andar, caminar (*LAm*); (= *put foot down*) • **to ~ (on)** pisar • **to ~ on sb's heels** pisar los talones a algn • **careful you don't ~ on it!** ¡ojo, que lo vas a pisar!, cuidado, no vas a pisarlo • **to ~ softly** pisar dulcemente, no hacer ruido al andar • IDIOMS: • **to ~ carefully** *or* **warily** andar con pies de plomo • **we must ~ very carefully in this matter** debemos andarnos con pies de plomo en este asunto • **to ~ on sb's toes** meterse con algn
▸ **tread down** (VT + ADV) pisar
▸ **tread in** (VT + ADV) [+ *root, seedling*] asegurar pisando la tierra alrededor

treadle ['tredl] (N) pedal *m*

treadmill ['tredmɪl] (N) rueda *f* de andar; (*fig*) rutina *f* • **back to the ~!** ¡volvamos al trabajo!

Treas. (ABBR) = **Treasurer**

treason ['tri:zn] (N) traición *f* • **high ~** alta traición *f*

treasonable ['tri:zənəbl] (ADJ) traidor, desleal

treasure ['treʒə^r] (N) (= *gold, jewels*) tesoro *m* • **buried ~** tesoro *m* enterrado *or* escondido; (= *valuable object, person*) joya *f* • **our charlady is a real ~** nuestra asistenta es una verdadera joya • **~s of Spanish art** joyas del arte español • **yes, my ~** sí, mi tesoro
(VT) **1** (= *value*) valorar
2 (*also* **treasure up**) (= *keep*) [+ *memories, mementos*] guardar, atesorar
(CPD) ▸ **treasure chest** (*lit*) cofre *m* del tesoro, tesoro *m*; (*fig*) [*of information, knowledge*] tesoro *m* ▸ **treasure house** (*fig*) mina *f* ▸ **treasure hunt** caza *f* del tesoro
▸ **treasure trove** tesoro *m* hallado

treasured ['treʒəd] (ADJ) [*memory*] entrañable; [*possession*] preciado

treasurer ['treʒərə^r] (N) tesorero/a *m/f*

treasury ['treʒərɪ] (N) **1** (*Pol*) • **the Treasury** la Secretaría de Hacienda
2 (*fig*) (= *anthology*) antología *f*
(CPD) ▸ **Treasury Bench** (*Brit*) (*Pol*) banco *m* azul, banco *m* del gobierno ▸ **treasury bill, treasury bond** (*US*) pagaré *m* del Tesoro, bono *m* del Tesoro ▸ **the Treasury Department** (*US*) (*Pol*) la Secretaría de Hacienda ▸ **Treasury promissory note** pagaré *m* del Tesoro ▸ **Treasury stock** (*Brit*) bonos *mpl* del Tesoro; (*US*) acciones *fpl* rescatadas ▸ **treasury warrant** autorización *f* para pago de fondos públicos

treat [tri:t] (N) **1** (= *something special*) • **I've bought a few little ~s for the children** les he comprado unas cosillas *or* unas chucherías a los niños • **a birthday/Christmas ~** un regalo de cumpleaños/Navidad • **as** *or* **for a (special) ~** como algo (muy) especial • **to give sb a ~** obsequiar a algn con algo especial • **you should give her a ~ as a reward for her good grades** deberías obsequiarla con algo especial en premio a sus buenas notas • **I wanted to give myself a ~** quería darme un gusto *or* permitirme un lujo • **viewers are in for a ~ this weekend** los televidentes se llevarán una agradable sorpresa este fin de semana • **the trip to the cinema was an unexpected ~** fue una agradable sorpresa que me llevara al cine
2 (= *offer to pay*) • **"I'll pay" — "no, this is my ~"** —yo pago —no, invito yo • **to stand sb a ~** invitar a algn; ▹ **Dutch**
3 (= *pleasure*) placer *m*, gusto *m* • **it was a ~ to see him happy again** era un placer *or* daba gusto volver a verle feliz
4 • **a ~*** (*as adv*) (*Brit*) • **the garden is coming on a ~** el jardín va de maravilla* • **this wine goes down a ~** este vino sienta de maravilla* • **take this powder for a headache, it works a ~** tómate estos polvos para el dolor de cabeza, hacen milagros *or* son mano de santo*
(VT) **1** (= *behave towards*) [+ *person, animal*] tratar; (= *handle*) [+ *object*] manejar • **we were ~ed with respect/contempt** nos trataron con respeto/desprecio • **to ~ sb well/badly** tratar bien/mal a algn • **the chemical should be ~ed with caution** este producto químico debería manejarse con cuidado • **to ~ sb like a child** tratar a algn como a un niño • **how's life ~ing you these days?** ¿cómo te va la vida últimamente? • IDIOM: • **to ~ sb like dirt*** tratar a algn a patadas*, tratar a algn como a un perro*
2 (= *consider, view*) tratar • **his statements should be ~ed with caution** hay que tomar sus declaraciones con cautela • **to ~ sth as a joke** tomarse algo a risa • **this is not a subject that should be ~ed lightly** este no es un asunto para ser tratado a la ligera • **police are ~ing the threats seriously** la policía está tratando las amenazas como un asunto serio
3 (= *deal with*) [+ *subject*] tratar • **the issues should be ~ed separately** los asuntos se deberían tratar por separado
4 (= *invite*) invitar • **I'm ~ing you** yo te invito • **to ~ sb to sth** invitar *or* convidar a algn a algo • **she was always ~ing him to ice cream** siempre le invitaba *or* convidaba a un helado, siempre le estaba comprando helados • **he ~ed us to a monologue on the virtues of abstinence** (*iro*) nos soltó un monólogo sobre las virtudes de la abstinencia • **to ~ o.s to sth** darse el gusto *or* permitirse el lujo de (hacer) algo • **we ~ed ourselves to a meal out** nos dimos el gusto *or* nos permitimos el lujo de comer fuera • **he ~ed himself to another drink** se permitió otra copa • **go on — ~ yourself!** ¡venga, date el gusto *or* el lujo!
5 (*Med*) [+ *patient*] tratar, atender; [+ *illness*] tratar • **which doctor is ~ing you?** ¿qué médico te atiende *or* trata? • **the condition can be ~ed successfully with antibiotics** la enfermedad se puede curar con antibióticos • **they were ~ed for shock** recibieron tratamiento por shock • **do not try and ~**

t

yourself no intente automedicarse
6 (= *process*) [+ *wood, crops, sewage*] tratar
VI (*frm*) **1** (= *negotiate*) • **to ~ with sb** negociar con algn
2 (= *deal with*) • **to ~ of sth** [*author*] tratar algo; [*book, article*] versar sobre algo

treatable ['tri:təbl] ADJ [*condition, illness*] tratable

treatise ['tri:tɪz] N tratado *m*

treatment ['tri:tmənt] N **1** (= *handling*) [*of people*] trato *m*; [*of object*] trato *m*, manejo *m*; [*of subject, idea*] tratamiento *m* • **our ~ of foreigners** el trato que damos a los extranjeros • **I wouldn't put up with such ~** yo no permitiría que me trataran así *or* que me dieran ese trato • **the judge was criticized for his harsh ~ of offenders** el juez fue criticado por su trato duro hacia los delincuentes • **his ~ of the subject is superficial** el tratamiento que da al tema es superficial • **for a more extensive ~ of this subject I refer the reader to ...** para ver este tema en más profundidad remito al lector a ... • **at that restaurant you get the full ~** en ese restaurante te tratan a cuerpo de rey* • **to give sb preferential ~** dar a algn un trato preferente • **to get preferential ~** recibir un trato preferente • **he has come in for some rough ~ from the press** ha recibido un trato duro por parte de la prensa • IDIOM: • **to give sb the ~*** (= *beat up*) dar caña a algn*; (= *treat*) tratar a algn a cuerpo de rey*
2 (*Med*) tratamiento *m* • **she has** *or* **receives** *or* **undergoes ~ twice a month** la someten a tratamiento dos veces al mes • **a course of ~** un tratamiento • **he needs medical ~** le hace falta atención médica *or* tratamiento médico • **I am still receiving ~ for the injury** todavía estoy en tratamiento por la lesión • **to respond to ~** responder al tratamiento
3 (= *processing*) [*of waste*] tratamiento *m*
CPD ▸ **treatment room** (*Med*) sala *f* de curas

treaty ['tri:tɪ] N tratado *m* • **Treaty of Accession** (*to EC*) Tratado *m* de Adhesión • **Treaty of Rome** Tratado *m* de Roma • **Treaty of Utrecht** Tratado *m* de Utrecht

treble ['trebl] N **1** (*Mus*) (= *voice*) voz *f* de tiple
2 (= *drink*) triple *m*
ADJ **1** (= *triple*) triple
2 (*Mus*) [*voice, note, instrument*] de tiple
VT triplicar
VI triplicarse
ADV (= *3 times*) tres veces
CPD ▸ **treble clef** clave *f* de sol ▸ **treble recorder** flauta *f* de pico

trebling ['treblɪŋ] N aumento *m* en tres veces

trebly ['treblɪ] ADV tres veces • **it is ~ dangerous to ...** es tres veces más peligroso ...

tree [tri:] N **1** (*Bot*) árbol *m* • **~ of knowledge** árbol *m* de la ciencia • IDIOMS: • **to be at the top of the ~** (*Brit*) estar en la cumbre de su carrera profesional • **to be out of one's ~*** (= *crazy*) estar como una cabra*, estar como una moto‡; (*on drugs, alcohol*) estar colocadísimo‡, haberse puesto como una moto‡ • **to be up a ~*** (= *in a fix*) estar en un aprieto; (= *mad*) estar chalado*, estar como una cabra *or* regadera* • **to be barking up the wrong ~** tomar el rábano por las hojas • **we can't see the wood** *or* (*US*) **the forest for the ~s** los árboles no dejan ver el bosque
2 (*for shoes*) horma *f*
3 [*of saddle*] arzón *m*
VT [+ *animal*] hacer refugiarse en un árbol
CPD ▸ **tree creeper** trepatroncos *mf inv* ▸ **tree frog** rana *f* de San Antonio, rana *f* arbórea ▸ **tree house** casita *f* en un árbol ▸ **tree hugger*** (*esp US*) (*hum*) fanático/a *m/f* del medioambiente ▸ **tree planting** plantación *f* de árboles ▸ **tree surgeon** arboricultor(a) *m/f* ▸ **tree trunk** tronco *m* (de árbol)

tree-covered ['tri:,kʌvəd] ADJ arbolado

treeless ['tri:lɪs] ADJ sin árboles, pelado

tree line ['tri:laɪn] N límite *m* forestal

tree-lined ['tri:laɪnd] ADJ bordeado de árboles

treetop ['tri:tɒp] N copa *f* (de árbol)

trefoil ['trefɔɪl] N trébol *m*

trek [trek] N **1** (= *hike*) expedición *f*
2* (= *long, tiring walk*) caminata *f* • **it's quite a ~ to the shops*** las tiendas quedan muy lejos
VI **1** (= *hike*) (*also Mil*) caminar • **we ~ked for days on end** caminamos día tras día
2* (= *traipse*) ir (penosamente) • **I had to ~ up to the top floor*** tuve que subir hasta el último piso

Trekkie* ['trekɪ] N trekker *mf*, trekkie *mf*, *fan de la serie televisiva "Star Trek"*

trekking ['trekɪŋ] N trekking *m*

trellis ['trelɪs] N espaldera *f*, enrejado *m*; (*Bot*) espaldera *f*, espaldar *m*

trelliswork ['trelɪswɜ:k] N enrejado *m*

tremble ['trembl] N temblor *m* • **to be all of a ~** estar tembloroso • **she said with a ~ in her voice** dijo con voz temblorosa
VI • **to ~ (with)** temblar (de) • **to ~ with fear** temblar de miedo • **to ~ at the thought of sth** temblar ante la idea de algo • **to ~ all over** estar todo tembloroso • **to ~ like a leaf** estar como un flan

trembling ['tremblɪŋ] ADJ tembloroso
N temblor *m*, estremecimiento *m*

tremendous [trə'mendəs] ADJ **1** (= *huge*) [*pressure, success, explosion, problem*] tremendo, enorme • **it cost a ~ amount of money** costó muchísimo dinero, costó una enorme *or* tremenda cantidad de dinero • **you've been a ~ help** me has ayudado enormemente *or* muchísimo • **~ progress has been made** se ha progresado enormemente *or* muchísimo • **at (a) ~ speed** a una velocidad increíble *or* tremenda
2 (= *wonderful*) [*person, goal, performance, achievement*] formidable, extraordinario; [*opportunity*] tremendo, estupendo • **the food is ~** la comida está estupenda *or* riquísima • **she has done a ~ job** ha hecho un trabajo formidable *or* magnífico *or* estupendo

tremendously [trə'mendəslɪ] ADV [*exciting, important, useful, satisfying*] tremendamente, enormemente; [*improve, vary, help*] enormemente, muchísimo • **he was ~ helpful** nos ayudó enormemente *or* muchísimo

tremolo ['treməlaʊ] N trémolo *m*

tremor ['tremə^r] N **1** (= *earthquake*) temblor *m* • **earth ~** temblor *m* de tierra
2 (= *tremble*) estremecimiento *m* • **he said without a ~** dijo sin inmutarse • **it sent ~s through the system** sacudió el sistema

tremulous ['tremjʊləs] ADJ trémulo (*liter*), tembloroso

tremulously ['tremjʊləslɪ] ADV trémulamente (*liter*), temblorosamente

trench [trentʃ] N (*gen*) zanja *f*; (*Mil*) trinchera *f*
VT (*gen*) hacer zanjas en; (*Mil*) hacer trincheras en, atrincherar; (*Agr*) excavar
CPD ▸ **trench coat** trinchera *f* ▸ **trench warfare** guerra *f* de trincheras

trenchant ['trentʃənt] ADJ mordaz

trenchantly ['trentʃəntlɪ] ADV mordazmente

trencher ['trentʃə^r] N tajadero *m*

trencherman ['trentʃəmæn] N (PL: **trenchermen**) • **to be a good ~** comer bien, tener siempre buen apetito

trend [trend] N (= *tendency*) tendencia *f*; (= *fashion*) moda *f* • **to set the ~** marcar la pauta • **a ~ towards (doing) sth** una tendencia hacia (hacer) algo • **a ~ away from (doing) sth** una tendencia en contra de (hacer) algo • **~s in popular music** tendencias *fpl* de la música popular • **to be on ~** estar de moda
VI **1** (= *tend*) tender
2 • **to be ~ing on Twitter** ser trending topic en Twitter
CPD ▸ **trend line** línea *f* de la tendencia

trendily ['trendɪlɪ] ADV a la moda • **to dress ~** vestirse a la moda

trendiness ['trendɪnɪs] N
1 (= *fashionableness*) lo moderno, modernidad *f*
2 (*pej*) (= *desire to be in fashion*) afán *m* de estar al día

trendsetter ['trend,setə^r] N iniciador(a) *m/f* de una moda

trendsetting ['trendsetɪŋ] ADJ que impone la moda

trendy* ['trendɪ] ADJ (COMPAR: **trendier**, SUPERL: **trendiest**) a la moda, moderno
N persona *f* de tendencias ultramodernas • **~ leftie*** progre* *mf*

Trent [trent] N Trento *m*

trepan [trɪ'pæn] VT trepanar

trephine [tre'fi:n] N trépano *m*
VT trepanar

trepidation [,trepɪ'deɪʃən] N (= *fear*) temor *m*; (= *anxiety*) inquietud *f*, agitación *f* • **in some ~** algo turbado, agitado

trespass ['trespəs] VI **1** (*on land*) entrar ilegalmente (**on en**) • **"no trespassing"** "prohibida la entrada" • **to ~ upon** (*fig*) abusar de • **may I ~ upon your kindness to ask that ...** (*frm*) permítame abusar de su amabilidad pidiendo que ... • **to ~ upon sb's privacy** invadir la vida íntima de algn
2 (= *do wrong*) (*Rel*) pecar (**against** contra) • **to ~ against** (*Jur*) infringir, violar
N **1** (*on land*) entrada *f* ilegal, invasión *f* (de propiedad ajena)
2 (= *transgression*) infracción *f*, violación *f*; (*Rel*) pecado *m* • **forgive us our ~es** perdónanos nuestras deudas

trespasser ['trespəsə^r] N intruso/a *m/f* • **"trespassers will be prosecuted"** "entrada terminantemente prohibida"

tress [tres] N **1** (= *lock of hair*) trenza *f*
2 tresses (= *head of hair*) cabellera *f*, pelo *m*

trestle ['tresl] N caballete *m*
CPD ▸ **trestle bridge** puente *m* de caballetes ▸ **trestle table** mesa *f* de caballete

trews [tru:z] NPL (*Scot*) pantalón *m* de tartán

tri... [traɪ] PREFIX tri...

triad ['traɪəd] N tríada *f*

triage ['tri:ɑ:ʒ] N (*in hospital*) clasificación *f*

trial ['traɪəl] N **1** (*Jur*) juicio *m*, proceso *m* • **the ~ continues today** el juicio *or* proceso se reanuda hoy • **to be awaiting ~** estar a la espera de juicio *or* de ser procesado • **to bring sb to ~** llevar a algn a juicio, procesar a algn • **the case never came to ~** el caso nunca se llevó a juicio • **~ by jury** proceso *m* *or m* juicio ante jurado • **murder ~** proceso *m* *or* juicio *m* por asesinato • **new ~** revisión *f* (de juicio) • **on ~**: • **he is on ~ for murder** se lo está procesando por asesinato • **to be on ~ for one's life** ser acusado de un crimen capital • **to go on ~** ser procesado • **to stand ~** ser procesado • **detention without ~** detención *f* sin procesamiento; ▹ **commit**, GRAND JURY
2 (= *test*) [*of drug, machine*] prueba *f*; [*of person*,

for job] periodo *m* de prueba, prueba *f* • **clinical ~s** ensayos *mpl* clínicos • **by** *or* **through ~ and error** a base de probar y cometer errores • **finding the right skin cream is a question of ~ and error** encontrar la crema apropiada para la piel es cuestión de probar *or* ir probando • **flight ~s** vuelos *mpl* de prueba, vuelos *mpl* experimentales • **to give sb a ~** (*for job*) ofrecer a algn un periodo de prueba • **to be on ~** (*lit, fig*) estar a prueba • **the fullback has been on ~ at the club for ten days** el defensa lleva diez días a prueba en el club • **I felt as if I was continually on ~** me sentía como si estuviera a prueba continuamente • **her reputation is on ~** su reputación está a prueba • **a ~ of strength** una prueba de fuerza
3 (= *hardship*) • **the ~s of old age** los padecimientos de la vejez • **a movie about the ~s of family life** una película sobre las dificultades de la vida familiar • **the interview was a great ~** la entrevista fue todo un suplicio • **the child is a great ~ to them** el niño les hace sufrir mucho • **~s and tribulations** tribulaciones *fpl* • **the ~s and tribulations of parenthood** las tribulaciones de ser padre
4 trials (*Sport*) pruebas *fpl* de selección • **the Olympic ~s** las pruebas de selección para los Juegos Olímpicos • **horse ~s** concurso *m* hípico • **sheepdog ~s** concurso *m* de perros pastores • **time ~s** pruebas *fpl* contrarreloj
VT (*Comm*) [+ *product*] poner a prueba • **products are ~led for six months before they go on the market** los productos se ponen a prueba durante seis meses antes de lanzarlos al mercado
CPD ▸ **trial balance** balance *m* de comprobación ▸ **trial balloon** (*US*) globo *m* sonda ▸ **trial basis** • **on a ~ basis** (en periodo) de prueba ▸ **trial flight** vuelo *m* de prueba ▸ **trial judge** juez *mf* de la causa ▸ **trial jury** (*US*) jurado *m* de juicio ▸ **trial offer** oferta *f* de prueba ▸ **trial period** periodo *m* de prueba ▸ **trial run** prueba *f* • **I took the car out for a ~ run** saqué el coche para probarlo *or* ponerlo a prueba ▸ **trial separation** periodo *m* de separación como prueba • **they are having a ~ separation** se han separado temporalmente como prueba

triangle ['traɪæŋgl] N (*also Mus*) triángulo *m*

triangular [traɪ'æŋgjʊləʳ] ADJ triangular

triangulate [traɪ'æŋgjʊleɪt] VT triangular

triangulation [traɪˌæŋgjʊ'leɪʃən] N triangulación *f*

triathlete [traɪ'æθliːt] N triatleta *mf*

triathlon [traɪ'æθlən] N triatlón *m*

tribal ['traɪbəl] ADJ tribal, de tribu

tribalism ['traɪbəlɪzəm] N tribalismo *m*

tribe [traɪb] N (*Anthropology, Zool*) tribu *f*; (*fig*) (= *family*) familia *f*; (*pej*) (= *group*) tribu *f*, pandilla *f*, horda *f*

tribesman ['traɪbzmən] N (PL: **tribesmen**) miembro *m* de una tribu

tribespeople ['traɪbzpiːpl] NPL (= *members of tribe*) miembros *mpl* de la/una tribu; (= *people living a tribal lifestyle*) tribus *fpl*

tribeswoman ['traɪbzˌwʊmən] N (PL: **tribeswomen**) miembro *f* de una tribu

tribulation [ˌtrɪbjʊ'leɪʃən] N **1** (*frm*) tribulación *f*
2 tribulations aflicciones *fpl*

tribunal [traɪ'bjuːnl] N tribunal *m*

tribune ['trɪbjuːn] N **1** (= *stand*) tribuna *f*
2 (= *person*) tribuno *m*

tributary ['trɪbjʊtərɪ] ADJ tributario
N **1** (*Geog*) afluente *m*
2 (= *state, ruler*) tributario *m*

tribute ['trɪbjuːt] N **1** (= *payment, tax*) tributo *m*
2 (*fig*) homenaje *m*, tributo *m* • **to pay ~ to sth/sb** rendir homenaje a algo/algn • **that is a ~ to his loyalty** eso acredita su lealtad, eso hace honor a su lealtad; ▹ **floral**
CPD ▸ **tribute band** grupo *m* de imitación

trice [traɪs] N • **in a ~** en un santiamén

tricentenary [ˌtraɪsen'tiːnərɪ] ADJ (de) tricentenario
N tricentenario *m*
CPD ▸ **tricentenary celebrations** celebraciones *fpl* de(l) tricentenario

triceps ['traɪseps] N (PL: **triceps** *or* **tricepses**) tríceps *m*

trick [trɪk] N **1** (= *joke, hoax*) broma *f*; (= *mischief*) travesura *f*; (= *ruse*) truco *m*, ardid *m* • **dirty** *or* **mean ~** mala pasada *f*, jugada *f* sucia • **the ~s of the trade** los trucos del oficio • **to play a ~ on sb** gastar una broma a algn • **unless my eyes are playing ~s on me** si los ojos no me engañan • **his memory played a ~ on him** le falló la memoria • **~ or treat!** *frase amenazante que pronuncian en tono jocoso los niños que rondan las casas en la noche de Halloween; quiere decir: —¡danos algo o te hacemos una trastada!*; ▹ **HALLOWE'EN** • **IDIOMS:** • **he's up to his old ~s again** ha vuelto a hacer de las suyas • **how's ~s?*** ¿cómo te va?
2 (= *card trick*) baza *f*; (= *conjuring trick*) truco *m*; (*in circus*) número *m* • **to take all the ~s** ganar *or* hacer todas las bazas • **IDIOMS:** • **he/she knows a ~ or two** se lo sabe todo • **I know a ~ worth two of that** yo me sé algo mucho mejor • **that should do the ~** esto servirá • **he/she doesn't miss a ~** no se pierde nada • **to try every ~ in the book** emplear todos los trucos • **that's the oldest ~ in the book** eso es un viejo truco • **the whole bag of ~s*** todo el rollo*
3 (= *special knack*) truco *m* • **there's a ~ to opening this door** esta puerta tiene truco para abrirla • **to get the ~ of it** coger el truco, aprender el modo de hacerlo
4 (= *peculiarity, strange habit*) manía *f*, peculiaridad *f* • **certain ~s of style** ciertas peculiaridades estilísticas, ciertos rasgos del estilo • **it's just a ~ he has** es una manía suya • **to have a ~ of doing sth** tener la manía de hacer algo • **history has a ~ of repeating itself** la historia tiene tendencia a repetirse • **it's a ~ of the light** es una ilusión óptica
5 (= *catch*) trampa *f* • **there must be a ~ in it** aquí seguro que hay trampa
6‡ [*of prostitute*] cliente *m* • **to turn ~s** ligarse clientes*
VT (= *deceive*) engañar; (= *swindle*) estafar, timar • **I've been ~ed!** ¡me han engañado! • **to ~ sb into doing sth** engañar a algn para que haga algo, conseguir con engaños que algn haga algo • **to ~ sb out of sth** quitar algo a algn con engaños
CPD ▸ **trick cyclist** ciclista *mf* acróbata ▸ **trick photography** trucaje *m* ▸ **trick question** pregunta *f* de pega ▸ **trick riding** acrobacia *f* ecuestre
▸ **trick out, trick up** VT + ADV (= *decorate*) ataviar (**with** de)

trickery ['trɪkərɪ] N engaño *m*, superchería *f* (*frm*) • **to obtain sth by ~** obtener algo fraudulentamente

trickle ['trɪkl] N **1** (*gen*) chorrito *m*; [*of blood*] hilo *m*
2 (*fig*) • **a ~ of people** un goteo de personas • **we received a ~ of news** nos llegaba alguna que otra noticia • **what was a ~ is now a flood** lo que era un goteo es ya un torrente
VI **1** [*liquid*] escurrir • **blood ~d down his cheek** la sangre le caía a gotas por la mejilla
2 (*fig*) (*slowly*) ir despacio; (*gradually*) poco a poco • **people kept trickling in** la gente seguía entrando poco a poco
VT (*lit*) gotear • **you're trickling blood** estás sangrando un poco
CPD ▸ **trickle charger** (*Elec*) cargador *m* de batería
▸ **trickle away** VI + ADV • **our money is trickling away** nuestro dinero se consume poco a poco

trickle-down economics [ˌtrɪkldaʊniːkə'nɒmɪks] N *efecto de filtración de la riqueza desde las capas sociales más altas hasta las más bajas*

trick-or-treat [ˌtrɪkɔː'triːt] VI • **to go trick-or-treating** *rondar de casa en casa disfrazados (los niños) en la noche de Halloween (víspera del día de Todos los Santos) pidiendo una propina o golosinas a cambio de no gastar una broma o hacer una trastada*

trickster ['trɪkstəʳ] N estafador(a) *m/f*, embustero/a *m/f*

tricksy ['trɪksɪ] ADJ **1** (= *playful*) juguetón
2 (= *crafty*) astuto, mañoso

tricky ['trɪkɪ] ADJ (COMPAR: **trickier**, SUPERL: **trickiest**) **1** [*situation*] complicado, difícil; [*problem*] delicado • **it's all rather ~** es un poco complicado, es un tanto difícil
2 [*person*] (= *sly*) tramposo, ladino; (= *difficult*) difícil

tricolour, tricolor (*US*) ['trɪkələʳ] N (= *flag*) bandera *f* tricolor, tricolor *f*

tricorn ['traɪkɔːn] ADJ tricornio
N tricornio *m*

tricuspid [traɪ'kʌspɪd] ADJ tricúspide

tricycle ['traɪsɪkl] N triciclo *m*

trident ['traɪdənt] N tridente *m*

Tridentine [traɪ'dentaɪn] ADJ tridentino

tried [traɪd] PT, PP *of* **try**
ADJ • **~ and tested** • **~ and trusted** probado

triennial [traɪ'enɪəl] ADJ trienal

triennially [traɪ'enɪəlɪ] ADV trienalmente, cada tres años

triennium [traɪ'enɪəm] N trienio *m*

trier ['traɪəʳ] N persona *f* aplicada

trifle ['traɪfl] N **1** (= *cheap object*) baratija *f*, fruslería *f* (*frm*)
2 (= *unimportant issue*) pequeñez *f*, nimiedad *f* (*frm*) • **he worries about ~s** se preocupa por nimiedades • **any ~ can distract her** le distrae cualquier tontería
3 (= *small amount*) insignificancia *f* • **£5 is a mere ~** cinco libras son una insignificancia • **you could have bought it for a ~** hubieras podido comprarlo por una insignificancia *or* por nada
4 • **a ~** (*as adv*) (= *somewhat*) algo, un poquito • **it's a ~ difficult** es un poco *or* poquito difícil • **we were a ~ put out** quedamos algo desconcertados, nos quedamos un poquito desconcertados
5 (*Culin*) dulce *m* de bizcocho borracho
▸ **trifle away** VT + ADV malgastar, desperdiciar
▸ **trifle with** VI + PREP jugar con • **to ~ with sb** jugar con algn, tratar a algn con poca seriedad • **he's not a person to be ~d with** con ese (es) mejor no meterse • **to ~ with sb's affections** jugar con los sentimientos de algn • **to ~ with one's food** hacer melindres *or* remilgos a la comida

trifler ['traɪfləʳ] N persona *f* frívola, persona *f* informal

trifling ['traɪflɪŋ] ADJ (= *insignificant*) sin importancia, frívolo

triforium [traɪ'fɔːrɪəm] N (PL: **triforia** [traɪ'fɔːrɪə]) triforio *m*

trigger ['trɪgəʳ] N [*of gun*] gatillo *m*; [*of bomb, machine*] disparador *m* • **to pull the ~** apretar el gatillo, disparar

VT (*also* **trigger off**) [+ *bomb*] hacer estallar; [+ *fight, explosion*] provocar; [+ *mechanism*] hacer funcionar, poner en movimiento; [+ *chain of events*] desencadenar
CPD ▸ **trigger finger** índice *m* de la mano derecha (empleado para apretar el gatillo)

trigger-happy* ['trɪgə,hæpɪ] ADJ pronto a disparar, que dispara a la mínima

trigonometric [,trɪgɒnə'metrɪk] ADJ trigonométrico

trigonometrical [,trɪgɒnə'metrɪkəl] ADJ = **trigonometric**

trigonometry [,trɪgə'nɒmɪtrɪ] N trigonometría *f*

trijet ['traɪdʒet] N trirreactor *m*

trike* [traɪk] N triciclo *m*

trilateral ['traɪ'lætərəl] ADJ trilátero

trilby ['trɪlbɪ] N (*Brit*) (*also* **trilby hat**) sombrero *m* flexible, sombrero *m* tirolés

trilingual ['traɪ'lɪŋgwəl] ADJ trilingüe

trill [trɪl] N [*of bird*] gorjeo *m*, trino *m*; [*of phone*] sonido *m*, ring-ring* *m*; (*Mus*) trino *m*; (*Phon*) [*of "R"*] vibración *f*
VI [*bird*] gorjear, trinar; [*phone*] sonar
VT **1** (*Phon*) hacer vibrar • **to ~ one's Rs** hacer vibrar las erres • **~ed R** erre vibrada
2 (= *say*) • **"how adorable!," she ~ed** —¡qué encantador! —gorjeó

trillion ['trɪlɪən] N trillón *m*; (*US*) billón *m* • **there are ~s of places I want to visit*** hay millones *or* montones de sitios a los que quiero ir

trilogy ['trɪlədʒɪ] N trilogía *f*

trim [trɪm] ADJ (COMPAR: **trimmer**, SUPERL: **trimmest**) **1** (= *neat*) [*garden*] bien cuidado, arreglado; [*person*] arreglado; [*clothes*] de corte elegante; [*moustache, beard*] bien cuidado • **a ~ little house** una casita bien cuidada
2 (= *slim*) [*person, figure*] esbelto; [*waist*] delgado • **to stay ~** conservar una figura esbelta
N **1** (= *cut*) • **to get** *or* **have a ~** cortarse un poco el pelo; (*on long hair*) cortarse solo las puntas • **to give one's beard a ~** recortarse la barba • **to give the lawn/hedge a ~** recortar el césped/el seto
2 (= *good physical condition*) • **to be in (good) ~** [*person*] estar en buena forma *or* en buen estado físico; [*car, house*] estar en buen estado *or* en buenas condiciones • **to get in** *or* **into ~** ponerse en forma • **to keep (o.s.) in (good) ~** mantenerse en buena forma *or* en buen estado físico • **to keep sth in (good) ~** mantener algo en buen estado *or* en buenas condiciones
3 (= *decoration*) **a** (*Sew*) adorno *m*; (*on edge*) ribete *m*, reborde *m* • **a coat with a fur ~** un abrigo con ribetes *or* rebordes de piel
b (*Aut*) (*on outside of car*) embellecedor *m* (*Sp*) • **leather ~** tapizado *m* de cuero • **wheel ~** tapacubos *m inv*, embellecedor *m* de la rueda (*Sp*)
VT **1** (= *clip*) [+ *hair, beard, moustache*] recortar; [+ *hedge*] cortar, podar; [+ *lamp, wick*] despabilar • **to ~ back** [+ *plant, shoot*] podar • **~ excess fat from** *or* **off the chops** quitar el exceso de grasa de las chuletas
2 (= *reduce*) [+ *costs, prices*] recortar, reducir; [+ *profits*] recortar; [+ *programme, policy*] hacer recortes en; (*also* **trim back**) [+ *workforce*] recortar, reducir
3 (= *slim*) [+ *hips, thighs*] adelgazar
4 (= *decorate*) [+ *dress, hat*] adornar; [+ *Christmas tree*] decorar • **a dress ~med with feathers/lace** un vestido adornado con plumas/con adornos de encaje
5 (*Naut*) [+ *sails*] orientar; [+ *boat*] equilibrar • IDIOM: • **to ~ one's sails** (*fig*) apretarse el cinturón
6 (*Aer*) equilibrar
7 (*Orn*) orientar
▸ **trim away** VT + ADV cortar, quitar
▸ **trim down** VT + ADV [+ *wick*] despabilar; [+ *workforce*] recortar, reducir; [+ *hips, thighs*] adelgazar
VI + ADV (= *get slimmer*) adelgazar
▸ **trim off** VT + ADV = **trim away**

trimaran ['traɪməræn] N trimarán *m*

trimester [trɪ'mestəʳ] N trimestre *m*

trimming ['trɪmɪŋ] N **1** (= *edging*) adorno *m*, guarnición *f*
2 trimmings: **a** (= *cuttings*) recortes *mpl*
b (= *extras, embellishments*) • **turkey with all the ~s** pavo con su guarnición • **without all the ~s** sin los adornos

trimness ['trɪmnɪs] N (= *elegance*) elegancia *f*; (= *good condition*) buen estado *m*

trimphone® ['trɪmfəʊn] N ≈ teléfono *m* góndola

Trinidad ['trɪnɪdæd] N Trinidad *f*
CPD ▸ **Trinidad and Tobago** Trinidad y Tobago *f*

Trinidadian [,trɪnɪ'dædɪən] ADJ de Trinidad
N nativo/a *m/f* de Trinidad, habitante *mf* de Trinidad

trinitrotoluene [traɪ'naɪtrəʊ'tɒljuːiːn] N trinitrotolueno *m*

Trinity ['trɪnɪtɪ] N (*Rel*) Trinidad *f*
CPD ▸ **Trinity Sunday** Domingo *m* de la Santísima Trinidad ▸ **Trinity term** (*Univ*) trimestre *m* de verano

trinket ['trɪŋkɪt] N chuchería *f*, baratija *f*

trinomial [traɪ'nəʊmɪəl] ADJ trinomio
N trinomio *m*

trio ['trɪəʊ] N trío *m*

trip [trɪp] N **1** (= *journey*) viaje *m*; (= *excursion*) excursión *f*; (= *visit*) visita *f*; (= *outing*) salida *f* • **it's her first ~ abroad** es su primer viaje al extranjero • **it's a 100-mile ~** es un recorrido *or* un viaje de 100 millas • **she's planning a ~ round the world** está planeando hacer un viaje por todo el mundo • **a ~ to the park/seaside** una excursión *or* una salida al parque/a la playa • **a ~ to the cinema** una visita *or* una salida al cine • **a ~ to the doctor** una visita al médico • **boat ~** paseo *m or* excursión *f* en barco • **fishing ~** excursión *f* de pesca • **to make a ~**: • **we made a ~ into town** fuimos a la ciudad • **he made several ~s to the toilet** fue varias veces al servicio • **she went on a ~ to Tasmania** (se) fue de viaje a Tasmania • **he's away on a ~** está de viaje • **school ~** excursión *f* del colegio • **shopping ~** visita *f* a las tiendas • **to take a ~**: • **they took a ~ to York** fueron de excursión a York • **they took a ~ to Canada** (se) fueron de viaje a Canadá • **take a ~ to your local library** hágale una visita a la biblioteca de su barrio, visite la biblioteca de su barrio • **weekend ~** viaje *m* de fin de semana • IDIOM: • **to take a ~ down memory lane** revivir el pasado; ▹ **business, coach, day, field, round**
2* (*on drugs*) viaje *m* • **acid ~** viaje *m* de ácido • **she had a bad ~** tuvo un mal viaje*; ▹ **ego, guilt**
3 (= *stumble*) tropezón *m*; (= *move to make sb trip*) zancadilla *f* • **he brought the other player down with a ~** hizo caer al otro jugador con una zancadilla
4 (*Elec*) (*also* **trip switch**) interruptor *m* de desconexión
VI **1** (= *stumble*) tropezar • **he ~ped and fell** tropezó y se cayó al suelo • **to ~ on/over sth** tropezar con algo; ▹ **trip over**
2 (*liter*) (= *step lightly*) • **she ~ped gracefully round the dance floor** se movía con paso ligero y grácil por la pista de baile • **to ~ along** • **go ~ping along** ir con paso ligero • IDIOM: • **to ~ off the tongue**: • **it doesn't exactly ~ off the tongue** no se puede decir que sea fácil de pronunciar • **the formula came ~ping off his tongue** pronunció la fórmula con la mayor facilidad; ▹ **tongue**
3* (*on drugs*) • **to be ~ping** estar colocado* • **they were all ~ping out on acid** todos estaban colocados con ácido*
VT **1** (*also* **trip up**) (= *cause to stumble*) (*intentionally*) poner *or* echar la zancadilla a; (*accidentally*) hacer tropezar • **he tried to ~ me** intentó ponerme *or* echarme la zancadilla • **don't leave things on the stairs where they may ~ you** no deje cosas en las escaleras donde se pueda tropezar
2 (*also* **trip up**) (= *catch out*) • **he was trying to ~ her into contradicting herself** estaba intentando tenderle una trampa para que se contradijera; ▹ **trip up**
3 (= *set off*) [+ *mechanism, switch*] activar
4 (= *dance*) • IDIOM: • **to ~ the light fantastic**†* mover el esqueleto*
CPD ▸ **trip switch** interruptor *m* de desconexión
▸ **trip over** VI + ADV (= *fall*) tropezar y caerse • **he ~ped over and fell flat on his face** tropezó y cayó de bruces
VI + PREP **1** (*lit*) tropezarse con, tropezar con • **he ~ped over a wire** tropezó *or* se tropezó con un cable • **she ~ped over her own feet** se tropezó con sus propios pies • **to ~ over one another to do sth** (*fig*) darse de tortas por hacer algo*
2 (*fig*) • **occasionally he would ~ over a word in his impatience to tell his story** a veces se le trababa la lengua en su impaciencia por contar su historia
▸ **trip up** VI + ADV **1** (= *stumble*) tropezar
2 (= *make a mistake*) equivocarse
VT + ADV **1** (= *cause to stumble*) (*intentionally*) poner *or* echar la zancadilla a; (*accidentally*) hacer tropezar
2 (= *cause to make a mistake*) • **she tried to ~ him up** intentó que se equivocase *or* que se confundiese • **the fourth question ~ped him up** la cuarta pregunta le hizo equivocarse *or* le confundió

tripartite ['traɪ'pɑːtaɪt] ADJ tripartito

tripe [traɪp] N **1** (*Culin*) callos *mpl*
2 (*esp Brit**) tonterías *fpl*, babosadas *fpl* (*LAm**), pendejadas *fpl* (*LAm**) • **what utter ~!** ¡tonterías! • **he talks a lot of ~** no habla más que bobadas
3 tripes* (*hum*) (= *guts*) tripas *fpl*

triphase ['traɪfeɪz] ADJ trifásico

triphthong ['trɪfθɒŋ] N triptongo *m*

triple ['trɪpl] ADJ triple
ADV el triple, tres veces • **~ the sum** el triple
N (= *jump*) triple *m*
VT triplicar
VI triplicarse
CPD ▸ **Triple Alliance** (*Hist*) Triple Alianza *f* ▸ **triple glazing** triple acristalamiento *m* ▸ **triple jump** triple salto *m*

triplet ['trɪplɪt] N **1** (= *person*) trillizo/a *m/f*, triate *mf* (*Mex*)
2 (*Mus*) tresillo *m*
3 (*Poetry*) terceto *m*

triplicate ADJ ['trɪplɪkɪt] triplicado
N ['trɪplɪkɪt] • **in ~** por triplicado
VT ['trɪplɪkeɪt] triplicar

triply ['trɪplɪ] ADV tres veces • **~ dangerous** tres veces más peligroso

tripod ['traɪpɒd] N trípode *m*

Tripoli ['trɪpəlɪ] N Trípoli *m*

tripper ['trɪpəʳ] N (*Brit*) turista *mf*, excursionista *mf*

tripping ['trɪpɪŋ] ADJ [*step*] ligero, airoso

trippy‡ ['trɪpɪ] ADJ flipante‡
triptych ['trɪptɪk] N tríptico *m*
tripwire ['trɪpwaɪəʳ] N cuerda *f* de trampa
trireme ['traɪri:m] N trirreme *m*
trisect [traɪ'sekt] VT trisecar
Tristan ['trɪstən], **Tristram** ['trɪstrəm] N Tristán
trisyllabic ['traɪsɪ'læbɪk] ADJ trisilábico
trisyllable ['traɪ'sɪləbl] N trisílabo *m*
trite [traɪt] ADJ trillado, manido
tritely ['traɪtlɪ] ADV con falta de originalidad
triteness ['traɪtnɪs] N lo trillado, lo manido, falta *f* de originalidad
tritium ['trɪtɪəm] N tritio *m*
Triton ['traɪtn] N Tritón
tritone ['traɪtəʊn] N tritono *m*
triturate ['trɪtʃəreɪt] VT triturar
trituration [,trɪtʃə'reɪʃən] N trituración *f*
triumph ['traɪʌmf] N **1** (= *victory*) triunfo *m* (over sobre) • **it is a ~ of man over nature** es un triunfo del hombre sobre la naturaleza • **to achieve a great ~** obtener un gran éxito • **a new ~ for industry** otro éxito para la industria
2 (= *emotion*) júbilo *m* • **in ~** con júbilo
VI triunfar • **to ~ over the enemy** triunfar sobre el enemigo • **to ~ over a difficulty** triunfar de una dificultad
triumphal [traɪ'ʌmfəl] ADJ triunfal, de triunfo
triumphalism [traɪ'ʌmfəlɪzəm] N triunfalismo *m*
triumphalist [traɪ'ʌmfəlɪst] ADJ triunfalista
triumphant [traɪ'ʌmfənt] ADJ (= *jubilant*) jubiloso, triunfante; (= *victorious*) victorioso, vencedor
triumphantly [traɪ'ʌmfəntlɪ] ADV triunfalmente, de modo triunfal • **he said ~** dijo en tono triunfal
triumvirate [traɪ'ʌmvɪrɪt] N triunvirato *m*
triune ['traɪju:n] ADJ trino
trivalent ['traɪveɪlənt] ADJ (*Chem*) trivalente
trivet ['trɪvɪt] N (*US*) salvamanteles *m inv*
trivia ['trɪvɪə] NPL trivialidades *fpl*, nimiedades *fpl*, banalidades *fpl*
CPD ▸ **trivia game, trivia quiz** *concurso de preguntas sobre temas variados*
trivial ['trɪvɪəl] ADJ [*details, matter*] trivial, banal; [*person*] frívolo; [*sum*] insignificante, nimio • **I found it all rather ~** me parecía todo muy trivial
triviality [,trɪvɪ'ælɪtɪ] N **1** (= *unimportance*) trivialidad *f*, banalidad *f*
2 (= *trivial detail*) trivialidad *f*
trivialization [,trɪvɪəlaɪ'zeɪʃən] N trivialización *f*, banalización *f*
trivialize ['trɪvɪəlaɪz] VT minimizar, trivializar
trivially ['trɪvɪəlɪ] ADV trivialmente, banalmente
trochaic [trɒ'keɪɪk] ADJ trocaico
trochee ['trɒki:] N troqueo *m*
trod [trɒd] PT *of* **tread**
trodden ['trɒdn] PP *of* **tread**
troglodyte ['trɒglədaɪt] N troglodita *mf*
troika ['trɔɪkə] N troica *f*
Trojan ['trəʊdʒən] ADJ troyano
N troyano/a *m/f* • IDIOM: • **to work like a ~** trabajar como un mulo/una mula
CPD ▸ **Trojan horse** (*lit*) caballo *m* de Troya; (*fig*) (*with devious intent*) tapadera *f*; (*Comput*) troyano *m* ▸ **Trojan War** Guerra *f* de Troya
troll [trɒl; trəʊl] N **1** (*Myth*) gnomo *m*, duende *m*
2 (*Internet*) trol *m*, troll *m*
VT, VI (*Internet*) trolear
trolley ['trɒlɪ] N **1** (*esp Brit*) (*in station, supermarket*) carrito *m*; (*in hospital*) camilla *f*; (*in mine*) vagoneta *f*; (= *tea trolley*) carrito *m*; (= *drinks trolley*) mesita *f* de ruedas • IDIOM: • **to be off one's ~** (*Brit**) estar chiflado*
2 (*US*) (= *tram*) tranvía *m*
3 (*Tech*) corredera *f* elevada
4 (*Elec*) trole *m*, arco *m* de trole
CPD ▸ **trolley bus** trolebús *m* ▸ **trolley car** (*US*) tranvía *m* ▸ **trolley pole** trole *m*
trolling ['trɒlɪŋ; 'trəʊlɪŋ] N (*Internet*) troleo *m*, trolleo *m*
trollop ['trɒləp] N (= *slut*) marrana *f*; (= *prostitute*) puta *f*
trombone [trɒm'bəʊn] N trombón *m*
trombonist [trɒm'bəʊnɪst] N (*orchestral*) trombón *mf*; (*jazz etc*) trombonista *mf*
trompe l'oeil [,trɒmp'lɔɪ] N (*Art*) ilusión *f* óptica, trampantojo *m*
troop [tru:p] N **1** (*Mil*) tropa *f*; [*of cavalry*] escuadrón *m*; **troops** tropas *fpl*
2 (*gen*) banda *f*, grupo *m*; (= *gang*) cuadrilla *f*; (*Theat*) = **troupe** • **to come in a ~** venir en tropel *or* en masa
3 (= *sound*) • **the steady ~ of feet** el ruido rítmico de pasos
VI (= *walk*) • **to ~ in/past/off/out** entrar/pasar/marcharse/salir en tropel, entrar/pasar/marcharse/salir atropelladamente
VT • **to ~ the colour** (*Brit*) presentar la bandera
CPD ▸ **troop carrier** (= *plane, ship*) transporte *m* (militar) ▸ **troop ship** (buque *m* de) transporte *m* ▸ **troop train** tren *m* militar
trooper ['tru:pəʳ] N **1** (*Mil*) soldado *mf* (de caballería) • IDIOM: • **to swear like a ~** jurar *or* hablar como un carretero
2 (*US*) (= *policeman*) policía *mf* montado/a
trope [trəʊp] N tropo *m*
trophy ['trəʊfɪ] N (*gen*) trofeo *m*
CPD ▸ **trophy wife*** *joven esposa de un hombre de éxito que este gusta de exhibir*
tropic ['trɒpɪk] N trópico *m* • **the ~s** el trópico • **the Tropic of Cancer/Capricorn** el Trópico de Cáncer/Capricornio
tropical ['trɒpɪkəl] ADJ tropical
tropism ['trəʊpɪzəm] N (*Bio*) tropismo *m*
troposphere ['trɒpəsfɪəʳ] N troposfera *f*
Trot* [trɒt] N ABBR = **Trotskyist**
trot [trɒt] N **1** (= *step*) trote *m* • **at an easy ~** • **at a slow ~** a trote corto • **to break into a ~** [*horse, rider*] echar a trotar; [*person*] echar a correr • **to go for a ~** (*on horse*) ir a montar a caballo • IDIOMS: • **to be always on the ~** no parar nunca, tener una vida ajetreada • **to keep sb on the ~** no dejar a algn descansar
2 • **on the ~*** seguidos, uno tras otro, uno detrás de otro • **for five days on the ~*** durante cinco días seguidos • **Barcelona won five times on the ~*** Barcelona ganó cinco veces seguidas
3 • **the ~s**‡ (= *diarrhoea*) diarrea *f* • **to have the ~s** tener diarrea
VI [*horse, rider*] trotar, ir al trote; [*person*] ir trotando
VT [+ *horse*] hacer trotar
▸ **trot along, trot off*** VI + ADV marcharse • **I must be ~ting along now** es hora de que me marche
▸ **trot out*** VT + ADV [+ *excuse, reason*] ensartar, recitar; [+ *names, facts*] echar mano de; [+ *arguments*] sacar a relucir, presentar otra vez
▸ **trot over***, **trot round*** VI + ADV • **he ~ted round to the shop** fue y volvió de la tienda en un santiamén
troth†† [trəʊθ] N ▹ **plight²**
Trotskyism ['trɒtskɪɪzəm] N trotskismo *m*
Trotskyist ['trɒtskɪɪst] ADJ trotskista
N trotskista *mf*
trotter ['trɒtəʳ] N **1** (= *horse*) trotón *m*, caballo *m* trotón
2 • **pig's ~s** manitas *fpl* (de cerdo *or* (*LAm*) chancho)
trotting ['trɒtɪŋ] N (*Sport*) trote *m*
troubadour ['tru:bədɔ:ʳ] N trovador *m*
trouble ['trʌbl] N **1** (= *problem*) problema *m*, dificultad *f*; (*for doing wrong*) problemas *mpl*, lío *m*; (= *difficult situation*) apuro *m*, aprieto *m* • **life is full of ~s** la vida está llena de problemas *or* aflicciones • **now your ~s are over** ya no tendrás de que preocuparte, se acabaron las preocupaciones • **what's the ~?** ¿cuál es el problema?, ¿qué pasa? • **the ~ is ...** el problema es ..., lo que pasa es ... • **that's just the ~** ahí está (la madre del cordero) • **it's just asking for ~** eso es buscarse problemas • **there'll be ~ if she finds out** se armará una buena si se entera • **there's ~ brewing** se va a armar lío* • **to get into ~**: • **he got into ~ with the police** se metió en un lío con la policía • **he got into ~ for saying that** se mereció una bronca diciendo eso • **to get sb into ~** meter a algn en un lío *or* problemas; (*euph*) (= *make pregnant*) dejar embarazada a algn • **to get out of ~** salir del apuro • **to get sb out of ~** ayudar a algn a salir del apuro, echar un cable a algn • **to give ~**: • **she never gave us any ~** nunca nos causó problemas • **to have ~ doing sth**: • **I had no ~ finding the house** encontré la casa sin problemas • **did you have any ~?** ¿tuviste algún problema *or* alguna dificultad? • **we had ~ getting here in time** nos costó trabajo llegar aquí a tiempo • **to be in ~** (= *having problems*) estar en un apuro *or* aprieto; (*for doing wrong*) tener problemas • **to be in great ~** estar muy apurado • **to lay up ~ for o.s.** crearse problemas • **don't go looking for ~** no busques camorra *or* problemas • **to make ~ for sb** crear un lío a algn • **money ~s** dificultades *fpl* económicas • **to stir up ~** meter cizaña, revolver el ajo • **to tell sb one's ~s** contar sus desventuras a algn • IDIOM: • **my/his ~ and strife** (*Brit*‡) la parienta
2 (= *effort, bother*) molestia *f* • **to go to (all) the ~ of doing sth** tomarse la molestia de hacer algo • **I went to a lot of ~ to get it for her** me tomé muchas molestias para conseguírselo • **we had all our ~ for nothing** todo aquello fue trabajo perdido • **it's no ~** no es molestia • **to put sb to the ~ of doing sth** molestar a algn pidiéndole que haga algo • **I fear I am putting you to a lot of ~** me temo que esto te vaya a molestar bastante • **to save o.s. the ~** ahorrarse el trabajo • **to spare no ~ in order to** (+ *infin*) no regatear medio para (+ *infin*) • **to take the ~ to do sth** tomarse la molestia de hacer algo • **he didn't even take the ~ to say thank you** ni se dignó siquiera darme las gracias • **to take a lot of ~ over sth** esmerarse en algo, hacer algo con el mayor cuidado • **nothing is too much ~ for her** para ella todo es poco • **it's more ~ than it's worth** • **it's not worth the ~** no vale la pena
3 (*Med*) • **heart ~** problemas *mpl* de corazón • **it's my old ~** ha vuelto lo de antes
4 (*Mech*) • **a mechanic put the ~ right** un mecánico reparó las piezas averiadas • **engine ~** problemas *mpl* con el motor
5 (= *unrest, fighting*) conflicto *m*, disturbio *m* • **the (Irish) ~s** los conflictos de los irlandeses • **there is constant ~ between them** riñen constantemente • **labour ~s** conflictos laborales • IDIOM: • **there's ~ at t'mill** (*Brit*) (*hum**) hay un disturbio en la fábrica; ▹ **brew**
VT **1** (= *worry*) preocupar • **it's not that that ~s me** no me preocupo por eso, eso me trae sin cuidado
2 (= *cause pain*) • **his eyes ~ him** tiene

problemas con la vista *or* los ojos • **if the tooth ~s you again call the dentist** si vuelves a tener molestias en el diente llama al dentista
3 (= *bother*) molestar • **I'm sorry to ~ you** disculpe la molestia • **maths never ~d me at all** las matemáticas no me costaron trabajo en absoluto • **to ~ o.s. about sth** preocuparse por algo • **to ~ o.s. to do sth** molestarse en *or* tomarse la molestia de hacer algo • **don't ~ yourself!** ¡no te molestes!, ¡no te preocupes! • **may I ~ you to hold this?** ¿te molestaría tener esto? • **may I ~ you for a light?** ¿le molestaría darme fuego, por favor? • **does it ~ you if I smoke?** ¿le molesta que fume? • **I won't ~ you with all the details** no le voy a aburrir con exceso de detalles
VI (= *make the effort*) preocuparse, molestarse • **please don't ~!** ¡no te molestes!, ¡no te preocupes! • **don't ~ to write** no te molestes en escribir • **he didn't ~ to shut the door** no se tomó la molestia de cerrar la puerta • **if you had ~d to find out** si te hubieras tomado la molestia de averiguarlo
CPD ▸ **trouble spot** (*esp Pol*) (= *area, country*) zona *f* conflictiva

troubled ['trʌbld] ADJ **1** (= *worried*) [*person*] preocupado, desazonado; [*mind*] preocupado, agitado; [*conscience*] intranquilo; [*expression, face, look*] de preocupación • **he was deeply ~** estaba profundamente preocupado *or* desazonado • **he was a lonely, ~ man** era un hombre que estaba solo y sin sosiego • **she fell into a ~ sleep** cayó en un sueño inquieto *or* agitado
2 (= *beset by problems*) [*life, marriage, relationship*] lleno de problemas, aquejado de problemas; [*period of time*] turbulento; [*area, country, region*] conflictivo; [*company, bank, industry*] aquejado de problemas • **these are ~ times** estos son tiempos difíciles; ▹ **oil**

trouble-free ['trʌblfri:] ADJ [*life*] sin problemas, tranquilo; [*demonstration, factory*] sin disturbios, pacífico; [*motoring*] sin problemas

troublemaker ['trʌbl,meɪkəʳ] N agitador(a) *m/f*

troublemaking ['trʌbl,meɪkɪŋ] ADJ alborotador, perturbador

troubleshooter ['trʌblʃu:təʳ] N apagafuegos *mf inv* (*profesional o consultor experto en la detección de problemas y el desarrollo de soluciones empresariales o administrativas*)

troubleshooting ['trʌblʃu:tɪŋ] N *detección de problemas y desarrollo de soluciones empresariales o administrativas*

troublesome ['trʌblsəm] ADJ [*person*] fastidioso, molesto, latoso; [*headache, toothache etc*] molesto; [*dispute, problem*] difícil, penoso • **now don't be ~** no seas difícil

troubling ['trʌblɪŋ] ADJ inquietante, alarmante

troublous ['trʌbləs] ADJ (*liter*) [*times*] turbulento, difícil

trough [trɒf] N **1** (= *depression*) depresión *f*, hoyo *m*; (*between waves, on graph*) seno *m*; (= *channel*) canal *m*; (*fig*) parte *f* baja, punto *m* más bajo; ▹ **peak**
2 (*Met*) zona *f* de bajas presiones
3 (*for animals*) (= *feeding trough*) comedero *m*, pesebre *m*; (= *drinking trough*) abrevadero *m*, bebedero *m*; (= *kneading trough*) artesa *f*

trounce [traʊns] VT **1** (= *defeat*) dar una paliza a*, derrotar
2 (= *thrash*) zurrar, dar una paliza a

trouncing ['traʊnsɪŋ] N paliza *f* • **to give sb a ~** dar una paliza a algn

troupe [tru:p] N (*Theat*) compañía *f* de teatro; (*Circus*) troupe *f*

trouper ['tru:pəʳ] N (*Theat*) miembro *mf* de una compañía de actores • **old ~** actor *m* veterano, actriz *f* veterana

trouser ['traʊzəʳ] (*esp Brit*) N **trousers** pantalón *m*, pantalones *mpl* • **short/long ~s** pantalones *mpl* cortos/largos • **a pair of ~s** un pantalón, unos pantalones • IDIOM: • **to wear the ~s** llevar los pantalones
CPD ▸ **trouser leg** pierna *f* de pantalón ▸ **trouser pocket** bolsillo *m* del pantalón ▸ **trouser press** prensa *f* para pantalones ▸ **trouser suit** traje-pantalón *m*

trousseau ['tru:səʊ] N (PL: **trousseaus, trousseaux** ['tru:səʊz]) ajuar *m*

trout [traʊt] (PL: **trout** *or* **trouts**) N **1** (= *fish*) trucha *f*
2 • **old ~*** (= *woman*) arpía *f*, bruja* *f*
CPD ▸ **trout farm** criadero *m* de truchas ▸ **trout fishing** pesca *f* de trucha

trove [trəʊv] N ▹ **treasure**

trowel ['traʊəl] N **1** (*Agr*) desplantador *m*
2 (*builder's*) paleta *f*, llana *f*

Troy [trɔɪ] N Troya *f*

troy ['trɔɪ] N (*also* **troy weight**) peso *m* troy

truancy ['trʊənsɪ] N ausencia *f* sin permiso

truant ['trʊənt] N (*Scol*) ausente *mf* • **to play ~** (*Scol*) hacer novillos, hacer la rabona*; (*fig*) ausentarse
VI (*Scol*) hacer novillos, hacer la rabona*; (*fig*) ausentarse (**from** de)
CPD ▸ **truant officer** *persona que se encarga de investigar los casos de ausentismo escolar*

truanting ['trʊəntɪŋ] N ausentismo *m* (escolar)

truce [tru:s] N (*Mil*) tregua *f* • **to call a ~** (*Mil*) (*also fig*) acordar una tregua

truck¹ [trʌk] N **1** (*esp US*) (= *lorry*) camión *m*
2 (*Rail*) (= *wagon*) vagón *m*
3 (= *hand trolley*) carretilla *f*
VT (*US*) llevar, transportar
CPD ▸ **truck driver** (*esp US*) camionero/a *m/f* ▸ **truck stop** (*US*) restaurante *m* de carretera

truck² [trʌk] N (= *dealings*) • IDIOM: • **to have no ~ with sb** no tener nada que ver con algn • **we want no ~ with that** no queremos tener nada que ver con eso
CPD ▸ **truck farm** (*US*) huerto *m* de hortalizas ▸ **truck farmer** (*US*) hortelano/a *m/f* ▸ **truck farming** (*US*) horticultura *f* ▸ **truck garden** = **truck farm** ▸ **truck system** (*Hist*) el trueque

truckage ['trʌkɪdʒ] N (*US*) acarreo *m*

trucker ['trʌkəʳ] N (*US*) camionero/a *m/f*, transportista *mf*

trucking ['trʌkɪŋ] N (*esp US*) acarreo *m*, transporte *m* (en camión)
CPD ▸ **trucking company** compañía *f* de transporte por carretera

truckle ['trʌkl] VI • **to ~ to sb** someterse servilmente a algn
CPD ▸ **truckle bed** carriola *f*

truckload ['trʌkləʊd] N carga *f* de camión • **by the ~** (*fig*) a carretadas

truckman ['trʌkmən] N (PL: **truckmen**) (*US*) camionero *m*, transportista *m*

truculence ['trʌkjʊləns] N agresividad *f*, mal humor *m*

truculent ['trʌkjʊlənt] ADJ agresivo, malhumorado

truculently ['trʌkjʊləntlɪ] ADV [*behave*] de modo agresivo; [*answer*] ásperamente

trudge [trʌdʒ] N caminata *f* (difícil, larga, penosa)
VT recorrer a pie (penosamente) • **we ~d the streets looking for him** nos cansamos buscándole por las calles
VI • **to ~ up/down/along** *etc* subir/bajar/caminar *etc* penosamente

true [tru:] ADJ (COMPAR: **truer**, SUPERL: **truest**) **1** (= *not false*) [*story*] real, verídico; [*account*] verídico; [*statement*] cierto, verídico; [*rumour*] cierto, verdadero • **it is ~ that …** es verdad *or* cierto que … • **is it ~?** ¿es (eso) verdad? • **it can't be ~!** ¡no me lo creo! • **I'm quite tired, it's ~** es verdad *or* cierto que estoy bastante cansado • **he's so jealous it's not ~*** es tan celoso que resulta difícil creerlo • **is it ~ about Harry?** ¿es verdad *or* cierto lo de Harry? • **~, but …** cierto, pero … • **to come ~** [*dream*] hacerse realidad; [*wish, prediction*] cumplirse, hacerse realidad • **it's a dream come ~** es un sueño hecho realidad • **~ or false?** ¿verdadero o falso? • **the reverse is ~** ocurre lo contrario • **it is ~ to say that …** puede afirmarse que … • **the film is based on a ~ story** la película está basada en un hecho real *or* verídico • **it's ~r than you know** es más verdad de lo que te imaginas • **that's ~** es cierto, es verdad • **too ~** eso es totalmente cierto • **it is only too ~ that …** es lamentablemente *or* desgraciadamente cierto que …; ▹ **good, ring²**
2 (= *genuine*) [*gentleman, romantic, genius*] verdadero, auténtico; [*friend, courage, happiness*] verdadero, de verdad, auténtico • **music is her ~ love** su verdadero amor es la música • **her ~ love†** (= *sweetheart*) su gran amor *m* • **then he was able to demonstrate his ~ worth** entonces pudo demostrar lo que valía realmente *or* su verdadera valía
3 (= *real, actual*) [*feelings, motives, meaning*] verdadero; [*value, cost*] verdadero, real • **the ~ meaning of love** el verdadero significado del amor • **this helps us to discover our ~ selves** esto nos ayuda a descubrir nuestra verdadera identidad • **in the ~ sense (of the word)** en el sentido estricto (de la palabra), propiamente dicho
4 (*Rel*) verdadero • **the one ~ God** el Dios único y verdadero
5 (= *relevant, applicable*) cierto • **to be ~ for sb/sth** ser cierto en el caso de algn/algo • **this is particularly ~ for single women** esto es cierto particularmente en el caso de las mujeres solteras • **this is ~ for nine out of ten cases** esto es cierto en nueve de cada diez casos • **to hold ~ (for sb/sth)** ser válido (para algn/algo) • **this is ~ of any new business venture** este es el caso con cualquier empresa nueva • **the same is ~ of nuclear power stations** el caso es el mismo con las centrales nucleares
6 (*frm*) (= *faithful*) • **I am a ~ believer in American values** creo firmemente en los valores americanos • **to be ~ to sb/sth** ser fiel a algn/algo • **to be ~ to o.s.** ser fiel a sí mismo • **~ to form** como es/era de esperar • **to be ~ to life** ser como la vida real • **to be ~ to one's promise** *or* **word** ser fiel a su palabra *or* promesa, cumplir con su palabra *or* promesa • **~ to type** como es/era de esperar
7 (= *accurate*) • **his aim was ~** dio en el blanco • **the portrait was a ~ likeness of her grandmother** el cuadro era un fiel retrato de su abuela
8 (= *straight*) derecho • **the window frame isn't quite ~** el marco de la ventana no está del todo derecho
9 (*Mus*) afinado • **his top notes were pure and ~** sus notas más altas eran puras y afinadas
N • **to be out of ~: the doorframe is out of ~** el marco de la puerta no cae a plomo • **the top of the window was out of ~** la parte superior de la ventana no estaba nivelada
ADV • **to breed ~** (*Bio*) reproducirse conforme con la raza

CPD ▸ **true colours, true colors** (*US*) • **to show one's ~ colours • show o.s. in one's ~ colours** mostrarse tal y como se es en realidad • **to see sb in their ~ colours** ver a algn tal y como es en realidad; ▹ **colour**
▸ **true north** (*Geog*) norte *m* geográfico
true-blue ['tru:'blu:] ADJ rancio, de lo más rancio
N partidario/a *m/f* de lo más leal, partidario/a *m/f* acérrimo/a
true-born ['tru:'bɔ:n] ADJ auténtico, verdadero
true-bred ['tru:'bred] ADJ de casta legítima, de pura sangre
true-life ['tru:laɪf] ADJ verdadero, conforme con la realidad
truffle ['trʌfl] N trufa *f*
trug [trʌg] N (*Brit*) *cesto para hortalizas o flores*
truism ['tru:ɪzəm] N (= *well-known truth*) perogrullada *f*; (*pej*) (= *cliché*) tópico *m*
truly ['tru:lɪ] ADV **1** (= *genuinely*) [*happy, democratic, international*] verdaderamente, realmente; [*understand, love*] de verdad • **the only man she ~ loved** el único hombre al que quería de verdad • **really and ~** de verdad
2 (*frm*) (= *sincerely*) [*grateful, worried*] verdaderamente, realmente, de verdad; [*believe, think, feel*] de verdad, realmente • **I ~ believe this** me lo creo de verdad, realmente me lo creo • **I was ~ hurt by what she said** lo que dijo me hizo realmente *or* verdadero daño • **it can ~ be said that ...** verdaderamente se puede decir que ..., realmente se puede decir que ... • **I am ~ sorry for what happened** siento de veras *or* muchísimo lo ocurrido • **it was ~ wrong of him to do that** lo que hizo estuvo verdaderamente *or* realmente mal • **yours ~** (*in letter*) le saluda atentamente • **nobody knows it better than yours ~*** nadie lo sabe mejor que un servidor*
3 (*as intensifier*) (= *absolutely*) [*amazing, remarkable*] verdaderamente, realmente; ▹ **well**
trump [trʌmp] N (*Cards*) triunfo *m* • **hearts are ~s** triunfan corazones, pintan corazones • **what's ~s?** ¿a qué pinta? • IDIOM: • **to turn up ~s** (*Brit*) salir *or* resultar bien • **he always turns up ~s** no nos falla nunca
VT (*Cards*) fallar; (*fig*) superar
VI (*Cards*) triunfar, poner un triunfo
CPD ▸ **trump card** triunfo *m* • IDIOM: • **to play one's ~ card** jugar su mejor carta
▸ **trump up** VT + ADV [+ *charge, excuse*] fabricar, inventar
trumped-up ['trʌmpt'ʌp] ADJ [*charge, excuse*] fabricado, inventado
trumpery ['trʌmpərɪ] ADJ (= *frivolous*) frívolo; (= *valueless*) inútil, sin valor; (= *insignificant*) sin importancia; (= *trashy*) de relumbrón
N oropel *m*
trumpet ['trʌmpɪt] N trompeta *f* • IDIOM: • **to blow one's own ~** darse bombo
VI [*elephant*] bramar
VT (*fig*) (*also* **trumpet forth**) pregonar, anunciar (a son de trompeta)
CPD ▸ **trumpet blast, trumpet call** trompetazo *m*; (*fig*) clarinazo *m* ▸ **trumpet player** trompetista *mf*
trumpeter ['trʌmpɪtəʳ] N (*orchestral*) trompetero *m*, trompeta *mf*; (*jazz*) trompetista *mf*
trumpeting ['trʌmpɪtɪŋ] N [*of elephant*] bramido *m*
truncate [trʌŋ'keɪt] VT [+ *report, speech*] truncar
truncated [trʌŋ'keɪtɪd] ADJ (= *shortened*) [*report*] truncado
truncating [trʌŋ'keɪtɪŋ] N (*Comput*) truncamiento *m*
truncation [trʌŋ'keɪʃən] N truncamiento *m*
truncheon ['trʌntʃən] N porra *f*
trundle ['trʌndl] VT (= *push*) empujar; (= *pull*) tirar, jalar (*LAm*)
VI [*cart etc*] rodar
▸ **trundle on** VI + ADV avanzar (con mucho ruido, pesadamente)
trunk [trʌŋk] N **1** [*of tree*] tronco *m*
2 (*Anat*) (= *human torso*) tronco *m*
3 [*of elephant*] trompa *f*
4 (= *big suitcase*) baúl *m*
5 (*US*) (= *boot of car*) maletero *m*, baúl *m* (*LAm*), cajuela *f* (*Mex*), maletera *f* (*S. Cone*)
CPD ▸ **trunk call** (*Brit*) (*Telec*) conferencia *f* (interurbana) • **to make a ~ call** llamar a larga distancia ▸ **trunk line** (*Rail*) línea *f* troncal; (*Telec*) línea *f* principal ▸ **trunk road** (*Brit*) carretera *f* principal
trunks [trʌŋks] NPL (*also* **swimming** *or* **bathing trunks**) bañador *m*, slip *m*
trunnion ['trʌnɪən] N muñón *m*
truss [trʌs] VT **1** (= *tie*) liar, atar; [+ *fowl*] espetar
2 (*Archit*) [+ *supporting wall*] apuntalar; [+ *supporting floor*] apoyar con entramado
N **1** (*Med*) braguero *m*
2 (*Archit*) entramado *m*, soporte *m* de puntales
3 (= *bundle*) lío *m*, paquete *m*; [*of hay etc*] haz *m*, lío *m*; [*of fruit*] racimo *m*
▸ **truss up** VT + ADV • **to ~ sb up** atar a algn (*con cuerdas etc*)
trust [trʌst] N **1** (= *faith, confidence*) confianza *f* (in en) • **you've betrayed their ~** has traicionado la confianza que tenían puesta en ti • **I have complete ~ in you** confío plenamente en ti, tengo absoluta confianza en ti • **to take sth/sb on ~** fiarse de algo/algn • **I'm not going to take what he says on ~** no me voy a fiar de lo que dice *or* de su palabra • **to put one's ~ in sth/sb** depositar su confianza en algo/algn
2 (= *responsibility*) • **to give sth into sb's ~** confiar algo a algn • **to be in a position of ~** tener un puesto de confianza *or* responsabilidad • **a sacred ~** un deber sagrado
3 (*Jur*) (= *money*) (*for third party*) fondo *m* fiduciario, fondo *m* de fideicomiso; (*Econ*) (= *investment*) fondo *m* de inversiones; (= *institution*) fundación *f* • **charitable ~** fundación *f* benéfica • **in ~** en fideicomiso • **the money will be held in ~ until she is 18** el dinero se mantendrá en fideicomiso hasta que cumpla los dieciocho años • **to put** *or* **place sth in ~** dejar algo en fideicomiso • **to set up a ~** crear un fondo fiduciario *or* de fideicomiso; ▹ **charitable, investment, unit**
4 (*Comm, Econ*) (*also* **trust company**) trust *m*, compañía *f* fiduciaria, compañía *f* de fideicomiso
5 (*also* **trust hospital**) fundación *f* hospitalaria
VT **1** (= *consider honest, reliable*) [+ *person, judgment, instincts*] fiarse de • **don't you ~ me?** ¿no te fías de mí? • **she is not to be ~ed** ella no es de fiar • **the government can't be ~ed** no se puede uno fiar del gobierno • **do you think we can ~ him?** ¿crees que nos podemos fiar de él?, ¿crees que podemos confiar *or* tener confianza en él? • **~ your own instincts** fíate de tus instintos • **to ~ sb to do sth: I ~ you to keep this secret** confío en que guardes este secreto • **her parents ~ her to make her own decisions** sus padres confían en ella y la dejan que tome sus propias decisiones • **do you think we can ~ him to give us our share?** ¿crees que podemos fiarnos de que nos va a dar nuestra parte? • **he did not ~ himself to speak** no se atrevió a hablar • **you can't ~ a word he says** es imposible creer ninguna palabra suya, no se puede uno fiar de nada de lo que dice • IDIOM: • **I wouldn't ~ him an inch** *or* **as far as I could throw him** no me fío de él ni un pelo
2 (= *have confidence in*) confiar en, tener confianza en • **~ me, I know what I'm doing** confía en mí, sé lo que estoy haciendo • **I ~ you completely** tengo plena confianza en ti • **"I forgot" — "~ you!"** —se me olvidó —¡mira por dónde! *or* —¡cómo no! • **~ you to break it!** ¡era de esperar que lo rompieses!
3 (= *entrust*) • **to ~ sth to sb** confiar algo a algn • **to ~ sb with sth:** • **he's not the sort of person to be ~ed with a gun** no es la clase de persona de la que se puede uno fiar con una pistola, no es la clase de persona a la que se puede confiar una pistola • **I'd ~ him with my life** pondría mi vida en sus manos
4 (*frm*) (= *hope*) esperar • **I ~ you are all well** espero que estéis todos bien • **I ~ you enjoyed your walk?** espero que haya disfrutado del paseo • **I ~ not** espero que no
VI • **to ~ in sth/sb** confiar en algo/algn • **to ~ to luck/fate** encomendarse a la suerte/al destino
CPD ▸ **trust account** cuenta *f* fiduciaria, cuenta *f* de fideicomiso ▸ **trust company** compañía *f* fiduciaria, compañía *f* de fideicomiso ▸ **trust fund** fondo *m* fiduciario, fondo *m* de fideicomiso ▸ **trust hospital** fundación *f* hospitalaria
trusted ['trʌstɪd] ADJ [*friend, adviser, servant*] de confianza; [*formula*] probado; ▹ **tried**
trustee [trʌs'ti:] N (*in bankruptcy*) síndico *m*; (= *holder of property for another*) fideicomisario/a *m/f*, depositario/a *m/f*, administrador(a) *m/f*; [*of college*] regente/a *m/f*
trusteeship [trʌs'ti:ʃɪp] N (*in bankruptcy*) cargo *m* de síndico; [*of property*] cargo *m* de fideicomisario, administración *f* fiduciaria
trustful ['trʌstfʊl] ADJ confiado
trusting ['trʌstɪŋ] ADJ [*person, nature*] confiado; [*relationship*] de confianza • **he has learned not to be too ~ of people** ha aprendido a no ser demasiado confiado con la gente
trustingly ['trʌstɪŋlɪ] ADV confiadamente
trustworthiness ['trʌst,wɜ:ðɪnɪs] N [*of person*] formalidad *f*; [*of source, news*] carácter *m* fidedigno, fiabilidad *f*; [*of statistics etc*] fiabilidad *f*, exactitud *f*
trustworthy ['trʌst,wɜ:ðɪ] ADJ [*person*] formal, de confianza; [*source of news*] fidedigno, fiable; [*statistics*] fiable, exacto
trusty ['trʌstɪ] ADJ (COMPAR: **trustier**, SUPERL: **trustiest**) [*servant*] fiel, leal; [*weapon*] seguro, bueno
N (*in prison*) recluso/a *m/f* de confianza
truth [tru:θ] (PL: **truths** [tru:ðz]) N verdad *f* • **there is some ~ in this** hay una parte de verdad en esto • **in ~** en verdad, a la verdad • **the plain ~** la pura verdad, la verdad lisa y llana • **the whole ~** toda la verdad • **to tell the ~** decir la verdad • **to tell (you) the ~** • **~ to tell** a decir verdad • **the ~ of the matter is that ...** si te digo la verdad *or* la verdad es que ... • **the ~ hurts** las verdades duelen • PROVERBS: • **~ will out** no hay mentira que no salga • **~ is stranger than fiction** la realidad sobrepasa a la ficción; ▹ **home**
CPD ▸ **truth drug** suero *m* de la verdad
truthful ['tru:θfʊl] ADJ [*account*] verídico, veraz; [*person*] veraz • **are you being ~?** ¿es esto la verdad?
truthfully ['tru:θfəlɪ] ADV sinceramente • **now tell me ~** ahora (bien), dime la verdad • **~, I don't know** de veras, no sé nada

t

truthfulness ['tru:θfʊlnɪs] N veracidad *f*
try [traɪ] N **1** (= *attempt*) intento *m*, tentativa *f* • **after several tries they gave up** tras varios intentos *or* varias tentativas, se dieron por vencidos • **it was a good try — better luck next time** no lo conseguiste pero no estuvo mal — otra vez será • **nice try Dave, but I know you're lying** no cuela, Dave, sé que estás mintiendo • **to give sth a try** intentar (hacer) algo • **she's out at the moment — give her a try in half an hour** en este momento ha salido, pero llámela dentro de media hora • **let me have a try** déjame intentarlo • **they're going to have another try at the summit when the weather improves** van a volver a intentar llegar a la cumbre cuando el tiempo mejore • **it's worth a try** vale *or* merece la pena intentarlo
2 (= *trial*) • **to give sth a try** [+ *product, food, experience*] probar algo • **you'll never know what snake is like if you don't give it a try** nunca sabrás a qué sabe la serpiente si no la pruebas • **to give sb a try** darle una oportunidad a algn, poner a algn a prueba • **we'll give her a try for a week** le daremos una semana de prueba • **these new burgers are worth a try** vale *or* merece la pena probar estas nuevas hamburguesas
3 (*Rugby*) ensayo *m* • **to score a try** marcar un ensayo
VT **1** (= *attempt*) intentar • **you've only tried three questions** solo has intentado hacer tres preguntas • **to try to do sth** intentar hacer algo, tratar de hacer algo • **he was shot while trying to escape** lo dispararon mientras intentaba escapar *or* trataba de escapar • **I tried not to think about it** intenté no pensar en ello, traté de no pensar en ello • **try not to cough** procura no toser, procura contener la tos • **he was trying his best not to laugh** estaba haciendo todo lo posible por no reírse • **it's trying to rain** tiene ganas como de llover
2 (= *try out, sample*) probar • **have you tried these olives?** ¿has probado estas aceitunas? • **to try doing sth** probar a hacer algo • **have you tried soaking the curtains in vinegar?** ¿has probado a poner las cortinas en remojo con vinagre? • **try turning the key** da vuelta a la llave y a ver qué pasa, prueba a *or* intenta darle la vuelta a la llave • **you try bringing up four children on your own!** ¡prueba tú a criar cuatro niños solo! • **I'll try anything once** siempre estoy dispuesto a probarlo todo, al menos una vez • **we've tried everything but the car still won't start** lo hemos intentado *or* probado todo, pero el coche todavía no arranca; ▹ **hand, size¹**
3 (= *attempt to work*) [+ *door handle*] tirar de; [+ *telephone number*] intentar llamar a • **he tried the phone but the line was dead** intentó usar el teléfono pero no había línea • **he tried the door — to his surprise it opened** intentó abrir la puerta — para su sorpresa se abrió
4 (= *inquire at*) • **we tried three hotels but they had no room** preguntamos en tres hoteles pero no tenían habitación • **have you tried the local music shops?** ¿lo has buscado en las tiendas de música del barrio?
5 (= *put to the test*) [+ *person, strength, patience*] poner a prueba • **why not try him for the job?** ¿por qué no ponerle a prueba en el puesto? • **he was tried and found wanting** fue sometido a prueba y resultó ser deficiente • **it would try the patience of a saint** pondría a prueba la paciencia de un santo • **to try one's luck** probar suerte • **to try sth on sb** probar algo con algn • **they haven't tried the drug on humans yet** todavía no han probado la droga con personas • **I tried the idea on a couple of people** le comenté la idea a un par de personas • **they have been sorely tried** (*liter*) han sufrido mucho • PROVERB: • **these things are sent to try us** estas cosas nos las manda el Señor para ponernos a prueba
6 (*Jur*) • **to try sb (for sth)** procesar *or* enjuiciar a algn (por algo) • **to try a case** ver una demanda
VI • **he didn't even try** ni siquiera lo intentó • **you're not trying!** ¡no estás poniendo todo tu empeño! • **try again!** ¡vuelve a intentarlo! • **try as I might I couldn't persuade her** por más que intenté persuadirla no lo conseguí • **I couldn't have done that (even) if I'd tried** no podría haber hecho eso ni (siquiera) queriendo • **you could do it if you tried** podrías hacerlo si lo intentaras • **(just) you try!** ¡hazlo y verás!, ¡atrévete (y verás)! • **to try and do sth*** intentar hacer algo, tratar de hacer algo • **I ought to try and get some sleep** debería tratar de *or* intentar dormir un rato • **to try one's (very) best** • **try one's (very) hardest** poner todo su empeño, hacer todo lo posible • **it is not for lack *or* want of trying** no será porque no se ha intentado; ▹ **succeed**
CPD ▸ **try line** (*Rugby*) línea *f* de marca
▸ **try for** VI + PREP intentar conseguir, tratar de conseguir • **he's going to try for a place at university** va tratar de *or* va intentar conseguir una plaza en la universidad • **they're trying for a baby** van a por un bebé
▸ **try on** VT + ADV **1** [+ *clothes, shoes*] probarse • **would you like to try it on?** ¿quiere probárselo?; ▹ **size¹**
2 (*Brit**) (*fig*) • **to try it on: she's trying it on to see how far she can push you** lo está haciendo para ver hasta cuánto aguantas • **take no notice, he's just trying it on** no le hagas caso, solo está intentando quedarse contigo* • **don't try anything on with me!** ¡no intentes quedarte conmigo!*
▸ **try out** VT + ADV [+ *machine, new product, method*] probar; [+ *new employee*] poner a prueba • **try it out on yourself first** pruébelo con usted mismo primero
VI + ADV • **to try out for sth** [*actor, singer, sportsperson*] intentar pasar las pruebas de algo
trying ['traɪɪŋ] ADJ [*time, situation, circumstances*] difícil; [*experience, day*] duro; [*person*] latoso, pesado
tryline ['traɪlaɪn] N (*Rugby*) línea *f* de marca
try-on* ['traɪɒn] N camelo* *m*
tryout ['traɪaʊt] N prueba *f* • **to give sb a ~** poner a algn a prueba • **to give sth a ~** probar algo
tryst [trɪst] N (*liter, hum*) **1** (= *meeting*) cita *f*
2 (*also* **trysting-place**) lugar *m* de encuentro
tsar [zɑːʳ] N zar *m*
tsarina [zɑː'riːnə] N zarina *f*
tsarism ['zɑːrɪsəm] N zarismo *m*
tsarist ['zɑːrɪst] ADJ, N zarista *mf*
tsetse fly ['tsetsɪflaɪ] N mosca *f* tsetsé
TSG ABBR (= **Traditional Speciality Guaranteed**) D.O.
T-shaped ['tiːʃeɪpt] ADJ en forma de T
T-shirt ['tiːʃɜːt] N camiseta *f* de manga corta, playera *f*, remera *f* (*Arg*), polera *f* (*Chile, Bol*)
tsp. ABBR (PL: **tsp.** *or* **tsps.**) = **teaspoon(ful)**
T-square ['tiːskwɛəʳ] N regla *f* en T
TSS N ABBR = **toxic shock syndrome**
tsunami [tsʊ'nɑːmɪ] N tsunami *m*
TT ADJ ABBR **1** = **teetotal, teetotaller**
2 (*Agr*) (= **tuberculin-tested**) a prueba de tuberculinas
N ABBR **1** (*Motorcycling*) = **Tourist Trophy**
2 (*Econ*) (= **telegraphic transfer**) transferencia *f* telegráfica
ABBR (*US*) = **Trust Territory**
TU N ABBR = **Trade(s) Union**
tub [tʌb] N **1** (= *large vessel*) cubo *m*, cuba *f*; (*for margarine etc*) tarrina *f*; (= *washtub*) tina *f*; [*of washing-machine*] tambor *m*
2 (*esp US*) (= *bathtub*) bañera *f*, tina *f* (*esp LAm*)
3 (*Naut**) carcamán *m*
tuba ['tjuːbə] N (PL: **tubas,** (*frm*) **tubae** ['tjuːbiː]) tuba *f*
CPD ▸ **tuba player** tuba *mf*
tubby* ['tʌbɪ] ADJ (COMPAR: **tubbier**, SUPERL: **tubbiest**) (= *fat*) gordito, rechoncho
tube [tjuːb] N **1** [*of toothpaste, paint etc*] tubo *m*; (*Anat*) trompa *f*; [*of tyre*] cámara *f* de aire; [*of television*] tubo *m*; (*US*) [*of radio*] lámpara *f* • IDIOM: • **to go down the ~**: • **it's all gone down the ~*** todo se ha perdido
2 • **the ~** (*US**) (= *television*) la tele*
3 (= *London underground*) metro *m* • **to go by ~** ir en el metro • **to travel by ~** viajar en metro
CPD ▸ **tube station** (*Brit*) estación *f* de metro ▸ **tube top** (*US*) camiseta *f* tubo ▸ **tube train** tren *m* del metro
tubeless ['tjuːblɪs] ADJ [*tyre*] sin cámara
tuber ['tjuːbəʳ] N (*Bot*) tubérculo *m*
tubercle ['tjuːbəkl] N (*all senses*) tubérculo *m*
tubercular [tjʊ'bɜːkjʊləʳ] ADJ tubercular; (*Med*) tuberculoso
tuberculin [tjʊ'bɜːkjʊlɪn] N tuberculina *f*
tuberculosis [tjʊˌbɜːkjʊ'ləʊsɪs] N tuberculosis *f*, tisis *f*
tuberculous [tjʊ'bɜːkjʊləs] ADJ tuberculoso
tubing ['tjuːbɪŋ] N tubería *f*, cañería *f* • **a piece of ~** un trozo de tubo
tub-thumper ['tʌbˌθʌmpəʳ] N (*Brit*) (*fig*) orador *m* demagógico
tub-thumping ['tʌbˌθʌmpɪŋ] (*Brit*) (*fig*) ADJ demagógico
N oratoria *f* demagógica
tubular ['tjuːbjʊləʳ] ADJ (*gen*) tubular, en forma de tubo; [*furniture*] de tubo
CPD ▸ **tubular bells** (*Mus*) campanas *fpl* tubulares
TUC N ABBR (*Brit*) = **Trades Union Congress**
tuck [tʌk] N **1** (*Sew*) (= *fold*) pinza *f*, pliegue *m* • **to make *or* put a ~ in sth** poner una pinza en algo
2 (*Brit**) (= *food*) comida *f*; (= *sweets*) dulces *fpl*, golosinas *fpl*
3 (*plastic surgery*) reducción *f* mediante cirugía plástica; ▹ **tummy**
VT **1** (= *put*) meter
2 (*Sew*) plegar
CPD ▸ **tuck shop** (*Brit*) (*Scol*) tienda *f* de golosinas
▸ **tuck away** VT + ADV **1** (= *hide*) esconder, ocultar • **~ it away out of sight** ocúltalo para que no se vea • **the village is ~ed away among the woods** la aldea se esconde en el bosque • **he ~ed it away in his pocket** se lo guardó en el bolsillo • **she has her money safely ~ed away** tiene su dinero bien guardado
2 (*Brit**) (= *eat*) devorar, zampar* • **he can certainly ~ it away** ese sí sabe comer • **I can't think where he ~s it all away** no entiendo dónde lo almacena *or* lo echa
▸ **tuck in** VI + ADV (*Brit**) (= *eat*) comer con apetito • **~ in!** ¡a comer!, ¡a ello!
VT + ADV **1** [+ *shirt, blouse*] remeter, meter dentro • **to ~ in a flap** meter una solapa para

dentro • **to ~ the bedclothes in** remeter la ropa de la cama
2 [+ *child*] (*in bed*) arropar
▸ **tuck into*** (VI + PREP) (*Brit*) [+ *meal*] comer con buen apetito
▸ **tuck under** (VT + PREP) • **to ~ one thing under another** remeter una cosa debajo de otra
▸ **tuck up** (VT + ADV) **1** (*Sew*) [+ *skirt, sleeves*] remangar
2 (*Brit*) [+ *child*] (*in bed*) arropar • **you'll soon be nicely ~ed up** pronto estarás a gustito en la cama

tucker* [ˈtʌkəʳ] (VT) (*US*) • **to be ~ed (out)** estar molido *or* rendido*

tuck-in* [ˈtʌkˈɪn] (N) (*Brit*) banquetazo* *m*, comilona* *f* • **to have a good tuck-in** darse un atracón*

Tudor [ˈtjuːdəʳ] (ADJ) [*monarch, house*] Tudor • **the ~ period** la época de los Tudor

Tues. (ABBR) (= **Tuesday**) mart.

Tuesday [ˈtjuːzdɪ] (N) martes *m inv* • **the date today is ~ 23 March** hoy es martes, 23 de marzo • **on ~** (*past or future*) el martes • **on ~s** los martes • **every ~** todos los martes • **every other ~** cada otro martes, un martes sí y otro no • **last ~** el martes pasado • **next ~** • **~ next** el martes próximo, el martes que viene • **this ~** este martes • **the following ~** el martes siguiente • **the ~ before last** el martes antepasado • **the ~ after next** el martes próximo no, el siguiente, el martes que viene no, el siguiente • **a week on ~** • **~ week** del martes en una semana • **a fortnight on ~** • **~ fortnight** del martes en una quincena • **~ morning/night** el martes por la mañana/por la noche • **~ afternoon/evening** el martes por la tarde • **~ lunchtime** el martes a mediodía • **the ~ film** (*TV*) la película del martes • **~'s newspaper** el periódico del martes; ▹ **Shrove Tuesday**

tufa [ˈtjuːfə] (N) toba *f*

tuft [tʌft] (N) [*of hair*] copete *m*, mechón *m*; [*of grass*] mata *f*; [*of feathers*] cresta *f*; (*on top of head*) copete *m*; (*on helmet*) penacho *m*

tufted [ˈtʌftɪd] (ADJ) copetudo

tug [tʌg] (N) **1** (= *pull*) tirón *m*, jalón *m* (*LAm*) • **to give sth a (good) tug** dar a algo un tirón (fuerte)
2 (*Naut*) (= *boat*) remolcador *m*
(VT) **1** (= *pull*) tirar de, jalar (*LAm*) • **to tug sth along** arrastrar algo, llevar algo arrastrándolo
2 (*Naut*) remolcar • **eventually they tugged the boat clear** por fin sacaron el barco a flote
(VI) tirar, jalar (*LAm*) • **to tug at sth** tirar de algo • **they tugged their hardest** se esforzaron muchísimo tirando de él • **somebody was tugging at my sleeve** alguien me tiraba de la manga

tugboat [ˈtʌgbəʊt] (N) remolcador *m*

tug-of-love* [ˌtʌgəvˈlʌv] (N) litigio *m* entre padres por la custodia de los hijos (*después de un divorcio etc*)

tug-of-war [ˈtʌgə(v)ˈwɔːʳ] (N) (*Sport*) juego *m* de tiro de cuerda; (*fig*) lucha *f*, tira y afloja *m*

tuition [tjʊˈɪʃən] (N) enseñanza *f*, instrucción *f*; (*US*) matrícula *f* • **private ~** clases *fpl* particulares (**in** de)
(CPD) ▸ **tuition fees** matrícula *fsing*, tasas *fpl* de matriculación

tulip [ˈtjuːlɪp] (N) tulipán *m*
(CPD) ▸ **tulip tree** tulipanero *m*, tulipero *m*

tulle [tjuːl] (N) tul *m*

tum* [tʌm] (N) (*Brit*) panza *f*

tumble [ˈtʌmbl] (N) (= *fall*) caída *f*; (= *somersault*) voltereta *f*, rodada *f* (*LAm*) • **to have** *or* **take a ~** caerse • **to have a ~ in the hay*** (*euph*) retozar, hacer el amor (en el pajar) • **to take a ~** (*fig*) bajar de golpe, dar un bajón; ▹ **rough-and-tumble**
(VI) **1** (= *fall*) caerse; (= *stumble*) tropezar • **to ~ downstairs/down a hill** rodar por la escalera/por una colina, rodar escaleras abajo/cuesta abajo • **to go tumbling over and over** ir rodando
2 [*water*] correr con fuerza; (*fig*) [*prices*] caer en picado, desplomarse
3 (= *rush*) • **to ~ into/out of bed** tirarse en/saltar de la cama • **the children ~d out of the room/car** los niños salieron de la habitación/del coche en tropel
4 (*Brit**) (= *suddenly understand*) • **to ~ to sth** caer en la cuenta de algo
(VT) (= *knock down*) derribar, abatir, tumbar; (*fig*) derrocar; (= *upset*) hacer caer; (= *disarrange*) desarreglar
(CPD) ▸ **tumble dryer** secadora *f*
▸ **tumble down** (VI + ADV) desplomarse, venirse abajo

tumbledown [ˈtʌmbldaʊn] (ADJ) [*building, shack*] ruinoso, desvencijado

tumble-dry [ˌtʌmblˈdraɪ] (VT) meter en la secadora

tumbler [ˈtʌmbləʳ] (N) **1** (= *glass*) vaso *m*
2 [*of lock*] seguro *m*, fiador *m*
3 (= *acrobat*) volteador(a) *m/f*, volatinero/a *mf*
4 (= *pigeon*) pichón *m* volteador
(CPD) ▸ **tumbler switch** interruptor *m* de resorte

tumbleweed [ˈtʌmblwiːd] (N) (*US*) planta *f* rodadora

tumbrel [ˈtʌmbrəl], **tumbril** [ˈtʌmbrɪl] (N) chirrión *m*, carreta *f*

tumefaction [ˌtjuːmɪˈfækʃən] (N) tumefacción *f*

tumescence [tjuːˈmesns] (N) (*frm*) tumefacción *f*

tumescent [tjuːˈmesnt] (ADJ) tumescente

tumid [ˈtjuːmɪd] (ADJ) túmido

tummy* [ˈtʌmɪ] (N) (= *stomach*) barriga* *f*, tripa* *f*
(CPD) ▸ **tummy ache** dolor *m* de barriga*, dolor *m* de tripa* ▸ **tummy bug*** trastorno *m* estomacal ▸ **tummy button*** ombligo *m* ▸ **tummy muscles*** abdominales *mpl* ▸ **tummy tuck** cirugía *f* plástica anti-michelines* ▸ **tummy upset** trastorno *m* estomacal • **to have a ~ upset** tener el estómago revuelto

tumour, tumor (*US*) [ˈtjuːməʳ] (N) tumor *m*

tumult [ˈtjuːmʌlt] (N) (= *uproar*) tumulto *m* • **to be in a ~** [*person*] estar agitado *or* alborotado • **her emotions were in a ~** tenía un conflicto emocional

tumultuous [tjuːˈmʌltjʊəs] (ADJ) [*applause*] tumultuoso

tumultuously [tjuːˈmʌltjʊəslɪ] (ADV) tumultuosamente

tumulus [ˈtjuːmjʊləs] (N) (PL: **tumuli** [ˈtjuːmjʊlaɪ]) túmulo *m*

tun [tʌn] (N) tonel *m*

tuna [ˈtjuːnə] (N) (PL: **tuna, tunas**) (*also* **tuna fish**) atún *m*

tundra [ˈtʌndrə] (N) tundra *f*

tune [tjuːn] (N) **1** (= *melody*) melodía *f*; (= *piece*) tema *m*; (= *song*) canción *f* • **can you remember the ~?** ¿te acuerdas de la melodía *or* la música? • **the cello has the ~ at that point** el chelo lleva la melodía en esa parte • **it hasn't got much ~** no es muy melódico, no tiene mucha melodía • **dance ~** canción *f* bailable • **come on, give us a ~!** (= *sing*) ¡vamos, cántanos algo! • **he gave us a ~ on the piano** nos tocó un tema al piano • **to hum a ~** tararear una melodía/canción • **to the ~ of sth** (*lit*): • **(sung) to the ~ of Rule Britannia** con la música de Rule Britannia; (*fig*) • **repairs to the ~ of £300** arreglos por la bonita suma de 300 libras • **he was in debt to the ~ of £4,000** tenía deudas que llegaban a 4.000 libras • IDIOMS: • **to call the ~** llevar la voz cantante • **to change one's ~** cambiar de parecer • **to sing another** *or* **a different ~** bailar a un son distinto • **the same old ~: I'm bored with politicians singing the same old ~** estoy harto de oír a los políticos siempre hablar de lo mismo; ▹ **dance, piper, signature**
2 (= *accurate pitch*) • **to be in ~** [*instrument*] estar afinado • **he can't sing in ~** no sabe cantar sin desafinar, no sabe cantar afinado • **to be out of ~** [*instrument*] estar desafinado • **to go out of ~** desafinar • **to sing out of ~** cantar desafinado, desafinar • **to be in/out of ~ with sth/sb**: • **he is in/out of ~ with the people** sintoniza con/está desconectado con el pueblo • **his ideas were in/out of ~ with the spirit of his age** sus ideas estaban a tono/desentonaban con el espíritu de su época
(VT) **1** (*Mus*) [+ *piano, guitar*] afinar
2 (*Mech*) [+ *engine, machine*] poner a punto, afinar
3 (*TV, Rad*) sintonizar • **you are ~d (in) to …** está usted sintonizando (la cadena) … • **stay ~d to this station for a further announcement** sigan en sintonía con esta emisora para escuchar otro anuncio
(VI) (*TV, Rad*) • **to ~ to sth** (*to programme, channel*) sintonizar algo
▸ **tune in** (VI + ADV) (*Rad, TV*) sintonizar • **~ in again tomorrow** sintonice con nosotros mañana • **to ~ in to sth** (*Rad, TV*) sintonizar (con) algo; (*fig*) (*to needs, feelings*) conectar con algo
(VT + ADV) **1** (*Rad, TV*) • **you are ~d in to …** está usted sintonizando (la cadena) …
2 (*fig*) • **to be ~d in to sth** (*to new developments*) estar al corriente de algo; (*to sb's feelings*) estar conectado con algo
▸ **tune out** (VI + ADV) (*US*) **1** (*lit*) desconectar la televisión/radio
2 (*fig*) desconectar, desconectarse • **he ~d out of the conversation** (se) desconectó de la conversación
(VT + ADV) **1** (*Rad, TV*) dejar de sintonizar
2 (*fig*) [+ *distractions, noises*] desconectar de, desconectarse de • **she yelled constantly so I learned to ~ her out** gritaba constantemente, así que aprendí a desconectar
▸ **tune up** (VT + ADV) **1** (*Mus*) afinar
2 (*Aut*) poner a punto, afinar
(VI + ADV) (*Mus*) afinar

tuneful [ˈtjuːnfʊl] (ADJ) [*voice, song*] melodioso, armonioso

tunefully [ˈtjuːnfəlɪ] (ADV) melodiosamente, armoniosamente

tunefulness [ˈtjuːnfʊlnɪs] (N) lo melodioso, lo armonioso

tuneless [ˈtjuːnlɪs] (ADJ) [*voice, song*] poco melodioso

tunelessly [ˈtjuːnlɪslɪ] (ADV) de forma poco melodiosa

tuner [ˈtjuːnəʳ] (N) **1** (*Rad*) (= *knob, equipment*) sintonizador *m*
2 (= *person*) afinador(a) *m/f*; ▹ **piano**
(CPD) ▸ **tuner amplifier** amplificador *m* sintonizador

tune-up [ˈtjuːnʌp] (N) **1** (*Mus*) afinación *f*
2 (*Aut*) puesta *f* a punto, afinado *m*

tungsten [ˈtʌŋstən] (N) tungsteno *m*

tunic [ˈtjuːnɪk] (N) túnica *f*; (*Brit*) (*Mil*) guerrera *f*, blusa *f*

tuning [ˈtjuːnɪŋ] (N) **1** (*Mus*) afinación *f*
2 (*Rad*) sintonización *f*
3 (*Aut*) afinado *m*
(CPD) ▸ **tuning coil** bobina *f* sintonizadora

t

▸ **tuning fork** diapasón *m* ▸ **tuning knob** sintonizador *m*

Tunis ['tju:nɪs] N Túnez *m*

Tunisia [tju:'nɪzɪə] N Túnez *m*

Tunisian [tju:'nɪzɪən] ADJ tunecino
N tunecino/a *m/f*

tunnel ['tʌnl] N (*gen*) túnel *m*; (*Min*) galería *f*; (= *underpass*) paso *m* subterráneo
VT [+ *one's way, a passage*] cavar • **they ~led their way out** escaparon excavando un túnel • **a mound ~led by rabbits** un montículo lleno de madrigueras de conejo • **shelters ~led out in the hillsides** refugios *mpl* horadados en las colinas
VI construir un túnel; [*animal*] excavar una madriguera • **they ~ into the hill** construyen un túnel bajo la colina • **to ~ down into the earth** perforar un túnel en la tierra • **the rabbits ~ under the fence** los conejos hacen madrigueras que pasan debajo de la valla
CPD ▸ **tunnel vision** visión *f* periférica restringida; (*fig*) estrechez *f* de miras

tunny ['tʌnɪ] N (PL: **tunny, tunnies**) atún *m* • **striped ~** bonito *m*

tuppence* ['tʌpəns] N = **twopence**

tuppenny* ['tʌpənɪ] ADJ (*Brit*) = **twopenny**

Tupperware® ['tʌpəwεəʳ] N tupperware® *m*
ADJ • **a ~ box** un tupperware

turban ['tɜ:bən] N turbante *m*

turbid ['tɜ:bɪd] ADJ túrbido

turbine ['tɜ:baɪn] N turbina *f*

turbo ['tɜ:bəʊ] N (= *fan*) turboventilador *m*; (*in cars*) turbo(compresor) *m*
CPD ▸ **turbo engine** motor *m* turbo

turbo... ['tɜ:bəʊ] PREFIX turbo...

turbocharged ['tɜ:bəʊtʃɑ:dʒd] ADJ turbocargado, turboalimentado

turbocharger ['tɜ:bəʊ,tʃɑ:dʒəʳ] N turbocompresor *m*, turbo *m*

turbofan ['tɜ:bəʊfæn] N turboventilador *m*

turbogenerator ['tɜ:bəʊ'dʒenəreɪtəʳ] N turbogenerador *m*

turbojet ['tɜ:bəʊ'dʒet] N turborreactor *m*
CPD turborreactor

turboprop ['tɜ:bəʊ'prɒp] N turbohélice *m*
CPD turbohélice

turbot ['tɜ:bət] N (PL: **turbot, turbots**) (= *fish*) rodaballo *m*

turbulence ['tɜ:bjʊləns] N **1** [*of air, water*] turbulencia *f* • **the plane ran into some ~** el avión entró en un área de turbulencias
2 (= *unrest*) (*social, political*) turbulencia *f*, agitación *f*

turbulent ['tɜ:bjʊlənt] ADJ **1** (= *confused, changing*) [*place, relationship*] turbulento • **these are ~ times** esta es una época turbulenta
2 (= *unruly*) [*person, character*] problemático; [*crowd*] alborotado, soliviantado
3 (= *unsettled*) [*water, sea, air*] turbulento

turd‡ [tɜ:d] N **1** (= *excrement*) cagada** *f*, zurullo** *m*
2 (= *person*) mierda** *mf*

tureen [tə'ri:n] N sopera *f*

turf [tɜ:f] N (PL: **turfs** *or* **turves** [tɜ:vz])
1 (= *grass*) césped *m*; (= *clod*) tepe *m*; (*in turfing*) pan *m* de hierba; (= *peat*) turba *f*
2 (*Horse racing*) • **the Turf** el turf, el hipódromo
3* [*of gang etc*] territorio *m*, zona *f* de influencia
VT (*also* **turf over**) cubrir con césped
CPD ▸ **turf accountant** (*Brit*) corredor(a) *m/f* de apuestas ▸ **turf war** lucha *f* por territorio

▸ **turf out*** VT + ADV (*Brit*) echar (de la casa), plantar en la calle

turgid ['tɜ:dʒɪd] ADJ [*prose etc*] inflado, rimbombante

turgidity [tɜ:'dʒɪdɪtɪ] N [*of prose etc*] rimbombancia *f*

Turin [tjʊ'rɪn] N Turín *m*

Turk [tɜ:k] N **1** (*from Turkey*) turco/a *m/f*
2 (*fig*) (*esp Pol*) elemento *m* alborotador • **young ~** joven reformista *mf*

Turkey ['tɜ:kɪ] N Turquía *f*

turkey ['tɜ:kɪ] N (PL: **turkey, turkeys**)
1 (= *bird*) pavo *m*, guajolote *m* (*Mex*), jolote *m* (*CAm*), chompipe *m* (*CAm*) • IDIOM: • **to talk ~** (*US**) hablar en serio; ▷ **cold**
2 (*esp US*) (*Cine, Theat**) (= *flop*) fiasco* *m*, fracaso *m*
3 (*US‡*) (= *person*) patoso/a *m/f*, pato *m* mareado*
CPD ▸ **turkey buzzard** (*US*) buitre *m*, zopilote *m* (*CAm, Mex*), aura *f* (*Carib*), gallinazo *m* (*Col, And*), zamuro *m* (*Ven*) ▸ **turkey cock** (*lit, fig*) pavo *m* ▸ **turkey shoot*** (*US*) • **to be (like) a ~ shoot** (*fig*) ser coser y cantar*, ser pan comido*

Turkish ['tɜ:kɪʃ] ADJ turco
N (= *language*) turco *m*
CPD ▸ **Turkish bath** baño *m* turco ▸ **Turkish coffee** café *m* turco ▸ **Turkish delight** lokum *m*, capricho *m* de reina ▸ **Turkish towel** (*US*) toalla *f*

Turkish-Cypriot ['tɜ:kɪʃ'sɪprɪət] ADJ turcochipriota
N turcochipriota *mf*

Turkmenistan [tɜ:k,menɪs'tɑ:n] N Turkmenistán *m*

turmeric ['tɜ:mərɪk] N cúrcuma *f*

turmoil ['tɜ:mɔɪl] N confusión *f*, desorden *m*; (*mental*) trastorno *m* • **we had complete ~ for a week** durante una semana reinó la confusión • **to be in ~** [*person*] estar totalmente confuso; [*house*] estar alborotado

turn [tɜ:n] N **1** (= *rotation*) vuelta *f*, revolución *f*; [*of spiral*] espira *f* • **with a quick ~ of the hand** con un movimiento rápido de la mano • **he gave the handle a ~** dio vuelta a la palanca • **to give a screw another ~** apretar un tornillo una vuelta más • IDIOM: • **he never does a hand's ~** no da golpe
2 (*Aut*) (*in road*) vuelta *f*, curva *f* • **a road full of twists and ~s** una carretera llena de curvas • **"no left turn"** "prohibido girar a la izquierda" • **to do a left ~** (*Aut*) doblar *or* girar a la izquierda
3 (*Aut*) (= *turn-off*) salida *f* • **I think we missed our ~ back there** creo que allí atrás nos hemos pasado de la salida
4 (*Naut*) viraje *m* • **to make a ~ to port** virar a babor
5 (*Swimming*) vuelta *f*
6 (= *change of direction*) • **at the ~ of the century** a finales del siglo • **this was a surprising ~ of events** esto suponía un giro inesperado de los acontecimientos • **at every ~** (*fig*) a cada paso • **to be on the ~**: • **the tide is on the ~** la marea está cambiando • **the milk is on the ~** la leche está a punto de cortarse • **the economy may at last be on the ~** puede que por fin la economía de un giro importante *or* cambie de signo • **~ of the tide** (*lit, fig*) cambio *m or* vuelta *f* de la marea • **things took a new ~** las cosas tomaron otro cariz *or* aspecto • **events took a tragic ~** los acontecimientos tomaron un cariz trágico • **events are taking a sensational ~** los acontecimientos vienen tomando un rumbo sensacional • **then things took a ~ for the better** entonces las cosas empezaron a mejorar • **the patient took a ~ for the worse** el paciente empeoró • **at the ~ of the year** a fin de año
7 (*in series etc*) turno *m*, vez *f* • **whose ~ is it?** ¿a quién le toca? • **it's your ~** te toca a ti • **it's her ~ next** le toca a ella después, ella es la primera en turno • **then it was my ~ to protest** luego protesté a mi vez • **your ~ will come** ya te tocará • **~ and ~ about** cada uno por turno, ahora esto y luego aquello • **by ~s** por turnos, sucesivamente • **I felt hot and cold by ~s** tuve calor y luego frío en momentos sucesivos • **to give up one's ~** ceder la vez • **in ~** por turnos, sucesivamente • **they spoke in ~** hablaron por turnos • **and they, in ~, said ...** y ellos a su vez dijeron ... • **to miss one's ~** perder la vez *or* el turno • **the player shall miss two ~s** el jugador deberá perder dos jugadas • **to go out of ~** (*in game*) jugar fuera de orden • **to speak out of ~** (*fig*) hablar fuera de lugar • **to take one's ~** llegarle (a algn) su turno • **to take ~s at doing sth** alternar *or* turnarse para hacer algo • **to take it in ~(s) to do sth** turnarse para hacer algo • **to take ~s at the wheel** conducir por turnos • **to take a ~ at the wheel** turnarse para conducir • **to wait one's ~** esperar (algn) su turno
8 (= *short walk*) vuelta *f* • **to take a ~ in the park** dar una vuelta por el parque
9 (*Med*) (= *fainting fit etc*) vahído *m*, desmayo *m*; (= *crisis*) crisis *f inv*, ataque *m* • **he had a bad ~ last night** anoche tuvo un ataque
10* (= *fright*) susto *m* • **the news gave me quite a ~** la noticia me asustó *or* dejó de piedra
11 (*esp Brit*) (*Theat*) número *m*, turno *m* • **he came on and did a funny ~** salió a escena y presentó un número cómico
12 (= *deed*) • **to do sb a bad ~** hacer una mala pasada a algn • **to do sb a good ~** hacerle un favor a algn • **his good ~ for the day** su buena acción del día • PROVERB: • **one good ~ deserves another** amor con amor se paga
13 (*Culin*) • **it's done to a ~** está en su punto
14 (= *inclination*) • **an odd ~ of mind** una manera retorcida *or* (*LAm*) chueca de pensar • **to be of** *or* **have a scientific ~ of mind** ser más dado a las ciencias
15 (= *expression*) • **~ of phrase** forma *f* de hablar, giro *m* • **that's a French ~ of phrase** eso es un modismo francés
VT **1** (= *rotate*) [+ *wheel, handle*] girar, dar vueltas a; [+ *screw*] atornillar, destornillar • **to ~ the key in the lock** dar vuelta a la llave en la cerradura • **the engine ~s the wheel** el motor hace girar la rueda • **you can ~ it through 90°** se puede girarlo hasta 90 grados • **~ it to the left** dale una vuelta hacia la izquierda
2 (*also* **turn over**) [+ *record, mattress, steak*] dar la vuelta a, voltear (*LAm*); [+ *page*] pasar; [+ *soil*] revolver; [+ *hay*] volver al revés • **the plough ~s the soil** el arado revuelve la tierra • **to ~ one's ankle** torcerse el tobillo • **to ~ a dress inside out** volver un vestido del revés • **it ~s my stomach** me revuelve el estómago • IDIOM: • **to ~ the page (on sth)** pasar la página (de algo), dar carpetazo (a algo)
3 (= *direct*) dirigir, volver • **they ~ed him against us** le pusieron en contra nuestra • **we managed to ~ his argument against him** pudimos volver su argumento contra él mismo • **to ~ one's attention to sth** concentrar su atención en algo • **to ~ one's back on sb/sth** (*also fig*) volver *or* dar la espalda a algn/algo • **as soon as his back is ~ed** en cuanto mira para otro lado • **to ~ one's eyes in sb's direction** volver la mirada hacia donde está algn • **to ~ a gun on sb** apuntar una pistola a algn • **to ~ one's head** volver la cabeza • **the fireman ~ed the hose on the building** el bombero dirigió la

manguera hacia el edificio • **to ~ the lights (down) low** poner la luz más baja • **to ~ one's steps homeward** dirigirse a casa, volver los pasos hacia casa • **to ~ one's thoughts to sth** concentrarse en algo • IDIOMS: • **to ~ the other cheek** ofrecer la otra mejilla • **without ~ing a hair** sin inmutarse • **to ~ one's hand to sth**: • **he ~ed his hand to cookery** se dedicó a la cocina • **to ~ sb's head: earning all that money has ~ed his/her head** se le han subido los humos con lo de ganar tanto dinero • **already in her first film she ~ed a few heads** ya en su primera película la gente se fijó en ella • **to ~ the tables** dar la vuelta a la tortilla

4 (= *pass*) doblar, dar la vuelta a • **the car ~ed the corner** el coche dobló la esquina • **he's ~ed 50** ha pasado los 50 años • **it's ~ed four o'clock** son las cuatro y pico *or* (*esp LAm*) las cuatro pasadas • IDIOM: • **to have ~ed the corner** haber salido del apuro, haber pasado lo peor

5 (= *change*) • **the heat ~ed the walls black** el calor volvió negras las paredes, el calor ennegreció las paredes • **the shock ~ed her hair white** del susto, el pelo se le puso blanco • **his goal ~ed the game** (*Brit*) su gol le dio un vuelco al partido • **an actor ~ed writer** un actor metido a escritor • **to ~ sth into sth** convertir algo en algo • **they ~ed the land into a park** convirtieron el terreno en un parque • **to ~ iron into gold** convertir el hierro en oro • **to ~ a play into a film** pasar una obra al cine • **to ~ verse into prose** verter verso en prosa • **to ~ English into Spanish** traducir el inglés al español • **it ~ed him into a bitter man** le volvió un resentido • **she ~ed her dreams to reality** hizo sus sueños realidad, realizó sus sueños

6 (= *deflect*) [+ *blow*] desviar • **nothing will ~ him from his purpose** nada le hará cambiar su intención

7 (= *shape*) [+ *wood, metal*] tornear • **to ~ wood on a lathe** labrar la madera en un torno; ▷ **well-turned**

8 (*Culin*) • **the heat has ~ed the milk** el calor ha cortado la leche

9 • **to ~ a profit** (*esp US*) sacar un beneficio, tener ganancias

VI **1** (= *rotate*) [*wheel etc*] girar, dar vueltas • **the object ~ed on a stand** el objeto giraba en un pedestal • **the earth ~s on its axis** la Tierra gira sobre su propio eje • **his stomach ~ed at the sight** al verlo se le revolvió el estómago, se le revolvieron las tripas al verlo* • IDIOMS: • **my head is ~ing** la cabeza me está dando vueltas • **to ~ in one's grave**: • **she would ~ in her grave if she knew** le daría un síncope si supiera; ▷ **toss**

2 (= *change direction*) [*person*] dar la vuelta, voltearse (*LAm*); [*tide*] repuntar • **to ~ and go back** volverse *or* dar la vuelta y regresar • **right ~!** (*Mil*) derecha … ¡ar! • **the game ~ed after half-time** (*Brit*) el partido dio un vuelco tras el descanso • **to ~ against sb** volverse contra algn • **to ~ against sth** coger aversión a algo • **to ~ for home** volver hacia casa • **farmers are ~ing from cows to pigs** los granjeros cambian de vacas a cerdos • **then our luck ~ed** luego mejoramos de suerte • **to ~ to sb/sth**: • **he ~ed to me and smiled** se volvió hacia mí y sonrió • **to ~ to sb for help** acudir a algn en busca de ayuda • **she has no-one to ~ to** no tiene a quién recurrir • **our thoughts ~ to those who …** pensamos ahora en los que … • **please ~ to page 34** vamos a la página 34 • **he ~ed to politics** se dedicó a la política • **he ~ed to drink** se dio a la bebida, le dio por el alcohol • **the conversation ~ed to religion** la conversación viró hacia la religión • **I don't know which way to ~** (*fig*) no sé qué hacer • **I don't know where to ~ for money** no sé en qué parte ir a buscar dinero • **the wind has ~ed** el viento ha cambiado de dirección • IDIOM: • **the tide is ~ing** (*lit*) está cambiando la marea; (*fig*) las cosas están cambiando

3 (*Aut*) torcer, girar; (*Aer, Naut*) virar • **to ~ left** (*Aut*) torcer *or* girar *or* doblar a la izquierda • **the car ~ed into a lane** el coche se metió en una bocacalle • **to ~ to port** (*Naut*) virar a babor

4 (= *change*) • **to ~ into sth** convertirse *or* transformarse en algo • **the whole thing has ~ed into a nightmare** todo el asunto se ha convertido en una pesadilla • **he ~ed into a cynic** se volvió cínico • **the princess ~ed into a toad** la princesa se transformó en sapo, la princesa quedó transformada en sapo • **the leaves were ~ing** se estaban descolorando *or* dorando las hojas • **the milk has ~ed** la leche se ha cortado • **it ~ed to stone** se convirtió en piedra • **his admiration ~ed to scorn** su admiración se tornó *or* se transformó en desprecio • **to wait for the weather to ~** esperar a que cambie el tiempo

5 (= *become*) • **then he began to ~ awkward** luego empezó a ponerse difícil • **he ~ed Catholic** se hizo católico • **the weather** *or* **it has ~ed cold** el tiempo se ha puesto frío, se ha echado el frío • **to ~ nasty** [*person*] ponerse *or* volverse antipático • **to ~ professional** hacerse profesional • **to ~ red** ponerse rojo • **matters are ~ing serious** las cosas se ponen graves

6 (= *depend*) • **everything ~s on his decision** todo depende de su decisión • **everything ~s on whether …** todo depende de si …

CPD ▸ **turn signal** (*US*) (*Aut*) indicador *m* (de dirección)

▸ **turn about, turn around** VT + ADV = **turn round**

VI + ADV **1** [*person, vehicle*] dar una vuelta completa; [*wind*] cambiar de dirección, soplar en la dirección contraria • **about ~!** (*Mil*) media vuelta … ¡ar!

2 (= *improve*) [*business, economy*] recuperarse

▸ **turn aside** VI + ADV desviarse, apartarse (**from** de)

VT + ADV desviar, apartar

▸ **turn away** VI + ADV apartarse (**from** de) • **I ~ed away in disgust** me aparté lleno de asco

VT + ADV **1** (= *move*) [+ *eyes, head, gun*] desviar, apartar

2 (= *reject*) [+ *person, offer, business, customer*] rechazar

▸ **turn back** VI + ADV **1** (*in journey etc*) volverse (atrás), desandar el camino • **there can be no ~ing back now** (*fig*) ahora no vale volverse atrás

2 (*in book*) volver

VT + ADV **1** (= *fold*) [+ *bedclothes*] doblar

2 (= *send back*) [+ *person*] hacer volver, hacer regresar, devolver; [+ *vehicle*] volver, dar la vuelta a • **they were ~ed back at the frontier** en la frontera les hicieron volver *or* regresar

3 [+ *clock*] retrasar • IDIOMS: • **to ~ the clock back**: • **we can't ~ the clock back** no podemos dar marcha atrás *or* volver al pasado • **to ~ the clock back 20 years** volver 20 años atrás

▸ **turn down** VT + ADV **1** (= *fold down*) [+ *bedclothes, collar, page*] doblar

2 (= *turn upside down*) [+ *playing card*] poner boca abajo

3 (= *reduce*) [+ *gas, heat, volume*] bajar

4 (= *refuse*) [+ *offer, suitor, candidate*] rechazar • **he was ~ed down for the job** no le dieron el puesto

▸ **turn in** VI + ADV **1** [*car, person*] entrar

2* (= *go to bed*) acostarse

VT + ADV **1** (= *hand over*) entregar • **to ~ sb in** entregar a algn a la policía • **to ~ o.s. in** entregarse

2 (= *submit*) [+ *essay, report*] entregar, presentar • **to ~ in a good performance** (*Sport*) tener una buena actuación

3 (= *fold*) doblarse hacia adentro, apuntar hacia adentro

▸ **turn off** VI + ADV **1** (*Aut*) [*person, vehicle*] doblar • **~ off at the next exit** toma la próxima (salida de la autopista)

2 [*appliance etc*] apagarse

VT + ADV **1** [+ *light*] apagar; [+ *appliance*] (= *switch off*) apagar; (= *plug out*) desenchufar; [+ *tap*] cerrar; [+ *engine*] parar; [+ *gas*] cerrar la llave de; [+ *central heating*] apagar; (*Elec*) (*at mains*) desconectar, cortar; [+ *TV programme, radio programme*] quitar • **the oven ~s itself off** el horno se apaga solo

2* [+ *person*] repugnar, repugnar; (= *fail to interest*) dejar frío; (*sexually*) matar el deseo a • **it ~s me right off** me repugna, me deja frío

▸ **turn on** VI + ADV **1** [*appliance*] encenderse, prender (*LAm*)

2 (*TV, Rad*) [*viewer, listener*] encender *or* (*LAm*) prender el receptor

VT + ADV **1** [+ *appliance, electricity*] encender, prender (*LAm*); [+ *tap*] abrir; [+ *light*] encender; [+ *central heating*] encender • **to leave the radio ~ed on** dejar la radio encendida • **to ~ on the charm*** (*fig*) desplegar todos sus encantos

2* (= *excite*) interesar, despertar; (*sexually*) excitar • **he doesn't ~ me on** no me chifla* • **whatever ~s you on** lo que te guste, lo que quieras

VI + PREP • **to ~ on sb** volverse contra algn

▸ **turn out** VI + ADV **1** (= *appear*) aparecer

2 (= *attend*) [*troops*] presentarse; [*doctor*] atender • **to ~ out for a meeting** asistir a una reunión

3 (= *prove*) resultar • **it ~ed out that …** resultó (ser) que … • **it ~s out to be harder than we thought** resulta más difícil de lo que pensábamos

4 (= *transpire*) salir • **how are things ~ing out?** ¿cómo van las cosas? • **it ~ed out well/badly** salió bien/mal • **as it ~s out I already have one** da la casualidad de que ya tengo uno • **as it ~ed out, nobody went** al final no fue nadie • **it's ~ed out nice again** [*weather*] vuelve a hacer bueno

5 (= *point outwards*) • **his toes ~ out** tiene los dedos de los pies levantados

VT + ADV **1** [+ *appliance, light*] apagar; [+ *gas*] cortar

2 (= *produce*) [+ *goods*] producir • **the college ~s out good secretaries** el colegio produce buenas secretarias

3 (= *empty*) [+ *pockets*] vaciar; (= *tip out*) [+ *cake*] sacar

4 (= *clean out*) [+ *room*] limpiar

5 (= *expel*) [+ *person*] expulsar, echar • **they ~ed him out of the house** lo expulsaron *or* echaron de la casa

6 [+ *guard, police*] llamar

7 • **to be well ~ed out** [*person*] ir elegante *or* bien vestido

8 • **to ~ one's toes out** caminar con los dedos de los pies levantados

▸ **turn over** VI + ADV **1** [*person, car etc*] volverse, voltearse (*LAm*); [*boat*] volcar(se) • **it ~ed over and over** fue dando tumbos • **my stomach ~ed over** se me revolvió el estómago

2 (*Aut*) [*engine*] girar

3 (*in reading*) pasar a la siguiente página; (*in letter*) volver la página • **please ~ over** véase al dorso, sigue …

4 (*TV*) (= *change channel*) cambiar de canal
VT + ADV **1** [+ *page*] volver; [+ *container, vehicle*] volcar; [+ *patient, mattress, card*] dar la vuelta a; [+ *tape, record*] dar la vuelta a, poner la otra cara de • **to ~ over an idea in one's mind** darle vueltas a una idea en la cabeza • **the thieves ~ed the place over*** los ladrones saquearon el local
2 [+ *engine*] hacer girar
3 (= *hand over*) [+ *object, business etc*] ceder, entregar (**to** a); [+ *person*] entregar (**to** a)
4 (*Comm*) [+ *sum*] mover, facturar • **they ~ over a million a year** su volumen de ventas *or* producción *etc* es de un millón al año
5 (= *destine, allocate*) • **the land has been ~ed over to sugar production** ahora la tierra está dedicada a la producción de azúcar
▸ **turn round** VI + ADV **1** (*back to front*) volverse, dar la espalda • **as soon as I ~ed round they were quarrelling again** en cuanto les volví la espalda se pusieron otra vez a reñir • **the government has ~ed right round** el gobierno ha cambiado completamente de rumbo • **he ~ed round and said ...*** (*fig*) fue y me dijo *or* me soltó ...*
2 (= *rotate*) girar, dar vueltas • **I could hardly ~ round** apenas podía volverme • **to ~ round and round** dar vueltas y más vueltas
3 (= *improve*) [*business, economy*] recuperarse
VT + ADV **1** [+ *person, object*] dar la vuelta a, voltear (*LAm*); [+ *vehicle, ship etc*] dar la vuelta a, girar
2 (*Comm*) • **to ~ an order round** tramitar un pedido
3 (= *make successful*) [+ *business, economy*] sacar a flote, hacer despegar; (= *make profitable*) [+ *company, school*] rentabilizar, sanear (las finanzas de); [+ *the economy*] sanear
4 (= *rework*) [+ *sentence, idea*] modificar, alterar
▸ **turn to** VI + ADV (= *assist, lend a hand*) • **everyone had to ~ to and help** todos tuvieron que ayudar • **we must all ~ to** todos tenemos que poner manos a la obra; ▹ **turn**
▸ **turn up** VI + ADV **1** (= *be found*) aparecer
2 (= *arrive, show up*) [*person*] llegar, aparecer; [*playing card etc*] salir • **we waited but she didn't ~ up** esperamos pero no apareció • **we'll see if anyone ~s up** veremos si viene alguien • **he ~ed up two hours late** llegó con dos horas de retraso • **he never ~s up at class** no asiste nunca a la clase • **something will ~ up** algo saldrá
3 (= *point upwards*) volverse hacia arriba • **his nose ~s up** tiene la nariz respingona
VT + ADV **1** [+ *collar, sleeve, hem*] subir; ▹ **nose**
2 [+ *heat, gas, sound*] subir; [+ *radio etc*] poner más fuerte, subir • IDIOM: • **to ~ up the heat (on sth/sb)*** meter más presión (a algo/algn)
3 (= *find*) descubrir, desenterrar; [+ *reference*] buscar, consultar; [+ *evidence, information*] sacar a la luz, revelar
4 (= *dig up*) [+ *earth*] revolver; [+ *buried object*] desenterrar, hacer salir a la superficie
5* (= *disgust*) • **it really ~s me up** me revuelve las tripas* *or* el estómago
6 (*Brit‡*) (= *desist*) • **~ it up!** ¡por favor!
turnabout [ˈtɜːnəbaʊt] N (= *change*) cambio *m* de rumbo, giro *m* radical
turnaround [ˈtɜːnəraʊnd] N **1** (= *change*) cambio *m* de rumbo, giro *m* radical
2 (= *improvement*) despegue *m*
3 (*also* **turnaround time**) (*Naut*) tiempo *m* de descarga y carga; (*Comm*) [*of goods*] plazo *m*
turncoat [ˈtɜːnkəʊt] N renegado/a *m/f*, chaquetero/a *m/f* • **to become a ~** cambiarse de chaqueta
turned-down [ˈtɜːndˈdaʊn] ADJ doblado hacia abajo
turned-up [ˈtɜːndˈʌp] ADJ doblado hacia arriba • **a turned-up nose** una nariz respingona
turner [ˈtɜːnəʳ] N tornero *m*
turnery [ˈtɜːnərɪ] N tornería *f*
turning [ˈtɜːnɪŋ] N (= *side road*) bocacalle *f*; (= *fork*) cruce *m*, esquina *f*; (= *bend*) curva *f* • **the first ~ on the right** la primera bocacalle a la derecha • **we parked in a side ~** aparcamos el coche en una calle que salía de la carretera
CPD ▸ **turning circle** (*Aut*) círculo *m* de viraje, diámetro *m* de giro ▸ **turning lathe** torno *m* ▸ **turning point** (*fig*) momento *m* decisivo, punto *m* de inflexión ▸ **turning radius** (*US*) capacidad *f* de giro, radio *m* de giro
turnip [ˈtɜːnɪp] N nabo *m*
turnkey [ˈtɜːnkiː] N **1** (*Hist*) llavero *m* (de una cárcel), carcelero *m*
2 (*Comput*) llave *f* de seguridad
CPD ▸ **turnkey system** (*Comput*) sistema *m* de seguridad
turn-off [ˈtɜːnɒf] N **1** (*in road*) desvío *m*, empalme *m*
2* • **he's a real turn-off** ese me cae gordo* • **the film was a complete turn-off** la película fue un rollo* • **his breath is a big turn-off** su aliento me repugna
turn-on* [ˈtɜːnɒn] N (= *girl*) tía *f* buena*; (= *guy*) tío *m* bueno* • **I don't find those sorts of film a turn-on at all** a mí esas películas no me ponen (cachondo) para nada
turnout [ˈtɜːnaʊt] N **1** (= *attendance*) concurrencia *f*, asistencia *f*; (= *paying spectators*) entrada *f*, público *m*; (*at election*) número *m* de votantes • **there was a poor ~** asistió poca gente • **we hope for a good ~ at the dance** esperamos que el baile sea muy concurrido
2 (= *clean*) limpieza *f* • **she gave the room a good ~** le hizo una buena limpieza al cuarto
3 (*Ind*) (= *output*) producción *f*
4 (= *dress*) atuendo *m*
turnover [ˈtɜːnˌəʊvəʳ] N **1** (*Comm*) [*of stock, goods*] renovación *f* de existencias; (= *total business*) movimiento *m* de mercancías • **he sold the goods cheaply, hoping for a quick ~** vendió barato las existencias, con la idea de renovarlas rápido • **a ~ of £6,000 a week** una facturación de 6000 libras a la semana • **there is a rapid ~ in staff** el personal cambia muy a menudo
2 (*Culin*) empanada *f*
turnpike [ˈtɜːnpaɪk] N **1** (*Hist*) barrera *f* de portazgo
2 (*US*) (*Aut*) autopista *f* de peaje
turnround [ˈtɜːnraʊnd] N = **turnaround**
turnspit [ˈtɜːnspɪt] N mecanismo *m* que da vueltas al asador
turnstile [ˈtɜːnstaɪl] N torniquete *m*
turntable [ˈtɜːnˌteɪbl] N (*for record player*) plato *m* (giratorio), giradiscos *m inv*; (*for trains, car etc*) placa *f* giratoria
CPD ▸ **turntable ladder** escalera *f* sobre plataforma giratoria
turn-up [ˈtɜːnʌp] (*Brit*) N **1** [*of trousers*] vuelta *f*
2* (= *piece of luck*) • **that was a turn-up for him** en eso tuvo mucha suerte • IDIOM: • **that was a turn-up for the books** eso sí que no se esperaba
turpentine [ˈtɜːpəntaɪn] N trementina *f*
CPD ▸ **turpentine substitute** aguarrás *m*
turpitude [ˈtɜːpɪtjuːd] N (= *liter*) infamia *f*, vileza *f* • **to be dismissed for gross moral ~** ser despedido por inmoralidad manifiesta, ser expulsado por conducta infame
turps* [tɜːps] N ABBR = **turpentine**
turquoise [ˈtɜːkwɔɪz] N **1** (= *stone*) turquesa *f*
2 (= *colour*) azul *m* turquesa
ADJ azul turquesa
turret [ˈtʌrɪt] N [*of castle*] torreón *m*; [*of tank, warship, aircraft*] torreta *f*; (*Mil, Hist*) torre *f*, torrecilla *f*; (*US*) (*Tech*) cabrestante *m*
turtle [ˈtɜːtl] N tortuga *f* (marina) • IDIOM: • **to turn ~*** volverse patas arriba; (*Naut*) volcar(se); (*Aut*) volcarse, dar una vuelta de campana
CPD ▸ **turtle soup** sopa *f* de tortuga
turtledove [ˈtɜːtldʌv] N tórtola *f*
turtleneck [ˈtɜːtlnek] N (*also* **turtleneck sweater**) jersey *m* de cuello alto *or* vuelto *or* de cisne
turves [tɜːvz] NPL *of* **turf**
Tuscan [ˈtʌskən] ADJ toscano
N **1** (= *person*) toscano/a *m/f*
2 (*Ling*) toscano *m*
Tuscany [ˈtʌskənɪ] N la Toscana
tush† [tʌʃ] EXCL ¡bah!
tusk [tʌsk] N colmillo *m*
tusker [ˈtʌskəʳ] N (= *elephant*) elefante *m*; (= *boar*) jabalí *m*
tussle [ˈtʌsl] N (= *struggle*) lucha *f* (**for** por); (= *scuffle*) pelea *f*, agarrada *f* • **to have a ~ with** pelearse con
VI pelearse (**with** con, **about, over** por) • **they ~d with the police** se pelearon con la policía
tussock [ˈtʌsək] N mata *f* (de hierba)
tut [tʌt] (*also* **tut-tut**) EXCL ¡vaya!
VI chasquear la lengua en señal de desaprobación
tutelage [ˈtjuːtɪlɪdʒ] N tutela *f* • **under the ~ of** bajo la tutela de
tutelary [ˈtjuːtɪlərɪ] ADJ tutelar
tutor [ˈtjuːtəʳ] N (= *private teacher*) profesor(a) *m/f* particular; (*Brit*) (*Univ*) tutor(a) *m/f*; (= *teaching assistant*) profesor(a) *m/f* auxiliar; (= *counsellor, supervisor*) profesor *m* consejero, profesora *f* consejera; (*eg for OU, also Jur*) tutor(a) *m/f*
VT • **to ~ sb in Latin** dar clases particulares de latín a algn
CPD ▸ **tutor group** (*Brit*) (*Scol*) grupo *m* de tutoría
tutorial [tjuːˈtɔːrɪəl] ADJ (*Jur*) tutelar
N (*Univ*) seminario *m*; (*eg for OU, UNED*) tutoría *f*
CPD ▸ **tutorial group** grupo *m* de tutoría ▸ **tutorial system** sistema *m* de tutorías
tutoring [ˈtjuːtərɪŋ] N clases *f* particulares (in de); (*remedial*) clases *fpl* de recuperación (in de)
Tutsi [ˈtʊtsɪ] ADJ tutsi
N tutsi *mf*
tutti-frutti [ˌtʊtɪˈfruːtɪ] N (PL: **tutti-fruttis**) tutti-frutti *m*
tutu [ˈtuːtuː] N tutú *m*
tuwhit-tuwhoo [tʊˈwɪttəˈwuː] N ulular *m*
tuxedo [tʌkˈsiːdəʊ], **tux*** [ˈtʌks] N (*esp US*) smoking *m*, esmoquin *m*
TV N ABBR (= **television**) tele *f*, TV *f*
CPD ▸ **TV dinner** *cena precocinada que se vende en el recipiente del que se come* ▸ **TV licence** (*Brit*) *licencia que se paga por el uso del televisor, destinada a financiar la BBC* ▸ **TV licence fee** (*Brit*) *impuesto que se paga por el uso del televisor, destinado a financiar la BBC* ▸ **TV movie** telefilm *m*
TVA N ABBR (*US*) = **Tennessee Valley Authority**
TVEI N ABBR (*Brit*) = **technical and vocational educational initiative**
TVP N ABBR (= **textured vegetable protein**) *sustituto de carne*
twaddle* [ˈtwɒdl] N tonterías *fpl*, chorradas* *fpl*, babosadas *fpl* (*LAm**), pendejadas *fpl* (*LAm**)

twain†† [tweɪn] N • **the ~** los dos • **to split sth in ~** partir algo en dos • PROVERB: • **and ne'er the ~ shall meet** sin que el uno se acerque al otro jamás

twang [twæŋ] N [*of wire, bow etc*] tañido *m*; [*of voice*] deje *m* • **to speak with a ~** ganguear
VT (*Mus*) tañer; [*+ bowstring*] estirar y soltar repentinamente
VI producir un sonido agudo; (*in speaking*) hablar con timbre nasal

twangy ['twæŋɪ] ADJ [*string etc*] elástico, muy estirado; [*accent*] nasal, gangoso

'twas†† [twɒz] = **it was**

twat** [twæt] N **1** (*Anat*) coño** *m*
2 (= *person*) gilipollas‡ *mf*

tweak [twi:k] N **1** (= *pull*) pellizco *m* • **to give sb's nose/ear a ~** pellizcar a algn la nariz/la oreja
2* (= *small alteration*) pequeño retoque *m*
VT **1** (= *pull*) pellizcar
2* (= *alter slightly*) retocar ligeramente

twee* [twi:] ADJ (*Brit*) (*pej*) cursi, afectado

tweed [twi:d] N **1** (= *cloth*) tweed *m*
2 tweeds (= *suit*) traje *msing* de tweed

tweedy ['twi:dɪ] ADJ con traje de tweed, vestido de tweed; (*fig*) aristocrático (y rural)

'tween (*liter*) [twi:n] PREP = **between**

tweet [twi:t] N **1** [*of bird*] pío pío *m*
2 (*on Twitter*) tuit *m*
VI **1** [*bird*] piar
2 (*on Twitter*) tuitear
VT (*on Twitter*) tuitear

tweeter ['twi:təʳ] N **1** (= *speaker*) altavoz *m* para frecuencias altas
2 (*Internet*) tuitero/a *m/f*

tweetup* ['twi:tʌp] N encuentro *m* tuitero • **to have a ~** celebrar un encuentro tuitero

tweezers ['twi:zəz] NPL pinzas *fpl* • **a pair of ~** unas pinzas

twelfth [twelfθ] ADJ duodécimo
N (*in series*) duodécimo/a *m/f*; (= *fraction*) doceavo *m*; ▷ **fifth**
CPD ▸ **Twelfth Night** Día *m* de Reyes, Reyes *mpl*

twelfth-grader [ˌtwelfθ'greɪdəʳ] N (*US*) alumno/a *m/f* de último curso (*de entre 17 y 18 años*)

twelve [twelv] ADJ, PRON doce
N (= *numeral*) doce *m*; ▷ **five**
CPD ▸ **twelve inch** (*Mus*) maxisingle *m*

twelvemonth†† ['twelvmʌnθ] N año *m* • **this day ~** de hoy en un año • **we've not seen him for a ~** hace un año que no le vemos

twelve-tone ['twelvtəʊn] ADJ dodecafónico

twentieth ['twentɪɪθ] ADJ vigésimo
N (*in series*) vigésimo/a *m/f*; (= *fraction*) veintésimo *m*; ▷ **fifth**

twenty ['twentɪ] ADJ, PRON veinte • **~-two metre line** (*Rugby*) línea *f* de veintidós metros • **twenty-twenty vision** visión *f* normal
N (= *numeral*) veinte *m* • **the twenties** (*eg 1920s*) los años veinte • **to be in one's twenties** tener veintitantos (años), ser un veinteañero; ▷ **fifty**

twenty-first ['twentɪfɜ:st] N (= *birthday*) veintiún cumpleaños *m inv*; (= *party*) fiesta *f* del veintiún cumpleaños

twentyfold ['twentɪfəʊld] ADV veinte veces
ADJ veinte veces mayor

twenty-four ['twentɪ'fɔ:ʳ] ADJ • **"twenty-four hour service"** "abierto 24 horas"

twenty-four-seven* [ˌtwentɪˌfɔ:'sevn] ADV (*esp US*) • **to do sth twenty-four-seven** hacer algo a todas horas, hacer algo las 24 horas del día

twentyish ['twentɪɪʃ] ADJ de unos veinte años

twerp* [twɜ:p] N idiota *mf*, bruto/a *m/f* • **you ~!** ¡imbécil!

twice [twaɪs] ADV dos veces • **to do sth ~** hacer algo dos veces • **~ as much/many** dos veces más • **~ a week** dos veces a la *or* por semana • **she is ~ your age** ella tiene dos veces tu edad, es dos veces mayor que tú • **~ the sum** • **~ the quantity** el doble • **at a speed ~ that of sound** a una velocidad dos veces superior a la del sonido • **A is ~ as big as B** A es el doble de B, A es dos veces más grande que B • **she's ~ the woman you are** como mujer ella vale dos veces lo que tú • **to go to a meeting ~ weekly** ir a una reunión dos veces por semana • **he didn't have to be asked ~** no se hizo de rogar, no se lo tuve que pedir dos veces

twiddle ['twɪdl] N vuelta *f* (ligera) • **to give a knob a ~** girar un botón
VT dar vueltas a • IDIOM: • **to ~ one's thumbs** estar de brazos cruzados, estar mano sobre mano
VI dar vueltas • **to ~ with sth** jugar con algo (entre los dedos)

twig¹ [twɪg] N **1** [*of wood*] ramita *f*
2 twigs (*for fire*) leña *f* menuda

twig²* [twɪg] (*Brit*) VT (= *understand*) caer en la cuenta de
VI caer en la cuenta

twilight ['twaɪlaɪt] N **1** (= *evening*) anochecer *m*, crepúsculo *m*; (= *morning*) madrugada *f* • **at ~** al anochecer • **in the ~** a media luz
2 (*fig*) crepúsculo *m*, ocaso *m*
CPD ▸ **twilight area** = **twilight zone** ▸ **twilight hours** (= *dusk*) crepúsculo *msing* • **during ~ hours** en el crepúsculo ▸ **a twilight world** un mundo crepuscular ▸ **twilight zone** zona *f* gris

twilit ['twaɪlɪt] ADJ • **in the ~ woods** en el bosque con luz crepuscular • **in some ~ area of the mind** en alguna zona crepuscular de la mente

twill [twɪl] N (= *fabric*) tela *f* cruzada

'twill [twɪl] = **it will**

twin [twɪn] N (*identical*) gemelo/a *m/f*; (*non-identical*) mellizo/a *m/f* • **they are ~s** son gemelos, son mellizos • **a pair of ~s** un par de gemelos, un par de mellizos
ADJ **1** [*brother, sister*] (*identical*) gemelo; (*non-identical*) mellizo • **she has ~ daughters** tiene dos hijas gemelas, tiene dos hijas mellizas
2 (= *linked*) [*town, city*] hermano • **Newlyn's ~ town is Concarneau** la ciudad hermana de Newlyn es Concarneau, Newlyn está hermanada con Concarneau
3 (= *double*) [*towers, peaks, engines*] gemelo; [*propellers*] doble; [*concepts*] hermano • **the ~ aims** *or* **goals of sth** el doble objetivo de algo • **the ~ evils of malnutrition and disease** la malnutrición y la enfermedad, dos males que siempre van juntos • **the ~ pillars of** (*fig*) el doble pilar de • **~ souls** almas *fpl* gemelas
VT **1** (= *link*) [*+ towns, cities*] hermanar (**with** con) • **to be ~ned with** estar hermanado con
2 (= *combine*) [*+ clothes*] combinar
CPD ▸ **twin beds** camas *fpl* gemelas ▸ **twin city** (*Brit*) ciudad *f* hermana *or* hermanada ▸ **twin cylinder** bicilindro *m*; ▷ **twin-cylinder** ▸ **twin jet** birreactor *m*; ▷ **twin-jet** ▸ **twin town** (*Brit*) ciudad *f* hermana *or* hermanada

twin-bedded ['twɪn'bedɪd] ADJ [*room*] con camas gemelas

twin-carburettor ['twɪnkɑ:bjʊ'retəʳ] N carburador *m* de doble cuerpo
ADJ [*engine*] por carburador de doble cuerpo

twin-cylinder ['twɪn'sɪlɪndəʳ] ADJ de dos cilindros, bicilíndrico
N bicilindro *m*

twine [twaɪn] N bramante *m*
VT [*+ fingers*] entrelazar; [*+ several strings, strands etc together*] trenzar; [*+ one string, strand etc around sth*] enroscar, enrollar • **she ~d the string round her finger** enroscó *or* enrolló la cuerda en el dedo • **to ~ one's arms round sb** abrazar a algn
VI [*spiral, plant*] enroscarse; [*fingers*] entrelazarse; [*road*] serpentear

twin-engined ['twɪn'endʒɪnd] ADJ bimotor

twinge [twɪndʒ] N (= *pain*) dolor *m* agudo • **a ~ of pain** una punzada de dolor, un dolor agudo • **I've been having ~s of conscience** he tenido remordimientos de conciencia

twining ['twaɪnɪŋ] ADJ [*plant*] sarmentoso, trepador

twin-jet ['twɪn'dʒet] ADJ birreactor

twinkle ['twɪŋkl] N centelleo *m*, parpadeo *m* • **in a ~*** en un instante • **"no," he said with a ~** —no, dijo maliciosamente *or* medio riendo • **he had a ~ in his eye** tenía un brillo en sus ojos • IDIOM: • **when you were only a ~ in your father's eye** cuando tú no eras más que una vida en potencia
VI [*light*] centellear, parpadear; [*eyes*] brillar; (*fig*) [*feet*] moverse rápidamente

twinkling ['twɪŋklɪŋ] ADJ [*light*] centelleante, titilante; [*eye*] brillante, risueño; (*fig*) [*feet*] rápido, ligero
N centelleo *m*, parpadeo *m* • **in the ~ of an eye*** en un abrir y cerrar de ojos

twinning ['twɪnɪŋ] N • **the ~ of Edinburgh and Kiev** el hacer a Edimburgo y Kiev ciudades hermanas

twinset ['twɪnset] N (*Brit*) conjunto *m*, juego *m*

twin-tub ['twɪn'tʌb] N lavadora *f* de dos tambores

twirl [twɜ:l] N **1** [*of body*] vuelta *f*, pirueta *f*
2 (*in writing*) rasgo *m*
VT dar vueltas rápidas a; [*+ baton, lasso*] dar vueltas a; [*+ knob*] girar; [*+ moustache*] atusarse
VI dar vueltas, piruetear

twirp* [twɜ:p] N = **twerp**

twist [twɪst] N **1** (= *coil*) [*of thread, yarn*] torzal *m*; [*of paper*] cucurucho *m*; [*of smoke*] voluta *f*; [*of tobacco*] rollo *m* • **a ~ of lemon** un pedacito *or* un rizo de limón
2 (= *loaf of bread*) trenza *f*
3 (= *kink*) (*in wire, cord, hose*) vuelta *f* • IDIOMS: • **to get (o.s.) into a ~*** • **get one's knickers in a ~‡** armarse *or* hacerse un lío*
4 (= *bend*) (*in road*) recodo *m*, curva *f*; (*in river*) recodo *m* • IDIOMS: • **to be round the ~*** estar chiflado* • **to go round the ~*** volverse loco* • **to drive sb round the ~*** volver loco a algn*
5 (= *turning action*) • **with a quick ~ of the wrist** torciendo *or* girando rápidamente la muñeca • **she smiled with a wry ~ of her mouth** sonrió torciendo la boca • **to give sth a ~** [*+ lid, top*] girar algo
6 (= *unexpected turn*) (*in plot, story*) giro *m* • **the plot has an unexpected ~** el argumento tiene un giro inesperado • **to put a new ~ on an old argument** darle un nuevo enfoque a un viejo argumento • **by a strange ~ of fate** por una de esas extrañas vueltas que da la vida • **the story has a ~ in the tail** la historia tiene un final inesperado
7 (= *dance*) twist *m* • **to do the ~** bailar el twist
VT **1** (= *coil*) enroscar, enrollar • **she ~ed her hair into a bun** se enrolló *or* enroscó el pelo en un moño • **the rope got ~ed round the pole** la cuerda se enroscó alrededor del palo • **the strands are ~ed together** las hebras están enrolladas unas a otras • IDIOM: • **to ~ sb round one's little finger** tener a algn en el bolsillo, hacer con algn lo que le da la gana

2 (= *turn*) [+ *knob, handle, top, lid*] girar; (= *turn round and round*) [+ *ring*] dar vueltas a • IDIOMS: • **to ~ sb's arm** (*lit*) retorcerle el brazo a algn; (*fig*) apretarle las tuercas a algn • **to ~ the knife** hurgar en la herida
3 (*Med*) (= *injure*) torcerse • **he ~ed his ankle** se torció el tobillo
4 (= *wrench*) • **she ~ed herself free** se retorció hasta soltarse
5 (= *distort, contort*) (*lit*) [+ *girder, metal*] retorcer; (*fig*) [+ *sense, words, argument*] tergiversar • **his face was ~ed with pain** tenía el rostro crispado por el dolor • **his limbs were ~ed by arthritis** sus miembros estaban torcidos por la artritis
VI 1 (= *coil*) enroscarse
2 (= *bend*) [*road, river*] serpentear
3 (= *turn*) [*person*] (*also* **twist round**) girar
4 (= *contort*) retorcerse • **his mouth ~ed into a sardonic smile** se le retorció la boca y soltó una sonrisa socarrona
5 (= *dance*) bailar el twist
▸ **twist off** VI + ADV [*top, lid*] desenroscarse VT + ADV [+ *top, lid*] desenroscar • **you ~ the top off like this** la tapa se desenrosca así • **to ~ a piece off** separar un trozo torciéndolo
▸ **twist round** VT + ADV (*lit*) dar vueltas a, girar; (*fig*) [+ *words*] tergiversar
VI + ADV girar
twisted [ˈtwɪstɪd] ADJ 1 (= *distorted*) [*metal, roots, smile*] retorcido; [*face, features*] torcido
2 (= *injured*) [*ankle, wrist*] torcido
3 (= *warped*) [*person, mind, logic*] retorcido
twister* [ˈtwɪstəʳ] N 1 (*US*) (= *tornado*) huracán *m*
2 (*Brit*) (= *crook*) estafador(a) *m/f*
twisting [ˈtwɪstɪŋ] N (*gen*) retorcimiento *m*; [*of meaning, words*] tergiversación *f*
ADJ [*lane, street*] con recodos *or* revueltas; [*staircase*] de caracol
twisty [ˈtwɪstɪ] ADJ [*road, path*] sinuoso, ondulante; [*river, stream*] ondulante, con meandros
twit* [twɪt] N (*esp Brit*) (= *fool*) imbécil *mf*
twitch [twɪtʃ] N 1 (= *slight pull*) tirón *m* • **to give sth a ~** dar un tirón a algo
2 (= *nervous tic*) tic *m*, contracción *f* nerviosa
VI [*hands, face, muscles*] crisparse; [*nose, ears, tail*] moverse nerviosamente
VT [+ *curtains, rope*] pegar un tirón de; [+ *hands*] crispar, retorcer; [+ *nose, ears etc*] mover nerviosamente • **to ~ sth away from sb** quitar algo a algn con un movimiento rápido
twitcher* [ˈtwɪtʃəʳ] N (*Brit*) observador(a) *m/f* de aves
twitchy* [ˈtwɪtʃɪ] ADJ (= *nervous*) nervioso, inquieto • **to get ~** ponerse nervioso, inquietarse
twitter [ˈtwɪtəʳ] N [*of bird*] pío *m* • **to be all of a ~*** • **be in a ~*** estar *or* andar agitado *or* nervioso
VI [*bird*] piar; [*person*] hablar nerviosamente; (*Internet*) tuitear
Twitterati* [ˌtwɪtəˈrɑːtɪ] NPL tuiteros/as *mpl/fpl*
Twitterer [ˈtwɪtərəʳ] N (*Internet*) tuitero/a *m/f*
Twittersphere* [ˈtwɪtəˌsfɪəʳ], **Twitterverse*** [ˈtwɪtəˌvɜːs] N **the ~** el universo Twitter®
ʼtwixt [twɪkst] (*poet*) PREP = **betwixt**
two [tuː] ADJ, PRON dos • **that makes two of us** ya somos dos
N (= *numeral*) dos *m* • **to break sth in two** romper algo en dos, partir algo por la mitad • **two by two** • **in twos** de dos en dos • **to arrive in twos and threes** llegar dos o tres a la vez • IDIOMS: • **they're/you're two of a kind** son/sois tal para cual • **to put two and two together** atar cabos • PROVERB: • **two's company, three's a crowd** dos son compañía, tres son multitud; ▹ **five**
two-bit* [ˈtuːbɪt] ADJ (*US*) de poca monta, de tres al cuarto
two-bits [ˌtuːˈbɪts] NPL (*US*) 25 centavos *mpl*
two-chamber [ˈtuːˈtʃeɪmbəʳ] ADJ [*parliament*] bicameral, de dos cámaras
two-colour [ˈtuːˈkʌləʳ] ADJ bicolor, de dos colores
two-cycle [ˈtuːˈsaɪkl] ADJ [*engine*] de dos tiempos
two-cylinder [ˈtuːˈsɪlɪndəʳ] ADJ bicilíndrico, de dos cilindros
two-dimensional [ˈtudaɪˈmenʃənl] ADJ bidimensional
two-door [ˈtuːˈdɔːʳ] ADJ [*car*] de dos puertas
two-edged [ˈtuːˈedʒd] ADJ de doble filo
two-engined [ˈtuːˈendʒɪnd] ADJ bimotor
two-faced [ˈtuːˈfeɪst] ADJ (*fig*) [*person*] falso, hipócrita
two-fisted* [ˌtuːˈfɪstɪd] ADJ (*US*) fortachón*, chicarrón
twofold [ˈtuːfəʊld] ADV dos veces
ADJ doble
two-handed [ˈtuːˈhændɪd] ADJ de dos manos; [*tool etc*] para dos manos
two-horse race [ˌtuːhɔːsˈreɪs] N • **the election was a two-horse race** la elección fue una lucha entre dos
two-legged [ˈtuːˈlegɪd] ADJ bípedo, de dos piernas
two-masted [ˈtuːˈmɑːstɪd] ADJ de dos palos
two-party [ˈtuːˈpɑːtɪ] ADJ bipartidista
twopence [ˈtʌpəns] N dos peniques; (= *coin*) moneda *f* de dos peniques • IDIOM: • **it's not worth ~*** no vale una perra gorda
twopenny [ˈtʌpənɪ] ADJ 1 (*Brit*) de dos peniques, que vale dos peniques
2 (*fig**) insignificante, de poca monta
twopenny-halfpenny* [ˈtʌpnɪˈheɪpnɪ] ADJ (*Brit*) (*fig*) insignificante, de poca monta
two-percent milk [ˈtuːpəˌsentˈmɪlk] N (*US*) leche *f* semidesnatada
two-phase [ˈtuːˈfeɪz] ADJ (*Elec*) bifásico
two-piece [ˈtuːˈpiːs] ADJ [*suit*] de dos piezas
N (= *suit*) conjunto *m* de dos piezas
two-ply [ˈtuːˈplaɪ] ADJ [*wool*] de dos hebras, doble; [*wood, tissue paper*] de dos capas
two-seater [ˈtuːˈsiːtəʳ] ADJ biplaza, de dos plazas
N (= *car, plane*) biplaza *m*
twosome [ˈtuːsəm] N (= *people*) pareja *f*
two-star [ˈtuːstɑːʳ], **two-star petrol** N (*Brit*) gasolina *f* normal
two-step [ˈtuːˌstep] N (= *dance*) paso *m* doble
two-storey, two-story (*US*) [ˈtuːˈstɔːrɪ] ADJ de dos pisos
two-stroke [ˈtuːstrəʊk] N (= *engine*) motor *m* de dos tiempos
ADJ [*engine*] de dos tiempos • **two-stroke oil** aceite *m* para motores de dos tiempos
two-thirds, two thirds [ˌtuːˈθɜːdz] PRON dos tercios *mpl* • **two thirds of sth** dos tercios de algo • **by two thirds** [*cut, increase*] en dos tercios
ADV • **do not fill the container more than two-thirds full** no llenes el contenedor más allá de los dos tercios • **a second book has already been commissioned and is two-thirds finished** ya ha sido encargado un segundo libro, que ya tiene dos tercios acabados
ADJ [*majority*] de dos tercios
two-time* [ˈtuːtaɪm] VT engañar con otro/a a, ser infiel con otro/a a
two-timer* [ˌtuːˈtaɪməʳ] N 1 (*gen*) (= *traitor*) traidor(a) *m/f*
2 (*in marriage*) (= *husband*) marido *m* infiel; (= *wife*) mujer *f* infiel
two-tone [ˈtuːˈtəʊn] ADJ (*in colour*) de dos tonos, bicolor
ʼtwould†† [twʊd] = **it would**
two-way [ˈtuːˈweɪ] ADJ [*radio*] emisor y receptor; [*street*] de doble sentido
CPD ▸ **two-way mirror** luna *f* de efecto espejo ▸ **two-way switch** conmutador *m* de dos direcciones ▸ **two-way traffic** circulación *f* en dos sentidos
two-wheeler [ˈtuːˈwiːləʳ] N bicicleta *f*
TX ABBR (*US*) = **Texas**
Tx ABBR = **telex**
tycoon [taɪˈkuːn] N magnate *m* • **an oil ~** un magnate del petróleo
tyke* [taɪk] N 1 (= *child*) chiquillo *m*; (= *dog*) perro *m* de la calle • **you little ~!** ¡tunante!
2 (*Brit*) (*pej*) (*also* **Yorkshire tyke**) hombre *m* de Yorkshire
tympani [ˈtɪmpənɪ] NPL (*Mus*) = **timpani**
tympanic [tɪmˈpænɪk] ADJ (*Anat*) • **~ bone** hueso timpánico • **~ membrane** membrana timpánica
tympanum [ˈtɪmpənəm] N (PL: **tympanums, tympana**) tímpano *m*
type [taɪp] N 1 (= *class, kind*) tipo *m*, clase *f* • **what ~ of desk did you want?** ¿qué tipo *or* clase de escritorio quería? • **what ~ of person is he?** ¿qué tipo *or* clase de persona es? • **I'm not the ~ to get carried away** no soy de la clase *or* del tipo de personas que se dejan llevar • **I know the ~ of thing you mean** tengo una idea de a qué te refieres • **nightclubs are not my ~ of thing** los clubes nocturnos no son lo mío • **she's/he's not my ~** no es mi tipo • **it's my ~ of film** es una película de las que a mí me gustan • **she's the motherly ~** es una madraza • **he's an outdoor ~** es el tipo *or* la clase de persona a la que le gusta la vida al aire • **a moisturizer suitable for all skin ~s** una crema hidratante apropiada para todo tipo de pieles
2 (= *character, essence*) tipo *m* • **she was the very ~ of Spanish beauty** era el tipo exacto de la belleza española • **to cast sb against ~** (*Theat, Cine*) darle a algn un papel atípico • **to revert to ~** (*Bio*) volver a su estado primitivo; (*fig*) volver a ser el mismo de siempre • **the government, true to ~, tried to make us believe nothing was wrong** el gobierno, como es característico en él *or* como siempre, intentó hacernos creer que no ocurría nada malo
3* (= *individual*) tipo/a* *m/f* • **she's a strange ~** es un bicho raro*, es una tipa rara*
4 (*Typ*) (= *typeface*) tipo *m*; (= *printed characters*) letra *f*; (= *blocks of characters*) tipos *mpl* • **in bold ~** en negrita • **in italic ~** en cursiva • **in large/small ~** en letra grande/pequeña
VT 1 (*also* **type out, type up**) escribir a máquina, pasar a máquina • **six closely ~d pages** seis hojas escritas a máquina *or* mecanografiadas con letra muy pequeña
2 (= *classify*) [+ *disease, blood*] clasificar
VI escribir a máquina
▸ **type in** VT + ADV (= *enter into computer*) [+ *information, command*] escribir, introducir • **to ~ sth into a computer** introducir algo en un ordenador
▸ **type out** VT + ADV escribir a máquina, pasar a máquina
▸ **type up** VT + ADV escribir a máquina, pasar a máquina
typecast [ˈtaɪpkɑːst] (PT, PP: **typecast**) VT • **to ~ an actor** encasillar a un actor
ADJ [*actor*] encasillado
typeface [ˈtaɪpfeɪs] N tipo *m*, tipo *m* de

letra, letra *f*
typescript ['taɪpskrɪpt] (ADJ) mecanografiado
(N) texto *m* mecanografiado
typeset ['taɪpset] (VT) componer
typesetter ['taɪp,setəʳ] (N) **1** (= *person*) cajista *mf*, compositor(a) *m/f*
2 (= *machine*) máquina *f* de componer
typesetting ['taɪp,setɪŋ] (N) composición *f* (tipográfica)
typewrite ['taɪpraɪt] (PT: **typewrote**, PP: **typewritten**) (VT) = **type**
typewriter ['taɪp,raɪtəʳ] (N) máquina *f* de escribir
(CPD) ▸ **typewriter ribbon** cinta *f* para máquina de escribir
typewriting ['taɪp,raɪtɪŋ] (N) mecanografía *f*
typewritten ['taɪp,rɪtn] (ADJ) escrito a máquina, mecanografiado
typhoid ['taɪfɔɪd] (N) tifoidea *f*, fiebre *f* tifoidea
typhoon [taɪ'fuːn] (N) tifón *m*
typhus ['taɪfəs] (N) tifus *m*
typical ['tɪpɪkəl] (ADJ) **1** (= *archetypal*) típico • **a ~ Canadian winter** un típico invierno canadiense • **the ~ Englishman** el inglés típico • **he is ~ of many people who ...** es un ejemplo típico de mucha gente que ...
2 (= *usual, characteristic*) [*behaviour, reaction, style*] típico • **with ~ modesty he said ...** con la modestia que le caracterizaba dijo ..., con una modestia típica en él dijo ... • **it was ~ of her to offer to pay** era típico en ella ofrecerse a pagar
3 (*expressing annoyance*) • **"typical!" she shouted** —¡cómo no! —gritó, —¡típico! —gritó • **that's ~ of him!** ¡eso es típico de él! • **it was ~ of our luck that it rained** con la mala suerte que nos caracteriza, llovió, con nuestra mala suerte de siempre, llovió
typically ['tɪpɪkəlɪ] (ADV) **1** (= *characteristically*) [*defiant, flamboyant, Spanish*] típicamente • **a spell of ~ British weather** un periodo de tiempo típicamente británico • **his letter was ~ humorous, but brief** su carta, como de costumbre, era graciosa pero breve
2 (= *usually*) por regla general, generalmente • **women ~ have lower cholesterol levels than men** por regla general *or* generalmente las mujeres tienen el colesterol más bajo que los hombres
3 (= *predictably*) (*iro*) como era de esperar, como suele ocurrir
typify ['tɪpɪfaɪ] (VT) [+ *thing*] representar, tipificar; [+ *person*] ser ejemplo de
typing ['taɪpɪŋ] (N) mecanografía *f*
(CPD) ▸ **typing agency** agencia *f* mecanográfica ▸ **typing error** error *m* mecanográfico ▸ **typing paper** papel *m* para máquina de escribir ▸ **typing pool** servicio *m* de mecanografía ▸ **typing speed** palabras *fpl* por minuto (mecanografiadas)
typist ['taɪpɪst] (N) mecanógrafo/a *m/f*
typo* ['taɪpəʊ] (N) errata *f*
typographer [taɪ'pɒgrəfəʳ] (N) tipógrafo/a *m/f*
typographic [,taɪpə'græfɪk] (ADJ) = **typographical**
typographical [,taɪpə'græfɪkəl] (ADJ) tipográfico
typography [taɪ'pɒgrəfɪ] (N) tipografía *f*
typology [taɪ'pɒlədʒɪ] (N) tipología *f*
tyrannic [tɪ'rænɪk] (ADJ) = **tyrannical**
tyrannical [tɪ'rænɪkəl] (ADJ) tiránico, tirano
tyrannically [tɪ'rænɪkəlɪ] (ADV) tiránicamente
tyrannicide [tɪ'rænɪsaɪd] (N) (= *act*) tiranicidio *m*; (= *person*) tiranicida *mf*
tyrannize ['tɪrənaɪz] (VT) tiranizar
(VI) • **to ~ over a people** tiranizar un pueblo
tyrannosaur [tɪ'rænəsɔːʳ] (N) tiranosaurio *m*
tyrannous ['tɪrənəs] (ADJ) tiránico
tyranny ['tɪrənɪ] (N) (*lit, fig*) tiranía *f*
tyrant ['taɪrənt] (N) tirano/a *m/f*
Tyre ['taɪəʳ] (N) Tiro *m*
tyre, tire (US) ['taɪəʳ] (N) [*of car, bus, bicycle etc*] neumático *m* (*Sp*), llanta *f* (*LAm*), caucho *m* (*S. Cone*); (= *outer cover*) cubierta *f*; (= *inner tube*) cámara *f* (de aire); [*of cart*] llanta *f*, calce *m*; [*of pram*] rueda *f* de goma • **to have a burst/flat ~** tener una rueda pinchada *or* (*Mex*) ponchada
(CPD) ▸ **tyre burst** pinchazo *m*, reventón *m* ▸ **tyre gauge** medidor *m* de presión ▸ **tyre lever** palanca *f* para desmontar neumáticos ▸ **tyre marks** marcas *fpl* de neumático ▸ **tyre pressure** presión *f* de los neumáticos ▸ **tyre valve** válvula *f* de neumático
tyro ['taɪərəʊ] (N) novicio/a *m/f*, principiante *mf*
Tyrol [tɪ'rəʊl] (N) el Tirol
Tyrolean [,tɪrə'lɪən], **Tyrolese** [,tɪrə'liːz] (ADJ) tirolés
(N) tirolés/esa *m/f*
Tyrrhenian [tɪ'riːnɪən] (ADJ) tirrénico
(N) • **the ~ (Sea)** el mar Tirreno
tzar [zɑːʳ] (N) zar *m*
tzarina [zɑː'riːnə] (N) zarina *f*
tzarist ['zɑːrɪst] (N) = **tsarist**

t

Uu

U, u [ju:] N (= *letter*) U, u *f* • **U for Uncle** U de Uruguay • **U-shaped** en forma de U; ▹ **U-turn**
ADJ ABBR (*Brit*) **1** = **upper-class**
2 (*Cine*) (= **universal**) todos los públicos
ABBR (= **University**) U.

UAE N ABBR (= **United Arab Emirates**) EAU *mpl*

UAR ABBR = **United Arab Republic**

UAW N ABBR (*US*) (= **United Automobile Workers**) *sindicato de los trabajadores de la industria automotriz*

UB40 [ˌju:bi:ˈfɔ:tɪ] N ABBR (*Brit*) (*formerly*) (= **Unemployment Benefit 40**) tarjeta *f* de desempleo, carné *m* del paro • **~s*** (= *unemployed people*) los parados

U-bend [ˈju:bend] N (*Brit*) codo *m*, curva *f* en U

uber- [ˈu:bə-] PREFIX súper-

ubiquitous [ju:ˈbɪkwɪtəs] ADJ ubicuo, omnipresente • **it is ~ in Spain** se encuentra en toda España • **the secretary has to be ~** el secretario tiene que estar constantemente en todas partes

ubiquity [ju:ˈbɪkwɪtɪ] N (*frm*) ubicuidad *f*, omnipresencia *f*

U-boat [ˈju:bəʊt] N submarino *m* alemán

UCAS [ˈju:kæs] N ABBR (*Brit*) = **Universities and Colleges Admissions Service**

UCCA [ˈʌkə] N ABBR (*Brit*) (*formerly*) = **Universities Central Council on Admissions**

UDA N ABBR (*Brit*) (= **Ulster Defence Association**) *organización paramilitar protestante en Irlanda del Norte*

UDC N ABBR (*Brit*) = **Urban District Council**

udder [ˈʌdəʳ] N ubre *f*

UDF ABBR = **Ulster Defence Force**

UDI N ABBR (*Brit*) = **Unilateral Declaration of Independence**

UDP N ABBR (*Brit*) = **Ulster Democratic Party**

UDR N ABBR (= **Ulster Defence Regiment**) *fuerza de seguridad de Irlanda del Norte*

UEFA [jʊˈeɪfə] N ABBR (= **Union of European Football Associations**) UEFA *f*

UFC N ABBR (*Brit*) (= **Universities' Funding Council**) *entidad que controla las finanzas de las universidades*

UFF N ABBR (*Brit*) (= **Ulster Freedom Fighters**) *organización paramilitar protestante en Irlanda del Norte*

UFO N ABBR (= **unidentified flying object**) ovni *m*, OVNI *m*
CPD ▸ **UFO sighting** aparición *f* de un ovni • **there has been a surge of UFO sightings in America** ha habido una oleada de apariciones de ovnis en los Estados Unidos

ufologist [ˌju:ˈfɒlədʒɪst] N ufólogo/a *m/f*

ufology [ˌju:ˈfɒlədʒɪ] N ufología *f*

Uganda [ju:ˈgændə] N Uganda *f*

Ugandan [ju:ˈgændən] ADJ ugandés
N ugandés/esa *m/f*

UGC N ABBR (*Brit*) (*formerly*) = **University Grants Committee**

ugh [ɜ:h] EXCL ¡uf!, ¡puf!

ugli fruit [ˈʌglɪˈfru:t] N *fruto parecido a un pomelo, híbrido de tres cítricos*

uglify* [ˈʌglɪfaɪ] VT afear

ugliness [ˈʌglɪnɪs] N fealdad *f*

ugly [ˈʌglɪ] ADJ (COMPAR: **uglier**, SUPERL: **ugliest**) **1** (= *not pretty*) [*appearance, person*] feo • IDIOM: • **to be as ~ as sin** ser feísimo, ser más feo que Picio*
2 (*fig*) (= *unpleasant*) desagradable; [*mood*] peligroso, violento; [*situation, wound*] peligroso; [*rumour etc*] nada grato, inquietante; [*custom, vice etc*] feo, repugnante • **an ~ customer*** un tipo de cuidado* • **to grow** *or* **turn ~** ponerse violento, amenazar violencia
CPD ▸ **ugly duckling** (*fig*) patito *m* feo

UHF N ABBR (= **ultra high frequency**) UHF *f*

uh-huh [ˈʌˌhʌ] EXCL (*agreeing*) ajá

UHT ADJ ABBR (= **ultra heat-treated**) uperizado

UK N ABBR (= **United Kingdom**) Reino *m* Unido, RU • **in the UK** en el Reino Unido • **the UK government** el gobierno del Reino Unido • **a UK citizen** un ciudadano del Reino Unido

Ukraine [ju:ˈkreɪn] N Ucrania *f*

Ukrainian [ju:ˈkreɪnɪən] ADJ ucranio
N ucranio/a *m/f*

ukulele [ˌju:kəˈleɪlɪ] N ukelele *m*

ULC N ABBR (*US*) (= **ultra-large carrier**) superpetrolero *m*

ulcer [ˈʌlsəʳ] N **1** (*Med*) (*internal*) úlcera *f*; (*external*) llaga *f* • **a mouth ~** una llaga en la boca
2 (*fig*) llaga *f*

ulcerate [ˈʌlsəreɪt] VT ulcerar
VI ulcerarse

ulcerated [ˈʌlsəreɪtɪd] ADJ ulcerado

ulceration [ˌʌlsəˈreɪʃən] N ulceración *f*

ulcerous [ˈʌlsərəs] ADJ ulceroso

ullage [ˈʌlɪdʒ] N (*Customs*) (= *loss*) merma *f*; (= *amount remaining*) atestadura *f*

'ullo* [əˈləʊ] EXCL (*Brit*) = **hello**

ulna [ˈʌlnə] N (PL: **ulnas** *or* **ulnae** [ˈʌlni:]) cúbito *m*

U-lock [ˈju:lɒk] N barra *f* antirrobo en forma de U

ULSI N ABBR = **ultra-large-scale integration**

Ulster [ˈʌlstəʳ] N Ulster *m*

Ulsterman [ˈʌlstəmən] N (PL: **Ulstermen**) nativo *m* de Ulster, habitante *m* de Ulster

Ulsterwoman [ˈʌlstəwʊmən] N (PL: **Ulsterwomen**) nativa *f or* habitante *f* de Ulster

ult. [ʌlt] ADV ABBR (*Comm*) (= **ultimo**) pdo. • **the 5th ~** el 5 del mes pdo., el 5 del mes pasado

ulterior [ʌlˈtɪərɪəʳ] ADJ • **~ motive** segunda intención *f*, motivo *m* oculto

ultimata [ˌʌltɪˈmeɪtə] NPL *of* **ultimatum**

ultimate [ˈʌltɪmɪt] ADJ **1** (= *final*) [*aim, decision, destination*] final • **she will retain ~ responsibility for budgets** ella será la responsable en última instancia de los presupuestos, ella tendrá la máxima responsabilidad sobre presupuestos
2 (= *greatest*) [*power, sacrifice*] máximo; [*control*] total; [*insult*] peor • **the ~ deterrent** (*Mil*) el mayor disuasivo • **it will be the ~ test of his abilities** supondrá la mayor prueba de su capacidad
3 (= *best*) • **the ~ sports car** lo último en coches deportivos
4 (= *basic*) [*purpose, truth, cause, source*] fundamental, principal
5 (= *furthest*) más remoto, extremo
N • **the ~ in luxury** lo último en lujos • **it's the ~ in hairstyling** es el último grito en estilos de peinado

ultimately [ˈʌltɪmɪtlɪ] ADV (= *eventually*) al final, finalmente; (= *in the end*) en última instancia; (= *in the long run*) a la larga; (= *fundamentally*) en el fondo • **they were ~ responsible for his death** eran responsables en última instancia de su muerte • **the more difficult, but ~ more satisfying, solution** la solución más difícil, pero a la larga la más satisfactoria • **we provide this sort of service because, ~, that's what people want** facilitamos esta clase de servicio porque, en el fondo, eso es lo que la gente quiere

ultimatum [ˌʌltɪˈmeɪtəm] N (PL: **ultimatums** *or* **ultimata**) (*Mil*) (*also fig*) ultimátum *m* • **to deliver** *or* **issue an ~** dar un ultimátum

ultimo [ˈʌltɪməʊ] ADV = **ult.**

ultra... [ˈʌltrə] PREFIX ultra...

ultraconservative [ˌʌltrəkənˈsɜ:vətɪv] ADJ ultraconservador

ultra-fashionable [ˈʌltrəˈfæʃnəbl] ADJ muy de moda, elegantísimo

ultrafine [ˌʌltrəˈfaɪn] ADJ ultrafino

ultralight [ˈʌltrəˈlaɪt] ADJ ultraligero
N (*Aer*) ultraligero *m*

ultramarine [ˌʌltrəməˈri:n] ADJ ultramarino
N azul *m* ultramarino *or* de ultramar

ultramodern [ˈʌltrəˈmɒdən] ADJ ultramoderno

ultramontane [ˌʌltrəmɒnˈteɪn] ADJ (*Rel*) ultramontano

ultra-red [ˌʌltrəˈred] ADJ ultrarrojo, infrarrojo

ultrasensitive [ˈʌltrəˈsensɪtɪv] ADJ ultrasensitivo

ultra-short wave [ˈʌltrəʃɔ:tˈweɪv] N onda *f* ultracorta
CPD de onda ultracorta

ultrasonic [ˈʌltrəˈsɒnɪk] ADJ ultrasónico

ultrasound [ˈʌltrəsaʊnd] N ultrasonido *m*
CPD ▸ **ultrasound scan** ecografía *f*

ultraviolet [ˈʌltrəˈvaɪəlɪt] ADJ ultravioleta (*inv*)
CPD ▸ **ultraviolet light** luz *f* ultravioleta ▸ **ultraviolet radiation** radiación *f* ultravioleta ▸ **ultraviolet rays** rayos *mpl*

ultravioleta ▸ **ultraviolet treatment** tratamiento *m* de onda ultravioleta
ululate ['ju:ljʊleɪt] VI ulular
ululation [,ju:ljʊ'leɪʃən] N ululato *m*
Ulysses [ju:'lɪsi:z] N Ulises
um [ʌm] EXCL (*in hesitation*) esto (*Sp*), este (*LAm*) • **to um and err** vacilar
umbel ['ʌmbəl] N umbela *f*
umber ['ʌmbəʳ] N (= *colour*) ocre *m or* pardo *m* oscuro; (= *earth*) tierra *f* de sombra
ADJ color ocre oscuro, pardo oscuro
umbilical [,ʌmbɪ'laɪkəl] ADJ umbilical
CPD ▸ **umbilical cord** cordón *m* umbilical
umbilicus [,ʌmbɪ'laɪkəs] N (PL: **umbilici** [,ʌmbə'laɪsaɪ]) ombligo *m*
umbra ['ʌmbrə] N (PL: **umbras** *or* **umbrae**) (*Astron*) umbra *f*
umbrage ['ʌmbrɪdʒ] N resentimiento *m* • **to take ~ (at sth)** ofenderse *or* quedarse resentido (por algo)
umbrella [ʌm'brelə] N **1** paraguas *m inv* • **beach/sun ~** sombrilla *f* • **under the ~ of** (*fig*) (= *protected*) al abrigo de; (= *incorporating*) comprendido en
2 (*Mil*) [*of fire*] cortina *f* de fuego antiaéreo; [*of aircraft*] sombrilla *f* protectora
CPD ▸ **umbrella organization** organización *f* paraguas ▸ **umbrella stand** paragüero *m*
umlaut ['ʊmlaʊt] N **1** (= *vowel change*) metafonía *f*, inflexión *f* vocálica
2 (= *symbol*) diéresis *f*
ump* [ʌmp] N (*US*) = **umpire**
umpire ['ʌmpaɪəʳ] N árbitro/a *m/f*
VT arbitrar
VI arbitrar, hacer de árbitro
umpteen* ['ʌmpti:n] ADJ tropecientos* • **I've told you ~ times** te lo he dicho tropecientas veces*, te lo he dicho miles de veces
umpteenth* ['ʌmpti:nθ] ADJ enésimo • **for the ~ time** por enésima vez
UMTS ABBR (*Telec*) (= **universal mobile telecommunications system**) UMTS *m*
UMW N ABBR (*US*) = **United Mineworkers of America**
UN N ABBR (= **United Nations**) ONU *f*
'un* [ʌn] PRON • **that's a good 'un!** (*joke etc*) ¡qué bueno! • **he did well, for an old 'un** lo hizo bien, para ser un viejo • **she's got two little 'uns** tiene dos críos
un... [ʌn] PREFIX in..., des..., no ..., poco ..., sin ..., anti...
unabashed ['ʌnə'bæʃt] ADJ (= *shameless*) descarado, desvergonzado; (= *unperturbed*) impertérrito • **"yes," he said quite ~** —sí —dijo sin alterarse
unabated ['ʌnə'beɪtɪd] ADJ sin disminución, no disminuido • **the storm continued ~** la tormenta siguió sin amainar
unabbreviated ['ʌnə'bri:vieɪtɪd] ADJ íntegro, completo
unable ['ʌn'eɪbl] ADJ • **to be ~ to do sth** (*gen*) no poder hacer algo; (= *be incapable of*) ser incapaz de hacer algo; (= *be prevented from*) verse imposibilitado de hacer algo • **unfortunately, he was ~ to come** desafortunadamente, no ha podido venir • **I am ~ to see why ...** no veo por qué ..., no comprendo por qué ... • **those ~ to go** los que no pueden ir
unabridged ['ʌnə'brɪdʒd] ADJ íntegro • **~ edition/version** edición *f*/versión *f* íntegra
unaccented ['ʌnæk'sentɪd] ADJ inacentuado, átono
unacceptable ['ʌnək'septəbl] ADJ inaceptable
unacceptably ['ʌnək'septəblɪ] ADV inaceptablemente
unaccommodating ['ʌnə'kɒmədeɪtɪŋ] ADJ poco amable, poco servicial
unaccompanied ['ʌnə'kʌmpənɪd] ADJ **1** solo, no acompañado • **to go somewhere ~** ir a un sitio sin compañía, ir solo a un sitio
2 (*Mus*) sin acompañamiento
unaccomplished ['ʌnə'kʌmplɪʃt] ADJ **1** [*task*] incompleto, sin acabar
2 [*person*] sin talento
unaccountable ['ʌnə'kaʊntəbl] ADJ **1** (= *inexplicable*) [*fear, pain*] inexplicable • **for some ~ reason** por alguna razón inexplicable *or* incomprensible
2 (= *not answerable*) [*institution, person*] no responsable (**to** ante)
unaccountably ['ʌnə'kaʊntəblɪ] ADV (= *inexplicably*) inexplicablemente; (= *strangely, incomprehensibly*) extrañamente • **she was ~ late** llegó inexplicablemente tarde • **he felt ~ depressed/cheerful** se sentía extrañamente deprimido/animado
unaccounted ['ʌnə'kaʊntɪd] ADJ • **two passengers are still ~ for** aún (nos) faltan dos pasajeros • **two books are ~ for** faltan dos libros
unaccustomed ['ʌnə'kʌstəmd] ADJ **1** • **to be ~ to sth** no estar acostumbrado a algo, no tener costumbre de algo • **to be ~ to doing sth** no tener costumbre de hacer algo, no acostumbrar hacer algo • **~ as I am to public speaking** aunque no tengo experiencia de hablar en público
2 (= *unusual*) • **with ~ zeal** con un entusiasmo insólito
unachievable [,ʌnə'tʃi:vəbl] ADJ [*task, quality*] imposible
unacknowledged ['ʌnək'nɒlɪdʒd] ADJ no reconocido; [*letter etc*] no contestado, sin contestar
unacquainted ['ʌnə'kweɪntɪd] ADJ • **to be ~ with** desconocer, ignorar
unadaptable ['ʌnə'dæptəbl] ADJ inadaptable
unadapted ['ʌnə'dæptɪd] ADJ inadaptado
unaddressed ['ʌnə'drest] ADJ [*letter*] sin señas
unadjusted [,ʌnə'dʒʌstɪd] ADJ no corregido • **seasonally ~ employment figures** estadísticas *fpl* de desempleo no desestacionalizadas
unadopted ['ʌnə'dɒptɪd] ADJ (*Brit*) [*road*] no oficial (*siendo de los vecinos la responsabilidad de su mantenimiento*)
unadorned ['ʌnə'dɔ:nd] ADJ sin adorno, sencillo • **beauty ~** la hermosura sin adorno • **the ~ truth** la verdad lisa y llana
unadulterated ['ʌnə'dʌltəreɪtɪd] ADJ sin mezcla, puro
unadventurous ['ʌnəd'ventʃərəs] ADJ poco atrevido
unadvisable ['ʌnəd'vaɪzəbl] ADJ poco aconsejable • **it is ~ to** (+ *infin*) es poco aconsejable (+ *infin*)
unaesthetic, unesthetic (*US*) [,ʌni:s'θetɪk] ADJ antiestético
unaffected ['ʌnə'fektɪd] ADJ **1** (= *sincere*) sin afectación, sencillo
2 (*emotionally*) no afectado, inmutable • **to be ~ by ...** no verse afectado por ...
unaffectedly ['ʌnə'fektɪdlɪ] ADV sin afectación, sencillamente
unaffiliated [,ʌnə'fɪlɪ,eɪtɪd] ADJ no afiliado
unafraid ['ʌnə'freɪd] ADJ sin temor *or* miedo, impertérrito • **to be ~ of (doing) sth** no temer (hacer) algo, no tener miedo de (hacer) algo
unaided ['ʌn'eɪdɪd] ADV sin ayuda, por sí solo
ADJ • **by his own ~ efforts** sin ayuda de nadie, por sí solo
unalike [,ʌnə'laɪk] ADJ no parecido • **to be ~** no parecerse (en nada) • **the two children are so ~** los dos niños no se parecen en nada
unallocated [ʌn'æləkeɪtɪd] ADJ [*funds*] sin adjudicar • **~ tickets** billetes sin vender
unalloyed ['ʌnə'lɔɪd] ADJ [*metal*] sin mezcla, puro; [*pleasure*] en estado puro
unalterable [ʌn'ɒltərəbl] ADJ inalterable
unalterably [ʌn'ɒltərəblɪ] ADV de modo inalterable • **we are ~ opposed to it** nos oponemos rotundamente a ello
unaltered ['ʌn'ɒltəd] ADJ inalterado, sin cambiar • **his appearance was ~** no había cambiado
unambiguous ['ʌnæm'bɪgjʊəs] ADJ inequívoco
unambiguously ['ʌnæm'bɪgjʊəslɪ] ADV de modo inequívoco
unambitious ['ʌnæm'bɪʃəs] ADJ [*person*] sin ambición, poco ambicioso; [*plan*] poco ambicioso, modesto
un-American ['ʌnə'merɪkən] ADJ **1** (*pej*) (= *anti-American*) antiamericano
2 (= *not typical*) poco americano
unamiable ['ʌn'eɪmɪəbl] ADJ poco simpático
unamused [,ʌnə'mju:zd] ADJ • **she was ~ (by this)** (eso) no le hizo ninguna gracia
unanimity [,ju:nə'nɪmɪtɪ] N unanimidad *f*
unanimous [ju:'nænɪməs] ADJ [*group, decision, vote*] unánime • **the committee was ~ in its condemnation of** *or* **in condemning this** el comité condenó esto unánimemente • **it was accepted by a ~ vote** fue aprobado por unanimidad
unanimously [ju:'nænɪməslɪ] ADV unánimemente, por unanimidad • **the motion was passed ~** la moción fue aprobada por unanimidad
unannounced ['ʌnə'naʊnst] ADJ [*visitor, visit*] inesperado
ADV • **to arrive ~** llegar sin dar aviso
unanswerable [ʌn'ɑ:nsərəbl] ADJ [*question*] incontestable; [*attack etc*] irrebatible, irrefutable
unanswered ['ʌn'ɑ:nsəd] ADJ [*question*] incontestado, sin contestar; [*letter*] sin contestar
unappealable ['ʌnə'pi:ləbl] ADJ inapelable
unappealing ['ʌnə'pi:lɪŋ] ADJ poco atractivo
unappeased [,ʌnə'pi:zd] ADJ insatisfecho
unappetizing ['ʌn'æpɪtaɪzɪŋ] ADJ poco apetitoso, poco apetecible; (*fig*) poco apetecible, nada atractivo
unappreciated [,ʌnə'pri:ʃɪeɪtɪd] ADJ poco valorado • **the ~ heroines of the war** las poco valoradas heroínas de la guerra • **she felt she was ~ by him** sentía que no la valoraba
unappreciative ['ʌnə'pri:ʃɪətɪv] ADJ desagradecido • **to be ~ of sth** no apreciar algo
unapproachable ['ʌnə'prəʊtʃəbl] ADJ **1** (= *inaccessible*) inaccesible
2 (= *aloof*) [*person*] intratable, inasequible
unappropriated [,ʌnə'prəʊprɪeɪtɪd] ADJ [*balance etc*] no asignado, sin asignar
unarguable [ʌn'ɑ:gjʊəbəl] ADJ indiscutible, incuestionable
unarguably [ʌn'ɑ:gjʊəblɪ] ADV indiscutiblemente • **it is ~ true that ...** es una verdad incuestionable que ...
unarmed ['ʌn'ɑ:md] ADJ desarmado; (= *defenceless*) inerme
CPD ▸ **unarmed combat** combate *m* sin armas
unashamed ['ʌnə'ʃeɪmd] ADJ desvergonzado, descarado • **she was quite ~ about it** no se avergonzó en lo más mínimo
unashamedly ['ʌnə'ʃeɪmɪdlɪ] ADV desvergonzadamente • **to be ~ proud of sth**

u

enorgullecerse desvergonzadamente de algo
unasked ['ʌn'ɑːskt] ADJ [*guest*] no invitado; [*advice*] no solicitado
ADV • **to do sth ~** hacer algo motu proprio • **they came to the party ~** vinieron a la fiesta sin ser invitados
unassailable [ˌʌnə'seɪləbl] ADJ [*proof*] incontestable; [*position, influence*] inatacable; [*argument*] irrefutable, irrebatible; [*fortress*] inexpugnable • **he is quite ~ on that score** no se le puede atacar por ese lado
unassisted ['ʌnə'sɪstɪd] ADJ, ADV sin ayuda, por sí solo
unassuming ['ʌnə'sjuːmɪŋ] ADJ modesto, sin pretensiones
unassumingly ['ʌnə'sjuːmɪŋlɪ] ADV modestamente
unattached ['ʌnə'tætʃt] ADJ **1** (= *loose*) suelto; (*fig*) (*gen*) libre; [*employee*] disponible
2 (= *unmarried*) soltero, libre
3 (*Mil*) de reemplazo
4 (*Jur*) no embargado
unattainable ['ʌnə'teɪnəbl] ADJ inaccesible; [*record, objective*] inalcanzable
unattended ['ʌnə'tendɪd] ADJ **1** (= *not looked after*) [*shop, machine, luggage*] desatendido, sin atender; [*child*] solo • **to leave sth ~** dejar algo desatendido • **please do not leave your luggage ~** por favor, no abandonen su equipaje
2 (= *unaccompanied*) [*king etc*] sin escolta
unattractive ['ʌnə'træktɪv] ADJ poco atractivo
unattractiveness ['ʌnə'træktɪvnɪs] N falta *f* de atractivo
unattributable ['ʌnə'trɪbjʊtəbl] ADJ de fuente que no se puede confirmar
unattributed [ˌʌnə'trɪbjʊtɪd] ADJ [*quote, remarks*] de fuente desconocida, anónimo; [*source*] anónimo, no confirmado
unauthenticated ['ʌnɔː'θentɪkeɪtɪd] ADJ no autentificado, no autenticado
unauthorized ['ʌn'ɔːθəraɪzd] ADJ (*gen*) no autorizado • **this was ~** esto no estaba autorizado
unavailable ['ʌnə'veɪləbl] ADJ **1** (*gen*) no disponible; (= *busy*) ocupado • **the Minister was ~ for comment** el ministro no se prestó a hacer comentarios
2 (*Comm*) (= *out of stock*) [*article*] agotado
unavailing ['ʌnə'veɪlɪŋ] ADJ inútil, vano
unavailingly ['ʌnə'veɪlɪŋlɪ] ADV inútilmente, en vano
unavoidable [ˌʌnə'vɔɪdəbl] ADJ inevitable, ineludible
unavoidably [ˌʌnə'vɔɪdəblɪ] ADV inevitablemente • **he was ~ detained** no pudo evitar retrasarse, se retrasó por causas ajenas a su voluntad
unaware ['ʌnə'wɛəʳ] ADJ • **to be ~ that …** ignorar que … • **she was ~ that she was being filmed** no se había dado cuenta de que la estaban filmando • **I am not ~ that …** no ignoro que … • **to be ~ of sth** ignorar algo, no darse cuenta de algo • **I was ~ of the regulations** ignoraba el reglamento
unawareness ['ʌnə'wɛənɪs] N inconsciencia *f* (**of** de)
unawares ['ʌnə'wɛəz] ADV sin saberlo, sin darse cuenta • **to catch** *or* **take sb ~** pillar a algn desprevenido
unbacked ['ʌn'bækt] ADJ sin respaldo; (*Econ*) al descubierto
unbalance ['ʌn'bæləns] N desequilibrio *m*
VT desequilibrar
unbalanced ['ʌn'bælənst] ADJ **1** (*physically*) desequilibrado; (*mentally*) trastornado, desequilibrado
2 (*Econ*) no conciliado
unban ['ʌn'bæn] VT levantar la prohibición de
unbandage ['ʌn'bændɪdʒ] VT desvendar, quitar las vendas a
unbaptized ['ʌnbæp'taɪzd] ADJ sin bautizar
unbar ['ʌn'bɑːʳ] VT [+ *door etc*] desatrancar; (*fig*) abrir, franquear
unbearable [ʌn'bɛərəbl] ADJ inaguantable, insoportable
unbearably [ʌn'bɛərəblɪ] ADV insoportablemente • **it is ~ hot** hace un calor insoportable • **she is ~ vain** es vanidosa hasta lo inaguantable
unbeatable ['ʌn'biːtəbl] ADJ [*team, opponent, army*] invencible; [*price, offer*] inmejorable
unbeaten ['ʌn'biːtn] ADJ [*team, opponent*] imbatido, invicto; [*army*] invicto; [*price*] insuperable
unbecoming ['ʌnbɪ'kʌmɪŋ] ADJ
1 (= *unseemly*) [*behaviour etc*] indecoroso, impropio
2 (= *unflattering*) [*dress etc*] poco favorecedor
unbeknown [ˌʌnbɪ'nəʊn], **unbeknownst** [ˌʌnbɪ'nəʊnst] ADV • **~ to me** sin yo saberlo
unbelief ['ʌnbɪ'liːf] N **1** (*Rel*) (*in general*) descreimiento *m*; [*of person*] falta *f* de fe
2 (= *astonishment*) incredulidad *f*
unbelievable [ˌʌnbɪ'liːvəbl] ADJ
1 (= *incredible*) increíble • **it is ~ that** es increíble que (+ *subjun*)
2* (= *fantastic*) increíble
unbelievably [ˌʌnbɪ'liːvəblɪ] ADV increíblemente • **they're ~ lucky** tienen una suerte increíble
unbeliever ['ʌnbɪ'liːvəʳ] N no creyente *mf*
unbelieving ['ʌnbɪ'liːvɪŋ] ADJ incrédulo
unbelievingly [ˌʌnbɪ'liːvɪŋlɪ] ADV [*watch, stare*] sin dar crédito a sus ojos
unbend ['ʌn'bend] (PT, PP: **unbent**) VT enderezar
VI (*fig*) [*person*] relajarse
unbending ['ʌn'bendɪŋ] ADJ inflexible, rígido; (*fig*) [*person, attitude*] inflexible; (= *strict*) estricto, severo
unbent ['ʌn'bent] PT, PP *of* **unbend**
unbiased, unbiassed ['ʌn'baɪəst] ADJ imparcial
unbidden ['ʌn'bɪdn] ADV (*liter*) • **to do sth ~** hacer algo espontáneamente
unbind ['ʌn'baɪnd] (PT, PP: **unbound**) VT desatar; (= *unbandage*) desvendar
unbleached ['ʌn'bliːtʃt] ADJ sin blanquear
unblemished [ʌn'blemɪʃt] ADJ sin tacha, sin mancha
unblinking [ʌn'blɪŋkɪŋ] ADJ imperturbable; (*pej*) desvergonzado
unblinkingly [ˌʌn'blɪŋkɪŋlɪ] ADV [*look, stare*] sin pestañear • **she looked at him ~** le miró imperturbable *or* sin pestañear
unblock ['ʌn'blɒk] VT [+ *sink, pipe*] desatascar; [+ *road etc*] despejar
unblushing [ʌn'blʌʃɪŋ] ADJ desvergonzado, fresco
unblushingly [ʌn'blʌʃɪŋlɪ] ADV desvergonzadamente • **he said ~** dijo tan fresco
unbolt ['ʌn'bəʊlt] VT desatrancar, quitar el cerrojo de
unborn ['ʌn'bɔːn] ADJ no nacido aún, nonato • **the ~ child** el feto • **generations yet ~** generaciones *fpl* que están todavía por nacer *or* que están por venir
unbosom [ʌn'bʊzəm] VT (*liter*) • **to ~ o.s. of sth** desahogarse de algo • **to ~ o.s. to sb** abrir su pecho a algn, desahogarse con algn
unbound ['ʌn'baʊnd] ADJ [*book*] sin encuadernar, en rústica
unbounded [ʌn'baʊndɪd] ADJ ilimitado, sin límites
unbowed ['ʌn'baʊd] ADJ • **with head ~** con la cabeza erguida
unbreakable ['ʌn'breɪkəbl] ADJ irrompible
unbribable ['ʌn'braɪbəbl] ADJ insobornable
unbridgeable [ˌʌn'brɪdʒəbl] ADJ insalvable, infranqueable
unbridled [ʌn'braɪdld] ADJ (*fig*) desenfrenado
unbroken [ˌʌn'brəʊkən] ADJ **1** (= *intact*) entero, intacto
2 (= *continuous*) ininterrumpido, continuo
3 (= *unbeaten*) no batido; [*spirit*] indómito • **his spirit remained ~** no se hundió
4 [*animal*] indomado
unbuckle ['ʌn'bʌkl] VT desabrochar
unbudgeted [ʌn'bʌdʒɪtɪd] ADJ no presupuestado
unburden [ʌn'bɜːdn] VT **1** (*lit*) [+ *person*] aliviar • **to ~ sb of a load** aliviar a algn quitándole un peso
2 (*fig*) • **to ~ one's heart to sb** abrir su pecho a algn • **to ~ o.s.** *or* **one's conscience to sb** desahogarse con algn • **to ~ o.s. of sth** desahogarse de algo
unburied ['ʌn'berɪd] ADJ insepulto
unbusinesslike [ʌn'bɪznɪslaɪk] ADJ (= *without method*) poco profesional; (*in appearance etc*) poco formal
unbutton ['ʌn'bʌtn] VT desabrochar, desabotonar
VI* hacerse más afable
uncalled-for [ʌn'kɔːldfɔːʳ] ADJ gratuito, impropio • **that was quite uncalled-for** eso fue totalmente gratuito *or* impropio
uncannily [ʌn'kænɪlɪ] ADV misteriosamente • **it is ~ like the other one** tiene un asombroso parecido con el otro, se parece extraordinariamente al otro
uncanny [ʌn'kænɪ] ADJ (COMPAR: **uncannier**, SUPERL: **uncanniest**) (= *peculiar*) raro, extraño; (= *ghostly*) misterioso • **it's quite ~** es extraordinario • **it's ~ how he does it** no llego a comprender cómo lo hace • **an ~ resemblance** un asombroso parecido
uncap ['ʌn'kæp] VT destapar
uncapped [ˌʌn'kæpt] ADJ (*Sport*) debutante • **~ player** debutante *mf* (*en la selección nacional*)
uncared-for ['ʌn'kɛədfɔːʳ] ADJ [*person*] abandonado, desamparado; [*appearance*] desaseado, de abandono; [*building etc*] abandonado
uncaring ['ʌnkɛərɪŋ] ADJ poco compasivo • **he went on all ~** (*liter*) siguió sin hacer caso
uncarpeted ['ʌn'kɑːpɪtɪd] ADJ no enmoquetado (*Sp*), no alfombrado (*LAm*)
uncashed ['ʌn'kæʃt] ADJ [*cheque*] no cobrado, sin cobrar
uncatalogued ['ʌn'kætəlɒgd] ADJ no catalogado
unceasing [ʌn'siːsɪŋ] ADJ incesante
unceasingly [ʌn'siːsɪŋlɪ] ADV incesantemente, sin cesar
uncensored ['ʌn'sensəd] ADJ no censurado
unceremonious ['ʌnˌserɪ'məʊnɪəs] ADJ (= *abrupt, rude*) brusco, hosco
unceremoniously ['ʌnˌserɪ'məʊnɪəslɪ] ADV bruscamente, sin cortesías
uncertain [ʌn'sɜːtn] ADJ **1** (= *unsure*) • **for a moment he looked ~** por un momento pareció no estar seguro • **to be ~ about/of sth** no estar seguro de algo • **she is ~ about the future/what to do next/how to proceed** no está segura sobre el futuro/de qué hacer ahora/de cómo proceder • **I am ~ as to whether she was involved in the accident** no estoy seguro si ella estuvo implicada en el accidente • **I am ~ whether to accept** no estoy seguro si aceptar

u

2 (= *doubtful*) [*future, outcome, destiny*] incierto • **the fate of the refugees remains ~** la suerte de los refugiados sigue siendo incierta *or* sigue sin conocerse • **in no ~ terms** sin dejar lugar a dudas, claramente
3 (= *changeable*) [*conditions*] inestable; [*weather, temper*] variable • **we live in ~ times** vivimos en unos tiempos muy inestables
4 (= *indecisive*) [*voice*] indeciso; [*smile*] tímido, indeciso; [*step*] vacilante
5 (= *indeterminate*) indeterminado • **a smartly-dressed man of ~ age** un hombre elegantemente vestido de edad indeterminada

uncertainly [ʌnˈsɜːtnlɪ] ADV • **he stood there ~ for a moment** por un momento se quedó allí de pie con aire indeciso *or* vacilante • **she smiled ~** sonrió con timidez, esbozó una sonrisa tímida *or* indecisa • **he said ~** dijo indeciso

uncertainty [ʌnˈsɜːtntɪ] N **1** (= *doubt*) duda *f*, incertidumbre *f* • **in view of this ~** *or* **these uncertainties** teniendo en cuenta estas dudas *or* este grado de incertidumbre • **there is ~ about the number of wounded** no se sabe con seguridad el número de heridos • **stress is caused by ~ about the future** el estrés está causado por la incertidumbre *or* inseguridad sobre el futuro
2 (= *indecision*) indecisión *f* • **he heard the ~ in her voice** notó la indecisión en su voz

uncertificated [ˈʌnsəˈtɪfɪkeɪtɪd] ADJ [*teacher etc*] sin título

unchain [ˈʌnˈtʃeɪn] VT desencadenar

unchallengeable [ˈʌnˈtʃælɪndʒəbl] ADJ incontestable, incuestionable

unchallenged [ˈʌnˈtʃælɪndʒd] ADJ (= *unnoticed*) inadvertido; (= *undeniable*) incontrovertible; (*Jur*) incontestado • **his ideas went ~** sus ideas no fueron cuestionadas • **we cannot let that go ~** eso no lo podemos dejar pasar sin protesta

unchangeable [ʌnˈtʃeɪndʒəbl] ADJ inalterable, inmutable

unchanged [ˈʌnˈtʃeɪndʒd] ADJ igual, sin cambiar • **everything is still ~** todo sigue igual

unchanging [ʌnˈtʃeɪndʒɪŋ] ADJ inalterable, inmutable

uncharacteristic [ˌʌnkærəktəˈrɪstɪk] ADJ [*hostility, politeness etc*] inusitado, nada típico • **to be ~ of sth** ser inusitado en algo • **to be ~ of sb** no ser propio de algn • **it's very ~ of her** no es nada propio de ella

uncharacteristically [ˌʌnkærɪktəˈrɪstɪklɪ] ADV • **~ rude/generous** de una grosería/generosidad inusitada • **to behave ~** comportarse de manera inusual

uncharged [ʌnˈtʃɑːdʒd] ADJ **1** (*Elec*) descargado
2 (*Econ*) [*account, service*] no cobrado

uncharitable [ʌnˈtʃærɪtəbl] ADJ poco caritativo

uncharitably [ʌnˈtʃærɪtəblɪ] ADV poco caritativamente

uncharted [ˈʌnˈtʃɑːtɪd] ADJ inexplorado, desconocido

unchaste [ˈʌnˈtʃeɪst] ADJ impúdico; [*spouse*] infiel

uncheck [ʌnˈtʃek] VT (*Comput*) [+ *control box*] desmarcar

unchecked [ˈʌnˈtʃekt] ADV [*continue etc*] libremente, sin estorbo *or* restricción • **the weeds had been allowed to grow ~** habían dejado que las malas hierbas crecieran descontroladamente • **left ~, the virus could spread throughout Africa** si no se controla, el virus podría extenderse por toda África
ADJ **1** (= *unrestrained*) [*growth, power, emotion, anger*] desenfrenado
2 (= *not verified*) [*data, statement*] no comprobado; (= *not examined*) [*text, manuscript*] sin revisar

unchivalrous [ˈʌnˈʃɪvəlrəs] ADJ poco caballeroso, poco caballeresco

unchristian [ˈʌnˈkrɪstɪən] ADJ poco cristiano, impropio de un cristiano

uncial [ˈʌnsɪəl] ADJ uncial
N uncial *f*

uncircumcised [ˈʌnˈsɜːkəmsaɪzd] ADJ incircunciso

uncivil [ˈʌnˈsɪvɪl] ADJ descortés • **to be ~ to sb** ser descortés con algn

uncivilized [ˈʌnˈsɪvɪlaɪzd] ADJ **1** (= *primitive*) [*people, country*] poco civilizado; (*fig*) bárbaro
2 (= *socially unacceptable*) [*conditions, activity*] inaceptable; [*person, behaviour*] grosero
3* (= *early*) • **at this ~ hour** a estas horas tan intempestivas

uncivilly [ˌʌnˈsɪvɪlɪ] ADV descortésmente

unclad [ˈʌnˈklæd] ADJ desnudo

unclaimed [ˈʌnˈkleɪmd] ADJ sin reclamar

unclasp [ˈʌnˈklɑːsp] VT [+ *dress etc*] desabrochar; [+ *hands*] soltar, separar

unclassifiable [ˌʌnˈklæsɪfaɪəbl] ADJ inclasificable

unclassified [ˈʌnˈklæsɪfaɪd] ADJ **1** (= *not arranged*) [*items, papers, waste, football results*] sin clasificar
2 (= *not secret*) [*information, document*] no confidencial

uncle [ˈʌŋkl] N **1** tío *m* • **my ~ and aunt** mis tíos • **Uncle Sam*** el tío Sam (*personificación de EE.UU.*) • **Uncle Tom** (*US**) (*pej*) *negro que trata de congraciarse con los blancos* • IDIOM: • **to cry** *or* **say ~** (*US**) rendirse, darse por vencido
2‡ (= *fence*) perista* *m*

unclean [ˈʌnˈkliːn] ADJ **1** (= *dirty*) [*person, hands, room*] sucio
2 (= *impure*) [*person, animal, activity, thoughts*] impuro

uncleanliness [ˈʌnˈklenlɪnɪs] N suciedad *f*

unclear [ˌʌnˈklɪəʳ] ADJ **1** (= *not obvious*) • **the reasons for this behaviour are ~** las razones de este comportamiento no están claras • **it is ~ what effect this will have** no se sabe muy bien qué efectos tendrá esto • **the impact of these changes remains ~** el impacto de estos cambios sigue sin conocerse con seguridad
2 (= *not specific*) • **he was ~ about the details of what had happened** no fue muy claro respecto a los detalles de lo que había sucedido
3 (= *confusing*) poco claro • **the wording of the contract is ~** los términos del contrato son poco claros
4 (= *unsure*) • **to be ~ about sth** no tener algo muy claro • **I'm still ~ about it** todavía no lo tengo muy claro

unclench [ˈʌnˈklentʃ] VT aflojar

unclimbed [ˈʌnˈklaɪmd] ADJ no escalado

unclog [ˈʌnˈklɒg] VT desatascar

unclothe [ˈʌnˈkləʊð] VT desnudar

unclothed [ˈʌnˈkləʊðd] ADJ desnudo

unclouded [ˈʌnˈklaʊdɪd] ADJ **1** [*sky etc*] despejado, sin nubes
2 (*fig*) (= *calm*) tranquilo

uncluttered [ˌʌnˈklʌtəd] ADJ [*room, house, picture*] despejado

uncoil [ˈʌnˈkɔɪl] VT desenrollar
VI desenrollarse; [*snake*] desenroscarse

uncollected [ˌʌnkəˈlektɪd] ADJ [*goods, luggage*] sin recoger; [*tax*] no recaudado, sin cobrar

uncoloured, uncolored (US) [ˈʌnˈkʌləd] ADJ **1** (= *colourless*) [*glass, plastic, liquid*] sin color, incoloro
2 (= *unbiased*) [*account, description, judgement*] objetivo

uncombed [ˈʌnˈkəʊmd] ADJ despeinado, sin peinar

uncomely [ˈʌnˈkʌmlɪ] ADJ desgarbado

uncomfortable [ʌnˈkʌmfətəbl] ADJ
1 (*physically*) incómodo • **to be/feel ~** [*chair, shoes, position*] ser *or* resultar incómodo; [*person*] estar/sentirse incómodo
2 (= *uneasy*) incómodo • **I had an ~ feeling that someone was watching me** tenía la incómoda sensación de que alguien me observaba • **to be ~ about sth** estar incómodo *or* a disgusto con algo • **he's always felt ~ with women** siempre se ha sentido incómodo *or* a disgusto con las mujeres • **to make sb ~** hacer a algn sentirse incómodo, hacer que algn se sienta incómodo • **to make life ~ for sb** ponérselo difícil a algn • **there was an ~ silence** se produjo un silencio muy incómodo
3 (= *worrying*) molesto • **it was an ~ dilemma** era una molesta disyuntiva
4 (= *disagreeable*) [*truth, fact*] desagradable

uncomfortably [ʌnˈkʌmfətəblɪ] ADV **1** (*lit*) • **she felt ~ hot** se encontraba incómoda del calor que tenía • **I'm feeling ~ full** estoy tan lleno que me siento incómodo • **he fidgeted ~** se movió incómodo • **the children were ~ dressed** los niños no llevaban ropa cómoda
2 (= *uneasily*) • **he shifted ~ in his chair** se removía incómodo *or* inquieto en su silla • **I was ~ aware that everyone was watching me** me daba cuenta de que todo el mundo me miraba, lo cual me hacía sentirme incómodo
3 (= *worryingly*) inquietantemente • **the shell fell ~ close** cayó el proyectil inquietantemente cerca

uncommitted [ˈʌnkəˈmɪtɪd] ADJ no comprometido; [*nation*] no alineado

uncommon [ʌnˈkɒmən] ADJ **1** (= *unusual*) poco común, nada frecuente
2 (= *outstanding*) insólito, extraordinario
ADV † sumamente, extraordinariamente

uncommonly [ʌnˈkɒmənlɪ] ADV
1† (= *exceptionally*) [*gifted, pretty, hot*] extraordinariamente • **that's ~ kind of you** ha sido usted amabilísimo
2 (= *rarely*) [*encountered*] raramente, rara vez • **not ~** con cierta frecuencia

uncommunicative [ˈʌnkəˈmjuːnɪkətɪv] ADJ poco comunicativo, reservado

uncompetitive [ˌʌnkəmˈpetɪtɪv] ADJ [*industry, prices*] no competitivo

uncomplaining [ˈʌnkəmˈpleɪnɪŋ] ADJ resignado, sumiso

uncomplainingly [ˈʌnkəmˈpleɪnɪŋlɪ] ADV sin protesta, sumisamente

uncompleted [ˈʌnkəmˈpliːtɪd] ADJ incompleto, inacabado

uncomplicated [ʌnˈkɒmplɪkeɪtɪd] ADJ sin complicaciones, sencillo

uncomplimentary [ˈʌnˌkɒmplɪˈmentərɪ] ADJ poco halagüeño *or* halagador, nada lisonjero

uncomprehending [ˈʌnˌkɒmprɪˈhendɪŋ] ADJ incomprensivo

uncompress [ʌnkəmˈpres] VT (*Comput*) [+ *data*] descomprimir

uncompromising [ʌnˈkɒmprəmaɪzɪŋ] ADJ intransigente, inflexible • **~ loyalty** lealtad *f* absoluta

uncompromisingly [ʌnˈkɒmprəmaɪzɪŋlɪ] ADV intransigentemente, inflexiblemente

unconcealed [ˈʌnkənˈsiːld] ADJ evidente, no disimulado • **with ~ glee** con abierta satisfacción

unconcern [ˈʌnkənˈsɜːn] N (= *calm*) calma *f*, tranquilidad *f*; (*in face of danger*) sangre *f* fría;

(= *lack of interest*) indiferencia *f*, despreocupación *f*

unconcerned [ˈʌnkənˈsɜːnd] ADJ (= *unworried*) despreocupado; (= *indifferent*) indiferente, despreocupado • **to be ~ about sth** no inquietarse *or* preocuparse por algo, mostrarse indiferente a algo

unconcernedly [ˈʌnkənˈsɜːnɪdlɪ] ADV sin preocuparse, sin inquietarse

unconditional [ˈʌnkənˈdɪʃənl] ADJ incondicional, sin condiciones • **~ surrender** rendición *f* sin condiciones

unconditionally [ˈʌnkənˈdɪʃnəlɪ] ADV incondicionalmente

unconditioned [ˌʌnkənˈdɪʃənd] ADJ (*Psych*) no condicionado

unconfessed [ˈʌnkənˈfest] ADJ [*sin*] no confesado; [*die*] sin confesar

unconfined [ˈʌnkənˈfaɪnd] ADJ ilimitado, no restringido, libre • **let joy be ~** (*liter*) que se regocijen todos, que la alegría no tenga límite

unconfirmed [ˈʌnkənˈfɜːmd] ADJ no confirmado, inconfirmado

uncongenial [ˈʌnkənˈdʒiːnɪəl] ADJ [*person*] antipático, poco amigable; [*company, work, surroundings*] desagradable, poco agradable • **to be ~ to sb** ser antipático *or* desagradable con algn

unconnected [ˈʌnkəˈnektɪd] ADJ
1 (= *unrelated*) no relacionado
2 (= *incoherent*) inconexo

unconquerable [ʌnˈkɒŋkərəbl] ADJ inconquistable, invencible

unconquered [ʌnˈkɒŋkəd] ADJ invicto

unconscionable [ʌnˈkɒnʃnəbl] ADJ (*frm*)
1 (= *disgraceful*) [*liar*] desvergonzado; [*behaviour, crime*] inadmisible
2 (= *excessive*) desmedido, desrazonable

unconscionably [ʌnˈkɒnʃnəblɪ] ADV (*frm*) desmesuradamente

unconscious [ʌnˈkɒnʃəs] ADJ **1** (*Med*) sin sentido, inconsciente • **to be ~** estar sin sentido *or* inconsciente • **to be ~ for three hours** pasar tres horas sin sentido • **to become ~** perder el sentido *or* conocimiento, desmayarse • **to fall ~** caer sin sentido • **they found him ~** lo encontraron inconsciente
2 (= *unaware*) inconsciente, insensible • **to be ~ of sth** no ser consciente de algo • **he remained blissfully ~ of the danger** continuó tan tranquilo, sin darse cuenta del peligro
3 (= *unintentional*) inconsciente
N • **the ~** (*Psych*) el inconsciente

unconsciously [ʌnˈkɒnʃəslɪ] ADV inconscientemente • **~ funny** cómico sin querer

unconsciousness [ʌnˈkɒnʃəsnɪs] N (*Med*) inconsciencia *f*

unconsidered [ˈʌnkənˈsɪdəd] ADJ (= *hasty*) [*comment, decision, action*] irreflexivo, precipitado • **~ trifles** pequeñeces *fpl* sin ninguna importancia

unconstitutional [ˈʌnˌkɒnstɪˈtjuːʃənl] ADJ inconstitucional, anticonstitucional

unconstitutionally [ʌnˌkɒnstɪˈtjuːʃnəlɪ] ADV inconstitucionalmente, anticonstitucionalmente

unconstrained [ˈʌnkənˈstreɪnd] ADJ libre, espontáneo

unconsummated [ʌnˈkɒnsəmeɪtɪd] ADJ [*marriage*] no consumado

uncontaminated [ˌʌnkənˈtæmɪneɪtɪd] ADJ sin contaminar, no contaminado

uncontested [ˈʌnkənˈtestɪd] ADJ (*Parl*) [*seat*] ganado sin oposición, no disputado

uncontrollable [ˈʌnkənˈtrəʊləbl] ADJ
1 (= *irrepressible*) [*rage, desire*] incontenible, incontrolable; [*urge*] irrefrenable, incontenible; [*laughter*] incontenible
2 (= *involuntary*) [*movement, spasm*] incontrolable
3 (= *unmanageable*) [*person, animal, situation*] incontrolable; [*car, boat, aeroplane*] fuera de control

uncontrollably [ˈʌnkənˈtrəʊləblɪ] ADV [*spread, increase*] incontrolablemente; [*laugh, cry, shake*] sin poder controlarse, inconteniblemente

uncontrolled [ˈʌnkənˈtrəʊld] ADJ (= *out of control*) descontrolado; [*passion*] desenfrenado; [*freedom etc*] irrestricto

uncontroversial [ˈʌnˌkɒntrəˈvɜːʃəl] ADJ no controvertido, nada conflictivo

unconventional [ˈʌnkənˈvenʃənl] ADJ poco convencional; [*person*] original, poco convencional

unconventionality [ˈʌnkənˌvenʃəˈnælɪtɪ] N originalidad *f*

unconventionally [ˌʌnkənˈvenʃənəlɪ] ADV poco convencionalmente

unconversant [ˈʌnkənˈvɜːsənt] ADJ • **to be ~ with** no estar al tanto de, estar poco versado en

unconverted [ˈʌnkənˈvɜːtɪd] ADJ no convertido (*also Fin*)

unconvertible [ˌʌnkənˈvɜːtɪbl] ADJ [*currency*] inconvertible

unconvinced [ˈʌnkənˈvɪnst] ADJ poco convencido • **I am *or* remain ~ by what she said** lo que dijo sigue sin convencerme

unconvincing [ˈʌnkənˈvɪnsɪŋ] ADJ poco convincente

unconvincingly [ˈʌnkənˈvɪnsɪŋlɪ] ADV [*argue etc*] de manera poco convincente

uncooked [ˈʌnˈkʊkt] ADJ (= *raw*) crudo, sin cocer; (= *not properly cooked*) a medio cocer

uncool* [ʌnˈkuːl] ADJ **1** (= *unsophisticated*) nada sofisticado; (= *unfashionable*) pasado de moda, anticuado
2 (= *excitable*) excitable; (= *tense*) nervioso

uncooperative [ˈʌnkəʊˈɒpərətɪv] ADJ poco dispuesto a cooperar, nada colaborador

uncoordinated [ˈʌnkəʊˈɔːdɪneɪtɪd] ADJ no coordinado, incoordinado

uncork [ˈʌnˈkɔːk] VT descorchar, destapar

uncorrected [ˈʌnkəˈrektɪd] ADJ sin corregir

uncorroborated [ˈʌnkəˈrɒbəreɪtɪd] ADJ no confirmado, sin corroborar

uncorrupted [ˈʌnkəˈrʌptɪd] ADJ incorrupto • **~ by** no corrompido por

uncount [ˈʌnˈkaʊnt] ADJ no contable
CPD ▸ **uncount noun** sustantivo *m* incontable, sustantivo *m* no contable

uncountable [ˈʌnˈkaʊntəbl] ADJ incontable
CPD ▸ **uncountable noun** sustantivo *m* incontable, sustantivo *m* no contable

uncounted [ˈʌnˈkaʊntɪd] ADJ sin cuenta

uncouple [ˈʌnˈkʌpl] VT desenganchar, desacoplar

uncouth [ʌnˈkuːθ] ADJ (= *unrefined*) grosero, inculto; (= *clumsy*) torpe, desmañado

uncover [ʌnˈkʌvəʳ] VT **1** (= *find out*) descubrir
2 (= *remove coverings of*) destapar; (= *disclose*) descubrir, dejar al descubierto

uncovered [ʌnˈkʌvəd] ADJ **1** (= *without a cover*) destapado, descubierto
2 (*Econ*) [*loan*] en descubierto; [*person*] sin seguro, no asegurado

uncritical [ˈʌnˈkrɪtɪkəl] ADJ falto de sentido crítico

uncritically [ˈʌnˈkrɪtɪkəlɪ] ADV sin sentido crítico

uncross [ˈʌnˈkrɒs] VT [+ *legs*] descruzar

uncrossed [ˈʌnˈkrɒst] ADJ [*cheque*] sin cruzar

uncrowded [ʌnˈkraʊdɪd] ADJ sin aglomeraciones

uncrowned [ˈʌnˈkraʊnd] ADJ sin corona • **the ~ king of Scotland** el rey sin corona de Escocia

UNCTAD [ˈʌŋktæd] N ABBR = **United Nations Conference on Trade and Development**

unction [ˈʌŋkʃən] N **1** (= *ointment*) unción *f* • **extreme ~** (*Rel*) extremaunción *f*
2 (*fig*) (= *suaveness*) unción *f*; (*pej*) (= *affected charm*) celo *m* fingido, afectación *f* • **he said with ~** dijo con afectación

unctuous [ˈʌŋktjʊəs] ADJ empalagoso, afectado • **in an ~ voice** en tono meloso, empalagosamente

unctuously [ˈʌŋktjʊəslɪ] ADV con afectación

unctuousness [ˈʌŋktjʊəsnɪs] N celo *m* fingido, afectación *f*

uncultivable [ˈʌnˈkʌltɪvəbl] ADJ incultivable

uncultivated [ˈʌnˈkʌltɪveɪtɪd] ADJ **1** (*Agr*) [*land*] sin cultivar, inculto (*frm*)
2 (= *uncultured*) [*person, mind*] sin cultivar; [*voice, accent*] no cultivado

uncultured [ˈʌnˈkʌltʃəd] ADJ [*person*] inculto, sin cultura; [*voice*] no cultivado; [*accent*] poco culto

uncurl [ˈʌnˈkɜːl] VT desenroscar
VI [*snake etc*] desenroscarse; (= *straighten out*) estirarse

uncut [ˈʌnˈkʌt] ADJ **1** [*grass, tree, hair, nails*] sin cortar; [*stone*] sin labrar
2 (= *not faceted*) [*diamond*] en bruto, sin tallar
3 (= *unabridged*) [*film, text*] integral, sin cortes
4 (= *pure*) [*heroin, cocaine*] puro

undamaged [ʌnˈdæmɪdʒd] ADJ (*gen*) en buen estado; (= *intact*) intacto

undamped [ˈʌnˈdæmpt] ADJ [*enthusiasm, courage*] no disminuido

undated [ˈʌnˈdeɪtɪd] ADJ sin fecha

undaunted [ˈʌnˈdɔːntɪd] ADJ impávido, impertérrito • **he carried on quite ~** siguió sin inmutarse • **with ~ bravery** con valor indomable • **to be ~ by** no dejarse desanimar por

undead [ʌnˈded] N • **the ~** los muertos vivientes

undeceive [ˈʌndɪˈsiːv] VT desengañar, desilusionar

undecided [ˈʌndɪˈsaɪdɪd] ADJ [*person*] indeciso; [*question*] pendiente, no resuelto • **we are still ~ whether to go** aún no sabemos si ir o no • **that is still ~** eso queda por resolver

undecipherable [ˌʌndɪˈsaɪfərəbl] ADJ indescifrable

undeclared [ˈʌndɪˈklɛəd] ADJ no declarado

undeclinable [ˈʌndɪˈklaɪnəbl] ADJ indeclinable

undefeated [ˈʌndɪˈfiːtɪd] ADJ invicto, imbatido • **he was ~ at the end** al final siguió invicto *or* imbatido

undefended [ˈʌndɪˈfendɪd] ADJ **1** (*Mil etc*) indefenso
2 (*Jur*) [*suit*] ganado por incomparecencia del demandado

undefiled [ˈʌndɪˈfaɪld] ADJ puro, inmaculado • **~ by any contact with …** no corrompido por contacto alguno con …

undefinable [ˌʌndɪˈfaɪnəbl] ADJ indefinible

undefined [ˌʌndɪˈfaɪnd] ADJ indefinido, indeterminado

undelete [ˈʌndɪˈliːt] VT (*Comput*) restaurar

undeliverable [ˌʌndɪˈlɪvərəbl] ADJ [*mail*] que no se puede entregar

undelivered [ˌʌndɪˈlɪvəd] ADJ no entregado al destinatario

undemanding [ˌʌndɪˈmɑːndɪŋ] ADJ [*person*] poco exigente; [*job*] que exige poco esfuerzo

undemocratic [ˌʌndeməˈkrætɪk] (ADJ) antidemocrático
undemonstrative [ˈʌndɪˈmɒnstrətɪv] (ADJ) poco expresivo
undeniable [ˌʌndɪˈnaɪəbl] (ADJ) innegable, indudable • **it is ~ that ...** es innegable *or* indudable que ...
undeniably [ˌʌndɪˈnaɪəblɪ] (ADV) innegablemente, indudablemente • **it is ~ true that ...** es innegable *or* indudable que ... • **an ~ successful trip** un viaje de éxito innegable *or* indudable
undenominational [ˈʌndɪˌnɒmɪˈneɪʃənl] (ADJ) no sectario
undependable [ˈʌndɪˈpendəbl] (ADJ) poco formal, poco confiable
under [ˈʌndəʳ] (ADV) **1** (= *beneath*) (*position*) debajo; (*direction*) abajo • **he stayed ~ for three minutes** (= *underwater*) estuvo sumergido durante tres minutos • **he lifted the rope and crawled ~** levantó la cuerda y se deslizó por debajo
2* (= *under anaesthetic*) • **he's been ~ for three hours** lleva tres horas bajo los efectos de la anestesia
3 (= *less*) menos • **children of 15 and ~** niños *mpl* de 15 años y menores • **ten degrees ~** diez grados bajo cero
(PREP) **1** (= *beneath*) debajo de • **~ the bed** debajo de la cama • **~ the microscope** bajo el microscopio • **~ the sky** bajo el cielo • **~ the water** bajo el agua • **the train passed ~ the bridge** el tren pasó por debajo del puente • **the tunnel goes ~ the Channel** el túnel pasa por debajo del Canal • **~ there** ahí debajo • **what's ~ there?** ¿qué hay ahí debajo?
2 (= *less than*) menos de • **~ 20 people** menos de 20 personas • **in ~ a minute** en menos de un minuto • **any number ~ 90** cualquier número inferior a 90 • **aged ~ 21** que tiene menos de 21 años • **children ~ ten** niños menores de diez años • **it sells at ~ £20** se vende a menos de 20 libras
3 (= *subject to*) bajo • **~ this government/the Romans** bajo este gobierno/los romanos • **~ Ferdinand VII** bajo Fernando VII, durante el reinado de Fernando VII • **he has 30 workers ~ him** tiene 30 obreros a su cargo • **to study ~ sb** estudiar con algn, tener a algn por profesor • **~ the command of** bajo el mando de • **~ construction** bajo construcción, en obras • **~ lock and key** bajo llave • **~ oath** bajo juramento • **~ pain/the pretext of** so pena/pretexto de • **~ full sail** a todo trapo, a vela llena
4 (*with names*) • **~ a false name** con nombre falso • **you'll find him ~ "plumbers" in the phone book** lo encontrarás en la sección de "fontaneros" en el listín
5 (= *according to, by*) de acuerdo con, según • **~ Article 25 of the Code** conforme al Artículo 25 del Código • **his rights ~ the contract** sus derechos según el contrato
6 (*Agr*) • **the field is ~ wheat** el campo está sembrado de trigo
under- [ˈʌndəʳ] (PREFIX) **1** (= *insufficiently*) poco, insuficientemente • **under-prepared** poco *or* insuficientemente preparado
2 (= *less than*) • **an under-15** (= *child*) un menor de 15 años • **the Spanish under-21 team** la selección española sub-21
3 [*part etc*] bajo, inferior; [*clothing*] interior; (*in rank*) subalterno, segundo • **the under-cook** el/la cocinero/a ayudante *or* auxiliar
under-achieve [ˌʌndərəˈtʃiːv] (VI) no desarrollar su potencial, no rendir (como se debe)
under-achievement [ˌʌndərəˈtʃiːvmənt] (N) bajo rendimiento *m*
under-achiever [ˌʌndərəˈtʃiːvəʳ] (N) (*Brit*) persona *f* que no desarrolla su potencial, persona *f* que no rinde (como podría)
underact [ˈʌndərˈækt] (VI) no dar de sí, hacer un papel sin el debido brío
underage [ˌʌndərˈeɪdʒ] (ADJ) menor de edad • **he's ~** es menor de edad
underarm [ˈʌndərɑːm] (N) axila *f*, sobaco *m*
(ADV) • **to serve ~** sacar sin levantar el brazo por encima
(CPD) (*Anat*) sobacal, del sobaco; [*service etc*] realizado sin levantar el brazo por encima
▸ **underarm deodorant** desodorante *m*
underbelly [ˈʌndəˌbelɪ] (N) (*Anat*) panza *f* • **the (soft) ~** (*fig*) la parte indefensa
underbid [ˈʌndəˈbɪd] (PT: **underbade** *or* **underbid**, PP: **underbidden** *or* **underbid**)
(VT) ofrecer un precio más bajo que
(VI) (*Bridge*) declarar por debajo de lo que se tiene
underbody [ˈʌndəbɒdɪ] (N) (*Aut*) bajos *mpl* (del chasis)
underbrush [ˈʌndəbrʌʃ] (N) (*US*) maleza *f*, monte *m* bajo
undercapitalized [ˈʌndəˈkæpɪtəlaɪzd] (ADJ) descapitalizado, subcapitalizado
undercarriage [ˈʌndəˌkærɪdʒ] (N) (*Aer*) tren *m* de aterrizaje
undercharge [ˈʌndəˈtʃɑːdʒ] (VT) cobrar de menos a • **he ~d me by £2** me cobró 2 libras de menos
underclass [ˈʌndəklɑːs] (N) clase *f* inferior
underclothes [ˈʌndəkləʊðz] (NPL), **underclothing** [ˈʌndəˌkləʊðɪŋ] (N) ropa *fsing* interior *or* (*esp LAm*) íntima • **to be in one's ~** estar en ropa interior, estar en paños menores*
undercoat [ˈʌndəkəʊt] (N) [*of paint*] primera capa *f*, primera mano *f*; (= *paint*) pintura *f* preparatoria
(VT) dar una primera capa a; (*US*) (*Aut*) proteger contra la corrosión
undercooked [ˈʌndəˈkʊkt] (ADJ) medio crudo, a medio cocer
undercover [ˈʌndəˌkʌvəʳ] (ADJ) [*operation, activity*] clandestino; [*agent*] secreto
(ADV) • **she was working ~ for the FBI** trabajaba como agente secreto para el FBI
undercurrent [ˈʌndəˌkʌrənt] (N) (*in sea*) corriente *f* submarina, contracorriente *f*; (*fig*) (*feeling etc*) trasfondo *m* • **an ~ of criticism** un trasfondo de críticas calladas
undercut [ˈʌndəkʌt] (PT, PP: **undercut**) (VT) (*Comm*) (= *sell cheaper than*) [+ *competitor*] vender más barato que
underdeveloped [ˈʌndədɪˈveləpt] (ADJ)
1 (*Econ*) [*country, society, economy*] subdesarrollado
2 (*Anat*) poco desarrollado
3 (*Phot*) insuficientemente revelado • **the image looks slightly ~** a la imagen le falta tiempo de revelación
underdevelopment [ˈʌndədɪˈveləpmənt] (N) subdesarrollo *m*
underdog [ˈʌndədɒg] (N) • **the ~ 1** (*in game, fight*) el/la más débil
2 (*economically, socially*) el/la desvalido/a, el/la desamparado/a
underdone [ˈʌndəˈdʌn] (ADJ) [*food*] a medio cocer; (*deliberately*) [*steak*] poco hecho
underdrawers [ˈʌndəˈdrɔːəz] (NPL) (*US*) calzoncillos *mpl*
underdressed [ˌʌndəˈdrest] (ADJ) • **to be ~** vestirse sin la debida elegancia, no vestirse de forma apropiada
underemphasize [ˌʌndərˈemfəsaɪz] (VT) subenfatizar
underemployed [ˈʌndərɪmˈplɔɪd] (ADJ) subempleado
underemployment [ˌʌndərɪmˈplɔɪmənt] (N) subempleo *m*
under-equipped [ʌndərɪˈkwɪpt] (ADJ) insuficientemente equipado
underestimate (N) [ˌʌndərˈestɪmɪt] estimación *f* demasiado baja, cálculo *m* demasiado bajo
(VT) [ˈʌndərˈestɪmeɪt] [+ *strength, importance, value, person*] subestimar, menospreciar • **you shouldn't ~ her** no deberías subestimarla • **I ~d the size of the sofa** al calcular las dimensiones del sofá me quedé corta • **they had ~d the size of the problem** no le habían dado al problema la importancia que merecía
underestimation [ˌʌndərestɪˈmeɪʃən] (N) infravaloración *f*
under-exploit [ʌndəreksˈplɔɪt] (VT) subexplotar
underexpose [ˈʌndərɪksˈpəʊz] (VT) (*Phot*) subexponer
underexposed [ˈʌndərɪksˈpəʊzd] (ADJ) (*Phot*) subexpuesto
underexposure [ˈʌnderɪksˈpəʊʒəʳ] (N) (*Phot*) subexposición *f*
underfed [ˈʌndəˈfed] (ADJ) subalimentado
underfeed [ˈʌndəˈfiːd] (PT, PP: **underfed**) (VT) alimentar insuficientemente
underfeeding [ˈʌndəˈfiːdɪŋ] (N) subalimentación *f*
underfelt [ˈʌndəfelt] (N) arpillera *f*
underfinanced [ˌʌndəfaɪˈnænst] (ADJ) insuficientemente financiado
underfloor [ˈʌndəflɔːʳ] (ADJ) de debajo del suelo
(CPD) ▸ **underfloor heating** calefacción *f* bajo el suelo
underfoot [ˈʌndəˈfʊt] (ADV) debajo de los pies • **it's wet ~** el suelo está mojado
underfund [ˌʌndəˈfʌnd] (VT) infradotar
underfunded [ˌʌndəˈfʌndɪd] (ADJ) infradotado
underfunding [ˌʌndəˈfʌndɪŋ] (N) infradotación *f*
undergarment [ˈʌndəˌgɑːmənt] (N) (*frm*) prenda *f* de ropa interior *or* (*LAm*) íntima; **undergarments** ropa *fsing* interior, ropa *fsing* íntima (*LAm*)
undergo [ˈʌndəˈgəʊ] (PT: **underwent**, PP: **undergone** [ˈʌndəˈgɒn]) (VT) sufrir, experimentar; [+ *treatment*] recibir; [+ *operation*] someterse a • **to ~ repairs** ser reparado
undergrad* [ˌʌndəˈgræd] (ADJ), (N) = **undergraduate**
undergraduate [ˈʌndəˈgrædjʊɪt] (N) estudiante *mf* universitario/a
(CPD) [*student*] no licenciado; [*course*] para universitarios (no licenciados)
▸ **undergraduate humour** humor *m* estudiantil
underground [ˈʌndəgraʊnd] (ADJ) **1** [*building, cave, mine*] subterráneo • **an ~ car park** un parking subterráneo
2 (*fig*) [*newspaper, movement*] clandestino
3 (= *alternative*) [*film, magazine, artist, culture*] underground (*inv*)
(ADV) **1** (= *under the ground*) bajo tierra • **moles live ~** los topos viven bajo tierra • **it's six feet ~** está a seis pies bajo tierra
2 (*fig*) (= *into hiding*) • **to go ~** (= *hide*) esconderse; (*Pol*) pasar a la clandestinidad
(N) **1** (*Brit*) (= *railway*) metro *m*, subterráneo *m* (*Arg*), subte *m* (*Arg**)
2 (*Mil*) resistencia *f* clandestina; (*Pol*) movimiento *m* clandestino; (*Art*) arte *m* marginal *or* underground
undergrowth [ˈʌndəgrəʊθ] (N) maleza *f*, matorrales *mpl*
underhand [ˈʌndəhænd] (ADJ) **1** (= *dishonest*) [*person*] solapado; [*behaviour, deals, tactics*]

turbio, poco limpio • **critics accuse the President of being ~** los críticos del presidente lo acusan de solapado
2 (*Sport*) [*throw*] por debajo del hombro
ADV • **to serve ~** sacar sin levantar el brazo por encima

underhanded ADJ [ˌʌndəˈhændɪd] = **underhand**

underhandedly [ˌʌndəˈhændɪdlɪ] ADV solapadamente

underinsure [ˌʌndərɪnˈʃʊəʳ] VT asegurar por debajo del valor real • **to be ~d** estar infraasegurado

underinvestment [ˌʌndərɪnˈvestmənt] N infrainversión *f*

underlay [ˈʌndəleɪ] N (*for carpet*) refuerzo *m*

underlie [ˌʌndəˈlaɪ] (PT: **underlay** [ˌʌndəˈleɪ]) (PP: **underlain** [ˌʌndəˈleɪn]) VT 1 (= *lie under*) estar debajo de, extenderse debajo de
2 (*fig*) sustentar

underline [ˌʌndəˈlaɪn] VT (*lit, fig*) subrayar

underling [ˈʌndəlɪŋ] N (*pej*) subordinado/a *m/f*, subalterno/a *m/f*

underlining [ˈʌndəˈlaɪnɪŋ] N subrayado *m*

underlip [ˈʌndəlɪp] N labio *m* inferior

underlying [ˈʌndəˈlaɪɪŋ] ADJ
1 (= *fundamental*) [*cause, theme*] subyacente • **the ~ problem is that …** el problema subyacente *or* de fondo es que …
2 [*rock, soil, bone*] subyacente
3 (*Econ*) [*rate, inflation, trend*] subyacente

undermanned [ˈʌndəˈmænd] ADJ • **to be ~** no tener (el) personal suficiente

undermanning [ˌʌndəˈmænɪŋ] N falta *f* de personal *or* mano de obra suficiente

undermentioned [ˈʌndəˈmenʃənd] ADJ abajo citado

undermine [ˌʌndəˈmaɪn] VT (*fig*) minar, socavar • **his health is being ~d by overwork** el exceso de trabajo le está minando la salud

undermost [ˈʌndəməʊst] ADJ (el) más bajo

underneath [ˈʌndəˈniːθ] PREP (*position*) bajo, debajo de • **the noise came from ~ the table** el ruido salía de debajo de la mesa • **~ the carpet** debajo de la moqueta • **I walked ~ a ladder** pasé por debajo de una escalera
ADV debajo, por debajo • **I got out of the car and looked ~** bajé del coche y miré (por) debajo
N parte *f* de abajo, fondo *m*
ADJ inferior, de abajo

undernourish [ˌʌndəˈnʌrɪʃ] VT subalimentar, desnutrir

undernourished [ˈʌndəˈnʌrɪʃt] ADJ subalimentado, desnutrido

undernourishment [ˈʌndəˈnʌrɪʃmənt] N subalimentación *f*, desnutrición *f*

underpaid [ˈʌndəˈpeɪd] ADJ mal pagado • **teachers are ~** los profesores están mal pagados

underpants [ˈʌndəpænts] NPL calzoncillos *mpl*, calzones *mpl* (*LAm*) • **a pair of ~** unos calzoncillos

underpart [ˈʌndəpɑːt] N parte *f* inferior

underpass [ˈʌndəpɑːs] N (*for cars*) paso *m* a desnivel; (*for pedestrians*) paso *m* subterráneo

underpay [ˈʌndəˈpeɪ] (PT, PP: **underpaid**) VT pagar mal

underpayment [ˌʌndəˈpeɪmənt] N pago *m* insuficiente • **because of ~ of tax** por un pago insuficiente de impuestos • **there was an ~ of £5 in your salary** se le pagaron 5 libras de menos en el sueldo

underperform [ˌʌndəpəˈfɔːm] VI 1 (*St Ex*) comportarse mal, tener un mal comportamiento • **the stock has ~ed on the Brussels stock market** las acciones han tenido un mal comportamiento en la bolsa de Bruselas
2 (*at work, in school*) rendir poco

underpin [ˌʌndəˈpɪn] VT 1 (*Archit*) apuntalar
2 (*fig*) [+ *argument, case*] sustentar, respaldar

underpinning [ˌʌndəˈpɪnɪŋ] N (*Archit*) apuntalamiento *m*

underplay [ˈʌndəˈpleɪ] VT 1 (= *play down*) [+ *importance*] minimizar; [+ *issue*] quitar *or* restar importancia a
2 (*Theat*) • **to ~ a part** hacer flojamente un papel
VI (*Theat*) hacer flojamente su papel, estar muy flojo en su papel

underpopulated [ˈʌndəˈpɒpjʊleɪtɪd] ADJ poco poblado, con baja densidad de población

underprice [ˈʌndəˈpraɪs] VT poner un precio demasiado bajo a • **at £10 this book is ~d** el precio de 10 libras es demasiado bajo para este libro

underpriced [ˈʌndəˈpraɪst] ADJ [*goods*] con un precio demasiado bajo

underpricing [ˈʌndəˈpraɪsɪŋ] N asignación *f* de precios demasiado bajos

underprivileged [ˈʌndəˈprɪvɪlɪdʒd] ADJ menos privilegiado, desfavorecido
NPL • **the ~** los menos privilegiados, los desfavorecidos

underproduction [ˈʌndəprəˈdʌkʃən] N producción *f* insuficiente

underqualified [ˈʌndəˈkwɒlɪˌfaɪd] ADJ • **to be ~** no estar suficientemente cualificado (**for** para)

underrate [ˌʌndəˈreɪt] VT [+ *strength, difficulty, person*] subestimar, menospreciar

underrated [ˌʌndəˈreɪtɪd] ADJ [*play, book, actor*] no debidamente valorado, infravalorado • **he's very ~** no se lo valora debidamente

under-represented [ˈʌndəreprɪˈzentɪd] ADJ • **to be under-represented** estar infrarrepresentado

underripe [ˈʌndəˈraɪp] ADJ poco maduro, verde

underscore [ˌʌndəˈskɔːʳ] VT subrayar, recalcar

undersea [ˈʌndəsiː] ADJ submarino
ADV bajo la superficie del mar

underseal [ˈʌndəsiːl] VT (*Brit*) impermeabilizar (*por debajo*), proteger contra la corrosión

undersealing [ˈʌndəsiːlɪŋ] N (*Brit*) impermeabilización *f* (*de los bajos*)

under-secretary [ˈʌndəˈsekrətərɪ] N subsecretario/a *m/f*

under-secretaryship [ˈʌndəˈsekrətərɪʃɪp] N subsecretaría *f*

undersell [ˈʌndəˈsel] (PT, PP: **undersold**) VT 1 (= *undercut*) [+ *competitor*] vender a precio más bajo que
2 (*fig*) • **to ~ o.s.** subestimarse, infravalorarse • **Burnley has been undersold as a tourist centre** no se ha hecho la debida publicidad de Burnley como centro turístico

undersexed [ˌʌndəˈsekst] ADJ de libido floja

undershirt [ˈʌndəʃɜːt] N (*US*) camiseta *f*

undershoot [ˌʌndəˈʃuːt] (PT, PP: **undershot**) VT [+ *target*] no alcanzar, no llegar a • **to ~ the runway** (*Aer*) aterrizar antes de llegar a la pista
VI no alcanzar el blanco • **we have undershot by £80** nos faltan 80 libras para alcanzar el objetivo

undershorts [ˈʌndəʃɔːts] NPL (*US*) calzoncillos *mpl*, calzones *mpl* (*LAm*)

underside [ˈʌndəsaɪd] N parte *f* inferior

undersigned [ˈʌndəsaɪnd] ADJ (*Jur*) (*frm*) • **the ~** el/la abajofirmante • **we, the ~** nosotros, los abajofirmantes

undersized [ˈʌndəˈsaɪzd] ADJ (= *too small*) demasiado pequeño

underskirt [ˈʌndəskɜːt] N (*Brit*) enaguas *fpl*

undersling [ˈʌndəslʌŋ] ADJ (*Aut*) colgante

undersoil [ˈʌndəˌsɔɪl] N subsuelo *m*
CPD ▸ **undersoil heating** calefacción *f* subterránea

undersold [ˈʌndəˈsəʊld] PT, PP *of* **undersell**

underspend [ˌʌndəˈspend] VI gastar menos de lo previsto

understaffed [ˈʌndəˈstɑːft] ADJ • **to be ~** no tener (el) personal suficiente, estar falto de personal

understaffing [ˈʌndəˈstɑːfɪŋ] N falta *f* de personal suficiente

understand [ˌʌndəˈstænd] (PT, PP: **understood**) VT 1 (= *comprehend*) (*gen*) entender; (*more formal, esp complex issues*) comprender • **I can't ~ it!** ¡no lo entiendo! • **I can't ~ your writing** no entiendo tu letra • **that's what I can't ~** eso es lo que no logro entender *or* comprender • **that is easily understood** eso se entiende fácilmente • **I don't want to hear another word about it, (is that) understood?** no quiero que se hable más del tema, ¿entendido *or* comprendido? • **the process is still not fully understood** el proceso todavía no se comprende *or* entiende del todo • **doctors are still trying to ~ the disease** los médicos siguen intentando comprender la enfermedad • **it must be understood that …** debe entenderse que … • **you must ~ that we're very busy** debes entender *or* comprender que estamos muy ocupados • **to ~ how/why** entender *or* comprender cómo/por qué
2 (= *follow, interpret*) entender • **did I ~ you correctly?** ¿te entendí bien? • **to make o.s. understood** hacerse entender • **he was trying to make himself understood** estaba intentando hacerse entender • **do I make myself understood?** ¿queda claro?
3 (= *empathize with*) [+ *person, point of view, attitude*] comprender, entender • **his wife doesn't ~ him** su mujer no le comprende *or* entiende • **she ~s children** comprende *or* entiende a los niños • **we ~ one another** nos comprendemos *or* entendemos • **I (fully) ~ your position** comprendo *or* entiendo (totalmente) su posición • **I quite ~ that you don't want to come** me hago cargo de que no quieres venir
4 (= *know*) [+ *language*] entender • **he can't ~ a word of Spanish** no entiende ni una palabra de español
5 (= *believe*) tener entendido • **I ~ you have been absent** tengo entendido que usted ha estado ausente • **as I ~ it, he's trying to set up a meeting** según tengo entendido *or* según creo está intentando convocar una reunión • **it's understood that he had a heart attack** se piensa *or* cree que sufrió un infarto • **am I to ~ that …?** ¿debo entender que …? • **we confirm our reservation and we ~ (that) the rental will be 500 euros** confirmamos nuestra reserva y entendemos que el alquiler será de 500 euros • **to give sb to ~ that** dar a algn a entender que • **we were given to ~ that …** se nos dio a entender que … • **it was understood that he would pay for it** se dio por sentado que él lo pagaría • **he let it be understood that …** dio a entender que …
VI 1 (= *comprehend*) entender; (*more emphatic*) comprender • **do you ~?** ¿entiendes *or* comprendes? • **now I ~!** ¡ahora entiendo!, ¡ahora comprendo! • **there's to be no noise, (do you) ~?** que no haya ruido, ¿entiendes *or* comprendes?
2 (= *believe*) • **she was, I ~, a Catholic** según

tengo entendido era católica
3 (= *accept sb's position*) entender; (*esp in more complex situation*) comprender • **he'll ~** lo entenderá *or* comprenderá • **don't worry, I quite ~** no te preocupes, lo entiendo *or* comprendo perfectamente

understandable [ˌʌndəˈstændəbl] ADJ
1 (= *comprehensible*) [*theory, statement*] comprensible • **he writes in a simple and ~ way** escribe de una forma simple y comprensible
2 (= *natural*) [*reaction, feeling*] comprensible • **an ~ desire to do sth** un deseo comprensible de hacer algo • **"his car broke down and he was late for work" — "well, that's ~"** —se le averió el coche y llegó tarde al trabajo —bueno, eso es comprensible • **it is ~ that …** se comprende que … • **it is very ~ that …** se comprende perfectamente que …

understandably [ˌʌndəˈstændəblɪ] ADV
1 (= *intelligibly*) [*speak, explain*] de manera clara *or* comprensible
2 (= *naturally*) • **~, he was very upset** tenía un disgusto muy grande, y era comprensible • **he's ~ reluctant to talk about the affair** se muestra reacio a hablar del asunto, y es comprensible

understanding [ˌʌndəˈstændɪŋ] ADJ [*person*] comprensivo; [*smile*] de comprensión • **to be ~ about sth** ser comprensivo (respecto a algo) • **she was very ~ about it** fue muy comprensiva
N 1 (= *faculty*) entendimiento *m* • **it was beyond my ~** iba más allá de mi entendimiento • **the peace that passeth all ~** (*Bible*) la paz que sobrepasa a todo entendimiento
2 [*of sth*] (= *comprehension*) comprensión *f*; (= *awareness*) conciencia *f* • **we need to test children's ~ of facts** hay que poner a prueba la comprensión que los niños tienen de los hechos • **our ~ of these processes is still poor** todavía no comprendemos muy bien estos procesos • **a basic ~ of computers is essential** se necesitan unos conocimientos básicos de informática • **to have a better** *or* **greater ~ of sth** (= *comprehend better*) entender *or* comprender mejor algo; (= *be more aware of*) tener mayor *or* más conciencia de algo • **to have little/no ~ of sth** saber muy poco/nada de algo • **a shift in public ~ of the issues of crime and punishment** un cambio de la conciencia pública con respecto a la cuestión de los crímenes y los castigos
3 (= *interpretation*) interpretación *f* • **what's your ~ of the Prime Minister's statement?** ¿cómo interpreta usted la declaración del Primer Ministro?, ¿cuál es su interpretación de la declaración del Primer Ministro? • **that's my ~ of the situation** esa es mi interpretación de la situación, así es como veo *or* interpreto la situación
4 (= *sympathy*) comprensión *f* • **thank you for your kindness and ~** le agradezco su amabilidad y comprensión • **to show no/little ~ of sth** no mostrar comprensión/mostrar muy poca comprensión hacia algo
5 (= *belief*) • **it was my ~ that …** • **my ~ was that …** tenía entendido que …, según yo creía …
6 (= *agreement*) acuerdo *m* • **to come to an ~ (with sb)** llegar a un acuerdo (con algn) • **to have an ~ (with sb)** tener un acuerdo (con algn) • **on the ~ that** a condición de que (+ *subjun*) • **on the ~ that he pays** a condición de que pague • **to reach an ~ (with sb)** llegar a un acuerdo (con algn)

understandingly [ˌʌndəˈstændɪŋlɪ] ADV con comprensión, de manera comprensiva

understate [ˈʌndəˈsteɪt] VT
1 (= *underestimate*) [+ *rate, level, growth*] subestimar • **these estimates ~ the size of the problem** estos pronósticos subestiman las dimensiones del problema
2 (= *underplay*) quitar importancia a • **the authorities originally ~d the disaster** las autoridades inicialmente quitaron importancia al desastre • **to describe it as a triumph is to ~ the orchestra's achievement** describirlo como un triunfo es no dar su merecida importancia a lo que ha logrado la orquesta

understated [ˌʌndəˈsteɪtɪd] ADJ [*style, clothes, elegance*] sencillo, discreto; [*writing, manner*] sencillo; [*performance, acting*] comedido

understatement [ˈʌndəˌsteɪtmənt] N
1 (= *underestimate*) [*of rate, level, growth*] subestimación *f* • **these figures are an ~** estas cifras son una subestimación
2 (= *not exaggeration*) • **I think that's something of an ~** creo que eso es quedarse corto • **to say I'm disappointed is an ~** decir que estoy desilusionado es quedarse corto • **interesting? that's the ~ of the year!** ¿interesante? ¡eso es quedarse corto!
3 (= *restraint*) moderación *f* • **typical British ~** la típica moderación británica, el típico comedimiento británico (*frm*)

understood [ˌʌndəˈstʊd] PT, PP *of* **understand**

understorey [ˈʌndəˌstɔːrɪ] N monte *m* bajo

understudy [ˈʌndəˌstʌdɪ] N suplente *mf*
VT prepararse para suplir a

undersubscribed [ˈʌndəsəbˈskraɪbd] ADJ
1 [*course*] que tiene plazas libres *or* vacantes
2 (*St Ex*) • **there is the possibility that the share issue will be ~** existe la posibilidad de que no se coloquen todas las acciones de la emisión

undersurface [ˈʌndəˌsɜːfɪs] N (= *underside*) parte *f* inferior
ADJ (= *under the surface*) bajo la superficie

undertake [ˌʌndəˈteɪk] (PT: **undertook**, PP: **undertaken** [ˌʌndəˈteɪkən]) VT [+ *task*] emprender; [+ *responsibility*] asumir • **to ~ to do sth** comprometerse a hacer algo • **to ~ that …** comprometerse a que …
VT (*Brit*) (*Aut**) adelantar por el lado contrario *or* el carril indebido
VI (*Brit*) (*Aut**) adelantar por el lado contrario *or* el carril indebido

undertaker [ˈʌndəˌteɪkəʳ] N (= *director*) director(a) *m/f* de funeraria *or* pompas fúnebres; (= *employee*) empleado/a *m/f* de una funeraria • **the ~'s** la funeraria

undertaking [ˌʌndəˈteɪkɪŋ] N 1 (= *enterprise*) empresa *f*; (= *task*) tarea *f*
2 (= *pledge*) garantía *f* • **to give an ~ that …** garantizar que … • **I can give no such ~** no puedo garantizar tal cosa, no puedo prometer eso
3 [ˈʌndəˌteɪkɪŋ] (*Brit*) (*Aut**) adelantamiento *m* por el lado contrario *or* el carril indebido
4 [ˈʌndəˌteɪkɪŋ] (*Brit*) (= *arranging funerals*) pompas *fpl* fúnebres

under-the-counter* [ˌʌndəðəˈkaʊntəʳ] ADJ [*goods etc*] adquirido por la trastienda*; [*deal*] turbio, poco limpio

underthings* [ˈʌndəθɪŋz] NPL paños *mpl* menores • **to be in one's ~** estar en paños menores

undertone [ˈʌndətəʊn] N 1 (= *low voice*) voz *f* baja
2 (= *suggestion, hint*) matiz *m*; [*of criticism*] trasfondo *m*
3 [*of perfume, taste, colour*] matiz *m*

undertook [ˌʌndəˈtʊk] PT *of* **undertake**

undertow [ˈʌndətəʊ] N resaca *f*

underuse N [ˌʌndəˈjuːs] infrautilización *f*
VT [ˌʌndəˈjuːz] infrautilizar

underused [ˌʌndəˈjuːzd] ADJ infrautilizado

underutilization [ˌʌndəˈjuːtəlaɪzeɪʃən] N infrautilización *f*

underutilize [ˌʌndəˈjuːtɪlaɪz] VT infrautilizar

underutilized [ˌʌndəˈjuːtəlaɪzd] ADJ infrautilizado

undervalue [ˈʌndəˈvæljuː] VT 1 (*Comm*) [+ *goods*] valorizar por debajo de su precio
2 (*fig*) subestimar • **he has been ~d as a writer** como escritor no se lo ha valorado debidamente

underwater [ˈʌndəˈwɔːtəʳ] ADJ submarino
ADV debajo del agua • **he swam ~ for several strokes before he surfaced** nadó varias brazas debajo del agua *or* bajo el agua antes de salir a la superficie • **this sequence was filmed ~** esta secuencia se filmó bajo el agua • **to stay ~** permanecer sumergido, permanecer bajo el agua
CPD [*exploration, fishing*] submarino; [*archaeology, photography*] submarino, subacuático ▸ **underwater camera** cámara *f* subacuática ▸ **underwater fisherman** submarinista *mf*

underway [ˌʌndəˈweɪ] ADJ ▹ **way**

underwear [ˈʌndəwɛəʳ] N ropa *f* interior, ropa *f* íntima (*LAm*)

underweight [ˌʌndəˈweɪt] ADJ de peso insuficiente • **to be ~** [*person*] pesar menos de lo debido • **she's 20lb ~** pesa 20 libras menos de lo que debiera

underwent [ˌʌndəˈwent] PT *of* **undergo**

underwhelm* [ˈʌndəˈwelm] VT (*hum*) impresionar muy poco • **this left us somewhat ~ed** eso apenas nos impresionó

underwhelming* [ˌʌndəˈwelmɪŋ] ADJ (*hum*) [*response, applause*] poco entusiasta; [*results, performance*] poco satisfactorio

underworld [ˈʌndəwɜːld] N 1 (= *hell*) • **the ~** el infierno
2 (*criminal*) • **the ~** el hampa
ADJ 1 (= *Hadian*) infernal
2 (= *criminal*) [*organization*] delictivo; [*personality*] del mundo del hampa; [*connections*] con el hampa

underwrite [ˈʌndəraɪt] (PT: **underwrote**, PP: **underwritten**) VT 1 (*Insurance*) asegurar (contra riesgos); (*on 2nd insurance*) reasegurar; (*Econ*) subscribir
2 (= *support*) aprobar, respaldar

underwriter [ˈʌndəˌraɪtəʳ] N (*Insurance*) asegurador(a) *m/f*, reasegurador(a) *m/f*

underwritten [ˈʌndəˌrɪtn] PP *of* **underwrite**

underwrote [ˈʌndərəʊt] PT *of* **underwrite**

undeserved [ˈʌndɪˈzɜːvd] ADJ inmerecido

undeservedly [ˈʌndɪˈzɜːvɪdlɪ] ADV inmerecidamente

undeserving [ˈʌndɪˈzɜːvɪŋ] ADJ [*person*] de poco mérito; [*cause*] poco meritorio • **to be ~ of sth** no ser digno de algo, no merecer algo

undesirable [ˈʌndɪˈzaɪərəbl] ADJ indeseable • **it is ~ that** no es recomendable que (+ *subjun*), es poco aconsejable que (+ *subjun*)
N indeseable *mf*

undetected [ˈʌndɪˈtektɪd] ADJ no descubierto • **to go ~** pasar inadvertido

undetermined [ˈʌndɪˈtɜːmɪnd] ADJ (= *unknown*) indeterminado; (= *uncertain*) incierto

undeterred [ˈʌndɪˈtɜːd] ADJ • **he was ~ by …** no se dejó intimidar por … • **he carried on ~** siguió sin inmutarse

undeveloped [ˈʌndɪˈveləpt] ADJ 1 [*country, nation*] no desarrollado; [*land, area, resources*] sin explotar

2 (= *immature*) [*person*] sin desarrollar
3 [*film*] sin revelar
undeviating [ʌn'diːvɪeɪtɪŋ] ADJ directo, constante • **to follow an ~ path** seguir un curso recto
undeviatingly [ʌn'diːvɪeɪtɪŋlɪ] ADV directamente, constantemente • **to hold ~ to one's course** seguir su curso sin apartarse en absoluto de él
undiagnosed [ʌn'daɪəɡ,nəʊzd] ADJ sin diagnosticar
undid [,ʌn'dɪd] PT *of* **undo**
undies* ['ʌndɪz] NPL ropa *fsing* interior, ropa *fsing* íntima (*LAm*)
undifferentiated [,ʌndɪfə'renʃɪeɪtɪd] ADJ sin diferenciar
undigested ['ʌndaɪ'dʒestɪd] ADJ indigesto
undignified [ʌn'dɪɡnɪfaɪd] ADJ [*behaviour*] indecoroso, poco digno; [*posture, position*] indecoroso; [*person*] poco digno
undiluted ['ʌndaɪ'luːtɪd] ADJ 1 (*lit*) [*fruit juice, chemical*] sin diluir, puro
2 (*fig*) [*pleasure, accent*] puro
undiminished ['ʌndɪ'mɪnɪʃt] ADJ no disminuido
undimmed ['ʌn'dɪmd] ADJ (*fig*) no empañado
undiplomatic ['ʌn,dɪplə'mætɪk] ADJ poco diplomático
undiscernible ['ʌndɪ'sɜːnəbl] ADJ imperceptible
undiscerning ['ʌndɪ'sɜːnɪŋ] ADJ sin criterio, sin discernimiento
undischarged ['ʌndɪs'tʃɑːdʒd] ADJ [*debt*] impagado, por pagar; [*promise*] no cumplido
CPD ▸ **undischarged bankrupt** (*Brit*) quebrado/a *m/f* no rehabilitado/a, persona *f* que sigue en estado de quiebra
undisciplined [ʌn'dɪsɪplɪnd] ADJ indisciplinado
undisclosed ['ʌndɪs'kləʊzd] ADJ no revelado, sin revelar
undiscovered ['ʌndɪs'kʌvəd] ADJ
1 (= *undetected*) [*treasure, country*] sin descubrir, no descubierto; [*planet*] no descubierto • **to lie ~** estar sin descubrir • **to remain ~** estar *or* permanecer sin ser descubierto • **he remained ~ for three days** estuvo *or* permaneció tres días sin ser descubierto
2 (= *unknown*) desconocido
undiscriminating ['ʌndɪs'krɪmɪneɪtɪŋ] ADJ sin discernimiento
undisguised ['ʌndɪs'ɡaɪzd] ADJ 1 (= *with no disguise*) sin disfraz
2 (*fig*) [*pleasure, relief, hostility*] manifiesto, indisimulado • **an ~ attempt to do sth** un intento manifiesto de hacer algo
undismayed ['ʌndɪs'meɪd] ADJ impávido • **he was ~ by this** no se dejó desanimar por esto • **... he said ~** ... dijo sin inmutarse
undisposed-of ['ʌndɪs'pəʊzdɒv] ADJ (*Comm*) no vendido
undisputed ['ʌndɪs'pjuːtɪd] ADJ
1 (= *irrefutable*) [*fact, authority*] innegable • **to have the ~ right to do sth** tener el derecho innegable de hacer algo
2 (= *unchallenged*) [*champion, leader*] indiscutible • **the ~ queen of fashion** la reina indiscutible de la moda
undistinguished ['ʌndɪs'tɪŋɡwɪʃt] ADJ mediocre
undistributed [,ʌndɪs'trɪbjʊtɪd] ADJ [*mail*] sin repartir
CPD ▸ **undistributed profit** beneficios *mpl* no distribuidos
undisturbed ['ʌndɪs'tɜːbd] ADJ
1 (= *untouched*) tranquilo • **to leave sth ~** dejar algo como está
2 (= *uninterrupted*) [*sleep*] ininterrumpido; [*person*] • **you need a quiet place where you will be ~** necesitas un lugar tranquilo donde no se te moleste • **he likes to be left ~** no le gusta que se le interrumpa, no quiere que le interrumpan las visitas *or* llamadas
3 (= *unconcerned*) • **to be ~** no dejarse perturbar *or* (*LAm*) alterar • **he was ~ by this** no se dejó perturbar *or* (*LAm*) alterar por ello
ADV [*work, play, sleep*] sin ser molestado • **he went on with his work ~** continuó su trabajo sin interrupciones
undivided ['ʌndɪ'vaɪdɪd] ADJ
1 (= *wholehearted*) [*admiration*] sin reservas • **I want your ~ attention** quiero que me prestes toda tu atención
2 (= *not split*) [*country, institution*] íntegro, entero
undo ['ʌn'duː] (PT: **undid**, PP: **undone**) VT
1 (= *unfasten*) [+ *button, blouse*] desabrochar; [+ *knot, parcel, shoe laces*] desatar; [+ *zipper*] abrir; (= *take to pieces*) desarmar
2 (= *reverse*) deshacer; [+ *damage etc*] reparar; [+ *arrangement etc*] anular
3 (*Comput*) [+ *command*] cancelar
undock [ʌn'dɒk] (*Space*) VT desacoplar
VI desacoplarse
undocumented [ʌn'dɒkjʊmentɪd] ADJ
1 [*event*] indocumentado
2 (*US*) [*person*] indocumentado
undoing ['ʌn'duːɪŋ] N ruina *f*, perdición *f* • **that was his ~** aquello fue su ruina *or* perdición
undomesticated ['ʌndə'mestɪkeɪtɪd] ADJ indomado, no domesticado
undone ['ʌn'dʌn] PP *of* **undo**
ADJ 1 (= *unfastened*) [*clasp, blouse*] desabrochado; [*zip, flies*] abierto; [*tie, shoelace, knot*] desatado; [*hair*] despeinado • **to come ~** [*button*] desabrocharse; [*parcel*] desatarse
2 (= *not yet done*) por hacer • **his desk was piled with work as yet ~** su escritorio estaba amontonado de trabajo por hacer • **to leave sth ~** dejar algo sin hacer
3 (= *cancelled out*) deshecho • **she has seen her life's work ~** ha visto el trabajo de toda su vida deshecho • **~ by ambition** destrozado por la ambición
4† (*liter*) (= *ruined*) • **I am ~!** ¡estoy perdido!, ¡es mi ruina!
undoubted [ʌn'daʊtɪd] ADJ indudable
undoubtedly [ʌn'daʊtɪdlɪ] ADV indudablemente, sin duda • **he is ~ the best man for the job** es sin duda alguna el mejor para el trabajo
undramatic [,ʌndrə'mætɪk] ADJ poco dramático
undreamed-of [ʌn'driːmdɒv] ADJ, **undreamt-of** [ʌn'dremtɒv] (*Brit*) ADJ inimaginable, nunca soñado
undress ['ʌn'dres] VT desnudar, desvestir (*LAm*) • **to get ~ed** desnudarse, desvestirse (*LAm*)
VI desnudarse, desvestirse (*LAm*) • **the doctor told me to ~** el médico me dijo que me desnudase
N 1 • **in a state of ~** desnudo
2 (*Mil*) uniforme *m* (de diario)
undressed [ʌn'drest] ADJ 1 (= *naked*) [*person*] desnudo
2 [*hide*] sin adobar, sin curtir
3 [*salad etc*] sin salsa
4 [*wound*] sin vendar
undrinkable ['ʌn'drɪŋkəbl] ADJ (= *unpalatable*) imbebible; (= *poisonous*) no potable
undue ['ʌn'djuː] ADJ indebido, excesivo
undulate ['ʌndjʊleɪt] VI ondular, ondear
undulating ['ʌndjʊleɪtɪŋ] ADJ ondulante, ondeante; [*land*] ondulado
undulation [,ʌndjʊ'leɪʃən] N ondulación *f*
undulatory ['ʌndjʊlətərɪ] ADJ ondulatorio
unduly ['ʌn'djuːlɪ] ADV (= *excessively*) excesivamente • **we are not ~ worried** no estamos demasiado preocupados
undying [ʌn'daɪɪŋ] ADJ (*fig*) imperecedero, inmarcesible
unearned ['ʌn'ɜːnd] ADJ no ganado
CPD ▸ **unearned income** renta *f* (no salarial) ▸ **unearned increment** plusvalía *f*
unearth ['ʌn'ɜːθ] VT 1 (= *dig up*) desenterrar
2 (= *uncover*) (*fig*) desenterrar, descubrir
unearthly [ʌn'ɜːθlɪ] ADJ 1 (= *otherworldly*) [*light, sound*] sobrenatural; [*beauty*] sobrenatural, de otro mundo
2* (= *ungodly*) [*noise*] tremendo* • **at some ~ hour** a unas horas intempestivas • **do you still get up at that ~ hour?** ¿todavía te levantas a esas horas (tan intempestivas)?
unease [ʌn'iːz] N (= *tension*) malestar *m*; (= *apprehension*) inquietud *f*, desasosiego *m*
uneasily [ʌn'iːzɪlɪ] ADV [*look, say*] con inquietud, inquietamente • **I noted ~ that ...** noté con inquietud que ... • **he shifted ~ in his chair** se removió inquieto en su silla • **she laughed ~** se rió nerviosa
uneasiness [ʌn'iːzɪnɪs] N inquietud *f*, desasosiego *m*
uneasy [ʌn'iːzɪ] ADJ 1 (= *worried*) inquieto; (= *ill at ease*) incómodo, molesto • **people are ~ about their future** la gente está preocupada por el futuro • **I felt ~ about doing it on my own** me inquietaba la idea de hacerlo solo • **to become ~ (about sth)** empezar a inquietarse (por algo) • **to make sb ~** dejar a algn intranquilo, inquietar a algn
2 (= *uncomfortable*) [*conscience*] intranquilo; [*silence*] incómodo
3 (= *fragile*) [*peace, truce, alliance*] frágil, precario
4 (= *restless*) [*sleep*] agitado; [*night*] intranquilo
uneatable ['ʌn'iːtəbl] ADJ incomible, que no se puede comer
uneaten ['ʌn'iːtn] ADJ sin comer, sin probar
uneconomic ['ʌn,iːkə'nɒmɪk] ADJ [*business, factory*] poco rentable, no económico • **it's ~ to put on courses for so few students** no es rentable organizar cursos para tan pocos alumnos
uneconomical ['ʌn,iːkə'nɒmɪkəl] ADJ antieconómico, poco económico
unedifying ['ʌn'edɪfaɪɪŋ] ADJ indecoroso, poco edificante
unedited [ʌn'edɪtɪd] ADJ inédito
uneducated ['ʌn'edjʊkeɪtɪd] ADJ inculto, ignorante
unemotional ['ʌnɪ'məʊʃənl] ADJ (*gen*) impasible, insensible; [*account*] objetivo
unemotionally ['ʌnɪ'məʊʃnəlɪ] ADV • **to look on ~** mirar impasible, mirar sin dejarse afectar
unemployable ['ʌnɪm'plɔɪəbl] ADJ inútil para el trabajo
unemployed ['ʌnɪm'plɔɪd] ADJ 1 [*person*] parado, en paro, desempleado (*LAm*), cesante (*Chile*) • **he's been ~ for a year** lleva parado un año
2 [*capital etc*] sin utilizar, no utilizado
NPL • **the ~** los parados, los desempleados (*LAm*)
unemployment ['ʌnɪm'plɔɪmənt] N desempleo *m*, paro *m* (*Sp*), cesantía *f* (*Chile*)
CPD ▸ **unemployment benefit** (*Brit*), **unemployment compensation** (*US*) subsidio *m* de desempleo *or* (*Sp*) paro ▸ **unemployment figures** cifras *fpl* de desempleo, cifras *fpl* del paro (*Sp*) ▸ **unemployment line** (*US*) fila *f* de parados,

u

cola *f* del paro (*Sp*) ▸ **unemployment rate** tasa *f* de desempleo, tasa *m* de paro (*Sp*)
unencumbered [ˌʌnɪnˈkʌmbəd] ADJ suelto, sin trabas; [*estate etc*] libre de gravamen • **~ by** sin el estorbo de
unending [ʌnˈendɪŋ] ADJ interminable, sin fin
unendurable [ˌʌnɪnˈdjʊərəbl] ADJ inaguantable, insoportable
unenforceable [ˌʌnɪnˈfɔːsɪbl] ADJ [*law, contract*] imposible de hacer cumplir; [*policy*] imposible de aplicar
unengaged [ˈʌnɪnˈgeɪdʒd] ADJ libre
un-English [ˈʌnˈɪŋglɪʃ] ADJ poco inglés
unenlightened [ˈʌnɪnˈlaɪtnd] ADJ [*person, age*] poco instruido; [*policy etc*] poco ilustrado
unenterprising [ˈʌnˈentəpraɪzɪŋ] ADJ [*person*] poco emprendedor, falto de iniciativa; [*character, policy, act*] tímido
unenthusiastic [ˈʌnɪnˌθuːzɪˈæstɪk] ADJ poco entusiasta • **everybody seemed rather ~ about it** nadie se mostró mayormente entusiasmado con la idea
unenthusiastically [ˈʌnɪnˌθuːzɪˈæstɪkəlɪ] ADV sin entusiasmo
unenviable [ˈʌnˈenvɪəbl] ADJ poco envidiable
unequal [ˈʌnˈiːkwəl] ADJ **1** (= *unfair*) desigual • **the ~ distribution of wealth** la distribución desigual de la riqueza
2 (= *differing*) [*size, length*] distinto • **her feet are of ~ sizes** tiene los pies de distinto tamaño
3 (= *inadequate*) • **to be ~ to a task** no estar a la altura de una tarea
unequalled, unequaled (*US*) [ˈʌnˈiːkwəld] ADJ inigualado, sin par • **a record ~ by anybody** un historial inigualado *or* sin par
unequally [ˈʌnˈiːkwəlɪ] ADV desigualmente
unequivocal [ˈʌnɪˈkwɪvəkəl] ADJ (= *unmistakeable*) [*response, message, proof*] inequívoco, claro; [*support*] incondicional; [*opposition*] rotundo • **to be ~ in one's support of sth** apoyar algo incondicionalmente
unequivocally [ˈʌnɪˈkwɪvəkəlɪ] ADV inequívocamente, de manera inequívoca • **they stated ~ that his heart disease began in childhood** manifestaron inequívocamente *or* de manera inequívoca que ha venido padeciendo del corazón desde la infancia • **the Minister has ~ rejected the idea** el ministro ha rechazado rotundamente la idea • **let's make it ~ clear that we support the president** dejemos bien claro que apoyamos al presidente
unerring [ˈʌnˈɜːrɪŋ] ADJ infalible
unerringly [ˌʌnˈɜːrɪŋlɪ] ADV de forma infalible
UNESCO [juːˈneskəʊ] N ABBR (= **United Nations Educational, Scientific and Cultural Organization**) UNESCO *f*
unescorted [ˌʌnɪsˈkɔːtɪd] ADJ **1** (*Mil, Naut*) sin escolta
2 (= *unaccompanied by a partner*) sin compañía, sin compañero/a
unessential [ˈʌnɪˈsenʃəl] ADJ no esencial
NPL • **the ~s** las cosas *or* los aspectos no esenciales
unesthetic [ˌʌniːsˈθetɪk] ADJ (*US*) antiestético
unethical [ˈʌnˈeθɪkəl] ADJ poco ético
unethically [ʌnˈeθɪkəlɪ] ADV poco éticamente
uneven [ˈʌnˈiːvən] ADJ **1** (= *not flat or straight*) [*surface, wall, road*] desigual, irregular; [*teeth*] desigual
2 (= *irregular*) [*breathing, rate*] irregular • **it was an ~ performance** fue una actuación irregular
3 (= *unfair*) [*distribution*] desigual, poco equitativo; [*contest*] desigual • **the ~ distribution of aid** la distribución desigual *or* poco equitativa de las ayudas
unevenly [ˈʌnˈiːvənlɪ] ADV **1** (*lit*) desigualmente, irregularmente • **she had cut his hair ~** se le había cortado el pelo de forma desigual • **apply the paint ~ in broad strokes** aplique la pintura a brochazos desiguales *or* irregulares • **microwaves heat food ~** las microondas no calientan todo el alimento por igual
2 (= *unfairly*) de manera poco equitativa • **the country's new wealth was ~ distributed** la nueva riqueza del país estaba distribuida de manera poco equitativa
unevenness [ˈʌnˈiːvənnɪs] N [*of surface*] desigualdad *f*, irregularidad *f*; [*of breathing*] irregularidad *f*; (= *unfairness*) [*of distribution*] desigualdad *f*; [*of contest*] lo desigual
uneventful [ˈʌnɪˈventfʊl] ADJ sin incidentes
uneventfully [ˈʌnɪˈventfʊlɪ] ADV • **the days passed ~** los días pasaban sin pena ni gloria • **the race progressed ~ until the fifth lap** la carrera transcurrió sin incidentes hasta la quinta vuelta
unexampled [ˈʌnɪgˈzɑːmpld] ADJ sin igual, sin precedente
unexceptionable [ˌʌnɪkˈsepʃnəbl] ADJ intachable, irreprochable
unexceptional [ˌʌnɪkˈsepʃənl] ADJ sin nada de extraordinario, común y corriente
unexciting [ˈʌnɪkˈsaɪtɪŋ] ADJ sin interés
unexpected [ˈʌnɪksˈpektɪd] ADJ [*death, arrival, appearance, visit*] inesperado, repentino; [*victory, success*] inesperado; [*problem, expense*] inesperado, imprevisto • **they turn up in the most ~ places** aparecen en los lugares más insospechados • **his arrival was an ~ bonus for the fans** su llegada fue un regalo inesperado para los fans • **it was all very ~** fue todo muy inesperado
unexpectedly [ˈʌnɪksˈpektɪdlɪ] ADV [*arrive*] de improviso, sin avisar; [*happen*] inesperadamente, de repente; [*die*] repentinamente, inesperadamente • **there was an ~ high turnout of voters** se produjo una asistencia de votantes inesperadamente alta • **not ~, he failed** como era de esperar, suspendió
unexpended [ˈʌnɪksˈpendɪd] ADJ no gastado
unexpired [ˈʌnɪksˈpaɪəd] ADJ [*bill*] no vencido; [*lease, ticket*] no caducado
unexplainable [ˌʌnɪkˈspleɪnəbl] ADJ inexplicable
unexplained [ˈʌnɪksˈpleɪnd] ADJ inexplicado
unexploded [ˈʌnɪksˈpləʊdɪd] ADJ sin explotar
unexploited [ˈʌnɪksˈplɔɪtɪd] ADJ inexplotado, sin explotar
unexplored [ˈʌnɪksˈplɔːd] ADJ inexplorado
unexposed [ˈʌnɪksˈpəʊzd] ADJ no descubierto; (*Phot*) inexpuesto
unexpressed [ˈʌnɪksˈprest] ADJ no expresado, tácito
unexpressive [ˈʌnɪksˈpresɪv] ADJ inexpresivo
unexpurgated [ˈʌnˈekspɜːgeɪtɪd] ADJ sin expurgar, íntegro
unfading [ʌnˈfeɪdɪŋ] ADJ (*fig*) inmarcesible, imperecedero
unfailing [ʌnˈfeɪlɪŋ] ADJ (*gen*) indefectible, infalible; [*supply*] inagotable
unfailingly [ʌnˈfeɪlɪŋlɪ] ADV • **to be ~ courteous** ser siempre cortés, no faltar en ningún momento a la cortesía
unfair [ˈʌnˈfɛəʳ] ADJ (COMPAR: **unfairer**, SUPERL: **unfairest**) [*system, treatment, decision*] injusto; [*comment, criticism*] injusto, improcedente; [*play*] sucio; [*tactics, practice, methods*] antirreglamentario; [*competition*] desleal • **you're being ~** estás siendo injusto • **how ~!** ¡no hay derecho! • **it's ~ to expect her to do that** no es justo *or* es injusto esperar que ella haga eso • **it's ~ on those who have paid** es injusto para los que han pagado • **to be ~ to sb** ser injusto con algn, no ser justo con algn
CPD ▸ **unfair dismissal** despido *m* improcedente, despido *m* injustificado
unfairly [ˈʌnˈfɛəlɪ] ADV [*treat, dismiss, judge, penalize*] injustamente; [*compete*] deslealmente
unfairness [ˈʌnˈfɛənɪs] N injusticia *f*
unfaithful [ˈʌnˈfeɪθfʊl] ADJ infiel (**to** a)
unfaithfulness [ˈʌnˈfeɪθfʊlnɪs] N infidelidad *f*
unfaltering [ʌnˈfɔːltərɪŋ] ADJ resuelto, firme
unfalteringly [ʌnˈfɔːltərɪŋlɪ] ADV resueltamente, firmemente
unfamiliar [ˈʌnfəˈmɪlɪəʳ] ADJ desconocido, extraño • **I heard an ~ voice** oí una voz desconocida *or* extraña • **to be ~ with sth** no estar familiarizado con algo
unfamiliarity [ˈʌnfəˌmɪlɪˈærɪtɪ] N falta *f* de familiaridad
unfashionable [ˈʌnˈfæʃnəbl] ADJ pasado de moda • **it is now ~ to talk of ...** no está de moda ahora hablar de ...
unfashionably [ʌnˈfæʃənəblɪ] ADV • **he wears his blonde hair ~ long** se deja el pelo rubio largo, sin hacer caso de la moda • **some people might consider this mobile** (*Brit*) *or* **cell** (*US*) **~ large** a algunos este móvil (*Sp*) *or* celular (*LAm*) les puede parecer demasiado grande para estar de moda • **rather ~, he still believes in marriage** bastante pasado de moda, todavía cree en el matrimonio
unfasten [ˈʌnˈfɑːsn] VT [*+ button etc*] desabrochar; [*+ rope etc*] desatar, aflojar (*LAm*); [*+ door*] abrir
unfathomable [ʌnˈfæðəməbl] ADJ insondable
unfathomed [ˈʌnˈfæðəmd] ADJ no sondado
unfavourable, unfavorable (*US*) [ˈʌnˈfeɪvərəbl] ADJ **1** (= *adverse*) [*situation*] adverso; [*conditions*] poco propicio, desfavorable; [*outlook, weather*] poco propicio; [*wind*] desfavorable • **to be ~ for sth** ser poco propicio para algo, no ser propicio para algo • **to be ~ to sb** no favorecer a algn, ser desfavorable para algn
2 (= *negative*) [*impression, opinion*] negativo, malo; [*comparison*] poco favorable • **to show sth/sb in an ~ light** presentar algo/a algn de forma negativa *or* poco favorable, dar una imagen negativa *or* poco favorable de algo/algn
unfavourably, unfavorably (*US*) [ˈʌnˈfeɪvərəblɪ] ADV [*react, impress*] de forma negativa • **he reviewed your book very ~** hizo una crítica muy negativa de tu libro • **she commented ~ on the way he was dressed** hizo comentarios desfavorables sobre la forma en que iba vestido • **he was compared ~ with his predecessors** se lo comparó desfavorablemente con sus predecesores • **to regard sth ~** no tener una opinión muy favorable *or* buena de algo
unfazed* [ˈʌnˈfeɪzd] ADJ (*esp US*) • **her criticism left him quite ~** sus críticas le dejaban tan pancho* • **she was completely ~**

u

by the extraordinary events se quedó como si nada ante unos sucesos tan extraordinarios

unfeasible [ʌn'fi:zɪbl] ADJ no factible, inviable

unfeeling [ʌn'fi:lɪŋ] ADJ insensible

unfeelingly [ʌn'fi:lɪŋlɪ] ADV insensiblemente

unfeigned [ʌn'feɪnd] ADJ no fingido, verdadero

unfeignedly [ʌn'feɪnɪdlɪ] ADV sin fingimiento, verdaderamente

unfeminine [ʌn'femɪnɪn] ADJ poco femenino

unfermented ['ʌnfə'mentɪd] ADJ no fermentado

unfettered ['ʌn'fetəd] ADJ sin trabas

unfilled ['ʌn'fɪld] ADJ • **~ orders** pedidos *mpl* pendientes

unfinished ['ʌn'fɪnɪʃt] ADJ inacabado, sin terminar • **I have three ~ letters** tengo tres cartas por terminar • **we have ~ business** tenemos asuntos pendientes

unfit ['ʌn'fɪt] ADJ **1** (= *unsuitable*) no apto (**for** para); (= *incompetent*) incapaz; (= *unworthy*) indigno (**to de**) • **he was considered an ~ parent** se lo consideró un padre inepto *or* incompetente • **he is quite ~ to hold office** no está capacitado en absoluto para ejercer ningún cargo • **to be ~ for sth: the road is ~ for lorries** el camino no es apto para el tránsito de camiones • **to be ~ for consumption/publication** no ser apto para el consumo/la publicación • **to be ~ for habitation** ser inhabitable • **complaints that he was ~ for the job** quejas *fpl* de que no estaba capacitado para el trabajo
2 (= *not physically fit*) en mala forma (física), bajo de forma; (= *ill*) indispuesto • **he is very ~** está en muy mala forma (física), está muy bajo de forma • **two of their players are ~** dos de sus jugadores no se encuentran en condiciones de jugar • **~ for military service** no apto para el servicio militar • **she is ~ to drive** no está en condiciones de conducir *or* (*LAm*) manejar
VT (*frm*) • **to ~ sb for sth/to do sth** inhabilitar *or* incapacitar a algn para algo/para hacer algo

unfitness ['ʌn'fɪtnɪs] N **1** (= *unsuitability*) (*for job*) incapacidad *f*, ineptitud *f*; (*for use, purpose*) lo poco apropiado
2 (*physical*) baja forma *f* (física)

unfitted [ʌn'fɪtɪd] ADJ • **to be ~ for sth** no reunir las condiciones para algo • **to be ~ to do sth** no reunir las condiciones para hacer algo

unfitting [ʌn'fɪtɪŋ] ADJ impropio

unfixed [ʌn'fɪkst] ADJ **1** (= *unrepaired*) sin reparar
2 (= *unsecured, loose*) suelto

unflagging [ʌn'flægɪŋ] ADJ incansable

unflaggingly [ʌn'flægɪŋlɪ] ADV incansablemente

unflappability* [ˌʌnflæpə'bɪlɪtɪ] N imperturbabilidad *f*

unflappable* ['ʌn'flæpəbl] ADJ imperturbable

unflattering ['ʌn'flætərɪŋ] ADJ [*person*] poco lisonjero; [*description*] poco halagüeño; [*clothes, haircut*] poco favorecedor

unflatteringly ['ʌn'flætərɪŋlɪ] ADV [*speak*] de modo poco lisonjero; [*describe*] de manera poco halagüeña

unfledged ['ʌn'fledʒd] ADJ implume

unflinching [ʌn'flɪntʃɪŋ] ADJ impávido, resuelto

unflinchingly ['ʌn'flɪntʃɪŋlɪ] ADV impávidamente, resueltamente

unfocused, unfocussed ['ʌn'fəʊkəst] ADJ [*eyes*] desenfocado; [*desires*] sin objetivo concreto, nada concreto; [*energies*] que carece de dirección

unfold [ʌn'fəʊld] VT **1** desplegar, desdoblar • **she ~ed the map** desplegó *or* desdobló el mapa
2 (*fig*) [+ *idea, plan*] exponer; [+ *secret*] revelar
VI desplegarse, desdoblarse; (*fig*) [*view etc*] revelarse

unforced [ʌn'fɔ:st] ADJ [*style etc*] natural, sin artificialidad; [*error*] no forzado

unforeseeable ['ʌnfɔ:'si:əbl] ADJ imprevisible

unforeseen ['ʌnfɔ:'si:n] ADJ imprevisto

unforgettable ['ʌnfə'getəbl] ADJ inolvidable

unforgettably ['ʌnfə'getəblɪ] ADV de manera inolvidable • **~ beautiful** tan hermoso que resulta inolvidable

unforgivable ['ʌnfə'gɪvəbl] ADJ imperdonable

unforgivably [ˌʌnfə'gɪvəblɪ] ADV imperdonable • **he said, quite ~, that ...** dijo, de forma imperdonable, que ...

unforgiven ['ʌnfə'gɪvən] ADJ no perdonado

unforgiving ['ʌnfə'gɪvɪŋ] ADJ implacable

unforgotten ['ʌnfə'gɒtn] ADJ no olvidado

unformatted ['ʌn'fɔ:mætɪd] ADJ (*Comput*) [*disk, text*] sin formatear, no formateado

unformed ['ʌn'fɔ:md] ADJ (= *shapeless*) informe; (= *immature*) inmaduro, sin formar aún

unforthcoming ['ʌnfɔ:θ'kʌmɪŋ] ADJ poco comunicativo

unfortified ['ʌn'fɔ:tɪfaɪd] ADJ no fortificado; [*town*] abierto

unfortunate [ʌn'fɔ:tʃnɪt] ADJ **1** (= *deserving of pity, unlucky*) • **how very ~!** ¡qué mala suerte!, ¡qué desgracia! • **you have been most ~** ha tenido usted muy mala suerte • **we must help these ~ people** debemos ayudar a estas personas tan desafortunadas • **he was ~ enough to be caught** tuvo la desgracia *or* mala suerte de que lo cogieran *or* pillaran • **it is most ~ that he left** es una lástima *or* muy de lamentar que se haya ido
2 (= *unsuitable, regrettable*) [*remark*] poco acertado, inoportuno; [*incident, consequences, tendency*] lamentable • **it was an ~ choice of words** las palabras que se eligieron fueron poco acertadas
N desgraciado/a *m/f*

unfortunately [ʌn'fɔ:tʃnɪtlɪ] ADV
1 (= *unluckily*) desgraciadamente, por desgracia • **~ for you** desgraciadamente para ti, por desgracia para ti
2 (= *regrettably*) lamentablemente
3 (= *inappropriately*) • **the statement was rather ~ phrased** la declaración estaba formulada con muy poco acierto

unfounded ['ʌn'faʊndɪd] ADJ infundado, sin fundamento

unframed ['ʌn'freɪmd] ADJ sin marco

unfreeze ['ʌn'fri:z] VT descongelar
VI descongelarse

unfrequented ['ʌnfrɪ'kwentɪd] ADJ poco frecuentado

unfriend ['ʌn'frend] VT (*Internet*) quitar de amigo a

unfriendliness ['ʌn'frendlɪnɪs] N hostilidad *f*

unfriendly ['ʌn'frendlɪ] ADJ (COMPAR: **unfriendlier**, SUPERL: **unfriendliest**) [*person*] poco amistoso; (*stronger*) antipático; [*voice*] poco amistoso; [*act, gesture*] poco amistoso; (*stronger*) hostil; [*place, atmosphere*] poco acogedor; [*country, territory*] hostil • **to be ~ to** *or* **towards sb** ser *or* mostrarse antipático *or* poco amistoso con algn

-unfriendly [-ʌn'frendlɪ] SUFFIX • **user-unfriendly** [*software, interface*] difícil de usar; [*instructions*] difícil de entender • **it's couched in such very user-unfriendly terminology** está formulado usando una terminología muy difícil de entender • **environmentally-unfriendly** antiecológico, que daña al medio ambiente

unfrock ['ʌn'frɒk] VT [+ *priest*] secularizar, exclaustrar

unfruitful ['ʌn'fru:tfʊl] ADJ infructuoso

unfulfilled ['ʌnfʊl'fɪld] ADJ **1** (= *unrealized*) [*ambition, hope*] frustrado; [*desire*] no hecho realidad; [*promise*] no cumplido; [*need*] insatisfecho; [*potential*] sin desarrollar
2 (= *dissatisfied*) insatisfecho • **to feel ~** sentirse insatisfecho, no sentirse realizado

unfulfilling ['ʌnfʊl'fɪlɪŋ] ADJ • **he finds his job ~** su trabaja no le llena (lo suficiente), no se siente realizado en su trabajo

unfunded [ʌn'fʌndɪd] ADJ (*Econ*) sin fondos

unfunny* ['ʌn'fʌnɪ] ADJ nada divertido

unfurl [ʌn'fɜ:l] VT desplegar

unfurnished ['ʌn'fɜ:nɪʃt] ADJ sin amueblar

ungainliness [ʌn'geɪnlɪnɪs] N desgarbo *m*, torpeza *f*

ungainly [ʌn'geɪnlɪ] ADJ [*person*] desgarbado; [*animal*] torpe; [*gait*] torpe, desgarbado

ungallant ['ʌn'gælənt] ADJ falto de cortesía, descortés

ungenerous ['ʌn'dʒenərəs] ADJ **1** (= *miserly*) poco generoso
2 (= *uncharitable*) mezquino • **I should not be ~ in my thoughts** no debería tener pensamientos mezquinos

ungentlemanly [ʌn'dʒentlmənlɪ] ADJ poco caballeroso, indigno de un caballero

un-get-at-able* ['ʌnget'ætəbl] ADJ inaccesible

ungifted [ʌn'gɪftɪd] ADJ sin talento

ungird ['ʌn'gɜ:d] (PT, PP: **ungirt**) VT (*liter*) desceñir

unglazed ['ʌn'gleɪzd] ADJ no vidriado; [*window*] sin cristales

unglued ['ʌn'glu:d] ADJ (*US*) = **unstuck**

ungodliness [ʌn'gɒdlɪnɪs] N impiedad *f*

ungodly [ʌn'gɒdlɪ] ADJ **1**† (= *sinful*) [*person, action, life*] impío, irreligioso
2* (= *unreasonable*) [*noise*] tremendo* • **at this ~ hour** a estas horas tan intempestivas

ungovernable [ʌn'gʌvənəbl] ADJ ingobernable; [*temper*] incontrolable, irrefrenable

ungracious ['ʌn'greɪʃəs] ADJ descortés • **it would be ~ to refuse** sería descortés no aceptar

ungraciously ['ʌn'greɪʃəslɪ] ADV descortésmente

ungrammatical ['ʌngrə'mætɪkəl] ADJ incorrecto desde el punto de vista gramatical

ungrammatically ['ʌngrə'mætɪkəlɪ] ADV incorrectamente • **to talk Spanish ~** hablar español con poca corrección

ungrateful [ʌn'greɪtfʊl] ADJ desagradecido, ingrato

ungratefully [ʌn'greɪtfəlɪ] ADV desagradecidamente, con ingratitud

ungrudging ['ʌn'grʌdʒɪŋ] ADJ liberal, generoso; [*support etc*] generoso

ungrudgingly [ʌn'grʌdʒɪŋlɪ] ADV liberalmente, generosamente; [*support etc*] desinteresadamente

unguarded ['ʌn'gɑ:dɪd] ADJ **1** (*Mil etc*) indefenso, sin protección
2 (*fig*) (= *open, careless*) descuidado; (= *thoughtless*) imprudente • **in an ~ moment** en un momento de descuido • **I caught him in an ~ moment** lo pillé *or* (*LAm*) agarré (en un momento en que estaba) desprevenido

unguent ['ʌŋgwənt] (N) ungüento *m*
ungulate ['ʌŋgjʊleɪt] (ADJ) ungulado (N) ungulado *m*
unhallowed [ʌn'hæləʊd] (ADJ) (*liter*) no consagrado
unhampered ['ʌn'hæmpəd] (ADJ) libre, sin estorbos • ~ **by** no estorbado por
unhand†† [ʌn'hænd] (VT) soltar • ~ **me, sir!** ¡suélteme, señor!
unhandy [ʌn'hændɪ] (ADJ) [*person*] desmañado; [*thing*] incómodo • **to be ~ with sth** ser desmañado en el manejo de algo
unhappily [ʌn'hæpɪlɪ] (ADV) **1** (= *miserably*) tristemente, con tristeza • **he stared ~ out of the window** miró tristemente *or* con tristeza por la ventana • **he was ~ married** no fue feliz *or* fue infeliz en su matrimonio
2 (= *unfortunately*) lamentablemente; (*stronger*) desgraciadamente, por desgracia • ~, **his plans didn't work out as he had wished** desgraciadamente *or* por desgracia, los planes no salieron como había deseado
unhappiness [ʌn'hæpɪnɪs] (N) **1** (= *sadness*) desdicha *f*, tristeza *f*; (= *absence of happiness*) infelicidad *f* • **he sensed her pain and ~** notó su dolor y su desdicha *or* tristeza • **I don't want to cause more ~ to you both** no quiero causarles más desdicha a los dos, no quiero ser más motivo de infelicidad para los dos • **the ~ of their marriage was public knowledge** la infelicidad de su matrimonio era del dominio público
2 (= *dissatisfaction*) descontento *m* • **they expressed their ~ with** *or* **over the decision** expresaron su descontento con respecto a la decisión
unhappy [ʌn'hæpɪ] (ADJ) (COMPAR: **unhappier**, SUPERL: **unhappiest**) **1** (= *sad*) [*person*] infeliz; (*stronger*) desdichado; [*childhood*] infeliz; (*stronger*) desgraciado, desdichado; [*marriage*] infeliz; [*memory*] desagradable • **that ~ time** aquella triste época • **I had an ~ time at school** lo pasé muy mal en la escuela • **she was ~ in her marriage** no fue feliz *or* fue infeliz en su matrimonio • **she looked so ~** se la veía tan triste • **don't look so ~!** ¡no pongas esa cara tan triste! • **to make sb ~**: • **other children at school were making him ~** otros niños en el colegio le estaban haciendo sufrir • **it makes me ~ to see you upset** me entristece *or* pone triste verte disgustada
2 (= *not pleased*) descontento • **to be ~ about sth** no estar contento con algo, estar descontento con algo • **to be ~ with sth/sb** no estar contento con algo/algn, estar descontento con algo/algn
3 (= *uneasy, worried*) • **I'm ~ about leaving him on his own** no estoy a gusto dejándolo solo, me preocupa dejarlo solo
4 (= *unfortunate*) [*remark*] poco acertado, inoportuno; [*experience, situation*] lamentable
5 (= *ill-fated*) [*day*] desafortunado
unharmed ['ʌn'hɑːmd] (ADJ) [*person, animal*] ileso; [*thing*] intacto • **the baby was found ~ in a bedroom** encontraron al bebé ileso en un dormitorio • **to escape/be released ~** escapar/ser liberado ileso
unharness ['ʌn'hɑːnɪs] (VT) desguarnecer
UNHCR (N ABBR) (= **United Nations High Commission for Refugees**) ACNUR *m*
unhealthy [ʌn'helθɪ] (ADJ) (COMPAR: **unhealthier**, SUPERL: **unhealthiest**)
1 (= *unwell*) [*person*] poco sano, enfermizo; [*complexion*] poco saludable • **he was an ~-looking fellow** era un tipo de aspecto poco sano *or* de aspecto enfermizo • **my finances are a bit ~ at the moment** no estoy lo que se dice muy boyante de dinero en estos momentos
2 (= *harmful*) [*climate, place, environment*] malsano, insalubre; [*diet, lifestyle, food*] poco sano; [*working conditions*] poco saludable, insalubre
3 (= *unwholesome*) [*interest, fascination, curiosity*] malsano, morboso; [*obsession*] enfermizo, malsano
unheard ['ʌn'hɜːd] (ADJ) **1** (= *ignored*) • **she condemned him ~** lo condenó sin escucharlo • **his pleas went ~** hicieron caso omiso de sus ruegos
2 (= *not heard*) • **his cries went ~** nadie oyó sus gritos • **a previously ~ opera** una ópera inédita
unheard-of [ʌn'hɜːdɒv] (ADJ) (= *unprecedented*) inaudito; (= *outrageous*) escandaloso
unheated ['ʌn'hiːtɪd] (ADJ) sin calefacción
unheeded ['ʌn'hiːdɪd] (ADJ) [*plea, warning*] desatendido • **the warning went ~** la advertencia fue desatendida, no se hizo caso de la advertencia
unheeding ['ʌn'hiːdɪŋ] (ADJ) desatento, sordo • **they passed by ~** pasaron sin prestar atención
unhelpful ['ʌn'helpfʊl] (ADJ) [*person*] poco servicial, poco dispuesto a ayudar; [*remark*] inútil; [*advice*] poco útil • **he didn't want to seem ~** no quería parecer poco servicial *or* poco dispuesto a ayudar • **it is ~ to pretend the problem does not exist** no se consigue nada pretendiendo que el problema no existe • **to be ~ to sth/sb** no ayudar a algo/algn
unhelpfully ['ʌn'helpfʊlɪ] (ADV) [*behave*] con poco espíritu de servicio; [*say, suggest*] con poco ánimo de ayudar
unhelpfulness ['ʌn'helpfʊlnɪs] (N) [*of person*] falta *f* de espíritu de servicio; [*of remark, advice, book, computer*] inutilidad *f*
unheralded ['ʌn'herəldɪd] (ADJ) (= *unannounced*) • **to arrive ~** llegar sin dar aviso
unhesitating [ʌn'hezɪteɪtɪŋ] (ADJ) (= *steadfast, unwavering*) resuelto, decidido; (= *prompt, immediate*) inmediato, pronto
unhesitatingly [ʌn'hezɪteɪtɪŋlɪ] (ADV) sin vacilar • **"yes," she answered ~** —sí —respondió sin vacilar
unhindered ['ʌn'hɪndəd] (ADJ) libre, sin estorbos • ~ **by** no estorbado por
unhinge [ʌn'hɪndʒ] (VT) desquiciar; (*fig*) [+ *mind*] trastornar; [+ *person*] trastornar el juicio de
unhinged ['ʌn'hɪndʒd] (ADJ) (= *mad*) trastornado
unhip* [ˌʌn'hɪp] (ADJ) fuera de onda*, que no está en la onda*
unhistorical ['ʌnhɪs'tɒrɪkəl] (ADJ) antihistórico, que no tiene nada de histórico
unhitch ['ʌn'hɪtʃ] (VT) desenganchar
unholy [ʌn'həʊlɪ] (ADJ) **1** (= *sinful*) [*activity*] impío
2* (= *terrible*) [*mess, row*] tremendo*; [*noise*] tremendo, de mil demonios*
unhook ['ʌn'hʊk] (VT) **1** (= *remove*) desenganchar, descolgar
2 (= *undo*) [+ *garment*] desabrochar
unhoped-for [ʌn'həʊptfɔːʳ] (ADJ) inesperado
unhopeful [ʌn'həʊpfʊl] (ADJ) [*prospect*] poco alentador, poco prometedor; [*person*] pesimista
unhorse ['ʌn'hɔːs] (VT) desarzonar
unhurried ['ʌn'hʌrɪd] (ADJ) [*pace*] pausado, lento; [*atmosphere, person*] tranquilo; [*activity*] tranquilo, pausado • **in an ~ way** de forma pausada
unhurriedly ['ʌn'hʌrɪdlɪ] (ADV) [*walk, speak*] lentamente, pausadamente
unhurt ['ʌn'hɜːt] (ADJ) ileso • **to escape ~** salir ileso
unhygienic ['ʌnhaɪ'dʒiːnɪk] (ADJ) antihigiénico
uni... ['juːnɪ] (PREFIX) uni...
unicameral ['juːnɪ'kæmərəl] (ADJ) unicameral
UNICEF ['juːnɪsef] (N ABBR) (= **United Nations International Children's Emergency Fund**) UNICEF *m*
unicellular ['juːnɪ'seljʊləʳ] (ADJ) unicelular
unicorn ['juːnɪkɔːn] (N) unicornio *m*
unicycle ['juːnɪˌsaɪkl] (N) monociclo *m*
unidentifiable ['ʌnaɪˌdentɪ'faɪəbl] (ADJ) no identificable
unidentified ['ʌnaɪ'dentɪfaɪd] (ADJ) sin identificar, no identificado
(CPD) ▸ **unidentified flying object** objeto *m* volante no identificado
unidiomatic [ˌʌnɪdɪə'mætɪk] (ADJ) nada natural
unidirectional [ˌjuːnɪdɪ'rekʃənl] (ADJ) unidireccional
UNIDO [juːniːdəʊ] (N ABBR) (= **United Nations Industrial Development Organization**) ONUDI *f*
unification [ˌjuːnɪfɪ'keɪʃən] (N) unificación *f*
unified ['juːnɪfaɪd] (ADJ) unificado
uniform ['juːnɪfɔːm] (ADJ) [*shape, size, colour*] uniforme; [*speed*] constante; [*rate, tariff*] fijo, invariable • **a ~ system of payments will be introduced** se introducirá un sistema uniforme de pagos • **to make sth ~** hacer algo uniforme, uniformar algo
(N) uniforme *m* • **school ~** uniforme *m* escolar *or* de colegio • **he was in full ~** llevaba el uniforme completo • **to be in/out of ~** ir con/sin uniforme • **to wear (a) ~** llevar uniforme, ir de uniforme; ▸ **dress**
uniformed ['juːnɪfɔːmd] (ADJ) uniformado, de uniforme
uniformity [ˌjuːnɪ'fɔːmɪtɪ] (N) [*of appearance, colour, standards*] uniformidad *f*; [*of attitudes, beliefs*] homogeneidad *f*
uniformly ['juːnɪfɔːmlɪ] (ADV) [*spread, distributed, applied*] uniformemente • **the book has had ~ bad reviews** el libro obtuvo malas críticas en general
unify ['juːnɪfaɪ] (VT) unificar, unir
unifying ['juːnɪfaɪɪŋ] (ADJ) [*factor etc*] unificador
unilateral ['juːnɪ'lætərəl] (ADJ) unilateral
(CPD) ▸ **unilateral disarmament** desarme *m* unilateral • ~ **nuclear disarmament** desarme *m* nuclear unilateral
unilateralism ['juːnɪ'lætərəlɪzəm] (N) unilateralismo *m*
unilateralist ['juːnɪ'lætərəlɪst] (N) persona *f* que está a favor del desarme unilateral, unilateralista *mf*
unilaterally ['juːnɪ'lætərəlɪ] (ADV) unilateralmente
unilingual [ˌjuːnɪ'lɪŋgwəl] (ADJ) monolingüe
unimaginable [ˌʌnɪ'mædʒɪnəbl] (ADJ) inimaginable, inconcebible
unimaginably [ˌʌnɪ'mædʒɪnəblɪ] (ADV) inimaginablemente, inconcebiblemente
unimaginative ['ʌnɪ'mædʒɪnətɪv] (ADJ) falto de imaginación, poco imaginativo
unimaginatively ['ʌnɪ'mædʒɪnətɪvlɪ] (ADV) de manera poco imaginativa
unimaginativeness ['ʌnɪ'mædʒɪnətɪvnɪs] (N) falta *f* de imaginación
unimpaired ['ʌnɪm'peəd] (ADJ) [*health, eyesight*] en perfectas condiciones; [*relationship*] intacto • **their faith remains ~** su fe no se ha visto afectada
unimpeachable [ˌʌnɪm'piːtʃəbl] (ADJ) irreprochable, intachable • **from an ~ source** de fuente fidedigna

u

unimpeded ['ʌnɪm'piːdɪd] ADJ [*access*] sin impedimentos, sin obstáculos; [*view*] perfecto
ADV sin impedimentos, libremente

unimportant ['ʌnɪm'pɔːtənt] ADJ sin importancia • **they talked of ~ things** hablaron de cosas sin importancia • **the problem itself is relatively ~** el problema en sí tiene relativamente poca importancia

unimposing ['ʌnɪm'pəʊzɪŋ] ADJ (= *not big*) poco impresionante; (= *drab, boring*) con poca gracia

unimpressed ['ʌnɪm'prest] ADJ • **I am ~ by the new building** el nuevo edificio no me impresiona • **she was ~ by Palm Beach** Palm Beach no le impresionó demasiado, Palm Beach la dejó igual* • **they were ~ by such arguments** tales argumentos les resultaron muy poco convincentes • **he remained ~** siguió sin convencerse

unimpressive ['ʌnɪm'presɪv] ADJ poco impresionante, poco convincente; [*person*] soso, insignificante

unimproved [,ʌnɪm'pruːvd] ADJ [*land*] (= *not drained*) sin drenar; (= *not treated*) sin abonar; [*property, house*] sin reformar

uninfluenced ['ʌn'ɪnfluənst] ADJ • **~ by any argument** no afectado por ningún argumento • **a style ~ by any other** un estilo no influido por ningún otro

uninformative ['ʌnɪn'fɔːmətɪv] ADJ poco informativo

uninformed ['ʌnɪn'fɔːmd] ADJ [*comment, rumour, criticism*] infundado; [*attitudes, prejudice*] ignorante • **I did not want to appear ~** no quería parecer ignorante • **well-meaning but ~ people** personas *fpl* de buenas intenciones pero sin conocimientos • **to be ~ about sth** no estar informado sobre algo, no estar al corriente *or* al tanto de algo • **he could not claim that he was ~ about the law** no podía afirmar que no estaba informado sobre la ley, no podía afirmar que no estaba al corriente *or* al tanto de la ley • **people are generally very ~ about the disease** la gente en general está muy poco informada sobre la enfermedad • **the ~ observer** el observador profano

uninhabitable ['ʌnɪn'hæbɪtəbl] ADJ inhabitable

uninhabited ['ʌnɪn'hæbɪtɪd] ADJ (= *deserted*) desierto, despoblado; [*house*] desocupado

uninhibited ['ʌnɪn'hɪbɪtɪd] ADJ [*person*] desinhibido, sin inhibiciones; [*behaviour*] desinhibido, desenfadado; [*emotion*] desbordante • **to be ~ by sth** no estar inhibido por algo, no tener inhibiciones con respecto a algo • **to be ~ in one's questions** hacer preguntas sin inhibiciones • **to be ~ in doing sth** no tener inhibiciones para hacer algo • **to be ~ about doing sth** no tener inhibiciones a la hora de hacer algo

uninitiated ['ʌnɪ'nɪʃɪeɪtɪd] ADJ no iniciado
NPL • **the ~** los no iniciados

uninjured ['ʌn'ɪndʒəd] ADJ ileso • **to escape ~** salir ileso

uninspired ['ʌnɪn'spaɪəd] ADJ [*person*] poco inspirado, sin inspiración; [*book, film, performance*] sin inspiración, falto de inspiración; [*food*] poco original

uninspiring ['ʌnɪn'spaɪərɪŋ] ADJ [*person, film, book, play*] poco estimulante, aburrido; [*view*] monótono

uninstall [,ʌnɪn'stɔːl] VT (*Comput*) [+ *program*] desinstalar

uninsured ['ʌnɪn'ʃʊəd] ADJ no asegurado

unintelligent ['ʌnɪn'telɪdʒənt] ADJ poco inteligente

unintelligibility ['ʌnɪn,telɪdʒə'bɪlɪtɪ] N ininteligibilidad *f*, incomprensibilidad *f*

unintelligible ['ʌnɪn'telɪdʒəbl] ADJ ininteligible, incomprensible • **she mumbled something ~** balbuceó algo ininteligible *or* incomprensible

unintelligibly ['ʌnɪn'telɪdʒəblɪ] ADV de modo ininteligible, de modo incomprensible

unintended ['ʌnɪn'tendɪd], **unintentional** ['ʌnɪn'tenʃənl] ADJ involuntario, no intencionado • **it was quite ~** fue totalmente involuntario

unintentionally ['ʌnɪn'tenʃnəlɪ] ADV sin querer, involuntariamente

uninterested [ʌn'ɪntrɪstɪd] ADJ (= *indifferent*) indiferente, desinteresado • **I am quite ~ in what he thinks** me es igual *or* indiferente lo que piensa • **to be ~ in a subject** no tener interés en un tema

uninteresting ['ʌn'ɪntrɪstɪŋ] ADJ [*person, book, film, speech*] poco interesante; [*city, building*] sin interés

uninterrupted ['ʌn,ɪntə'rʌptɪd] ADJ ininterrumpido

uninterruptedly ['ʌn,ɪntə'rʌptɪdlɪ] ADV ininterrumpidamente

uninvited ['ʌnɪn'vaɪtɪd] ADJ [*guest etc*] sin invitación; [*criticism, comment*] gratuito • **to do sth ~** hacer algo sin que nadie se lo pida • **they came to the party ~** vinieron a la fiesta sin haber sido invitados • **she helped herself ~ to cake** se sirvió pastel sin esperar que le ofreciesen

uninviting ['ʌnɪn'vaɪtɪŋ] ADJ [*appearance, offer*] poco atractivo; [*food*] poco apetitoso

union ['juːnjən] N **1** unión *f*; (= *marriage*) enlace *m* • **the Union** (*US*) la Unión
2 (= *trade union*) sindicato *m*, gremio *m*
3 (= *club, society*) club *m*, sociedad *f*
4 (*Mech*) (*for pipes etc*) unión *f*, manguito *m* de unión
CPD (*Ind*) [*leader, movement, headquarters*] sindical ▸ **union card** carnet *m* de afiliado ▸ **union catalog(ue)** catálogo *m* colectivo *or* conjunto ▸ **Union Jack** bandera *f* del Reino Unido ▸ **union member** miembro *mf* del sindicato, sindicalista *mf* ▸ **union membership** (= *numbers*) afiliados *mpl* al sindicato • **~ membership has declined** el número de afiliados a los sindicatos ha disminuido; (= *being a member*) afiliación *f* a un/al sindicato • **~ membership is compulsory** es obligatorio afiliarse a *or* hacerse miembro del sindicato ▸ **Union of Soviet Socialist Republics** (*formerly*) Unión *f* de Repúblicas Socialistas Soviéticas ▸ **Union of South Africa** (*formerly*) Unión *f* Sudafricana ▸ **union shop** (*US*) taller *m* de afiliación (sindical) obligatoria ▸ **union suit** (*US*) prenda *f* interior de cuerpo entero

unionism ['juːnjənɪzəm] N **1** (*Ind*) sindicalismo *m*
2 • **Unionism** (*Brit*) (*Pol*) unionismo *m*

unionist ['juːnjənɪst] ADJ (*Brit*) (*Pol*) unionista
N **1** (*Ind*) (*also* **trade unionist**) sindicalista *mf*, miembro *mf* de un sindicato
2 • **Unionist** (*Brit*) (*Pol*) unionista *mf*

unionization [,juːnjənaɪ'zeɪʃən] N sindicación *f*, sindicalización *f*

unionize ['juːnjənaɪz] VT sindicar, sindicalizar
VI sindicarse, sindicalizarse

unique [juː'niːk] ADJ **1** (= *exclusive*) [*style, collection, combination*] único • **to be ~ to sth/sb: it is a species ~ to these islands** es una especie que se da únicamente en estas islas • **the experience is ~ to each individual** la experiencia es única (e irrepetible) en cada individuo • **this behaviour is not ~ to men** este comportamiento no se da únicamente en los hombres
2 (= *exceptional*) [*opportunity*] único; [*ability, talent*] sin igual, excepcional; [*insight*] único, de excepción; [*relationship*] especial
CPD ▸ **unique selling point** argumento *m* de venta diferenciador, proposición *f* única de venta

uniquely [juː'niːklɪ] ADV • **she is ~ qualified for the job** está excepcionalmente capacitada para el puesto • **to be ~ placed to do sth** encontrarse en una posición de excepción para hacer algo • **a ~ British characteristic** una característica exclusivamente británica

uniqueness [juː'niːknɪs] N singularidad *f*

unisex ['juːnɪseks] ADJ unisex (*inv*)

UNISON ['juːnɪsn] N ABBR (*Brit*) *gran sindicato de funcionarios*

unison ['juːnɪzn] N armonía *f*; (*Mus*) unisonancia *f* • **in ~** (*Mus*) al unísono • **to sing in ~** cantar al unísono • **to act in ~ with sb** obrar al unísono con algn • **"yes," they said in ~** —sí —dijeron al unísono

unissued ['ʌn'ɪʃuːd] ADJ • **~ capital** capital *m* no emitido

unit ['juːnɪt] N **1** (*Admin, Elec, Mech, Math, Mil*) unidad *f*; (*Univ*) (*for marking purposes*) unidad *f* de valor; (*Tech*) (= *mechanism*) conjunto *m* • **administrative/linguistic/monetary ~** unidad *f* administrativa/lingüística/monetaria • **~ of account** unidad *f* de cuenta • **a ~ of measurement** una unidad de medida
2 (= *complete section, part*) [*of textbook*] módulo *m*, unidad *f*; (= *device*) aparato *m* • **a kitchen ~** un módulo de cocina
3 (= *building*) • **intensive care ~** unidad *f* de cuidados intensivos • **sports ~** polideportivo *m* • **the shop ~s remain unlet** los locales comerciales siguen sin traspasarse • **the staff accommodation ~** las viviendas de los empleados
4 (= *group of people*) unidad *f*; (*in firm*) centro *m* • **army ~** unidad *f* militar • **research/information ~** centro *m* de investigación/información • **family ~** núcleo *m* familiar, familia *f*
CPD ▸ **unit charge, unit cost** (*Brit*) (*Econ*) costo *m* unitario *or* por unidad ▸ **unit furniture** muebles *mpl* de elementos adicionables, muebles *mpl* combinados ▸ **unit price** precio *m* unitario *or* por unidad ▸ **unit trust** (*Brit*) (*Econ*) (= *fund*) fondo *m* de inversión mobiliaria; (= *company*) sociedad *f* de inversiones

UNITA [juː'niːtə] N ABBR (= **União Nacional para a Independencia Total de Angola**) UNITA *f*, Unita *f*

Unitarian [,juːnɪ'tɛərɪən] ADJ unitario
N unitario/a *m/f*

Unitarianism [,juːnɪ'tɛərɪənɪzəm] N unitarismo *m*

unitary ['juːnɪtərɪ] ADJ unitario
CPD ▸ **unitary labour costs** costes *mpl* laborales unitarios

unite [juː'naɪt] VT (= *join*) [+ *people, organizations*] unir; [+ *parts of country*] unificar, unir
VI unirse • **to ~ against sb** unirse para hacer frente a algn • **we must ~ in defence of our rights** debemos unirnos para defender nuestros derechos

united [juː'naɪtɪd] ADJ [*country, group*] unido; [*effort*] conjunto • **they were ~ by a common enemy** los unía un enemigo común • **to present a ~ front (to sb)** presentar un frente unido (ante algn) • **to be ~ in sth**: • **the family was ~ in grief** la familia estaba unida por el dolor • **they are**

~ in their belief that ... comparten la creencia de que ... • **they are ~ in their opposition to the plan** los une su oposición al plan • **we are ~ on the need to solve the problem** compartimos la necesidad de resolver el problema • PROVERB: • **~ we stand, divided we fall** unidos venceremos
CPD ▸ **United Arab Emirates** Emiratos *mpl* Árabes Unidos ▸ **United Arab Republic** República *f* Árabe Unida ▸ **United Kingdom** Reino *m* Unido (*Inglaterra, Gales, Escocia, Irlanda del Norte*) ▸ **United Nations (Organization)** (Organización *f* de las) Naciones *fpl* Unidas ▸ **United States (of America)** Estados *mpl* Unidos (de América)

unity ['ju:nɪtɪ] N (= *oneness*) unidad *f*; (= *harmony*) armonía *f*, acuerdo *m* • **~ of place** unidad *f* de lugar • **~ of time** unidad *f* de tiempo • PROVERB: • **~ is strength** la unión hace la fuerza

Univ. ABBR (= **University**) U

univalent [ˈju:nɪ'veɪlənt] ADJ univalente

univalve ['ju:nɪvælv] ADJ univalvo
N molusco *m* univalvo

universal [ˌju:nɪ'vɜ:səl] ADJ **1** (= *general*) [*agreement, acceptance*] general, global • **the closures met with ~ condemnation** los cierres provocaron la condena general *or* unánime • **its use has been ~ since 1900** se usa en todas partes *or* globalmente desde 1900 • **her writing has ~ appeal** su forma de escribir atrae a todo el mundo • **a ~ truth** una verdad universal, una verdad aceptada por todos *or* por todo el mundo • **to become ~** generalizarse
2 (= *worldwide*) [*law, language*] universal • **the threat of ~ destruction** la amenaza de la destrucción mundial
CPD ▸ **universal donor** donante *mf* universal ▸ **universal joint** (*Tech*) junta *f* cardán *or* universal ▸ **universal product code** (*US*) código *m* de barras ▸ **universal suffrage** sufragio *m* universal

universality [ˌju:nɪvɜ:'sælɪtɪ] N universalidad *f*

universalize [ˌju:nɪ'vɜ:səlaɪz] VT universalizar

universally [ˌju:nɪ'vɜ:səlɪ] ADV [*accepted, acknowledged*] universalmente, generalmente; [*popular, available*] en todas partes; [*known*] mundialmente; [*applicable*] para todo; [*condemned*] unánimemente • **there is no ~ accepted definition** no existe una definición aceptada universalmente *or* generalmente aceptada • **he was ~ liked** caía bien a todo el mundo, todo el mundo lo apreciaba

universe ['ju:nɪvɜ:s] N universo *m* • **he's the funniest writer in the ~*** es el escritor más divertido del mundo

university [ˌju:nɪ'vɜ:sɪtɪ] N universidad *f* • **to be at ~** estar en la universidad • **to go to ~** ir a la universidad • **to study at ~** estudiar en la universidad • **a ~ place** una plaza universitaria • **he has a ~ education** ha cursado estudios universitarios • **Lancaster University** la Universidad de Lancaster
CPD [*degree, year, professor, student*] universitario; [*library*] de la universidad ▸ **university degree** título *m* universitario ▸ **university entrance** acceso *m* a la universidad • **~ entrance examination** examen *m* de ingreso a la universidad ▸ **university faculty** facultad *f* universitaria ▸ **university fees** matrícula *fsing* universitaria ▸ **university hospital** hospital *m* universitario ▸ **university student** estudiante *mf* universitario/a, universitario(a) *m/f* ▸ **university town** ciudad *f* que tiene universidad

unjust ['ʌn'dʒʌst] ADJ injusto • **she had been so ~** había sido muy injusta • **to be ~ to sb** ser injusto con algn

unjustifiable [ʌn'dʒʌstɪfaɪəbl] ADJ injustificable

unjustifiably [ʌn'dʒʌstɪfaɪəblɪ] ADV injustificadamente • **they have been ~ treated by the media** los medios de comunicación los han tratado injustificadamente *or* de forma injustificada

unjustified ['ʌn'dʒʌstɪfaɪd] ADJ **1** (= *unfair*) [*action, attack, reputation*] injustificado • **he described their action as inappropriate and ~** calificó su acción de impropia e injustificada
2 (*Typ*) [*text*] no alineado, no justificado

unjustly ['ʌn'dʒʌstlɪ] ADV injustamente • **they had ~ accused him of lying** lo habían acusado injustamente de mentir

unkempt ['ʌn'kempt] ADJ [*clothes, appearance*] descuidado, desaliñado; [*hair*] despeinado, descuidado; [*beard, garden, park*] descuidado

unkind [ʌn'kaɪnd] ADJ (COMPAR: **unkinder**, SUPERL: **unkindest**) **1** (= *cruel, nasty*) [*person*] poco amable; (*stronger*) cruel; [*criticism*] duro; [*remark*] cruel; [*words*] desagradable • **that was very ~ of him** eso fue muy poco amable de su parte • **I've never known him to be ~** nunca ha sido desagradable, que yo sepa • **she never has an ~ word to say about anyone** nunca dice nada malo de nadie • **it would be ~ to say that ...** sería cruel decir que ... • **to be ~ to sb** portarse mal con algn
2 [*climate*] riguroso • **the weather was ~ to us** el tiempo nos jugó una mala pasada

unkindly [ʌn'kaɪndlɪ] ADV [*say, behave*] cruelmente, con crueldad • **it wasn't meant ~** no iba con malas intenciones • **to speak ~ of sb** hablar mal de algn • **don't take it ~ if ...** no lo tome a mal si ... • **to treat sb ~** tratar con poca amabilidad a algn; (*stronger*) tratar mal a algn

unkindness [ʌn'kaɪndnɪs] N **1** (= *quality*) falta *f* de amabilidad; (= *cruelty*) crueldad *f*
2 (= *act*) acto *m* de crueldad • **to do sb an ~** portarse mal con algn

unknowable ['ʌn'nəʊəbl] ADJ (*esp liter*) inconocible • **the ~** lo inconocible

unknowing ['ʌn'nəʊɪŋ] ADJ inconsciente • **she was the ~ cause** ella fue la causa, inconscientemente

unknowingly ['ʌn'nəʊɪŋlɪ] ADV (= *involuntarily*) inconscientemente, sin querer; (= *in ignorance*) sin darse cuenta, sin saberlo • **he did it all ~** lo hizo sin darse cuenta

unknown ['ʌn'nəʊn] ADJ [*identity, destination, territory, writer*] desconocido • **the Cazorla Sierra is almost ~ outside Spain** la sierra de Cazorla casi no se conoce fuera de España • **it's ~ for him to refuse a sweet** nunca ha dicho que no a un caramelo que se sepa • **it's not ~ for him to be wrong** (*iro*) no es precisamente que no se haya equivocado nunca (*iro*) • **she's a bit of an ~ quantity** ella es una incógnita • **for some ~ reason** por alguna razón desconocida • **the Unknown Soldier** el soldado desconocido • **to be ~ to sb**: • **the name is ~ to me** el nombre no me resulta conocido • **a substance ~ to science** una sustancia no conocida por la ciencia, una sustancia que la ciencia desconoce; ▹ **person**
ADV • **~ to me** si yo saberlo
N (= *person*) desconocido/a *m/f*; (*Math*) (*also fig*) incógnita *f* • **the ~** lo desconocido • **a journey into the ~** un viaje a lo desconocido

unlabelled, unlabeled (*US*) [ʌn'leɪbld] ADJ sin etiquetar

unlace ['ʌn'leɪs] VT desenlazar; [+ *shoes*] desatar los cordones de

unladen ['ʌn'leɪdn] ADJ vacío, sin cargamento

unladylike ['ʌn'leɪdɪlaɪk] ADJ impropio de una dama

unlamented ['ʌnlə'mentɪd] ADJ no llorado, no lamentado

unlatch ['ʌn'lætʃ] VT [+ *door*] alzar el pestillo de, abrir levantando el picaporte de

unlawful ['ʌn'lɔ:fʊl] ADJ ilegal, ilícito

unlawfully ['ʌn'lɔ:fəlɪ] ADV ilegalmente, ilícitamente

unleaded [ˌʌn'ledɪd] ADJ [*petrol*] sin plomo
N gasolina *f* sin plomo

unlearn ['ʌn'lɜ:n] (PT, PP: **unlearned** *or* **unlearnt**) VT desaprender, olvidar

unlearned ['ʌn'lɜ:nɪd] ADJ indocto, ignorante

unleash ['ʌn'li:ʃ] VT [+ *dog*] desatar, soltar; (*fig*) [+ *anger, imagination etc*] desencadenar, desatar

unleavened ['ʌn'levnd] ADJ ázimo, sin levadura
CPD ▸ **unleavened bread** pan *m* ázimo *or* sin levadura

unless [ən'les] CONJ a menos que (+ *subjun*), a no ser que (+ *subjun*) • **~ he comes tomorrow** a menos que venga mañana, a no ser que venga mañana • **~ I hear to the contrary** a menos que me digan lo contrario, a no ser que me digan lo contrario • **I won't come ~ you phone me** no vendré a menos que me llames, no vendré a no ser que me llames • **~ I am mistaken, we're lost** si no me equivoco, estamos perdidos • **~ otherwise stated** de no especificarse lo contrario

unlettered ['ʌn'letəd] ADJ indocto

unlicensed ['ʌn'laɪsənst] ADJ sin permiso, sin licencia

unlike ['ʌn'laɪk] PREP a diferencia de • **~ him, I really enjoy flying** a diferencia de él, a mí me encanta viajar en avión • **I, ~ others ...** yo, a diferencia de otros ... • **it's quite ~ him** no es nada característico de él • **the photo is quite ~ him** la foto no se le parece en absoluto
ADJ distinto; (*Math*) de signo contrario • **they are quite ~** son muy distintos, no se parecen en nada

unlikeable ['ʌn'laɪkəbl] ADJ antipático

unlikelihood [ʌn'laɪklɪhʊd], **unlikeliness** [ʌn'laɪklɪnɪs] N improbabilidad *f*

unlikely [ʌn'laɪklɪ] ADJ (COMPAR: **unlikelier**, SUPERL: **unlikeliest**) **1** (= *improbable*) poco probable, improbable • **it is most ~** es muy poco probable • **he is an ~ candidate for promotion** no tiene muchas probabilidades de que lo asciendan • **it is ~ that he will come** • **he is ~ to come** es poco probable que venga, no es probable que venga • **he's ~ to survive** tiene pocas posibilidades de sobrevivir, es poco probable que sobreviva • **in the ~ event that we win** en el caso improbable de que ganáramos, en el caso de que ganáramos, lo cual es poco probable
2 (= *implausible*) [*explanation, excuse*] inverosímil, increíble • **that sounds an ~ story** me parece una historia inverosímil
3 (= *odd*) insólito, extraño • **he and Paula made an ~ couple** *or* **pair** él y Paula hacían una pareja insólita *or* extraña • **they turn up in the most ~ places** aparecen en los lugares más insospechados *or* extraños

unlimited [ʌn'lɪmɪtɪd] ADJ [*travel, amount, access, use*] ilimitado; [*patience*] inagotable • **we have not got ~ funds** no tenemos fondos ilimitados • **they had ~ time** no tenían límite de tiempo

u

CPD ▸ **unlimited company** (*Comm, Jur*) compañía *f* ilimitada ▸ **unlimited liability** (*Comm, Jur*) responsabilidad *f* ilimitada ▸ **unlimited mileage** ≈ kilometraje *m* ilimitado

unlined [ˈʌnˈlaɪnd] ADJ **1** (= *without lines*) [*paper*] sin pautar; [*face*] sin arrugas
2 (= *without lining*) [*garment, curtain*] sin forro

unlisted [ˈʌnˈlɪstɪd] ADJ **1** (*St Ex*) • **~ company** sociedad *f* sin cotización oficial, compañía *f* no cotizable • **~ securities** valores *mpl* no inscritos en bolsa
2 (*US*) (*Telec*) • **~ number** número *m* que no figura en la guía telefónica
3 • **~ building** (*Brit*) *edificio no catalogado como de interés histórico o arquitectónico*

unlit [ˈʌnˈlɪt] ADJ **1** (= *not burning*) [*fire, cigarette, pipe*] sin encender, apagado
2 (= *dark*) [*place*] no iluminado, oscuro

unload [ˈʌnˈləʊd] VT **1** descargar • **we ~ed the furniture** descargamos los muebles
2* (= *get rid of*) deshacerse de
VI descargar

unloaded [ˈʌnˈləʊdɪd] ADJ [*gun*] descargado; [*truck, ship*] descargado, sin carga

unloading [ˈʌnˈləʊdɪŋ] N descarga *f*

unlock [ˈʌnˈlɒk] VT **1** [+ *door, box*] abrir (con llave) • **the door is ~ed** la puerta no está cerrada con llave • **he ~ed the door of the car** abrió la puerta del coche
2 (*fig*) [+ *heart*] ganarse; [+ *mystery*] resolver; [+ *secret*] descubrir; [+ *potential*] liberar
VI [*lock, box, door*] abrirse

unlooked-for [ʌnˈlʊktfɔːʳ] ADJ inesperado, inopinado

unloose [ˈʌnˈluːs], **unloosen** [ˈʌnˈluːsn] VT aflojar, soltar

unlovable [ˈʌnˈlʌvəbl] ADJ antipático

unloved [ˈʌnˈlʌvd] ADJ no amado • **to feel ~** sentirse rechazado

unlovely [ˈʌnˈlʌvlɪ] ADJ feo, sin atractivo

unloving [ˈʌnˈlʌvɪŋ] ADJ nada cariñoso

unluckily [ʌnˈlʌkɪlɪ] ADV lamentablemente, desgraciadamente • **~, she herself had no creative talent** lamentablemente *or* desgraciadamente, ella no tenía talento creativo • **~ for her** lamentablemente *or* desgraciadamente para ella • **the day started ~** el día empezó sin suerte

unluckiness [ʌnˈlʌkɪnɪs] N mala suerte *f*

unlucky [ʌnˈlʌkɪ] ADJ (COMPAR: **unluckier**, SUPERL: **unluckiest**) **1** (= *luckless*) [*person*] desafortunado; [*day*] de mala suerte • **the ~ ones had to wait another hour** los menos afortunados tuvieron que esperar otra hora • **how very ~!** ¡qué mala suerte! • **to be ~** [*person*] tener mala suerte • **he was ~ enough to meet him** tuvo la mala suerte *or* la desgracia de encontrarse con él • **to be ~ in love** no tener suerte en el amor • **he was ~ not to score a second goal** no tuvo la suerte de marcar un segundo gol
2 (= *causing bad luck*) [*number, object*] que trae mala suerte • **that dress is ~ for me** ese vestido me trae mala suerte • **it's ~ to break a mirror** romper un espejo trae mala suerte
3 (= *ill-omened*) [*day, omen*] funesto, nefasto • **1990 was an ~ year for me** 1990 fue un año de mala suerte para mí

unmade [ˈʌnˈmeɪd] ADJ [*bed*] sin hacer; (*Brit*) (= *unsurfaced*) [*road*] sin pavimentar, sin asfaltar

unmake [ˈʌnˈmeɪk] (PT, PP: **unmade**) VT deshacer

unman [ˈʌnˈmæn] VT **1** (*liter*) amedrentar (*liter*), acobardar
2 [+ *post etc*] desguarnecer

unmanageable [ʌnˈmænɪdʒəbl] ADJ
1 (= *overwhelming*) [*problem, system, situation, size, number*] imposible de controlar; [*hair*] difícil de peinar, rebelde
2 (= *unruly*) [*person*] rebelde; [*animal*] difícil de controlar, rebelde

unmanly [ˈʌnˈmænlɪ] ADJ impropio de un hombre • **it is ~ to cry** los hombres no lloran, llorar no es propio de un hombre

unmanned [ˈʌnˈmænd] ADJ no tripulado

unmannerly [ʌnˈmænəlɪ] ADJ (*frm*) descortés

unmarked [ˈʌnˈmɑːkt] ADJ **1** (= *unscratched*) [*person*] sin ningún rasguño; [*face*] sin señales
2 (= *anonymous*) [*grave*] sin nombre; [*police car*] particular, camuflado (*Sp*); [*container, envelope*] sin marcar
3 (*Educ*) (= *uncorrected*) [*essay, exam etc*] sin corregir
4 (*Sport*) [*player*] desmarcado
5 (*Ling*) no marcado

unmarketable [ˈʌnˈmɑːkɪtəbl] ADJ invendible

unmarriageable [ˈʌnˈmærɪdʒəbl] ADJ incasable

unmarried [ˈʌnˈmærɪd] ADJ soltero • **an ~ mother** una madre soltera • **an ~ couple** una pareja no casada • **the ~ state** el estado de soltero, la soltería

unmask [ˈʌnˈmɑːsk] VT (*lit, fig*) desenmascarar
VI quitarse la máscara, descubrirse

unmasking [ʌnˈmɑːskɪŋ] N (*fig*) desenmascaramiento *m*

unmast [ˈʌnˈmɑːst] VT desarbolar

unmatched [ˈʌnˈmætʃt] ADJ incomparable, sin par

unmemorable [ˈʌnˈmemərəbəl] ADJ nada memorable, indigno de ser recordado

unmentionable [ʌnˈmenʃnəbl] ADJ que no se puede *or* quiere mencionar *or* nombrar
NPL **unmentionables**† (*hum*) prendas *fpl* íntimas

unmerciful [ʌnˈmɜːsɪfʊl] ADJ despiadado

unmercifully [ʌnˈmɜːsɪfəlɪ] ADV despiadadamente

unmerited [ˈʌnˈmerɪtɪd] ADJ inmerecido

unmet [ʌnˈmet] ADJ [*needs, demands*] insatisfecho • **basic needs that are going ~** necesidades *fpl* básicas que no están siendo satisfechas

unmetered [ʌnˈmiːtəd] ADJ [*access*] ilimitado; [*supply*] sin contador

unmethodical [ˈʌnmɪˈθɒdɪkəl] ADJ poco metódico, desordenado

unmindful [ʌnˈmaɪndfʊl] ADJ • **to be ~ of sth** no hacer caso de algo, hacer caso omiso de algo • **~ of the danger, he ...** él, haciendo caso omiso del peligro ...

unmissable* [ˌʌnˈmɪsəbəl] ADJ (*Brit*) [*event, film*] que no se puede perder, que hay que ver/coger *etc* • **it was an ~ chance/ opportunity** era una oportunidad que no podía/podíamos perder, era una oportunidad que había que coger

unmistakable [ˈʌnmɪsˈteɪkəbl] ADJ inconfundible, inequívoco

unmistakably [ˈʌnmɪsˈteɪkəblɪ] ADV de modo inconfundible • **it is ~ mine** sin duda alguna es mío

unmitigated [ʌnˈmɪtɪgeɪtɪd] ADJ [*disaster, failure*] auténtico, verdadero; [*success*] rotundo; [*delight*] puro, verdadero; [*nonsense*] puro; [*liar, rogue*] redomado, rematado • **it was an ~ disaster** fue un auténtico *or* verdadero desastre

unmixed [ˈʌnˈmɪkst] ADJ sin mezcla, puro

unmodified [ʌnˈmɒdɪfaɪd] ADJ sin modificar

unmolested [ˈʌnməˈlestɪd] ADJ tranquilo, seguro • **to do sth ~** hacer algo sin ser molestado por otros

unmotivated [ˈʌnˈməʊtɪveɪtɪd] ADJ sin motivo, inmotivado

unmounted [ˈʌnˈmaʊntɪd] ADJ **1** (= *without horse*) [*rider*] desmontado
2 (= *without mounting*) [*gem*] sin engastar; [*photo, stamp*] sin pegar; [*picture*] sin enmarcar

unmourned [ˈʌnˈmɔːnd] ADJ no llorado

unmoved [ˈʌnˈmuːvd] ADJ impasible • **to remain ~ by** seguir indiferente ante, permanecer impasible frente a • **it leaves me ~** no me conmueve, me deja frío

unmoving [ˈʌnˈmuːvɪŋ] ADJ inmóvil

unmusical [ˈʌnˈmjuːzɪkəl] ADJ [*sound, rendition*] inarmónico; [*person*] poco musical, sin oído para la música

unmuzzle [ˌʌnˈmʌzl] VT [+ *dog*] quitar el bozal a; (*fig*) [+ *press etc*] quitar la mordaza a • **~d** sin bozal; (*fig*) libre, sin mordaza

unnamed [ˈʌnˈneɪmd] ADJ (= *nameless*) sin nombre; (= *anonymous*) anónimo

unnatural [ʌnˈnætʃrəl] ADJ **1** (= *unusual, abnormal*) poco normal, poco natural • **her arm was twisted into an ~ position** tenía el brazo torcido en una postura poco normal *or* natural • **it was ~ for her to be so talkative** era extraño *or* raro en ella hablar tanto • **it's ~ to eat so much** no es normal comer tanto • **~ death** muerte *f* por causas no naturales • **it is not ~ to think that ...** es normal pensar que ... • **there was an ~ silence** se hizo un silencio irreal
2 (= *affected*) [*smile, voice, manner*] poco natural, forzado
3 (= *perverted*) [*habit, vice, practice*] antinatural

unnaturally [ʌnˈnætʃrəlɪ] ADV
1 (= *unusually, abnormally*) extrañamente • **she was ~ subdued that day** estaba extrañamente apagada aquel día • **not ~, he was cross** como es natural *or* lógico se enfadó
2 (= *affectedly*) [*speak, act*] de manera poco natural, afectadamente

unnavigable [ˈʌnˈnævɪgəbl] ADJ innavegable

unnecessarily [ʌnˈnesɪsərɪlɪ] ADV innecesariamente, sin necesidad • **I don't want him to suffer ~** no quiero que sufra innecesariamente *or* sin necesidad

unnecessary [ʌnˈnesɪsərɪ] ADJ innecesario • **it is ~ to add that ...** no hace falta añadir que ..., no es necesario añadir que ...

unneighbourly, unneighborly (*US*) [ˈʌnˈneɪbəlɪ] ADJ [*person*] poco amistoso; [*attitude, behaviour*] impropio de un buen vecino

unnerve [ˈʌnˈnɜːv] VT desconcertar

unnerving [ˈʌnˈnɜːvɪŋ] ADJ desconcertante

unnervingly [ʌnˈnɜːvɪŋlɪ] ADV • **~ quiet/calm** de una frialdad/calma desconcertante

unnoticed [ˈʌnˈnəʊtɪst] ADJ inadvertido, desapercibido • **to go** *or* **pass ~** pasar inadvertido *or* desapercibido

unnumbered [ˈʌnˈnʌmbəd] ADJ sin numerar; (= *countless*) innumerable

UNO N ABBR (= **United Nations Organization**) ONU *f*

unobjectionable [ˈʌnəbˈdʒekʃnəbl] ADJ inofensivo

unobservant [ˈʌnəbˈzɜːvənt] ADJ [*person etc*] distraído, poco atento

unobserved [ˈʌnəbˈzɜːvd] ADJ **1** (= *not seen*) inadvertido, desapercibido • **to get away ~** lograr pasar inadvertido *or* desapercibido
2 (= *not celebrated*) sin celebrar *or* (*LAm*) festejar

unobstructed [ˈʌnəbˈstrʌktɪd] ADJ [*pipe etc*] despejado; [*view etc*] perfecto

unobtainable [ˈʌnəbˈteɪnəbl] ADJ
1 (= *unavailable*) [*goods*] imposible de conseguir
2 (= *unrealizable*) [*goal, objective*] inalcanzable, imposible de conseguir *or* realizar
3 (*Telec*) [*number*] desconectado • **his number was ~** su número estaba desconectado
4 (*sexually*) [*person*] imposible de conseguir
unobtrusive [ˈʌnəbˈtruːsɪv] ADJ discreto, modesto
unobtrusively [ˈʌnəbˈtruːsɪvlɪ] ADV discretamente, modestamente
unoccupied [ˈʌnˈɒkjʊpaɪd] ADJ 1 (= *empty*) [*building*] desocupado, vacío; [*room*] vacío; [*seat, table*] libre; [*post*] vacante
2 (*Mil*) [*country, zone*] no ocupado
3 (= *not busy*) [*person*] desocupado
unofficial [ˈʌnəˈfɪʃəl] ADJ 1 (= *informal*) [*visit, tour*] no oficial, extraoficial • **in an ~ capacity** de forma *or* manera extraoficial *or* no oficial • **from an ~ source** de fuente oficiosa • **~ strike** huelga *f* no oficial
2 (= *de facto*) [*leader, spokesperson*] no oficial
3 (= *unconfirmed*) [*report, results*] no oficial
unofficially [ˈʌnəˈfɪʃəlɪ] ADV extraoficialmente • **I have already asked him ~** ya le he preguntado extraoficialmente
unopened [ˈʌnˈəʊpənd] ADJ sin abrir
unopposed [ˈʌnəˈpəʊzd] ADJ sin oposición; (*Mil*) sin encontrar resistencia • **to be returned ~** (*Parl*) ganar un escaño sin oposición
unorganized [ˈʌnˈɔːgənaɪzd] ADJ (= *spontaneous*) no organizado; (= *untidy*) desorganizado
unoriginal [ˈʌnəˈrɪdʒɪnəl] ADJ poco original
unorthodox [ˈʌnˈɔːθədɒks] ADJ
1 (= *unconventional*) poco ortodoxo, poco convencional
2 (*Rel*) heterodoxo
unostentatious [ˈʌnˌɒstenˈteɪʃəs] ADJ modesto, sin ostentación
unpack [ˈʌnˈpæk] VT deshacer, desempacar (*LAm*) • **I ~ed my suitcase** deshice la maleta • **I haven't ~ed my clothes yet** todavía no he sacado la ropa de la maleta
VI deshacer las maletas, desempacar (*LAm*) • **I went to my room to ~** fui a mi habitación a deshacer la(s) maleta(s)
unpacking [ˈʌnˈpækɪŋ] N • **to do one's ~** deshacer las maletas, desempacar (*LAm*)
unpaid [ˈʌnˈpeɪd] ADJ [*staff, worker, overtime*] no remunerado, no retribuido; [*leave*] sin paga, sin sueldo; [*debts, bills*] sin pagar, pendiente; [*taxes, rent*] sin pagar
unpalatable [ʌnˈpælɪtəbl] ADJ 1 (*in taste*) [*food*] de mal sabor
2 (*fig*) (= *difficult*) [*truth, fact*] difícil de aceptar
unparalleled [ʌnˈpærəleld] ADJ [*opportunity, prosperity, event*] sin precedentes, sin paralelo; [*beauty, wit*] sin par, incomparable • **this is ~ in our history** esto no tiene precedentes en nuestra historia
unpardonable [ʌnˈpɑːdnəbl] ADJ imperdonable, indisculpable
unpardonably [ʌnˈpɑːdnəblɪ] ADV imperdonablemente
unparliamentary [ˈʌnˌpɑːləˈmentərɪ] ADJ antiparlamentario
unpatented [ˈʌnˌpeɪtntɪd] ADJ sin patentar
unpatriotic [ˈʌnˌpætrɪˈɒtɪk] ADJ antipatriótico, poco patriótico
unpatriotically [ˈʌnˌpætrɪˈɒtɪkəlɪ] ADV de modo antipatriótico
unpaved [ˈʌnˈpeɪvd] ADJ sin pavimentar, sin asfaltar
unperceived [ˈʌnpəˈsiːvd] ADJ inadvertido, desapercibido
unperturbed [ˈʌnpəˈtɜːbd] ADJ impertérrito • **he carried on ~** siguió sin inmutarse *or* (*LAm*) alterarse • **~ by this disaster …** sin dejarse desanimar por esta catástrofe …
unpick [ˈʌnˈpɪk] VT descoser
unpin [ˈʌnˈpɪn] VT desprender, quitar los alfileres a
unplaced [ˈʌnˈpleɪst] ADJ (*Sport*) no colocado
unplanned [ˈʌnˈplænd] ADJ [*pregnancy*] sin planear; [*visit*] imprevisto
unplayable [ˈʌnˈpleɪəbl] ADJ [*pitch*] en condiciones tan malas que está inservible
unpleasant [ʌnˈpleznt] ADJ (*gen*) desagradable; [*person*] desagradable, antipático • **to be ~ to sb** ser desagradable *or* antipático con algn
unpleasantly [ʌnˈplezntlɪ] ADV de manera poco agradable • **"no," he said ~** —no —dijo en tono nada amistoso • **the bomb fell ~ close** la bomba cayó lo bastante cerca como para inquietarnos
unpleasantness [ʌnˈplezntnɪs] N (*gen*) lo desagradable; [*of person*] lo antipático, lo desagradable; (= *bad feeling, quarrel*) desavenencia *f*, disgusto *m* • **there has been a lot of ~** ha habido muchos disgustos *or* muchas desavenencias
unpleasing [ʌnˈpliːzɪŋ] ADJ poco atractivo, antiestético • **~ to the ear** poco grato al oído
unplug [ˈʌnˈplʌg] VT desenchufar, desconectar
unplugged [ˌʌnˈplʌgd] ADJ (*Mus*) unplugged, *sin efectos acústicos ni elementos electrónicos*
unplumbed [ˈʌnˈplʌmd] ADJ no sondado, insondable
unpoetic [ˈʌnpəʊˈetɪk] ADJ poco poético
unpoetical [ˈʌnpəʊˈetɪkəl] ADJ = **unpoetic**
unpolished [ˈʌnˈpɒlɪʃt] ADJ 1 sin pulir; [*diamond*] en bruto
2 (*fig*) tosco, inculto
unpolitical [ˌʌnpəˈlɪtɪkəl] ADJ no político
unpolluted [ˈʌnpəˈluːtɪd] ADJ no contaminado, impoluto
unpopular [ˈʌnˈpɒpjʊləʳ] ADJ (*gen*) impopular, poco popular; (= *unacceptable*) inaceptable, mal visto • **it was an ~ decision** fue una decisión impopular • **she's an ~ child** tiene muy pocos amigos • **it is ~ with the miners** los mineros no lo aceptan, los mineros lo ven mal • **to make o.s. ~** hacerse impopular • **you will be very ~ with me** no te lo agradeceré
unpopularity [ˈʌnˌpɒpjʊˈlærɪtɪ] N impopularidad *f*
unpopulated [ˈʌnˈpɒpjʊleɪtɪd] ADJ deshabitado, desierto
unpractical [ˈʌnˈpræktɪkəl] ADJ [*plan, scheme, idea*] poco práctico; [*person*] falto de sentido práctico
unpractised, unpracticed (*US*) [ʌnˈpræktɪst] ADJ inexperto
unprecedented [ʌnˈpresɪdəntɪd] ADJ sin precedentes, inaudito
unpredictability [ˈʌnprɪˌdɪktəˈbɪlɪtɪ] N [*of situation*] lo imprevisible, imprevisibilidad *f*; [*of person*] carácter *m* caprichoso, volubilidad *f*
unpredictable [ˈʌnprɪˈdɪktəbl] ADJ [*event*] imprevisible; [*situation*] impredecible, incierto; [*weather*] variable; [*person*] caprichoso, de reacción imprevisible
unpredictably [ˈʌnprɪˈdɪktəblɪ] ADV de manera imprevisible, imprevisiblemente; [*behave*] caprichosamente, de manera voluble
unprejudiced [ʌnˈpredʒʊdɪst] ADJ (= *not biased*) imparcial; (= *having no prejudices*) sin prejuicios
unpremeditated [ˈʌnprɪˈmedɪteɪtɪd] ADJ impremeditado
unprepared [ˈʌnprɪˈpɛəd] ADJ 1 (= *unready*) • **the student who comes to an exam ~** el estudiante que viene al examen sin estar preparado *or* sin preparación • **to catch sb ~** pillar a algn desprevenido • **to be ~ for sth** (= *not expect*) no contar con algo, no esperar algo; (= *be unequipped*) no estar preparado para algo • **she was totally ~ for motherhood** no estaba preparada para ser madre en absoluto
2 (= *improvised*) [*speech, lecture*] improvisado
3 (= *unwilling*) • **to be ~ to do sth** no estar dispuesto a hacer algo
unpreparedness [ˈʌnprɪˈpɛərɪdnɪs] N falta *f* de preparación
unprepossessing [ˈʌnˌpriːpəˈzesɪŋ] ADJ poco atractivo
unpresentable [ˈʌnprɪˈzentəbl] ADJ mal apersonado
unpretentious [ˈʌnprɪˈtenʃəs] ADJ sin pretensiones, modesto
unpriced [ˈʌnˈpraɪst] ADJ sin precio
unprincipled [ʌnˈprɪnsɪpld] ADJ sin escrúpulos, cínico
unprintable [ˈʌnˈprɪntəbl] ADJ
1 (= *unpublishable*) [*article*] impublicable
2 (*hum*) (= *shocking*) [*story*] impublicable; [*remark, comment*] irrepetible
unproductive [ˈʌnprəˈdʌktɪv] ADJ [*capital, soil etc*] improductivo; [*meeting etc*] infructuoso
unprofessional [ˈʌnprəˈfeʃənl] ADJ [*person, behaviour, attitude*] poco profesional • **it was ~ of her** fue poco profesional de su parte • **~ conduct** comportamiento *m* contrario a la ética profesional
unprofitable [ʌnˈprɒfɪtəbl] ADJ
1 (= *uneconomic*) [*business, industry, route*] poco rentable
2 (= *fruitless*) [*argument, activity, day*] inútil
UNPROFOR, Unprofor [ˈʌnprəʊfɔːʳ] N ABBR (= **United Nations Protection Force**) FORPRONU *f*, Unprofor *f*
unpromising [ˈʌnˈprɒmɪsɪŋ] ADJ poco prometedor • **it looks ~** no promete mucho
unprompted [ˈʌnˈprɒmptɪd] ADJ espontáneo
unpronounceable [ˈʌnprəˈnaʊnsəbl] ADJ impronunciable
unpropitious [ˈʌnprəˈpɪʃəs] ADJ impropicio, poco propicio
unprotected [ˈʌnprəˈtektɪd] ADJ
1 (= *defenceless*) [*person*] indefenso • **to leave sth ~** dejar algo sin protección • **to be ~ by the law** no estar protegido por la ley
2 (= *uncovered*) [*skin, eyes, plants*] sin protección • **to be ~ from the sun** no estar protegido del sol
3 • **~ sex** • **~ intercourse** relaciones *fpl* sexuales sin protección
unprovable [ʌnˈpruːvəbl] ADJ que no se puede probar
unproved [ˈʌnˈpruːvd], **unproven** [ʌnˈpruːvən] ADJ no probado
unprovided-for [ʌnprəˈvaɪdɪdˌfɔːʳ] ADJ [*person*] desamparado, desvalido
unprovoked [ˈʌnprəˈvəʊkt] ADJ no provocado, sin provocación
unpublished [ˈʌnˈpʌblɪʃt] ADJ inédito, no publicado
unpunctual [ˈʌnˈpʌŋktjʊəl] ADJ poco puntual • **this train is always ~** este tren siempre llega con retraso
unpunctuality [ˈʌnˌpʌŋktjʊˈælɪtɪ] N falta *f* de puntualidad, atraso *m*

unpunished ['ʌn'pʌnɪʃt] ADJ • **to go ~** [*crime*] quedar sin castigo, quedar impune; [*person*] escapar sin castigo, salir impune
unputdownable* ['ʌnpʊt'daʊnəbl] ADJ absorbente, que no se puede dejar de la mano
unqualified ['ʌn'kwɒlɪfaɪd] ADJ **1** (= *without qualifications*) [*person, staff, pilot*] no calificado, no cualificado; [*teacher*] sin título, no titulado • **to be ~ to do sth** no estar capacitado para hacer algo
2 (= *unmitigated*) [*success, disaster*] rotundo, total y absoluto; [*acceptance, support, approval*] incondicional
unquenchable [ʌn'kwentʃəbl] ADJ (*fig*) inextinguible; [*thirst*] inapagable; [*desire etc*] insaciable
unquestionable [ʌn'kwestʃənəbl] ADJ indiscutible, incuestionable
unquestionably [ʌn'kwestʃənəblɪ] ADV indiscutiblemente, incuestionablemente
unquestioned [ʌn'kwestʃənd] ADJ (= *unchallenged*) indiscutido, incontestable
unquestioning [ʌn'kwestʃənɪŋ] ADJ [*acceptance*] incondicional, ciego; [*loyalty*] incondicional; [*faith etc*] ciego
unquestioningly [ʌn'kwestʃənɪŋlɪ] ADV incondicionalmente; [*accept, obey*] ciegamente
unquiet ['ʌn'kwaɪət] ADJ inquieto
unquote ['ʌn'kwəʊt] N ▸ **quote**
unquoted ['ʌn'kwəʊtɪd] ADJ [*share etc*] no cotizado, sin cotización oficial
unravel [ʌn'rævəl] VT desenredar, desenmarañar
VI desenredarse, desenmarañarse
unread ['ʌn'red] ADJ no leído • **to leave sth ~** dejar algo sin leer
unreadable ['ʌn'ri:dəbl] ADJ **1** (= *turgid*) [*book*] imposible de leer • **I found the book ~** el libro me resultó pesadísimo
2 (= *illegible*) [*handwriting etc*] ilegible
3 (*Comput*) [*data*] ilegible
4 (*liter*) (= *impenetrable*) [*face, eyes*] impenetrable
unreadiness ['ʌn'redɪnɪs] N desprevención *f*
unready ['ʌn'redɪ] ADJ desprevenido
unreal ['ʌn'rɪəl] ADJ **1** (= *not real*) [*situation, world*] irreal
2* (= *excellent*) increíble*; (= *unbelievable*) increíble
unrealistic ['ʌnrɪə'lɪstɪk] ADJ poco realista • **it is ~ to expect that ...** no es realista esperar que ...
unrealistically ['ʌnrɪə'lɪstɪkəlɪ] ADV • **the prices are ~ high** los precios son tan altos que no son realistas
unreality ['ʌnrɪ'ælɪtɪ] N irrealidad *f*
unrealizable ['ʌnrɪə'laɪzəbl] ADJ irrealizable
unrealized ['ʌn'ri:əlaɪzd] ADJ [*ambition*] no realizado, que ha quedado sin realizar; [*objective*] no logrado
unreason ['ʌn'ri:zn] N insensatez *f*
unreasonable [ʌn'ri:znəbl] ADJ [*person, behaviour*] irrazonable, poco razonable; [*price, amount*] excesivo • **he was most ~ about it** reaccionó en forma irracional • **I think her attitude is ~** creo que su actitud es poco razonable
unreasonableness [ʌn'ri:znəblnɪs] N irracionalidad *f*, lo irrazonable
unreasonably [ʌn'ri:znəblɪ] ADV • **to be ~ difficult about sth** porfiar estúpidamente en algo
unreasoning [ʌn'ri:znɪŋ] ADJ irracional
unreceptive ['ʌnrɪ'septɪv] ADJ poco receptivo
unreclaimed ['ʌnrɪ'kleɪmd] ADJ [*land*] no rescatado, no utilizado
unrecognizable ['ʌn'rekəgnaɪzəbl] ADJ irreconocible
unrecognized ['ʌn'rekəgnaɪzd] ADJ
1 (= *unnoticed*) [*talent, genius*] desapercibido, no reconocido • **to go ~** pasar desapercibido • **he walked along the road ~ by passers-by** fue por la calle sin que los transeúntes le reconocieran
2 (*Pol*) [*government, party, country*] no reconocido
unreconstructed [,ʌnri:kən'strʌktɪd] ADJ [*system, idea, policy*] no reformado, inamovible; [*person*] recalcitrante
unrecorded ['ʌnrɪ'kɔ:dɪd] ADJ no registrado, ignorado
unredeemed ['ʌnrɪ'di:md] ADJ no redimido; [*promise*] sin cumplir, incumplido; [*pledge*] no desempeñado; [*bill*] sin redimir; [*debt*] sin amortizar
unreel [ʌn'rɪəl] VT desenrollar
unrefined ['ʌnrɪ'faɪnd] ADJ **1** (= *not processed*) [*oil, sugar etc*] crudo, sin refinar
2 (= *coarse*) [*person, manners*] poco refinado
unreflecting ['ʌnrɪ'flektɪŋ] ADJ irreflexivo
unreformed ['ʌnrɪ'fɔ:md] ADJ no reformado
unregarded ['ʌnrɪ'gɑ:dɪd] ADJ desatendido, no estimado • **those ~ aspects** aquellos aspectos de los que nadie hace caso
unregenerate ['ʌnrɪ'dʒenərɪt] ADJ empedernido
unregistered ['ʌn'redʒɪstəd] ADJ no registrado; [*letter*] sin certificar
unregretted ['ʌnrɪ'gretɪd] ADJ no llorado, no lamentado
unregulated [ʌn'regjʊleɪtɪd] ADJ no regulado
unrehearsed ['ʌnrɪ'hɜ:st] ADJ (*Theat etc*) no ensayado; (= *spontaneous*) improvisado
unrelated ['ʌnrɪ'leɪtɪd] ADJ **1** (= *unconnected*) inconexo
2 (*by family*) no emparentado • **they are ~ to each other** no están emparentados
unrelenting ['ʌnrɪ'lentɪŋ] ADJ [*rain, heat, attack*] implacable; [*person*] despiadado
unreliability ['ʌnrɪ,laɪə'bɪlɪtɪ] N falta *f* de fiabilidad
unreliable ['ʌnrɪ'laɪəbl] ADJ [*person*] informal, poco de fiar; [*machine, service*] poco fiable, que no es de fiar; [*information, statistics*] poco fiable; [*weather, climate*] variable, inestable • **they thought British workers were ~** opinaban que a los trabajadores británicos les faltaba formalidad, opinaban que los trabajadores británicos eran muy informales *or* no eran muy de fiar • **the phones here are ~** los teléfonos aquí son poco fiables *or* no son de fiar • **my memory is so ~ these days** mi memoria no es muy de fiar últimamente
unrelieved ['ʌnrɪ'li:vd] ADJ [*work etc*] continuo • **~ by** no aliviado por, no mitigado por • **sadness ~ by hope** tristeza *f* sin alivio de esperanza • **three hours of ~ boredom** tres horas de aburrimiento total
unremarkable ['ʌnrɪ'mɑ:kəbl] ADJ ordinario, corriente
unremarked ['ʌnrɪ'mɑ:kt] ADJ inadvertido
unremitting ['ʌnrɪ'mɪtɪŋ] ADJ incansable; (= *continuous*) continuo
unremittingly ['ʌnrɪ'mɪtɪŋlɪ] ADV incansablemente
unremunerative ['ʌnrɪ'mju:nərətɪv] ADJ poco remunerador, poco lucrativo
unrepealed ['ʌnrɪ'pi:ld] ADJ no revocado
unrepeatable ['ʌnrɪ'pi:təbl] ADJ irrepetible, que no puede repetirse • **what he said is quite ~** no me atrevo a repetir lo que dijo • **an ~ bargain** una ganga única
unrepentant ['ʌnrɪ'pentənt] ADJ impenitente
unreported [,ʌnrɪ'pɔ:tɪd] ADJ [*crime*] no denunciado, sin denunciar • **the news went ~** la noticia no fue comunicada
unrepresentative ['ʌn,reprɪ'zentətɪv] ADJ (= *untypical*) poco representativo • **to be ~ of sth** no ser representativo de algo • **he holds an ~ view** mantiene una opinión poco representativa
unrepresented ['ʌn,reprɪ'zentɪd] ADJ sin representación • **they are ~ in the House** no tienen representación en la Cámara
unrequited ['ʌnrɪ'kwaɪtɪd] ADJ no correspondido
unreserved ['ʌnrɪ'zɜ:vd] ADJ **1** (= *not booked*) no reservado
2 (= *frank*) franco, directo
3 (= *complete*) total, completo
unreservedly ['ʌnrɪ'zɜ:vɪdlɪ] ADV sin reserva, incondicionalmente
unresisting ['ʌnrɪ'zɪstɪŋ] ADJ sumiso
unresolved ['ʌnrɪ'zɒlvd] ADJ [*problem*] no resuelto, pendiente
unresponsive ['ʌnrɪs'pɒnsɪv] ADJ insensible, sordo (**to** a)
unrest [ʌn'rest] N **1** (*Pol*) malestar *m*; (= *riots*) disturbios *mpl* • **the ~ in the Congo** los disturbios del Congo
2 (= *unease*) malestar *m*, inquietud *f*
unrestrained ['ʌnrɪ'streɪnd] ADJ
1 (= *uncontrolled*) [*joy, laughter, violence*] desenfrenado, incontrolado; [*enthusiasm*] desbordante • **to be ~ by morality** no estar frenado por la moralidad • **to be ~ in one's views** expresar su opinión sin reservas
2 (= *not held physically*) [*car passenger*] sin cinturón; [*patient, prisoner*] sin maniatar
unrestrainedly ['ʌnrɪ'streɪnɪdlɪ] ADV desenfrenadamente, incontroladamente
unrestricted ['ʌnrɪ'strɪktɪd] ADJ
1 (= *unlimited*) [*use, right*] ilimitado • **~ access** libre acceso *m*
2 (= *unobstructed*) [*view*] perfecto
unrevealed ['ʌnrɪ'vi:ld] ADJ no revelado
unrewarded ['ʌnrɪ'wɔ:dɪd] ADJ sin recompensa • **to go ~** quedar sin recompensa
unrewarding ['ʌnrɪ'wɔ:dɪŋ] ADJ ingrato; (*financially*) improductivo
unrighteous [ʌn'raɪtʃəs] ADJ malo, perverso
NPL • **the ~** los malos, los perversos
unripe ['ʌn'raɪp] ADJ verde
unrivalled, unrivaled (*US*) [ʌn'raɪvəld] ADJ sin par, incomparable • **Bilbao is ~ for food** la cocina bilbaína es incomparable
unroadworthy ['ʌn'rəʊd,wɜ:ðɪ] ADJ no apto para circular
unrobe ['ʌn'rəʊb] (*frm*) VI desvestirse, desnudarse
VT desvestir, desnudar
unroll ['ʌn'rəʊl] VT desenrollar
VI desenrollarse
unromantic ['ʌnrə'mæntɪk] ADJ poco romántico
unroof ['ʌn'ru:f] VT destechar, quitar el techo de
unrope ['ʌn'rəʊp] VT desatar
VI desatarse
UNRRA N ABBR (*formerly*) = **United Nations Relief and Rehabilitation Administration**
unruffled ['ʌn'rʌfld] ADJ **1** [*person*] sereno, imperturbable • **he carried on quite ~** siguió sin inmutarse
2 [*hair, surface*] liso
unruled ['ʌn'ru:ld] ADJ [*paper*] sin rayar, sin pautar
unruliness [ʌn'ru:lɪnɪs] N rebeldía *f*
unruly [ʌn'ru:lɪ] ADJ (COMPAR: **unrulier**,

SUPERL: **unruliest**) **1** [*behaviour*] rebelde; [*child*] revoltoso; [*mob*] alterado
2 (*liter*) [*hair*] rebelde
UNRWA (N ABBR) = **United Nations Relief and Works Agency**
unsaddle ['ʌn'sædl] (VT) [+ *rider*] desarzonar; [+ *horse*] desensillar, quitar la silla a
unsafe ['ʌn'seɪf] (ADJ) **1** (= *dangerous*) [*building, neighbourhood*] peligroso, poco seguro; [*machine, vehicle, wiring*] poco seguro, peligroso; [*working conditions*] peligroso • **the car is ~ to drive** el coche no está en condiciones de conducirlo • **it is ~ to walk there at night** es peligroso caminar por ahí de noche • **to declare a building ~** declarar un edificio un peligro
2 (= *in danger*) • **to be ~** [*person*] estar en peligro • **to feel ~** no sentirse seguro
3 (*Jur*) (= *dubious*) [*evidence, conviction, verdict*] abierto a revisión judicial
4 (= *unprotected*) • **~ sex** relaciones *fpl* sexuales sin protección
unsaid ['ʌn'sed] (ADJ) sin decir • **to leave sth ~** callar algo, dejar de decir algo • **to leave nothing ~** no dejar nada en el tintero • **much was left ~** muchas cosas se quedaron por decir
unsalable ['ʌn'seɪləbl] (ADJ) (*US*) = unsaleable
unsalaried ['ʌn'sælərɪd] (ADJ) sin sueldo, no remunerado
unsaleable, **unsalable** (*US*) ['ʌn'seɪləbl] (ADJ) invendible
unsalted [ˌʌn'sɒltɪd] (ADJ) sin sal
unsanitary [ˌʌn'sænɪtərɪ] (ADJ) insalubre, antihigiénico
unsatisfactory ['ʌnˌsætɪs'fæktərɪ] (ADJ) poco satisfactorio; [*work*] insatisfactorio
unsatisfied ['ʌn'sætɪsfaɪd] (ADJ) insatisfecho
unsatisfying ['ʌn'sætɪsfaɪɪŋ] (ADJ) poco satisfactorio; (= *insufficient*) insuficiente
unsaturated ['ʌn'sætʃəreɪtɪd] (ADJ) no saturado, insaturado
unsavoury, **unsavory** (*US*) ['ʌn'seɪvərɪ] (ADJ) [*person*] indeseable; [*remark etc*] desagradable, repugnante
unsay ['ʌn'seɪ] (PT, PP: **unsaid**) (VT) desdecirse de
unscaled [ʌn'skeɪld] (ADJ) [*heights, peak*] no escalado
unscathed ['ʌn'skeɪðd] (ADJ) ileso • **to escape/get out ~** salir ileso
unscented [ʌn'sentɪd] (ADJ) sin perfumar
unscheduled ['ʌn'ʃedju:ld] (ADJ) no programado
unscholarly ['ʌn'skɒləlɪ] (ADJ) [*person*] nada erudito; [*work*] indigno de un erudito
unschooled ['ʌn'sku:ld] (ADJ) indocto • **to be ~ in a technique** no haber aprendido nada de una técnica
unscientific ['ʌnˌsaɪən'tɪfɪk] (ADJ) poco científico
unscramble ['ʌn'skræmbl] (VT) (*Telec*) [+ *message*] descifrar; (*TV*) descodificar
unscratched [ʌn'skrætʃt] (ADJ) (= *unhurt*) ileso; [*record*] sin rayar
unscrew ['ʌn'skru:] (VT) destornillar; [+ *lid*] desenroscar
(VI) destornillarse; [*lid*] desenroscar
unscripted ['ʌn'skrɪptɪd] (ADJ) [*speech, remark*] improvisado; (*Rad, TV*) [*programme*] sin guión
unscrupulous [ʌn'skru:pjʊləs] (ADJ) sin escrúpulos, poco escrupuloso
unscrupulously [ʌn'skru:pjʊləslɪ] (ADV) de modo poco escrupuloso
unscrupulousness [ʌn'skru:pjʊləsnɪs] (N) falta *f* de escrúpulos
unseal ['ʌn'si:l] (VT) desellar, abrir
unsealed [ʌn'si:ld] (ADJ) [*envelope, jar*] sin cerrar; (= *without wax seal*) sin sellar
unseasonable [ʌn'si:znəbl] (ADJ) [*weather*] impropio de la estación; [*clothes, food*] fuera de estación
unseasonably [ʌn'si:znəblɪ] (ADV) • **we had an ~ warm spring** tuvimos una primavera calurosa para esa época del año • **it was ~ mild for late January** hacía un tiempo muy moderado para estar a últimos de enero
unseasoned ['ʌn'si:znd] (ADJ) no sazonado
unseat ['ʌn'si:t] (VT) **1** [+ *rider*] derribar, desarzonar; [+ *passenger etc*] echar de su asiento
2 (*Parl*) [+ *MP*] hacer perder su escaño
unseaworthy ['ʌn'si:ˌwɜ:ðɪ] (ADJ) innavegable
unsecured ['ʌnsɪ'kjʊəd] (ADJ) (*Econ*) no respaldado, sin aval
(CPD) ▸ **unsecured creditor** acreedor(a) *m/f* común ▸ **unsecured debt** deuda *f* sin respaldo
unseeded ['ʌn'si:dɪd] (ADJ) [*player, team*] que no es cabeza de serie
unseeing ['ʌn'si:ɪŋ] (ADJ) (*fig*) ciego • **he stared, ~, out of the window** miraba por la ventana, con la mirada perdida • **to gaze at sth with ~ eyes** mirar algo sin verlo
unseemliness [ʌn'si:mlɪnɪs] (N) lo indecoroso, falta *f* de decoro, impropiedad *f*
unseemly [ʌn'si:mlɪ] (ADJ) (*gen*) mal visto; [*behaviour*] impropio, indecoroso
unseen ['ʌn'si:n] (ADJ) (= *hidden*) oculto; (= *unknown*) desconocido; [*translation*] hecho a primera vista • **he managed to get through ~** logró pasar inadvertido
(N) **1** (*Scol*) traducción *f* (al idioma materno) hecha a primera vista
2 • **the ~** lo invisible, lo oculto
unsegregated ['ʌn'segrɪgeɪtɪd] (ADJ) no segregado, sin segregación (racial *etc*)
unselfconscious ['ʌnˌself'kɒnʃəs] (ADJ) natural
unselfconsciously ['ʌnˌself'kɒnʃəslɪ] (ADV) de manera desenfadada
unselfish ['ʌn'selfɪʃ] (ADJ) desinteresado
unselfishly ['ʌn'selfɪʃlɪ] (ADV) desinteresadamente
unselfishness ['ʌn'selfɪʃnɪs] (N) desinterés *m*
unsentimental ['ʌnsentɪ'mentəl] (ADJ) nada sentimental
unserviceable ['ʌn'sɜ:vɪsəbl] (ADJ) inservible, inútil
unsettle ['ʌn'setl] (VT) [+ *opponent*] desconcertar; [+ *relationship*] desestabilizar • **if this gets into the papers it will only ~ people** si esto se publica en los periódicos lo único que hará es poner nerviosa *or* inquietar a la gente • **don't let her comments ~ you** no dejes que sus comentarios te pongan nervioso
unsettled ['ʌn'setld] (ADJ) **1** (= *uneasy, restless*) [*person*] intranquilo; [*sleep, night*] agitado • **he's feeling ~ in his job** no está del todo contento *or* a gusto en su trabajo
2 (= *undecided*) [*matter, question*] pendiente, sin resolver
3 (= *changeable*) [*weather*] inestable, variable; [*situation, market*] inestable
4 (= *not populated*) [*land*] sin colonizar
5 (= *unpaid*) [*account, bill*] pendiente, sin saldar
unsettling ['ʌn'setlɪŋ] (ADJ) [*influence, effect*] desestabilizador; [*experience, dream*] perturbador; [*thought*] inquietante • **this is an ~ time for us all** esta época es preocupante para todos nosotros • **it is ~ to know he could be watching me** me inquieta saber que podría estar vigilándome
unsex ['ʌn'seks] (VT) (*liter*) privar de la sexualidad, suprimir el instinto sexual de
unsexy* ['ʌn'seksɪ] (ADJ) nada sexy
unshackle ['ʌn'ʃækl] (VT) desencadenar, quitar los grillos a
unshaded ['ʌn'ʃeɪdɪd] (ADJ) [*place*] sin sombra; [*bulb*] sin pantalla
unshakable, **unshakeable** [ʌn'ʃeɪkəbl] (ADJ) [*belief*] inquebrantable • **he was ~ in his resolve** se mostró totalmente resuelto • **after three hours he was still ~** después de tres horas seguía tan resuelto como antes
unshaken ['ʌn'ʃeɪkən] (ADJ) impertérrito • **he was ~ by what had happened** no se dejó amedrentar por lo que había pasado
unshaven ['ʌn'ʃeɪvn] (ADJ) sin afeitar
unsheathe ['ʌn'ʃi:ð] (VT) desenvainar
unship ['ʌn'ʃɪp] (VT) [+ *goods*] desembarcar; [+ *rudder, mast etc*] desmontar
unshockable ['ʌn'ʃɒkəbl] (ADJ) • **she's ~** no se escandaliza por nada
unshod ['ʌn'ʃɒd] (ADJ) descalzo; [*horse*] desherrado
unshrinkable ['ʌn'ʃrɪŋkəbl] (ADJ) que no encoge, inencogible
unshrinking [ʌn'ʃrɪŋkɪŋ] (ADJ) impávido
unsighted ['ʌn'saɪtɪd] (ADJ) (= *blind*) invidente; (= *with no view*) • **I was ~ for a moment** por un momento no pude ver
(CPD) ▸ **unsighted person** invidente *mf*
unsightliness [ʌn'saɪtlɪnɪs] (N) fealdad *f*
unsightly [ʌn'saɪtlɪ] (ADJ) feo
unsigned ['ʌn'saɪnd] (ADJ) (= *without signature*) [*letter, article, contract*] sin firmar
unsinkable ['ʌn'sɪŋkəbl] (ADJ) insumergible
unskilful, **unskillful** (*US*) ['ʌn'skɪlfʊl] (ADJ) inexperto, desmañado
unskilled ['ʌn'skɪld] (ADJ) [*work*] no especializado
(CPD) ▸ **unskilled worker** trabajador(a) *m/f* no cualificado/a, trabajador(a) *m/f* no calificado/a (*LAm*)
unskimmed ['ʌn'skɪmd] (ADJ) sin desnatar, sin descremar (*LAm*)
unsmiling ['ʌn'smaɪlɪŋ] (ADJ) adusto
unsmilingly ['ʌn'smaɪlɪŋlɪ] (ADV) sin sonreír
unsociability ['ʌnˌsəʊʃə'bɪlɪtɪ] (N) insociabilidad *f*
unsociable [ʌn'səʊʃəbl] (ADJ) insociable; [*person*] poco sociable, huraño
unsocial [ʌn'səʊʃəl] (ADJ) antisocial • **to work ~ hours** trabajar fuera de las horas normales
unsold ['ʌn'səʊld] (ADJ) por vender, sin venderse • **to remain ~** quedar por vender *or* sin venderse
unsoldierly ['ʌn'səʊldʒəlɪ] (ADJ) indigno de un militar, impropio de un militar
unsolicited ['ʌnsə'lɪsɪtɪd] (ADJ) no solicitado
unsolvable ['ʌn'sɒlvəbl] (ADJ) irresoluble, insoluble
unsolved ['ʌn'sɒlvd] (ADJ) no resuelto, sin resolver • **~ crime** crimen *m* que sigue sin resolver
unsophisticated ['ʌnsə'fɪstɪkeɪtɪd] (ADJ) sencillo, cándido; (*pej*) burdo
unsought ['ʌn'sɔ:t] (ADJ) no solicitado • **the offer came quite ~** se hizo la oferta sin que se hubiera pedido nada
unsound ['ʌn'saʊnd] (ADJ) (*in health*) malo; (*in construction*) defectuoso; (= *unstable*) poco sólido *or* estable; [*argument*] poco sólido • **of ~ mind** (*Jur*) mentalmente incapacitado • **the book is ~ on some points** el libro yerra en algunos puntos, no hay que fiarse del libro en ciertos aspectos
unsoundness ['ʌn'saʊndnɪs] (N) lo defectuoso; [*of argument*] falta *f* de solidez

unsparing [ʌn'spɛərɪŋ] ADJ (= *generous*) pródigo, generoso; (= *untiring*) incansable; (= *unmerciful*) despiadado • **to be ~ in one's praise** no escatimar las alabanzas • **to be ~ in one's efforts to** (+ *infin*) no regatear esfuerzo por (+ *infin*)

unsparingly [ʌn'spɛərɪŋlɪ] ADV (= *generously*) generosamente, pródigamente; (= *untiringly*) incansablemente

unspeakable [ʌn'spi:kəbl] ADJ (= *terrible*) [*pain etc*] horrible; (= *dreadful*) incalificable

unspeakably [ʌn'spi:kəblɪ] ADV • **to suffer ~** sufrir lo indecible • **it was ~ bad** fue horroroso

unspecified ['ʌn'spesɪfaɪd] ADJ no especificado

unspectacular [ˌʌnspek'tækjʊlə^r] ADJ poco espectacular

unspent ['ʌn'spent] ADJ no gastado

unsplinterable ['ʌn'splɪntərəbl] ADJ inastillable

unspoiled ['ʌn'spɔɪld], **unspoilt** ['ʌn'spɔɪlt] ADJ [*place*] que no ha perdido su belleza natural; [*child*] nada mimado • **~ by tourism** no echado a perder por el turismo • **to remain ~** conservar la belleza natural

unspoken ['ʌn'spəʊkən] ADJ tácito, sobreentendido • **to leave sth ~** no expresar algo, dejar de decir algo • **to remain ~** dejarse sin decir

unsporting ['ʌn'spɔ:tɪŋ], **unsportsmanlike** ['ʌn'spɔ:tsmənlaɪk] ADJ antideportivo

unstable ['ʌn'steɪbl] ADJ **1** (= *unsafe*) [*building, construction*] inestable, poco firme, poco sólido
2 (= *unpredictable*) [*condition, economy, prices*] inestable • **the country is politically ~** el país es inestable desde el punto de vista político
3 [*weather*] inestable, variable
4 (*Psych*) [*person, character*] inestable • **mentally/emotionally ~** mentalmente/ emocionalmente inestable
5 (*Phys*) [*matter, molecule*] inestable

unstamped ['ʌn'stæmpt] ADJ sin sello, sin franquear

unstated [ʌn'steɪtɪd] ADJ [*wish etc*] no expresado; [*understanding*] tácito

unstatesmanlike ['ʌn'steɪtsmənlaɪk] ADJ indigno *or* impropio de un estadista

unsteadily ['ʌn'stedɪlɪ] ADV de manera insegura; [*walk*] con paso vacilante

unsteadiness ['ʌn'stedɪnɪs] N [*of chair, ladder, structure*] inestabilidad *f*, inseguridad *f*; [*of sb's steps, walk*] lo vacilante, inseguridad *f*; [*of voice, hand*] temblor *m*

unsteady ['ʌn'stedɪ] ADJ [*chair, ladder structure*] inestable, inseguro; [*walk*] vacilante; [*voice, hand*] tembloroso • **to be ~ on one's feet** caminar con paso vacilante

unstick ['ʌn'stɪk] VT despegar

unstinted [ʌn'stɪntɪd] ADJ [*effort*] incansable

unstinting [ʌn'stɪntɪŋ] ADJ pródigo • **to be ~ in one's praise** no escatimar las alabanzas, prodigar las alabanzas • **to be ~ in one's efforts to** (+ *infin*) no regatear esfuerzo por (+ *infin*)

unstintingly [ˌʌn'stɪntɪŋlɪ] ADV sin escatimar esfuerzos, de manera infatigable y generosa

unstitch ['ʌn'stɪtʃ] VT descoser • **to come ~ed** descoserse

unstop ['ʌn'stɒp] VT desobstruir, desatascar

unstoppable ['ʌn'stɒpəbl] ADJ incontenible, irrefrenable; (*Sport*) [*shot etc*] imparable

unstrap [ʌn'stræp] VT quitar la correa de

unstressed ['ʌn'strest] ADJ (*Ling*) átono, inacentuado

unstring ['ʌn'strɪŋ] (PT, PP: **unstrung**) VT (*Mus*) desencordar; [+ *pearls*] desensartar; (*fig*) [+ *nerves*] trastornar

unstructured ['ʌn'strʌktʃəd] ADJ sin estructura, no estructurado

unstuck ['ʌn'stʌk] ADJ • **to come ~** [*label etc*] despegarse, desprenderse; (*fig**) fracasar, sufrir un revés • **where he comes ~ is ...** a él lo que le pierde es ...

unstudied ['ʌn'stʌdɪd] ADJ natural, sin afectación

unstylish [ʌn'staɪlɪʃ] ADJ sin estilo

unsubdued ['ʌnsəb'dju:d] ADJ indomado

unsubmissive ['ʌnsəb'mɪsɪv] ADJ insumiso

unsubscribe ['ʌnsəb'skraɪb] VI (*Internet*) borrarse

unsubsidized [ʌn'sʌbsɪdaɪzd] ADJ no subvencionado

unsubstantial ['ʌnsəb'stænʃəl] ADJ insustancial

unsubstantiated ['ʌnsəb'stænʃɪeɪtɪd] ADJ no comprobado, no demostrado

unsubtle [ʌn'sʌtl] ADJ nada sutil • **how ~ can you get!** ¡qué poca sutileza!

unsuccessful ['ʌnsək'sesfʊl] ADJ [*attempt, effort*] inútil, infructuoso; [*appeal, search, job application*] infructuoso • **he embarked on an ~ business venture** se embarcó en un negocio que no tuvo éxito *or* que fracasó • **an ~ writer** un escritor que no consiguió el éxito, un escritor fracasado • **to be ~** no tener éxito, fracasar • **their marriage was ~** el matrimonio fracasó • **we regret to inform you that your application for the post has been ~** lamentamos informarle que no ha sido seleccionado para el puesto de trabajo solicitado • **they were ~ in their efforts to reach an agreement** fracasaron en sus esfuerzos por llegar a un acuerdo • **to be ~ in (doing) sth: he was ~ in getting a job** no consiguió *or* logró encontrar trabajo • **a search for the weapon proved ~** la búsqueda del arma resultó ser infructuosa

unsuccessfully ['ʌnsək'sesfəlɪ] ADV [*try, argue*] sin éxito, en vano; [*compete*] sin éxito

unsuitability ['ʌnˌsu:tə'bɪlɪtɪ] N [*of clothes, shoes*] lo inadecuado, lo inapropiado; [*of moment*] lo inoportuno; [*of behaviour, answer, book, reading*] impropiedad *f*

unsuitable ['ʌn'su:təbl] ADJ [*clothes, shoes*] inadecuado, inapropiado; [*accommodation, job, site*] inadecuado; [*candidate*] poco idóneo; [*moment*] inoportuno, inconveniente • **the building was ~ as an office** el edificio no reunía las condiciones necesarias para hacer de oficina • **these shoes are ~ for walking** estos zapatos no son los adecuados *or* apropiados para caminar • **the film is ~ for children** la película no es apta para menores • **this book is ~ for children** este libro no es apropiado para niños *or* es impropio para niños • **he is ~ for the post** no es la persona indicada para el puesto • **she always went for ~ men** siempre escogía a hombres que no le convenían • **he married a most ~ girl** se casó con una chica que no le convenía nada

unsuitably ['ʌn'su:təblɪ] ADV [*dressed*] de manera inapropiada

unsuited ['ʌn'su:tɪd] ADJ • **to be ~ for/to sth** no estar hecho para algo, no servir para algo • **he is ~ to be king** no está hecho *or* no sirve para ser rey • **it was a job to which I was totally ~** era un trabajo para el que no estaba hecha *or* no servía en absoluto • **they are ~ to each other** son incompatibles (el uno con el otro) • **the vehicles are ~ for use in the desert** los vehículos no son adecuados para su utilización en el desierto

unsullied ['ʌn'sʌlɪd] ADJ (*liter*) inmaculado, no corrompido • **~ by** no corrompido por

unsung ['ʌn'sʌŋ] ADJ [*person, achievement*] no reconocido; [*hero, heroine*] olvidado

unsupportable [ˌʌnsə'pɔ:təbl] ADJ [*statement*] indefendible

unsupported ['ʌnsə'pɔ:tɪd] ADJ
1 (= *unsubstantiated*) [*allegation*] sin pruebas que lo respalden; [*claim, statement*] sin base
2 (= *without backup*) [*troops*] sin refuerzos, sin apoyo; [*expedition*] sin apoyo; (*Pol*) [*candidate*] sin apoyo, no respaldado por nadie; (*financially*) [*mother*] sin ayuda económica
3 (*physically*) [*person*] sin ayuda • **he was too weak to walk ~** estaba demasiado débil para andar sin ayuda
4 (*Archit, Constr*) [*structure, wall*] sin sujeción

unsure ['ʌn'ʃʊə^r] ADJ **1** (= *doubtful, undecided*) • **to be ~ about/of sth** no estar seguro de algo • **he seemed very ~ about it** no parecía estar muy seguro de ello • **she looked at him, ~ of his reaction** lo miró, sin estar segura de su reacción • **he was ~ of his welcome** no estaba seguro de la bienvenida que recibiría • **I was ~ what to expect** no estaba segura de qué esperar • **he was ~ whether he would be able to do it** no estaba seguro de si sería capaz de hacerlo
2 (= *lacking confidence*) inseguro, poco seguro • **she seemed nervous and ~** parecía nerviosa e insegura, parecía nerviosa y poco segura • **to be ~ of o.s.** no estar seguro de uno mismo, no tener confianza en sí mismo
3 (= *unreliable*) [*situation, economic climate*] poco seguro; [*loyalty, commitment*] poco fiable

unsurmountable ['ʌnsə'maʊntəbl] ADJ insuperable

unsurpassable ['ʌnsə'pɑ:səbl] ADJ inmejorable, insuperable

unsurpassed ['ʌnsə'pɑ:st] ADJ no superado, sin par • **~ in quality** de calidad inmejorable • **~ by anybody** no superado por nadie

unsurprising ['ʌnsə'praɪzɪŋ] ADJ nada sorprendente

unsurprisingly ['ʌnsə'praɪzɪŋlɪ] ADV como era de esperar • **~, they decided not to pursue the deal** como era de esperar, decidieron no seguir con el trato

unsuspected ['ʌnsəs'pektɪd] ADJ insospechado

unsuspecting ['ʌnsəs'pektɪŋ] ADJ confiado

unsweetened ['ʌn'swi:tnd] ADJ sin azúcar

unswerving [ʌn'swɜ:vɪŋ] ADJ [*resolve*] inquebrantable; [*loyalty*] inquebrantable, firme

unswervingly [ʌn'swɜ:vɪŋlɪ] ADV • **to be ~ loyal to sb** ser totalmente leal a algn • **to hold ~ to one's course** no apartarse ni un ápice de su rumbo

unsympathetic ['ʌnˌsɪmpə'θetɪk] ADJ poco comprensivo • **he was totally ~** no mostró la más mínima comprensión • **they were ~ to my plea** no hicieron caso de mi ruego • **I am not ~ to your request** me parece totalmente comprensible su petición

unsystematic ['ʌnˌsɪstɪ'mætɪk] ADJ poco sistemático, poco metódico

unsystematically ['ʌnˌsɪstɪ'mætɪkəlɪ] ADV de modo poco metódico

untainted ['ʌn'teɪntɪd] ADJ inmaculado, no corrompido; [*food*] no contaminado • **~ by** no corrompido por

untalented [ʌn'tæləntɪd] ADJ sin talento

untamable, **untameable** ['ʌn'teɪməbl] ADJ indomable

untamed ['ʌn'teɪmd] ADJ indomado

untangle ['ʌn'tæŋgl] VT desenredar, desenmarañar

u

untanned ['ʌn'tænd] (ADJ) sin curtir
untapped ['ʌn'tæpt] (ADJ) sin explotar
untarnished ['ʌn'tɑ:nɪʃt] (ADJ) *[reputation etc]* sin tacha
untasted ['ʌn'teɪstɪd] (ADJ) sin probar
untaught ['ʌn'tɔ:t] (ADJ) no enseñado; (= *ignorant*) sin instrucción
untaxed ['ʌn'tækst] (ADJ) libre de impuestos, no sujeto a contribuciones
unteachable ['ʌn'ti:tʃəbl] (ADJ) *[subject, syllabus]* imposible de enseñar
untempered ['ʌn'tempəd] (ADJ) *[steel etc]* sin templar
untenable ['ʌn'tenəbl] (ADJ) insostenible
untenanted ['ʌn'tenəntɪd] (ADJ) desocupado, vacío
untended [ʌn'tendɪd] (ADJ) desatendido, no vigilado • **he left the car ~** dejó el coche sin vigilar
untested ['ʌn'testɪd] (ADJ) no probado
unthinkable [ʌn'θɪŋkəbl] (ADJ)
1 (= *inconceivable*) inconcebible, impensable • **it is ~ that** es inconcebible *or* impensable que (+ *subjun*)
2 (= *unbearable*) insoportable
(N) • **the ~** lo inconcebible
unthinking ['ʌn'θɪŋkɪŋ] (ADJ) irreflexivo
unthinkingly ['ʌn'θɪŋkɪŋlɪ] (ADV) irreflexivamente, sin pensar
unthoughtful [ʌn'θɔ:tfʊl] (ADJ) (= *inconsiderate*) desconsiderado; (= *careless*) descuidado
unthought-of [ʌn'θɔ:tɒv] (ADJ) inimaginable, inconcebible
unthread ['ʌn'θred] (VT) *[+ cloth]* deshebrar, descoser; *[+ needle]* desenhebrar; *[+ pearls]* desensartar
unthrifty ['ʌn'θrɪftɪ] (ADJ) manirroto*
untidily [ʌn'taɪdɪlɪ] (ADV) *[piled, stacked]* sin orden, de manera desordenada; *[dressed]* de forma desaliñada • **the boxes were piled ~ around the room** las cajas estaban amontonadas sin orden *or* de manera desordenada por la habitación
untidiness [ʌn'taɪdɪnɪs] (N) **1** *[of room, person's habits]* desorden *m*; *[of person's dress]* desaliño *m*
2 (*fig*) *[of ideas]* falta *f* de método
untidy [ʌn'taɪdɪ] (ADJ) (COMPAR: **untidier**, SUPERL: **untidiest**) **1** (*lit*) *[room, desk, heap, person]* desordenado; *[garden]* descuidado; *[appearance]* desaliñado, descuidado; *[clothes]* desarreglado; *[hair]* despeinado; *[work, writing]* poco metódico, descuidado
2 (*fig*) • **the film has an ~ ending** la película tiene un final poco coherente • **an ~ mind** una mente poco metódica
untie ['ʌn'taɪ] (VT) *[+ shoelace, shoe, animal]* desatar; *[+ knot, parcel]* deshacer
until [ən'tɪl] (PREP) hasta • **~ ten** hasta las diez • **~ his arrival** hasta su llegada • **he won't be back ~ tomorrow** no volverá hasta mañana • **from morning ~ night** desde la mañana hasta la noche • **~ now** hasta ahora • **it's never been a problem ~ now** hasta ahora nunca ha sido un problema • **~ then** hasta entonces • **~ then I'd never been to Italy** hasta entonces no había estado nunca en Italia
(CONJ) **1** (*in future*) hasta que (+ *subjun*) • **wait ~ I get back** espera hasta que yo vuelva • **~ they build the new road** hasta que construyan la nueva carretera • **~ they come/sleep** hasta que vengan/se duerman • **he won't come ~ you invite him** no vendrá hasta que (no) lo invites • **they did nothing ~ we came** no hicieron nada hasta que (no) vinimos nosotros • **I don't get up ~ eight o'clock** no me levanto antes de las ocho
2 (*in past*) hasta que (+ *indic*) • **he did nothing ~ I told him to** no hizo nada hasta que yo se lo dije, no hizo nada hasta que no se lo dije • **~ they built the new road** hasta que construyeron la nueva carretera • **we stayed there ~ the doctor came** nos quedamos allí hasta que vino el médico • **we didn't stop ~ we reached York** no paramos hasta llegar a York

UNTIL

▷ *As with other time conjunctions,* **hasta que** *is used with the subjunctive if the action which follows hasn't happened yet or hadn't happened at the time of speaking:*
Go on stirring until the sauce is cold
Sigue removiendo hasta que se enfríe la salsa
I shan't be happy until you come
No estaré contenta hasta que (no) vengas

When the main clause is negative, **no** *can optionally be given in the* **hasta que** *clause without changing the meaning.*

▷ **Hasta que** *is used with the indicative when the action in the* **hasta que** *clause has already taken place:*
He lived in this house until he died
Vivió en esta casa hasta que murió
I didn't see her again until she returned to London
No volví a verla hasta que (no) regresó a Londres

▷ **Hasta que** *is also used with the indicative when describing habitual actions:*
I never wake up until the alarm goes off
Nunca me despierto hasta que (no) suena el despertador

▷ *Instead of* **hasta que** *+ verb, you can use* **hasta** *with an infinitive when the subject of both clauses is the same:*
Go on stirring until you get a thick creamy mixture
Sigue removiendo hasta obtener una crema espesa

For further uses and examples, see main entry.

untilled ['ʌn'tɪld] (ADJ) sin cultivar
untimely [ʌn'taɪmlɪ] (ADJ) (= *premature*) prematuro; (= *inopportune*) inoportuno
untiring [ʌn'taɪərɪŋ] (ADJ) incansable
untiringly [ʌn'taɪərɪŋlɪ] (ADV) incansablemente
untitled [ʌn'taɪtəld] (ADJ) *[painting]* sin título; *[person]* sin título
unto†† ['ʌntʊ] (PREP) (*liter*) = **to, toward**
untold ['ʌn'təʊld] (ADJ) **1** (= *not recounted*) *[story]* nunca contado; *[secret]* nunca revelado
2 (= *indescribable, incalculable*) *[suffering]* indecible; *[loss, wealth etc]* incalculable, fabuloso
untouchable [ʌn'tʌtʃəbl] (ADJ) intocable
(N)** intocable *mf*
untouched ['ʌn'tʌtʃt] (ADJ) **1** (= *not used etc*) intacto, sin tocar • **to leave one's food ~** dejar su comida sin probar • **she left her breakfast ~** no tocó el desayuno • **a product ~ by human hand** un producto no manipulado, un producto que no ha sido tocado por la mano del hombre
2 (= *safe*) indemne, incólume
3 (= *unaffected*) insensible, indiferente • **he is ~ by any plea** es insensible a cualquier súplica • **those peoples ~ by civilization** esos pueblos no alcanzados por la civilización
untoward [,ʌntə'wɔ:d] (ADJ) (= *adverse*) adverso; (= *inapt*) impropio; (= *unfortunate*) desafortunado
untraceable [,ʌn'treɪsəbl] (ADJ) imposible de rastrear
untrained ['ʌn'treɪnd] (ADJ) *[person]* sin formación, no capacitado; *[teacher etc]* sin título; (*Sport*) no entrenado; *[animal]* sin amaestrar • **to the ~ ear/eye** para el oído/ojo de alguien que no es experto
untrammelled, **untrameled** (US) [ʌn'træməld] (ADJ) (*liter*) ilimitado
untransferable ['ʌntræns'fɜ:rəbl] (ADJ) intransferible
untranslatable ['ʌntrænz'leɪtəbl] (ADJ) intraducible
untravelled, **untraveled** (US) ['ʌn'trævld] (ADJ) **1** *[road etc]* no trillado, poco frecuentado; *[place]* inexplorado
2 *[person]* que no ha viajado
untreated [ʌn'tri:tɪd] (ADJ) **1** (*Med*) *[patient, injury, illness]* sin tratar
2 (= *unprocessed*) *[sewage, wood, cotton]* no tratado, sin tratar
untried ['ʌn'traɪd] (ADJ) **1** (= *untested*) *[product, method]* no probado
2 (= *inexperienced*) *[person]* no puesto a prueba; *[soldier]* bisoño
3 (*Jur*) *[person]* no procesado, sin procesar; *[case]* no visto, no juzgado
untrimmed ['ʌn'trɪmd] (ADJ) *[hedge]* sin recortar, sin podar; *[wood]* sin desbastar; *[dress]* sin guarnición
untrodden ['ʌn'trɒdn] (ADJ) no trillado, sin pisar
untroubled ['ʌn'trʌbld] (ADJ) tranquilo • **she was ~ by the news** la noticia no pareció preocuparle • **~ by thoughts of her** sin preocuparse en absoluto por ella
untrue ['ʌn'tru:] (ADJ) **1** (= *inaccurate*) falso • **it is ~ that** no es cierto *or* verdad que, es falso que • **that is wholly ~** eso es completamente falso
2 (*liter*) (= *unfaithful*) infiel • **to be ~ to sb** ser infiel a algn • **to be ~ to one's principles** no ser fiel a sus principios
untrustworthy ['ʌn'trʌst,wɜ:ðɪ] (ADJ) *[person]* de poca confianza, no muy de fiar; *[leadership, results, information, evidence]* poco fiable; *[book etc]* de dudosa autoridad; *[machine, car]* inseguro, no muy de fiar
untruth ['ʌn'tru:θ] (N) (PL: **untruths** ['ʌn'tru:ðz]) mentira *f*
untruthful ['ʌn'tru:θfʊl] (ADJ) *[person]* mentiroso, falso; *[account]* falso
untruthfully ['ʌn'tru:θfəlɪ] (ADV) falsamente
untruthfulness ['ʌn'tru:θfʊlnɪs] (N) falsedad *f*
unturned [ʌn'tɜ:nd] (ADJ) ▷ **stone**
untutored ['ʌn'tju:təd] (ADJ) indocto, poco instruido; *[mind, taste]* no formado
untwine ['ʌn'twaɪn], **untwist** ['ʌn'twɪst] (VT) destorcer
untypical ['ʌn'tɪpɪkəl] (ADJ) atípico
unusable ['ʌn'ju:zəbl] (ADJ) inservible, inútil
unused¹ ['ʌn'ju:zd] (ADJ) (= *new*) nuevo, sin estrenar; (= *not made use of*) sin usar *or* utilizar
unused² ['ʌn'ju:st] (ADJ) (= *unaccustomed*) • **to be ~ to sth** no estar acostumbrado a algo • **to be ~ to doing sth** no estar acostumbrado a hacer algo
unusual [ʌn'ju:ʒʊəl] (ADJ) **1** (= *uncommon*) *[sight, circumstances, name]* poco común, poco corriente; *[amount, number]* fuera de lo normal, fuera de lo corriente • **the case has received an ~ amount of publicity** el caso ha

U

recibido una cantidad de publicidad fuera de lo normal *or* lo corriente • **here are some ~ gift ideas** aquí tiene unas ideas para regalos poco corrientes *or* que salen de lo corriente • **I didn't feel hungry, which was ~ for me** no me sentía con hambre, lo cual era raro en mí • **it's ~ for him to be late** no suele llegar tarde • **it's not ~ to see snow in June here** no es raro ver nieve aquí en junio • **there's nothing ~ in that** no hay nada de raro *or* extraordinario en ello
2 (= *odd*) raro, extraño • **don't you find it ~ that he never tells you where he's been?** ¿no te parece raro *or* extraño que nunca te diga dónde ha estado?
3 (= *exceptional*) excepcional, poco común *or* corriente • **a man of ~ intelligence** un hombre de inteligencia excepcional, un hombre de una inteligencia poco común *or* corriente

unusually [ʌn'ju:ʒʊəlɪ] ADV
1 (= *unaccustomedly*) • **he arrived ~ late** llegó más tarde que de costumbre • **the streets were ~ quiet** las calles estaban extrañamente silenciosas • **~ for her, she didn't say goodbye** no se despidió, lo cual es raro en ella
2 (= *exceptionally*) excepcionalmente, extraordinariamente • **this year's ~ harsh winter** el invierno excepcionalmente *or* extraordinariamente riguroso de este año • **an ~ gifted man** un hombre de excepcional talento, un hombre de un talento poco común *or* corriente

unutterable [ʌn'ʌtərəbl] ADJ indecible

unutterably [ʌn'ʌtərəblɪ] ADV indeciblemente

unvaried [ʌn'vɛərɪd] ADJ (*gen*) invariable; (= *unchanged*) sin cambiar, constante; (= *monotonous*) monótono

unvarnished ['ʌn'vɑ:nɪʃt] ADJ **1** (= *not varnished*) sin barnizar
2 (*fig*) (= *plain*) [*account, description*] llano • **the ~ truth** la verdad lisa y llana, la verdad sin adornos

unvarying [ʌn'vɛərɪɪŋ] ADJ invariable, constante

unveil [ʌn'veɪl] VT quitar el velo a; [+ *statue, painting etc*] descubrir

unveiling [ʌn'veɪlɪŋ] N descubrimiento *m*; (= *ceremony*) inauguración *f*

unventilated ['ʌn'ventɪleɪtɪd] ADJ sin ventilación, sin aire

unverifiable ['ʌn'verɪfaɪəbl] ADJ no comprobable, que no puede verificarse

unverified ['ʌn'verɪfaɪd] ADJ sin verificar

unversed ['ʌn'vɜ:st] ADJ • **~ in** no versado en, poco ducho en*

unvisited ['ʌn'vɪzɪtɪd] ADJ no visitado, no frecuentado

unvoiced ['ʌn'vɔɪst] ADJ **1** [*opinion, sentiment*] no expresado
2 (*Ling*) [*consonant*] sordo

unwaged [ʌn'weɪdʒd] ADJ sin sueldo
N • **the ~** (= *the unemployed*) los no asalariados

unwanted ['ʌn'wɒntɪd] ADJ [*item*] superfluo; [*visitor, guest*] poco grato, inoportuno; [*child, pregnancy, advances, attention*] no deseado • **to feel ~** sentirse de más • **an ~ gift** un regalo sin estrenar • **to remove ~ hair** quitar el vello superfluo

unwarily [ʌn'wɛərɪlɪ] ADV imprudentemente, incautamente

unwariness [ʌn'wɛərɪnɪs] N imprudencia *f*

unwarlike ['ʌn'wɔ:laɪk] ADJ pacífico, poco belicoso

unwarranted [ʌn'wɒrəntɪd] ADJ injustificado

unwary [ʌn'wɛərɪ] ADJ imprudente, incauto

unwashed ['ʌn'wɒʃt] ADJ sin lavar, sucio
NPL • **the Great Unwashed*** (*hum*) la plebe

unwavering [ʌn'weɪvərɪŋ] ADJ [*loyalty, resolve*] inquebrantable, firme; [*course*] firme; [*gaze*] fijo

unwaveringly [ʌn'weɪvərɪŋlɪ] ADV firmemente • **to hold ~ to one's course** no apartarse ni un ápice de su rumbo

unweaned ['ʌn'wi:nd] ADJ no destetado

unwearable ['ʌn'wɛərəbl] ADJ [*clothes, colour*] imposible de llevar

unwearying [ʌn'wɪərɪɪŋ] ADJ incansable

unwed† [ʌn'wed] ADJ soltero

unwedded [ʌn'wedɪd] ADJ • **to live in ~ bliss** vivir felizmente sin estar legítimamente casado(s)

unwelcome [ʌn'welkəm] ADJ [*news, surprise*] desagradable, poco grato; [*visitor, guest, intruder*] poco grato, inoportuno; [*visit*] inoportuno; [*reminder, advances, attention*] poco grato • **the change is not ~** el cambio no nos resulta del todo molesto • **I felt ~** sentí que allí sobraba • **to make sb feel ~** hacer que algn sienta que sobra

unwelcoming [ʌn'welkəmɪŋ] ADJ [*person*] nada simpático, poco cordial; [*place*] poco acogedor

unwell ['ʌn'wel] ADJ • **to be ~** estar indispuesto • **to feel ~** sentirse mal • **I felt ~ on the ship** me mareé en el barco

unwholesome ['ʌn'həʊlsəm] ADJ
1 (= *unhealthy*) [*food*] poco sano, poco saludable; [*air*] malsano, poco saludable; [*smell*] desagradable
2 (*morally*) [*lifestyle, desire, habit*] malsano, pernicioso; [*thoughts*] malsano • **to have an ~ interest in sth** tener un interés malsano en algo

unwieldy [ʌn'wi:ldɪ] ADJ **1** (= *difficult to handle*) [*object*] difícil de manejar
2 (= *difficult to manage*) [*system, structure, bureaucracy*] rígido

unwilling ['ʌn'wɪlɪŋ] ADJ poco dispuesto • **to be ~ to do sth** estar poco dispuesto a hacer algo, no estar dispuesto a hacer algo • **he was ~ to help me** no estaba dispuesto a ayudarme • **to be ~ for sb to do sth** no estar dispuesto a permitir que algn haga algo

unwillingly ['ʌn'wɪlɪŋlɪ] ADV de mala gana, a regañadientes

unwillingness ['ʌn'wɪlɪŋnɪs] N falta *f* de inclinación, desgana *f* • **his ~ to help us** lo poco dispuesto que está/estaba a ayudarnos, su desgana para ayudarnos

unwind ['ʌn'waɪnd] (PT, PP: **unwound**) VT desenrollar; [+ *wool, thread*] desovillar
VI **1** desenrollarse; [*wool, thread*] desovillarse
2* (*fig*) (= *relax*) relajarse

unwisdom ['ʌn'wɪzdəm] N imprudencia *f*

unwise ['ʌn'waɪz] ADJ (= *careless*) imprudente; (= *inadvisable*) poco aconsejable • **it would be ~ to** (+ *infin*) sería poco aconsejable (+ *infin*) • **that was ~ of you** lo que hiciste fue imprudente • **that was most ~ of you** en eso has sido muy imprudente

unwisely ['ʌn'waɪzlɪ] ADV imprudentemente

unwitting [ʌn'wɪtɪŋ] ADJ involuntario • **I was the ~ cause** sin querer, yo fui la causa • **an ~ instrument of sth/sb** un instrumento involuntario de algo/algn

unwittingly [ʌn'wɪtɪŋlɪ] ADV inconscientemente, sin darse cuenta

unwomanly [ʌn'wʊmənlɪ] ADJ poco femenino

unwonted [ʌn'wəʊntɪd] ADJ insólito, inusitado

unworkable ['ʌn'wɜ:kəbl] ADJ **1** [*plan, suggestion*] impracticable, no viable
2 [*mine*] inexplotable

unworkmanlike [ʌn'wɜ:kmənlaɪk] ADJ [*job*] poco profesional

unworldly ['ʌn'wɜ:ldlɪ] ADJ
1 (= *unmaterialistic*) [*person*] nada materialista
2 (= *naïve*) [*person, attitude*] ingenuo, poco realista
3 (= *not of this world*) [*beauty, silence*] de otro mundo

unworn ['ʌn'wɔ:n] ADJ nuevo, sin estrenar

unworried [ʌn'wʌrɪd] ADJ despreocupado, sin preocupaciones • **he was ~ by my criticism** no le preocupaban mis críticas

unworthiness [ʌn'wɜ:ðɪnɪs] N falta *f* de valía, indignidad *f*

unworthy [ʌn'wɜ:ðɪ] ADJ **1** (= *undeserving*) [*person*] indigno, poco digno • **to be ~ to do sth** no ser digno de hacer algo, no merecer hacer algo • **I feel she is ~ to judge them** me parece que no es digna de juzgarlos • **to be ~ of sth/sb** no ser digno de algo/algn, no merecerse algo/a algn • **he felt himself ~ of her** sentía que no era digno de ella, sentía que no se la merecía • **it is ~ of attention/comment** no merece atención/comentario alguno
2 (= *ignoble*) [*activity, thought*] impropio • **his accusations are ~ of a gentleman** sus acusaciones no son dignas *or* son impropias de un caballero

unwound [ˌʌn'waʊnd] PT, PP *of* **unwind**

unwounded ['ʌn'wu:ndɪd] ADJ ileso

unwrap ['ʌn'ræp] VT abrir • **after the meal we ~ped the presents** después de comer abrimos los regalos

unwritten ['ʌn'rɪtn] ADJ no escrito • **~ law** ley *f* consuetudinaria

unyielding [ʌn'ji:ldɪŋ] ADJ inflexible

unyoke ['ʌn'jəʊk] VT desuncir

unzip ['ʌn'zɪp] VT **1** (= *open zip of*) abrir la cremallera *or* (*LAm*) el cierre de • **can you ~ me?** ¿me puedes bajar la cremallera?
2 (*Comput*) [+ *file*] descomprimir

up [ʌp]

ADVERB
PREPOSITION
NOUN
ADJECTIVE
INTRANSITIVE VERB
TRANSITIVE VERB

*When **up** is the second element in a phrasal verb, eg **come up, throw up, walk up**, look up the verb. When it is part of a set combination, eg **the way up, close up**, look up the other word.*

ADVERB
1 *direction* hacia arriba, para arriba • **he looked up** (*towards sky*) miró hacia *or* para arriba • **to walk up and down** pasearse de un lado para otro *or* de arriba abajo • **he's been up and down all evening** no ha parado quieto en toda la tarde • **she's still a bit up and down** todavía tiene sus altibajos • **to stop halfway up** pararse a mitad de la subida • **to throw sth up in the air** lanzar algo al aire • **he walked/ran up to the house** caminó/corrió hasta la casa • **a blond boy went up to her** un chico rubio le acercó
2 *position* • **the people three floors up (from me)** los que viven tres pisos más arriba • **up above (us) we could see a ledge** por encima (de nosotros) *or* sobre nuestras cabezas

podíamos ver una cornisa • **from up above** desde arriba • **my office is five floors up** mi oficina está en el quinto piso • **higher up** más arriba • **up in the mountains** montaña arriba • **up in the sky** en lo alto del cielo • **the jug's up there, on the freezer** la jarra está ahí arriba, en el congelador • **the castle's up there, on top of the hill** el castillo está allí arriba, en la cima del monte

3 (*in northern place, capital etc*) • **we're up for the day** hemos venido a pasar el día • **when you're next up this way** la próxima vez que pases por aquí • **how long have you lived up here?** ¿cuánto tiempo llevas viviendo aquí? • **when you're next up here** la próxima vez que pases por aquí • **he lives up in Scotland** vive en Escocia • **up in London** (allá) en Londres • **up north** en el norte • **how long did you live up there?** ¿cuánto tiempo estuviste viviendo allí *or* allá? • **the next time you're up there** la próxima vez que pases por allí *or* allá • **to go up to London/to university** ir a Londres/a la universidad

4 (*= standing*) de pie • **while you're up, can you get me a glass of water?** ya que estás de pie, ¿me puedes traer un vaso de agua? • **the ladder was up against the wall** la escalera estaba apoyada en *or* contra la pared

5 (*= out of bed*) • **to be up** (*= get up*) levantarse; (*= be active*) estar levantado • **we were up at 7** nos levantamos a las 7 • **what time will you be up** ¿a qué hora te levantarás? • **is Peter up yet?** ¿está levantado Peter? • **I'm usually up by 7 o'clock** normalmente a las 7 estoy levantado • **we were still up at midnight** a medianoche seguíamos sin acostarnos, a medianoche todavía estábamos levantados • **she was up and about at 6 a.m.** lleva en pie desde las 6 de la mañana • **to be up and about again** [*sick person*] estar repuesto • **to be up all night** no acostarse en toda la noche • **get up!** ¡levántate!

6 (*= raised*) • **with his head up (high)** con la cabeza bien levantada *or* erguida • **several children had their hands up** varios niños habían levantado la mano • **the blinds were up** las persianas estaban subidas *or* levantadas • **he sat in the car with the windows up** se sentó en el coche con las ventanillas subidas • **"this side up"** "este lado hacia arriba" • **look, the flag is up!** mira, la bandera está izada

7 (*in price, value*) • **potatoes are up** han subido las patatas • **the thermometer is up 2 degrees** el termómetro ha subido 2 grados • **the interest rate has risen sharply, up from 3% to 5%** los tipos de interés han subido bruscamente del 3% al 5% • **the temperature was up in the forties** la temperatura estaba por encima de los cuarenta • **prices are up on last year** los precios han subido desde el año pasado, del año pasado a este los precios han subido

8 (*in score*) • **we're a goal up** llevamos un tanto de ventaja • **we were 20 points up on them** les llevábamos una ventaja de 20 puntos

9 (*in terms of excellence*) • **to be up among** *or* **with the leaders** estar a la altura de los líderes • **she's right up there with the jazz greats** está en la cumbre con los grandes del jazz

10 (*= built, installed*) • **the new building isn't up yet** el nuevo edificio no está construido todavía, no han levantado el nuevo edificio todavía • **the tent isn't up yet** la tienda todavía no está puesta • **the scaffolding is now up** el andamio está puesto ahora • **the notice about the outing is up** el cartel de la excursión está puesto • **we've got the pictures up at last** por fin hemos puesto *or* colgado los cuadros • **the curtains are up** las cortinas están colocadas

11 (*= finished*) [*contract etc*] vencido, caducado • **when the period is up** cuando termine el plazo, cuando venza el plazo • **his holiday is up** han terminado ya sus vacaciones • **time is up** se ha acabado el tiempo • **time is up, put down your pens** se ha acabado el tiempo, dejen los bolígrafos sobre la mesa • **time is up for the people living here, their homes are to be demolished** a la gente que vive aquí le toca marcharse, están derribando sus casas • **our time here is up** no podemos quedarnos más tiempo aquí

12 (*= and over*) • **from £2 up** de 2 libras para arriba • **from the age of 13 up** a partir de los 13 años

13 (*= knowledgeable*) • **he's well up in** *or* **on British politics** está muy al corriente *or* al día en lo referente a la política británica • **how are you up on your military history?** ¿cómo andan tus conocimientos de historia militar?

14* (*= wrong*) • **there's something up with him** algo le pasa • **there's something up with the TV** le pasa algo a la tele • **what's up?** ¿qué pasa? • **what's up with him?** ¿que le pasa?

15 (*in running order*) • **first up** el primero (de la lista) • **next up** el siguiente (de la lista)

16 (*Jur*) • **her case isn't due up until next week** su caso no se verá hasta la próxima semana • **to be up before the judge/board** [*person*] (tener que) comparecer ante el juez/el consejo; [*case, matter*] verse ante el juez/en el consejo

17 (*= risen*) • **the river is up** el río ha subido • **the sun is up** ha salido el sol • **the tide is up** la marea está alta • IDIOM: • **his blood is up** le hierve la sangre

18 (*Brit*) (*= under repair*) • **the road is up** la calle está en obras

19 (*US*) (*Culin**) • **two fried eggs, up** un par de huevos fritos boca arriba • **a bourbon (straight) up** un bourbon sin hielo

20 (*= mounted*) • **a horse with Dettori up** un caballo montado por Dettori

21 (*in exclamations*) • **up (with) Celtic!** ¡arriba el Celtic!

22 (*in set expressions*) **up against** • **he's really up against it** ahora sí que está en un aprieto • **to be up against sb** tener que habérselas con algn, tener que enfrentarse a algn

up and running • **to be up and running** estar en funcionamiento • **to get sth up and running** poner algo en funcionamiento

up for sth • **three seats are up for election** tres escaños salen a elecciones • **most politicians up for reelection know this** (*= seeking*) la mayoría de los políticos que se presentan a la reelección lo saben • **every two years, a third of the Senate comes up for election** cada dos años se renueva una tercera parte del Senado • **to be up for sth*** (*= ready, willing*) tener ganas de algo • **are you up for it?** ¿estás dispuesto?

up to (*= till, as far as*) hasta • **up to now** hasta ahora, hasta la fecha • **up to this week** hasta esta semana • **up to here** hasta aquí • **up to £10** hasta 10 libras nada más • **to count up to 100** contar hasta 100 • **we were up to our knees/waist in water** el agua nos llegaba por *or* hasta las rodillas/la cintura • **what page are you up to?** ¿por qué página vas? • **to be up to a task** (*= capable of*) estar a la altura de una tarea, estar en condiciones de realizar una tarea • **to be up to doing sth** estar en condiciones de hacer algo • **they weren't up to running a company** no estaban en condiciones de gestionar una empresa, no estaban a la altura necesaria para gestionar una empresa

to be *or* **feel up to sth** • **are you (feeling) up to going for a walk?** ¿te sientes con ganas de dar un paseo? • **I don't feel up to going out** no tengo ánimos para salir; ▷ **including**

to be up to sth* (*= doing*) • **what are you up to?** ¿qué andas haciendo? • **what are you up to with that knife?** ¿qué haces con ese cuchillo? • **he's up to something** está tramando algo • **what does he think he's up to?** ¿qué diablos piensa hacer? • **I see what you're up to** te veo venir • **what have you been up to lately?** ¿qué has estado haciendo últimamente?

to be up to a standard/to much (*= equal to*) • **it isn't up to his usual standard** no está a su nivel de siempre • **the book isn't up to much** (*Brit**) el libro no vale mucho

to be up to sb (*= depend on*) • **it's up to you to decide** te toca (a ti) decidir • **I feel it is up to me to tell him** creo que me corresponde a mí decírselo • **I wouldn't do it but it's up to you** yo (que tú) no lo haría, pero allá tú *or* tú verás • **I'd go, but it's up to you** por mí iría, pero depende de ti • **if it were** *or* **was up to me** si dependiera de mí

PREPOSITION

1 (*= on top of*) en lo alto de, arriba de (*LAm*) • **he was up a ladder pruning the apple trees** estaba subido a una escalera *or* en lo alto de una escalera podando los manzanos • **to be up a tree** estar en lo alto de *or* (*LAm*) arriba de un árbol

2 (*= along, towards the top*) • **he went off up the road** se fue calle arriba • **put your handkerchief up your sleeve** guárdate el pañuelo dentro de la manga • **the heat disappears straight up the chimney** el calor se escapa chimenea arriba, el calor se escapa por lo alto de la chimenea • **to travel up and down the country** viajar por todo el país • **people up and down the country are saying ...** la gente por todo el país dice ... • **they live further up the road** viven en esta calle pero más arriba • **further up the page** en la misma página, más arriba • **halfway up the stairs** a mitad de la escalera • **halfway up the mountain** a mitad de la subida de la montaña • **up north** en el norte • **up river** río arriba

3 • **up yours!**** ¡vete a hacer puñetas!**

NOUN

1 • **ups and downs** altibajos *mpl*, vicisitudes *fpl* • **the ups and downs that every politician is faced with** los altibajos a que se enfrenta todo político, las vicisitudes a que está sometido todo político • **after many ups and downs** después de mil peripecias

2 • **it's on the up and up** (*Brit*) (*= improving*) va cada vez mejor; (*US*) (*= above board*) está en regla

ADJECTIVE

1 (*Rail*) [*train, line*] ascendente

2 (*= elated*) • **to be up*** estar en plena forma

INTRANSITIVE VERB*

1 (*= jump up*) • **he upped and hit him** se levantó (de un salto) y le pegó

2 (*emphatic*) • **she upped and left** (*= stood up*) se levantó y se marchó, se levantó y se largó*; (*= went*) fue y se marchó, fue y se largó* • **he upped and offed** se largó sin más*

TRANSITIVE VERB

(*= raise†*) [*+ price, offer*] subir, aumentar • **to up anchor** levar el ancla

up-and-coming [ˈʌpəndˈkʌmɪŋ] (ADJ) prometedor, con futuro

up-and-down [ˈʌpənˈdaʊn] (ADJ) [*movement*] de arriba a abajo, vertical; (*fig*) [*career,*

business, progress, relationship] inestable
up-and-under [ˌʌpən'ʌndəʳ] N (*Rugby*) patada *f* a seguir
upbeat ['ʌp'bi:t] ADJ* (= *positive*) optimista
N (*Mus*) tiempo *m* débil, tiempo *m* no acentuado; (*fig*) (*in prosperity*) aumento *m*
up-bow ['ʌpbəʊ] N (*Mus*) movimiento *m* ascendente del arco
upbraid [ʌp'breɪd] VT censurar, reprender • **to ~ sb with sth** censurar algo a algn
upbringing ['ʌpˌbrɪŋɪŋ] N educación *f*
upcast ['ʌpkɑ:st] N (*Min*) (*also* **upcast shaft**) pozo *m* de ventilación
upchuck‡ ['ʌptʃʌk] VI (*US*) echar los hígados por la boca*
upcoming ['ʌpkʌmɪŋ] ADJ [*elections, holidays*] próximo
upcountry ['ʌp'kʌntrɪ] ADV • **to go ~** ir hacia el interior, ir tierra adentro • **to be ~** estar tierra adentro, estar en el interior
ADJ [*town, school, accent*] del interior; [*trip, tour*] hacia el interior, al interior
up-current ['ʌp'kʌrənt] N (*Aer*) corriente *f* ascendente
upcycle ['ʌpˌsaɪkl] VT reciclar creativamente
upcycling ['ʌpˌsaɪklɪŋ] N reciclado *m* creativo
update VT [ʌp'deɪt] poner al día • **to ~ sb on sth** poner a algn al corriente *or* al tanto de algo
N ['ʌpdeɪt] puesta *f* al día; (*updated version*) versión *f* actualizada • **news ~** últimas noticias *fpl* • **he gave me an ~ on ...** me puso al día con respecto a ..., me puso al corriente *or* al tanto de ...
updating [ʌp'deɪtɪŋ] N puesta *f* al día
updraught, updraft (*US*) ['ʌpdræft] N corriente *f* ascendente
upend [ʌp'end] VT **1** (= *stand on its end*) poner vertical
2* (= *knock over*) [+ *person*] volcar
upfront [ʌp'frʌnt] ADJ **1*** (= *frank*) abierto, franco
2 [*payment*] inicial
ADV **1** (= *in advance*) por adelantado • **to pay ~ for sth** pagar algo por adelantado
2 (*esp US**) (= *frankly*) sinceramente, francamente
upgradability, upgradeability [ʌpgreɪdə'bɪlɪtɪ] N [*of computer, system*] capacidad *f* de expansión; [*of software*] capacidad *f* de actualización
upgradable, upgradeable [ʌp'greɪdəbl] ADJ [*computer, system*] expandible; [*software*] actualizable
upgrade N ['ʌpgreɪd] **1** (= *slope*) cuesta *f*, pendiente *f* • **to be on the ~** (*fig*) ir cuesta arriba, prosperar, estar en auge; (*Med*) estar mejor, estar reponiéndose
2 [*of system etc*] mejoramiento *m*, reforma *f*
3 (*Comput*) [*of computer, computer system*] expansión *f*; [*of software*] actualización *f*
VT [ʌp'greɪd] **1** (= *promote*) [+ *person*] ascender; [+ *job*] asignar a un grado más alto
2 [+ *system etc*] mejorar, reformar
3 (*Comput*) (= *update*) actualizar; (= *modernize*) modernizar, mejorar las prestaciones de
upgradeability [ʌpgreɪdə'bɪlɪtɪ] N = **upgradability**
upgradeable [ʌp'greɪdəbl] ADJ = **upgradable**
upheaval [ʌp'hi:vəl] N **1** (*emotional*) trastorno *m*
2 (*in home, office etc*) trastorno *m*
3 (*Pol*) agitación *f*
4 (*Geol*) levantamiento *m*
upheld [ʌp'held] PT, PP *of* **uphold**
uphill ['ʌp'hɪl] ADV • **to go ~** ir cuesta arriba • **the road goes ~ for two miles** la carretera sube durante dos millas
ADJ en cuesta, en pendiente; (*fig*) arduo, penoso • **it's ~ all the way** (*lit*) el camino es todo cuesta arriba; (*fig*) es una tarea laboriosa • **it was an ~ struggle** fue muy difícil • **it's an ~ task** es una tarea laboriosa
uphold [ʌp'həʊld] (PT, PP: **upheld**) VT
1 (= *sustain*) mantener, sostener; (= *support*) apoyar, defender
2 (*Jur*) confirmar
upholder [ʌp'həʊldəʳ] N defensor(a) *m/f*
upholster [ʌp'həʊlstəʳ] VT tapizar, entapizar (**with** de) • **well ~ed*** (*euph*) rellenito*
upholsterer [ʌp'həʊlstərəʳ] N tapicero/a *m/f*
upholstery [ʌp'həʊlstərɪ] N **1** (*cushioning etc*) tapizado *m*, almohadillado *m*; (*in car*) tapizado *m*
2 (= *trade*) tapicería *f*
upkeep ['ʌpki:p] N **1** (= *care*) mantenimiento *m*
2 (= *cost*) gastos *mpl* de mantenimiento
upland ['ʌplənd] N tierra *f* alta, meseta *f*; **uplands** tierras *fpl* altas
ADJ de la meseta
uplift N ['ʌplɪft] (= *edification*) inspiración *f*, edificación *f* • **moral ~** edificación *f*
VT [ʌp'lɪft] (*fig*) (= *encourage*) animar; (= *raise*) mejorar, elevar
uplifted [ʌp'lɪftɪd] ADJ **1** (= *raised*) [*hand, arm*] levantado, en alto; [*face*] vuelto hacia arriba, mirando hacia arriba
2 (= *edified*) • **to feel ~ (by sth)** sentirse animado (por algo)
uplifting [ʌp'lɪftɪŋ] ADJ inspirador, edificante
uplink ['ʌplɪŋk] N enlace *m* ascendente
upload [ʌp'ləʊd] VT (*Comput*) subir, poner
up-market [ʌp'mɑ:kɪt] (*Brit*) ADJ [*image, shop, hotel, person*] de categoría; [*product*] de primera calidad, de calidad superior; [*magazine*] para un público de categoría
ADV • **to go/move up-market** [*company*] (*for clients*) subir de categoría, buscar una clientela más selecta
upmost ['ʌpməʊst] = **uppermost**
upon [ə'pɒn] PREP **1** (*with place, position*) sobre • **he placed the tray ~ the table** puso la bandeja sobre la mesa • **I saw pictures of him walking ~ the moon** vi fotos de él caminando sobre la luna • **he had a suspicious look ~ his face** en su rostro había una mirada sospechosa • **he recalled the attacks ~ him** recordó los ataques que recibió • **~ my word!†** ¡caramba!
2 (*with time*) • **he emigrated ~ the death of his son** emigró tras la muerte de su hijo • **~ hearing this she wept** al oír esto, lloró • **~ entering the church, take the door on the left** al entrar en la iglesia, siga por la puerta de la izquierda • **Christmas is almost ~ us again** las Navidades ya están otra vez encima
3 (*with large numbers*) • **row ~ row of women surged forwards** hilera tras hilera de mujeres iban avanzando • **thousands ~ thousands of people were arriving** iban llegando miles y miles de personas; ▹ **on**
upper ['ʌpəʳ] ADJ **1** (*in level*) [*deck, floor*] de arriba; (*more frm*) superior • **the ~ atmosphere** la atmósfera superior • **the ~ slopes of Illimani** las pendientes más altas del Illimani; ▹ **hand, reach, stiff**
2 (*in importance, rank*) [*echelons, ranks, caste*] superior • **~ management** los altos cargos de la administración
3 (*on scale*) [*limit*] máximo • **properties at the ~ end of the market** inmuebles de la sección más cara del mercado • **people in the ~ income bracket** las personas con un nivel de ingresos superior
4 (*in Geog names*) alto • **the Upper Nile** el alto Nilo
N **1 uppers** [*of shoe*] pala *fsing* • IDIOM: • **to be (down) on one's ~s** estar en las últimas *or* (*Sp*) sin un duro
2* (= *drug*) anfeta* *f*
3 (*Dentistry*) dentadura *f* postiza (*superior*)
4 (*US*) (*Rail*) litera *f* de arriba
CPD ▸ **upper arm** brazo *m* superior ▸ **upper atmosphere** • **the ~ atmosphere** la termosfera ▸ **upper case** (*Typ*) mayúsculas *fpl* • **in ~ case** en mayúsculas ▸ **upper chamber** (*Pol*) cámara *f* alta ▸ **the upper circle** (*Theat*) la galería superior ▸ **upper class** • **the ~ classes** la(s) clase(s) alta(s) ▸ **the upper crust*** la flor y nata ▸ **Upper Egypt** alto Egipto *m* ▸ **upper house** (*Pol*) cámara *f* alta ▸ **upper jaw** maxilar *m* superior ▸ **upper lip** labio *m* superior ▸ **upper middle class** clase *f* media alta; (*used as adjective*) de la clase media alta ▸ **upper school** cursos *mpl* superiores; (*in names*) instituto *m* de enseñanza media ▸ **upper sixth** ≈ último curso *m* de bachillerato • **she's in the ~ sixth** ≈ está en el último curso de bachillerato ▸ **Upper Volta** alto Volta *m*
upper-case ['ʌpə'keɪs] ADJ mayúsculo, de letra mayúscula
upper-class ['ʌpə'klɑ:s] ADJ de clase alta • **an upper-class twit** un señorito de clase alta
upper-crust* ['ʌpə'krʌst] ADJ de categoría (social) superior, de buen tono; ▹ **upper**
uppercut ['ʌpəkʌt] N uppercut *m*, gancho *m* a la cara
upper-division [ˌʌpədɪ'vɪʒən] ADJ • **upper-division student** (*US*) estudiante *mf* de tercer *or* cuarto año
uppermost ['ʌpəməʊst] ADJ **1** el/la más alto/a • **to put sth face ~** poner algo cara arriba
2 (*fig*) principal, predominante • **what is ~ in sb's mind** lo que más le preocupa a algn • **it was ~ in my mind** me preocupaba más que cualquier otra cosa
ADV encima
uppish* ['ʌpɪʃ], **uppity*** ['ʌpɪtɪ] ADJ (*Brit*) presumido, engreído • **to get ~** presumir, darse aires de importancia
upraise [ʌp'reɪz] VT levantar • **with arm ~d** con el brazo levantado
upright ['ʌpraɪt] ADJ **1** (*lit*) derecho, recto
2 (*fig*) honrado, íntegro
ADV erguido, derecho, recto • **to hold o.s. ~** mantenerse erguido • **to sit bolt ~** sentarse muy derecho, sentarse muy erguido
N **1** (= *post*) montante *m*, poste *m*; (= *goalpost*) poste *m*
2 (= *piano*) piano *m* vertical *or* recto
CPD ▸ **upright piano** piano *m* vertical *or* recto ▸ **upright vacuum cleaner** aspirador *m* vertical
uprightly ['ʌpˌraɪtlɪ] ADV (*fig*) honradamente, rectamente
uprightness ['ʌpˌraɪtnɪs] N (*fig*) honradez *f*, rectitud *f*
uprising ['ʌpraɪzɪŋ] N alzamiento *m*, sublevación *f*
up-river ['ʌp'rɪvəʳ] ADV = **upstream**
uproar ['ʌprɔ:ʳ] N alboroto *m*, jaleo *m* • **this caused an ~** • **at this there was (an) ~** (= *shouting*) en esto se armó un alboroto; (= *protesting*) en esto estallaron ruidosas las protestas • **the hall was in (an) ~** (= *shouting*) había alboroto en la sala; (= *protesting*) se oían protestas airadas en la sala

uproarious [ʌp'rɔːrɪəs] ADJ **1** (= *noisy*) [*laughter*] escandaloso; [*meeting*] alborotado, ruidoso; [*success*] clamoroso
2 (= *hilarious*) [*occasion*] divertidísimo; [*comedy*] desternillante; [*personality*] divertidísimo

uproariously [ʌp'rɔːrɪəslɪ] ADV • **to laugh ~** reírse a carcajadas • **he told me an ~ funny story** me contó una historia para desternillarse *or* troncharse de risa

uproot [ʌp'ruːt] VT desarraigar, arrancar (de raíz); (= *destroy*) eliminar, extirpar • **whole families have been ~ed** familias enteras se han visto desarraigadas

upsa-daisy* ['ʌpsə,deɪzɪ] EXCL ¡aúpa!

upscale* [ʌp'skeɪl] ADJ (US) [*image, store, hotel, person*] de categoría; [*product*] de primera calidad, de calidad superior

upset [ʌp'set] (VB: PT, PP: **upset**) VT
1 (= *knock over*) [+ *object*] volcar, tirar; [+ *liquid*] derramar, tirar; [+ *boat*] volcar • IDIOM: • **to ~ the applecart** desbaratar los planes, desbaratar el tinglado*
2 (= *distress*) afectar; (= *hurt, make sad*) disgustar; (= *offend*) ofender, disgustar • **the news ~ her a lot** la noticia la afectó mucho • **it ~ me that he forgot my birthday** me disgustó que se olvidara de mi cumpleaños • **I didn't mean to ~ her** no quería ofenderla *or* disgustarla • **people who are easily ~ may prefer not to watch** puede que las personas que se impresionen fácilmente prefieran no mirar • **to ~ o.s.**: • **you'll only ~ yourself if you see him** no harás más que cogerte un disgusto si te ves con él • **there now, don't ~ yourself** venga, no te disgustes
3 (= *disrupt*) [+ *plans, calculations*] dar al traste con, desbaratar • **this could ~ the balance of power in the region** esto podría alterar el equilibrio de poderes en la región
4 (= *make ill*) sentar mal a, enfermar (*LAm*) • **garlic ~s me/my stomach** el ajo no me sienta bien
ADJ **1** (= *distressed*) alterado; (= *hurt, sad*) disgustado; (= *offended*) ofendido, disgustado; (= *annoyed*) molesto • **he's ~ that you didn't tell him** se disgustó *or* se molestó porque no se lo dijiste • **she's ~ about failing** está disgustada por haber suspendido • **what are you so ~ about?** ¿qué es lo que te ha disgustado tanto? • **to get ~** (= *distressed*) alterarse; (= *hurt*) disgustarse; (= *offended*) ofenderse; (= *annoyed*) enfadarse • **don't get ~, they didn't take anything** no te alteres, no se llevaron nada • **she gets ~ when she sees anyone suffering** la afecta mucho ver a alguien sufriendo, lo pasa muy mal *or* sufre mucho si ve a alguien sufriendo • **he gets very ~ if I don't ring him every day** se pone fatal *or* lo pasa fatal si no lo llamo todos los días*
2 ['ʌpset] (= *sick*) • **I have an ~ stomach** tengo el estómago revuelto
N ['ʌpset] **1** (= *disturbance*) contratiempo *m* • **she has had to deal with many ~s in her personal life** su vida ha estado llena de contratiempos *or* reveses • **she has had her fair share of ~s in the past few weeks** ya ha tenido bastantes disgustos en las últimas semanas • **people who are prone to emotional ~s** las personas propensas a trastornos emocionales
2 (*Sport, Pol*) (= *unexpected result*) derrota *f* sorpresa
3 (= *illness*) malestar *m* • **stomach ~** malestar *m* de estómago • **to have a stomach ~** tener el estómago revuelto
CPD ['ʌpset] ▸ **upset price** (*esp Scot, US*) precio *m* mínimo, precio *m* de reserva

upsetting [ʌp'setɪŋ] ADJ (= *distressing*) [*experience, incident*] terrible; [*image*] sobrecogedor; (= *saddening*) triste; (= *offending*) [*language, remark*] ofensivo; (= *annoying*) fastidioso, molesto • **the whole incident was very ~ for me** todo el incidente me afectó *or* disgustó mucho • **it is ~ for him to talk about it** lo pasa mal *or* se pone mal al hablar de ello • **parts of the film may be ~ to some viewers** algunas partes de la película pueden resultarles sobrecogedoras a algunos espectadores

upshot ['ʌpʃɒt] N resultado *m* • **the ~ of it all was ...** el resultado fue que ... • **in the ~** al fin y al cabo

upside-down ['ʌpsaɪd'daʊn] ADV al revés; (= *untidily*) patas arriba • **to turn sth upside-down** volver algo al revés; (*fig*) revolverlo todo • **we turned everything upside-down looking for it** al buscarlo lo revolvimos todo, en la búsqueda lo registramos todo de arriba abajo
ADJ al revés • **to be upside-down** estar al revés • **the room was upside-down** reinaba el desorden en el cuarto, en el cuarto todo estaba patas arriba*

upstage ['ʌp'steɪdʒ] ADV (*Theat*) • **to be ~** estar en el fondo del escenario • **to go ~** ir hacia el fondo del escenario
VT • **to ~ sb** (*fig*) eclipsar a algn

upstairs ['ʌp'stɛəz] ADV arriba • **"where's your coat?" — "it's ~"** —¿dónde está tu abrigo? —está arriba • **the people ~** los de arriba • **to go ~** subir (al piso superior) • **he went ~ to bed** subió para irse a la cama • **to walk slowly ~** subir lentamente la escalera
ADJ de arriba • **we looked out of an ~ window** nos asomamos a una ventana del piso superior *or* de arriba
N piso *m* superior *or* de arriba

upstanding [ʌp'stændɪŋ] ADJ
1 (= *respectable*) honrado • **a fine ~ young man** un joven distinguido y honrado
2 (*frm*) (= *erect*) [*person*] recto
3 (*Jur*) (*frm*) • **be ~!** ¡pónganse de pie!

upstart ['ʌpstɑːt] (*pej*) ADJ **1** (= *socially ambitious*) arribista, advenedizo
2 (= *arrogant*) presuntuoso • **some ~ youth** un joven presuntuoso
N **1** (= *social climber*) arribista *mf*, advenedizo/a *m/f*
2 (= *arrogant person*) presuntuoso/a *m/f*

upstate ['ʌp'steɪt] (US) N interior *m*
ADJ interior, septentrional
ADV [*be*] en el interior; [*go*] al interior

upstream ['ʌp'striːm] ADV río arriba • **to go ~** ir río arriba • **to swim ~** nadar contra la corriente • **a town ~ from Windsor** una ciudad más arriba de Windsor • **about three miles ~ from Windsor** unas tres millas más arriba de Windsor

upstretched ['ʌpstretʃt] ADJ extendido hacia arriba

upstroke ['ʌpstrəʊk] N **1** (*with pen*) trazo *m* ascendente
2 (*Mech*) (*of piston*) carrera *f* ascendente

upsurge ['ʌpsɜːdʒ] N (*in violence, fighting*) recrudecimiento *m*; (*in demand*) fuerte aumento *m* • **a great ~ of interest in Góngora** un gran renacimiento del interés por Góngora • **there has been an ~ of feeling about this question** ha aumentado de pronto la preocupación por esta cuestión

upswept ['ʌpswept] ADJ [*wing*] elevado, inclinado hacia arriba • **with ~ hair** con peinado alto

upswing ['ʌpswɪŋ] N (*lit*) movimiento *m* hacia arriba; (*fig*) alza *f*, mejora *f* notable (**in** en) • **an ~ in sales** una alza/mejora notable en las ventas • **an ~ in the economy** una notable mejora en la economía • **to be on the ~** estar en alza

uptake ['ʌpteɪk] N **1** (= *understanding*) • **to be quick on the ~*** ser muy listo, agarrar las cosas al vuelo* • **to be slow on the ~*** ser corto (de entendederas)*
2 (= *intake*) consumo *m*
3 (= *acceptance*) aceptación *f*; (= *number accepted*) cantidad *f* admitida

up-tempo [,ʌp'tempəʊ] ADJ [*tune*] con ritmo rápido

upthrust ['ʌp'θrʌst] ADJ **1** (*gen*) (*Tech*) empujado hacia arriba, dirigido hacia arriba
2 (*Geol*) solevantado
N **1** (*gen*) (*Tech*) empuje *m* hacia arriba
2 (*Geol*) solevantamiento *m*

uptight* [ʌp'taɪt] ADJ nervioso, tenso • **she's very ~ today** está muy nerviosa *or* tensa hoy • **to get (all) ~ about sth** ponerse nervioso por algo • **don't get so ~!** ¡no te pongas tan nervioso!, ¡no te pongas tan neura!*

uptime ['ʌptaɪm] N tiempo *m* de operación

up-to-date ['ʌptə'deɪt] ADJ [*information, edition, report*] al día, actualizado; [*clothes, equipment, technology*] moderno • **to be up-to-date with one's payments** llevar sus pagos al día • **to bring/keep sth/sb up-to-date** poner/mantener algo/a algn al día *or* al corriente • **we'll keep you up-to-date with any news** le mantendremos al día *or* al corriente de las noticias • **I like to keep up-to-date with all the latest fashions** me gusta mantenerme al día *or* al corriente de la última moda

up-to-the-minute ['ʌptəðə'mɪnɪt] ADJ de última hora

uptown ['ʌp'taʊn] (US) ADV hacia las afueras, hacia los barrios exteriores
ADJ exterior, de las afueras

uptrend ['ʌptrend] N (*Econ*) tendencia *f* al alza • **in** *or* **on an ~** en alza

upturn N ['ʌptɜːn] (= *improvement*) mejora *f*, aumento *m* (**in** de); (*Econ etc*) repunte *m*
VT [ʌp'tɜːn] (= *turn over*) volver hacia arriba; (= *overturn*) volcar

upturned ['ʌptɜːnd] ADJ [*box etc*] vuelto hacia arriba; [*nose*] respingón

UPU N ABBR (= **Universal Post Union**) UPU *f*

UPVC ABBR = **unplasticized polyvinyl chloride**

upward ['ʌpwəd] ADJ [*slope*] ascendente, hacia arriba; [*tendency*] al alza • **~ mobility** ascenso *m* social, movilidad *f* social ascendente
ADV (*also* **upwards**) **1** (*gen*) hacia arriba • **face ~** boca arriba • **to lay sth face ~** poner algo boca arriba • **to look ~** mirar hacia arriba
2 (*with numbers*) • **£50 and ~** de 50 libras para arriba • **from the age of 13 ~** desde los 13 años • **~ of 500** más de 500

upwardly ['ʌpwədlɪ] ADV • **~ mobile** [*person*] ambicioso

upwards ['ʌpwədz] ADV (*esp Brit*) = **upward**

upwind ['ʌp'wɪnd] ADV • **to stay ~** quedarse en la parte de donde sopla el viento

URA N ABBR (US) = **Urban Renewal Administration**

uraemia [jʊ'riːmɪə] N uremia *f*

uraemic [jʊ'riːmɪk] ADJ urémico

Urals ['jʊərəlz] N (*also* **Ural Mountains**) (Montes *mpl*) Urales *mpl*

uranalysis [jʊərə'nælɪsɪs] N (PL: **uranalyses** [,jʊərə'nælɪsiːz]) = **urinalysis**

uranium [jʊə'reɪnɪəm] N uranio *m*

Uranus ['jʊərənəs] N Urano *m*

urban ['ɜːbən] ADJ urbano
CPD ▸ **urban blight** desertización *f* urbana ▸ **urban clearway** calle *f* en la que está

prohibido parar ▸ **urban conservation area** área *f* de conservación urbana ▸ **urban development** desarrollo *m* urbano ▸ **urban development zone** ≈ área *f* de urbanización prioritaria ▸ **urban guerrilla** guerrillero/a *m/f* urbano/a ▸ **urban myth** leyenda *f* urbana ▸ **urban planner** urbanista *mf* ▸ **urban planning** urbanismo *m* ▸ **urban renewal** renovación *f* urbana ▸ **urban sprawl** extensión *f* urbana ▸ **urban warfare** guerrilla *f* urbana

urbane [3:'beɪn] (ADJ) urbano, cortés

urbanity [3:'bænɪtɪ] (N) urbanidad *f*, cortesía *f*

urbanization ['3:bənaɪ'zeɪʃən] (N) urbanización *f*

urbanize ['3:bənaɪz] (VT) urbanizar

urchin ['3:tʃɪn] (N) pilluelo/a *m/f*, golfillo/a *m/f* • **sea ~** erizo *m* de mar

Urdu ['ʊədu:] (N) (*Ling*) urdu *m*

urea ['jʊərɪə] (N) urea *f*

uremia [jʊə'ri:mɪə] (*US*) = **uraemia**

uremic [jʊə'ri:mɪk] (*US*) = **uraemic**

ureter [jʊə'ri:təʳ] (N) uréter *m*

urethra [jʊə'ri:θrə] (N) (PL: **urethras** *or* **urethrae** [jʊ'ri:θri:]) uretra *f*

urge [3:dʒ] (N) impulso *m*; (*sexual etc*) deseo *m* • **the ~ to write** el deseo apremiante de escribir, la ambición de hacerse escritor • **to feel an ~ to do sth** sentir fuertes deseos *or* ganas de hacer algo • **to get** *or* **have the ~ (to do sth): when you get** *or* **have the ~ to eat something exotic ...** cuando te entren ganas de comer algo exótico • **he had the sudden ~ to take all his clothes off** de repente le entraron ganas de desnudarse

(VT) **1** (= *try to persuade*) animar, alentar • **to ~ sb to do sth** animar *or* instar a algn a hacer algo • **to ~ that sth should be done** recomendar encarecidamente que se haga algo

2 (= *advocate*) recomendar, abogar por • **to ~ sth on** *or* **upon sb** insistir en algo con algn • **to ~ a policy on the government** hacer presión en el gobierno para que adopte una política

▸ **urge on** (VT + ADV) animar, alentar; (*fig*) animar, instar

urgency ['3:dʒənsɪ] (N) **1** (= *haste*) urgencia *f* • **not everyone had the same sense of ~** no todo el mundo tenía el mismo sentido de la urgencia • **it is a matter of ~** es un asunto urgente • **the problem must be tackled as a matter of ~** el problema debe tratarse con la máxima urgencia

2 [*of tone of voice, pleas*] urgencia *f* • **with a note of ~ in his voice** con un tono de urgencia

urgent ['3:dʒənt] (ADJ) **1** (= *imperative*) [*matter, business, case, message*] urgente • **he needs ~ medical treatment** necesita tratamiento médico urgente *or* urgentemente • **is this ~?** ¿es urgente?, ¿corre prisa esto? • **it is ~ that I see him** tengo que verlo urgentemente • **there is an ~ need for water** se necesita urgentemente agua, hay una necesidad apremiante de agua • **to be in ~ need of sth** necesitar algo urgentemente

2 (= *earnest, persistent*) [*tone*] de urgencia, insistente; [*voice*] insistente; [*plea, appeal*] urgente

urgently ['3:dʒəntlɪ] (ADV) **1** (= *immediately*) [*need, seek*] urgentemente, con urgencia • **he ~ needs help** necesita ayuda urgentemente *or* con urgencia

2 (= *earnestly, persistently*) (*gen*) con insistencia; [*speak*] con tono de urgencia

uric ['jʊərɪk] (ADJ) úrico • **~ acid** ácido *m* úrico

urinal [jʊə'raɪnl] (N) (= *building*) urinario *m*; (= *vessel*) orinal *m*

urinalysis [jʊərə'nælɪsɪs] (N) (PL: **urinalyses** [ˌjʊərɪ'nælɪsi:z]) análisis *m inv* de orina

urinary ['jʊərɪnərɪ] (ADJ) urinario

urinate ['jʊərɪneɪt] (VT) orinar

(VI) orinar(se)

urine ['jʊərɪn] (N) orina *f*, orines *mpl*

URL (N ABBR) (*Internet*) (= **uniform resource locator**) URL *m*

urn [3:n] (N) **1** (= *vase*) urna *f*

2 (= *tea urn*) tetera *f*; (= *coffee urn*) cafetera *f*

urogenital [ˌjʊərəʊ'dʒenɪtl] (ADJ) urogenital

urological [ˌjʊərəʊ'lɒdʒɪkl] (ADJ) urológico

urologist [jʊə'rɒlədʒɪst] (N) urólogo/a *m/f*

urology [jʊə'rɒlədʒɪ] (N) urología *f*

Ursa Major ['3:sə'meɪdʒəʳ] (N) Osa *f* Mayor

Ursa Minor ['3:sə'maɪnəʳ] (N) Osa *f* Menor

urticaria [ˌ3:tɪ'keərɪə] (N) urticaria *f*

Uruguay ['jʊərəgwaɪ] (N) Uruguay *m*

Uruguayan [ˌjʊərə'gwaɪən] (ADJ) uruguayo

(N) uruguayo/a *m/f*

US (N ABBR) = **United States** • **the US** EE.UU., Estados Unidos • **in the US** en Estados Unidos • **the US Army/government** el Ejército/gobierno estadounidense

us [ʌs] (PRON) **1** (*direct/indirect object*) nos • **they helped us** nos ayudaron • **look at us!** ¡míranos! • **give it to us** dánoslo • **they gave us some brochures** nos dieron unos folletos • **see if you can find us some food** mira a ver si nos encuentras algo de comer

2 (*after prepositions, in comparisons, with the verb to be*) nosotros/as • **why don't you come with us?** ¿por qué no vienes con nosotros? • **several of us** varios de nosotros • **he is one of us** es uno de nosotros • **both of us** los dos • **they are older than us** son mayores que nosotros • **as for us English, we ...** en cuanto a nosotros los ingleses, ... • **it's us** somos nosotros

3 (*Brit*‡) (= *me*) me • **give us a bit!** ¡dame un poco! • **give us a look!** ¡déjame ver!

USA (N ABBR) **1** = **United States of America** • **the USA** Estados Unidos, EE.UU. • **in the USA** en Estados Unidos

2 = **United States Army**

usable ['ju:zəbl] (ADJ) utilizable • **~ space** espacio *m* útil • **it is no longer ~** ya no sirve

USAF (N ABBR) = **United States Air Force**

usage ['ju:zɪdʒ] (N) **1** (= *custom*) costumbre *f*, usanza *f* • **an ancient ~ of the Celts** una antigua usanza de los celtas

2 (*Ling*) (= *use, way of using*) uso *m* • **in the ~ of railwaymen** en el lenguaje de los ferroviarios, en el uso ferroviario

3 (= *handling*) manejo *m*; (= *treatment*) tratos *mpl* • **ill ~** mal tratamiento *m* • **it's had some rough ~** ha sido manejado con bastante dureza

USB (*Comput*) (= **Universal Serial Bus**) (N) USB *m*

(CPD) [*port, hub, cable, driver*] USB (*inv*)

USCG (N ABBR) (*US*) = **United States Coast Guard**

USD (ABBR) = **US Dollars**

USDA (N ABBR) (= **United States Department of Agriculture**) ≈ MAPA *m*

USDAW ['ʌzdɔ:] (N ABBR) (*Brit*) = **Union of Shop, Distributive and Allied Workers**

USDI (N ABBR) = **United States Department of the Interior**

use [ju:s] (N) **1** (= *act of using*) uso *m*, empleo *m*, utilización *f*; (= *handling*) manejo *m* • **the use of steel in industry** el empleo *or* la utilización *or* el uso del acero en la industria • **for the use of the blind** para (uso de) los ciegos • **for use in case of emergency** para uso en caso de emergencia • **care in the use of guns** cuidado *m* en el manejo de las armas de fuego • **a new use for old tyres** un nuevo método para utilizar los neumáticos viejos • **"directions for use"** "modo de empleo" • **fit for use** servible, en buen estado • **in use**: • **word in use** palabra *f* en uso *or* que se usa • **to be in daily use** ser de uso diario • **to be no longer in use** estar fuera de uso • **it is not now in use** ya no se usa • **it has not been in use for five years** hace cinco años que no se usa • **an article in everyday use** un artículo de uso diario • **to make use of** hacer uso de, usar; [+ *right etc*] valerse de, ejercer • **to make good use of** sacar partido *or* provecho de • **out of use** en desuso • **it is now out of use** ya no se usa, está en desuso • **to go** *or* **fall out of use** caer en desuso • **to put sth to good use** hacer buen uso de algo, sacar partido *or* provecho de algo • **to put sth into use** poner algo en servicio • **ready for use** listo (para ser usado) • **it improves with use** mejora con el uso

2 (= *way of using*) modo *m* de empleo; (= *handling*) manejo *m* • **we were instructed in the use of firearms** se nos instruyó en el manejo de armas de fuego

3 (= *function*) uso *m* • **it has many uses** tiene muchos usos • **can you find a use for this?** ¿te sirve esto?

4 (= *usefulness*) utilidad *f* • **it has its uses** tiene su utilidad • **to be of use** servir, tener utilidad • **can I be of any use?** ¿puedo ayudar? • **to be no use**: • **he's no use as a teacher** no vale para profesor, no sirve como profesor • **it's (of) no use** es inútil, no sirve para nada • **it's no use discussing it further** es inútil *or* no vale la pena seguir discutiendo • **I have no further use for it** ya no lo necesito, ya no me sirve para nada • **to have no use for sb*** no aguantar a algn • **I've no use for those who ...** no aguanto a los que ... • **what's the use of all this?** ¿de qué sirve todo esto?

5 (= *ability to use, access*) • **he gave me the use of his car** me dejó que usara su coche • **to have the use of**: • **to have the use of a garage** tener acceso a un garaje • **I have the use of it on Sundays** me permiten usarlo los domingos, lo puedo usar los domingos • **I have the use of the kitchen until 6p.m.** puedo *or* tengo permitido usar la cocina hasta las seis • **he lost the use of his arm** se le quedó inútil el brazo

6 (*Ling*) (= *sense*) uso *m*, sentido *m*

7 (*frm*) (= *custom*) uso *m*, costumbre *f*

(VT) [ju:z] **1** (*gen*) usar, emplear, utilizar • **he used a knife** empleó *or* usó *or* utilizó un cuchillo • **are you using this book?** ¿te hace falta este libro? • **which book did you use?** ¿qué libro consultaste? • **it isn't used any more** ya no se usa • **have you used a gun before?** ¿has manejado alguna vez una escopeta? • **"use only in emergencies"** "usar solo en caso de emergencia" • **to use sth as a hammer** emplear *or* usar algo como martillo • **to be used**: • **what's this used for?** ¿para qué sirve esto?, ¿para qué se utiliza esto? • **the money is used for the poor** el dinero se dedica a los pobres • **the word is no longer used** la palabra ya no se usa • **this room could use some paint*** a este cuarto no le vendría mal una mano de pintura • **I could use a drink!*** ¡no me vendría mal un trago! • **to use sth for**: • **to use sth for a purpose** servirse de algo con un propósito • **to use force** emplear la fuerza • **careful how you use that razor!** ¡cuidado con la navaja esa! • **to use every means** emplear todos los medios a su alcance (**to do sth** para hacer algo)

2 (= *make use of, exploit*) usar, utilizar • **he said I could use his car** dijo que podía usar *or* utilizar su coche • **I don't use my Spanish**

much no uso mucho el español • **you can use the leftovers in a soup** puedes usar las sobras para una sopa • **he wants to use the bathroom** quiere usar el cuarto de baño; (= *go to the toilet*) quiere ir al lavabo *or* (*LAm*) al baño • **someone is using the bathroom** el lavabo *or* (*LAm*) el baño está ocupado • **use your head** *or* **brains!*** ¡usa el coco!*
3 (= *consume*) [+ *fuel*] consumir • **have you used all the milk?** ¿has terminado toda la leche?
4† (= *treat*) tratar • **she had been cruelly used by …** había sido tratada con crueldad por … • **to use sb roughly** maltratar a algn • **to use sb well** tratar bien a algn
(VI) (*Drugs*‡) drogarse
(AUX VB) [juːs] (*gen*) soler, acostumbrar (a) • **I used to go camping as a child** de pequeño solía *or* acostumbraba ir de acampada • **I used to live in London** (antes) vivía en Londres • **I didn't use to like maths, but now I love it** antes no me gustaban las matemáticas, pero ahora me encantan • **but I used not to** pero antes no • **things aren't what they used to be** las cosas ya no son lo que eran
▸ **use up** (VT + ADV) [+ *supplies*] agotar; [+ *money*] gastar • **we've used up all the paint** hemos acabado toda la pintura • **when we've used up all our money** cuando hayamos gastado todo el dinero • **please use up all the coffee** terminaos el café

USED TO

▹ *To describe what someone* **used to do** *or what* **used to happen**, *you should generally just use the imperfect tense of the main verb:*
We used to buy our food at the corner shop
Comprábamos la comida en la tienda de la esquina
… as my mother used to say …
… como decía mi madre …

▹ *Alternatively, to describe someone's habits you can use* **solía** + *infinitive or* **acostumbraba (a)** + *infinitive:*
He used to go for a walk every day
Solía *or* Acostumbraba (a) dar un paseo todos los días

▹ *To emphasize the contrast between what* **used to** *happen previously and what happens now, use* **antes** + *imperfect:*
He used to be a journalist
Antes era periodista
She didn't use to *or* **She used not to drink alcohol**
Antes no tomaba alcohol

For further uses and examples, see **use**

useable [ˈjuːzəbl] (ADJ) = **usable**
used¹ [juːzd] (ADJ) **1** (= *finished with*) [*stamp, syringe*] usado; [*battery, tyre*] gastado, usado
2 (= *second-hand*) [*clothing, car*] usado • **a ~ car** un coche de segunda mano
used² [juːst] (ADJ) • **to be ~ to sth** estar acostumbrado a algo • **he wasn't ~ to driving on the right** no estaba acostumbrado a conducir por la derecha • **don't worry, I'm ~ to it** no te preocupes, estoy acostumbrado • **to be ~ to doing sth** estar acostumbrado a hacer algo • **to get ~ to** acostumbrarse a • **I still haven't got ~ to the lifts** todavía no me he acostumbrado a los ascensores
used-car salesman [ˌjuːzdˈkɑːˌseɪlzmən] (N) vendedor *m* de coches de segunda mano
useful [ˈjuːsfʊl] (ADJ) **1** (= *valuable*) [*information, advice, tool*] útil; [*discussion, meeting*] fructífero; [*experience*] provechoso, útil • **beans are a ~ source of protein** las judías son una buena fuente de proteína • **a ~ player** un buen jugador, un jugador que vale • **the time we spent in Spain was very ~** nuestra estancia en España fue muy provechosa • **he's a ~ person to know** es una persona que conviene conocer • **it is very ~ to be able to drive** es muy útil saber conducir • **~ capacity** capacidad *f* útil • **to come in ~** ser útil, venir bien • **the machine has reached the end of its ~ life** la máquina ha llegado al final de su periodo de funcionamiento • **he lived a ~ life** tuvo una vida provechosa • **to make o.s. ~** ayudar, echar una mano* • **come on, make yourself ~!** ¡venga, haz algo!, ¡vamos, echa una mano!* • **this discussion is not serving any ~ purpose** esta discusión no está sirviendo para nada útil *or* provechoso • **I feel I am ~ to the company** me parece que le soy de utilidad a *or* útil a la empresa
2* (= *capable*) • **he's ~ with his fists** sabe defenderse con los puños • **he's ~ with a gun** sabe manejar un fusil
usefully [ˈjuːsfəlɪ] (ADV) de manera provechosa, provechosamente • **you could spend your time more ~ in the library** podrías emplear el tiempo de manera más provechosa *or* más provechosamente en la biblioteca • **the staff are not being ~ employed** la plantilla no se está empleando de manera provechosa *or* provechosamente • **there was nothing that could ~ be said** nada de lo que podía decirse servía de nada
usefulness [ˈjuːsfʊlnɪs] (N) utilidad *f* • **it has outlived its ~** ha dejado de tener utilidad
useless [ˈjuːslɪs] (ADJ) **1** (= *ineffective*) [*object*] que no sirve para nada; [*person*] inútil • **this can opener's ~** este abrelatas no sirve para nada • **compasses are ~ in the jungle** las brújulas no sirven para *or* de nada en la selva • **she's ~** es una inútil • **he's ~ as a forward** no vale para delantero, no sirve como delantero • **I was always ~ at maths** siempre fui (un) negado *or* un inútil para las matemáticas
2 (= *unusable*) [*object, vehicle*] inservible; [*limb*] inutilizado, inútil • **he's a mine of ~ information!** (*hum*) se sabe todo tipo de datos y chorraditas que no sirven de nada* • **to render** *or* **make sth ~** inutilizar algo
3 (= *pointless*) inútil • **it's ~ to shout** de nada sirve gritar, es inútil gritar
uselessly [ˈjuːslɪslɪ] (ADV) (= *ineffectually*) inútilmente; (= *in vain, pointlessly*) inútilmente, en vano
uselessness [ˈjuːslɪsnɪs] (N) (= *ineffectualness*) inutilidad *f*; (= *pointlessness*) lo inútil
Usenet [ˈjuːznet] (N) Usenet *f or m*
user [ˈjuːzəʳ] (N) **1** usuario/a *m/f* • **computer ~s** usuarios *mpl* de ordenadores
2 (*Drugs*) • **drug ~** drogadicto/a *m/f* • **heroin ~** heroinómano/a *m/f*
(CPD) ▸ **user group** [*of product, service*] grupo *m* de usuarios ▸ **user identification** identificación *f* del usuario ▸ **user interface** interfaz *m or f* de usuario, interface *m or f* de usuario • **the development of better ~ interfaces** el desarrollo de mejores interfaces de usuario ▸ **user language** lenguaje *m* del usuario ▸ **user name** (*Comput*) nombre *m* de usuario ▸ **user's guide** guía *m* del usuario ▸ **user software** software *m* del usuario
user-definable [ˌjuːzədɪˈfaɪnəbl], **user-defined** [ˌjuːzədɪˈfaɪnd] (ADJ) definido por el usuario
user-friendliness [ˌjuːzəˈfrendlɪnɪs] (N) facilidad *f* de uso, facilidad *f* de manejo
user-friendly [ˌjuːzəˈfrendlɪ] (ADJ) [*computer, software, system, dictionary*] fácil de utilizar *or* usar *or* manejar • **to make sth more user-friendly** hacer algo más fácil de manejar, hacer algo más accesible para el usuario
USES (N ABBR) = **United States Employment Service**
USGS (N ABBR) = **United States Geological Survey**
usher [ˈʌʃəʳ] (N) (*in court etc*) ujier *mf*; (*in theatre, cinema etc*) acomodador(a) *m/f*; (*at public meeting etc*) guardia *mf* de sala, encargado/a *m/f* del orden
(VT) • **to ~ sb into a room** hacer pasar a algn a un cuarto • **to ~ sb to the door** • **~ sb out** acompañar a algn a la puerta • **to ~ sb out** [+ *unwanted individual*] hacer salir a algn
▸ **usher in** (VT + ADV) [+ *person*] hacer pasar a; (*Theat etc*) acomodar a, conducir su sitio • **I was ~ed in by the butler** el mayordomo me hizo pasar • **it ~ed in a new reign** anunció un nuevo reinado, marcó el comienzo de un nuevo reinado • **summer was ~ed in by storms** el verano empezó con tormentas
usherette [ˌʌʃəˈret] (N) acomodadora *f*
USIA (N ABBR) = **United States Information Agency**
USM (N ABBR) **1** = **United States Mail**
2 (*Econ*) (= **unlisted securities market**) mercado *m* de valores no cotizados en la Bolsa
3 = **United States Mint**
USMC (N ABBR) = **United States Marine Corps**
USN (N ABBR) = **United States Navy**
USO (N ABBR) (*US*) = **United Service Organization**
USP (N ABBR) **1** = **unique sales** *or* **selling proposition**
2 = **unique selling point**
USPHS (N ABBR) = **United States Public Health Service**
USPO (N ABBR) (= **United States Post Office**) *los Correos de los Estados Unidos*
USPS (N ABBR) = **United States Postal Service**
USS (N ABBR) = **United States Ship** *or* **Steamer**
USSR (N ABBR) (= **Union of Soviet Socialist Republics**) URSS *f* • **in the ~** en la URSS, en la Unión Soviética
usu. (ABBR) = **usual(ly)**
usual [ˈjuːʒʊəl] (ADJ) (= *customary*) [*method, answer*] acostumbrado, habitual, usual; [*place, time, excuse*] de siempre • **more than ~** más que de costumbre • **to come earlier than ~** venir más temprano que de costumbre, venir antes de la hora acostumbrada • **it's ~ to give a tip** es costumbre *or* (*esp LAm*) se acostumbra dar una propina • **as (per) ~** como de costumbre, como siempre • **it's not ~ for her to be late** no suele llegar tarde • **it is not our ~ practice to allow this** no acostumbramos *or* solemos permitir esto • **it's not contagious in the ~ sense of the word** no es contagioso en el sentido normal de la palabra • **he came home late, drunk, the ~ thing** llegó a casa tarde y borracho, lo de siempre • **boil the potatoes in the ~ way** cueza las patatas como de costumbre *or* como siempre
(N) • **the ~ please!*** (= *drink*) lo de siempre, por favor
usually [ˈjuːʒʊəlɪ] (ADV) normalmente, por lo general • **we ~ go on a Friday** normalmente *or* por lo general vamos un viernes • **what do you ~ do?** ¿qué hacen ustedes normalmente? • **we have to be more than ~ careful** tenemos que tomar más cuidado que de costumbre • **not ~** por lo general *or* normalmente no • **the ~ crowded**

streets were deserted las calles normalmente atiborradas de gente estaban desiertas

usufruct ['ju:zjʊfrʌkt] (N) usufructo *m*

usufructuary [,ju:zjʊ'frʌktərɪ] (N) usufructuario/a *m/f*

usurer ['ju:ʒərəʳ] (N) usurero/a *m/f*

usurious [ju:'zjʊərɪəs] (ADJ) usurario

usurp [ju:'zɜ:p] (VT) usurpar

usurpation [,ju:zɜ:'peɪʃən] (N) usurpación *f*

usurper [ju:'zɜ:pəʳ] (N) usurpador(a) *m/f*

usurping [ju:'zɜ:pɪŋ] (ADJ) usurpador

usury ['ju:ʒʊrɪ] (N) usura *f*

UT (ABBR) (US) = **Utah**

UTC (ABBR) = **Universal Time Coordinated**

ute [ju:t] (N) (*Australia*) (= *utility vehicle*) furgoneta *f*, camioneta *f*

utensil [ju:'tensl] (N) utensilio *m* • **kitchen ~s** utensilios *mpl* de cocina; (= *set*) batería *f* de cocina

uterine ['ju:təraɪn] (ADJ) uterino

uterus ['ju:tərəs] (N) (PL: **uteri** ['ju:tərai]) útero *m*

utilitarian [,ju:tɪlɪ'tɛərɪən] (ADJ) utilitario (N) utilitarista *mf*

utilitarianism [,ju:tɪlɪ'tɛərɪənɪzəm] (N) utilitarismo *m*

utility [ju:'tɪlɪtɪ] (N) **1** (= *usefulness*) utilidad *f* **2** (*also* **public utility**) servicio *m* público (CPD) utilitario ▸ **utility player** (*Sport*) jugador(a) *m/f* polivalente ▸ **utility room** lavadero *m* ▸ **utility vehicle** furgoneta *f*, camioneta *f*

utilizable ['ju:tɪ,laɪzəbl] (ADJ) utilizable

utilization [,ju:tɪlaɪ'zeɪʃən] (N) utilización *f*

utilize ['ju:tɪlaɪz] (VT) utilizar, aprovecharse de

utmost ['ʌtməʊst] (ADJ) **1** (= *greatest*) sumo • **of the ~ importance** de la mayor importancia, de suma importancia • **with the ~ ease** con suma facilidad **2** (= *furthest*) más lejano (N) • **the ~ that one can do** todo lo que puede hacer uno • **200 at the ~** 200 a lo más, 200 a lo sumo • **to do one's ~ (to do sth)** hacer todo lo posible (por hacer algo) • **to the ~** al máximo, hasta más no poder • **to the ~ of one's ability** lo mejor que pueda *or* sepa uno

Utopia [ju:'təʊpɪə] (N) Utopía *f*

Utopian [ju:'təʊpɪən] (ADJ) [*dream etc*] utópico; [*person*] utopista (N) utopista *mf*

Utopianism [ju:'təʊpɪənɪzəm] (N) utopismo *m*

utricle ['ju:trɪkl] (N) utrículo *m*

utter¹ ['ʌtəʳ] (ADJ) completo, total; [*madness*] puro; [*fool*] perfecto • **~ nonsense!** ¡tonterías! • **it was an ~ disaster** fue un desastre total • **he was in a state of ~ depression** estaba completamente deprimido

utter² ['ʌtəʳ] (VT) **1** [+ *words*] pronunciar; [+ *cry*] dar, soltar; [+ *threat, insult etc*] proferir; [+ *libel*] publicar • **she never ~ed a word** no dijo nada *or* (ni una) palabra • **don't ~ a word about it** no le digas nada a nadie **2** (*Jur*) [+ *counterfeit money*] poner en circulación, expender

utterance ['ʌtərəns] (N) **1** (= *remark*) palabras *fpl*, declaración *f* **2** (= *expression*) expresión *f* • **to give ~ to** expresar, manifestar, declarar **3** (= *style*) pronunciación *f*, articulación *f*

utterly ['ʌtəlɪ] (ADV) totalmente, completamente

uttermost ['ʌtəməʊst] (ADJ) = **utmost**

U-turn ['ju:tɜ:n] (N) (*lit, fig*) cambio *m* de sentido, giro *m* de 180 grados • **to do a U-turn** cambiar de sentido • **"no U-turns"** "prohibido cambiar de sentido"

UV (ADJ ABBR) (= **ultraviolet**) UV, UVA

UVA, UV-A (ADJ ABBR) • **UVA rays** rayos *mpl* UVA

UVB, UV-B (ADJ ABBR) • **UVB rays** rayos *mpl* UVB

UVF (N ABBR) (*Brit*) (= **Ulster Volunteer Force**) *organización paramilitar protestante en Irlanda del Norte*

uvula ['ju:vjələ] (N) (PL: **uvulas, uvulae** ['ju:vjəli:]) úvula *f*

uvular ['ju:vjələʳ] (ADJ) uvular

uxorious [ʌk'sɔ:rɪəs] (ADJ) muy enamorado de su mujer, enamorado con exceso *or* con ostentación de su mujer

Uzbek ['ʊzbek] (ADJ) uzbeko (N) **1** (= *person*) uzbeko/a *m/f* **2** (*Ling*) uzbeko

Uzbekistan [,ʊzbekɪs'tɑ:n] (N) Uzbekistán *m*

Vv

V, v¹ [viː] N (= letter) V, v *f* • **V for victory** V de la victoria • **V1** (= *flying bomb*) bomba *f* volante (1944-45) • **V2** (= *rocket*) cohete *m* (1944-45); ▹ **V-sign, V-neck**
v² ABBR **1** (*Literat*) (= **verse**) v.
2 (*Bible*) (= **verse**) vers.º
3 (*Sport, Jur*) (= **versus**) v., vs.
4 (*Elec*) = **volt(s)**
5 (= **vide**) (= *see*) vid., v.
6 = **very**
7 = **volume**
VA (*US*) ABBR = **Virginia**
N ABBR = **Veterans Administration**
Va. ABBR = **Virginia**
vac* [væk] N **1** (*Brit*) (*Univ*) = **vacation**
2 (*esp Brit*) = **vacuum cleaner**
vacancy [ˈveɪkənsɪ] N **1** (= *job*) vacante *f* • **"vacancies"** "ofertas de trabajo" • **"vacancy for keen young man"** "se busca joven enérgico" • **to fill a ~** proveer una vacante
2 (*in boarding house etc*) habitación *f* libre, cuarto *m* libre • **have you any vacancies?** ¿tiene *or* hay alguna habitación *or* algún cuarto libre? • **we have no vacancies for August** para agosto no hay nada disponible, en agosto todo está lleno • **"no vacancies"** "completo" • **"vacancies"** "hay habitaciones"
3 (= *emptiness*) lo vacío; [*of mind*] vaciedad *f*, vacuidad *f*
vacant [ˈveɪkənt] ADJ **1** (= *unoccupied*) [*seat*] libre, desocupado; [*room*] libre, disponible; [*house*] desocupado, vacío; [*space*] vacío • **is this seat ~?** ¿está libre (este asiento)? • **~ lot** (*US*) solar *m* • **~ post** vacante *f* • **to become** *or* **fall ~** [*post*] quedar(se) vacante; ▹ **situation**
2 (= *expressionless*) [*look*] ausente, vacío
3 (= *stupid*) [*person*] alelado
vacantly [ˈveɪkəntlɪ] ADV **1** [*look*] con gesto ausente, distraídamente
2 (= *stupidly*) sin comprender, boquiabierto
vacate [vəˈkeɪt] VT (*frm*) [+ *seat, room*] dejar libre; [+ *premises*] desocupar, desalojar; [+ *post*] dejar; [+ *throne*] renunciar a
vacation [vəˈkeɪʃən] N **1** (*esp Brit*) (*Jur*) receso *m* vacacional (*frm*), periodo *m* vacacional
2 (*Univ*) • **the long ~** las vacaciones de verano
3 (*US*) (= *holiday*) vacaciones *fpl* • **to be on ~** estar de vacaciones • **to take a ~** tomarse unas vacaciones
4 (= *vacating*) [*of premises*] desalojo *m*
VI (*US*) pasar las vacaciones
CPD ▸ **vacation course** curso *m* extracurricular (*durante las vacaciones*); (*in summer*) curso *m* de verano ▸ **vacation job** empleo *m* de verano ▸ **vacation pay** paga *f* de las vacaciones ▸ **vacation resort** centro *m* turístico ▸ **vacation season** temporada *f* de las vacaciones ▸ **vacation work** trabajo *m* para las vacaciones
vacationer [vəˈkeɪʃənəʳ], **vacationist** [vəˈkeɪʃənɪst] N (*US*) (*gen*) turista *mf*; (*in summer*) veraneante *mf*
vaccinate [ˈvæksɪneɪt] VT vacunar
vaccination [ˌvæksɪˈneɪʃən] N vacunación *f* • **you must have the ~ a month before you travel** debes vacunarte un mes antes de viajar
vaccine [ˈvæksiːn] N vacuna *f*
vacillate [ˈvæsɪleɪt] VI (= *hesitate*) vacilar, dudar; (= *waver*) oscilar (**between** entre)
vacillating [ˈvæsɪleɪtɪŋ] ADJ vacilante, irresoluto
vacillation [ˌvæsɪˈleɪʃən] N vacilación *f*
vacua [ˈvækjʊə] NPL *of* **vacuum**
vacuity [væˈkjuːɪtɪ] N (*frm*) **1** (= *vapidity*) vacuidad *f*
2 vacuities (= *silly remarks*) vaciedades *fpl*
vacuous [ˈvækjʊəs] ADJ (*frm*) [*expression*] vacío, ausente; [*face*] alelado, de pasmo; [*comment*] vacuo, vacío; [*person*] alelado, bobo
vacuum [ˈvækjʊm] N (PL: **vacuums** *or* (*frm*) **vacua**) **1** (*gen*) vacío *m* • **it can't exist in a ~** no puede existir en el vacío
2 (= *hoover*) • **to give a room a ~** limpiar un cuarto con aspiradora
VT pasar la aspiradora por
VI pasar la aspiradora
CPD ▸ **vacuum bottle** (*US*) = **vacuum flask** ▸ **vacuum cleaner** aspiradora *f* ▸ **vacuum flask** termo *m* ▸ **vacuum pump** bomba *f* de vacío
vacuum-packed [ˈvækjʊmˈpækt] ADJ envasado al vacío
vade mecum [ˈvɑːdɪˈmeɪkʊm] N vademécum *m*
vagabond [ˈvægəbɒnd] ADJ vagabundo
N vagabundo/a *m/f*
vagary [ˈveɪgərɪ] N (= *whim*) capricho *m*, antojo *m*; (= *strange idea*) manía *f*, capricho *m* • **the vagaries of love** los caprichos del amor • **the vagaries of the weather** los caprichos del tiempo • **it can't be left to the vagaries of chance** no se puede dejar al azar *or* en manos del azar
vagina [vəˈdʒaɪnə] N (PL: **vaginas** *or* **vaginae** [vəˈdʒaɪniː]) vagina *f*
vaginal [vəˈdʒaɪnəl] ADJ vaginal • **~ smear** frotis *m* vaginal
CPD ▸ **vaginal discharge** flujo *m* vaginal
vagrancy [ˈveɪgrənsɪ] N vagancia *f*, vagabundeo *m*
vagrant [ˈveɪgrənt] N vagabundo/a *m/f*
ADJ vagabundo, vagante; (*fig*) errante
vague [veɪg] ADJ (COMPAR: **vaguer**, SUPERL: **vaguest**) **1** (= *imprecise*) [*concept*] impreciso, vago; [*description*] impreciso; [*outline*] borroso; [*feeling*] indefinido, indeterminado; [*person*] (*in giving details etc*) impreciso; (*by nature*) de ideas poco precisas • **the outlook is somewhat ~** el futuro es algo incierto • **there have been ~ hints of a reconciliation** ha habido ligeros atisbos de reconciliación • **my memories of that time are very ~** mis recuerdos de aquella época son muy vagos, aquella época la recuerdo muy vagamente • **the ~ outline of a ship** el perfil borroso de un buque • **he made some ~ promises** hacía promesas, pero sin concretar • **I haven't the ~st idea** no tengo la más remota idea • **he was ~ about the date** no quiso precisar la fecha • **you mustn't be so ~** hay que decir las cosas con claridad, hay que concretar • **I'm a bit ~ on that subject** sé poco en concreto sobre ese tema • **then he went all ~** luego comenzó a decir vaguedades
2 (= *absent-minded*) [*person*] despistado, distraído; [*expression, look*] ausente • **he's terribly ~** tiene un tremendo despiste, es un despistado • **to look ~** tener aire distraído
vaguely [ˈveɪglɪ] ADV **1** (= *imprecisely*) [*define, remember*] vagamente; [*embarrassed, guilty*] ligeramente, levemente • **a ~ worded agreement** un acuerdo expresado de forma imprecisa *or* en términos poco claros • **he talks very ~** habla en términos muy vagos • **she was ~ aware of someone else in the room** tenía la ligera *or* vaga impresión de que había alguien más en la habitación • **he gestured ~ towards the hills** señaló con gesto impreciso hacia las colinas • **his face looked ~ familiar** su rostro me resultaba ligeramente familiar • **her style is ~ reminiscent of Jane Austen** su estilo recuerda vagamente a *or* tiene un cierto parecido con Jane Austen
2 (= *absent-mindedly*) distraídamente • **she looked at me ~** me miró distraída • **I thought ~ of ringing him up** se me pasó por la cabeza la idea de llamarle
vagueness [ˈveɪgnɪs] N **1** (= *imprecision*) vaguedad *f*, imprecisión *f*
2 (= *absent-mindedness*) distracción *f*
vain [veɪn] ADJ **1** (= *useless*) vano, inútil • **in ~** [*try, struggle*] en vano, inútilmente; [*search*] sin éxito, en vano • **all our efforts were in ~** todos nuestros esfuerzos fueron en vano *or* resultaron inútiles • **I stayed, in the ~ hope that ...** me quedé con la vana esperanza de que ... • IDIOM: • **to take sb's name in ~** hablar con poco respeto de algn • **to take the Lord's name in ~** tomar el nombre de Dios en vano
2 (COMPAR: **vainer**, SUPERL: **vainest**) (= *conceited*) vanidoso, presumido • **she is very ~ about her hair** siempre está arreglándose el pelo
vainglorious [veɪnˈglɔːrɪəs] ADJ vanaglorioso
vainglory [veɪnˈglɔːrɪ] N vanagloria *f*
vainly [ˈveɪnlɪ] ADV **1** (= *to no effect*) [*try, struggle*] en vano, inútilmente; [*search*] sin éxito, en vano
2 (= *conceitedly*) vanidosamente
valance [ˈvæləns] N (*on bed*) cenefa *f*; (*on curtains*) [*of wood*] galería *f*; [*of fabric*] cenefa *f*
vale [veɪl] N (*poet*) valle *m* • **~ of tears** valle *m* de lágrimas
valediction [ˌvælɪˈdɪkʃən] N despedida *f*
valedictorian [ˌvælɪdɪkˈtɔːrɪən] N (*US*) *el mejor estudiante de su promoción que realiza el*

discurso de despedida al final de la ceremonia de graduación
valedictory [ˌvælɪˈdɪktərɪ] ADJ [*address*] de despedida
N (*US*) oración *f* de despedida
valence [ˈveɪləns] N valencia *f*
Valencian [vəˈlensɪən] ADJ valenciano
N **1** (= *person*) valenciano/a *m/f*
2 (*Ling*) valenciano *m*
valency [ˈveɪlənsɪ] N valencia *f*
valentine [ˈvæləntaɪn] N **1** • **(St) Valentine's Day** día *m* de San Valentín, día *m* de los enamorados (*14 febrero*)
2 (*also* **valentine card**) tarjeta *f* del día de San Valentín, tarjeta *f* de los enamorados (*enviada por jóvenes, sin firmar, de tono amoroso o jocoso*)
3 (= *person*) novio/a *m/f* (*escogido el día de San Valentín*)
valerian [vəˈlɪərɪən] N valeriana *f*
valet [ˈvæleɪ] N **1** (= *person*) (*in hotel or household*) ayuda *m* de cámara
2 (*for car*) lavado *m* y limpieza *f*, limpieza *f* completa
VT [+ *car*] lavar y limpiar, hacer una limpieza completa de
CPD ▸ **valet parking** (*US*) servicio *m* de aparcamiento a cargo del hotel
valeting service [ˈvælɪtɪŋˌsɜːvɪs] N (*in hotel*) servicio *m* de planchado; (*for car*) servicio *m* de limpieza
valetudinarian [ˈvælɪˌtjuːdɪˈnɛərɪən] ADJ valetudinario
N valetudinario/a *m/f*
Valhalla [vælˈhælə] N Valhala *m*
valiant [ˈvælɪənt] ADJ (*poet*) [*person*] valiente, valeroso; [*effort*] valeroso
valiantly [ˈvælɪəntlɪ] ADV valientemente, con valor
valid [ˈvælɪd] ADJ **1** [*argument, point, question*] válido; [*excuse, claim, objection*] válido, legítimo • **that argument is not ~** ese argumento no es válido *or* no vale
2 [*ticket, passport, licence, contract*] válido, valedero • **a ticket ~ for three months** un billete válido *or* valedero para tres meses • **that ticket is no longer ~** ese billete ya no vale *or* ha caducado ya
validate [ˈvælɪdeɪt] VT (*gen*) validar, dar validez a; [+ *document*] convalidar
validation [ˌvælɪˈdeɪʃən] N convalidación *f*
validity [vəˈlɪdɪtɪ] N (*all senses*) validez *f*
valise [vəˈliːz] N valija *f*, maleta *f*
Valium® [ˈvælɪəm] N valium® *m*
Valkyrie [ˈvælkɪrɪ] N Valquiria *f*
valley [ˈvælɪ] N valle *m*
valor [ˈvæləʳ] N (*US*) = **valour**
valorous [ˈvælərəs] ADJ (*liter*) valiente, valeroso
valour, **valor** (*US*) [ˈvæləʳ] N (*frm*) valor *m*, valentía *f*
valuable [ˈvæljʊəbl] ADJ **1** (*in monetary terms*) valioso • **is it ~?** ¿vale mucho?
2 (= *extremely useful*) [*information, assistance, advice*] valioso • **a ~ contribution** una valiosa aportación • **the experience taught me a ~ lesson** aquella experiencia me enseñó una valiosa lección • **we are wasting your ~ time** le estamos haciendo perder su valioso *or* precioso tiempo
N **valuables** objetos *mpl* de valor
valuation [ˌvæljʊˈeɪʃən] N **1** (= *evaluation*) [*of property, house, assets, antique*] tasación *f*, valoración *f* • **to make a ~ of sth** tasar *or* valorar algo
2 (*fig*) [*of person's character*] valoración *f* • **to take sb at his own ~** aceptar todo lo que dice algn acerca de sí mismo
valuator [ˈvæljʊˌeɪtəʳ] N valuador(a) *m/f*, tasador(a) *m/f*
value [ˈvæljuː] N **1** (*monetary*) valor *m* • **property/land ~s** valores *mpl* de propiedad/tierras • **it's good ~** sale a cuenta, está bien de precio • **Spanish wines are still the best ~** los vinos españoles todavía son los que más salen a cuenta *or* los que mejor están de precio • **to go down** *or* **decrease in ~** bajar de valor, depreciarse • **to go up** *or* **increase in ~** subir de valor, revalorizarse • **a rise/drop in the ~ of the pound** una subida/bajada del valor de la libra • **market ~** valor *m* en el mercado • **the company offers good service and ~ for money** la compañía ofrece un buen servicio a buen precio • **it might contain something of ~** puede que contenga algo de valor • **you can't put** *or* **set a ~ on it** (*lit, fig*) no se le puede poner precio • **surplus ~** plusvalía *f* • **goods to the ~ of £100** bienes por valor de 100 libras; ▹ **book, cash, face**
2 (= *merit*) valor *m* • **literary/artistic/scientific ~** valor *m* literario/artístico/científico • **his visit to the country will have huge symbolic ~** su visita al país tendrá un gran valor simbólico • **to attach a great deal of ~ to sth** conceder gran valor *or* importancia a algo, valorar mucho algo • **to attach no ~ to sth** no dar importancia a algo, no valorar algo • **something of ~** algo valioso *or* de valor • **to be of ~ (to sb)** ser útil *or* de utilidad (para algn), servir (a algn) • **strategically, the city was of little ~ to the British** desde el punto de vista estratégico, la ciudad era de poca utilidad *or* tenía poco valor para los británicos • **her education has been of no ~ to her** su educación no le ha servido de *or* para nada • **to put** *or* **place** *or* **set a high ~ on sth** valorar mucho algo • **sentimental ~** valor *m* sentimental
3 (*moral*) **values** valores *mpl* (morales) • **family ~s** valores *mpl* de familia
4 (*Math, Mus, Gram*) valor *m* • **what is the ~ of x when y is 5?** ¿qué valor tiene x cuando y es igual a 5?
VT **1** (= *estimate worth of*) [+ *property, jewellery, painting*] valorar, tasar • **to ~ sth at £200** valorar *or* tasar algo en 200 libras • **I had to have my jewellery ~d for insurance purposes** tuve que valorar *or* tasar mis joyas para poder asegurarlas
2 (= *appreciate*) [+ *health, life, independence,*] valorar; [+ *sb's work, opinion, friendship*] valorar, apreciar
CPD ▸ **value judgment** juicio *m* de valor ▸ **value system** sistema *m* de valores, escala *f* de valores
value-added tax [ˈvæljuːˈædɪdˈtæks] N (*Brit*) impuesto *m* sobre el valor agregado, impuesto *m* sobre el valor añadido (*Sp*)
valued [ˈvæljuːd] ADJ [*friend, customer*] estimado, apreciado; [*contribution*] valioso
valueless [ˈvæljʊlɪs] ADJ sin valor
valuer [ˈvæljʊəʳ] N (*Brit*) tasador(a) *m/f*
valve [vælv] N (*Anat, Mech*) válvula *f*; (*Rad, TV*) lámpara *f*, válvula *f*; (*Bot, Zool*) valva *f*; [*of musical instrument*] llave *f*
CPD ▸ **valve tester** comprobador *m* de válvulas
valvular [ˈvælvjʊləʳ] ADJ **1** (= *shaped like valve*) en forma de válvula
2 (*Med*) valvular • **~ inflammation** inflamación *f* valvular
vamoose* [vəˈmuːs] VI largarse*
vamp [væmp] N **1** (= *woman*) vampiresa *f*, vampi* *f*
2 [*of shoe*] empeine *m*
3 (= *patch*) remiendo *m*
4 (*Mus*) (= *improvised accompaniment*) acompañamiento *m* improvisado
VT **1** (= *flirt with*) coquetear con, flirtear con • **to ~ sb into doing sth** engatusar a algn para que haga algo
2 [+ *shoe*] poner empella a
3 (*Mus*) improvisar, improvisar un acompañamiento para
VI (*Mus*) improvisar (un acompañamiento)
▸ **vamp up** VT + ADV (= *make more attractive*) [+ *dress, room*] arreglar • **to ~ up an engine** (= *repair*) componer un motor; (= *supercharge*) sobrealimentar un motor
vampire [ˈvæmpaɪəʳ] N **1** (*Zool*) vampiro *m*
2 (*fig*) vampiro *m*; (= *woman*) vampiresa *f*
CPD ▸ **vampire bat** vampiro *m*
vampirism [ˈvæmpaɪərɪzəm] N vampirismo *m*
van[1] [væn] N (*Brit*) (*Aut*) camioneta *f*, furgoneta *f*; (*for removals*) camión *m* de mudanzas; (*Brit*) (*Rail*) furgón *m*
CPD ▸ **van driver** conductor(a) *m/f* de camioneta ▸ **van pool** (*US*) parque *m* (móvil) de furgonetas
van[2] [væn] N (*Mil*) (*also fig*) vanguardia *f*
vanadium [vəˈneɪdɪəm] N vanadio *m*
V & A N ABBR (*Brit*) = **Victoria and Albert Museum**
Vandal [ˈvændəl] (*Hist*) ADJ vándalo, vandálico
N vándalo/a *m/f*
vandal [ˈvændəl] N vándalo/a *m/f*, gamberro/a *m/f*
Vandalic [vænˈdælɪk] ADJ vándalo, vandálico
vandalism [ˈvændəlɪzəm] N vandalismo *m*
vandalize [ˈvændəlaɪz] VT destrozar
vane [veɪn] N (= *weather vane*) veleta *f*; [*of mill*] aspa *f*; [*of propeller*] paleta *f*; [*of feather*] barbas *fpl*
vanguard [ˈvæŋgɑːd] N vanguardia *f* • **to be in the ~** ir a la vanguardia, estar en la vanguardia • **to be in the ~ of progress** ir a *or* estar en la vanguardia del progreso
vanilla [vəˈnɪlə] N vainilla *f*
ADJ de vainilla
CPD ▸ **vanilla essence** esencia *f* de vainilla
vanish [ˈvænɪʃ] VI desaparecer • **to ~ without trace** desaparecer sin dejar rastro • **to ~ into thin air** esfumarse
vanishing [ˈvænɪʃɪŋ] CPD ▸ **vanishing act*** • IDIOM: • **to do a ~ act** desaparecer ▸ **vanishing cream** crema *f* de día ▸ **vanishing point** punto *m* de fuga ▸ **vanishing trick** truco *m* de desaparecer
vanity [ˈvænɪtɪ] N **1** (= *conceit*) vanidad *f* • **to do sth out of ~** hacer algo por vanidad
2 (= *pride*) orgullo *m*
3 (= *emptiness*) vanidad *f* • **all is ~** todo es vanidad
CPD ▸ **vanity box, vanity case** neceser *m* ▸ **vanity (license) plate** (*esp US*) (*Aut*) matrícula *f* personalizada ▸ **vanity unit** lavabo *m* empotrado
vanquish [ˈvæŋkwɪʃ] VT (*poet*) vencer, derrotar
vantage [ˈvɑːntɪdʒ] N **1** ventaja *f*
2 = **vantage point**
CPD ▸ **vantage point** posición *f* ventajosa, lugar *m* estratégico; (*for views*) punto *m* panorámico • **from our modern ~ point we can see that …** desde nuestra atalaya moderna vemos que …, desde la perspectiva del tiempo presente se ve que …
vape [veɪp] VI, VT vapear
vaper [ˈveɪpəʳ] N fumador(a) *m/f* de cigarrillos electrónicos
vapid [ˈvæpɪd] ADJ insípido, soso
vapidity [væˈpɪdɪtɪ] N insipidez *f*, sosería *f*
vaping [ˈveɪpɪŋ] N cigarrillos *mpl* electrónicos
vapor [ˈveɪpəʳ] N (*US*) = **vapour**
vaporization [ˌveɪpəraɪˈzeɪʃən] N vaporización *f*

vaporize ['veɪpəraɪz] (VT) vaporizar, volatilizar
(VI) vaporizarse, volatilizarse
vaporizer ['veɪpəraɪzəʳ] (N) vaporizador *m*; (*for inhalation*) inhalador *m*; (*for perfume*) atomizador *m*
vaporous ['veɪpərəs] (ADJ) vaporoso
vapour, **vapor** (US) ['veɪpəʳ] (N) (= *steam*) vapor *m*; (*on breath, window*) vaho *m* • **the ~s** (*Med*†) los vapores
(CPD) ▸ **vapour trail** (*Aer*) estela *f* (de humo)
Varanasi [və'rɑːnəsɪ] (N) Benarés *f*
variability [ˌvɛərɪə'bɪlɪtɪ] (N) variabilidad *f*
variable ['vɛərɪəbl] (ADJ) (*gen*) variable; [*person*] variable, voluble • **~ costs** costes *mpl* variables
(N) variable *f*
variance ['vɛərɪəns] (N) • **to be at ~ (with sb over sth)** estar en desacuerdo *or* discrepar (con algn en algo) • **his statement is at ~ with the facts** sus afirmaciones no concuerdan con los hechos
variant ['vɛərɪənt] (ADJ) variante • **there are several ~ spellings of this word** esta palabra se escribe de varias formas, hay distintas variantes ortográficas de esta palabra
(N) variante *f*
variation [ˌvɛərɪ'eɪʃən] (N) (*gen*) variación *f* (*also Mus*); (= *variant form*) variedad *f*
varicoloured, **varicolored** (US) ['værɪ'kʌləd] (ADJ) abigarrado, multicolor
varicose veins ['værɪkəʊs'veɪnz] (NPL) varices *fpl*
varied ['vɛərɪd] (ADJ) variado
variegated ['vɛərɪgeɪtɪd] (ADJ) [*plant, plumage, markings*] multicolor; [*colour*] abigarrado; [*leaf*] jaspeado, abigarrado (*Bot*)
variegation [ˌvɛərɪ'geɪʃən] (N) [*of plants, plumage, markings*] multiplicidad *f* de colores, variedad *f* de colores; [*of colour*] abigarramiento *m*; [*of leaves*] jaspeado *m*, abigarramiento *m* (*Bot*)
variety [və'raɪətɪ] (N) (*gen*) variedad *f*; (= *range, diversity*) diversidad *f*; (*Comm*) [*of stock*] surtido *m* • **he likes a ~ of food** le gustan diversas comidas • **a ~ of opinions was expressed** se expresaron diversas opiniones • **it comes in a ~ of colours** lo hay en varios colores *or* de diversos colores • **for a ~ of reasons** por varias *or* diversas razones • **in a ~ of ways** de diversas maneras • **for ~** por variar • **to lend ~ to sth** dar variedad a algo • PROVERB: • **~ is the spice of life** en la variedad está el gusto
(CPD) ▸ **variety artist** artista *mf* de variedades ▸ **variety show** espectáculo *m* de variedades ▸ **variety store** (US) bazar *m* (*tienda barata que vende de todo*) ▸ **variety theatre** teatro *m* de variedades
varifocal ['vɛərɪ'fəʊkəl] (ADJ) progresivo
(N) **varifocals** gafas *fpl* progresivas, lentes *fpl* progresivas
variola [və'raɪələ] (N) viruela *f*
various ['vɛərɪəs] (ADJ) (*gen*) varios, diversos; (= *different*) distintos • **for ~ reasons** por diversas razones • **in ~ ways** de diversos modos • **at ~ times** a distintas horas • **on ~ occasions in the past** en varias ocasiones antes
variously ['vɛərɪəslɪ] (ADV) • **the phrase has been ~ interpreted** la frase se ha interpretado de varias *or* diversas maneras • **a pile of ~ coloured socks** un montón de calcetines de distintos *or* diversos colores • **the caravan served ~ as an office, bedroom and changing room** según los casos la caravana hacía de oficina, dormitorio o vestuario
varmint ['vɑːmɪnt] (N) **1** (*Hunting*) bicho *m* **2*** golfo *m*, bribón *m*
varnish ['vɑːnɪʃ] (N) (*for wood*) barniz *m*; (*for nails*) esmalte *m* (para las uñas), laca *f* (para las uñas); (*fig*) barniz *m*, apariencia *f*
(VT) [+ *wood*] barnizar; [+ *nails*] pintar, laquear
varnishing ['vɑːnɪʃɪŋ] (N) barnizado *m*
varsity ['vɑːsɪtɪ] (N) (*Brit**) universidad *f*
(CPD) ▸ **Varsity Match** partido *m* entre las Universidades de Oxford y Cambridge
vary ['vɛərɪ] (VT) **1** (= *make variable*) [+ *routine, diet*] variar
2 (= *change*) [+ *temperature, speed*] cambiar, modificar
(VI) **1** (= *differ*) [*amounts, sizes, conditions*] variar • **prices ~ from area to area** los precios varían con la zona • **to ~ according to sth** variar según *or* dependiendo de algo • **they ~ enormously in quality** la calidad varía enormemente • **they ~ in price** los hay de diversos precios • **it varies** depende, según
2 (= *be at odds*) • **designs may ~ from the illustration on the box** los diseños pueden diferir de la ilustración del paquete • **authors ~ about the date** los autores discrepan con respecto a la fecha • **opinions ~ on this point** las opiniones varían en este punto
3 (= *change, fluctuate*) [*weight, temperature, number*] oscilar • **my weight varies between 70 and 73 kilos** mi peso oscila entre los 70 y los 73 kilos
varying ['vɛərɪɪŋ] (ADJ) [*amounts*] distinto; [*periods of time*] variado; [*ages, shades, sizes*] diverso • **with ~ degrees of success** con más o menos éxito • **in** *or* **to ~ degrees** en mayor o menor grado
vascular ['væskjʊləʳ] (ADJ) vascular
vasculitis [ˌvæskjʊ'laɪtɪs] (N) (*Med*) vasculitis *f*
vase [vɑːz] (N) florero *m*, jarrón *m*
vasectomy [væ'sektəmɪ] (N) vasectomía *f*
Vaseline® ['væsɪliːn] (N) vaselina® *f*
vasoconstriction [ˌveɪzəʊkən'strɪkʃən] (N) vasoconstricción *f*
vasoconstrictor [ˌveɪzəʊkən'strɪktəʳ] (N) vasoconstrictor *m*
vasodilation [ˌveɪzəʊdaɪ'leɪʃən] (N) vasodilatación *f*
vasodilator [ˌveɪzəʊdaɪ'leɪtəʳ] (N) vasodilatador *m*
vassal ['væsəl] (N) vasallo *m*
vassalage ['væsəlɪdʒ] (N) vasallaje *m*
vast [vɑːst] (ADJ) (COMPAR: **vaster**, SUPERL: **vastest**) [*building, quantity, organization*] enorme, inmenso; [*area*] vasto, extenso; [*range, selection*] enorme, amplísimo; [*knowledge, experience*] vasto • **at ~ expense** gastando enormes cantidades de dinero • **it's a ~ improvement on his previous work** es muchísimo mejor que su trabajo anterior • **the ~ majority (of people)** la inmensa mayoría (de la gente)
vastly ['vɑːstlɪ] (ADV) inmensamente, enormemente • **two women from ~ different backgrounds** dos mujeres de orígenes enormemente diferentes • **a ~ improved quality of life** una calidad de vida muchísimo *or* infinitamente mejor • **I think he's ~ overrated** creo que está enormemente sobreestimado • **~ superior to** infinitamente superior a
vastness ['vɑːstnɪs] (N) inmensidad *f*
VAT [viːeɪ'tiː, væt] (N ABBR) (*Brit*) (= **value-added tax**) IVA *m*, impuesto *m* sobre el valor añadido
(CPD) ▸ **VAT man** recaudador *m* del IVA ▸ **VAT return** declaración *f* del IVA
vat [væt] (N) tina *f*, tinaja *f*; [*of cider*] cuba *f*
Vatican ['vætɪkən] (N) • **the ~** el Vaticano
(ADJ) vaticano, del Vaticano
(CPD) ▸ **Vatican City** Ciudad *f* del Vaticano
VAT-registered ['væt,redʒɪstəd] (N) • **VAT-registered company** compañía *f* declarante del IVA
vaudeville ['vəʊdəvɪl] (N) vodevil *m*
vault¹ [vɔːlt] (N) (*Archit*) bóveda *f*; (= *cellar*) sótano *m*; (*for wine*) bodega *f*; [*of bank*] cámara *f* acorazada; (= *tomb*) panteón *m*; [*of church*] cripta *f* • **family ~** panteón *m* familiar • **~ of heaven** bóveda *f* celeste
vault² [vɔːlt] (N) salto *m* • **at one ~** • **with one ~** de un solo salto
(VI) saltar • **to ~ over a stream** cruzar un arroyo de un salto, saltar un arroyo • **to ~ into the saddle** colocarse de un salto en la silla
(VT) saltar
vaulted ['vɔːltɪd] (ADJ) abovedado
vaulting ['vɔːltɪŋ] (N) **1** (*Archit*) abovedado *m* **2** (*Sport*) salto *m* con pértiga
(CPD) ▸ **vaulting horse** potro *m* (de madera)
vaunt [vɔːnt] (VT) (= *boast of*) jactarse de, hacer alarde de; (= *display*) lucir, ostentar
(VI) jactarse
vaunted ['vɔːntɪd] (ADJ) cacareado • **much ~** tan cacareado
vaunting ['vɔːntɪŋ] (ADJ) jactancioso
(N) jactancia *f*
vb (ABBR) (= **verb**) v.
VC (N ABBR) **1** (*Brit*) (*Mil*) (= **Victoria Cross**) *condecoración británica*
2 (*Univ*) = **Vice-Chancellor**
3 = **vice-chairman**
4 (US) (*in Vietnam*) = **Vietcong**
V-chip ['viːtʃɪp] (N) chip *m* antiviolencia, *chip para que los padres puedan censurar el contenido de la programación televisiva*
VCR (N ABBR) = **video cassette recorder**
VD (N ABBR) (= **venereal disease**) enfermedad *f* venérea
VDT (N ABBR) (*esp US*) (= **visual display terminal**) UDV *f*
(CPD) ▸ **VDT operator** operador(a) *m/f* de UDV
VDU (N ABBR) (*Comput*) (= **visual display unit**) UDV *f*
(CPD) ▸ **VDU operator** operador(a) *m/f* de UDV
veal [viːl] (N) ternera *f*
(CPD) ▸ **veal crate** *cajón en el que son criados los terneros*
vector ['vektəʳ] (N) vector *m*
Veda ['veɪdə] (N) Veda *m*
V-E Day [ˌviː'iːdeɪ] (N ABBR) (= **Victory in Europe Day**) día *m* de la victoria en Europa

> **V-E DAY**
> El 8 de mayo se celebra en el Reino Unido y Estados Unidos el Día de la Victoria Europea o **V-E Day**: **Victory in Europe Day**. En este día se conmemora la victoria del ejército aliado en Europa en la Segunda Guerra Mundial en 1945. El 15 de agosto se conmemora el Día de la Victoria sobre Japón o **V-J Day**: **Victory over Japan Day**, que ocurrió también en 1945.

Vedic ['veɪdɪk] (ADJ) védico
veep* [viːp] (N) (US) vicepresidente/a *m/f*
veer [vɪəʳ] (VI) (*also* **veer round**) [*ship*] virar; [*car*] girar, torcer; [*wind*] cambiar de dirección, rolar (*Met, Naut*); (*fig*) cambiar (de rumbo) • **the car ~ed off the road** el coche se salió de la carretera • **the wind ~ed to the east** el viento cambió hacia el este, el viento roló al este • **the country has ~ed to the left** el país ha dado un giro hacia *or* a la izquierda • **it ~s from one extreme to the other** oscila desde un extremo al otro • **people are ~ing round to our point of view**

la gente está empezando a aceptar nuestro criterio
veg* [vedʒ] (N ABBR) (= **vegetable(s)**) verdura *f*, vegetales *mpl*
▸ **veg out‡** (VI + ADV) relajarse
vegan ['vi:gən] (N) vegetariano/a *m/f* estricto/a
veganism ['vi:gənɪzəm] (N) vegetarianismo *m* estricto
vegeburger ['vedʒɪ,bɜ:gəʳ] (N) hamburguesa *f* vegetariana
vegetable ['vedʒɪtəbl] (N) **1** (*Bot*) vegetal *m*, planta *f*; (*Culin*) (= *food*) hortaliza *f*, verdura *f* • **we grow a few ~s in our garden** tenemos plantadas algunas verduras *or* hortalizas en el jardín • **green ~s** verdura(s) *f(pl)* • **diced ~s** menestra *f* de verduras • **~s are an important part of the diet** la verdura es *or* las hortalizas son una parte importante de la dieta • **come along, eat up your ~s!** ¡vamos, cómete la verdura!; ▹ **root**
2‡ (= *human vegetable*) vegetal *m*
(CPD) ▸ **vegetable dish** (= *food*) plato *m* de verdura(s); (= *vessel*) fuente *f* de verdura(s) ▸ **vegetable fat** grasa *f* vegetal ▸ **vegetable garden** (*big*) huerta *f*; (*small*) huerto *m* ▸ **the vegetable kingdom** el reino vegetal ▸ **vegetable marrow** (*esp Brit*) calabacín *m* ▸ **vegetable matter** materia *f* vegetal ▸ **vegetable oil** aceite *m* vegetal ▸ **vegetable patch** huerto *m*, huertecito *m* ▸ **vegetable salad** ensalada *f* verde, macedonia *f* de verduras con mayonesa, ≈ ensaladilla *f* rusa ▸ **vegetable soup** sopa *f* de verduras
vegetarian [,vedʒɪ'tɛərɪən] (ADJ) vegetariano (N) vegetariano/a *m/f*
vegetarianism [,vedʒɪ'tɛərɪənɪzəm] (N) vegetarianismo *m*
vegetate ['vedʒɪteɪt] (VI) (*lit, fig*) vegetar
vegetated ['vedʒɪteɪtɪd] (ADJ) • **the land is sparsely ~** la tierra tiene escasa vegetación
vegetation [,vedʒɪ'teɪʃən] (N) vegetación *f*
vegetative ['vedʒɪtətɪv] (ADJ) vegetativo (CPD) ▸ **vegetative state** estado *m* vegetativo
veggie* ['vedʒɪ] (ADJ) vegetariano • **~ burger** hamburguesa *f* vegetal, hamburguesa *f* vegetariana (N) vegetariano/a *m/f*
veggies* ['vedʒɪz] (NPL) (*esp US*) (= *vegetables*) verdura *fsing*
vehemence ['vi:ɪməns] (N) [*of words, person, criticism, protest*] vehemencia *f*; [*of attack*] violencia *f*; [*of opposition*] fuerza *f*, radicalidad *f*; [*of denial*] rotundidad *f*; [*of dislike*] intensidad *f*
vehement ['vi:ɪmənt] (ADJ) [*person, tone, criticism, protest*] vehemente; [*denial*] rotundo, categórico; [*dislike*] intenso; [*attack*] violento • **there was ~ opposition** hubo una fuerte *or* radical oposición
vehemently ['vi:ɪməntlɪ] (ADV) [*say, curse*] vehementemente, con vehemencia; [*deny*] rotundamente, categóricamente; [*reject, shake one's head*] ostensiblemente; [*oppose*] radicalmente; [*attack*] violentamente • **to be ~ opposed to sth** oponerse radicalmente a algo, estar radicalmente en contra de algo
vehicle ['vi:ɪkl] (N) **1** (= *form of transport*) vehículo *m*
2 (*fig*) (= *means*) vehículo *m*, medio *m*, instrumento *m* (**for** para) • **the programme was a ~ for promoting himself** el programa era un vehículo *or* medio *or* instrumento para promocionarse • **they see the new constitution as a ~ for change** ven la nueva constitución como un instrumento de cambio
(CPD) ▸ **vehicle emissions** emisiones *fpl* de los vehículos
vehicular [vɪ'hɪkjʊləʳ] (ADJ) [*road*] de vehículos, para coches • **the roadworks made ~ access difficult** las obras en la calzada complicaban el acceso de los vehículos • **~ traffic** circulación *f* rodada
veil [veɪl] (N) (*lit, fig*) velo *m* • **a ~ of secrecy surrounded the project** un halo de misterio rodeaba el proyecto • **under a ~ of secrecy** en el mayor secreto • **to draw a ~ over sth** (*fig*) correr un (tupido) velo sobre algo • **IDIOM:** • **to take the ~** (*Rel*) tomar el hábito, meterse monja
(VT) (*lit*) cubrir con un velo; (*fig*) (= *disguise*) [+ *truth, facts*] velar, encubrir; [+ *dislike, hatred*] disimular • **eyes ~ed by tears** ojos *mpl* empañados por lágrimas • **the town was ~ed in mist** la ciudad estaba cubierta por un velo de niebla
veiled [veɪld] (ADJ) [*threat, hint, criticism, insult*] velado; [*reference*] encubierto • **thinly-veiled dislike** antipatía *f* apenas disimulada • **with ~ irony** con velada ironía
veiling ['veɪlɪŋ] (N) (*Phot*) velo *m*
vein [veɪn] (N) **1** (*Anat, Bot*) vena *f*
2 (*Min*) [*of ore*] filón *m*, veta *f*; (*in stone*) vena *f*
3 (*fig*) (= *streak*) vena *f* • **there is a ~ of anti-semitism running through his writing** hay una vena antisemita en todos sus escritos
4 (= *mood, tone*) vena *f* • **she went on in this ~ for some time** continuó de esta guisa *or* en este tono durante un rato • **the next two speakers continued in the same ~** los dos siguientes conferenciantes se expresaron en la misma línea
veined [veɪnd] (ADJ) [*hands, eyes*] venoso; [*leaves*] nervado • **blue-veined cheese** queso *m* azul
veining ['veɪnɪŋ] (N) **1** (*Anat, Bot*) venas *fpl*
2 (*Min*) vetas *fpl*, veteado *m*
velar ['vi:ləʳ] (ADJ) velar
Velasquez, Velazquez [vɪ'læskwɪz] (N) Velázquez
Velcro® ['velkrəʊ] (N) velcro® *m*
(CPD) ▸ **Velcro strip®** tira *f* de velcro®
veld, veldt [velt] (N) veld *m* (*meseta esteparia sudafricana*)
vellum ['veləm] (N) (= *writing paper*) papel *m* vitela
velocipede†† [və'lɒsɪpi:d] (N) velocípedo *m*
velocity [vɪ'lɒsɪtɪ] (N) velocidad *f*
velodrome ['velə,drəʊm] (N) velódromo *m*
velour, velours [və'lʊəʳ] (N) velvetón *m*
velum ['vi:ləm] (N) (PL: **vela** ['vi:lə]) velo *m* del paladar
velvet ['velvɪt] (N) terciopelo *m*; (*on antlers*) piel *f* velluda, vello *m* • **she had skin like ~** tenía una piel aterciopelada
(ADJ) (= *of velvet*) de terciopelo; (= *velvety*) aterciopelado • **the Velvet Revolution** la revolución de terciopelo
velveteen ['velvɪti:n] (N) pana *f*
velvety ['velvɪtɪ] (ADJ) aterciopelado
venal ['vi:nl] (ADJ) [*person*] venal, sobornable; [*action*] corrupto, corrompido
venality [vi:'nælɪtɪ] (N) venalidad *f*
vend [vend] (VT) vender
vendee [ven'di:] (N) comprador(a) *m/f*
vendetta [ven'detə] (N) vendetta *f* • **to carry on *or* pursue a ~ against sb** (*public*) hacer una campaña contra algn; (*personal*) hostigar *or* perseguir a algn
vending ['vendɪŋ] (N) venta *f*, distribución *f*
(CPD) ▸ **vending machine** máquina *f* expendedora, vendedora *f* automática
vendor ['vendɔ:ʳ] (N) vendedor(a) *m/f*; (= *pedlar*) vendedor(a) *m/f* ambulante
veneer [və'nɪəʳ] (N) chapa *f*, enchapado *m*; (*fig*) barniz *m*, apariencia *f* • **to give *or* lend sth a ~ of respectability** dar a algo un barniz *or* una apariencia de respetabilidad
(VT) chapear
venerable ['venərəbl] (ADJ) venerable
venerate ['venəreɪt] (VT) venerar, reverenciar
veneration [,venə'reɪʃən] (N) veneración *f* • **his ~ for …** la veneración que sentía por … • **to hold sb in ~** reverenciar a algn
venereal [vɪ'nɪərɪəl] (ADJ) venéreo • **~ disease** enfermedad *f* venérea
Venetian [vɪ'ni:ʃən] (ADJ) veneciano (N) veneciano/a *m/f*
(CPD) ▸ **Venetian blind** persiana *f*
Venezuela [,vene'zweɪlə] (N) Venezuela *f*
Venezuelan [,vene'zweɪlən] (ADJ) venezolano
(N) venezolano/a *m/f*
vengeance ['vendʒəns] (N) venganza *f* • **to take ~ on sb** vengarse de algn • **it started raining with a ~*** empezó a llover de verdad, empezó a llover de lo lindo*
vengeful ['vendʒfʊl] (ADJ) vengativo
venial ['vi:nɪəl] (ADJ) venial; [*error, fault*] leve
veniality [,vi:nɪ'ælɪtɪ] (N) venialidad *f*
Venice ['venɪs] (N) Venecia *f*
venison ['venɪzn] (N) carne *f* de venado
venom ['venəm] (N) (*lit*) veneno *m*; (*fig*) veneno *m*, malicia *f* • **he spoke with real ~** habló con veneno *or* malicia, habló con palabras envenenadas
venomous ['venəməs] (ADJ) (*lit*) venenoso; (*fig*) [*look*] maligno; [*tongue*] viperino
venomously ['venəməslɪ] (ADV) (*fig*) con malignidad
venous ['vi:nəs] (ADJ) (*Med*) venoso
vent [vent] (N) **1** (*Mech*) agujero *m*; (= *valve*) válvula *f*; (= *airhole*) respiradero *m*; (= *grille*) rejilla *f* de ventilación; (= *pipe*) ventosa *f*, conducto *m* de ventilación
2 (= *opening*) (*in jacket, skirt*) abertura *f*
3 (*Zool*) cloaca *f*
4 (= *expression*) • **to give ~ to one's feelings** desahogarse • **to give ~ to one's anger** dar rienda suelta a su ira, desahogar su ira
(VT) **1** (*Mech*) purgar; (= *discharge*) descargar, emitir, dejar escapar
2 (= *release*) [+ *feelings*] desahogar, descargar • **to ~ one's anger on sth/sb** desahogar la ira con algo/algn • **to ~ one's spleen (on)** descargar la bilis (contra)
ventilate ['ventɪleɪt] (VT) [+ *room*] ventilar, airear; (*fig*) [+ *grievance, question*] ventilar
ventilation [,ventɪ'leɪʃən] (N) ventilación *f*
(CPD) ▸ **ventilation shaft** pozo *m* de ventilación
ventilator ['ventɪleɪtəʳ] (N) **1** (*Constr*) ventilador *m*
2 (*Med*) respirador *m*
ventral ['ventrəl] (ADJ) ventral
ventricle ['ventrɪkl] (N) ventrículo *m*
ventriloquism [ven'trɪləkwɪzəm] (N) ventriloquia *f*
ventriloquist [ven'trɪləkwɪst] (N) ventrílocuo/a *m/f*
(CPD) ▸ **ventriloquist's dummy** muñeco *m* de ventrílocuo
venture ['ventʃəʳ] (N) (= *enterprise*) empresa *f*; (= *exploit, adventure*) aventura *f* • **a business ~** una empresa comercial • **his ~ into business** su aventura en el mundo de los negocios • **a new ~ in publishing** (= *new direction*) un nuevo rumbo en la edición de libros; (= *new company*) una nueva empresa editorial; ▹ **joint**
(VT) [+ *money, reputation, life*] arriesgar, jugar(se); [+ *opinion, guess*] aventurar • **they ~d everything** arriesgaron *or* se lo jugaron todo • **if I may ~ an opinion** si se me permite expresar *or* si puedo aventurar una opinión • **may I ~ a guess?** ¿puedo hacer *or* aventurar

V

una conjetura? • **to ~ to do sth** osar *or* atreverse a hacer algo • **he ~d to remark that ...** se permitió observar que ... • **but he did not ~ to speak** pero no osó hablar • PROVERB: • **nothing ~d, nothing gained** quien no se arriesga no pasa la mar
VI • **to ~ into a wood** (osar) penetrar en un bosque • **they did not ~ onto the streets after dark** no se aventuraban a salir a la calle de noche • **to ~ out (of doors)** aventurarse a salir (fuera)
CPD ▸ **venture capital** capital-riesgo *m* ▸ **venture capitalist** capitalista *mf* de riesgo ▸ **Venture Scout** *boy scout de aproximadamente entre 14 y 18 años*
▸ **venture forth** VI + ADV (*liter*) aventurarse a salir
venturesome ['ventʃəsəm] ADJ [*person*] atrevido, audaz; [*enterprise*] arriesgado, azaroso
venue ['venju:] N **1** (*for concert*) local *m* • **the ~ for the next match** el escenario del próximo partido • **there has been a change of ~ for the rehearsal** se ha cambiado de lugar para el ensayo
2 (= *meeting place*) lugar *m* de reunión, punto *m* de reunión
3 (*Jur*) • **change of ~** cambio *m* de jurisdicción
Venus ['vi:nəs] N (*Myth*) Venus *f*; (*Astron*) Venus *m*
Venusian [vɪ'nju:zɪən] N venusiano/a *m/f*
ADJ venusiano • **~ landscape** paisaje venusiano
veracious [və'reɪʃəs] ADJ (*frm*) veraz
veracity [və'ræsɪtɪ] N (*frm*) veracidad *f*
veranda, verandah [və'rændə] N galería *f*, veranda *f*, terraza *f*
verb [vɜ:b] N verbo *m*
verbal ['vɜ:bəl] ADJ verbal • **a ~ agreement** un acuerdo verbal
CPD ▸ **verbal abuse** insultos *mpl* ▸ **verbal diarrhoea*** verborrea *f*
verbalize ['vɜ:bəlaɪz] VT expresar verbalmente, expresar en palabras
VI expresarse en palabras
verbally ['vɜ:bəlɪ] ADV [*communicate, abuse*] verbalmente; [*agree*] de palabra
verbatim [vɜ:'beɪtɪm] ADJ textual, literal
ADV textualmente, palabra por palabra
verbena [vɜ:'bi:nə] N verbena *f*
verbiage ['vɜ:bɪɪdʒ] N verborrea *f*, palabrería *f*
verbose [vɜ:'bəʊs] ADJ [*person*] verboso, hablador; [*writing, style*] prolijo, verboso
verbosely [vɜ:'bəʊslɪ] ADV con verbosidad, prolijamente
verbosity [vɜ:'bɒsɪtɪ] N verbosidad *f*, prolijidad *f*
verdant ['vɜ:dənt] ADJ verde
verdict ['vɜ:dɪkt] N (*Jur*) (= *judgment*) veredicto *m*, fallo *m*; [*of judge*] sentencia *f*; (*fig*) opinión *f*, juicio *m* • **~ of guilty/not guilty** veredicto *m* de culpabilidad/inocencia • **to bring in** *or* **return a ~** (*Jur*) emitir *or* pronunciar un veredicto, emitir un fallo • **the inquest recorded an open ~** las pesquisas judiciales no determinaban las causas del fallecimiento • **to give one's ~ (on sb/sth)** dar un veredicto (sobre algn/algo), dar su juicio *or* opinión (sobre algn/algo) • **what's your ~?** ¿qué opinas de esto? • **his ~ on the wine was unfavourable** dio un juicio desfavorable sobre el vino
verdigris ['vɜ:dɪgrɪ:s] N verdete *m*, cardenillo *m*
verdure ['vɜ:djʊə^r] N verdor *m*
verge [vɜ:dʒ] N **1** [*of road*] borde *m*; [*of motorway*] arcén *m*
2 (*fig*) borde *m*, margen *m* • **to be on the ~ of disaster/a nervous breakdown** estar al borde de la catástrofe/de una crisis nerviosa • **we are on the ~ of war** estamos al borde de la guerra • **to be on the ~ of a great discovery** estar en la antesala de un gran descubrimiento • **she was on the ~ of tears** estaba a punto de llorar • **to be on the ~ of doing sth** estar a punto *or* al borde de hacer algo
▸ **verge on, verge upon** VI + PREP rayar en; [*colour*] tirar a • **a state verging on madness** un estado que raya en la locura
verger ['vɜ:dʒə^r] N (*in church*) sacristán *m*
Vergil ['vɜ:dʒɪl] N Virgilio
Vergilian [və'dʒɪlɪən] ADJ virgiliano
verifiability [,verɪfaɪə'bɪlɪtɪ] N verificabilidad *f*
verifiable ['verɪfaɪəbl] ADJ verificable, comprobable
verification [,verɪfɪ'keɪʃən] N (*gen*) verificación *f*, comprobación *f*; [*of result*] confirmación *f*; (= *document*) comprobante *m*
verifier ['verɪfaɪə^r] N (*Comput*) verificador *m*
verify ['verɪfaɪ] VT verificar, comprobar; [+ *result*] confirmar; (*Comput*) verificar
verily† ['verɪlɪ] ADV en verdad • **~ I say unto you ...** en verdad os digo ...
verisimilitude [,verɪsɪ'mɪlɪtju:d] N verosimilitud *f*
veritable ['verɪtəbl] ADJ verdadero, auténtico • **a ~ monster** un verdadero monstruo
veritably ['verɪtəblɪ] ADV verdaderamente
verity ['verɪtɪ] N verdad *f* • **the eternal verities** las verdades eternas
vermicelli [,vɜ:mɪ'selɪ] N fideos *mpl* de cabello de ángel
vermicide ['vɜ:mɪsaɪd] N vermicida *m*
vermifuge ['vɜ:mɪfju:dʒ] N vermífugo *m*
vermilion [və'mɪlɪən] N bermellón *m*
ADJ bermejo
vermin ['vɜ:mɪn] N **1** (*lit*) (= *insects*) bichos *mpl*, sabandijas *fpl*; (= *mammals*) alimañas *fpl*
2 (*fig*) (*pej*) (= *people*) chusma *f*
verminous ['vɜ:mɪnəs] ADJ verminoso, piojoso; (*fig*) vil
vermouth ['vɜ:məθ] N vermut *m*, vermú *m*
vernacular [və'nækjʊlə^r] ADJ **1** (*Ling*) vernáculo, vulgar • **in ~ Persian** en persa vulgar, en la lengua vernácula de Persia
2 [*architecture*] típico, local, regional
N (*Ling*) lengua *f* vernácula; (*fig*) lenguaje *m* corriente, lenguaje *m* vulgar
vernal ['vɜ:nl] ADJ [*equinox*] de primavera; (*liter*) [*flowers*] de primavera, primaveral
Veronica [və'rɒnɪkə] N Verónica
veronica [və'rɒnɪkə] N (*Bot*) verónica *f*
verruca [və'ru:kə] N (PL: **verrucas** *or* **verrucae** [və'ru:si:]) (*esp Brit*) verruga *f*
Versailles [veə'saɪ] N Versalles *m*
versatile ['vɜ:sətaɪl] ADJ [*person*] polifacético, versátil; [*material*] versátil, que se presta a usos distintos • **eggs are very ~** los huevos dan mucho juego
versatility [,vɜ:sə'tɪlɪtɪ] N [*of person*] carácter *m* polifacético, versatilidad *f*; [*of tool, machine, material*] versatilidad *f*, múltiple funcionalidad *f*
verse [vɜ:s] N **1** (= *stanza*) estrofa *f*; [*of Bible*] versículo *m*
2 (= *genre*) verso *m*; (= *poetry*) verso *m*, poesía *f* • **in ~** en verso • **a ~ version of the "Celestina"** una versión en verso de la "Celestina"
CPD ▸ **verse drama** teatro *m* en verso, drama *m* poético
versed [vɜ:st] ADJ • **to be well ~ in** ser *or* estar versado en, ser experto en
versification [,vɜ:sɪfɪ'keɪʃən] N versificación *f*
versifier ['vɜ:sɪfaɪə^r] N versificador(a) *m/f*, versista *mf*
versify ['vɜ:sɪfaɪ] VT versificar
VI versificar, escribir versos
version ['vɜ:ʃən] N (*gen*) versión *f*; (= *translation*) traducción *f*; [*of car etc*] modelo *m* • **in Lope's ~ of the story** en la versión que hizo Lope de la historia • **my ~ of events is as follows ...** esta es mi versión de los hechos ... • **according to his ~** según su versión, según lo que él cuenta
verso ['vɜ:səʊ] N [*of page*] dorso *m*; (*Tech*) verso *m*; [*of coin*] reverso *m*
versus ['vɜ:səs] PREP (*Jur, Sport*) contra
vertebra ['vɜ:tɪbrə] N (PL: **vertebras** *or* **vertebrae** ['vɜ:tɪbri:]) vértebra *f*
vertebral ['vɜ:tɪbrəl] ADJ vertebral
vertebrate ['vɜ:tɪbrɪt] ADJ vertebrado
N vertebrado *m*
vertex ['vɜ:teks] N (PL: **vertexes** *or* **vertices** ['vɜ:tɪsi:z]) (*Math, Archit*) vértice *m*
vertical ['vɜ:tɪkəl] ADJ vertical
N vertical *f*
CPD ▸ **vertical integration** integración *f* vertical ▸ **vertical section** sección *f* vertical, corte *m* vertical ▸ **vertical take-off aircraft** avión *m* de despegue vertical
vertically ['vɜ:tɪkəlɪ] ADV verticalmente • **~ challenged** (*hum*) de estatura menuda
vertiginous [vɜ:'tɪdʒɪnəs] ADJ vertiginoso
vertigo ['vɜ:tɪgəʊ] N (PL: **vertigoes, vertigines** [vɜ:'tɪdʒɪni:z]) vértigo *m*
verve [vɜ:v] N (= *drive*) energía *f*, empuje *m*; (= *vitality*) brío *m*; (= *enthusiasm*) entusiasmo *m*
very ['verɪ] ADV **1** (= *extremely*) muy • **it is ~ cold** [*object*] está muy frío; [*weather*] hace mucho frío • **the food was ~ good** la comida estuvo muy buena • **"that will be all" — "~ good, sir"** —nada más —muy bien, señor • **you're not being ~ helpful** me ayudas bien poco, no me estás siendo de gran ayuda • **~ high frequency** (*Rad*) (*abbr VHF*) frecuencia *f* muy alta • **that's ~ kind of you** eres muy amable • **~ much** mucho • **"did you enjoy it?" — "~ much (so)"** —¿te ha gustado? —sí, mucho • **she feels ~ much better** se encuentra muchísimo mejor • **I was ~ (much) surprised** me sorprendió mucho, para mí fue una gran sorpresa • **I didn't like it ~ much** no me gustó mucho • **he ~ nearly missed the bus** por muy poco pierde el autobús • **we don't see each other ~ often** nos vemos poco, no nos vemos mucho • **he's so ~ poor** es tan pobre • **it's not so ~ difficult** no es tan difícil • **~ well, I'll do what I can** muy bien *or* bueno, haré lo que pueda • **he couldn't ~ well refuse** no pudo negarse a hacerlo
2 (= *absolutely*) • **the ~ best**: • **she eats nothing but the ~ best** solo come lo mejor de lo mejor • **we did our ~ best** hicimos todo lo que pudimos • **at the ~ earliest** como muy pronto • **the ~ first** el primero de todos • **try your ~ hardest** esfuérzate al máximo • **the ~ last** el último de todos • **at the ~ latest** a más tardar, como muy tarde • **at the ~ least** como mínimo • **at the ~ most** a lo sumo, como mucho, como máximo • **that is the ~ most we can offer** eso es todo lo más que podemos ofrecer • **the ~ next day** precisamente el día siguiente • **she was given her ~ own TV show** le dieron su propio programa de televisión • **it's my ~ own** es el mío • **the ~ same hat** el mismísimo sombrero
3 (*alone, in reply to question*) mucho • **"are you tired?" — "(yes,) ~"** —¿estás cansado? —(sí,) mucho
ADJ **1** (= *precise*) mismo • **the ~ bishop himself was there** el mismísimo obispo estaba allí • **from the ~ beginning** desde el

comienzo mismo • **that ~ day** ese mismo día • **in this ~ house** en esta misma casa • **he's the ~ man we want** es justo el hombre que buscamos • **at that ~ moment** en ese mismo momento • **it's the ~ thing!** ¡es justo lo que necesitamos! • **those were his ~ words** eso fue exactamente lo que dijo
2 (= *mere*) • **the ~ idea!** ¡qué cosas dices!, ¡cómo se te ocurre! • **the ~ thought (of it) makes me feel sick** con solo pensarlo me da náuseas
3 (= *extreme*) • **at the ~ bottom** abajo del todo • **at the ~ end** justo al final, al final de todo • **at the ~ top** arriba del todo
4 (*liter*) • **the veriest rascal** el mayor bribón • **the veriest simpleton** el más bobo
vesicle [ˈvesɪkl] N vesícula *f*
vespers [ˈvespəz] NPL vísperas *fpl*
vessel [ˈvesl] N 1 (= *ship*) barco *m*, buque *m*, embarcación *f*
2 (= *receptacle*) vasija *f*, recipiente *m*
3 (*Anat, Bot*) vaso *m*; ▸ **blood**
vest[1] [vest] N 1 (*Brit*) (= *undergarment*) camiseta *f*
2 (*US*) (= *waistcoat*) chaleco *m*
CPD ▸ **vest pocket** (*US*) bolsillo *m* del chaleco
vest[2] [vest] VT • **to ~ sb with sth** investir a algn de algo • **to ~ rights/authority in sb** conferir *or* conceder derechos/autoridad a algn • **by the authority ~ed in me** en virtud de la autoridad que se me ha concedido • **to ~ property in sb** ceder una propiedad a algn, hacer a algn titular de una propiedad
vesta [ˈvestə] N cerilla *f*
vestal [ˈvestl] ADJ vestal • **~ virgin** vestal *f*
N vestal *f*
vested [ˈvestɪd] ADJ [*right*] inalienable • **~ interest** interés *m* personal • **to have a ~ interest in sth** tener un interés personal en algo • **~ interests** intereses *mpl* creados
vestibule [ˈvestɪbjuːl] N (*frm*) vestíbulo *m*
vestige [ˈvestɪdʒ] N 1 (= *trace*) vestigio *m*, rastro *m* • **not a ~ of it remains** no queda rastro de ello, de ello no queda ni el menor vestigio • **without a ~ of decency** sin la menor decencia • **if there is a ~ of doubt** si hay una sombra de duda • **a ~ of truth** un elemento *or* un tanto de verdad
2 (*Bio*) rudimento *m*
vestigial [vesˈtɪdʒɪəl] ADJ vestigial; (*Bio*) rudimentario
vestment [ˈvestmənt] N vestiduras *fpl*; **vestments** (*esp Rel*) vestiduras *fpl*
vestry [ˈvestrɪ] N sacristía *f*
vesture [ˈvestʃəʳ] N (*liter*) vestidura *f*
Vesuvius [vɪˈsuːvɪəs] N Vesubio *m*
vet[1] [vet] N ABBR 1 (= **veterinary surgeon, veterinarian**) veterinario/a *m/f*
2 (*US**) (= **veteran**) excombatiente *mf*
vet[2] [vet] (*esp Brit*) VT 1 [+ *article, speech*] repasar, revisar
2 (= *examine*) [+ *application*] examinar, investigar • **he was vetted by Security** fue sometido a una investigación por los servicios de seguridad
vetch [vetʃ] N arveja *f* (*planta*)
veteran [ˈvetərən] ADJ (*gen*) veterano; (= *battleworn*) aguerrido
N (= *war veteran*) veterano/a *m/f*; (= *ex-serviceman*) excombatiente *mf*; (= *experienced person*) veterano/a *m/f* • **she is a ~ of the anti-nuclear movement** es una veterana del movimiento antinuclear • **a ~ UN diplomat** un veterano diplomático de la ONU
CPD ▸ **veteran car** (*Brit*) *coche fabricado antes de 1919, especialmente antes de 1905* ▸ **Veterans Day** (*US*) *día de los veteranos de guerra estadounidenses*
veterinarian [ˌvetərɪˈneərɪən] N (*US*) veterinario/a *m/f*
veterinary [ˈvetərɪnərɪ] ADJ veterinario
CPD ▸ **veterinary medicine** medicina *f* veterinaria, veterinaria *f* ▸ **veterinary school** escuela *f* de veterinaria ▸ **veterinary science** = **veterinary medicine** ▸ **veterinary surgeon** veterinario/a *m/f*
veto [ˈviːtəʊ] N (PL: **vetoes**) veto *m* • **to have a ~** tener veto • **to put a ~ on sth** vetar algo, poner veto a algo • **to use** *or* **exercise one's ~** ejercer el (derecho a) veto
VT [+ *bill, application*] vetar, prohibir • **the president ~ed it** el presidente lo vetó *or* le puso su veto • **I suggested it but he ~ed the idea** yo lo sugerí pero el rechazó la idea
vetting [ˈvetɪŋ] N (= *check*) examen *m* previo; (= *investigation*) investigación *f*; ▸ **positive**
vex [veks] VT 1 (= *anger*) fastidiar, irritar; (= *make impatient*) impacientar, sacar de quicio
2 (= *afflict*) afligir • **the problems that are vexing the country** los problemas que afligen el país
vexation [vekˈseɪʃən] N 1 (= *anger*) irritación *f*
2 (= *trouble*) aflicción *f*, disgusto *m* • **he had to put up with numerous ~s** tuvo que soportar muchos disgustos
vexatious [vekˈseɪʃəs], **vexing** [ˈveksɪŋ] ADJ fastidioso, molesto, enojoso (*LAm*)
vexed [vekst] ADJ 1 (= *angry*) enfadado, enojado (*LAm*) • **to be ~ (with sb) (about sth)** estar enfadado *or* (*LAm*) enojado (con algn) (por algo) • **to get ~ (with sb) (about sth)** enfadarse *or* (*LAm*) enojarse (con algn) (por algo) • **in a ~ tone** en tono ofendido, en tono de enojo
2 [*question*] reñido, controvertido
3 (= *puzzled*) perplejo, confuso
vexing [ˈveksɪŋ] ADJ fastidioso, molesto, enojoso (*LAm*) • **it's very ~** da mucha rabia
VFD N ABBR (*US*) = **voluntary fire department**
VG ABBR (*Scol etc*) (= **very good**) S
v.g. ABBR = **very good**
VGA N ABBR = **video graphics array**
vgc ABBR = **very good condition**
VHF N ABBR (= **very high frequency**) VHF
VHS N ABBR = **video home system**
VI ABBR (*US*) = **Virgin Islands**
via [ˈvaɪə] PREP por; (*esp by plane*) vía • **we drove to Lisbon via Salamanca** fuimos a Lisboa por Salamanca • **a flight via Brussels** un vuelo vía Bruselas
viability [ˌvaɪəˈbɪlɪtɪ] N viabilidad *f*
viable [ˈvaɪəbl] ADJ viable
viaduct [ˈvaɪədʌkt] N viaducto *m*
Viagra® [vaɪˈægrə] N Viagra® *m*
vial [ˈvaɪəl] N frasquito *m*
viands [ˈvaɪəndz] NPL (*liter*) viandas *fpl*
viaticum [vaɪˈætɪkəm] N (PL: **viaticums** *or* **viatica** [vaɪˈætɪkə]) viático *m*
vibes [vaɪbz] NPL ABBR 1‡ (= **vibrations**) (*from band, singer*) vibraciones *fpl*, ambiente *m* • **I got good ~ from her** me cayó muy bien
2* (= **vibraphone**) vibráfono *m*
vibrancy [ˈvaɪbrənsɪ] N [*of colour*] viveza *f*; [*of person*] dinamismo *m*, vitalidad *f*; [*of voice*] sonoridad *f*
vibrant [ˈvaɪbrənt] ADJ [*colour*] vivo; [*person*] animado; [*personality*] vibrante; [*voice*] vibrante, sonoro
N (*Phon*) vibrante *f*
vibrantly [ˈvaɪbrəntlɪ] ADV • **~ coloured** de colores vivos *or* brillantes
vibraphone [ˈvaɪbrəˌfəʊn] N vibráfono *m*
vibrate [vaɪˈbreɪt] VI vibrar • **the room ~d with tension** se palpaba la tensión en la sala • **her voice ~d with sorrow** la voz le temblaba de pena
VT hacer vibrar
vibration [vaɪˈbreɪʃən] N 1 (= *movement*) vibración *f*
2* **vibrations** vibraciones* *fpl*
vibrato [vɪˈbrɑːtəʊ] N vibrato *m*
vibrator [vaɪˈbreɪtəʳ] N vibrador *m*
vibratory [ˈvaɪbrətərɪ] ADJ vibratorio
viburnum [vaɪˈbɜːnəm] N viburno *m*
Vic [vɪk] N *familiar form of* **Victor, Victoria**
vicar [ˈvɪkəʳ] N (*gen*) vicario *m*; (*Anglican*) cura *m*, párroco *m*
vicarage [ˈvɪkərɪdʒ] N casa *f* del párroco
vicar-general [ˈvɪkəˈdʒenərəl] N (PL: **vicars-general**) vicario *m* general
vicarious [vɪˈkeərɪəs] ADJ (= *indirect*) indirecto; [*substitute*] por referencias • **to get ~ pleasure out of sth** disfrutar indirectamente de algo • **I got a ~ thrill** me emocioné mucho sin tener nada que ver con lo que pasaba
vicariously [vɪˈkeərɪəslɪ] ADV indirectamente • **he filled his emotional needs ~, through those around him** satisfacía sus necesidades emocionales indirectamente, a través de los que lo rodeaban • **she brought glamour into my life, but only ~** le dio sofisticación a mi vida, aunque solo de forma indirecta
vice[1] [vaɪs] N vicio *m* • **a life of ~** una vida de vicio y desenfreno • **smoking is his only ~** el tabaco es su único vicio
CPD ▸ **vice ring** asociación *f* criminal ▸ **vice squad** brigada *f* antivicio
vice[2], **vise** (*US*) [vaɪs] N (*esp Brit*) (*Mech*) torno *m* de banco, tornillo *m* de banco
vice[3] [ˈvaɪsɪ] PREP en lugar de, sustituyendo a
vice- [vaɪs] PREFIX vice-
vice-admiral [ˈvaɪsˈædmərəl] N vicealmirante *mf*
vice-captain [ˈvaɪsˈkæptɪn] N segundo capitán *m*
vice-chairman [ˈvaɪsˈtʃeəmən] N (PL: **vice-chairmen**) vicepresidente/a *m/f*
vice-chairmanship [ˈvaɪsˈtʃeəmənʃɪp] N vicepresidencia *f*
vice-chancellor [ˈvaɪsˈtʃɑːnsələʳ] N (*Univ*) rector(a) *m/f*
vice-consul [ˈvaɪsˈkɒnsəl] N vicecónsul *mf*
vice-presidency [ˈvaɪsˈprezɪdənsɪ] N vicepresidencia *f*
vice-president [ˈvaɪsˈprezɪdənt] N vicepresidente/a *m/f*
vice-presidential [ˈvaɪsprezɪˈdenʃəl] ADJ [*nomination, contender, campaign*] a la vicepresidencia; [*salary, residence*] del vicepresidente
CPD ▸ **vice-presidential candidate** candidato/a *m/f* a la vicepresidencia
vice-principal [ˈvaɪsˈprɪnsɪpəl] N (*US*) (*Scol*) subdirector(a) *m/f*
viceroy [ˈvaɪsrɔɪ] N virrey *m*
viceroyalty [ˈvaɪsˈrɔɪəltɪ] N virreinato *m*
vice versa [ˈvaɪsɪˈvɜːsə] ADV viceversa, al revés
vicinity [vɪˈsɪnɪtɪ] N 1 (= *neighbourhood*) cercanías *fpl*, alrededores *mpl*, inmediaciones *fpl* • **there has been heavy fighting in the ~ of Tel Aviv** ha habido fuertes enfrentamientos en las cercanías *or* en los alrededores *or* en las inmediaciones de Tel Aviv • **houses in the immediate ~ of the blast were damaged** las viviendas más cercanas a la explosión sufrieron daños • **and other towns in the ~** y otras ciudades de las inmediaciones *or* de la zona *or* cercanas • **he denied being anywhere in the ~** negó encontrarse cerca del lugar • **in the ~ of 20** alrededor de 20, unos 20

2 (= *nearness*) proximidad *f* (**to** a)
vicious [ˈvɪʃəs] (ADJ) **1** (= *brutal*) [*person, gang*] despiadado; [*attack, assault, crime*] atroz, brutal; [*animal*] agresivo, fiero • **a ~-looking knife** un cuchillo de aspecto horrorífico
2 (= *malicious*) [*criticism, campaign*] despiadado, cruel; [*remark*] malicioso • **to have a ~ temper** tener muy mal genio • **to have a ~ tongue** tener una lengua viperina
(CPD) ▸ **vicious circle** círculo *m* vicioso • **to be caught in a ~ circle** estar atrapado en un círculo vicioso
viciously [ˈvɪʃəslɪ] (ADV) **1** (= *brutally*) [*attack, beat, stab*] brutalmente, con saña
2 (= *maliciously*) [*say, speak*] con malicia
viciousness [ˈvɪʃəsnɪs] (N) **1** (= *brutality, fierceness*) [*of person, attack*] brutalidad *f*; [*of animal*] fiereza *f*, agresividad *f*
2 (= *maliciousness*) [*of words*] malicia *f*, malevolencia *f*; [*of criticism, campaign*] lo despiadado, crueldad *f*
vicissitudes [vɪˈsɪsɪtjuːdz] (NPL) vicisitudes *fpl*, peripecias *fpl*
vicissitudinous [vɪˌsɪsɪˈtjuːdɪnəs] (ADJ) agitado, accidentado
Vicky [ˈvɪkɪ] (N) *familiar form of* **Victoria**
victim [ˈvɪktɪm] (N) (= *subject of attack*) víctima *f* • **the ~s** (= *survivors of disaster*) los damnificados • **to be the ~ of** [+ *attack, hoax*] ser víctima de • **to fall ~ to** [+ *desire, sb's charms*] sucumbir a, dejarse llevar por
(CPD) ▸ **Victim Support** (*Brit*) *organización de ayuda a las víctimas de actos delictivos*
victimhood [ˈvɪktɪmhʊd] (N) estatus *m* de víctima
victimization [ˌvɪktɪmaɪˈzeɪʃən] (N) persecución *f*; (= *retaliation, punishment*) castigo *m*, represalias *fpl*
victimize [ˈvɪktɪmaɪz] (VT) (= *pursue*) perseguir; (= *punish*) escoger y castigar, tomar represalias contra • **to be ~d** ser víctima de una persecución • **the strikers should not be ~d** no hay por qué castigar a los huelguistas • **she feels she has been ~d** ella cree que ha sido escogida como víctima
victimless [ˈvɪktɪmlɪs] (ADJ) sin víctimas
victimology [ˌvɪktɪˈmɒlədʒɪ] (N) (= *branch of criminology*) victimología *f*
Victor [ˈvɪktəʳ] (N) Víctor
victor [ˈvɪktəʳ] (N) vencedor(a) *m/f*
Victoria [vɪkˈtɔːrɪə] (N) Victoria
Victoria Cross [vɪkˈtɔːrɪəˈkrɒs] (N) (*Brit*) *la condecoración más alta de las fuerzas armadas británicas y de la Commonwealth*
Victoria Falls [vɪkˈtɔːrɪəˈfɔːlz] (NPL) Cataratas *fpl* de Victoria
Victorian [vɪkˈtɔːrɪən] (ADJ) victoriano (N) victoriano/a *m/f*

VICTORIAN
El adjetivo **Victorian** se usa tanto en Gran Bretaña como en EE.UU. para referirse a las personas, la arquitectura y la cultura de la época de la reina Victoria (1837-1901). Asimismo, las actitudes o cualidades llamadas victorianas son las que se consideran características de su época, tales como el interés por el respeto social y la moral estricta acompañada de la falta de sentido del humor, la intolerancia y la hipocresía. El término **Victorian values** (valores victorianos) se usa positivamente en política para referirse a la honestidad, la superación personal, el respeto a la autoridad y la importancia de la familia.

Victoriana [vɪkˌtɔːrɪˈɑːnə] (NPL) objetos *mpl* victorianos, antigüedades *fpl* victorianas
victorious [vɪkˈtɔːrɪəs] (ADJ) [*army*] victorioso, triunfante; [*person, team*] vencedor, triunfador; [*campaign*] triunfal, victorioso • **the ~ team** el equipo vencedor *or* triunfador, los vencedores • **he gave a ~ shout** lanzó un grito triunfal *or* de triunfo • **to be ~** triunfar, salir victorioso, vencer • **he was ~ over his enemies** triunfó sobre sus enemigos, venció a sus enemigos
victoriously [vɪkˈtɔːrɪəslɪ] (ADV) victoriosamente, triunfalmente
victory [ˈvɪktərɪ] (N) victoria *f*, triunfo *m* (**over** sobre) • **they celebrated their ~ over Arsenal/the Labour Party** celebraron su victoria *or* triunfo sobre el Arsenal/el Partido Laborista • **~ V** la V de la victoria • **to win a famous ~** obtener un triunfo señalado
(CPD) ▸ **victory lap** vuelta *f* de honor
victual [ˈvɪtl] (VT) avituallar, abastecer
(VI) avituallarse, abastecerse
(NPL) **victuals** víveres *mpl*, vituallas *fpl*
victualler [ˈvɪtləʳ] (N) ▸ **licensed**
vicuña [vɪˈkjuːnə] (N) vicuña *f*
vid* [vɪd] (N ABBR) (= **video**) vídeo *f*, video *m* (*LAm*)
vide [ˈvɪdeɪ] (VT) vea, véase
videlicet [vɪˈdiːlɪset] (ADV) a saber
video [ˈvɪdɪəʊ] (N) **1** (*also* **video recorder**) aparato *m* de vídeo, vídeo *m*, video *m* (*LAm*)
2 (*also* **video cassette**) videocinta *f*, cinta *f* de vídeo *or* (*LAm*) video, vídeo *m*, video *m* (*LAm*) • **it's out on ~** ha salido en vídeo
(VT) grabar en vídeo *or* (*LAm*) video
(CPD) ▸ **video arcade** salón *m* recreativo de videojuegos ▸ **video blog** videoblog *m* ▸ **video call** videollamada *f* ▸ **video camera** videocámara *f* ▸ **video cassette** = **video** ▸ **video cassette recorder** = **video** ▸ **video clip** videoclip *m* ▸ **video club** videoclub *m* ▸ **video conference** videoconferencia *f* ▸ **video conferencing** videoconferencia *f* ▸ **video diary** (*TV*) diario *m* en vídeo ▸ **video disk** videodisco *m* ▸ **video disk player** reproductor *m* de videodisco ▸ **video film** película *f* de vídeo, videofilm *m* ▸ **video frequency** videofrecuencia *f* ▸ **video game** videojuego *m* ▸ **video gamer** videojugador(a) *m/f*, jugador(a) *m/f* de videojuegos ▸ **video installation** instalación *f* de vídeo ▸ **video library** videoteca *f* ▸ **video nasty*** (= *horror film*) videofilm *m* de horror; (= *pornography*) videofilm *m* porno* ▸ **video piracy** videopiratería *f* ▸ **video player** reproductor *m* de vídeo, magnetoscopio *m* ▸ **video recorder** aparato *m* de vídeo, vídeo *m*, video *m* (*LAm*) ▸ **video recording** (= *act*) videograbación *f*; (= *object*) grabación *f* de vídeo ▸ **video screen** pantalla *f* de vídeo ▸ **video shop** videoclub *m* ▸ **video surveillance** vigilancia *f* por vídeo ▸ **video wall** vídeo-panel *m* (*Sp*), panel *m* de vídeo
videofit [ˈvɪdɪəʊfɪt] (N) retrato *m* robot (*informatizado*)
videophone [ˈvɪdɪəʊˌfəʊn] (N) videoteléfono *m*
videotape [ˈvɪdɪəʊˌteɪp] (N) (= *tape*) cinta *f* de vídeo *or* (*LAm*) video; (= *recording*) vídeo *m*, video *m* (*LAm*)
(VT) grabar en vídeo *or* (*LAm*) video
(CPD) ▸ **videotape library** videoteca *f*
videotaping [ˈvɪdɪəʊˌteɪpɪŋ] (N) videograbación *f*
Videotex® [ˈvɪdɪəʊˌteks] (N) vídeotex® *m*
videotext [ˈvɪdɪəʊˌtekst] (N) videotexto *m*
vie [vaɪ] (VI) • **to vie for sth** disputarse algo • **to vie with sb** competir con algn, rivalizar con algn • **to vie with sb for sth** disputar algo a algn, competir con algn por algo
Vienna [vɪˈenə] (N) Viena *f*
Viennese [ˌvɪəˈniːz] (ADJ) vienés (N) vienés/esa *m/f*
Vietcong [ˌvjetˈkɒŋ] (ADJ) del Vietcong (N) vietcong *mf*
Vietnam, Viet Nam [ˈvjetˈnæm] (N) Vietnam *m*
Vietnamese [ˌvjetnəˈmiːz] (ADJ) vietnamita (N) **1** (= *person*) vietnamita *mf*
2 (*Ling*) vietnamita *m*
vieux jeu [ˈvjɜːˈʒɜː] (ADJ) anticuado, fuera de moda
view [vjuː] (N) **1** (= *prospect*) vista *f* • **most rooms have ~s over the gardens** la mayoría de las habitaciones tienen vistas a los jardines • **he stood up to get a better ~** se puso de pie para ver mejor • **to have/get a good ~ of sth/sb** ver algo/a algn bien; ▹ **back, front, side**
2 (= *line of vision*) • **he stopped in the doorway, blocking her ~** se paró en la entrada, tapándole la vista • **am I blocking your ~?** ¿te estoy tapando? • **a cyclist came into ~** apareció un ciclista • **as we rounded the bend the hospital came into ~** al salir de la curva apareció el hospital • **to disappear from ~** perderse de vista • **to be hidden from ~** estar oculto, estar escondido • **to keep sth/sb in ~** no perder de vista algo/a algn • **in full ~ of the crowd** bien a la vista de la multitud • **to be on ~** estar expuesto al público • **the paintings will go on ~ next month** los cuadros se expondrán al público el mes próximo • **the pond was within ~ of my bedroom window** el estanque se veía desde la ventana de mi habitación
3 (= *picture*) vista *f* • **50 ~s of Venice** 50 vistas de Venecia
4 (= *mind*) • **to have sth in ~** tener algo en mente *or* en perspectiva • **he has only one objective in ~** tiene solo un objetivo en mente, solo persigue un objetivo • **with this in ~** con este propósito *or* fin • **with a ~ to doing sth** con miras *or* vistas a hacer algo
5 (= *opinion*) opinión *f* • **you should make your ~s known to your local MP** debería hacerle saber sus opiniones *or* ideas al diputado de su zona • **my (personal) ~ is that ...** mi opinión (personal) es que ... • **an opportunity for people to express their ~s** una oportunidad para que la gente exprese su opinión • **to express the ~ that ...** opinar que ... • **in my ~** a mi parecer, en mi opinión • **to take** *or* **hold the ~ that** opinar que • **I take a similar/different ~** opino de forma parecida/de distinta forma • **to take the long(-term) ~** adoptar una perspectiva a largo plazo; ▹ **dim, point**
6 (= *understanding*) visión *f* • **an overall ~ of the situation** una visión de conjunto de la situación • **an idealistic ~ of the world** una visión idealista del mundo
7 • **in ~ of (the fact that)** en vista de (que) • **in ~ of this** en vista de esto
(VT) **1** (= *regard*) ver • **how does the government ~ it?** ¿cómo lo ve el gobierno? • **they ~ the United States as a land of golden opportunity** consideran a los Estados Unidos un país lleno de oportunidades, ven a los Estados Unidos como un país lleno de oportunidades • **we would ~ favourably any sensible suggestion** cualquier sugerencia razonable sería bien acogida • **he is ~ed with suspicion by many MPs** muchos parlamentarios lo miran *or* tratan con recelo
2 (= *look at, observe*) ver • **mourners were allowed to ~ the body** a los dolientes se les permitió ver el cadáver • **London ~ed from the air** Londres vista desde arriba
3 (= *inspect, see*) [+ *property, sights, goods, slides*] ver; [+ *accounts*] examinar • **when can we ~ the house?** ¿cuándo podemos ver la casa?

V

4 (*frm*) [+ *television*] ver
VI (*TV*) (*frm*) ver la televisión • **the ~ing public** los telespectadores, la audiencia televisiva
viewable ['vju:əbl] ADJ (= *visible*) visible; [*film etc*] que se puede ver
Viewdata® ['vju:,deɪtə] N vídeodatos *mpl*, videodatos *mpl* (*LAm*)
viewer ['vju:əʳ] N **1** (= *onlooker*) espectador(a) *m/f*; (*TV*) televidente *mf*, telespectador(a) *m/f*
2 (*for viewing slides*) visor *m*
viewership ['vju:əʃɪp] N teleaudiencia *f*
viewfinder ['vju:,faɪndəʳ] N (*Phot*) visor *m* (de imagen), objetivo *m*
viewing ['vju:ɪŋ] N **1** [*of property, gallery*] visita *f*; (*prior to auction*) exposición *f*, inspección *f* • **"viewing by appointment only"** "estrictamente visitas concertadas" • **the gallery will be open for a private ~ this evening** la galería estará abierta esta noche para una visita privada
2 (*TV*) **a** (= *act*) • **"unsuitable for family ~"** "no apto para ver en familia" • **films sold for home ~** películas que se venden para ver en casa • **we strictly limit our children's TV ~** limitamos el tiempo que nuestros hijos ven la televisión de manera estricta
b (= *programmes*) programas *mpl*, programación *f* • **your weekend ~** sus programas *or* su programación para el fin de semana • **the series has become compulsive ~** la serie se ha convertido en un programa que no debe perderse
CPD ▸ **TV viewing figures** cifras *fpl* de audiencia televisiva ▸ **viewing gallery** (*gen*) galería *f* para observadores; (*balcony-shaped*) palco *m* para observadores ▸ **viewing habits** hábitos *mpl* de los telespectadores *or* televidentes ▸ **viewing platform** plataforma *f* de observación; ▹ **peak** ▸ **viewing public** telespectadores *mpl*, televidentes *mpl*
viewpoint ['vju:pɔɪnt] N **1** (*on hill etc*) mirador *m*, punto *m* panorámico
2 (*fig*) punto *m* de vista • **from the ~ of the economy** desde el punto de vista de la economía
vigil ['vɪdʒɪl] N vigilia *f*, vela *f* • **to keep ~ (over sth/sb)** velar (algo/a algn)
vigilance ['vɪdʒɪləns] N vigilancia *f* • **to escape sb's ~** burlar la vigilancia de algn • **to relax one's ~** disminuir la vigilancia, bajar la guardia
CPD ▸ **vigilance committee** (*US*) comité *m* de autodefensa
vigilant ['vɪdʒɪlənt] ADJ vigilante, alerta • **staff have been instructed to be extra ~** se ha ordenado a todo el personal que extreme la vigilancia • **under his ~ eye** bajo su atenta mirada • **to be ~ against** [+ *danger, threat*] mantenerse alerta *or* vigilante frente a
vigilante [,vɪdʒɪ'læntɪ] N vigilante *mf*
vigilantism [,vɪdʒɪ'læntɪzəm] N vigilancia *f* callejera
vigilantly ['vɪdʒɪləntlɪ] ADV vigilantemente
vignette [vɪ'njet] N (*Phot, Typ*) viñeta *f*; (= *character sketch*) esbozo *m* en miniatura, esbocito *m*, estampa *f*
vigor ['vɪgəʳ] N (*US*) = **vigour**
vigorous ['vɪgərəs] ADJ **1** (= *energetic*) [*exercise, activity, training*] enérgico; (= *lively*) [*debate*] enérgico • **she is a ~ 75 year-old** es una mujer de 75 años llena de vigor *or* energía
2 (= *strong*) [*opponent, campaign, defence*] enérgico; [*denial*] categórico, rotundo; [*growth*] (*Bot, Econ*) vigoroso; [*economy*] pujante
vigorously ['vɪgərəslɪ] ADV **1** (= *energetically*) [*nod, shake*] enérgicamente, vigorosamente; [*exercise*] enérgicamente
2 (= *strongly*) [*deny*] categóricamente, rotundamente; [*defend, oppose, protest*] enérgicamente • **to campaign ~** realizar una enérgica campaña • **to grow ~** [*plant*] crecer con vigor; [*economy, company*] crecer con vigor *or* vigorosamente
vigour, vigor (*US*) ['vɪgəʳ] N vigor *m*, energía *f* • **with great ~** con mucho vigor, con mucha energía • **with renewed ~** con renovado vigor, con renovada energía
Viking ['vaɪkɪŋ] N vikingo/a *m/f*
ADJ vikingo
vile [vaɪl] ADJ **1** (= *base, evil*) [*person, behaviour, attack, regime*] vil, infame; [*language*] abominable • **he was ~ to her** se portó de un modo infame con ella
2* (= *disgusting*) [*conditions*] miserable, infame; [*weather*] pésimo, infame; [*smell, taste*] repugnante • **it smelled/tasted ~** tenía un olor/sabor repugnante • **to be in a ~ mood** estar de pésimo humor, estar de un humor de mil demonios* • **he has a ~ temper** tiene un genio muy violento, tiene un genio de mil demonios*
vilely ['vaɪllɪ] ADV [*behave*] vilmente, de modo infame
vileness ['vaɪlnɪs] N [*of person, behaviour, action*] vileza *f*
vilification [,vɪlɪfɪ'keɪʃən] N vilipendio *m*
vilify ['vɪlɪfaɪ] VT vilipendiar
villa ['vɪlə] N (*Roman*) villa *f*; (= *country house*) casa *f* de campo, quinta *f*; (*for holiday*) chalet *m*
village ['vɪlɪdʒ] N pueblo *m*; (= *small*) aldea *f*, pueblito *m* (*LAm*)
CPD ▸ **village church** iglesia *f* del pueblo ▸ **village cricket** críquet *m* pueblerino ▸ **village green** prado *m* comunal, campo *m* comunal ▸ **village hall** sala *f* del pueblo ▸ **village idiot** tonto *m* del lugar ▸ **village life** la vida rural, la vida de pueblo ▸ **village school** escuela *f* del pueblo ▸ **village shop**, **village store** tienda *f* del pueblo
villager ['vɪlɪdʒəʳ] N (= *inhabitant*) vecino/a *m/f* del pueblo; [*of small village*] aldeano/a *m/f*
villain ['vɪlən] N **1*** (= *wrongdoer*) maleante *mf*, delincuente *mf*
2 (*hum*) (= *rascal*) bribón/ona *m/f*, tunante/a *m/f*
3 (*in novel, film*) malo/a *m/f* • **the ~ of the piece is Malone** (*hum*) el malo de la historia es Malone
villainous ['vɪlənəs] ADJ (= *evil*) malvado, vil; (= *very bad*) malísimo, horrible • **he was a ~-looking character** era un tipo de mala catadura (*frm*), era un tipo de aspecto malvado
villainously ['vɪlənəslɪ] ADV vilmente • **~ ugly** feísimo
villainy ['vɪlənɪ] N (*esp poet*) maldad *f*, vileza *f*
villein ['vɪlɪn] N (*Hist*) villano/a *m/f*
vim [vɪm] N energía *f*, empuje *m*
VIN N ABBR = **vehicle identification number**
vinaigrette [,vɪneɪ'gret] N vinagreta *f*
Vincent ['vɪnsənt] N Vicente
vindaloo [,vɪndə'lu:] N *plato indio muy picante*
vindicate ['vɪndɪkeɪt] VT [+ *decision, action*] justificar; [+ *claim, right*] reivindicar, hacer valer • **I feel totally ~d by this decision** me siento totalmente resarcido por esta decisión, siento que con esta decisión se me hace justicia • **to ~ o.s.** justificarse
vindication [,vɪndɪ'keɪʃən] N justificación *f*; [*of claim, right*] reivindicación *f*, defensa *f*; (= *means of exoneration*) vindicación *f* (*frm*) • **it was a ~ of all she had fought for** suponía una justificación de todo aquello por lo que había luchado
vindictive [vɪn'dɪktɪv] ADJ vengativo; (= *spiteful*) rencoroso • **to be ~ towards sb** ser vengativo con algn
vindictively [vɪn'dɪktɪvlɪ] ADV (= *vengefully*) vengativamente, con afán de venganza; (= *unforgivingly*) con rencor, rencorosamente
vindictiveness [vɪn'dɪktɪvnɪs] N (= *desire for revenge*) afán *m* de venganza, revanchismo *m*; (= *spitefulness*) rencor *m*
vine [vaɪn] N vid *f*; (= *climbing, trained*) parra *f*; (= *climber*) enredadera *f*
CPD ▸ **vine grower** viticultor(a) *m/f*, viñador(a) *m/f* ▸ **vine growing** viticultura *f*; ▹ **vine-growing** ▸ **vine leaf** hoja *f* de parra, hoja *f* de vid, pámpana *f*
vinegar ['vɪnɪgəʳ] N vinagre *m*
vinegary ['vɪnɪgərɪ] ADJ vinagroso
vine-growing ['vaɪn,grəʊɪŋ] ADJ [*region*] viticultor; ▹ **vine**
vineyard ['vɪnjəd] N viña *f*, viñedo *m*
viniculture ['vɪnɪkʌltʃəʳ] N vinicultura *f*
vino* ['vi:nəʊ] N vinacho* *m*, morapio *m* (*Sp**)
vinous ['vaɪnəs] ADJ vinoso
vintage ['vɪntɪdʒ] N (= *season, harvest*) vendimia *f*; (= *year*) cosecha *f*, añada *f* • **the 1970 ~** la cosecha de 1970 • **it will be a good ~** la cosecha será buena • **it was a ~ performance** fue una actuación memorable • **this film is ~ Chaplin** esta es una película clásica de Chaplin, esta película es un clásico de Chaplin • **it has been a ~ year for plays** ha sido un año destacado en lo que a teatro se refiere
CPD ▸ **vintage car** coche *m* de época, coche *m* antiguo (*fabricado entre 1919 y 1930*) ▸ **vintage wine** vino *m* añejo
vintner ['vɪntnəʳ] N (= *merchant*) vinatero/a *m/f*; (= *wine-maker*) vinicultor(a) *m/f*
vinyl ['vaɪnl] N vinilo *m*
ADJ de vinilo, vinílico
CPD ▸ **vinyl acetate** acetato *m* de vinilo
viol ['vaɪəl] N viola *f*
viola¹ [vɪ'əʊlə] N (*Mus*) viola *f* • **~ da gamba** viola *f* de gamba • **~ d'amore** viola *f* de amor
CPD ▸ **viola player** viola *mf*
viola² ['vaɪələ] N (*Bot*) viola *f*, violeta *f*
violate ['vaɪəleɪt] VT **1** (= *breach*) [+ *law*] violar, infringir, quebrantar; [+ *constitution, agreement, treaty*] violar, infringir, vulnerar; (*Comm, Pol*) [+ *sanctions*] incumplir, desobedecer; [+ *contract*] no cumplir, incumplir; [+ *rights*] violar, vulnerar; [+ *privacy*] invadir • **to ~ sb's trust** abusar de la confianza de algn
2 (= *defile*) [+ *grave*] profanar
3 (*liter*) (= *rape*) violar
violation [,vaɪə'leɪʃən] N **1** [*of law*] violación *f*, infracción *f*; [*of rights*] violación *f* • **~ of privacy** entrometimiento *m*, intromisión *f* • **it was in ~ of the law/agreement** violaba la ley/el acuerdo • **it was in ~ of sanctions** incumplía *or* desobedecía las sanciones
2 (*US*) (= *minor offence*) infracción *f*, falta *f* leve • **a minor traffic ~** una infracción de tráfico
3 (*liter*) (= *rape*) violación *f*
violator ['vaɪəleɪtəʳ] N [*of law*] infractor(a) *m/f*, violador(a) *m/f*; [*of agreement, rights*] violador(a) *m/f*
violence ['vaɪələns] N (*gen*) violencia *f* • **an act of ~** un acto de violencia • **crimes of ~** delitos *mpl* violentos • **to do ~ to sb** agredir a algn • **to do ~ to sth** estropear algo • **to resort to ~** recurrir a la violencia *or* a la fuerza • **robbery with ~** robo *m* con violencia
violent ['vaɪələnt] ADJ [*person, quarrel, storm,*

V

language] violento; [*kick*] violento, fuerte; [*pain*] intenso, agudo; [*colour*] chillón • **to become** *or* **turn ~** mostrarse violento • **to die a ~ death** morir de muerte violenta • **~ crimes** delitos *mpl* violentos • **to come to a ~ halt** detenerse *or* (*LAm*) parar bruscamente • **he has a ~ temper** tiene un genio terrible • **to take a ~ dislike to sb** coger *or* (*LAm*) agarrar una profunda antipatía a algn • **to take a ~ dislike to sth** tomar una tremenda *or* profunda aversión a algo • **by ~ means** por la fuerza, por la violencia

violently ['vaɪələntlɪ] ADV [*act*] con violencia, de manera violenta; [*tremble*] violentamente; [*brake*] bruscamente • **she shook the child ~** sacudió al niño con violencia • **to die ~** morir violentamente • **to react ~ to sth** reaccionar violentamente *or* con violencia ante algo • **to fall ~ in love with sb** enamorarse perdidamente de algn • **to be ~ opposed to sth** oponerse radicalmente a algo • **he is ~ anti-Communist** es un anticomunista furibundo • **to be ~ sick** vomitar mucho

violet ['vaɪəlɪt] N 1 (*Bot*) violeta *f*
2 (= *colour*) violado *m*, violeta *f*
ADJ violado, violeta • **~ colour** • **~ color** (*US*) color *m* violeta

violin [ˌvaɪə'lɪn] N violín *m*
CPD ▸ **violin case** estuche *m* de violín ▸ **violin concerto** concierto *m* para violín ▸ **violin player** violinista *mf* ▸ **violin section** sección *f* de violines

violinist [ˌvaɪə'lɪnɪst] N violinista *mf*

violist [vɪ'əʊlɪst] N (*US*) viola *mf*

violoncellist [ˌvaɪələn'tʃelɪst] N violonchelista *mf*

violoncello [ˌvaɪələn'tʃeləʊ] N violonchelo *m*

VIP N ABBR (= **very important person**) VIP *mf*, persona *f* de categoría
CPD ▸ **VIP lounge** sala *f* de VIPs ▸ **VIP treatment** • **to give sb the VIP treatment** tratar a algn como a un VIP • **to get the VIP treatment** ser tratado como un VIP

viper ['vaɪpəʳ] N (*lit, fig*) víbora *f*

viperish ['vaɪpərɪʃ] ADJ (*fig*) viperino

virago [vɪ'rɑːgəʊ] N (PL: **viragoes** *or* **viragos**) fiera *f*, arpía *f*

viral ['vaɪərəl] ADJ 1 vírico • **a ~ infection** una infección vírica
2 (*Marketing*) • **to go ~** hacerse viral

Virgil ['vɜːdʒɪl] N Virgilio

Virgilian [vɜː'dʒɪlɪən] ADJ virgiliano

virgin ['vɜːdʒɪn] N (*lit*) virgen *mf* • **to be a ~** ser virgen • **the Blessed Virgin** la Santísima Virgen
ADJ (*fig*) [*forest, soil etc*] virgen
CPD ▸ **virgin birth** partenogénesis *f inv* ▸ **the Virgin Isles** las islas Vírgenes ▸ **virgin oil** aceite *m* virgen

virginal ['vɜːdʒɪnl] ADJ virginal
N • **the ~** (*Mus*) la espineta

Virginian [və'dʒɪnɪən] ADJ virginiano
N 1 (= *person*) virginiano/a *m/f*
2 (*also* **Virginian tobacco**) tabaco *m* rubio

virginity [vɜː'dʒɪnɪtɪ] N virginidad *f*

Virgo ['vɜːgəʊ] N 1 (= *sign, constellation*) Virgo *m*
2 (= *person*) virgo *mf* • **she's (a) ~** es virgo

Virgoan ['vɜːgəʊən] N (= *person*) virgo *mf* • **he's a ~** es virgo

virgule ['vɜːgjuːl] N (*US*) (*Typ*) barra *f* oblicua

virile ['vɪraɪl] ADJ [*man*] viril; [*looks*] varonil

virility [vɪ'rɪlɪtɪ] N virilidad *f*

virologist [ˌvaɪə'rɒlədʒɪst] N virólogo/a *m/f*

virology [ˌvaɪə'rɒlədʒɪ] N virología *f*

virtual ['vɜːtjʊəl] ADJ real, verdadero • **he's the ~ star of the show** en realidad *or* en la práctica, la estrella del espectáculo es él • **it was a ~ defeat/failure** en realidad fue una derrota/un fracaso
CPD ▸ **virtual memory** memoria *f* virtual ▸ **virtual memory storage** memoria *f* virtual ▸ **virtual reality** realidad *f* virtual

virtuality [vɜːtjʊ'ælɪtɪ] N realidad *f* virtual, virtualidad *f*

virtually ['vɜːtjʊəlɪ] ADV prácticamente • **it is ~ impossible to do anything** es prácticamente imposible hacer nada • **it ~ destroyed the building** destruyó prácticamente el edificio • **I've ~ finished the work** casi he terminado el trabajo • **he started with ~ nothing** empezó prácticamente *or* casi sin nada

virtue ['vɜːtjuː] N 1 (= *good quality*) virtud *f* • **to extol sb's ~s** alabar *or* ensalzar las virtudes de algn • IDIOM: • **to make a ~ of necessity** hacer de la necesidad virtud
2 (= *advantage*) virtud *f*, ventaja *f* • **it has the ~ of simplicity** *or* **of being simple** tiene la virtud *or* ventaja de ser sencillo • **I see no ~ in (doing) that** no veo ninguna ventaja en (hacer) eso
3 (= *chastity*) castidad *f*, honra *f* • **her ~ was in no danger** su castidad *or* honra no corría peligro • **he had designs on her ~** iba a tratar de seducirla • **a woman of easy ~** una mujer de vida alegre, una mujer de moralidad laxa
4 • **by ~ of** • **in ~ of** en virtud de, debido a

virtuosity [ˌvɜːtjʊ'ɒsɪtɪ] N virtuosismo *m*

virtuoso [ˌvɜːtjʊ'əʊzəʊ] N (PL: **virtuosos** *or* **virtuosi** [ˌvɜːtjʊ'əʊziː]) virtuoso/a *m/f*
ADJ de virtuoso/a • **a ~ performance** una interpretación de auténtico virtuoso *or* llena de virtuosismo

virtuous ['vɜːtjʊəs] ADJ virtuoso
CPD ▸ **virtuous circle** círculo *m* virtuoso

virtuously ['vɜːtjʊəslɪ] ADV virtuosamente

virulence ['vɪrʊləns] N virulencia *f*

virulent ['vɪrʊlənt] ADJ (*Med*) (*also fig*) virulento

virulently ['vɪrʊləntlɪ] ADJ con virulencia

virus ['vaɪərəs] N (PL: **viruses**) (*Med, Comput*) virus *m inv* • **the AIDS ~** el virus del SIDA • **a computer ~** un virus informático
CPD ▸ **virus disease** enfermedad *f* vírica

visa ['viːzə] N (PL: **visas**) visado *m*, visa *f* (*LAm*)
VT visar

visage ['vɪzɪdʒ] N (*liter*) semblante *m*

vis-à-vis ['viːzɑːviː] PREP (= *with regard to*) con respecto a, en relación con, con relación a • **Switzerland's position vis-à-vis the EU** la posición de Suiza con respecto a *or* en relación con *or* con relación a la UE • **the government's policy vis-à-vis the unions** la política del gobierno frente a los sindicatos

viscera ['vɪsərə] NPL vísceras *fpl*

visceral ['vɪsərəl] ADJ (*liter*) visceral

viscid ['vɪsɪd] ADJ viscoso

viscose ['vɪskəʊs] ADJ viscoso
N viscosa *f*

viscosity [vɪs'kɒsɪtɪ] N viscosidad *f*

viscount ['vaɪkaʊnt] N vizconde *m*

viscountcy ['vaɪkaʊntsɪ] N vizcondado *m*

viscountess ['vaɪkaʊntɪs] N vizcondesa *f*

viscous ['vɪskəs] ADJ viscoso

vise [vaɪs] N (*US*) = **vice**[2]

vishing ['vɪʃɪŋ] N *llamadas fraudulentas para obtener información confidencial*

visibility [ˌvɪzɪ'bɪlɪtɪ] N 1 (*Met*) visibilidad *f* • **good/poor ~** buena/poca visibilidad *f*
2 (= *level of recognition*) • **the company needs to improve its ~** la compañía necesita darse más a conocer

visible ['vɪzəbl] ADJ 1 (= *able to be seen*) • **~ to the human eye** perceptible a simple vista, visible al ojo humano • **to be ~: your identity card must be ~ at all times** su carné de identidad tiene que estar siempre a la vista • **the house is ~ from the road** la casa puede verse desde la carretera
2 (= *obvious*) [*effect, sign, result*] evidente • **there was no ~ damage** no se veía ningún daño aparente • **the effects were clearly ~** los efectos saltaban a la vista, eran muy evidentes • **he was showing ~ signs of distress** mostraba evidentes *or* claras señales de agitación • **with a ~ effort** con un esfuerzo evidente • **with no ~ means of support** (*Jur*) sin ninguna fuente de ingresos aparente
3 (= *prominent*) [*person*] destacado, prominente • **at management level women are becoming increasingly ~** a niveles directivos, las mujeres ocupan lugares cada vez más destacados *or* prominentes
CPD ▸ **visible exports** (*Econ*) exportaciones *fpl* visibles

visibly ['vɪzəblɪ] ADV visiblemente • **many were ~ moved by what they saw** muchos estaban visiblemente emocionados por lo que habían visto • **he was ~ shaken by his ordeal** estaba visiblemente afectado por la terrible experiencia vivida • **she was ~ thinner** estaba visiblemente más delgada

Visigoth ['vɪzɪgɒθ] N visigodo/a *m/f*

Visigothic [ˌvɪzɪ'gɒθɪk] ADJ visigodo, visigótico

vision ['vɪʒən] N 1 (= *eyesight*) vista *f* • **to have normal ~** tener la vista normal • **field of ~** campo *m* visual; ▹ **double, tunnel**
2 (= *farsightedness*) clarividencia *f*, visión *f* de futuro; (= *imagination*) imaginación *f* • **we need ~ to make this idea work** nos hace falta clarividencia *or* visión de futuro para hacer que esta idea funcione • **he had the ~ to see that ...** tenía la suficiente visión de futuro como para ver que ... • **a man of (broad) ~** un hombre de miras amplias
3 (= *dream, hope*) visión *f* • **he outlined his ~ of the company over the next decade** esbozó su visión de la empresa para la siguiente década • **a ~ of the future** una visión del futuro
4 (= *image*) • **I had ~s of having to walk home** ya me veía volviendo a casa a pie
5 (*Rel*) visión *f* • **to have a ~** tener una visión • **Christ appeared to her in a ~** tuvo una visión de Cristo, se le apareció Cristo

visionary ['vɪʒənərɪ] N 1 (= *original thinker*) visionario/a *m/f*
2 (= *dreamer*) soñador(a) *m/f*
ADJ 1 (= *farsighted*) [*person, plan*] con visión de futuro, visionario
2 (= *impractical*) [*idea, plan*] utópico, quimérico
3 (= *idealistic*) [*person*] idealista
4 (= *religious, supernatural*) [*experience*] sobrenatural

vision-mixer ['vɪʒənˌmɪksəʳ] N (*TV*) mezclador(a) *m/f* de imágenes

visit ['vɪzɪt] N (*gen*) visita *f* • **to go on** *or* **make a ~ to** [+ *person, place*] ir de visita a, visitar a • **to pay sb a ~** • **pay a ~ to sb** hacer una visita *or* visitar a algn, pasar a ver a algn (*esp LAm*) • **on a private/an official ~** de *or* en visita privada/oficial • **he was taken ill on** *or* **during a ~ to Amsterdam** cayó enfermo durante una visita a Amsterdam • **to return a ~** devolver una visita • **a ~ to the lavatory** *or* **toilet** una visita al servicio, una visita al señor Roca*
VT 1 (= *go and see*) [+ *person*] visitar, hacer una visita a; [+ *place*] ir a, visitar • **to ~ the sick** visitar a los enfermos • **to ~ a patient** ir a ver a un paciente, visitar a un paciente • **he never ~s the doctor** nunca va al médico

• **we're hoping to ~ Tarragona** esperamos poder ir a *or* visitar Tarragona • **when we first ~ed the town** la primera vez que fuimos a *or* visitamos la ciudad
2 (*= stay with*) [*+ person*] visitar, pasar un tiempo con; (*= stay in*) [*+ town, area*] visitar, pasar un tiempo en
3 (*frm*) (*= inflict, afflict*) • **to ~ a punishment on sb** castigar a algn con algo, mandar un castigo a algn • **they were ~ed with the plague**†† sufrieron el azote de la peste • **the sins of the fathers are ~ed on the children** los hijos sufren los pecados de los padres
VI 1 (*= make a visit*) hacer una visita; (*= make visits*) hacer visitas • **they always ~ when they're in town** siempre nos hacen una visita cuando vienen a la ciudad • **she has promised to ~ next year** ha prometido venir de visita el año que viene • **to go ~ing** hacer visitas
2 (*US*) • **to ~ with sb** (*= go and see*) visitar a algn; (*= chat with*) charlar con algn

visitation [ˌvɪzɪˈteɪʃən] N 1 (*= visit*) (*by official*) inspección *f*; (*by bishop, cardinal*) visita *f* pastoral • **we had a ~ from her** (*hum*) nos cayó encima una de sus visitas
2 (*Rel*) visitación *f* • **the Visitation of the Blessed Virgin Mary** la Visitación de la Santísima Virgen María
3 (*= punishment*) castigo *m*
CPD ▸ **visitation rights** derecho *msing* de visita

visiting [ˈvɪzɪtɪŋ] ADJ [*speaker, professor*] invitado; [*team*] visitante, de fuera • **we're on ~ terms** nos visitamos
CPD ▸ **visiting card** tarjeta *f* de visita ▸ **visiting hours** horas *fpl* de visita ▸ **visiting nurse** (*US*) enfermera *f* que visita a domicilio ▸ **visiting professor** profesor(a) *m/f* invitado/a ▸ **visiting rights** derecho *msing* de visita ▸ **visiting time** horas *fpl* de visita

visitor [ˈvɪzɪtəʳ] N 1 (*to one's home*) visita *f* • **she had a ~ earlier** tuvo una visita antes • **we had a constant stream of ~s** no paraba de visitarnos gente • **to have ~s** tener visita • **we can't invite you because we've got ~s** no podemos invitarte porque tenemos visita
2 (*in hotel*) huésped(a) *m/f*
3 (*to place*) (*= tourist*) turista *mf*, visitante *mf*; (*= tripper*) excursionista *mf*; (*to zoo, exhibition*) visitante *mf*; (*to hospital, prison*) visita *f* • **~s to this country must be made to feel welcome** los que visitan este país deben sentirse bien recibidos • **the museum had 900 ~s** el museo recibió a 900 visitantes • **sorry, we're just ~s here** lo siento, estamos aquí de visita nada más • **the summer ~s bring a lot of money** los veraneantes aportan mucho dinero • **he's only allowed two ~s** [*patient, prisoner*] solo puede recibir dos visitas
CPD ▸ **visitor centre, visitor center** (*US*) centro *m* de información ▸ **visitors' book** libro *m* de visitas

visor [ˈvaɪzəʳ] N visera *f*

VISTA [ˈvɪstə] N ABBR (*US*) (= **Volunteers in Service to America**) *programa de ayuda voluntaria a los necesitados*

vista [ˈvɪstə] N (*lit*) vista *f*, panorama *m*; (*fig*) perspectiva *f*, horizonte *m* • **to open up new ~s** abrir nuevas perspectivas *or* nuevos horizontes

visual [ˈvɪzjʊəl] ADJ visual
CPD ▸ **visual aids** (*in teaching*) medios *mpl* visuales ▸ **the visual arts** las artes plásticas ▸ **visual display unit** unidad *f* de despliegue visual, monitor *m* ▸ **visual effects** efectos *mpl* visuales ▸ **visual proof** pruebas *fpl* oculares

visualization [ˌvɪzjʊəlaɪˈzeɪʃən] N visualización *f*

visualize [ˈvɪzjʊəlaɪz] VT 1 (*= imagine*) imaginarse • **he tried to ~ the scene** intentó imaginarse la escena • **he could not ~ her as old** no podía hacerse una idea de ella *or* no podía imaginársela de mayor • **she ~d him working at his desk** se lo imaginó trabajando en su mesa • **try to ~ yourself sitting calmly on a plane** imagínate que vas tranquilamente sentado en un avión
2 (*= call to mind*) [*+ person, sb's face*] recordar • **he found it difficult to ~ her now** ahora le resultaba difícil recordarla
3 (*= foresee*) prever • **we do not ~ any great change** no prevemos ningún cambio de importancia • **that is not how we ~d it** eso no corresponde a lo que nosotros preveíamos

visually [ˈvɪzjʊəlɪ] ADV visualmente • **~ impaired** con discapacidad visual

vital [ˈvaɪtl] ADJ 1 (*= crucial*) [*part, component, element*] vital, indispensable; [*ingredient*] esencial, indispensable, imprescindible; [*factor*] decisivo; [*link, role*] fundamental; [*question*] vital; [*information*] vital, esencial • **it is ~ to keep accurate records** es imprescindible *or* esencial llevar un registro detallado • **is it really ~ for her to have a new dress?** ¿es realmente imprescindible que se compre un vestido nuevo? • **it is ~ that this be kept secret** es esencial que se mantenga en secreto • **to be of ~ importance (to sth/sb)** ser de suma *or* vital importancia (para algo/algn) • **at the ~ moment** en el momento crítico *or* clave • **these meetings are ~ to a successful outcome** estas reuniones son esenciales para un resultado positivo
2 (*= dynamic*) [*person, organization*] vital, lleno de vitalidad • **~ spark** chispa *f* vital
3 (*Physiol*) [*organ, function*] vital
N **vitals** (*Anat*) (*esp hum*) (*= internal organs*) órganos *mpl* vitales; (*= male genitals*) órganos *mpl* sexuales, partes *fpl* (*hum*)
CPD ▸ **vital signs** (*Med*) signos *mpl* vitales ▸ **vital statistics** (*Sociol*) estadísticas *fpl** demográficas; [*of woman's body*] medidas *fpl*

vitality [vaɪˈtælɪtɪ] N vitalidad *f*

vitalize [ˈvaɪtəlaɪz] VT 1 (*lit*) vitalizar, vivificar
2 (*fig*) [*+ person*] animar; [*+ economy, organization*] vitalizar

vitally [ˈvaɪtəlɪ] ADV 1 (*= extremely*) [*interested, concerned*] sumamente; [*affect*] de forma vital • **it is ~ important that ...** es de vital *or* suma importancia que ... (*+ subjun*) • **it is ~ necessary that ...** es indispensable que ... (*+ subjun*) • **~ needed** [*food, tents, money*] indispensable • **this statement ~ ignores a number of issues** estas manifestaciones ignoran de forma fundamental una serie de cuestiones
2 (*= intensely*) • **music which remains ~ fresh today** música que sigue fresca y llena de vitalidad

vitamin [ˈvɪtəmɪn] N vitamina *f* • **with added ~s** vitaminado, reforzado con vitaminas
CPD ▸ **vitamin content** contenido *m* vitamínico ▸ **vitamin deficiency** avitaminosis *f*, déficit *m* vitamínico ▸ **vitamin pill** pastilla *f* de vitaminas ▸ **vitamin supplement** suplemento *m* vitamínico ▸ **vitamin tablet** pastilla *f* de vitaminas

vitamin-enriched [ˌvɪtəmɪnɪnˈrɪtʃt] ADJ enriquecido con vitaminas

vitaminize [ˈvɪtəmɪnaɪz] VT vitaminar

vitaminized [ˈvɪtəmɪnaɪzd] ADJ vitamin(iz)ado, reforzado con vitaminas

vitiate [ˈvɪʃɪeɪt] VT (*frm*) (*= weaken*) afectar negativamente; (*= spoil*) estropear, arruinar; (*= devalue*) quitar valor a; (*Jur*) [*+ contract, deed*] invalidar

viticulture [ˈvɪtɪkʌltʃəʳ] N viticultura *f*

vitreous [ˈvɪtrɪəs] ADJ vítreo

vitrifaction [ˌvɪtrɪˈfækʃən], **vitrification** [ˌvɪtrɪfɪˈkeɪʃən] N vitrificación *f*

vitrify [ˈvɪtrɪfaɪ] VT vitrificar
VI vitrificarse

vitriol [ˈvɪtrɪəl] N vitriolo *m*

vitriolic [ˌvɪtrɪˈɒlɪk] ADJ [*attack, speech, criticism*] corrosivo, mordaz; [*abuse, outburst*] virulento

vitro [ˈviːtrəʊ] ▹ **in vitro**

vituperate [vɪˈtjuːpəreɪt] (*frm*) VT vituperar, llenar de injurias
VI • **to ~ against sth/sb** vituperar algo/a algn

vituperation [vɪˌtjuːpəˈreɪʃən] (*frm*) N vituperio *m*, injurias *fpl*

vituperative [vɪˈtjuːpərətɪv] ADJ (*frm*) injurioso

viva¹ [ˈvaɪvə] N (*also* **viva voce**) examen *m* oral

viva² [ˈviːvə] EXCL • **~ Caroline!** ¡viva Caroline!

vivacious [vɪˈveɪʃəs] ADJ vivaz, animado

vivaciously [vɪˈveɪʃəslɪ] ADJ con vivacidad, animadamente

vivacity [vɪˈvæsɪtɪ] N vivacidad *f*, animación *f*

vivarium [vɪˈvɛərɪəm] N (PL: **vivariums** *or* **vivaria** [vɪˈvɛərɪə]) vivero *m*

viva voce [ˈvaɪvəˈvəʊsɪ] ADV de viva voz
ADJ [*exam*] oral
N (*Brit*) examen *m* oral

vivid [ˈvɪvɪd] ADJ [*colour*] vivo, intenso; [*impression, recollection, memory*] vivo, fuerte; [*dream*] clarísimo; [*description*] gráfico, realista • **to have a ~ imagination** tener una imaginación muy viva *or* despierta

vividly [ˈvɪvɪdlɪ] ADV (*gen*) vivamente; [*describe*] gráficamente

vividness [ˈvɪvɪdnɪs] N [*of colours*] intensidad *f*, viveza *f*; [*of description*] lo gráfico; [*of impression, memory*] fuerza *f*

vivify [ˈvɪvɪfaɪ] VT vivificar

viviparous [vɪˈvɪpərəs] ADJ vivíparo

vivisection [ˌvɪvɪˈsekʃən] N vivisección *f*

vivisectionist [ˌvɪvɪˈsekʃənɪst] N vivisector(a) *m/f*

vixen [ˈvɪksn] N 1 (*= fox*) zorra *f*, raposa *f*
2 (*pej*) (*= bad-tempered woman*) arpía *f*, bruja *f*

viz. [vɪz] ADV ABBR (= **videlicet**) (*= namely*) v.g., v.gr.

vizier [vɪˈzɪəʳ] N visir *m* • **grand ~** gran visir *m*

V-J Day [ˌviːˈdʒeɪdeɪ] N ABBR (= **Victory over Japan Day**) *Brit: 15 agosto 1945; US: 2 setiembre 1945;* ▹ V-E DAY

VLF N ABBR = **very low frequency**

vlog [vlɒg] N vlog *m*, vídeo *m* blog
VI publicar un vlog

vlogger [ˈvlɒgəʳ] N autor(a) *m/f* de un vlog

VLSI N ABBR (= **very large-scale integration**) integración *f* a muy gran escala

V-neck [ˈviːnek] N (*= neckline*) cuello *m* en pico; (*= sweater*) jersey *m* de cuello de pico
ADJ (*also* **V-necked**) de cuello de pico

V-necked [ˈviːnekt] ADJ = **V-neck**

VOA N ABBR (= **Voice of America**) Voz *f* de América

vocab* [ˈvəʊkæb] N ABBR = **vocabulary**

vocable [ˈvəʊkəbl] N (*Phon*) vocablo *m*

vocabulary [vəʊˈkæbjʊlərɪ] N 1 [*of person, language, subject*] vocabulario *m*, léxico *m* • **a new word in the German ~** una palabra nueva en el vocabulario *or* léxico alemán

2 (= *glossary*) glosario *m*
vocal ['vəʊkəl] ADJ **1** (*Anat, Mus*) vocal
2 (= *vociferous*) ruidoso • **a small but ~ minority** una minoría pequeña pero ruidosa • **there was some ~ opposition** se dejaron oír voces fuertemente discrepantes • **they are getting rather ~ about it** están empezando a protestar
N ▹ **vocals**
CPD ▸ **vocal cords** cuerdas *fpl* vocales ▸ **vocal music** música *f* vocal ▸ **vocal organs** órganos *mpl* vocales ▸ **vocal score** partitura *f* vocal
vocalic [vəʊ'kælɪk] ADJ vocálico
vocalist ['vəʊkəlɪst] N (*in cabaret*) vocalista *mf*; (*in pop group*) cantante *mf*
vocalization [,vəʊkəlaɪ'zeɪʃən] N vocalización *f*
vocalize ['vəʊkəlaɪz] VT vocalizar
VI vocalizarse
vocally ['vəʊkəlɪ] ADV **1** (*Mus*) vocalmente
2 (= *vociferously*) ruidosamente
vocals ['vəʊkəlz] NPL voz *fsing*, canto *msing* • **backing ~** coros *mpl* • **lead ~** voz *f* principal
vocation [vəʊ'keɪʃən] N (= *calling*) vocación *f*; (= *profession*) profesión *f*, carrera *f* • **to have a ~ for art** tener vocación por el arte • **he has missed his ~** se ha equivocado de carrera
vocational [vəʊ'keɪʃənl] ADJ [*subject, course*] de formación profesional; [*qualification, skill*] profesional • **~ guidance** orientación *f* profesional • **~ training** formación *f* or capacitación *f* profesional
CPD ▸ **vocational school** (*in US*) centro *m* de formación profesional
vocationally [vəʊ'keɪʃənlɪ] ADV [*train*] vocacionalmente, de manera vocacional • **~ oriented** orientado vocacionalmente *or* de manera vocacional
vocative ['vɒkətɪv] ADJ • **~ case** vocativo *m*
N vocativo *m*
vociferate [vəʊ'sɪfəreɪt] VI vociferar, gritar
VT vociferar, gritar
vociferation [vəʊ,sɪfə'reɪʃən] N vociferación *f*
vociferous [vəʊ'sɪfərəs] ADJ **1** (= *forceful, energetic*) ruidoso • **there were ~ protests** hubo ruidosas protestas, se protestó ruidosamente
2 (= *noisy*) vociferante
vociferously [vəʊ'sɪfərəslɪ] ADV
1 (= *forcefully, energetically*) [*protest, campaign*] ruidosamente; [*oppose, deny*] terminantemente, categóricamente
2 (= *noisily*) [*cheer*] a gritos
VOD ABBR (= **video on demand**) vídeo *m* bajo demanda *or* a la carta (*Sp*), video *m* bajo demanda *or* a la carta (*LAm*)
vodka ['vɒdkə] N vodka *m*
vogue [vəʊg] N moda *f* • **to be in ~** • **be the ~** estar en boga *or* de moda • **the ~ for short skirts** la moda de la falda corta
CPD ▸ **vogue word** palabra *f* que está de moda
voice [vɔɪs] N **1** (= *sound, faculty of speech*) voz *f* • **I didn't recognize your ~** no he reconocido tu voz • **her ~ sounded cold** se notaba un dejo de frialdad en su voz • **man's/woman's ~** voz de hombre/mujer • **if you carry on shouting, you won't have any ~ left** si sigues gritando te vas a quedar afónica *or* sin voz • **he is a ~ (crying) in the wilderness** está predicando en el desierto • **he added his ~ to opposition critics** unió su voz a las críticas de la oposición • **to find one's ~** (*lit*) recuperar el habla; (*fig*) encontrar su medio de expresión • **to give ~ to sth** (*frm*) dar expresión a algo • **to hear ~s** oír voces • **human ~** voz *f* humana • **in a deep ~** en tono grave • **in a loud/low ~** en voz alta/baja • **in a small ~** con voz queda • **inner ~** voz *f* interior • **a ~ inside me** una voz en mi interior • **if you don't keep your ~s down, you'll have to leave** si no hablan más bajo tendrán que irse • **keep your ~ down!** ¡no levantes la voz! • **to lose one's ~** quedarse afónico *or* sin voz • **to lower one's ~** bajar la voz • **to raise one's ~** alzar *or* levantar la voz • **the ~ of reason** la voz de la razón • **at the top of one's ~** a voz en grito, a voz en cuello • **he yelled at the top of his ~** gritó con todas sus fuerzas *or* a voz en cuello • IDIOMS: • **to speak with one ~ (about sth)** expresar una opinión unánime (con respecto a algo) • **to like the sound of one's own ~**: • **he does like the sound of his own ~** cómo le gusta oírse hablar; ▹ **throw, tone**
2 (*Mus*) voz *f* • **she has a beautiful (singing) ~** tiene una voz preciosa (para el canto), canta muy bien • **a piece for ~ and piano** una pieza para voz y piano • **bass/contralto/soprano/tenor ~** voz *f* de bajo/contralto/soprano/tenor • **to be in good ~** estar bien de voz
3 (= *opinion*) voz *f* • **the ~ of the people/nation** la voz del pueblo/de la nación • **to have a/no ~ in the matter** tener/no tener voz en el asunto • **there were no dissenting ~s** no hubo opiniones en contra • **she is a respected ~ in the women's movement** es una voz respetada dentro del movimiento feminista
4 (= *spokesperson*) portavoz *mf*
5 (*Phon*) sonoridad *f*
6 (*Gram*) • **active/passive ~** voz *f* activa/pasiva • **in the active/passive ~** en (voz) activa/pasiva
VT **1** [+ *opinion, feelings, concern, support*] expresar • **he felt obliged to ~ his opposition to the war** se sintió obligado a expresar su oposición a la guerra
2 (*Phon*) [+ *consonant*] sonorizar
3 (*Mus*) [+ *wind instrument*] templar
CPD ▸ **voice box** laringe *f* ▸ **voice mail** (*Telec*) buzón *m* de voz ▸ **voice part** (*Mus*) parte *f* cantable ▸ **voice production** producción *f* de voz ▸ **voice range** registro *m* de voz ▸ **voice recognition** reconocimiento *m* de la voz ▸ **voice synthesis** síntesis *f* de voz ▸ **voice synthesizer** sintetizador *m* de voz ▸ **voice training** educación *f* de la voz ▸ **voice vote** (*US*) (*Pol*) voto *m* oral
voice-activated ['vɔɪs'æktɪveɪtəd] ADJ activado por voz
voiced [vɔɪst] ADJ (*Phon*) [*consonant*] sonoro
voiceless ['vɔɪslɪs] ADJ (*Ling*) [*consonant*] sordo
voice-over ['vɔɪs,əʊvəʳ] N voz *f* en off
voiceprint ['vɔɪs,prɪnt] N impresión *f* vocal
voicing ['vɔɪsɪŋ] N sonorización *f*
void [vɔɪd] ADJ **1** (*Jur*) (= *invalid*) nulo, inválido • **to make** *or* **render a contract ~** anular *or* invalidar un contrato; ▹ **null**
2 (*frm*) (= *empty*) vacío • **~ of interest** carente *or* desprovisto de interés • **to make sb's efforts ~** hacer inútiles los esfuerzos de algn
N **1** (= *emptiness*) (*lit*) vacío *m*; (*fig*) (= *sense of emptiness*) vacío *m* • **the ~** la nada • **to fill the ~** llenar el hueco *or* vacío
2 (= *hole*) hueco *m*
3 (*Cards*) fallo *m* • **to have a ~ in hearts** tener fallo a corazones
VT **1** (*Med*) evacuar, vaciar
2 (*Jur*) anular, invalidar
voile [vɔɪl] N gasa *f*
vol. ABBR (= **volume**) t.
volatile ['vɒlətaɪl] ADJ **1** (*Chem*) volátil
2 (= *unstable*) [*person*] voluble; [*situation, atmosphere, market*] inestable, volátil
3 (*Comput*) • **~ memory** memoria *f* no permanente
volatility [,vɒlə'tɪlɪtɪ] N **1** (*Chem*) volatilidad *f*
2 (= *instability*) [*of person*] volubilidad *f*; [*of situation, atmosphere, market*] inestabilidad *f*, volatilidad *f*
volatilize [vɒ'lætəlaɪz] (*Chem*) VT volatilizar
VI volatilizarse
vol-au-vent ['vɒləʊvɑ̃] N volován *m*
volcanic [vɒl'kænɪk] ADJ volcánico
volcano [vɒl'keɪnəʊ] N (PL: **volcanoes** *or* **volcanos**) volcán *m*
volcanologist [,vɒlkə'nɒlədʒɪst] N vulcanólogo/a *m/f*
volcanology [,vɒlkə'nɒlədʒɪ] N vulcanología *f*
vole [vəʊl] N campañol *m*, ratón *m* de campo
volition [və'lɪʃən] N • **of one's own ~** (*frm*) por voluntad (propia), de libre albedrío
volitional [və'lɪʃənl] ADJ volitivo • **~ act** acto volitivo
volley ['vɒlɪ] N **1** [*of shots*] descarga *f* (cerrada); [*of applause*] salva *f*; [*of stones, objects*] lluvia *f*; [*of insults*] torrente *m*
2 (*Tennis*) volea *f*
VT **1** [+ *abuse, insults*] dirigir (**at** a)
2 (*Tennis*) volear
VI (*Mil*) lanzar una descarga
volleyball ['vɒlɪbɔ:l] N balonvolea *m*, voleibol *m*, volibol *m* (*LAm*)
CPD ▸ **volleyball player** jugador(a) *m/f* de balonvolea, jugador(a) *m/f* de voleibol, jugador(a) *m/f* de volibol (*LAm*)
volleyer ['vɒlɪəʳ] N especialista *mf* en voleas
vols. ABBR (= **volumes**) t.
volt [vəʊlt] N voltio *m*
voltage ['vəʊltɪdʒ] N voltaje *m*, tensión *f*
voltaic [vɒl'teɪɪk] ADJ voltaico
volte-face ['vɒlt'fɑ:s] N viraje *m*, cambio *m* súbito de opinión
voltmeter ['vəʊlt,mi:təʳ] N voltímetro *m*
volubility [,vɒljʊ'bɪlɪtɪ] N locuacidad *f*
voluble ['vɒljʊbl] ADJ [*person*] locuaz; [*speech*] prolijo
volubly ['vɒljʊblɪ] ADV [*speak, talk*] locuazmente; [*write*] prolijamente
volume ['vɒlju:m] N **1** (= *book*) libro *m*, volumen *m*; (= *one of series*) volumen *m*, tomo *m* • **a 125-page ~** un libro *or* volumen de 125 páginas • **in the third ~** en el tercer tomo *or* volumen • **an edition in four ~s** una edición en cuatro tomos *or* volúmenes
2 (= *sound*) volumen *m* • **to turn the ~ up** subir el volumen *or* sonido
3 (*Phys, Math*) volumen *m*; (*when measuring liquids*) capacidad *f*
4 (= *size, bulk*) volumen *m*; [*of water*] cantidad *f*, volumen *m*
5 (= *amount*) [*of work, sales*] volumen *m* • **production ~** volumen *m* de producción
6 volumes (of) (= *great quantities*) gran cantidad (de) • **~s of smoke** gran cantidad de humo • **to write ~s** escribir mucho • **his expression spoke ~s** su expresión lo decía todo • **it speaks ~s for him** eso lo dice todo de él
CPD ▸ **volume business** empresa *f* que comercia solo en grandes cantidades ▸ **volume control** control *m* de volumen ▸ **volume discount** descuento *m* por volumen de compras ▸ **volume sales** ventas *fpl* a granel
volumetric [,vɒljʊ'metrɪk] ADJ volumétrico
voluminous [və'lu:mɪnəs] ADJ (= *large, capacious*) voluminoso; (= *prolific*) prolífico;

(= *overlong*) prolijo
voluntarily ['vɒləntərɪlɪ] (ADV) **1** (= *freely*) voluntariamente, por voluntad propia
2 (= *for no payment*) [*work*] como voluntario
voluntarism ['vɒləntərɪzəm] (N) voluntariado *m*
voluntary ['vɒləntərɪ] (ADJ) **1** (= *not compulsory*) [*contribution, attendance, scheme*] voluntario • **attendance is on a ~ basis** la asistencia es voluntaria
2 (= *unpaid*) [*work, helper*] voluntario • **he does ~ work in his spare time** trabaja de voluntario en su tiempo libre • **he works at the school on a ~ basis** trabaja en el colegio como voluntario
3 (= *charitable*) [*organization*] voluntario
(N) (*Mus*) solo *m* musical • **an organ/trumpet ~** un solo de órgano/trompeta
(CPD) ▸ **voluntary euthanasia** eutanasia *f* voluntaria ▸ **voluntary hospital** (*US*) hospital *m* benéfico ▸ **voluntary liquidation** (*Comm, Econ*) liquidación *f* voluntaria, disolución *f* • **to go into ~ liquidation** entrar en liquidación voluntaria, disolverse voluntariamente ▸ **voluntary manslaughter** (*US*) (*Jur*) homicidio *m* con circunstancias atenuantes ▸ **voluntary helper** voluntario/a *m/f* ▸ **voluntary layoff** (*US*) retiro *m* voluntario, baja *f* voluntaria (*Sp*) ▸ **voluntary organization** organización *f* voluntaria ▸ **voluntary redundancy** retiro *m* voluntario, baja *f* voluntaria (*Sp*) • **to take ~ redundancy** tomar el retiro voluntario, coger la baja voluntaria (*Sp*) ▸ **voluntary repatriation** repatriación *f* voluntaria ▸ **voluntary school** (*Brit*) ≈ colegio *m* concertado ▸ **the voluntary sector** el voluntariado ▸ **Voluntary Service Overseas** (*Brit*) Servicio *m* de Voluntarios en el Extranjero ▸ **voluntary work** trabajo *m* voluntario • **to do ~ work** trabajar como voluntario/a ▸ **voluntary worker** voluntario/a *m/f*
volunteer [ˌvɒlən'tɪəʳ] (N) (*gen*) voluntario/a *m/f*
(ADJ) [*forces*] voluntario, de voluntarios; [*helper*] voluntario
(VT) **1** (= *offer*) [+ *one's help, services*] ofrecer; [+ *remark, suggestion*] hacer; [+ *information*] dar
2 (= *put forward**) • **they ~ed him for the job** le señalaron contra su voluntad para la tarea
(VI) (*for a task*) ofrecerse; (*for the army*) alistarse como voluntario • **to ~ for service overseas** ofrecerse para servir en ultramar • **to ~ to do sth** ofrecerse (voluntario) para hacer algo • **he wasn't forced to, he ~ed** nadie le obligó a ello, se ofreció libremente
volunteerism [ˌvɒlən'tɪərɪzəm] (N) (*esp US*) (= *willingness to help*) voluntad *f* de ayudar; (= *voluntary work*) voluntariado *m*
voluptuary [və'lʌptjʊərɪ] (N) voluptuoso/a *m/f*
voluptuous [və'lʌptjʊəs] (ADJ) voluptuoso
voluptuously [və'lʌptjʊəslɪ] (ADJ) voluptuosamente
voluptuousness [və'lʌptjʊəsnɪs] (N) voluptuosidad *f*
vomit ['vɒmɪt] (N) vómito *m*
(VI) devolver, vomitar
(VT) **1** (*lit*) (*also* **vomit up**) vomitar
2 (*fig*) (= *pour out*) arrojar, echar
vomiting ['vɒmɪtɪŋ] (N) vómito *m*
voodoo ['vu:du:] (N) vudú *m*
voracious [və'reɪʃəs] (ADJ) [*appetite, person, animal*] voraz; (*fig*) [*reader*] insaciable, ávido
voraciously [və'reɪʃəslɪ] (ADV) (*lit*) [*eat*] vorazmente; (*fig*) [*read*] con avidez
voracity [vɒ'ræsɪtɪ] (N) (*lit*) voracidad *f*; (*fig*) avidez *f* (**for** de)
vortex ['vɔ:teks] (N) (PL: **vortexes** *or* **vortices** ['vɔ:tɪsi:z]) **1** (*lit*) vórtice *m*, torbellino *m*
2 (*fig*) [*of activity*] torbellino, remolino *m*
Vosges [vəʊʒ] (NPL) Vosgos *mpl*
votary ['vəʊtərɪ] (N) **1** (*Rel*) devoto/a *m/f*
2 (*fig*) partidario/a *m/f*
vote [vəʊt] (N) **1** (= *single vote*) voto *m* (**for** a favor, **against** en contra de) • **he was elected by 102 ~s to 60** salió elegido con 102 votos a favor y 60 en contra • **he gets my ~ any day!** ¡cuenta con mi voto incondicional! • **to count the ~s** escrutar *or* computar los votos • **one person, one ~** una persona, un voto; ▹ **cast**
2 (= *votes cast*) votos *mpl* • **they captured 13 per cent of the ~** se hicieron con un 13 por ciento de los votos • **the middle class ~** los votos de la clase media • **as the 1931 ~ showed** según demostraron las elecciones de 1931 • **the ~ was overwhelmingly in favour of the Democratic Party** el partido demócrata obtuvo una aplastante mayoría • **the protest was rejected by a majority ~** la protesta fue rechazada por voto mayoritario
3 (= *right to vote*) derecho *m* al voto *or* a votar, sufragio *m* • **to give sb the ~** dar a algn el derecho al voto • **to have the ~** tener (el) derecho al voto • **~s for women!** ¡el sufragio para las mujeres!
4 (= *act*) votación *f* • **to have** *or* **take a ~ on sth** decidir algo por votación, someter algo a votación (*more frm*) • **a ~ of confidence** un voto de confianza • **to pass a ~ of confidence (in sb)** dar un voto de confianza (a algn) • **to allow a free ~** dejar libertad de voto • **a ~ of no confidence** un voto de censura • **by popular ~** (*lit*) por votación popular; (*fig*) en la opinión de muchos • **to put sth to the ~** someter algo a votación • **a ~ of thanks** un voto de gracias
(VT) **1** (= *cast one's vote for*) votar • **to ~ Labour/Conservative** votar por *or* a los laboristas/conservadores • **~ Ross at the next election!** ¡vote por *or* a Ross en las próximas elecciones! • **to ~ no** votar no • **to ~ sb into office** votar por *or* a algn para un cargo • **to ~ sb out of office** votar para reemplazar a algn (en un cargo) • **to ~ a bill/measure through parliament** aprobar una ley/una medida en el parlamento • **to ~ yes** votar sí
2 (= *elect*) elegir (por votación) • **she was ~d Miss Granada 1995** fue elegida (por votación) Miss Granada 1995
3 (= *approve*) aprobar (por votación) • **MPs have today ~d themselves a pay increase** hoy, los diputados parlamentarios se han aprobado (por votación) un aumento de sueldo
4 (= *suggest*) • **I ~ we turn back** sugiero *or* propongo que regresemos
5 (= *judge*) • **we ~d it a failure** opinamos que fue un fracaso
(VI) votar • **how did you ~?** ¿a *or* por quién votaste? • **which way will you be voting?** ¿a quién votarás? • **the country ~s in three weeks** el país acudirá a las urnas dentro de tres semanas • **to ~ to do sth** votar por hacer algo • **to ~ against sth** votar en contra de algo • **to ~ in favour of sth** votar a favor de algo • **to ~ for sb** votar por *or* a algn • **to ~ on sth** someter algo a votación • IDIOM: • **to ~ with one's feet**: • **if the bank goes on like this, customers may start voting with their feet** si el banco sigue así, es posible que los clientes empiecen a prescindir de sus servicios
(CPD) ▸ **vote loser*** lastre *m* electoral • **it's a ~ loser for us** nos hace perder votos, nos supone un lastre electoral ▸ **vote winner*** triunfo *m* electoral
▸ **vote down** (VT + ADV) (= *reject*) [+ *proposal, motion, amendment*] rechazar por mayoría de votos • **I often get ~d down in my house** en casa a menudo tengo que ceder y hacer lo que deciden los demás
▸ **vote in** (VT + ADV) [+ *candidate, party*] elegir (por votación); [+ *law*] aprobar (por votación)
▸ **vote out** (VT + ADV) [+ *person, party*] no reelegir
▸ **vote through** (VT + ADV) [+ *bill, motion*] aprobar
vote-catching ['vəʊtkætʃɪŋ] (ADJ) electoralista
(N) electoralismo *m*
voter ['vəʊtəʳ] (N) (*gen*) votante *mf*; (*in election*) elector(a) *m/f*
voting ['vəʊtɪŋ] (N) votación *f*
(CPD) ▸ **voting booth** cabina *f* electoral ▸ **voting machine** (*US*) máquina *f* de votar ▸ **voting paper** papeleta *f* de votación ▸ **voting pattern** tendencia *f* de la votación ▸ **voting power** potencia *f* electoral ▸ **voting precinct** (*US*) circunscripción *f* electoral ▸ **voting right** derecho *m* a voto ▸ **voting share** acción *f* con derecho a voto ▸ **voting slip** = **voting paper**
votive ['vəʊtɪv] (ADJ) votivo • **~ offering** ofrenda *f* votiva, exvoto *m*
(CPD) ▸ **votive candle** (*in church*) cirio *m*
vouch [vaʊtʃ] (VI) • **to ~ for sth** responder de algo, garantizar algo • **I cannot ~ for its authenticity** no puedo responder de *or* garantizar su autenticidad • **to ~ for sb** responder por *or* salir como fiador de algn
(VT) • **to ~ that ...** afirmar que ..., asegurar que ...
voucher ['vaʊtʃəʳ] (N) vale *m*; (*Comm*) bono *m* • **luncheon/travel ~** vale *m* de comida/viaje
vouchsafe [vaʊtʃ'seɪf] (VT) [+ *privilege, favour*] conceder; [+ *reply*] servirse hacer, dignarse hacer • **to ~ to** (+ *infin*) dignarse (+ *infin*)
vow [vaʊ] (N) (*Rel*) voto *m*; (= *promise*) promesa *f*, compromiso *m* • **lovers' vows** promesas *fpl* solemnes de los amantes • **to take** *or* **make a vow that ...** jurar *or* prometer que ... • **to take** *or* **make a vow to do sth** jurar hacer algo, comprometerse a hacer algo • **to break one's vow** faltar a un compromiso • **to take one's vows** (*Rel*) hacer sus votos (monásticos) • **to take a vow of poverty/chastity** hacer voto de pobreza/castidad
(VT) [+ *obedience, allegiance*] jurar, prometer • **to vow to do sth** jurar hacer algo, comprometerse a hacer algo • **to vow that ...** jurar *or* prometer que ...
vowel [vaʊəl] (N) vocal *f*
(CPD) ▸ **vowel shift** cambio *m* vocálico ▸ **vowel sound** sonido *m* vocálico ▸ **vowel system** sistema *m* vocálico
vox pop* ['vɒks'pɒp] (N) (*Brit*) voz *f* de la calle
voyage ['vɔɪɪdʒ] (N) viaje *m* (*por mar, por el espacio*); (= *crossing*) travesía *f* • **the ~ out** el viaje de ida • **the ~ home** el viaje de regreso *or* de vuelta
(VI) viajar (*por mar, por el espacio*) • **to ~ across unknown seas** viajar por mares desconocidos
voyager ['vɔɪədʒəʳ] (N) viajero/a *m/f* (*por mar*)
voyeur [vwɑ:'jɜ:ʳ] (N) voyeur *mf*, voyer *mf*, mirón/ona *m/f*
voyeurism [vwɑ:'jɜ:rɪzəm] (N) voyeurismo *m*, voyerismo *m*, mironismo *m*
voyeuristic [ˌvwɑ:jɜ:'rɪstɪk] (ADJ) voyeurista, de voyeur
V.P. (N ABBR) (= **Vice-President**) V.P. *mf*
VPL* (N ABBR) = **visible panty line**
VR (N ABBR) (= **virtual reality**) realidad *f* virtual

V

vroom [vru:m] (EXCL) ¡burrum!
vs (ABBR) (= **versus**) vs.
V-sign ['vi:saɪn] (N) V *f* de la victoria; (*obscene*) corte *m* de mangas • **to give sb the V-sign** hacer un corte de mangas a algn
VSO (N ABBR) (*Brit*) = **Voluntary Service Overseas**
VSOP (N ABBR) (*sherry*) = **very special** *or* **superior old pale**
VT, **Vt.** (ABBR) (*US*) = **Vermont**
VTOL ['vi:tɒl] (N ABBR) (= **vertical take-off and landing**) ADAC *m*
VTR (N ABBR) = **videotape recorder**
Vulcan ['vʌlkən] (N) Vulcano
vulcanite ['vʌlkənaɪt] (N) vulcanita *f*, ebonita *f*
vulcanization [,vʌlkənaɪ'zeɪʃən] (N) vulcanización *f*
vulcanize ['vʌlkənaɪz] (VT) vulcanizar
vulcanologist [,vʌlkən'ɒlədʒɪst] (N) vulcanólogo/a *m/f*
vulcanology [,vʌlkə'nɒlədʒɪ] (N) vulcanología *f*
vulgar ['vʌlgəʳ] (ADJ) **1** (= *unrefined, coarse*) [*person, taste*] ordinario, vulgar • **it is ~ to talk about money** hablar de dinero es una ordinariez *or* vulgaridad, hablar de dinero es de mala educación
2 (= *tasteless*) de mal gusto, vulgar
3 (= *indecent*) [*joke*] verde, colorado (*LAm*); [*song*] grosero; [*person, comedian*] grosero, ordinario
4 (*of the people*) vulgar • **Vulgar Latin** latín *m* vulgar • **in the ~ tongue** en la lengua vulgar *or* vernácula
5 (*Math*) • **~ fraction** fracción *f* común
vulgarian [vʌl'gɛərɪən] (N) (= *unrefined*) ordinario/a *m/f*; (= *wealthy*) ricacho/a *m/f*
vulgarism ['vʌlgərɪzəm] (N) vulgarismo *m*
vulgarity [vʌl'gærɪtɪ] (N) **1** (= *lack of refinement*) ordinariez *f*, vulgaridad *f*
2 (= *tastelessness*) mal gusto *m*, vulgaridad *f*
3 (= *indecency*) grosería *f*, obscenidad *f*; (= *crude remark*) grosería *f*
vulgarize ['vʌlgəraɪz] (VT) vulgarizar
vulgarly ['vʌlgəlɪ] (ADV) **1** (= *in an unrefined way*) de un modo ordinario, vulgarmente
2 (= *tastelessly*) con mal gusto
3 (= *indecently*) groseramente
4 (= *in ordinary parlance*) • **sodium chloride, ~ known as salt** cloruro de sodio, vulgarmente conocido como sal
Vulgate ['vʌlgɪt] (N) Vulgata *f*
vulnerability [,vʌlnərə'bɪlɪtɪ] (N) vulnerabilidad *f*
vulnerable ['vʌlnərəbl] (ADJ) vulnerable
vulpine ['vʌlpaɪn] (ADJ) (*lit, fig*) vulpino
vulture ['vʌltʃəʳ] (N) **1** (*Orn*) buitre *m*, zopilote *m* (*CAm, Mex*), aura *f* (*Carib*), carancho *m* (*S. Cone*), gallinazo *m* (*Col, And*), urubú *m* (*Peru, Uru*), zamuro *m* (*Ven*) • **black ~** buitre *m* negro
2 (*fig*) buitre *m* • **as the ~s from the press descended** cuando los buitres de la prensa se acercaron • **they're like a lot of ~s** son una panda de buitres; ▹ **culture**
vulva ['vʌlvə] (N) (PL: **vulvas** *or* **vulvae** ['vʌlvi:]) vulva *f*
vv. (ABBR) = **verses**
v.v. (ABBR) = **vice versa**
vying ['vaɪɪŋ] ▹ **vie**

Ww

W[1], w[1] ['dʌblju] N (= *letter*) W, w *f* • **W for William** W de Washington
W[2] ABBR (= **west**) O
w[2] ABBR (= **watt(s)**) w
W. ABBR = **Wales, Welsh**
WA ABBR (US) = **Washington**
WAAF [wæf] N ABBR = **Women's Auxiliary Air Force**
wacko* ['wækəʊ] ADJ colgado*, excéntrico
wacky* ['wækɪ] ADJ (COMPAR: **wackier**, SUPERL: **wackiest**) [*person*] chiflado*; [*idea*] disparatado • **~ baccy** (*Brit*) (*hum*‡) chocolate* *m*, costo‡ *m*
wad [wɒd] N (= *stuffing*) taco *m*, tapón *m*; (*in gun, cartridge*) taco *m*; [*of cotton wool*] bolita *f*; [*of papers*] fajo *m*, lío *m*; [*of banknotes*] fajo *m* • **wads of money** un dineral
VT (*stuff*) rellenar; (*Sew*) acolchar
wadding ['wɒdɪŋ] N (*for packing*) relleno *m*; (*for quilting*) entretela *f*, forro *m*; (*Med*) algodón *m* hidrófilo
waddle ['wɒdl] N andares *mpl* de pato • **to walk with a ~** andar como un pato
VI andar como un pato • **she ~d over to the window** fue andando como un pato a la ventana • **to ~ in/out** entrar/salir andando como un pato
wade [weɪd] VI **1** (*also* **wade along**) caminar (por el agua/la nieve/el barro *etc*) • **to ~ across a river** vadear un río • **to ~ ashore** llegar a tierra vadeando • **to ~ through the water/snow** caminar por el agua/la nieve • **to ~ through the mud** caminar por el barro • **to ~ through a book** leer(se) un libro con dificultad (*por lo aburrido/lo difícil que es*) • **it took me an hour to ~ through your essay** tardé una hora en leer tu ensayo
2 • **to ~ into sb** (*physically*) abalanzarse sobre algn; (*fig*) emprenderla con algn, arremeter contra algn • **to ~ into a meal** ponerse a comer
VT [+ *river*] vadear
▸ **wade in** VI + ADV (*lit*) entrar en el agua • **he ~d in and helped us** (*fig*) se puso a ayudarnos
wader ['weɪdəʳ] N **1** (= *bird*) ave *f* zancuda
2 waders (= *boots*) botas *fpl* altas de goma
wadge [wɒdʒ] N = **wodge**
wadi ['wɒdɪ] N (PL: **wadies**) *cauce de río en el norte de África*
wading ['weɪdɪŋ] CPD ▸ **wading bird** ave *f* zancuda ▸ **wading pool** (US) estanque *m* or piscina *f* para niños
wafer ['weɪfəʳ] N **1** (= *biscuit*) galleta *f*; (*Rel*) hostia *f*; (*eaten with ice cream*) barquillo *m*
2 (*Comput*) oblea *f*
3 (*for sealing*) oblea *f*
wafer-thin ['weɪfə'θɪn] ADJ **1** (*lit*) finísimo
2 (*fig*) [*majority*] muy estrecho
wafery ['weɪfərɪ] ADJ delgado, ligero
waffle ['wɒfl] N **1** (*Culin*) gofre *m*
2* (= *talk*) palabrería *f*; (*in essay*) paja *f*
VI * (*also* **waffle on**) enrollarse; (*in essay*) poner mucha paja • **he ~s on endlessly about the state of the economy** se enrolla como una persiana cuando habla sobre el estado de la economía*
CPD ▸ **waffle iron** molde *m* para hacer gofres
waffler* ['wɒfləʳ] N (*Brit*) charlatán/ana *m/f*, pico *m* de oro*
waffling ['wɒflɪŋ] N palabrería *f*
waft [wɑ:ft] N soplo *m*, ráfaga *f*
VT llevar por el aire
VI flotar, moverse
wag[1] [wæg] N [*of tail*] sacudida *f*, meneo *m*; [*of finger*] movimiento *m* • **the dog gave a wag of its tail** el perro sacudió *or* meneó la cola
VT [+ *tail*] sacudir, menear • **the dog wagged its tail** el perro sacudió *or* meneó la cola • **he wagged a finger at me, "naughty, naughty!" he said** me apuntó agitando el dedo —¡pillín, pillín! —dijo
VI [*tail*] sacudirse, menearse • IDIOM: • **tongues will wag** se dará que hablar • **tongues were wagging about their relationship** las malas lenguas hablaban de sus relaciones
wag[2]† [wæg] N (= *joker*) bromista *mf*
wage [weɪdʒ] N **1** (= *rate per week, year etc*) sueldo *m*, salario *m* • **a basic ~ of £55 a week** un sueldo *or* salario base de 55 libras semanales • **he gets a good ~** gana un buen sueldo • **those on high/low ~s** las personas que ganan sueldos *or* salarios altos/bajos • **minimum ~** salario mínimo; ▹ **living**
2 wages (= *money received*) paga *f*, sueldo *m* • **a day's ~s** la paga *or* el sueldo de un día; (*Agr*) un jornal • **I get my ~s on Fridays** me pagan los viernes • PROVERB: • **the ~s of sin is death** el pecado se paga con la muerte
VT [+ *war*] hacer; [+ *campaign*] llevar a cabo, hacer • **to ~ war against** *or* **on sb** hacer la guerra a algn • **to ~ war against** *or* **on inflation** luchar contra la inflación, hacer la guerra a la inflación
CPD ▸ **wage agreement** convenio *m* salarial ▸ **wage bill** gastos *mpl* de nómina, gastos *mpl* salariales ▸ **wage claim** (*Brit*) reivindicación *f* salarial ▸ **wage clerk** = **wages clerk** ▸ **wage contract** = **wage agreement** ▸ **wage costs** costes *mpl* del factor trabajo ▸ **wage demand** reivindicación *f* salarial ▸ **wage differential** diferencia *f* salarial ▸ **wage earner** asalariado/a *m/f* • **we are both ~ earners** los dos somos asalariados • **she is the family ~ earner** ella es la que mantiene a la familia ▸ **wage freeze** congelación *f* salarial ▸ **wage increase** aumento *m* salarial ▸ **wage levels** salarios *mpl*, niveles *mpl* salariales ▸ **wage negotiations** negociaciones *fpl* salariales ▸ **wage packet** (*esp Brit*) (= *envelope with pay*) sobre *m* de la paga; (*fig*) paga *f* ▸ **wage restraint** moderación *f* salarial ▸ **wage rise** aumento *m* salarial ▸ **wages bill** = **wage bill** ▸ **wage scale** escala *f* salarial ▸ **wages clerk** habilitado/a *m/f* ▸ **wage settlement** acuerdo *m* salarial ▸ **wage slave*** currante* *mf* ▸ **wage slip** nómina *f*, hoja *f* salarial ▸ **wages snatch** robo *m* de nóminas ▸ **wage talks** negociaciones *fpl* salariales ▸ **wage worker** (US) asalariado/a *m/f*
waged [weɪdʒd] ADJ [*person*] asalariado; [*employment*] remunerado
wager ['weɪdʒəʳ] N apuesta *f* (**on a**) • **to lay a ~ on sth** apostar por algo
VT [+ *sum of money*] apostar • **to ~ £20 on a horse** apostar 20 libras por un caballo • **I'll ~ that he already knew** apostaría a que ya lo sabía • **he won't do it, I ~!** ¡a que no lo hace!, ¡apuesto a que no lo hace!
waggish† ['wægɪʃ] ADJ bromista, zumbón
waggishly† ['wægɪʃlɪ] ADV • **he said ~** dijo zumbón
waggle ['wægl] N [*of finger*] movimiento *m*; [*of hips*] contoneo *m*, meneo *m*
VT [+ *finger*] agitar; [+ *hips*] contonear, menear; [+ *tail*] sacudir, menear • **he can ~ his ears** puede mover las orejas
waggon *etc* ['wægən] N (*esp Brit*) = **wagon**
Wagnerian [vɑ:g'nɪərɪən] ADJ wagneriano
wagon ['wægən] N **1** (*horse-drawn*) carro *m*; (= *truck*) camión *m*; (*Brit*) (*Rail*) vagón *m*; (US) (*also* **station wagon**) furgoneta *f*, camioneta *f*; (US) (= *police van*) furgón *m* policial • IDIOMS: • **to be on the ~*** no beber • **he decided to go on the ~** se resolvió a no beber • **to hitch one's ~ to a star** picar muy alto
2 (*also* **tea wagon**) carrito *m*
wagonload ['wægənləʊd] N carretada *f*, carga *f* de un carro • **50 ~s of coal** 50 vagones de carbón
wagtail ['wægteɪl] N lavandera *f*
waif [weɪf] N (= *child*) niño/a *m/f* abandonado/a, niño/a *m/f* desamparado/a; (= *animal*) animal *m* abandonado • **~s and strays** (= *children*) niños *mpl* abandonados *or* desamparados; (= *animals*) animales *mpl* abandonados
waif-like ['weɪflaɪk] ADJ [*girl, model*] esquelético
wail [weɪl] N **1** (= *moan*) lamento *m*, gemido *m*; [*of new-born*] vagido *m*; (= *complaint*) queja *f*, protesta *f* • **a great ~ went up** pusieron el grito en el cielo
2 [*of siren, wind*] gemido *m*
VI **1** (= *moan*) lamentarse, gemir; [*child*] llorar; (= *complain*) quejarse, protestar
2 [*siren, wind, bagpipes*] gemir
wailing ['weɪlɪŋ] N **1** (= *moaning*) lamentaciones *fpl*, gemidos *mpl*; [*of child*] llanto *m*; (= *complaints*) quejas *fpl*, protestas *fpl*
2 [*of siren, wind, bagpipes*] gemido *m*
CPD ▸ **the Wailing Wall** el Muro de las Lamentaciones
wain [weɪn] N (*liter*) carro *m* • **the Wain** (*Astron*) el Carro
wainscot ['weɪnskət], **wainscotting**

['weɪnskəʊtɪŋ] N revestimiento *m* (de la pared)

waist [weɪst] N [*of person*] cintura *f*, talle *m*; [*of dress, skirt*] talle *m*; (*Naut*) combés *m*; (*fig*) (= *narrow part*) cuello *m*
CPD ▸ **waist measurement**, **waist size** (talla *f* de) cintura *f*

waistband ['weɪstbænd] N pretina *f*, cinturilla *f*

waistcoat ['weɪskəʊt] N (*Brit*) chaleco *m*

waist-deep ['weɪst'di:p] ADJ hasta la cintura

-waisted ['weɪstɪd] ADJ (*ending in compounds*) • **slim-waisted** de cintura delgada, de talle delgado • **high-/low-waisted** de talle alto/bajo

waist-high ['weɪst'haɪ] ADJ hasta la cintura • **the water was waist-high** el agua cubría *or* llegaba hasta la cintura
ADV • **the ball bounced waist-high** la pelota dio un bote al nivel de la cintura

waistline ['weɪstlaɪn] N [*of person*] cintura *f*, talle *m*; [*of dress, skirt*] talle *m*

wait [weɪt] VI **1** (= *hold on*) **a** [*person*] esperar • **just ~ a moment while I fetch you a chair** espere un momento que voy a traerle una silla • **"repairs while you wait"** "reparaciones en el acto" • **reporters were ~ing to interview her** los reporteros estaban esperando para entrevistarla • **I can't ~ to see his face** estoy deseando ver su cara • **they can't ~ for us to go** están deseando que nos vayamos • **to ~ for sth/sb** esperar algo/a algn • **I'll ~ for you outside** te espero fuera • **what are you ~ing for?** (= *hurry up*) ¡a qué esperas!, ¡venga ya! • **the best things in life are worth ~ing for** en esta vida las cosas buenas merecen la espera • **to ~ for sb to do sth** esperar (a) que algn haga algo • **they ~ed for him to finish** esperaron (a) que terminara • **I'm ~ing for them to make a decision** estoy esperando (a) que tomen una decisión, estoy pendiente de que tomen una decisión • **I can hardly ~!** ¡me muero de impaciencia! • **to keep sb ~ing** hacer esperar a algn • **sorry to keep you ~ing** • **sorry to have kept you ~ing** siento haberle hecho esperar • **~ a minute!** ¡un momento!, ¡momentito! (*esp LAm*), ¡aguarde! (*LAm*) • **now ~ a minute, Dave, you never told me that** eh, un momento, Dave, tú nunca me dijiste eso • **~ and see!** ¡espera, ya verás! • **I ~ed till two o'clock** esperé hasta las dos • **~ till you're asked** espera a que te inviten • **just you ~ till your father finds out!** ¡ya verás cuando se entere tu padre! • IDIOM: • **to be ~ing in the wings** esperar entre bastidores
b [*thing*] • **the dishes can ~** los platos pueden esperar • **there's a parcel ~ing to be collected** hay un paquete que hay que recoger • **there is a big market just ~ing to be opened up** hay un mercado grande para abrir • **the ferry tragedy was a disaster ~ing to happen** la tragedia del ferry se veía venir
2 (*as servant*) • **to ~ at table** servir a *or* atender la mesa
VT **1** (= *await*) • **to ~ one's chance** esperar la oportunidad • **can't you ~ your turn like everyone else?** ¿no puedes esperar a que llegue tu turno como los demás?
2* (= *delay*) [+ *dinner, lunch etc*] • **don't ~ dinner for me** no me esperen para cenar
3 (= *serve*) • **to ~ table** (*US*) servir a la mesa, atender la mesa
N espera *f* • **it was a long ~ for the train** fue una larga espera hasta la llegada del tren • **patients face a 28-week ~ for operations** los pacientes tienen que esperar 28 semanas a que les operen • **to lie in ~ (for sb)** andar *or* estar al acecho (de algn) • **you may have quite a ~** puede que tengas que esperar bastante • **dinner was worth the ~** la cena mereció la espera
▸ **wait around, wait about** VI + ADV quedarse esperando • **to ~ around for sb** quedarse esperando a algn • **to ~ around for sth to happen** quedarse esperando a que pase algo
▸ **wait behind** VI + ADV esperarse • **to ~ behind for sb** quedarse para esperar a algn
▸ **wait in** (*esp Brit*) VI + ADV quedarse en casa (esperando) • **to ~ in for sb** quedarse en casa esperando a algn
▸ **wait on** VI + PREP [*waiter, servant*] servir, atender (*esp LAm*) • IDIOM: • **to ~ on sb hand and foot** atender el menor deseo de algn
▸ **wait out** VT + ADV **1** (= *wait till end of*) [+ *storm*] esperar a que pase • **we have enough capital to ~ it out until the economy improves** tenemos suficiente capital para aguantar hasta que mejore la economía
2 (*US*) **a** (= *wait longer than*) • **we can ~ you out indefinitely, why don't you surrender?** podemos esperar indefinidamente *or* tenemos todo el tiempo del mundo, ¿por qué no te rindes?
b (= *wait for*) • **we have to ~ out the results of the vote** tenemos que esperar a que se conozcan los resultados de la votación
▸ **wait up** VI + ADV **1** (= *stay up*) • **to ~ up for sb** quedarse despierto esperando a algn • **don't ~ up for me** no te quedes despierto esperándome
2 (*US**) (= *wait*) esperar
▸ **wait upon** VI + PREP • **to ~ upon sb 1** (*frm*) [*ambassador, envoy*] presentar sus respetos a algn, cumplimentar a algn
2 = **wait on**

waiter ['weɪtə^r] N camarero *m*, mesero *m* (*Mex*), garzón *m* (*S. Cone*), mesonero *m* (*Ven*)

waiting ['weɪtɪŋ] N **1** espera *f* • **the ~ seemed endless** la espera parecía interminable • **he decided that the ~ had gone on long enough** decidió que ya se había esperado bastante • **"no waiting"** "prohibido aparcar", "prohibido estacionarse (*esp LAm*)" • **a prime minister/government in ~** un primer ministro/gobierno en potencia
2 (*frm*) (= *service*) servicio *m* • **to be in ~ on sb** estar de servicio con algn
CPD ▸ **waiting game** • **to play a ~ game** esperar la ocasión apropiada ▸ **waiting list** lista *f* de espera ▸ **waiting room** sala *f* de espera

waitlist ['weɪtlɪst] (*US*) N lista *f* de espera
VT • **to be ~ed** ser colocado en una lista de espera

waitress ['weɪtrɪs] N camarera *f*, mesera *f* (*Mex*), mesonera *f* (*Ven*)

waitressing ['weɪtrɪsɪŋ] N • **to do ~** trabajar de camarera • **to get a job ~** obtener un trabajo de camarera

waive [weɪv] VT **1** (= *not claim*) [+ *right, claim, fee*] renunciar a
2 (= *exonerate from*) [+ *payment of loan, interest*] exonerar de
3 (= *suspend*) [+ *regulation*] no aplicar; [+ *condition, restriction*] no exigir

waiver ['weɪvə^r] N **1** (= *renouncement*) [*of right, claim, fee*] renuncia *f*
2 (= *exoneration*) (*from payment*) exoneración *f*
3 (= *suspension*) [*of regulation, condition, restriction*] exención *f*
4 (= *disclaimer*) [*of responsibility*] descargo *m*

wake¹ [weɪk] N **1** (*Naut*) estela *f*
2 (*fig*) • **the tornado brought/left a trail of destruction in its ~** el tornado dejó una estela de destrucción a su paso • **in the ~ of the storm/riots** tras la tormenta/los disturbios • **to come** *or* **follow in the ~ of sth** producirse a raíz de algo

wake² [weɪk] N (*over corpse*) velatorio *m*, vela *f*, velorio *m* (*esp LAm*)

wake³ [weɪk] (VB: PT: **woke, waked**, PP: **woken, waked**) VI (*also* **wake up**) despertar, despertarse • **to ~ from a dream/deep sleep/coma** despertar(se) de un sueño/sueño profundo/coma • **on waking** al despertar
VT (*also* **wake up**) despertar • **they were making enough noise to ~ the dead** hacían un ruido que despertaría a los muertos
▸ **wake up** VI + ADV **1** (*lit*) despertar, despertarse • **~ up!** ¡despierta!, ¡despiértate! • **to ~ up from a nightmare** despertar(se) de una pesadilla • **to ~ up with a hangover/a headache** despertar(se) con resaca/dolor de cabeza • **he woke up (to find himself) in prison** amaneció en la cárcel • **she woke up to find them gone** cuando (se) despertó se encontró con que se habían ido • IDIOM: • **~ up and smell the coffee!** (*esp US*) ¡abre los ojos!, ¡pon los pies en la tierra!
2 (*fig*) despertar(se), despabilar(se) • **companies had better ~ up** a las empresas les convendría despertar(se) • **~ up, Ian! we've already discussed point 12** ¡despierta *or* despabila Ian! ya hemos discutido el punto 12, ¡despiértate *or* despabílate Ian! ya hemos discutido el punto • **to ~ up to the truth** darse cuenta de la verdad • **to ~ up to reality** darse cuenta de la realidad, despertar a la realidad
VT + ADV **1** (*lit*) despertar • **I was woken up by the phone** el teléfono me despertó, me desperté con el teléfono • **you need a coffee to ~ you up** te hace falta una taza de café para despertarte
2 (*fig*) despertar • **to ~ one's ideas up*** despabilarse • **to ~ sb up to sth** hacer ver algo a algn, hacer que algn se dé cuenta de algo • **someone needs to ~ him up to the risks involved** alguien tiene que hacerle ver los riesgos que implica

wakeful ['weɪkfʊl] ADJ **1** (= *unable to sleep*) [*person*] desvelado
2 (= *sleepless*) • **to have a ~ night** pasar la noche en vela
3 (*frm*) (= *vigilant*) alerta, vigilante (**to** a)

wakefulness ['weɪkfʊlnɪs] N
1 (= *sleeplessness*) insomnia *f*, desvelo *m*
2 (*frm*) (= *watchfulness*) vigilancia *f*

waken ['weɪkən] (*liter*) VT despertar
VI despertar, despertarse

wake-up call ['weɪkʌp,kɔ:l] N **1** (*lit*) • **ask the hotel staff for an early wake-up call** pídele al personal del hotel que te despierten temprano
2 (*fig*) aviso *m*

wakey-wakey* ['weɪkɪ'weɪkɪ] EXCL ¡despierta! • **wakey-wakey, rise and shine!** ¡levanta levanta, que los pajarillos cantan!

waking ['weɪkɪŋ] ADJ • **I spent my early childhood in a kind of ~ dream** pasé los primeros años de mi infancia como soñando despierto • **one's ~ hours** las horas en que se está despierto • **he spent every ~ moment in the kitchen** pasaba cada minuto del día en la cocina • **this experience has been a ~ nightmare** esta experiencia ha sido como vivir una pesadilla

Waldorf salad [,wɔ:ldɔ:f'sæləd] N ensalada *f* Waldorf (*ensalada de manzanas, nueces y apio con mayonesa*)

Wales [weɪlz] N (el país de) Gales *m*

walk [wɔ:k] N **1** (= *stroll, ramble*) paseo *m*; (= *hike*) caminata *f*, excursión *f* a pie; (= *race*) marcha *f* atlética • **there's a nice ~ by the**

W

river hay un paseo agradable por el río • **this is my favourite ~** este es mi paseo favorito • **it's only a ten-minute ~ from here** está a solo diez minutos de aquí a pie • **from there it's a short ~ to his house** desde allí a su casa se va a pie en muy poco tiempo • **to go for** *or* **take a ~** ir de paseo • **we went for a ~ around** fuimos a dar una vuelta • **take a ~!*** ¡lárgate*! • **to take sb for a ~** llevar a algn de paseo • IDIOM: • **it was a ~ in the park** (*esp US*) fue coser y cantar, fue pan comido
2 (= *avenue*) paseo *m*
3 (= *pace*) paso *m* • **he went at a quick ~** caminó a (un) paso rápido • **the cavalry advanced at a ~** la caballería avanzaba al paso
4 (= *gait*) paso *m*, andar *m* • **he has an odd sort of ~** tiene un modo de andar algo raro • **to know sb by his ~** conocer a algn por su modo de andar
5 • **~ of life: I meet people from all ~s of life** me encuentro con gente de todas las profesiones y condiciones sociales
VT 1 [+ *distance*] andar, caminar (*esp LAm*) • **we ~ed 40 kilometres yesterday** ayer anduvimos 40 kilómetros • **to ~ the streets** andar por las calles; (*aimlessly*) vagar por las calles; (= *be homeless*) no tener hogar, estar sin techo; [*prostitute*] hacer la calle *or* la carrera • **to ~ the wards** (*Med*) hacer prácticas de clínica • **you can ~ it in five minutes** está a cinco minutos andando *or* a pie de aquí • **I had to ~ it** tuve que ir a pie *or* ir andando • **don't worry, you'll ~ it*** (*fig*) no te preocupes, será facilísimo
2 (= *lead*) [+ *dog*] pasear, sacar a pasear; [+ *horse*] llevar al paso • **she ~s the dog every day** pasea *or* saca a pasear al perro todos los días • **I'll ~ you to the station** te acompaño a la estación • IDIOM: • **to ~ sb into the ground** *or* **off his feet** dejar a algn rendido de tanto caminar
VI 1 andar, caminar (*esp LAm*); (*as opposed to riding etc*) ir a pie, ir andando, ir caminando (*esp LAm*); (*Sport*) marchar • **can your little boy ~ yet?** ¿ya anda tu niño? • **to ~ slowly** andar despacio • **don't ~ so fast!** ¡no andes tan deprisa! • **you can ~ there in five minutes** está a cinco minutos andando de aquí • **are you ~ing or going by bus?** ¿vas a ir a pie o en autobús? • **"walk"** (*US*) (*on traffic signal*) "cruzar" • **"don't walk"** (*US*) (*on traffic signal*) "no cruzar" • **~ a little with me** acompáñame un rato • **to ~ in one's sleep** ser sonámbulo, andar dormido • **to ~ downstairs/upstairs** bajar/subir la escalera • **we had to ~** tuvimos que ir a pie *or* andando • **to ~ home** ir andando a casa, volver andando a casa • **we were out ~ing in the hills/in the park** estábamos paseando por la montaña/el parque • **to ~ across sth** cruzar algo • **to ~ slowly up/down the stairs** subir/bajar lentamente la escalera • **to ~ up and down** pasearse (de acá para allá) • IDIOM: • **to ~ tall** andar con la cabeza alta
2 [*ghost*] andar, aparecer
3* (= *disappear*) volar* • **my camera's ~ed** mi cámara ha volado *or* desaparecido
4* (= *be acquitted*) salir sin cargos

▸ **walk about, walk around** VI + ADV pasearse (de acá para allá)
▸ **walk away** VI + ADV irse, marcharse • **he just got up and ~ed away** simplemente se levantó y se fue *or* se marchó • **she watched him ~ away** lo vio alejarse • **to ~ away unhurt** salir ileso • **to ~ away from a problem** huir de un problema • **you can't just ~ away from it!** ¡no puedes desentenderte! • **to ~ away with** [+ *prize*] llevarse; (= *steal*) robar
▸ **walk back** VI + ADV volver a pie, regresar andando
▸ **walk in** VI + ADV entrar • **who should ~ in but Joe** ¿a que no te imaginas quién entró? ¡Joe! • **to ~ in on sb** interrumpir a algn
▸ **walk into** VI + PREP 1 (= *enter*) [+ *room*] entrar en
2 (= *fall into*) [+ *trap*] caer en • **you really ~ed into that one!*** ¡te has dejado embaucar por las buenas!
3 (= *collide with*) chocar con, dar con, dar contra
4* (= *meet*) topar, tropezar con
5* • **to ~ into a job** conseguir fácilmente un puesto
▸ **walk off** VI + ADV irse, marcharse • **he ~ed off angrily** se fue enfadado
VT + ADV • **we ~ed off our lunch** dimos un paseo para bajar la comida
▸ **walk off with** VI + PREP (= *take, win*) • **to ~ off with sth** llevarse algo
▸ **walk on** VI + ADV (= *go on walking*) seguir andando *or* (*esp LAm*) caminando; (*Theat*) (= *come on stage*) salir a escena; (= *have a walk-on part*) hacer de figurante *or* comparsa
▸ **walk out** VI + ADV (= *go out*) salir; (*from meeting*) salir, retirarse (**of** de); (*on strike*) abandonar el trabajo • **you can't ~ out now!** ¡no puedes marcharte ahora!
▸ **walk out on** VI + PREP [+ *spouse, family*] abandonar, dejar; [+ *business partner*] dejar; (= *leave in the lurch*) dejar plantado a* • **she ~ed out on her husband** abandonó *or* dejó a su marido
▸ **walk out with**† VI + PREP • **to ~ out with sb** (*Brit*) (= *court*) salir con algn
▸ **walk over** VI + PREP (= *defeat*) derrotar • **to ~ all over sb** (= *dominate*) tratar a algn a patadas*, atropellar a algn • **they ~ed all over us in the second half** nos dieron una paliza en el segundo tiempo
▸ **walk up** VI + ADV (= *ascend*) subir (a pie); (= *approach*) acercarse (**to a**) • **~ up, ~ up!** ¡vengan!, ¡acérquense! • **to ~ up to sb** acercarse a algn

walkable ['wɔːkəbl] ADJ 1 [*distance, route*] (= *able to be walked*) que se puede hacer a pie • **to be ~** poderse hacer a pie
2 [*city, neighbourhood, town*] (= *suitable for walking*) apropiado para pasear; (= *good for walking*) bueno para pasear

walkabout ['wɔːkəbaʊt] N (*Brit*) (= *walk*) paseo *m*; (*Australia*) *excursión de un aborigen al bosque interior australiano* • **to go on a ~** [*monarch, politician*] pasearse entre el público • **to go ~** (*Australia*) irse de excursión al bosque; (= *disappear**) desaparecer

walkaway* ['wɔːkəweɪ] N (*US*) victoria *f* fácil, paseo *m*, pan *m* comido*

walker ['wɔːkəʳ] N 1 (= *person*) (*gen*) paseante *mf*, transeúnte *mf*; (= *pedestrian*) peatón *m*; (*Sport*) marchador(a) *m/f*; (= *hiker*) excursionista *mf* • **to be a great ~** ser gran andarín, ser aficionado a las excursiones a pie
2 (*also* **baby walker**) andador *m*, tacatá *m* (*Sp**)

walker-on ['wɔːkər'ɒn] N (*Theat*) figurante/a *m/f*, comparsa *mf*; (*Cine*) extra *mf*

walkies* ['wɔːkɪz] NSING paseo *m* • **to go ~** dar un paseo • **to take the dog ~** llevar al perro de paseo

walkie-talkie ['wɔːkɪ'tɔːkɪ] N transmisor-receptor *m* portátil, walkie-talkie *m*

walk-in ['wɔːkɪn] CPD ▸ **walk-in closet** (*US*) alacena *f* ropera ▸ **walk-in customer** • **a lot of our business is from walk-in customers** hacemos mucho negocio con los clientes que entran de la calle ▸ **walk-in clinic** *clínica donde no hay que pedir hora para ver al médico* ▸ **walk-in condition** • **in walk-in condition** en condiciones de habitabilidad, habitable ▸ **walk-in pantry** despensa *f* ▸ **walk-in wardrobe** (*US*) alacena *f* ropera

walking ['wɔːkɪŋ] N (= *act*) andar *m*, caminar *m*; (*as pastime*) excursionismo *m*; (= *hill walking*) senderismo *m*; (*Sport*) marcha *f* (atlética) • **~ is very good for you** andar *or* caminar es muy sano • **she found ~ painful** le resultaba doloroso andar • **I did some ~ in the Alps last summer** el verano pasado hice senderismo por los Alpes
ADJ ambulante • **he's a ~ encyclopaedia** es una enciclopedia ambulante • **the ~ wounded** los heridos que pueden/podían ir a pie *or* andar
CPD ▸ **walking boots** botas *fpl* de trekking ▸ **walking distance** • **it's within ~ distance** se puede ir andando ▸ **walking frame** andador *m* ▸ **walking holiday** • **they went on a ~ holiday to Wales** fueron a Gales de vacaciones para caminar • **a hotel which offers ~ holidays** un hotel que ofrece vacaciones con excursiones a pie ▸ **walking pace** • **at a ~ pace** a paso de peatón, a paso normal • **to slow to a ~ pace** aminorar la marcha a paso normal ▸ **walking papers*** (*US*) pasaporte* *m*, aviso *m* de despido ▸ **walking race** carrera *f* pedestre ▸ **walking shoes** zapatos *mpl* para andar *or* (*esp LAm*) caminar ▸ **walking stick** bastón *m* ▸ **walking tour** viaje *m* a pie, excursión *f* a pie

walking-on [ˌwɔːkɪŋ'ɒn] ADJ = **walk-on**

Walkman® ['wɔːkmən] N (PL: **Walkmans** ['wɔːkmənz]) Walkman® *m*

walk-on ['wɔːkɒn] ADJ • **walk-on part** (*Theat*) papel *m* de figurante *or* de comparsa; (*Cine*) papel *m* de extra

walkout ['wɔːkaʊt] N (*from conference*) retirada *f*, abandono *m* (de la sala); (= *strike*) abandono *m* del trabajo

walkover ['wɔːkˌəʊvəʳ] N 1 (*Horse racing*) walkover *m*
2 (*fig*) victoria *f* fácil, paseo *m*, pan *m* comido*

walk-through ['wɔːkθruː] N ensayo *m*

walk-up ['wɔːkʌp] N (*US*) (= *building*) edificio *m* sin ascensor; (= *flat*) piso *m* *or* (*LAm*) departamento *m* en un edificio sin ascensor

walkway ['wɔːkweɪ] N (*raised*) pasarela *f*; (= *passageway*) pasaje *m* (entre edificios)

wall [wɔːl] N 1 (*interior*) (*also Anat*) pared *f*; (*outside*) muro *m*; [*of city*] muralla *f*; (= *garden wall*) tapia *f* • **the Great Wall of China** la Gran Muralla China • **the north ~ of the Eiger** la pared norte del Eiger • IDIOMS: • **to come up against a brick ~** tener por delante una barrera infranqueable • **talking to him is like talking to a brick ~** hablar con él es como hablar a la pared • **to do sth off the ~** (*esp US**) hacer algo espontáneamente *or* de improviso • **to climb** *or* **crawl up the ~s*** (*from boredom, frustration*) subirse por las paredes* • **it drives me up the ~*** me saca de quicio • **to go up the ~*** (= *get angry*) ponerse furioso • **to go to the ~** [*firm*] ir a la bancarrota, quebrar • PROVERB: • **~s have ears** las paredes oyen
2 (*Sport*) [*of players*] barrera *f*
3 (*fig*) barrera *f* • IDIOM: • **to break the ~ of silence** romper el muro *or* la barrera del silencio
CPD [*cupboard, light, clock*] de pared; [*map, painting*] mural ▸ **wall bars** (*Sport*) espalderas *fpl* ▸ **wall chart** gráfico *m* mural ▸ **wall hanging** tapiz *m* ▸ **wall socket** enchufe *m* de pared
▸ **wall in** VT + ADV [+ *area of land*] cerrar con muro; [+ *garden*] tapiar, cercar con tapia

▸ **wall off** VT + ADV separar con un muro
▸ **wall up** VT + ADV [+ *person*] emparedar; [+ *opening, entrance*] tapiar, cerrar con muro, tabicar; [+ *window*] condenar

wallaby ['wɒləbɪ] N (PL: **wallabies** *or* **wallaby**) ualabi *m*

wallah* ['wɒlə] N hombre *m*; (*pej*) tío* *m*, sujeto* *m* • **the ice-cream ~** el hombre de los helados • **the ~ with the beard** él de la barba

wallboard ['wɔ:lbɔ:d] N fibra *f* prensada (para paredes)

wall-covering ['wɔ:l,kʌvərɪŋ] N material *m* de decoración de paredes

walled [wɔ:ld] ADJ [*city*] amurallado; [*garden*] tapiado

-walled ['wɔ:ld] SUFFIX • **a glass-walled elevator** un ascensor de cristal • **a white-walled room** una habitación con paredes blancas

wallet ['wɒlɪt] N cartera *f*, billetera *f* (*esp LAm*)

wall-eyed ['wɔ:l'aɪd] ADJ (= *with white iris*) de ojos incoloros; (= *with squint*) estrábico

wallflower ['wɔ:l,flaʊəʳ] N alhelí *m* • IDIOM: • **to be a ~** comer pavo, ser la fea del baile

wall-mounted ['wɔ:l,maʊntɪd] ADJ fijado a la pared

Walloon [wɒ'lu:n] ADJ valón
N **1** (= *person*) valón/ona *m/f*
2 (*Ling*) valón *m*

wallop* ['wɒləp] N **1** (= *blow*) golpe *m* fuerte, golpazo* *m* • **wallop!** (= *sound*) ¡zas! • **to give sb a ~** pegar fuerte a algn • **it packs a ~*** es muy fuerte, tiene mucho efecto
2 (*Brit*‡) (= *beer*) cerveza *f*
VT (= *strike*) golpear fuertemente; (= *punish*) dar una paliza a, zurrar*

walloping* ['wɒləpɪŋ] N • **to give sb a ~** dar una paliza a algn, zurrar a algn*
ADJ enorme, colosal
ADV • **a ~ great portion of ice-cream** una porción enorme de helado

wallow ['wɒləʊ] N • **I had a good ~ in the bath** descansé bañándome largamente
VI (*in water, mud*) revolcarse (**in** en); [*boat*] bambolearse • **to ~ in guilt** regodearse *or* deleitarse en el remordimiento • **to ~ in luxury/money** nadar en la opulencia/abundancia

wallpaper ['wɔ:l,peɪpəʳ] N **1** (*for walls*) papel *m* pintado
2 (*Comput*) fondo *m* de escritorio
VT empapelar
CPD ▸ **wallpaper paste** cola *f* de empapelar

Wall Street ['wɔ:lstri:t] N (*US*) *calle de la Bolsa y de muchos bancos en Nueva York*; (*fig*) mundo *m* bursátil • **shares rose sharply on ~** las acciones subieron bruscamente en la Bolsa de Nueva York

wall-to-wall ['wɔ:ltə'wɔ:l] ADJ
1 • **wall-to-wall carpeting** moqueta *f*, alfombra *f* de pared a pared
2 (*fig*) [*football, music etc*] a todas horas • **there were wall-to-wall people** había gente a rebosar, estaba abarrotado de gente
ADV • **the room was filled wall-to-wall with people** la sala estaba atestada *or* repleta de gente

wally* ['wɒlɪ] (*Brit*) N gili* *mf*

walnut ['wɔ:lnʌt] N (= *nut*) nuez *f*; (= *tree, wood*) nogal *m*
ADJ (= *wooden*) de nogal
CPD ▸ **walnut oil** aceite *m* de nuez
▸ **walnut tree** nogal *m*

walrus ['wɔ:lrəs] N (PL: **walruses** *or* **walrus**) morsa *f*
CPD ▸ **walrus moustache** bigotes *mpl* de foca

Walter ['wɔ:ltəʳ] N Gualterio

waltz [wɔ:lts] N vals *m*
VI bailar el vals • **to ~ in/out*** entrar/salir tan fresco*
▸ **waltz off with*** VI + PREP **1** (*also* **waltz away with**) [+ *title, championship, prize*] hacerse fácilmente con
2 [+ *object, person*] largarse con* • **she ~ed off with my boyfriend** se largó con mi novio*
▸ **waltz through*** VT + PREP [+ *match, game*] ganar sin mover un dedo

waltzer ['wɔ:ltsəʳ] N bailarín/ina *m/f* de vals

WAN [wæn] N ABBR (*Comput*) = **wide area network**

wan [wɒn] ADJ [*complexion, face*] pálido; [*light*] tenue, pálido; [*smile*] lánguido • **she was feeling rather wan** se sentía un poco indispuesto

wand [wɒnd] N (= *magic wand*) varita *f* mágica; [*of office*] bastón *m* de mando;
▹ wave

wander ['wɒndəʳ] N paseo *m* • **to go for** *or* **have a ~** pasearse, dar un paseo, dar una vuelta
VI **1** (*for pleasure*) pasear; (*aimlessly*) deambular, vagar, errar • **we spent the morning ~ing round the old town** pasamos la mañana paseando por el casco antiguo • **they ~ed aimlessly through the streets** iban deambulando *or* vagando por las calles • **to ~ round the shops** curiosear *or* pasearse por las tiendas
2 (= *stray*) • **to ~ from the path** desviarse *or* alejarse del camino • **the sheep had ~ed into the next field** las ovejas se habían metido en el prado de al lado
3 (*fig*) [*person*] (*in speech*) divagar • **to ~ from** *or* **off the point** salirse del tema • **to let one's mind ~** dejar vagar la imaginación • **his eyes ~ed round the room** paseó la mirada por la habitación • **his attention ~ed for a moment and the milk boiled over** se distrajo *or* despistó un momento y se le salió la leche • **my attention ~ed a bit in the second half of the film** perdí un poco la concentración *or* me distraje *or* me despisté en la segunda mitad de la película
VT [+ *streets, hills*] recorrer, vagar por • **to ~ the world** recorrer el mundo entero • **he had ~ed the seven seas in search of it** (*liter*) había surcado los siete mares en su busca (*liter*)
▸ **wander about, wander around** VI + ADV deambular
▸ **wander off** VI + ADV • **the children ~ed off into the woods** los niños se alejaron sin rumbo y entraron en el bosque • **don't go ~ing off** no te alejes demasiado
VI + PREP ▸ **wander**

wanderer ['wɒndərəʳ] N (= *traveller*) viajero/a *m/f*; (*pej*) vagabundo/a *m/f*; (= *tribesman, nomad*) nómada *mf* • **the ~ returns!** (*hum*) ¡ha vuelto el viajero! • **I've always been a ~** nunca he querido establecerme de fijo en un sitio

wandering ['wɒndərɪŋ] ADJ [*person*] errante; [*tribe*] nómada, errante; [*minstrel*] itinerante; [*path, river*] sinuoso; [*eyes, mind*] distraído • **he suffers from ~ hands** (*hum*) es un sobón*

wanderings ['wɒndərɪŋz] NPL (= *travels*) viajes *mpl*, andanzas *fpl*; [*of mind, speech*] divagaciones *fpl* • **let me know if you see one on your ~** avísame si encuentras uno por ahí

wanderlust ['wɒndəlʌst] N pasión *f* de viajar, ansia *f* de ver mundo

wane [weɪn] VI [*moon*] menguar; (*fig*) [*strength*] decaer; [*popularity, power, enthusiasm, interest, support*] disminuir
N • **to be on the ~** [*moon*] estar menguando; [*strength*] estar decayendo; [*popularity, support, power, interest*] estar disminuyendo

wangle* ['wæŋgl] VT [+ *job, ticket*] agenciarse • **I've ~d an invitation to the reception** me he agenciado una invitación para la recepción • **he ~d his way in** se las arregló para entrar • **can you ~ me a free ticket?** ¿puedes conseguirme una entrada gratis?
N chanchullo* *m*, truco *m*

wangler* ['wæŋgləʳ] N chanchullero* *m*, trapisondista* *mf*

wangling* ['wæŋglɪŋ] N chanchullos* *mpl*, trucos *mpl*

waning ['weɪnɪŋ] ADJ [*moon*] menguante; (*fig*) [*popularity, power, enthusiasm, interest, support*] decreciente
N [*of moon*] menguante *f*; (*fig*) [*of popularity, power*] disminución *f*, mengua *f*; [*of enthusiasm, interest, support*] disminución *f*

wank** [wæŋk] (*Brit*) N **1** • **to have a ~** hacerse una paja**
2 (= *person*) = **wanker**
VI hacerse una paja**

wanker** ['wæŋkəʳ] N (*Brit*) gilipollas** *mf*

wankered** ['wæŋkəd] ADJ (*Brit*) (= *drunk*) pedo‡

wanky** ['wæŋkɪ] ADJ (*Brit*) de puta pena**, mierdoso‡, cutre*

wanly ['wɒnlɪ] ADV [*shine*] tenuemente, pálidamente; [*look, smile, say*] lánguidamente

wanna* ['wɒnə] = **want to**

wannabe* ['wɒnəbi:] N • **an Elvis ~** un imitador barato de Elvis
ADJ amateur, aspirante

wanness ['wɒnnɪs] N palidez *f*

want [wɒnt] VT **1** (= *desire, wish for*) **a** querer • **I don't ~ anything more to do with him** no quiero tener nada más que ver con él • **I ~ my mummy!** ¡quiero que venga mi mamá! • **he ~s a lot of attention** quiere que le presten mucha atención • **I don't ~ you interfering!** ¡no quiero que te entrometas! • **I've always ~ed a car like this** siempre he querido un coche como este • **we only ~ the best/what's best for you** solo queremos lo mejor para ti • **what do you ~ for your birthday?** ¿qué quieres por tu cumpleaños? • **what I ~ from a computer is ...** lo que quiero de un ordenador es ... • **I ~ an explanation from you** quiero que me des una explicación • **she was everything he ~ed in a woman** era todo lo que él quería en una mujer • **food was the last thing I ~ed** comida era lo último que quería • **I know when I'm not ~ed** sé muy bien cuando sobro *or* estoy de más • **where do you ~ the table?** ¿dónde quieres que pongamos la mesa? • **what does he ~ with/of me?** ¿qué quiere de mí? • IDIOM: • **you've got him where you ~ him** lo tienes donde tú quieres
b (*with complement*) • **I ~ my son alive** quiero a mi hijo vivo • **you ~ her back, don't you?** quieres que vuelva, ¿no? • **I ~ him dead!** ¡lo quiero muerto! • **I ~ her sacked!** ¡quiero que se la despida!, ¡quiero que la despidan!
c (*with infinitive*) • **to ~ to do sth** querer hacer algo • **I was ~ing to leave anyway** de todas formas yo ya quería marcharme • **if you really ~ to know** si de verdad lo quieres saber • **I don't ~ to** no quiero • **to ~ sb to do sth** querer que algn haga algo • **the last thing we ~ is for them to feel obliged to help** lo último que queremos es que se sientan obligados a ayudar • **without ~ing to sound big-headed, I think I'll succeed** no quiero parecer engreído pero pienso que voy a tener éxito • **I wouldn't ~ to hurt their feelings/cause them any problems** no

W

quisiera herir sus sentimientos/causarles ningún problema
d (*sexually*) • **to ~ sb** desear a algn
2 (= *ask for*) [+ *money*] querer, pedir • **she ~s £500 for the car** quiere *or* pide 500 libras por el coche • **how much do you ~ for it?** ¿cuánto quiere *or* pide? • **you don't ~ much!** (*iro*) ¡anda que no pides nada! (*iro*)
3 (= *seek*) [*police*] buscar • **"wanted (dead or alive)"** "se busca (vivo o muerto)" • **"wanted: general maid"** "se necesita asistenta" • **he is ~ed for robbery** se le busca por robo • **you're ~ed in the kitchen** te buscan en la cocina • **the boss ~s you in his office** el jefe quiere verte en su oficina • **you're ~ed on the phone** te llaman al teléfono
4 (= *need, require*) [*person*] necesitar • **children ~ lots of sleep** los niños necesitan *or* requieren muchas horas de sueño • **this car ~s cleaning** a este coche le hace falta una limpieza, a este coche hay que limpiarlo • **he ~s locking up!** está loco de atar* • **that's the last thing I ~!*** ¡solo me faltaba eso!* • **you ~ to be more careful when you're driving** tienes que tener más cuidado al conducir • **you ~ to see his new boat!** ¡tienes que ver su nuevo barco! • **what you ~ is a good hiding** lo que necesitas *or* te hace falta es una buena paliza* • **what do you ~ with a house that size?** ¿para qué quieres una casa tan grande?
5 (= *lack*) • **the contract ~s only her signature** al contrato solo le falta su firma • **it only ~ed the parents to come in** solo faltaba que llegaran los padres
(VI) **1** (= *wish, desire*) querer • **you're welcome to stay if you ~** te puedes quedar si quieres • **I ~ for you to be happy** (*US*) quiero que seas feliz
2 (= *lack*) • **they will not ~ for money or food** no les faltará ni dinero ni comida • **they ~ for nothing** no les falta de nada; ▹ **waste**
(N) **1** (= *lack*) falta *f* • **it showed a ~ of good manners** demostró una falta de educación • **for ~ of sth** (*at beginning of clause*) a falta de algo; (*at end of clause*) por falta de algo • **for ~ of anything better to do, I decided to go home** a falta de algo mejor que hacer, decidí irme a casa • **I decided to go home for ~ of anything better to do** decidí irme a casa por falta de algo mejor que hacer • **for ~ of a better word** a/por falta de una palabra más apropiada • **he never did become a minister, but it was not for ~ of trying** nunca llegó a ministro, pero no fue por falta de intentarlo
2 (= *need*) necesidad *f* • **she had servants to attend to her every ~** tenía sirvientes que atendían todas y cada una de sus necesidades • **my ~s are few** necesito poco • **to be in ~ of sth** necesitar algo
3 (= *poverty*) necesidad *f*, penuria *f* • **to be in ~** estar necesitado • **to live in ~** pasar necesidades, vivir en la penuria
(CPD) ▸ **want ad*** (*US*) anuncio *m* clasificado
▸ **want in*** (VI + ADV) **1** (*to house, building, room*) querer entrar (**to** en)
2 (*on scheme, project*) querer meterse* • **we're playing cards tonight, do you ~ in?** esta noche jugamos a las cartas, ¿te quieres apuntar? • **it's a huge market and every company ~s in** es un mercado enorme y todas las empresas quieren meterse* • **to ~ in on sth** querer participar en algo
▸ **want out*** (VI + ADV) **1** (*of house, room*) querer salir
2 • **he ~s out** (*of scheme, project, job*) quiere dejarlo • **to ~ out of** [+ *scheme, project, job*] querer dejar; [+ *relationship*] querer dejar, querer terminar con
wanting [ˈwɒntɪŋ] (ADJ) • **all the applicants proved ~ in some respect** todos los aspirantes resultaron deficientes en algún aspecto • **he was tried and found ~** fue puesto a prueba y le encontraron carencias *or* deficiencias • **he looked at his life and found it ~** examinó su vida y se dio cuenta de que faltaba algo • **to be ~ in sth** carecer de algo
wanton [ˈwɒntən] (ADJ) **1** (= *wilful, gratuitous*) [*neglect*] displicente; [*destruction*] sin sentido, gratuito; [*violence*] gratuito
2† (*pej*) (= *dissolute*) [*woman*] lascivo, libertino; [*behaviour*] disipado, inmoral
3 (= *unrestrained*) [*spending*] desenfrenado
wantonly [ˈwɒntənlɪ] (ADV) **1** (= *wilfully, gratuitously*) [*neglect*] con displicencia; [*destroy*] gratuitamente, sin sentido; [*cruel*] gratuitamente
2 (= *dissolutely*) lascivamente
wantonness [ˈwɒntənnɪs] (N)
1 (= *gratuitousness*) lo gratuito; (= *senselessness*) falta *f* de sentido
2 (= *dissoluteness*) [*of person*] lascivia *f*; [*of behaviour*] disipación *f*, inmoralidad *f*
WAP [wæp] (N ABBR) (= **Wireless Application Protocol**) WAP *f*
(CPD) ▸ **WAP phone** teléfono *m* WAP
war [wɔːʳ] (N) guerra *f*; (*fig*) lucha *f* • **the war against inflation** la lucha contra la inflación • **to be at war (with)** estar en guerra (con) • **the period between the wars** el período de entreguerras • **to declare war (on)** declarar la guerra (a) • **to go to war (with sb) (over sth)** entrar en guerra (con algn) (por algo) • **they went off to war singing** fueron a la guerra cantando • **the Great War** la Primera Guerra Mundial • **war to the knife** guerra *f* a muerte • **to make war (on)** hacer la guerra (a) • **war of nerves** guerra *f* de nervios • **to wage war with sb** hacer la guerra a algn • **war of words** guerra de palabras • **the First/Second World War** la Primera/Segunda Guerra Mundial • IDIOM: • **you've been in the wars!** (*hum*) ¡parece que vienes de la guerra!
(VI) (*lit*) combatir, luchar (**with** con) • **revulsion and guilt warred within him** (*liter*) la repugnancia y el sentimiento de culpabilidad luchaban en su interior
(CPD) de guerra ▸ **war chest** (*esp US*) *dinero destinado a apoyar una causa* ▸ **war clouds** nubes *fpl* de guerra ▸ **war correspondent** corresponsal *mf* de guerra ▸ **war crime** crimen *m* de guerra ▸ **war criminal** criminal *mf* de guerra ▸ **war cry** grito *m* de guerra ▸ **war dance** danza *f* guerrera ▸ **the war dead** los muertos en campaña ▸ **war debt** deuda *f* de guerra ▸ **war effort** esfuerzo *m* bélico ▸ **war fever** psicosis *f inv* de guerra ▸ **war footing** • **on a war footing** en pie de guerra ▸ **war game** (*Mil*) simulacro *m* de guerra; (= *game*) juego *m* de guerra ▸ **war grave** tumba *f* de guerra ▸ **war hero** héroe *m* de guerra ▸ **war loan** empréstito *m* de guerra ▸ **war material** material *m* bélico ▸ **war memorial** monumento *m* a los caídos ▸ **War Office** (*Hist*) Ministerio *m* de Guerra ▸ **war paint** pintura *f* de guerra; (*hum*) (= *make-up*) maquillaje *m* ▸ **war widow** viuda *f* de guerra ▸ **the war wounded** los heridos de guerra ▸ **war zone** zona *f* de guerra; ▹ **record**
warble [ˈwɔːbl] (N) [*of bird*] trino *m*, gorjeo *m*
(VT) cantar trinando, cantar gorjeando
(VI) gorjear, trinar
warbler [ˈwɔːbləʳ] (N) (= *bird*) curruca *f*
warbling [ˈwɔːblɪŋ] (N) gorjeo *m*
ward [wɔːd] (N) **1** (*Jur*) (= *person*) pupilo/a *m/f* • **he is her ~** (él) está bajo su tutela • **to make sb a ~ of court** poner a algn bajo la protección *or* el amparo del tribunal
2 (*Pol*) distrito *m* electoral
3 (*in hospital*) sala *f*, pabellón *m*
4 [*of key*] guarda *f*
(CPD) ▸ **ward heeler** (*US*) (*Pol*) muñidor *m* ▸ **ward round** (*Med*) visita *f* de salas ▸ **ward sister** (*Med*) enfermera *f* jefe de sala
▸ **ward off** (VT + ADV) [+ *attack*] rechazar; [+ *blow*] parar, desviar; [+ *infection*] protegerse de; [+ *danger*] protegerse contra, conjurar; [+ *evil spirits*] conjurar • **to ~ off the cold** protegerse del frío
...ward [wəd] (SUFFIX) hacia • **they looked seaward** miraron hacia el mar • **the homeward journey** el viaje de vuelta a casa *or* de regreso
warden [ˈwɔːdn] (N) [*of castle*] guardián/ana *m/f*, alcaide† *m*; (*in institution*) encargado/a *m/f*; (*Univ*) rector(a) *m/f*; (*Aut*) (*also* **traffic warden**) controlador(a) *m/f* de estacionamiento; (*also* **church warden**) coadjutor(a) *m/f*; (*US*) [*of prison*] celador(a) *m/f*
warder [ˈwɔːdəʳ] (N) (*esp Brit*) celador(a) *m/f*
wardress [ˈwɔːdrɪs] (N) celadora *f*
wardrobe [ˈwɔːdrəʊb] (N) **1** (= *cupboard*) guardarropa *m*, armario *m* (ropero), ropero *m* (*LAm*)
2 (= *clothes*) vestuario *m*
(CPD) ▸ **wardrobe assistant** (*Cine, Theat etc*) ayudante *mf* de vestuario ▸ **wardrobe mistress** (*Theat*) encargada *f* del vestuario ▸ **wardrobe trunk** baúl *m* ropero
wardroom [ˈwɔːdrʊm] (N) (*Naut*) cámara *f* de oficiales
...wards [wədz] (SUFFIX) (*esp Brit*) hacia • **they looked seawards** miraron hacia el mar
wardship [ˈwɔːdʃɪp] (N) tutela *f*
warehouse (N) [ˈwɛəhaʊs] (PL: **warehouses** [ˈwɛəhaʊzɪz]) almacén *m*, depósito *m*
(VT) [ˈwɛəhaʊz] almacenar
(CPD) [ˈwɛəhaʊs] ▸ **warehouse club** (*esp US*) (*Comm*) economato *m* ▸ **warehouse manager** gerente *mf* de almacén ▸ **warehouse price** • **at ~ prices** a precios de mayorista
warehouseman [ˈwɛəhaʊsmən] (N) (PL: **warehousemen**) almacenista *m*
warehousing [ˈwɛəhaʊzɪŋ] (N) almacenamiento *m*
wares [wɛəz] (NPL) mercancías *fpl* • **to cry one's ~** pregonar sus mercancías
warfare [ˈwɔːfɛəʳ] (N) (= *fighting*) guerra *f*; (= *techniques*) artes *mpl* militares • **chemical/germ ~** guerra *f* química/bacteriológica • **trench ~** guerra *f* de trincheras
warfarin [ˈwɔːfərɪn] (N) warfarina *f*
warhead [ˈwɔːhed] (N) [*of torpedo*] cabeza *f* explosiva; [*of rocket*] cabeza *f* de guerra • **nuclear ~** cabeza *f* nuclear
warhorse [ˈwɔːhɔːs] (N) caballo *m* de guerra; (*fig*) veterano *m*
warily [ˈwɛərɪlɪ] (ADV) con cautela, cautelosamente • **she answered his questions ~** contestó con cautela *or* cautelosamente a sus preguntas • **she looked at him ~** lo miró con recelo • IDIOM: • **to tread ~** (*fig*) andar con cuidado *or* cautela
wariness [ˈwɛərɪnɪs] (N) cautela *f*, recelo *m*
Warks (ABBR) (*Brit*) = **Warwickshire**
warlike [ˈwɔːlaɪk] (ADJ) [*activity*] bélico; [*people, tribe*] guerrero, belicoso
warlock [ˈwɔːlɒk] (N) brujo *m*, hechicero *m*
warlord [ˈwɔːlɔːd] (N) caudillo *m*
warm [wɔːm] (ADJ) (COMPAR: **warmer**, SUPERL: **warmest**) **1** (= *hot*) [*bath, hands, feet*] caliente; [*water*] templado, tibio; [*air*] templado, cálido; [*room, place, weather*] cálido • **to be ~** [*person*] tener calor • **it's very ~ today** hace calor hoy • **to get ~** [*person*]

W

entrar en calor; [*object, surface*] calentarse • **he started jumping to get ~** empezó a saltar para entrar en calor • **come and get ~** ven a calentarte • **it's getting ~er** [*weather*] ya empieza a hacer más calor • **to be getting ~** (*in guessing game*) ir acercándose a la respuesta • **you're getting ~(er)!** ¡caliente, caliente! • **to keep sb ~** mantener caliente a algn, mantener a algn abrigado • **to keep (o.s.) ~** mantenerse abrigado • **wear thick gloves to keep your hands ~** usa guantes gruesos para mantener las manos calientes • **keep the sauce ~** mantén la salsa caliente • IDIOM: • **to be as ~ as toast** estar bien calentito*

2 (= *thick*) [*clothes*] de abrigo, abrigado (*S. Cone*) • **take something ~ to put on** llévate algo de abrigo *or* abrigado para ponerte • **this blanket's nice and ~** esta manta es muy calentita

3 (= *cosy, homely*) [*colour, shade, sound*] cálido

4 (= *kindly*) [*person, smile, face*] simpático, afable, cálido • **the two leaders exchanged ~ greetings** los dos líderes intercambiaron cordiales saludos • **her speech was received with ~ applause** su discurso fue recibido con un caluroso aplauso • **~est congratulations to ...** la más cordial *or* sincera enhorabuena a ... • **~est thanks to ...** mi/nuestro más sincero agradecimiento a ... • **to give sb a ~ welcome** dar a algn una cordial *or* calurosa bienvenida • **with ~est wishes** (*in letter*) con mis/nuestros mejores deseos

(VT) **1** (= *heat*) [+ *one's hands, feet*] calentarse • **I ~ed my hands on the radiator** me calenté las manos en el radiador • **to ~ o.s.** calentarse; ▹ **cockle**

2 = **warm up**

(VI) = **warm up**

(N) • **the ~: come into the ~!** ¡entra aquí que hace calorcito!*

(ADV)* • **to wrap up ~** abrigarse bien

(CPD) ▸ **warm front** (*Met*) frente *m* cálido

▸ **warm down** (VI + ADV) (*after exercise*) hacer ejercicios suaves de recuperación (*tras un esfuerzo*)

▸ **warm over** (VT + ADV) (*US*) **1** [+ *food*] (re)calentar

2* (*fig*) • **it's just a ~ed over version of the measures he suggested last year** simplemente es un refrito de las medidas que sugirió el año pasado*

▸ **warm through** (VT + ADV) [+ *food*] (re)calentar

▸ **warm to** (VI + PREP) • **I began to ~ to him** empecé a encontrarle agradable • **she was beginning to ~ to the idea** estaba empezando a gustarle la idea • **he began to ~ to his subject** *or* **theme** empezó a entusiasmarse con su tema

▸ **warm up** (VI + ADV) **1** (= *get warm*) [*person*] entrar en calor; [*room, engine*] calentarse

2 (*fig*) **a** [*athlete, singer*] calentarse

b [*party, game*] animarse

(VT + ADV) **1** [+ *food*] (re)calentar; [+ *engine*] calentar

2 (*fig*) [+ *party, audience*] animar

warm-blooded ['wɔːm'blʌdɪd] (ADJ) de sangre caliente

warm-down ['wɔːmdaʊn] (N) ejercicios *mpl* suaves de recuperación (*tras un esfuerzo*)

warmed-up ['wɔːmd'ʌp] (ADJ) recalentado

warm-hearted ['wɔːm'hɑːtɪd] (ADJ) cariñoso, afectuoso

warming ['wɔːmɪŋ] (ADJ) [*drink*] que hace entrar en calor

(N) **1** recalentamiento *m*; ▹ **global**

2†* (= *hiding*) zurra* *f*

(CPD) ▸ **warming pan** calentador *m* (de cama)

warmish ['wɔːmɪʃ] (ADJ) templado • **~ weather** tiempo templado

warmly ['wɔːmlɪ] (ADV) **1** (= *cosily*) • **to be ~ dressed** ir *or* estar bien abrigado • **remember to wrap up ~** acuérdate de abrigarte bien

2 (= *affectionately*) [*greet, smile*] calurosamente, afectuosamente; [*say, speak*] cariñosamente; [*thank*] cordialmente • **he embraced her ~** la abrazó con ternura

3 (= *enthusiastically*) [*congratulate*] efusivamente; [*welcome*] calurosamente; [*endorse, recommend*] sin reservas • **to be ~ applauded** recibir un caluroso aplauso • **the plan was ~ received** el plan fue recibido con entusiasmo

4 [*shine*] con fuerza • **the sun was shining ~** el sol brillaba con fuerza

warmonger ['wɔːˌmʌŋgəʳ] (N) belicista *mf*

warmongering ['wɔːˌmʌŋgərɪŋ] (ADJ) belicista

(N) belicismo *m*

warmth [wɔːmθ] (N) **1** [*of sun, fire*] calor *m*

2 [*of clothing, blanket*] • **a blanket will provide extra ~** una manta proporcionará más abrigo • **wear a jacket for ~** ponte una chaqueta para ir bien abrigado

3 [*of greeting, welcome*] cordialidad *f*; [*of smile*] simpatía *f*, afabilidad *f*

warm-up ['wɔːmʌp] (N) **1** (*Sport*) precalentamiento *m*, ejercicios *mpl* de calentamiento

2 (= *preparatory activity*) actividad *f* preliminar, preparativos *mpl*

(CPD) ▸ **warm-up suit** (*US*) chandal *m*

warn [wɔːn] (VT) **1** (= *put on guard, urge caution to*) advertir; (= *notify, tell*) avisar, advertir • **children must be ~ed about** *or* **of the dangers of smoking** debe advertirse a los niños de los peligros que conlleva fumar • **I did ~ you that this would happen** ya te avisé *or* advertí que esto pasaría • **I must ~ you that my men are armed** debo avisarle *or* advertirle que mis hombres van armados • **we must ~ them that the police are on their way** debemos avisarles *or* advertirles que la policía está de camino • **you have been ~ed!** ¡ya estás avisado!, ¡quedas advertido! • **but, be ~ed, this is not a cheap option** pero, quedas avisado *or* advertido, esta no es una opción barata

2 (= *counsel*) advertir • **"don't do anything yet," he ~ed** —no hagas nada todavía —advirtió • **to ~ sb to do sth** advertir *or* aconsejar a algn que haga algo • **people have been ~ed to stay indoors** se ha advertido *or* aconsejado a la gente que no salga • **she ~ed me not to go out alone at night** me advirtió *or* me aconsejó que no saliera sola por la noche • **I ~ed you not to interfere** te advertí que no te entrometieras • **to ~ sb against sth** prevenir a algn contra algo • **he ~ed us against complacency** nos previno contra la autocomplacencia • **to ~ sb against doing sth** aconsejar a algn que no haga algo

3 (= *admonish*) • **to ~ sb about sth** llamar la atención a algn por algo • **I've ~ed you about your behaviour before** ya te he llamado la atención por tu comportamiento antes

(VI) • **to ~ about** *or* **of sth** advertir de algo • **he ~ed against complacency** advirtió de las consecuencias de la autocomplacencia • **some doctors ~ against vitamin supplements during pregnancy** algunos médicos desaconsejan el consumo de suplementos vitamínicos durante el embarazo

▸ **warn away** (VT + ADV) • **a lighthouse was built to ~ sailors away from the area** se construyó un faro para advertir a los marineros que se mantuvieran alejados de la zona • **analysts ~ us away from drawing any conclusions** los analistas nos advierten que no intentemos sacar conclusiones

▸ **warn off** (VT + ADV) • **he pressed for an investigation but was ~ed off** presionó para que se llevara a cabo una investigación, pero le advirtieron que no lo hiciera *or* se lo desaconsejaron • **the dogs ~ed the intruder off** los perros ahuyentaron al intruso

(VT + PREP) • **he ~ed the children off the grass** advirtió a los niños que no pisaran el césped • **to ~ sb off doing sth** advertir a algn que no haga algo • **I was ~ed off trying to help her** me advirtieron que no intentara ayudarla

warning ['wɔːnɪŋ] (N) (= *caution*) advertencia *f*; (= *advance notice*) aviso *m*, advertencia *f* • **this is a final ~** esta es la última advertencia • **let me just add a note of ~** quisiera añadir una nota de advertencia • **to be a ~ to sb** ser una advertencia para algn • **let this be a ~ to you** que te sirva de advertencia • **his employer gave him a ~ about lateness** el patrón le advirtió que no debía seguir llegando tarde • **his heart attack was a ~** su ataque al corazón fue un aviso *or* una advertencia • **they only had five minutes' ~ before the bomb went off** les dieron un aviso solo cinco minutos antes de que la bomba hiciese explosión, solo les avisaron *or* advirtieron cinco minutos antes de que la bomba hiciese explosión • **you could have given me a bit more ~** me podrías haber avisado *or* advertido con más tiempo • **without (any) ~** sin previo aviso; ▹ **gale, word, advance, early, fair¹**

(ADJ) [*sign, signal*] de aviso, de advertencia; [*look, label*] de advertencia • **to sound a ~ note** (*fig*) dar una señal de advertencia • **the ~ signs of depression** los indicios de la depresión

(CPD) ▸ **warning bell** • IDIOM: • **to set off ~ bells** enviar señales de alarma ▸ **warning device** dispositivo *m* de alarma ▸ **warning light** señal *f* luminosa ▸ **warning shot** (*lit*) disparo *m* de advertencia • **to deliver** *or* **fire a ~ shot** (*fig*) hacer una advertencia ▸ **warning triangle** (*Aut*) triángulo *m* de advertencia

warp [wɔːp] (N) **1** (*in weaving*) urdimbre *f*

2 [*of wood*] alabeo *m*, comba *f*

(VT) **1** [+ *wood*] alabear, combar

2 (*fig*) [+ *mind*] pervertir

(VI) [*wood*] alabearse, combarse

warpath ['wɔːpɑːθ] (N) • **to be on the ~** (*lit*) estar en pie de guerra; (*fig**) estar dispuesto a armar un lío*

warped [wɔːpt] (ADJ) **1** [*wood*] alabeado, combado

2 (*fig*) [*mind, sense of humour*] pervertido

warping ['wɔːpɪŋ] (N) [*of wood*] deformación *f*, alabeo *m*; (*Aer*) torsión *f*

warplane ['wɔːpleɪn] (N) avión *m* de combate

warrant ['wɒrənt] (N) **1** (= *justification*) justificación *f*

2 (*Comm, Econ*) (= *certificate, bond*) cédula *f*, certificado *m*; (= *guarantee*) garantía *f*

3 (*for travel*) (= *permission*) autorización *f*; (= *permit*) permiso *m*

4 (*Jur*) (*for seizure of goods*) mandamiento *m* judicial; (*also* **search warrant**) orden *f* de registro; (*also* **arrest warrant**) orden *f* de detención • **there is a ~ out for his arrest** se ha ordenado su detención; ▹ **death**

(VT) **1** (= *justify, merit*) merecer • **his complaint ~s further investigation** su queja merece una investigación más a fondo • **her condition did not ~ calling the doctor** su condición no justificaba llamar al médico

• **the facts do not ~ it** los hechos no lo justifican
2 (*Comm*) (= *guarantee*) garantizar
3 (= *assure*) asegurar, garantizar • **he didn't do it legally, I'll ~ (you)** no lo hizo por la vía legal, te lo aseguro *or* garantizo
CPD ▸ **warrant officer** (*Mil*) suboficial *mf*; (*Naut*) contramaestre *mf*

warrantable ['wɒrəntəbl] ADJ justificable

warranted ['wɒrəntɪd] ADJ **1** (= *justified*) [*action, remark*] justificado • **that wasn't ~!** ¡ese comentario está de sobra!
2 (*Comm*) [*goods*] garantizado • **"warranted 18 carat gold"** "certificado de oro de 18 quilates"

warrantee [ˌwɒrən'ti:] N titular *mf* de una garantía

warrantor ['wɒrəntɔ:ʳ] N garante *mf*

warranty ['wɒrəntɪ] N garantía *f*

warren ['wɒrən] N **1** (*also* **rabbit warren**) madriguera *f* (de conejos)
2 (*fig*) (= *place, area*) laberinto *m*; (= *house*) conejera *f* • **it is a ~ of little streets** es un laberinto de callejuelas

warring ['wɔ:rɪŋ] ADJ [*interests*] opuesto; [*nations, armies*] en guerra; [*factions, parties*] enfrentado; [*parents, families*] enfrentado; [*emotions*] contradictorio, encontrado

warrior ['wɒrɪəʳ] N guerrero/a *m/f*

Warsaw ['wɔ:sɔ:] N Varsovia *f*
CPD ▸ **Warsaw Pact** Pacto *m* de Varsovia

warship [wɔ:ʃɪp] N buque *m or* barco *m* de guerra

wart [wɔ:t] N (*Med*) verruga *f* • IDIOM: • **~s and all** con todas sus imperfecciones

warthog ['wɔ:thɒg] N jabalí *m* verrugoso, facochero *m*

wartime ['wɔ:taɪm] N tiempo *m* de guerra • **in ~** en tiempos de guerra
CPD [*regulations, rationing*] de guerra

war-torn ['wɔ:ˌtɔ:n] ADJ destrozado por la guerra, devastado por la guerra

warty ['wɔ:tɪ] ADJ verrugoso

war-weary ['wɔ:ˌwɪərɪ] ADJ cansado de la guerra

wary ['wɛərɪ] ADJ (COMPAR: **warier**, SUPERL: **wariest**) [*person*] receloso; [*manner*] cauteloso, precavido • **she seems very ~** parece estar muy recelosa • **banks are becoming increasingly ~** los bancos están volviéndose cada vez más precavidos • **to keep a ~ eye on sth/sb**: • **I kept a ~ eye on the gathering stormclouds** observaba con cierta preocupación los nubarrones que se acercaban • **the president had to keep a ~ eye on the radical faction of his party** el presidente tenía que vigilar de cerca al sector más radical de su partido • **he gave her a ~ look** la miró con recelo • **the question made her ~** la pregunta la puso en guardia • **to be ~ of sth/sb** desconfiar de algo/algn, no fiarse de algo/algn • **to be ~ of strangers** desconfiar *or* no fiarse de los desconocidos • **they were very ~ of his violent temper** se mostraban muy cautelosos debido a su temperamento violento

was [wɒz, wəz] PT *of* **be**

wash [wɒʃ] N **1** (= *act of washing*) • **that jacket could do with a ~** a esa chaqueta no le vendría mal un lavado • **to give sth a ~** (*gen*) lavar algo • **to give one's hands/face a ~** lavarse las manos/la cara • **to have a ~** lavarse; ▹ **brush-up**
2 (*in washing-machine*) lavado *m* • **this setting gives you a cool ~** en esta posición la máquina hace un lavado en frío
3 (= *laundry*) colada *f* • **I do a big ~ on Mondays** los lunes hago una colada grande • **I had two ~es on the line** tenía dos coladas en el tendedero • **your jeans are in the ~** (= *being washed*) tus vaqueros se están lavando; (= *with dirty clothes*) tus vaqueros están con la ropa sucia • **the colours run in the ~** los colores destiñen con el lavado • IDIOM: • **it'll all come out in the ~** al final, todo se arreglará
4 [*of ship, plane*] estela *f*
5 [*of paint, distemper*] capa *f*; (*Art*) aguada *f*
VT **1** (= *clean*) [+ *clothes, car*] lavar; [+ *floor*] fregar • **to ~ the dishes** fregar (los platos), lavar los platos • **the rain had ~ed the verandah clean** la lluvia había limpiado la terraza • **to get ~ed** lavarse • **to ~ one's hands/hair** lavarse las manos/el pelo • IDIOMS: • **to ~ one's hands of sth** lavarse las manos de algo, desentenderse de algo • **to ~ one's hands of sb** despreocuparse de algn; ▹ **linen**
2 (= *paint*) • **to ~ the walls with distemper** dar una mano de pintura (al temple) a las paredes
3 (*liter*) (= *lap*) [*sea, waves*] bañar • **an island ~ed by a blue sea** una isla bañada por el mar azul
4 (= *sweep, carry*) arrastrar • **the sea ~ed it ashore** el mar lo arrastró hasta la playa • **the house was ~ed downstream** la casa fue arrastrada río abajo • **he was ~ed overboard** cayó del barco arrastrado por las olas
VI **1** (= *have a wash*) lavarse; (= *wash the dishes*) fregar; (= *do the washing*) lavar (la) ropa • **I'll ~ and you dry** yo friego y tú secas
2 (= *be washable*) [*fabric*] • **will it ~?** ¿se puede lavar? • **man-made fabrics usually ~ well** los tejidos sintéticos suelen lavarse bien • IDIOM: • **that excuse won't ~!*** ¡esa excusa no cuela!*
3 [*sea, waves*] • **the sea ~ed against the cliffs** el mar batía contra los acantilados • **small waves gently ~ed over the coral reef** las pequeñas olas bañaban suavemente el arrecife de coral • **the oil ~ed ashore quite near here** el petróleo fue arrastrado a la orilla bastante cerca de aquí
CPD ▸ **wash bag** (*US*) neceser *m* ▸ **wash cycle** ciclo *m* de lavado ▸ **wash house** lavadero *m* ▸ **wash leather** gamuza *f* ▸ **wash sale** (*US*) venta *f* ficticia

▸ **wash away** VT + ADV **1** [+ *bridge, house, vehicle*] llevarse por delante, arrastrar; [+ *dirt*] quitar (lavando); [+ *taste*] quitar • **several cars were ~ed away in the flood** durante la inundación las aguas se llevaron varios coches por delante, durante la inundación varios coches fueron arrastrados por las aguas
2 (*fig*) • **Christ who ~es away the sins of the world** Cristo que quita los pecados del mundo
VI + ADV • **terraces prevent the soil from ~ing away** los bancales evitan que el agua se lleve la tierra

▸ **wash down** VT + ADV **1** (= *clean*) [+ *walls, car*] lavar
2 (= *take with*) • **he ~ed the tablets down with a glass of water** se tragó las pastillas con ayuda de un vaso de agua • **a cheese sandwich ~ed down with a bottle of beer** un bocadillo de queso acompañado con una botella de cerveza

▸ **wash off** VT + ADV [+ *stain, dirt*] quitar (lavando)
VI + ADV (= *disappear*) quitarse, limpiarse • **it ~es off easily** se quita *or* se limpia fácilmente • **it won't ~ off** no se quita *or* no sale al lavarlo

▸ **wash out** VT + ADV **1** [+ *stain*] quitar (lavando); [+ *container*] lavar; [+ *paintbrush*] lavar, enjuagar • **you ought to ~ your mouth out with soap!** ¡con jabón tendrían que lavarte a ti la boca!
2 (*Sport*) • **the game was ~ed out** el partido fue cancelado debido a la lluvia • **rain ~ed out the last four games** los últimos cuatro partidos tuvieron que cancelarse debido a la lluvia
3 • **to feel ~ed out** sentirse rendido *or* agotado • **to look ~ed out** tener aspecto de estar rendido *or* agotado
VI + ADV **1** (= *disappear*) [*stain, mark*] quitarse, limpiarse • **the paint will ~ out** la pintura saldrá *or* se limpiará al lavarlo
2 (= *fade*) [*dye, colour*] descolorarse, desteñirse • **the colours won't ~ out** los colores no se descolorán *or* desteñirán (con el lavado)

▸ **wash over** VI + PREP **1** (= *take hold of*) invadir • **a feeling of relief ~ed over her** la invadió una sensación de alivio • **waves of panic ~ed over her** se sentía invadida por oleadas de pánico
2 (= *pass by*) • **I just let all this criticism ~ over me** todas estas críticas simplemente me resbalan
3 (= *envelop*) • **relax and let the music ~ over you** relájese y déjese llevar por la música; ▹ **wash**

▸ **wash through** VT + ADV [+ *clothes*] lavar rápidamente

▸ **wash up** VI + ADV **1** (*Brit*) (= *wash dishes*) fregar (los platos), lavar los platos
2 (*US*) (= *have a wash*) lavarse
3 (= *come ashore*) • **it ~ed up with the tide** lo trajo la marea, la marea lo arrastró a la playa
VT + ADV **1** (*Brit*) [+ *dishes*] fregar, lavar
2 (*onto beach*) arrastrar • **the sea ~ed it up** el mar lo arrastró a la playa • **a body had been ~ed up on the beach** un cuerpo había aparecido en la playa, arrastrado por el mar
3* • IDIOM: • **to be all ~ed up** [*person, marriage*] estar acabado

Wash. ABBR (*US*) = **Washington**

washable ['wɒʃəbl] ADJ lavable

wash-and-wear ['wɒʃən'wɛəʳ] ADJ que no necesita planchado, de lava y pon

washbasin ['wɒʃbeɪsn] N lavabo *m*, lavamanos *m inv*, lavatorio *m* (*S. Cone*); (= *bowl*) palangana *f*, jofaina *f*

washboard ['wɒʃbɔ:d] N tabla *f* de lavar; (*US*) rodapié *m*, zócalo *m*

washbowl ['wɒʃbəʊl] N (*esp US*) = **washbasin**

washcloth ['wɒʃklɒθ] N (*US*) paño *m* para lavarse, manopla *f*

washday ['wɒʃdeɪ] N día *m* de lavado *or* de colada

washed-out* ['wɒʃtaʊt] ADJ (= *faded, pale*) [*fabric*] decolorado, desteñido; [*colour*] pálido • **his washed-out blue eyes** sus pálidos ojos azules

washed-up* [ˌwɒʃt'ʌp] ADJ ▹ **wash up**

washer ['wɒʃəʳ] N **1** (*Tech*) arandela *f*
2 (= *washing machine*) lavadora *f*; (= *dishwasher*) lavavajillas *m inv*

washer-dryer, washer-drier ['wɔ:ʃə'draɪəʳ] N lavadora-secadora *f*

washerwoman ['wɒʃəˌwʊmən] N (PL: **washerwomen**) lavandera *f*

wash-hand basin ['wɒʃˌhænd,beɪsn] N lavabo *m*, lavamanos *m inv*, lavatorio *m* (*S. Cone*)

washing ['wɒʃɪŋ] N **1** (= *act*) lavado *m* • **some fabrics don't stand up to repeated ~s** algunos tejidos no aguantan constantes lavados
2 (= *clothes*) (*dirty*) ropa *f* sucia; (*hung to dry*) colada *f* • **to take in ~** [*woman*] ser lavandera
CPD ▸ **washing day** día *m* de lavado, día *m* de colada ▸ **washing line** tendedero *m* ▸ **washing machine** lavadora *f* ▸ **washing**

powder jabón *m* en polvo, detergente *m* ▸ **washing soda** sosa *f*, carbonato *m* sódico
Washington ['wɒʃɪŋtən] (N) Washington *m*
washing-up ['wɒʃɪŋ'ʌp] (N) (= *act*) fregado *m*; (= *dishes*) platos *mpl* (para fregar) • **to do the washing-up** fregar (los platos), lavar los platos
(CPD) ▸ **washing-up bowl** barreño *m*, palangana *f* ▸ **washing-up liquid** lavavajillas *m inv*
washout* ['wɒʃaʊt] (N) • **it was a ~** [*match*] se suspendió debido a la lluvia; [*plan, party etc*] fue un fracaso *or* desastre • **you're a ~ as a father!** ¡como padre eres un desastre!
washrag ['wɒʃræg] (N) (US) **1** (= *dishcloth*) paño *m* de cocina
2 (= *flannel*) = **washcloth**
washroom ['wɒʃrʊm] (N) servicios *mpl*, aseos *mpl*, baño *m*
washstand ['wɒʃstænd] (N) lavabo *m*, lavamanos *m inv*
washtub ['wɒʃtʌb] (N) (= *container*) tina *f* de lavar; (= *bath*) bañera *f*
wash-wipe ['wɒʃwaɪp] (N) (*on windscreen*) limpiaparabrisas *m inv*; (= *polishing cloth*) paño *m* abrillantador
washy ['wɒʃɪ] (ADJ) (*of food, drink*) aguado
wasn't ['wɒznt] = **was not**
WASP [wɒsp] (N ABBR) (US*) = **White Anglo-Saxon Protestant**

> **WASP**
> La expresión **WASP** o **White Anglo-Saxon Protestant** se usa para referirse a los norteamericanos originarios del norte de Europa. Esta expresión fue acuñada en los años sesenta por E. Digby Baltzell, un escritor de Philadelphia. Es un término peyorativo para los miembros de este grupo étnico y religioso, a los que se considera como los más poderosos, privilegiados e influyentes en Estados Unidos. Este término también se utiliza por extensión para hacer referencia a toda persona blanca de clase media descendiente de los primeros colonos y que cree en los valores tradicionales estadounidenses.

wasp [wɒsp] (N) avispa *f* • **~s' nest** (*also fig*) avispero *m*
(CPD) ▸ **wasp waist** (*fig*) talle *m* de avispa
waspish ['wɒspɪʃ] (ADJ) [*character, person*] irritable, irascible; [*remark*] mordaz, punzante
waspishly ['wɒspɪʃlɪ] (ADV) [*remark*] mordazmente
wasp-waisted ['wɒsp'weɪstɪd] (ADJ) (*fig*) con talle de avispa
wassail†† ['wɒseɪl] (N) (= *drink*) cerveza *f* especiada; (= *festivity*) juerga *f*, fiesta *f* de borrachos
(VI) beber mucho
wast†† [wɒst] (PT) *thou form of* **be**
wastage ['weɪstɪdʒ] (N) (= *loss*) desperdicio *m*; (= *amount wasted*) pérdidas *fpl*; (*from container*) merma *f*; (= *wear and tear*) desgaste *m* • **the country cannot afford this ~ of human resources** el país no puede permitirse este desperdicio de los recursos humanos • **there is a very high ~ rate among students** existe un porcentaje muy elevado de estudiantes que no terminan sus estudios • **the ~ rate among entrants to the profession** el porcentaje de los que abandonan la profesión poco tiempo después de ingresar en ella; ▹ **natural**
waste [weɪst] (N) **1** (= *misuse*) desperdicio *m*, derroche *m* • **I hate ~** odio el desperdicio *or* el derroche • **what a ~!** ¡qué desperdicio *or* derroche! • **her death is a terrible ~** su muerte es una terrible pérdida • **there was no ~ on that meat** esa carne no tenía desperdicio • **an effort to locate and eliminate government ~** una campaña para identificar y eliminar las áreas de ineficacia en el gobierno • **to go to ~** echarse a perder, desperdiciarse • **it's a ~ of money** es dinero perdido, es tirar *or* derrochar el dinero • **it's a ~ of time** es una pérdida de tiempo • **it's a ~ of effort** es un esfuerzo inútil • **that man's a ~ of space!*** ¡ese hombre es un inútil!*
2 (= *rubbish*) basura *f*, desperdicios *mpl*; (= *waste material, substance*) desechos *mpl*, residuos *mpl* • **household ~** basura *f* doméstica • **human ~** excrementos *mpl* • **nuclear ~** desechos *mpl or* residuos *mpl* nucleares • **toxic ~** desechos *mpl or* residuos *mpl* tóxicos
3 (= *leftover material*) material *m* sobrante
4 wastes • **the barren ~s of the Sahara** las áridas y baldías inmensidades del Sáhara
(VT) **1** (= *use inefficiently, squander*) [+ *water, electricity, gas*] derrochar; [+ *money*] malgastar, derrochar; [+ *time*] perder; [+ *life*] echar a perder; [+ *space, opportunity*] desaprovechar, desperdiciar; [+ *food*] desperdiciar, echar a perder; [+ *talent*] desaprovechar • **I ~d a whole day on that journey** perdí un día entero haciendo ese viaje • **don't ~ your time trying to persuade her** no pierdas el tiempo intentando persuadirla • **to ~ no time in doing sth** no tardar en hacer algo • **don't ~ your efforts on him** no derroches tus esfuerzos *or* energías con él • **all my efforts were ~d** todos mis esfuerzos fueron inútiles • **sarcasm is ~d on him** con él el sarcasmo es inútil • **caviar is ~d on him** no sabe apreciar el caviar • **nothing is ~d** no se desperdicia nada, no se echa a perder nada • IDIOM: • **you're wasting your breath!** ¡estás gastando saliva!
2 (= *weaken*) [+ *muscles*] atrofiar • **cancer was wasting his body** el cáncer lo estaba consumiendo *or* debilitando
3 (US‡) (= *kill*) cargarse*, liquidar*
(VI) **1** • PROVERB: • **~ not, want not** quien no malgasta no pasa necesidades
2 = **waste away**
(ADJ) **1** (= *for disposal*) [*material*] de desecho; [*gas, oil*] residual
2 (= *leftover*) [*paper, fabric*] sobrante; [*heat*] residual
3 (= *unused*) [*ground*] baldío, yermo
4 • **to lay ~** [+ *country, area, town*] devastar, asolar • **to lay ~ to sth** devastar algo, asolar algo
(CPD) ▸ **waste disposal** (*industrial*) eliminación *f* de los desechos *or* residuos; [*of household waste*] eliminación *f* de la basura doméstica; (= *device*) = **waste disposal unit** ▸ **waste disposal unit** triturador *m* de basura ▸ **waste heat** calor *m* residual ▸ **waste management** tratamiento *m* de desechos, tratamiento *m* de residuos ▸ **waste material** material *m* de desecho ▸ **waste matter** (*industrial*) residuos *mpl*; (*from body*) excrementos *mpl* ▸ **waste paper** papel *m* de desecho ▸ **waste pipe** tubería *f* de desagüe ▸ **waste products** (*industrial*) residuos *mpl*; (*from body*) excrementos *mpl* ▸ **waste water** aguas *fpl* residuales
▸ **waste away** (VI + ADV) [*person*] consumirse; [*muscles*] atrofiarse • **you're not exactly wasting away** (*iro*) no es que te hayas consumido precisamente
wastebasket ['weɪstbɑːskɪt] (N) (US) cesto *m* de los papeles, papelera *f*
waste-bin ['weɪstbɪn] (N) (*Brit*) cubo *m* de la basura
wasted ['weɪstɪd] (ADJ) **1** (= *lost, useless*) [*opportunity*] desaprovechado, desperdiciado; [*effort*] inútil; [*years*] perdido • **at least it hadn't been an entirely ~ day** por lo menos no había sido un día completamente perdido • **I'm afraid you've had a ~ journey** me temo que has hecho un viaje inútil *or* en vano • **a vote for them is a ~ vote** votar por ellos es desaprovechar el voto
2 (= *thin*) [*person*] consumido; [*muscle*] atrofiado; [*arm, leg, hand*] atrofiado, inútil
3* a (*from drugs*) destrozado
b (*from drink*) borracho • **to get ~** emborracharse
wasteful ['weɪstfʊl] (ADJ) [*person*] despilfarrador, derrochador; [*process, method*] antieconómico; [*expenditure*] pródigo, excesivo • **to be ~ with sth** despilfarrar algo, desperdiciar algo • **the government is ~ of taxpayers' money** el gobierno despilfarra *or* derrocha los impuestos de los contribuyentes • **war is ~ of human lives** la guerra supone un desperdicio de vidas humanas
wastefully ['weɪstfəlɪ] (ADV) [*use*] antieconómicamente, excesivamente
wastefulness ['weɪstfʊlnɪs] (N) [*of war*] desperdicio *m*; [*of system*] derroche *m*, despilfarro *m*; [*of person*] falta *f* de economía, prodigalidad *f*
wasteland ['weɪstlænd] (N) **1** (*undeveloped*) terreno *m* baldío *or* yermo, tierra *f* baldía *or* yerma; (*uncultivated*) erial *m* • **industrial ~** terreno *m* industrial baldío
2 (*fig*) desierto *m* • **a cultural ~** un desierto cultural
wastepaper basket [ˌweɪst'peɪpəˌbɑːskɪt], **wastepaper bin** [ˌweɪst'peɪpəbɪn] (N) cesto *m* de los papeles, papelera *f*
waster ['weɪstəʳ] (N) **1** (= *good-for-nothing*) gandul *mf*
2 (= *spendthrift*) derrochador(a) *m/f*
wasting ['weɪstɪŋ] (ADJ) [*disease*] debilitante; [*asset*] amortizable
wastrel† ['weɪstrəl] (N) gandul *mf*, derrochador(a) *m/f*
watch¹ [wɒtʃ] (N) (= *wristwatch*) reloj (de pulsera) *m*; (= *pocket watch*) reloj de bolsillo, leontina *f* (*frm*) • **what does your ~ say?** ¿qué hora tienes?
(CPD) ▸ **watch stem** (US) = **watchstem**
watch² [wɒtʃ] (N) **1** (= *vigilance*) vigilancia *f* • **to keep ~** hacer guardia, vigilar • **to keep ~ for sth/sb** estar al acecho de algo/algn • **to keep a (close) ~ on sth/sb** (*lit*) vigilar algo/a algn (de cerca) • **our task was to keep a ~ on the suspect** nuestra tarea consistía en vigilar al sospechoso *or* mantener al sospechoso bajo vigilancia • **US officials have been keeping a close ~ on the situation** los representantes del gobierno estadounidense han estado siguiendo la situación de cerca • **I keep a close ~ on my expenditure** controlo mucho los gastos • **to be on the ~ for danger** estar atento *or* alerta por si hay peligro • **can you keep a ~ out for Daphne?** ¿puedes estar al tanto para ver cuándo viene Daphne? • **to keep ~ over sth/sb** (= *keep a check on*) vigilar algo/a algn; (= *look after*) cuidar algo/a algn
2 (= *period of duty*) guardia *f* • **you take the first ~** monta *or* haz tú la primera guardia • **the long ~es of the night** (*liter*) las largas vigilias • **officer of the ~** oficial *mf* de guardia • **to be on ~** estar de guardia, hacer guardia; ▹ **night**
3 (= *guard*) **a** (*Mil*) (= *individual*) centinela *mf*, guardia *mf*; (= *pair, group*) guardia *f*
b (*Naut*) (= *individual*) vigía *mf*; (= *pair, group*) guardia *f*, vigía *f*

c† (= *watchman*) • **the night ~** (*in streets, flats*) el sereno; (*in factory*) el vigilante nocturno
VT **1** (= *view, spectate at*) [+ *television, programme, game, play*] ver • **some children ~ too much television** algunos niños ven demasiada televisión
2 (= *observe, look at*) (*gen*) mirar; (*more attentively*) observar • **Sue was ~ing me curiously** Sue me miraba/observaba con curiosidad • **now ~ this closely** ahora observen esto detenidamente • **~ what I do** mira/observa lo que hago • **~ how I do it** mira/observa cómo lo hago • **to ~ sth/sb do sth: we ~ed the car turn the corner and disappear from view** vimos cómo el coche torcía la esquina y desaparecía de nuestra vista, vimos al coche torcer la esquina y desaparecer de nuestra vista • **she ~ed me clean the gun** miraba/observaba cómo limpiaba yo la pistola • **just ~ him run!** ¡mira cómo corre! • **"you can't do that" — "just you ~ (me)!"** —no puedes hacer eso —¿que no? ¡ya verás (como puedo)! • **to ~ sth/sb doing sth: I ~ed the gulls hovering overhead** miraba/observaba las gaviotas cerniéndose en lo alto • IDIOMS: • **to ~ the clock** estar pendiente del reloj • **to ~ sb like a hawk** no quitar el ojo *or* la vista de encima a algn • **it's about as exciting as ~ing paint dry** *or* **grass grow** es para morirse de aburrimiento • PROVERB: • **a ~ed pot** *or* **kettle never boils** quien espera desespera
3 (= *mind*) [+ *children, luggage, shop*] cuidar; [+ *soup, frying pan*] echar un ojo a • **~ that knife/your head/your language!** ¡(ten) cuidado con ese cuchillo/la cabeza/esas palabrotas! • **~ your speed** ten cuidado con la velocidad, atención a la velocidad • **~ you don't burn yourself** ten cuidado de no quemarte • **~ he does his homework** mira de que haga los deberes • **~ how you go!** ¡ve con cuidado! • **~ what you're doing!** ¡cuidado con lo que haces! • **he wasn't ~ing where he was going** no miraba por donde iba • **~ it!** (= *careful!*) ¡ojo!*, ¡cuidado!, ¡abusado! (*Mex**); (*threatening*) ¡cuidadito!* • **to ~ one's step** (*lit, fig*) ir con cuidado
4 (= *be mindful of*) [+ *weight, health*] cuidar; [+ *time*] estar pendiente de • **I have to ~ what I eat** tengo que tener cuidado con lo que como • **we shall have to ~ our spending** tendremos que vigilar *or* tener cuidado con los gastos
5 (= *monitor*) [+ *situation, developments*] seguir; [+ *case*] seguir, vigilar; [+ *suspect, house, sb's movements*] vigilar • **we are being ~ed** nos están vigilando • **Big Brother is ~ing you** el Gran Hermano te vigila • **he needs ~ing** hay que vigilarlo • **a new actor to be ~ed** un nuevo actor muy prometedor • **~ this space** (*lit*) estén pendientes, les mantendremos informados • **"so is the row over?" — "~ this space"** —¿se ha terminado la pelea? —eso habrá que verlo
VI **1** (= *observe*) mirar; (*attentively*) observar • **somebody was ~ing at the window** alguien estaba mirando/observando desde la ventana • **he could only sit and ~ as his team lost 2-0** no pudo hacer más que sentarse y ver como su equipo perdía 2 a 0
2 (= *wait, be alert*) • **I was ~ing for the plumber** estaba atento esperando a que llegara el fontanero • **he's ~ing to see what you're going to do** está pendiente de lo que vas a hacer
3 (= *keep watch*) • **to ~ by sb's bedside** velar a algn
CPD ▸ **Watch Night** (*in Protestant church*) Nochevieja *f* ▸ **watch night service** misa *f* de fin de año

▸ **watch out** VI + ADV tener cuidado, ir con cuidado • **you'll get fat if you don't ~ out** te pondrás gordo como no tengas cuidado • **~ out!** (= *be careful*) ¡(ten) cuidado!, ¡abusado! (*Mex**); (*threatening*) ¡cuidadito! • **~ out for thieves** cuidado con los ladrones • **to ~ out for trouble** estar alerta *or* al acecho por si hay problemas
▸ **watch over** VI + PREP **1** (= *look after*) [+ *person*] velar por; [+ *sb's rights, safety*] velar por, mirar por • **God is ~ing over me** Dios vela por mí • **to ~ over sb's interests** velar *or* mirar por los intereses de algn
2 (= *monitor*) supervisar
3 (= *guard*) vigilar
watchable ['wɒtʃəbl] ADJ [*programme*] que se deja ver • **the film is eminently ~** la película es sumamente entretenida
watchband ['wɒtʃbænd] N (*esp US*) pulsera *f* de reloj, correa *f* de reloj
watchcase ['wɒtʃkeɪs] N caja *f* de reloj
watchdog ['wɒtʃdɒg] N **1** (= *guard dog*) perro *m* guardián
2 (*fig*) (= *person*) guardián/ana *m/f*; (= *organization*) organismo *m* protector • **a consumer ~** un organismo que protege los intereses del consumidor
CPD ▸ **watchdog committee** comisión *f* protectora
watcher ['wɒtʃəʳ] N [*of situation*] observador(a) *m/f*; [*of event*] espectador(a) *m/f*; (*pej*) mirón/ona *m/f* • **China ~** especialista *mf* en asuntos chinos, sinólogo/a *m/f* • **royal ~** *periodista que escribe sobre la familia real*; ▹ **bird-watcher, weight watcher**
watchful ['wɒtʃfʊl] ADJ [*eyes, face*] atento; (*stronger*) vigilante • **to be ~ (for sth)** estar atento (a algo); (*stronger*) mantener una actitud vigilante (ante algo) • **to keep a ~ eye on sth/sb** vigilar algo/a algn de cerca • **under the ~ eye of** bajo la atenta mirada de, bajo la mirada vigilante de
watchfully ['wɒtʃfəlɪ] ADV vigilantemente
watchfulness ['wɒtʃfʊlnɪs] N vigilancia *f*
watchglass ['wɒtʃglɑːs] N cristal *m* de reloj
watchmaker ['wɒtʃˌmeɪkəʳ] N relojero/a *m/f* • **~'s (shop)** relojería *f*
watchman ['wɒtʃmən] N (PL: **watchmen**) (= *security guard*) guardián *m*, vigilante *m*; (*also* **night watchman**) (*in factory*) vigilante *m* nocturno; (*in street*) sereno *m*
watchstem ['wɒtʃstəm] N (*US*) cuerda *f*
watchstrap ['wɒtʃstræp] N correa *f* de reloj
watchtower ['wɒtʃˌtaʊəʳ] N atalaya *f*, torre *f* de vigilancia
watchword ['wɒtʃwɜːd] N (*Mil, Pol*) contraseña *f*; (= *motto*) lema *m*, consigna *f*
water ['wɔːtəʳ] N **1** agua *f* • **to back ~** ciar • **bottled ~** agua *f* mineral • **by ~** por mar • **fresh ~** agua *f* dulce • **hard ~** agua *f* dura • **high ~** marea *f* alta • **on land and ~** por tierra y por mar • **low ~** marea *f* baja • **salt ~** agua *f* salada • **soft ~** agua *f* blanda • **to turn on the ~** • **turn the ~ on** (*at main*) hacer correr el agua; (*at tap*) abrir el grifo • **under ~**: • **the High Street is under ~** la Calle Mayor está inundada • **to swim under ~** nadar bajo el agua, bucear • IDIOMS: • **a lot of ~ has flowed under the bridge since then** ha llovido mucho desde entonces • **that's all ~ under the bridge now** todo eso ya ha pasado a la historia • **to pour cold ~ on an idea** echar un jarro de agua fría a una idea • **like ~ off a duck's back** como si nada, como quien oye llover • **that theory doesn't hold ~** esa teoría carece de fundamento • **to be in hot ~*** estar metido en un lío* • **to get into hot ~*** meterse en un lío* • **to spend money like ~** despilfarrar *or* tirar el dinero • **to test the ~(s)** probar la temperatura del agua; ▹ **drinking, running, still**
2 waters (*at spa, of sea, river*) aguas *fpl* • **to drink** *or* **take the ~s at Harrogate** tomar las aguas en Harrogate • **the ~s of the Amazon** las aguas del Amazonas • **British ~s** aguas británicas
3 (= *urine*) aguas *fpl* menores, orina *f* • **to make** *or* **pass ~** orinar, hacer aguas (menores)
4 (*Med*) • **~ on the brain** hidrocefalia *f* • **her ~s broke** rompió aguas • **~ on the knee** derrame *m* sinovial
5 (= *essence*) • **lavender/rose ~** agua *f* de lavanda/rosa
6 • IDIOM: • **of the first ~** de lo mejor, de primerísima calidad
VT [+ *garden, plant*] regar; [+ *horses, cattle*] abrevar, dar de beber a; [+ *wine*] aguar, diluir, bautizar* (*hum*) • **the river ~s the provinces of …** el río riega las provincias de … • **to ~ capital** emitir un número excesivo de acciones
VI (*Physiol*) • **her eyes started ~ing** empezaron a llorarle los ojos • **her mouth ~ed** se le hizo agua la boca • **it's enough to make your mouth ~** se hace la boca agua
CPD ▸ **water bed** cama *f* de agua ▸ **water bird** ave *f* acuática ▸ **water biscuit** galleta *f* de agua ▸ **water blister** ampolla *f* ▸ **water bomb** bomba *f* de agua ▸ **water bottle** (*for drinking*) cantimplora *f*; (*also* **hot-water bottle**) bolsa *f* de agua caliente, guatona *f* (*Chile*) ▸ **water buffalo** búfalo *m* de agua, carabao *m* ▸ **water butt** (*Brit*) tina *f* para recoger el agua de la lluvia ▸ **water cannon** cañón *m* de agua ▸ **water carrier** aguador *m* ▸ **water cart** cuba *f* de riego, carro *m* aljibe; (*motorized*) camión *m* de agua ▸ **water chestnut** castaña *f* de agua ▸ **water closet** (*frm*) wáter *m*, baño *m* ▸ **water cooler** enfriadora *f* de agua ▸ **water cooling** refrigeración *f* por agua ▸ **water diviner** zahorí *mf* ▸ **water divining** arte *m* del zahorí ▸ **water feature** fuente *f* ornamental ▸ **water heater** calentador *m* de agua ▸ **water hole** ▹ **waterhole** ▸ **water ice** (*Brit*) sorbete *m*, helado *m* de agua (*LAm*) ▸ **water inlet** entrada *f* de agua ▸ **water jacket** camisa *f* de agua ▸ **water jump** foso *m* (de agua) ▸ **water level** nivel *m* del agua; (*Naut*) línea *f* de agua ▸ **water lily** nenúfar *m* ▸ **water line** línea *f* de flotación ▸ **water main** cañería *f* principal ▸ **water meadow** (*esp Brit*) vega *f*, ribera *f* ▸ **water meter** contador *m* de agua ▸ **water metering** *control del agua mediante instalación de un contador de agua* ▸ **water mill** molino *m* de agua ▸ **water park** parque *m* acuático ▸ **water pipe** caño *m* de agua ▸ **water pistol** pistola *f* de agua ▸ **water plant** planta *f* acuática ▸ **water polo** waterpolo *m*, polo *m* acuático ▸ **water power** energía *f* hidráulica ▸ **water pressure** presión *f* del agua ▸ **water pump** bomba *f* de agua ▸ **water purification plant** estación *f* depuradora de aguas residuales ▸ **water rat** rata *f* de agua ▸ **water rate** (*Brit*) tarifa *f* de agua ▸ **water snake** culebra *f* de agua ▸ **water softener** ablandador *m* de agua ▸ **water sports** deportes *mpl* acuáticos ▸ **water supply** abastecimiento *m* de agua ▸ **water table** capa *f* freática, nivel *m* freático ▸ **water tank** (*for village, in house*) depósito *m* de agua; (*on lorry*) cisterna *f* ▸ **water tower** depósito *f* de agua ▸ **water vapour, water vapor** (*US*) vapor *m* de agua ▸ **water vole** rata *f* de agua ▸ **water wagon** (*US*) vagón-cisterna *m* ▸ **water wheel** rueda *f* hidráulica; (*Agr*) noria *f* ▸ **water wings**

manguitos *mpl*, flotadores *mpl* para los brazos
▸ **water down** (VT + ADV) **1** (*lit*) [+ *wine*] aguar, bautizar*; [+ *juice, milk, paint*] diluir
2 (*fig*) [+ *reform, proposal, report*] suavizar
waterage ['wɔːtərɪdʒ] (N) transporte *m* por barco
waterboarding ['wɔːtə,bɔːdɪŋ] (N) (= *form of torture*) submarino *m*
waterborne ['wɔːtəbɔːn] (ADJ) [*disease*] transmitido a través del agua; [*traffic, trade*] (*by river*) fluvial; (*by sea*) marítimo
waterbuck ['wɔːtə,bʌk] (N) cobo *m* untuoso
watercolour, watercolor (US) ['wɔːtə,kʌləʳ] (N) acuarela *f* • **to paint in ~s** pintar a la acuarela
watercolourist, watercolorist (US) ['wɔːtə,kʌlərɪst] (N) acuarelista *mf*
water-cooled ['wɔːtəkuːld] (ADJ) refrigerado (por agua)
watercourse ['wɔːtəkɔːs] (N) (= *river bed*) lecho *m*, cauce *m*; (= *canal*) canal *m*, conducto *m*
watercress ['wɔːtəkres] (N) berro *m*
watered ['wɔːtəd] (ADJ) aguado
(CPD) ▸ **watered silk** muaré *m* ▸ **watered stock** acciones *fpl* diluidas
watered-down ['wɔːtəd'daʊn] (ADJ) **1** [*wine*] aguado, bautizado*; [*juice, milk, paint*] diluido
2 (*fig*) [*account, version*] suavizado; [*bill, reform, compromise*] suavizado
waterfall ['wɔːtəfɔːl] (N) cascada *f*, salto *m* de agua; (*larger*) catarata *f*
waterfowl ['wɔːtəfaʊl] (PL) (**waterfowl**) (N) ave *f* acuática
waterfront ['wɔːtəfrʌnt] (N) (= *harbour area*) puerto *m*, muelle *m* • **a ~ restaurant** *un restaurante situado a orillas de un río/lago etc*
Watergate ['wɔːtə,geɪt] (N) Watergate *m*
waterhole ['wɔːtəhəʊl] (N) charco *m*; (*for animals*) abrevadero *m*
watering ['wɔːtərɪŋ] (N) riego *m* • **frequent ~ is needed** hay que regar con frecuencia
(CPD) ▸ **watering can** regadera *f* ▸ **watering hole** (*for animals*) abrevadero *m*;* (= *pub*) pub *m* ▸ **watering place** (= *spa*) balneario *m*; (= *seaside resort*) playa *f*, ciudad *f* marítima, ciudad *f* de veraneo; (*for animals*) abrevadero *m*
waterless ['wɔːtəlɪs] (ADJ) sin agua, árido
waterlogged ['wɔːtəlɒgd] (ADJ) [*ground*] anegado, inundado; [*pitch*] encharcado, inundado; [*boat, ship*] inundado; [*wood, paper*] empapado • **to get ~** [*ground*] anegarse, inundarse; [*wood, paper*] empaparse
Waterloo [,wɔːtə'luː] (N) Waterloo *m* • IDIOM: • **he met his ~** se le llegó su San Martín
waterman ['wɔːtəmən] (N) (PL: **watermen**) barquero *m*
watermark ['wɔːtəmɑːk] (N) (*on paper*) filigrana *f*; (*left by tide*) marca *f* del nivel del agua
watermelon ['wɔːtə,melən] (N) sandía *f*
waterproof ['wɔːtəpruːf] (ADJ) [*material*] impermeable; [*watch, torch*] sumergible; [*mascara, sunscreen, glue*] resistente al agua
(N) (*Brit*) impermeable *m*
(VT) impermeabilizar
waterproofing ['wɔːtə'pruːfɪŋ] (N) (= *process*) impermeabilización *f*; (= *material*) impermeabilizante *m*
water-repellent ['wɔːtərɪ'pelənt] (ADJ) [*material, clothing*] hidrófugo
(N) hidrófugo *m*
water-resistant ['wɔːtərɪ'zɪstənt] (ADJ) [*material*] impermeable; [*sunscreen*] a prueba de agua
watershed ['wɔːtəʃed] (N) **1** (*Geog*) línea *f* divisoria de las aguas; (= *basin*) cuenca *f* • **the ~ of the Duero** la cuenca del Duero
2 (*fig*) (= *decisive moment*) momento *m* clave, momento *m* decisivo; (= *landmark*) hito *m* • **she had reached a ~ in her career** había llegado a un momento clave *or* decisivo en su carrera profesional • **the talks marked a ~ in the peace process** las negociaciones marcaron un hito en el proceso de paz
3 (*Brit*) (*TV*) • **the nine o'clock ~** *comienzo de la programación televisiva para adultos a las nueve de la noche*
waterside ['wɔːtəsaɪd] (N) (= *river, lake*) orilla *f*, ribera *f*; (= *harbour*) muelle *m*
(ADJ) ribereño
water-ski ['wɔːtəskiː] (VI) esquiar en el agua
water-skier ['wɔːtə,skiːəʳ] (N) esquiador(a) *m/f* acuático/a
water-skiing ['wɔːtə,skiːɪŋ] (N) esquí *m* acuático
water-soluble ['wɔːtə'sɒljʊbl] (ADJ) soluble en agua
waterspout ['wɔːtəspaʊt] (N) **1** (= *tornado*) tromba *f* marina
2 (= *drainage pipe*) tubo *m* de desagüe
watertight ['wɔːtətaɪt] (ADJ) **1** [*bottle, container, seal*] hermético; [*compartment, boat, ship*] estanco; [*door*] de cierre hermético
2 (*fig*) [*alibi*] perfecto; [*agreement*] sin lagunas; [*guarantee, embargo*] sólido; [*argument, theory*] irrefutable
waterway ['wɔːtəweɪ] (N) vía *f* fluvial *or* navegable; (= *inland waterway*) canal *m* (navegable)
waterweed ['wɔːtə'wiːd] (N) alga *f*
waterworks ['wɔːtəwɜːks] (N) **1** (*for water purification*) central *f* depuradora
2* (= *tears*) • IDIOM: • **to turn on the ~** echarse a llorar
3‡ (= *urinary tract*) vías *fpl* urinarias • **to have trouble with one's ~** tener problemas de orina
watery ['wɔːtərɪ] (ADJ) **1** (= *like or containing water*) [*fluid, discharge, solution*] acuoso; [*blood*] líquido; [*paint, ink*] aguado
2 (*pej*) (= *containing excessive water*) [*tea, soup*] aguado
3 (= *producing water*) [*eyes*] lloroso
4 (= *insipid*) [*smile*] tímido; [*sun*] débil; [*light*] desvaído, tenue
5 (= *pale*) [*colour*] pálido, desvaído
6 (= *relating to water*) acuático • **to go to a ~ grave** (*liter*) encontrar su lecho de muerte en el fondo del mar (*liter*)
WATS ['wɒts] (N ABBR) (US) = **Wide Area Telecommunications Service**
watt [wɒt] (N) vatio *m*
wattage ['wɒtɪdʒ] (N) vatiaje *m*
wattle¹ ['wɒtl] (N) (*Constr*) zarzo *m* • **~ and daub** zarzos *mpl* y barro
wattle² ['wɒtl] (N) (*Orn*) barba *f*
wave [weɪv] (N) **1** (*in sea, lake*) ola *f* • **life on the ocean ~** la vida en el *or* la mar • IDIOM: • **to make ~s** (= *make an impression*) causar sensación; (= *stir up trouble*) crear problemas; ▹ **tidal**
2 (*in hair*) onda *f* • **her hair has a natural ~ (in it)** tiene el pelo ondulado por naturaleza; ▹ **permanent**
3 (*on surface*) ondulación *f*; ▹ **shock**
4 (*Phys, Rad*) onda *f* • **long/medium/short ~** onda larga/media/corta; ▹ **light, radio, sound**
5 (*in brain*) onda *f*
6 (= *surge*) [*of strikes, refugees, enthusiasm*] oleada *f* • **the recent ~ of bombings** la reciente oleada de bombardeos • **a ~ of panic swept over me** me invadió el pánico • **in the first ~ of the attack** en la primera oleada del ataque • **the pain comes in ~s** el dolor va y viene; ▹ **crime, Mexican, new**
7 (= *wave of hand*) gesto *m* de la mano • **he dismissed me with a ~ of the hand** me echó con un gesto de la mano • **with a ~ he was gone** hizo un gesto con la mano para despedirse y se fue • **to give sb a ~** (*in greeting*) saludar a algn con la mano; (*saying goodbye*) decir adiós a algn con la mano
8 (US) = **Mexican wave**
(VT) **1** (= *shake, brandish*) [+ *flag, handkerchief, placard*] agitar; [+ *weapon, spear, stick*] blandir, agitar • **he was waving his arms in the air** agitaba los brazos en el aire • **he saw Jarvis, and ~d a hand** (*to catch attention*) vio a Jarvis y le hizo señas con la mano • **she ~d her hand for silence** hizo un gesto con la mano para que se callaran • **he ~d a piece of paper at her** le hizo señas agitando un papel que llevaba en la mano • **he ~d the ticket under my nose** agitó el billete delante de mis narices • **to ~ one's/a magic wand** agitar su varita mágica
2 (= *gesture*) • **to ~ sb goodbye** • **~ goodbye to sb** decir adiós a algn con la mano • **he ~d the car through the gates** le indicó al coche que entrara por el portón
3 (*Hairdressing*) • **it's used for waving hair** se utiliza para hacer ondas (en el pelo) • **to have one's hair ~d** hacerse ondas (en el pelo)
(VI) **1** [*person*] • **I saw her and ~d** la vi y la saludé con la mano • **we ~d as the train drew out** cuando partió el tren nos dijimos adiós con la mano • **Ralph ~d for silence** Ralph hizo un gesto con la mano para que se callaran • **to ~ to** *or* **at sb** (= *sign to*) hacer señas a algn con la mano; (= *greet*) saludar a algn con la mano; (= *say goodbye to*) decir adiós a algn con la mano
2 (= *sway*) [*flag*] ondear; [*branches, grass*] mecerse
(CPD) ▸ **wave energy** energía *f* mareomotriz ▸ **wave frequency** frecuencia *f* de las ondas ▸ **wave mechanics** mecánica *f* ondulatoria ▸ **wave power** energía *f* mareomotriz ▸ **wave range** (*Rad*) gama *f* de ondas
▸ **wave about, wave around** (VT + ADV) [+ *object, arms*] agitar
▸ **wave aside** (VT + ADV) (= *dismiss*) [+ *suggestion, objection*] (*verbally*) rechazar, desechar; (*with gesture*) rechazar con (un gesto de) la mano • **I told her how much I appreciated her help but she ~d aside my thanks** le dije cuánto apreciaba su ayuda, pero ella le quitó importancia (con un gesto de la mano)
▸ **wave away** (VT + ADV) [+ *sth offered*] rechazar con (un gesto de) la mano • **he ~d the waiter away** con un gesto de la mano le indicó al camarero que se fuera
▸ **wave down** (VT + ADV) • **to ~ a car down** (= *sign to stop*) hacer señales a un coche para que pare • **we ~d down a passing car** paramos a un coche que pasaba haciéndole señas con las manos
▸ **wave off** (VT + ADV) • **to ~ sb off** decir adiós a algn con la mano • **she came to the pier to ~ us off** vino al muelle para decirnos adiós
▸ **wave on** (VT + ADV) • **to ~ sb on** indicar a algn que siga adelante, hacer señas a algn para que siga adelante
waveband ['weɪvbænd] (N) banda *f* de frecuencia • **long ~** onda *f* larga
wavelength ['weɪvleŋθ] (N) longitud *f* de onda • IDIOM: • **we're not on the same ~** no estamos en la misma onda
wavelet ['weɪvlɪt] (N) pequeña ola *f*, olita *f*
waver ['weɪvəʳ] (VI) **1** (= *oscillate*) [*needle*] oscilar; [*flame*] temblar
2 (*fig*) (= *hesitate*) vacilar, dudar (**between** entre); (= *weaken*) [*courage, support*] flaquear; (= *falter*) [*voice*] temblar • **he's beginning to ~** está empezando a vacilar *or* dudar • **his gaze**

W

never ~ed no apartó la mirada ni por un momento • **she never ~ed in her belief** siempre se mantuvo firme en sus creencias
waverer ['weɪvərəʳ] (N) indeciso/a *m/f*, irresoluto/a *m/f*
wavering ['weɪvərɪŋ] (ADJ) indeciso, irresoluto, vacilante
(N) (= *flickering*) temblor *m*; (= *indecisiveness*) vacilación *f*, indecisión *f*, irresolución *f*
wavy ['weɪvɪ] (ADJ) (COMPAR: **wavier**, SUPERL: **waviest**) [*hair, surface, line*] ondulado
wavy-haired ['weɪvɪ'hɛəd] (ADJ) de pelo ondulado
wax¹ [wæks] (N) cera *f*; (*in ear*) cera *f* (de los oídos), cerumen *m*, cerilla *f*
(ADJ) de cera
(VT) [+ *furniture, car*] encerar
(CPD) ▸ **wax bean** (*US*) judía *f* amarilla ▸ **wax museum** museo *m* de cera ▸ **wax paper** papel *m* encerado ▸ **wax seal** sello *m* de lacre
wax² [wæks] (VI) [*moon*] crecer • **to wax and wane** crecer y decrecer • **to wax enthusiastic** (*liter*) entusiasmarse • **to wax eloquent about sth** ponerse elocuente acerca de algo; ▹ **lyrical**
waxed [wækst] (ADJ) [*paper, jacket*] encerado (CPD) ▸ **waxed cotton** algodón *m* encerado
waxen ['wæksən] (ADJ) **1**† (= *made of wax*) de cera, céreo
2 (*liter*) (= *pale*) ceroso
waxing ['wæksɪŋ] (ADJ) [*moon*] creciente
(N) crecimiento *m*
waxwork ['wækswɜːk] (N) figura *f* de cera
waxworks ['wækswɜːks] (N) (PL) (**waxworks**) museo *m* de cera
waxy ['wæksɪ] (ADJ) (COMPAR: **waxier**, SUPERL: **waxiest**) ceroso
way [weɪ] (N) **1** (= *road, lane*) camino *m*; (*in street names*) calle *f*, avenida *f* • **Way of the Cross** Vía *f* Crucis, viacrucis *m* • **across** *or* **over the way (from)** enfrente (de), frente (a) • **permanent way** vía *f* • **the public way** la vía pública
2 (= *route*) camino *m* (**to** de) • **the way to the station** el camino de la estación • **which is the way to the station?** ¿cómo se va *or* cómo se llega a la estación? • **this isn't the way to Lugo!** ¡por aquí no se va a Lugo! • **he walked all the way here** vino todo el camino andando • **it rained all the way there** llovió durante todo el viaje • **he ran all the way home** hizo todo el camino a casa corriendo • **to ask one's way to the station** preguntar el camino *or* cómo se va a la estación • **we came a back way** vinimos por los caminos vecinales • **she went by way of Birmingham** fue por *or* vía Birmingham • **if the chance comes my way** si se me presenta la oportunidad • **way down** bajada *f*, ruta *f* para bajar • **to take the easy way out** optar por la solución más fácil • **to feel one's way** (*lit*) andar a tientas • **he's still feeling his way in the new job** todavía se está familiarizando con el nuevo trabajo • **to find one's way** orientarse, ubicarse (*esp LAm*) • **to find one's way into a building** encontrar la entrada de un edificio, descubrir cómo entrar en un edificio • **the cat found the way into the pantry** el gato logró introducirse en la despensa • **I had to find my own way home** me las tuve que arreglar para volver a casa • **the way is hard** el camino es duro • **the way in** (= *entrance*) la entrada • **I don't know the way to his house** no sé el camino a su casa, no sé cómo se va *or* llega a su casa • **do you know the way to the hotel?** ¿sabes el camino del *or* al hotel?, ¿sabes cómo llegar al hotel? • **I know my way about town** conozco la ciudad • **she knows her way around** (*fig*) tiene bastante experiencia, no es que sea una inocente • **to lead the way** (*lit*) ir primero; (*fig*) marcar la pauta, abrir el camino • **to go the long way round** ir por el camino más largo • **to lose one's way** extraviarse • **to make one's way to** dirigirse a • **to make one's way home** volver a casa • **to make one's way in the world** abrirse camino en la vida • **the middle way** el camino de en medio • **on the way here** de camino hacia aquí, mientras veníamos aquí • **on the way to London** rumbo a Londres, camino de Londres • **it's on the way to Murcia** está en la carretera de Murcia • **we're on our way!** ¡vamos para allá! • **he's on his way** está de camino • **they have another child on the way** tienen otro niño en camino • **you pass it on your way home** te pilla de camino a casa • **your house is on my way** tu casa me viene de camino • **he is well on the way to finishing it** lo tiene casi terminado • **he's on the way to becoming an alcoholic** va camino de hacerse un alcohólico • **the way out** la salida • **you'll find it on the way out** lo encontrarás cerca de la salida • **I'll find my own way out** no hace falta que me acompañen a la puerta • **to find a way out of a problem** encontrar una solución a un problema • **there's no way out** (*fig*) no hay salida *or* solución, esto no tiene solución • **there's no other way out** (*fig*) no hay más remedio • **it's on its way out** está en camino de desaparecer, ya está pasando de moda • **to go out of one's way** (*lit*) desviarse del camino • **to go out of one's way to help sb** desvivirse por ayudar a algn • **I don't want to take you out of your way** no quiero apartarle del camino • **the village I live in is rather out of the way** mi pueblo está un poco retirado • **that's nothing out of the way these days** eso no es nada extraordinario hoy día • **to pay one's way** (*in restaurant*) pagar su parte • **the company isn't paying its way** la compañía no rinde *or* no da provecho • **he put me in the way of some good contracts** me conectó *or* enchufó para que consiguiera buenos contratos • **to see one's way (clear) to helping sb** ver la forma de ayudar a algn • **could you possibly see your way clear to lending him some money?** ¿tendrías la amabilidad de prestarle algo de dinero? • **to go the shortest way** ir por el camino más corto • **to start on one's way** ponerse en camino • **way up** subida *f*, ruta *f* para subir • **the way of virtue** el camino de la virtud • IDIOMS: • **to go the way of all flesh** fenecer como todo ser humano • **I'm with you all the way** te apoyo en todo • **to go one's own way** seguir su propio camino • **she always goes her own sweet way** hace lo que le da la gana; ▹ **prepare**
3 (= *space sb wants to go through*) camino *m* • **to bar the way** ponerse en medio del camino • **to clear a way for** abrir camino para • **to clear the way** despejar el camino • **he crawled his way to the gate** llegó arrastrándose hasta la puerta • **to elbow one's way through the crowd** abrirse paso por la multitud a codazos • **to fight one's way out** lograr salir luchando • **to force one's way in** introducirse a la fuerza • **to hack one's way through sth** abrirse paso por algo a fuerza de tajos • **to be/get in sb's way** estorbar a algn • **to get in the way** estorbar • **am I in the way?** ¿estorbo? • **you can watch, but don't get in the way** puedes mirar, pero no estorbes • **to put difficulties in sb's way** crear dificultades a algn • **to stand in sb's way** (*lit*) cerrar el paso a algn; (*fig*) ser un obstáculo para algn • **now nothing stands in our way** ahora no hay obstáculo alguno • **to stand in the way of progress** impedir *or* entorpecer el progreso • **to make way (for sth/sb)** (*lit, fig*) dejar paso (a algo/algn) • **make way!** ¡abran paso! • **to leave the way open for further talks** dejar la puerta abierta a posteriores conversaciones • **this law leaves the way open to abuse** esta ley deja vía libre a toda clase de desafueros • **to get out of the way** quitarse de en medio • **out of my way!** ¡quítate de en medio! • **I should keep out of his way if I were you** yo que tú evitaría el trato con él • **I try to keep out of his way** procuro evitar cualquier contacto con él • **I kept well out of the way** me mantuve muy lejos • **to get** *or* **move sth out of the way** quitar algo de en medio *or* del camino • **put it somewhere out of the way** ponlo donde no estorbe • **it's out of the way of the wind** está al abrigo del viento • **as soon as I've got this essay out of the way** en cuanto termine este ensayo • **keep those matches out of his way** no dejes esas cerillas a su alcance • **to push one's way through the crowd** abrirse paso por la multitud a empujones • **to work one's way to the front** abrirse camino hacia la primera fila • **he worked his way up in the company** ascendió en la compañía a fuerza de trabajo • **he worked his way up from nothing** empezó sin nada y fue muy lejos a fuerza de trabajo; ▹ **give**
4 (= *direction*) • **down our way** por nuestra zona, en nuestro barrio • **are you going my way?** ¿vas por dónde voy yo? • **everything is going my way** (*fig*) todo me está saliendo a pedir de boca • **to look the other way** (*lit*) mirar para otro lado; (*fig*) mirar para otro lado, hacer la vista gorda • **turn it the other way round** vuélvelo al revés • **it was you who invited her, not the other way round** eres tú quien la invitaste, no al revés • **it's out Windsor way** está cerca de Windsor • **turn the map the right way up** pon el mapa mirando hacia arriba • **the car landed the right way up** el coche cayó sobre las ruedas • **to split sth three ways** dividir algo en tres partes iguales • **come this way** pase por aquí • **"this way for the lions"** "a los leones" • **this way and that** por aquí y por allá • **which way did it go?** ¿hacia dónde fue?, ¿por dónde se fue? • **which way do we go from here?** (*lit, fig*) ¿desde aquí adónde vamos ahora? • **which way is the wind blowing?** ¿de dónde sopla el viento? • **she didn't know which way to look** no sabía dónde mirar, no sabía dónde poner los ojos
5 (= *distance*) • **a little way off** no muy lejos, a poca distancia • **a little way down the road** bajando la calle, no muy lejos • **it's a long** *or* **good way away** *or* **off** está muy lejos • **spring is a long way off** la primavera queda muy lejos • **it's a long** *or* **good way** es mucho camino • **we have a long way to go** tenemos mucho camino por delante • **he'll go a long way** (*fig*) llegará lejos • **a little of that flavouring goes a long way** un poco de ese condimento cunde mucho • **a little of her company goes a long way** (*iro*) solo se le puede aguantar en pequeñas dosis • **we've come a long way since those days** hemos avanzado mucho desde entonces • **it should go a long way towards convincing him** (esto) seguramente contribuirá mucho a convencerlo • **that's a long way from the truth** eso queda muy lejos de la verdad • **better by a long way** mucho mejor, mejor pero con mucho • **not by a long way** ni con

mucho • **I can swim quite a way now** ahora puedo nadar bastante distancia • **a short way off** no muy lejos, a poca distancia
6 (= *means*) manera *f*, forma *f*, modo *m* • **we'll find a way of doing it** encontraremos la manera *or* forma *or* modo de hacerlo • **love will find a way** el amor encontrará el camino • **it's the only way of doing it** es la única manera *or* forma *or* modo de hacerlo • **my way is to** (+ *infin*) mi sistema consiste en (+ *infin*) • **that's the way!** ¡así!, ¡eso es! • **that way it won't disturb anybody** así no molestará a nadie • **every which way** (*esp US*) (= *in every manner*) de muchísimas maneras; (= *in every direction*) por todas partes • **he re-ran the experiment every which way he could** reprodujo el experimento de todas las maneras habidas y por haber • **ways and means** medios *mpl* • **that's not the right way** así no se hace • IDIOM: • **there are no two ways about it** no hay vuelta de hoja
7 (= *manner*) manera *f*, forma *f*, modo *m* • **the way things are going we shall have nothing left** si esto continúa así nos vamos a quedar sin nada • **she looked at me in a strange way** me miró de manera *or* forma extraña *or* de modo extraño • **it's a strange way to thank someone** ¡vaya manera *or* forma *or* modo de mostrar gratitud *or* darle las gracias a alguien! • **without in any way wishing to** (+ *infin*) sin querer en lo más mínimo (+ *infin*), sin tener intención alguna de (+ *infin*) • **in a big way*** en grande* • **they like to celebrate their birthdays in a big way** les gusta celebrar sus cumpleaños en grande • **we lost in a really big way*** perdimos de manera *or* forma *or* modo realmente espectacular • **you can't have it both ways** tienes que optar por lo uno o lo otro • **each way** (*Racing*) (a) ganador y colocado • **either way I can't help you** de todas formas no puedo ayudarle • **I will help you in every way possible** haré todo lo posible por ayudarte • **he insulted us in every possible way** nos ha insultado en todos los sentidos • **the British way of life** el estilo de vida británico • **no way!*** ¡ni pensarlo!, ¡ni hablar! • **no way was that a goal*** ¡imposible que fuera eso un gol! • **there is no way I am going to agree*** de ninguna manera *or* forma *or* de ningún modo lo voy a consentir • **(in) one way or another** de una u otra manera *or* forma *or* modo • **it doesn't matter to me one way or the other** me es igual, me da lo mismo • **a week one way or the other won't matter** no importa que sea una semana más o una semana menos • **in the ordinary way (of things)** por lo general, en general • **he has his own way of doing it** tiene su manera *or* forma *or* modo de hacerlo • **I'll do it (in) my own way** lo haré a mi manera *or* forma *or* modo • **he's a good sort in his own way** tiene sus rarezas pero es buena persona • **in the same way** de la misma manera *or* forma, del mismo modo • **to go on in the same old way** seguir como siempre • **we help in a small way** ayudamos un poco • **she's clever that way** para esas cosas es muy lista • **to my way of thinking** a mi parecer, a mi manera *or* forma *or* modo de ver • **do it this way** hazlo así • **in this way** así, de esta manera *or* forma *or* modo • **it was this way ...** pasó lo siguiente ... • **that's always the way with him** siempre le pasa igual
8 [*of will*] • **to get one's own way** salirse con la suya • **have it your own way!** ¡como quieras! • **they've had it all their own way too long** hace tiempo que hacen lo que les da la gana • **they didn't have things all their own way** (*in football match*) no dominaron el partido completamente • **he had his wicked** *or* **evil way with her** (*hum*) se la llevó al huerto*, la sedujo
9 (= *custom*) costumbre *f* • **the ways of the Spaniards** las costumbres de los españoles • **that is our way with traitors** así tratamos a los traidores • **he has his little ways** tiene sus manías *or* rarezas • **to get into the way of doing sth** adquirir la costumbre de hacer algo • **to be/get out of the way of doing sth** haber perdido/perder la costumbre de hacer algo • IDIOM: • **to mend one's ways** enmendarse, reformarse
10 (= *gift, special quality*) • **he has a way with people** tiene don de gentes • **he has a way with children** sabe manejar a los niños • **he has a way with him** tiene su encanto
11 (= *respect, aspect*) sentido *m* • **in a way** en cierto sentido • **in many ways** en muchos sentidos • **he's like his father in more ways than one** se parece a su padre en muchos sentidos • **in no way** • **not in any way** de ninguna manera, de manera alguna • **in some ways** en algunos sentidos
12 (= *state*) estado *m* • **the way things are** tal como están *or* van las cosas • **to leave things the way they are** dejar las cosas como están • **things are in a bad way** las cosas van *or* marchan mal • **the car is in a bad way** el coche está en mal estado • **he's in a bad way** (= *sick*) está grave; (= *troubled*) está muy mal • **he's in a fair way to succeed** tiene buenas posibilidades de lograrlo • **it looks that way** así parece • IDIOM: • **to be in the family way*** estar embarazada
13 (= *speed*) • **to gather way** [*ship*] empezar a moverse; (*fig*) [*enthusiasm*] encenderse
14 (*in set expressions with preposition*) • **by the way** a propósito, por cierto • **how was your holiday, by the way?** a propósito *or* por cierto, ¿qué tal tus vacaciones? • **Jones, which, by the way, is not his real name** Jones que, a propósito *or* por cierto, no es su verdadero nombre • **oh, and by the way** antes que se me olvide • **all this is by the way** todo esto no viene al caso • **by way of a warning** a modo de advertencia • **that was all I got by way of an answer** eso es todo lo que conseguí por respuesta • **she's by way of being an artist** tiene sus ribetes de artista • **he had little in the way of formal education** tuvo poca educación formal • **to be under way** estar en marcha • **the job is now well under way** el trabajo ya está muy avanzado • **to get under way** [*ship*] zarpar; [*person, group*] partir, ponerse en camino; [*work, project*] ponerse en marcha, empezar a moverse • **things are getting under way at last** por fin las cosas están empezando a moverse
(ADV)* • **that was way back** eso fue hace mucho tiempo ya • **way back in 1900** allá en 1900 • **way down (below)** muy abajo • **it's way out in Nevada** está allá en Nevada • **way out to sea** mar afuera • **he was way out in his estimate** se equivocó (en) mucho en su presupuesto • **it's way past your bedtime** hace rato que deberías estar en la cama • **it's way too big** es demasiado grande • **way up high** muy alto • **way up in the sky** muy alto en el cielo
(CPD) ▸ **way station** (*US*) apeadero *m*; (*fig*) paso *m* intermedio

-way [weɪ] (ADJ) (*ending in compounds*) • **a five-way split** una división en cinco partes • **a two-way street** una calle de doble sentido

waybill [ˈweɪbɪl] (N) hoja *f* de ruta

wayfarer† [ˈweɪˌfɛərəʳ] (N) caminante *mf*, viajero/a *m/f*

wayfaring [ˈweɪfɛərɪŋ] (ADJ) (*liter*) caminante
(CPD) ▸ **wayfaring man** caminante *m* ▸ **wayfaring tree** viburno *m*

waylay [weɪˈleɪ] (PT, PP: **waylaid** [weɪˈleɪd]) (VT) abordar, detener • **I was waylaid by the manager** me detuvo el gerente • **they were waylaid by thieves** les atacaron unos ladrones

waymarked [ˈweɪmɑːkt] (ADJ) [*path, trail*] señalizado

way-out* [ˈweɪˈaʊt] (ADJ) ultramoderno

wayside [ˈweɪsaɪd] (N) borde *m* del camino • **by the ~** al borde del camino • IDIOM: • **to fall by the ~** [*project*] quedarse en aguas de borraja; [*person*] quedarse a mitad de camino
(CPD) [*inn*] de carretera; [*flowers*] al borde del camino

wayward [ˈweɪwəd] (ADJ) 1 (= *wilful*) [*person*] rebelde; [*behaviour*] díscolo, rebelde; [*horse*] caprichoso, rebelde • **she separated from her ~ husband** se separó del rebelde de su marido
2 (= *unmanageable*) [*hair*] rebelde; [*satellite, missile*] rebelde, incontrolable

waywardness [ˈweɪwədnɪs] (N) (= *wilfulness*) rebeldía *f*; (= *capriciousness*) lo caprichoso

WB (N ABBR) (= **World Bank**) BM

W/B (ABBR) = **waybill**

WBA (N ABBR) = **World Boxing Association**

WC (N ABBR) (*Brit*) (= **water closet**) wáter *m*, WC *m*

WCC (N ABBR) = **World Council of Churches**

wdv (ABBR) (= **written-down value**) valor *m* amortizado

we [wiː] (PRON) (*for emphasis, to avoid ambiguity*) nosotros/as • **you've got kids but we haven't** vosotros tenéis hijos pero nosotros no • **we English** nosotros los ingleses • **it's we who ...** somos nosotros quienes ... • **they work harder than we do** trabajan más que nosotros

Don't translate the subject pronoun when not emphasizing or clarifying:

• **we were in a hurry** teníamos prisa • **we were dissatisfied with the service** estábamos insatisfechos con el servicio

w/e (ABBR) = **week ending** • **w/e 28 Oct** semana que termina el día 28 de octubre

WEA (N ABBR) (*Brit*) = **Workers' Educational Association**

weak [wiːk] (ADJ) (COMPAR: **weaker**, SUPERL: **weakest**) 1 (*physically*) [*person, limb, constitution*] débil • **he was too ~ to stand up** estaba demasiado débil para levantarse, no tenía fuerzas para levantarse • **to have ~ eyesight** tener mala vista • **to feel ~** sentirse débil • **my legs/arms felt ~** no tenía fuerza en las piernas/los brazos • **to be ~ from hunger** estar debilitado por el hambre • **to grow** *or* **get ~(er)** debilitarse • **to have a ~ heart** padecer del corazón • **the ~er sex**† el sexo débil • **to have a ~ stomach** marearse con facilidad • **to be ~ with hunger** estar debilitado por el hambre • **to be ~ with fear** estar débil por el miedo • IDIOMS: • **to be ~ in the head*** ser cortito de arriba* • **to go ~ at the knees**: • **I went ~ at the knees** se me flaquearon las piernas
2 (= *fragile*) [*bone, fingernail, bond*] frágil; [*structure*] endeble, frágil; [*material*] endeble • **that chair's got a ~ leg** a esa silla le falla una pata, esa silla tiene una pata floja • **the ~ link (in the chain)** (*fig*) el eslabón flojo (de la cadena)
3 (= *ineffectual*) [*person, voice, smile, currency, government*] débil; [*economy*] débil, flojo;

W

[*market*] flojo • **they believe it is ~ to cry** creen que llorar es signo de debilidad, creen que llorar es de débiles • **the dollar is ~ against the pound** el dólar está débil en comparación con la libra • **to have a ~ chin** tener una barbilla poco pronunciada
4 (= *poor*) [*subject, student, team*] flojo • **geography is my ~ subject** estoy flojo en geografía, la geografía es mi asignatura floja • **to be ~ at** *or* **in sth** flojear en algo, estar flojo en algo • **the course was very ~ on grammar** el curso era muy flojo en lo referente a gramática • **~ point** punto *m* débil; ▹ **spot**
5 (= *unconvincing*) [*argument, evidence*] poco sólido, poco convincente; [*case*] poco sólido; [*excuse, answer*] poco convincente • **the film had a ~ plot** el argumento de la película era muy flojo
6 (= *faint*) [*light*] débil, tenue; [*sun, signal, electric current*] débil; [*tide, current*] flojo; [*pulse*] débil, flojo
7 (= *watery*) [*coffee, tea, alcoholic drink*] poco cargado; [*solution*] diluido
NPL • **the ~** los débiles

weaken ['wi:kən] VT [+ *person, heart, structure, economy*] debilitar; [+ *power, influence, resolve*] menguar, debilitar; [+ *case, argument*] quitar fuerza a; [+ *solution, mixture*] diluir • **he ~ed his grip on her arm** dejó de apretarle el brazo con tanta fuerza • **he doesn't want to do anything that might ~ his grip on power** no quiere hacer nada que pueda menguar el control que tiene sobre el país
VI **1** (= *grow weaker*) [*person, muscle, structure, economy*] debilitarse; [*power, influence, resolve*] menguarse, debilitarse • **the pound ~ed against the dollar today** hoy la libra ha bajado frente al dólar
2 (= *give way*) flaquear • **we must not ~ now** no debemos flaquear, ahora menos que nunca

weakening ['wi:kənɪŋ] N [*of muscles, structure, currency, economy, power*] debilitamiento *m* • **we have seen a ~ of government resolve** hemos observado un debilitamiento en la resolución del gobierno
ADJ [*effect*] debilitante

weak-kneed ['wi:k'ni:d] ADJ (*fig*) [*person*] sin carácter, débil

weakling ['wi:klɪŋ] N (*physically*) debilucho/a *m/f*; (*morally*) pelele *m*

weakly ['wi:klɪ] ADV **1** (= *without physical strength*) [*move, lean*] sin fuerzas • **his heart was beating ~** su corazón latía con poca fuerza *or* débilmente • **she struggled ~** forcejeó con pocas fuerzas
2 (= *ineffectually*) [*act, respond*] sin firmeza; [*say, smile*] débilmente, tímidamente; [*laugh*] tímidamente; [*give in*] sin oponer resistencia
ADJ [*person, child*] enfermizo, enclenque

weak-minded ['wi:k'maɪndɪd] ADJ (= *irresolute*) sin carácter; (= *not sane*) mentecato

weakness ['wi:knɪs] N **1** (*in body*) debilidad *f*; [*of bone, fingernail*] fragilidad *f*; [*of structure*] falta *f* de solidez, lo endeble
2 (= *ineffectuality*) [*of person*] falta *f* de carácter; [*of government, management*] flaqueza *f*, debilidad *f*
3 (= *weak point*) punto *m* débil
4 (= *soft spot*) debilidad *f* • **I'm afraid doughnuts are my ~** me temo que los donuts son mi debilidad • **to have a ~ for sth** tener debilidad por algo

weak-willed ['wi:k'wɪld] ADJ sin voluntad, indeciso

weal¹ [wi:l] N (*esp Brit*) (= *wound*) verdugón *m*

weal²†† [wi:l] N (= *well-being*) bienestar *m* • **the common ~** el bien común

wealth [welθ] N **1** (*lit*) riqueza *f* • **for all his ~** a pesar de su riqueza • **the country's mineral ~** las riquezas minerales del país
2 (*fig*) (= *abundance*) abundancia *f* (**of** de) • **the report provides a ~ of detail/new information** el informe contiene una abundancia de detalles/de información nueva
CPD ▸ **wealth tax** impuesto *m* sobre el patrimonio

wealthy ['welθɪ] ADJ (COMPAR: **wealthier**, SUPERL: **wealthiest**) rico, acaudalado
NPL • **the ~** los ricos

wean [wi:n] VT [+ *child*] destetar • **to ~ sb (away) from sth** (*fig*) alejar a algn de algo

weaning ['wi:nɪŋ] N destete *m*, ablactación *f*

weapon ['wepən] N arma *f*
CPD ▸ **weapons inspector** inspector(a) *m/f* de armas ▸ **weapons of mass destruction** armas *fpl* de destrucción masiva ▸ **weapons testing** pruebas *fpl* con armas

weaponize ['wepənaɪz] (*Brit*) VT utilizar como arma

weaponry ['wepənrɪ] N armas *fpl*

weapons-grade ['wepənz,greɪd] ADJ [*uranium, plutonium*] (de uso) militar

wear [wεəʳ] (VB: PT: **wore**, PP: **worn**) N
1 (= *use*) uso *m* • **this material will stand up to a lot of ~** este tejido resistirá mucho uso • **I've had a lot of ~ out of this jacket** le he dado mucho uso a esta chaqueta, esta chaqueta ha aguantado mucho trote* • **there is still some ~ left in it** todavía le queda vida • **clothes for evening ~** ropa *f* para la noche • **clothes for everyday ~** ropa *f* para todos los días, ropa *f* para uso diario
2 (= *deterioration through use*) desgaste *m* • **the ~ on the engine** el desgaste del motor • **to show signs of ~** [*clothes, furniture, tyres*] dar muestras de desgaste, mostrar señales de desgaste • **~ and tear** desgaste natural • **one has to allow for ~ and tear** hay que tener en cuenta el desgaste natural • IDIOM: • **the worse for ~***: • **his suit looked decidedly the worse for ~** el traje se le veía muy deslucido • **she looks the worse for ~** se la ve algo desmejorada • **he returned from the pub rather the worse for ~** volvió del bar algo ajumado*
3 (= *dress, clothing*) ropa *f* • **what is the correct ~ for these occasions?** ¿qué es lo que se debe poner uno en tal ocasión?, ¿qué ropa es la apropiada para tal ocasión? • **casual ~** ropa *f* informal • **children's ~** ropa *f* de niños • **evening ~** ropa *f* para la noche • **ladies'** *or* **women's ~** ropa *f* de señora • **summer ~** ropa *f* de verano
VT **1** (= *have on*) [+ *clothing, jewellery*] llevar, llevar puesto; [+ *spectacles, hairstyle, perfume*] llevar; [+ *beard*] tener; [+ *smile*] lucir; (= *put on*) [+ *clothes, shoes, perfume*] ponerse • **she was ~ing high-heeled shoes** llevaba (puestos) zapatos de tacón alto • **can you describe what he was ~ing?** ¿puede describir lo que llevaba (puesto)? • **were you ~ing a watch?** ¿llevabas reloj?, ¿llevabas un reloj puesto? • **what the well-dressed woman is ~ing this year** lo que lleva *or* se pone este año la mujer bien vestida • **she wore blue** iba de azul • **what shall I ~?** ¿qué me pongo? • **I have nothing to ~ to the dinner** no tengo qué ponerme para ir a la cena • **I haven't worn that for ages** hace siglos que no me pongo eso • **why don't you ~ your black dress?** ¿por qué no te pones el vestido negro? • **hats are rarely worn nowadays** hoy día apenas se llevan los sombreros • **I never ~ perfume/make-up** nunca llevo *or* me pongo perfume/maquillaje • **what size do you ~?** (*clothes*) ¿qué talla usa? • **what size shoes do you ~?** ¿qué número calza? • **does she ~ glasses/a wig?** ¿usa gafas/peluca? • **to ~ the crown** ceñir la corona • **to ~ one's hair long/short** llevar el pelo largo/corto • IDIOMS: • **she ~s her age** *or* **her years well** se conserva muy bien • **she's the one who ~s the trousers** *or* (*US*) **pants in that house*** en esa casa los pantalones los lleva ella*; ▹ **heart**
2 (= *make worn*) • **to ~ a path across the lawn** hacer un camino pisando la hierba • **the carpet had been worn threadbare** la alfombra estaba muy desgastada del uso • **to ~ o.s. to death** matarse (trabajando etc) • **to ~ a hole in sth** hacer un agujero en algo • **he had worn holes in his socks** les había hecho agujeros a los calcetines • **the flagstones had been worn smooth by centuries of use** tantos siglos de uso habían alisado las losas
3* (= *tolerate*) permitir, consentir • **your father won't ~ it** tu padre no lo va a permitir *or* consentir
VI **1** (= *last*) durar, aguantar • **that dress/carpet has worn well** ese vestido/esa alfombra ha durado *or* aguantado mucho • **it's a friendship that has worn very well** es una amistad que ha resistido *or* aguantado muy bien el paso del tiempo • **she's worn well*** se ha conservado muy bien
2 (= *become worn*) desgastarse • **the trousers have worn at the knees** los pantalones se han desgastado por la rodillas • **the rock has worn smooth** la roca se ha alisado por el desgaste • **to ~ thin** [*material*] desgastarse • **that excuse is ~ing a bit thin** esa excusa está ya muy pasada • **my patience is ~ing thin** se me está agotando la paciencia, estoy perdiendo la paciencia
3 [*day, year, sb's life*] • **to ~ to its end** *or* **a close** acercarse a su fin
▸ **wear away** VT + ADV [+ *rock*] erosionar; [+ *pattern*] desgastar, borrar
VI + ADV [*wood, metal*] desgastarse, gastarse; [*cliffs*] erosionarse; [*inscription, design*] borrarse
▸ **wear down** VT + ADV **1** (*lit*) [+ *heels, tyre tread, pencil*] gastar, desgastar
2 (*fig*) [+ *opposition, resistance, patience*] agotar; [+ *person*] (*physically*) agotar, cansar; (*mentally*) cansar
VI + ADV [*heels, tyre tread*] desgastarse, gastarse
▸ **wear off** VI + ADV [*excitement, novelty*] pasar; [*anaesthetic, effects, pain*] pasarse; [*colour, design, inscription*] borrarse • **when the novelty ~s off** cuando pase la novedad • **the pain is ~ing off** se me está pasando el dolor
VT + ADV [+ *design, inscription*] quitar, borrar
▸ **wear on** VI + ADV [*year, war*] transcurrir, pasar • **the years wore on** transcurrían *or* pasaban los años • **as the evening wore on** a medida que transcurría la noche
▸ **wear out** VT + ADV **1** (= *ruin*) [+ *clothes, battery, engine, clutch*] gastar, desgastar • **you'll ~ your eyes out doing that** como hagas eso te vas a cansar la vista
2 (= *exhaust*) agotar • **you'll ~ me out!** ¡me vas a agotar!, ¡me vas a matar!* • **I'm worn out** estoy agotado *or* rendido • **to ~ o.s. out** agotarse, matarse*
VI + ADV [*clothes, shoes, battery, engine, clutch*] gastarse, desgastarse; [*knee, elbow of garment*] gastarse
▸ **wear through** VT + ADV • **the sole of his**

boot was completely worn through con el uso la suela de la bota se le había agujereado
VI + ADV [*clothing*] romperse *or* agujerearse con el uso • **it has worn through at the elbows** con el uso se ha roto *or* agujereado por los codos

WEAR

▹ *Don't translate the* **a** *in sentences like* **was she wearing a hat?, he wasn't wearing a coat** *if the number of such items is not significant since people normally only wear one at a time:*

Was he wearing a hat?
¿Llevaba sombrero?
He wasn't wearing a coat
No llevaba abrigo

▹ *Do translate the* **a** *if the garment, item of jewellery etc is qualified:*

Queen Sofía is wearing a long dress
Doña Sofía lleva un vestido largo

For further uses and examples, see main entry.

wearable ['wɛərəbl] ADJ que se puede llevar, ponible • **it's still ~** todavía está ponible • **I haven't got anything ~ for the wedding** no tengo nada apropiado que ponerme para la boda
wearer ['wɛərəʳ] N • **contact lens/denture ~s** personas que usan lentillas/dentadura postiza • **spectacle ~s** personas que llevan gafas • **this device can improve the ~'s hearing considerably** este dispositivo puede mejorar considerablemente la audición del usuario • **~s of bowler hats** los que llevan sombrero de hongo • **a mask grants the ~ anonymity** una máscara da anonimato a quien la lleva
wearily ['wɪərɪlɪ] ADV (= *with tiredness*) con cansancio; (= *dispiritedly*) con desaliento • **she smiled/sighed ~** sonrió/suspiró cansada
weariness ['wɪərɪnɪs] N (*physical, mental*) cansancio *m*, fatiga *f*; (*emotional*) hastío *m*
wearing ['wɛərɪŋ] ADJ (= *exhausting*) [*journey*] cansado, pesado; [*activity*] pesado • **it was a ~ time for us** fue una época muy pesada para nosotros • **the loud music was ~ on the ear** la música tan alta estaba resultando pesada *or* cansina
wearisome ['wɪərɪsəm] ADJ (*frm*) (= *tiring*) fatigoso, pesado; (= *boring*) aburrido
weary ['wɪərɪ] ADJ (COMPAR: **wearier**, SUPERL: **weariest**) **1** [*person*] cansado; [*sigh, smile, voice*] de cansancio • **to be ~ of sth/sb** estar cansado *or* harto de algo/algn • **to be ~ of doing sth** estar cansado *or* harto de hacer algo • **to grow ~** cansarse • **he had grown ~ of travelling** se había cansado de viajar
2 (*liter*) (= *tiring*) [*wait, day*] pesado • **five ~ hours** cinco agotadoras horas
VT (*frm*) cansar, agotar
VI (*frm*) • **to ~ of sth/sb** cansarse *or* hartarse de algo/algn
weasel ['wi:zl] N (PL: **weasel** *or* **weasels**) **1** (*Zool*) comadreja *f*
2* (= *person*) zorro/a* *m/f*
VI • **to ~ out of sth** escabullirse de algo
CPD ▸ **weasel words** ambages *mpl*, palabras *fpl* equívocas
weather ['weðəʳ] N tiempo *m* • **~ permitting** si el tiempo lo permite, si el tiempo no lo impide • **in this ~** con el tiempo que hace, con este tiempo • **it's very comfortable to wear in hot ~** es muy cómodo de llevar (puesto) cuando hace calor • **what's the ~ like?** ¿qué tiempo hace? • **he has to go out in all ~s** tiene que salir haga el tiempo que haga • **it gets left outside in all ~s** se deja siempre a la intemperie • IDIOMS: • **to keep a ~ eye on sth** observar algo con atención • **to make heavy ~ of sth** complicar algo, hacer algo más difícil de lo que es • **he only needed to change the bulb but he made such heavy ~ of it** ¡solo tenía que cambiar la bombilla pero lo complicó de una manera! • **to be under the ~** (= *ill*) estar indispuesto, estar pachucho*
VT **1** [+ *storm*] aguantar • **we've ~ed worse criticism than this** hemos superado peores críticas que estas, hemos hecho frente a peores críticas que estas • IDIOM: • **to ~ the storm** capear el temporal
2 (*Geol*) [+ *rock*] erosionar; [+ *wood*] curar; [+ *skin, face*] curtir • **the rocks had been ~ed into fantastic shapes** las rocas tenían formas fantásticas debido a la erosión
3 (*Naut*) [+ *cape*] doblar
VI [*rocks*] erosionarse; [*wood*] curarse; [*skin, face*] curtirse
CPD [*station, balloon*] meteorológico ▸ **Weather Bureau** (*US*), **Weather Centre** (*Brit*) Instituto *m* Nacional de Meteorología ▸ **weather chart** (= *map*) mapa *m* del tiempo, mapa *m* meteorológico; (= *other type of chart*) gráfico *m* del tiempo ▸ **weather conditions** estado *m* del tiempo ▸ **weather forecast** pronóstico *m* del tiempo, boletín *m* meteorológico ▸ **weather forecaster** meteorólogo/a *m/f* ▸ **weather girl** mujer *f* del tiempo, meteoróloga *f* ▸ **weather map** mapa *m* del tiempo, mapa *m* meteorológico ▸ **weather report** boletín *m* meteorológico ▸ **weather ship** barco *m* del servicio meteorológico ▸ **weather side** (*Naut*) costado *m* de barlovento ▸ **weather strip** burlete *m* ▸ **weather vane** veleta *f*
weather-beaten ['weðə,bi:tn] ADJ [*skin, face*] curtido; [*wood*] deteriorado; [*stone*] erosionado • **the houses have a weather-beaten look** en las casas se nota el efecto de los elementos
weatherboard ['weðəbɔ:d] N tabla *f* de chilla • **~ house** (*US*) casa *f* de madera
weather-bound ['weðəbaʊnd] ADJ bloqueado por el mal tiempo
weathercast ['weðə,kɑ:st] N (*US*) pronóstico *m* del tiempo, boletín *m* meteorológico
weathercaster ['weðə,kɑ:stəʳ] N (*US*) meteorólogo/a *m/f*
weathercock ['weðəkɒk] N veleta *f*
weathered ['weðəd] ADJ [*rocks*] erosionado; [*skin, face*] curtido; [*wood*] curado, maduro
weathering ['weðərɪŋ] N (*Geol*) erosión *f*
weatherman ['weðəmæn] N (PL: **weathermen**) hombre *m* del tiempo
weatherproof ['weðəpru:f] ADJ [*building*] impermeabilizado; [*clothing*] impermeable, impermeabilizado
VT impermeabilizar
weatherwise ['weðə,waɪz] ADV en lo que se refiere al tiempo
weatherwoman ['weðə,wʊmən] (PL: **weatherwomen**) N mujer *f* del tiempo
weave [wi:v] (VB: PT: **wove**, PP: **woven**) N tejido *m*
VT **1** (*lit*) [+ *fabric, basket*] tejer
2 (*fig*) [+ *story*] urdir • **he wove a story round these experiences** urdió una historia con estas experiencias • **he wove these details into the story** entretejó *or* intercaló estos detalles en el cuento
3 (PT: **weaved** *or* **wove**, PP: **weaved** *or* **woven**) (= *zigzag*) • **to ~ one's way through the crowd** abrirse paso entre la multitud • **he ~d** *or* **wove his way to the bathroom** fue hasta el baño haciendo eses
VI **1** (*lit*) tejer
2 (PT, PP: **weaved**) (*fig*) (= *move in and out*) zigzaguear • **he ~s from side to side, trying to dodge his opponent** va zigzagueando *or* se mueve de lado a lado intentando esquivar a su rival • **the motorbike was weaving in and out of the traffic** la motocicleta zigzagueaba *or* se abría paso entre los coches • **the road ~s about a lot** el camino tiene muchas curvas, el camino serpentea mucho (*liter*) • IDIOM: • **to get weaving**† poner manos a la obra • **let's get weaving!** ¡pongamos manos a la obra!
weaver ['wi:vəʳ] N tejedor(a) *m/f*
weaving ['wi:vɪŋ] N tejido *m* • **basket ~** cestería *f*
CPD ▸ **weaving machine** telar *m* ▸ **weaving mill** tejeduría *f*
web [web] N **1** [*of spider*] telaraña *f*
2 (= *fabric*) tela *f*, tejido *m*
3 (*between toes*) membrana *f*
4 (= *network*) red *f* • **a complex web of relationships** una complicada maraña *or* red de relaciones • **a web of intrigue** una red *or* un tejido de intrigas • **a web of deceit/lies** una maraña de engaños/mentiras
5* (*also* **Web**) (*Internet*) • **the web** el *or* la web
CPD ▸ **web address** dirección *f* de Internet ▸ **web browser** navegador *m* de Internet ▸ **web feet** = webbed feet ▸ **web page** página *f* web ▸ **web ring, webring** (*Internet*) anillo *m* web, webring *m* ▸ **web surfer** internauta *mf*, cibernauta *mf*
webbed [webd] ADJ palmeado
CPD ▸ **webbed feet** • **to have ~ feet** [*animal*] tener (los) pies palmeados
webbing ['webɪŋ] N (= *material*) cincha *f*; [*of chair*] cinchas *fpl*
CPD ▸ **webbing belt** pretina *f* de reps
webcam ['webkæm] N webcam *f*
webcast ['webkɑ:st] N transmisión *f* por Internet
web-footed [,web'fʊtɪd] ADJ palmípedo
webinar ['webɪnɑ:ʳ] N seminario *m* web, webinario *m*
weblog ['weblɒg] N weblog *m*
weblogging ['weblɒgɪŋ] N blogueo *m*, weblogging *m*
webmail ['webmeɪl] N correo *m* web
webmaster ['webmɑ:stəʳ] N administrador(a) *m/f* de web
website ['websaɪt] N web site *m*, sitio *m* web
CPD ▸ **website designer** diseñador(a) *m/f* de páginas web
webspace ['webspeɪs] N espacio *m* disponible en la Red *or* el Web
webzine ['webzi:n] N (*Internet*) revista *f* electrónica, revista *f* digital
wed [wed] (*frm*) VT • **to wed sb** [*bride, bridegroom*] desposarse con algn, casarse con algn; [*priest*] desposar a algn, casar a algn
VI† desposarse, casarse
we'd [wi:d] = **we would, we had**
Wed. ABBR (= **Wednesday**) miérc.
wedded ['wedɪd] ADJ **1** (*frm*) [*wife, husband*] desposado, casado; [*bliss, life*] conyugal • **his lawful ~ wife** su legítima esposa
2 (*fig*) • **to be ~ to** (= *linked to*) estar ligado *or* unido a • **to be ~ to an idea** [*person*] aferrarse *or* estar aferrado a una idea • **she's ~ to her work** está casada con su trabajo
wedding ['wedɪŋ] N boda *f*, casamiento *m* • **silver/ruby ~** bodas de plata/de rubí • **to have a church ~** casarse por la iglesia • **civil ~** boda *f* civil • **to have a civil ~** casarse por lo civil • **to have a quiet ~**

casarse en la intimidad
CPD ▸ **wedding anniversary** aniversario *m* de boda ▸ **wedding band** = **wedding ring** ▸ **wedding banquet** banquete *m* de boda(s) ▸ **wedding breakfast** (*frm*) banquete *m* de boda(s) ▸ **wedding cake** tarta *f or* pastel *m* de boda ▸ **wedding day** día *m* de la boda • **on her ~ day** el día de su boda ▸ **wedding dress** traje *m* de novia ▸ **wedding feast** banquete *m* de boda(s) ▸ **wedding invitation** invitación *f* de boda ▸ **wedding march** marcha *f* nupcial ▸ **wedding night** noche *f* de bodas ▸ **wedding present** regalo *m* de boda ▸ **wedding reception** banquete *m* de bodas ▸ **wedding ring** alianza *f*, anillo *m* de boda ▸ **wedding service** boda *f*, ceremonia *f* nupcial; ▹ BEST MAN

wedge [wedʒ] N **1** (*for keeping in position*) cuña *f*, calza *f* • **to drive a ~ between two people** abrir una brecha entre dos personas • IDIOM: • **this is the thin end of the ~** esto puede ser el principio de muchos males
2 (= *piece*) [*of cheese, cake*] porción *f*, pedazo *m* (grande)
3 (*Golf*) wedge *m*, cucharilla *f*
4 (= *shoe*) zapato *m* de cuña
VT • **to ~ sth in place** asegurar algo • **to ~ a door open** mantener abierta una puerta con una cuña *or* una calza • **I was ~d between two other passengers** me estuve apretado *or* inmovilizado entre otros dos pasajeros • **it's ~d** no se puede mover
CPD ▸ **wedge heel** (= *heel*) tacón *m* de cuña; (= *shoe*) zapato *m* de cuña
▸ **wedge in** VT + ADV • **the car was ~d in between two lorries** el coche quedó encajado entre dos camiones • **a short documentary ~d in between sports programmes** un documental corto encasillado entre programas deportivos

wedge-heeled shoes ['wedʒhiːld'ʃuːz] NPL zapatos *mpl* de cuña

wedge-shaped ['wedʒʃeɪpt] ADJ en forma de cuña

wedlock ['wedlɒk] N (*frm*) matrimonio *m* • **to be born out of ~** nacer fuera del matrimonio

Wednesday ['wenzdeɪ] N miércoles *m inv*; ▹ Tuesday

wee[1]* [wiː] ADJ (COMPAR: **weer**, SUPERL: **weest**) (*Scot*) pequeñito, chiquito (*LAm*) • **I was a wee boy when it happened** era pequeñito cuando ocurrió • **a wee bit** (= *small amount*) un poquitín, un poquito • **I'm a wee bit worried** estoy un poco inquieto • **poor wee thing!** ¡pobrecito! • **we were up till the wee hours (of the morning)** *or* **the wee small hours** no nos acostamos hasta las altas horas de la madrugada

wee[2]* [wiː] N pipí* *m* • **to (have a) wee** hacer pipí* • **I need a wee** tengo que hacer pipí*
VI hacer pipí*

weed [wiːd] N **1** mala hierba *f*, hierbajo *m*; (= *waterweed*) alga *f* • **the garden was full of ~s** el jardín estaba lleno de malas hierbas *or* hierbajos
2* (= *person*) pelele* *m*
3 • **the ~*** (*hum*) (= *tobacco*) el tabaco
4* (= *marihuana*) hierba* *f*
5 • **(widow's) ~s** ropa *f* de luto
VT [+ *flowerbed*] desherbar
VI desherbar
▸ **weed out** VT + ADV [+ *plant*] arrancar; (*fig*) eliminar

weeding [wiːdɪŋ] N • **to do the ~** desherbar

weedkiller ['wiːd,kɪləʳ] N herbicida *m*

weedy ['wiːdɪ] ADJ (COMPAR: **weedier**, SUPERL: **weediest**) **1** [*ground*] lleno de malas hierbas *or* hierbajos
2 (*Brit**) (*pej*) (= *scrawny*) [*person*] debilucho*, desmirriado*, enclenque

week [wiːk] N semana *f* • **allow four ~s for delivery** la entrega se realiza dentro de cuatro semanas • **twice a ~** dos veces a la semana • **this day ~** • **a ~ today** de hoy en ocho días, dentro de ocho días • **tomorrow ~** de mañana en ocho días • **Tuesday ~** • **a ~ on Tuesday** del martes en ocho días, este martes no, el otro • **in a ~ or so** dentro de una semana • **in the middle of the ~** a mitad de semana • **I don't have time during the ~** entre semana no tengo tiempo • **it changes from ~ to ~** esto cambia cada semana • **~ in, ~ out** semana tras semana • **I haven't seen her for** *or* **in ~s** hace tiempo que no la veo • IDIOM: • **to knock sb into the middle of next ~*** dar a algn un golpe que le pone en órbita; ▹ working

weekday ['wiːkdeɪ] N día *m* laborable • **on a ~** • **on ~s** entre semana • **I go every ~ morning** entre semana voy todas las mañanas

weekend ['wiːk'end] N **1** fin *m* de semana • **to stay over the ~** pasar el fin de semana • **a long ~** un puente • **to take a long ~** • **make a long ~ of it** hacer puente
2 (*as adv*) • **they are away ~s** los fines de semana se van fuera
VI pasar el fin de semana
CPD [*cottage, trip, visit*] de fin de semana ▸ **weekend case** maletín *m* de viaje ▸ **weekend return** *billete de ida y vuelta para el fin de semana*

weekender [,wiːk'endəʳ] N *persona que va a pasar solamente el fin de semana*

weekly ['wiːklɪ] ADJ semanal
ADV semanalmente, cada semana • **they meet ~** se reúnen semanalmente *or* cada semana • **I am paid ~** me pagan semanalmente *or* por semana • **£15 ~** 15 libras por semana • **twice/three times ~** dos/tres veces por semana *or* a la semana • **the novel was published ~ in instalments** la novela se publicó en fascículos semanales
N (= *magazine*) semanario *m*

weeknight ['wiːknaɪt] N noche *f* de entresemana

weenie* ['wiːnɪ] N (*US*) = **wienie**

weeny* ['wiːnɪ] ADJ chiquitito*, minúsculo

weeny-bopper* ['wiːnɪ'bɒpəʳ] N doceañera *f* (aficionada de la música pop)

weep [wiːp] (VB: PT, PP: **wept**) VI **1** (= *cry*) llorar • **to ~ for joy** llorar de alegría • **to ~ for sb** llorar a algn • **to ~ for one's sins** llorar sus pecados • **to ~ to see sth** llorar al ver algo • **I could have wept** era para desesperarse
2 (*Med*) [*wound*] supurar
VT [+ *tears*] llorar
N • **to have a good ~** llorar a lágrima viva

weeping ['wiːpɪŋ] N (= *crying*) llanto *m*
ADJ lloroso
CPD ▸ **weeping willow** sauce *m* llorón

weepy ['wiːpɪ] ADJ **1** (= *tearful*) [*person*] llorón; [*eyes*] lloroso • **to feel ~** sentir *or* tener ganas de llorar • **to get** *or* **become ~ (about sth)** ponerse a llorar (por algo)
2* (= *sentimental*) [*film, novel, song*] lacrimógeno
N* (= *film*) película *f* lacrimógena, melodrama *m*; (= *novel*) novela *f* lacrimógena

weever ['wiːvəʳ] N peje *m* araña

weevil ['wiːvl] N gorgojo *m*

wee-wee* ['wiːwiː] N pipí* *m*
VI hacer pipí*

w.e.f. ABBR = **with effect from**

weft [weft] N **1** (*lit*) trama *f*
2 (*fig*) red *f*

weigh [weɪ] VT **1** (= *measure weight of*) pesar • **to ~ o.s.** pesarse
2 (= *consider*) [+ *evidence, options, risks*] sopesar, considerar • **the advantages of surgery have to be ~ed against possible risks** las ventajas de la cirugía se tienen que contraponer a los posibles riesgos • **to ~ the pros and cons (of sth)** sopesar *or* considerar los pros y los contras (de algo); ▹ **word**
3 • **to ~ anchor** levar anclas
VI **1** (= *tip the scales at*) pesar • **it ~s four kilos** pesa cuatro kilos • **how much** *or* **what do you ~?** ¿cuánto pesas? • **this ~s a ton!*** ¡esto pesa un quintal!*
2 (*fig*) **a** (= *be influential*) influir • **to ~ against sth/sb** ser un factor en contra de algo/algn • **there are many factors ~ing against the meeting happening** hay muchos factores en contra de que tenga lugar la reunión • **to ~ in favour of sth/sb** ser un factor a favor de algo/algn, inclinar la balanza a favor de algo/algn • **all these factors will ~ heavily with voters** todos estos factores influirán mucho en los votantes
b (= *be a burden*) • **to ~ on sb** agobiar a algn • **her absence began to ~ on me** su ausencia comenzó a agobiarme • **to ~ on sb's conscience** pesar sobre la conciencia de algn • **it ~s (heavily) on her mind** le preocupa (mucho) • **eat something that won't ~ on your stomach** come algo que no te resulte pesado al estómago
▸ **weigh down** VT + ADV **1** (*lit*) **a** (= *hold down*) sujetar (con un peso/una piedra *etc*)
b (= *encumber*) • **don't take anything with you that will ~ you down** no te lleves nada que te suponga demasiado peso • **she was ~ed down with parcels** iba muy cargada de paquetes • **a branch ~ed down with fruit** una rama muy cargada de fruta
2 (*fig*) agobiar, abrumar (*more liter*) • **to be ~ed down with** *or* **by sorrow** estar abrumado por la pena • **he felt ~ed down with** *or* **by responsibilities** se sentía agobiado por las responsabilidades • **I was ~ed down by guilt** me pesaba el sentimiento de culpabilidad • **the government is ~ed down with** *or* **by debt** el gobierno está cargado de deudas
VI + ADV • **to ~ down on sb** agobiar a algn, abrumar a algn (*more liter*) • **sorrow ~ed down on her** la pena la abrumaba
▸ **weigh in** VI + ADV **1** [*boxer, jockey*] pesarse • **to ~ in at 65 kilos** pesar 65 kilos
2 (*at airport desk*) facturar el equipaje
3 (= *contribute*) intervenir • **he ~ed in with his opinion** intervino con *or* expresando su opinión • **he ~ed in with the argument that …** intervino afirmando que …
VT + ADV **1** [+ *boxer, jockey*] pesar
2 [+ *luggage*] pesar, facturar
▸ **weigh out** VT + ADV [+ *goods, ingredients, kilo*] pesar
▸ **weigh up** (*esp Brit*) VT + ADV [+ *situation, risks, alternatives, evidence*] sopesar, considerar; [+ *person*] sondear, tantear • **we looked at each other, ~ing each other up** nos miramos, sondeándonos *or* tanteándonos el uno al otro • **I'm ~ing up whether to go or not** estoy considerando si ir o no

weighbridge ['weɪbrɪdʒ] N báscula-puente *f*, báscula *f* de puente

weigh-in ['weɪɪn] N pesaje *m*

weighing machine ['weɪɪŋmə,ʃiːn] N báscula *f*

weighing scales ['weɪɪŋ,skeɪlz] NPL balanza *fsing*

weight [weɪt] N **1** (= *heaviness*) peso *m* • **sold by ~** vendido a peso • **to gain ~** engordar, ganar peso • **a package three kilos in ~** un paquete que pesa tres kilos, un paquete de tres kilos • **to lose ~** adelgazar, perder peso

• **to put on ~** engordar, ganar peso • **the fence couldn't take his ~ and collapsed** la valla no aguantó su peso y se vino abajo • **to take the ~ off one's feet** sentarse a descansar • IDIOMS: • **to chuck** *or* **throw one's ~ about*** ir de sargento* • **to throw one's ~ behind sb** apoyar a algn con toda su fuerza • **the government is throwing its ~ behind the reforms** el gobierno está apoyando con toda su fuerza las reformas • **it is worth its ~ in gold** vale su peso en oro • **that's a ~ off my mind** eso me quita un peso de encima • **he doesn't pull his ~** no hace su parte *or* lo que le corresponde
2 (*in clock, for scales*) pesa *f*; (= *heavy object*) peso *m* • **~s and measures** pesas *fpl* y medidas • **the doctor has forbidden me to lift heavy ~s** el médico me ha prohibido levantar peso
3 (*fig*) (= *importance*) peso *m* • **these are arguments of some ~** son argumentos de cierto peso • **those arguments carry great ~ with the minister** esos argumentos influyen poderosamente en el ministro • **those arguments carry no ~ with the minister** esos argumentos no influyen en el ministro • **they won by sheer ~ of numbers** ganaron simplemente porque eran más • **to give due ~ to sth** dar la debida importancia a algo • **to lend ~ to sth** darle más peso a algo
(VT) (= *add weight to*) cargar, dar peso a; (= *hold down*) sujetar con un peso
(CPD) ▸ **weight gain** aumento *m* de peso ▸ **weight limit** límite *m* de peso ▸ **weight loss** pérdida *f* de peso ▸ **weight problem** • **to have a ~ problem** tener problemas de peso ▸ **weight training** entrenamiento *m* con pesas ▸ **weight watcher** persona *f* que vigila el peso *or* cuida la línea

▸ **weight down** (VT + ADV) sujetar con un peso/una piedra *etc*

weighted [ˈweɪtɪd] (ADJ) [*clothing, object*] con peso • **~ average** media *f* ponderada • **~ index** índice *m* compensado • **to be ~ in favour of sb** favorecer a algn • **to be ~ against sb** perjudicar a algn

weightiness [ˈweɪtɪnɪs] (N) **1** (*lit*) peso *m*
2 (*fig*) [*of matter, problem*] gravedad *f*; [*of argument, reason*] peso *m*, importancia *f*

weighting [ˈweɪtɪŋ] (N) **1** (*on salary*) plus *m* (salarial) por coste de vida • **London ~** plus *m* (salarial) por residir en Londres
2 (*Scol*) factor *m* de valoración
3 (*Statistics*) ponderación *f*

weightless [ˈweɪtlɪs] (ADJ) ingrávido

weightlessness [ˈweɪtlɪsnɪs] (N) ingravidez *f*

weightlifter [ˈweɪtˌlɪftəʳ] (N) levantador(a) *m/f* de pesas, halterófilo/a *m/f*

weightlifting [ˈweɪtˌlɪftɪŋ] (N) levantamiento *m* de pesas, halterofilia *f*

weight-train [ˈweɪtˌtreɪn] (VI) entrenar con pesas

weighty [ˈweɪtɪ] (ADJ) (COMPAR: **weightier**, SUPERL: **weightiest**) **1** (*lit*) [*load*] pesado • **a ~ tome** *or* **volume** un tomo de peso
2 (*fig*) [*matter, problem*] grave; [*argument, reason*] importante, de peso; [*burden*] pesado; [*responsibility*] grande

weir [wɪəʳ] (N) **1** (= *dam*) presa *f*
2 (= *fish trap*) encañizada *f*, cañal *m*

weird [wɪəd] (ADJ) (COMPAR: **weirder**, SUPERL: **weirdest**) raro, extraño • **the ~ thing is that …** lo raro es que … • **all sorts of ~ and wonderful things** todo tipo de cosas extraordinarias

weirdly [ˈwɪədlɪ] (ADV) (= *strange as it may seem*) extrañamente • **it was ~ quiet** reinaba una extraña calma • **he grunted ~** gruñó de una manera rara *or* extraña • **~ enough …** por raro *or* extraño que parezca …

weirdness [ˈwɪədnɪs] (N) rareza *f*, extrañeza *f*

weirdo* [ˈwɪədəʊ] (N) persona *f* rara

welch [welʃ] (VI) = **welsh**

welcome [ˈwelkəm] (VT) (= *receive gladly*) [+ *person*] dar la bienvenida a; [+ *news*] alegrarse de • **he ~d me in** me dio la bienvenida al entrar • **her marriage was not ~d by the family** su matrimonio no fue bien recibido en la familia • **we'd ~ your suggestions** nos alegraría recibir sus sugerencias • IDIOM: • **to ~ sb with open arms** recibir a algn con los brazos abiertos
(N) bienvenida *f*, recibimiento *m* • **to give sb a warm/frosty ~** dar a algn una calurosa/fría bienvenida, dar a algn un caluroso/frío recibimiento • **let's give a warm ~ to Ed Lilly!** ¡demos una calurosa bienvenida a Ed Lilly! • **to bid sb ~** (*frm*) dar la bienvenida a algn; ▷ **outstay, overstay**
(ADJ) **1** [*person, guest, visitor*] bienvenido, bien recibido • **everyone is ~** todo el mundo es bienvenido *or* bien recibido • **he's not ~ here any more** aquí ya no es bienvenido • **you're ~** (*esp US*) (*in reply to thanks*) de nada, no hay de qué • **you're ~ to it!** (*iro*) ¡te lo puedes quedar! • **I didn't feel very ~** no me sentí muy bien recibido • **to make sb ~** hacer que algn se sienta acogido • **you're ~ to visit any time** puedes venir cuando quieras • **you're ~ to try** puedes probar si quieres • **you're ~ to use my car** puedes usar mi coche con toda libertad, el coche está a tu disposición • IDIOM: • **to roll** *or* **put out the ~ mat for sb** dar un recibimiento de reyes a algn
2 (= *acceptable*) [*decision*] bienvenido • **the recent changes are very ~** los recientes cambios son muy bienvenidos • **a cup of tea is always ~** una taza de té siempre se agradece • **to be ~ news** ser una noticia grata • **shelters provide ~ relief from the sun and flies** los refugios proporcionan un grato alivio del sol y de las moscas • **the bags of flour were a ~ sight to the refugees** los refugiados recibieron con alegría las bolsas de harina
(EXCL) • **~!** ¡bienvenido! • **~ back!** ¡bienvenido! • **~ home!** ¡bienvenido a casa! • **~ to Scotland!** ¡bienvenido a Escocia!

▸ **welcome back** (VT + ADV) • **to ~ sb back** dar una buena acogida a algn cuando regresa; ▷ **welcome**

welcoming [ˈwelkəmɪŋ] (ADJ) **1** [*smile*] amable, cordial; [*place, atmosphere*] acogedor • **to be ~ to sb** ser acogedor *or* cordial con algn
2 [*ceremony, banquet, speech*] de bienvenida • **~ party** *or* **committee** comité *m* de bienvenida

weld [weld] (N) soldadura *f*
(VT) (*Tech*) soldar • **the hull is ~ed throughout** el casco es totalmente soldado • **to ~ together** (*lit*) soldar; (*fig*) unir, unificar • **to ~ parts together** soldar unas piezas • **we must ~ them together into a new body** hemos de unirlos *or* unificarlos para formar un nuevo organismo
(VI) soldarse

welder [ˈweldəʳ] (N) soldador(a) *m/f*

welding [ˈweldɪŋ] (N) soldadura *f*
(CPD) [*process*] de soldar, soldador ▸ **welding torch** soplete *m* soldador

welfare [ˈwelfɛəʳ] (N) **1** (= *well-being*) bienestar *m* • **physical/spiritual ~** bienestar físico/espiritual • **you've got to think about the ~ of the children** tienes que pensar en el bienestar de los niños • **animal ~** la protección de los animales • **child ~** la protección a *or* de la infancia
2 (= *social aid*) asistencia *f* social • **to be on ~** recibir asistencia social • **to live on ~** vivir a cargo de la asistencia social
(CPD) [*programme, provision*] de asistencia social ▸ **welfare centre, welfare center** (US) centro *m* de asistencia social ▸ **welfare check** (US) cheque *m* social ▸ **welfare hotel** (US) albergue *m* social ▸ **welfare mother** *madre que recibe asistencia social* ▸ **welfare officer** asistente *mf* social ▸ **welfare organization** organización *f* de asistencia social • **animal ~ organization** una organización para la protección de los animales ▸ **welfare payments** prestaciones *fpl* sociales ▸ **welfare services** asistencia *fsing* social ▸ **welfare state** estado *m* de bienestar social ▸ **welfare work** trabajos *mpl* de asistencia social ▸ **welfare worker** asistente *mf* social

Welfarism [ˈwelfɛərɪzəm] (N) (US) *teoría y práctica de la protección de la salud y del bienestar públicos*

well¹ [wel] (N) **1** (= *bore*) (*for water*) pozo *m*, fuente *f*; (*for oil*) pozo *m* • **to sink a ~** perforar un pozo
2 [*of stairs*] hueco *m*, caja *f*
3 (*in auditorium*) estrado *m*
(VI) (*also* **well out, well up**) brotar, manar

well² [wel] (COMPAR: **better**, SUPERL: **best**)
(ADV) **1** (= *in a good manner*) bien • **I remember it ~** lo recuerdo bien • **I know the place ~** conozco bien el lugar • **(and) ~ I know it!** ¡(y) bien que lo sé! • **to eat/live ~** comer/vivir bien • **he sings as ~ as she does** canta tan bien como ella • **as ~ as he could** lo mejor que pudo • **to do ~ at school** sacar buenas notas en el colegio • **to do ~ in an exam** sacar buena nota en un examen • **the patient is doing ~** el paciente evoluciona bien • **you would do ~ to think seriously about our offer** le convendría considerar seriamente nuestra oferta • **you did ~ to come at once** hizo bien en venir enseguida • **~ done!** ¡bien hecho! • **to go ~** ir bien • **everything is going ~** todo va bien • **~ and good** muy bien • **~ played!** (*Sport*) ¡bien hecho! • **to speak ~ of sb** hablar bien de algn • **to think ~ of sb** tener una buena opinión de algn • **he is ~ thought of here** aquí se le estima mucho
2 (= *thoroughly, considerably*) **a** bien • **it was ~ deserved** estuvo bien merecido • **he's ~ away*** (= *drunk*) está borracho perdido • **to be ~ in with sb** llevarse muy bien con algn • **it continued ~ into 1996** siguió hasta bien entrado 1996 • **he is ~ over** *or* **past fifty** tiene cincuenta y muchos años • **~ over a thousand** muchos más de mil, los mil bien pasados • **it's ~ past ten o'clock** son las diez y mucho • **she knows you too ~ to think that** te conoce demasiado bien para pensar eso de ti • **she loved him too ~** lo quería demasiado • **as we know all** *or* **only too ~** como sabemos perfectamente • **~ and truly** (*esp Brit*) de verdad, realmente • **we got ~ and truly wet** nos mojamos de verdad • **to wish sb ~** desear todo lo mejor a algn • **it was ~ worth the trouble** realmente valió la pena
b • **~ dodgy/annoyed‡** bien chungo*/enfadado
3 (= *probably, reasonably*) • **you may ~ be surprised to learn that …** puede que te sorprenda mucho saber que … • **it may ~ be that …** es muy posible que (+ *subjun*) • **they may ~ be lying** es muy posible que mientan • **we may as ~ begin now** ya podemos empezar, ¿no? • **you might as ~ tell me the truth** más valdría decirme la verdad • **"shall I go?" — "you may** *or* **might as ~"** "¿voy?" — "por qué no" • **we might (just) as ~ have stayed at home** para lo que hemos hecho, nos podíamos haber quedado en casa • **she**

W

cried, as ~ she might lloró, y con razón • **you may ~ ask!** ¡buena pregunta! • **I couldn't very ~ leave** me resultaba imposible marcharme
4 (*in set expressions*) **a** • **as ~** (= *in addition*) también • **I'll take those as ~** me llevo esos también • **and it rained as ~!** ¡y además llovió! • **by night as ~ as by day** tanto de noche como de día • **as ~ as his dog he has two rabbits** además de un perro tiene dos conejos • **I had Paul with me as ~ as Lucy** Paul estaba conmigo, así como Lucy *or* además de Lucy • **could you manage to eat mine as ~ as yours?** ¿podrías comerte el mío y el tuyo? • **all sorts of people, rich as ~ as poor** gente de toda clase, tanto rica como pobre
b • **to leave ~ alone**: • **my advice is to leave ~ alone** te aconsejo que no te metas • **this sort of wound is best left ~ alone** lo mejor es ni tocar este tipo de herida
ADJ **1** (= *healthy*) bien • **I'm very ~ thank you** estoy muy bien, gracias • **I hope you're ~** espero que te encuentres bien • **are you ~?** ¿qué tal estás? • **she's not been ~ lately** recientemente ha estado algo indispuesta • **to get ~** mejorarse • **get ~ soon!** ¡que te mejores!
2 (= *acceptable, satisfactory*) bien • **that's all very ~, but ...** todo eso está muy bien, pero ... • **it** *or* **we would be ~ to start early** mejor si salimos temprano • **it would be as ~ to ask** más vale *or* valdría preguntar • **it's as ~ not to offend her** más te vale no ofenderla • **it would be just as ~ for you to stay** mejor si te quedas • **it's as ~ for you that nobody saw you** menos mal que nadie te vio • **it's just as ~ we asked** menos mal que preguntamos • PROVERB: • **all's ~ that ends ~** bien está lo que bien acaba
EXCL **1** (*introducing topic, resuming*) bueno • **~, it was like this** bueno, pues así ocurrió • **~, as I was saying ...** bueno, como iba diciendo • **~, that's that!** ¡bueno, asunto concluido!
2 (*expressing resignation*) • **~, if we must go, let's get going** bueno, si nos tenemos que ir, vayámonos • **~ then?** ¿y qué?
3 (*concessive, dismissive*) pues • **~, if you're worried, why don't you call her?** pues si estás tan preocupada ¿por qué no la llamas? • **~, I think she's a fool** pues yo pienso que es tonta
4 (*expressing relief*) • **~, thank goodness for that!** (pues) ¡gracias a Dios!
5 (*expressing surprise*) ¡vaya! • **~, what do you know!*** ¡anda, quién lo diría! • **~, who would have thought it!** ¡anda, quién lo diría! • **~, ~!** ¡vaya, vaya!

we'll [wi:l] = **we will, we shall**
well- [wel] PREFIX bien-
well-adjusted [ˌweləˈdʒʌstɪd] ADJ equilibrado
well-advised, well advised [ˌweləd'vaɪzd] ADJ [*action, decision*] acertado • **you would be well advised to attend** sería aconsejable que asistieses
well-aimed [ˌwel'eɪmd] ADJ certero
well-appointed [ˌweləˈpɔɪntɪd] ADJ bien amueblado
well-argued [ˌwel'ɑ:gju:d] ADJ razonado
well-assorted [ˌweləˈsɔ:tɪd] ADJ [*range, store*] bien surtido; [*couple*] bien combinado
well-attended [ˌweləˈtendɪd] ADJ muy concurrido
well-baby clinic [wel'beɪbɪklɪnɪk] N clínica *f* de revisión pediátrica
well-balanced [ˌwel'bælənst] ADJ bien equilibrado
well-behaved [ˌwelbɪ'heɪvd] ADJ que se porta bien
well-being ['welˌbi:ɪŋ] N bienestar *m*
well-born [ˌwel'bɔ:n] ADJ bien nacido
well-bred [ˌwel'bred] ADJ [*person*] educado, cortés; [*accent*] culto; [*animal*] de raza, pura sangre
well-brought-up [ˌwelˌbrɔ:t'ʌp] ADJ [*child*] educado
well-built [ˌwel'bɪlt] ADJ [*house*] de construcción sólida; [*person*] fornido
well-chosen [ˌwel'tʃəʊzn] ADJ [*remark, words*] acertado
well-connected, well connected [ˌwelkə'nektɪd] ADJ bien relacionado
well-cooked [ˌwel'kʊkt] ADJ (= *tasty*) bien preparado; (= *well-done*) muy hecho
well-defined [ˌweldɪ'faɪnd] ADJ bien definido
well-deserved [ˌweldɪ'zɜ:vd] ADJ merecido
well-designed [ˌweldɪ'zaɪnd] ADJ bien diseñado
well-developed [ˌweldɪ'veləpt] ADJ [*arm, muscle*] bien desarrollado; [*sense*] agudo, fino
well-disciplined [ˌwel'dɪsɪplɪnd] ADJ bien disciplinado
well-disposed [ˌweldɪs'pəʊzd] ADJ bien dispuesto (**to, towards** hacia)
well-documented [ˌwel'dɒkjʊˌmentɪd] ADJ documentado
well-dressed [ˌwel'drest] ADJ bien vestido
well-earned [ˌwel'ɜ:nd] ADJ merecido
well-educated [ˌwel'edjʊkeɪtɪd] ADJ instruido, culto
well-endowed [ˌwelɪn'daʊd] ADJ
1 [*institution*] bien dotado de fondos, con buena dotación monetaria
2* (*euph*) [*man, woman*] bien dotado, bien despachado*
well-equipped [ˌwelɪ'kwɪpt] ADJ bien equipado
well-established [ˌwelɪ'stæblɪʃt] ADJ (*gen*) sólidamente establecido; [*custom*] muy arraigado; [*firm*] (= *of long standing*) sólido; (= *with good reputation*) de buena reputación
well-favoured, well-favored (US) [ˌwel'feɪvəd] ADJ bien parecido
well-fed [ˌwel'fed] ADJ (*lit*) bien alimentado; (*in appearance*) regordete
well-fixed* [ˌwel'fɪkst] ADJ (US) • **to be well-fixed** nadar en la abundancia, estar boyante • **we're well-fixed for food** tenemos comida de sobra
well-formed [ˌwel'fɔ:md] ADJ (*Ling*) gramatical
well-formedness [ˌwel'fɔ:mdnɪs] N gramaticalidad *f*
well-founded [ˌwel'faʊndɪd] ADJ fundamentado
well-groomed [ˌwel'gru:md] ADJ acicalado
well-grown ['wel'grəʊn] ADJ grande, maduro, adulto
wellhead ['welhed] N fuente *f*, manantial *m*
well-heeled* [ˌwel'hi:ld] ADJ ricacho*
well-hung [ˌwel'hʌŋ] ADJ **1‡** [*man*] bien dotado, bien despachado*, con un buen paquete‡
2 (*Culin*) [*game*] bien manido
well-informed [ˌwelɪn'fɔ:md] ADJ bien informado, al corriente
Wellington ['welɪŋtən] N Wellington *m*
wellington ['welɪŋtən] N (*Brit*) (*also* **wellington boot**) bota *f* de goma
well-intentioned [ˌwelɪn'tenʃnd] ADJ [*person*] con buenas intenciones; [*act*] bienintencionado; [*lie*] piadoso
well-judged [ˌwel'dʒʌdʒd] ADJ bien calculado
well-kept [ˌwel'kept] ADJ [*secret,*] bien guardado; [*garden*] bien cuidado; [*house*] bien conservado
well-knit [ˌwel'nɪt] ADJ [*body*] robusto, fornido; [*scheme*] lógico, bien razonado; [*speech*] bien pensado, de estructura lógica
well-known [ˌwel'nəʊn] ADJ [*name, brand, person*] muy conocido, famoso • **it's a well-known fact that ...** • **it's well-known that ...** es bien sabido que ...
well-liked [ˌwel'laɪkt] ADJ querido
well-loved [ˌwel'lʌvd] ADJ muy querido, amado
well-made [ˌwel'meɪd] ADJ bien hecho, fuerte
well-managed [ˌwel'mænɪdʒd] ADJ bien administrado
well-man clinic [wel'mænklɪnɪk] N clínica *f* de salud (*para hombres*)
well-mannered [ˌwel'mænəd] ADJ educado, cortés
well-marked [ˌwel'mɑ:kt] ADJ bien marcado
well-matched [ˌwel'mætʃt] ADJ muy iguales
well-meaning [ˌwel'mi:nɪŋ] ADJ bienintencionado
well-meant [ˌwel'ment] ADJ bienintencionado
wellness ['welnəs] N (= *well-being*) bienestar *m*; (= *health*) salud *f*
well-nigh ['welnaɪ] ADV • **well-nigh impossible** casi imposible
well-nourished [ˌwel'nʌrɪʃt] ADJ bien alimentado
well-off [ˌwel'ɒf] ADJ **1** (*financially*) acomodado, pudiente • **the less well-off** las gentes menos pudientes
2 (*in circumstances*) • **she's well-off without him** está mejor sin él • **you don't know when you're well-off** no sabes los muchos beneficios que tienes
NPL • **the well-off** las clases acomodadas
well-oiled* [ˌwel'ɔɪld] ADJ hecho una cuba*
well-padded* [ˌwel'pædɪd] ADJ bien rellenito
well-paid [ˌwel'peɪd] ADJ bien pagado, bien retribuido
well-preserved [ˌwelprɪ'zɜ:vd] ADJ [*person*] bien conservado
well-proportioned [ˌwelprə'pɔ:ʃnd] ADJ bien proporcionado, de forma elegante; [*person*] de talle elegante
well-read [ˌwel'red] ADJ culto, instruido • **to be well-read in history** haber leído mucha historia, estar muy documentado en historia
well-respected [ˌwelrɪ'spektɪd] ADJ respetado, estimado
well-rounded [ˌwel'raʊndɪd] ADJ [*person*] polifacético; [*education*] equilibrado
well-spent [ˌwel'spent] ADJ bien empleado, fructuoso
well-spoken [ˌwel'spəʊkən] ADJ bienhablado, con acento culto
wellspring ['welˌsprɪŋ] N (*fig*) fuente *f*
well-stacked* [ˌwel'stækt] ADJ de buen tipo, curvilínea
well-stocked [ˌwel'stɒkt] ADJ bien surtido, bien provisto • **well-stocked shelves** estantes *mpl* llenos
well-thought-of [ˌwel'θɔ:təv] ADJ bien reputado, de buena reputación
well-thought-out [ˌwelθɔ:t'aʊt] ADJ bien planeado
well-thumbed [ˌwel'θʌmd] ADJ [*book*] muy usado, manoseado; [*pages*] manoseado
well-timed [ˌwel'taɪmd] ADJ oportuno
well-to-do [ˌweltə'du:] ADJ acomodado
NPL • **the well-to-do** las clases acomodadas
well-travelled, well-traveled (US) [ˌwel'trævld] ADJ [*person*] que ha viajado mucho, que ha visto mucho mundo

• **a well-travelled path** un camino muy trillado
well-tried [ˌwelˈtraɪd] (ADJ) [*method*] comprobado
well-trodden [ˌwelˈtrɒdn] (ADJ) trillado
• **a well-trodden path** un camino muy trillado
well-turned [ˌwelˈtɜːnd] (ADJ) elegante
• **a well-turned phrase** una frase elegante
• **a well-turned ankle** un tobillo bien formado
well-versed, **well versed** [ˌwelˈvɜːst] (ADJ)
• **to be well versed in sth** estar bien versado en algo
well-wisher [ˈwelˌwɪʃəʳ] (N) admirador(a) *m/f*
well-woman clinic [ˈwelwʊmənˌklɪnɪk] (N) clínica *f* de salud (*para mujeres*)
well-worn [ˌwelˈwɔːn] (ADJ) [*garment*] raído; [*path, cliché*] trillado
well-written [ˌwelˈrɪtn] (ADJ) bien escrito
welly* [ˈwelɪ] (N) (*Brit*) • **~ boots** • **wellies** botas *fpl* de goma
Welsh [welʃ] (ADJ) galés
(N) **1** (= *language*) galés *m*
2 • **the ~** (= *people*) los galeses
(CPD) ▸ **the Welsh Assembly** el parlamento galés ▸ **Welsh dresser** *aparador con estantes en la mitad de arriba* ▸ **Welsh rabbit**, **Welsh rarebit** pan *m* con queso tostado
welsh [welʃ] (VI) [*bookmaker*] largarse sin pagar* • **to ~ on a promise** no cumplir una promesa • **they ~ed on the agreement** no respetaron el acuerdo
Welshman [ˈwelʃmən] (N) (PL: **Welshmen**) galés *m*
Welshwoman [ˈwelʃˌwʊmən] (N) (PL: **Welshwomen**) galesa *f*
welt [welt] (N) **1** (= *weal*) verdugón *m*
2 [*of garment*] ribete *m*
3 [*of shoe*] vira *f*
(VT) **1** [+ *shoe*] poner vira a
2 (= *beat*) pegar, zurrar
welter [ˈweltəʳ] (N) confusión *f*, mezcla *f* confusa, mescolanza *f*, revoltijo *m* • **in a ~ of blood** en un mar de sangre
(VI) revolcarse • **to ~ in** estar bañado en, bañarse en
welterweight [ˈweltəweɪt] (N) wélter *m* • **light ~** wélter *m* ligero
wen [wen] (N) lobanillo *m*, quiste *m* sebáceo • **the Great Wen** el gran tumor (*Londres*)
wench†† [wentʃ] (N) moza *f*; (= *whore*) puta *f*
(VI) (*also* **go wenching**) putañear††, ir de fulanas
wend [wend] (VT) (*liter*) • **to ~ one's way to** enderezar sus pasos a • **to ~ one's way home** (*hum*) encaminarse a casa
Wendy house [ˈwendɪhaʊs] (N) (PL: **Wendy houses** [ˈwendɪhaʊzɪz]) (*Brit*) casa *f* de juguete (*suficientemente grande para jugar dentro*)
went [went] (PT) *of* **go**
wept [wept] (PT), (PP) *of* **weep**
we're [wɪəʳ] = **we are**
were [wɜːʳ] (PT) *of* **be**
weren't [wɜːnt] = **were not**
werewolf [ˈwɪəwʊlf] (N) (PL: **werewolves**) hombre *m* lobo
wert†† [wɜːt] (PT) *thou form of* **be**
Wesleyan [ˈwezlɪən] (ADJ) metodista
(N) metodista *mf*
Wesleyanism [ˈwezlɪənɪzəm] (N) metodismo *m*
west [west] (N) oeste *m*, occidente *m* • **the West** (*Pol*) el Oeste, (el) Occidente • **tales of the American West** cuentos *mpl* del Oeste americano • **in the ~ of the country** al oeste *or* en el oeste del país • **the wind is from the** *or* **in the ~** el viento sopla *or* viene del oeste • **to the ~ of** al oeste de
(ADJ) [*part, coast*] oeste, del oeste, occidental; [*wind*] del oeste
(ADV) (= *westward*) hacia el oeste; (= *in the west*) al oeste, en el oeste • **we were travelling ~** viajábamos hacia el oeste • **~ of the border** al oeste de la frontera • **it's ~ of London** está al oeste *or* en el oeste de Londres • IDIOM: • **to go ~*** [*object, machine*] cascarse*, estropearse; [*plan*] irse al garete; [*person*] estirar la pata*
(CPD) ▸ **West Africa** África *f* Occidental ▸ **the West Bank** Cisjordania *f* ▸ **West Berlin** (*Hist*) Berlín *m* Oeste ▸ **the West Country** (*Brit*) el West Country (*el sudoeste de Inglaterra, esp. los condados de Cornualles, Devon y Somerset*) ▸ **the West End** (*of London*) el West End (de Londres) (*zona del centro de Londres donde hay muchas tiendas y locales de ocio*) ▸ **West Germany** (*formerly*) Alemania *f* Occidental; ▹ **West German**, **West Indian** ▸ **West Indies** Antillas *fpl* ▸ **West Point** *academia militar de Estados Unidos* ▸ **West Virginia** Virginia *f* Occidental
westbound [ˈwestbaʊnd] (ADJ) [*traffic, carriageway*] con rumbo al oeste
westerly [ˈwestəlɪ] (ADJ) [*wind*] del oeste • **in a ~ direction** hacia el oeste, rumbo al oeste, en dirección oeste • **the most ~ point in Europe** el punto más occidental *or* más al oeste de Europa
(N) (= *wind*) viento *m* del oeste
western [ˈwestən] (ADJ) occidental
• **Western** (*Pol*) occidental, del Oeste • **the ~ part of the island** la parte occidental *or* oeste de la isla • **in ~ Spain** en la España occidental • **the ~ coast** la costa occidental *or* oeste
(N) (= *film*) western *m*, película *f* del oeste
(CPD) ▸ **Western Isles** (*Brit*) las Hébridas
westerner [ˈwestənəʳ] (N) habitante *mf* del Oeste; (*Pol etc*) occidental *mf*
westernization [ˈwestənaɪˈzeɪʃən] (N) occidentalización *f*
westernize [ˈwestənaɪz] (VT) occidentalizar
westernized [ˈwestənaɪzd] (ADJ) occidentalizado • **to become ~** occidentalizarse
westernmost [ˈwestənməʊst] (ADJ) más occidental, más al oeste • **the ~ point of Spain** el punto más occidental *or* más al oeste de España
west-facing [ˈwestˈfeɪsɪŋ] (ADJ) con cara al oeste, orientado hacia el oeste • **west-facing slope** vertiente *f* oeste
West German [ˌwestˈdʒɜːmən] (*formerly*)
(ADJ) de Alemania Occidental
(N) alemán/ana *m/f* (de Alemania Occidental)
West Indian [ˌwestˈɪndɪən] (ADJ) antillano
(N) antillano/a *m/f*
Westminster [ˈwestˌmɪnstəʳ] (N) (*Brit*) Westminster *m*

> **WESTMINSTER**
> **Westminster**, también llamado **City of Westminster**, es el distrito del centro de Londres que comprende el Parlamento (**Houses of Parliament**), la Abadía de Westminster (**Westminster Abbey**) y el Palacio de Buckingham (**Buckingham Palace**). Este nombre se usa también normalmente en los medios de comunicación para referirse al Parlamento o a los parlamentarios británicos.

west-northwest [ˌwestnɔːθˈwest] (N) oesnoroeste *m*, oesnorueste *m*
(ADJ) oesnoroeste, oesnorueste
(ADV) (= *toward west-northwest*) hacia el oesnoroeste *or* oesnorueste; [*situated*] al oesnoroeste *or* oesnorueste, en el oesnoroeste *or* oesnorueste
west-southwest [ˌwestsaʊθˈwest] (N) oesuroeste *m*, oesurueste *m*
(ADJ) oesuroeste, oesurueste
(ADV) (= *toward west-southwest*) hacia el oesuroeste *or* oesurueste; [*situated*] al oesuroeste *or* oesurueste, en el oesuroeste *or* oesurueste
westward [ˈwestwəd] (ADJ) [*movement, migration*] hacia el oeste, en dirección oeste
(ADV) hacia el oeste, en dirección oeste
westwards [ˈwestwədz] (ADV) (*esp Brit*) = **westward**
wet [wet] (ADJ) (COMPAR: **wetter**, SUPERL: **wettest**) **1** [*person, clothes, nappy, bed*] mojado; (= *sopping*) calado; [*paint, ink, plaster*] fresco • **the baby was wet** el niño se había hecho pis* • **"wet paint"** "recién pintado" • **to get wet** mojarse • **to get one's feet/shoes wet** mojarse los pies/zapatos • **to be soaking** *or* **wringing wet** estar chorreando • **to be wet through** estar empapado, estar calado • **the grass was wet with dew** la hierba estaba mojada de rocío • IDIOM: • **to be wet behind the ears*** estar verde*
2 (*from crying*) [*eyes*] lloroso, lleno de lágrimas; [*cheeks, face*] lleno de lágrimas • **her cheeks were wet with tears** las lágrimas le corrían por las mejillas
3 (= *rainy*) [*day, month, winter, climate*] lluvioso • **take a raincoat if it's wet** llévate un impermeable si llueve • **we've had a lot of wet weather** hemos tenido un tiempo muy lluvioso • **it's been very wet** ha llovido mucho • **the wet season** la estación lluviosa *or* de las lluvias
4* (*pej*) (= *feeble*) soso, blandengue; (*Brit*) (*Pol*) *término aplicado a los políticos conservadores de tendencias centristas, desdeñados por la parte más radicalmente conservadora del partido*
5 (*US*) (= *against prohibition*) antiprohibicionista
(N) **1** • **the wet** (= *rain, wet weather*) la lluvia • **the bike had been left out in the wet** habían dejado la bicicleta bajo la lluvia
2 (*Brit*) (*Pol**) *político conservador de tendencias centristas, desdeñado por la parte más radicalmente conservadora del partido*
(VT) **1** (= *make wet*) mojar • **to wet one's lips** humedecerse los labios • IDIOM: • **to wet one's whistle**† mojar el gaznate
2 (= *urinate on*) • **he's wet his trousers** se ha orinado en los pantalones, se ha hecho pis en los pantalones*, se ha meado en los pantalones‡ • **to wet the bed** orinarse en la cama, hacerse pis en la cama*, mearse en la cama‡ • **to wet o.s.** orinarse encima, hacerse pis encima*, mearse encima‡ • IDIOM: • **to wet o.s.*** (*with amusement*) mearse de risa‡; (*with terror*) mearse de miedo‡
(CPD) ▸ **wet blanket*** aguafiestas* *mf inv* ▸ **wet dream** polución *f* nocturna • **to have a wet dream** tener una polución nocturna, correrse dormido** ▸ **wet fish** (*Culin*) pescado *m* fresco • **he's a bit of a wet fish** (*fig*) es un poco soso ▸ **wet nurse** nodriza *f*, ama *f* de cría ▸ **wet suit** traje *m* isotérmico
wetback‡ [ˈwetbæk] (N) (*US*) inmigrante *mf* (mexicano) ilegal, espalda *mf* mojada
wether [ˈweðəʳ] (N) carnero *m* castrado
wetland [ˈwetlənd] (N) pantano *m*, zona *f* húmeda *or* acuosa • **~s** pantanos *mpl*, tierras *fpl* pantanosas
wet-look [ˈwetlʊk] (ADJ) [*material, jeans, boots*] con un acabado abrillantado
wetness [ˈwetnɪs] (N) [*of surface, road*] estado *m* mojado; [*of substance*] lo mojado; [*of weather*] lo lluvioso
wetting [ˈwetɪŋ] (N) • **to get a ~** mojarse, empaparse • **to give sb a ~** mojar *or* empapar a algn
WEU (N ABBR) (= **Western European Union**) UEO *f*

we've [wi:v] = **we have**

WFP (N ABBR) (= **World Food Programme**) PMA *m*

WFTU (N ABBR) (= **World Federation of Trade Unions**) FSM *f*

whack [wæk] (N) **1** (= *blow*) golpe *m* fuerte, porrazo *m* • **to give sb a ~** dar un golpe fuerte *or* un porrazo a algn • **to give sth a ~** golpear algo ruidosamente
2* (= *attempt*) • **to have a ~ at sth** intentar algo, probar algo • **let's have a ~ (at it)** probemos, intentemos
3* (= *share*) parte *f*, porción *f* • **you'll get your ~** recibirás tu parte
4* • **the car does 200kph top ~** a toda máquina, el coche alcanza una velocidad de 200km/h
5 • **out of ~** (*US**) fastidiado
(EXCL) • **~!** ¡zas!
(VT) **1** (= *beat*) golpear, aporrear; (= *defeat*) dar una paliza a* • **he ~ed me with a cane** me dio con una palmeta
2 (*fig*) • **the problem has me ~ed** el problema me trae perplejo • **we've got the problem ~ed at last** por fin hemos resuelto el problema

whacked* ['wækt] (ADJ) (*Brit*) • **to be ~** estar agotado, estar hecho polvo*

whacking ['wækɪŋ] (ADJ) (*esp Brit**) (*also* **whacking great**) grandote*, enorme • **a ~ (great) book** un tocho de libro*
(N) zurra *f* • **to give sb a ~** zurrar a algn, pegar a algn

whacky* ['wækɪ] (ADJ) (*US*) = **wacky**

whale [weɪl] (N) (PL: **whales** *or* **whale**) ballena *f* • **IDIOMS**: • **a ~ of a difference*** una enorme diferencia • **to have a ~ of a time*** pasarlo bomba *or* (*S. Cone*) regio
(CPD) ▸ **whale oil** aceite *m* de ballena ▸ **whale watching** avistaje *m* de ballenas • **to go ~ watching** ir a avistar ballenas

whalebone ['weɪlbəʊn] (N) barba *f* de ballena; (*in haberdashery*) ballena *f*

whaler ['weɪləʳ] (N) (= *person, ship*) ballenero *m*

whaling ['weɪlɪŋ] (N) pesca *f* de ballenas • **to go ~** ir a pescar ballenas
(CPD) ▸ **whaling ship** ballenero *m* ▸ **whaling station** estación *f* ballenera

wham [wæm] (EXCL) • **~!** ¡zas!
(N) golpe *m* resonante
(VT) golpear de modo resonante
(VI) • **to ~ against/into sth** chocar ruidosamente con algo

whammy* ['wæmɪ] (N) (*US*) mala sombra *f*, mala suerte *f*, mala pata *f*; ▹ **double**

whang [wæŋ] (N) golpe *m* resonante
(VT) golpear de modo resonante
(VI) • **to ~ against/into sth** chocar ruidosamente con algo

wharf [wɔ:f] (N) (PL: **wharfs** *or* **wharves** [wɔ:vz]) muelle *m*, embarcadero *m* • **ex ~** franco en el muelle • **price ex ~** precio *m* franco de muelle

wharfage ['wɔ:fɪdʒ] (N) muellaje *m*

---

what [wɒt]

PRONOUN
ADJECTIVE
EXCLAMATION

(PRONOUN)

1 (*in direct questions*) **a**

*In direct questions, **what** can generally be translated by **qué** with an accent:*

qué • **~ do you want now?** ¿qué quieres ahora? • **~'s in here?** ¿qué hay aquí dentro? • **~ is it now?** y ahora ¿qué? • **~ does he owe his success to?** • **to ~ does he owe his success?** (*frm*) ¿a qué debe su éxito? • **~'s a tractor, Daddy?** ¿qué es un tractor, papá? • **~ are capers?** ¿qué son las alcaparras?

*Only use **¿qué es...?/¿qué son...?** to translate **what is/are** when asking for a **definition**. In other contexts use **¿cuál es?/¿cuáles son?**:*

• **~'s the capital of Finland?** ¿cuál es la capital de Finlandia? • **~'s her telephone number?** ¿cuál es su número de teléfono? • **~ were the greatest problems?** ¿cuáles eran los mayores problemas?

*However, not all expressions with **what** should be translated literally. Some require **qué** used adjectivally:*

• **~ is the difference?** ¿qué diferencia hay? • **~ are your plans?** ¿qué planes tienes? • **~'s the Spanish for "pen"?** ¿cómo se dice "pen" en español? • **~'s your name?** ¿cómo te llamas?
b (= *how much*) cuánto • **~ will it cost?** ¿cuánto va a costar? • **~ does it weigh?** ¿cuánto pesa? • **~'s nine times five?** ¿cuánto es nueve por cinco?
c (= *what did you say*) cómo, qué • **~? I didn't catch that** ¿cómo? *or* ¿qué?, no he entendido eso • **~ did you say?** ¿cómo *or* qué dices?, ¿qué has dicho?, ¿qué dijiste? (*LAm*)
d (*Brit*†) (*as question tag*) verdad • **it's getting late, ~?** se está haciendo tarde ¿no? *or* ¿verdad?

2 (*in indirect questions*) **a**

*In most cases, translate the pronoun **what** using either **qué** with an accent or **lo que** without an accent:*

qué, lo que • **he asked her ~ she thought of it** le preguntó qué *or* lo que pensaba de ello • **I asked him ~ DNA was** le pregunté qué *or* lo que era el ADN

*Use **cuál era/cuáles son** etc instead of **lo que era/lo que son** etc if **what was/are** etc does not relate to a definition:*

• **she asked me ~ my hobbies were** me preguntó cuáles eran mis hobbys • **please explain ~ you saw** por favor, explique qué *or* lo que vio • **can you explain ~'s happening?** ¿me puedes explicar (qué es) lo que está pasando? • **he explained ~ it was** explicó qué era *or* lo que era • **do you know ~'s happening?** ¿sabes qué *or* lo que está pasando? • **I don't know ~'s happening** no sé qué está pasando, no sé (qué es) lo que está pasando • **tell me ~ happened** cuéntame qué *or* lo que ocurrió
b (= *how much*) cuánto • **he asked her ~ she had paid for it** le preguntó cuánto había pagado por ello

3 (*before an infinitive*) qué • **I don't know ~ to do** no sé qué hacer

4 (*relative use*) lo que • **~ I want is a cup of tea** lo que quiero es una taza de té • **it wasn't ~ I was expecting** no era lo que yo me esperaba • **do ~ you like** haz lo que quieras • **business isn't ~ it was** los negocios ya no son lo que eran • **I've no clothes except ~ I'm wearing** no tengo ropa, aparte de lo que llevo puesto • **I saw ~ happened** vi lo que pasó • **she told him ~ she thought of it** le dijo lo que pensaba de ello

5 (*in exclamations*) • **~ it is to be rich and famous!** ¡lo que es ser rico y famoso! • **PROVERB**: • **~'s done is done** lo hecho hecho está

6 (*in set expressions*)
and what have you *or* **what not*** y qué sé yo qué más, y qué sé yo cuántas cosas más
to give sb what for* regañar a algn
know what • **it was full of cream, jam, chocolate and I don't know ~** estaba lleno de nata, mermelada, chocolate y no sé cuántas cosas más • **you know ~? I think he's drunk** creo que está borracho, ¿sabes? • **I know ~, let's ring her up** se me ocurre una idea, vamos a llamarla por teléfono
to know what's what* saber cuántas son cinco*
or what?* • **do you want it or ~?** ¿lo quieres o qué? • **are you coming or ~?** entonces ¿vienes o no? • **I mean, is this sick, or ~?** vamos, que es de verdadero mal gusto, ¿o no? • **is this luxury or ~?** esto sí que es lujo, ¿eh?
say what you like, ... digas lo que digas, ..., se diga lo que se diga, ...
so what?* ¿y qué? • **so ~ if it does rain?** ¿y qué, si llueve? • **so ~ if he is gay?** ¿y qué (pasa) si es gay?, ¿y qué importa que sea gay?
(I'll) tell you what se me ocurre una idea, tengo una idea
what about • **~ about me?** y yo ¿qué? • **~ about next week?** ¿qué te parece la semana que viene? • **"your car ..." — "~ about it?"*** —tu coche ... —¿qué pasa con mi coche? • **~ about going to the cinema?** ¿qué tal si vamos al cine?, ¿y si vamos al cine? • **~ about lunch, shall we go out?** ¿y para comer? ¿salimos fuera? *or* ¿qué tal si salimos fuera? • **~ about people who haven't got cars?** ¿y la gente que no tiene coche?
what for? (= *why*) ¿por qué?; (= *to what purpose*) ¿para qué? • **~ are you doing that for?** ¿por *or* para qué haces eso? • **~'s that button for?** ¿para qué es ese botón?
what if ...? ¿y si ...? • **~ if this doesn't work out?** ¿y si esto no funciona? • **~ if he says no?** ¿y si dice que no?
what of • **but ~ of the political leaders?** pero, ¿y qué hay de los líderes políticos? • **~ of it?*** y eso ¿qué importa?
what's ... • **~'s surprising is that we hadn't heard of this before** lo sorprendente es que no nos habíamos enterado antes
what's it like? (*asking for description*) ¿cómo es?; (*asking for evaluation*) ¿qué tal es? • **~'s their new house like?** ¿cómo es su nueva casa? • **~'s his first novel like?** ¿qué tal es su primera novela? • **~ will the weather be like tomorrow?** ¿qué tal tiempo va a hacer mañana?
and what's more ... y, además, ...
what's that? (*asking about sth*) ¿qué es eso?; (= *what did you say?*) ¿qué has dicho? • **~'s that to you?*** ¿eso qué tiene que ver contigo?, ¿a ti qué te importa?*
what's worse • **and ~'s worse ...** y lo que es peor ...
what with • **~ with one thing and another** entre una cosa y otra • **~ with the stress and lack of sleep, I was in a terrible state** entre la tensión y la falta de sueño me encontraba fatal

(ADJECTIVE)

1 (*in direct and indirect questions*) qué • **~ dress shall I wear?** ¿qué vestido me pongo? • **~ colour is it?** ¿de qué color es? • **she asked me ~ day she should come** me preguntó qué día tenía que venir • **he explained ~ ingredients are used** explicó qué ingredientes se usan • **~ good would that do?** ¿de qué serviría eso? • **do you know ~ music they're going to play?** ¿sabes

qué música van a tocar? • **did they tell you ~ time they'd be arriving?** ¿te dijeron a qué hora llegarían?
2 (*relative*) • **~ savings we had are now gone** los ahorros que teníamos ya han desaparecido • **I will give you ~ information we have** te daré la información que tenemos • **I gave him ~ money/coins I had** le di todo el dinero/todas las monedas que tenía • **I gave her ~ comfort I could** la consolé en lo que pude • **they packed ~ few belongings they had** hicieron la maleta con las pocas pertenencias que tenían • **~ little I had** lo poco que tenía
3 (*in exclamations*)

*Remember to put an accent on **qué** in exclamations as well as in direct and indirect questions:*

• **~ a nuisance!** ¡qué lata! • **~ a fool I was!** ¡qué tonto fui! • **~ an ugly dog!** ¡qué perro más *or* tan feo! • **~ a lot of people!** ¡qué cantidad de gente! • **~ an excuse!** (*iro*) ¡buen pretexto!, ¡vaya excusa!
EXCLAMATION
¡qué! • **~! you sold it!** ¿qué? ¡lo has vendido! • **~! you expect me to believe that!** ¿qué? ¿esperas que me crea eso? • **~! he can't be a spy!** ¿qué? ¿cómo va a ser un espía? • **you told him ~?** ¿que le has dicho qué? • **"he's getting married" — "what!"** se casa — ¿cómo dices?
you what? • **"I'm going to be an actress" — "you what?"*** —voy a hacerme actriz —¿cómo *or* qué dices? • **I'm going to have a baby — you ~?** —voy a tener un niño —¡¿que vas a tener un qué?!

what-d'you-call-her* ['wɒtdʒʊˌkɔːləʳ] PRON fulana *f*, cómo-se-llame *f* • **I bumped into what-d'you-call-her from next door at the party** en la fiesta me encontré con esa chica de al lado, ¿cómo se llame?
what-d'you-call-him* ['wɒtdʒʊˌkɔːlɪm] PRON fulano *m*, cómo-se-llame *m* • **I bumped into what-d'you-call-him from next door at the party** en la fiesta me encontré con ese chico de al lado, ¿cómo se llame? • **old what-d'you-call-him with the red nose** ese que tiene la nariz tan coloradota
what-d'you-call-it* ['wɒtdʒʊˌkɔːlɪt] PRON cosa *f*, chisme *m* • **he does it with the what-d'you-call-it** lo hace con el chisme ese • **that green what-d'you-call-it on the front** esa cosa verde en la parte delantera
whatever [wɒt'evəʳ] PRON **1** (= *no matter what*) • **~ it may be** sea lo que sea • **~ he says** diga lo que diga • **~ happens** pase lo que pase • **get it, ~ it costs** cómpralo, cueste lo que cueste • **~ the weather** haga el tiempo que haga
2 (= *anything that*) lo que; (= *everything that*) todo lo que • **~ you like** lo que quieras • **do ~ you want** haz lo que quieras • **we'll do ~'s necessary** haremos lo que haga falta • **~ you say** (*acquiescing*) lo que quieras • **"I tell you I'm ill" — "~ you say"** (*iro*) —te digo que estoy enfermo —sí, sí *or* —sí, lo que tú quieras • **~ I have is yours** todo lo que tengo es tuyo • **~ you find** todo lo que *or* cualquier cosa que encuentres • **or ~ they're called** o como quiera que se llamen
3 (*in questions*) qué • **~ do you mean?** ¿qué quieres decir? • **~ did you do?** ¿pero qué hiciste? • **~ did you say that for?** ¿a santo de qué dijiste eso?
4 (= *other similar things*) • **you can put your pyjamas, sponge bag and ~ in here** aquí puedes guardar el pijama, el neceser y todas esas cosas
ADJ **1** (= *any*) cualquier; (= *all*) todo • **~ book you choose** cualquier libro que elijas • **~ books you choose** cualquier libro de los que elijas • **give me ~ change you've got** dame todo el cambio que tengas
2 (= *no matter what*) • **~ problems you've got, we'll help** nosotros te ayudaremos, tengas el problema que tengas
3 (*in questions*) qué • **~ time is it?** ¿qué hora podrá ser? • **~ help will that be?** ¿para qué servirá eso?
ADV (*with negative*) en absoluto • **nothing ~** nada en absoluto • **it's no use ~** no sirve para nada • **he said nothing ~ of interest** no dijo nada en absoluto que tuviera interés
what-ho†* ['wɒt'həʊ] EXCL (*surprise*) ¡caramba!, ¡vaya!; (*greeting*) ¡hola!, ¡oye!
whatnot ['wɒtnɒt] N **1*** (*whatsit*) chisme *m*
2 (= *furniture*) estantería *f* portátil
PRON • **and ~*** y qué sé yo, y todas esas cosas
what's-her-name* ['wɒtsənem] PRON fulana *f*, cómo-se-llame *f* • **I ran into what's-her-name from the hairdresser's** me encontré con fulana, la de la peluquería
what's-his-name* ['wɒtsɪzneɪm] PRON fulano *m*, cómo-se-llame *m* • **I ran into what's-his-name from the hairdresser's** me encontré con fulano, el de la peluquería • **old what's-his-name with the limp** fulano el cojo
whatsit* ['wɒtsɪt] N chisme *m*
what's-its-name* ['wɒtsɪtsneɪm] N chisme* *m*
whatsoever [ˌwɒtsəʊ'evəʳ], **whatsoe'er** (*poet*) ADV, PRON, ADJ = **whatever**
wheat [wiːt] N trigo *m* • **IDIOM:** • **to separate the ~ from the chaff** separar la cizaña *or* la paja del buen grano
CPD de trigo, trigueño ▸ **wheat loaf** pan *m* de trigo
wheatear ['wiːtɪəʳ] N (*Orn*) collalba *f*
wheaten ['wiːtn] ADJ de trigo
wheatfield ['wiːtfiːld] N trigal *m*
wheatgerm ['wiːtdʒɜːm] N germen *m* de trigo
wheatmeal ['wiːtmiːl] N harina *f* negra
wheatsheaf ['wiːtʃiːf] N gavilla *f* de trigo
wheedle ['wiːdl] VT • **to ~ sb into doing sth** engatusar a algn para que haga algo • **to ~ sth out of sb** sonsacar algo a algn
wheedling ['wiːdlɪŋ] ADJ mimoso
N mimos *mpl*, halagos *mpl*
wheel [wiːl] N **1** (*lit*) rueda *f*; (= *steering wheel*) volante *m*; (*Naut*) timón *m*; (*potter's*) torno *m* • **a basket on ~s** una cesta con ruedas • **to be at** *or* **behind the ~** estar al volante • **to take the ~** tomar el volante; ▹ **big**
2 (*Mil*) vuelta *f*, conversión *f* • **a ~ to the right** una vuelta hacia la derecha
3 wheels coche *msing* • **do you have ~s?*** ¿tienes coche?
4 (*in fig phrases*) • **the ~ of fortune** la rueda de fortuna • **the ~s of government** el mecanismo del gobierno • **IDIOM:** • **there are ~s within ~s** esto es más complicado de lo que parece, esto tiene su miga
VT (= *push*) [+ *bicycle, pram*] empujar; [+ *child*] pasear en cochecito • **we ~ed it over to the window** lo empujamos hasta la ventana • **when it broke down I had to ~ it** cuando se averió tuve que empujarlo
VI **1** (= *roll*) rodar
2 (= *turn*) girar; [*bird*] revolotear • **to ~ left** (*Mil*) dar una vuelta hacia la izquierda • **to ~ round** [+ *person*] girar sobre los talones
3 • **IDIOM:** • **to ~ and deal*** andar en trapicheos*, hacer chanchullos*
CPD ▸ **wheel horse*** (*US*) trabajador(a) *m/f* infatigable, mula *f* de carga ▸ **wheel trim** tapacubos *m inv*
▸ **wheel out*** VT + ADV [+ *supporter, expert*] traer; [+ *idea, cliché*] desempolvar
wheelbarrow ['wiːlˌbærəʊ] N carretilla *f*
wheelbase ['wiːlbeɪs] N batalla *f*, distancia *f* entre ejes
wheelbrace ['wiːlbreɪs] N llave *f* de ruedas en cruz
wheelchair ['wiːltʃɛəʳ] N silla *f* de ruedas
wheelchair-bound ['wiːltʃɛəbaʊnd] ADJ [*person*] en silla de ruedas
wheel-clamp ['wiːlklæmp] N cepo *m*
VT poner cepo a, inmovilizar con el cepo • **I found I'd been wheel-clamped** me encontré inmovilizado con el cepo
wheeled [wiːld] ADJ [*traffic, transport*] rodado
-wheeled [wiːld] ADJ (*ending in compounds*) • **three-wheeled** de tres ruedas
wheeler-dealer ['wiːləˌdiːləʳ] N chanchullero/a *m/f*
wheelhouse ['wiːlhaʊs] N timonera *f*, cámara *f* del timonel
wheelie* ['wiːlɪ] N • **to do a ~** hacer el caballito
wheelie-bin ['wiːlibɪn] N (*Brit*) contenedor *m* (de basura)
wheeling ['wiːlɪŋ] N • **~ and dealing** trapicheos* *mpl*, chanchullos* *mpl*
wheelwright ['wiːlraɪt] N ruedero *m*, carretero *m*
wheeze [wiːz] VI resollar, respirar con silbido
VT • **"yes," he ~d** —sí —dijo casi sin voz
N **1** (*lit*) resuello *m* (asmático), respiración *f* sibilante
2 (*Brit**) (= *trick*) truco *m*, treta *f*; (= *idea*) idea *f* • **that's a good ~** es buena idea • **to think up a ~** idear una treta
wheezing ['wiːzɪŋ] ADJ, **wheezy** ['wiːzɪ] ADJ [*breath*] ruidoso, difícil; [*pronunciation*] sibilante
whelk [welk] N buccino *m*
whelp [welp] N cachorro *m*
VI [*bitch*] parir

when [wen]

ADVERB
CONJUNCTION

ADVERB
1 (*in direct and indirect questions, reported speech*)

*When in direct and indirect questions as well as after expressions of (un)certainty and doubt (e.g. **no sé**) translates as **cuándo** (with an accent) and is used with the indicative:*

cuándo • **~ did it happen?** ¿cuándo ocurrió? • **he asked me ~ I had seen it** me preguntó cuándo lo había visto • **do you know ~ he died?** ¿sabes cuándo murió? • **I know ~ it happened** yo sé cuándo ocurrió • **he told me ~ the wedding would be** me dijo cuándo sería la boda • **he told me ~ to come in** me indicó cuándo entrar
say when! (*when serving food, drink*) ¡dime cuánto!
since when • **since ~ do you like** *or* **have you liked Indian food?** ¿desde cuándo te gusta la comida india?
till when? ¿hasta cuándo?
2 (*in exclamations*) cuándo • **~ will we learn to**

keep our mouths shut! ¡cuándo aprenderemos a callar la boca!

3 *(in other statements)* **a** (*= the time, day, moment etc*) cuando • **that was ~ the trouble started** entonces fue cuando empezaron los problemas • **Monday? that's ~ Ted gets back** ¿el lunes? ese día es cuando vuelve Ted • **that's ~ the programme starts** a esa hora es cuando empieza el programa • **1958: that's ~ I was born** 1958: (en) ese año nací yo • **she told me about ~ she was in London** me contó lo que le pasó cuando estuvo en Londres

b (*relative use*)

> *If* **when** *follows a noun (e.g.* **day, time***) and defines the noun, translate using* **(en) que** *not* **cuando***:*

(en) que • **during the time ~ she lived abroad** durante el tiempo (en) que vivió en el extranjero • **the year ~ you were born** el año (en) que naciste • **she can't remember a time ~ she wasn't happy** no recuerda una época (en) que no fuese feliz • **there are times ~ I wish I'd never met him** hay momentos en los que desearía no haberlo conocido nunca

c

> *If the* **when** *clause following a noun provides additional information which does not define or restrict the noun — in English as in Spanish commas are obligatory here — translate using* **cuando***:*

cuando • **some days, ~ we're very busy, we don't finish work till very late** algunos días, cuando tenemos mucho trabajo, no acabamos hasta muy tarde

CONJUNCTION

1 *(= at, during or after the time that)*

> *As a conjunction,* **when** *can be translated by* **cuando** *(without an accent) followed by either the indicative or the subjunctive. Use the indicative when talking about the past or making general statements about the present. Use the subjunctive when the action is or was in the future:*

cuando • **~ I came in** cuando entré • **~ I was young** cuando era joven • **he had just sat down ~ the phone rang** acababa de sentarse cuando sonó el teléfono • **everything looks nicer ~ the sun is shining** todo está más bonito cuando brilla el sol • **he arrived at 8 o'clock, ~ traffic is at its peak** llegó a las ocho en punto, en lo peor del tráfico • **call me ~ you get there** llámame cuando llegues • **~ the bridge is built** cuando se construya el puente • **you can go ~ we have finished** puedes irte cuando hayamos terminado • **he said he'd tell me ~ I was older** dijo que me lo diría cuando fuera mayor

> *If* **when** *+ verb can be substituted by* **on** *+ '-ing' in English and describes an action that takes place at the same time as another one or follows it very closely, you can use* **al** *+ infinitive:*

• **be careful ~ crossing** *or* **~ you cross the road** ten cuidado al cruzar la calle • **~ he went out he saw it was raining** al salir vio que estaba lloviendo • **~ a student at Oxford, she ...** cuando era estudiante *or* estudiaba en Oxford ... • **my father, ~ young, had a fine tenor voice** mi padre, de joven *or* cuando era joven, tenía una buena voz de tenor • **~ just three years old, he was ...** cuando tenía solo tres años, era ... • **the floor is slippery ~ wet** el suelo resbala cuando está mojado • **hardly had the film begun ~ there was a power cut** apenas había empezado la película cuando se fue la corriente • **even ~** aun cuando

2 *(= if)* si, cuando • **this sounds expensive ~ compared with other cars** este parece caro si *or* cuando se compara con otros coches • **how can I relax ~ I've got loads of things to do?** ¿cómo puedo relajarme si *or* cuando tengo montones de cosas que hacer? • **I wouldn't walk ~ I could get the bus** no iría a pie si pudiese tomar el autobús

3 *(= whereas)* cuando • **he thought he was recovering, ~ in fact ...** pensaba que se estaba recuperando, cuando de hecho ... • **she made us study ~ all we wanted to do was play** nos hacía estudiar cuando lo único que queríamos hacer era jugar

whence [wens] ADV **1** (*poet*) (*= from where*) de donde; (*interrog*) ¿de dónde?
2 (*frm*) (*= from which*) por lo cual; (*= therefore*) y por consiguiente • **~ I conclude that ...** por lo cual concluyo que ...

whenever [wen'evəʳ] CONJ **1** (*= at whatever time*) cuando • **we can leave ~ it suits you** nos podemos ir cuando quieras • **come ~ you like** ven cuando quieras
2 (*= every time*) siempre que, cuando, cada vez que, cada que (*Mex**) • **~ I smell roses I think of Mary** siempre que *or* cada vez que *or* cuando huele a rosas me acuerdo de Mary • **~ you see one of those, stop** siempre que *or* cada vez que *or* cuando veas uno de esos, párate • **I go ~ I can** voy siempre que puedo • **we will help ~ possible** ayudaremos siempre cuando *or* que sea posible
ADV **1** • **Monday, Tuesday, or ~** el lunes o el martes o cuando sea
2 (*in questions*) cuándo • **~ did I say that?** ¿cuándo dije yo eso? • **~ can he have done it?** ¿cuándo demonios ha podido hacerlo? • **~ do I have the time for such things?** ¿cuándo crees que tengo tiempo para estas cosas?

where [wɛəʳ]

ADVERB
CONJUNCTION

ADVERB

1 *(in direct and indirect questions, reported speech)*

> **Where** *in direct questions as well as after report verbs and expressions of (un)certainty and doubt (e.g.* **no sé***) usually translates as* **dónde** *(with an accent), sometimes preceded by a preposition:*

dónde • **~ am I?** ¿dónde estoy? • **~ are you going (to)?** ¿a dónde *or* adónde vas?, ¿dónde vas? • **~ have you come from?** ¿de dónde has venido? • **~ can I have put my keys (down)?** ¿dónde *or* en dónde puedo haber puesto las llaves? • **~ should we be if ...?** ¿a dónde *or* adónde habríamos ido a parar si ...? • **~ did we go wrong?** ¿en qué nos equivocamos? • **can you tell me ~ there's a chemist's?** ¿puede decirme dónde hay una farmacia? • **I don't know ~ she lives** no sé dónde vive

2 *(in other statements)* **a** (*= the place that*)

> **Where** *in other statements is usually translated as* **donde** *(without an accent), again often preceded by a preposition:*

donde • **there's a telephone box near ~ I live** hay una cabina cerca de donde vivo • **this is ~ we found it** aquí es donde lo encontramos • **that's ~ we got to in the last lesson** hasta aquí llegamos en la última clase • **that's just ~ you're wrong!** ¡en eso te equivocas!, ¡ahí es donde te equivocas! • **that's ~ I disagree with you** en eso no estoy de acuerdo contigo, ahí es donde no estoy de acuerdo contigo • **~ this book is dangerous is in suggesting that ...** el aspecto peligroso de este libro es la sugerencia de que ...
b (*after noun*) donde • **this is the hotel ~ we stayed** este es el hotel donde *or* en el que estuvimos • **the beach ~ we picnicked** la playa donde *or* a la que *or* adonde fuimos de picnic • **we went to visit the house ~ Diego was born** fuimos a visitar la casa (en) donde nació Diego

CONJUNCTION

1 *(= if)* • **~ husband and wife both work, benefits are ...** en el caso de que los dos esposos trabajen, los beneficios son ... • **~ possible** en lo posible

2 *(= whereas)* mientras que, cuando • **sometimes a teacher will be listened to ~ a parent might not** a veces a un maestro se le hace caso, mientras que *or* cuando a un padre tal vez no

whereabouts ADV [,wɛərə'baʊts] dónde • **~ did you first see it?** ¿dónde lo viste por primera vez?
NSING OR NPL ['wɛərəbaʊts] paradero *msing* • **nobody knows his ~** se desconoce su paradero actual

whereas [wɛər'æz] CONJ (*= on the other hand*) mientras; (*Jur*) considerando que

whereat [wɛər'æt] ADV (*liter*) con lo cual

whereby [wɛə'baɪ] ADV (*frm*) por lo cual, por donde • **the rule ~ it is not allowed to** (*+ infin*) la regla según *or* mediante la cual no se permite (*+ infin*)

wherefore ['wɛəfɔː'] ADV †† (*= why*) por qué; (*= and for this reason*) y por tanto, por lo cual
N ▹ **why**

wherein [wɛər'ɪn] ADV (*frm or liter*) en donde

whereof [wɛər'ɒv] ADV (*frm or liter*) de que

whereon [wɛər'ɒn] ADV (*frm or liter*) en que

wheresoever [,wɛəsəʊ'evəʳ] ADV (*liter*) dondequiera que

whereto [,wɛə'tuː] ADV (*frm or liter*) adonde

whereupon ['wɛərəpɒn] ADV (*frm or liter*) con lo cual, después de lo cual

wherever [wɛər'evəʳ] CONJ **1** (*= no matter where*) dondequiera que • **he follows me ~ I go** me sigue dondequiera que *or* por donde vaya • **~ you go I'll go too** (a)dondequiera que vayas *or* vayas donde vayas yo te acompañaré • **~ I am** (esté) donde esté • **~ they went they were cheered** les recibían con aplausos dondequiera que fueran *or* fueran a donde fueran • **I'll buy them ~ they come from** los compraré no importa su procedencia, los compraré vengan de donde vengan
2 (*= anywhere*) donde • **sit ~ you like** siéntate donde te parezca bien • **~ possible** donde sea posible
ADV **1** • **in Madrid, London, or ~** en Madrid, Londres o donde sea • **he comes from Laxey, ~ that is** es de Laxey, a saber dónde está eso
2 (*in questions*) ¿dónde demonios *or* diablos? • **~ did you put it?** ¿dónde demonios lo pusiste? • **~ can they have got to?** ¿dónde diablos se habrán metido?

wherewith [wɛə'wɪθ] ADV (*frm or liter*) con lo cual

W

wherewithal ['wɛəwɪðɔːl] (N) • **the ~ (to do sth)** los medios (para hacer algo), los recursos (para hacer algo)
wherry ['werɪ] (N) chalana *f*
whet [wet] (VT) [*+ tool*] afilar, amolar; [*+ appetite, curiosity*] estimular, despertar
whether ['weðə^r] (CONJ) si • **I don't know ~ ...** no sé si ... • **I doubt ~ ...** dudo que (*+ subjun*) • **I am not certain ~ he'll come (or not)** no estoy seguro de que venga • **~ it is ... or not** sea ... o no (sea) • **~ you like it or not** tanto si quieres como si no • **~ they come or not** vengan o no (vengan)
whetstone ['wetstəʊn] (N) piedra *f* de amolar, afiladera *f*
whew [hwjuː] (EXCL) ¡vaya!, ¡caramba!
whey [weɪ] (N) suero *m*
whey-faced ['weɪ'feɪst] (ADJ) pálido
whf (ABBR) = **wharf**

which [wɪtʃ]

PRONOUN
ADJECTIVE

PRONOUN

1 (*in direct and indirect questions, reported speech*)

> *Which/which one/which ones in direct and indirect questions and after expressions of (un)certainty and doubt (e.g.* ***no sé****) usually translate as* ***cuál/cuáles****:*

cuál • **~ do you want?** (*offering one*) ¿cuál quieres?; (*offering two or more*) ¿cuáles quieres? • **I can't tell ~ is ~** no sé cuál es cuál • **~ of you did it?** ¿cuál de vosotros lo hizo? • **~ of you is Kathleen?** ¿cuál de vosotras es Kathleen? • **I don't know ~ to choose** no sé cuál escoger • **tell me ~ you like best** dime cuáles te gustan más • **I don't mind ~** no me importa cuál

2 (*relative*) **a** (*replacing noun*)

> *In relative clauses where* ***which*** *defines the noun it refers to, you can usually translate it as* ***que****. Note that in this type of sentence* ***which*** *can be substituted by* ***that*** *in English:*

que • **the letter ~ came this morning was from my niece** la carta que llegó esta mañana era de mi sobrina • **it's an illness ~ causes nerve damage** es una enfermedad que daña los nervios • **do you remember the house ~ we saw last week?** ¿te acuerdas de la casa que vimos la semana pasada? • **the bear ~ I saw** el oso que vi

> *If* ***which*** *is the object of a preposition, you can either translate it as* ***que*** *(usually preceded by the definite article) or as article +* ***cual/cuales****. Use the second option particularly in formal language or after long prepositions or prepositional phrases:*

• **your letter, ~ I received this morning, cheered me up** tu carta, que *or* (*more frm*) la cual he recibido esta mañana, me ha levantado el ánimo • **the bull ~ I'm talking about** el toro del que *or* (*more frm*) del cual estoy hablando • **the meeting ~ we attended** la reunión a la que *or* (*more frm*) a la cual asistimos • **the hotel at ~ we stayed** el hotel en el que *or* (*more frm*) en el cual nos hospedamos • **the cities to ~ we are going** las ciudades a las que *or* (*more frm*) a las cuales vamos • **he explained the means by ~ we could achieve our objective** explicó los medios a través de los cuales podíamos alcanzar nuestro objetivo

> *If instead of defining the noun the* ***which*** *clause merely adds additional information, you can translate* ***which*** *using either* ***que*** *or article +* ***cual/cuales****:*

• **the oak dining-table, ~ was a present from my father, seats 10 people comfortably** la mesa de roble, que *or* la cual fue un regalo de mi padre, admite cómodamente diez comensales

b (*replacing clause*)

> *When* ***which*** *refers to the whole of a preceding sentence or idea, translate as* ***lo que*** *or* ***lo cual****:*

• **it rained hard ~ upset her** llovió mucho, lo que *or* lo cual le disgustó • **they left early, ~ my wife did not like at all** se marcharon pronto, lo cual *or* lo que no agradó nada a mi mujer

> *After a preposition only* ***lo cual*** *can be used:*

• **after ~ we went to bed** después de lo cual nos acostamos • **from ~ we deduce that ...** de lo cual deducimos que ...

ADJECTIVE

1 (*in direct and indirect questions, reported speech*)

> *When* ***which*** *is used as an interrogative adjective, translate using* ***qué*** *+ noun when the possibilities are very open or* ***cuál/cuáles de*** *+ article + plural noun when the possibilities are limited:*

qué • **~ house do you live in?** ¿en qué casa vives? • **~ day are they coming?** ¿qué día vienen? • **I don't know ~ tie he wants** no sé qué corbata quiere • **~ picture do you prefer?** ¿qué cuadro prefieres?, ¿cuál de los cuadros prefieres? • **~ option do you prefer?** ¿cuál de las alternativas prefieres? • **~ way did she go?** ¿por dónde se fue? • **~ one?** ¿cuál? • **I don't know ~ one to choose** no sé cuál escoger • **tell me ~ ones you like best** dime cuáles te gustan más

2 (*relative*) • **look ~ way you will ...** mires por donde mires ... • **he used "peradventure", ~ word is now archaic** (*frm*) dijo "peradventure", palabra que ha quedado ahora anticuada • **in ~ case** en cuyo caso • **he didn't get here till 10, by ~ time Jane had already left** no llegó hasta las 10 y para entonces Jane ya se había ido

whichever [wɪtʃ'evə^r] (PRON) **1** (*= no matter which*) • **~ of the methods you choose** cualquiera de los métodos que escojas, no importa el método que escojas
2 (*= the one which*) el/la que • **choose ~ is easiest** elige el que sea más fácil
(ADJ) **1** (*= no matter which*) • **~ system you have there are difficulties** no importa el sistema que tengas, hay problemas, cualquiera que sea el sistema que tengas, hay problemas • **~ way you look at it** se mire como se mire
2 (*= any, the ... which*) el ... que/la ... que • **you can choose ~ system you want** puedes elegir el sistema que quieras
whiff [wɪf] (N) **1** (*= smell*) olorcito *m*; (*= nasty*) tufillo • **a faint ~ of mothballs** un leve olorcito a bolas de naftalina • **to catch a ~ of sth** oler algo • **a ~ of grapeshot** un poco de metralla • **what a ~!** ¡qué tufo!
2 (*= sniff, mouthful*) • **to go out for a ~ of air** salir a tomar el fresco • **not a ~ of wind** ni el menor soplo de viento
3 (*fig*) [*of scandal, corruption*] indicio *m*
(VI)* oler (mal) • **to ~ of** oler a; (*= stink of*) apestar a
whiffy* ['wɪfɪ] (ADJ) • **to be ~** apestar • **it's a bit ~ here** aquí apesta
Whig [wɪg] (*Pol, Hist*) (N) *político liberal de los siglos XVII y XVIII*
(ADJ) liberal
while [waɪl] (N) **1** • **a ~** (*= some moments*) un ratito; (*= some minutes, hours*) un rato; (*= some weeks, months*) un tiempo • **after a ~** al cabo de un rato, al rato • **all the ~** todo el tiempo • **I lived in Paris for a ~** viví un tiempo en París • **let it simmer for a ~** deje que hierva un rato a fuego lento • **it will be a good ~ before he gets here** tardará (un rato) en venir aún, todavía falta (un rato) para que venga (*LAm*) • **a little ~ ago** hace poco • **a long ~ ago** hace mucho • **once in a ~** de vez en cuando • **it takes quite a ~** lleva tiempo • **in a short ~** dentro de poco, al rato (*LAm*) • **stay a ~ with us** quédate un rato con nosotros • **the ~** entretanto, mientras tanto • **he looked at me the ~** mientras tanto me estaba mirando
2 • **it is worth ~ to ask whether ...** vale la pena preguntar si ... • **we'll make it worth your ~** te compensaremos generosamente • **it's not worth my ~** no me vale la pena
(CONJ) **1** (*= during the time that*) mientras • **~ this was happening** mientras pasaba esto • **she fell asleep ~ reading** se durmió mientras leía • **~ you are away** mientras estés fuera • **to drink ~ on duty** beber estando de servicio
2 (*= as long as*) mientras (que) • **it won't happen ~ I'm here** no pasará mientras (que) yo esté aquí
3 (*= although*) aunque • **~ I admit it is awkward** aunque reconozco que es difícil
4 (*= whereas*) mientras que • **I enjoy sport, ~ he prefers reading** a mí me gusta el deporte, mientras que él prefiere la lectura
▸ **while away** (VT + ADV) • **to ~ away the time** *or* **the hours** pasar el tiempo *or* el rato
whilst [waɪlst] (CONJ) (*esp Brit*) = **while**
whim [wɪm] (N) capricho *m*, antojo *m* • **a passing ~** un capricho pasajero, un antojo • **it's just a ~ of hers** es un capricho suyo • **as the ~ takes me** según se me antoja
whimbrel ['wɪmbrəl] (N) zarapito *m*
whimper ['wɪmpə^r] (N) [*of from dog, sick person*] gemido *m*, quejido *m* • **without a ~** sin un quejido, sin una queja; ▹ **bang**
(VT) • **"yes," she ~ed** —sí —dijo lloriqueando *or* gimoteando
(VI) [*dog*] gemir, gimotear; [*sick person*] gemir; [*child*] lloriquear
whimpering ['wɪmpərɪŋ] (ADJ) [*dog*] que gime, que gimotea; [*sick person*] que gime; [*child*] lloriqueante
(N) [*of dog*] gemidos *mpl*, gimoteo *m*; [*of sick person*] gemidos *mpl*; [*of child*] lloriqueo *m*
whimsical ['wɪmzɪkəl] (ADJ) [*person*] caprichoso; [*idea, suggestion*] caprichoso, fantástico; [*smile*] enigmático • **to be in a ~ mood** estar de humor para dejar volar la fantasía
whimsicality [wɪmzɪ'kælɪtɪ] (N) [*of person*] capricho *m*, fantasía *f*; [*of idea*] lo fantástico • **a novel of a pleasing ~** una novela de agradable fantasía
whimsically ['wɪmzɪkəlɪ] (ADV) [*describe, muse*] caprichosamente; [*smile, laugh*] enigmáticamente
whimsy ['wɪmzɪ] (N) (*= whim*) capricho *m*, antojo *m*; (*= whimsicality*) fantasía *f*
whin [wɪn] (N) tojo *m*

whine [waɪn] (N) [*of dog*] gemido *m*; (*louder*) gañido *m*; [*of child*] quejido *m*; [*of siren, bullet*] silbido *m* • **... he said in a ~** [*child*] ... dijo lloriqueando; [*adult*] ... dijo quejumbroso *or* quejándose
(VI) **1** (= *make noise*) [*dog*] gemir; (*louder*) gañir; [*child*] lloriquear, gimotear; [*siren, bullet*] silbar
2* (= *complain*) quejarse • **it's just a scratch, stop whining** no es más que un arañazo, deja de quejarte • **to ~ about sth** [*adult*] quejarse de algo; [*child*] lloriquear *or* gimotear por algo • **don't come whining to me about it** no vengas a quejarte a mí
(VT) [*adult*] decir quejumbroso *or* quejándose; [*child*] decir lloriqueando *or* gimoteando

whiner ['waɪnəʳ] (N) (= *complainer*) quejica *mf*

whiney* ['waɪnɪ] (ADJ) = **whiny**

whinge* [wɪndʒ] (N) • **to have a ~ (about sth)** quejarse (de algo)
(VI) quejarse • **to ~ about sth** quejarse de algo
(VT) • **"but I want to go too," he ~d** —pero yo también quiero ir —dijo en tono de queja

whingeing* ['wɪndʒɪŋ] (Brit) (ADJ) [*voice*] quejumbroso; [*person*] protestón, quejica*
(N) gimoteo *m*, lloriqueo *m*

whinger* ['wɪndʒəʳ] (N) (Brit) quejica* *mf*, llorica* *mf*

whining ['waɪnɪŋ] (ADJ) **1** (= *complaining*) [*voice*] quejumbroso; [*person*] quejica*
2 • **a ~ sound** (*made by engine, machine*) un sonido chirriante
(N) **1** (= *complaining*) quejidos *mpl*, gimoteo *m*
2 (= *sound*) [*of engine, machine*] chirrido *m*; [*of siren*] silbido *m*; [*of dog*] gemido(s) *m(pl)*; (*louder*) gañido(s) *m(pl)*

whinny ['wɪnɪ] (N) relincho *m*
(VI) relinchar

whiny* ['waɪnɪ] (ADJ) quejica*

whip [wɪp] (N) **1** (*for training, driving animals*) látigo *m*; (= *riding crop*) fusta *f*, fuete *m* (*LAm*); (*for punishment*) azote *m* • **he was given 20 lashes of the ~** le dieron 20 latigazos con el azote; ▷ **crack**
2 (Brit) (Parl) **a** (= *person*) *diputado encargado de la disciplina del partido en el parlamento* • **chief ~** *diputado jefe encargado de la disciplina del partido en el parlamento*
b (= *call*) • **(two-line/three-line) ~** *citación (con subrayado doble/triple) para que un diputado acuda a votar en una cuestión importante*; ▷ **LEADER OF THE HOUSE**
3 (Culin) batido *m* (*de claras de huevo o nata*)
(VT) **1** (*with whip, stick*) [+ *horse*] fustigar; [+ *person*] azotar; [+ *child*] dar un azote a, dar una paliza a • **IDIOM:** • **to ~ into a frenzy:** • **he was ~ping the crowd into a frenzy** estaba provocando el frenesí en la multitud; ▷ **shape**
2 (*liter*) [*wind*] azotar • **the wind ~ped her skirts around her legs** el viento hacía que la falda le azotara las piernas
3 (Culin) [+ *cream*] montar; [+ *mixture, egg white*] batir
4* (= *defeat*) dar una paliza a*
5* (= *remove*) • **he ~ped a gun out of his pocket** en un abrir y cerrar de ojos sacó un revólver del bolsillo • **he ~ped the letter out of my hand** me quitó la carta de la mano de un tirón, me arrebató la carta
6 (= *rush*) • **they ~ped her into hospital** la llevaron al hospital a toda prisa
7 (Brit*) (= *steal*) mangar*, birlar*
8 (= *strengthen*) [+ *rope*] reforzar
9 (Sew) [+ *hem, seam*] sobrehilar
(VI) **1** (= *speed, rush*) • **I ~ped into a parking space** me metí enseguida en un hueco para aparcar • **I'll just ~ into the chemist's** voy en un segundo a la farmacia
2 (= *lash*) • **the rope broke and ~ped across his face** la cuerda se rompió y le azotó la cara
3 (= *flap*) batir • **the rigging was ~ping against the mast of the yacht** las jarcias batían contra el mástil del yate
(CPD) ▸ **whip hand** • **IDIOMS:** • **to have the ~ hand** llevar la voz cantante • **to have the ~ hand over sb** llevar ventaja a algn

▸ **whip around** (VI + ADV) (= *turn*) [*person*] volverse *or* darse la vuelta de repente

▸ **whip back** (VI + ADV) (= *return*) volverse de golpe; (= *bounce back*) rebotar de repente hacia atrás

▸ **whip in** (VT + ADV) **1** (Hunting) [+ *hounds*] llamar, reunir
2 (Parl) [+ *member*] llamar para que vote; [+ *electors*] hacer que acudan a las urnas

▸ **whip off** (VT + ADV) [+ *lid*] quitar con un movimiento brusco; [+ *dress, trousers, gloves*] quitarse rápidamente

▸ **whip on** (VT + ADV) [+ *lid*] poner con un movimiento brusco; [+ *dress, trousers, gloves*] ponerse rápidamente

▸ **whip out** (VT + ADV) sacar de repente • **we'll soon ~ that tooth out** te sacaremos ese diente antes de que te des cuenta; ▷ **whip**

▸ **whip round** (VI + ADV) (= *turn*) [*person*] volverse *or* darse la vuelta de repente • **his head ~ped round in astonishment** volvió *or* giró la cabeza asombrado

▸ **whip through** (VI + PREP) [+ *book*] leer rápidamente; [+ *task, homework*] realizar de un tirón

▸ **whip up*** (VT + ADV) **1** (= *make*) [+ *meal*] preparar rápidamente; [+ *dress*] hacer rápidamente
2 (Culin) [+ *cream*] montar; [+ *egg white*] batir
3 (= *stir up*) [+ *support*] procurar, conseguir; [+ *enthusiasm, interest, excitement*] despertar; [+ *hatred*] provocar • **I couldn't ~ up any enthusiasm for the idea** (*among other people*) no pude despertar entusiasmo por la idea; (*in myself*) la idea no me entusiasmaba • **the proposed measure has ~ped up a storm of protest among students** la medida propuesta ha levantado una ola de protestas entre los estudiantes
4 (= *rouse*) [+ *crowd*] exaltar • **he ~ped the crowd up into a frenzy of hate** exaltó a la multitud hasta despertar en ellos un odio febril
5 (= *spur on*) [+ *horses*] azotar
6 (= *lift*) [+ *dust*] levantar

> **WHIP**
> En el Parlamento británico la disciplina de partido está a cargo de un grupo de parlamentarios llamados **whips**, encabezados por el **Chief Whip**. Están encargados de informar al resto de miembros del partido de los asuntos del Parlamento, comunicar a los líderes las opiniones de los parlamentarios y asegurarse de que todos ellos asistan a la Cámara de los Comunes (**House of Commons**) y acudan a las votaciones importantes, lo que puede ser crucial cuando el gobierno no tiene mayoría absoluta. Tanto el gobierno como la oposición tienen sus propios **whips** y por lo general todos ellos ostentan también altos cargos en la Administración del Estado, si pertenecen al partido del gobierno.

whipcord ['wɪpkɔːd] (N) tralla *f*

whiplash ['wɪplæʃ] (N) **1** tralla *f*, latigazo *m*
2 (Med) (*also* **whiplash injury**) traumatismo *m* cervical

whipped [wɪpt] (ADJ) (Culin) batido
(CPD) ▸ **whipped cream** nata *f* montada

whipper-in ['wɪpər'ɪn] (N) (PL: **whippers-in**) (Hunting) montero/a *m/f* que cuida los perros de caza

whippersnapper ['wɪpə,snæpəʳ] (N) (*also* **young whippersnapper**) mequetrefe *m*

whippet ['wɪpɪt] (N) perro *m* lebrel

whipping ['wɪpɪŋ] (N) **1** (= *hiding*) tunda* *f*, azotaina* *f*; (*more serious*) paliza* *f* • **you'll get a ~ if your dad finds out** como tu padre se entere te van a dar una tunda *or* azotaina • **to give sb a ~** dar una tunda *or* azotaina a algn
2* (= *defeat*) paliza* *f*
(CPD) ▸ **whipping boy** cabeza *f* de turco, chivo *m* expiatorio ▸ **whipping cream** nata *f* para montar ▸ **whipping post** *poste donde se apoya el infractor para ser azotado* ▸ **whipping top** peonza *f*, trompo *m*

whippoorwill ['wɪpʊəwɪl] (N) chotacabras *mf inv*

whippy ['wɪpɪ] (ADJ) flexible, dúctil

whip-round* ['wɪpraʊnd] (N) colecta *f* • **to have a whip-round (for sb)** hacer una colecta (para algn)

whipsaw ['wɪpsɔː] (N) sierra *f* cabrilla

whir [wɜːʳ] = **whirr**

whirl [wɜːl] (N) (= *spin*) giro *m*, vuelta *f*; [*of dust, water etc*] remolino *m*; [*of cream*] rizo *m* • **my head is in a ~** la cabeza me está dando vueltas • **the social ~** la actividad social • **a ~ of pleasures** un torbellino de placeres • **IDIOM:** • **let's give it a ~*** ¡nada se pierde con intentar!
(VT) **1** (= *spin*) hacer girar • **he ~ed Anne round the dance floor** hizo girar a Anne por la pista • **as the wind ~ed leaves into the air** mientras el aire hacia revolotear *or* girar las hojas en el aire • **he ~ed his sword round his head** esgrimió su espada haciéndola girar sobre su cabeza
2 (*fig*) (= *transport*) llevar rápidamente • **the train ~ed us off to Paris** el tren nos llevó rápidamente a París • **he ~ed us off to the theatre** nos llevó volando al teatro
(VI) [*wheel, merry-go-round*] girar; [*leaves, dust, water*] arremolinarse; (*fig*) (= *move quickly*) • **the dancers ~ed past** los bailarines pasaron girando vertiginosamente • **my head was ~ing** me daba vueltas la cabeza

▸ **whirl around, whirl round** (VI + ADV) [*wheel, merry-go-round*] girar, dar vueltas; [*dust, water*] arremolinarse • **she ~ed round to face me** se volvió rápidamente para mirarme
(VT + ADV) hacer girar • **he was ~ing something round on the end of a string** hacía girar algo al extremo de un hilo
(VT + PREP) ▷ **whirl**

whirligig ['wɜːlɪgɪg] (N) **1** (= *toy*) molinete *m*
2 (= *merry-go-round*) tiovivo *m*
3 (*also* **whirligig beetle**) girino *m*
4 (*fig*) vicisitudes *fpl*; (= *confusion*) movimiento *m* confuso

whirlpool ['wɜːlpuːl] (N) **1** (*lit*) remolino *m*; (*fig*) vorágine *f*
2 (*also* **whirlpool bath**) (= *tub*) bañera *f* de hidromasaje; (= *pool*) piscina *f* de hidromasaje

whirlwind ['wɜːlwɪnd] (N) (*lit, fig*) torbellino *m* • **IDIOMS:** • **like a ~** como un torbellino, como una tromba • **to reap the ~** segar lo que se ha sembrado, padecer las consecuencias
(CPD) [*romance*] apasionado, arrollador • **a ~ courtship** un noviazgo brevísimo • **they took us on a ~ tour** nos llevaron de gira relámpago

whirlybird* ['wɜːlɪbɜːd] (N) (US) helicóptero *m*

W

whirr [wɜːʳ] (N) [*of insect wings*] zumbido *m*; [*of machine*] (*quiet*) zumbido *m*, runrún *m*; (*louder*) rechino *m*
(VI) [*insect wings*] zumbar; [*machine*] (*quietly*) zumbar, runrunear; (*more loudly*) rechinar
whirring [ˈwɜːrɪŋ] (N) zumbido *m*
whisk [wɪsk] (N) **1** (= *fly whisk*) matamoscas *m inv*
2 (*Culin*) (= *hand whisk*) batidor *m*; (= *electric whisk*) batidora *f*
(VT) **1** (*Culin*) batir
2* (= *move quickly*) • **they ~ed him off to a meeting** se lo llevaron volando a una reunión • **we were ~ed up in the lift to the ninth floor** el ascensor nos llevó con toda rapidez al piso nueve; ▷ **whisk off, whisk up**
(VI)* • **he ~ed past me as I was coming in** cuando entraba, le vi pasar de largo a toda velocidad
▸ **whisk away** (VT + ADV) **1** (= *shake off*) [+ *dust*] quitar con un movimiento brusco • **the horse ~ed the flies away with its tail** el caballo ahuyentó las moscas con la cola
2 (= *take*) • **the waiter ~ed the dishes away** el camarero se llevó los platos en seguida • **she ~ed it away from me** me lo arrebató
(VI + ADV) desaparecer de repente
▸ **whisk off** (VT + ADV) [+ *dust*] quitar con un movimiento brusco; ▷ **whisk**
▸ **whisk up** (VT + ADV) (*Culin*) batir; ▷ **whisk**
whisker [ˈwɪskəʳ] (N) [*of animal*] bigote *m*; (= *hair*) pelo *m* • **~s** (*Zool*) bigotes *mpl*; (= *side whiskers*) patillas *fpl*; (= *beard*) barba *fsing*; (= *moustache*) bigote(s) *m(pl)* • **IDIOMS:** • **by a ~** por un pelo • **within a ~ of:** • **he was within a ~ of falling down** le faltó un pelo para caer, faltó un pelo para que cayera
whiskered [ˈwɪskəd] (ADJ) bigotudo
whisky, whiskey (*US, Irl*) [ˈwɪskɪ] (N) whisky *m* • **~ and soda** whisky *m* con sifón, whisky *m* con soda
whisper [ˈwɪspəʳ] (N) **1** (*lit*) (= *low tone*) cuchicheo *m*, susurro *m*; [*of leaves*] susurro *m* • **to speak in a ~** hablar en voz baja, susurrar • **to say sth in a ~** decir algo en voz baja, susurrar algo • **her voice was scarcely more than a ~** su voz no era más que un susurro
2 (= *rumour*) rumor *m*, voz *f* • **there is a ~ that** ... corre el rumor *or* la voz de que ..., se rumorea que ... • **at the least ~ of scandal** al menor indicio del escándalo
(VT) **1** (*lit*) decir en voz baja, susurrar • **to ~ sth to sb** decir algo al oído de algn, susurrar algo a algn
2 (*fig*) • **it is ~ed that** ... corre la voz de que ..., se rumorea que ...
(VI) (= *talk*) cuchichear, susurrar, hablar muy bajo; [*leaves*] susurrar • **to ~ to sb** cuchichear a algn • **it's rude to ~ in company** es de mala educación cuchichear en compañía, secretos en reunión es falta de educación • **stop ~ing!** ¡silencio!
whispering [ˈwɪspərɪŋ] (N) **1** (= *talking*) cuchicheo *m*; [*of leaves*] susurro *m*
2 (= *gossip*) chismes *mpl*, chismografía *f*; (= *rumours*) rumores *mpl*
(CPD) ▸ **whispering campaign** campaña *f* de murmuraciones
whist [wɪst] (N) whist *m*
(CPD) ▸ **whist drive** certamen *m* de whist
whistle [ˈwɪsl] (N) **1** (= *sound*) silbido *m*, chiflido *m* (*esp LAm*) • **final ~** pitido *m* final
2 (= *instrument*) silbato *m*, pito *m* • **blast on the ~** pitido *m* • **the referee blew his ~** el árbitro pitó • **IDIOM:** • **to blow the ~ on sb** (= *denounce*) delatar a algn; (= *put a stop to*) poner fin a las actividades de algn
(VT) silbar • **to ~ a tune** silbar una melodía • **IDIOM:** • **I'm not just whistling Dixie** (*US*) no hablo en broma, no me estoy marcando ningún farol*
(VI) silbar, chiflar (*esp LAm*); (*Sport*) pitar, silbar • **the boys ~ at the girls** los chicos silban a las chicas • **the crowd ~d at the referee** el público silbó al árbitro • **he ~d for his dog** llamó a su perro con un silbido • **the referee ~d for a foul** el árbitro pitó una falta • **the bullet ~d past my ear** la bala pasó silbando muy cerca de mi oreja • **IDIOM:** • **he can ~ for it*** lo pedirá en vano
▸ **whistle up** (VT + ADV) **1** • **to ~ up one's dog** llamar a su perro con un silbido
2 (= *find*) encontrar, hacer aparecer
3 (= *rustle up*) [+ *meal*] preparar, servir
4 (= *get together*) [+ *people*] reunir
whistle-blower* [ˈwɪslbləʊəʳ] (N) *persona que desvela una situación interna ilegal*
whistle-blowing, whistleblowing [wɪslbləʊɪŋ] (N) denuncia *f* (*interna*)
whistle-stop [ˈwɪslstɒp] (N) (*US*) (= *station*) apeadero *m*
(CPD) ▸ **whistle-stop tour** (*US*) (*Pol*) gira *f* electoral rápida; (*fig*) recorrido *m* rápido
whistling [ˈwɪslɪŋ] (N) silbido *m*
Whit [wɪt] (N) Pentecostés *m*
(CPD) [*holiday, weekend*] de Pentecostés
▸ **Whit Monday** lunes *m* de Pentecostés
▸ **Whit Sunday** día *m* de Pentecostés ▸ **Whit week** semana *f* de Pentecostés
whit [wɪt] (N) (*liter*) • **not a ~** ni un ápice • **without a ~ of** sin pizca de • **every ~ as good as** de ningún modo inferior a
white [waɪt] (ADJ) (COMPAR: **whiter**, SUPERL: **whitest**) **1** (*gen*) blanco; [*wine, grape, chocolate*] blanco; [*coffee*] (= *milky*) con leche; (= *with dash of milk*) cortado • **to go** *or* **turn ~** (*in face*) ponerse blanco *or* pálido, palidecer • **IDIOMS:** • **whiter than white** [*person, way of life*] sin tacha, angelical • **"Bleacho" washes whiter than white** "Bleacho" deja la colada blanca como la nieve • **he went ~ at the age of 30** el pelo se le puso blanco a los 30 años, encaneció a los 30 años • **she was ~ with rage** estaba pálida de la rabia • **to show the ~ feather** mostrarse cobarde • **to be as ~ as a sheet** *or* **ghost** estar pálido como la muerte; ▷ **bleed**
2 (*racially*) [*person*] blanco; [*area*] de raza blanca; [*vote*] de los blancos
(N) **1** (= *colour*) blanco *m* • **his face was a deathly ~** su rostro estaba blanco *or* pálido como la muerte • **the sheets were a dazzling ~** las sábanas eran de un blanco deslumbrante • **to be dressed in ~** ir vestido de blanco; ▷ **black**
2 (= *white person*) blanco/a *m/f*
3 (*also* **white wine**) blanco *m* • **a glass of ~** un blanco
4 [*of egg*] clara *f*
5 [*of eye*] blanco *m*
6 whites (*Sport*) • **cricket/tennis ~s** equipo *m* blanco de cricket/tennis
(CPD) ▸ **white blood cell** glóbulo *m* blanco
▸ **white bread** pan *m* blanco ▸ **white chocolate** chocolate *m* blanco ▸ **white Christmas** Navidades *fpl* blancas *or* con nieve ▸ **white coffee** (*milky*) café *m* con leche; (*with dash of milk*) café *m* cortado ▸ **white dwarf** (*Astron*) enana *f* blanca ▸ **white elephant** (*fig*) elefante *m* blanco • **~ elephant stall** *tenderete donde se venden cachivaches*
▸ **white ensign** (*Brit*) enseña *f* blanca ▸ **white flag** (*Mil*) bandera *f* blanca ▸ **white fox** = **arctic fox** ▸ **white gold** oro *m* blanco
▸ **white goods** electrodomésticos *mpl*
▸ **white grape** uva *f* blanca ▸ **white heat** (*Phys*) calor *m* blanco ▸ **white hope** • **the great ~ hope** la gran esperanza dorada
▸ **white horses** (*on waves*) cabrillas *fpl* ▸ **the White House** (*in US*) la Casa Blanca ▸ **white knight** (*Econ*) caballero *m* blanco ▸ **white lead** (*Chem*) albayalde *m* ▸ **white lie** mentira *f* piadosa • **to tell a ~ lie** decir una mentira piadosa ▸ **white light** (*Phys*) luz *f* blanca
▸ **white line** (*on road*) línea *f* blanca ▸ **white list** (= *list of "safe" websites, email addresses*) lista *f* blanca; (*Brit*) (= *list of "safe" countries*) lista *f* blanca, lista *f* de países seguros
▸ **white magic** magia *f* blanca ▸ **white meat** (*Culin*) carne *f* blanca ▸ **white meter** • **~ meter heating** calefacción *f* por acumulador ▸ **White Nile** = **Nile** ▸ **white noise** (*Acoustics*) ruido *m* blanco *or* uniforme
▸ **white owl** búho *m* blanco ▸ **White Pages** (*US*) (*Telec*) Páginas *fpl* Blancas ▸ **White Paper** (*Brit, Australia, Canada*) (*Parl*) libro *m* blanco ▸ **white pepper** pimienta *f* blanca
▸ **White Russia** (*Hist*) la Rusia Blanca
▸ **White Russian** (*Hist*) ruso/a *m/f* blanco/a
▸ **white sale** (*Comm*) rebajas *fpl* de ropa blanca ▸ **white sapphire** zafiro *m* blanco
▸ **white sauce** salsa *f* bechamel, besamel *f*
▸ **the White Sea** el mar Blanco ▸ **white shark** tiburón *m* blanco ▸ **white slave trade** trata *f* de blancas ▸ **white spirit** (*Brit*) trementina *f* ▸ **white tie** (= *tie*) pajarita *f* blanca; (= *outfit*) traje *m* de etiqueta con pajarita blanca; ▷ **white-tie** ▸ **white trash**** (*US*) (*pej*) *término ofensivo contra la clase blanca pobre estadounidense* ▸ **white water** aguas *fpl* rápidas • **~ water rafting** piragüismo *m* en aguas rápidas, rafting *m* ▸ **white wedding** • **to have a ~ wedding** casarse de blanco (y por la iglesia) ▸ **white whale** ballena *f* blanca ▸ **white wine** vino *m* blanco ▸ **white wood** madera *f* blanca; ▷ **supremacist**
whitebait [ˈwaɪtbeɪt] (N) morralla *f*, pescadito *m* frito
whitebeam [ˈwaɪtbiːm] (N) mojera *f*
whiteboard [ˈwaɪtbɔːd] (N) pizarra *f* vileda®, pizarra *f* blanca
white-collar [ˈwaɪtˌkɒləʳ] (ADJ) • **white-collar worker** oficinista *mf* • **white-collar crime** crímenes *mpl* de guante blanco
white-faced [ˈwaɪtˈfeɪst] (ADJ) blanco (como papel)
whitefish [ˈwaɪtfɪʃ] (N) (= *species*) corégono *m*; (*collectively*) pescado *m* magro, pescado *m* blanco
whitefly [ˈwaɪtˌflaɪ] (N) mosca *f* blanca
white-haired [ˈwaɪtˈhɛəd] (ADJ) canoso, con canas, de pelo cano
Whitehall [ˌwaɪtˈhɔːl] (N) *calle de Londres en la cual hay muchos ministerios*; (*fig*) el gobierno británico

> **WHITEHALL**
> **Whitehall** es la calle de Londres que va desde **Trafalgar Square** al Parlamento (**Houses of Parliament**), calle en la que se hallan la mayoría de los ministerios. Su nombre se usa con frecuencia para referirse conjuntamente a la Administración (**Civil Service**) y a los ministerios, cuando se trata de sus funciones administrativas.

white-headed [ˈwaɪtˈhedɪd] (ADJ) canoso, con canas, de pelo cano • **white-headed boy*** (*fig*) favorito *m*, protegido *m*
white-hot [ˈwaɪtˈhɒt] (ADJ) [*metal*] calentado al blanco, candente
white-knuckle [ˌwaɪtˈnʌkl] (ADJ) **1** [*ride*] (*in fairground*) para los amantes de sensaciones fuertes • **white-knuckle rides such as the rollercoaster** atracciones para los amantes de sensaciones fuertes como la montaña rusa
2 (*fig*) [*experience*] cargado de adrenalina • **a hellish white-knuckle ride through the heavy London traffic** una vuelta infernal

cargada de adrenalina por el denso tráfico de Londres

whiten ['waɪtn] (VT) blanquear
(VI) blanquear; [*person*] palidecer, ponerse pálido

whitener ['waɪtnəʳ] (N) blanqueador *m*

whiteness ['waɪtnɪs] (N) blancura *f*

whitening ['waɪtnɪŋ] (N) = whiting[2]

whiteout ['waɪtaʊt] (N) **1** (*Met*) resplandor *m* sin sombras
2 (= *block*) bloqueo *m* total causado por la nieve
3 (*fig*) masa *f* confusa

whitethorn ['waɪtθɔːn] (N) espino *m*

whitethroat ['waɪtθrəʊt] (N) curruca *f* zarcera

white-tie ['waɪt,taɪ] (ADJ) de etiqueta
• **a white-tie dinner** una cena de etiqueta; ▹ white

whitewash ['waɪtwɒʃ] (N) **1** (*lit*) cal *f*, jalbegue *m*
2 (*fig*) encubrimiento *m*
(VT) **1** (*lit*) encalar, enjalbegar
2 (*fig*) encubrir
3 (*Sport**) dejar en blanco, dar un baño a*

whitey‡ ['waɪtɪ] (N) (*pej*) blanco/a *m/f*

whither ['wɪðəʳ] (ADV) (*poet*) ¿adónde?

whiting[1] ['waɪtɪŋ] (N) (PL: **whiting**) (= *fish*) pescadilla *f*

whiting[2] ['waɪtɪŋ] (N) (= *colouring*) tiza *f*, blanco *m* de España; (*for shoes*) blanco *m* para zapatos; (= *whitewash*) jalbegue *m*

whitish ['waɪtɪʃ] (ADJ) blanquecino, blancuzco

whitlow ['wɪtləʊ] (N) panadizo *m*

Whitsun ['wɪtsn] (N) Pentecostés *m*
(CPD) de Pentecostés

Whitsuntide ['wɪtsntaɪd] (N) Pentecostés *m*
(CPD) de Pentecostés

whittle ['wɪtl] (VT) [+ *wood, shape*] tallar (con cuchillo)

▸ **whittle away** (VT + ADV) (= *reduce*) [+ *savings, amount*] ir reduciendo • **our sovereignty is gradually being ~d away** poco a poco está mermando nuestra soberanía
(VI + ADV) • **to ~ away at sth** (*lit*) tallar algo; (*fig*) ir reduciendo algo

▸ **whittle down** (VT + ADV) [+ *workforce, amount*] reducir • **the short-list has been ~d down to three** hemos reducido el número de candidatos preseleccionados a tres

whiz, whizz [wɪz] (N) **1*** (= *ace*) as* *m* • **he's a ~ at tennis** es un as del tenis*
2 (= *sound*) silbido *m*, zumbido *m*
(VI) • **to ~ by** *or* **past** [*bullet, arrow*] pasar zumbando; [*car*] pasar a gran velocidad • **it ~zed past my head** pasó (silbando) muy cerca de mi cabeza • **to ~ along** • **go ~zing along** ir como una bala • **the sledge ~zed down the slope** el trineo bajó la cuesta a gran velocidad
(CPD) ▸ **whiz(z) kid*** prodigio *m*

whizzy* ['wɪzɪ] (ADJ) sofisticado (y llamativo)

WHO (N ABBR) (= **World Health Organization**) OMS *f*

who [huː] (PRON) **1** (*in direct and indirect questions*) quién (*sing*), quiénes (*pl*) • **who is it?** ¿quién es? • **who are they?** ¿quiénes son? • **who are you looking for?** ¿a quién buscas? • **who does she think she is?*** ¿quién se cree que es? • **I know who it was** (yo) sé quién fue • **you'll soon find out who's who** pronto sabrás quién es quién
2 (*in exclamations*) quién • **guess who!** ¡a ver si adivinas quién soy! • **who should it be but Neil!** ¿a que no sabes quién era? ¡Neil!, ¡no era otro que Neil!
3 (*relative*) que; (*after preposition*) el/la que, quien, el/la cual (*more frm*) • **my cousin who lives in New York** mi primo que vive en Nueva York • **the girl who you saw** la chica que viste • **the girl who you spoke to has since left the company** la chica con la que *or* con quien *or* (*more frm*) con la cual hablaste ya no trabaja en la empresa • **those who can swim** los que saben nadar • **he who wishes to ...** el que desee ... • **deny it who may** aunque habrá quien lo niegue
(CPD) ▸ **Who's Who** (= *book*) *libro que contiene una lista de británicos famosos y destacados* • **their client list reads like a celebrity Who's Who** su lista de clientes incluye a todos los que son alguien en el mundo de la fama

WHO, WHOM

In direct and indirect questions

▹ *In direct and indirect questions as well as after expressions of (un)certainty and doubt (e.g.* **no sé***), translate* **who** *using* **quién/quiénes** *when it is the subject of a verb:*

Who broke the window?
¿Quién rompió la ventana?
She had no idea who her real parents were
Ignoraba quiénes eran sus verdaderos padres

▹ *When* **who/whom** *is the object of a verb or preposition, translate using* **quién/quiénes** *preceded by personal* **a** *or another preposition as relevant:*

Who(m) did you call?
¿A quién llamaste?
Who(m) is she going to marry?
¿Con quién se va a casar?
You must tell me who you are going to go out with
Tienes que decirme con quién/quiénes vas a salir

In exclamations

▹ *Translate using* **quién/quiénes** *with an accent as in the interrogative form:*

Who would have thought it!
¡Quién lo hubiera pensado!

As relative

▹ *When* **who/whom** *follows the noun it refers to, the most common translation is* **que***:*

Do you recognize the three girls who have just come in?
¿Reconoces a las tres chicas que acaban de entrar?
Peter, who was at the match, has told me all about it
Peter, que estuvo en el partido, me lo ha contado todo
That man (who(m you saw wasn't my father
El hombre que viste no era mi padre

NOTE: Personal **a** *is not used before* **que***.*

"Who" as subject of a verb

▹ *When* **who** *is the subject,* **que** *can sometimes be substituted by* **el cual/la cual** *or* **quien** *(singular) and* **los cuales/las cuales** *or* **quienes** *(plural). This can help avoid ambiguity:*

I bumped into Ian and Sue, who had just come back from Madrid
Me encontré con Ian y con Sue, la cual *or* quien acababa de regresar de Madrid

▹ *Only* **que** *is possible in cases where subject* **who** *can be substituted by* **that***, i.e. where* **who** *defines the person in question and the sentence does not make sense if you omit the* **who** *clause:*

The little boy who won the cycle race is Sarah's nephew
El niñito que ganó la carrera ciclista es el sobrino de Sarah

"Who(m)" as object of a verb or preposition

▹ *When* **who(m)** *is the object of a verb, you can translate it using* **que** *as above. Alternatively, especially in formal language, use personal* **a** *+ article +* **quien/quienes** *or personal* **a** *+ article +* **cual/cuales** *etc or personal* **a** *+ article +* **que***:*

The woman (who *or* **whom) you're describing is my music teacher**
La señora que *or* a quien *or* a la cual *or* a la que describes es mi profesora de música

"Who(m)" as object of a preposition

▹ *After prepositions, you should usually use* **que** *or* **cual** *preceded by the article or* **quien***:*

This is the girl (who *or* **whom) I talked to you about**
esta es la chica de la que *or* de la cual *or* de quien te hablé

For further uses and examples, see **who, whom**

whoa [wəʊ] (EXCL) ¡so!

who'd [huːd] = who would, who had

whodunit, whodunnit* [huː'dʌnɪt] (N) novela *f* policíaca

whoever [huː'evəʳ] (PRON) **1** (= *no matter who, anyone that*) • **it won't be easy, ~ does it** no será fácil, no importa quién lo haga • **~ finds it can keep it** quienquiera que lo encuentre puede quedarse con él, el/la que lo encuentre que se lo quede • **I'll talk to ~ it is** hablaré con quien sea • **ask ~ you like** pregúntaselo a cualquiera
2 (= *the person that*) • **~ said that is an idiot** quien haya dicho eso es un imbécil, quienquiera que haya dicho eso es un imbécil
3 (*in questions*) quién • **~ told you that?** ¿quién te dijo eso?

whole [həʊl] (N) (= *complete unit*) todo *m* • **the ~ may be greater than the sum of the** *or* **its parts** el todo puede ser mayor que la suma de las partes • **four quarters make a ~** cuatro cuartos hacen una unidad • **as a ~:** • **the estate is to be sold as a ~** la propiedad va a venderse como una unidad • **Europe should be seen as a ~** Europa debería considerarse como un todo *or* una unidad • **taken as a ~, the project is a success** si se considera en su totalidad, el proyecto es un éxito • **is this true just in India, or in the world as a ~?** ¿es ese el caso solo en la India o en todo el mundo? • **the ~ of** todo • **the ~ of Glasgow was talking about it** todo Glasgow hablaba de ello • **the ~ of our output this year** toda nuestra producción de este año • **the ~ of July** todo el mes de julio • **the ~ of the time** todo el tiempo • **the ~ of Europe** toda Europa, Europa entera • **the ~ of the morning** toda la mañana, la mañana entera • **on the ~** en general
(ADJ) **1** (= *entire*) todo • **the ~ family was there** toda la familia estaba allí • **we spent the ~ summer in Italy** pasamos todo el verano *or* el verano entero en Italia • **a ~ hour** toda una hora, una hora entera • **it rained for three ~ days** llovió durante tres días enteros *or*

W

seguidos • **~ towns were destroyed** pueblos enteros fueron destruidos • **along its ~ length** todo a lo largo • **I've never told anyone in my ~ life** nunca se lo he dicho a nadie en toda mi vida • **a ~ load of people were there*** había un montón de gente allí* • **he took the ~ lot*** se lo llevó todo • **I'm fed up with the ~ lot of them*** estoy harto de todos ellos • **a ~ lot better/worse*** muchísimo mejor/peor • **it's a ~ new world to me*** es un mundo completamente nuevo para mí • **I've bought myself a ~ new wardrobe*** me he comprado un vestuario completamente nuevo • **the ~ point was to avoid that happening** el propósito era evitar que eso pasara • **the ~ point of coming here was to relax** el objetivo de venir aquí era relajarse • **the figures don't tell the ~ story** las cifras no nos dicen toda la verdad • **let's forget the ~ thing** olvidemos todo el asunto, olvidémoslo todo • **he didn't tell the ~ truth** no dijo toda la verdad • **the ~ world** todo el mundo, el mundo entero • IDIOMS: • **to go the ~ hog*** liarse la manta a la cabeza* • **this is a ~ new ball game*** es una historia distinta por completo, es algo completamente distinto

2 (= *intact*) entero • **not a glass was left ~ following the party** no quedó ni un vaso entero tras la fiesta • **keep the egg yolks ~** procure que no se rompan las yemas de huevo • **the seal on the letter was still ~** el sello de la carta no estaba roto • **to make sth ~** (*liter*) (= *heal*) curar algo • **he swallowed it ~** se lo tragó entero

CPD ▸ **whole grains** cereales *mpl* integrales ▸ **whole milk** leche *f* entera ▸ **whole note** (*US*) (*Mus*) semibreve *f* ▸ **whole number** número *m* entero

wholefood ['həʊlfu:d] (*Brit*) N (*also* **wholefoods**) comida *f* naturista, alimentos *mpl* integrales

CPD ▸ **wholefood restaurant** restaurante *m* naturista

whole-grain ['həʊlgreɪn] ADJ [*bread, cereal*] integral

wholegrains ['həʊlgreɪnz] NPL cereales *mpl* integrales

wholehearted ['həʊl'hɑ:tɪd] ADJ [*approval, support*] incondicional

wholeheartedly ['həʊl'hɑ:tɪdlɪ] ADV [*approve, support, accept*] incondicionalmente

wholeheartedness ['həʊl'hɑ:tɪdnɪs] N entusiasmo *m*

wholemeal ['həʊlmi:l] ADJ [*bread, flour*] integral

wholeness ['həʊlnɪs] N (*gen*) totalidad *f*, integridad *f*; [*of mind, body*] integridad *f*

wholesale ['həʊlseɪl] ADJ **1** [*price, trade*] al por mayor

2 (*fig*) (= *on a large scale*) en masa; (= *indiscriminate*) general, total • **~ destruction** destrucción *f* total *or* sistemática

ADV **1** (*lit*) al por mayor • **to buy/sell ~** comprar/vender al por mayor

2 (*fig*) en masa • **the books were burnt ~** los libros fueron quemados en masa

N venta *f* al por mayor, mayoreo *m* (*Mex*)

CPD ▸ **wholesale dealer** = **wholesaler** ▸ **wholesale price index** índice *m* de precios al por mayor ▸ **wholesale trader** = **wholesaler**

wholesaler ['həʊlseɪlə^r] N comerciante *mf* al por mayor, mayorista *mf*

wholesaling ['həʊlseɪlɪŋ] N venta *f* al por mayor, mayoreo *m* (*Mex*)

wholesome ['həʊlsəm] ADJ sano, saludable

wholesomeness ['həʊlsəmnɪs] N lo sano, lo saludable

whole-wheat ['həʊlwi:t] ADJ (*esp US*) de trigo integral, hecho con trigo entero

who'll [hu:l] = **who will**

wholly ['həʊlɪ] ADV totalmente, completamente • **not ~ successful** no todo un éxito, no un éxito completo

wholly-owned subsidiary [ˌhəʊlɪˌəʊnd-səb'sɪdɪərɪ] N filial *f* de plena propiedad

whom [hu:m] PRON (*frm*) **1** (*in direct and indirect questions*) • **~ did you see?** ¿a quién viste? • **from ~ did you receive it?** ¿de quién lo recibiste? • **I know of ~ you are talking** sé de quién hablas

2 (*relative*) • **the gentleman ~ I saw** el señor a quien *or* al cual *or* al que vi; (*less formal*) el señor que vi • **the lady ~ I saw** la señora a quien *or* a la cual *or* a la que vi; (*less formal*) la señora que vi • **the lady with ~ I was talking** la señora con la que *or* con la cual *or* con quien hablaba • **three policemen, none of ~ wore a helmet** tres policías, ninguno de los cuales llevaba casco • **three policemen, two of ~ were drunk** tres policías, dos de los cuales estaban borrachos • **three policemen, all of ~ were drunk** tres policías, que estaban todos borrachos; ▹ WHO, WHOM

whomever [hu:m'evə^r] PRON *an accusative form of* **whoever**

whomp* [wɒmp] (*US*) VT (= *hit*) dar un tortazo a; (= *defeat*) dar una paliza a

N paliza *f*

whomsoever [ˌhu:msəʊ'evə^r] PRON *an emphatic accusative form of* **whosoever**

whoop [hu:p] N grito *m*, alarido *m* • **with a ~ of joy** con un grito de alegría

VI gritar, dar alaridos; (*when coughing*) toser

VT • **to ~ it up**†* (= *make merry*) divertirse ruidosamente; (= *let hair down*) echar una cana al aire

whoopee [wʊ'pi:] EXCL ¡estupendo!

N • **to make ~**†* divertirse una barbaridad*

CPD ▸ **whoopee cushion*** cojín *m* de ventosidades

whooping cough ['hu:pɪŋˌkɒf] N tos *f* ferina, coqueluche *f*

whoops [wu:ps] EXCL ¡epa!, ¡lep!

whoosh [wʊʃ] N *ruido del agua que sale bajo presión, o del viento fuerte* • **it came out with a ~** salió con mucha fuerza

whop‡ [wɒp] VT pegar

whopper* ['wɒpə^r] N **1** (= *big thing*) monstruo *m* • **that fish is a ~** ese pez es enorme • **what a ~!** ¡qué enorme!

2 (= *lie*) bola *f*

whopping* ['wɒpɪŋ] ADJ (*also* **whopping great**) enorme, grandísimo

whore ['hɔ:^r] N (*pej*) puta *f*

VI (*also* **go whoring**) putear, putañear††

who're ['hu:ə^r] = **who are**

whorehouse ['hɔ:haʊs] N (PL: **whorehouses** ['hɔ:haʊzɪz]) (*US*) casa *f* de putas

whorl [wɜ:l] N [*of shell*] espira *f*; [*of fingerprint*] espiral *m*; (*Bot*) verticilo *m*

whortleberry ['wɜ:tlˌbərɪ] N arándano *m*

who's [hu:z] = **who is, who has**

whose [hu:z] PRON (*in direct and indirect questions*) de quién • **~ is this?** ¿de quién es esto? • **~ are these?** (*1 owner expected*) ¿de quién son estos?; (*2 or more owners expected*) ¿de quiénes son estos? • **I don't know ~ it is** no sé de quién es

ADJ **1** (*in direct and indirect questions*) de quién • **~ purse is this?** ¿de quién es este monedero? • **~ cars are these?** (*1 owner expected*) ¿de quién son estos coches?; (*2 or more owners expected*) ¿de quiénes son estos coches? • **~ fault was it?** ¿quién tuvo la culpa? • **~ car did you go in?** ¿en qué coche fuiste? • **do you know ~ hat this is?** ¿sabes de quién es este sombrero? • **I don't know ~ watch this is** no sé de quién es este reloj

2 (*relative*) cuyo • **those ~ passports I have** aquellas personas cuyos pasaportes tengo, *or* de las que tengo pasaportes • **the man ~ hat I took** el hombre cuyo sombrero tomé • **the man ~ seat I sat in** el hombre en cuya silla me senté • **the cup ~ handle you broke** la taza a la que le rompiste el asa

> **WHOSE**
>
> **In direct and indirect questions**
>
> ▹ **Whose** *in direct questions as well as after report verbs and expressions of (un)certainty and doubt (e.g.* **no sé***) translates as* **de quién/de quiénes**, *never* **cuyo**:
>
> **Whose coat is this?**
> ¿De quién es este abrigo?
> **He asked us whose coats they were**
> Nos preguntó de quiénes eran los abrigos
> **I don't know whose umbrella this is**
> No sé de quién es este paraguas
>
> **As a relative**
>
> ▹ *In relative clauses* **whose** *can be translated by* **cuyo/cuya/cuyos/cuyas** *and must agree with the following noun:*
>
> **The man whose daughter is a friend of Emily's works for the Government**
> El señor cuya hija es amiga de Emily trabaja para el Gobierno
> **... the house whose roof collapsed ...**
> ... la casa cuyo tejado se hundió ...
>
> *When* **whose** *refers to more than one noun, make* **cuyo** *agree with the first:*
>
> **... a party whose policies and strategies are very extremist ...**
> ... un partido cuya política y tácticas son muy extremistas ...
>
> ▹ *However,* **cuyo** *is not much used in spoken Spanish. Try using another structure instead:*
>
> **... the house whose roof collapsed ...**
> ... la casa a la que se le hundió el tejado ...
> **My daughter, whose short story won a prize in the school competition, wants to be a journalist**
> Mi hija, a quien premiaron por su relato en el concurso de la escuela, quiere ser periodista
>
> *NOTE: There is no accent on* **quien** *here, as it is a relative pronoun.*
>
> *For further uses and examples, see main entry.*

whosis* ['hu:zɪs] N (*US*) **1** (= *thing*) chisme *m*, cosa *f*

2 (= *person*) fulano/a *m/f*, cómo-se-llame *mf*

whosoever [ˌhu:səʊ'evə^r] = **whoever**

who've [hu:v] = **who have**

whozis* ['hu:zɪs] N (*US*) = **whosis**

whse ABBR = **warehouse**

why [waɪ] ADV por qué • **why not?** ¿por qué no? • **why on earth didn't you tell me?** ¿por qué demonios no me lo dijiste? • **I know why you did it** sé por qué lo hiciste • **why he did it we shall never know** no sabremos nunca por qué razón lo hizo • **that's why I couldn't come** por eso no pude venir • **which is why I am here** que es por lo que estoy aquí

EXCL ¡toma!, ¡anda! • **why, it's you!** ¡toma, eres tú!, ¡anda, eres tú! • **why, what's the matter?** bueno, ¿qué pasa? • **why, there are**

W

8 of us! ¡si somos 8! • **why, it's easy!** ¡vamos, es muy fácil!
(N) • **the whys and (the) wherefores** el porqué

WHY

▷ **Why** *can usually be translated by* **por qué**:
Why didn't you come?
¿Por qué no viniste?
They asked her why she hadn't finished her report
Le preguntaron por qué no había terminado el informe

NOTE: Remember the difference in spelling between **por qué** *(why) and* **porque** *(because).*

▷ *To ask specifically about the purpose of something, you can translate* **why** *using* **para qué**:
Why go if we are not needed?
¿Para qué vamos a ir si no nos necesitan?

▷ *In statements, you can translate* **(the reason) why** *using* **por qué, la razón (por la que)** *or* **el motivo (por el que)**:
Tell me (the reason) why you don't want to accept the proposal
Dime por qué *or* la razón por la que *or* el motivo por el que no quieres aceptar la propuesta

▷ *Translate* **that's why** *using* **por eso**:
That's why they wouldn't pay
Por eso no querían pagar

▷ *Like all question words in Spanish,* **porqué** *can function as a masculine noun. Note that in* **el porqué, porqué** *is written as one word:*
I'd like to know why he's absent *or* **the reason for his absence**
Me gustaría saber el porqué de su ausencia

For further uses and examples, see main entry.

whyever [ˌwaɪ'evəʳ] (ADV) • **~ did you do it?** ¿por qué demonios lo hiciste?

WI (ABBR) **1** = **West Indies**
2 (US) = **Wisconsin**
(N ABBR) (Brit) (= **Women's Institute**) ≈ IM *m*

Wicca ['wɪkə] (N) Wicca *f*

wick [wɪk] (N) mecha *f* • **IDIOMS**: • **he gets on my ~*** me hace subir por las paredes* • **to dip one's ~**‡ echar un polvo‡

wicked ['wɪkɪd] (ADJ) **1** (= *evil*) malvado, cruel • **that was a ~ thing to do** eso no se perdona
2 (= *naughty*) [*grin, look, suggestion*] pícaro • **he gave a ~ grin** sonrió con picardía • **a ~ sense of humour** un sentido del humor socarrón
3* (*fig*) [*price*] escandaloso; [*satire*] muy mordaz, cruel; [*temper*] terrible; (= *very bad*) horroroso, horrible • **a ~ waste** un despilfarro escandaloso • **it's ~ weather** hace un tiempo horrible • **it's a ~ car to start** este coche es horrible para arrancar
4‡ (= *brilliant*) de puta madre‡, estupendo*, guay*
(N) • **IDIOM**: • **no rest** *or* **peace for the ~** no hay descanso para los malvados

wickedly ['wɪkɪdlɪ] (ADV) **1** (= *evilly*) [*behave, destroy*] malvadamente, cruelmente
2 (= *naughtily*) [*grin, laugh, suggest*] con picardía • **a ~ funny play** una obra para desternillarse de risa

wickedness ['wɪkɪdnɪs] (N) **1** (= *evil*) maldad *f*, crueldad *f* • **all manner of ~** toda clase de maldades
2 (= *naughtiness*) [*of grin, laugh, suggestion*] picardía *f*

wicker ['wɪkəʳ] (N) mimbre *m or f*
(CPD) de mimbre

wickerwork ['wɪkəwɜːk] (N) **1** (= *objects*) artículos *mpl* de mimbre
2 [*of chair etc*] rejilla *f*
3 (= *craft*) cestería *f*
(CPD) de mimbre

wicket ['wɪkɪt] (N) **1** (*Cricket*) (= *stumps*) palos *mpl*; (= *pitch*) terreno *m*; (= *fallen wicket*) entrada *f*, turno *m* • **IDIOM**: • **to be on a sticky ~** estar en un aprieto*; ▷ **CRICKET**
2 (*also* **wicket gate**) postigo *m*, portillo *m*
(CPD) ▸ **wicket keeper** (*Cricket*) guardameta *mf*

wide [waɪd] (ADJ) (COMPAR: **wider**, SUPERL: **widest**) **1** [*street, river, trousers*] ancho; [*area*] extenso; [*ocean, desert*] vasto; [*space, circle, valley*] amplio • **he was a tall man with ~ shoulders** era un hombre alto de hombros anchos • **it's ten centimetres ~** tiene diez centímetros de ancho *or* de anchura • **a three-mile-wide crater** un cráter de tres millas de ancho *or* de anchura • **how ~ is it?** ¿cuánto tiene de ancho?, ¿qué anchura tiene? • **her eyes were ~ with amazement** tenía los ojos como platos de asombro* • **IDIOM**: • **to give sb a ~ berth** evitar a algn
2 (= *extensive*) [*support, variety*] gran; [*range, selection*] amplio • **a ~ choice of bulbs is available** hay una gran variedad de bulbos donde escoger, hay una gran variedad de bulbos disponible • **there is a ~ choice of colours** hay muchos colores para escoger • **he has a ~ following** tiene un gran número de seguidores • **a ~ range of** una amplia gama de • **in the wider context of** dentro del contexto más amplio de • **the story received ~ coverage** el suceso recibió una amplia cobertura • **to have (a) ~ knowledge of sth** tener amplios conocimientos de algo • **this ruling could have wider implications** esta decisión podría tener implicaciones más amplias • **the incident raises wider issues** el incidente hace plantearse cuestiones de mayor envergadura
3 (= *large*) [*gap, differences*] grande • **to win by a ~ margin** ganar por un margen amplio
4 (= *off target*) • **his first shot was ~** (*Ftbl*) su primer tiro *or* chute pasó de largo; (*Shooting*) su primer disparo no dio en el blanco • **to be ~ of the target** desviarse mucho del blanco • **IDIOM**: • **to be ~ of the mark** encontrarse lejos de la realidad • **their accusations may not be so ~ of the mark** puede que sus acusaciones no se encuentren tan lejos de la realidad
(ADV) **1** (= *fully*) • **he opened the window ~** abrió la ventana de par en par • **~ apart** bien separados • **to be ~ awake** (*lit*) estar completamente despierto • **we'll have to be ~ awake for this meeting** tendremos que estar con los ojos bien abiertos en esta reunión, tendremos que estar muy al tanto en esta reunión • **~ open** [*window, door*] de par en par, completamente abierto • **with his eyes (open) ~** *or* **~ open** con los ojos muy abiertos • **she went into marriage with her eyes ~ open** se casó sabiendo muy bien lo que hacía • **the ~ open spaces** los espacios abiertos • **we were left ~ open to attack** quedamos totalmente expuestos a un ataque
2 (= *off target*) • **the shot went ~** (*Ftbl*) el tiro *or* chute pasó de largo; (*Shooting*) el disparo no dio en el blanco • **Fleming shot ~** (*Ftbl*) Fleming realizó un disparo que pasó de largo a la portería; ▷ **far**
(N) (*Cricket*) *pelota que el bateador no puede golpear porque la han lanzado muy lejos y que cuenta como una carrera para el equipo del bateador*
(CPD) ▸ **wide boy**‡ buscón‡ *m*, ratero* *m*
▸ **wide area network** red *f* de área amplia

-wide [waɪd] (ADJ), (ADV) (*ending in compounds*) • **a Community-wide ballot** una votación a escala comunitaria; ▷ **countrywide, nationwide**

wide-angle ['waɪdˌæŋgl] (ADJ) • **wide-angle lens** gran angular *m*

wide-awake ['waɪdə'weɪk] (ADJ) **1** (*lit*) completamente *or* bien despierto
2 (*fig*) (= *on the ball*) despabilado; (= *alert*) vigilante, alerta

wide-bodied ['waɪd'bɒdɪd] (ADJ) (*Aer*) de fuselaje ancho

wide-eyed ['waɪd'aɪd] (ADJ) con los ojos muy abiertos, con los ojos como platos*; (*fig*) inocente, cándido

widely ['waɪdlɪ] (ADV) **1** (= *over wide area, far apart*) • **debris from the blast was scattered ~** los restos de la explosión quedaron esparcidos por una amplia zona • **the trees were ~ spaced** los árboles estaban muy separados los unos de los otros
2 (= *extensively*) [*travel*] mucho • **to be ~ available** poder conseguirse con facilidad • **it is ~ believed that ...** mucha gente cree que ... • **the cabinet reshuffle had been ~ expected** la remodelación del gabinete ministerial había sido esperada por muchos • **a ~ held belief** una creencia generalizada • **to be ~ read** [*reader*] tener una amplia cultura, haber leído mucho; [*author*] contar con un gran número de lectores • **his books are ~ read** sus libros cuentan con un gran número de lectores, sus libros se leen mucho • **it is ~ regarded as ...** es considerado por la mayoría como ... • **to be ~ travelled** haber viajado mucho • **to be ~ used** ser de uso extendido *or* generalizado
3 (= *greatly*) [*vary, differ*] mucho
4 (= *broadly*) [*smile*] abiertamente

widen ['waɪdn] (VT) **1** (*lit*) [+ *road, river, sleeve*] ensanchar
2 (*fig*) [+ *knowledge, circle of friends*] extender, ampliar
(VI) **1** (*lit*) (*also* **widen out**) ensancharse • **the passage ~s out into a cave** el pasillo se ensancha para formar una caverna
2 (*fig*) • **the gap between rich and poor has ~ed** ha aumentado la diferencia entre ricos y pobres • **the ~ing gap between the rich and the poor** el creciente abismo entre los ricos y los pobres

wideness ['waɪdnɪs] (N) anchura *f*, amplitud *f*

widening ['waɪdnɪŋ] (N) **1** [*of road*] ensanche *m*
2 [*of gap, difference*] aumento *m*

wide-ranging ['waɪdˌreɪndʒɪŋ] (ADJ) [*survey, report*] de gran alcance; [*interests*] muy diversos

wide-screen ['waɪdskriːn] (ADJ) [*film*] para pantalla ancha; [*television set*] de pantalla ancha, con pantalla panorámica

widespread ['waɪdspred] (ADJ) [*use*] generalizado, extendido; [*belief, concern*] generalizado; [*support, criticism*] a nivel general; [*fraud, corruption*] muy extendido • **to become ~** extenderse, generalizarse • **rain will become ~ across the whole of the British Isles** las lluvias se extenderán por todas las islas Británicas • **there is ~ fear that ...** muchos temen que ...

widgeon ['wɪdʒən] (N) ánade *m* silbón

widget* ['wɪdʒɪt] (N) (= *device*) artilugio *m*; (= *thingummy*) ingenio *m*, cacharro* *m*

widow ['wɪdəʊ] (N) **1** viuda *f* • **to be left a ~** quedar viuda, enviudar • **Widow Newson**†† la viuda de Newson • **~'s pension** viudedad *f*,

pensión *f* de viudedad
2 (*fig*) • **I'm a golf ~** paso mucho tiempo sola mientras mi marido juega al golf • **all the cricket ~s got together for tea** todas las mujeres cuyos maridos estaban jugando al críquet se reunieron para tomar el té
(VT) • **to be ~ed** enviudar, quedar viudo/a • **she was twice ~ed** ha enviudado dos veces, quedó viuda dos veces • **she has been ~ed for five years** enviudó hace cinco años, quedó viuda hace cinco años
(CPD) ▸ **widow's peak** pico *m* de viuda
widowed ['wɪdəʊd] (ADJ) viudo • **his ~ mother** su madre viuda
widower ['wɪdəʊəʳ] (N) viudo *m*
widowhood ['wɪdəʊhʊd] (N) viudez *f*
width [wɪdθ] (N) **1** [*of street, river*] ancho *m*, anchura *f* • **what ~ is the room?** ¿qué ancho *or* anchura tiene la habitación? • **it is five metres in ~** • **it has a ~ of five metres** tiene cinco metros de ancho *or* anchura, tiene un ancho *or* una anchura de cinco metros
2 [*of fabric, swimming pool*] ancho *m* • **to swim a ~** hacer un ancho (de la piscina)
widthways ['wɪdθweɪz] (ADV), **widthwise** ['wɪdθwaɪz] (ADV) a lo ancho
wield [wi:ld] (VT) [+ *sword, axe, pen*] manejar; [+ *power, influence*] ejercer
wiener ['wi:nəʳ] (N) (*US*) (= *frankfurter*) salchicha *f* de Frankfurt
wiener schnitzel ['vi:nə'ʃnɪtsəl] (N) escalope *m* de ternera con guarnición
wienie ['wi:nɪ] (N) (*US*) (*Culin*) salchicha *f* de Frankfurt
wife [waɪf] (N) (PL: **wives**) mujer *f*, esposa *f* • **this is my ~** esta es mi esposa *or* mujer • **my boss and his ~** mi jefe y su esposa *or* mujer • **the ~*** la parienta*, la jefa* • **"The Merry Wives of Windsor"** "Las alegres comadres de Windsor" • **~'s earned income** ingresos *mpl* de la mujer • **to take a ~†** desposarse • **to take sb to ~†** desposarse con algn
(CPD) ▸ **wife beater** *hombre que maltrata a su mujer* ▸ **wife swapping** cambio *m* de pareja
wifely† ['waɪflɪ] (ADJ) de esposa
wifey* ['waɪfɪ] (N) mujercita* *f*
Wi-Fi, wifi ['waɪfaɪ] (N) (= **wireless fidelity**) wifi *m*
(CPD) [*hotspot, network*] wifi
wig [wɪg] (N) peluca *f*
wigeon ['wɪdʒən] (N) ánade *m* silbón
wigged [wɪgd] (ADJ) con peluca
wigging* ['wɪgɪŋ] (N) (*Brit*) rapapolvo* *m*, bronca *f* • **to give sb a ~** echar un rapapolvo *or* una bronca a algn*
wiggle ['wɪgl] (N) meneo *m* • **to walk with a ~** caminar contoneándose
(VT) [+ *toes, fingers*] mover (mucho); [+ *hips*] contonear, menear
(VI) [*person*] contonearse; [*hips*] contonearse, menearse
(CPD) ▸ **wiggle room*** (= *room for manoeuvre*) margen *m* de maniobra
wiggly ['wɪglɪ] (ADJ) [*line*] ondulado
wigmaker ['wɪg,meɪkəʳ] (N) peluquero/a *m/f* (*que se dedica a hacer pelucas*)
wigwam ['wɪgwæm] (N) tipi *m*, tienda *f* india
wiki ['wɪkɪ] (N) wiki *f*
(CPD) [*entry, site, software*] de wiki
wilco [,wɪl'kəʊ] (ADV ABBR) (*Telec*) (= **I will comply**) ¡procedo!
wild [waɪld] (ADJ) (COMPAR: **wilder**, SUPERL: **wildest**) **1** (= *not domesticated*) **a** [*animal, bird*] salvaje; (= *fierce*) feroz • **~ duck** pato *m* salvaje • IDIOM: • **~ horses wouldn't drag me there** tendrían que llevarme a rastras, no iría ni por todo el oro del mundo
b [*plant*] silvestre • **~ flowers** flores *fpl* silvestres • **~ strawberries** fresas *fpl* silvestres • IDIOM: • **to sow one's ~ oats** correrla*
c [*countryside*] salvaje, agreste • **a ~ stretch of coastline** un tramo salvaje *or* agreste de costa
2 (= *stormy*) [*wind*] furioso, violento; [*weather*] tormentoso; [*sea*] bravo • **it was a ~ night** fue una noche tormentosa *or* de tormenta
3 (= *unrestrained, disorderly*) [*party*] loco; [*enthusiasm*] desenfrenado; [*hair*] revuelto; [*appearance*] desastrado; [*look, eyes*] de loco • **he invited a bunch of his ~ friends round** invitó a un grupo de amigos locos • **he had a ~ youth** hizo muchas locuras en su juventud • **we had some ~ times together** ¡hicimos cada locura juntos! • IDIOM: • **~ and woolly**: • **a member of some ~ and woolly activist group** un miembro de un grupo de esos de activistas locos
4* (*emotionally*) **a** (= *angry*) • **it drives** *or* **makes me ~** me saca de quicio • **he went ~ when he found out** se puso como loco cuando se enteró • **to be ~ with sb** estar furioso con algn
b (= *distraught*) • **I was ~ with jealousy** estaba loco de celos
c (= *ecstatic*) [*cheers, applause*] exaltado, apasionado • **to be ~ about sth/sb: he's just ~ about Inga** está loco por Inga • **I'm not exactly ~ about the idea** no es que la idea me entusiasme demasiado • **Anthea drives men ~ with desire** Anthea vuelve a los hombres locos de deseo • **the crowd went ~ (with excitement)** la multitud se puso loca de entusiasmo • **to be ~ with joy** estar loco de alegría
5 (= *crazy, rash*) [*idea, plan, rumour*] descabellado, disparatado • **it's a ~ exaggeration** es una enorme exageración • **they made some ~ promises** hicieron unas promesas disparatadas • **they have succeeded beyond their ~est dreams** han tenido más éxito del que jamás habían soñado • **never in my ~est dreams did I imagine winning this much** nunca imaginé, ni soñando, que ganaría tanto
6 (= *haphazard*) • **it's just a ~ guess** no es más que una conjetura al azar *or* una suposición muy aventurada • **I made a ~ guess** dije lo primero que se me vino a la cabeza
7 (*Cards*) • **aces are ~** los ases sirven de comodines
(ADV) **1** • **to grow ~** crecer en estado silvestre
2 • **to run ~ a** (= *roam freely*) [*animal*] correr libremente; [*child*] corretear libremente
b (= *get out of control*) • **the garden had run ~** las plantas del jardín habían crecido de forma descontrolada • **Molly has let that girl run ~** Molly ha dejado que esa niña haga lo que quiera • **you've let your imagination run ~** te has dejado llevar por la imaginación • **the inevitable result of fanaticism run ~** la inevitable consecuencia del fanatismo desenfrenado
(N) **1** • **the ~: animals caught in the ~** animales capturados en su hábitat natural • **untended fields returning to the ~** campos descuidados que vuelven a su estado silvestre • **the call of the ~** el atractivo de lo salvaje *or* de la naturaleza
2 • **the ~s** tierras *fpl* inexploradas • **the ~s of Canada** las tierras inexploradas de Canadá • **to live out in the ~s** (*hum*) vivir en el quinto pino* • **they live out in the ~s of Berkshire** viven en lo más remoto de Berkshire
(CPD) ▸ **wild beast** fiera *f*, bestia *f* salvaje ▸ **wild boar** jabalí *m* ▸ **wild card** (*Comput, Cards*) comodín *m*; (*Sport*) *invitación para participar en un torneo a pesar de no reunir los requisitos establecidos* • **the ~ card in the picture is Eastern Europe** la gran incógnita dentro de este conjunto es Europa Oriental ▸ **wild cherry** cereza *f* silvestre ▸ **wild child** (*Brit*) adolescente *mf* rebelde ▸ **wild goose chase** • **he sent me off on a ~ goose chase** me mandó de la Ceca a la Meca* • **it proved to be a ~ goose chase** resultó ser una búsqueda inútil ▸ **wild rice** arroz *m* silvestre ▸ **the Wild West** el oeste americano
wildcat ['waɪld'kæt] (N) (PL: **wildcats** *or* **wildcat**) **1** (*Zool*) gato *m* montés
2 (*for oil*) perforación *f* de sondaje en tierra virgen
(VI) (*US*) hacer perforaciones para extraer petróleo
(CPD) [*scheme, venture*] descabellado ▸ **wildcat strike** huelga *f* salvaje *or* no autorizada
wildebeest ['wɪldɪbi:st] (N) (PL: **wildebeests** *or* **wildebeest**) ñu *m*
wilderness ['wɪldənɪs] (N) (= *desert*) desierto *m*; (= *hills*) monte *m*; (= *virgin land*) tierra *f* virgen • **a ~ of ruins** un desierto de ruinas • **he spent four years in the ~ before returning to power** (*fig*) pasó cuatro años al margen de la política antes de volver al poder
wild-eyed ['waɪld'aɪd] (ADJ) de mirada salvaje
wildfire ['waɪld,faɪəʳ] (N) • **to spread like ~** correr como un reguero de pólvora
wildfowl ['waɪldfaʊl] (NPL) (*gen*) aves *fpl* de caza; (= *ducks*) ánades *mpl*
wildfowler ['waɪld,faʊləʳ] (N) cazador(a) *m/f* de ánades
wildfowling ['waɪld,faʊlɪŋ] (N) caza *f* de ánades
wildlife ['waɪldlaɪf] (N) fauna *f*
(CPD) ▸ **wildlife park** parque *m* natural ▸ **wildlife photographer** fotógrafo/a *m/f* de naturaleza ▸ **wildlife preserve** reserva *f* natural ▸ **wildlife programme** programa *m* de naturaleza ▸ **wildlife reserve** reserva *f* natural ▸ **wildlife sanctuary** santuario *m* natural ▸ **wildlife trust** asociación *f* protectora de la naturaleza
wildly ['waɪldlɪ] (ADV) **1** (= *ecstatically*) [*shout*] como loco; [*applaud*] a rabiar, como loco • **the Democrats were cheering ~ for their nominee** los demócratas vitoreaban como locos a su candidato nominado
2 (= *frantically*) [*stare, look*] con cara de espanto; [*gesture*] como loco, violentamente • **the driver was gesticulating ~** el conductor gesticulaba como loco *or* violentamente
3 (= *violently*) [*hit out, throw*] violentamente, como loco
4 (= *crazily, rashly*) [*guess*] sin pensarlo mucho; [*promise*] en un arrebato; [*exaggerated*] muy
5 (= *haphazardly*) [*shoot*] a lo loco, a tontas y a locas*; [*fluctuate, vary*] muchísimo
6 (= *extremely*) • **~ happy/enthusiastic** loco de felicidad/entusiasmo • **Naomi was ~ jealous of her sister** Naomi sentía unos celos locos de su hermana • **a ~ improbable story** una historia disparatadísima • **a ~ inaccurate estimate** un cálculo que dista/distaba muchísimo de la realidad
wildness ['waɪldnɪs] (N) **1** (= *undomesticated state*) [*of animal, tribe, landscape*] estado *m* salvaje, lo salvaje; [*of place*] estado *m* salvaje *or* agreste, lo salvaje, lo agreste
2 (= *storminess*) [*of weather*] furia *f*; [*of sea*] bravura *f*
3 (= *lack of restraint*) desenfreno *m*; [*of appearance*] lo desordenado • **there was a look of ~ in his eyes** había algo de locura en su mirada
4 (= *craziness, rashness*) [*of idea, plan, rumour*] lo descabellado, lo disparatado

5 (= *haphazardness*) [*of shot*] lo errático

wiles ['waɪlz] (NPL) artimañas *fpl*, ardides *mpl*

wilful, **willful** (*US*) ['wɪlfʊl] (ADJ)
1 (= *obstinate*) testarudo, terco
2 (= *deliberate*) intencionado, deliberado, premeditado; [*murder etc*] premeditado

wilfully, **willfully** (*US*) ['wɪlfəlɪ] (ADV)
1 (= *obstinately*) voluntariosamente, tercamente • **you have ~ ignored ...** te has obstinado en no hacer caso de ...
2 (= *intentionally*) a propósito, adrede

wilfulness, **willfulness** (*US*) ['wɪlfʊlnɪs] (N)
1 (= *obstinacy*) testarudez *f*, terquedad *f*
2 (= *premeditation*) lo intencionado, lo premeditado

wiliness ['waɪlɪnɪs] (N) astucia *f*

will¹ [wɪl] (PT: **would**) (MODAL VB) 1 (*talking about the future*) **a** • **I ~** *or* **I'll finish it tomorrow** lo terminaré mañana • **I ~** *or* **I'll have finished it by tomorrow** lo habré terminado para mañana • **you won't lose it, ~ you?** no lo perderás ¿verdad?; (*stronger*) no lo vayas a perder • **you ~ come to see us, won't you?** vendrás a vernos, ¿no? • **it won't take long** no llevará mucho tiempo • **we'll probably go out later** seguramente saldremos luego • **I'll always love you** te querré siempre • **what ~ you do?** ¿qué vas a hacer? • **we'll be having lunch late** vamos a comer tarde • **we'll talk about it later** hablamos luego
b (*emphatic language*) • **I ~ do it!** ¡sí lo haré! • **no he won't!** ¡no lo hará!
2 (*in conjectures*) • **he ~** *or* **he'll be there by now** ya debe de haber llegado *or* ya habrá llegado • **she'll be about 50** tendrá como 50 años • **that ~ be the postman** será el cartero
3 (*expressing willingness*) **a** (*in commands, insistence*) • **~ you sit down!** ¡siéntate! • **~ you be quiet!** ¿te quieres callar? • **he ~ have none of it** no quiere ni siquiera pensarlo • **"I won't go" — "oh yes you ~"** —no voy —¿cómo que no? • **I ~ not** *or* **I won't put up with it!** ¡no lo voy a consentir! • **I ~ not have it that ...** no permito que se diga que ... (+ *subjun*) • **I ~** (*marriage service*) sí quiero
b (*in offers, requests, invitations, refusals*) • **come on, I'll help you** venga, te ayudo • **~ you help me?** ¿me ayudas? • **wait a moment, ~ you?** espera un momento, ¿quieres? • **~ you have some tea?** ¿quieres tomar un té? • **~ you sit down?** ¿quiere usted sentarse?, tome usted asiento (*more frm*) • **won't you come with us?** ¿no quieres venir con nosotros? • **Tom won't help me** Tom no me quiere ayudar
4 (*expressing habits*) **a** soler, acostumbrar a • **she ~ read for hours on end** suele leer *or* acostumbra a leer durante horas y horas
b (*expressing persistence*) • **she ~ smoke, despite what the doctor says** a pesar de lo que dice el médico, se empeña en fumar • **accidents ~ happen** son cosas que pasan • **boys ~ be boys** así son los chicos • **he ~ keep leaving the door open** siempre tiene que dejar la puerta abierta • **if you ~ eat so much, you can hardly expect to be slim** si insistes en comer tanto, no pensarás adelgazar
5 (*expressing capability*) • **the car won't start** el coche no arranca • **the car ~ cruise at 100mph** el coche podrá alcanzar las 100 millas por hora • **a man who ~ do that ~ do anything** un hombre que es capaz de eso es capaz de todo
(VI) (= *wish*) querer • **(just) as you ~!** ¡como quieras! • **if God ~s** si lo quiere Dios • **say what you ~** di lo que quieras • **do as you ~** haz lo que quieras, haz lo que te parezca bien • **look where you ~, you won't find one** mires donde mires, no vas a encontrar uno

will² [wɪl] (N) 1 (= *inclination, wish*) voluntad *f* • **against sb's ~** contra la voluntad de algn • **at ~** a voluntad • **to do sb's ~** hacer la voluntad de algn • **Thy ~ be done** hágase tu voluntad • **to do sth of one's own free ~** hacer algo por voluntad propia • **the ~ of God** la voluntad de Dios • **iron ~** • **~ of iron** voluntad *f* de hierro • **to have a ~ of one's own** tener voluntad propia • **it is my ~ that you should do it** (*frm*) quiero que lo hagas • **the ~ to win/live** el deseo de ganar/vivir • **to work with a ~** trabajar con ahínco • **with the best ~ in the world** por mucho que se quiera • PROVERB: • **where there's a ~ there's a way** querer es poder; ▹ **ill**
2 (= *testament*) testamento *m* • **the last ~ and testament of ...** la última voluntad de ... • **to make a ~** hacer testamento
(VT) 1 (= *urge on by willpower*) lograr a fuerza de voluntad • **he ~ed himself to stay awake** consiguió quedarse despierto a fuerza de voluntad • **I was ~ing you to win** estaba deseando que ganaras
2 (= *ordain*) ordenar, disponer • **God has so ~ed it** Dios lo ha ordenado así
3 (= *leave in one's will*) • **to ~ sth to sb** legar algo a algn, dejar algo (en herencia) a algn • **he ~ed his pictures to the nation** legó sus cuadros a la nación

Will [wɪl] (N) *familiar form of* **William**

willful ['wɪlfʊl] (ADJ) (*US*) = **wilful**

willfully ['wɪlfəlɪ] (ADV) (*US*) = **wilfully**

willfulness ['wɪlfʊlnɪs] (N) (*US*) = **wilfulness**

William ['wɪljəm] (N) Guillermo • **~ the Conqueror** Guillermo el Conquistador

willie* ['wɪlɪ] (N) (*Brit*) = **willy**

willies* ['wɪlɪz] (NPL) • **it gives me the ~** me da horror • **I get the ~ whenever I think about it** me horroriza pensar en ello

willing ['wɪlɪŋ] (ADJ) 1 (= *enthusiastic*) [*helper*] voluntarioso • **she proved to be a ~ helper in their campaign** demostró ser una ayudante voluntariosa en su campaña • **there were plenty of ~ hands** había mucha gente dispuesta a ayudar • **he was a ~ participant in the scheme** participó en el programa por su propia voluntad • **we're looking for a few ~ volunteers** estamos buscando unos cuantos voluntarios con buena disposición • **his pronouncements found a ~ audience** sus opiniones tuvieron una buena acogida
2 (= *disposed*) • **to be ~ to do sth** estar dispuesto a hacer algo • **are you ~?** ¿estás dispuesto (a hacerlo)? • **to show ~** mostrarse dispuesto; ▹ **god**

willingly ['wɪlɪŋlɪ] (ADV) 1 (= *with pleasure*) con gusto, de buena gana • **"will you help us?" — "willingly!"** —¿nos ayudas? —¡con mucho gusto! *or* ¡cómo no!
2 (= *voluntarily*) por voluntad propia

willingness ['wɪlɪŋnɪs] (N) buena voluntad *f*, buena disposición *f* • **I don't doubt his ~, just his competence** no dudo de su buena voluntad *or* disposición, solo de su capacidad • **I had to prove my ~ to work** tuve que probar mi buena disposición para trabajar • **I was grateful for his ~ to help** agradecí su interés por ayudar

will-o'-the-wisp ['wɪləðə'wɪsp] (N) (*lit*) fuego *m* fatuo; (*fig*) quimera *f*

willow ['wɪləʊ] (N) (*also* **willow tree**) sauce *m*
(CPD) ▸ **willow pattern** *dibujos de aspecto chinesco para la cerámica*; ▹ **willow-pattern**
▸ **willow warbler** mosquitero *m* musical

willowherb ['wɪləʊhɜːb] (N) adelfa *f*

willow-pattern ['wɪləʊˌpætən] (ADJ) • **willow-pattern plate** plato *m* de estilo chino; ▹ **willow**

willowy ['wɪləʊɪ] (ADJ) esbelto

willpower ['wɪlpaʊəʳ] (N) fuerza *f* de voluntad

Willy ['wɪlɪ] (N) *familiar form of* **William**

willy* ['wɪlɪ] (N) 1 (*Anat*) colita* *f*, pito* *m*
2 • **the willies** ▹ **willies**

willy-nilly ['wɪlɪ'nɪlɪ] (ADV)
1 (= *unsystematically*) de cualquier manera
2 (= *willingly or not*) quiérase o no, guste o no guste

wilt¹ [wɪlt] (VI) 1 [*flower*] marchitarse
2 (*fig*) (= *lose strength*) debilitarse; (= *lose courage*) perder el ánimo, desanimarse • **we were beginning to ~ in the heat** el calor estaba empezando a hacernos desfallecer
(VT) 1 (*lit*) marchitar
2 (*fig*) debilitar
3 (*Culin*) rehogar

wilt²†† [wɪlt] (VB) *2nd pers: 'thou' form of* **will¹**

wilted ['wɪltɪd] (ADJ) 1 [*flower*] marchitado
2 (*Culin*) rehogado

Wilts [wɪlts] (N ABBR) = **Wiltshire**

wily ['waɪlɪ] (ADJ) (COMPAR: **wilier**, SUPERL: **wiliest**) astuto, taimado

WIMP [wɪmp] (ABBR) (*Comput*) = **windows, icons, menu** *or* **mice, pointers**

wimp* [wɪmp] (N) • **he's a ~** (*physically*) es un debilucho*; (*in character*) es un parado*
▸ **wimp out*** (VI + ADV) rajarse*

wimpish* ['wɪmpɪʃ] (ADJ) [*behaviour*] ñoño; [*person*] (*physically*) debilucho*; (*in character*) parado*

wimpishness* ['wɪmpɪʃnɪs] (N) debilidad *f*

wimple ['wɪmpl] (N) griñón *m*

wimpy ['wɪmpɪ] = **wimpish**

win [wɪn] (VB: PT, PP: **won**) (N) victoria *f*, triunfo *m* • **another win for Castroforte** otra victoria *or* otro triunfo para el Castroforte • **their fifth win in a row** su quinta victoria consecutiva, su quinto triunfo consecutivo • **last Sunday's win against** *or* **over Pakistan** la victoria del domingo frente a *or* sobre Pakistán • **to back a horse for a win** apostar dinero por un caballo para que gane la/una carrera • **I had a win on the lottery** gané la lotería; ▹ **no-win**
(VT) 1 (= *be victorious in*) [+ *competition, bet, war, election*] ganar • IDIOMS: • **you can't win them all** no siempre se puede ganar • **to win the day** (*Mil*) triunfar; (*fig*) triunfar, imponerse • **pragmatism will probably win the day** al final triunfará *or* se impondrá el pragmatismo • **the government finally won the day after a heated debate** finalmente el gobierno triunfó *or* se impuso tras un debate acalorado; ▹ **spur**
2 (= *be awarded*) [+ *cup, award, prize, title*] ganar; [+ *contract, order*] obtener, conseguir • **the party won a convincing victory at the polls** el partido consiguió *or* obtuvo una victoria convincente en las elecciones
3 (= *obtain*) [+ *pay rise, promotion*] conseguir, ganarse; [+ *support, friendship, recognition*] ganarse; [+ *metal, ore*] extraer (**from** de) • **how to win friends and influence people** cómo ganarse amigos e influenciar a las personas • **to win a reputation for honesty** granjearse *or* ganarse una reputación de persona honrada • **to win sb sth: it won him first prize** le valió *or* le ganó el primer premio • **this manoeuvre won him the time he needed** esta maniobra le ganó el tiempo que necesitaba • **to win sth from sb** ganar algo a algn • **he won five pounds from her at cards** le ganó cinco libras jugando a cartas • **new land won from the marshes** nuevas tierras ganadas a los pantanos • **to win sb's hand (in marriage)** obtener la mano de algn (en matrimonio) (*frm*) • **to win sb's heart** conquistar a algn • **to win sb to one's cause** ganar a algn para la causa de uno, atraer a algn a la causa de uno

4 (= *reach*) [+ *shore*] llegar a, alcanzar; [+ *goal*] conseguir • **he won his way to the top of his profession** (a base de trabajar duro) consiguió llegar a la cima de su profesión
5 (*Mil*) (= *capture*) tomar
VI (*in war, sport, competition*) ganar • **who's winning?** ¿quién va ganando? • **go in and win!** ¡a ganar! • **he has a good chance of winning** tiene muchas posibilidades de hacerse con la victoria *or* de ganar • **OK, you win*** vale, ganas tú • **Evans won 2-6, 6-4, 6-3** Evans ganó 2-6, 6-4, 6-3 • **she always wins at cards** siempre gana a las cartas • **to win by a head/a length** ganar por una cabeza/un largo • **to play to win** jugar a ganar • IDIOMS: • **you can't win**: • **whatever you say, you're always wrong, you can't win** digas lo que digas, ellos siempre tienen razón, ¡no hay manera! • **to win hands down** ganar de forma aplastante
▸ **win back** VT + ADV [+ *trophy*] recobrar; [+ *support, confidence*] volver a ganarse; [+ *land*] reconquistar, volver a conquistar; [+ *gambling loss, job*] recuperar; [+ *voters, girlfriend, boyfriend*] volver a conquistar a • **I won the money back from him** recuperé el dinero que me ganó
▸ **win out** VI + ADV triunfar, imponerse • **tiredness won out** triunfó *or* se impuso el cansancio • **she won out over six other candidates** se impuso a otros seis candidatos
▸ **win over, win round** VT + ADV convencer • **eventually we won him over to our point of view** por fin lo convencimos de que teníamos razón • **they are hoping to win over undecided voters** esperan ganarse a los votantes indecisos
▸ **win through** VI + ADV 1 (= *succeed*) triunfar • **stick to your principles and you will win through** mantente firme a tus principios y al final triunfarás
2 (*Sport*) • **she won through to the second round** ganó y pasó a la segunda ronda

wince [wɪns] N [*of revulsion*] mueca *f*; [*of pain*] mueca *f* de dolor • **he said with a ~** dijo con una mueca
VI (= *shudder*) estremecerse • **he ~d in pain** hizo una mueca de dolor • **he ~d at the thought of dining with Camilla** la idea de cenar con Camilla le hacía estremecer

winceyette [ˌwɪnsɪˈet] N (*Brit*) franela *f* de algodón

winch [wɪntʃ] N torno *m*, cabrestante *m*
VT (*also* **winch up**) levantar (con un torno *or* cabrestante) • **he was ~ed up by the helicopter** lo levantaron con el helicóptero • **to ~ sth down** bajar algo (con un torno *or* cabrestante)

Winchester disk® [ˈwɪntʃɪstəˈdɪsk] N disco *m* Winchester®

wind¹ [wɪnd] N 1 viento *m* • **which way is the ~ blowing?** ¿de dónde sopla el viento? • **against the ~** contra el viento • **to run before the ~** (*Naut*) navegar viento en popa • **high ~** viento fuerte • **into the ~** contra el viento • IDIOMS: • **to see which way the ~ blows** esperar para ver por dónde van los tiros • **~s of change** aires *mpl* de cambio, aires *mpl* nuevos • **to get ~ of sth** enterarse de algo • **to get the ~ up*** preocuparse • **to have the ~ up*** estar preocupado • **there's something in the ~** algo se está cociendo • **to put the ~ up sb** (*Brit**) dar un susto a algn • **it really put the ~ up me** me dio un susto de los buenos • **to take the ~ out of sb's sails** cortar las alas a algn • PROVERB: • **it's an ill ~ that blows nobody any good** no hay mal que por bien no venga; ▹ **sail**
2 (*Physiol*) gases *mpl*; [*of baby*] flato *m* • **to break ~** ventosear • **to bring up ~** [*baby*] eructar
3 (= *breath*) aliento *m* • **to be short of ~** estar sin aliento; ▹ **second¹**
4* (= *talk*) • **that's all a lot of ~** todo eso son chorradas*
5 (*Mus*) • **the ~(s)** los instrumentos *mpl* de viento
VT • **to ~ sb** (*with punch etc*) dejar a algn sin aliento • **to ~ a baby** hacer eructar a un niño • **to be ~ed by a ball** quedar sin aliento por el golpe de un balón • **to be ~ed after a race** quedar sin aliento después de una carrera
CPD ▸ **wind chimes** móvil *m* de campanillas ▸ **wind cone** = **windsock** ▸ **wind energy** = **wind power** ▸ **wind farm** parque *m* eólico ▸ **wind instrument** instrumento *m* de viento ▸ **wind machine** máquina *f* de viento ▸ **wind power** energía *f* eólica *or* del viento ▸ **wind tunnel** túnel *m* aerodinámico *or* de pruebas aerodinámicas ▸ **wind turbine** aerogenerador *m*

wind² [waɪnd] (PT, PP: **wound** [waʊnd]) VT
1 (= *roll, coil*) [+ *rope, wire*] enrollar • **the rope wound itself round a branch** la cuerda se enrolló en *or* alrededor de una rama • **with a rope wound tightly round his waist** con una cuerda que le ceñía estrechamente la cintura • **to ~ wool into a ball** ovillar lana, hacer un ovillo de lana • **~ this round your head** envuélvete la cabeza con esto, líate esto a la cabeza • **to ~ one's arms round sb** rodear a algn con los brazos, abrazar a algn estrechamente
2 (*also* **wind up**) [+ *clock, watch, toy*] dar cuerda a; [+ *key, handle*] dar vueltas a
3 (= *twist*) • **the road ~s its way through the valley** la carretera serpentea por el valle
VI (= *snake*) serpentear • **the road ~s up the valley** el camino serpentea por el valle • **the car wound slowly up the hill** el coche subió lentamente la sinuosa colina
N 1 (= *bend*) curva *f*, recodo *m*
2 • **to give one's watch a ~** dar cuerda al reloj • **give the handle another ~** dale otra vuelta a la manivela
▸ **wind back** VT + ADV [+ *tape, film*] rebobinar
▸ **wind down** VT + ADV [+ *car window*] bajar; (= *scale down*) [+ *production, business*] disminuir poco a poco, reducir poco a poco
VI + ADV 1 (*lit*) [*clock*] pararse
2* (= *relax*) relajarse
3* (= *come to an end*) [*activity, event*] tocar a su fin
▸ **wind forward** VT + ADV [+ *tape, film*] correr
▸ **wind in** VT + ADV • **to ~ in a fishing line** ir cobrando sedal
▸ **wind on** VT + ADV [+ *film*] enrollar
VI + ADV [*film*] enrollarse
▸ **wind up** VT + ADV 1 (*lit*) [+ *car window*] subir; [+ *clock, toy*] dar cuerda a
2 (= *close*) [+ *meeting, debate*] cerrar, dar por terminado; [+ *company*] liquidar • **he wound up his speech by saying that ...** terminó su discurso diciendo que ...
3 • **to be wound up** (= *tense*) estar tenso • **she's dreadfully wound up** está muy tensa • **it gets me all wound up (inside)** me pone nerviosísimo
4 (*Brit**) • **to ~ sb up** (= *provoke*) provocar a algn; (= *tease*) tomar el pelo a algn
VI + ADV 1 (= *finish*) [*meeting, debate, speaker*] concluir, terminar • **how does the play ~ up?** ¿cómo concluye *or* termina la obra?
2* (= *end up*) acabar • **we wound up in Rome** acabamos en Roma, fuimos a parar a Roma

windbag* [ˈwɪndbæg] N (= *person*) hablador(a) *m/f*

windblown [ˈwɪndbləʊn] ADJ [*leaf etc*] llevado *or* arrancado por el viento; [*hair*] despeinado por el viento

windborne [ˈwɪndbɔːn] ADJ llevado por el viento

windbreak [ˈwɪndbreɪk] N (*natural*) abrigada *f*, barrera *f* contra el viento; (*for plants*) pantalla *f* cortavientos; (*at seaside*) cortavientos *m inv*

windbreaker [ˈwɪndˌbreɪkəʳ] N (*esp US*) cazadora *f*

windburn [ˈwɪndˌbɜːn] N • **to get ~** curtirse al viento

windcheater [ˈwɪndˈtʃiːtəʳ] N cazadora *f*

windchill [ˈwɪndtʃɪl] N sensación *f* térmica, *efecto térmico producido por un viento frío y una baja temperatura*
CPD ▸ **the windchill factor** *factor que determina la sensación térmica producida por un viento frío y una baja temperatura*

winder [ˈwaɪndəʳ] N (*on watch etc*) cuerda *f*

windfall [ˈwɪndfɔːl] N 1 (= *apple etc*) fruta *f* caída
2 (*fig*) dinero *m* caído del cielo
CPD ▸ **windfall profits** beneficios *mpl* imprevistos ▸ **windfall tax** *impuesto sobre determinados beneficios extraordinarios*

windgauge [ˈwɪndgeɪdʒ] N anemómetro *m*

winding [ˈwaɪndɪŋ] ADJ [*road, path*] tortuoso, serpenteante
N [*of road*] tortuosidad *f* • **the ~s of a river** las vueltas *or* los meandros de un río
CPD ▸ **winding sheet** mortaja *f* ▸ **winding staircase** escalera *f* de caracol

winding-gear [ˈwaɪndɪŋgɪəʳ] N manubrio *m*, cabrestante *m*

winding-up [ˈwaɪndɪŋˈʌp] N conclusión *f*; (*Comm*) liquidación *f*

windjammer [ˈwɪndˌdʒæməʳ] N buque *m* de vela (grande y veloz)

windlass [ˈwɪndləs] N torno *m*

windless [ˈwɪndlɪs] ADJ sin viento

windmill [ˈwɪndmɪl] N molino *m* de viento; (= *toy*) molinete *m*

window [ˈwɪndəʊ] N 1 (*also Comput*) ventana *f*; (= *shop window*) escaparate *m*, vitrina *f* (*LAm*), vidriera *f* (*S. Cone*); [*of booking office, car, envelope*] ventanilla *f* • **to lean out of the ~** asomarse a la ventana • **to look out of the ~** mirar por la ventana • **to break a ~** romper un cristal *or* (*LAm*) un vidrio • IDIOM: • **to fly out of the ~**: **common sense flies out of the ~** el sentido común se va al traste, se pierde todo atisbo de sentido común
2 (= *period of time*) espacio *m*
CPD ▸ **window box** jardinera *f* de ventana ▸ **window cleaner** (= *liquid*) limpiacristales *m inv*; (= *person*) limpiacristales *mf inv* ▸ **window display** escaparate *m* ▸ **window dresser** escaparatista *mf*, decorador(a) *m/f* de escaparates ▸ **window dressing** escaparatismo *m*, decoración *f* de escaparates; (*in accounts etc*) presentación *f* de información especiosa • **it's all just ~ dressing** (*fig*) es pura fachada ▸ **window envelope** sobre *m* de ventanilla ▸ **window frame** marco *m* de ventana ▸ **window ledge** antepecho *m*, alféizar *m* de la ventana ▸ **window of opportunity** excelente oportunidad *f*, oportunidad *f* única ▸ **window pane** cristal *m*, vidrio *m* (*LAm*) ▸ **window seat** asiento *m* junto a la ventana; (*Rail etc*) asiento *m* junto a una ventanilla ▸ **window shade** (*US*) (*in one-piece*) estor *m*; (*slatted*) persiana *f*

window-shop [ˈwɪndəʊʃɒp] VI ir a mirar escaparates

window-shopping [ˈwɪndəʊˌʃɒpɪŋ] N • **to go window-shopping** ir a mirar escaparates • **I like window-shopping** me gusta mirar escaparates

windowsill [ˈwɪndəʊsɪl] N antepecho *m*,

W

alféizar *m* de la ventana

windpipe ['wɪndpaɪp] (N) tráquea *f*

wind-powered ['wɪnd,paʊəd] (ADJ) impulsado por el viento

windproof ['wɪndpru:f] (ADJ) a prueba de viento

windscreen ['wɪndskri:n], **windshield** ['wɪndʃi:ld] (*US*) (N) parabrisas *m inv*
(CPD) ▸ **windscreen washer** lavaparabrisas *m inv* ▸ **windscreen wiper** limpiaparabrisas *m inv*

windsleeve ['wɪndsli:v] (N) = **windsock**

windsock ['wɪndsɒk] (N) (*Aer*) manga *f* (de viento)

windstorm ['wɪndstɔ:m] (N) ventarrón *m*, huracán *m*

windsurf ['wɪndsɜ:f] (VI) hacer windsurf

windsurfer ['wɪndsɜ:fəʳ] (N) tablista *mf*, surfista *mf*

windsurfing ['wɪndsɜ:fɪŋ] (N) windsurf *m* • **to go ~** hacer windsurf

windswept ['wɪndswept] (ADJ) [*place*] azotado por el viento • **he came in looking very ~** entró con el pelo muy revuelto

wind-up* ['waɪndʌp] (N) **1** (*Brit*) (= *joke*) tomadura *f* de pelo*
2 = **winding-up**

windward ['wɪndwəd] (ADJ) de barlovento
(N) barlovento *m* • **to ~** a barlovento

Windward Isles ['wɪndwəd,aɪlz] (NPL) islas *fpl* de Barlovento

windy ['wɪndɪ] (ADJ) (COMPAR: **windier**, SUPERL: **windiest**) **1** [*day*] de mucho viento, ventoso; [*place*] (= *exposed to wind*) expuesto al viento • **it's ~ today** hoy hace viento • **Edinburgh's a very ~ city** en Edimburgo hace mucho viento • **the Windy City** Chicago *m*; ▷ CITY NICKNAMES
2 (*Brit**) (= *afraid, nervous*) miedoso, temeroso (**about** por) • **to be ~** pasar miedo • **to get ~** asustarse
(CPD) ▸ **windy conditions** condiciones *fpl* de viento • **in ~ conditions** en condiciones de viento

wine [waɪn] (N) vino *m* • **red/white/rosé ~** vino tinto/blanco/rosado
(VT) • **to ~ and dine sb** agasajar a algn
(VI) • **to ~ and dine** comer y beber (en restaurantes)
(CPD) ▸ **wine bar** bar *m* especializado en servir vinos ▸ **wine bottle** botella *f* de vino ▸ **wine box** caja *f* de vino ▸ **wine cask** tonel *m* de vino, barril *m* de vino ▸ **wine cellar** bodega *f* ▸ **wine expert** experto/a *m/f* en vinos ▸ **wine glass** = **wineglass** ▸ **wine grower** viñador(a) *m/f* ▸ **wine growing** vinicultura *f*; ▸ **wine-growing** ▸ **wine list** lista *f or* carta *f* de vinos ▸ **wine merchant** (*Brit*) vinatero/a *m/f* ▸ **wine press** prensa *f* de uvas, lagar *m* ▸ **wine rack** botellero *m* ▸ **wine taster** catador(a) *m/f* de vinos ▸ **wine tasting** cata *f* de vinos ▸ **wine vinegar** vinagre *m* de vino ▸ **wine waiter** sumiller *m*, escanciador *m*

winebibber ['waɪn,bɪbəʳ] (N) bebedor(a) *m/f*

wine-coloured, **wine-colored** (*US*) ['waɪnkʌləd] (ADJ) de color vino (*inv*), burdeos (*inv*)

wineglass ['waɪnglɑ:s] (N) copa *f* (de vino)

wine-growing ['waɪn,grəʊɪŋ] (ADJ) vinícola; ▷ **wine**

winemanship ['waɪnmənʃɪp] (N) pericia *f* en vinos, enofilia *f*

winery ['waɪnərɪ] (N) (*esp US*) bodega *f*

wineskin ['waɪnskɪn] (N) pellejo *m*, odre *m*

wing [wɪŋ] (N) **1** [*of bird*] ala *f* • **the bird spread its ~s** el pájaro extendió las alas • **to be on the ~** estar volando • **to shoot a bird on the ~** matar un pájaro al vuelo • **on the ~s of fantasy** en alas de la fantasía • **to take ~** (*liter*) irse volando, alzar el vuelo • IDIOMS: • **to clip sb's ~s** cortar las alas a algn • **to do sth on a ~ and a prayer** hacer algo con Dios y ayuda • **to stretch** *or* **spread one's ~s** empezar a volar • **to take sb under one's ~** dar amparo a algn, tomar a algn bajo su protección
2 [*of chair*] orejera *f*, oreja *f*
3 (*Sport*) (= *position*) extremo *m*, ala *f*; (= *player*) extremo/a *m/f*, alero/a *m/f*
4 (*Archit*) ala *f* • **the east/west ~** el ala este/oeste
5 (= *section*) ala *f* • **the left ~ of the party** el ala izquierda del partido
6 (*Brit*) (*Aut*) aleta *f*
7 wings (*Theat*) bastidores *mpl* • IDIOM: • **to be waiting in the ~s** esperar entre bastidores
(VT) **1** • **to ~ one's way: soon they were airborne and ~ing their way south** poco tiempo después iban (transportados) por aire en dirección sur
2 (= *wound*) [+ *bird*] tocar en el ala, herir en el ala; [+ *person*] herir en el brazo/hombro
3 • **to ~ it** (*Theat*) (*also fig**) improvisar sobre la marcha
(CPD) ▸ **wing back** (*Ftbl*) lateral *mf* ▸ **wing case** (*Zool*) élitro *m* ▸ **wing chair** butaca *f* de orejas, butaca *f* orejera ▸ **wing collar** cuello *m* de puntas ▸ **wing commander** teniente *mf* coronel de aviación ▸ **wing forward** (*Rugby*) ala *mf* ▸ **wing mirror** retrovisor *m* ▸ **wing nut** tuerca *f* mariposa ▸ **wing tip** punta *f* del ala

wingding‡ ['wɪŋ,dɪŋ] (N) (*US*) fiesta *f* animada, guateque *m* divertido

winged [wɪŋd] (ADJ) (*Zool*) alado; [*seed*] con alas

-winged [wɪŋd] (ADJ) (*ending in compounds*) de alas • **brown-winged** de alas pardas • **four-winged** de cuatro alas

winger ['wɪŋəʳ] (N) (*Sport*) extremo/a *m/f*, alero/a *m/f*

wingless ['wɪŋlɪs] (ADJ) sin alas

wingspan ['wɪŋspæn], **wingspread** ['wɪŋspred] (N) envergadura *f*

wink [wɪŋk] (N) **1** (= *blink*) pestañeo *m*; (*meaningful*) guiño *m* • **to give sb a ~** guiñar el ojo a algn • **he said with a ~** dijo guiñando el ojo • IDIOMS: • **to have 40 ~s** echarse una siesta *or* cabezada • **to tip sb the ~*** avisar a algn secretamente
2 (= *instant*) • **I didn't sleep a ~** • **I didn't get a ~ of sleep** no pegué ojo
(VI) **1** (*meaningfully*) guiñar el ojo • **to ~ at sb** guiñar el ojo a algn • **to ~ at sth** (*fig*) hacer la vista gorda a algo
2 [*light, star*] centellear, parpadear
(VT) [+ *eye*] guiñar

winker ['wɪŋkəʳ] (N) (*Brit*) (*Aut*) intermitente *m*

winking ['wɪŋkɪŋ] (N) pestañeo *m* • IDIOM: • **it was as easy as ~** era facilísimo
(ADJ) pestañeante

winkle ['wɪŋkl] (N) bígaro *m*, bigarro *m*
(VT) • **to ~ a secret out of sb** sacar un secreto a algn

winkle-pickers* ['wɪnkl,pɪkəz] (NPL) (*Brit*) *zapatos o botas de puntera muy estrecha*

winnable ['wɪnəbl] (ADJ) que se puede ganar

winner ['wɪnəʳ] (N) **1** (*in race, competition*) vencedor(a) *m/f*, ganador(a) *m/f*; [*of prize, lottery*] ganador(a) *m/f* • **~ takes all** el ganador se lo lleva todo
2 (*Ftbl*) (= *goal*) gol *m* de la victoria, gol *m* decisivo
3 (*fig*) **a*** (= *sth successful*) • **this record is a ~!** ¡este disco es un exitazo!* • **I think you're on to a ~ there** creo que con esto tienes la ganancia asegurada
b (= *beneficiary*) • **the ~s will be the shareholders** los que saldrán ganando serán los accionistas
(CPD) ▸ **winner's enclosure** (*at race course*) recinto *m* de ganadores

winning ['wɪnɪŋ] (ADJ) **1** [*person, horse, team*] ganador, vencedor; [*number, entry*] ganador; [*goal, shot*] de la victoria, decisivo
2 (= *engaging*) [*smile*] encantador, irresistible; [*personality*] encantador, cautivador
(CPD) ▸ **winning post** meta *f*

winningly ['wɪnɪŋlɪ] (ADV) [*smile*] encantadoramente

winnings ['wɪnɪŋz] (NPL) ganancias *fpl*

winnow ['wɪnəʊ] (VT) aventar

winnower ['wɪnəʊəʳ], **winnowing machine** ['wɪnəʊɪŋmə,ʃi:n] (N) aventadora *f*

wino* ['waɪnəʊ] (N) alcohólico/a *m/f*

winsome ['wɪnsəm] (ADJ) encantador, cautivador

winsomely ['wɪnsəmlɪ] (ADV) de forma encantadora, de forma cautivadora

winsomeness ['wɪnsəmnɪs] (N) encanto *m*

winter ['wɪntəʳ] (N) invierno *m* • **in ~** en invierno • **I like to go skiing in (the) ~** me gusta ir a esquiar en invierno • **in the ~ of 1998** en el invierno de 1998 • **a ~'s day** un día de invierno
(VI) invernar
(CPD) ▸ **winter blues*** depresión *f* invernal, depresión *f* del invierno ▸ **winter clothes** ropa *f* de invierno ▸ **winter Olympics** Olimpiada *f* de invierno, Juegos *mpl* Olímpicos de invierno ▸ **winter quarters** cuarteles *mpl* de invierno ▸ **winter solstice** solsticio *m* de invierno ▸ **winter sports** deportes *mpl* de invierno

wintergreen ['wɪntəgri:n] (N) gaulteria *f* • **oil of ~** aceite *m* de gaulteria

winterize ['wɪntəraɪz] (VT) (*US*) adaptar para el invierno

winterkill ['wɪntə'kɪl] (*US*) (VT) matar de frío
(VI) perecer a causa del frío

wintertime ['wɪntətaɪm] (N) invierno *m* • **in (the) ~** en invierno

winterwear ['wɪntə,wɛəʳ] (N) ropa *f* de invierno

wintry, **wintery** ['wɪntrɪ] (ADJ) invernal; (*fig*) glacial

win-win [,wɪn'wɪn] (ADJ) [*situation, opportunity*] beneficioso para todos

wipe [waɪp] (N) **1** (= *action*) • **to give sth a ~ (down** *or* **over)** pasar un trapo a algo, dar una pasada con un trapo a algo
2 (= *product*) toallita *f* • **baby ~s** toallitas *fpl* húmedas para el bebé • **face ~s** toallitas húmedas para la cara
(VT) **1** (= *clean, dry*) [+ *table, floor, surface*] pasar un trapo a, limpiar (con un trapo); [+ *blackboard*] borrar, limpiar; [+ *dishes*] secar; [+ *one's nose, shoes*] limpiarse; [+ *one's face, hands*] secarse • **to ~ one's eyes/one's brow** enjugarse *or* secarse las lágrimas/la frente • **~ your feet before you come in** límpiate los pies antes de entrar • **to ~ one's bottom** limpiarse el trasero • **to ~ sth clean** limpiar algo • **to ~ sth dry** secar algo (con un trapo/una toalla *etc*) • IDIOMS: • **to ~ the floor with sb*** dar una paliza a algn* • **to ~ the slate clean** hacer borrón y cuenta nueva
2 (= *remove*) • **she ~d the sweat from** *or* **off her face** se secó *or* se limpió el sudor de la cara • **she ~d the tears from her eyes** se secó *or* se limpió las lágrimas de los ojos • **he stood up, wiping the crumbs from around his mouth** se levantó, limpiándose *or* quitándose las migas de alrededor de la boca • **ten billion pounds was ~d off shares** el valor de las acciones bajó en diez mil millones de libras • IDIOM: • **that will ~ the smile off her face!*** ¡eso le quitará las ganas

W

de sonreír!, ¡con eso se le quitarán las ganas de sonreír!
3 (= move, pass) • **to ~ sth over sth**: • **he ~d a handkerchief over his forehead** se enjugó *or* se secó la frente con un pañuelo • **he ~d his hand across his eyes** se pasó la mano por los ojos
4 (= erase) [+ tape, disk, data] borrar • **they had ~d what had happened from their minds** habían borrado de la memoria lo sucedido • **the village was ~d from** *or* **off the map in a bombing raid** los bombardeos borraron la aldea del mapa
VI secar • **you wash, I'll ~** tú friega, yo seco
▸ **wipe at** VI + PREP (= dry) secar; (= clean) limpiar • **she ~d at her nose with (the back of) her hand** se secó/limpió la nariz con (el dorso de) la mano
▸ **wipe away** VT + ADV 1 (lit) [+ one's tears] enjugarse, secarse; [+ sb's tears] enjugar, secar; [+ marks] quitar, limpiar • **he ~d away the blood with a handkerchief** limpió la sangre con un pañuelo
2 (fig) [+ guilt, hurt, memory] borrar
▸ **wipe down** VT + ADV [+ surface, wall] limpiar
▸ **wipe off** VT + ADV (= remove) [+ stain, marks] quitar, limpiar; [+ recording, data] borrar
VI + ADV [stain, marks] salir, limpiarse
▸ **wipe out** VT + ADV 1 (= clean) [+ container] limpiar
2 (= eliminate) [+ town, people, army] aniquilar; [+ species] exterminar; [+ disease] erradicar; [+ opposition] derrotar de forma aplastante, aniquilar
3 (= erase) [+ past, memory] borrar
4 (= cancel) [+ debt] liquidar; [+ gains] cancelar
5* (= exhaust) dejar hecho polvo*
6* (= bankrupt) dejar en la ruina *or* bancarrota
7* (= kill) liquidar*, borrar del mapa*
▸ **wipe up** VT + ADV limpiar
VI + ADV 1 (= dry the dishes) secar
2 (= clean up) limpiar
wipe-out ['waɪpaʊt] N 1 (= destruction) [of town] destrucción *f*; [of army, people] aniquilación *f*
2 (in competition, election) derrota *f* aplastante
3 (Surfing) caída *f*
wiper ['waɪpəʳ] N 1 (= cloth) paño *m*, trapo *m*
2 (Brit) (Aut) limpiaparabrisas *m inv*
wire ['waɪəʳ] N 1 (metal) alambre *m*; (Elec) cable *m* • **copper ~** hilo *m* de cobre • **the telephone ~** el cable del teléfono • IDIOMS: • **to get one's ~s crossed*** tener un malentendido • **to pull ~s** (US*) tocar resortes • **he can pull ~s** (US*) tiene enchufes*, tiene buenas agarraderas (Chile*)
2 (US) (Telec) telegrama *m* • **to send sb a ~** enviar un telegrama a algn
3 (Police) (= hidden microphone) micrófono *m* oculto
VT 1 (also **wire up**) (Elec) [+ house] poner la instalación eléctrica en; [+ fence] electrificar • **it's ~d (up) for sound** tiene la instalación eléctrica para el sonido • **it's all ~d (up) for cable television** se ha completado la instalación eléctrica para la televisión por cable • **to be ~d up** (US*) (= tense) estar tenso
2 (US) (Telec) • **to ~ sb** comunicar con algn (por telegrama) • **to ~ money to sb** enviar un giro telegráfico a algn • **to ~ information to sb** enviar información a algn por telegrama
3 (= connect) conectar (**to** a) • **it's ~d to the alarm** está conectado a la alarma
CPD ▸ **wire brush** cepillo *m* de alambre ▸ **wire cutters** cortaalambres *m inv*, cizalla *fsing* ▸ **wire fence** alambrado *m* ▸ **wire mesh, wire netting** tela *f* metálica, malla *f* metálica ▸ **wire service** (esp US) agencia *f* de noticias ▸ **wire wool** lana *f* de alambre
▸ **wire up** VT + ADV ▹ **wire**

wired ['waɪəd] ADJ 1* (esp US) (also **wired up**) (= edgy, uptight) con los nervios de punta
2* (= connected to the internet) conectado
CPD ▸ **wired ribbon** cinta *f* con alambre
wire-haired ['waɪəhɛəd] ADJ [dog] de pelo áspero
wireless ['waɪəlɪs] ADJ (= without wires) inalámbrico; [technology, communication] sin cables, inalámbrico
N (esp Brit†) radio *f* • **by ~** por radio • **to talk on the ~** hablar por radio
CPD ▸ **Wireless Application Protocol** (Telec) Protocolo *m* de aplicaciones inalámbricas ▸ **wireless hotspot** punto *m* caliente, hotspot *m* ▸ **wireless message**† radiograma *m* ▸ **wireless operator**† radiotelegrafista *mf*, radio *mf* ▸ **wireless router** router *m* inalámbrico ▸ **wireless set**† radio *f*, receptor *m* de radio, transistor *m* ▸ **wireless station**† emisora *f* ▸ **wireless technology** tecnología *f* inalámbrica
wirepuller* ['waɪə,pʊləʳ] N (US) enchufista* *mf*
wirepulling* ['waɪə,pʊlɪŋ] N (US) empleo *m* de resortes, enchufismo* *m*
wire-rimmed ['waɪə'rɪmd] ADJ [glasses] de montura metálica
wiretap ['waɪətæp] (US) VI intervenir las conexiones telefónicas, practicar escuchas telefónicas
VT [+ telephone] intervenir; [+ room] poner escuchas telefónicas en
wiretapping ['waɪə'tæpɪŋ] N (US) intervención *f* electrónica
wirewalker ['waɪəwɔːkəʳ] N (US) = **tightrope walker**
wireworm ['waɪəwɜːm] N gusano *m* de elatérido
wiring ['waɪərɪŋ] N (Elec) (= wiring system) instalación *f* eléctrica; (= wires) cables *mpl* • **the cause of the fire was faulty ~** la causa del incendio fue la instalación eléctrica defectuosa
CPD ▸ **wiring diagram** diagrama *m* de la instalación eléctrica
wiry ['waɪərɪ] ADJ (COMPAR: **wirier**, SUPERL: **wiriest**) [person, animal, build] enjuto y fuerte; [hair] áspero, tieso; [hand] nervudo
Wis., Wisc. ABBR (US) = **Wisconsin**
wisdom ['wɪzdəm] N sabiduría *f* • **he is a man of great ~** es un hombre de gran sabiduría • **I question the ~ of that decision** dudo que sea una decisión acertada • **I would question the ~ of attempting such a thing** no me parece acertado intentarlo • **in my ~, I decided to ignore their advice** (iro) dando muestras de mi gran sabiduría, decidí hacer caso omiso de su consejo
CPD ▸ **wisdom tooth** muela *f* del juicio
wise[1] [waɪz] ADJ (COMPAR: **wiser**, SUPERL: **wisest**) 1 (= learned) [person] sabio; [words] sabio, acertado • **he's a very ~ man** es un hombre muy sabio • **the Three Wise Men** los Reyes Magos • **she's very ~ in the ways of the world** tiene mucha experiencia de la vida • **she had grown ~r with age** se había vuelto más prudente *or* juiciosa con los años • **to get ~** (esp US*) darse cuenta, caer en la cuenta* • **the police got ~ to them** la policía los caló* • **to get ~ with sb** (esp US*) hacerse el listo con algn • **a ~ move** una idea acertada • **I'm none the wiser** me he quedado igual • **nobody will be any the ~r** nadie se dará cuenta • **to put sb ~ to sth*** poner a algn al corriente *or* al tanto de algo • IDIOM: • **to be ~ after the event** criticar una vez que las cosas ya han pasado, criticar a posteriori
2 (= prudent) [precaution] sabio; [decision, choice] sabio, acertado • **a map of the area would be a ~ investment** sería aconsejable comprar un mapa del área • **it would be ~ to** (+ infin) sería prudente (+ infin), sería aconsejable (+ infin) • **you'd be ~ to accept** harías bien en aceptar • **he was ~ enough to refuse** tuvo la suficiente sensatez como para negarse
CPD ▸ **wise guy*** listillo/a* *m/f* (pej) • **~ guy, huh?** ¿tú te lo sabes todo, eh?, eres muy listo, ¿verdad? ▸ **wise man** (= sage) sabio *m*; (= witch doctor) hechicero *m* ▸ **Wise Men** • **the (Three) Wise Men** los (Tres) Reyes Magos ▸ **wise woman** (= sage) sabia *f*; (= witch doctor) hechicera *f*
▸ **wise up** VI + ADV espabilarse*, avisparse* • **~ up!** ¡espabílate! • **to ~ up to sth** caer en la cuenta de algo
wise[2]† [waɪz] N (frm) • **in this ~** de esta guisa • **in no ~** de ningún modo
-wise [waɪz] ADV (ending in compounds) en cuanto a, respecto a • **how are you off money-wise?** ¿de dinero cómo estás?
wiseacre ['waɪz,eɪkəʳ] N sabihondo/a *m/f*
wisecrack* ['waɪzkræk] N salida *f* graciosa • **to make a ~** tener una salida graciosa
VT • **"you weigh a ton," he ~ed** —pesas más que un burro en brazos —dijo bromeando
VI bromear
wisecracking ['waɪzkrækɪŋ] ADJ bromista
wisely ['waɪzlɪ] ADV 1 (= prudently) sabiamente, prudentemente • **she chose ~** escogió sabiamente *or* prudentemente • **he had ~ brought an umbrella with him** había tenido la prudencia de traerse un paraguas
2 (= sagaciously) sabiamente • **we all nodded ~** (iro, hum) todos asentimos con aire de entendidos
wish [wɪʃ] N 1 (= desire, will) deseo *m* • **they are sincere in their ~ to make amends for the past** son sinceros en su deseo de enmendar el pasado • **their ~ for peace is sincere** • **they are sincere in their ~ for peace** son sinceros en sus deseos de paz • **it has long been my ~ to do that** desde hace mucho tiempo vengo deseando hacer eso • **he did it against my ~es** lo hizo en contra de mis deseos *or* mi voluntad • **to go against sb's ~es** ir en contra de los deseos *or* la voluntad de algn • **his ~ came true** su deseo se hizo realidad • **your ~ is my command** sus deseos son órdenes para mí • **it is her dearest ~ to go there one day** su mayor deseo es ir allí un día • **his dying ~ was to be buried here** su última voluntad fue que lo enterraran aquí • **she expressed a ~ that the money be donated to charity** manifestó su deseo de que el dinero se donara a instituciones benéficas • **the fairy granted her three ~es** el hada le concedió tres deseos • **I have no great ~ to go** no tengo muchas ganas de ir, no me apetece mucho ir • **you shall have** *or* **get your ~** tu deseo se hará realidad, tu deseo se cumplirá • **to make a ~** pedir un deseo • PROVERB: • **if ~es were horses, beggars would ride** no se puede pedir la luna; ▹ **death**
2 (in letters, greetings) • **(with) best ~es** saludos, recuerdos • **with best ~es from Peter** recuerdos de Peter • **best ~es** *or* **all good ~es for a happy birthday** te deseamos un feliz cumpleaños, nuestros mejores deseos para un feliz cumpleaños • **(with) best ~es for Christmas and the New Year** (con) nuestros mejores deseos *or* (frm) augurios para la Navidad y el Año Nuevo • **please give him my best ~es** dale recuerdos míos • **I went to give him my best ~es** fui a darle la enhorabuena • **the Prime Minister has sent a message of good ~es to the French president** el Primer Ministro ha

mandado un mensaje de buena voluntad al presidente francés

(VT) **1 • I ~** (= *if only*) **a** (*in unrealizable or unlikely situations*) • **I ~ I were rich** ojalá fuese rico • **I ~ it weren't true** ojalá no fuera así • **I only ~ I'd known that before** ojalá lo hubiera sabido antes • **I ~ I could!** ¡ojalá pudiera! • **"did you go?" — "I ~ I had"** —¿fuiste? —¡ya me hubiera gustado! *or* —¡ojalá! • **I ~ I hadn't said that** siento haber dicho eso, ojalá no hubiera dicho eso

b (*when change is possible*) • **I ~ you'd hurry up** a ver si te das prisa • **I do ~ you'd let me help** ¿por qué no me dejas que te ayude? • **I ~ you wouldn't shout** me gustaría que no gritaras, a ver si dejas de gritar

2 (*other subjects, other tenses*) • **she ~es that she could go to school like other children** le gustaría poder ir a la escuela como otros niños • **I bet you ~ you were still working here!** ¡apuesto a que te gustaría seguir trabajando aquí todavía!

3 • to ~ sb sth: to ~ sb good luck/a happy Christmas desear buena suerte/felices pascuas a algn • **~ me luck!** ¡deséame suerte! • **I ~ you all possible happiness** os/te deseo la más completa felicidad • **to ~ sb good morning** dar los buenos días a algn • **to ~ sb goodbye** despedirse de algn • **to ~ sb well/ill:** • **we ~ her well in her new job** le deseamos todo lo mejor en su nuevo trabajo • **I don't ~ her ill** *or* **any harm** no le deseo ningún mal

4 • to ~ sth on sb desear algo a algn • **I wouldn't ~ that on anybody** eso no se lo desearía a nadie

5 (*frm*) (= *want*) querer, desear (*frm*) • **I do not ~ it** no lo quiero, no lo deseo (*frm*) • **to ~ to do sth** querer *or* (*frm*) desear hacer algo • **I ~ to be alone** quiero *or* (*frm*) deseo estar solo • **I ~ to be told when he comes** quiero *or* (*frm*) deseo que se me avisen cuando llegue • **I don't ~ to sound mean, but ...** no quisiera parecer tacaño, pero ... • **without ~ing to be unkind, you must admit she's not the most interesting company** sin ánimo de ser cruel, tienes que admitir que no es una persona muy interesante • **to ~ sb to do sth** querer *or* (*frm*) desear que algn haga algo • **what do you ~ me to do?** ¿qué quieres *or* (*frm*) deseas que haga?

(VI) **1** (= *make a wish*) pedir un deseo • **to ~ for sth** desear algo • **she has everything she could ~ for** tiene todo lo que pudiera desear • **what more could one ~ for?** ¿qué más se puede pedir *or* desear? • **I couldn't have ~ed for a nicer birthday** no podía haber soñado con un día de cumpleaños mejor • **"of course you're earning a lot, aren't you?" — "I ~!"** —claro que ganas un montón, ¿verdad? —¡ojalá!

2 (*frm*) (= *want*) • **(just) as you ~** como quieras, como usted desee (*frm*) • **you may stay here as long as you ~** te puedes quedar todo el tiempo que quieras *or* desees

(CPD) ▸ **wish fulfilment** • **daydreams are a sort of ~ fulfilment** las fantasías son una especie de satisfacción de los deseos ▸ **wish list** lista *f* de deseos • **top of my ~ list is ...** mi deseo principal es ...

▸ **wish away** (VT + ADV) • **these problems/people can't just be ~ed away** estos problemas/estas personas no desaparecen solo con desearlo • **the son he would ~ away if he could** el hijo que desearía no haber tenido nunca

wishbone [ˈwɪʃbəʊn] (N) espoleta *f*

wishful [ˈwɪʃfʊl] (ADJ) • **to be ~ to do** *or* **of doing sth** (*frm*) estar deseoso de hacer algo

(CPD) ▸ **wishful thinking** ilusiones *fpl* • **that's just ~ thinking** eso es querer hacerse ilusiones

wishing well [ˈwɪʃɪŋ,wel] (N) pozo *m* de los deseos

wish-wash* [ˈwɪʃwɒʃ] (N) aguachirle *f*

wishy-washy* [ˈwɪʃɪ,wɒʃɪ] (ADJ) [*colour*] soso; [*beer*] insípido; [*answer, solution*] a medias; [*thinking, ideas*] vago; [*person*] sin carácter

wisp [wɪsp] (N) [*of hair*] mechón *m*; [*of cloud, smoke*] voluta *f*; [*of straw*] manojo *m*

wispy [ˈwɪspɪ] (ADJ) [*hair*] ralo, fino; [*cloud*] tenue

wisteria [wɪsˈtɪərɪə] (N) glicina *f*, vistaria *f*

wistful [ˈwɪstfʊl] (ADJ) (= *thoughtful*) pensativo; (= *sad*) melancólico, triste

wistfully [ˈwɪstfəlɪ] (ADV) (= *thoughtfully*) pensativamente; (= *sadly*) con melancolía, tristemente • **she looked at me ~** (= *thoughtfully*) me miró pensativa; (= *sadly*) me miró melancólica *or* triste

wistfulness [ˈwɪstfʊlnɪs] (N) (= *thoughtfulness*) lo pensativo; (= *sadness*) melancolía *f*, tristeza *f*

wit¹ [wɪt] (N) **1** (= *understanding*) inteligencia *f* • **a battle of wits** una contienda entre dos inteligencias • **to collect one's wits** reconcentrarse • **to be at one's wits' end** no saber qué hacer, estar desesperado • **to gather one's wits** reconcentrarse • **to have** *or* **keep one's wits about one** no perder la cabeza • **he hadn't the wit to see that ...** no tenía bastante inteligencia para comprender que ... • **to live by one's wits** vivir del cuento • **to be out of one's wits** estar fuera de sí • **to be frightened** *or* **scared out of one's wits** estar profundamente asustado • **to sharpen one's wits** aguzar el ingenio, despabilarse • **to use one's wits** usar su sentido común

2 (= *humour, wittiness*) ingenio *m*, agudeza *f* • **in a flash of wit he said ...** en un golpe de ingenio dijo ... • **to have a ready wit** ser ingenioso • **the wit and wisdom of Joe Soap** las agudezas y sabiduría de Joe Soap • **a story told without wit** un cuento narrado sin gracia

3 (= *person*) persona *f* ingeniosa; (*Hist*) ingenio *m* • **an Elizabethan wit** un ingenio de la época isabelina

wit² [wɪt] (N) (*frm*) (*also Jur*) • **to wit ...** a saber ..., esto es ...

witch [wɪtʃ] (N) bruja *f*

(CPD) ▸ **witch doctor** hechicero *m* ▸ **witch hazel** olmo *m* escocés ▸ **witch hunt** caza *f* de brujas

witchcraft [ˈwɪtʃkrɑːft] (N) brujería *f*

witchery [ˈwɪtʃərɪ] (N) **1** (*lit*) brujería *f* **2** (*fig*) encanto *m*, magia *f*

witching hour [ˈwɪtʃɪŋ,aʊəʳ] (N) (*hum*) hora *f* de las brujas

---

with [wɪð, wɪθ]

(PREPOSITION)

> *When **with** is part of a set combination, eg **good with**, **pleased with**, **to agree with**, look up the other word.*

> *The commonest translation of **with** is **con**. Note that whenever it combines with **mí**, **ti** or **sí** the forms **conmigo**, **contigo**, **consigo** are used.*

1 con • **he had an argument ~ his brother** tuvo una discusión con su hermano • **she mixed the sugar ~ the eggs** mezcló el azúcar con los huevos • **I'll be ~ you in a moment** un momento y estoy con vosotros, en un momento *or* enseguida estoy con vosotros • **come ~ me!** ven conmigo • **he took it away ~ him** se lo llevó consigo • **~ the Alcántara it is the biggest ship in** *or* **of its class** junto con el Alcántara es el mayor buque de esa clase; ▹ **down, off, out**

along *or* **together with** junto con • **he was arrested along** *or* **together ~ four other terrorists** fue detenido junto con otros cuatro terroristas

to be with sb (= *in the company of*) estar con algn • **I was ~ him** yo estaba con él • **I'm ~ you there** en eso estoy de acuerdo contigo • **are you ~ us or against us?** ¿estás a favor nuestro o en contra? • **I'm not ~ you*** (= *able to understand*) no te entiendo *or* sigo • **are you ~ me?*** ¿me entiendes? • **it's a problem that will always be ~ us** es un problema que siempre nos va a afectar, es un problema que no se va a resolver

to be with it* (= *up-to-date*) estar al tanto *or* al día; (= *fashionable*) [*person*] estar al tanto de lo que se lleva; [*thing*] estar de moda; (= *mentally alert*) estar lúcido *or* despabilado • **sorry, I'm just not ~ it today** lo siento, hoy estoy atontado

to get with it* ponerse al día • **get ~ it!** ¡ponte al día!

2 (*in descriptions*) con • **we're looking for a house ~ a garden** buscamos una casa con jardín • **I don't like men ~ beards** no me gustan los hombres con barba • **a man ~ checked trousers** un hombre con pantalones de cuadros • **a car ~ the latest features** un coche con las últimas novedades *or* prestaciones • **passengers ~ tickets** los pasajeros que tienen *or* con billetes • **you can't speak to the queen ~ your hat on** no se puede hablar con la reina con el sombrero puesto

> *Note: when the **with** description pinpoints the particular person or thing you are talking about, **with** is usually translated by **de**.*

• **the man ~ the checked trousers** el hombre de los pantalones de cuadros • **the girl ~ the blue eyes** la chica de los ojos azules

3 (*indicating manner, means*) con • **to walk ~ a walking stick** andar con bastón • **to cut wood ~ a knife** cortar madera con un cuchillo • **~ one blow** de un golpe • **she took off her shoes ~ a sigh** se quitó los zapatos dando un suspiro • **... and ~ these words of advice, he left us** ... y tras darnos este consejo nos dejó • **to fill a glass ~ wine** llenar una copa de vino • **~ no trouble at all** sin dificultad alguna, sin ninguna dificultad • **~ that, he closed the door** luego *or* a continuación, cerró la puerta, luego, cerró la puerta

4 (*indicating cause*) de • **to shiver ~ cold** tiritar *or* temblar de frío • **to shake ~ fear** temblar de miedo • **the hills are white ~ snow** las colinas están cubiertas de nieve • **to be ill ~ measles** tener sarampión • **I spent a week in bed ~ flu** estuve una semana en (la) cama con la gripe

5 (= *as regards*) con • **it's the same ~ most team sports** lo mismo ocurre con la mayoría de los deportes de equipo • **it's a habit ~ him** es una costumbre que tiene, es algo típico de él • **how are things ~ you?** ¿qué tal?, ¿cómo te va? (*esp LAm*), ¿qué hubo? (*Mex, Chile*)

6 (= *owing to*) con • **I couldn't see him ~ so many people there** no lo vi con tanta gente como había • **~ so much happening it was difficult to arrange a date** con todo lo que estaba pasando era difícil acordar una cita • **~ the approach of winter, trade began to fall off** al acercarse el invierno, el comercio

empezó a declinar
7 (*= according to*) [*increase, change, improve*] con • **the risk of developing heart disease increases ~ the number of cigarettes smoked** el riesgo de sufrir enfermedades coronarias aumenta con el número de cigarrillos que se fume • **it varies ~ the time of year** varía según la estación
8 (*= in the house of*) con • **he lives ~ his aunt** vive con su tía • **she stayed ~ friends** se quedó con *or* en casa de unos amigos
9 (*= working for*) • **he's ~ IBM** trabaja para *or* en IBM • **a scientist ~ ICI** un científico de ICI • **I've been ~ this company for eight years** llevo ocho años en esta empresa
10 (*= in the care of*) • **to leave sth ~ sb** dejar algo en manos de algn *or* con algn • **to leave a child ~ sb** dejar a un niño al cuidado de algn *or* con algn
11 (*= on, about*) • **he had no money ~ him** no llevaba dinero (encima) • **luckily, she had an umbrella ~ her** afortunadamente, llevaba (encima) un paraguas
12 (*= in the same direction as*) con • **I was swimming ~ the current** nadaba con *or* a favor de la corriente; ▸ **flow**
13 (*= in spite of*) con • **~ all his faults** con todos sus defectos

withal†† [wɪ'ðɔːl] ADV además, también
withdraw [wɪθ'drɔː] (PT: **withdrew**, PP: **withdrawn**) VT **1** (*= take out*) [*+ money*] retirar, sacar (**from** de)
2 (*= recall*) [*+ troops, ambassador, team*] retirar (**from** de); [*+ product, advertisement, banknotes*] retirar (**from** de)
3 (*= cancel*) [*+ application, permission, support, licence*] retirar • **to ~ one's labour** ponerse en huelga
4 (*= retract*) [*+ words, remark*] retractarse de, retirar; [*+ charge*] retirar • **to ~ one's hand (from sth/sb)** apartar la mano (de algo/algn)
VI **1** (*= move away*) apartarse, alejarse
2 (*= leave room*) retirarse
3 (*= move back, retreat*) [*troops, forces, police*] retirarse (**from** de) • **to ~ to a new position** retirarse a una nueva posición
4 (*= pull out*) (*from deal, game, talks*) retirarse (**from** de)
5 (*= withdraw application, candidacy*) retirarse (**from** de) • **to ~ in favour of sb** retirarse en favor de algn
6 (*during lovemaking*) dar marcha atrás*
7 (*Psych*) • **to ~ into o.s.** retraerse, encerrarse en sí mismo
withdrawal [wɪθ'drɔːəl] N **1** (*from bank*) • **to make a ~** retirar dinero *or* fondos
2 (*= recall, removal*) [*of troops, ambassador, team, services, advertisement*] retirada *f* (**from** de); [*of banknote*] retirada *f* de la circulación • **his party has announced its ~ of support for the government** su partido ha anunciado la retirada de su apoyo al gobierno • **they may be contemplating a partial ~ from the country** puede que estén considerando una retirada parcial del país
3 (*= cancellation*) [*of application, permission, support, licence*] retirada *f*
4 (*= retraction*) [*of allegation, remark*] retractación *f*; [*of charge*] retirada *f*
5 (*Psych*) (*from sb, sth*) retraimiento *m* (**from** de)
6 (*after drug addiction*) síndrome *m* de abstinencia • **to be suffering from ~** padecer el síndrome de abstinencia
7 (*during lovemaking*) (*= act*) retirada *f* (del pene); (*as contraception*) marcha *f* atrás*, coitus *m* interruptus
CPD ▸ **withdrawal method** método *m* de la marcha atrás*, coitus *m* interruptus ▸ **withdrawal notice** (*Econ*) aviso *m* de retirada de fondos ▸ **withdrawal slip** comprobante *m* (*de retirada de fondos*) ▸ **withdrawal symptoms** síndrome *msing* de abstinencia
withdrawn [wɪθ'drɔːn] PP *of* **withdraw**
ADJ (*= introverted*) reservado, introvertido; (*= detached, absent*) retraído, encerrado en sí mismo
withdrew [wɪθ'druː] PT *of* **withdraw**
withe [wɪθ] N mimbre *m or f*
wither ['wɪðəʳ] VT [*+ flower, plant*] marchitar • **to ~ sb with a look** aplastar *or* fulminar a algn con la mirada
VI [*flower, plant, beauty*] marchitarse; [*limb*] debilitarse, atrofiarse; [*person*] debilitarse; [*hope*] desvanecerse
▸ **wither away** VI + ADV [*flower, plant*] marchitarse; [*hope*] desvanecerse
withered ['wɪðəd] ADJ [*flower, plant*] marchito; [*limb*] debilitado, atrofiado
withering ['wɪðərɪŋ] ADJ [*heat*] abrasador; [*tone, look, remark*] fulminador
witheringly ['wɪðərɪŋlɪ] ADV [*say, look*] desdeñosamente
withers ['wɪðəz] NPL cruz *fsing* (de caballo)
withhold [wɪθ'həʊld] (PT, PP: **withheld** [wɪθ'held]) VT **1** [*+ information*] ocultar; [*+ money*] retener; [*+ decision*] aplazar • **to ~ the truth from sb** no revelar la verdad a algn • **to ~ a pound of sb's pay** retener una libra del pago a algn
2 (*= refuse*) negar • **to ~ one's consent** negar el consentimiento • **a parent's right to grant or ~ permission** el derecho de un padre a dar o (de)negar su permiso • **to ~ one's help** negarse a ayudar a algn
withholding tax [wɪθ'həʊldɪŋ,tæks] N
1 *impuesto que se grava a aquellos que tienen una fuente de ingresos en el país pero residen en otro, y que se puede reclamar si existe un acuerdo entre ambos países*
2 (*US*) *porción de los impuestos de un empleado que la empresa paga directamente al gobierno*
within [wɪð'ɪn] PREP dentro de • **I want it back ~ three days** quiero que me lo devuelvas dentro de tres días • **here ~ the town** aquí dentro de la ciudad • **to be ~ call** estar al alcance de la voz • **to live ~ one's income** vivir conforme a los ingresos • **to be ~ the law** no rebasar los límites de la ley, atenerse a la legalidad • **a voice ~ me said ...** una voz interior me dijo ... • **the police arrived ~ minutes** la policía llegó a los pocos minutos • **the village is ~ a mile of the river** el pueblo dista poco menos de una milla del pueblo • **we were ~ 100 metres of the summit** faltaban 100 metros para que llegáramos a la cumbre • **~ a year of her death** a poco menos de un año de su muerte • **~ a radius of ten kilometres** en un radio de diez kilómetros • **the shops are ~ easy reach** las tiendas están cerca • **~ the stipulated time** dentro del plazo señalado • **~ the week** antes de terminar la semana • IDIOM: • **to be ~ an inch of** estar a dos dedos de
ADV dentro • **"car for sale - apply within"** "se vende coche - razón dentro *or* (*LAm*) infórmese adentro" • **from ~** desde dentro, desde el interior
with-it* ['wɪðɪt] ADJ (*= up-to-date*) moderno; ▸ **with 1**
without [wɪð'aʊt]

When **without** *is an element in a phrasal verb, eg* **do without, go without**, *look up the verb.*

PREP **1** sin • **~ a coat** sin abrigo • **three days ~ food** tres días sin comer • **~ speaking** sin hablar, sin decir nada • **he did it ~ telling me** lo hizo sin decírmelo • **~ my noticing it** sin verlo yo, sin que yo lo notase • **not ~ some difficulty** no sin cierta dificultad • **times ~ number** un sinfín de veces
2†† (*= outside*) fuera de
ADV (*liter*) fuera • **from ~** desde fuera
with-profits [wɪθ'prɒfɪts] ADJ
• **with-profits endowment assurance** seguro *m* dotal con beneficios
withstand [wɪθ'stænd] (PT, PP: **withstood** [wɪθ'stʊd]) VT resistir, aguantar
withy ['wɪðɪ] N mimbre *m or f*
witless ['wɪtlɪs] ADJ estúpido, tonto • **to scare sb ~** dar un susto mortal a algn
witness ['wɪtnɪs] N **1** (*= person*) testigo *mf* • **eye ~** testigo ocular • **~ for the prosecution/defence** testigo de cargo/ descargo • **there were no ~es** no hubo testigos • **to call sb as a ~** citar a algn como testigo • **we want no ~es to this** no queremos que nadie vea esto, no queremos que haya testigos • **I was (a) ~ to this event** yo presencié este suceso, yo fui testigo de este suceso
2 (*= evidence*) testimonio *m* • **to give ~ for/against sb** atestiguar a favor de/en contra de algn • **to bear ~ to sth** (*lit*) atestiguar algo; (*fig*) demostrar *or* probar algo • **in ~ of** en fe de
VT **1** (*= be present at*) presenciar, asistir a; (*= see*) ver • **to ~ sb doing sth** ver a algn hacer algo, ver cómo algn hace algo • **the accident was ~ed by two people** hay dos testigos del accidente • **to ~ a document** firmar un documento como testigo • **this period ~ed important changes** (*liter*) este periodo fue testigo de cambios importantes
2 (*= attest by signature*) atestiguar la veracidad de
3 (*= consider as evidence*) ver, mirar
VI (*= testify*) dar testimonio, atestiguar • **to ~ to sth** dar testimonio de *or* atestiguar algo
CPD ▸ **witness box** (*Brit*), **witness stand** (*US*) tribuna *f* de los testigos, estrado *m* ▸ **witness statement** declaración *f* de testigo
witter* ['wɪtəʳ] VI (*Brit*) parlotear • **to ~ on about sth** hablar de algo sin parar • **stop ~ing (on)!** ¿quieres callarte de una vez?
witticism ['wɪtɪsɪzəm] N dicho *m* ingenioso, agudeza *f*, ocurrencia *f*
wittily ['wɪtɪlɪ] ADV (*= cleverly*) ingeniosamente; (*= amusingly*) con gracia, de modo divertido
wittiness ['wɪtɪnɪs] N [*of person*] agudeza *f*, ingenio *m*; [*of remarks, script*] lo agudo, lo ingenioso • **I loved the ~ of the script** me encantó lo agudo *or* ingenioso del guión
wittingly ['wɪtɪŋlɪ] ADV (*frm*) a sabiendas
witty ['wɪtɪ] ADJ (COMPAR: **wittier**, SUPERL: **wittiest**) [*person, remark, speech*] agudo, ingenioso • **he's very ~** (*= clever*) es muy agudo *or* ingenioso; (*= funny*) tiene mucha gracia
wives [waɪvz] NPL *of* **wife**
wizard ['wɪzəd] N **1** (*= sorcerer*) mago *m*, brujo *m*, hechicero *m*
2* (*= genius*) genio *mf*, as *m* • **he's a financial ~** es un genio de las finanzas • **he's a ~ at chess** es un genio jugando al ajedrez
ADJ (*esp Brit*†*) estupendo*, maravilloso
wizardry ['wɪzədrɪ] N **1** (*= sorcery*) hechicería *f*, brujería *f*
2* (*= skill*) • **his financial ~** su genio financiero • **a piece of technical ~** una maravilla de la técnica
wizened ['wɪznd] ADJ arrugado, marchito

wk (ABBR) (= **week**) sem.
wkly (= **weekly**) (ADJ ABBR) semanal (ADV ABBR) semanalmente
W/L (ABBR) = **wavelength**
WLTM* (ABBR) = **would like to meet**
Wm (ABBR) = **William**
WMD, **WMDs** (NPL ABBR) = **weapons of mass destruction**
WMO (N ABBR) (= **World Meteorological Organization**) OMM *f*
WNW (ABBR) (= **west-northwest**) ONO
WO (N ABBR) (*Mil*) = **warrant officer**
wo, **woa** [wəʊ] (EXCL) = **whoa**
w/o (ABBR) (= **without**) sin
woad [wəʊd] (N) hierba *f* pastel, glasto *m*
wobble ['wɒbl] (N) [*of chair, table etc*] tambaleo *m*, bamboleo *m*; [*of voice*] temblor *m* • **to walk with a ~** tambalearse al andar, andar tambaleándose
(VI) **1** (= *move unsteadily*) tambalearse, bambolearse; [*voice*] temblar
2 (= *hesitate*) vacilar
wobbly ['wɒblɪ] (ADJ) (COMPAR: **wobblier**, SUPERL: **wobbliest**) [*chair, table*] cojo, que se tambalea; [*tooth, wheel*] flojo, que se mueve; [*cyclist*] inseguro; [*voice, jelly*] temblón; [*bottom, thighs*] flácido • **his legs are a bit ~** • **he's a bit ~ on his legs** tiene las piernas un poco flojas • **she drew a ~ line** trazó una línea irregular
(N) • **to throw a ~*** ponerse histérico
wodge* [wɒdʒ] (N) trozo *m* grande
woe [wəʊ] (N) (*poet, hum*) desgracia *f*, aflicción *f* • **woe is me!** ¡ay de mí! • **woe betide you if you're lying!** ¡pobre de ti como sea mentira! • **a tale of woe** una historia triste
woebegone ['wəʊbɪ,gɒn] (ADJ) (*liter*) desconsolado, angustiado
woeful ['wəʊfʊl] (ADJ) **1** (= *lamentable*) [*lack, ignorance, state*] lamentable, deplorable
2 (*liter*) (= *sad*) [*person*] afligido, desconsolado; [*look, expression*] de desconsuelo, de congoja; [*tale*] triste
woefully ['wəʊfəlɪ] (ADV) **1** (= *lamentably*) • **the level of funding is ~ inadequate** el nivel de financiación es de una insuficiencia lamentable *or* deplorable • **he is ~ out of touch with public opinion** está lamentablemente desconectado de la opinión pública • **to be ~ short of sth** andar sumamente escaso de algo
2 (*liter*) (= *sadly*) tristemente • **she shook her head ~** sacudió la cabeza afligida, sacudió la cabeza tristemente
Wog** [wɒg] (N) (*Brit*) (*offensive*) negro/a *m/f*
wok [wɒk] (N) *cazuela china de base redonda*
woke [wəʊk] (PT) *of* **wake**[3]
woken ['wəʊkn] (PP) *of* **wake**[3]
wold [wəʊld] (N) rasa *f* ondulada
wolf [wʊlf] (N) (PL: **wolves** [wʊlvz])
1 (= *animal*) lobo *m* • **lone ~** (*fig*) lobo *m* solitario • IDIOMS: • **to cry ~** dar una falsa alarma • **to keep the ~ from the door** defenderse de *or* contra la miseria • **a ~ in sheep's clothing** un lobo disfrazado de cordero • **to throw sb to the wolves** arrojar a algn a los lobos
2* (= *womanizer*) tenorio *m*
(VT) (*also* **wolf down**) zamparse*, engullir
(CPD) ▸ **wolf whistle** silbido *m* de admiración
wolfcub ['wʊlfkʌb] (N) lobato *m*
wolfhound ['wʊlfhaʊnd] (N) (*also* **Irish wolfhound**) lebrel *m* irlandés
wolfish ['wʊlfɪʃ] (ADJ) lobuno
wolfpack ['wʊlfpæk] (N) manada *f* de lobos
wolfram ['wʊlfrəm] (N) volframio *m*, wolfram *m*
wolf-whistle ['wʊlf,wɪsl] (VI) silbar (con admiración) • **to wolf-whistle at sb** silbar (con admiración) a algn • **they wolf-whistled at me** me silbaron (con admiración); ▸ **wolf whistle**
wolverine ['wʊlvəri:n] (N) carcayú *m*, glotón *m*
wolves [wʊlvz] (NPL) *of* **wolf**
woman ['wʊmən] (N) (PL: **women** ['wɪmɪn]) mujer *f* • **~ is very different from man** la mujer es muy distinta del hombre • **I have a ~ who comes in to do the cleaning** tengo una mujer que me hace la limpieza • **the ~ in his life** su compañera • **his ~*** (= *lover*) su querida • **~ to ~** de mujer a mujer • **women's doubles** dobles *mpl* femeninos • **women's football** fútbol *m* femenino • **women's group** grupo *m* femenino • **women's lib*** la liberación de la mujer • **women's libber*** feminista *mf* • **women's liberation**† liberación *f* de la mujer • **women's movement** movimiento *m* feminista • **she's her own ~** es una mujer muy fiel a sí misma • **women's page** sección *f* femenina • **women's refuge** hogar *m* para mujeres maltratadas • **women's rights** derechos *mpl* de la mujer • **women's room** (*US*) servicio *m* de señoras • **women's studies** (*Univ*) estudios *mpl* de la mujer • **women's team** equipo *m* femenino • **~ of the town** (*euph*) prostituta *f* • **it's women's work** es un trabajo de mujeres • **a ~ of the world** una mujer de mundo • **young ~** joven *f*; ▸ **honest**, **little**[1], **old**
(CPD) ▸ **woman doctor** doctora *f* ▸ **woman driver** conductora *f* ▸ **woman engineer** ingeniera *f* ▸ **woman friend** amiga *f* ▸ **woman pilot** piloto *f* ▸ **woman police constable** (*Brit*) (mujer *f*) agente *f* de policía ▸ **woman priest** mujer *f* sacerdote ▸ **woman teacher** profesora *f* ▸ **woman writer** escritora *f*
woman-hater ['wʊmən,heɪtəʳ] (N) misógino *m*
womanhood ['wʊmənhʊd] (N) **1** (= *women in general*) mujeres *fpl*, sexo *m* femenino
2 (= *age*) edad *f* adulta (de mujer) • **to reach ~** llegar a la edad adulta (de mujer)
3 (= *womanliness*) feminidad *f*
womanish ['wʊmənɪʃ] (ADJ) mujeril, propio de mujer; [*man*] afeminado
womanize ['wʊmənaɪz] (VI) dedicarse a la caza de mujeres
womanizer ['wʊmənaɪzəʳ] (N) mujeriego *m*, donjuán *m*
womankind ['wʊmən'kaɪnd] (N) mujeres *fpl*, sexo *m* femenino
womanlike ['wʊmənlaɪk] (ADJ) mujeril
womanliness ['wʊmənlɪnɪs] (N) feminidad *f*
womanly ['wʊmənlɪ] (ADJ) femenino
womb [wu:m] (N) matriz *f*, útero *m*; (*fig*) cuna *f*
wombat ['wɒmbæt] (N) wombat *m*
women ['wɪmɪn] (NPL) *of* **woman**
womenfolk ['wɪmɪnfəʊk] (NPL) mujeres *fpl*
won [wʌn] (PT), (PP) *of* **win**
wonder ['wʌndəʳ] (N) **1** (= *feeling*) asombro *m* • **in ~** asombrado, maravillado • **to be lost in ~** quedar maravillado
2 (= *object of wonder*) maravilla *f*; (= *cause of wonder*) milagro *m* • **the ~s of science** las maravillas de la ciencia • **the Seven Wonders of the World** las Siete Maravillas del Mundo • **the ~ of it was that ...** lo (más) asombroso fue que ... • **a nine-day ~** un prodigio que deja pronto de serlo • **it's a ~ that ...** es un milagro que ... • **~s will never cease!** ¡todavía hay milagros! • **to do ~s** obrar milagros • **it did ~s for her health** obró milagros en su salud • **it's little** *or* **no** *or* **small ~ that he left** no es de extrañarse que se haya marchado • **no ~!** ¡no me extraña! • **he promised ~s** prometió el oro y el moro • **to work ~s** obrar milagros
(VT) preguntarse • **if you're ~ing how to do it** si te estás preguntando cómo hacerlo • **I was just ~ing if you knew ...** me preguntaba si tu sabrías ... • **I ~ what he'll do now** me pregunto qué hará ahora • **I ~ where Caroline is** ¿dónde estará Caroline?, ¿me pregunto dónde estará Caroline? • **I ~ whether the milkman's been** a ver si el lechero ha venido • **she ~ed whether to go on** no sabía si seguir adelante • **I ~ why she said that** ¿por qué diría eso?, me pregunto por qué dijo eso
(VI) **1** (= *ask o.s., speculate*) preguntarse, pensar • **"does she know about it?" — "I ~"** —¿se habrá enterado ella? —eso mismo me pregunto yo • **I ~ed about that for a long time** le di muchas vueltas a eso • **I was ~ing if you could help** te agradecería que me ayudaras • **I often ~** me lo pregunto a menudo • **it set me ~ing** me hizo pensar
2 (= *be surprised*) asombrarse, maravillarse • **to ~ at sth** asombrarse de algo, maravillarse de algo • **that's hardly to be ~ed at** eso no tiene nada de extraño, no hay que asombrarse de eso • **can you ~?** natural, ¿no? • **I shouldn't ~!** ¡sería lógico! • **I shouldn't ~ if ...** no me sorprendería que (+ *subjun*) • **she's married by now, I shouldn't ~** se habrá casado ya como sería lógico, cabe presumir que está casada ya
(CPD) ▸ **wonder boy** joven *m* prodigio ▸ **wonder drug** remedio *m* milagroso ▸ **wonder girl** niña *f* prodigio
wonderful ['wʌndəfʊl] (ADJ) **1** (= *excellent*) [*person, experience, surprise*] maravilloso, estupendo; [*painting, piece of music*] maravilloso, precioso; [*opportunity*] estupendo; [*feeling*] maravilloso • **it would be ~ to be able to sing well** sería maravilloso tener buena voz • **she looks ~ for her age** está estupenda para la edad que tiene • **isn't it ~!** • **how ~!** ¡qué estupendo!, ¡qué maravilla! • **we had a ~ time** (nos) lo pasamos de maravilla *or* estupendamente
2 (= *amazing*) [*memory, achievement*] increíble
wonderfully ['wʌndəfəlɪ] (ADV) **1** (= *extremely*) • **she was always ~ kind to me** siempre fue amabilísima conmigo • **it's a ~ funny play** es una obra increíblemente divertida, es una obra divertidísima • **he looks ~ well** está de maravilla, tiene un aspecto estupendo
2 (= *very well*) [*sleep, adapt, work*] de maravilla • **the doctor says she is doing ~** el médico dice que se está recuperando de maravilla *or* estupendamente
wondering ['wʌndərɪŋ] (ADJ) [*tone, look*] (= *questioning*) perplejo; (= *amazed*) sorprendido
wonderingly ['wʌndərɪŋlɪ] (ADV) • **to look ~ at sb** (= *questioningly*) mirar a algn perplejo; (= *in amazement*) mirar a algn sorprendido
wonderland ['wʌndəlænd] (N) país *m* de la maravilla, país *m* de las aventuras • **a ~ of amusement parks** un paraíso de parques de atracciones
wonderment ['wʌndəmənt] (N) = **wonder**
wonderstruck ['wʌndəstrʌk] (ADJ) (*liter*) asombrado, pasmado
wonder-worker ['wʌndə,wɜ:kəʳ] (N) (*Med*) remedio *m* milagroso
wondrous ['wʌndrəs] (*liter*) (ADJ) maravilloso
(ADV)†† = **wondrously**
wondrously ['wʌndrəslɪ] (ADV) (*liter*) maravillosamente • **~ beautiful** extraordinariamente hermoso, hermoso

en extremo

wonga‡ ['wɒŋgə] (N) (Brit) pasta* f, guita‡ f

wonky* ['wɒŋkɪ] (ADJ) (COMPAR: **wonkier**, SUPERL: **wonkiest**) (Brit) **1** (= *wobbly*) [*chair, table*] cojo, que se tambalea
2 (= *crooked*) torcido, chueco (*LAm*)
3 (= *broken down*) estropeado, descompuesto (*esp Mex*) • **to go ~** [*car, machine*] estropearse; [*TV picture*] descomponerse

wont [wəʊnt] (*frm*) (ADJ) • **to be ~ to do sth** soler hacer algo, acostumbrar a hacer algo • **as he was ~ (to)** como solía (hacer) *or* acostumbraba a hacer
(N) costumbre f • **as was my ~** como era mi costumbre, como solía hacer *or* acostumbraba a hacer • **it is his ~ to read after dinner** tiene por costumbre leer después de cenar, suele leer *or* acostumbra a leer después de cenar

won't [wəʊnt] = **will not**

wonted ['wəʊntɪd] (ADJ) (*liter*) acostumbrado

woo [wu:] (VT) **1** (*lit*) cortejar
2 (*fig*) buscarse

wood [wʊd] (N) **1** (= *material*) madera f • **it's made of ~** es de madera • **dead ~** (*lit*) ramas *fpl* muertas • **touch ~!** ¡toca madera!
2 (= *firewood*) leña f
3 (= *forest*) bosque m; **woods** bosque *msing* • **we went for a walk in the ~(s)** fuimos a pasear por el bosque • **to take to the ~s** echarse al monte • IDIOMS: • **we're not out of the ~(s) yet** aún no estamos fuera de peligro • **he can't see the ~ for the trees** (*Brit*) los árboles no le dejan ver el bosque, aún no le encuentra el chiste (*LAm*)
4 (*Golf*) palo m de madera
5 (*Bowls*) bola f
6 (*in brewing*) • **beer drawn from the ~** cerveza f de barril
7 (*Mus*) • **the ~s** los instrumentos de viento de madera
(CPD) ▸ **wood alcohol** alcohol m metílico ▸ **wood anemone** anémona f silvestre ▸ **wood block** bloque m de madera; (= *woodcut*) grabado m en madera; (*in paving*) adoquín m de madera, tarugo m ▸ **wood carving** talla f de madera ▸ **wood engraving** grabado m en madera ▸ **wood pulp** pasta f de madera ▸ **wood shavings** virutas *fpl* ▸ **wood spirit** alcohol m metílico ▸ **wood stove** estufa f de leña

woodbine ['wʊdbaɪn] (N) **1** (= *honeysuckle*) madreselva f
2 (*US*) (= *Virginia creeper*) viña f loca

wood-burning stove ['wʊdbɜ:nɪŋ'stəʊv] (N) estufa f de leña

woodchuck ['wʊdtʃʌk] (N) marmota f de América; ▷ GROUNDHOG DAY

woodcock ['wʊdkɒk] (N) chocha f perdiz

woodcraft ['wʊdkrɑ:ft] (N) conocimiento m de la vida del bosque

woodcut ['wʊdkʌt] (N) grabado m en madera

woodcutter ['wʊd,kʌtəʳ] (N) leñador m

wooded ['wʊdɪd] (ADJ) arbolado

wooden ['wʊdn] (ADJ) **1** (= *made of wood*) de madera
2 (*fig*) (= *lacking expression*) [*actor, performance*] acartonado, inexpresivo; [*face, person*] rígido, inexpresivo; [*style*] seco, poco expresivo
(CPD) ▸ **wooden horse** caballo m de madera ▸ **wooden leg** pierna f de madera, pata f de palo* ▸ **wooden spoon** cuchara f de palo; (*fig*) premio m de consolación

wooden-headed ['wʊdn'hedɪd] (ADJ) cabezahueca

woodenly ['wʊdnlɪ] (ADV) [*say, react*] de manera poco expresiva; [*act*] de forma acartonada

woodland ['wʊdlənd] (N) bosque m
(CPD) de los bosques

woodlark ['wʊdlɑ:k] (N) totovía f, cogujada f

woodlouse ['wʊdlaʊs] (N) (PL: **woodlice** ['wʊdlaɪs]) cochinilla f

woodman ['wʊdmən] (N) (PL: **woodmen**) (= *woodcutter*) leñador m; (= *forester*) trabajador m forestal

woodpecker ['wʊd,pekəʳ] (N) pájaro m carpintero • **green ~** pito m real • **lesser spotted ~** pico m menor

woodpigeon ['wʊd,pɪdʒən] (N) paloma f torcaz

woodpile ['wʊdpaɪl] (N) montón m de leña

woodshed ['wʊdʃed] (N) leñera f

woodsman ['wʊdzmən] (N) (PL: **woodsmen**) leñador m

woodstove [wʊdstəʊv] (N) (*US*) estufa f de leña

woodsy ['wʊdzɪ] (ADJ) (*US*) selvático

woodwind ['wʊdwɪnd] (N) • **the ~s** • **the ~ section** los instrumentos *mpl* de viento de madera

woodwork ['wʊdwɜ:k] (N) **1** (= *craft*) carpintería f
2 (= *wooden parts*) enmaderado m, maderaje m • **they come crawling out of the ~** (*fig*) aparecen de no se sabe dónde

woodworm ['wʊdwɜ:m] (N) carcoma f • **the table has ~** la mesa está carcomida

woody ['wʊdɪ] (ADJ) (COMPAR: **woodier**, SUPERL: **woodiest**) **1** [*plant, stem, texture*] leñoso; [*odour*] a madera
2 (= *wooded*) [*countryside*] lleno de bosque

woof[1] [wʊf] (N) (= *bark*) ladrido m
(EXCL) ¡guau!
(VI) ladrar

woof[2] [wu:f] (N) (*Textiles*) trama f

woofer ['wu:fəʳ] (N) altavoz m para sonidos graves

woofter‡, **wooftah**‡ ['wʊftə] (N) (*Brit*) (*pej*) marica‡ m

wooing ['wu:ɪŋ] (N) galanteo m

wool [wʊl] (N) [*of sheep*] lana f • **all ~** • **pure ~** lana pura • **it's made of ~** es de lana • IDIOM: • **to pull the ~ over sb's eyes** dar a algn gato por liebre
(ADJ) de lana
(CPD) ▸ **wool merchant** comerciante *mf* de lanas, lanero/a *m/f* ▸ **wool trade** comercio m de lana

woolen ['wʊlən] (ADJ), (N) (*US*) = **woollen**

woolgathering ['wʊl,gæðərɪŋ] (N) (*fig*) • **to be ~** andar distraído

wooliness ['wʊlɪnɪs] (N) (*US*) = **woolliness**

woollen, woolen (*US*) ['wʊlən] (ADJ) de lana
(NPL) **woollens** géneros *mpl* de lana
(CPD) ▸ **woollen industry** industria f de la lana

woolliness, wooliness (*US*) ['wʊlɪnɪs] (N) **1** [*of material, garment, sheep*] lanosidad f, lo lanoso
2 (= *vagueness*) [*of ideas, thinking, essay*] vaguedad f, imprecisión f; [*of person*] confusión f

woolly, wooly (*US*) ['wʊlɪ] (ADJ) (COMPAR: **woollier**, SUPERL: **woolliest**) **1** [*jumper etc*] de lana; [*animal*] lanudo
2 (= *vague*) [*ideas, thinking, essay*] vago, impreciso; [*person*] confuso
(N) **1** (= *sweater*) jersey m de lana
2 woollies*, **woolies** (*US**) (= *clothing*) ropa *fsing* de lana
(CPD) ▸ **woolly mammoth** mamut m lanudo

woolly-minded ['wʊlɪ'maɪndɪd] (ADJ) confuso

woolman ['wʊlmæn] (N) (PL: **woolmen**) (= *trader*) comerciante m en lanas; (= *manufacturer*) dueño m de una fábrica textil, lanero m

Woolsack ['wʊlsæk] (N) • **the ~** (*Brit*) (*Parl*) saco m de lana (*silla del Gran Canciller en la Cámara de los Lores*)

wooly ['wʊlɪ] (ADJ), (N) (*US*) = **woolly**

woops* [wʊps] = **whoops**

woozy* ['wu:zɪ] (ADJ) (COMPAR: **woozier**, SUPERL: **wooziest**) mareado

Wop** [wɒp] (N) (*offensive*) italiano/a *m/f*

Worcester sauce [,wʊstə'sɔ:s], **Worcestershire sauce** [,wʊstəʃə'sɔ:s] (N) salsa f Worcester, salsa f Worcestershire

Worcs. (ABBR) = **Worcestershire**

word [wɜ:d] (N) **1** (*gen*) palabra f; (= *remark*) palabra f; (*Ling*) voz f, vocablo m • **I remember every ~ he said** recuerdo todas y cada una de sus palabras • **that's not the ~ I would have chosen** yo no me hubiera expresado así • **the ~s** (= *lyrics*) la letra • **I won't hear a ~ against him** no permito que se le critique • **a big ~*** una palabra difícil • **in ~ and deed** de palabra y hecho • **~s fail me** no me lo puedo creer • **~s failed me** me quedé sin habla • **a man of few ~s** un hombre nada locuaz • **I can't find (the) ~s to tell you …** no encuentro palabras para decirte … • **fine ~s** palabras elocuentes (pero quizá poco sinceras) • **~ for ~** palabra por palabra • **too stupid for ~s** de lo más estúpido • **what's the ~ for "shop" in Spanish?** ¿cómo se dice "shop" en español? • **the Spanish have a ~ for it** en español existe una palabra para eso • **there is no other ~ for it** no se puede llamar de otro modo • **silly isn't the ~ for it** ¡llamarle estúpido es poco! • **I can't get a ~ out of him** no logro sacarle una palabra • **in a ~** en pocas palabras, en una palabra • **in other ~s** en otros términos, es decir, esto es • **in the ~s of Calderón** con palabras de Calderón, como dice Calderón • **in his own ~s** con sus propias palabras • **she didn't say so in so many ~s** no lo dijo exactamente así, no lo dijo así concretamente • **to have the last ~ in an argument** decir la última palabra en una discusión • **to measure one's ~s** medir las palabras • **by ~ of mouth** verbalmente, de palabra • **a ~ of advice** un consejo • **a ~ of thanks** unas palabras de agradecimiento • **a ~ of warning** una advertencia • **I can't put my feelings into ~s** no tengo palabras para expresar lo que siento • **to put in a (good) ~ for sb** avalar a algn, interceder por algn • **don't say a ~ about it** no digas nada de eso • **he never said a ~** no dijo una sola palabra • **he didn't say a ~ about it to me** ni me lo mencionó • **nobody had a good ~ to say about him** nadie quería defenderle, nadie habló en su favor • **I now call on Mr Allison to say a few ~s** ahora le cedo la palabra al Sr. Allison, ahora le invito al Sr. Allison a hacer uso de la palabra • **to weigh one's ~s** medir las palabras • **with these ~s, he sat down** y tras pronunciar estas palabras se sentó • **without a ~** sin decir palabra *or* ni pío • IDIOMS: • **from the ~ go** desde el principio mismo • **it's the last ~ in luxury** es el último grito en lo que a lujo se refiere • **you're putting ~s into my mouth** te refieres a cosas que yo no he dicho • **you took the ~s right out of my mouth** me quitaste la palabra de la boca • **the ~ on the street is that …** los que saben del tema dicen que … • PROVERBS: • **many a true ~ is spoken in jest** las bromas a veces pueden ser veras • **a ~ to the wise (is sufficient)** al buen entendedor pocas palabras le bastan; ▷ **breathe, eat, edgeways, mince**
2 (= *talk*) • **to have a ~ with sb** hablar (dos palabras) con algn, tener unas palabras con algn • **I'll have a ~ with him about it** lo hablaré con él, se lo mencionaré • **could I**

W

have a (short) ~ with you? ¿puedo hablar un momento contigo? • **I had a few ~s with him yesterday** tuve unas palabras con él ayer • **to have a ~ in sb's ear** (*Brit*) decir algo a algn en confianza
3 (= *angry words*) • **to have ~s with sb** reñir *or* (*esp LAm*) pelear(se) con algn • **the referee had ~s with him** el árbitro le dijo cuatro palabras • **~s passed between them** cambiaron algunas palabras injuriosas
4 (*no pl*) (= *message*) recado *m*; (= *news*) noticia *f*, aviso *m* • **to bring ~ of sth to sb** informar a algn de algo • **~ came that ...** llegó noticia de que ..., se supo que ... • **if ~ gets out that ...** si sale a la luz que ..., si llega a saberse que ... • **the ~ is going round that ...** se dice que ..., corre la voz de que ... • **~ has it that ...** • **the ~ is that ...** se dice que ... • **to leave ~ (with/for sb) that ...** dejar recado (con/para algn) de que ..., dejar dicho (con/para algn) que ... • **there's still no ~ from John** todavía no sabemos nada de John • **pass the ~ that it's time to go** diles que es hora de marcharnos • **to send ~** mandar recado • **to send sb ~ of sth** avisar a algn de algo • **to spread the ~** propagar la noticia
5 (*no pl*) (= *promise, assurance*) palabra *f* (de honor) • **it's his ~ against mine** es su palabra contra la mía • **to take sb at his ~** aceptar lo que algn dice • **to break one's ~** faltar a *or* no cumplir la palabra • **to give sb one's ~ (that ...)** dar la palabra a algn (de que ...) • **to go back on one's ~** faltar a la palabra • **you have my ~** tienes mi palabra • **we only have** *or* **we've only got her ~ for it** todo lo que sabemos es lo que ella dice • **to hold** *or* **keep sb to his ~** hacer que algn cumpla su palabra • **~ of honour** palabra *f*, palabra *f* de honor • **to keep one's ~** cumplir (lo prometido) • **(upon) my ~!** ¡caramba! • **he's a man of his ~** es hombre de palabra • **I take your ~ for it** te creo, ¡basta con que me lo digas!* • **take my ~ for it** te lo aseguro • IDIOMS: • **his ~ is (as good as) his bond** su palabra merece entera confianza • **to be as good as one's ~** cumplir (lo prometido)
6 (*no pl*) (= *command*) orden *f* • **to give the ~ to do sth** dar la orden de hacer algo • **you have only to say the ~** solamente hace falta que des la orden • **his ~ is law** su palabra es ley • **~ of command** voz *f* de mando
7 (*Rel*) verbo *m*, palabra *f* • **the Word of God** el Verbo de Dios
(VT) [+ *letter etc*] redactar • **it's not very clearly ~ed** está mal redactado • **how shall we ~ it?** ¿cómo lo expresamos? • **a simply ~ed refusal** una negativa sencilla • **a well ~ed declaration** una declaración bien expresada
(CPD) ▸ **word association** (*Psych*) asociación *f* de palabras ▸ **word blindness** alexia *f* ▸ **word class** categoría *f* gramatical (de las palabras) ▸ **word count** recuento *m* de vocabulario ▸ **word formation** formación *f* de palabras ▸ **word game** juego *m* de formación de palabras ▸ **word list** lista *f* de palabras, vocabulario *m* ▸ **word order** orden *m* de palabras ▸ **word picture** descripción *f* ▸ **word processing** procesamiento *m* de textos ▸ **word processor** procesador *m* de textos

wordage [ˈwɜːdɪdʒ] (N) número *m or* recuento *m* de palabras
word-blind [ˈwɜːdblaɪnd] (ADJ) aléxico
wordbook [ˈwɜːdbʊk] (N) vocabulario *m*
word-for-word [ˌwɜːdfəˈwɜːd] (ADJ) [*translation*] literal; [*quotation*] textual
wordiness [ˈwɜːdɪnɪs] (N) verbosidad *f*, prolijidad *f*
wording [ˈwɜːdɪŋ] (N) • **the ~ is unclear** está mal redactado
wordless [ˈwɜːdlɪs] (ADJ) **1** (= *silent*) silencioso **2** (= *without words*) sin palabras
wordlessly [ˈwɜːdləslɪ] (ADV) sin decir una (sola) palabra
word-of-mouth [ˈwɜːdəvˈmaʊθ] (ADJ) verbal, oral; ▹ **word**
word-perfect [ˈwɜːdˈpɜːfɪkt] (ADJ) (*Brit*) sin falta de expresión • **to be word-perfect** saber perfectamente su papel
wordplay [ˈwɜːdpleɪ] (N) juego *m* de palabras
word-process [ˈwɜːdˈprəʊses] (VT) pasar a máquina
wordsmith [ˈwɜːdsmɪθ] (N) (= *writer*) artífice *mf* de la palabra; (= *poet*) poeta *mf*
wordwrap [ˈwɜːdræp] (N) salto *m* de línea automático
wordy [ˈwɜːdɪ] (ADJ) (COMPAR: **wordier**, SUPERL: **wordiest**) verboso, prolijo
wore [wɔːʳ] (PT) *of* **wear**
work [wɜːk] (N) **1** (= *activity*) trabajo *m*; (= *effort*) esfuerzo *m* • **"work in progress"** "trabajo en proceso" • **to be at ~ on sth** estar trabajando sobre algo • **there are forces at ~** hay fuerzas en movimiento • **~ has begun on the new dam** se han comenzado las obras del nuevo embalse • **~ has begun on the new project** ha comenzado el trabajo en el nuevo proyecto • **it's all in a day's ~** es pan de cada día • **to do one's ~** hacer su trabajo • **he did some good ~ at head office** hizo un buen trabajo en la oficina central • **the medicine had done its ~** la medicina había surtido efecto • **to get some ~ done** hacer algo (de trabajo) • **to get on with one's ~** seguir trabajando • **good ~!** (= *well done*) ¡buen trabajo! • **it's hard ~** es mucho trabajo, cuesta (trabajo) • **he's hard ~*** es una persona difícil • **a piece of ~** un trabajo • **she's put a lot of ~ into it** le ha puesto grandes esfuerzos • **to make quick ~ of sth/sb** despachar algo/a algn con rapidez • **to set to ~** ponerse a trabajar • **to set sb to ~** poner a algn a trabajar • **to make short ~ of sth/sb** despachar algo/a algn con rapidez • **to start ~** ponerse a trabajar • IDIOM: • **to have one's ~ cut out**: • **I have my ~ cut out as it is** ya tengo trabajo hasta por encima de las cejas • **I had my ~ cut out to stop it** me costó detenerlo • **you'll have your ~ cut out trying to stop him** te costará muchísimo trabajo impedirle; ▹ **nasty**
2 (= *employment, place of employment*) trabajo *m* • **"~ wanted"** (*US*) "demandas de empleo" • **to be at ~** estar trabajando • **accidents at ~** accidentes *mpl* laborales • **to go to ~** ir a trabajar • **to go out to ~** (= *have a job*) tener un trabajo • **to be in ~** tener trabajo • **she's looking for ~** está buscando trabajo • **it's nice ~ if you can get it** es muy agradable para los que tienen esa suerte • **I'm off ~ for a week** tengo una semana de permiso • **a day off ~** un día libre • **to take time off ~** tomarse tiempo libre • **to be out of ~** estar desempleado *or* parado *or* en paro • **to put sb out of ~** dejar a algn sin trabajo • **on her way to ~** camino del trabajo
3 (= *product, deed*) obra *f*; (= *efforts*) trabajo • **the ~s of God** las obras de Dios • **this is the ~ of a professional/madman** esto es trabajo de un profesional/loco • **what do you think of his ~?** ¿qué te parece su trabajo? • **the dictator and all his ~s** el dictador y todo lo suyo • **good ~s** obras *fpl* de caridad • **his life's ~** el trabajo al que ha dedicado su vida
4 (*Art, Literat etc*) obra *f* • **the ~s of Dickens** las obras de Dickens • **a ~ of art** una obra de arte • **a literary ~** una obra literaria • **a ~ of reference** un libro de consulta
5 works [*of machine, clock etc*] mecanismo *msing* • IDIOM: • **to bung** *or* **gum up the ~s** fastidiarlo todo; ▹ **spanner**
6 works (*Mil*) obras *fpl*, fortificaciones *fpl* • **road ~s** obras • **Ministry of Works** Ministerio *m* de Obras Públicas
(VI) **1** (*gen*) trabajar; (= *be in a job*) tener trabajo • **to ~ to achieve sth** dirigir todos sus esfuerzos a lograr algo • **he is ~ing at his German** está dándole al alemán • **to ~ hard** trabajar mucho *or* duro • **she ~s in a bakery** trabaja en una panadería • **he ~s in education/publishing** trabaja en la enseñanza/el campo editorial • **he prefers to ~ in wood/oils** prefiere trabajar la madera/con óleos • **to ~ to rule** (*Ind*) estar en huelga de celo • **to ~ towards sth** trabajar *or* realizar esfuerzos para conseguir algo • IDIOM: • **to ~ like a slave** *or* **Trojan** *etc* trabajar como un demonio
2 (= *function*) [*machine, car*] funcionar • **the heating isn't ~ing** la calefacción no funciona • **it won't ~** no funciona • **"not working"** "no funciona" • **my brain doesn't seem to be ~ing today** (*hum*) mi cerebro no funciona hoy como es debido • **it may ~ against us** podría sernos desfavorable • **this can ~ both ways** esto puede ser un arma de doble filo • **this may ~ in our favour** puede que esto nos venga bien • **to get sth ~ing** hacer funcionar algo • **it ~s off the mains** funciona con la electricidad de la red • **my plan ~ed perfectly** mi plan funcionó a la perfección
3 (= *be effective*) [*plan*] salir, marchar; [*drug, medicine, spell*] surtir efecto, ser eficaz; [*yeast*] fermentar • **how long does it take to ~?** ¿cuánto tiempo hace falta para que empiece a surtir efecto? • **the scheme won't ~** el proyecto no es práctico, esto no será factible • **it won't ~, I tell you!** ¡te digo que no se puede (hacer)!
4 [*mouth, face, jaws*] moverse, torcerse
5 (= *move gradually*) • **she ~ed methodically down the list** repasó metódicamente la lista • **to ~ loose** desprenderse • **to ~ round to a question** preparar el terreno para preguntar algo • **eventually he ~ed round to the price** por fin llegó a mencionar el precio • **what are you ~ing round to?** ¿adónde va a parar todo esto?, ¿qué propósito tiene todo esto?
(VT) **1** (= *make work*) hacer trabajar • **he ~s his staff too hard** hace trabajar demasiado al personal • **to ~ o.s. to death** matarse trabajando
2 (= *operate*) • **can you ~ it?** ¿sabes manejarlo? • **it is ~ed by electricity** funciona con electricidad
3 (= *achieve*) [+ *change*] producir, motivar; [+ *cure*] hacer, efectuar; [+ *miracle*] hacer • **he has managed to ~ his promotion*** ha conseguido asegurarse el ascenso • **they ~ed it so that she could come*** lo arreglaron para que viniera; ▹ **wonder**
4 (*Sew*) coser; (*Knitting*) [+ *row*] hacer • **~ed with blue thread** bordado de hilo azul
5 (= *shape*) [+ *dough, clay*] trabajar; [+ *stone, marble*] tallar, grabar • **~ed flint** piedra *f* tallada • **~ the butter and sugar together** amasar el azúcar y la mantequilla juntos
6 (= *exploit*) [+ *mine*] explotar; [+ *land*] cultivar • **this land has not been ~ed for many years** estas tierras hace mucho tiempo que no se cultivan • **he ~s the eastern part of the province** trabaja en la parte este de la provincia
7 (= *manoeuvre*) • **he gradually ~ed the rope through the hole** poco a poco fue metiendo la cuerda por el agujero • **to ~ one's hands free** lograr soltar las manos • **he ~ed the**

lever up and down movió la palanca hacia arriba y hacia abajo • **to ~ o.s. into a rage** ponerse furioso, enfurecerse • **he ~ed the crowd (up) into a frenzy** exaltó los ánimos de la multitud • **the screw had ~ed itself loose** el tornillo se había soltado solo • **to ~ one's way along** ir avanzando poco a poco • **to ~ one's way up a cliff** escalar poco a poco *or* a duras penas un precipicio • **to ~ one's way up to the top of a company** llegar a la dirección de una compañía por sus propios esfuerzos • **he ~ed his way up in the firm** ascendió en la compañía mediante sus propios esfuerzos
8 (= *finance*) • **to ~ one's passage on a ship** costearse un viaje trabajando • **to ~ one's way through college** costearse los estudios universitarios trabajando
(CPD) ▸ **work area** área *f* de trabajo ▸ **work camp** campamento *m* laboral ▸ **work ethic** ética *f* del trabajo ▸ **work experience** experiencia *f* laboral ▸ **work file** fichero *m* de trabajo ▸ **work force** (= *labourers*) mano *f* de obra; (= *personnel*) plantilla *f* ▸ **work in progress** trabajo *m* en proceso ▸ **work permit** permiso *m* de trabajo ▸ **work prospects** [*of student*] perspectivas *fpl* de trabajo ▸ **work study** práctica *f* estudiantil ▸ **work surface** = **worktop** ▸ **work therapy** laborterapia *f*, terapia *f* laboral ▸ **work week** (*US*) semana *f* laboral

▸ **work away** (VI + ADV) seguir trabajando, trabajar sin parar • **to ~ away at sth** darle (duro) a algo*

▸ **work in** (VI + ADV) (= *fit in*) ajustarse a, cuadrar con • **it ~s in quite well with our plans** esto se ajusta bastante bien a nuestros planes, esto cuadra bastante bien con nuestros planes
(VT + ADV) **1** [+ *screw etc*] (*slowly*) introducir poco a poco; (*with difficulty*) meter con esfuerzo
2 [+ *quotation, reference, subject*] meter • **we'll try to ~ in a reference somewhere** trataremos de meter una referencia en alguna parte
3 (= *mix in*) agregar, añadir • **~ the flour in gradually** agregar *or* añadir la harina poco a poco

▸ **work off** (VI + ADV) [*nut, handle*] desprenderse, soltarse (con el uso)
(VT + ADV) **1** [+ *debt*] pagar con su trabajo
2 • **to ~ off one's feelings** desahogarse • **to ~ off surplus fat** quitarse las grasas excesivas trabajando • **I must try to ~ off all the weight I've put on** tengo que moverme para ver si adelgazo lo que he engordado

▸ **work on** (VI + PREP) **1** [+ *project etc*] trabajar en • **they're ~ing on the car now** están trabajando en el coche ahora • **they will get ~ing on it at once** se pondrán enseguida manos a la obra • **the police are ~ing on it** la policía lo está investigando
2 (= *act on*) • **we've no clues to ~ on** no tenemos pistas en qué basarnos • **we're ~ing on the principle that ...** nos atenemos al *or* nos basamos en el principio de que ...
3 (= *try to persuade*) • **he hasn't agreed yet but I'm ~ing on him** todavía no está de acuerdo pero le estoy tratando de convencer

▸ **work out** (VT + ADV) **1** (= *calculate*) [+ *cost, profit*] calcular; [+ *answer*] encontrar • **I ~ed it out in my head** lo calculé mentalmente
2 (= *solve*) [+ *problem*] resolver • **things will ~ themselves out** al final, todo saldrá bien *or* se solucionará
3 (= *devise*) idear • **to ~ out a plan** idear *or* (*frm*) urdir un plan
4 (= *understand*) lograr entender • **I just couldn't ~ it out** no lograba entenderlo • **can you ~ out where we are on the map?** ¿puedes determinar *or* averiguar dónde estamos en el mapa? • **I can't ~ him out*** no puedo entenderle
5 (= *exhaust*) [+ *mine, land*] agotar
6 (*in job*) • **to ~ out one's notice** trabajar hasta que se acabe el tiempo de preaviso
7 (= *get rid of*) [+ *anger, frustration*] librarse de
(VI + ADV) **1** (= *allow solution*) resolverse • **it doesn't ~ out** [*sum*] no sale
2 (= *amount to*) • **the cost ~ed out at five pounds** los costos ascendieron a cinco libras • **how much does it ~ out at?** ¿cuánto suma?, ¿a cuánto sale? • **it ~s out at ten pounds each** sale a diez libras esterlinas por persona • **gas heating would ~ out cheaper** la calefacción de gas saldría más barata
3 (= *succeed*) salir bien • **I hope it will ~ out well** espero que salga bien • **everything ~ed out well** todo *or* la cosa salió bien • **how did it ~ out?** ¿qué tal salió? • **it hasn't ~ed out that way** no ha sido así
4 (= *exercise*) hacer ejercicio • **I ~ out twice a week** hago ejercicio dos veces a la semana

▸ **work over** (VT + ADV) (= *beat up*) dar una paliza a

▸ **work through** (VI + PREP) (*Psych*) [+ *problem, conflict*] tratar

▸ **work up** (VT + ADV) **1** (= *develop*) [+ *energy, courage*] conseguir • **I can't ~ up much enthusiasm for the plan** no consigo entusiasmarme con el plan • **together they ~ed the business up from nothing** entre los dos levantaron el negocio de la nada • **you could ~ this story up into a film** podrías desarrollar este cuento para hacer una película • **to ~ up an appetite** abrir el apetito • **I've ~ed up quite a thirst, carrying those boxes** me ha entrado mucha sed cargando esas cajas
2 (= *excite*) • **he ~ed the crowd up into a frenzy** exaltó los ánimos de la multitud • **to ~ o.s. up into a rage** ponerse furioso, enfurecerse • **to be ~ed up** excitarse, exaltarse, emocionarse (*esp LAm*) • **don't get all ~ed up!** ¡cálmate!

▸ **work up to** (VI + PREP) preparar el terreno para • **events were ~ing up to a crisis** los sucesos estaban preparando el terreno para una crisis • **what are you ~ing up to?** ¿qué propósito tiene todo esto?, ¿adónde va a parar todo esto? • **I thought he was ~ing up to a proposal** creía que estaba preparando el terreno para hacerme una declaración

workable ['wɜːkəbl] (ADJ) práctico, factible
workaday ['wɜːkədeɪ] (ADJ) rutinario
workaholic [ˌwɜːkə'hɒlɪk] (N) trabajador(a) *m/f* obsesivo/a, adicto/a *m/f* al trabajo
workbasket ['wɜːkˌbɑːskɪt] (N) neceser *m* de costura
workbench ['wɜːkbentʃ] (N) banco *m* de trabajo, mesa *f* de trabajo
workbook ['wɜːkbʊk] (N) libro *m* de trabajo; (*Scol*) cuaderno *m*
workbox ['wɜːkbɒks] (N) (*Sew*) neceser *m* de costura
workday ['wɜːkdeɪ] (N) (*US*) día *m* laborable
worker ['wɜːkə[r]] (N) **1** (= *person*) (*gen*) trabajador(a) *m/f*; (*Agr, Ind*) obrero/a *m/f* • **he's a fast ~** trabaja deprisa; (*euph**) va deprisa con las mujeres* • **she's a hard ~** es muy trabajadora • **she's a good ~** trabaja bien; ▹ **office, research**
2 (= *ant, bee*) obrera *f*
(CPD) ▸ **worker ant** hormiga *f* obrera ▸ **worker bee** abeja *f* obrera ▸ **worker priest** sacerdote *m* obrero
workflow ['wɜːkfləʊ] (N) volumen *m* de trabajo
workforce ['wɜːkfɔːs] (N) **1** (*in country, region*) población *f* activa
2 (*in company*) (= *personnel*) plantilla *f*; (= *labourers*) mano *f* de obra
workhorse ['wɜːkˌhɔːs] (N) caballo *m* de tiro; (*fig*) persona *f* muy trabajadora
workhouse ['wɜːkhaʊs] (N) (PL: **workhouses** ['wɜːkhaʊzɪz]) (*Brit*) (*Hist*) asilo *m* de pobres
work-in ['wɜːkɪn] (N) encierro *m* (en una fábrica *etc*)
working ['wɜːkɪŋ] (ADJ) **1** (= *economically active*) [*person*] trabajador, que trabaja; [*population*] activo • **~ mothers** madres *fpl* trabajadoras, madres *fpl* que trabajan • **the ~ man** el hombre trabajador *or* que trabaja • **the ~ woman** la mujer trabajadora *or* que trabaja • **ordinary ~ people** gente trabajadora normal y corriente • **he's a ~ dog** es un perro de trabajo *or* labor
2 (= *relating to work*) [*conditions, practice, environment, week*] laboral; [*life*] laboral, activo; [*day*] laborable; [*breakfast, lunch*] de trabajo; [*clothes*] de faena, de trabajo • **your order will be sent within three ~ days** (*Brit*) su pedido será despachado en un plazo de tres días laborales • **my ~ day begins at eight a.m.** mi jornada (laboral *or* de trabajo) empieza a las ocho de la mañana • **during ~ hours** durante horas de trabajo • **~ patterns** pautas *fpl* laborales, pautas *fpl* de trabajo
3 (= *provisional*) [*title, definition*] momentáneo, provisional • **~ hypothesis** hipótesis *f inv* de trabajo
4 (= *functioning*) [*farm, mill, steam train*] en funcionamiento • **to have a ~ knowledge of sth** tener conocimientos básicos de algo • **to be in ~ order** funcionar perfectamente
(N) **1** (= *operation*) [*of machine, engine, computer*] funcionamiento *m*; [*of mine*] explotación *f*
2 workings: **a** [*of organization, parliament*] forma *f* de funcionar; [*of machine, engine, computer*] (= *operation, way of working*) funcionamiento *m*; (= *mechanism*) mecanismo *m* • **the ~s of his mind** su forma de pensar
b (= *mine*) mina *fsing*; (= *excavations*) excavaciones *fpl*
(CPD) ▸ **working assets** (*Comm, Econ*) activo *m* circulante ▸ **working capital** (*Comm, Econ*) capital *m* circulante, capital *m* de explotación ▸ **the working class(es)** la clase obrera, la clase trabajadora; ▹ **working-class** ▸ **working expenses** gastos *mpl* de explotación ▸ **working face** cara *f* de trabajo ▸ **working group** grupo *m* de trabajo (on sobre) ▸ **working holiday** *vacaciones en las que se combina el trabajo con el ocio* ▸ **working majority** (*Pol*) mayoría *f* suficiente ▸ **working model** modelo *m* articulado ▸ **working paper** documento *m* de trabajo ▸ **working parts** partes *fpl* activas ▸ **working partner** socio *m* activo ▸ **working party** = **working group** ▸ **working relationship** relación *f* de trabajo • **they have a good ~ relationship** tienen una buena relación de trabajo, trabajan bien juntos ▸ **working vacation** (*US*) = **working holiday**
working-class ['wɜːkɪŋklɑːs] (ADJ) [*person, family*] de clase obrera, de clase trabajadora; [*neighbourhood*] obrero • **a self-educated man from a working-class background** un autodidacta de familia de clase obrera *or* trabajadora • **to be working-class** ser de clase obrera *or* trabajadora; ▹ **working**
work/life balance [ˌwɜːklaɪf'bæləns] (N) equilibrio *m* entre el trabajo y la vida privada
workload ['wɜːkləʊd] (N) cantidad *f* de trabajo, trabajo *m* • **we've taken on more staff to cope with the extra ~** hemos

contratado más personal para dar abasto con el trabajo extra

workman ['wɜ:kmən] (N) (PL: **workmen**) obrero *m* • **to be a good ~** ser buen trabajador, trabajar bien • PROVERB: • **a bad** *or* **poor ~ always blames his tools** el mal trabajador siempre echa la culpa a sus herramientas

workmanlike ['wɜ:kmənlaɪk] (ADJ) competente, bien hecho

workmanship ['wɜ:kmənʃɪp] (N) [*of craftsman*] (= *work*) trabajo *m*; (= *skill*) habilidad *f*; [*of artefact*] factura *f*, fabricación *f* • **he prides himself on the quality of his ~** presume de la calidad de su trabajo • **he has been accused of shoddy ~** le acusan de hacer un trabajo de mala calidad • **the chest was of Arab ~** el arcón era de factura *or* fabricación árabe • **the finish and ~ of the woodwork was excellent** el acabado y la factura *or* fabricación de la caja eran excelentes • **of fine ~** esmerado, exquisito • **this is just poor ~** esto no es más que un ejemplo de falta de habilidad profesional

workmate ['wɜ:kmeɪt] (N) compañero/a *m/f* de trabajo

workout ['wɜ:kaʊt] (N) (*Sport*) sesión *f* de ejercicios, sesión *f* de entrenamiento

workpeople ['wɜ:k,pi:pl] (N) (= *workers*) obreros *mpl*; (= *staff*) personal *m*, mano *f* de obra

workplace ['wɜ:kpleɪs] (N) lugar *m* de trabajo

workroom ['wɜ:krʊm] (N) taller *m*

works [wɜ:ks] (N) (*pl inv*) **1** (*Brit*) (= *factory etc*) fábrica *f*

2 • **the ~*** (= *the lot*) todo, la totalidad • IDIOM: • **to give sb the ~** (= *treat harshly*) dar a algn una paliza; (= *treat generously*) tratar a algn a cuerpo de rey

3‡ (= *syringe*) chuta‡ *f*

(CPD) ▸ **works canteen** comedor *m* de la fábrica ▸ **works council** consejo *m* de obreros, comité *m* de empresa ▸ **works manager** gerente *mf* de fábrica ▸ **works outing** excursión *f* del personal

work-sharing ['wɜ:k,ʃɛərɪŋ] (N) repartimiento *m* del trabajo

worksheet ['wɜ:kʃi:t] (N) **1** (*Ind*) hoja *f* de trabajo

2 (*Scol*) hoja *f* de ejercicios

workshop ['wɜ:kʃɒp] (N) taller *m* • **a music ~** un taller de música • **a drama ~** un taller de teatro

workshy ['wɜ:kʃaɪ] (ADJ) perezoso, flojo (*esp LAm*)

workspace ['wɜ:kspeɪs] (N) **1** (= *area to work in*) espacio *m* para trabajar

2 (*Comput*) área *f* de trabajo

workstation ['wɜ:k,steɪʃən] (N) (*Comput*) terminal *f* de trabajo

worktable ['wɜ:k,teɪbl] (N) mesa *f* de trabajo

worktop ['wɜ:ktɒp] (N) encimera *f*

work-to-rule ['wɜ:ktə'ru:l] (N) huelga *f* de brazos caídos

workwear ['wɜ:kwɛəʳ] (N) ropa *f* de trabajo

work-worn ['wɜ:kwɔ:n] (ADJ) agotado (por el trabajo)

world [wɜ:ld] (N) **1** (= *planet*) mundo *m* • **Australia is on the other side of the ~** Australia está al otro lado del mundo • **the ~ we live in** el mundo en el que vivimos • **the ~'s worst cook** el peor cocinero del mundo • **our company leads the ~ in shoe manufacturing** nuestra empresa es líder mundial en la confección de calzado • **since the ~ began** desde que el mundo es mundo • **in the best of all possible ~s** en el mejor de los mundos • **it's not the end of the ~!*** ¡no es el fin del mundo! • **the tallest man in the ~** el hombre más alto del mundo • **it's what he wants most in (all) the ~** es lo que más quiere en el mundo • **the New World** el Nuevo Mundo • **the Old World** el Viejo Mundo • **she has travelled all over the ~** ha viajado por todo el mundo • **people came from all over the ~** vino gente de todas partes del mundo • **it's the same the ~ over** es igual en todo el mundo, es igual vayas a donde vayas • **in a perfect ~ this would be possible** en un mundo ideal *or* perfecto esto sería posible • **you have to start living in the real ~** tienes que empezar a afrontar la vida *or* la realidad • **to go round the ~** dar la vuelta al mundo • **on a ~ scale** a escala mundial • **to see the ~** ver mundo • **to take the ~ as it is** aceptar la realidad, aceptar las cosas como son • **the worst of all possible ~s** el peor de todos los mundos posibles • IDIOMS: • **to have the ~ at one's feet** tener el mundo a sus pies • **it's out of this ~*** es una maravilla • **to live in a ~ of one's own** vivir en su propio mundo • **you seem to be in a ~ of your own today** hoy parece que estás en otro mundo • **the ~ is your oyster** tienes el mundo a tus pies • **it's a small ~!** ¡el mundo es un pañuelo! • **to feel on top of the ~** sentirse de maravilla; ▹ **dead, money, third**

2 (= *realm*) mundo *m* • **the ~ of dreams** el mundo de los sueños • **the animal ~** el reino animal • **the Arab ~** el mundo árabe • **the business ~** el mundo de los negocios • **the English-speaking ~** el mundo de habla inglesa • **the plant ~** el reino vegetal • **the ~ of sport** el mundo deportivo, el mundo de los deportes • **the sporting ~** el mundo deportivo, el mundo de los deportes • **the Western ~** el mundo occidental

3 (= *society*) mundo *m* • **her blouse was undone for all the ~ to see** tenía la blusa desabrochada a la vista de todo el mundo • **to be alone in the ~** estar solo en el mundo, no tener a nadie en el mundo • IDIOMS: • **to come down in the ~** venir a menos • **to go up in the ~** prosperar, medrar • **the ~ and his wife** el ciento y la madre*, todo Dios*; ▹ **man, outside, way**

4 (= *life*) mundo *m* • **in this ~** en esta vida, en este mundo • **to bring a child into the ~** traer a un niño al mundo • **to come into the ~** venir al mundo • **in the next ~** en la otra vida, en el otro mundo • **the other ~** el otro mundo • IDIOMS: • **to have the best of both ~s** tenerlo todo • **he's not long for this ~** no le queda mucha vida, le queda poco de vida

5 (*in emphatic expressions*) • **for all the ~ as if it had never happened** como si nunca hubiera ocurrido • **she looked for all the ~ as if she were dead** cualquiera hubiera dicho que estaba muerta • **they're ~s apart** son totalmente opuestos *or* diferentes, no tiene nada que ver el uno con el otro • **they're ~s apart politically** políticamente los separa un abismo, mantienen posiciones políticas totalmente diferentes • **their views are ~s apart** sus opiniones son totalmente distintas • **there's a ~ of difference between ...** hay un mundo *or* abismo entre ... • **I'd give the ~ to know** daría todo el oro del mundo por saberlo • **it did him the ~ of good** le sentó de maravilla, le hizo la mar de bien* • **nothing in the ~ would make me do it** no lo haría por nada del mundo • **how in the ~ did you manage to do it?*** ¿cómo demonios *or* diablos conseguiste hacerlo? • **what in the ~ were you thinking of!*** ¡qué demonios *or* diablos estabas pensando!* • **where in the ~ has he got to?*** ¿dónde demonios *or* diablos se ha metido?* • **why in the ~ did you do that?*** ¿por qué demonios *or* diablos hiciste eso?* • **she means the ~ to me** ella significa muchísimo para mí • **not for all the ~** por nada del mundo • **he promised me the ~** me prometió la luna • **to think the ~ of sb** tener a algn en gran estima

(CPD) [*economy, proportions*] mundial; [*events, news*] internacional; [*trade*] internacional, mundial; [*tour*] mundial, alrededor del mundo ▸ **World Bank** Banco *m* Mundial ▸ **world beater** campeón/ona *m/f* mundial ▸ **world champion** campeón/ona *m/f* del mundo, campeón/ona *m/f* mundial ▸ **world championship** campeonato *m* mundial, campeonato *m* del mundo ▸ **the World Council of Churches** el Concilio Mundial de las Iglesias ▸ **the World Court** el Tribunal Internacional de Justicia ▸ **the World Cup** (*Ftbl*) la Copa Mundial, la Copa del Mundo ▸ **world fair** feria *f* universal ▸ **the World Health Organization** la Organización Mundial de la Salud ▸ **World Heritage Site** lugar *m* patrimonio de la humanidad • **to be a World Heritage Site** ser patrimonio de la humanidad ▸ **world language** lengua *f* universal ▸ **world leader** [*of country, company*] líder *m* mundial; (= *politician*) jefe/a *m/f* de estado ▸ **world market** mercado *m* mundial ▸ **world market price** precio *m* (del mercado) mundial ▸ **world music** músicas *fpl* del mundo, world music *f* ▸ **world order** orden *m* mundial ▸ **world power** (= *country*) potencia *f* mundial ▸ **world premiere** estreno *m* mundial ▸ **world record** récord *m* mundial ▸ **world's champion** (*US*) campeón/ona *m/f* del mundo, campeón/ona *m/f* mundial ▸ **World Series** (*US*) campeonato *m* mundial de béisbol; ▹ BASEBALL ▸ **World Service** (*Brit*) *servicio internacional de la BBC* ▸ **world title** título *m* mundial ▸ **World Trade Organization** • **the World Trade Organization** la Organización Mundial del Comercio ▸ **world view** cosmovisión *f* ▸ **world war** guerra *f* mundial • **World War One/Two** la Primera/Segunda Guerra Mundial ▸ **the World Wide Web** el World Wide Web

world-class ['wɜ:ld'klɑ:s] (ADJ) de talla mundial

world-famous ['wɜ:ld'feɪməs] (ADJ) de fama mundial, mundialmente conocido

worldliness ['wɜ:ldlɪnɪs] (N) mundanería *f*; (= *sophistication*) sofisticación *f*

worldly ['wɜ:ldlɪ] (ADJ) (COMPAR: **worldlier**, SUPERL: **worldliest**) **1** (= *material*) [*success, pleasures*] mundano, material • **all my ~ goods** todos mis bienes materiales

2 (= *experienced*) con (mucho) mundo • **he was more ~ than other boys his age** tenía más mundo que otros muchachos de su edad • **~ wisdom** mundo *m*, saber *m* mundano

3 (= *sophisticated*) sofisticado

worldly-wise ['wɜ:ldlɪ'waɪz] (ADJ) de mundo, que conoce mundo

world-shaking ['wɜ:ld,ʃeɪkɪŋ], **world-shattering** ['wɜ:ld,ʃætərɪŋ] (ADJ) pasmoso

world-weariness ['wɜ:ld'wɪərɪnɪs] (N) hastío *m*

world-weary ['wɜ:ld'wɪərɪ] (ADJ) hastiado, cansado de la vida

worldwide ['wɜ:ld'waɪd] (ADJ) mundial, universal

(ADV) mundialmente, en todo el mundo • **it's known ~** es mundialmente conocido, es conocido en todo el mundo • **to travel ~** viajar por todo el mundo

(CPD) ▸ **the Worldwide Web** (*Internet*) el World Wide Web, el WWW

WORM [wɜ:m] (ABBR) = **write once read**

many times
worm [wɜːm] (N) **1** (= *earthworm*) gusano *m*, lombriz *f* • IDIOM: • **the ~ will turn** la paciencia tiene un límite; ▹ **glow**
2 (*in fruit, vegetable*) gusano *m* (*also Comput*)
3 (*Med*) • **to have ~s** tener lombrices
4 (*pej*) (= *person*) gusano *m*
(VT) **1** (= *wriggle*) • **he ~ed his way out through the narrow window** salió arrastrándose por la estrecha ventana • **to ~ one's way into a group** (*pej*) infiltrarse en un grupo • **to ~ one's way into sb's confidence** (*pej*) ganarse la confianza de algn
2 (*pej*) (= *extract*) • **to ~ a secret out of sb** arrancarle un secreto a algn
3 (= *treat*) [+ *dog, cat, horse*] desparasitar
(CPD) ▸ **worm powder** polvos *mpl* antiparasitarios ▸ **worm tablet** tableta *f* antiparasitaria
worm-eaten ['wɜːmˌiːtn] (ADJ) [*wood*] carcomido, apolillado; [*cloth*] apolillado; [*fruit*] con gusanos
wormhole ['wɜːmhəʊl] (N) (*left by earthworm*) agujero *m* de gusano; (*left by woodworm*) agujero *m* de polilla
worming ['wɜːmɪŋ] (CPD) ▸ **worming powder** polvos *mpl* antiparasitarios ▸ **worming tablet** tableta *f* antiparasitaria
wormwood ['wɜːmwʊd] (N) **1** ajenjo *m*
2 (*fig*) hiel *f*, amargura *f*
wormy ['wɜːmɪ] (ADJ) **1** (= *worm-eaten*) [*fruit*] con gusanos; [*furniture*] carcomido, apolillado
2 (= *full of worms*) [*soil*] lleno de gusanos
worn [wɔːn] (PP) *of* **wear**
(ADJ) **1** (= *deteriorated*) [*garment, furniture, tyre, component*] gastado; [*steps, stone, surface*] desgastado • **the carpet is a bit ~** la moqueta está un poco gastada
2 (= *tired*) [*person*] rendido, agotado; [*face*] cansado • **he's looking very ~** tiene aspecto de muy cansado
worn-out ['wɔːn'aʊt] (ADJ) **1** [*garment, furniture, tyre, component*] gastado
2 (= *exhausted*) [*person*] rendido, agotado • **we were worn out after the long walk** estábamos rendidos *or* agotados después de andar tanto
3 (*fig*) [*argument, idea*] gastado
worried ['wʌrɪd] (ADJ) **1** (= *anxious*) [*person*] preocupado; [*look*] de preocupación • **to be ~** estar preocupado • **to be ~ about sth** estar preocupado por algo • **if I'm late he gets ~** si llego tarde se preocupa • **I was getting ~** estaba empezando a preocuparme • **you had me ~** me tenías preocupado • **to be ~ sick** *or* **to death (about sth)*** estar preocupadísimo *or* muy preocupado (por algo) • **he was ~ that she would report him to the police** tenía miedo de que ella lo delatase a la policía
2 (= *bothered*) • **I'm not ~** me da igual*, me tiene sin cuidado • **I'm not ~ either way** me da igual una cosa que otra*
worriedly ['wʌrɪdlɪ] (ADV) [*say*] con preocupación
worrier ['wʌrɪə^r] (N) • **to be a ~** ser un/una agonías*, ser un preocupón/una preocupona*
worrisome ['wʌrɪsəm] (ADJ) (*esp US*) inquietante, preocupante
worry ['wʌrɪ] (N) **1** (= *thing to worry about*) preocupación *f* • **he hasn't any worries** no tiene ninguna preocupación • **his worries were completely unfounded** estaba preocupado sin razón • **he may have damaged his spine, which is a ~** puede que se haya dañado la columna, lo que es causa *or* motivo de preocupación • **my son has always been a ~ to me** mi hijo siempre me ha causado preocupaciones • **it's a great ~ to us all** es una gran preocupación para todos nosotros, nos preocupa mucho a todos • **financial worries** problemas *mpl* económicos, problemas *mpl* de dinero • **that's the least of my worries** eso es lo que menos me preocupa, eso es lo de menos
2 (= *anxiety*) preocupación *f*, inquietud *f* • **she has caused me a great deal** *or* **a lot of ~** me ha tenido muy preocupado *or* inquieto, me ha dado muchas preocupaciones • **to make o.s. sick with ~** preocuparse muchísimo • **to be frantic** *or* **out of one's mind** *or* **sick with ~*** estar preocupadísimo • **source of ~** motivo *m* de preocupación
(VT) **1** (= *cause concern to*) preocupar • **what's ~ing you?** ¿qué es lo que te preocupa? • **that phone call has been ~ing me all day** esa llamada de teléfono me ha tenido preocupado todo el día • **that doesn't ~ me in the least** eso no me preocupa en absoluto • **to ~ o.s. about sth** preocuparse por algo • **don't ~ your head!*** ¡no le des muchas vueltas!, ¡no te calientes la cabeza!* • **to ~ o.s. over sth** preocuparse por algo • **to ~ o.s. sick about sth*** preocuparse muchísimo por algo
2 (= *bother*) molestar • **the cold doesn't ~ me** el frío no me molesta • **that doesn't ~ me in the least** eso me trae absolutamente sin cuidado • **I don't want to ~ you with my problems but ...** no te quiero cargar *or* molestar con mis problemas pero ... • **don't ~ yourself with the details** no te preocupes por los detalles
3 (= *fear*) • **they ~ that extremists might gain control** temen que los extremistas se hagan con el control, los preocupa que los extremistas se hagan con el control
4 (= *play with, harry*) [*dog*] [+ *bone*] mordisquear, juguetear con; [+ *sheep*] acosar
5 (= *fiddle with*) [+ *object*] juguetear con; [+ *problem*] dar vueltas a • **he kept ~ing the loose tooth with his tongue** no dejaba de toquetearse con la lengua el diente que tenía flojo
(VI) **1** (= *be anxious*) preocuparse • **he worries a lot** se preocupa mucho • **don't ~!** ¡no te preocupes! • **I'll punish him if I catch him, don't you ~!** ¡si lo pillo lo castigaré, que no te quepa duda! • **to ~ about sth/sb** preocuparse por algo/algn • **there's nothing to ~ about** no hay por qué preocuparse • **that's nothing to ~ about** no hay que preocuparse por eso • **don't ~ about me** no te preocupes por mí • **I've got quite enough to ~ about without that** tengo ya bastantes problemas para preocuparme por eso • **she worries about her health** le preocupa su salud • **not to ~!*** ¡no pasa nada!, ¡no te preocupes! • **to ~ over sth/sb** preocuparse por algo/algn
2 (= *bother*) molestarse • **don't ~, I'll do it** no te molestes, yo lo haré
3 • **to ~ at sth** [*dog*] mordisquear algo, juguetear con algo; [*person*] (= *fiddle with*) juguetear con algo • **to ~ at a problem** dar vueltas a un problema
(CPD) ▸ **worry beads** *sarta de cuentas con la que se juguetea para calmar los nervios* ▸ **worry lines** *arrugas en la frente debidas a la preocupación*
worrying ['wʌrɪɪŋ] (ADJ) [*situation, news, sign*] preocupante, inquietante
(N) • **all this ~ has aged him** todas estas preocupaciones lo han envejecido
worrywart* ['wʌrɪˌwɔːt] (N) angustias* *mf inv*
worse [wɜːs] (ADJ) (*compar of* **bad**) peor • **his essay is ~ than yours** su trabajo es peor que el tuyo • **it could be ~** podría ser peor • **it's even ~ than we'd predicted** es todavía peor de lo que habíamos pronosticado • **to get ~** [*weather, situation, crime*] empeorar; [*patient*] empeorar, ponerse peor • **my cold is getting ~** mi resfriado va a peor • **my eyesight is getting ~** mi vista va a peor, cada vez veo peor, cada vez tengo peor vista • **his behaviour is getting ~** su comportamiento es cada vez peor • **to get ~ and ~** ponerse cada vez peor, ir de mal en peor • **things will get ~ before they get better** las cosas empeorarán antes de que se les vea la punta • **it gets ~** (*preparing sb for bad news*) lo peor no es eso • **to make sth ~** empeorar algo • **it'll only make matters** *or* **things ~** sólo empeorará las cosas • **and, to make matters ~, ...** y, para colmo de desgracia, ... • **he appeared none the ~ for his ordeal** no parecía desmejorado a pesar de su terrible experiencia • **there's nothing ~ than ...** no hay nada peor que ... • **to be ~ off** (*lit, fig*) estar peor • **he is now ~ off than before** está peor ahora que antes • **she's now ~ off than before she changed jobs** está peor ahora que cuando cambió de trabajo • **he'd be two pounds a week ~ off** tendría dos libras menos a la semana • **it's like last time, only ~** es como la última vez, solo que peor • **to be the ~ for drink** ir cargado de copas* • **what was ~** para colmo (de males); ▹ **bad, bark, better, wear**
(ADV) (*compar of* **badly**) peor • **I sang ~ than he did** *or* **than him** yo cantaba peor que él • **you could** *or* **might do ~ than give her a call** sería aconsejable que la llamarás
(N) • **it's a change for the ~** es un cambio a peor • **there was ~ to come** • **~ was to come** lo peor todavía estaba por verse, aún quedaba lo peor; ▹ **turn**
worsen ['wɜːsn] (VT) empeorar
(VI) empeorar
worsening ['wɜːsnɪŋ] (ADJ) [*situation*] que empeora, que va de mal en peor
(N) empeoramiento *m*
worship ['wɜːʃɪp] (N) **1** (= *adoration*) adoración *f*; (= *reverence*) veneración *f*; (= *organized worship*) culto *m* • **place of ~** lugar *m* de culto • **hours of ~** horario *m* de cultos
2 (*Brit*) (*in titles*) • **Your Worship** (*to judge*) su Señoría; (*to mayor*) señor(a) alcalde(sa) • **His Worship the Mayor** el señor alcalde
(VT) [+ *God, money, success*] adorar, rendir culto a; [+ *film star, singer*] adorar, idolatrar • **she ~s her children** (*fig*) adora a sus hijos • IDIOM: • **he ~ped the ground she walked on** besaba la tierra que ella pisaba, sentía verdadera adoración por ella
(VI) (*Rel*) hacer sus devociones
worshiper ['wɜːʃɪpə^r] (N) (*US*) = **worshipper**
worshipful ['wɜːʃɪpfʊl] (ADJ) (*esp Brit*) (*in titles*) excelentísimo
worshipper, worshiper (*US*) ['wɜːʃɪpə^r] (N) devoto/a *m/f*; **worshippers** (*collectively*) fieles *mpl*
worst [wɜːst] (ADJ) (*superl of* **bad**) **1** (*gen*) peor • **it was the ~ film I've ever seen** fue la peor película de mi vida, fue la película más mala que he visto en mi vida • **~ of all** lo que es peor • **it was the ~ winter for 20 years** fue el peor invierno en 20 años • **the ~ storm in years** la peor tormenta en años • **that's the ~ part (of it)** eso es lo peor • **at the ~ possible time** en el peor momento posible • **it was the ~ thing he ever did** fue lo peor que hizo nunca; ▹ **fear**
2 (= *most badly affected*) [*victim*] más afectado • **the ~ sufferers are children** los más afectados son los niños
(ADV) (*superl of* **badly**) **1** (*gen*) peor • **the ~-dressed man in England** el hombre

peor vestido de Inglaterra • they all sing badly but he sings ~ (of all) todos cantan mal, pero él peor que nadie • to come off ~: • they had a punch-up and he came off ~ tuvieron una pelea y él fue el que salió peor parado

2 [affected, hit] más • he visited some of the ~ affected areas visitó algunas de las zonas más afectadas

N 1 • the ~ lo peor • the ~ that can happen is that ... lo peor que puede pasar es que ... • we threw away the ~ of them los peores los tiramos a la basura • to fear the ~ temerse lo peor • the ~ of it is that ... lo peor de todo es que ... • that's not the ~ of it eso no es lo peor • to get the ~ of it* llevarse la peor parte • IDIOM: • if the ~ comes to the ~ en el peor de los casos

2 • at ~ en el peor de los casos • at ~, they can only say no en el peor de los casos, nos dirán que no • the situation is at its ~ in urban centres en los núcleos urbanos es donde la situación es más grave • things or matters were at their ~ las cosas estaban peor que nunca • he's at his ~ in the evenings por las tardes es cuando está más insoportable

VT † [+ person] (in fight) derrotar; (in conflict) vencer

worst-case ['wɜːstkeɪs] ADJ [hypothesis, projection, guess] más pesimista • the worst-case scenario el peor de los casos

worsted ['wʊstɪd] N (= cloth) estambre m

worth [wɜːθ] ADJ 1 (= equal in value to) • to be ~ sth valer algo • it's ~ five pounds vale cinco libras • it's ~ a lot of money vale mucho dinero • what or how much is it ~? ¿cuánto vale? • it's not ~ much no vale mucho • it's ~ a great deal to me (sentimentally) para mí tiene gran valor sentimental • he was ~ a million when he died murió millonario, murió dejando una fortuna de un millón • what's the old man ~? ¿cuánto dinero tiene el viejo? • "don't tell anybody" — "what's it ~ to you?"* —no se lo digas a nadie —¿cuánto me das si no digo nada? • to run for all one is ~ correr como si le llevara a uno el diablo • to sing for all one is ~ cantar con toda el alma • it must be ~ a fortune debe valer una fortuna • it's more than my job's ~ to tell you me costaría mi empleo decirte eso • it's not ~ the paper it's written on vale menos que el papel en que está escrito • she's ~ ten of him ella vale diez veces más que él • I tell you this for what it's ~ te digo esto por si te interesa

2 (= deserving of) • it's ~ reading vale or merece la pena leerlo • it's ~ the effort vale or merece la pena molestarse en hacerlo • it's ~ having vale or merece la pena tenerlo • it's (not) ~ it (no) vale or merece la pena • life isn't ~ living la vida no tiene sentido para mí • the cathedral is ~ a look la catedral merece la pena, merece la pena ver la catedral • it's ~ mentioning that ... merece la pena mencionar que ..., es digno de mención el hecho de que ... • it's ~ supporting es digno de apoyo • it's ~ thinking about vale or merece la pena pensarlo • it's not ~ the trouble no vale or merece la pena • the meal was ~ the wait la comida estaba tan rica que mereció la pena esperar, la comida mereció or compensó la espera • it's well ~ doing bien vale or merece la pena hacerlo; ▹ job, while

N [of thing] valor m; [of person] valía f • ten pounds' ~ of books libros por valor de diez libras, diez libras de libros • he had no chance to show his true ~ no tuvo oportunidad de mostrar su valía; ▹ money

worthily ['wɜːðɪlɪ] ADV dignamente • he ~ represented his country representó a su país dignamente • to respond ~ to an occasion estar a la altura de las circunstancias

worthiness ['wɜːðɪnɪs] N [of person] valía f; [of cause] mérito m

worthless ['wɜːθlɪs] ADJ (= of no monetary value) sin ningún valor; (= useless) inútil; (= despicable) despreciable • the painting was quite ~ la pintura apenas tenía ningún valor • a ~ individual un tipo despreciable

worthlessness ['wɜːθlɪsnɪs] N [of object] (in money terms) falta f de valor; [of effort, advice] lo inútil; [of person] lo despreciable • feelings of ~ sensación f de inutilidad

worthwhile ['wɜːθ'waɪl] ADJ [activity, enterprise, job] que vale la pena; [cause] loable • a ~ film una película seria or que merece atención • it makes it all ~ le da sentido a todo • to be ~ (= worthy) valer or merecer la pena • it would be ~ seeing or to see him convendría verlo • I had nothing ~ to say no tenía nada interesante que decir; ▹ while

worthy ['wɜːðɪ] ADJ (COMPAR: worthier, SUPERL: worthiest) 1 (= deserving) [winner, champion] merecido; [successor] digno • she found a ~ opponent in Sabatini encontró en Sabatini a una oponente de su categoría • ~ cause buena causa f, causa f noble • to be ~ of sth/sb ser digno de algo/algn • ~ of attention digno de atención • a greatest hits album ~ of the name un disco de grandes éxitos digno de su nombre • she wanted so much to be ~ of her father ansiaba ser digna hija de su padre • that comment was not ~ of you esa observación fue indigna de usted • that remark is not ~ of a reply ese comentario no (se) merece una respuesta

2 (= good) [person] respetable; [motive, aim] encomiable

3 (iro) [person] honorable, venerable

N (hum) ilustre personaje m

wot‡ [wɒt] PRON (Brit) = what

wotcha‡ ['wɒtʃə], **wotcher‡** ['wɒtʃəʳ] EXCL (Brit) ¡hola!

would [wʊd] MODAL VB 1 (conditional tense) • if you asked him he ~ do it si se lo pidieras lo haría • if you had asked him he ~ have done it si se lo hubieras pedido lo habría hecho • you ~ never know she was not a native Spanish speaker nadie diría que el español no es su lengua materna • ~ you go there by yourself? ¿irías allí sola? • I ~ have a word with him (if I were you) sería aconsejable discutirlo con él • I ~n't worry too much if I were you yo en tu lugar no me preocuparía demasiado

2 (in indirect speech) • I said I ~ do it te dije que lo haría or hacía • I thought you ~ want to know pensé que querrías saber

3 (emphatic) • you ~ be the one to forget! ¡quién más si no tú se iba a olvidar!, ¡tú tenías que ser el que se olvidase! • it ~ be you! ¡tú tenías que ser! • he ~ say that, ~n't he? es lógico que dijera eso

4 (conjecture) • what ~ this be? ¿qué será esto? • it ~ have been about eight o'clock serían las ocho • it ~ seem so así parece ser

5 (indicating willingness) a (in invitations) querer • ~ you like some tea? • ~ you care for some tea? ¿quiere tomar un té? • ~ you come this way? pase por favor or (esp LAm) si hace favor

b (requests, wishes) • ~ you close the door please? ¿puedes cerrar la puerta, por favor? • please ~ you wake me up at seven o'clock? ¿podría despertarme a las siete, por favor? • ~ you mind? si no le importa, si no tiene inconveniente • what ~ you have me do? ¿qué quieres que haga?

c (insistence) • I told her not to but she ~ do it le dije que no, pero insistió en hacerlo

d (refusal) • he ~n't do it no quería hacerlo, se negó a hacerlo • he ~n't say if it was true no quiso decir si era verdad • the car ~n't start el coche se negó or negaba a arrancar, el coche no quería arrancar

6 (habit) • he ~ paint it each year solía pintarlo cada año, lo pintaba cada año

7 (in set expressions) • ~ that it were not so!† (poet) ¡ojalá (y) no fuera así! • ~ to God! • ~ to heaven! (liter) ¡ojalá! • try as he ~ por mucho que se esforzara, por más que intentase

would-be ['wʊdbiː] ADJ • a would-be poet/politician un aspirante a poeta/político

wouldn't ['wʊdnt] = would not

would've ['wʊdəv] = would have

wound¹ [wuːnd] N herida f • a bullet/knife ~ una herida de bala/cuchillo • a chest/head ~ una herida en el pecho/la cabeza • IDIOMS: • to lick one's ~s lamer sus heridas • to open up old ~s abrir viejas heridas; ▹ salt

VT herir • he was ~ed in the leg fue herido en la pierna • to ~ sb's feelings (fig) herir los sentimientos de algn • she was deeply ~ed by this remark (fig) su comentario la hirió profundamente

wound² [waʊnd] PT, PP of wind²

wounded ['wuːndɪd] ADJ herido • there were six dead and fifteen ~ hubo seis muertos y quince heridos

NPL • the ~ los heridos

wounding ['wuːndɪŋ] ADJ [remark, tone] hiriente

wound up [,waʊnd'ʌp] ADJ ▹ wind up

wove [wəʊv] PT of weave

woven ['wəʊvən] PP of weave

wow* [waʊ] EXCL ¡vaya!, ¡anda!, ¡mira nomás! (LAm)

VT chiflar*, cautivar

N (Acoustics) lloro m, bajón m del volumen

CPD ▸ wow factor* efecto m impresionante (impresión inicial)

WP N ABBR 1 = word processing

2 = word processor

ABBR (= weather permitting) si lo permite el tiempo

wpb* N ABBR = wastepaper basket

WPC N ABBR = Woman Police Constable

WPI N ABBR = wholesale price index

wpm ABBR (= words per minute) p.p.m.

WR N ABBR (Sport) = World Record

WRAC [ræk] N ABBR (Brit) = Women's Royal Army Corps

wrack¹ [ræk] VT = rack¹

wrack² [ræk] N = rack²

wrack³ [ræk] N (Bot) fuco m, alga f

WRAF [wæf] N ABBR (Brit) = Women's Royal Air Force

wraith [reɪθ] N fantasma m

wrangle ['ræŋgl] N riña f, disputa f, pleito m (esp LAm) • legal ~ disputa f legal

VI • to ~ (about or over sth) reñir or pelear (por or sobre algo)

wrangling ['ræŋglɪŋ] N riña f, discusión f

wrap [ræp] N 1 (= garment) chal m, rebozo m (LAm)

2 (around parcel) envoltorio m • under ~s (fig) en secreto, tapado (esp LAm) • to keep sth under ~s (fig) guardar algo en secreto • to take the ~s off sth (fig) desvelar or revelar algo, sacar algo a la luz pública

VT (also wrap up) envolver • shall I ~ it for you? ¿se lo envuelvo? • she ~ped the child in a blanket envolvió al niño en una manta • the scheme is ~ped in secrecy (fig) el proyecto está envuelto en el misterio

▸ **wrap around, wrap round** VT + PREP • to ~ sth around sth [+ paper, cloth, tape] envolver

algo con algo • **to ~ sth around o.s.** [*+ scarf, blanket, coat*] liarse algo • **~ the rug round your legs** enróllate la manta alrededor de las piernas • **to ~ one's arms around sb** abrazar a algn
▸ **wrap up** (VT + ADV) **1** = **wrap**
2* (= *conclude*) concluir, poner punto final a • **that just about ~s it up** eso prácticamente lo concluye *or* le pone punto final • **to ~ up a deal** cerrar un trato
3 • **to be ~ped up in sb/sth** estar embelesado con algn/absorto en algo • **they're ~ped up in each other** están embelesados el uno con el otro, están absortos el uno en el otro
(VI + ADV) **1** (= *dress warmly*) abrigarse • **~ up warm!** ¡abrígate bien!
2* (= *be quiet*) callarse • **~ up!*** ¡cállate!
wraparound [ˈræpəˌraʊnd] (N) reciclado *m*, bucle *m*
(CPD) ▸ **wraparound shades** = **wraparound sunglasses** ▸ **wraparound skirt** falda *f* cruzada ▸ **wraparound sunglasses** gafas *fpl* de sol envolventes
wrapper [ˈræpəʳ] (N) [*of goods*] envoltura *f*, envase *m*; [*of sweet*] envoltorio *m*; [*of book*] sobrecubierta *f*; (*postal: round newspaper*) faja *f*
wrapping [ˈræpɪŋ] (N) envoltura *f*, envase *m*
(CPD) ▸ **wrapping paper** (*gen*) papel *m* de envolver; (= *gift-wrap*) papel *m* de regalo
wrath [rɒθ] (N) (*poet*) [*of person*] cólera *f*; [*of storm*] ira *f*, furia *f*; ▹ **incur**
wrathful [ˈrɒθfʊl] (ADJ) (*liter*) colérico, iracundo
wrathfully [ˈrɒθfəlɪ] (ADV) (*liter*) coléricamente
wreak [riːk] (VT) [*+ destruction, vengeance*] hacer, causar • **to ~ havoc** causar estragos
wreath [riːθ] (N) (PL: **wreaths** [riːðz]) [*of flowers*] guirnalda *f*; (*for funeral*) corona *f*; [*of smoke, mist*] espiral *m* • **laurel ~** corona *f* de laurel
wreathe [riːð] (*esp liter*) (VT) **1** (= *encircle*) ceñir, rodear (**with** de) • **a face ~d in smiles** una cara muy risueña *or* sonriente • **trees ~d in mist** árboles *mpl* envueltos en niebla
2 (= *garland*) [*+ person*] engalanar, enguirnaldar (**with** con) • **to ~ flowers into one's hair** ponerse flores en el pelo
(VI) [*smoke*] • **to ~ upwards** elevarse en espirales
wreck [rek] (N) **1** (= *destruction*) [*of ship*] naufragio *m*; (*fig*) [*of hopes, plans*] fracaso *m*, frustración *f*
2 (= *wrecked ship*) restos *mpl* de un naufragio, buque *m* hundido
3* (= *old car*) tartana* *f*; (= *old boat, plane*) cacharro* *m* • **that car is a ~!** ¡ese coche es una tartana!* • **the car was a complete ~** el coche estaba hecho polvo* • **I'm a ~** • **I feel a ~** estoy hecho polvo* • **he's an old ~** es un carcamal* • **she's a nervous ~** tiene los nervios destrozados • **she looks a ~** está hecha una pena*
(VT) **1** (*Naut*) [*+ ship*] hundir, hacer naufragar • **to be ~ed** naufragar • **the ship was ~ed on those rocks** el buque naufragó en aquellas rocas
2 (= *break*) estropear, destrozar; (*into pieces*) destruir, hacer pedazos • **the explosion ~ed the whole house** la explosión destruyó toda la casa • **he ~ed his Dad's car** dejó el coche de su padre destrozado
3 (= *ruin*) [*+ health, happiness*] arruinar, hundir; [*+ marriage*] destrozar • **it ~ed my life** me arruinó la vida • **the bad weather ~ed our plans** el mal tiempo echó por tierra nuestros planes
wreckage [ˈrekɪdʒ] (N) **1** (= *remains*) [*of ship*] restos *mpl* de un naufragio, pecios *mpl* de un naufragio (*frm*); [*of car, aeroplane, train*] restos *mpl*; [*of house, building*] escombros *mpl*, ruinas *fpl*
2 (= *act*) [*of ship*] naufragio *m*; (*fig*) naufragio *m*, ruina *f*, destrucción *f*
wrecked [rekt] (ADJ) **1** (= *destroyed*) destruido; (= *broken down*) estropeado, averiado; [*ship*] naufragado, hundido
2‡ [*person*] (= *exhausted*) hecho polvo; (= *drunk*) cocido‡; (*from drugs*) (= *high*) colocado‡ • **he got really ~ at the party** se coció bien en la fiesta‡, se cogió una buena borrachera en la fiesta
wrecker [ˈrekəʳ] (N) **1** (= *destroyer*) (*gen*) destructor(a) *m/f*; (*Hist*) [*of ships*] saboteador(a) *m/f*, *persona que se dedicaba a provocar naufragios*
2 (*US*) (= *breaker, salvager*) demoledor *m*
3 (*US*) (= *breakdown van*) camión-grúa *m*
wrecking ball [ˈrekɪŋˌbɔːl] (N) martillo *m* de demolición
Wren* [ren] (N) (*Brit*) (*Navy*) *miembro de la sección femenina de la marina británica*
wren [ren] (N) (*Orn*) reyezuelo *m*, troglodito *m*
wrench [rentʃ] (N) **1** (= *tug*) tirón *m*, jalón *m* (*LAm*) • **to give sth a ~** tirar *or* (*LAm*) jalar algo (con violencia *or* fuerza)
2 (*Med*) torcedura *f*
3 (= *tool*) llave *f* inglesa, llave *f* de tuerca
4 (*fig*) • **it was a ~ to see her go** dolió mucho verla partir
(VT) **1** • **to ~ sth off/(away) from/out of** arrancar algo de • **he ~ed himself free** haciendo un gran esfuerzo se soltó • **to ~ a door open** abrir una puerta de un tirón *or* (*LAm*) jalón
2 (*Med*) torcerse
(VI) • **he ~ed free** haciendo un gran esfuerzo se soltó
wrest [rest] (VT) • **to ~ sth from sb** arrebatar *or* arrancar algo a algn • **to ~ gold from the rocks** extraer a duras penas oro de las rocas • **to ~ a living from the soil** vivir penosamente cultivando la tierra • **to ~ o.s. free** (lograr) liberarse tras grandes esfuerzos
wrestle [ˈresl] (N) • **to have a ~ with sb** luchar con algn
(VI) luchar (a brazo partido); (*Sport*) (*also fig*) luchar (**with** con) • **we are wrestling with the problem** estamos luchando con el problema • **the pilot ~d with the controls** el piloto luchaba con los mandos
(VT) (*Sport*) luchar con, luchar contra • **to ~ sb to the ground** tumbar a algn, derribar a algn
wrestler [ˈresləʳ] (N) (*Sport*) luchador(a) *m/f*
wrestling [ˈreslɪŋ] (N) (*Sport*) lucha *f* libre
(CPD) ▸ **wrestling match** partido *m* de lucha libre
wretch [retʃ] (N) desgraciado/a *m/f*, miserable *mf* • **little ~** (*esp hum*) pícaro/a *m/f*, granuja *mf* • **some poor ~** algún desgraciado, algún pobre diablo
wretched [ˈretʃɪd] (ADJ) **1** (= *unhappy*) desdichado, desgraciado
2 (= *abject, poor*) [*condition*] miserable, lamentable; [*slum*] lamentable; [*life, existence*] miserable, desgraciado, infeliz • **to live in ~ poverty** vivir en la miseria más absoluta
3* (= *very bad*) horrible, espantoso • **what ~ luck!** ¡maldita la suerte! • **where's that ~ dog!** ¡dónde está ese maldito *or* condenado perro! • **to feel ~** (= *miserable*) sentirse infeliz; (= *ill*) sentirse muy mal
wretchedly [ˈretʃɪdlɪ] (ADV) **1** (*as intensifier*) terriblemente • **she felt ~ alone** se sentía terriblemente sola • **his marriage was ~ unhappy** era muy infeliz en su matrimonio • **to be ~ unlucky** tener malísima suerte • **to be ~ poor** vivir en la miseria más absoluta
2 (= *miserably*) • **"I made it all up," she said ~** —me lo inventé todo —dijo desconsolada • **they treated her ~** la trataron de modo infame
3†* (= *very badly*) [*play, sing etc*] pésimamente, fatal*
wretchedness [ˈretʃɪdnɪs] (N)
1 (= *unhappiness*) desdicha *f*
2 (= *abjectness*) [*of conditions*] miseria *f*; [*of life, existence*] desgracia *f*, infelicidad *f*; (= *poverty*) miseria *f*
wrick [rɪk] (N) torcedura *f*
(VT) (*Brit*) torcer • **to ~ one's neck** torcerse el cuello
wriggle [ˈrɪgl] (VT) mover • **to ~ one's toes/fingers** mover los dedos de los pies/de las manos • **to ~ one's way through sth** avanzar con dificultad a través de algo
(VI) (*also* **wriggle about** *or* **around**) [*person, animal*] (*restlessly*) moverse, revolverse; (*in pain*) retorcerse; [*worm, snake, eel*] serpentear; [*fish*] colear • **to ~ along** moverse serpenteando • **to ~ away** escaparse serpenteando • **to ~ down** bajarse serpenteando • **to ~ free** escaparse, escurrirse • **to ~ through a hole** deslizarse por un agujero • **to ~ out of a difficulty** escabullirse, escaparse de un apuro
wriggly [ˈrɪglɪ] (ADJ) (COMPAR: **wrigglier**, SUPERL: **wriggliest**) sinuoso
wring [rɪŋ] (PT, PP: **wrung**) (VT) **1** (*also* **wring out**) [*+ clothes, washing*] escurrir
2 (= *twist*) torcer, retorcer • **I'll ~ your neck for that!*** ¡te voy a retorcer el pescuezo!* • **she wrung my hand** me dio un apretón de manos • IDIOM: • **to ~ one's hands** (*in distress*) retorcerse las manos
3 (*fig*) • **eventually we wrung the truth out of them** al final les sacamos la verdad • **to ~ money out of sb** sacar dinero a algn
(N) • **to give the clothes a ~** escurrir la ropa
wringer [ˈrɪŋəʳ] (N) escurridor *m*
wringing [ˈrɪŋɪŋ] (ADJ) (*also* **wringing wet**) empapado
wrinkle¹ [ˈrɪŋkl] (N) arruga *f*
(VT) (*also* **wrinkle up**) [*+ fabric, clothes*] arrugar; [*+ brow, forehead*] fruncir
(VI) (*also* **wrinkle up**) arrugarse
wrinkle²‡ [ˈrɪŋkl] (N) (= *idea*) idea *f*, noción *f*; (= *tip*) indicación *f*; (= *dodge*) truco *m*
wrinkled [ˈrɪŋkld] (ADJ) arrugado
wrinkly [ˈrɪŋklɪ] (ADJ) (COMPAR: **wrinklier**, SUPERL: **wrinkliest**) = **wrinkled**
(N) (*Brit**) (*pej*) viejo/a *m/f*
wrist [rɪst] (N) muñeca *f*
(CPD) ▸ **wrist joint** articulación *f* de la muñeca
wristband [ˈrɪstbænd] (N) [*of shirt*] puño *m*; [*of watch*] pulsera *f*; (*Sport*) muñequera *f*
wristlet [ˈrɪstlɪt] (N) pulsera *f*, muñequera *f*, brazalete *m*
(CPD) ▸ **wristlet watch** reloj *m* de pulsera
wrist-rest [ˈrɪstrest] (N) reposamuñecas *m inv*
wristwatch [ˈrɪstwɒtʃ] (N) reloj *m* de pulsera
writ¹ [rɪt] (N) (*Jur*) mandato *m* judicial • **to serve a ~ on sb** notificar un mandato judicial a algn • **to issue a ~ against sb** demandar a algn
writ² [rɪt] (PT), (PP) *of* **write**
(ADJ) (*liter*) • **it's just the old policy ~ large** es la misma política en forma exagerada • **guilt was ~ large on his face** se hacía patente la culpa en su cara
writable, writeable [ˈraɪtəbl] (ADJ) (*Comput*) grabable
write [raɪt] (PT: **wrote**, PP: **written**) (VT)
1 (*gen*) [*+ letter, book, essay, article*] escribir;

W

[+ *music, song*] escribir, componer • **he's just written another novel** acaba de escribir otra novela • **~ your name here** escribe *or* pon tu nombre aquí • **how do you ~ his name?** ¿cómo se escribe su nombre? • **he's got an essay to ~** tiene que escribir una redacción • **she ~s that she is very happy in her new life** dice en la carta que está muy contenta con su nueva vida • **it is written that …** está escrito que … • **to ~ sb a cheque** hacer un cheque a algn, extender un cheque a algn (*more frm*) • **to ~ a letter to sb** • **~ sb a letter** escribir (una carta) a algn • **to ~ a note to/for sb** escribir una nota a algn • **to ~ sb a prescription** • **~ a prescription for sb** hacer una receta a algn • IDIOM: • **to have sth written all over one:** • **he had "policeman" written all over him*** se le notaba a la legua que era policía • **his guilt was written all over him*** se le veía *or* notaba en la cara que era culpable • **you're lying, it's written all over your face!*** estás mintiendo, se te nota a la legua *or* en la cara

2 (= *write a letter to*) (*US*) • **to ~ sb** escribir a algn

3 (*Comput*) [+ *program, software*] escribir • **to ~ sth to disk** pasar algo a un disco

(VI) **1** (*in longhand*) escribir • **~ on both sides of the paper** escribe por los dos lados del papel • **this pen ~s well** esta pluma escribe muy bien

2 (= *correspond*) escribir • **she wrote to say that she'd be late** escribió para avisar que llegaría tarde • **I am writing in reply to your advertisement** les escribo en respuesta a su anuncio • **I'll ~ for a catalogue** escribiré pidiendo un catálogo • **to ~ to sb** escribir a algn • IDIOM: • **it's nothing to ~ home about*** no es nada del otro mundo*

3 (*as author, journalist*) escribir • **he ~s for a living** se gana la vida escribiendo • **he ~s about social policy** escribe sobre política social • **he ~s for the "Times"** escribe *or* colabora en el "Times" • **he ~s on foreign policy for the "Guardian"** escribe sobre política internacional para el "Guardian"

▸ **write away** (VI + ADV) • **to ~ away for sth** escribir pidiendo algo

▸ **write back** (VI + ADV) • **to ~ back to sb** contestar a algn • **he wrote in April but I still haven't written back** me escribió en abril pero aún no le he contestado

▸ **write down** (VT + ADV) **1** (= *note down*) [+ *address, number, details*] apuntar, anotar

2 (= *decrease value of*) [+ *asset*] amortizar (por depreciación); [+ *value*] depreciar; [+ *goods*] rebajar el valor en libros

▸ **write in** (VI + ADV) escribir, mandar una carta • **a lot of people have written in to complain** mucha gente ha escrito *or* ha mandado cartas quejándose • **to ~ in for sth** escribir pidiendo algo

(VT + ADV) (= *include*) [+ *word, item, part, scene*] añadir, agregar; [+ *clause in contract*] incluir; (*US*) (*Pol*) [+ *candidate's name*] añadir a la lista oficial

▸ **write into** (VT + PREP) **1** (*Jur*) incluir en • **to ~ sth into an agreement/contract** (*at the outset*) incluir algo en un acuerdo/contrato; (*later*) añadir algo en un acuerdo/contrato

2 [+ *character, scene, item*] incluir en

▸ **write off** (VI + ADV) • **to ~ off for** [+ *information, application form, details, goods*] escribir pidiendo

(VT + ADV) **1** (*Econ*) [+ *debt*] cancelar (por considerarla incobrable) • **to ~ £1000 off for depreciation** amortizar 1000 libras por depreciación • **to ~ sth off against tax** desgravar algo de los impuestos

2 [+ *vehicle*] [*insurer*] declarar siniestro total; [*driver*] destrozar • **the car had to be written off** el coche fue declarado siniestro total • **he has just written off his new car** acaba de tener un accidente con el coche nuevo y ha quedado destrozado

3 (= *reject*) [+ *idea, scheme*] desechar • **to ~ sth off as a total loss** considerar algo como totalmente perdido • **I've written off the whole thing as a dead loss** ese asunto lo considero un fracaso que es mejor olvidar • **it would be unwise to ~ off the former minister just yet** sería prematuro considerar acabado al anterior ministro • **many people wrote them off as cranks** mucha gente los rechazó considerándolos unos chalados

4 (= *write quickly*) [+ *letter, postcard*] escribir (rápidamente)

▸ **write out** (VT + ADV) **1** (= *put on paper*) [+ *word, name, speech, list*] escribir

2 (= *make out*) [+ *cheque*] hacer, extender (*more frm*); [+ *receipt*] hacer; [+ *prescription*] escribir

3 (= *copy*) [+ *notes, essay*] pasar en limpio, pasar a limpio (*Sp*); [+ *recipe*] copiar

4 (*of TV or radio series*) [+ *character, part*] suprimir • **he was written out of the series** suprimieron el papel que tenía en la serie, lo eliminaron de la serie

▸ **write up** (VT + ADV) **1** (= *make*) [+ *report*] redactar; [+ *notes*] pasar en limpio, pasar a limpio (*Sp*); [+ *diary*] poner al día

2 (= *record*) [+ *experiment, one's findings, visit*] describir (por escrito)

3 (= *report on*) [+ *event*] escribir una crónica sobre, hacer un reportaje sobre • **she wrote it up for the local paper** escribió una crónica *or* hizo un reportaje sobre ello en el periódico local

4 (= *review*) escribir una reseña de, escribir una crítica de

writeable ['raɪtəbəl] (ADJ) = **writable**

write-off ['raɪtɒf] (N) **1** (= *vehicle*) siniestro *m* total • **his car was a complete write-off** el coche fue declarado siniestro total, el coche quedó siniestro total

2 (*Comm*) anulación *f* en libros, cancelación *f* en libros

3 (*Econ*) cancelación *f* (*de una deuda considerada incobrable*) • **he proposed a complete write-off of debt** propuso cancelar totalmente la deuda

4 (= *disaster*) desastre *m*, fracaso *m* • **the whole afternoon was a write-off** la tarde entera fue un desastre *or* fracaso

write-protect ['raɪtprə'tekt] (VT) proteger contra escritura

writer ['raɪtəʳ] (N) [*of letter, report*] escritor(a) *m/f*; (*as profession*) escritor(a) *m/f*, autor(a) *m/f* • **a ~ of detective stories** un escritor *or* autor de novelas policíacas • **to be a good ~** (*handwriting*) tener buena letra; (*content*) escribir bien, ser buen escritor(a) • **to be a poor ~** (*handwriting*) tener mala letra • **~'s cramp** calambre *m* de los escribientes

write-up ['raɪtʌp] (N) **1** (= *report*) crónica *f*, reportaje *m*

2 (= *review*) crítica *f*, reseña *f*

writhe [raɪð] (VI) retorcerse • **to ~ with** *or* **in pain** retorcerse de dolor • **to ~ with embarrassment** morirse de vergüenza *or* (*LAm*) pena

▸ **writhe about, writhe around** (VI + ADV) retorcerse

writing ['raɪtɪŋ] (N) **1** (= *handwriting*) letra *f* • **I can't read your ~** no entiendo tu letra

2 (= *system*) escritura *f* • **before the invention of ~** antes de la invención de la escritura

3 (= *letters, words*) • **there was some ~ on the page** había algo escrito en la página • **I could see the ~ but couldn't read it** podía ver que había algo escrito pero no podía leerlo • **in ~** por escrito • **I'd like to have that in ~** me gustaría tenerlo por escrito • **to put sth in ~** poner algo por escrito • IDIOM: • **to see the ~ on the wall** vérsela venir* • **he had seen the ~ on the wall** vio lo que se le venía encima* • **the ~ is on the wall for the president/the company** el presidente/la compañia tiene los días contados

4 (= *written work*) • **the essay contains some imaginative ~** el ensayo tiene secciones redactadas con imaginación • **Aubrey's biographical ~s** las obras biográficas de Aubrey • **it's a brilliant piece of ~** está maravillosamente escrito

5 (= *activity*) escritura *f* • **~ is his hobby** su hobby es la escritura, su hobby es escribir • **he earns quite a lot from ~** gana bastante escribiendo • **a course in novel ~** un curso sobre redacción de novelas

(CPD) ▸ **writing case** estuche *m* para material de correspondencia ▸ **writing desk** escritorio *m* ▸ **writing materials** artículos *mpl* de escritorio ▸ **writing pad** bloc *m* ▸ **writing paper** papel *m* de escribir ▸ **writing table** escritorio *m*

written ['rɪtn] (PP) *of* **write**

(ADJ) [*test, agreement, exam*] escrito; [*permission, guarantee, offer*] por escrito • **her ~ English is excellent** su inglés escrito es excelente • **Somali has been a ~ language for over 25 years** la lengua somalí ha tenido escritura desde hace más de 25 años • **the power of the ~ word** el poder de la palabra escrita • **~ statement** declaración *f* escrita • **~ evidence/proof** (*Admin*) pruebas *fpl* documentales

(CPD) ▸ **written word** • **the ~ word** lo escrito

WRNS [renz] (N ABBR) (*Brit*) = **Women's Royal Naval Service**

wrong [rɒŋ] (ADJ) **1** (*morally*) (= *bad*) malo; (= *unfair*) injusto • **it's ~ to steal** • **stealing is ~** robar está mal • **there's nothing ~ in that** no hay nada malo en eso • **that was very ~ of you** ahí *or* en eso has hecho muy mal • **you were ~ to do that** hacer eso estuvo mal por tu parte • **what's ~ with a drink now and again?** ¿qué tiene de malo tomarse una copa de vez en cuando? • **there's nothing ~ with that** no hay nada malo en eso

2 (= *incorrect, mistaken*) [*answer*] incorrecto; [*calculation, belief*] equivocado • **the ~ answer** la respuesta incorrecta • **he made a number of ~ assumptions** se equivocó al hacer ciertas suposiciones • **to be ~** [*person*] equivocarse, estar equivocado • **that is ~** eso no es exacto *or* cierto • **the information they gave us was ~** la información que nos dieron era incorrecta • **you're ~ about that** ahí *or* en eso estás equivocado • **that clock is ~** ese reloj anda *or* marcha mal • **the letter has the ~ date on it** la carta tiene la fecha equivocada • **you've opened the packet at the ~ end** has abierto el paquete por el lado que no es, has abierto el paquete al revés • **I was ~ in thinking that …** me equivoqué al pensar que … • **I'm in the ~ job** tengo un puesto que no me conviene • **he's got the ~ kind of friends** no tiene los amigos apropiados • **that's the ~ kind of plug** se necesita otro tipo de enchufe • **she married the ~ man** se equivocó al casarse con él • **to play a ~ note** tocar una nota falsa • **you have the ~ number** (*Telec*) se ha equivocado de número • **it's the ~ one** no es el/la que hace falta • **I think you're talking to the ~ person** creo que no es conmigo con quien debería hablar • **it's in the ~ place** está mal situado, está mal colocado • **is this the ~ road?** ¿nos habremos equivocado de camino? • **~ side** [*of cloth*] revés *m*, envés *m* • **he was driving on**

the ~ side (of the road) iba por el carril contrario • **to say/do the ~ thing** decir/hacer algo inoportuno • **at the ~ time** inoportunamente • **we were on the ~ train** nos habíamos equivocado de tren • **the ~ way round** al revés • **to go the ~ way** (*on route*) equivocarse de camino • **that's the ~ way to go about it** esa no es la forma de enfocarlo • **a piece of bread went down the ~ way** se me fue un pedazo de pan por el otro camino *or* por el camino viejo; ▹ **rub up**
3 (= *amiss*) • **is anything** *or* **something ~?** ¿pasa algo? • **what's ~?** ¿qué pasa? • **what's ~ with you?** ¿qué te pasa? • **what's ~ with the car?** ¿qué le pasa al coche? • **nothing's ~** • **there's nothing ~** no pasa nada • **there's nothing ~ with it/him** no le pasa nada • **something's ~** • **there's something ~** hay algo mal *or* que no está bien • **there's something ~ with my lights** • **something's ~ with my lights** algo les pasa a mis faros • **something was very ~** había algo que no iba nada bien
4 • **to be ~ in the head*** estar chiflado*
(ADV) mal • **to answer ~** contestar mal, contestar incorrectamente • **you did ~ to insult him** hiciste mal en insultarle • **you're doing it all ~** lo estás haciendo todo mal • **you've done it ~** lo has hecho mal • **to get sth ~** equivocarse en algo • **the accountant got his sums ~*** el contable se equivocó al hacer las cuentas • **don't get me ~*** no me malinterpretes • **you've got it all ~*** (= *misunderstood*) no has entendido nada • **to go ~** [*person*] (*on route*) equivocarse de camino; (*in calculation*) equivocarse; (*morally*) ir por el mal camino; [*plan*] salir mal, malograrse (*Peru*), cebarse (*Mex**); (*Mech*) fallar, estropearse • **the robbery went ~ and they got caught** el atraco fracasó y los pillaron • **something went ~ with the gears** las marchas empezaron a funcionar mal • **something went ~ with their plans** algo falló en sus planes • **you can't go ~** (*with choice*) no te equivocarás, puedes estar seguro (**with** con); (*in directions*) no tiene pérdida • **well, in that case you thought ~** bueno, en ese caso pensaste mal
(N) mal *m* • **to do sb a ~** hacer mal a algn • **he can do no ~** es incapaz de hacer mal a nadie • **he did her ~** se portó mal con ella • **to be in the ~** (= *guilty*) obrar mal; (= *mistaken*) estar equivocado • **to put sb in the ~** dejar en mal lugar a algn, poner en evidencia a algn • **to right a ~** deshacer un agravio, acabar con un abuso • PROVERB: • **two ~s don't make a right** no se subsana un error cometiendo otro; ▹ **right**
(VT) ser injusto con • **you ~ me** eso no es justo • **to feel that one has been ~ed** sentirse agraviado

wrongdoer ['rɒŋ,duːəʳ] (N) malhechor(a) *m/f*, delincuente *mf*

wrongdoing ['rɒŋ,duːɪŋ] (N) maldad *f*; (*Rel*) pecado *m* • **he will be punished for his ~s** se le castigará por su maldad

wrong-foot ['rɒŋ'fʊt] (VT) poner en situación violenta, poner en situación desfavorable • **that left us wrong-footed** eso nos dejó en una situación violenta

wrongful ['rɒŋfʊl] (ADJ) **1** (= *unjust*) injusto • **~ dismissal** despido *m* improcedente
2 (= *unlawful*) ilegal • **~ arrest** arresto *m* ilegal

wrongfully ['rɒŋfəlɪ] (ADV) **1** [*accused, convicted*] injustamente
2 [*arrested*] ilegalmente

wrong-headed ['rɒŋ'hedɪd] (ADJ) [*ideas, opinions, policies*] desatinado, desacertado; [*person*] obcecado

wrong-headedness ['rɒŋ'hedɪdnɪs] (N) obcecación *f*

wrongly ['rɒŋlɪ] (ADV) **1** (= *incorrectly*) [*believe, assume, diagnose*] equivocadamente • **you have been ~ informed** le han informado mal
2 (= *unjustly*) [*accuse, convict*] injustamente; ▹ **rightly**

wrongness ['rɒŋnɪs] (N) **1** (= *unfairness*) injusticia *f*
2 (= *incorrectness*) [*of answer*] lo incorrecto
3 (= *evil*) maldad *f*

wrote [rəʊt] (PT) *of* **write**

wrought [rɔːt] (VB) †† (*pt, pp of* **work**) • **great changes have been ~** se han efectuado grandes cambios • **destruction ~ by the floods** daños *mpl* causados por las inundaciones
(ADJ) • **~ iron** hierro *m* forjado

wrought-iron [,rɔːt'aɪən] (ADJ) [*gate*] de hierro forjado

wrought-up ['rɔːt'ʌp] (ADJ) • **to be wrought-up** estar nervioso

WRU (N ABBR) (*in Wales*) = **Welsh Rugby Union**

wrung [rʌŋ] (PT), (PP) *of* **wring**

WRVS (N ABBR) (*Brit*) = **Women's Royal Voluntary Service**

wry [raɪ] (ADJ) [*person, sense of humour, remark*] irónico • **to make a wry face** hacer una mueca, torcer el gesto

wryly ['raɪlɪ] (ADV) irónicamente, con ironía

wryneck ['raɪnek] (N) torcecuello *m*

WS (N ABBR) (*Scot*) (*Jur*) = **Writer to the Signet**

WSW (ABBR) (= **west-southwest**) OSO

wt (ABBR) = **weight**

W/T (ABBR) (= **wireless telegraphy**) radiotelegrafía *f*

WTO (N ABBR) (= **World Trade Organization**) OMC *f*

wuss* [wʊs] (N) (*US*) pavo/a* *m/f*, gallina* *mf*

WV (ABBR) (*US*) = **West Virginia**

W. Va. (ABBR) (*US*) = **West Virginia**

WWF (N ABBR) = **Worldwide Fund for Nature**

WWI (N ABBR) = **World War One**

WWII (N ABBR) = **World War Two**

WWW (N ABBR) (*Internet*) = **World Wide Web** • **the WWW** el Web

WY (ABBR) (*US*) = **Wyoming**

wych-elm ['wɪtʃelm] (N) olmo *m* escocés, olmo *m* de montaña

Wyo. (ABBR) (*US*) = **Wyoming**

WYSIWYG ['wɪzɪ,wɪg] (ABBR) (*Comput*) = **what you see is what you get**

Xx

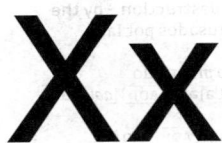

X, x [eks] (N) (= *letter*) (*also Math*) X, x *f* • **if you have X dollars a year** si uno tiene X dólares al año • **for X number of years** durante X años • **X marks the spot** el sitio está señalado con una X • **X for Xmas** X de Xiquena
(CPD) ▸ **X chromosome** cromosoma *m* X
Xavier ['zeɪvɪəʳ] (N) Javier
X-certificate ['eksə,tɪfɪkɪt] (ADJ) (*Brit*) (*Cine*) no apto para menores de 18 años
xenon ['ziːnɒn] (N) xenón *m*
xenophobe ['zenəfəʊb] (N) xenófobo/a *m/f*
xenophobia [,zenə'fəʊbɪə] (N) xenofobia *f*
xenophobic [,zenə'fəʊbɪk] (ADJ) xenófobo
Xenophon ['zenəfən] (N) Jenofonte
xerography [zɪə'rɒgrəfɪ] (N) xerografía *f*
Xerox® ['zɪərɒks] (N) (= *machine*) fotocopiadora *f*; (= *copy*) fotocopia *f*
(VT) fotocopiar
Xerxes ['zɜːksiːz] (N) Jerjes
XL (ABBR) = **extra large**
Xmas ['eksməs] (N ABBR) = **Christmas**
X-rated ['eks'reɪtɪd] (ADJ) (*US*) (*Cine*) = **X-certificate**
X-ray ['eks'reɪ] (N) (= *ray*) rayo-X *m*; (= *photo*) radiografía *f* • **I had an X-ray taken** me hicieron una radiografía
(VT) hacer una radiografía a, radiografiar • **they X-rayed my arm** me hicieron una radiografía del brazo, me radiografiaron el brazo
(CPD) ▸ **X-ray examination** examen *m* con rayos X ▸ **X-ray photograph** radiografía *f* ▸ **X-ray treatment** tratamiento *m* de rayos X
xylograph ['zaɪləgrɑːf] (N) xilografía *f*, grabado *m* en madera
xylographic [zaɪlə'græfɪk] (ADJ) xilográfico
xylography [zaɪ'lɒgrəfɪ] (N) xilografía *f*
xylophone ['zaɪləfəʊn] (N) xilófono *m*
xylophonist [zaɪ'lɒfənɪst] (N) xilofonista *mf*

Yy

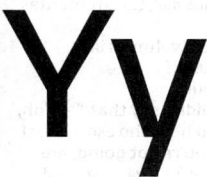

Y, y [waɪ] N (= *letter*) Y, y *f* • **Y for Yellow** Y de Yegua
CPD ▸ **Y chromosome** cromosoma *m* Y; ▹ **Y-fronts**

Y2K [ˌwaɪtuː'keɪ] ABBR = **Year 2000** • **the Y2K problem** (*Comput*) el (problema del) efecto 2000

yacht [jɒt] N (*esp Sport*) barco *m* de vela, velero *m*; (*luxury*) yate *m*; (*small, model*) balandro *m*, balandra *f*
VI pasear a vela, navegar a vela • **to go ~ing** ir a pasear *or* navegar a vela
CPD ▸ **yacht club** club *m* náutico ▸ **yacht race** regata *f* de veleros

yachting ['jɒtɪŋ] N navegación *f* a vela, balandrismo *m* • **the ~ fraternity** los aficionados al deporte de la vela • **a ~ trip** una excursión en barco de vela

yachtsman ['jɒtsmən] N (PL: **yachtsmen**) balandrista *m*, deportista *m* náutico

yachtsmanship ['jɒtsmənʃɪp] N arte *m* de navegar en yate *or* balandro

yachtswoman ['jɒtswʊmən] N (PL: **yachtswomen**) balandrista *f*, deportista *f* náutica

yack* [jæk], **yackety-yak*** ['jækɪtɪ'jæk] N (= *chatter*) cháchara* *f* • **to have a ~** estar de cháchara*
VI (*pej*) hablar como una cotorra*

yah [jɑː] EXCL ¡bah!

yahoo EXCL [jɑː'huː] ¡yupi!
N ['jɑːhuː] (*Brit**) (*pej*) niñato/a* *m/f*

yak [jæk] N (= *animal*) yac *m*, yak *m*

Yakuza [jə'kuːzə] N • **the ~** los yakuzas

Yale® [jeɪl] CPD ▸ **Yale key** llave *f* de seguridad ▸ **Yale lock** cerradura *f* de cilindro

y'all* [yɔːl] PRON (*US*) = **you all**

yam [jæm] N ñame *m*; (= *sweet potato*) batata *f*, camote *m* (*LAm*)

yammer* ['jæmə^r] VI quejarse, gimotear

yang [jæŋ] N yang *m*

Yank‡ [jæŋk] N (*sometimes pej*) yanqui *mf*, gringo/a *m/f* (*LAm*)

yank [jæŋk] N tirón *m*, jalón *m* (*LAm*) • **to give sth a ~** tirar de *or* (*LAm*) jalar algo
VT tirar de, jalar (*LAm*)
▸ **yank off*** VT + ADV (= *detach*) arrancar de un tirón • **he ~ed the button off** arrancó el botón de un tirón • **to ~ one's clothes off** quitarse la ropa precipitadamente • **to ~ sb off to jail** pillar *or* (*LAm*) agarrar y meter a algn en la cárcel
▸ **yank out*** VT + ADV sacar de un tirón • **to ~ a nail out** sacar un clavo de un tirón

Yankee ['jæŋkɪ] ADJ yanqui
N yanqui *mf*

> **YANKEE**
> El término **Yankee** o el peyorativo **Yank** se utilizan fuera de EE.UU. para referirse a los estadounidenses en general. Sin embargo, desde la guerra de Secesión, en el sur de Estados Unidos un **Yankee** es un habitante de un estado del norte, y a su vez, en el norte se considera un verdadero **Yankee** al oriundo de Nueva Inglaterra. El nombre procede de la canción **Yankee Doodle**, escrita inicialmente por un inglés para burlarse de los colonos americanos y adoptada después como himno patriótico por los soldados del general Washington durante la lucha por la independencia.

yap [jæp] N [*of dog*] pequeño ladrido *m*
VI **1** [*dog*] dar pequeños ladridos, ladrar
2* (= *chat*) charlar

yapping ['jæpɪŋ] N **1** (*of dog*) pequeños ladridos *mpl*
2* (= *chatting*) charla* *f*, palique* *m*

yappy ['jæpɪ] ADJ [*dog*] ladrador • **a ~ little dog** un perrito ladrador

yard¹ [jɑːd] N (= *measure*) yarda *f* (*91,44cm*) • **a few ~s off** ≈ a unos metros • **he pulled out ~s of handkerchief** sacó un enorme pañuelo • **with a face a ~ long** con una cara muy larga

yard² [jɑːd] N **1** (= *courtyard, farmyard*) patio *m*; (*US*) (= *garden*) jardín *m*; (*for livestock*) corral *m*; (*Scol*) patio *m* (de recreo); (= *worksite*) taller *m*; (*for storage*) depósito *m*, almacén *m*; (*for shipping, boats*) astillero *m*; (*Rail*) estación *f* • **Scotland Yard** • **the Yard** (*Brit*) *oficina central de la policía de Londres*
2 (*Naut*) (= *spar*) verga *f*
CPD ▸ **yard sale** (*US*) *venta de objetos usados en el jardín del vendedor*

yardage ['jɑːdɪdʒ] N ≈ metraje *m*

yardarm ['jɑːdɑːm] N (*Naut*) verga *f*, penol *m*

Yardie ['jɑːdɪ] N (*Brit*) Yardy *m* (*miembro de una organización criminal de Jamaica*)

yardstick ['jɑːdstɪk] N (*fig*) patrón *m*, criterio *m*, medida *f*

yarmulke ['jɑːmʊlkə] N kipá *f*

yarn [jɑːn] N **1** (= *wool*) hilo *m*
2 (= *tale*) cuento *m*, historia *f* • IDIOM: • **to spin a ~** soltar una historia • **she spun them a ~ about how she'd masterminded the whole project** les soltó una historia de cómo había estado al frente de todo el proyecto
VI contar historias

yarrow ['jærəʊ] N milenrama *f*

yashmak ['jæʃmæk] N velo *m* (de musulmana)

yaw [jɔː] (*Naut*) N guiñada *f*
VI guiñar, hacer una guiñada

yawl [jɔːl] N yol *m*, yola *f*

yawn [jɔːn] N bostezo *m* • **to give a ~** bostezar • **to say sth with a ~** decir algo bostezando • **it was a ~ from start to finish*** fue aburridísimo, fue un plomo*
VI bostezar; (*fig*) [*gap, abyss*] abrirse
VT • **to ~ one's head off** bostezar mucho

yawning ['jɔːnɪŋ] ADJ (*fig*) [*gap, abyss*] enorme • **there is a ~ gap between the moderates and the left wing of the party** existe un enorme abismo entre los moderados y el ala izquierda del partido

yd ABBR (= **yard**) yda

ye [jiː] PRON (*liter, dialect*) vosotros, vosotras
DEF ART †† = **the**

yea†† [jeɪ] ADV (= *yes*) sí; (= *indeed*) sin duda, ciertamente; (= *moreover*) además
N (= *yes*) sí • **the yeas and the nays** los votos a favor y los votos en contra • **let your yea be yea and your nay be nay** sé consecuente con lo que dices

yeah* [jɛə] ADV = yes

year ['jɪə^r] N **1** (= *twelve months*) año *m* • **it takes ~s** es cosa de años, se tarda años • **we waited ~s** esperamos una eternidad • **in the ~ (of our Lord) 1869** en el año (del Señor) 1869 • **he died in his 89th ~** murió a los 89 años • **he got ten ~s** le condenaron a diez años de prisión • **three times a ~** tres veces al año • **100 dollars a ~** 100 dólares al año • **in after ~s** (*liter*) en los años siguientes, años después • **to reckon sth by the ~** calcular algo por años • **~ end** final *m* del año • **we never see her from one ~'s end to the other** no la vemos en todo el año • **~ of grace** año *m* de gracia • **~ in, ~ out** año tras año, todos los años sin falta • **to reckon sth in ~s** calcular algo por años • **last ~** el año pasado • **the ~ before last** el año antepasado • **next ~** (*looking to future*) el año que viene • **the next ~** (*in past time*) el año siguiente • **she's three ~s old** tiene tres años • **an eight-year-old child** un niño de ocho años • **the work has put ~s on him** el trabajo lo ha envejecido • **all (the) ~ round** durante todo el año • **that hairstyle takes ~s off you*** ese peinado te quita un montón de años* • IDIOM: • **in the ~ dot** en el año de la nana* • **since the ~ dot** desde el año de la nana*, desde siempre
2 (= *age*) • **in my early ~s** en mi infancia, en mi juventud • **from her earliest ~s** desde muy joven • **he looks old/young for his ~s** aparenta más/menos años de los que tiene • **she's very spry for a woman of her ~s** para una mujer de su edad está muy ágil • **he's getting on in ~s** va para viejo • **in his later ~s** en sus últimos años
3 (*Brit*) (*Scol, Univ*) curso *m*, año *m* • **she's in the fifth** • está en quinto • **the kids in my ~** los chicos de mi curso • **he's in fourth ~ Law** estudia cuarto (curso de) de Derecho
4 [*of wine*] cosecha *f*, vendimia *f* • **1982 was a good/bad ~** 1982 fue una buena/mala cosecha *or* vendimia, 1982 fue un buen/mal año

yearbook ['jɪəbʊk] N anuario *m*;
▹ YEARBOOK, HIGH SCHOOL

yearling ['jɪəlɪŋ] ADJ primal
N primal(a) *m/f*

yearlong ['jɪə'lɒŋ] ADJ que dura un año (entero); [*ban, moratorium*] de un año

yearly ['jɪəlɪ] ADJ anual • **~ payment** anualidad *f*

YEARBOOK
En los centros de educación secundaria (**high schools**) y universidades estadounidenses se suele publicar un anuario (**yearbook**) al final de cada curso académico, en el que se registran muchos aspectos de su vida académica y social. El libro contiene fotografías de cada uno de los alumnos, profesores y demás personal de la administración, además de fotografías de grupos y organizaciones estudiantiles. Una sección se dedica a las estudiantes más atractivas, entre las cuales se incluye la **Homecoming Queen**, reina de las fiestas de antiguos alumnos. También hay secciones dedicadas a los estudiantes con más probabilidades de éxito en la vida y a aquellos que gozan de mayor popularidad. Es tradición que los estudiantes escriban dedicatorias en los anuarios de sus compañeros de clase.
▷ **HIGH SCHOOL**

(ADV) anualmente, cada año • **(once) ~** una vez al año
yearn [jɜ:n] (VI) • **to ~ for** [+ *native land, person*] añorar; [+ *freedom*] anhelar • **to ~ to do sth** anhelar hacer algo, ansiar hacer algo
yearning ['jɜ:nɪŋ] (ADJ) [*desire*] ansioso, vehemente; [*look, tone*] de ansia, anhelante
(N) (= *desire*) ansia *f*, anhelo *m*; (= *longing*) añoranza *f* (**for** de) • **to have a ~ to do sth** tener ansias *or* muchas ganas de hacer algo, anhelar hacer algo (*liter*)
yearningly ['jɜ:nɪŋlɪ] (ADV) con ansia, ansiosamente
year-round ['jɪə'raʊnd] (ADJ) que dura todo el año, de todo el año
yeast [ji:st] (N) levadura *f*
(CPD) ▸ **yeast extract** extracto *m* de levadura ▸ **yeast infection** (= *fungal infection*) *infección causada por un hongo oportunista*; (= *candida infection*) candidiasis *f*
yeasty ['ji:stɪ] (ADJ) **1** [*smell, taste*] a levadura
2 (*fig*) frívolo, superficial
yeh* [jɛə] (ADV) (*Brit*) ya • **yeh, whatever** ya, lo que digas
yell [jel] (N) grito *m*, chillido *m* • **to let out** *or* **give a ~** soltar *or* pegar un grito • **~s of laughter** carcajadas *fpl*
(VI) (*also* **yell out**) gritar, chillar
(VT) (*also* **yell out**) [+ *order, name*] gritar
yelling ['jelɪŋ] (N) gritos *mpl*, chillidos *mpl*
yellow ['jeləʊ] (ADJ) (COMPAR: **yellower**, SUPERL: **yellowest**) **1** (*in colour*) [*ribbon, paint, colour*] amarillo; [*hair*] rubio; [*teeth, fingers*] amarillo, amarillento • **to go** *or* **turn ~** volverse *or* ponerse amarillo, volverse *or* ponerse amarillento • **the fields were ~ with buttercups** los campos estaban amarillos, llenos de ranúnculos • **his fingers were ~ with nicotine** tenía los dedos amarillos *or* amarillentos de la nicotina
2 (*by race*) amarillo
3* (= *cowardly*) gallina*, miedica*, cagueta‡ • **to have a ~ streak** ser un poco gallina *or* miedica*
(N) **1** (= *colour*) amarillo *m*
2 (= *yolk*) yema *f*
(VI) volverse amarillo, ponerse amarillo • **the paper had ~ed with age** el papel se había vuelto *or* puesto amarillo con el paso del tiempo • **~ing leaves/pages** hojas *fpl* amarillentas
(VT) • **~ed newspapers** periódicos amarillentos (por el paso del tiempo) • **grass verges ~ed by weeks of sunshine** la hierba seca y amarillenta al borde del camino tras semanas de sol
(CPD) ▸ **yellow belly*** gallina* *mf*, cagueta‡ *mf* ▸ **yellow card** (*Ftbl*) tarjeta *f* amarilla ▸ **yellow fever** fiebre *f* amarilla ▸ **yellow jersey** maillot *m* amarillo ▸ **yellow line** línea *f* amarilla (de estacionamiento limitado) • **a double ~ line** una línea amarilla doble • **a single ~ line** una línea amarilla ▸ **yellow ochre** ocre *m* amarillo ▸ **Yellow Pages®** (*Telec*) páginas *fpl* amarillas ▸ **the yellow peril*** la amenaza amarilla ▸ **the yellow press** la prensa amarilla, la prensa sensacionalista ▸ **the Yellow River** el río Amarillo ▸ **the Yellow Sea** el mar Amarillo ▸ **yellow wagtail** lavandera *f* boyera
yellow-card ['jeləʊ,kɑ:d] (VT) (*Sport*) amonestar, mostrar la tarjeta amarilla a
yellowhammer ['jeləʊ,hæməʳ] (N) escribano *m* cerillo
yellowish ['jeləʊɪʃ] (ADJ) amarillento
yellowness ['jeləʊnɪs] (N) color *m* amarillo, amarillez *f*
yellowy ['jeləʊɪ] (ADJ) amarillento, que tira a amarillo
yelp [jelp] (N) [*of animal*] gañido *m*; [*of person*] grito *m*, chillido *m*
(VI) [*animal*] gañir; [*person*] gritar, chillar
yelping ['jelpɪŋ] (N) [*of animal*] gañidos *mpl*; [*of person*] gritos *mpl*, chillidos *mpl*
Yemen ['jemən] (N) Yemen *m*
Yemeni ['jemənɪ] (ADJ) yemenita
(N) yemenita *mf*
yen [jen] (N) **1** (= *currency*) yen *m*
2* • **to have a yen to do sth** morirse de ganas de hacer algo*, tener muchas ganas de hacer algo
yeoman ['jəʊmən] (N) (PL: **yeomen**) (*Brit*) (*Hist*) **1** (*also* **yeoman farmer**) pequeño propietario *m*, terrateniente *m* rural
2 (*Mil*) soldado *m* (voluntario) de caballería • **~ of the guard** alabardero *m* de la Casa Real • IDIOM: • **to give ~ service** prestar grandes servicios
yeomanry ['jəʊmənrɪ] (N) **1** (= *landowners*) pequeños propietarios *mpl*, terratenientes *mpl* rurales
2 (*Brit*) (*Mil*) caballería *f* voluntaria
yep* [jep] (ADV) (*esp US*) sí
yer* [jɜ:ʳ] (PRON) = **your**
yes [jes] (ADV) sí • **"I didn't say that!" — "oh, yes, you did"** —¡yo no he dicho eso! —sí, sí que lo has dicho • **"you're not going, are you?" — "yes, I am"** —tú no vas, ¿verdad? —sí sí, (que) voy • **yes?** (*doubtfully*) ¿de verdad?, ¿ah sí?; (*awaiting further reply*) ¿y qué más?, y ¿luego? (*LAm*); (*answering knock at door*) ¿sí?, ¡adelante! • **to say yes** decir que sí, aceptar; (*to marriage proposal*) dar el sí • **he says yes to everything** a todo dice que sí, se conforma con cualquier cosa • **yes and no** (= *sort of*) sí y no • **yes yes, but what if it doesn't?** de acuerdo, pero ¿y si no es así?
(N) sí *m* • **he gave a reluctant yes** asintió pero de mala gana
(CPD) ▸ **yes man*** adulador *m*, pelotillero *m* (*Sp**)
yes-no question [,jes'nəʊ,kwestʃən] (N) pregunta *f* de sí o no
yesterday ['jestədeɪ] (ADV) ayer • **~ afternoon** ayer por la tarde • **~ morning/evening** ayer por la mañana/tarde • **all day ~** todo el día de ayer • **late ~** ayer a última hora • IDIOM: • **I wasn't born ~** no me chupo el dedo*
(N) ayer *m* • **the day before ~** anteayer • **~ was Monday** ayer era lunes • **all our ~s** todos nuestros ayeres
yesteryear ['jestə,jɪəʳ] (ADV) (*poet*) antaño
yet [jet] (ADV) **1** (= *now, up to now, by now*) todavía, aún • **he hasn't come yet** todavía *or* aún no ha llegado, no ha llegado todavía *or* aún • **don't go (just) yet** no te vayas todavía,

YET

In questions

▷ *When* **yet** *is used in affirmative questions, translate using* **ya**:
Is Mary here yet?
¿Está aquí María ya?
Have they arrived yet?
¿Han llegado ya?

In negatives

▷ *When* **not ... yet** *is used in statements or questions, translate using* **todavía no** *or* **aún no**, *both of which can go at either the beginning or the end of the sentence:*
My parents haven't got up yet
Mis padres no se han levantado todavía *or* aún, Todavía *or* Aún no se han levantado mis padres
Haven't they done it yet?
¿No lo han hecho todavía *or* aún?, ¿Todavía *or* Aún no lo han hecho?

Meaning "to date"

▷ *When* **yet** *follows a superlative or* **never** *and means "to date", translate using* **hasta ahora**:
It's the best (one) yet
Es el mejor hasta ahora
I've never been late yet
Hasta ahora no he llegado nunca con retraso

Meaning "still"

In predictions

▷ *When* **yet** *is used in predictions about the future, translate using* **todavía** *or* **aún**:
The economic crisis will go on for some time yet
La crisis económica continuará todavía *or* aún algún tiempo
They will be a long time yet
Todavía *or* Aún tardarán bastante en venir

With to + infinitive

▷ *When* **yet** *is followed by* **to** *+ verb, translate using* **todavía por** *or* **sin** *+ infinitive or* **aún por** *or* **sin** *+ infinitive:*
The house is yet to be cleaned
La casa está todavía por *or* sin limpiar
La casa está aún por *or* sin limpiar

Meaning "even"

▷ *When* **yet** *precedes a comparative and means "even", translate using* **todavía** *or* **aún**:
There is yet more rain to come in the north
Todavía *or* Aún habrá más precipitaciones en el norte
Yet bigger satellites will be sent up into orbit
Se pondrán en órbita satélites todavía *or* aún más grandes

quédate un rato • **need you go yet?** ¿tienes que irte ya? • **as yet** todavía, por ahora • **we haven't heard anything as yet** todavía *or* por ahora no sabemos nada • **not yet** todavía *or* aún no • **"are you coming?" — "not just yet"** —¿vienes? —todavía *or* aún no
2 (*= to date*) hasta ahora • **this is his best film yet** es su mejor película hasta ahora
3 (*= still*) todavía, aún • **there's hope for me yet** todavía *or* aún tengo esperanzas • **that question is yet to be decided** está todavía por *or* sin decidir, aún está por *or* sin decidir • **he may yet succeed** todavía puede que lo consiga, puede que aún lo consiga • **it won't be dark for half an hour yet** todavía *or* aún queda media hora para que anochezca
4 (*= even*) todavía, aún • **the queues are likely to grow longer yet** es probable que las colas se hagan aún *or* todavía más largas • **better yet, let him buy them for you for Christmas** mejor aún, deja que te los regale por Navidad • **yet again** otra *or* una vez más • **they are celebrating yet another victory** están celebrando otra *or* una victoria más • **many were killed, yet more have been left homeless** muchos resultaron muertos y aún *or* todavía más han perdido sus hogares
5 (*frm*) • **nor yet** ni
CONJ (*= in spite of everything*) sin embargo, con todo; (*= but*) pero • **I told him several times, yet he still hasn't done it** se lo dije varias veces, (y) sin embargo no lo ha hecho • **a powerful yet fragile piece of equipment** un equipo potente pero frágil

yeti ['jetɪ] N yeti *m*
yew [juː] N (*also* **yew tree**) tejo *m*
Y-fronts® ['waɪfrʌnts] NPL (*Brit*) calzoncillos *mpl*
YHA N ABBR (*Brit*) = **Youth Hostels Association**
Yid*! [jɪd] N (*offensive*) judío/a *m/f*
Yiddish ['jɪdɪʃ] ADJ judío
N (*Ling*) yíd(d)ish *m*, judeo-alemán *m*
yield [jiːld] N (*from crop, mine, investment*) rendimiento *m* • **~ per hectare** el rendimiento por hectárea • **high-yield bonds** bonos *mpl* de alto rendimiento • **this year, grain ~s have trebled** este año la producción de cereales se ha triplicado • **how to improve milk ~s** cómo mejorar la producción de leche
VT **1** (*= produce*) [*+ crop, minerals, results*] producir; [*+ interest*] rendir, producir; [*+ profit, benefits*] producir, reportar; [*+ opportunity*] brindar, ofrecer • **the shares ~ five per cent** las acciones producen *or* reportan *or* rinden un cinco por ciento de beneficios
2 (*frm*) (*= surrender*) [*+ territory, power, control*] ceder (**to** a) • **to ~ the floor to sb** ceder la palabra a algn • **to ~ ground to sb** (*Mil*) (*also fig*) ceder terreno a algn • **to ~ the right of way to sb** (*US*) (*Aut*) ceder el paso a algn
VI **1** (*Agr*) (*= produce*) • **land that ~s well/poorly** una tierra que produce mucho/poco • **a variety of strawberry that ~s well** una variedad de fresa que da mucha producción
2 (*frm*) (*= surrender*) rendirse, ceder • **we shall never ~** nunca nos rendiremos, nunca cederemos • **to ~ to sth** ceder a *or* ante algo • **we will not ~ to threats** no vamos a ceder a *or* ante las amenazas • **he refused to ~ to temptation** se negó a caer en la tentación, se negó a ceder a *or* ante la tentación • **the disease ~ed to treatment** la enfermedad remitió con el tratamiento
3 (*= give way*) [*ice, door, branch*] ceder • **he felt the floor ~ beneath his feet** notó cómo el suelo cedía *or* hundía bajo sus pies • **to ~ under pressure** ceder *or* hundirse ante la presión
4 (*US*) (*Aut*) ceder el paso • **"yield"** "ceda el paso"
▸ **yield up** VT + ADV (*liter*) [*+ territory, power, control*] ceder (**to** a); [*+ secret*] revelar • **nature ~s up its bounty** (*liter*) la naturaleza da su recompensa

yielding ['jiːldɪŋ] ADJ **1** (*= soft*) [*ground, surface, substance*] flexible, blando
2 (*= compliant, submissive*) [*person*] (*in temperament*) complaciente; (*physically*) tierno
yin [jɪn] N yin *m*
yip ['jɪp] (*esp US*) VI (*= yelp*) gañir
N gañido *m*
yippee* [jɪ'piː] EXCL yupi*
YMCA N ABBR = **Young Men's Christian Association**
yo ['jəʊ] EXCL (*as greeting*) ¡hola!; (*to attract attention*) ¡eh!, ¡oye!
yob* [jɒb], **yobbo** ['jɒbəʊ] N (*Brit*) vándalo *m*, gamberro *m* (*Sp*)
yobbish ['jɒbɪʃ] ADJ (*Brit*) [*behaviour*] de gamberro; [*person*] salvaje, incívico
yod [jɒd] N yod *f*
yodel, **yodle** ['jəʊdl] VI cantar a la tirolesa
VT cantar a la tirolesa
N canto *m* a la tirolesa
yoga ['jəʊgə] N yoga *m*
CPD [*meditation, technique, position*] yóguico, de yoga ▸ **yoga mat** colchoneta *f* para yoga
yoghurt ['jəʊgət] N = **yogurt**
yogi ['jəʊgɪ] N (PL: **yogis** *or* **yogin** ['jəʊgɪn]) yogui *m*
yogic flying [ˌjəʊgɪk'flaɪɪŋ] N levitación *f* yóguica
yogurt ['jəʊgət] N yogur *m*
CPD ▸ **yogurt pot** bote *m* de yogur, tarro *m* de yogur
yo-heave-ho [jəʊ'hiːv'həʊ] EXCL = **heave-ho**
yoke [jəʊk] N (PL: **yokes** *or* **yoke**) **1** [*of oxen*] yunta *f*; (*carried on shoulder*) balancín *m*, percha *f*; (*fig*) yugo *m* • **under the ~ of the Nazis** bajo el yugo de los nazis • **to throw off the ~** sacudir el yugo
2 (*on dress, blouse*) canesú *m*
VT (*also* **yoke together**) [*+ oxen*] uncir; (*fig*) unir
yokel ['jəʊkəl] N palurdo/a *m/f*, pueblerino/a *m/f*
yolk [jəʊk] N yema *f* (de huevo)
Yom Kippur [ˌjɒmkɪ'pʊəʳ] N Yom Kip(p)ur *m*
yomp [jɒmp] VI *caminar penosamente (por un terreno difícil)*
yon [jɒn] ADV (*poet or dialect*) aquel
yonder ['jɒndəʳ] ADJ aquel
ADV allá, a lo lejos • (**over**) **~** allá
yonks* [jɒŋks] N (*Brit*) • **for ~** hace siglos* • **I haven't seen you for ~** hace siglos que no te veo*
yoo-hoo* ['juː'huː] EXCL ¡yu-hu!*
yore [jɔːʳ] N (*liter*) • **of ~** de antaño, de otro tiempo, de hace siglos • **the days of ~** los tiempos de antaño, otros tiempos
Yorks [jɔːks] N ABBR (*Brit*) = **Yorkshire**
Yorkshire pudding [ˈjɔːkʃɪəˈpʊdɪŋ] N (*Brit*) *especie de buñuelo que se sirve acompañando al rosbif*
you [juː] PRON

Note that subject pronouns are used less in Spanish than in English – mainly for emphasis or to avoid ambiguity.

1 (*sing*) **a** (*familiar*) (*= as subject*) tú; (*as direct/indirect object*) te; (*after prep*) ti • **what do you think about it?** ¿y tú que piensas? • **you and I will go** iremos tú y yo • **you're very strong** eres muy fuerte • **you don't understand me** no me entiendes • **I know you** te conozco • **I'll send you a postcard** te mandaré una postal • **I gave the letter to you yesterday** te di la carta ayer • **I gave it to you** te lo di • **I told you to do it** te dije a ti que lo hicieras, es a ti a quien dije que lo hicieras • **it's for you** es para ti • **she's taller than you** es más alta que tú • **can I come with you** ¿puedo ir contigo?
b (*frm*) (*= as subject*) usted, Ud, Vd; (*as direct object*) lo/la, le (*Sp*); (*as indirect object*) le; (*after prep*) usted, Ud, Vd • **you're very kind** es usted muy amable • **I saw you, Mrs Jones** la vi, señora Jones • **I gave you the keys** le di las llaves

*Change **le** to **se** before a direct object pronoun:*

• **I gave it to you** se lo di • **I gave them to you** se las di • **this is for you** esto es para usted • **they're taller than you** son más altos que usted
2 (*pl*) **a** (*familiar*) (*= as subject*) vosotros/as (*Sp*), ustedes (*LAm*); (*as direct object*) os (*Sp*), los/las (*LAm*); (*as indirect object*) os (*Sp*), les (*LAm*); (*after prep*) vosotros/as (*Sp*), ustedes (*LAm*) • **you've got kids but we haven't** vosotros tenéis hijos pero nosotros no • **you're sisters, aren't you?** vosotras sois hermanas, ¿no? • **you have all been here before** todos (vosotros) habéis estado aquí antes • **you all know why we are here** todos sabéis por qué estamos aquí • **you stay here, and I'll go and get the key** (vosotros) quedaos aquí, que yo iré a por la llave • **I know you both** yo os conozco a los dos • **I gave it to you** os lo di • **I gave them to you** os los di • **I'd like to speak to you** quiero hablar con vosotros • **I live upstairs from you** vivo justo encima de vosotros • **they've done it better than you** lo han hecho mejor que vosotros • **they'll go without you** irán sin vosotros
b (*frm*) (*= as subject*) ustedes, Uds, Vds; (*as direct object*) los/las, les (*Sp*); (*as indirect object*) les; (*after prep*) ustedes, Uds, Vds • **you are very kind** son ustedes muy amables • **are you brothers?** ¿son (ustedes) hermanos? • **may I help you?** ¿puedo ayudarlos? • **I gave you the keys** les di las llaves

*Change **les** to **se** before a direct object pronoun:*

• **I gave it to you** se lo di • **I gave them to you** se las di • **we arrived after you** llegamos después de ustedes
3 (*general*)

*When **you** means "one" or "people" in general, the impersonal **se** is often used:*

• **you can't do that** no se puede hacer eso, eso no se hace, eso no se permite • **you can't smoke here** no se puede fumar aquí, no se permite fumar aquí, se prohíbe fumar aquí • **when you need one it's not here** cuando se necesita uno no está aquí • **you never know** • **you never can tell** nunca se sabe

*A further possibility is **uno**:*

• **you never know whether …** uno nunca sabe si …

Impersonal constructions are also used:

• **you need to check it every day** hay que comprobarlo cada día, conviene comprobarlo cada día • **you must paint it**

Y

hace falta pintarlo • **fresh air does you good** el aire puro (te) hace bien
4 (*phrases and special uses*) • **you Spaniards** vosotros los españoles • **you doctors!** ¡vosotros, los médicos! • **between you and me** entre tú y yo • **you fool!** ¡no seas tonto! • **that's lawyers for you!** ¡para que te fíes de los abogados! • **there's a pretty girl for you!** ¡mira que chica más guapa! • **if I were** *or* **was you** yo que tú, yo en tu lugar • **you there!** ¡oye, tú! • **that dress just isn't you** ese vestido no te sienta bien • **poor you!** • **poor old you!** • **you poor old thing!** ¡pobrecito!

YOU

When translating **you**, *even though you often need not use the pronoun itself, you will have to choose between using familiar* **tú/vosotros** *verb forms and the polite* **usted/ustedes** *ones.*

▷ *In Spain, use* **tú** *and the plural* **vosotros/vosotras** *with anyone you call by their first name, with children and younger adults. Use* **usted/ustedes** *with people who are older than you, those in authority and in formal contexts.*

▷ *In Latin America usage varies depending on the country and in some places only the* **usted** *forms are used. Where the* **tú** *form does exist, only use it with people you know very well. In other areas* **vos**, *used with verb forms that are similar to the* **vosotros** *ones, often replaces* **tú**. *This is standard in Argentina and certain Central American countries while in other countries it is considered substandard. Use* **ustedes** *for all cases of* **you** *in the plural.*

For further uses and examples, see main entry.

you'd [ju:d] = **you would, you had**
you-know-who* [ju:nəʊ'hu:] (N) tú ya sabes quien, fulano
you'll [ju:l] = **you will, you shall**
young [jʌŋ] (ADJ) (COMPAR: **younger**, SUPERL: **youngest**) **1** (= *not old*) [*person, animal*] joven; [*child*] pequeño, de corta edad • **my ~er brother** mi hermano menor *or* pequeño • **she is two years ~er than me** es dos años más joven que yo, tiene dos años menos que yo • **if I were ten years ~er** si tuviera diez años menos, si fuera diez años más joven • **I'm not so ~ as I was, I'm not getting any ~er** los años no perdonan *or* no pasan en balde • **~ Britain** la juventud británica • **Pitt the ~er** Pitt el joven • **she started writing poetry at a very ~ age** comenzó a escribir poesía siendo muy joven • **at a very ~ age he was sent to boarding school** siendo muy pequeño lo mandaron a un internado • **in my ~(er) days** cuando era joven, en mi juventud • **they have a ~ family** tienen niños pequeños • **she looks quite ~ for her age** aparenta bastante menos edad de la que tiene, parece bastante más joven de lo que es • **the ~er generation** la generación de los más jóvenes • **the ~er generation of film-makers** la generación de cineastas jóvenes • **~ hopeful** joven aspirante *mf* • **a ~ lady** una joven • **why thank you, ~ lady!** ¡muchas gracias, señorita *or* joven! • **now look here, ~ lady!** ¡atiende, jovencita! • **a ~ man** un joven • **you've done well, ~ man** muy bien hecho, muchacho • **she's out with her ~ man** ha salido con su novio *or* chico* • **to marry ~** casarse joven • **it is enjoyed by millions, ~ and old** millones lo disfrutan, grandes y pequeños • **a ~ person** una persona joven • IDIOMS: • **you're as ~ as you feel** la edad se lleva dentro • **~ at heart** joven de espíritu • **the night is ~** la noche es joven • **you're only ~ once** solo se vive una vez; ▷ **Turk**
2 (= *youthful*) • **that dress is too ~ for her** ese vestido es para alguien más joven • **the family business was in need of ~ blood** el negocio familiar necesitaba savia nueva • **he has a very ~ outlook** piensa como los jóvenes, tiene mentalidad de joven
3 (= *new*) [*moon*] nuevo; [*plant, spinach, wheat*] tierno; [*wine, country*] joven • **the 20th century was still ~** el siglo XX estaba todavía en sus comienzos
(NPL) **1** (= *offspring*) [*of animals*] crías *fpl* • **a mother defending her ~** una madre protegiendo a sus crías • **to be with ~** estar preñada
2 (= *young people*) • **the ~** los jóvenes, la juventud
(CPD) ▸ **young gun** (= *actor, sportsman etc*) joven valor *m* ▸ **young offender** (*Brit*) delincuente *mf* juvenil
youngish ['jʌŋɪʃ] (ADJ) bastante joven, más bien joven
young-looking ['jʌŋ,lʊkɪŋ] (ADJ) de aspecto joven
youngster ['jʌŋstəʳ] (N) joven *mf*
your ['jʊəʳ] (POSS ADJ) **1** (*belonging to one person*) **a** (*familiar*) (= *with singular noun*) tu; (*with plural noun*) tus • **~ book/table** tu libro/mesa • **~ friends** tus amigos • **it's ~ go** te toca, es tu turno • **have you washed ~ hair?** ¿te has lavado el pelo? • **he's ~ son, not mine!** ¡es hijo tuyo, no mío!
b (*frm*) (*with singular noun*) su; (*with plural noun*) sus • **~ book/table** su libro/mesa • **~ friends** sus amigos • **it's ~ go** es su turno, le toca a usted • **can I see ~ passport, sir?** ¿me enseña su pasaporte, señor? • **is this ~ luggage?** ¿es de usted este equipaje?
2 (*belonging to more than one person*) **a** (*familiar*) (*with singular noun*) vuestro/a (*Sp*), su (*LAm*); (*with plural noun*) vuestros/as (*Sp*), sus (*LAm*) • **~ house** vuestra casa (*Sp*), su casa (*LAm*) • **you can leave ~ bags in this room** podéis dejar las *or* vuestras bolsas en esta habitación (*Sp*), pueden dejar las *or* sus bolsas en esta habitación (*LAm*) • **would you like to wash ~ hands?** ¿queréis lavaros las manos?
b (*frm*) (*with singular noun*) su; (*with plural noun*) sus • **~ house** su casa • **you can leave ~ bags in this room** pueden dejar las *or* sus bolsas en esta habitación • **is this ~ dog?** ¿es de ustedes este perro?
3 (= *one's*) • **it's bad for ~ health** perjudica la salud
you're ['jʊəʳ] = **you are**
yours ['jʊəz] (POSS PRON) **1** (*belonging to one person*) **a** (*familiar*) (*referring to singular possession*) (el/la) tuyo/a; (*referring to plural possession*) (los/las) tuyos/as • **is that box ~?** ¿esa caja es tuya? • **I've lost my pen, can I use ~?** he perdido el bolígrafo, ¿puedo usar el tuyo? • **that dog of ~!** ¡ese perro tuyo! • **which is ~?** ¿cuál es el tuyo? • **these are my keys and those are ~** estas son mis llaves y esas son las tuyas • **what's ~?*** (*offering drink*) ¿qué vas a tomar?
b (*frm*) (*referring to singular possession*) (el/la) suyo/a, (el/la) de usted; (*referring to plural possession*) (los/las) suyos/as, (los/las) de usted • **you and ~** usted y los suyos • **is that box ~?** ¿esa caja es suya? • **I've lost my pen, can I use ~?** he perdido el bolígrafo, ¿puedo usar el suyo? • **these are my keys and those are ~** estas son mis llaves y esas son las suyas • **Yours** (*in letter*) le saluda atentamente; ▷ **truly**
2 (*belonging to more than one person*) **a** (*familiar*) (*referring to singular possession*) (el/la) vuestro/a, (el/la) suyo/a (*LAm*), (el/la) de ustedes (*LAm*); (*referring to plural possession*) (los/las) vuestros/as, (los/las) suyos /as (*LAm*), (los/las) de ustedes (*LAm*) • **that's ~** eso es vuestro
b (*frm*) (*referring to singular possession*) (el/la) suyo/a, (el/la) de ustedes; (*referring to plural possession*) (los/las) suyos/as, (los/las) de ustedes
yourself [jə'self] (PRON) (PL: **yourselves** [jə'selvz]) **1** (*reflexive*) **a** (*familiar*) te • **have you hurt ~?** ¿te has hecho daño?
b (*frm*) se • **have you hurt ~?** ¿se ha hecho daño?
2 (*for emphasis*) **a** (*familiar*) tú mismo/a • **you did it ~** tú mismo lo hiciste • **do it ~!** ¡hazlo tú mismo! • **you ~ said so** tú mismo lo dijiste
b (*frm*) usted mismo/a • **you did it ~** usted mismo lo hizo • **you ~ said so** usted mismo lo dijo
3 (*after a preposition*) **a** (*familiar*) ti mismo/a • **you did it for ~** lo hiciste para ti mismo
b (*frm*) usted mismo/a • **you did it for ~** lo hizo para usted mismo
c • **(all) by ~** sin ayuda de nadie • **did you come by ~?** ¿viniste solo?
4 = oneself
yourselves [jə'selvz] (PRON) **1** (*reflexive*) **a** (*familiar*) os (*Sp*), se (*LAm*) • **did you enjoy ~?** ¿os divertisteis?, ¿se divirtieron? (*LAm*) • **help ~ to vegetables** servíos las verduras
b (*frm*) se • **help ~ to vegetables** sírvanse las verduras
2 (*after prep, for emphasis*) **a** (*familiar*) vosotros/as mismos/as, ustedes mismos/as (*LAm*) • **you'll have to pay for taxis ~** vosotros mismos tendréis que pagar los taxis
b (*frm*) ustedes mismos/as • **you'll have to pay for taxis ~** ustedes mismos tendrán que pagar los taxis
youth [ju:θ] (N) **1** (= *young age*) juventud *f* • **in my ~** en mi juventud
2 (PL: **youths** [ju:ðz]) (= *boy*) joven *m*
3 (= *young people*) jóvenes *mpl*, juventud *f* • **the ~ of today** los jóvenes *or* la juventud de hoy
(CPD) ▸ **youth centre, youth center** (*US*) centro *m* de ocio juvenil ▸ **youth club** club *m* juvenil ▸ **youth crime** delincuencia *f* juvenil ▸ **youth culture** cultura *f* juvenil ▸ **youth employment scheme** plan *m* de empleo juvenil ▸ **youth hostel** albergue *m* juvenil ▸ **youth hostelling** • **to go ~ hostelling** pasar las vacaciones en albergues juveniles ▸ **youth movement** movimiento *m* juvenil ▸ **youth worker** (*Brit*) (= *social worker*) *asistente social que se encarga de adolescentes menores de 18 años*; (= *community worker*) *empleado del municipio que trabaja con grupos de jóvenes en la comunidad*
youthful ['ju:θfʊl] (ADJ) [*looks, appearance*] joven, juvenil; [*enthusiasm, energy*] juvenil; [*ambition, indiscretion, inexperience*] de juventud • **a group of ~ newcomers** un grupo de jóvenes aún desconocidos • **to look ~** tener aspecto joven, parecer joven
youthfulness ['ju:θfʊlnɪs] (N) juventud *f*
you've [ju:v] = **you have**
yowl [jaʊl] (N) [*of animal*] aullido *m*; [*of person*] alarido *m*
(VI) [*animal*] aullar; [*person*] dar alaridos
yo-yo ['jəʊjəʊ] (N) (PL: **yo-yos**) **1** ® (= *toy*) yoyó® *m*
2 (*US‡*) bobo/a *m/f*, imbécil *mf*
yr (ABBR) **1** = **year**
2 = **your**
yrs (ABBR) **1** = **years**
2 = **yours**
YT (ABBR) (*Canada*) = **Yukon Territory**
YTS (N ABBR) (*Brit*) (*formerly*) (= **Youth Training**

Scheme) *plan de promoción de empleo para jóvenes*
ytterbium [ɪ'tɜ:bɪəm] (N) iterbio *m*, yterbio *m*
yttrium ['ɪtrɪəm] (N) itrio *m*
yuan ['ju:'æn] (N) yuan *m*
yucca ['jʌkə] (N) yuca *f*
yuck* [jʌk] (EXCL) ¡puaj!*
yucky* ['jʌkɪ] (ADJ) asqueroso
Yugoslav ['ju:gəʊ'slɑ:v] (ADJ) yugoeslavo, yugoslavo
(N) yugoeslavo/a *m/f*, yugoslavo/a *m/f*
Yugoslavia ['ju:gəʊ'slɑ:vɪə] (N) Yugoslavia *f*
Yugoslavian ['ju:gəʊ'slɑ:vɪən] (ADJ) yugoeslavo, yugoslavo
yuk* [jʌk] (EXCL) = **yuck**
Yule [ju:l] (N) (*liter*) Navidad *f*
(CPD) ▸ **Yule log** (= *wood*) leño *m* de Navidad; (= *cake*) tronco *m* de Navidad
Yuletide ['ju:ltaɪd] (N) (*liter*) Navidad *f* • **at ~** por Navidades, en Navidad
yum* [jʌm] (EXCL) • **yum yum!** ¡ñam ñam!*
yummy* ['jʌmɪ] (ADJ) (COMPAR: **yummier**, SUPERL: **yummiest**) de rechupete*
yup* [jʌp] (ADV) (*US*) sí
yuppie* ['jʌpɪ] (N ABBR) (= **young upwardly mobile professional**) yuppie *mf*
(CPD) [*car, clothes*] de yuppie; [*bar, restaurant, area*] de yuppies ▸ **yuppie flu** síndrome *m* vírico
yuppified* ['jʌpɪfaɪd] (ADJ) [*bar, restaurant, area, flat*] de yuppies • **he is becoming more and more ~** se está haciendo cada vez más yuppie
yuppy* ['jʌpɪ] (N) = **yuppie**
YWCA (N ABBR) = **Young Women's Christian Association**

Zz

Z, z [zed], *(US)* [zi:] N *(= letter)* Z, z *f* • **Z for Zebra** Z de Zaragoza
zaftig* ['zæftɪg] ADJ *(US)* [*woman*] regordeta y mona
Zaire [zɑ:'i:əʳ] N Zaire *m*
Zairean [zɑ:'i:ərɪən] ADJ zaireño
N zaireño/a *m/f*
Zambesi [zæm'bi:zɪ] N Zambeze *m*
Zambia ['zæmbɪə] N Zambia *f*
Zambian ['zæmbɪən] ADJ zambiano
N zambiano/a *m/f*
zany ['zeɪnɪ] ADJ (COMPAR: **zanier**, SUPERL: **zaniest**) estrafalario, surrealista
Zanzibar ['zænzɪbɑ:ʳ] N Zanzíbar *m*
zap* [zæp] EXCL ¡zas!
VT **1** *(= destroy)* [*+ person*] cargarse*
2 *(= delete)* [*+ word, data*] borrar, suprimir
3 *(TV)* • **to zap the TV channels** zapear
VI *(= move quickly)* ir corriendo
▸ **zap along*** VI + ADV ir a toda pastilla*
zapper* ['zæpəʳ] N *(= remote control)* mando *m* (a distancia)
zappy* ['zæpɪ] ADJ [*car*] alegre, respondón; [*computer*] veloz; [*prose, style*] ágil
Z-bed ['zedbed] N cama *f* plegable
zeal [zi:l] N celo *m*, entusiasmo *m* (**for** por)
zealot ['zelət] N fanático/a *m/f*
zealotry ['zelətrɪ] N fanatismo *m*
zealous ['zeləs] ADJ entusiasta (**for** de)
zealously ['zeləslɪ] ADV con entusiasmo
zebra ['zi:brə] N (PL: **zebras** *or* **zebra**) cebra *f*
CPD ▸ **zebra crossing** *(Brit)* paso *m* de peatones, paso *m* de cebra
zebu ['zi:bu:] N cebú *m*
zed [zed], **zee** [zi:] *(US)* N zeta *f*
zeitgeist ['zaɪtgaɪst] N espíritu *m* de la era
Zen [zen] N Zen *m*
CPD ▸ **Zen Buddhism** budismo *m* Zen ▸ **Zen Buddhist** budista *mf* Zen
zenana [ze'nɑ:nə] N harén *m* indio
zenith ['zenɪθ] N **1** *(Astron)* cenit *m*
2 *(fig)* cenit *m*, apogeo *m* • **to be at the ~ of one's power** estar en el apogeo de su poder
Zeno ['zi:nəʊ] N Zenón *m*
Zephaniah [,zefə'naɪə] N Sofonías *m*
zephyr ['zefəʳ] N céfiro *m*
zeppelin ['zeplɪn] N zepelín *m*
zero ['zɪərəʊ] N (PL: **zeros** *or* **zeroes**) cero *m* • **absolute ~** cero *m* absoluto • **5° below ~** 5 grados bajo cero
CPD [*altitude*] cero; [*interest, hope**] nulo ▸ **zero emissions** • **the only car with ~ emissions is the electric car** el único coche sin emisiones es el eléctrico ▸ **zero gravity** gravedad *f* nula ▸ **zero growth** crecimiento *m* cero ▸ **zero hour** hora *f* cero, hora *f* H ▸ **zero option** opción *f* cero ▸ **zero rating** tasa *f* cero ▸ **zero tolerance** • **a policy of ~ tolerance** una política de mano dura *(en el mantenimiento del orden público)*
▸ **zero in on** VI + PREP **1** *(Mil)* *(= aim at)* [*+ target*] apuntar a; *(= move in on)* dirigirse de cabeza a
2 *(fig)* *(= identify)* identificar; *(= concentrate on)* dirigir todos sus esfuerzos a • **he raised the binoculars and ~ed in on an eleventh-floor room** elevó los prismáticos y los dirigió *or* enfocó hacia una habitación de la undécima planta • **he ~ed in on those who ...** reservó sus críticas más acérrimas para los que ...

ZERO
Existen varias palabras que pueden usarse en lugar de **zero** según el contexto. **Zero** es el término más general en inglés americano, que se usa en la mayoría de los casos. En inglés británico se usa normalmente en matemáticas y ciencias para referirse a temperaturas u otras escalas de valores, como por ejemplo en las frases **zero population growth** (crecimiento de población cero), o **zero inflation** (índice de inflación cero).
Nought se usa en inglés británico para leer números decimales, como por ejemplo **nought point nought seven: 0.07** (en inglés se usa el punto en vez de la coma como separador decimal) y en las calificaciones: **nought out of ten** (cero sobre diez).
O (pronunciado igual que la letra **o**) se usa en inglés británico en los números de teléfono: **O one four one**: 0141. También se usa en secuencias de dígitos que no representan cantidades numéricas, como por ejemplo en tarjetas de crédito o números de cuentas bancarias.
Nil se usa normalmente en el Reino Unido en los tanteos deportivos: **Liverpool won five nil** (Liverpool ganó cinco a cero).
Nothing es el equivalente americano de **nil**, aunque también se usa a veces en inglés británico.

zero-emission [,zɪərəʊɪ'mɪʃən] ADJ sin emisiones
zero-hour(s) contract ['zɪərəʊ'aʊə(z)'kɒntrækt] N *(Brit)* contrato *m* de cero horas • **to be on a ~** tener un contrato de cero horas
zero-rated ['zɪərəʊ,reɪtɪd] ADJ • **to be zero-rated for VAT** tener tipo cero del IVA
zest [zest] N **1** *(= enthusiasm)* gusto *m*, entusiasmo *m* (**for** por) • **to do sth with ~** hacer algo con entusiasmo • **to eat with ~** comer con gusto • **her ~ for life** sus ganas de vivir, su gusto por la vida
2 *(= excitement)* ánimo *m*
zester ['zestəʳ] N pelador *m*
zestful ['zestfʊl] ADJ entusiasta
zestfully ['zestfəlɪ] ADV con entusiasmo
zesty ['zestɪ] ADJ [*wine*] garboso, enérgico
Zeus [zju:s] N Zeus
ZIFT [zɪft] N ABBR = **Zygote Intrafallopian Transfer**
zigzag ['zɪgzæg] N zigzag *m*
VI zigzaguear, serpentear
ADJ en zigzag
zilch‡ [zɪltʃ] N nada de nada • **these shares are worth ~** estas acciones no valen nada de nada*, estas acciones no valen ni cinco* • **Mark knows ~ about art** Mark no sabe absolutamente nada sobre arte • **he's a real ~** *(US)* es un cero a la izquierda
zillion* ['zɪljən] ADJ • **a ~ dollars** tropecientos dólares* • **a ~ problems** tropecientos problemas*, problemas a montones*
N (PL: **zillions** *or* **zillion**) • **~s of dollars** tropecientos dólares*
Zimbabwe [zɪm'bɑ:bwɪ] N Zimbabue *m*
Zimbabwean [zɪm'bɑ:bwɪən] ADJ zimbabuo
N zimbabuo/a *m/f*
Zimmer® ['zɪmə] N *(Brit)* (*also* **Zimmer frame**) andador *m*
zinc [zɪŋk] N zinc *m*, cinc *m*
CPD ▸ **zinc ointment** pomada *f* de zinc ▸ **zinc oxide** óxido *m* de zinc
zine*, **'zine*** [zi:n] N fanzine *m*, revistilla *f*
zing [zɪŋ] N **1** *(= noise of bullet)* silbido *m*, zumbido *m*
2* *(= zest)* gusto *m*, entusiasmo *m*
VI [*bullet, arrow*] silbar • **the bullet ~ed past his ear** la bala le pasó silbando cerca de la oreja • **the cars ~ed past** los coches pasaron estruendosamente
zinnia ['zɪnɪə] N rascamoño *m*, zinnia *f*
Zion ['zaɪən] N Sión *m*
Zionism ['zaɪənɪzəm] N sionismo *m*
Zionist ['zaɪənɪst] ADJ sionista
N sionista *mf*
zip [zɪp] N **1** *(Brit)* (*also* **zip fastener**) cremallera *f*, cierre *m* relámpago *(LAm)*
2* *(= energy)* vigor *m*, energía *f*
3‡ *(= nothing)* nada de nada*
4 *(= sound of bullet)* silbido *m*, zumbido *m*
VT **1** *(= close)* [*+ dress, bag*] cerrar la cremallera de
2 • **to zip open** abrir la cremallera de
3 *(Computing)* [*+ file*] comprimir
VI • **to zip in** entrar volando *or* zumbando • **to zip past** pasar volando *or* zumbando
CPD ▸ **zip code** *(US)* código *m* postal ▸ **zip fastener** cremallera *f*, cierre *m* relámpago *(LAm)* ▸ **zip file** archivo *m* zip, archivo *m* comprimido ▸ **zip gun** *(US)* arma *f* de fuego de fabricación casera ▸ **zip line**, **zip wire** tirolina *f*
▸ **zip up** VT + ADV [*+ dress, bag*] cerrar la cremallera de • **can you zip me up please?** ¿me subes *or* cierras la cremallera?
VI + ADV cerrar
zipper ['zɪpəʳ] N *(esp US)* = **zip**
zippy* ['zɪpɪ] ADJ (COMPAR: **zippier**, SUPERL: **zippiest**) enérgico, vigoroso
zircon ['zɜ:kən] N circón *m*
zirconium [zɜ:'kəʊnɪəm] N circonio *m*
zit* [zɪt] N grano *m*
zither ['zɪðəʳ] N cítara *f*
zloty ['zlɒtɪ] N (PL: **zlotys** *or* **zloty**) zloty *m*
zodiac ['zəʊdɪæk] N zodíaco *m*

zodiacal [zəʊ'daɪəkəl] (ADJ) zodiacal, del zodíaco
zombie ['zɒmbɪ] (N) **1** (= *monster*) zombi *m*
2 (*fig*) zombi *mf*
zonal ['zəʊnl] (ADJ) zonal
zone [zəʊn] (N) (*gen*) zona *f* • **postal ~** (*US*) zona *f* postal
(VT) dividir en *or* por zonas, distribuir en zonas
(CPD) ▸ **zone therapy** reflexoterapia *f*, reflejoterapia *f*
zoning ['zəʊnɪŋ] (N) división *f* por zonas, distribución *f* en zonas
zonked‡ [zɒŋkt] (ADJ) (*also* **zonked out**)
1 (= *exhausted*) agotado, reventado*, hecho polvo*
2 (*on drugs*) colgado*, colocado (*Sp**); (*on drink*) como una cuba*, curda (*inv*) (*Sp‡*)
zonk out‡ [,zɒŋk'aʊt] (VI + ADV) quedarse como un tronco*
zoo [zu:] (N) zoo *m*, zoológico *m*, jardín *m* zoológico, parque *m* zoológico
zookeeper ['zu:ki:pə^r] (N) guarda *mf* de jardín zoológico, guarda *mf* de parque zoológico
zoological [,zəʊə'lɒdʒɪkəl] (ADJ) zoológico
• **~ gardens** = **zoo**
zoologist [zəʊ'ɒlədʒɪst] (N) zoólogo/a *m/f*
zoology [zəʊ'ɒlədʒɪ] (N) zoología *f*
zoom [zu:m] (N) **1** (= *sound*) zumbido *m*
2 (*Phot*) (*also* **zoom lens**) zoom *m*
3 (*Aer*) (= *upward flight*) empinadura *f*
(VI) **1** [*engine*] zumbar • **it ~ed past my ear** me pasó zumbando por la oreja
2 (= *go fast*) ir zumbando* • **he ~ed past at 120kph** pasó zumbando a 120kph*
3 (*Aer*) empinarse
(CPD) ▸ **zoom lens** (*Phot*) zoom *m*
▸ **zoom in** (VI + ADV) (*Phot, Cine*) • **to ~ in (on sb/sth)** enfocar (a algn/algo) con el zoom
▸ **zoom out** (VI + ADV) (*Cine*) pasar a un plano general con el zoom
zoomorph ['zəʊəʊmɒ:f] (N) zoomorfo *m*
zoomorphic [,zəʊəʊ'mɒ:fɪk] (ADJ) zoomórfico
zoophyte ['zəʊə,faɪt] (N) zoófito *m*
zooplankton [,zəʊəʊ'plæŋktən] (N) zooplancton *m*
zoot-suit* ['zu:tsu:t] (N) *traje de espaldas anchas y de pantalones anchos de los años 40*
Zoroaster [,zɒrəʊ'æstə^r] (N) Zoroastro
Zoroastrianism [,zɒrəʊ'æstrɪənɪzəm] (N) zoroastrismo *m*
zouk [zu:k] (N) (*Mus*) zouk *m*
zucchini [zu:'ki:nɪ] (N) (PL: **zucchini** *or* **zucchinis**) (*US*) calabacín *m*, calabacita *f* (*LAm*)
Zulu ['zu:lu:] (ADJ) zulú
(N) zulú *mf*
Zululand ['zu:lu:lænd] (N) Zululandia *f*
Zürich ['zjʊərɪk] (N) Zurich *f*
zygote ['zaɪgəʊt] (N) cigoto *m*, zigoto *m*

The Spanish verb

Each verb entry in the Spanish-English section of the Dictionary includes a reference by number and letter to the tables below, in which the simple tenses and parts of the three conjugations and of irregular verbs are set out. For verbs having only a slight irregularity the indication of it is given in the main text of the dictionary (*eg* **arder** ▷ CONJUG 2a), and is not repeated here. Certain other verbs have been marked in the main text as *defective* and in some cases indications of usage have been given there, but for further information it is best to consult a full grammar of the language.

Certain general points may be summarized here:

The **imperfect** is regular for all verbs except *ser* (*era* etc) and *ir* (*iba* etc).

The **conditional** is formed by adding to the stem of the future tense (in most cases the infinitive) the endings of the imperfect tense of *haber*: *contaría etc*. If the stem of the future tense is irregular, the conditional will have the same irregularity: *decir – diré, diría*; *poder – podré, podría*.

Compound tenses are formed with the auxiliary *haber* and the past participle:

perfect	he cantado (*subj*: haya cantado)
pluperfect	había cantado (*subj*: hubiera cantado, hubiese cantado)
future perfect	habré cantado
conditional perfect	habría cantado
perfect infinitive	haber cantado
perfect gerund	habiendo cantado

The **imperfect subjunctives** I and II can be seen as being formed from the 3rd person plural of the preterite, using as a stem what remains after removing the final *-ron* syllable and adding to it *-ra* (I) or *-se* (II), *eg*:

cantar: canta/ron – cantara, cantase
perder: perdie/ron – perdiera, perdiese
reducir: reduje/ron – redujera, redujese

The form of the **imperative** depends not only on number but also on whether the person(s) addressed is (are) treated in familiar or in formal terms. The 'true' imperative is used only in familiar address in the affirmative:

cantar: canta (tú), cantad (vosotros)
vender: vende (tú), vended (vosotros)
partir: parte (tú), partid (vosotros)

(There are a few irregular imperatives in the singular – *salir – sal, hacer – haz*, etc, but all the plurals are regular.) The imperative affirmative in formal address requires the subjunctive: *envíemelo, háganlo, conduzca Vd con más cuidado, ¡oiga!* The imperative negative in both familiar and formal address also requires the subjunctive: *no me digas, no os preocupéis, no grite tanto Vd, no se desanimen Vds.*

Continuous tenses are formed with *estar* and the gerund: *está leyendo, estaba lloviendo, estábamos hablando de eso*. Other auxiliary verbs may occasionally replace *estar* in certain senses: *según voy viendo, va mejorando, iba cogiendo flores, lo venía estudiando desde hacía muchos años*. Usage of the continuous tenses does not exactly coincide with that of English.

The **passive** is formed with tenses of *ser* and the past participle, which agrees in number and gender with the subject: *las casas fueron construidas, será firmado mañana el tratado, después de haber sido vencido*. The passive is much less used in Spanish than in English, its function often being taken over by a reflexive construction, by *uno*, etc.

SPANISH VERB CONJUGATIONS

INFINITIVE	PRESENT INDICATIVE	PRESENT SUBJUNCTIVE	PRETERITE
[1a] **cantar** (regular: see table at end of list) Gerund: *cantando*			
[1b] **cambiar** **i** of the stem is not stressed and the verb is regular Gerund: *cambiando*	cambio cambias cambia cambiamos cambiáis cambian	cambie cambie cambie cambiemos cambiéis cambien	cambié cambiaste cambió cambiamos cambiasteis cambiaron
[1c] **enviar** **i** of the stem stressed in parts of the present tenses Gerund: *enviando*	env**í**o env**í**as env**í**a enviamos enviáis env**í**an	env**í**e env**í**es env**í**e enviemos enviéis env**í**en	envié enviaste envió enviamos enviasteis enviaron
[1d] **evacuar** **u** of the stem is not stressed and the verb is regular Gerund: *evacuando*	evacuo evacuas evacua evacuamos evacuáis evacuan	evacue evacues evacue evacuemos evacuéis evacuen	evacué evacuaste evacuó evacuamos evacuasteis evacuaron
[1e] **situar** **u** of the stem stressed in parts of the present tenses Gerund: *situando*	sit**ú**o sit**ú**as sit**ú**a situamos situáis sit**ú**an	sit**ú**e sit**ú**es sit**ú**e situemos situéis sit**ú**en	situé situaste situó situamos situasteis situaron
[1f] **cruzar** Stem consonant **z** written **c** before **e** Gerund: *cruzando*	cruzo cruzas cruza cruzamos cruzáis cruzan	cru**c**e cru**c**es cru**c**e cru**c**emos cru**c**éis cru**c**en	cru**c**é cruzaste cruzó cruzamos cruzasteis cruzaron
[1g] **picar** Stem consonant **c** written **qu** before **e** Gerund: *picando*	pico picas pica picamos picáis pican	pi**qu**e pi**qu**es pi**qu**e pi**qu**emos pi**qu**éis pi**qu**en	pi**qu**é picaste picó picamos picasteis picaron
[1h] **pagar** Stem consonant **g** written **gu** (with **u** silent) before **e** Gerund: *pagando*	pago pagas paga pagamos pagáis pagan	pa**gu**e pa**gu**es pa**gu**e pa**gu**emos pa**gu**éis pa**gu**en	pa**gu**é pagaste pagó pagamos pagasteis pagaron
[1i] **averiguar** **u** of the stem written **ü** (so that it is pronounced) before **e** Gerund: *averiguando*	averiguo averiguas averigua averiguamos averiguáis averiguan	averi**gü**e averi**gü**es averi**gü**e averi**gü**emos averi**gü**éis averi**gü**en	averi**gü**é averiguaste averiguó averiguamos averiguasteis averiguaron
[1j] **cerrar** Stem vowel **e** becomes **ie** when stressed Gerund: *cerrando*	c**ie**rro c**ie**rras c**ie**rra cerramos cerráis c**ie**rran	c**ie**rre c**ie**rres c**ie**rre cerremos cerréis c**ie**rren	cerré cerraste cerró cerramos cerrasteis cerraron

INFINITIVE	PRESENT INDICATIVE	PRESENT SUBJUNCTIVE	PRETERITE
[1k] **errar**	**ye**rro	**ye**rre	erré
As [1j], but diphthong written **ye-** at the start of the word	**ye**rras	**ye**rres	erraste
Gerund: *errando*	**ye**rra	**ye**rre	erró
	erramos	erremos	erramos
	erráis	erréis	errasteis
	yerran	**ye**rren	erraron
[1l] **contar**	c**ue**nto	c**ue**nte	conté
Stem vowel **o** becomes **ue** when stressed	c**ue**ntas	c**ue**ntes	contaste
Gerund: *contando*	c**ue**nta	c**ue**nte	contó
	contamos	contemos	contamos
	contáis	contéis	contasteis
	c**ue**ntan	c**ue**nten	contaron
[1m] **agorar**	ag**üe**ro	ag**üe**re	agoré
As [1l], but diphthong written **üe** (so that the **u** is pronounced)	ag**üe**ras	ag**üe**res	agoraste
Gerund: *agorando*	ag**üe**ra	ag**üe**re	agoró
	agoramos	agoremos	agoramos
	agoráis	agoréis	agorasteis
	ag**üe**ran	ag**üe**ren	agoraron
[1n] **jugar**	**jue**go	**juegu**e	ju**gu**é
Stem vowel **u** becomes **ue** when stressed; stem consonant **g** written **gu** (with **u** silent) before **e**	**jue**gas	**juegu**es	jugaste
Gerund: *jugando*	**jue**ga	**juegu**e	jugó
	jugamos	ju**gu**emos	jugamos
	jugáis	ju**gu**éis	jugasteis
	juegan	**juegu**en	jugaron
[1o] **estar**	estoy	esté	estuve
Irregular.	estás	estés	estuviste
Imperative: *está (tú)*	está	esté	estuvo
Gerund: *estando*	estamos	estemos	estuvimos
	estáis	estéis	estuvisteis
	están	estén	estuvieron
[1p] **andar**	ando	ande	anduve
Irregular.	andas	andes	anduviste
Gerund: *andando*	anda	ande	anduvo
	andamos	andemos	anduvimos
	andáis	andéis	anduvisteis
	andan	anden	anduvieron
[1q] **dar**	doy	dé	di
Irregular.	das	des	diste
Gerund: *dando*	da	dé	dio
	damos	demos	dimos
	dais	deis	disteis
	dan	den	dieron
[2a] **temer** (regular: see table at end of list)			
[2b] **vencer**	ven**z**o	ven**z**a	vencí
Stem consonant **c** written **z** before **a** and **o**	vences	ven**z**as	venciste
Gerund: *venciendo*	vence	ven**z**a	venció
	vencemos	ven**z**amos	vencimos
	vencéis	ven**z**áis	vencisteis
	vencen	ven**z**an	vencieron
[2c] **coger**	co**j**o	co**j**a	cogí
Stem consonant **g** written **j** before **a** and **o**	coges	co**j**as	cogiste
Gerund: *cogiendo*	coge	co**j**a	cogió
	cogemos	co**j**amos	cogimos
	cogéis	co**j**áis	cogisteis
	cogen	co**j**an	cogieron
[2d] **conocer**	cono**zc**o	cono**zc**a	conocí
Stem consonant **c** becomes **zc** before **a** and **o**	conoces	cono**zc**as	conociste
Gerund: *conociendo*	conoce	cono**zc**a	conoció
	conocemos	cono**zc**amos	conocimos
	conocéis	cono**zc**áis	conocisteis
	conocen	cono**zc**an	conocieron

INFINITIVE	PRESENT INDICATIVE	PRESENT SUBJUNCTIVE	PRETERITE
[2e] **leer**	leo	lea	leí
Unstressed **i** between vowels is written **y**	lees	leas	leíste
Past Participle: *leído*	lee	lea	le**y**ó
Gerund: *leyendo*	leemos	leamos	leímos
	leéis	leáis	leísteis
	leen	lean	le**y**eron
[2f] **tañer**	taño	taña	tañí
Unstressed **i** after **ñ** (and also after **ll**) is omitted	tañes	tañas	tañiste
Gerund: *tañendo*	tañe	taña	ta**ñ**ó
	tañemos	tañamos	tañimos
	tañéis	tañáis	tañisteis
	tañen	tañan	ta**ñ**eron
[2g] **perder**	p**ie**rdo	p**ie**rda	perdí
Stem vowel **e** becomes **ie** when stressed	p**ie**rdes	p**ie**rdas	perdiste
Gerund: *perdiendo*	p**ie**rde	p**ie**rda	perdió
	perdemos	perdamos	perdimos
	perdéis	perdáis	perdisteis
	p**ie**rden	p**ie**rdan	perdieron
[2h] **mover**	m**ue**vo	m**ue**va	moví
Stem vowel **o** becomes **ue** when stressed	m**ue**ves	m**ue**vas	moviste
Gerund: *moviendo*	m**ue**ve	m**ue**va	movió
	movemos	movamos	movimos
	movéis	mováis	movisteis
	m**ue**ven	m**ue**van	movieron
[2i] **oler**	**hue**lo	**hue**la	olí
As [2h], but diphthong is written **hue-** at the start of the word	**hue**les	**hue**las	oliste
Gerund: *oliendo*	**hue**le	**hue**la	olió
	olemos	olamos	olimos
	oléis	oláis	olisteis
	huelen	**hue**lan	olieron
[2j] **haber** (see table at end of list)			
[2k] **tener**	tengo	tenga	tuve
Irregular.	tienes	tengas	tuviste
Future: *tendré*	tiene	tenga	tuvo
Imperative: *ten (tú)*	tenemos	tengamos	tuvimos
Gerund: *teniendo*	tenéis	tengáis	tuvisteis
	tienen	tengan	tuvieron
[2l] **caber**	quepo	quepa	cupe
Irregular.	cabes	quepas	cupiste
Future: *cabré*	cabe	quepa	cupo
Gerund: *cabiendo*	cabemos	quepamos	cupimos
	cabéis	quepáis	cupisteis
	caben	quepan	cupieron
[2m] **saber**	sé	sepa	supe
Irregular.	sabes	sepas	supiste
Future: *sabré*	sabe	sepa	supo
Gerund: *sabiendo*	sabemos	sepamos	supimos
	sabéis	sepáis	supisteis
	saben	sepan	supieron
[2n] **caer**	caigo	caiga	caí
Unstressed **i** between vowels written **y**, as [2e]	caes	caigas	caíste
Past Participle: *caído*	cae	caiga	ca**y**ó
Gerund: *cayendo*	caemos	caigamos	caímos
	caéis	caigáis	caísteis
	caen	caigan	ca**y**eron
[2o] **traer**	traigo	traiga	traje
Irregular.	traes	traigas	trajiste
Past Participle: *traído*	trae	traiga	trajo
Gerund: *trayendo*	traemos	traigamos	trajimos
	traéis	traigáis	trajisteis
	traen	traigan	trajeron

INFINITIVE	PRESENT INDICATIVE	PRESENT SUBJUNCTIVE	PRETERITE
[2p] **valer**	valgo	valga	valí
Irregular.	vales	valgas	valiste
Future: *valdré*	vale	valga	valió
Gerund: *valiendo*	valemos	valgamos	valimos
	valéis	valgáis	valisteis
	valen	valgan	valieron
[2q] **poner**	pongo	ponga	puse
Irregular.	pones	pongas	pusiste
Future: *pondré*	pone	ponga	puso
Past Participle: *puesto*	ponemos	pongamos	pusimos
Imperative: *pon (tú)*	ponéis	pongáis	pusisteis
Gerund: *poniendo*	ponen	pongan	pusieron
[2r] **hacer**	hago	haga	hice
Irregular.	haces	hagas	hiciste
Future: *haré*	hace	haga	hizo
Past Participle: *hecho*	hacemos	hagamos	hicimos
Imperative: *haz (tú)*	hacéis	hagáis	hicisteis
Gerund: *haciendo*	hacen	hagan	hicieron
[2s] **poder**	puedo	pueda	pude
Irregular.	puedes	puedas	pudiste
In present tenses like [2h]	puede	pueda	pudo
Future: *podré*	podemos	podamos	pudimos
Gerund: *pudiendo*	podéis	podáis	pudisteis
	pueden	puedan	pudieron
[2t] **querer**	quiero	quiera	quise
Irregular.	quieres	quieras	quisiste
In present tenses like [2g]	quiere	quiera	quiso
Future: *querré*	queremos	queramos	quisimos
Gerund: *queriendo*	queréis	queráis	quisisteis
	quieren	quieran	quisieron
[2u] **ver**	veo	vea	vi
Irregular.	ves	veas	viste
Imperfect: *veía*	ve	vea	vio
Past Participle: *visto*	vemos	veamos	vimos
Gerund: *viendo*	veis	veáis	visteis
	ven	vean	vieron

[2v] **ser** (see table at end of list)

[2w] **placer.** Exclusively 3rd person singular. Irregular forms: Present subj. *plazca* (less commonly *plega* or *plegue*); Preterite *plació* (less commonly *plugo*); Imperfect subj. I *placiera*, II *placiese* (less commonly *plugiera*, *plugiese*).

[2x] **yacer.** Archaic. Irregular forms: Present indic. *yazco* (less commonly *yazgo* or *yago*), *yaces* etc; Present subj. *yazca* (less commonly *yazga* or *yaga*), *yazcas* etc; Imperative *yace (tú)* (less commonly *yaz*).

[2y] **raer.** Present indic. usually *raigo*, *raes* etc (like *caer* [2n]), but *rayo* occasionally found; Present subj. usually *raiga*, *raigas* etc (also like *caer*), but *raya*, *rayas* etc occasionally found.

[2z] **roer.** Alternative forms in present tenses: Indicative, *roo*, *roigo* or *royo*; *roes*, *roe* etc. Subjunctive, *roa*, *roiga* or *roya*. First persons usually avoided because of the uncertainty. The gerund is *royendo*.

[3a] **partir** (regular: see table at end of list)

INFINITIVE	PRESENT INDICATIVE	PRESENT SUBJUNCTIVE	PRETERITE
[3b] **esparcir**	espar**z**o	espar**z**a	esparcí
Stem consonant **c** written **z** before **a** and **o**	esparces	espar**z**as	esparciste
Gerund: *esparciendo*	esparce	espar**z**a	esparció
	esparcimos	espar**z**amos	esparcimos
	esparcís	espar**z**áis	esparcisteis
	esparcen	espar**z**an	esparcieron
[3c] **dirigir**	diri**j**o	diri**j**a	dirigí
Stem consonant **g** written **j** before **a** and **o**	diriges	diri**j**as	dirigiste
Gerund: *dirigiendo*	dirige	diri**j**a	dirigió
	dirigimos	diri**j**amos	dirigimos
	dirigís	diri**j**áis	dirigisteis
	dirigen	diri**j**an	dirigieron

INFINITIVE	PRESENT INDICATIVE	PRESENT SUBJUNCTIVE	PRETERITE
[3d] **distinguir** **u** after the stem consonant **g** omitted before **a** and **o** Gerund: *distinguendo*	distingo distingues distingue distinguimos distinguís distinguen	distinga distingas distinga distingamos distingáis distingan	distinguí distinguiste distinguió distinguimos distinguisteis distinguieron
[3e] **delinquir** Stem consonant **qu** written **c** before **a** and **o** Gerund: *delinquiendo*	delinco delinques delinque delinquimos delinquís delinquen	delinca delincas delinca delincamos delincáis delincan	delinquí delinquiste delinquió delinquimos delinquisteis delinquieron
[3f] **lucir** Stem consonant **c** becomes **zc** before **a** and **o** Gerund: *luciendo*	luzco luces luce lucimos lucís lucen	luzca luzcas luzca luzcamos luzcáis luzcan	lucí luciste lució lucimos lucisteis lucieron
[3g] **huir** A **y** is inserted before endings not beginning with **i** Gerund: *huyendo*	huyo huyes huye huimos huís huyen	huya huyas huya huyamos huyáis huyan	huí huiste huyó huimos huisteis huyeron
[3h] **gruñir** Unstressed **i** after **ñ** (and also after **ch** and **ll**) omitted Gerund: *gruñendo*	gruño gruñes gruñe gruñimos gruñís gruñen	gruña gruñas gruña gruñamos gruñáis gruñan	gruñí gruñiste gruñó gruñimos gruñisteis gruñeron
[3i] **sentir** The stem vowel **e** becomes **ie** when stressed; **e** becomes **i** in 3rd persons of Preterite, 1st and 2nd persons pl. of Present Subjunctive. Gerund: *sintiendo* In *adquirir* the stem vowel **i** becomes **ie** when stressed	siento sientes siente sentimos sentís sienten	sienta sientas sienta sintamos sintáis sientan	sentí sentiste sintió sentimos sentisteis sintieron
[3j] **dormir** The stem vowel **o** becomes **ue** when stressed; **o** becomes **u** in 3rd persons of Preterite, 1st and 2nd persons pl. of Present Subjunctive. Gerund: *durmiendo*	duermo duermes duerme dormimos dormís duermen	duerma duermas duerma durmamos durmáis duerman	dormí dormiste durmió dormimos dormisteis durmieron
[3k] **pedir** The stem vowel **e** becomes **i** when stressed, and in 3rd persons of Preterite, 1st and 2nd persons pl. of Present Subjunctive. Gerund: *pidiendo*	pido pides pide pedimos pedís piden	pida pidas pida pidamos pidáis pidan	pedí pediste pidió pedimos pedisteis pidieron
[3l] **reír** Irregular. Past Participle: *reído* Gerund: *riendo* Imperative: *ríe (tú)*	río ríes ríe reímos reís ríen	ría rías ría riamos riáis rían	reí reíste rió reímos reísteis rieron
[3m] **erguir** Irregular. Gerund: *irguiendo* Imperative: *yergue (tú)* and less commonly *irgue (tú)*	yergo yergues yergue erguimos erguís yerguen	yerga yergas yerga yergamos yergáis yergan	erguí erguiste irguió erguimos erguisteis irguieron

INFINITIVE	PRESENT INDICATIVE	PRESENT SUBJUNCTIVE	PRETERITE
[3n] **reducir** The stem consonant **c** becomes **zc** before **a** and **o** as [3f]; irregular preterite in **-uj-** Gerund: *reduciendo*	redu**zc**o reduces reduce reducimos reducís reducen	redu**zc**a redu**zc**as redu**zc**a redu**zc**amos redu**zc**áis redu**zc**an	red**uj**e red**uj**iste red**uj**o red**uj**imos red**uj**isteis red**uj**eron
[3o] **decir** Irregular. Future: *diré* Past Participle: *dicho* Gerund: *diciendo* Imperative: *di (tú)*	digo dices dice decimos decís dicen	diga digas diga digamos digáis digan	dije dijiste dijo dijimos dijisteis dijeron
[3p] **oír** Irregular. Unstressed **i** between vowels becomes **y** Past Participle: *oído* Gerund: *oyendo*	oigo o**y**es o**y**e oímos oís o**y**en	oiga oigas oiga oigamos oigáis oigan	oí oíste o**y**ó oímos oísteis o**y**eron
[3q] **salir** Irregular. Future: *saldré* Imperative: *sal (tú)* Gerund: *saliendo*	salgo sales sale salimos salís salen	salga salgas salga salgamos salgáis salgan	salí saliste salió salimos salisteis salieron
[3r] **venir** Irregular. Future: *vendré* Gerund: *viniendo* Imperative: *ven (tú)*	vengo vienes viene venimos venís vienen	venga vengas venga vengamos vengáis vengan	vine viniste vino vinimos vinisteis vinieron
[3s] **ir** Irregular. Imperfect: *iba* Gerund: *yendo* Imperative: *ve (tú), id (vosotros)*	voy vas va vamos vais van	vaya vayas vaya vayamos vayáis vayan	fui fuiste fue fuimos fuisteis fueron

[1a] **cantar** (regular verb)

INDICATIVE

Present
canto
cantas
canta
cantamos
cantáis
cantan

Imperfect
cantaba
cantabas
cantaba
cantábamos
cantabais
cantaban

Preterite
canté
cantaste
cantó
cantamos
cantasteis
cantaron

Future
cantaré
cantarás
cantará
cantaremos
cantaréis
cantarán

Gerund
cantando

CONDITIONAL
cantaría
cantarías
cantaría
cantaríamos
cantaríais
cantarían

Imperative
canta (tú)
cantad (vosotros)

Past Participle
cantado

SUBJUNCTIVE

Present
cante
cantes
cante
cantemos
cantéis
canten

Imperfect
cantara/-ase
cantaras/-ases
cantara/-ase
cantáramos/-ásemos
cantarais/-aseis
cantaran/-asen

[2a] **temer** (regular verb)

INDICATIVE

Present
temo
temes
teme
tememos
teméis
temen

Imperfect
temía
temías
temía
temíamos
temíais
temían

Future
temeré
temerás
temerá
temeremos
temeréis
temerán

Preterite
temí
temiste
temió
temimos
temisteis
temieron

Gerund
temiendo

CONDITIONAL
temería
temerías
temería
temeríamos
temeríais
temerían

Imperative
teme (tú)
temed (vosotros)

Past Participle
temido

SUBJUNCTIVE

Present
tema
temas
tema
temamos
temáis
teman

Imperfect
temiera/-iese
temieras/-ieses
temiera/-iese
temiéramos/-iésemos
temierais/-ieseis
temieran/-iesen

[3a] **partir** (regular verb)

INDICATIVE

Present
parto
partes
parte
partimos
partís
parten

Imperfect
partía
partías
partía
partíamos
partíais
partían

Preterite
partí
partiste
partió
partimos
partisteis
partieron

Future
partiré
partirás
partirá
partiremos
partiréis
partirán

Gerund
partiendo

CONDITIONAL
partiría
partirías
partiría
partiríamos
partiríais
partirían

Imperative
parte (tú)
partid (vosotros)

Past Participle
partido

SUBJUNCTIVE

Present
parta
partas
parta
partamos
partáis
partan

Imperfect
partiera/-iese
partieras/-ieses
partiera/-iese
partiéramos/-iésemos
partierais/-ieseis
partieran/-iesen

[2j] **haber**

INDICATIVE

Present
he
has
ha
hemos
habéis
han

Imperfect
había
habías
había
habíamos
habíais
habían

Preterite
hube
hubiste
hubo
hubimos
hubisteis
hubieron

Future
habré
habrás
habrá
habremos
habréis
habrán

Gerund
habiendo

Past Participle
habido

CONDITIONAL
habría
habrías
habría
habríamos
habríais
habrían

SUBJUNCTIVE

Present
haya
hayas
haya
hayamos
hayáis
hayan

Imperfect
hubiera/-iese
hubieras/-ieses
hubiera/-iese
hubiéramos/-iésemos
hubierais/-ieseis
hubieran/-iesen

[2v] **ser**

INDICATIVE

Present
soy
eres
es
somos
sois
son

Imperfect
era
eras
era
éramos
erais
eran

Preterite
fui
fuiste
fue
fuimos
fuisteis
fueron

Future
seré
serás
será
seremos
seréis
serán

Gerund
siendo

Past Participle
sido

CONDITIONAL
sería
serías
sería
seríamos
seríais
serían

Imperative
sé (tú)
sed (vosotros)

SUBJUNCTIVE

Present
sea
seas
sea
seamos
seáis
sean

Imperfect
fuera/-ese
fueras/-eses
fuera/-ese
fuéramos/-ésemos
fuerais/-eseis
fueran/-esen

El verbo inglés

El verbo inglés es bastante más sencillo que el español, a lo menos en cuanto a su forma. Hay muchos verbos fuertes o irregulares (damos una lista de ellos a continuación) y varias clases de irregularidad ortográfica (véanse las notas al final); pero hay una sola conjugación, y dentro de cada tiempo no hay variación para las seis personas excepto en el presente (tercera persona de singular). Por tanto, no es necesario ofrecer para el verbo inglés los cuadros y paradigmas con que se suele explicar el verbo español; la estructura general y las formas del verbo inglés se resumen en las siguientes notas.

Indicativo

(a) Presente: tiene la misma forma que el infinitivo en todas las personas menos la tercera del singular; en ésta, se añade una **-s** al infinitivo, p.ej. **he sells**, o se añade **-es** si el infinitivo termina en sibilante (los sonidos [s], [z], [ʃ] y [tʃ]; en la escritura **-ss, -zz, -sh** y **-ch**, etc). Esta **-s** añadida tiene dos pronunciaciones: tras consonante sorda se pronuncia sorda [s], p.ej. **scoffs** [skɒfs], **likes** [laɪks], **taps** [tæps], **waits** [weɪts], **baths** [bɑːθs]; tras consonante sonora se pronuncia sonora, p.ej. **robs** [rɒbz], **bends** [bendz], **seems** [siːmz], **gives** [gɪvz], **bathes** ['beɪðz]; **-es** se pronuncia también sonora tras sibilante o consonante sonora, o letra final del infinitivo, p.ej. **races** ['reɪsɪz], **urges** ['ɜːdʒɪz], **lashes** ['læʃɪz], **passes** ['pɑːsɪz].

Los verbos que terminan en **-y** la cambian en **-ies** en la tercera persona del singular, p.ej. **tries**, **pities**, **satisfies**; pero son regulares los verbos que en el infinitivo tienen una vocal delante de la **-y**, p.ej. **pray – he prays, annoy – she annoys**.

El verbo **be** es irregular en todas las personas:

I am	we are
you are	you are
he is	they are

Tres verbos más tienen forma irregular en la tercera persona del singular:

do – he does [dʌz]	go – he goes [gəʊz]
have – he has [hæz]	

(b) Pretérito (o **pasado simple**) **y participio de pasado:** tienen la misma forma en inglés; se forman añadiendo **-ed** al infinitivo, p.ej. **paint – I painted – painted**, o bien añadiendo **-d** a los infinitivos terminados en **-e** muda, p.ej. **bare – I bared – bared, move – I moved – moved, revise – I revised – revised.** (Para los muchos verbos irregulares, véase la lista abajo.) Esta **-d** o **-ed** se pronuncia por lo general [t]: **raced** [reɪst], **passed** [pɑːst]; pero cuando se añade a un infinitivo terminado en consonante sonora o en **r**, se pronuncia [d], p.ej. **bared** [bɛəd], **moved** [muːvd], **seemed** [siːmd], **buzzed** [bʌzd]. Si el infinitivo termina en **-d** o **-t**, la desinencia **-ed** se pronuncia como una sílaba más, [ɪd], p.ej. **raided** [ˈreɪdɪd], **dented** [ˈdentɪd]. Para los verbos cuyo infinitivo termina en **-y**, véase **Verbos débiles** **(e)** abajo.

(c) Tiempos compuestos del pasado: se forman como en español con el verbo auxiliar **to have** y el participio de pasado: perfecto **I have painted**, pluscuamperfecto **I had painted**.

(d) Futuro y condicional (o **potencial**): se forma el futuro con el auxiliar **will** o **shall** y el infinitivo, p.ej.**I will do it, they shall not pass**; se forma el condicional (o potencial) con el auxiliar **would** o **should** y el infinitivo, p.ej. **I would go, if she should come**. Como en español y de igual formación existen los tiempos compuestos llamados futuro perfecto, p.ej. **I shall have finished**, y potencial compuesto, p.ej. **I would have paid**.

(e) Para cada tiempo del indicativo existe una forma continua que se forma con el tiempo apropiado del verbo **to be** (equivalente en este caso al español **estar**) y el participio de presente (véase abajo): **I am waiting, we were hoping, they will be buying it, they would still have been waiting, I had been painting all day.** Conviene subrayar que el modo de emplear estas formas continuas no corresponde siempre al sistema español.

Subjuntivo

Este modo tiene muy poco uso en inglés. En el presente tiene la misma forma que el infinitivo en todas las personas, **(that) I go**, **(that) she go** etc. En el pasado simple el único verbo que tiene forma especial es **to be**, que es **were** en todas las personas, **(that) I were**, **(that) we were** etc. En los demás casos donde la lógica de los tiempos en español pudiera parecer exigir una forma de subjuntivo en pasado, el inglés emplea el presente, p.ej. **he had urged that we do it at once**. El subjuntivo se emplea obligatoriamente en inglés en **if I were you, if he were to do it, were I to attempt it** (el indicativo **was** es tenido por vulgar en estas frases y análogas); se encuentra también en la frase fosilizada **so be it,** y en el lenguaje oficial de las actas, etc, p.ej. **it is agreed that nothing be done, it was resolved that the pier be painted** (pero son igualmente correctos **should be done, should be painted**).

Gerundio y participio de presente

Tienen la misma forma en inglés; se añade al infinitivo la desinencia **-ing**, p.ej. **washing, sending, passing**. Para las muchas irregularidades ortográficas de esta desinencia, véase la sección **Verbos débiles** abajo.

Voz pasiva

Se forma exactamente como en español, con el tiempo apropiado del verbo **to be** (equivalente en este caso a **ser**) y el participio de pasado: **we are forced to, he was killed, they had been injured, the company will be taken over, it ought to have been rebuilt, were it to be agreed**.

Imperativo

Hay solamente una forma, que es la del infinitivo: **tell me, come here, don't do that**.

VERBOS FUERTES (O IRREGULARES)

INFINITIVO	PRETÉRITO	PARTICIPIO DE PASADO
abide	abode *or* abided	abode *or* abided
arise	arose	arisen
awake	awoke *or* awaked	awoken *or* awaked
be	was, were	been
bear	bore	(*llevado*) borne, (*nacido*) born
beat	beat	beaten
become	became	become
beget	begot, (††) begat	begotten
begin	began	begun
bend	bent	bent
beseech	besought	besought
bet	bet *or* betted	bet *or* betted
bid (*ordenar*)	bade	bidden
(*licitar* etc)	bid	bid
bind	bound	bound
bite	bit	bitten
bleed	bled	bled
blow	blew	blown
break	broke	broken
breed	bred	bred
bring	brought	brought
build	built	built
burn	burned *or* burnt	burned *or* burnt
burst	burst	burst
buy	bought	bought
can	could	–
cast	cast	cast
catch	caught	caught
choose	chose	chosen
cleave[1] (*vt*)	clove *or* cleft	cloven *or* cleft
cleave[2] (*vi*)	cleaved, (††) clave	cleaved
cling	clung	clung
come	came	come
cost (*vt*)	costed	costed
(*vi*)	cost	cost
creep	crept	crept
cut	cut	cut
deal	dealt	dealt
dig	dug	dug
do	did	done
draw	drew	drawn
dream	dreamed *or* dreamt	dreamed *or* dreamt
drink	drank	drunk
drive	drove	driven
dwell	dwelt	dwelt
eat	ate	eaten
fall	fell	fallen
feed	fed	fed
feel	felt	felt
fight	fought	fought
find	found	found
flee	fled	fled
fling	flung	flung
fly	flew	flown
forbid	forbad(e)	forbidden
forget	forgot	forgotten
forsake	forsook	forsaken
freeze	froze	frozen
get	got	got, (*US*) gotten
gild	gilded	gilded *or* gilt
gird	girded *or* girt	girded *or* girt
give	gave	given
go	went	gone

INFINITIVO	PRETÉRITO	PARTICIPIO DE PASADO
grind	ground	ground
grow	grew	grown
hang	hung, (*Law*) hanged	hung, (*Law*) hanged
have	had	had
hear	heard	heard
heave	heaved, (*Naut*) hove	heaved, (*Naut*) hove
hew	hewed	hewed *or* hewn
hide	hid	hidden
hit	hit	hit
hold	held	held
hurt	hurt	hurt
keep	kept	kept
kneel	knelt	knelt
know	knew	known
lade	laded	laden
lay	laid	laid
lead	led	led
lean	leaned *or* leant	leaned *or* leant
leap	leaped *or* leapt	leaped *or* leapt
learn	learned *or* learnt	learned *or* learnt
leave	left	left
lend	lent	lent
let	let	let
lie	lay	lain
light	lit *or* lighted	lit *or* lighted
lose	lost	lost
make	made	made
may	might	–
mean	meant	meant
meet	met	met
mow	mowed	mown *or* mowed
pay	paid	paid
put	put	put
quit	quit *or* quitted	quit *or* quitted
read [riːd]	read [red]	read [red]
rend	rent	rent
rid	rid	rid
ride	rode	ridden
ring	rang	rung
rise	rose	risen
run	ran	run
saw	sawed	sawed *or* sawn
say	said	said
see	saw	seen
seek	sought	sought
sell	sold	sold
send	sent	sent
set	set	set
sew	sewed	sewn
shake	shook	shaken
shave	shaved	shaved *or* shaven
shear	sheared	sheared *or* shorn
shed	shed	shed
shine	shone	shone
shoe	shod	shod
shoot	shot	shot
show	showed	shown *or* showed
shrink	shrank	shrunk
shut	shut	shut
sing	sang	sung
sink	sank	sunk
sit	sat	sat
slay	slew	slain
sleep	slept	slept

INFINITIVO	PRETÉRITO	PARTICIPIO DE PASADO
slide	slid	slid
sling	slung	slung
slink	slunk	slunk
slit	slit	slit
smell	smelled *or* smelt	smelled *or* smelt
smite	smote	smitten
sow	sowed	sowed *or* sown
speak	spoke	spoken
speed (*vt*)	speeded	speeded
(*vi*)	sped	sped
spell	spelled *or* spelt	spelled *or* spelt
spend	spent	spent
spill	spilled *or* spilt	spilled *or* spilt
spin	spun, (††) span	spun
spit	spat	spat
split	split	split
spoil	spoiled *or* spoilt	spoiled *or* spoilt
spread	spread	spread
spring	sprang	sprung
stand	stood	stood
stave	stove *or* staved	stove *or* staved
steal	stole	stolen
stick	stuck	stuck
sting	stung	stung
stink	stank	stunk
strew	strewed	strewed *or* strewn

INFINITIVO	PRETÉRITO	PARTICIPIO DE PASADO
stride	strode	stridden
strike	struck	struck
string	strung	strung
strive	strove	striven
swear	swore	sworn
sweep	swept	swept
swell	swelled	swollen
swim	swam	swum
swing	swung	swung
take	took	taken
teach	taught	taught
tear	tore	torn
tell	told	told
think	thought	thought
thrive	throve *or* thrived	thriven *or* thrived
throw	threw	thrown
thrust	thrust	thrust
tread	trod	trodden
wake	woke *or* waked	woken *or* waked
wear	wore	worn
weave	wove	woven
weep	wept	wept
win	won	won
wind	wound	wound
wring	wrung	wrung
write	wrote	written

N.B. No constan en esta lista los verbos compuestos con prefijo etc; para ellos véase el verbo básico, p.ej. para **forbear** véase **bear**, para **understand** véase **stand**.

VERBOS DÉBILES CON IRREGULARIDAD ORTOGRÁFICA

(a) Hay muchos verbos cuya ortografía varía ligeramente en el participio de pasado y en el gerundio. Son los que terminan en consonante simple precedida de vocal simple acentuada; antes de añadirles la desinencia **-ed** o **-ing**, se dobla la consonante:

Infinitivo	*Participio de pasado*	*Gerundio*
sob	sobbed	sobbing
wed	wedded	wedding
lag	lagged	lagging
control	controlled	controlling
dim	dimmed	dimming
tan	tanned	tanning
tap	tapped	tapping
prefer	preferred	preferring
pat	patted	patting

(pero **cook-cooked-cooking**, **fear-feared-fearing**, **roar-roared-roaring**, donde la vocal no es simple y por tanto no se dobla la consonante).

(b) Los verbos que terminan en **-c** la cambian en **-ck** al añadirse las desinencias **-ed**, **-ing**:

frolic	frolicked	frolicking
traffic	trafficked	trafficking

(c) Los verbos terminados en **-l**, **-p**, aunque precedida de vocal átona, tienen doblada la consonante en el participio de pasado y en el gerundio en el inglés británico, pero simple en el de Estados Unidos:

grovel	*(Brit)* grovelled *(US)* groveled	*(Brit)* grovelling *(US)* groveling
travel	*(Brit)* travelled *(US)* traveled	*(Brit)* travelling *(US)* traveling
worship	*(Brit)* worshipped *(US)* worshiped	*(Brit)* worshipping *(US)* worshiping

Nota – existe la misma diferencia en los sustantivos formados sobre tales verbos: *(Brit)* traveller = *(US)* traveler, *(Brit)* worshipper = *(US)* worshiper.

(d) Si el verbo termina en **-e** muda, se suprime ésta al añadir las desinencias **-ed**, **-ing**:

rake	raked	raking
care	cared	caring
smile	smiled	smiling
move	moved	moving
invite	invited	inviting

(Pero se conserva esta **-e** muda delante de **-ing** en los verbos **dye**, **singe** y otros, y en los pocos que terminan en **-oe**: **dyeing**, **singeing**, **hoeing**.)

(e) Si el verbo termina en **-y** (con las dos pronunciaciones de [ɪ] y [aɪ]) se cambia ésta en **-ied** (con las pronunciaciones respectivas de [ɪd] y [aɪd]) para formar el pretérito y el participio de pasado: **worry-worried-worried**; **pity-pitied-pitied**; **falsify-falsified-falsified**; **try-tried-tried**. El gerundio de tales verbos es regular: **worrying**, **trying** etc. Pero el gerundio de los verbos monosílabos **die**, **lie**, **vie** se escribe **dying**, **lying**, **vying**.

Aspects of Word Formation in Spanish

Processes of word formation in Spanish are in some respects far richer and more complex than those of English, and users of the dictionary may find the following notes of interest as guides which both draw together and extend information conveyed in the main alphabetic list.

1 Prefixes and prefixed elements

These very largely correspond to those of English when drawn, as so many are, from the common Graeco-Latin stock: **contra-**, **des-**, **dis-**, **ex-**, **hiper-**, **hipo-**, **para-**, **re-**, **ultra-** and so on, with **auto-** representing both English **auto-** and **self-**. There is normally total correspondence also in the immense range of scientific elements, allowance being made for phonetic and orthographic adjustments such as **lympho-/linfo-**. Elements may build up in blinding-with-science advertisements such as that for **electrofisiohidroterapias**. There are a few traditional Spanish intensifying prefixes which have no corresponding English forms: see **re-**, **requete-**, **recontra-**, also **archi-** which is much more used than **arch-** in English. These may be combined for exce tional emphasis: **archirrequetedicho** 'oft-repeated'.

2 Formation by suffix

(a) In both languages many suffixes of Latin origin correspond perfectly and will not be discussed here: **-al/-al**, **-ific(al)/-ífico**, **-ity/-idad**, **-ous/-oso**, **-tion/-ción**, and others. It is probable but not wholly predictable that in both languages on any one base the full range of forms can be built: for example **-izar**, **-izado**, **-izante**, **-izaje**, **-ización**, **-izacionar**, **-izacionismo**, though Spanish with its greater degree of latinity may much exceed English in this regard (**tecnocratizarse** 'to become technocratic'; 'to become dominated by technocrats'; **desgubernamentalización**, **destrascendentalización**). See further remarks below on **-able**, **-abilidad**.

(b) For other suffixes, hundreds of items have been listed in the main body of the dictionary because they are sufficiently common to warrant this. They are of two types. In the first group are those words which have become fully 'lexicalized' and need separate treatment, such as **lentillas**, **mesilla**, **mujerzuela**, **palabrota**, **plazoleta**. In the second group, an occasional series has been included in the main dictionary as an illustration of the process here under discussion: see for example **amigacho-amigazo-amiguete-amigote-amiguito**. In any case, the notion of what may be considered 'lexicalized' is very unsure.

(c) Identification of the base word is easy in most cases. Normally, but far from always, the suffixed form retains the gender of the original noun. Certain changes of what is or becomes with suffix a medial consonant need to be borne in mind: **lazo-lacito**, **voz-vocecita**, **barco-barquito**, **loco-loquillo**. Sometimes two or even more suffixes are built on a base: **facilonería** consists of **fácil** + **-ón** + **-ería**, **hombrachón** consists of **hombre** + **-acho** + **-ón**, **tristoncete** consists of **triste** + **-ón** + **ete**, **gentucilla** consists of **gente** + **-uza** + **-illa**, while real complexities are offered by **es una marisabidilla** and **hay peces pero son chiquititecillos**. The need for a compounding consonant is seen in some formations: **hombre** will not make ***hombrito** or ***hombrillo**, but **hombrecito**, **hombrecillo**.

(d) Nearly all the suffixes to be listed below are nouns and adjectives. There is little one can say about the formation of verbs except to note that it is less free than in English (in which one can all too readily say 'the troops will be helicoptered in', 'the match was weathered off', 'please have this text word-processed and the data accessed'). New verbs almost always belong to the first **-ar** conjugation (including **-ear**, **-ificar**, **-izar**) and may themselves be built on noun or adjectival suffixes or related to them (eg **mariconear** supposing noun suffix **-eo**).

(e) Few adverbs are listed below; they are readily formed in the standard way from the feminine form of the adjective + **-mente**. Speakers and writers of Spanish in ordinary colloquial registers tend to avoid these forms (this does not refer to such ordinary forms as eg **rápidamente**), preferring less pretentious circumlocutions ('de una manera ...', etc), but the **-mente** forms appear powerfully in literary and journalistic writing and are often much more expressive than the English adverbial form in **-ly**. Thus we find **obrar maquiavélicamente** 'to act in a Machiavellian fashion', **pintar goyescamente** 'to paint in the manner of Goya', **una fruta gustativamente superior** 'a fruit which is superior in terms of flavour', **generacionalmente hablando** 'speaking in terms of generations', **solicitar improrrogablemente** 'apply with no possible extension of the deadline', **una republiquilla organizada mafiosamente** 'a potty republic organized on Mafia lines', and even as an imaginative nonce-word **huyó gacelamente** 'she fled with the grace of a gazelle' (there being no base adjective ***gacelo**).

(f) The usage discussed below is that of Spain. Latin-American Spanish offers notable differences from this: some suffixes of Spain are hardly used in Latin America, while **-ito** is used far more and often without any perceptible diminutive or emotive function (eg **Con permiso** 'May I come in?' in Spain may be **Con permisito** in Venezuela). See eg **ahorita**, **lueguito**.

(g) While some of the suffixes listed below present no semantic problem, being wholly objective or neutral (when designating largeness or smallness), some of these and many others may carry an emotive charge (intensifying, belittling, self-deprecatory, ironical, admiring ...) for the speaker or writer and this is often a subtle one. It follows that to give an English translation or even an impression in a few words is difficult: the reader should try to form his own sense by inspecting a wide range of examples of the same suffix, including some which are cross-referenced to the main dictionary. The expressive wealth of formation by suffix can be illustrated by the following collection of forms all based on **rojo** in its political sense and gathered from the press in recent years: **rojamen**, **rojazo**, **rojeras**, **rojería**, **rojerío**, **rojete**, **rojillo**, **rojismo**, **rojista**, **rojoide**.

-able, -abilidad (*also* -ible, -ibilidad)

This suffix often expresses more than the corresponding English **-able**, **-ability** (or English does not tolerate the corresponding forms). Examples are **idolatrable** 'that can be idolatrized', **improrrogable** 'that cannot be extended', **jubilable** 'of pensionable age'. The latinate nature of Spanish permits such formations as **inasequibilidad**, **inconsultabilidad**, **la indescarrilabilidad del nuevo tren**.

-acho, -acha

Pejorative noun suffix: **vulgacho** 'the common herd'. Compare in the dictionary **hombracho**, **populacho**, **ricacho**.

-aco, -aca

Pejorative noun suffix: **hombraco** 'contemptible fellow, horrible chap', **tiparraco** 'odious individual, creep'. Compare in the dictionary **libraco**, **pajarraco**.

-ada

(i) A noun suffix expressing 'an act by or typical of': **carlistada** 'Carlist uprising', **payasada** 'clownish trick'; compare in the dictionary **bobada**, **perrada**, **puñalada**.

(ii) A noun suffix implying some notion of collectivity, as in **extranjerada** 'group of foreigners', **parrafada** 'good long chat', and compare in the dictionary **camada**, **hornada**, **indiada**, **muslada**. Beyond these one finds also an intensifying function, as in **gozada**, **liada**, **riada**, with which perhaps belong **panzada**, **tripada** 'bellyful'.

-ado, -aje

These noun suffixes of similar function are enjoying some popularity at the moment in new formations which express a process (often rendered by English **-ing**): **blanqueado** and **lavado (del dinero)** 'laundering (of money)', **lastrado** 'ballasting', **clonaje** 'cloning', **reciclaje** 'recycling'. A particular function of **-ado** is to express a collectivity, in English 'the body of...': see in the dictionary **alumnado**, **campesinado**, **estudiantado**, **profesorado**.

-ajo, -aja

Strongly pejorative noun suffix: **muñecajo** 'rotten old doll', **papelajo** 'dirty old bit of paper'; see further in the dictionary **pintarrajo**. Among adjectives one finds **pequeñajo** 'wretchedly small'.

-amen

A humorous augmentative: **barrigamen** 'grossly fat belly', **labiamen** 'great red gash of a made-up mouth', **papelamen** 'lots of paper'. Compare in the dictionary **caderamen**, **culamen**, **tetamen**, whose tone is warmly appreciative.

-ante

A neutral adjectival suffix which generally corresponds to English **-ing**. Self-explanatory are eg **destripante**, **gimoteante**, **lastrante**, **masificante**, **mistificante**, **mitificante**: less transparent are the **crónicas masacrantes** 'vicious reports' which a journalist wrote about an event. Compare in the dictionary **golfante**, **hilarante**, **pimpante**, **preocupante**, and see also **-izante**.

-ata

See in the dictionary the group **bocata**, **drogata**, **fumata**, **tocata**, colloquial variations created by young people.

-azo, -aza

(i) Augmentative of more or less neutral tone: **animalazo** 'huge creature, whacking great brute', **generalazo** 'important general', **golpazo** 'heavy blow'.

(ii) Augmentative of favourable tone: **golazo** 'great goal', **morenazo** 'man with dark good looks'; 'man with a lovely tan', **talentazo** 'immense talent'.

(iii) Augmentative of unfavourable tone: **cochinaza** 'dirty sow of a woman', **locaza** 'outrageous old queen', **melenaza** 'great mop of long hair'.

(iv) The suffix may signify 'a blow with ...': **ladrillazo** 'blow with a brick', **misilazo** 'missile strike'; compare in the dictionary **aldabonazo**, **codazo**, etc.

(v) The suffix may signify 'a sound made with ...': **cornetazo** 'bugle-call, blast on the bugle'; compare in the dictionary **telefonazo** and (with probable sounds) **frenazo**.

(vi) The (attempted) blow may be a military one, a coup or attack: in the past a **gibraltarazo** may have been contemplated, and there was certainly a **malvinazo**. See in the dictionary **cuartelazo**, **decretazo**, **tejerazo**.

-e

This is increasingly used as a noun suffix to refer to a process: **manduque** 'eating', **tueste** 'roasting' (of coffee). Compare in the dictionary **cuelgue**, **derrame**, **desfase**, **desmadre**.

-ejo, -eja

Mostly a pejorative suffix: **discursejo** 'rotten speech', **grupejo** 'insignificant little group', **nos costó un milloncejo** 'it cost us all of a million', **todo por unas cuantas pesetejas** 'all for a few measly pesetas'. See in the dictionary **animalejo**, **caballejo**, **palabreja**. Sometimes the sense is simply diminutive, eg **gracejo**, **rinconcejo**.

-eo

This like **-e** refers to a process or continuing act, and is much commoner: **guitarreo** 'strumming on the guitar', **ligoteo** 'chatting-up', **mariposeo** 'flirting', **marisqueo** 'gathering shellfish'. See in the dictionary **cachondeo**, **gimoteo**, **musiqueo**, **papeleo**.

-eras

A strongly intensifying masculine singular suffix: **guarreras** 'filthy person', **macheras** 'over-the-top macho man'. Compare **boceras**, **golferas**, **guaperas**.

-ería

Among a very wide variety of applications of this common suffix one may distinguish a general notion of quality inherent in the base noun or adjective: **marchosería**, **matonería**, **mitinería**, **milagrería**, **pelmacería** (compare in the dictionary **chiquillería**, **nadería**, **patriotería**, **tontería**). The suffix may also indicate 'place where', as in **floristería**, **frutería**; a recent invention is **bocatería** 'sandwich bar'.

-ero

The wide application of this mainly adjectival suffix may be gauged from eg **cafetero**, **carero**, **faldero**, **futbolero**, **patriotero**, **pesetero** in the dictionary. A **barco atunero/bacaladero/camaronero/marisquero** will fish for tunny, cod, shrimps, and shellfish respectively.

-esco

English **-esque** is only a pale equivalent of this adjectival suffix. Self-explanatory are **chaplinesco**, **tarzanesco**, and in the dictionary **goyesco**, **mitinesco**, **oficinesco**.

-ete, -eta

Mildly diminutive noun and adjectival suffix: **alegrete** 'a bit merry', **guapete** 'quite handsome'; **unos duretes** 'a few measly pesetas', **tartaleta** 'small cake'. Compare in the dictionary **galancete**, **palacete**, **pobrete**.

-ez

A noun suffix which can often be translated by the English abstract **-ness**: **grisez**, **majez**, **menudez**, **modernez**, **muchachez**, and in the dictionary eg **gelidez**, **morenez**, **testarudez**.

-iano

A common adjectival suffix which English **-ian** might but usually cannot represent when attached to personal names: not only, in the dictionary, native **calderoniano**, **galdosiano**, **lorquiano**, but also **galbraithiano**, **goethiano**, **grouchiano**, **joyciano** (and **joyceano**), **una novela lampedusiana**. Some forms may puzzle foreign learners: eg **la poesía juanramoniana** refers to the work of the Spanish poet Juan Ramón Jiménez.

-ico, -ica

As an adjective, this is a regional (Aragon and Navarre, Granada, Murcia) variant of **-ito**: **me duele un tantico**, **¿te han dejado solico?** As a noun it is a contemptuous diminutive: **cobardica**, **llorica**, **miedica**, **mierdica**, **sólo me pidió medio milloncico**. Compare in the dictionary **acusica**, **roñica**.

-il

An adjectival suffix which is not specially pejorative but conveys a mildly ironical tone. Senses are transparent: **caciquil**, **curanderil**, **una dieta garbancil**, **machil** 'a bit too macho', **ministeril**, **ratonil**. Very expressive are **urraquil**, which depends on the word **urraca**, 'magpie', with its thievish propensities, and **sus encantos cleopatriles** 'her femme fatale (-like) charms'.

-illo, -illa

A noun and adjectival suffix, gently diminutive and often implying a degree of good-humoured condescension. For adjectives, consider **un vino ligerillo** 'a pleasantly light wine', **es dificilillo** 'it's a wee bit tricky'. For nouns, **un lugarcillo** 'a nice little place', **jefecillo** 'local boss, petty boss', **jequecillo** 'petty sheik', **un olorcillo a corrupción** 'a slight smell of corruption'. More plainly pejorative are **empleadillo**, **ministrillo**, **personajillo**.

-ín, -ina

A mildly approving suffix for nouns and adjectives, quite widely used but specially attached to Asturias and Granada: **guapín**, **guapina**, **jovencina**, **monín**, **pequeñín; cafetín** is in part demeaning but also affectionate, and **tontín** to a child will not cause alarm.

-ísimo

This suffix is not one of the degrees of comparison but implies 'very' with various nuances:

(i) 'Very', neutral in tone: **un asunto importantísimo** 'a very important matter, a most important matter'; **una cuestión discutidísima** 'a highly controversial question'; **un desarrolladísimo sentido de orgullo** 'a very highly developed sense of pride'; **es dificilísimo** 'it is extremely difficult'.

(ii) More emotionally: **es simpatiquísimo** 'he's terribly nice, he's awfully kind'; **es guapísima** 'she really is pretty'.

(iii) Exaggerating somewhat in order to impress: **un libro grandísimo** 'an enormous great book, a megatome'; **una comida costosísima**. There may be humour or irony, depending on context: **la superfinísima actriz**, **esta cursilísima costumbre**.

(iv) Passionately patriotic: **aquel españolísimo plato** 'that most Spanish of all dishes'; **la madrileñísima plaza de Santa Ana** 'St Anne's Square which is so (endearingly) typical of Madrid'.

(v) Exceptionally, one finds this suffix attached to a noun: **aquí ella es la jefísima** 'she's the only real boss round here'.

(vi) Adverbs may be formed in the usual way on some of these forms, eg **brillantísimamente**, **riquísimamente**.

-ismo

In hundreds of simple cases, Spanish words in **-ismo** naturally correspond to English **-ism**. But Spanish uses the suffix much more and in creations which English has to express in a circumlocutory way: while **japonesismo** might just be 'Japanese-ness', and **ilegalismo** is hardly more than **ilegalidad** 'illegality',

el guitarrismo moderno has to be 'modern guitar-playing' and **gorilismo** 'rule by bully-boys'. **El felipismo** sums up criticism of the former Spanish Prime Minister Felipe González.

Real complications start with such examples as **gaudinismo** 'style and practices of the architect Gaudí', **gubernamentalismo** 'government interventionism, tendency for the government to intervene in everything', **el paragüismo de los gallegos** 'devotion of the Galicians to their umbrellas' and in America **quemimportismo** 'couldn't-care-less attitude'.

-ista

This forms nouns of common gender and adjectives also. Simple cases such as **comunista** again correspond precisely to English, but many do not: an **independentista** supports an independence movement, that is **un movimiento independentista**; a **madridista** is a supporter of Real Madrid football club, and many Spanish teams acquire similarly-designated supporters; a **plusmarquista** is a record-holder and a **mariposista** specializes in the butterfly stroke. Compare in the dictionary **congresista**, **juerguista**, **ordenancista**.

-itis

A few formations on this adopt the suffix of eg **bronquitis** and humorously imply a medical condition: **barriguitis** 'tendency to get a paunch, paunchiness', **concursitis** 'obsessive wish to enter competitions', **empatitis** 'tendency to draw games', **mudancitis** 'disease which leads one to move house perpetually'. See in the dictionary **gandulitis**, **holgazanitis**.

-ito, -ita

This suffix is the commonest of all. One can discern at least three categories:

(i) The purely diminutive: **Juanito** 'Johnny', **su hijito** 'her small son, her baby', **es más bien bajita** 'she's rather on the short side'. Among adverbs one finds **salimos tempranito**, **pues hazlo prontito**.

(ii) Diminutive with added affective (usually kindly) nuance: **jugosito** 'nice and juicy', **limpito** 'clean as a new pin', **un golito** 'a nice little goal', **iban cogiditos de la mano**, **¡pobrecito!** 'poor old chap!', 'poor little fellow!', etc. One may be self-deprecating: **te traigo un regalito**, **ofrecemos una fiestecita en casa**, or one may need to apologize for troubling others: **¿me echas una firmita aquí?** 'could you please sign here?' To small children it is natural to say **hay que ser educaditos** 'we must be on our best behaviour'.

(iii) Other uses express a kind of superlative: **ahora mismito** 'this very instant', **estaba solito** 'he was all on his own', **están calentitos** 'they're piping hot', **lo mejorcito que haya** 'the very best there is'.

-izante

This adjectival and noun suffix may correspond to English **-izing**, as in **medida liberalizante**, **tendencia modernizante**, but sometimes goes beyond this: **idiotizante** 'stupefying', **colores mimetizantes**, **hormona masculinizante**. Compare **teorizante** and others in the dictionary.

-izo

This adjectival suffix expresses the 'quality' of the base word: see in the dictionary eg **acomodadizo**, **huidizo**, **quebradizo**, **rollizo**.

-ocracia

Spanish **meritocracia** = English 'meritocracy', but Spanish seems to have a greater capacity for rather bitterly humorous formations with this suffix: **dedocracia**, **falocracia**, **yernocracia**.

-oide

This adjectival and noun suffix implies 'somewhat, rather', and is always pejorative: **extranjeroide** 'somewhat foreign', **liberaloide** 'pseudo-liberal', **estas tramas fascistoides** 'these quasi-fascist schemes'.

-ón, -ona

This very frequent noun and adjectival suffix has several differing connotations:

(i) purely augmentative: **muchachón**, **generalón** 'really important general', **pistolón**, **liberalón**, **lingotón** 'big shot of whisky' (etc); among adjectives, **grandón** 'tall and solidly built', **gastón** 'free-spending', **docilón** 'extremely placid'.

(ii) augmentative with a strongly approving tone: **mimosón**, **simpaticón**, **guapetón**.

(iii) augmentative with unpleasant or strongly ironic nuances: **facilón** 'trite', **pegarse un madrugón** 'to get up at the crack of dawn', **hombrón** 'hulking great brute', **milagrón** 'great miracle', **movidón** (see **movida** in the dictionary).

-osis

Like **-itis**, this is for jocular formations which echo the common suffix of medical terms: **ligosis** 'obsessive womanizing'.

-ote, -ota

An adjectival and noun augmentative, with varying nuances. Among adjectives, **gordote**, **guapote**, **liberalote**, **mansote** (of a bull) carry little extra charge, as is the case also with nouns **drogota**, **muchachote**, **pasota**. Stronger feelings emerge with **presumidote** 'impossibly vain', **militarote** 'overblown braggart soldier'. One man who stole a glance at an attractive girl took a longer look, explaining that his **miradita** became a **miradota**.

-ucho, -ucha

Much like **-uco**, **-uca**, and commoner: **debilucho** 'weakish', **delicaducho** 'rather delicate', **delgaducho** 'terribly thin, scrawny', **morenucho** 'extremely swarthy'; a **hotelucho** would be classed as minus two stars. See in the dictionary **cuartucho**, **novelucha**.

-uco, -uca

This is a diminutive suffix, not common except perhaps in Santander province (**niñuco** 'very small boy'), and more especially a pejorative one: **frailuco** 'contemptible little priest', **mujeruca** 'very odd little woman'.

-udo, -uda

This adjectival suffix expresses the notion of 'possessing (the base quality) in abundance': **mostachudo**, **patilludo**, **talentudo; una caligrafía garrapatuda** 'nasty scrawled writing'. Compare in the dictionary **concienzudo**, **huesudo**, **linajudo**, **melenudo**, **suertudo**.

-uelo, -uela

A diminutive and sometimes affectionate suffix: **gordezuelo**, **pequeñuelo**, **muchachuelo**, **tontuela**.

-ujo, -uja

A strongly pejorative suffix for adjective and noun: **papelujo** 'wretched bit of paper'; **estrechujo**, **pequeñujo**.

-uzo, -uza

A very strongly pejorative suffix for adjective and noun: **marranuzo** 'filthy, stinking'; **carnuza** 'rotten awful meat'.

3 Designations of women in the professions etc.

(a) In recent decades the entry of women into many professions previously more or less closed to them has caused developments and problems for Spanish with its consistent gender-marking of nouns (in contrast to English with its very restricted perception of gender in such usages as 'she will dock tomorrow' and 'she's been a very good car', together, naturally, with the full range of biological pairs 'fox/vixen', 'bull/cow' and so on). What follows is an attempt to outline aspects of usage and problems in Spanish, without recommendations which it would be perilous to offer in a time of rapid change. Alternative possibilities have been offered in many entries in the main text of the dictionary. The remarks relate to Peninsular Spanish; usage in Latin America, especially in countries with strongly conservative social structures, is very varied and often different from that of Spain.

(b) There is generally no problem about the morphology (forms) of the feminine. A noun whose masculine ends in **-o** has a feminine in **-a: la médica**, **la ministra**, **la bióloga**, **la bioquímica**. The same is true of **-or** and **-ora**: **la instructora**, **la lectora**, **la embajadora**, **la conductora**, and of other pairs such as **alcalde/alcaldesa**, **coronel/coronela**, **capitán/capitana**, **presidente/presidenta**, **jefe/jefa**, while all nouns in **-ista** are of common gender anyway: **el/la periodista** etc. (note however the special case of **el modisto**). There is doubt as between **la juez** and **la jueza**.

(c) Usage, however, often invalidates any automatic application of forms mentioned above. On the one hand, some women in the professions may feel that they have attained full status and equality with men colleagues only when the established standard word is applied to them: one may expect **la abogada** and this will often be correct, but sometimes a woman prefers to be **la médico** and equally **la arquitecto, la dramaturgo**.

As the presence of women increases in posts originally held only by men, the feminine form seems to take over the masculine when applied to women, becoming more acceptable and widely used.

(d) There is a special problem when a feminine form already exists in a pejorative sense which may for a time preclude, for some speakers and writers, its use about a woman with a newly-attained professional or other status: such words as **jefa** and **socia** are concerned here. It was noticed that the woman circulation manager of a Spanish newspaper sent out subscription forms for some years signing her name over the words **Jefe de Márketing** and then changing the first to **Jefa**. The women members of a society will more likely be **las miembros** but one notes a tendency for them to be **las socias**, showing that the old pejorative sense is no longer a bar to this. There is also a group of words for sciences whose existence may in some contexts cause doubt: because **la física** is 'physics' there may be uncertainty about whether a woman physicist should be **una física** or **una físico**. A few special cases cause difficulties of other kinds: since **la policía** is established as 'the police force', it is not readily applicable to a policewoman in case confusion should arise, and informants specify that while they will refer to **una policía** 'a policewoman' and **unas policías** 'several policewomen', they would avoid such usage with the definite article and say **la mujer policía** 'the policewoman' or possibly take refuge in the safely bi-gender **la agente**. If there is doubt a woman should naturally be asked which designation she herself prefers.

(e) In the category of military and similar ranks older senses have been relegated as archaisms: **la coronela** was 'the colonel's lady' but is now '(woman) colonel', **la embajadora** is not 'the ambassador's wife' but '(woman) ambassador', and **la alcaldesa** is '(woman) mayor'. A woman minister in a nonconformist church may safely be called **la pastora**, but it is wholly unsure by what term women priests in the Anglican Church are or will be known.

4 Attributive use of nouns

(a) Examples of such formations as **el patrón oro** go back to the 17th century, but remained rare until recent times when there has been an explosion of the attributive use of nouns (defined as the use of a noun in a qualifying or adjectival function but without concord of number or gender). Much of this is owed to the influence of English, but some formations now go well beyond any possible pattern existing in English. **Buque fantasma** translates English 'ghost ship' and **gobierno fantasma** was once formed as a calque on English 'shadow cabinet', but the usage then develops a momentum of its own in Spanish and we find **empresa fantasma**, **gol fantasma** and other expressive formations.

(b) Well-established usages are covered in many cases by entries in the dictionary. Such are **acuerdo marco**, **cuestión clave**, **cárcel modelo**, **emisión pirata**, **fecha límite**, **niño prodigio**, **país satélite**, **peso pluma**, **piso piloto**, **programa coloquio**, **reunión cumbre**. There is a range of attributives which may go with eg **efecto**: **efecto boomerang/dominó/embudo/escoba/invernadero**. Formations such as **faros antiniebla**, **manifestaciones antihuelga**, **medidas antipolución** are now standard, as are many others in the domains of fashion (**falda pantalón**, **falda tubo**) and cuisine, etc. These correspond closely to English models. Statements about colour in attributive form are also standard usage, eg **un vestido color lila**, **uniformes verde oliva**, **cortinas verde oscuro** (but naturally **cortinas verdes** with concord). The same is true of phrases with **modelo**, **tipo**, and similar words: **un coche modelo Tiburón 1500**, **aviones tipo Concorde**, **un sombrero estilo Bogart**, and also of biological definitions such as **el pájaro hembra**, **las musarañas macho**.

(c) Creativity in this aspect in journalistic Spanish has now gone well beyond any possible English model, however: examples are **un jugador promesa**, **horas punta**, **tecnología punta**, **el grupo revelación del año**, **una teoría puente**. Abbreviations may figure too in a kind of journalistic shorthand: **tres aviones USA**, **dos agentes CIA**.

(d) While the principle of non-concord is the soundest one, as above, speakers may occasionally treat the attributive element as an adjective and assign it concord for number (but never for gender): **hay dos palabras claves**, **pedimos pagos extras**. One finds both **hombres rana** and **hombres ranas**.

Note: *preceding a word denotes an invented form.

Numerals

CARDINAL NUMBERS / NÚMEROS CARDINALES

nought, zero	**0**	cero
one	**1**	(*m*) uno, (*f*) una
two	**2**	dos
three	**3**	tres
four	**4**	cuatro
five	**5**	cinco
six	**6**	seis
seven	**7**	siete
eight	**8**	ocho
nine	**9**	nueve
ten	**10**	diez
eleven	**11**	once
twelve	**12**	doce
thirteen	**13**	trece
fourteen	**14**	catorce
fifteen	**15**	quince
sixteen	**16**	dieciséis
seventeen	**17**	diecisiete
eighteen	**18**	dieciocho
nineteen	**19**	diecinueve
twenty	**20**	veinte
twenty-one	**21**	veintiuno (*see note* **B**)
twenty-two	**22**	veintidós
twenty-three	**23**	veintitrés
thirty	**30**	treinta
thirty-one	**31**	treinta y uno
thirty-two	**32**	treinta y dos
forty	**40**	cuarenta
fifty	**50**	cincuenta
sixty	**60**	sesenta
seventy	**70**	setenta
eighty	**80**	ochenta
ninety	**90**	noventa
ninety-nine	**99**	noventa y nueve
a (*or* one) hundred	**100**	cien, ciento (*see note* **C**)
a hundred and one	**101**	ciento uno
a hundred and two	**102**	ciento dos
a hundred and ten	**110**	ciento diez
a hundred and eighty-two	**182**	ciento ochenta y dos
two hundred	**200**	(*m*) doscientos, (*f*) –as
three hundred	**300**	(*m*) trescientos, (*f*) –as
four hundred	**400**	(*m*) cuatrocientos, (*f*) –as
five hundred	**500**	(*m*) quinientos, (*f*) –as
six hundred	**600**	(*m*) seiscientos, (*f*) –as
seven hundred	**700**	(*m*) setecientos, (*f*) –as
eight hundred	**800**	(*m*) ochocientos, (*f*) –as
nine hundred	**900**	(*m*) novecientos, (*f*) –as
a (*or* one) thousand	**1000**	mil
a thousand and two	**1002**	mil dos
two thousand	**2000**	dos mil
ten thousand	**10000**	diez mil
a (*or* one) hundred thousand	**100000**	cien mil
a (or one) million	**1000000**	un millón (*see note* **D**)
two million	**2000000**	dos millones (*see note* **D**)

Los números

Notes on usage of the cardinal numbers

A **One,** and the other numbers ending in one, agree in Spanish with the noun (stated or implied): *una casa, un coche, si se trata de pagar en libras ello viene a sumar treinta y una, había ciento una personas.*

B **21:** In Spanish there is some uncertainty when the number is accompanied by a feminine noun. In the spoken language both *veintiuna peseta* and *veintiuna pesetas* are heard; in 'correct' literary language only *veintiuna pesetas* is found. With a masculine noun the numeral is shortened in the usual way: *veintiún perros rabiosos.* These remarks apply also to 31, 41 etc.

C **100:** When the number is spoken alone or in counting a series of numbers both *cien* and *ciento* are heard. When there is an accompanying noun the form is always *cien: cien hombres, cien chicas.* In the compound numbers note 101 = *ciento uno*, 110 = *ciento diez*, but 100000 = *cien mil*.

D **1000000:** In Spanish the word *millón* is a noun, so the numeral takes *de* when there is a following noun: *un millón de fichas, tres millones de árboles quemados.*

E In Spanish the cardinal numbers may be used as nouns, as in English; they are always masculine: *jugó el siete de corazones, el once nacional de Ruritania, éste es el trece y nosotros buscamos el quince.*

F To divide the larger numbers clearly a point is traditionally used in Spanish where English places a comma: English 1,000 = Spanish 1.000, English 2,304,770 = Spanish 2.304.770. (This does not apply to dates: see below.)

ORDINAL NUMBERS / NÚMEROS ORDINALES

first	**1**	primero (*see note* **B**)
second	**2**	segundo
third	**3**	tercero (*see note* **B**)
fourth	**4**	cuarto
fifth	**5**	quinto
sixth	**6**	sexto
seventh	**7**	séptimo
eighth	**8**	octavo
ninth	**9**	noveno, nono
tenth	**10**	décimo
eleventh	**11**	undécimo
twelfth	**12**	duodécimo
thirteenth	**13**	decimotercio, decimotercero
fourteenth	**14**	decimocuarto
fifteenth	**15**	decimoquinto
sixteenth	**16**	decimosexto
seventeenth	**17**	decimoséptimo
eighteenth	**18**	decimoctavo
nineteenth	**19**	decimonoveno, decimonono
twentieth	**20**	vigésimo
twenty-first	**21**	vigésimo primero, vigésimo primo
twenty-second	**22**	vigésimo segundo
thirtieth	**30**	trigésimo
thirty-first	**31**	trigésimo primero, trigésimo primo
fortieth	**40**	cuadragésimo
fiftieth	**50**	quincuagésimo
sixtieth	**60**	sexagésimo

seventieth	**70**	septuagésimo
eightieth	**80**	octogésimo
ninetieth	**90**	nonagésimo
hundredth	**100**	centésimo
hundred and first	**101**	centésimo primero
hundred and tenth	**110**	centésimo décimo
two hundredth	**200**	ducentésimo
three hundredth	**300**	trecentésimo
four hundredth	**400**	cuadringentésimo
five hundredth	**500**	quingentésimo
six hundredth	**600**	sexcentésimo
seven hundredth	**700**	septingentésimo
eight hundredth	**800**	octingentésimo
nine hundredth	**900**	noningentésimo
thousandth	**1000**	milésimo
two thousandth	**2000**	dos milésimo
millionth	**1000000**	millonésimo
two millionth	**2000000**	dos millonésimo

Notes on usage of the ordinal numbers

A All these numbers are adjectives in *-o*, and therefore agree with the noun in number and gender: *la quinta vez, en segundas nupcias, en octavo lugar.*

B *Primero* and *tercero* are shortened to *primer, tercer* when they directly precede a masculine singular noun: *en el primer capítulo, l tercer hombre* (but *los primeros coches en llegar, el primero y más importante hecho*).

C In Spanish the ordinal numbers from 1 to 10 are commonly used; from 11 to 20 rather less; above 21 they are rarely written and almost never heard in speech (except for *milésimo*, which is frequent). The custom is to replace the forms for 21 and above by the cardinal number: *en el capítulo treinta y seis, celebran el setenta aniversario* (or *el aniversario setenta*), *en el poste ciento cinco contando desde la esquina.*

D **Kings, popes and centuries.** The ordinal numbers from 1 to 9 are employed for these in Spanish as in English: *en el siglo cuarto, Eduardo octavo, Pío nono, Enrique primero.* For 10 either the cardinal or the ordinal may be used: *siglo diez* or *siglo décimo, Alfonso diez* or *Alfonso décimo.* For 11 and above it is now customary to use only the cardinal number: *Alfonso once* (but *onceno* in the Middle Ages), *Juan veintitrés, en el siglo dieciocho.*

E **Abbreviations.** English 1st, 2nd, 3rd, 4th, 5th etc = Spanish 1° or 1er, 2°, 3° or 3er, 4°, 5° and so on (*f*: 1^{era}, 2^{a}).

F See also the notes on Dates, below.

DECIMALS — LAS DECIMALES

In Spanish a comma is written where English writes a point: English 3·56 (*three point five six*) = Spanish 3,56 (*tres coma cinco seis*); English ·07 (*point zero seven*) = Spanish ,07 (*coma cero siete*). The recurring decimal 3·3333 may be written in English as 3·3 and in Spanish as 3,3.

FRACTIONS — NÚMEROS QUEBRADOS

one half, a half	½	(m) *medio*, (f) *media*
one and a half helpings	1½	*(una) porción y media*
two and a half kilos	2½	*dos kilos y medio*
one third, a third	⅓	*un tercio, la tercera parte*
two thirds	⅔	*dos tercios, las dos terceras partes*
one quarter, a quarter	¼	*un cuarto, la cuarta parte*
three quarters	¾	*tres cuartos, las tres cuartas partes*
one sixth, a sixth	⅙	*un sexto, la sexta parte*
five and five sixths	5⅚	*cinco y cinco sextos*
one twelfth, a twelfth	1/12	*un duodécimo; un dozavo, la duodécima parte*
seven twelfths	7/12	*siete dozavos*
one hundredth, a hundredth	1/100	*un centésimo, una centésima parte*
one thousandth, a thousandth	1/1000	*un milésimo*

UNITS — NOMENCLATURA

3,684 is a four-digit number.	*3.684 es un número de cuatro dígitos (or guarismos).*
It contains 4 units, 8 tens, 6 hundreds and 3 thousands.	*Contiene 4 unidades, 8 decenas, 6 centenas y 3 unidades de millar.*
The decimal ·234 contains 2 tenths, 3 hundredths and 4 thousandths.	*La fracción decimal ,234 contiene 2 décimas, 3 centésimas y 4 milésimas.*

PERCENTAGES — LOS PORCENTAJES

2½% two and a half per cent	*2½ por 100*, (less frequently) *2½%; dos y medio por cien, dos y medio por ciento* (in spoken usage and among the authorities there is disagreement about *cien/ciento* here).
18% of the people here are over 65.	*El dieciocho por ciento de la gente aquí tienen mas de 65 años.*
Production has risen by 8%.	*La producción ha aumentado en un 8 por 100.*
(*See also* per, hundred *in the main text.*)	(*Véase también* por, cien/ciento *en el diccionario.*)

CALCULATIONS

8 + 6 = 14 eight and (*or* plus) six are (*or* make) fourteen
15 − 3 = 12 fifteen take away three are (*or* equals) twelve, three from fifteen leaves twelve
3 x 3 = 9 three threes are nine, three times three is nine
32 ÷ 8 = 4 thirty-two divided by eight is (*or* equals) four
3^2 = 9 three squared is nine
2^5 = 32 two to the fifth (*or* to the power of five) is (*or* equals) thirty-two
√16 = 4 the square root of sixteen is four

EL CÁLCULO

8 + 6 = 14 *ocho y (or más) seis son catorce*
15 − 3 = 12 *quince menos tres resta doce, de tres a quince van doce*
3 x 3 = 9 *tres por tres son nueve*
32 ÷ 8 = 4 *treinta y dos dividido por ocho es cuatro*
3^2 = 9 *tres al cuadrado son nueve*
2^5 = 32 *dos a la quinta potencia son treinta y dos*
√16 = 4 *la raíz cuadrada de dieciséis es cuatro.*

SIGNS

+	addition sign
+	plus sign (*eg* +7 = plus seven)
−	subtraction sign
−	minus sign (*eg* −3 = minus three)
x	multiplication sign
÷	division sign
√	square root sign
∞	infinity
≡	sign of identity, is exactly equal to
=	sign of equality, equals
≈	is approximately equal to
≠	sign of inequality, is not equal to
>	is greater than
<	is less than

LOS SIGNOS

+	signo de adición
+	signo de más (*p.ej.* +7 = 7 de más)
−	signo de sustracción
−	signo de menos (*p.ej.* −3 = 3 de menos)
x	signo de multiplicación
:	signo de división
√	signo de raíz cuadrada
∞	infinito
≡	signo de identidad, es exactamente igual a
=	signo de igualdad, es igual a
≈	es aproximadamente igual a
≠	signo de no identidad, no es igual a
>	es mayor que
<	es menor que

METRIC SYSTEM — SISTEMA MÉTRICO

Measures formed with the following prefixes are mostly omitted:

Se omiten la mayor parte de las medidas formadas con los siguientes prefijos:

deca-	10 times	10 veces	*deca-*
hecto-	100 times	100 veces	*hecto-*
kilo-	1000 times	1000 veces	*kilo-*
deci-	one tenth	una décima	*deci-*
centi-	one hundredth	una centésima	*centi-*
mil(l)i-	one thousandth	una milésima	*mili-*

Linear measures — medidas de longitud

1 millimetre (milímetro)	=	0·03937 inch (pulgada)
1 centimetre (centímetro)	=	0·3937 inch (pulgada)
1 metre (metro)	=	39·37 inches (pulgadas)
	=	1.094 yards (yardas)
1 kilometre (kilómetro)	=	0·6214 mile (milla) *or* almost exactly five-eighths of a mile

Square measures — medidas cuadradas o de superficie

1 square centimetre (centímetro cuadrado)	=	0·155 square inch (pulgada cuadrada)
1 square metre (metro cuadrado)	=	10·764 square feet (pies cuadrados)
	=	1·196 square yards (yardas cuadradas)
1 square kilometre (kilómetro cuadrado)	=	0·3861 square mile (milla cuadrada)
	=	247·1 acres (acres)
1 are = 100 square metres (área)	=	119·6 square yards (yardas cuadradas)
1 hectare = 100 ares (hectárea)	=	2·471 acres (acres)

Cubic measures — medidas cúbicas

1 cubic centimetre (centímetro cúbico)	=	0·061 cubic inch (pulgada cubica)
1 cubic metre (metro cúbico)	=	35·315 cubic feet (pies cubicos)
	=	1·308 cubic yards (yardas cubicas)

Measures of capacity — medidas de capacidad

1 litre (litro) = 1000 cubic centimetres	=	1·76 pints (pintas)
	=	0·22 gallon (galón)

Weights — pesos

1 gramme (gramo)	=	15·4 grains (granos)
1 kilogramme (kilogramo)	=	2·2046 pounds (libras)
1 quintal (quintal métrico) = 100 kilogrammes	=	220·46 pounds (libras)
1 metric ton (tonelada métrica) = 1000 kilogrammes	=	0·9842 ton (tonelada)

BRITISH SYSTEM — SISTEMA BRITÁNICO

Linear measures — medidas de longitud

1 inch (pulgada)	=	2,54 centímetros
1 foot (pie) = 12 inches	=	30,48 centímetros
1 yard (yarda) = 3 feet	=	91,44 centímetros
1 furlong (estadio) = 220 yards	=	201,17 metros
1 mile (milla) = 1760 yards	=	1.609,33 metros
	=	1,609 kilómetros

Surveyors' measures — medidas de agrimensura

1 link = 7·92 inches	=	20,12 centímetros
1 rod (*or* pole, perch) = 25 links	=	5,029 metros
1 chain = 22 yards = 4 rods	=	20,12 metros

Square measures — medidas cuadradas o de superficie

1 square inch (pulgada cuadrada)	=	6,45 cm^2
1 square foot (pie cuadrado) = 144 square inches	=	929,03 cm^2
1 square yard (yarda cuadrada) = 9 square feet	=	0,836 m^2
1 square rod = 30·25 square yards	=	25,29 m^2
1 acre = 4840 square yards	=	40,47 areas
1 square mile (milla cuadrada) = 640 acres	=	2,59 km^2

Cubic measures — medidas cúbicas

1 cubic inch (pulgada cúbica)	=	16,387 cm^3
1 cubic foot (pie cúbico) = 1728 cubic inches	=	0,028 m^3
1 cubic yard (yarda cúbica) = 27 cubic feet	=	0,765 m^3
1 register ton (tonelada de registro) = 100 cubic feet	=	2,832 m^3

Measures of capacity — medidas de capacidad

(a) Liquid – para líquidos

1 gill	=	0,142 litro
1 pint (pinta) = 4 gills	=	0,57 litro
1 quart = 2 pints	=	1,136 litros
1 gallon (galon) = 4 quarts	=	4,546 litros

(b) Dry – para áridos

1 peck = 2 gallons	=	9,087 litros
1 bushel = 4 pecks	=	36,37 litros
1 quarter = 8 bushels	=	290,94 litros

Weights — pesos (Avoirdupois system — sistema avoirdupois)

1 grain (grano)	=	0,0648 gramo
1 drachm *or* dram = 27,34 grains	=	1,77 gramos
1 ounce (onza) = 16 dra(ch)ms	=	28,35 gramos
1 pound (libra) = 16 ounces	=	453,6 gramos
	=	0,453 kilogramo
1 stone = 14 pounds	=	6,35 kilogramos
1 quarter = 28 pounds	=	12,7 kilogramos
1 hundredweight = 112 pounds	=	50,8 kilogramos
1 ton (tonelada) = 2240 pounds = 20 hundredweight	=	1.016,06 kilogramos

US MEASURES — MEDIDAS NORTEAMERICANAS

In the US the same system as that which applies in Great Britain is used for the most part; the main differences are mentioned below.
En EE.UU. se emplea en general el mismo sistema que en Gran Bretaña; las principales diferencias son las siguientes:

Measures of capacity — medidas de capacidad

(a) Liquid – para líquidos		
1 US liquid gill	=	0,118 litro
1 US liquid pint = 4 gills	=	0,47 litro
1 US liquid quart = 2 pints	=	0,946 litro
1 US gallon = 4 quarts	=	3,785 litros
(b) Dry – para áridos		
1 US dry pint	=	0,550 litro
1 US dry quart = 2 dry pints	=	1,1 litros
1 US peck = 8 dry quarts	=	8,81 litros
1 US bushel = 4 pecks	=	35,24 litros

Weights — pesos

1 hundredweight (or short hundredweight) = 100 pounds	=	45,36 kilogramos
1 ton (or short ton) = 2000 pounds = 20 short hundredweights	=	907,18 kilogramos

TRADITIONAL SPANISH WEIGHTS AND MEASURES — PESOS Y MEDIDAS ESPAÑOLES TRADICIONALES

These are the measures which were standard until the introduction of the metric system in Spain in 1871, and they are still in use in some provinces and in agriculture.

Son éstas las medidas que se emplearon hasta la introducción del sistema métrico en España en 1871. Se emplean todavía en algunas provincias y en la agricultura.

Linear measures — medidas de longitud

1 vara	=	0·836 metre
1 braza	=	1·67 metres
1 milla	=	1·852 kilometres
1 legua	=	5·5727 kilometres

Square measure — medida cuadrada o de superficie

1 fanega = 6460 square metres = 1·59 acres

Measures of capacity — medidas de capacidad

(a) Liquid – para líquidos		
1 cuartillo	=	0·504 litre
1 azumbre = 4 cuartillos	=	2·016 litres
1 cántara = 8 azumbres	=	16·13 litres
(b) Dry – para áridos		
1 celemín	=	4·625 litres
1 fanega = 12 celemines	=	55·5 litres = 1·58 bushels

Weights — pesos

1 onza	=	28·7 grammes
1 libra = 16 onzas	=	460 grammes
1 arroba = 25 libras	=	11·502 kilogrammes = 25 pounds
1 quintal = 4 arrobas	=	46 kilogrammes

TIME / LA HORA

TIME	LA HORA
2 hours 33 minutes and 14 seconds	*2 horas 33 minutos y 14 segundos*
half an hour	*media hora*
a quarter of an hour	*un cuarto de hora*
three quarters of an hour	*tres cuartos de hora*
what's the time?	*¿qué hora es?*
what do you make the time?	*¿qué hora tienes?*
have you the right time?	*¿tiene Vd la hora exacta?*
I make it 2.20	*yo tengo las dos veinte*
my watch says 3.37	*mi reloj marca las tres treinta y siete*
it's 1 o'clock	*es la una*
it's 2 o'clock	*son las dos*
it's 5 past 4	*son las cuatro y cinco*
it's 10 to 6	*son las seis menos diez*
it's half-past 8	*son las ocho y media*
it's a quarter past 9	*son las nueve y cuarto*
it's a quarter to 2	*son las dos menos cuarto*
at 10 a.m.	*a las diez de la mañana*
at 4 p.m.	*a las cuatro de la tarde*
at 11 p.m.	*a las once de la noche*
at exactly 3 o'clock, at 3 sharp, at 3 on the dot	*a las tres en punto*
the train leaves at 19.32	*el tren sale a las diecinueve treinta y dos*
(at) what time does it start?	*¿a qué hora comienza?*
it is just after 3	*son un poco más de las tres*
it is nearly 9	*son casi las nueve*
about 8 o'clock	*cerca de las ocho, hacia las ocho, a eso de las ocho*
at (*or* by) 6 o'clock at the latest	*a las seis a más tardar*
have it ready for 5 o'clock	*téngalo listo para las cinco*
it is full each night from 7 to 9	*está lleno todas las noches de siete a nueve*
"closed from 1.30 to 4.30"	*"cerrado de 1.30 a 4.30"*
until 8 o'clock	*hasta las ocho*
it would be about 11	*serán las once*
it would have been about 10	*serían las diez*
at midnight	*a medianoche*
before midday, before noon	*antes del mediodía*

DATES / LAS FECHAS

N.B. The days of the week and the months are written with small letters in Spanish: *lunes, martes, febrero, mayo.*
N.B. *Los días de la semana y los meses empiezan con mayúscula en inglés*: Monday, Tuesday, February, May.

DATES	LAS FECHAS
the 1st of July, 1 July	*el 1º de julio, el primero de julio*
the 2nd of May, 2 May	*el 2 de mayo, el dos de mayo* (the cardinal numbers are used in Spanish for dates from 2nd to 31st)
on the 21st (of) June, on 21 June	*el 21 de junio, el día veintiuno de junio*
on Monday	*el lunes*
he comes on Mondays	*viene los lunes*
"closed on Fridays"	*"cerrado los viernes"*
he lends it to me from Monday to Friday	*me lo presta de lunes a viernes*
from the 14th to the 18th	*desde el 14 hasta el 18, desde el catorce hasta el dieciocho*
what's the date?, what date is it today?	*¿qué día es hoy?*
today's the 12th	*hoy es el doce, estamos a doce*
one Thursday in October	*un jueves en octubre*
about the 4th of July	*hacia el cuatro de julio*
In letters: 19 May 2016	En cartas: *19 de mayo de 2016*
1975, nineteen (hundred and) seventy-five	*mil novecientos setenta y cinco*
2015, two thousand (and) fifteen, twenty fifteen	*2015, dos mil quince*
4 BC, BC 4	*4 a. de C.*
70 AD, AD 70	*70 d. de C.*
in the 13th Century	*en el siglo XIII, en el siglo trece*
in (*or* during) the 1930s	*en el decenio de 1930 a 40, durante los años treinta*
in 1940 something	*en el año 1940 y tantos*

Abreviaturas e indicaciones semánticas y estilísticas		Abbreviations, field labels and style labels
abreviatura	*abr, abbr*	abbreviation
adjetivo	*adj*	adjective
administración	*Admin*	administration
adverbio	*adv*	adverb
aeronáutica	*Aer*	aeronautics
agricultura	*Agr*	agriculture
alguien	*algn*	somebody, someone
anatomía	*Anat*	anatomy
Andes	*And*	Andes
arqueología	*Archeol*	archeology
arquitectura	*Archit*	architecture
Argentina	*Arg*	Argentina
arquitectura	*Arquit*	architecture
artículo	*art*	article
astrología	*Astrol*	astrology
astronomía	*Astron*	astronomy
automóviles, automovilismo	*Aut*	automobiles
auxiliar	*aux*	auxiliary
las Islas Baleares	*Baleares*	Balearic Islands
biología	*Bio, Biol*	biology
Bolivia	*Bol*	Bolivia
botánica	*Bot*	botany
británico, Gran Bretaña	*Brit*	British, Great Britain
Centroamérica	*CAm*	Central America
química	*Chem*	chemistry
cine	*Cine*	cinema
Colombia	*Col*	Colombia
comercio	*Com, Comm*	commerce, business
comparativo	*compar*	comparative
informática	*Comput*	computing
condicional	*cond*	conditional
conjunción	*conj*	conjunction
conjugación	*conjug*	conjugation
construcción	*Constr*	construction
costura	*Cos*	sewing
compuesto	*cpd*	compound
Costa Rica	*C. Rica*	Costa Rica
culinario, cocina	*Culin*	culinary, cooking
definido	*def*	definite
demostrativo	*dem*	demonstrative
deportes	*Dep*	sport
ecología	*Ecol*	ecology
economía	*Econ*	economy
Ecuador	*Ecu*	Ecuador
educación	*Educ*	education
Estados Unidos	*EEUU*	United States
por ejemplo	*eg*	for example
electricidad	*Elec*	electricity
escolar	*Escol*	school
España	*Esp*	Spain
especialmente	*esp*	especially
etcétera	*etc*	etcetera
eufemismo	*euf, euph*	euphemism
exclamación	*excl*	exclamation
femenino	*f*	feminine
farmacia	*Farm*	pharmacy
femenino	*fem*	feminine
ferrocarriles	*Ferro*	railways
figurado	*fig*	figurative
filosofía	*Fil*	philosophy
finanzas	*Fin*	finance
física	*Fís*	physics
fisiología	*Fisiol*	physiology
fotografía	*Fot*	photography
femenino plural	*fpl*	feminine plural
frecuentemente	*frec, freq*	frequently
uso formal	*frm*	formal usage
femenino singular	*fsing*	feminine singular
fútbol	*Ftbl*	football
generalmente	*gen*	generally
geografía	*Geog*	geography
geología	*Geol*	geology
geometría	*Geom*	geometry
gobierno	*Govt*	government
gramática	*Gram*	grammar
Guatemala	*Guat*	Guatemala
historia	*Hist*	history
Honduras	*Hond*	Honduras
horticultura	*Hort*	horticulture
humorístico	*hum*	humorous
impersonal	*impers*	impersonal
industria	*Ind*	industry
indefinido	*indef*	indefinite
indicativo	*indic*	indicative
infinitivo	*infin*	infinitive
informática	*Inform*	computing
interrogativo	*interrog*	interrogative
invariable	*inv*	invariable
Irlanda	*Irl*	Ireland
irónico	*iró, iro*	ironic
irregular	*irr*	irregular
derecho, jurídico	*Jur*	law, legal
Latinoamérica	*LAm*	Latin America
lingüística	*Ling*	linguistics
literalmente	*lit*	literally
literario	*liter*	literary
literatura	*Literat*	literature
masculino	*m, masc*	masculine